NORTHERN EUROPEAN RUSSIA pp 124-125
THE BALTIC STATES AND BELARUS pp 118-119
SOUTHERN EUROPEAN RUSSIA pp 126-127
ROMANIA, MOLDOVA & UKRAINE pp 116-117
BULGARIA & GREECE pp 114-115

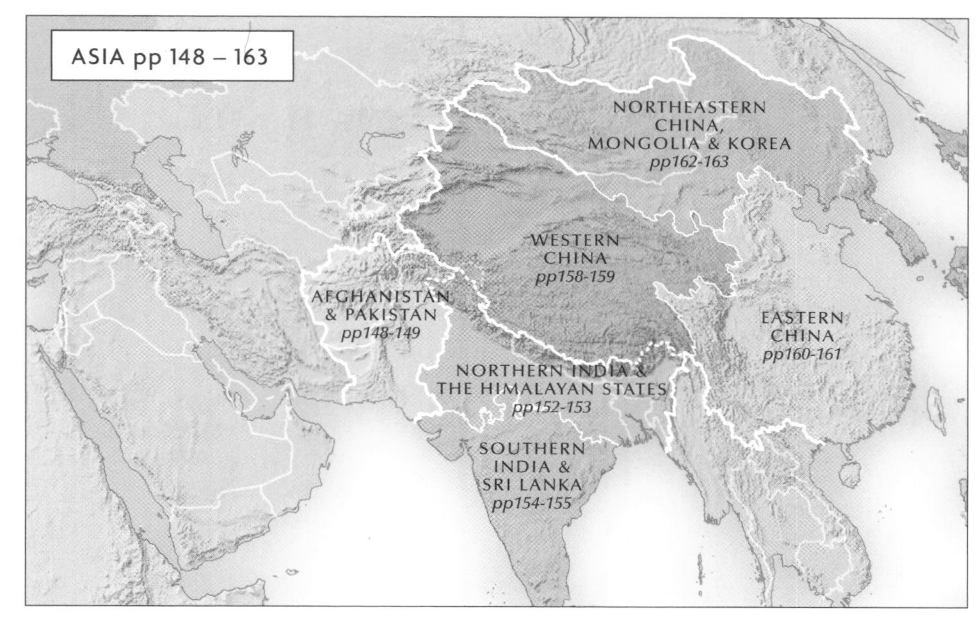
ASIA pp 148 – 163
NORTHEASTERN CHINA, MONGOLIA & KOREA pp162-163
WESTERN CHINA pp158-159
AFGHANISTAN & PAKISTAN pp148-149
EASTERN CHINA pp160-161
NORTHERN INDIA & THE HIMALAYAN STATES pp152-153
SOUTHERN INDIA & SRI LANKA pp154-155

Svalbard *p 92*

SCANDINAVIA, FINLAND & ICELAND *pp92-93*

THE RUSSIAN FEDERATION *pp122-123*

EUROPE *pp 84-127* *(also see inset)*

KAZAKHSTAN *pp144-145*

ASIA *pp 128-173* *(also see inset)*

TURKEY & THE CAUCASUS *pp136-137*

CENTRAL ASIA *pp146-147*

THE MEDITERRANEAN *pp 120-121*

Cyprus *pp 121*

THE NEAR EAST *pp138-139*

IRAN & THE GULF STATES *pp142-143*

MAINLAND EAST ASIA *pp 156-157*

JAPAN *pp 164-165*

Izu-shoto, Ogasawara-shoto & Kazan-retto *p 165*

THE PACIFIC OCEAN *pp 192-193*

NORTH AFRICA *pp 74-75*

Ryukyu Islands *p 165*

Sakishima-shoto *p 165*

THE ARABIAN PENINSULA *pp140-141*

SOUTH ASIA *pp150-151*

Mariana Islands *p 188*

Wake Island *p 189*

Saipan *p 188*

MICRONESIA *pp 188-189*

MAINLAND SOUTHEAST ASIA *pp 166-167*

Guam *p 188*

AFRICA *pp 66-83*

Yap *p 188*

Chuuk Islands *p 189*

Pohnpei *p 189*

Marshall Islands *p 189*

Babeldaob *p 188*

Majuro Atoll *p 189*

EAST AFRICA *pp 80-81*

Palau *p 188*

Micronesia *pp 188-189*

Kosrae *p 189*

Maldives *p 151*

CENTRAL AFRICA *pp 78-79*

WESTERN MARITIME SOUTHEAST ASIA *pp 168-169*

EASTERN MARITIME SOUTHEAST ASIA *pp 170-171*

Nauru *p 189*

Tarawa *p 190*

Kiribati *p 191*

Seychelles *p 172*

Tuvalu *p 190*

Funafuti Atoll *p 190*

Comoro Islands *p 172*

THE INDIAN OCEAN *pp 172-173*

MELANESIA *pp 186-187*

Madagascar *p 172*

AUSTRALASIA & OCEANIA *pp 174-193*

Mauritius *p 173*

SOUTHERN AFRICA *pp 82-83*

Réunion *p 173*

AUSTRALIA *pp 180-181*

SOUTHEAST AUSTRALIA *pp 182-183*

NEW ZEALAND *pp 184-18*

ANTARCTICA *pp 194-195*

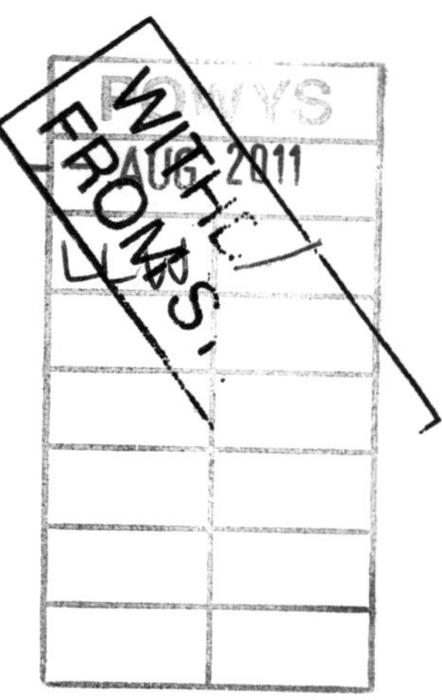

WORLD ATLAS

REFERENCE

London • New York • Melbourne • Munich • Delhi

WORLD ATLAS

REFERENCE

LONDON, NEW YORK, MELBOURNE, MUNICH, DELHI

FOR THE EIGHTH EDITION

Publisher Jonathan Metcalf **Art Director** Philip Ormerod **Associate Publisher** Liz Wheeler
Managing Cartographer David Roberts **Senior Cartographic Editor** Simon Mumford **Designers** Encompass Graphics Ltd, Brighton, UK • Philip Rowles
Cartographers Paul Eames • Iorwerth Watkins **Jacket Designer** Philip Ormerod **Production Controller** Inderjit Bhullar **Production Editor** Joanna Byrne

General Geographical Consultants

Physical Geography Denys Brunsden, Emeritus Professor, Department of Geography, King's College, London
Human Geography Professor J Malcolm Wagstaff, Department of Geography, University of Southampton
Place Names Caroline Burgess, Permanent Committee on Geographical Names, London
Boundaries International Boundaries Research Unit, Mountjoy Research Centre, University of Durham

Digital Mapping Consultants

DK Cartopia developed by George Galfalvi and XMap Ltd, London
Professor Jan-Peter Muller, Department of Photogrammetry and Surveying, University College, London
Cover globes, planets and information on the Solar System provided by Philip Eales and Kevin Tildsley, Planetary Visions Ltd, London

Regional Consultants

North America Dr David Green, Department of Geography, King's College, London • Jim Walsh, Head of Reference, Wessell Library, Tufts University, Medford, Massachussetts
South America Dr David Preston, School of Geography, University of Leeds **Europe** Dr Edward M Yates, formerly of the Department of Geography, King's College, London
Africa Dr Philip Amis, Development Administration Group, University of Birmingham • Dr Ieuan Ll Griffiths, Department of Geography, University of Sussex
Dr Tony Binns, Department of Geography, University of Sussex
Central Asia Dr David Turnock, Department of Geography, University of Leicester **South and East Asia** Dr Jonathan Rigg, Department of Geography, University of Durham
Australasia and Oceania Dr Robert Allison, Department of Geography, University of Durham

Acknowledgments

Digital terrain data created by Eros Data Center, Sioux Falls, South Dakota, USA. Processed by GVS Images Inc, California, USA and Planetary Visions Ltd, London, UK
Cambridge International Reference on Current Affairs (CIRCA), Cambridge, UK • Digitization by Robertson Research International, Swanley, UK • Peter Clark
British Isles maps generated from a dataset supplied by Map Marketing Ltd/European Map Graphics Ltd in combination with DK Cartopia copyright data

DORLING KINDERSLEY CARTOGRAPHY

Editor-in-Chief Andrew Heritage **Managing Cartographer** David Roberts **Senior Cartographic Editor** Roger Bullen
Editorial Direction Louise Cavanagh **Database Manager** Simon Lewis **Art Direction** Chez Picthall

Cartographers
Pamela Alford • James Anderson • Caroline Bowie • Dale Buckton • Tony Chambers • Jan Clark • Bob Croser • Martin Darlison • Damien Demaj • Claire Ellam • Sally Gable
Jeremy Hepworth • Geraldine Horner • Chris Jackson • Christine Johnston • Julia Lunn • Michael Martin • Ed Merritt • James Mills-Hicks • Simon Mumford • John Plumer
John Scott • Ann Stephenson • Gail Townsley • Julie Turner • Sarah Vaughan • Jane Voss • Scott Wallace • Iorwerth Watkins • Bryony Webb • Alan Whitaker • Peter Winfield

Digital Maps Created in DK Cartopia by
Tom Coulson • Thomas Robertshaw
Philip Rowles • Rob Stokes
Managing Editor
Lisa Thomas
Editors
Thomas Heath • Wim Jenkins • Jane Oliver
Siobhan Ryan • Elizabeth Wyse
Editorial Research
Helen Dangerfield • Andrew Rebeiro-Hargrave
Additional Editorial Assistance
Debra Clapson • Robert Damon • Ailsa Heritage
Constance Novis • Jayne Parsons • Chris Whitwell

Placenames Database Team
Natalie Clarkson • Ruth Duxbury • Caroline Falce • John Featherstone • Dan Gardiner
Ciárán Hynes • Margaret Hynes • Helen Rudkin • Margaret Stevenson • Annie Wilson
Senior Managing Art Editor
Philip Lord
Designers
Scott David • Carol Ann Davis • David Douglas • Rhonda Fisher
Karen Gregory • Nicola Liddiard • Paul Williams
Illustrations
Ciárán Hughes • Advanced Illustration, Congleton, UK
Picture Research
Melissa Albany • James Clarke • Anna Lord
Christine Rista • Sarah Moule • Louise Thomas

First published in Great Britain in 1997 as the DK World Atlas, and subsequent editions as the Reference Atlas of the World,
by Dorling Kindersley Limited, 80 Strand, London WC2R 0RL.

A Penguin Company

Reprinted with revisions 1998, 1999. Second Edition (revised) 2001. Third Edition (revised) 2003.
Reprinted with revisions 2004. Sixth Edition 2005. Seventh Edition 2007. Eighth Edition 2010.

A CIP catalogue record for this book is available from the British Library.

ISBN: 978-1-4053-3706-9

Reprographics by MDP Ltd, Wiltshire, UK.
Printed and bound by Neografia, Slovakia.

Discover more at **www.dk.com**

Introduction

EVERYTHING YOU NEED TO KNOW ABOUT OUR PLANET TODAY

For many, the outstanding legacy of the twentieth century was the way in which the Earth shrank. In the third millennium, it is increasingly important for us to have a clear vision of the world in which we live. The human population has increased fourfold since 1900. The last scraps of *terra incognita* – the polar regions and ocean depths – have been penetrated and mapped. New regions have been colonized and previously hostile realms claimed for habitation. The growth of air transport and mass tourism allows many of us to travel further, faster, and more frequently than ever before. In doing so we are given a bird's-eye view of the Earth's surface denied to our forebears.

At the same time, the amount of information about our world has grown enormously. Our multimedia environment hurls uninterrupted streams of data at us, on the printed page, through the airwaves and across our television, computer, and phone screens; events from all corners of the globe reach us instantaneously, and are witnessed as they unfold. Our sense of stability and certainty has been eroded; instead, we are aware that the world is in a constant state of flux and change. Natural disasters, man-made cataclysms, and conflicts between nations remind us daily of the enormity and fragility of our domain. The ongoing threat of international terrorism throws into very stark relief the difficulties that arise when trying to 'know' or 'understand' our planet and its many cultures.

The current crisis in our 'global' culture has made the need greater than ever before for everyone to possess an atlas. The **REFERENCE** WORLD **ATLAS** has been conceived to meet this need. At its core, like all atlases, it seeks to define where places are, to describe their main characteristics, and to locate them in relation to other places. Every attempt has been made to make the information on the maps as clear, accurate, and accessible as possible using the latest digital cartographic techniques. In addition, each page of the atlas provides a wealth of further information, bringing the maps to life. Using photographs, diagrams, 'at-a-glance' maps, introductory texts, and captions, the atlas builds up a detailed portrait of those features – cultural, political, economic, and geomorphological – that make each region unique and which are also the main agents of change.

This eighth edition of the **REFERENCE** WORLD **ATLAS** incorporates hundreds of revisions and updates affecting every map and every page, distilling the burgeoning mass of information available through modern technology into an extraordinarily detailed and reliable view of our world.

CONTENTS

Introduction v
Contents ..... vi–vii
How to use this Atlas ..... viii–ix

THE WORLD

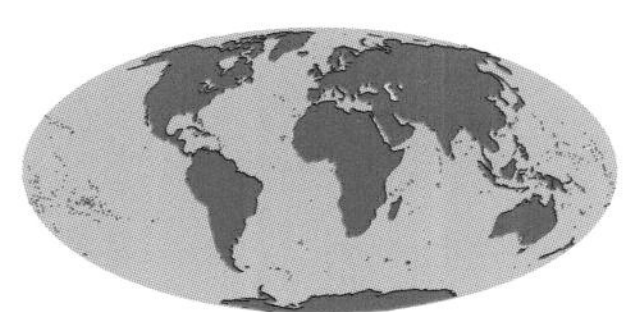

The solar system ..... x–xi
The physical world ..... xii–xiii
Structure of the Earth ..... xiv–xv
Shaping the landscape ..... xvi–xvii
The world's oceans ..... xviii–xix
The global climate ..... xx–xxi
Life on Earth ..... xxii–xxiii
Population and settlement ..... xxiv–xxv
The economic system ..... xxvi–xxvii
The political world ..... xxviii–xxix
States and boundaries ..... xxx–xxxi
International disputes xxxii

THE BRITISH ISLES

Political British Isles xxxiv
Wales xxxv
Southern England ..... xxxvi–xxxvii
Central England ..... xxxviii–xxxix
Northern England ..... xl–xli
Scotland ..... xlii–xliii
Ireland xliv

ATLAS OF THE WORLD

North America

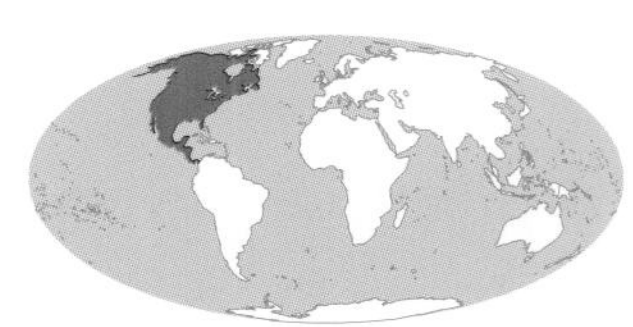

NORTH AMERICA 1
PHYSICAL NORTH AMERICA 2–3
POLITICAL NORTH AMERICA 4–5
NORTH AMERICAN RESOURCES 6–7
Canada 8–9
Canada: Western Provinces 10–11
Alberta, British Columbia, Manitoba, Saskatchewan, Yukon
Canada: Eastern Provinces 12–13
New Brunswick, Newfoundland & Labrador, Nova Scotia, Ontario, Prince Edward Island, Québec, St Pierre & Miquelon
Southeastern Canada 14–15
Southern Ontario, Southern Québec
United States of America 16–17
USA: Northeastern States 18–19
Connecticut, Maine, Massachussetts, New Hampshire, New Jersey, New York, Pennsylvania, Rhode Island, Vermont
USA: Mid-Eastern States 20–21
Delaware, District of Columbia, Kentucky, Maryland, North Carolina, South Carolina, Tennessee, Virginia, West Virginia
USA: Southern States 22–23
Alabama, Florida, Georgia, Louisiana, Mississippi
USA: Texas 24–25
USA: South Midwestern States 26–27
Arkansas, Kansas, Missouri, Oklahoma
USA: Upper Plains States 28–29
Iowa, Minnesota, Nebraska, North Dakota, South Dakota
USA: Great Lakes States 30–31
Illinois, Indiana, Michigan, Ohio, Wisconsin
USA: North Mountain States 32–33
Idaho, Montana, Oregon, Washington, Wyoming
USA: California & Nevada 34–35
USA: South Mountain States 36–37
Arizona, Colorado, New Mexico, Utah
USA: Hawaii & Alaska 38–39
Mexico 40–41
Central America 42–43
Belize, Costa Rica, El Salvador, Guatemala, Honduras, Nicaragua, Panama
The Caribbean 44–45
Anguilla, Antigua & Barbuda, Aruba, Bahamas, Barbados, British Virgin Islands, Cayman Islands, Cuba, Dominica, Dominican Republic, Grenada, Guadeloupe, Haiti, Jamaica, Martinique, Montserrat, Navassa Island, Netherlands Antilles, Puerto Rico, St Kitts & Nevis, St Lucia, St Vincent & the Grenadines, Trinidad & Tobago, Turks & Caicos Islands, Virgin Islands (US)

South America

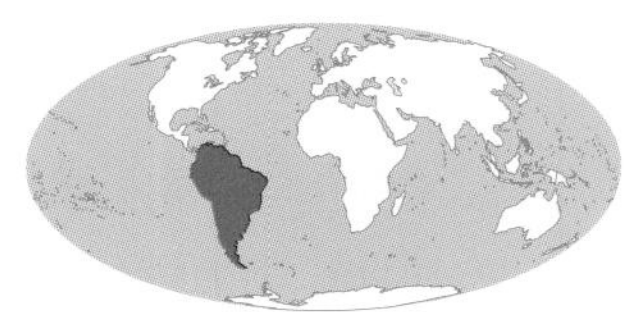

SOUTH AMERICA 46–47
PHYSICAL SOUTH AMERICA 48–49
POLITICAL SOUTH AMERICA 50–51
SOUTH AMERICAN RESOURCES 52–53
Northern South America 54–55
Colombia, French Guiana, Guyana, Surinam, Venezuela
Western South America 56–57
Bolivia, Ecuador, Peru
Brazil 58–59
Eastern South America 60–61
Southeast Brazil, Northeast Argentina, Uruguay
Southern South America 62–63
Argentina, Chile, Paraguay
The Atlantic Ocean 64–65

Africa

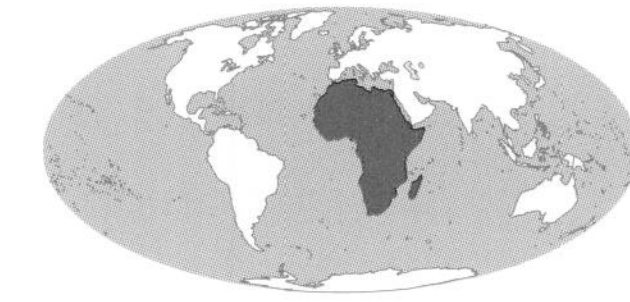

AFRICA 66–67
PHYSICAL AFRICA 68–69
POLITICAL AFRICA 70–71
AFRICAN RESOURCES 72–73
North Africa 74–75
Algeria, Egypt, Libya, Morocco, Tunisia, Western Sahara
West Africa 76–77
Benin, Burkina, Cape Verde, Gambia, Ghana, Guinea, Guinea-Bissau, Ivory Coast, Liberia, Mali, Mauritania, Niger, Nigeria, Senegal, Sierra Leone, Togo
Central Africa 78–79
Cameroon, Central African Republic, Chad, Congo, Dem. Rep. Congo, Equatorial Guinea, Gabon, Sao Tome & Principe
East Africa 80–81
Burundi, Djibouti, Eritrea, Ethiopia, Kenya, Rwanda, Somalia, Sudan, Tanzania, Uganda
Southern Africa 82–83
Angola, Botswana, Lesotho, Malawi, Mozambique, Namibia, South Africa, Swaziland, Zambia, Zimbabwe

Europe

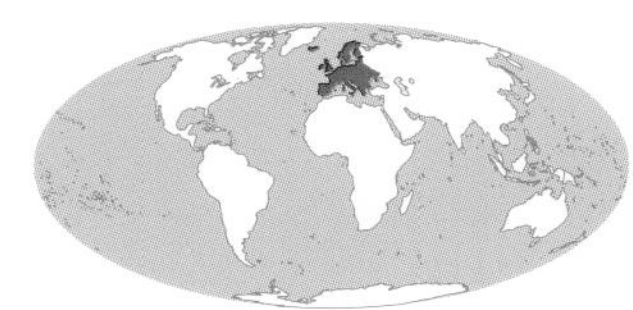

EUROPE 84–85

PHYSICAL EUROPE 86–87

POLITICAL EUROPE 88–89

EUROPEAN RESOURCES 90–91

Scandinavia, Finland & Iceland 92–93
Denmark, Finland, Iceland, Norway, Svalbard, Sweden

Southern Scandinavia 94–95
Denmark, Faeroe Islands, Southern Norway, Southern Sweden

The British Isles 96–97
Channel Islands, Ireland, Isle of Man, United Kingdom

The Low Countries 98–99
Belgium, Luxembourg, Netherlands

Germany 100–101

France 102–103
France, Monaco

The Iberian Peninsula 104–105
Andorra, Gibraltar, Portugal, Spain

The Italian Peninsula 106–107
Italy, San Marino, Vatican City

The Alpine States 108–109
Austria, Liechtenstein, Slovenia, Switzerland

Central Europe 110–111
Czech Republic, Hungary, Poland, Slovakia

Southeast Europe 112–113
Albania, Bosnia & Herzegovina, Croatia, Kosovo, Macedonia, Montenegro, Serbia

Bulgaria & Greece 114–115
(including European Turkey)

Romania, Moldova & Ukraine 116–117

The Baltic States & Belarus 118–119
Belarus, Estonia, Latvia, Lithuania, Kaliningrad

The Mediterranean 120–121

The Russian Federation 122–123

Northern European Russia 124–125

Southern European Russia 126–127

Asia

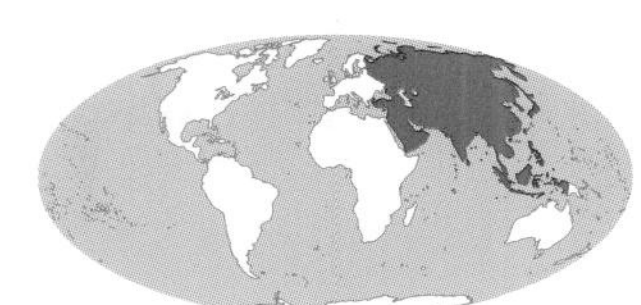

ASIA 128–129

PHYSICAL ASIA 130–131

POLITICAL ASIA 132–133

ASIAN RESOURCES 134–135

Turkey & the Caucasus 136–137
Armenia, Azerbaijan, Georgia, Turkey

The Near East 138–139
Iraq, Israel, Jordan, Lebanon, Syria

The Arabian Peninsula 140–141
Bahrain, Kuwait, Oman, Qatar, Saudi Arabia, United Arab Emirates, Yemen

Iran & the Gulf States 142–143
Bahrain, Iran, Kuwait, Qatar, United Arab Emirates

Kazakhstan 144–145

Central Asia 146–147
Kyrgyzstan, Tajikistan, Turkmenistan, Uzbekistan

Afghanistan & Pakistan 148–149

South Asia 150–151
Bangladesh, Bhutan, India, Maldives, Nepal, Pakistan, Sri Lanka

Northern India & the Himalayan States 152–153
Bangladesh, Bhutan, Nepal, Northern India

Southern India & Sri Lanka 154–155

Mainland East Asia 156–157
China, Mongolia, North Korea, South Korea, Taiwan

Western China 158–159

Eastern China 160–161
Eastern China, Taiwan

Northeastern China, Mongolia & Korea 162–163
Mongolia, Northeastern China, North Korea, South Korea

Japan 164–165

Mainland Southeast Asia 166–167
Burma, Cambodia, Laos, Paracel Islands, Thailand, Vietnam

West Maritime Southeast Asia 168–169
Brunei, Indonesia, Malaysia, Singapore

East Maritime Southeast Asia 170–171
East Timor, Indonesia, Philippines

The Indian Ocean 172–173

Australasia & Oceania

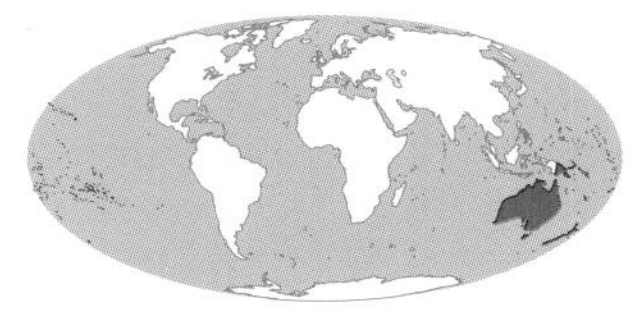

AUSTRALASIA & OCEANIA 174–175

POLITICAL AUSTRALASIA & OCEANIA 176–177

AUSTRALASIAN & OCEANIAN RESOURCES 178–179

Australia 180–181

Southeast Australia 182–183
New South Wales, South Australia, Tasmania, Victoria

New Zealand 184–185

Melanesia 186–187
Fiji, New Caledonia, Papua New Guinea, Solomon Islands, Vanuatu

Micronesia 188–189
Guam, Marshall Islands, Micronesia, Nauru, Northern Mariana Islands, Palau, Wake Island

Polynesia 190–191
Cook Islands, Easter Island, French Polynesia, Kiribati, Niue, Pitcairn Islands, Tokelau, Tuvalu, Wallis & Futuna

The Pacific Ocean 192–193

Antarctica 194–195

The Arctic 196–197

INDEX–GAZETTEER

Geographical comparisons 198–199

Countries of the world including The time zones 200–207

Geographical glossary 208–210

Geographical names 211

Index 212–349

Acknowledgements 350

Key to maps

Regional

Physical features

elevation

6000m / 19,686ft
4000m / 13,124ft
3000m / 9843ft
2000m / 6562ft
1000m / 3281ft
500m / 1640ft
250m / 820ft
100m / 328ft
sea level
below sea level

▲ elevation above sea level (mountain height)
volcano
pass
▼ elevation below sea level (depression depth)

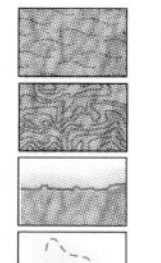

sand desert
lava flow
coastline
reef
atoll

sea depth

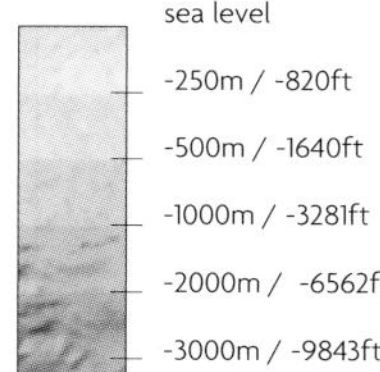

sea level
-250m / -820ft
-500m / -1640ft
-1000m / -3281ft
-2000m / -6562ft
-3000m / -9843ft

▲ seamount / guyot symbol
▼ undersea spot depth

Drainage features

main river
secondary river
tertiary river
minor river
main seasonal river
secondary seasonal river
canal
waterfall
rapids
dam
perennial lake
seasonal lake
perennial salt lake
seasonal salt lake
reservoir
salt flat / salt pan
marsh / salt marsh
mangrove
wadi
spring / well / waterhole / oasis

Ice features

ice cap / sheet
ice shelf
glacier / snowfield
summer pack ice limit
winter pack ice limit

Communications

motorway / highway
motorway / highway (under construction)
major road
minor road
tunnel (road)
main line
minor line
tunnel (rail)
international airport

Borders

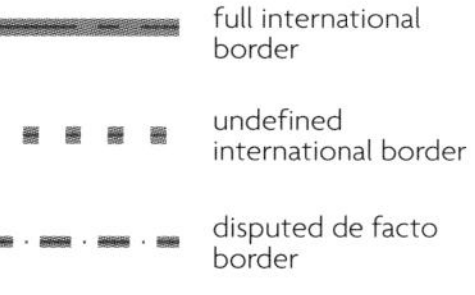

full international border
undefined international border
disputed de facto border
disputed territorial claim border
indication of country extent (Pacific only)
indication of dependent territory extent (Pacific only)
demarcation/ cease fire line
autonomous / federal region border
2nd order internal administrative border
3rd order internal administrative border

Settlements

built up area

settlement population symbols

more than 5 million
1 million to 5 million
500,000 to 1 million
100,000 to 500,000
50,000 to 100,000
10,000 to 50,000
fewer than 10,000
country/dependent territory capital city
autonomous / federal region / 2nd order internal administrative centre
3rd order internal administrative centre

Miscellaneous features

ancient wall
site of interest
scientific station

Graticule features

lines of latitude and longitude / Equator
Tropics / Polar circles
45° degrees of longitude / latitude

Typographic key

Physical features

landscape features ... *Namib Desert* *Massif Central* *ANDES*
headland .... *Nordkapp*
elevation / volcano / pass .... Mount Meru 4556 m
drainage features .... *Lake Geneva*
rivers / canals spring / well / waterhole / oasis / waterfall / rapids / dam .... *Mekong*
ice features .... *Vatnajökull*
sea features........... *Golfe de Lion* *Andaman Sea* *INDIAN OCEAN*
undersea features ... *Barracuda Fracture Zone*

Regions

country .... ARMENIA
dependent territory with parent state ..... NIUE (to NZ)
region outside feature area .... ANGOLA
autonomous / federal region .... MINAS GERAIS
2nd order internal administrative region .... MINSKAYA VOBLASTS'
3rd order internal administrative region .... Vaucluse
cultural region .... New England

Settlements

capital city .... BEIJING
dependent territory capital city .... FORT-DE-FRANCE
other settlements ··· Chicago Adana Tizi Ozou Yonezawa Farnham

Miscellaneous

sites of interest / miscellaneous .... Valley of the Kings
Tropics / Polar circles .... *Antarctic Circle*

How to use this Atlas

The atlas is organized by continent, moving eastwards from the International Date Line. The opening section describes the world's structure, systems and its main features. The Atlas of the World which follows, is a continent-by-continent guide to today's world, starting with a comprehensive insight into the physical, political and economic structure of each continent, followed by integrated mapping and descriptions of each region or country.

The world

The introductory section of the Atlas deals with every aspect of the planet, from physical structure to human geography, providing an overall picture of the world we live in. Complex topics such as the landscape of the Earth, climate, oceans, population and economic patterns are clearly explained with the aid of maps, diagrams drawn from the latest information.

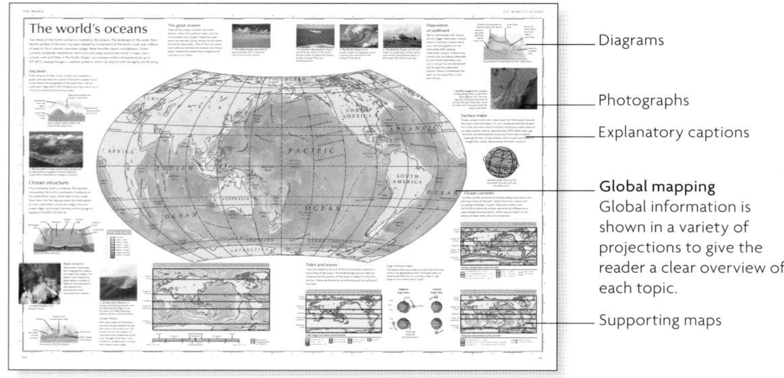
The world's oceans
Diagrams
Photographs
Explanatory captions
Global mapping
Global information is shown in a variety of projections to give the reader a clear overview of each topic.
Supporting maps

The political continent

The political portrait of the continent is a vital reference point for every continental section, showing the position of countries relative to one another, and the relationship between human settlement and geographic location. The complex mosaic of languages spoken in each continent is mapped, as is the effect of communications networks on the pattern of settlement.

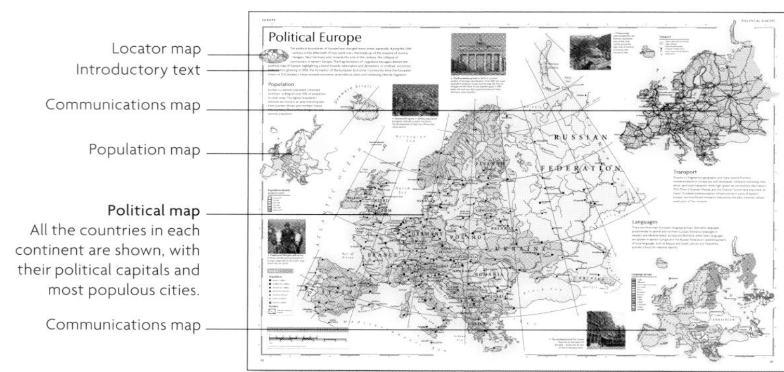
Political Europe
Locator map
Introductory text
Communications map
Population map
Political map
All the countries in each continent are shown, with their political capitals and most populous cities.
Communications map

Continental resources

The Earth's rich natural resources, including oil, gas, minerals and fertile land, have played a key role in the development of society. These pages show the location of minerals and agricultural resources on each continent, and how they have been instrumental in dictating industrial growth and the varieties of economic activity across the continent.

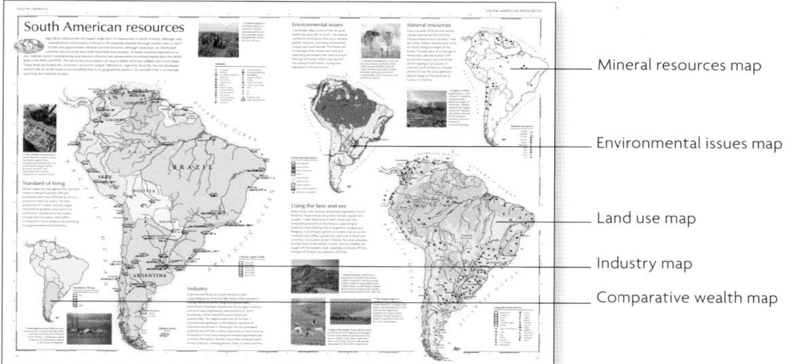
South American resources
Mineral resources map
Environmental issues map
Land use map
Industry map
Comparative wealth map

The physical continent

The astonishing variety of landforms, and the dramatic forces that created and continue to shape the landscape, are explained in the continental physical spread. Cross-sections, illustrations and terrain maps highlight the different parts of the continent, showing how nature's forces have produced the landscapes we see today.

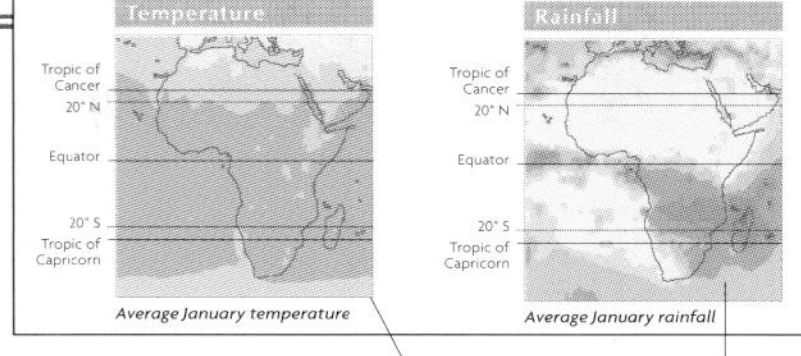

Temperature
Rainfall
Tropic of Cancer 20° N
Equator
20° S Tropic of Capricorn
Average January temperature
Average January rainfall

Climate charts
Rainfall and temperature charts clearly show the continental patterns of rainfall and temperature.

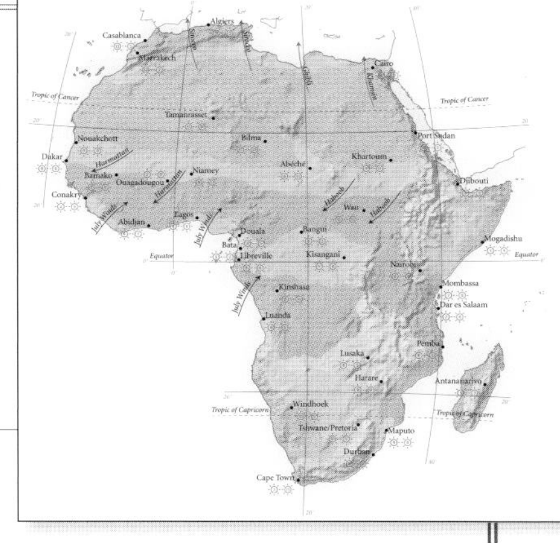

Climate map
Climatic regions vary across each continent. The map displays the differing climatic regions, as well as daily hours of sunshine at selected weather stations.

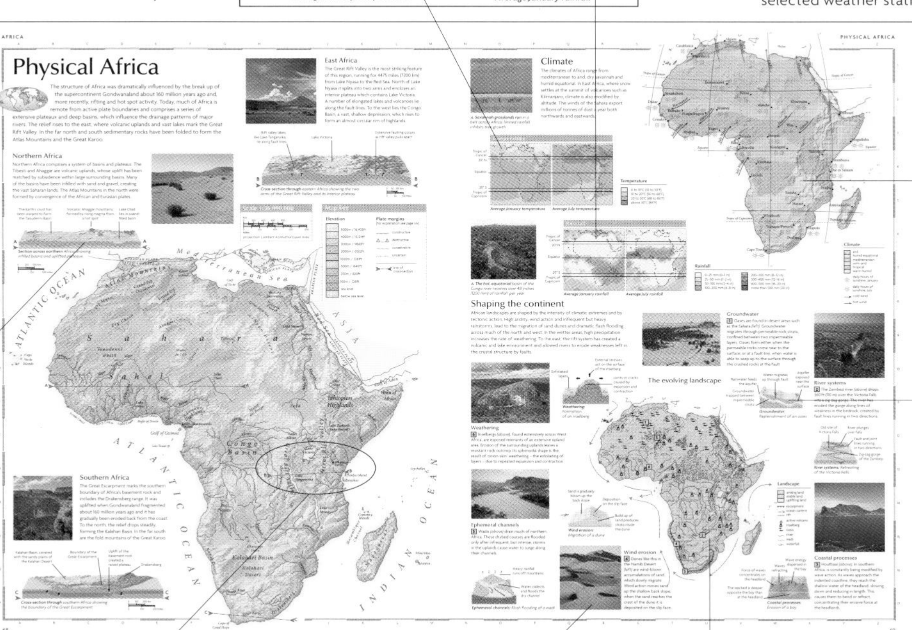

Physical Africa

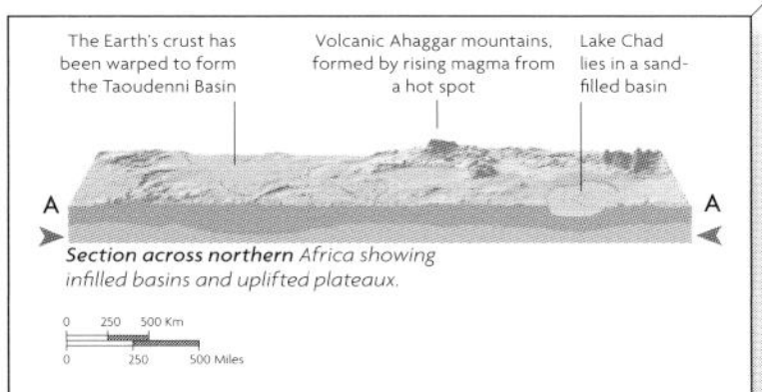

The Earth's crust has been warped to form the Taoudenni Basin
Volcanic Ahaggar mountains, formed by rising magma from a hot spot
Lake Chad lies in a sand-filled basin
A
A
Section across northern Africa showing infilled basins and uplifted plateaux.

Cross-sections
Detailed cross-sections through selected parts of the continent show the underlying geomorphic structure.

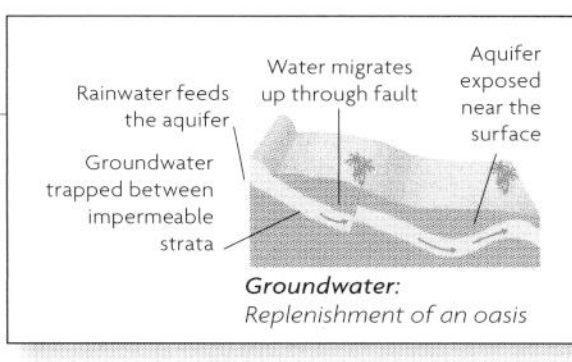

Rainwater feeds the aquifer
Water migrates up through fault
Aquifer exposed near the surface
Groundwater trapped between impermeable strata
Groundwater: Replenishment of an oasis

Landform diagrams
The complex formation of many typical landforms is summarized in these easy-to-understand illustrations.

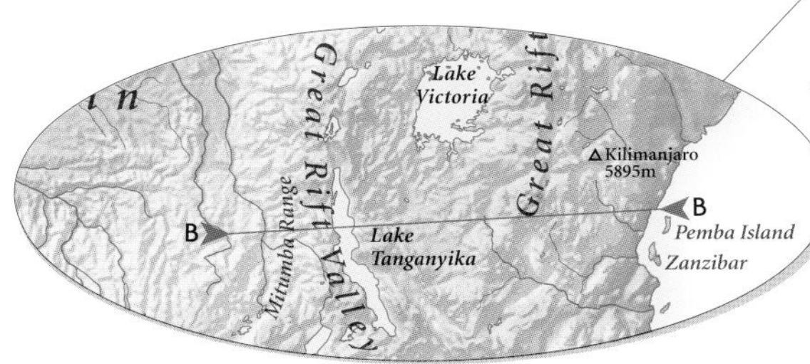

Lake Victoria
Great Rift
Kilimanjaro 5895m
B
B
Pemba Island
Zanzibar
Lake Tanganyika
Great Rift Valley
Mitumba Range

Main physical map
Detailed satellite data has been used to create an accurate and visually striking picture of the surface of the continent.

Photographs
A wide range of beautiful photographs bring the world's regions to life.

Landscape evolution map
The physical shape of each continent is affected by a variety of forces which continually sculpt and modify the landscape. This map shows the major processes which affect different parts of the continent.

Regional mapping

The main body of the Atlas is a unique regional map set, with detailed information on the terrain, the human geography of the region and its infrastructure. Around the edge of the map, additional 'at-a-glance' maps, give an instant picture of regional industry, land use and agriculture. The detailed terrain map (shown in perspective), focuses on the main physical features of the region, and is enhanced by annotated illustrations, and photographs of the physical structure.

Key to transport symbols
❶ Extent of national paved road network.
❷ Extent of motorways, freeways or major national highways.
❸ Extent of commercial rail network.
❹ Extent of inland waterways navigable by commercial craft.

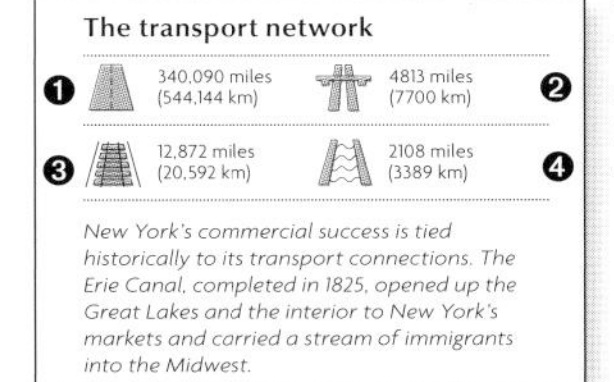

The transport network

❶	340,090 miles (544,344 km)	4813 miles (7700 km)	❷
❸	12,872 miles (20,592 km)	2108 miles (3389 km)	❹

New York's commercial success is tied historically to its transport connections. The Erie Canal, completed in 1825, opened up the Great Lakes and the interior to New York's markets and carried a stream of immigrants into the Midwest.

Transport network
The differing extent of the transport network for each region is shown here, along with key facts about the transport system.

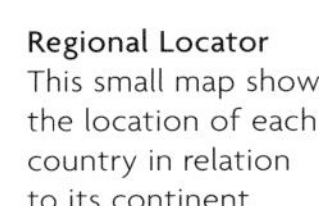

Regional Locator
This small map shows the location of each country in relation to its continent.

Key to main map
A key to the population symbols and land heights accompanies the main map.

World locator
This locates the continent in which the region is found on a small world map.

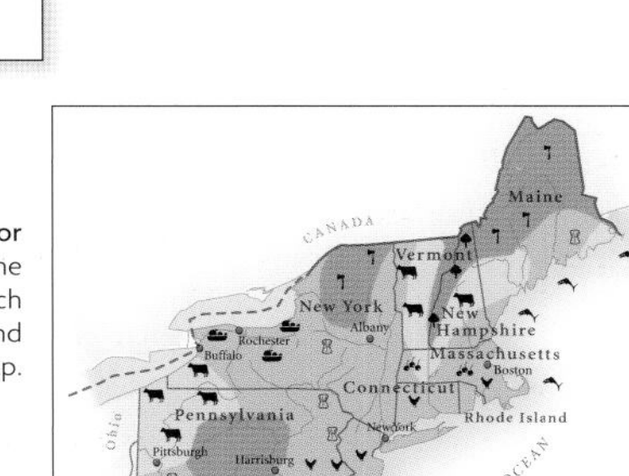

CANADA
Maine
Vermont
New Hampshire
New York
Massachusetts
Connecticut
Rhode Island
Pennsylvania
New Jersey
West Virginia
ATLANTIC OCEAN

Land use map
This shows the different types of land use which characterize the region, as well as indicating the principal agricultural activities.

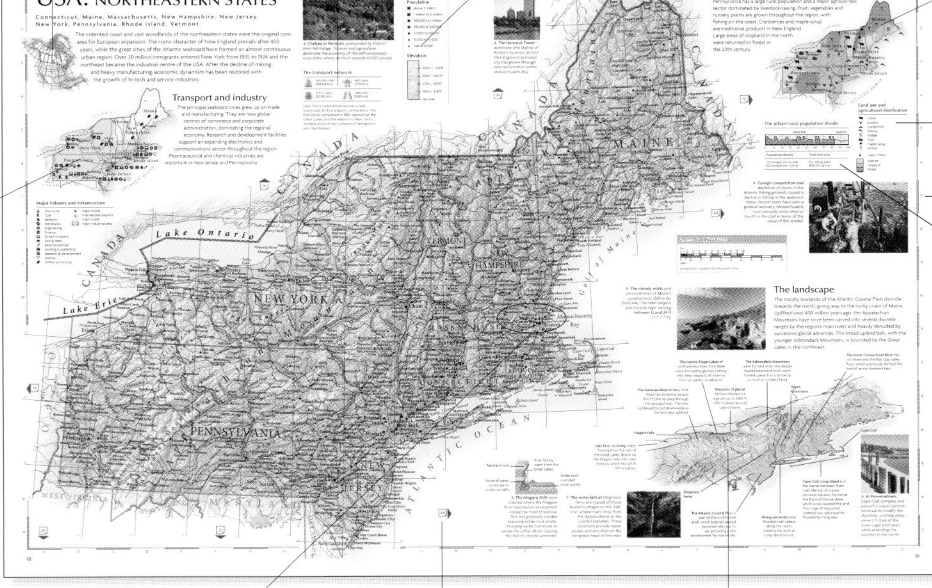

USA: NORTHEASTERN STATES

Map keys
Each supporting map has its own key.

Grid reference
The framing grid provides a location reference for each place listed in the Index.

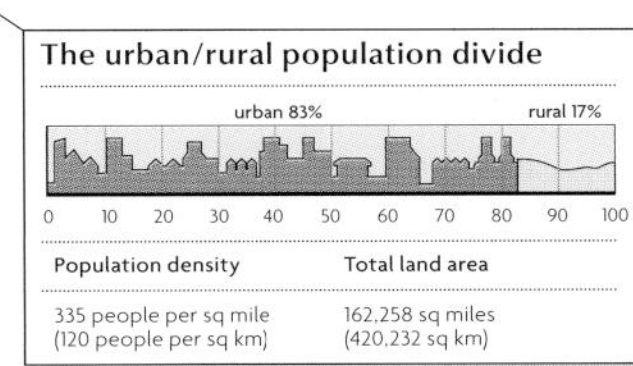

The urban/rural population divide

urban 83% — rural 17%

0 10 20 30 40 50 60 70 80 90 100

Population density	Total land area
335 people per sq mile (120 people per sq km)	162,258 sq miles (420,232 sq km)

Urban/rural population divide
The proportion of people in the region who live in urban and rural areas, as well as the overall population density and land area are clearly shown in these simple graphics.

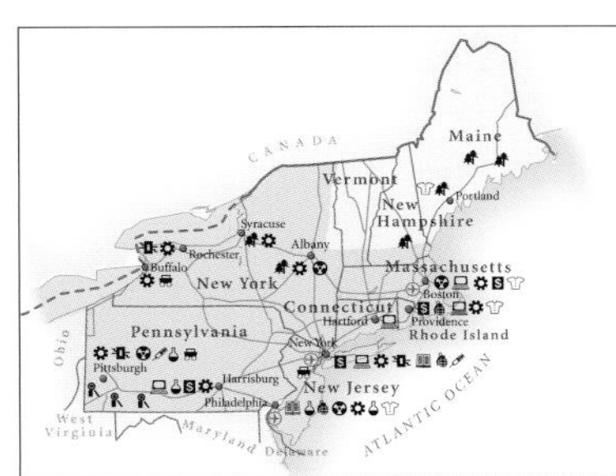

CANADA
Maine
Vermont
New Hampshire
New York
Massachusetts
Connecticut
Rhode Island
Pennsylvania
New Jersey
West Virginia
ATLANTIC OCEAN

Transport and industry map
The main industrial areas are mapped, and the most important industrial and economic activities of the region are shown.

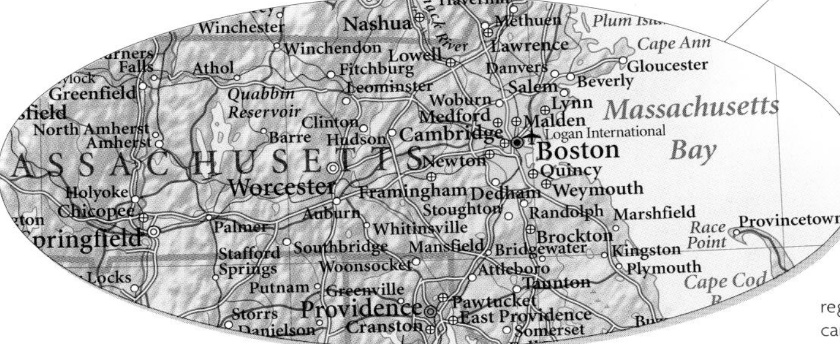

Nashua
Winchester
Methuen
Lawrence
Lowell
Cape Ann
Gloucester
Fitchburg
Leominster
Danvers
Beverly
Salem
Lynn
Massachusetts
Woburn
Medford
Malden
Greenfield
Athol
Quabbin Reservoir
North Amherst
Amherst
Clinton
Barre
Hudson
Cambridge
Logan International
Boston
Bay
Quincy
Weymouth
Newton
Holyoke
Chicopee
Springfield
Worcester
Framingham
Dedham
Auburn
Whitinsville
Randolph
Marshfield
Stoughton
Brockton
Provincetown
Palmer
Southbridge
Mansfield
Bridgewater
Kingston
Race Point
Stafford Springs
Woonsocket
Attleboro
Plymouth
Taunton
Cape Cod
Putnam
Greenville
Pawtucket
Providence
East Providence
Cranston
Somerset

Continuation symbols
These symbols indicate where adjacent maps can be found.

Main regional map
A wealth of information is displayed on the main map, building up a rich portrait of the interaction between the physical landscape and the human and political geography of each region. The key to the regional maps can be found on page viii.

Landscape map
The computer-generated terrain model accurately portrays an oblique view of the landscape. Annotations highlight the most important geographic features of the region.

The Solar System

Nine major planets, their satellites and countless minor planets (asteroids) orbit the Sun to form the Solar System. The Sun, our nearest star, creates energy from nuclear reactions deep within its interior, providing all the light and heat which make life on Earth possible. The Earth is unique in the Solar System in that it supports life: its size, gravitational pull and distance from the Sun have all created the optimum conditions for the evolution of life. The planetary images seen here are composites derived from actual spacecraft images (not shown to scale).

Orbits

All the Solar System's planets and dwarf planets orbit the Sun in the same direction and (apart from Pluto) roughly in the same plane. All the orbits have the shapes of ellipses (stretched circles). However in most cases, these ellipses are close to being circular: only Pluto and Eris have very elliptical orbits. Orbital period (the time it takes an object to orbit the Sun) increases with distance from the Sun. The more remote objects not only have further to travel with each orbit, they also move more slowly.

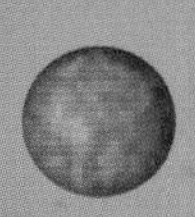

Mercury

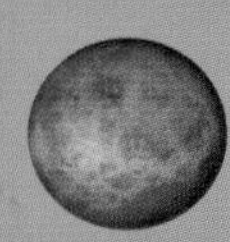

Venus

Earth

Mars

Ceres *(dwarf planet)*

Jupiter

The Sun

⊖ ***Diameter:*** *864,948 miles (1,392,000 km)*
● ***Mass:*** *1990 million million million million tons*

The Sun was formed when a swirling cloud of dust and gas contracted, pulling matter into its centre. When the temperature at the centre rose to 1,000,000°C, nuclear fusion – the fusing of hydrogen into helium, creating energy – occurred, releasing a constant stream of heat and light.

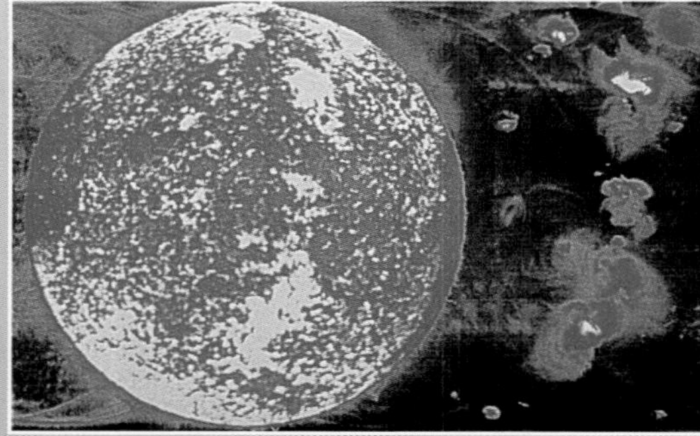

▲ ***Solar flares are*** *sudden bursts of energy from the Sun's surface. They can be 125,000 miles (200,000 km) long.*

The formation of the Solar System

The cloud of dust and gas thrown out by the Sun during its formation cooled to form the Solar System. The smaller planets nearest the Sun are formed of minerals and metals. The outer planets were formed at lower temperatures, and consist of swirling clouds of gases.

Solar eclipse

A solar eclipse occurs when the Moon passes between Earth and the Sun, casting its shadow on Earth's surface. During a total eclipse *(below)*, viewers along a strip of Earth's surface, called the area of totality, see the Sun totally blotted out for a short time, as the umbra (Moon's full shadow) sweeps over them. Outside this area is a larger one, where the Sun appears only partly obscured, as the penumbra (partial shadow) passes over.

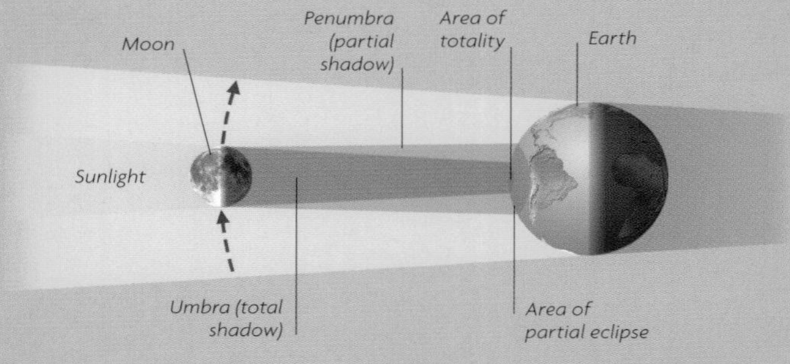
Moon
Penumbra (partial shadow)
Area of totality
Earth
Sunlight
Umbra (total shadow)
Area of partial eclipse

N O P Q R S T U V W X Y Z

PLANETS	MERCURY	VENUS	EARTH	MARS	JUPITER	SATURN	URANUS	NEPTUNE
DIAMETER	3029 miles (4875 km)	7521 miles (12,104 km)	7928 miles (12,756 km)	4213 miles (6780 km)	88,846 miles (142,984 km)	74,898 miles (120,536 km)	31,763 miles (51,118 km)	30,775 miles (49,528 km)
AVERAGE DISTANCE FROM THE SUN	36 mill. miles (57.9 mill. km)	67.2 mill. miles (108.2 mill. km)	93 mill. miles (149.6 mill. km)	141.6 mill. miles (227.9 mill. km)	483.6 mill. miles (778.3 mill. km)	889.8 mill. miles (1431 mill. km)	1788 mill. miles (2877 mill. km)	2795 mill. miles (4498 mill. km)
ROTATION PERIOD	58.6 days	243 days	23.93 hours	24.62 hours	9.93 hours	10.65 hours	17.24 hours	16.11 hours
ORBITAL PERIOD	88 days	224.7 days	365.26 days	687 days	11.86 years	29.37 years	84.1 years	164.9 years
SURFACE TEMPERATURE	-180°C to 430°C (-292°F to 806°F)	480°C (896°F)	-70°C to 55°C (-94°F to 131°F)	-120°C to 25°C (-184°F to 77 °F)	-110°C (-160°F)	-140°C (-220°F)	-200°C (-320°F)	-200°C (-320°F)

DWARF PLANETS	CERES	PLUTO	ERIS
DIAMETER	590 miles (950 km)	1432 miles (2304 km)	1429-1553 miles (2300-2500 km)
AVERAGE DISTANCE FROM THE SUN	257 mill. miles (414 mill. km)	3675 mill. miles (5915 mill. km)	6344 mill. miles (10,210 mill. km)
ROTATION PERIOD	9.1 hours	6.38 days	not known
ORBITAL PERIOD	4.6 years	248.6 years	557 years
SURFACE TEMPERATURE	-107°C (-161°F)	-230°C (-380°F)	-243°C (-405°F)

AVERAGE DISTANCE FROM THE SUN

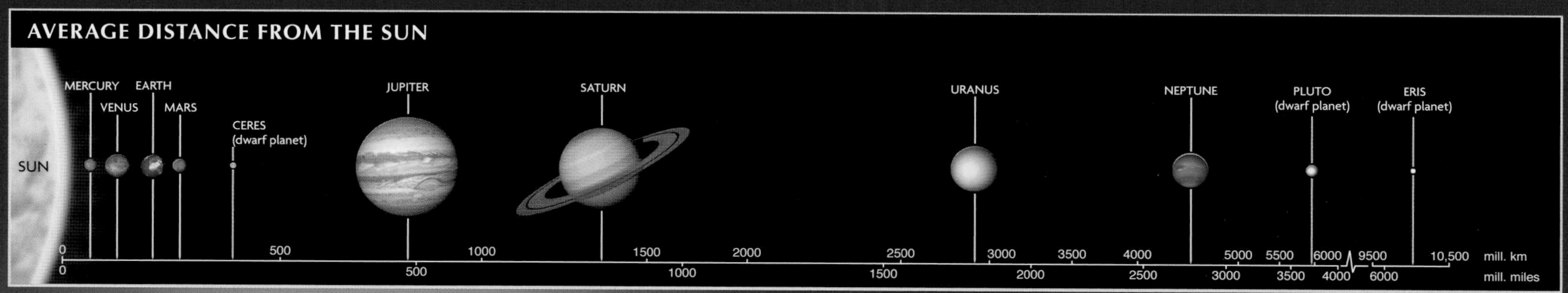

SUN
MERCURY
VENUS
EARTH
MARS
CERES (dwarf planet)
JUPITER
SATURN
URANUS
NEPTUNE
PLUTO (dwarf planet)
ERIS (dwarf planet)
0 500 1000 1500 2000 2500 3000 3500 4000 5000 5500 6000 9500 10,500 mill. km
0 500 1000 1500 2000 2500 3000 3500 4000 6000 mill. miles

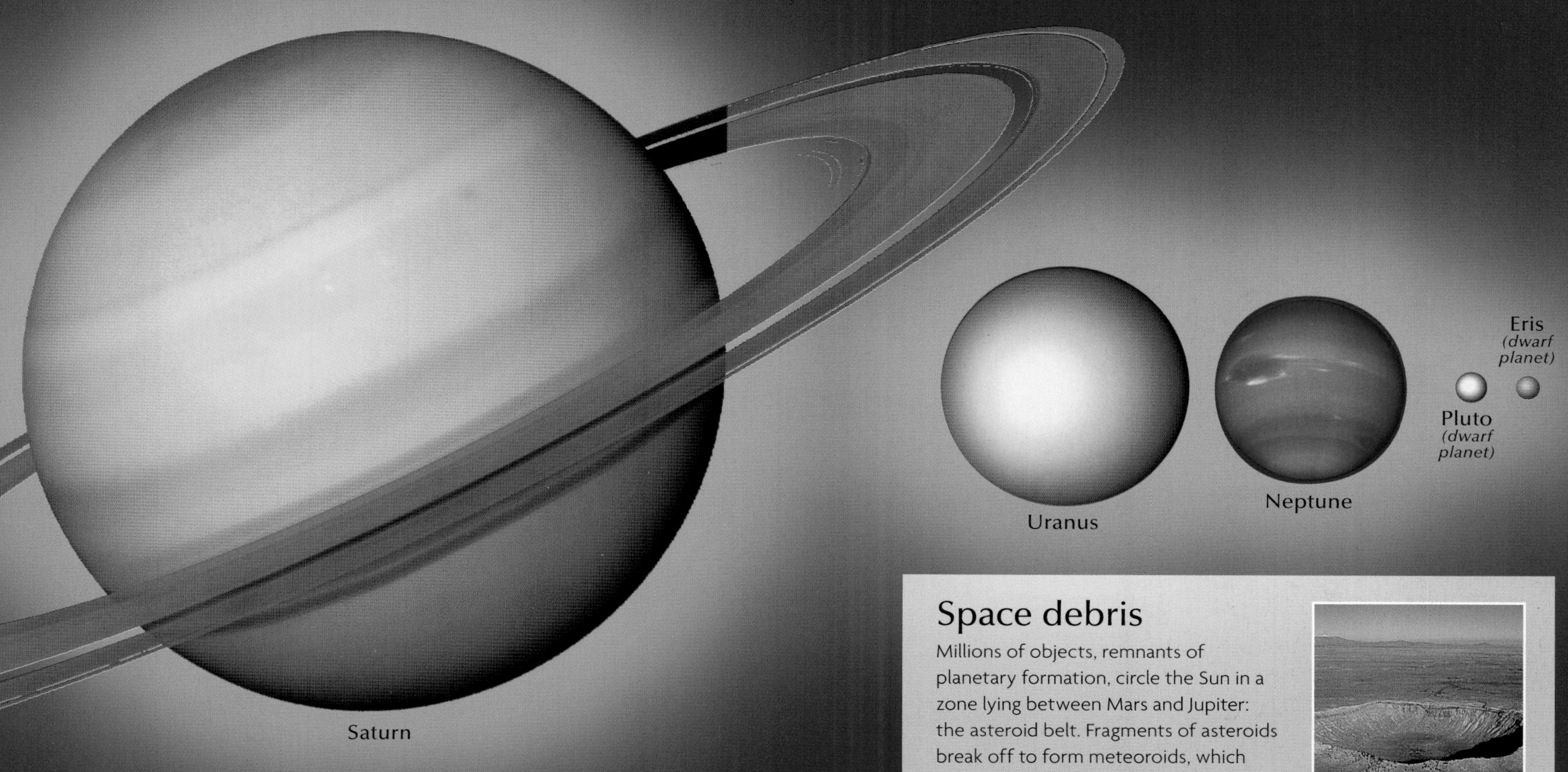

Saturn
Uranus
Neptune
Pluto (dwarf planet)
Eris (dwarf planet)

Space debris

Millions of objects, remnants of planetary formation, circle the Sun in a zone lying between Mars and Jupiter: the asteroid belt. Fragments of asteroids break off to form meteoroids, which can reach the Earth's surface. Comets, composed of ice and dust, originated outside our Solar System. Their elliptical orbit brings them close to the Sun and into the inner Solar System.

▲ ***Meteor Crater** in Arizona is 4200 ft (1300 m) wide and 660 ft (200 m) deep. It was formed over 10,000 years ago.*

Possible and actual meteorite craters

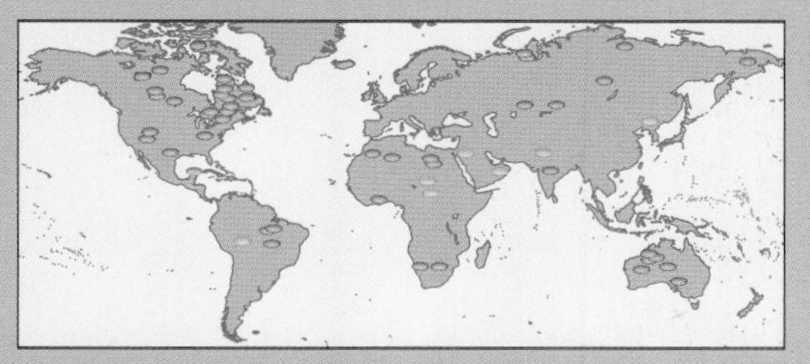

Map key
Possible impact craters
Meteorite impact craters

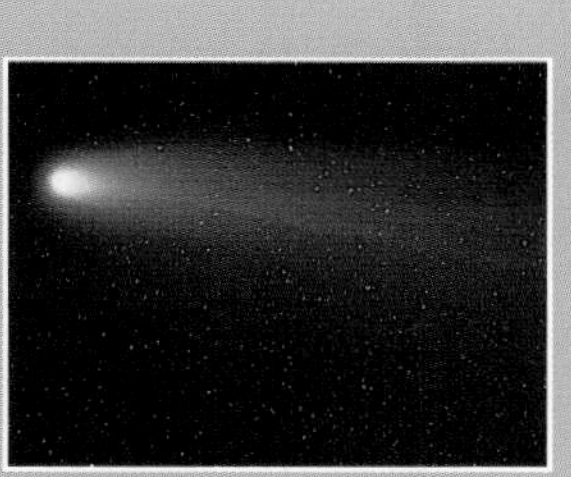

▲ ***The orbit of** Halley's Comet brings it close to the Earth every 76 years. It last visited in 1986.*

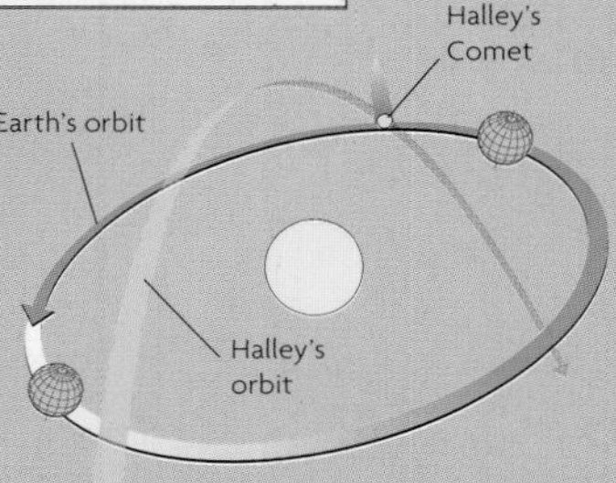

Halley's Comet
Earth's orbit
Halley's orbit

Orbit of Halley's Comet around the Sun

The Earth's atmosphere

During the early stages of the Earth's formation, ash, lava, carbon dioxide and water vapour were discharged onto the surface of the planet by constant volcanic eruptions. The water formed the oceans, while carbon dioxide entered the atmosphere or was dissolved in the oceans. Clouds, formed of water droplets, reflected some of the Sun's radiation back into space. The Earth's temperature stabilized and early life forms began to emerge, converting carbon dioxide into life-giving oxygen.

▲ ***It is thought** that the gases that make up the Earth's atmosphere originated deep within the interior, and were released many millions of years ago during intense volcanic actvity, similar to this eruption at Mount St. Helens.*

N O P Q R S T U V W X Y Z

The physical world

The Earth's surface is constantly being transformed: it is uplifted, folded and faulted by tectonic forces; weathered and eroded by wind, water and ice. Sometimes change is dramatic, the spectacular results of earthquakes or floods. More often it is a slow process lasting millions of years. A physical map of the world represents a snapshot of the ever-evolving architecture of the Earth. This terrain map shows the whole surface of the Earth, both above and below the sea.

The world in section

These cross-sections around the Earth, one in the northern hemisphere; one straddling the Equator, reveal the limited areas of land above sea level in comparison with the extent of the sea floor. The greater erosive effects of weathering by wind and water limit the upward elevation of land above sea level, while the deep oceans retain their dramatic mountain and trench profiles.

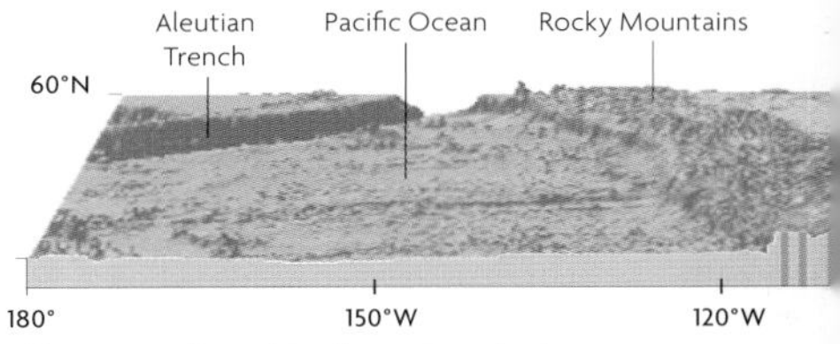

Aleutian Trench
Pacific Ocean
Rocky Mountains
60°N
180°
150°W
120°W

Cross-section: Northern hemisphere

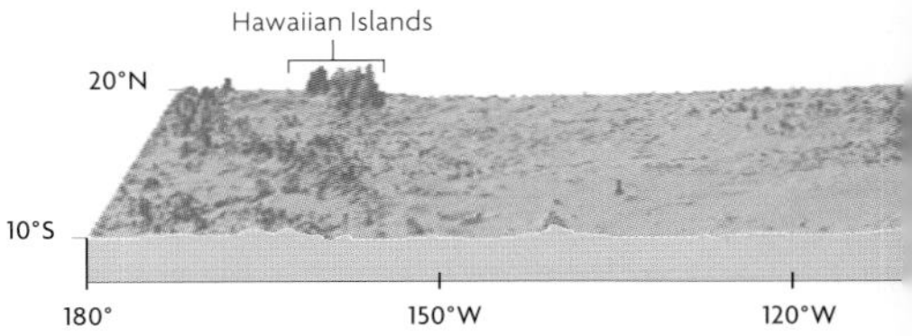

Hawaiian Islands
20°N
10°S
180°
150°W
120°W

Cross-section: Southern hemisphere

Map key

Geographical regions

- ice
- tundra
- needleleaf forest
- broadleaf forest
- cultivated land
- hot desert
- cold desert
- tropical grassland
- tropical rainforest
- mountain
- submarine regions

Scale 1:66,000,000

Km 0 250 500 1000 1500 2000

0 250 500 1000 1500 2000 Miles

projection: Wagner VII

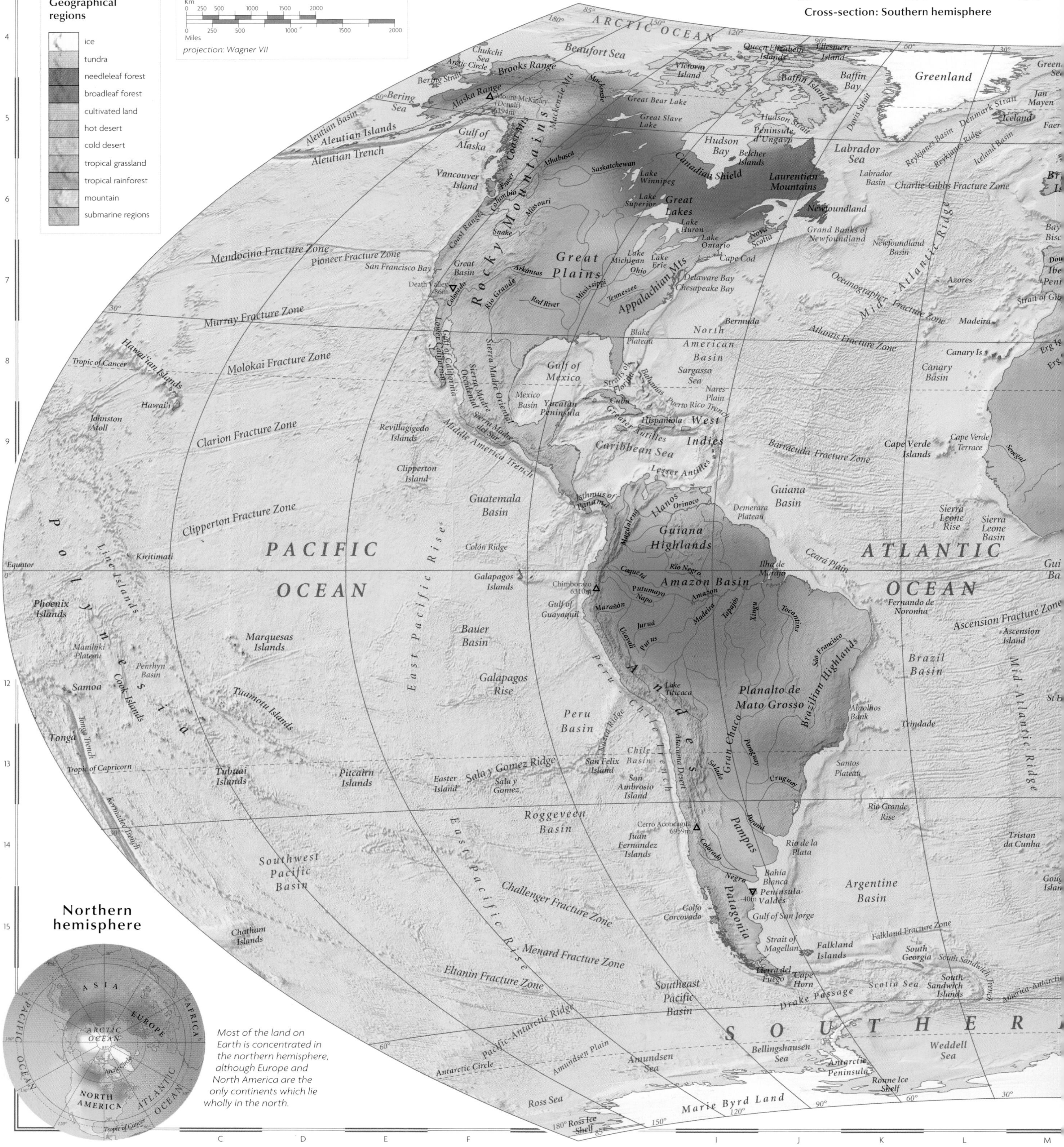

Northern hemisphere

ASIA
EUROPE
AFRICA
ARCTIC OCEAN
PACIFIC OCEAN
ATLANTIC OCEAN
NORTH AMERICA

Most of the land on Earth is concentrated in the northern hemisphere, although Europe and North America are the only continents which lie wholly in the north.

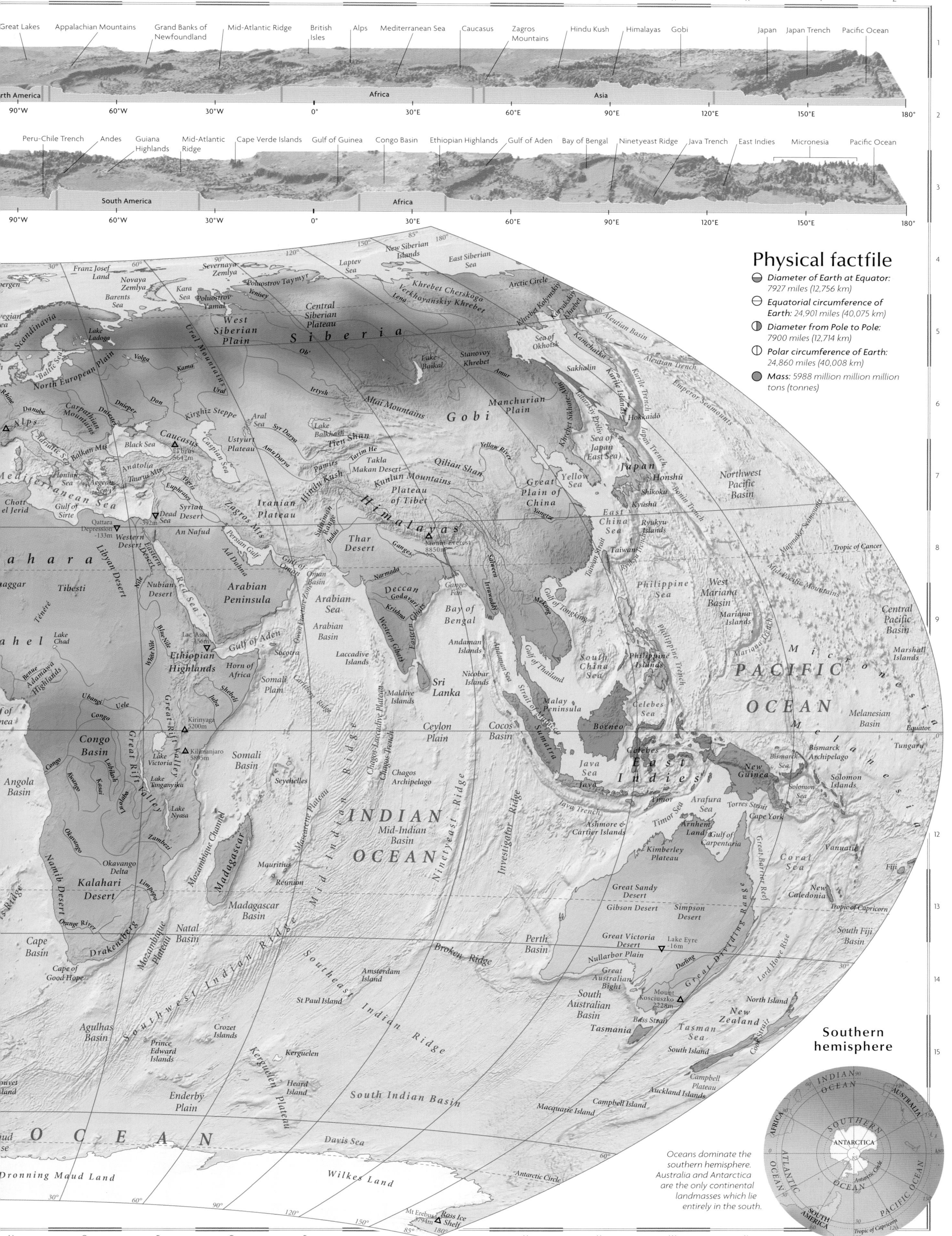
N O P Q R S T U V W X Y Z
Great Lakes
Appalachian Mountains
Grand Banks of Newfoundland
Mid-Atlantic Ridge
British Isles
Alps
Mediterranean Sea
Caucasus
Zagros Mountains
Hindu Kush
Himalayas
Gobi
Japan
Japan Trench
Pacific Ocean
North America
Africa
Asia
90°W 60°W 30°W 0° 30°E 60°E 90°E 120°E 150°E 180°
Peru-Chile Trench
Andes
Guiana Highlands
Mid-Atlantic Ridge
Cape Verde Islands
Gulf of Guinea
Congo Basin
Ethiopian Highlands
Gulf of Aden
Bay of Bengal
Ninetyeast Ridge
Java Trench
East Indies
Micronesia
Pacific Ocean
South America
Africa
Siberia
West Siberian Plain
Central Siberian Plateau
Gobi
Himalayas
Plateau of Tibet
Arabian Peninsula
Ethiopian Highlands
Congo Basin
Kalahari Desert
Madagascar
INDIAN OCEAN
PACIFIC OCEAN
East Indies
Borneo
Sumatra
New Guinea
Great Sandy Desert
Great Victoria Desert
Tasmania
New Zealand
Wilkes Land
Dronning Maud Land
Mt Everest 8850m
Kilimanjaro 5895m
Lake Eyre -16m
Mount Kosciuszko 2228m
Mt Erebus 3794m
Physical factfile
Diameter of Earth at Equator: 7927 miles (12,756 km)
Equatorial circumference of Earth: 24,901 miles (40,075 km)
Diameter from Pole to Pole: 7900 miles (12,714 km)
Polar circumference of Earth: 24,860 miles (40,008 km)
Mass: 5988 million million million tons (tonnes)
Southern hemisphere
INDIAN OCEAN
AUSTRALIA
SOUTHERN OCEAN
ANTARCTICA
ATLANTIC OCEAN
PACIFIC OCEAN
AFRICA
SOUTH AMERICA

Oceans dominate the southern hemisphere. Australia and Antarctica are the only continental landmasses which lie entirely in the south.

Structure of the Earth

The Earth as it is today is just the latest phase in a constant process of evolution which has occurred over the past 4.5 billion years. The Earth's continents are neither fixed nor stable; over the course of the Earth's history, propelled by currents rising from the intense heat at its centre, the great plates on which they lie have moved, collided, joined together, and separated. These processes continue to mould and transform the surface of the Earth, causing earthquakes and volcanic eruptions and creating oceans, mountain ranges, deep ocean trenches and island chains.

Inside the Earth

The Earth's hot inner core ismade up of solid iron, while the outer core is composed of liquid iron and nickel. The mantle nearest the core is viscous, whereas the rocky upper mantle is fairly rigid. The crust is the rocky outer shell of the Earth. Together, the upper mantle and the crust form the lithosphere.

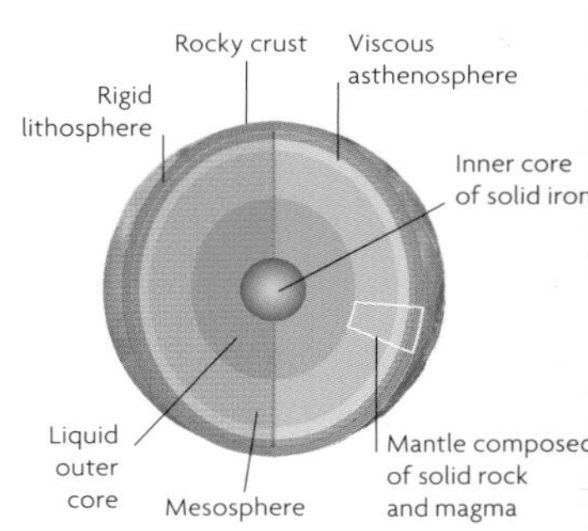
Rocky crust
Viscous asthenosphere
Rigid lithosphere
Inner core of solid iron
Liquid outer core
Mesosphere
Mantle composed of solid rock and magma

The dynamic Earth

The Earth's crust is made up of eight major (and several minor) rigid continental and oceanic tectonic plates, which fit closely together. The positions of the plates are not static. They are constantly moving relative to one another. The type of movement between plates affects the way in which they alter the structure of the Earth. The oldest parts of the plates, known as shields, are the most stable parts of the Earth and little tectonic activity occurs here.

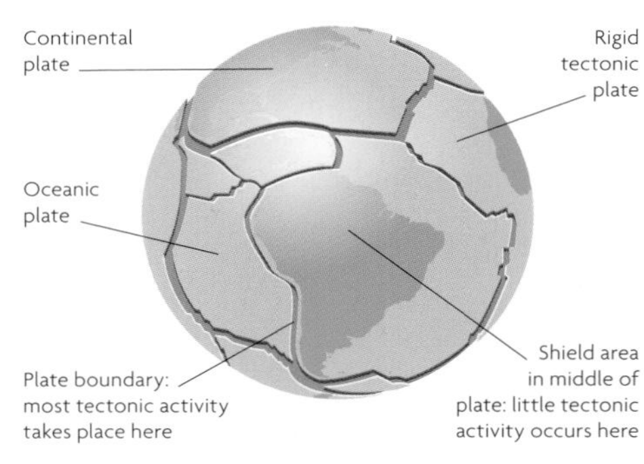
Continental plate
Rigid tectonic plate
Oceanic plate
Plate boundary: most tectonic activity takes place here
Shield area in middle of plate: little tectonic activity occurs here

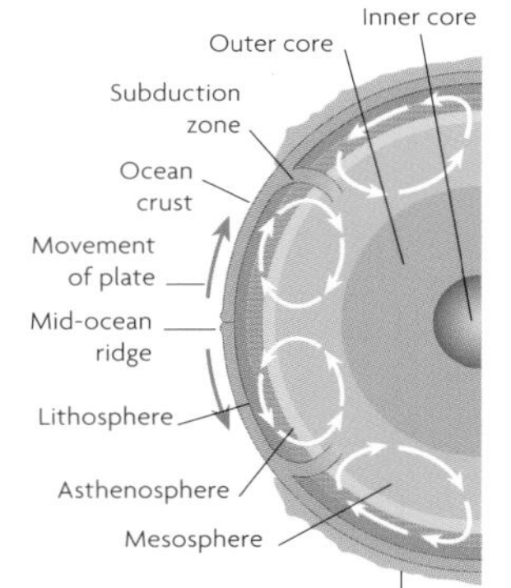
Inner core
Outer core
Subduction zone
Ocean crust
Movement of plate
Mid-ocean ridge
Lithosphere
Asthenosphere
Mesosphere
Continental crust

Convection currents

Deep within the Earth, at its inner core, temperatures may exceed 8100°F (4500°C). This heat warms rocks in the mesosphere which rise through the partially molten mantle, displacing cooler rocks just below the solid crust, which sink, and are warmed again by the heat of the mantle. This process is continually repeated, creating convection currents which form the moving force beneath the Earth's crust.

Plate boundaries

The boundaries between the plates are the areas where most tectonic activity takes place. Three types of movement occur at plate boundaries: the plates can either move towards each other, move apart, or slide past each other. The effect this has on the Earth's structure depends on whether the margin is between two continental plates, two oceanic plates or an oceanic and continental plate.

▲ *The Mid-Atlantic Ridge rises above sea level in Iceland, producing geysers and volcanoes.*

Mid-ocean ridges

—— Mid-ocean ridges are formed when two adjacent oceanic plates pull apart, allowing magma to force its way up to the surface, which then cools to form solid rock. Vast amounts of volcanic material are discharged at these mid-ocean ridges which can reach heights of 10,000 ft (3000 m).

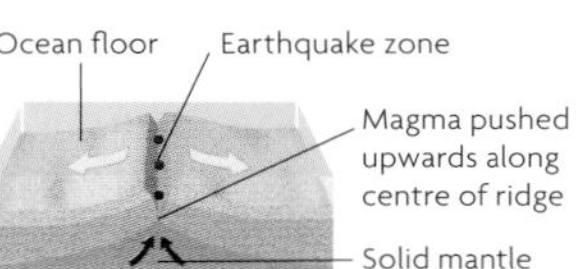
Ocean floor
Earthquake zone
Magma pushed upwards along centre of ridge
Solid mantle

Formation of a mid-ocean ridge

▲ *Mount Pinatubo is an active volcano, lying on the Pacific 'Ring of Fire'.*

Ocean plates meeting

△△ Oceanic crust is denser and thinner than continental crust; on average it is 3 miles (5 km) thick, while continental crust averages 18–24 miles (30–40 km). When oceanic plates of similar density meet, the crust is contorted as one plate overrides the other, forming deep sea trenches and volcanic island arcs above sea level.

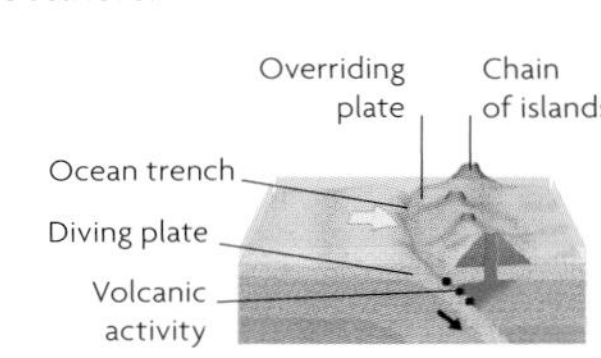
Overriding plate
Chain of islands
Ocean trench
Diving plate
Volcanic activity

Ocean plates meeting to form an island arc

Tectonic activity

- - - - uncertain plate boundary
▲ volcanic zone
● earthquake zone
● hot spot
rift valley

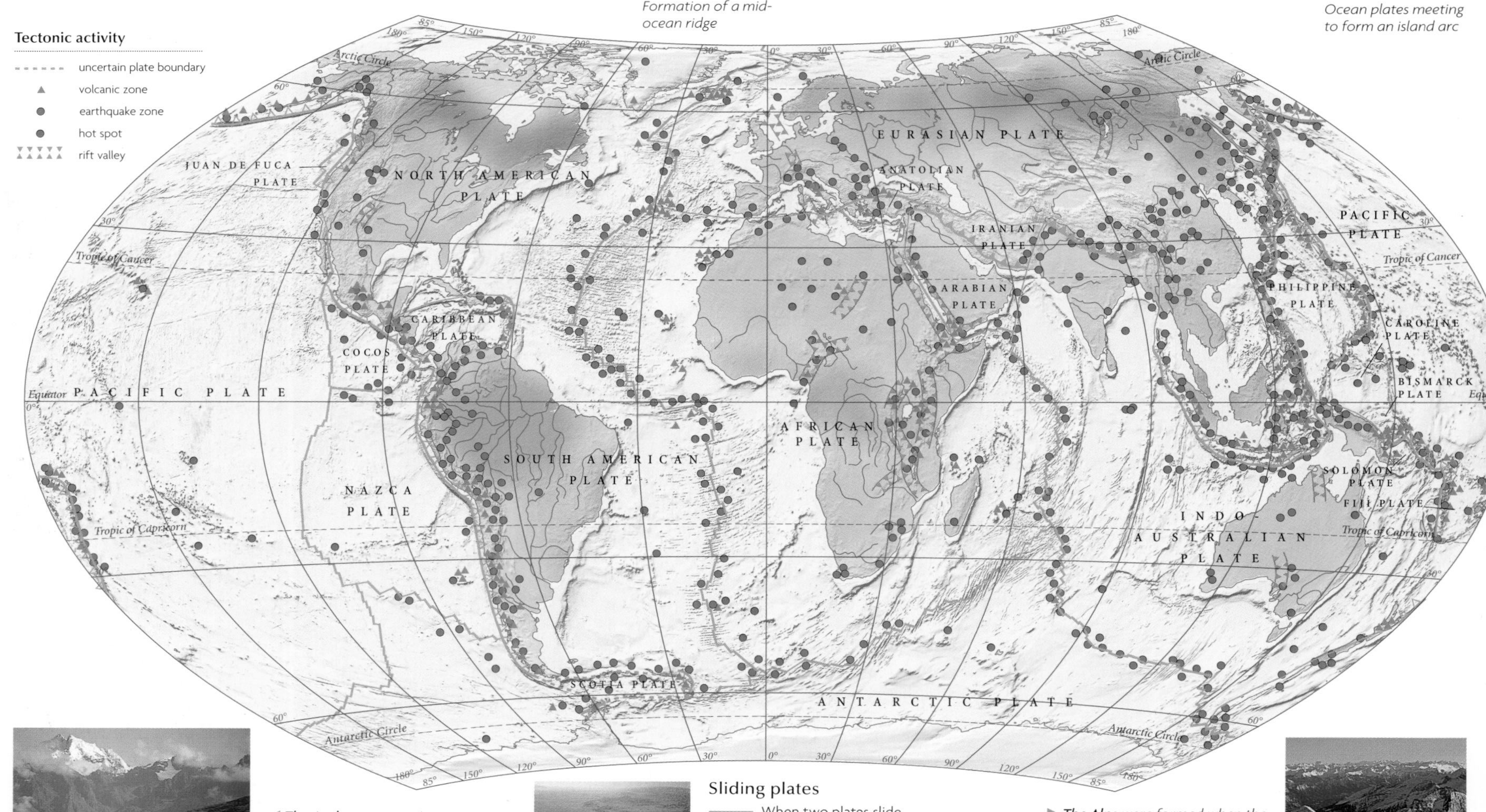
Arctic Circle
JUAN DE FUCA PLATE
NORTH AMERICAN PLATE
EURASIAN PLATE
ANATOLIAN PLATE
IRANIAN PLATE
ARABIAN PLATE
PACIFIC PLATE
PHILIPPINE PLATE
CAROLINE PLATE
BISMARCK PLATE
Tropic of Cancer
CARIBBEAN PLATE
COCOS PLATE
Equator
PACIFIC PLATE
AFRICAN PLATE
SOUTH AMERICAN PLATE
NAZCA PLATE
SOLOMON PLATE
FIJI PLATE
INDO-AUSTRALIAN PLATE
Tropic of Capricorn
SCOTIA PLATE
ANTARCTIC PLATE
Antarctic Circle

Diving plates

△△ When an oceanic and a continental plate meet, the denser oceanic plate is driven underneath the continental plate, which is crumpled by the collision to form mountain ranges. As the ocean plate plunges downward, it heats up, and molten rock (magma) is forced up to the surface.

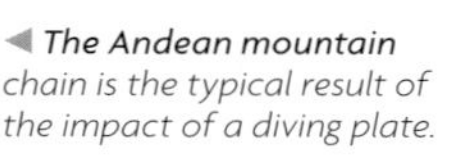

◀ *The Andean mountain chain is the typical result of the impact of a diving plate.*

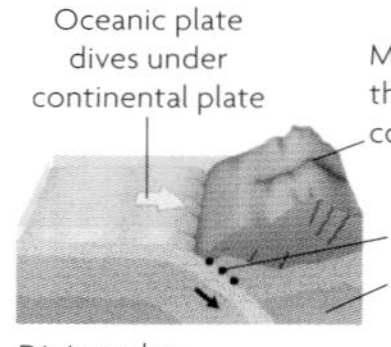
Oceanic plate dives under continental plate
Mountains thrust up by collision
Earthquake zone
Continental plate

Diving plate

▲ *The deep fracture caused by the sliding plates of the San Andreas Fault can be clearly seen in parts of California.*

Sliding plates

—— When two plates slide past each other, friction is caused along the fault line which divides them. The plates do not move smoothly, and the uneven movement causes earthquakes.

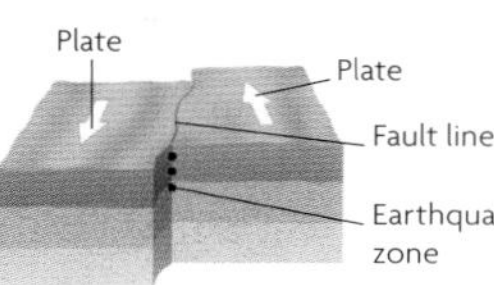
Plate
Plate
Fault line
Earthquake zone

Sliding plates

▶ *The Alps were formed when the African Plate collided with the Eurasian Plate, about 65 million years ago.*

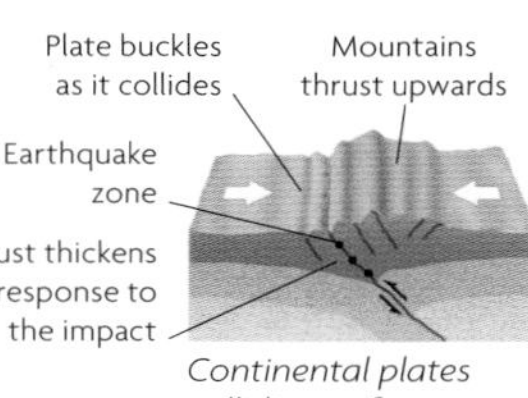
Plate buckles as it collides
Mountains thrust upwards
Earthquake zone
Crust thickens in response to the impact

Continental plates colliding to form a mountain range

Colliding plates

▲▲▲ When two continental plates collide, great mountain chains are thrust upwards as the crust buckles and folds under the force of the impact.

Continental drift

Although the plates which make up the Earth's crust move only a few centimetres in a year, over the millions of years of the Earth's history, its continents have moved many thousands of kilometres, to create new continents, oceans and mountain chains.

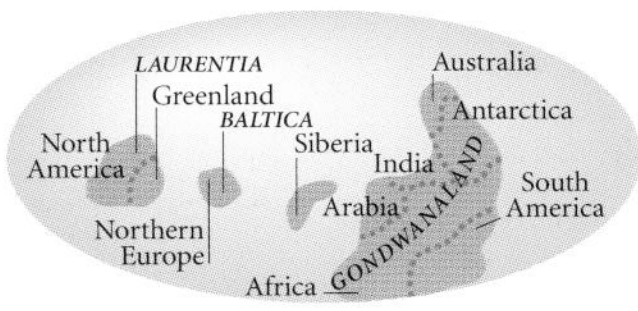
LAURENTIA
Greenland
BALTICA
North America
Siberia
India
Australia
Antarctica
South America
Arabia
Northern Europe
Africa
GONDWANALAND

1: Cambrian period

570–510 million years ago. Most continents are in tropical latitudes. The supercontinent of Gondwanaland reaches the South Pole.

Greenland
SIBERIA
LAURENTIA
/BALTICA
North America
Northern Europe
South Asia
Kazakhstania
Africa
Arabia
Australia
South America
India
Antarctica
GONDWANALAND

2: Devonian period

408–362 million years ago. The continents of Gondwanaland and Laurentia are drifting northwards.

ANGARALAND
Siberia
LAURENTIA
Northwest China
North America
Greenland
Northern Europe
Antarctica
Australia
South America
Arabia
Africa
GONDWANALAND

3: Carboniferous period

362–290 million years ago. The Earth is dominated by three continents; Laurentia, Angaraland and Gondwanaland.

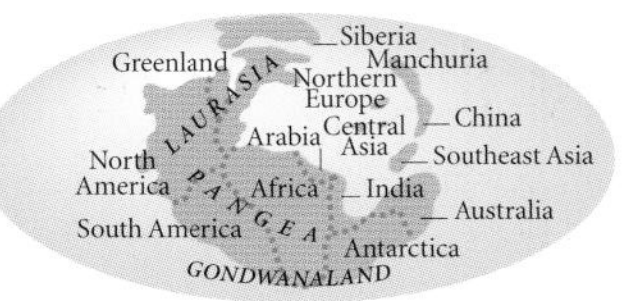
Greenland
Siberia
Manchuria
Northern Europe
LAURASIA
China
North America
Arabia
Central Asia
Southeast Asia
Africa
India
South America
PANGEA
Australia
Antarctica
GONDWANALAND

4: Triassic period

245–208 million years ago. All three major continents have joined to form the super-continent of Pangea.

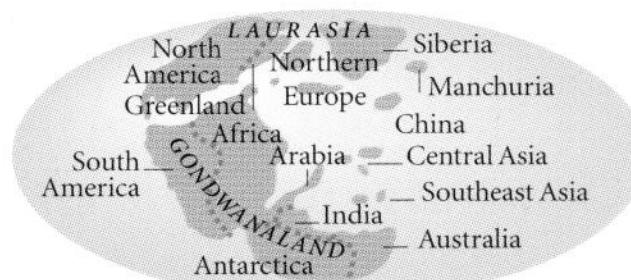
LAURASIA
North America
Greenland
Northern Europe
Siberia
Manchuria
China
Africa
Arabia
Central Asia
Southeast Asia
South America
India
Australia
GONDWANALAND
Antarctica

5: Jurassic period

208–145 million years ago. The super-continent of Pangea begins to break up, causing an overall rise in sea levels.

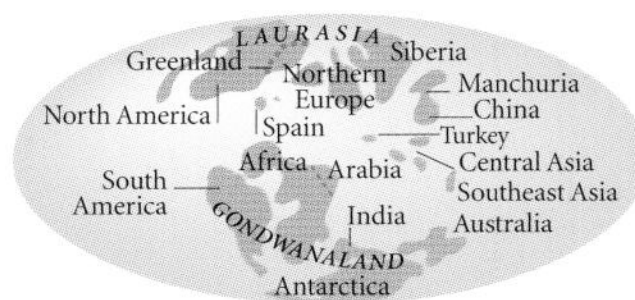
Greenland
LAURASIA
Siberia
Northern Europe
Manchuria
North America
Spain
China
Turkey
Africa
Arabia
Central Asia
Southeast Asia
South America
India
Australia
GONDWANALAND
Antarctica

6: Cretaceous period

145–65 million years ago. Warm shallow seas cover much of the land: sea levels are about 80 ft (25 m) above present levels.

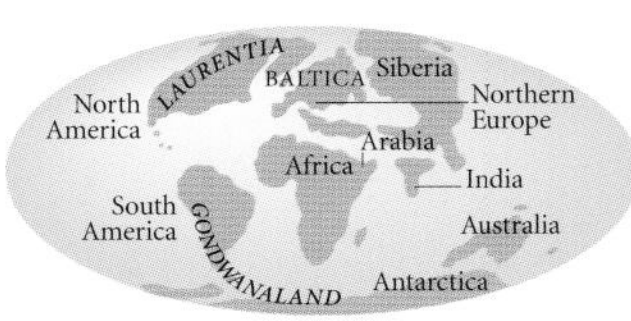
LAURENTIA
BALTICA
Siberia
North America
Northern Europe
Arabia
Africa
India
South America
Australia
GONDWANALAND
Antarctica

7: Tertiary period

65–2 million years ago. Although the world's geography is becoming more recognizable, major events such as the creation of the Himalayan mountain chain, are still to occur during this period.

Continental shields

The centres of the Earth's continents, known as shields, were established between 2500 and 500 million years ago; some contain rocks over three billion years old. They were formed by a series of turbulent events: plate movements, earthquakes and volcanic eruptions. Since the Pre-Cambrian period, over 570 million years ago, they have experienced little tectonic activity, and today, these flat, low-lying slabs of solidified molten rock form the stable centres of the continents. They are bounded or covered by successive belts of younger sedimentary rock.

Canadian (Laurentian)
Scandinavian (Fenno-Scandian)
Siberian
Korean
Indian
African
Guyana (Venezuelan)
Brazilian
Australian
Antarctic

The Hawai'ian island chain

A hot spot lying deep beneath the Pacific Ocean pushes a plume of magma from the Earth's mantle up through the Pacific Plate to form volcanic islands. While the hot spot remains stationary, the plate on which the islands sit is moving slowly. A long chain of islands has been created as the plate passes over the hot spot.

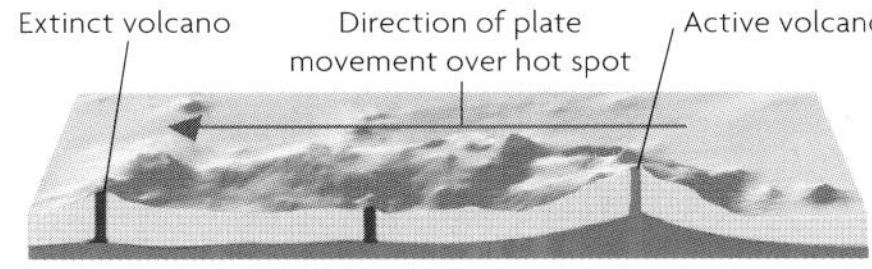
Extinct volcano
Direction of plate movement over hot spot
Active volcano

Cross-section through the Hawai'ian Islands

Evolution of the Hawai'ian Islands

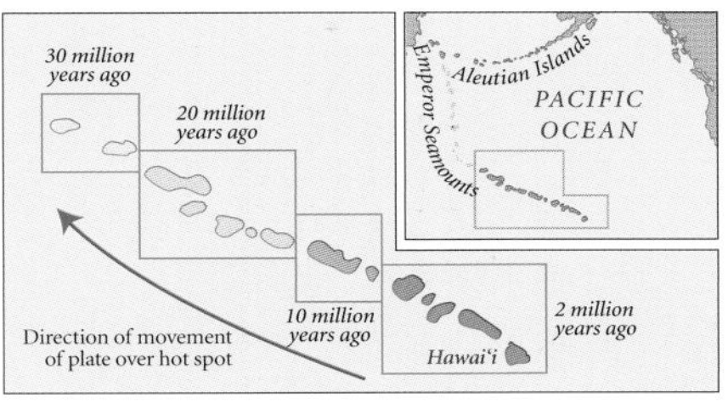
30 million years ago
20 million years ago
10 million years ago
2 million years ago
Hawai'i
Direction of movement of plate over hot spot
Emperor Seamounts
Aleutian Islands
PACIFIC OCEAN

Creation of the Himalayas

Between 10 and 20 million years ago, the Indian subcontinent, part of the ancient continent of Gondwanaland, collided with the continent of Asia. The Indo-Australian Plate continued to move northwards, displacing continental crust and uplifting the Himalayas, the world's highest mountain chain.

Movements of India

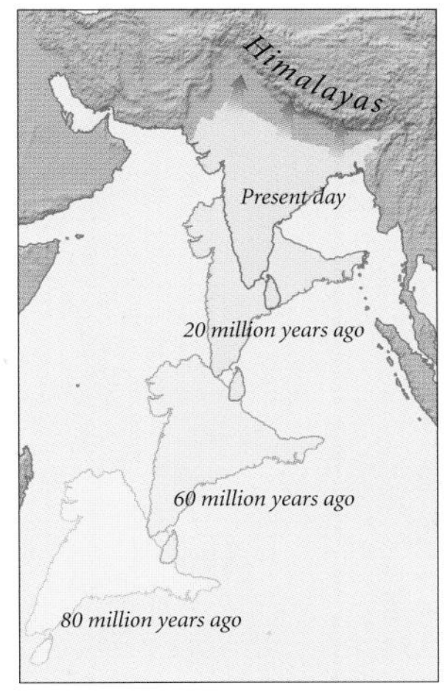
Himalayas
Present day
20 million years ago
60 million years ago
80 million years ago

Force of collision pushes up mountains

Cross-section through the Himalayas

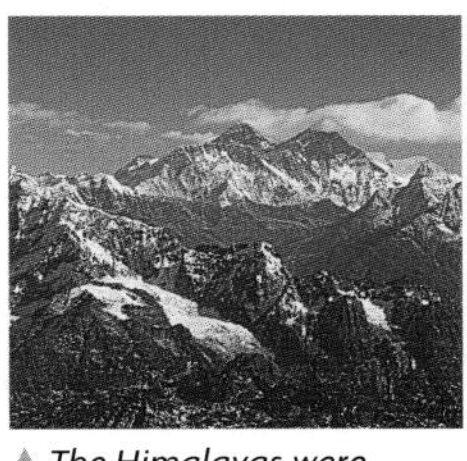

▲ *The Himalayas were uplifted when the Indian subcontinent collided with Asia.*

The Earth's geology

The Earth's rocks are created in a continual cycle. Exposed rocks are weathered and eroded by wind, water and chemicals and deposited as sediments. If they pass into the Earth's crust they will be transformed by high temperatures and pressures into metamorphic rocks or they will melt and solidify as igneous rocks.

Sandstone

8 Sandstones are sedimentary rocks formed mainly in deserts, beaches and deltas. Desert sandstones are formed of grains of quartz which have been well rounded by wind erosion.

▲ ***Rock stacks** of desert sandstone, at Bryce Canyon National Park, Utah, USA.*

◀ ***Extrusive igneous rocks** are formed during volcanic eruptions, as here in Hawai'i.*

Andesite

7 Andesite is an extrusive igneous rock formed from magma which has solidified on the Earth's crust after a volcanic eruption.

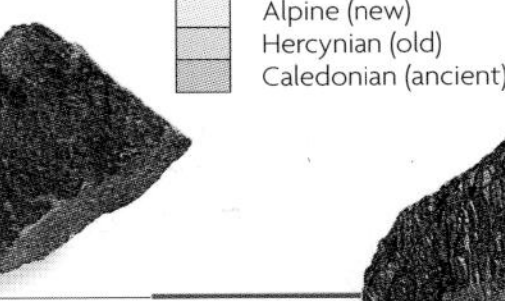

▲ ***Gneiss formations in** Norway's Jotunheimen Mountains.*

Gneiss

1 Gneiss is a metamorphic rock made at great depth during the formation of mountain chains, when intense heat and pressure transform sedimentary or igneous rocks.

◀ ***Basalt columns at** Giant's Causeway, Northern Ireland, UK.*

Basalt

2 Basalt is an igneous rock, formed when small quantities of magma lying close to the Earth's surface cool rapidly.

Limestone

3 Limestone is a sedimentary rock, which is formed mainly from the calcite skeletons of marine animals which have been compressed into rock.

▲ ***Limestone hills, Guilin,** China.*

Coral

4 Coral reefs are formed from the skeletons of millions of individual corals.

▲ ***Great Barrier Reef,** Australia.*

Geological regions

- continental shield
- sedimentary cover
- coral formation
- igneous rock types

Mountain ranges

- Alpine (new)
- Hercynian (old)
- Caledonian (ancient)

Schist

6 Schist is a metamorphic rock formed during mountain building, when temperature and pressure are comparatively high. Both mudstones and shales reform into schist under these conditions.

▶ ***Schist formations in** the Atlas Mountains, northwestern Africa.*

Granite

5 Granite is an intrusive igneous rock formed from magma which has solidified deep within the Earth's crust. The magma cools slowly, producing a coarse-grained rock.

▶ ***Namibia's Namaqualand Plateau** is formed of granite.*

Shaping the landscape

The basic material of the Earth's surface is solid rock: valleys, deserts, soil, and sand are all evidence of the powerful agents of weathering, erosion, and deposition which constantly shape and transform the Earth's landscapes. Water, either flowing continually in rivers or seas, or frozen and compacted into solid sheets of ice, has the most clearly visible impact on the Earth's surface. But wind can transport fragments of rock over huge distances and strip away protective layers of vegetation, exposing rock surfaces to the impact of extreme heat and cold.

Coastal water

The world's coastlines are constantly changing; every day, tides deposit, sift and sort sand, and gravel on the shoreline. Over longer periods, powerful wave action erodes cliffs and headlands and carves out bays.

▶ ***A low, wide** sandy beach on South Africa's Cape Peninsula is continually re-shaped by the action of the Atlantic waves.*

▲ ***The sheer chalk** cliffs at Seven Sisters in southern England are constantly under attack from waves.*

Water

Less than 2% of the world's water is on the land, but it is the most powerful agent of landscape change. Water, as rainfall, groundwater and rivers, can transform landscapes through both erosion and deposition. Eroded material carried by rivers forms the world's most fertile soils.

▲ ***Waterfalls such as** the Iguaçu Falls on the border between Argentina and southern Brazil, erode the underlying rock, causing the falls to retreat.*

Groundwater

In regions where there are porous rocks such as chalk, water is stored underground in large quantities; these reservoirs of water are known as aquifers. Rain percolates through topsoil into the underlying bedrock, creating an underground store of water. The limit of the saturated zone is called the water table.

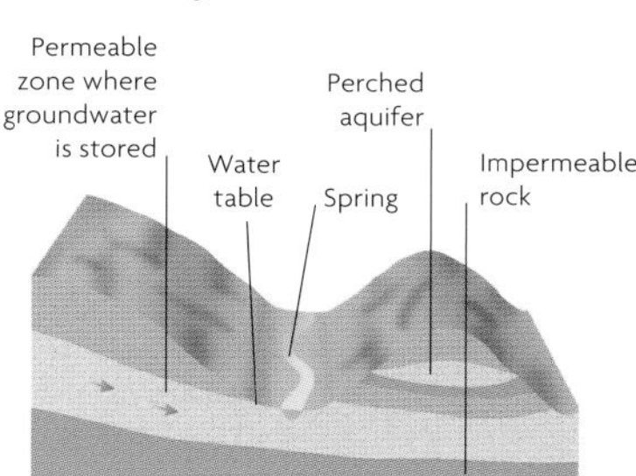
Permeable zone where groundwater is stored
Water table
Spring
Perched aquifer
Impermeable rock

Storage of groundwater in an aquifer

World river systems

drainage basin

World river systems: Sediment deposited annually per drainage basin

tons per sq mile per year: 9120, 6080, 1520, 760

tonnes per sq km per year: 2400, 1600, 400, 200 and less

ARCTIC OCEAN · PACIFIC OCEAN · ATLANTIC OCEAN · INDIAN OCEAN · Arctic Circle · Tropic of Cancer · Equator · Tropic of Capricorn · Antarctic Circle

Yukon · Mackenzie · Nelson · Columbia · St. Lawrence · Mississippi/Missouri · Colorado · Rio Grande · Orinoco · Amazon · São Francisco · Paraná · Niger · Nile · Congo · Zambezi · Orange · Rhine · Danube · Volga · Tigris/Euphrates · Ob' · Yenisey · Lena · Amur · Indus · Ganges/Brahmaputra · Yellow River · Yangtze · Mekong · Murray/Darling

Rivers

Rivers erode the land by grinding and dissolving rocks and stones. Most erosion occurs in the river's upper course as it flows through highland areas. Rock fragments are moved along the river bed by fast-flowing water and deposited in areas where the river slows down, such as flat plains, or where the river enters seas or lakes.

River valleys

Over long periods of time rivers erode uplands to form characteristic V-shaped valleys with smooth sides.

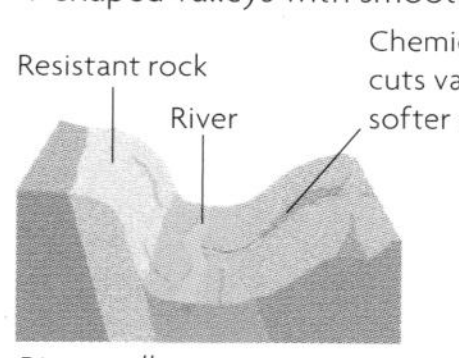
Resistant rock
River
Chemical erosion cuts valley in softer rock

River valley erosion

Deltas

When a river deposits its load of silt and sediment (alluvium) on entering the sea, it may form a delta. As this material accumulates, it chokes the mouth of the river, forcing it to create new channels to reach the sea.

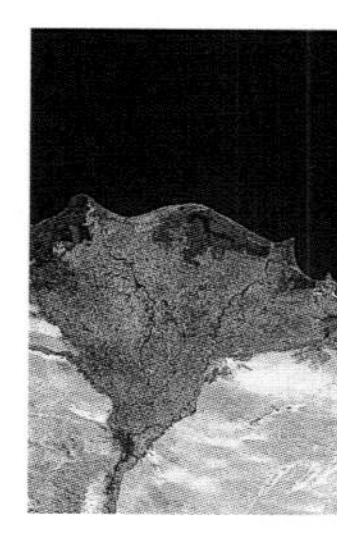

▶ ***The Nile forms** a broad delta as it flows into the Mediterranean.*

Drainage basins

The drainage basin is the area of land drained by a major trunk river and its smaller branch rivers or tributaries. Drainage basins are separated from one another by natural boundaries known as watersheds.

Watershed · Major trunk river · Alps · Dolomites · Apennines · Tributary river · Delta · River mouth · Po Valley

The drainage basin of the Po river, northern Italy.

Meanders

In their lower courses, rivers flow slowly. As they flow across the lowlands, they form looping bends called meanders.

▲ ***The Mississippi River** forms meanders as it flows across the southern US.*

▲ ***The meanders of** Utah's San Juan River have become deeply incised.*

◀ ***Mud is deposited** by China's Yellow River in its lower course.*

Deposition

When rivers have deposited large quantities of fertile alluvium, they are forced to find new channels through the alluvium deposits, creating braided river systems.

Landslides

Heavy rain and associated flooding on slopes can loosen underlying rocks, which crumble, causing the top layers of rock and soil to slip.

▶ ***A huge landslide** in the Swiss Alps has left massive piles of rocks and pebbles called scree.*

▲ ***A deep gully** in the French Alps caused by the scouring of upper layers of turf.*

Gullies

In areas where soil is thin, rainwater is not effectively absorbed, and may flow overland. The water courses downhill in channels, or gullies, and may lead to rapid erosion of soil.

Ice

During its long history, the Earth has experienced a number of glacial episodes when temperatures were considerably lower than today. During the last Ice Age, 18,000 years ago, ice covered an area three times larger than it does today. Over these periods, the ice has left a remarkable legacy of transformed landscapes.

Glaciers

Glaciers are formed by the compaction of snow into 'rivers' of ice. As they move over the landscape, glaciers pick up and carry a load of rocks and boulders which erode the landscape they pass over, and are eventually deposited at the end of the glacier.

▲ ***A massive glacier*** *advancing down a valley in southern Argentina.*

Post-glacial features

When a glacial episode ends, the retreating ice leaves many features. These include depositional ridges called moraines, which may be eroded into low hills known as drumlins; sinuous ridges called eskers; kames, which are rounded hummocks; depressions known as kettle holes; and windblown loess deposits.

Kame terrace
Retreating glacier
Kettle hole
Esker
Drumlin
Braided river
Terminal moraine
Windblown loess
Glacial till
Bedrock

Post-glacial landscape features

Glacial valleys

Glaciers can erode much more powerfully than rivers. They form steep-sided, flat-bottomed valleys with a typical U-shaped profile. Valleys created by tributary glaciers, whose floors have not been eroded to the same depth as the main glacial valley floor, are called hanging valleys

▲ ***The U-shaped profile*** *and piles of morainic debris are characteristic of a valley once filled by a glacier.*

▲ ***A series of*** *hanging valleys high up in the Chilean Andes.*

Past and present world ice-cover and glacial features

Past and present world ice cover and glacial features

extent of last Ice Age
loess deposits
post-glacial feature
glacial feature
present day ice cover
glacial field

Ice shattering

Water drips into fissures in rocks and freezes, expanding as it does so. The pressure weakens the rock, causing it to crack, and eventually to shatter into polygonal patterns.

▲ ***Irregular polygons show*** *through the sedge-grass tundra in the Yukon, Canada.*

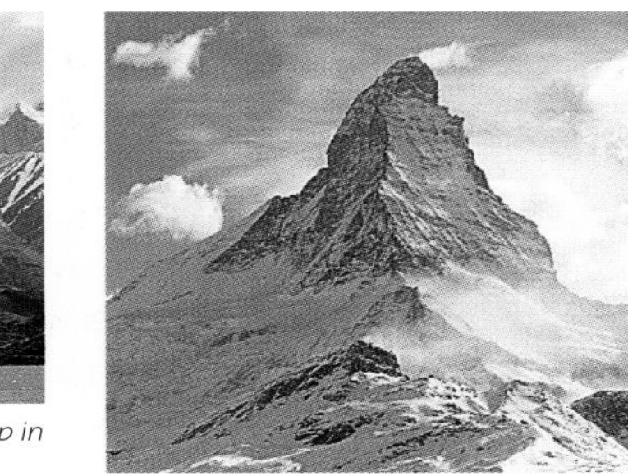

▲ ***The profile of*** *the Matterhorn has been formed by three cirques lying 'back-to-back'.*

Cirques

Cirques are basin-shaped hollows which mark the head of a glaciated valley. Where neighboring cirques meet, they are divided by sharp rock ridges called arêtes. It is these arêtes which give the Matterhorn its characteristic profile.

Fjords

Fjords are ancient glacial valleys flooded by the sea following the end of a period of glaciation. Beneath the water, the valley floor can be 4000 ft (1300 m) deep.

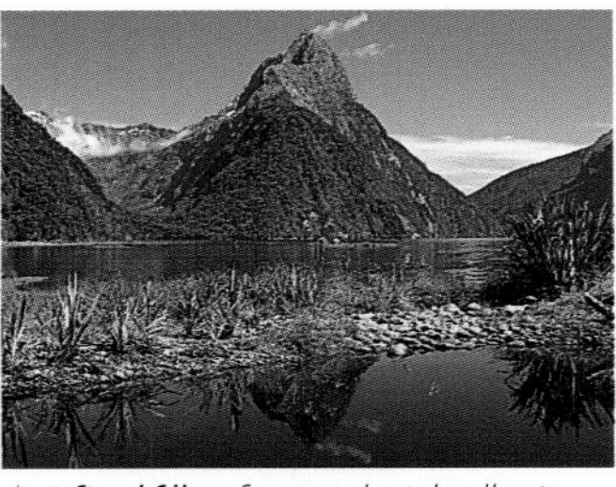

▲ ***A fjord fills*** *a former glacial valley in southern New Zealand.*

Periglaciation

Periglacial areas occur near to the edge of ice sheets. A layer of frozen ground lying just beneath the surface of the land is known as permafrost. When the surface melts in the summer, the water is unable to drain into the frozen ground, and so 'creeps' downhill, a process known as solifluction.

Wind

Strong winds can transport rock fragments great distances, especially where there is little vegetation to protect the rock. In desert areas, wind picks up loose, unprotected sand particles, carrying them over great distances. This powerfully abrasive debris is blasted at the surface by the wind, eroding the landscape into dramatic shapes.

Prevailing winds and dust trajectories

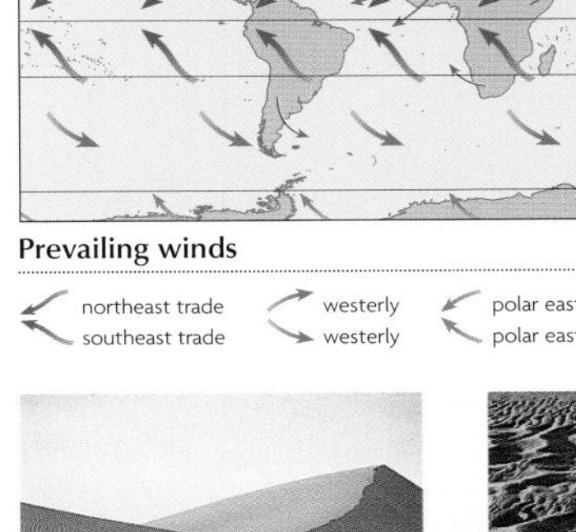

Prevailing winds: northeast trade, southeast trade; westerly, westerly; polar easterly, polar easterly
Dust trajectories: trajectory of aeolian dust

Deposition

The rocky, stony floors of the world's deserts are swept and scoured by strong winds. The smaller, finer particles of sand are shaped into surface ripples, dunes, or sand mountains, which rise to a height of 650 ft (200 m). Dunes usually form single lines, running perpendicular to the direction of the prevailing wind. These long, straight ridges can extend for over 100 miles (160 km).

▲ ***Barchan dunes in*** *the Arabian Desert.*

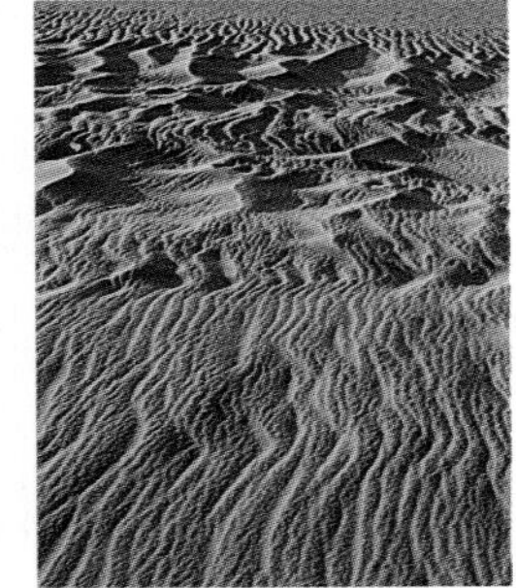

▲ ***Complex dune system*** *in the Sahara.*

Dunes

Dunes are shaped by wind direction and sand supply. Where sand supply is limited, crescent-shaped barchan dunes are formed.

Types of dune

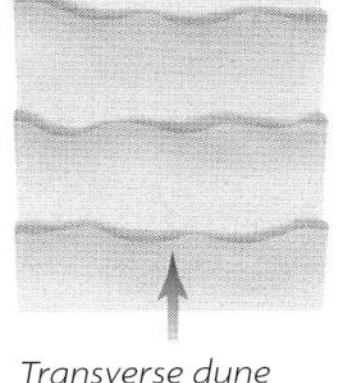

Wind direction

Transverse dune

Barchan dune

Linear dune

Star dune

Hot and cold deserts

Main desert types: hot arid; semi-arid; cold polar

Temperature

Most of the world's deserts are in the tropics. The cold deserts which occur elsewhere are arid because they are a long way from the rain-giving sea. Rock in deserts is exposed because of lack of vegetation and is susceptible to changes in temperature; extremes of heat and cold can cause both cracks and fissures to appear in the rock.

Heat

Fierce sun can heat the surface of rock, causing it to expand more rapidly than the cooler, underlying layers. This creates tensions which force the rock to crack or break up. In arid regions, the evaporation of water from rock surfaces dissolves certain minerals within the water, causing salt crystals to form in small openings in the rock. The hard crystals force the openings to widen into cracks and fissures.

▲ ***The cracked and*** *parched floor of Death Valley, California. This is one of the hottest deserts on Earth.*

Desert abrasion

Abrasion creates a wide range of desert landforms from faceted pebbles and wind ripples in the sand, to large-scale features such as yardangs (low, streamlined ridges), and scoured desert pavements.

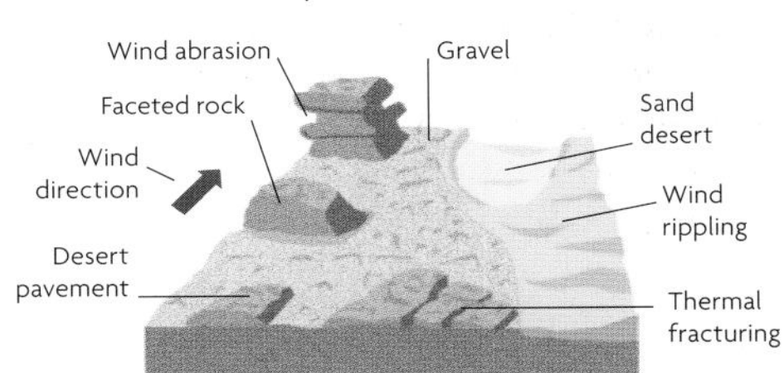
Wind abrasion
Gravel
Faceted rock
Sand desert
Wind direction
Wind rippling
Desert pavement
Thermal fracturing

Features of a desert surface

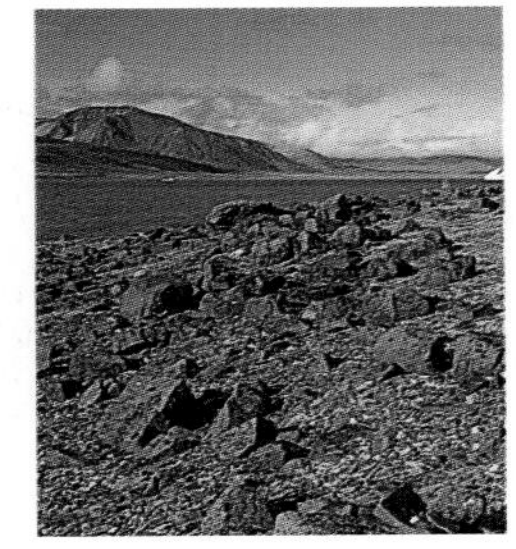

◀ ***This dry valley*** *at Ellesmere Island in the Canadian Arctic is an example of a cold desert. The cracked floor and scoured slopes are features also found in hot deserts.*

The world's oceans

Two-thirds of the Earth's surface is covered by the oceans. The landscape of the ocean floor, like the surface of the land, has been shaped by movements of the Earth's crust over millions of years to form volcanic mountain ranges, deep trenches, basins and plateaux. Ocean currents constantly redistribute warm and cold water around the world. A major warm current, such as El Niño in the Pacific Ocean, can increase surface temperature by up to 10°F (8°C), causing changes in weather patterns which can lead to both droughts and flooding.

The great oceans

There are five oceans on Earth: the Pacific, Atlantic, Indian and Southern oceans, and the much smaller Arctic Ocean. These five ocean basins are relatively young, having evolved within the last 80 million years. One of the most recent plate collisions, between the Eurasian and African plates, created the present-day arrangement of continents and oceans.

▲ ***The Indian Ocean** accounts for approximately 20% of the total area of the world's oceans.*

Sea level

If the influence of tides, winds, currents and variations in gravity were ignored, the surface of the Earth's oceans would closely follow the topography of the ocean floor, with an underwater ridge 3000 ft (915 m) high producing a rise of up to 3 ft (1 m) in the level of the surface water.

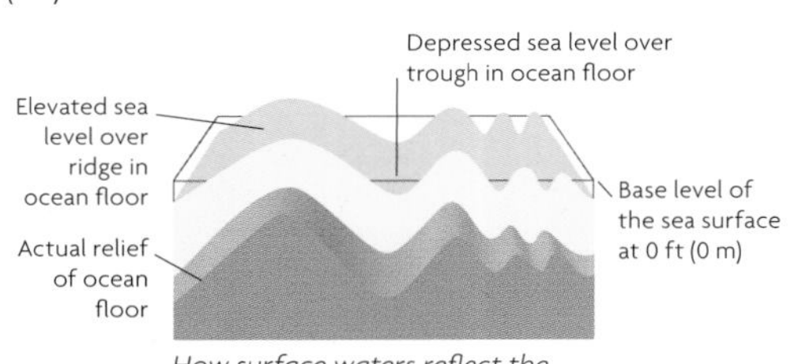

Depressed sea level over trough in ocean floor
Elevated sea level over ridge in ocean floor
Base level of the sea surface at 0 ft (0 m)
Actual relief of ocean floor

How surface waters reflect the relief of the ocean floor

▲ ***The low relief** of many small Pacific islands such as these atolls at Huahine in French Polynesia makes them vulnerable to changes in sea level.*

Ocean structure

The continental shelf is a shallow, flat sea-bed surrounding the Earth's continents. It extends to the continental slope, which falls to the ocean floor. Here, the flat abyssal plains are interrupted by vast, underwater mountain ranges, the mid-ocean ridges, and ocean trenches which plunge to depths of 35,828 ft (10,920 m).

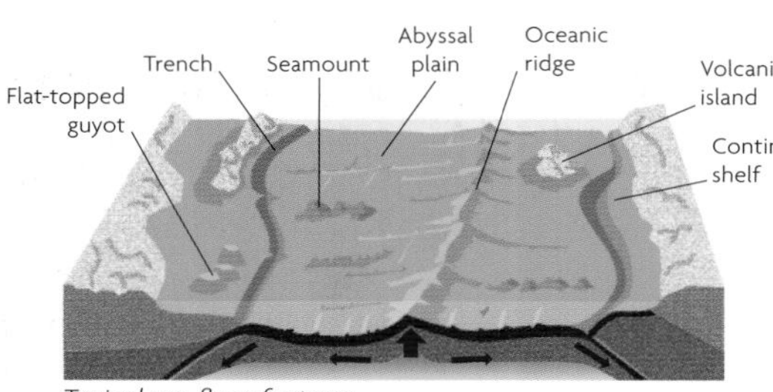
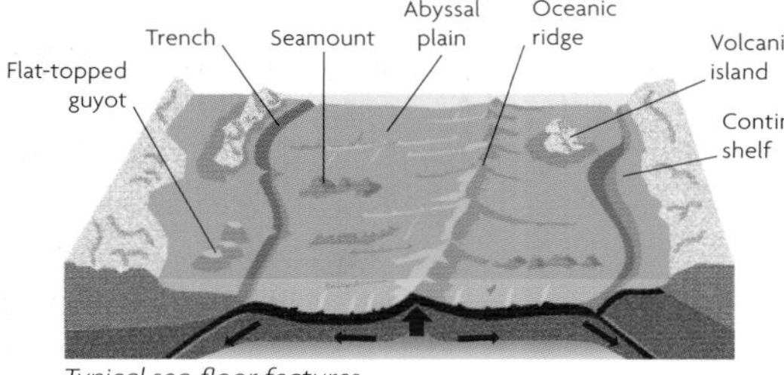

Flat-topped guyot
Trench
Seamount
Abyssal plain
Oceanic ridge
Volcanic island
Continental shelf

Typical sea-floor features

Arctic Circle
Barents Sea
Kara Sea
Laptev Sea
ARCTI
East Siber Sea
North Sea
Baltic Sea
EUROPE
ASIA
Sea of Okhotsk
Mediterranean Sea
Adriatic Sea
Black Sea
Caspian Sea
Kurile Trench
Emperor Seamounts
Sea of Japan (East Sea)
Japan Trench
Northwest Pacific Basin
Yellow Sea
East China Sea
Tropic of Cancer
Persian Gulf
Red Sea
Arabian Sea
Taiwan Strait
Mid-Pacific Mountains
Bay of Bengal
AFRICA
Philippine Sea
Mariana Trench
Gulf of Thailand
South China Sea
Sunda Shelf
Carlsberg Ridge
Chagos-Laccadive Plateau
Strait of Malacca
Celebes Sea
Gulf of Guinea
Equator
Somali Basin
INDIAN
Melanesian Basin
Bismarck Sea
Solomon Sea
Mid-Indian Basin
Mid-Indian Ridge
Ninetyeast Ridge
Arafura Sea
Timor Sea
Angola Basin
Mozambique Channel
Mascarene Plateau
Coral Sea
Great Barrier Reef
Tropic of Capricorn
Walvis Ridge
AUSTRALIA
Madagascar Basin
Perth Basin
Cape Basin
Mozambique Plateau
Southwest Indian Ridge
OCEAN
South Australian Basin
Bass Strait
Tasman Sea
Agulhas Basin
Southeast Indian Ridge
Kerguelen Plateau
South Indian Basin
SOUTHERN
Enderby Plain
Antarctic Circle
ANTARCTICA

Ocean depth
Sea level
200m / 656ft
1000m / 3281ft
2000m / 6562ft
3000m / 9843ft
4000m / 13,124ft
5000m / 16,400ft
6000m / 19,686ft

Black smokers

These vents in the ocean floor disgorge hot, sulphur-rich water from deep in the Earth's crust. Despite the great depths, a variety of lifeforms have adapted to the chemical-rich environment which surrounds black smokers.

▲ ***A black smoker** in the Atlantic Ocean.*

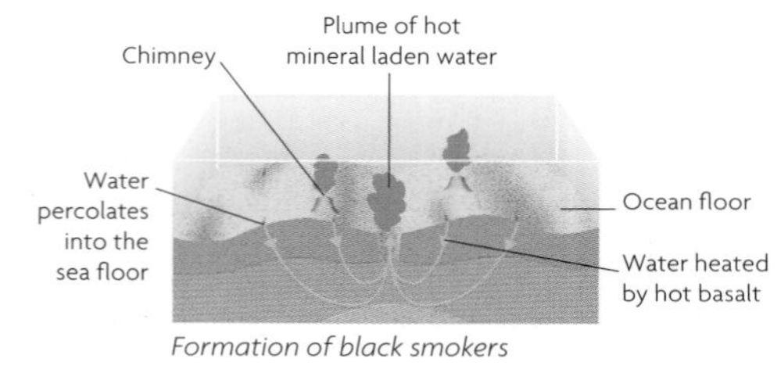

Chimney
Plume of hot mineral laden water
Water percolates into the sea floor
Ocean floor
Water heated by hot basalt

Formation of black smokers

▲ ***Surtsey, near Iceland,** is a volcanic island lying directly over the Mid-Atlantic Ridge. It was formed in the 1960s following intense volcanic activity nearby.*

Ocean floors

Mid-ocean ridges are formed by lava which erupts beneath the sea and cools to form solid rock. This process mirrors the creation of volcanoes from cooled lava on the land. The ages of sea floor rocks increase in parallel bands outwards from central ocean ridges.

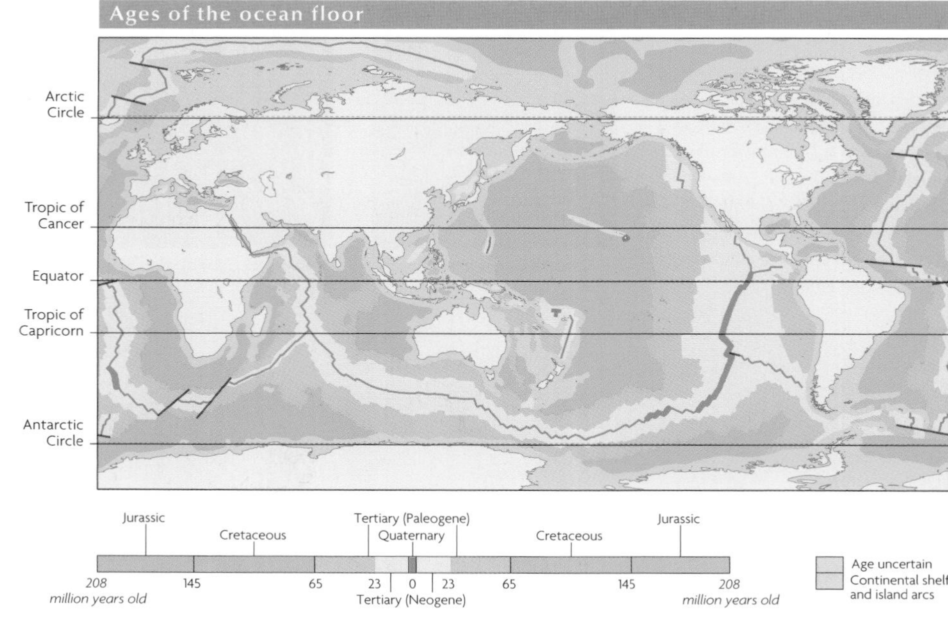

Ages of the ocean floor
Arctic Circle
Tropic of Cancer
Equator
Tropic of Capricorn
Antarctic Circle
Jurassic
Cretaceous
Tertiary (Paleogene)
Quaternary
Cretaceous
Jurassic
208 million years old
145
65
23
0
23
65
145
208 million years old
Tertiary (Neogene)
Age uncertain
Continental shelf and island arcs

▲ ***Currents in the*** *Southern Ocean are driven by some of the world's fiercest winds, including the Roaring Forties, Furious Fifties and Shrieking Sixties.*

▲ ***The Pacific Ocean*** *is the world's largest and deepest ocean, covering over one-third of the surface of the Earth.*

▲ ***The Atlantic Ocean*** *was formed when the landmasses of the eastern and western hemispheres began to drift apart 180 million years ago.*

Deposition of sediment

Storms, earthquakes, and volcanic activity trigger underwater currents known as turbidity currents which scour sand and gravel from the continental shelf, creating underwater canyons. These strong currents pick up material deposited at river mouths and deltas, and carry it across the continental shelf and through the underwater canyons, where it is eventually laid down on the ocean floor in the form of fans.

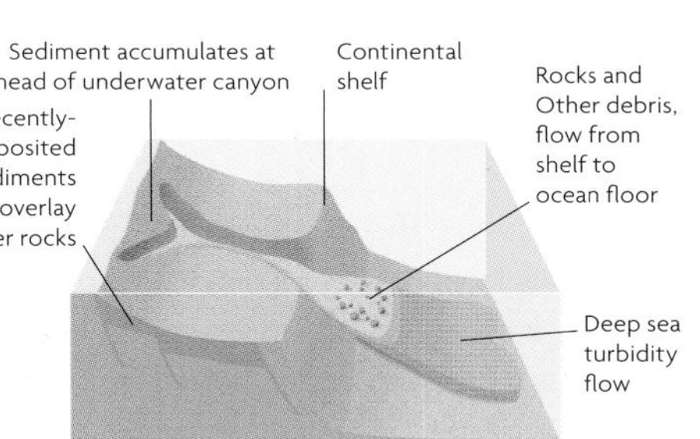
Sediment accumulates at head of underwater canyon
Continental shelf
Rocks and Other debris, flow from shelf to ocean floor
Recently-deposited sediments overlay older rocks
Deep sea turbidity flow

How sediment is deposited on the ocean floor

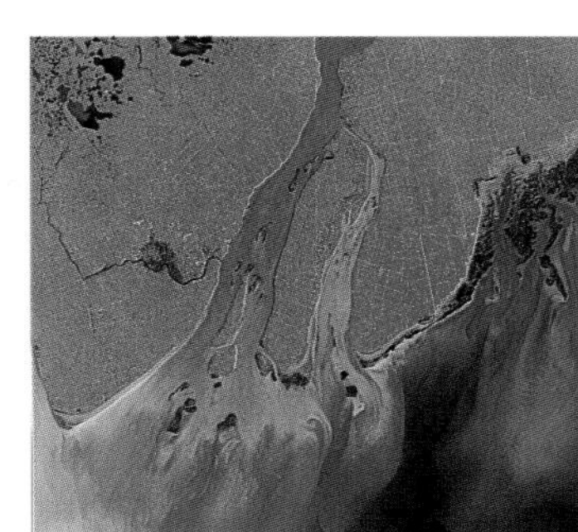

► ***Satellite image of*** *the Yangtze (Chang Jiang) Delta, in which the land appears red. The river deposits immense quantities of silt into the East China Sea, much of which will eventually reach the deep ocean floor.*

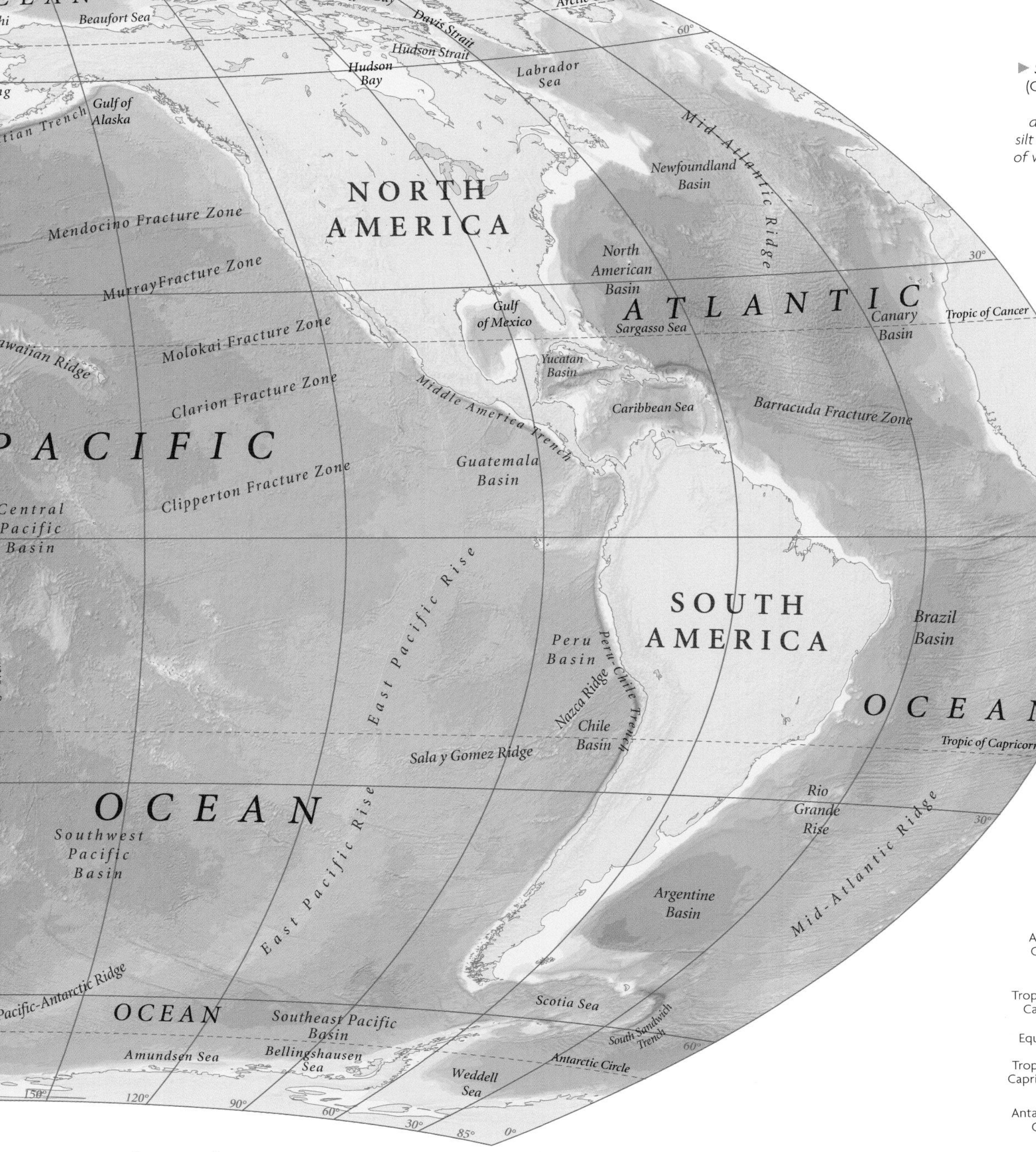
NORTH AMERICA
SOUTH AMERICA
PACIFIC OCEAN
ATLANTIC OCEAN
OCEAN
Beaufort Sea
Baffin Bay
Davis Strait
Hudson Strait
Hudson Bay
Greenland Sea
Arctic Circle
Labrador Sea
Gulf of Alaska
Newfoundland Basin
Mid-Atlantic Ridge
Mendocino Fracture Zone
Murray Fracture Zone
Molokai Fracture Zone
Hawaiian Ridge
Clarion Fracture Zone
Clipperton Fracture Zone
Central Pacific Basin
North American Basin
Gulf of Mexico
Sargasso Sea
Canary Basin
Tropic of Cancer
Yucatan Basin
Middle America Trench
Caribbean Sea
Barracuda Fracture Zone
Guatemala Basin
Equator
East Pacific Rise
Peru Basin
Peru-Chile Trench
Nazca Ridge
Chile Basin
Brazil Basin
Tropic of Capricorn
Sala y Gomez Ridge
Rio Grande Rise
Southwest Pacific Basin
Tonga Trench
Argentine Basin
Mid-Atlantic Ridge
Pacific-Antarctic Ridge
Southeast Pacific Basin
Scotia Sea
South Sandwich Trench
Amundsen Sea
Bellingshausen Sea
Antarctic Circle
Weddell Sea

Surface water

Ocean currents move warm water away from the Equator towards the poles, while cold water is, in turn, moved towards the Equator. This is the main way in which the Earth distributes surface heat and is a major climatic control. Approximately 4000 million years ago, the Earth was dominated by oceans and there was no land to interrupt the flow of the currents, which would have flowed as straight lines, simply influenced by the Earth's rotation.

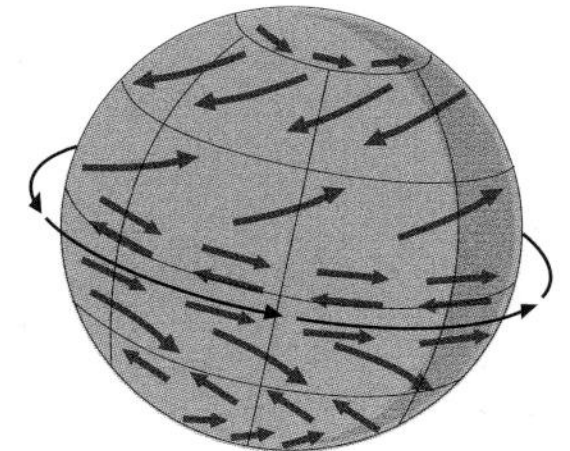

Idealized globe showing the movement of water around a landless Earth.

Ocean currents

Surface currents are driven by the prevailing winds and by the spinning motion of the Earth, which drives the currents into circulating whirlpools, or gyres. Deep sea currents, over 330 ft (100 m) below the surface, are driven by differences in water temperature and salinity, which have an impact on the density of deep water and on its movement.

Surface temperature and currents

Arctic Circle
Tropic of Cancer
Equator
Tropic of Capricorn
Antarctic Circle

Surface temperature and currents

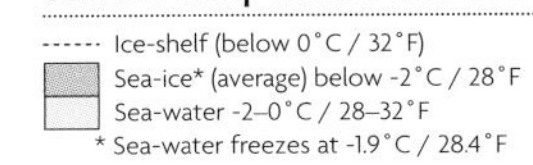
Ice-shelf (below 0°C / 32°F)
Sea-ice* (average) below -2°C / 28°F
Sea-water -2–0°C / 28–32°F
* Sea-water freezes at -1.9°C / 28.4°F
0–10°C / 32–50°F
10–20°C / 50–68°F
20–30°C / 68–86°F

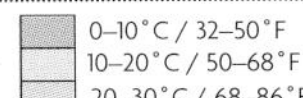
warm current
cold current

Tides and waves

Tides are created by the pull of the Sun and Moon's gravity on the surface of the oceans. The levels of high and low tides are influenced by the position of the Moon in relation to the Earth and Sun. Waves are formed by wind blowing over the surface of the water.

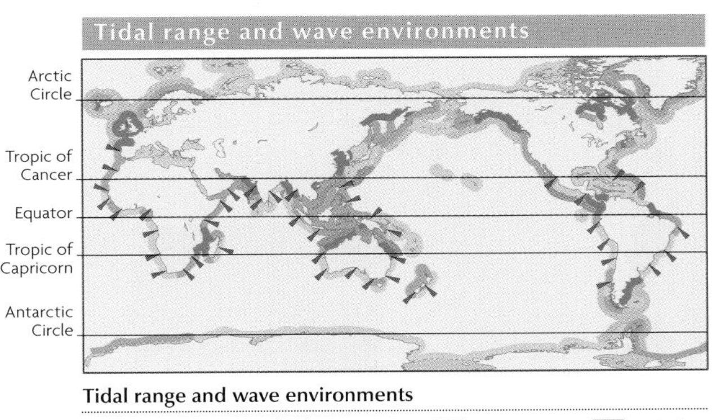
Tidal range and wave environments
Arctic Circle
Tropic of Cancer
Equator
Tropic of Capricorn
Antarctic Circle

Tidal range and wave environments

less than 2m / 7ft
2–4m / 7–13ft
greater than 4m / 13ft
east coast swell
west coast swell
tropical cyclone storm wave
ice-shelf

High and low tides

The highest tides occur when the Earth, the Moon and the Sun are aligned *(below left)*. The lowest tides are experienced when the Sun and Moon align at right angles to one another *(below right)*.

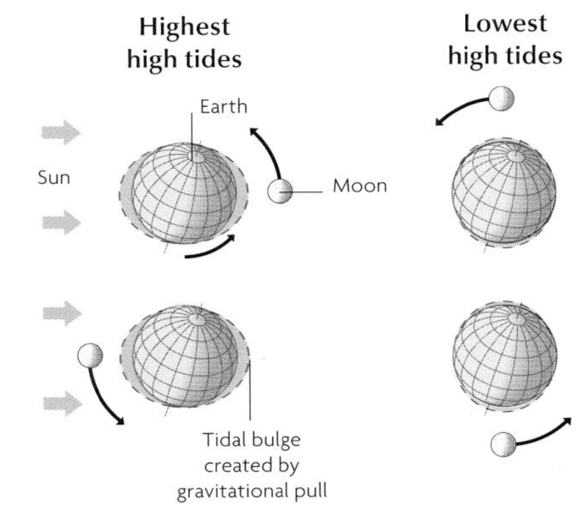
Highest high tides
Lowest high tides
Earth
Sun
Moon
Tidal bulge created by gravitational pull

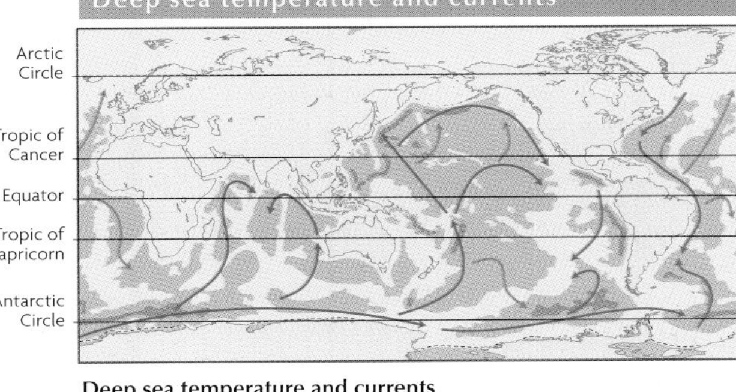
Deep sea temperature and currents
Arctic Circle
Tropic of Cancer
Equator
Tropic of Capricorn
Antarctic Circle

Deep sea temperature and currents

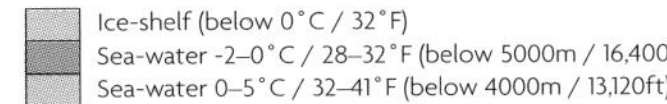
Ice-shelf (below 0°C / 32°F)
Sea-water -2–0°C / 28–32°F (below 5000m / 16,400ft)
Sea-water 0–5°C / 32–41°F (below 4000m / 13,120ft)

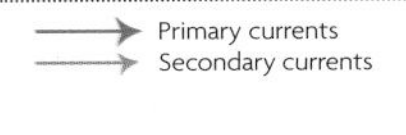
Primary currents
Secondary currents

The global climate

The Earth's climatic types consist of stable patterns of weather conditions averaged out over a long period of time. Different climates are categorized according to particular combinations of temperature and humidity. By contrast, weather consists of short-term fluctuations in wind, temperature and humidity conditions. Different climates are determined by latitude, altitude, the prevailing wind and circulation of ocean currents. Longer-term changes in climate, such as global warming or the onset of ice ages, are punctuated by shorter-term events which comprise the day-to-day weather of a region, such as frontal depressions, hurricanes and blizzards.

The atmosphere, wind and weather

The Earth's atmosphere has been compared to a giant ocean of air which surrounds the planet. Its circulation patterns are similar to the currents in the oceans and are influenced by three factors; the Earth's orbit around the Sun and rotation about its axis, and variations in the amount of heat radiation received from the Sun. If both heat and moisture were not redistributed between the Equator and the poles, large areas of the Earth would be uninhabitable.

◀ *Heavy fogs, as here in southern England, form as moisture-laden air passes over cold ground.*

Temperature

The world can be divided into three major climatic zones, stretching like large belts across the latitudes: the tropics which are warm; the cold polar regions and the temperate zones which lie between them. Temperatures across the Earth range from above 30°C (86°F) in the deserts to as low as -55°C (-70°F) at the poles. Temperature is also controlled by altitude; because air becomes cooler and less dense the higher it gets, mountainous regions are typically colder than those areas which are at, or close to, sea level.

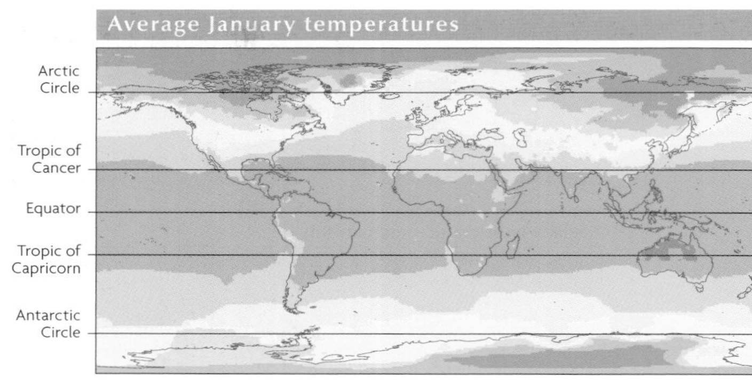
Average January temperatures
Arctic Circle
Tropic of Cancer
Equator
Tropic of Capricorn
Antarctic Circle

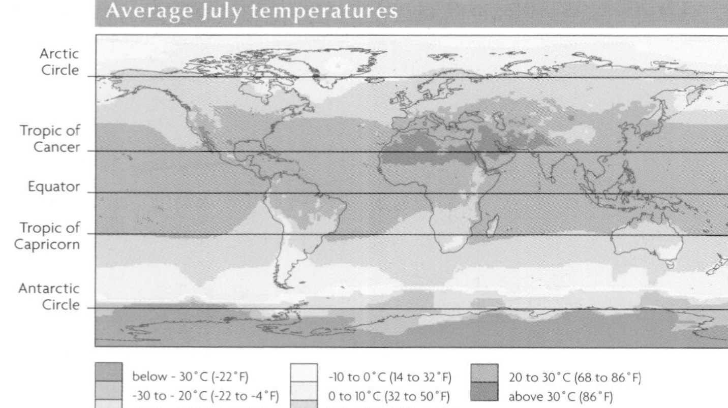
Average July temperatures
Arctic Circle
Tropic of Cancer
Equator
Tropic of Capricorn
Antarctic Circle

below - 30°C (-22°F)
-30 to - 20°C (-22 to -4°F)
-20 to - 10°C (-4 to 14°F)
-10 to 0°C (14 to 32°F)
0 to 10°C (32 to 50°F)
10 to 20°C (50 to 68°F)
20 to 30°C (68 to 86°F)
above 30°C (86°F)

Global air circulation

Air does not simply flow from the Equator to the poles, it circulates in giant cells known as Hadley and Ferrel cells. As air warms it expands, becoming less dense and rising; this creates areas of low pressure. As the air rises it cools and condenses, causing heavy rainfall over the tropics and slight snowfall over the poles. This cool air then sinks, forming high pressure belts. At surface level in the tropics these sinking currents are deflected polewards as the westerlies and towards the equator as the trade winds. At the poles they become the polar easterlies.

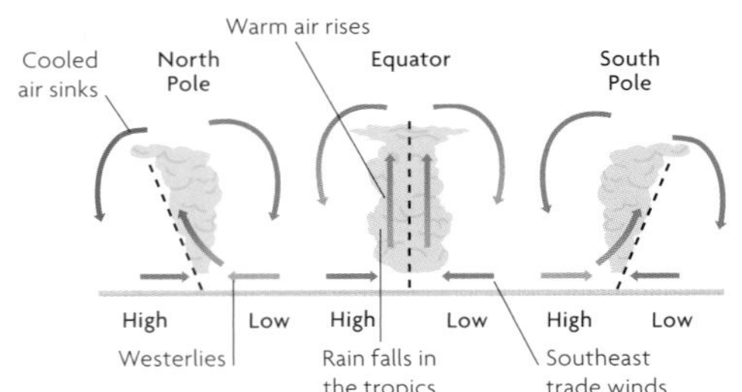
Warm air rises
Cooled air sinks
North Pole
Equator
South Pole
High
Low
High
Low
High
Low
Westerlies
Rain falls in the tropics
Southeast trade winds

▲ *The Antarctic pack ice expands its area by almost seven times during the winter as temperatures drop and surrounding seas freeze.*

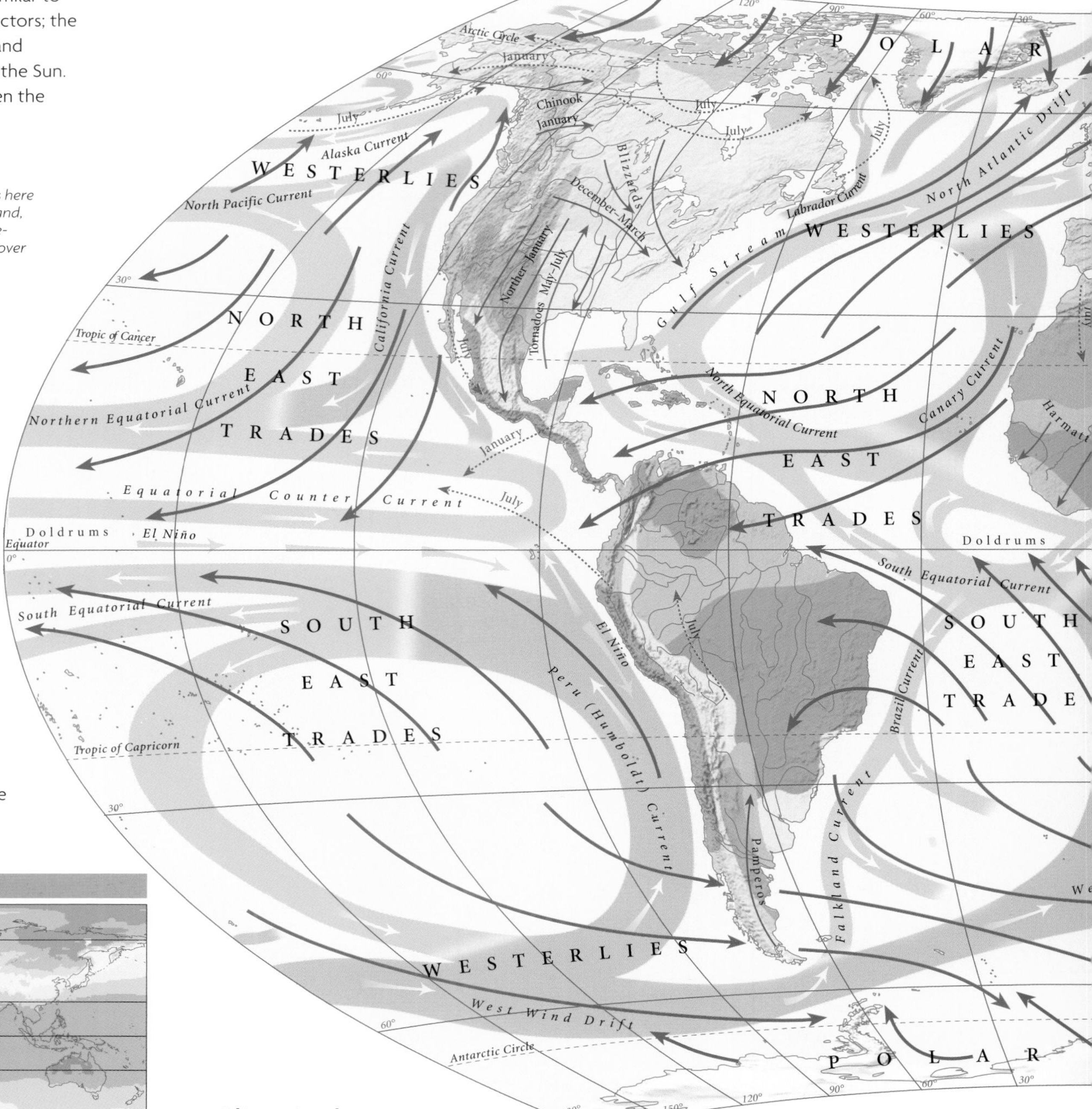
POLAR
WESTERLIES
NORTH EAST TRADES
SOUTH EAST TRADES
WESTERLIES
POLAR
Arctic Circle
Tropic of Cancer
Equator
Tropic of Capricorn
Antarctic Circle
Doldrums
El Niño
Alaska Current
North Pacific Current
California Current
Northern Equatorial Current
Equatorial Counter Current
South Equatorial Current
Peru (Humboldt) Current
Gulf Stream
Labrador Current
North Atlantic Drift
North Equatorial Current
Canary Current
Brazil Current
Falkland Current
West Wind Drift
Chinook
January
July
Blizzards
December-March
Norther January
Tornadoes May-July
Pampero
Harmattan

Climatic change

The Earth is currently in a warm phase between ice ages. Warmer temperatures result in higher sea levels as more of the polar ice caps melt. Most of the world's population lives near coasts, so any changes which might cause sea levels to rise, could have a potentially disastrous impact.

▲ *This ice fair, painted by Pieter Brueghel the Younger in the 17th century, shows the Little Ice Age which peaked around 300 years ago.*

The greenhouse effect

Gases such as carbon dioxide are known as 'greenhouse gases' because they allow shortwave solar radiation to enter the Earth's atmosphere, but help to stop longwave radiation from escaping. This traps heat, raising the Earth's temperature. An excess of these gases, such as that which results from the burning of fossil fuels, helps trap more heat and can lead to global warming.

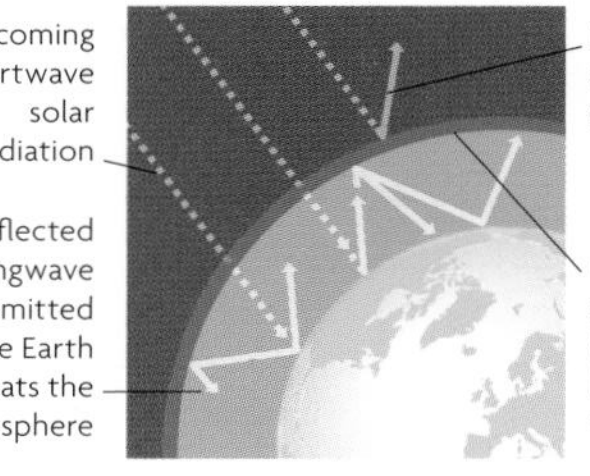
Incoming shortwave solar radiation
Deflected longwave radiation emitted by the Earth heats the atmosphere
Deflected shortwave solar radiation
Greenhouse gases prevent the escape of longwave radiation

◀ *The islands of the Caribbean, Mexico's Gulf coast and the southeastern USA are often hit by hurricanes formed far out in the Atlantic.*

Oceanic water circulation

In general, ocean currents parallel the movement of winds across the Earth's surface. Incoming solar energy is greatest at the Equator and least at the poles. So, water in the oceans heats up most at the Equator and flows polewards, cooling as it moves north or south towards the Arctic or Antarctic. The flow is eventually reversed and cold water currents move back towards the Equator. These ocean currents act as a vast system for moving heat from the Equator towards the poles and are a major influence on the distribution of the Earth's climates.

▲ ***In marginal climatic** zones years of drought can completely dry out the land and transform grassland to desert.*

Tilt and rotation

The tilt and rotation of the Earth during its annual orbit largely control the distribution of heat and moisture across its surface, which correspondingly controls its large-scale weather patterns. As the Earth annually rotates around the Sun, half its surface is receiving maximum radiation, creating summer and winter seasons. The angle of the Earth means that on average the tropics receive two and a half times as much heat from the Sun each day as the poles.

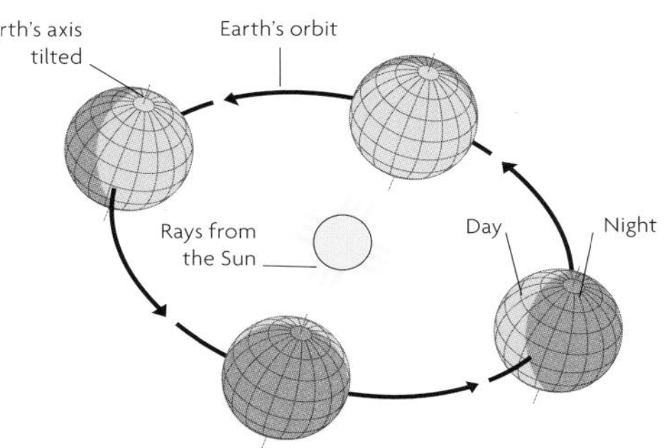
Earth's axis tilted
Earth's orbit
Rays from the Sun
Day
Night

Map key

Climate zones: ice cap; subarctic; tundra; continental; temperate; warm temperate; mediterranean; semi-arid; arid; hot humid; humid equatorial; tropical

Ocean currents: warm; cold

Prevailing winds: warm; cold

Local winds: warm; cold; June seasonal*

* (seasonal winds which can either be warm or cold)

▲ ***The wide range** of environments found in the Andes is strongly related to their altitude, which modifies climatic influences. While the peaks are snow-capped, many protected interior valleys are semi-tropical.*

The Coriolis effect

The rotation of the Earth influences atmospheric circulation by deflecting winds and ocean currents. Winds blowing in the northern hemisphere are deflected to the right and those in the southern hemisphere are deflected to the left, creating large-scale patterns of wind circulation, such as the northeast and southeast trade winds and the westerlies. This effect is greatest at the poles and least at the Equator.

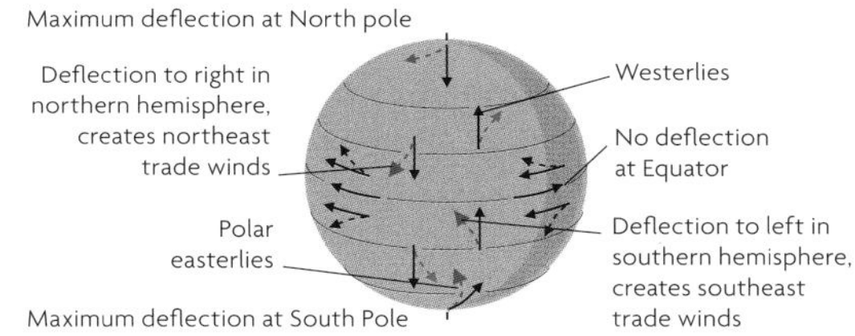
Maximum deflection at North pole
Deflection to right in northern hemisphere, creates northeast trade winds
Polar easterlies
Maximum deflection at South Pole
Westerlies
No deflection at Equator
Deflection to left in southern hemisphere, creates southeast trade winds

Precipitation

When warm air expands, it rises and cools, and the water vapour it carries condenses to form clouds. Heavy, regular rainfall is characteristic of the equatorial region, while the poles are cold and receive only slight snowfall. Tropical regions have marked dry and rainy seasons, while in the temperate regions rainfall is relatively unpredictable.

▲ ***Monsoon rains, which** affect southern Asia from May to September, are caused by sea winds blowing across the warm land.*

▲ ***Heavy tropical rainstorms** occur frequently in Papua New Guinea, often causing soil erosion and landslides in cultivated areas.*

Average January rainfall

Arctic Circle · Tropic of Cancer · Equator · Tropic of Capricorn · Antarctic Circle

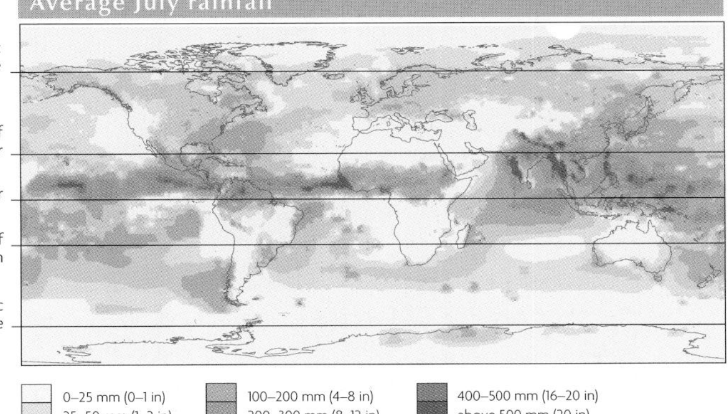
Average July rainfall
Arctic Circle
Tropic of Cancer
Equator
Tropic of Capricorn
Antarctic Circle
0–25 mm (0–1 in)
25–50 mm (1–2 in)
50–100 mm (2–4 in)
100–200 mm (4–8 in)
200–300 mm (8–12 in)
300–400 mm (12–16 in)
400–500 mm (16–20 in)
above 500 mm (20 in)

▲ ***The intensity of** some blizzards in Canada and the northern USA can give rise to snowdrifts as high as 10 ft (3 m).*

▲ ***The Atacama Desert** in Chile is one of the driest places on Earth, with an average rainfall of less than 2 inches (50 mm) per year.*

▲ ***Violent thunderstorms occur** along advancing cold fronts, when cold, dry air masses meet warm, moist air, which rises rapidly, its moisture condensing into thunderclouds. Rain and hail become electrically charged, causing lightning.*

The rainshadow effect

When moist air is forced to rise by mountains, it cools and the water vapour falls as precipitation, either as rain or snow. Only the dry, cold air continues over the mountains, leaving inland areas with little or no rain. This is called the rainshadow effect and is one reason for the existence of the Mojave Desert in California, which lies east of the Coast Ranges.

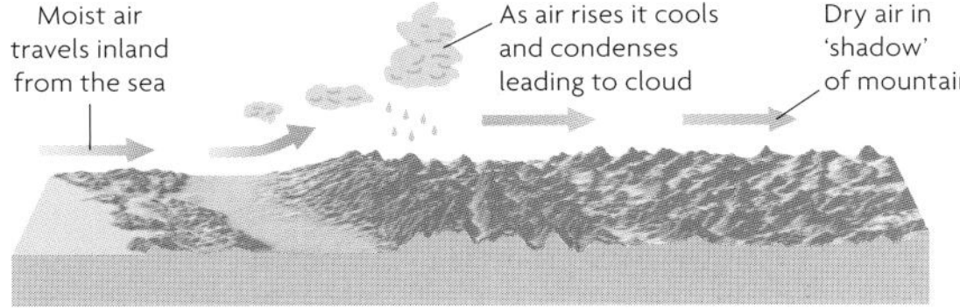
Moist air travels inland from the sea
As air rises it cools and condenses leading to cloud
Dry air in 'shadow' of mountain

The rainshadow effect

Life on Earth

A unique combination of an oxygen-rich atmosphere and plentiful water is the key to life on Earth. Apart from the polar ice caps, there are few areas which have not been colonized by animals or plants over the course of the Earth's history. Plants process sunlight to provide them with their energy, and ultimately all the Earth's animals rely on plants for survival. Because of this reliance, plants are known as primary producers, and the availability of nutrients and temperature of an area is defined as its primary productivity, which affects the quantity and type of animals which are able to live there. This index is affected by climatic factors – cold and aridity restrict the quantity of life, whereas warmth and regular rainfall allow a greater diversity of species.

Biogeographical regions

The Earth can be divided into a series of biogeographical regions, or biomes, ecological communities where certain species of plant and animal co-exist within particular climatic conditions. Within these broad classifications, other factors including soil richness, altitude and human activities such as urbanization, intensive agriculture and deforestation, affect the local distribution of living species within each biome.

Polar regions

A layer of permanent ice at the Earth's poles covers both seas and land. Very little plant and animal life can exist in these harsh regions.

Tundra

A desolate region, with long, dark freezing winters and short, cold summers. With virtually no soil and large areas of permanently frozen ground known as permafrost, the tundra is largely treeless, though it is briefly clothed by small flowering plants in the summer months.

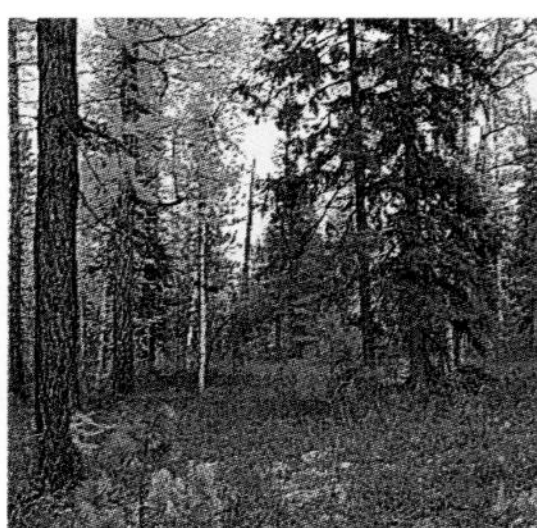

Needleleaf forests

With milder summers than the tundra and less wind, these areas are able to support large forests of coniferous trees.

Broadleaf forests

Much of the northern hemisphere was once covered by deciduous forests, which occurred in areas with marked seasonal variations. Most deciduous forests have been cleared for human settlement.

Temperate rainforests

In warmer wetter areas, such as southern China, temperate deciduous forests are replaced by evergreen forest.

Deserts

Deserts are areas with negligible rainfall. Most hot deserts lie within the tropics; cold deserts are dry because of their distance from the moisture-providing sea.

Mediterranean

Hot, dry summers and short winters typify these areas, which were once covered by evergreen shrubs and woodland, but have now been cleared by humans for agriculture.

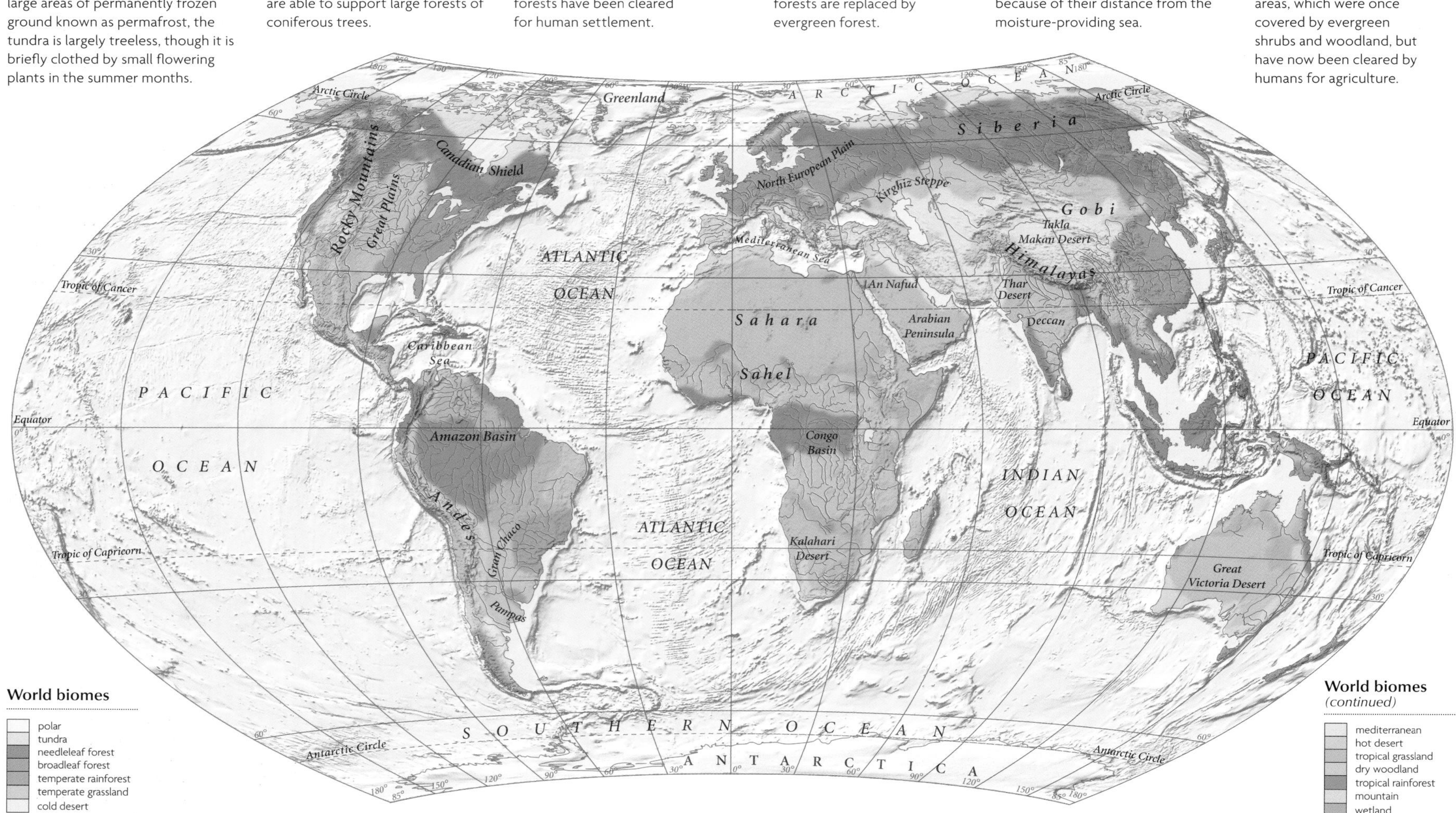
Arctic Circle
Greenland
A R C T I C O C E A N
Siberia
Canadian Shield
Rocky Mountains
Great Plains
North European Plain
Kirghiz Steppe
Gobi
Takla Makan Desert
Mediterranean Sea
Himalayas
ATLANTIC OCEAN
Tropic of Cancer
An Nafud
Thar Desert
Arabian Peninsula
Deccan
Sahara
Caribbean Sea
Sahel
PACIFIC OCEAN
Equator
Amazon Basin
Congo Basin
INDIAN OCEAN
Andes
Gran Chaco
ATLANTIC OCEAN
Kalahari Desert
Tropic of Capricorn
Great Victoria Desert
Pampas
SOUTHERN OCEAN
Antarctic Circle
ANTARCTICA

World biomes

- polar
- tundra
- needleleaf forest
- broadleaf forest
- temperate rainforest
- temperate grassland
- cold desert

World biomes *(continued)*

- mediterranean
- hot desert
- tropical grassland
- dry woodland
- tropical rainforest
- mountain
- wetland

Tropical and temperate grasslands

The major grassland areas are found in the centres of the larger continental landmasses. In Africa's tropical savannah regions, seasonal rainfall alternates with drought. Temperate grasslands, also known as steppes and prairies are found in the northern hemisphere, and in South America, where they are known as the pampas.

Dry woodlands

Trees and shrubs, adapted to dry conditions, grow widely spaced from one another, interspersed by savannah grasslands.

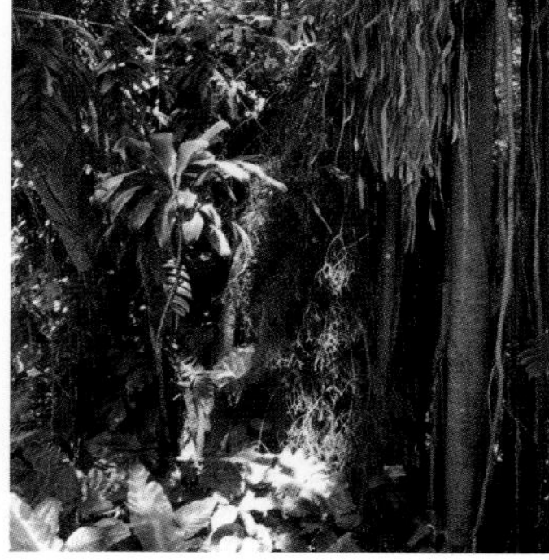

Tropical rainforests

Characterized by year-round warmth and high rainfall, tropical rainforests contain the highest diversity of plant and animal species on Earth.

Mountains

Though the lower slopes of mountains may be thickly forested, only ground-hugging shrubs and other vegetation will grow above the tree line which varies according to both altitude and latitude.

Wetlands

Rarely lying above sea level, wetlands are marshes, swamps and tidal flats. Some, with their moist, fertile soils, are rich feeding grounds for fish and breeding grounds for birds. Others have little soil structure and are too acidic to support much plant and animal life.

Biodiversity

The number of plant and animal species, and the range of genetic diversity within the populations of each species, make up the Earth's biodiversity. The plants and animals which are endemic to a region – that is, those which are found nowhere else in the world – are also important in determining levels of biodiversity. Human settlement and intervention have encroached on many areas of the world once rich in endemic plant and animal species. Increasing international efforts are being made to monitor and conserve the biodiversity of the Earth's remaining wild places.

Animal adaptation

The degree of an animal's adaptability to different climates and conditions is extremely important in ensuring its success as a species. Many animals, particularly the largest mammals, are becoming restricted to ever-smaller regions as human development and modern agricultural practices reduce their natural habitats. In contrast, humans have been responsible – both deliberately and accidentally – for the spread of some of the world's most successful species. Many of these introduced species are now more numerous than the indigenous animal populations.

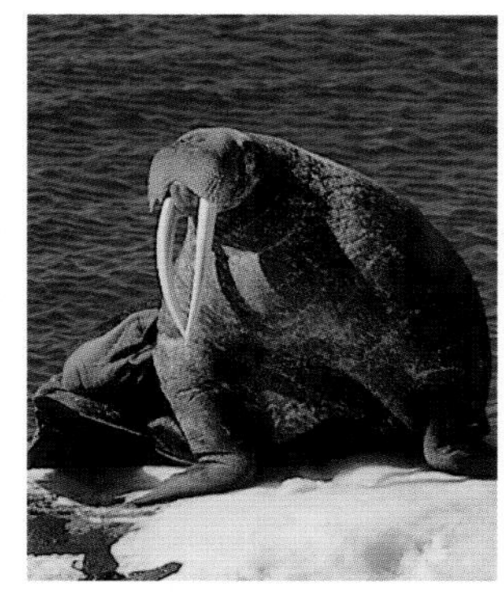

Polar animals

The frozen wastes of the polar regions are able to support only a small range of species which derive their nutritional requirements from the sea. Animals such as the walrus *(left)* have developed insulating fat, stocky limbs and double-layered coats to enable them to survive in the freezing conditions.

Desert animals

Many animals which live in the extreme heat and aridity of the deserts are able to survive for days and even months with very little food or water. Their bodies are adapted to lose heat quickly and to store fat and water. The Gila monster *(above)* stores fat in its tail.

Diversity of animal species

Number of animal species per country

- more than 2000
- 1000–1999
- 700–999
- 400–699
- 200–399
- 100–199
- 0–99
- data not available

Marine biodiversity

The oceans support a huge variety of different species, from the world's largest mammals like whales and dolphins down to the tiniest plankton. The greatest diversities occur in the warmer seas of continental shelves, where plants are easily able to photosynthesize, and around coral reefs, where complex ecosystems are found. On the ocean floor, nematodes can exist at a depth of more than 10,000 ft (3000 m) below sea level.

Amazon rainforest

The vast Amazon Basin is home to the world's greatest variety of animal species. Animals are adapted to live at many different levels from the treetops to the tangled undergrowth which lies beneath the canopy. The sloth *(below)* hangs upside down in the branches. Its fur grows from its stomach to its back to enable water to run off quickly.

High altitudes

Few animals exist in the rarefied atmosphere of the highest mountains. However, birds of prey such as eagles and vultures *(above)*, with their superb eyesight can soar as high as 23,000 ft (7000 m) to scan for prey below.

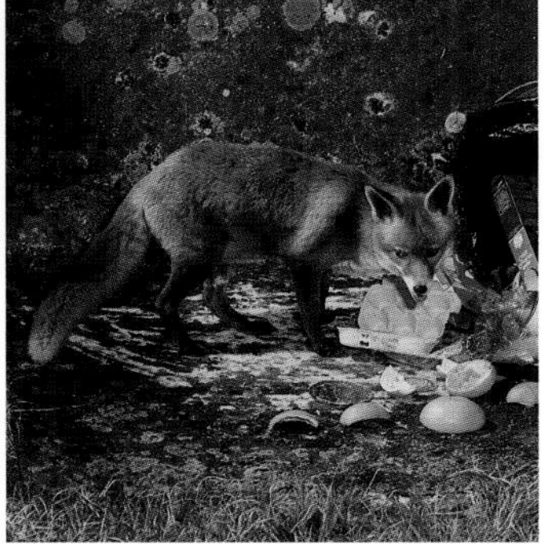

Urban animals

The growth of cities has reduced the amount of habitat available to many species. A number of animals are now moving closer into urban areas to scavenge from the detritus of the modern city *(left)*. Rodents, particularly rats and mice, have existed in cities for thousands of years, and many insects, especially moths, quickly develop new colouring to provide them with camouflage.

Endemic species

Isolated areas such as Australia and the island of Madagascar, have the greatest range of endemic species. In Australia, these include marsupials such as the kangaroo *(below)*, which carry their young in pouches on their bodies. Destruction of habitat, pollution, hunting, and predators introduced by humans, are threatening this unique biodiversity.

Plant adaptation

Environmental conditions, particularly climate, soil type and the extent of competition with other organisms, influence the development of plants into a number of distinctive forms. Similar conditions in quite different parts of the world create similar adaptations in the plants, which may then be modified by other, local, factors specific to the region.

Cold conditions

In areas where temperatures rarely rise above freezing, plants such as lichens *(left)* and mosses grow densely, close to the ground.

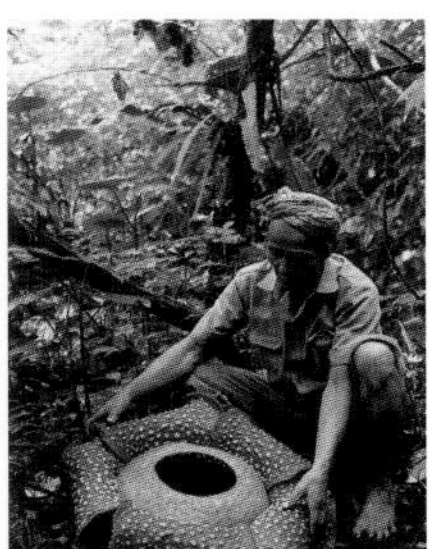

Rainforests

Most of the world's largest and oldest plants are found in rainforests; warmth and heavy rainfall provide ideal conditions for vast plants like the world's largest flower, the rafflesia *(left)*.

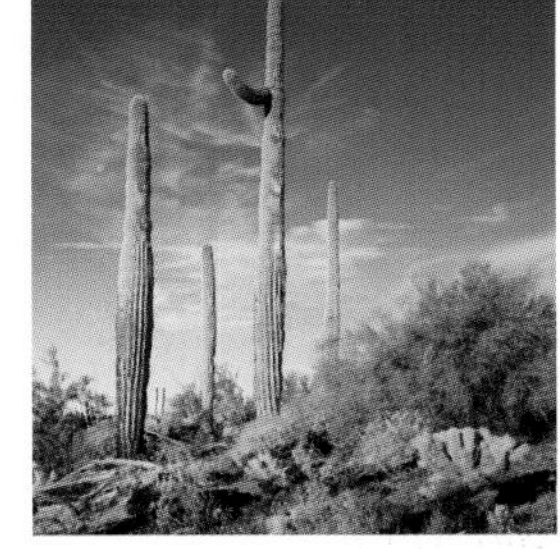

Hot, dry conditions

Arid conditions lead to the development of plants whose surface area has been reduced to a minimum to reduce water loss. In cacti *(above)*, which can survive without water for months, leaves are minimal or not present at all.

Ancient plants

Some of the world's most primitive plants still exist today, including algae, cycads and many ferns *(above)*, reflecting the success with which they have adapted to changing conditions.

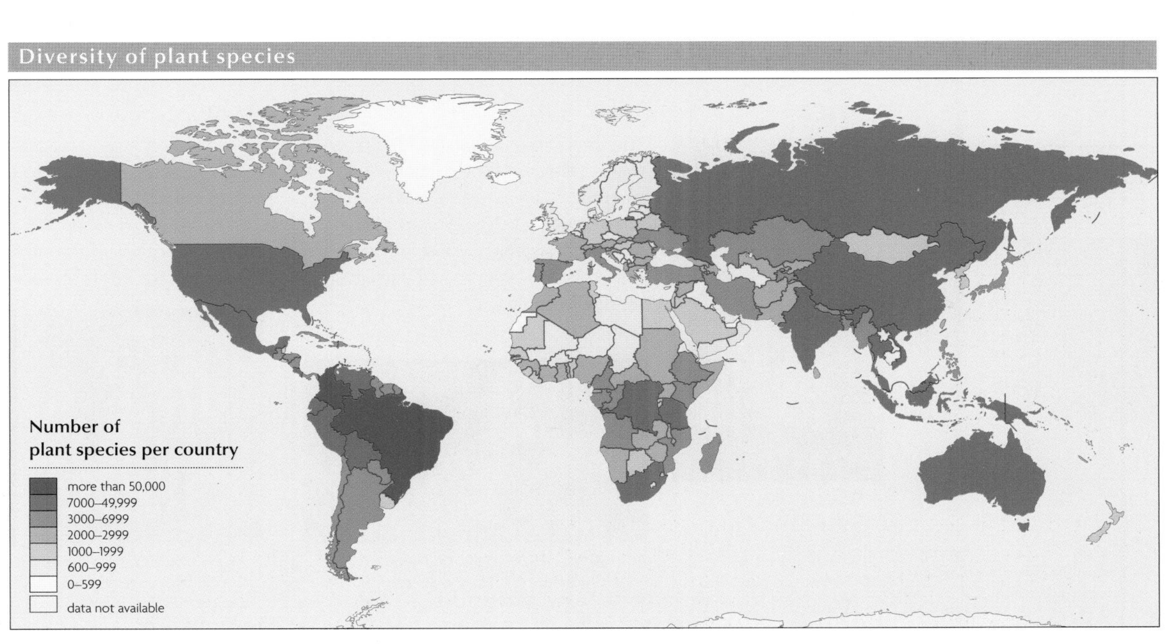
Diversity of plant species
Number of plant species per country
more than 50,000
7000–49,999
3000–6999
2000–2999
1000–1999
600–999
0–599
data not available

Resisting predators

A great variety of plants have developed devices including spines *(above)*, poisons, stinging hairs and an unpleasant taste or smell to deter animal predators.

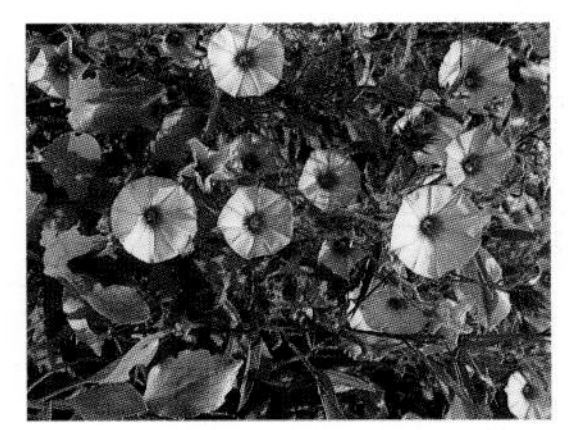

Weeds

Weeds such as bindweed *(above)* are fast-growing, easily dispersed, and tolerant of a number of different environments, enabling them to quickly colonize suitable habitats. They are among the most adaptable of all plants.

Population and settlement

The Earth's population is projected to rise from its current level of about 6.5 billion to reach some 10 billion by 2025. The global distribution of this rapidly growing population is very uneven, and is dictated by climate, terrain and natural and economic resources. The great majority of the Earth's people live in coastal zones, and along river valleys. Deserts cover over 20% of the Earth's surface, but support less than 5% of the world's population. It is estimated that over half of the world's population live in cities – most of them in Asia – as a result of mass migration from rural areas in search of jobs. Many of these people live in the so-called 'megacities', some with populations as great as 40 million.

Patterns of settlement

The past 200 years have seen the most radical shift in world population patterns in recorded history.

Nomadic life

All the world's peoples were hunter-gatherers 10,000 years ago. Today nomads, who live by following available food resources, account for less than 0.0001% of the world's population. They are mainly pastoral herders, moving their livestock from place to place in search of grazing land.

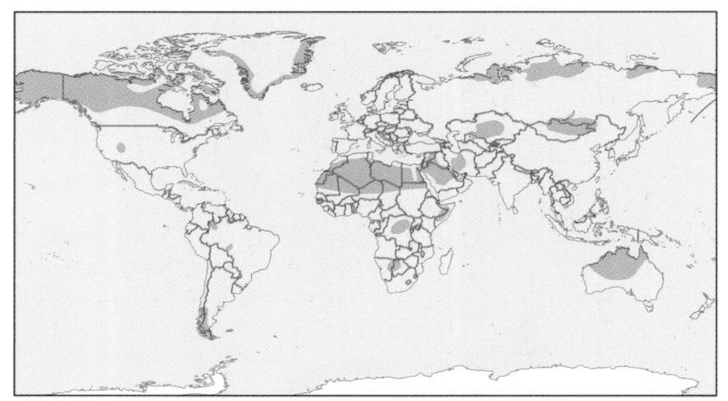

Nomadic population

Nomadic population area

The growth of cities

In 1900 there were only 14 cities in the world with populations of more than a million, mostly in the northern hemisphere. Today, as more and more people in the developing world migrate to towns and cities, there are 29 cities whose population exceeds 5 million, and around 440 million-cities.

Million-cities in 1900

Million-cities in 1900

• Cities over 1 million population

Million-cities in 2005

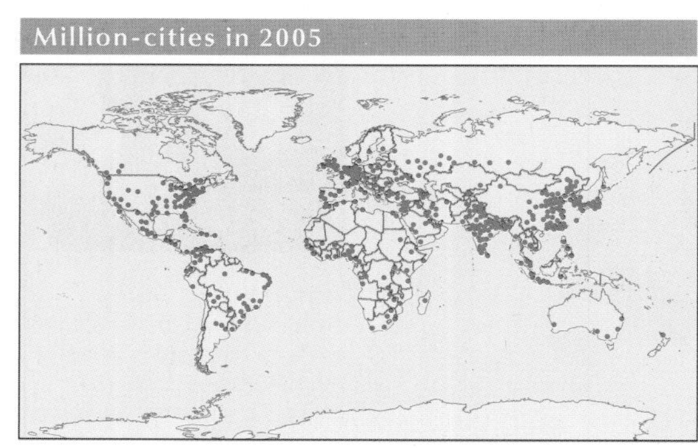

Million-cities in 2005

• Cities over 1 million population

North America

The eastern and western seaboards of the USA, with huge expanses of interconnected cities, towns and suburbs, are vast, densely-populated megalopolises. Central America and the Caribbean also have high population densities. Yet, away from the coasts and in the wildernesses of northern Canada the land is very sparsely settled.

▲ *Vancouver on Canada's west coast, grew up as a port city. In recent years it has attracted many Asian immigrants, particularly from the Pacific Rim.*

▲ *North America's central plains, the continent's agricultural heartland, are thinly populated and highly productive.*

Europe

With its temperate climate, and rich mineral and natural resources, Europe is generally very densely settled. The continent acts as a magnet for economic migrants from the developing world, and immigration is now widely restricted. Birth rates in Europe are generally low, and in some countries, such as Germany, the populations have stabilized at zero growth, with a fast-growing elderly population.

▲ *Many European cities, like Siena, once reflected the 'ideal' size for human settlements. Modern technological advances have enabled them to grow far beyond the original walls.*

▲ *Within the densely-populated Netherlands the reclamation of coastal wetlands is vital to provide much-needed land for agriculture and settlement.*

Population density (inhabitants per sq km)

- 200–1000
- 100–200
- 50–100
- 20–50
- 10–20
- 5–10
- 1–5
- Less than 1

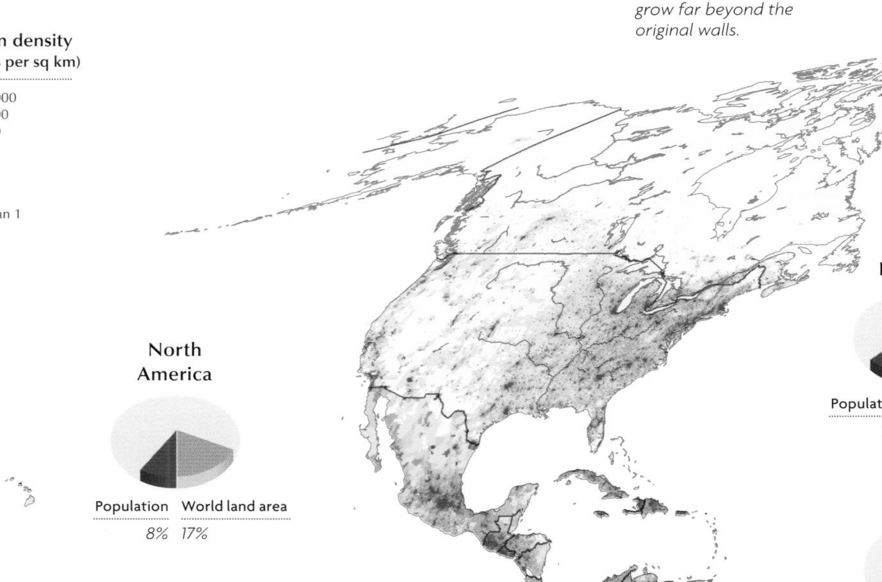

Europe
Population World land area
11% 7.1%
North America
Population World land area
8% 17%
Africa
Population World land area
14% 20.2%
South America
Population World land area
6% 11.8%

South America

Most settlement in South America is clustered in a narrow belt in coastal zones and in the northern Andes. During the 20th century, cities such as São Paulo and Buenos Aires grew enormously, acting as powerful economic magnets to the rural population. Shanty towns have grown up on the outskirts of many major cities to house these immigrants, often lacking basic amenities.

▲ *Many people in western South America live at high altitudes in the Andes, both in cities and in villages such as this one in Bolivia.*

▲ *Venezuela is one of the most highly urbanized countries in South America, with nearly 90% of the population living in cities such as Caracas.*

Africa

▲ *Cities such as Nairobi (above), Cairo and Johannesburg have grown rapidly in recent years, although only Cairo has a significant population on a global scale.*

The arid climate of much of Africa means that settlement of the continent is sparse, focusing in coastal areas and fertile regions such as the Nile Valley. Africa still has a high proportion of nomadic agriculturalists, although many are now becoming settled, and the population is predominantly rural.

▲ *Traditional lifestyles and homes persist across much of Africa, which has a higher proportion of rural or village-based population than any other continent.*

Asia

Most Asian settlement originally centred around the great river valleys such as the Indus, the Ganges and the Yangtze. Today, almost 60% of the world's population lives in Asia, many in burgeoning cities – particularly in the economically-buoyant Pacific Rim countries. Even rural population densities are high in many countries; practices such as terracing in Southeast Asia making the most of the available land.

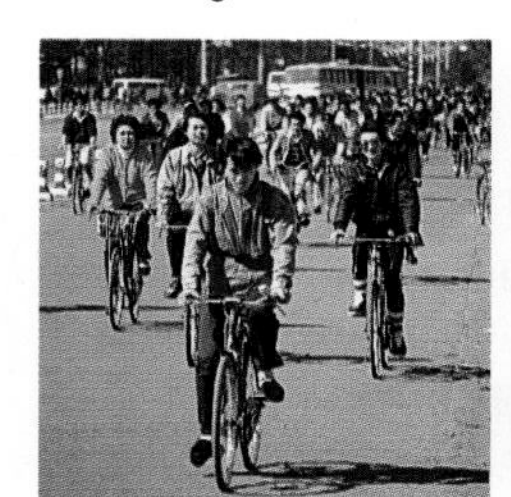

▲ *Many of China's cities are now vast urban areas with populations of more than 5 million people.*

▲ *This stilt village in Bangladesh is built to resist the regular flooding. Pressure on land, even in rural areas, forces many people to live in marginal areas.*

Population structures

Population pyramids are an effective means of showing the age structures of different countries, and highlighting changing trends in population growth and decline. The typical pyramid for a country with a growing, youthful population, is broad-based *(left)*, reflecting a high birth rate and a far larger number of young rather than elderly people. In contrast, countries with populations whose numbers are stabilizing have a more balanced distribution of people in each age band, and may even have lower numbers of people in the youngest age ranges, indicating both a high life expectancy, and that the population is now barely replacing itself *(right)*. The Russian Federation *(centre)* shows a marked decline in population due to a combination of a high death rate and low birth rate. The government has taken steps to reverse this trend by providing improved child support and health care. Immigration is also seen as vital to help sustain the population.

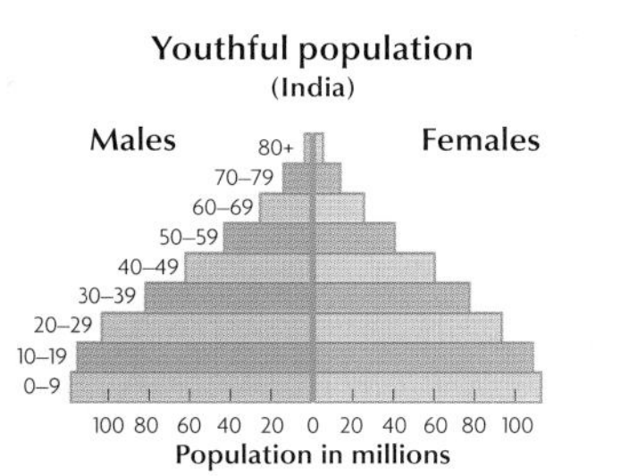
Youthful population
(India)
Males
Females
80+
70–79
60–69
50–59
40–49
30–39
20–29
10–19
0–9
100 80 60 40 20 0 20 40 60 80 100
Population in millions

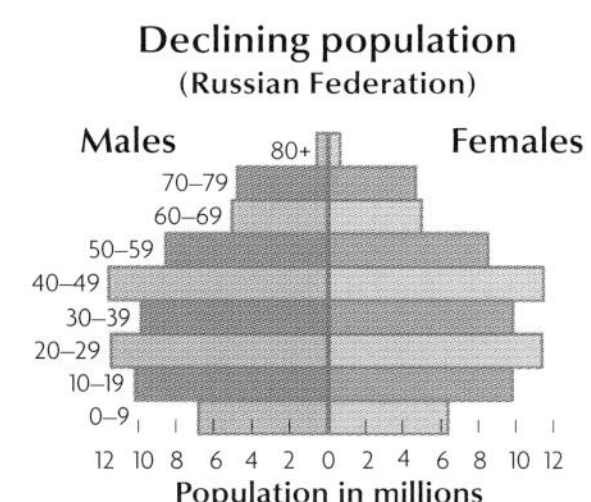
Declining population
(Russian Federation)
Males
Females
80+
70–79
60–69
50–59
40–49
30–39
20–29
10–19
0–9
12 10 8 6 4 2 0 2 4 6 8 10 12
Population in millions

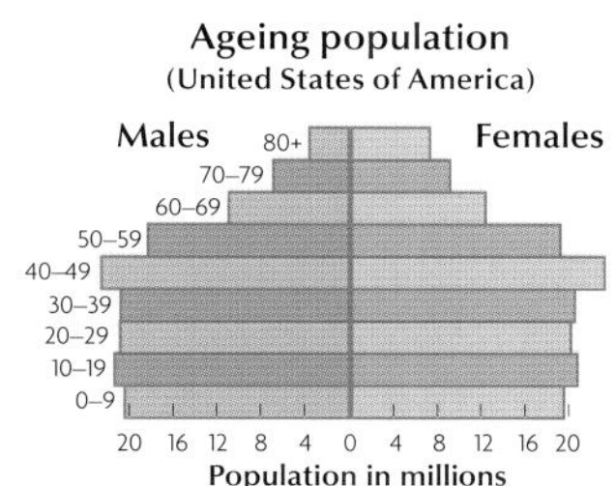
Ageing population
(United States of America)
Males
Females
80+
70–79
60–69
50–59
40–49
30–39
20–29
10–19
0–9
20 16 12 8 4 0 4 8 12 16 20
Population in millions

Population growth

Improvements in food supply and advances in medicine have both played a major role in the remarkable growth in global population, which has increased five-fold over the last 150 years. Food supplies have risen with the mechanization of agriculture and improvements in crop yields. Better nutrition, together with higher standards of public health and sanitation, have led to increased longevity and higher birth rates.

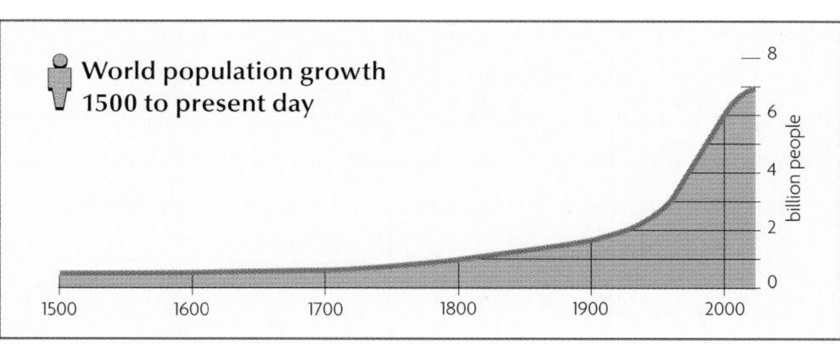
World population growth
1500 to present day
billion people
8
6
4
2
0
1500
1600
1700
1800
1900
2000

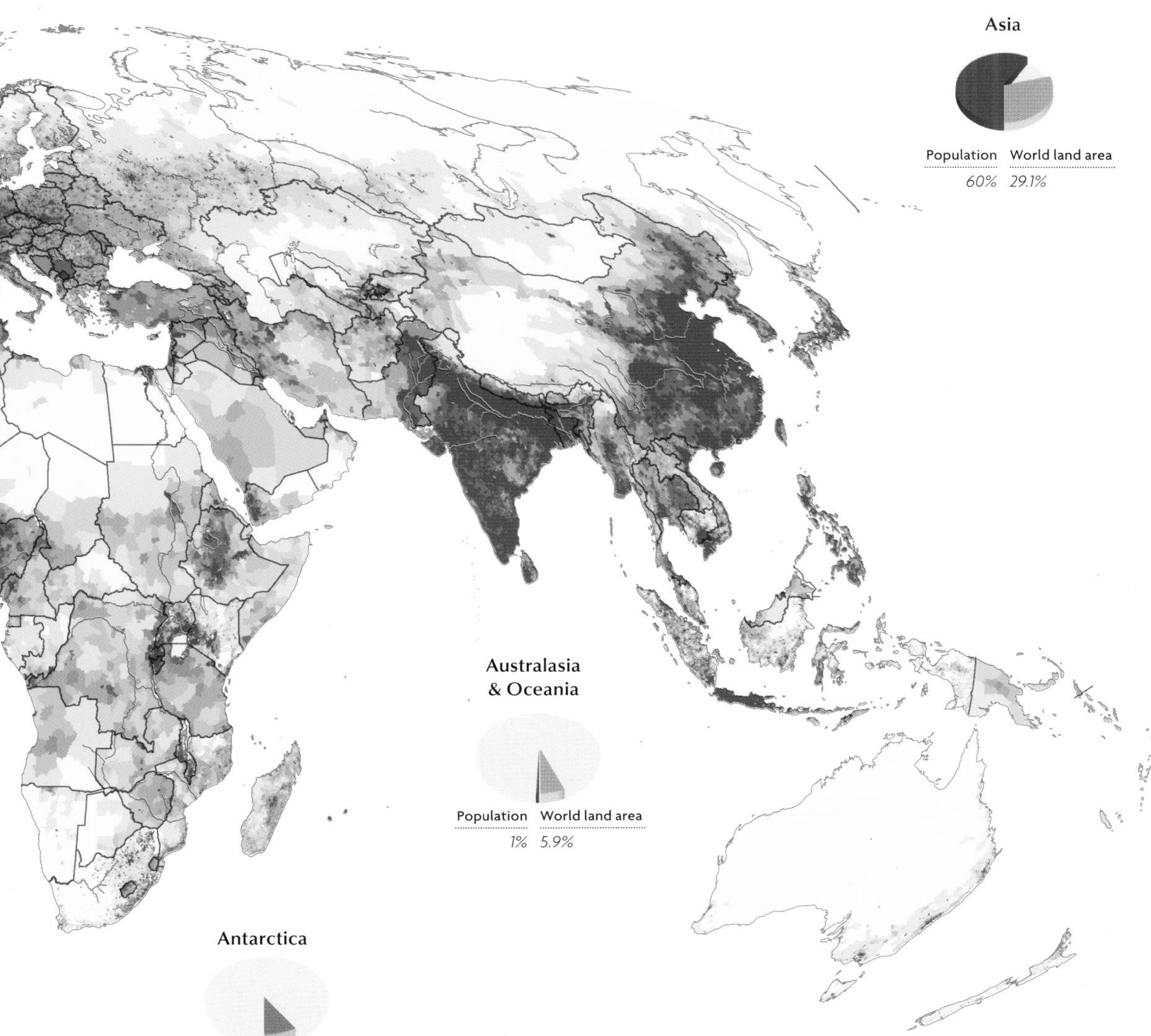
Asia
Population
World land area
60%
29.1%
Australasia
& Oceania
Population
World land area
1%
5.9%
Antarctica
Population
World land area
0%
8.9%

World nutrition

Two-thirds of the world's food supply is consumed by the industrialized nations, many of which have a daily calorific intake far higher than is necessary for their populations to maintain a healthy body weight. In contrast, in the developing world, about 800 million people do not have enough food to meet their basic nutritional needs.

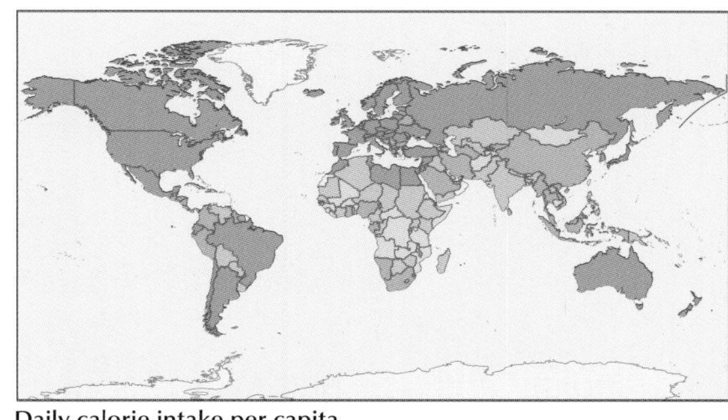

Daily calorie intake per capita

above 3000 | 2500–2999 | 2000–2499 | below 2000 | data not available

World life expectancy

Improved public health and living standards have greatly increased life expectancy in the developed world, where people can now expect to live twice as long as they did 100 years ago. In many of the world's poorest nations, inadequate nutrition and disease, means that the average life expectancy still does not exceed 45 years.

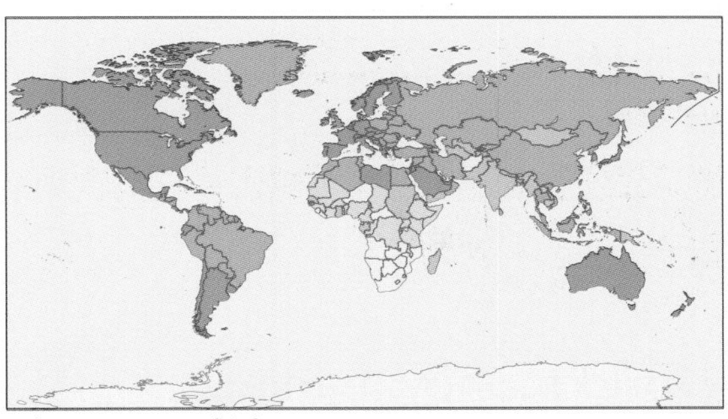

Life expectancy at birth

above 75 years | 65–74 years | 55–64 years | 45–54 years | below 44 years | data not available

Australasia and Oceania

This is the world's most sparsely settled region. The peoples of Australia and New Zealand live mainly in the coastal cities, with only scattered settlements in the arid interior. The Pacific islands can only support limited populations because of their remoteness and lack of resources.

► *Brisbane, on Australia's Gold Coast is the most rapidly expanding city in the country. The great majority of Australia's population lives in cities near the coasts.*

◄ *The remote highlands of Papua New Guinea are home to a wide variety of peoples, many of whom still subsist by traditional hunting and gathering.*

Average world birth rates

Birth rates are much higher in Africa, Asia and South America than in Europe and North America. Increased affluence and easy access to contraception are both factors which can lead to a significant decline in a country's birth rate.

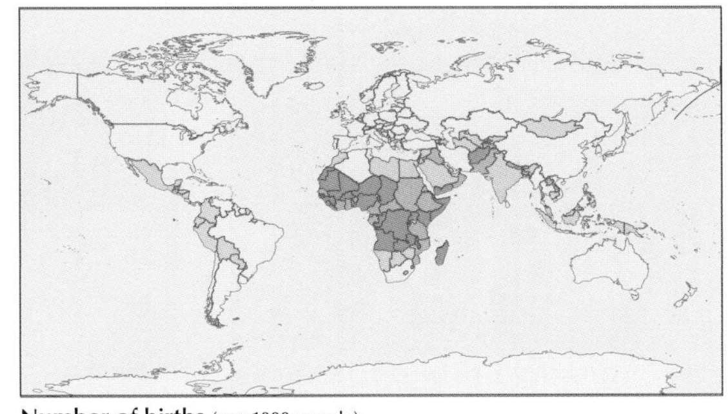

Number of births (per 1000 people)

above 40 | 30–39 | 20–29 | below 20 | data not available

World infant mortality

In parts of the developing world infant mortality rates are still high; access to medical services such as immunization, adequate nutrition and the promotion of breast-feeding have been important in combating infant mortality.

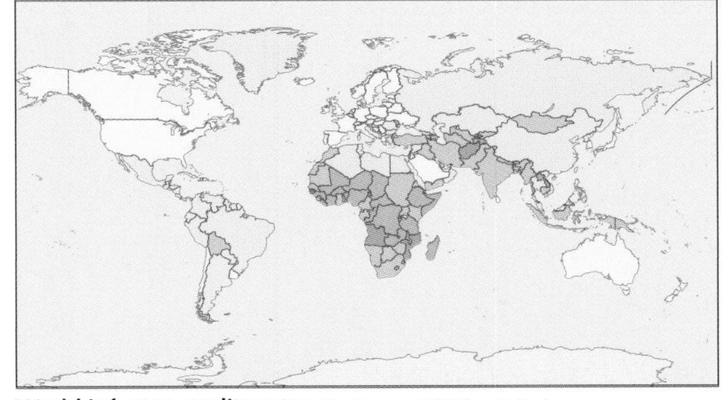

World infant mortality rates (deaths per 1000 live births)

above 125 | 75–124 | 35–74 | 15–34 | below 15 | data not available

The economic system

The wealthy countries of the developed world, with their aggressive, market-led economies and their access to productive new technologies and international markets, dominate the world economic system. At the other extreme, many of the countries of the developing world are locked in a cycle of national debt, rising populations and unemployment. The state-managed economies of the former communist bloc began to be dismantled during the 1990s, and China is emerging as a major economic power following decades of isolation.

Trade blocs

EU / CACM — NAFTA / SADC — ASEAN / ECOWAS — LAIA / CEEAC

Trade blocs

International trade blocs are formed when groups of countries, often already enjoying close military and political ties, join together to offer mutually preferential terms of trade for both imports and exports. Increasingly, global trade is dominated by three main blocs: the EU, NAFTA, and ASEAN. They are supplanting older trade blocs such as the Commonwealth, a legacy of colonialism.

International trade flows

World trade acts as a stimulus to national economies, encouraging growth. Over the last three decades, as heavy industries have declined, services – banking, insurance, tourism, airlines and shipping – have taken an increasingly large share of world trade. Manufactured articles now account for nearly two-thirds of world trade; raw materials and food make up less than a quarter of the total.

Shipping

Ships carry 80% of international cargo, and extensive container ports, where cargo is stored, are vital links in the international transport network.

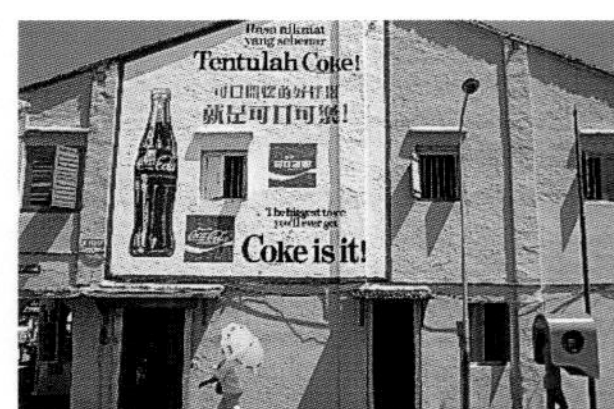
Tentulah Coke!
Coke is it!

Multinationals

Multinational companies are increasingly penetrating inaccessible markets. The reach of many American commodities is now global.

Primary products

Many countries, particularly in the Caribbean and Africa, are still reliant on primary products such as rubber and coffee, which makes them vulnerable to fluctuating prices.

Service industries

Service industries such as banking, tourism and insurance were the fastest-growing industrial sector in the last half of the 20th century. Lloyds of London is the centre of the world insurance market.

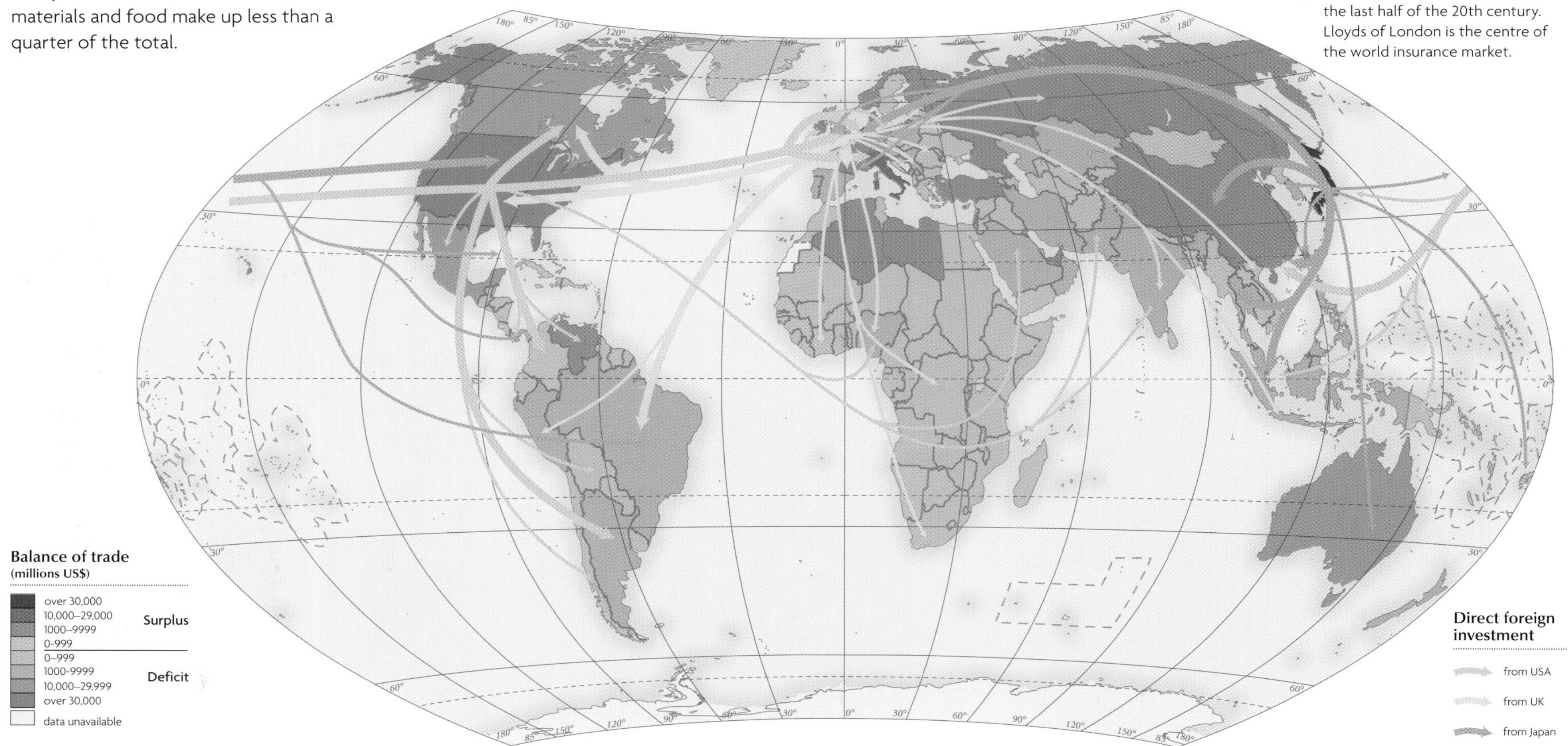
Balance of trade
(millions US$)
Surplus
over 30,000
10,000–29,000
1000–9999
0–999
Deficit
0–999
1000–9999
10,000–29,999
over 30,000
data unavailable
Direct foreign investment
from USA
from UK
from Japan

World money markets

The financial world has traditionally been dominated by three major centres – Tokyo, New York and London, which house the headquarters of stock exchanges, multinational corporations and international banks. Their geographic location means that, at any one time in a 24-hour day, one major market is open for trading in shares, currencies and commodities. Since the late 1980s, technological advances have enabled transactions between financial centres to occur at ever-greater speed, and new markets have sprung up throughout the world.

Major money markets

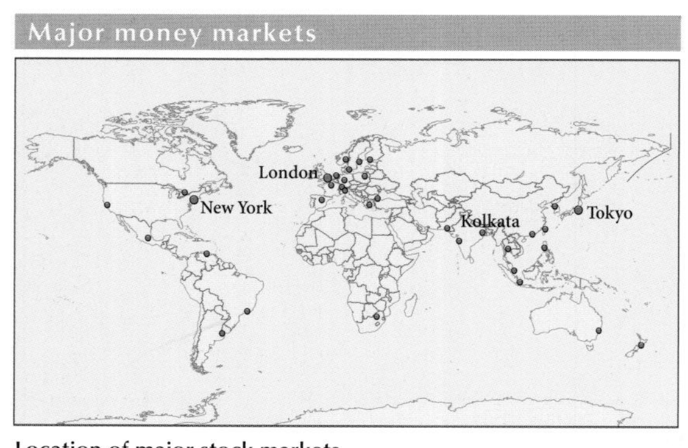
London
New York
Kolkata
Tokyo

Location of major stock markets

● Major stock markets

▲ ***The Tokyo Stock Market** crashed in 1990, leading to slow-down in the growth of the world's most powerful economy, and a refocusing on economic policy away from export-led growth and towards the domestic market.*

New stock markets

New stock markets are now opening in many parts of the world, where economies have recently emerged from state controls. In Moscow and Beijing, and several countries in eastern Europe, newly-opened stock exchanges reflect the transition to market-driven economies.

▲ ***Dealers at the** Kolkata Stock Market. The Indian economy has been opened up to foreign investment and many multinationals now have bases there.*

The developing world

International trade in capital and currency is dominated by the rich nations of the northern hemisphere. In parts of Africa and Asia, where exports of any sort are extremely limited, home-produced commodities are simply sold in local markets.

▲ ***Markets have thrived** in communist Vietnam since the introduction of a liberal economic policy.*

World wealth disparity

A global assessment of Gross Domestic Product (GDP) by nation reveals great disparities. The developed world, with only a quarter of the world's population, has 80% of the world's manufacturing income. Civil war, conflict and political instability further undermine the economic self-sufficiency of many of the world's poorest nations.

▲ **Cities such as** *Detroit have been badly hit by the decline in heavy industry.*

Urban decay

Although the USA still dominates the global economy, it faces deficits in both the federal budget and the balance of trade. Vast discrepancies in personal wealth, high levels of unemployment, and the dismantling of welfare provisions throughout the 1980s have led to severe deprivation in several of the inner cities of North America's industrial heartland.

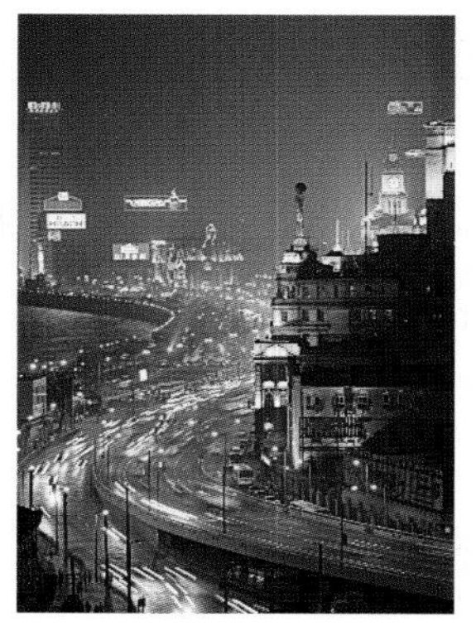

◄ **Foreign investment has** *encouraged new infrastructure development in cities like Shanghai.*

Booming cities

Since the 1980s the Chinese government has set up special industrial zones, such as Shanghai, where foreign investment is encouraged through tax incentives. Migrants from rural China pour into these regions in search of work, creating 'boomtown' economies.

Urban sprawl

Cities are expanding all over the developing world, attracting economic migrants in search of work and opportunities. In cities such as Rio de Janeiro, housing has not kept pace with the population explosion, and squalid shanty towns *(favelas)* rub shoulders with middle-class housing.

▲ **The favelas of** *Rio de Janeiro sprawl over the hills surrounding the city.*

Comparative world wealth

World economies - average GDP per capita (US$)

- above 20,000
- 5000–20,000
- 2000–5000
- below 2000
- data unavailable

Economic 'tigers'

The economic 'tigers' of the Pacific Rim – China, Singapore, and South Korea – have grown faster than Europe and the USA over the last decade. Their export- and service-led economies have benefited from stable government, low labour costs, and foreign investment.

▲ **Hong Kong, with** *its fine natural harbour, is one of the most important ports in Asia.*

Agricultural economies

In parts of the developing world, people survive by subsistence farming – only growing enough food for themselves and their families. With no surplus product, they are unable to exchange goods for currency, the only means of escaping the poverty trap. In other countries, farmers have been encouraged to concentrate on growing a single crop for the export market. This reliance on cash crops leaves farmers vulnerable to crop failure and to changes in the market price of the crop.

▲ ***The Ugandan uplands*** *are fertile, but poor infrastructure hampers the export of cash crops.*

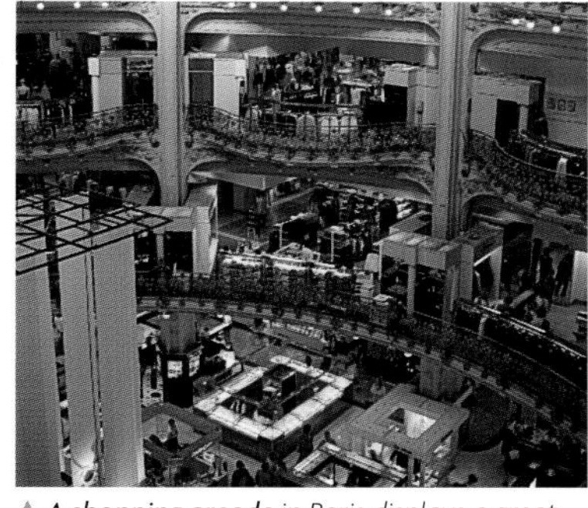

▲ ***A shopping arcade*** *in Paris displays a great profusion of luxury goods.*

The affluent West

The capital cities of many countries in the developed world are showcases for consumer goods, reflecting the increasing importance of the service sector, and particularly the retail sector, in the world economy. The idea of shopping as a leisure activity is unique to the western world. Luxury goods and services attract visitors, who in turn generate tourist revenue.

Tourism

In 2004, there were over 700 million tourists worldwide. Tourism is now the world's biggest single industry, employing 130 million people, though frequently in low-paid unskilled jobs. While tourists are increasingly exploring inaccessible and less-developed regions of the world, the benefits of the industry are not always felt at a local level. There are also worries about the environmental impact of tourism, as the world's last wildernesses increasingly become tourist attractions.

▲ ***Botswana's Okavango Delta*** *is an area rich in wildlife. Tourists make safaris to the region, but the impact of tourism is controlled.*

Money flows

Foreign investment in the developing world during the 1970s led to a global financial crisis in the 1980s, when many countries were unable to meet their debt repayments. The International Monetary Fund (IMF) was forced to reschedule the debts and, in some cases, write them off completely. Within the developing world, austerity programmes have been initiated to cope with the debt, leading in turn to high unemployment and galloping inflation. In many parts of Africa, stricken economies are now dependent on international aid.

◄ ***In rural Southeast Asia,*** *babies are given medical checks by UNICEF as part of a global aid programme sponsored by the UN.*

Tourist arrivals

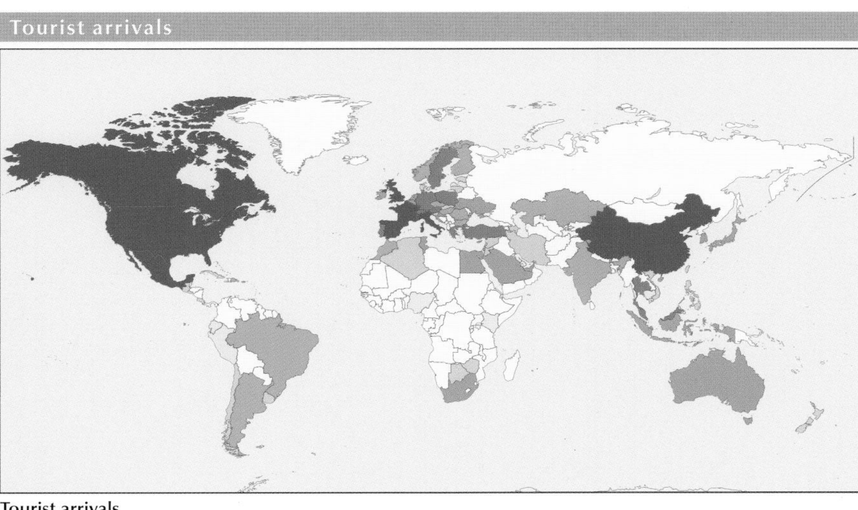

Tourist arrivals

- over 20 million
- 10–20 million
- 5–10 million
- 2.5–5 million
- 1–2.5 million
- 700,000–999,000
- under 700,000
- data unavailable

International debt

International debt (as percentage of GNI)

- over 100%
- 70–99%
- 50–69%
- 30–49%
- 10–29%
- below 10%
- data unavailable

The political world

There are 195 independent countries in the world today. With the exception of Antarctica, where territorial claims have been deferred by international treaty, every land area of the Earth's surface either belongs to, or is claimed by, one country or another. The largest country in the world is the Russian Federation, the smallest is Vatican City. Some 60 overseas dependent territories remain, administered variously by France, Australia, Denmark, New Zealand, Norway, Portugal, the UK, the US and the Netherlands.

Most densely populated country
Monaco: 43,561 people per sq mile (16,754 people per sq km)

Smallest country
Vatican City: 0.17 sq miles (0.44 sq km)

Longest land borders
Russian Federation: 12,427 miles (20,000 km)

Longest single land border
Canada/USA: 5526 miles (8893 km)

Largest country
Russian Federation: 6,592,735 sq miles (17,075,200 sq km)

Most populous City
Tokyo: 34,200,000 people

Most sparsely populated country
Mongolia: 4 people per sq mile (2 people per sq km)

Most populous country
China: 1,331,400,000 people

Largest island country
Australia: 2,967,893 sq miles (7,686,850 sq km)

Smallest island country
Nauru: 8.2 sq miles (21.2 sq km)

International borders

The map shows three main types of boundary between states. Full borders represent internationally agreed and recognized territorial boundaries. Undefined borders exist where no fixed boundary between states has been demarcated; the boundaries indicated in this way show approximate areas of sovereignty. A disputed border is indicated where a *de facto* territorial boundary exists, which is not agreed or is subject to arbitration.

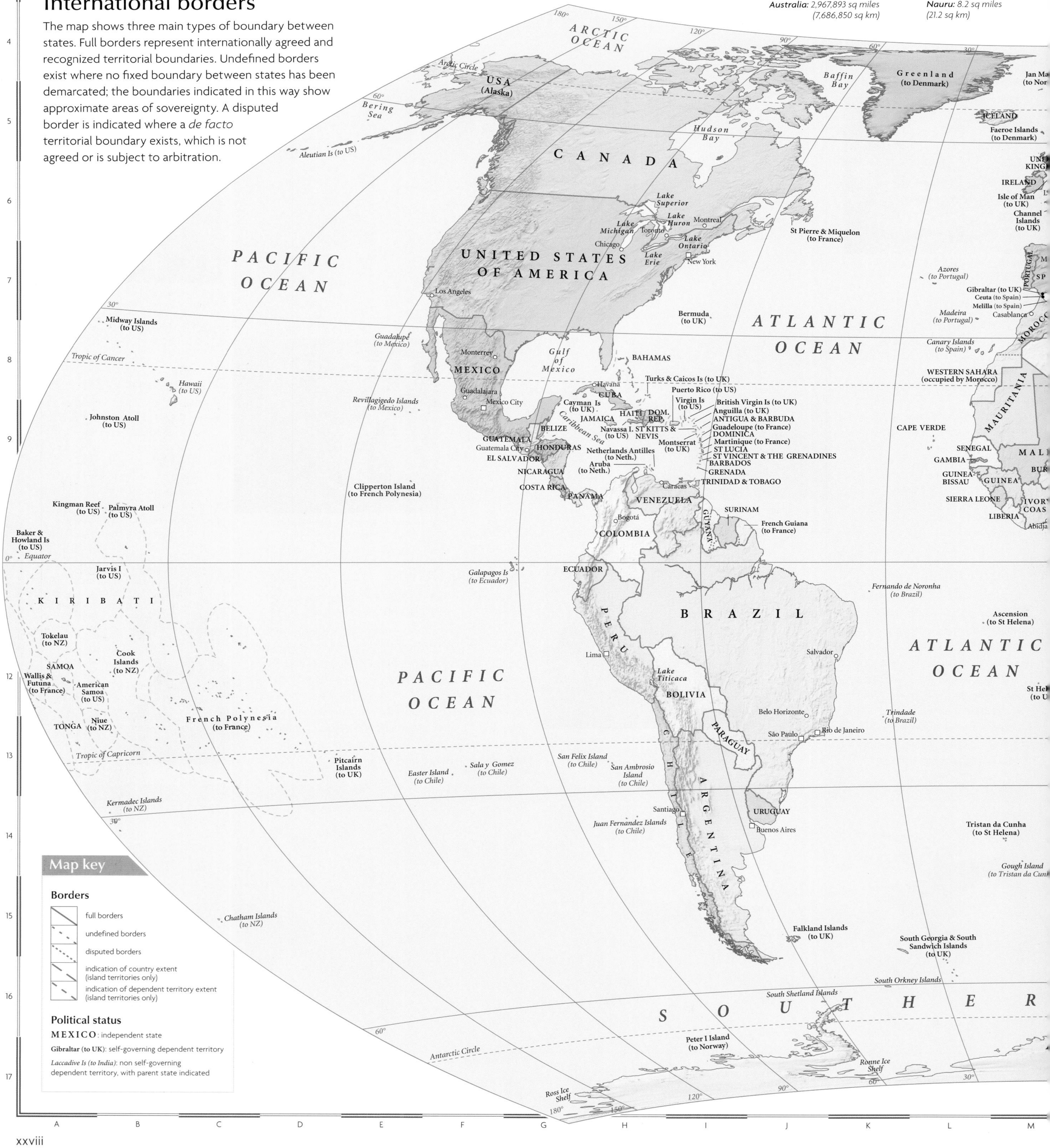

Map key

Borders

- full borders
- undefined borders
- disputed borders
- indication of country extent (island territories only)
- indication of dependent territory extent (island territories only)

Political status

MEXICO: independent state

Gibraltar (to UK): self-governing dependent territory

Laccadive Is (to India): non self-governing dependent territory, with parent state indicated

The world in 1914

The early years of the 20th century saw the mainly European colonial empires reaching their greatest extents by 1914. Two world wars inaugurated their disintegration, but even in 1950 there were only 82 independent countries. Since then, over 100 have gained their independence, culminating in the breakup of the Soviet Union and former Yugoslavia in the early 1990s.

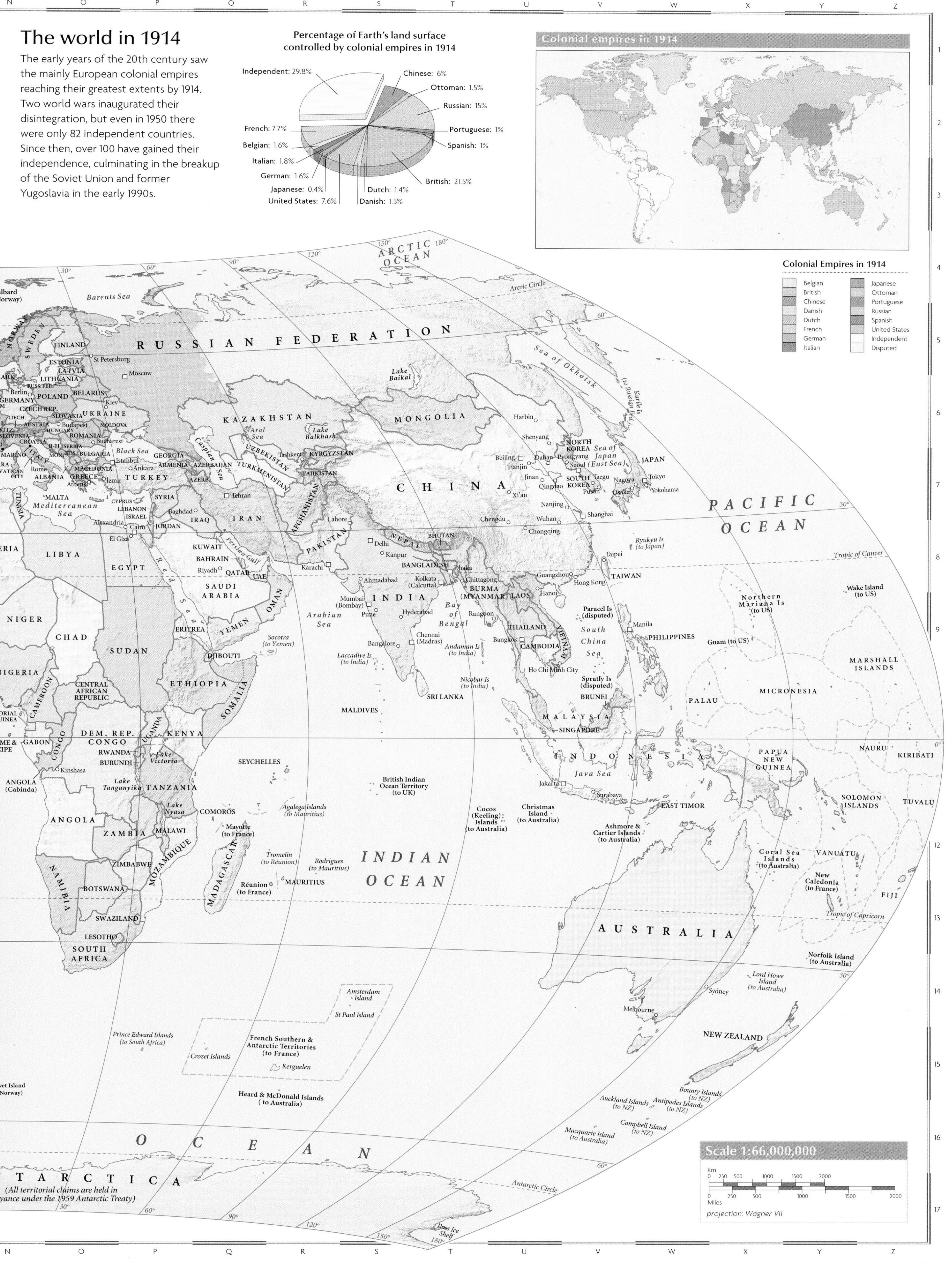
Percentage of Earth's land surface controlled by colonial empires in 1914
Independent: 29.8%
Chinese: 6%
Ottoman: 1.5%
Russian: 15%
French: 7.7%
Portuguese: 1%
Belgian: 1.6%
Spanish: 1%
Italian: 1.8%
German: 1.6%
British: 21.5%
Japanese: 0.4%
Dutch: 1.4%
United States: 7.6%
Danish: 1.5%
Colonial empires in 1914
Colonial Empires in 1914
Belgian
British
Chinese
Danish
Dutch
French
German
Italian
Japanese
Ottoman
Portuguese
Russian
Spanish
United States
Independent
Disputed
ARCTIC OCEAN
Arctic Circle
Barents Sea
RUSSIAN FEDERATION
FINLAND
SWEDEN
NORWAY
St Petersburg
Moscow
ESTONIA
LATVIA
LITHUANIA
BELARUS
POLAND
UKRAINE
MOLDOVA
ROMANIA
BULGARIA
TURKEY
GEORGIA
ARMENIA
AZERBAIJAN
KAZAKHSTAN
Aral Sea
Lake Balkhash
UZBEKISTAN
TURKMENISTAN
KYRGYZSTAN
TAJIKISTAN
AFGHANISTAN
PAKISTAN
IRAN
IRAQ
SYRIA
LEBANON
ISRAEL
JORDAN
KUWAIT
BAHRAIN
QATAR
UAE
SAUDI ARABIA
OMAN
YEMEN
Black Sea
Caspian Sea
Mediterranean Sea
Persian Gulf
Red Sea
LIBYA
EGYPT
NIGER
CHAD
SUDAN
NIGERIA
ERITREA
DJIBOUTI
ETHIOPIA
SOMALIA
CENTRAL AFRICAN REPUBLIC
CAMEROON
GABON
CONGO
DEM. REP. CONGO
UGANDA
KENYA
RWANDA
BURUNDI
Lake Victoria
Lake Tanganyika
TANZANIA
Lake Nyasa
ANGOLA
ANGOLA (Cabinda)
ZAMBIA
MALAWI
MOZAMBIQUE
ZIMBABWE
NAMIBIA
BOTSWANA
SWAZILAND
LESOTHO
SOUTH AFRICA
MADAGASCAR
COMOROS
SEYCHELLES
Mayotte (to France)
Réunion (to France)
MAURITIUS
Tromelin (to Réunion)
Rodrigues (to Mauritius)
Agalega Islands (to Mauritius)
Socotra (to Yemen)
MONGOLIA
Lake Baikal
CHINA
NEPAL
BHUTAN
INDIA
BANGLADESH
BURMA (MYANMAR)
LAOS
THAILAND
CAMBODIA
VIETNAM
MALAYSIA
SINGAPORE
BRUNEI
INDONESIA
PHILIPPINES
TAIWAN
NORTH KOREA
SOUTH KOREA
JAPAN
Sea of Okhotsk
Sea of Japan (East Sea)
Kurile Is (to Russian Fed.)
Ryukyu Is (to Japan)
Arabian Sea
Bay of Bengal
South China Sea
Java Sea
Andaman Is (to India)
Nicobar Is (to India)
Laccadive Is (to India)
SRI LANKA
MALDIVES
British Indian Ocean Territory (to UK)
Cocos (Keeling) Islands (to Australia)
Christmas Island (to Australia)
Paracel Is (disputed)
Spratly Is (disputed)
INDIAN OCEAN
PACIFIC OCEAN
Tropic of Cancer
Tropic of Capricorn
Northern Mariana Is (to US)
Guam (to US)
Wake Island (to US)
MARSHALL ISLANDS
MICRONESIA
PALAU
NAURU
KIRIBATI
PAPUA NEW GUINEA
SOLOMON ISLANDS
TUVALU
VANUATU
FIJI
New Caledonia (to France)
Coral Sea Islands (to Australia)
EAST TIMOR
Ashmore & Cartier Islands (to Australia)
AUSTRALIA
Norfolk Island (to Australia)
Lord Howe Island (to Australia)
Sydney
Melbourne
NEW ZEALAND
Bounty Islands (to NZ)
Antipodes Islands (to NZ)
Auckland Islands (to NZ)
Campbell Island (to NZ)
Macquarie Island (to Australia)
Amsterdam Island
St Paul Island
Prince Edward Islands (to South Africa)
Crozet Islands
French Southern & Antarctic Territories (to France)
Kerguelen
Heard & McDonald Islands (to Australia)
OCEAN
ANTARCTICA
(All territorial claims are held in abeyance under the 1959 Antarctic Treaty)
Antarctic Circle
Ross Ice Shelf
Scale 1:66,000,000
Km
Miles
projection: Wagner VII

States and boundaries

There are over 190 sovereign states in the world today; in 1950 there were only 82. Over the last half-century national self-determination has been a driving force for many states with a history of colonialism and oppression. As more borders have been added to the world map, the number of international border disputes has increased.

In many cases, where the impetus towards independence has been religious or ethnic, disputes with minority groups have also caused violent internal conflict. While many newly-formed states have moved peacefully towards independence, successfully establishing government by multiparty democracy, dictatorship by military regime or individual despot is often the result of the internal power-struggles which characterize the early stages in the lives of new nations.

The nature of politics

Democracy is a broad term: it can range from the ideal of multiparty elections and fair representation to, in countries such as Singapore, a thin disguise for single-party rule. In despotic regimes, on the other hand, a single, often personal authority has total power; institutions such as parliament and the military are mere instruments of the dictator.

◄ **The stars and** stripes of the US flag are a potent symbol of the country's status as a federal democracy.

The changing world map

Decolonization

In 1950, large areas of the world remained under the control of a handful of European countries *(page xxviii)*. The process of decolonization had begun in Asia, where, following the Second World War, much of south and southeast Asia sought and achieved self-determination. In the 1960s, a host of African states achieved independence, so that by 1965, most of the larger tracts of the European overseas empires had been substantially eroded. The final major stage in decolonization came with the break-up of the Soviet Union and the Eastern bloc after 1990. The process continues today as the last toeholds of European colonialism, often tiny island nations, press increasingly for independence.

▲ ***Icons of communism,** including statues of former leaders such as Lenin and Stalin, were destroyed when the Soviet bloc was dismantled in 1989, creating several new nations.*

New nations 1945–1965

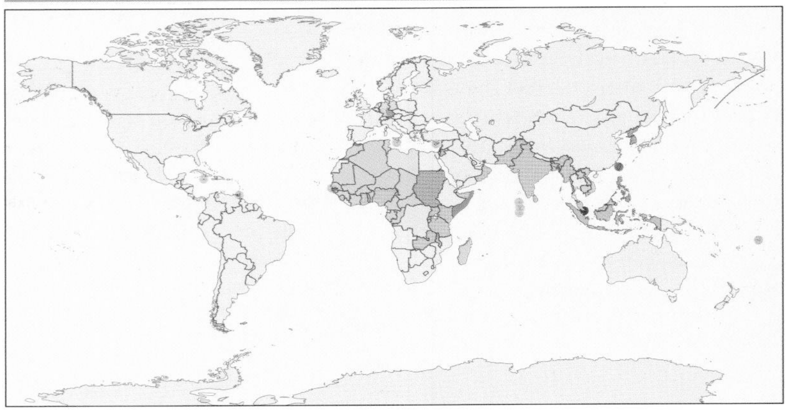

New nations 1965–present

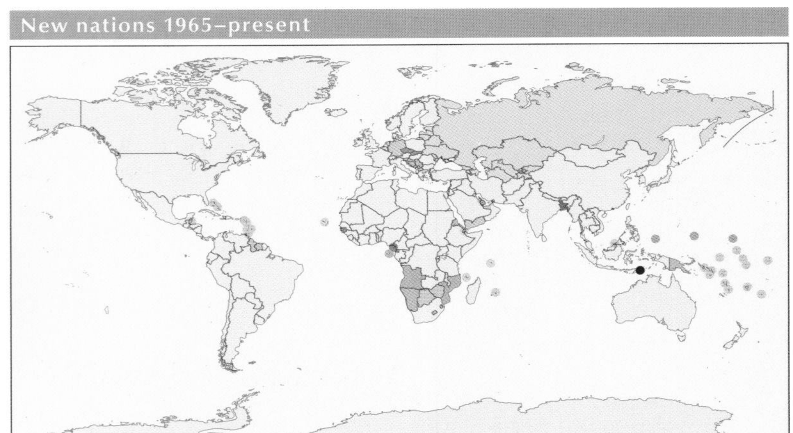

▲ ***Iran has been** one of the modern world's few true theocracies; Islam has an impact on every aspect of political life.*

▲ ***North Korea is** an independent communist republic. Power is concentrated in the hands of Kim Jong Il.*

Administration at the time of independence

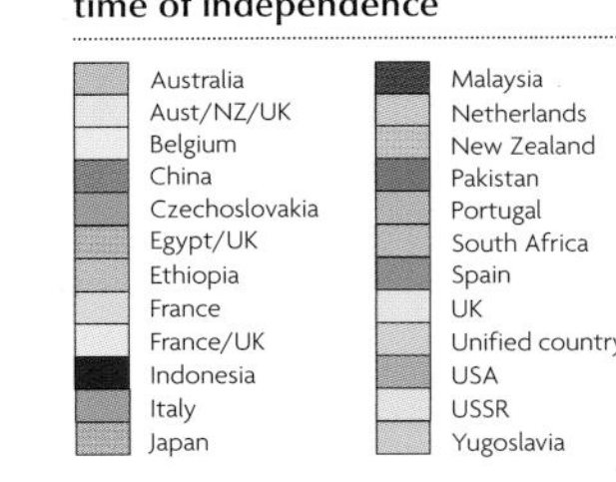
Australia
Aust/NZ/UK
Belgium
China
Czechoslovakia
Egypt/UK
Ethiopia
France
France/UK
Indonesia
Italy
Japan
Malaysia
Netherlands
New Zealand
Pakistan
Portugal
South Africa
Spain
UK
Unified country
USA
USSR
Yugoslavia

◄ ***Saddam Hussein,** former autocratic leader of Iraq, promoted an extreme personality cult for over 20 years. He was ousted by a US-led coalition in 2003.*

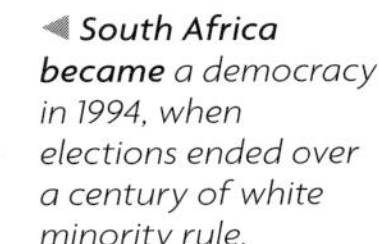

◄ ***South Africa** became a democracy in 1994, when elections ended over a century of white minority rule.*

▲ ***In Brunei the** Sultan has ruled by decree since 1962; power is closely tied to the royal family. The Sultan's brothers are responsible for finance and foreign affairs.*

Types of government

- Multiparty democracy for more than 10 yrs
- Multiparty democracy within last 10 yrs
- Single-party government
- Military regime
- Theocracy
- Monarchy
- Non-party system
- Transitional regime
- Current civil unrest

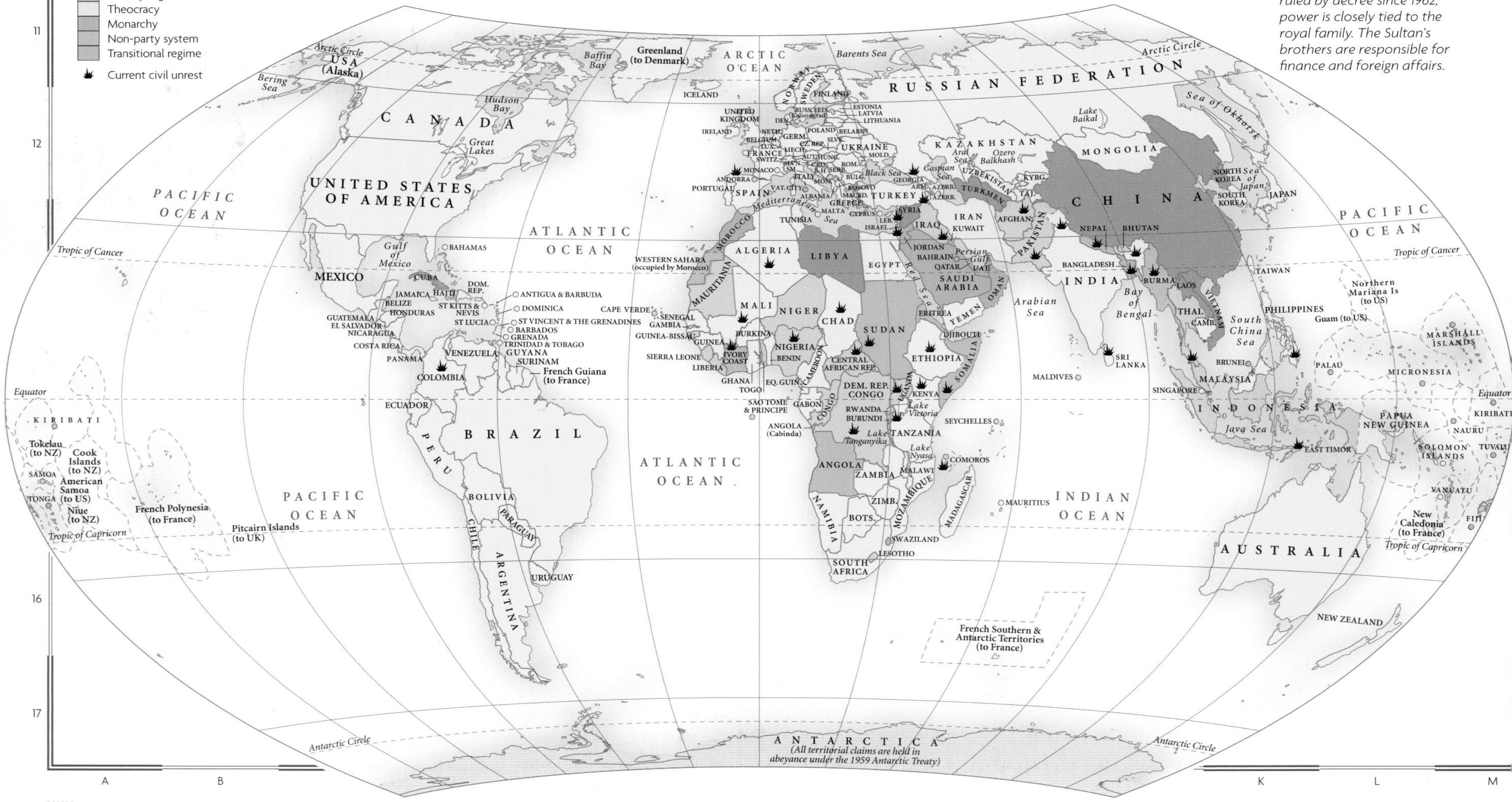

ARCTIC OCEAN
RUSSIAN FEDERATION
CANADA
UNITED STATES OF AMERICA
PACIFIC OCEAN
ATLANTIC OCEAN
INDIAN OCEAN
BRAZIL
CHINA
INDIA
AUSTRALIA
ANTARCTICA
(All territorial claims are held in abeyance under the 1959 Antarctic Treaty)
French Southern & Antarctic Territories (to France)
Greenland (to Denmark)
Arctic Circle
Tropic of Cancer
Equator
Tropic of Capricorn
Antarctic Circle

Lines on the map

The determination of international boundaries can use a variety of criteria. Many of the borders between older states follow physical boundaries; some mirror religious and ethnic differences; others are the legacy of complex histories of conflict and colonialism, while others have been imposed by international agreements or arbitration.

Post-colonial borders

When the European colonial empires in Africa were dismantled during the second half of the 20th century, the outlines of the new African states mirrored colonial boundaries. These boundaries had been drawn up by colonial administrators, often based on inadequate geographical knowledge. Such arbitrary boundaries were imposed on people of different languages, racial groups, religions and customs. This confused legacy often led to civil and international war.

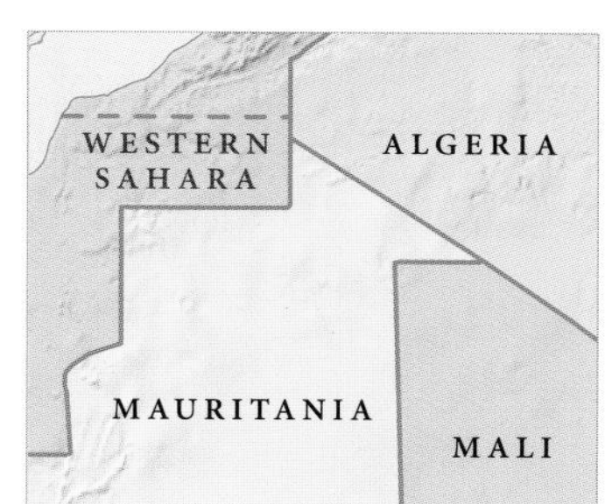
WESTERN SAHARA
ALGERIA
MAURITANIA
MALI

▲ *The conflict that has plagued many African countries since independence has caused millions of people to become refugees.*

Enclaves

The shifting political map over the course of history has frequently led to anomalous situations. Parts of national territories may become isolated by territorial agreement, forming an enclave. The West German part of the city of Berlin, which until 1989 lay a hundred miles (160 km) within East German territory, was a famous example.

Baltic Sea
ESTONIA
RUSSIAN FEDERATION
LATVIA
LITHUANIA
RUSS. FED. (Kaliningrad)
POLAND
BELARUS

▲ ***Since the independence** of Lithuania and Belarus, the peoples of the Russian enclave of Kaliningrad have become physically isolated.*

Antarctica

When Antarctic exploration began a century ago, seven nations, Australia, Argentina, Britain, Chile, France, New Zealand and Norway, laid claim to the new territory. In 1961 the Antarctic Treaty, now signed by 45 nations, agreed to hold all territorial claims in abeyance.

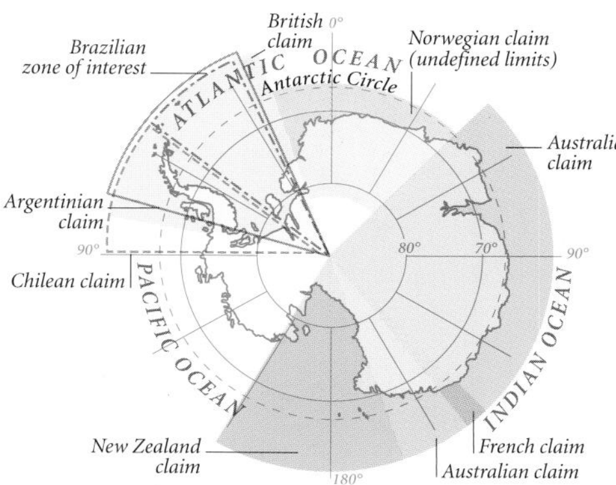
Brazilian zone of interest
British claim
Norwegian claim (undefined limits)
ATLANTIC OCEAN
Antarctic Circle
Australian claim
Argentinian claim
Chilean claim
PACIFIC OCEAN
INDIAN OCEAN
New Zealand claim
French claim
Australian claim
0°
90°
80°
70°
180°

Geometric borders

Straight lines and lines of longitude and latitude have occasionally been used to determine international boundaries; and indeed the world's second longest continuous international boundary, between Canada and the USA, follows the 49th Parallel for over one-third of its course. Many Canadian, American and Australian internal administrative boundaries are similarly determined using a geometric solution.

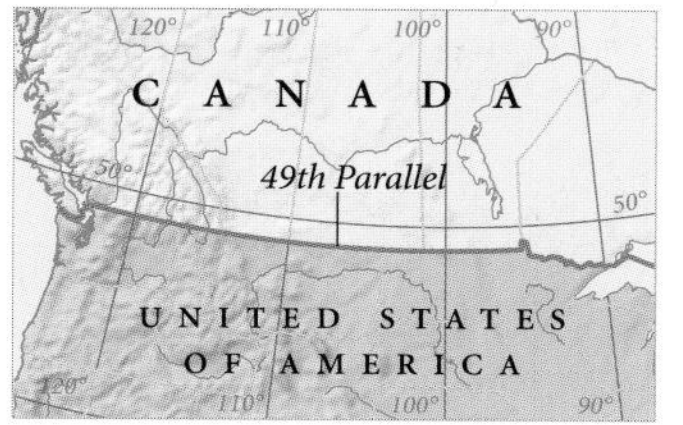
CANADA
49th Parallel
UNITED STATES OF AMERICA
120°
110°
100°
90°
50°

▲ ***Different farming techniques** in Canada and the USA clearly mark the course of the international boundary in this satellite map.*

World boundaries

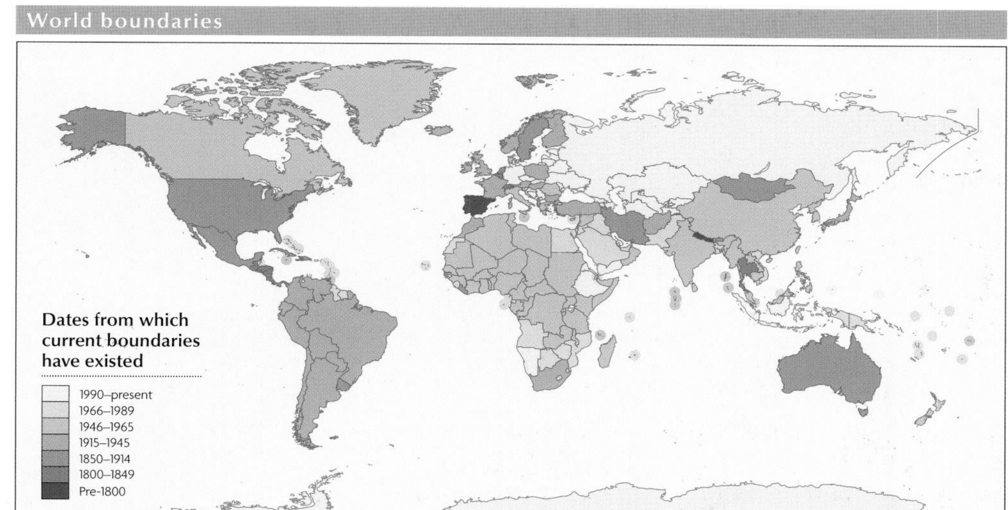
Dates from which current boundaries have existed
1990–present
1966–1989
1946–1965
1915–1945
1850–1914
1800–1849
Pre-1800

Physical borders

Many of the world's countries are divided by physical borders: lakes, rivers, mountains. The demarcation of such boundaries can, however, lead to disputes. Control of waterways, water supplies and fisheries are frequent causes of international friction.

Lake borders

Countries which lie next to lakes usually fix their borders in the middle of the lake. Unusually the Lake Nyasa border between Malawi and Tanzania runs along Tanzania's shore.

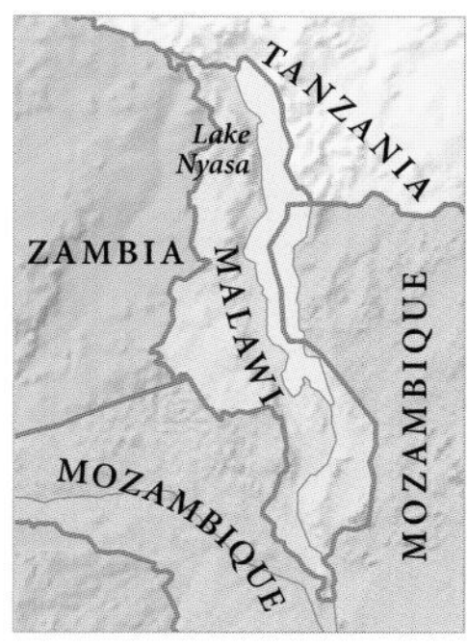
TANZANIA
Lake Nyasa
ZAMBIA
MALAWI
MOZAMBIQUE
MOZAMBIQUE

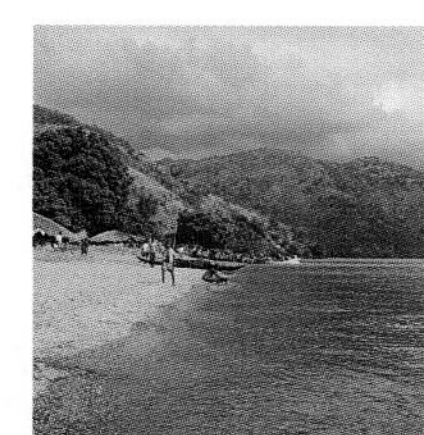

▲ ***Complicated agreements between** colonial powers led to the awkward division of Lake Nyasa.*

River borders

Rivers alone account for one-sixth of the world's borders. Many great rivers form boundaries between a number of countries. Changes in a river's course and interruptions of its natural flow can lead to disputes, particularly in areas where water is scarce. The centre of the river's course is the nominal boundary line.

GERMANY
Danube
SLOVAKIA
UKRAINE
AUSTRIA
HUNGARY
ROMANIA
CROATIA
Danube
SERBIA
BULGARIA

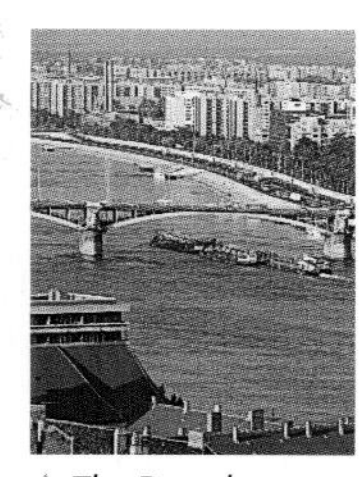

▲ ***The Danube forms** all or part of the border between nine European nations.*

Mountain borders

Mountain ranges form natural barriers and are the basis for many major borders, particularly in Europe and Asia. The watershed is the conventional boundary demarcation line, but its accurate determination is often problematic.

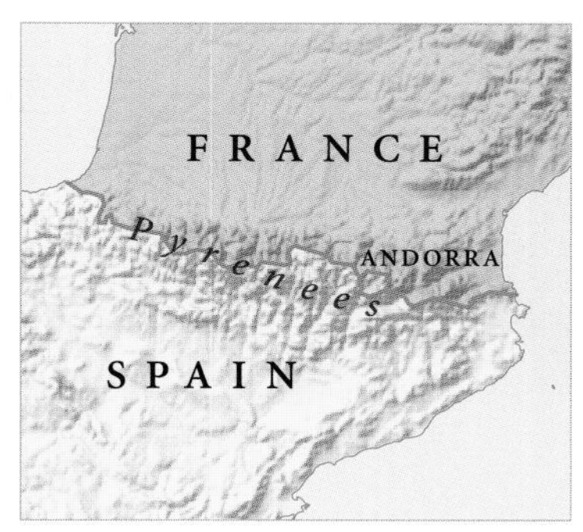
FRANCE
Pyrenees
ANDORRA
SPAIN

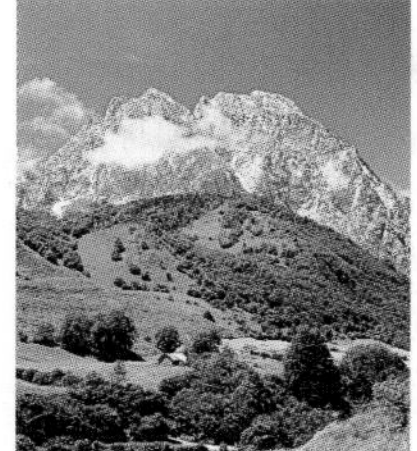

▲ ***The Pyrenees form** a natural mountain border between France and Spain.*

Shifting boundaries – Poland

Borders between countries can change dramatically over time. The nations of eastern Europe have been particularly affected by changing boundaries. Poland is an example of a country whose boundaries have changed so significantly that it has literally moved around Europe. At the start of the 16th century, Poland was the largest nation in Europe. Between 1772 and 1795, it was absorbed into Prussia, Austria and Russia, and it effectively ceased to exist. After the First World War, Poland became an independent country once more, but its borders changed again after the Second World War following invasions by both Soviet Russia and Nazi Germany.

Moscow
POLAND
Warsaw
Kiev

▲ ***In 1634, Poland** was the largest nation in Europe, its eastern boundary reaching towards Moscow.*

Moscow
RUSSIA
PRUSSIA
Warsaw
Kiev
AUSTRIA

▲ ***From 1772–1795, Poland** was gradually partitioned between Austria, Russia and Prussia. Its eastern boundary receded by over 100 miles (160 km).*

Moscow
POLAND
Warsaw
Kiev

▲ ***Following the First** World War, Poland was reinstated as an independent state, but it was less than half the size it had been in 1634.*

Moscow
POLAND
Warsaw
Kiev

▲ ***After the Second** World War the Baltic Sea border was extended westwards, but much of the eastern territory was annexed by Russia.*

International disputes

There are more than 60 disputed borders or territories in the world today. Although many of these disputes can be settled by peaceful negotiation, some areas have become a focus for international conflict. Ethnic tensions have been a major source of territorial disagreement throughout history, as has the ownership of, and access to, valuable natural resources. The turmoil of the post-colonial era in many parts of Africa is partly a result of the 19th century 'carve-up' of the continent, which created potential for conflict by drawing often arbitrary lines through linguistic and cultural areas.

Jammu and Kashmir

Disputes over Jammu and Kashmir have caused three serious wars between India and Pakistan since 1947. Pakistan wishes to annex the largely Muslim territory, while India refuses to cede any territory or to hold a referendum, and also lays claim to the entire territory. Most international maps show the 'line of control' agreed in 1972 as the *de facto* border. In addition India has territorial disputes with neighbouring China. The situation is further complicated by a Kashmiri independence movement, active since the late 1980s.

▲ ***Indian army troops** maintain their positions in the mountainous terrain of northern Kashmir.*

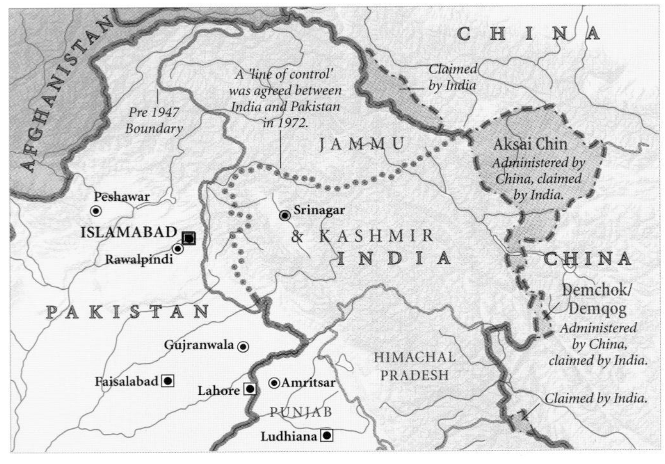
AFGHANISTAN
CHINA
A 'line of control' was agreed between India and Pakistan in 1972.
Claimed by India
Pre 1947 Boundary
JAMMU
& KASHMIR
Aksai Chin
Administered by China, claimed by India.
Peshawar
Srinagar
ISLAMABAD
Rawalpindi
INDIA
CHINA
Demchok/ Demqog
Administered by China, claimed by India.
PAKISTAN
Gujranwala
HIMACHAL PRADESH
Faisalabad
Lahore
Amritsar
PUNJAB
Ludhiana
Claimed by India.

North and South Korea

Since 1953, the *de facto* border between North and South Korea has been a ceasefire line which straddles the 38th Parallel and is designated as a demilitarized zone. Both countries have heavy fortifications and troop concentrations behind this zone.

CHINA
NORTH KOREA
Sea of Japan
PYONGYANG
SEOUL
SOUTH KOREA
Yellow Sea

▲ ***Heavy fortifications** on the border between North and South Korea.*

Cyprus

Cyprus was partitioned in 1974, following an invasion by Turkish troops. The south is now the Greek Cypriot Republic of Cyprus, while the self-proclaimed Turkish Republic of Northern Cyprus is recognized only by Turkey.

▲ ***The so-called** 'green line' divides Cyprus into Greek and Turkish sectors.*

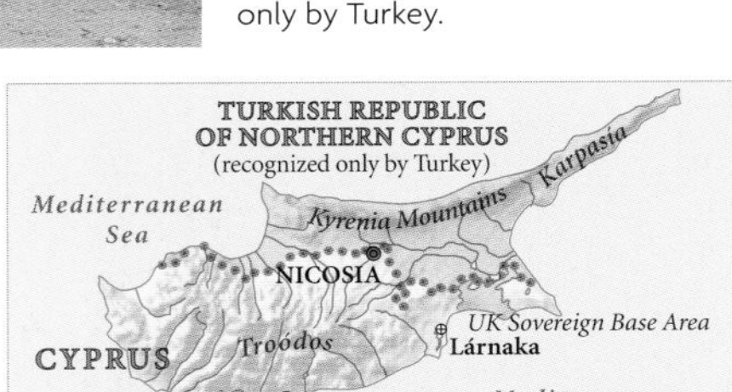
TURKISH REPUBLIC OF NORTHERN CYPRUS
(recognized only by Turkey)
Mediterranean Sea
Kyrenia Mountains
Karpasia
NICOSIA
CYPRUS
Troodos
UK Sovereign Base Area
Lárnaka
UK Sovereign Base Area
Lemesós (Limassol)
Mediterranean Sea

Conflicts and international disputes

- Countries contributing troops to coalition force in Iraq (as of 2008)
- Major active territorial or border disputes
- Countries involved in internal conflict
- Active territorial or border disputes and internal conflict

The Falkland Islands

The British dependent territory of the Falkland Islands was invaded by Argentina in 1982, sparking a full-scale war with the UK. In 1995, the UK and Argentina reached an agreement on the exploitation of oil reserves around the islands.

◀ ***British warships** in Falkland Sound during the 1982 war with Argentina.*

Former Yugoslavia

Following the disintegration in 1991 of the communist state of Yugoslavia, the breakaway states of Croatia and Bosnia and Herzegovina came into conflict with the 'parent' state (consisting of Serbia and Montenegro). Warfare focused on ethnic and territorial ambitions in Bosnia. The tenuous Dayton Accord of 1995 sought to recognize the post-1990 borders, whilst providing for ethnic partition and required international peace-keeping troops to maintain the terms of the peace.

CROATIA
Sava
Bosna
Brčko
Bihać
Banja Luka
Tuzla
Jajce
BOSNIA &
HERZEGOVINA
Drina
Srebrenica
SERBIA
Gornji Vakuf
SARAJEVO
Goražde
Adriatic Sea
Split
Mostar
Republika Srpska
Federacija Bosna i Hercegovina
MONTENEGRO
Dubrovnik

The Spratly Islands

The site of potential oil and natural gas reserves, the Spratly Islands in the South China Sea have been claimed by China, Vietnam, Taiwan, Malaysia and the Philippines since the Japanese gave up a wartime claim in 1951.

▲ ***Most claimant states** have small military garrisons on the Spratly Islands.*

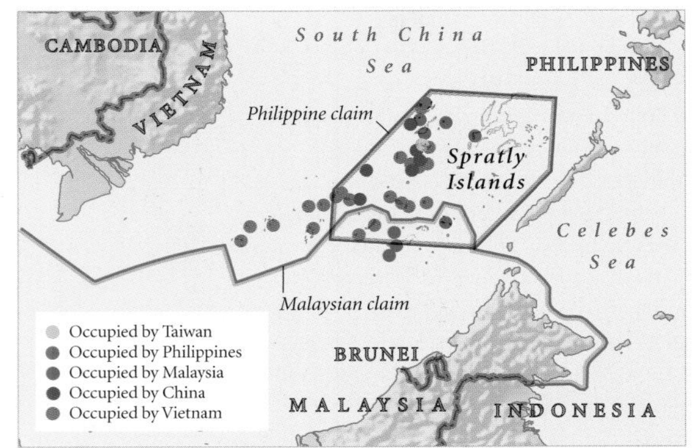
CAMBODIA
South China Sea
PHILIPPINES
VIETNAM
Philippine claim
Spratly Islands
Celebes Sea
Malaysian claim
Occupied by Taiwan
Occupied by Philippines
Occupied by Malaysia
Occupied by China
Occupied by Vietnam
BRUNEI
MALAYSIA
INDONESIA

Israel

Israel was created in 1948 following the 1947 UN Resolution (147) on Palestine. Until 1979 Israel had no borders, only ceasefire lines from a series of wars in 1948, 1967 and 1973. Treaties with Egypt in 1979 and Jordan in 1994 led to these borders being defined and agreed. Negotiations over Israeli settlements and Palestinian self-government have seen little effective progress since 2000.

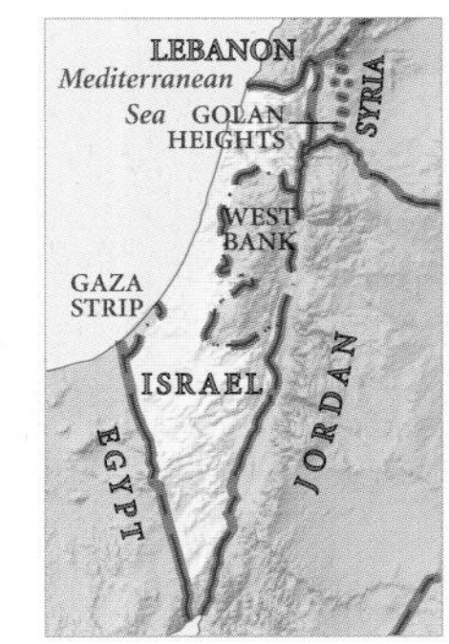
Jenin
ISRAEL
Tulkarm
Jordan
Qalqiliya
Nablus
WEST BANK
Ramallah
Auja et Tahta
Nu'eima
Jericho
JORDAN
JERUSALEM
Bethlehem
Hebron
(Israel retains 15% control)
Dead Sea
Israeli settlement
Palestinian settlement
West Bank fence
Palestinian control
Mixed control
Israeli settlement block

LEBANON
Mediterranean Sea
GOLAN HEIGHTS
SYRIA
WEST BANK
GAZA STRIP
ISRAEL
JORDAN
EGYPT

▲ ***Barbed-wire fences** surround a settlement in the Golan Heights.*

The British Isles

Lying in the north atlantic ocean, the British Isles were once joined to continental Europe. Rugged mountains in the north and west are the continuation of a Scandinavian mountain chain. Chalk landscapes in southern England were formed over 80 million years ago when flooding seas deposited a thick layer of chalk in the region. The British Isles also bear the imprint of the last Ice Age, which ended 10,000 years ago. Ice sheets eroded highlands, carved deep valleys and indented the Scottish coastline.

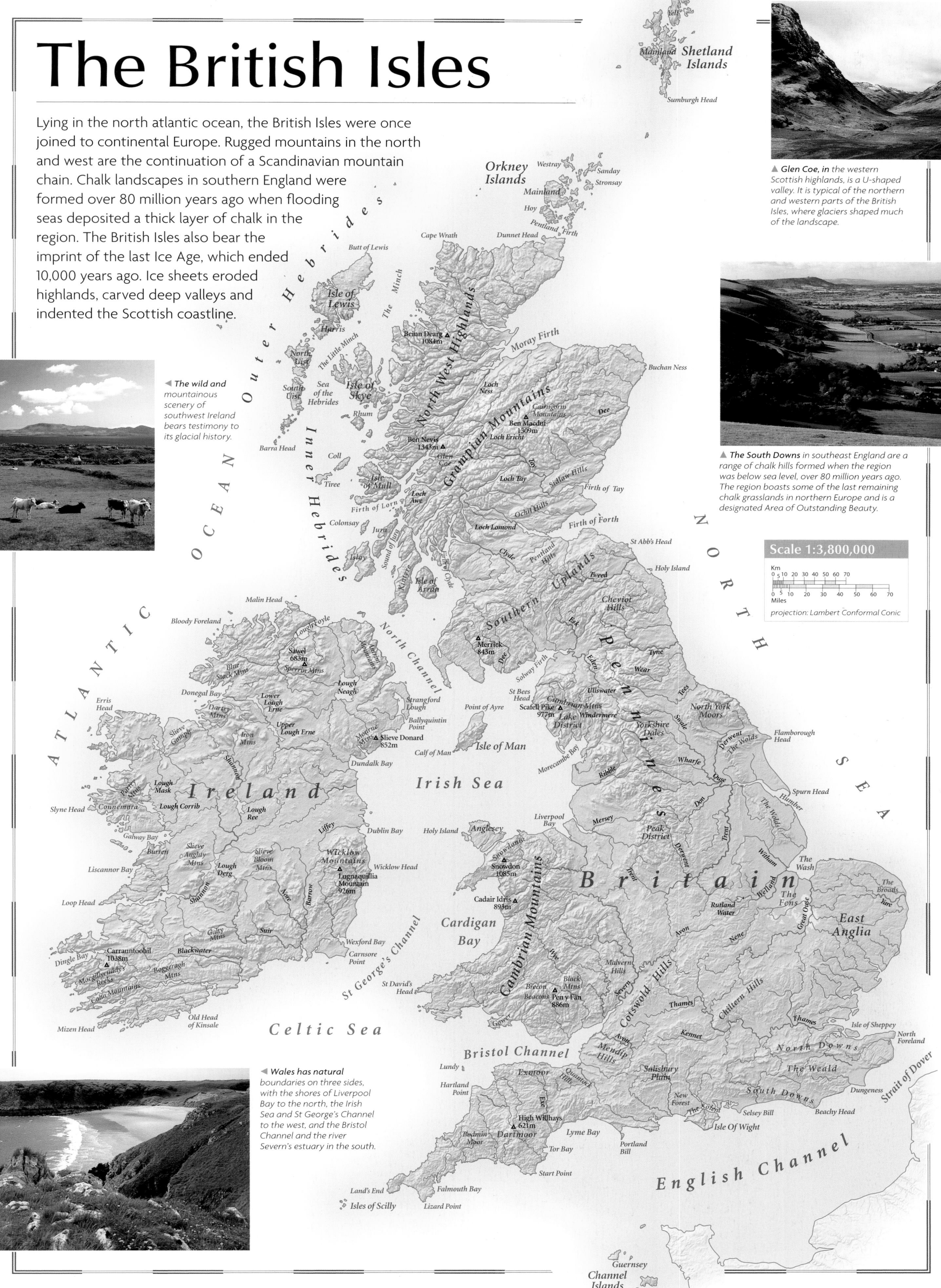

Herma Ness
Unst
Yell
Mainland
Shetland Islands
Sumburgh Head
Orkney Islands
Westray
Sanday
Stronsay
Mainland
Hoy
Pentland Firth
Dunnet Head
Cape Wrath
Butt of Lewis
Outer Hebrides
The Minch
Isle of Lewis
Harris
The Little Minch
North Uist
South Uist
Sea of the Hebrides
Isle of Skye
Rhum
Barra Head
Coll
Tiree
Isle of Mull
Firth of Lorn
Colonsay
Jura
Sound of Jura
Islay
Kintyre
Isle of Arran
Firth of Clyde
Inner Hebrides
North West Highlands
Beinn Dearg 1084m
Moray Firth
Buchan Ness
Loch Ness
Grampian Mountains
Cairngorm Mountains
Ben Macdui 1309m
Dee
Ben Nevis 1343m
Glen Coe
Loch Ericht
Tay
Loch Tay
Sidlaw Hills
Firth of Tay
Ochil Hills
Loch Lomond
Firth of Forth
St Abb's Head
Clyde
Pentland Hills
Southern Uplands
Tweed
Holy Island
Cheviot Hills
Esk
Merrick 843m
Dee
Solway Firth
Tyne
Wear
Tees
Pennines
Eden
Ullswater
St Bees Head
Cumbrian Mtns
Scafell Pike 977m
Lake District
Windermere
North York Moors
Swale
Yorkshire Dales
Derwent
The Wolds
Flamborough Head
Morecambe Bay
Ribble
Wharfe
Ouse
Spurn Head
Humber
The Wolds
Malin Head
Bloody Foreland
Lough Foyle
Sawel 683m
Sperrin Mtns
Antrim Mountains
North Channel
Blue Stack Mtns
Lough Neagh
Donegal Bay
Lower Lough Erne
Strangford Lough
Ballyquintin Point
Point of Ayre
Erris Head
Dartry Mtns
Upper Lough Erne
Slieve Gamph
Iron Mtns
Mourne Mtns
Slieve Donard 852m
Isle of Man
Calf of Man
Shannon
Dundalk Bay
Irish Sea
Lough Mask
Partry Mtns
Ireland
Slyne Head
Connemara
Lough Corrib
Lough Ree
Liffey
Dublin Bay
Holy Island
Anglesey
Liverpool Bay
Mersey
Don
Peak District
Trent
Witham
The Wash
Galway Bay
Burren
Slieve Aughty Mtns
Slieve Bloom Mtns
Wicklow Mountains
Wicklow Head
Lugnaquillia Mountain 926m
Snowdonia
Snowdon 1085m
Derwent
Trent
Britain
Liscannor Bay
Lough Derg
Shannon
Nore
Barrow
Loop Head
Cadair Idris 893m
Welland
The Fens
Rutland Water
Great Ouse
The Broads
Yare
East Anglia
Galty Mtns
Suir
Cardigan Bay
Cambrian Mountains
Avon
Nene
Carrauntoohil 1038m
Dingle Bay
Blackwater
Macgillycuddy's Reeks
Boggeragh Mtns
Caha Mountains
Wexford Bay
Carnsore Point
St George's Channel
St David's Head
Wye
Malvern Hills
Severn
Cotswold Hills
Chiltern Hills
Black Mtns
Brecon Beacons
Pen y Fan 886m
Thames
Old Head of Kinsale
Mizen Head
Celtic Sea
Gower
Bristol Channel
Kennet
Thames
Isle of Sheppey
North Foreland
Avon
Mendip Hills
North Downs
Lundy
Exmoor
Quantock Hills
Salisbury Plain
The Weald
Hartland Point
Exe
New Forest
The Solent
South Downs
Dungeness
Strait of Dover
High Willhays 621m
Selsey Bill
Beachy Head
Bodmin Moor
Dartmoor
Lyme Bay
Isle Of Wight
Tor Bay
Portland Bill
Start Point
English Channel
Land's End
Falmouth Bay
Isles of Scilly
Lizard Point
Guernsey
Channel Islands
Jersey
ATLANTIC OCEAN
NORTH SEA
Scale 1:3,800,000
Km
0 5 10 20 30 40 50 60 70
0 5 10 20 30 40 50 60 70
Miles
projection: Lambert Conformal Conic

▲ **Glen Coe, in** *the western Scottish highlands, is a U-shaped valley. It is typical of the northern and western parts of the British Isles, where glaciers shaped much of the landscape.*

◄ **The wild and** *mountainous scenery of southwest Ireland bears testimony to its glacial history.*

▲ **The South Downs** *in southeast England are a range of chalk hills formed when the region was below sea level, over 80 million years ago. The region boasts some of the last remaining chalk grasslands in northern Europe and is a designated Area of Outstanding Beauty.*

◄ **Wales has natural** *boundaries on three sides, with the shores of Liverpool Bay to the north, the Irish Sea and St George's Channel to the west, and the Bristol Channel and the river Severn's estuary in the south.*

Political British Isles

The United Kingdom's system of government has evolved over a long period, uninterrupted by any successful foreign invasion since 1066. Democracy takes the form of a constitutional monarchy, in which the monarch is a passive figurehead. The identity of the UK is being challenged by the prospect of a federal Europe, by the establishment of national assemblies in Scotland and Wales and by the introduction of an assembly in Northern Ireland which represents Unionist and Republican views. Ireland grew out of the Irish Free State, established in 1921, and has become an independent democracy with membership of the UN and the EU. The Anglo-Irish Accord of 1985 established a permanent cabinet-level channel for dialogue between Britain and Ireland.

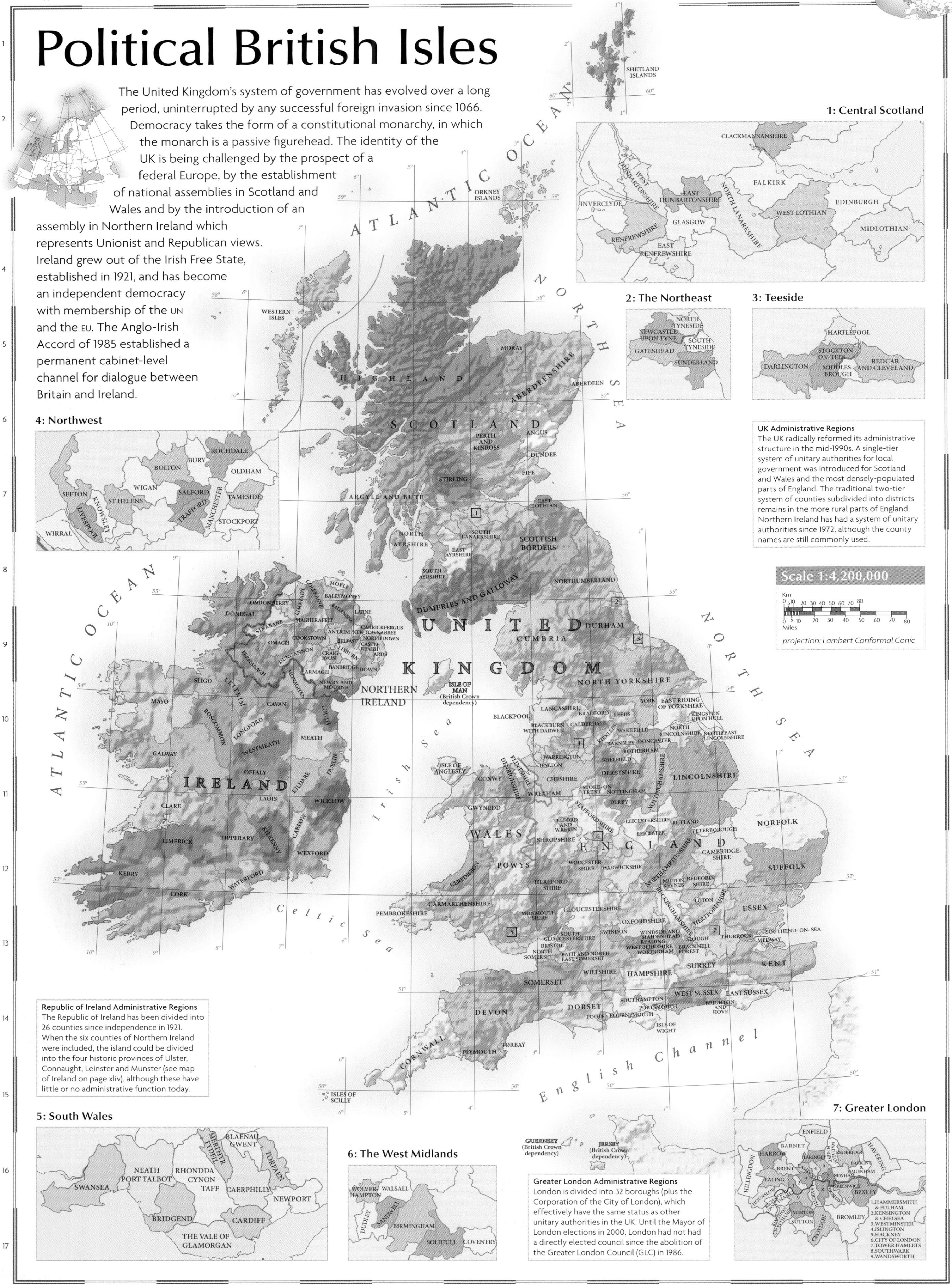

1: Central Scotland

2: The Northeast

3: Teeside

4: Northwest

UK Administrative Regions

The UK radically reformed its administrative structure in the mid-1990s. A single-tier system of unitary authorities for local government was introduced for Scotland and Wales and the most densely-populated parts of England. The traditional two-tier system of counties subdivided into districts remains in the more rural parts of England. Northern Ireland has had a system of unitary authorities since 1972, although the county names are still commonly used.

Scale 1:4,200,000

projection: Lambert Conformal Conic

Republic of Ireland Administrative Regions

The Republic of Ireland has been divided into 26 counties since independence in 1921. When the six counties of Northern Ireland were included, the island could be divided into the four historic provinces of Ulster, Connaught, Leinster and Munster (see map of Ireland on page xliv), although these have little or no administrative function today.

5: South Wales

6: The West Midlands

7: Greater London

Greater London Administrative Regions

London is divided into 32 boroughs (plus the Corporation of the City of London), which effectively have the same status as other unitary authorities in the UK. Until the Mayor of London elections in 2000, London had not had a directly elected council since the abolition of the Greater London Council (GLC) in 1986.

Wales

The ancient Cambrian mountains form the backbone of this green, mountainous country, which has been a stronghold of Celtic culture for about 3000 years. Wales had been incorporated with England from 1535 until a pro-devolution majority vote in a referendum in 1997. Over one-fifth of the people speak Welsh, a Celtic language with a rich poetic tradition. About 60 per cent of the country's 2.8 million population live in the south or extreme northeast. The old coal-based industries that transformed these areas last century have since given way to a service-led economy.

Transport and Industry

The mining industries, particularly slate and coal, have declined greatly this century. Factories in South Wales are served by deepwater ports such as Milford Haven, which has a large oil refinery and steel works. Electronics and light manufacturing industries, supported by government incentives, have grown rapidly in the south and also in central rural areas.

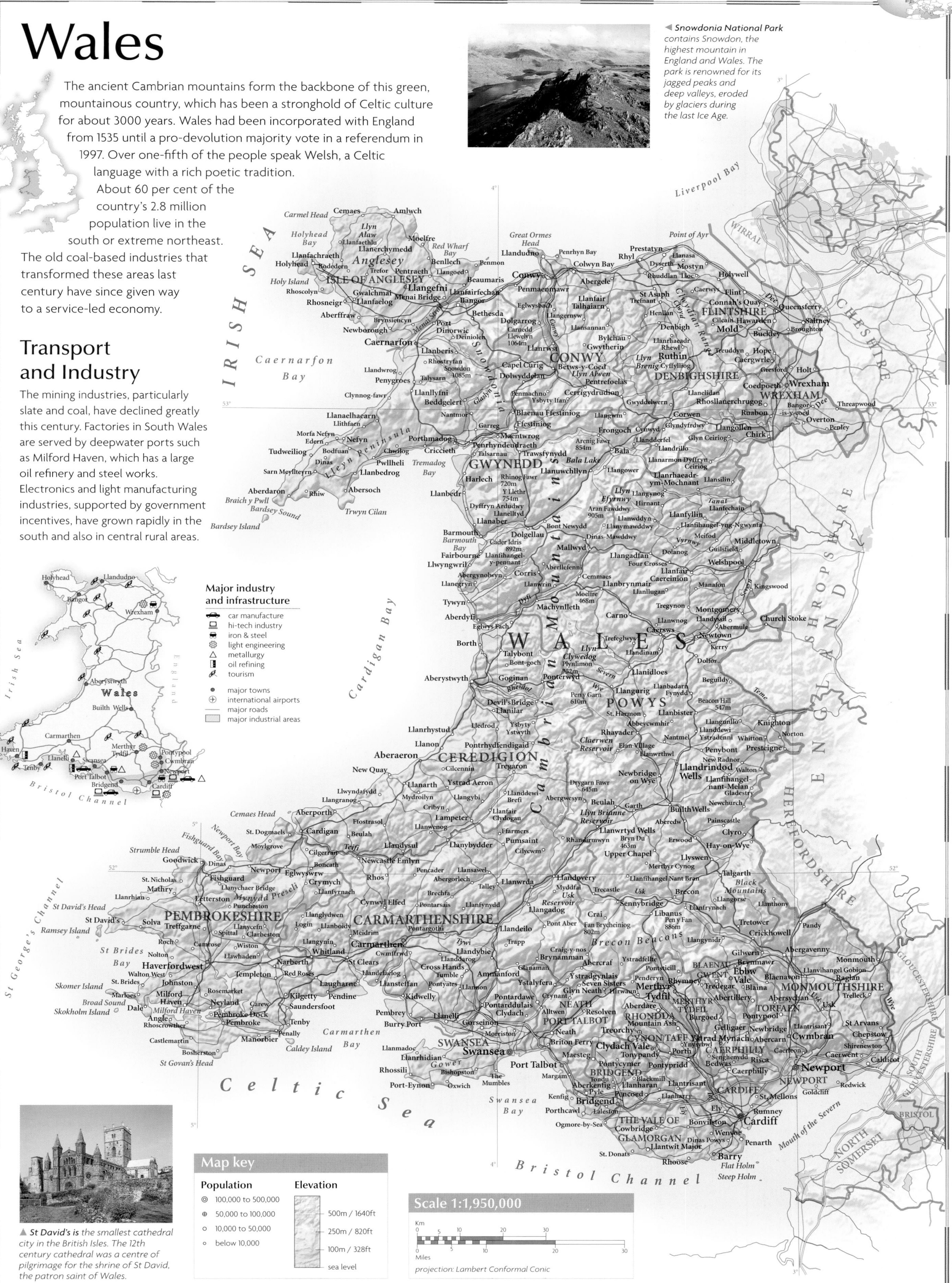
Major industry and infrastructure
car manufacture
hi-tech industry
iron & steel
light engineering
metallurgy
oil refining
tourism
major towns
international airports
major roads
major industrial areas
Map key
Population
100,000 to 500,000
50,000 to 100,000
10,000 to 50,000
below 10,000
Elevation
500m / 1640ft
250m / 820ft
100m / 328ft
sea level
Scale 1:1,950,000
projection: Lambert Conformal Conic
WALES
Irish Sea
Celtic Sea
Bristol Channel
Cardigan Bay
Liverpool Bay
St George's Channel
Cambrian Mountains
Snowdonia
Brecon Beacons
ENGLAND

◄ **Snowdonia National Park** contains Snowdon, the highest mountain in England and Wales. The park is renowned for its jagged peaks and deep valleys, eroded by glaciers during the last Ice Age.

▲ **St David's is** the smallest cathedral city in the British Isles. The 12th century cathedral was a centre of pilgrimage for the shrine of St David, the patron saint of Wales.

Southern England

Southern England is the most affluent part of the British Isles, benefiting from close proximity to Europe, fertile agricultural land, and the capital, London, as a focus of wealth, political power and population. The physical landscape varies dramatically from the bleak uplands of the southwestern Cornish peninsula through the rolling Cotswold Hills to the flat, often marshy, expanses of Essex. The southeast of England is the most densely populated region of the UK, and the growth of industries such as communications and financial services since the 1980s, has put considerable strain on transport and housing provision, with the building of new infrastructure becoming an issue of political controversy in the 1990s.

◀ ***The city of** Bath is built on the site of the Roman spa, Aquae Sulis. It is one of the most architecturally distinguished of British cities, noted for its elegant Georgian crescents built from the distinctive honey-coloured local stone.*

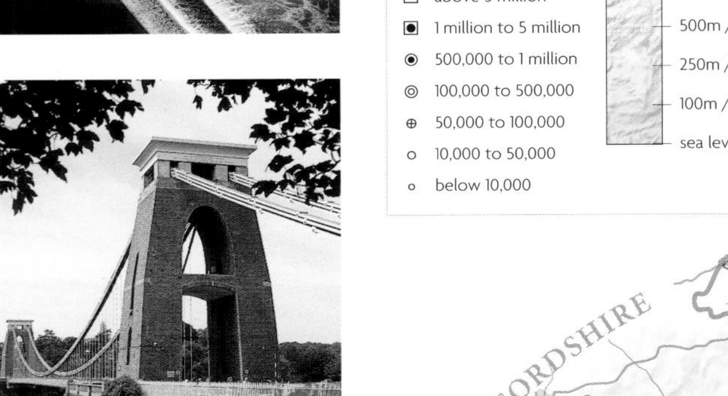

Map key

Population

- above 5 million
- 1 million to 5 million
- 500,000 to 1 million
- 100,000 to 500,000
- 50,000 to 100,000
- 10,000 to 50,000
- below 10,000

Elevation

- 500m / 1640ft
- 250m / 820ft
- 100m / 328ft
- sea level

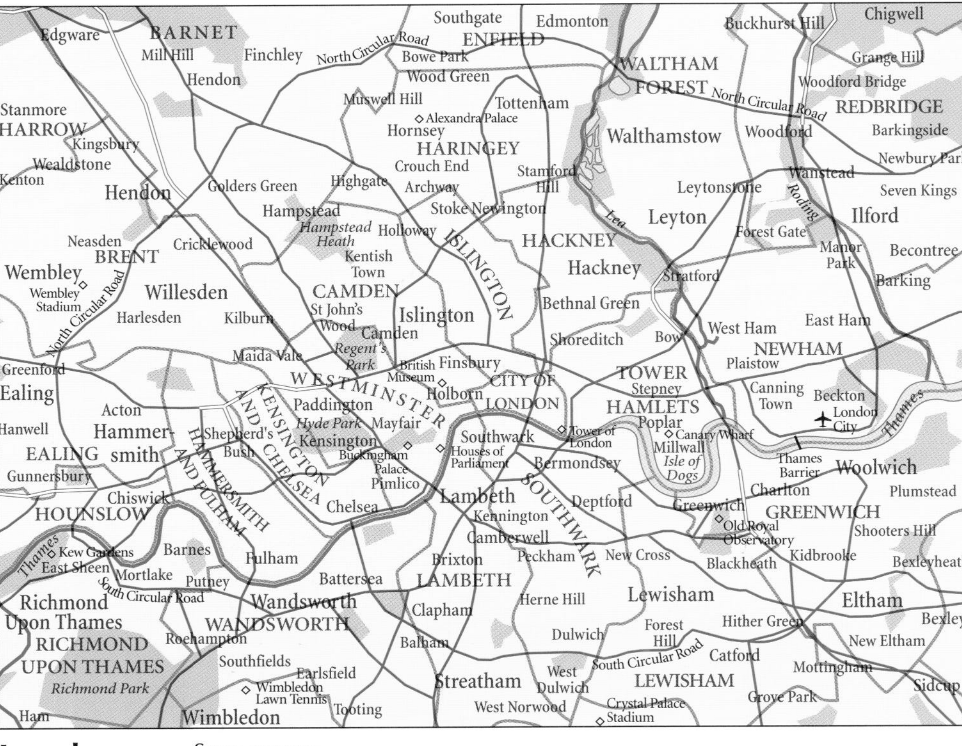
BARNET
ENFIELD
WALTHAM FOREST
REDBRIDGE
HARROW
HARINGEY
BRENT
CAMDEN
ISLINGTON
HACKNEY
NEWHAM
WESTMINSTER
CITY OF LONDON
TOWER HAMLETS
KENSINGTON AND CHELSEA
HAMMERSMITH AND FULHAM
EALING
HOUNSLOW
SOUTHWARK
LAMBETH
GREENWICH
LEWISHAM
WANDSWORTH
RICHMOND UPON THAMES
Thames
Wimbledon
Woolwich
Eltham

London

SCALE 1:230,000

0 5 Km

0 5 Miles

▲ ***Clifton Suspension Bridge,** which spans the Avon Gorge, was designed by the great Victorian engineer, Isambard Kingdom Brunel and completed in 1864. It served as an important transport link for Bristol's then growing import and export trade in meat, tobacco and fruit.*

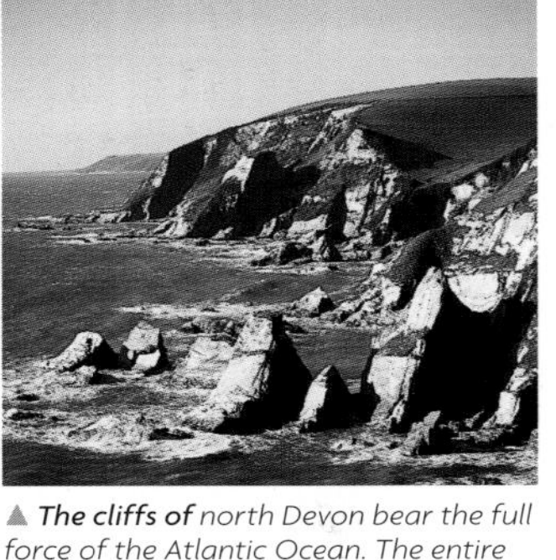

▲ ***The cliffs of** north Devon bear the full force of the Atlantic Ocean. The entire British land mass is gradually tilting, with uplift continuing on the west coast, while the east faces the increasing threat of flooding by the sea.*

ATLANTIC OCEAN

Bristol Channel

English Channel

WALES

HEREFORDSHIRE

MONMOUTHSHIRE

SOUTH GLOUCESTERSHIRE

NORTH SOMERSET

BATH AND NORTHEAST SOMERSET

SOMERSET

DEVON

CORNWALL

DORSET

TORBAY

PLYMOUTH

Bristol

Exeter

Plymouth

Taunton

Dartmoor

Exmoor

Lyme Bay

Isles of Scilly

(same scale as main map)

Transport and industry

Throughout the southeast, service industries are growing, most notably in the areas of tourism, business support and retailing. At the heart of the capital, the City of London is one of the world's leading financial centres. In contrast to the flourishing service sector, engineering industries such as aerospace and car manufacture have faced long-term decline. Lightweight manufacturing industries such as pharmaceuticals and electronics are expanding around cities and along major transport corridors such as the M4. The southwest remains far less industrialized.

▲ *The luxury homes and offices at Canary Wharf are part of the Docklands development project, an attempt to revitalize east London following the decline of the dockyards and provide space for the expansion of the City of London.*

Major industry and infrastructure

aerospace
car manufacture
chemicals
engineering
finance
food processing
hi-tech industry
light engineering
printing & publishing
tourism
capital cities
major towns
international airports
major roads
major industrial areas

▲ *Leeds Castle, near Maidstone, is one of a number of important castles in the southeast. First started in the 12th century, the castle has been inhabited continuously, and has been extended and rebuilt countless times.*

CHANNEL ISLANDS (to UK)

(same scale as main map)

Scale 1:1,000,000

Km 0 5 10 20 30

Miles 0 5 10 20 30

projection: Lambert Conformal Conic

Central England

The industrial regions around Birmingham, Coventry and the Potteries of Stoke-on-Trent, the dramatic hills of the Derbyshire's Peak District, and the windy fenlands of Lincolnshire and Norfolk, all illustrate the great diversity of England's central counties. Many of the most important developments of the Industrial Revolution occurred in this area, including the construction of the canal system. The traditional industrial heartland remains the most populous part of this region with far lower densities in East Anglia, although counties such as Cambridgeshire have recently seen large influxes of people from the crowded southeast.

Scale 1:9,000,000

Km 0 5 10 20 30

Miles 0 5 10 20 30

projection: Lambert Conformal Conic

Transport and Industry

The mass production of iron and steel, ceramics and textiles was important in this region from the end of the 18th century onwards. This great industrial base provided an ideal location for automotive manufacturing throughout much of the 20th century, particularly around Coventry and Birmingham. In recent years, the growth of hi-tech and service industries, particularly in and around Cambridge, has attracted new investment, while agriculture remains important in both Hereford and the East Anglian counties.

Major industry and infrastructure

- aerospace
- brewing
- car manufacture
- ceramics
- chemicals
- engineering
- fish processing
- food processing
- hi-tech industry
- metallurgy
- pharmaceuticals
- printing & publishing
- textiles
- major towns
- international airports
- major roads
- major industrial areas

The West Midlands

SCALE 1:560,000

0 5 10 Km

0 5 10 Miles

One of the most important developments of the Industrial Revolution took place at Ironbridge. In 1709, Abraham Darby I discovered how to smelt iron ore using local coke, rather than charcoal, of which there was a shortage. This paved the way for the mass production of iron, used for bridges, ships and buildings.

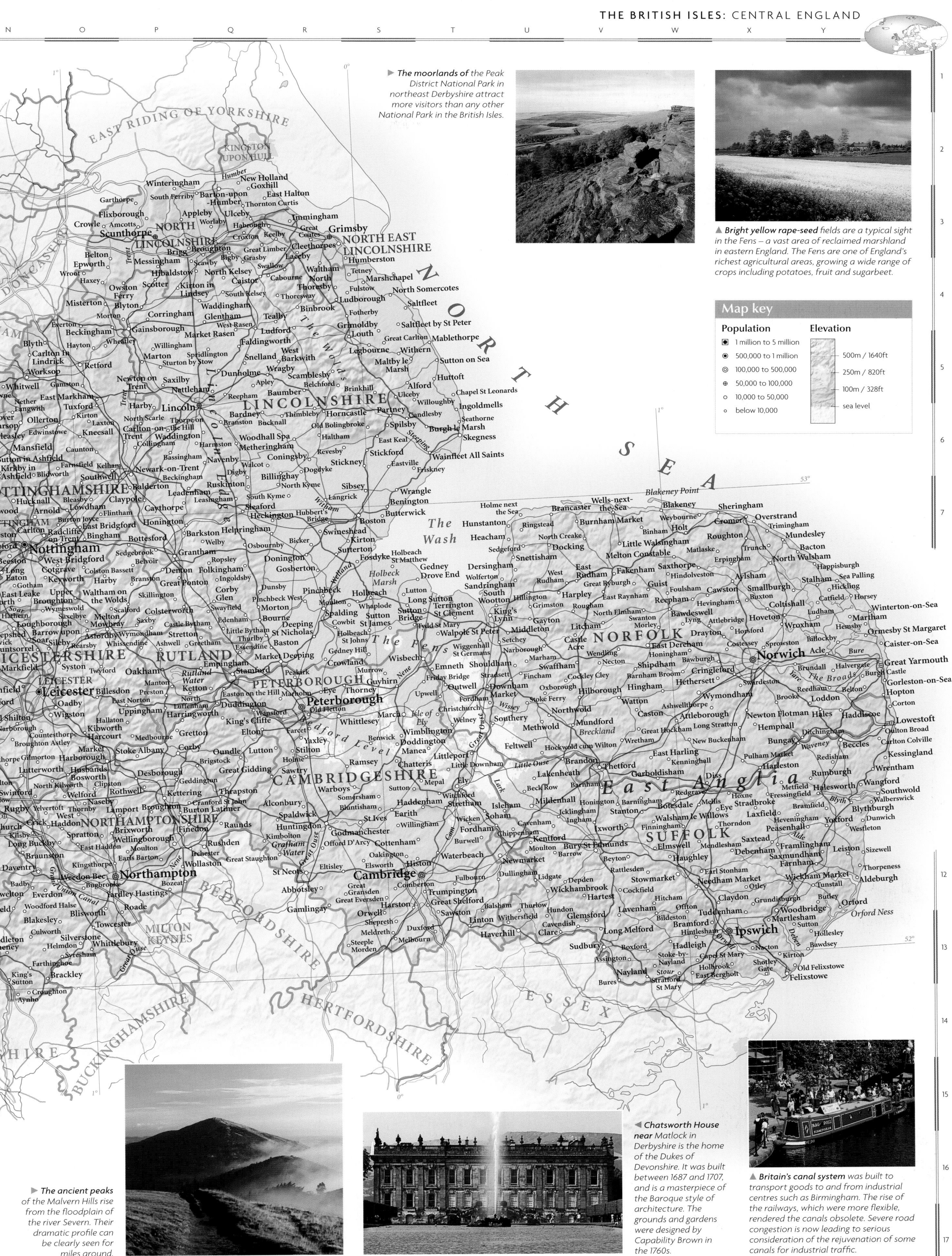

N O P Q R S T U V W X Y Z
EAST RIDING OF YORKSHIRE
KINGSTON UPON HULL
NORTH LINCOLNSHIRE
NORTH EAST LINCOLNSHIRE
LINCOLNSHIRE
NOTTINGHAMSHIRE
LEICESTERSHIRE
RUTLAND
PETERBOROUGH
CAMBRIDGESHIRE
NORTHAMPTONSHIRE
MILTON KEYNES
BEDFORDSHIRE
HERTFORDSHIRE
BUCKINGHAMSHIRE
ESSEX
NORFOLK
SUFFOLK
East Anglia
NORTH SEA
The Wash
The Fens
The Broads
Lincoln Edge
The Wolds
Bedford Level
Holbeck Marsh
Breckland
Rutland Water
Grafham Water
Blakeney Point
Orford Ness
Grimsby
Scunthorpe
Lincoln
Nottingham
Leicester
Peterborough
Northampton
Cambridge
Norwich
Ipswich
Great Yarmouth
Lowestoft
King's Lynn
Boston
Skegness
Mansfield
Newark-on-Trent
Gainsborough
Loughborough
Kettering
Huntingdon
Bury St Edmunds
Felixstowe
Map key
Population
1 million to 5 million
500,000 to 1 million
100,000 to 500,000
50,000 to 100,000
10,000 to 50,000
below 10,000
Elevation
500m / 1640ft
250m / 820ft
100m / 328ft
sea level

▶ ***The moorlands of** the Peak District National Park in northeast Derbyshire attract more visitors than any other National Park in the British Isles.*

▲ ***Bright yellow rape-seed** fields are a typical sight in the Fens – a vast area of reclaimed marshland in eastern England. The Fens are one of England's richest agricultural areas, growing a wide range of crops including potatoes, fruit and sugarbeet.*

▶ ***The ancient peaks** of the Malvern Hills rise from the floodplain of the river Severn. Their dramatic profile can be clearly seen for miles around.*

◀ ***Chatsworth House** near Matlock in Derbyshire is the home of the Dukes of Devonshire. It was built between 1687 and 1707, and is a masterpiece of the Baroque style of architecture. The grounds and gardens were designed by Capability Brown in the 1760s.*

▲ ***Britain's canal system** was built to transport goods to and from industrial centres such as Birmingham. The rise of the railways, which were more flexible, rendered the canals obsolete. Severe road congestion is now leading to serious consideration of the rejuvenation of some canals for industrial traffic.*

Northern England

The dramatic Pennine range provides a central upland spine for northern England's fine and varied landscape, flanked to the west by the famous Lake District. The modern world's first industrial cities, including Manchester, Sheffield and Bradford, rose to greatness across this region from the mid 18th century, fuelled by local coal fields, with each specializing in particular trades including textiles, metal products and shipbuilding. The decline of manufacturing – particularly in the heavy industries – in the 20th century hit northern England hard, leading to prolonged economic depression. However, following major economic restructuring in the late 1980s, the north has been highly successful in attracting foreign investment. The great industrial cities such as Manchester, Liverpool, Leeds and Newcastle have maintained their position at the centre of northern England's cultural and economic life.

◀ *Blackpool's famous tower, built in 1895, stands as a testament to the rise of the tourist industry in late 19th century Britain, as workers from the nearby Lancashire cotton mills and Yorkshire woollen mills flocked to the town on their annual holidays. Blackpool remains a popular tourist resort today.*

Transport and Industry

Once the centre of heavy manufacturing, service industries now dominate the northern economy, following a difficult period of transition. Massive inward investment by multinational companies has helped northern England retain a majority share of current manufacturing activity in the UK. New light engineering and car production plants have developed in and around the region's cities, alongside more traditional industries such as iron and steel, and textiles.

Scale 1:9,000,000

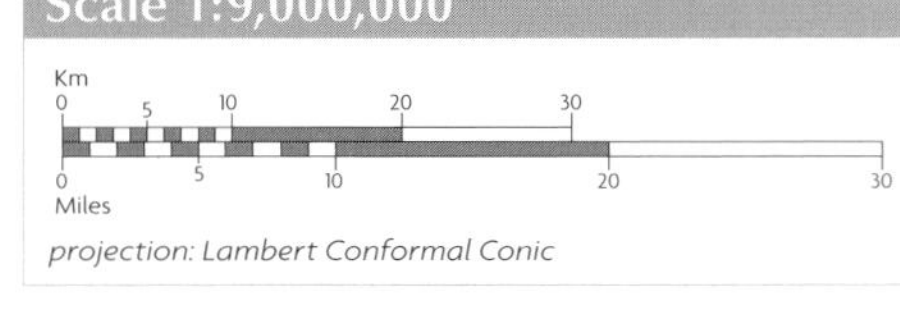
Km
0 10 20 30
Miles
0 5 10 20 30

projection: Lambert Conformal Conic

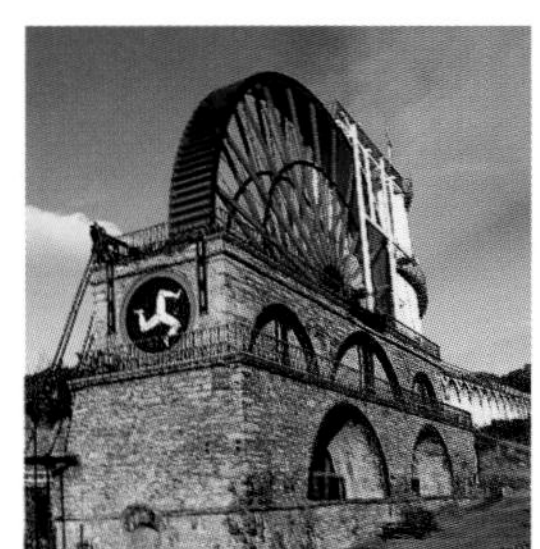

▲ *The Laxey Wheel on the Isle of Man – 72 ft (22 m) high is the largest waterwheel in the world. During the 19th century it was used to pump water from the nearby iron ore mines. The 'Three Legs of Man' on the front of the wheel is an ancient symbol, first thought to have been used by the Vikings.*

Map key

Population
- 500,000 to 1 million
- 100,000 to 500,000
- 50,000 to 100,000
- 10,000 to 50,000
- below 10,000

Elevation
- 500m / 1640ft
- 250m / 820ft
- 100m / 328ft
- sea level

Major industry and infrastructure

aerospace	iron & steel	major towns
brewing	metallurgy	international airports
car manufacture	printing & publishing	major roads
chemicals	shipbuilding	major industrial areas
engineering	textiles	
food processing	tourism	
hi-tech industry		

Point of Ayre
Rue Point
Bride
Jurby West
Andreas
Ballaugh
Sulby
Ramsey Bay
Ramsey
Maughold
Kirk Michael
Isle of Man
Snaefell 620m
Peel
St. John's
Laxey
Laxey Bay
Clay Head
Patrick
Crosby
Foxdale
Onchan
Dalby
South Barrule 483m
St. Mark's
DOUGLAS
ISLE OF MAN (to UK)
Colby
Port Erin
Ballasalla
Castletown
Calf of Man
Port St Mary
Irish Sea

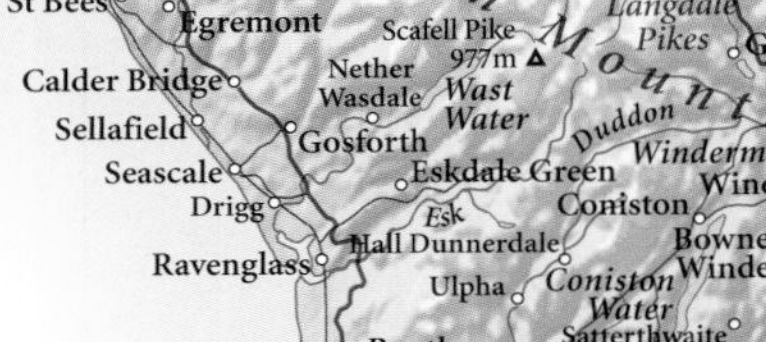

The Northwest

SCALE 1:560,000

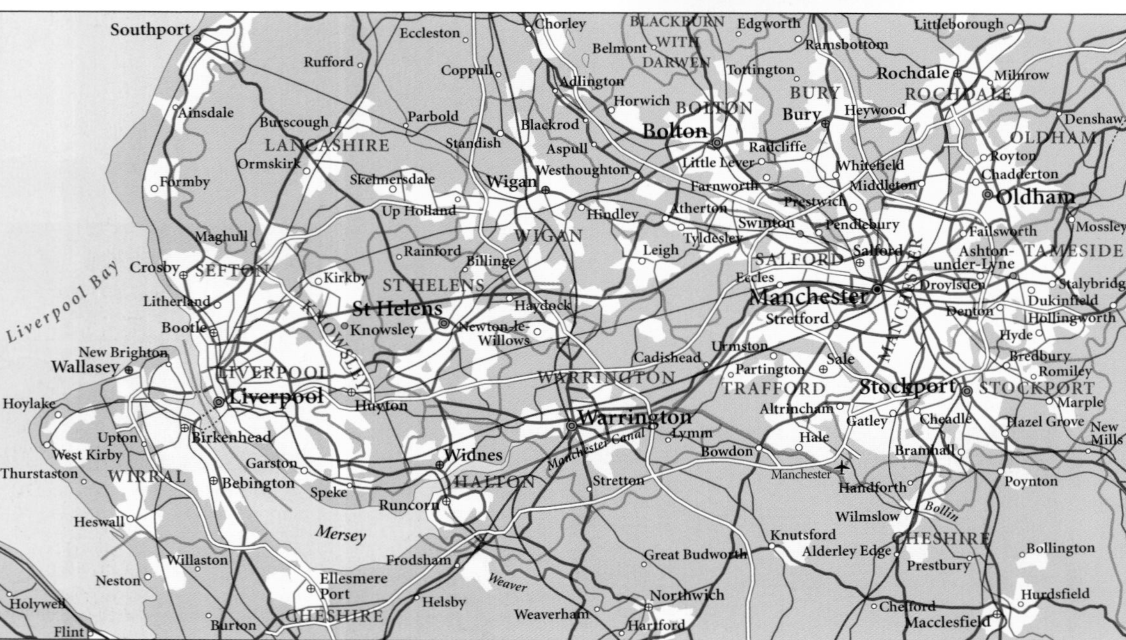
Southport
Eccleston
Chorley
Edgworth
Littleborough
Rufford
Coppull
BLACKBURN WITH DARWEN
Belmont
Ramsbottom
Ainsdale
Burscough
Parbold
Adlington
Horwich
Westhoughton
Little Lever
Radcliffe
Whitefield
Middleton
Royton
Chadderton
Hindley
Atherton
Farnworth
Prestwich
Swinton
Pendlebury
Failsworth
Mossley
TAMESIDE
SEFTON
Kirkby
Rainford
Billinge
Leigh
Tyldesley
Haydock
Newton-le-Willows
Droylsden
Dukinfield
Bootle
Stretford
Denton
Hyde
Hollingworth
New Brighton
Liverpool Bay
North Sea

SCOTLAND
DUMFRIES AND GALLOWAY
Solway Firth
Bowness-on-Solway
Skinburness
Silloth
Kirkbride
Kirkbampton
Abbey Town
Newton Arlosh
Carlisle
Beckfoot
Wigton
Mawbray
Rosley
Allonby
Westnewton
Mealsgate
Caldbeck
Maryport
Aspatria
Bothel
Uldale
Flimby
Dearham
Skiddaw
Workington
Bassenthwaite
Keswick
High Harrington
Lowеswater
Crummock Water
Loweswater
Distington
Whinlatter Pass
Braithwaite
Parton
Kirkland
CUMBRIA
Whitehaven
Ennerdale Water
Cumbrian Mountains
St Bees Head
Cleator Moor
Frizington
Helvellyn
Lake District
St Bees
Egremont
Scafell Pike
977m
Coniston
Calder Bridge
Nether Wasdale
Wast Water
Windermere
Sellafield
Gosforth
Eskdale Green
Seascale
Drigg
Windermere
Ravenglass
Ulpha
Broughton in Furness
Bootle
Coniston Water
Whitbeck
Grizebeck
Greenodd
Silecroft
Millom
Cartmel
Haverigg
Ulverston
Askam in Furness
Dalton-in-Furness
Barrow-in-Furness
Aldingham
Vickerstown
Isle of Walney
Morecambe
Heysham
Morecambe Bay

Fleetwood
Cleveleys
Poulton-le-Fylde
Blackpool
BLACKPOOL
Lytham St. Anne's
Liverpool
Wallasey
Birkenhead
WIRRAL
St Helens
Warrington
Wigan
Bolton
Bury
Rochdale
Oldham
Salford
Manchester
Stockport
Widnes
Runcorn
Macclesfield
Northwich
CHESHIRE
LANCASHIRE
Mersey

▲ *The spectacular gothic-revival architecture of Manchester Town Hall recalls the great wealth and civic pride of the city at the height of the Industrial Revolution.*

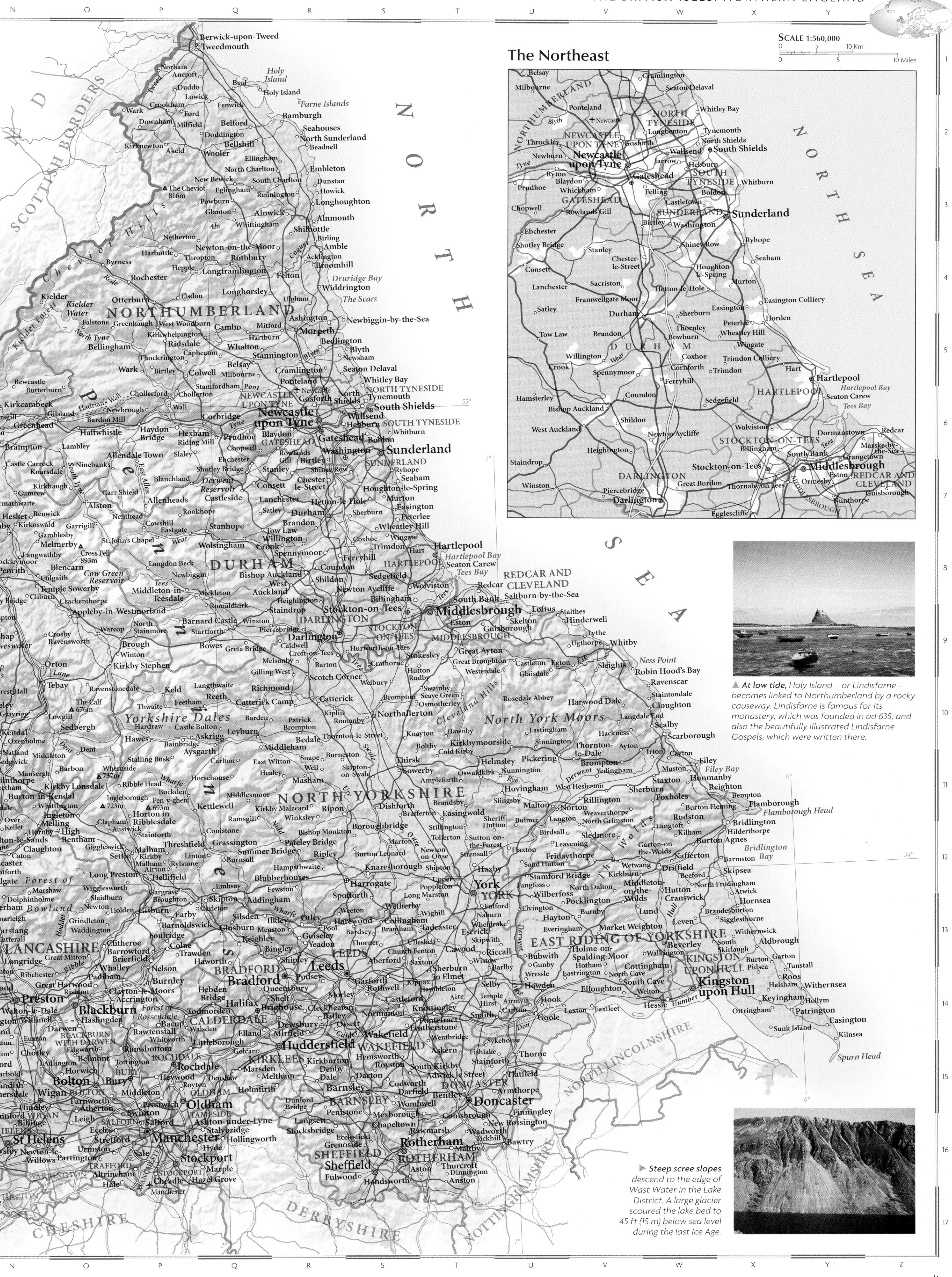
The Northeast
SCALE 1:560,000
0 5 10 Km
0 5 10 Miles
NORTH SEA
NORTHUMBERLAND
DURHAM
NORTH YORKSHIRE
EAST RIDING OF YORKSHIRE
LANCASHIRE
CHESHIRE
DERBYSHIRE
NOTTINGHAMSHIRE
NORTH LINCOLNSHIRE
SCOTTISH BORDERS
REDCAR AND CLEVELAND
NORTH TYNESIDE
SOUTH TYNESIDE
NEWCASTLE UPON TYNE
GATESHEAD
SUNDERLAND
HARTLEPOOL
STOCKTON-ON-TEES
MIDDLESBROUGH
DARLINGTON
YORK
LEEDS
BRADFORD
CALDERDALE
KIRKLEES
WAKEFIELD
BARNSLEY
DONCASTER
SHEFFIELD
ROTHERHAM
KINGSTON UPON HULL
Berwick-upon-Tweed
Newcastle upon Tyne
Sunderland
Middlesbrough
Darlington
Hartlepool
Durham
York
Leeds
Bradford
Kingston upon Hull
Preston
Blackburn
Bolton
Wigan
Oldham
Manchester
Stockport
St Helens
Huddersfield
Doncaster
Rotherham
Sheffield
Scarborough
Whitby
Harrogate
Yorkshire Dales
North York Moors
Cheviot Hills
Holy Island
Farne Islands
Flamborough Head
Spurn Head
Hartlepool Bay
Tees Bay
Filey Bay
Bridlington Bay
The Cheviot 816m
Cross Fell 893m

▲ **At low tide,** Holy Island – or Lindisfarne – becomes linked to Northumberland by a rocky causeway. Lindisfarne is famous for its monastery, which was founded in ad 635, and also the beautifully illustrated Lindisfarne Gospels, which were written there.

► **Steep scree slopes** descend to the edge of Wast Water in the Lake District. A large glacier scoured the lake bed to 45 ft (15 m) below sea level during the last Ice Age.

Scotland

This rugged northern region of Britain was an independent state until the Act of Union with England in 1707. Almost three quarters of the people live in the heavily industrialized central lowlands, which lie between the high moors of the southern uplands and the rugged highlands and islands of the north. English is the main language, with Gaelic also spoken, especially in highland areas. Since the 1970s, development of the North Sea oilfields has given Scotland a critical role in the British energy industry, lending potency to the 'Home Rule' campaign for a Scottish parliament, which was finally realized in 1999.

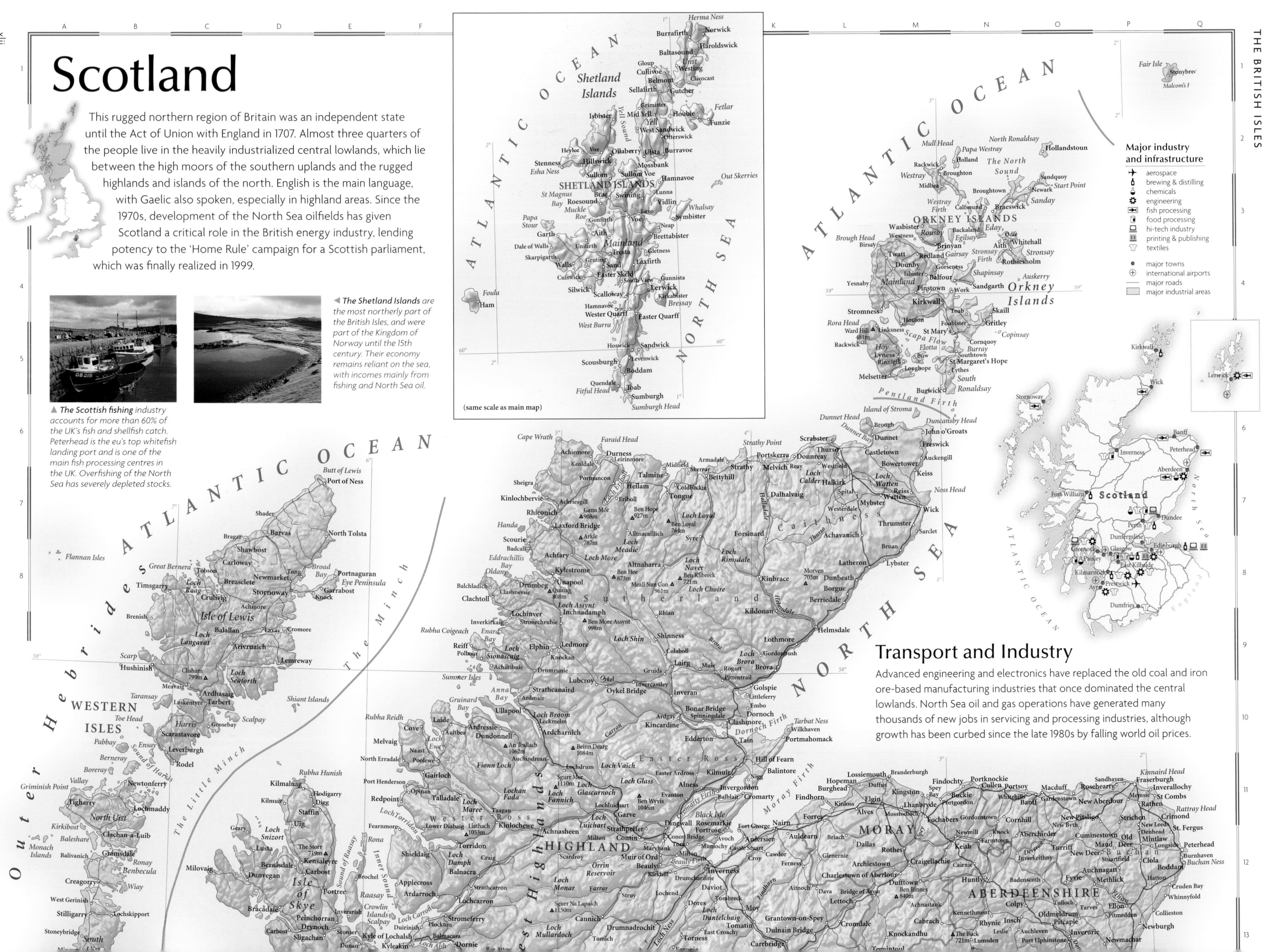

Major industry and infrastructure
aerospace
brewing & distilling
chemicals
engineering
fish processing
food processing
hi-tech industry
printing & publishing
textiles
major towns
international airports
major roads
major industrial areas
Scotland
ATLANTIC OCEAN
NORTH SEA
Shetland Islands
SHETLAND ISLANDS
ORKNEY ISLANDS
Orkney Islands
WESTERN ISLES
Outer Hebrides
HIGHLAND
MORAY
ABERDEENSHIRE
Sutherland
Caithness
Isle of Lewis
Isle of Skye
The Minch
The Little Minch
Pentland Firth
Moray Firth
(same scale as main map)

▲ *The Scottish fishing industry accounts for more than 60% of the UK's fish and shellfish catch. Peterhead is the EU's top whitefish landing port and is one of the main fish processing centres in the UK. Overfishing of the North Sea has severely depleted stocks.*

◀ *The Shetland Islands are the most northerly part of the British Isles, and were part of the Kingdom of Norway until the 15th century. Their economy remains reliant on the sea, with incomes mainly from fishing and North Sea oil.*

Transport and Industry

Advanced engineering and electronics have replaced the old coal and iron ore-based manufacturing industries that once dominated the central lowlands. North Sea oil and gas operations have generated many thousands of new jobs in servicing and processing industries, although growth has been curbed since the late 1980s by falling world oil prices.

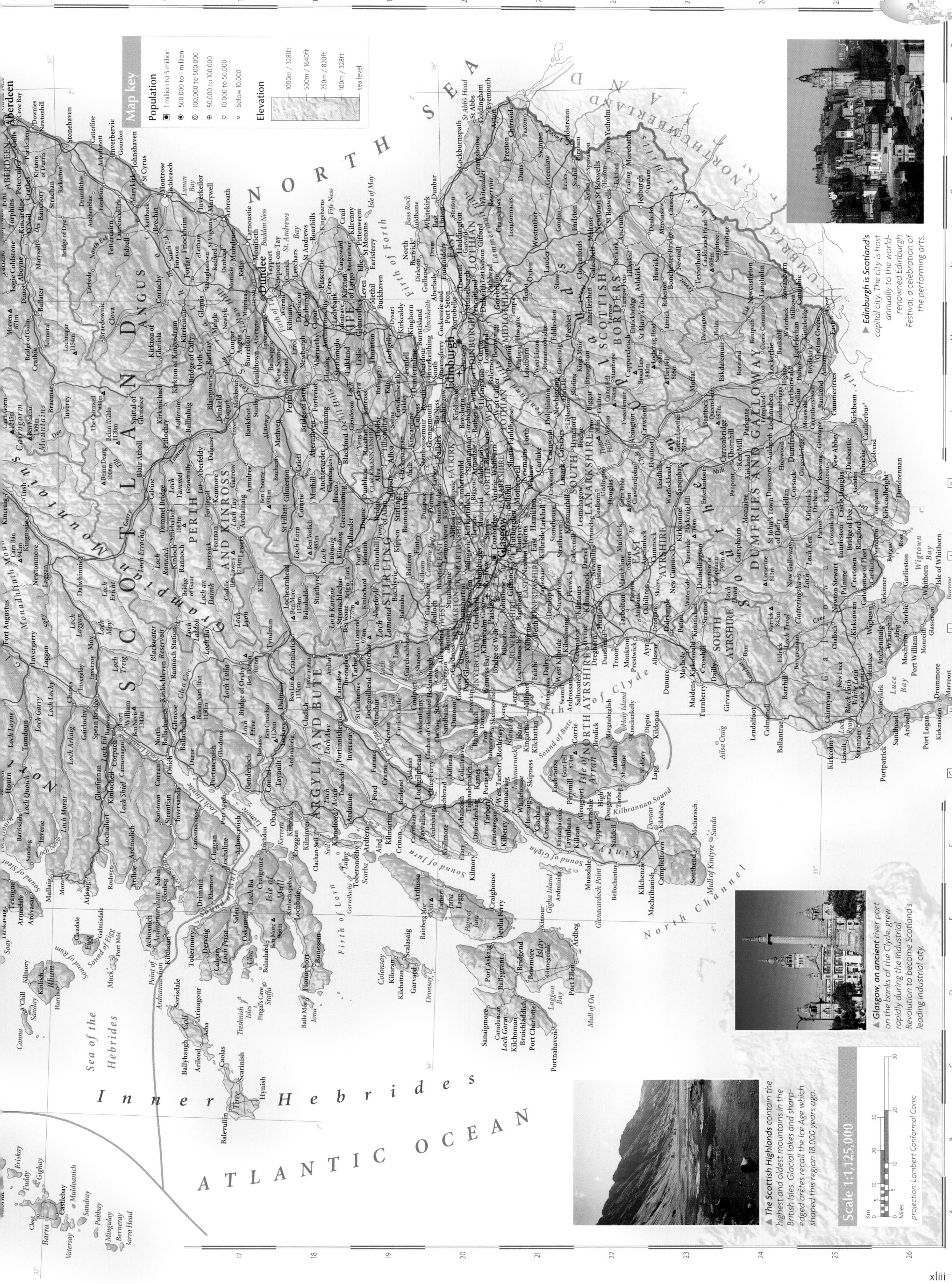

Map key

Population

- 1 million to 5 million
- 500,000 to 1 million
- 100,000 to 500,000
- 50,000 to 100,000
- 10,000 to 50,000
- below 10,000

Elevation

- 1000m / 3281ft
- 500m / 1640ft
- 250m / 820ft
- 100m / 328ft
- sea level

Scale 1:1,125,000

Km 0 5 10 20 30

Miles 0 5 10 20 30

projection: Lambert Conformal Conic

▲ **The Scottish Highlands** contain the highest and oldest mountains in the British Isles. Glacial lakes and sharp-edged arêtes recall the Ice Age which shaped this region 18,000 years ago.

▲ **Glasgow, an ancient** river port on the banks of the Clyde, grew rapidly during the Industrial Revolution to become Scotland's leading industrial city.

▶ **Edinburgh is Scotland's** capital city. The city is host annually to the world-renowned Edinburgh Festival, a celebration of the performing arts.

Ireland

The unspoilt scenery and folk culture of Ireland reflect its remote position on the western fringe of Europe, and contrast with the so-called 'troubles' which have long hindered its development. Ireland emerged from British rule as a free state in 1921 and is separated from Northern Ireland by the UK's only land border. Coastal hill ranges encircle a central undulating plain, strewn with many lakes and bogs. Ireland has benefited from EU grants since the 1980s, which have contributed to the growth of industry and infrastructure.

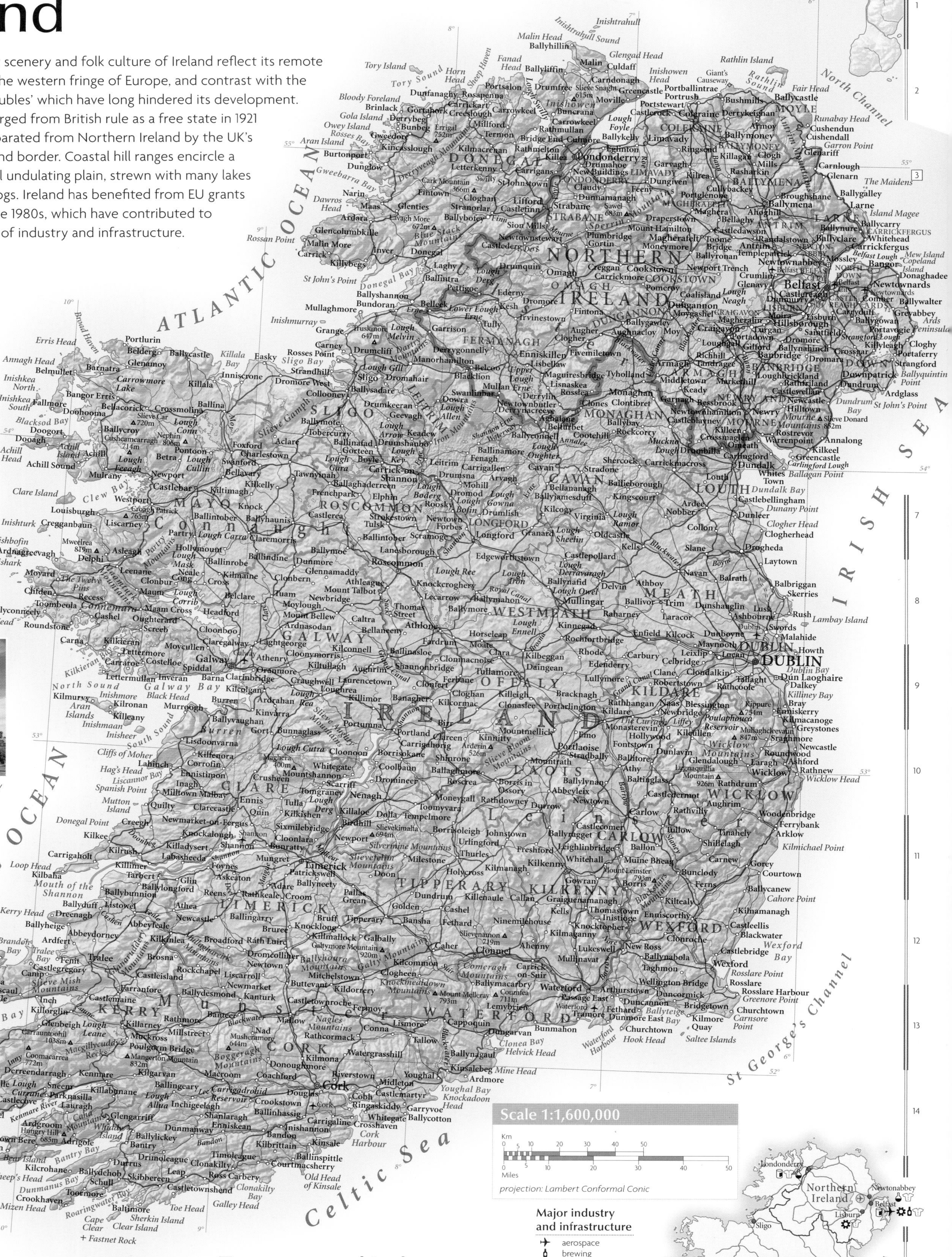

Map key

Population

- ◎ 100,000 to 500,000
- ⊕ 50,000 to 100,000
- ○ 10,000 to 50,000
- ○ below 10,000

Elevation

- 500m / 1640ft
- 250m / 820ft
- 100m / 328ft
- sea level

▲ *The Campanile in Trinity College, Dublin, was built by Sir Charles Lanyon, architect of Queen's College, Belfast. It is 98 ft (30 m) high.*

Scale 1:1,600,000

Km 0 5 10 20 30 40 50

Miles 0 5 10 20 30 40 50

projection: Lambert Conformal Conic

► *The Burren is a massive limestone plateau in the northwest of County Clare. A wide range of Mediterranean and Alpine plants flourish in the pastures, near shallow lakes and in the cracks in the limestone pavement.*

Transport and Industry

Northern Ireland's industries are concentrated in Belfast, once a great textiles and shipbuilding centre which has faced chronic recession since the 1970s. Industrialization in Ireland began properly in the 1950s. A broad range of goods are now produced for export near Dublin, and in many other larger towns.

Major industry and infrastructure

- aerospace
- brewing
- chemicals
- engineering
- food processing
- hi-tech industry
- textiles
- tourism
- capital cities
- major towns
- international airports
- major roads
- major industrial areas

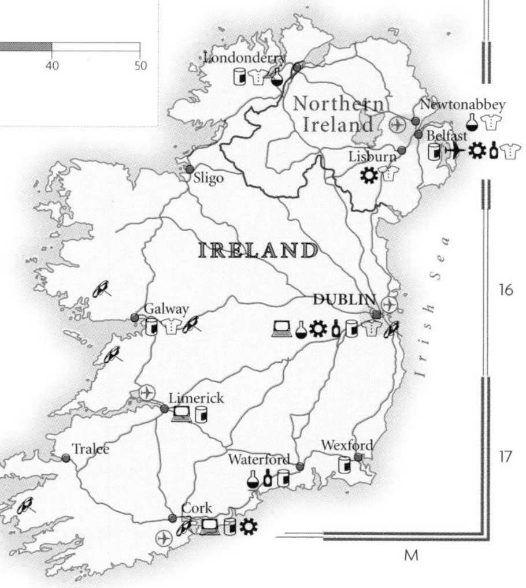

Index: British Isles & Ireland

The place names of the British Isles reflect the languages of both the present and the past. The distribution of these settlement names on maps indicates where these languages are now, and where they were once spoken. The early inhabitants of the British Isles were Celts. Their names now survive in the west; the region to which they were driven by successive invasions of Romans, Anglo-Saxons and Norwegian Vikings. The most immediately recognisable of these names are Welsh names. These are found both in north Wales, where the language is still the mother tongue of more than half a million people, and in the south, where the language generally spoken is now English. The familiar initial elements Llan– (church) and Aber– (river mouth, confluence) are found throughout Wales and many anglicised names on maps and signposts are now accompanied by their original Welsh forms: Cardiff (Caerdydd), Swansea (Abertawe), Carmarthen (Caerfyrddin).

Less than 100,000 people in Scotland still speak Gaelic. They are found principally in the Hebrides and the northwest highlands. Surviving Gaelic names are more widely dispersed throughout western Scotland as a whole. Some physical feature names are preserved in their Gaelic spelling, for example, Sgurr a 'Choire Ghlais – but most settlement names, and the names of prominent features such as Oban and Ben Nevis, have long been anglicised. However as in Wales, there is now increasing recognition of Gaelic spellings: Benbecula (Beinn na Faoghlia) and North Uist (Uibhist a'Tuath).

Most of the Irish Gaelic names in Ireland were systematically anglicised during the years of British rule and the language itself all but disappeared; barely 60,000 people in the western extremities of the country still speak Irish as their mother tongue. Since independence in 1922, the Irish government has tried to remedy this situation by decreeing Irish the official national language and making it a compulsory subject in schools. As a result, over half a million people in the island of Ireland now claim to be able to speak some Irish. A commission has also been set up by the Irish government to determine the true Irish form of every place name in the country and many of these are now being given recognition on maps, for example, Dublin (Baile Átha Cliath), Cork (Corcaigh) and Limerick (Luimneach). Very few names exist in Irish only. Examples are Dun Laoghaire (formerly Kingstown) and Cobh (formerly Queenstown). Typical anglicised Irish elements in place names are Bally- (Town) and Inish- (island).

Two lesser Celtic languages, both now dead, survive in a few place names: Cornish, with names beginning with Tre- (Village), and Manx with names prefaced by Balla-.

Little place name evidence remains of the Roman occupation of Britain. Though the Romans latinized the mainly Celtic names they found throughout the country, these soon disappeared as later Anglo-Saxon and Norwegian newcomers imposed their own names. Old Sarum is a rare example of a surviving Latin name. The Language continued to be used occasionally; Magna (big), Parva (little) and Super-Mare (on the sea) were added to place names to differentiate villages of the same name.

Anglo-Saxons began their invasion of southern Britain only thirty years after the Romans left in ad 410. Norwegian Viking invasions of Scotland and northern Britain followed in the late eighth and early ninth centuries. Thus it came about that Norwegian and Anglo-Saxon place names spread across the country from Shetland in the north, to Hampshire in the south and westwards to the Celtic fringe. These are the names that survive today, though their spellings are very different from the Old English forms recorded in the Domesday Book of 1086. The dividing line between the two linguistic strands is geographically complex but as a general rule it can be stated that names ending in –by and –thorpe are Norwegian in origin, while those with –ham and –ton are Anglo-Saxon.

The Norman Invasion of 1066 brought the French language with it. French, therefore, contributed in a minor way to the formation of place names in southern England; names with Beau- and Bel- (beautiful) being the most conspicuous. Norman French prepositions survive in such names as Ashby de la Zouch and Chapel en le Frith.

A

xxxv *J10* **Abbeycwmhir** Powys, C Wales, UK
xxxviii *G14* **Abbey Dore** Herefordshire, W England, UK
xliv *C12* **Abbeydorney** Kerry, SW Ireland
xliv *D12* **Abbeyfeale** ***Ir.*** Mainistir na Féile. Limerick, SW Ireland
xliv *I10* **Abbeyleix** Laois, C Ireland
xl *L7* **Abbey Town** Cumbria, NW England, UK
xxxvi *L14* **Abbotsbury** Dorset, S England, UK
xxxvii *S8* **Abbots Langley** Hertfordshire, E England, UK
xxxix *R12* **Abbotsley** Cambridgeshire, E England, UK
xxxv *F10* **Aberaeron** Ceredigion, SW Wales, UK
xxxv *K14* **Abercarn** Caerphilly, S Wales, UK
xlii *N11* **Aberchirder** Aberdeenshire, NE Scotland, UK
xxxv *H13* **Abercraf** Powys, C Wales, UK
xxxv *I14* **Aberdare** Rhondda Cynon Taff, S Wales, UK
xxxv *E7* **Aberdaron** Gwynedd, NW Wales, UK
xliii *P14* **Aberdeen** ***anc.*** Devana. City of Aberdeen, NE Scotland, UK
xliii *O14* **Aberdeen, City of** ⬖ *unitary authority* NE Scotland, UK
xlii *M12* **Aberdeenshire** ⬖ *unitary authority* NE Scotland, UK
xliii *M19* **Aberdour** Fife, E Scotland, UK
xxxv *G9* **Aberdyfi** Gwynedd, NW Wales, UK
xxxv *J11* **Aberedw** Powys, C Wales, UK
xliii *K16* **Aberfeldy** Perth and Kinross, C Scotland, UK
xxxv *E5* **Aberffraw** Isle of Anglesey, NW Wales, UK
xli *S14* **Aberford** Leeds, N England, UK
xliii *I18* **Aberfoyle** Stirling, C Scotland, UK
xxxv *K13* **Abergavenny** ***anc.*** Gobannium. Monmouthshire, SE Wales, UK
xxxv *I4* **Abergele** Conwy, N Wales, UK
xxxv *G12* **Abergorlech** Carmarthenshire, S Wales, UK
xxxv *H11* **Abergwesyn** Powys, C Wales, UK
xxxv *G8* **Abergynolwyn** Gwynedd, NW Wales, UK
xxxv *I15* **Aberkenfig** Bridgend, S Wales, UK
xliii *N19* **Aberlady** East Lothian, SE Scotland, UK
xxxv *H8* **Aberllefenni** Gwynedd, NW Wales, UK
xxxv *J9* **Abermule** Powys, C Wales, UK
xliii *L18* **Abernethy** Perth and Kinross, C Scotland, UK
xliii *M17* **Abernyte** Perth and Kinross, C Scotland, UK
xxxv *E11* **Aberporth** Ceredigion, W Wales, UK
xxxv *E7* **Abersoch** Gwynedd, NW Wales, UK
xxxv *K14* **Abersychan** Torfaen, SE Wales, UK
xxxv *K14* **Abertillery** Blaenau Gwent, SE Wales, UK
xliii *L18* **Aberuthven** Perth and Kinross, C Scotland, UK
xxxv *G9* **Aberystwyth** Ceredigion, W Wales, UK
xxxvii *P8* **Abingdon** ***anc.*** Abindonia. Oxfordshire, S England, UK
xliii *K22* **Abington** South Lanarkshire, C Scotland, UK
xliii *N14* **Aboyne** Aberdeenshire, NE Scotland, UK
xli *O14* **Accrington** Lancashire, NW England, UK
xliii *C16* **Acha** Argyll and Bute, W Scotland, UK
xliii *F20* **Achahoish** Argyll and Bute, W Scotland, UK
xlii *L7* **Achavanich** Highland, N Scotland, UK
xlii *H8* **Achfary** Highland, NW Scotland, UK
xliii *D14* **A'Chill** Highland, NW Scotland, UK
xliv *B6* **Achill** Mayo, NW Ireland
xliv *C6* **Achill Head** ***Ir.*** Ceann Acla. *headland* W Ireland
xliv *C6* **Achill Island** ***Ir.*** Acaill. *island* W Ireland
xliv *C6* **Achill Sound** Mayo, W Ireland
xlii *G9* **Achiltibuie** Highland, NW Scotland, UK
xlii *D8* **Achmore** Western Isles, NW Scotland, UK
xliii *F17* **Achnacroish** Argyll and Bute, W Scotland, UK
xlii *H11* **Achnasheen** Highland, NW Scotland, UK
xlii *M12* **Achnastank** Moray, N Scotland, UK
xliii *E16* **Achosnich** Highland, NW Scotland, UK
xlii *H7* **Achriesgill** Highland, NW Scotland, UK
xli *R4* **Acklington** Northumberland, N England, UK
xliv *F6* **Aclare** Sligo, N Ireland
xxxix *Y9* **Acle** Norfolk, E England, UK
xxxvi *B7* **Acton** Ealing, SE England, UK
xliv *F11* **Adare** Limerick, SW Ireland
xxxviii *I8* **Adderley** Shropshire, W England, UK
xli *Q13* **Addingham** Bradford, N England, UK
xli *N15* **Adlington** Lancashire, NW England, UK
xliv *C14* **Adrigole** Cork, S Ireland
xxxvii *T12* **Adur** ≈ SE England, UK
xlii *G13* **Affric, Loch** ◎ NW Scotland, UK
xliv *I6* **Aghalane** Fermanagh, W Northern Ireland, UK
xliv *I12* **Ahenny** Tipperary, S Ireland
xliv *K3* **Ahoghill** Ballymena, NE Northern Ireland, UK
xliii *G23* **Ailsa Craig** *island* SW Scotland, UK
xl *M15* **Ainsdale** Sefton, NW England, UK
xliii *F19* **Aird** Argyll and Bute, W Scotland, UK
xliii *K20* **Airdrie** North Lanarkshire, S Scotland, UK
xli *T14* **Aire** ≈ N England, UK
xli *U14* **Airmyn** North Yorkshire, N England, UK
xliii *K19* **Airth** Falkirk, C Scotland, UK
xli *P12* **Airton** North Yorkshire, N England, UK
xlii *I3* **Aith** Orkney Islands, N Scotland, UK
xlii *N3* **Aith** Shetland Islands, NE Scotland, UK
xlii *K12* **Aitnoch** Moray, N Scotland, UK
xli *P2* **Akeld** Northumberland, N England, UK
xxxvii *Q6* **Akeley** Buckinghamshire, C England, UK
xxxv *E3* **Alaw, Llyn** ***var.*** Alaw Reserv***oir.*** ◎ NW Wales, UK
xxxviii *A13* **Albrighton** Shropshire, W England, UK
xxxviii *K12* **Alcester** Warwickshire, C England, UK
xxxix *R11* **Alconbury** Cambridgeshire, E England, UK
xxxvii *O9* **Aldbourne** Wiltshire, S England, UK
xli *X13* **Aldbrough** East Riding of Yorkshire, N England, UK
xxxix *X12* **Alde** ≈ E England, UK
xxxix *Y12* **Aldeburgh** Suffolk, E England, UK
xxxvii *O12* **Alderbury** Wiltshire, S England, UK
xl *G17* **Alderley Edge** Cheshire, W England, UK
xxxvii *Q10* **Aldermaston** West Berkshire, S England, UK
xxxvii *W14* **Alderney** island Channel Islands
xxxvii *R11* **Aldershot** Hampshire, S England, UK
xxxviii *G6* **Aldford** Cheshire, W England, UK
xl *L12* **Aldingham** Cumbria, NW England, UK
xxxviii *C14* **Aldridge** Walsall, C England, UK
xxxvii *O8* **Aldsworth** Gloucestershire, C England, UK
xli *T15* **Aldwick le Street** Doncaster, N England, UK
xliii *H19* **Alexandria** West Dunbartonshire, W Scotland, UK
xxxix *S5* **Alford** Lincolnshire, E England, UK
xlii *N13* **Alford** Aberdeenshire, NE Scotland, UK
xxxviii *M7* **Alfreton** Derbyshire, C England, UK
xxxvii *U13* **Alfriston** East Sussex, SE England, UK
xxxvii *Y11* **Alkham** Kent, SE England, UK
xli *P7* **Allendale** Town Northumberland, N England, UK
xli *P7* **Allenheads** Northumberland, N England, UK
xliv *H6* **Allen, Lough** ***Ir.*** Loch Aillionn. ◎ NW Ireland
xxxviii *E15* **Allesley** Coventry, C England, UK
xxxviii *K6* **Allgreave** Cheshire, C England, UK
xxxvii *W9* **Allhallows** Kent, SE England, UK
xliii *K19* **Alloa** Clackmannan, C Scotland, UK
xl *K8* **Allonby** Cumbria, NW England, UK
xliii *I22* **Alloway** South Ayrshire, W Scotland, UK
xlii *I7* **Alltnacaillich** Highland, NW Scotland, UK
xxxv *H14* **Alltwen** Neath Port Talbot, S Wales, UK
xliv *D14* **Allua,** Lough ◎ S Ireland
xxxviii *G13* **Almeley** Herefordshire, W England, UK
xliii *K17* **Almond** ≈ C Scotland, UK
xxxvi *L9* **Almondsbury** South Gloucestershire, SW England, UK
xli *Q3* **Aln** ≈ N England, UK
xlii *J11* **Alness** Highland, NW Scotland, UK
xli *R3* **Alnmouth** Northumberland, N England, UK
xli *R3* **Alnwick** Northumberland, N England, UK
xxxviii *D12* **Alrewas** Staffordshire, C England, UK
xxxviii *I7* **Alsager** Cheshire, W England, UK
xlii *F13* **Alsh,** Loch inlet NW Scotland, UK
xli *O7* **Alston** Cumbria, NW England, UK
xlii *I8* **Altnaharra** Highland, NW Scotland, UK
xxxvii *Q11* **Alton** Hampshire, S England, UK
xxxviii *K7* **Alton** Staffordshire, C England, UK
xxxvii *N10* **Alton** Priors Wiltshire, S England, UK
xli *P17* **Altrincham** Trafford, NW England, UK
xliii *K19* **Alva** Clackmannan, C Scotland, UK
xxxviii *C16* **Alvechurch** Worcestershire, W England, UK
xlii *L11* **Alves** Moray, N Scotland, UK
xxxvi *L9* **Alveston** South Gloucestershire, SW England, UK
xxxviii *L12* **Alveston** Warwickshire, C England, UK
xlii *K13* **Alvie** Highland, NW Scotland, UK
xxxv *H5* **Alwen,** Llyn ◎ N Wales, UK
xliii *M16* **Alyth** Perth and Kinross, C Scotland, UK
xxxvii *S13* **Amberley** West Sussex, SE England, UK
xli *R4* **Amble** Northumberland, N England, UK
xxxviii *A15* **Amblecote** Dudley, C England, UK
xl *M10* **Ambleside** Cumbria, NW England, UK
xxxix *P3* **Amcotts** North Lincolnshire, N England, UK
xxxvii *S8* **Amersham** Buckinghamshire, SE England, UK
xxxvii *O11* **Amesbury** Wiltshire, S England, UK
xxxv *F3* **Amlwch** Isle of Anglesey, NW Wales, UK
xxxv *G13* **Ammanford** Carmarthenshire, S Wales, UK
xli *T11* **Ampleforth** North Yorkshire, N England, UK
xxxvii *S6* **Ampthill** Bedfordshire, C England, UK
xliii *K17* **Amulree** Perth and Kinross, C Scotland, UK
xliv *C13* **Anascaul** Kerry, SW Ireland
xli *P1* **Ancroft** Northumberland, N England, UK
xliii *O22* **Ancrum** The Borders, S Scotland, UK
xxxvii *P11* **Andover** Hampshire, S England, UK
xl *G10* **Andreas** N Isle of Man
xxxv *C14* **Angle** Pembrokeshire, SW Wales, UK
xxxv *E4* **Anglesey** *island* NW Wales, UK
xxxvii *S13* **Angmering** West Sussex, SE England, UK
xliii *M15* **Angus** ⬖ *unitary authority* E Scotland, UK
xliv *C6* **Annagh Head** *headland* NW Ireland
xliv *I6* **Annalee** ≈ N Ireland
xliv *L6* **Annalong** Newry and Mourne, S Northern Ireland, UK
xliii *M24* **Annan** Dumfries and Galloway, S Scotland, UK
xlii *G9* **Annat** Bay bay NW Scotland, UK
xliii *I22* **Annbank** South Ayrshire, W Scotland, UK
xli *T17* **Anston** Rotherham, N England, UK
xliii *N18* **Anstruther** Fife, E Scotland, UK
xxxviii *M11* **Ansty** Warwickshire, C England, UK
xlii *G10* **An Teallach** ▲ NW Scotland, UK
xliv *L4* **Antrim** ***Ir.*** Aontroim. Antrim, NE Northern Ireland, UK
xliv *K4* **Antrim** ***Ir.*** Aontroim. ⬖ district NE Northern Ireland, UK
xliv *L3* **Antrim** Mountains ▲▲ NE Northern Ireland, UK
xxxix *Q5* **Apley** Lincolnshire, E England, UK
xxxix *P3* **Appleby** North Lincolnshire, N England, UK
xli *O9* **Appleby-in-Westmorland** Cumbria, NW England, UK
xlii *F12* **Applecross** Highland, NW Scotland, UK
xxxvi *F12* **Appledore** Devon, SW England, UK
xxxvii *X12* **Appledore** Kent, SE England, UK
xxxv *H7* **Aran** Fawddwy l NW Wales, UK
xliv *F3* **Aran Island** ***Ir.*** Árainn Mhór. *island* NW Ireland
xliv *C9* **Aran Islands** *island group* W Ireland
xliii *N16* **Arbroath** ***anc.*** Aberbrothock. Angus, E Scotland, UK
xliii *O15* **Arbuthnott** Aberdeenshire, NE Scotland, UK
xlii *H6* **Archiemore** Highland, NW Scotland, UK
xlii *M12* **Archiestown** Moray, N Scotland, UK
xxxvi *D6* **Archway** Islington, SE England, UK
xliii *G17* **Ardanaiseig** Argyll and Bute, W Scotland, UK
xliv *G4* **Ardara** ***Ir.*** Ard an Rátha. Donegal, N Ireland
xlii *F12* **Ardarroch** Highland, NW Scotland, UK
xliii *E21* **Ardbeg** Argyll and Bute, W Scotland, UK
xlii *H10* **Ardcharnich** Highland, NW Scotland, UK
xliv *K7* **Ardee** ***Ir.*** Baile Átha Fhirdhia. Louth, NE Ireland
xliii *I19* **Arden** Argyll and Bute, W Scotland, UK
xliii *H19* **Ardentinny** Argyll and Bute, W Scotland, UK
xliv *H10* **Arderin** ▲ C Ireland
xlii *J11* **Ardersier** Highland, NW Scotland, UK
xliii *F18* **Ardfern** Argyll and Bute, W Scotland, UK
xliv *C12* **Ardfert** Kerry, SW Ireland
xlii *J10* **Ardgay** Highland, NW Scotland, UK
xliv *M6* **Ardglass** Down, E Northern Ireland, UK
xliv *C14* **Ardgroom** Cork, S Ireland
xlii *C9* **Ardhasaig** Western Isles, NW Scotland, UK
xxxvii *U11* **Ardingly Reservoir** ▣ SE England, UK
xxxvii *X6* **Ardleigh** Essex, SE England, UK
xxxvii *Q7* **Ardley** Oxfordshire, C England, UK
xliii *I18* **Ardlui** Argyll and Bute, W Scotland, UK
xliii *F19* **Ardlussa** Argyll and Bute, W Scotland, UK
xlii *G9* **Ardmair** Highland, NW Scotland, UK
xliii *F21* **Ardminish** Argyll and Bute, W Scotland, UK
xliii *F15* **Ardmolich** Highland, NW Scotland, UK
xliv *H14* **Ardmore** Waterford, S Ireland
xliv *C8* **Ardnagreevagh** Galway, W Ireland
xliii *E16* **Ardnamurchan** *peninsula* NW Scotland, UK
xliii *D15* **Ardnamurchan, Point of** *headland* N Scotland, UK
xliv *F8* **Ardnasodan** Galway, W Ireland
xliv *F9* **Ardrahan** Galway, W Ireland
xlii *G10* **Ardressie** Highland, NW Scotland, UK
xliii *F19* **Ardrishaig** Argyll and Bute, W Scotland, UK
xliii *H21* **Ardrossan** North Ayrshire, W Scotland, UK
xliv *M5* **Ards** ⬖ *district* E Northern Ireland, UK
xliv *M5* **Ards Peninsula** *peninsula* E Northern Ireland, UK
xliii *J17* **Ardtalnaig** Perth and Kinross, C Scotland, UK
xliii *E15* **Ardtoe** Highland, NW Scotland, UK
xliii *F18* **Arduaine** Argyll and Bute, W Scotland, UK
xliii *E14* **Ardvasar** Highland, NW Scotland, UK
xliii *H25* **Ardwell** Dumfries and Galloway, SW Scotland, UK
xxxv *H6* **Arenig Fawr** ▲ NW Wales, UK
xliii *F18* **Argyll and Bute** ⬖ *unitary authority* W Scotland, UK
xliii *C16* **Arileod** Argyll and Bute, W Scotland, UK
xliii *D16* **Arinagour** Argyll and Bute, W Scotland, UK
xliii *E15* **Arisaig** Highland, NW Scotland, UK
xlii *C9* **Arivruaich** Western Isles, NW Scotland, UK
xliii *G14* **Arkaig,** Loch c NW Scotland, UK
xliv *L11* **Arklow** ***Ir.*** An tInbhear Mór. Wicklow, SE Ireland
xlii *J6* **Armadale** Highland, NW Scotland, UK
xliii *E14* **Armadale** Highland, NW Scotland, UK
xliii *K20* **Armadale** West Lothian, SE Scotland, UK
xliv *K5* **Armagh** ***Ir.*** Ard Mhacha. Armagh, S Northern Ireland, UK
xliv *K5* **Armagh** ⬖ *district* S Northern Ireland, UK
xli *N7* **Armathwaite** Cumbria, NW England, UK
xxxviii *K9* **Armitage** Staffordshire, C England, UK
xliv *L2* **Armoy** Moyle, N Northern Ireland, UK
xli *T15* **Armthorpe** Doncaster, N England, UK
xxxix *N7* **Arnold** Nottinghamshire, C England, UK
xl *M11* **Arnside** Cumbria, NW England, UK
xliii *G21* **Arran, Isle of** *island* SW Scotland, UK
xliii *H18* **Arrochar** Argyll and Bute, W Scotland, UK
xxxviii *K12* **Arrow** Warwickshire, C England, UK
xliv *G6* **Arrow,** Lough ◎ N Ireland
xliv *J13* **Arthurstown** Wexford, SE Ireland
xxxvii *S12* **Arun** ≈ SE England, UK
xxxvii *S13* **Arundel** West Sussex, SE England, UK
xliv *I7* **Arvagh** Cavan, N Ireland
xliii *H20* **Ascog** Argyll and Bute, W Scotland, UK
xxxvii *S10* **Ascot** Windsor and Maidenhead, S England, UK
xxxix *O9* **Asfordby** Leicestershire, C England, UK
xxxvii *Z10* **Ash** Kent, SE England, UK
xxxvii *V10* **Ash** Kent, SE England, UK
xxxvi *R11* **Ash** Surrey, SE England, UK
xliv *K8* **Ashbourne** Meath, E Ireland
xxxviii *L7* **Ashbourne** Derbyshire, C England, UK
xxxvi *H15* **Ashburton** Devon, SW England, UK
xxxvii *O9* **Ashbury** Oxfordshire, C England, UK
xxxviii *L9* **Ashby de la Zouch** Leicestershire, C England, UK
xliv *L10* **Ashford** Wicklow, E Ireland
xxxvi *F12* **Ashford** Devon, SW England, UK
xxxvii *X11* **Ashford** Kent, SE England, UK
xxxviii *L6* **Ashford in the Water** Derbyshire, C England, UK
xxxvii *X8* **Ashingdon** Essex, E England, UK
xli *R4* **Ashington** Northumberland, N England, UK
xliii *N22* **Ashkirk** The Borders, S Scotland, UK
xxxviii *I8* **Ashley** Staffordshire, C England, UK
xxxvii *N8* **Ashton** Keynes Wiltshire, S England, UK
xli *P16* **Ashton-under-Lyne** ***var.*** Ashton. Tameside, NW England, UK
xxxvi *F14* **Ashwater** Devon, SW England, UK
xxxvii *T6* **Ashwell** Hertfordshire, SE England, UK
xxxix *P9* **Ashwell** Rutland, C England, UK
xxxix *W10* **Ashwellthorpe** Norfolk, E England, UK
xl *L11* **Askam-in-Furness** Cumbria, NW England, UK
xliv *E11* **Askeaton** Limerick, SW Ireland
xli *T15* **Askern** Doncaster, N England, UK
xliii *G19* **Asknish** Argyll and Bute, W Scotland, UK
xli *P11* **Askrigg** North Yorkshire, N England, UK
xliv *D8* **Asleagh** Mayo, NW Ireland
xl *K8* **Aspatria** Cumbria, NW England, UK
xl *E14* **Aspull** Bolton, NW England, UK
xxxix *V13* **Assington** Suffolk, E England, UK
xlii *H8* **Assynt, Loch** ◎ NW Scotland, UK
xxxviii *I7* **Aston** Cheshire, W England, UK
xli *S17* **Aston** Rotherham, N England, UK
xxxvii *R7* **Aston Clinton** Buckinghamshire, C England, UK
xxxviii *C17* **Astwood Bank** Worcestershire, W England, UK
xliv *J8* **Athboy** ***Ir.*** Baile Átha Buí. Meath, E Ireland
xliv *D12* **Athea** Limerick, SW Ireland
xliv *F9* **Athenry** ***Ir.*** Baile Átha an Rí. Galway, W Ireland
xxxvi *G12* **Atherington** Devon, E England, UK
xxxviii *E14* **Atherstone** Warwickshire, C England, UK
xli *O16* **Atherton** Wigan, NW England, UK
xliv *G8* **Athleague** Roscommon, C Ireland
xliv *H8* **Athlone** ***Ir.*** Baile Átha Luain. Westmeath, C Ireland
xliv *J10* **Athy** ***Ir.*** Baile Átha Í. Kildare, C Ireland
xxxix *W10* **Attleborough** Norfolk, E England, UK
xxxix *W9* **Attlebridge** Norfolk, E England, UK
xli *X13* **Atwick** East Riding of Yorkshire, N England, UK
xxxvi *M10* **Atworth** Wiltshire, S England, UK
xliii *F19* **Auchbraad** Argyll and Bute, W Scotland, UK
xliii *O15* **Auchenblae** Aberdeenshire, NE Scotland, UK
xliii *H25* **Auchenmaig** Dumfries and Galloway, SW Scotland, UK
xlii *H10* **Auchindrean** Highland, NW Scotland, UK
xliii *J22* **Auchinleck** East Ayrshire, W Scotland, UK
xlii *N13* **Auchleven** Aberdeenshire, NE Scotland, UK
xlii *P12* **Auchnagatt** Aberdeenshire, NE Scotland, UK
xliii *K18* **Auchterarder** Perth and Kinross, C Scotland, UK
xliii *M18* **Auchtermuchty** Fife, E Scotland, UK
xlii *M6* **Auckengill** Highland, N Scotland, UK
xxxviii *I7* **Audlem** Cheshire, W England, UK
xxxviii *J7* **Audley** Staffordshire, C England, UK
xliv *J5* **Augher** Dungannon, C Northern Ireland, UK
xliv *J5* **Aughnacloy** Dungannon, C Northern Ireland, UK
xliv *G9* **Aughrim** Galway, W Ireland
xliv *K10* **Aughrim** Wicklow, E Ireland
xlii *K11* **Auldearn** Highland, NW Scotland, UK
xliii *K24* **Auldgirth** Dumfries and Galloway, SW Scotland, UK
xliii *N19* **Auldhame** East Lothian, SE Scotland, UK
xlii *F10* **Aultbea** Highland, NW Scotland, UK
xlii *N4* **Auskerry** *island* N Scotland, UK
xli *O12* **Austwick** North Yorkshire, N England, UK
xxxvii *N10* **Avebury** Wiltshire, S England, UK
xxxvi *G16* **Aveton Gifford** Devon, SW England, UK
xliii *G18* **Avich, Loch** ◎ W Scotland, UK
xlii *K13* **Aviemore** Highland, N Scotland, UK
xlii *J11* **Avoch** Highland, NW Scotland, UK
xxxvi *L9* **Avon** ≈ C England, UK
xxxvii *O13* **Avon** ≈ S England, UK
xxxvi *G15* **Avon** ≈ SW England, UK
xxxvi *K9* **Avonmouth** City of Bristol, SW England, UK
xliii *G18* **Awe, Loch** ◎ W Scotland, UK
xxxvi *K10* **Axbridge** Somerset, SW England, UK
xxxvi *K10* **Axe** ≈ SW England, UK
xxxvi *J14* **Axe** ≈ SW England, UK
xxxvi *J13* **Axminster** Devon, SW England, UK
xxxvii *R7* **Aylesbury** Buckinghamshire, SE England, UK
xxxvii *Y10* **Aylesham** Kent, SE England, UK
xxxix *X8* **Aylsham** Norfolk, E England, UK
xxxix *N14* **Aynho** Northamptonshire, C England, UK
xliii *I22* **Ayr** South Ayrshire, W Scotland, UK
xliii *J22* **Ayr** ≈ W Scotland, UK
xl *G10* **Ayre, Point of** *headland* N Isle of Man
xxxv *J4* **Ayr, Point of** *headland* N Wales, UK
xli *Q11* **Aysgarth** North Yorkshire, N England, UK
xli *V11* **Ayton** North Yorkshire, N England, UK
xliii *P20* **Ayton** The Borders, S Scotland, UK

B

xxxvi *I15* **Babbacombe Bay** *bay* SW England, UK
xlii *N3* **Backaland** Orkney Islands, N Scotland, UK
xxxix *Y8* **Bacton** Norfolk, E England, UK
xli *P15* **Bacup** Lancashire, NW England, UK
xxxix *N12* **Badby** Northamptonshire, C England, UK
xlii *G7* **Badcall** Highland, NW Scotland, UK
xlii *O12* **Badenscoth** Aberdeenshire, NE Scotland, UK
xxxvi *M9* **Badminton** South Gloucestershire, SW England, UK
xxxvii *S10* **Bagshot** Surrey, SE England, UK
xliii *D18* **Baile Mór** Argyll and Bute, W Scotland, UK
xliv *J7* **Bailieborough** Cavan, N Ireland
xli *P11* **Bainbridge** North Yorkshire, N England, UK
xxxviii *L6* **Bakewell** Derbyshire, C England, UK
xxxv *I6* **Bala** Gwynedd, NW Wales, UK
xxxv *H7* **Bala Lake** ◎ NW Wales, UK
xlii *C9* **Balallan** Western Isles, NW Scotland, UK
xliii *L17* **Balbeggie** Perth and Kinross, C Scotland, UK
xlii *J11* **Balblair** Highland, NW Scotland, UK
xliv *L8* **Balbriggan** ***Ir.*** Baile Brigín. Dublin, E Ireland
xlii *G8* **Balchladich** Highland, NW Scotland, UK
xxxvii *U12* **Balcombe** West Sussex, SE England, UK
xxxix *P7* **Balderton** Nottinghamshire, C England, UK
xxxvii *T6* **Baldock** Hertfordshire, E England, UK
xliii *L20* **Balerno** City of Edinburgh, SE Scotland, UK
xlii *A11* **Baleshare** *island* NW Scotland, UK
xliii *B17* **Balevullin** Argyll and Bute, W Scotland, UK
xlii *M4* **Balfour** Orkney Islands, N Scotland, UK
xliii *J19* **Balfron** Stirling, C Scotland, UK
xxxvi *D9* **Balham** Wandsworth, SE England, UK
xlii *K10* **Balintore** Highland, N Scotland, UK

◆ Country
● Country Capital
◇ Dependent Territory
○ Dependent Territory Capital
⬖ Administrative Region
✈ International Airport
▲ Mountain
▲▲ Mountain Range
◎ Lake
▣ Reservoir
≈ River

xlii A12 Balivanich Western Isles, NW Scotland, UK
xliii G16 Ballachulish Highland, NW Scotland, UK
xliv L7 Ballagan Point headland NE Ireland
xliv F7 Ballaghaderreen Ir. Bealach an Doirín. Roscommon, C Ireland
xliv H10 Ballaghmore Laois, C Ireland
xliii H24 Ballantrae South Ayrshire, W Scotland, UK
xl F12 Ballasalla S Isle of Man
xliii M14 Ballater Aberdeenshire, NE Scotland, UK
xl G11 Ballaugh NE Isle of Man
xliv E6 Ballina Ir. Béal an Átha. Mayo, W Ireland
xliv G6 Ballinafad Sligo, N Ireland
xliv H6 Ballinamore Ir. Béal an Átha Móir. Leitrim, NW Ireland
xliv G9 Ballinasloe Ir. Béal Átha na Sluaighe. Galway, W Ireland
xliv E7 Ballindine Mayo, NW Ireland
xliv E12 Ballingarry Limerick, SW Ireland
xliv D14 Ballingeary Cork, S Ireland
xliii L18 Ballingry Fife, E Scotland, UK
xliv F14 Ballinhassig Cork, S Ireland
xliii L16 Ballinluig Perth and Kinross, C Scotland, UK
xliv E8 Ballinrobe Ir. Baile an Róba. Mayo, W Ireland
xliv B14 Ballinskelligs Kerry, SW Ireland
xliv B14 Ballinskelligs Bay Ir. Bá na Scealg. inlet SW Ireland
xliv F15 Ballinspittle Cork, S Ireland
xliv E7 Ballintober Mayo, NW Ireland
xliv G7 Ballintober Roscommon, C Ireland
xliv G4 Ballintra Ir. Baile an tSratha. Donegal, NW Ireland
xliii L16 Ballintuim Perth and Kinross, C Scotland, UK
xliv J10 Ballitore Kildare, E Ireland
xliv J8 Ballivor Meath, E Ireland
xliii I19 Balloch West Dunbartonshire, W Scotland, UK
xliv J11 Ballon Carlow, SE Ireland
xliv J6 Ballybay Ir. Béal Átha Beithe. Monaghan, N Ireland
xliv H4 Ballybofey Ir. Bealach Féich. Donegal, NW Ireland
xliv D11 Ballybunnion Kerry, SW Ireland
xliv L11 Ballycanew Wexford, SE Ireland
xliv M4 Ballycarry Carrickfergus, E Northern Ireland, UK
xliv E5 Ballycastle Mayo, NW Ireland
xliv L2 Ballycastle Ir. Baile an Chaistil. Moyle, N Northern Ireland, UK
xliv L4 Ballyclare Ir. Bealach Cláir. Newtownabbey, E Northern Ireland, UK
xliv C8 Ballyconneely Galway, W Ireland
xliv G14 Ballycotton Cork, S Ireland
xliv C6 Ballycroy Mayo, NW Ireland
xliv D15 Ballydehob Cork, S Ireland
xliv D13 Ballydesmond Cork, S Ireland
xliv B15 Ballydonegan Cork, S Ireland
xliv D12 Ballyduff Kerry, SW Ireland
xliv B13 Ballyferriter Kerry, SW Ireland
xliv M3 Ballygalley Larne, E Northern Ireland, UK
xliv J5 Ballygawley Dungannon, C Northern Ireland, UK
xliv M5 Ballygowan Ards, E Northern Ireland, UK
xliii D20 Ballygrant Argyll and Bute, W Scotland, UK
xliii C16 Ballyhaugh Argyll and Bute, W Scotland, UK
xliv F7 Ballyhaunis Ir. Beál Átha hAmhnais. Mayo, W Ireland
xliv C12 Ballyheige Kerry, SW Ireland
xliv I1 Ballyhillin Donegal, N Ireland
xliv F12 Ballyhoura Mountains ▲▲ S Ireland
xliv I7 Ballyjamesduff Cavan, N Ireland
xliv J3 Ballykelly Limavady, N Northern Ireland, UK
xliv D14 Ballylickey Cork, S Ireland
xliv I2 Ballyliffin Donegal, N Ireland
xliv D11 Ballylongford Kerry, SW Ireland
xliv J10 Ballylynan Laois, C Ireland
xliv H13 Ballymacarbry Waterford, S Ireland
xliv H8 Ballymahon Longford, C Ireland
xliv L3 Ballymena Ir. An Baile Meánach. Ballymena, NE Northern Ireland, UK
xliv K3 Ballymena ◐ district NE Northern Ireland, UK
xliv G7 Ballymoe Galway, W Ireland
xliv K2 Ballymoney Ir. Baile Monaidh. Ballymoney, NE Northern Ireland, UK
xliv K3 Ballymoney ◐ district N Northern Ireland, UK
xliv H8 Ballymore Westmeath, C Ireland
xliv F6 Ballymote Sligo, N Ireland
xliv J12 Ballynabola Wexford, SE Ireland
xliv I8 Ballynafid Westmeath, C Ireland
xliv H13 Ballynagaul Waterford, S Ireland
xliv L5 Ballynahinch Ir. Baile na hInse. Down, SE Northern Ireland, UK
xliv B13 Ballynana Kerry, SW Ireland
xliv F11 Ballyneety Limerick, SW Ireland
xliv L4 Ballynure Newtownabbey, E Northern Ireland, UK
xliv M6 Ballyquintin Point headland E Northern Ireland, UK
xliv I11 Ballyragget Kilkenny, SE Ireland
xliv K4 Ballyronan Cookstown, C Northern Ireland, UK
xliv F6 Ballysadare Ir. Baile Easa Dara. Sligo, NW Ireland
xliv G4 Ballyshannon Ir. Béal Átha Seanaidh. Donegal, NW Ireland
xliv J13 Ballyteige Bay bay SE Ireland
xliv E9 Ballyvaughan Clare, W Ireland
xliv M5 Ballywalter Ards, E Northern Ireland, UK
xliii F13 Balmacara Highland, NW Scotland, UK
xliii J24 Balmaclellan Dumfries and Galloway, SW Scotland, UK
xliii I19 Balmaha Stirling, C Scotland, UK
xliii P13 Balmedie Aberdeenshire, NE Scotland, UK
xlii G12 Balnacra Highland, NW Scotland, UK
xliii E17 Balnahard Argyll and Bute, W Scotland, UK
xliii E17 Ba, Loch ◎ W Scotland, UK
xliii H16 Ba, Loch ◎ NW Scotland, UK
xliii J17 Balquhidder Stirling, C Scotland, UK
xliv K8 Balrath Meath, E Ireland
xxxviii E16 Balsall Solihull, C England, UK
xxxix T13 Balsham Cambridgeshire, E England, UK
xli J1 Baltasound Shetland Islands, NE Scotland, UK
xliv D15 Baltimore Cork, S Ireland
xliv K10 Baltinglass Wicklow, E Ireland
xxxvi K11 Baltonsborough Somerset, SW England, UK
xli R2 Bamburgh Northumberland, N England, UK
xxxviii L5 Bamford Derbyshire, C England, UK
xli N9 Bampton Cumbria, NW England, UK
xxxvi H12 Bampton Devon, SW England, UK
xxxvii O8 Bampton Oxfordshire, C England, UK
xliv H9 Banagher Ir. Beannchar. Offaly, C Ireland
xliii H15 Banavie Highland, NW Scotland, UK
xliv L5 Banbridge Ir. Droichead na Banna. Banbridge, SE Northern Ireland, UK
xliv L5 Banbridge ◐ district SE Northern Ireland, UK
xxxvii P6 Banbury Oxfordshire, S England, UK
xliii O14 Banchory Aberdeenshire, NE Scotland, UK
xliv F14 Bandon Ir. Droicheadna Bandan. Cork, SW Ireland
xliv E14 Bandon ≈ S Ireland
xlii O11 Banff Aberdeenshire, NE Scotland, UK
xliv M4 Bangor Ir. Beannchar. North Down, E Northern Ireland, UK
xxxv G5 Bangor Gwynedd, NW Wales, UK
xliv D6 Bangor Erris Mayo, NW Ireland
xxxv K6 Bangor-is-y-coed Wrexham, NE Wales, UK
xliii L24 Bankend Dumfries and Galloway, SW Scotland, UK
xliii L17 Bankfoot Perth and Kinross, C Scotland, UK
xl M15 Banks Lancashire, NW England, UK
xliii M24 Bankshill Dumfries and Galloway, SW Scotland, UK
xliv K5 Bann var. Lower Bann, Upper Bann. ≈ N Northern Ireland, UK
xliii K19 Bannockburn Stirling, C Scotland, UK
xliv G12 Bansha Tipperary, S Ireland
xxxvii T10 Banstead Surrey, SE England, UK
xliv E13 Banteer Cork, S Ireland
xliv D14 Bantry Ir. Beanntraí. Cork, SW Ireland
xliv C15 Bantry Bay Ir. Bá Bheanntraí. bay SW Ireland
xli O11 Barbon Cumbria, NW England, UK
xli Q10 Barden North Yorkshire, N England, UK
xxxix Q6 Bardney Lincolnshire, E England, UK
xli O6 Bardon Mill Northumberland, N England, UK
xl M12 Bardsea Cumbria, NW England, UK
xli S13 Bardsey Leeds, N England, UK
xxxv D7 Bardsey Island island NW Wales, UK
xxxv G5 Bardsey Sound sound NW Wales, UK
xxxviii M12 Barford Warwickshire, C England, UK
xxxv J14 Bargoed Caerphilly, S Wales, UK
xxxvii Y10 Barham Kent, SE England, UK
xxxvi G6 Barking Barking and Dagenham, SE England, UK
xxxiv L16 Barking and Dagenham ◐ London borough SE England, UK
xxxvi G5 Barkingside Redbridge, SE England, UK
xxxix P7 Barkston Lincolnshire, E England, UK
xxxvii U6 Barkway Hertfordshire, SE England, UK
xxxviii J8 Barlaston City of Stoke-on-Trent, C England, UK
xli T14 Barlby North Yorkshire, N England, UK
xxxviii M9 Barlestone Leicestershire, C England, UK
xxxvii U6 Barley Hertfordshire, SE England, UK
xxxv G8 Barmouth Gwynedd, NW Wales, UK
xxxv G8 Barmouth Bay bay NW Wales, UK
xli W12 Barmston East Riding of Yorkshire, N England, UK
xliv E9 Barna Galway, W Ireland
xli Q9 Barnard Castle Durham, N England, UK
xliv D5 Barnatra Mayo, NW Ireland
xxxvi B8 Barnes Richmond upon Thames, SE England, UK
xxxvii T8 Barnet Barnet, SE England, UK
xxxiv K16 Barnet ◐ London borough SE England, UK
xxxix V11 Barnham Suffolk, E England, UK
xxxix W9 Barnham Broom Norfolk, E England, UK
xxxix V11 Barningham Suffolk, E England, UK
xli P13 Barnoldswick Lancashire, NW England, UK
xli S15 Barnsley Barnsley, N England, UK
xxxvii N8 Barnsley Gloucestershire, C England, UK
xli R16 Barnsley ◐ unitary authority N England, UK
xxxvi F12 Barnstaple Devon, SW England, UK
xxxvi E12 Barnstaple Bay bay SW England, UK
xliii I23 Barr South Ayrshire, W Scotland, UK
xlii A14 Barra island NW Scotland, UK
xlii A15 Barra Head headland NW Scotland, UK
xliii I24 Barrgrennan Dumfries and Galloway, SW Scotland, UK
xliii I20 Barrhead East Renfrewshire, W Scotland, UK
xliii H24 Barrhill South Ayrshire, W Scotland, UK
xliii F14 Barrisdale Highland, NW Scotland, UK
xliv J12 Barrow Ir. An Bhearú. ≈ SE Ireland
xxxix U12 Barrow Suffolk, E England, UK
xli P14 Barrowford Lancashire, NW England, UK
xl L12 Barrow-in-Furness Cumbria, NW England, UK
xxxix O9 Barrow upon Soar Leicestershire, C England, UK
xxxv J16 Barry The Vale of Glamorgan, S Wales, UK
xli R9 Barton North Yorkshire, N England, UK
xxxvii S6 Barton-le-Clay Bedfordshire, C England, UK
xxxix P3 Barton-upon-Humber North Lincolnshire, N England, UK
xlii D7 Barvas Western Isles, NW Scotland, UK
xxxviii G9 Baschurch Shropshire, W England, UK
xxxvi W9 Basildon Essex, E England, UK
xxxvii Q11 Basingstoke Hampshire, S England, UK
xxxviii L6 Baslow Derbyshire, C England, UK
xl L8 Bassenthwaite Cumbria, NW England, UK
xl L8 Bassenthwaite Lake ◎ NW England, UK
xxxix P6 Bassingham Lincolnshire, E England, UK
xliii N19 Bass Rock island E Scotland, UK
xxxix Q9 Baston Lincolnshire, E England, UK
xxxvi L10 Bath hist. Akermanceaster, anc. Aquae Calidae, Aquae Solis. Bath and North East Somerset, SW England, UK
xxxvi K10 Bath and North East Somerset ◐ unitary authority W England, UK
xliii L20 Bathgate West Lothian, SE Scotland, UK
xli R14 Batley Kirklees, N England, UK
xxxvi C9 Battersea Wandsworth, SE England, UK
xxxvii W12 Battle East Sussex, SE England, UK
xxxix R5 Baumber Lincolnshire, E England, UK
xxxix X9 Bawburgh Norfolk, E England, UK
xxxix W8 Bawdeswell Norfolk, E England, UK
xxxix Y13 Bawdsey Suffolk, E England, UK
xli U16 Bawtry Doncaster, N England, UK
xxxvii O9 Baydon Wiltshire, S England, UK
xxxvii R6 Beachampton Buckinghamshire, C England, UK
xxxvii V13 Beachy Head headland SE England, UK
xxxv J10 Beacon Hill hill E Wales, UK
xxxvii R9 Beaconsfield Buckinghamshire, C England, UK
xli R2 Beadnell Northumberland, N England, UK
xxxvi F13 Beaford Devon, SW England, UK
xli Q1 Beal Northumberland, N England, UK
xxxvi K13 Beaminster Dorset, S England, UK
xliv C15 Bear Island island S Ireland
xxxviii D17 Bearley Warwickshire, C England, UK
xliii J20 Bearsden East Dunbartonshire, S Scotland, UK
xliii L23 Beattock Dumfries and Galloway, SW Scotland, UK
xxxvii P13 Beaulieu Hampshire, S England, UK
xxxvii P13 Beaulieu ≈ S England, UK
xlii J12 Beauly Highland, N Scotland, UK
xlii J12 Beauly Firth inlet N Scotland, UK
xxxv G4 Beaumaris Isle of Anglesey, NW Wales, UK
xl B16 Bebington Wirral, NW England, UK
xxxix Y10 Beccles Suffolk, E England, UK
xxxvi U9 Beckenham Bromley, SE England, UK
xl K7 Beckfoot Cumbria, NW England, UK
xxxvii N10 Beckhampton Wiltshire, S England, UK
xxxix P7 Beckingham Lincolnshire, E England, UK
xxxix O4 Beckingham Nottinghamshire, C England, UK
xxxvi M11 Beckington Somerset, SW England, UK
xxxix U11 Beck Row Suffolk, E England, UK
xxxvi F7 Beckton Newham, SE England, UK
xxxvi G6 Becontree Redbridge, SE England, UK
xli R11 Bedale North Yorkshire, N England, UK
xxxv G6 Beddgelert Gwynedd, NW Wales, UK
xxxvii S6 Bedford Bedfordshire, E England, UK
xxxix R10 Bedford Level physical region E England, UK
xxxvii S6 Bedfordshire ◐ county E England, UK
xli R5 Bedlington Northumberland, N England, UK
xxxv J14 Bedwas Caerphilly, S Wales, UK
xxxviii E15 Bedworth Warwickshire, C England, UK
xli W12 Beeford East Riding of Yorkshire, N England, UK
xxxvi J14 Beer Devon, SW England, UK
xxxix N8 Beeston Nottinghamshire, C England, UK
xliii K24 Beeswing Dumfries and Galloway, SW Scotland, UK
xli N11 Beetham Cumbria, NW England, UK
xxxv J9 Beguildy Powys, C Wales, UK
xliii K15 Beinn A'Ghlo ▲ C Scotland, UK
xliii K15 Beinn Dearg ▲ C Scotland, UK
xliii H10 Beinn Dearg ▲ N Scotland, UK
xliii I21 Beith North Ayrshire, W Scotland, UK
xxxviii B16 Belbroughton Worcestershire, W England, UK
xxxix R5 Belchford Lincolnshire, E England, UK
xliv E8 Belclare Galway, W Ireland
xliv H5 Belcoo Fermanagh, W Northern Ireland, UK
xliv D5 Belderg Mayo, NW Ireland
xliv L4 Belfast Ir. Béal Feirste. political division capital E Northern Ireland, UK
xliv L4 Belfast International ✕ Antrim, E Northern Ireland, UK
xliv L4 Belfast City ✕ Belfast City, E Northern Ireland, UK
xliv L4 Belfast City ◐ district E Northern Ireland, UK
xliv M4 Belfast Lough Ir. Loch Lao. inlet E Northern Ireland, UK
xli Q2 Belford Northumberland, N England, UK
xliv D6 Bellacorick Mayo, NW Ireland
xliv K3 Bellaghy Magherafelt, C Northern Ireland, UK
xliv I7 Bellananagh var. Ballinagh. Cavan, N Ireland
xliv G8 Bellaneeny Roscommon, C Ireland
xliv E7 Bellavary Mayo, NW Ireland
xliv H5 Belleek Fermanagh, W Northern Ireland, UK
xli P5 Bellingham Northumberland, N England, UK
xliii F22 Bellochantuy Argyll and Bute, W Scotland, UK
xli Q2 Bellshill Northumberland, N England, UK
xliii K20 Bellshill North Lanarkshire, C Scotland, UK
xli O15 Belmont Lancashire, NW England, UK
xli J1 Belmont Shetland Islands, NE Scotland, UK
xliv C5 Belmullet Ir. Béal an Mhuirhead. Mayo, W Ireland
xxxviii M7 Belper Derbyshire, C England, UK
xli Q5 Belsay Northumberland, N England, UK
xxxix Y10 Belton Norfolk, E England, UK
xxxix O4 Belton North Lincolnshire, N England, UK
xliv I6 Belturbet Ir. Béal Tairbirt. Cavan, N Ireland
xxxix P8 Belvoir Leicestershire, C England, UK
xxxvii Q14 Bembridge Isle of Wight, S England, UK
xli X11 Bempton East Riding of Yorkshire, N England, UK
xliii H7 Ben Arkle ▲ NW Scotland, UK
xliii G13 Ben Attow ▲ NW Scotland, UK
xliii B12 Benbecula island NW Scotland, UK
xliii K17 Ben Chonzie ▲ C Scotland, UK
xliii G17 Ben Cruachan ▲ W Scotland, UK
xliii G17 Benderloch Argyll and Bute, W Scotland, UK
xliii I17 Ben Dórain ▲ W Scotland, UK
xliii I8 Ben Hee ▲ NW Scotland, UK
xliii I7 Ben Hope ▲ N Scotland, UK
xxxix S7 Benington Lincolnshire, E England, UK
xliii J8 Ben Klibreck ▲ N Scotland, UK
xliii J17 Ben Lawers ▲ C Scotland, UK
xxxv F4 Benllech Isle of Anglesey, NW Wales, UK
xliii I7 Ben Loyal ▲ NW Scotland, UK
xliii H17 Ben Lui ▲ C Scotland, UK
xliii L14 Ben Macdui var. Beinn MacDuibh. ▲ C Scotland, UK
xliii I17 Ben More ▲ C Scotland, UK
xliii E17 Ben More ▲ W Scotland, UK
xliii H8 Ben More Assynt ▲ N Scotland, UK
xliii H15 Ben Nevis ▲ N Scotland, UK
xliii M12 Ben Rinnes ▲ N Scotland, UK
xxxvii O8 Benson Oxfordshire, C England, UK
xli T15 Bentley Doncaster, N England, UK
xxxvii R11 Bentley Hampshire, S England, UK
xliii M23 Bentpath Dumfries and Galloway, SW Scotland, UK
xliii I18 Ben Venue ▲ C Scotland, UK
xliii J18 Ben Vorlich ▲ C Scotland, UK
xxxix S10 Benwick Cambridgeshire, E England, UK
xliii I11 Ben Wyvis ▲ NW Scotland, UK
xxxvi F15 Bere Alston Devon, SW England, UK
xxxvi F15 Bere Ferrers Devon, SW England, UK
xxxvi M14 Bere Regis Dorset, S England, UK
xxxvi L8 Berkeley Gloucestershire, C England, UK
xxxvii S8 Berkhamsted Hertfordshire, SE England, UK
xxxvi D8 Bermondsey Southwark, SE England, UK
xliii A15 Berneray island NW Scotland, UK
xliii B10 Berneray island NW Scotland, UK
xliii D12 Bernisdale Highland, NW Scotland, UK
xliii L8 Berriedale Highland, N Scotland, UK
xxxvi J11 Berrow Somerset, SW England, UK
xli P1 Berwick-upon-Tweed Northumberland, N England, UK
xliv K6 Bessbrook Newry and Mourne, S Northern Ireland, UK
xxxv G5 Bethesda Gwynedd, NW Wales, UK
xxxvi E7 Bethnal Green Tower Hamlets, SE England, UK
xliv D6 Betra Mayo, NW Ireland
xlii I6 Bettyhill Highland, N Scotland, UK
xxxv H5 Betws-y-Coed Conwy, N Wales, UK
xxxv E11 Beulah Ceredigion, W Wales, UK
xxxv I11 Beulah Powys, C Wales, UK
xxxvii W11 Beult ≈ SE England, UK
xli W13 Beverley East Riding of Yorkshire, E England, UK
xli N6 Bewcastle Cumbria, NW England, UK
xxxviii I11 Bewdley Worcestershire, W England, UK
xxxvii W11 Bewl Water ⊡ SE England, UK
xxxvii W13 Bexhill var. Bexhill-on-Sea. East Sussex, SE England, UK
xxxiv L16 Bexley ◐ London borough SE England, UK
xxxvi G9 Bexley Bexley, SE England, UK
xxxvi G8 Bexleyheath London borough capital Bexley, SE England, UK
xxxix V12 Beyton Suffolk, E England, UK
xxxvii N8 Bibury Gloucestershire, C England, UK
xxxvii Q7 Bicester Oxfordshire, C England, UK
xxxix R8 Bicker Lincolnshire, E England, UK
xxxvi H15 Bickington Devon, SW England, UK
xxxvi H13 Bickleigh Devon, SW England, UK
xxxviii H7 Bickley Moss Cheshire, W England, UK
xxxvii W11 Biddenden Kent, SE England, UK
xxxviii J7 Biddulph Staffordshire, C England, UK
xliii H16 Bidean Nam Bian ▲ NW Scotland, UK
xxxvi E12 Bideford Devon, SW England, UK
xxxviii K13 Bidford-on-Avon Warwickshire, C England, UK
xxxvi G16 Bigbury Bay bay SW England, UK
xxxix Q3 Bigby Lincolnshire, E England, UK
xliii L21 Biggar South Lanarkshire, C Scotland, UK
xxxvi U10 Biggin Hill Bromley, SE England, UK
xxxvii T6 Biggleswade Bedfordshire, C England, UK
xxxix W13 Bildeston Suffolk, E England, UK
xxxvi W8 Billericay Essex, SE England, UK
xxxix O10 Billesdon Leicestershire, C England, UK
xli N16 Billinge St Helens, NW England, UK
xli S8 Billingham Redcar and Cleveland, N England, UK
xxxix R7 Billinghay Lincolnshire, E England, UK
xxxvii S12 Billingshurst West Sussex, SE England, UK
xxxviii I11 Billingsley Shropshire, W England, UK
xxxix Y9 Billockby Norfolk, E England, UK
xxxviii B14 Bilston Wolverhampton, C England, UK
xxxix R4 Binbrook Lincolnshire, E England, UK
xxxix O7 Bingham Nottinghamshire, C England, UK
xli Q14 Bingley Bradford, N England, UK
xxxix V7 Binham Norfolk, E England, UK
xliv F11 Birdhill Tipperary, S Ireland
xxxviii M6 Birdholme Derbyshire, C England, UK
xxxvi M7 Birdlip Gloucestershire, C England, UK
xli U12 Birdsall North Yorkshire, N England, UK
xliii O21 Birgham The Borders, S Scotland, UK
xli B16 Birkenhead Wirral, NW England, UK
xli R4 Birling Northumberland, N England, UK
xxxviii C14 Birmingham Birmingham, C England, UK
xxxviii C14 Birmingham ◐ unitary authority C England, UK
xxxviii D15 Birmingham ✕ Birmingham, C England, UK
xliv H10 Birr var. Parsonstown, Ir. Biorra. Offaly, C Ireland
xlii L3 Birsay Orkney Islands, N Scotland, UK
xli V3 Birtley Gateshead, NE England, UK
xli P5 Birtley Northumberland, N England, UK
xxxviii K13 Bishampton Worcestershire, W England, UK
xli R8 Bishop Auckland Durham, N England, UK
xliii J20 Bishopbriggs East Dunbartonshire, C Scotland, UK
xli S12 Bishop Monkton North Yorkshire, N England, UK
xxxvii N10 Bishops Cannings Wiltshire, S England, UK
xxxviii G11 Bishop's Castle Shropshire, W England, UK
xxxvi L13 Bishop's Caundle Dorset, S England, UK
xxxvi M7 Bishop's Cleeve Gloucestershire, C England, UK
xxxvii V7 Bishop's Stortford Hertfordshire, E England, UK
xxxv G15 Bishopston Swansea, S Wales, UK
xxxvii Q12 Bishop's Waltham Hampshire, S England, UK
xxxvi M8 Bisley Gloucestershire, C England, UK
xxxvii S10 Bisley Surrey, SE England, UK
xxxvi F11 Bittadon Devon, SW England, UK
xxxviii H11 Bitterley Shropshire, W England, UK
xli O14 Blackburn Lancashire, NW England, UK
xlii O13 Blackburn Aberdeenshire, NE Scotland, UK
xliii L20 Blackburn West Lothian, SE Scotland, UK
xl C14 Blackburn ◐ unitary authority NW England, UK
xliii J23 Blackcraig Hill ▲ W Scotland, UK
xliii K18 Blackford Perth and Kinross, C Scotland, UK
xliv D9 Black Head headland W Ireland
xxxvi F8 Blackheath Lewisham, SE England, UK
xlii J11 Black Isle peninsula NW Scotland, UK
xliv H5 Blacklion Cavan, N Ireland
xliii H25 Black Loch ◎ Dumfries and Galloway, SW Scotland, UK
xxxv I15 Blackmill Bridgend, S Wales, UK
xxxv K12 Black Mountains ▲▲ SE Wales, UK
xl M14 Blackpool Lancashire, NW England, UK
xl L14 Blackpool ◐ unitary authority NW England, UK
xl E14 Blackrod Bolton, NW England, UK
xliv C6 Blacksod Bay Ir. Cuan an Fhóid Duibh. inlet W Ireland
xliv J12 Blackstairs Mountains ▲▲ SE Ireland
xxxvii Q7 Blackthorn Oxfordshire, C England, UK
xliv J7 Blackwater ≈ E Ireland
xliv K12 Blackwater Wexford, SE Ireland
xliv H13 Blackwater Ir. An Abhainn Mhór. ≈ S Ireland
xliv J5 Blackwater ≈ Ireland/Northern Ireland, UK
xxxix X8 Blackwater ≈ E England, UK
xliii H16 Blackwater Reservoir ⊡ NW Scotland, UK
xxxv G6 Blaenau Ffestiniog Gwynedd, NW Wales, UK
xxxv J13 Blaenau Gwent ◐ unitary authority SE Wales, UK
xxxv K13 Blaenavon Torfaen, SE Wales, UK
xxxvi K10 Blagdon North West Somerset, SW England, UK
xxxv K13 Blaina Blaenau Gwent, SE Wales, UK
xliii K15 Blair Atholl Perth and Kinross, C Scotland, UK
xliii L16 Blairgowrie Perth and Kinross, C Scotland, UK
xxxviii G13 Blakemere Herefordshire, W England, UK
xxxvi L8 Blakeney Gloucestershire, C England, UK
xxxix W7 Blakeney Norfolk, E England, UK
xxxix W7 Blakeney Point headland E England, UK
xxxix O13 Blakesley Northamptonshire, C England, UK
xli P7 Blanchland Northumberland, N England, UK
xxxvi M13 Blandford Forum Dorset, S England, UK
xliii J19 Blanefield Stirling, C Scotland, UK
xliv A13 Blasket Islands island group W Ireland
xli R6 Blaydon Gateshead, NE England, UK
xxxvi J10 Bleadon North West Somerset, SW England, UK
xxxix O7 Bleasby Nottinghamshire, C England, UK
xxxvii O7 Bledington Gloucestershire, C England, UK
xli N8 Blencarn Cumbria, NW England, UK
xliv K9 Blessington Wicklow, E Ireland
xxxvii R6 Bletchley Buckinghamshire, SE England, UK
xxxvii Q9 Blewbury Oxfordshire, C England, UK
xxxix N7 Blidworth Nottinghamshire, C England, UK
xxxix O13 Blisworth Northamptonshire, C England, UK
xxxvii O6 Blockley Gloucestershire, C England, UK
xliv G2 Bloody Foreland Ir. Cnoc Fola. headland NW Ireland
xxxvii P6 Bloxham Oxfordshire, C England, UK
xxxviii C14 Bloxwich Walsall, C England, UK
xli R13 Blubberhouses North Yorkshire, N England, UK
xliv G4 Blue Stack Mountains ▲▲ N Ireland
xxxix S11 Bluntisham Cambridgeshire, E England, UK
xli R5 Blyth Northumberland, N England, UK
xxxix N5 Blyth Nottinghamshire, C England, UK
xli R5 Blyth ≈ N England, UK
xxxix Y11 Blyth ≈ E England, UK
xxxix Y11 Blythburgh Suffolk, E England, UK
xxxix P4 Blyton Lincolnshire, E England, UK
xliii N18 Boarhills Fife, E Scotland, UK
xliii K13 Boat of Garten Highland, N Scotland, UK
xxxvii V6 Bocking Churchstreet Essex, SE England, UK
xlii Q12 Boddam Aberdeenshire, NE Scotland, UK
xlii I5 Boddam Shetland Islands, NE Scotland, UK
xxxv E4 Bodedern Isle of Anglesey, NW Wales, UK
xliv G7 Boderg, Lough ◎ C Ireland
xxxv E6 Bodfuan Gwynedd, NW Wales, UK
xxxvii W12 Bodiam East Sussex, SE England, UK
xxxvi D15 Bodmin Cornwall, SW England, UK
xxxvi D15 Bodmin Moor moorland SW England, UK
xliv H7 Bofin, Lough ◎ N Ireland
xliv E13 Boggeragh Mountains ▲▲ S Ireland
xxxvii S13 Bognor Regis West Sussex, SE England, UK
xli S6 Boldon South Tyneside, NE England, UK
xxxvii P13 Boldre Hampshire, S England, UK
xl G16 Bollin ≈ Cheshire, C England, UK
xl H17 Bollington Cheshire, W England, UK
xxxix N6 Bolsover Derbyshire, C England, UK
xli S11 Boltby North Yorkshire, N England, UK
xl E14 Bolton prev. Bolton-le-Moors. Bolton, NW England, UK
xli O15 Bolton ◐ unitary authority NW England, UK
xli N12 Bolton-le-Sands Lancashire, NW England, UK
xliv A14 Bolus Head headland SW Ireland
xlii J10 Bonar Bridge Highland, NW Scotland, UK
xliii G17 Bonawe Argyll and Bute, W Scotland, UK
xxxv E12 Boncath Pembrokeshire, SW Wales, UK
xliii N22 Bonchester Bridge The Borders, S Scotland, UK
xliii L19 Bo'Ness Falkirk, C Scotland, UK
xliii K19 Bonnybridge Falkirk, C Scotland, UK
xliii M20 Bonnyrigg Midlothian, SE Scotland, UK
xxxv H9 Bont-goch Ceredigion, W Wales, UK
xxxv H7 Bont Newydd Gwynedd, NW Wales, UK
xxxv J15 Bonvilston The Vale of Glamorgan, S Wales, UK
xl K11 Bootle Cumbria, NW England, UK
xl B15 Bootle Sefton, NW England, UK
xxxvii R11 Bordon Hampshire, S England, UK
xxxvii T8 Borehamwood Hertfordshire, E England, UK
xliii M23 Boreland Dumfries and Galloway, SW Scotland, UK
xliii A10 Boreray island NW Scotland, UK
xliii J25 Borgue Dumfries and Galloway, SW Scotland, UK
xlii L8 Borgue Highland, N Scotland, UK
xli S12 Boroughbridge North Yorkshire, N England, UK
xliv J11 Borris Carlow, SE Ireland
xliv H10 Borris in Ossory Laois, C Ireland
xliv G10 Borrisokane Tipperary, S Ireland
xliv H11 Borrisoleigh Tipperary, S Ireland
xxxv G9 Borth Ceredigion, W Wales, UK
xxxviii I13 Bosbury Herefordshire, W England, UK
xxxvi D14 Boscastle Cornwall, SW England, UK
xxxvii R13 Bosham West Sussex, S England, UK
xxxv D14 Bosherston Pembrokeshire, SW Wales, UK
xxxix S7 Boston prev. St Botolph's Town. Lincolnshire, E England, UK
xxxvi D17 Boswinger Cornwall, SW England, UK
xxxix W11 Botesdale Suffolk, E England, UK
xl L8 Bothel Cumbria, NW England, UK
xxxvii P13 Botley Hampshire, S England, UK
xxxix P8 Bottesford Leicestershire, C England, UK
xxxvii X10 Boughton Street Kent, SE England, UK
xliii M13 Boultenstone Aberdeenshire, NE Scotland, UK
xxxix Q9 Bourne Lincolnshire, E England, UK
xxxvii S8 Bourne End Buckinghamshire, C England, UK
xxxvii N14 Bournemouth Bournemouth, S England, UK
xxxvii N14 Bournemouth ◐ unitary authority S England, UK
xxxviii C15 Bournville Birmingham, C England, UK
xxxvi M12 Bourton Dorset, S England, UK
xxxvii O7 Bourton-on-the-Water Gloucestershire, C England, UK
xxxvi H15 Bovey Tracey Devon, SW England, UK
xxxvi G13 Bow Devon, SW England, UK
xxxvi E7 Bow Tower Hamlets, SE England, UK
xlii M5 Bow Orkney Islands, N Scotland, UK
xli W5 Bowburn Durham, N England, UK
xl F16 Bowdon Cheshire, C England, UK
xxxvi D5 Bowe Park Enfield, SE England, UK
xlii I6 Bowertower Highland, N Scotland, UK
xli Q9 Bowes Durham, N England, UK
xli N13 Bowland, Forest of forest N England, UK
xliii D20 Bowmore Argyll and Bute, W Scotland, UK
xl L6 Bowness-on-Solway Cumbria, NW England, UK
xl M10 Bowness-on-Windermere Cumbria, NW England, UK
xxxvi M10 Box Wiltshire, S England, UK
xxxix W13 Boxford Suffolk, E England, UK
xliv G6 Boyle Ir. Mainistirna Búille. Roscommon, C Ireland
xliv K8 Boyne Ir. An Bhóinn. ≈ E Ireland
xxxvi E14 Boyton Cornwall, SW England, UK
xxxix P12 Bozeat Northamptonshire, C England, UK
xxxvii Y11 Brabourne Kent, SE England, UK
xlii D12 Bracadale Highland, NW Scotland, UK
xxxix N14 Brackley Northamptonshire, C England, UK
xliv J9 Bracknagh Offaly, C Ireland
xxxvii R10 Bracknell Bracknell Forest, S England, UK
xxxvii R9 Bracknell Forest ◐ unitary authority SE England, UK
xliii K18 Braco Perth and Kinross, C Scotland, UK
xli R14 Bradford Bradford, N England, UK
xli Q14 Bradford ◐ unitary authority N England, UK
xxxvi L10 Bradford-on-Avon Wiltshire, S England, UK
xxxvii Q14 Brading Isle of Wight, S England, UK
xxxvi I13 Bradninch Devon, SW England, UK
xxxviii L5 Bradwell Derbyshire, C England, UK
xxxvii X8 Bradwell-on-Sea Essex, SE England, UK
xxxvi E13 Bradworthy Devon, SW England, UK
xlii I3 Brae Shetland Islands, NE Scotland, UK
xliii M15 Braedownie Angus, E Scotland, UK
xliii L14 Braemar Aberdeenshire, NE Scotland, UK
xlii N3 Braeswick Orkney Islands, N Scotland, UK
xli S12 Brafferton North Yorkshire, N England, UK
xlii C7 Bragar Western Isles, NW Scotland, UK
xxxv D7 Braich y Pwll headland NW Wales, UK
xxxviii L7 Brailsford Derbyshire, C England, UK
xxxvii W7 Braintree Essex, SE England, UK
xxxvii P12 Braishfield Hampshire, S England, UK
xl L9 Braithwaite Cumbria, NW England, UK
xxxvii Q12 Bramdean Hampshire, S England, UK
xxxix Y11 Bramfield Suffolk, E England, UK
xxxix W13 Bramford Suffolk, E England, UK
xl H16 Bramhall Stockport, NW England, UK
xli S13 Bramham Leeds, N England, UK
xxxvii Q10 Bramley Hampshire, S England, UK
xli N6 Brampton Cumbria, NW England, UK
xxxvii O12 Bramshaw Hampshire, S England, UK
xxxix U7 Brancaster Norfolk, E England, UK
xliii M11 Branderburgh Moray, N Scotland, UK
xli W13 Brandesburton East Riding of Yorkshire, N England, UK
xliv B12 Brandon Kerry, SW Ireland
xli R8 Brandon Durham, N England, UK
xxxix U11 Brandon Suffolk, E England, UK
xliv B12 Brandon Bay bay SW Ireland
xliv B12 Brandon Head headland SW Ireland
xliv B12 Brandon Mountain Ir. Cnoc Bréanainn. ▲ SW Ireland
xli T11 Brandsby North Yorkshire, N England, UK
xxxix P8 Branston Leicestershire, C England, UK
xxxix Q6 Branston Lincolnshire, E England, UK
xxxviii L7 Brassington Derbyshire, C England, UK
xxxvi F14 Bratton Clovelly Devon, SW England, UK
xxxix N12 Braunston Northamptonshire, C England, UK
xxxvi F12 Braunton Devon, SW England, UK
xliv L10 Bray Ir. Bré. Wicklow, E Ireland
xxxvi G12 Brayford Devon, SW England, UK
xxxvi B17 Breage Cornwall, SW England, UK
xxxvi L8 Bream Gloucestershire, C England, UK
xxxvi J10 Brean Somerset, SW England, UK
xlii C8 Breasclete Western Isles, NW Scotland, UK
xxxv G12 Brechfa Carmarthenshire, S Wales, UK
xliii N16 Brechin Angus, E Scotland, UK
xxxix V10 Breckland heathland E England, UK
xxxv J12 Brecon Powys, E Wales, UK
xxxv I13 Brecon Beacons ▲▲ S Wales, UK
xl H15 Bredbury Stockport, NW England, UK
xxxvii W12 Brede East Sussex, SE England, UK
xxxvii W10 Bredhurst Kent, SE England, UK
xxxviii K14 Bredon Worcestershire, W England, UK
xxxviii M9 Breedon on the Hill Leicestershire, C England, UK
xxxvi G11 Brendon Devon, SW England, UK
xxxvi I12 Brendon Hills hill range SW England, UK
xxxv I5 Brenig, Llyn ◎ N Wales, UK
xlii B8 Brenish Western Isles, NW Scotland, UK
xxxiv K16 Brent ◐ London borough SE England, UK
xxxvii U6 Brent Pelham Hertfordshire, SE England, UK
xxxvii V8 Brentwood Essex, E England, UK
xlii I4 Bressay island NE Scotland, UK
xlii I3 Brettabister Shetland Islands, NE Scotland, UK
xxxviii B13 Brewood Staffordshire, C England, UK
xlii L11 Briach Moray, N Scotland, UK
xxxv H11 Brianne Reservoir, Llyn ⊡ E Wales, UK
xl G10 Bride N Isle of Man
xxxvi F14 Bridestowe Devon, SW England, UK
xxxvi Y10 Bridge Kent, SE England, UK
xliv I3 Bridgend Donegal, N Ireland
xliii D20 Bridgend Argyll and Bute, W Scotland, UK
xliii G19 Bridgend Argyll and Bute, W Scotland, UK
xliii L17 Bridgend Perth and Kinross, C Scotland, UK
xxxv I15 Bridgend Bridgend, S Wales, UK
xxxv I15 Bridgend ◐ unitary authority S Wales, UK
xliii K19 Bridge of Allan Stirling, C Scotland, UK
xliii L12 Bridge of Avon Moray, N Scotland, UK
xliii L16 Bridge of Cally Perth and Kinross, C Scotland, UK
xliii K25 Bridge of Dee Dumfries and Galloway, SW Scotland, UK
xlii P13 Bridge of Don City of Aberdeen, NE Scotland, UK
xlii O14 Bridge of Dye Aberdeenshire, NE Scotland, UK
xliii L18 Bridge of Earn Perth and Kinross, C Scotland, UK
xlii M14 Bridge of Gairn Aberdeenshire, NE Scotland, UK
xliii I16 Bridge of Gaur Perth and Kinross, C Scotland, UK
xliii H17 Bridge of Orchy Argyll and Bute, W Scotland, UK
xliii I20 Bridge of Weir Renfrewshire, W Scotland, UK
xliv K13 Bridgetown Wexford, SE Ireland
xxxviii I10 Bridgnorth Shropshire, W England, UK
xxxvi J11 Bridgwater Somerset, SW England, UK
xxxvi I11 Bridgwater Bay bay SW England, UK
xli X12 Bridlington East Riding of Yorkshire, E England, UK
xli X12 Bridlington Bay bay E England, UK
xxxvi K14 Bridport Dorset, S England, UK
xli P14 Brierfield Lancashire, NW England, UK
xxxix Q3 Brigg North Lincolnshire, N England, UK
xli R14 Brighouse Calderdale, N England, UK
xxxvii P14 Brighstone Isle of Wight, S England, UK
xxxvii Y7 Brightlingsea Essex, SE England, UK
xxxvii U13 Brighton Brighton and Hove, SE England, UK
xxxvii T13 Brighton and Hove ◐ unitary authority SE England, UK
xliii J18 Brig o'Turk Stirling, C Scotland, UK
xxxix P11 Brigstock Northamptonshire, C England, UK
xxxvii Q7 Brill Buckinghamshire, C England, UK
xxxix S5 Brinkhill Lincolnshire, E England, UK
xxxviii M11 Brinklow Warwickshire, C England, UK
xxxvii N9 Brinkworth Wiltshire, S England, UK
xliv G2 Brinlack Donegal, N Ireland

◆ Country ● Country Capital ◇ Dependent Territory ○ Dependent Territory Capital ◐ Administrative Region ✕ International Airport ▲ Mountain ▲▲ Mountain Range ◎ Lake ⊡ Reservoir ≈ River

xlii M3 **Brinyan** Orkney Islands, N Scotland, UK
xxxvi L10 **Bristol** ***anc.*** Bricgstow. City of Bristol, SW England, UK
xxxv H16 **Bristol Channel** *inlet* England/Wales, UK
xxxvi K9 **Bristol, City of** ⬖ *unitary authority* SW England, UK
xxxv H14 **Briton Ferry** Neath Port Talbot, S Wales, UK
xxxvi H16 **Brixham** Devon, SW England, UK
xxxvi D8 **Brixton** Lambeth, SE England, UK
xxxix O12 **Brixworth** Northamptonshire, C England, UK
xlii D8 **Broad Bay** *bay* NW Scotland, UK
xxxvii N12 **Broad Chalke** Wiltshire, S England, UK
xxxvi I14 **Broad Clyst** Devon, SW England, UK
xliv E12 **Broadford** Limerick, SW Ireland
xlii E13 **Broadford** Highland, N Scotland, UK
xliv C5 **Broad Haven** *inlet* NW Ireland
xxxvi I13 **Broadhembury** Devon, SW England, UK
xxxvii N9 **Broad Hinton** Wiltshire, S England, UK
xliii L22 **Broad Law** ▲ S Scotland, UK
xxxvi L14 **Broadmayne** Dorset, S England, UK
xxxv B14 **Broad Sound** *sound* SW Wales, UK
xxxvii Z10 **Broadstairs** Kent, SE England, UK
xxxix Y9 **Broads, The** *wetland* E England, UK
xxxvii N13 **Broadstone** Poole, S England, UK
xxxvi J13 **Broadway** Somerset, SW England, UK
xxxviii L14 **Broadway** Worcestershire, W England, UK
xxxvi L14 **Broadwey** Dorset, S England, UK
xxxvi K13 **Broadwindsor** Dorset, S England, UK
xlii E12 **Brochel** Highland, NW Scotland, UK
xxxvii O13 **Brockenhurst** Hampshire, S England, UK
xli N8 **Brockleymoor** Cumbria, NW England, UK
xliii G21 **Brodick** North Ayrshire, W Scotland, UK
xxxviii H11 **Bromfield** Shropshire, W England, UK
xxxvii U9 **Bromley** Bromley, SE England, UK
xxxiv L17 **Bromley** ⬖ *London borough* SE England, UK
xli V11 **Brompton** North Yorkshire, N England, UK
xli S11 **Brompton** North Yorkshire, N England, UK
xxxvi I12 **Brompton Ralph** Somerset, SW England, UK
xxxvi H12 **Brompton Regis** Somerset, SW England, UK
xxxviii B16 **Bromsgrove** Worcestershire, W England, UK
xxxviii I12 **Bromyard** Herefordshire, W England, UK
xxxvii P14 **Brook** Isle of Wight, S England, UK
xxxix X10 **Brooke** Norfolk, E England, UK
xxxvii X12 **Brookland** Kent, SE England, UK
xli R4 **Broomhill** Northumberland, N England, UK
xlii G10 **Broom, Loch** *inlet* NW Scotland, UK
xlii K9 **Brora** Highland, N Scotland, UK
xlii J9 **Brora** ≈ N Scotland, UK
xlii K9 **Brora, Loch** ◎ N Scotland, UK
xxxviii I10 **Broseley** Shropshire, W England, UK
xliv D12 **Brosna** Kerry, SW Ireland
xliv I9 **Brosna** ≈ Westmeath, C Ireland
xli O9 **Brough** Cumbria, NW England, UK
xlii L6 **Brough** Highland, N Scotland, UK
xlii L3 **Brough Head** *island* N Scotland, UK
xliv L3 **Broughshane** Ballymena, NE Northern Ireland, UK
xli N14 **Broughton** Lancashire, NW England, UK
xxxix P11 **Broughton** Northamptonshire, C England, UK
xxxix P3 **Broughton** North Lincolnshire, N England, UK
xli P13 **Broughton** North Yorkshire, N England, UK
xlii M2 **Broughton** Orkney Islands, N Scotland, UK
xliii L21 **Broughton** The Borders, S Scotland, UK
xxxv K5 **Broughton** Flintshire, N Wales, UK
xxxix N10 **Broughton Astley** Leicestershire, C England, UK
xl L11 **Broughton in Furness** Cumbria, NW England, UK
xlii N3 **Broughtown** Orkney Islands, N Scotland, UK
xxxviii C13 **Brownhills** Walsall, C England, UK
xxxvi D14 **Brown Willy** *hill* SW England, UK
xxxvii T8 **Broxbourne** Hertfordshire, E England, UK
xliii L20 **Broxburn** City of Edinburgh, E Scotland, UK
xxxviii H7 **Broxton** Cheshire, W England, UK
xlii M7 **Bruan** Highland, N Scotland, UK
xxxvi J11 **Brue** ≈ SW England, UK
xliv F12 **Bruff** Limerick, SW Ireland
xliii D20 **Bruichladdich** Argyll and Bute, W Scotland, UK
xxxix Y9 **Brundall** Norfolk, E England, UK
xliv F12 **Bruree** Limerick, SW Ireland
xxxvi L12 **Bruton** Somerset, SW England, UK
xliii M24 **Brydekirk** Dumfries and Galloway, SW Scotland, UK
xxxv H13 **Brynamman** Carmarthenshire, S Wales, UK
xxxv I12 **Bryn Du** *hill* E Wales, UK
xxxv J13 **Brynmawr** Blaenau Gwent, SE Wales, UK
xxxv F5 **Brynsiencyn** Isle of Anglesey, NW Wales, UK
xli U14 **Bubwith** East Riding of Yorkshire, N England, UK
xlii Q12 **Buchan Ness** *headland* NE Scotland, UK
xliii K17 **Buchanty** Perth and Kinross, C Scotland, UK
xliii J19 **Buchlyvie** Stirling, C Scotland, UK
xli P11 **Buckden** North Yorkshire, N England, UK
xxxvi G15 **Buckfastleigh** Devon, SW England, UK
xliii M18 **Buckhaven** Fife, E Scotland, UK
xxxvi F5 **Buckhurst Hill** Redbridge, SE England, UK
xlii M11 **Buckie** Moray, NE Scotland, UK
xxxvii Q6 **Buckingham** Buckinghamshire, C England, UK
xxxvii Q7 **Buckinghamshire** ⬖ *county* SE England, UK
xxxvii O8 **Buckland** Oxfordshire, C England, UK
xxxvi F12 **Buckland Brewer** Devon, SW England, UK
xxxvii P13 **Bucklers Hard** Hampshire, S England, UK
xxxv K5 **Buckley** Flintshire, N Wales, UK
xxxix R6 **Bucknall** Lincolnshire, E England, UK
xxxviii G12 **Bucknell** Shropshire, W England, UK
xlii P13 **Bucksburn** City of Aberdeen, NE Scotland, UK
xxxvi E12 **Buck's Cross** Devon, SW England, UK
xlii M13 **Buck, The** ▲ N Scotland, UK
xliii N17 **Buddon Ness** *headland* E Scotland, UK
xxxvi E13 **Bude** Cornwall, SW England, UK
xxxvi D13 **Bude Bay** *bay* SW England, UK
xxxvi I14 **Budleigh Salterton** Devon, SW England, UK
xxxix O12 **Bugbrooke** Northamptonshire, C England, UK
xxxvi D16 **Bugle** Cornwall, SW England, UK
xxxv J11 **Builth Wells** Powys, E Wales, UK
xxxvii O11 **Bulford** Wiltshire, S England, UK
xliv A15 **Bull, The** *island* S Ireland
xli U12 **Bulmer** North Yorkshire, N England, UK
xliv G2 **Bunbeg** Donegal, N Ireland
xxxviii H7 **Bunbury** Cheshire, W England, UK
xliv K11 **Bunclody** Wexford, SE Ireland
xliv I2 **Buncrana** ***Ir.*** Bun Cranncha. Donegal, NW Ireland
xliv G5 **Bundoran** ***Ir.*** Bun Dobhráin. Donegal, NW Ireland
xliii D18 **Bunessan** Argyll and Bute, W Scotland, UK
xxxix Y10 **Bungay** Suffolk, E England, UK
xliv I13 **Bunmahon** Waterford, S Ireland
xliv F10 **Bunnaglass** Galway, W Ireland
xliv F11 **Bunratty** Clare, W Ireland
xxxvii U6 **Buntingford** Hertfordshire, SE England, UK
xxxviii K6 **Burbage** Derbyshire, C England, UK
xxxvii O10 **Burbage** Wiltshire, S England, UK
xxxix Y9 **Bure** ≈ E England, UK
xxxix V14 **Bures** Essex, E England, UK
xxxviii I7 **Burfard** Cheshire, C England, UK
xxxvii O7 **Burford** Oxfordshire, C England, UK
xxxvii T12 **Burgess Hill** West Sussex, SE England, UK
xxxix Y9 **Burgh Castle** Norfolk, E England, UK
xlii L11 **Burghead** Moray, N Scotland, UK
xxxvii Q10 **Burghfield** West Berkshire, S England, UK
xxxix T6 **Burgh le Marsh** Lincolnshire, E England, UK
xxxvii O13 **Burley** Hampshire, S England, UK
xxxviii H8 **Burlton** Shropshire, W England, UK
xli V13 **Burnby** East Riding of Yorkshire, N England, UK
xli R11 **Burneston** North Yorkshire, N England, UK
xxxix V7 **Burnham** Market Norfolk, E England, UK
xxxvii X8 **Burnham-on-Crouch** Essex, SE England, UK
xxxvi J11 **Burnham-on-Sea** Somerset, SW England, UK
xlii Q12 **Burnhaven** Aberdeenshire, NE Scotland, UK
xli P14 **Burnley** Lancashire, NW England, UK
xli Q12 **Burnsall** North Yorkshire, N England, UK
xliii J23 **Burnside** East Ayrshire, W Scotland, UK
xliii M19 **Burntisland** Fife, E Scotland, UK
xxxviii C13 **Burntwood** Staffordshire, C England, UK
xlii J1 **Burrafirth** Shetland Islands, NE Scotland, UK
xlii I2 **Burravoe** Shetland Islands, NE Scotland, UK
xlii N5 **Burray** *island* NE Scotland, UK
xliii M17 **Burrelton** Perth and Kinross, C Scotland, UK
xliv E9 **Burren** Clare, W Ireland
xliv E10 **Burren** *physical region* W Ireland
xliii I26 **Burrow Head** *headland* SW Scotland, UK
xxxv F14 **Burry Port** Carmarthenshire, S Wales, UK
xl M15 **Burscough** Lancashire, NW England, UK
xl B17 **Burton** Cheshire, W England, UK
xli W12 **Burton Agnes** East Riding of Yorkshire, N England, UK
xxxvi K14 **Burton Bradstock** Dorset, S England, UK
xli W11 **Burton Fleming** East Riding of Yorkshire, N England, UK
xli N11 **Burton-in-Kendal** Cumbria, NW England, UK
xxxix O7 **Burton Joyce** Nottinghamshire, C England, UK
xxxix P11 **Burton Latimer** Northamptonshire, C England, UK
xli S12 **Burton Leonard** North Yorkshire, N England, UK
xli X14 **Burton Pidsea** East Riding of Yorkshire, N England, UK
xliv G3 **Burtonport** Donegal, N Ireland
xxxviii L9 **Burton upon Trent** ***var.*** Burton on Trent, Burton-upon-Trent. Staffordshire, C England, UK
xxxviii H7 **Burwardsley** Cheshire, W England, UK
xxxix T12 **Burwell** Cambridgeshire, E England, UK
xlii M5 **Burwick** Orkney Islands, N Scotland, UK
xl G14 **Bury** Bury, NW England, UK
xxxvii S13 **Bury** West Sussex, SE England, UK
xl F14 **Bury** ⬖ *unitary authority* NW England, UK
xxxix U12 **Bury St Edmunds** ***hist.*** Beodericsworth. Suffolk, E England, UK
xliv K2 **Bushmills** Moyle, N Northern Ireland, UK
xliii G20 **Bute, Island of** *island* SW Scotland, UK
xliii G21 **Bute, Sound of** *sound* W Scotland, UK
xxxvi K12 **Butleigh** Somerset, SW England, UK
xxxix Y13 **Butley** Suffolk, SW England, UK
xli O6 **Butterburn** Cumbria, NW England, UK
xl L9 **Buttermere** Cumbria, NW England, UK
xxxix S7 **Butterwick** Lincolnshire, E England, UK
xliv F13 **Buttevant** Cork, S Ireland
xxxviii K6 **Buxton** Derbyshire, C England, UK
xxxix X8 **Buxton** Norfolk, E England, UK
xxxix N13 **Byfield** Northamptonshire, C England, UK
xxxvii S10 **Byfleet** Surrey, SE England, UK
xxxv I5 **Bylchau** Conwy, N Wales, UK
xli O4 **Byrness** Northumberland, N England, UK

C

xxxix Q4 **Cabourne** Lincolnshire, E England, UK
xlii M13 **Cabrach** Moray, N Scotland, UK
xxxv H8 **Cader Idris** ▲ NW Wales, UK
xl F15 **Cadishead** Salford, NW England, UK
xxxvii O13 **Cadnam** Hampshire, S England, UK
xxxv K5 **Caergwrle** Flintshire, N Wales, UK
xxxv K14 **Caerleon** Newport, SE Wales, UK
xxxv F5 **Caernarfon** ***var.*** Caernarvon, Carnarvon. Gwynedd, NW Wales, UK
xxxv D5 **Caernarfon Bay** *bay* NW Wales, UK
xxxv J15 **Caerphilly** Caerphilly, S Wales, UK
xxxv J14 **Caerphilly** ⬖ *unitary authority* S Wales, UK
xxxv I9 **Caersws** Powys, C Wales, UK
xxxv L14 **Caerwent** Monmouthshire, SE Wales, UK
xxxv J4 **Caerwys** Flintshire, N Wales, UK
xliv C14 **Caha Mountains** ***Ir.*** An Cheacha. ▲▲ SW Ireland
xliv H12 **Caher** ***Ir.*** An Cathai*r*. Tipperary, S Ireland
xliv B13 **Caherciveen** ***Ir.*** Cathair Saidhbhín. Kerry, SW Ireland
xliv B14 **Caherdaniel** Kerry, SW Ireland
xliv L12 **Cahore Point** ***Ir.*** Rinn Chathói*r*. *headland* SE Ireland
xliii F19 **Cairnbaan** Argyll and Bute, W Scotland, UK
xliii H18 **Cairndow** Argyll and Bute, W Scotland, UK
xliii L14 **Cairn Gorm** ▲ C Scotland, UK
xliii L14 **Cairngorm Mountains** ▲▲ C Scotland, UK
xlii N12 **Cairnie** Aberdeenshire, NE Scotland, UK
xliii H24 **Cairnryan** Dumfries and Galloway, SW Scotland, UK
xliii J23 **Cairnsmore of Carsphairn** ▲ SW Scotland, UK
xliii K22 **Cairn Table** ▲ C Scotland, UK
xliii L15 **Cairnwell, The** ▲ C Scotland, UK
xxxix Z9 **Caister-on-Sea** Norfolk, E England, UK
xxxix Q4 **Caistor** Lincolnshire, E England, UK
xl M8 **Caldbeck** Cumbria, NW England, UK
xli R15 **Calder** ≈ N England, UK
xl K10 **Calder Bridge** Cumbria, NW England, UK
xliii K20 **Caldercruix** North Lanarkshire, C Scotland, UK
xli P15 **Calderdale** ⬖ *unitary authority* N England, UK
xlii K6 **Calder, Loch** ◎ N Scotland, UK
xliii J21 **Caldermill** South Lanarkshire, C Scotland, UK
xxxv D14 **Caldey Island** *island* SW Wales, UK
xxxv L14 **Caldicot** Monmouthshire, SE Wales, UK
xli R9 **Caldwell** North Yorkshire, N England, UK
xl F12 **Calf of Man** *island* SW Isle of Man
xlii N3 **Calfsound** Orkney Islands, N Scotland, UK
xli O10 **Calf, The** ▲ NW England, UK
xliii D16 **Calgary** Argyll and Bute, W Scotland, UK
xliv I12 **Callan** ***Ir.*** Callain. Kilkenny, S Ireland
xliii J18 **Callander** Stirling, C Scotland, UK
xxxvi E15 **Callington** Cornwall, SW England, UK
xxxvii N9 **Calne** Wiltshire, S England, UK
xxxvii P13 **Calshot** Hampshire, S England, UK
xliv G8 **Caltra** Galway, W Ireland
xliii K15 **Calvine** Perth and Kinross, C Scotland, UK
xxxix T12 **Cam** ≈ E England, UK
xliii F16 **Camasnacroise** Highland, NW Scotland, UK
xxxvii X12 **Camber** East Sussex, SE England, UK
xxxvii R10 **Camberley** Surrey, SE England, UK
xxxvi D8 **Camberwell** Southwark, SE England, UK
xli Q5 **Cambo** Northumberland, N England, UK
xxxvi B17 **Camborne** Cornwall, SW England, UK
xxxv H11 **Cambrian Mountains** ▲▲ C Wales, UK
xxxix S12 **Cambridge** ***Lat.*** Cantabrigia. Cambridgeshire, E England, UK
xxxix Q11 **Cambridgeshire** ⬖ *county* E England, UK
xxxiv K16 **Camden** ⬖ *London borough* SE England, UK
xxxvi C7 **Camden** Camden, SE England, UK
xxxvi D15 **Camel** ≈ SW England, UK
xxxvi D14 **Camelford** Cornwall, SW England, UK
xliii P14 **Cammachmore** Aberdeenshire, NE Scotland, UK
xliv C12 **Camp** Kerry, SW Ireland
xliii F22 **Campbeltown** Argyll and Bute, W Scotland, UK
xliii J19 **Campsie Fells** ▲▲ Stirling, C Scotland, UK
xxxv C13 **Camrose** Pembrokeshire, SW Wales, UK
xliii G15 **Camusnagaul** Highland, NW Scotland, UK
xxxix S6 **Candlesby** Lincolnshire, E England, UK
xliii C14 **Canna** *island* NW Scotland, UK
xlii H12 **Cannich** Highland, NW Scotland, UK
xxxvi J11 **Cannington** Somerset, SW England, UK
xxxvi F7 **Canning Town** Newham, SE England, UK
xxxviii B13 **Cannock** Staffordshire, C England, UK
xxxviii K9 **Cannock Chase** *forest* C England, UK
xliii N24 **Canonbie** Dumfries and Galloway, SW Scotland, UK
xxxvii X10 **Canterbury** ***hist.*** Cantwaraburh, ***anc.*** Durovernum, ***Lat.*** Cantuaria. Kent, SE England, UK
xxxvii W9 **Canvey Island** Essex, SE England, UK
xliii C16 **Caolas** Argyll and Bute, W Scotland, UK
xxxvii T11 **Capel** Surrey, SE England, UK
xxxv H5 **Capel Curig** Conwy, N Wales, UK
xxxix W13 **Capel St Mary** Suffolk, E England, UK
xli Q5 **Capheaton** Northumberland, N England, UK
xliii M22 **Cappercleuch** The Borders, S Scotland, UK
xliv H13 **Cappoquin** Waterford, S Ireland
xliii L17 **Caputh** Perth and Kinross, C Scotland, UK
xxxvi L16 **Carbis Bay** Cornwall, SW England, UK
xlii D13 **Carbost** Highland, NW Scotland, UK
xlii D12 **Carbost** Highland, NW Scotland, UK
xliv J9 **Carbury** Kildare, E Ireland
xxxv J15 **Cardiff** ⬖ *unitary authority* S Wales, UK
xxxv K15 **Cardiff** ***Wel.*** Caerdydd. *national region capital* Cardiff, S Wales, UK
xxxv E11 **Cardigan** ***Wel.*** Aberteifi. Ceredigion, SW Wales, UK
xxxv E10 **Cardigan Bay** *bay* W Wales, UK
xxxviii H10 **Cardington** Shropshire, W England, UK
xxxvii T6 **Cardington** Bedfordshire, C England, UK
xliii I19 **Cardross** Argyll and Bute, W Scotland, UK
xxxv D14 **Carew** Pembrokeshire, SW Wales, UK
xliii L24 **Cargenbridge** Dumfries and Galloway, SW Scotland, UK
xl M11 **Cark** Cumbria, NW England, UK
xliv H3 **Cark Mountain** *hill* N Ireland
xli P13 **Carleton** North Yorkshire, N England, UK
xliv L6 **Carlingford** Louth, NE Ireland
xliv L6 **Carlingford Lough** *inlet* Ireland/Northern Ireland, UK
xl M7 **Carlisle** ***anc.*** Caer Luel, Luguvallium, Luguvallum. Cumbria, NW England, UK
xliii L20 **Carlops** The Borders, S Scotland, UK
xliv J11 **Carlow** ***Ir.*** Ceatharlach. Carlow, SE Ireland
xliv J11 **Carlow** ***Ir.*** Cheatharlach. ⬖ *county* SE Ireland
xlii C8 **Carloway** Western Isles, NW Scotland, UK
xli U14 **Carlton** North Yorkshire, N England, UK
xli Q11 **Carlton** North Yorkshire, N England, UK
xxxix N7 **Carlton** Nottinghamshire, C England, UK
xxxix Z10 **Carlton Colville** Suffolk, E England, UK
xxxix N5 **Carlton in Lindrick** Nottinghamshire, C England, UK
xxxix P6 **Carlton-on-Trent** Nottinghamshire, C England, UK
xliii K21 **Carluke** South Lanarkshire, C Scotland, UK
xxxv F13 **Carmarthen** Carmarthenshire, SW Wales, UK
xxxv E14 **Carmarthen Bay** *bay* S Wales, UK
xxxv E13 **Carmarthenshire** ⬖ *unitary authority* S Wales, UK
xxxv E3 **Carmel Head** *headland* NW Wales, UK
xliv C9 **Carna** Galway, W Ireland
xliii J14 **Carn Bàn** ▲ NW Scotland, UK
xliv I2 **Carndonagh** ***Ir.*** Carn Domhnach. Donegal, NW Ireland
xliii D20 **Carnduncan** Argyll and Bute, W Scotland, UK
xxxv G5 **Carnedd Llywelyn** ▲ NW Wales, UK
xlii H13 **Carn Eige** ▲ N Scotland, UK
xliv K11 **Carnew** Wicklow, E Ireland
xliv F5 **Carney** Sligo, N Ireland
xliv L3 **Carnlough** Larne, E Northern Ireland, UK
xxxv I9 **Carno** Powys, C Wales, UK
xliii N17 **Carnoustie** Angus, E Scotland, UK
xliv K13 **Carnsore Point** ***Ir.*** Ceann an Chairn. headland SE Ireland
xliii L21 **Carnwath** South Lanarkshire, C Scotland, UK
xliii F21 **Carradale** Argyll and Bute, W Scotland, UK
xliv E7 **Carra, Lough** ◎ NW Ireland
xliv D9 **Carraroe** Galway, W Ireland
xliv C13 **Carrauntoohil** ***Ir.*** Carrantual, Carrauntohil, Corrán Tuathail. ▲ SW Ireland
xlii K13 **Carrbridge** Highland, NW Scotland, UK
xliii N17 **Carrick** Fife, E Scotland, UK
xliv F4 **Carrick** Donegal, N Ireland
xliv H2 **Carrickart** ***var.*** Carrigart, ***Ir.*** Carraig *Airt*. Donegal, N Ireland
xliii H19 **Carrick Castle** Argyll and Bute, W Scotland, UK
xliv M4 **Carrickfergus** ⬖ *district* E Northern Ireland, UK
xliv M4 **Carrickfergus** ***Ir.*** Carraig Fhearghais. Carrickfergus, NE Northern Ireland, UK
xliv J6 **Carrickmacross** ***Ir.*** Carraig Mhachaire Rois. Monaghan, N Ireland
xliv J4 **Carrickmore** Omagh, W Northern Ireland, UK
xliv G7 **Carrick-on-Shannon** ***Ir.*** Cora Droma Rúisc. Leitrim/Roscommon, NW Ireland
xliv I12 **Carrick-on-Suir** ***Ir.*** Carraig na Siúire. Tipperary, S Ireland
xliv E14 **Carrigadrohid Reservoir** ⊡ S Ireland
xliv C11 **Carrigaholt** Clare, W Ireland
xliv G10 **Carrigahorig** Tipperary, S Ireland
xliv F14 **Carrigaline** Cork, S Ireland
xliv H7 **Carrigallen** Leitrim, N Ireland
xliv I3 **Carrigans** Donegal, N Ireland
xlii H10 **Carron** ≈ NW Scotland, UK
xliii K23 **Carronbridge** Dumfries and Galloway, SW Scotland, UK
xlii F12 **Carron, Loch** *inlet* NW Scotland, UK
xliv J2 **Carrowkeel** ***var.*** Kerrykeel. Donegal, N Ireland
xliv D5 **Carrowmore Lake** ◎ NW Ireland
xli O7 **Carr Shield** Northumberland, N England, UK
xliii L24 **Carrutherstown** Dumfries and Galloway, SW Scotland, UK
xliv L5 **Carryduff** Castlereagh, E Northern Ireland, UK
xliii J25 **Carsluith** Dumfries and Galloway, SW Scotland, UK
xliii J23 **Carsphairn** Dumfries and Galloway, SW Scotland, UK
xliii K21 **Carstairs** South Lanarkshire, C Scotland, UK
xxxvii O8 **Carterton** Oxfordshire, C England, UK
xl M11 **Cartmel** Cumbria, NW England, UK
xl M11 **Cartmel Fell** Cumbria, NW England, UK
xliv C9 **Cashel** Galway, W Ireland
xliv H12 **Cashel** ***Ir.*** Caiseal. Tipperary, S Ireland
xliv D12 **Cashen** ≈ SW Ireland
xliii I17 **Cashlie** Perth and Kinross, C Scotland, UK
xxxix V9 **Castle Acre** Norfolk, E England, UK
xliv E7 **Castlebar** ***Ir.*** Caisleán an Bharraigh. Mayo, W Ireland
xliii A14 **Castlebay** Western Isles, NW Scotland, UK
xliv K7 **Castlebellingham** Louth, NE Ireland
xliv K6 **Castleblayney** ***Ir.*** Baile na Lorgan. Monaghan, N Ireland
xli Q10 **Castle Bolton** North Yorkshire, N England, UK
xliv K12 **Castlebridge** Wexford, SE Ireland
xxxviii D15 **Castle Bromwich** Birmingham, C England, UK
xxxix Q9 **Castle Bytham** Lincolnshire, E England, UK
xli N7 **Castle Carrock** Cumbria, NW England, UK
xxxvi L12 **Castle Cary** Somerset, SW England, UK
xxxvi M9 **Castle Combe** Wiltshire, S England, UK
xliv I11 **Castlecomer** Kilkenny, SE Ireland
xliv B14 **Castlecove** Kerry, SW Ireland
xliii L21 **Castlecraig** The Borders, S Scotland, UK
xliv K3 **Castledawson** Magherafelt, C Northern Ireland, UK
xliv I4 **Castlederg** Strabane, W Northern Ireland, UK
xliv J10 **Castledermot** Kildare, E Ireland
xliii K25 **Castle Douglas** Dumfries and Galloway, S Scotland, UK
xliv K12 **Castleellis** Wexford, SE Ireland
xliv I3 **Castlefinn** ***Ir.*** Caisleán na Finne. Donegal, NW Ireland
xli S14 **Castleford** Wakefield, N England, UK
xliv C12 **Castlegregory** Kerry, SW Ireland
xliv D12 **Castleisland** ***Ir.*** Oileán Ciarral. Kerry, SW Ireland
xliii H25 **Castle Kennedy** Dumfries and Galloway, SW Scotland, UK
xliv C13 **Castlemaine** Kerry, SW Ireland
xxxv C14 **Castlemartin** Pembrokeshire, SW Wales, UK
xliv G14 **Castlemartyr** Cork, S Ireland
xliv I8 **Castlepollard** Westmeath, C Ireland
xliv F7 **Castlerea** ***Ir.*** An Caisleán Riabhach. Roscommon, W Ireland
xliv L4 **Castlereagh** ***Ir.*** An Caisleán Riabhach. Castlereagh, N Northern Ireland, UK
xliv L4 **Castlereagh** ⬖ *district* E Northern Ireland, UK
xliv J2 **Castlerock** Coleraine, N Northern Ireland, UK
xli Q7 **Castleside** Durham, N England, UK
xlii J12 **Castle Stuart** Highland, NW Scotland, UK
xli U9 **Castleton** North Yorkshire, N England, UK
xl F12 **Castletown** SE Isle of Man
xli W3 **Castletown** Sunderland, NE England, UK
xlii L6 **Castletown** Highland, N Scotland, UK
xliv C14 **Castletown Bere** Cork, S Ireland
xliv F13 **Castletownroche** Cork, S Ireland
xliv D15 **Castletownshend** Cork, S Ireland
xliv L6 **Castlewellan** Down, E Northern Ireland, UK
xxxix V10 **Caston** Norfolk, E England, UK
xxxvii U10 **Caterham** Surrey, SE England, UK
xxxix Y8 **Catfield** Norfolk, E England, UK
xxxvi F9 **Catford** Lewisham, SE England, UK
xl M5 **Catlowdy** Cumbria, NW England, UK
xli N12 **Caton** Lancashire, NW England, UK
xliii J22 **Catrine** East Ayrshire, SW Scotland, UK
xxxviii B16 **Catshill** Worcestershire, W England, UK
xli N13 **Catterall** Lancashire, NW England, UK
xli R10 **Catterick** North Yorkshire, N England, UK
xli R10 **Catterick Camp** North Yorkshire, N England, UK
xliii N23 **Cauldcleuch Head** ▲ S Scotland, UK
xliii L25 **Caulkerbush** Dumfries and Galloway, SW Scotland, UK
xxxix O6 **Caunton** Nottinghamshire, C England, UK
xliv I7 **Cavan** ***Ir.*** Cabhán. Cavan, N Ireland
xliv I6 **Cavan** ***Ir.*** An Cabhán. ⬖ *county* N Ireland
xxxix U13 **Cavendish** Suffolk, E England, UK
xxxix U11 **Cavenham** Suffolk, E England, UK
xli T14 **Cawood** North Yorkshire, N England, UK
xxxix W8 **Cawston** Norfolk, E England, UK
xxxix P7 **Caythorpe** Lincolnshire, E England, UK
xli W11 **Cayton** North Yorkshire, N England, UK
xliv K9 **Celbridge** Kildare, E Ireland
xxxviii K7 **Cellarhead** Staffordshire, C England, UK
xxxv E3 **Cemaes** Isle of Anglesey, NW Wales, UK
xxxv D11 **Cemaes Head** *headland* SW Wales, UK
xxxv H8 **Cemmaes** Powys, C Wales, UK
xxxv F10 **Ceredigion** ⬖ *unitary authority* W Wales, UK
xliii M18 **Ceres** Fife, E Scotland, UK
xxxvi L13 **Cerne Abbas** Dorset, S England, UK
xxxv I6 **Cerrigydrudion** Conwy, N Wales, UK
xl H14 **Chadderton** Oldham, NW England, UK
xxxviii B16 **Chaddesley Corbett** Worcestershire, W England, UK
xxxvii P9 **Chaddleworth** West Berkshire, S England, UK
xxxvi G14 **Chagford** Devon, SW England, UK
xxxvii P14 **Chale** Isle of Wight, S England, UK
xxxvii S8 **Chalfont St Giles** Buckinghamshire, C England, UK
xxxvi G11 **Challacombe** Devon, SW England, UK
xliii I24 **Challoch** Dumfries and Galloway, SW Scotland, UK
xxxvii X10 **Challock** Kent, SE England, UK
xxxvii X15 **Channel Islands** ***Fr.*** Îles Normandes. *island group* S English Channel
xxxvii Z11 **Channel Tunnel** *tunnel* France/UK
xxxviii K5 **Chapel-en-le-Frith** Derbyshire, C England, UK
xxxix T5 **Chapel St Leonards** Lincolnshire, E England, UK
xli S16 **Chapeltown** Sheffield, N England, UK
xxxvi K13 **Chard** Somerset, SW England, UK
xxxvi J13 **Chardstock** Devon, SW England, UK
xxxvii X11 **Charing** Kent, SE England, UK
xxxvii P7 **Charlbury** Oxfordshire, C England, UK
xlii M12 **Charlestown of Aberlour** Moray, N Scotland, UK
xliv F6 **Charlestown** Mayo, NW Ireland
xxxvi F8 **Charlton** Greenwich, SE England, UK
xxxvii N9 **Charlton** Wiltshire, S England, UK
xxxvii N7 **Charlton Kings** Gloucestershire, C England, UK
xxxvii T11 **Charlwood** Surrey, SE England, UK
xxxvi K14 **Charmouth** Dorset, S England, UK
xxxix N12 **Charwelton** Northamptonshire, C England, UK
xxxvii W10 **Chatham** Kent, SE England, UK
xxxix S11 **Chatteris** Cambridgeshire, E England, UK
xxxvi G13 **Chawleigh** Devon, SW England, UK
xxxvii Q11 **Chawton** Hampshire, S England, UK
xxxviii K7 **Cheadle** Staffordshire, C England, UK
xli P17 **Cheadle** Stockport, NW England, UK
xxxvi K11 **Cheddar** Somerset, SW England, UK
xxxviii K7 **Cheddleton** Staffordshire, C England, UK
xl G17 **Chelford** Cheshire, W England, UK
xxxviii M8 **Chellaston** City of Derby, C England, UK
xxxvii W7 **Chelmer** ≈ E England, UK
xxxvii W8 **Chelmsford** Essex, E England, UK
xxxvi C8 **Chelsea** Kensington and Chelsea, SE England, UK
xxxvi M7 **Cheltenham** Gloucestershire, C England, UK
xxxv M14 **Chepstow** Monmouthshire, SE Wales, UK
xxxvii Q12 **Cheriton** Hampshire, S England, UK
xxxvi H13 **Cheriton Fitzpaine** Devon, SW England, UK
xxxvii S10 **Chertsey** Surrey, SE England, UK
xxxvii S8 **Chesham** Buckinghamshire, C England, UK
xl H17 **Cheshire** ⬖ *county* C England, UK
xxxvii U8 **Cheshunt** Hertfordshire, SE England, UK
xxxviii B13 **Cheslyn Hay** Staffordshire, C England, UK
xxxviii G6 **Chester** ***Wel.*** Caerleon; ***hist.*** Legaceaster, ***Lat.*** Deva, Devana Castra. Cheshire, C England, UK
xxxviii M6 **Chesterfield** Derbyshire, C England, UK
xli R7 **Chester-le-Street** Durham, N England, UK
xliii O22 **Chesters** The Borders, S Scotland, UK
xxxviii I8 **Cheswardine** Shropshire, W England, UK
xxxvi L13 **Chetnole** Dorset, S England, UK
xliii O23 **Cheviot Hills** *hill range* England/Scotland, UK
xli P3 **Cheviot, The** ▲ NE England, UK
xxxvi L10 **Chew Magna** Bath and North East Somerset, SW England, UK
xxxvi L11 **Chewton Mendip** Somerset, SW England, UK
xxxvii R13 **Chichester** West Sussex, SE England, UK
xxxvi L14 **Chickerell** Dorset, S England, UK
xxxvii S11 **Chiddingfold** Surrey, SE England, UK
xxxvi K14 **Chideock** Dorset, S England, UK
xxxvii P9 **Chieveley** West Berkshire, S England, UK
xxxvi G5 **Chigwell** Essex, SE England, UK
xxxviii I8 **Child's Ercall** Shropshire, W England, UK
xxxvii Y10 **Chilham** Kent, SE England, UK
xxxvi F14 **Chillaton** Devon, SW England, UK
xxxvii R8 **Chiltern Hills** *hill range* S England, UK
xxxvii R8 **Chinnor** Oxfordshire, C England, UK
xxxix U12 **Chippenham** Cambridgeshire, E England, UK
xxxvi M9 **Chippenham** Wiltshire, S England, UK
xxxvii N6 **Chipping Campden** Gloucestershire, C England, UK
xxxvii O7 **Chipping Norton** Oxfordshire, C England, UK
xxxvii V8 **Chipping Ongar** Essex, SE England, UK
xxxvi M9 **Chipping Sodbury** South Gloucestershire, SW England, UK
xxxviii G10 **Chirbury** Shropshire, W England, UK
xxxv K6 **Chirk** Wrexham, NE Wales, UK
xliii P20 **Chirnside** The Borders, S Scotland, UK
xxxvi B8 **Chiswick** Hounslow, SE England, UK
xxxvii N11 **Chitterne** Wiltshire, S England, UK
xxxvi G12 **Chittlehampton** Devon, SW England, UK
xxxvii S10 **Chobham** Surrey, SE England, UK
xlii J8 **Choire, Loch** ◎ NW Scotland, UK
xxxvii O11 **Cholderton** Wiltshire, S England, UK
xli P6 **Chollerford** Northumberland, N England, UK
xli P6 **Chollerton** Northumberland, N England, UK
xxxvii Q9 **Cholsey** Oxfordshire, C England, UK
xli Q7 **Chopwell** Gateshead, NE England, UK
xli N15 **Chorley** Lancashire, NW England, UK
xxxix T10 **Christchurch** Cambridgeshire, E England, UK
xxxvii O14 **Christchurch** Dorset, S England, UK
xxxvi H14 **Chudleigh** Devon, SW England, UK
xxxvi G13 **Chulmleigh** Devon, SW England, UK
xxxvi M7 **Churchdown** Gloucestershire, C England, UK
xxxviii J9 **Church Eaton** Staffordshire, C England, UK
xli T14 **Church Fenton** North Yorkshire, N England, UK
xxxviii H6 **Church Minshull** Cheshire, W England, UK
xxxv K9 **Church Stoke** Powys, C Wales, UK
xxxviii H10 **Church Stretton** Shropshire, W England, UK
xliv K13 **Churchtown** Wexford, SE Ireland
xliv J13 **Churchtown** Wexford, SE Ireland
xxxv F6 **Chwilog** Gwynedd, NW Wales, UK
xxxv J5 **Cilcain** Flintshire, N Wales, UK
xxxv G11 **Cilcennin** Ceredigion, W Wales, UK
xxxv E12 **Cilgerran** Pembrokeshire, SW Wales, UK
xxxv H12 **Cilycwm** Carmarthenshire, S Wales, UK
xxxvi L7 **Cinderford** Gloucestershire, C England, UK
xxxvii N8 **Cirencester** ***anc.*** Corinium, Corinium Dobunorum. Gloucestershire, C England, UK
xliii H19 **Clachaig** Argyll and Bute, W Scotland, UK
xliii F21 **Clachan** Argyll and Bute, W Scotland, UK
xlii A11 **Clachan-a-Luib** Western Isles, NW Scotland, UK
xliii G19 **Clachan of Glendaruel** Argyll and Bute, W Scotland, UK
xliii F18 **Clachan-Seil** Argyll and Bute, W Scotland, UK
xlii G8 **Clachtoll** Highland, NW Scotland, UK
xliii K19 **Clackmannan** Clackmannan, C Scotland, UK
xliii K18 **Clackmannan** ⬖ *unitary authority* C Scotland, UK
xxxvii Y7 **Clacton-on-Sea** ***var.*** Clacton. Essex, E England, UK
xliii H18 **Cladich** Argyll and Bute, W Scotland, UK
xxxv H10 **Claerwen Reservoir** ⊡ E Wales, UK
xliii F16 **Claggan** Highland, NW Scotland, UK
xliv K9 **Clane** Kildare, E Ireland
xxxvii O8 **Clanfield** Oxfordshire, C England, UK
xliii G20 **Claonaig** Argyll and Bute, W Scotland, UK
xxxvi D9 **Clapham** Lambeth, SE England, UK
xli O12 **Clapham** North Yorkshire, N England, UK
xxxv D13 **Clarbeston** Pembrokeshire, SW Wales, UK
xxxix V13 **Clare** Suffolk, E England, UK
xliv E10 **Clare** ***Ir.*** An Clár. ⬖ *county* W Ireland
xliv F8 **Clare** ≈ W Ireland
xliv E10 **Clarecastle** Clare, W Ireland
xliv H10 **Clareen** Offaly, C Ireland
xliv E9 **Claregalway** Galway, W Ireland
xliv C7 **Clare Island** ***Ir.*** Cliara. *island* W Ireland
xliv E7 **Claremorris** ***Ir.*** Clár Chlainne Mhuiris. Mayo, W Ireland
xliv F9 **Clarinbridge** Galway, W Ireland
xlii J10 **Clashmore** Highland, NW Scotland, UK
xlii G8 **Clashnessie** Highland, NW Scotland, UK
xliii J24 **Clatteringshaws Loch** ◎ SW Scotland, UK
xliv J3 **Claudy** Londonderry, NW Northern Ireland, UK
xli N12 **Claughton** Lancashire, NW England, UK
xxxviii D17 **Claverdon** Warwickshire, C England, UK
xxxvi E13 **Clawton** Devon, SW England, UK
xxxviii M6 **Clay Cross** Derbyshire, C England, UK
xxxix W13 **Claydon** Suffolk, E England, UK
xl G11 *headland* C Isle of Man
xxxix P7 **Claypole** Lincolnshire, E England, UK
xli O14 **Clayton-le-Moors** Lancashire, NW England, UK
xliii E15 **Cleadale** Highland, NW Scotland, UK
xliv C15 **Clear, Cape** ***var.*** The Bill of Cape Clear, ***Ir.*** Ceann Cléire. *headland* SW Ireland
xliv D15 **Clear Island** *island* S Ireland
xliii A14 **Cleat** Western Isles, NW Scotland, UK
xl K9 **Cleator Moor** Cumbria, NW England, UK
xli R14 **Cleckheaton** Kirklees, N England, UK
xxxviii H11 **Clee St Margaret** Shropshire, W England, UK
xxxix R3 **Cleethorpes** North East Lincolnshire, E England, UK
xxxviii I11 **Cleobury Mortimer** Shropshire, W England, UK
xxxvi K10 **Clevedon** North West Somerset, SW England, UK
xli T10 **Cleveland Hills** *hill range* N England, UK
xl M13 **Cleveleys** Lancashire, NW England, UK
xliv C7 **Clew Bay** ***Ir.*** Cuan Mó. *inlet* W Ireland
xli N9 **Cliburn** Cumbria, NW England, UK
xxxvii Q11 **Cliddesden** Hampshire, S England, UK
xliv C8 **Clifden** ***Ir.*** An Clochán. Galway, W Ireland
xxxvii W9 **Cliffe** Kent, SE England, UK
xxxviii G13 **Clifford** Herefordshire, W England, UK
xxxviii I12 **Clifton upon Teme** Worcestershire, W England, UK
xxxix O11 **Clipston** Northamptonshire, C England, UK
xlii C9 **Clisham** ▲ NW Scotland, UK
xli O13 **Clitheroe** Lancashire, NW England, UK
xxxviii H9 **Clive** Shropshire, W England, UK
xlii J1 **Clivocast** Shetland Islands, NE Scotland, UK
xliv H3 **Cloghan** Donegal, N Ireland
xliv H9 **Cloghan** Offaly, C Ireland
xliv G12 **Clogheen** Tipperary, S Ireland
xliv I5 **Clogher** Dungannon, C Northern Ireland, UK
xliv L7 **Clogher Head** *headland* E Ireland
xliv L7 **Clogherhead** Louth, NE Ireland
xliv M5 **Cloghy Ards**, E Northern Ireland, UK
xliv L3 **Clog Mills** Ballymena, NE Northern Ireland, UK
xlii P12 **Clola** Aberdeenshire, NE Scotland, UK
xliv E15 **Clonakilty** ***Ir.*** Cloich na Coillte. Cork, SW Ireland
xliv E15 **Clonakilty Bay** *bay* S Ireland
xliv I9 **Clonaslee** Laois, C Ireland
xliv F8 **Clonbern** Galway, W Ireland
xliv D8 **Clonbur** Galway, W Ireland
xliv K9 **Clondalkin** ***Ir.*** Cluain Dolcáin. Dublin, E Ireland
xliv I13 **Clonea Bay** *bay* S Ireland
xliv I5 **Clones** ***Ir.*** Cluain Eois. Monaghan, N Ireland
xliv G9 **Clonfert** Galway, W Ireland
xliv H9 **Clonmacnoise** Offaly, C Ireland
xliv H12 **Clonmel** ***Ir.*** Cluain Meala. Tipperary, S Ireland
xliv K12 **Clonroche** Wexford, SE Ireland
xliv J6 **Clontibret** Monaghan, NE Ireland
xliv E8 **Cloonboo** Galway, W Ireland
xliv F11 **Cloonlara** Clare, W Ireland
xliv G10 **Cloonoon** Galway, W Ireland
xliv F9 **Cloonymorris** Galway, W Ireland
xxxvii S6 **Clophill** Bedfordshire, C England, UK
xli W10 **Cloughton** North Yorkshire, N England, UK
xliii M15 **Clova** Angus, E Scotland, UK
xxxvi E12 **Clovelly** Devon, SW England, UK
xliii N21 **Clovenfords** The Borders, S Scotland, UK
xxxix N5 **Clowne** Derbyshire, C England, UK
xxxviii J11 **Clows Top** Worcestershire, W England, UK
xlii G13 **Cluanie, Loch** ◎ NW Scotland, UK
xxxviii G11 **Clun** Shropshire, W England, UK
xliii H14 **Clunes** Highland, NW Scotland, UK
xxxviii G11 **Clungunford** Shropshire, W England, UK
xxxvi L10 **Clutton** Bath and North East Somerset, SW England, UK
xxxv J4 **Clwyd** ≈ N Wales, UK
xxxv J4 **Clwydian Range** ▲▲ N Wales, UK
xxxv H14 **Clydach** Swansea, S Wales, UK
xxxv I14 **Clydach Vale** Rhondda Cynon Taff, S Wales, UK
xliii K22 **Clyde** ≈ W Scotland, UK
xliii I20 **Clydebank** West Dunbartonshire, W Scotland, UK
xliii H20 **Clyde, Firth of** *inlet* S Scotland, UK
xxxv F6 **Clynnog-fawr** Gwynedd, NW Wales, UK
xxxv K11 **Clyro** Powys, C Wales, UK
xxxvi I13 **Clyst** ≈ SW England, UK
xxxvi I14 **Clyst St Mary** Devon, SW England, UK

◆ Country ● Country Capital ◇ Dependent Territory ○ Dependent Territory Capital ⬖ Administrative Region ✕ International Airport ▲ Mountain ▲▲ Mountain Range ◎ Lake ⊡ Reservoir ≈ River

xxxv I9 **Clywedog, Llyn** var. Clywedog Reservoir. ⊟ E Wales, UK
xliv E14 **Coachford** Cork, S Ireland
xliii K21 **Coalburn** South Lanarkshire, C Scotland, UK
xliv K4 **Coalisland** Dungannon, C Northern Ireland, UK
xxxviii M9 **Coalville** Leicestershire, C England, UK
xliii K20 **Coatbridge** North Lanarkshire, S Scotland, UK
xliv G14 **Cobh** Ir. An Cóbh; prev. Cove of Cork, Queenstown. Cork, SW Ireland
xliii O20 **Cockburnspath** The Borders, S Scotland, UK
xliii N19 **Cockenzie and Port Seton** East Lothian, SE Scotland, UK
xli N13 **Cockerham** Lancashire, NW England, UK
xl K8 **Cockermouth** Cumbria, NW England, UK
xxxix V12 **Cockfield** Suffolk, E England, UK
xxxvii R12 **Cocking** West Sussex, SE England, UK
xxxix U9 **Cockley Cley** Norfolk, E England, UK
xxxviii H8 **Cockshutt** Shropshire, W England, UK
xxxvi N11 **Codford St Peter** Wiltshire, S England, UK
xxxviii J10 **Codsall** Staffordshire, C England, UK
xxxv K5 **Coedpoeth** Wrexham, NE Wales, UK
xxxvii W7 **Coggeshall** Essex, SE England, UK
xlii F9 **Coigeach, Rubha** headland NW Scotland, UK
xlii I9 **Colabol1** Highland, NW Scotland, UK
xl F12 **Colby** S Isle of Man
xxxvii X7 **Colchester** hist. Colneceaste, anc. Camulodunum. Essex, E England, UK
xlii J7 **Coldbackie** Highland, N Scotland, UK
xliii P20 **Coldingham** The Borders, S Scotland, UK
xli T11 **Cold Kirby** North Yorkshire, N England, UK
xxxvii W8 **Cold Norton** Essex, SE England, UK
xliii P21 **Coldstream** The Borders, SE Scotland, UK
xxxvi L8 **Coleford** Gloucestershire, C England, UK
xliv K2 **Coleraine** Ir. Cúil Raithin. Coleraine, N Northern Ireland, UK
xliv J2 **Coleraine** ◐ district N Northern Ireland, UK
xxxvi N7 **Colesbourne** Gloucestershire, C England, UK
xxxviii D15 **Coleshill** Warwickshire, C England, UK
xliii G20 **Colintraive** Argyll and Bute, W Scotland, UK
xliii C16 **Coll** island W Scotland, UK
xlii P12 **Collieston** Aberdeenshire, NE Scotland, UK
xxxvi E15 **Colliford Reservoir** ⊟ SW England, UK
xliii L24 **Collin** Dumfries and Galloway, SW Scotland, UK
xli S13 **Collingham** Leeds, N England, UK
xxxix P6 **Collingham** Nottinghamshire, C England, UK
xliv K7 **Collon** Louth, NE Ireland
xliv F6 **Collooney** Ir. Cúil Mhuine. Sligo, NW Ireland
xliii H24 **Colmonell** South Ayrshire, W Scotland, UK
xlii M13 **Colnabaichin** Aberdeenshire, NE Scotland, UK
xli P13 **Colne** Lancashire, NW England, UK
xxxvii X7 **Colne** ⩫ SE England, UK
xliii D19 **Colonsay** island W Scotland, UK
xlii N12 **Colpy** Aberdeenshire, NE Scotland, UK
xxxix P8 **Colsterworth** Lincolnshire, E England, UK
xxxix O8 **Colston Bassett** Nottinghamshire, C England, UK
xxxix X8 **Coltishall** Norfolk, E England, UK
xliii K25 **Colvend** Dumfries and Galloway, SW Scotland, UK
xli P5 **Colwell** Northumberland, N England, UK
xxxv H4 **Colwyn Bay** Conwy, N Wales, UK
xxxvi J14 **Colyford** Devon, SW England, UK
xxxvi J14 **Colyton** Devon, SW England, UK
xxxvi G11 **Combe Martin** Devon, SW England, UK
xliv M5 **Comber** Ir. An Comar. Ards, E Northern Ireland, UK
xxxix S12 **Comberton** Cambridgeshire, E England, UK
xxxvi J13 **Combe St Nicholas** Somerset, SW England, UK
xliv H12 **Comeragh Mountains** ▲▲ S Ireland
xxxvii R12 **Compton** West Sussex, SE England, UK
xliii K17 **Comrie** Perth and Kinross, C Scotland, UK
xliv E8 **Cong** Mayo, NW Ireland
xxxviii I6 **Congleton** Cheshire, W England, UK
xxxvi K10 **Congresbury** North West Somerset, SW England, UK
xxxix R6 **Coningsby** Lincolnshire, E England, UK
xli T16 **Conisbrough** Doncaster, N England, UK
xl M10 **Coniston** Cumbria, NW England, UK
xli Q12 **Conistone** North Yorkshire, N England, UK
xl L10 **Coniston Water** ◎ NW England, UK
xliv G13 **Conna** Cork, S Ireland
xxxv K5 **Connah's Quay** Flintshire, N Wales, UK
xliv D7 **Connaught** var. Connacht, Ir. Chonnacht, Cúige. province W Ireland
xliii G17 **Connel** Argyll and Bute, W Scotland, UK
xliv C8 **Connemara** Ir. Conamara. physical region W Ireland
xliv E6 **Conn, Lough** Ir. Loch Con. ◎ W Ireland
xlii I11 **Conon Bridge** Highland, NW Scotland, UK
xli U4 **Consett** Durham, N England, UK
xlii I11 **Contin** Highland, NW Scotland, UK
xxxv H4 **Conwy** Conwy, N Wales, UK
xxxv H5 **Conwy** ◐ unitary authority N Wales, UK
xxxv H5 **Conwy** ⩫ N Wales, UK
xxxvii R9 **Cookham** Windsor and Maidenhead, S England, UK
xliv K4 **Cookstown** Ir. An Chorr Chríochach. Cookstown, C Northern Ireland, UK
xliv J4 **Cookstown** ◐ district C Northern Ireland, UK
xliv G10 **Coolbaun** Tipperary, S Ireland
xxxvii T12 **Coolham** West Sussex, SE England, UK
xlv C13 **Coomacarrea** ▲ SW Ireland
xxxvi N12 **Coombe Bissett** Wiltshire, S England, UK
xliv J6 **Cootehill** Ir. Muinchille. Cavan, N Ireland
xliv M4 **Copeland Island** island E Northern Ireland, UK
xlii N5 **Copinsay** island N Scotland, UK
xxxvi G13 **Copplestone** Devon, SW England, UK
xl D13 **Coppull** Lancashire, N England, UK
xli R4 **Coquet** ⩫ N England, UK
xxxvii W17 **Corbiere Point** headland Jersey, Channel Islands
xli Q6 **Corbridge** Northumberland, N England, UK
xxxix P10 **Corby** Northamptonshire, C England, UK
xxxix Q8 **Corby Glen** Lincolnshire, E England, UK
xxxvi J12 **Corfe** Somerset, SW England, UK
xxxvii N14 **Corfe Castle** Dorset, S England, UK
xlii M13 **Corgarff** Aberdeenshire, NE Scotland, UK
xliv F14 **Cork** Ir. Corcaigh. Cork, S Ireland
xliv F13 **Cork** Ir. Corcaigh. ◐ county SW Ireland
xliv F14 **Cork** ✕ Cork, SW Ireland
xliv G14 **Cork Harbour** Ir. Cuan Chorcaí. inlet SW Ireland
xli W5 **Cornforth** Durham, N England, UK
xlii N11 **Cornhill** Aberdeenshire, NE Scotland, UK
xlii N5 **Cornquoy** Orkney Islands, N Scotland, UK
xxxvi C16 **Cornwall** ◐ county SW England, UK
xxxvi C16 **Cornwall, Cape** headland SW England, UK
xliii G15 **Corpach** Highland, NW Scotland, UK
xliii F14 **Corran** Highland, NW Scotland, UK
xliii G16 **Corran** Highland, NW Scotland, UK
xliv D8 **Corrib, Lough** Ir. Loch Coirib. ◎ W Ireland
xliii G21 **Corrie** North Ayrshire, W Scotland, UK
xliii M24 **Corrie Common** Dumfries and Galloway, SW Scotland, UK
xxxix P4 **Corringham** Lincolnshire, E England, UK
xxxv H8 **Corris** Gwynedd, NW Wales, UK
xliv E10 **Corrofin** Clare, W Ireland
xlii E13 **Corry** Highland, NW Scotland, UK
xliii J24 **Corserine** ▲ SW Scotland, UK
xxxvi M10 **Corsham** Wiltshire, S England, UK
xliii K24 **Corsock** Dumfries and Galloway, SW Scotland, UK
xliii M16 **Cortachy** Angus, E Scotland, UK
xxxix Z10 **Corton** Suffolk, E England, UK
xxxv J6 **Corwen** Denbighshire, N Wales, UK
xxxvii W9 **Coryton** Essex, SE England, UK
xliv D9 **Costelloe** Galway, W Ireland
xxxix X9 **Costessey** Norfolk, E England, UK
xxxix O8 **Cotgrave** Nottinghamshire, C England, UK
xxxvii N7 **Cotswold Hills** var. Cotswolds. hill range S England, UK
xxxix S12 **Cottenham** Cambridgeshire, E England, UK
xli W14 **Cottingham** East Riding of Yorkshire, N England, UK
xliii H19 **Coulport** Argyll and Bute, W Scotland, UK
xliii L21 **Coulter** South Lanarkshire, C Scotland, UK
xliv H13 **Coumfea** ▲ S Ireland
xli R8 **Coundon** Durham, N England, UK
xxxix N10 **Countesthorpe** Leicestershire, C England, UK
xliii M17 **Coupar Angus** Perth and Kinross, C Scotland, UK
xliv F15 **Courtmacsherry** Cork, S Ireland
xliv L11 **Courtown** var. Courtown Harbour. Wexford, SE Ireland
xliii H19 **Cove** Argyll and Bute, W Scotland, UK
xlii F10 **Cove** Highland, NW Scotland, UK
xlii P14 **Cove Bay** City of Aberdeen, NE Scotland, UK
xxxviii F15 **Coventry** anc. Couentrey. Coventry, C England, UK
xxxviii E15 **Coventry** ◐ unitary authority C England, UK
xxxviii E14 **Coventry Canal** canal C England, UK
xxxvi C17 **Coverack** Cornwall, SW England, UK
xxxix R9 **Cowbit** Lincolnshire, E England, UK
xxxv I15 **Cowbridge** The Vale of Glamorgan, S Wales, UK
xliii L19 **Cowdenbeath** Fife, E Scotland, UK
xxxvii P13 **Cowes** Isle of Wight, S England, UK
xxxvii T12 **Cowfold** West Sussex, SE England, UK
xli O8 **Cow Green Reservoir** ⊟ NW England, UK
xxxvii Q8 **Cowley** Oxfordshire, S England, UK
xli P8 **Cowshill** Durham, N England, UK
xli S8 **Coxhoe** Durham, N England, UK
xlii K13 **Coylumbridge** Highland, NW Scotland, UK
xli O9 **Crackenthorpe** Cumbria, NW England, UK
xxxvi C14 **Crackington Haven** Cornwall, SW England, UK
xxxv I13 **Crai** Powys, C Wales, UK
xlii G12 **Craig** Highland, NW Scotland, UK
xliv K5 **Craigavon** Craigavon, C Northern Ireland, UK
xliv K5 **Craigavon** ◐ district C Northern Ireland, UK
xlii M12 **Craigellachie** Moray, N Scotland, UK
xliii E20 **Craighouse** Argyll and Bute, W Scotland, UK
xliii F17 **Craignure** Argyll and Bute, W Scotland, UK
xxxv H13 **Craig-y-nos** Powys, C Wales, UK
xliii N18 **Crail** Fife, E Scotland, UK
xliii O22 **Crailing** The Borders, S Scotland, UK
xli R5 **Cramlington** Northumberland, N England, UK
xxxvii N13 **Cranbourne** Dorset, S England, UK
xxxvii N12 **Cranbourne Chase** hill range S England, UK
xxxvii W11 **Cranbrook** Kent, SE England, UK
xxxix P11 **Cranford St John** Northamptonshire, C England, UK
xxxvii S11 **Cranleigh** Surrey, SE England, UK
xliii O20 **Cranshaws** The Borders, S Scotland, UK
xliii G19 **Crarae** Argyll and Bute, W Scotland, UK
xlii O14 **Crathes** Aberdeenshire, NE Scotland, UK
xlii M14 **Crathie** Aberdeenshire, NE Scotland, UK
xli S10 **Crathorne** North Yorkshire, N England, UK
xliv F9 **Craughwell** Galway, W Ireland
xxxviii H11 **Craven Arms** Shropshire, W England, UK
xliii L22 **Crawford** South Lanarkshire, C Scotland, UK
xliii K22 **Crawfordjohn** South Lanarkshire, C Scotland, UK
xxxvii P11 **Crawley** Hampshire, S England, UK
xxxvii T11 **Crawley** West Sussex, SE England, UK
xlii E12 **Crawlin Islands** island group NW Scotland, UK
xlii A12 **Creagorry** Western Isles, NW Scotland, UK
xxxviii H13 **Credenhill** Herefordshire, W England, UK
xxxvi H13 **Crediton** Devon, SW England, UK
xliii I24 **Cree** ⩫ SW Scotland, UK
xliv D11 **Creegh** Clare, W Ireland
xliv H2 **Creeslough** Donegal, N Ireland
xliii I25 **Creetown** Dumfries and Galloway, SW Scotland, UK
xliv J4 **Creggan** Omagh, W Northern Ireland, UK
xliv C7 **Cregganbaun** Mayo, NW Ireland
xxxviii H10 **Cressage** Shropshire, W England, UK
xliii F20 **Cretshengan** Argyll and Bute, W Scotland, UK
xxxviii I7 **Crewe** Cheshire, C England, UK
xxxvi K13 **Crewkerne** Somerset, SW England, UK
xliii I17 **Crianlarich** Stirling, C Scotland, UK
xxxv G11 **Cribyn** Ceredigion, W Wales, UK
xxxv F6 **Criccieth** Gwynedd, NW Wales, UK
xxxviii M7 **Crich** Derbyshire, C England, UK
xxxix N11 **Crick** Northamptonshire, C England, UK
xxxv K13 **Crickhowell** Powys, C Wales, UK
xxxvi N8 **Cricklade** Wiltshire, S England, UK
xxxvi B6 **Cricklewood** Brent, SE England, UK
xliii K17 **Crieff** Perth and Kinross, C Scotland, UK
xlii P11 **Crimond** Aberdeenshire, NE Scotland, UK
xliii F19 **Crinan** Argyll and Bute, W Scotland, UK
xxxix X9 **Cringleford** Norfolk, E England, UK
xliv D7 **Croagh Patrick** Ir. Cruach Phádraig. ▲ W Ireland
xxxvi U11 **Crockham Hill** Kent, SE England, UK
xli R9 **Croft-on-Tees** Darlington, N England, UK
xliii F17 **Croggan** Argyll and Bute, W Scotland, UK
xlii J11 **Cromarty** Highland, N Scotland, UK
xlii J11 **Cromarty Firth** inlet N Scotland, UK
xlii L13 **Cromdale** Highland, NW Scotland, UK
xxxix X7 **Cromer** Norfolk, E England, UK
xlii D9 **Cromore** Western Isles, NW Scotland, UK
xxxvii R11 **Crondall** Hampshire, S England, UK
xli R8 **Crook** Durham, N England, UK
xli P2 **Crookham** Northumberland, N England, UK
xliv C15 **Crookhaven** Cork, S Ireland
xliv E14 **Crookstown** Cork, S Ireland
xliv F12 **Croom** Limerick, SW Ireland
xxxvii P6 **Cropredy** Oxfordshire, C England, UK
xl C13 **Crosby** C Isle of Man
xl B15 **Crosby** var. Great Crosby. Sefton, NW England, UK
xli N9 **Crosby Ravensworth** Cumbria, NW England, UK
xliv E8 **Cross** Mayo, NW Ireland
xliii F21 **Crossaig** Argyll and Bute, W Scotland, UK
xli O8 **Cross Fell** ▲ N England, UK
xliii K21 **Crossford** South Lanarkshire, C Scotland, UK
xliv M5 **Crossgar Down**, E Northern Ireland, UK
xxxv G13 **Cross Hands** Carmarthenshire, S Wales, UK
xliv G14 **Crosshaven** Cork, S Ireland
xliii I23 **Crosshill** South Ayrshire, W Scotland, UK
xliv K6 **Crossmaglen** Newry and Mourne, S Northern Ireland, UK
xliii K24 **Crossmichael** Dumfries and Galloway, SW Scotland, UK
xliv E6 **Crossmolina** Mayo, NW Ireland
xl M11 **Crosthwaite** Cumbria, NW England, UK
xli N15 **Croston** Lancashire, NW England, UK
xxxvi X8 **Crouch** ⩫ E England, UK
xxxvi D6 **Crouch End** Haringey, SE England, UK
xxxix N14 **Croughton** Northamptonshire, C England, UK
xxxvii V12 **Crowborough** East Sussex, SE England, UK
xxxix R9 **Crowland** Lincolnshire, E England, UK
xxxix O3 **Crowle** North Lincolnshire, N England, UK
xxxviii K13 **Crowle** Worcestershire, W England, UK
xxxvii R10 **Crowthorne** Bracknell Forest, S England, UK
xxxix Q3 **Croxton** North Lincolnshire, N England, UK
xli K12 **Croy** Highland, NW Scotland, UK
xxxvi F11 **Croyde** Devon, SW England, UK
xxxvi U10 **Croydon** Croydon, SE England, UK
xxxvi L17 **Croydon** ◐ London borough SE England, UK
xlii P12 **Cruden Bay** Aberdeenshire, NE Scotland, UK
xxxviii I9 **Crudgington** Shropshire, W England, UK
xxxvii N8 **Crudwell** Wiltshire, S England, UK
xli C8 **Crulivig** Western Isles, NW Scotland, UK
xliv L4 **Crumlin** Antrim, NE Northern Ireland, UK
xl L9 **Crummock Water** ◎ NW England, UK
xliv E10 **Crusheen** Clare, W Ireland
xxxv E12 **Crymych** Pembrokeshire, SW Wales, UK
xxxv H14 **Crynant** Neath Port Talbot, S Wales, UK
xxxviii F16 **Cubbington** Warwickshire, C England, UK
xxxvi U12 **Cuckfield** West Sussex, SE England, UK
xli S15 **Cudworth** Barnsley, N England, UK
xxxvi U8 **Cuffley** Hertfordshire, E England, UK
xliv J2 **Culdaff** Donegal, N Ireland
xli N8 **Culgaith** Cumbria, NW England, UK
xlii N11 **Cullen** Moray, N Scotland, UK
xliv E6 **Cullin, Lough** ◎ NW Ireland
xlii I1 **Cullivoe** Shetland Islands, NE Scotland, UK
xxxvi I13 **Cullompton** Devon, SW England, UK
xliv K3 **Cullybackey** Ballymena, NE Northern Ireland, UK
xliv I3 **Culmore** Donegal, N Ireland
xxxvi I13 **Culmstock** Devon, SW England, UK
xliii L19 **Culross** Fife, E Scotland, UK
xlii H4 **Culswick** Shetland Islands, NE Scotland, UK
xliii L22 **Culter Fell** ▲ C Scotland, UK
xlii P14 **Cults** City of Aberdeen, NE Scotland, UK
xxxix N13 **Culworth** Northamptonshire, C England, UK
xliii K20 **Cumbernauld** North Lanarkshire, S Scotland, UK
xl L8 **Cumbria** ◐ county NW England, UK
xl L9 **Cumbrian Mountains** ▲▲ NW England, UK
xlii O11 **Cuminestown** Aberdeenshire, NE Scotland, UK
xl M7 **Cummersdale** Cumbria, NW England, UK
xliii L24 **Cummertrees** Dumfries and Galloway, SW Scotland, UK
xliii J22 **Cumnock** East Ayrshire, W Scotland, UK
xxxvii P8 **Cumnor** Oxfordshire, S England, UK
xli N7 **Cumrew** Cumbria, NW England, UK
xliii M18 **Cupar** Fife, E Scotland, UK
xliv J9 **Curragh, The** physical region E Ireland
xliv B14 **Currane, Lough** ◎ SW Ireland
xliii M20 **Currie** City of Edinburgh, SE Scotland, UK
xliv C6 **Cushcamcarragh** ▲ NW Ireland
xliv L3 **Cushendall** Moyle, N Northern Ireland, UK
xliv L2 **Cushendun** Moyle, N Northern Ireland, UK
xliv F10 **Cutra, Lough** ◎ W Ireland
xxxv K13 **Cwmbran** Wel. Cwmbrân. Torfaen, SW Wales, UK
xxxv F13 **Cwmffrwd** Carmarthenshire, S Wales, UK
xxxv I5 **Cyffylliog** Denbighshire, N Wales, UK
xxxv I6 **Cynwyd** Denbighshire, N Wales, UK
xxxv F12 **Cynwyl Elfed** Carmarthenshire, S Wales, UK

D

xl M8 **Dacre** Cumbria, NW England, UK
xxxvi V9 **Dagenham** Barking and Dagenham, SE England, UK
xxxvii S7 **Dagnall** Buckinghamshire, S England, UK
xliii H23 **Dailly** South Ayrshire, W Scotland, UK
xliii I16 **Daimh, Loch an** ◎ C Scotland, UK
xliv I9 **Daingean** Offaly, C Ireland
xliii N18 **Dairsie** Fife, E Scotland, UK
xliii G18 **Dalavich** Argyll and Bute, W Scotland, UK
xliii K25 **Dalbeattie** Dumfries and Galloway, SW Scotland, UK
xl F12 **Dalby** W Isle of Man
xlii H13 **Dalchreichart** Highland, NW Scotland, UK
xxxv C14 **Dale** Pembrokeshire, SW Wales, UK
xlii H3 **Dale of Walls** Shetland Islands, NE Scotland, UK
xliii L16 **Dalguise** Perth and Kinross, C Scotland, UK
xlii K7 **Dalhalvaig** Highland, N Scotland, UK
xlii A13 **Daliburgh** Western Isles, NW Scotland, UK
xliii M20 **Dalkeith** Midlothian, SE Scotland, UK
xliv L9 **Dalkey** Dublin, E Ireland
xlii L11 **Dallas** Moray, N Scotland, UK
xliii H17 **Dalmally** Argyll and Bute, W Scotland, UK
xliii I23 **Dalmellington** East Ayrshire, W Scotland, UK
xliii I21 **Dalry** North Ayrshire, W Scotland, UK
xliii I22 **Dalrymple** South Ayrshire, W Scotland, UK
xl M7 **Dalston** Cumbria, NW England, UK
xliii L24 **Dalton** Dumfries and Galloway, SW Scotland, UK
xl L12 **Dalton-in-Furness** Cumbria, NW England, UK
xliii J15 **Dalwhinnie** Highland, NW Scotland, UK
xxxvi J13 **Dalwood** Devon, SW England, UK
xxxvii N12 **Damerham** Hampshire, S England, UK
xli F12 **Damph, Loch** ◎ NW Scotland, UK
xxxvii W8 **Danbury** Essex, SE England, UK
xli S16 **Darfield** Barnsley, N England, UK
xli W7 **Darlington** Darlington, N England, UK
xli R9 **Darlington** ◐ unitary authority N England, UK
xxxvi H15 **Dart** ⩫ SW England, UK
xxxvi V9 **Dartford** Kent, SE England, UK
xxxvi H15 **Dartington** Devon, SW England, UK
xxxvi G15 **Dartmoor** moorland SW England, UK
xxxvi H16 **Dartmouth** Devon, SW England, UK
xli S15 **Darton** Barnsley, N England, UK
xliv G5 **Dartry Mountains** ▲▲ N Ireland
xliii J21 **Darvel** East Ayrshire, W Scotland, UK
xli O15 **Darwen** Lancashire, NW England, UK
xlii L12 **Dava** Moray, N Scotland, UK
xliii F22 **Davaar** island W Scotland, UK
xxxviii I6 **Davenham** Cheshire, W England, UK
xxxix N12 **Daventry** Northamptonshire, C England, UK
xliii M23 **Davington** Dumfries and Galloway, SW Scotland, UK
xlii J12 **Daviot** Highland, NW Scotland, UK
xxxviii I10 **Dawley** Shropshire, W England, UK
xxxvi J15 **Dawlish** Devon, SW England, UK
xliv F3 **Dawros Head** headland N Ireland
xxxvi Z10 **Deal** Kent, SE England, UK
xxxvi L8 **Dean, Forest of** forest C England, UK
xl K8 **Dearham** Cumbria, NW England, UK
xxxix X13 **Deben** ⩫ E England, UK
xxxix X12 **Debenham** Suffolk, E England, UK
xxxvii P6 **Deddington** Oxfordshire, C England, UK
xxxv K4 **Dee** Wel. Afon Dyfrdwy. ⩫ England/Wales, UK
xliii J25 **Dee** ⩫ S Scotland, UK
xlii N14 **Dee** ⩫ NE Scotland, UK
xliv E11 **Deel** ⩫ W Ireland
xxxix Q9 **Deeping St Nicholas** Lincolnshire, E England, UK
xliv I8 **Deeravaragh, Lough** ◎ C Ireland
xxxviii J13 **Defford** Worcestershire, W England, UK
xxxv G5 **Deiniolen** Gwynedd, NW Wales, UK
xxxvi D14 **Delabole** Cornwall, SW England, UK
xliv D8 **Delphi** Mayo, NW Ireland
xliv J8 **Delvin** Westmeath, C Ireland
xxxv I5 **Denbigh** Wel. Dinbych. Denbighshire, NE Wales, UK
xxxv I5 **Denbighshire** ◐ unitary authority N Wales, UK
xli R15 **Denby Dale** Kirklees, N England, UK
xliii N16 **Denhead** Aberdeenshire, NE Scotland, UK
xlii P11 **Denhead** Angus, E Scotland, UK
xlii N22 **Denholm** The Borders, S Scotland, UK
xliii K19 **Denny** Falkirk, C Scotland, UK
xli Q15 **Denshaw** Oldham, NW England, UK
xli O11 **Dent** Cumbria, NW England, UK
xli O11 **Dent** ⩫ NW England, UK
xxxix P8 **Denton** Lincolnshire, E England, UK
xli H15 **Denton** Tameside, NW England, UK
xxxix U12 **Depden** Suffolk, E England, UK
xxxvi E8 **Deptford** Lewisham, SE England, UK
xxxviii M8 **Derby** City of Derby, C England, UK
xxxviii M8 **Derby, City of** ◐ unitary authority C England, UK
xxxviii L6 **Derbyshire** ◐ county C England, UK
xliv I4 **Derg** ⩫ Ireland/Northern Ireland, UK
xliv F10 **Derg, Lough** Ir. Loch Deirgeirt. ◎ W Ireland
xliv H4 **Derg, Lough** ◎ N Ireland
xxxvii W14 **Déroute, Passage de la** strait Channel Islands/France
xliv C14 **Derreendarragh** Kerry, SW Ireland
xliv G2 **Derrybeg** Donegal, N Ireland
xliv H5 **Derrygonnelly** Fermanagh, W Northern Ireland, UK
xliv K2 **Derrykeighan** Ballymoney, N Northern Ireland, UK
xliv I6 **Derrylin** Fermanagh, W Northern Ireland, UK
xliv H6 **Derrynacreeve** Cavan, N Ireland
xliv G3 **Derryveagh Mountains** ▲▲ N Ireland
xxxix U8 **Dersingham** Norfolk, E England, UK
xliii D16 **Dervaig** Argyll and Bute, W Scotland, UK
xl L8 **Derwent** ⩫ NW England, UK
xli U13 **Derwent** ⩫ N England, UK
xxxviii L6 **Derwent Reservoir** ⊟ C England, UK
xli Q7 **Derwent Reservoir** ⊟ N England, UK
xxxix P11 **Desborough** Northamptonshire, C England, UK
xxxix N10 **Desford** Leicestershire, C England, UK
xlii N12 **Deveron** ⩫ NE Scotland, UK
xxxv H10 **Devil's Bridge** Ceredigion, W Wales, UK
xxxvii N10 **Devizes** Wiltshire, S England, UK
xxxvi G14 **Devon** ◐ county SW England, UK
xli R15 **Dewsbury** Kirklees, N England, UK
xxxvii P9 **Didcot** Oxfordshire, C England, UK
xxxix Q7 **Digby** Lincolnshire, E England, UK
xlii D11 **Digg** Highland, NW Scotland, UK
xxxv E7 **Dinas** Gwynedd, NW Wales, UK
xxxv D12 **Dinas** Pembrokeshire, SW Wales, UK
xxxv H8 **Dinas-Mawddwy** Gwynedd, NW Wales, UK
xxxv J15 **Dinas Powys** The Vale of Glamorgan, S Wales, UK
xliv B13 **Dingle** Ir. An Daingean. Kerry, SW Ireland
xliv B13 **Dingle Bay** Ir. Bá an Daingin. bay SW Ireland
xlii I11 **Dingwall** Highland, N Scotland, UK
xliii N14 **Dinnet** Aberdeenshire, NE Scotland, UK
xli T17 **Dinnington** Rotherham, N England, UK
xxxvii N12 **Dinton** Wiltshire, S England, UK
xliii F21 **Dippen** Argyll and Bute, W Scotland, UK
xliii G22 **Dippin** North Ayrshire, W Scotland, UK
xliii N19 **Dirleton** East Lothian, SE Scotland, UK
xli S12 **Dishforth** North Yorkshire, N England, UK
xxxix W11 **Diss** Norfolk, E England, UK
xl K9 **Distington** Cumbria, NW England, UK
xxxix Y10 **Ditchingham** Norfolk, E England, UK
xxxvii U12 **Ditchling** East Sussex, SE England, UK
xxxvi H16 **Dittisham** Devon, SW England, UK
xxxviii I11 **Ditton Priors** Shropshire, W England, UK
xxxvi E15 **Dobwalls** Cornwall, SW England, UK
xxxix U8 **Docking** Norfolk, E England, UK
xxxix S10 **Doddington** Cambridgeshire, E England, UK
xxxvii X10 **Doddington** Kent, SE England, UK
xli P2 **Doddington** Northumberland, N England, UK
xxxv K5 **Dodleston** Flintshire, NE Wales, UK
xxxvi D17 **Dodman Point** headland SW England, UK
xxxix R6 **Dogdyke** Lincolnshire, E England, UK
xxxv J8 **Dolanog** Powys, C Wales, UK
xxxv J9 **Dolfor** Powys, C Wales, UK
xxxv H5 **Dolgarrog** Conwy, N Wales, UK
xxxv H7 **Dolgellau** Gwynedd, NW Wales, UK
xliv G11 **Dolla** Tipperary, S Ireland
xliii L18 **Dollar** Clackmannan, C Scotland, UK
xliii L21 **Dolphinton** The Borders, S Scotland, UK
xxxvi F13 **Dolton** Devon, SW England, UK
xxxv H6 **Dolwyddelan** Conwy, N Wales, UK
xli U14 **Don** ⩫ N England, UK
xlii O13 **Don** ⩫ NE Scotland, UK
xliv M4 **Donaghadee** Ards, E Northern Ireland, UK
xli T16 **Doncaster** anc. Danum. Doncaster, N England, UK
xli T15 **Doncaster** ◐ unitary authority N England, UK
xliv G4 **Donegal** Ir. Dún na nGall. Donegal, NW Ireland
xliv H3 **Donegal** Ir. Dún na nGall. ◐ county NW Ireland
xliv H4 **Donegal Bay** Ir. Bá Dhún na nGall. bay NW Ireland
xliv C11 **Donegal Point** headland W Ireland
xxxix R8 **Donington** Lincolnshire, E England, UK
xxxviii I9 **Donnington** Shropshire, W England, UK
xliv F13 **Donoughmore** Cork, S Ireland
xliv C6 **Dooagh** Mayo, NW Ireland
xliv C6 **Doogort** var. Dugort. Mayo, NW Ireland
xliv C6 **Doohooma** Mayo, NW Ireland
xliv G11 **Doon** Limerick, SW Ireland
xliv D11 **Doonbeg** ⩫ W Ireland
xliii I23 **Doon, Loch** ◎ W Scotland, UK
xli N13 **Dophinholme** Lancashire, NW England, UK
xxxvi M14 **Dorchester** anc. Durnovaria. Dorset, S England, UK
xxxvii Q8 **Dorchester** Oxfordshire, C England, UK
xlii J12 **Dores** Highland, NW Scotland, UK
xxxvii T11 **Dorking** Surrey, SE England, UK
xli Y6 **Dormanstown** Redcar and Cleveland, N England, UK
xlii F13 **Dornie** Highland, NW Scotland, UK
xlii J10 **Dornoch** Highland, N Scotland, UK
xlii J10 **Dornoch Firth** inlet N Scotland, UK
xxxviii D16 **Dorridge** Solihull, C England, UK
xxxvi L13 **Dorset** ◐ county S England, UK
xxxviii G13 **Dorstone** Herefordshire, W England, UK
xliii G21 **Dougarie** North Ayrshire, W Scotland, UK
xliv F14 **Douglas** Cork, S Ireland
xl G12 **Douglas** ○ (Isle of Man) E Isle of Man
xliii K22 **Douglas** South Lanarkshire, C Scotland, UK
xliii N16 **Douglastown** Angus, E Scotland, UK
xlii M4 **Dounby** Orkney Islands, N Scotland, UK
xliii J18 **Doune** Stirling, C Scotland, UK
xlii K6 **Dounreay** Highland, NW Scotland, UK
xxxviii K5 **Dove Holes** Derbyshire, C England, UK
xxxvii Z11 **Dover** Fr. Douvres; Lat. Dubris Portus. Kent, SE England, UK
xxxviii L8 **Doveridge** Derbyshire, C England, UK
xxxvii Z12 **Dover, Strait of** var. Straits of Dover, Fr. Pas de Calais. strait England, UK/France
xliv M5 **Down** ◐ district SE Northern Ireland, UK
xli P2 **Downham** Northumberland, N England, UK
xxxix T10 **Downham Market** Norfolk, E England, UK
xliii P14 **Downies** Aberdeenshire, NE Scotland, UK
xliv M5 **Downpatrick** Ir. Dún Pádraig. Down, SE Northern Ireland, UK
xxxvii O12 **Downton** Wiltshire, S England, UK
xliv H6 **Dowra** Leitrim, N Ireland
xliv K4 **Draperstown** Magherafelt, C Northern Ireland, UK
xxxviii L8 **Draycott in the Clay** Staffordshire, C England, UK
xxxix X9 **Drayton** Norfolk, E England, UK
xliv C12 **Dreenagh** Kerry, SW Ireland
xliii I21 **Dreghorn** North Ayrshire, W Scotland, UK
xliii N19 **Drem** East Lothian, SE Scotland, UK
xli W12 **Driffield** East Riding of Yorkshire, E England, UK
xl K10 **Drigg** Cumbria, NW England, UK
xliii E16 **Drimnin** Highland, NW Scotland, UK
xliv D15 **Drimoleague** Cork, S Ireland
xliv K7 **Drogheda** Ir. Droichead Átha. Louth, NE Ireland
xliv J9 **Droichead Nua** var. An Droichead Nua, Newbridge, C Ireland
xxxviii B17 **Droitwich** Worcestershire, W England, UK
xliv G5 **Dromahair** Leitrim, N Ireland
xliv L5 **Dromara** Banbridge, SE Northern Ireland, UK
xliv E12 **Dromcolliher** Limerick, SW Ireland
xliv G10 **Dromineer** Tipperary, S Ireland
xliv H7 **Dromod** Leitrim, N Ireland
xliv L5 **Dromore** Ir. Droim Mór. Banbridge, SE Northern Ireland, UK
xliv I4 **Dromore** Omagh, W Northern Ireland, UK
xliv F5 **Dromore West** Sligo, N Ireland
xxxviii L5 **Dronfield** Derbyshire, C England, UK
xliii I22 **Drongan** East Ayrshire, W Scotland, UK
xl H15 **Droylsden** Tameside, NW England, UK
xliii F20 **Druimdrishaig** Argyll and Bute, W Scotland, UK
xliv I3 **Drumahoe** Londonderry, NW Northern Ireland, UK
xlii G8 **Drumbeg** Highland, NW Scotland, UK
xliv K6 **Drumbilla** Louth, NE Ireland
xlii J12 **Drumchardine** Highland, NW Scotland, UK
xliv G5 **Drumcliff** Sligo, N Ireland
xliii J21 **Drumclog** South Lanarkshire, C Scotland, UK
xlii E13 **Drumfearn** Highland, NW Scotland, UK
xliv I2 **Drumfree** Donegal, N Ireland
xliv G6 **Drumkeeran** Leitrim, N Ireland
xliv H7 **Drumlish** Longford, C Ireland
xliii O15 **Drumlithie** Aberdeenshire, NE Scotland, UK
xliii H26 **Drummore** Dumfries and Galloway, SW Scotland, UK
xlii I13 **Drumnadrochit** Highland, NW Scotland, UK
xliv I4 **Drumquin** Omagh, W Northern Ireland, UK
xlii H9 **Drumrunie** Highland, NW Scotland, UK
xliv H7 **Drumshanbo** Leitrim, N Ireland
xliv H7 **Drumsna** Leitrim, N Ireland
xli R4 **Druridge Bay** bay N England, UK
xxxv I11 **Drygarn Fawr** ▲ E Wales, UK
xlii D13 **Drynoch** Highland, NW Scotland, UK
xliv L9 **Dublin** Ir. Baile Átha Cliath; anc. Eblana. ● (Ireland) Dublin, E Ireland
xliv K9 **Dublin** Ir. Baile Átha Cliath; anc. Eblana. ◐ county E Ireland
xliv L8 **Dublin** ✕ Dublin, E Ireland
xliv L9 **Dublin Bay** bay E Ireland
xxxvii P8 **Ducklington** Oxfordshire, C England, UK
xxxix Q10 **Duddington** Northamptonshire, C England, UK
xli P1 **Duddo** Northumberland, N England, UK
xl L10 **Duddon** ⩫ NW England, UK
xxxviii B15 **Dudley** Dudley, C England, UK
xxxviii J11 **Dudley** ◐ unitary authority C England, UK
xxxviii M7 **Duffield** Derbyshire, C England, UK
xlii M12 **Dufftown** Moray, N Scotland, UK
xlii M11 **Duffus** Moray, N Scotland, UK
xlii F13 **Duirinish** Highland, NW Scotland, UK
xlii F13 **Duisdalemore** Highland, NW Scotland, UK
xl H15 **Dukinfield** Tameside, NW England, UK
xxxix U12 **Dullingham** Cambridgeshire, E England, UK
xlii K13 **Dulnain Bridge** Highland, NW Scotland, UK
xxxvi H12 **Dulverton** Somerset, SW England, UK
xxxvi E9 **Dulwich** Southwark, SE England, UK
xliii I19 **Dumbarton** West Dunbartonshire, W Scotland, UK
xliii L24 **Dumfries** Dumfries and Galloway, S Scotland, UK
xliii J24 **Dumfries and Galloway** ◐ unitary authority SW Scotland, UK
xliii H20 **Dunan** Argyll and Bute, W Scotland, UK
xlii E13 **Dunan** Highland, NW Scotland, UK
xliv L7 **Dunany Point** headland NE Ireland
xliii O19 **Dunbar** East Lothian, SE Scotland, UK
xlii L8 **Dunbeath** Highland, N Scotland, UK
xliii K18 **Dunblane** Stirling, C Scotland, UK
xliv K8 **Dunboyne** Meath, E Ireland
xliv J13 **Duncannon** Wexford, SE Ireland
xlii M6 **Duncansby Head** headland N Scotland, UK
xxxix N11 **Dunchurch** Warwickshire, C England, UK
xliv K13 **Duncormick** Wexford, SE Ireland
xliv K7 **Dundalk** Ir. Dún Dealgan. Louth, NE Ireland
xliv L7 **Dundalk Bay** Ir. Cuan Dhún Dealgan. bay NE Ireland
xliii M17 **Dundee** City of Dundee, E Scotland, UK
xliii M17 **Dundee, City of** ◐ unitary authority E Scotland, UK
xliii I22 **Dundonald** South Ayrshire, W Scotland, UK
xlii G10 **Dundonnell** Highland, NW Scotland, UK
xliii K25 **Dundrennan** Dumfries and Galloway, SW Scotland, UK
xliv G11 **Dundrum** Tipperary, S Ireland
xliv M5 **Dundrum Down**, E Northern Ireland, UK
xliv M6 **Dundrum Bay** Ir. Cuan Dhún Droma. inlet NW Irish Sea
xlii O13 **Dunecht** Aberdeenshire, NE Scotland, UK
xliv H2 **Dunfanaghy** Ir. Dún Fionnachaidh. Donegal, NW Ireland
xliii L19 **Dunfermline** Fife, C Scotland, UK
xli R16 **Dunford Bridge** Barnsley, N England, UK
xliv J5 **Dungannon** Ir. Dún Geanainn. Dungannon, C Northern Ireland, UK
xliv J5 **Dungannon** ◐ district C Northern Ireland, UK
xliv H13 **Dungarvan** Ir. Dun Garbháin. Waterford, S Ireland
xxxvii Y12 **Dungeness** headland SE England, UK
xliv J3 **Dungiven** Limavady, N Northern Ireland, UK
xliv G3 **Dunglow** var. Dungloe, Ir. An Clochán Liath. NW Ireland
xxxix Q5 **Dunholme** Lincolnshire, E England, UK
xliii K19 **Dunipace** Falkirk, C Scotland, UK
xliii L16 **Dunkeld** Perth and Kinross, C Scotland, UK
xxxvi H11 **Dunkery Beacon** ▲ SW England, UK
xliv L9 **Dún Laoghaire** Eng. Dunleary; prev. Kingstown. Dublin, E Ireland
xliv K10 **Dunlavin** Wicklow, E Ireland
xliv K7 **Dunleer** Louth, NE Ireland
xliii I21 **Dunlop** East Ayrshire, W Scotland, UK
xliv C15 **Dunmanus Bay** bay S Ireland
xliv E14 **Dunmanway** Ir. Dún Mánmhaí. Cork, SW Ireland
xliv F8 **Dunmore** Galway, W Ireland
xliv J13 **Dunmore East** Waterford, S Ireland
xliv L5 **Dunmurry** Lisburn, E Northern Ireland, UK
xliv I3 **Dunnamanagh** Strabane, W Northern Ireland, UK
xlii L6 **Dunnet** Highland, N Scotland, UK
xlii L6 **Dunnet Bay** bay N Scotland, UK
xlii L6 **Dunnet Head** headland N Scotland, UK
xliii L18 **Dunning** Perth and Kinross, C Scotland, UK
xliii H20 **Dunoon** Argyll and Bute, W Scotland, UK
xliv B13 **Dunquin** Kerry, SW Ireland
xliii O20 **Duns** The Borders, SE Scotland, UK
xxxix Q8 **Dunsby** Lincolnshire, E England, UK
xliii K24 **Dunscore** Dumfries and Galloway, SW Scotland, UK
xxxvi H14 **Dunsford** Devon, SW England, UK
xliv K8 **Dunshauglin** Meath, E Ireland
xxxvii S7 **Dunstable** Lat. Durocobrivae. Bedfordshire, E England, UK
xli R3 **Dunstan** Northumberland, N England, UK
xxxvi I11 **Dunster** Somerset, SW England, UK
xlii J12 **Duntelchaig, Loch** ◎ N Scotland, UK
xliii H22 **Dunure** South Ayrshire, W Scotland, UK
xlii D12 **Dunvegan** Highland, NW Scotland, UK
xxxix Y11 **Dunwich** Suffolk, E England, UK
xxxvi M14 **Durdle Door** natural arch S England, UK
xli V4 **Durham** hist. Dunholme. Durham, N England, UK
xli Q8 **Durham** ◐ county N England, UK
xlii I6 **Durness** Highland, N Scotland, UK
xlii G16 **Duror** Highland, NW Scotland, UK
xxxvii O11 **Durrington** Wiltshire, S England, UK
xliv I10 **Durrow** Laois, C Ireland
xliv D15 **Durrus** Cork, S Ireland
xliv B15 **Dursey Head** Ir. Ceann Baoi. headland S Ireland
xliv B15 **Dursey Island** Ir. Oileán Baoi. island SW Ireland
xxxvi L8 **Dursley** Gloucestershire, C England, UK
xxxix T13 **Duxford** Cambridgeshire, E England, UK
xlii P13 **Dyce** City of Aberdeen, NE Scotland, UK
xxxv G7 **Dyffryn Ardudwy** Gwynedd, NW Wales, UK
xxxv H8 **Dyfi** ⩫ W Wales, UK
xxxvi Y12 **Dymchurch** Kent, SE England, UK
xxxvi L6 **Dymock** Gloucestershire, C England, UK
xliii M19 **Dysart** Fife, E Scotland, UK
xxxv I4 **Dyserth** Denbighshire, N Wales, UK

E

xliii J21 **Eaglesham** East Renfrewshire, W Scotland, UK
xxxvi A7 **Ealing** Ealing, SE England, UK
xxxvi K16 **Ealing** ◐ London borough SE England, UK
xli P13 **Earby** Lancashire, NW England, UK
xxxix S11 **Earith** Cambridgeshire, E England, UK
xxxvii R9 **Earley** Reading, S England, UK
xxxvii P12 **Earls Barton** Northamptonshire, C England, UK
xxxvii W6 **Earls Colne** Essex, SE England, UK

◆ Country ● Country Capital ◇ Dependent Territory ○ Dependent Territory Capital ◐ Administrative Region ✕ International Airport ▲ Mountain ▲▲ Mountain Range ◎ Lake ⊟ Reservoir ⩫ River

xliii N18 **Earlsferry** Fife, E Scotland, UK
xxxvi C9 **Earlsfield** Wandsworth, SE England, UK
xxxix N10 **Earl Shilton** Leicestershire, C England, UK
xliii N21 **Earlston** The Borders, S Scotland, UK
xxxix W12 **Earl Stonham** Suffolk, E England, UK
xliii K17 **Earn** ~ N Scotland, UK
xliii J17 **Earn, Loch** ◎ C Scotland, UK
xxxvii R12 **Easebourne** West Sussex, SE England, UK
xli W4 **Easington** Durham, N England, UK
xli Y14 **Easington** East Riding of Yorkshire, N England, UK
xli X4 **Easington Colliery** Durham, N England, UK
xli T12 **Easingwold** North Yorkshire, N England, UK
xliv F5 **Easky** Sligo, N Ireland
xli P7 **East Allen** ~ N England, UK
xxxix V11 **East Anglia** *physical region* E England, UK
xliii I22 **East Ayrshire** ◐ *unitary authority* SW Scotland, UK
xxxix W14 **East Bergholt** Suffolk, E England, UK
xxxvii V13 **Eastbourne** East Sussex, SE England, UK
xxxvi J11 **East Brent** Somerset, SW England, UK
xxxix O7 **East Bridgford** Nottinghamshire, C England, UK
xxxvii P9 **East Challow** Oxfordshire, C England, UK
xxxvi L13 **East Chinnock** Somerset, SW England, UK
xxxvii X9 **Eastchurch** Kent, SE England, UK
xxxvii P13 **East Cowes** Isle of Wight, S England, UK
xlii J13 **East Croachy** Highland, NW Scotland, UK
xxxvii V13 **East Dean** East Sussex, SE England, UK
xxxix W9 **East Dereham** Norfolk, E England, UK
xliii I19 **East Dunbartonshire** ◐ *unitary authority* C Scotland, UK
xlii J11 **Easter Ardross** Highland, NW Scotland, UK
xliii M14 **Easter Balmoral** Aberdeenshire, NE Scotland, UK
xlii I4 **Easter Quarff** Shetland Islands, NE Scotland, UK
xlii H4 **Easter Skeld** Shetland Islands, NE Scotland, UK
xli P8 **Eastgate** Durham, N England, UK
xxxvii O10 **East Grafton** Wiltshire, S England, UK
xxxvii U11 **East Grinstead** West Sussex, SE England, UK
xxxix O12 **East Haddon** Northamptonshire, C England, UK
xxxix Q3 **East Halton** North Lincolnshire, N England, UK
xxxvi F7 **East Ham** Newham, SE England, UK
xxxvii P8 **East Hanney** Oxfordshire, C England, UK
xxxix W11 **East Harling** Norfolk, E England, UK
xxxvii T10 **East Horsley** Surrey, SE England, UK
xxxvii P9 **East Ilsley** West Berkshire, S England, UK
xxxvi M8 **Eastington** Gloucestershire, C England, UK
xxxix S6 **East Keal** Lincolnshire, E England, UK
xliii J20 **East Kilbride** South Lanarkshire, S Scotland, UK
xxxvi M12 **East Knoyle** Wiltshire, S England, UK
xxxix N8 **East Leake** Nottinghamshire, C England, UK
xxxvii P12 **Eastleigh** Hampshire, S England, UK
xliii N19 **East Linton** East Lothian, SE Scotland, UK
xxxvi E16 **East Looe** Cornwall, SW England, UK
xliii N20 **East Lothian** ◐ *unitary authority* SE Scotland, UK
xxxix O5 **East Markham** Nottinghamshire, C England, UK
xxxvii Q12 **East Meon** Hampshire, S England, UK
xxxviii I14 **Eastnor** Herefordshire, W England, UK
xxxix P10 **East Norton** Rutland, C England, UK
xxxvi L15 **Easton** Dorset, S England, UK
xxxvii P12 **Easton** Hampshire, S England, UK
xxxix Q10 **Easton on the Hill** Northamptonshire, C England, UK
xxxvi H17 **East Prawle** Devon, SW England, UK
xxxix V8 **East Raynham** Norfolk, E England, UK
xliii I21 **East Renfrewshire** ◐ *unitary authority* C Scotland, UK
xli U13 **East Riding of Yorkshire** ◐ *unitary authority* N England, UK
xliii M24 **Eastriggs** Dumfries and Galloway, SW Scotland, UK
xli U14 **Eastrington** East Riding of Yorkshire, N England, UK
xxxix V8 **East Rudham** Norfolk, E England, UK
xxxvii Z10 **Eastry** Kent, SE England, UK
xliii N20 **East Saltoun** East Lothian, SE Scotland, UK
xxxvi A8 **East Sheen** Richmond upon Thames, SE England, UK
xxxvii U12 **East Sussex** ◐ *county* SE England, UK
xli S6 **Eastville** Lincolnshire, E England, UK
xxxvii R13 **East Wittering** West Sussex, SE England, UK
xli Q11 **East Witton** North Yorkshire, N England, UK
xxxix N7 **Eastwood** Nottinghamshire, C England, UK
xxxv J13 **Ebbw Vale** Blaenau Gwent, SE Wales, UK
xli Q7 **Ebchester** Durham, N England, UK
xliii M24 **Ecclefechan** Dumfries and Galloway, SW Scotland, UK
xli O16 **Eccles** Salford, NW England, UK
xliii O21 **Eccles** The Borders, S Scotland, UK
xli S16 **Ecclesfield** Sheffield, N England, UK
xxxviii J8 **Eccleshall** Staffordshire, C England, UK
xxxviii G6 **Eccleston** Cheshire, W England, UK
xli N15 **Eccleston** Lancashire, NW England, UK
xliii O13 **Echt** Aberdeenshire, NE Scotland, UK
xliii O22 **Eckford** The Borders, S Scotland, UK
xxxviii M5 **Eckington** Derbyshire, C England, UK
xli N3 **Eday** *island* NE Scotland, UK
xlii J10 **Edderton** Highland, NW Scotland, UK
xliii M21 **Eddleston** The Borders, S Scotland, UK
xlii G8 **Eddrachillis Bay** *bay* NW Scotland, UK
xxxvi F17 **Eddystone Rocks** *rocks* SW England, UK
xl M6 **Eden** ~ NW England, UK
xxxvii V11 **Edenbridge** Kent, SE England, UK
xliv J9 **Edenderry** *Ir.* Éadan Doire. Offaly, C Ireland
xxxix Q9 **Edenham** Lincolnshire, E England, UK
xxxviii L6 **Edensor** Derbyshire, C England, UK
xliv I4 **Ederny** Fermanagh, W Northern Ireland, UK
xli O15 **Edgeworth** Lancashire, NW England, UK
xliv H7 **Edgeworthstown** Longford, C Ireland
xxxviii I9 **Edgmond** Shropshire, W England, UK
xxxvi A5 **Edgware** Harrow, SE England, UK
xliii M20 **Edinburgh** *national region capital* City of Edinburgh, S Scotland, UK
xliii L20 **Edinburgh** ✕ City of Edinburgh, S Scotland, UK
xliii L20 **Edinburgh, City of** ◐ *unitary authority* E Scotland, UK
xxxvi D5 **Edmonton** Enfield, SE England, UK
xxxix N6 **Edwinstowe** Nottinghamshire, C England, UK
xliii N15 **Edzell** Angus, E Scotland, UK
xli X7 **Egglescliffe** Stockton-on-Tees, N England, UK
xxxvii S10 **Egham** Surrey, SE England, UK
xli M3 **Egilsay** *island* N Scotland, UK
xli Q3 **Eglingham** Northumberland, N England, UK
xliv J3 **Eglinton** Londonderry, NW Northern Ireland, UK
xxxvi E14 **Egloskerry** Cornwall, SW England, UK
xxxv H5 **Eglwysbach** Conwy, N Wales, UK
xxxv H9 **Eglwys Fach** Ceredigion, W Wales, UK
xxxv D12 **Eglwyswrw** Pembrokeshire, SW Wales, UK
xl K9 **Egremont** Cumbria, NW England, UK
xli V9 **Egton** North Yorkshire, N England, UK
xliii E15 **Eigg** *island* W Scotland, UK
xliii D15 **Eigg, Sound of** *strait* NW Scotland, UK
xliii G15 **Eil, Loch** *inlet* NW Scotland, UK
xxxv I10 **Elan Village** Powys, C Wales, UK
xliii I24 **Eldrick** South Ayrshire, W Scotland, UK
xxxviii D13 **Elford** Staffordshire, C England, UK
xlii L11 **Elgin** Moray, NE Scotland, UK
xli E13 **Elgol** Highland, NW Scotland, UK
xxxvii Y11 **Elham** Kent, SE England, UK
xliii N18 **Elie** Fife, E Scotland, UK
xli Q15 **Elland** Calderdale, N England, UK
xli F20 **Ellary** Argyll and Bute, W Scotland, UK
xxxviii L7 **Ellastone** Staffordshire, C England, UK
xxxviii G8 **Ellesmere** Shropshire, W England, UK
xl C17 **Ellesmere Port** Cheshire, C England, UK
xli R2 **Ellingham** Northumberland, N England, UK
xlii P12 **Ellon** Aberdeenshire, NE Scotland, UK
xli V14 **Elloughton** East Riding of Yorkshire, N England, UK
xxxvi U6 **Elmdon** Essex, SE England, UK
xxxix W12 **Elmswell** Suffolk, E England, UK
xliv G7 **Elphin** Roscommon, C Ireland
xli H9 **Elphin** Highland, NW Scotland, UK
xliii I25 **Elrig** Dumfries and Galloway, SW Scotland, UK
xli P4 **Elsdon** Northumberland, N England, UK
xliii L21 **Elsrickle** South Lanarkshire, C Scotland, UK
xxxvii R11 **Elstead** Surrey, SE England, UK
xxxvii S8 **Elstree** Hertfordshire, SE England, UK
xl M14 **Elswick** Lancashire, NW England, UK
xxxix S12 **Elsworth** Cambridgeshire, E England, UK
xxxvi G9 **Eltham** Greenwich, SE England, UK
xxxix R12 **Eltisley** Cambridgeshire, E England, UK
xxxix Q10 **Elton** Cambridgeshire, E England, UK
xliii L22 **Elvanfoot** South Lanarkshire, C Scotland, UK
xli U13 **Elvington** York, N England, UK
xxxviii I6 **Elworth** Cheshire, C England, UK
xxxix T11 **Ely** Cambridgeshire, E England, UK
xxxv J15 **Ely** Cardiff, S Wales, UK
xxxv J15 **Ely** ~ S Wales, UK
xxxix S10 **Ely, Isle of** *physical region* E England, UK
xli R3 **Embleton** Northumberland, N England, UK
xli K10 **Embo** Highland, N Scotland, UK
xli Q13 **Embsay** North Yorkshire, N England, UK
xxxvi T9 **Emneth** Norfolk, E England, UK
xliv I10 **Emo** Laois, C Ireland
xxxix Q9 **Empingham** Rutland, C England, UK
xxxvii R13 **Emsworth** West Sussex, SE England, UK
xli G9 **Enard Bay** *bay* NW Scotland, UK
xxxviii J7 **Endon** Staffordshire, C England, UK
xliv J8 **Enfield** Meath, E Ireland
xxxvi U8 **Enfield** Enfield, SE England, UK
xxxvi K15 **Enfield** ◐ *London borough* SE England, UK
xliv I8 **Ennell, Lough** ◎ C Ireland
xl K9 **Ennerdale Water** ◎ NW England, UK
xliv E10 **Ennis** *Ir.* Inis. Clare, W Ireland
xliv K12 **Enniscorthy** *Ir.* Inis Córthaidh. Wexford, SE Ireland
xliv E14 **Enniskean** Cork, S Ireland
xliv L10 **Enniskerry** Wicklow, E Ireland
xliv I5 **Enniskillen** *var.* Inniskilling, *Ir.* Inis Ceithleann. Fermanagh, SW Northern Ireland, UK
xliv E10 **Ennistimon** *Ir.* Inis Díomáin. Clare, W Ireland
xlii B10 **Ensay** *island* NW Scotland, UK
xxxvii P7 **Enstone** Oxfordshire, C England, UK
xliii K23 **Enterkinfoot** Dumfries and Galloway, SW Scotland, UK
xxxvii V8 **Epping** Essex, SE England, UK
xxxvii T10 **Epsom** Surrey, SE England, UK
xxxix O4 **Epworth** North Lincolnshire, N England, UK
xli I7 **Eriboll** Highland, NW Scotland, UK
xlii I7 **Eriboll, Loch** *inlet* NW Scotland, UK
xliii I15 **Ericht, Loch** ◎ C Scotland, UK
xliii B14 **Eriskay** *island* NW Scotland, UK
xxxvii U9 **Erith** Bexley, SE England, UK
xxxvi G16 **Erme** ~ SW England, UK
xliv G4 **Erne** Donegal, N Ireland
xliv G6 **Erne** ~ Ireland/Northern Ireland, UK
xxxix X8 **Erpingham** Norfolk, E England, UK
xliv H2 **Errigal** *Ir.* An Earagail. ▲ N Ireland
xliv C5 **Erris Head** *Ir.* Ceann Iorrais. *headland* W Ireland
xliii I15 **Errochty, Loch** ◎ C Scotland, UK
xliii I13 **Errogie** Highland, N Scotland, UK
xliii M17 **Errol** Perth and Kinross, C Scotland, UK
xxxv J12 **Erwood** Powys, C Wales, UK
xli T13 **Escrick** North Yorkshire, N England, UK
xli H2 **Esha Ness** *headland* NE Scotland, UK
xxxvii T10 **Esher** Surrey, SE England, UK
xli V9 **Esk** ~ N England, UK
xl L10 **Esk** ~ NW England, UK
xliii M23 **Esk** ~ England/Scotland, UK
xl L10 **Eskdale Green** Cumbria, NW England, UK
xliii M23 **Eskdalemuir** Dumfries and Galloway, SW Scotland, UK
xxxix Q9 **Essendine** Rutland, C England, UK
xxxvii V7 **Essex** ◐ *county* E England, UK
xli T9 **Eston** Redcar and Cleveland, N England, UK
xxxvii W12 **Etchingham** East Sussex, SE England, UK
xliii G17 **Etive, Loch** *inlet* W Scotland, UK
xxxvii S9 **Eton** Windsor and Maidenhead, S England, UK
xxxviii M13 **Ettington** Warwickshire, C England, UK
xliii M22 **Ettrick** The Borders, S Scotland, UK
xliii N22 **Ettrickbridge** The Borders, S Scotland, UK
xxxviii L8 **Etwall** Derbyshire, C England, UK
xli N15 **Euxton** Lancashire, NW England, UK
xlii J11 **Evanton** Highland, NW Scotland, UK
xxxvii O7 **Evenlode** ~ C England, UK
xxxvi L11 **Evercreech** Somerset, SW England, UK
xxxix N12 **Everdon** Northamptonshire, C England, UK
xli U13 **Everingham** East Riding of Yorkshire, N England, UK
xxxvii O10 **Everleigh** Wiltshire, S England, UK
xxxvi L13 **Evershot** Dorset, S England, UK
xxxix O4 **Everton** Nottinghamshire, C England, UK
xxxviii K13 **Evesham** Worcestershire, C England, UK
xlii F10 **Ewe, Loch** *inlet* NW Scotland, UK
xxxvii S11 **Ewhurst** Surrey, SE England, UK
xxxvi G13 **Exbourne** Devon, SW England, UK
xxxvii P13 **Exbury** Hampshire, S England, UK
xxxvi H14 **Exe** ~ SW England, UK
xxxvi H14 **Exeter** *anc.* Isca Damnoniorum. Devon, SW England, UK
xxxvi H11 **Exford** Somerset, SW England, UK
xxxvi H12 **Exmoor** *moorland* SW England, UK
xxxvi I14 **Exmouth** Devon, SW England, UK
xxxvi I14 **Exton** Devon, SW England, UK
xxxvi H12 **Exton** Somerset, SW England, UK
xxxviii L5 **Eyam** Derbyshire, C England, UK
xxxix R10 **Eye** Cambridgeshire, E England, UK
xxxix W11 **Eye** Suffolk, E England, UK
xliii P20 **Eyemouth** The Borders, SE Scotland, UK
xlii E8 **Eye Peninsula** *peninsula* NW Scotland, UK
xxxvii P8 **Eynsham** Oxfordshire, C England, UK
xxxvii Z11 **Eythorne** Kent, SE England, UK

F

xliii G11 **Fada, Lochan** ◎ NW Scotland, UK
xl H14 **Failsworth** Tameside, NW England, UK
xxxv G8 **Fairbourne** Gwynedd, NW Wales, UK
xxxvii O8 **Fairford** Gloucestershire, C England, UK
xliv L2 **Fair Head** *headland* N Northern Ireland, UK
xlii P1 **Fair Isle** *island* NE Scotland, UK
xliii H21 **Fairlie** North Ayrshire, W Scotland, UK
xxxvii W13 **Fairlight** East Sussex, SE England, UK
xxxvi I14 **Fairmile** Devon, SW England, UK
xxxvii P12 **Fair Oak** Hampshire, S England, UK
xxxix V8 **Fakenham** Norfolk, E England, UK
xxxvi C16 **Fal** ~ SW England, UK
xliii N20 **Fala** Midlothian, SE Scotland, UK
xxxix Q5 **Faldingworth** Lincolnshire, E England, UK
xxxvi L8 **Falfield** South Gloucestershire, SW England, UK
xliii K19 **Falkirk** Falkirk, C Scotland, UK
xliii K19 **Falkirk** ◐ *unitary authority* C Scotland, UK
xliii M18 **Falkland** Fife, E Scotland, UK
xliv C6 **Fallmore** Mayo, NW Ireland
xxxvi C17 **Falmouth** Cornwall, SW England, UK
xxxvi C17 **Falmouth Bay** *bay* SW England, UK
xli O5 **Falstone** Northumberland, N England, UK
xliv I2 **Fanad Head** *headland* N Ireland
xxxv H13 **Fan Brycheiniog** *var.* Carmarthen Van. ▲ E Wales, UK
xli U13 **Fangfoss** East Riding of Yorkshire, N England, UK
xli H11 **Fannich, Loch** ◎ NW Scotland, UK
xli H6 **Faraid Head** *headland* NW Scotland, UK
xxxix R10 **Farcet** Cambridgeshire, E England, UK
xliv H8 **Fardrum** Westmeath, C Ireland
xxxvii Q13 **Fareham** Hampshire, S England, UK
xxxvii O8 **Faringdon** Oxfordshire, C England, UK
xxxv G11 **Farmers** Carmarthenshire, S Wales, UK
xlii N11 **Farmtown** Moray, N Scotland, UK
xxxvii S10 **Farnborough** Hampshire, S England, UK
xli R2 **Farne Islands** *island group* N England, UK
xxxix Y12 **Farnham** Suffolk, E England, UK
xxxvii R11 **Farnham** Surrey, S England, UK
xxxvii V10 **Farningham** Kent, SE England, UK
xxxix O6 **Farnsfield** Nottinghamshire, C England, UK
xli O16 **Farnworth** Bolton, NW England, UK
xliv D13 **Farranfore** Kerry, SW Ireland
xlii H12 **Farrar** ~ NW Scotland, UK
xxxix N13 **Farthinghoe** Northamptonshire, C England, UK
xliv C15 **Fastnet Rock** *Ir.* Carraig Aonair. *island* SW Ireland
xliii K20 **Fauldhouse** West Lothian, SE Scotland, UK
xxxvii X10 **Faversham** Kent, SE England, UK
xxxvii P13 **Fawley** Hampshire, S England, UK
xli V14 **Faxfleet** East Riding of Yorkshire, N England, UK
xxxviii D14 **Fazeley** Staffordshire, C England, UK
xliv D12 **Feale** ~ SW Ireland
xliii J16 **Fearnan** Perth and Kinross, C Scotland, UK
xlii F11 **Fearnmore** Highland, NW Scotland, UK
xli S15 **Featherstone** Wakefield, N England, UK
xxxviii K12 **Feckenham** Worcestershire, W England, UK
xliv D6 **Feeagh, Lough** ◎ NW Ireland
xliv J3 **Feeny** Limavady, N Northern Ireland, UK
xli Q10 **Feetham** North Yorkshire, N England, UK
xxxix X14 **Felixstowe** Suffolk, E England, UK
xli V3 **Felling** Gateshead, NE England, UK
xli R4 **Felton** Northumberland, N England, UK
xxxix U10 **Feltwell** Norfolk, E England, UK
xliv H6 **Fenagh** Leitrim, N Ireland
xliv C12 **Fenit** Kerry, SW Ireland
xxxix S9 **Fens, The** *wetland* E England, UK
xliii I21 **Fenwick** East Ayrshire, W Scotland, UK
xli Q2 **Fenwick** Northumberland, N England, UK
xxxvi C17 **Feock** Cornwall, SW England, UK
xliv B12 **Feohanagh** Kerry, SW Ireland
xliii E20 **Feolin Ferry** Argyll and Bute, W Scotland, UK
xliv H9 **Ferbane** Offaly, C Ireland
xliv H5 **Fermanagh** ◐ *district* SW Northern Ireland, UK
xliv G13 **Fermoy** *Ir.* Mainistir Fhear Maí. Cork, SW Ireland
xxxvii N13 **Ferndown** Dorset, S England, UK
xlii K12 **Ferness** Highland, NW Scotland, UK
xxxvii R12 **Fernhurst** West Sussex, SE England, UK
xliv K11 **Ferns** Wexford, SE Ireland
xliv L11 **Ferrybank** Wicklow, E Ireland
xli R8 **Ferryhill** Durham, N England, UK
xliv H12 **Fethard** Tipperary, S Ireland
xliv J13 **Fethard** Wexford, SE Ireland
xlii J2 **Fetlar** *island* NE Scotland, UK
xliii O15 **Fettercairn** Aberdeenshire, NE Scotland, UK
xli R13 **Fewston** North Yorkshire, N England, UK
xxxv H6 **Ffestiniog** Gwynedd, NW Wales, UK
xxxv F11 **Ffostrasol** Ceredigion, W Wales, UK
xliii M18 **Fife** *var.* Kingdom of Fife. ◐ *unitary authority* E Scotland, UK
xliii O18 **Fife Ness** *headland* E Scotland, UK
xli W11 **Filey** North Yorkshire, N England, UK
xli W11 **Filey Bay** *bay* N England, UK
xxxviii E15 **Fillongley** Warwickshire, C England, UK
xxxvi L9 **Filton** South Gloucestershire, SW England, UK
xliii N16 **Finavon** Angus, E Scotland, UK
xxxix U9 **Fincham** Norfolk, E England, UK
xxxvii V6 **Finchingfield** Essex, SE England, UK
xxxvi C5 **Finchley** Barnet, SE England, UK
xlii L11 **Findhorn** Moray, N Scotland, UK
xlii K12 **Findhorn** ~ N Scotland, UK
xlii N11 **Findochty** Moray, N Scotland, UK
xxxvii T13 **Findon** West Sussex, SE England, UK
xxxix P11 **Finedon** Northamptonshire, C England, UK
xliii D17 **Fingal's Cave** *cave* W Scotland, UK
xliv I4 **Finn** ~ Ireland/Northern Ireland, UK
xxxix W12 **Finningham** Suffolk, E England, UK
xli U16 **Finningley** Doncaster, N England, UK
xxxvi D7 **Finsbury** Islington, SE England, UK
xlii M4 **Finstown** Orkney Islands, N Scotland, UK
xliv I5 **Fintona** Omagh, W Northern Ireland, UK
xliv H3 **Fintown** Donegal, N Ireland
xliii J19 **Fintry** Stirling, C Scotland, UK
xliii G10 **Fionn Loch** ◎ NW Scotland, UK
xliii D18 **Fionnphort** Argyll and Bute, W Scotland, UK
xxxvii P14 **Fishbourne** Isle of Wight, S England, UK
xxxv C12 **Fishguard** *Wel.* Abergwaun. Pembrokeshire, SW Wales, UK
xxxv C11 **Fishguard Bay** *bay* SW Wales, UK
xli U15 **Fishlake** Doncaster, N England, UK
xli H5 **Fitful Head** *headland* NE Scotland, UK
xxxvi E14 **Fivelanes** Cornwall, SW England, UK
xliv I5 **Fivemiletown** Dungannon, C Northern Ireland, UK
xxxvii T12 **Five Oaks** West Sussex, SE England, UK
xli X12 **Flamborough** East Riding of Yorkshire, N England, UK
xli X12 **Flamborough Head** *headland* E England, UK
xlii A8 **Flannan Isles** *island group* NW Scotland, UK
xxxviii K6 **Flash** Staffordshire, C England, UK
xxxvii O14 **Flat Holm** *island* S England, UK
xli U12 **Flaxton** North Yorkshire, N England, UK
xxxvii R10 **Fleet** Hampshire, S England, UK
xl L13 **Fleetwood** Lancashire, NW England, UK
xl K8 **Flimby** Cumbria, NW England, UK
xl B17 **Flint** Flintshire, NE Wales, UK
xxxix O7 **Flintham** Nottinghamshire, C England, UK
xxxv J5 **Flintshire** ◐ *unitary authority* N Wales, UK
xxxvii S6 **Flitwick** Bedfordshire, C England, UK
xxxix P3 **Flixborough** North Lincolnshire, N England, UK
xlii D11 **Flodigarry** Highland, NW Scotland, UK
xlii M5 **Flotta** *island* N Scotland, UK
xli M11 **Fochabers** Moray, N Scotland, UK
xxxvii Y11 **Folkestone** Kent, SE England, UK
xxxix Q8 **Folkingham** Lincolnshire, E England, UK
xxxvi F14 **Folly Gate** Devon, SW England, UK
xliv J10 **Fontstown** Kildare, E Ireland
xli P2 **Ford** Northumberland, N England, UK
xliii G18 **Ford** Argyll and Bute, W Scotland, UK
xliii L19 **Fordell** Fife, E Scotland, UK
xxxix U11 **Fordham** Cambridgeshire, E England, UK
xxxix T10 **Fordham** Norfolk, E England, UK
xxxvii O13 **Fordingbridge** Hampshire, S England, UK
xliii O15 **Fordoun** Aberdeenshire, NE Scotland, UK
xxxvii N14 **Foreland, The** *headland* SW England, UK
xxxvi F6 **Forest Gate** Newham, SE England, UK
xli N10 **Forest Hall** Cumbria, NW England, UK
xxxvi E9 **Forest Hill** Lewisham, SE England, UK
xxxvii U11 **Forest Row** East Sussex, SE England, UK
xliii N16 **Forfar** Angus, E Scotland, UK
xl L16 **Formby** Sefton, NW England, UK
xlii L11 **Forres** Moray, NE Scotland, UK
xli K7 **Forsinard** Highland, N Scotland, UK
xliii I14 **Fort Augustus** Highland, N Scotland, UK
xliii L18 **Forteviot** Perth and Kinross, C Scotland, UK
xlii J11 **Fort George** Highland, NW Scotland, UK
xliii J19 **Forth** ~ C Scotland, UK
xliii K20 **Forth** South Lanarkshire, C Scotland, UK
xliii N19 **Forth, Firth of** *estuary* E Scotland, UK
xliii J16 **Fortingall** Perth and Kinross, C Scotland, UK
xli J11 **Fortrose** Highland, NW Scotland, UK
xxxvi L15 **Fortuneswell** Dorset, S England, UK
xliii H15 **Fort William** Highland, N Scotland, UK
xxxix S8 **Fosdyke** Lincolnshire, E England, UK
xxxix R4 **Fotherby** Lincolnshire, E England, UK
xli N4 **Foubister** Orkney Islands, N Scotland, UK
xlii G4 **Foula** *island* NE Scotland, UK
xxxix X8 **Foulness Island** *island* SE England, UK
xli P13 **Foulridge** Lancashire, NW England, UK
xxxix W8 **Foulsham** Norfolk, E England, UK
xxxv J8 **Four Crosses** Powys, C Wales, UK
xxxvi D16 **Fowey** Cornwall, SW England, UK
xxxvi D15 **Fowey** ~ SW England, UK
xxxviii I14 **Fownhope** Herefordshire, W England, UK
xl F12 **Foxdale** Isle of Man
xliv E6 **Foxford** Mayo, NW Ireland
xli W11 **Foxholes** North Yorkshire, N England, UK
xli I13 **Foyers** Highland, NW Scotland, UK
xliv I3 **Foyle** ~ Ireland/Northern Ireland, UK
xliv J2 **Foyle, Lough** *Ir.* Loch Feabhail. *inlet* N Ireland
xliv E11 **Foynes** Limerick, SW Ireland
xxxix X12 **Framlingham** Suffolk, E England, UK
xxxvi L14 **Frampton** Dorset, S England, UK
xxxvi L8 **Frampton on Severn** Gloucestershire, C England, UK
xli V4 **Framwellgate Moor** Durham, N England, UK
xxxvii V11 **Frant** East Sussex, SE England, UK
xli P11 **Fraserburgh** Aberdeenshire, NE Scotland, UK
xl M14 **Freckleton** Lancashire, NW England, UK
xxxvi F12 **Fremington** Devon, SW England, UK
xliv G7 **Frenchpark** Roscommon, C Ireland
xxxvii R11 **Frensham** Surrey, SE England, UK
xliv I11 **Freshford** Kilkenny, SE Ireland
xxxvii P14 **Freshwater** Isle of Wight, S England, UK
xxxix X11 **Fressingfield** Suffolk, E England, UK
xli M6 **Freswick** Highland, N Scotland, UK
xxxix T9 **Friday Bridge** Cambridgeshire, E England, UK
xli V12 **Fridaythorpe** East Riding of Yorkshire, N England, UK
xxxvii Y7 **Frinton-on-Sea** Essex, SE England, UK
xliii N16 **Friockheim** Angus, E Scotland, UK
xliii E17 **Frisa, Loch** ◎ W Scotland, UK
xxxix S6 **Friskney** Lincolnshire, E England, UK
xl K9 **Frizington** Cumbria, NW England, UK
xl D17 **Frodsham** Cheshire, W England, UK
xxxvi M11 **Frome** Somerset, SW England, UK
xxxvi M14 **Frome** ~ S England, UK
xxxv I6 **Frongoch** Gwynedd, NW Wales, UK
xxxvii O10 **Froxfield** Wiltshire, S England, UK
xlii A14 **Fuday** *island* NW Scotland, UK
xxxix T12 **Fulbourn** Cambridgeshire, E England, UK
xli T13 **Fulford** York, N England, UK
xxxvi C8 **Fulham** Hammersmith and Fulham, SE England, UK
xxxix S4 **Fulstow** Lincolnshire, E England, UK
xli N14 **Fulwood** Lancashire, NW England, UK
xli S17 **Fulwood** Sheffield, N England, UK
xlii J2 **Funzie** Shetland Islands, NE Scotland, UK
xliii G18 **Furnace** Argyll and Bute, W Scotland, UK
xxxvii V8 **Fyfield** Essex, SE England, UK
xlii G19 **Fyne, Loch** *inlet* W Scotland, UK
xlii O12 **Fyvie** Aberdeenshire, NE Scotland, UK

G

xxxviii B13 **Gailey** Staffordshire, C England, UK
xxxix O4 **Gainsborough** Lincolnshire, E England, UK
xlii F10 **Gairloch** Highland, NW Scotland, UK
xlii H15 **Gairlochy** Highland, NW Scotland, UK
xli M4 **Gairsay** *island* N Scotland, UK
xliii N21 **Galashiels** The Borders, SE Scotland, UK
xliv G12 **Galbally** Limerick, SW Ireland
xli N13 **Galgate** Lancashire, NW England, UK
xliv E15 **Galley Head** *headland* S Ireland
xli H26 **Galloway, Mull of** *headland* S Scotland, UK
xliii E15 **Galmisdale** Highland, NW Scotland, UK
xliii I21 **Galston** East Ayrshire, W Scotland, UK
xliv G12 **Galtymore Mountain** *Ir.* Cnoc Mór na nGaibhlte. ▲ S Ireland
xliv G12 **Galty Mountains** *Ir.* Na Gaibhlte. ▲▲ S Ireland
xliv E9 **Galway** *Ir.* Gaillimh. Galway, W Ireland
xliv F8 **Galway** *Ir.* Gaillimh. ◐ *county* W Ireland
xliv E9 **Galway** ✕ Galway, W Ireland
xliv D9 **Galway Bay** *Ir.* Cuan na Gaillimhe. *bay* W Ireland
xli N8 **Gamblesby** Cumbria, NW England, UK
xxxix R13 **Gamlingay** Cambridgeshire, E England, UK
xxxix O5 **Gamston** Nottinghamshire, C England, UK
xlii H7 **Ganu Mòr** ▲ NW Scotland, UK
xliv F6 **Gara, Lough** ◎ N Ireland
xxxvi W11 **Garboldisham** Norfolk, E England, UK
xlii O11 **Gardenstown** Aberdeenshire, NE Scotland, UK
xliii H19 **Garelochead** Argyll and Bute, W Scotland, UK
xli S14 **Garforth** Leeds, N England, UK
xli P13 **Gargrave** North Yorkshire, N England, UK
xliii I25 **Garlieston** Dumfries and Galloway, SW Scotland, UK
xliv K6 **Garnagh** Armagh, S Northern Ireland, UK
xlii E8 **Garrabost** Western Isles, NW Scotland, UK
xxxv G6 **Garreg** Gwynedd, NW Wales, UK
xli O8 **Garrigill** Cumbria, NW England, UK
xliv G5 **Garrison** Fermanagh, W Northern Ireland, UK
xliv L3 **Garron Point** *headland* E Northern Ireland, UK
xliii K17 **Garrow** Perth and Kinross, C Scotland, UK
xliii J15 **Garry** ~ C Scotland, UK
xliii G14 **Garry, Loch** ◎ NW Scotland, UK
xliv G14 **Garryvoe** Cork, S Ireland
xli N13 **Garstang** Lancashire, NW England, UK
xl C16 **Garston** Liverpool, NW England, UK
xlii H3 **Garth** Shetland Islands, NE Scotland, UK
xxxv I11 **Garth** Powys, C Wales, UK
xli P3 **Garthorpe** North Lincolnshire, N England, UK
xliii I19 **Gartocharn** West Dunbartonshire, W Scotland, UK
xli X14 **Garton** East Riding of Yorkshire, N England, UK
xli V12 **Garton-on-the-Wolds** East Riding of Yorkshire, N England, UK
xliv K3 **Garvagh** Coleraine, N Northern Ireland, UK
xliii N20 **Garvald** East Lothian, SE Scotland, UK
xliii D19 **Garvard** Argyll and Bute, W Scotland, UK
xlii I11 **Garve** Highland, NW Scotland, UK
xliii E18 **Garvellachs** *island group* W Scotland, UK
xliii J25 **Gatehouse of Fleet** Dumfries and Galloway, SW Scotland, UK
xli V2 **Gateshead** Gateshead, NE England, UK
xli V3 **Gateshead** ◐ *unitary authority* NE England, UK
xl G16 **Gatley** Manchester, NW England, UK
xxxvii T11 **Gatwick** ✕ (London) SE England, UK
xxxix U9 **Gayton** Norfolk, E England, UK
xlii D11 **Geary** Highland, NW Scotland, UK
xxxix P11 **Geddington** Northamptonshire, C England, UK
xxxix S8 **Gedney Drove End** Lincolnshire, E England, UK
xxxix S9 **Gedney Hill** Lincolnshire, E England, UK
xliv G6 **Geevagh** Sligo, N Ireland
xxxv J14 **Gelligaer** Caerphilly, S Wales, UK
xliii K25 **Gelston** Dumfries and Galloway, SW Scotland, UK
xxxvi F11 **Georgeham** Devon, SW England, UK
xxxvii S9 **Gerrards Cross** Buckinghamshire, C England, UK
xliv K2 **Giant's Causeway** *Ir.* Clochán an Aifir. *lava flow* N Northern Ireland, UK
xliii J20 **Giffnock** East Renfrewshire, C Scotland, UK
xliii N20 **Gifford** East Lothian, SE Scotland, UK
xli O12 **Giggleswick** North Yorkshire, N England, UK
xliii E21 **Gigha Island** *island* SW Scotland, UK
xliii F21 **Gigha, Sound of** *strait* W Scotland, UK
xlii A14 **Gighay** *island* NW Scotland, UK
xl K8 **Gilcrux** Cumbria, NW England, UK
xliv K5 **Gilford** Banbridge, SE Northern Ireland, UK
xxxvi M12 **Gillingham** Dorset, S England, UK
xxxvii W10 **Gillingham** Kent, SE England, UK
xli R10 **Gilling West** North Yorkshire, N England, UK
xliv G5 **Gill, Lough** ◎ N Ireland
xliii K17 **Gilmerton** Perth and Kinross, C Scotland, UK
xxxix N11 **Gilmorton** Leicestershire, C England, UK
xli N6 **Gilsland** Cumbria, NW England, UK
xxxv K13 **Gilwern** Monmouthshire, SE Wales, UK
xli P13 **Girdle Ness** *headland* NE Scotland, UK
xliii H23 **Girvan** South Ayrshire, W Scotland, UK
xli P13 **Gisburn** Lancashire, NW England, UK
xxxv K11 **Gladestry** Powys, C Wales, UK
xli U10 **Glaisdale** North Yorkshire, N England, UK
xliii M16 **Glamis** Angus, E Scotland, UK
xxxv H13 **Glanaman** Carmarthenshire, S Wales, UK
xliv D12 **Glanaruddery Mountains** *hill range* W Ireland
xli Q3 **Glanton** Northumberland, N England, UK
xlii H11 **Glascarnoch, Loch** ◎ NW Scotland, UK
xliii M14 **Glascorrie** Aberdeenshire, NE Scotland, UK
xlii G16 **Glasdrum** Argyll and Bute, W Scotland, UK
xliii J20 **Glasgow** City of Glasgow, S Scotland, UK
xliii I20 **Glasgow** ✕ Renfrewshire, W Scotland, UK
xliii J20 **Glasgow, City of** ◐ *unitary authority* C Scotland, UK
xxxv G6 **Glaslyn** ~ NW Wales, UK
xliii I26 **Glasserton** Dumfries and Galloway, SW Scotland, UK
xliii I11 **Glass, Loch** ◎ NW Scotland, UK
xl M13 **Glasson** Lancashire, NW England, UK
xxxvi K11 **Glastonbury** Somerset, SW England, UK
xxxix V13 **Glemsford** Suffolk, E England, UK
xliii E21 **Glenacardoch Point** *headland* W Scotland, UK
xliv D5 **Glenamoy** Mayo, NW Ireland
xliv L3 **Glenariff** Moyle, N Northern Ireland, UK
xliv L3 **Glenarm** Larne, E Northern Ireland, UK
xliv L5 **Glenavy** Lisburn, E Northern Ireland, UK
xliii E16 **Glenbeg** Highland, NW Scotland, UK
xliv C13 **Glenbeigh** Kerry, SW Ireland
xliii L24 **Glencaple** Dumfries and Galloway, SW Scotland, UK
xliii H16 **Glen Coe** *valley* N Scotland, UK
xliv F4 **Glencolumbkille** Donegal, N Ireland
xliii G16 **Glencoe** Highland, NW Scotland, UK
xliv K10 **Glendalough** Wicklow, E Ireland
xliii L18 **Glendevon** Perth and Kinross, C Scotland, UK
xlii I13 **Glendoebeg** Highland, NW Scotland, UK
xliii K18 **Gleneagles** Perth and Kinross, C Scotland, UK
xliii D21 **Glenegedale** Argyll and Bute, W Scotland, UK
xlii F13 **Glenelg** Highland, NW Scotland, UK
xliii L12 **Glenernie** Moray, N Scotland, UK
xliii L18 **Glenfarg** Perth and Kinross, C Scotland, UK
xxxix N9 **Glenfield** Leicestershire, C England, UK
xliii G15 **Glenfinnan** Highland, NW Scotland, UK
xliv J2 **Glengad Head** *headland* N Ireland
xliv D14 **Glengarriff** Cork, S Ireland
xliii M13 **Glenkindie** Aberdeenshire, NE Scotland, UK
xliii H25 **Glenluce** Dumfries and Galloway, SW Scotland, UK
xlii I13 **Glen Mor** *valley* NW Scotland, UK
xliv F8 **Glennamaddy** Galway, W Ireland
xliii M18 **Glenrothes** Fife, E Scotland, UK
xxxix Q4 **Glentham** Lincolnshire, E England, UK
xliv G5 **Glenties** *Ir.* Na Gleannta. Donegal, NW Ireland
xlii I3 **Gletness** Shetland Islands, NE Scotland, UK
xliv D11 **Glin** Limerick, SW Ireland
xxxviii K4 **Glossop** Derbyshire, C England, UK
xxxvi M7 **Gloucester** *hist.* Caer Glou, *Lat.* Glevum. Gloucestershire, C England, UK
xxxvi L7 **Gloucestershire** ◐ *county* C England, UK
xlii I1 **Gloup** Shetland Islands, NE Scotland, UK
xli Q13 **Glusburn** North Yorkshire, N England, UK
xxxv J6 **Glyn Ceiriog** Wrexham, NE Wales, UK
xxxvii U13 **Glyndebourne** East Sussex, SE England, UK
xxxv J6 **Glyndyfrdwy** Denbighshire, N Wales, UK
xxxv I13 **Glyn-Neath** Neath Port Talbot, S Wales, UK
xxxviii J9 **Gnosall** Staffordshire, C England, UK
xliii G21 **Goat Fell** ▲ W Scotland, UK
xxxvii S11 **Godalming** Surrey, SE England, UK
xxxix R11 **Godmanchester** Cambridgeshire, E England, UK
xxxvi L14 **Godmanstone** Dorset, S England, UK
xxxvii Q14 **Godshill** Isle of Wight, S England, UK
xxxvii U11 **Godstone** Surrey, SE England, UK
xxxv H10 **Goginan** Ceredigion, W Wales, UK
xliii H19 **Goil, Loch** *inlet* W Scotland, UK
xliv G2 **Gola Island** *island* N Ireland
xli Q15 **Golcar** Kirklees, N England, UK
xxxv L15 **Goldcliff** Newport, SE Wales, UK
xliv G12 **Golden** Tipperary, S Ireland
xxxvi B6 **Golders Green** Barnet, SE England, UK
xlii K9 **Golspie** Highland, N Scotland, UK
xlii I3 **Gonfirth** Shetland Islands, NE Scotland, UK
xxxvi L7 **Goodrich** Gloucestershire, C England, UK
xxxv C12 **Goodwick** Pembrokeshire, SW Wales, UK
xli U14 **Goole** East Riding of Yorkshire, E England, UK
xxxvi C16 **Goonhavern** Cornwall, SW England, UK
xliii O21 **Gordon** The Borders, S Scotland, UK
xlii K9 **Gordonbush** Highland, N Scotland, UK
xli N11 **Gordonstown** Aberdeenshire, NE Scotland, UK
xliii M20 **Gorebridge** Midlothian, SE Scotland, UK
xliv L11 **Gorey** *Ir.* Guaire. Wexford, SE Ireland
xxxvii X17 **Gorey** Jersey, Channel Islands
xxxvii Q9 **Goring** Oxfordshire, C England, UK
xxxvii T13 **Goring-by-Sea** West Sussex, SE England, UK
xxxix Z9 **Gorleston-on-Sea** Norfolk, E England, UK
xliii C20 **Gorm, Loch** ◎ W Scotland, UK
xxxvi D17 **Gorran Haven** Cornwall, SW England, UK
xxxv G14 **Gorseinon** Swansea, S Wales, UK
xlii M4 **Gorseness** Orkney Islands, N Scotland, UK
xliv F10 **Gort** Galway, W Ireland
xliv H2 **Gortahork** Donegal, N Ireland
xliv F6 **Gorteen** Sligo, N Ireland
xliv I4 **Gortin** Omagh,
xliv I4 **Gortin** Omagh, W Northern Ireland, UK
xxxix R8 **Gosberton** Lincolnshire, E England, UK
xl K10 **Gosforth** Cumbria, NW England, UK
xli V2 **Gosforth** Newcastle upon Tyne, NE England, UK
xxxvii Q13 **Gosport** Hampshire, S England, UK
xxxix N8 **Gotham** Nottinghamshire, C England, UK
xxxvii W11 **Goudhurst** Kent, SE England, UK
xliii H20 **Gourock** Inverclyde, W Scotland, UK
xxxv F14 **Gower** *peninsula* S Wales, UK
xliv H7 **Gowna, Lough** ◎ N Ireland
xliv J11 **Gowran** Kilkenny, SE Ireland
xxxix Q3 **Goxhill** North Lincolnshire, N England, UK
xxxix R12 **Grafham Water** ⊡ E England, UK
xliv J12 **Graiguenamanagh** Kilkenny, SE Ireland
xxxvii X9 **Grain** Kent, SE England, UK
xliii J15 **Grampian Mountains** ▲▲ C Scotland, UK
xxxvi C16 **Grampound** Cornwall, SW England, UK
xlii A12 **Gramsdale** Western Isles, NW Scotland, UK
xliv I7 **Granard** *Ir.* Gránard. Longford, C Ireland
xliv J9 **Grand Canal** *Ir.* An Chanáil Mhór. *canal* C Ireland
xliii K16 **Grandtully** Perth and Kinross, C Scotland, UK
xxxix O12 **Grand Union Canal** *canal* SE England, UK
xliv G5 **Grange** Sligo, N Ireland
xxxvi G5 **Grange Hill** Essex, SE England, UK

◆ Country ● Country Capital ◇ Dependent Territory ○ Dependent Territory Capital ◐ Administrative Region ✕ International Airport ▲ Mountain ▲▲ Mountain Range ◎ Lake ⊡ Reservoir ~ River

xliii K19 **Grangemouth** Falkirk, C Scotland, UK
xl M11 **Grange-over-Sands** Cumbria, NW England, UK
xli Y6 **Grangetown** Redcar and Cleveland, N England, UK
xxxix P8 **Grantham** Lincolnshire, E England, UK
xliii L13 **Grantown-on-Spey** Highland, N Scotland, UK
xliii O20 **Grantshouse** The Borders, S Scotland, UK
xxxix Q4 **Grasby** Lincolnshire, E England, UK
xl M10 **Grasmere** Cumbria, NW England, UK
xli Q12 **Grassington** North Yorkshire, N England, UK
xxxvii O11 **Grateley** Hampshire, S England, UK
xxxviii G10 **Gravels** Shropshire, W England, UK
xxxvii V9 **Gravesend** Kent, SE England, UK
xli N10 **Grayrigg** Cumbria, NW England, UK
xxxvii V9 **Grays** Essex, SE England, UK
xli T9 **Great Ayton** North Yorkshire, N England, UK
xxxvii W8 **Great Baddow** Essex, SE England, UK
xxxvii V6 **Great Bardfield** Essex, SE England, UK
xxxvii S5 **Great Barford** Bedfordshire, C England, UK
xxxvii O10 **Great Bedwyn** Wiltshire, S England, UK
xliii B8 **Great Bernera** *island* NW Scotland, UK
xliv A13 **Great Blasket Island** *Ir.* An Blascaod Mór. *island* SW Ireland
xxxvii R6 **Great Brickhill** Buckinghamshire, C England, UK
xli T10 **Great Broughton** North Yorkshire, N England, UK
xl E17 **Great Budworth** Cheshire, W England, UK
xli W7 **Great Burdon** Darlington, N England, UK
xxxix S5 **Great Carlton** Lincolnshire, E England, UK
xxxvii V6 **Great Chesterford** Essex, SE England, UK
xxxix R3 **Great Coates** North East Lincolnshire, E England, UK
xxxvii V7 **Great Dunmow** Essex, SE England, UK
xl M14 **Great Eccleston** Lancashire, NW England, UK
xxxix S12 **Great Eversden** Cambridgeshire, E England, UK
xxxix Q11 **Great Gidding** Cambridgeshire, E England, UK
xxxix S12 **Great Gransden** Cambridgeshire, E England, UK
xli O14 **Great Harwood** Lancashire, NW England, UK
xxxix V10 **Great Hockham** Norfolk, E England, UK
xxxix Q3 **Great Limber** Lincolnshire, E England, UK
xxxviii J13 **Great Malvern** Worcestershire, W England, UK
xxxvii R8 **Great Missenden** Buckinghamshire, C England, UK
xli O14 **Great Mitton** Lancashire, NW England, UK
xxxvii Y6 **Great Oakley** Essex, SE England, UK
xxxvii T7 **Great Offley** Hertfordshire, SE England, UK
xxxv H4 **Great Ormes Head** *headland* N Wales, UK
xl M7 **Great Orton** Cumbria, NW England, UK
xxxix T10 **Great Ouse** *var.* Ouse. *river*
xxxix P8 **Great Ponton** Lincolnshire, E England, UK
xxxvii O7 **Great Rissington** Gloucestershire, C England, UK
xxxix V8 **Great Ryburgh** Norfolk, E England, UK
xxxvii V6 **Great Sampford** Essex, SE England, UK
xxxvii P9 **Great Shefford** West Berkshire, S England, UK
xxxix T13 **Great Shelford** Cambridgeshire, E England, UK
xxxvii N9 **Great Somerford** Wiltshire, S England, UK
xxxix R12 **Great Staughton** Cambridgeshire, E England, UK
xxxvii Y12 **Greatstone-on-Sea** Kent, SE England, UK
xxxvii P7 **Great Tew** Oxfordshire, C England, UK
xxxvi F12 **Great Torrington** Devon, SW England, UK
xxxvii X9 **Great Wakering** Essex, SE England, UK
xxxvii W7 **Great Waltham** Essex, SE England, UK
xxxvii N11 **Great Wishford** Wiltshire, S England, UK
xxxviii I12 **Great Witley** Worcestershire, W England, UK
xxxix Z9 **Great Yarmouth** *var.* Yarmouth. Norfolk, E England, UK
xxxvii V6 **Great Yeldham** Essex, SE England, UK
xliv J2 **Greencastle** Donegal, N Ireland
xliv L6 **Greencastle** Newry and Mourne, S Northern Ireland, UK
xxxvi A7 **Greenford** Ealing, SE England, UK
xli O5 **Greenhaugh** Northumberland, N England, UK
xli N6 **Greenhead** Northumberland, N England, UK
xliii O21 **Greenlaw** The Borders, S Scotland, UK
xliii K18 **Greenloaning** Perth and Kinross, C Scotland, UK
xliii K22 **Green Lowther** ▲ C Scotland, UK
xliii H19 **Greenock** Inverclyde, W Scotland, UK
xl M11 **Greenodd** Cumbria, NW England, UK
xliv L13 **Greenore Point** *headland* SE Ireland
xxxiv L16 **Greenwich** ◐ *London borough* SE England, UK
xxxvii U9 **Greenwich** *hist.* Grenawic. Greenwich, SE England, UK
xxxix P9 **Greetham** Rutland, C England, UK
xli S16 **Grenoside** Sheffield, N England, UK
xxxv K5 **Gresford** Wrexham, NE Wales, UK
xli Q9 **Greta Bridge** Durham, N England, UK
xliii M24 **Gretna** Dumfries and Galloway, SW Scotland, UK
xliii M24 **Gretna Green** Dumfries and Galloway, SW Scotland, UK
xxxix P10 **Gretton** Northamptonshire, C England, UK
xliv M5 **Greyabbey** Ards, E Northern Ireland, UK
xl M8 **Greystoke** Cumbria, NW England, UK
xliv L10 **Greystones** *Ir.* Na Clocha Liatha. Wicklow, E Ireland
xlii A11 **Griminish Point** *headland* NW Scotland, UK
xlii I2 **Grimister** Shetland Islands, NE Scotland, UK
xxxix S5 **Grimoldby** Lincolnshire, E England, UK
xxxix R3 **Grimsby** *prev.* Great Grimsby. North East Lincolnshire, E England, UK
xxxix U8 **Grimston** Norfolk, E England, UK
xli O13 **Grindleton** Lancashire, NW England, UK
xlii N4 **Gritley** Orkney Islands, N Scotland, UK
xl L11 **Grizebeck** Cumbria, NW England, UK
xliii F21 **Grogport** Argyll and Bute, W Scotland, UK
xlii C10 **Grosebay** Western Isles, NW Scotland, UK
xxxvii Y10 **Grove** Kent, SE England, UK
xxxvi F9 **Grove Park** Lewisham, SE England, UK
xxxvii W16 **Groznez Point** *headland* Jersey, Channel Islands
xlii I9 **Gruids** Highland, NW Scotland, UK
xlii F10 **Gruinard Bay** *bay* NW Scotland, UK
xxxix X13 **Grundisburgh** Suffolk, E England, UK
xlii H4 **Gruting** Shetland Islands, NE Scotland, UK
xxxiv H16 **Guernsey** *off.* Bailiwick of Guernsey. ◇ *UK crown dependency* NW Europe
xxxvii V15 **Guernsey** *island* Channel Islands, NW Europe
xxxvii W12 **Guestling Green** East Sussex, SE England, UK
xxxvii S11 **Guildford** Surrey, SE England, UK
xliii L17 **Guildtown** Perth and Kinross, C Scotland, UK
xxxv K8 **Guilsfield** Powys, C Wales, UK
xli T9 **Guisborough** Redcar and Cleveland, N England, UK
xli R13 **Guiseley** Leeds, N England, UK
xxxix W8 **Guist** Norfolk, E England, UK
xliii N19 **Gullane** East Lothian, SE Scotland, UK
xli U14 **Gunby** East Riding of Yorkshire, N England, UK
xxxvi A8 **Gunnersbury** Hounslow, SE England, UK
xxxvi F15 **Gunnislake** Cornwall, SW England, UK
xlii I4 **Gunnista** Shetland Islands, NE Scotland, UK
xxxvi B17 **Gunwalloe** Cornwall, SW England, UK
xlii I1 **Gutcher** Shetland Islands, NE Scotland, UK
xxxix S9 **Guyhirn** Cambridgeshire, E England, UK
xxxv F4 **Gwalchmai** Isle of Anglesey, NW Wales, UK
xliv F3 **Gweebarra Bay** *Ir.* Béal an Bheara. *inlet* W Ireland
xliv G2 **Gweedore** *Ir.* Gaoth Dobhair. Donegal, NW Ireland
xxxv J6 **Gwyddelwern** Denbighshire, N Wales, UK
xxxv G7 **Gwynedd** ◐ *unitary authority* NW Wales, UK
xxxv H5 **Gwytherin** Conwy, N Wales, UK

H

xxxix Q3 **Habrough** North East Lincolnshire, E England, UK
xxxvii Z10 **Hacklinge** Kent, SE England, UK
xli V10 **Hackness** North Yorkshire, N England, UK
xxxvi E6 **Hackney** Hackney, SE England, UK
xxxiv L16 **Hackney** ◐ *London borough* SE England, UK
xxxvii R8 **Haddenham** Buckinghamshire, C England, UK
xxxix T11 **Haddenham** Cambridgeshire, E England, UK
xliii N19 **Haddington** East Lothian, SE Scotland, UK
xxxix Y10 **Haddiscoe** Norfolk, E England, UK
xxxix W9 **Hadleigh** Essex, SE England, UK
xxxix W13 **Hadleigh** Suffolk, E England, UK
xxxviii I9 **Hadley** Shropshire, W England, UK
xxxviii H9 **Hadnall** Shropshire, W England, UK
xli O6 **Hadrian's Wall** *ancient wall* N England, UK
xxxviii B17 **Hadzor** Worcestershire, W England, UK
xl M6 **Haggbeck** Cumbria, NW England, UK
xxxviii B15 **Hagley** Worcestershire, W England, UK
xliv D10 **Hag's Head** *Ir.* Ceann Caillí. *headland* W Ireland
xxxvii V13 **Hailsham** East Sussex, SE England, UK
xli O17 **Hale** Trafford, NW England, UK
xxxix Y10 **Hales** Norfolk, E England, UK
xxxviii B15 **Halesowen** Dudley, C England, UK
xxxix Y11 **Halesworth** Suffolk, E England, UK
xxxviii M13 **Halford** Warwickshire, C England, UK
xli Q14 **Halifax** Calderdale, N England, UK
xlii L6 **Halkirk** Highland, N Scotland, UK
xli K7 **Halladale** *river* N Scotland, UK
xxxix P10 **Hallaton** Leicestershire, C England, UK
xl L10 **Hall Dunnerdale** Cumbria, NW England, UK
xxxviii J13 **Hallow** Worcestershire, W England, UK
xxxvi H17 **Hallsands** Devon, SW England, UK
xxxvi D14 **Hallworthy** Cornwall, SW England, UK
xli X14 **Halsham** East Riding of Yorkshire, N England, UK
xxxvii W6 **Halstead** Essex, SE England, UK
xxxix R6 **Haltham** Lincolnshire, E England, UK
xl D16 **Halton** ◐ *unitary authority* NW England, UK
xli O6 **Haltwhistle** Northumberland, N England, UK
xxxix Y9 **Halvergate** Norfolk, E England, UK
xxxvi H16 **Halwell** Devon, SW England, UK
xxxvi F13 **Halwill** Devon, SW England, UK
xxxvi A9 **Ham** Richmond upon Thames, SE England, UK
xlii G4 **Ham** Shetland Islands, NE Scotland, UK
xxxvii Q12 **Hambledon** Hampshire, S England, UK
xli T14 **Hambleton** North Yorkshire, N England, UK
xliii J20 **Hamilton** South Lanarkshire, S Scotland, UK
xxxvi A7 **Hammersmith** *London borough capital* Hammersmith and Fulham, SE England, UK
xxxiv K16 **Hammersmith and Fulham** ◐ *London borough* SE England, UK
xlii I3 **Hamnavoe** Shetland Islands, NE Scotland, UK
xlii I4 **Hamnavoe** Shetland Islands, NE Scotland, UK
xxxvii P11 **Hampshire** ◐ *county* S England, UK
xxxvi C6 **Hampstead** Camden, SE England, UK
xli R12 **Hampsthwaite** North Yorkshire, N England, UK
xli U5 **Hamsterley** Durham, N England, UK
xxxvii X11 **Hamstreet** Kent, SE England, UK
xlii G7 **Handa Island** *island* NW Scotland, UK
xxxvii T12 **Handcross** West Sussex, SE England, UK
xl G16 **Handforth** Cheshire, W England, UK
xli S17 **Handsworth** Rotherham, N England, UK
xxxviii J7 **Hanley** City of Stoke-on-Trent, C England, UK
xxxvii Q10 **Hannington** Hampshire, S England, UK
xxxvii R6 **Hanslope** Milton Keynes, C England, UK
xxxvi A7 **Hanwell** Ealing, SE England, UK
xxxix Y8 **Happisburgh** Norfolk, E England, UK
xli P4 **Harbottle** Northumberland, N England, UK
xxxviii M12 **Harbury** Warwickshire, C England, UK
xxxix O8 **Harby** Leicestershire, C England, UK
xxxix P6 **Harby** Nottinghamshire, C England, UK
xli P10 **Hardrow** North Yorkshire, N England, UK
xli S13 **Harewood** Leeds, N England, UK
xxxiv K16 **Haringey** ◐ *London borough* SE England, UK
xxxv G7 **Harlech** Gwynedd, NW Wales, UK
xxxvi B7 **Harlesden** Brent, SE England, UK
xxxix X11 **Harleston** Norfolk, E England, UK
xxxvii U7 **Harlow** Essex, E England, UK
xxxix P6 **Harmston** Lincolnshire, E England, UK
xxxvii N12 **Harnham** Wiltshire, S England, UK
xxxvii S5 **Harold** Bedfordshire, C England, UK
xlii J1 **Haroldswick** Shetland Islands, NE Scotland, UK
xxxvii S7 **Harpenden** Hertfordshire, E England, UK
xxxix U8 **Harpley** Norfolk, E England, UK
xxxvii W10 **Harrietsham** Kent, SE England, UK
xxxix P10 **Harringworth** Northamptonshire, C England, UK
xliii D14 **Harris** Highland, NW Scotland, UK
xlii C10 **Harris** *physical region* NW Scotland, UK
xlii B10 **Harris, Sound of** *strait* NW Scotland, UK
xli S12 **Harrogate** North Yorkshire, N England, UK
xxxvii T8 **Harrow** Harrow, SE England, UK
xxxiv K16 **Harrow** ◐ *London borough* SE England, UK
xxxix S13 **Harston** Cambridgeshire, E England, UK
xli S8 **Hart** Hartlepool, N England, UK
xli Q5 **Hartburn** Northumberland, N England, UK
xxxix V12 **Hartest** Suffolk, E England, UK
xliii L22 **Hart Fell** ▲ SW Scotland, UK
xl E17 **Hartford** Cheshire, C England, UK
xxxviii L6 **Hartington** Derbyshire, C England, UK
xxxvi E12 **Hartland** Devon, SW England, UK
xxxvi D12 **Hartland Point** *headland* SW England, UK
xxxviii A16 **Hartlebury** Worcestershire, W England, UK
xli Y5 **Hartlepool** Hartlepool, N England, UK
xli X5 **Hartlepool** ◐ *unitary authority* NE England, UK
xli T8 **Hartlepool Bay** *bay* N England, UK
xxxvii R10 **Hartley Wintney** Hampshire, S England, UK
xxxvii M7 **Hartpury** Gloucestershire, C England, UK
xxxviii K13 **Harvington** Worcestershire, W England, UK
xxxvii P9 **Harwell** Oxfordshire, C England, UK
xxxvii Y6 **Harwich** Essex, E England, UK
xli V10 **Harwood Dale** North Yorkshire, N England, UK
xxxvii S12 **Haslemere** Surrey, SE England, UK
xli O15 **Haslingden** Lancashire, NW England, UK
xxxvii W13 **Hastings** East Sussex, SE England, UK
xxxvi J12 **Hatch Beauchamp** Somerset, SW England, UK
xli U15 **Hatfield** Doncaster, N England, UK
xxxviii I12 **Hatfield** Herefordshire, W England, UK
xxxvii T7 **Hatfield** Hertfordshire, E England, UK
xxxvii V7 **Hatfield Broad Oak** Essex, SE England, UK
xxxvii W7 **Hatfield Peverel** Essex, SE England, UK
xxxvi F13 **Hatherleigh** Devon, SW England, UK
xxxix N9 **Hathern** Leicestershire, C England, UK
xxxvii N8 **Hatherop** Gloucestershire, C England, UK
xxxviii L5 **Hathersage** Derbyshire, C England, UK
xxxviii L8 **Hatton** Derbyshire, C England, UK
xlii P12 **Hatton** Aberdeenshire, NE Scotland, UK
xxxix W12 **Haughley** Suffolk, E England, UK
xxxviii J9 **Haughton** Staffordshire, C England, UK
xxxvii R13 **Havant** Hampshire, S England, UK
xxxv C13 **Haverfordwest** Pembrokeshire, SW Wales, UK
xxxix U13 **Haverhill** Suffolk, E England, UK
xl K11 **Haverigg** Cumbria, NW England, UK
xxxiv M16 **Havering** ◐ *London borough* SE England, UK
xxxv K5 **Hawarden** Flintshire, N Wales, UK
xli P11 **Hawes** North Yorkshire, N England, UK
xli N9 **Haweswater** ◎ NW England, UK
xliii N22 **Hawick** The Borders, SE Scotland, UK
xxxvii W11 **Hawkhurst** Kent, SE England, UK
xli T11 **Hawnby** North Yorkshire, N England, UK
xli Q14 **Haworth** Bradford, N England, UK
xli T12 **Haxby** York, N England, UK
xxxix O4 **Haxey** North Lincolnshire, N England, UK
xl D15 **Haydock** St Helens, NW England, UK
xli P6 **Haydon Bridge** Northumberland, N England, UK
xxxviii K5 **Hayfield** Derbyshire, C England, UK
xxxvi M16 **Hayle** Cornwall, SW England, UK
xxxvi M16 **Hayle** *river* SW England, UK
xxxv K12 **Hay-on-Wye** Powys, E Wales, UK
xli V13 **Hayton** East Riding of Yorkshire, N England, UK
xxxix O5 **Hayton** Nottinghamshire, C England, UK
xxxvii U12 **Haywards Heath** West Sussex, SE England, UK
xxxvi L13 **Hazelbury Bryan** Dorset, S England, UK
xli P17 **Hazel Grove** Stockport, NW England, UK
xxxvii R8 **Hazlemere** Buckinghamshire, SE England, UK
xxxix U7 **Heacham** Norfolk, E England, UK
xxxvii W11 **Headcorn** Kent, SE England, UK
xliv E8 **Headford** Galway, W Ireland
xxxvii Q8 **Headington** Oxfordshire, S England, UK
xxxvii R11 **Headley** Hampshire, S England, UK
xli R11 **Healey** North Yorkshire, N England, UK
xxxviii M7 **Heanor** Derbyshire, C England, UK
xxxvi H15 **Heathfield** Devon, SW England, UK
xxxvii V12 **Heathfield** East Sussex, SE England, UK
xxxviii C13 **Heath Hayes** Staffordshire, C England, UK
xxxvii S9 **Heathrow** ✕ (London)SE England, UK
xli R6 **Hebburn** South Tyneside, NE England, UK
xli Q14 **Hebden Bridge** Calderdale, N England, UK
xliii C15 **Hebrides, Sea of the** *sea* NW Scotland, UK
xxxix Q7 **Heckington** Lincolnshire, E England, UK
xxxviii C13 **Hednesford** Staffordshire, C England, UK
xli R9 **Heighington** Darlington, N England, UK
xlii I7 **Heilam** Highland, N Scotland, UK
xliii O21 **Heiton** The Borders, S Scotland, UK
xliii H19 **Helensburgh** Argyll and Bute, W Scotland, UK
xli P13 **Hellifield** North Yorkshire, N England, UK
xxxvii V13 **Hellingly** East Sussex, SE England, UK
xxxvii N13 **Helmdon** Northamptonshire, C England, UK
xlii L9 **Helmsdale** Highland, N Scotland, UK
xli K8 **Helmsdale** *river* N Scotland, UK
xli T11 **Helmsley** North Yorkshire, N England, UK
xxxix Q7 **Helpringham** Lincolnshire, E England, UK
xl D17 **Helsby** Cheshire, W England, UK
xxxvi B17 **Helston** Cornwall, SW England, UK
xl M9 **Helvellyn** ▲ NW England, UK
xliv H13 **Helvick Head** *headland* S Ireland
xxxvii S8 **Hemel Hempstead** Hertfordshire, E England, UK
xxxix X10 **Hempnall** Norfolk, E England, UK
xxxix Y9 **Hemsby** Norfolk, E England, UK
xli S15 **Hemsworth** Wakefield, N England, UK
xxxvi B6 **Hendon** Barnet, SE England, UK
xxxvii T12 **Henfield** West Sussex, SE England, UK
xxxviii G8 **Hengoed** Shropshire, W England, UK
xxxviii D17 **Henley-in-Arden** Warwickshire, C England, UK
xxxvii Q9 **Henley-on-Thames** Oxfordshire, C England, UK
xxxv I5 **Henllan** Conwy, N Wales, UK
xxxvii T6 **Henlow** Bedfordshire, C England, UK
xxxvi L12 **Henstridge** Somerset, SW England, UK
xli P4 **Hepple** Northumberland, N England, UK
xxxviii H13 **Hereford** Herefordshire, W England, UK
xxxvi K6 **Herefordshire** ◐ *unitary authority* W England, UK
xliii N20 **Heriot** The Borders, S Scotland, UK
xxxvii W15 **Herm** *island* Channel Islands
xlii J1 **Herma Ness** *headland* NE Scotland, UK
xxxvii P9 **Hermitage** West Berkshire, S England, UK
xliii N23 **Hermitage** The Borders, S Scotland, UK
xxxvii Y10 **Herne Bay** Kent, SE England, UK
xxxvi D9 **Herne Hill** Southwark, SE England, UK
xxxvii Q11 **Herriard** Hampshire, S England, UK
xxxvii V12 **Herstmonceux** East Sussex, SE England, UK
xxxvii T7 **Hertfordshire** ◐ *county* E England, UK
xl M15 **Hesketh Bank** Lancashire, NW England, UK
xli W14 **Hessle** East Riding of Yorkshire, N England, UK
xl B16 **Heswall** Wirral, NW England, UK
xxxix X8 **Hethersett** Norfolk, E England, UK
xl M6 **Hethersgill** Cumbria, NW England, UK
xli W4 **Hetton-le-Hole** Sunderland, NE England, UK
xxxix Y11 **Heveningham** Suffolk, E England, UK
xxxix X8 **Hevingham** Norfolk, E England, UK
xli Q6 **Hexham** Northumberland, N England, UK
xxxvii W8 **Heybridge** Essex, SE England, UK
xlii H2 **Heylor** Shetland Islands, NE Scotland, UK
xl M12 **Heysham** Lancashire, NW England, UK
xxxvi M11 **Heytesbury** Wiltshire, S England, UK
xli P15 **Heywood** Rochdale, NW England, UK
xxxix P4 **Hibaldstow** North Lincolnshire, N England, UK
xxxix Y8 **Hickling** Norfolk, E England, UK
xxxviii M6 **Higham** Derbyshire, C England, UK
xxxvii W9 **Higham** Kent, SE England, UK
xxxvi F13 **Highampton** Devon, SW England, UK
xli O12 **High Bentham** North Yorkshire, N England, UK
xxxvi J11 **Highbridge** Somerset, SW England, UK
xxxvii P10 **Highclere** Hampshire, S England, UK
xxxviii I9 **High Ercall** Shropshire, W England, UK
xxxvi I17 **Higher Town** Isles of Scilly, SW England, UK
xxxvi C6 **Highgate** Haringey, SE England, UK
xxxvii X11 **High Halden** Kent, SE England, UK
xl K8 **High Harrington** Cumbria, NW England, UK
xl M7 **High Hesket** Cumbria, NW England, UK
xli H12 **Highland** ◐ *unitary authority* NW Scotland, UK
xxxviii I11 **Highley** Shropshire, W England, UK
xxxvii V7 **High Roding** Essex, SE England, UK
xliii L24 **Hightae** Dumfries and Galloway, SW Scotland, UK
xxxvi G14 **High Willhays** ▲ SW England, UK
xxxvii O8 **Highworth** Swindon, S England, UK
xxxvii R8 **High Wycombe** *prev.* Chepping Wycombe, Chipping Wycombe. Buckinghamshire, SE England, UK
xxxix V10 **Hilborough** Norfolk, E England, UK
xxxviii J8 **Hilderstone** Staffordshire, C England, UK
xli X12 **Hilderthorpe** East Riding of Yorkshire, N England, UK
xxxiv K16 **Hillingdon** ◐ *London borough* SE England, UK
xxxix U8 **Hillington** Norfolk, E England, UK
xlii K10 **Hill of Fearn** Highland, N Scotland, UK
xliv L5 **Hillsborough** Lisburn, E Northern Ireland, UK
xliii H2 **Hillswick** Shetland Islands, NE Scotland, UK
xliv L6 **Hilltown** Newry and Mourne, S Northern Ireland, UK
xxxvii N9 **Hilmarton** Wiltshire, S England, UK
xxxviii M10 **Hinckley** Leicestershire, C England, UK
xli U9 **Hinderwell** North Yorkshire, N England, UK
xxxvii R11 **Hindhead** Surrey, SE England, UK
xli N16 **Hindley** Wigan, NW England, UK
xxxix W8 **Hindolveston** Norfolk, E England, UK
xxxvi M12 **Hindon** Wiltshire, S England, UK
xxxix W10 **Hingham** Norfolk, E England, UK
xxxix W13 **Hintlesham** Suffolk, E England, UK
xxxv I7 **Hirnant** Powys, C Wales, UK
xxxv I14 **Hirwaun** Rhondda Cynon Taff, S Wales, UK
xxxix S12 **Histon** Cambridgeshire, E England, UK
xxxix W13 **Hitcham** Suffolk, E England, UK
xxxvii T6 **Hitchin** Hertfordshire, E England, UK
xxxvi F9 **Hither Green** Lewisham, SE England, UK
xxxix U10 **Hockwold cum Wilton** Norfolk, E England, UK
xli O13 **Hodder** *river* NW England, UK
xxxvii U8 **Hoddesdon** Hertfordshire, SE England, UK
xxxviii I8 **Hodnet** Shropshire, W England, UK
xxxix S8 **Holbeach** Lincolnshire, E England, UK
xxxix S9 **Holbeach St Johns** Lincolnshire, E England, UK
xxxix S8 **Holbeach St Matthew** Lincolnshire, E England, UK
xxxix S8 **Holbeck Marsh** *physical region* E England, UK
xxxvi D7 **Holborn** Camden, SE England, UK
xxxix X13 **Holbrook** Suffolk, E England, UK
xxxvi I12 **Holcombe Rogus** Devon, SW England, UK
xli O13 **Holden** Lancashire, NW England, UK
xxxvi I11 **Holford** Somerset, SW England, UK
xlii M2 **Holland** Orkney Islands, N Scotland, UK
xxxvii Y7 **Holland-on-Sea** Essex, SE England, UK
xli O2 **Hollandstoun** Orkney Islands, N Scotland, UK
xxxix Y13 **Hollesley** Suffolk, E England, UK
xl I15 **Hollingworth** Tameside, NW England, UK
xxxvi C6 **Holloway** Islington, SE England, UK
xxxvi Y14 **Hollym** East Riding of Yorkshire, N England, UK
xliv E7 **Hollymount** Mayo, NW Ireland
xliv K10 **Hollywood** Wicklow, E Ireland
xliii M23 **Holm** Dumfries and Galloway, SW Scotland, UK
xxxix R10 **Holme** Cambridgeshire, E England, UK
xxxix U7 **Holme next the Sea** Norfolk, E England, UK
xli U13 **Holme on Spalding Moor** East Riding of Yorkshire, N England, UK
xxxviii I6 **Holmes Chapel** Cheshire, W England, UK
xli R15 **Holmfirth** Kirklees, N England, UK
xxxvi E13 **Holsworthy** Devon, SW England, UK
xxxix W7 **Holt** Norfolk, E England, UK
xxxv L5 **Holt** Wrexham, NE Wales, UK
xliv H11 **Holycross** Tipperary, S Ireland
xxxv E4 **Holyhead** *Wel.* Caer Gybi. Isle of Anglesey, NW Wales, UK
xxxv E4 **Holyhead Bay** *bay* NW Wales, UK
xli Q1 **Holy Island** Northumberland, N England, UK
xli Q1 **Holy Island** *island* NE England, UK
xliii H22 **Holy Island** *island* W Scotland, UK
xxxv D4 **Holy Island** *island* NW Wales, UK
xxxvi L13 **Holywell** Dorset, S England, UK
xl A17 **Holywell** Flintshire, N Wales, UK
xliii L24 **Holywood** Dumfries and Galloway, SW Scotland, UK
xxxix W9 **Honingham** Norfolk, E England, UK
xxxix P7 **Honington** Lincolnshire, E England, UK
xxxix V11 **Honington** Suffolk, E England, UK
xxxvi J13 **Honiton** Devon, SW England, UK
xxxvii W9 **Hoo** Kent, SE England, UK
xli U14 **Hook** East Riding of Yorkshire, N England, UK
xxxvii R10 **Hook** Hampshire, S England, UK
xliv J13 **Hook Head** *Ir.* Rinn Duáin. *headland* SE Ireland
xxxvii P6 **Hook Norton** Oxfordshire, C England, UK
xxxviii L5 **Hope** Derbyshire, C England, UK
xxxv K5 **Hope** Flintshire, N Wales, UK
xxxviii H10 **Hope Bowdler** Shropshire, W England, UK
xlii L11 **Hopeman** Moray, N Scotland, UK
xxxvi H15 **Hope's Nose** *headland* SW England, UK
xxxviii H13 **Hope under Dinmore** Herefordshire, W England, UK
xxxix Z10 **Hopton** Norfolk, E England, UK
xli X4 **Horden** Durham, N England, UK
xxxvii U11 **Horley** Surrey, SE England, UK
xli N12 **Hornby** Lancashire, NW England, UK
xxxix R6 **Horncastle** Lincolnshire, E England, UK
xxxvii Q13 **Horndean** Hampshire, S England, UK
xliv H2 **Horn Head** *headland* N Ireland
xxxvii W12 **Horns Cross** East Sussex, SE England, UK
xli X13 **Hornsea** East Riding of Yorkshire, E England, UK
xxxvi C5 **Hornsey** Haringey, SE England, UK
xxxvi F15 **Horrabridge** Devon, SW England, UK
xli Q11 **Horsehouse** North Yorkshire, N England, UK
xliv H9 **Horseleap** Westmeath, C Ireland
xxxix Y8 **Horsey** Norfolk, E England, UK
xxxix X9 **Horsford** Norfolk, E England, UK
xxxvii T12 **Horsham** West Sussex, SE England, UK
xxxvi M8 **Horsley** Gloucestershire, C England, UK
xli P12 **Horton in Ribblesdale** North Yorkshire, N England, UK
xli O15 **Horwich** Bolton, NW England, UK
xlii I5 **Hoswick** Shetland Islands, NE Scotland, UK
xli V14 **Hotham** East Riding of Yorkshire, N England, UK
xlii J2 **Houbie** Shetland Islands, NE Scotland, UK
xl M7 **Houghton** Cumbria, NW England, UK
xli S7 **Houghton-le-Spring** Sunderland, NE England, UK
xxxvi S9 **Hounslow** Hounslow, SE England, UK
xxxiv K16 **Hounslow** ◐ *London borough* SE England, UK
xliii F14 **Hourn, Loch** *inlet* NW Scotland, UK
xlii M4 **Houton** Orkney Islands, N Scotland, UK
xxxvii T13 **Hove** Brighton and Hove, SE England, UK
xxxix X9 **Hoveton** Norfolk, E England, UK
xli U11 **Hovingham** North Yorkshire, N England, UK
xli U14 **Howden** East Riding of Yorkshire, N England, UK
xliii M20 **Howgate** Midlothian, SE Scotland, UK
xli R3 **Howick** Northumberland, N England, UK
xliv L9 **Howth** Dublin, E Ireland
xxxix X11 **Hoxne** Suffolk, E England, UK
xlii L5 **Hoy** *island* N Scotland, UK
xl A16 **Hoylake** Wirral, NW England, UK
xxxix R7 **Hubbert's Bridge** Lincolnshire, E England, UK
xxxix N7 **Hucknall** Nottinghamshire, C England, UK
xli R15 **Huddersfield** Kirklees, N England, UK
xxxvi I17 **HughTown** Isles of Scilly, SW England, UK
xxxvi I12 **Huish Champflower** Somerset, SW England, UK
xli W13 **Hull** *river* N England, UK
xxxvi M9 **Hullavington** Wiltshire, S England, UK
xli W14 **Humber** *estuary* E England, UK
xxxix R4 **Humberston** North East Lincolnshire, E England, UK
xxxix U13 **Hundon** Suffolk, E England, UK
xxxvii P10 **Hungerford** West Berkshire, S England, UK
xliv C14 **Hungry Hill** ▲ SW Ireland
xliii D11 **Hunish, Rubha** *headland* NW Scotland, UK
xli W11 **Hunmanby** North Yorkshire, N England, UK
xxxix U7 **Hunstanton** Norfolk, E England, UK
xxxix R12 **Huntingdon** Cambridgeshire, E England, UK
xxxvi L7 **Huntley** Gloucestershire, C England, UK
xlii N12 **Huntly** Aberdeenshire, NE Scotland, UK
xxxvi J11 **Huntspill** Somerset, SW England, UK
xl H17 **Hurdsfield** Cheshire, C England, UK
xliii I21 **Hurlford** East Ayrshire, W Scotland, UK
xxxvi N13 **Hurn** Dorset, S England, UK
xxxvii P12 **Hursley** Hampshire, S England, UK
xxxvii P11 **Hurstbourne Priors** Hampshire, S England, UK
xxxvii P11 **Hurstbourne Tarrant** Hampshire, S England, UK
xxxvii U12 **Hurstpierpoint** West Sussex, SE England, UK
xli R9 **Hurworth-on-Tees** Darlington, N England, UK
xxxix O11 **Husbands Bosworth** Leicestershire, C England, UK
xlii B9 **Hushinish** Western Isles, NW Scotland, UK
xxxix T5 **Huttoft** Lincolnshire, E England, UK
xli W13 **Hutton Cranswick** East Riding of Yorkshire, N England, UK
xli S10 **Hutton Rudby** North Yorkshire, N England, UK
xl C16 **Huyton Knowsley**, NW England, UK
xli P16 **Hyde** Tameside, NW England, UK
xliii K21 **Hyndford Bridge** South Lanarkshire, C Scotland, UK
xliii B17 **Hynish** Argyll and Bute, W Scotland, UK
xxxvii P13 **Hythe** Hampshire, S England, UK
xxxvii Y11 **Hythe** Kent, SE England, UK

I

xxxvii O13 **Ibsley** Hampshire, S England, UK
xxxviii M9 **Ibstock** Leicestershire, C England, UK
xxxix U11 **Icklingham** Suffolk, E England, UK
xxxvi H15 **Ideford** Devon, SW England, UK
xxxvii O11 **Idmiston** Wiltshire, S England, UK
xxxviii H8 **Ightfield** Shropshire, W England, UK
xxxvii V10 **Ightham** Kent, SE England, UK
xxxvi K12 **Ilchester** Somerset, SW England, UK
xxxvi G6 **Ilford** Redbridge, SE England, UK
xxxvi F11 **Ilfracombe** Devon, SW England, UK
xxxix N7 **Ilkeston** Derbyshire, C England, UK
xli R13 **Ilkley** Bradford, N England, UK
xxxviii L13 **Ilmington** Warwickshire, C England, UK
xxxvi J12 **Ilminster** Somerset, SW England, UK
xxxix R3 **Immingham** North East Lincolnshire, E England, UK
xliv E10 **Inagh** Clare, W Ireland
xliv C13 **Inch** Kerry, SW Ireland
xliii O16 **Inchbraoch** Angus, E Scotland, UK
xliv E14 **Inchigeelagh** Cork, S Ireland
xliii M19 **Inchkeith** *island* C Scotland, UK
xliii G20 **Inchmarnock** *island* W Scotland, UK
xlii H8 **Inchnadamph** Highland, NW Scotland, UK
xxxvii V8 **Ingatestone** Essex, SE England, UK
xxxix V11 **Ingham** Suffolk, E England, UK
xli O11 **Ingleborough** ▲ N England, UK
xli O12 **Ingleton** North Yorkshire, N England, UK
xxxix T6 **Ingoldmells** Lincolnshire, E England, UK
xxxix Q8 **Ingoldsby** Lincolnshire, E England, UK
xliv F14 **Inishannon** Cork, S Ireland
xliv B8 **Inishark** *island* W Ireland
xliv B7 **Inishbofin** *Ir.* Inis Bó Finne. *island* W Ireland
xliv D10 **Inisheer** *var.* Inishere, *Ir.* Inis Oírr. *island* W Ireland
xliv B6 **Inishkea North** *island* NW Ireland
xliv B6 **Inishkea South** *island* NW Ireland
xliv C9 **Inishmaan** *Ir.* Inis Meáin. *island* W Ireland
xliv D9 **Inishmore** *Ir.* Árainn. *island* W Ireland
xliv F5 **Inishmurray** *island* N Ireland
xliv J2 **Inishowen Head** *headland* N Ireland
xliv J1 **Inishtrahull** *Ir.* Inis Trá Tholl. *island* NW Ireland
xliv I1 **Inishtrahull Sound** *sound* N Ireland
xliv B8 **Inishturk** *Ir.* Inis Toirc. *island* W Ireland
xliv J12 **Inistioge** Kilkenny, SE Ireland
xxxviii K12 **Inkberrow** Worcestershire, W England, UK
xliii B17 **Inner Hebrides** *island group* W Scotland, UK
xliii M21 **Innerleithen** The Borders, S Scotland, UK
xlii E12 **Inner Sound** *strait* NW Scotland, UK
xliii J16 **Innerwick** Perth and Kinross, C Scotland, UK
xliv E5 **Inniscrone** Sligo, N Ireland
xliv B14 **Inny** *river* SW Ireland
xlii N12 **Insch** Aberdeenshire, NE Scotland, UK
xliii K14 **Insh** Highland, NW Scotland, UK
xxxvi F12 **Instow** Devon, SW England, UK
xliii I18 **Inversnaid** Stirling, C Scotland, UK
xliv G4 **Inver** Donegal, N Ireland
xliii L17 **Inver** Perth and Kinross, C Scotland, UK
xlii P11 **Inverallochy** Aberdeenshire, NE Scotland, UK
xliv D9 **Inveran** Galway, W Ireland
xlii I9 **Inveran** Highland, NW Scotland, UK
xliii H18 **Inveraray** Argyll and Bute, W Scotland, UK
xlii E12 **Inverarish** Highland, NW Scotland, UK
xliii O15 **Inverbervie** Aberdeenshire, NE Scotland, UK
xlii I9 **Invercassley** Highland, NW Scotland, UK
xliii H20 **Inverclyde** ◐ *unitary authority* C Scotland, UK
xlii L14 **Inverey** Aberdeenshire, NE Scotland, UK
xliii H14 **Invergarry** Highland, NW Scotland, UK
xliii H15 **Invergloy** Highland, NW Scotland, UK
xliii J11 **Invergordon** Highland, N Scotland, UK
xliii M17 **Invergowrie** City of Dundee, E Scotland, UK
xliii F14 **Inverie** Highland, NW Scotland, UK
xliii G13 **Inverinate** Highland, NW Scotland, UK
xliii O16 **Inverkeilor** Angus, E Scotland, UK
xliii L19 **Inverkeithing** Fife, E Scotland, UK
xlii N12 **Inverkeithny** Aberdeenshire, NE Scotland, UK
xliii H20 **Inverkip** Inverclyde, W Scotland, UK
xlii G8 **Inverkirkaig** Highland, NW Scotland, UK
xlii I13 **Invermoriston** Highland, NW Scotland, UK
xlii J12 **Inverness** Highland, N Scotland, UK
xliii H15 **Inverroy** Highland, NW Scotland, UK
xliii G16 **Inversanda** Highland, NW Scotland, UK
xliii I18 **Inveruglas** Argyll and Bute, W Scotland, UK
xlii O13 **Inverurie** Aberdeenshire, NE Scotland, UK
xliii D18 **Iona** *island* W Scotland, UK
xxxviii K7 **Ipstones** Staffordshire, C England, UK
xxxix X13 **Ipswich** *hist.* Gipeswic. Suffolk, E England, UK
xxxix P12 **Irchester** Northamptonshire, C England, UK
xl L8 **Ireby** Cumbria, NW England, UK
xliv F8 **Ireland** *off.* Ireland, *prev.* Ireland, Republic of, *Ir.* Éire. ◆ *republic* NW Europe
xxxvi L9 **Iron Acton** South Gloucestershire, SW England, UK
xxxviii I10 **Ironbridge** The Wrekin, W England, UK
xliv I8 **Iron, Lough** ◎ C Ireland
xliv H6 **Iron Mountains** ▲ N Ireland
xli W11 **Irton** North Yorkshire, N England, UK
xliii I21 **Irvine** North Ayrshire, W Scotland, UK
xliv I5 **Irvinestown** Fermanagh, W Northern Ireland, UK
xlii M4 **Isbister** Orkney Islands, N Scotland, UK
xlii I2 **Isbister** Shetland Islands, NE Scotland, UK
xliii L17 **Isla** *river* C Scotland, UK
xliii D21 **Islay** *island* SW Scotland, UK
xxxix U11 **Isleham** Cambridgeshire, E England, UK
xxxv E4 **Isle of Anglesey** ◐ *unitary authority* NW Wales, UK
xl G12 **Isle of Man** ◇ *UK crown dependency* NW Europe
xliii I26 **Isle of Whithorn** Dumfries and Galloway, SW Scotland, UK
xxxvii P14 **Isle of Wight** ◐ *unitary authority* S England, UK
xxxiv L16 **Islington** ◐ *London borough* SE England, UK
xxxvi D7 **Islington** *London borough capital* Islington, SE England, UK
xxxvii P7 **Islip** Oxfordshire, C England, UK
xxxvii P12 **Itchen** *river* S England, UK
xxxvii S7 **Ivinghoe** Buckinghamshire, C England, UK
xxxvi G16 **Ivybridge** Devon, SW England, UK
xxxix V11 **Ixworth** Suffolk, E England, UK

J

xli W2 **Jarrow** South Tyneside, NE England, UK
xxxvii Y7 **Jaywick** Essex, SE England, UK
xliii O22 **Jedburgh** The Borders, SE Scotland, UK
xxxiv I16 **Jersey** ◇ *UK crown dependency* NW Europe
xxxvii X16 **Jersey** *island* NW Europe
xlii M6 **John o'Groats** Highland, N Scotland, UK
xliii O15 **Johnshaven** Aberdeenshire, NE Scotland, UK
xxxv C13 **Johnston** Pembrokeshire, SW Wales, UK
xliii I20 **Johnstone** Renfrewshire, W Scotland, UK
xliv H11 **Johnstown** Kilkenny, SE Ireland
xliii E19 **Jura** *island* SW Scotland, UK
xliii E20 **Jura, Paps of** ▲ W Scotland, UK

◆ Country
● Country Capital
◇ Dependent Territory
○ Dependent Territory Capital
◐ Administrative Region
✕ International Airport
▲ Mountain
▲ Mountain Range
◎ Lake
▣ Reservoir
river River

xliii *E20* **Jura, Sound of** *strait* W Scotland, UK
xl *G10* **Jurby** West NW Isle of Man

K

xliii *G20* **Kames** Argyll and Bute, W Scotland, UK
xliv *E13* **Kanturk** *Ir.* Ceann Toirc. Cork, SW Ireland
xliii *I18* **Katrine, Loch** ◎ C Scotland, UK
xliv *G6* **Keadew** Roscommon, C Ireland
xliv *K5* **Keady** Armagh, S Northern Ireland, UK
xxxix *R3* **Keelby** Lincolnshire, E England, UK
xxxix *N8* **Kegworth** Leicestershire, C England, UK
xli *Q13* **Keighley** Bradford, N England, UK
xliii *F19* **Keillmore** Argyll and Bute, W Scotland, UK
xliii *K23* **Keir Mill** Dumfries and Galloway, SW Scotland, UK
xlii *M6* **Keiss** Highland, N Scotland, UK
xlii *M11* **Keith** Moray, NE Scotland, UK
xliii *N15* **Keithock** Angus, E Scotland, UK
xli *P10* **Keld** North Yorkshire, N England, UK
xxxix *O6* **Kelham** Nottinghamshire, C England, UK
xliii *N17* **Kellas** Angus, E Scotland, UK
xliv *I12* **Kells** Kilkenny, S Ireland
xliv *J7* **Kells** *Ir.* Ceanannas. Meath, E Ireland
xliii *O21* **Kelso** The Borders, SE Scotland, UK
xliii *L19* **Kelty** Fife, E Scotland, UK
xxxvii *W7* **Kelvedon** Essex, SE England, UK
xxxvii *V8* **Kelvedon Hatch** Essex, SE England, UK
xxxvii *N8* **Kemble** Gloucestershire, C England, UK
xlii *O13* **Kemnay** Aberdeenshire, NE Scotland, UK
xxxviii *J13* **Kempsey** Worcestershire, W England, UK
xxxvii *S6* **Kempston** Bedfordshire, E England, UK
xli *N11* **Kendal** Cumbria, NW England, UK
xxxv *H15* **Kenfig** Bridgend, S Wales, UK
xxxviii *E16* **Kenilworth** Warwickshire, C England, UK
xliii *J24* **Ken, Loch** ◎ SW Scotland, UK
xliv *D14* **Kenmare** *Ir.* Neidín. Kerry, S Ireland
xliv *B14* **Kenmare River** *Ir.* An Ribhéar. *inlet* NE Atlantic Ocean
xliii *K16* **Kenmore** Perth and Kinross, C Scotland, UK
xliii *F20* **Kennacraig** Argyll and Bute, W Scotland, UK
xxxvii *O10* **Kennet** ≈ S England, UK
xxxvii *O10* **Kennet and Avon Canal** *canal* S England, UK
xlii *N12* **Kennethmont** Aberdeenshire, NE Scotland, UK
xxxvi *H14* **Kennford** Devon, SW England, UK
xxxix *W11* **Kenninghall** Norfolk, E England, UK
xxxvii *X11* **Kennington** Kent, SE England, UK
xxxvi *D8* **Kennington** Lambeth, SE England, UK
xlii *D12* **Kensaleyre** Highland, NW Scotland, UK
xxxvi *C7* **Kensington** *London borough capital* Kensington and Chelsea, SE England, UK
xxxiv *K16* **Kensington and Chelsea** *var.* Royal Borough of Kensington and Chelsea. ⬖ *London borough* SE England, UK
xxxvii *W11* **Kent** ⬖ *county* SE England, UK
xl *M10* **Kent** ≈ NW England, UK
xxxix *U11* **Kentford** Suffolk, E England, UK
xxxvi *G11* **Kentisbury** Devon, SW England, UK
xxxvi *C6* **Kentish Town** Camden, SE England, UK
xxxvi *A6* **Kenton** Harrow, SE England, UK
xlii *H6* **Keoldale** Highland, NW Scotland, UK
xliii *F17* **Kerrera** *island* W Scotland, UK
xxxv *J9* **Kerry** Powys, C Wales, UK
xliv *C13* **Kerry** *Ir.* Ciarraí. ⬖ *county* SW Ireland
xliv *C12* **Kerry Head** *headland* SW Ireland
xliv *H4* **Kesh** Fermanagh, W Northern Ireland, UK
xxxix *Z11* **Kessingland** Suffolk, E England, UK
xl *L9* **Keswick** Cumbria, NW England, UK
xxxix *P11* **Kettering** Northamptonshire, C England, UK
xli *P12* **Kettlewell** North Yorkshire, N England, UK
xxxix *Q10* **Ketton** Rutland, C England, UK
xli *X14* **Keyingham** East Riding of Yorkshire, N England, UK
xliv *G6* **Key, Lough** ◎ C Ireland
xxxvi *L10* **Keynsham** Bath and North East Somerset, SW England, UK
xxxix *N8* **Keyworth** Nottinghamshire, C England, UK
xxxix *P10* **Kibworth Harcourt** Leicestershire, C England, UK
xxxvi *F8* **Kidbrooke** Greenwich, SE England, UK
xxxviii *A16* **Kidderminster** Worcestershire, C England, UK
xxxvii *P8* **Kidlington** Oxfordshire, C England, UK
xxxviii *J7* **Kidsgrove** Staffordshire, C England, UK
xxxv *F14* **Kidwelly** Carmarthenshire, S Wales, UK
xli *N4* **Kielder** Northumberland, N England, UK
xli *N5* **Kielder Forest** *forest* N England, UK
xli *O5* **Kielder Water** ◎ N England, UK
xliv *C11* **Kilbaha** Clare, W Ireland
xliii *I20* **Kilbarchan** Renfrewshire, W Scotland, UK
xliv *I9* **Kilbeggan** Westmeath, C Ireland
xliii *F20* **Kilberry** Argyll and Bute, W Scotland, UK
xliii *H21* **Kilbirnie** North Ayrshire, W Scotland, UK
xliii *F22* **Kilbrannan Sound** *sound* W Scotland, UK
xlii *A13* **Kilbride** Argyll and Bute, W Scotland, UK
xliii *F17* **Kilbride** Western Isles, NW Scotland, UK
xliv *F14* **Kilbrittain** Cork, S Ireland
xxxvi *B7* **Kilburn** Brent, SE England, UK
xliii *H21* **Kilchattan** Argyll and Bute, W Scotland, UK
xliii *D19* **Kilchattan** Argyll and Bute, W Scotland, UK
xliii *F22* **Kilchenzie** Argyll and Bute, W Scotland, UK
xliii *E16* **Kilchoan** Highland, NW Scotland, UK
xliii *D20* **Kilchoman** Argyll and Bute, W Scotland, UK
xliv *K9* **Kilcock** *Ir.* Cill Choca. Kildare, E Ireland
xliv *I7* **Kilcogy** Cavan, N Ireland
xliv *F9* **Kilcolgan** Galway, W Ireland
xliv *H12* **Kilcommon** Tipperary, S Ireland
xliv *G9* **Kilconnell** Galway, W Ireland
xliv *H9* **Kilcormac** Offaly, C Ireland
xliii *H19* **Kilcreggan** Argyll and Bute, W Scotland, UK
xliv *C15* **Kilcrohane** Cork, S Ireland
xliv *K10* **Kilcullen** Kildare, E Ireland
xliii *F22* **Kildalloig** Argyll and Bute, W Scotland, UK
xliv *K9* **Kildare** *Ir.* Cill Dara. Kildare, E Ireland
xliv *J9* **Kildare** *Ir.* Cill Dara. ⬖ *county* E Ireland
xlii *K8* **Kildonan** Highland, N Scotland, UK
xliii *G22* **Kildonan** North Ayrshire, W Scotland, UK
xliv *F13* **Kildorrery** Cork, S Ireland
xliv *E10* **Kilfenora** Clare, W Ireland
xliii *G19* **Kilfinan** Argyll and Bute, W Scotland, UK
xliv *D14* **Kilgarvan** Kerry, SW Ireland
xxxv *D14* **Kilgetty** Pembrokeshire, SW Wales, UK
xli *W12* **Kilham** East Riding of Yorkshire, N England, UK
xliv *D11* **Kilkee** *Ir.* Cill Chaoi. Clare, W Ireland
xliv *L6* **Kilkeel** Newry and Mourne, S Northern Ireland, UK
xliv *F6* **Kilkelly** Mayo, NW Ireland
xliv *I11* **Kilkenny** *Ir.* Cill Chainnigh. Kilkenny, S Ireland
xliv *I11* **Kilkenny** *Ir.* Cill Chainnigh. ⬖ *county* S Ireland
xxxvi *E13* **Kilkhampton** Cornwall, SW England, UK
xliv *D9* **Kilkieran** Galway, W Ireland
xliv *C9* **Kilkieran Bay** *Ir.* Cuan Chill Chiaráin. *bay* W Ireland
xliv *D12* **Kilkinlea** Kerry, SW Ireland
xliv *F11* **Kilkishen** Clare, W Ireland
xliv *D14* **Killabunane** Kerry, SW Ireland
xliv *E11* **Killadysert** Clare, W Ireland
xliv *K3* **Killagan** Ballymoney, N Northern Ireland, UK
xliv *E5* **Killala** Mayo, NW Ireland
xliv *E5* **Killala Bay** *Ir.* Cuan Chill Ala. *inlet* NW Ireland
xliv *F11* **Killaloe** Clare, W Ireland
xliv *D13* **Killarney** *Ir.* Cill Airne. Kerry, SW Ireland
xliv *I3* **Killea** Donegal, N Ireland
xliv *I3* **Killea** Londonderry, NW Northern Ireland, UK
xliii *F21* **Killean** Argyll and Bute, W Scotland, UK
xliv *D9* **Killeany** Galway, W Ireland
xliii *J19* **Killearn** Stirling, C Scotland, UK
xliv *K6* **Killeen** Newry and Mourne, S Northern Ireland, UK
xliv *I9* **Killeigh** Offaly, C Ireland
xliv *I11* **Killenaule** Tipperary, S Ireland
xliv *D11* **Killimer** Clare, W Ireland
xliv *G9* **Killimor** Galway, W Ireland
xliii *J17* **Killin** Stirling, C Scotland, UK
xliv *L9* **Killiney Bay** *bay* E Ireland
xliv *F12* **Killmallock** Limerick, SW Ireland
xliv *C13* **Killorglin** Kerry, SW Ireland
xliv *G4* **Killybegs** *Ir.* Na Cealla Beaga. Donegal, NW Ireland
xliv *M5* **Killyleagh** Down, E Northern Ireland, UK
xliv *L10* **Kilmacanoge** Wicklow, E Ireland
xliii *I20* **Kilmacolm** Inverclyde, W Scotland, UK
xliv *H3* **Kilmacrenan** Donegal, N Ireland
xliv *I12* **Kilmaganny** Kilkenny, SE Ireland
xliii *J18* **Kilmahog** Stirling, C Scotland, UK
xliv *E8* **Kilmaine** Mayo, NW Ireland
xlii *D11* **Kilmaluag** Highland, NW Scotland, UK
xliv *I11* **Kilmanagh** Kilkenny, SE Ireland
xliii *M17* **Kilmany** Fife, E Scotland, UK
xliii *I21* **Kilmarnock** East Ayrshire, W Scotland, UK
xliii *F19* **Kilmartin** Argyll and Bute, W Scotland, UK
xliii *I21* **Kilmaurs** East Ayrshire, W Scotland, UK
xliii *F18* **Kilmelford** Argyll and Bute, W Scotland, UK
xliv *L11* **Kilmichael Point** *peninsula* E Ireland
xliv *F13* **Kilmona** Cork, S Ireland
xliv *K13* **Kilmore Quay** Wexford, SE Ireland
xliii *F20* **Kilmory** Argyll and Bute, W Scotland, UK
xliii *D14* **Kilmory** Highland, NW Scotland, UK
xlii *D11* **Kilmuir** Highland, NW Scotland, UK
xlii *J11* **Kilmuir** Highland, NW Scotland, UK
xliv *C9* **Kilmurvy** Galway, W Ireland
xliv *K12* **Kilnamanagh** Wexford, SE Ireland
xliii *F18* **Kilninver** Argyll and Bute, W Scotland, UK
xli *Y15* **Kilnsea** East Riding of Yorkshire, N England, UK
xliii *D19* **Kiloran** Argyll and Bute, W Scotland, UK
xliv *K3* **Kilrea** Coleraine, N Northern Ireland, UK
xliii *N18* **Kilrenny** Fife, E Scotland, UK
xliv *D9* **Kilronan** Galway, W Ireland
xliv *D11* **Kilrush** *Ir.* Cill Rois. Clare, W Ireland
xxxix *N12* **Kilsby** Northamptonshire, C England, UK
xliii *J19* **Kilsyth** North Lanarkshire, C Scotland, UK
xliv *J12* **Kiltealy** Wexford, SE Ireland
xliv *E6* **Kiltimagh** Mayo, NW Ireland
xliv *F9* **Kiltullagh** Galway, W Ireland
xliii *I21* **Kilwinning** North Ayrshire, W Scotland, UK
xxxix *Q12* **Kimbolton** Cambridgeshire, E England, UK
xxxvi *M14* **Kimmeridge** Dorset, S England, UK
xxxvii *T7* **Kimpton** Hertfordshire, SE England, UK
xlii *K8* **Kinbrace** Highland, N Scotland, UK
xliii *K19* **Kincardine** Fife, E Scotland, UK
xlii *J10* **Kincardine** Highland, NW Scotland, UK
xliv *G3* **Kincaslough** Donegal, N Ireland
xliii *K14* **Kincraig** Highland, NW Scotland, UK
xxxviii *K5* **Kinder Scout** ▲ C England, UK
xxxviii *M13* **Kineton** Warwickshire, C England, UK
xliii *H20* **Kingarth** Argyll and Bute, W Scotland, UK
xliii *M19* **Kinghorn** Fife, E Scotland, UK
xliii *N18* **Kingsbarns** Fife, E Scotland, UK
xxxvi *G16* **Kingsbridge** Devon, SW England, UK
xxxviii *L9* **King's Bromley** Staffordshire, C England, UK
xxxviii *D14* **Kingsbury** Warwickshire, C England, UK
xxxvi *A5* **Kingsbury** Brent, SE England, UK
xxxvi *K12* **Kingsbury Episcopi** Somerset, SW England, UK
xxxviii *H14* **Kings Caple** Herefordshire, W England, UK
xxxvii *Q10* **Kingsclere** Hampshire, S England, UK
xxxix *Q10* **King's Cliffe** Northamptonshire, C England, UK
xliv *J7* **Kingscourt** Cavan, N Ireland
xxxvi *H15* **Kingskerswell** Devon, SW England, UK
xxxviii *H12* **Kingsland** Herefordshire, W England, UK
xxxviii *K7* **Kingsley** Staffordshire, C England, UK
xxxix *T9* **King's Lynn** *var.* Bishop's Lynn, Kings Lynn, Lynn, Lynn Regis. Norfolk, E England, UK
xxxvii *V15* **King's Mills** Guernsey, Channel Islands
xliii *M21* **Kings Muir** The Borders, S Scotland, UK
xxxvii *X11* **Kingsnorth** Kent, SE England, UK
xxxviii *C16* **Kings Norton** Birmingham, C England, UK
xxxvi *G13* **King's Nympton** Devon, SW England, UK
xxxvii *P12* **King's Somborne** Hampshire, S England, UK
xxxix *N14* **King's Sutton** Northamptonshire, C England, UK
xxxviii *H14* **Kings Thorn** Herefordshire, W England, UK
xxxix *O12* **Kingsthorpe** Northamptonshire, C England, UK
xlii *M11* **Kingston** Moray, N Scotland, UK
xxxvii *P8* **Kingston Bagpuize** Oxfordshire, C England, UK
xxxviii *H14* **Kingstone** Herefordshire, W England, UK
xxxvi *K10* **Kingston Seymour** North West Somerset, SW England, UK
xli *W14* **Kingston upon Hull** *var.* Hull. City of Kingston upon Hull, E England, UK
xli *W13* **Kingston upon Hull, City of** ⬖ *unitary authority* N England, UK
xxxvii *T9* **Kingston upon Thames** Kingston upon Thames, SE England, UK
xxxiv *K17* **Kingston upon Thames** *var.* Kingston-upon-Thames. ⬖ *London borough* SE England, UK
xxxvi *H16* **Kingswear** Devon, SW England, UK
xxxviii *B15* **Kingswinford** Dudley, C England, UK
xxxvi *L10* **Kingswood** South Gloucestershire, SW England, UK
xxxv *K8* **Kingswood** Powys, C Wales, UK
xxxvii *P11* **Kings Worthy** Hampshire, S England, UK
xxxviii *G13* **Kington** Herefordshire, W England, UK
xliii *J14* **Kingussie** Highland, NW Scotland, UK
xliii *D14* **Kinloch** Highland, NW Scotland, UK
xliii *I18* **Kinlochard** Stirling, C Scotland, UK
xlii *H7* **Kinlochbervie** Highland, NW Scotland, UK
xliii *G15* **Kinlocheil** Highland, NW Scotland, UK
xlii *G11* **Kinlochewe** Highland, NW Scotland, UK
xliii *G14* **Kinloch Hourn** Highland, NW Scotland, UK
xliii *H16* **Kinlochleven** Highland, NW Scotland, UK
xliii *J16* **Kinloch** Rannoch Perth and Kinross, C Scotland, UK
xliii *F17* **Kinlochspelve** Argyll and Bute, W Scotland, UK
xlii *L11* **Kinloss** Moray, N Scotland, UK
xlii *P11* **Kinnaird Head** *var.* Kinnairds Head. *headland* NE Scotland, UK
xliv *J8* **Kinnegad** Westmeath, C Ireland
xxxviii *G9* **Kinnerley** Shropshire, W England, UK
xliv *H10* **Kinnitty** Offaly, C Ireland
xliii *L18* **Kinross** Perth and Kinross, C Scotland, UK
xliv *F14* **Kinsale** *Ir.* Cionn tSáile. Cork, SW Ireland
xliv *H14* **Kinsalebeg** Waterford, S Ireland
xxxvii *P10* **Kintbury** West Berkshire, S England, UK
xlii *O13* **Kintore** Aberdeenshire, NE Scotland, UK
xliii *E21* **Kintour** Argyll and Bute, W Scotland, UK
xliii *F22* **Kintyre** *peninsula* W Scotland, UK
xliii *E23* **Kintyre, Mull of** *headland* W Scotland, UK
xliv *E9* **Kinvarra** Galway, W Ireland
xxxviii *A15* **Kinver** Staffordshire, C England, UK
xli *R10* **Kiplin** North Yorkshire, N England, UK
xli *T14* **Kippax** Leeds, N England, UK
xliii *J19* **Kippen** Stirling, C Scotland, UK
xliv *K9* **Kippure** *Ir.* Cipiúr. l E Ireland
xlii *I4* **Kirkabister** Shetland Islands, NE Scotland, UK
xl *L7* **Kirkbampton** Cumbria, NW England, UK
xliii *L25* **Kirkbean** Dumfries and Galloway, SW Scotland, UK
xl *L7* **Kirkbride** Cumbria, NW England, UK
xli *V12* **Kirkburn** East Riding of Yorkshire, N England, UK
xli *R15* **Kirkburton** Kirklees, N England, UK
xl *C15* **Kirkby** Knowsley, NW England, UK
xxxix *N7* **Kirkby in Ashfield** Nottinghamshire, C England, UK
xli *N11* **Kirkby Lonsdale** Cumbria, NW England, UK
xli *P12* **Kirkby Malham** North Yorkshire, N England, UK
xli *R11* **Kirkby Malzeard** North Yorkshire, N England, UK
xli *U11* **Kirkbymoorside** North Yorkshire, N England, UK
xli *O9* **Kirkby Stephen** Cumbria, NW England, UK
xliii *M19* **Kirkcaldy** Fife, E Scotland, UK
xli *N6* **Kirkcambeck** Cumbria, NW England, UK
xliii *K22* **Kirkconnel** Dumfries and Galloway, SW Scotland, UK
xliii *I25* **Kirkcowan** Dumfries and Galloway, SW Scotland, UK
xliii *J25* **Kirkcudbright** Dumfries and Galloway, S Scotland, UK
xliii *K24* **Kirkgunzeon** Dumfries and Galloway, SW Scotland, UK
xl *M14* **Kirkham** Lancashire, NW England, UK
xli *O7* **Kirkhaugh** Northumberland, N England, UK
xlii *I12* **Kirkhill** Highland, NW Scotland, UK
xlii *A11* **Kirkibost** *island* NW Scotland, UK
xliii *I25* **Kirkinner** Dumfries and Galloway, SW Scotland, UK
xliii *J20* **Kirkintilloch** East Dunbartonshire, C Scotland, UK
xl *K9* **Kirkland** Cumbria, NW England, UK
xliii *K23* **Kirkland** Dumfries and Galloway, SW Scotland, UK
xli *Q14* **Kirklees** ⬖ *unitary authority* N England, UK
xliii *L20* **Kirkliston** City of Edinburgh, SE Scotland, UK
xliii *H26* **Kirkmaiden** Dumfries and Galloway, SW Scotland, UK
xl *G11* **Kirk** Michael W Isle of Man
xliii *L16* **Kirkmichael** Perth and Kinross, C Scotland, UK
xliii *I23* **Kirkmichael** South Ayrshire, W Scotland, UK
xliii *K21* **Kirkmuirhill** South Lanarkshire, C Scotland, UK
xli *P2* **Kirknewton** Northumberland, N England, UK
xliii *G24* **Kirkolm** Dumfries and Galloway, SW Scotland, UK
xli *N8* **Kirkoswald** Cumbria, NW England, UK
xliii *H23* **Kirkoswald** South Ayrshire, W Scotland, UK
xliii *K24* **Kirkpatrick Durham** Dumfries and Galloway, SW Scotland, UK
xl *M9* **Kirkstone Pass** *pass* NW England, UK
xliii *O14* **Kirkton of Durris** Aberdeenshire, NE Scotland, UK
xliii *M16* **Kirkton of Glenisla** Angus, E Scotland, UK
xliii *M16* **Kirkton of Kingoldrum** Angus, E Scotland, UK
xliii *M18* **Kirkton of Largo** Fife, E Scotland, UK
xlii *O13* **Kirkton of Skene** Aberdeenshire, NE Scotland, UK
xlii *M4* **Kirkwall** Orkney Islands, NE Scotland, UK
xli *Q5* **Kirkwhelpington** Northumberland, N England, UK
xliii *M16* **Kirriemuir** Angus, E Scotland, UK
xliii *M24* **Kirtlebridge** Dumfries and Galloway, SW Scotland, UK
xxxvii *P7* **Kirtlington** Oxfordshire, C England, UK
xxxix *S7* **Kirton** Lincolnshire, E England, UK
xxxix *O6* **Kirton** Nottinghamshire, C England, UK
xxxix *X13* **Kirton** Suffolk, E England, UK
xxxix *P4* **Kirton in Lindsey** North Lincolnshire, N England, UK
xxxvii *S10* **Knaphill** Surrey, SE England, UK
xli *T12* **Knaresborough** North Yorkshire, N England, UK
xli *O7* **Knarsdale** Northumberland, N England, UK
xli *S11* **Knayton** North Yorkshire, N England, UK
xxxvii *T7* **Knebworth** Hertfordshire, SE England, UK
xxxix *O6* **Kneesall** Nottinghamshire, C England, UK
xxxv *K10* **Knighton** Powys, E Wales, UK
xliv *B13* **Knightstown** Kerry, SW Ireland
xxxviii *L7* **Kniveton** Derbyshire, C England, UK
xliv *E7* **Knock** Mayo, NW Ireland
xlii *N11* **Knock** Moray, N Scotland, UK
xxlii *D8* **Knock** Western Isles, NW Scotland, UK
xliv *H14* **Knockadoon Head** *headland* S Ireland
xliv *E11* **Knockalough** Clare, W Ireland
xlii *H9* **Knockan** Highland, NW Scotland, UK
xlii *L13* **Knockandhu** Moray, N Scotland, UK
xliv *G8* **Knockcroghery** Roscommon, C Ireland
xliii *G22* **Knockenkelly** North Ayrshire, W Scotland, UK
xliv *F12* **Knocklong** Limerick, SW Ireland
xliv *G13* **Knockmealdown Mountains** ▲▲ S Ireland
xliv *I12* **Knocktopher** Kilkenny, SE Ireland
xli *S14* **Knottingley** Wakefield, N England, UK
xxxviii *D16* **Knowle** Solihull, C England, UK
xl *C15* **Knowsley** Knowsley, NW England, UK
xl *M17* **Knowsley** ⬖ *unitary authority* NW England, UK
xl *F17* **Knutsford** Cheshire, W England, UK
xlii *F13* **Kyleakin** Highland, NW Scotland, UK
xlii *F13* **Kyle of Lochalsh** Highland, N Scotland, UK
xlii *H8* **Kylestrome** Highland, NW Scotland, UK

L

xliv *E11* **Labasheeda** Clare, W Ireland
xxxix *R3* **Laceby** North East Lincolnshire, E England, UK
xxxvi *M10* **Lacock** Wiltshire, S England, UK
xliii *M18* **Ladybank** Fife, E Scotland, UK
xliii *E20* **Lagg** Argyll and Bute, W Scotland, UK
xliii *G22* **Lagg** North Ayrshire, W Scotland, UK
xliii *H14* **Laggan** Highland, NW Scotland, UK
xliii *J14* **Laggan** Highland, NW Scotland, UK
xliii *D21* **Laggan Bay** *bay* W Scotland, UK
xliii *I14* **Laggan, Loch** ◎ NW Scotland, UK
xliv *E9* **Laghtgeorge** Galway, W Ireland
xliv *H4* **Laghy** Donegal, N Ireland
xliv *D10* **Lahinch** Clare, W Ireland
xlii *F10* **Laide** Highland, NW Scotland, UK
xliii *I16* **Laidon, Loch** ◎ C Scotland, UK
xlii *I9* **Lairg** Highland, N Scotland, UK
xl *L9* **Lake District** *physical region* NW England, UK
xxxix *U11* **Lakenheath** Suffolk, E England, UK
xxxv *I15* **Laleston** Bridgend, S Wales, UK
xliv *L8* **Lambay Island** *Ir.* Reachrainn. *island* E Ireland
xxxvii *V11* **Lamberhurst** Kent, SE England, UK
xxxvi *D8* **Lambeth** Lambeth, SE England, UK
xxxiv *L16* **Lambeth** ⬖ *London borough* SE England, UK
xli *O7* **Lambley** Northumberland, N England, UK
xxxvii *O9* **Lambourn** West Berkshire, S England, UK
xliii *G22* **Lamlash** North Ayrshire, W Scotland, UK
xliii *N20* **Lammermuir Hills** ▲▲ SE Scotland, UK
xxxv *G11* **Lampeter** Ceredigion, SW Wales, UK
xxxix *O11* **Lamport** Northamptonshire, C England, UK
xliii *K21* **Lanark** South Lanarkshire, S Scotland, UK
xli *N14* **Lancashire** ⬖ *county* N England, UK
xli *N12* **Lancaster** Lancashire, NW England, UK
xli *R7* **Lanchester** Durham, N England, UK
xxxvi *B17* **Landewednack** Cornwall, SW England, UK
xxxvi *L16* **Land's End** *headland* SW England, UK
xliv *H8* **Lanesborough** Roscommon, C Ireland
xlii *C9* **Langavat, Loch** ◎ NW Scotland, UK
xli *V10* **Langdale End** North Yorkshire, N England, UK
xl *L9* **Langdale Pikes** ▲▲ NW England, UK
xli *P8* **Langdon Beck** Durham, N England, UK
xxxvi *I12* **Langford Budville** Somerset, SW England, UK
xliii *M24* **Langholm** Dumfries and Galloway, S Scotland, UK
xxxvii *U6* **Langley** Essex, SE England, UK
xxxvii *W10* **Langley** Kent, SE England, UK
xxxvi *K12* **Langport** Somerset, SW England, UK
xxxix *R7* **Langrick** Lincolnshire, E England, UK
xli *R16* **Langsett** Barnsley, N England, UK
xli *Q10* **Langthwaite** North Yorkshire, N England, UK
xli *W12* **Langtoft** East Riding of Yorkshire, N England, UK
xli *U12* **Langton** North Yorkshire, N England, UK
xli *N8* **Langwathby** Cumbria, NW England, UK
xxxvi *E16* **Lanreath** Cornwall, SW England, UK
xliv *I10* **Laois** *prev.* Leix, Queen's County. ⬖ *county* C Ireland
xxxvi *G13* **Lapford** Devon, SW England, UK
xliv *J8* **Laracor** Meath, E Ireland
xliv *L10* **Laragh** Wicklow, E Ireland
xliii *K19* **Larbert** Falkirk, C Scotland, UK
xliii *N18* **Largoward** Fife, E Scotland, UK
xliii *H20* **Largs** North Ayrshire, W Scotland, UK
xxxix *T11* **Lark** ≈ E England, UK
xliii *K21* **Larkhall** South Lanarkshire, C Scotland, UK
xliv *M3* **Larne** *Ir.* Latharna. Larne, E Northern Ireland, UK
xliv *L3* **Larne** ⬖ *district* E Northern Ireland, UK
xxxvii *Q11* **Lasham** Hampshire, S England, UK
xli *U10* **Lastingham** North Yorkshire, N England, UK
xlii *L8* **Latheron** Highland, N Scotland, UK
xliii *N21* **Lauder** The Borders, S Scotland, UK
xxxv *E13* **Laugharne** Carmarthenshire, S Wales, UK
xxxvi *E14* **Launceston** *anc.* Dunheved. Cornwall, SW England, UK
xliv *C13* **Laune** ≈ SW Ireland
xliv *C14* **Lauragh** Kerry, SW Ireland
xliii *O15* **Laurencekirk** Aberdeenshire, NE Scotland, UK
xliv *G9* **Laurencetown** Galway, W Ireland
xliii *J25* **Laurieston** Dumfries and Galloway, SW Scotland, UK
xliv *H4* **Lavagh More** ▲ N Ireland
xxxvii *R5* **Lavendon** Milton Keynes, C England, UK
xxxix *V13* **Lavenham** Suffolk, E England, UK
xliii *J17* **Lawers** Perth and Kinross, C Scotland, UK
xlii *D9* **Laxay** Western Isles, NW Scotland, UK
xl *G11* **Laxey** E Isle of Man
xl *G11* **Laxey Bay** *bay* E Isle of Man
xxxix *X11* **Laxfield** Suffolk, E England, UK
xlii *I4* **Laxfirth** Shetland Islands, NE Scotland, UK
xlii *H7* **Laxford Bridge** Highland, NW Scotland, UK
xlii *I3* **Laxo** Shetland Islands, NE Scotland, UK
xli *U14* **Laxton** East Riding of Yorkshire, N England, UK
xxxix *O6* **Laxton** Nottinghamshire, C England, UK
xxxvii *X7* **Layer-de-la-Haye** Essex, SE England, UK
xliv *L8* **Laytown** Meath, E Ireland
xli *N8* **Lazonby** Cumbria, NW England, UK
xxxviii *I15* **Lea** Herefordshire, W England, UK
xliii *M20* **Leadburn** Midlothian, SE Scotland, UK
xxxix *P7* **Leadenham** Lincolnshire, E England, UK
xxxvii *V7* **Leaden Roding** Essex, SE England, UK
xliii *K22* **Leadhills** South Lanarkshire, C Scotland, UK
xliv *C13* **Leane, Lough** *Ir.* Loch Léin. ◎ SW Ireland
xliv *E15* **Leap** Cork, S Ireland
xxxix *Q7* **Leasingham** Lincolnshire, E England, UK
xxxvii *T10* **Leatherhead** Surrey, SE England, UK
xli *U12* **Leavening** North Yorkshire, N England, UK
xliv *G8* **Lecarrow** Roscommon, C Ireland
xxxvii *O8* **Lechlade** Gloucestershire, C England, UK
xlii *H10* **Leckmelm** Highland, NW Scotland, UK
xxxviii *I14* **Ledbury** Herefordshire, W England, UK
xlii *H9* **Ledmore** Highland, NW Scotland, UK
xliv *E14* **Lee** *Ir.* An Laoi. ≈ SW Ireland
xxxviii *H10* **Leebotwood** Shropshire, W England, UK
xli *R14* **Leeds** Leeds, N England, UK
xli *R14* **Leeds** ⬖ *unitary authority* N England, UK
xxxvi *B17* **Leedstown** Cornwall, SW England, UK
xxxviii *K7* **Leek** Staffordshire, C England, UK
xliv *D8* **Leenane** Galway, W Ireland
xxxix *S5* **Legbourne** Lincolnshire, E England, UK
xxxix *N9* **Leicester** *Lat.* Batae Coritanorum. City of Leicester, C England, UK
xxxviii *M9* **Leicester, City of** ⬖ *unitary authority* C England, UK
xxxviii *E13* **Leicestershire** ⬖ *county* C England, UK
xxxvi *M7* **Leigh** Gloucestershire, C England, UK
xxxvii *V11* **Leigh** Kent, SE England, UK
xli *O16* **Leigh** Wigan, NW England, UK
xliv *J11* **Leighlinbridge** Carlow, SE Ireland
xxxvii *S7* **Leighton** Buzzard Bedfordshire, E England, UK
xliv *H11* **Leinster** *Ir.* Cúige Laighean. *province* E Ireland
xliv *J11* **Leinster, Mount** *Ir.* Stua Laighean. ▲ SE Ireland
xxxviii *G11* **Leintwardine** Herefordshire, W England, UK
xlii *I6* **Leirinmore** Highland, NW Scotland, UK
xxxix *Y12* **Leiston** Suffolk, E England, UK
xxxvii *T11* **Leith Hill** *hill* SE England, UK
xliv *G6* **Leitrim** Leitrim, N Ireland
xliv *G6* **Leitrim** *Ir.* Liatroim. ⬖ *county* NW Ireland
xliv *K9* **Leixlip** *Eng.* Salmon Leap, *Ir.* Léim an Bhradáin. Kildare, E Ireland
xxxvi *M16* **Lelant** Cornwall, SW England, UK
xlii *D9* **Lemreway** Western Isles, NW Scotland, UK
xliv *I13* **Lemybrien** Waterford, S Ireland
xliii *H23* **Lendalfoot** South Ayrshire, W Scotland, UK
xliv *I8* **Lene, Lough** ◎ C Ireland
xxxvii *X10* **Lenham** Kent, SE England, UK
xliii *J19* **Lennoxtown** East Dunbartonshire, C Scotland, UK
xliii *J20* **Lenzie** East Dunbartonshire, C Scotland, UK
xxxviii *H13* **Leominster** Herefordshire, W England, UK
xlii *I4* **Lerwick** Shetland Islands, NE Scotland, UK
xlii *N13* **Leslie** Aberdeenshire, NE Scotland, UK
xliii *M18* **Leslie** Fife, E Scotland, UK
xliii *K21* **Lesmahagow** South Lanarkshire, C Scotland, UK
xliii *G25* **Leswalt** Dumfries and Galloway, SW Scotland, UK
xxxvii *T6* **Letchworth** Hertfordshire, E England, UK
xliii *N16* **Letham** Angus, E Scotland, UK
xliv *H3* **Letterkenny** *Ir.* Leitir Ceanainn. Donegal, NW Ireland
xliv *D9* **Lettermore** Galway, W Ireland
xliv *D9* **Lettermullan** Galway, W Ireland
xxxv *C12* **Letterston** Pembrokeshire, SW Wales, UK
xlii *L12* **Lettoch** Highland, NW Scotland, UK
xliii *N17* **Leuchars** Fife, E Scotland, UK
xli *W13* **Leven** East Riding of Yorkshire, N England, UK
xliii *M18* **Leven** Fife, E Scotland, UK
xliii *L18* **Leven, Loch** ◎ C Scotland, UK
xli *N11* **Levens** Cumbria, NW England, UK
xlii *I5* **Levenwick** Shetland Islands, NE Scotland, UK
xlii *B10* **Leverburgh** Western Isles, NW Scotland, UK
xxxvi *E14* **Lewannick** Cornwall, SW England, UK
xxxvii *U13* **Lewes** East Sussex, SE England, UK
xlii *E6* **Lewis, Butt of** *headland* NW Scotland, UK
xxxiv *L16* **Lewisham** ⬖ *London borough* SE England, UK
xxxvi *E8* **Lewisham** Lewisham, SE England, UK
xlii *C8* **Lewis, Isle of** *island* NW Scotland, UK
xxxvi *F14* **Lewtrenchard** Devon, SW England, UK
xli *Q11* **Leyburn** North Yorkshire, N England, UK
xli *N15* **Leyland** Lancashire, NW England, UK
xxxvii *Y10* **Leysdown-on-sea** Kent, SE England, UK
xxxvi *E6* **Leyton** Waltham Forest, SE England, UK
xxxvi *E6* **Leytonstone** Waltham Forest, SE England, UK
xlii *M11* **Lhanbryde** Moray, N Scotland, UK
xlii *G11* **Liathach** ▲ NW Scotland, UK
xxxv *I12* **Libanus** Powys, C Wales, UK
xliii *L21* **Libberton** South Lanarkshire, C Scotland, UK
xxxviii *C13* **Lichfield** Staffordshire, C England, UK
xxxix *U12* **Lidgate** Suffolk, E England, UK
xliv *K9* **Liffey** ≈ E Ireland
xliv *I3* **Lifford** *Ir.* Leifear. Donegal, NW Ireland
xxxvi *F14* **Lifton** Devon, SW England, UK
xxxvi *B16* **Ligger Bay** *var.* Perran Bay. *bay* SW England, UK
xliii *N22* **Lilliesleaf** The Borders, S Scotland, UK
xliv *J3* **Limavady** *Ir.* Léim an Mhadaidh. Limavady, NW Northern Ireland, UK
xliv *J3* **Limavady** ⬖ *district* N Northern Ireland, UK
xliv *F11* **Limerick** *Ir.* Luimneach. Limerick, SW Ireland
xliv *E12* **Limerick** *Ir.* Luimneach. ⬖ *county* SW Ireland
xxxix *Q6* **Lincoln** *anc.* Lindum, Lindum Colonia. Lincolnshire, E England, UK
xxxix *Q6* **Lincoln Edge** *ridge* E England, UK
xxxix *Q6* **Lincolnshire** ⬖ *county* E England, UK
xxxviii *G12* **Lingen** Herefordshire, W England, UK
xxxvii *U11* **Lingfield** Surrey, SE England, UK
xlii *L4* **Linksness** Orkney Islands, N Scotland, UK
xliii *L20* **Linlithgow** West Lothian, SE Scotland, UK
xliii *F16* **Linnhe, Loch** *inlet* W Scotland, UK
xxxvii *R6* **Linslade** Bedfordshire, C England, UK
xxxix *T13* **Linton** Cambridgeshire, E England, UK
xli *Q12* **Linton** North Yorkshire, N England, UK
xxxvii *R12* **Liphook** Hampshire, S England, UK
xliv *I5* **Lisbellaw** Fermanagh, W Northern Ireland, UK
xliv *L5* **Lisburn** *Ir.* Lios na gCearrbhach. Lisburn, E Northern Ireland, UK
xliv *L5* **Lisburn** ⬖ *district* E Northern Ireland, UK
xliv *D10* **Liscannor Bay** *Ir.* Bá Lios Ceannúir. *inlet* W Ireland
xliv *D7* **Liscarney** Mayo, NW Ireland
xliv *F12* **Liscarroll** Cork, S Ireland
xliv *E10* **Lisdoonvarna** Clare, W Ireland
xxxvi *E15* **Liskeard** Cornwall, SW England, UK
xliv *H13* **Lismore** *Ir.* Lios Mór. Waterford, S Ireland
xliv *I5* **Lisnaskea** Fermanagh, W Northern Ireland, UK
xxxvii *R12* **Liss** Hampshire, S England, UK
xliv *D12* **Listowel** *Ir.* Lios Tuathail. Kerry, SW Ireland
xxxix *V9* **Litcham** Norfolk, E England, UK
xl *M16* **Litherland** Sefton, NW England, UK
xli *P15* **Littleborough** Rochdale, NW England, UK
xxxix *Q9* **Little Bytham** Lincolnshire, E England, UK
xxxvi *G13* **Little Dart** ≈ SW England, UK
xxxix *T10* **Little Downham** Cambridgeshire, E England, UK
xlii *K9* **Littleferry** Highland, N Scotland, UK
xxxvii *S13* **Littlehampton** West Sussex, SE England, UK
xl *F14* **Little Lever** Bolton, NW England, UK
xlii *C11* **Little Minch, The** *strait* NW Scotland, UK
xxxvii *S8* **Little Missenden** Buckinghamshire, C England, UK
xxxix *U11* **Little Ouse** ≈ E England, UK
xxxix *T10* **Littleport** Cambridgeshire, E England, UK
xxxix *V8* **Little** Walsingham Norfolk, E England, UK
xxxvi *L14* **Litton Cheney** Dorset, S England, UK
xl *B16* **Liverpool** Liverpool, NW England, UK
xl *M16* **Liverpool** ⬖ *unitary authority* NW England, UK
xl *L16* **Liverpool Bay** *bay* England/Wales, UK
xliii *L20* **Livingston** West Lothian, C Scotland, UK
xxxvi *B17* **Lizard** Cornwall, SW England, UK
xxxvi *B17* **Lizard Point** *headland* SW England, UK
xxxv *G7* **Llanaber** Gwynedd, NW Wales, UK
xxxv *F6* **Llanaelhaearn** Gwynedd, NW Wales, UK
xxxv *J7* **Llanarmon Dyffryn Ceiriog** Wrexham, NE Wales, UK
xxxv *F11* **Llanarth** Ceredigion, W Wales, UK
xxxv *J4* **Llanasa** Flintshire, N Wales, UK
xxxv *J10* **Llanbadarn Fynydd** Powys, C Wales, UK
xxxv *G7* **Llanbedr** Gwynedd, NW Wales, UK
xxxv *E7* **Llanbedrog** Gwynedd, NW Wales, UK
xxxv *G5* **Llanberis** Gwynedd, NW Wales, UK
xxxv *J10* **Llanbister** Powys, C Wales, UK
xxxv *E13* **Llanboidy** Carmarthenshire, S Wales, UK
xxxv *I8* **Llanbrynmair** Powys, C Wales, UK
xxxv *G13* **Llanddarog** Carmarthenshire, S Wales, UK
xxxv *I6* **Llandderfel** Gwynedd, NW Wales, UK
xxxv *G11* **Llanddewi-Brefi** Ceredigion, W Wales, UK
xxxv *J10* **Llanddewi Ystradenni** Powys, C Wales, UK
xxxv *F13* **Llandefaelog** Carmarthenshire, S Wales, UK
xxxv *G13* **Llandeilo** Carmarthenshire, S Wales, UK
xxxv *I9* **Llandinam** Powys, C Wales, UK
xxxv *H12* **Llandovery** Carmarthenshire, S Wales, UK
xxxv *I6* **Llandrillo** Denbighshire, N Wales, UK
xxxv *J11* **Llandrindod Wells** Powys, E Wales, UK
xxxv *H4* **Llandudno** Conwy, N Wales, UK
xxxv *F5* **Llandwrog** Gwynedd, NW Wales, UK
xxxv *G13* **Llandybie** Carmarthenshire, S Wales, UK
xxxv *J9* **Llandyssil** Powys, C Wales, UK
xxxv *F12* **Llandysul** Ceredigion, W Wales, UK
xxxv *G8* **Llanegryn** Gwynedd, NW Wales, UK
xxxv *J6* **Llanelidan** Denbighshire, N Wales, UK
xxxv *G14* **Llanelli** *prev.* Llanelly. Carmarthenshire, SW Wales, UK
xxxv *H7* **Llanelltyd** Gwynedd, NW Wales, UK
xxxv *F4* **Llanerchymedd** Isle of Anglesey, NW Wales, UK
xxxv *E4* **Llanfachraeth** Isle of Anglesey, NW Wales, UK
xxxv *E4* **Llanfaelog** Isle of Anglesey, NW Wales, UK
xxxv *E4* **Llanfaethlu** Isle of Anglesey, NW Wales, UK
xxxv *J8* **Llanfair Caereinion** Powys, C Wales, UK
xxxv *G11* **Llanfair Clydogau** Ceredigion, W Wales, UK
xxxv *G4* **Llanfairfechan** Conwy, N Wales, UK
xxxv *I5* **Llanfair Talhaiarn** Conwy, N Wales, UK
xxxv *J7* **Llanfechain** Powys, C Wales, UK
xxxv *I12* **Llanfihangel Nant Bran** Powys, C Wales, UK
xxxv *J11* **Llanfihangel-nant-Melan** Powys, C Wales, UK
xxxv *J7* **Llanfihangel-yng-Ngwynfa** Powys, C Wales, UK
xxxv *G8* **Llanfihangel-y-pennant** Gwynedd, NW Wales, UK
xxxv *E12* **Llanfrynach** Pembrokeshire, SW Wales, UK
xxxv *J7* **Llanfyllin** Powys, C Wales, UK
xxxv *G12* **Llanfynydd** Carmarthenshire, S Wales, UK
xxxv *J12* **Llanfyrnach** Powys, C Wales, UK
xxxv *I8* **Llangadfan** Powys, C Wales, UK
xxxv *H12* **Llangadog** Carmarthenshire, S Wales, UK
xxxv *F4* **Llangefni** Isle of Anglesey, NW Wales, UK
xxxv *H5* **Llangernyw** Conwy, N Wales, UK
xxxv *E13* **Llanglydwen** Carmarthenshire, S Wales, UK
xxxv *G4* **Llangoed** Isle of Anglesey, NW Wales, UK
xxxv *J6* **Llangollen** Denbighshire, NE Wales, UK
xxxv *J12* **Llangorse** Powys, C Wales, UK
xxxv *I7* **Llangower** Gwynedd, NW Wales, UK
xxxv *E11* **Llangranog** Ceredigion, W Wales, UK
xxxv *K10* **Llangunllo** Powys, C Wales, UK
xxxv *I10* **Llangurig** Powys, C Wales, UK
xxxv *I6* **Llangwm** Conwy, N Wales, UK
xxxv *G11* **Llangybi** Ceredigion, W Wales, UK
xxxv *J13* **Llangynidr** Powys, C Wales, UK
xxxv *E13* **Llangynin** Carmarthenshire, S Wales, UK
xxxv *J7* **Llangynog** Powys, C Wales, UK
xxxv *I15* **Llanharan** Rhondda Cynon Taff, S Wales, UK
xxxv *I15* **Llanharry** Rhondda Cynon Taff, S Wales, UK
xxxv *I9* **Llanidloes** Powys, C Wales, UK
xxxv *G10* **Llanilar** Ceredigion, W Wales, UK
xxxv *J8* **Llanllugan** Powys, C Wales, UK
xxxv *F6* **Llanllyfni** Gwynedd, NW Wales, UK
xxxv *F14* **Llanmadoc** Swansea, S Wales, UK
xxxv *G13* **Llannon** Carmarthenshire, S Wales, UK
xxxv *G10* **Llanon** Ceredigion, W Wales, UK
xxxv *J5* **Llanrhaeadr** Denbighshire, N Wales, UK
xxxv *J7* **Llanrhaeadr-ym-Mochnant** Powys, C Wales, UK
xxxv *G14* **Llanrhidian** Swansea, S Wales, UK
xxxv *G10* **Llanrhystud** Ceredigion, W Wales, UK
xxxv *C12* **Llanrian** Pembrokeshire, SW Wales, UK
xxxv *H5* **Llanrwst** Conwy, N Wales, UK
xxxv *I5* **Llansannan** Conwy, N Wales, UK
xxxv *G12* **Llansawel** Carmarthenshire, S Wales, UK
xxxv *J7* **Llansilin** Powys, C Wales, UK
xxxv *F13* **Llansteffan** Carmarthenshire, S Wales, UK
xxxv *K12* **Llanthony** Monmouthshire, SE Wales, UK
xxxv *L14* **Llantrisant** Monmouthshire, SE Wales, UK
xxxv *J15* **Llantrisant** Rhondda Cynon Taff, S Wales, UK

◆ Country ● Country Capital ◇ Dependent Territory ○ Dependent Territory Capital ⬖ Administrative Region ✈ International Airport ▲ Mountain ▲▲ Mountain Range ◎ Lake ⊠ Reservoir ≈ River

xxxv *I16* **Llantwit Major** The Vale of Glamorgan, S Wales, UK
xxxv *I7* **Llanuwchllyn** Gwynedd, NW Wales, UK
xxxv *K13* **Llanvihangel Gobion** Monmouthshire, SE Wales, UK
xxxv *I7* **Llanwddyn** Powys, C Wales, UK
xxxv *F11* **Llanwenog** Ceredigion, W Wales, UK
xxxv *I9* **Llanwnog** Powys, C Wales, UK
xxxv *H12* **Llanwrda** Carmarthenshire, S Wales, UK
xxxv *H8* **Llanwrin** Powys, C Wales, UK
xxxv *I10* **Llanwrthwl** Powys, C Wales, UK
xxxv *I11* **Llanwrtyd Wells** Powys, C Wales, UK
xxxv *G12* **Llanybydder** Carmarthenshire, S Wales, UK
xxxv *D13* **Llanycefn** Pembrokeshire, SW Wales, UK
xxxv *D12* **Llanychaer Bridge** Pembrokeshire, SW Wales, UK
xxxv *I7* **Llanymawddwy** Gwynedd, NW Wales, UK
xxxv *D13* **Llawhaden** Pembrokeshire, SW Wales, UK
xxxv *G10* **Lledrod** Ceredigion, W Wales, UK
xxxv *E7* **Lleyn Peninsula** *peninsula* NW Wales, UK
xxxv *F6* **Llithfaen** Gwynedd, NW Wales, UK
xxxv *J4* **Lloc** Flintshire, N Wales, UK
xxxv *F11* **Llwyndafydd** Ceredigion, W Wales, UK
xxxv *G8* **Llwyngwril** Gwynedd, NW Wales, UK
xxxv *J12* **Llyswen** Powys, C Wales, UK
xliii *M20* **Loanhead** Midlothian, SE Scotland, UK
xliii *F15* **Lochailort** Highland, NW Scotland, UK
xliii *F16* **Lochaline** Highland, NW Scotland, UK
xliii *H25* **Lochans** Dumfries and Galloway, SW Scotland, UK
xliii *L24* **Locharbriggs** Dumfries and Galloway, SW Scotland, UK
xliii *H17* **Lochawe** Argyll and Bute, W Scotland, UK
xlii *A13* **Lochboisdale** Western Isles, NW Scotland, UK
xliii *E17* **Lochbuie** Argyll and Bute, W Scotland, UK
xlii *F12* **Lochcarron** Highland, NW Scotland, UK
xliii *M22* **Lochcraig Head** ▲ S Scotland, UK
xliii *F17* **Lochdon** Argyll and Bute, W Scotland, UK
xlii *H10* **Lochdrum** Highland, NW Scotland, UK
xliii *J17* **Lochearnhead** Stirling, C Scotland, UK
xlii *J12* **Lochend** Highland, NW Scotland, UK
xliii *M19* **Lochgelly** Fife, E Scotland, UK
xliii *G19* **Lochgilphead** Argyll and Bute, W Scotland, UK
xliii *H18* **Lochgoilhead** Argyll and Bute, W Scotland, UK
xlii *G8* **Lochinver** Highland, N Scotland, UK
xlii *H11* **Lochluichart** Highland, NW Scotland, UK
xliii *L24* **Lochmaben** Dumfries and Galloway, SW Scotland, UK
xlii *B11* **Lochmaddy** Western Isles, NW Scotland, UK
xliii *M14* **Lochnagar** ▲ C Scotland, UK
xliii *G21* **Lochranza** North Ayrshire, W Scotland, UK
xliii *I21* **Lochwinnoch** Renfrewshire, W Scotland, UK
xliii *H14* **Lochy, Loch** ◎ N Scotland, UK
xliii *L24* **Lockerbie** Dumfries and Galloway, S Scotland, UK
xxxix *Y10* **Loddon** Norfolk, E England, UK
xli *U9* **Loftus** Redcar and Cleveland, N England, UK
xliii *N14* **Logie Coldstone** Aberdeenshire, NE Scotland, UK
xxxv *E13* **Login** Carmarthenshire, S Wales, UK
xliii *I19* **Lomond, Loch** ◎ C Scotland, UK
xxxvii *U9* **London** *anc.* Augusta, ***Lat.*** Londinium. ● (UK) SE England, UK
xxxvi *G7* **London City** ✈ City of London, SE England, UK
xxxiv *L16* **London, City of** ⬖ *London borough* SE England, UK
xliv *I3* **Londonderry** ***var.*** Derry, ***Ir.*** Doire. Londonderry, NW Northern Ireland, UK
xliv *I3* **Londonderry** ⬖ *district* NW Northern Ireland, UK
xxxvi *K10* **Long Ashton** North West Somerset, SW England, UK
xli *V2* **Longbenton** North Tyneside, NE England, UK
xxxviii *C16* **Longbridge** Birmingham, C England, UK
xxxvi *M11* **Longbridge Deverill** Wiltshire, S England, UK
xxxix *O12* **Long Buckby** Northamptonshire, C England, UK
xxxvii *Q8* **Long Crendon** Buckinghamshire, C England, UK
xxxix *N8* **Long Eaton** Derbyshire, C England, UK
xliv *H7* **Longford** ***Ir.*** An Longfort. Longford, C Ireland
xxxviii *M11* **Longford** Coventry, C England, UK
xxxviii *L8* **Longford** Derbyshire, C England, UK
xliv *H7* **Longford** ***Ir.*** An Longfort. ⬖ *county* C Ireland
xliii *O20* **Longformacus** The Borders, S Scotland, UK
xli *Q4* **Longframlington** Northumberland, N England, UK
xlii *M5* **Longhope** Orkney Islands, N Scotland, UK
xli *Q4* **Longhorsley** Northumberland, N England, UK
xli *R3* **Longhoughton** Northumberland, N England, UK
xliii *H19* **Long, Loch** *inlet* W Scotland, UK
xli *T13* **Long Marston** North Yorkshire, N England, UK
xxxviii *L13* **Long Marston** Warwickshire, C England, UK
xxxix *V13* **Long Melford** Suffolk, E England, UK
xxxviii *H10* **Long Mynd, The** *hill range* W England, UK
xxxvi *L7* **Longney** Gloucestershire, C England, UK
xliii *N19* **Longniddry** East Lothian, SE Scotland, UK
xxxviii *K6* **Longnor** Staffordshire, C England, UK
xli *P12* **Long Preston** North Yorkshire, N England, UK
xli *N14* **Longridge** Lancashire, NW England, UK
xlii *P12* **Longside** Aberdeenshire, NE Scotland, UK
xxxix *X10* **Long Stratton** Norfolk, E England, UK
xxxix *S8* **Long Sutton** Lincolnshire, E England, UK
xxxvi *K12* **Long Sutton** Somerset, SW England, UK
xli *N14* **Longton** Lancashire, NW England, UK
xl *M6* **Longtown** Cumbria, NW England, UK
xxxviii *G14* **Longtown** Herefordshire, W England, UK
xliv *C11* **Loop Head** ***Ir.*** Ceann Léime. *headland* W Ireland
xxxvii *W10* **Loose** Kent, SE England, UK
xliii *E18* **Lorn, Firth of** *inlet* W Scotland, UK
xlii *L11* **Lossiemouth** Moray, NE Scotland, UK
xxxvi *D16* **Lostwithiel** Cornwall, SW England, UK
xlii *K9* **Lothmore** Highland, N Scotland, UK
xxxix *N9* **Loughborough** Leicestershire, C England, UK
xliv *L5* **Loughbrickland** Banbridge, SE Northern Ireland, UK
xliv *F9* **Loughrea** ***Ir.*** Baile Locha Riach. Galway, W Ireland
xliv *C7* **Louisburgh** Mayo, NW Ireland
xliv *K7* **Louth** Louth, NE Ireland
xxxix *S5* **Louth** Lincolnshire, E England, UK
xliv *K7* **Louth** ***Ir.*** Lú. ⬖ *county* NE Ireland
xliv *K5* **Louthgall** Armagh, S Northern Ireland, UK
xxxix *O7* **Lowdham** Nottinghamshire, C England, UK
xlii *F11* **Lower Diabaig** Highland, NW Scotland, UK
xxxvii *P7* **Lower Heyford** Oxfordshire, C England, UK
xliv *I5* **Lower Lough Erne** ◎ SW Northern Ireland, UK
xxxix *Z10* **Lowestoft** Suffolk, E England, UK
xl *K9* **Loweswater** Cumbria, NW England, UK
xli *N10* **Lowgill** Cumbria, NW England, UK
xl *M7* **Low Hesket** Cumbria, NW England, UK
xli *Q2* **Lowick** Northumberland, N England, UK
xlii *I7* **Loyal, Loch** ◎ N Scotland, UK
xliii *G14* **Loyne, Loch** ◎ NW Scotland, UK
xlii *H9* **Lubcroy** Highland, NW Scotland, UK
xliii *J18* **Lubnaig, Loch** ◎ C Scotland, UK
xliv *K9* **Lucan** ***Ir.*** Leamhcán. Dublin, E Ireland
xxxvi *H11* **Luccombe** Somerset, SW England, UK
xliii *H26* **Luce Bay** *inlet* SW Scotland, UK
xxxix *R4* **Ludborough** Lincolnshire, E England, UK
xxxix *R4* **Ludford** Lincolnshire, E England, UK
xxxvii *O11* **Ludgershall** Wiltshire, S England, UK
xxxvi *A17* **Ludgvan** Cornwall, SW England, UK
xxxix *Y9* **Ludham** Norfolk, E England, UK
xxxviii *H11* **Ludlow** Shropshire, W England, UK
xliv *K10* **Lugnaquillia Mountain** ***Ir.*** Log na Coille. ▲ E Ireland
xlii *H11* **Luichart, Loch** ◎ NW Scotland, UK
xliii *F18* **Luing** *island* W Scotland, UK
xliv *I12* **Lukeswell** Kilkenny, SE Ireland
xliv *J9* **Lullymore** Kildare, E Ireland
xliii *N14* **Lumphanan** Aberdeenshire, NE Scotland, UK
xlii *N13* **Lumsden** Aberdeenshire, NE Scotland, UK
xliii *O16* **Lunan Bay** *bay* E Scotland, UK
xli *V13* **Lund** East Riding of Yorkshire, N England, UK
xxxvi *D11* **Lundy** *island* SW England, UK
xli *N10* **Lune** ≈ NW England, UK
xlii *I3* **Lunna** Shetland Islands, NE Scotland, UK
xliv *L5* **Lurgan** ***Ir.*** An Lorgain. Craigavon, S Northern Ireland, UK
xxxvii *S12* **Lurgashall** West Sussex, SE England, UK
xliv *L8* **Lusk** Dublin, E Ireland
xlii *C10* **Luskentyre** Western Isles, NW Scotland, UK
xliii *I19* **Luss** Argyll and Bute, W Scotland, UK
xlii *D12* **Lusta** Highland, NW Scotland, UK
xxxvi *H14* **Lustleigh** Devon, SW England, UK
xxxvii *T7* **Luton** Luton, E England, UK
xxxvii *S7* **Luton** ⬖ *unitary authority* C England, UK
xxxvii *T7* **Luton** ✈ (London) Luton, SE England, UK
xxxix *N11* **Lutterworth** Leicestershire, C England, UK
xxxix *S8* **Lutton** Lincolnshire, E England, UK
xxxix *R10* **Lutton** Northamptonshire, C England, UK
xxxvi *H11* **Luxborough** Somerset, SW England, UK
xlii *L8* **Lybster** Highland, N Scotland, UK
xxxvii *X12* **Lydd** Kent, SE England, UK
xxxvi *F14* **Lydford** Devon, SW England, UK
xxxviii *G11* **Lydham** Shropshire, W England, UK
xxxvi *L8* **Lydney** Gloucestershire, C England, UK
xxxvi *J15* **Lyme Bay** *bay* S England, UK
xxxvi *K14* **Lyme Regis** Dorset, S England, UK
xxxvii *Y11* **Lyminge** Kent, SE England, UK
xxxvii *P14* **Lymington** Hampshire, S England, UK
xl *E16* **Lymm** Cheshire, W England, UK
xxxvii *Y11* **Lympne** Kent, SE England, UK
xxxvii *O13* **Lyndhurst** Hampshire, S England, UK
xxxvii *N9* **Lyneham** Wiltshire, S England, UK
xlii *M5* **Lyness** Orkney Islands, N Scotland, UK
xxxix *W9* **Lyng** Norfolk, E England, UK
xxxvi *E15* **Lynher** ≈ SW England, UK
xxxvi *G11* **Lynmouth** Devon, SW England, UK
xxxvi *G11* **Lynton** Devon, SW England, UK
xliii *I17* **Lyon, Loch** ◎ C Scotland, UK
xl *M14* **Lytham St Anne's** Lancashire, NW England, UK
xli *V9* **Lythe** North Yorkshire, N England, UK
xlii *M5* **Lythes** Orkney Islands, N Scotland, UK

M

xliv *D8* **Maam Cross** Galway, W Ireland
xliv *D8* **Maamturk Mountains** ▲▲ W Ireland
xliv *G3* **Maas** Donegal, N Ireland
xxxix *T5* **Mablethorpe** Lincolnshire, E England, UK
xl *H17* **Macclesfield** Cheshire, C England, UK
xlii *O11* **Macduff** Aberdeenshire, NE Scotland, UK
xliv *C13* **Macgillycuddy's Reeks** ***var.*** Macgillicuddy's Reeks Mountains, ***Ir.*** Na Cruacha Dubha. ▲▲ SW Ireland
xliii *F23* **Macharioch** Argyll and Bute, W Scotland, UK
xliii *F22* **Machrihanish** Argyll and Bute, W Scotland, UK
xxxv *H8* **Machynlleth** Powys, C Wales, UK
xliv *E14* **Macroom** ***Ir.*** Maigh Chromtha. Cork, SW Ireland
xxxviii *I7* **Madeley** Staffordshire, C England, UK
xxxv *G6* **Maentwrog** Gwynedd, NW Wales, UK
xxxv *I14* **Maesteg** Bridgend, S Wales, UK
xliv *M4* **Magee, Island** *island* E Northern Ireland, UK
xliv *K3* **Maghera** ***Ir.*** Machaire Rátha. Magherafelt, C Northern Ireland, UK
xliv *F10* **Maghera** *hill* W Ireland
xliv *K3* **Magherafelt** ***Ir.*** Machaire Fíolta. Magherafelt, C Northern Ireland, UK
xliv *K4* **Magherafelt** ⬖ *district* C Northern Ireland, UK
xliv *L5* **Magheralin** Craigavon, C Northern Ireland, UK
xl *M16* **Maghull** Sefton, NW England, UK
xliv *I6* **Maguiresbridge** Fermanagh, W Northern Ireland, UK
xxxvi *B7* **Maida Vale** Westminster, SE England, UK
xxxvi *L11* **Maiden Bradley** Wiltshire, S England, UK
xxxvii *R9* **Maidenhead** Windsor and Maidenhead, S England, UK
xxxvi *L13* **Maiden Newton** Dorset, S England, UK
xliii *H23* **Maidens** South Ayrshire, W Scotland, UK
xliv *M3* **Maidens, The** *island group* E Northern Ireland, UK
xxxvii *W10* **Maidstone** Kent, SE England, UK
xliv *F11* **Maigue** ≈ W Ireland
xlii *L4* **Mainland** *island* Orkney, N Scotland, UK
xlii *I3* **Mainland** *island* Shetland, NE Scotland, UK
xliv *L8* **Malahide** ***Ir.*** Mullach Íde. Dublin, E Ireland
xxxvi *G17* **Malborough** Devon, SW England, UK
xlii *P1* **Malcom's Head** *headland* NE Scotland, UK
xxxvii *W8* **Maldon** Essex, E England, UK
xli *P12* **Malham** North Yorkshire, N England, UK
xliv *I2* **Malin** ***Ir.*** Málainn. Donegal, NW Ireland
xliv *I1* **Malin Head** ***Ir.*** Cionn Mhálanna. *headland* NW Ireland
xliv *F4* **Malin More** Donegal, N Ireland
xliii *F14* **Mallaig** Highland, N Scotland, UK
xliv *F13* **Mallow** ***Ir.*** Mala. Cork, SW Ireland
xxxv *I8* **Mallwyd** Gwynedd, NW Wales, UK
xxxvi *M9* **Malmesbury** Wiltshire, S England, UK
xxxviii *H7* **Malpas** Cheshire, W England, UK
xli *T16* **Maltby** Rotherham, N England, UK
xxxix *S5* **Maltby le Marsh** Lincolnshire, E England, UK
xli *U11* **Malton** North Yorkshire, N England, UK
xxxviii *I13* **Malvern Hills** *hill range* W England, UK
xxxviii *J13* **Malvern Link** Worcestershire, W England, UK
xxxv *J8* **Manafon** Powys, C Wales, UK
xl *G15* **Manchester** ***Lat.*** Mancunium. Manchester, NW England, UK
xli *P16* **Manchester** ⬖ *unitary authority* NW England, UK
xl *E16* **Manchester Canal** *canal* NW England, UK
xxxix *S10* **Manea** Cambridgeshire, E England, UK
xliv *D13* **Mangerton Mountain** ▲ SW Ireland
xxxvi *L9* **Mangotsfield** South Gloucestershire, SW England, UK
xl *G11* **Man, Isle of** *island* British Isles
xxxvii *Y6* **Manningtree** Essex, SE England, UK
xxxv *D14* **Manorbier** Pembrokeshire, SW Wales, UK
xliv *G5* **Manorhamilton** ***Ir.*** Cluainín. Leitrim, NW Ireland
xxxvi *F6* **Manor Park** Newham, SE England, UK
xli *N11* **Mansergh** Cumbria, NW England, UK
xxxix *N6* **Mansfield** Nottinghamshire, C England, UK
xxxix *P9* **Manton** Rutland, C England, UK
xxxvi *L16* **Marazion** Cornwall, SW England, UK
xxxix *S10* **March** Cambridgeshire, E England, UK
xxxvii *W11* **Marden** Kent, SE England, UK
xlii *F11* **Maree, Loch** ◎ N Scotland, UK
xxxv *H15* **Margam** Neath Port Talbot, S Wales, UK
xxxvii *Z9* **Margate** ***prev.*** Mergate. Kent, SE England, UK
xliii *G22* **Margnaheglish** North Ayrshire, W Scotland, UK
xxxix *U9* **Marham** Norfolk, E England, UK
xxxvi *E13* **Marhamchurch** Cornwall, SW England, UK
xxxix *R10* **Marholm** Cambridgeshire, E England, UK
xxxvi *K11* **Mark** Somerset, SW England, UK
xxxviii *M10* **Market Bosworth** Leicestershire, C England, UK
xxxix *R9* **Market Deeping** Lincolnshire, E England, UK
xxxviii *I8* **Market Drayton** Shropshire, W England, UK
xxxix *O10* **Market Harborough** Leicestershire, C England, UK
xliv *K5* **Markethill** Armagh, S Northern Ireland, UK
xxxix *Q5* **Market Rasen** Lincolnshire, E England, UK
xli *V13* **Market Weighton** East Riding of Yorkshire, N England, UK
xxxix *N9* **Markfield** Leicestershire, C England, UK
xxxvi *L10* **Marksbury** Bath and North East Somerset, SW England, UK
xxxvii *S7* **Markyate** Hertfordshire, E England, UK
xxxvii *O10* **Marlborough** Wiltshire, S England, UK
xxxv *C14* **Marloes** Pembrokeshire, SW Wales, UK
xxxvii *R9* **Marlow** Buckinghamshire, C England, UK
xli *Q17* **Marple** Stockport, NW England, UK
xli *Q15* **Marsden** Kirklees, N England, UK
xli *N13* **Marshaw** Lancashire, NW England, UK
xxxix *S4* **Marshchapel** Lincolnshire, E England, UK
xxxvi *M9* **Marshfield** South Gloucestershire, SW England, UK
xxxvi *D14* **Marshgate** Cornwall, SW England, UK
xxxvii *Q7* **Marsh Gibbon** Buckinghamshire, C England, UK
xli *Z6* **Marske-by-the-Sea** Redcar and Cleveland, N England, UK
xxxvi *L12* **Marston Magna** Somerset, SW England, UK
xxxix *Y9* **Martham** Norfolk, E England, UK
xxxvii *N12* **Martin** Hampshire, S England, UK
xxxvi *G11* **Martinhoe** Devon, SW England, UK
xxxix *X13* **Martlesham** Suffolk, E England, UK
xxxviii *I12* **Martley** Worcestershire, W England, UK
xxxvi *K12* **Martock** Somerset, SW England, UK
xxxix *P5* **Marton** Lincolnshire, E England, UK
xli *S12* **Marton** North Yorkshire, N England, UK
xxxvi *F12* **Marwood** Devon, SW England, UK
xlii *I11* **Marybank** Highland, NW Scotland, UK
xliii *O15* **Marykirk** Aberdeenshire, NE Scotland, UK
xl *K8* **Maryport** Cumbria, NW England, UK
xliii *H26* **Maryport** Dumfries and Galloway, SW Scotland, UK
xxxvi *F14* **Mary Tavy** Devon, SW England, UK
xliii *N14* **Marywell** Aberdeenshire, NE Scotland, UK
xliii *O16* **Marywell** Angus, E Scotland, UK
xli *R11* **Masham** North Yorkshire, N England, UK
xliv *D8* **Mask, Lough** ***Ir.*** Loch Measca. ◎ W Ireland
xxxv *C12* **Mathry** Pembrokeshire, SW Wales, UK
xxxix *X8* **Matlaske** Norfolk, E England, UK
xxxviii *M6* **Matlock** Derbyshire, C England, UK
xxxviii *L6* **Matlock Bath** Derbyshire, C England, UK
xliii *I22* **Mauchline** East Ayrshire, W Scotland, UK
xlii *P12* **Maud** Aberdeenshire, NE Scotland, UK
xl *H11* **Maughold** E Isle of Man
xliv *D8* **Maum** Galway, W Ireland
xl *K7* **Mawbray** Cumbria, NW England, UK
xxxvi *C17* **Mawgan** Cornwall, SW England, UK
xxxvi *C17* **Mawnan Smith** Cornwall, SW England, UK
xliii *I23* **Maybole** South Ayrshire, W Scotland, UK
xxxvi *C7* **Mayfair** Westminster, SE England, UK
xxxvii *V12* **Mayfield** East Sussex, SE England, UK
xxxviii *L7* **Mayfield** Staffordshire, C England, UK
xliii *O18* **May, Isle of** *island* E Scotland, UK
xliv *K9* **Maynooth** Kildare, E Ireland
xliv *E7* **Mayo** ***Ir.*** Maigh Eo. ⬖ *county* W Ireland
xlii *I7* **Meadie, Loch** ◎ NW Scotland, UK
xlii *I8* **Meall Nom Con** ▲ NW Scotland, UK
xl *L8* **Mealsgate** Cumbria, NW England, UK
xxxviii *F13* **Measham** Leicestershire, C England, UK
xliv *J8* **Meath** ***Ir.*** An Mhí. ⬖ *county* E Ireland
xlii *C9* **Meavaig** Western Isles, NW Scotland, UK
xxxix *P10* **Medbourne** Leicestershire, C England, UK
xxxvii *Q11* **Medstead** Hampshire, S England, UK
xxxvii *V11* **Medway** ≈ SE England, UK
xxxv *E13* **Meidrim** Carmarthenshire, S Wales, UK
xxxv *J8* **Meifod** Powys, C Wales, UK
xliii *M16* **Meigle** Perth and Kinross, C Scotland, UK
xliii *L17* **Meikleour** Perth and Kinross, C Scotland, UK
xxxviii *M8* **Melbourne** Derbyshire, C England, UK
xxxix *S13* **Meldreth** Cambridgeshire, E England, UK
xxxvi *M10* **Melksham** Wiltshire, S England, UK
xliv *H13* **Melleray, Mount** ▲ S Ireland
xli *N12* **Melling** Lancashire, NW England, UK
xxxix *W11* **Mellis** Suffolk, E England, UK
xxxvi *L11* **Mells** Somerset, SW England, UK
xli *N8* **Melmerby** Cumbria, NW England, UK
xliii *N21* **Melrose** The Borders, S Scotland, UK
xlii *M5* **Melsetter** Orkney Islands, N Scotland, UK
xli *R9* **Melsonby** North Yorkshire, N England, UK
xli *Q15* **Meltham** Kirklees, N England, UK
xxxix *W8* **Melton Constable** Norfolk, E England, UK
xxxix *P9* **Melton Mowbray** Leicestershire, C England, UK
xlii *F10* **Melvaig** Highland, NW Scotland, UK
xlii *K6* **Melvich** Highland, N Scotland, UK
xliv *G5* **Melvin, Lough** ***Ir.*** Loch Meilbhe. ◎ S Northern Ireland, UK/Ireland
xlii *P11* **Memsie** Aberdeenshire, NE Scotland, UK
xxxv *G4* **Menai Bridge** Isle of Anglesey, NW Wales, UK
xxxv *F5* **Menai Strait** *strait* NW Wales, UK
xxxvi *K11* **Mendip Hills** ***var.*** Mendips. *hill range* S England, UK
xxxix *W12* **Mendlesham** Suffolk, E England, UK
xli *Q13* **Menston** Leeds, N England, UK
xxxvii *Q12* **Meon** ≈ S England, UK
xxxvii *Q12* **Meonstoke** Hampshire, S England, UK
xxxvii *W10* **Meopham** Kent, SE England, UK
xxxix *T11* **Mepal** Cambridgeshire, E England, UK
xxxvi *M12* **Mere** Wiltshire, S England, UK
xxxvii *V10* **Mereworth** Kent, SE England, UK
xxxviii *E15* **Meriden** Solihull, C England, UK
xliii *I24* **Merrick** ▲ S Scotland, UK
xxxvi *K13* **Merriott** Somerset, SW England, UK
xl *M17* **Mersey** ≈ NW England, UK
xxxv *I12* **Merthyr** Cynog Powys, C Wales, UK
xxxv *J13* **Merthyr Tydfil** Merthyr Tydfil, S Wales, UK
xxxv *J14* **Merthyr Tydfil** ⬖ *unitary authority* S Wales, UK
xxxvi *F13* **Merton** Devon, SW England, UK
xxxvii *T9* **Merton** Merton, SE England, UK
xxxiv *K17* **Merton** ⬖ *London borough* SE England, UK
xliii *O22* **Mervinslaw** The Borders, S Scotland, UK
xxxvi *G12* **Meshaw** Devon, SW England, UK
xxxix *P4* **Messingham** North Lincolnshire, N England, UK
xxxix *X11* **Metfield** Suffolk, E England, UK
xxxix *Q6* **Metheringham** Lincolnshire, E England, UK
xliii *M18* **Methil** Fife, E Scotland, UK
xlii *O12* **Methlick** Aberdeenshire, NE Scotland, UK
xliii *L17* **Methven** Perth and Kinross, C Scotland, UK
xxxix *U10* **Methwold** Norfolk, E England, UK
xxxvi *D16* **Mevagissey** Cornwall, SW England, UK
xliv *M4* **Mew Island** *island* E Northern Ireland, UK
xli *S16* **Mexborough** Doncaster, N England, UK
xlii *I13* **Mhor, Loch** ◎ NW Scotland, UK
xxxviii *G14* **Michaelchurch Escley** Herefordshire, W England, UK
xxxvii *P11* **Micheldever** Hampshire, S England, UK
xli *P9* **Mickleton** Durham, N England, UK
xxxvii *N6* **Mickleton** Gloucestershire, C England, UK
xlii *M3* **Midbea** Orkney Islands, N Scotland, UK
xxxvii *P7* **Middle Barton** Oxfordshire, C England, UK
xli *Q11* **Middleham** North Yorkshire, N England, UK
xli *Y6* **Middlesbrough** Middlesborough, N England, UK
xli *Y7* **Middlesbrough** ⬖ *unitary authority* N England, UK
xli *Q11* **Middlesmoor** North Yorkshire, N England, UK
xli *N11* **Middleton** Cumbria, NW England, UK
xxxix *U9* **Middleton** Norfolk, E England, UK
xl *G14* **Middleton** Rochdale, NW England, UK
xxxix *N13* **Middleton Cheney** Northamptonshire, C England, UK
xli *P8* **Middleton in Teesdale** Durham, N England, UK
xxxvii *S13* **Middleton-on-Sea** West Sussex, SE England, UK
xli *V13* **Middleton-on-the-Wolds** East Riding of Yorkshire, N England, UK
xliv *J5* **Middletown** Armagh, S Northern Ireland, UK
xxxv *K8* **Middletown** Powys, C Wales, UK
xxxviii *M13* **Middle Tysoe** Warwickshire, C England, UK
xxxvii *O11* **Middle Wallop** Hampshire, S England, UK
xxxviii *I6* **Middlewich** Cheshire, W England, UK
xlii *I6* **Midfield** Highland, N Scotland, UK
xxxvii *R12* **Midhurst** West Sussex, SE England, UK
xliv *G14* **Midleton** ***Ir.*** Mainistir na Corann. Cork, SW Ireland
xliii *M20* **Midlothian** ⬖ *unitary authority* S Scotland, UK
xxxvi *L10* **Midsomer Norton** Bath and North East Somerset, SW England, UK
xlii *I2* **Mid Yell** Shetland Islands, NE Scotland, UK
xxxvi *L12* **Milborne Port** Somerset, SW England, UK
xli *Q5* **Milbourne** Northumberland, N England, UK
xxxix *U11* **Mildenhall** Suffolk, E England, UK
xxxvii *X6* **Mile End** Essex, SE England, UK
xliv *G11* **Milestone** Tipperary, S Ireland
xli *P2* **Milfield** Northumberland, N England, UK
xxxvii *S11* **Milford** Surrey, SE England, UK
xxxv *C14* **Milford Haven** ***prev.*** Milford. Pembrokeshire, SW Wales, UK
xxxv *C14* **Milford Haven** *inlet* SW Wales, UK
xxxvi *F16* **Millbrook** Cornwall, SW England, UK
xliv *I2* **Millford** ***Ir.*** Baile na nGallóglach. Donegal, NW Ireland
xxxvi *B5* **Mill Hill** Barnet, SE England, UK
xliii *P15* **Mill of Uras** Aberdeenshire, NE Scotland, UK
xl *L11* **Millom** Cumbria, NW England, UK
xliii *H21* **Millport** North Ayrshire, W Scotland, UK
xliv *E13* **Millstreet** Cork, S Ireland
xliii *M24* **Milltown** Dumfries and Galloway, SW Scotland, UK
xliv *D10* **Milltown Malbay** ***Ir.*** Sráid na Cathrach. Clare, W Ireland
xxxvi *E8* **Millwall** Tower Hamlets, SE England, UK
xliii *J20* **Milngavie** East Dunbartonshire, C Scotland, UK
xl *H13* **Milnow** Rochdale, NW England, UK
xli *N11* **Milnthorpe** Cumbria, NW England, UK
xlii *C12* **Milovaig** Highland, NW Scotland, UK
xlii *H11* **Milton** Highland, NW Scotland, UK
xlii *J12* **Milton** Highland, NW Scotland, UK
xxxvi *F15* **Milton Abbot** Devon, SW England, UK
xxxvii *S5* **Milton Ernest** Bedfordshire, C England, UK
xxxvii *R6* **Milton Keynes** Milton Keynes, SE England, UK
xxxvii *R5* **Milton Keynes** ⬖ *unitary authority* C England, UK
xliii *J19* **Milton of Campsie** East Dunbartonshire, C Scotland, UK
xxxvi *I12* **Milverton** Somerset, SW England, UK
xlii *E9* **Minch, The** ***var.*** North Minch. *strait* NW Scotland, UK
xliv *H14* **Mine Head** ***Ir.*** Mionn Ard. *headland* S Ireland
xxxvi *I11* **Minehead** Somerset, SW England, UK
xxxvii *N9* **Minety** Wiltshire, S England, UK
xlii *A13* **Mingary** Western Isles, NW Scotland, UK
xliii *A15* **Mingulay** *island* NW Scotland, UK
xxxvii *O13* **Minstead** Hampshire, S England, UK
xxxvii *X9* **Minster** Kent, SE England, UK
xxxvii *Z10* **Minster** Kent, SE England, UK
xxxviii *G10* **Minsterley** Shropshire, W England, UK
xlii *P11* **Mintlaw** Aberdeenshire, NE Scotland, UK
xli *R15* **Mirfield** Kirklees, N England, UK
xxxix *O4* **Misterton** Nottinghamshire, C England, UK
xxxvi *K13* **Misterton** Somerset, SW England, UK
xliv *G12* **Mitchelstown** ***Ir.*** Baile Mhistéala. Cork, SW Ireland
xli *R5* **Mitford** Northumberland, N England, UK
xliv *C15* **Mizen Head** ***Ir.*** Carn Uí Néid. *headland* SW Ireland
xliv *H9* **Moate** Westmeath, C Ireland
xliii *I25* **Mochrum** Dumfries and Galloway, SW Scotland, UK
xxxvi *G16* **Modbury** Devon, SW England, UK
xxxv *F4* **Moelfre** Isle of Anglesey, NW Wales, UK
xxxv *H8* **Moelfre** *hill* E Wales, UK
xliii *L23* **Moffat** Dumfries and Galloway, S Scotland, UK
xliv *D10* **Moher, Cliffs of** *cliff* W Ireland
xliv *H7* **Mohill** Leitrim, N Ireland
xliv *L5* **Moira** Craigavon, C Northern Ireland, UK
xlii *D13* **Mol-chlach** Highland, NW Scotland, UK
xxxv *J5* **Mold** Flintshire, NE Wales, UK
xxxvii *T11* **Mole** ≈ SE England, UK
xxxvi *H12* **Molland** Devon, SW England, UK
xlii *A11* **Monach Islands** *island group* NW Scotland, UK
xliii *J14* **Monadhliath Mountains** ▲▲ N Scotland, UK
xliv *J5* **Monaghan** ***Ir.*** Muineachán. Monaghan, N Ireland
xliv *J6* **Monaghan** ***Ir.*** Muineachán. ⬖ *county* N Ireland
xlii *H12* **Monar, Loch** ◎ NW Scotland, UK
xliv *J9* **Monasterevin** Kildare, E Ireland
xliv *H10* **Moneygall** Offaly, C Ireland
xliv *K4* **Moneymore** Cookstown, C Northern Ireland, UK
xliii *K23* **Moniaive** Dumfries and Galloway, SW Scotland, UK
xliii *N17* **Monifieth** Angus, E Scotland, UK
xliii *N17* **Monikie** Angus, E Scotland, UK
xxxviii *H13* **Monkland** Herefordshire, W England, UK
xxxvii *T12* **Monk's Gate** West Sussex, SE England, UK
xxxvi *I11* **Monksilver** Somerset, SW England, UK
xliii *I22* **Monkton** South Ayrshire, W Scotland, UK
xxxv *L13* **Monmouth** ***Wel.*** Trefynwy. Monmouthshire, SE Wales, UK
xxxv *K13* **Monmouthshire** ⬖ *unitary authority* SE Wales, UK
xliii *I26* **Monreith** Dumfries and Galloway, SW Scotland, UK
xxxv *K9* **Montgomery** Powys, E Wales, UK
xliii *M18* **Montrave** Fife, E Scotland, UK
xliii *O16* **Montrose** Angus, E Scotland, UK
xlii *O13* **Monymusk** Aberdeenshire, NE Scotland, UK
xxxvi *K11* **Moorlinch** Somerset, SW England, UK
xliii *F14* **Morar** Highland, NW Scotland, UK
xliii *F14* **Morar, Loch** ◎ N Scotland, UK
xlii *L11* **Moray** ⬖ *unitary authority* N Scotland, UK
xlii *K11* **Moray Firth** *inlet* N Scotland, UK
xxxvi *G13* **Morchard Bishop** Devon, SW England, UK
xxxviii *H14* **Mordiford** Herefordshire, W England, UK
xliii *O22* **Morebattle** The Borders, S Scotland, UK
xl *M12* **Morecambe** Lancashire, NW England, UK
xl *M12* **Morecambe Bay** *inlet* NW England, UK
xlii *H8* **More, Loch** ◎ NW Scotland, UK
xxxvi *M14* **Moreton** Dorset, S England, UK
xxxvii *V8* **Moreton** Essex, SE England, UK
xxxvi *H14* **Moretonhampstead** Devon, SW England, UK
xxxvii *O6* **Moreton-in-Marsh** Gloucestershire, C England, UK
xxxvi *E13* **Morewenstow** Cornwall, SW England, UK
xxxv *E6* **Morfa Nefyn** Gwynedd, NW Wales, UK
xlii *I13* **Mor, Glen** ***var.*** Glen Albyn, Great Glen. *valley* N Scotland, UK
xli *R14* **Morley** Leeds, N England, UK
xli *R5* **Morpeth** Northumberland, N England, UK
xxxv *H14* **Morriston** Swansea, S Wales, UK
xxxvi *F11* **Mortehoe** Devon, SW England, UK
xxxviii *H12* **Mortimer's Cross** Herefordshire, W England, UK
xxxvi *B8* **Mortlake** Richmond upon Thames, SE England, UK
xxxix *Q8* **Morton** Lincolnshire, E England, UK
xxxix *O4* **Morton** Lincolnshire, E England, UK
xxxvi *L16* **Morvah** Cornwall, SW England, UK
xliii *M14* **Morven** ▲ NE Scotland, UK
xlii *K8* **Morven** ▲ N Scotland, UK
xxxviii *I10* **Morville** Shropshire, W England, UK
xlii *I2* **Mossbank** Shetland Islands, NE Scotland, UK
xliv *L4* **Mossley** Newtownabbey, E Northern Ireland, UK
xl *H14* **Mossley** Tameside, NW England, UK
xlii *M11* **Mosstodloch** Moray, N Scotland, UK
xxxv *J4* **Mostyn** Flintshire, N Wales, UK
xliii *K20* **Motherwell** North Lanarkshire, C Scotland, UK
xxxvi *F9* **Mottingham** Bromley, SE England, UK
xxxix *R8* **Moulton** Lincolnshire, E England, UK
xxxix *P12* **Moulton** Northamptonshire, C England, UK
xxxix *U12* **Moulton** Suffolk, E England, UK
xxxv *J14* **Mountain Ash** Rhondda Cynon Taff, S Wales, UK
xliv *F8* **Mount Bellew** Galway, W Ireland
xxxvii *W12* **Mountfield** East Sussex, SE England, UK
xliv *J4* **Mount Hamilton** Strabane, W Northern Ireland, UK
xxxvi *C16* **Mountjoy** Cornwall, SW England, UK
xliv *I10* **Mountmellick** ***Ir.*** Móinteach Mílic. Laois, C Ireland
xliv *I10* **Mountrath** Laois, C Ireland
xxxvi *M17* **Mount's Bay** *inlet* SW England, UK
xliv *F10* **Mountshannon** Clare, W Ireland
xxxix *N9* **Mountsorrel** Leicestershire, C England, UK
xliv *G8* **Mount Talbot** Roscommon, C Ireland
xliv *I4* **Mourne** ≈ W Northern Ireland, UK
xliv *L6* **Mourne Mountains** ***Ir.*** Beanna Boirche. ▲▲ SE Northern Ireland, UK
xxxvi *M16* **Mousehole** Cornwall, SW England, UK
xliii *L24* **Mouswald** Dumfries and Galloway, SW Scotland, UK
xliv *J2* **Moville** Donegal, N Ireland
xxxviii *J7* **Mow Cop** Staffordshire, C England, UK
xliv *K5* **Moy** Dungannon, C Northern Ireland, UK
xlii *J12* **Moy** Highland, NW Scotland, UK
xliii *I15* **Moy** Highland, NW Scotland, UK
xliv *E6* **Moy** ≈ NW Ireland
xliv *C8* **Moyard** Galway, W Ireland
xliv *E9* **Moycullen** Galway, W Ireland
xliv *K5* **Moygashel** Dungannon, C Northern Ireland, UK
xliv *L2* **Moyle** ⬖ *district* N Northern Ireland, UK
xxxv *D12* **Moylgrove** Pembrokeshire, SW Wales, UK
xliii *I15* **Moy, Loch** ◎ NW Scotland, UK
xliv *F8* **Moylough** Galway, W Ireland
xliii *F21* **Muasdale** Argyll and Bute, W Scotland, UK
xxxvii *U7* **Much Hadham** Hertfordshire, SE England, UK
xxxviii *I14* **Much Marcle** Herefordshire, W England, UK
xxxviii *I10* **Much Wenlock** Shropshire, W England, UK
xliii *D15* **Muck** *island* W Scotland, UK
xlii *H3* **Muckle Roe** *island* NE Scotland, UK
xliv *J6* **Muckno Lough** ◎ NE Ireland
xliv *D13* **Muckross** Kerry, SW Ireland
xlii *J9* **Muie** Highland, NW Scotland, UK
xliv *J11* **Muine Bheag** ***Eng.*** Bagenalstown. Carlow, SE Ireland
xliii *N17* **Muirdrum** Angus, E Scotland, UK
xliii *J20* **Muirhead** Angus, E Scotland, UK
xliii *M17* **Muirhead** North Lanarkshire, C Scotland, UK
xliii *J22* **Muirkirk** East Ayrshire, W Scotland, UK
xlii *I12* **Muir of Ord** Highland, NW Scotland, UK
xliii *A14* **Muldoanich** *island* NW Scotland, UK
xliv *F11* **Mulkear** ≈ W Ireland
xliv *E12* **Mullaghareirk Mountains** *hill range* W Ireland
xliv *K10* **Mullaghcleevaun** ▲ E Ireland
xliv *G5* **Mullaghmore** Sligo, N Ireland
xliv *H6* **Mullan** Fermanagh, W Northern Ireland, UK
xlii *H13* **Mullardoch, Loch** ◎ NW Scotland, UK
xlii *M2* **Mull Head** *headland* N Scotland, UK
xliv *I12* **Mullinavat** Kilkenny, SE Ireland
xliv *I8* **Mullingar** ***Ir.*** An Muileann gCearr. Westmeath, C Ireland
xxxvi *B17* **Mullion** Cornwall, SW England, UK
xliii *E17* **Mull, Isle of** *island* W Scotland, UK
xliii *E16* **Mull, Sound of** *strait* NW Scotland, UK
xliv *D7* **Mulrany** Mayo, NW Ireland
xxxix *X7* **Mundesley** Norfolk, E England, UK
xxxix *V10* **Mundford** Norfolk, E England, UK
xliv *F11* **Mungret** Limerick, SW Ireland
xlii *J11* **Munlochy** Highland, NW Scotland, UK
xliv *D13* **Munster** ***Ir.*** Cúige Mumhan. *province* S Ireland
xliv *E9* **Murroogh** Clare, W Ireland
xxxix *S9* **Murrow** Cambridgeshire, E England, UK
xli *S7* **Murton** Durham, N England, UK
xxxvi *J14* **Musbury** Devon, SW England, UK
xliv *E13* **Musheramore** ▲ S Ireland
xliii *M20* **Musselburgh** East Lothian, SE Scotland, UK
xli *W11* **Muston** North Yorkshire, N England, UK
xxxvi *C5* **Muswell Hill** Haringey, SE England, UK
xliii *K18* **Muthill** Perth and Kinross, C Scotland, UK
xliv *D10* **Mutton Island** *island* W Ireland.
xliv *C7* **Mweelrea** ***Ir.*** Caoc Maol Réidh. ▲ W Ireland
xlii *L7* **Mybster** Highland, N Scotland, UK
xxxv *H12* **Myddfai** Carmarthenshire, S Wales, UK
xxxviii *H9* **Myddle** Shropshire, W England, UK
xxxv *F11* **Mydroilyn** Ceredigion, W Wales, UK

N

xliv *K9* **Naas** ***Ir.*** An Nás, Nás na Ríogh. Kildare, C Ireland
xlii *F10* **Naast** Highland, NW Scotland, UK
xli *T13* **Naburn** York, N England, UK
xxxix *X13* **Nacton** Suffolk, E England, UK
xliv *E13* **Nad** Cork, S Ireland
xli *W12* **Nafferton** East Riding of Yorkshire, N England, UK
xliv *F13* **Nagles Mountains** ▲▲ S Ireland
xxxvi *K10* **Nailsea** North West Somerset, SW England, UK
xxxvi *M8* **Nailsworth** Gloucestershire, C England, UK
xlii *K11* **Nairn** Highland, N Scotland, UK
xxxv *J10* **Nantmel** Powys, C Wales, UK
xxxv *G6* **Nantmor** Gwynedd, NW Wales, UK
xxxviii *H7* **Nantwich** Cheshire, W England, UK
xxxv *D13* **Narberth** Pembrokeshire, SW Wales, UK
xxxix *N10* **Narborough** Leicestershire, C England, UK
xxxix *U9* **Narborough** Norfolk, E England, UK
xliv *G3* **Narin** Donegal, N Ireland
xxxix *O11* **Naseby** Northamptonshire, C England, UK
xli *N11* **Natland** Cumbria, NW England, UK
xliv *K8* **Navan** ***Ir.*** An Uaimh. Meath, E Ireland
xxxix *Q6* **Navenby** Lincolnshire, E England, UK
xlii *J8* **Naver, Loch** ◎ NW Scotland, UK
xxxix *W14* **Nayland** Suffolk, E England, UK
xliv *K5* **Neagh, Lough** ◎ E Northern Ireland, UK
xliv *E8* **Neale** Mayo, NW Ireland
xlii *I3* **Neap** Shetland Islands, NE Scotland, UK
xxxvi *A6* **Neasden** Brent, SE England, UK
xxxv *H14* **Neath** Neath Port Talbot, S Wales, UK
xxxv *H14* **Neath Port Talbot** ⬖ *unitary authority* S Wales, UK
xxxix *V9* **Necton** Norfolk, E England, UK
xxxix *W12* **Needham Market** Suffolk, E England, UK
xxxvii *O14* **Needles, The** *rocks* Isle of Wight, S England, UK
xxxv *E6* **Nefyn** Gwynedd, NW Wales, UK
xli *P14* **Nelson** Lancashire, NW England, UK
xliv *G10* **Nenagh** ***Ir.*** An tAonach. Tipperary, C Ireland
xxxix *S9* **Nene** ≈ E England, UK
xli *O7* **Nenthead** Cumbria, NW England, UK
xliv *D6* **Nephin** ***Ir.*** Néifinn. ▲ W Ireland
xxxviii *G9* **Nesscliffe** Shropshire, W England, UK
xlii *I13* **Ness, Loch** ◎ N Scotland, UK
xli *V9* **Ness Point** *headland* N England, UK
xl *B17* **Neston** Cheshire, W England, UK
xxxvii *O11* **Netheravon** Wiltshire, S England, UK
xxxix *N6* **Nether Langwith** Nottinghamshire, C England, UK
xxxvi *J11* **Nether Stowey** Somerset, SW England, UK
xli *P4* **Netherton** Northumberland, N England, UK
xl *K10* **Nether Wasdale** Cumbria, NW England, UK
xlii *K13* **Nethy Bridge** Highland, NW Scotland, UK
xxxvii *Q9* **Nettlebed** Oxfordshire, C England, UK
xxxix *Q5* **Nettleham** Lincolnshire, E England, UK
xliii *F14* **Nevis, Loch** *inlet* NW Scotland, UK
xliii *L24* **New Abbey** Dumfries and Galloway, SW Scotland, UK

◆ Country ● Country Capital ◇ Dependent Territory ○ Dependent Territory Capital ⬖ Administrative Region ✈ International Airport ▲ Mountain ▲▲ Mountain Range ◎ Lake ⊠ Reservoir ≈ River

xlii P11 **New Aberdour** Aberdeenshire, NE Scotland, UK
xxxvii Q12 **New Alresford** Hampshire, S England, UK
xlii O3 **Newark** Orkney Islands, N Scotland, UK
xxxix P7 **Newark-on-Trent** ***var.*** Newark. Nottinghamshire, C England, UK
xli Q3 **New Bewick** Northumberland, N England, UK
xli P8 **Newbiggin** Durham, N England, UK
xli R5 **Newbiggin-by-the-Sea** Northumberland, N England, UK
xliii L21 **Newbigging** South Lanarkshire, C Scotland, UK
xxxv F5 **Newborough** Isle of Anglesey, NW Wales, UK
xliv G8 **Newbridge** Galway, W Ireland
xxxv K14 **Newbridge** Caerphilly, S Wales, UK
xxxv I11 **Newbridge on Wye** Powys, C Wales, UK
xl B15 **New Brighton** Wirral, NW England, UK
xli P6 **Newbrough** Northumberland, N England, UK
xxxix W10 **New Buckenham** Norfolk, E England, UK
xliv I3 **New Buildings** Londonderry, NW Northern Ireland, UK
xlii P13 **Newburgh** Aberdeenshire, NE Scotland, UK
xliii M18 **Newburgh** Fife, E Scotland, UK
xli U2 **Newburn** Newcastle upon Tyne, NE England, UK
xxxvii P10 **Newbury** West Berkshire, S England, UK
xxxvii P10 **West Berkshire** ⬖ *unitary authority* S England, UK
xxxvi G6 **Newbury Park** Redbridge, SE England, UK
xl M11 **Newby Bridge** Cumbria, NW England, UK
xlii O11 **New Byth** Aberdeenshire, NE Scotland, UK
xliv L10 **Newcastle** Wicklow, E Ireland
xxxviii G11 **Newcastle** Shropshire, W England, UK
xliv L6 **Newcastle** ***Ir.*** An Caisleán Nua. Down, SE Northern Ireland, UK
xli V2 **Newcastle** ✕ NE England, UK
xxxv E12 **Newcastle Emlyn** Carmarthenshire, S Wales, UK
xliii N23 **Newcastleton** The Borders, S Scotland, UK
xxxviii J7 **Newcastle-under-Lyme** Staffordshire, C England, UK
xli V2 **Newcastle upon Tyne** ***var.*** Newcastle; ***hist.*** Monkchester, ***Lat.*** Pons Aelii. Newcastle upon Tyne, NE England, UK
xli U2 **Newcastle upon Tyne** ⬖ *unitary authority* NE England, UK
xliv E12 **Newcastle West** ***Ir.*** An Caisleán Nua. Limerick, SW Ireland
xxxv K11 **Newchurch** Powys, C Wales, UK
xxxvi E8 **New Cross** Lewisham, SE England, UK
xliii J22 **New Cumnock** East Ayrshire, W Scotland, UK
xlii P12 **New Deer** Aberdeenshire, NE Scotland, UK
xxxvi G9 **New Eltham** Greenwich, SE England, UK
xxxvi L7 **Newent** Gloucestershire, C England, UK
xxxvii O13 **New Forest** *physical region* S England, UK
xliii J24 **New Galloway** Dumfries and Galloway, SW Scotland, UK
xxxvi I17 **New Grimsby** Isles of Scilly, SW England, UK
xxxiv L16 **Newham** ⬖ *London borough* SE England, UK
xxxvii V13 **Newhaven** East Sussex, SE England, UK
xxxix Q2 **New Holland** North Lincolnshire, N England, UK
xxxvii U12 **Newick** East Sussex, SE England, UK
xlii P11 **New Leeds** Aberdeenshire, NE Scotland, UK
xliii H25 **New Luce** Dumfries and Galloway, SW Scotland, UK
xxxvi L16 **Newlyn** Cornwall, SW England, UK
xxxvi C16 **Newlyn** East Cornwall, SW England, UK
xlii P13 **Newmachar** Aberdeenshire, NE Scotland, UK
xliii K20 **Newmains** North Lanarkshire, C Scotland, UK
xliv E11 **Newmarket-on-Fergus** Clare, W Ireland
xliv E13 **Newmarket** Cork, S Ireland
xxxix U12 **Newmarket** Suffolk, E England, UK
xlii D8 **Newmarket** Western Isles, NW Scotland, UK
xlii M11 **Newmill** Moray, N Scotland, UK
xliii N22 **Newmill** The Borders, S Scotland, UK
xxxviii K5 **New Mills** Derbyshire, C England, UK
xl H16 **New Mills** Cheshire, C England, UK
xliii J21 **Newmilns** East Ayrshire, W Scotland, UK
xxxvii P13 **New Milton** Hampshire, S England, UK
xxxvi L8 **Newnham** Gloucestershire, C England, UK
xlii P11 **New Pitsligo** Aberdeenshire, NE Scotland, UK
xliv D7 **Newport** Mayo, NW Ireland
xliv G11 **Newport** Tipperary, S Ireland
xxxvii V6 **Newport** Essex, SE England, UK
xxxvii Q14 **Newport** Isle of Wight, S England, UK
xxxviii I9 **Newport** Shropshire, W England, UK
xxxv K14 **Newport** Newport, SE Wales, UK
xxxv D12 **Newport** Pembrokeshire, SE Wales, UK
xxxv K15 **Newport** ⬖ *unitary authority* SE Wales, UK
xxxv D11 **Newport Bay** *bay* SW Wales, UK
xliii N17 **Newport-on-Tay** Fife, E Scotland, UK
xxxvii R6 **Newport Pagnell** Milton Keynes, SE England, UK
xliv K4 **Newport Trench** Cookstown, C Northern Ireland, UK
xxxv F11 **New Quay** Ceredigion, SW Wales, UK
xxxv K10 **New Radnor** Powys, C Wales, UK
xxxvi B16 **Newquay** Cornwall, SW England, UK
xxxvii Y12 **New Romney** Kent, SE England, UK
xliv J12 **New Ross** ***Ir.*** Ros Mhic Thriúin. Wexford, SE Ireland
xli U16 **New Rossington** Doncaster, N England, UK
xliv K6 **Newry** ***Ir.*** An tIúr. Newry and Mourne, SE Northern Ireland, UK
xliv K6 **Newry and Mourne** ⬖ *district* S Northern Ireland, UK
xliii L17 **New Scone** Perth and Kinross, C Scotland, UK
xli R5 **Newsham** Northumberland, N England, UK
xli O13 **Newton** Lancashire, NW England, UK
xliii G19 **Newton** Argyll and Bute, W Scotland, UK
xxxvi H15 **Newton Abbot** Devon, SW England, UK
xl L7 **Newton Arlosh** Cumbria, NW England, UK
xli R9 **Newton Aycliffe** Durham, N England, UK
xxxvi F16 **Newton Ferrers** Devon, SW England, UK
xlii B11 **Newtonferry** Western Isles, NW Scotland, UK
xxxix X10 **Newton Flotman** Norfolk, E England, UK
xli N16 **Newton-le-Willows** St Helens, NW England, UK
xliii J20 **Newton Mearns** East Renfrewshire, W Scotland, UK
xliii J14 **Newtonmore** Highland, NW Scotland, UK
xli T12 **Newton-on-Ouse** North Yorkshire, N England, UK
xli R4 **Newton-on-the-Moor** Northumberland, N England, UK
xxxix P5 **Newton on Trent** Lincolnshire, E England, UK
xliii I25 **Newton Stewart** Dumfries and Galloway, S Scotland, UK
xxxvi F12 **Newton Tracey** Devon, SW England, UK
xliv F12 **Newtown** Cork, S Ireland
xliv J10 **Newtown** Laois, C Ireland
xxxv J9 **Newtown** Powys, E Wales, UK
xliv L4 **Newtownabbey** ***Ir.*** Baile na Mainistreach. Newtownabbey, E Northern Ireland, UK
xliv L4 **Newtownabbey** ⬖ *district* E Northern Ireland, UK
xliv M4 **Newtownards** ***Ir.*** Baile Nua na hArda. Ards, SE Northern Ireland, UK
xliv M4 **Newtownards** ✕ Ards, E Northern Ireland, UK
xliv I6 **Newtownbutler** Fermanagh, SW Northern Ireland, UK
xliv H7 **Newtown Forbes** Longford, C Ireland
xliv K6 **Newtownhamilton** Newry and Mourne, S Northern Ireland, UK
xliii N21 **Newtown St Boswells** The Borders, S Scotland, UK
xliv I4 **Newtownstewart** Strabane, W Northern Ireland, UK
xliii M16 **Newtyle** Angus, E Scotland, UK
xxxv C14 **Neyland** Pembrokeshire, SW Wales, UK
xli Q12 **Nidd** ≈ N England, UK
xlii K11 **Nigg** Highland, NW Scotland, UK
xli O7 **Ninebanks** Northumberland, N England, UK
xliv I12 **Ninemilehouse** Tipperary, S Ireland
xxxvii W13 **Ninfield** East Sussex, SE England, UK
xliii K23 **Nith** ≈ S Scotland, UK
xxxvii P14 **Niton** Isle of Wight, S England, UK
xliv J7 **Nobber** Meath, E Ireland
xxxv C13 **Nolton** Pembrokeshire, SW Wales, UK
xliv J12 **Nore** ***Ir.*** An Fheoir. ≈ S Ireland
xxxix V9 **Norfolk** ⬖ *county* E England, UK
xli P1 **Norham** Northumberland, N England, UK
xxxviii M8 **Normanton** City of Derby, C England, UK
xli S14 **Normanton** Wakefield, N England, UK
xli S10 **Northallerton** North Yorkshire, N England, UK
xxxix O12 **Northampton** Northamptonshire, C England, UK
xxxix O11 **Northamptonshire** ⬖ *county* C England, UK
xliii G21 **North Ayrshire** ⬖ *unitary authority* W Scotland, UK
xliii G16 **North Ballachulish** Highland, NW Scotland, UK
xliii N19 **North Berwick** East Lothian, SE Scotland, UK
xxxvi F14 **North Brentor** Devon, SW England, UK
xli V14 **North Cave** East Riding of Yorkshire, N England, UK
xxxvii S12 **Northchapel** West Sussex, SE England, UK
xli R3 **North Charlton** Northumberland, N England, UK
xxxix V7 **North Creake** Norfolk, E England, UK
xxxvi J12 **North Curry** Somerset, SW England, UK
xli V13 **North Dalton** East Riding of Yorkshire, N England, UK
xliv M4 **North Down** ⬖ *district* E Northern Ireland, UK
xxxvii U10 **North Downs** *hill range* SE England, UK
xxxix R3 **North East Lincolnshire** ⬖ *unitary authority* N England, UK
xxxix V8 **North Elmham** Norfolk, E England, UK
xliv I4 **Northern Ireland** ***var.*** The Six Counties. *political division* Northern Ireland, UK
xlii F10 **North Erradale** Highland, NW Scotland, UK
xliii N15 **North Esk** ≈ E Scotland, UK
xxxvii Z9 **North Foreland** *headland* SE England, UK
xli W13 **North Frodingham** East Riding of Yorkshire, N England, UK
xli V12 **North Grimston** North Yorkshire, N England, UK
xxxvi E15 **North Hill** Cornwall, SW England, UK
xxxvii W12 **Northiam** East Sussex, SE England, UK
xxxix Q4 **North Kelsey** Lincolnshire, E England, UK
xxxix O11 **North Kilworth** Leicestershire, C England, UK
xxxix R7 **North Kyme** Lincolnshire, E England, UK
xliii J20 **North Lanarkshire** ⬖ *unitary authority* C Scotland, UK
xxxvii N7 **Northleach** Gloucestershire, C England, UK
xxxvi F14 **Northlew** Devon, SW England, UK
xxxix O3 **North Lincolnshire** ⬖ *unitary authority* N England, UK
xxxix P10 **North Luffenham** Rutland, C England, UK
xxxvii Q7 **North Marston** Buckinghamshire, C England, UK
xxxvi G12 **North Molton** Devon, SW England, UK
xxxvi L8 **North Nibley** Gloucestershire, C England, UK
xxxvi J12 **North Petherton** Somerset, SW England, UK
xlii N2 **North Ronaldsay** *island* NE Scotland, UK
xxxix P6 **North Scarle** Lincolnshire, E England, UK
xli S6 **North Shields** North Tyneside, NE England, UK
xxxix S4 **North Somercotes** Lincolnshire, E England, UK
xliv C9 **North Sound** *sound* W Ireland
xlii N2 **North Sound, The** *sound* N Scotland, UK
xli P9 **North Stainmore** Cumbria, NW England, UK
xli R2 **North Sunderland** Northumberland, N England, UK
xxxvi G13 **North Tawton** Devon, SW England, UK
xxxix R4 **North Thoresby** Lincolnshire, E England, UK
xxxvii O11 **North Tidworth** Wiltshire, S England, UK
xlii E7 **North Tolsta** Western Isles, NW Scotland, UK
xli O5 **North Tyne** ≈ N England, UK
xli S6 **North Tyneside** ⬖ *unitary authority* NE England, UK
xlii A11 **North Uist** *island* NW Scotland, UK
xli O5 **Northumberland** ⬖ *county* N England, UK
xxxix X8 **North Walsham** Norfolk, E England, UK
xlii G13 **North West Highlands** ▲▲ N Scotland, UK
xxxvi K10 **North West Somerset** ⬖ *unitary authority* SW England, UK
xl E17 **Northwich** Cheshire, C England, UK
xxxix U10 **Northwold** Norfolk, E England, UK
xxxviii H8 **Northwood** Shropshire, W England, UK
xli T10 **North York Moors** *moorland* N England, UK
xli R11 **North Yorkshire** ⬖ *county* N England, UK
xli U12 **Norton** North Yorkshire, N England, UK
xxxv K10 **Norton** Powys, C Wales, UK
xxxvi J12 **Norton Fitzwarren** Somerset, SW England, UK
xxxvi M10 **Norton St Philip** Somerset, SW England, UK
xxxix X9 **Norwich** Norfolk, E England, UK
xlii J1 **Norwick** Shetland Islands, NE Scotland, UK
xlii M7 **Noss Head** *headland* N Scotland, UK
xxxix N8 **Nottingham** Nottinghamshire, C England, UK
xxxix N7 **Nottingham, City of** ⬖ *unitary authority* C England, UK
xxxix N7 **Nottinghamshire** ⬖ *county* C England, UK
xxxviii E14 **Nuneaton** Warwickshire, C England, UK
xxxvi L11 **Nunney** Somerset, SW England, UK
xli U11 **Nunnington** North Yorkshire, N England, UK
xli Y7 **Nunthorpe** Middlesborough, NE England, UK
xxxvii V12 **Nutley** East Sussex, SE England, UK

O

xxxix O10 **Oadby** Leicestershire, C England, UK
xxxviii I9 **Oakengates** Shropshire, W England, UK
xxxvi H12 **Oakford** Devon, SW England, UK
xxxix P9 **Oakham** Rutland, C England, UK
xxxix S12 **Oakington** Cambridgeshire, E England, UK
xxxvii Q7 **Oakley** Buckinghamshire, C England, UK
xliii L19 **Oakley** Fife, E Scotland, UK
xliii D21 **Oa, Mull of** *headland* W Scotland, UK
xliii F17 **Oban** Argyll and Bute, W Scotland, UK
xliii L18 **Ochil Hills** ▲▲ C Scotland, UK
xliii J22 **Ochiltree** East Ayrshire, W Scotland, UK
xlii N3 **Odie** Orkney Islands, N Scotland, UK
xxxvii R11 **Odiham** Hampshire, S England, UK
xliv H9 **Offaly** ***Ir.*** Ua Uíbh Fhailí; ***prev.*** King's County. ⬖ *county* C Ireland
xxxix R12 **Offord d'Arcy** Cambridgeshire, E England, UK
xxxix W13 **Offton** Suffolk, E England, UK
xxxvii O9 **Ogbourne St George** Wiltshire, S England, UK
xxxv I15 **Ogmore by Sea** Bridgend, S Wales, UK
xxxvi G14 **Okehampton** Devon, SW England, UK
xlii P13 **Old Aberdeen** City of Aberdeen, NE Scotland, UK
xlii G8 **Oldany** *island* NW Scotland, UK
xxxvii Q10 **Old Basing** Hampshire, S England, UK
xxxix S6 **Old Bolingbroke** Lincolnshire, E England, UK
xxxviii B15 **Oldbury** Sandwell, C England, UK
xliv J7 **Oldcastle** Meath, E Ireland
xlii P11 **Old Deer** Aberdeenshire, NE Scotland, UK
xxxix Y13 **Old Felixstowe** Suffolk, E England, UK
xxxix R10 **Old Fletton** Cambridgeshire, E England, UK
xl H14 **Oldham** Oldham, NW England, UK
xli P15 **Oldham** ⬖ *unitary authority* NW England, UK
xliv F15 **Old Head of Kinsale** ***Ir.*** An Seancheann. *headland* SW Ireland
xlii O12 **Oldmeldrum** Aberdeenshire, NE Scotland, UK
xlii I2 **Ollaberry** Shetland Islands, NE Scotland, UK
xxxix O6 **Ollerton** Nottinghamshire, C England, UK
xxxvii R5 **Olney** Milton Keynes, C England, UK
xxxviii D15 **Olton** Solihull, C England, UK
xliv I4 **Omagh** ***Ir.*** An Ómaigh. Omagh, W Northern Ireland, UK
xliv I4 **Omagh** ⬖ *district* W Northern Ireland, UK
xxxviii A17 **Ombersley** Worcestershire, W England, UK
xliv L6 **Omeath** Louth, NE Ireland
xl G11 **Onchan** E Isle of Man
xliii G16 **Onich** Highland, NW Scotland, UK
xlii F11 **Opinan** Highland, NW Scotland, UK
xliv E9 **Oranmore** Galway, W Ireland
xlii E13 **Ord** Highland, NW Scotland, UK
xxxvii W13 **Ore** East Sussex, SE England, UK
xxxix Y13 **Orford** Suffolk, E England, UK
xxxix Y13 **Orford Ness** *headland* E England, UK
xlii M3 **Orkney Islands** ⬖ *unitary authority* N Scotland, UK
xlii N4 **Orkney Islands** ***var.*** Orkney, Orkneys. *island group* N Scotland, UK
xxxviii H12 **Orleton** Herefordshire, W England, UK
xli Y6 **Ormesby** Redcar and Cleveland, N England, UK
xxxix Y9 **Ormesby St Margaret** Norfolk, E England, UK
xl C14 **Ormskirk** Lancashire, NW England, UK
xliii D19 **Oronsay** *island* W Scotland, UK
xxxvii U10 **Orpington** Bromley, SE England, UK
xlii H12 **Orrin Reservoir** ⊡ NW Scotland, UK
xli N10 **Orton** Cumbria, NW England, UK
xxxix S13 **Orwell** Cambridgeshire, E England, UK
xxxix X13 **Orwell** ≈ E England, UK
xxxix Q8 **Osbournby** Lincolnshire, E England, UK
xliii E17 **Oskamull** Argyll and Bute, W Scotland, UK
xxxvi L14 **Osmington** Dorset, S England, UK
xli S10 **Osmotherley** North Yorkshire, N England, UK
xli R15 **Ossett** Wakefield, N England, UK
xli T11 **Oswaldkirk** North Yorkshire, N England, UK
xxxviii G8 **Oswestry** Shropshire, W England, UK
xli R13 **Otley** Leeds, N England, UK
xxxix X12 **Otley** Suffolk, E England, UK
xxxvi I14 **Otter** ≈ SW England, UK
xli P4 **Otterburn** Northumberland, N England, UK
xliii G19 **Otter Ferry** Argyll and Bute, W Scotland, UK
xlii I2 **Otterswick** Shetland Islands, NE Scotland, UK
xxxvi I14 **Otterton** Devon, SW England, UK
xxxvi I14 **Ottery St Mary** Devon, SW England, UK
xli X14 **Ottringham** East Riding of Yorkshire, N England, UK
xliv D8 **Oughterard** Galway, W Ireland
xliv I6 **Oughter, Lough** ◎ N Ireland
xxxix Z10 **Oulton Broad** Suffolk, E England, UK
xxxix Q10 **Oundle** Northamptonshire, C England, UK
xli U14 **Ouse** ≈ N England, UK
xxxvii U12 **Ouse** ≈ SE England, UK
xlii A10 **Outer Hebrides** ***var.*** Western Isles. *island group* NW Scotland, UK
xlii J2 **Out Skerries** *island group* NE Scotland, UK
xxxix T9 **Outwell** Norfolk, E England, UK
xxxvii U11 **Outwood** Surrey, SE England, UK
xli N12 **Over Kellet** Lancashire, NW England, UK
xxxviii M9 **Overseal** Derbyshire, C England, UK
xxxix X7 **Overstrand** Norfolk, E England, UK
xxxvii P11 **Overton** Hampshire, S England, UK
xl M12 **Overton** Lancashire, NW England, UK
xxxv K6 **Overton** Wrexham, NE Wales, UK
xliv I8 **Owel, Lough** ◎ C Ireland
xxxvi M14 **Owermoigne** Dorset, S England, UK
xliv G2 **Owey Island** *island* N Ireland
xxxix O4 **Owston Ferry** North Lincolnshire, N England, UK
xxxix U10 **Oxborough** Norfolk, E England, UK
xli N11 **Oxenholme** Cumbria, NW England, UK
xxxvii P8 **Oxford** ***Lat.*** Oxonia. Oxfordshire, S England, UK
xxxix N12 **Oxford Canal** *canal* S England, UK
xxxvii O7 **Oxfordshire** ⬖ *county* S England, UK
xliii O22 **Oxnam** The Borders, S Scotland, UK
xxxvii U10 **Oxted** Surrey, SE England, UK
xliii N20 **Oxton** The Borders, S Scotland, UK
xxxv G15 **Oxwich** Swansea, S Wales, UK
xlii H9 **Oykel** ≈ N Scotland, UK
xlii I9 **Oykel Bridge** Highland, NW Scotland, UK

P

xliii A15 **Pabbay** *island* NW Scotland, UK
xlii A10 **Pabbay** *island* NW Scotland, UK
xxxvii Q6 **Padbury** Buckinghamshire, C England, UK
xxxvi C7 **Paddington** City of Westminster, SE England, UK
xxxvii V11 **Paddock Wood** Kent, SE England, UK
xli O14 **Padiham** Lancashire, NW England, UK
xxxvi C15 **Padstow** Cornwall, SW England, UK
xxxvii R13 **Pagham** West Sussex, S England, UK
xxxvi H15 **Paignton** Devon, SW England, UK
xxxix N11 **Pailton** Warwickshire, C England, UK
xxxv J11 **Painscastle** Powys, C Wales, UK
xxxvi M8 **Painswick** Gloucestershire, C England, UK
xliii I20 **Paisley** Renfrewshire, W Scotland, UK
xliv G11 **Pallas Grean** Limerick, SW Ireland
xliii K25 **Palnackie** Dumfries and Galloway, SW Scotland, UK
xliii I25 **Palnure** Dumfries and Galloway, SW Scotland, UK
xxxv K13 **Pandy** Monmouthshire, SE Wales, UK
xxxvii Q9 **Pangbourne** West Berkshire, S England, UK
xxxviii G9 **Pant** Shropshire, W England, UK
xlii H3 **Papa Stour** *island* NE Scotland, UK
xlii N2 **Papa Westray** *island* NE Scotland, UK
xli N15 **Parbold** Lancashire, NW England, UK
xxxvii Y6 **Parkeston** Essex, SE England, UK
xliii L23 **Parkgate** Dumfries and Galloway, SW Scotland, UK
xliv C14 **Parknasilla** Kerry, SW Ireland
xxxvi G11 **Parracombe** Devon, SW England, UK
xxxvi K12 **Parrett** ≈ SW England, UK
xli O16 **Partington** Trafford, NW England, UK
xxxix S6 **Partney** Lincolnshire, E England, UK
xl K9 **Parton** Cumbria, NW England, UK
xliii J24 **Parton** Dumfries and Galloway, SW Scotland, UK
xliv E7 **Partry** Mayo, NW Ireland
xliv D7 **Partry** Mountains m W Ireland
xxxviii L7 **Parwich** Derbyshire, C England, UK
xliv J13 **Passage East** Waterford, S Ireland
xxxvi L9 **Patchway** South Gloucestershire, W England, UK
xli R12 **Pateley Bridge** North Yorkshire, N England, UK
xliii M20 **Pathhead** Midlothian, SE Scotland, UK
xliii I23 **Patna** East Ayrshire, W Scotland, UK
xl F11 **Patrick** W Isle of Man
xli R10 **Patrick Brompton** North Yorkshire, N England, UK
xliv F11 **Patrickswell** Limerick, SW Ireland
xli X14 **Patrington** East Riding of Yorkshire, N England, UK
xxxvi J11 **Pawlett** Somerset, SW England, UK
xliii P20 **Paxton** The Borders, S Scotland, UK
xxxvii U13 **Peacehaven** East Sussex, SE England, UK
xxxviii L5 **Peak District** *physical region* C England, UK
xxxix R9 **Peakirk** Cambridgeshire, E England, UK
xxxix Y12 **Peasenhall** Suffolk, E England, UK
xxxvii X12 **Peasmarsh** East Sussex, SE England, UK
xxxvi D8 **Peckham** Southwark, SE England, UK
xliii M21 **Peebles** The Borders, SE Scotland, UK
xl F11 **Peel** W Isle of Man
xxxvii Z10 **Pegwell Bay** *bay* SE England, UK
xlii E13 **Peinchorran** Highland, NW Scotland, UK
xxxv F14 **Pembrey** Carmarthenshire, S Wales, UK
xxxviii G12 **Pembridge** Herefordshire, W England, UK
xxxv D14 **Pembroke** Pembrokeshire, SW Wales, UK
xxxv C14 **Pembroke Dock** Pembrokeshire, SW Wales, UK
xxxv C13 **Pembrokeshire** ⬖ *unitary authority* SW Wales, UK
xxxvii V11 **Pembury** Kent, SE England, UK
xxxv D14 **Penally** Pembrokeshire, SW Wales, UK
xxxv K15 **Penarth** The Vale of Glamorgan, S Wales, UK
xxxv F12 **Pencader** Carmarthenshire, S Wales, UK
xliii N20 **Pencaitland** East Lothian, SE Scotland, UK
xxxv I15 **Pencoed** Bridgend, S Wales, UK
xxxv I13 **Penderyn** Rhondda Cynon Taff, S Wales, UK
xxxv E14 **Pendine** Carmarthenshire, S Wales, UK
xl G14 **Pendlebury** Salford, NW England, UK
xliii M20 **Penicuik** Midlothian, SE Scotland, UK
xli R16 **Penistone** Barnsley, N England, UK
xxxviii B13 **Penkridge** Staffordshire, C England, UK
xxxv L6 **Penley** Wrexham, NE Wales, UK
xxxv H6 **Penmachno** Conwy, N Wales, UK
xxxv H4 **Penmaenmawr** Conwy, N Wales, UK
xxxv G4 **Penmon** Isle of Anglesey, NW Wales, UK
xli P8 **Pennines** ***var.*** Pennine Chain. ▲▲ N England, UK
xliii K23 **Penpont** Dumfries and Galloway, SW Scotland, UK
xxxv H4 **Penrhyn Bay** Conwy, N Wales, UK
xxxv G6 **Penrhyndeudraeth** Gwynedd, NW Wales, UK
xli N8 **Penrith** Cumbria, NW England, UK
xl M8 **Penruddock** Cumbria, NW England, UK
xxxvi C17 **Penryn** Cornwall, SW England, UK
xxxvii U11 **Penshurst** Kent, SE England, UK
xxxvi E15 **Pensilva** Cornwall, SW England, UK
xlii M5 **Pentland Firth** *strait* N Scotland, UK
xliii L20 **Pentland Hills** *hill range* S Scotland, UK
xxxv F4 **Pentraeth** Isle of Anglesey, NW Wales, UK
xxxv H6 **Pentrefoelas** Conwy, N Wales, UK
xxxv J10 **Penybont** Powys, C Wales, UK
xxxv I13 **Pen y Fan** ▲ SE Wales, UK
xxxv H10 **Pen y Garn** ▲ W Wales, UK
xli P12 **Pen-y-ghent** ▲ N England, UK
xxxv F6 **Penygroes** Gwynedd, NW Wales, UK
xxxvi L16 **Penzance** Cornwall, SW England, UK
xxxvi B16 **Perranporth** Cornwall, SW England, UK
xxxviii K13 **Pershore** Worcestershire, W England, UK
xliii L17 **Perth** Perth and Kinross, C Scotland, UK
xliii I16 **Perth and Kinross** ⬖ *unitary authority* C Scotland, UK
xxxix R10 **Peterborough** ***prev.*** Medeshamstede. Cambridgeshire, E England, UK
xxxix Q10 **Peterborough** ⬖ *unitary authority* E England, UK
xliii O14 **Peterculter** City of Aberdeen, NE Scotland, UK
xlii Q12 **Peterhead** Aberdeenshire, NE Scotland, UK
xli X4 **Peterlee** Durham, N England, UK
xxxvii R12 **Petersfield** Hampshire, S England, UK
xxxviii H14 **Peterstow** Herefordshire, W England, UK
xxxvii Y10 **Petham** Kent, SE England, UK
xxxvi F13 **Petrockstow** Devon, SW England, UK
xliv H4 **Pettigoe** Donegal, N Ireland
xxxvii S12 **Petworth** West Sussex, SE England, UK
xxxvii V13 **Pevensey** East Sussex, SE England, UK
xxxvii O10 **Pewsey** Wiltshire, S England, UK
xli U11 **Pickering** North Yorkshire, N England, UK
xxxvi M14 **Piddle** ≈ S England, UK
xxxvi L13 **Piddletrenthide** Dorset, S England, UK
xli R9 **Piercebridge** Darlington, N England, UK
xl M13 **Pilling** Lancashire, NW England, UK
xxxvi L11 **Pilton** Somerset, SW England, UK
xxxvi C8 **Pimlico** Westminster, SE England, UK
xxxix R8 **Pinchbeck** Lincolnshire, E England, UK
xxxix Q8 **Pinchbeck** West Lincolnshire, E England, UK
xxxvi H14 **Pinhoe** Devon, SW England, UK
xxxvii S10 **Pirbright** Surrey, SE England, UK
xliii G21 **Pirnmill** North Ayrshire, W Scotland, UK
xlii O13 **Pitcaple** Aberdeenshire, NE Scotland, UK
xliii K16 **Pitlochry** Perth and Kinross, C Scotland, UK
xlii P12 **Pitmedden** Aberdeenshire, NE Scotland, UK
xliii N18 **Pitscottie** Fife, E Scotland, UK
xlii J9 **Pittentrail** Highland, NW Scotland, UK
xliii N18 **Pittenweem** Fife, E Scotland, UK
xxxvi F7 **Plaistow** Newham, SE England, UK
xxxix N6 **Pleasley** Derbyshire, C England, UK
xlii F12 **Plockton** Highland, NW Scotland, UK
xliv I4 **Plumbridge** Strabane, W Northern Ireland, UK
xxxvi G8 **Plumstead** Greenwich, SE England, UK
xxxvi G15 **Plym** ≈ SW England, UK
xxxvi F16 **Plymouth** Devon, SW England, UK
xxxvi F16 **Plymouth** ⬖ *unitary authority* SW England, UK
xxxvi F16 **Plympton** Devon, SW England, UK
xxxvi F16 **Plymstock** Devon, SW England, UK
xxxv H9 **Plynlimon** ▲ C Wales, UK
xli U13 **Pocklington** East Riding of Yorkshire, N England, UK
xlii G9 **Polbain** Highland, NW Scotland, UK
xxxvii V13 **Polegate** East Sussex, SE England, UK
xxxviii E14 **Polesworth** Warwickshire, C England, UK
xxxvi E16 **Polperro** Cornwall, SW England, UK
xxxvi D16 **Polruan** Cornwall, SW England, UK
xxxvi C15 **Polzeath** Cornwall, SW England, UK
xliv J4 **Pomeroy** Cookstown, C Northern Ireland, UK
xli Q6 **Pont** ≈ N England, UK
xxxv H13 **Pont Aber** Carmarthenshire, S Wales, UK
xxxv H14 **Pontardawe** Neath Port Talbot, S Wales, UK
xxxv G14 **Pontardulais** Swansea, S Wales, UK
xxxv G13 **Pontargothi** Carmarthenshire, S Wales, UK
xxxv F12 **Pontarsais** Carmarthenshire, S Wales, UK
xli T14 **Pontefract** Wakefield, N England, UK
xli Q5 **Ponteland** Northumberland, N England, UK
xxxv H9 **Ponterwyd** Ceredigion, W Wales, UK
xxxviii G10 **Pontesbury** Shropshire, W England, UK
xliv E6 **Pontoon** Mayo, NW Ireland
xxxv H10 **Pontrhydfendigaid** Ceredigion, W Wales, UK
xxxviii G14 **Pontrilas** Herefordshire, W England, UK
xxxv J13 **Pontsticill** Merthyr Tydfil, S Wales, UK
xxxv F13 **Pontyates** Carmarthenshire, S Wales, UK
xxxv I14 **Pontycymer** Bridgend, S Wales, UK
xxxv K14 **Pontypool** ***Wel.*** Pontypŵl. Torfaen, SE Wales, UK
xxxv J14 **Pontypridd** Rhondda Cynon Taff, S Wales, UK
xli R13 **Pool** Leeds, N England, UK
xxxvii N14 **Poole** Poole, S England, UK
xxxvii N14 **Poole** ⬖ *unitary authority* S England, UK
xxxvii N14 **Poole Bay** *bay* S England, UK
xlii F10 **Poolewe** Highland, NW Scotland, UK
xl M9 **Pooley Bridge** Cumbria, NW England, UK
xxxvi E7 **Poplar** *london borough capital* Tower Hamlets, SE England, UK
xxxvi H11 **Porlock** Somerset, SW England, UK
xxxvi H11 **Porlock Bay** *bay* SW England, UK
xliv K5 **Portadown** ***Ir.*** Port An Dúnáin. Craigavon, S Northern Ireland, UK
xliv M5 **Portaferry** Ards, E Northern Ireland, UK
xliii G16 **Port Appin** Argyll and Bute, W Scotland, UK
xliv I9 **Portarlington** ***Ir.*** Cúil an tSúdaire. Laois/Offaly, C Ireland
xliii E20 **Port Askaig** Argyll and Bute, W Scotland, UK
xliii G20 **Portavadie** Argyll and Bute, W Scotland, UK
xliv M5 **Portavogie** Ards, E Northern Ireland, UK
xliv K2 **Portballintrae** Coleraine, N Northern Ireland, UK
xliii H20 **Port Bannatyne** Argyll and Bute, W Scotland, UK
xxxvii Q13 **Portchester** Hampshire, S England, UK
xxxv F5 **Port Dinorwic** Gwynedd, NW Wales, UK
xliii D21 **Port Ellen** Argyll and Bute, W Scotland, UK
xlii N13 **Port Elphinstone** Aberdeenshire, NE Scotland, UK
xliii H21 **Portencross** North Ayrshire, W Scotland, UK
xl F12 **Port Erin** SW Isle of Man
xxxvi L14 **Portesham** Dorset, S England, UK
xxxv F15 **Port-Eynon** Swansea, S Wales, UK
xliii H20 **Port Glasgow** Inverclyde, W Scotland, UK
xliv K3 **Portglenone** Ballymena, NE Northern Ireland, UK
xlii M11 **Portgordon** Moray, N Scotland, UK
xxxv J14 **Porth** Rhondda Cynon Taff, S Wales, UK
xxxvi C17 **Porthallow** Cornwall, SW England, UK
xxxv H15 **Porthcawl** Bridgend, S Wales, UK
xlii F11 **Port Henderson** Highland, NW Scotland, UK
xxxvi B17 **Porthleven** Cornwall, SW England, UK
xxxv G6 **Porthmadog** ***var.*** Portmadoc. Gwynedd, NW Wales, UK
xxxvi L16 **Porthmeor** Cornwall, SW England, UK
xxxvi B16 **Porthtowan** Cornwall, SW England, UK
xliii G18 **Portinnisherrich** Argyll and Bute, W Scotland, UK
xxxvi D14 **Port Isaac Bay** *bay* SW England, UK
xxxvi J9 **Portishead** North West Somerset, SW England, UK
xxxvi D14 **Port Issac** Cornwall, SW England, UK
xlii N11 **Portknockie** Moray, N Scotland, UK
xliv G10 **Portland** Tipperary, S Ireland
xxxvi L15 **Portland Bill** ***var.*** Bill of Portland. *headland* S England, UK
xxxvi L15 **Portland, Isle of** *island* SW England, UK
xliv I10 **Portlaoise** ***var.*** Port Laoise, ***Ir.*** Portlaoighise; ***prev.*** Maryborough. Laois, C Ireland
xliii P14 **Portlethen** Aberdeenshire, NE Scotland, UK
xliii H26 **Port Logan** Dumfries and Galloway, SW Scotland, UK
xliv D5 **Portlurin** Mayo, NW Ireland
xliv B14 **Portmagee** Kerry, SW Ireland
xlii K10 **Portmahomack** Highland, N Scotland, UK
xliii D15 **Port Mor** Highland, NW Scotland, UK
xliii G16 **Portnacroish** Argyll and Bute, W Scotland, UK
xlii E8 **Portnaguran** Western Isles, NW Scotland, UK
xliii C21 **Portnahaven** Argyll and Bute, W Scotland, UK
xlii I7 **Portnancon** Highland, NW Scotland, UK
xliii M20 **Portobello** City of Edinburgh, SE Scotland, UK
xliii J18 **Port of Mentieth** Stirling, C Scotland, UK
xlii E7 **Port of Ness** Western Isles, NW Scotland, UK
xliii G25 **Portpatrick** Dumfries and Galloway, SW Scotland, UK
xxxvi B16 **Portreath** Cornwall, SW England, UK
xlii E12 **Portree** Highland, N Scotland, UK
xliv K2 **Portrush** ***Ir.*** Port Rois. Coleraine, N Northern Ireland, UK
xl F12 **Port St Mary** SW Isle of Man
xliv I2 **Portsalon** Donegal, N Ireland
xlii K6 **Portskerra** Highland, N Scotland, UK
xxxvii Q13 **Portsmouth** City of Portsmouth, S England, UK
xxxvii Q13 **Portsmouth, City of** ⬖ *unitary authority* S England, UK
xlii N11 **Portsoy** Aberdeenshire, NE Scotland, UK
xliv K2 **Portstewart** ***Ir.*** Port Stíobhaird. Coleraine, N Northern Ireland, UK
xxxv H14 **Port Talbot** Neath Port Talbot, S Wales, UK
xliv G10 **Portumna** ***Ir.*** Port Omna. Galway, W Ireland
xliii I26 **Port William** Dumfries and Galloway, SW Scotland, UK
xxxvii T8 **Potter's Bar** Hertfordshire, SE England, UK
xxxvii T5 **Potton** Bedfordshire, C England, UK
xliv K9 **Poulaphouca Reservoir** ⊡ E Ireland
xliv D13 **Poulgorm Bridge** Kerry, SW Ireland
xxxvii N8 **Poulton** Gloucestershire, C England, UK
xl M14 **Poulton-le-Fylde** Lancashire, NW England, UK
xxxvi E14 **Poundstock** Cornwall, SW England, UK
xli Q3 **Powburn** Northumberland, N England, UK
xxxvi K14 **Powerstock** Dorset, S England, UK
xxxviii J13 **Powick** Worcestershire, W England, UK
xxxv I10 **Powys** ⬖ *unitary authority* E Wales, UK
xl H16 **Poynton** Cheshire, N England, UK
xxxvi H17 **Prawle Point** *headland* SW England, UK
xxxviii H8 **Prees** Shropshire, W England, UK
xl M13 **Preesall** Lancashire, NW England, UK
xxxv D12 **Preseli, Mynydd** ▲▲ SW Wales, UK
xxxv I4 **Prestatyn** Denbighshire, N Wales, UK
xl G17 **Prestbury** Cheshire, W England, UK
xxxv K10 **Presteigne** Powys, C Wales, UK
xxxvi L14 **Preston** Dorset, S England, UK
xli N14 **Preston** Lancashire, NW England, UK
xxxix P10 **Preston** Rutland, C England, UK
xliii O20 **Preston** The Borders, S Scotland, UK
xxxvii Q11 **Preston Candover** Hampshire, S England, UK
xli P16 **Prestwich** Bury, NW England, UK
xliii I22 **Prestwick** South Ayrshire, W Scotland, UK
xxxvii R8 **Princes Risborough** Buckinghamshire, C England, UK
xxxviii M12 **Princethorpe** Warwickshire, C England, UK
xxxvi G15 **Princetown** Devon, SW England, UK
xli Q7 **Prudhoe** Northumberland, N England, UK
xxxvii U7 **Puckeridge** Hertfordshire, SE England, UK
xxxvi M14 **Puddletown** Dorset, S England, UK
xli R14 **Pudsey** Leeds, N England, UK
xxxvii S12 **Pulborough** West Sussex, SE England, UK
xxxix X11 **Pulham Market** Norfolk, E England, UK
xxxv G12 **Pumsaint** Carmarthenshire, S Wales, UK
xxxv D12 **Puncheston** Pembrokeshire, SW Wales, UK
xxxvii V9 **Purfleet** Essex, SE England, UK
xxxvi J11 **Puriton** Somerset, SW England, UK
xxxvii U10 **Purley** Croyden, SE England, UK
xxxvii N9 **Purton** Swindon, S England, UK
xxxvi B9 **Putney** Wandsworth, SE England, UK
xxxv F7 **Pwllheli** Gwynedd, NW Wales, UK
xxxv H15 **Pyle** Bridgend, S Wales, UK

Q

xxxvi J12 **Quantock Hills** *hill range* SW England, UK
xxxviii M7 **Quarndon** Derbyshire, C England, UK
xxxviii J11 **Quatt** Shropshire, W England, UK
xliii L23 **Queensberry** ▲ SW Scotland, UK
xli Q14 **Queensbury** Bradford, N England, UK
xxxv K5 **Queensferry** Flintshire, N Wales, UK
xlii I5 **Quendale** Shetland Islands, NE Scotland, UK
xxxvii U6 **Quendon** Essex, SE England, UK
xxxvii X14 **Quesnard Point** *headland* Alderney, Channel Islands
xliv D10 **Quilty** Clare, W Ireland
xliv E10 **Quin** Clare, W Ireland
xlii H8 **Quinag** ▲ NW Scotland, UK
xliii F14 **Quoich, Loch** ◎ NW Scotland, UK

R

xlii E12 **Raasay** *island* NW Scotland, UK
xlii E12 **Raasay, Sound of** *sound* NW Scotland, UK
xxxvi H12 **Rackenford** Devon, SW England, UK
xlii L5 **Rackwick** Orkney Islands, N Scotland, UK
xlii M2 **Rackwick** Orkney Islands, N Scotland, UK
xl F14 **Radcliffe** Bury, NW England, UK
xxxix O8 **Radcliffe on Trent** Nottinghamshire, C England, UK
xxxvi L10 **Radstock** Bath and North East Somerset, SW England, UK
xxxv L13 **Raglan** Monmouthshire, SE Wales, UK
xliv J8 **Raharney** Westmeath, C Ireland
xliii E19 **Rainberg Mór** *hill* W Scotland, UK
xli N16 **Rainford** St Helens, NW England, UK
xxxvii V10 **Rainham** Havering, SE England, UK
xxxvii W9 **Rainham** The Medway Towns, SE England, UK
xxxvii R12 **Rake** West Sussex, SE England, UK
xxxvi F16 **Rame** Cornwall, SW England, UK
xliv J7 **Ramor, Lough** ◎ N Ireland
xli O15 **Ramsbottom** Bury, NW England, UK
xxxvii O10 **Ramsbury** Wiltshire, S England, UK
xl G11 **Ramsey** NE Isle of Man
xxxix R11 **Ramsey** Cambridgeshire, E England, UK
xxxvii Y6 **Ramsey** Essex, SE England, UK
xl H10 **Ramsey Bay** *bay* NE Isle of Man
xxxv A13 **Ramsey Island** *island* SW Wales, UK
xxxvii Z10 **Ramsgate** Kent, SE England, UK
xli Q12 **Ramsgill** North Yorkshire, N England, UK
xliv K4 **Randalstown** Antrim, NE Northern Ireland, UK

◆ Country ● Country Capital ◇ Dependent Territory ○ Dependent Territory Capital ⬖ Administrative Region ✕ International Airport ▲ Mountain ▲▲ Mountain Range ◎ Lake ⊡ Reservoir ≈ River

xliii J16 **Rannoch, Loch** ◎ C Scotland, UK
xliii I16 **Rannoch Station** Perth and Kinross, C Scotland, UK
xliv K3 **Rasharkin** Ballymoney, N Northern Ireland, UK
xliv K9 **Rathcoole** Dublin, E Ireland
xliv G13 **Rathcormack** Cork, S Ireland
xliv H10 **Rathdowney** Laois, C Ireland
xliv L10 **Rathdrum** Wicklow, E Ireland
xlii P11 **Rathen** Aberdeenshire, NE Scotland, UK
xliv L5 **Rathfriland** Banbridge, SE Northern Ireland, UK
xliv J9 **Rathangan** Kildare, E Ireland
xliv E11 **Rathkeale** *Ir.* Ráth Caola. Limerick, SW Ireland
xliv K2 **Rathlin Island** *Ir.* Reachlainn. *island* N Northern Ireland, UK
xliv L2 **Rathlin Sound** *strait* NE Northern Ireland, UK
xliv F12 **Ráth Luirc** *Ir.* An Ráth. Cork, S Ireland
xliv I3 **Rathmelton** *Ir.* Ráth Mealtain. Donegal, N Ireland
xliv D13 **Rathmore** Kerry, SW Ireland
xliv I2 **Rathmullan** *Ir.* Ráth Maoláin. Donegal, N Ireland
xliv L10 **Rathnew** Wicklow, E Ireland
xliv K10 **Rathvilly** Carlow, SE Ireland
xxxix V12 **Rattlesden** Suffolk, E England, UK
xliii I16 **Rattray** Perth and Kinross, C Scotland, UK
xlii Q11 **Rattray Head** *headland* NE Scotland, UK
xxxix Q11 **Raunds** Northamptonshire, C England, UK
xl K10 **Ravenglass** Cumbria, NW England, UK
xli W10 **Ravenscar** North Yorkshire, N England, UK
xli O10 **Ravenstonedale** Cumbria, NW England, UK
xli S16 **Rawmarsh** Rotherham, N England, UK
xli P15 **Rawtenstall** Lancashire, NW England, UK
xxxvii W8 **Rayleigh** Essex, SE England, UK
xxxvii Q9 **Reading** Reading, S England, UK
xxxvii Q9 **Reading** ◐ *unitary authority* S England, UK
xliv F9 **Rea, Lough** ◎ Galway, W Ireland
xxxix O9 **Rearsby** Leicestershire, C England, UK
xlii K6 **Reay** Highland, N Scotland, UK
xliv D8 **Recess** Galway, W Ireland
xxxvii Y10 **Reculver** Kent, SE England, UK
xxxiv L16 **Redbridge** ◐ *London borough* SE England, UK
xli T8 **Redcar** Redcar and Cleveland, N England, UK
xli T8 **Redcar and Cleveland** ◐ *unitary authority* N England, UK
xxxviii C17 **Redditch** Worcestershire, W England, UK
xli O4 **Rede** ≈ N England, UK
xliii N16 **Redford** Angus, E Scotland, UK
xxxix W11 **Redgrave** Suffolk, E England, UK
xxxvii U11 **Redhill** Surrey, SE England, UK
xxxix Y11 **Redisham** Suffolk, E England, UK
xlii M3 **Redland** Orkney Islands, N Scotland, UK
xlii F11 **Redpoint** Highland, NW Scotland, UK
xxxv E13 **Red Roses** Carmarthenshire, S Wales, UK
xxxvi B17 **Redruth** Cornwall, SW England, UK
xxxv F4 **Red Wharf Bay** *bay* N Wales, UK
xxxv L15 **Redwick** Newport, SE Wales, UK
xxxix Y10 **Reedham** Norfolk, E England, UK
xliv H8 **Ree, Lough** *Ir.* Loch Rí. ◎ C Ireland
xliv E12 **Reens** Limerick, SW Ireland
xxxix Q5 **Reepham** Lincolnshire, E England, UK
xxxix W8 **Reepham** Norfolk, E England, UK
xli Q10 **Reeth** North Yorkshire, N England, UK
xlii E10 **Reidh, Rubha** *headland* NW Scotland, UK
xlii G9 **Reiff** Highland, NW Scotland, UK
xxxvii T11 **Reigate** Surrey, SE England, UK
xli W11 **Reighton** North Yorkshire, N England, UK
xlii M7 **Reiss** Highland, N Scotland, UK
xliii J20 **Renfrew** Renfrewshire, W Scotland, UK
xliii H20 **Renfrewshire** ◐ *unitary authority* W Scotland, UK
xli R3 **Rennington** Northumberland, N England, UK
xliii I19 **Renton** West Dunbartonshire, W Scotland, UK
xli N7 **Renwick** Cumbria, NW England, UK
xxxv H14 **Resolven** Neath Port Talbot, S Wales, UK
xxxix O5 **Retford** Nottinghamshire, C England, UK
xxxvii W8 **Rettendon** Essex, SE England, UK
xxxix R6 **Revesby** Lincolnshire, E England, UK
xxxv H11 **Rhandirmwyn** Carmarthenshire, S Wales, UK
xxxv I10 **Rhayader** Powys, C Wales, UK
xxxv G10 **Rheidol** ≈ W Wales, UK
xliii E16 **Rhemore** Highland, W Scotland, UK
xxxv J5 **Rhewl** Denbighshire, N Wales, UK
xlii I8 **Rhian** Highland, NW Scotland, UK
xlii H7 **Rhiconich** Highland, NW Scotland, UK
xxxv G7 **Rhinog Fawr** ▲ NW Wales, UK
xxxv E7 **Rhiw** Gwynedd, NW Wales, UK
xliv I9 **Rhode** Offaly, E Ireland
xxxv I14 **Rhondda Cynon Taff** ◐ *unitary authority* S Wales, UK
xxxv J16 **Rhoose** The Vale of Glamorgan, S Wales, UK
xxxv F12 **Rhos** Carmarthenshire, S Wales, UK
xxxv E4 **Rhoscolyn** Isle of Anglesey, NW Wales, UK
xxxv C14 **Rhoscrowther** Pembrokeshire, SW Wales, UK
xxxv K6 **Rhosllanerchrugog** Wrexham, NE Wales, UK
xxxv E4 **Rhosneigr** Isle of Anglesey, NW Wales, UK
xxxv F15 **Rhossili** Swansea, S Wales, UK
xxxv F5 **Rhostryfan** Gwynedd, NW Wales, UK
xliii G20 **Rhubodach** Argyll and Bute, W Scotland, UK
xxxv I4 **Rhuddlan** Denbighshire, N Wales, UK
xlii D14 **Rhum** *var.* Rum. *island* W Scotland, UK
xliii F21 **Rhunahaorine** Argyll and Bute, W Scotland, UK
xxxv J7 **Rhydycroesau** Powys, C Wales, UK
xxxv I4 **Rhyl** Denbighshire, NE Wales, UK
xxxv J13 **Rhymney** Caerphilly, S Wales, UK
xlii N13 **Rhynie** Aberdeenshire, NE Scotland, UK
xli O14 **Ribble** ≈ NW England, UK
xli O11 **Ribble Head** North Yorkshire, N England, UK
xli O14 **Ribchester** Lancashire, NW England, UK
xli U13 **Riccall** North Yorkshire, N England, UK
xliv K5 **Richhill** Armagh, S Northern Ireland, UK
xli R10 **Richmond** North Yorkshire, N England, UK
xxxvi A9 **Richmond upon Thames** Richmond upon Thames, SE England, UK
xxxiv K16 **Richmond upon Thames** *var.* Richmond-upon-Thames. ◐ *London borough* SE England, UK
xliii O14 **Rickarton** Aberdeenshire, NE Scotland, UK
xxxvii S8 **Rickmansworth** Hertfordshire, SE England, UK
xxxvii W6 **Ridgewell** Essex, SE England, UK
xxxvii U12 **Ridgewood** East Sussex, SE England, UK
xxxvii S6 **Ridgmont** Bedfordshire, C England, UK
xli P6 **Riding Mill** Northumberland, N England, UK
xli P5 **Ridsdale** Northumberland, N England, UK
xliii K20 **Riggend** North Lanarkshire, C Scotland, UK
xli V11 **Rillington** North Yorkshire, N England, UK
xlii J8 **Rimsdale, Loch** ◎ N Scotland, UK
xliv G14 **Ringaskiddy** Cork, S Ireland
xliii J25 **Ringford** Dumfries and Galloway, SW Scotland, UK
xxxvii U13 **Ringmer** East Sussex, SE England, UK
xliv K3 **Ringsend** Coleraine, N Northern Ireland, UK
xxxix U7 **Ringstead** Norfolk, E England, UK
xxxvii O13 **Ringwood** Dorset, S England, UK
xlii M5 **Rinnigill** Orkney Islands, N Scotland, UK
xxxviii M7 **Ripley** Derbyshire, C England, UK
xli R12 **Ripley** North Yorkshire, N England, UK
xxxvii S10 **Ripley** Surrey, SE England, UK
xli R12 **Ripon** North Yorkshire, N England, UK
xxxv K14 **Risca** Caerphilly, S Wales, UK
xli O14 **Rishton** Lancashire, NW England, UK
xliv F14 **Riverstown** Cork, S Ireland
xxxix O13 **Roade** Northamptonshire, C England, UK
xxxvi F14 **Roadford Reservoir** ⊞ SW England, UK
xlii C8 **Roag, Loch** *inlet* NW Scotland, UK
xliv C15 **Roaringwater Bay** *bay* S Ireland
xliii N22 **Roberton** The Borders, S Scotland, UK
xxxvii W12 **Robertsbridge** East Sussex, SE England, UK
xliv J9 **Robertstown** Kildare, E Ireland
xli V10 **Robin Hood's Bay** North Yorkshire, N England, UK
xxxvi F13 **Roborough** Devon, SW England, UK
xxxviii K8 **Rocester** Staffordshire, C England, UK
xxxv C13 **Roch** Pembrokeshire, SW Wales, UK
xl G13 **Rochdale** Rochdale, NW England, UK
xl P14 **Rochdale** ◐ *unitary authority* NW England, UK
xxxvii V10 **Rochester** *anc.* Durobrivae. Kent, SE England, UK
xli O4 **Rochester** Northumberland, N England, UK
xxxvii X8 **Rochford** Essex, SE England, UK
xliv I8 **Rochfortbridge** Westmeath, C Ireland
xxxvi I14 **Rockbeare** Devon, SW England, UK
xliv E12 **Rockchapel** Cork, S Ireland
xl M6 **Rockcliffe** Cumbria, NW England, UK
xliv J6 **Rockcorry** Monaghan, NE Ireland
xlii B10 **Rodel** Western Isles, NW Scotland, UK
xxxvii V8 **Roding** ≈ SE England, UK
xxxviii H9 **Rodington** Shropshire, W England, UK
xliv J3 **Roe** ≈ N Northern Ireland, UK
xxxvii B9 **Roehampton** Wandsworth, SE England, UK
xlii H3 **Roesound** Shetland Islands, NE Scotland, UK
xlii J9 **Rogart** Highland, NW Scotland, UK
xli Q9 **Romaldkirk** Durham, N England, UK
xli S10 **Romanby** North Yorkshire, N England, UK
xliii L21 **Romannobridge** The Borders, S Scotland, UK
xxxvii V9 **Romford** Havering, SE England, UK
xl H15 **Romiley** Stockport, NW England, UK
xxxvii X12 **Romney Marsh** *physical region* SE England, UK
xxxvii O12 **Romsey** Hampshire, S England, UK
xlii E11 **Rona** *island* NW Scotland, UK
xlii B12 **Ronay** *island* NW Scotland, UK
xli P7 **Rookhope** Durham, N England, UK
xli X14 **Roos** East Riding of Yorkshire, N England, UK
xliv H7 **Roosky** Roscommon, C Ireland
xxxvii Q12 **Ropley** Hampshire, S England, UK
xxxix Q8 **Ropsley** Lincolnshire, E England, UK
xlii L4 **Rora Head** *headland* N Scotland, UK
xliv H2 **Rosapenna** Donegal, N Ireland
xliv G8 **Roscommon** *Ir.* Ros Comáin. Roscommon, C Ireland
xliv F7 **Roscommon** *Ir.* Ros Comáin. ◐ *county* C Ireland
xliv H10 **Roscrea** *Ir.* Ros Cré. Tipperary, C Ireland
xli U10 **Rosedale Abbey** North Yorkshire, N England, UK
xlii P11 **Rosehearty** Aberdeenshire, NE Scotland, UK
xxxv C14 **Rosemarket** Pembrokeshire, SW Wales, UK
xlii J11 **Rosemarkie** Highland, NW Scotland, UK
xlii F15 **Roshven** Highland, NW Scotland, UK
xl M7 **Rosley** Cumbria, NW England, UK
xliii J25 **Ross** Dumfries and Galloway, SW Scotland, UK
xliv F4 **Rossan Point** *headland* N Ireland
xliv E15 **Ross Carbery** Cork, S Ireland
xli P14 **Rossendale, Forest of** *forest* N England, UK
xliv G2 **Rosses Bay** *bay* N Ireland
xliv F5 **Rosses Point** Sligo, N Ireland
xliv K13 **Rosslare** *Ir.* Ros Láir. Wexford, SE Ireland
xliv K13 **Rosslare Harbour** Wexford, SE Ireland
xliv K12 **Rosslare Point** *headland* SE Ireland
xliv J6 **Rosslea** Fermanagh, W Northern Ireland, UK
xxxviii I14 **Ross-on-Wye** Herefordshire, W England, UK
xliv L6 **Rostrevor** Newry and Mourne, S Northern Ireland, UK
xliii L19 **Rosyth** Fife, E Scotland, UK
xli Q4 **Rothbury** Northumberland, N England, UK
xxxvii S12 **Rother** ≈ S England, UK
xxxvii V12 **Rother** ≈ SE England, UK
xxxvii V12 **Rotherfield** East Sussex, SE England, UK
xli S16 **Rotherham** Rotherham, N England, UK
xli S16 **Rotherham** ◐ *unitary authority* N England, UK
xlii M12 **Rothes** Moray, N Scotland, UK
xliii H20 **Rothesay** Argyll and Bute, W Scotland, UK
xlii N4 **Rothiesholm** Orkney Islands, N Scotland, UK
xli S14 **Rothwell** Leeds, N England, UK
xxxix P11 **Rothwell** Northamptonshire, C England, UK
xxxvii U13 **Rottingdean** Brighton and Hove, SE England, UK
xxxix V8 **Rougham** Norfolk, E England, UK
xxxix X7 **Roughton** Norfolk, E England, UK
xliv C8 **Roundstone** Galway, W Ireland
xliv L10 **Roundwood** Wicklow, E Ireland
xlii M3 **Rousay** *island* N Scotland, UK
xliii N24 **Rowanburn** Dumfries and Galloway, SW Scotland, UK
xxxvii R13 **Rowland's Castle** Hampshire, S England, UK
xli R6 **Rowlands Gill** Gateshead, NE England, UK
xxxvii T5 **Roxton** Bedfordshire, C England, UK
xxxvii V8 **Roxwell** Essex, SE England, UK
xliv H8 **Royal Canal** *Ir.* An Chanáil Ríoga. *canal* C Ireland
xxxviii E17 **Royal Leamington Spa** *var.* Leamington, Leamington Spa. Warwickshire, C England, UK
xxxvii X12 **Royal Military Canal** *canal* SE England, UK
xxxvii V11 **Royal Tunbridge Wells** *var.* Tunbridge Wells. Kent, SE England, UK
xli S15 **Royston** Barnsley, N England, UK
xxxvii U6 **Royston** Hertfordshire, E England, UK
xli P15 **Royton** Oldham, NW England, UK
xxxvii X16 **Rozel** Jersey, Channel Islands
xxxv K6 **Ruabon** Wrexham, NE Wales, UK
xxxvi B17 **Ruan Minor** Cornwall, SW England, UK
xxxvii S11 **Rudgwick** West Sussex, SE England, UK
xli W12 **Rudston** East Riding of Yorkshire, N England, UK
xl G10 **Rue Point** *headland* N Isle of Man
xl N15 **Rufford** Lancashire, NW England, UK
xxxviii M11 **Rugby** Warwickshire, C England, UK
xxxviii K9 **Rugeley** Staffordshire, C England, UK
xxxix Y11 **Rumburgh** Suffolk, E England, UK
xxxv K15 **Rumney** Cardiff, S Wales, UK
xlii D15 **Rùm, Sound of** *strait* NW Scotland, UK
xliv L2 **Runabay Head** *headland* N Northern Ireland, UK
xl D16 **Runcorn** Cheshire, C England, UK
xliv L8 **Rush** *Ir.* An Ros. Dublin, E Ireland
xxxix Q12 **Rushden** Northamptonshire, C England, UK
xxxix Q7 **Ruskington** Lincolnshire, E England, UK
xliii J20 **Rutherglen** City of Glasgow, C Scotland, UK
xxxv J5 **Ruthin** *Wel.* Rhuthun. Denbighshire, NE Wales, UK
xxxix P9 **Rutland** ◐ *unitary authority* C England, UK
xxxix P9 **Rutland Water** ◎ C England, UK
xliii G25 **Ryan, Loch** *inlet* SW Scotland, UK
xxxvii Q14 **Ryde** Isle of Wight, S England, UK
xxxvii X12 **Rye** East Sussex, SE England, UK
xli T11 **Rye** ≈ N England, UK
xli S7 **Ryhope** Sunderland, NE England, UK
xli P12 **Rylstone** North Yorkshire, N England, UK
xli U2 **Ryton** Gateshead, NE England, UK

S

xli V4 **Sacriston** Durham, N England, UK
xliii F22 **Saddell** Argyll and Bute, W Scotland, UK
xlii G13 **Saddle, The** ▲ NW Scotland, UK
xxxvii V6 **Saffron Walden** Essex, SE England, UK
xliii P20 **St Abbs** The Borders, S Scotland, UK
xliii P20 **St Abb's Head** *headland* SE Scotland, UK
xxxvi B16 **St Agnes** Cornwall, SW England, UK
xxxvi I17 **St Agnes** *island* SW England, UK
xxxvii T8 **St Albans** *anc.* Verulamium. Hertfordshire, E England, UK
xxxvii N15 **St Alban's Head** *var.* St Aldhelm's Head. *headland* S England, UK
xliii N18 **St Andrews** Fife, E Scotland, UK
xliii N17 **St Andrews Bay** *bay* E Scotland, UK
xxxvii X14 **St Anne** Alderney, N Guernsey
xxxv L14 **St Arvans** Monmouthshire, SE Wales, UK
xxxv I4 **St Asaph** Denbighshire, N Wales, UK
xxxvii X17 **St Aubin** Jersey, Channel Islands
xxxvi D16 **St Austell** Cornwall, SW England, UK
xxxvi D16 **St Austell Bay** *bay* SW England, UK
xl K9 **St Bees** Cumbria, NW England, UK
xl J9 **St Bees Head** *headland* NW England, UK
xxxvi D16 **St Blazey** Cornwall, SW England, UK
xliii N21 **St Boswells** The Borders, S Scotland, UK
xxxvi K8 **St Briavels** Gloucestershire, C England, UK
xxxv C13 **St Brides** Pembrokeshire, SW Wales, UK
xxxv B13 **St Brides Bay** *inlet* SW Wales, UK
xliii H18 **St Catherines** Argyll and Bute, W Scotland, UK
xxxvii P15 **St Catherine's Point** *headland* S England, UK
xxxv E13 **St Clears** Carmarthenshire, S Wales, UK
xxxvi C15 **St Columb Major** Cornwall, SW England, UK
xlii P11 **St Combs** Aberdeenshire, NE Scotland, UK
xliii O15 **St Cyrus** Aberdeenshire, NE Scotland, UK
xxxv B13 **St David's** Pembrokeshire, SW Wales, UK
xxxv A12 **St David's Head** *headland* SW Wales, UK
xxxvi B17 **St Day** Cornwall, SW England, UK
xxxvi C16 **St Dennis** Cornwall, SW England, UK
xxxv E11 **St Dogmaels** Ceredigion, W Wales, UK
xxxv I16 **St Donats** The Vale of Glamorgan, S Wales, UK
xlii P11 **St Fergus** Aberdeenshire, NE Scotland, UK
xliv M5 **Saintfield** Down, E Northern Ireland, UK
xliii J17 **St Fillans** Perth and Kinross, C Scotland, UK
xxxvi E16 **St Germans** Cornwall, SW England, UK
xxxv C14 **St Govan's Head** *headland* SW Wales, UK
xxxv I10 **St Harmon** Powys, C Wales, UK
xl D15 **St Helens** St Helens, NW England, UK
xli N16 **St Helens** ◐ *unitary authority* NW England, UK
xxxvii X17 **St Helier** ○ (Jersey) S Jersey, Channel Islands
xxxvi C15 **St Issey** Cornwall, SW England, UK
xxxix S11 **St Ives** Cambridgeshire, E England, UK
xxxvi L16 **St Ives** Cornwall, SW England, UK
xxxvi M16 **St Ives Bay** *bay* SW England, UK
xxxvii X16 **St John** Jersey, Channel Islands
xl F11 **St John's** C Isle of Man
xli P8 **St John's Chapel** Durham, N England, UK
xliv F4 **St John's Point** *headland* N Ireland
xliv M6 **St John's Point** *headland* E Northern Ireland, UK
xliv I3 **St Johnstown** Donegal, N Ireland
xliii J24 **St John's Town of Dalry** Dumfries and Galloway, SW Scotland, UK
xxxvi C7 **St John's Wood** Westminster, SE England, UK
xxxvi L16 **St Just** Cornwall, SW England, UK
xxxvi C17 **St Keverne** Cornwall, SW England, UK
xlii H3 **St Magnus Bay** *bay* N Scotland, UK
xxxvii Z11 **St Margaret's at Cliffe** Kent, SE England, UK
xlii M5 **St Margaret's Hope** Orkney Islands, NE Scotland, UK
xl G12 **St Mark's** S Isle of Man
xxxvii X17 **St Mary** Jersey, Channel Islands
xlii M5 **St Mary's** Orkney Islands, N Scotland, UK
xxxvi I17 **St Mary's** *island* SW England, UK
xliii M22 **St Mary's Loch** ◎ S Scotland, UK
xxxvi C17 **St Mawes** Cornwall, SW England, UK
xxxvi C15 **St Mawgan** Cornwall, SW England, UK
xxxvi F15 **St Mellion** Cornwall, SW England, UK
xxxv K15 **St Mellons** Cardiff, S Wales, UK
xxxvi C15 **St Minver** Cornwall, SW England, UK
xliii N18 **St Monans** Fife, E Scotland, UK
xxxvi E15 **St Neot** Cornwall, SW England, UK
xxxix R12 **St Neots** Cambridgeshire, E England, UK
xxxv C12 **St Nicholas** Pembrokeshire, SW Wales, UK
xxxvii Y7 **St Osyth** Essex, SE England, UK
xxxvii X17 **St Peter** Jersey, Channel Islands
xxxvii V15 **St Peter Port** ○ (Guernsey) C Guernsey, Channel Islands
xxxvii W15 **St Sampson** Guernsey, Channel Islands
xxxvi D15 **St Teath** Cornwall, SW England, UK
xliii O16 **St Vigeans** Angus, E Scotland, UK
xxxvi C15 **St Wenn** Cornwall, SW England, UK
xxxviii H14 **St Weonards** Herefordshire, W England, UK
xxxvi G17 **Salcombe** Devon, SW England, UK
xxxvii X7 **Salcott** Essex, SE England, UK
xli P16 **Sale** Trafford, NW England, UK
xliii E17 **Salen** Argyll and Bute, W Scotland, UK
xliii F16 **Salen** Highland, NW Scotland, UK
xl G15 **Salford** Salford, NW England, UK
xli O15 **Salford** ◐ *unitary authority* NW England, UK
xliii L19 **Saline** Fife, E Scotland, UK
xxxvii O12 **Salisbury** *var.* New Sarum. Wiltshire, S England, UK
xxxvii N11 **Salisbury Plain** *plain* S England, UK
xxxvi E16 **Saltash** Cornwall, SW England, UK
xli U9 **Saltburn-by-the-Sea** Redcar and Cleveland, N England, UK
xliii H21 **Saltcoats** North Ayrshire, W Scotland, UK
xliv K13 **Saltee Islands** *island group* SE Ireland
xxxix S4 **Saltfleet** Lincolnshire, E England, UK
xxxix S4 **Saltfleetby St Peter** Lincolnshire, E England, UK
xxxvi L10 **Saltford** Bath and North East Somerset, SW England, UK
xxxviii G6 **Saltney** Cheshire, W England, UK
xxxvi I13 **Sampford Peverell** Devon, SW England, UK
xliii D20 **Sanaigmore** Argyll and Bute, W Scotland, UK
xlii I4 **Sand** Shetland Islands, NE Scotland, UK
xliii F23 **Sanda** *island* W Scotland, UK
xliii F14 **Sandaig** Highland, NW Scotland, UK
xlii C14 **Sanday** *island* NW Scotland, UK
xlii O3 **Sanday** *island* NE Scotland, UK
xxxviii I6 **Sandbach** Cheshire, W England, UK
xliii H19 **Sandbank** Argyll and Bute, W Scotland, UK
xxxvi K10 **Sandford** North West Somerset, SW England, UK
xlii N4 **Sandgarth** Orkney Islands, N Scotland, UK
xlii P11 **Sandhaven** Aberdeenshire, NE Scotland, UK
xliii H25 **Sandhead** Dumfries and Galloway, SW Scotland, UK
xxxvii R10 **Sandhurst** Bracknell Forest, S England, UK
xli U12 **Sand Hutton** North Yorkshire, N England, UK
xxxviii K8 **Sandon** Staffordshire, C England, UK
xxxvii Q14 **Sandown** Isle of Wight, S England, UK
xxxvi E16 **Sandplace** Cornwall, SW England, UK
xlii O2 **Sandquoy** Orkney Islands, N Scotland, UK
xlii A15 **Sandray** *island* NW Scotland, UK
xxxix U8 **Sandringham** Norfolk, E England, UK
xxxviii B14 **Sandwell** ◐ *unitary authority* C England, UK
xxxvii Z10 **Sandwich** Kent, SE England, UK
xxxvii Z10 **Sandwich Bay** *bay* SE England, UK
xl M9 **Sandwick** Cumbria, NW England, UK
xlii I5 **Sandwick** Shetland Islands, NE Scotland, UK
xxxvii T5 **Sandy** Bedfordshire, C England, UK
xliii K23 **Sanquhar** Dumfries and Galloway, SW Scotland, UK
xlii M7 **Sarclet** Highland, N Scotland, UK
xxxvii W15 **Sark** *Fr.* Sercq. *island* Channel Islands
xxxviii G13 **Sarnesfield** Herefordshire, W England, UK
xxxv E7 **Sarn Meyllteyrn** Gwynedd, NW Wales, UK
xxxvii Y10 **Sarre** Kent, SE England, UK
xli Q7 **Satley** Durham, N England, UK
xl M11 **Satterthwaite** Cumbria, NW England, UK
xliii N23 **Saughtree** The Borders, S Scotland, UK
xxxv D14 **Saundersfoot** Pembrokeshire, SW Wales, UK
xxxvii U7 **Sawbridgeworth** Hertfordshire, SE England, UK
xliv J3 **Sawel** ▲ C Northern Ireland, UK
xxxix T13 **Sawston** Cambridgeshire, E England, UK
xxxix R11 **Sawtry** Cambridgeshire, E England, UK
xxxix P9 **Saxby** Leicestershire, C England, UK
xxxix O9 **Saxelbye** Leicestershire, C England, UK
xxxix P5 **Saxilby** Lincolnshire, E England, UK
xxxix Y12 **Saxmundham** Suffolk, E England, UK
xxxix X12 **Saxtead** Suffolk, E England, UK
xxxix W8 **Saxthorpe** Norfolk, E England, UK
xli S14 **Saxton** North Yorkshire, N England, UK
xl L10 **Scafell Pike** ▲ NW England, UK
xliii D19 **Scalasaig** Argyll and Bute, W Scotland, UK
xli W10 **Scalby** North Yorkshire, N England, UK
xl M9 **Scales** Cumbria, NW England, UK
xxxix O8 **Scalford** Leicestershire, C England, UK
xlii I4 **Scalloway** Shetland Islands, N Scotland, UK
xlii C10 **Scalpay** *island* NW Scotland, UK
xlii E13 **Scalpay** *island* NW Scotland, UK
xxxix R5 **Scamblesby** Lincolnshire, E England, UK
xlii M5 **Scapa Flow** *sea basin* N Scotland, UK
xlii B10 **Scarastavore** Western Isles, NW Scotland, UK
xliii E18 **Scarba** *island* W Scotland, UK
xli W10 **Scarborough** North Yorkshire, N England, UK
xlii H12 **Scardroy** Highland, NW Scotland, UK
xliv A14 **Scariff Island** *island* SW Ireland
xliii C17 **Scarinish** Argyll and Bute, W Scotland, UK
xlii B9 **Scarp** *island* NW Scotland, UK
xliv F10 **Scarriff** Clare, W Ireland
xli R4 **Scars, The** *headland* N England, UK
xxxix P4 **Scawby** North Lincolnshire, N England, UK
xliii J16 **Schiehallion** ▲ C Scotland, UK
xliv D15 **Schull** Cork, S Ireland
xxxvi I17 **Scilly, Isles of** *island group* SW England, UK
xlii E13 **Sconser** Highland, NW Scotland, UK
xli R10 **Scotch Corner** North Yorkshire, N England, UK
xli N12 **Scotforth** Lancashire, NW England, UK
xliii H15 **Scotland** *national region* Scotland, UK
xliii F16 **Scotstown** Highland, NW Scotland, UK
xxxix P4 **Scotter** Lincolnshire, E England, UK
xlii G7 **Scourie** Highland, NW Scotland, UK
xlii I5 **Scousburgh** Shetland Islands, NE Scotland, UK
xlii L6 **Scrabster** Highland, N Scotland, UK
xliv H8 **Scramoge** Roscommon, C Ireland
xliv D8 **Screeb** Galway, W Ireland
xxxix P3 **Scunthorpe** North Lincolnshire, E England, UK
xxxvii V13 **Seaford** East Sussex, SE England, UK
xlii C9 **Seaforth, Loch** *inlet* NW Scotland, UK
xli S7 **Seaham** Durham, N England, UK
xli R2 **Seahouses** Northumberland, N England, UK
xliii H21 **Seamill** North Ayrshire, W Scotland, UK
xxxix Y8 **Sea Palling** Norfolk, E England, UK
xl K10 **Seascale** Cumbria, NW England, UK
xxxix T6 **Seathorne** Lincolnshire, E England, UK
xl K8 **Seaton** Cumbria, NW England, UK
xxxvi J14 **Seaton** Devon, SW England, UK
xli T8 **Seaton Carew** Hartlepool, N England, UK
xli R5 **Seaton Delaval** Northumberland, N England, UK
xli T10 **Seave Green** North Yorkshire, N England, UK
xxxvii Q14 **Seaview** Isle of Wight, S England, UK
xl M8 **Sebergham** Cumbria, NW England, UK
xli O10 **Sedbergh** Cumbria, NW England, UK
xxxix P8 **Sedgebrook** Lincolnshire, E England, UK
xli S8 **Sedgefield** Durham, N England, UK
xxxix U8 **Sedgeford** Norfolk, E England, UK
xxxviii A14 **Sedgley** Dudley, C England, UK
xli N11 **Sedgwick** Cumbria, NW England, UK
xxxvii M10 **Seend** Wiltshire, S England, UK
xli L15 **Sefton** ◐ *unitary authority* NW England, UK
xlii F18 **Seil** *island* W Scotland, UK
xxxviii G8 **Selattyn** Shropshire, W England, UK
xxxvii R11 **Selborne** Hampshire, S England, UK
xli T14 **Selby** North Yorkshire, N England, UK
xliii N22 **Selkirk** SE Scotland, UK
xli K10 **Sellafield Station** Cumbria, NW England, UK
xlii I1 **Sellafirth** Shetland Islands, NE Scotland, UK
xxxvii R14 **Selsey** West Sussex, SE England, UK
xxxvii R14 **Selsey Bill** *headland* S England, UK
xxxvii M10 **Semington** Wiltshire, S England, UK
xxxvii S10 **Send** Surrey, SE England, UK
xxxv J14 **Senghenydd** Caerphilly, S Wales, UK
xxxvi L16 **Sennen** Cornwall, SW England, UK
xxxv I12 **Sennybridge** Powys, C Wales, UK
xxxix U9 **Setchey** Norfolk, E England, UK
xli P12 **Settle** North Yorkshire, N England, UK
xxxvi G6 **Seven Kings** Redbridge, SE England, UK
xxxvii U10 **Sevenoaks** Kent, SE England, UK
xxxv H13 **Seven Sisters** Neath Port Talbot, S Wales, UK
xxxvi J10 **Severn, Mouth of the** *estuary* England/Wales, UK
xlii D13 **Sgurr Alasdair** ▲ NW Scotland, UK
xlii H11 **Sgurr Mor** *cliff* NW Scotland, UK
xlii H12 **Sgurr Na Lapaich** ▲ Highland, NW Scotland, UK
xlii D7 **Shader** Western Isles, NW Scotland, UK
xxxvi M12 **Shaftesbury** Dorset, S England, UK
xxxvii O10 **Shalbourne** Wiltshire, S England, UK
xxxvii P14 **Shalfleet** Isle of Wight, S England, UK
xxxvii S11 **Shalford** Surrey, SE England, UK
xliii H19 **Shandon** Argyll and Bute, W Scotland, UK
xxxvii Q14 **Shanklin** Isle of Wight, S England, UK
xliv E14 **Shanlaragh** Cork, S Ireland
xliv E11 **Shannon** Clare, W Ireland
xliv G9 **Shannon** *Ir.* An tSionainn. ≈ W Ireland
xliv E11 **Shannon** ✕ Clare, W Ireland
xliv G9 **Shannonbridge** Offaly, C Ireland
xliv H6 **Shannon Erne Waterway** *canal* N Ireland
xliv C11 **Shannon, Mouth of the** *estuary* W Ireland
xli N9 **Shap** Cumbria, NW England, UK
xli N10 **Shap Fells** ⛰ NW England, UK
xlii N4 **Shapinsay** *island* NE Scotland, UK
xxxix S5 **Sharnbrook** Bedfordshire, C England, UK
xxxvi L8 **Sharpness** Gloucestershire, C England, UK
xxxviii I7 **Shavington** Cheshire, W England, UK
xlii C7 **Shawbost** Western Isles, NW Scotland, UK
xxxviii H9 **Shawbury** Shropshire, W England, UK
xxxvi F13 **Shebbear** Devon, SW England, UK
xliv I7 **Sheelin, Lough** ◎ C Ireland
xliv H2 **Sheep Haven** *Ir.* Cuan nag Caorach. *inlet* N Ireland
xliv B15 **Sheep's Head** *headland* S Ireland
xxxvi F13 **Sheepwash** Devon, SW England, UK
xxxvii X9 **Sheerness** Kent, SE England, UK
xli S17 **Sheffield** Sheffield, N England, UK
xli R17 **Sheffield** ◐ *unitary authority* N England, UK
xxxvii T6 **Shefford** Bedfordshire, C England, UK
xlii H7 **Sheigra** Highland, NW Scotland, UK
xl Q14 **Shelf** Bradford, N England, UK
xxxviii G10 **Shelve** Shropshire, W England, UK
xxxvi B7 **Shepherd's Bush** Hammersmith and Fulham, SE England, UK
xxxvii Y11 **Shepherdswell** Kent, SE England, UK
xxxvii X9 **Sheppey, Isle of** *island* SE England, UK
xxxix S13 **Shepreth** Cambridgeshire, E England, UK
xxxix N9 **Shepshed** Leicestershire, C England, UK
xxxvi L11 **Shepton Mallet** Somerset, SW England, UK
xxxvi L12 **Sherborne** Dorset, S England, UK
xli W4 **Sherburn** Durham, N England, UK
xli V11 **Sherburn** North Yorkshire, N England, UK
xli T14 **Sherburn in Elmet** North Yorkshire, N England, UK
xliv J6 **Shercock** Cavan, N Ireland
xxxviii I9 **Sheriffhales** Shropshire, W England, UK
xli T12 **Sheriff Hutton** North Yorkshire, N England, UK
xxxix X7 **Sheringham** Norfolk, E England, UK
xxxviii R6 **Sherington** Milton Keynes, C England, UK
xliv D15 **Sherkin Island** *island* S Ireland
xxxvi M9 **Sherston** Wiltshire, S England, UK
xlii H3 **Shetland Islands** ◐ *unitary authority* NE Scotland, UK
xlii H1 **Shetland Islands** *island group* NE Scotland, UK
xlii D10 **Shiant Islands** *island group* NW Scotland, UK
xlii G13 **Shiel Bridge** Highland, NW Scotland, UK
xlii F12 **Shieldaig** Highland, NW Scotland, UK
xliii F15 **Shiel, Loch** ◎ N Scotland, UK
xxxviii I9 **Shifnal** Shropshire, W England, UK
xli R3 **Shilbottle** Northumberland, N England, UK
xli R8 **Shildon** Durham, N England, UK
xliv K11 **Shillelagh** Wicklow, E Ireland
xxxvi M13 **Shillingstone** Dorset, S England, UK
xli S7 **Shiney Row** Sunderland, NE England, UK
xlii I9 **Shin, Loch** ◎ N Scotland, UK
xlii I9 **Shinness** Highland, NW Scotland, UK
xliv H10 **Shinrone** Offaly, C Ireland
xxxvii V10 **Shipbourne** Kent, SE England, UK
xxxix V9 **Shipdham** Norfolk, E England, UK
xli R13 **Shipley** Bradford, N England, UK
xxxviii M13 **Shipston on Stour** Warwickshire, C England, UK
xli T12 **Shipton** North Yorkshire, N England, UK
xxxvii O7 **Shipton-under-Wychwood** Oxfordshire, C England, UK
xxxv L14 **Shirenewton** Monmouthshire, SE Wales, UK
xxxviii D16 **Shirley** Solihull, C England, UK
xliii G22 **Shiskine** North Ayrshire, W Scotland, UK
xxxvii X9 **Shoeburyness** Southend-on-Sea, SE England, UK
xxxvi G8 **Shooters Hill** Greenwich, SE England, UK
xxxvi E7 **Shoreditch** Hackney, SE England, UK
xxxvii S13 **Shoreham-by-Sea** West Sussex, SE England, UK
xxxvii P14 **Shorwell** Isle of Wight, S England, UK
xli Q7 **Shotley Bridge** Durham, N England, UK
xxxix X13 **Shotley Gate** Suffolk, E England, UK
xliii K20 **Shotts** North Lanarkshire, C Scotland, UK
xxxix U9 **Shouldham** Norfolk, E England, UK
xxxviii H9 **Shrewsbury** *hist.* Scrobesbyrig'. Shropshire, W England, UK
xxxvii O9 **Shrivenham** Oxfordshire, C England, UK
xxxviii G10 **Shropshire** ◐ *county* W England, UK
xxxviii B13 **Shropshire Union Canal** *canal* W England, UK
xxxvi J14 **Shute** Devon, SW England, UK
xxxvii W6 **Sible Hedingham** Essex, E England, UK
xxxix S7 **Sibsey** Lincolnshire, E England, UK
xxxvi I14 **Sidbury** Devon, SW England, UK
xxxvi G9 **Sidcup** Bexley, SE England, UK
xliii M17 **Sidlaw Hills** ⛰ E Scotland, UK
xxxvi J14 **Sidmouth** Devon, SW England, UK
xli W13 **Sigglesthorne** East Riding of Yorkshire, N England, UK
xxxix N9 **Sileby** Leicestershire, C England, UK
xl K11 **Silecroft** Cumbria, NW England, UK
xl K7 **Silloth** Cumbria, NW England, UK
xli Q13 **Silsden** Bradford, N England, UK
xli N11 **Silverdale** Lancashire, NW England, UK
xliv G11 **Silvermine Mountains** *hill range* Tipperary, C Ireland
xxxix O13 **Silverstone** Northamptonshire, C England, UK
xxxvi H13 **Silverton** Devon, SW England, UK
xlii H4 **Silwick** Shetland Islands, NE Scotland, UK
xxxvi G11 **Simonsbath** Somerset, SW England, UK
xxxvii R13 **Singleton** West Sussex, SE England, UK
xli U11 **Sinnington** North Yorkshire, N England, UK
xlii G9 **Sionascaig, Loch** ◎ NW Scotland, UK
xliv I3 **Sion Mills** Strabane, W Northern Ireland, UK
xxxvii X10 **Sittingbourne** Kent, SE England, UK
xliv F11 **Sixmilebridge** Clare, W Ireland
xxxvii N12 **Sixpenny Handley** Dorset, S England, UK
xxxix Y12 **Sizewell** Suffolk, E England, UK
xlii N4 **Skaill** Orkney Islands, N Scotland, UK
xliii J22 **Skares** East Ayrshire, W Scotland, UK
xlii H4 **Skarpigarth** Shetland Islands, NE Scotland, UK
xxxix T6 **Skegness** Lincolnshire, E England, UK
xli N16 **Skelmersdale** Lancashire, NW England, UK
xliii H20 **Skelmorlie** North Ayrshire, W Scotland, UK
xl M8 **Skelton** Cumbria, NW England, UK
xli U9 **Skelton** Redcar and Cleveland, N England, UK
xlii J6 **Skerray** Highland, N Scotland, UK
xliv L8 **Skerries** *Ir.* Na Sceirí. Dublin, E Ireland
xliv D15 **Skibbereen** *Ir.* An Sciobairín. Cork, SW Ireland
xl L8 **Skiddaw** ▲ NW England, UK
xxxix P8 **Skillington** Lincolnshire, E England, UK
xl K7 **Skinburness** Cumbria, NW England, UK
xliii G20 **Skipness** Argyll and Bute, W Scotland, UK
xli X12 **Skipsea** East Riding of Yorkshire, N England, UK
xli Q13 **Skipton** North Yorkshire, N England, UK
xli S11 **Skipton-on-Swale** North Yorkshire, N England, UK
xli T13 **Skipwith** North Yorkshire, N England, UK
xliii L21 **Skirling** The Borders, S Scotland, UK
xxxv A14 **Skokholm Island** *island* SW Wales, UK
xxxv A13 **Skomer Island** *island* SW Wales, UK
xlii D12 **Skye, Isle of** *island* NW Scotland, UK
xli O13 **Slaidburn** Lancashire, NW England, UK
xli P7 **Slaley** Northumberland, N England, UK
xliii K20 **Slamannan** Falkirk, C Scotland, UK
xliv K7 **Slane** Meath, E Ireland
xliv K11 **Slaney** *Ir.* An tSláine. ≈ SE Ireland
xxxvi H16 **Slapton** Devon, SW England, UK
xxxix Q7 **Sleaford** Lincolnshire, E England, UK
xliv B13 **Slea Head** *Ir.* Ceann Sléibhe. *headland* SW Ireland
xliii F14 **Sleat, Sound of** *strait* NW Scotland, UK
xli V12 **Sledmere** East Riding of Yorkshire, N England, UK
xli V10 **Sleights** North Yorkshire, N England, UK
xliii G22 **Sliddery** North Ayrshire, W Scotland, UK
xliv F9 **Slieve Aughty Mountains** ⛰ W Ireland
xliv H10 **Slieve Bloom Mountains** ⛰ C Ireland
xliv D6 **Slieve Car** ▲ NW Ireland
xliv L6 **Slieve Donard** ▲ SE Northern Ireland, UK
xliv G11 **Slievefelim Mountains** ⛰ C Ireland
xliv F6 **Slieve Gamph** *var.* Ox Mountains. ⛰ N Ireland
xliv G11 **Slievekimalta** ▲ C Ireland
xliv C13 **Slieve Mish Mountains** ⛰ SW Ireland
xliv H12 **Slievenamon** ▲ S Ireland
xliv I2 **Slieve Snaght** ▲ N Ireland
xliii E13 **Sligachan** Highland, NW Scotland, UK
xliv G5 **Sligo** *Ir.* Sligeach. Sligo, NW Ireland
xliv F6 **Sligo** *Ir.* Sligeach. ◐ *county* NW Ireland
xliv F5 **Sligo Bay** *Ir.* Cuan Shligigh. *inlet* NW Ireland
xxxvii S13 **Slindon** West Sussex, SE England, UK
xli T11 **Slingsby** North Yorkshire, N England, UK
xxxvii S9 **Slough** Slough, S England, UK
xxxvii S9 **Slough** ◐ *unitary authority* S England, UK
xliv B8 **Slyne Head** *Ir.* Ceann Léime. *headland* W Ireland
xxxix Y8 **Smallburgh** Norfolk, E England, UK
xxxvii Y11 **Smeeth** Kent, SE England, UK
xxxviii B15 **Smethwick** Sandwell, C England, UK
xl M6 **Smithfield** Cumbria, NW England, UK
xl G11 **Snaefell** ▲ C Isle of Man
xli T14 **Snaith** East Riding of Yorkshire, N England, UK
xli R11 **Snape** North Yorkshire, N England, UK
xliv C14 **Sneem** Kerry, SW Ireland
xxxix Q5 **Snelland** Lincolnshire, E England, UK
xxxix U8 **Snettisham** Norfolk, E England, UK
xxxviii L12 **Snitterfield** Warwickshire, C England, UK
xlii D11 **Snizort, Loch** *inlet* NW Scotland, UK
xxxvii W10 **Snodland** Kent, SE England, UK
xxxv G5 **Snowdon** ▲ NW Wales, UK
xxxv G5 **Snowdonia** ⛰ NW Wales, UK
xxxix N8 **Soar** ≈ C England, UK
xlii D14 **Soay** *island* NW Scotland, UK
xxxix T11 **Soham** Cambridgeshire, E England, UK
xxxvii P13 **Solent, The** *channel* S England, UK
xxxviii D15 **Solihull** Solihull, C England, UK
xxxviii L11 **Solihull** ◐ *unitary authority* C England, UK
xxxv C13 **Solva** Pembrokeshire, SW Wales, UK
xxxvi J12 **Somerset** ◐ *county* SW England, UK
xxxix S11 **Somersham** Cambridgeshire, E England, UK
xxxvii P7 **Somerton** Oxfordshire, C England, UK
xxxvi K12 **Somerton** Somerset, SW England, UK
xxxvii O13 **Sopley** Hampshire, S England, UK

◆ Country ● Country Capital ◇ Dependent Territory ○ Dependent Territory Capital ◐ Administrative Region ✕ International Airport ▲ Mountain ⛰ Mountain Range ◎ Lake ⊞ Reservoir ≈ River

xliii I25 **Sorbie** Dumfries and Galloway, SW Scotland, UK
xliii D16 **Sorisdale** Argyll and Bute, W Scotland, UK
xliii J22 **Sorn** East Ayrshire, W Scotland, UK
xxxvii T9 **Southall** Ealing, SE England, UK
xxxviii M12 **Southam** Warwickshire, C England, UK
xxxvii P13 **Southampton** ***hist.*** Hamwih, ***Lat.*** Clausentum. City of Southampton, S England, UK
xxxvii P12 **Southampton, City of** ⬖ *unitary authority* S England, UK
xliii H23 **South** Ayrshire ⬖ *unitary authority* W Scotland, UK
xli U9 **South Bank** Redcar and Cleveland, N England, UK
xl F12 **South Barrule** *hill* S Isle of Man
xxxvii W9 **South Benfleet** Essex, SE England, UK
xxxvii V11 **Southborough** Kent, SE England, UK
xxxvi G16 **South Brent** Devon, SW England, UK
xli V14 **South Cave** East Riding of Yorkshire, N England, UK
xxxvii N8 **South Cerney** Gloucestershire, C England, UK
xli R3 **South Charlton** Northumberland, N England, UK
xxxvii R12 **South Downs** *hill range* SE England, UK
xliii F23 **Southend** Argyll and Bute, W Scotland, UK
xxxvii X9 **Southend-on-Sea** Essex, E England, UK
xxxvii W9 **Southend-on-Sea** ⬖ *unitary authority* SE England, UK
xliii K23 **Southern Uplands** ▲▲ S Scotland, UK
xxxix T10 **Southery** Norfolk, E England, UK
xliii N16 **South Esk** ≈ E Scotland, UK
xxxix P3 **South Ferriby** North Lincolnshire, N England, UK
xxxvi B9 **Southfields** Wandsworth, SE England, UK
xxxvii Z11 **South Foreland** *headland* SE England, UK
xxxvi D5 **Southgate** Enfield, SE England, UK
xxxvi L8 **South Gloucestershire** ⬖ *unitary authority* W England, UK
xxxvii R12 **South Harting** West Sussex, SE England, UK
xxxvii Q13 **South Hayling** Hampshire, S England, UK
xxxvii T11 **South Holmwood** Surrey, SE England, UK
xxxix Q4 **South Kelsey** Lincolnshire, E England, UK
xli S15 **South Kirkby** Wakefield, N England, UK
xxxix R7 **South Kyme** Lincolnshire, E England, UK
xliii J21 **South Lanarkshire** ⬖ *unitary authority* C Scotland, UK
xxxviii K13 **South Littleton** Worcestershire, C England, UK
xxxvii U13 **South Malling** East Sussex, SE England, UK
xxxvii X8 **Southminster** Essex, SE England, UK
xxxvi G12 **South Molton** Devon, SW England, UK
xxxvi K12 **South Petherton** Somerset, SW England, UK
xl B13 **Southport** Sefton, NW England, UK
xliii L19 **South Queensferry** City of Edinburgh, SE Scotland, UK
xlii N5 **South Ronaldsay** *island* NE Scotland, UK
xli W2 **South Shields** South Tyneside, NE England, UK
xli W13 **South Skirlaugh** East Riding of Yorkshire, N England, UK
xliv D10 **South Sound** *sound* W Ireland
xlii N5 **Southtown** Orkney Islands, N Scotland, UK
xli O7 **South Tyne** ≈ N England, UK
xli S6 **South Tyneside** ⬖ *unitary authority* NE England, UK
xlii A13 **South Uist** *island* NW Scotland, UK
xlii I4 **South View** Shetland Islands, NE Scotland, UK
xxxiv L16 **Southwark** ⬖ *London borough* SE England, UK
xxxvi D8 **Southwark** *London borough capital* Southwark, SE England, UK
xxxix O7 **Southwell** Nottinghamshire, C England, UK
xxxix Z11 **Southwold** Suffolk, E England, UK
xxxvii W8 **South Woodham Ferrers** Essex, E England, UK
xxxix T8 **South Wootton** Norfolk, E England, UK
xxxvi G14 **South Zeal** Devon, SW England, UK
xli S11 **Sowerby** North Yorkshire, N England, UK
xxxix R8 **Spalding** Lincolnshire, E England, UK
xxxix R11 **Spaldwick** Cambridgeshire, E England, UK
xliv D10 **Spanish Point** *headland* W Ireland
xxxvi L12 **Sparkford** Somerset, SW England, UK
xliii H15 **Spean Bridge** Highland, NW Scotland, UK
xl M17 **Speke** Liverpool, NW England, UK
xli R8 **Spennymoor** Durham, N England, UK
xliv J3 **Sperrin Mountains** ▲▲ N Northern Ireland, UK
xxxviii J13 **Spetchley** Worcestershire, W England, UK
xlii M11 **Spey** ≈ NE Scotland, UK
xlii M11 **Spey Bay** Moray, N Scotland, UK
xliv E9 **Spiddle** Galway, W Ireland
xxxix S6 **Spilsby** Lincolnshire, E England, UK
xlii J10 **Spinningdale** Highland, NW Scotland, UK
xlii L7 **Spital** Highland, N Scotland, UK
xxxv D13 **Spittal** Pembrokeshire, SW Wales, UK
xliii L15 **Spittal of Glenshee** Perth and Kinross, C Scotland, UK
xli R13 **Spofforth** North Yorkshire, N England, UK
xxxix O12 **Spratton** Northamptonshire, C England, UK
xxxix Q5 **Spridlington** Lincolnshire, E England, UK
xliii O21 **Sprouston** The Borders, S Scotland, UK
xxxix X9 **Sprowston** Norfolk, E England, UK
xli Y15 **Spurn Head** *headland* E England, UK
xliv L10 **Sraghmore** Wicklow, E Ireland
xlii J4 **Stack Skerry** *island* N Scotland, UK
xxxvii Q8 **Stadhampton** Oxfordshire, C England, UK
xliii D17 **Staffa** *island* W Scotland, UK
xlii E11 **Staffin** Highland, NW Scotland, UK
xxxviii J9 **Stafford** Staffordshire, C England, UK
xxxviii C13 **Staffordshire** ⬖ *county* C England, UK
xli Q9 **Staindrop** Durham, N England, UK
xxxvii S9 **Staines** Surrey, SE England, UK
xli T15 **Stainforth** Doncaster, N England, UK
xli P12 **Stainforth** North Yorkshire, N England, UK
xli W10 **Staintondale** North Yorkshire, N England, UK
xli U9 **Staithes** Redcar and Cleveland, N England, UK
xxxvi L12 **Stalbridge** Dorset, S England, UK
xxxix Y8 **Stalham** Norfolk, E England, UK
xli P11 **Stalling Busk** North Yorkshire, N England, UK
xli Q16 **Stalybridge** Tameside, NW England, UK
xxxix Q9 **Stamford** Lincolnshire, E England, UK
xli U12 **Stamford Bridge** East Riding of Yorkshire, N England, UK
xli Q6 **Stamfordham** Northumberland, N England, UK
xxxvi D6 **Stamford Hill** Hackney, SE England, UK
xli N15 **Standish** Wigan, NW England, UK
xxxviii J8 **Standon** Staffordshire, C England, UK
xxxvii W9 **Stanford-le-Hope** Essex, SE England, UK
xli Q8 **Stanhope** Durham, N England, UK
xliii L22 **Stanhope** The Borders, S Scotland, UK
xli Q7 **Stanley** Durham, N England, UK
xliii L17 **Stanley** Perth and Kinross, C Scotland, UK
xxxvi A5 **Stanmore** Harrow, SE England, UK
xli R5 **Stannington** Northumberland, N England, UK
xxxvii V7 **Stansted** ✕ (London) Essex, E England, UK
xxxvii V7 **Stansted** Mountfitchet Hertfordshire, E England, UK
xxxix V11 **Stanton** Suffolk, E England, UK
xxxvii Q8 **Stanton St John** Oxfordshire, C England, UK
xxxvii X7 **Stanway** Essex, SE England, UK
xxxvii N6 **Stanway** Gloucestershire, C England, UK
xxxvi J12 **Staple Fitzpaine** Somerset, SW England, UK
xxxix N8 **Stapleford** Nottinghamshire, C England, UK
xxxvii N11 **Stapleford** Wiltshire, S England, UK
xxxvii W11 **Staplehurst** Kent, SE England, UK
xxxvi I14 **Starcross** Devon, SW England, UK
xxxvi H16 **Start Bay** *bay* SW England, UK
xli Q9 **Startforth** Durham, N England, UK
xxxvi H17 **Start Point** *headland* SW England, UK
xlii O3 **Start Point** *headland* N Scotland, UK
xxxvi M7 **Staunton** Gloucestershire, C England, UK
xxxvi K7 **Staunton** Gloucestershire, C England, UK
xxxviii G13 **Staunton on Wye** Herefordshire, W England, UK
xli N10 **Staveley** Cumbria, NW England, UK
xxxviii M5 **Staveley** Derbyshire, C England, UK
xxxvi M7 **Staverton** Gloucestershire, C England, UK
xli W11 **Staxton** North Yorkshire, N England, UK
xxxvi I10 **Steep Holm** *island* S England, UK
xxxix S6 **Steeping** ≈ E England, UK
xxxvii W6 **Steeple Bumpstead** Essex, SE England, UK
xxxvii R7 **Steeple Claydon** Buckinghamshire, C England, UK
xxxix R13 **Steeple Morden** Cambridgeshire, E England, UK
xliii K19 **Stenhousemuir** Falkirk, C Scotland, UK
xlii H2 **Stenness** Shetland Islands, NE Scotland, UK
xliii O19 **Stenton** East Lothian, SE Scotland, UK
xxxvi E7 **Stepney** Tower Hamlets, SE England, UK
xliii J20 **Stepps** North Lanarkshire, C Scotland, UK
xxxvii T7 **Stevenage** Hertfordshire, E England, UK
xliii I21 **Stevenston** North Ayrshire, W Scotland, UK
xxxvii P8 **Steventon** Oxfordshire, C England, UK
xliii I21 **Stewarton** East Ayrshire, W Scotland, UK
xxxvii T13 **Steyning** West Sussex, SE England, UK
xxxvi F13 **Stibb Cross** Devon, SW England, UK
xliii O21 **Stichill** The Borders, S Scotland, UK
xxxix S6 **Stickford** Lincolnshire, E England, UK
xxxix S6 **Stickney** Lincolnshire, E England, UK
xlii A12 **Stilligarry** Western Isles, NW Scotland, UK
xli T12 **Stillington** North Yorkshire, N England, UK
xxxix R10 **Stilton** Cambridgeshire, E England, UK
xliii H23 **Stinchar** ≈ W Scotland, UK
xliii K19 **Stirling** Stirling, C Scotland, UK
xliii I19 **Stirling** ⬖ *unitary authority* C Scotland, UK
xxxvi B17 **Stithians** Cornwall, SW England, UK
xxxvii W8 **Stock** Essex, SE England, UK
xxxvii P11 **Stockbridge** Hampshire, S England, UK
xxxvi J13 **Stockland** Devon, SW England, UK
xl H16 **Stockport** Stockport, NW England, UK
xli P16 **Stockport** ⬖ *unitary authority* NW England, UK
xli R16 **Stocksbridge** Sheffield, N England, UK
xli X6 **Stockton-on-Tees** ***var.*** Stockton on Tees. Stockton-on-Tees, N England, UK
xli S9 **Stockton-on-Tees** ⬖ *unitary authority* NE England, UK
xxxvii W9 **Stoke** Kent, SE England, UK
xxxix P10 **Stoke Albany** Northamptonshire, C England, UK
xxxix W13 **Stoke-by-Nayland** Suffolk, E England, UK
xxxix U10 **Stoke Ferry** Norfolk, E England, UK
xxxvi H16 **Stoke Fleming** Devon, SW England, UK
xxxviii M10 **Stoke Golding** Leicestershire, C England, UK
xxxvii R7 **Stoke Hammond** Buckinghamshire, C England, UK
xxxvii R8 **Stokenchurch** Buckinghamshire, C England, UK
xxxvi D6 **Stoke Newington** Hackney, SE England, UK
xxxviii J7 **Stoke-on-Trent** ***var.*** Stoke. City of Stoke-on-Trent, C England, UK
xxxviii J7 **Stoke-on-Trent, City of** ⬖ *unitary authority* C England, UK
xxxvii S9 **Stoke Poges** Buckinghamshire, C England, UK
xxxviii B17 **Stoke Prior** Worcestershire, W England, UK
xli T9 **Stokesley** North Yorkshire, N England, UK
xxxvii R7 **Stone** Buckinghamshire, C England, UK
xxxvi L8 **Stone** Gloucestershire, C England, UK
xxxviii J8 **Stone** Staffordshire, C England, UK
xliii P14 **Stonehaven** Aberdeenshire, NE Scotland, UK
xxxvii N11 **Stonehenge** *ancient monument* Wiltshire, S England, UK
xliii J21 **Stonehouse** South Lanarkshire, C Scotland, UK
xlii A13 **Stoneybridge** Western Isles, NW Scotland, UK
xliii H25 **Stoneykirk** Dumfries and Galloway, SW Scotland, UK
xlii Q1 **Stonybreck** Shetland Islands, NE Scotland, UK
xxxvii R6 **Stony Stratford** Milton Keynes, C England, UK
xlii D8 **Stornoway** Western Isles, NW Scotland, UK
xxxvii S12 **Storrington** West Sussex, S England, UK
xlii E12 **Storr, The** ▲ NW Scotland, UK
xxxvii T6 **Stotfold** Bedfordshire, E England, UK
xxxix W13 **Stour** ≈ E England, UK
xxxvi L12 **Stour** ≈ S England, UK
xxxvii Z10 **Stour** ≈ SE England, UK
xxxviii B15 **Stourbridge** Dudley, C England, UK
xxxviii A16 **Stourport-on-Severn** Worcestershire, W England, UK
xliii N21 **Stow** The Borders, S Scotland, UK
xxxix W12 **Stowmarket** Suffolk, E England, UK
xxxvii N7 **Stow-on-the-Wold** Gloucestershire, C England, UK
xliv I3 **Strabane** ***Ir.*** An Srath Bán. Strabane, W Northern Ireland, UK
xliv I3 **Strabane** ⬖ *district* W Northern Ireland, UK
xliii O14 **Strachan** Aberdeenshire, NE Scotland, UK
xliii H18 **Strachur** Argyll and Bute, W Scotland, UK
xliv J10 **Stradbally** Laois, C Ireland
xxxix X11 **Stradbroke** Suffolk, E England, UK
xliv I6 **Stradone** Cavan, N Ireland
xxxix U9 **Stradsett** Norfolk, E England, UK
xliii I23 **Straiton** South Ayrshire, W Scotland, UK
xliv F5 **Strandhill** Sligo, N Ireland
xliv M5 **Strangford** Down, E Northern Ireland, UK
xliv M5 **Strangford Lough** ***Ir.*** Loch Cuan. *inlet* E Northern Ireland, UK
xliv H3 **Stranorlar** ***Ir.*** Srath an Urlá***ir.*** Donegal, NW Ireland
xliii H25 **Stranraer** Dumfries and Galloway, S Scotland, UK
xxxvi E6 **Stratford** Newham, SE England, UK
xxxix W14 **Stratford St Mary** Suffolk, E England, UK
xxxviii K13 **Stratford-upon-Avon** ***var.*** Stratford. Warwickshire, C England, UK
xxxviii D17 **Stratford upon Avon Canal** *canal* C England, UK
xliii J21 **Strathaven** South Lanarkshire, C Scotland, UK
xliii J19 **Strathblane** Stirling, C Scotland, UK
xlii H9 **Strathcanaird** Highland, NW Scotland, UK
xlii G12 **Strathcarron** Highland, NW Scotland, UK
xlii M13 **Strathdon** Aberdeenshire, NE Scotland, UK
xliii M18 **Strathmiglo** Fife, E Scotland, UK
xlii I11 **Strathpeffer** Highland, NW Scotland, UK
xlii K6 **Strathy** Highland, N Scotland, UK
xlii J6 **Strathy Point** *headland* N Scotland, UK
xliii J18 **Strathyre** Stirling, C Scotland, UK
xxxvi E13 **Stratton** Cornwall, SW England, UK
xxxvii Q7 **Stratton Audley** Oxfordshire, C England, UK
xxxvi D9 **Streatham** Lambeth, SE England, UK
xxxvii S6 **Streatley** Bedfordshire, C England, UK
xxxvii Q9 **Streatley** West Berkshire, S England, UK
xxxvi K11 **Street** Somerset, SW England, UK
xli T12 **Strensall** York, N England, UK
xli P16 **Stretford** Trafford, NW England, UK
xxxix T11 **Stretham** Cambridgeshire, E England, UK
xl E16 **Stretton** Cheshire, W England, UK
xxxix Q9 **Stretton** Rutland, C England, UK
xlii P11 **Strichen** Aberdeenshire, NE Scotland, UK
xliv G7 **Strokestown** Roscommon, C Ireland
xlii L6 **Stroma, Island of** *island* N Scotland, UK
xlii F12 **Stromeferry** Highland, N Scotland, UK
xlii L4 **Stromness** Orkney Islands, N Scotland, UK
xliii I18 **Stronachlachar** Stirling, C Scotland, UK
xliii H19 **Strone** Argyll and Bute, W Scotland, UK
xlii H8 **Stronechrubie** Highland, NW Scotland, UK
xlii N3 **Stronsay** *island* NE Scotland, UK
xlii N3 **Stronsay Firth** *inlet* N Scotland, UK
xliii F16 **Strontian** Highland, NW Scotland, UK
xxxvi M8 **Stroud** Gloucestershire, C England, UK
xxxvii R12 **Stroud** Hampshire, S England, UK
xxxv C12 **Strumble Head** *headland* SW Wales, UK
xlii I12 **Struy** Highland, NW Scotland, UK
xlii P12 **Stuartfield** Aberdeenshire, NE Scotland, UK
xxxvii N14 **Studland** Dorset, S England, UK
xxxviii C17 **Studley** Warwickshire, C England, UK
xxxvi M13 **Sturminster Newton** Dorset, S England, UK
xxxvii Y10 **Sturry** Kent, SE England, UK
xxxix P5 **Sturton by Stow** Lincolnshire, E England, UK
xliv G8 **Suck** ≈ C Ireland
xxxviii L8 **Sudbury** Derbyshire, C England, UK
xxxix V13 **Sudbury** Suffolk, E England, UK
xxxix W12 **Suffolk** ⬖ *county* E England, UK
xliv H12 **Suir** ***Ir.*** An tSiú***ir.*** ≈ S Ireland
xl G11 **Sulby** N Isle of Man
xlii J4 **Sule Skerry** *island* N Scotland, UK
xlii I2 **Sullom** Shetland Islands, NE Scotland, UK
xlii I5 **Sumburgh** Shetland Islands, NE Scotland, UK
xlii I6 **Sumburgh Head** *headland* NE Scotland, UK
xli R12 **Summer Bridge** North Yorkshire, N England, UK
xxxvi C16 **Summercourt** Cornwall, SW England, UK
xlii F9 **Summer Isles** *island group* NW Scotland, UK
xliii F16 **Sunart, Loch** *inlet* NW Scotland, UK
xli X3 **Sunderland** ***var.*** Wearmouth. Sunderland, NE England, UK
xli W3 **Sunderland** ⬖ *unitary authority* NE England, UK
xli X15 **Sunk Island** East Riding of Yorkshire, N England, UK
xxxvii S10 **Sunningdale** Surrey, SE England, UK
xxxvii S11 **Surrey** ⬖ *county* SE England, UK
xxxix R8 **Sutterton** Lincolnshire, E England, UK
xxxix S11 **Sutton** Cambridgeshire, E England, UK
xxxix Y13 **Sutton** Suffolk, E England, UK
xxxvii T10 **Sutton** Sutton, SE England, UK
xxxiv K17 **Sutton** ⬖ *London borough* SE England, UK
xxxvi M9 **Sutton Benger** Wiltshire, S England, UK
xxxix T8 **Sutton Bridge** Lincolnshire, E England, UK
xxxviii D14 **Sutton Coldfield** Birmingham, C England, UK
xxxix N6 **Sutton in Ashfield** Nottinghamshire, C England, UK
xxxix T5 **Sutton on Sea** Lincolnshire, E England, UK
xli T12 **Sutton-on-the-Forest** North Yorkshire, N England, UK
xxxix S9 **Sutton St James** Lincolnshire, E England, UK
xxxvii P11 **Sutton Scotney** Hampshire, S England, UK
xxxvii W11 **Sutton Valence** Kent, SE England, UK
xxxviii L9 **Swadlincote** Derbyshire, C England, UK
xxxix V9 **Swaffham** Norfolk, E England, UK
xli S10 **Swainby** North Yorkshire, N England, UK
xxxvi M10 **Swainswick** Bath and North East Somerset, SW England, UK
xxxvii P6 **Swalcliffe** Oxfordshire, C England, UK
xli S11 **Swale** ≈ N England, UK
xliv H6 **Swalinbar** Cavan, N Ireland
xxxix Q4 **Swallow** Lincolnshire, E England, UK
xxxvii N12 **Swallowcliffe** Wiltshire, S England, UK
xxxvii R10 **Swallowfield** Wokingham, S England, UK
xxxvii N14 **Swanage** Dorset, S England, UK
xxxvii V9 **Swanley** Kent, SE England, UK
xxxv G14 **Swansea** ***Wel.*** Abertawe. Swansea, S Wales, UK
xxxv G14 **Swansea** ⬖ *unitary authority* S Wales, UK
xxxv G15 **Swansea Bay** *bay* S Wales, UK
xxxix W9 **Swanton Morley** Norfolk, E England, UK
xxxix X10 **Swardeston** Norfolk, E England, UK
xxxix Q8 **Swayfield** Lincolnshire, E England, UK
xliv H3 **Swilly** ≈ N Ireland
xliv I2 **Swilly, Lough** ***Ir.*** Loch Súilí. *inlet* N Ireland
xxxvi G12 **Swimbridge** Devon, SW England, UK
xxxvii O9 **Swindon** Thamesdown, S England, UK
xxxvii N9 **Swindon** ⬖ *unitary authority* C England, UK
xxxvii S5 **Swineshead** Bedfordshire, C England, UK
xxxix R7 **Swineshead** Lincolnshire, E England, UK
xliv E6 **Swinford** Mayo, NW Ireland
xxxix N11 **Swinford** Leicestershire, C England, UK
xlii I3 **Swining** Shetland Islands, NE Scotland, UK
xli O16 **Swinton** Salford, NW England, UK
xliii P21 **Swinton** The Borders, S Scotland, UK
xliv L8 **Swords** ***Ir.*** Sord, Sórd Choluim Chille. Dublin, E Ireland
xli T15 **Sykehouse** Doncaster, N England, UK
xlii I3 **Symbister** Shetland Islands, NE Scotland, UK
xxxviii H15 **Symonds Yat** Herefordshire, W England, UK
xlii J7 **Syre** Highland, N Scotland, UK
xxxix O13 **Syresham** Northamptonshire, C England, UK
xxxix O9 **Syston** Leicestershire, C England, UK

T

xli S13 **Tadcaster** North Yorkshire, N England, UK
xxxvii Q10 **Tadley** Hampshire, S England, UK
xxxvii T11 **Tadworth** Surrey, SE England, UK
xxxv J15 **Taff** ≈ SE Wales, UK
xliv K12 **Taghmon** Wexford, SE Ireland
xlii J10 **Tain** Highland, N Scotland, UK
xxxvii V7 **Takeley** Essex, SE England, UK
xxxv J12 **Talgarth** Powys, C Wales, UK
xlii F11 **Talladale** Highland, NW Scotland, UK
xliv L9 **Tallaght** Dublin, E Ireland
xxxv G12 **Talley** Carmarthenshire, S Wales, UK
xliv G13 **Tallow** Waterford, S Ireland
xlii I6 **Talmine** Highland, N Scotland, UK
xxxv G6 **Talsarnau** Gwynedd, NW Wales, UK
xxxv G9 **Talybont** Ceredigion, W Wales, UK
xxxv F6 **Talysarn** Gwynedd, NW Wales, UK
xxxviii D14 **Tam** ≈ C England, UK
xxxvi E14 **Tamar** ≈ SW England, UK
xxxvi F15 **Tamerton Foliot** Devon, SW England, UK
xli P16 **Tameside** ⬖ *unitary authority* NW England, UK
xxxviii D13 **Tamworth** Staffordshire, C England, UK
xxxv J7 **Tanat** ≈ E Wales, UK
xliv K5 **Tandragee** Armagh, S Northern Ireland, UK
xlii B9 **Taransay** *island* NW Scotland, UK
xlii K10 **Tarbat Ness** *headland* N Scotland, UK
xliv D11 **Tarbert** Kerry, SW Ireland
xliii G20 **Tarbert** Argyll and Bute, W Scotland, UK
xliii E19 **Tarbert** Argyll and Bute, W Scotland, UK
xlii C10 **Tarbert** Western Isles, NW Scotland, UK
xliii I18 **Tarbet** Argyll and Bute, W Scotland, UK
xliii I22 **Tarbolton** South Ayrshire, W Scotland, UK
xliii N15 **Tarfside** Angus, E Scotland, UK
xliii N14 **Tarland** Aberdeenshire, NE Scotland, UK
xxxviii I6 **Tarporley** Cheshire, W England, UK
xliii E14 **Tarskavaig** Highland, NW Scotland, UK
xxxviii H6 **Tarvin** Cheshire, W England, UK
xxxviii H6 **Tattenhall** Cheshire, W England, UK
xxxvi J12 **Taunton** Somerset, SW England, UK
xxxvi F15 **Tavistock** Devon, SW England, UK
xxxvi F15 **Tavy** ≈ SW England, UK
xxxvi G12 **Taw** ≈ SW England, UK
xliv F7 **Tawnyinah** Mayo, NW Ireland
xliii L17 **Tay** ≈ C Scotland, UK
xliii M17 **Tay, Firth of** *inlet* E Scotland, UK
xliii F21 **Tayinloan** Argyll and Bute, W Scotland, UK
xliii J17 **Tay, Loch** ◎ C Scotland, UK
xliii G17 **Taynuilt** Argyll and Bute, W Scotland, UK
xliii N17 **Tayport** Fife, E Scotland, UK
xliii F19 **Tayvallich** Argyll and Bute, W Scotland, UK
xxxix R4 **Tealby** Lincolnshire, E England, UK
xliii E14 **Teangue** Highland, NW Scotland, UK
xli N10 **Tebay** Cumbria, NW England, UK
xxxvi G14 **Tedburn St Mary** Devon, SW England, UK
xli R9 **Tees** ≈ N England, UK
xli T8 **Tees Bay** *bay* N England, UK
xxxv E12 **Teifi** ***var.*** River Teif. ≈ SW Wales, UK
xxxvi H14 **Teign** ≈ SW England, UK
xxxvi H15 **Teignmouth** Devon, SW England, UK
xxxviii I9 **Telford** Shropshire, W England, UK
xxxviii J13 **Teme** ≈ England/Wales, UK
xliv H11 **Tempelmore** Tipperary, S Ireland
xliii L24 **Templand** Dumfries and Galloway, SW Scotland, UK
xxxvi D15 **Temple** Cornwall, SW England, UK
xliii M20 **Temple** Midlothian, SE Scotland, UK
xxxvi L12 **Templecombe** Somerset, SW England, UK
xli T14 **Temple Hirst** North Yorkshire, N England, UK
xliv L4 **Templepatrick** Antrim, NE Northern Ireland, UK
xli N8 **Temple Sowerby** Cumbria, NW England, UK
xxxv D13 **Templeton** Pembrokeshire, SW Wales, UK
xxxviii I12 **Tenbury Wells** Worcestershire, W England, UK
xxxv E14 **Tenby** Pembrokeshire, SW Wales, UK
xxxvii X11 **Tenterden** Kent, SE England, UK
xxxvii W7 **Terling** Essex, SE England, UK
xliv H2 **Termon** Donegal, N Ireland
xxxix T8 **Terrington St Clement** Norfolk, E England, UK
xxxvii P11 **Test** ≈ S England, UK
xxxvi M8 **Tetbury** Gloucestershire, C England, UK
xxxix S4 **Tetney** Lincolnshire, E England, UK
xxxvii Q8 **Tetsworth** Oxfordshire, C England, UK
xxxviii A14 **Tettenhall** Wolverhampton, C England, UK
xliii M23 **Teviot** ≈ SE Scotland, UK
xliii N23 **Teviothead** The Borders, S Scotland, UK
xxxvi M6 **Tewkesbury** Gloucestershire, C England, UK
xxxvii Q8 **Thame** Oxfordshire, C England, UK
xxxvii T9 **Thames** ≈ S England, UK
xxxvii P10 **Thatcham** West Berkshire, S England, UK
xxxvii V6 **Thaxted** Essex, SE England, UK
xxxvii Q10 **Theale** West Berkshire, S England, UK
xliii M22 **The Borders** ⬖ *unitary authority* S Scotland, UK
xxxvii V9 **The Medway Towns** ⬖ *unitary authority* SE England, UK
xxxv G15 **The Mumbles** Swansea, S Wales, UK
xxxvii U6 **Therfield** Hertfordshire, SE England, UK
xxxix V11 **Thetford** Norfolk, E England, UK
xxxv I15 **The Vale of Glamorgan** ⬖ *unitary authority* S Wales, UK
xxxviii H9 **The Wrekin** ⬖ *unitary authority* C England, UK
xxxix R6 **Thimbleby** Lincolnshire, E England, UK
xli S11 **Thirsk** North Yorkshire, N England, UK
xli P5 **Thockrington** Northumberland, N England, UK
xliv G8 **Thomas Street** Roscommon, C Ireland
xliv I12 **Thomastown** Kilkenny, SE Ireland
xxxix R4 **Thoresway** Lincolnshire, E England, UK
xli X7 **Thornaby on Tees** Middlesborough, NE England, UK
xxxvi L9 **Thornbury** South Gloucestershire, SW England, UK
xxxix O11 **Thornby** Northamptonshire, C England, UK
xxxvi K13 **Thorncombe** Dorset, S England, UK
xxxix W12 **Thorndon** Suffolk, E England, UK
xli U15 **Thorne** Doncaster, N England, UK
xli S13 **Thorner** Leeds, N England, UK
xxxix R9 **Thorney** Cambridgeshire, E England, UK
xliii K23 **Thornhill** Dumfries and Galloway, S Scotland, UK
xliii J18 **Thornhill** Stirling, C Scotland, UK
xli W5 **Thornley** Durham, N England, UK
xl M13 **Thornton** Lancashire, NW England, UK
xliii M18 **Thornton** Fife, E Scotland, UK
xxxix Q3 **Thornton Curtis** North Lincolnshire, N England, UK
xli V11 **Thornton Dale** North Yorkshire, N England, UK
xli S11 **Thornton-le-Street** North Yorkshire, N England, UK
xxxix Y12 **Thorpeness** Suffolk, E England, UK
xxxix P6 **Thorpe on the Hill** Lincolnshire, E England, UK
xxxvii Y7 **Thorrington** Essex, SE England, UK
xxxvi H13 **Thorverton** Devon, SW England, UK
xxxix Q11 **Thrapston** Northamptonshire, C England, UK
xxxvii U11 **Three Bridges** West Sussex, S England, UK
xli P12 **Threshfield** North Yorkshire, N England, UK
xli U2 **Throckley** Newcastle upon Tyne, NE England, UK
xli Q4 **Thropton** Northumberland, N England, UK
xlii M7 **Thrumster** Highland, N Scotland, UK
xxxvii O11 **Thruxton** Hampshire, S England, UK
xli T16 **Thurcroft** Rotherham, N England, UK
xxxix Q9 **Thurlby** Lincolnshire, E England, UK
xliv H11 **Thurles** ***Ir.*** Durlas. Tipperary, S Ireland
xxxvi G16 **Thurlestone** Devon, SW England, UK
xxxix U13 **Thurlow** Suffolk, E England, UK
xxxvii V9 **Thurrock** ⬖ *unitary authority* SE England, UK
xl M7 **Thursby** Cumbria, NW England, UK
xlii L6 **Thurso** Highland, N Scotland, UK
xlii K7 **Thurso** ≈ NW Scotland, UK
xl B16 **Thurstaston** Wirral, NW England, UK
xli P10 **Thwaite** North Yorkshire, N England, UK
xxxvi L7 **Tibberton** Gloucestershire, C England, UK
xxxvii W12 **Ticehurst** East Sussex, SE England, UK
xli T16 **Tickhill** Doncaster, N England, UK
xxxvi K8 **Tidenham** Gloucestershire, C England, UK
xxxviii L5 **Tideswell** Derbyshire, C England, UK
xlii A11 **Tigharry** Western Isles, NW Scotland, UK
xliii G20 **Tighnabruaich** Argyll and Bute, W Scotland, UK
xxxvii V9 **Tilbury** Essex, SE England, UK
xxxvii Q9 **Tilehurst** Reading, S England, UK
xliii K19 **Tillicoultry** Clackmannan, C Scotland, UK
xxxvii X8 **Tillingham** Essex, SE England, UK
xxxvii N11 **Tilshead** Wiltshire, S England, UK
xxxviii H8 **Tilstock** Shropshire, W England, UK
xxxviii H7 **Tilston** Cheshire, W England, UK
xliii K15 **Tilt** ≈ C Scotland, UK
xliv E15 **Timoleague** Cork, S Ireland
xlii B8 **Timsgarry** Western Isles, NW Scotland, UK
xliv K11 **Tinahely** Wicklow, E Ireland
xxxvii Q6 **Tingewick** Buckinghamshire, C England, UK
xxxvi D14 **Tintagel** Cornwall, SW England, UK
xliii L21 **Tinto** ▲ C Scotland, UK
xliii K22 **Tinto Hills** ▲▲ South Lanarkshire, C Scotland, UK
xliv G12 **Tipperary** ***Ir.*** Tiobraid Árann. Tipperary, S Ireland
xliv G11 **Tipperary** ***Ir.*** Tiobraid Árann. ⬖ *county* S Ireland
xxxviii B14 **Tipton** Sandwell, C England, UK
xxxvii X7 **Tiptree** Essex, SE England, UK
xliii B17 **Tiree** *island* W Scotland, UK
xxxvii N12 **Tisbury** Wiltshire, S England, UK
xxxviii L7 **Tissington** Derbyshire, C England, UK
xxxvii Q13 **Titchfield** Hampshire, S England, UK
xxxvi I13 **Tiverton** Devon, SW England, UK
xlii N4 **Toab** Orkney Islands, N Scotland, UK
xlii I5 **Toab** Shetland Islands, NE Scotland, UK
xliv F6 **Tobercurry** Sligo, N Ireland
xliii E16 **Tobermory** Argyll and Bute, W Scotland, UK
xliii F18 **Toberonochy** Argyll and Bute, W Scotland, UK
xlii C8 **Tobson** Western Isles, NW Scotland, UK
xxxvii S6 **Toddington** Bedfordshire, C England, UK
xli P14 **Todmorden** Calderdale, N England, UK
xliv D15 **Toe Head** *headland* SW Ireland
xlii B10 **Toe Head** *headland* NW Scotland, UK
xli T12 **Tollerton** North Yorkshire, N England, UK
xxxvii X7 **Tollesbury** Essex, SE England, UK
xxxvii X7 **Tolleshunt d'Arcy** Essex, SE England, UK
xlii K13 **Tomatin** Highland, NW Scotland, UK
xlii J12 **Tombreck** Highland, NW Scotland, UK
xliii H14 **Tomdoun** Highland, NW Scotland, UK
xliv F10 **Tomgraney** Clare, W Ireland
xlii H13 **Tomich** Highland, NW Scotland, UK
xlii L13 **Tomintoul** Moray, N Scotland, UK
xxxvii V11 **Tonbridge** Kent, SE England, UK
xxxv I15 **Tondu** Bridgend, S Wales, UK
xlii D8 **Tong** Western Isles, NW Scotland, UK
xliii J25 **Tongland** Dumfries and Galloway, SW Scotland, UK
xlii I7 **Tongue** Highland, N Scotland, UK
xxxv I14 **Tonypandy** Rhondda Cynon Taff, S Wales, UK
xliv C8 **Toombeola** Galway, W Ireland
xliv K4 **Toome Bridge** Antrim, NE Northern Ireland, UK
xliv G10 **Toomyvara** Tipperary, S Ireland
xliv C15 **Toormore** Cork, S Ireland
xxxvi C9 **Tooting** Wandsworth, SE England, UK
xxxvi I14 **Topsham** Devon, SW England, UK
xxxvi H16 **Tor Bay** *bay* SW England, UK
xxxvi H15 **Torbay** ⬖ *unitary authority* SW England, UK
xliii G22 **Torbeg** North Ayrshire, W Scotland, UK
xxxvi H16 **Torcross** Devon, SW England, UK
xlii J11 **Tore** Highland, NW Scotland, UK
xxxv K14 **Torfaen** ⬖ *unitary authority* SE Wales, UK
xxxvi M9 **Tormarton** South Gloucestershire, SW England, UK
xlii J13 **Torness** Highland, NW Scotland, UK
xliii L20 **Torphichen** West Lothian, SE Scotland, UK
xliii N14 **Torphins** Aberdeenshire, NE Scotland, UK
xxxvi F16 **Torpoint** Cornwall, SW England, UK
xxxvi H15 **Torquay** Devon, SW England, UK
xxxvi F12 **Torridge** ≈ SW England, UK
xlii F11 **Torridon** Highland, NW Scotland, UK
xlii F11 **Torridon, Loch** *inlet* NW Scotland, UK
xlii E13 **Torrin** Highland, NW Scotland, UK
xxxvii V16 **Torteval** Guernsey, Channel Islands
xliii L24 **Torthorwald** Dumfries and Galloway, SW Scotland, UK
xliv G2 **Tory Island** ***Ir.*** Toraigh. island NW Ireland
xliv G2 **Tory Sound** *sound* N Ireland
xxxvii P14 **Totland** Isle of Wight, S England, UK
xxxvi H15 **Totnes** Devon, SW England, UK
xxxvi D5 **Tottenham** Haringey, SE England, UK
xli O15 **Tottington** Bury, NW England, UK
xxxvii P13 **Totton** Hampshire, S England, UK
xxxix O13 **Towcester** Northamptonshire, C England, UK
xxxiv L16 **Tower Hamlets** ⬖ *London borough* SE England, UK
xli Q8 **Tow Law** Durham, N England, UK
xliii O22 **Town Yetholm** The Borders, S Scotland, UK
xli O17 **Trafford** ⬖ *unitary authority* NW England, UK
xliv C12 **Tralee** ***Ir.*** Trá Lí. Kerry, SW Ireland
xliv C12 **Tralee Bay** ***Ir.*** Bá Thrá Lí. *bay* SW Ireland
xliv I13 **Tramore** ***Ir.*** Tráigh Mhór, Trá Mhór. Waterford, S Ireland
xliii N20 **Tranent** East Lothian, SE Scotland, UK
xxxv G13 **Trapp** Carmarthenshire, S Wales, UK
xli P14 **Trawden** Lancashire, NW England, UK
xxxv H6 **Trawsfynydd** Gwynedd, NW Wales, UK
xxxv I12 **Trecastle** Powys, C Wales, UK
xxxv J13 **Tredegar** Blaenau Gwent, SE Wales, UK
xxxvi L17 **Treen** Cornwall, SW England, UK
xxxv I9 **Trefeglwys** Powys, C Wales, UK
xxxv C13 **Treffgarne** Pembrokeshire, SW Wales, UK
xxxv I4 **Trefnant** Denbighshire, N Wales, UK
xxxviii G8 **Trefonen** Shropshire, W England, UK
xxxv F4 **Trefor** Isle of Anglesey, NW Wales, UK
xxxv H11 **Tregaron** Ceredigion, W Wales, UK
xxxvi C16 **Tregony** Cornwall, SW England, UK
xxxv J8 **Tregynon** Powys, C Wales, UK
xliii H15 **Treig, Loch** ◎ NW Scotland, UK
xxxv L14 **Trelleck** Monmouthshire, SE Wales, UK
xxxv F7 **Tremadog Bay** *bay* NW Wales, UK
xxxvi L12 **Trent** Somerset, SW England, UK
xxxviii M8 **Trent** ≈ C England, UK
xxxv I14 **Treorchy** Rhondda Cynon Taff, S Wales, UK
xxxvi I17 **Tresco** *island* SW England, UK
xliii D17 **Treshnish Isles** *island group* W Scotland, UK
xxxvi C16 **Tresillian** Cornwall, SW England, UK
xlii I4 **Tresta** Shetland Islands, NE Scotland, UK
xxxv J13 **Tretower** Powys, C Wales, UK
xxxv K5 **Treuddyn** Flintshire, N Wales, UK
xxxvi B15 **Trevose Head** *headland* SW England, UK
xliv J8 **Trim** ***Ir.*** Baile Átha Troim. Meath, E Ireland
xli S8 **Trimdon** Durham, N England, UK
xli X5 **Trimdon Colliery** Durham, N England, UK
xxxix X7 **Trimingham** Norfolk, E England, UK
xxxvii S7 **Tring** Hertfordshire, SE England, UK
xxxvii X17 **Trinity** Jersey, Channel Islands
xliii I24 **Trool, Loch** ◎ Dumfries and Galloway, SW Scotland, UK
xliii H22 **Troon** South Ayrshire, W Scotland, UK
xxxvi M10 **Trowbridge** Wiltshire, S England, UK
xxxix T12 **Trumpington** Cambridgeshire, E England, UK
xxxix X8 **Trunch** Norfolk, E England, UK
xxxvi C16 **Truro** Cornwall, SW England, UK
xliv G5 **Truskmore** ▲ N Ireland
xxxv E7 **Trwyn Cilan** *headland* NW Wales, UK
xliv F8 **Tuam** ***Ir.*** Tuaim. Galway, W Ireland
xxxix X13 **Tuddenham** Suffolk, E England, UK
xxxv E6 **Tudweiliog** Gwynedd, NW Wales, UK
xliv F10 **Tulla** Clare, W Ireland
xliii H16 **Tulla, Loch** ◎ W Scotland, UK
xliv I9 **Tullamore** ***Ir.*** Tulach Mhór. Offaly, C Ireland
xliii K19 **Tullibody** Clackmannan, C Scotland, UK
xlii O12 **Tulloch** Aberdeenshire, NE Scotland, UK
xliv J11 **Tullow** ***Ir.*** An Tullach. Carlow, SE Ireland
xliv H5 **Tully** Fermanagh, SW Northern Ireland, UK
xliv G7 **Tulsk** Roscommon, C Ireland
xxxv G13 **Tumble** Carmarthenshire, S Wales, UK
xliii K16 **Tummel** ≈ C Scotland, UK
xliii K16 **Tummel Bridge** Perth and Kinross, C Scotland, UK
xliii K16 **Tummel, Loch** ◎ C Scotland, UK
xxxviii J7 **Tunstall** City of Stoke-on-Trent, C England, UK
xli X14 **Tunstall** East Riding of Yorkshire, N England, UK
xxxix Y12 **Tunstall** Suffolk, E England, UK
xliii H23 **Turnberry** South Ayrshire, W Scotland, UK
xlii O11 **Turriff** Aberdeenshire, NE Scotland, UK
xxxviii L8 **Tutbury** Staffordshire, C England, UK
xxxix O6 **Tuxford** Nottinghamshire, C England, UK
xlii M4 **Twatt** Orkney Islands, N Scotland, UK
xliii P21 **Tweed** ≈ England/Scotland, UK
xli P1 **Tweedmouth** Northumberland, N England, UK
xliii L22 **Tweedsmuir** The Borders, S Scotland, UK
xliv C8 **Twelve Pins, The** ▲▲ W Ireland
xxxvi A9 **Twickenham** Richmond upon Thames, SE England, UK
xxxvi G15 **Two Bridges** Devon, SW England, UK
xxxviii E13 **Twycross** Leicestershire, C England, UK
xxxvii P12 **Twyford** Hampshire, S England, UK
xxxix O9 **Twyford** Leicestershire, C England, UK
xxxvii R9 **Twyford** Wokingham, S England, UK
xliii J25 **Twynholm** Dumfries and Galloway, SW Scotland, UK
xxxix S9 **Tydd St Mary** Lincolnshire, E England, UK
xliv J5 **Tyholland** Monaghan, NE Ireland
xl E14 **Tyldesley** Wigan, NW England, UK
xliii I17 **Tyndrum** Stirling, C Scotland, UK
xli Q6 **Tyne** ≈ N England, UK
xli S6 **Tynemouth** North Tyneside, NE England, UK
xxxv G13 **Tywi** ≈ S Wales, UK
xxxv G8 **Tywyn** Gwynedd, W Wales, UK

U

xxxvii U12 **Uckfield** East Sussex, SE England, UK
xliii K21 **Uddington** South Lanarkshire, C Scotland, UK
xxxvi I13 **Uffculme** Devon, SW England, UK
xxxvii O9 **Uffington** Oxfordshire, C England, UK
xli U9 **Ugthorpe** North Yorkshire, N England, UK
xlii D11 **Uig** Highland, N Scotland, UK
xxxix S5 **Ulceby** Lincolnshire, E England, UK
xxxix Q3 **Ulceby** North Lincolnshire, N England, UK
xl L8 **Uldale** Cumbria, NW England, UK

◆ Country ● Country Capital ◇ Dependent Territory ○ Dependent Territory Capital ⬖ Administrative Region ✕ International Airport ▲ Mountain ▲▲ Mountain Range ◎ Lake ⊡ Reservoir ≈ River

xxxvi *M8* **Uley** Gloucestershire, C England, UK
xli *R4* **Ulgham** Northumberland, N England, UK
xlii *G10* **Ullapool** Highland, N Scotland, UK
xli *T13* **Ulleskelf** North Yorkshire, N England, UK
xxxix *N11* **Ullesthorpe** Leicestershire, C England, UK
xl *M9* **Ullswater** ◎ NW England, UK
xl *L10* **Ulpha** Cumbria, NW England, UK
xlii *I2* **Ulsta** Shetland Islands, NE Scotland, UK
xliv *H4* **Ulster** *province* Northern Ireland, UK/Ireland
xliv *J5* **Ulster Canal** *canal* Ireland/ Northern Ireland, UK
xliii *D17* **Ulva** *island* W Scotland, UK
xl *L11* **Ulverston** Cumbria, NW England, UK
xlii *H8* **Unapool** Highland, NW Scotland, UK
xlii *H3* **Unifirth** Shetland Islands, NE Scotland, UK
xlii *J1* **Unst** *island* NE Scotland, UK
xxxvii *N10* **Upavon** Wiltshire, S England, UK
xl *D14* **Up Holland** Lancashire, NW England, UK
xxxvi *J13* **Upottery** Devon, SW England, UK
xxxix *O8* **Upper Broughton** Nottinghamshire, C England, UK
xxxv *I12* **Upper Chapel** Powys, C Wales, UK
xliv *H5* **Upper Lough Erne** ◎ SW Northern Ireland, UK
xli *T13* **Upper Poppleton** York, N England, UK
xxxviii *K8* **Upper Tean** Staffordshire, C England, UK
xxxix *P10* **Uppingham** Rutland, C England, UK
xxxvii *Y10* **Upstreet** Kent, SE England, UK
xl *B16* **Upton** Wirral, NW England, UK
xxxviii *J13* **Upton upon Severn** Worcestershire, W England, UK
xxxix *T10* **Upwell** Cambridgeshire, E England, UK
xxxvii *N10* **Urchfont** Wiltshire, S England, UK
xli *R11* **Ure** ≈ N England, UK
xliv *H11* **Urlingford** Kilkenny, SE Ireland
xli *O16* **Urmston** Salford, NW England, UK
xxxv *L14* **Usk** Monmouthshire, SE Wales, UK
xxxv *L14* **Usk** *Wel.* Wysg. ≈ SE Wales,UK
xxxv *H12* **Usk Reservoir** ⊟ S Wales, UK
xxxviii *K8* **Uttoxeter** Staffordshire, C England, UK
xxxvii *S9* **Uxbridge** Hillingdon, SE England, UK

V

xlii *H10* **Vaich, Loch** ◎ NW Scotland, UK
xliv *A13* **Valencia Island** *Ir.* Dairbhre. *island* SW Ireland
xlii *A11* **Vallay** *island* NW Scotland, UK
xliii *A14* **Vatersay** *island* NW Scotland, UK
xxxvii *Q14* **Ventnor** Isle of Wight, S England, UK
xxxvii *P10* **Vernham Dean** Hampshire, S England, UK
xxxvii *N13* **Verwood** Dorset, S England, UK
xxxvi *C17* **Veryan** Cornwall, SW England, UK
xl *L12* **Vickerstown** Cumbria, NW England, UK
xlii *I3* **Vidlin** Shetland Islands, NE Scotland, UK
xliv *J7* **Virginia** Cavan, N Ireland
xlii *I3* **Voe** Shetland Islands, NE Scotland, UK
xlii *H2* **Voe** Shetland Islands, NE Scotland, UK
xxxviii *G14* **Vowchurch** Herefordshire, W England, UK
xxxv *J8* **Vyrnwy** *Wel.* Afon Efyrnwy. ≈ E Wales, UK

W

xxxvii *R7* **Waddesdon** Buckinghamshire, C England, UK
xxxix *Q4* **Waddingham** Lincolnshire, E England, UK
xli *O13* **Waddington** Lancashire, NW England, UK
xxxix *Q6* **Waddington** Lincolnshire, E England, UK
xxxvi *D15* **Wadebridge** Cornwall, SW England, UK
xli *T16* **Wadworth** Doncaster, N England, UK
xxxix *T6* **Wainfleet All Saints** Lincolnshire, E England, UK
xli *S15* **Wakefield** Wakefield, N England, UK
xli *R15* **Wakefield** ⬖ *unitary authority* N England, UK
xxxvii *X6* **Wakes Colne** Essex, SE England, UK
xxxix *Z11* **Walberswick** Suffolk, E England, UK
xxxix *Q6* **Walcot** Lincolnshire, E England, UK
xxxv *H9* **Wales** *Wel.* Cymru. *national region* Wales, UK
xxxviii *G12* **Walford** Herefordshire, W England, UK
xxxviii *I7* **Walgherton** Cheshire, W England, UK
xxxvii *T7* **Walkern** Hertfordshire, SE England, UK
xli *V14* **Walkington** East Riding of Yorkshire, N England, UK
xli *P6* **Wall** Northumberland, N England, UK
xl *B15* **Wallasey** Wirral, NW England, UK
xxxvii *Q9* **Wallingford** Oxfordshire, C England, UK
xlii *H4* **Walls** Shetland Islands, NE Scotland, UK
xli *R6* **Wallsend** North Tyneside, NE England, UK
xxxvii *Z10* **Walmer** Kent, SE England, UK
xl *L12* **Walney, Isle of** *island* NW England, UK
xxxix *T9* **Walpole St Peter** Norfolk, E England, UK
xxxviii *C14* **Walsall** Walsall, C England, UK
xxxviii *K10* **Walsall** ⬖ *unitary authority* C England, UK
xli *P15* **Walsden** Calderdale, N England, UK
xxxix *W11* **Walsham le Willows** Suffolk, E England, UK
xxxix *R4* **Waltham** North East Lincolnshire, E England, UK
xxxvii *U8* **Waltham Abbey** Essex, SE England, UK
xxxiv *L16* **Waltham Forest** ⬖ *London borough* SE England, UK
xxxix *P8* **Waltham on the Wolds** Leicestershire, C England, UK
xxxvi *E5* **Walthamstow** *London borough capital* Waltham Forest, SE England, UK
xli *N6* **Walton** Cumbria, NW England, UK
xxxv *K11* **Walton** Powys, C Wales, UK
xli *N14* **Walton-le-Dale** Lancashire, NW England, UK
xxxvii *Y7* **Walton-on-The-Naze** Essex, SE England, UK
xxxv *C13* **Walton** West Pembrokeshire, SW Wales, UK
xxxiv *K16* **Wandsworth** ⬖ *London borough* SE England, UK
xxxvi *C8* **Wandsworth** *London borough capital* Wandsworth, SE England, UK
xxxix *Y11* **Wangford** Suffolk, E England, UK
xliii *K22* **Wanlockhead** Dumfries and Galloway, SW Scotland, UK
xxxix *Q10* **Wansford** Cambridgeshire, E England, UK
xxxvi *F6* **Wanstead** Redbridge, SE England, UK
xxxvii *P9* **Wantage** Oxfordshire, C England, UK
xxxix *S11* **Warboys** Cambridgeshire, E England, UK
xli *O9* **Warcop** Cumbria, NW England, UK
xlii *L4* **Ward Hill** *hill* N Scotland, UK
xxxvii *U7* **Ware** Hertfordshire, SE England, UK
xxxvi *M14* **Wareham** Dorset, S England, UK
xxxvii *R9* **Wargrave** Wokingham, S England, UK
xli *P5* **Wark** Northumberland, N England, UK
xli *O2* **Wark** Northumberland, N England, UK
xxxvii *T10* **Warlingham** Surrey, SE England, UK
xxxvi *M11* **Warminster** Wiltshire, S England, UK
xliv *L6* **Warrenpoint** *Ir.* An Pointe. Newry and Mourne, SE Northern Ireland, UK
xl *E16* **Warrington** Cheshire, C England, UK
xl *E16* **Warrington** ⬖ *unitary authority* NW England, UK
xxxix *N6* **Warsop** Nottinghamshire, C England, UK
xxxviii *E17* **Warwick** Warwickshire, C England, UK
xxxviii *E16* **Warwickshire** ⬖ *county* C England, UK
xlii *M3* **Wasbister** Orkney Islands, N Scotland, UK
xli *R7* **Washington** Sunderland, NE England, UK
xxxix *T7* **Wash, The** *bay* E England, UK
xl *L10* **Wast Water** ◎ NW England, UK
xxxvi *I11* **Watchet** Somerset, SW England, UK
xxxix *T12* **Waterbeach** Cambridgeshire, E England, UK
xliii *M24* **Waterbeck** Dumfries and Galloway, SW Scotland, UK
xliv *J13* **Waterford** *Ir.* Port Láirge. Waterford, S Ireland
xliv *H13* **Waterford** *Ir.* Port Láirge. ⬖ *county* S Ireland
xliv *J13* **Waterford** ✕ Waterford, S Ireland
xliv *J13* **Waterford Harbour** *Ir.* Cuan Phort Láirge. *inlet* S Ireland
xxxvi *C15* **Watergate Bay** *bay* SW England, UK
xliv *G13* **Watergrasshill** Cork, S Ireland
xxxvii *Q13* **Waterlooville** Hampshire, S England, UK
xliii *I23* **Waterside** East Ayrshire, W Scotland, UK
xliv *B14* **Waterville** Kerry, SW Ireland
xxxvii *S8* **Watford** Hertfordshire, E England, UK
xxxvii *Q8* **Watlington** Oxfordshire, S England, UK
xlii *L7* **Watten** Highland, NW Scotland, UK
xlii *L7* **Watten, Loch** ◎ N Scotland, UK
xxxix *V10* **Watton** Norfolk, E England, UK
xxxix *Y10* **Waveney** ≈ E England, UK
xxxvi *A6* **Wealdstone** Harrow, SE England, UK
xxxvii *U11* **Weald, The** *lowlands* SE England, UK
xli *W4* **Wear** ≈ N England, UK
xl *D17* **Weaver** ≈ W England, UK
xl *E17* **Weaverham** Cheshire, W England, UK
xli *V12* **Weaverthorpe** North Yorkshire, N England, UK
xxxvi *K11* **Wedmore** Somerset, SW England, UK
xxxviii *B14* **Wednesbury** Sandwell, C England, UK
xxxviii *B14* **Wednesfield** Wolverhampton, C England, UK
xxxix *O12* **Weedon Bec** Northamptonshire, C England, UK
xxxvi *E14* **Week St Mary** Cornwall, SW England, UK
xxxvii *Y7* **Weeley** Essex, SE England, UK
xxxviii *K9* **Weeping Cross** Staffordshire, C England, UK
xli *S13* **Weeton** North Yorkshire, N England, UK
xxxix *Q7* **Welby** Lincolnshire, E England, UK
xxxix *O11* **Welford** Northamptonshire, C England, UK
xli *R11* **Well** North Yorkshire, N England, UK
xxxviii *J13* **Welland** Worcestershire, W England, UK
xxxix *R8* **Welland** ≈ C England, UK
xli *S10* **Wellbury** North Yorkshire, N England, UK
xxxviii *M13* **Wellesbourne** Warwickshire, C England, UK
xxxix *P12* **Wellingborough** Northamptonshire, C England, UK
xxxviii *I9* **Wellington** Shropshire, W England, UK
xxxvi *I12* **Wellington** Somerset, SW England, UK
xliv *J13* **Wellington Bridge** Wexford, SE Ireland
xxxvi *L10* **Wellow** Bath and North East Somerset, SW England, UK
xxxvi *K11* **Wells** Somerset, SW England, UK
xxxix *V7* **Wells-next-the-Sea** Norfolk, E England, UK
xxxix *T10* **Welney** Norfolk, E England, UK
xxxviii *H8* **Welshampton** Shropshire, W England, UK
xxxv *K8* **Welshpool** *Wel.* Y Trallwng. Powys, E Wales, UK
xli *V14* **Welton** East Riding of Yorkshire, N England, UK
xxxvii *T7* **Welwyn Garden City** Hertfordshire, E England, UK
xxxviii *H8* **Wem** Shropshire, W England, UK
xxxvi *A6* **Wembley** Brent, SE England, UK
xliii *H20* **Wemyss Bay** Inverclyde, W Scotland, UK
xxxix *V9* **Wendling** Norfolk, E England, UK
xxxvii *V6* **Wendons Ambo** Essex, SE England, UK
xxxvii *R8* **Wendover** Buckinghamshire, C England, UK
xxxviii *H11* **Wenlock Edge** *hill range* W England, UK
xli *T15* **Wentbridge** Wakefield, N England, UK
xxxv *J15* **Wenvoe** The Vale of Glamorgan, S Wales, UK
xxxviii *G13* **Weobley** Herefordshire, W England, UK
xli *O11* **Wernside** ▲ N England, UK
xli *R8* **West Auckland** Durham, N England, UK
xxxix *R5* **West Barkwith** Lincolnshire, E England, UK
xxxviii *C15* **West Bromwich** Sandwell, C England, UK
xlii *H5* **West Burra** *island* NE Scotland, UK
xxxviii *G9* **Westbury** Shropshire, W England, UK
xxxvi *M11* **Westbury** Wiltshire, S England, UK
xxxvi *K11* **Westbury-sub-Mendip** Somerset, SW England, UK
xliii *L20* **West Calder** West Lothian, SE Scotland, UK
xxxvii *O12* **West Dean** Wiltshire, S England, UK
xxxvi *F11* **West Down** Devon, SW England, UK
xxxvi *D9* **West Dulwich** Lambeth, SE England, UK
xliii *H19* **West Dunbartonshire** ⬖ *unitary authority* W Scotland, UK
xli *U10* **Westerdale** North Yorkshire, N England, UK
xlii *L7* **Westerdale** Highland, N Scotland, UK
xxxvii *V10* **Westerham** Kent, SE England, UK
xlii *A10* **Western Isles** ⬖ *unitary authority* NW Scotland, UK
xlii *I4* **Wester Quarff** Shetland Islands, NE Scotland, UK
xxxviii *G8* **West Felton** Shropshire, W England, UK
xlii *L6* **Westfield** Highland, N Scotland, UK
xxxvii *Z9* **Westgate on Sea** Kent, SE England, UK
xlii *A12* **West Gerinish** Western Isles, NW Scotland, UK
xxxix *O11* **West Haddon** Northamptonshire, C England, UK
xxxvi *F7* **West Ham** Newham, SE England, UK
xxxvi *K10* **West Harptree** Bath and North East Somerset, SW England, UK
xli *V11* **West Heslerton** North Yorkshire, N England, UK
xlii *O13* **Westhill** Aberdeenshire, NE Scotland, UK
xxxvii *U12* **West Hoathly** West Sussex, SE England, UK
xl *E14* **Westhoughton** Bolton, NW England, UK
xlii *J1* **Westing** Shetland Islands, NE Scotland, UK
xliii *H21* **West Kilbride** North Ayrshire, W Scotland, UK
xl *A16* **West Kirby** Wirral, NW England, UK
xxxix *Y11* **Westleton** Suffolk, E England, UK
xliii *L21* **West Linton** The Borders, S Scotland, UK
xxxvi *E16* **West Looe** Cornwall, SW England, UK
xliii *K20* **West Lothian** ⬖ *unitary authority* S Scotland, UK
xxxvi *M14* **West Lulworth** Dorset, S England, UK
xxxvii *W10* **West Malling** Kent, SE England, UK
xliv *H9* **Westmeath** *Ir.* An Iarmhí, Na h-Iarmhidhe. ⬖ *county* C Ireland
xxxvii *Q12* **West Meon** Hampshire, S England, UK
xxxvii *X7* **West Mersea** Essex, SE England, UK
xxxiv *K16* **Westminster, City of** ⬖ *London borough* SE England, UK
xlii *M3* **Westness** Orkney Islands, N Scotland, UK
xl *K7* **Westnewton** Cumbria, NW England, UK
xxxvi *D9* **West Norwood** Lambeth, SE England, UK
xxxviii *K8* **Weston** Staffordshire, C England, UK
xxxvi *M9* **Westonbirt** Gloucestershire, C England, UK
xxxvi *J10* **Weston-super-Mare** North West Somerset, SW England, UK
xxxviii *L7* **Weston Underwood** Derbyshire, C England, UK
xxxvi *J12* **Westonzoyland** Somerset, SW England, UK
xxxvii *N10* **West Overton** Wiltshire, S England, UK
xxxvi *K11* **West Pennard** Somerset, SW England, UK
xliv *D7* **Westport** *Ir.* Cathair na Mart. Mayo, W Ireland
xxxix *Q5* **West Rasen** Lincolnshire, E England, UK
xlii *M2* **Westray** *island* NE Scotland, UK
xlii *M3* **Westray Firth** *inlet* N Scotland, UK
xxxix *U8* **West Rudham** Norfolk, E England, UK
xliii *O21* **Westruther** The Borders, S Scotland, UK
xlii *I2* **West Sandwick** Shetland Islands, NE Scotland, UK
xxxvii *S12* **West Sussex** ⬖ *county* S England, UK
xliii *F20* **West Tarbert** Argyll and Bute, W Scotland, UK
xxxvi *F12* **Westward Ho** Devon, SW England, UK
xxxvii *O12* **West Wellow** Hampshire, S England, UK
xli *P5* **West Woodburn** Northumberland, N England, UK
xl *M7* **Wetheral** Cumbria, NW England, UK
xli *S13* **Wetherby** Leeds, N England, UK
xli *V12* **Wetwang** East Riding of Yorkshire, N England, UK
xliv *K12* **Wexford** *Ir.* Loch Garman. Wexford, SE Ireland
xliv *J12* **Wexford** *Ir.* Loch Garman. ⬖ *county* SE Ireland
xliv *L12* **Wexford Bay** *bay* SE Ireland
xxxvii *S10* **Wey** ≈ SE England, UK
xxxix *W7* **Weybourne** Norfolk, E England, UK
xxxvii *S10* **Weybridge** Surrey, SE England, UK
xxxvii *O11* **Weyhill** Hampshire, S England, UK
xxxvi *L14* **Weymouth** Dorset, S England, UK
xxxvi *M15* **Weymouth Bay** *bay* S England, UK
xxxviii *K5* **Whaley Bridge** Derbyshire, C England, UK
xli *O14* **Whalley** Lancashire, NW England, UK
xlii *J3* **Whalsay** *island* NE Scotland, UK
xli *Q5* **Whalton** Northumberland, N England, UK
xxxix *S8* **Whaplode** Lincolnshire, E England, UK
xli *R12* **Wharfe** ≈ N England, UK
xliii *I25* **Whauphill** Dumfries and Galloway, SW Scotland, UK
xxxvii *T7* **Wheathampstead** Hertfordshire, SE England, UK
xxxix *O5* **Wheatley** Nottinghamshire, C England, UK
xxxvii *Q8* **Wheatley** Oxfordshire, C England, UK
xli *S8* **Wheatley Hill** Durham, N England, UK
xxxvi *H11* **Wheddon Cross** Somerset, SW England, UK
xli *U13* **Wheldrake** York, N England, UK
xl *O11* **Whernside** ▲ N England, UK
xli *V3* **Whickham** Gateshead, NE England, UK
xxxvi *G14* **Whiddon Down** Devon, SW England, UK
xliv *D14* **Whiddy Island** *island* S Ireland
xl *L9* **Whinlatter Pass** *pass* NW England, UK
xlii *P12* **Whinneyfold** Aberdeenshire, NE Scotland, UK
xxxvii *S7* **Whipsnade** Bedfordshire, C England, UK
xxxix *P9* **Whissendine** Rutland, C England, UK
xl *K11* **Whitbeck** Cumbria, NW England, UK
xxxviii *I13* **Whitbourne** Herefordshire, W England, UK
xli *S6* **Whitburn** South Tyneside, NE England, UK
xliii *K20* **Whitburn** West Lothian, SE Scotland, UK
xli *V9* **Whitby** North Yorkshire, N England, UK
xxxvii *R7* **Whitchurch** Buckinghamshire, C England, UK
xxxvii *P11* **Whitchurch** Hampshire, S England, UK
xxxviii *H15* **Whitchurch** Herefordshire, W England, UK
xxxviii *H7* **Whitchurch** Shropshire, W England, UK
xliii *O20* **Whiteadder Reservoir** ⊟ S Scotland, UK
xl *G14* **Whitefield** Bury, NW England, UK
xliv *G10* **Whitegate** Clare, W Ireland
xliv *G14* **Whitegate** Cork, S Ireland
xliv *J11* **Whitehall** Kilkenny, SE Ireland
xlii *N3* **Whitehall** Orkney Islands, N Scotland, UK
xl *K9* **Whitehaven** Cumbria, NW England, UK
xliv *M4* **Whitehead** Carrickfergus, E Northern Ireland, UK
xlii *N11* **Whitehills** Aberdeenshire, NE Scotland, UK
xxxvii *P8* **White Horse, Vale of** *valley* S England, UK
xlii *N13* **Whitehouse** Aberdeenshire, NE Scotland, UK
xliii *F20* **Whitehouse** Argyll and Bute, W Scotland, UK
xliii *N19* **Whitekirk** East Lothian, SE Scotland, UK
xliii *H25* **White Loch** ◎ Dumfries and Galloway, SW Scotland, UK
xxxvii *W7* **White Notley** Essex, SE England, UK
xxxvii *O12* **Whiteparish** Wiltshire, S England, UK
xxxvi *H14* **Whitestone** Devon, SW England, UK
xliv *L7* **Whites Town** Louth, NE Ireland
xxxvii *Z11* **Whitfield** Kent, SE England, UK
xliii *I26* **Whithorn** Dumfries and Galloway, S Scotland, UK
xxxv *E13* **Whitland** Carmarthenshire, S Wales, UK
xli *S6* **Whitley Bay** North Tyneside, NE England, UK
xxxviii *J8* **Whitmore** Staffordshire, C England, UK
xxxvi *F16* **Whitsand Bay** *bay* SW England, UK
xxxvii *X9* **Whitstable** Kent, SE England, UK
xli *Q3* **Whittingham** Northumberland, N England, UK
xxxviii *M5* **Whittington** Derbyshire, C England, UK
xli *N11* **Whittington** Lancashire, NW England, UK
xxxviii *G8* **Whittington** Shropshire, W England, UK
xxxviii *D13* **Whittington** Staffordshire, C England, UK
xxxix *O13* **Whittlebury** Northamptonshire, C England, UK
xxxix *R10* **Whittlesey** Cambridgeshire, E England, UK
xxxvi *A9* **Whitton** Richmond upon Thames, SE England, UK
xxxv *K10* **Whitton** Powys, C Wales, UK
xxxix *N5* **Whitwell** Derbyshire, C England, UK
xxxvii *T7* **Whitwell** Hertfordshire, SE England, UK
xxxviii *M9* **Whitwick** Leicestershire, C England, UK
xli *P15* **Whitworth** Lancashire, NW England, UK
xlii *B12* **Wiay** *island* NW Scotland, UK
xxxvi *L10* **Wick** South Gloucestershire, SW England, UK
xlii *M7* **Wick** Highland, N Scotland, UK
xxxix *T11* **Wicken** Cambridgeshire, E England, UK
xxxvii *W8* **Wickford** Essex, SE England, UK
xxxvii *Q13* **Wickham** Hampshire, S England, UK
xxxix *U12* **Wickhambrook** Suffolk, E England, UK
xxxix *X12* **Wickham Market** Suffolk, E England, UK
xliv *L10* **Wicklow** *Ir.* Cill Mhantáin. Wicklow, E Ireland
xliv *K10* **Wicklow** *Ir.* Cill Mhantáin. ⬖ *county* E Ireland
xliv *L10* **Wicklow Head** *Ir.* Ceann Chill Mhantáin. *headland* E Ireland
xliv *K10* **Wicklow Mountains** *Ir.* Sléibhte Chill Mhantáin. ▲▲ E Ireland
xxxvi *L9* **Wickwar** South Gloucestershire, SW England, UK
xxxvi *G15* **Widecombe in the Moor** Devon, SW England, UK
xl *D16* **Widnes** Halton, C England, UK
xl *E14* **Wigan** Wigan, NW England, UK
xli *N16* **Wigan** ⬖ *unitary authority* NW England, UK
xxxix *T9* **Wiggenhall St Germans** Norfolk, E England, UK
xli *O13* **Wigglesworth** North Yorkshire, N England, UK
xli *S13* **Wighill** North Yorkshire, N England, UK
xxxviii *H12* **Wigmore** Herefordshire, W England, UK
xxxix *O10* **Wigston** Leicestershire, C England, UK
xl *L7* **Wigton** Cumbria, NW England, UK
xliii *I25* **Wigtown** Dumfries and Galloway, S Scotland, UK
xliii *J26* **Wigtown Bay** *bay* SW Scotland, UK
xli *U13* **Wilberfoss** East Riding of Yorkshire, N England, UK
xlii *K10* **Wilkhaven** Highland, N Scotland, UK
xliii *L20* **Wilkieston** City of Edinburgh, SE Scotland, UK
xxxvi *I13* **Willand** Devon, SW England, UK
xl *B17* **Willaston** Cheshire, W England, UK
xxxviii *B14* **Willenhall** Walsall, C England, UK
xxxvi *B6* **Willesden** Brent, SE England, UK
xxxvii *V13* **Willingdon** East Sussex, SE England, UK
xxxix *P5* **Willingham** Lincolnshire, E England, UK
xxxviii *M8* **Willington** Derbyshire, C England, UK
xli *Q8* **Willington** Durham, N England, UK
xxxvi *I11* **Williton** Somerset, SW England, UK
xxxix *S5* **Willoughby** Lincolnshire, E England, UK
xl *G17* **Wilmslow** Cheshire, W England, UK
xxxvii *N12* **Wilton** Wiltshire, S England, UK
xxxvi *M11* **Wiltshire** ⬖ *county* S England, UK
xxxvi *B10* **Wimbledon** Merton, SE England, UK
xxxix *S10* **Wimblington** Cambridgeshire, E England, UK
xxxvii *N13* **Wimborne Minster** Dorset, S England, UK
xxxvi *L12* **Wincanton** Somerset, SW England, UK
xxxvii *N7* **Winchcombe** Gloucestershire, C England, UK
xxxvii *X12* **Winchelsea** East Sussex, SE England, UK
xxxvii *P12* **Winchester** *hist.* Wintanceaster, *Lat.* Venta Belgarum. Hampshire, S England, UK
xl *M10* **Windermere** Cumbria, NW England, UK
xl *L10* **Windermere** ◎ NW England, UK
xxxvii *S9* **Windsor** Windsor and Maidenhead, S England, UK
xxxvii *R9* **Windsor and Maidenhead** ⬖ *unitary authority* S England, UK
xxxvii *R7* **Wing** Buckinghamshire, C England, UK
xli *S8* **Wingate** Durham, N England, UK
xxxvii *Y10* **Wingham** Kent, SE England, UK
xxxvi *G13* **Winkleigh** Devon, SW England, UK
xli *R12* **Winksley** North Yorkshire, N England, UK
xli *N13* **Winmarleigh** Lancashire, NW England, UK
xxxvi *K10* **Winscombe** North West Somerset, SW England, UK
xxxviii *H6* **Winsford** Cheshire, W England, UK
xxxvi *H12* **Winsford** Somerset, SW England, UK
xxxvi *K13* **Winsham** Somerset, SW England, UK
xxxviii *M9* **Winshill** Staffordshire, C England, UK
xxxvii *Q7* **Winslow** Buckinghamshire, C England, UK
xl *M10* **Winster** Cumbria, NW England, UK
xxxviii *L6* **Winster** Derbyshire, C England, UK
xli *U7* **Winston** Durham, N England, UK
xxxvi *M8* **Winstone** Gloucestershire, C England, UK
xxxvi *M13* **Winterborne Stickland** Dorset, S England, UK
xxxvi *L14* **Winterbourne Abbas** Dorset, S England, UK
xxxvii *O11* **Winterbourne Earls** Wiltshire, S England, UK
xxxix *P3* **Winteringham** North Lincolnshire, N England, UK
xxxix *Z8* **Winterton-on-Sea** Norfolk, E England, UK
xli *O9* **Winton** Cumbria, NW England, UK
xxxviii *L7* **Wirksworth** Derbyshire, C England, UK
xl *L17* **Wirral** ⬖ *unitary authority* NW England, UK
xxxix *S9* **Wisbech** Cambridgeshire, E England, UK
xxxvii *S12* **Wisborough Green** West Sussex, SE England, UK
xliii *K20* **Wishaw** North Lanarkshire, W Scotland, UK
xxxix *U10* **Wissey** ≈ E England, UK
xxxviii *H11* **Wistanstow** Shropshire, W England, UK
xliii *L21* **Wiston** South Lanarkshire, C Scotland, UK
xxxv *D13* **Wiston** Pembrokeshire, SW Wales, UK
xli *T14* **Wistow** North Yorkshire, N England, UK
xxxix *T11* **Witchford** Cambridgeshire, E England, UK
xxxvii *W7* **Witham** Essex, SE England, UK
xxxix *R7* **Witham** ≈ E England, UK
xxxvi *L11* **Witham Friary** Somerset, SW England, UK
xxxvi *H13* **Witheridge** Devon, SW England, UK
xxxix *S5* **Withern** Lincolnshire, E England, UK
xli *Y14* **Withernsea** East Riding of Yorkshire, E England, UK
xli *X13* **Withernwick** East Riding of Yorkshire, N England, UK
xxxix *U13* **Withersfield** Suffolk, E England, UK
xxxvii *N7* **Withington** Gloucestershire, C England, UK
xxxviii *H13* **Withington** Herefordshire, W England, UK
xli *O15* **Withnell** Lancashire, NW England, UK
xxxvi *H12* **Withypool** Somerset, SW England, UK
xxxvii *S11* **Witley** Surrey, SE England, UK
xxxvii *P8* **Witney** Oxfordshire, S England, UK
xxxvii *W12* **Wittersham** Kent, SE England, UK
xxxvi *I12* **Wiveliscombe** Somerset, SW England, UK
xxxvii *X7* **Wivenhoe** Essex, SE England, UK
xxxvii *Y6* **Wix** Essex, SE England, UK
xxxvii *S6* **Woburn** Bedfordshire, C England, UK
xxxvii *S6* **Woburn Sands** Bedfordshire, C England, UK
xxxvii *S10* **Woking** Surrey, SE England, UK
xxxvii *R10* **Wokingham** Wokingham, S England, UK
xxxvii *Q10* **Wokingham** ⬖ *unitary authority* S England, UK
xxxix *R4* **Wolds, The** *hill range* E England, UK
xl *V12* **Wolds, The** *hill range* N England, UK
xxxix *U8* **Wolferton** Norfolk, E England, UK
xxxix *P12* **Wollaston** Northamptonshire, C England, UK
xli *Q8* **Wolsingham** Durham, N England, UK
xxxviii *B14* **Wolverhampton** Wolverhampton, C England, UK
xxxviii *B13* **Wolverhampton** ⬖ *unitary authority* C England, UK
xxxvii *R6* **Wolverton** Milton Keynes, C England, UK
xxxviii *M11* **Wolvey** Warwickshire, C England, UK
xli *S9* **Wolviston** Stockton-on-Tees, N England, UK
xxxviii *A14* **Wombourne** Staffordshire, C England, UK
xli *S16* **Wombwell** Barnsley, N England, UK
xxxvii *S11* **Wonersh** Surrey, SE England, UK
xxxix *X13* **Woodbridge** Suffolk, E England, UK
xxxvii *X11* **Woodchurch** Kent, SE England, UK
xliv *L11* **Woodenbridge** Wicklow, E Ireland
xxxvi *F5* **Woodford** Redbridge, SE England, UK
xxxvi *F5* **Woodford Bridge** Redbridge, SE England, UK
xxxix *N13* **Woodford Halse** Northamptonshire, C England, UK
xxxvi *D5* **Wood Green** Haringey, SE England, UK
xxxix *R6* **Woodhall Spa** Lincolnshire, E England, UK
xxxviii *J8* **Woodseaves** Staffordshire, C England, UK
xxxvii *P7* **Woodstock** Oxfordshire, C England, UK
xxxvi *G11* **Woody Bay** *bay* SW England, UK
xxxviii *H12* **Woofferton** Shropshire, W England, UK
xxxvi *K11* **Wookey** Somerset, SW England, UK
xxxvi *M14* **Wool** Dorset, S England, UK
xxxvi *F11* **Woolacombe** Devon, SW England, UK
xli *P2* **Wooler** Northumberland, N England, UK
xxxvi *E12* **Woolfardisworthy** Devon, SW England, UK
xxxvi *G7* **Woolwich** Greenwich, SE England, UK
xxxvii *I7* **Woore** Shropshire, W England, UK
xxxvii *Y11* **Wootton** Kent, SE England, UK
xxxvii *P7* **Wootton** Oxfordshire, C England, UK
xxxvii *N9* **Wootton Bassett** Wiltshire, S England, UK
xxxviii *D17* **Wootton Wawen** Warwickshire, C England, UK
xxxviii *J13* **Worcester** *hist.* Wigorna Ceaster. Worcestershire, W England, UK
xxxviii *C16* **Worcester and Birmingham Canal** *canal* C England, UK
xxxviii *B16* **Worcestershire** ⬖ *county* C England, UK
xlii *M4* **Work** Orkney Islands, N Scotland, UK
xl *K9* **Workington** Cumbria, NW England, UK
xxxix *N5* **Worksop** Nottinghamshire, C England, UK
xxxix *Q3* **Worlaby** North Lincolnshire, N England, UK
xxxvi *G13* **Worlington** Devon, SW England, UK
xliii *M17* **Wormit** Fife, E Scotland, UK
xxxvii *X10* **Wormshill** Kent, SE England, UK
xxxvii *T13* **Worthing** West Sussex, SE England, UK
xxxvi *L8* **Wotton-under-Edge** Gloucestershire, C England, UK
xxxvii *V10* **Wouldham** Kent, SE England, UK
xxxix *Q5* **Wragby** Lincolnshire, E England, UK
xxxix *S7* **Wrangle** Lincolnshire, E England, UK
xlii *G6* **Wrath, Cape** *headland* N Scotland, UK
xl *M14* **Wrea Green** Lancashire, NW England, UK
xxxix *Z11* **Wrentham** Suffolk, E England, UK
xli *U14* **Wressle** East Riding of Yorkshire, N England, UK
xxxix *V10* **Wretham** Norfolk, E England, UK
xxxv *K6* **Wrexham** Wrexham, NE Wales, UK
xxxv *K6* **Wrexham** ⬖ *unitary authority* NE Wales, UK
xxxvi *K10* **Wrington** North West Somerset, SW England, UK
xxxvii *V10* **Wrotham** Kent, SE England, UK
xxxvii *O9* **Wroughton** Swindon, S England, UK
xxxviii *H10* **Wroxeter** Shropshire, W England, UK
xxxix *X9* **Wroxham** Norfolk, E England, UK
xxxvii *P6* **Wroxton** Oxfordshire, C England, UK
xxxvii *X11* **Wye** Kent, SE England, UK
xxxix *N8* **Wymeswold** Leicestershire, C England, UK
xxxix *O9* **Wymondham** Leicestershire, C England, UK
xxxix *W10* **Wymondham** Norfolk, E England, UK
xl *M13* **Wyre** ≈ NW England, UK

Y

xxxvii *W11* **Yalding** Kent, SE England, UK
xxxvi *J13* **Yarcombe** Devon, SW England, UK
xxxix *P12* **Yardley** Hastings Northamptonshire, C England, UK
xxxix *X9* **Yare** ≈ E England, UK
xxxvi *L12* **Yarlington** Somerset, SW England, UK
xxxvii *P14* **Yarmouth** Isle of Wight, S England, UK
xxxvi *M10* **Yarnbrook** Wiltshire, S England, UK
xliii *M22* **Yarrow** The Borders, S Scotland, UK
xliii *M22* **Yarrow Feus** The Borders, S Scotland, UK
xxxvi *L9* **Yate** South Gloucestershire, SW England, UK
xxxvii *Q9* **Yattendon** West Berkshire, S England, UK
xxxvi *K10* **Yatton** North West Somerset, SW England, UK
xxxix *R10* **Yaxley** Cambridgeshire, E England, UK
xli *R13* **Yeadon** Leeds, N England, UK
xxxvi *G16* **Yealm** ≈ SW England, UK
xxxvi *G16* **Yealmpton** Devon, SW England, UK
xli *V11* **Yedingham** North Yorkshire, N England, UK
xlii *I2* **Yell** *island* NE Scotland, UK
xlii *I2* **Yell Sound** *strait* N Scotland, UK
xxxix *N11* **Yelvertoft** Northamptonshire, C England, UK
xxxvi *F15* **Yelverton** Devon, SW England, UK
xxxvi *H13* **Yeoford** Devon, SW England, UK
xxxvi *L12* **Yeovil** Somerset, SW England, UK
xlii *L4* **Yesnaby** Orkney Islands, N Scotland, UK
xxxvi *L13* **Yetminster** Dorset, S England, UK
xliii *L18* **Yetts o'Muckhart** Clackmannan, C Scotland, UK
xxxv *G7* **Y Llethr** ▲ NW Wales, UK
xxxv *J14* **Ynysybwl** Rhondda Cynon Taff, S Wales, UK
xli *T13* **York** *anc.* Eboracum, Eburacum. York, N England, UK
xli *T13* **York** ⬖ *unitary authority* N England, UK
xli *P10* **Yorkshire Dales** *physical region* N England, UK
xliv *H14* **Youghal** *Ir.* Eochaill. Cork, S Ireland
xliv *H14* **Youghal Bay** *Ir.* Cuan Eochaille. *inlet* S Ireland
xxxviii *L6* **Youlgreave** Derbyshire, C England, UK
xxxviii *L9* **Yoxall** Staffordshire, C England, UK
xxxix *Y11* **Yoxford** Suffolk, E England, UK
xxxv *H6* **Ysbyty Ifan** Conwy, N Wales, UK
xxxv *H10* **Ysbyty Ystwyth** Ceredigion, W Wales, UK
xxxv *H13* **Ystalyfera** Neath Port Talbot, S Wales, UK
xxxv *G11* **Ystrad Aeron** Ceredigion, W Wales, UK
xxxv *I13* **Ystradfellte** Powys, C Wales, UK
xxxv *H13* **Ystradgynlais** Powys, C Wales, UK
xxxv *J14* **Ystrad Mynach** *var.* Ystradmynach. Caerphilly, SE Wales, UK
xlii *P12* **Ythan** ≈ NE Scotland, UK

◆ Country ● Country Capital ◇ Dependent Territory ○ Dependent Territory Capital ⬖ Administrative Region ✕ International Airport ▲ Mountain ▲▲ Mountain Range ◎ Lake ⊟ Reservoir ≈ River

ATLAS OF THE WORLD

THE MAPS IN THIS ATLAS ARE ARRANGED CONTINENT BY CONTINENT, STARTING FROM THE INTERNATIONAL DATE LINE, AND MOVING EASTWARDS. THE MAPS PROVIDE A UNIQUE VIEW OF TODAY'S WORLD, COMBINING TRADITIONAL CARTOGRAPHIC TECHNIQUES WITH THE LATEST REMOTE-SENSED AND DIGITAL TECHNOLOGY.

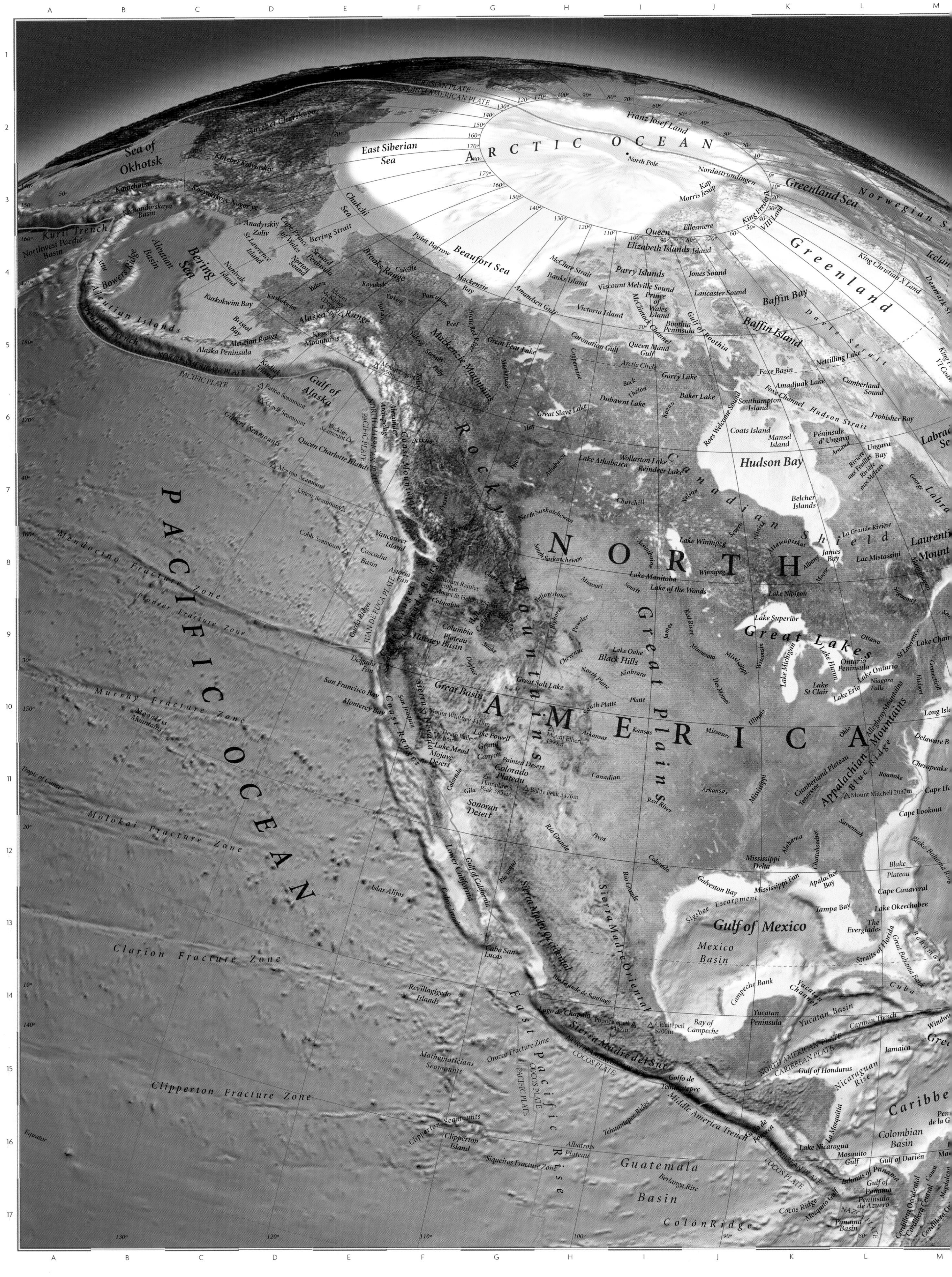

A B C D E F G H I J K L M

ARCTIC OCEAN
EURASIAN PLATE
NORTH AMERICAN PLATE
Franz Josef Land
North Pole
Nordostrundingen
Kap Morris Jesup
Greenland Sea
Norwegian Sea
Greenland
King Frederik VIII Land
King Christian X Land
East Siberian Sea
Sea of Okhotsk
Khrebet Cherskogo
Khrebet Kolymskiy
Kamchatka
Koryakskoye Nagor'ye
Komandorskaya Basin
Kuril Trench
Northwest Pacific Basin
Chukchi Sea
Anadyrskiy Zaliv
Cape Prince of Wales
Bering Strait
St Lawrence Island
Seward Peninsula
Norton Sound
Point Barrow
Beaufort Sea
Brooks Range
Colville
Bering Sea
Aleutian Basin
Bowers Ridge
Nunivak Island
Kuskokwim Bay
Kuskokwim
Yukon
Koyukuk
Tanana
Porcupine
Mackenzie Bay
Alaska Range
Bristol Bay
Aleutian Islands
Aleutian Trench
Aleutian Range
Alaska Peninsula
Kenai Mountains
Kodiak Island
NORTH AMERICAN PLATE
PACIFIC PLATE
Gulf of Alaska
Patton Seamount
Cowie Seamount
Gilbert Seamounts
Dickins Seamount
Alexander Archipelago
Queen Charlotte Islands
Morton Seamount
Union Seamount
Cobb Seamount
Vancouver Island
Cascadia Basin
Astoria Fan
Gorda Ridges
JUAN DE FUCA PLATE
Delgado Fan
San Francisco Bay
Monterey Bay
Coast Ranges
Coast Mountains
Skeena
Peel
Arctic Red River
Mackenzie Mountains
Mackenzie
Great Bear Lake
Great Slave Lake
Hay
Peace
Athabasca
Lake Athabasca
Fraser
Rocky Mountains
McClure Strait
Banks Island
Amundsen Gulf
Victoria Island
Queen Elizabeth Islands
Ellesmere Island
Parry Islands
Viscount Melville Sound
McClintock Channel
Prince of Wales Island
Boothia Peninsula
Gulf of Boothia
Jones Sound
Lancaster Sound
Baffin Bay
Baffin Island
Davis Strait
Coronation Gulf
Coppermine
Queen Maud Gulf
Arctic Circle
Back
Thelon
Garry Lake
Dubawnt Lake
Baker Lake
Kazan
Roes Welcome Sound
Southampton Island
Foxe Basin
Foxe Channel
Amadjuak Lake
Nettilling Lake
Cumberland Sound
Hudson Strait
Frobisher Bay
Coats Island
Mansel Island
Péninsule d'Ungava
Ungava Bay
Hudson Bay
Wollaston Lake
Reindeer Lake
Canadian Shield
Churchill
Nelson
Belcher Islands
North Saskatchewan
South Saskatchewan
Assiniboine
Lake Winnipeg
Severn
Winisk
Attawapiskat
Albany
James Bay
Moose
La Grande Rivière
Lac Mistassini
Laurentian Mountains
NORTH AMERICA
Lake Manitoba
Winnipeg
Lake of the Woods
Lake Nipigon
Missouri
Souris
Red River
Yellowstone
Bighorn
Powder
Clark Fork
Mount Rainier
Mount St Helens
Columbia
Snake
Columbia Plateau
Harney Basin
Great Basin
Great Salt Lake
Great Plains
Lake Oahe
Black Hills
Cheyenne
North Platte
Niobrara
Platte
South Platte
Kansas
Arkansas
Mount Elbert
Lake Superior
Great Lakes
Lake Michigan
Lake Huron
Lake Ontario
Lake St Clair
Lake Erie
Ontario Peninsula
Niagara Falls
Ottawa
St Lawrence
Saguenay
Minnesota
Mississippi
Wisconsin
Des Moines
Illinois
Ohio
Allegheny Mountains
Appalachian Mountains
Blue Ridge
Cumberland Plateau
Tennessee
Mount Mitchell
Roanoke
Long Island
Delaware Bay
Chesapeake Bay
Cape Hatteras
Cape Lookout
Savannah
Alabama
Chattahoochee
Sierra Nevada
Mount Whitney
San Joaquin
Death Valley
Lake Powell
Grand Canyon
Lake Mead
Mojave Desert
Painted Desert
Colorado Plateau
Colorado
Humphreys Peak
Baldy Peak
Gila
Sonoran Desert
Canadian
Red River
Arkansas
Rio Grande
Pecos
Lower California
Gulf of California
Rio Yaqui
Sierra Madre Occidental
Sierra Madre Oriental
Galveston Bay
Mississippi Delta
Mississippi Fan
Sigsbee Escarpment
Gulf of Mexico
Mexico Basin
Apalachee Bay
Tampa Bay
Blake Plateau
Blake-Bahama Ridge
Cape Canaveral
Lake Okeechobee
The Everglades
Straits of Florida
Great Bahama Bank
Bahamas
Cuba
Campeche Bank
Yucatan Channel
Yucatan Basin
Yucatan Peninsula
Bay of Campeche
Cayman Trench
Jamaica
Cabo San Lucas
Revillagigedo Islands
Río Grande de Santiago
Lago de Chapala
Popocatépetl
Citlaltépetl
Sierra Madre del Sur
NORTH AMERICAN PLATE
CARIBBEAN PLATE
COCOS PLATE
Golfo de Tehuantepec
Gulf of Honduras
Nicaraguan Rise
Middle America Trench
Tehuantepec Ridge
Golfo de Fonseca
La Mosquitia
Lake Nicaragua
Mosquito Gulf
Colombian Basin
Gulf of Darién
Isthmus of Panama
Gulf of Panama
Península de Azuero
Panama Basin
NAZCA PLATE
Cocos Ridge
Colón Ridge
Berlanga Rise
Guatemala Basin
Albatross Plateau
East Pacific Rise
Orozco Fracture Zone
PACIFIC PLATE
Mathematicians Seamounts
Clipperton Seamounts
Clipperton Island
Siqueiros Fracture Zone
Clipperton Fracture Zone
Clarion Fracture Zone
Islas Alijos
Molokai Fracture Zone
Murray Fracture Zone
Moonless Mountains
Pioneer Fracture Zone
Mendocino Fracture Zone
PACIFIC OCEAN
Tropic of Cancer
Equator
Caribbean Sea
Labrador Sea
Iceland
Denmark Strait

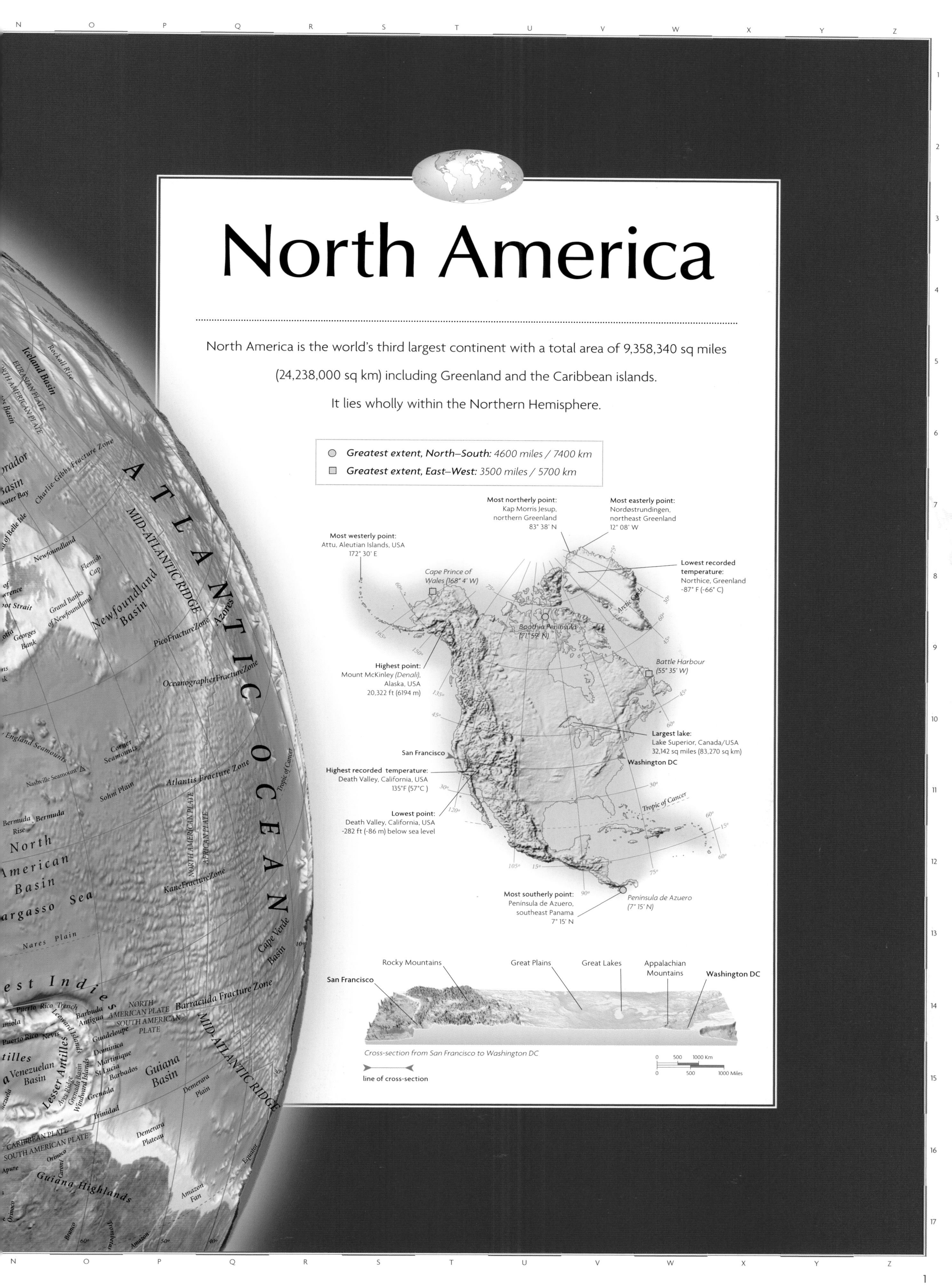
North America
North America is the world's third largest continent with a total area of 9,358,340 sq miles
(24,238,000 sq km) including Greenland and the Caribbean islands.
It lies wholly within the Northern Hemisphere.
Greatest extent, North–South: 4600 miles / 7400 km
Greatest extent, East–West: 3500 miles / 5700 km
Most northerly point: Kap Morris Jesup, northern Greenland 83° 38' N
Most easterly point: Nordøstrundingen, northeast Greenland 12° 08' W
Most westerly point: Attu, Aleutian Islands, USA 172° 30' E
Cape Prince of Wales (168° 4' W)
Lowest recorded temperature: Northice, Greenland -87° F (-66° C)
Boothia Peninsula (71° 59' N)
Arctic Circle
Highest point: Mount McKinley (Denali), Alaska, USA 20,322 ft (6194 m)
Battle Harbour (55° 35' W)
Largest lake: Lake Superior, Canada/USA 32,142 sq miles (83,270 sq km)
San Francisco
Washington DC
Highest recorded temperature: Death Valley, California, USA 135°F (57°C)
Tropic of Cancer
Lowest point: Death Valley, California, USA -282 ft (-86 m) below sea level
Most southerly point: Peninsula de Azuero, southeast Panama 7° 15' N
Peninsula de Azuero (7° 15' N)
Rocky Mountains
Great Plains
Great Lakes
Appalachian Mountains
Washington DC
San Francisco
Cross-section from San Francisco to Washington DC
line of cross-section
0 500 1000 Km
0 500 1000 Miles
ATLANTIC OCEAN
MID-ATLANTIC RIDGE
Newfoundland Basin
North American Basin
Sargasso Sea
Nares Plain
West Indies
Lesser Antilles
Guiana Basin
Guiana Highlands
Cape Verde Basin
Atlantis Fracture Zone
Kane Fracture Zone
Barracuda Fracture Zone
Oceanographer Fracture Zone
Azores
Iceland Basin
Rockall Rise
Charlie-Gibbs Fracture Zone
Grand Banks of Newfoundland
Flemish Cap
Sohm Plain
Corner Seamounts
Bermuda Rise
Demerara Plain
Demerara Plateau
Amazon Fan
Equator

Physical North America

The North American continent can be divided into a number of major structural areas: the Western Cordillera, the Canadian Shield, the Great Plains and Central Lowlands, and the Appalachians. Other smaller regions include the Gulf Atlantic Coastal Plain which borders the southern coast of North America from the southern Appalachians to the Great Plains. This area includes the expanding Mississippi Delta. A chain of volcanic islands, running in an arc around the margin of the Caribbean Plate, lie to the east of the Gulf of Mexico.

The Western Cordillera

About 80 million years ago the Pacific and North American plates collided, uplifting the Western Cordillera. This consists of the Aleutian, Coast, Cascade and Sierra Nevada mountains, and the inland Rocky Mountains. These run parallel from the Arctic to Mexico.

The weight of the ice sheet, 1.8 miles (3 km) thick, has depressed the land to 0.6 miles (1 km) below sea level

▲ *This computer-generated view shows the ice-covered island of Greenland without its ice cap.*

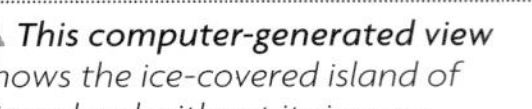

Strata have been thrust eastward along fault lines

Volcanic rock

The Rocky Mountain Trench is the longest linear fault on the continent

B B

***Cross-section through the** Western Cordillera showing direction of mountain building.* →

0 50 100 Km
0 50 100 Miles

The Canadian Shield

Spanning northern Canada and Greenland, this geologically stable plain forms the heart of the continent, containing rocks over two billion years old. A long history of weathering and repeated glaciation has scoured the region, leaving flat plains, gentle hummocks, numerous small basins and lakes, and the bays and islands of the Arctic.

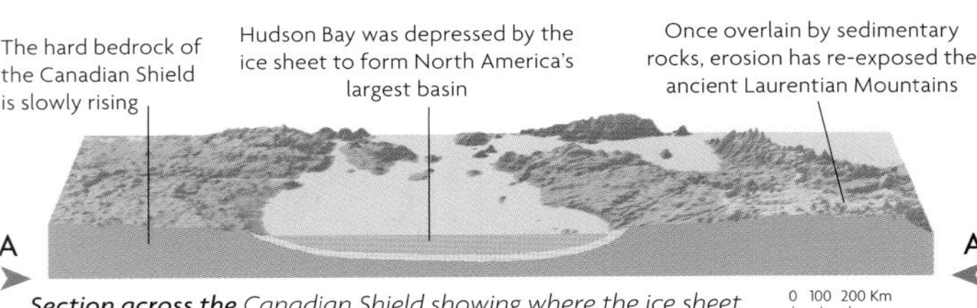
The hard bedrock of the Canadian Shield is slowly rising
Hudson Bay was depressed by the ice sheet to form North America's largest basin
Once overlain by sedimentary rocks, erosion has re-exposed the ancient Laurentian Mountains
A
A

***Section across the** Canadian Shield showing where the ice sheet has depressed the underlying rock and formed bays and islands.*

0 100 200 Km
0 100 200 Miles

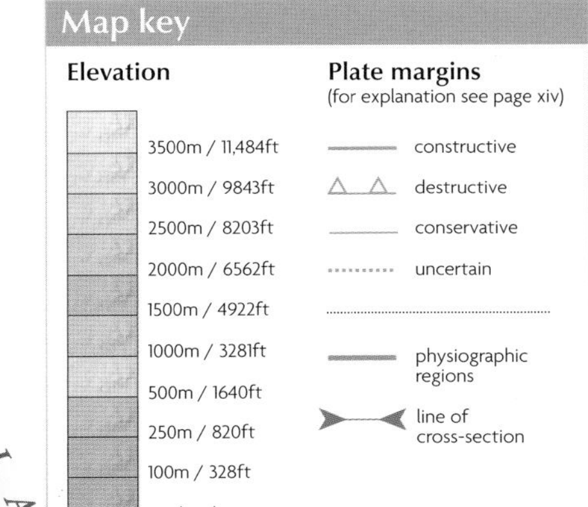
Map key
Elevation
3500m / 11,484ft
3000m / 9843ft
2500m / 8203ft
2000m / 6562ft
1500m / 4922ft
1000m / 3281ft
500m / 1640ft
250m / 820ft
100m / 328ft
sea level
Plate margins
(for explanation see page xiv)
constructive
destructive
conservative
uncertain
physiographic regions
line of cross-section

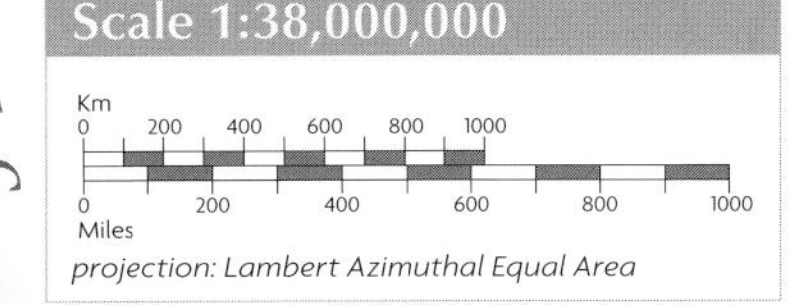
Scale 1:38,000,000
Km
0 200 400 600 800 1000
0 200 400 600 800 1000
Miles
projection: Lambert Azimuthal Equal Area

Greenland · Baffin Bay · Davis Strait · ATLANTIC OCEAN · Beaufort Sea · Bering Sea · Bering Strait · ASIA · Aleutian Islands · Aleutian Range · Alaska Range · Mount McKinley 6194m · Brooks Range · Mackenzie Delta · Mackenzie Mountains · Mackenzie · Baffin Island · Foxe Basin · Hudson Strait · Labrador Sea · Gulf of Alaska · NORTH AMERICAN PLATE · PACIFIC PLATE · Coast Mountains · Great Bear Lake · Great Slave Lake · Lake Athabasca · Reindeer Lake · Hudson Bay · Labrador · Laurentian Mountains · Newfoundland · CANADIAN SHIELD · ROCKY MOUNTAINS · WESTERN CORDILLERA · CENTRAL LOWLANDS · GREAT PLAINS · Lake Winnipeg · Lake Manitoba · Lake Superior · Lake Huron · Lake Michigan · Lake Ontario · Lake Erie · Great Lakes · St Lawrence · Nova Scotia · Cape Cod · Missouri · Mount Rainier 4392m · Mount St Helens 2549m · Cascade Range · Coast Ranges · Great Basin · Great Salt Lake · Sierra Nevada · San Joaquin Valley · San Andreas Fault · Colorado · Colorado Plateau · Death Valley -86m · Grand Canyon · Mojave Desert · Sonoran Desert · Arkansas · Mississippi · Ohio · Appalachian Mountains · APPALACHIANS · GULF ATLANTIC COASTAL PLAIN · Mississippi Delta · Lower California · Gulf of California · Sierra Madre Occidental · Sierra Madre Oriental · Rio Grande · Gulf of Mexico · Volcán Pico de Orizaba 5700m · Sierra Madre del Sur · Yucatan Peninsula · West Indies · Greater Antilles · Lesser Antilles · Caribbean Sea · NORTH AMERICAN PLATE · CARIBBEAN PLATE · COCOS PLATE · Lake Nicaragua · Isthmus of Panama · SOUTH AMERICAN PLATE · SOUTH AMERICA · PACIFIC OCEAN · A · B · C · D

The Appalachians

The Appalachian Mountains, uplifted about 400 million years ago, are some of the oldest in the world. They have been lowered and rounded by erosion and now slope gently towards the Atlantic across a broad coastal plain.

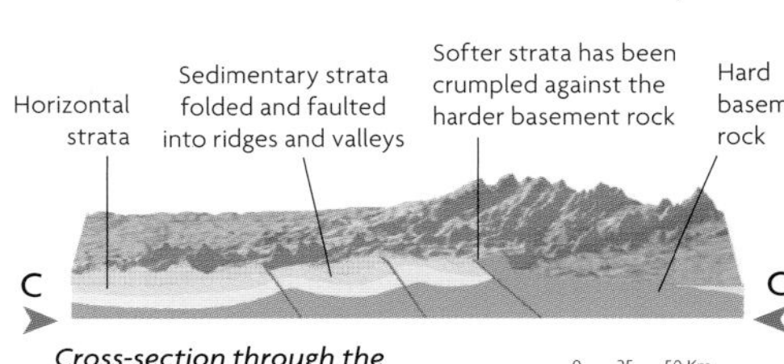
Horizontal strata
Sedimentary strata folded and faulted into ridges and valleys
Softer strata has been crumpled against the harder basement rock
Hard basement rock
C
C

***Cross-section through the** Appalachians showing the numerous folds, which have subsequently been weathered to create a rounded relief.*

0 25 50 Km
0 25 50 Miles

The Great Plains and Central Lowlands

Deposits left by retreating glaciers and rivers have made this vast flat area very fertile. In the north this is the result of glaciation, with deposits up to one mile (1.7 km) thick, covering the basement rock. To the south and west, the massive Missouri/Mississippi river system has for centuries deposited silt across the plains, creating broad, flat flood plains and deltas.

Sedimentary layers overlay domed basement rock

Upland rivers drain south towards the Mississippi Basin

Confluence of the Missouri and Mississippi rivers

D D

***Section across the** Great Plains and Central Lowlands showing river systems and structure.*

0 200 400 Km
0 200 400 Miles

Climate

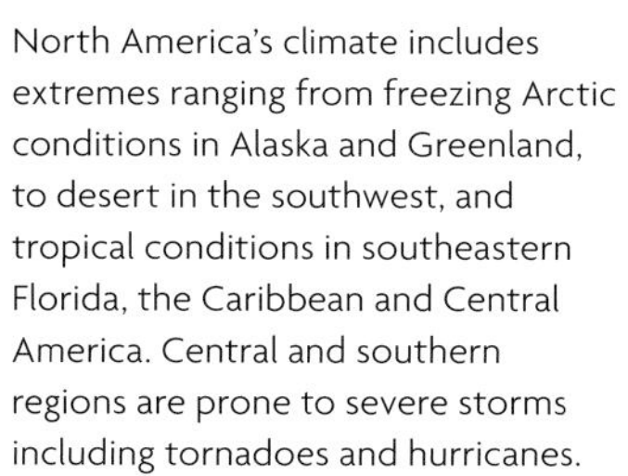

North America's climate includes extremes ranging from freezing Arctic conditions in Alaska and Greenland, to desert in the southwest, and tropical conditions in southeastern Florida, the Caribbean and Central America. Central and southern regions are prone to severe storms including tornadoes and hurricanes.

▲ *'Tornado alley' in the Mississippi Valley suffers frequent tornadoes.*

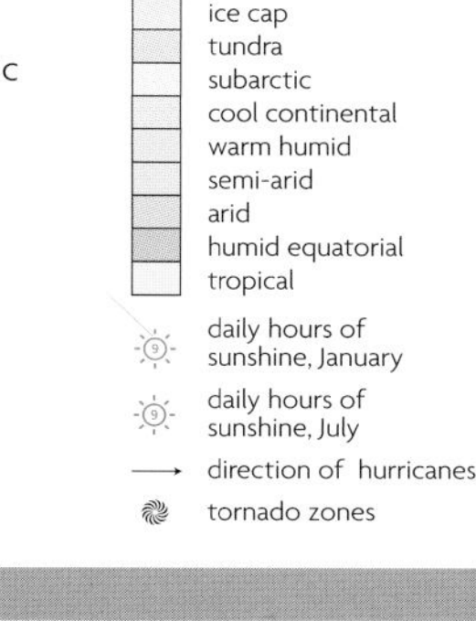
Climate
ice cap
tundra
subarctic
cool continental
warm humid
semi-arid
arid
humid equatorial
tropical
daily hours of sunshine, January
daily hours of sunshine, July
direction of hurricanes
tornado zones

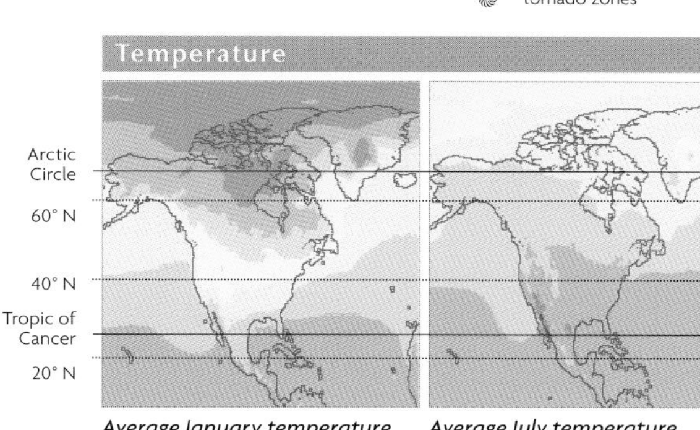
Temperature
Arctic Circle
60° N
40° N
Tropic of Cancer
20° N

Average January temperature *Average July temperature*

Temperature

below -30°C (-22°F)
-30 to -20°C (-22 to -4°F)
-20 to -10°C (-4 to 14°F)
-10 to 0°C (14 to 32°F)
0 to 10°C (32 to 50°F)
10 to 20°C (50 to 68°F)
20 to 30°C (68 to 86°F)
above 30°C (86°F)

▲ *Much of the southwest is semi-desert; receiving less than 12 inches (300 mm) of rainfall a year.*

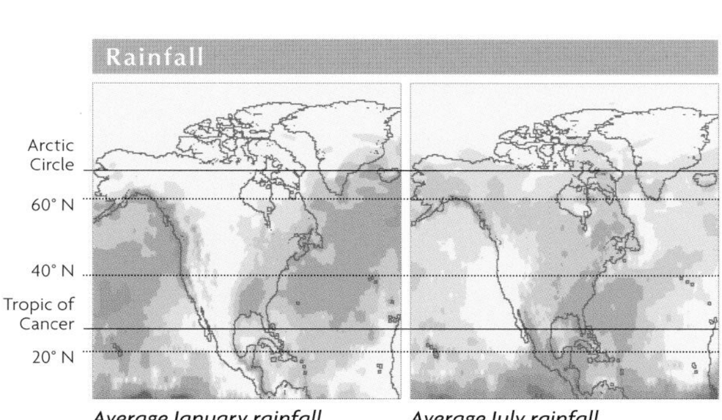
Rainfall
Arctic Circle
60° N
40° N
Tropic of Cancer
20° N

Average January rainfall *Average July rainfall*

Rainfall

0–25 mm (0–1 in)
25–50 mm (1–2 in)
50–100 mm (2–4 in)
100–200 mm (4–8 in)
200–300 mm (8–12 in)
300–400 mm (12–16 in)
400–500 mm (16–20 in)
more than 500 mm (20 in)

◀ *The lush, green mountains of the Lesser Antilles receive annual rainfalls of up to 360 inches (9000 mm).*

Nome · Fairbanks · Aklavik · Resolute · Eismitte · Kugluktuk · Iqaluit · Haines Junction · Juneau · Fort Vermillon · Fort St John · Churchill · Happy Valley - Goose Bay · Torbay · Vancouver · Medicine Hat · Winnipeg · Montréal · Toronto · Boise · Sioux City · New York · Salt Lake City · San Francisco · Denver · Las Vegas · Phoenix · Cape Hatteras · Los Angeles · Atlanta · Little Rock · Guaymas · Houston · Chihuahua · New Orleans · Miami · Nassau · Santo Domingo · Fort-de-France · Mérida · Kingston · Acapulco · San Salvador · San José · Arctic Circle · Tropic of Cancer

Shaping the continent

Glacial processes affect much of northern Canada, Greenland and the Western Cordillera. Along the western coast of North America, Central America and the Caribbean, underlying plates moving together lead to earthquakes and volcanic eruptions. The vast river systems, fed by mountain streams, constantly erode and deposit material along their paths.

Volcanic activity

1 Mount St Helens volcano *(right)* in the Cascade Range erupted violently in May 1980, killing 57 people and levelling large areas of forest. The lateral blast filled a valley for 15 miles (25 km) with debris.

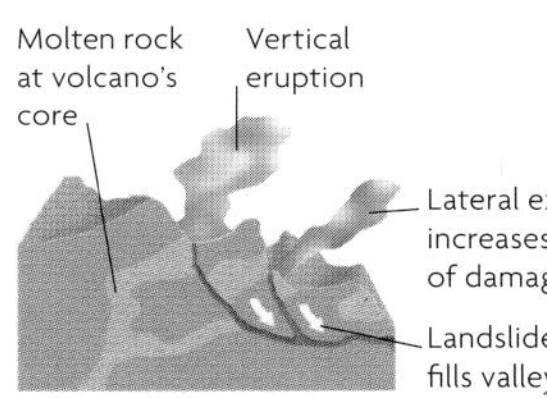
Molten rock at volcano's core
Vertical eruption
Lateral explosion increases extent of damage
Landslide fills valley

***Volcanic activity:** Eruption of Mount St Helens*

Seismic activity

5 The San Andreas Fault *(above)* places much of the North America's west coast under constant threat from earthquakes. It is caused by the Pacific Plate grinding past the North American Plate at a faster rate, though in the same direction.

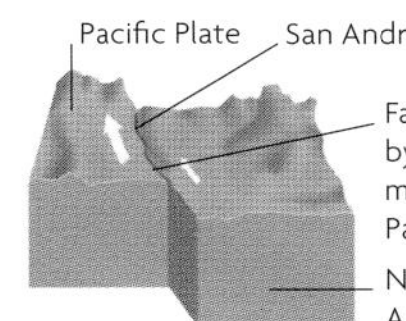
Pacific Plate
San Andreas Fault
Fault is caused by faster movement of Pacific Plate
North American Plate

***Seismic activity:** Action of the San Andreas Fault*

River erosion

6 The Grand Canyon *(above)* in the Colorado Plateau was created by the downward erosion of the Colorado River, combined with the gradual uplift of the plateau, over the past 30 million years. The contours of the canyon formed as the softer rock layers eroded into gentle slopes, and the hard rock layers into cliffs. The depth varies from 3855–6560 ft (1175–2000 m).

Periglaciation

2 The ground in the far north is nearly always frozen: the surface thaws only in summer. This freeze-thaw process produces features such as pingos *(left)*; formed by the freezing of groundwater. With each successive winter ice accumulates producing a mound with a core of ice.

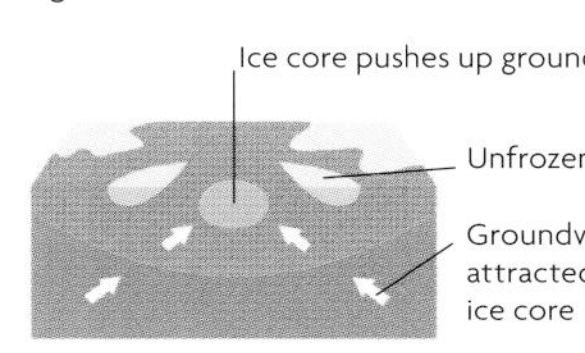
Ice core pushes up ground to form pingo
Unfrozen lake
Groundwater attracted to ice core

***Periglaciation:** Formation of a pingo in the Mackenzie Delta*

Post-glacial lakes

3 A chain of lakes from Great Bear Lake to the Great Lakes *(above)* was created as the ice retreated northwards. Glaciers scoured hollows in the softer lowland rock. Glacial deposits at the lip of the hollows, and ridges of harder rock, trapped water to form lakes.

Retreating glacier
Ice-scoured hollow filled with glacial meltwater to form a lake
Harder rock creates a barrier between lakes
Softer lowland rock

***Post-glacial lakes:** Formation of the Great Lakes*

The evolving landscape

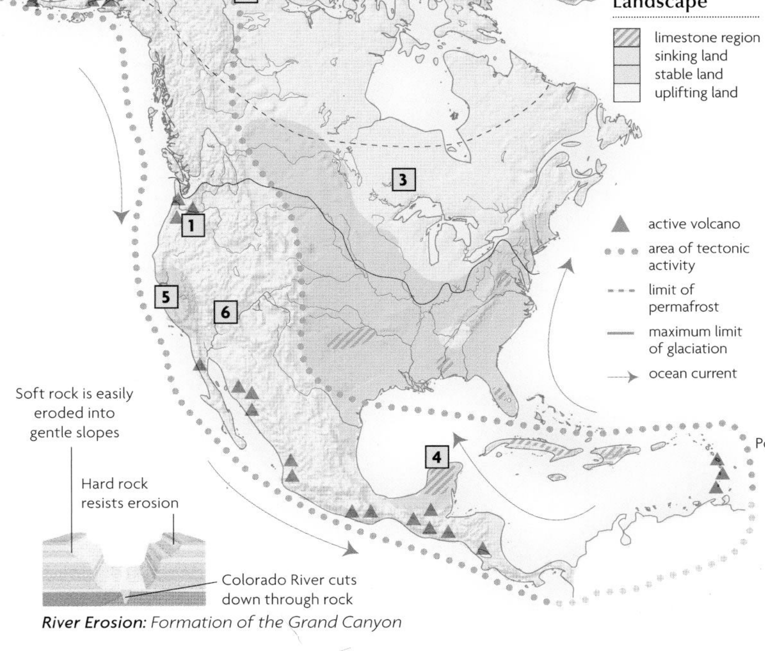
2
3
1
5
6
4
Landscape
limestone region
sinking land
stable land
uplifting land
active volcano
area of tectonic activity
limit of permafrost
maximum limit of glaciation
ocean current
Soft rock is easily eroded into gentle slopes
Hard rock resists erosion
Colorado River cuts down through rock

***River Erosion:** Formation of the Grand Canyon*

Weathering

4 The Yucatan Peninsula is a vast, flat limestone plateau in southern Mexico. Weathering action from both rainwater and underground streams has enlarged fractures in the rock to form caves and hollows, called sinkholes *(above)*.

Porous limestone plateau
Rainwater erodes porous rock forming sinkholes
Sea level
Underground stream further erodes rock

***Weathering:** Water erosion on the Yucatan Peninsula*

Political North America

Democracy is well established in some parts of the continent but is a recent phenomenon in others. The economically dominant nations of Canada and the USA have a long democratic tradition but elsewhere, notably in the countries of Central America, political turmoil has been more common. In Nicaragua and Haiti, harsh dictatorships have only recently been superseded by democratically-elected governments. North America's largest countries, Canada, Mexico and the USA have federal state systems, sharing political power between national and state governments. The USA has intervened militarily on several occasions in Central America and the Caribbean to protect its strategic interests.

Transport

In the 19th century, railways were used to open up the North American continent. Air transport is now more common for long distance passenger travel, although railways are still extensively used for bulk freight transport. Waterways, like the Mississippi River, are important for the transport of bulk materials, and the Panama Canal is a vital link between the Pacific Ocean and the Caribbean. In the 20th century, road transport increased massively in North America, with the introduction of cheap, mass-produced motor cars and extensive highway construction.

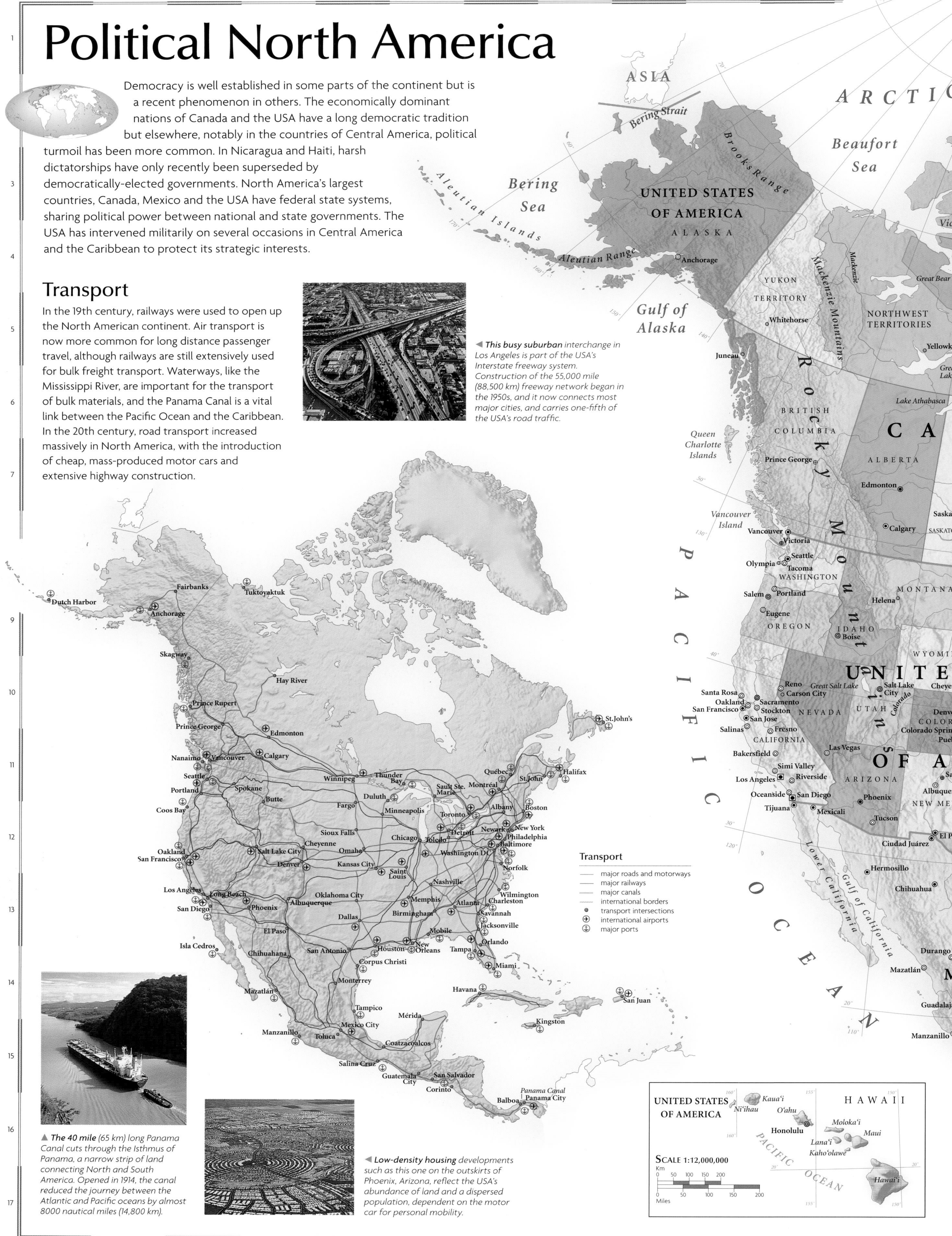
ASIA
Bering Strait
ARCTIC
Beaufort Sea
Bering Sea
Aleutian Islands
Aleutian Range
Brooks Range
UNITED STATES OF AMERICA
ALASKA
Anchorage
Gulf of Alaska
YUKON TERRITORY
Whitehorse
Mackenzie Mountains
NORTHWEST TERRITORIES
Juneau
Rocky Mountains
BRITISH COLUMBIA
Queen Charlotte Islands
Prince George
ALBERTA
Edmonton
Calgary
Vancouver Island
Vancouver
Victoria
Seattle
Olympia
Tacoma
WASHINGTON
Salem
Portland
Eugene
OREGON
MONTANA
Helena
IDAHO
Boise
PACIFIC OCEAN
Reno
Carson City
Great Salt Lake
Salt Lake City
Santa Rosa
Oakland
San Francisco
Sacramento
Stockton
San Jose
NEVADA
UTAH
Salinas
Fresno
CALIFORNIA
Bakersfield
Las Vegas
Simi Valley
Los Angeles
Riverside
ARIZONA
Oceanside
San Diego
Phoenix
Tijuana
Mexicali
Tucson
Ciudad Juárez
Hermosillo
Chihuahua
Lower California
Gulf of California
Durango
Mazatlán
Guadalajara
Manzanillo
Transport
major roads and motorways
major railways
major canals
international borders
transport intersections
international airports
major ports
UNITED STATES OF AMERICA
HAWAII
Kaua'i
Ni'ihau
O'ahu
Honolulu
Moloka'i
Maui
Lana'i
Kaho'olawe
Hawai'i
PACIFIC OCEAN
SCALE 1:12,000,000

◀ *This busy suburban* interchange in Los Angeles is part of the USA's Interstate freeway system. Construction of the 55,000 mile (88,500 km) freeway network began in the 1950s, and it now connects most major cities, and carries one-fifth of the USA's road traffic.

▲ *The 40 mile* (65 km) long Panama Canal cuts through the Isthmus of Panama, a narrow strip of land connecting North and South America. Opened in 1914, the canal reduced the journey between the Atlantic and Pacific oceans by almost 8000 nautical miles (14,800 km).

◀ *Low-density housing* developments such as this one on the outskirts of Phoenix, Arizona, reflect the USA's abundance of land and a dispersed population, dependent on the motor car for personal mobility.

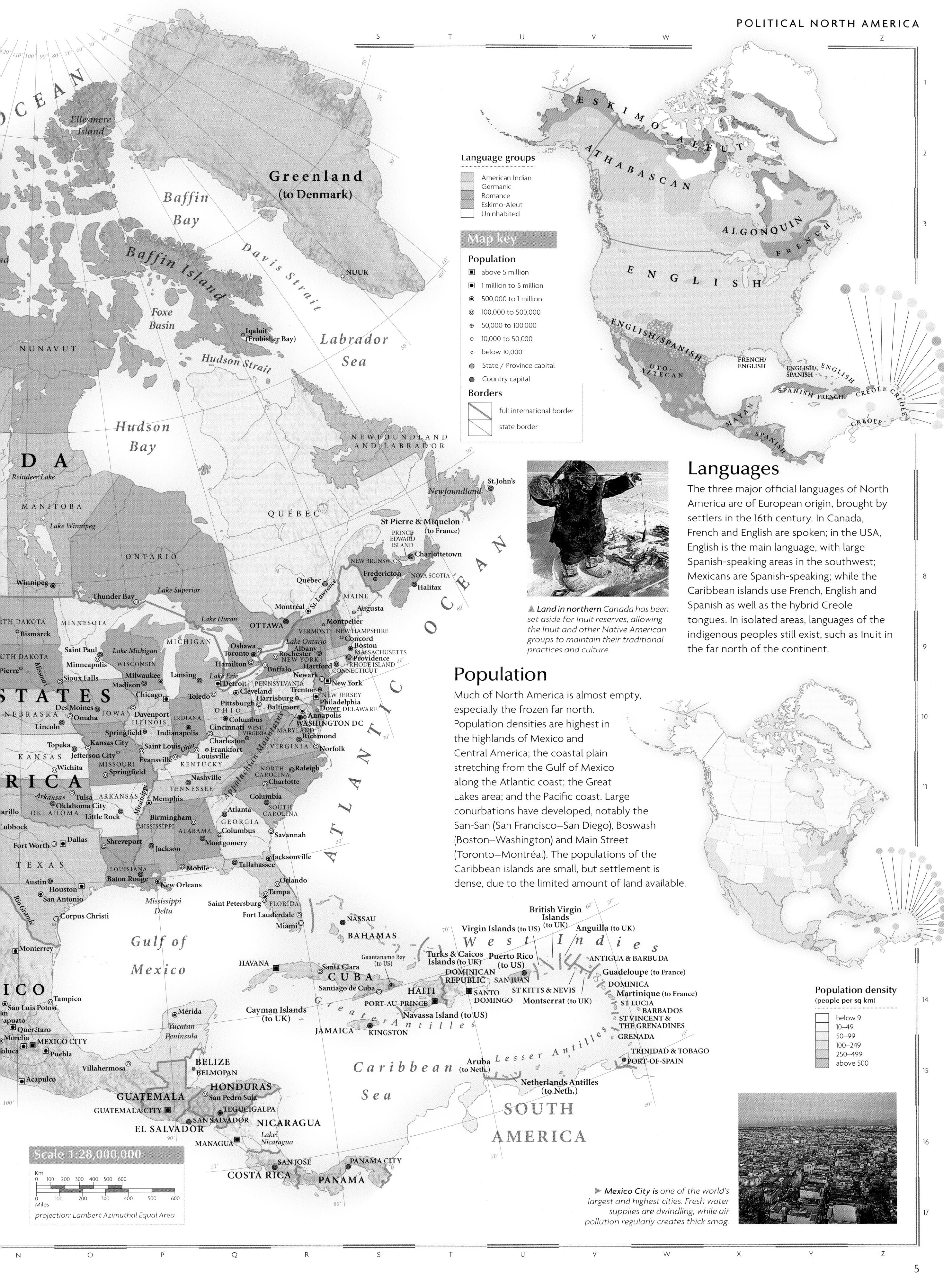

Language groups
American Indian
Germanic
Romance
Eskimo-Aleut
Uninhabited
ESKIMO-ALEUT
ATHABASCAN
ALGONQUIN
FRENCH
ENGLISH
ENGLISH/SPANISH
UTO-AZTECAN
FRENCH/ENGLISH
ENGLISH/SPANISH
ENGLISH
SPANISH
FRENCH
CREOLE
MAYAN
SPANISH
Map key
Population
above 5 million
1 million to 5 million
500,000 to 1 million
100,000 to 500,000
50,000 to 100,000
10,000 to 50,000
below 10,000
State / Province capital
Country capital
Borders
full international border
state border
Population density
(people per sq km)
below 9
10–49
50–99
100–249
250–499
above 500
Scale 1:28,000,000
projection: Lambert Azimuthal Equal Area
Greenland
(to Denmark)
Ellesmere Island
Baffin Bay
Baffin Island
Davis Strait
NUUK
Foxe Basin
Iqaluit (Frobisher Bay)
Labrador Sea
NUNAVUT
Hudson Strait
Hudson Bay
NEWFOUNDLAND AND LABRADOR
Reindeer Lake
MANITOBA
Lake Winnipeg
QUÉBEC
Newfoundland
St.John's
St Pierre & Miquelon (to France)
PRINCE EDWARD ISLAND
Charlottetown
NEW BRUNSWICK
Fredericton
NOVA SCOTIA
Halifax
ONTARIO
Winnipeg
Thunder Bay
Lake Superior
Québec
St. Lawrence
MAINE
Augusta
Montréal
OTTAWA
Lake Huron
VERMONT
NEW HAMPSHIRE
Montpelier
Concord
Boston
MASSACHUSETTS
Providence
RHODE ISLAND
CONNECTICUT
Hartford
Lake Ontario
Albany
Rochester
NEW YORK
Oshawa
Toronto
Hamilton
Buffalo
MINNESOTA
MICHIGAN
Bismarck
Saint Paul
Minneapolis
Lake Michigan
WISCONSIN
Sioux Falls
Milwaukee
Lansing
Lake Erie
Detroit
Madison
Chicago
Toledo
Cleveland
PENNSYLVANIA
Harrisburg
Pittsburgh
Newark
New York
Trenton
NEW JERSEY
Philadelphia
Dover
DELAWARE
Baltimore
Annapolis
WASHINGTON DC
MARYLAND
Richmond
Norfolk
VIRGINIA
WEST VIRGINIA
OHIO
Columbus
Cincinnati
Charleston
Frankfort
Louisville
KENTUCKY
INDIANA
Indianapolis
ILLINOIS
Springfield
Davenport
IOWA
Des Moines
Omaha
NEBRASKA
Lincoln
Topeka
Kansas City
KANSAS
Jefferson City
Saint Louis
Ohio
Evansville
MISSOURI
Wichita
Springfield
Nashville
TENNESSEE
NORTH CAROLINA
Raleigh
Charlotte
Appalachian Mountains
Tulsa
Oklahoma City
OKLAHOMA
ARKANSAS
Memphis
Mississippi
Little Rock
Columbia
SOUTH CAROLINA
Atlanta
GEORGIA
Birmingham
MISSISSIPPI
ALABAMA
Columbus
Savannah
Dallas
Fort Worth
Shreveport
Jackson
Montgomery
TEXAS
Jacksonville
Tallahassee
LOUISIANA
Baton Rouge
Mobile
Austin
Houston
San Antonio
New Orleans
Orlando
Tampa
Mississippi Delta
Saint Petersburg
FLORIDA
Fort Lauderdale
Miami
Rio Grande
Corpus Christi
Gulf of Mexico
Monterrey
NASSAU
BAHAMAS
HAVANA
Santa Clara
Guantanamo Bay (to US)
CUBA
Santiago de Cuba
Turks & Caicos Islands (to UK)
DOMINICAN REPUBLIC
Puerto Rico (to US)
SAN JUAN
SANTO DOMINGO
HAITI
PORT-AU-PRINCE
Navassa Island (to US)
Cayman Islands (to UK)
JAMAICA
KINGSTON
Greater Antilles
British Virgin Islands (to UK)
Virgin Islands (to US)
Anguilla (to UK)
West Indies
ANTIGUA & BARBUDA
Guadeloupe (to France)
DOMINICA
ST KITTS & NEVIS
Montserrat (to UK)
Martinique (to France)
ST LUCIA
BARBADOS
ST VINCENT & THE GRENADINES
GRENADA
TRINIDAD & TOBAGO
PORT-OF-SPAIN
Lesser Antilles
Aruba (to Neth.)
Netherlands Antilles (to Neth.)
Caribbean Sea
SOUTH AMERICA
Tampico
San Luis Potosí
Querétaro
Morelia
MEXICO CITY
Puebla
Mérida
Yucatan Peninsula
Acapulco
Villahermosa
BELIZE
BELMOPAN
HONDURAS
San Pedro Sula
TEGUCIGALPA
GUATEMALA
GUATEMALA CITY
SAN SALVADOR
EL SALVADOR
NICARAGUA
Lake Nicaragua
MANAGUA
SAN JOSÉ
COSTA RICA
PANAMA CITY
PANAMA
ATLANTIC OCEAN

▲ *Land in northern Canada has been set aside for Inuit reserves, allowing the Inuit and other Native American groups to maintain their traditional practices and culture.*

Languages

The three major official languages of North America are of European origin, brought by settlers in the 16th century. In Canada, French and English are spoken; in the USA, English is the main language, with large Spanish-speaking areas in the southwest; Mexicans are Spanish-speaking; while the Caribbean islands use French, English and Spanish as well as the hybrid Creole tongues. In isolated areas, languages of the indigenous peoples still exist, such as Inuit in the far north of the continent.

Population

Much of North America is almost empty, especially the frozen far north. Population densities are highest in the highlands of Mexico and Central America; the coastal plain stretching from the Gulf of Mexico along the Atlantic coast; the Great Lakes area; and the Pacific coast. Large conurbations have developed, notably the San-San (San Francisco–San Diego), Boswash (Boston–Washington) and Main Street (Toronto–Montréal). The populations of the Caribbean islands are small, but settlement is dense, due to the limited amount of land available.

► *Mexico City is one of the world's largest and highest cities. Fresh water supplies are dwindling, while air pollution regularly creates thick smog.*

North American resources

The two northern countries of Canada and the USA are richly endowed with natural resources which have helped to fuel economic development. The USA is the world's largest economy, although today it is facing stiff competition from the Far East. Mexico has relied on oil revenues but there are hopes that the North American Free Trade Agreement (NAFTA), will encourage trade growth with Canada and the USA. The poorer countries of Central America and the Caribbean depend largely on cash crops and tourism.

Industry

The modern, industrialized economies of the USA and Canada contrast sharply with those of Mexico, Central America and the Caribbean. Manufacturing is especially important in the USA; vehicle production is concentrated around the Great Lakes, while electronic and hi-tech industries are increasingly found in the western and southern states. Mexico depends on oil exports and assembly work, taking advantage of cheap labour. Many Central American and Caribbean countries rely heavily on agricultural exports.

◀ ***After its purchase*** *from Russia in 1867, Alaska's frozen lands were largely ignored by the USA. Oil reserves similar in magnitude to those in eastern Texas were discovered in Prudhoe Bay, Alaska in 1968. Freezing temperatures and a fragile environment hamper oil extraction.*

Standard of living

The USA and Canada have one of the highest overall standards of living in the world. However, many people still live in poverty, especially in inner city ghettos and some rural areas. Central America and the Caribbean are markedly poorer than their wealthier northern neighbours. Haiti is the poorest country in the western hemisphere.

Standard of living
(UN human development index)
high
low

▲ ***Fish such as*** *cod, flounder and plaice are caught in the Grand Banks, off the Newfoundland coast, and processed in many North Atlantic coastal settlements.*

▲ ***South of San Francisco,*** *'Silicon Valley' is both a national and international centre for hi-tech industries, electronic industries and research institutions.*

▲ ***The health of*** *the Wall Street stock market in New York is the standard measure of the state of the world's economy.*

▲ ***Multinational companies rely*** *on cheap labour and tax benefits to facilitate the assembly of vehicle parts in Mexican factories.*

Industry

- aerospace
- brewing
- car/vehicle manufacture
- chemicals
- defence
- electronics
- engineering
- film industry
- finance
- food processing
- hi-tech industry
- iron & steel
- pharmaceuticals
- printing & publishing
- research & development
- shipbuilding
- sugar processing
- textiles
- timber processing
- tobacco processing
- coal
- oil
- gas
- industrial cities
- major industrial areas

GNI per capita (US$)

- below 1999
- 2000–4999
- 5000–9999
- 10,000–19,999
- 20,000–24,999
- above 25,000

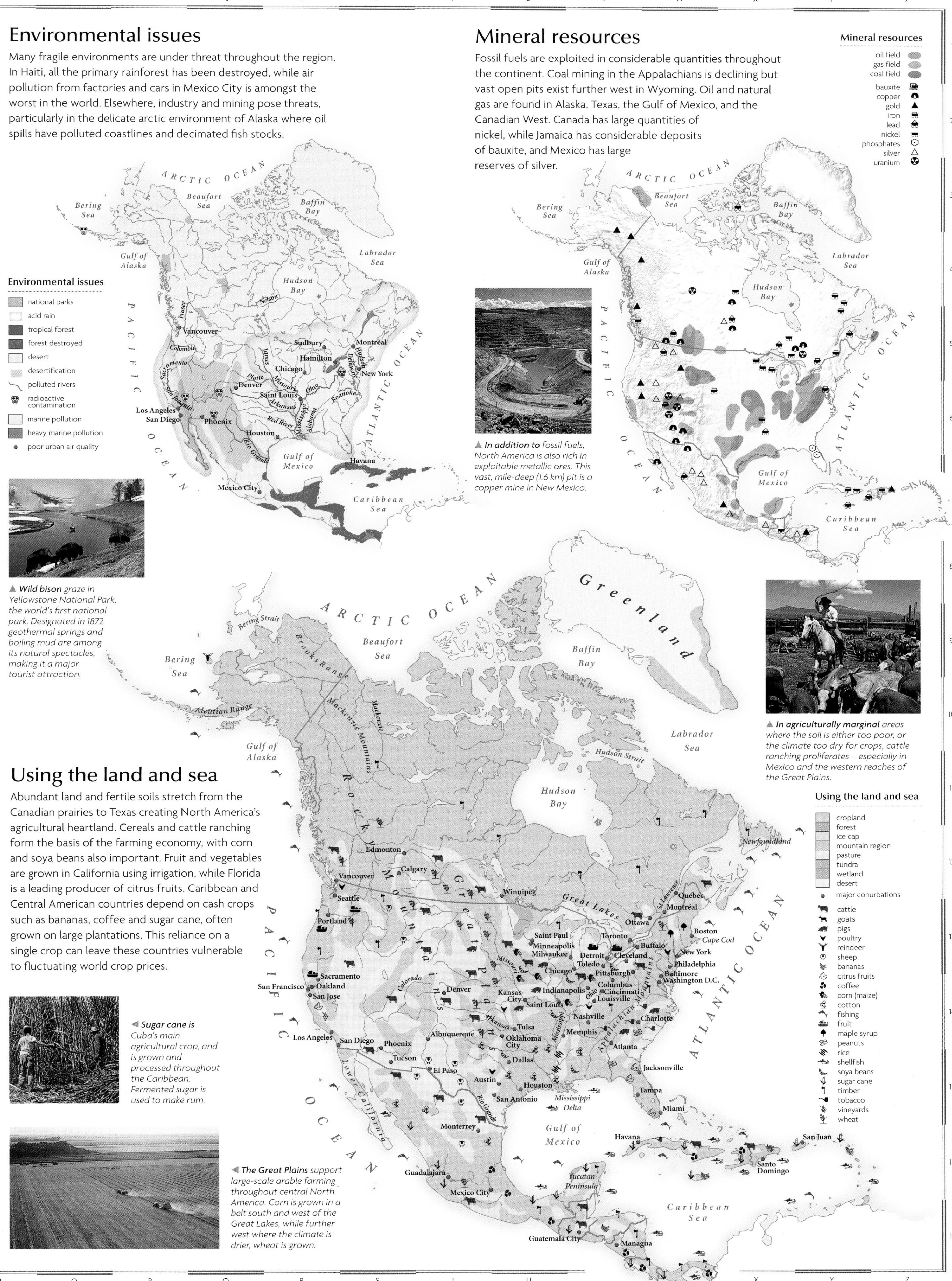

N O P Q R S T U V W X Y Z
1 2 3 4 5 6 8 9 10 11 12 13 14 15 16 17

Environmental issues

Many fragile environments are under threat throughout the region. In Haiti, all the primary rainforest has been destroyed, while air pollution from factories and cars in Mexico City is amongst the worst in the world. Elsewhere, industry and mining pose threats, particularly in the delicate arctic environment of Alaska where oil spills have polluted coastlines and decimated fish stocks.

Environmental issues
national parks
acid rain
tropical forest
forest destroyed
desert
desertification
polluted rivers
radioactive contamination
marine pollution
heavy marine pollution
poor urban air quality
ARCTIC OCEAN
Beaufort Sea
Bering Sea
Baffin Bay
Gulf of Alaska
Labrador Sea
Hudson Bay
PACIFIC OCEAN
ATLANTIC OCEAN
Gulf of Mexico
Caribbean Sea
Nelson
Fraser
Vancouver
Columbia
Sacramento
San Joaquin
Sudbury
Hamilton
Montreal
Hudson
Delaware
New York
Chicago
James
Missouri
Platte
Denver
Saint Louis
Ohio
Roanoke
Arkansas
Mississippi
Alabama
Red River
Los Angeles
San Diego
Phoenix
Houston
Rio Grande
Havana
Mexico City

▲ ***Wild bison*** *graze in Yellowstone National Park, the world's first national park. Designated in 1872, geothermal springs and boiling mud are among its natural spectacles, making it a major tourist attraction.*

Mineral resources

Fossil fuels are exploited in considerable quantities throughout the continent. Coal mining in the Appalachians is declining but vast open pits exist further west in Wyoming. Oil and natural gas are found in Alaska, Texas, the Gulf of Mexico, and the Canadian West. Canada has large quantities of nickel, while Jamaica has considerable deposits of bauxite, and Mexico has large reserves of silver.

Mineral resources
oil field
gas field
coal field
bauxite
copper
gold
iron
lead
nickel
phosphates
silver
uranium
ARCTIC OCEAN
Beaufort Sea
Bering Sea
Baffin Bay
Gulf of Alaska
Labrador Sea
Hudson Bay
PACIFIC OCEAN
ATLANTIC OCEAN
Gulf of Mexico
Caribbean Sea

▲ ***In addition to*** *fossil fuels, North America is also rich in exploitable metallic ores. This vast, mile-deep (1.6 km) pit is a copper mine in New Mexico.*

Using the land and sea

Abundant land and fertile soils stretch from the Canadian prairies to Texas creating North America's agricultural heartland. Cereals and cattle ranching form the basis of the farming economy, with corn and soya beans also important. Fruit and vegetables are grown in California using irrigation, while Florida is a leading producer of citrus fruits. Caribbean and Central American countries depend on cash crops such as bananas, coffee and sugar cane, often grown on large plantations. This reliance on a single crop can leave these countries vulnerable to fluctuating world crop prices.

Using the land and sea
cropland
forest
ice cap
mountain region
pasture
tundra
wetland
desert
major conurbations
cattle
goats
pigs
poultry
reindeer
sheep
bananas
citrus fruits
coffee
corn (maize)
cotton
fishing
fruit
maple syrup
peanuts
rice
shellfish
soya beans
sugar cane
timber
tobacco
vineyards
wheat
Greenland
ARCTIC OCEAN
Beaufort Sea
Bering Strait
Bering Sea
Brooks Range
Aleutian Range
Mackenzie Mountains
Mackenzie
Gulf of Alaska
Baffin Bay
Hudson Strait
Labrador Sea
Hudson Bay
Newfoundland
ROCKY MOUNTAINS
GREAT PLAINS
Edmonton
Calgary
Vancouver
Seattle
Winnipeg
Great Lakes
St Lawrence
Québec
Montréal
Ottawa
Portland
Boston
Cape Cod
Toronto
Saint Paul
Minneapolis
Milwaukee
Buffalo
Detroit
Cleveland
New York
Toledo
Philadelphia
Chicago
Pittsburgh
Baltimore
Washington D.C.
Sacramento
San Francisco
Oakland
San Jose
Colorado
Denver
Kansas City
Indianapolis
Columbus
Cincinnati
Louisville
Saint Louis
Ohio
Missouri
Appalachian Mountains
Nashville
Charlotte
Arkansas
Tulsa
Memphis
Mississippi
Los Angeles
San Diego
Phoenix
Albuquerque
Oklahoma City
Atlanta
Tucson
El Paso
Dallas
Jacksonville
Austin
Houston
Tampa
San Antonio
Mississippi Delta
Miami
Lower California
Rio Grande
Monterrey
Gulf of Mexico
Havana
San Juan
Santo Domingo
Guadalajara
Yucatan Peninsula
Mexico City
Caribbean Sea
Guatemala City
Managua
PACIFIC OCEAN
ATLANTIC OCEAN

▲ ***In agriculturally marginal*** *areas where the soil is either too poor, or the climate too dry for crops, cattle ranching proliferates – especially in Mexico and the western reaches of the Great Plains.*

◀ ***Sugar cane is*** *Cuba's main agricultural crop, and is grown and processed throughout the Caribbean. Fermented sugar is used to make rum.*

◀ ***The Great Plains*** *support large-scale arable farming throughout central North America. Corn is grown in a belt south and west of the Great Lakes, while further west where the climate is drier, wheat is grown.*

Canada

Canada is the second largest country in the world, and with only about one-tenth of its land area inhabited, it is one of the most sparsely populated. Canada became a confederation in 1867, though Newfoundland did not join until 1949. As a founding member of the UN and of the Commonwealth, Canada has played an important role in international affairs. A constitutional crisis, focusing on the French-speaking Québécois, and Inuit and Native American land rights, dominated politics in the 1990s. In 1999, part of the Northwest Territories, Nunavut, became a self-governing homeland for the Inuit.

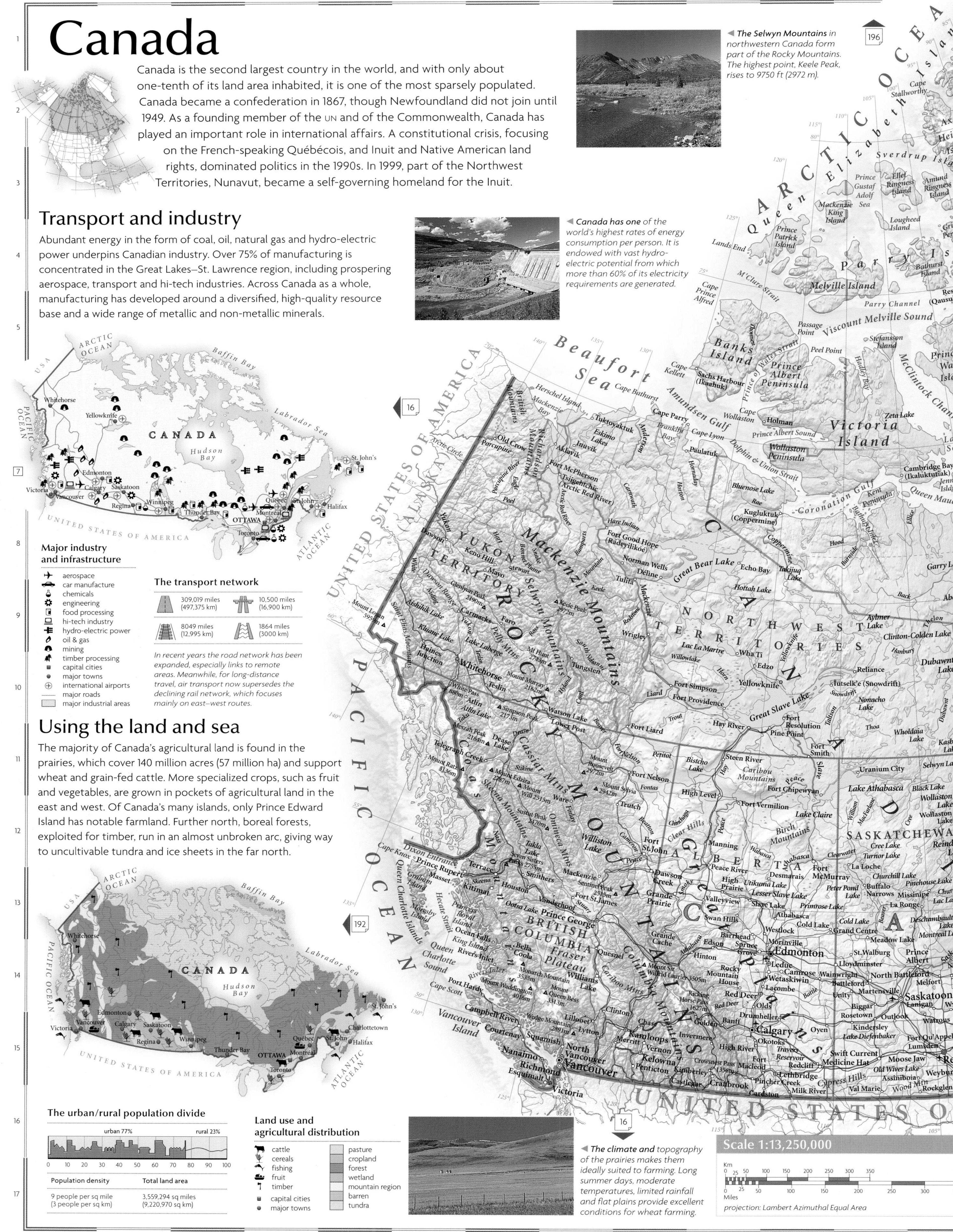

ARCTIC OCEAN
Beaufort Sea
PACIFIC OCEAN
UNITED STATES OF AMERICA (ALASKA)
YUKON TERRITORY
NORTHWEST TERRITORIES
BRITISH COLUMBIA
ALBERTA
SASKATCHEWAN
ROCKY MOUNTAINS
Mackenzie Mountains
Victoria Island
Banks Island
Melville Island
Queen Elizabeth Islands
Parry Islands
Great Bear Lake
Great Slave Lake
Lake Athabasca
Whitehorse
Yellowknife
Edmonton
Calgary
Vancouver
Victoria
Saskatoon
Scale 1:13,250,000
projection: Lambert Azimuthal Equal Area

The Selwyn Mountains in northwestern Canada form part of the Rocky Mountains. The highest point, Keele Peak, rises to 9750 ft (2972 m).

Transport and industry

Abundant energy in the form of coal, oil, natural gas and hydro-electric power underpins Canadian industry. Over 75% of manufacturing is concentrated in the Great Lakes–St. Lawrence region, including prospering aerospace, transport and hi-tech industries. Across Canada as a whole, manufacturing has developed around a diversified, high-quality resource base and a wide range of metallic and non-metallic minerals.

Canada has one of the world's highest rates of energy consumption per person. It is endowed with vast hydro-electric potential from which more than 60% of its electricity requirements are generated.

Major industry and infrastructure

- aerospace
- car manufacture
- chemicals
- engineering
- food processing
- hi-tech industry
- hydro-electric power
- oil & gas
- mining
- timber processing
- capital cities
- major towns
- international airports
- major roads
- major industrial areas

The transport network

309,019 miles (497,375 km)	10,500 miles (16,900 km)
8049 miles (12,995 km)	1864 miles (3000 km)

In recent years the road network has been expanded, especially links to remote areas. Meanwhile, for long-distance travel, air transport now supersedes the declining rail network, which focuses mainly on east–west routes.

Using the land and sea

The majority of Canada's agricultural land is found in the prairies, which cover 140 million acres (57 million ha) and support wheat and grain-fed cattle. More specialized crops, such as fruit and vegetables, are grown in pockets of agricultural land in the east and west. Of Canada's many islands, only Prince Edward Island has notable farmland. Further north, boreal forests, exploited for timber, run in an almost unbroken arc, giving way to uncultivable tundra and ice sheets in the far north.

The urban/rural population divide

urban 77% | rural 23%

Population density	Total land area
9 people per sq mile (3 people per sq km)	3,559,294 sq miles (9,220,970 sq km)

Land use and agricultural distribution

- cattle
- cereals
- fishing
- fruit
- timber
- capital cities
- major towns
- pasture
- cropland
- forest
- wetland
- mountain region
- barren
- tundra

The climate and topography of the prairies makes them ideally suited to farming. Long summer days, moderate temperatures, limited rainfall and flat plains provide excellent conditions for wheat farming.

Permanently frozen ground
Top layer thaws in the summer
Marginal areas of permafrost thaw in summer
Unfrozen ground where temperature is more moderate
Great Bear Lake
Baffin Bay
Baffin Island
Hudson Bay
James Bay
Hudson Strait
Labrador Sea
Davis Strait
Gulf of St. Lawrence
Atlantic Ocean
Great Lakes
Lake Superior
Lake Huron
Lake Michigan
Lake Ontario
Lake Erie
Laurentian Mountains
Newfoundland & Labrador
Québec
Ontario
Manitoba
Nova Scotia
New Brunswick
Prince Edward Island
Ottawa
Montréal
Québec
Toronto
Winnipeg
Halifax
St. John's
196
64
16
Map key
Population
1 million to 5 million
500,000 to 1 million
100,000 to 500,000
50,000 to 100,000
10,000 to 50,000
below 10,000
Elevation
6000m / 19,686ft
4000m / 13,124ft
3000m / 9843ft
2000m / 6562ft
1000m / 3281ft
500m / 1640ft
250m / 820ft
100m / 328ft
sea level

The landscape

Glaciers on islands in the Arctic Ocean are the last remnants of the ice sheet that once covered and shaped Canada. Hudson Bay is the centre of the Canadian Shield, a huge, eroded plateau marked at its southern extremity by a string of lakes running southeastwards from Great Bear Lake to the Great Lakes. In contrast to the rolling relief of the Shield and the central lowland region, the Rocky Mountains rise to peaks of over 13,000 ft (4000 m), stretching 500 miles (800 km) along the west coast.

► ***Permanently frozen ground*** *known as permafrost is common in Canada's northern tundra. It thickens further north, becoming hundreds of metres deep in parts of the Arctic.*

The Mackenzie river, flowing north over the permafrost, forms a wide river channel with many tributaries. Together with the Peel river it has created a long, narrow delta at its mouth. The entire river freezes during the winter.

Fertile prairies stretch from the southern rim of the Canadian Shield, south into the USA.

Exposure to three phases of mountain-building and subsequent erosion over millions of years has moulded the ancient Canadian Shield into a series of basins and ridges.

▲ ***Along the northeastern*** *coast of Baffin Island the mountains rise to 8000 ft (2440 m). Glaciers move down through the valleys to the sea, eroding wide U-shaped valleys.*

The Rocky Mountains were formed some 80 million years ago, when the Pacific plate was driven under the North American plate, forcing up the land.

The Great Lakes lie on the Canada–USA border. The basins they now occupy were fashioned by repeated ice advance. At one time, Lakes Superior, Huron and Michigan formed a single large lake, Lake Nipissing.

The St. Lawrence River is 2350 miles (3782 km) long. It flows from the western shore of Lake Superior through the Great Lakes and on to the Atlantic Ocean. From December to April, the St. Lawrence Seaway freezes between Lake Ontario and Montréal.

► ***The Great Lakes*** *are drained by the St. Lawrence River which flows down through a wide tectonic depression. It forms a broad estuary for much of its course, the width varying from 1.2 miles (1.9 km) in the upper reaches to 90 miles (145 km) at its mouth.*

► ***Isolated pillars, known*** *as hoodos near Red Deer river in the badlands of Alberta are a product of wind and water erosion, especially flash floods. The badlands lie in the rain shadow of the Rocky Mountains, which creates a semi-arid climate.*

Canada: WESTERN PROVINCES

Alberta, British Columbia, Manitoba, Saskatchewan, Yukon Territory

The mountains of the west coast, incorporating British Columbia and the Yukon Territory, descend into the vast, flat prairies of Alberta, Saskatchewan and Manitoba. The empty lands and fertile soils of the prairie provinces attracted migrants, and the descendants of early European immigrants still make up a large proportion of the population. The mechanization of agriculture has reduced the need for labour, and rural population densities remain low. The majority of the people live within 100 miles (160 km) of the southern Canada–USA border, and in British Columbia, one of the leading Canadian provinces in terms of economic wealth. The Yukon Territory, in the far north, remains a relatively unspoilt wilderness, containing large, untapped mineral reserves. This province has a significant population of Native Americans, many of whom maintain a traditional lifestyle.

16

Using the land and sea

Wheat farming is the economic mainstay of Alberta, Manitoba and Saskatchewan, which contain 82% of farmland in Canada. Cattle are also raised on the prairies. Forestry and fishing are the most prominent resource-based industries in British Columbia. Despite the mountainous terrain, fruit and specialized grains can be grown in the Okanagan and Fraser valleys.

Land use and agricultural distribution

- cattle
- cereals
- fishing
- fruit
- timber
- major towns
- pasture
- cropland
- forest
- wetland
- barren
- tundra

▲ *Large, highly-mechanized and often very specialized farms, requiring huge investment but little labour, characterize modern farming in the prairies.*

The urban/rural population divide

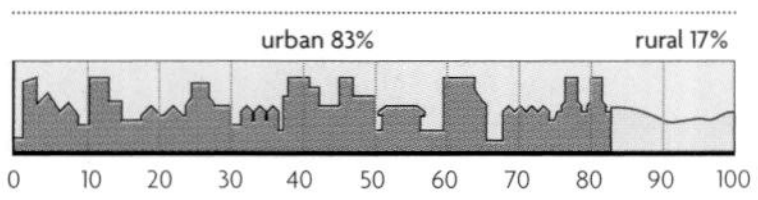

urban 83% · rural 17%

Population density	Total land area
8 people per sq mile (3 people per sq km)	1,230,547 sq miles (3,187,120 sq km)

Transport and industry

The western provinces contain a wealth of mineral resources. Alberta holds the bulk of Canada's fossil fuels; the other provinces contain reserves of metallic ores, such as zinc, lead and silver. Isolation from markets has slowed the development of manufacturing, restricting it to the large cities like Vancouver, Winnipeg and Calgary. Hydro-electric power is widely exploited, although there is increasing concern about potential ecological damage.

The transport network

- 82,438 miles (135,145 km)
- 6459 miles (10,401 km)
- 24,041 miles (38,694 km)
- None

The transport network of the western provinces is dominated by east–west routes that weave through mountain passes and spread across the plains. Access to some northern areas is restricted to air travel.

Major industry and infrastructure

- aerospace
- chemicals
- coal
- engineering
- food processing
- hydro-electric power
- mining
- oil & gas
- timber processing
- major towns
- international airports
- major roads
- major industrial areas

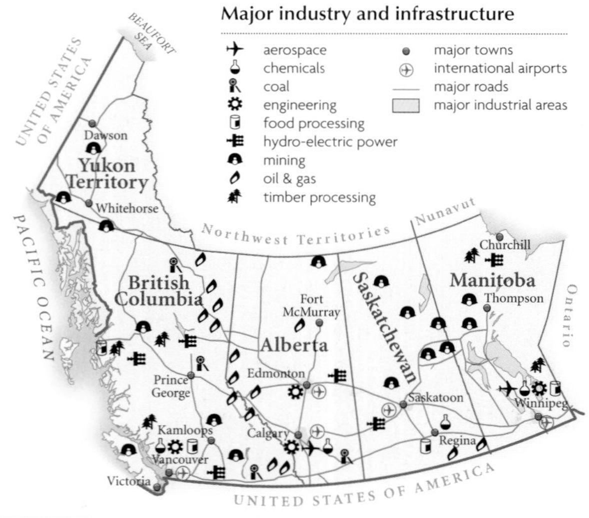

◄ *Much of the Yukon Territory is uninhabited tundra. Industry is based on the extraction of mineral resources, and to a lesser extent, on the scattered forests of the south.*

192

▲ *The Fraser River valley is a major area of settlement in British Columbia. Railways cross the Rocky Mountains via this valley.*

▲ *Established in 1907, Jasper National Park lies in the heart of the Rocky Mountains. It is noted for its spectacular alpine scenery and contains part of the large Columbia Icefield.*

The landscape

The massive Rocky Mountains form a continental divide between rivers flowing eastward and westward. East of the mountains, stretching from the Arctic Circle south into the USA, lie the interior plains. Covered with glacial deposits from the last Ice Age, these are interspersed with hilly regions and long, steep escarpments.

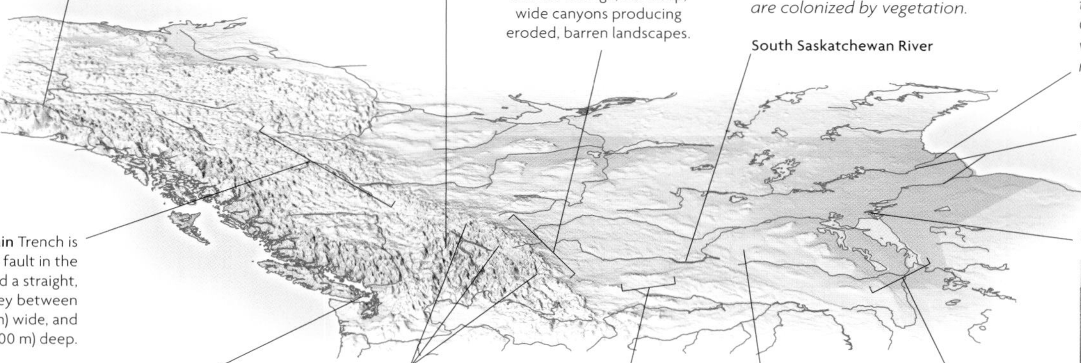

Mount Logan rises 19,551 ft (5959 m). It is the highest peak in Canada.

The Columbia Icefield in the Rocky Mountains is the source of two major rivers, the Athabasca and the North Saskatchewan.

Vegetated island

Bar

River flow is diverted by deposited sediments

Sand flat

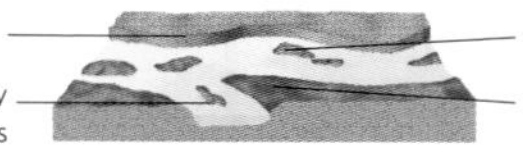

▲ ***Braided rivers are*** *shallow and fast-flowing. The interlaced branches are formed when excess sediments, which can no longer be transported, are deposited. The sediments collect in the river channel forming bars and sand flats. Islands form when the bars are colonized by vegetation.*

▲ ***Across the tundra*** *of northern Manitoba, widespread permafrost inhibits water from permeating the soil. This causes rivers like the Churchill to flow in many channels, which can be frozen for up to six months during the winter.*

The badlands of Alberta were created when east-flowing rivers, swollen by meltwater at the end of the last Ice Age, cut deep, wide canyons producing eroded, barren landscapes.

South Saskatchewan River

The Nelson and Churchill rivers drain northward across the Canadian Shield to Hudson Bay. The shield covers three-fifths of Saskatchewan.

Setting Lake

▲ ***Ancient granite outcrops,*** *part of the Canadian Shield, rise above the surface of Setting Lake, which was initially formed by meltwater from the last Ice Age.*

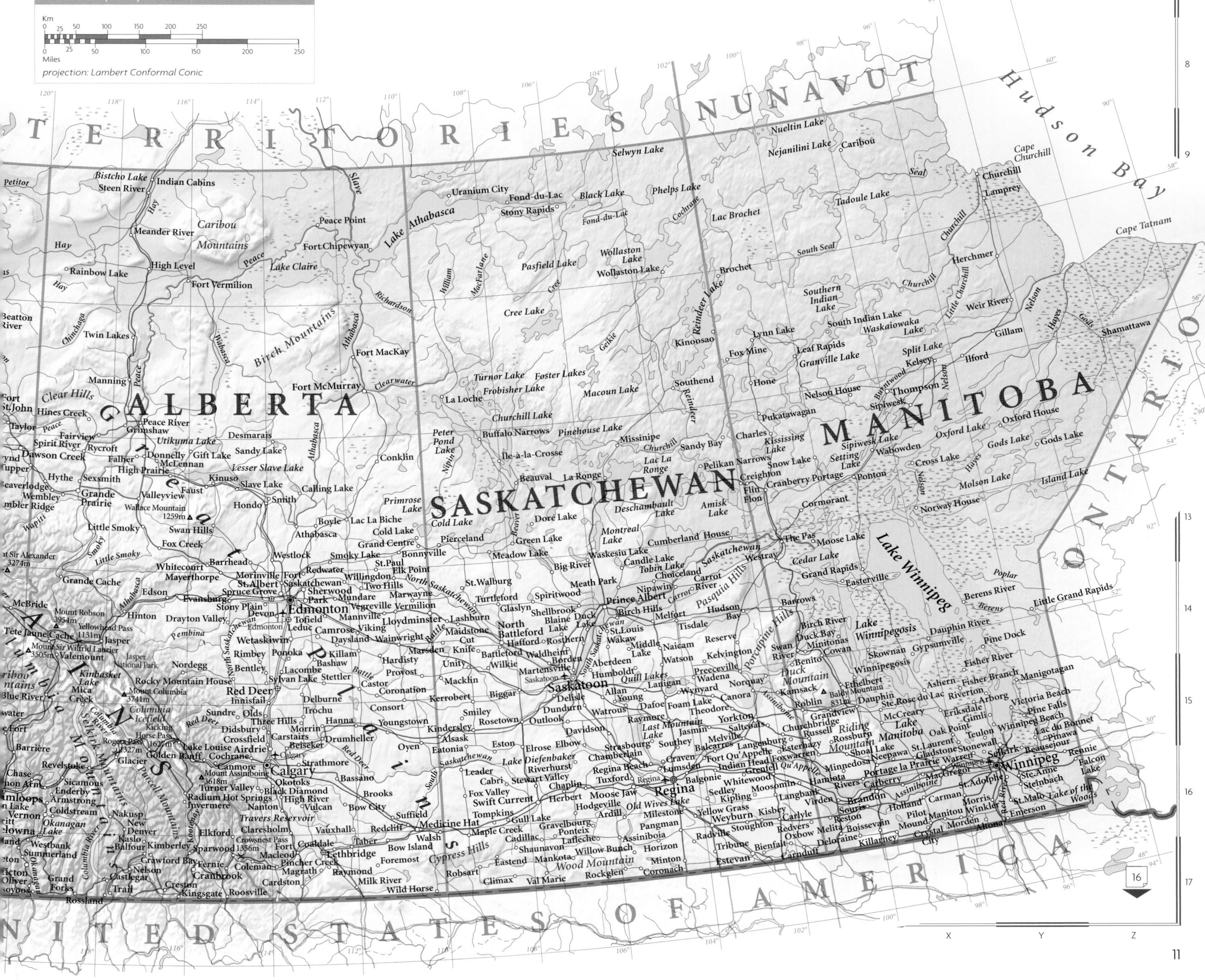

The Rocky Mountain Trench is the longest linear fault in the world. It has formed a straight, flat-bottomed valley between 2–9 miles (4–15 km) wide, and up to 3280 ft (1000 m) deep.

Hundreds of islands dot the fjord-indented coast of British Columbia; the largest is Vancouver Island.

Three major passes cut through the Rocky Mountains: Yellowhead, Kicking Horse and Crowsnest. They are all used as transport routes through the mountains.

The Cypress Hills rise to 4806 ft (1465 m) above the surrounding plain. Having escaped the last glaciation they contain unique plant and animal life. The silvery lupine, bunchberry and lodgepole pine all grow in the cool, moist climate of the hills.

The Alberta and Saskatchewan plains bear strong testament to past glaciations. The Assiniboine, Saskatchewan and Qu'Appelle rivers occupy flat-bottomed, steep-sided valleys eroded during the last Ice Age by glacial meltwater.

The lowlands of Manitoba are a basin that once held the vast post-glacial Lake Agassiz, remnants of which include Lake Winnipeg, Lake Winnipegosis and Lake Manitoba.

Map key

Population

- 500,000 to 1 million
- 100,000 to 500,000
- 50,000 to 100,000
- 10,000 to 50,000
- below 10,000

Elevation

- 6000m / 19,686ft
- 4000m / 13,124ft
- 3000m / 9843ft
- 2000m / 6562ft
- 1000m / 3281ft
- 500m / 1640ft
- 250m / 820ft
- 100m / 328ft
- sea level

Scale 1:7,500,000

Km 0 25 50 100 150 200 250

Miles 0 25 50 100 150 200 250

projection: Lambert Conformal Conic

16

Canada: EASTERN PROVINCES

New Brunswick, Newfoundland & Labrador, Nova Scotia, Ontario, Prince Edward Island, Québec, ***St Pierre & Miquelon (to France)***

Colonized by both the English and the French during the 16th century, Canada's eastern provinces are still marked by their dual influences. They contain the last fragment of once-sizeable French territories, the islands of St Pierre and Miquelon. French remains Canada's second official language and Québec's first language. The population of the eastern provinces is highly concentrated in the south, especially along the border with the USA. A recent decline in fishing in the Atlantic provinces has encouraged a steady flow of westerly migration to more prosperous regions. The north, around Hudson Bay, remains snow-covered for most of the year and the indigenous Inuit people make up the bulk of its sparse population.

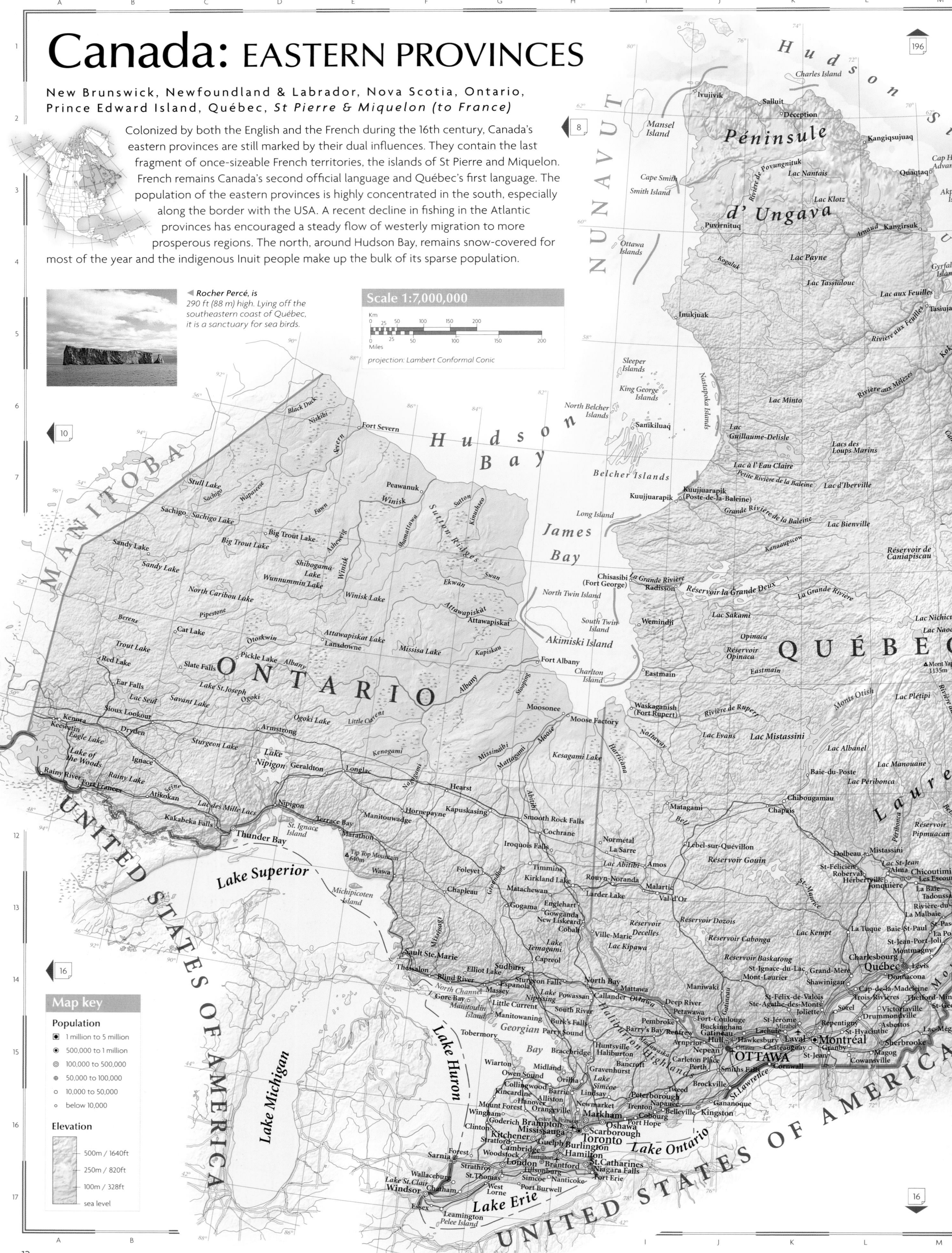
Scale 1:7,000,000
Km 0 25 50 100 150 200
Miles 0 25 50 100 150 200
projection: Lambert Conformal Conic
Map key
Population
1 million to 5 million
500,000 to 1 million
100,000 to 500,000
50,000 to 100,000
10,000 to 50,000
below 10,000
Elevation
500m / 1640ft
250m / 820ft
100m / 328ft
sea level
Hudson Bay
James Bay
Péninsule d' Ungava
NUNAVUT
MANITOBA
ONTARIO
QUÉBEC
UNITED STATES OF AMERICA
Lake Superior
Lake Michigan
Lake Huron
Lake Ontario
Lake Erie
Georgian Bay
Akimiski Island
Belcher Islands
OTTAWA
Toronto
Montréal
Québec

◀ *Rocher Percé, is 290 ft (88 m) high. Lying off the southeastern coast of Québec, it is a sanctuary for sea birds.*

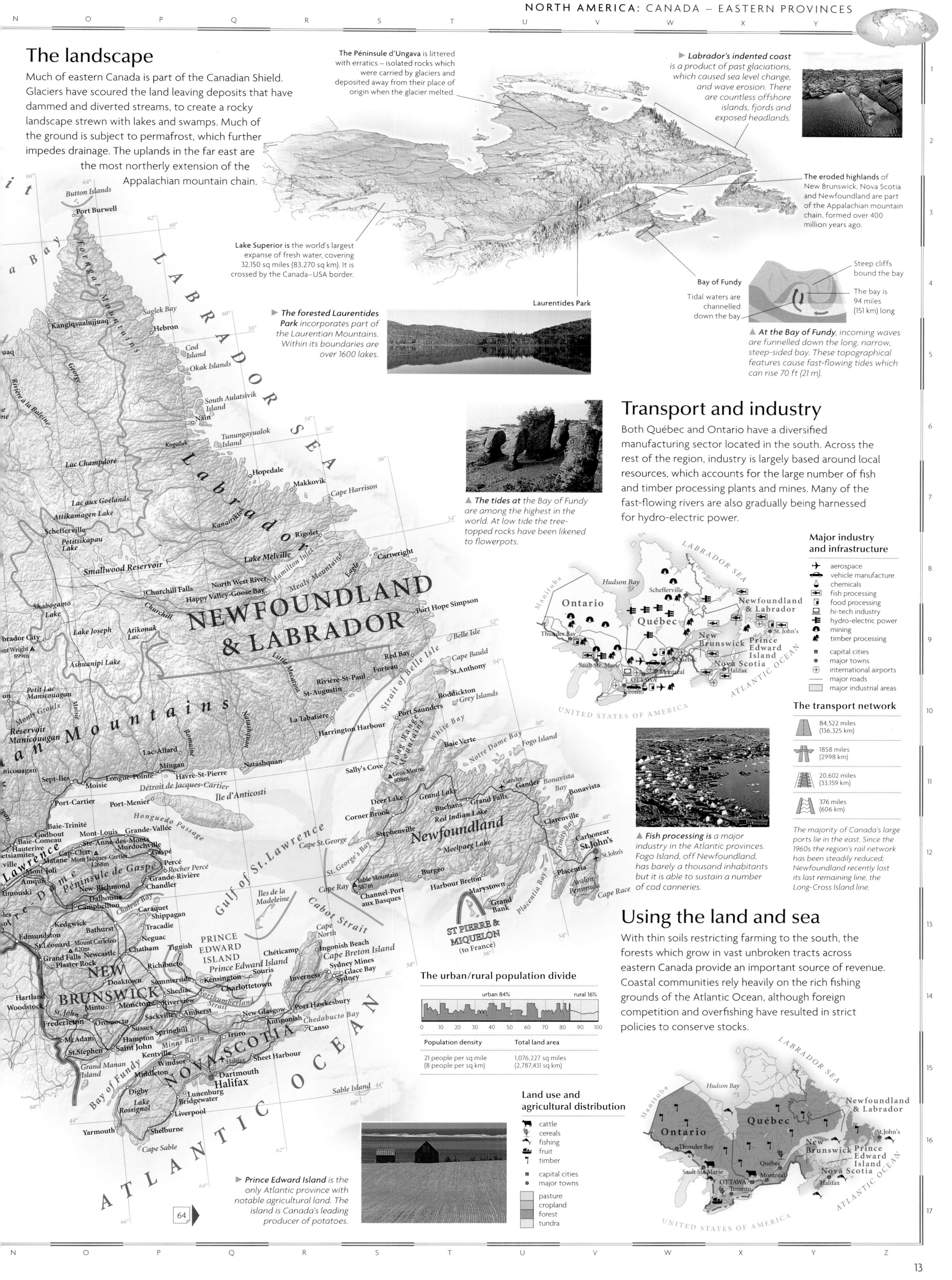

N O P Q R S T U V W X Y Z
1 2 3 4 5 6 7 8 9 10 11 12 13 14 15 16 17
Lake Superior
Laurentides Park
Bay of Fundy
Tidal waters are channelled down the bay
Steep cliffs bound the bay
The bay is 94 miles (151 km) long
NEWFOUNDLAND & LABRADOR
LABRADOR SEA
Labrador
Newfoundland
Québec
Ontario
NEW BRUNSWICK
NOVA SCOTIA
PRINCE EDWARD ISLAND
ATLANTIC OCEAN
Gulf of St. Lawrence
Cabot Strait
Strait of Belle Isle
ST PIERRE & MIQUELON (to France)
UNITED STATES OF AMERICA
Hudson Bay
Major industry and infrastructure
aerospace
vehicle manufacture
chemicals
fish processing
food processing
hi-tech industry
hydro-electric power
mining
timber processing
capital cities
major towns
international airports
major roads
major industrial areas
The transport network
84,522 miles (136,325 km)
1858 miles (2998 km)
20,602 miles (33,159 km)
376 miles (606 km)
The urban/rural population divide
urban 84%
rural 16%
0 10 20 30 40 50 60 70 80 90 100
Population density
21 people per sq mile (8 people per sq km)
Total land area
1,076,227 sq miles (2,787,431 sq km)
Land use and agricultural distribution
cattle
cereals
fishing
fruit
timber
capital cities
major towns
pasture
cropland
forest
tundra

The landscape

Much of eastern Canada is part of the Canadian Shield. Glaciers have scoured the land leaving deposits that have dammed and diverted streams, to create a rocky landscape strewn with lakes and swamps. Much of the ground is subject to permafrost, which further impedes drainage. The uplands in the far east are the most northerly extension of the Appalachian mountain chain.

The Péninsule d'Ungava is littered with erratics – isolated rocks which were carried by glaciers and deposited away from their place of origin when the glacier melted.

▶ *Labrador's indented coast is a product of past glaciations, which caused sea level change, and wave erosion. There are countless offshore islands, fjords and exposed headlands.*

The eroded highlands of New Brunswick, Nova Scotia and Newfoundland are part of the Appalachian mountain chain, formed over 400 million years ago.

Lake Superior is the world's largest expanse of fresh water, covering 32,150 sq miles (83,270 sq km). It is crossed by the Canada–USA border.

▶ ***The forested Laurentides Park** incorporates part of the Laurentian Mountains. Within its boundaries are over 1600 lakes.*

▲ ***At the Bay of Fundy**, incoming waves are funnelled down the long, narrow, steep-sided bay. These topographical features cause fast-flowing tides which can rise 70 ft (21 m).*

▲ ***The tides at** the Bay of Fundy are among the highest in the world. At low tide the tree-topped rocks have been likened to flowerpots.*

Transport and industry

Both Québec and Ontario have a diversified manufacturing sector located in the south. Across the rest of the region, industry is largely based around local resources, which accounts for the large number of fish and timber processing plants and mines. Many of the fast-flowing rivers are also gradually being harnessed for hydro-electric power.

▲ ***Fish processing is** a major industry in the Atlantic provinces. Fogo Island, off Newfoundland, has barely a thousand inhabitants but it is able to sustain a number of cod canneries.*

The majority of Canada's large ports lie in the east. Since the 1960s the region's rail network has been steadily reduced; Newfoundland recently lost its last remaining line, the Long-Cross Island line.

Using the land and sea

With thin soils restricting farming to the south, the forests which grow in vast unbroken tracts across eastern Canada provide an important source of revenue. Coastal communities rely heavily on the rich fishing grounds of the Atlantic Ocean, although foreign competition and overfishing have resulted in strict policies to conserve stocks.

▶ ***Prince Edward Island** is the only Atlantic province with notable agricultural land. The island is Canada's leading producer of potatoes.*

64

Southeastern Canada

Southern Ontario, Southern Québec

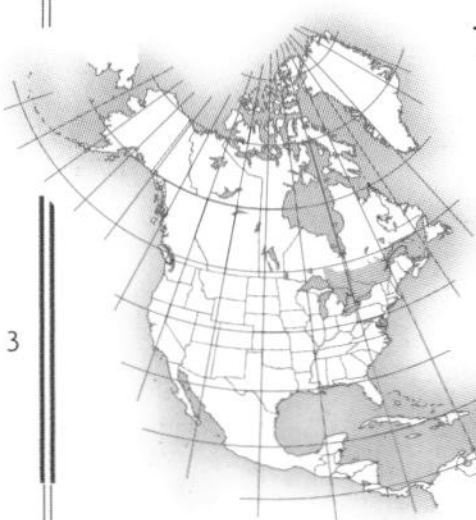

The southern parts of Québec and Ontario form the economic heart of Canada. The two provinces are divided by their language and culture; in Québec, French is the main language, whereas English is spoken in Ontario. Separatist sentiment in Québec has led to a provincial referendum on the question of a sovereignty association with Canada. The region contains Canada's capital, Ottawa and its two largest cities: Toronto, the centre of commerce and Montréal, the cultural and administrative heart of French Canada.

▲ *The port at Montréal is situated on the St. Lawrence Seaway. A network of 16 locks allows sea-going vessels access to routes once plied by fur-trappers and early settlers.*

Transport and industry

The cities of southern Québec and Ontario, and their hinterlands, form the heart of Canadian manufacturing industry. Toronto is Canada's leading financial centre, and Ontario's motor and aerospace industries have developed around the city. A major centre for nickel mining lies to the north of Toronto. Most of Québec's industry is located in Montréal, the oldest port in North America. Chemicals, paper manufacture and the construction of transport equipment are leading industrial activities.

► ***Niagara Falls lies*** *on the border between Canada and the USA. It comprises a system of two falls: American Falls, in New York, is separated from Horseshoe Falls, in Ontario, by Goat Island. Horseshoe Falls, seen here, plunges 184 ft (56 m) and is 2500 ft (762 m) wide.*

Major industry and infrastructure

- car manufacture
- chemicals
- engineering
- finance
- food processing
- hi-tech industry
- mining
- iron & steel
- textiles
- paper industry
- timber processing
- capital cities
- major towns
- international airports
- major roads
- major industrial areas

Sault Ste.Marie
North Bay
Québec
Québec
New Brunswick
Lake Huron
Ontario
Montreal
OTTAWA
Toronto
Lake Ontario
Lake Erie
UNITED STATES OF AMERICA

The transport network

The opening of the St. Lawrence Seaway in 1959 finally allowed ocean-going ships (up to 24,000 tons (tonnes)) access to the interior of Canada, creating a vital trading route.

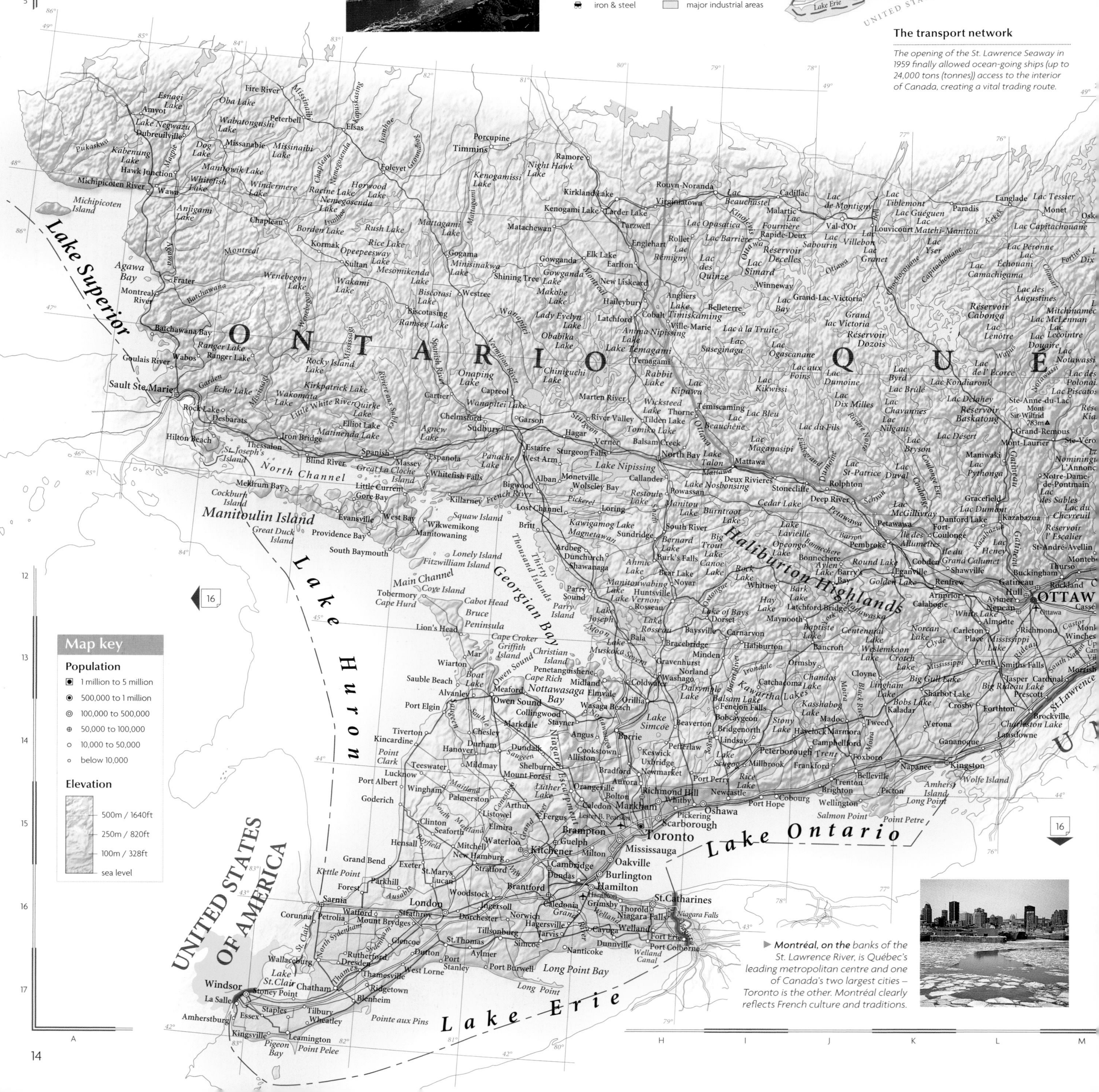

Map key

Population

- 1 million to 5 million
- 500,000 to 1 million
- 100,000 to 500,000
- 50,000 to 100,000
- 10,000 to 50,000
- below 10,000

Elevation

- 500m / 1640ft
- 250m / 820ft
- 100m / 328ft
- sea level

16

16

► ***Montréal, on the*** *banks of the St. Lawrence River, is Québec's leading metropolitan centre and one of Canada's two largest cities – Toronto is the other. Montréal clearly reflects French culture and traditions.*

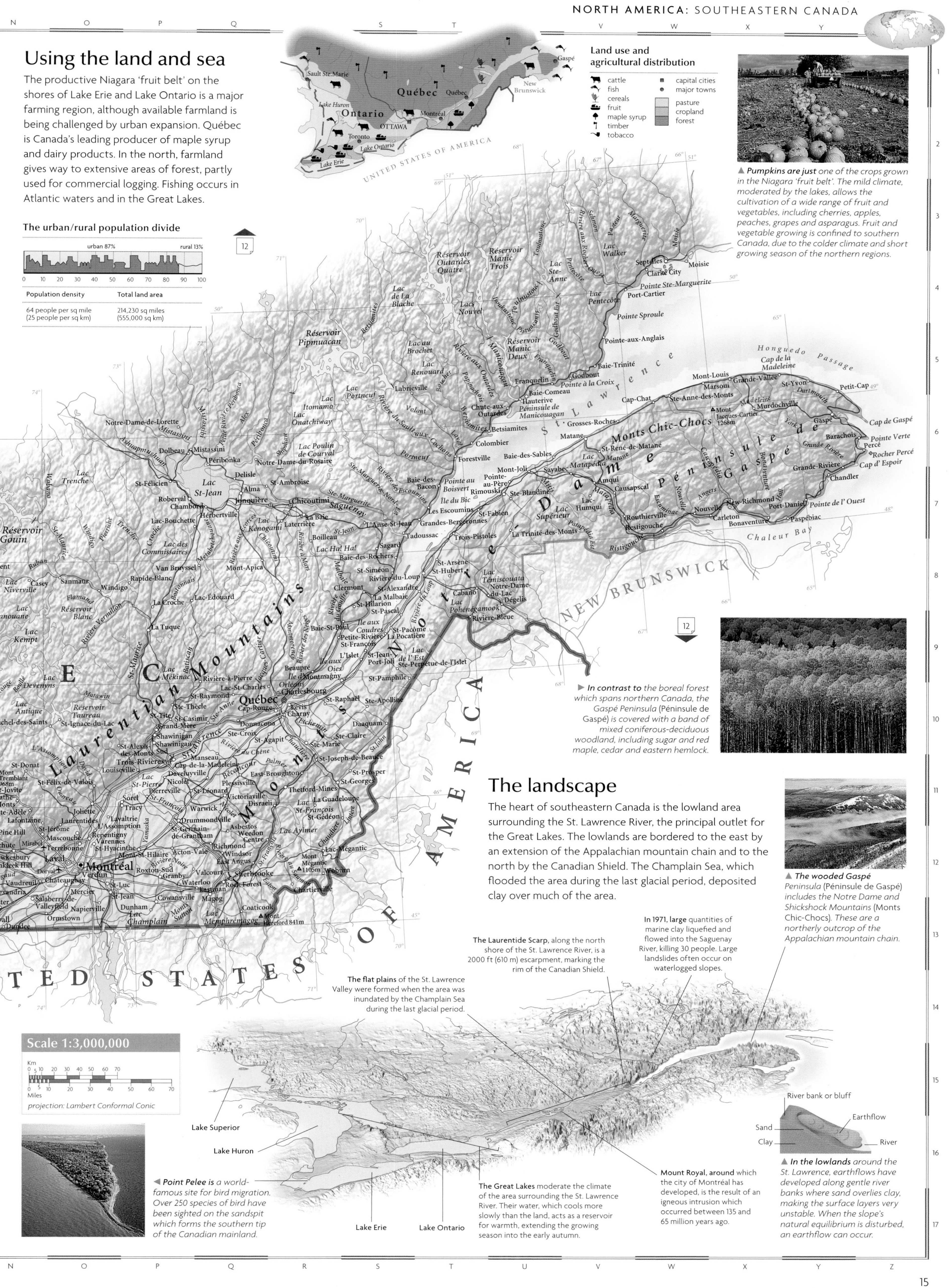

Using the land and sea

The productive Niagara 'fruit belt' on the shores of Lake Erie and Lake Ontario is a major farming region, although available farmland is being challenged by urban expansion. Québec is Canada's leading producer of maple syrup and dairy products. In the north, farmland gives way to extensive areas of forest, partly used for commercial logging. Fishing occurs in Atlantic waters and in the Great Lakes.

The urban/rural population divide

urban 87%
rural 13%
0 10 20 30 40 50 60 70 80 90 100

Population density	Total land area
64 people per sq mile (25 people per sq km)	214,230 sq miles (555,000 sq km)

Land use and agricultural distribution

cattle
fish
cereals
fruit
maple syrup
timber
tobacco
capital cities
major towns
pasture
cropland
forest
Québec
Ontario
OTTAWA
Toronto
Montréal
Québec
Sault Ste.Marie
Lake Huron
Lake Ontario
Lake Erie
Gaspé
New Brunswick
UNITED STATES OF AMERICA

▲ *Pumpkins are just one of the crops grown in the Niagara 'fruit belt'. The mild climate, moderated by the lakes, allows the cultivation of a wide range of fruit and vegetables, including cherries, apples, peaches, grapes and asparagus. Fruit and vegetable growing is confined to southern Canada, due to the colder climate and short growing season of the northern regions.*

▶ *In contrast to the boreal forest which spans northern Canada, the Gaspé Peninsula (Péninsule de Gaspé) is covered with a band of mixed coniferous-deciduous woodland, including sugar and red maple, cedar and eastern hemlock.*

Laurentian Mountains
Monts Notre-Dame
Monts Chic-Chocs
Péninsule de Gaspé
St Lawrence
NEW BRUNSWICK
UNITED STATES OF AMERICA
Québec
Montréal
Lac St-Jean
Chaleur Bay
Honguedo Passage

The landscape

The heart of southeastern Canada is the lowland area surrounding the St. Lawrence River, the principal outlet for the Great Lakes. The lowlands are bordered to the east by an extension of the Appalachian mountain chain and to the north by the Canadian Shield. The Champlain Sea, which flooded the area during the last glacial period, deposited clay over much of the area.

▲ *The wooded Gaspé Peninsula (Péninsule de Gaspé) includes the Notre Dame and Shickshock Mountains (Monts Chic-Chocs). These are a northerly outcrop of the Appalachian mountain chain.*

Scale 1:3,000,000

Km
0 5 10 20 30 40 50 60 70
Miles
0 5 10 20 30 40 50 60 70

projection: Lambert Conformal Conic

The Laurentide Scarp, along the north shore of the St. Lawrence River, is a 2000 ft (610 m) escarpment, marking the rim of the Canadian Shield.

In 1971, large quantities of marine clay liquefied and flowed into the Saguenay River, killing 30 people. Large landslides often occur on waterlogged slopes.

The flat plains of the St. Lawrence Valley were formed when the area was inundated by the Champlain Sea during the last glacial period.

Lake Superior
Lake Huron
Lake Erie
Lake Ontario
River bank or bluff
Earthflow
Sand
Clay
River

◀ *Point Pelee is a world-famous site for bird migration. Over 250 species of bird have been sighted on the sandspit which forms the southern tip of the Canadian mainland.*

The Great Lakes moderate the climate of the area surrounding the St. Lawrence River. Their water, which cools more slowly than the land, acts as a reservoir for warmth, extending the growing season into the early autumn.

Mount Royal, around which the city of Montréal has developed, is the result of an igneous intrusion which occurred between 135 and 65 million years ago.

▲ *In the lowlands around the St. Lawrence, earthflows have developed along gentle river banks where sand overlies clay, making the surface layers very unstable. When the slope's natural equilibrium is disturbed, an earthflow can occur.*

The United States of America

COTERMINOUS USA (FOR ALASKA AND HAWAII SEE PAGES 38-39)

The USA's progression from frontier territory to economic and political superpower has taken less than 200 years. The 48 coterminous states, along with the outlying states of Alaska and Hawaii, are part of a federal union, held together by the guiding principles of the US Constitution, which enshrines the ideals of democracy and liberty for all. Abundant fertile land and a rich resource-base fuelled and sustained the USA's economic development. With the spread of agriculture and the growth of trade and industry came the need for a larger workforce, which was supplied by millions of immigrants, many seeking an escape from poverty and political or religious persecution. Immigration continues today, particularly from Central America and Asia.

▲ *Washington DC was established as the site for the nation's capital in 1790. It is home to the seat of national government, on Capitol Hill, as well as the President's official residence, the White House.*

► *The clear waters of Niagara Falls cascade 190 ft (58 m) into the gorge below. It is one of America's most famous spectacles and a leading tourist attraction. The falls are slowly receding and the gorge may one day stretch from Lake Ontario to Lake Erie.*

▲ *Mount Rainier is a dormant volcano in the Cascade Range, Washington. This 14,090 ft (4392 m) peak is flanked by the most extensive glacier outside Alaska.*

Scale 1:11,450,000

Km 0 25 50 100 150 200 250 300 350 400

Miles 0 25 50 100 150 200 250 300 350 400

projection: Lambert Azimuthal Equal Area

8

192

40

Transport and industry

The USA has been the industrial powerhouse of the world since the Second World War, pioneering mass-production and the consumer lifestyle. Initially, heavy engineering and manufacturing in the northeast led the economy. Today, heavy industry has declined and the USA's economy is driven by service and financial industries, with the most important being defence, hi-tech and electronics.

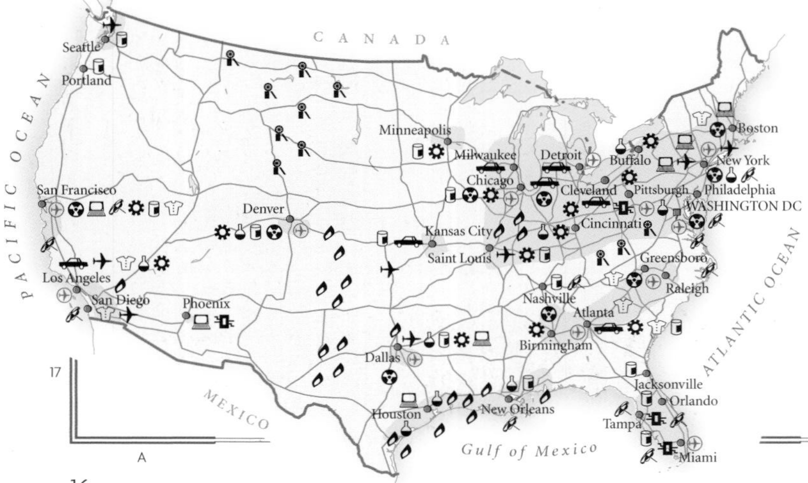

The transport network

3,875,040 miles (6,240,000 km)	52,388 miles (84,361 km)
148,308 miles (235,238 km)	25,467 miles (41,009 km)

Transport in the USA is dominated by the car which, with the extensive Interstate Highway system, allows great personal mobility. Today, internal air flights between major cities provide the most rapid cross-country travel.

Major industry and infrastructure

- aerospace
- car manufacture
- chemicals
- coal
- electronics
- engineering
- food processing
- hi-tech industry
- oil & gas
- research & development
- textiles
- tourism
- capital cities
- major towns
- international airports
- major roads
- major industrial areas

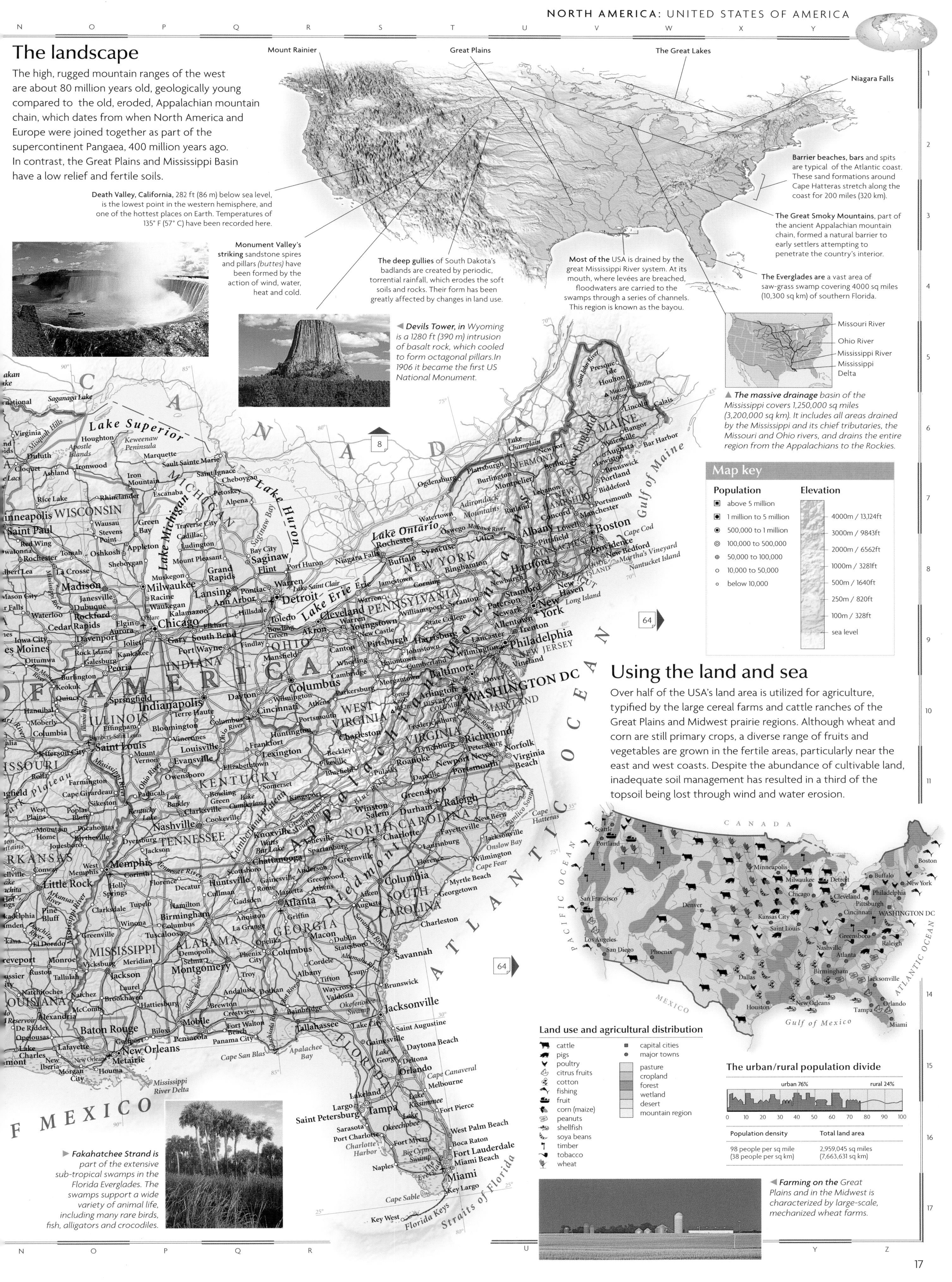

The landscape

The high, rugged mountain ranges of the west are about 80 million years old, geologically young compared to the old, eroded, Appalachian mountain chain, which dates from when North America and Europe were joined together as part of the supercontinent Pangaea, 400 million years ago. In contrast, the Great Plains and Mississippi Basin have a low relief and fertile soils.

Mount Rainier

Great Plains

The Great Lakes

Niagara Falls

Death Valley, California, 282 ft (86 m) below sea level, is the lowest point in the western hemisphere, and one of the hottest places on Earth. Temperatures of 135° F (57° C) have been recorded here.

Monument Valley's striking sandstone spires and pillars *(buttes)* have been formed by the action of wind, water, heat and cold.

The deep gullies of South Dakota's badlands are created by periodic, torrential rainfall, which erodes the soft soils and rocks. Their form has been greatly affected by changes in land use.

Most of the USA is drained by the great Mississippi River system. At its mouth, where levées are breached, floodwaters are carried to the swamps through a series of channels. This region is known as the bayou.

Barrier beaches, bars and spits are typical of the Atlantic coast. These sand formations around Cape Hatteras stretch along the coast for 200 miles (320 km).

The Great Smoky Mountains, part of the ancient Appalachian mountain chain, formed a natural barrier to early settlers attempting to penetrate the country's interior.

The Everglades are a vast area of saw-grass swamp covering 4000 sq miles (10,300 sq km) of southern Florida.

◀ ***Devils Tower, in** Wyoming is a 1280 ft (390 m) intrusion of basalt rock, which cooled to form octagonal pillars.In 1906 it became the first US National Monument.*

Missouri River
Ohio River
Mississippi River
Mississippi Delta

▲ ***The massive drainage** basin of the Mississippi covers 1,250,000 sq miles (3,200,000 sq km). It includes all areas drained by the Mississippi and its chief tributaries, the Missouri and Ohio rivers, and drains the entire region from the Appalachians to the Rockies.*

Map key

Population

- ▣ above 5 million
- ◙ 1 million to 5 million
- ◉ 500,000 to 1 million
- ◎ 100,000 to 500,000
- ⊕ 50,000 to 100,000
- ○ 10,000 to 50,000
- ∘ below 10,000

Elevation

- 4000m / 13,124ft
- 3000m / 9843ft
- 2000m / 6562ft
- 1000m / 3281ft
- 500m / 1640ft
- 250m / 820ft
- 100m / 328ft
- sea level

Using the land and sea

Over half of the USA's land area is utilized for agriculture, typified by the large cereal farms and cattle ranches of the Great Plains and Midwest prairie regions. Although wheat and corn are still primary crops, a diverse range of fruits and vegetables are grown in the fertile areas, particularly near the east and west coasts. Despite the abundance of cultivable land, inadequate soil management has resulted in a third of the topsoil being lost through wind and water erosion.

Land use and agricultural distribution

cattle, pigs, poultry, citrus fruits, cotton, fishing, fruit, corn (maize), peanuts, shellfish, soya beans, timber, tobacco, wheat

capital cities, major towns

pasture, cropland, forest, wetland, desert, mountain region

The urban/rural population divide

urban 76% | rural 24%

Population density	Total land area
98 people per sq mile (38 people per sq km)	2,959,045 sq miles (7,663,631 sq km)

▶ ***Fakahatchee Strand is** part of the extensive sub-tropical swamps in the Florida Everglades. The swamps support a wide variety of animal life, including many rare birds, fish, alligators and crocodiles.*

◀ ***Farming on the** Great Plains and in the Midwest is characterized by large-scale, mechanized wheat farms.*

USA: NORTHEASTERN STATES

Connecticut, Maine, Massachusetts, New Hampshire, New Jersey, New York, Pennsylvania, Rhode Island, Vermont

The indented coast and vast woodlands of the northeastern states were the original core area for European expansion. The rustic character of New England prevails after 400 years, while the great cities of the Atlantic seaboard have formed an almost continuous urban region. Over 20 million immigrants entered New York from 1855 to 1924 and the northeast became the industrial centre of the USA. After the decline of mining and heavy manufacturing, economic dynamism has been restored with the growth of hi-tech and service industries.

▲ *Chelsea in Vermont, surrounded by trees in their fall foliage. Tourism and agriculture dominate the economy of this self-consciously rural state, where no town exceeds 40,000 people.*

Transport and industry

The principal seaboard cities grew up on trade and manufacturing. They are now global centres of commerce and corporate administration, dominating the regional economy. Research and development facilities support an expanding electronics and communications sector throughout the region. Pharmaceutical and chemical industries are important in New Jersey and Pennsylvania.

Major industry and infrastructure

- chemicals
- coal
- defence
- electronics
- engineering
- finance
- hi-tech industry
- iron & steel
- pharmaceuticals
- printing & publishing
- research & development
- textiles
- timber processing
- major towns
- international airports
- major roads
- major industrial area

The transport network

340,090 miles (544,144 km)	4813 miles (7700 km)
12,872 miles (20,592 km)	2108 miles (3389 km)

New York's commercial success is tied historically to its transport connections. The Erie Canal, completed in 1825, opened up the Great Lakes and the interior to New York's markets and carried a stream of immigrants into the Midwest.

Map key

Population

- above 5 million
- 1 million to 5 million
- 500,000 to 1 million
- 100,000 to 500,000
- 50,000 to 100,000
- 10,000 to 50,000
- below 10,000

Elevation

- 1000m / 3281ft
- 500m / 1640ft
- 250m / 820ft
- 100m / 328ft
- sea level

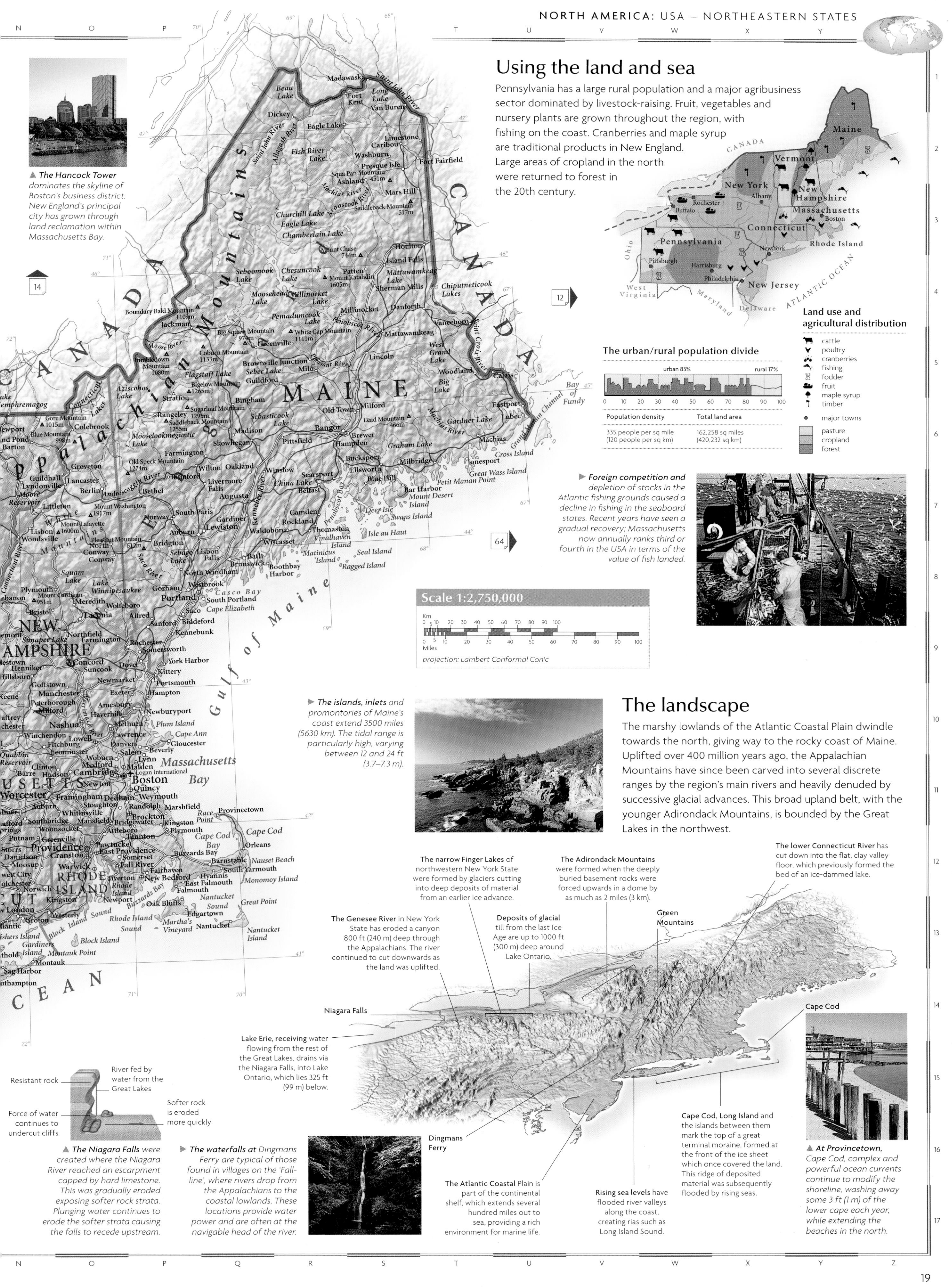

Using the land and sea

Pennsylvania has a large rural population and a major agribusiness sector dominated by livestock-raising. Fruit, vegetables and nursery plants are grown throughout the region, with fishing on the coast. Cranberries and maple syrup are traditional products in New England. Large areas of cropland in the north were returned to forest in the 20th century.

Land use and agricultural distribution

- cattle
- poultry
- cranberries
- fishing
- fodder
- fruit
- maple syrup
- timber
- major towns
- pasture
- cropland
- forest

The urban/rural population divide

urban 83% | rural 17%

Population density	Total land area
335 people per sq mile (120 people per sq km)	162,258 sq miles (420,232 sq km)

▲ **The Hancock Tower** dominates the skyline of Boston's business district. New England's principal city has grown through land reclamation within Massachusetts Bay.

▶ **Foreign competition and** depletion of stocks in the Atlantic fishing grounds caused a decline in fishing in the seaboard states. Recent years have seen a gradual recovery; Massachusetts now annually ranks third or fourth in the USA in terms of the value of fish landed.

Scale 1:2,750,000

projection: Lambert Conformal Conic

▶ **The islands, inlets** and promontories of Maine's coast extend 3500 miles (5630 km). The tidal range is particularly high, varying between 12 and 24 ft (3.7–7.3 m).

The landscape

The marshy lowlands of the Atlantic Coastal Plain dwindle towards the north, giving way to the rocky coast of Maine. Uplifted over 400 million years ago, the Appalachian Mountains have since been carved into several discrete ranges by the region's main rivers and heavily denuded by successive glacial advances. This broad upland belt, with the younger Adirondack Mountains, is bounded by the Great Lakes in the northwest.

The narrow Finger Lakes of northwestern New York State were formed by glaciers cutting into deep deposits of material from an earlier ice advance.

The Adirondack Mountains were formed when the deeply buried basement rocks were forced upwards in a dome by as much as 2 miles (3 km).

The lower Connecticut River has cut down into the flat, clay valley floor, which previously formed the bed of an ice-dammed lake.

The Genesee River in New York State has eroded a canyon 800 ft (240 m) deep through the Appalachians. The river continued to cut downwards as the land was uplifted.

Deposits of glacial till from the last Ice Age are up to 1000 ft (300 m) deep around Lake Ontario.

Green Mountains

Niagara Falls

Cape Cod

Lake Erie, receiving water flowing from the rest of the Great Lakes, drains via the Niagara Falls, into Lake Ontario, which lies 325 ft (99 m) below.

Resistant rock

River fed by water from the Great Lakes

Force of water continues to undercut cliffs

Softer rock is eroded more quickly

▲ **The Niagara Falls** were created where the Niagara River reached an escarpment capped by hard limestone. This was gradually eroded exposing softer rock strata. Plunging water continues to erode the softer strata causing the falls to recede upstream.

▶ **The waterfalls at** Dingmans Ferry are typical of those found in villages on the 'Fall-line', where rivers drop from the Appalachians to the coastal lowlands. These locations provide water power and are often at the navigable head of the river.

Dingmans Ferry

The Atlantic Coastal Plain is part of the continental shelf, which extends several hundred miles out to sea, providing a rich environment for marine life.

Rising sea levels have flooded river valleys along the coast, creating rias such as Long Island Sound.

Cape Cod, Long Island and the islands between them mark the top of a great terminal moraine, formed at the front of the ice sheet which once covered the land. This ridge of deposited material was subsequently flooded by rising seas.

▲ **At Provincetown,** Cape Cod, complex and powerful ocean currents continue to modify the shoreline, washing away some 3 ft (1 m) of the lower cape each year, while extending the beaches in the north.

USA: MID-EASTERN STATES

Delaware, District of Columbia, Kentucky, Maryland, North Carolina, South Carolina, Tennessee, Virginia, West Virginia

Key events in the history of the USA took place in this diverse region, which became the front line in the Civil War of 1861–65 between North and South. Strong regional contrasts exist between the fertile coastal plains, the isolated upcountry of the Appalachian Mountains and the cotton-growing areas of the Mississippi lowlands to the west. Whilst coal mining, a traditional industry in the Appalachians, has declined in recent years leaving much rural poverty, service industries elsewhere have increased, especially in the US federal capital, Washington DC.

Map key

Population

- 500,000 to 1 million
- 100,000 to 500,000
- 50,000 to 100,000
- 10,000 to 50,000
- below 10,000

Elevation

- 6000m / 19,686ft
- 4000m / 13,124ft
- 3000m / 9843ft
- 2000m / 6562ft
- 1000m / 3281ft
- 500m / 1640ft
- 250m / 820ft
- 100m / 328ft
- sea level

Scale 1:3,000,000

projection: Lambert Conformal Conic

▲ ***The Bluegrass region** of Kentucky centres on the town of Lexington. This exceptionally fertile rolling plain is well known for its thoroughbred horse-breeding ranches.*

Transport and industry

In the urbanized northeast, manufacturing remains important, alongside a burgeoning service sector. North Carolina is a major centre for industrial research and development. Traditional industries include Tennessee whiskey, and textiles in South Carolina. The decline of open-cast coal mining in the Appalachians has been hastened by environmental controls, although adventure-tourism is a flourishing new industry.

Major industry and infrastructure

- adventure-tourism
- car manufacture
- coal
- electronics
- engineering
- finance
- food processing
- hi-tech industry
- mining
- research & development
- textiles
- capital cities
- major towns
- international airports
- major roads
- major industrial areas

The transport network

452,218 miles (723,548 km)	5737 miles (8267 km)
18,336 miles (29,503 km)	4404 miles (7081 km)

Tennessee's rivers are part of an important inland bulk-transport network. Memphis is connected with New Orleans in the south, and with cities as distant as Minneapolis, Sioux City, Chicago and Pittsburgh, via the Mississippi and its tributaries.

The landscape

The eastern tributaries of the Mississippi drain the interior lowlands. The Cumberland Plateau and the parallel ranges of the Appalachians have been successively uplifted and eroded over time, with the eastern side reduced to a series of foothills known as the Piedmont. The broad coastal plain gradually falls away into salt marshes, lagoons and offshore bars, broken by flooded estuaries along the shores of the Atlantic.

Natural Bridge in eastern Kentucky is an arch 78 ft (26 m) long and 65 ft (20 m) high. It has been shaped from resistant sandstone by gradual weathering processes, which removed the softer rock lying underneath.

The Allegheny Mountains form the northwestern edge of the Appalachian mountain chain. Continuous folding has formed rich seams of bituminous coal.

◄ ***Farmland on the** eastern shores of Chesapeake Bay is sustained by artificial drainage. The area also provides refuge for a variety of waterfowl.*

Appalachian Mountains

The many inlets of Chesapeake Bay are the flooded tributaries of the main river valley, which have been inundated by rising sea levels.

The Mammoth Cave is part of an extensive cave system in the limestone region of southwestern Kentucky. It stretches for over 300 miles (485 km) on five different levels and contains three rivers and three lakes.

Salt marshes such as Great Dismal Swamp, develop where the coast is sheltered. Vast areas of such marshland have been reclaimed for farmland and settlement.

The Mississippi River and its tributary the Ohio River form the western border of the region.

Cape Hatteras is the easternmost point of an offshore barrier island; a wave-deposited sand-bar which has become permanent, establishing its own vegetation.

Barrier islands

Tidal inlet

Barrier island

These intertidal mudflats become submerged at high tide

▲ ***Barrier islands are** common along the coasts of North and South Carolina. As sea levels rise, wave action builds up ridges of sand and pebbles parallel to the coast, separated by lagoons or intertidal mudflats, which are flooded at high tide.*

The Cumberland Plateau is the most southwesterly part of the Appalachians. Big Black Mountain at 4180 ft (1274 m) is the highest point in the range.

The Blue Ridge mountains are a steep ridge, culminating in Mount Mitchell, the highest point in the Appalachians, at 6684 ft (2037 m).

◄ ***The Great Smoky Mountains** form the western escarpment of the Appalachians. The region is heavily forested, with over 130 species of tree.*

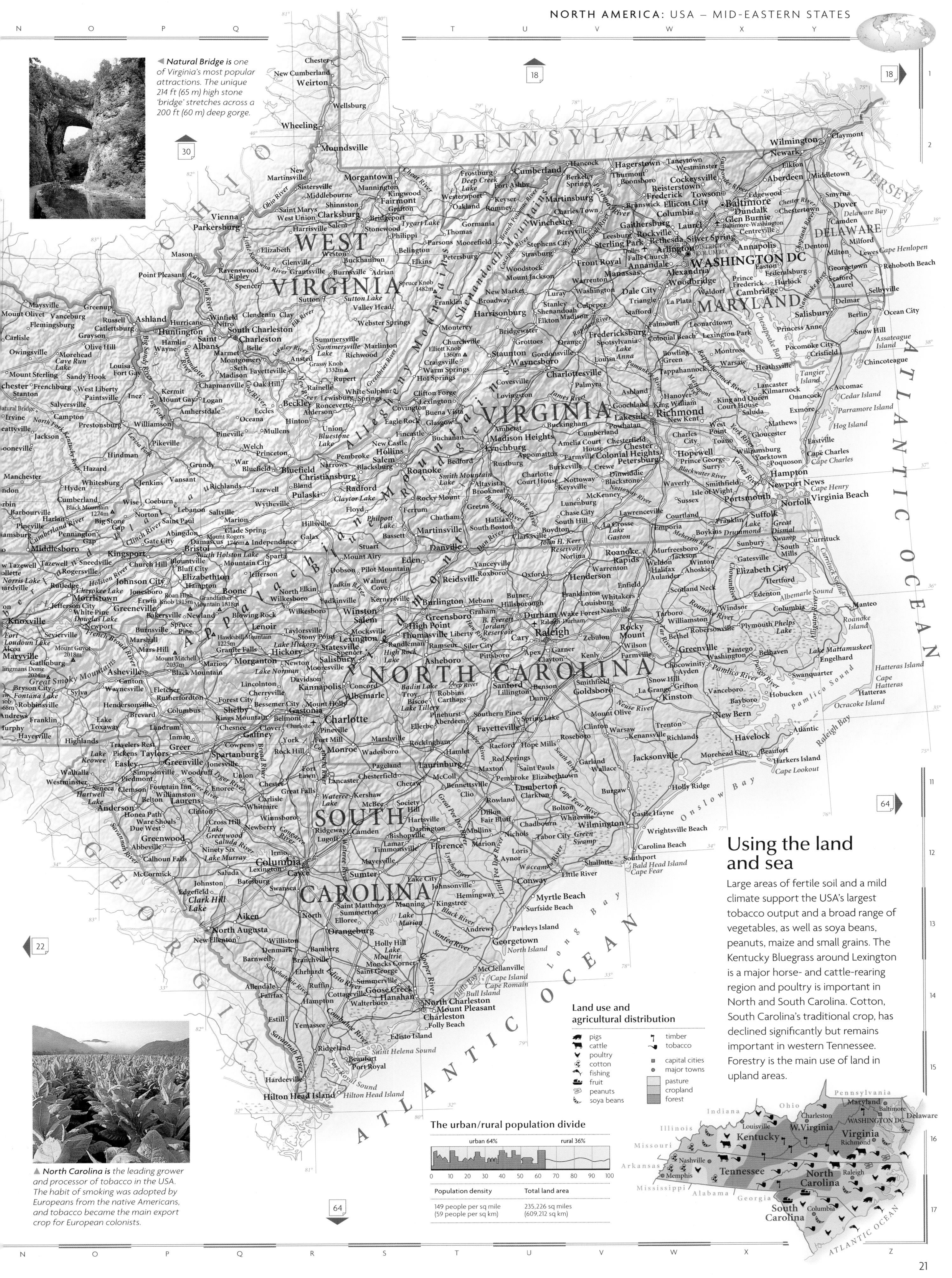
PENNSYLVANIA
OHIO
WEST VIRGINIA
VIRGINIA
MARYLAND
DELAWARE
NEW JERSEY
NORTH CAROLINA
SOUTH CAROLINA
GEORGIA
ATLANTIC OCEAN
WASHINGTON DC
Shenandoah Mountains
Allegheny Mountains
Appalachian Mountains
Blue Ridge
Piedmont
Great Smoky Mountains
Chesapeake Bay
Albemarle Sound
Pamlico Sound
Onslow Bay
Long Bay
Raleigh Bay
Richmond
Baltimore
Norfolk
Virginia Beach
Raleigh
Charlotte
Columbia
Charleston
Greensboro
Wilmington
Land use and agricultural distribution
pigs
cattle
poultry
cotton
fishing
fruit
peanuts
soya beans
timber
tobacco
capital cities
major towns
pasture
cropland
forest
Pennsylvania
Ohio
Indiana
Illinois
Missouri
Arkansas
Mississippi
Alabama
Georgia
Kentucky
W.Virginia
Virginia
Maryland
Delaware
Tennessee
North Carolina
South Carolina
Louisville
Nashville
Memphis
Charleston
Baltimore
WASHINGTON DC
Richmond
Raleigh
Columbia
ATLANTIC OCEAN
The urban/rural population divide
urban 64%
rural 36%
0 10 20 30 40 50 60 70 80 90 100
Population density
149 people per sq mile (59 people per sq km)
Total land area
235,226 sq miles (609,212 sq km)

◀ **Natural Bridge is** *one of Virginia's most popular attractions. The unique 214 ft (65 m) high stone 'bridge' stretches across a 200 ft (60 m) deep gorge.*

▲ **North Carolina is** *the leading grower and processor of tobacco in the USA. The habit of smoking was adopted by Europeans from the native Americans, and tobacco became the main export crop for European colonists.*

Using the land and sea

Large areas of fertile soil and a mild climate support the USA's largest tobacco output and a broad range of vegetables, as well as soya beans, peanuts, maize and small grains. The Kentucky Bluegrass around Lexington is a major horse- and cattle-rearing region and poultry is important in North and South Carolina. Cotton, South Carolina's traditional crop, has declined significantly but remains important in western Tennessee. Forestry is the main use of land in upland areas.

USA: SOUTHERN STATES

Alabama, Florida, Georgia, Louisiana, Mississippi

The South has maintained a separate identity and outlook throughout the history of the USA. Defeat in the American Civil War (1861–65) brought chronic poverty to the Confederate states, while the subsequent liberation of four million black slaves began a struggle not resolved until the 1960s, when the Civil Rights movement achieved an end to legal racial segregation. Since then many parts of the region have experienced rapid change: tourism and retirement communities, together with agriculture, have fuelled growth in Florida whilst defence-related industries have boosted the growth of cities such as Miami and Atlanta. Despite these changes, many people retain a strong attachment to their history: in Louisiana, French is still spoken in Cajun communities near the coast.

ARKANSAS
MISSISSIPPI
LOUISIANA
TEXAS
Shreveport
Monroe
Alexandria
Lake Charles
Lafayette
Baton Rouge
New Orleans
Jackson
Vicksburg
Hattiesburg
Gulfport
Natchez
Greenville
26
24
40

Transport and industry

Florida's tourist trade is only part of a flourishing service sector, which has swelled the principal cities of the south. Petroleum and mineral extraction has made the Gulf coast a major industrial region. Traditional textile production remains important in Georgia, while advanced new industries have grown from the NASA Space Program.

The transport network

Roads	441,625 miles (706,600 km)
Motorways	5116 miles (8186 km)
Railways	16,597 miles (26,555 km)
Waterways	6179 miles (9942 km)

Atlanta's Hartsfield International airport is one of the busiest in the world. A dramatic rise in the use of regional air transport has helped to integrate the major cities of the southern states.

◄ ***The French Quarter*** *is the traditional cultural centre of New Orleans. The city, extensively damaged by Hurricane Katrina in 2005, once thrived on the cotton trade but now relies mainly on tourism and on oil from the Gulf of Mexico.*

Tennessee
Arkansas
Mississippi
Alabama
Georgia
Florida
Louisiana
Texas
South Carolina
N. Carolina
Huntsville
Birmingham
Atlanta
Montgomery
Savannah
Jackson
Baton Rouge
New Orleans
Mobile
Tallahassee
Jacksonville
Daytona Beach
Orlando
Tampa
Melbourne
Miami
Key West
Gulf of Mexico
ATLANTIC OCEAN

Major industry and infrastructure

- aerospace
- car manufacture
- chemicals
- coal
- defence
- electronics
- engineering
- food processing
- oil
- textiles
- tourism
- major towns
- international airports
- major roads
- major industrial areas

The Yazoo River flows parallel to the Mississippi through a common flood plain. The confluence of the rivers is deferred downstream because flood deposition has built the Mississippi channel up above the level of the Yazoo.
Cathedral Caverns near Huntsville in Alabama is a system of vast limestone caves, with a main opening 1000 ft (300 m) high and 150 ft (50 m) wide.
At De Soto Falls, Alabama, the Little River descends into the deepest canyon east of the Mississippi, with sheer cliff walls up to 700 ft (230 m) high.
Brasstown Bald in the Blue Ridge mountains of Georgia is the region's highest point, at 4784 ft (1458 m).
The Mississippi is the world's third longest river and moves over 1000 million tonnes of sediment a year, creating deep alluvial plains. Flooding is a constant threat in lowland areas.
Piedmont
Sand bars, deposited by waves breaking offshore, form barrier beaches along much of the coastline, creating sheltered lagoons and salt marshes behind them.
Mississippi Delta
Atchafalaya Bay
Delta lobe
The delta of the Mississippi over 5000 years ago
Present-day delta
Lake Okeechobee is actually a shallow, slow-moving river, 150 miles (240 km) long and 50 miles (80 km) wide.
Across Florida the coastal plain is mostly less than 75 ft (25 m) above sea level. The land is underlain by limestone, pitted with hollows which have been filled by over 10,000 lakes.
The Everglades lie in a limestone hollow formed over two million years ago, which has gradually become in-filled with swamp deposits.
Florida Keys

▲ ***In Providence Canyon,*** *Georgia, the Chattahoochee River has cut straight down through the sandy bedrock, to leave sheer rock faces and pinnacles, which have been smoothed by subsequent weathering.*

▲ ***The cypress swamps*** *of the Mississippi Delta form in the backswamps behind the levées of the river and in the multitude of subsiding delta basins.*

▲ ***Over the last*** *5000 years the lower course of the Mississippi has moved back and forth over great distances. These changes, caused by varying sediment loads and human modification, have resulted in a 'bird's foot' delta with several lobes, each reflecting the river's different historic position.*

The landscape

The Blue Ridge mountains in the north are skirted by the gentle hills of the Piedmont, whose rivers drain south on to the great flat expanse of the coastal plain. Sandy barrier beaches and islands dominate the sea shore, tracing round the swampy limestone arm of Florida. In the west, the Mississippi meanders towards its delta, crossing the thickly mantled alluvial plain of the interior lowlands.

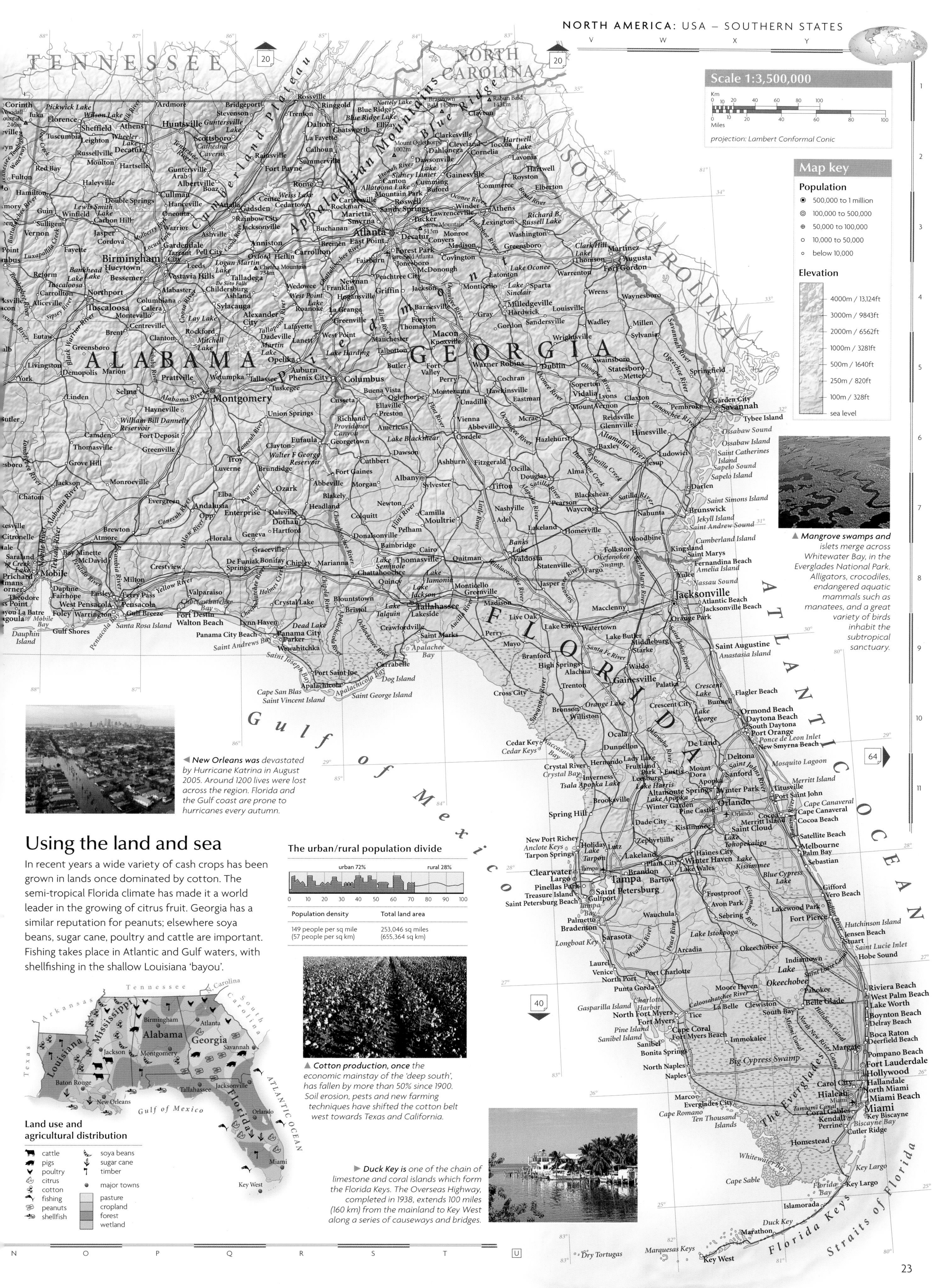
V W X Y
Scale 1:3,500,000
Km 0 10 20 40 60 80 100
Miles 0 10 20 40 60 80 100
projection: Lambert Conformal Conic
Map key
Population
500,000 to 1 million
100,000 to 500,000
50,000 to 100,000
10,000 to 50,000
below 10,000
Elevation
4000m / 13,124ft
3000m / 9843ft
2000m / 6562ft
1000m / 3281ft
500m / 1640ft
250m / 820ft
100m / 328ft
sea level
TENNESSEE
NORTH CAROLINA
SOUTH CAROLINA
ALABAMA
GEORGIA
FLORIDA
Gulf of Mexico
ATLANTIC OCEAN
Straits of Florida
Florida Keys
Appalachian Mountains
Blue Ridge
Cumberland Plateau
Piedmont
The Everglades
Atlanta
Birmingham
Montgomery
Columbus
Macon
Savannah
Jacksonville
Tallahassee
Orlando
Tampa
Saint Petersburg
Miami
Mobile
Key West
20
20
40
64
The urban/rural population divide
urban 72%
rural 28%
0 10 20 30 40 50 60 70 80 90 100
Population density
149 people per sq mile (57 people per sq km)
Total land area
253,046 sq miles (655,364 sq km)
Tennessee
Carolina
South Carolina
Arkansas
Mississippi
Alabama
Georgia
Louisiana
Texas
Birmingham
Atlanta
Montgomery
Jackson
Savannah
Baton Rouge
Tallahassee
Jacksonville
New Orleans
Gulf of Mexico
ATLANTIC OCEAN
Florida
Orlando
Miami
Key West
Land use and agricultural distribution
cattle
pigs
poultry
citrus
cotton
fishing
peanuts
shellfish
soya beans
sugar cane
timber
major towns
pasture
cropland
forest
wetland
N O P Q R S T U

▲ Mangrove swamps and islets merge across Whitewater Bay, in the Everglades National Park. Alligators, crocodiles, endangered aquatic mammals such as manatees, and a great variety of birds inhabit the subtropical sanctuary.

◀ New Orleans was devastated by Hurricane Katrina in August 2005. Around 1200 lives were lost across the region. Florida and the Gulf coast are prone to hurricanes every autumn.

Using the land and sea

In recent years a wide variety of cash crops has been grown in lands once dominated by cotton. The semi-tropical Florida climate has made it a world leader in the growing of citrus fruit. Georgia has a similar reputation for peanuts; elsewhere soya beans, sugar cane, poultry and cattle are important. Fishing takes place in Atlantic and Gulf waters, with shellfishing in the shallow Louisiana 'bayou'.

▲ Cotton production, once the economic mainstay of the 'deep south', has fallen by more than 50% since 1900. Soil erosion, pests and new farming techniques have shifted the cotton belt west towards Texas and California.

▶ Duck Key is one of the chain of limestone and coral islands which form the Florida Keys. The Overseas Highway, completed in 1938, extends 100 miles (160 km) from the mainland to Key West along a series of causeways and bridges.

USA: Texas

First explored by Spaniards moving north from Mexico in search of gold, Texas was controlled by Spain and then Mexico, before becoming an independent republic in 1836, and joining the Union of States in 1845. During the 19th century, many of the migrants who came to Texas raised cattle on the abundant land; in the 20th century, they were joined by prospectors attracted by the promise of oil riches. Today, although natural resources, especially oil, still form the basis of its wealth, the diversified Texan economy includes thriving hi-tech and finance industries. The major urban centres, home to 80% of the population, lie in the south and east, and include Houston, the 'oil-city', and Dallas–Fort Worth. Hispanic influences remain strong, especially in the south and west.

▲ ***Dallas was founded*** *in 1841 as a prairie trading post and its development was stimulated by the arrival of railroads. Cotton and then oil funded the town's early growth. Today, the modern, high-rise skyline of Dallas reflects the city's position as a leading centre of banking, insurance and the petroleum industry in the southwest.*

36

Using the land

Cotton production and livestock-raising, particularly cattle, dominate farming, although crop failures and the demands of local markets have led to some diversification. Following the introduction of modern farming techniques, cotton production spread out from the east to the plains of western Texas. Cattle ranches are widespread, while sheep and goats are raised on the dry Edwards Plateau.

Land use and agricultural distribution

cattle
goats
sheep
cereals
cotton
major towns

pasture
cropland
forest
barren

The urban/rural population divide

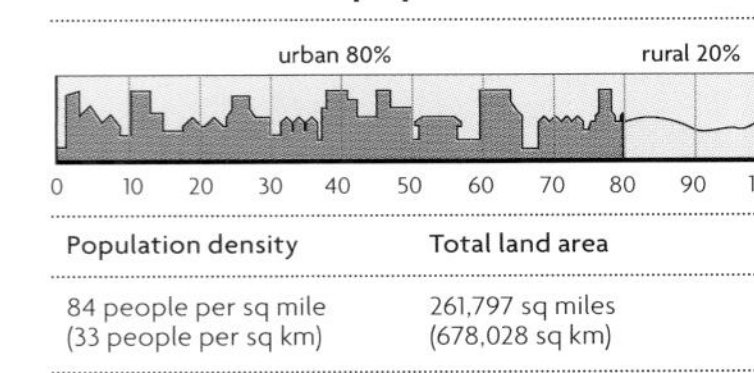

urban 80%
rural 20%
0 10 20 30 40 50 60 70 80 90 100

Population density	Total land area
84 people per sq mile (33 people per sq km)	261,797 sq miles (678,028 sq km)

▲ ***The huge cattle*** *ranches of Texas developed during the 19th century when land was plentiful and could be acquired cheaply. Today, more cattle and sheep are raised in Texas than in any other state.*

The landscape

Texas is made up of a series of massive steps descending from the mountains and high plains of the west and northwest to the coastal lowlands in the southeast. Many of the state's borders are delineated by water. The Rio Grande flows from the Rocky Mountains to the Gulf of Mexico, marking the border with Mexico.

▲ ***Cap Rock Escarpment*** *juts out from the plains, running 200 miles (320 km) from north to south. Its height varies from 300 ft (90 m) rising to sheer cliffs up to 1000 ft (300 m).*

40

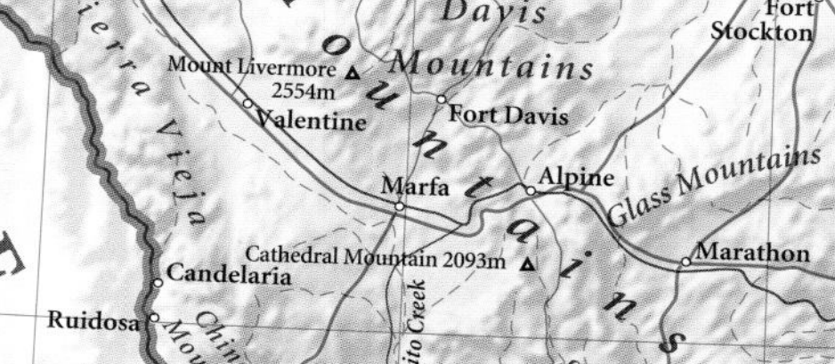

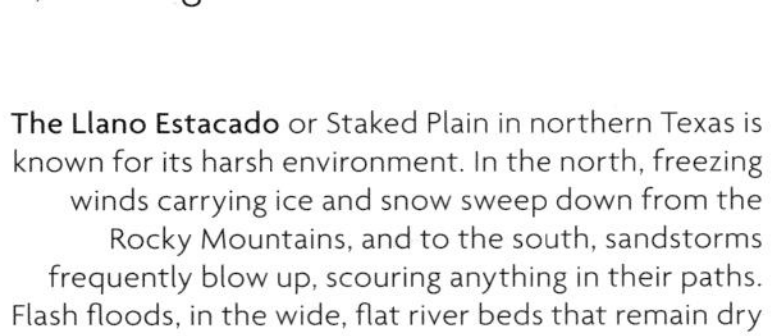

The Llano Estacado or Staked Plain in northern Texas is known for its harsh environment. In the north, freezing winds carrying ice and snow sweep down from the Rocky Mountains, and to the south, sandstorms frequently blow up, scouring anything in their paths. Flash floods, in the wide, flat river beds that remain dry for most of the year, are another hazard.

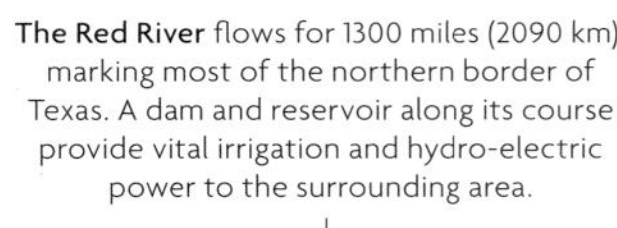

The Red River flows for 1300 miles (2090 km), marking most of the northern border of Texas. A dam and reservoir along its course provide vital irrigation and hydro-electric power to the surrounding area.

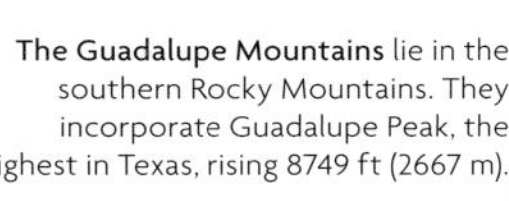

The Guadalupe Mountains lie in the southern Rocky Mountains. They incorporate Guadalupe Peak, the highest in Texas, rising 8749 ft (2667 m).

Sabine River

Extensive forests of pine and cypress grow in the eastern corner of the coastal lowlands where the average rainfall is 45 inches (1145 mm) a year. This is higher than the rest of the state and over twice the average in the west.

The Rio Grande flows from the Rocky Mountains through semi-arid land, supporting sparse vegetation. The river actually shrinks along its course, losing more water through evaporation and seepage than it gains from its tributaries and rainfall.

In the coastal lowlands of southeastern Texas the Earth's crust is warping, causing the land to subside and allowing the sea to invade. Around Galveston, the rate of downward tilting is 6 inches (15 cm) per year. Erosion of the coast is also exacerbated by hurricanes.

Big Bend National Park

Edwards Plateau is a limestone outcrop. It is part of the Great Plains, bounded to the southeast by the Balcones Escarpment, which marks the southerly limit of the plains.

◄ ***Flowing through*** *1500 ft (450 m) high gorges, the shallow, muddy Rio Grande makes a 90° bend, which marks the southern border of Big Bend National Park, giving it its name. The area is a mixture of forested mountains, deserts and canyons.*

Padre Island

Laguna Madre in southern Texas has been almost completely cut off from the sea by Padre Island. This sand bank was created by wave action, carrying and depositing material along the coast. The process is known as longshore drift.

Oil deposits

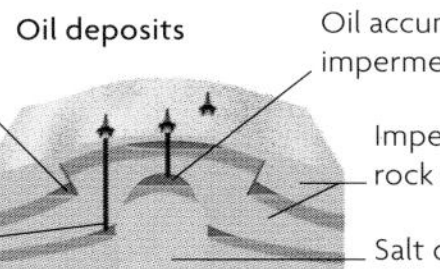

Oil accumulates beneath impermeable cap rock
Oil trapped by fault
Oil deposits migrate through reservoir rocks such as shale
Impermeable rock strata
Salt dome

▲ ***Oil deposits are*** *found beneath much of Texas. They collect as oil migrates upwards through porous layers of rock until it is trapped, either by a cap of rock above a salt dome, or by a fault line which exposes impermeable rock through which the oil cannot rise.*

Transport and industry

Industry in the 20th century was largely concentrated on the processing of local raw materials, especially oil – deposits were discovered under 65% of the state's area. The technological demands of the oil industry and defence-related institutions, particularly NASA, have stimulated the development of numerous electronics and hi-tech firms which, alongside many national corporate headquarters, are based in Dallas–Fort Worth and Houston.

Major industry and infrastructure

- chemicals
- defence
- engineering
- finance
- food processing
- gas
- hi-tech industry
- mining
- oil
- textiles
- major towns
- international airports
- major roads
- major industrial areas

The transport network

293,509 miles (496,614 km)	3229 miles (5166 km)
10,681 miles (17,089 km)	845 miles (1359 km)

The sheer size of Texas promoted the development of an extensive road and rail network. The highway system, although well-developed, is concentrated in the east.

▲ ***Padre Island is** a sand bank. It extends 113 miles (182 km) along the southern coast of Texas.*

▲ ***The Texas hill** country is the most southerly extension of the Great Plains. Although farming is the primary source of income, the beautiful hills, valleys and lakes are a major tourist attraction.*

Scale 1:3,250,000

Km 0 10 20 40 60 80 100
Miles 0 10 20 40 60 80 100

projection: Lambert Conformal Conic

Map key

Population

- 1 million to 5 million
- 500,000 to 1 million
- 100,000 to 500,000
- 50,000 to 100,000
- 10,000 to 50,000
- below 10,000

Elevation

- 2000m / 6562ft
- 1000m / 3281ft
- 500m / 1640ft
- 250m / 820ft
- 100m / 328ft
- sea level

USA: SOUTH MIDWESTERN STATES

Arkansas, Kansas, Missouri, Oklahoma

The expansion of the USA focused on this region in the mid-19th century. Settlers spread from the confluence of the Missouri and Mississippi rivers up onto the Great Plains. This treeless expanse, which early explorers had called the 'Great American Desert', was turned into one of the world's richest agricultural regions; but periodic droughts, coupled with over-intensive farming, led to the 'Dustbowl' soil erosion crisis of the 1930s, the abandonment of many farms, and a mass exodus to the west coast. The land has since recovered, although the mechanization of agriculture has led to a decline in the rural population. In recent years, suburban residential development has spread rapidly across the wooded Ozark Plateau in the east of the region.

Transport and industry

The processing of agricultural products, such as brewing and meat packing, has been traditionally important in these states. In Kansas and Oklahoma, diversified manufacturing now supplements income from fossil fuels; Wichita has become a world centre for aeronautical engineering, an industry which also employs many people in neighbouring Missouri.

Major industry and infrastructure

- aerospace
- engineering
- finance
- food processing
- gas
- mining
- oil
- vehicle manufacture
- major towns
- international airports
- major roads
- major industrial areas

Agricultural produce from the plains is moved by barges along the Mississippi. The river now carries a far greater tonnage of freight than any other waterway system in the USA.

The transport network

380,307 miles (608,491 km)	4068 miles (6508 km)
16,185 miles (25,896 km)	1994 miles (3208 km)

The Arkansas River and its tributaries allow access to over half of the USA's navigable inland waterways. A system of locks and dams along the river provides Tulsa in Oklahoma with a navigable water route to the Gulf of Mexico.

Map key

Population

- 100,000 to 500,000
- 50,000 to 100,000
- 10,000 to 50,000
- below 10,000

Elevation

- 1000m / 3281ft
- 500m / 1640ft
- 250m / 820ft
- 100m / 328ft
- sea level

Scale 1:3,000,000

projection: Lambert Conformal Conic

The landscape

Most of the region consists of high, treeless plains, which gradually descend east from the Rocky Mountains. Drainage follows this slope, with rivers flowing towards the alluvial lowlands of the Mississippi in the southeast. Between the plains and the lowlands lie various ranges of wooded hills, including the deeply incised Ozark Plateau.

The Mississippi, North America's longest river, is joined by the Missouri, its main tributary, on a flood plain which spreads south to the Gulf of Mexico.

Collapsed limestone caverns led to the formation of Big Basin in Kansas; a depression 100 ft (33 m) deep and 1 mile (1.6 km) wide.

The Great Salt Plains of northern Oklahoma cover 45 sq mile (116 sq km). The arid, white flats were left by the gradual evaporation of an ancient salt lake.

Underground water reserves

Flint Hills is the region's easternmost major escarpment. Steep, grassy uplands are interspersed with rocky, wooded ravines and outcrops of limestone and chert.

Missouri River

The Ozark Plateau is a wooded, hilly region of rivers and narrow, winding lakes. The Lake of the Ozarks was created by the damming of the Osage River in 1930.

Crowleys Ridge is a long, sandy ridge, rising from the Mississippi flood plain. It was formed over thousands of years by the deposition of sand blown eastwards from the Great Plains.

Lake Ouachita, in Arkansas is one of a number of irregularly-shaped lakes found among the ridges of the Ouachita Mountains.

Extent of the aquifer

Kansas

Oklahoma

Red River

The Ogallala Aquifer, beneath the Great Plains, is the largest known source of underground water in the world. There is concern about the rapid depletion of this finite water supply by irrigation schemes.

Devil's Den is a dry badland area. The rugged landscape, strewn with large boulders, is the eroded remnant of a spur extending from the Arbuckle mountains to the west.

Ouachita Mountains

Mississippi River

The landscape of northeast Kansas is interlaced by rivers which have cut broad wooded valleys through the gentle hills. All the rivers in Kansas form part of the massive Missouri/Mississippi drainage basin.

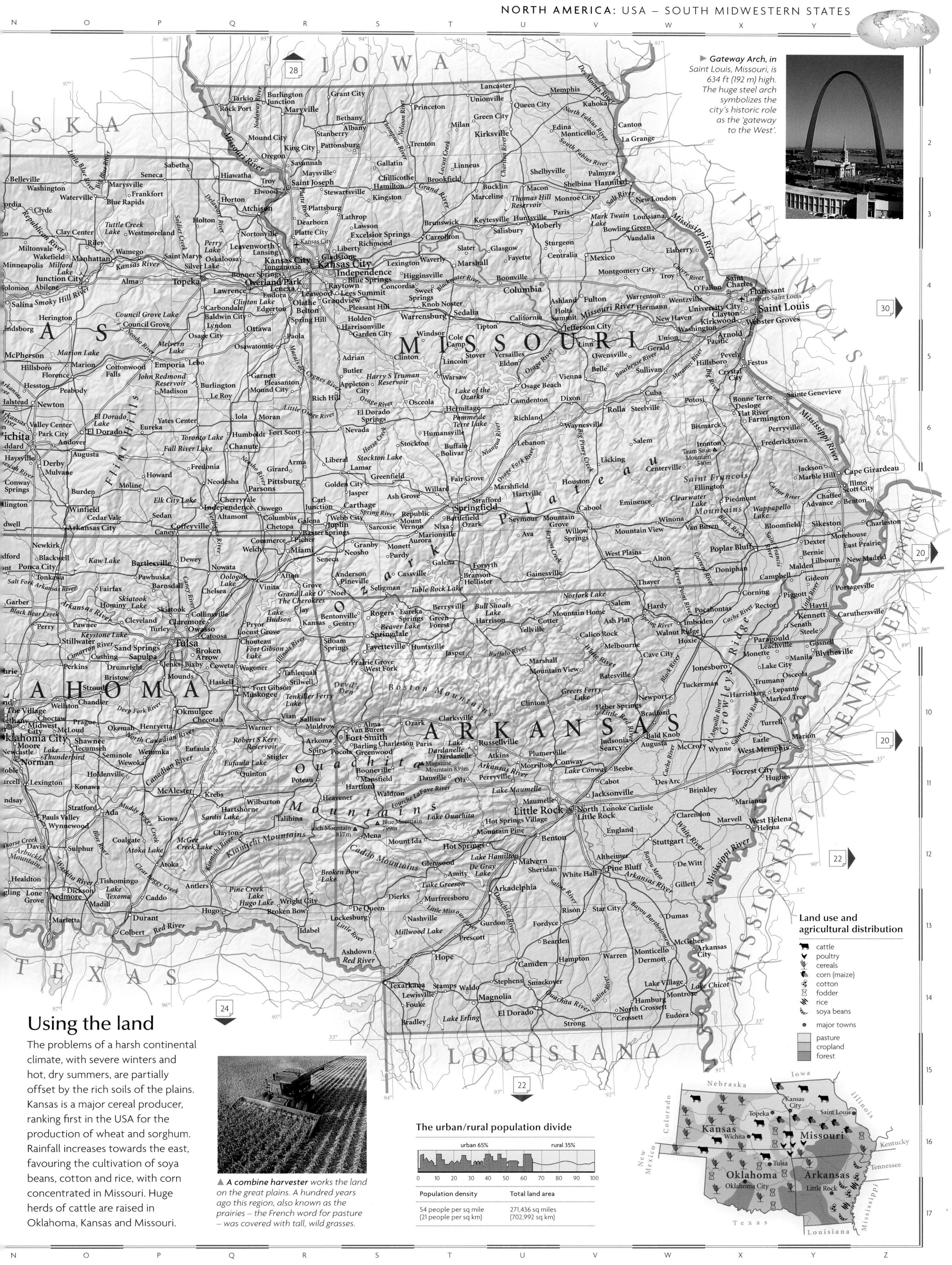
IOWA
MISSOURI
ARKANSAS
KANSAS
OKLAHOMA
TEXAS
LOUISIANA
ILLINOIS
KENTUCKY
TENNESSEE
MISSISSIPPI
Ozark Plateau
Boston Mountains
Ouachita Mountains
Flint Hills
Crowley's Ridge
Saint Louis
Kansas City
Springfield
Little Rock
Fort Smith
Tulsa
Topeka
Jefferson City
Oklahoma City

► ***Gateway Arch***, *in Saint Louis, Missouri, is 634 ft (192 m) high. The huge steel arch symbolizes the city's historic role as the 'gateway to the West'.*

Using the land

The problems of a harsh continental climate, with severe winters and hot, dry summers, are partially offset by the rich soils of the plains. Kansas is a major cereal producer, ranking first in the USA for the production of wheat and sorghum. Rainfall increases towards the east, favouring the cultivation of soya beans, cotton and rice, with corn concentrated in Missouri. Huge herds of cattle are raised in Oklahoma, Kansas and Missouri.

▲ ***A combine harvester*** *works the land on the great plains. A hundred years ago this region, also known as the prairies – the French word for pasture – was covered with tall, wild grasses.*

The urban/rural population divide

urban 65% | rural 35%

0 10 20 30 40 50 60 70 80 90 100

Population density	Total land area
54 people per sq mile (21 people per sq km)	271,436 sq miles (702,992 sq km)

Land use and agricultural distribution

- cattle
- poultry
- cereals
- corn (maize)
- cotton
- fodder
- rice
- soya beans
- major towns
- pasture
- cropland
- forest

USA: UPPER PLAINS STATES

Iowa, Minnesota, Nebraska, North Dakota, South Dakota

Lying at the very heart of the North American continent, much of this region was acquired from France as part of the Louisiana Purchase in 1803. The area was largely by-passed by the early waves of westward migrants. When Europeans did settle, during the 19th century, they displaced the Native Americans who lived on the plains. The settlers planted arable crops and raised cattle on the immensely fertile prairie land, founding an agrarian tradition which flourishes today. Most of this region remains rural; of the five states, only in Minnesota has there been significant diversification away from agriculture and resource-based industries into the hi-tech and service sectors.

Using the land

The popular image of these states as agricultural is entirely justified; prairies stretch uninterrupted across most of the area. Croplands fall into two regions: the wheat belt of the plains, and the corn belt of the central USA. Cash crops, such as soya beans, are grown to supplement incomes. Livestock, particularly pigs and cattle, are raised throughout this region.

The urban/rural population divide

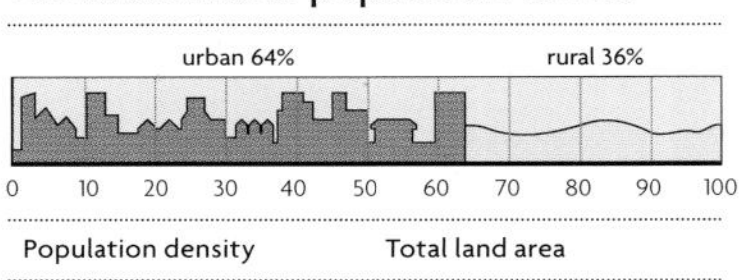
urban 64%
rural 36%
0 10 20 30 40 50 60 70 80 90 100

Population density	Total land area
31 people per sq mile (12 people per sq km)	357,212 sq miles (925,143 sq km)

► ***Dark, fertile prairie*** *soils in the southeast provide Minnesota's most productive farmland. Hot, humid summers create a long growing season for corn cultivation.*

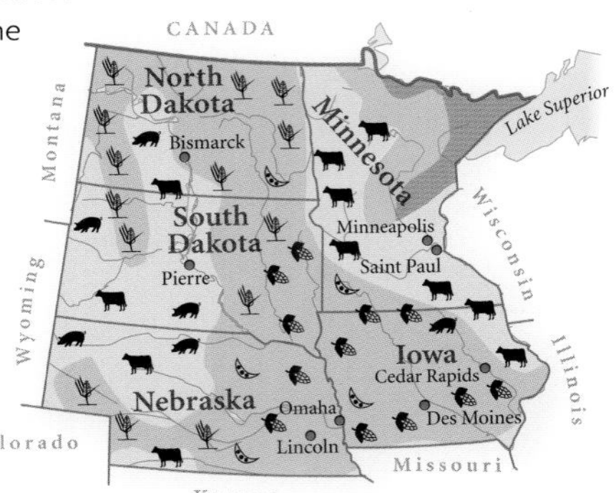
CANADA
North Dakota
Bismarck
Minnesota
Lake Superior
South Dakota
Pierre
Minneapolis
Saint Paul
Wisconsin
Montana
Wyoming
Iowa
Cedar Rapids
Des Moines
Nebraska
Omaha
Lincoln
Illinois
Colorado
Missouri
Kansas

Land use and agricultural distribution

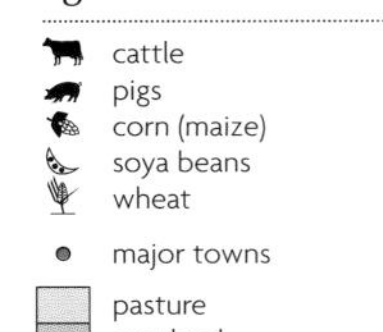
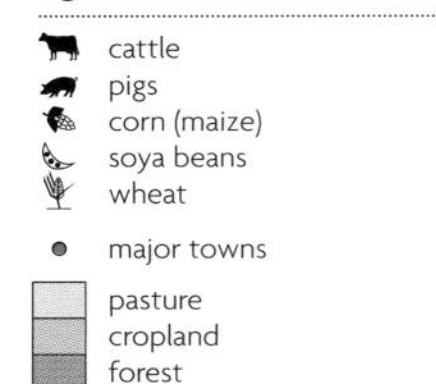
cattle
pigs
corn (maize)
soya beans
wheat
major towns
pasture
cropland
forest
wetland

Beach
Sentinel Butte 1045m
Medora
Belfield
Dickinson
Richardton
Hebron
Glen Ullin
Heart River
Lake Tschida
New Salem
Amidon
New England
Marmarth
White Butte 1069m
Mott
Elgin
Carson
New Leipzig
Cannonball River
Bowman
Reeder
Bowman-Haley Lake
Hettinger
North Fork Grand River
Ludlow
Lemmon
McIntosh
South Fork Grand River
Shadehill Reservoir
Buffalo
Reva
Bison
Little Missouri River
Cedar Creek
Selfridge

Transport and industry

Food processing and the production of farm machinery are supported by the large agricultural sector. Mineral exploitation is also an important activity: gold is mined in the ore-rich Black Hills of South Dakota, and both North Dakota and Nebraska are emerging as major petroleum producers.

The transport network

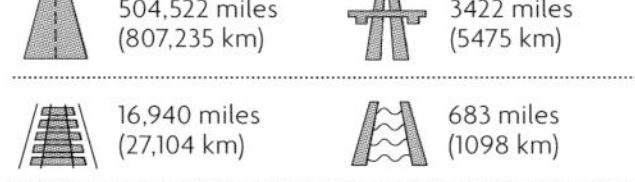

504,522 miles (807,235 km)	3422 miles (5475 km)
16,940 miles (27,104 km)	683 miles (1098 km)

Nebraska's central location has made it an important transport artery for east–west traffic. Minnesota's road network radiates out from the hub of the twin cities, Minneapolis–Saint Paul.

► ***Water erosion along*** *the Little Missouri River has carried away sedimentary deposits, creating rugged landscapes known as badlands.*

CANADA
North Dakota
Fargo
Bismarck
Minnesota
Duluth
Lake Superior
South Dakota
Pierre
Sioux Falls
Minneapolis
Saint Paul
Wisconsin
Montana
Wyoming
Iowa
Cedar Rapids
Des Moines
Nebraska
Omaha
Lincoln
Illinois
Colorado
Missouri
Kansas

Major industry and infrastructure

coal
engineering
electronics
finance
food processing
oil & gas
mining
major towns
international airports
major roads
major industrial areas

The landscape

These states straddle the Great Plains and the lowlands of the central USA, with Minnesota lying in a transition zone between the eastern forests and the prairies. The region was shaped by repeated ice advances and retreats, leaving a flat relief, broken only by the numerous lakes and broad river networks which drain the prairies.

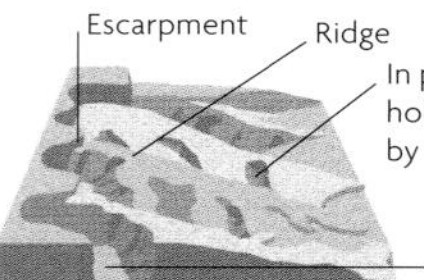
Escarpment
Ridge
In permeable strata hollows are formed by small mudslides
Water flowing into gullies erodes back the escarpment

▲ ***Badlands are formed*** *by stormwater run-off which flows down the impermeable strata of the escarpment and saturates the permeable strata leading to mudslides and the formation of gullies.*

▲ ***In the badlands*** *of North and South Dakota, horizontal layers of sandstone have been eroded by rivers, leaving a landscape of narrow gullies, sharp crests and pinnacles.*

North Dakota Badlands

South Dakota Badlands

The Minnesota landscape contains many post-glacial features, including its numerous lakes, boulder-strewn hills and mineral-rich deposits.

Although it escaped the last glaciation, the limestone bedrock of southeastern Minnesota has been eroded by surface and subterranean streams, leaving a network of underground caverns and steepsided valleys.

▲ ***Chimney Rock is*** *a remnant of an ancient land surface, eroded by the North Platte River. The tip of its spire stands 500 ft (150 m) above the plain.*

Missouri River

Mississippi River

◄ ***In northeastern Iowa,*** *the Mississippi and its tributaries have deeply incised the underlying bedrock creating a hilly terrain, with bluffs standing 300 ft (90 m) above the valley.*

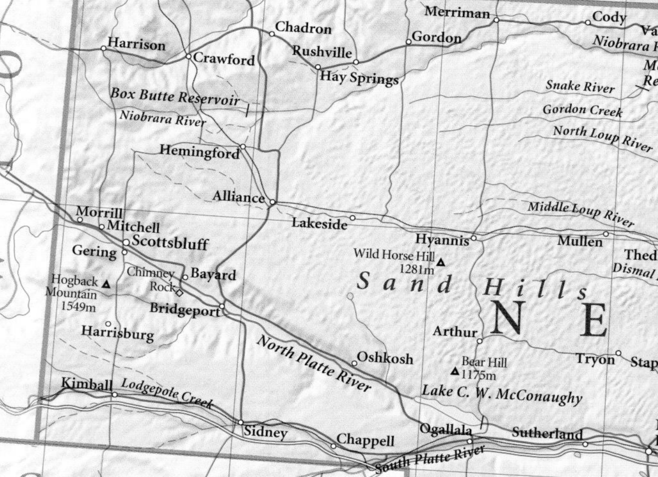
Harrison
Chadron
Crawford
Rushville
Hay Springs
Gordon
Merriman
Box Butte Reservoir
Niobrara River
Hemingford
Alliance
Lakeside
Morrill
Mitchell
Scottsbluff
Gering
Hogback Mountain 1549m
Chimney Rock
Bayard
Bridgeport
Wild Horse Hill 1281m
Sand Hills
Hyannis
Mullen
Harrisburg
Oshkosh
Arthur
Bear Hill 1175m
Tryon
Lake C. W. McConaughy
North Platte River
Kimball
Lodgepole Creek
Sidney
Chappell
Ogallala
Sutherland
South Platte River
Snake River
Gordon Creek
North Loup River
Middle Loup River
WYOMING
NE

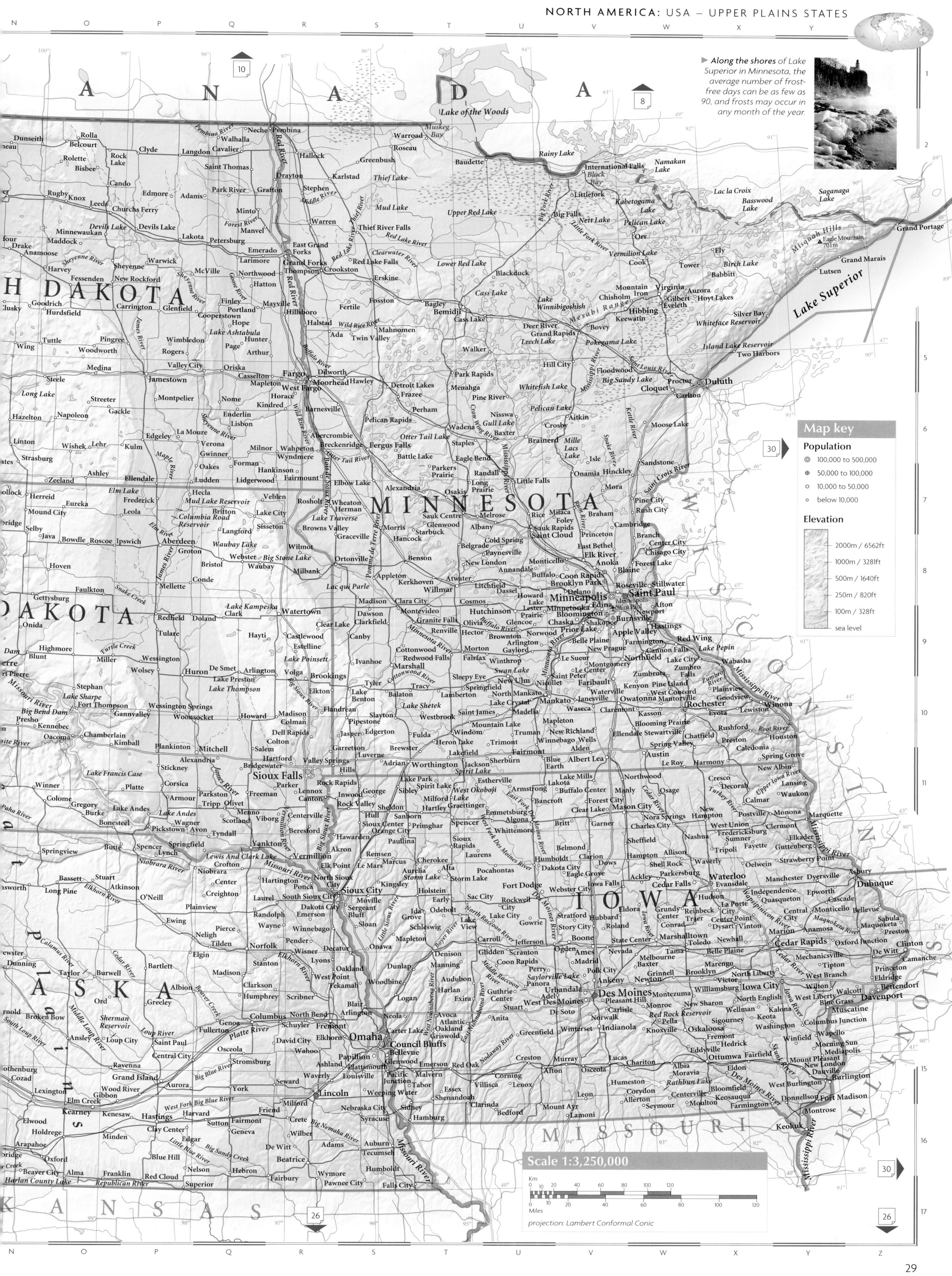
Along the shores of Lake Superior in Minnesota, the average number of frost-free days can be as few as 90, and frosts may occur in any month of the year.
Map key
Population
100,000 to 500,000
50,000 to 100,000
10,000 to 50,000
below 10,000
Elevation
2000m / 6562ft
1000m / 3281ft
500m / 1640ft
250m / 820ft
100m / 328ft
sea level
Scale 1:3,250,000
Km
Miles
projection: Lambert Conformal Conic
CANADA
MINNESOTA
IOWA
MISSOURI
KANSAS
WISCONSIN
ILLINOIS
Lake of the Woods
Lake Superior
Minneapolis
Saint Paul
Duluth
Des Moines
Sioux Falls
Omaha
Lincoln
Fargo
Rochester
Cedar Rapids
Davenport
Sioux City
Mississippi River
Missouri River
Red River

USA: GREAT LAKES STATES

Illinois, Indiana, Michigan, Ohio, Wisconsin

The states bordering the Great Lakes developed rapidly in the second half of the 19th century as a result of improvements in communications: rail to the west and waterways to the south and east. Fertile land and good links with growing eastern seaboard cities encouraged the development of agriculture and food processing. Migrants from Europe and other parts of the USA flooded into the region and for much of the 20th century the region's economy boomed. However, in recent years heavy industry has declined, earning the region the unwanted label the 'Rustbelt'.

Transport and industry

The Great Lakes region is the centre of the USA's car industry. Since the early part of the 20th century, its prosperity has been closely linked to the fortunes of automobile manufacturing. Iron and steel production has expanded to meet demand from this industry. In the 1970s, nationwide recession, cheaper foreign competition in the automobile sector, pollution in and around the Great Lakes and the collapse of the meat-packing industry, centred on Chicago, forced these states to diversify their industrial base. New industries have emerged, notably electronics, service and finance industries.

The transport network

540,682 miles (865,091 km)	6550 miles (10,480 km)
24,928 miles (39,884 km)	2330 miles (3748 km)

Few areas of the USA have a comparable transport system. Chicago is a principal transport terminus with a dense network of roads, railways and Interstate freeways radiating from the city.

Major industry and infrastructure

- car manufacture
- coal
- electronics
- engineering
- finance
- food processing
- iron & steel
- oil
- research & development
- textiles
- major towns
- international airports
- major roads
- major industrial areas

▶ ***Ever since Ransom Olds** and Henry Ford started mass-producing automobiles in Detroit early in the 20th century, the city's name has become synonymous with the American automotive industry.*

The landscape

Much of this region shows the impact of glaciation which lasted until about 10,000 years ago, and extended as far south as Illinois and Ohio. Although the relief of the region slopes towards the Great Lakes, because the ice sheets blocked northerly drainage, most of the rivers today flow southwards, forming part of the massive Mississippi/Missouri drainage basin.

◀ ***The dunes near** Sleeping Bear Point rise 400 ft (120 m) from the banks of Lake Michigan. They are constantly being resculpted by wind action.*

Lake Michigan

The many lakes and marshes of Wisconsin and Michigan are the result of glacial erosion and deposition which occurred during the last Ice Age.

Southwestern Wisconsin is known as a 'driftless' area. Unlike most of the region, low hills protected it from erosion by the advancing ice sheet.

Most of the water used in northern Illinois is pumped from underground reservoirs. Due to increased demand, many areas now face a water shortage. Around Joliet, the water table was lowered by more than 700 ft (210 m) over the last century.

Illinois plains

Lake Erie is the shallowest of the five Great Lakes. Its average depth is about 62 ft (19 m). Storms sweeping across from Canada erode its shores and cause the silting of its harbours.

The Appalachian plateau stretches eastward from Ohio. It is dissected by streams flowing west into the Mississippi and Ohio rivers.

Mississippi River

Ohio River

Relic landforms from the last glaciation, such as shallow basins and ridges, cover all but the south of this region. Ridges, known as moraines, up to 300 ft (100 m) high, lie to the south of Lake Michigan.

Unlike the level prairie to the north, southern Indiana is relatively rugged. Limestone in the hills has been dissolved by water, producing features such as sinkholes and underground caves.

▲ ***The plains of** Illinois are characteristic of drift landscapes, scoured and flattened by glacial erosion and covered with fertile glacial deposits.*

Glacial till

Present-day river or stream

Channels caused by outwash from melting glacier

Most recent till deposits

Older till sheet

Bedrock

▲ ***As a result** of successive glacial depositions, the total depth of till along the former southern margin of the Laurentide ice sheet can exceed 1300 ft (400 m).*

28

28

26

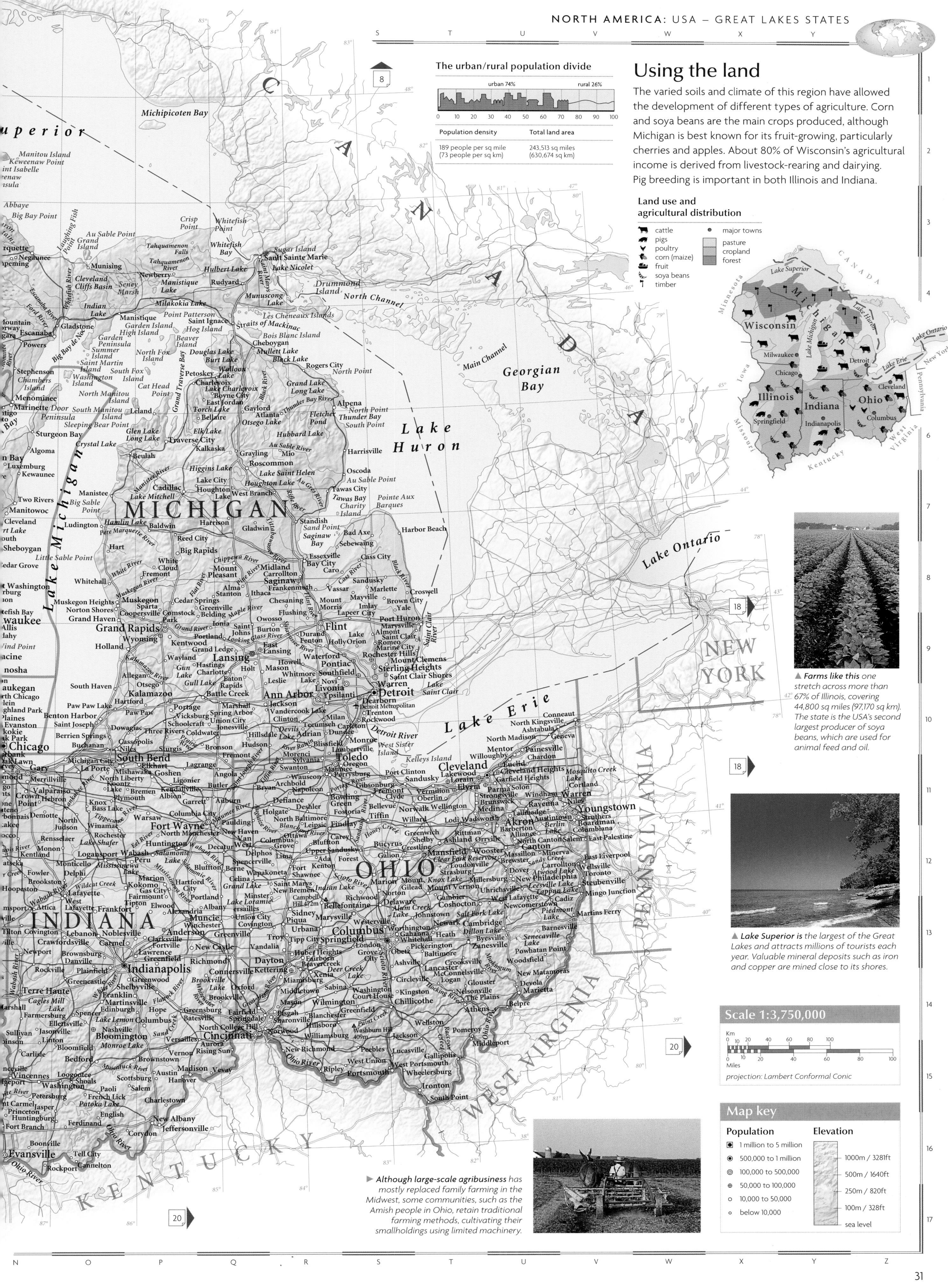

The urban/rural population divide
urban 74%
rural 26%
0 10 20 30 40 50 60 70 80 90 100
Population density
189 people per sq mile
(73 people per sq km)
Total land area
243,513 sq miles
(630,674 sq km)
Land use and agricultural distribution
cattle
pigs
poultry
corn (maize)
fruit
soya beans
timber
major towns
pasture
cropland
forest
Scale 1:3,750,000
Km
Miles
projection: Lambert Conformal Conic
Map key
Population
1 million to 5 million
500,000 to 1 million
100,000 to 500,000
50,000 to 100,000
10,000 to 50,000
below 10,000
Elevation
1000m / 3281ft
500m / 1640ft
250m / 820ft
100m / 328ft
sea level
MICHIGAN
INDIANA
OHIO
NEW YORK
PENNSYLVANIA
WEST VIRGINIA
KENTUCKY
CANADA
Lake Huron
Lake Erie
Lake Ontario
Lake Michigan
Georgian Bay
Chicago
Detroit
Cleveland
Toledo
Columbus
Indianapolis
Cincinnati
Grand Rapids
Fort Wayne
Dayton

Using the land

The varied soils and climate of this region have allowed the development of different types of agriculture. Corn and soya beans are the main crops produced, although Michigan is best known for its fruit-growing, particularly cherries and apples. About 80% of Wisconsin's agricultural income is derived from livestock-rearing and dairying. Pig breeding is important in both Illinois and Indiana.

▲ ***Farms like this** one stretch across more than 67% of Illinois, covering 44,800 sq miles (97,170 sq km). The state is the USA's second largest producer of soya beans, which are used for animal feed and oil.*

▲ ***Lake Superior** is the largest of the Great Lakes and attracts millions of tourists each year. Valuable mineral deposits such as iron and copper are mined close to its shores.*

► ***Although large-scale agribusiness** has mostly replaced family farming in the Midwest, some communities, such as the Amish people in Ohio, retain traditional farming methods, cultivating their smallholdings using limited machinery.*

USA: NORTH MOUNTAIN STATES

Idaho, Montana, Oregon, Washington, Wyoming

The remoteness of the northwestern states, coupled with the rugged landscape, ensured that this was one of the last areas settled by Europeans in the 19th century. Fur-trappers and gold-prospectors followed the Snake River westwards as it wound its way through the Rocky Mountains. The states of the northwest have pioneered many conservationist policies, with the USA's first national park opened at Yellowstone in 1872. More recently, the Cascades and Rocky Mountains have become havens for adventure tourism. The mountains still serve to isolate the western seaboard from the rest of the continent. This isolation has encouraged west coast cities to expand their trade links with countries of the Pacific Rim.

▲ *The Snake River has cut down into the basalt of the Columbia Basin to form Hells Canyon, the deepest in the USA, with cliffs up to 7900 ft (2408 m) high.*

Map key

Population
- ◉ 500,000 to 1 million
- ◎ 100,000 to 500,000
- ⊕ 50,000 to 100,000
- ○ 10,000 to 50,000
- ∘ below 10,000

Elevation
- 4000m / 13,124ft
- 3000m / 9843ft
- 2000m / 6562ft
- 1000m / 3281ft
- 500m / 1640ft
- 250m / 820ft
- 100m / 328ft
- sea level

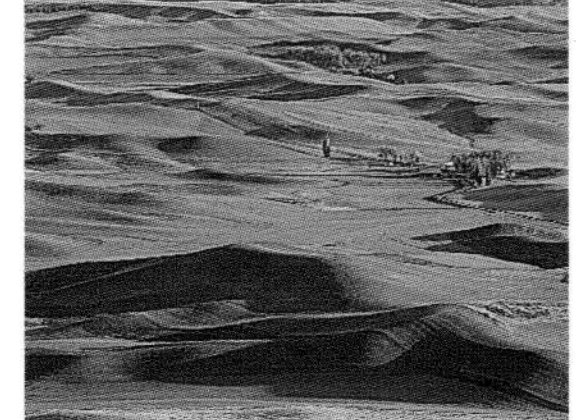

► *Fine-textured, volcanic soils in the hilly Palouse region of eastern Washington are susceptible to erosion.*

Scale 1:3,750,000

Km 0 10 20 40 60 80 100
Miles 0 10 20 40 60 80 100

projection: Lambert Conformal Conic

Using the land

Wheat farming in the east gives way to cattle ranching as rainfall decreases. Irrigated farming in the Snake River valley produces large yields of potatoes and other vegetables. Dairying and fruit-growing take place in the wet western lowlands between the mountain ranges.

The urban/rural population divide

urban 74% rural 26%

0 10 20 30 40 50 60 70 80 90 100

Population density	Total land area
26 people per sq mile (10 people per sq km)	487,970 sq miles (1,263,716 sq km)

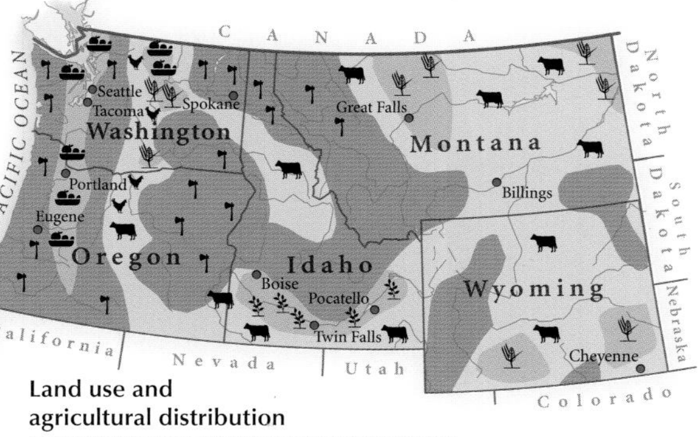
CANADA
PACIFIC OCEAN
Seattle
Tacoma
Spokane
Washington
Great Falls
Montana
North Dakota
South Dakota
Billings
Portland
Eugene
Oregon
Idaho
Boise
Pocatello
Twin Falls
Wyoming
Nebraska
Cheyenne
California
Nevada
Utah
Colorado

Land use and agricultural distribution

- cattle
- poultry
- cereals
- fruit
- potatoes
- timber
- major towns
- pasture
- cropland
- forest

Transport and industry

Minerals and timber are extremely important in this region. Uranium, precious metals, copper and coal are all mined, the latter in vast open-cast pits in Wyoming; oil and natural gas are extracted further north. Manufacturing, notably related to the aerospace and electronics industries, is important in western cities.

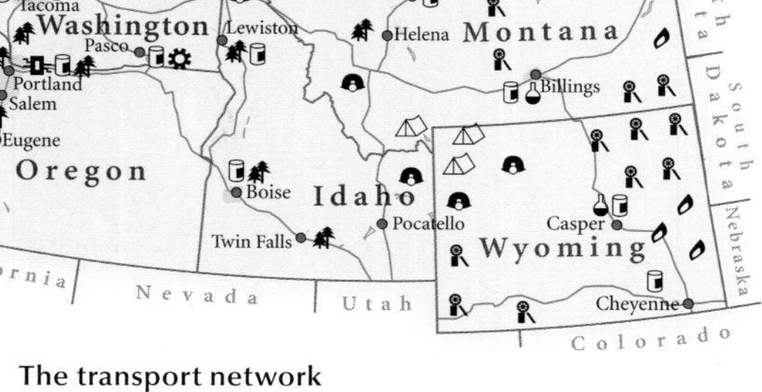
CANADA
PACIFIC OCEAN
Seattle
Tacoma
Spokane
Washington
Pasco
Lewiston
Great Falls
Helena
Montana
North Dakota
South Dakota
Billings
Portland
Salem
Eugene
Oregon
Boise
Idaho
Pocatello
Twin Falls
Casper
Wyoming
Cheyenne
Nebraska
California
Nevada
Utah
Colorado

The transport network

- 347,857 miles (556,571 km)
- 4200 miles (6720 km)
- 12,354 miles (19,766 km)
- 1108 miles (1782 km)

The Union Pacific Railroad has been in service across Wyoming since 1867. The route through the Rocky Mountains is now shared with the Interstate 80, a major east–west highway.

Major industry and infrastructure

- adventure tourism
- aerospace
- coal
- chemicals
- electronics
- food processing
- mining
- oil & gas
- timber processing
- major towns
- international airports
- major roads
- major industrial areas

◄ *Seattle lies in one of Puget Sound's many inlets. The city receives oil and other resources from Alaska, and benefits from expanding trade across the Pacific.*

◄ *Crater Lake, Oregon, is 6 miles (10 km) wide and 1800 ft (600 m) deep. It marks the site of a volcanic cone, which collapsed after an eruption within the last 7000 years.*

8

192

34

34

The landscape

The Rocky Mountains are flanked by lower parallel ranges, which spread onto the Great Plains in the east and surmount the broad lava plateau which extends westwards. The Cascade Range divides the Columbia Basin from the coastlands, where the low areas skirting Puget Sound are broken by the steep, volcanic Olympic Mountains and the wooded hills of the Coast Ranges.

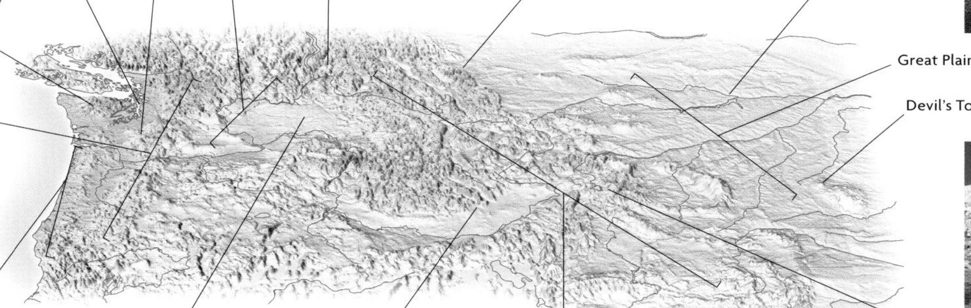

Glacial valleys on the seaward side of the Olympic Mountains receive about 142 inches (3600 mm) of rain per year, supporting the only true rainforest of the northern hemisphere.

Puget Sound

Mount St Helens erupted in 1980, killing 57 people and devastating a huge area.

Columbia Basin

Grand Coulee and the lesser *coulées* (ravines) were cut by cataclysmic floods, from the release of an ice-dammed lake, at the end of the last Ice Age.

The Continental Divide, or watershed, crosses the Lewis Range. From here, rivers flow east to Hudson Bay, south to the Gulf of Mexico and west to the Pacific Ocean.

▶ ***Piney Buttes are*** *the remnants of an older, higher land surface gradually weathered and eroded into isolated outcrops with flat tops and steep sides.*

Great Plains

Devil's Tower

The Cascades are glacially scoured volcanic mountains, the highest of which is Mount Rainier, a dormant volcano at 14,409 ft (4392 m).

Molten rock cools, forming parallel columns

Surrounding strata eroded away

Molten rock wells up from the Earth's core

▲ ***Devil's Tower in*** *Wyoming is an igneous intrusion, formed below the Earth's surface. Molten rock intruded through cracks in the overlying strata and cooled. Over time, the softer rock layers have been eroded away, leaving only the tower standing.*

Coast Ranges

The plateaus of the Columbia and Snake rivers represent one of the world's largest accumulations of lava. Over 5 million years ago, successive flows of molten basalt buried the existing land surface by up to 450 ft (150 m).

The contorted rock shapes at 'Craters of the Moon' National Monument in Idaho were left 2000 years ago by the sporadic upwelling of viscous lava from fissures in the basalt plateau.

Rocky Mountains

▲ ***Water from the*** *hot springs in Yellowstone National Park deposits minerals as it cools in rock pools. Long periods of deposition have created these rock terraces.*

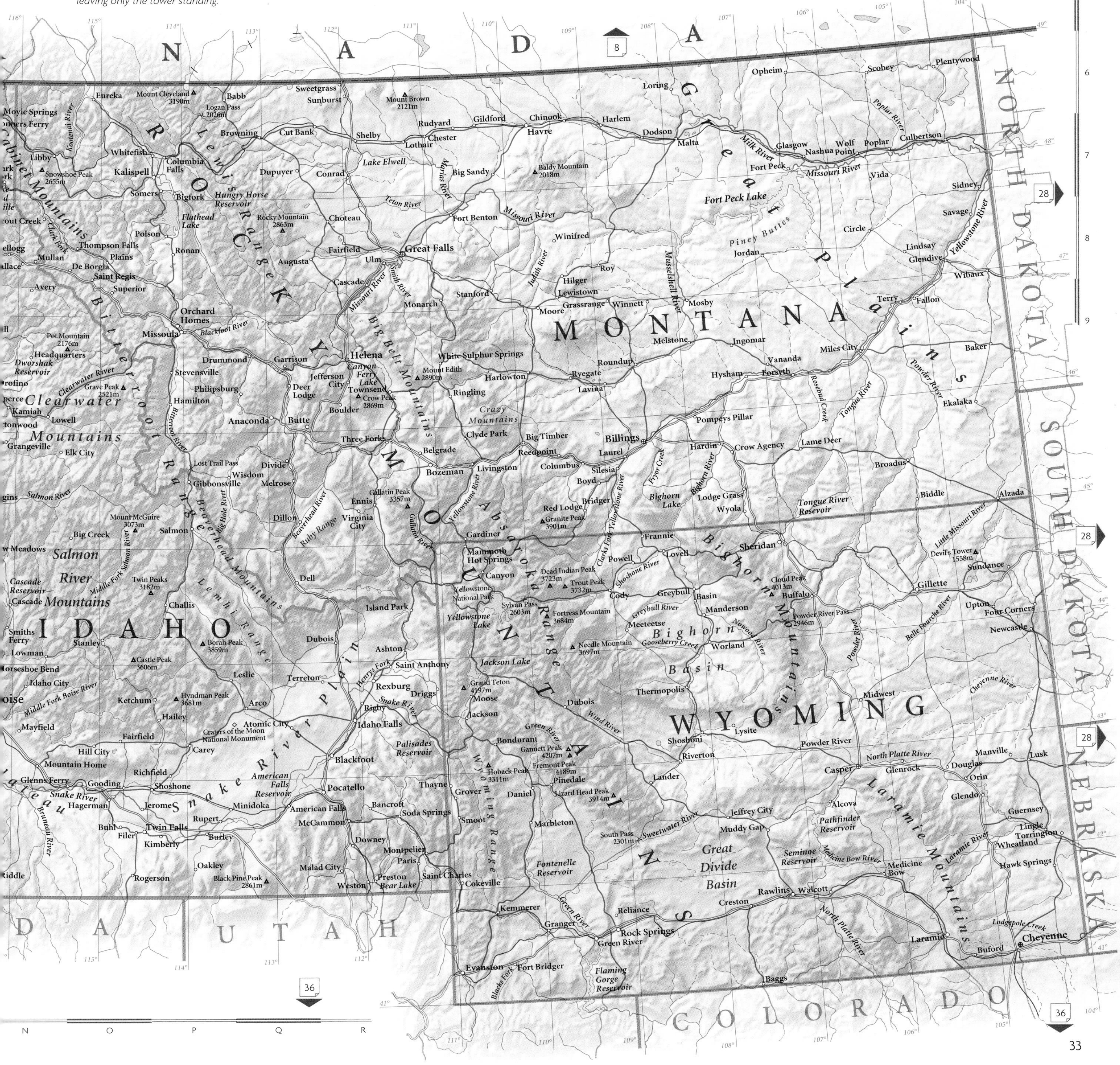

MONTANA

WYOMING

IDAHO

USA: CALIFORNIA & NEVADA

The 'Gold Rush' of 1849 attracted the first major wave of European settlers to the USA's west coast. The pleasant climate, beautiful scenery and dynamic economy continue to attract immigrants – despite the ever-present danger of earthquakes – and California has become the USA's most populous state. The population is concentrated in the vast conurbations of Los Angeles, San Francisco and San Diego; new immigrants include people from South Korea, the Philippines, Vietnam and Mexico. Nevada's arid lands were initially exploited for minerals; in recent years, revenue from mining has been superseded by income from the tourist and gambling centres of Las Vegas and Reno.

Map key

Population

- 1 million to 5 million
- 500,000 to 1 million
- 100,000 to 500,000
- 50,000 to 100,000
- 10,000 to 50,000
- below 10,000

Elevation

- 4000m / 13,124ft
- 3000m / 9843ft
- 2000m / 6562ft
- 1000m / 3281ft
- 500m / 1640ft
- 250m / 820ft
- 100m / 328ft
- sea level

Scale 1:3,000,000

Km 0 5 10 20 30 40 50 60 70 80
Miles 0 5 10 20 30 40 50 60 70 80

projection: Lambert Conformal Conic

Transport and industry

Nevada's rich mineral reserves ushered in a period of mining wealth which has now been replaced by revenue generated from gambling. California supports a broad set of activities including defence-related industries and research and development facilities. 'Silicon Valley', near San Francisco, is a world leading centre for micro-electronics, while tourism and the Los Angeles film industry also generate large incomes.

◄ **Gambling was legalized** in Nevada in 1931. Las Vegas has since become the centre of this multi-million dollar industry.

Oregon
Idaho
Utah
Arizona
Nevada
California
Reno
Carson City
Ely
Sacramento
San Francisco
Oakland
San Jose
Las Vegas
Bakersfield
Los Angeles
San Diego
PACIFIC OCEAN
MEXICO

Major industry and infrastructure

- aerospace
- car manufacture
- defence
- film industry
- finance
- food processing
- gambling
- hi-tech industry
- mining
- pharmaceuticals
- research & development
- textiles
- tourism
- major towns
- international airports
- major roads
- major industrial areas

The transport network

- 211,459 miles (338,334 km)
- 2944 miles (4710 km)
- 7822 miles (12,595 km)
- 190 miles (360 km)

In California, the motor vehicle is a vital part of daily life, and an extensive freeway system runs throughout the state, cementing its position as the most important mode of transport.

The landscape

The broad Central Valley divides California's coastal mountains from the Sierra Nevada. The San Andreas Fault, running beneath much of the state, is the site of frequent earth tremors and sometimes more serious earthquakes. East of the Sierra Nevada, the landscape is characterized by the basin and range topography with stony deserts and many salt lakes.

Rising molten rock causes stretching of the Earth's crust

Extensive cracking (faulting) uplifted a series of ridges

As ridges are eroded they fill intervening valleys with sediments

▲ ***Molten rock (magma)*** *welling up to form a dome in the Earth's interior, causes the brittle surface rocks to stretch and crack. Some areas were uplifted to form mountains (ranges), while others sunk to form flat valleys (basins).*

◄ ***The General Sherman*** *sequoia tree in Sequoia National Park is 2500 years old and at 275 ft (84 m) is one of the largest living things on earth.*

Most of California's agriculture is confined to the fertile and extensively irrigated Central Valley, running between the Coast Ranges and the Sierra Nevada. It incorporates the San Joaquin and Sacramento valleys.

The dramatic granitic rock formations of Half Dome and El Capitan, and the verdant coniferous forests, attract millions of visitors annually to Yosemite National Park in the Sierra Nevada.

Sierra Nevada

The Great Basin dominates most of Nevada's topography containing large open basins, punctuated by eroded features such as *buttes* and *mesas*. River flow tends to be seasonal, dependent upon spring showers and winter snow melt.

Wheeler Peak is home to some of the world's oldest trees, bristlecone pines, which live for up to 5000 years.

When the Hoover Dam across the Colorado River was completed in 1936, it created Lake Mead, one of the largest artificial lakes in the world, extending for 115 miles (285 km) upstream.

Amargosa Desert

The San Andreas Fault is a transverse fault which extends for 650 miles (1050 km) through California. Major earthquakes occur when the land either side of the fault moves at different rates. San Francisco was devastated by an earthquake in 1906.

Death Valley

► ***Named by migrating*** *settlers in 1849, Death Valley is the driest, hottest place in North America, as well as being the lowest point on land in the western hemisphere, at 282 ft (86 m) below sea level.*

The sparsely populated Mojave Desert receives less than 8 inches (200 mm) of rainfall a year. It is used extensively for weapons-testing and military purposes.

The Salton Sea was created accidentally between 1905 and 1907 when an irrigation channel from the Colorado River broke out of its banks and formed this salty 300 sq mile (777 sq km), land-locked lake.

▲ ***The Sierra Nevada*** *create a 'rainshadow', preventing rain from reaching much of Nevada. Pacific air masses, passing over the mountains, are stripped of their moisture.*

Using the land

California is the USA's leading agricultural producer, although low rainfall makes irrigation essential. The long growing season and abundant sunshine allow many crops to be grown in the fertile Central Valley including grapes, citrus fruits, vegetables and cotton. Almost 17 million acres (6.8 million hectares) of California's forests are used commercially. Nevada's arid climate and poor soil are largely unsuitable for agriculture; 85% of its land is state owned and large areas are used for underground testing of nuclear weapons.

Land use and agricultural distribution

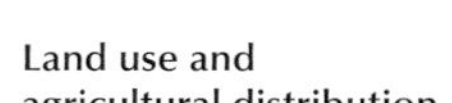

- cattle
- citrus fruits
- fruit
- irrigation
- timber
- vineyards
- major towns
- pasture
- cropland
- forest
- desert

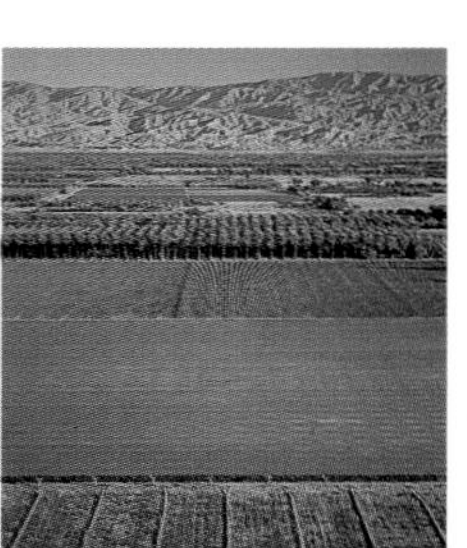

▲ ***Without considerable irrigation***, *this fertile valley at Palm Springs would still be part of the Sonoran Desert. California's farmers account for about 80% of the state's total water usage.*

The urban/rural population divide

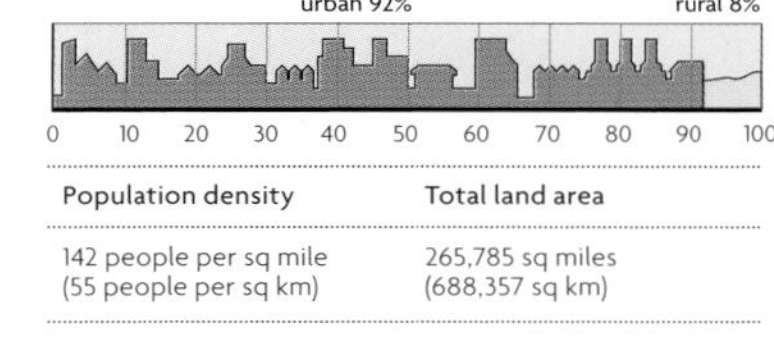

urban 92%
rural 8%
0 10 20 30 40 50 60 70 80 90 100

Population density	Total land area
142 people per sq mile (55 people per sq km)	265,785 sq miles (688,357 sq km)

192

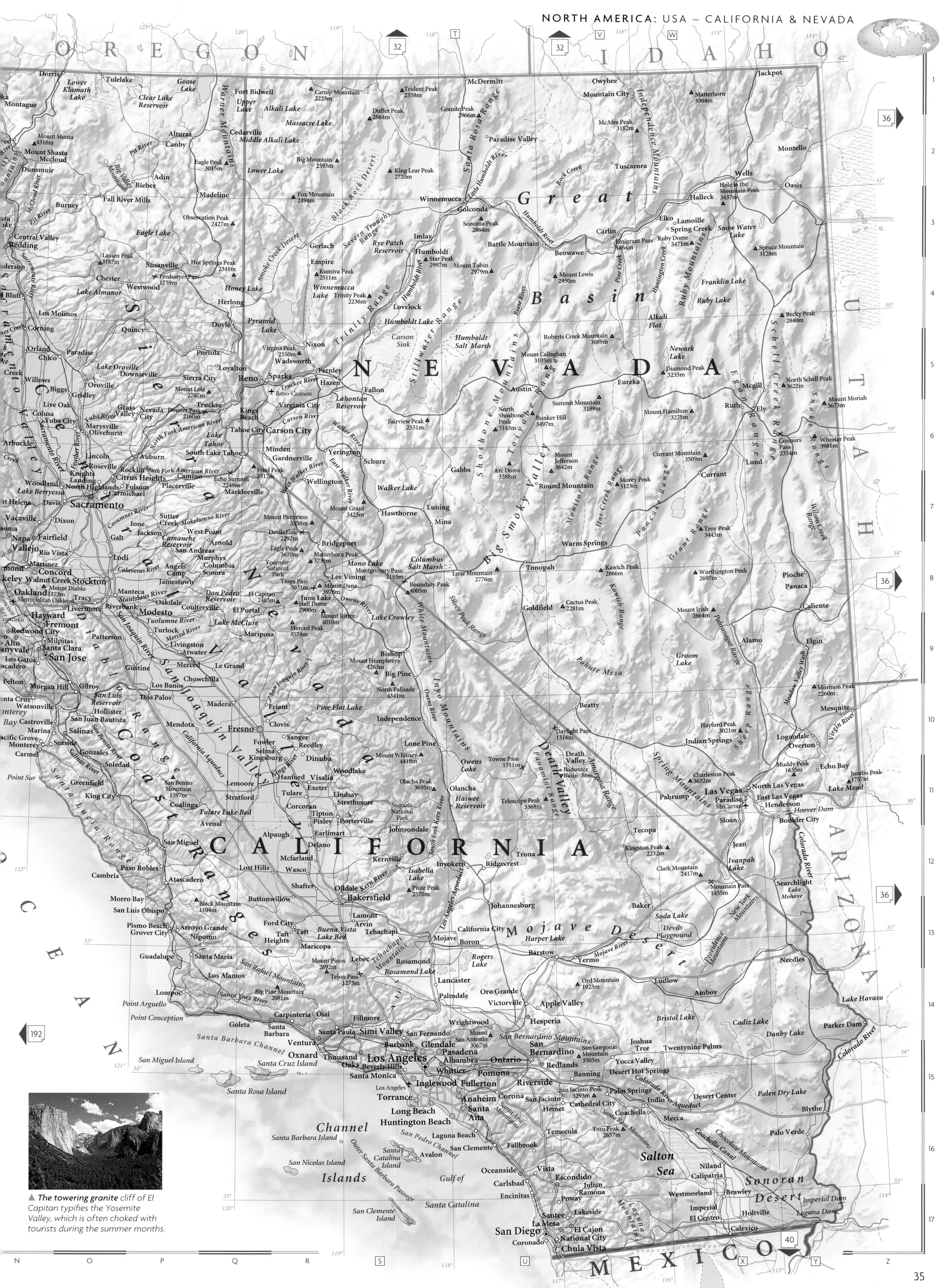

▲ ***The towering granite** cliff of El Capitan typifies the Yosemite Valley, which is often choked with tourists during the summer months.*

USA: SOUTH MOUNTAIN STATES

Arizona, Colorado, New Mexico, Utah

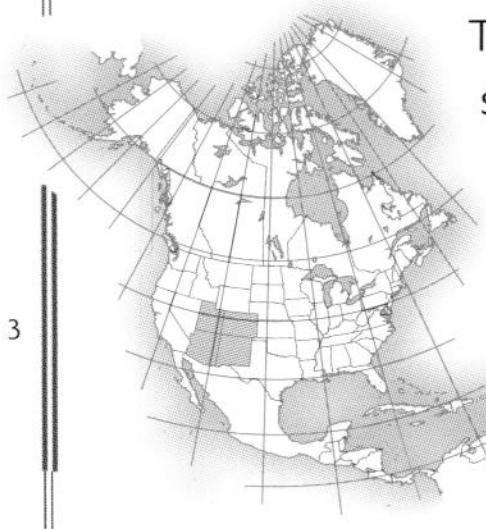

This arid region, characterized by expansive plateaux and spectacular canyons is home to several distinct peoples. The ruins of cliff dwellings built a thousand years ago by the Anasazi people still exist today, and native Americans own one-third of the land in Arizona. Spanish and Mexican conquest and settlement left a hispanic presence which is strongest in New Mexico. The Mormons, who came to the Great Salt Lake seeking religious freedom in 1847, were among the earliest Anglo-American settlers and now make up over 70% of Utah's population. The region's mineral wealth drove rapid development in the 20th century, yet the constraints of a fragile environment, including widespread water shortages, may limit prospects for growth.

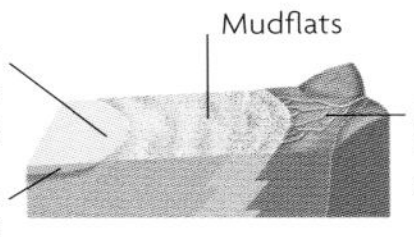

When water evaporates it leaves a salt pan

Mudflats

Lake is fed by seasonal snow melt

Water level of lake varies according to quantity of run-off received from snow melt

▲ *The Great Salt Lake is an ephemeral lake; it can remain dry for extended periods, leaving a pan of evaporated mineral salts in its centre.*

The landscape

The arid, rocky expanse of the Colorado Plateau is dissected by immense canyons of the Colorado River. Desert lies to the north and south and branches of the Rocky Mountains run to the east and west. The Great Salt Lake and Desert lie within the Great Basin, a barren region of parallel mountain ranges which extends into Arizona.

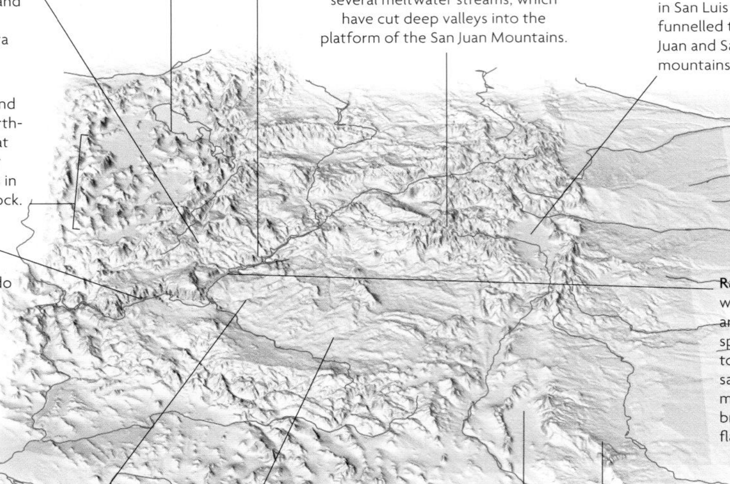

Over 13 million years of weathering has created thousands of spires and pinnacles from the alternating rock strata of Bryce Canyon.

Lake Powell

The Rio Grande has its source in several meltwater streams, which have cut deep valleys into the platform of the San Juan Mountains.

Sand dunes, 600 ft (180 m) high, have been deposited in San Luis Valley, by winds funnelled through the San Juan and Sangre de Cristo mountains in the Rockies.

The parallel basins and ridges, which run north-south along the Great Basin, reflect a major series of block-faults in the underlying bedrock.

Parts of the Grand Canyon, which cuts through the Colorado Plateau, are 16 miles (25 km) wide. The Colorado River has cut down 6262 ft (2000 m), exposing rock strata more than 2 billion years old.

Rainbow Bridge is the world's largest natural arch. The 309 ft (94 m) span probably began to grow when the sandstone spur of a meandering creek was breached during a flash flood.

The striking colour effects seen in the Painted Desert come from minerals such as gypsum and haematite, combined with ambient heat and dust.

Petrified Forest

Shifting gypsum sands produce a constantly changing land surface, overwhelming plants and any other obstacles in Tularosa Valley.

Carlsbad Caverns

► *In the arid landscape of Petrified Forest National Park in Arizona, the grain of prehistoric trees has been preserved as a fossil imprint in the rocks. The bog-preserved trees were gradually turned to stone by seeping mineral-rich water.*

► *The intricate stalactites of Carlsbad Caverns have grown with the seepage of calcium-rich water, over the last 100,000 years. The huge caves are home to around 100,000 Mexican freetail bats.*

Transport and industry

New industries have helped reduce the region's dependence on the extraction of minerals and fossil fuels. Precision manufacture has grown rapidly, particularly in Arizona and Colorado. Salt Lake City and Denver are well-established financial centres and New Mexico, the USA's main producer of uranium, is a prominent region for nuclear research. Colorado is the USA's most important centre for winter sports.

The transport network

232,434 miles (373,986 km)	4059 miles (6515 km)
8627 miles (13,881 km)	none

The Colorado Rockies are crossed by 32 mountain passes, some as high as 12,183 ft (3713 m). The Eisenhower Tunnel west of Denver carries Interstate Highway 70 straight through the Continental Divide.

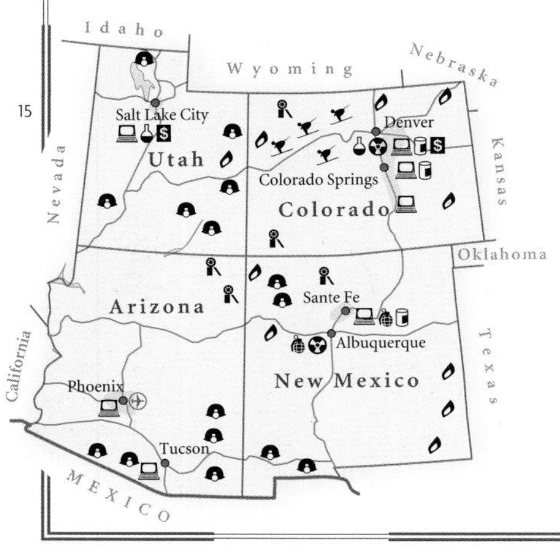

Major industry and infrastructure

- chemicals
- coal
- defence
- finance
- food processing
- hi-tech industry
- oil & gas
- mining
- research & development
- winter sports
- major towns
- international airports
- major roads
- major industrial areas

▲ *Glen Canyon Dam on the Colorado river was completed in 1964. It provides hydro-electric power and irrigation water as part of a long-term federal project to harness the river.*

◄ *The flat tablelands (mesas), and the isolated pinnacles (buttes) which rise from the floor of Monument Valley are the resistant remnants of an earlier land surface, gradually cut back by erosion under arid conditions.*

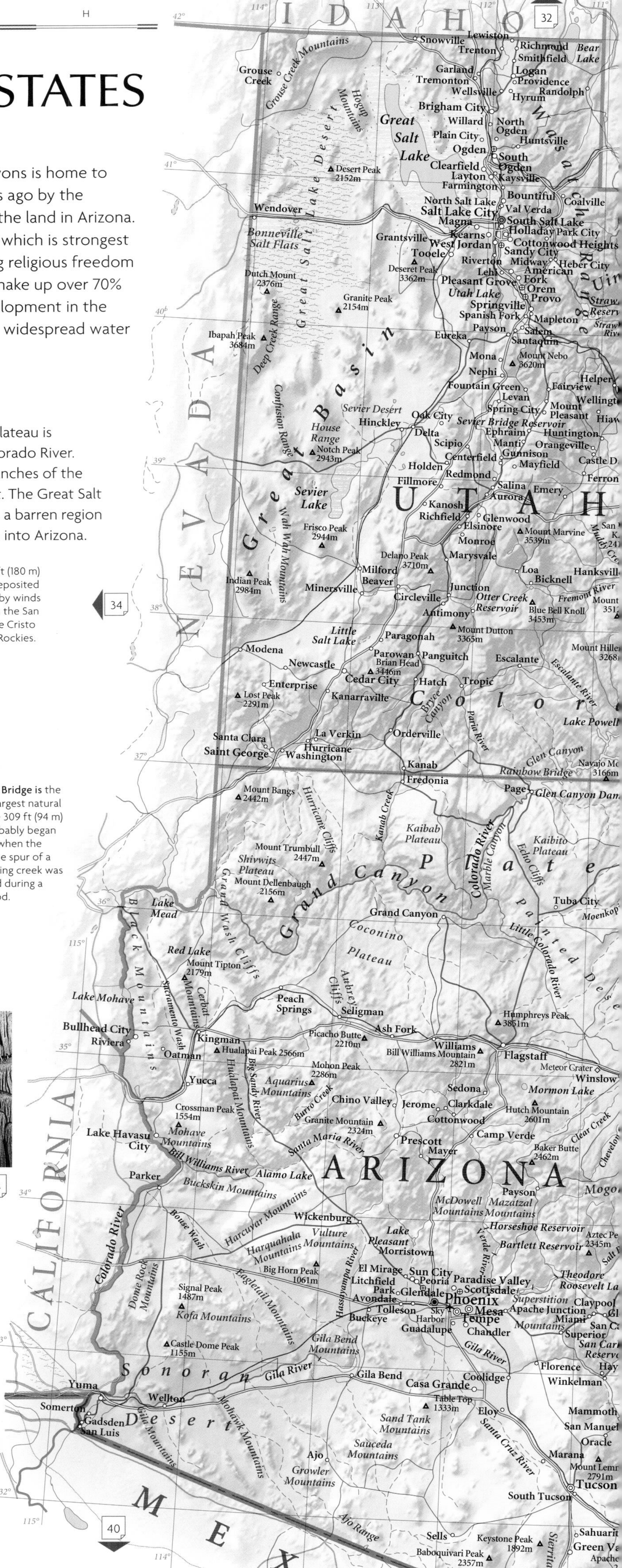

32
34
40

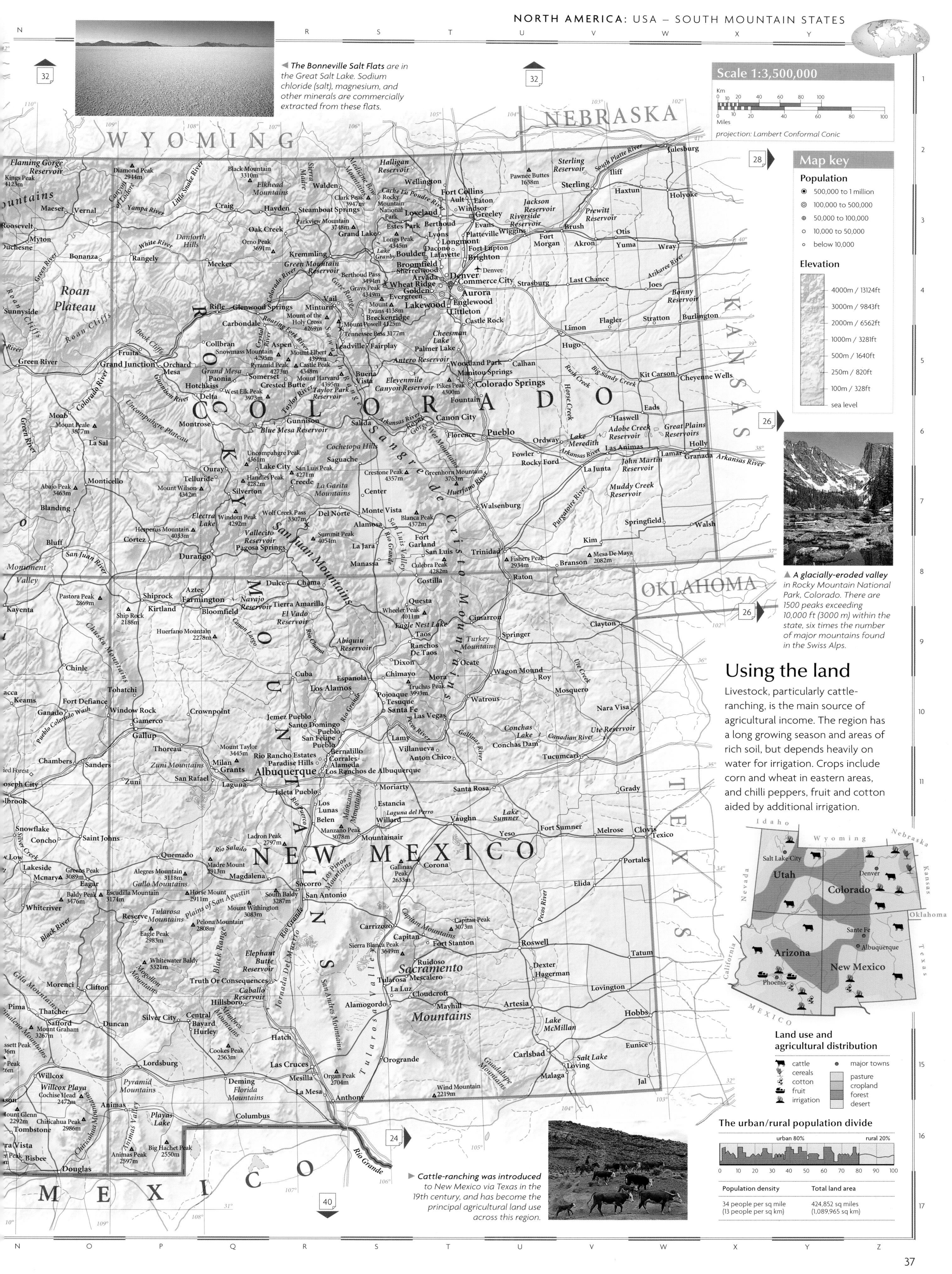
WYOMING
NEBRASKA
KANSAS
OKLAHOMA
TEXAS
MEXICO
COLORADO
NEW MEXICO
ROCKY MOUNTAINS
San Juan Mountains
Sangre de Cristo Mountains
Sacramento Mountains
Roan Plateau
Denver
Colorado Springs
Pueblo
Albuquerque
Santa Fe
Las Cruces
Rio Grande
Scale 1:3,500,000
projection: Lambert Conformal Conic
Map key
Population
500,000 to 1 million
100,000 to 500,000
50,000 to 100,000
10,000 to 50,000
below 10,000
Elevation
4000m / 13124ft
3000m / 9843ft
2000m / 6562ft
1000m / 3281ft
500m / 1640ft
250m / 820ft
100m / 328ft
sea level
Land use and agricultural distribution
cattle
cereals
cotton
fruit
irrigation
major towns
pasture
cropland
forest
desert

◀ *The Bonneville Salt Flats* are in the Great Salt Lake. Sodium chloride (salt), magnesium, and other minerals are commercially extracted from these flats.

▲ *A glacially-eroded valley* in Rocky Mountain National Park, Colorado. There are 1500 peaks exceeding 10,000 ft (3000 m) within the state, six times the number of major mountains found in the Swiss Alps.

Using the land

Livestock, particularly cattle-ranching, is the main source of agricultural income. The region has a long growing season and areas of rich soil, but depends heavily on water for irrigation. Crops include corn and wheat in eastern areas, and chilli peppers, fruit and cotton aided by additional irrigation.

The urban/rural population divide

urban 80% — rural 20%

Population density	Total land area
34 people per sq mile (13 people per sq km)	424,852 sq miles (1,089,965 sq km)

▶ *Cattle-ranching was introduced* to New Mexico via Texas in the 19th century, and has become the principal agricultural land use across this region.

USA: HAWAII

The 122 islands of the Hawai'ian archipelago – which are part of Polynesia – are the peaks of the world's largest volcanoes. They rise approximately 6 miles (9.7 km) from the floor of the Pacific Ocean. The largest, the island of Hawai'i, remains highly active. Hawaii became the USA's 50th state in 1959. A tradition of receiving immigrant workers is reflected in the islands' ethnic diversity, with peoples drawn from around the rim of the Pacific. Only 9% of the current population are native Polynesians.

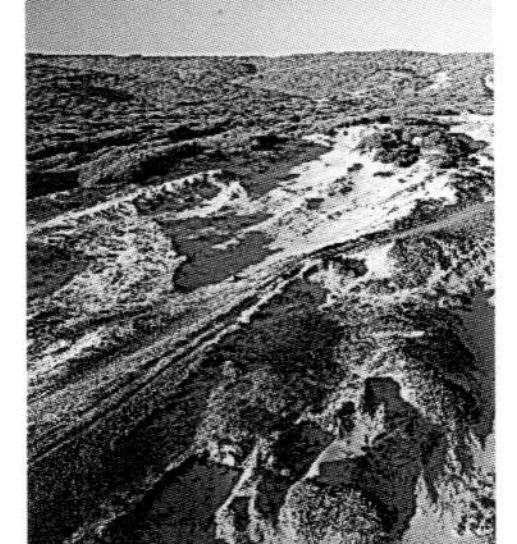

▲ *The island of Moloka'i is formed from volcanic rock. Mature sand dunes cover the rocks in coastal areas.*

Transport and industry

Tourism dominates the economy, with over 90% of the population employed in services. The naval base at Pearl Harbor is also a major source of employment. Industry is concentrated on the island of O'ahu and relies mostly on imported materials, while agricultural produce is processed locally.

The transport network

Road	Rail	Air	Water
4102 miles (6600 km)	none	43 miles (69 km)	none

Hawaii relies on ocean-surface transportation. Honolulu is the main focus of this network, bringing foreign trade and the markets of mainland USA to Hawaii's outer islands.

◀ *Haleakala's extinct volcanic crater is the world's largest. The giant caldera, containing many secondary cones, is 2000 ft (600 m) deep and 20 miles (32 km) in circumference.*

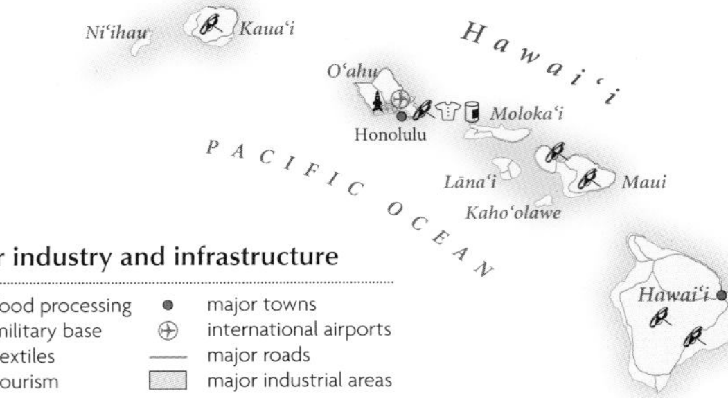

Ni'ihau
Kaua'i
O'ahu
Honolulu
Moloka'i
Lāna'i
Maui
Kaho'olawe
Hawai'i
Hilo
Hawai'i
PACIFIC OCEAN

Major industry and infrastructure

- food processing
- military base
- textiles
- tourism
- major towns
- international airports
- major roads
- major industrial areas

Using the land and sea

The volcanic soils are extremely fertile and the climate hot and humid on the lower slopes, supporting large commercial plantations growing sugar cane, bananas, pineapples and other tropical fruit, as well as nursery plants and flowers. Some land is given to pasture, particularly for beef and dairy cattle.

Land use and agricultural distribution

- cattle
- fishing
- fruit
- sugar cane
- major towns
- pasture
- cropland
- forest
- mountain region

▶ *The island of Kaua'i is one of the wettest places in the world, receiving some 450 inches (11,500 mm) of rain a year.*

Scale 1:3,500,000

projection: Lambert Conformal Conic

Map key

Population

- 100,000 to 500,000
- 50,000 to 100,000
- 10,000 to 50,000
- below 10,000

Elevation

- 4000m / 13,124ft
- 3000m / 9843ft
- 2000m / 6562ft
- 1000m / 3281ft
- 500m / 1640ft
- 250m / 820ft
- 100m / 328ft
- sea level

192

The urban/rural population divide

urban 89% — rural 11%

Population density	Total land area
189 people per sq mile (73 people per sq km)	6,423 sq miles (16,636 sq km)

Using the land and sea

The ice-free coastline of Alaska provides access to salmon fisheries and more than 129 million acres (52.2 million ha) of forest. Most of Alaska is uncultivable, and around 90% of food is imported. Barley, hay and hothouse products are grown around Anchorage, where dairy farming is also concentrated.

The urban/rural population divide

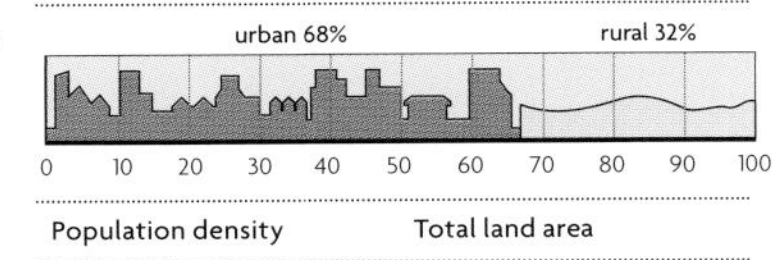

urban 68%
rural 32%
0 10 20 30 40 50 60 70 80 90 100

Population density	Total land area
1 person per sq mile (0.4 people per sq km)	571,951 sq miles (1,481,296 sq km)

◀ *A raft of timber from the Tongass forest is hauled by a tug, bound for the pulp mills of the Alaskan coast between Juneau and Ketchikan.*

122

192

Map key

Population

- 100,000 to 500,000
- 50,000 to 100,000
- 10,000 to 50,000
- below 10,000

Elevation

- 4000m / 13,124ft
- 3000m / 9843ft
- 2000m / 6562ft
- 1000m / 3281ft
- 500m / 1640ft
- 250m / 820ft
- 100m / 328ft
- sea level

Scale 1:8,000,000

projection: Lambert Conformal Conic

USA: ALASKA

Almost 650,000 people live in Alaska, a wilderness of ice, forest, mountains and plains, purchased from Russia in 1867 and twice the size of Texas. The discovery of large oil reserves has brought prosperity to the USA's 'last frontier', while advancing the need to preserve natural habitats and the traditional livelihoods of indigenous peoples such as the Aleuts and Inupiaq.

Land use and agricultural distribution

- fishing
- reindeer
- fruit
- major towns
- forest
- barren
- tundra

The landscape

The mountains of the Pacific coast culminate in the heavily glaciated Alaska Range and extend west, to the Alaska Peninsula and the great volcanic arc of the Aleutian Islands. The interior plains are drained by the Yukon River and bounded by the bare, jagged peaks of the Brooks Range to the north.

The Yukon Delta is a fan of alluvial material eroded by the Yukon River and its tributaries. It is approximately twice the size of the Mississippi Delta.

Brooks Range

The ten highest mountains in the USA are all in the Alaska Range, Mount McKinley *(Denali)*, at 20,321 ft (6194 m) is the highest.

West Fork Glacier

Yukon River

The arc of the Aleutian Islands marks the boundary between the Eurasian and Pacific tectonic plates.

Fjords are found along the coast where valleys, deeply excavated by large glaciers, were inundated by rising seas.

Alaska Range

▲ ***By August, the** Alaska Range is covered with autumnal tundra vegetation.*

West Fork Glacier

The surging ice mass shears along the glacier margin

Deep crevasses divide the front of the surging glacier into large ice blocks

▲ ***Surging glaciers make** rapid and dramatic advances, normally after periods of snow accumulation. West Fork Glacier in the Susitna River Basin travelled 2.5 miles (4 km) in 1987.*

Transport and industry

Large areas of Alaska are undeveloped, and much of the existing infrastructure is a legacy of Cold War military investment. Mineral ores, including gold, have been mined for over a century, but the oil business now dominates the economy. Processing industries such as paper-pulp mills supply Japan and other markets on the Pacific Rim.

The transport network

13,524 miles (21,760 km)	49 miles (78 km)
482 miles (772 km)	none

Over 40 million gallons (182 million litres) of oil are pumped through the Trans-Alaska Pipeline every day. The oil takes six days to travel the 789 miles (1262 km) from Prudhoe Bay to Valdez.

Major industry and infrastructure

- fish processing
- gold mining
- oil
- timber processing
- major towns
- international airports
- major roads

▲ ***The Trans-Alaska Pipeline** has carried crude oil from Prudhoe Bay since 1977. The oilfield is the USA's largest and is estimated to be equal in size to the biggest oilfields of the Persian Gulf.*

196
8
192
192

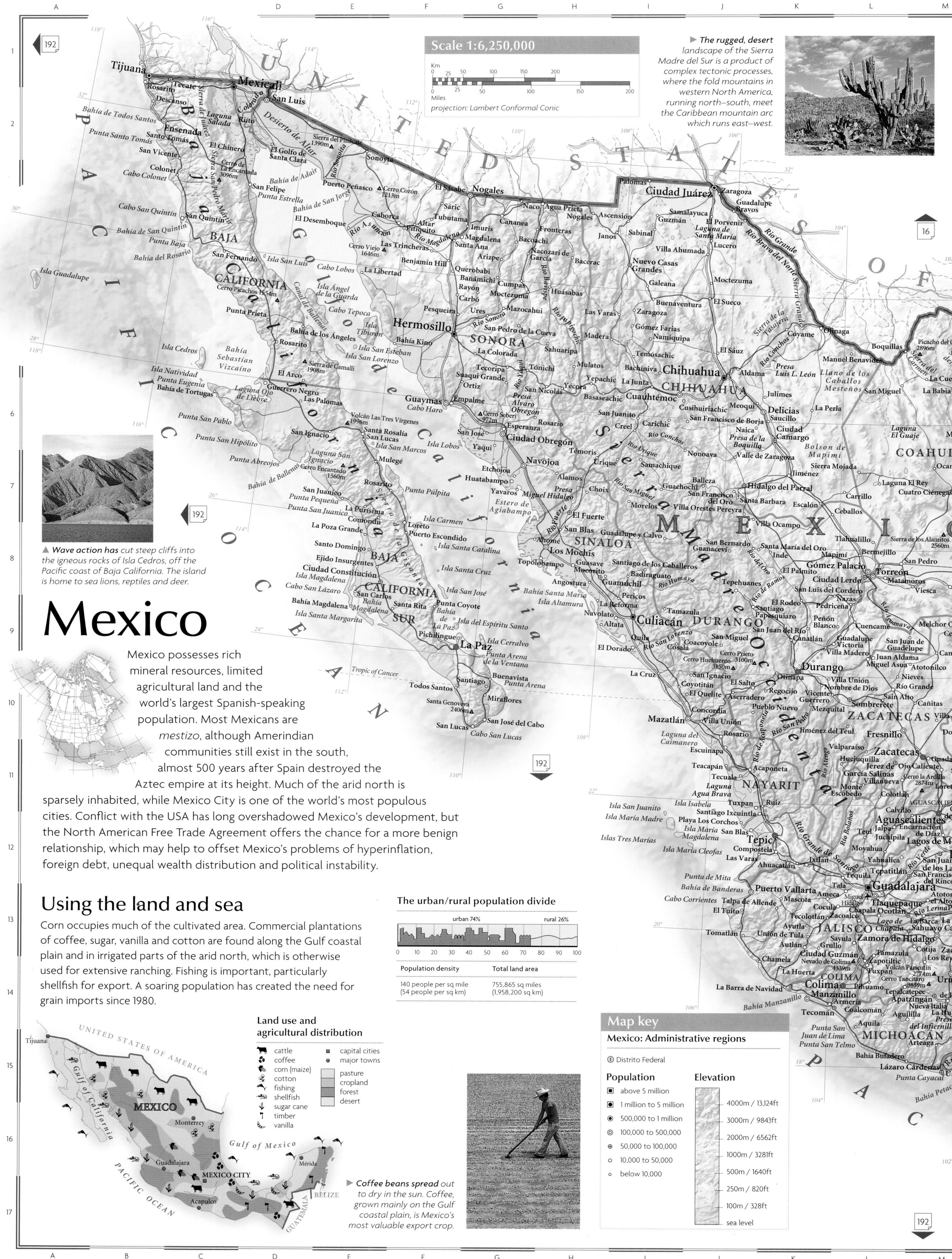

Scale 1:6,250,000
Km 0 25 50 100 150 200
Miles 0 25 50 100 150 200
projection: Lambert Conformal Conic
UNITED STATES OF AMERICA
PACIFIC OCEAN
Gulf of California
MEXICO
Sierra Madre Occidental
Map key
Mexico: Administrative regions
① Distrito Federal
Population
above 5 million
1 million to 5 million
500,000 to 1 million
100,000 to 500,000
50,000 to 100,000
10,000 to 50,000
below 10,000
Elevation
4000m / 13,124ft
3000m / 9843ft
2000m / 6562ft
1000m / 3281ft
500m / 1640ft
250m / 820ft
100m / 328ft
sea level

▶ ***The rugged, desert*** *landscape of the Sierra Madre del Sur is a product of complex tectonic processes, where the fold mountains in western North America, running north–south, meet the Caribbean mountain arc which runs east–west.*

▲ ***Wave action has*** *cut steep cliffs into the igneous rocks of Isla Cedros, off the Pacific coast of Baja California. The island is home to sea lions, reptiles and deer.*

Mexico

Mexico possesses rich mineral resources, limited agricultural land and the world's largest Spanish-speaking population. Most Mexicans are *mestizo*, although Amerindian communities still exist in the south, almost 500 years after Spain destroyed the Aztec empire at its height. Much of the arid north is sparsely inhabited, while Mexico City is one of the world's most populous cities. Conflict with the USA has long overshadowed Mexico's development, but the North American Free Trade Agreement offers the chance for a more benign relationship, which may help to offset Mexico's problems of hyperinflation, foreign debt, unequal wealth distribution and political instability.

Using the land and sea

Corn occupies much of the cultivated area. Commercial plantations of coffee, sugar, vanilla and cotton are found along the Gulf coastal plain and in irrigated parts of the arid north, which is otherwise used for extensive ranching. Fishing is important, particularly shellfish for export. A soaring population has created the need for grain imports since 1980.

The urban/rural population divide

urban 74%
rural 26%
0 10 20 30 40 50 60 70 80 90 100

Population density	Total land area
140 people per sq mile (54 people per sq km)	755,865 sq miles (1,958,200 sq km)

Land use and agricultural distribution

cattle
coffee
corn (maize)
cotton
fishing
shellfish
sugar cane
timber
vanilla
capital cities
major towns
pasture
cropland
forest
desert
Tijuana
UNITED STATES OF AMERICA
Gulf of California
MEXICO
Monterrey
Gulf of Mexico
Guadalajara
MEXICO CITY
Mérida
PACIFIC OCEAN
Acapulco
BELIZE
GUATEMALA

▶ ***Coffee beans spread*** *out to dry in the sun. Coffee, grown mainly on the Gulf coastal plain, is Mexico's most valuable export crop.*

Formation of the Gulf of California
Direction of plate movement
Baja California
Transform fault
Gulf of California
Edge of continental crust
Spreading oceanic ridge
Sierra Madre Oriental
Rio Grande
Sierra Madre Occidental
Río Balsas
Popocatépetl
Major industry and infrastructure
brewing
car manufacture
chemicals
electronics
fish processing
maquiladoras
mining
oil & gas
textiles
capital cities
major towns
international airports
major roads
major industrial areas
The transport network
67,564 miles (108,746 km)
3994 miles (6429 km)
16,561 miles (26,656 km)
1801 miles (2900 km)

The landscape

The great central plateau rises gently southwards from the Rio Grande, isolated from the coastal plains by the Sierra Madre Oriental and Occidental. The two ranges converge from east and west respectively, culminating in high volcanic peaks around Mexico City. Further ranges of the Sierra Madre rise to the south of the Balsas basin, skirted by the low-lying Isthmus of Tehuantepec *(Istmo de Tehuantepec)* and Yucatan Peninsula.

The long, narrow, extremely arid peninsula of Baja (lower) California is an elongated granite block, separated from the mainland by the flooded rift valley of the Gulf of California *(Golfo de California).*

Wave action has constructed sand bars which shelter lagoons along the shore of the Gulf coastal plain.

The dormant cone of Volcán Pico de Orizaba is, at 18,700 ft (5700 m), the highest peak in Mexico. In North America, only Mount McKinley and Mount Logan are taller.

▲ ***Tropical rainforest abounds** in the Yucatan Peninsula, a broad, low limestone shelf. Rivers are rare due to the porous nature of limestone, so the forest is mostly fed by streams and underground water.*

The heavily-forested Isthmus of Tehuantepec *(Istmo de Tehuantepec)* is a graben; a low-lying trough created by downward movement of the bedrock between two fault lines.

▲ ***The Gulf of California*** (Golfo de California) *began to open out about 4 million years ago as a result of rifting and plate displacement along transform faults.*

▲ ***Popocatépetl is a** dormant volcano, part of the Pacific 'Ring of Fire'. The crater is over half a mile (1 km) wide.*

The unstable, earthquake-prone, upland basin around Mexico City was once a region of shallow lakes. Flood control measures and domestic consumption over the last four centuries have caused the virtual disappearance of this surface water.

The highlands of Chiapas are a series of *horsts*, blocks of land thrust upwards between two fault lines. Volcanic cones have developed where lava has flowed out from the faults.

Transport and industry

Oil and gas on the Gulf coast are Mexico's main sources of export income. Metal mining has declined but the country remains a leading global producer of silver. Manufacturing is heavily concentrated around the Mexico City metropolitan area, while the duty-free movement of goods in the USA border region, under the *Maquiladora* (twin plant) scheme, has created new hi-tech and service growth centres.

Fast, modern highways or autopistas now link Mexico City with Toluca, Puebla and other satellite cities, yet distant centres like Chihuahua are still served by narrow roads and an outdated rail network.

▲ ***A stone figure** reclines by the Temple of Warriors, within the Mayan city of Chichén-Itzá. The Maya civilization flourished across the Yucatan Peninsula between 200 and 900 AD.*

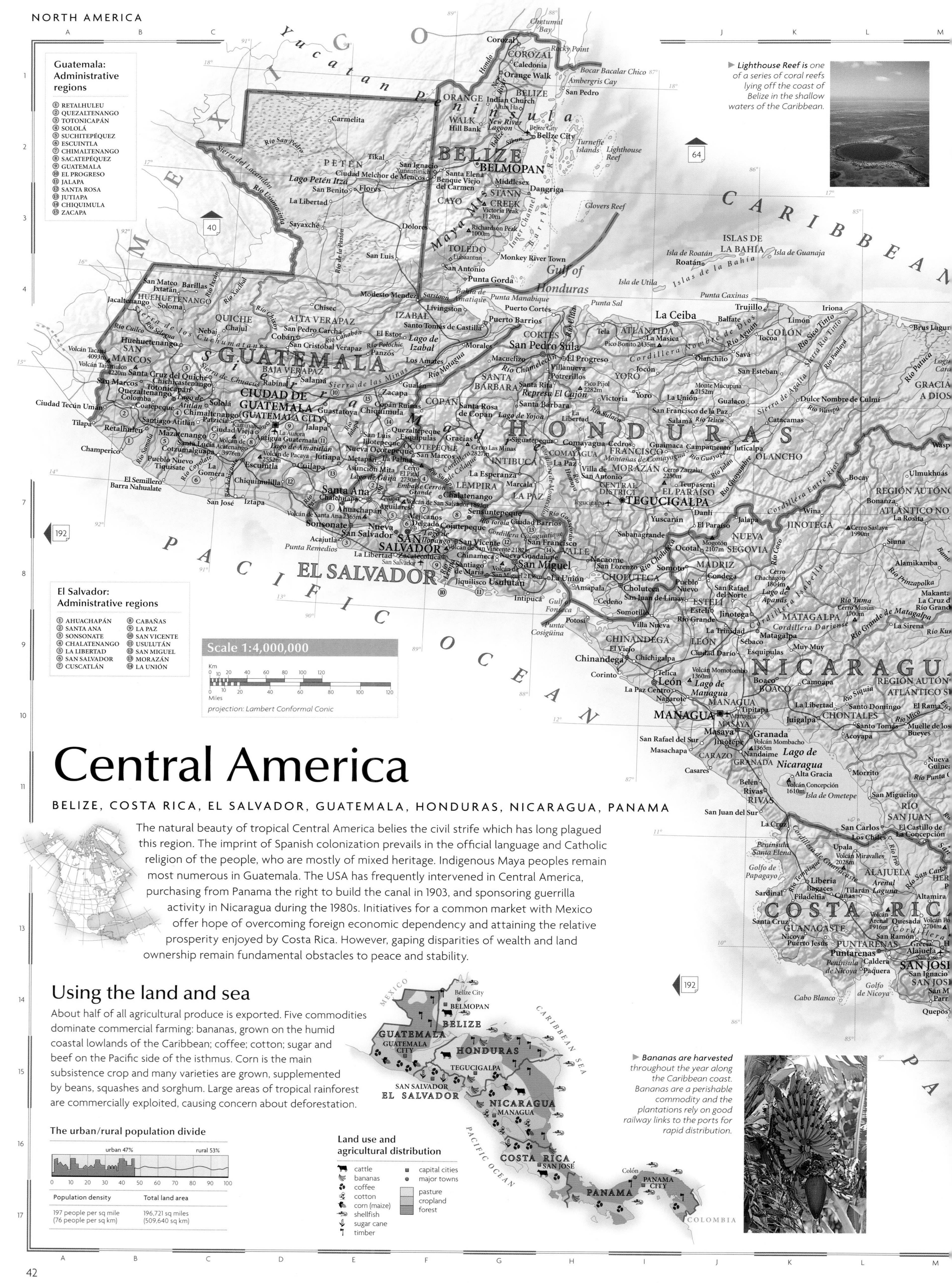
Guatemala: Administrative regions
① RETALHULEU
② QUEZALTENANGO
③ TOTONICAPÁN
④ SOLOLÁ
⑤ SUCHITEPÉQUEZ
⑥ ESCUINTLA
⑦ CHIMALTENANGO
⑧ SACATEPÉQUEZ
⑨ GUATEMALA
⑩ EL PROGRESO
⑪ JALAPA
⑫ SANTA ROSA
⑬ JUTIAPA
⑭ CHIQUIMULA
⑮ ZACAPA
El Salvador: Administrative regions
① AHUACHAPÁN
② SANTA ANA
③ SONSONATE
④ CHALATENANGO
⑤ LA LIBERTAD
⑥ SAN SALVADOR
⑦ CUSCATLÁN
⑧ CABAÑAS
⑨ LA PAZ
⑩ SAN VICENTE
⑪ USULUTÁN
⑫ SAN MIGUEL
⑬ MORAZÁN
⑭ LA UNIÓN
Scale 1:4,000,000
projection: Lambert Conformal Conic
MEXICO
Yucatan Peninsula
BELIZE
BELMOPAN
GUATEMALA
CIUDAD DE GUATEMALA (GUATEMALA CITY)
EL SALVADOR
SAN SALVADOR
HONDURAS
TEGUCIGALPA
NICARAGUA
MANAGUA
COSTA RICA
SAN JOSÉ
CARIBBEAN SEA
PACIFIC OCEAN
Gulf of Honduras
Gulf of Fonseca
Lago de Nicaragua
Lago de Managua
40
64
192
The urban/rural population divide
urban 47%
rural 53%
Population density
197 people per sq mile (76 people per sq km)
Total land area
196,721 sq miles (509,640 sq km)
Land use and agricultural distribution
cattle
bananas
coffee
cotton
corn (maize)
shellfish
sugar cane
timber
capital cities
major towns
pasture
cropland
forest

▶ **Lighthouse Reef** *is one of a series of coral reefs lying off the coast of Belize in the shallow waters of the Caribbean.*

Central America

BELIZE, COSTA RICA, EL SALVADOR, GUATEMALA, HONDURAS, NICARAGUA, PANAMA

The natural beauty of tropical Central America belies the civil strife which has long plagued this region. The imprint of Spanish colonization prevails in the official language and Catholic religion of the people, who are mostly of mixed heritage. Indigenous Maya peoples remain most numerous in Guatemala. The USA has frequently intervened in Central America, purchasing from Panama the right to build the canal in 1903, and sponsoring guerrilla activity in Nicaragua during the 1980s. Initiatives for a common market with Mexico offer hope of overcoming foreign economic dependency and attaining the relative prosperity enjoyed by Costa Rica. However, gaping disparities of wealth and land ownership remain fundamental obstacles to peace and stability.

Using the land and sea

About half of all agricultural produce is exported. Five commodities dominate commercial farming: bananas, grown on the humid coastal lowlands of the Caribbean; coffee; cotton; sugar and beef on the Pacific side of the isthmus. Corn is the main subsistence crop and many varieties are grown, supplemented by beans, squashes and sorghum. Large areas of tropical rainforest are commercially exploited, causing concern about deforestation.

▶ **Bananas are harvested** *throughout the year along the Caribbean coast. Bananas are a perishable commodity and the plantations rely on good railway links to the ports for rapid distribution.*

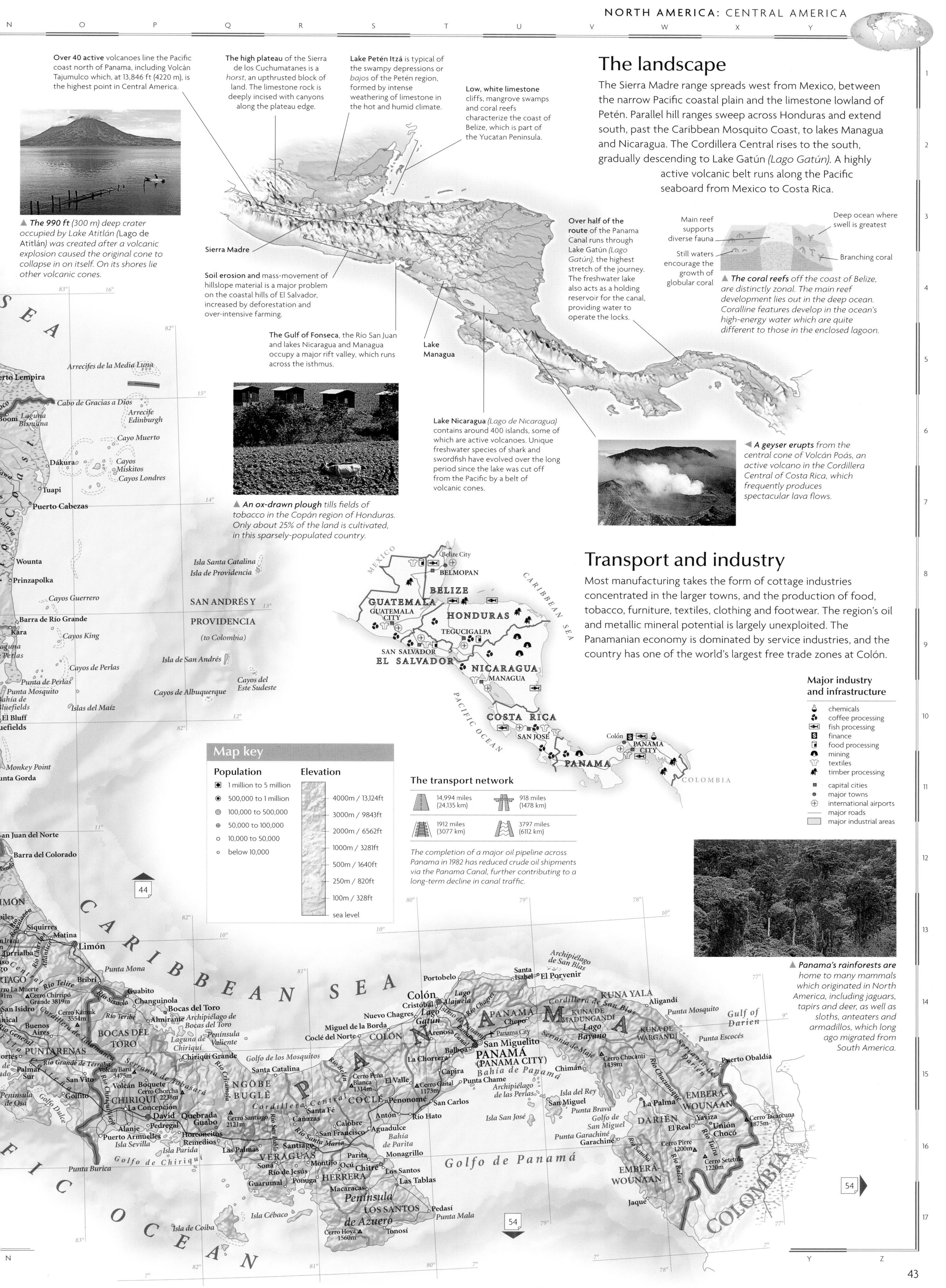

The landscape

The Sierra Madre range spreads west from Mexico, between the narrow Pacific coastal plain and the limestone lowland of Petén. Parallel hill ranges sweep across Honduras and extend south, past the Caribbean Mosquito Coast, to lakes Managua and Nicaragua. The Cordillera Central rises to the south, gradually descending to Lake Gatún *(Lago Gatún)*. A highly active volcanic belt runs along the Pacific seaboard from Mexico to Costa Rica.

Over 40 active volcanoes line the Pacific coast north of Panama, including Volcán Tajumulco which, at 13,846 ft (4220 m), is the highest point in Central America.

The high plateau of the Sierra de los Cuchumatanes is a *horst*, an upthrusted block of land. The limestone rock is deeply incised with canyons along the plateau edge.

Lake Petén Itzá is typical of the swampy depressions or *bajos* of the Petén region, formed by intense weathering of limestone in the hot and humid climate.

Low, white limestone cliffs, mangrove swamps and coral reefs characterize the coast of Belize, which is part of the Yucatan Peninsula.

▲ ***The 990 ft** (300 m) deep crater occupied by Lake Atitlán (*Lago de Atitlán*) was created after a volcanic explosion caused the original cone to collapse in on itself. On its shores lie other volcanic cones.*

Sierra Madre

Soil erosion and mass-movement of hillslope material is a major problem on the coastal hills of El Salvador, increased by deforestation and over-intensive farming.

The Gulf of Fonseca, the Río San Juan and lakes Nicaragua and Managua occupy a major rift valley, which runs across the isthmus.

Lake Managua

Over half of the route of the Panama Canal runs through Lake Gatún *(Lago Gatún)*, the highest stretch of the journey. The freshwater lake also acts as a holding reservoir for the canal, providing water to operate the locks.

Main reef supports diverse fauna

Still waters encourage the growth of globular coral

Deep ocean where swell is greatest

Branching coral

▲ ***The coral reefs** off the coast of Belize, are distinctly zonal. The main reef development lies out in the deep ocean. Coralline features develop in the ocean's high-energy water which are quite different to those in the enclosed lagoon.*

Lake Nicaragua *(Lago de Nicaragua)* contains around 400 islands, some of which are active volcanoes. Unique freshwater species of shark and swordfish have evolved over the long period since the lake was cut off from the Pacific by a belt of volcanic cones.

▲ ***An ox-drawn plough** tills fields of tobacco in the Copán region of Honduras. Only about 25% of the land is cultivated, in this sparsely-populated country.*

◄ ***A geyser erupts** from the central cone of Volcán Poás, an active volcano in the Cordillera Central of Costa Rica, which frequently produces spectacular lava flows.*

Transport and industry

Most manufacturing takes the form of cottage industries concentrated in the larger towns, and the production of food, tobacco, furniture, textiles, clothing and footwear. The region's oil and metallic mineral potential is largely unexploited. The Panamanian economy is dominated by service industries, and the country has one of the world's largest free trade zones at Colón.

Major industry and infrastructure

- chemicals
- coffee processing
- fish processing
- finance
- food processing
- mining
- textiles
- timber processing
- capital cities
- major towns
- international airports
- major roads
- major industrial areas

The transport network

14,994 miles (24,135 km)	918 miles (1478 km)
1912 miles (3077 km)	3797 miles (6112 km)

The completion of a major oil pipeline across Panama in 1982 has reduced crude oil shipments via the Panama Canal, further contributing to a long-term decline in canal traffic.

Map key

Population

- 1 million to 5 million
- 500,000 to 1 million
- 100,000 to 500,000
- 50,000 to 100,000
- 10,000 to 50,000
- below 10,000

Elevation

- 4000m / 13,124ft
- 3000m / 9843ft
- 2000m / 6562ft
- 1000m / 3281ft
- 500m / 1640ft
- 250m / 820ft
- 100m / 328ft
- sea level

▲ *Panama's rainforests are home to many mammals which originated in North America, including jaguars, tapirs and deer, as well as sloths, anteaters and armadillos, which long ago migrated from South America.*

44

54

54

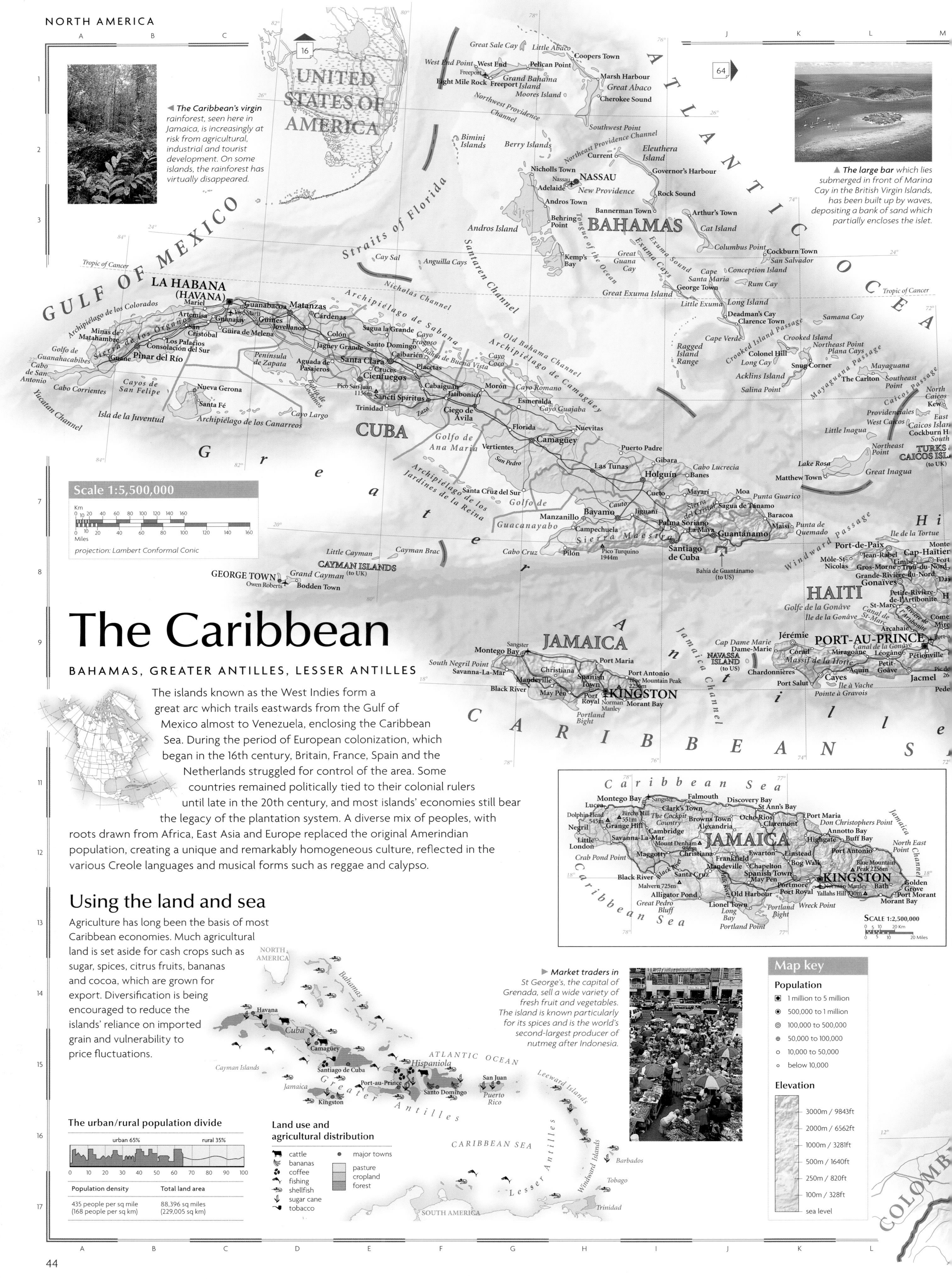

◄ The Caribbean's virgin rainforest, seen here in Jamaica, is increasingly at risk from agricultural, industrial and tourist development. On some islands, the rainforest has virtually disappeared.

▲ The large bar which lies submerged in front of Marina Cay in the British Virgin Islands, has been built up by waves, depositing a bank of sand which partially encloses the islet.

Scale 1:5,500,000

projection: Lambert Conformal Conic

The Caribbean

BAHAMAS, GREATER ANTILLES, LESSER ANTILLES

The islands known as the West Indies form a great arc which trails eastwards from the Gulf of Mexico almost to Venezuela, enclosing the Caribbean Sea. During the period of European colonization, which began in the 16th century, Britain, France, Spain and the Netherlands struggled for control of the area. Some countries remained politically tied to their colonial rulers until late in the 20th century, and most islands' economies still bear the legacy of the plantation system. A diverse mix of peoples, with roots drawn from Africa, East Asia and Europe replaced the original Amerindian population, creating a unique and remarkably homogeneous culture, reflected in the various Creole languages and musical forms such as reggae and calypso.

Using the land and sea

Agriculture has long been the basis of most Caribbean economies. Much agricultural land is set aside for cash crops such as sugar, spices, citrus fruits, bananas and cocoa, which are grown for export. Diversification is being encouraged to reduce the islands' reliance on imported grain and vulnerability to price fluctuations.

► Market traders in St George's, the capital of Grenada, sell a wide variety of fresh fruit and vegetables. The island is known particularly for its spices and is the world's second-largest producer of nutmeg after Indonesia.

The urban/rural population divide

urban 65% | rural 35%

Population density	Total land area
435 people per sq mile (168 people per sq km)	88,396 sq miles (229,005 sq km)

Land use and agricultural distribution

cattle, bananas, coffee, fishing, shellfish, sugar cane, tobacco, major towns, pasture, cropland, forest

Map key

Population

- 1 million to 5 million
- 500,000 to 1 million
- 100,000 to 500,000
- 50,000 to 100,000
- 10,000 to 50,000
- below 10,000

Elevation

- 3000m / 9843ft
- 2000m / 6562ft
- 1000m / 3281ft
- 500m / 1640ft
- 250m / 820ft
- 100m / 328ft
- sea level

Transport and industry

Caribbean industry remains, with few exceptions, agricultural and export-led, or service-based, supporting the flourishing tourist industry. However, several countries including Jamaica, Barbados, Trinidad and Tobago and Puerto Rico have developed important mineral industries, and Cuba is attempting to diversify its economy by importing capital goods to start up new manufacturing businesses.

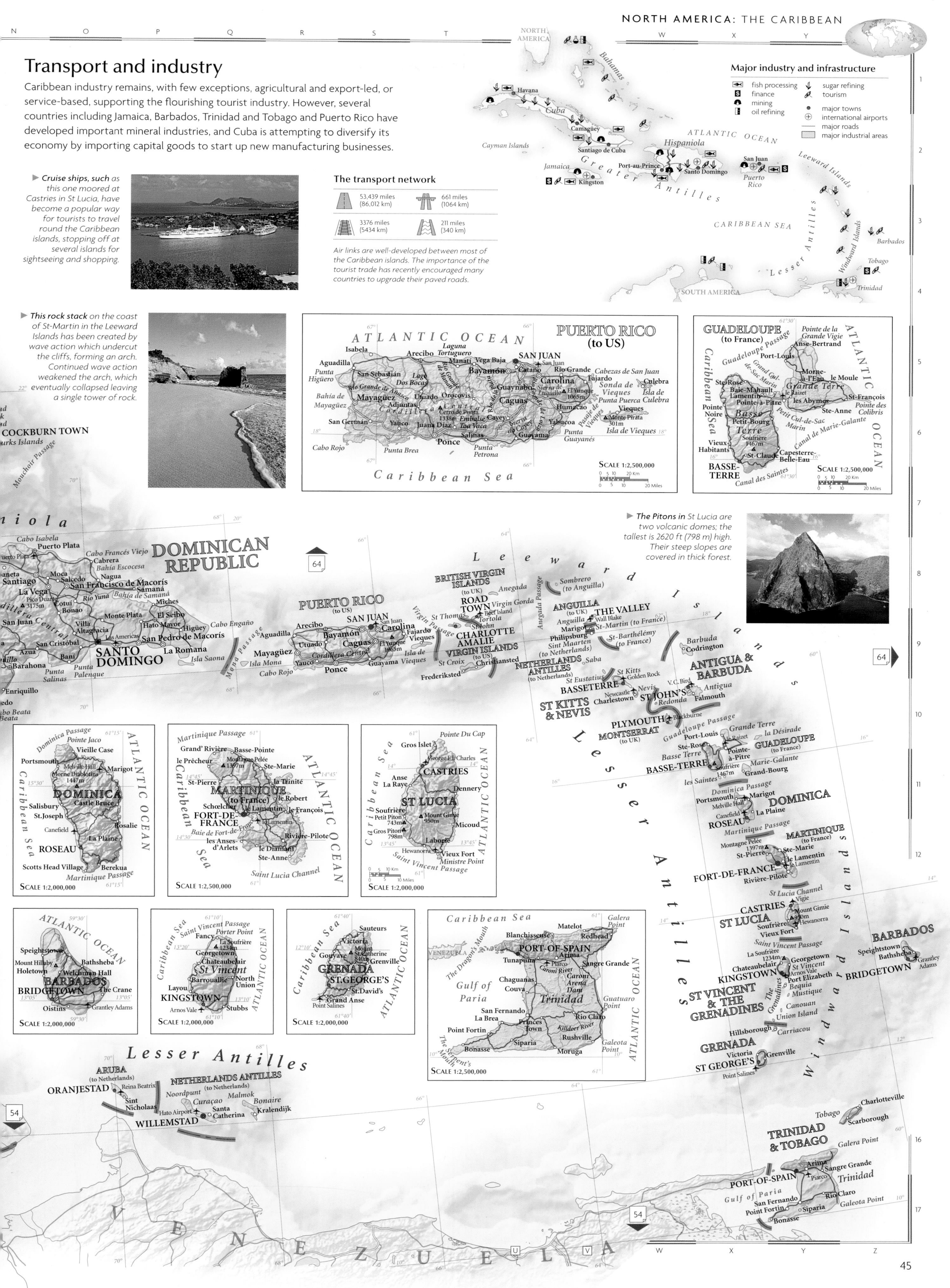

Major industry and infrastructure
fish processing
finance
mining
oil refining
sugar refining
tourism
major towns
international airports
major roads
major industrial areas
The transport network
53,439 miles (86,012 km)
661 miles (1064 km)
3376 miles (5434 km)
211 miles (340 km)
Air links are well-developed between most of the Caribbean islands. The importance of the tourist trade has recently encouraged many countries to upgrade their paved roads.
ATLANTIC OCEAN
CARIBBEAN SEA
Greater Antilles
Lesser Antilles
Leeward Islands
Windward Islands
Havana
Cuba
Camagüey
Santiago de Cuba
Cayman Islands
Jamaica
Kingston
Hispaniola
Port-au-Prince
Santo Domingo
San Juan
Puerto Rico
Barbados
Tobago
Trinidad
SOUTH AMERICA
PUERTO RICO (to US)
SCALE 1:2,500,000
GUADELOUPE (to France)
SCALE 1:2,500,000
DOMINICAN REPUBLIC
SANTO DOMINGO
BRITISH VIRGIN ISLANDS (to UK)
ROAD TOWN
VIRGIN ISLANDS (to US)
CHARLOTTE AMALIE
ANGUILLA (to UK)
THE VALLEY
NETHERLANDS ANTILLES (to Netherlands)
ANTIGUA & BARBUDA
ST JOHN'S
ST KITTS & NEVIS
BASSETERRE
PLYMOUTH
MONTSERRAT (to UK)
GUADELOUPE (to France)
BASSE-TERRE
DOMINICA
ROSEAU
MARTINIQUE (to France)
FORT-DE-FRANCE
CASTRIES
ST LUCIA
BARBADOS
BRIDGETOWN
KINGSTOWN
ST VINCENT & THE GRENADINES
GRENADA
ST GEORGE'S
TRINIDAD & TOBAGO
PORT-OF-SPAIN
DOMINICA
SCALE 1:2,000,000
MARTINIQUE (to France)
SCALE 1:2,500,000
ST LUCIA
SCALE 1:2,000,000
BARBADOS
SCALE 1:2,000,000
St Vincent
KINGSTOWN
SCALE 1:2,000,000
GRENADA
ST.GEORGE'S
SCALE 1:2,000,000
Trinidad
PORT-OF-SPAIN
SCALE 1:2,500,000
Lesser Antilles
ARUBA (to Netherlands)
ORANJESTAD
NETHERLANDS ANTILLES (to Netherlands)
WILLEMSTAD
Curaçao
Bonaire
VENEZUELA
COCKBURN TOWN
64
54

► Cruise ships, such as this one moored at Castries in St Lucia, have become a popular way for tourists to travel round the Caribbean islands, stopping off at several islands for sightseeing and shopping.

► This rock stack on the coast of St-Martin in the Leeward Islands has been created by wave action which undercut the cliffs, forming an arch. Continued wave action weakened the arch, which eventually collapsed leaving a single tower of rock.

► The Pitons in St Lucia are two volcanic domes; the tallest is 2620 ft (798 m) high. Their steep slopes are covered in thick forest.

South America

Reaching from the humid tropics down into the cold south Atlantic, South America has an area of 6,886,000 sq miles (17,835,000 sq km). There are 12 separate countries, with the largest, Brazil, covering almost half the continent.

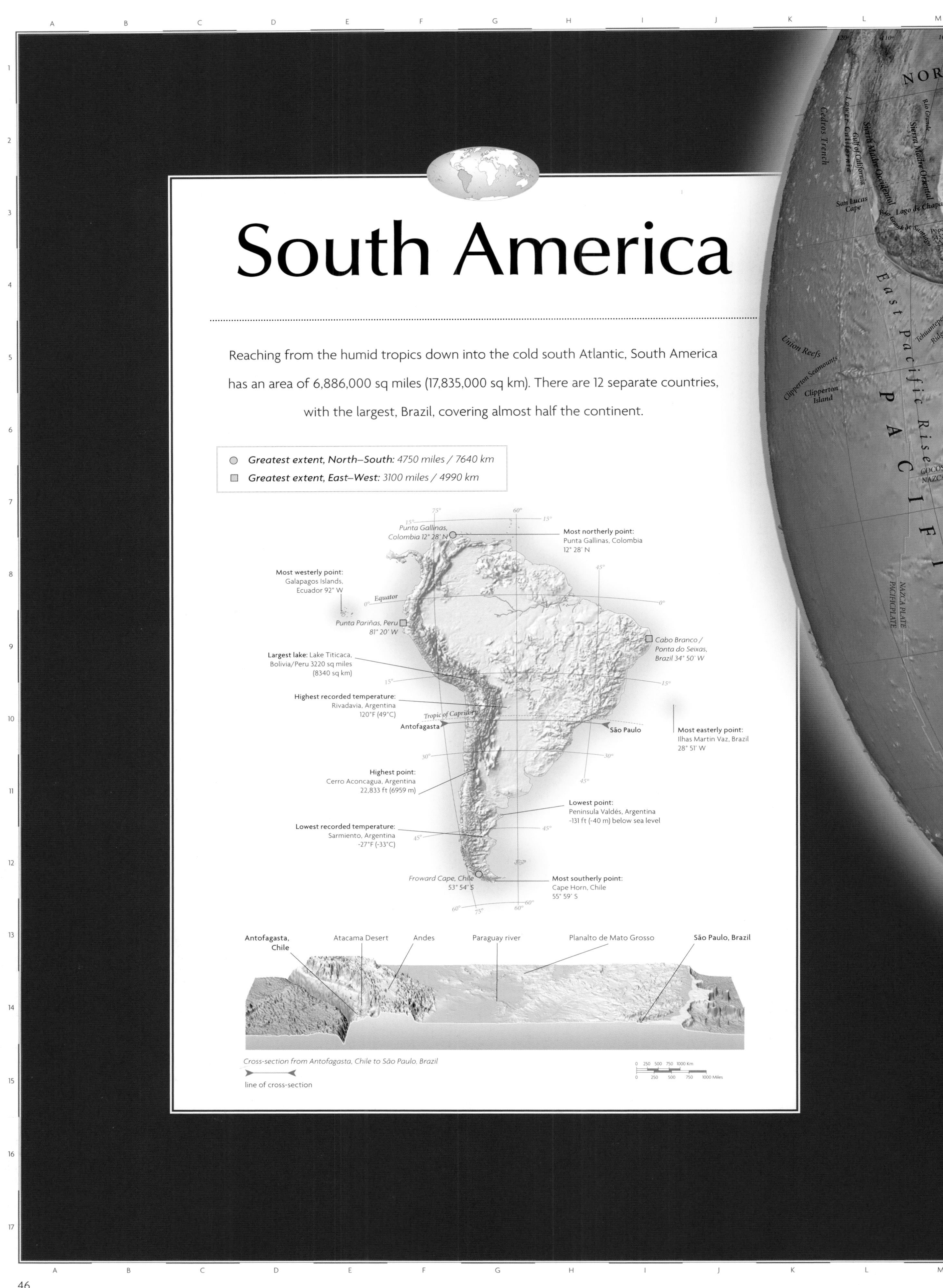

Greatest extent, North–South: 4750 miles / 7640 km
Greatest extent, East–West: 3100 miles / 4990 km
Punta Gallinas, Colombia 12° 28' N
Most northerly point: Punta Gallinas, Colombia 12° 28' N
Most westerly point: Galapagos Islands, Ecuador 92° W
Equator
Punta Pariñas, Peru 81° 20' W
Cabo Branco / Ponta do Seixas, Brazil 34° 50' W
Largest lake: Lake Titicaca, Bolivia/Peru 3220 sq miles (8340 sq km)
Highest recorded temperature: Rivadavia, Argentina 120°F (49°C)
Tropic of Capricorn
Antofagasta
São Paulo
Most easterly point: Ilhas Martin Vaz, Brazil 28° 51' W
Highest point: Cerro Aconcagua, Argentina 22,833 ft (6959 m)
Lowest point: Peninsula Valdés, Argentina -131 ft (-40 m) below sea level
Lowest recorded temperature: Sarmiento, Argentina -27°F (-33°C)
Froward Cape, Chile 53° 54' S
Most southerly point: Cape Horn, Chile 55° 59' S
Antofagasta, Chile
Atacama Desert
Andes
Paraguay river
Planalto de Mato Grosso
São Paulo, Brazil
Cross-section from Antofagasta, Chile to São Paulo, Brazil
line of cross-section
NORT
Cedros Trench
Lower California
Gulf of California
Sierra Madre Occidental
Sierra Madre Oriental
Rio Grande
San Lucas Cape
Lago de Chapala
East Pacific Rise
Tehuantepec Ridge
Union Reefs
Clipperton Seamounts
Clipperton Island
PACIFIC
COCOS PL
NAZCA P
NAZCA PLATE
PACIFIC PLATE

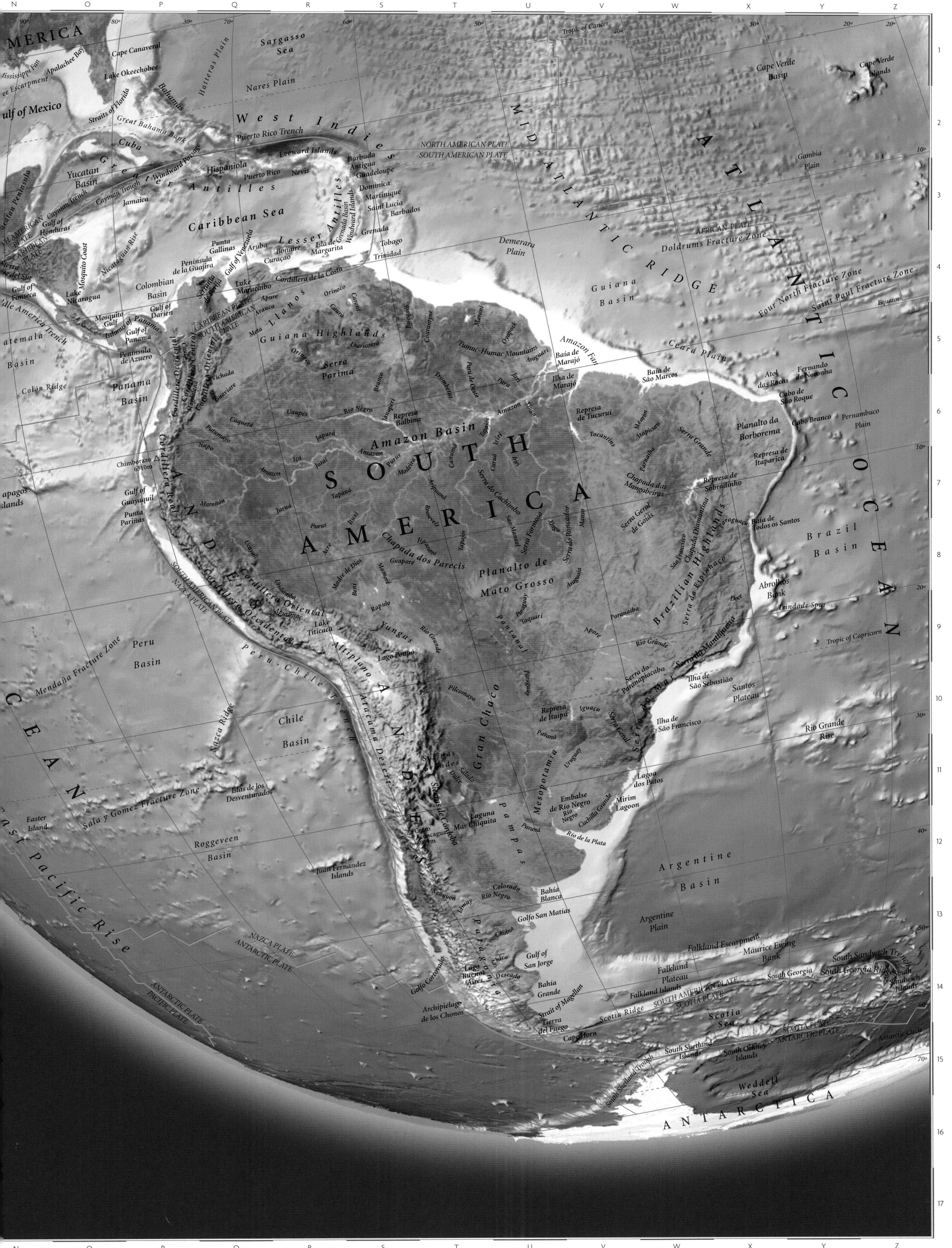

SOUTH AMERICA
ATLANTIC OCEAN
MID-ATLANTIC RIDGE
West Indies
Greater Antilles
Lesser Antilles
Caribbean Sea
Sargasso Sea
Nares Plain
Hatteras Plain
Gulf of Mexico
Cape Canaveral
Lake Okeechobee
Apalachee Bay
Bahamas
Straits of Florida
Great Bahama Bank
Cuba
Yucatan Basin
Cayman Trench
Cayman Trough
Windward Passage
Jamaica
Hispaniola
Puerto Rico
Puerto Rico Trench
Leeward Islands
Nevis
Barbuda
Antigua
Guadeloupe
Dominica
Martinique
Saint Lucia
Barbados
Grenada
Tobago
Trinidad
Windward Islands
Grenada Basin
Gulf of Honduras
Nicaraguan Rise
Mosquito Coast
Lake Nicaragua
Gulf of Fonseca
Punta Gallinas
Peninsula de la Guajira
Gulf of Venezuela
Aruba
Curaçao
Bonaire
Isla de Margarita
Lake Maracaibo
Cordillera de la Costa
Colombian Basin
Gulf of Darien
Mosquito Gulf
Isthmus of Panama
Gulf of Panama
Peninsula de Azuero
Panama Basin
Colón Ridge
Middle America Trench
Guatemala Trench
NORTH AMERICAN PLATE
SOUTH AMERICAN PLATE
CARIBBEAN PLATE
AFRICAN PLATE
Tropic of Cancer
Cape Verde Basin
Cape Verde Islands
Gambia Plain
Doldrums Fracture Zone
Four North Fracture Zone
Saint Paul Fracture Zone
Equator
Demerara Plain
Guiana Basin
Amazon Fan
Ceará Plain
Baía de Marajó
Ilha de Marajó
Baía de São Marcos
Atol das Rocas
Fernando de Noronha
Cabo de São Roque
Cabo Branco
Pernambuco Plain
Planalto da Borborema
Represa de Itaparica
Represa de Sobradinho
Baía de Todos os Santos
Brazil Basin
Abrolhos Bank
Trindade Spur
Tropic of Capricorn
Llanos
Guiana Highlands
Serra Parima
Tumuc-Humac Mountains
Orinoco
Apure
Meta
Caroni
Caura
Essequibo
Courantyne
Maroni
Oyapock
Araguari
Uraricoera
Branco
Trombetas
Paru de Oeste
Jari
Paru
Rio Negro
Uaupés
Japurá
Caquetá
Putumayo
Napo
Amazon
Amazon Basin
Represa Balbina
Uatumã
Xingu
Represa de Tucuruí
Tocantins
Mearim
Itapicuru
Parnaíba
Serra Grande
Chapada das Mangabeiras
Serra Geral de Goiás
Chapada Diamantina
São Francisco
Paraguaçu
Brazilian Highlands
Serra do Espinhaço
Doce
Cordillera Occidental
Cordillera Central
Cordillera Oriental
Magdalena
Cauca
Vichada
Guaviare
Chimborazo 6310m
Gulf of Guayaquil
Punta Pariñas
Cordillera Real
Marañón
Ucayali
Juruá
Içá
Jutaí
Purus
Madeira
Tapauá
Ituxi
Acre
Canumã
Aripuanã
Roosevelt
Curuá
Iriri
Serra do Cachimbo
Teles Pires
Juruena
Ji-Paraná
Serra Formosa
Serra do Roncador
Manso
Chapada dos Parecis
Planalto de Mato Grosso
Mamoré
Guaporé
Madre de Dios
Beni
Rapulo
Urubamba
Apurimac
Cordillera Oriental
Cordillera Occidental
ANDES
Lake Titicaca
Yungas
Rio Grande
Lago Poopó
Altiplano
Atacama Desert
Paraguay
Taquari
pantanal
Araguaia
Paranaíba
Aporé
Rio Grande
Serra da Mantiqueira
Serra do Paranapiacaba
Serra do Mar
Ilha de São Sebastião
Santos Plateau
Represa de Itaipu
Iguaçu
Serra Geral
Paraná
Ilha de São Francisco
Rio Grande Rise
Pilcomayo
Bermejo
Gran Chaco
Salado
Dulce
Uruguay
Mesopotamia
Lagoa dos Patos
Embalse de Río Negro
Cuchilla Grande
Mirim Lagoon
Laguna Mar Chiquita
Cerro Aconcagua 6959m
Sierras de Córdoba
pampas
Río de la Plata
Argentine Basin
Argentine Plain
Colorado
Río Negro
Neuquén
Limay
Bahía Blanca
Golfo San Matías
Chubut
Chico
Deseado
Gulf of San Jorge
Patagonia
Lago Buenos Aires
Golfo Corcovado
Archipiélago de los Chonos
Bahía Grande
Strait of Magellan
Tierra del Fuego
Cape Horn
Falkland Escarpment
Maurice Ewing Bank
Falkland Plateau
Falkland Islands
South Georgia
South Georgia Ridge
South Sandwich Trench
South Sandwich Islands
Scotia Ridge
Scotia Sea
SCOTIA PLATE
ANTARCTIC PLATE
Antarctic Circle
South Shetland Islands
South Shetland Trough
South Orkney Islands
Weddell Sea
ANTARCTICA
Peru Basin
Peru-Chile Trench
SOUTH AMERICAN PLATE
NAZCA PLATE
Mendaña Fracture Zone
Nazca Ridge
Chile Basin
Islas de los Desventurados
Sala y Gomez Fracture Zone
Easter Island
Roggeveen Basin
Juan Fernandez Islands
East Pacific Rise
PACIFIC PLATE
Galapagos Islands

Physical South America

Three major physiographic regions characterize South America. The oldest, the ancient Brazilian Shield and the smaller Guiana and Patagonian shields, form the stable core of the continent. Stretching along the entire west coast are the younger Andean fold mountains with many summits rising to 20,000 ft (6100 m). These two diverse regions are separated by a number of sedimentary basins carrying South America's large river systems to the sea. These include the massive Amazon Basin and the basin of the Gran Chaco.

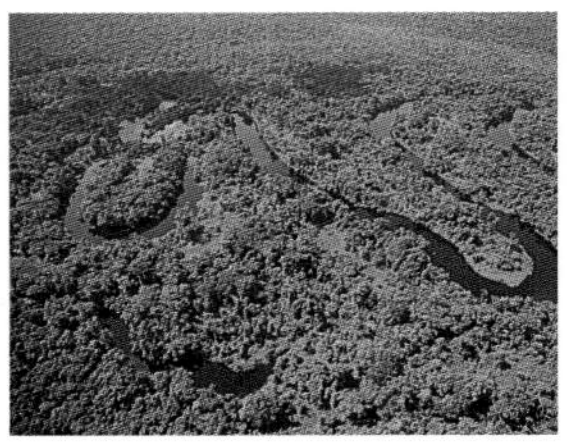

The Amazon Basin and Guiana Shield

The Amazon river occupies a large depression in the Earth's crust, formed by the uplift of the Andes. It is covered by thick volcanic deposits and layers of alluvium – these have been laid down by the Amazon's many tributaries. To the north is the smaller Guiana Shield.

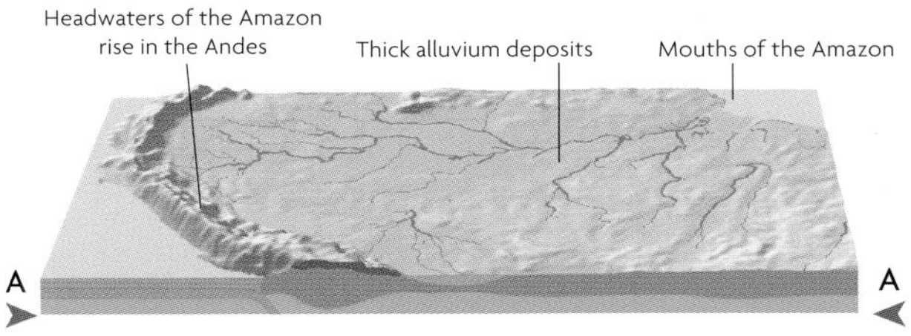

Headwaters of the Amazon rise in the Andes
Thick alluvium deposits
Mouths of the Amazon

***Section across northern** South America showing Amazon Basin and its drainage pattern.*

Scale 1:27,500,000

projection: Lambert Azimuthal Equal Area

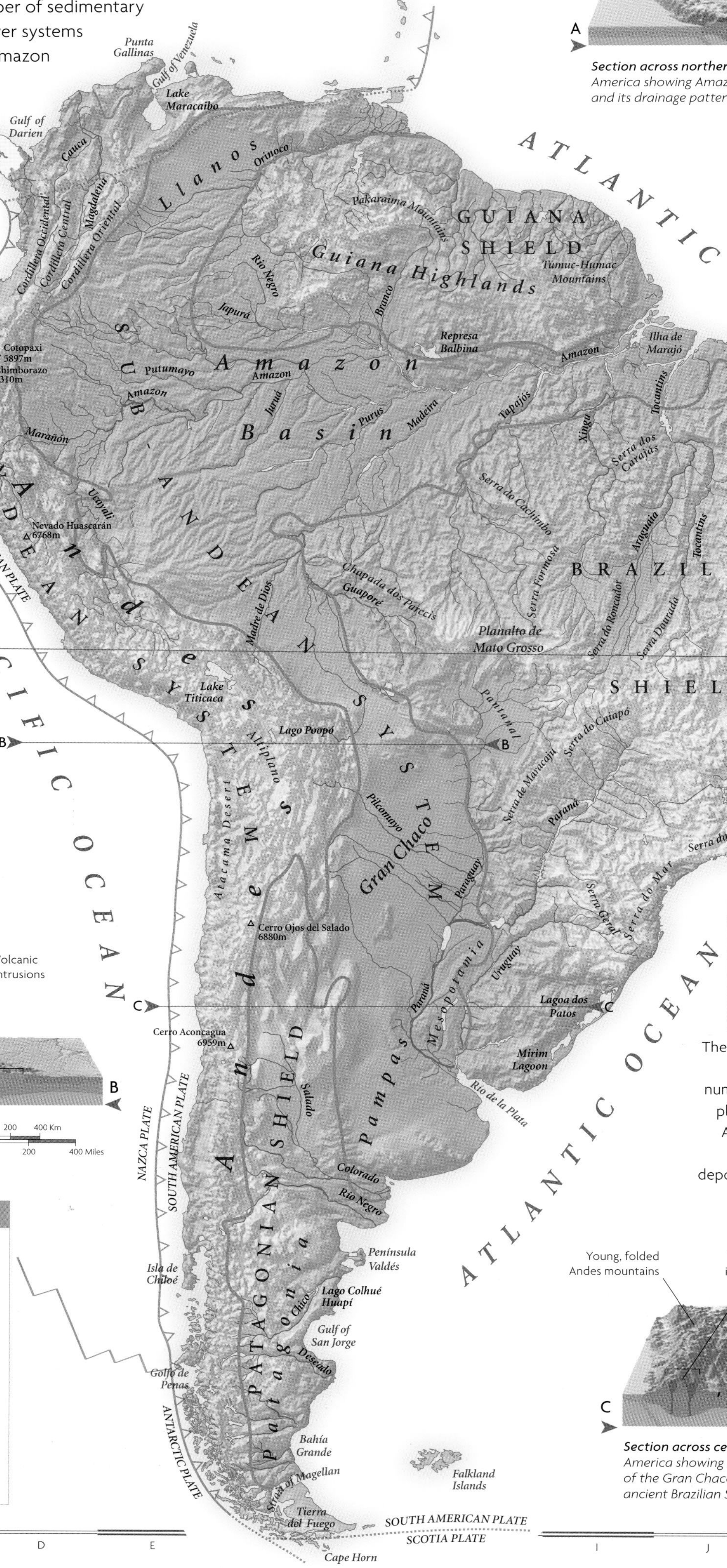

The Andean Uplands

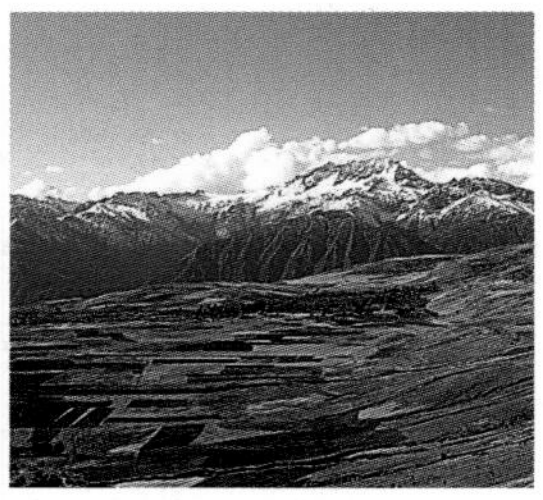

The Andean Uplands run along the west coast of South America. They are being uplifted as the Nazca Plate is subducted beneath the South American Plate. They contain some of the world's largest volcanoes, such as Cotopaxi, and Lake Titicaca which occupies a dormant site. The far south has many large ice-sheets and a fragmented coastline.

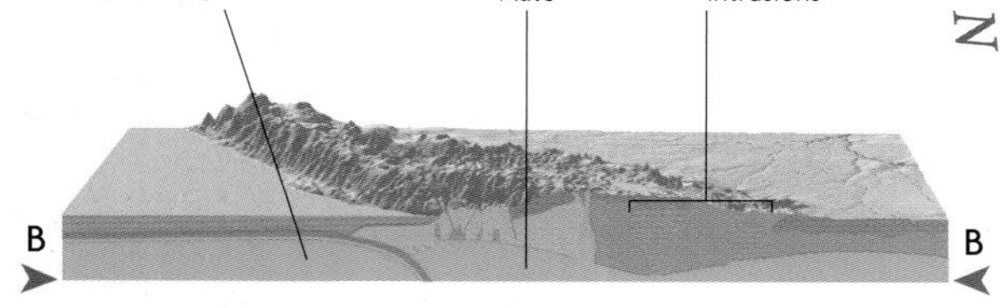

Nazca Plate
South American Plate
Volcanic intrusions

***Cross-section through the** Andes showing the subduction of the Nazca Plate beneath the South American Plate.*

The Brazilian Shield and Gran Chaco

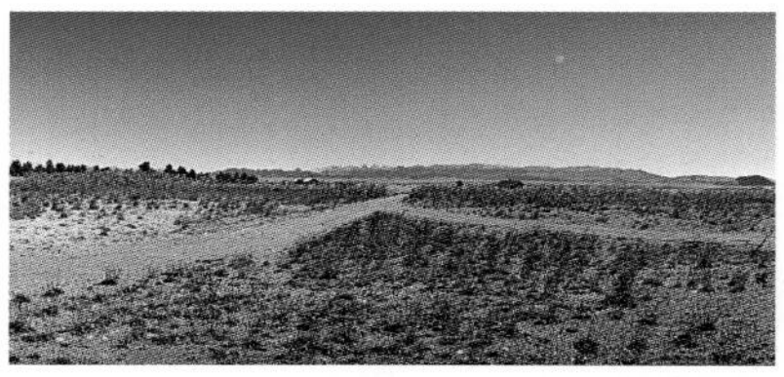

The immense Brazilian Shield underlies more than one-third of South America. It is pitted with numerous volcanic intrusions, and a large basaltic plateau exists between the Paraná river and the Atlantic Ocean. The flat Gran Chaco lies to the west of the shield, covered by sedimentary deposits eroded from the Andes, and transported by South America's mighty rivers.

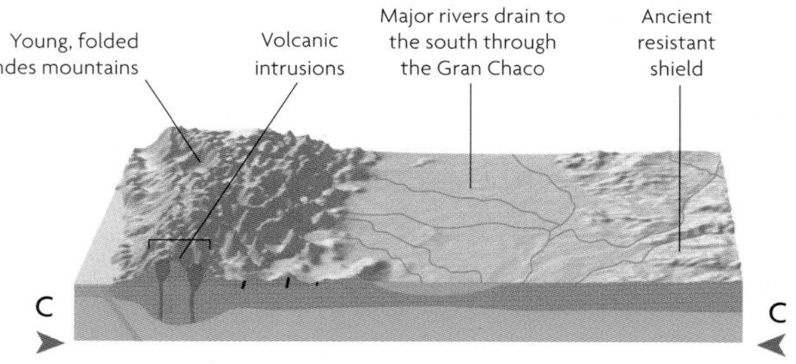

Young, folded Andes mountains
Volcanic intrusions
Major rivers drain to the south through the Gran Chaco
Ancient resistant shield

***Section across central** South America showing the flat basin of the Gran Chaco and the ancient Brazilian Shield.*

Map key

Elevation

- 6000m / 19,686ft
- 4000m / 13,124ft
- 3000m / 9843ft
- 2000m / 6562ft
- 1000m / 3281ft
- 500m / 1640ft
- 250m / 820ft
- 100m / 328ft
- sea level

Plate margins (for explanation see page xiv)

- constructive
- destructive
- conservative
- uncertain
- physiographic regions
- line of cross-section

ATLANTIC OCEAN
PACIFIC OCEAN
GUIANA SHIELD
Guiana Highlands
Amazon Basin
BRAZILIAN SHIELD
Brazilian Highlands
ANDEAN SYSTEM
SUBANDEAN SYSTEM
PATAGONIAN SHIELD
Patagonia
Llanos
Gran Chaco
Pampas
Mesopotamia
Punta Gallinas
Gulf of Venezuela
Lake Maracaibo
Gulf of Darien
Gulf of Panama
COCOS PLATE
NAZCA PLATE
SOUTH AMERICAN PLATE
ANTARCTIC PLATE
SCOTIA PLATE
Cotopaxi 5897m
Chimborazo 6310m
Nevado Huascarán 6768m
Cerro Ojos del Salado 6880m
Cerro Aconcagua 6959m
Gulf of Guayaquil
Punta Negra
Lake Titicaca
Lago Poopó
Altiplano
Atacama Desert
Planalto de Mato Grosso
Planalto da Borborema
Cabo de São Roque
Represa de Sobradinho
Represa Balbina
Ilha de Marajó
Tumuc-Humac Mountains
Pakaraima Mountains
Lagoa dos Patos
Mirim Lagoon
Río de la Plata
Península Valdés
Lago Colhué Huapí
Gulf of San Jorge
Golfo de Penas
Isla de Chiloé
Bahía Grande
Strait of Magellan
Tierra del Fuego
Cape Horn
Falkland Islands

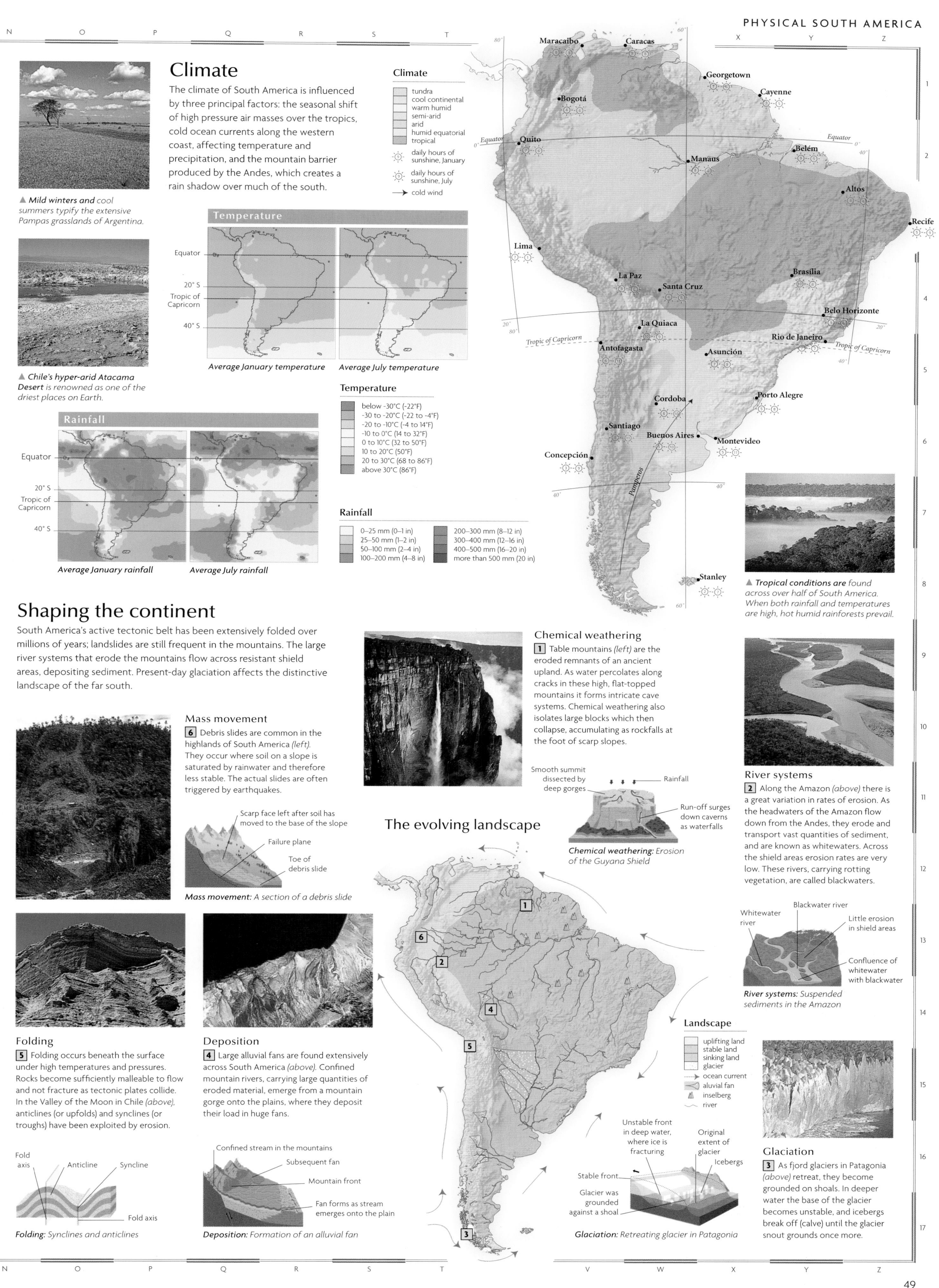
Climate
The climate of South America is influenced by three principal factors: the seasonal shift of high pressure air masses over the tropics, cold ocean currents along the western coast, affecting temperature and precipitation, and the mountain barrier produced by the Andes, which creates a rain shadow over much of the south.
▲ Mild winters and cool summers typify the extensive Pampas grasslands of Argentina.
▲ Chile's hyper-arid Atacama Desert is renowned as one of the driest places on Earth.
Climate
tundra
cool continental
warm humid
semi-arid
arid
humid equatorial
tropical
daily hours of sunshine, January
daily hours of sunshine, July
cold wind
Temperature
Equator
20° S
Tropic of Capricorn
40° S
Average January temperature
Average July temperature
Temperature
below -30°C (-22°F)
-30 to -20°C (-22 to -4°F)
-20 to -10°C (-4 to 14°F)
-10 to 0°C (14 to 32°F)
0 to 10°C (32 to 50°F)
10 to 20°C (50°F)
20 to 30°C (68 to 86°F)
above 30°C (86°F)
Rainfall
Equator
20° S
Tropic of Capricorn
40° S
Average January rainfall
Average July rainfall
Rainfall
0–25 mm (0–1 in)
25–50 mm (1–2 in)
50–100 mm (2–4 in)
100–200 mm (4–8 in)
200–300 mm (8–12 in)
300–400 mm (12–16 in)
400–500 mm (16–20 in)
more than 500 mm (20 in)
Maracaibo
Caracas
Georgetown
Cayenne
Bogotá
Equator
Quito
Belém
Manaus
Altos
Recife
Lima
La Paz
Santa Cruz
Brasília
Belo Horizonte
La Quiaca
Tropic of Capricorn
Antofagasta
Rio de Janeiro
Asunción
Porto Alegre
Cordoba
Santiago
Buenos Aires
Montevideo
Concepción
Pamperos
Stanley
▲ Tropical conditions are found across over half of South America. When both rainfall and temperatures are high, hot humid rainforests prevail.
Shaping the continent
South America's active tectonic belt has been extensively folded over millions of years; landslides are still frequent in the mountains. The large river systems that erode the mountains flow across resistant shield areas, depositing sediment. Present-day glaciation affects the distinctive landscape of the far south.
Chemical weathering
1 Table mountains (left) are the eroded remnants of an ancient upland. As water percolates along cracks in these high, flat-topped mountains it forms intricate cave systems. Chemical weathering also isolates large blocks which then collapse, accumulating as rockfalls at the foot of scarp slopes.
Smooth summit dissected by deep gorges
Rainfall
Run-off surges down caverns as waterfalls
Chemical weathering: Erosion of the Guyana Shield
Mass movement
6 Debris slides are common in the highlands of South America (left). They occur where soil on a slope is saturated by rainwater and therefore less stable. The actual slides are often triggered by earthquakes.
Scarp face left after soil has moved to the base of the slope
Failure plane
Toe of debris slide
Mass movement: A section of a debris slide
The evolving landscape
River systems
2 Along the Amazon (above) there is a great variation in rates of erosion. As the headwaters of the Amazon flow down from the Andes, they erode and transport vast quantities of sediment, and are known as whitewaters. Across the shield areas erosion rates are very low. These rivers, carrying rotting vegetation, are called blackwaters.
Whitewater river
Blackwater river
Little erosion in shield areas
Confluence of whitewater with blackwater
River systems: Suspended sediments in the Amazon
Folding
5 Folding occurs beneath the surface under high temperatures and pressures. Rocks become sufficiently malleable to flow and not fracture as tectonic plates collide. In the Valley of the Moon in Chile (above), anticlines (or upfolds) and synclines (or troughs) have been exploited by erosion.
Fold axis
Anticline
Syncline
Fold axis
Folding: Synclines and anticlines
Deposition
4 Large alluvial fans are found extensively across South America (above). Confined mountain rivers, carrying large quantities of eroded material, emerge from a mountain gorge onto the plains, where they deposit their load in huge fans.
Confined stream in the mountains
Subsequent fan
Mountain front
Fan forms as stream emerges onto the plain
Deposition: Formation of an alluvial fan
Landscape
uplifting land
stable land
sinking land
glacier
ocean current
aluvial fan
inselberg
river
Unstable front in deep water, where ice is fracturing
Original extent of glacier
Icebergs
Stable front
Glacier was grounded against a shoal
Glaciation: Retreating glacier in Patagonia
Glaciation
3 As fjord glaciers in Patagonia (above) retreat, they become grounded on shoals. In deeper water the base of the glacier becomes unstable, and icebergs break off (calve) until the glacier snout grounds once more.

Political South America

Modern South America's political boundaries have their origins in the territorial endeavours of explorers during the 16th century, who claimed almost the entire continent for Portugal and Spain. The Portuguese land in the east later evolved into the federal states of Brazil, while the Spanish vice-royalties eventually emerged as separate independent nation-states in the early 19th century. South America's growing population has become increasingly urbanized, with the expansion of coastal cities into large conurbations like Rio de Janeiro and Buenos Aires. In Brazil, Argentina, Chile and Uruguay, a succession of military dictatorships has given way to fragile, but strengthening, democracies.

◀ ***Europe retains a*** *small foothold in South America. Kourou in French Guiana was the site chosen by the European Space Agency to launch the Ariane rocket. As a result of its status as a French overseas department, French Guiana is actually part of the European Union.*

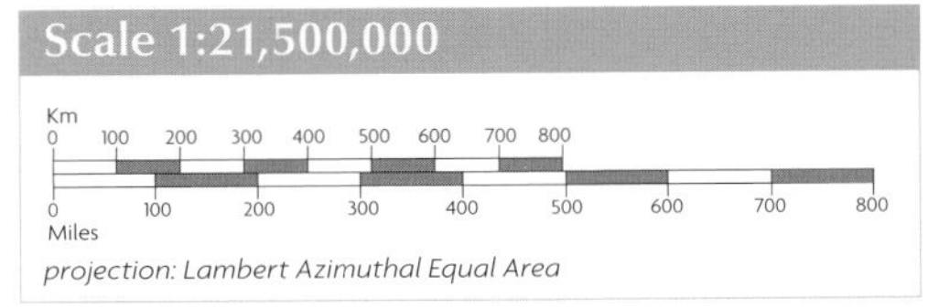
Scale 1:21,500,000
Km
0 100 200 300 400 500 600 700 800
0 100 200 300 400 500 600 700 800
Miles
projection: Lambert Azimuthal Equal Area

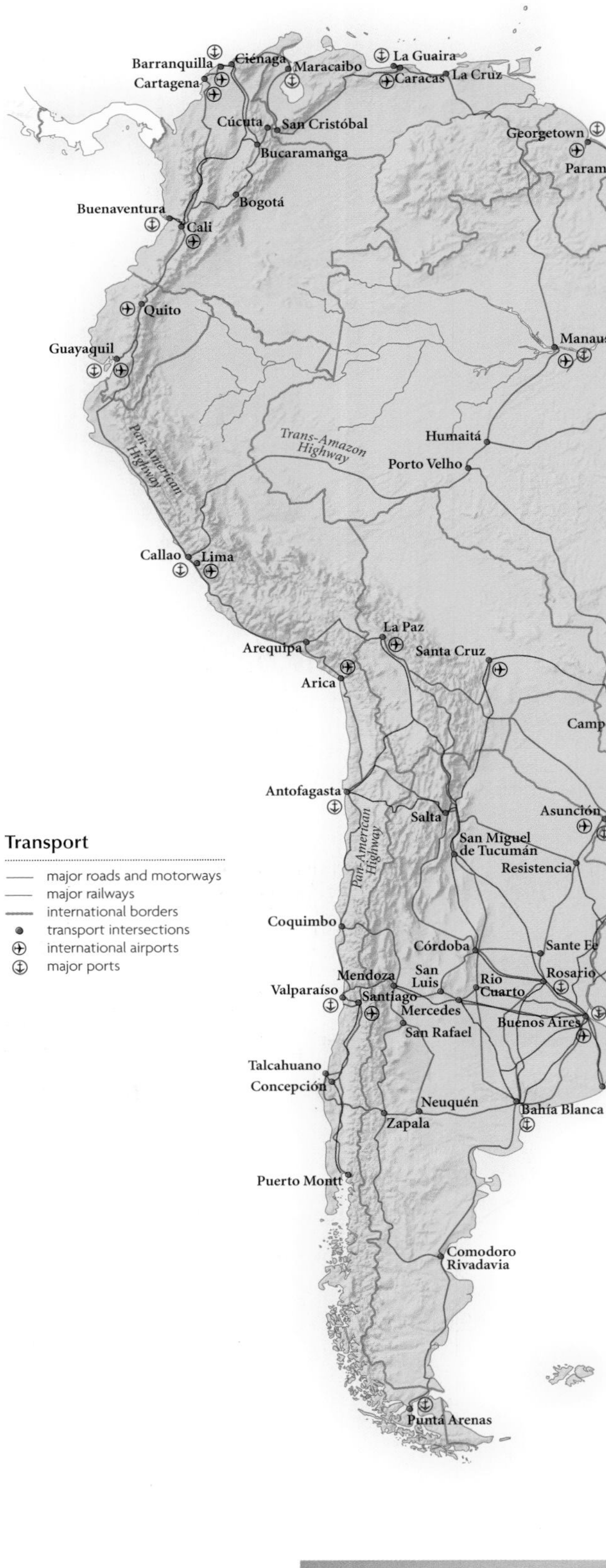

Transport

Most major road and rail routes are confined to the coastal regions by the forbidding natural barriers of the Andes mountains and the Amazon Basin. Few major cross-continental routes exist, although Buenos Aires serves as a transport centre for the main rail links to La Paz and Valparaíso, while the construction of the Trans-Amazon and Pan-American Highways have made direct road travel possible from Recife to Lima and from Puerto Montt up the coast into central America. A new waterway project is proposed to transform the Paraguay river into a major shipping route, although it involves considerable wetland destruction.

▶ ***South America's most*** *extensive rail network is centred on the Argentinian capital, Buenos Aires.The construction of new rail lines from this important port, allowed the colonization of the Pampas lands for agriculture.*

Transport

- major roads and motorways
- major railways
- international borders
- transport intersections
- international airports
- major ports

Languages

Prior to European exploration in the 16th century, a diverse range of indigenous languages were spoken across the continent. With the arrival of Iberian settlers, Spanish became the dominant language, with Portuguese spoken in Brazil, and Native American languages such as Quechua and Guaraní, becoming concentrated in the continental interior. Today this pattern persists, although successive European colonization has led to Dutch being spoken in Surinam, English in Guyana, and French in French Guiana, while in large urban areas, Japanese and Chinese are increasingly common.

Language groups

- American Indian
- Germanic
- Romance

▶ ***Chile's main port,*** *Valparaíso, is a vital national shipping centre, in addition to playing a key role in the growing trade with Pacific nations. The country's awkward, elongated shape means that sea transport is frequently used for internal travel and communications in Chile.*

▲ ***Indigenous South American*** *lifestyles have not been totally submerged by European cultures and languages. The continental interior, and particularly the Amazon Basin, is still home to many different ethnic peoples.*

▶ ***Lima's magnificent cathedral*** *reflects South America's colonial past with its unmistakably Spanish style. In July 1821, Peru became the last Spanish colony on the mainland to declare independence.*

In April 1960, Brazil's government began the move from Rio de Janeiro to Brasília, a futuristic new city built in the sparsely populated interior. Brasília is now the federal capital of Brazil.

Rapid urbanization was a feature of most South American countries in the latter half of the 20th century. In many cases, this unchecked growth has led to the development of sprawling slums, lacking adequate water and sewerage facilities.

Perched high in the Andes like many of the cities in western South America, La Paz, Bolivia is the world's highest capital city at over 11,500 ft (3500 m).

Map key

Population

- above 5 million
- 1 million to 5 million
- 500,000 to 1 million
- 100,000 to 500,000
- 50,000 to 100,000
- 10,000 to 50,000
- below 10,000
- Country capital
- State capital

Borders

- full international border
- disputed de facto border
- disputed territorial claim border
- state border

Population

Almost half of South America's population lives in Brazil but, due to the large uninhabited expanses of the Amazon Basin, its overall population density is much lower than in other countries. During the 20th century the most important population trend was the movement from rural to urban areas, giving rise to great population concentrations in large cities like São Paulo, Rio de Janeiro, Caracas, Lima, Bogotá and Buenos Aires.

Population density
(people per sq km)

- below 4
- 5–9
- 10–14
- 15–19
- 20–29
- above 30

South American resources

Agriculture still provides the largest single form of employment in South America, although rural unemployment and poverty continue to drive people towards the huge coastal cities in search of jobs and opportunities. Mineral and fuel resources, although substantial, are distributed unevenly; few countries have both fossil fuels and minerals. To break industrial dependence on raw materials, boost manufacturing, and improve infrastructure, governments borrowed heavily from the World Bank in the 1960s and 1970s. This led to the accumulation of massive debts which are unlikely ever to be repaid. Today, Brazil dominates the continent's economic output, followed by Argentina. Recently, the less-developed western side of South America has benefited due to its geographical position; for example Chile is increasingly exporting raw materials to Japan.

◀ *Ciudad Guayana is a planned industrial complex in eastern Venezuela, built as an iron and steel centre to exploit the nearby iron ore reserves.*

Industry

- aerospace
- brewing
- car/vehicle manufacture
- chemicals
- electronics
- engineering
- finance
- fish processing
- food processing
- hi-tech industry
- iron & steel
- meat processing
- metal refining
- narcotics
- pharmaceuticals
- printing & publishing
- shipbuilding
- sugar processing
- textiles
- timber processing
- tobacco processing
- wine
- oil
- gas
- industrial cities
- major industrial areas

▲ ***The cold Peru Current** flows north from the Antarctic along the Pacific coast of Peru, providing rich nutrients for one of the world's largest fishing grounds. However, over-exploitation has severely reduced Peru's anchovy catch.*

Standard of living

Wealth disparities throughout the continent create a wide gulf between affluent landowners and those afflicted by chronic poverty in inner-city slums. The illicit production of cocaine, and the hugely influential drug barons who control its distribution, contribute to the violent disorder and corruption which affect northwestern South America, de-stabilizing local governments and economies.

Standard of living
(UN human development index)

- low
- high

▶ ***Both Argentina and Chile** are now exploring the southernmost tip of the continent in search of oil. Here in Punta Arenas, a drilling rig is being prepared for exploratory drilling in the Strait of Magellan.*

GNI per capita (US$)

- below 999
- 1000–1999
- 2000–2999
- 3000–3999
- 4000–4999
- above 5000

Industry

Argentina and Brazil are South America's most industrialized countries and São Paulo is the continent's leading industrial centre. Long-term government investment in Brazilian industry has encouraged a diverse industrial base; engineering, steel production, food processing, textile manufacture and chemicals predominate. The illegal production of cocaine is economically significant in the Andean countries of Colombia and Bolivia. In Venezuela, the oil-dominated economy has left the country vulnerable to world oil price fluctuations. Food processing and mineral exploitation are common throughout the less industrially developed parts of the continent, including Bolivia, Chile, Ecuador and Peru.

Environmental issues

The Amazon Basin is one of the last great wilderness areas left on Earth. The tropical rainforests which grow there are a valuable genetic resource, containing innumerable unique plants and animals. The forests are increasingly under threat from new and expanding settlements and 'slash and burn' farming techniques, which clear land for the raising of beef cattle, causing land degradation and soil erosion.

▲ ***Clouds of smoke** billow from the burning Amazon rainforest. Over 11,500 sq miles (30,000 sq km) of virgin rainforest are being cleared annually, destroying an ancient, irreplaceable, natural resource and biodiverse habitat.*

Environmental issues

- national parks
- tropical forest
- forest destroyed
- desert
- desertification
- polluted rivers
- marine pollution
- heavy marine pollution
- poor urban air quality

Mineral resources

Over a quarter of the world's known copper reserves are found at the Chuquicamata mine in northern Chile, and other metallic minerals such as tin are found along the length of the Andes. The discovery of oil and gas at Venezuela's Lake Maracaibo in 1917 turned the country into one of the world's leading oil producers. In contrast, South America is virtually devoid of coal, the only significant deposit being on the peninsula of Guajira in Colombia.

◀ ***Copper** is Chile's largest export, most of which is mined at Chuquicamata. Along the length of the Andes, metallic minerals like copper and tin are found in abundance, formed by the excessive pressures and heat involved in mountain-building.*

Mineral resources

- oil field
- gas field
- coal field
- bauxite
- copper
- diamonds
- gold
- iron
- lead
- silver
- tin

Using the land and sea

Many foods now common worldwide originated in South America. These include the potato, tomato, squash, and cassava. Today, large herds of beef cattle roam the temperate grasslands of the Pampas, supporting an extensive meat-packing trade in Argentina, Uruguay and Paraguay. Corn (maize) is grown as a staple crop across the continent and coffee is grown as a cash crop in Brazil and Colombia. Coca plants grown in Bolivia, Peru and Colombia provide most of the world's cocaine. Fish and shellfish are caught off the western coast, especially anchovies off Peru, shrimps off Ecuador and pilchards off Chile.

◀ ***South America, and** Brazil in particular, now leads the world in coffee production, mainly growing* Coffea Arabica *in large plantations. Coffee beans are harvested, roasted and brewed to produce the world's second most popular drink, after tea.*

◀ ***High in the Andes,** hardy alpacas graze on the barren land. Alpacas are thought to have been domesticated by the Incas, whose nobility wore robes made from their wool. Today, they are still reared and prized for their soft, warm fleeces.*

◀ ***The Pampas region** of southeast South America is characterized by extensive, flat plains, and populated by cattle and ranchers (gauchos). Argentina is a major world producer of beef, much of which is exported to the USA for use in hamburgers.*

Using the land and sea

- barren land
- cropland
- desert
- forest
- mountain region
- pasture
- major conurbations
- cattle
- pigs
- sheep
- bananas
- corn (maize)
- citrus fruits
- cocoa
- cotton
- coffee
- fishing
- oil palms
- peanuts
- rubber
- shellfish
- soya beans
- sugar cane
- vineyards
- wheat

Northern South America

COLOMBIA, GUYANA, SURINAM, VENEZUELA, French Guiana (to France)

Fringed by the Pacific and Atlantic oceans and the Caribbean Sea, South America's northern region has a rich range of natural resources, some exploited for centuries by colonial powers including the Spanish, French, Dutch and British, others still to be fully explored. The prospects for further economic development in Colombia, Guyana and Surinam are blighted by drug-related violence and political instability. Venezuela, despite huge incomes from its oil reserves, remains less developed in other industrial sectors. French Guiana is an overseas *département* of France, now seeking greater autonomy. Most of the major population centres, such as Bogotá, have grown up in the temperate conditions of the high Andes or, like Caracas, at strategic points along the Caribbean coast.

▶ **Flowers grown in** *Colombia are exported all over the world, and include fine carnations and roses. Here, workers are cutting roses which have been grown in plastic greenhouses.*

Map key

Population

- 1 million to 5 million
- 500,000 to 1 million
- 100,000 to 500,000
- 50,000 to 100,000
- 10,000 to 50,000
- below 10,000

Elevation

- 4000m / 13,124ft
- 3000m / 9843ft
- 2000m / 6562ft
- 1000m / 3281ft
- 500m / 1640ft
- 250m / 820ft
- 100m / 328ft
- sea level

42

192

56

▲ **Large open squares** *like the Plaza de Bolívar in Bogotá are characteristic of many cities founded by the Spanish.*

◀ **Scattered farms and** *villages have grown up on the gentle slopes of this Colombian river valley, utilizing the fertile soils for farming.*

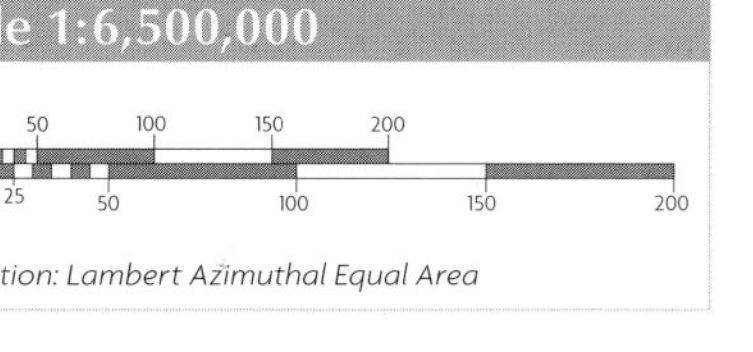
Scale 1:6,500,000
Km
0 25 50 100 150 200
0 25 50 100 150 200
Miles
projection: Lambert Azimuthal Equal Area

56

58

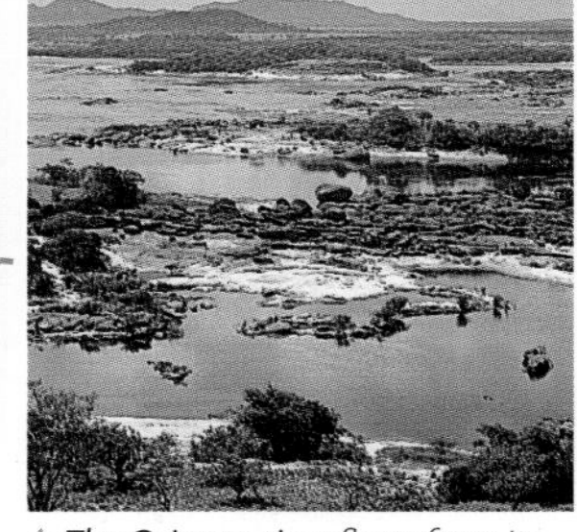

▲ **The Orinoco river** *flows from its source in the southern Guiana Highlands to form a broad delta on Venezuela's Atlantic coast. One of its distributary channels opens into a wide bay called the Serpent's Mouth.*

Transport and industry

Many mineral resources are mined in Colombia, including fuels, gold and precious and semi-precious stones. Revenues from coffee and exports of illegal narcotics are crucial to the economy. Venezuela's major economic activity is the oil industry around Lake Maracaibo *(Lago de Maracaibo)*. Sugar and bauxite are exported from Guyana and Surinam.

The transport network
31,720 miles (51,054 km)
3411 miles (5490 km)
2448 miles (3940 km)
22,429 miles (36,100 km)
Major industry and infrastructure
chemicals
finance
food processing
iron & steel
narcotics
mining
oil
oil refining
pharmaceuticals
textiles
timber processing
capital cities
major towns
international airports
major roads
major industrial areas
Land use and agricultural distribution
cattle
goats
bananas
cereals
coffee
cotton
sugar cane
capital cities
major towns
pasture
cropland
forest
wetlands
mountain region
The urban/rural population divide
urban 80%
rural 20%
Population density
78 people per sq mile (30 people per sq km)
Total land area
1,111,317 sq miles (2,879,060 sq km)
Caribbean Sea
ATLANTIC OCEAN
PACIFIC OCEAN
VENEZUELA
COLOMBIA
GUYANA
SURINAM
FRENCH GUIANA (to France)
BRAZIL
PERU
ECUADOR
PANAMA
CARACAS
BOGOTÁ
GEORGETOWN
PARAMARIBO
CAYENNE
TRINIDAD & TOBAGO
Guiana Highlands
Pakaraima Mountains
Acarai Mountains
Tumuc-Humac Mountains
(Venezuela claims all of Guyana west of Essequibo river)
(Claimed by Surinam)
Guiana Shield
Alluvial plains
Inselbergs
Table mountains
Cordillera Occidental
Cordillera Central
Cordillera Oriental
Potaru river

Rivers are an important means of transport in Colombia; many are extensively navigable. The Pan-American Highway runs through Colombia. In Venezuela, much infrastructure investment is linked to the oil industry.

▲ ***Vast oil reserves*** *around Lake Maracaibo (Lago de Maracaibo) form the focus of Venezuelan industry. Incomes from oil are used to invest in other industries and in the development of infrastructure.*

Using the land

The Andean basins support cereals and potatoes. Livestock graze at higher altitudes and on the drier tropical grasslands known as the *llanos*; hardy goats are reared in scrubland areas. Grown at higher elevations, coffee is an important cash crop, as is cotton, sugar cane, bananas, citrus fruits, cocoa and rice, farmed on the Caribbean lowlands. Coca is the most widely-grown narcotic plant, with heroin poppies grown in Colombia and marijuana in lowland areas throughout the region.

▲ ***The Sierra Nevada*** *de Santa Marta is a granite massif which rises sharply from the Caribbean lowlands to snow-covered peaks, the tallest of which is 18,947 ft (5775 m) high.*

Lake Maracaibo *(Lago de Maracaibo)* is not a true lake but a shallow inlet of the Caribbean Sea. It is the main source of Venezuela's oil.

The drainage basin of the Magdalena River and the Cauca, its main tributary, covers over 20% of Colombia's total surface area.

In the Guiana Highlands, Venezuela's most remote region, the ancient crystalline rocks contain deposits of iron ore, gold and diamonds.

Angel Falls *(Salto Ángel)*, at 3212 ft (979 m), is the world's highest waterfall.

Igneous intrusions into the crystalline plateau which forms most of central Guyana have led to the formation of the many rapids which characterize Guyana's rivers.

▲ ***The Guiana Shield*** *is one of the oldest land surfaces in the world – probably formed more than 4 billion years ago. Chemical weathering over millions of years has created flat-topped table mountains and large numbers of inselbergs.*

Over 80% of Surinam is covered by tropical rainforest.

The landscape

At its northernmost reaches, in western Colombia and Venezuela, the great Andean mountain chain splits into three distinct ranges: the Cordillera Oriental, Cordillera Central and Cordillera Occidental, intercut by a complex series of lesser ranges and basins. The relief becomes lower toward the coast and the interior plains of the northern Amazon Basin, rising again into the tropical hills of the Guiana Highlands.

Colombia's eastern lowlands are known locally as *llanos*, meaning grasslands.

► ***The Potaru*** *river descends 741 ft (226 m) over a sandstone ledge at the Kaieteur Falls in Guyana.*

Most of the land in French Guiana is low-lying; here, the rocks of the Guiana Highlands have been eroded by rivers flowing towards the sea.

Western South America

BOLIVIA, ECUADOR, PERU

The three states of Western South America share a similar geography and recent history. Dominated by the Inca empire until Spanish conquest in the 16th century, they achieved independence from Spain in the early 19th century. The precipitous terrain of the Andes presents severe difficulties for overland transport and continues to be a barrier to national unity and stability. Although Ecuador is now a relatively stable democracy, the military is highly influential in Peru and Bolivia, while the drug trade and associated corruption discourages external aid and economic progress. Wealth and power are still largely concentrated in the hands of a small elite of families, who attained their position during the Spanish colonial period. Energy resources and political recognition for the indigenous peoples are becoming increasingly important issues, particularly in Bolivia.

▶ *Ecuador's capital city, Quito, lies high in the Andes, nestling between snow-capped peaks. At 9350 ft (2850 m), Quito is the second highest capital in the world – La Paz in Bolivia is the highest.*

The landscape

Bolivia, Peru and Ecuador each possess a high Andean mountain region and an eastern region consisting of tropical lowlands and the Andean slope leading down to them. Towards the south of the region, the mountains widen to form the high plateau of the Altiplano. Peru and Ecuador also have fertile, lowland coastal plains. A wide variety of environments include *selva* (tropical rainforest), *montaña* (mountain forest) and grassland.

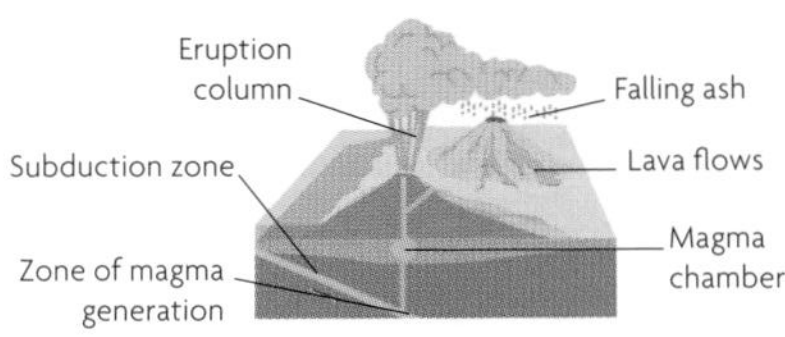

Eruption column
Subduction zone
Zone of magma generation
Falling ash
Lava flows
Magma chamber

▲ ***There are many** large and active volcanoes in the Andes. Magma generated in the heart of the volcano erupts in a huge cloud of ash. Ash-fall deposits are common throughout the Andes and the rock produced is known as andesite. This is rapidly soaked by heavy rain, causing massive debris flows.*

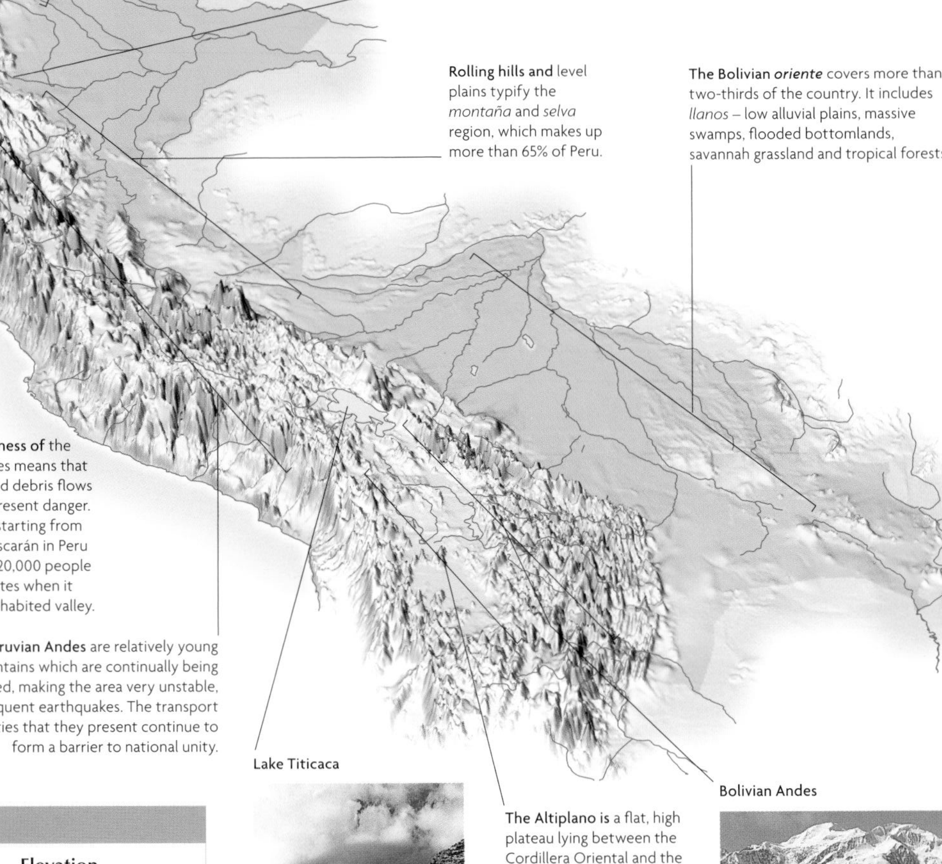

Cotopaxi is the world's highest active volcano, with a peak 19,347 ft (5897 m) high. A massive eruption in 1877 caused a mudflow which destroyed everything in its path for 150 miles (240 km).

Much of eastern Ecuador is covered by the tropical rainforest of the Amazon Basin.

Fast-flowing tributaries of the Amazon, which rise in the Andes, run eastwards through the front ranges to reach the tropical lowlands. They cut valleys so deep that tropical environments can be found extending well into mountainous areas.

Rolling hills and level plains typify the *montaña* and *selva* region, which makes up more than 65% of Peru.

The Bolivian *oriente* covers more than two-thirds of the country. It includes *llanos* – low alluvial plains, massive swamps, flooded bottomlands, savannah grassland and tropical forests.

The coastal flood plains are the source of Ecuador's richest soils, enabling the cultivation of a wide range of crops.

The steepness of the Andean slopes means that avalanches and debris flows are an ever-present danger. A landslide starting from Nevado Huascarán in Peru in 1970 killed 20,000 people in 2.5 minutes when it engulfed an inhabited valley.

The Peruvian Andes are relatively young mountains which are continually being uplifted, making the area very unstable, with frequent earthquakes. The transport difficulties that they present continue to form a barrier to national unity.

Lake Titicaca

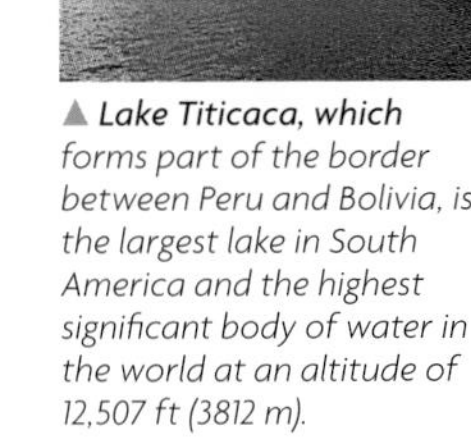

▲ ***Lake Titicaca, which** forms part of the border between Peru and Bolivia, is the largest lake in South America and the highest significant body of water in the world at an altitude of 12,507 ft (3812 m).*

The Altiplano is a flat, high plateau lying between the Cordillera Oriental and the Cordillera Occidental at a height of up to 12,500 ft (3800 m). At its margins lie many spurs and alluvial fans.

Bolivian Andes

▲ ***Nevado de Illampu** and Nevado de Ancohuma, at 21,275 ft (6485 m) and 21,490 ft (6550 m) respectively, form Illampu, the highest mountain in the Bolivian Andes.*

Map key

Population

- above 5 million
- 1 million to 5 million
- 500,000 to 1 million
- 100,000 to 500,000
- 50,000 to 100,000
- 10,000 to 50,000
- below 10,000

Elevation

- 6000m / 19,686ft
- 4000m / 13,124ft
- 3000m / 9843ft
- 2000m / 6562ft
- 1000m / 3281ft
- 500m / 1640ft
- 250m / 820ft
- 100m / 328ft
- sea level

Scale 1:7,750,000

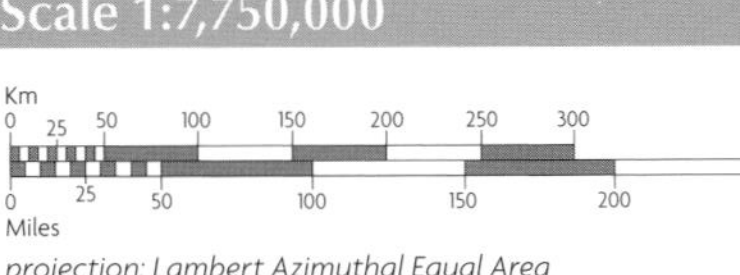

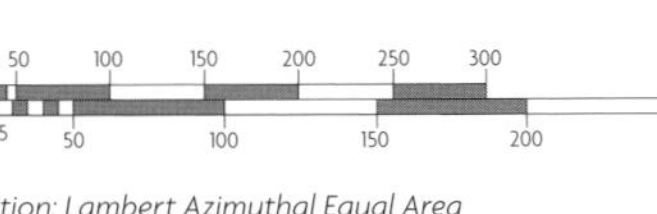

Km 0 25 50 100 150 200 250 300
Miles 0 25 50 100 150 200 250 300

projection: Lambert Azimuthal Equal Area

Ecuador: Administrative regions

1. CARCHI
2. TUNGURAHUA
3. BOLÍVAR
4. CHIMBORAZO
5. ZAMORA CHINCHIPE

COLOMBIA
ECUADOR
PERU
BRAZIL
Esmeraldas
QUITO
Guayaquil
Cuenca
Iquitos
Pucallpa
Trujillo
Chiclayo
Piura

192
54
58

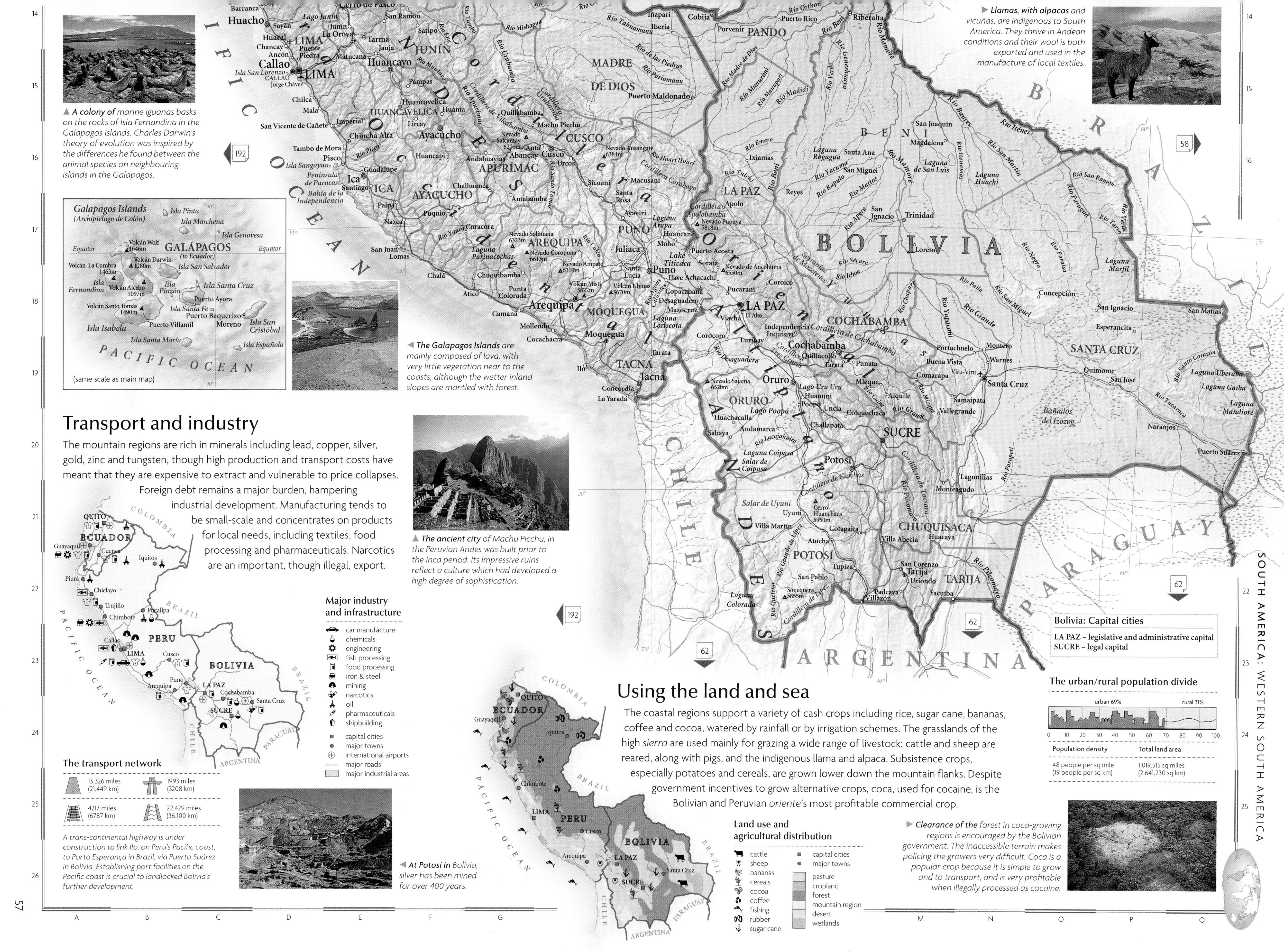

▲ **A colony of** marine iguanas basks on the rocks of Isla Fernandina in the Galapagos Islands. Charles Darwin's theory of evolution was inspired by the differences he found between the animal species on neighbouring islands in the Galapagos.

▶ **Llamas, with alpacas** and vicuñas, are indigenous to South America. They thrive in Andean conditions and their wool is both exported and used in the manufacture of local textiles.

Galapagos Islands (Archipiélago de Colón)

(same scale as main map)

◀ **The Galapagos Islands** are mainly composed of lava, with very little vegetation near to the coasts, although the wetter inland slopes are mantled with forest.

Transport and industry

The mountain regions are rich in minerals including lead, copper, silver, gold, zinc and tungsten, though high production and transport costs have meant that they are expensive to extract and vulnerable to price collapses. Foreign debt remains a major burden, hampering industrial development. Manufacturing tends to be small-scale and concentrates on products for local needs, including textiles, food processing and pharmaceuticals. Narcotics are an important, though illegal, export.

▲ **The ancient city** of Machu Picchu, in the Peruvian Andes was built prior to the Inca period. Its impressive ruins reflect a culture which had developed a high degree of sophistication.

Major industry and infrastructure

- car manufacture
- chemicals
- engineering
- fish processing
- food processing
- iron & steel
- mining
- narcotics
- oil
- pharmaceuticals
- shipbuilding
- capital cities
- major towns
- international airports
- major roads
- major industrial areas

The transport network

13,326 miles (21,449 km)	1993 miles (3208 km)
4217 miles (6787 km)	22,429 miles (36,100 km)

A trans-continental highway is under construction to link Ilo, on Peru's Pacific coast, to Porto Esperança in Brazil, via Puerto Suárez in Bolivia. Establishing port facilities on the Pacific coast is crucial to landlocked Bolivia's further development.

◀ **At Potosí in** Bolivia, silver has been mined for over 400 years.

Bolivia: Capital cities

LA PAZ – legislative and administrative capital
SUCRE – legal capital

Using the land and sea

The coastal regions support a variety of cash crops including rice, sugar cane, bananas, coffee and cocoa, watered by rainfall or by irrigation schemes. The grasslands of the high *sierra* are used mainly for grazing a wide range of livestock; cattle and sheep are reared, along with pigs, and the indigenous llama and alpaca. Subsistence crops, especially potatoes and cereals, are grown lower down the mountain flanks. Despite government incentives to grow alternative crops, coca, used for cocaine, is the Bolivian and Peruvian *oriente*'s most profitable commercial crop.

The urban/rural population divide

urban 69% — rural 31%

Population density	Total land area
48 people per sq mile (19 people per sq km)	1,019,515 sq miles (2,641,230 sq km)

Land use and agricultural distribution

- cattle
- sheep
- bananas
- cereals
- cocoa
- coffee
- fishing
- rubber
- sugar cane
- capital cities
- major towns
- pasture
- cropland
- forest
- mountain region
- desert
- wetlands

▶ **Clearance of the** forest in coca-growing regions is encouraged by the Bolivian government. The inaccessible terrain makes policing the growers very difficult. Coca is a popular crop because it is simple to grow and to transport, and is very profitable when illegally processed as cocaine.

Brazil

Brazil is the largest country in South America, with a population of 191 million – almost half the combined total of the continent. The 26 states which make up the federal republic of Brazil are administered from the purpose-built capital, Brasília. Tropical rainforest, covering more than one-third of the country, contains rich natural resources, but great tracts are sacrificed to agriculture, industry and urban expansion on a daily basis. Most of Brazil's multi-ethnic population now live in cities, some of which are vast areas of urban sprawl; São Paulo is one of the world's biggest conurbations, with more than 20 million inhabitants. Although prosperity is a reality for some, many people still live in great poverty, and mounting foreign debts continue to damage Brazil's prospects of economic advancement.

Using the land

Brazil has immense natural resources, including minerals and hardwoods, many of which are found in the fragile rainforest. Brazil is the world's leading coffee grower and a major producer of livestock, sugar and orange juice concentrate. Soya beans for animal feed, particularly for poultry feed, have become the country's most significant crop.

The urban/rural population divide

urban 78% · rural 22%

Population density	Total land area
55 people per sq mile (21 people per sq km)	3,286,472 sq miles (8,511,970 sq km)

Land use and agricultural distribution

cattle · pigs · sheep · citrus fruits · coffee · cotton · soya beans · sugar cane · timber · capital cities · major towns · pasture · cropland · forest

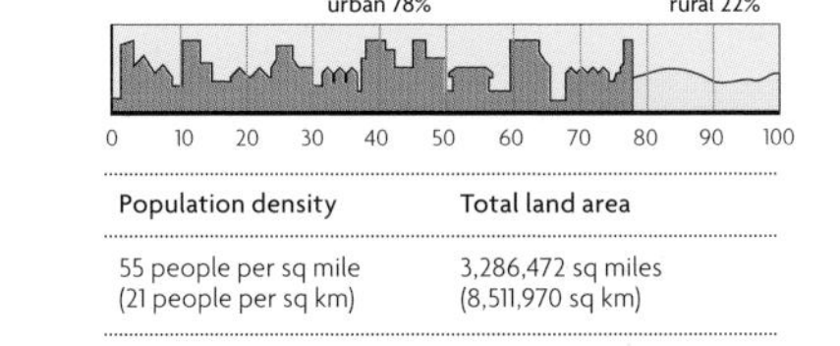

The fecundity of parts of Brazil's rainforest results from exceptionally high levels of rainfall and the quantities of silt deposited by the Amazon river system.

The landscape

The Amazon Basin, containing the largest area of tropical rainforest on Earth, covers nearly half of Brazil. It is bordered by two shield areas: in the south by the Brazilian Highlands, and in the north by the Guiana Highlands. The east coast is dominated by a great escarpment which runs for 1600 miles (2565 km).

Brazil's highest mountain is the Pico da Neblina which was only discovered in 1962. It is 9888 ft (3014 m) high.

The flood plains which border the Amazon river are made up of a variety of different features including shallow lakes and swamps, mangrove forests in the tidal delta area and fertile leveés on river banks and point bars.

The Amazon Basin is the largest river basin in the world. The Amazon river and over a thousand tributaries drain an area of 2,375,000 sq miles (6,150,000 sq km) and carry one-fifth of the world's fresh water out to sea.

Guiana Highlands

The ancient Brazilian Highlands have a varied topography. Their plateaux, hills and deep valleys are bordered by highly-eroded mountains containing important mineral deposits. They are drained by three great river systems, the Amazon, the Paraguay–Paraná and the São Francisco.

The São Francisco Basin has a climate unique in Brazil. Known as the 'drought polygon', it has almost no rain during the dry season, leading to regular disastrous droughts.

The northeastern scrublands are known as the *caatinga*, a virtually impenetrable thorny woodland, sometimes intermixed with cacti where water is scarce.

Pantanal wetlands

The Pantanal region *in the south of Brazil is an extension of the Gran Chaco plain. The swamps and marshes of this area are renowned for their beauty, and abundant and unique wildlife, including wildfowl and these caimans, a type of crocodile.*

The famous Sugar Loaf Mountain (*Pão de Açúcar*) which overlooks Rio de Janeiro is a fine example of a volcanic plug a domed core of solidified lava left after the slopes of the original volcano have eroded away.

Deep natural harbours such as Baia de Guanabara were created where the steep slopes of the Serra da Mantiqueira plunge directly into the ocean.

The Iguaçu river *surges over the spectacular Iguaçu Falls (Saltos do Iguaçu) towards the Paraná river. Falls like these are increasingly under pressure from large-scale hydro-electric projects such as that at Itaipú.*

Hillslope gullying

Rainfall · Direction of growth · Overland water flow · Water seeps through hillslope · Gully

Large-scale gullies are *common in Brazil, particularly on hillslopes from which vegetation has been removed. Gullies grow headwards (up the slope), aided by a combination of erosion through water seepage and rainwater runoff.*

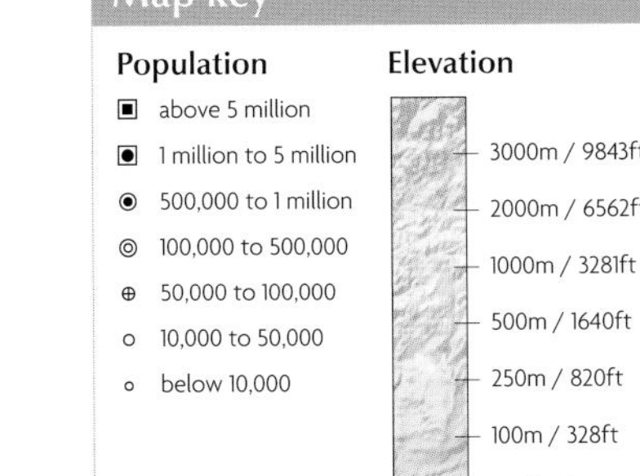
Map key
Population
above 5 million
1 million to 5 million
500,000 to 1 million
100,000 to 500,000
50,000 to 100,000
10,000 to 50,000
below 10,000
Elevation
3000m / 9843ft
2000m / 6562ft
1000m / 3281ft
500m / 1640ft
250m / 820ft
100m / 328ft
sea level

54 · 54 · 64 · 54 · 56

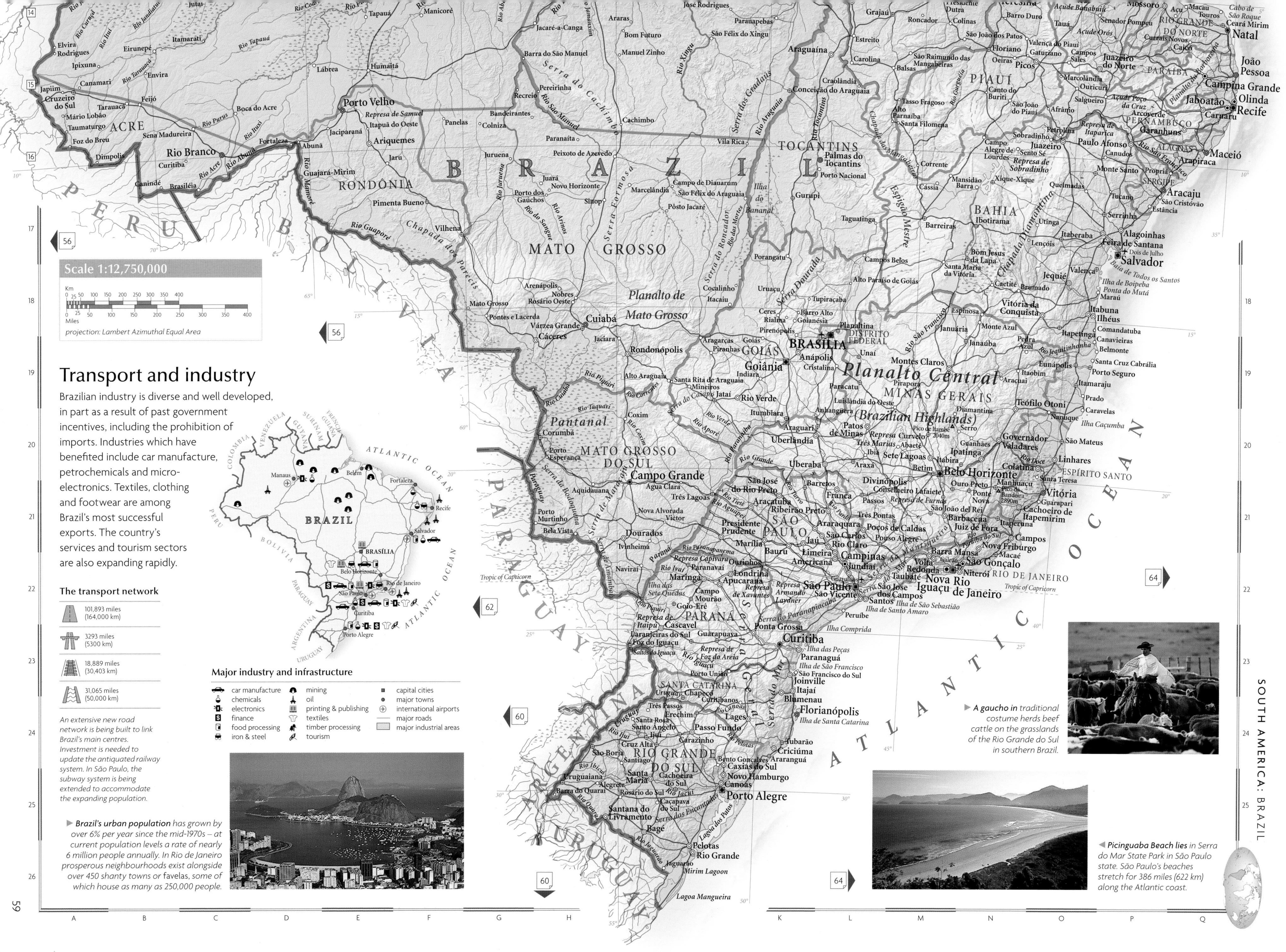
BRAZIL
ATLANTIC OCEAN
PERU
BOLIVIA
PARAGUAY
ARGENTINA
URUGUAY
ACRE
RONDÔNIA
MATO GROSSO
MATO GROSSO DO SUL
TOCANTINS
GOIÁS
DISTRITO FEDERAL
MINAS GERAIS
BAHIA
PIAUÍ
SÃO PAULO
PARANÁ
SANTA CATARINA
RIO GRANDE DO SUL
RIO DE JANEIRO
ESPÍRITO SANTO
SERGIPE
ALAGOAS
PERNAMBUCO
PARAÍBA
RIO GRANDE DO NORTE
Planalto Central
(Brazilian Highlands)
Planalto de Mato Grosso
Pantanal
Serra Geral
Tropic of Capricorn
Brasília
São Paulo
Rio de Janeiro
Salvador
Recife
Belo Horizonte
Porto Alegre
Curitiba

56

Scale 1:12,750,000

Km 0 25 50 100 150 200 250 300 350 400

Miles 0 25 50 100 150 200 250 300 350 400

projection: Lambert Azimuthal Equal Area

56

Transport and industry

Brazilian industry is diverse and well developed, in part as a result of past government incentives, including the prohibition of imports. Industries which have benefited include car manufacture, petrochemicals and micro-electronics. Textiles, clothing and footwear are among Brazil's most successful exports. The country's services and tourism sectors are also expanding rapidly.

The transport network

- 101,893 miles (164,000 km)
- 3293 miles (5300 km)
- 18,889 miles (30,403 km)
- 31,065 miles (50,000 km)

An extensive new road network is being built to link Brazil's main centres. Investment is needed to update the antiquated railway system. In São Paulo, the subway system is being extended to accommodate the expanding population.

Major industry and infrastructure

- car manufacture
- chemicals
- electronics
- finance
- food processing
- iron & steel
- mining
- oil
- printing & publishing
- textiles
- timber processing
- tourism
- capital cities
- major towns
- international airports
- major roads
- major industrial areas

▶ ***Brazil's urban population** has grown by over 6% per year since the mid-1970s – at current population levels a rate of nearly 6 million people annually. In Rio de Janeiro prosperous neighbourhoods exist alongside over 450 shanty towns or favelas, some of which house as many as 250,000 people.*

62

60

60

64

64

▶ ***A gaucho** in traditional costume herds beef cattle on the grasslands of the Rio Grande do Sul in southern Brazil.*

◀ ***Picinguaba Beach lies** in Serra do Mar State Park in São Paulo state. São Paulo's beaches stretch for 386 miles (622 km) along the Atlantic coast.*

Eastern South America

URUGUAY, NORTHEAST ARGENTINA, SOUTHEAST BRAZIL

The vast conurbations of Rio de Janeiro, São Paulo and Buenos Aires form the core of South America's highly-urbanized eastern region. São Paulo state, with over 40 million inhabitants, is among the world's 20 most powerful economies, and São Paulo is the fastest growing city on the continent. Rio de Janeiro and Buenos Aires, transformed in the last hundred years from port cities to great metropolitan areas each with more than 10 million inhabitants, typify the unstructured growth and wealth disparities of South America's great cities. In Uruguay, two fifths of the population lives in the capital, Montevideo, which faces Buenos Aires across the River Plate *(Río de la Plata)*. Immigration from the countryside has created severe pressure on the urban infrastructure, particularly on available housing, leading to a profusion of crowded shanty settlements *(favelas* or *barrios)*.

Using the land

Most of Uruguay and the Pampas of northern Argentina are devoted to the rearing of livestock, especially cattle and sheep, which are central to both countries' economies. Soya beans, first produced in Brazil's Rio Grande do Sul, are now more widely grown for large-scale export, as are cereals, sugar cane and grapes. Subsistence crops, including potatoes, corn and sugar beet, are grown on the remaining arable land.

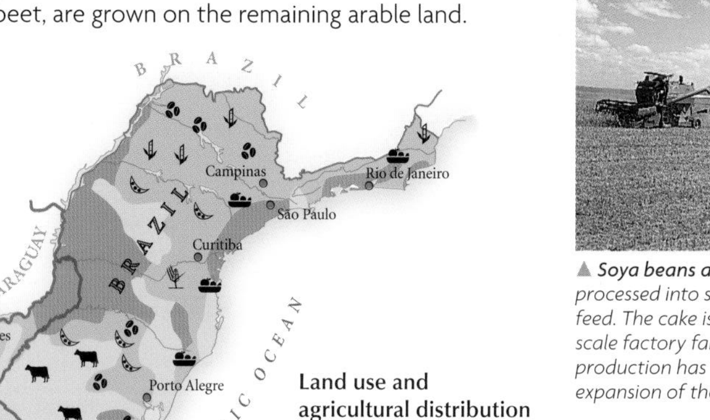
Land use and agricultural distribution
cattle
sheep
cereals
coffee
fruit
soya beans
sugar cane
capital cities
major towns
pasture
cropland
forest
wetlands
barren land

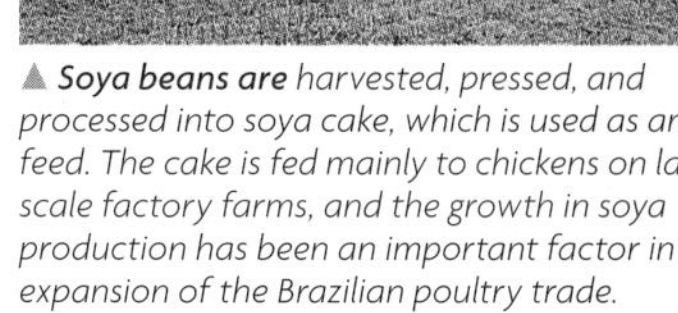

▲ *The rolling grasslands of Uruguay are ideally suited to the rearing of cattle, which are concentrated in great herds throughout the region.*

Scale 1:6,250,000

projection: Lambert Azimuthal Equal Area

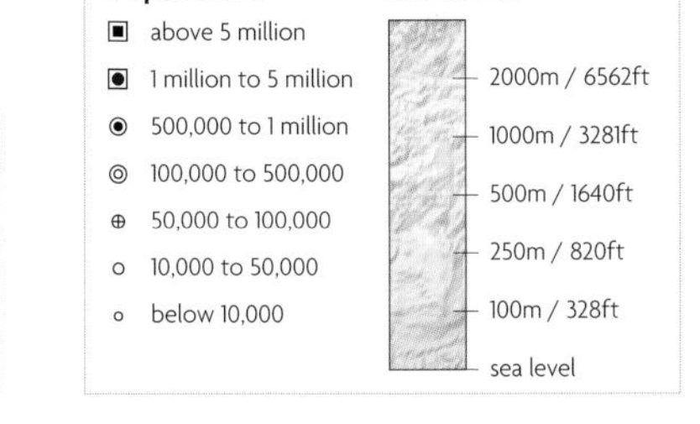

▲ ***Soya beans are** harvested, pressed, and processed into soya cake, which is used as animal feed. The cake is fed mainly to chickens on large-scale factory farms, and the growth in soya production has been an important factor in the expansion of the Brazilian poultry trade.*

Transport and industry

Southeast Brazil is home to much of the important motor and capital goods industry, largely based around São Paulo; iron and steel production is also concentrated in this region. Uruguay's economy continues to be based mainly on the export of livestock products including meat and leather goods. Buenos Aires is Argentina's chief port, and the region has a varied and sophisticated economic base including service-based industries such as finance and publishing, as well as primary processing.

Major industry and infrastructure
car manufacture
chemicals
engineering
finance
food processing
iron & steel
meat processing
printing & publishing
shipbuilding
textiles
timber processing
capital cities
major towns
international airports
major roads
major industrial areas

The transport network

Throughout the region, road networks need to be expanded to cope with urban development. Plans are underway to build a bridge over the River Plate (Río de la Plata) to link Colonia and Buenos Aires.

Map key

Population	Elevation
above 5 million	2000m / 6562ft
1 million to 5 million	1000m / 3281ft
500,000 to 1 million	500m / 1640ft
100,000 to 500,000	250m / 820ft
50,000 to 100,000	100m / 328ft
10,000 to 50,000	sea level
below 10,000	

▲ ***The Itaipú dam** on the Paraná river is one of the largest hydro-electric projects in the world, jointly financed by Brazil and Paraguay.*

58
62
64

▶ ***Rio de Janeiro's** annual carnival, Mardi Gras, which ushers in the start of Lent, is an extravagant five-day parade through the city, characterized by fantastically decorated floats, exuberant dancing and samba music.*

The landscape

The southern reaches of the Brazilian Highlands follow the Atlantic coast to form low, rolling hills in the northeast of Uruguay. Much of South America's mid-eastern region and all of Uruguay has a gentle relief with land rarely rising above 300 ft (100 m). Argentina's northeast comprises two main regions: a long, narrow lowland known as Mesopotamia; and part of the Pampas grasslands.

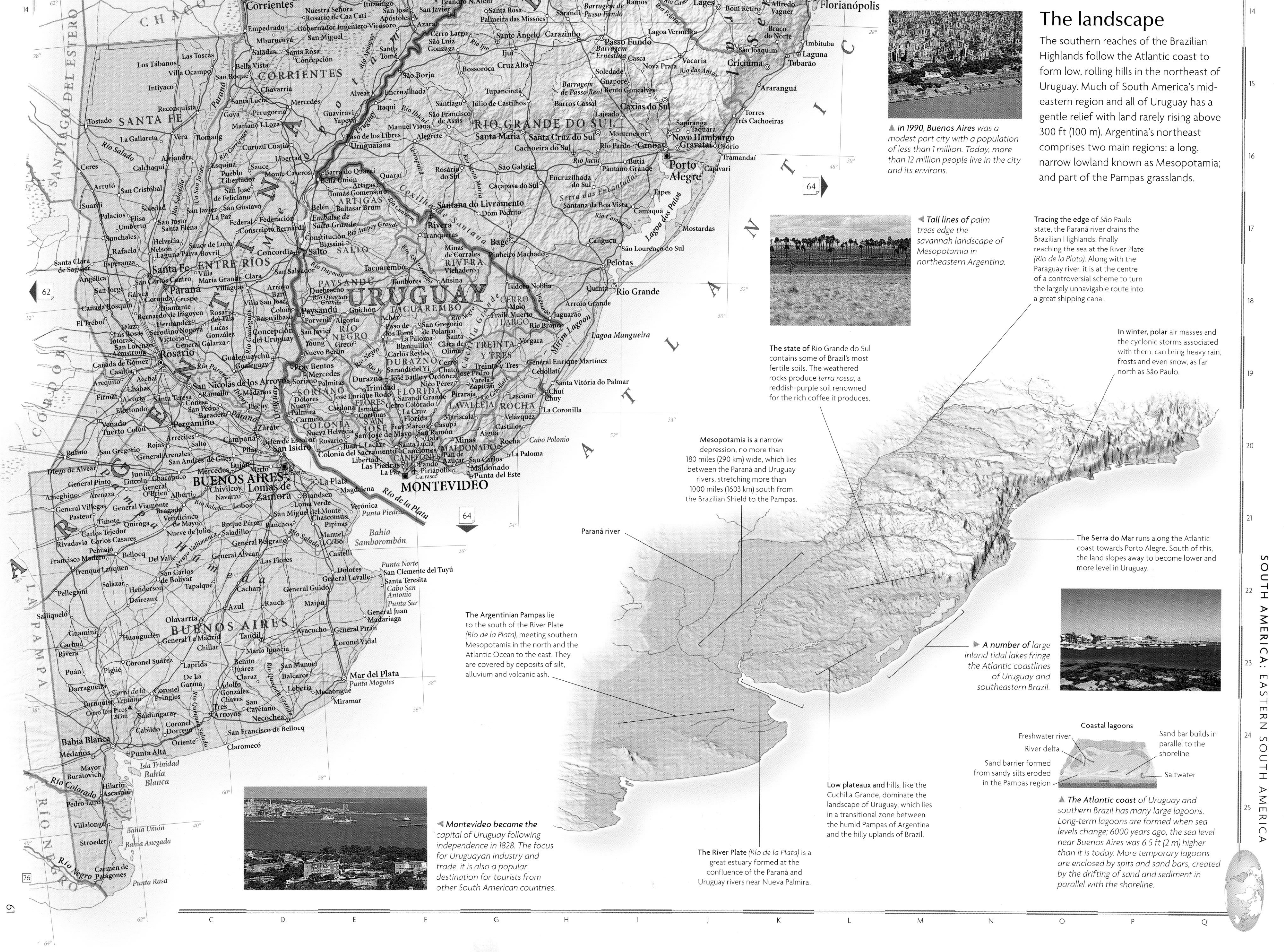

ARGENTINA
URUGUAY
RIO GRANDE DO SUL
SANTA FE
CORRIENTES
ENTRE RÍOS
BUENOS AIRES
MONTEVIDEO
Río de la Plata
ATLANTIC
Pampa Húmeda
Paraná river
Tracing the edge of São Paulo state, the Paraná river drains the Brazilian Highlands, finally reaching the sea at the River Plate (Río de la Plata). Along with the Paraguay river, it is at the centre of a controversial scheme to turn the largely unnavigable route into a great shipping canal.
In winter, polar air masses and the cyclonic storms associated with them, can bring heavy rain, frosts and even snow, as far north as São Paulo.
The state of Rio Grande do Sul contains some of Brazil's most fertile soils. The weathered rocks produce terra rossa, a reddish-purple soil renowned for the rich coffee it produces.
Mesopotamia is a narrow depression, no more than 180 miles (290 km) wide, which lies between the Paraná and Uruguay rivers, stretching more than 1000 miles (1603 km) south from the Brazilian Shield to the Pampas.
The Serra do Mar runs along the Atlantic coast towards Porto Alegre. South of this, the land slopes away to become lower and more level in Uruguay.
The Argentinian Pampas lie to the south of the River Plate (Río de la Plata), meeting southern Mesopotamia in the north and the Atlantic Ocean to the east. They are covered by deposits of silt, alluvium and volcanic ash.
Low plateaux and hills, like the Cuchilla Grande, dominate the landscape of Uruguay, which lies in a transitional zone between the humid Pampas of Argentina and the hilly uplands of Brazil.
The River Plate (Río de la Plata) is a great estuary formed at the confluence of the Paraná and Uruguay rivers near Nueva Palmira.
Coastal lagoons
Freshwater river
River delta
Sand barrier formed from sandy silts eroded in the Pampas region
Sand bar builds in parallel to the shoreline
Saltwater

▲ *In 1990, Buenos Aires was a modest port city with a population of less than 1 million. Today, more than 12 million people live in the city and its environs.*

◀ ***Tall lines of** palm trees edge the savannah landscape of Mesopotamia in northeastern Argentina.*

▶ ***A number of** large inland tidal lakes fringe the Atlantic coastlines of Uruguay and southeastern Brazil.*

▲ ***The Atlantic coast** of Uruguay and southern Brazil has many large lagoons. Long-term lagoons are formed when sea levels change; 6000 years ago, the sea level near Buenos Aires was 6.5 ft (2 m) higher than it is today. More temporary lagoons are enclosed by spits and sand bars, created by the drifting of sand and sediment in parallel with the shoreline.*

◀ ***Montevideo became the** capital of Uruguay following independence in 1828. The focus for Uruguayan industry and trade, it is also a popular destination for tourists from other South American countries.*

Southern South America

ARGENTINA, CHILE, PARAGUAY

South America's cone-shaped southern region is shared by Argentina and Chile, two overwhelmingly urbanized nations whose populations live mainly in or around the capital cities, Buenos Aires and Santiago. The people are largely *mestizo* or of European origin; in the early 20th century Argentina absorbed waves of new European immigrants, many from Italy and Germany. Paraguay is far less urbanized than its neighbours, with a homogeneous population of mixed Spanish and Guaraní origin, who retain their Indian roots through the Guaraní language. Though most Paraguayans live in the southeast, near Asunción, the indigenous Indians live in the sparsely populated Gran Chaco. The Gran Chaco is also home to some of Argentina's minority indigenous peoples, who otherwise live mainly in Andean regions. Chile's estimated 800,000 Mapauche Indians live almost exclusively in the south.

Transport and industry

Food processing and agricultural exports remain a fundamental part of Argentina's economy. The growth of manufacturing is regularly hampered by hyper-inflation and massive foreign debts. The world's most important copper-producer and one of the top twenty gold producers, Chile also has a thriving wine and grape industry. Most Paraguayan exports involve primary processing, although domestic goods are produced for home markets.

▲ ***Chuquicamata copper mine,** lies on a desert plateau near Calama in the Andes of northern Chile. It is the world's largest open-cast copper mine.*

▲ ***Boiling water and** steam emerge from a volcanic vent, one of the Tatio geysers which lie at the foot of Cerro de Tocorpuri near Chile's border with Bolivia.*

▶ ***Floodwaters cover the** land in the Gran Chaco, partly submerging its vegetation of fan palms and hyacinths.*

Major industry and infrastructure

- chemicals
- engineering
- food processing
- meat processing
- mining
- oil
- textiles
- timber processing
- capital cities
- major towns
- international airports
- major roads
- major industrial areas

The transport network

55,062 miles (93,453 km)		3038 miles (4889 km)	
26,811 miles (43,153 km)		9180 miles (14,775 km)	

Argentina's state transport system is undergoing privatization, though the outmoded rail network requires updating. Paraguay requires foreign investment to upgrade its roads and railways. Essential internal air routes, especially across the Andes, are well developed in all three countries.

Map key

Population

- 1 million to 5 million
- 500,000 to 1 million
- 100,000 to 500,000
- 50,000 to 100,000
- 10,000 to 50,000
- below 10,000

Elevation

- 6000m / 19,686ft
- 4000m / 13,124ft
- 3000m / 9843ft
- 2000m / 6562ft
- 1000m / 3281ft
- 500m / 1640ft
- 250m / 820ft
- 100m / 328ft
- sea level

56

58

The landscape

The Andes run from north to south, forming a precipitous natural border between Chile and Argentina. East of the Andes are the scrublands of the Gran Chaco and the plains of the Pampas, which extend northward towards Paraguay. In the far southwest, Chile's indented Pacific coastline has many features typical of areas which have been affected by glaciation.

▲ *The Atacama Desert* (Desierto de Atacama) *in Chile is one of the driest places on Earth where some areas have never recorded any rain. It contains a number of salt lakes.*

The Gran Chaco combines poor drainage, extremely hot temperatures and thorn-infested scrub to make it one of South America's most inhospitable regions.

Landlocked Paraguay relies on its river system for access to the sea and to produce hydro-electric power. The most important river system is the Paraguay–Paraná which provides links into neighbouring countries including Brazil, Uruguay and Argentina.

Most of the highest mountains in Chile's northern Andes are volcanoes like Volcán Lascar and Volcán Rutana.

The Pampas derive their name from an Indian word meaning flat surface. The dry western region is largely desert, whereas the east is well-watered, supporting temperate grasses.

Cerro Aconcagua in the central Andes is the tallest mountain in the whole chain, rising to 22,834 ft (6959 m).

Alluvial deposits from the many rivers in central Chile have created rich soils, ideal for a wide range of agriculture.

Andes

Patagonia divides into two zones, with the Andes in the west, and the lower main plateau, extending east towards the Atlantic. It is a desolate area with climatic extremes; dark lava fields scattered with light bunchgrass give a 'leopard skin' effect to the landscape.

The Patagonian ice sheet is the world's third largest ice field, covering 6560 sq miles (17,000 sq km). Patagonia also contains many typical features from past glaciations. These include glacial lakes, U-shaped valleys, fjords and deep-cut channels.

Cape Horn is the most southerly point of South America. The severity of the Roaring Forties winds makes the Horn one of the world's most treacherous shipping regions.

Argentinian Pampas
Jet stream
Rainfall
Windblown particles
Ice-capped Andes are source of loess
Thick layer of loess sediments

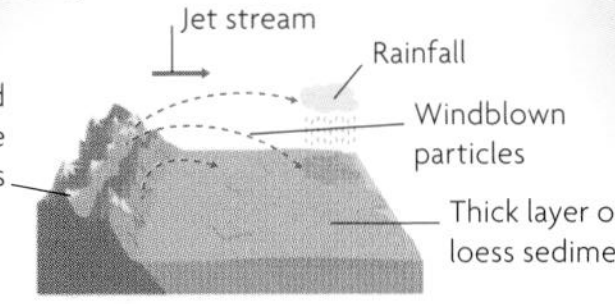

▲ *A thick, fertile layer of loess lies in the basin underlying the Argentinian Pampas. It has been laid down following successive periods of glaciation. The minute loess particles are transported as dust and deposited by a downward air motion, or following rainfall.*

192

64

▲ *Great blocks of ice break away from the jagged blue peaks of these ice mountains to form icebergs off the coast of Patagonia, Argentina's most southerly region.*

Using the land and sea

The rich plains of the Pampas support massive herds of cattle, producing meat, milk and hides essential to the domestic and export markets of both Argentina and Paraguay. Wheat and fruit are Argentina's other major agricultural products. A wide range of soft fruits, citrus fruits and more specialized crops such as walnuts, and grapes for wine and the table, are grown in Chile's fertile Central Valley, while the landscape to the south is dominated by forestry, mainly growing commercial radiata pine. Paraguay is self-sufficient in wheat and other staples. Cotton, coffee, tobacco and oilseeds such as soya, are the major export crops.

The urban/rural population divide

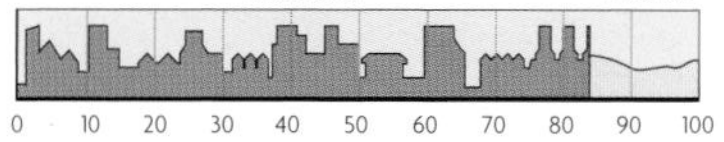

urban 84% rural 16%

0 10 20 30 40 50 60 70 80 90 100

Population density	Total land area
40 people per sq mile (15 people per sq km)	1,498,757 sq miles (3,882,790 sq km)

Land use and agricultural distribution

cattle, sheep, cereals, fruit, grapes, timber, fishing
capital cities, major towns
pasture, cropland, forest, barren land, mountain region, desert

▲ *Charred tree stumps surround a cattle enclosure on the island of Tierra del Fuego in southern Argentina. Forest clearance to provide grazing land for cattle is of major environmental concern.*

Scale 1:8,750,000

projection: Lambert Azimuthal Equal Area

The Atlantic Ocean

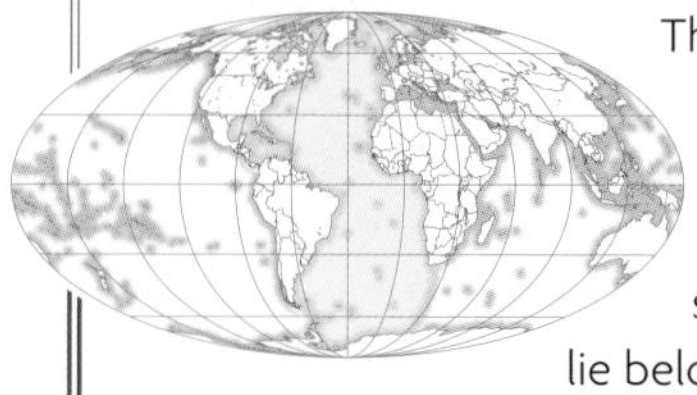

The Atlantic is the youngest of the world's oceans, formed about 180 million years ago when the landmasses of the eastern and western hemispheres separated. Its underwater topography is dominated by the Mid-Atlantic Ridge, a huge mountain system running north to south along the centre of the ocean. Although most of the ridge's peaks lie below the sea, some emerge as volcanic islands, like Iceland and the Azores. The Atlantic contains a wealth of resources, including substantial oil and gas reserves and rich fishing grounds. Until the 1950s, the north Atlantic was the world's busiest shipping route; cheaper air transport and alternative routes have shifted patterns of world trade.

▲ **Surtsey near Iceland,** *lies on the Mid-Atlantic Ridge. The island was formed in 1963 following a volcanic eruption caused by sea-floor spreading.*

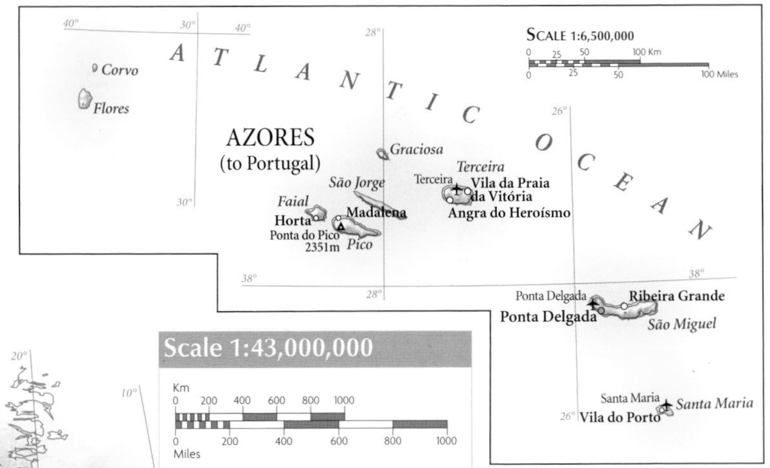

Resources

Development of the oil and gas reserves in the Atlantic began in the 1940s around the Gulf of Mexico. Since then other areas have been exploited, including the North Sea, the west coast of Africa and the area east of Newfoundland and Nova Scotia. There is also extensive mining of sand, gravel and shell deposits by the USA and UK. For centuries, the north Atlantic's fishing grounds have been utilized more heavily than other oceans, leading to a serious decline in many fish stocks.

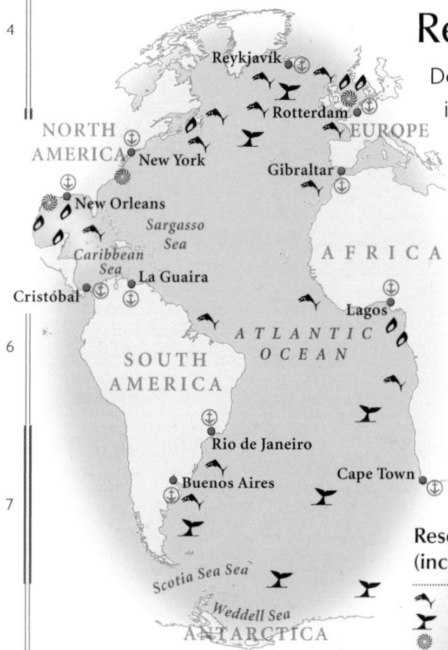

Resources (including wildlife)

- fish
- whales
- aggregates
- oil & gas
- major towns
- major ports

▲ **Fishing in the** *seas around northwestern Europe dates back over 1500 years. The high nutrient content of the seas makes them ideal breeding grounds for many species of fish.*

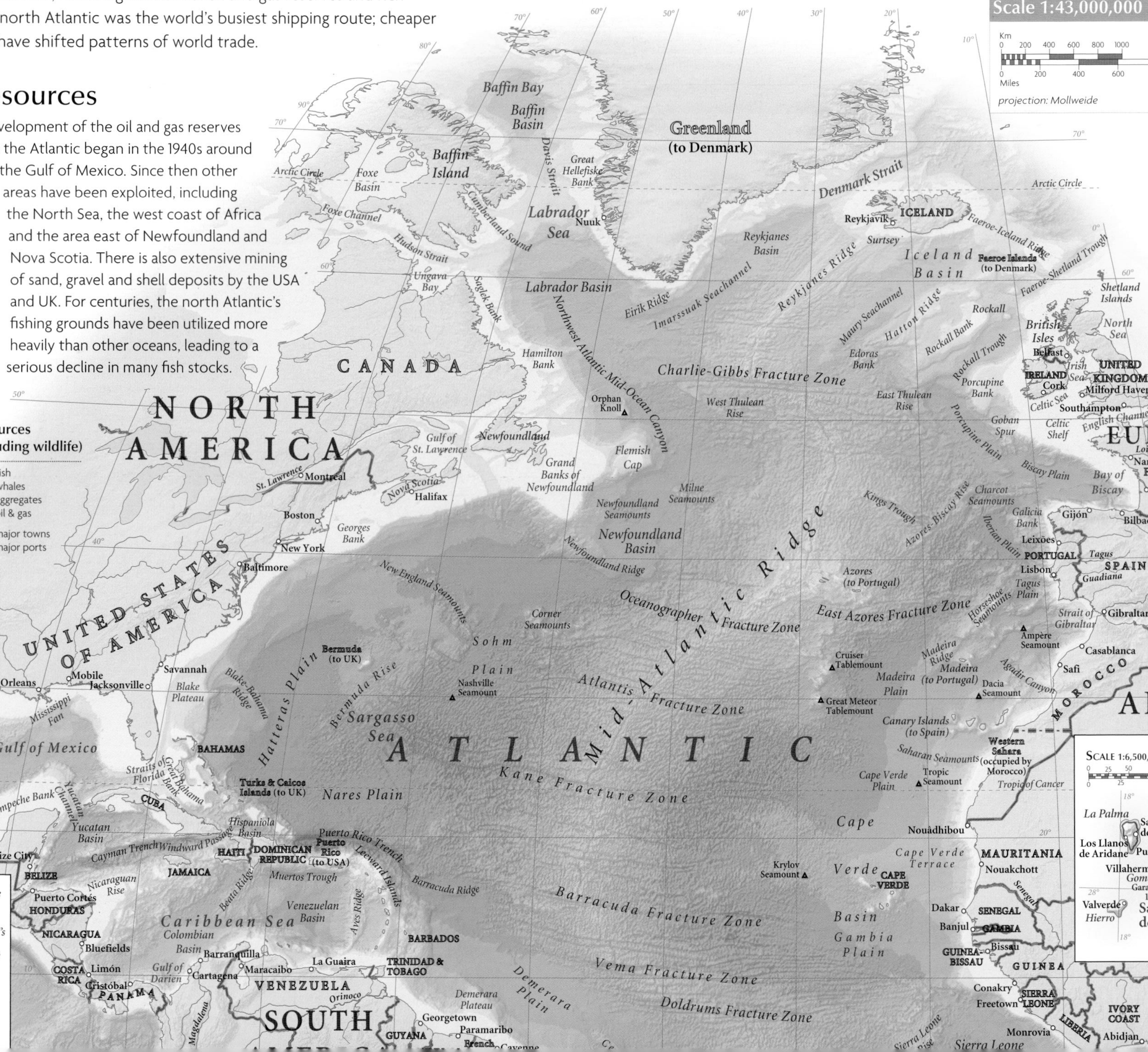

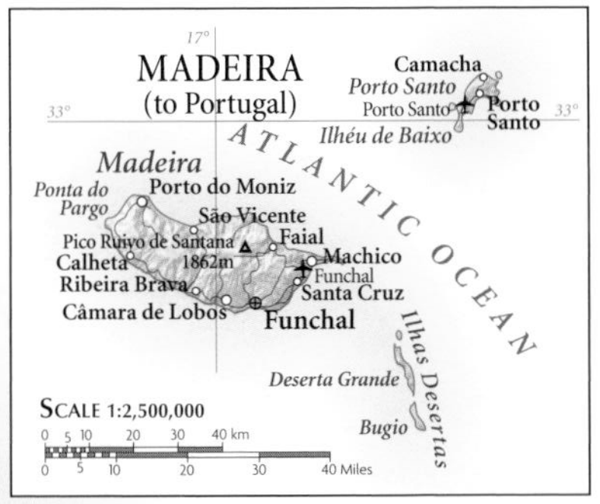

Scale 1:43,000,000

projection: Mollweide

▲ **On 5 January 1993,** *the oil tanker Braer ran aground in the Shetland Islands, spilling 83,660 tons (85,000 tonnes) of light crude oil into the ocean, devastating the local marine ecosystem.*

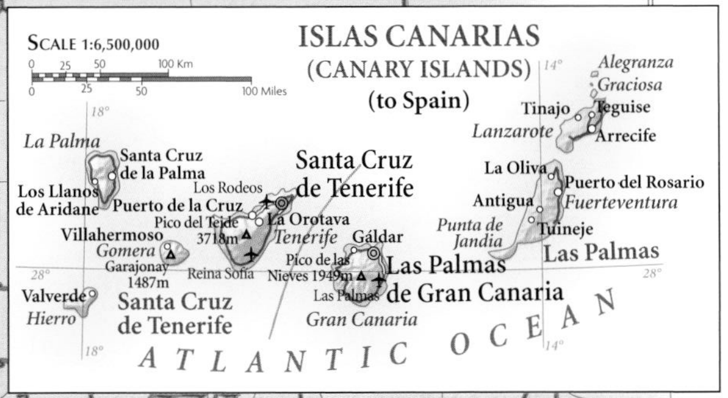

The landscape

The floor of the Atlantic is spreading by about one inch (2.5 cm) a year. The South American and African plates are moving apart drawing molten rock up from the Earth's core. The Mid-Atlantic Ridge lies along the boundary of the two plates, forming the world's longest mountain range and dividing the Atlantic floor into two parallel troughs. These troughs are subdivided into numerous smaller basins by transform faults. Most of the oceanic islands in the Atlantic are volcanic in origin; either part of the Mid-Atlantic Ridge or the Caribbean arc.

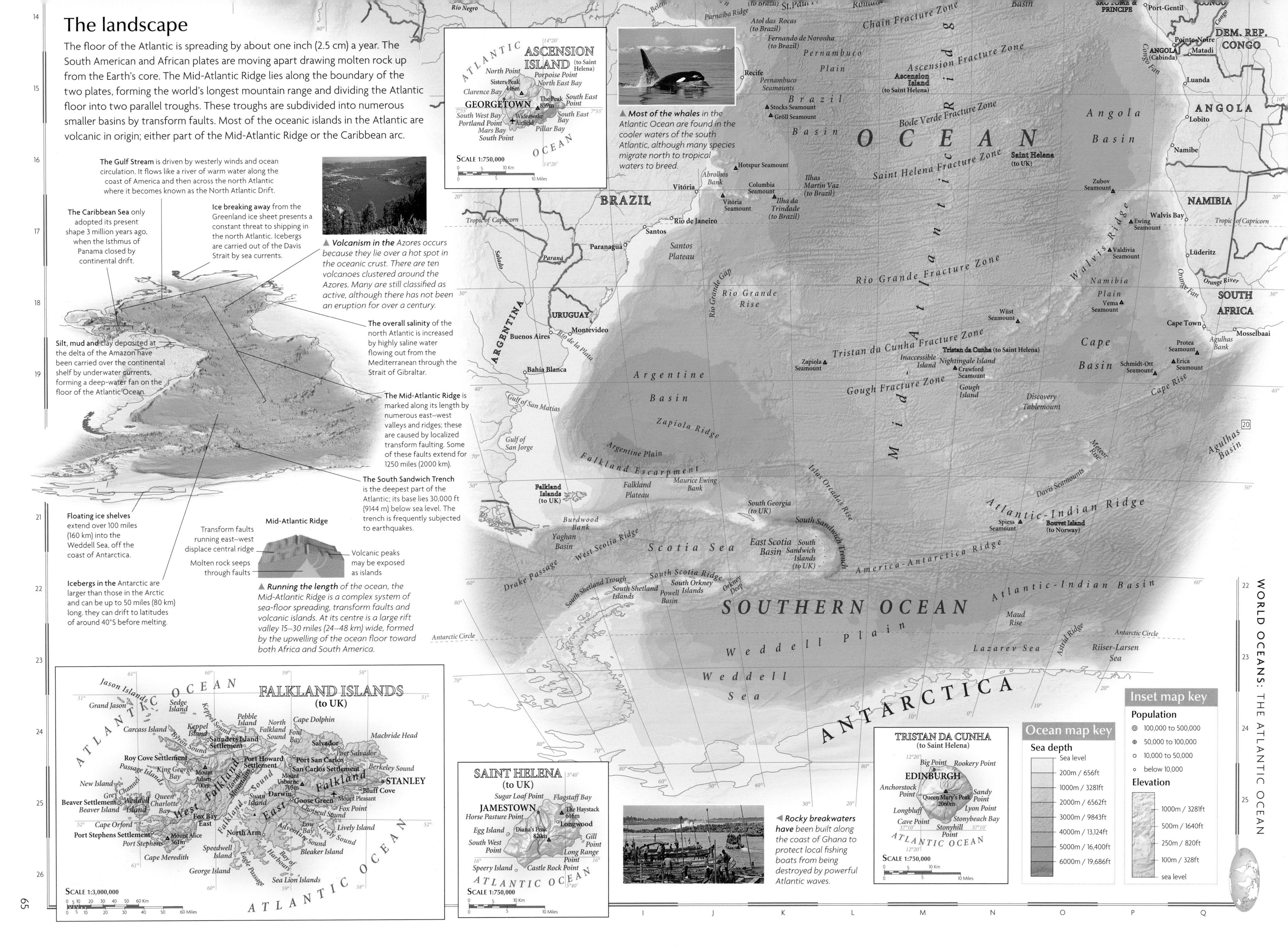

Mid-Atlantic Ridge
Transform faults running east–west displace central ridge
Molten rock seeps through faults
Volcanic peaks may be exposed as islands
ASCENSION ISLAND (to Saint Helena)
GEORGETOWN
SCALE 1:750,000
BRAZIL
ARGENTINA
URUGUAY
NAMIBIA
ANGOLA
SOUTH AFRICA
DEM. REP. CONGO
OCEAN
SOUTHERN OCEAN
ANTARCTICA
Argentine Basin
Brazil Basin
Angola Basin
Cape Basin
Scotia Sea
Weddell Sea
Weddell Plain
Mid-Atlantic Ridge
Atlantic-Indian Ridge
America-Antarctica Ridge
Atlantic-Indian Basin
FALKLAND ISLANDS (to UK)
STANLEY
SCALE 1:3,000,000
SAINT HELENA (to UK)
JAMESTOWN
TRISTAN DA CUNHA (to Saint Helena)
EDINBURGH
Ocean map key
Sea depth
Sea level
200m / 656ft
1000m / 3281ft
2000m / 6562ft
3000m / 9843ft
4000m / 13,124ft
5000m / 16,400ft
6000m / 19,686ft
Inset map key
Population
100,000 to 500,000
50,000 to 100,000
10,000 to 50,000
below 10,000
Elevation
1000m / 3281ft
500m / 1640ft
250m / 820ft
100m / 328ft
sea level

The Gulf Stream is driven by westerly winds and ocean circulation. It flows like a river of warm water along the coast of America and then across the north Atlantic where it becomes known as the North Atlantic Drift.

The Caribbean Sea only adopted its present shape 3 million years ago, when the Isthmus of Panama closed by continental drift.

Ice breaking away from the Greenland ice sheet presents a constant threat to shipping in the north Atlantic. Icebergs are carried out of the Davis Strait by sea currents.

▲ ***Volcanism in the** Azores occurs because they lie over a hot spot in the oceanic crust. There are ten volcanoes clustered around the Azores. Many are still classified as active, although there has not been an eruption for over a century.*

Silt, mud and clay deposited at the delta of the Amazon have been carried over the continental shelf by underwater currents, forming a deep-water fan on the floor of the Atlantic Ocean.

The overall salinity of the north Atlantic is increased by highly saline water flowing out from the Mediterranean through the Strait of Gibraltar.

The Mid-Atlantic Ridge is marked along its length by numerous east–west valleys and ridges; these are caused by localized transform faulting. Some of these faults extend for 1250 miles (2000 km).

The South Sandwich Trench is the deepest part of the Atlantic; its base lies 30,000 ft (9144 m) below sea level. The trench is frequently subjected to earthquakes.

Floating ice shelves extend over 100 miles (160 km) into the Weddell Sea, off the coast of Antarctica.

Icebergs in the Antarctic are larger than those in the Arctic and can be up to 50 miles (80 km) long. they can drift to latitudes of around 40°S before melting.

▲ ***Running the length** of the ocean, the Mid-Atlantic Ridge is a complex system of sea-floor spreading, transform faults and volcanic islands. At its centre is a large rift valley 15–30 miles (24–48 km) wide, formed by the upwelling of the ocean floor toward both Africa and South America.*

▲ ***Most of the whales** in the Atlantic Ocean are found in the cooler waters of the south Atlantic, although many species migrate north to tropical waters to breed.*

◀ ***Rocky breakwaters have** been built along the coast of Ghana to protect local fishing boats from being destroyed by powerful Atlantic waves.*

Africa

The world's second largest continent, Africa covers an area of 11,712,434 sq miles (30,335,000 sq km). It has 53 separate countries, including Madagascar in the Indian Ocean – the highest number of any continent.

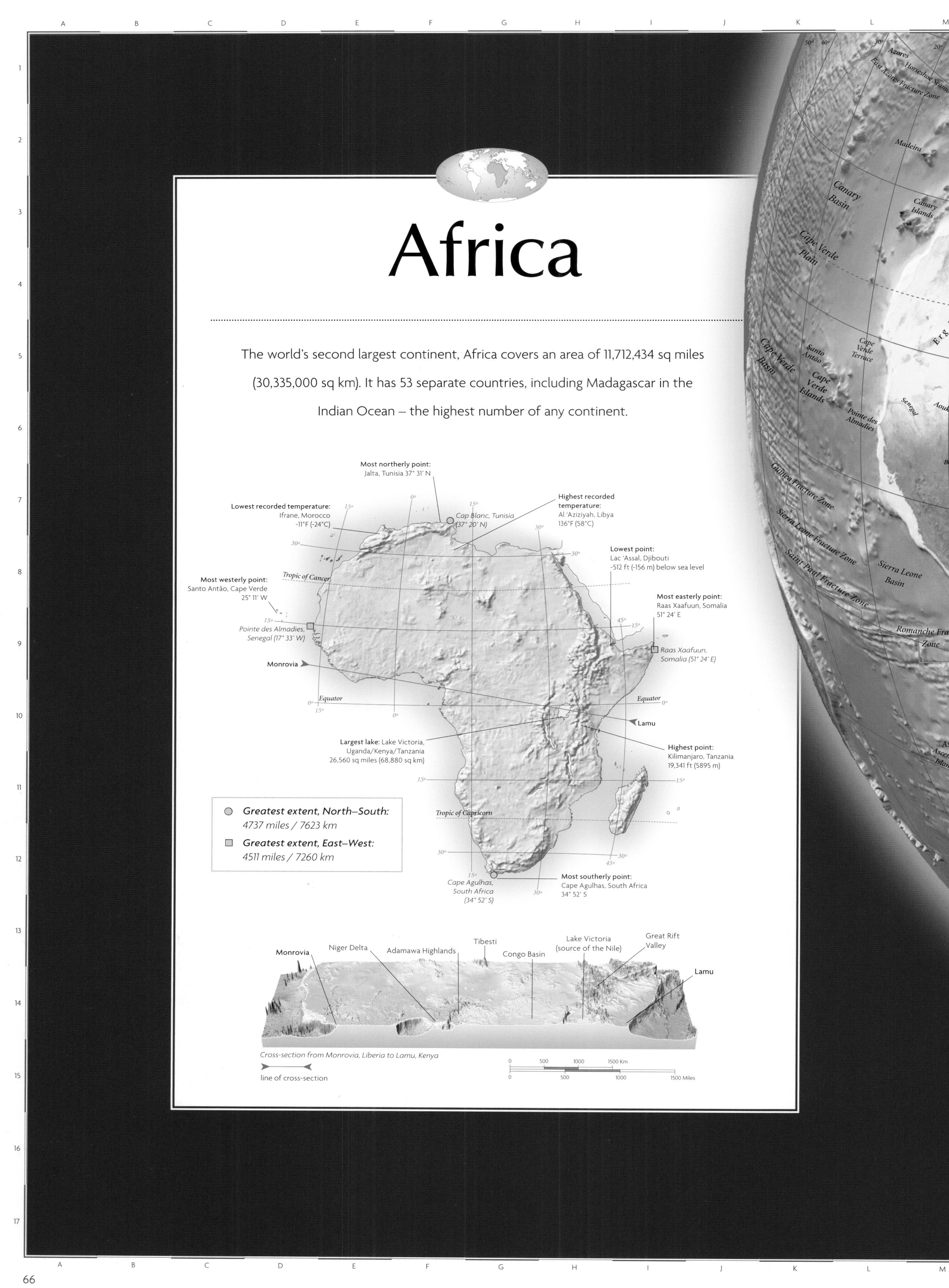

Most northerly point:
Jalta, Tunisia 37° 31' N
Lowest recorded temperature:
Ifrane, Morocco
-11°F (-24°C)
Cap Blanc, Tunisia
(37° 20' N)
Highest recorded temperature:
Al 'Aziziyah, Libya
136°F (58°C)
Lowest point:
Lac 'Assal, Djibouti
-512 ft (-156 m) below sea level
Most westerly point:
Santo Antão, Cape Verde
25° 11' W
Tropic of Cancer
Most easterly point:
Raas Xaafuun, Somalia
51° 24' E
Pointe des Almadies,
Senegal (17° 33' W)
Raas Xaafuun,
Somalia (51° 24' E)
Monrovia
Equator
Lamu
Largest lake: Lake Victoria,
Uganda/Kenya/Tanzania
26,560 sq miles (68,880 sq km)
Highest point:
Kilimanjaro, Tanzania
19,341 ft (5895 m)
Greatest extent, North–South:
4737 miles / 7623 km
Greatest extent, East–West:
4511 miles / 7260 km
Tropic of Capricorn
Cape Agulhas,
South Africa
(34° 52' S)
Most southerly point:
Cape Agulhas, South Africa
34° 52' S
Monrovia
Niger Delta
Adamawa Highlands
Tibesti
Congo Basin
Lake Victoria
(source of the Nile)
Great Rift Valley
Lamu
Cross-section from Monrovia, Liberia to Lamu, Kenya
line of cross-section
0 500 1000 1500 Km
0 500 1000 1500 Miles
Azores
Horseshoe Seamounts
East Azores Fracture Zone
Madeira
Canary Basin
Canary Islands
Cape Verde Plain
Cape Verde Basin
Santo Antão
Cape Verde Terrace
Cape Verde Islands
Pointe des Almadies
Senegal
Guinea Fracture Zone
Sierra Leone Fracture Zone
Saint Paul Fracture Zone
Sierra Leone Basin
Romanche Fracture Zone

N O P Q R S T U V W X Y Z

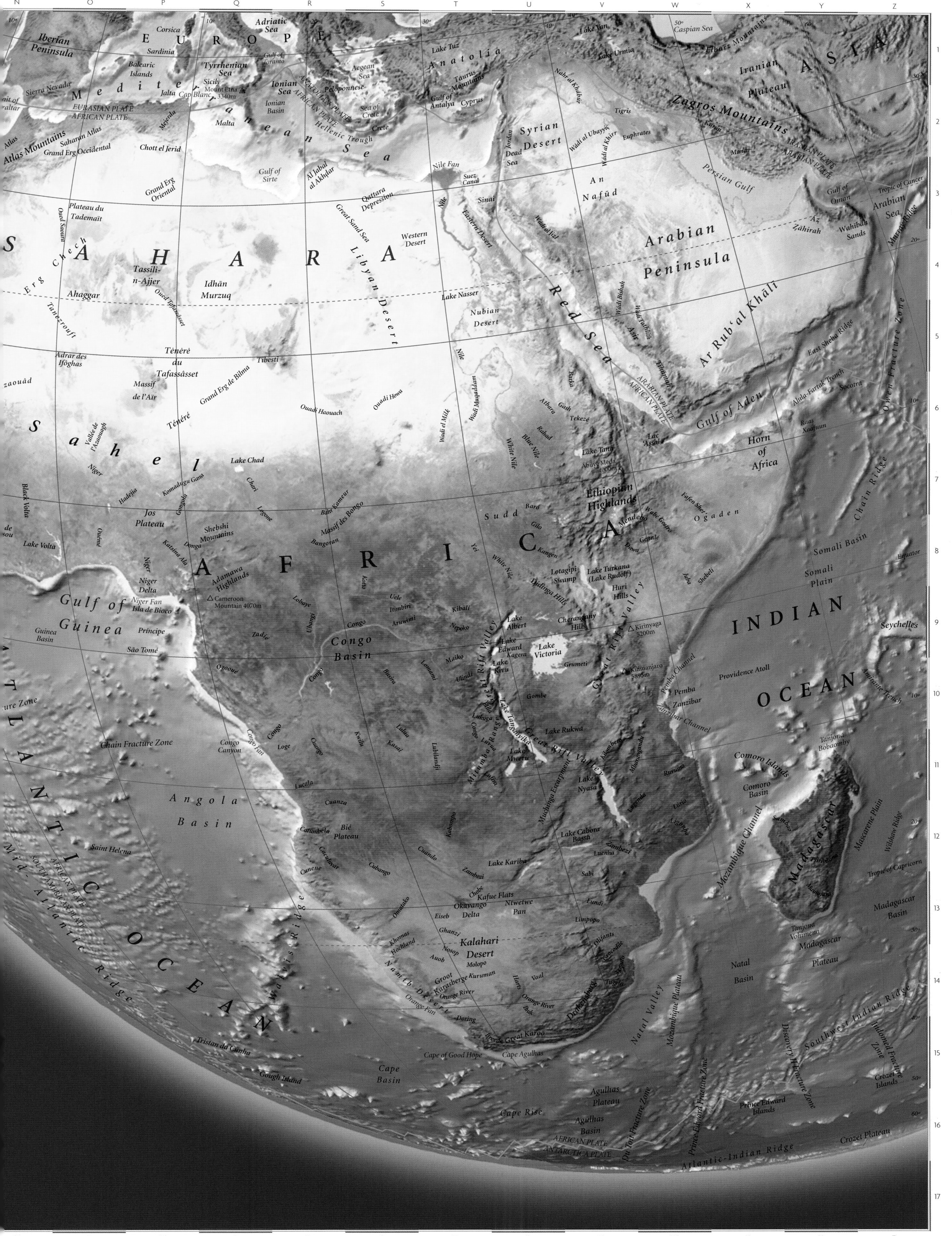

Iberian Peninsula
Corsica
Sardinia
EUROPE
Adriatic Sea
Balearic Islands
Tyrrhenian Sea
Sicily
Mount Etna 3340m
Ionian Sea
Ionian Basin
Aegean Sea
Peloponnese
Sea of Crete
Crete
Lake Tuz
Anatolia
Taurus Mountains
Gulf of Antalya
Cyprus
Lake Van
Lake Urmia
Caspian Sea
Elburz Mountains
Iranian Plateau
ASIA
Zagros Mountains
Tigris
Euphrates
Sierra Nevada
Mediterranean Sea
EURASIAN PLATE
AFRICAN PLATE
Malta
Atlas Mountains
Saharan Atlas
Grand Erg Occidental
Chott el Jerid
Hellenic Trough
Syrian Desert
Jordan
Dead Sea
Nile Fan
Suez Canal
Sinai
Gulf of Sirte
Al Jabal al Akhdar
Qattara Depression
Grand Erg Oriental
Plateau du Tademaït
Oued Saoura
Great Sand Sea
Western Desert
Eastern Desert
An Nafūd
Persian Gulf
Gulf of Oman
Tropic of Cancer
Arabian Sea
Az Zāhirah
Wahibah Sands
SAHARA
Erg Chech
Tassili-n-Ajjer
Idhān Murzuq
Libyan Desert
Arabian Peninsula
Ahaggar
Tanezrouft
Lake Nasser
Nubian Desert
Red Sea
Ar Rub'al Khālī
Adrar des Ifôghas
Ténéré du Tafassâsset
Tibesti
Massif de l'Aïr
Grand Erg de Bilma
Ténéré
Ouadi Haouach
Ouadi Howa
Wadi el Milk
Wadi Muqaddam
Atbara
Tekezē
Gulf of Aden
Horn of Africa
Socotra
Sahel
Lake Chad
Chari
Niger
Blue Nile
White Nile
Lake Tana
Ethiopian Highlands
Ogaden
Black Volta
Jos Plateau
Shebshi Mountains
Adamawa Highlands
Sudd
AFRICA
Lake Volta
Massif des Bongo
Lotagipi Swamp
Lake Turkana (Lake Rudolf)
Huri Hills
Somali Basin
Somali Plain
Equator
Gulf of Guinea
Niger Delta
Niger Fan
Isla de Bioco
Cameroon Mountain 4070m
Príncipe
São Tomé
Guinea Basin
Congo
Congo Basin
Lake Albert
Lake Edward
Lake Victoria
Lake Kivu
Kirinyaga 5200m
Kilimanjaro 5895m
Great Rift Valley
Western Rift Valley
INDIAN OCEAN
Seychelles
Providence Atoll
Pemba
Zanzibar
Pemba Channel
Zanzibar Channel
Lake Tanganyika
Lake Rukwa
Lake Mweru
Chain Fracture Zone
Congo Canyon
Congo Fan
Lake Nyasa
Comoro Islands
Comoro Basin
Tanjona Bobaomby
Angola Basin
Bié Plateau
Lake Cabora Bassa
Mozambique Channel
Madagascar
Mascarene Plain
Saint Helena
Lake Kariba
Zambezi
Kafue Flats
Okavango Delta
Ntwetwe Pan
Limpopo
Tropic of Capricorn
Madagascar Basin
Kalahari Desert
Khomas Hochland
Groot Karasberge
Orange River
Namib Desert
Walvis Ridge
Tanjona Vohimena
Madagascar Plateau
Natal Basin
Drakensberg
Great Karoo
Natal Valley
Mozambique Plateau
Southwest Indian Ridge
ATLANTIC OCEAN
Mid-Atlantic Ridge
Tristan da Cunha
Gough Island
Cape of Good Hope
Cape Agulhas
Cape Basin
Agulhas Plateau
Agulhas Basin
Cape Rise
Prince Edward Islands
Crozet Islands
Crozet Plateau
AFRICAN PLATE
ANTARCTICA PLATE
Atlantic-Indian Ridge
Du Toit Fracture Zone
Prince Edward Fracture Zone
Discovery II Fracture Zone

N O P Q R S T U V W X Y Z

Physical Africa

The structure of Africa was dramatically influenced by the break up of the supercontinent Gondwanaland about 160 million years ago and, more recently, rifting and hot spot activity. Today, much of Africa is remote from active plate boundaries and comprises a series of extensive plateaux and deep basins, which influence the drainage patterns of major rivers. The relief rises to the east, where volcanic uplands and vast lakes mark the Great Rift Valley. In the far north and south sedimentary rocks have been folded to form the Atlas Mountains and the Great Karoo.

Northern Africa

Northern Africa comprises a system of basins and plateaux. The Tibesti and Ahaggar are volcanic uplands, whose uplift has been matched by subsidence within large surrounding basins. Many of the basins have been infilled with sand and gravel, creating the vast Saharan lands. The Atlas Mountains in the north were formed by convergence of the African and Eurasian plates.

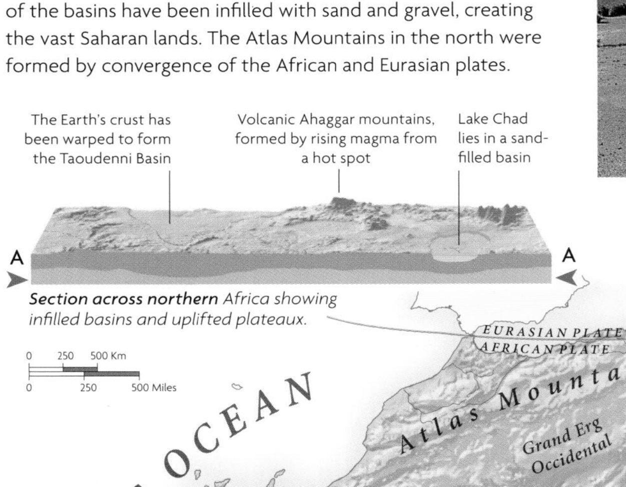

The Earth's crust has been warped to form the Taoudenni Basin
Volcanic Ahaggar mountains, formed by rising magma from a hot spot
Lake Chad lies in a sand-filled basin
A
A
0 250 500 Km
0 250 500 Miles

Section across northern *Africa showing infilled basins and uplifted plateaux.*

East Africa

The Great Rift Valley is the most striking feature of this region, running for 4475 miles (7200 km) from Lake Nyasa to the Red Sea. North of Lake Nyasa it splits into two arms and encloses an interior plateau which contains Lake Victoria. A number of elongated lakes and volcanoes lie along the fault lines. To the west lies the Congo Basin, a vast, shallow depression, which rises to form an almost circular rim of highlands.

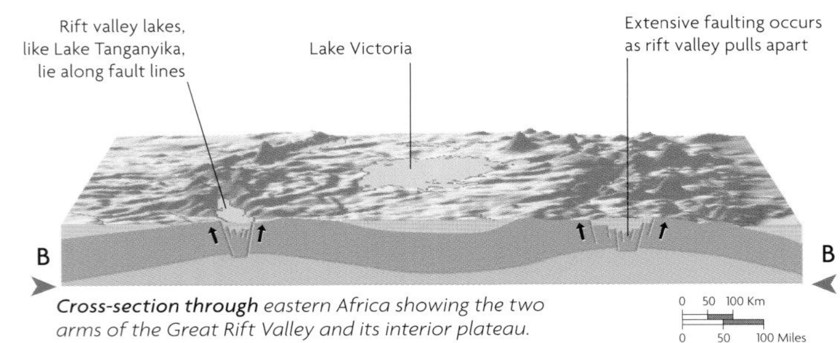

Rift valley lakes, like Lake Tanganyika, lie along fault lines
Lake Victoria
Extensive faulting occurs as rift valley pulls apart
B
B
0 50 100 Km
0 50 100 Miles

Cross-section through *eastern Africa showing the two arms of the Great Rift Valley and its interior plateau.*

Scale 1:36,000,000

Km 0 200 400 600 800

Miles 0 200 400 600 800

projection: Lambert Azimuthal Equal Area

Map key

Elevation

- 5000m / 16,405ft
- 4000m / 13,124ft
- 3000m / 9843ft
- 2000m / 6562ft
- 1000m / 3281ft
- 500m / 1640ft
- 250m / 820ft
- 100m / 328ft
- sea level
- below sea level

Plate margins (for explanation see page xiv)

- constructive
- destructive
- conservative
- uncertain
- line of cross-section

Mediterranean Sea
EURASIAN PLATE
AFRICAN PLATE
ANATOLIAN PLATE
AFRICAN PLATE
ARABIAN PLATE
ARABIAN PLATE
AFRICAN PLATE
ATLANTIC OCEAN
Atlas Mountains
Chott el Jerid
Grand Erg Occidental
Grand Erg Oriental
Gulf of Sirte
Erg Iguidi
Erg Chech
Ahaggar
Sahara
Tibesti
Qattara Depression
Nile Delta
Western Desert
Great Sand Sea
Libyan Desert
Eastern Desert
Nile
Red Sea
ASIA
Lake Nasser
Nubian Desert
Cape Verde Islands
Taoudenni Basin
Niger
Senegal
Massif de l'Aïr
Ténéré
Sahel
Lake Chad
Blue Nile
White Nile
Gulf of Aden
Lake Tana
Horn of Africa
White Volta
Lake Volta
Ethiopian Highlands
Benue
Adamawa Highlands
Massif des Bongo
Sudd
Grain Coast
Ivory Coast
Gold Coast
Slave Coast
Bight of Benin
Niger Delta
Cameroon Mountain 4070m
Ubangi
Shebeli
Lake Turkana (Lake Rudolf)
Gulf of Guinea
Congo
Lake Albert
Juba
São Tomé
Congo Basin
Great Rift Valley
Lake Victoria
Kilimanjaro 5895m
Seychelles
Mitumba Range
Lake Tanganyika
Pemba Island
Zanzibar
Bié Plateau
Lake Nyasa
Comoro Islands
Zambezi
Mozambique Channel
Madagascar
INDIAN OCEAN
Okavango Delta
Namib Desert
Kalahari Basin
Kalahari Desert
Limpopo
Mauritius
Réunion
Orange River
Drakensberg
Great Karoo
Cape of Good Hope

Southern Africa

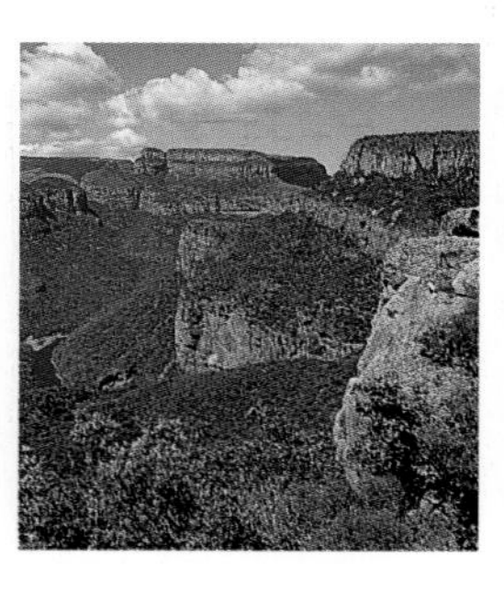

The Great Escarpment marks the southern boundary of Africa's basement rock and includes the Drakensberg range. It was uplifted when Gondwanaland fragmented about 160 million years ago and it has gradually been eroded back from the coast. To the north, the relief drops steadily, forming the Kalahari Basin. In the far south are the fold mountains of the Great Karoo.

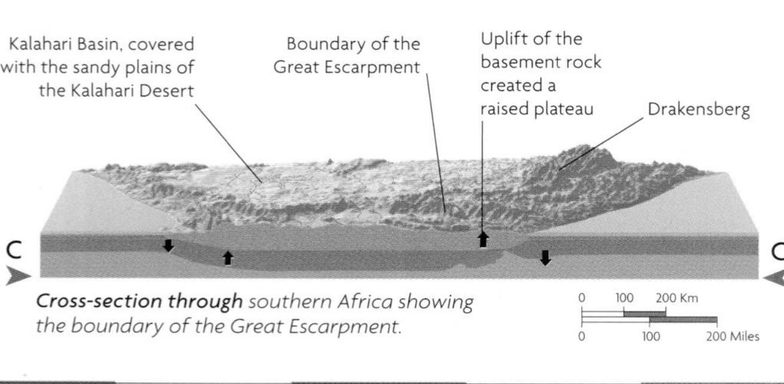

Kalahari Basin, covered with the sandy plains of the Kalahari Desert
Boundary of the Great Escarpment
Uplift of the basement rock created a raised plateau
Drakensberg
C
C
0 100 200 Km
0 100 200 Miles

Cross-section through *southern Africa showing the boundary of the Great Escarpment.*

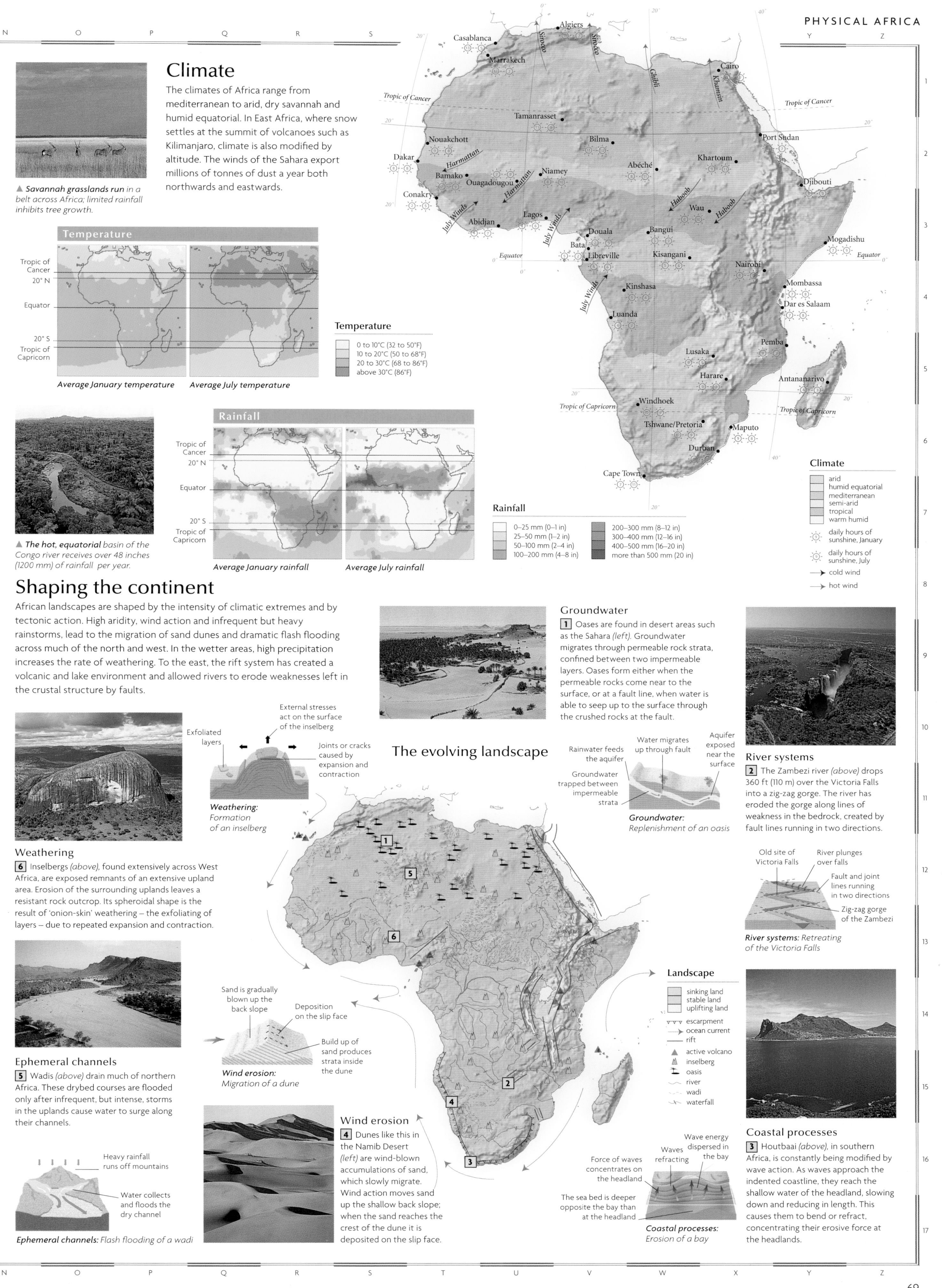

N O P Q R S Y Z
1 2 3 4 5 6 7 8 9 10 11 12 13 14 15 16 17
Algiers
Casablanca
Marrakech
Sirocco
Ghibli
Cairo
Khamsin
Tropic of Cancer
Tamanrasset
Port Sudan
Nouakchott
Bilma
Dakar
Harmattan
Khartoum
Bamako
Niamey
Abéché
Ouagadougou
Djibouti
Conakry
Haboob
July Winds
Wau
Abidjan
Lagos
Douala
Bangui
Mogadishu
Bata
Libreville
Kisangani
Equator
Nairobi
Kinshasa
Mombassa
Dar es Salaam
Luanda
Pemba
Lusaka
Harare
Antananarivo
Tropic of Capricorn
Windhoek
Tshwane/Pretoria
Maputo
Durban
Cape Town
Temperature
Tropic of Cancer
20° N
Equator
20° S
Tropic of Capricorn
Average January temperature
Average July temperature
Temperature
0 to 10°C (32 to 50°F)
10 to 20°C (50 to 68°F)
20 to 30°C (68 to 86°F)
above 30°C (86°F)
Rainfall
Average January rainfall
Average July rainfall
Rainfall
0–25 mm (0–1 in)
25–50 mm (1–2 in)
50–100 mm (2–4 in)
100–200 mm (4–8 in)
200–300 mm (8–12 in)
300–400 mm (12–16 in)
400–500 mm (16–20 in)
more than 500 mm (20 in)
Climate
arid
humid equatorial
mediterranean
semi-arid
tropical
warm humid
daily hours of sunshine, January
daily hours of sunshine, July
cold wind
hot wind

Climate

The climates of Africa range from mediterranean to arid, dry savannah and humid equatorial. In East Africa, where snow settles at the summit of volcanoes such as Kilimanjaro, climate is also modified by altitude. The winds of the Sahara export millions of tonnes of dust a year both northwards and eastwards.

▲ *Savannah grasslands run in a belt across Africa; limited rainfall inhibits tree growth.*

▲ ***The hot, equatorial** basin of the Congo river receives over 48 inches (1200 mm) of rainfall per year.*

Shaping the continent

African landscapes are shaped by the intensity of climatic extremes and by tectonic action. High aridity, wind action and infrequent but heavy rainstorms, lead to the migration of sand dunes and dramatic flash flooding across much of the north and west. In the wetter areas, high precipitation increases the rate of weathering. To the east, the rift system has created a volcanic and lake environment and allowed rivers to erode weaknesses left in the crustal structure by faults.

The evolving landscape

Exfoliated layers
External stresses act on the surface of the inselberg
Joints or cracks caused by expansion and contraction
Sand is gradually blown up the back slope
Deposition on the slip face
Build up of sand produces strata inside the dune
Rainwater feeds the aquifer
Water migrates up through fault
Aquifer exposed near the surface
Groundwater trapped between impermeable strata
Old site of Victoria Falls
River plunges over falls
Fault and joint lines running in two directions
Zig-zag gorge of the Zambezi
Heavy rainfall runs off mountains
Water collects and floods the dry channel
Force of waves concentrates on the headland
Waves refracting
Wave energy dispersed in the bay
The sea bed is deeper opposite the bay than at the headland
Landscape
sinking land
stable land
uplifting land
escarpment
ocean current
rift
active volcano
inselberg
oasis
river
wadi
waterfall
1 2 3 4 5 6

Weathering: *Formation of an inselberg*

Groundwater

1 Oases are found in desert areas such as the Sahara *(left)*. Groundwater migrates through permeable rock strata, confined between two impermeable layers. Oases form either when the permeable rocks come near to the surface, or at a fault line, when water is able to seep up to the surface through the crushed rocks at the fault.

***Groundwater:** Replenishment of an oasis*

River systems

2 The Zambezi river *(above)* drops 360 ft (110 m) over the Victoria Falls into a zig-zag gorge. The river has eroded the gorge along lines of weakness in the bedrock, created by fault lines running in two directions.

***River systems:** Retreating of the Victoria Falls*

Weathering

6 Inselbergs *(above)*, found extensively across West Africa, are exposed remnants of an extensive upland area. Erosion of the surrounding uplands leaves a resistant rock outcrop. Its spheroidal shape is the result of 'onion-skin' weathering – the exfoliating of layers – due to repeated expansion and contraction.

Ephemeral channels

5 Wadis *(above)* drain much of northern Africa. These drybed courses are flooded only after infrequent, but intense, storms in the uplands cause water to surge along their channels.

***Ephemeral channels:** Flash flooding of a wadi*

***Wind erosion:** Migration of a dune*

Wind erosion

4 Dunes like this in the Namib Desert *(left)* are wind-blown accumulations of sand, which slowly migrate. Wind action moves sand up the shallow back slope; when the sand reaches the crest of the dune it is deposited on the slip face.

***Coastal processes:** Erosion of a bay*

Coastal processes

3 Houtbaai *(above)*, in southern Africa, is constantly being modified by wave action. As waves approach the indented coastline, they reach the shallow water of the headland, slowing down and reducing in length. This causes them to bend or refract, concentrating their erosive force at the headlands.

Political Africa

The political map of modern Africa only emerged following the end of the Second World War. Over the next half-century, all of the countries formerly controlled by European powers gained independence from their colonial rulers – only Liberia and Ethiopia were never colonized.

The post-colonial era has not been an easy period for many countries, but there have been moves towards multi-party democracy across much of the continent. In South Africa, democratic elections replaced the internationally-condemned apartheid system only in 1994. Other countries have still to find political stability; corruption in government and ethnic tensions are serious problems. National infrastructures, based on the colonial transport systems built to exploit Africa's resources, are often inappropriate for independent economic development.

Languages

Three major world languages act as *lingua francas* across the African continent: Arabic in North Africa; English in southern and eastern Africa and Nigeria; and French in Central and West Africa, and in Madagascar. A huge number of African languages are spoken as well – over 2000 have been recorded, with more than 400 in Nigeria alone – reflecting the continuing importance of traditional cultures and values. In the north of the continent, the extensive use of Arabic reflects Middle Eastern influences while Bantu is widely-spoken across much of southern Africa.

BERBER ARABIC TUAREG TEDA ARABIC BEJA FULANI MANDINGO MOSI HAUSA KANURI AKAN YORUBA EVE IBO TIGRAI AMHARA GALLA DINKA SOMALI AZANDE MASAI SWAHILI BANTU SAN KHOI AFRIKAANS MALAGASY

Language groups

- Afro-Asiatic (Hamito-Semitic)
- Niger-Congo
- Nilo-Saharan
- Khoisan
- Indo-European
- Austronesian

Official African languages

- French
- English
- Arabic
- Portuguese
- Swahili
- Amharic
- Spanish
- French/English
- French/Arabic
- French/Malagasy
- English/Swahili
- Arabic/Somali

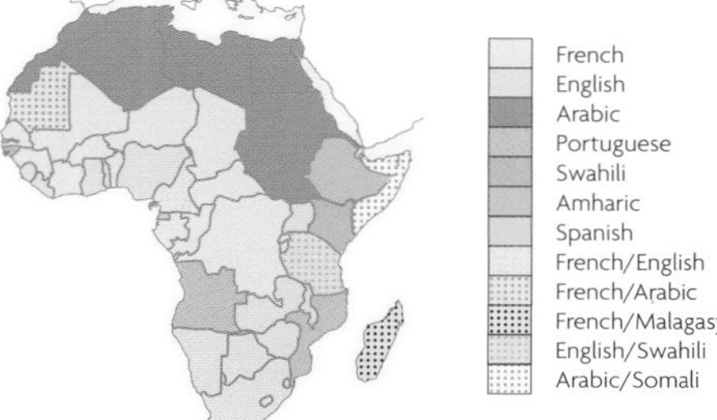

▲ *Islamic influences are evident throughout North Africa. The Great Mosque at Kairouan, Tunisia, is Africa's holiest Islamic place.*

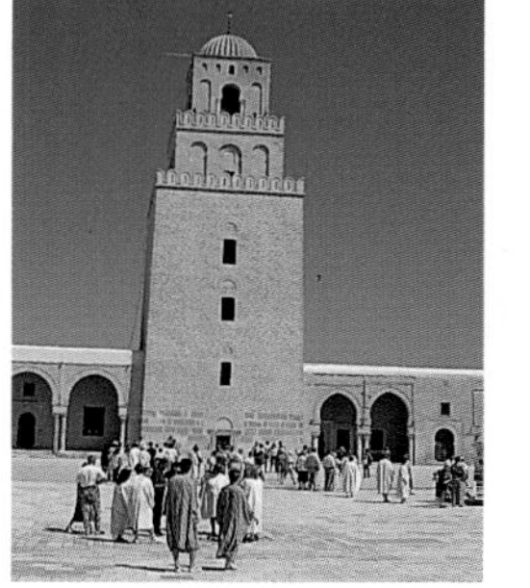

▲ *In northeastern Nigeria, people speak Kanuri – a dialect of the Nilo-Saharan language group.*

Transport

African railways were built to aid the exploitation of natural resources, and most offer passage only from the interior to the coastal cities, leaving large parts of the continent untouched – five land-locked countries have no railways at all. The Congo, Nile and Niger river networks offer limited access to land within the continental interior, but have a number of waterfalls and cataracts which prevent navigation from the sea. Many roads were developed in the 1960s and 1970s, but economic difficulties are making the maintenance and expansion of the networks difficult.

► *South Africa has the largest concentration of railways in Africa. Over 20,000 miles (32,000 km) of routes have been built since 1870.*

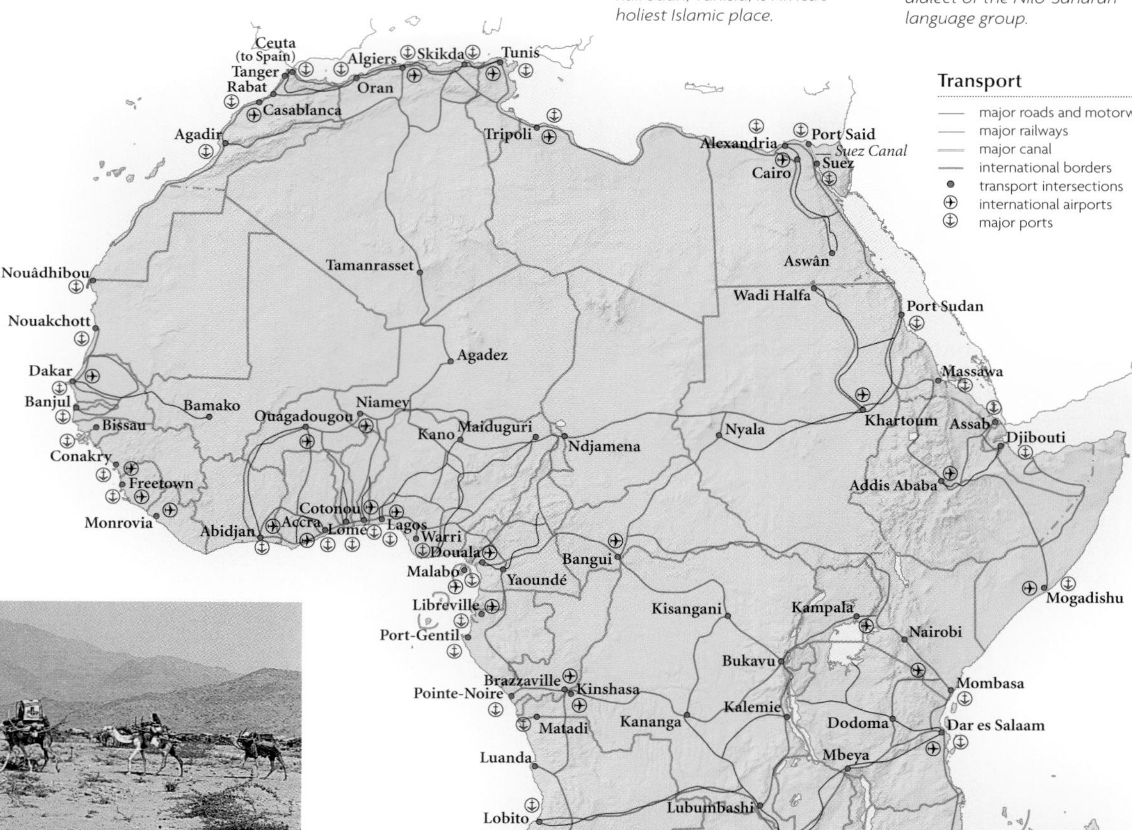
Transport
major roads and motorways
major railways
major canal
international borders
transport intersections
international airports
major ports
Ceuta (to Spain)
Tanger
Rabat
Casablanca
Algiers
Skikda
Tunis
Oran
Agadir
Tripoli
Alexandria
Port Said
Suez Canal
Cairo
Suez
Aswân
Wadi Halfa
Port Sudan
Tamanrasset
Nouâdhibou
Nouakchott
Agadez
Dakar
Banjul
Bissau
Bamako
Niamey
Ouagadougou
Kano
Maiduguri
Ndjamena
Nyala
Khartoum
Massawa
Assab
Djibouti
Addis Ababa
Conakry
Freetown
Monrovia
Abidjan
Accra
Lomé
Cotonou
Lagos
Warri
Douala
Malabo
Yaoundé
Bangui
Libreville
Port-Gentil
Kisangani
Kampala
Nairobi
Mogadishu
Bukavu
Mombasa
Brazzaville
Kinshasa
Pointe-Noire
Matadi
Kananga
Kalemie
Dodoma
Dar es Salaam
Mbeya
Luanda
Lobito
Lubumbashi
Namibe
Nampula
Lusaka
Livingstone
Harare
Tsumeb
Bulawayo
Beira
Antananarivo
Toamasina
Walvis Bay
Windhoek
Tshwane/Pretoria
Johannesburg
Maputo
Keetmanshoop
Durban
Cape Town
Port Elizabeth

▲ *Traditional means of transport, such as the camel, are still widely used across the less accessible parts of Africa.*

◄ *The Congo river, though not suitable for river transport along its entire length, forms a vital link for people and goods in its navigable inland reaches.*

PORTUGAL Madeira (to Portugal) Canary Islands (to Spain) Casablanca Safi Marrakech MOROCCO Agadir LAÂYOUNE Western Sahara (Occupied by Morocco) Tropic of Cancer MAURITANIA NOUAKCHOTT CAPE VERDE PRAIA Senegal SENEGAL DAKAR Kaolack BANJUL GAMBIA GUINEA-BISSAU BISSAU BAMAKO GUINEA CONAKRY FREETOWN Koidu SIERRA LEONE YAMOUSSOUKRO MONROVIA LIBERIA

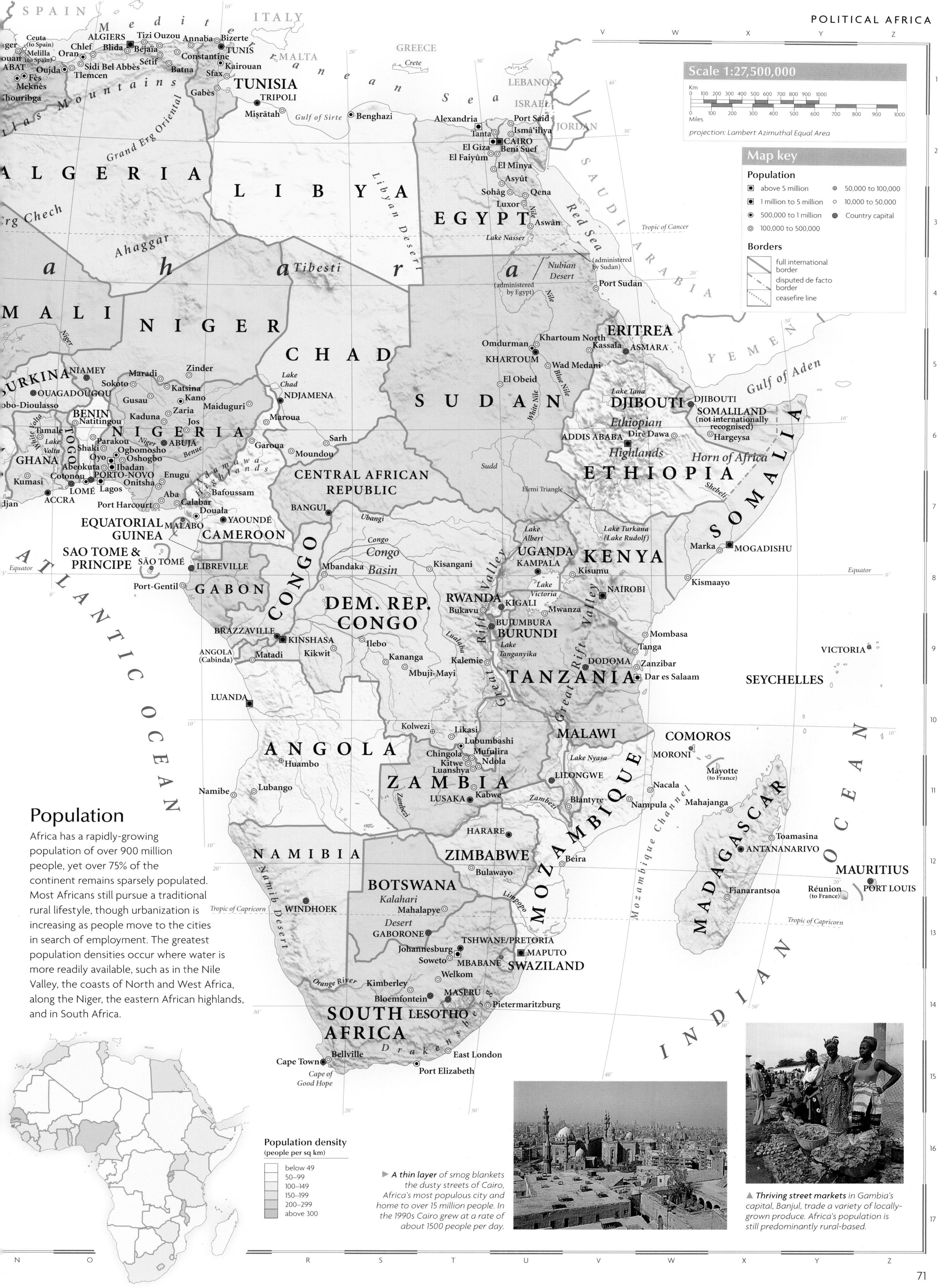
Scale 1:27,500,000
projection: Lambert Azimuthal Equal Area
Map key
Population
above 5 million
1 million to 5 million
500,000 to 1 million
100,000 to 500,000
50,000 to 100,000
10,000 to 50,000
Country capital
Borders
full international border
disputed de facto border
ceasefire line
Population density
(people per sq km)
below 49
50–99
100–149
150–199
200–299
above 300
ATLANTIC OCEAN
INDIAN OCEAN
ALGERIA
LIBYA
EGYPT
MALI
NIGER
CHAD
SUDAN
ERITREA
DJIBOUTI
SOMALILAND (not internationally recognised)
ETHIOPIA
SOMALIA
NIGERIA
CENTRAL AFRICAN REPUBLIC
CAMEROON
EQUATORIAL GUINEA
SAO TOME & PRINCIPE
GABON
CONGO
DEM. REP. CONGO
UGANDA
KENYA
RWANDA
BURUNDI
TANZANIA
SEYCHELLES
COMOROS
MALAWI
ANGOLA
ZAMBIA
MOZAMBIQUE
ZIMBABWE
NAMIBIA
BOTSWANA
MADAGASCAR
MAURITIUS
SWAZILAND
LESOTHO
SOUTH AFRICA
TUNISIA
BENIN
TOGO
GHANA

Population

Africa has a rapidly-growing population of over 900 million people, yet over 75% of the continent remains sparsely populated. Most Africans still pursue a traditional rural lifestyle, though urbanization is increasing as people move to the cities in search of employment. The greatest population densities occur where water is more readily available, such as in the Nile Valley, the coasts of North and West Africa, along the Niger, the eastern African highlands, and in South Africa.

▶ *A thin layer* of smog blankets the dusty streets of Cairo, Africa's most populous city and home to over 15 million people. In the 1990s Cairo grew at a rate of about 1500 people per day.

▲ *Thriving street markets* in Gambia's capital, Banjul, trade a variety of locally-grown produce. Africa's population is still predominantly rural-based.

African resources

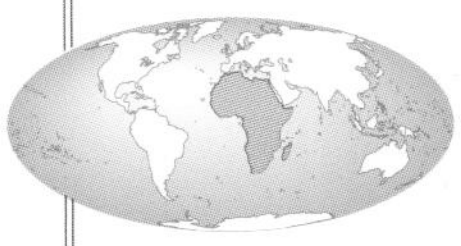

The economies of most African countries are dominated by subsistence and cash crop agriculture, with limited industrialization. Manufacturing industry is largely confined to South Africa. Many countries depend on a single resource, such as copper or gold, or a cash crop, such as coffee, for export income, which can leave them vulnerable to fluctuations in world commodity prices. In order to diversify their economies and develop a wider industrial base, investment from overseas is being actively sought by many African governments.

Standard of living

Since the 1960s most countries in Africa have seen significant improvements in life expectancy, healthcare and education. However, 28 of the 30 most deprived countries in the world are African, and the continent as a whole lies well behind the rest of the world in terms of meeting many basic human needs.

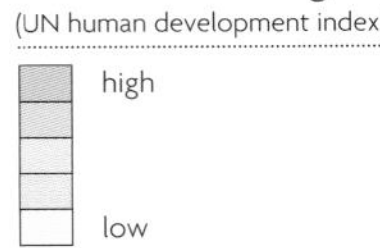
Standard of living
(UN human development index)
high
low

Industry

Many African industries concentrate on the extraction and processing of raw materials. These include the oil industry, food processing, mining and textile production. South Africa accounts for over half of the continent's industrial output with much of the remainder coming from the countries along the northern coast. Over 60% of Africa's workforce is employed in agriculture.

◀ ***The unspoilt natural** splendour of wildlife reserves, like the Serengeti National Park in Tanzania, attract tourists to Africa from around the globe. The tourist industry in Kenya and Tanzania is particularly well developed, where it accounts for almost 10% of GNI*

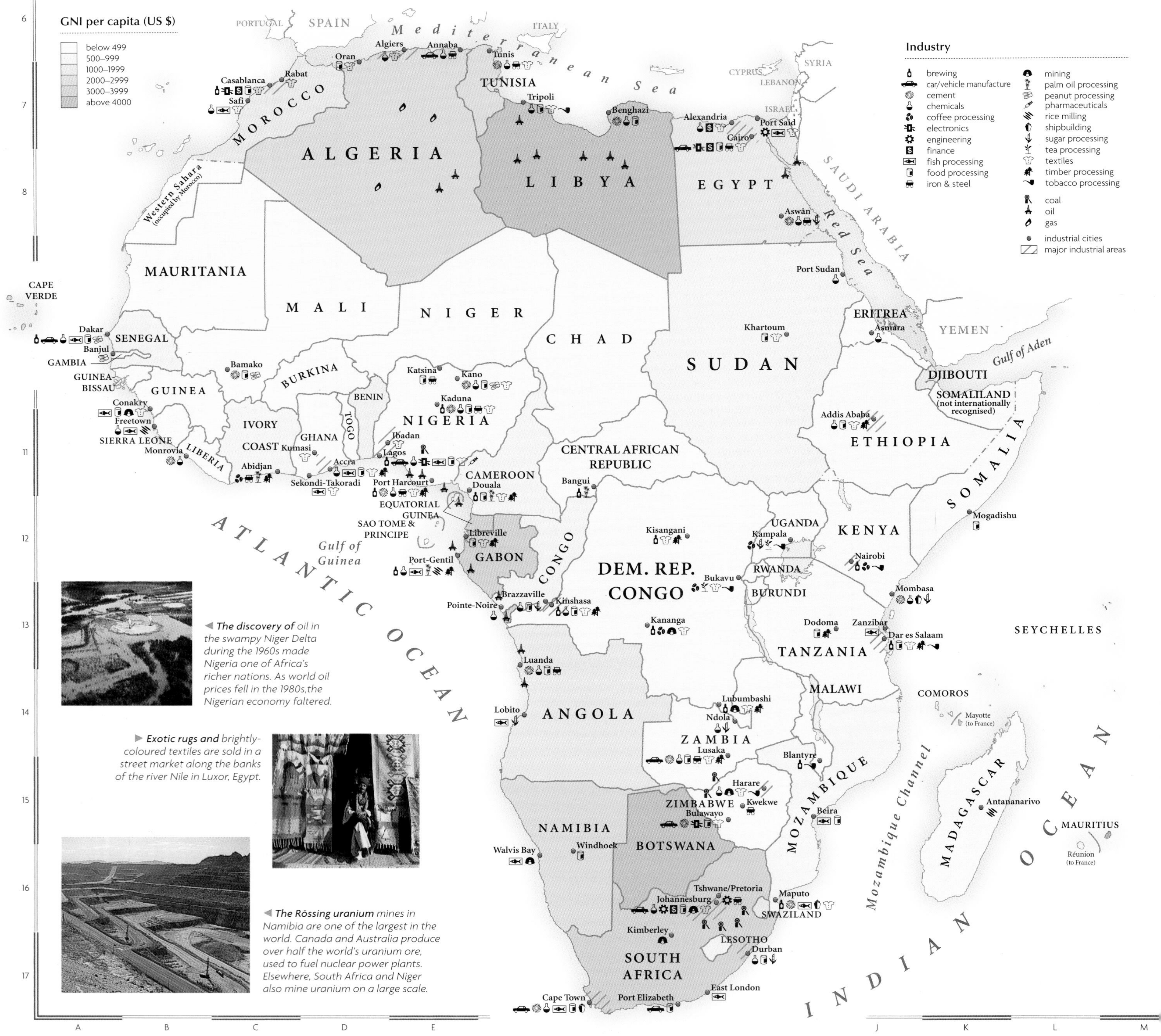

GNI per capita (US $)

- below 499
- 500–999
- 1000–1999
- 2000–2999
- 3000–3999
- above 4000

Industry

- brewing
- car/vehicle manufacture
- cement
- chemicals
- coffee processing
- electronics
- engineering
- finance
- fish processing
- food processing
- iron & steel
- mining
- palm oil processing
- peanut processing
- pharmaceuticals
- rice milling
- shipbuilding
- sugar processing
- tea processing
- textiles
- timber processing
- tobacco processing
- coal
- oil
- gas
- industrial cities
- major industrial areas

PORTUGAL SPAIN ITALY Mediterranean Sea CYPRUS SYRIA LEBANON ISRAEL SAUDI ARABIA Red Sea YEMEN Gulf of Aden

Casablanca Rabat Safi MOROCCO Western Sahara (occupied by Morocco) Oran Algiers Annaba ALGERIA Tunis TUNISIA Tripoli Benghazi LIBYA Alexandria Port Said Cairo EGYPT Aswân Port Sudan Khartoum SUDAN ERITREA Asmara DJIBOUTI SOMALILAND (not internationally recognised) Addis Ababa ETHIOPIA SOMALIA Mogadishu

MAURITANIA MALI NIGER CHAD CAPE VERDE Dakar SENEGAL Banjul GAMBIA GUINEA-BISSAU GUINEA Conakry Freetown SIERRA LEONE Monrovia LIBERIA Bamako BURKINA IVORY COAST Abidjan Kumasi GHANA Accra Sekondi-Takoradi TOGO BENIN Katsina Kano Kaduna NIGERIA Ibadan Lagos Port Harcourt CAMEROON Douala CENTRAL AFRICAN REPUBLIC Bangui EQUATORIAL GUINEA SAO TOME & PRINCIPE Gulf of Guinea Libreville GABON Port-Gentil CONGO Brazzaville Pointe-Noire Kinshasa Kisangani DEM. REP. CONGO Bukavu Kananga UGANDA Kampala RWANDA BURUNDI KENYA Nairobi Mombasa SEYCHELLES TANZANIA Dodoma Zanzibar Dar es Salaam

ATLANTIC OCEAN Luanda Lobito ANGOLA Lubumbashi Ndola ZAMBIA Lusaka MALAWI Blantyre COMOROS Mayotte (to France) MOZAMBIQUE Mozambique Channel Harare Kwekwe ZIMBABWE Bulawayo Beira MADAGASCAR Antananarivo MAURITIUS Réunion (to France) NAMIBIA Windhoek Walvis Bay BOTSWANA Tshwane/Pretoria Johannesburg Maputo SWAZILAND Kimberley LESOTHO Durban SOUTH AFRICA East London Cape Town Port Elizabeth INDIAN OCEAN

◀ ***The discovery of** oil in the swampy Niger Delta during the 1960s made Nigeria one of Africa's richer nations. As world oil prices fell in the 1980s,the Nigerian economy faltered.*

▶ ***Exotic rugs and** brightly-coloured textiles are sold in a street market along the banks of the river Nile in Luxor, Egypt.*

◀ ***The Rössing uranium** mines in Namibia are one of the largest in the world. Canada and Australia produce over half the world's uranium ore, used to fuel nuclear power plants. Elsewhere, South Africa and Niger also mine uranium on a large scale.*

Environmental issues

One of Africa's most serious environmental problems occurs in marginal areas such as the Sahel where scrub and forest clearance, often for cooking fuel, combined with overgrazing, are causing desertification. Game reserves in southern and eastern Africa have helped to preserve many endangered animals, although the needs of growing populations have led to conflict over land use, and poaching is a serious problem.

Environmental issues

- national parks
- tropical forest
- forest destroyed
- desert
- desertification
- polluted rivers
- radioactive contamination
- marine pollution
- heavy marine pollution
- poor urban air quality

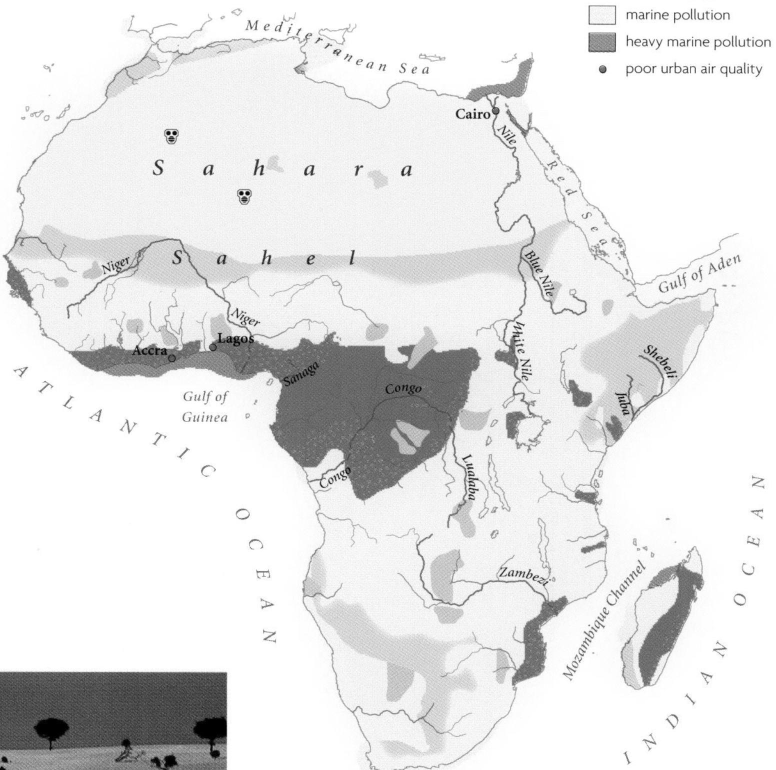

▲ ***The Sahel's delicate*** *natural equilibrium is easily destroyed by the clearing of vegetation, drought and overgrazing. This causes the Sahara to advance south, engulfing the savannah grasslands.*

Mineral resources

Africa's ancient plateaux contain some of the world's most substantial reserves of precious stones and metals. About 15% of the world's gold is mined in South Africa; Zambia has great copper deposits; and diamonds are mined in Botswana, Dem. Rep. Congo and South Africa. Oil has brought great economic benefits to Algeria, Libya and Nigeria.

Mineral resources

- oil field
- gas field
- coal field
- bauxite
- copper
- diamonds
- gold
- iron
- phosphates
- tin
- uranium

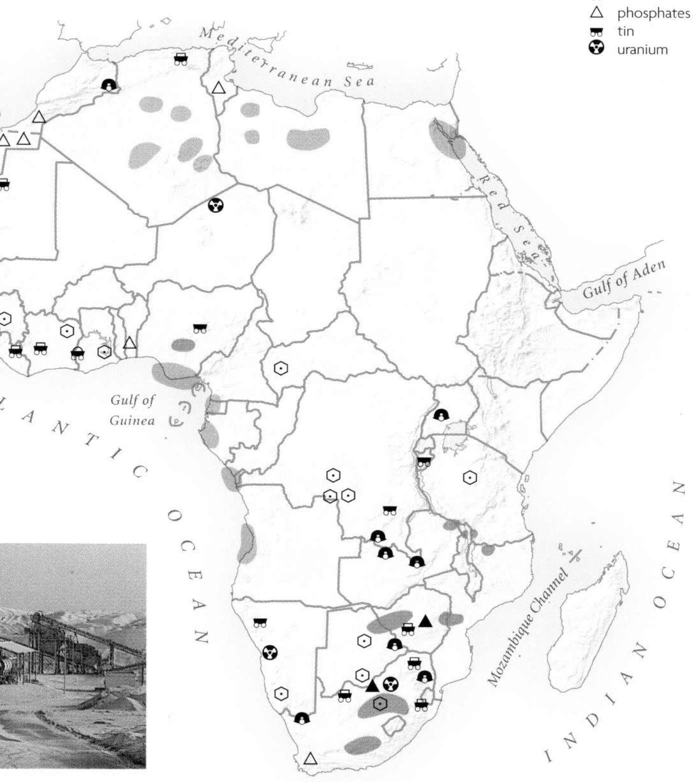

▲ ***North and West Africa*** *have large deposits of white phosphate minerals, which are used in making fertilizers. Morocco, Senegal, and Tunisia are among the continent's leading producers.*

▲ ***Workers on a tea plantation*** *gather one of Africa's most important cash crops, providing a valuable source of income. Coffee, rubber, bananas, cotton and cocoa are also widely grown as cash crops.*

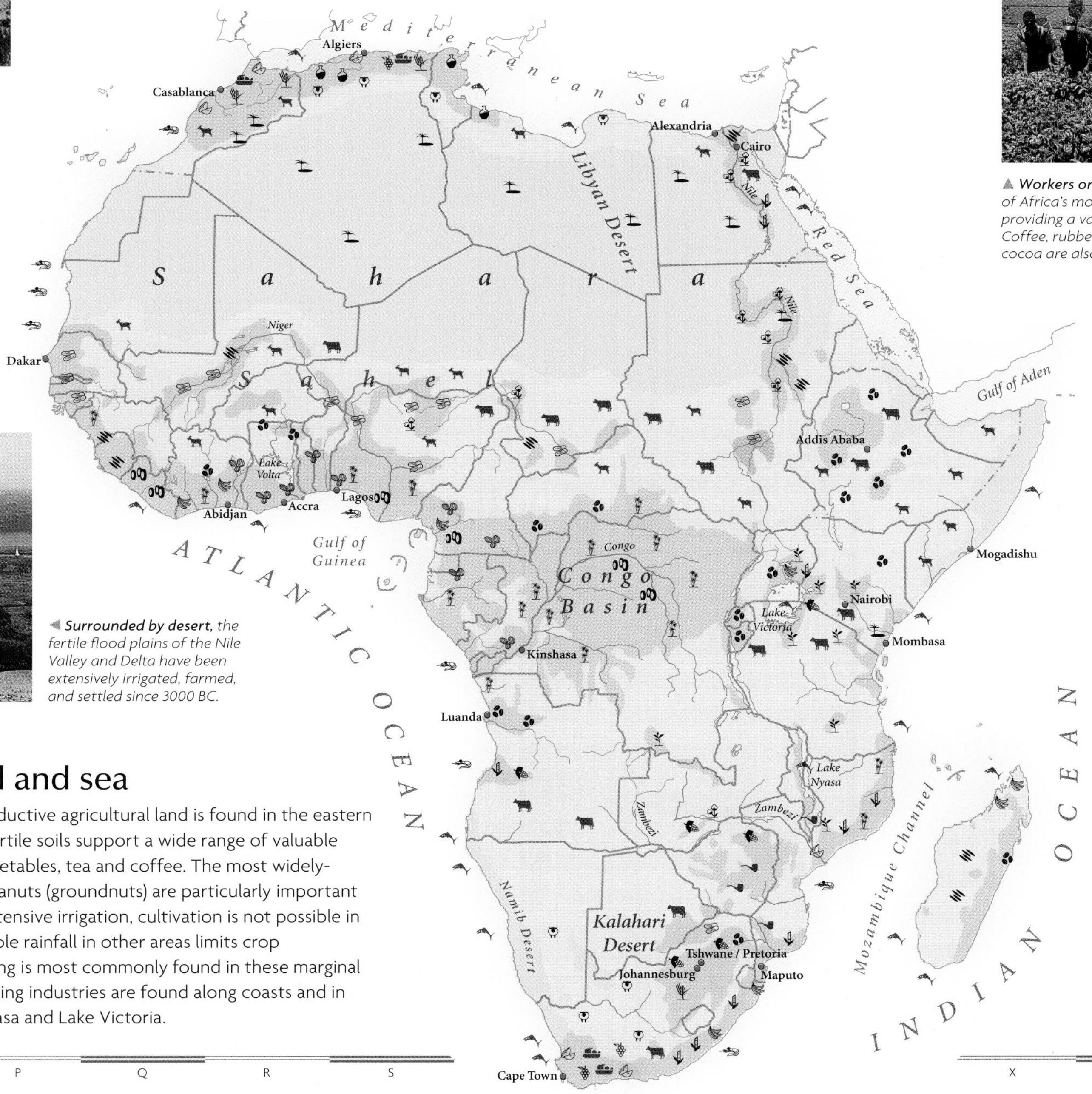

◀ ***Surrounded by desert,*** *the fertile flood plains of the Nile Valley and Delta have been extensively irrigated, farmed, and settled since 3000 BC.*

Using the land and sea

Some of Africa's most productive agricultural land is found in the eastern volcanic uplands, where fertile soils support a wide range of valuable export crops including vegetables, tea and coffee. The most widely-grown grain is corn and peanuts (groundnuts) are particularly important in West Africa. Without intensive irrigation, cultivation is not possible in desert regions and unreliable rainfall in other areas limits crop production. Pastoral herding is most commonly found in these marginal lands. Substantial local fishing industries are found along coasts and in vast lakes such as Lake Nyasa and Lake Victoria.

Using the land and sea

- cropland
- desert
- forest
- pasture
- wetland
- major conurbations
- cattle
- goats
- cereals
- sheep
- bananas
- corn (maize)
- citrus fruits
- cocoa
- cotton
- coffee
- dates
- fishing
- fruit
- oil palms
- olives
- peanuts
- rice
- rubber
- shellfish
- sugar cane
- tea
- tobacco
- vineyards
- wheat

North Africa

ALGERIA, EGYPT, LIBYA, MOROCCO, TUNISIA, WESTERN SAHARA

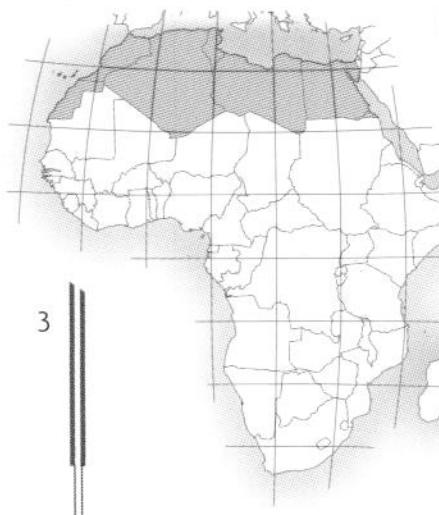

Fringed by the Mediterranean along the northern coast and by the arid Sahara in the south, North Africa reflects the influence of many invaders, both European and, most importantly, Arab, giving the region an almost universal Islamic flavour and a common Arabic language. The countries lying to the west of Egypt are often referred to as the Maghreb, an Arabic term for 'west'. Today, Morocco and Tunisia exploit their culture and landscape for tourism, while rich oil and gas deposits aid development in Libya and Algeria, despite political turmoil. Egypt, with its fertile, Nile-watered agricultural land and varied industrial base, is the most populous nation.

▲ *These rock piles in Algeria's Ahaggar mountains are the result of weathering caused by extremes of temperature. Great cracks or joints appear in the rocks, which are then worn and smoothed by the wind.*

The landscape

The Atlas Mountains, which extend across much of Morocco, northern Algeria and Tunisia, are part of the fold mountain system which also runs through much of southern Europe. They recede to the south and east, becoming a steppe landscape before meeting the Sahara desert which covers more than 90% of the region. The sediments of the Sahara overlie an ancient plateau of crystalline rock, some of which is more than four billion years old.

Map key

Population

- above 5 million
- 1 million to 5 million
- 500,000 to 1 million
- 100,000 to 500,000
- 50,000 to 100,000
- 10,000 to 50,000
- below 10,000

Elevation

- 4000m / 13,124ft
- 3000m / 9843ft
- 2000m / 6562ft
- 1000m / 3281ft
- 500m / 1640ft
- 250m / 820ft
- 100m / 328ft
- sea level

Scale 1:11,000,000

projection: Lambert Azimuthal Equal Area

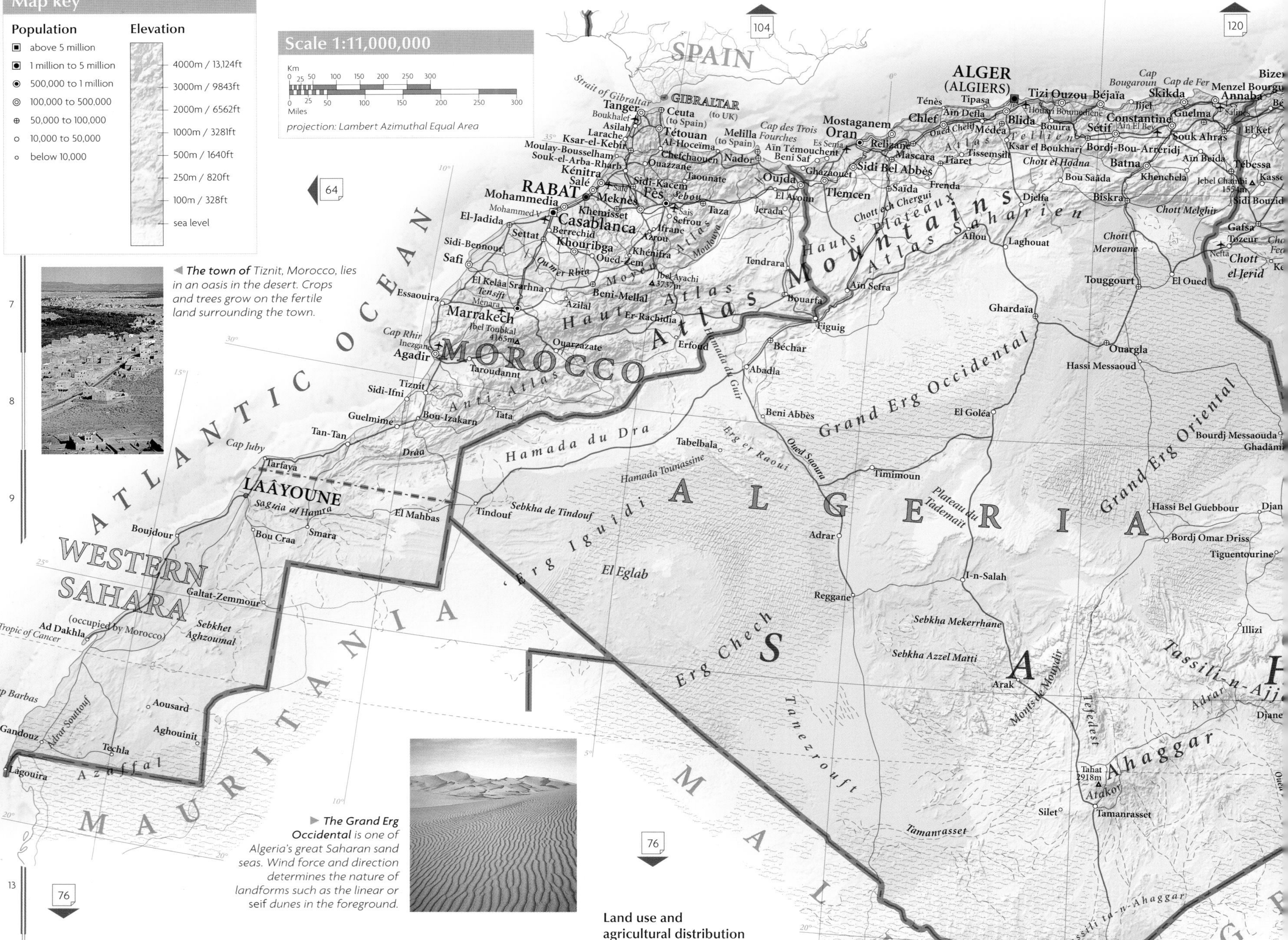

◀ *The town of Tiznit, Morocco, lies in an oasis in the desert. Crops and trees grow on the fertile land surrounding the town.*

▶ *The Grand Erg Occidental is one of Algeria's great Saharan sand seas. Wind force and direction determines the nature of landforms such as the linear or seif dunes in the foreground.*

Using the land and sea

Sheltered valleys in the Atlas Mountains, the Nile Valley and Delta, and the Mediterranean coast are the main sources of good farming land. A wide variety of valuable crops including cereals, rice and cotton, and woods such as cedar and cork, are grown. Typical Mediterranean crops such as olives, figs, dates and citrus fruits also thrive in these areas. The Nile Valley is particularly fertile, and most of Egypt's population lives close to the river. Elsewhere, irrigation is essential to improve crop yields on the desert margins.

The urban/rural population divide

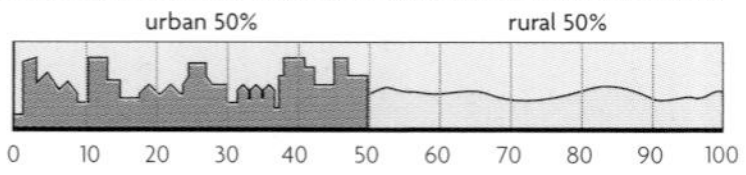

urban 50% | rural 50%

Population density	Total land area
65 people per sq mile (25 people per sq km)	2,215,020 sq miles (5,738,394 sq km)

Land use and agricultural distribution

- goats
- sheep
- cereals
- citrus fruits
- cork
- cotton
- dates
- fishing
- olives
- vineyards
- capital cities
- major towns
- pasture
- cropland
- forest
- desert

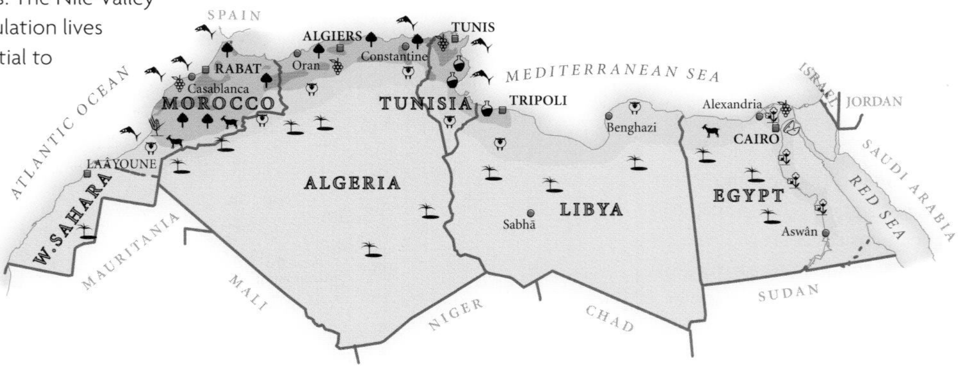

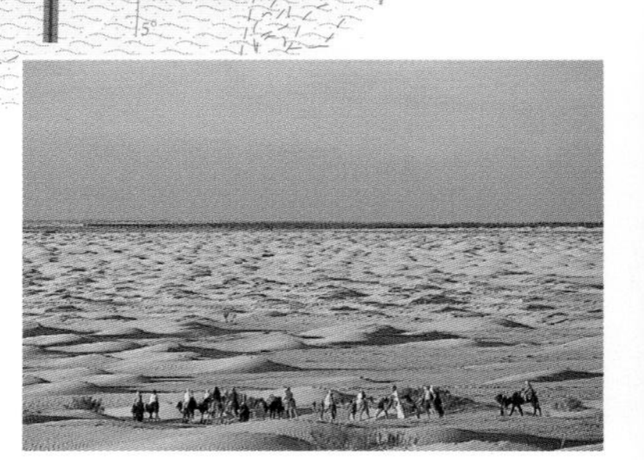

▲ *Many North African nomads, such as the Bedouin, maintain a traditional pastoral lifestyle on the desert fringes, moving their herds of sheep, goats and camels from place to place – crossing country borders in order to find sufficient grazing land.*

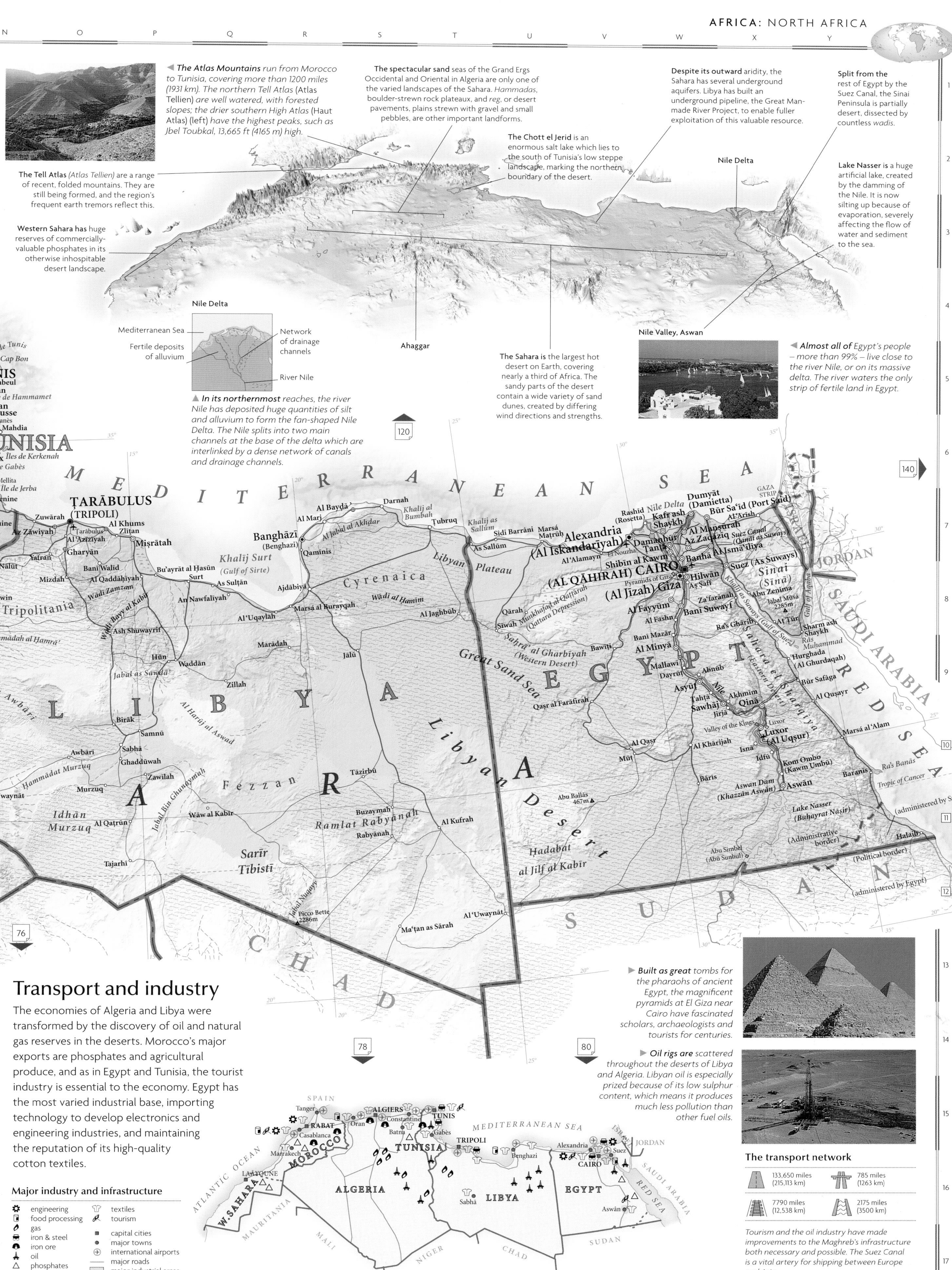

Nile Delta
Ahaggar
Nile Valley, Aswan
Mediterranean Sea
Fertile deposits of alluvium
Network of drainage channels
River Nile
120
140
76
78
80
MEDITERRANEAN SEA
TUNISIA
Tunis
Cap Bon
Nabeul
Golfe de Hammamet
Sousse
Mahdia
Sfax
Îles de Kerkenah
Golfe de Gabès
Île de Jerba
Medenine
ṬARĀBULUS (TRIPOLI)
Zuwārah
Az Zāwiyah
Al Khums
Zlīṭan
Miṣrātah
Tarābulus
Al 'Azīzīyah
Yafran
Gharyān
Nālūt
Bani Walid
Al Qaddāḥiyah
Mizdah
Tripolitania
Ash Shuwayrif
Khalīj Surt (Gulf of Sirte)
Bu'ayrāt al Ḥasūn
Surt
As Sulṭān
An Nawfalīyah
Banghāzī (Benghazi)
Qaminis
Al Bayḍā'
Al Marj
Darnah
Al Jabal al Akhḍar
Khalij al Bumbah
Tubruq
Khalij as Sallum
Ajdābiyā
Cyrenaica
Marsá al Burayqah
Al 'Uqaylah
Wādī al Ḥamīm
Al Jaghbūb
Marādah
Jālū
Hūn
Waddān
Zillah
Jabal as Sawdā'
Al Harūj al Aswad
LIBYA
Birāk
Samnū
Sabhā
Ghaddūwah
Awbārī
Ḥammādat Murzuq
Zawīlah
Murzuq
Idhān Murzuq
Al Qaṭrūn
Wāw al Kabīr
Fezzan
Tāzirbū
Buzaymah
Ramlat Rabyānah
Rabyānah
Al Kufrah
Sarīr Tibistī
Tajarhī
Picco Bette 2286m
Ma'ṭan as Sārah
Al 'Uwaynāt
Libyan Desert
Libyan Plateau
Great Sand Sea
Sidi Barrāni
Marsá Maṭrūḥ
As Sallūm
Alexandria (Al Iskandarīyah)
Rashīd (Rosetta)
Kafr ash Shaykh
Dumyāṭ (Damietta)
Būr Sa'īd (Port Said)
Al Manṣūrah
Az Zaqāzīq
Al 'Arīsh
Damanhūr
Ṭanṭā
El Nouzha
Al 'Alamayn
Shibin al Kawm
Banhā
Al Ismā'īlīya
CAIRO (AL QĀHIRAH)
Giza (Al Jīzah)
Ḥilwān
Aṣ Ṣaff
Suez (As Suways)
Suez Canal (Qanat as Suways)
Sinai (Sīnā)
Abu Zenima
Jabal Mūsā 2285m
Qārah
Sīwah
Munkhafaḍ al Qaṭṭārah (Qattara Depression)
Al Fayyūm
Al Fashn
Bani Suwayf
Za'farānah
Ra's Ghārib
Sharm ash Shaykh
Aṭ Ṭūr
Gulf of Aqaba
Gulf of Suez
Ṣaḥrā' al Gharbīyah (Western Desert)
Bawīṭī
Bani Mazār
Al Minyā
Mallawi
Dayrūṭ
Abnūb
Asyūṭ
EGYPT
Ṣaḥrā' ash Sharqīyah (Eastern Desert)
Ras Muḥammad
Hurghada (Al Ghurdaqah)
Būr Safāga
Al Quṣayr
Qaṣr al Farāfirah
Ṭahṭā
Sawhāj
Akhmīm
Qinā
Jirjā
Valley of the Kings
Luxor (Al Uqṣur)
Al Qaṣr
Al Khārijah
Mūṭ
Isnā
Idfū
Kom Ombo (Kawm Umbū)
Bārīs
Aswan Dam (Khazzān Aswān)
Aswān
Marsá al 'Alam
Baranis
Ra's Banās
Tropic of Cancer
Abu Ballās 467m
Hadabat al Jilf al Kabīr
Lake Nasser (Buḥayrat Nāṣir)
Abu Simbel (Abū Sunbul)
(administered by Sudan)
(Administrative border)
Ḥalā'ib
(Political border)
(administered by Egypt)
GAZA STRIP
ISRAEL
JORDAN
SAUDI ARABIA
RED SEA
SUDAN
CHAD
SPAIN
Tanger
RABAT
Casablanca
Marrakech
MOROCCO
LAÂYOUNE
W. SAHARA
ATLANTIC OCEAN
MAURITANIA
MALI
NIGER
ALGIERS
Oran
Constantine
Batna
ALGERIA
TUNIS
Gabès
TUNISIA
TRIPOLI
Benghazi
Sabhā
LIBYA
Alexandria
CAIRO
Suez
Aswān
MEDITERRANEAN SEA

◄ *The Atlas Mountains run from Morocco to Tunisia, covering more than 1200 miles (1931 km). The northern Tell Atlas (Atlas Tellien) are well watered, with forested slopes; the drier southern High Atlas (Haut Atlas) (left) have the highest peaks, such as Jbel Toubkal, 13,665 ft (4165 m) high.*

The spectacular sand seas of the Grand Ergs Occidental and Oriental in Algeria are only one of the varied landscapes of the Sahara. *Hammadas*, boulder-strewn rock plateaux, and *reg*, or desert pavements, plains strewn with gravel and small pebbles, are other important landforms.

Despite its outward aridity, the Sahara has several underground aquifers. Libya has built an underground pipeline, the Great Man-made River Project, to enable fuller exploitation of this valuable resource.

Split from the rest of Egypt by the Suez Canal, the Sinai Peninsula is partially desert, dissected by countless *wadis*.

The Chott el Jerid is an enormous salt lake which lies to the south of Tunisia's low steppe landscape, marking the northern boundary of the desert.

The Tell Atlas (*Atlas Tellien*) are a range of recent, folded mountains. They are still being formed, and the region's frequent earth tremors reflect this.

Lake Nasser is a huge artificial lake, created by the damming of the Nile. It is now silting up because of evaporation, severely affecting the flow of water and sediment to the sea.

Western Sahara has huge reserves of commercially-valuable phosphates in its otherwise inhospitable desert landscape.

▲ *In its northernmost reaches, the river Nile has deposited huge quantities of silt and alluvium to form the fan-shaped Nile Delta. The Nile splits into two main channels at the base of the delta which are interlinked by a dense network of canals and drainage channels.*

The Sahara is the largest hot desert on Earth, covering nearly a third of Africa. The sandy parts of the desert contain a wide variety of sand dunes, created by differing wind directions and strengths.

◄ *Almost all of Egypt's people – more than 99% – live close to the river Nile, or on its massive delta. The river waters the only strip of fertile land in Egypt.*

► *Built as great tombs for the pharaohs of ancient Egypt, the magnificent pyramids at El Giza near Cairo have fascinated scholars, archaeologists and tourists for centuries.*

► *Oil rigs are scattered throughout the deserts of Libya and Algeria. Libyan oil is especially prized because of its low sulphur content, which means it produces much less pollution than other fuel oils.*

Transport and industry

The economies of Algeria and Libya were transformed by the discovery of oil and natural gas reserves in the deserts. Morocco's major exports are phosphates and agricultural produce, and as in Egypt and Tunisia, the tourist industry is essential to the economy. Egypt has the most varied industrial base, importing technology to develop electronics and engineering industries, and maintaining the reputation of its high-quality cotton textiles.

Major industry and infrastructure

- engineering
- food processing
- gas
- iron & steel
- iron ore
- oil
- phosphates
- textiles
- tourism
- capital cities
- major towns
- international airports
- major roads
- major industrial areas

The transport network

- 133,650 miles (215,113 km)
- 785 miles (1263 km)
- 7790 miles (12,538 km)
- 2175 miles (3500 km)

Tourism and the oil industry have made improvements to the Maghreb's infrastructure both necessary and possible. The Suez Canal is a vital artery for shipping between Europe and Asia.

West Africa

BENIN, BURKINA, CAPE VERDE, GAMBIA, GHANA, GUINEA, GUINEA-BISSAU, IVORY COAST, LIBERIA, MALI, MAURITANIA, NIGER, NIGERIA, SENEGAL, SIERRA LEONE, TOGO

▶ *The dry scrub of the Sahel is only suitable for grazing herd animals like these cattle in Mali.*

West Africa is an immensely diverse region, encompassing the desert landscapes and mainly Muslim populations of the southern Saharan countries, and the tropical rainforests of the more humid south, with a great variety of local languages and cultures. The rich natural resources and accessibility of the area were quickly exploited by Europeans; most of the Africans taken by slave traders came from this region, causing serious depopulation. The very different influences of West Africa's leading colonial powers, Britain and France, remain today, reflected in the languages and institutions of the countries they once governed.

Scale 1:9,000,000

Km 0 25 50 100 150 200 250

Miles 0 25 50 100 150 200 250

projection: Lambert Azimuthal Equal Area

Transport and industry

Abundant natural resources including oil and metallic minerals are found in much of West Africa, although investment is required for their further exploitation. Nigeria experienced an oil boom during the 1970s but subsequent growth has been sporadic. Most industry in other countries has a primary basis, including mining, logging and food processing.

The transport network

62,154 miles (100,038 km)	1037 miles (1669 km)
6752 miles (10,867 km)	10,192 miles (16,405 km)

The road and rail systems are most developed near the coasts. Some of the land-locked countries remain disadvantaged by the difficulty of access to ports, and their poor road networks.

Major industry and infrastructure

- chemicals
- cotton spinning
- food processing
- mining
- oil
- palm oil processing
- peanut processing
- textiles
- vehicle manufacture
- capital cities
- major towns
- international airports
- major roads
- major industrial areas

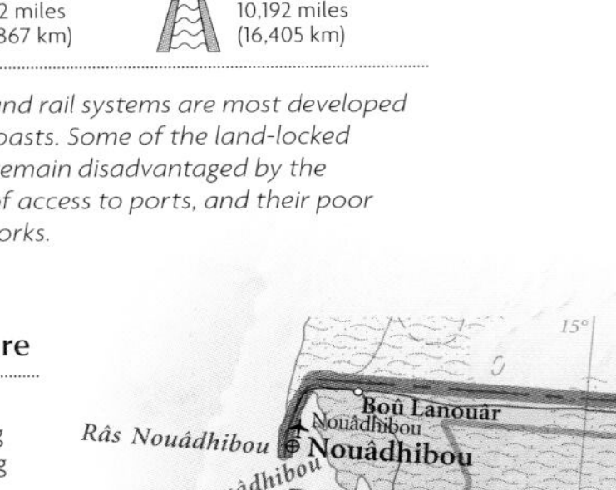

CAPE VERDE

(same scale as main map)

Map key

Population

- 1 million to 5 million
- 500,000 to 1 million
- 100,000 to 500,000
- 50,000 to 100,000
- 10,000 to 50,000
- below 10,000

Elevation

- 2000m / 6562ft
- 1000m / 3281ft
- 500m / 1640ft
- 250m / 820ft
- 100m / 328ft
- sea level

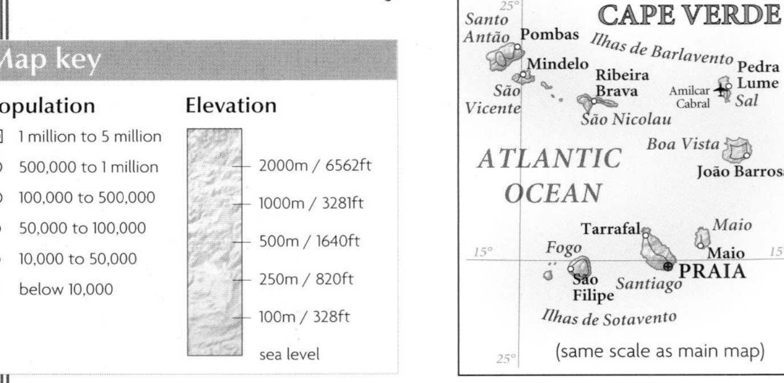

◀ *The southern regions of West Africa still contain great swathes of tropical rainforest, including some of the world's most prized hardwood trees, such as mahogany and iroko.*

Using the land and sea

The humid southern regions are most suitable for cultivation; in these areas, cash crops such as coffee, cotton, cocoa and rubber are grown in large quantities. Peanuts (groundnuts) are grown throughout West Africa. In the north, advancing desertification has made the Sahel increasingly unviable for cultivation, and pastoral farming is more common. Great herds of sheep, cattle and goats are grazed on the savannah grasses, and fishing is important in coastal and delta areas.

▲ *The Gambia, mainland Africa's smallest country, produces great quantities of peanuts (groundnuts). Winnowing is used to separate the nuts from their stalks.*

Land use and agricultural distribution

- goats
- sheep
- cocoa
- coffee
- cotton
- oil palms
- peanuts
- rubber
- shellfish
- capital cities
- major towns
- pasture
- cropland
- forest
- desert

The urban/rural population divide

urban 36% · rural 64%

0 10 20 30 40 50 60 70 80 90 100

Population density	Total land area
104 people per sq mile (40 people per sq km)	2,337,137 sq miles (6,054,760 sq km)

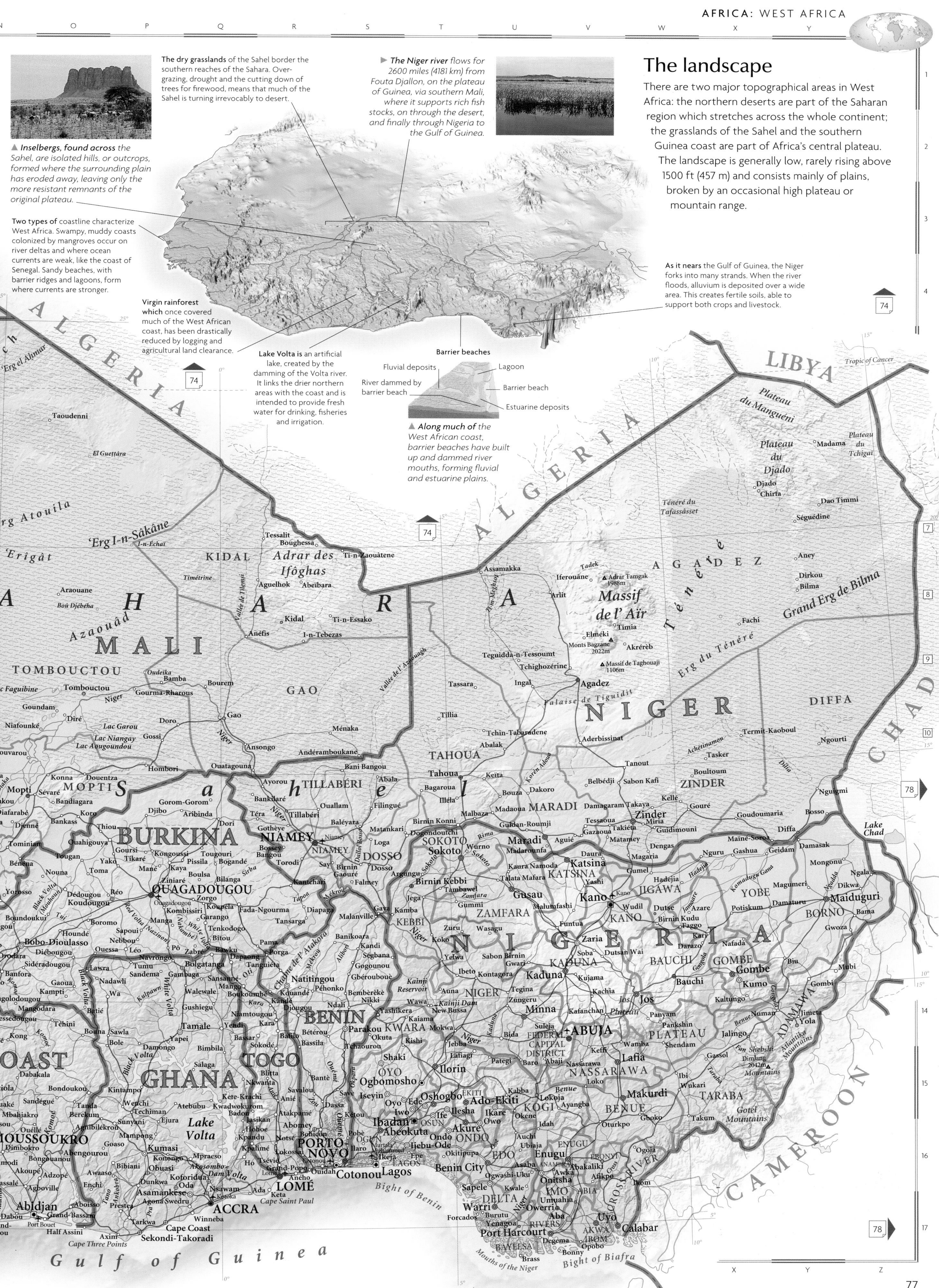
Fluvial deposits
Lagoon
River dammed by barrier beach
Barrier beach
Estuarine deposits
Barrier beaches
ALGERIA
LIBYA
MALI
NIGER
CHAD
NIGERIA
BURKINA
BENIN
TOGO
GHANA
CAMEROON
Gulf of Guinea
Bight of Benin
Bight of Biafra
Lake Chad
Lake Volta
Massif de l'Aïr
Grand Erg de Bilma
Ténéré
Adrar des Ifôghas
NIAMEY
OUAGADOUGOU
PORTO-NOVO
LOMÉ
ACCRA
ABUJA
Lagos
Cotonou
Kano
Agadez
Tombouctou
Gao
Kaduna
Ibadan
Port Harcourt

The landscape

There are two major topographical areas in West Africa: the northern deserts are part of the Saharan region which stretches across the whole continent; the grasslands of the Sahel and the southern Guinea coast are part of Africa's central plateau. The landscape is generally low, rarely rising above 1500 ft (457 m) and consists mainly of plains, broken by an occasional high plateau or mountain range.

▲ ***Inselbergs, found across** the Sahel, are isolated hills, or outcrops, formed where the surrounding plain has eroded away, leaving only the more resistant remnants of the original plateau.*

The dry grasslands of the Sahel border the southern reaches of the Sahara. Overgrazing, drought and the cutting down of trees for firewood, means that much of the Sahel is turning irrevocably to desert.

► ***The Niger river** flows for 2600 miles (4181 km) from Fouta Djallon, on the plateau of Guinea, via southern Mali, where it supports rich fish stocks, on through the desert, and finally through Nigeria to the Gulf of Guinea.*

Two types of coastline characterize West Africa. Swampy, muddy coasts colonized by mangroves occur on river deltas and where ocean currents are weak, like the coast of Senegal. Sandy beaches, with barrier ridges and lagoons, form where currents are stronger.

Virgin rainforest which once covered much of the West African coast, has been drastically reduced by logging and agricultural land clearance.

Lake Volta is an artificial lake, created by the damming of the Volta river. It links the drier northern areas with the coast and is intended to provide fresh water for drinking, fisheries and irrigation.

As it nears the Gulf of Guinea, the Niger forks into many strands. When the river floods, alluvium is deposited over a wide area. This creates fertile soils, able to support both crops and livestock.

▲ ***Along much of** the West African coast, barrier beaches have built up and dammed river mouths, forming fluvial and estuarine plains.*

Central Africa

CAMEROON, CENTRAL AFRICAN REPUBLIC, CHAD, CONGO, DEM. REP. CONGO, EQUATORIAL GUINEA, GABON, SAO TOME & PRINCIPE

The great rainforest basin of the Congo river embraces most of remote Central Africa. The interior was largely unknown to Europeans until late in the 19th century, when its tribal kingdoms were split – principally between France and Belgium – with Sao Tome and Principe the lone Portuguese territory, and Equatorial Guinea controlled by Spain. Open democracy and regional economic integration are important goals for these nations – several of which have only recently emerged from restrictive regimes – and investment is needed to improve transport infrastructures. Many of the small, but fast-growing and increasingly urban population, speak French, the regional *lingua franca*, along with several hundred Pygmy, Bantu and Sudanic dialects.

Transport and industry

Large reserves of valuable minerals are found in Central Africa: copper, cobalt and diamonds are mined in Dem. Rep. Congo and manganese in Gabon. Congo, Cameroon, Gabon and Equatorial Guinea have oil deposits and oil has also been recently discovered in Chad. Goods such as palm oil and rubber are processed for export.

▲ ***The ancient rocks*** *of Dem. Rep. Congo hold immense and varied mineral reserves. This open pit copper mine is at Kolwezi in the far south.*

Major industry and infrastructure

- brewing
- chemicals
- cobalt
- copper
- diamonds
- food processing
- manganese
- oil
- palm oil processing
- textiles
- tin
- capital cities
- major towns
- international airports
- major roads
- major industrial areas

The transport network

102,747 miles (165,774 km)	37 miles (60 km)
3985 miles (6414 km)	14,110 miles (22,710 km)

The Trans-Gabon railway, which began operating in 1987, has opened up new sources of timber and manganese. Elsewhere, much investment is needed to update and improve road, rail and water transport.

The landscape

Lake Chad lies in a desert basin bounded by the volcanic Tibesti mountains in the north, plateaux in the east and, in the south, the broad watershed of the Congo basin. The vast circular depression of the Congo is isolated from the coastal plain by the granite Massif du Chaillu. To the northwest, the volcanoes and fold mountains of the Cameroon Ridge *(Dorsale Camerounaise)* extend as islands into the Gulf of Guinea. The high fold mountains fringing the east of the Congo Basin fall steeply to the lakes of the Great Rift Valley.

◀ ***A plug of*** *resistant lava, at the southwestern end of the Cameroon Ridge (Dorsale Camerounaise), is all that remains of an eroded volcano.*

The volcanic massif of Cameroon Mountain occupies an area which remains volcanically active.

Gulf of Guinea

Massif du Chaillu

Lake Chad is the remnant of an inland sea, which once occupied much of the surrounding basin. A series of droughts since the 1970s has reduced the area of this shallow freshwater lake to about 1000 sq miles (2599 sq km).

The lake-like expansion of the Congo river at Stanley Pool is the lowest point of the interior basin, although the river still descends more than 1000 ft (300 m) to reach the sea.

The Tibesti mountains are the highest in the Sahara. They were pushed up by the movement of the African Plate over a hot spot, which first formed the northern Ahaggar mountains and is now thought to lie under the Great Rift Valley.

The Congo river is second only to the Amazon in the volume of water it carries, and in the size of its drainage basin.

Lake Tanganyika, the world's second deepest lake, is the largest of a series of linear 'ribbon' lakes occupying a trench within the Great Rift Valley.

Rich mineral deposits in the 'Copper Belt' of Dem. Rep. Congo were formed under intense heat and pressure when the ancient African Shield was uplifted to form the region's mountains.

Broad, shallow basin · Waterfalls and cataracts · Submarine canyon

▲ ***The Congo river*** *flows sluggishly through the rainforest of the interior basin. Towards the coast, the river drops steeply in a series of waterfalls and cataracts. At this point, the erosional power of the river becomes so great that it has formed a deep submarine canyon offshore.*

▲ ***Virgin tropical rainforest*** *covers the Ruwenzori range on the borders of Dem. Rep. Congo and Uganda.*

▲ ***The vast sand*** *flats surrounding Lake Chad were once covered by water. Changing climatic patterns caused the lake to shrink, and desert now covers much of its previous area.*

Map key

Population

- 1 million to 5 million
- 500,000 to 1 million
- 100,000 to 500,000
- 50,000 to 100,000
- 10,000 to 50,000
- below 10,000

Elevation

- 4000m / 13,124ft
- 3000m / 9843ft
- 2000m / 6562ft
- 1000m / 3281ft
- 500m / 1640ft
- 250m / 820ft
- 100m / 328ft
- sea level

Scale 1:9,500,000

projection: Lambert Azimuthal Equal Area

74

76

CENTRAL AFRICAN REPUBLIC
CAMEROON
CONGO
GABON
DEM. REP. CONGO
EQUATORIAL GUINEA
SAO TOME & PRINCIPE
ANGOLA (CABINDA)
ANGOLA
ZAMBIA
TANZANIA
UGANDA
RWANDA
BURUNDI
ATLANTIC OCEAN
Gulf of Guinea
Bight of Biafra
BANGUI
YAOUNDÉ
LIBREVILLE
MALABO
SÃO TOMÉ
BRAZZAVILLE
KINSHASA
Douala
Pointe-Noire
Kisangani
Mbandaka
Lubumbashi
Kananga
Mbuji-Mayi
Matadi
Lake Tanganyika
Lake Kivu
Lake Albert
Lake Edward
Lake Mweru
Congo Basin
Great Rift Valley
Equator
64
80
82
Land use and agricultural distribution
cattle
cocoa
coffee
cotton
palms
peanuts
rubber
timber
capital cities
major towns
pasture
cropland
forest
desert
The urban/rural population divide
urban 33%
rural 67%
0 10 20 30 40 50 60 70 80 90 100
Population density
43 people per sq mile (17 people per sq km)
Total land area
2,023,939 sq miles (5,243,364 sq km)

▲ ***The great Congo** river forms part of the border between Congo and Dem. Rep. Congo. The river is fast-flowing, and a series of falls and rapids means that it is only partly navigable.*

Using the land

Cash crops for export include cocoa, coffee and rubber. Shifting cultivation is widely practised, and plantains are the staple food of the equatorial region, grown with yam and taro. Cassava, guinea corn (sorghum), and millet are the main subsistence crops in savanna areas. Cattle farming is limited to areas free of tsetse fly, and fish from the interior rivers are an important protein source.

▲ ***High-quality timber is** floated to Port-Gentil, Gabon, via the Ogooué river. Timber provides important export revenue for several countries, although there has been concern about the uncontrolled logging of rare tropical woods.*

East Africa

BURUNDI, DJIBOUTI, ERITREA, ETHIOPIA, KENYA, RWANDA, SOMALIA, SUDAN, TANZANIA, UGANDA

The countries of East Africa divide into two distinct cultural regions. Sudan and the 'Horn' nations have been influenced by the Middle East; Ethiopia was the home of one of the earliest Christian civilizations, and Sudan reflects both Muslim and Christian influences, while the southern countries share a closer cultural affinity with other sub-Saharan nations. Some of Africa's most densely populated countries lie in this region, and the needs of a growing number of people have put pressure on marginal lands and fragile environments. Although most East African economies remain strongly agricultural, Kenya has developed a varied industrial base.

The landscape

East Africa's most significant landscape feature is the Great Rift Valley, which formed during the most recent phase of continental movement when the rigid basement rocks cracked and buckled. Great blocks of land were raised and lowered, creating huge flat-bottomed valleys and steep escarpments, sometimes covered by volcanic extrusions in highland areas.

◀ ***This dome at** Gonder, in Ethiopia, is a volcanic intrusion, formed when molten rock pushed up the surface of the Earth and then solidified, leaving an outcrop of igneous rock.*

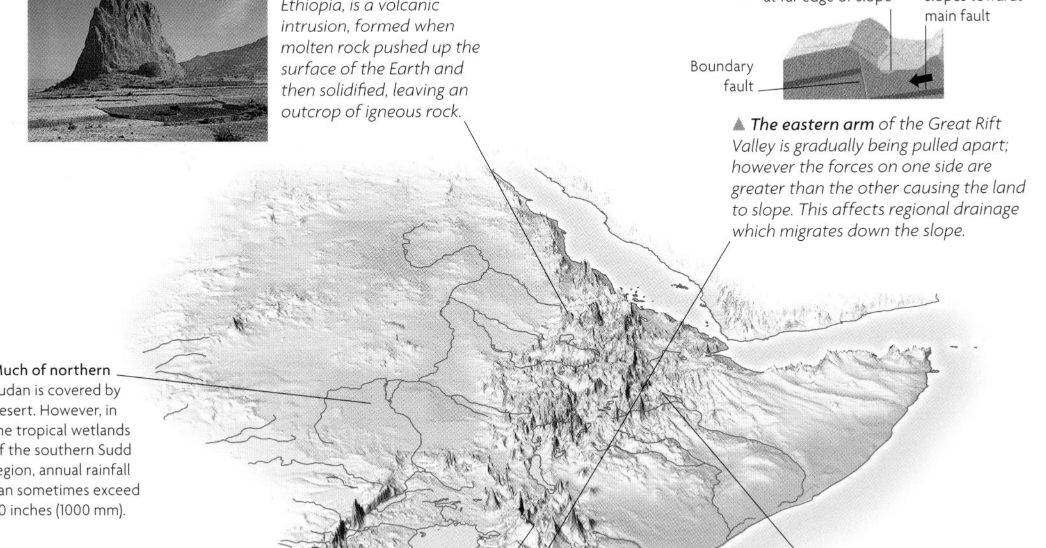

Ephemeral lake forms at far edge of slope

Central block slopes towards main fault

Boundary fault

▲ ***The eastern arm** of the Great Rift Valley is gradually being pulled apart; however the forces on one side are greater than the other causing the land to slope. This affects regional drainage which migrates down the slope.*

Much of northern Sudan is covered by desert. However, in the tropical wetlands of the southern Sudd region, annual rainfall can sometimes exceed 40 inches (1000 mm).

The tiny countries of Rwanda and Burundi are mainly mountainous, with large areas of inaccessible tropical rainforest.

Lake Tanganyika lies 8202 ft (2500 m) above sea level. It has a depth of nearly 4700 ft (1435 m). The lake traces the valley floor for some 400 miles (644 km) of the western arm of the Great Rift Valley.

Lake Victoria occupies a vast basin between the two arms of the Great Rift Valley. It is the world's second largest lake in terms of surface area, extending 26,560 sq miles (68,880 sq km). The lake contains numerous islands and coral reefs.

A vast plateau lies between the eastern and western rift valleys in Kenya, Uganda and western Tanzania. It has been levelled by long periods of erosion to form a peneplain, but is dotted with inselbergs – outcrops of more resistant rocks.

Lava flows on uplifted areas either side of the eastern branch of the Great Rift Valley gave the Ethiopian Highlands – a series of high, wide plateaux – their distinctive rounded appearance and fertile soils.

Kilimanjaro

▲ ***An extinct volcano,** Kilimanjaro is Africa's highest mountain, rising 19,340 ft (5895 m). Once famed for its snow-capped peak, this has almost completely melted due to changing climatic conditions.*

▶ ***The Kassala region** in eastern Sudan is watered by the Atbara river, an important tributary of the Nile. Most of the population is engaged in agriculture, growing cotton and cereals.*

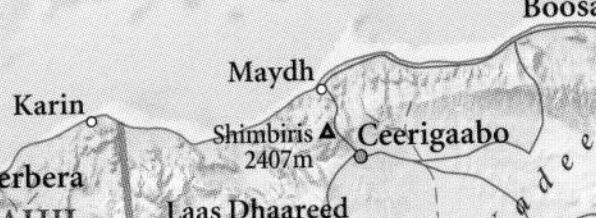

74 78 140

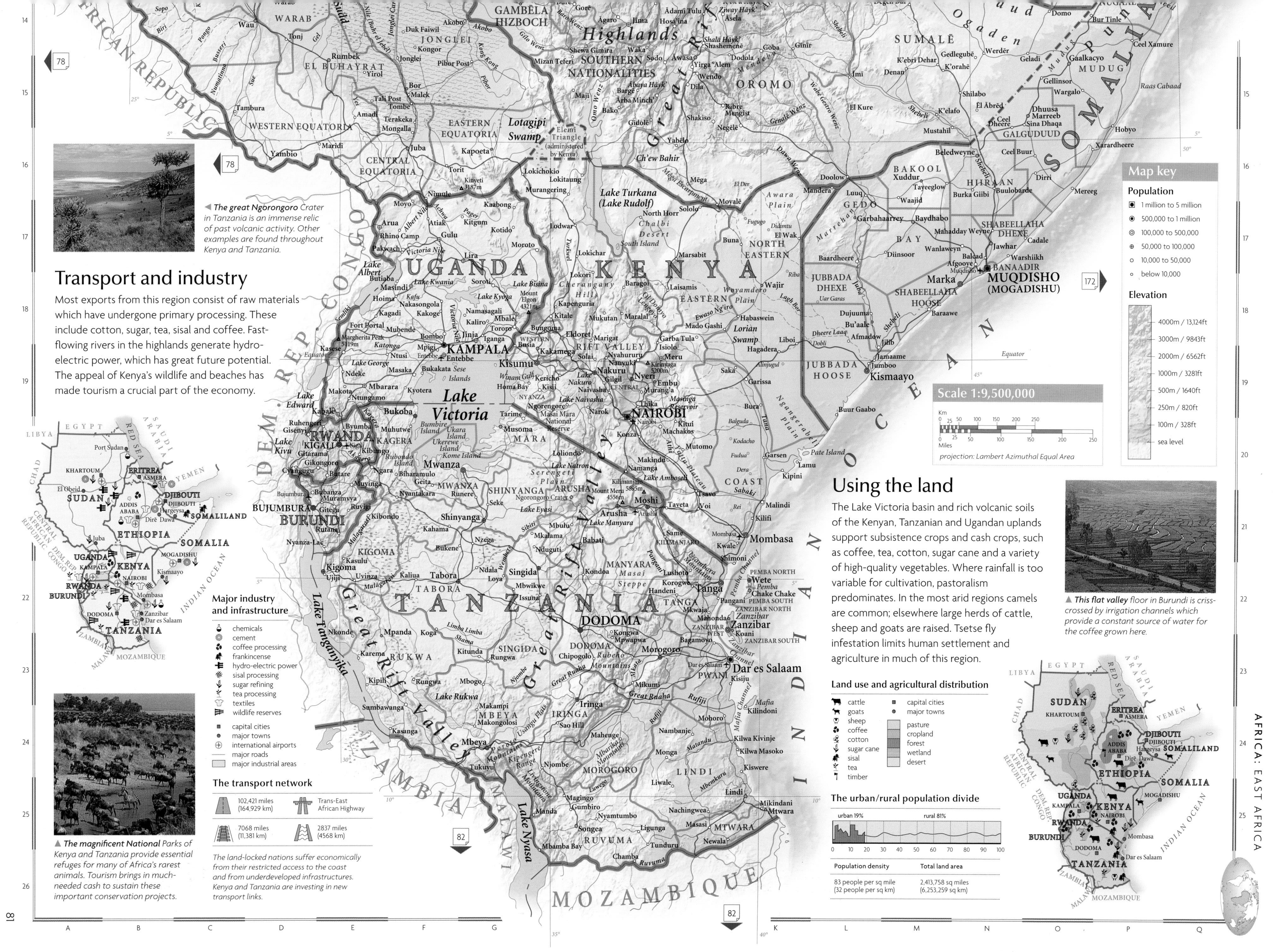

SUDAN
UGANDA
KENYA
TANZANIA
SOMALIA
RWANDA
BURUNDI
DEM. REP. CONGO
ZAMBIA
MALAWI
MOZAMBIQUE
INDIAN OCEAN
Lake Victoria
Lake Turkana (Lake Rudolf)
Lake Tanganyika
Lake Nyasa
Great Rift Valley
NAIROBI
KAMPALA
DODOMA
Dar es Salaam
MUQDISHO (MOGADISHU)
Mombasa
Kismaayo
Scale 1:9,500,000
projection: Lambert Azimuthal Equal Area
Map key
Population
1 million to 5 million
500,000 to 1 million
100,000 to 500,000
50,000 to 100,000
10,000 to 50,000
below 10,000
Elevation
4000m / 13,124ft
3000m / 9843ft
2000m / 6562ft
1000m / 3281ft
500m / 1640ft
250m / 820ft
100m / 328ft
sea level

▲ *The great Ngorongoro* Crater in Tanzania is an immense relic of past volcanic activity. Other examples are found throughout Kenya and Tanzania.

Transport and industry

Most exports from this region consist of raw materials which have undergone primary processing. These include cotton, sugar, tea, sisal and coffee. Fast-flowing rivers in the highlands generate hydro-electric power, which has great future potential. The appeal of Kenya's wildlife and beaches has made tourism a crucial part of the economy.

Major industry and infrastructure
chemicals
cement
coffee processing
frankincense
hydro-electric power
sisal processing
sugar refining
tea processing
textiles
wildlife reserves
capital cities
major towns
international airports
major roads
major industrial areas
The transport network
102,421 miles (164,929 km)
Trans-East African Highway
7068 miles (11,381 km)
2837 miles (4568 km)

The land-locked nations suffer economically from their restricted access to the coast and from underdeveloped infrastructures. Kenya and Tanzania are investing in new transport links.

▲ *The magnificent National* Parks of Kenya and Tanzania provide essential refuges for many of Africa's rarest animals. Tourism brings in much-needed cash to sustain these important conservation projects.

Using the land

The Lake Victoria basin and rich volcanic soils of the Kenyan, Tanzanian and Ugandan uplands support subsistence crops and cash crops, such as coffee, tea, cotton, sugar cane and a variety of high-quality vegetables. Where rainfall is too variable for cultivation, pastoralism predominates. In the most arid regions camels are common; elsewhere large herds of cattle, sheep and goats are raised. Tsetse fly infestation limits human settlement and agriculture in much of this region.

▲ *This flat valley* floor in Burundi is criss-crossed by irrigation channels which provide a constant source of water for the coffee grown here.

Land use and agricultural distribution
cattle
goats
sheep
coffee
cotton
sugar cane
sisal
tea
timber
capital cities
major towns
pasture
cropland
forest
wetland
desert
The urban/rural population divide
urban 19%
rural 81%
Population density
83 people per sq mile (32 people per sq km)
Total land area
2,413,758 sq miles (6,253,259 sq km)

Southern Africa

ANGOLA, BOTSWANA, LESOTHO, MALAWI, MOZAMBIQUE, NAMIBIA, SOUTH AFRICA, SWAZILAND, ZAMBIA, ZIMBABWE

Africa's vast southern plateau has been a contested homeland for disparate peoples for many centuries. The European incursion began with the slave trade and quickened in the 19th century, when the discovery of enormous mineral wealth secured South Africa's regional economic dominance. The struggle against white minority rule led to strife in Namibia, Zimbabwe, and the former Portuguese territories of Angola and Mozambique. South Africa's notorious apartheid laws, which denied basic human rights to more than 75% of the people, led to the state being internationally ostracized until 1994, when the first fully democratic elections inaugurated a new era of racial justice.

Transport and industry

South Africa, the world's largest exporter of gold, has a varied economy which generates about 75% of the region's income and draws migrant labour from neighbouring states. Angola exports petroleum; Botswana and Namibia rely on diamond mining; and Zambia is seeking to diversify its economy to compensate for declining copper reserves.

◀ *Almost all new mining ventures in Zimbabwe are now subject to government control. This mine at Bindura in northeastern Zimbabwe produces nickel, one of the country's top three minerals in terms of economic value.*

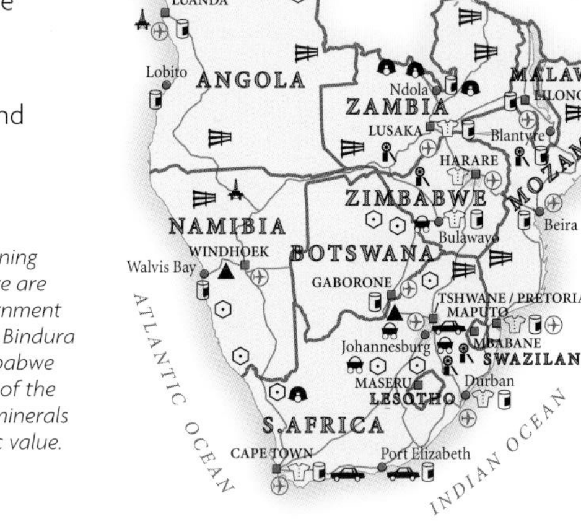
DEM. REP. CONGO
TANZANIA
ANGOLA
LUANDA
Lobito
ZAMBIA
Ndola
LUSAKA
MALAWI
LILONGWE
Blantyre
HARARE
MOZAMBIQUE
ZIMBABWE
Bulawayo
Beira
NAMIBIA
WINDHOEK
Walvis Bay
BOTSWANA
GABORONE
TSHWANE/PRETORIA
MAPUTO
Johannesburg
MBABANE
SWAZILAND
MASERU
LESOTHO
Durban
S. AFRICA
CAPE TOWN
Port Elizabeth
ATLANTIC OCEAN
INDIAN OCEAN

Major industry and infrastructure

- car manufacture
- coal
- copper
- diamonds
- food processing
- gold
- oil
- textiles
- uranium
- wildlife reserves
- capital cities
- major towns
- international airports
- major roads
- major industrial areas

The landscape

Most of southern Africa rests on a concave plateau comprising the Kalahari basin and a mountainous fringe, skirted by a coastal plain which widens out in Mozambique. The plateau extends north, towards the Planalto de Bié in Angola, the Congo Basin and the lake-filled troughs of the Great Rift Valley. The eastern region is drained by the Zambezi and Limpopo rivers, and the Orange is the major western river.

Thousands of years of evaporating water have produced the Etosha Pan, one of the largest salt flats in the world. Lake and river sediments in the area indicate that the region was once less arid.

Khorixas, Namibia

Planalto de Bié

The Okavango/Cubango river flows from the Planalto de Bié to the swamplands of the Okavango Delta, one of the world's largest inland deltas, where it divides into countless distributary channels, feeding out into the desert.

At Victoria Falls, the Zambezi river has cut a spectacular gorge taking advantage of large joints in the basalt, which were first formed as the lava cooled and contracted.

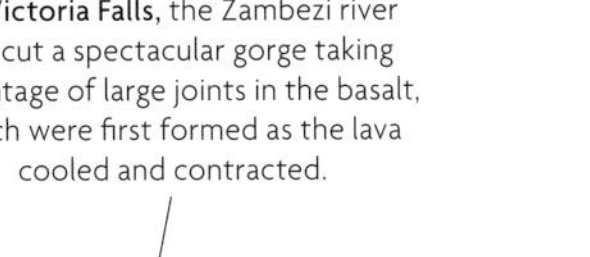

▶ *The fast-flowing Zambezi river cuts a deep, wide channel as it flows along the Zimbabwe/Zambia border.*

Lake Nyasa occupies one of the deep troughs of the Great Rift Valley, where the land has been displaced downwards by as much as 3000 ft (920 m).

Great Rift Valley

Limpopo river

Bushveld intrusion

Volcanic lava, over 250 million years old, caps the peaks of the Drakensberg range, which lie on the mountainous rim of southern Africa's interior plateau.

Namib Desert

The Kalahari Desert is the largest continuous sand surface in the world. Iron oxide gives a distinctive red colour to the windblown sand, which, in eastern areas covers the bedrock by over 200 ft (60 m).

The Orange River, one of the longest in Africa, rises in Lesotho and is the only major river in the south which flows westward, rather than to the east coast.

The mountains of the Little Karoo are composed of sedimentary rocks which have been substantially folded and faulted.

Broad, flat-topped mountains characterize the Great Karoo, which have been cut from level rock strata under extremely arid conditions.

▲ *Finger Rock, near Khorixas, Namibia is a remnant of a former land surface, which has been denuded by erosion over the last 5 million years. These occasional stacks of partially weathered rocks interrupt the plains of the dry southern interior.*

The transport network

84,213 miles (135,609 km)	746 miles (1202 km)
23,208 miles (37,372 km)	3815 miles (6144 km)

Southern Africa's Cape-gauge rail network is by far the largest in the continent. About two-thirds of the 20,000 mile (32,000 km) system lies within South Africa. Lines such as the Harare–Bulawayo route have become corridors for industrial growth.

▲ *Following a series of droughts, this baobab tree in Zimbabwe now stands alone in a field once filled by sugar cane. The thick trunk and small leaves of the baobab help it to conserve water, enabling it to survive even in drought conditions.*

Scale 1:9,500,000

Km 0 25 50 100 150 200 250 300
Miles 0 25 50 100 150 200 250 300

projection: Lambert Azimuthal Equal Area

Bushveld intrusion

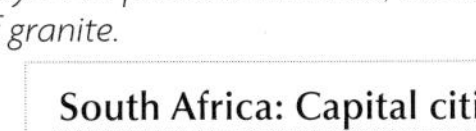
Gabbro and peridotite
Magnetite
Platinum minerals
Granite
Chromite

▲ *The Bushveld intrusion lies on South Africa's high 'veld'. Molten magma intruded into the Earth's crust creating a saucer-shaped feature, more than 180 miles (300 km) across, containing regular layers of precious minerals, overlain by a dome of granite.*

South Africa: Capital cities

TSHWANE / PRETORIA – administrative capital
CAPE TOWN – legislative capital
BLOEMFONTEIN – judicial capital

Map key

Population

- 1 million to 5 million
- 500,000 to 1 million
- 100,000 to 500,000
- 50,000 to 100,000
- 10,000 to 50,000
- below 10,000

Elevation

- 3000m / 9843ft
- 2000m / 6562ft
- 1000m / 3281ft
- 500m / 1640ft
- 250m / 820ft
- 100m / 328ft
- sea level

78
80

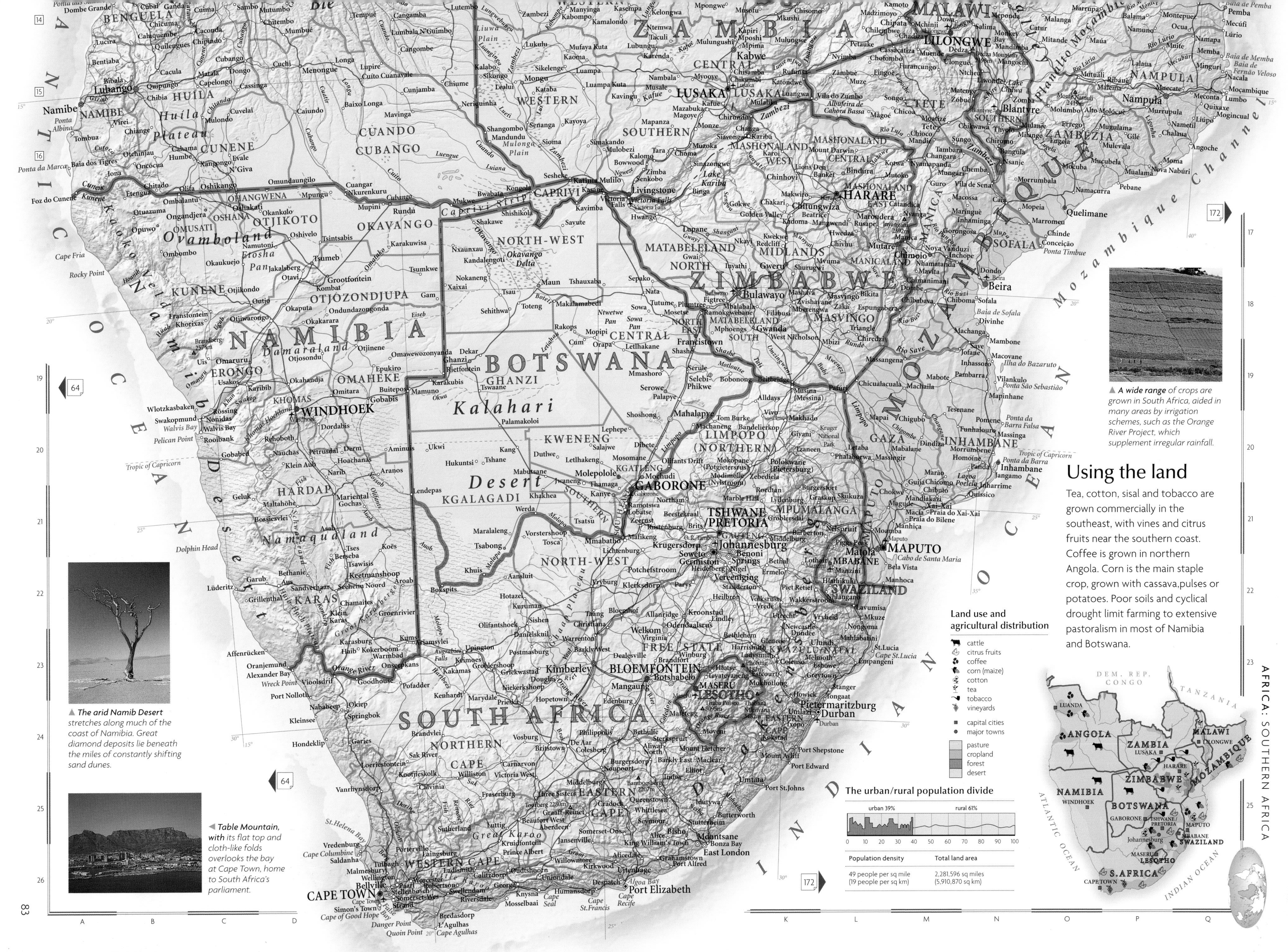
NAMIBIA
BOTSWANA
ZIMBABWE
ZAMBIA
MOZAMBIQUE
SOUTH AFRICA
MALAWI
LESOTHO
SWAZILAND
WINDHOEK
GABORONE
HARARE
LUSAKA
LILONGWE
MAPUTO
MBABANE
MASERU
TSHWANE PRETORIA
BLOEMFONTEIN
CAPE TOWN
Kalahari
Desert
Namib Desert
ATLANTIC OCEAN
INDIAN OCEAN
Mozambique Channel
Land use and agricultural distribution
cattle
citrus fruits
coffee
corn (maize)
cotton
tea
tobacco
vineyards
capital cities
major towns
pasture
cropland
forest
desert
The urban/rural population divide
urban 39%
rural 61%
0 10 20 30 40 50 60 70 80 90 100
Population density
49 people per sq mile (19 people per sq km)
Total land area
2,281,596 sq miles (5,910,870 sq km)

▲ **A wide range** *of crops are grown in South Africa, aided in many areas by irrigation schemes, such as the Orange River Project, which supplement irregular rainfall.*

Using the land

Tea, cotton, sisal and tobacco are grown commercially in the southeast, with vines and citrus fruits near the southern coast. Coffee is grown in northern Angola. Corn is the main staple crop, grown with cassava,pulses or potatoes. Poor soils and cyclical drought limit farming to extensive pastoralism in most of Namibia and Botswana.

▲ **The arid Namib Desert** *stretches along much of the coast of Namibia. Great diamond deposits lie beneath the miles of constantly shifting sand dunes.*

◀ **Table Mountain, with** *its flat top and cloth-like folds overlooks the bay at Cape Town, home to South Africa's parliament.*

A B C D E F G H I J K L M

1 2 3 4 5 6 7 8 9 10 11 12 13 14 15 16 17

ARCTIC OCEAN
North Pole
Ellesmere Island
Laptey Sea
Severnaya Zemlya
Poluostrov Taymyr
Ostrov Rudol'fa
Kara Sea
King Frederik VIII Land
Franz Josef Land
Greenland
Mys Flissingskiy
Spitsbergen
NORTH AMERICAN PLATE
EURASIAN PLATE
Novaya Zemlya
Greenland Sea
King Christian X Land
Barents Sea
Bjørnøya
Poluostrov Yamal
Yenisey
Baydaratskaya Guba
Gulf of Ob
Barents Trough
Kara Strait
Jan Mayen Fracture Zone
Jan Mayen
Kolbeinsey Ridge
Denmark Strait
Iceland Plateau
Jan Mayen Ridge
North Cape
Nordkinn
Tromsøflaket
Fugløya Bank
Murmansk Rise
Ostrov Kolguyev
Poluostrov Kanin
Pechora
West Siberian Plain
Ob'
Arctic Circle
Norwegian Sea
Norwegian Basin
Vesterålen
Lofoten
Kebnekaise 2117m
Inarijärvi
Kola Peninsula
Ozero Imandra
Ural Mountains
Bjargtangar
Iceland
Vatnajökull
Voring Plateau
Torneälven
Timanskiy Kryazh
Mezen'
White Sea
ASIA
Reykjanes Ridge
Faeroe-Iceland Ridge
Traena Bank
Kölen
Scandinavia
Kemijoki
Oulujoki
Onega Bay
Northern Dvina
Umeälven
Ozero Vygozero
Iceland Basin
Faeroe Islands
Gulf of Bothnia
Lake Onega
Lake Ladoga
ATLANTIC OCEAN
Bill Baileys Bank
Galdhøpiggen 2469m
Ljungan
Svir
Ozero Beloye
Rybinsk Reservoir
Votkinsk Reservoir
Hatton Ridge
Faeroe-Shetland Trough
Shetland Islands
Viking Bank
Åland
Gulf of Finland
Outer Hebrides
Orkney Islands
Norwegian Trench
Vänern
Lake Peipus
Lake Ilmen
Gor'kiy Reservoir
Kuybyshev Reservoir
Rockall Rise
Ben Nevis 1343m
Grampian Mountains
North Sea
Jutland Bank
Skagerrak
Vättern
Gotland
Gulf of Riga
Lake Pskov
Feni Ridge
Rockall Trough
North Channel
Kattegat
Jylland
Great Fisher Bank
Sjælland
Baltic Sea
Western Dvina
Moskva
Volga Upland
British Isles
Ireland
Irish Sea
Pennines
Dogger Bank
Neman
North European Plain
Porcupine Plain
Shannon
Snowdon 1085m
Trent
Frisian Islands
Elbe
Byerezino
Dnieper
Central Russian Upland
Celtic Sea
St. George's Channel
Britain
Severn
Vistula
Bug
Pripet Marshes
Oder
Warta
Seym
Don
Khoper
Celtic Shelf
Bristol Channel
Thames
Strait of Dover
Harz
EUROPE
Desna
Dnieper Lowlands
Land's End
English Channel
Channel Islands
Ardennes
Rhine
Kiev Reservoir
Kremenchuk Reservoir
Tsimlyansk Reservoir
Seine
Marne
Meuse
Moselle
Dniester
Podil's'ka Vysochina
Pridennyy Bug
Donets
Manych
Yergeni
Vosges
Black Forest
Danube
Tisza
Carpathian Mountains
Black Sea Lowland
Loire
Vienne
Cher
Lake Constance
Prut
Siret
Sea of Azov
Charcot Seamounts
Bay of Biscay
Saône
Lake Geneva
Lake Balaton
Great Hungarian Plain
Crimea
Biscay Plain
Massif Central
Mont Blanc 4807m
Drava
Tisza
Transylvanian Alps
Kerch Strait
Azores-Biscay Rise
Dordogne
Lot
Garonne
Lake Garda
Po
Sava
Theta Gap
Galicia Bank
Cévennes
Rhône
Adriatic Sea
Dinaric Alps
Danube
Black Sea
Miño
Cordillera Cantábrica
Iberian Peninsula
Aragón
Ebro
Gulf of Lion
Ligurian Sea
Apennines
Balkan Mountains
Maritsa
Rhodope Mountains
Iberian Plain
Douro
Duero
Sistema Central
Sistema Ibérico
Corsica
Corno Grande 2912m
Tiber
Lake Scutari
Bosporus
EURASIAN PLATE
ANATOLIAN PLATE
Strait of Bonifacio
Adriatic Basin
Lake Ohrid
Lake Prespa
Sea of Marmara
Cabo da Roca
Tagus
Guadiana
Júcar
Gulf of Valencia
Sardinia
Tyrrhenian Sea
Gulf of Taranto
Strait of Otranto
Anatolia
Tagus Plain
Sierra Morena
Guadalquivir
Segura
Balearic Islands
Algerian Basin
Tyrrhenian Basin
Aegean Sea
Lake Tuz
Gorringe Ridge
Cape Saint Vincent
Sistemas Béticos
Sierra Nevada
Mediterranean Sea
Strait of Messina
Mount Etna 3340m
Ionian Sea
Peloponnese
Taurus Mountains
Horseshoe Seamounts
Punta de Tarifa
Strait of Sicily
Mirtoan Sea
Gulf of Antalya
Ampère Seamount
Strait of Gibraltar
Alboran Sea
Oued Chelif
EURASIAN PLATE
AFRICAN PLATE
Sicily
Rhodes Basin
Seine Plain
Seine Seamount
Rif
Sebou
Tell Atlas
Malta
Ionian Basin
Sea of Crete
Karpathos Strait
Crete
Gavdos
Cyprus
Madeira
Atlas Mountains
Middle Atlas
Moulouya
Oum er Rbia
Mediterranean Ridge
Cyprus Basin
Agadir Canyon
Dacia Seamount
Saharan Atlas
Chott el Jerid
Levantine Basin
High Atlas
Gulf of Sirte
Nile Fan
Canary Islands
Suez Canal
Grand Erg Occidental
Grand Erg Oriental
Qattara Depression -133m
Nile
Gulf of Suez
Sinai
Libyan Desert
Western Desert
AFRICA
SAHARA
'Erg Iguidi
Erg Chech

A B C D E F G H I J K L M

Europe

Europe is the world's second smallest continent, covering 4,053,309 sq miles (10,498,000 sq km). It comprises 46 separate countries, including Turkey and the Russian Federation, although the greater parts of these nations lie in Asia.

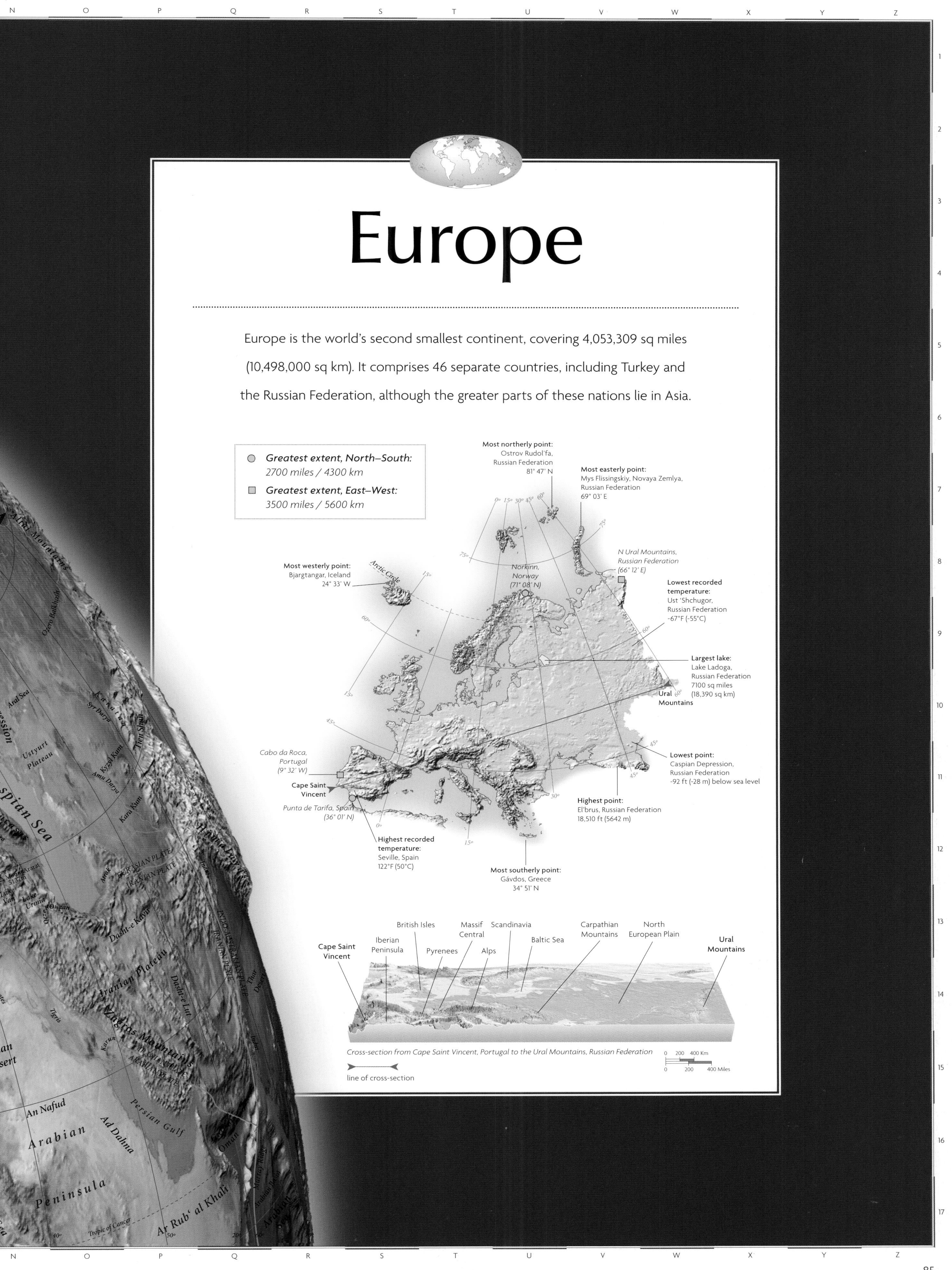

Greatest extent, North–South: 2700 miles / 4300 km
Greatest extent, East–West: 3500 miles / 5600 km
Most northerly point: Ostrov Rudol'fa, Russian Federation 81° 47' N
Most easterly point: Mys Flissingskiy, Novaya Zemlya, Russian Federation 69° 03' E
N Ural Mountains, Russian Federation (66° 12' E)
Most westerly point: Bjargtangar, Iceland 24° 33' W
Arctic Circle
Nordkinn, Norway (71° 08' N)
Lowest recorded temperature: Ust 'Shchugor, Russian Federation -67°F (-55°C)
Largest lake: Lake Ladoga, Russian Federation 7100 sq miles (18,390 sq km)
Ural Mountains
Cabo da Roca, Portugal (9° 32' W)
Cape Saint Vincent
Punta de Tarifa, Spain (36° 01' N)
Lowest point: Caspian Depression, Russian Federation -92 ft (-28 m) below sea level
Highest point: El'brus, Russian Federation 18,510 ft (5642 m)
Highest recorded temperature: Seville, Spain 122°F (50°C)
Most southerly point: Gávdos, Greece 34° 51' N
Cape Saint Vincent
Iberian Peninsula
British Isles
Pyrenees
Massif Central
Alps
Scandinavia
Baltic Sea
Carpathian Mountains
North European Plain
Ural Mountains
Cross-section from Cape Saint Vincent, Portugal to the Ural Mountains, Russian Federation
0 200 400 Km
0 200 400 Miles
line of cross-section
Aral Sea
Ustyurt Plateau
Caspian Sea
Zagros Mountains
Iranian Plateau
Dasht-e Kavir
Dasht-e Lut
Persian Gulf
An Nafud
Arabian Peninsula
Ad Dahna
Ar Rub' al Khali
Tropic of Cancer

Physical Europe

The physical diversity of Europe belies its relatively small size. To the northwest and south it is enclosed by mountains. The older, rounded Atlantic Highlands of Scandinavia and the British Isles lie to the north and the younger, rugged peaks of the Alpine Uplands to the south. In between lies the North European Plain, stretching 2485 miles (4000 km) from The Fens in England to the Ural Mountains in Russia. South of the plain lies a series of gently folded sedimentary rocks separated by ancient plateaux, known as massifs.

The Atlantic Highlands

The Atlantic Highlands were formed by compression against the Scandinavian Shield during the Caledonian mountain-building period over 500 million years ago. The highlands were once part of a continuous mountain chain, now divided by the North Sea and a submerged rift valley.

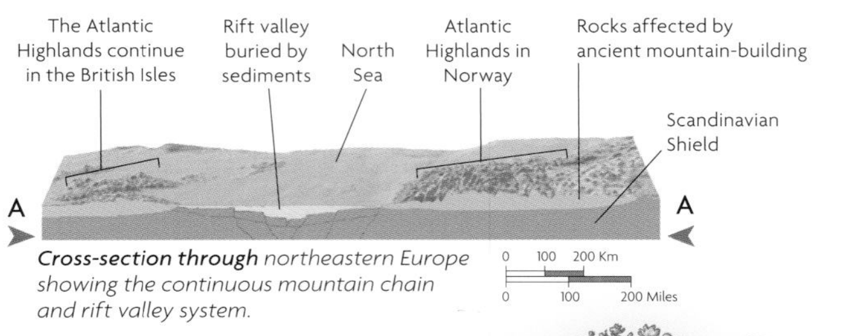
The Atlantic Highlands continue in the British Isles
Rift valley buried by sediments
North Sea
Atlantic Highlands in Norway
Rocks affected by ancient mountain-building
Scandinavian Shield
A
A
0 100 200 Km
0 100 200 Miles

Cross-section through northeastern Europe showing the continuous mountain chain and rift valley system.

The North European Plain

Rising less than 1000 ft (300 m) above sea level, the North European Plain strongly reflects past glaciation. Ridges of both coarse moraine and finer, windblown deposits have accumulated over much of the region. The ice sheet also diverted a number of river channels from their original courses.

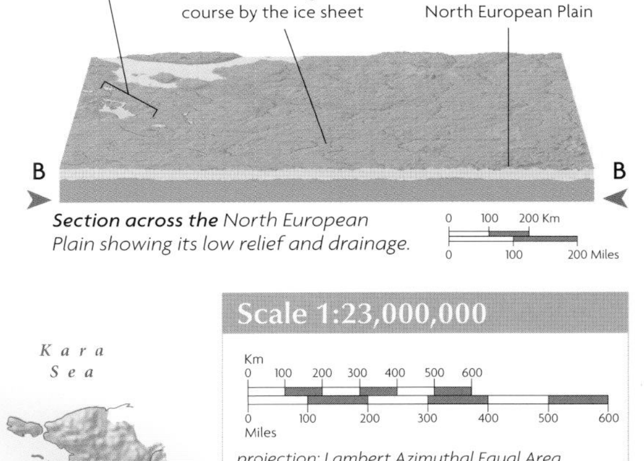
Glacial lakes
Rivers were diverted from their original course by the ice sheet
A layer of glacial sediments covers the North European Plain
B
B
0 100 200 Km
0 100 200 Miles

Section across the North European Plain showing its low relief and drainage.

Scale 1:23,000,000

Km 0 100 200 300 400 500 600

Miles 0 100 200 300 400 500 600

projection: Lambert Azimuthal Equal Area

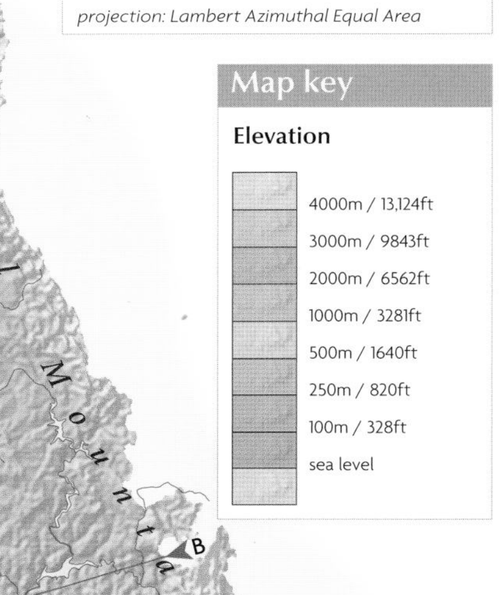
Map key
Elevation
4000m / 13,124ft
3000m / 9843ft
2000m / 6562ft
1000m / 3281ft
500m / 1640ft
250m / 820ft
100m / 328ft
sea level

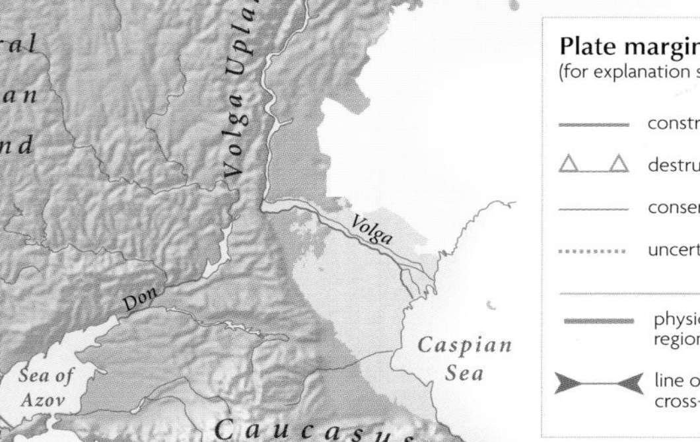

Plate margins (for explanation see page xiv)

- constructive
- destructive
- conservative
- uncertain
- physiographic regions
- line of cross-section

The plateaux and lowlands

The uplifted plateaux or massifs of southern central Europe are the result of long-term erosion, later followed by uplift. They are the source areas of many of the rivers which drain Europe's lowlands. In some of the higher reaches, fractures have enabled igneous rocks from deep in the Earth to reach the surface.

Igneous rocks have intruded into the Massif Central — Older, eroded massifs lie behind the arc of the Alps — Po Valley — Tectonically formed basins — Great Hungarian Plain

D — D

0 100 100 Km / 0 100 100 Miles

Cross-section through the plateaux and lowlands showing the lower elevation of the ancient massifs.

The Alpine Uplands

The collision of the African and European continents, which began about 65 million years ago, folded and then uplifted a series of mountain ranges running across southern Europe and into Asia. Two major lines of folding can be traced: one includes the Pyrenees, the Alps and the Carpathian Mountains; the other incorporates the Apennines and the Dinaric Alps.

European basement rock — Alps — Weak sedimentary strata have been folded — African Plate moved northwards — The Apennines

C — C

0 50 100 Km / 0 50 100 Miles

Cross-section through the Alps showing folding and faulting caused by plate tectonics.

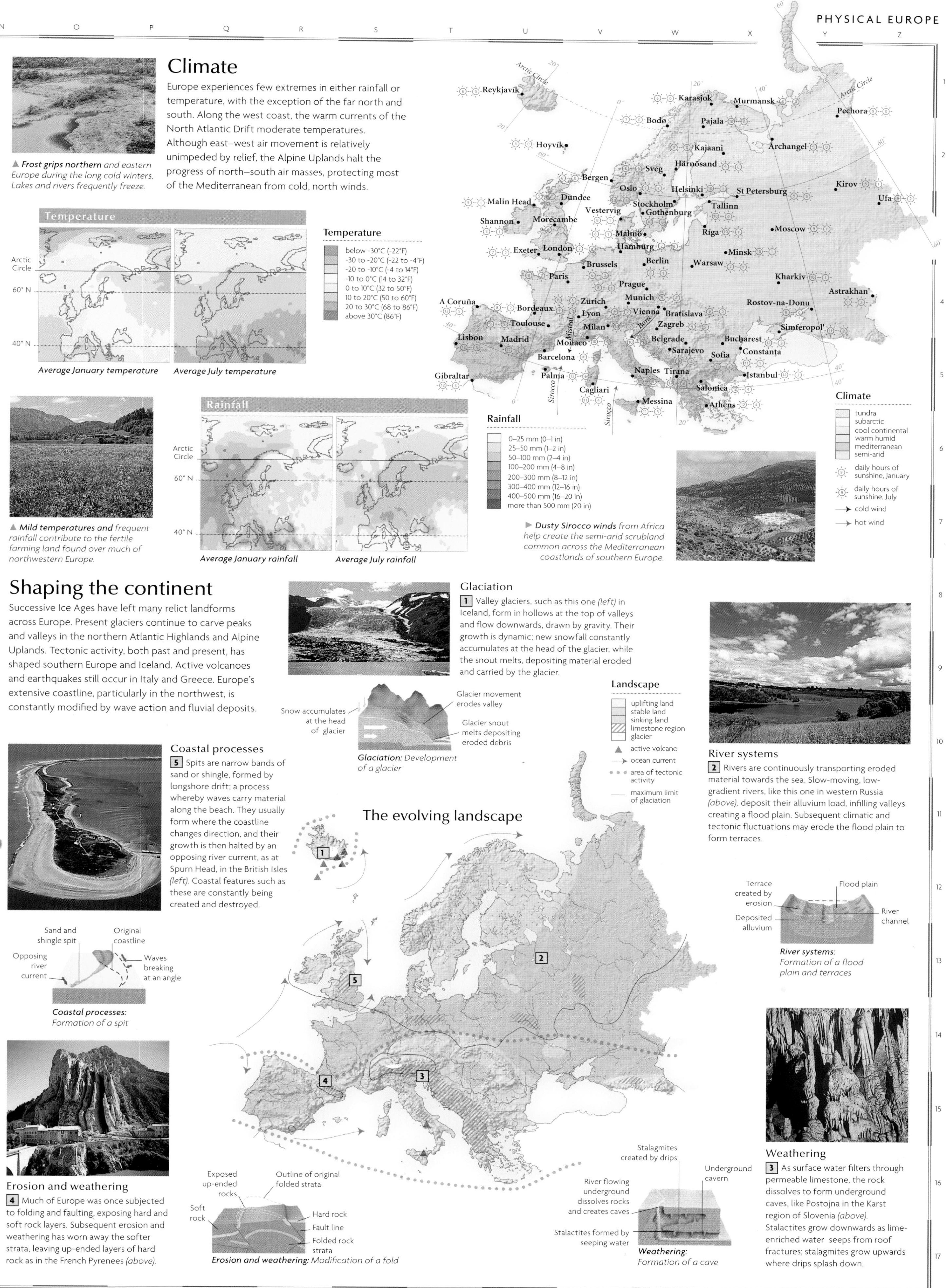

Temperature
Arctic Circle
60° N
40° N
Temperature
below -30°C (-22°F)
-30 to -20°C (-22 to -4°F)
-20 to -10°C (-4 to 14°F)
-10 to 0°C (14 to 32°F)
0 to 10°C (32 to 50°F)
10 to 20°C (50 to 60°F)
20 to 30°C (68 to 86°F)
above 30°C (86°F)
Rainfall
Arctic Circle
60° N
40° N
Rainfall
0–25 mm (0–1 in)
25–50 mm (1–2 in)
50–100 mm (2–4 in)
100–200 mm (4–8 in)
200–300 mm (8–12 in)
300–400 mm (12–16 in)
400–500 mm (16–20 in)
more than 500 mm (20 in)
Reykjavík
Karasjok
Murmansk
Pechora
Bodø
Pajala
Hoyvík
Kajaani
Archangel
Härnösand
Sveg
Bergen
Oslo
Helsinki
St Petersburg
Kirov
Malin Head
Dundee
Stockholm
Tallinn
Ufa
Vestervig
Gothenburg
Shannon
Morecambe
Malmö
Riga
Moscow
Exeter
London
Hamburg
Minsk
Brussels
Berlin
Warsaw
Paris
Kharkiv
Prague
Astrakhan'
A Coruña
Bordeaux
Zürich
Munich
Rostov-na-Donu
Lyon
Vienna
Bratislava
Toulouse
Milan
Zagreb
Simferopol'
Lisbon
Madrid
Monaco
Belgrade
Bucharest
Sarajevo
Constanța
Barcelona
Sofia
Mistral
Bora
Palma
Naples
Tirana
Istanbul
Gibraltar
Cagliari
Salonica
Sirocco
Messina
Athens
Arctic Circle
Climate
tundra
subarctic
cool continental
warm humid
mediterranean
semi-arid
daily hours of sunshine, January
daily hours of sunshine, July
cold wind
hot wind
Snow accumulates at the head of glacier
Glacier movement erodes valley
Glacier snout melts depositing eroded debris
Landscape
uplifting land
stable land
sinking land
limestone region
glacier
active volcano
ocean current
area of tectonic activity
maximum limit of glaciation
The evolving landscape
Terrace created by erosion
Flood plain
River channel
Deposited alluvium
Sand and shingle spit
Original coastline
Opposing river current
Waves breaking at an angle
Exposed up-ended rocks
Outline of original folded strata
Soft rock
Hard rock
Fault line
Folded rock strata
Stalagmites created by drips
Underground cavern
River flowing underground dissolves rocks and creates caves
Stalactites formed by seeping water

Climate

Europe experiences few extremes in either rainfall or temperature, with the exception of the far north and south. Along the west coast, the warm currents of the North Atlantic Drift moderate temperatures. Although east–west air movement is relatively unimpeded by relief, the Alpine Uplands halt the progress of north–south air masses, protecting most of the Mediterranean from cold, north winds.

▲ *Frost grips northern and eastern Europe during the long cold winters. Lakes and rivers frequently freeze.*

Average January temperature *Average July temperature*

▲ *Mild temperatures and frequent rainfall contribute to the fertile farming land found over much of northwestern Europe.*

Average January rainfall *Average July rainfall*

▶ *Dusty Sirocco winds from Africa help create the semi-arid scrubland common across the Mediterranean coastlands of southern Europe.*

Shaping the continent

Successive Ice Ages have left many relict landforms across Europe. Present glaciers continue to carve peaks and valleys in the northern Atlantic Highlands and Alpine Uplands. Tectonic activity, both past and present, has shaped southern Europe and Iceland. Active volcanoes and earthquakes still occur in Italy and Greece. Europe's extensive coastline, particularly in the northwest, is constantly modified by wave action and fluvial deposits.

Glaciation

1 Valley glaciers, such as this one *(left)* in Iceland, form in hollows at the top of valleys and flow downwards, drawn by gravity. Their growth is dynamic; new snowfall constantly accumulates at the head of the glacier, while the snout melts, depositing material eroded and carried by the glacier.

***Glaciation:** Development of a glacier*

River systems

2 Rivers are continuously transporting eroded material towards the sea. Slow-moving, low-gradient rivers, like this one in western Russia *(above)*, deposit their alluvium load, infilling valleys creating a flood plain. Subsequent climatic and tectonic fluctuations may erode the flood plain to form terraces.

***River systems:** Formation of a flood plain and terraces*

Coastal processes

5 Spits are narrow bands of sand or shingle, formed by longshore drift; a process whereby waves carry material along the beach. They usually form where the coastline changes direction, and their growth is then halted by an opposing river current, as at Spurn Head, in the British Isles *(left)*. Coastal features such as these are constantly being created and destroyed.

***Coastal processes:** Formation of a spit*

Erosion and weathering

4 Much of Europe was once subjected to folding and faulting, exposing hard and soft rock layers. Subsequent erosion and weathering has worn away the softer strata, leaving up-ended layers of hard rock as in the French Pyrenees *(above)*.

***Erosion and weathering:** Modification of a fold*

Weathering

3 As surface water filters through permeable limestone, the rock dissolves to form underground caves, like Postojna in the Karst region of Slovenia *(above)*. Stalactites grow downwards as lime-enriched water seeps from roof fractures; stalagmites grow upwards where drips splash down.

***Weathering:** Formation of a cave*

Political Europe

The political boundaries of Europe have changed many times, especially during the 20th century in the aftermath of two world wars, the break-up of the empires of Austria-Hungary, Nazi Germany and, towards the end of the century, the collapse of communism in eastern Europe. The fragmentation of Yugoslavia has again altered the political map of Europe, highlighting a trend towards nationalism and devolution. In contrast, economic federalism is growing. In 1958, the formation of the European Economic Community (now the European Union or EU) started a move towards economic and political union and increasing internal migration.

▲ ***The Brandenburg Gate*** *in Berlin is a potent symbol of German reunification. From 1961, the road beneath it ended in a wall, built to stop the flow of refugees to the West. It was opened again in 1989 when the wall was destroyed and East and West Germany were reunited.*

Population

Europe is a densely populated, urbanized continent; in Belgium over 90% of people live in urban areas. The highest population densities are found in an area stretching east from southern Britain and northern France, into Germany. The northern fringes are only sparsely populated.

Denmark Strait
Arctic Circle
REYKJAVÍK
ICELAND

▲ ***Demand for space*** *in densely populated European cities like London has led to the development of high-rise offices and urban sprawl.*

Population density
(people per sq km)

- below 49
- 50–99
- 100–149
- 150–199
- 200–299
- above 300

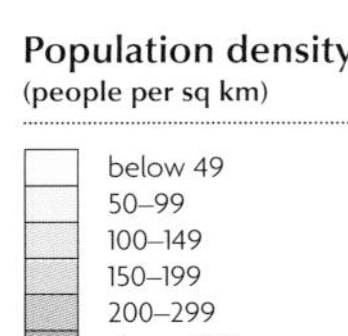
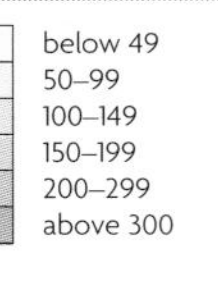
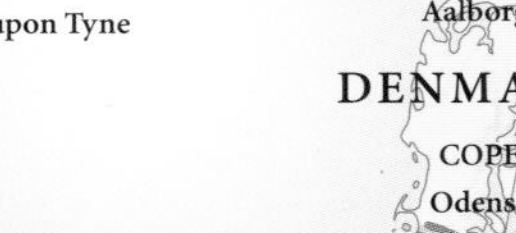

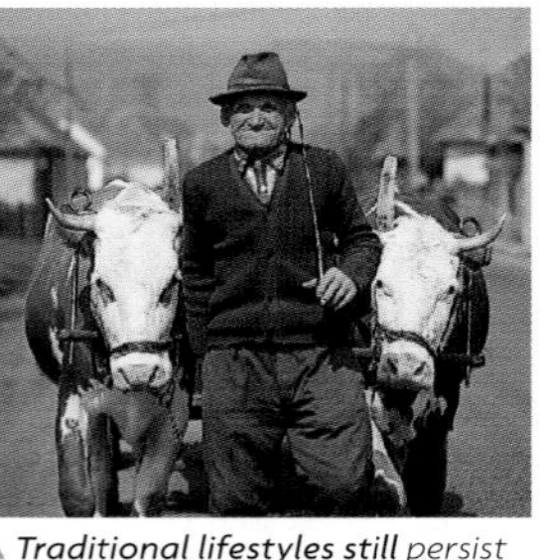

▲ ***Traditional lifestyles still*** *persist in many remote and rural parts of Europe, especially in the south, east, and in the far north.*

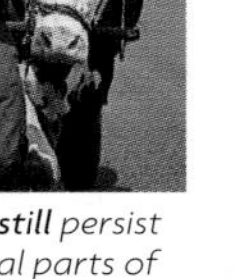

Map key

Population

- ■ above 5 million
- ◙ 1 million to 5 million
- ◉ 500,000 to 1 million
- ◎ 100,000 to 500,000
- ⊕ 50,000 to 100,000
- ○ 10,000 to 50,000
- ● Country capital

Borders

- full international border

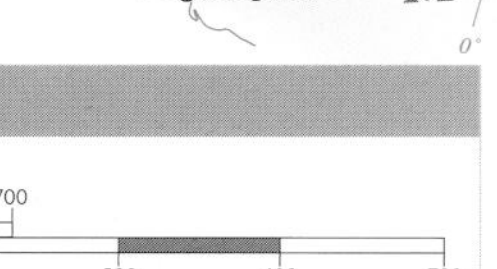
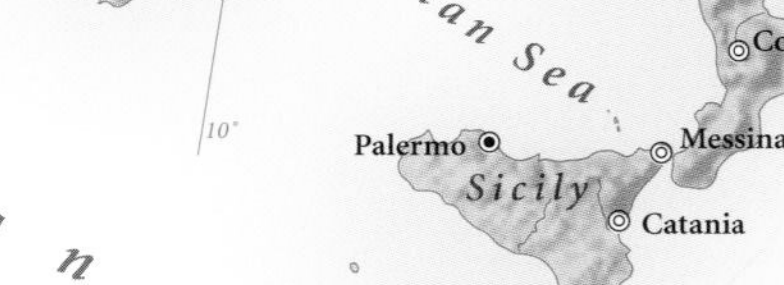

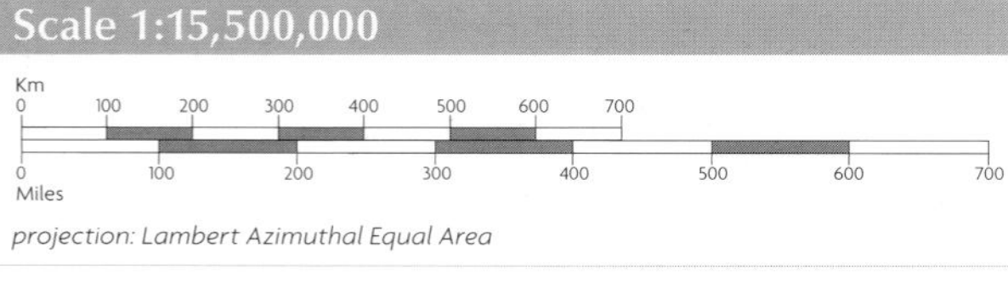

Scale 1:15,500,000

Km 0 100 200 300 400 500 600 700

Miles 0 100 200 300 400 500 600 700

projection: Lambert Azimuthal Equal Area

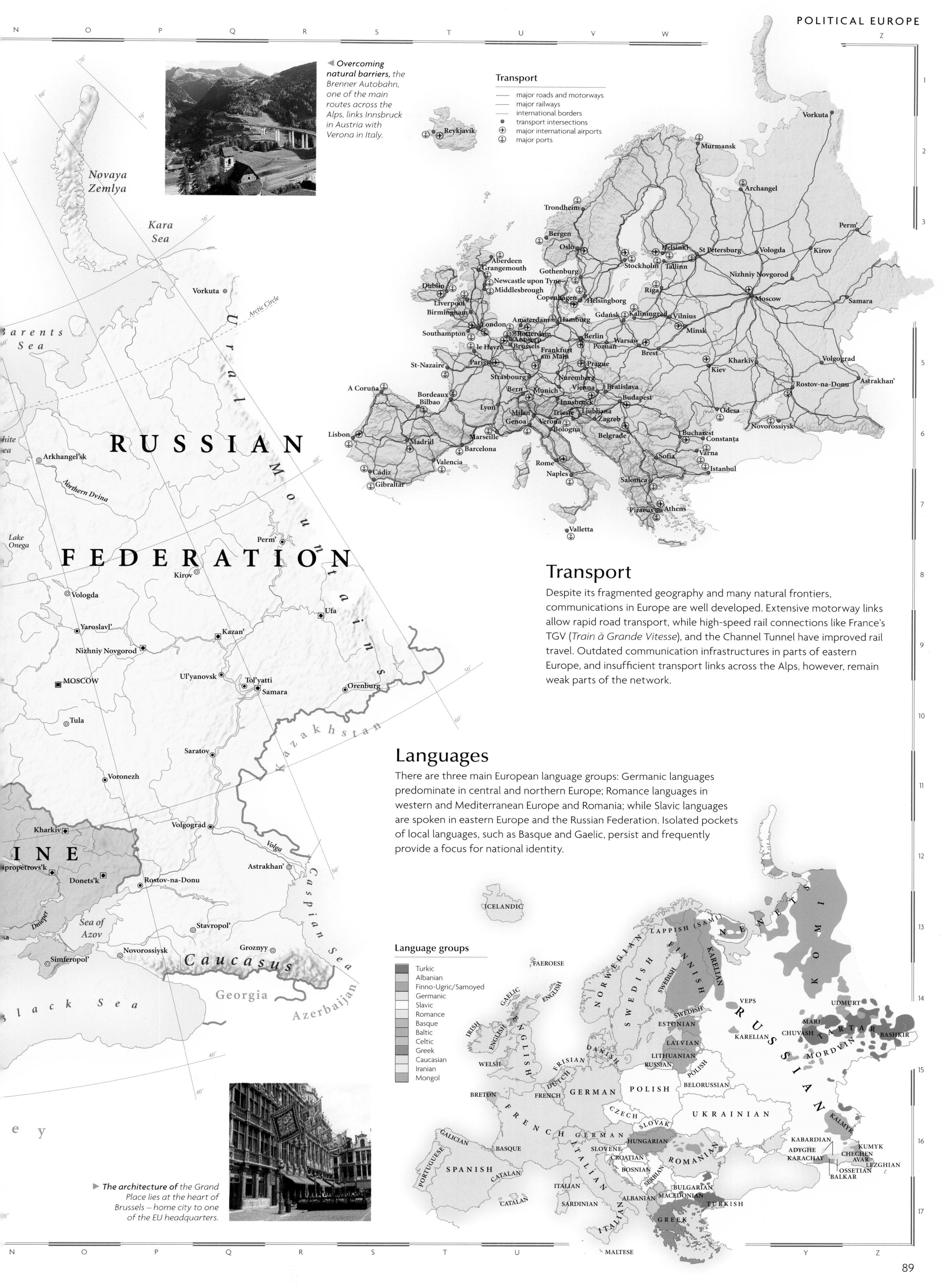

N O P Q R S T U V W Z
1 2 3 4 5 6 7 8 9 10 11 12 13 14 15 16 17
Novaya Zemlya
Kara Sea
Barents Sea
Vorkuta
Arctic Circle
Ural Mountains
RUSSIAN FEDERATION
Arkhangel'sk
Northern Dvina
Lake Onega
Perm'
Kirov
Vologda
Ufa
Yaroslavl'
Kazan'
Nizhniy Novgorod
MOSCOW
Ul'yanovsk
Tol'yatti
Samara
Orenburg
Tula
Kazakhstan
Saratov
Voronezh
Volgograd
Kharkiv
Volga
Astrakhan'
Dnipropetrovs'k
Donets'k
Rostov-na-Donu
Caspian Sea
Dnieper
Sea of Azov
Stavropol'
Groznyy
Novorossiysk
Simferopol'
Caucasus
Georgia
Azerbaijan
Black Sea
Transport
major roads and motorways
major railways
international borders
transport intersections
major international airports
major ports
Reykjavik
Murmansk
Vorkuta
Archangel
Trondheim
Perm'
Bergen
Oslo
Helsinki
St Petersburg
Vologda
Kirov
Aberdeen
Grangemouth
Stockholm
Tallinn
Gothenburg
Nizhniy Novgorod
Dublin
Newcastle upon Tyne
Middlesbrough
Riga
Moscow
Samara
Liverpool
Copenhagen
Helsingborg
Birmingham
Gdańsk
Kaliningrad
Vilnius
Amsterdam
Hamburg
Minsk
London
Rotterdam
Southampton
Antwerp
Berlin
Warsaw
le Havre
Brussels
Poznań
Brest
Frankfurt am Main
St-Nazaire
Paris
Prague
Kharkiv
Volgograd
Kiev
Strasbourg
Nuremberg
A Coruña
Bratislava
Bern
Munich
Vienna
Rostov-na-Donu
Astrakhan'
Bordeaux
Bilbao
Budapest
Innsbruck
Lyon
Milan
Trieste
Ljubljana
Odesa
Genoa
Verona
Zagreb
Novorossiysk
Bologna
Lisbon
Belgrade
Bucharest
Constanța
Marseille
Madrid
Barcelona
Sofia
Varna
Valencia
Rome
Istanbul
Cádiz
Naples
Salonica
Gibraltar
Piraeus
Athens
Valletta
Language groups
Turkic
Albanian
Finno-Ugric/Samoyed
Germanic
Slavic
Romance
Basque
Baltic
Celtic
Greek
Caucasian
Iranian
Mongol
ICELANDIC
FAEROESE
NENETS
KOMI
LAPPISH (SAMI)
KARELIAN
FINNISH
SWEDISH
NORWEGIAN
GAELIC
ENGLISH
VEPS
UDMURT
IRISH
ESTONIAN
MARI
CHUVASH
TARTAR
BASHKIR
KARELIAN
RUSSIAN
LATVIAN
DANISH
MORDVIN
WELSH
LITHUANIAN
RUSSIAN
FRISIAN
POLISH
DUTCH
BELORUSSIAN
BRETON
FRENCH
GERMAN
POLISH
CZECH
UKRAINIAN
KALMYK
SLOVAK
GALICIAN
HUNGARIAN
KABARDIAN
KUMYK
ADYGHE
CHECHEN
BASQUE
SLOVENE
KARACHAY
AVAR
ROMANIAN
CROATIAN
LEZGHIAN
PORTUGUESE
OSSETIAN
BALKAR
SPANISH
BOSNIAN
CATALAN
SERBIAN
BULGARIAN
ITALIAN
MACEDONIAN
ALBANIAN
TURKISH
SARDINIAN
CATALAN
GREEK
MALTESE

◀ *Overcoming natural barriers, the Brenner Autobahn, one of the main routes across the Alps, links Innsbruck in Austria with Verona in Italy.*

Transport

Despite its fragmented geography and many natural frontiers, communications in Europe are well developed. Extensive motorway links allow rapid road transport, while high-speed rail connections like France's TGV (*Train à Grande Vitesse*), and the Channel Tunnel have improved rail travel. Outdated communication infrastructures in parts of eastern Europe, and insufficient transport links across the Alps, however, remain weak parts of the network.

Languages

There are three main European language groups: Germanic languages predominate in central and northern Europe; Romance languages in western and Mediterranean Europe and Romania; while Slavic languages are spoken in eastern Europe and the Russian Federation. Isolated pockets of local languages, such as Basque and Gaelic, persist and frequently provide a focus for national identity.

▶ *The architecture of the Grand Place lies at the heart of Brussels – home city to one of the EU headquarters.*

European resources

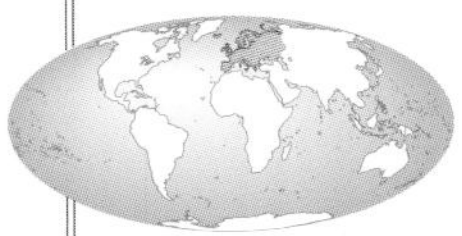

Europe's large tracts of fertile, accessible land, combined with its generally temperate climate, have allowed a greater percentage of land to be used for agricultural purposes than in any other continent. Extensive coal and iron ore deposits were used to create steel and manufacturing industries during the 19th and 20th centuries. Today, although natural resources have been widely exploited, and heavy industry is of declining importance, the growth of hi-tech and service industries has enabled Europe to maintain its wealth.

Industry

Europe's wealth was generated by the rise of industry and colonial exploitation during the 19th century. The mining of abundant natural resources made Europe the industrial centre of the world. Adaptation has been essential in the changing world economy, and a move to service-based industries has been widespread except in eastern Europe, where heavy industry still dominates.

▲ *Countries like Hungary are still struggling to modernize inefficient factories left over from extensive, centrally-planned industrialization during the communist era.*

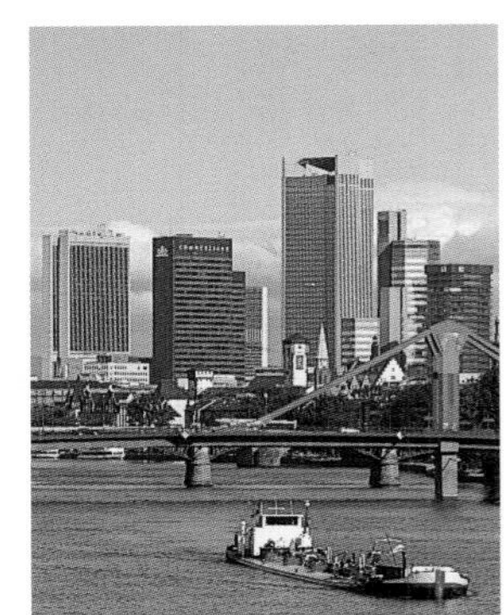

◄ *Frankfurt am Main is an example of a modern service-based city. The skyline is dominated by headquarters from the worlds of banking and commerce.*

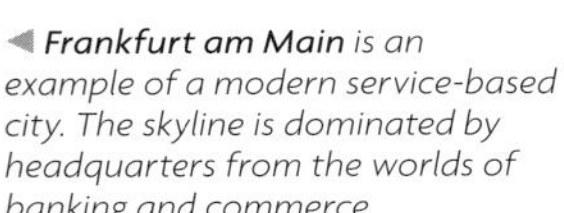

▲ *Other power sources are becoming more attractive as fossil fuels run out; 16% of Europe's electricity is now provided by hydro-electric power.*

Standard of living

Living standards in western Europe are among the highest in the world, although there is a growing sector of homeless, jobless people. Eastern Europeans have lower overall standards of living – a legacy of stagnated economies.

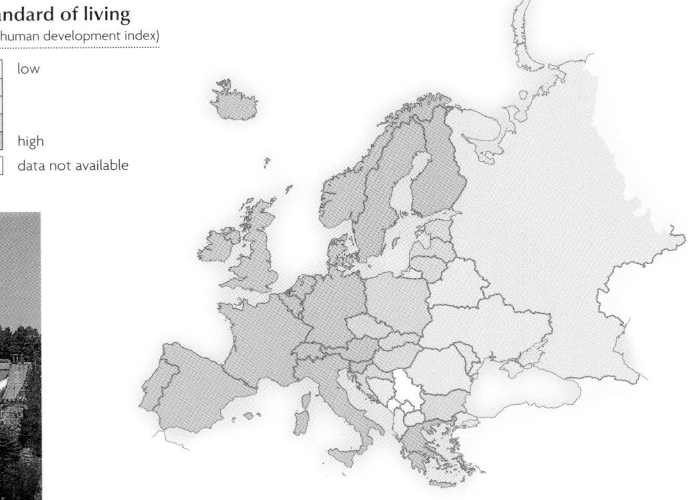

Standard of living
(UN human development index)
low
high
data not available

► *Skiing brings millions of tourists to the slopes each year, which means that even unproductive, marginal land is used to create wealth in the French, Swiss, Italian and Austrian Alps.*

GNI per capita (US $)

- below 1999
- 2000–4999
- 5000–9999
- 10,000–19,999
- 20,000–24,999
- above 25,000

ICELAND · Reykjavík · Faeroe Islands (to Denmark) · Norwegian Sea · ATLANTIC OCEAN · NORWAY · Trondheim · Bergen · Oslo · SWEDEN · Stockholm · Gothenburg · Malmö · FINLAND · Turku · Helsinki · Gulf of Bothnia · Baltic Sea · DENMARK · Copenhagen · North Sea · IRELAND · Dublin · Belfast · Isle of Man (to UK) · UNITED KINGDOM · Glasgow · Newcastle upon Tyne · Liverpool · Manchester · Birmingham · Cardiff · London · Channel Islands (to UK) · NETH. · Amsterdam · Rotterdam · BELG. · Antwerp · Brussels · Liège · LUX. · Lille · Rouen · Paris · Nantes · FRANCE · Bay of Biscay · Bordeaux · Lyon · Toulouse · Marseille · MONACO · ANDORRA · GERMANY · Hamburg · Essen · Cologne · Berlin · Leipzig · Dresden · Frankfurt am Main · Metz · Strasbourg · Stuttgart · Munich · SWITZ. · Zürich · LIECH. · AUSTRIA · Linz · Vienna · ITALY · Turin · Milan · Venice · Genoa · Bologna · SAN MARINO · VATICAN CITY · Rome · Naples · Taranto · Palermo · Sicily · Sardinia · Corsica · MALTA · SPAIN · A Coruña · Bilbao · Madrid · Barcelona · Seville · Balearic Islands · PORTUGAL · Porto · Lisbon · Gibraltar (to UK) · Ceuta (to Spain) · Melilla (to Spain) · MOROCCO · Mediterranean Sea · Tyrrhenian Sea · Adriatic Sea · Ionian Sea · POLAND · Gdańsk · Poznań · Łódź · Warsaw · Kraków · Katowice · RUSS. FED. (Kaliningrad) · CZECH REP. · Prague · SLOVAKIA · Bratislava · HUNGARY · Budapest · SLVN. · Zagreb · CROATIA · BOSNIA & HERZ. · SERBIA · Belgrade · MONT. · KOSOVO · ALBANIA · MACED. · GREECE · Salonica · Piraeus · Athens · Aegean Sea · Crete · ROMANIA · Ploieşti · Bucharest · Constanţa · BULGARIA · Sofia · Varna · TURKEY · Istanbul · Black Sea · MOLDOVA · Odesa · UKRAINE · Kiev · Kharkiv · Dnipropetrovs'k · Donets'k · Kryvyy Rih · BELARUS · Minsk · LITHUANIA · Vilnius · LATVIA · Riga · ESTONIA · Tallinn · RUSSIAN FEDERATION · St Petersburg · Murmansk · Barents Sea · Ostrov Kolguyev · Novaya Zemlya · Archangel · Cherepovets · Yaroslavl' · Ivanovo · Nizhniy Novgorod · Moscow · Ryazan' · Tula · Kursk · Voronezh · Saratov · Volgograd · Rostov-na-Donu · Kazan' · Perm' · Ufa · Tol'yatti · Samara · KAZAKHSTAN · Caspian Sea · GEORGIA · AZERBAIJAN

Industry

- aerospace
- brewing
- car/vehicle manufacture
- chemicals
- defence
- electronics
- engineering
- finance
- food processing
- hi-tech industry
- iron & steel
- pharmaceuticals
- printing & publishing
- shipbuilding
- textiles
- timber processing
- wine
- coal
- oil
- gas
- industrial cities
- major industrial areas

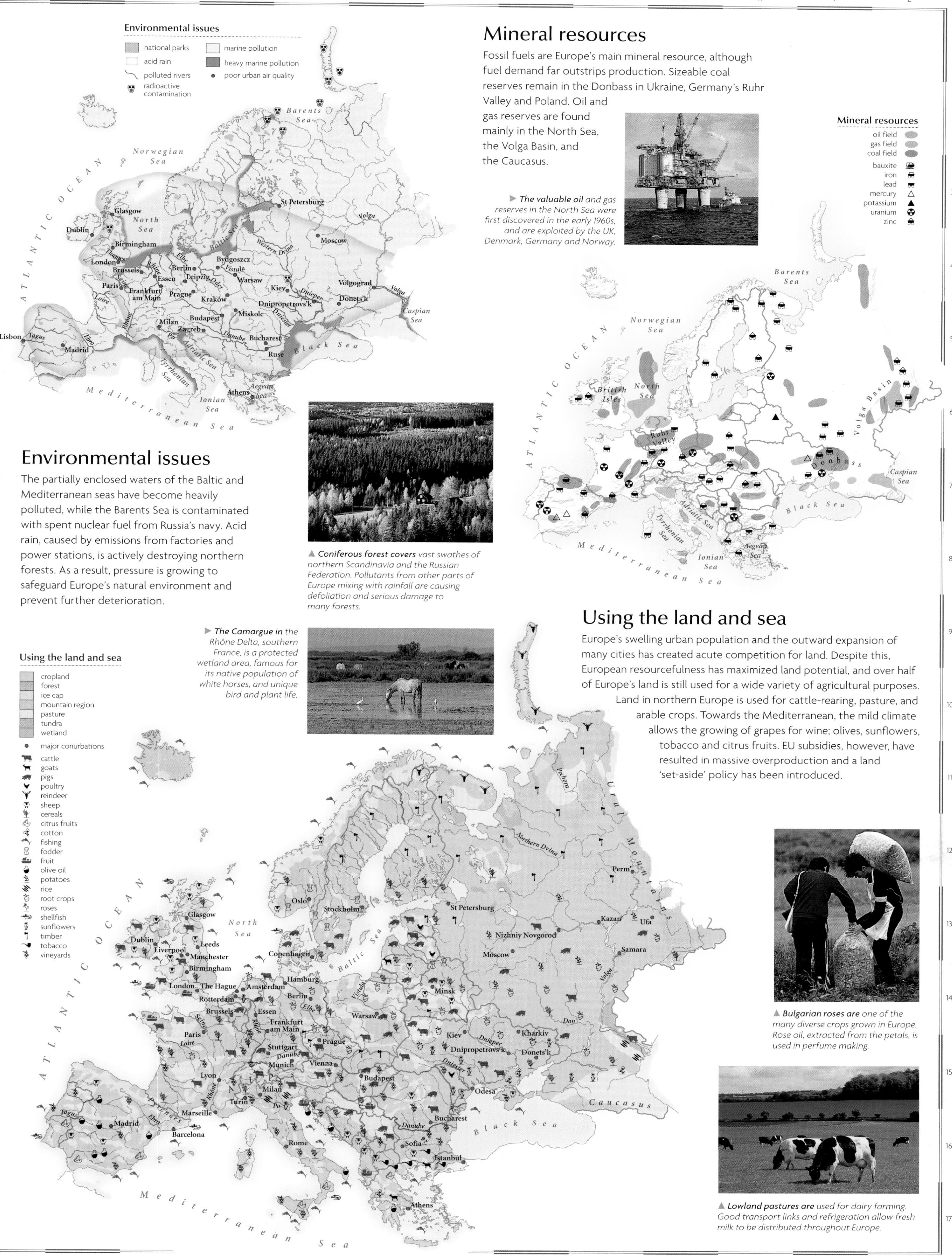
Environmental issues
national parks
acid rain
polluted rivers
radioactive contamination
marine pollution
heavy marine pollution
poor urban air quality
Barents Sea
Norwegian Sea
North Sea
ATLANTIC OCEAN
Glasgow
Dublin
Birmingham
London
Brussels
Paris
Frankfurt am Main
Essen
Berlin
Leipzig
Bydgoszcz
Warsaw
Prague
Kraków
St Petersburg
Moscow
Kiev
Volgograd
Donets'k
Dnipropetrovs'k
Miskolc
Budapest
Zagreb
Milan
Bucharest
Ruse
Madrid
Lisbon
Athens
Caspian Sea
Black Sea
Mediterranean Sea
Ionian Sea
Aegean Sea
Adriatic Sea
Tyrrhenian Sea
Mineral resources
oil field
gas field
coal field
bauxite
iron
lead
mercury
potassium
uranium
zinc
British Isles
Ruhr Valley
Donbass
Volga Basin
Using the land and sea
cropland
forest
ice cap
mountain region
pasture
tundra
wetland
major conurbations
cattle
goats
pigs
poultry
reindeer
sheep
cereals
citrus fruits
cotton
fishing
fodder
fruit
olive oil
potatoes
rice
root crops
roses
shellfish
sunflowers
timber
tobacco
vineyards
Ural Mountains
Caucasus
Oslo
Stockholm
Copenhagen
Hamburg
Amsterdam
The Hague
Rotterdam
Liverpool
Leeds
Manchester
Nizhniy Novgorod
Kazan'
Ufa
Perm'
Samara
Kharkiv
Minsk
Odesa
Vienna
Munich
Stuttgart
Lyon
Marseille
Turin
Barcelona
Rome
Sofia
Istanbul

Mineral resources

Fossil fuels are Europe's main mineral resource, although fuel demand far outstrips production. Sizeable coal reserves remain in the Donbass in Ukraine, Germany's Ruhr Valley and Poland. Oil and gas reserves are found mainly in the North Sea, the Volga Basin, and the Caucasus.

▶ *The valuable oil and gas reserves in the North Sea were first discovered in the early 1960s, and are exploited by the UK, Denmark, Germany and Norway.*

Environmental issues

The partially enclosed waters of the Baltic and Mediterranean seas have become heavily polluted, while the Barents Sea is contaminated with spent nuclear fuel from Russia's navy. Acid rain, caused by emissions from factories and power stations, is actively destroying northern forests. As a result, pressure is growing to safeguard Europe's natural environment and prevent further deterioration.

▲ *Coniferous forest covers vast swathes of northern Scandinavia and the Russian Federation. Pollutants from other parts of Europe mixing with rainfall are causing defoliation and serious damage to many forests.*

▶ *The Camargue in the Rhône Delta, southern France, is a protected wetland area, famous for its native population of white horses, and unique bird and plant life.*

Using the land and sea

Europe's swelling urban population and the outward expansion of many cities has created acute competition for land. Despite this, European resourcefulness has maximized land potential, and over half of Europe's land is still used for a wide variety of agricultural purposes. Land in northern Europe is used for cattle-rearing, pasture, and arable crops. Towards the Mediterranean, the mild climate allows the growing of grapes for wine; olives, sunflowers, tobacco and citrus fruits. EU subsidies, however, have resulted in massive overproduction and a land 'set-aside' policy has been introduced.

▲ *Bulgarian roses are one of the many diverse crops grown in Europe. Rose oil, extracted from the petals, is used in perfume making.*

▲ *Lowland pastures are used for dairy farming. Good transport links and refrigeration allow fresh milk to be distributed throughout Europe.*

Scandinavia, Finland & Iceland

DENMARK, NORWAY, SWEDEN, FINLAND, ICELAND

Jutting into the Arctic Circle, this northern swathe of Europe has some of the continent's harshest environments, but benefits from great reserves of oil, gas and natural evergreen forests. While most early settlers came from the south, migrants to Finland came from the east, giving it a distinct language and culture. Since the late 19th century, the Scandinavian states have developed strong egalitarian traditions. Today, their welfare benefits systems are among the most extensive in the world, and standards of living are high. The Lapps, or Sami, maintain their traditional lifestyle in the northern regions of Norway, Sweden and Finland.

The landscape

Glaciers up to 10,000 ft (3000 m) deep covered most of Scandinavia and Finland during the last Ice Age. The effects of glaciation mark the entire landscape, from the mountains to the lowlands, across the tundra landscape of Lapland, and the lake districts of Sweden and Finland.

Geysers are a by-product of Iceland's volcanic activity. Geysir, Iceland's largest spring, gives them their name.

The Lofoten Islands were one of the first areas exposed as the ice sheet melted.

Halti mountain is Finland's highest point, at 4356 ft (1328 m).

Lapland, north of the Arctic Circle, is an area of undulating fells and plains known as tundra. The subsoil is permanently frozen and therefore impermeable. There are many peat bogs. Pools reappear in the summer when the surface thaws.

Oulujärvi

◀ *Finland's landscape was fashioned by ice action. Glaciers gouged out its distinctive shallow lake basins, such as Oulujärvi, and left debris called moraines in their wake.*

Fjords

▲ ***The fjords on*** *the western coast of Norway were once gentle river valleys. Their deep floors and steep sides were carved out by glaciers during the last Ice Age, and they were later flooded by the sea.*

Sjælland coast

▲ ***On the coast*** *of Sjælland, these cliffs have been eroded by the sea, exposing layers of chalk and limestone.*

Slower rates of uplift 0.1 in/yr (3 mm/yr)

Area of maximum yearly uplift 0.3 in/yr (9 mm/yr)

▲ ***Scandinavia is still*** *recovering from the last Ice Age, when ice depressed the land by 2000 ft (600 m). This gradual uplift is known as isostatic rebound.*

SCALE 1:8,000,000

projection: Lambert Conformal Conic

(same scale as main map)

Scale 1:5,000,000

projection: Lambert Conformal Conic

Using the land and sea

The cold climate, short growing season, poorly developed soil, steep slopes, and exposure to high winds across northern regions means that most agriculture is concentrated, with the population, in the south. Most of Finland and much of Norway and Sweden are covered by dense forests of pine, spruce and birch, which supply the timber industries.

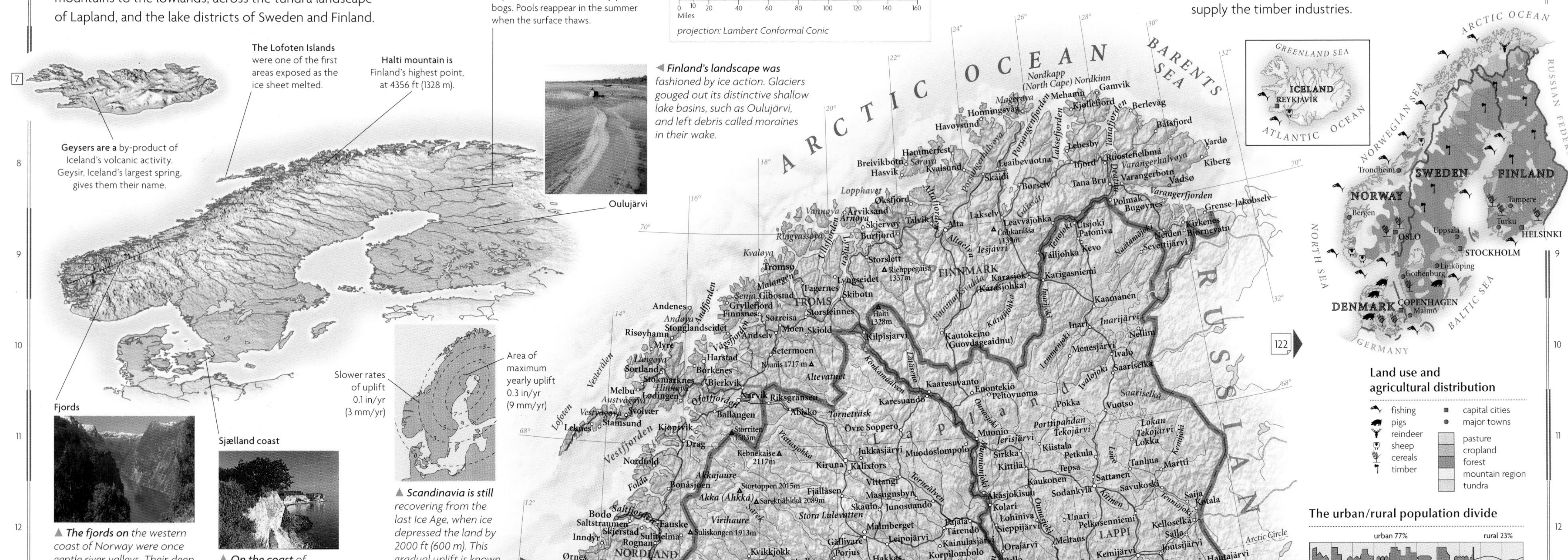

ARCTIC OCEAN
BARENTS SEA
NORWEGIAN SEA
RUSSIAN FEDERATION
LAPPI
FINNMARK
TROMS
NORDLAND
NORRBOTTEN
Lappland
Nordkapp (North Cape)
Halti 1328m
Kebnekaise 2117m
Hammerfest
Tromsø
Kiruna
Arctic Circle

Land use and agricultural distribution

fishing, pigs, reindeer, sheep, cereals, timber

capital cities, major towns

pasture, cropland, forest, mountain region, tundra

The urban/rural population divide

urban 77% | rural 23%

Population density	Total land area
51 people per sq mile	473,970 sq miles

7

122

▲ **Many Lappish people,** in addition to traditional reindeer herding, now also make their living from fishing and farming, or working in cities. Tourism provides some with an extra source of income.

▲ **Sweden is one** of the world's largest producers of wood and wood-based products. The traditional movement of logs by floating them down rivers has now been largely replaced by the use of trucks.

Map key

Population

- 500,000 to 1 million
- 100,000 to 500,000
- 50,000 to 100,000
- 10,000 to 50,000
- below 10,000

Elevation

- 2000m / 6562ft
- 1000m / 3281ft
- 500m / 1640ft
- 250m / 820ft
- 100m / 328ft
- sea level

Transport and industry

Norway derives its premier industry, the production of oil and gas, from the North Sea, while Denmark exploits its own oil and gas reserves. Hydro-electric power is a major industry, particularly in Sweden and Iceland. Timber processing remains significant in Finland and Sweden, but metal and engineering industries are increasingly important. In Iceland, fish products are the main source of export earnings.

The transport network

- 226,735 miles (364,936 km)
- 2042 miles (3286 km)
- 13,704 miles (22,057 km)
- 6,661 miles (10,721 km)

Although roads now reach most areas, the railways are markedly less developed. Much of the north is not served by rail and must rely on air and sea services for long distance travel and freight transportation.

Major industry and infrastructure

- car manufacture
- engineering
- fish processing
- hydro-electric power
- nuclear power
- oil & gas
- timber processing
- capital cities
- major towns
- international airports
- major roads
- major industrial areas

▶ **The use of** geothermal power in Iceland began half a century ago. Today geothermal power stations supply 89% of the country's domestic heating requirements.

100

Southern Scandinavia

SOUTHERN NORWAY, SOUTHERN SWEDEN, DENMARK

Scandinavia's economic and political hub is the more habitable and accessible southern region. Many of the area's major cities are on the southern coasts, including Oslo and Stockholm, the capitals of Norway and Sweden. In Denmark, most of the population and the capital, Copenhagen, are located on its many islands. A cultural unity links the three Scandinavian countries. Their main languages, Danish, Swedish and Norwegian, are mutually intelligible, and they all retain their monarchies, although the parliaments have legislative control.

Using the land

Agriculture in southern Scandinavia is highly mechanized although farms are small. Denmark is the most intensively farmed country and its western pastureland is used mainly for pig farming. Cereal crops including wheat, barley and oats, predominate in eastern Denmark and in the far south of Sweden. Southern Norway and Sweden have large tracts of forest which are exploited for logging.

The urban/rural population divide

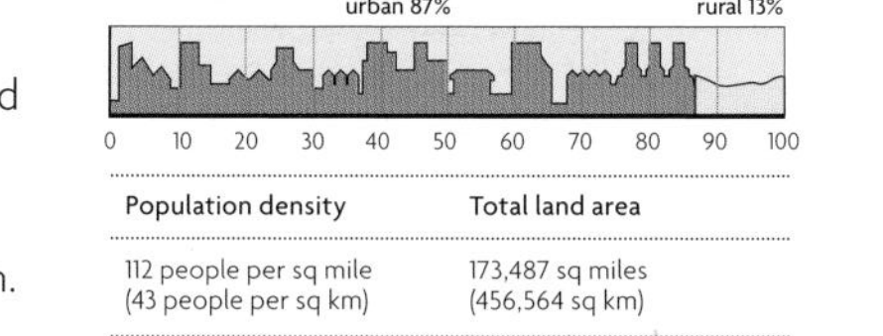
urban 87%
rural 13%
0 10 20 30 40 50 60 70 80 90 100

Population density	Total land area
112 people per sq mile (43 people per sq km)	173,487 sq miles (456,564 sq km)

Land use and agricultural distribution

- cattle
- pigs
- sheep
- cereals
- fodder
- root crops
- timber
- capital cities
- major towns
- pasture
- cropland
- forest
- mountain region

▲ *In Norway winters are longer and colder inland than in coastal areas, where the warm current of the North Atlantic Drift moderates the climate.*

The landscape

Southern Scandinavia, with the exception of Norway, has a flatter terrain than the rest of the region. Denmark and southern Sweden are both extensions of the North European Plain. In this area, because of glacial deposition rather than erosion, the soils are deeper and more fertile.

Acid rain, caused by industrial pollution carried north from elsewhere in Europe, harms plant and animal life in Scandinavian forests and lakes. The region's surface rocks lack lime to neutralize the acid, so making the problem more serious.

◀ ***In the past,*** *glaciers such as this one in Olden, Norway, were much larger. Today, many are retreating to yield the spectacular glacial scenery.*

Olden

The peak of Glittertind in the Jotunheimen mountains is 8110 ft (2472 m) high.

Distinctive low ridges, called eskers, are found across southern Sweden. They are formed from sand and gravel deposits left by retreating glaciers.

▲ ***Limestone pillars eroded*** *by the sea dot the coast of Gotland and surrounding islands.*

The lakes of southern Sweden remain from a period when the land was completely flooded. As the ice which covered the area melted, the land rose, leaving lakes in shallow, ice-scoured depressions. Sweden has over 90,000 lakes.

Vänern in Sweden is the largest lake in Scandinavia. It covers an area of 2080 sq miles (5390 sq km).

Denmark's flat and fertile soils are formed on glacial deposits between 100–160 ft (30–50 m) deep.

Sognefjorden

Erosion by glaciers deepened existing river valleys

Sea level

When the ice retreated the valley was flooded by the sea

Old valley floor

▲ ***Sognefjorden is the*** *deepest of Norway's many fjords. It drops to 4291 ft (1308 m) below sea level.*

96

92

92

Scale 1:2,900,000

Km 0 5 10 20 30 40 50 60 70 80 90 100

Miles 0 5 10 20 30 40 50 60 70 80 90 100

projection: Lambert Conformal Conic

Map key

Population

- 500,000 to 1 million
- 100,000 to 500,000
- 50,000 to 100,000
- 10,000 to 50,000
- below 10,000

Elevation

- 2000m / 6562ft
- 1000m / 3281ft
- 500m / 1640ft
- 250m / 820ft
- 100m / 328ft
- sea level

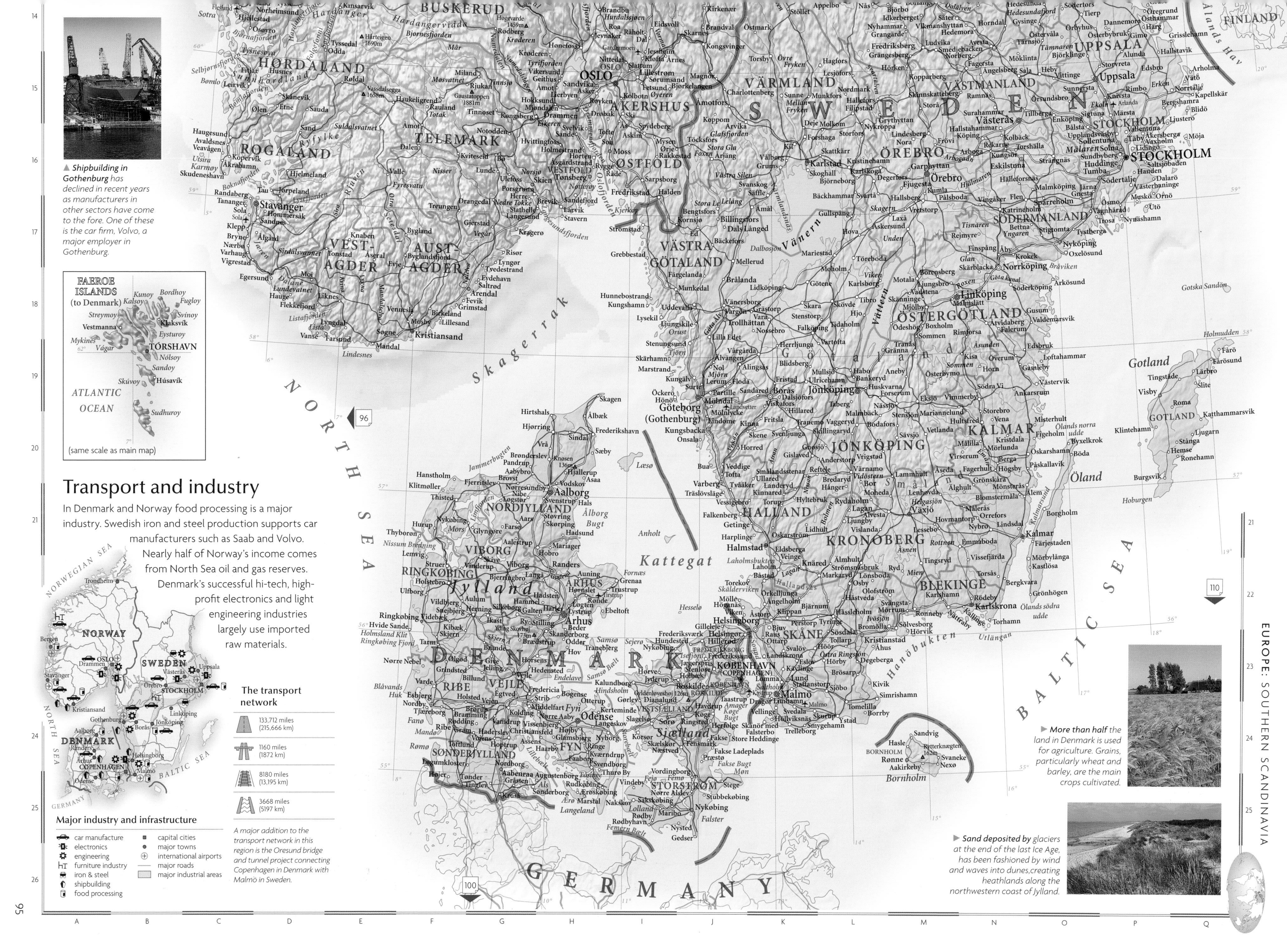
FINLAND
Ålands Hav
SWEDEN
NORWAY
DENMARK
GERMANY
NORTH SEA
BALTIC SEA
Skagerrak
Kattegat
BUSKERUD
HORDALAND
ROGALAND
TELEMARK
VEST-AGDER
AUST-AGDER
AKERSHUS
ØSTFOLD
VESTFOLD
OSLO
VÄRMLAND
VÄSTMANLAND
UPPSALA
STOCKHOLM
ÖREBRO
SÖDERMANLAND
ÖSTERGÖTLAND
VÄSTRA GÖTALAND
JÖNKÖPING
KALMAR
HALLAND
KRONOBERG
BLEKINGE
SKÅNE
NORDJYLLAND
VIBORG
ÅRHUS
RINGKØBING
VEJLE
RIBE
FYN
SØNDERJYLLAND
STORSTRØM
VESTSJÆLLAND
KØBENHAVN
Jylland
Sjælland
Gotland
Öland
Bornholm
Vänern
Vättern
FAEROE ISLANDS (to Denmark)
TÓRSHAVN
ATLANTIC OCEAN
(same scale as main map)
96
100
110
NORWEGIAN SEA
Major industry and infrastructure
car manufacture
electronics
engineering
furniture industry
iron & steel
shipbuilding
food processing
capital cities
major towns
international airports
major roads
major industrial areas
The transport network
133,712 miles (215,666 km)
1160 miles (1872 km)
8180 miles (13,195 km)
3668 miles (5197 km)

▲ **Shipbuilding in Gothenburg** has declined in recent years as manufacturers in other sectors have come to the fore. One of these is the car firm, Volvo, a major employer in Gothenburg.

Transport and industry

In Denmark and Norway food processing is a major industry. Swedish iron and steel production supports car manufacturers such as Saab and Volvo. Nearly half of Norway's income comes from North Sea oil and gas reserves. Denmark's successful hi-tech, high-profit electronics and light engineering industries largely use imported raw materials.

A major addition to the transport network in this region is the Oresund bridge and tunnel project connecting Copenhagen in Denmark with Malmö in Sweden.

► **More than half** the land in Denmark is used for agriculture. Grains, particularly wheat and barley, are the main crops cultivated.

► **Sand deposited by** glaciers at the end of the last Ice Age, has been fashioned by wind and waves into dunes,creating heathlands along the northwestern coast of Jylland.

The British Isles

UNITED KINGDOM, IRELAND

The British Isles have for centuries played a central role in European and world history. England, Wales, Scotland and Northern Ireland together form the United Kingdom (UK), while the southern portion of Ireland is an independent country, self-governing since 1921. Although England has tended to be the politically and economically dominant partner in the UK, the Scots, Welsh and Irish maintain independent cultures, distinct national identities and languages. Southeastern England is the most densely populated part of this crowded region, with over eight million people living in and around the London area.

▲ **The valley of** Glen Coe in the Scottish Highlands is a U-shaped valley, typical of the north and west of the British Isles, where glaciers shaped much of the landscape.

Transport and industry

The British Isles' industrial base was founded primarily on coal, iron and textiles, based largely in the north. Today, the most productive sectors include hi-tech industries clustered mainly in southeastern England, chemicals, finance and the service sector, particularly tourism.

Major industry and infrastructure

- car manufacture
- chemicals
- engineering
- hi-tech industry
- iron & steel
- tourism
- capital cities
- major towns
- international airports
- major roads
- major industrial areas

The transport network

285,947 miles (460,240 km)	2023 miles (3578 km)
11,825 miles (19,032km)	3976 miles (6400 km)

The UK's congested roads have become a major focus of environmental concern in recent years. No longer an island, the UK was finally linked to continental Europe by the Channel Tunnel in 1994.

◀ **Clew Bay in** western Ireland, is characteristic of the heavily indented west coast, where deep wide-mouthed bays separate the mountains of Mayo, Donegal and Kerry as they thrust out into the Atlantic Ocean.

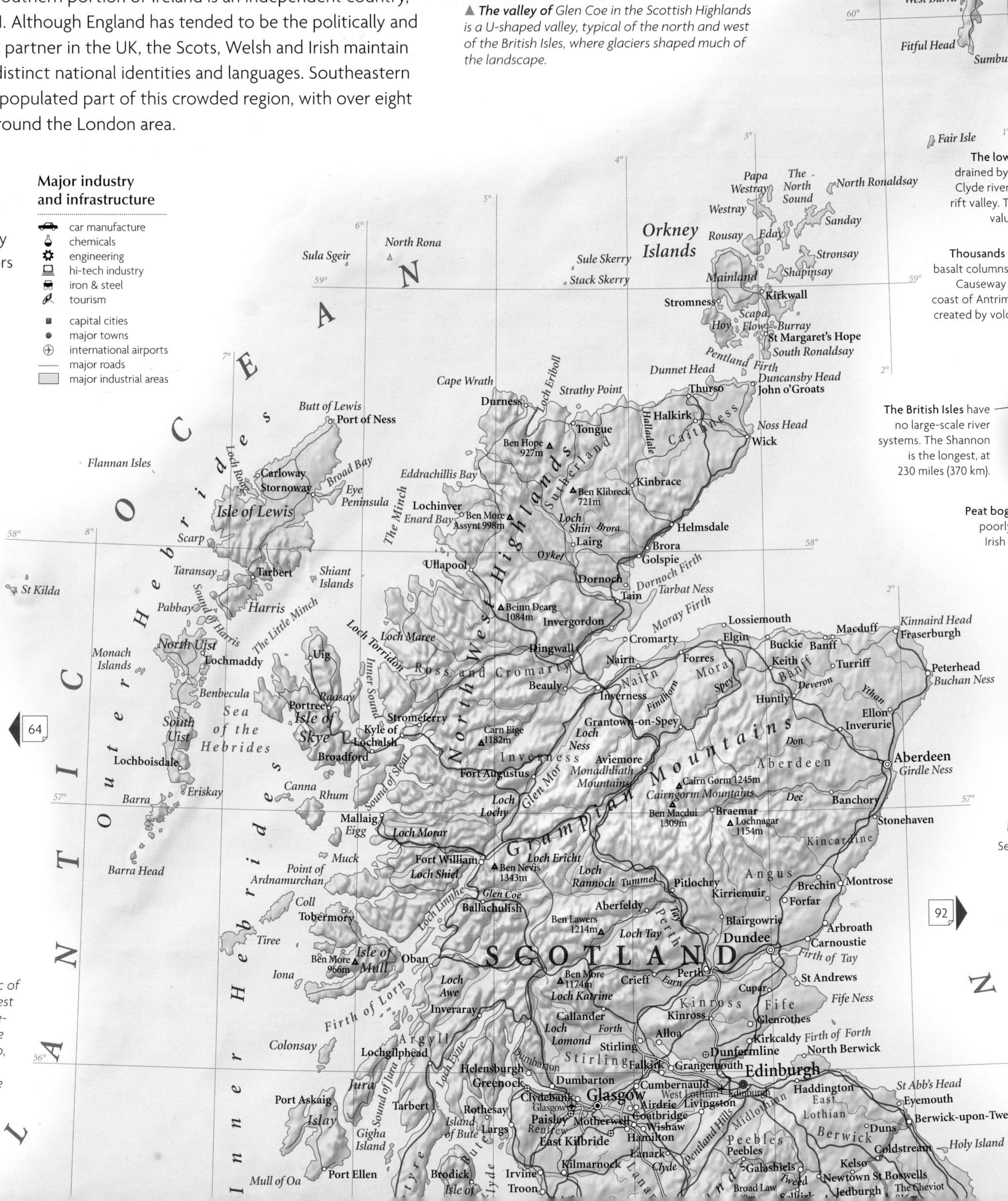

64

92

The landscape

Rugged uplands dominate the landscape of Scotland, Wales and northern England. All the peaks in the British Isles over 4000 ft (1219 m) lie in highland Scotland. Lowland England rises into several ranges of rolling hills, including the older Mendips, and the Cotswolds and the Chilterns, which were formed at the same time as the Alps in southern Europe.

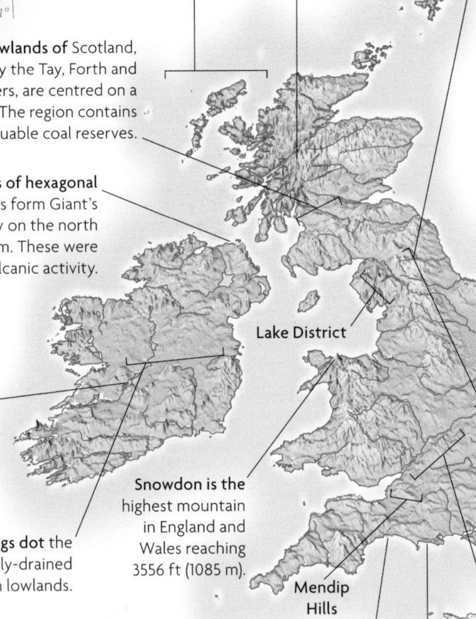

Over 600 islands, mostly uninhabited, lie west and north of the Scottish mainland.

Ben Nevis at 4409 ft (1343 m) is the highest peak in the UK.

The Pennines, sometimes called 'the backbone of England', are formed of limestones and grits.

The lowlands of Scotland, drained by the Tay, Forth and Clyde rivers, are centred on a rift valley. The region contains valuable coal reserves.

Thousands of hexagonal basalt columns form Giant's Causeway on the north coast of Antrim. These were created by volcanic activity.

▲ **Ullswater in the** Lake District fills a deep valley formed by glacial erosion.

The Fens are a low-lying area reclaimed from the sea.

Lake District

The British Isles have no large-scale river systems. The Shannon is the longest, at 230 miles (370 km).

Snowdon is the highest mountain in England and Wales reaching 3556 ft (1085 m).

Peat bogs dot the poorly-drained Irish lowlands.

Mendip Hills

Chiltern Hills

The Cotswold Hills are characterized by a series of limestone ridges overlooking clay vales.

Durdle Door

◀ **Dartmoor, studded with** tors, is an exposed part of a vast granite dome, formed when molten rock intruded into the Earth's crust.

Black Ven, Lyme Regis

Water, Mudslide, Sea, Cracks, Sandstone, Clay, Limestone

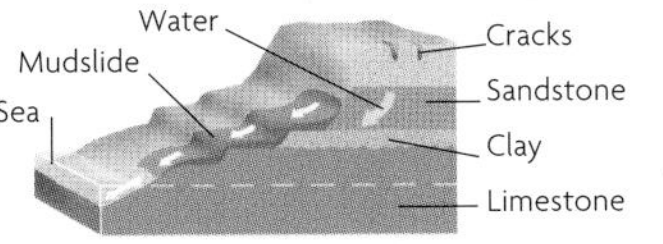

▲ **Much of the** south coast is subject to landslides. Following rain, porous sandstones feed water into the underlying, less permeable clays which then crumble and slide into the sea.

▲ **Coastal erosion around** the British Isles forms striking features such as this limestone arch, Durdle Door in Dorset.

Map key

Population

- above 5 million
- 1 million to 5 million
- 500,000 to 1 million
- 100,000 to 500,000
- 50,000 to 100,000
- 10,000 to 50,000
- below 10,000

Elevation

- 1000m / 3281ft
- 500m / 1640ft
- 250m / 820ft
- 100m / 328ft
- sea level

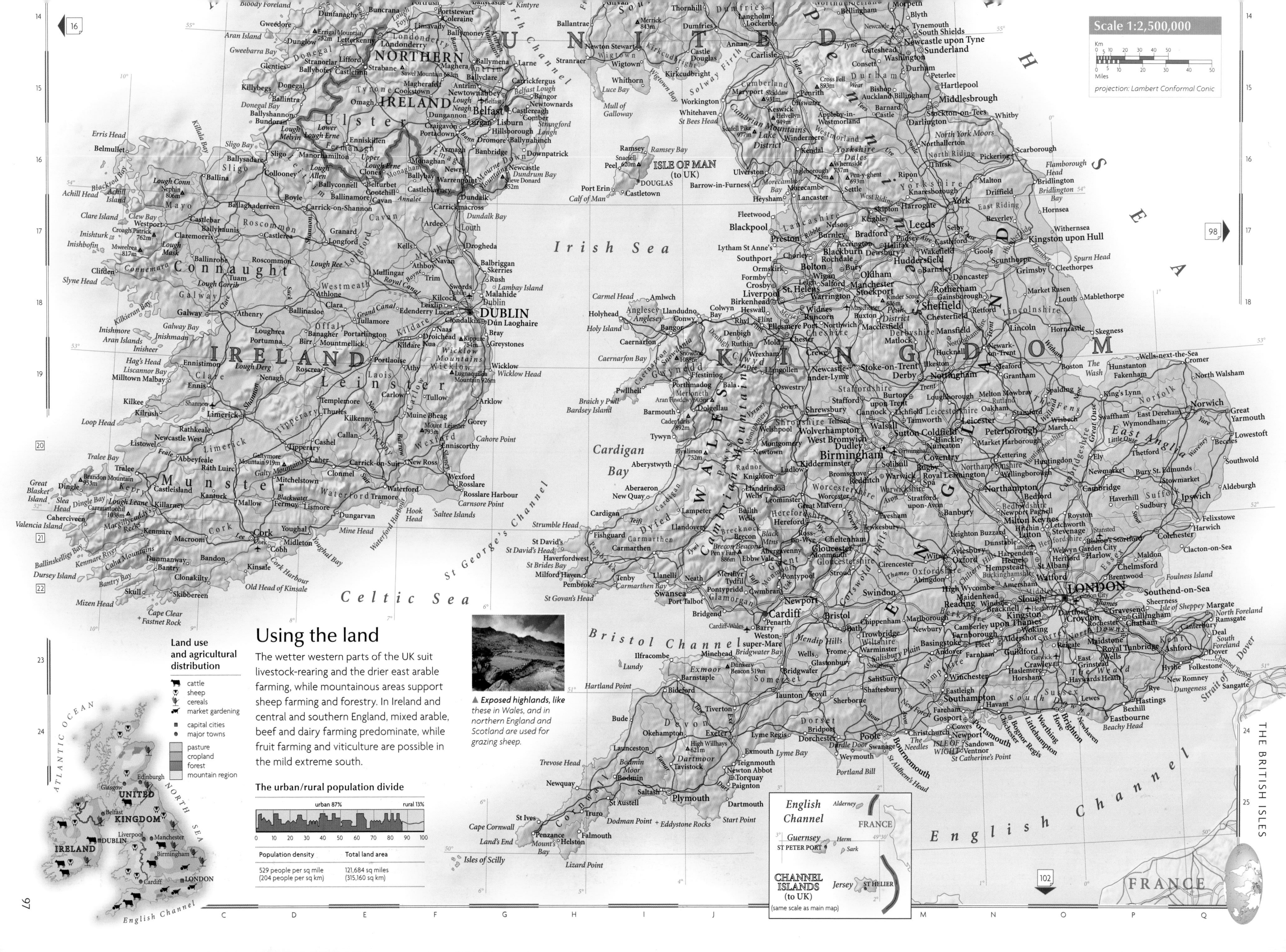
Scale 1:2,500,000
projection: Lambert Conformal Conic
Land use and agricultural distribution
cattle
sheep
cereals
market gardening
capital cities
major towns
pasture
cropland
forest
mountain region
English Channel
CHANNEL ISLANDS (to UK)
(same scale as main map)

Using the land

The wetter western parts of the UK suit livestock-rearing and the drier east arable farming, while mountainous areas support sheep farming and forestry. In Ireland and central and southern England, mixed arable, beef and dairy farming predominate, while fruit farming and viticulture are possible in the mild extreme south.

▲ *Exposed highlands, like these in Wales, and in northern England and Scotland are used for grazing sheep.*

The urban/rural population divide

urban 87% | rural 13%

Population density	Total land area
529 people per sq mile (204 people per sq km)	121,684 sq miles (315,160 sq km)

The Low Countries

BELGIUM, LUXEMBOURG, NETHERLANDS

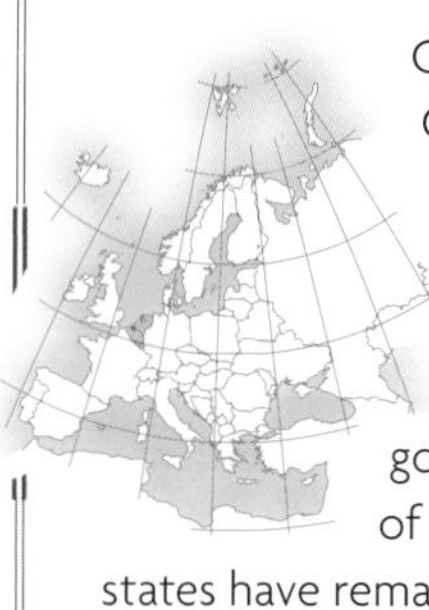

One of northwestern Europe's strategic crossroads, the Low Countries are united by a common history in which they have often been a battleground in European wars. For over a thousand years they were ruled by foreign powers. Even after they achieved independence, the three countries maintained close links, later forming the world's first totally free labour and goods market, the Benelux Economic Union, which became the core of the European Community (now the European Union or EU). These states have remained at the forefront of wider European co-operation; Brussels, The Hague and Luxembourg are hosts to major institutions of the EU.

Transport and industry

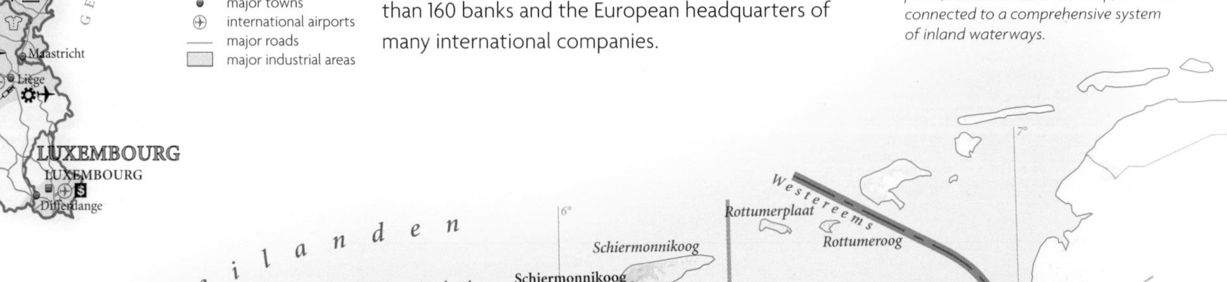

In the western Netherlands, a massive, sprawling industrialized zone encompasses many new hi-tech and service industries. Belgium's central region has emerged as the country's light manufacturing and services centre. Luxembourg city is home to more than 160 banks and the European headquarters of many international companies.

Major industry and infrastructure

- aerospace
- finance
- engineering
- hi-tech industry
- pharmaceuticals
- textiles
- capital cities
- major towns
- international airports
- major roads
- major industrial areas

The transport network

140,588 miles (226,281 km)

2565 miles (4129 km)

4099 miles (6598 km)

4134 miles (6653 km)

The Low Countries hold a key position on the North Sea, containing Europe's two largest ports, Rotterdam and Antwerp, which are connected to a comprehensive system of inland waterways.

The landscape

The main geographical regions of the Netherlands are the northern glacial heathlands, the low-lying lands of the Rhine and Maas/Meuse, the reclaimed polders, and the dune coast and islands. Belgium includes part of the Ardennes, together with the coalfields on its northern flanks, and the fertile Flanders plain.

Schoorl

◀ ***Heathlands, like these** at Schoorl, are found along the coast of the Netherlands. Much of the coast was breached by the sea in the 5th century, creating its distinctive inlets and islands.*

▲ ***One-third of the** Netherlands lies below sea level and flooding is a constant threat. Barrages have been built across the mouths of many rivers to contain floodwaters.*

Dune system — Polder — Drainage ditch — Sea

▲ ***Extensive sand dune** systems along the coast have prevented flooding of the land. Behind the dunes, marshy land is drained to form polders, usable land suitable for agriculture.*

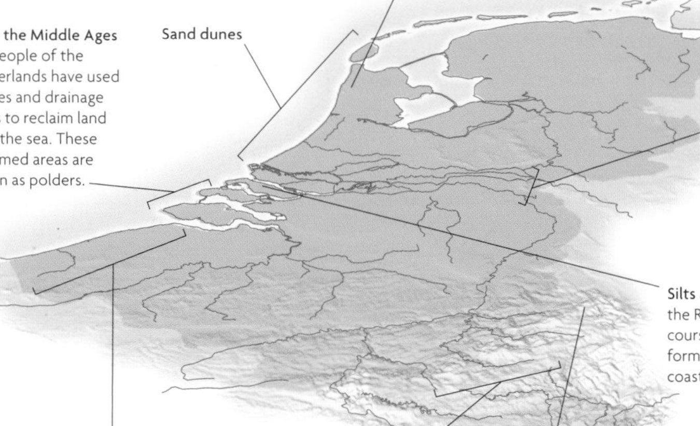

Since the Middle Ages the people of the Netherlands have used ditches and drainage dykes to reclaim land from the sea. These reclaimed areas are known as polders.

Sand dunes

The parallel valleys of the Maas/Meuse and Rhine rivers were created when the Rhine was deflected from its previous course by the ice sheet which formed during the last Ice Age.

Silts and sands eroded by the Rhine throughout its course are deposited to form a delta on the west coast of the Netherlands.

The loess soils of the Flanders Plain in western Belgium provide excellent conditions for arable farming.

Ardennes

Hautes Fagnes is the highest part of Belgium. The bogs and streams in this upland region result from high rainfall and low temperatures.

▶ ***Uplifted and folded** 220 million years ago, the Ardennes have since been reduced to relatively level plateaux, then sharply incised by rivers such as the Maas/Meuse.*

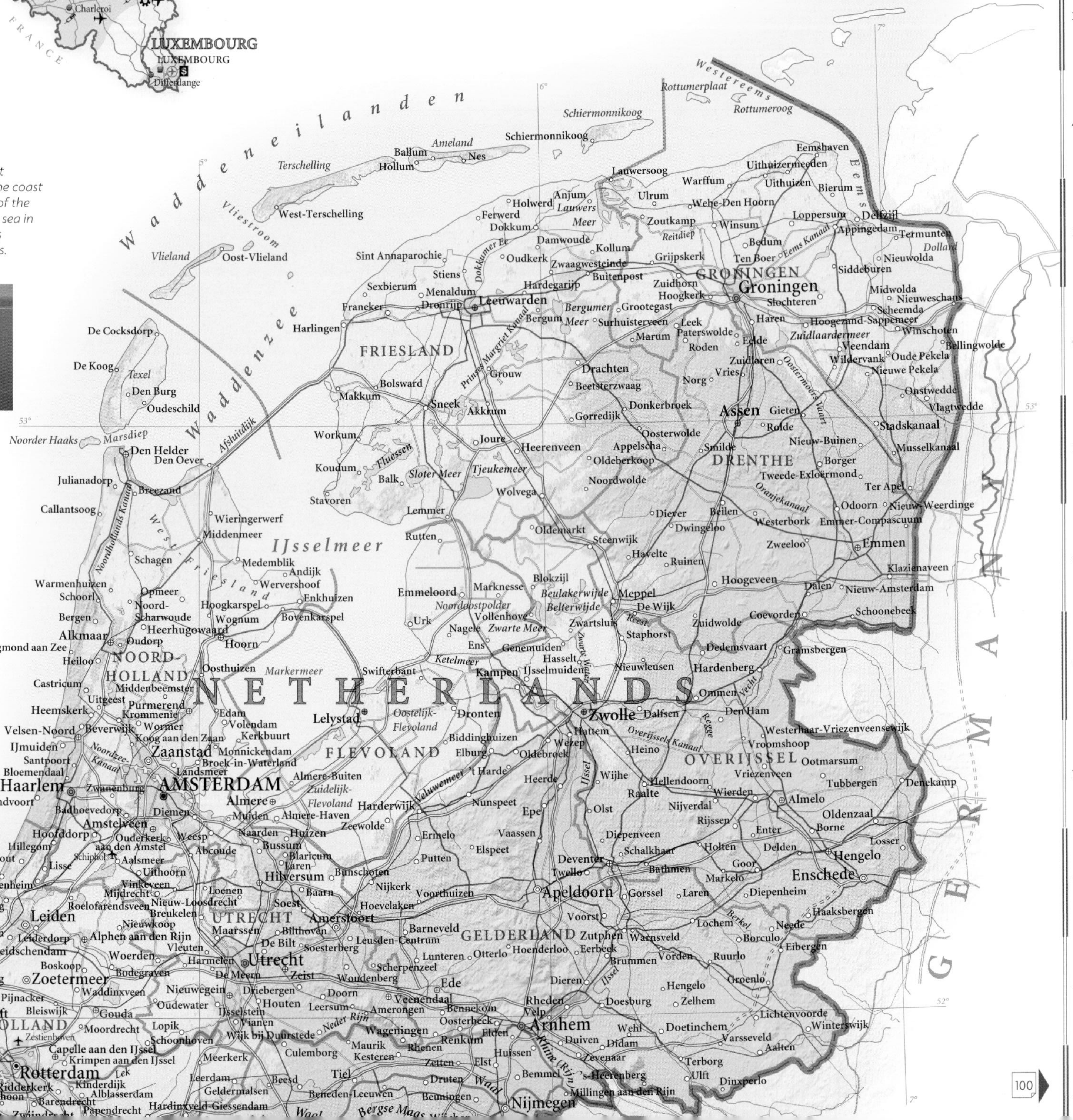

100

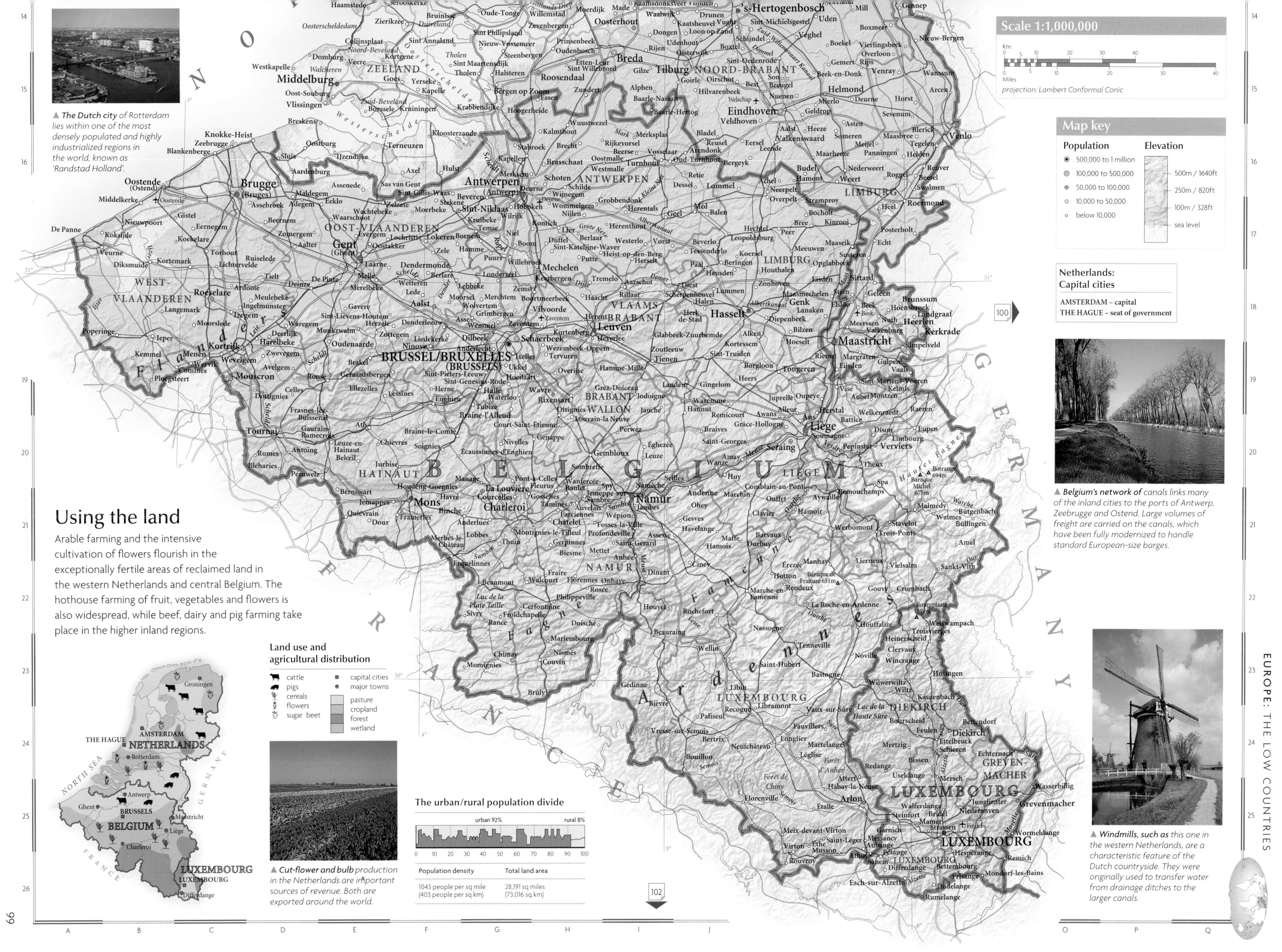
Scale 1:1,000,000
Km
Miles
projection: Lambert Conformal Conic
Map key
Population
500,000 to 1 million
100,000 to 500,000
50,000 to 100,000
10,000 to 50,000
below 10,000
Elevation
500m / 1640ft
250m / 820ft
100m / 328ft
sea level
Netherlands: Capital cities
AMSTERDAM – capital
THE HAGUE – seat of government
BELGIUM
GERMANY
FRANCE
NORTH SEA
LUXEMBOURG
BRUSSEL/BRUXELLES (BRUSSELS)
Antwerpen (Antwerp)
Gent (Ghent)
Brugge (Bruges)
Liège
Namur
Charleroi
Mons
Leuven
Hasselt
Maastricht
Eindhoven
's-Hertogenbosch
Breda
Tilburg
Middelburg
Oostende (Ostend)
ZEELAND
NOORD-BRABANT
LIMBURG
WEST-VLAANDEREN
OOST-VLAANDEREN
ANTWERPEN
VLAAMS BRABANT
BRABANT WALLON
HAINAUT
NAMUR
LIÈGE
LUXEMBOURG
DIEKIRCH
GREVENMACHER
Flanders
Famenne
Fagne
Ardennes
100
102
Land use and agricultural distribution
cattle
pigs
cereals
flowers
sugar beet
capital cities
major towns
pasture
cropland
forest
wetland
The urban/rural population divide
urban 92%
rural 8%
0 10 20 30 40 50 60 70 80 90 100
Population density
1043 people per sq mile (403 people per sq km)
Total land area
28,191 sq miles (73,016 sq km)

▲ **The Dutch city** of Rotterdam lies within one of the most densely populated and highly industrialized regions in the world, known as 'Randstad Holland'.

▲ **Belgium's network of** canals links many of the inland cities to the ports of Antwerp, Zeebrugge and Ostend. Large volumes of freight are carried on the canals, which have been fully modernized to handle standard European-size barges.

▲ **Windmills, such as** this one in the western Netherlands, are a characteristic feature of the Dutch countryside. They were originally used to transfer water from drainage ditches to the larger canals.

Using the land

Arable farming and the intensive cultivation of flowers flourish in the exceptionally fertile areas of reclaimed land in the western Netherlands and central Belgium. The hothouse farming of fruit, vegetables and flowers is also widespread, while beef, dairy and pig farming take place in the higher inland regions.

▲ **Cut-flower and bulb** production in the Netherlands are important sources of revenue. Both are exported around the world.

Germany

Despite the devastation of its industry and infrastructure during the Second World War and its separation from eastern Germany during the Cold War, West Germany made a rapid recovery in the following generation to become Europe's most formidable economic power. When the Berlin Wall was dismantled in 1989, the two halves of Germany were politically united for the first time in 40 years. Complete social and economic unity remain a longer term goal, as East German industry and society adapt to a free market. Germany has been a key player in the creation of the European Union (EU) and in moves toward a single European currency.

Using the land

Germany has a large, efficient agricultural sector, and produces more than three-quarters of its own food. The major crops grown are cereals and sugar beet on the more fertile soils, and root crops, rye, oats and fodder on the poorer soils of the northern plains and central uplands. Southern Germany is also a principal producer of high quality wines. Vineyards cover the slopes surrounding the Rhine and its tributaries.

Land use and agricultural distribution

- cattle
- pigs
- cereals
- sugar beet
- vineyards
- capital cities
- major towns
- pasture
- cropland
- forest

The urban/rural population divide

urban 87% — rural 13%

Population density	Total land area
612 people per sq mile (236 people per sq km)	13,804 sq miles (356,910 sq km)

▲ *The Moselle river flows through the Rhine State Uplands* (Rheinisches Schiefergebirge). *During a period of uplift, pre-existing river meanders were deeply incised, to form its present dramatic contours.*

▶ ***The heathlands of** northern Germany are covered by glacial deposits of sandy outwash soil which makes them largely infertile. They support only sheep and solitary trees.*

Much of the landscape of northern Germany has been shaped by glaciation. During the last Ice Age, the ice sheet advanced as far the northern slopes of the central uplands.

Fault lines / Rhine / Downfaulted block

▲ ***Part of the** floor of the Rhine Rift Valley was let down between two parallel faults in the Earth's crust.*

The Rhine is Germany's principal waterway and one of Europe's longest rivers, flowing 820 miles (1320 km).

Rhine Rift Valley

Lüneburg Heath (*Lüneburger Heide*)

Müritz lake covers 45 sq miles (117 sq km), but is only 108 ft (33 m) deep. It lies in a shallow valley formed by meltwater flowing out from a retreating ice sheet. These valleys are known as Urstromtäler.

Zugspitze, the highest peak in Germany at 9719 ft (2962 m), was formed during the Alpine mountain-building period, 30 million years ago.

The Danube rises in the Black Forest (*Schwarzwald*) and flows east, across a wide valley, on its course to the Black Sea.

The Harz Mountains were formed 300 million years ago. They are block-faulted mountains, formed when a section of the Earth's crust was thrust up between two faults.

Elbe river

◀ ***The Elbe flows** in wide meanders across the north German plain to the North Sea. At its mouth it is 10 miles (16 km) wide.*

The landscape

The plains of northern Germany, the volcanic plateaux and mountains of the central uplands, and the Bavarian Alps are the three principal geographic regions in Germany. North to south the land rises steadily from barely 300 ft (90 m) in the plains to 6500 ft (2000 m) in the Bavarian Alps, which are a small but distinct region in the far south.

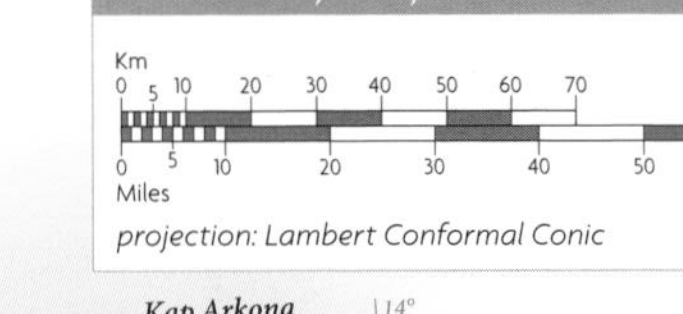
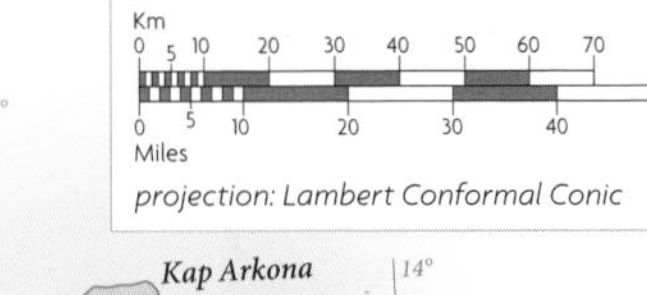
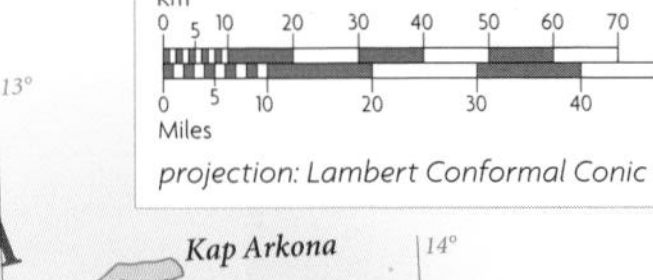
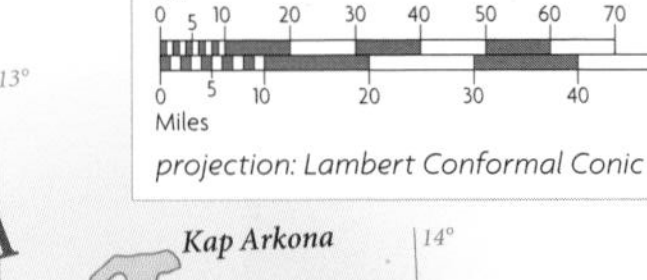
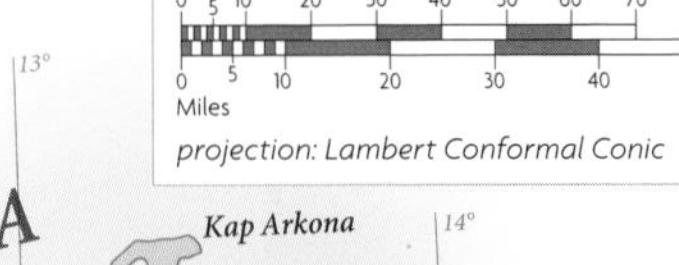
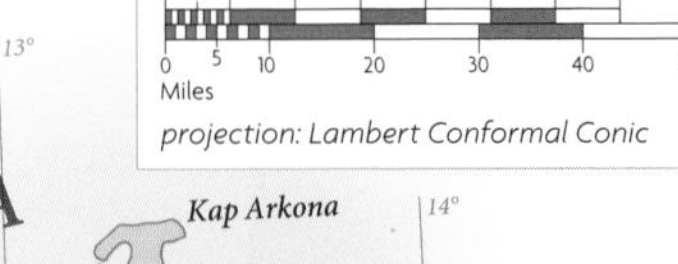
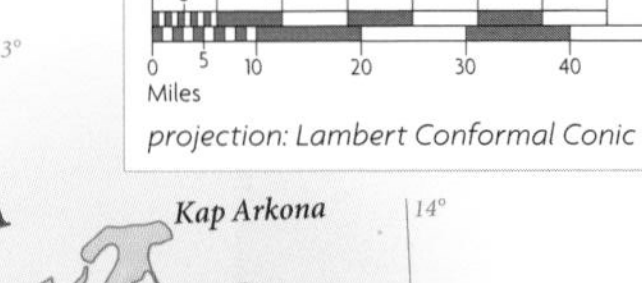
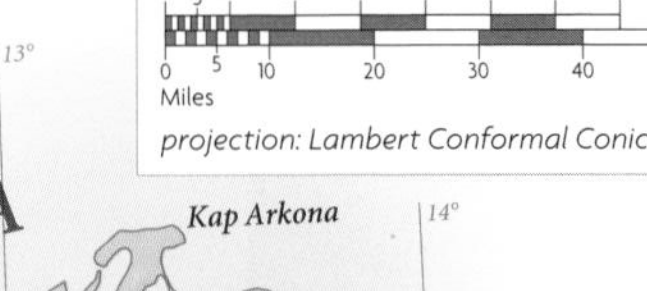
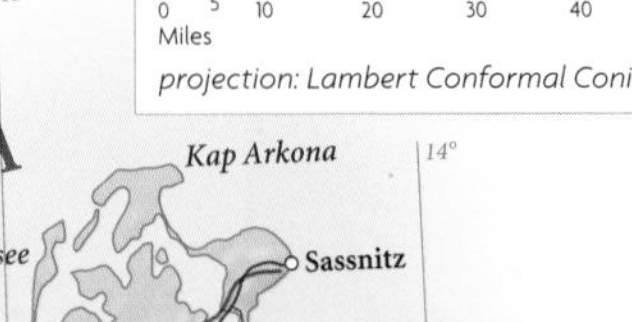
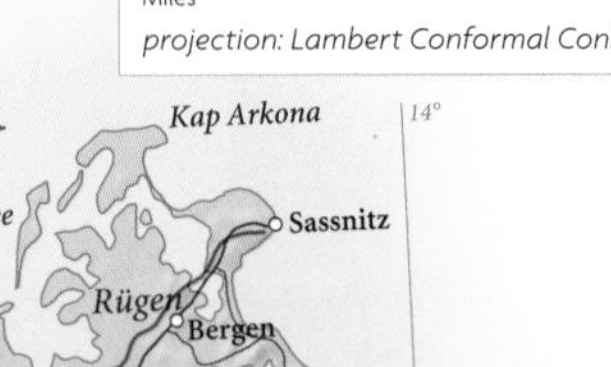

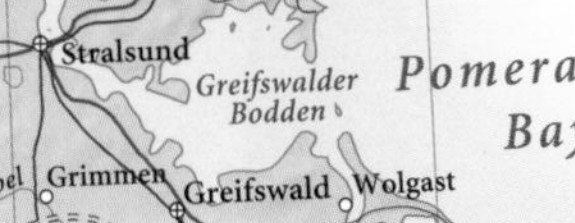
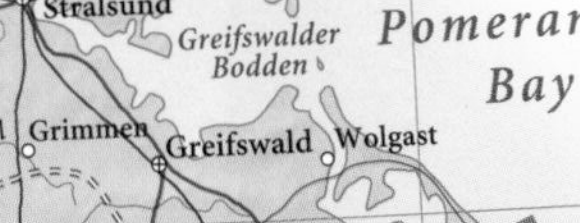
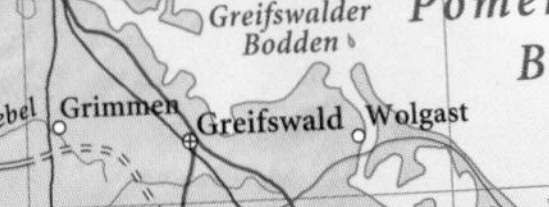
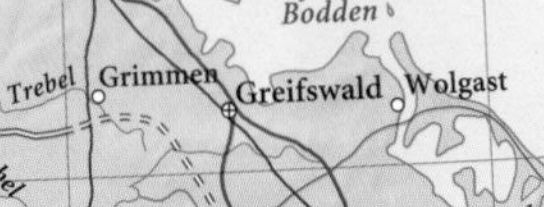

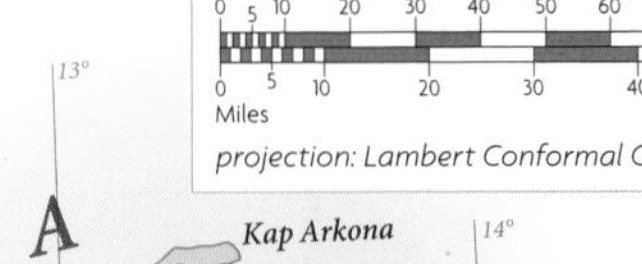

Scale 1:2,250,000

projection: Lambert Conformal Conic

92
96
98
110

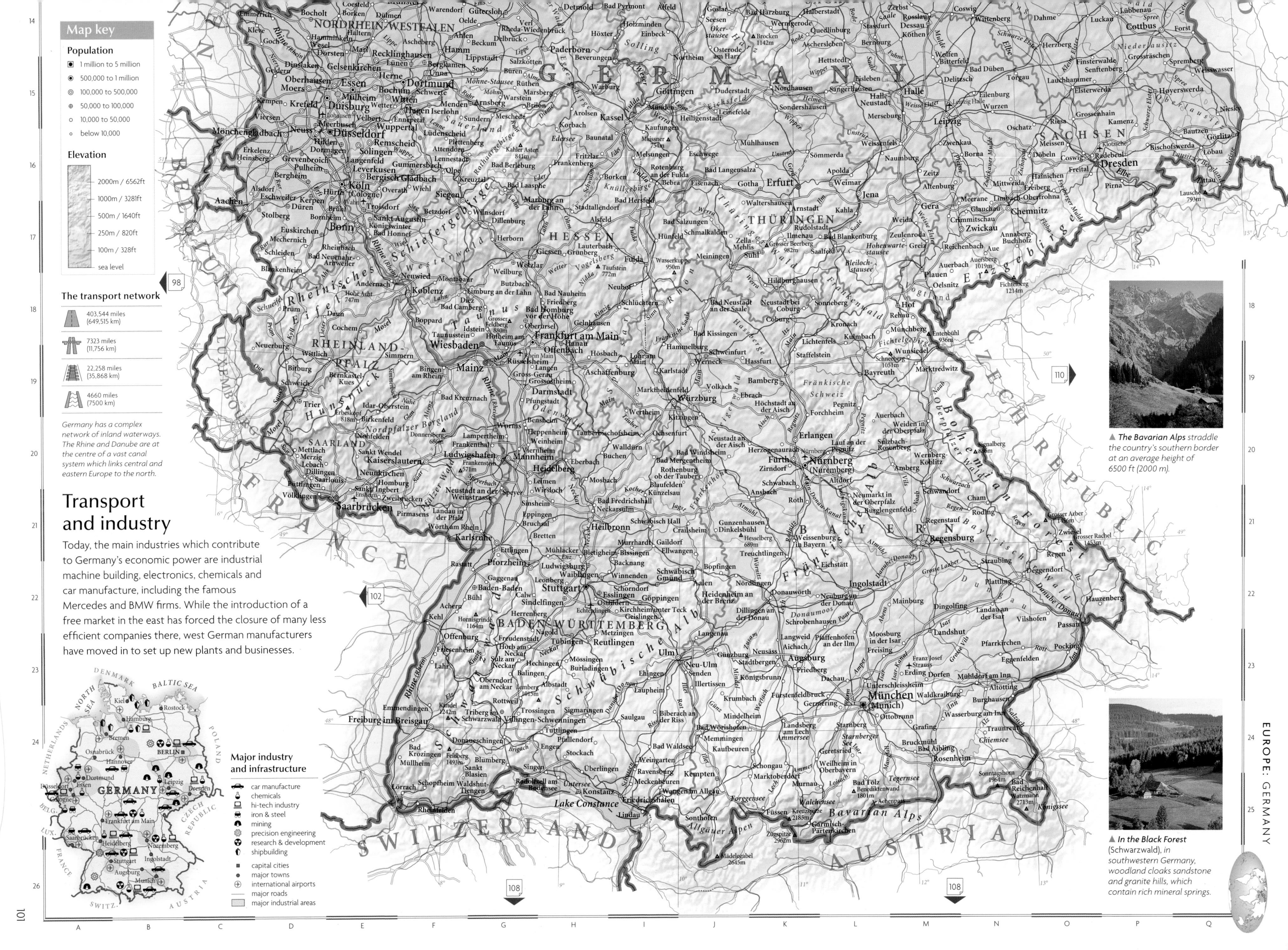

Map key
Population
1 million to 5 million
500,000 to 1 million
100,000 to 500,000
50,000 to 100,000
10,000 to 50,000
below 10,000
Elevation
2000m / 6562ft
1000m / 3281ft
500m / 1640ft
250m / 820ft
100m / 328ft
sea level
The transport network
403,544 miles (649,515 km)
7323 miles (11,756 km)
22,258 miles (35,868 km)
4660 miles (7500 km)
Major industry and infrastructure
car manufacture
chemicals
hi-tech industry
iron & steel
mining
precision engineering
research & development
shipbuilding
capital cities
major towns
international airports
major roads
major industrial areas
GERMANY
CZECH REPUBLIC
SWITZERLAND
AUSTRIA
FRANCE
BELGIUM
LUXEMBOURG

Germany has a complex network of inland waterways. The Rhine and Danube are at the centre of a vast canal system which links central and eastern Europe to the north.

Transport and industry

Today, the main industries which contribute to Germany's economic power are industrial machine building, electronics, chemicals and car manufacture, including the famous Mercedes and BMW firms. While the introduction of a free market in the east has forced the closure of many less efficient companies there, west German manufacturers have moved in to set up new plants and businesses.

▲ ***The Bavarian Alps*** *straddle the country's southern border at an average height of 6500 ft (2000 m).*

▲ ***In the Black Forest*** *(Schwarzwald), in southwestern Germany, woodland cloaks sandstone and granite hills, which contain rich mineral springs.*

France

FRANCE, MONACO

A major centre of culture and fashion, and a leading producer of both industrial and agricultural goods, France is a key player in the push towards European unity. The founder of modern Republican government in the 18th century, France has been closely involved in European events for many centuries. The Paris Basin is the most highly populated area; Île de France is home to over 11 million people. Large parts of rural France remain thinly populated, particularly the mountainous Massif Central, Pyrenees and southern Alps.

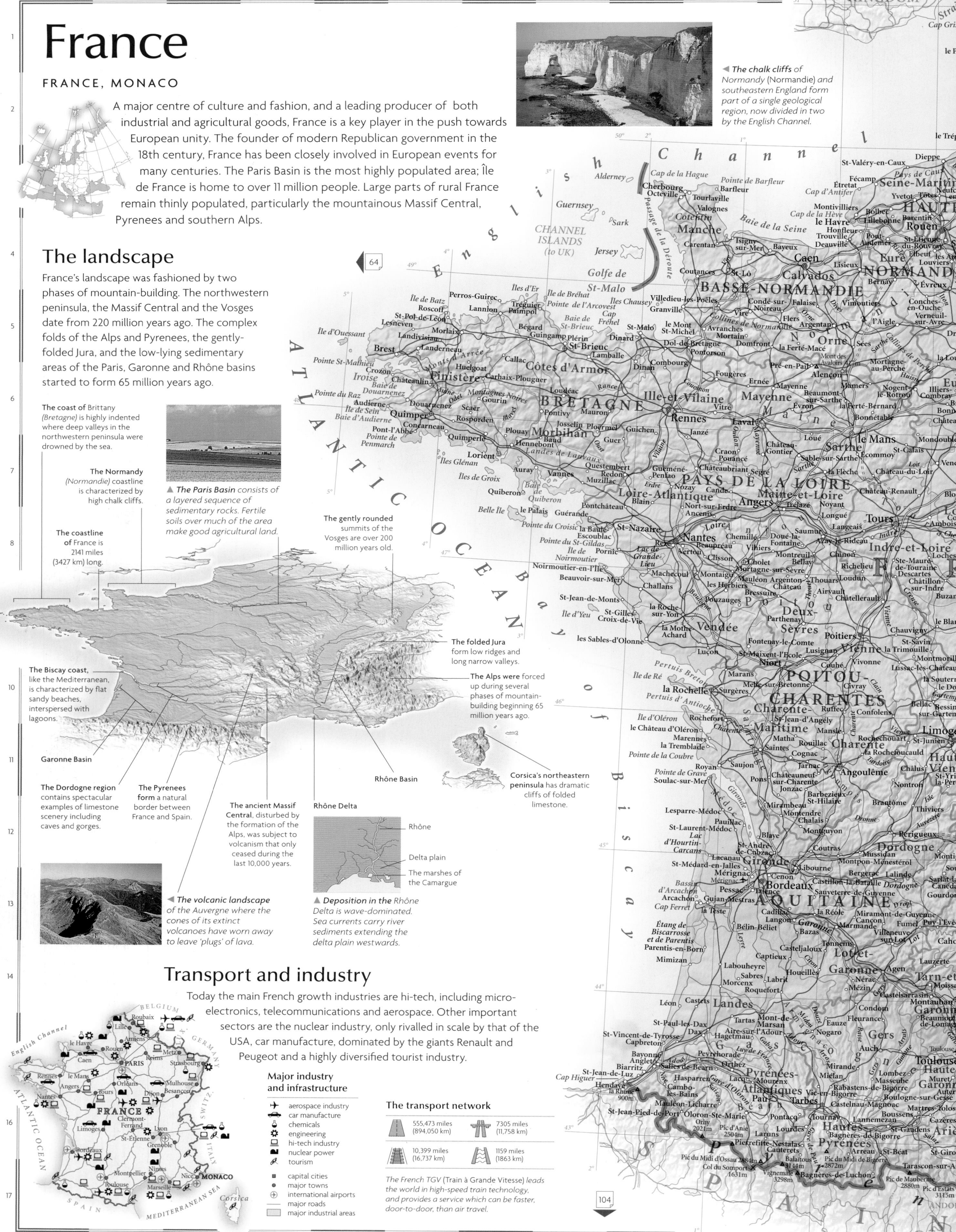

◀ *The chalk cliffs of Normandy (Normandie) and southeastern England form part of a single geological region, now divided in two by the English Channel.*

The landscape

France's landscape was fashioned by two phases of mountain-building. The northwestern peninsula, the Massif Central and the Vosges date from 220 million years ago. The complex folds of the Alps and Pyrenees, the gently-folded Jura, and the low-lying sedimentary areas of the Paris, Garonne and Rhône basins started to form 65 million years ago.

The coast of Brittany *(Bretagne)* is highly indented where deep valleys in the northwestern peninsula were drowned by the sea.

The Normandy *(Normandie)* coastline is characterized by high chalk cliffs.

▲ ***The Paris Basin*** *consists of a layered sequence of sedimentary rocks. Fertile soils over much of the area make good agricultural land.*

The coastline of France is 2141 miles (3427 km) long.

The gently rounded summits of the Vosges are over 200 million years old.

The folded Jura form low ridges and long narrow valleys.

The Biscay coast, like the Mediterranean, is characterized by flat sandy beaches, interspersed with lagoons.

The Alps were forced up during several phases of mountain-building beginning 65 million years ago.

Garonne Basin

Rhône Basin

Corsica's northeastern peninsula has dramatic cliffs of folded limestone.

The Dordogne region contains spectacular examples of limestone scenery including caves and gorges.

The Pyrenees form a natural border between France and Spain.

The ancient Massif Central, disturbed by the formation of the Alps, was subject to volcanism that only ceased during the last 10,000 years.

Rhône Delta

Rhône

Delta plain

The marshes of the Camargue

◀ ***The volcanic landscape*** *of the Auvergne where the cones of its extinct volcanoes have worn away to leave 'plugs' of lava.*

▲ ***Deposition in the** Rhône Delta is wave-dominated. Sea currents carry river sediments extending the delta plain westwards.*

Transport and industry

Today the main French growth industries are hi-tech, including micro-electronics, telecommunications and aerospace. Other important sectors are the nuclear industry, only rivalled in scale by that of the USA, car manufacture, dominated by the giants Renault and Peugeot and a highly diversified tourist industry.

Major industry and infrastructure

- aerospace industry
- car manufacture
- chemicals
- engineering
- hi-tech industry
- nuclear power
- tourism
- capital cities
- major towns
- international airports
- major roads
- major industrial areas

The transport network

555,473 miles (894,050 km)	7305 miles (11,758 km)
10,399 miles (16,737 km)	1159 miles (1863 km)

The French TGV (Train à Grande Vitesse) leads the world in high-speed train technology, and provides a service which can be faster, door-to-door, than air travel.

64

104

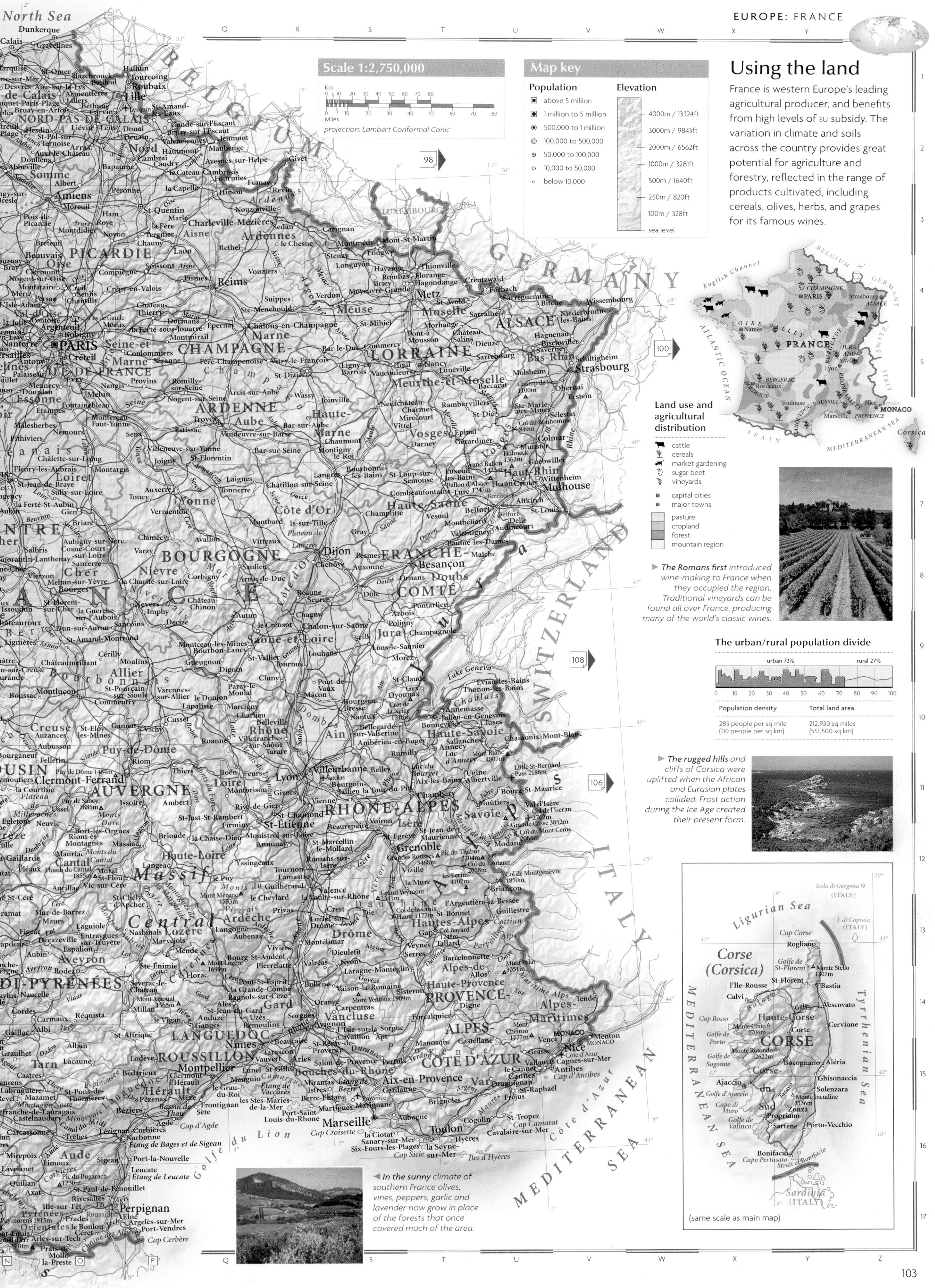
Scale 1:2,750,000
Km 0 5 10 20 30 40 50 60 70 80
Miles 0 5 10 20 30 40 50 60 70 80
projection: Lambert Conformal Conic
Map key
Population
above 5 million
1 million to 5 million
500,000 to 1 million
100,000 to 500,000
50,000 to 100,000
10,000 to 50,000
below 10,000
Elevation
4000m / 13,124ft
3000m / 9843ft
2000m / 6562ft
1000m / 3281ft
500m / 1640ft
250m / 820ft
100m / 328ft
sea level
98
100
108
106
North Sea
BELGIUM
LUXEMBOURG
GERMANY
SWITZERLAND
ITALY
MEDITERRANEAN SEA
Golfe du Lion
PARIS
ÎLE-DE-FRANCE
CHAMPAGNE-ARDENNE
LORRAINE
ALSACE
PICARDIE
NORD-PAS-DE-CALAIS
BOURGOGNE
FRANCHE-COMTÉ
AUVERGNE
RHÔNE-ALPES
PROVENCE-ALPES-CÔTE D'AZUR
LANGUEDOC-ROUSSILLON
MIDI-PYRÉNÉES
Massif Central
Alps
Jura
Lyon
Marseille
Strasbourg
Grenoble
Nice
Montpellier
Dijon
Reims
Lille
Toulon
Land use and agricultural distribution
cattle
cereals
market gardening
sugar beet
vineyards
capital cities
major towns
pasture
cropland
forest
mountain region
The urban/rural population divide
urban 73%
rural 27%
0 10 20 30 40 50 60 70 80 90 100
Population density
285 people per sq mile (110 people per sq km)
Total land area
212,930 sq miles (551,500 sq km)
Corse (Corsica)
Ligurian Sea
Tyrrhenian Sea
MEDITERRANEAN SEA
(same scale as main map)

Using the land

France is western Europe's leading agricultural producer, and benefits from high levels of EU subsidy. The variation in climate and soils across the country provides great potential for agriculture and forestry, reflected in the range of products cultivated, including cereals, olives, herbs, and grapes for its famous wines.

▶ ***The Romans first** introduced wine-making to France when they occupied the region. Traditional vineyards can be found all over France, producing many of the world's classic wines.*

▶ ***The rugged hills** and cliffs of Corsica were uplifted when the African and Eurasian plates collided. Frost action during the Ice Age created their present form.*

◀ ***In the sunny** climate of southern France olives, vines, peppers, garlic and lavender now grow in place of the forests that once covered much of the area.*

The Iberian peninsula

ANDORRA, GIBRALTAR, PORTUGAL, SPAIN (Azores, Canary Islands, Madeira on p.64)

The Iberian peninsula is separated from the rest of Europe by the Pyrenees, and at its most southerly point is only 5 miles (8 km) from North Africa. The location of Iberia has been central to its diverse history. The Greeks, Carthaginians, Romans, Visigoths and most recently the Moors, invaded Iberia at various times. For much of the 20th century, both Spain and Portugal were governed by right-wing dictators. Since the establishment of democratic governments in the mid-1970s, modernization has been rapid and both countries are now among the most popular of European holiday destinations.

Using the land

The principal crops grown in Iberia are cereals, especially wheat and barley. Both countries are major wine producers, most notably of Rioja, sherry and port. Sheep are kept throughout the region, and citrus fruits thrive on the Mediterranean coast. The successful forest industry in Iberia produces 84% of the world's cork.

▲ *The steep, terraced* slopes of the Douro Valley in northern Portugal, are used to cultivate vines. The grapes harvested produce Portugal's famous port wine.

Land use and agricultural distribution

- sheep
- cereals
- citrus fruit
- olives
- vineyards
- cork
- capital cities
- major towns
- pasture
- cropland
- forest
- mountain region

The urban/rural population divide

urban 68% · rural 32%

Population density	Total land area
215 people per sq mile (83 people per sq km)	230,569 sq miles (597,170 sq km)

Transport and industry

Since the 1970s, the economies of Spain and Portugal have expanded and diversified. In both countries, tourism has outstripped agriculture in economic importance. Spain's resource base is varied, including coal, iron and the world's largest reserves of mercury. Portugal is a leading producer of tungsten ore.

Major industry and infrastructure

- car manufacture
- chemicals
- engineering
- fish processing
- mining
- textiles
- tourism
- capital cities
- major towns
- international airports
- major roads
- major industrial areas

The transport network

241,720 miles (388,990 km)	1552 miles (2529 km)
11,793 miles (18,979 km)	1159 miles (1865 km)

Radiating from Madrid, the road network in Spain dates from the 18th century, but now includes many motorways. Portugal's road system has been completely modernized in recent years.

◄ *The eroded cliffs* of the Algarve in southern Portugal were carved by Atlantic waves. The numerous rocky bays and beaches, and the region's pleasant climate, have made it a popular tourist destination.

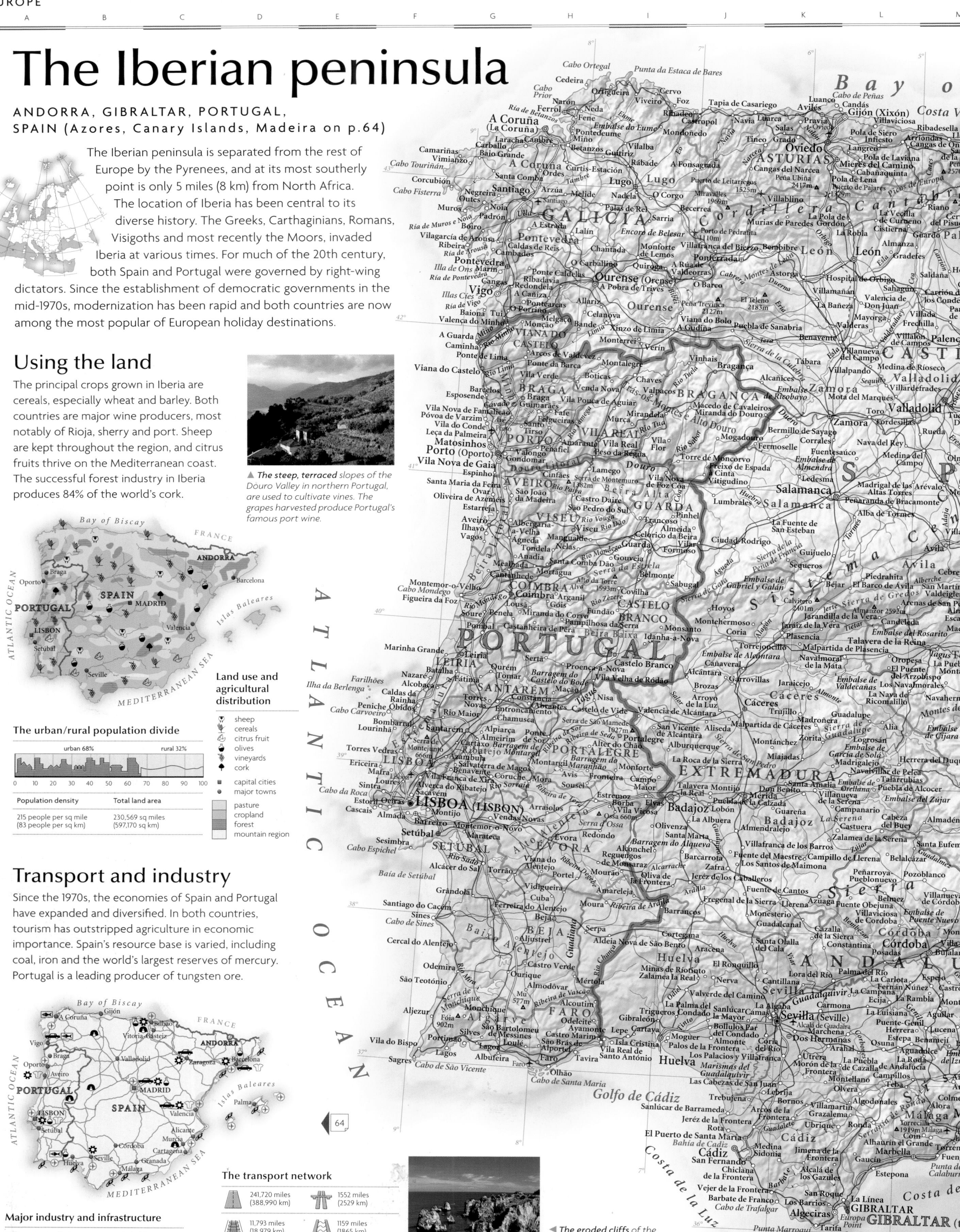

Bay of Biscay
ATLANTIC OCEAN
PORTUGAL
GALICIA
ASTURIAS
Cordillera Cantábrica
EXTREMADURA
Sistema Central
Golfo de Cádiz
Costa de la Luz
Strait of Gibraltar
GIBRALTAR
MOROCCO
LISBOA (LISBON)
Porto (Oporto)
Sevilla (Seville)
Salamanca
Valladolid
Córdoba
Cádiz

64

74

102

▶ *The climate in northwestern Spain is milder in both summer and winter than in the rest of the country, creating a verdant environment, more commonly associated with northwestern Europe.*

Map key

Population

- 1 million to 5 million
- 500,000 to 1 million
- 100,000 to 500,000
- 50,000 to 100,000
- 10,000 to 50,000
- below 10,000

Elevation

- 3000m / 9843ft
- 2000m / 6562ft
- 1000m / 3281ft
- 500m / 1640ft
- 250m / 820ft
- 100m / 328ft
- sea level

Scale 1:2,750,000

Km 0 5 10 20 30 40 50 60 70 80

Miles 0 5 10 20 30 40 50 60 70 80

projection: Lambert Conformal Conic

The landscape

A vast plateau, the Meseta dominates the centre of the peninsula, enclosed by the Cordillera Cantábrica to the north and the Sierra Morena to the south. It is drained by three major rivers, the Douro/Duero, the Tagus, and the Guadalquivir. The peninsula experiences great variations in climate and rainfall, both regionally and locally.

▲ *The Pyrenees form Iberia's northeastern boundary, running for 270 miles (440 km), dividing the peninsula from the rest of Europe.*

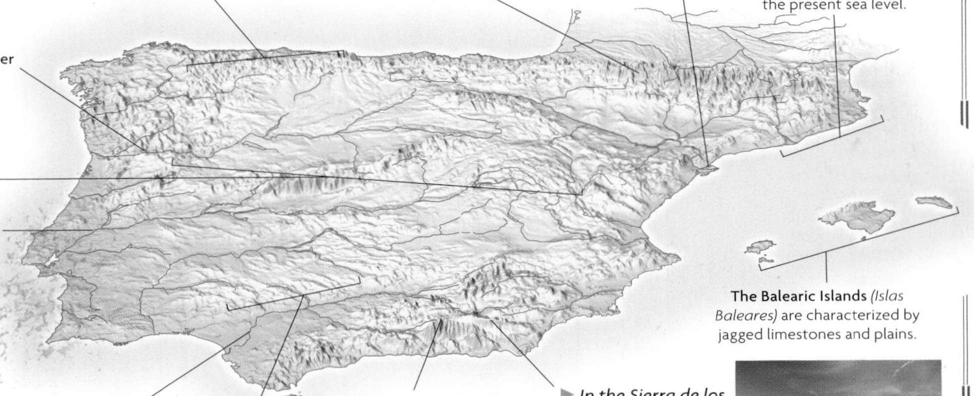

The Ebro river has formed the peninsula's largest delta. Recently, sediment flows have been seriously disturbed by nearby reservoirs.

On the northeastern coast sea level changes are evident from wave-cut beaches which rise up to 200 ft (60 m) above the present sea level.

Cordillera Cantábrica

Douro/Duero river

The Meseta plateau averages 1970 ft (600 m) in height and is now largely dry and treeless.

Tagus River

Mountain front

Weathered material

Pediment

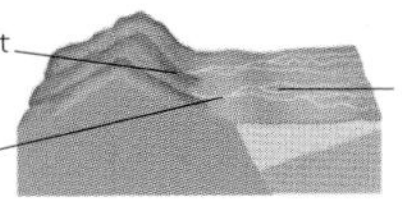

▲ *Pediments are characteristic of semi-arid lands across Iberia. A pediment is a flat, low-lying, eroded platform, cut into the bedrock. Weathered material is transported by streams and deposited in broad fan shapes on the pediment.*

The Guadalquivir river brings vital irrigation water to the plains, and like many of Iberia's rivers, is prone to flooding.

Sierra Morena

The Sierra Nevada in southern Spain contain Iberia's highest peak, Mulhacén, which rises 11,418 ft (3481 m).

▶ *In the Sierra de los Filabres deforestation and overgrazing, which cause soil erosion, have created semi-desert badlands.*

The Balearic Islands *(Islas Baleares)* are characterized by jagged limestones and plains.

The Italian peninsula

ITALY, SAN MARINO, VATICAN CITY

The Italian peninsula is a land of great contrasts. Until unification in 1861, Italy was a collection of independent states, whose competitiveness during the Renaissance resulted in the architectural and artistic magnificence of cities such as Rome, Florence and Venice. The majority of Italy's population and economic activity is concentrated in the north, centred on the sophisticated industrial city of Milan. Southern Italy, the *Mezzogiorno*, has a harsh and difficult terrain, and remains far less developed than the north. Attempts to attract industry and investment in the south are frequently deterred by the entrenched network of organized crime and corruption.

The landscape

The mainly mountainous and hilly Italian peninsula took its present form following a collision between the African and Eurasian tectonic plates. The Alps in the northwest rise to a high point of 15,772 ft (4807 m) at Mont Blanc *(Monte Bianco)* on the French border, while the Apennines *(Appennino)* form a rugged backbone, running along the entire length of the country.

▶ *The island of Sardinia is an ancient land mass; an uplifted section of very old igneous rocks. Its rugged mountainous regions provide pasture for sheep and goats, while its valleys support some agriculture.*

Mont Blanc (*Monte Bianco*)

▲ ***The Dolomites*** (Alpi Dolomitiche) *are formed of thick limestones, overlying weaker marine strata. They have distinctive serrated peaks and many massive landslides occur.*

The Po Valley once formed part of the Adriatic Sea. Sediments of gravel, sand and clay washed down from the Alps gradually filling the bay and forming a broad, cultivable plain.

The distinctive square shape of the Gulf of Taranto (*Golfo di Taranto*) was defined by numerous block faults. Earthquakes are common in this region.

Costa Smeralda

The Apennines (*Appennino*) are the source of most of Italy's rivers. They run 823 miles (1324 km) down the length of the peninsula.

The Pontine Marshes (*Agro Pontino*) are bounded by low sand hills which prevent natural drainage.

Vesuvius (*Vesuvio*)

Sardinia is the second largest island in the Mediterranean Sea. The highest point is Punta La Marmora at 6017 ft (1834 m).

The southwestern tip of Sicily lies 95 miles (152 km) from the north African mainland and is part of the same geological region.

The Strait of Messina (*Stretto di Messina*) is between 2 and 12 miles (3–19 km) wide, and is a rich fishing ground.

Sicily is the largest island in the Mediterranean at 9926 sq miles (25,708 sq km).

Vesuvius (*Vesuvio*)

Monte Somma

Old crater

Present-day crater has developed within the old crater of Monte Somma

▲ ***There have been** four volcanoes on the site of Vesuvius since volcanic activity began here more than 10,000 years ago.*

Using the land

Italy produces 95% of its own food. The best farming land is in the Po Valley in northern Italy, where soft wheat and rice are grown. Irrigation is essential to agriculture in much of the south. Italy is a major producer and exporter of citrus fruits, olives, tomatoes and wine.

The urban/rural population divide

urban 67% rural 33%

0 10 20 30 40 50 60 70 80 90 100

Population density	Total land area
506 people per sq mile (195 people per sq km)	116,320 sq miles (301,270 sq km)

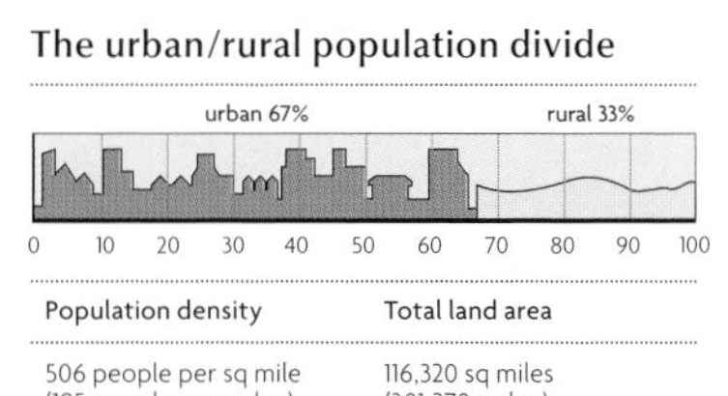
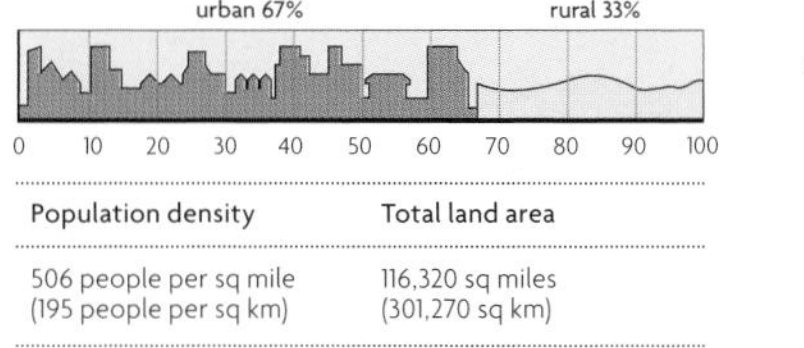
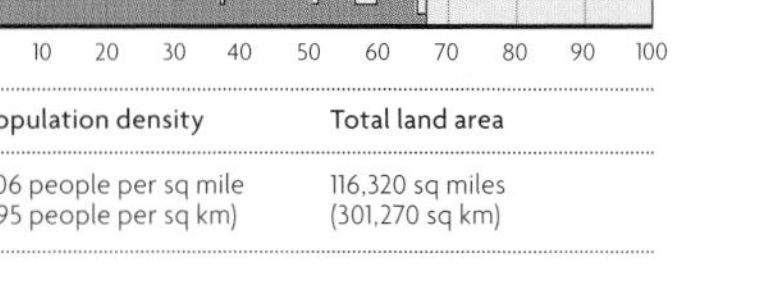

Land use and agricultural distribution

- cattle
- cereals
- citrus fruits
- olive oil
- rice
- vineyards
- capital cities
- major towns
- pasture
- cropland
- forest
- mountain region

Scale 1:2,500,000

projection: Lambert Conformal Conic

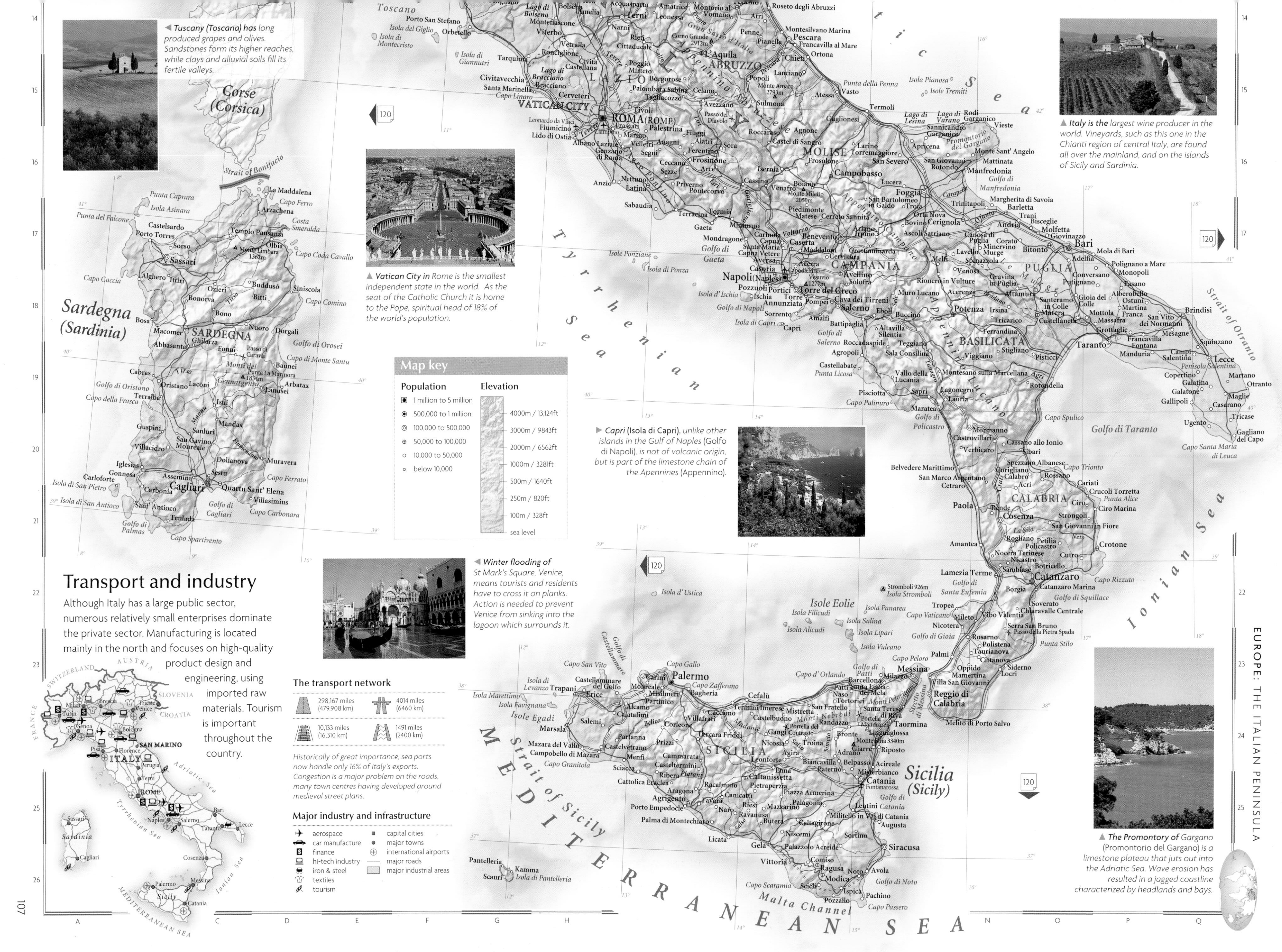

Corse (Corsica)
Sardegna (Sardinia)
SARDEGNA
LAZIO
ABRUZZO
MOLISE
CAMPANIA
PUGLIA
BASILICATA
CALABRIA
SICILIA
Sicilia (Sicily)
Tyrrhenian Sea
Ionian Sea
MEDITERRANEAN SEA
Strait of Sicily
Strait of Otranto
Strait of Bonifacio
Malta Channel
Golfo di Taranto
ROMA (ROME)
VATICAN CITY
Napoli (Naples)
Palermo
Cagliari
Bari
Taranto
Reggio di Calabria
Messina
Catania
Siracusa
Isole Eolie
120

◀ **Tuscany (Toscana) has** long produced grapes and olives. Sandstones form its higher reaches, while clays and alluvial soils fill its fertile valleys.

▲ **Vatican City in** Rome is the smallest independent state in the world. As the seat of the Catholic Church it is home to the Pope, spiritual head of 18% of the world's population.

▲ **Italy is the** largest wine producer in the world. Vineyards, such as this one in the Chianti region of central Italy, are found all over the mainland, and on the islands of Sicily and Sardinia.

Map key

Population

- 1 million to 5 million
- 500,000 to 1 million
- 100,000 to 500,000
- 50,000 to 100,000
- 10,000 to 50,000
- below 10,000

Elevation

- 4000m / 13,124ft
- 3000m / 9843ft
- 2000m / 6562ft
- 1000m / 3281ft
- 500m / 1640ft
- 250m / 820ft
- 100m / 328ft
- sea level

▶ **Capri (Isola di Capri),** unlike other islands in the Gulf of Naples (Golfo di Napoli), is not of volcanic origin, but is part of the limestone chain of the Apennines (Appennino).

◀ **Winter flooding of** St Mark's Square, Venice, means tourists and residents have to cross it on planks. Action is needed to prevent Venice from sinking into the lagoon which surrounds it.

Transport and industry

Although Italy has a large public sector, numerous relatively small enterprises dominate the private sector. Manufacturing is located mainly in the north and focuses on high-quality product design and engineering, using imported raw materials. Tourism is important throughout the country.

The transport network

298,167 miles (479,908 km)		4014 miles (6460 km)	
10,133 miles (16,310 km)		1491 miles (2400 km)	

Historically of great importance, sea ports now handle only 16% of Italy's exports. Congestion is a major problem on the roads, many town centres having developed around medieval street plans.

Major industry and infrastructure

- aerospace
- car manufacture
- finance
- hi-tech industry
- iron & steel
- textiles
- tourism
- capital cities
- major towns
- international airports
- major roads
- major industrial areas

▲ **The Promontory of** Gargano (Promontorio del Gargano) is a limestone plateau that juts out into the Adriatic Sea. Wave erosion has resulted in a jagged coastline characterized by headlands and bays.

The Alpine states

AUSTRIA, LIECHTENSTEIN, SLOVENIA, SWITZERLAND

The Alpine countries of Austria, Switzerland, Liechtenstein and Slovenia form a narrow strip across western Europe's geographical core, lying on the main north–south trading routes across the Alps. Switzerland, politically neutral since 1815, is an important international meeting place and houses one of the headquarters of the United Nations, although it only became a member in 2002. Austria, once at the heart of the great Habsburg Empire has been a fully independent nation since 1955, and maintains a deserved reputation as an international centre of culture. Slovenia declared independence from the former Yugoslavia in 1991 and despite initial economic hardship, is now starting to achieve the prosperity enjoyed by its Alpine neighbours.

Using the land

The Alpine region's mountainous terrain discourages cultivation over much of the land area. The primary agricultural activity is the raising of dairy and beef cattle on the pasture land of the lower mountain slopes. Austria is self-supporting in grains, and crops such as wheat, barley and grapes are grown on the east Austrian lowlands. Woodlands are more prevalent in the eastern Alps; both Austria and Slovenia have large tracts of forest.

Land use and agricultural distribution

cattle · pigs · cereals · vineyards · capital cities · major towns · pasture · cropland · forest · mountain region

◀ *The Matterhorn, on the Swiss-Italian border, is one of the highest mountains in the Alps, at 14,692 ft (4478 m). The term 'horn' refers to its distinctive peak, formed by three glaciers eroding hollows, known as cirques, in each of its sides.*

100
102
106
102

The landscape

The Alps occupy three-fifths of Switzerland, most of southern Austria and the northwest of Slovenia. They were formed by the collision of the African and Eurasian tectonic plates, which began 65 million years ago. Their complex geology is reflected in the differing heights and rock types of the various ranges. The Rhine flows along Liechtenstein's border with Switzerland, creating a broad flood plain in the north and west of Liechtenstein. In the far northeast and east are a number of lowland regions, including the Vienna Basin, Burgenland and the plain of the Danube. Slovenia's major rivers flow across the lower eastern regions; in the west, the rivers flow largely underground through the limestone Karst region.

Original height after uplift and folding
Folded strata are overturned creating a *nappe*
Eurasian Plate
Present-day height of Alps
African Plate

▲ *The convergence of the African and Eurasian plates compressed and folded huge masses of rock strata. As the plates continued to move together, the folded strata were overturned, creating complex nappes. Much of the rock strata has since been eroded, resulting in the current topography of the Alps.*

▲ *Constricted as it cuts through ridges in the Alps, the Danube meanders across the lowlands, where uplift combined with river erosion has deepened meanders.*

The Vienna Basin lies mainly below 390 ft (120 m). It gradually subsided and filled with sediment as the Alps were uplifted.

Neusiedler See straddles the border of Austria and Hungary; the area around it provides some of the best wine-growing land in Austria.

The Austrian Alps comprise three distinct mountain ranges, separated by deep trenches. The northern and southern ranges are rugged limestones, while the Tauern range is formed of crystalline rocks.

The mountains of the Jura form a natural border between Switzerland and France. Their marine limestones date from over 200 million years ago. When the Alps were formed the Jura were folded into a series of parallel ridges and troughs.

Tectonic activity has resulted in dramatic changes in land height over very short distances. Lake Geneva, lying at 1221 ft (372 m) is only 43 miles (70 km) away from the 15,772 ft (4807 m) peak of Mont Blanc, on the France–Italy border.

The Bernese Alps *(Berner Alpen)* contain the Aletsch, which at 15 miles (24 km) is the longest Alpine glacier.

The Rhine, like other major Alpine rivers, follows a broad, flat trough between the mountains. Along part of its course, the Rhine forms the boundary between Switzerland and Liechtenstein.

The first road through the Brenner Pass was built in 1772, although it has been used as a mountain route since Roman times. It is the lowest of the main Alpine passes at 4298 ft (1374 m).

Karst region

▶ *The deep, blue lakes of the Karst region are part of a drainage network which runs largely underground through this limestone area.*

The limestone cave system at Postojna extends for more than 10 miles (16 km) and includes caverns reaching 125 ft (40 m) in height and width.

The Tauern range in the central Austrian Alps contains the highest mountain in Austria, the towering Grossglockner, rising 12,461 ft (3798 m).

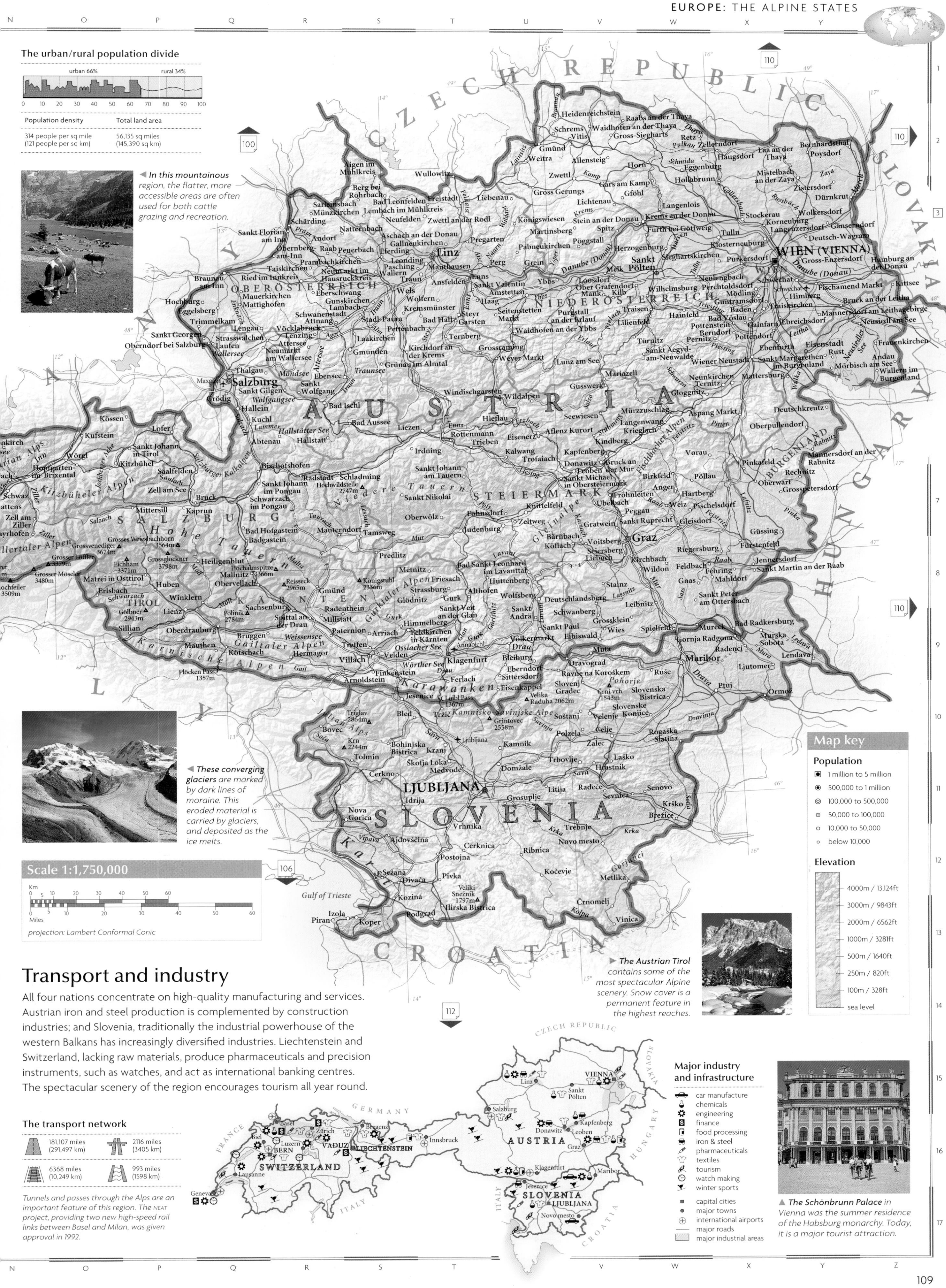

The urban/rural population divide
urban 66%
rural 34%
0 10 20 30 40 50 60 70 80 90 100
Population density
314 people per sq mile (121 people per sq km)
Total land area
56,135 sq miles (145,390 sq km)
CZECH REPUBLIC
SLOVAKIA
HUNGARY
CROATIA
ITALY
AUSTRIA
SLOVENIA
OBERÖSTERREICH
NIEDERÖSTERREICH
STEIERMARK
KÄRNTEN
SALZBURG
TIROL
BURGENLAND
WIEN (VIENNA)
LJUBLJANA
Linz
Graz
Salzburg
Klagenfurt
Innsbruck
Sankt Pölten
Villach
Maribor
Hohe Tauern
Niedere Tauern
Karawanken
Karnische Alpen
Kitzbüheler Alpen
Gailtaler Alpen
Julian Alps
Danube (Donau)
Drau
Mur
Enns
Sava
Großglockner 3798m
Grossvenediger 3674m
Triglav 2864m
Gulf of Trieste
Map key
Population
1 million to 5 million
500,000 to 1 million
100,000 to 500,000
50,000 to 100,000
10,000 to 50,000
below 10,000
Elevation
4000m / 13,124ft
3000m / 9843ft
2000m / 6562ft
1000m / 3281ft
500m / 1640ft
250m / 820ft
100m / 328ft
sea level
Scale 1:1,750,000
projection: Lambert Conformal Conic
The transport network
181,107 miles (291,497 km)
2116 miles (3405 km)
6368 miles (10,249 km)
993 miles (1598 km)
Major industry and infrastructure
car manufacture
chemicals
engineering
finance
food processing
iron & steel
pharmaceuticals
textiles
tourism
watch making
winter sports
capital cities
major towns
international airports
major roads
major industrial areas
SWITZERLAND
LIECHTENSTEIN
BERN
VADUZ
Zürich
Basel
Luzern
Biel
Lausanne
Geneva
Bregenz
Donawitz
Leoben
Kapfenberg
Jesenice
Novo mesto
GERMANY
FRANCE

◀ In this mountainous region, the flatter, more accessible areas are often used for both cattle grazing and recreation.

◀ These converging glaciers are marked by dark lines of moraine. This eroded material is carried by glaciers, and deposited as the ice melts.

▶ The Austrian Tirol contains some of the most spectacular Alpine scenery. Snow cover is a permanent feature in the highest reaches.

Transport and industry

All four nations concentrate on high-quality manufacturing and services. Austrian iron and steel production is complemented by construction industries; and Slovenia, traditionally the industrial powerhouse of the western Balkans has increasingly diversified industries. Liechtenstein and Switzerland, lacking raw materials, produce pharmaceuticals and precision instruments, such as watches, and act as international banking centres. The spectacular scenery of the region encourages tourism all year round.

Tunnels and passes through the Alps are an important feature of this region. The NEAT project, providing two new high-speed rail links between Basel and Milan, was given approval in 1992.

▲ The Schönbrunn Palace in Vienna was the summer residence of the Habsburg monarchy. Today, it is a major tourist attraction.

Central Europe

CZECH REPUBLIC, HUNGARY, POLAND, SLOVAKIA

When Slovakia and the Czech Republic became separate countries in 1993, they joined Hungary and Poland in a new role as independent nation states, following centuries of shifting boundaries and imperial strife. This turbulent history bequeathed the region a rich cultural heritage, shared through the works of its many great writers and composers, and celebrated in the vibrant historic capitals of Prague, Budapest and Warsaw. Having shaken off years of Soviet domination in 1989, these states are confronting the challenge of winning commercial investment to modernize outmoded industries as they integrate their economies with those of the European Union.

Transport and industry

Heavy industry has dominated post-war life in Central Europe. Poland has large coal reserves, having inherited the Silesian coalfield from Germany after the Second World War, allowing the export of large quantities of coal, along with other minerals. Hungary specializes in consumer goods and services, while Slovakia's industrial base is still relatively small. The Czech Republic's traditional glassworks and breweries bring some stability to its precarious Soviet-built manufacturing sector.

Major industry and infrastructure

- car manufacture
- chemicals
- engineering
- food processing
- mining
- shipbuilding
- tourism
- capital cities
- major towns
- international airports
- major roads
- major industrial areas

The transport network

213,997 miles (344,600 km)

817 miles (1315 km)

27,479 miles (44,249 km)

3784 miles (6094 km)

The huge growth of tourism and business has prompted major investment in the transport infrastructure, with new road-building schemes within and between the main cities of the region.

▲ ***Budapest, the capital** of Hungary, straddles the Danube. It comprises the historic towns of Buda, on the west bank, and Pest, which contains the Parliament Building, seen here on the far bank.*

The landscape

The forested Carpathian Mountains, uplifted with the Alps, lie southeast of the older Bohemian Massif, which contains the Sudeten and Krusné Hory *(Erzgebirge)* ranges. They divide the fertile plains of the Danube to the south and the Vistula *(Wisla)*, which flows north across vast expanses of glacial deposits into the Baltic Sea.

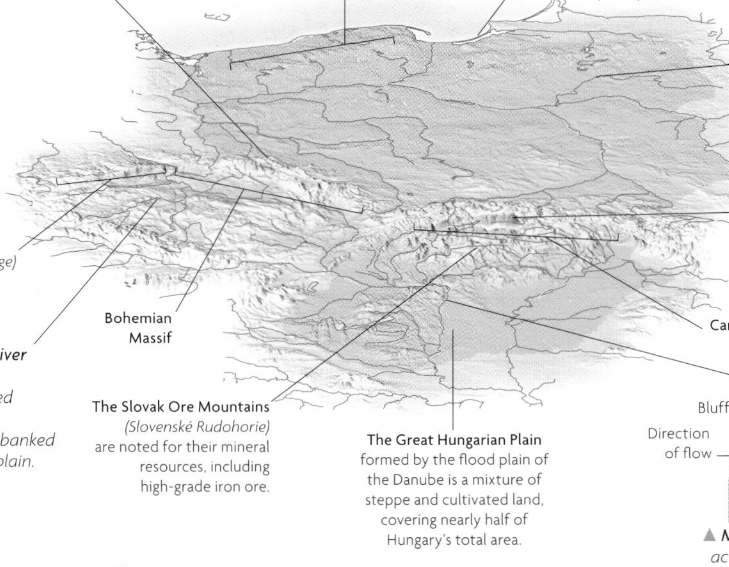

◀ ***The Berounka river** cuts through the precipitous wooded landscape of the Bohemian Massif, banked by a broad flood plain.*

Hot mineral springs occur where geothermally heated water wells up through faults and fractures in the rocks of the Sudeten Mountains.

Pomerania is a sandy coastal region of glacially-formed lakes stretching west from the Vistula *(Wisla)*.

Longshore currents moving east along the Baltic coast have built a 40 mile (65 km) spit composed of material from the Vistula *(Wisla)* river.

▲ ***The Biebrza river** has left meanders and oxbow lakes as it flows across low-lying ground.*

Gerlachovsky stit, in the Tatra Mountains, is Slovakia's highest mountain, at 8711ft (2655 m).

Krusné Hory *(Erzgebirge)*

Bohemian Massif

Carpathian Mountains

Danube river

The Slovak Ore Mountains *(Slovenské Rudohorie)* are noted for their mineral resources, including high-grade iron ore.

The Great Hungarian Plain formed by the flood plain of the Danube is a mixture of steppe and cultivated land, covering nearly half of Hungary's total area.

Bluff

Direction of flow

Slip-off slope

▲ ***Meanders form as** rivers flow across plains at a low gradient. A steep cliff or bluff, forms on the outside curve, and a gentler slip-off slope on the inside bend.*

BALTIC SEA

Gulf of Danzig

Pomeranian Bay

RUSSIAN FEDERATION (Kaliningrad)

LITHUANIA

BELARUS

POLAND

118

118

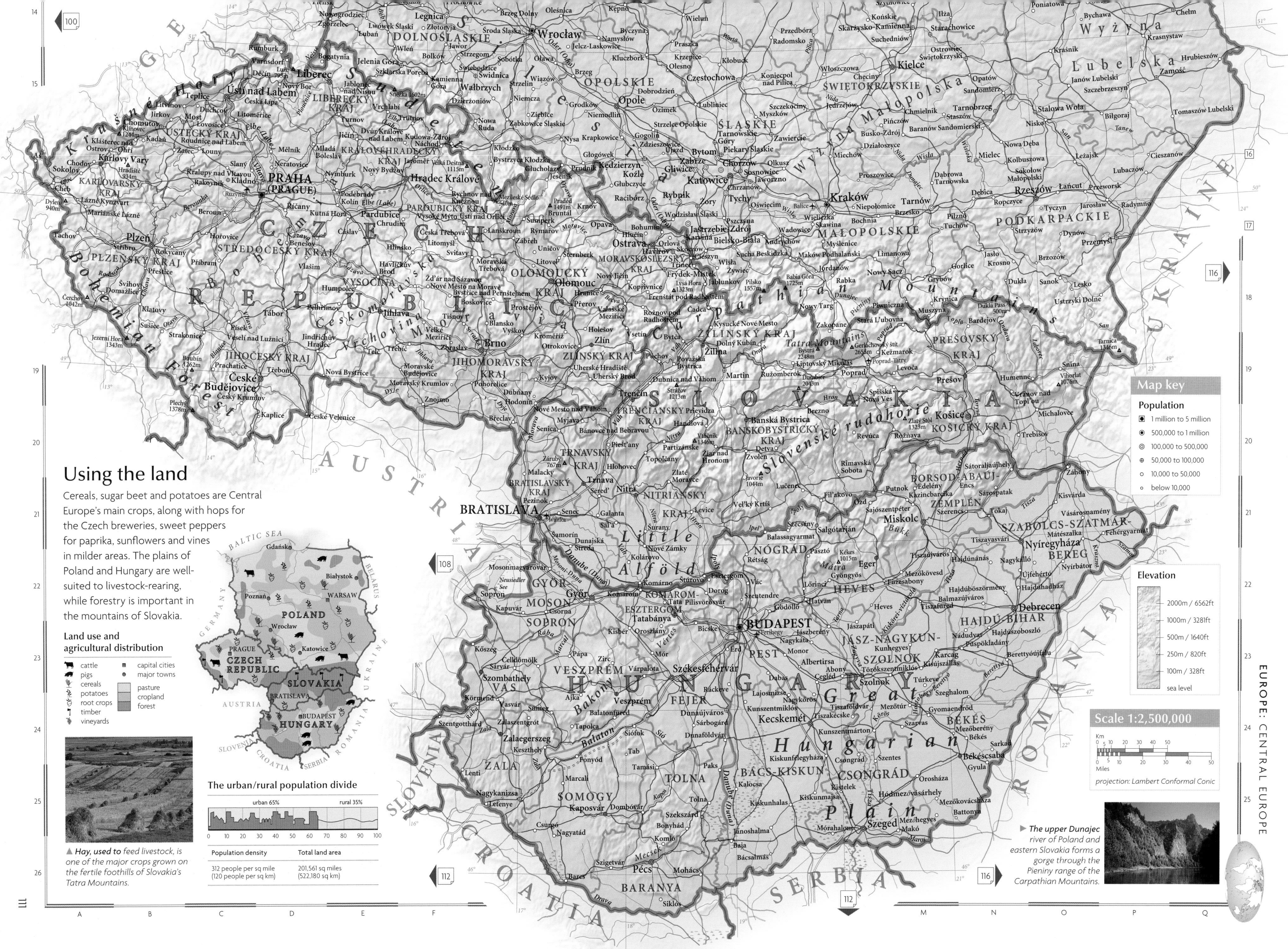
CZECH REPUBLIC
SLOVAKIA
HUNGARY
POLAND
GERMANY
AUSTRIA
UKRAINE
ROMANIA
SERBIA
CROATIA
SLOVENIA
PRAHA (PRAGUE)
BRATISLAVA
BUDAPEST
Map key
Population
1 million to 5 million
500,000 to 1 million
100,000 to 500,000
50,000 to 100,000
10,000 to 50,000
below 10,000
Elevation
2000m / 6562ft
1000m / 3281ft
500m / 1640ft
250m / 820ft
100m / 328ft
sea level
Scale 1:2,500,000
Km
Miles
projection: Lambert Conformal Conic
Land use and agricultural distribution
cattle
pigs
cereals
potatoes
root crops
timber
vineyards
capital cities
major towns
pasture
cropland
forest
BALTIC SEA
The urban/rural population divide
urban 65%
rural 35%
Population density
312 people per sq mile (120 people per sq km)
Total land area
201,561 sq miles (522,180 sq km)

Using the land

Cereals, sugar beet and potatoes are Central Europe's main crops, along with hops for the Czech breweries, sweet peppers for paprika, sunflowers and vines in milder areas. The plains of Poland and Hungary are well-suited to livestock-rearing, while forestry is important in the mountains of Slovakia.

▲ *Hay, used to feed livestock, is one of the major crops grown on the fertile foothills of Slovakia's Tatra Mountains.*

▶ *The upper Dunajec river of Poland and eastern Slovakia forms a gorge through the Pieniny range of the Carpathian Mountains.*

Southeast Europe

ALBANIA, BOSNIA & HERZEGOVINA, CROATIA, KOSVOVO, MACEDONIA, MONTENEGRO, SERBIA

For 46 years the federation of Yugoslavia held together the most diverse ethnic region in Europe, along the picturesque mountain hinterland of the Dalmatian coast. Economic collapse resulted in internal tensions. In the early 1990s, civil war broke out in both Croatia and Bosnia as the ethnic populations struggled to establish their own exclusive territories. Peace was only restored by the UN after NATO launched air strikes in 1995. Montenegro voted to split from Serbia in 2006. More recently, Kosovo controversially declared independence from Serbia in 2008, although this may take some time to be fully recognized. Neighbouring Albania is slowly improving its fragile economy but remains one of Europe's poorest nations.

▲ ***Hot, dry summers** and mild winters offer excellent conditions for viticulture in Montenegro. The precipitous Dinaric Alps have kept this region relatively isolated for centuries.*

Scale 1:2,500,000

Km 0 5 10 20 30 40 50 60 70
Miles 0 5 10 20 30 40 50 60 70

projection: Lambert Conformal Conic

The landscape

The Tisza, Sava and Drava rivers drain the broad northern lowland, meeting the Danube after it crosses the Hungarian border. In the west, the Dinaric Alps divide the Adriatic Sea from the interior. Mainland valleys and elongated islands run parallel to the steep Dalmatian *(Dalmacija)* coastline, following alternating bands of resistant limestone.

At least 70% of the fresh water in the western Balkans drains eastwards into the Black Sea, mostly via the Danube *(Dunav)*.

The river flood plains of the Pannonian Basin are flanked by terraces of gravel and wind-blown glacial deposits known as loess.

Drava river

Tisza river

Sava river

The elongated islands, promontories and straits of the Dalmatian *(Dalmacija)* coast were formed as the Adriatic Sea rose to flood valleys running parallel to the shore.

At Iron Gate *(Derdap)*, on the border with Romania, the Danube narrows and cuts through foothills of the Balkan and Carpathian mountains, forming the deepest gorge in Europe.

A major earthquake at Skopje, Macedonia, in 1963 killed 1000 people. The whole region lies on an active crustal plate margin.

A series of river valleys breaking through the Dinaric Alps from the lowlands of western Albania, give access to the interior.

Dalmatian *(Dalmacija)* coast

Lake Ohrid

***Poljes* in the Kosovo region**

Underground drainage along joints in the rock

Spring at foot of cliff

Sheer limestone walls enclose all sides

Flat *polje* floor

▲ ***Rain and underground** water dissolve limestone along massive vertical joints (cracks). This creates* poljes: *depressions several miles across with steep walls and broad, flat floors.*

► ***Limestone cliffs along** the Dalmatian* (Dalmacija) *shoreline are heavily eroded, as salt water dissolves the rock along existing horizontal cracks, or joints. This tends to form a platform of rock at the foot of the cliff.*

▲ ***Lake Ohrid borders** Albania and Macedonia. Ohrid is the deepest lake in the western Balkans, reaching depths of 938 ft (286 m).*

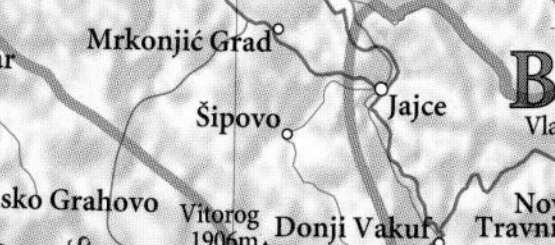

108 110 116 120 114

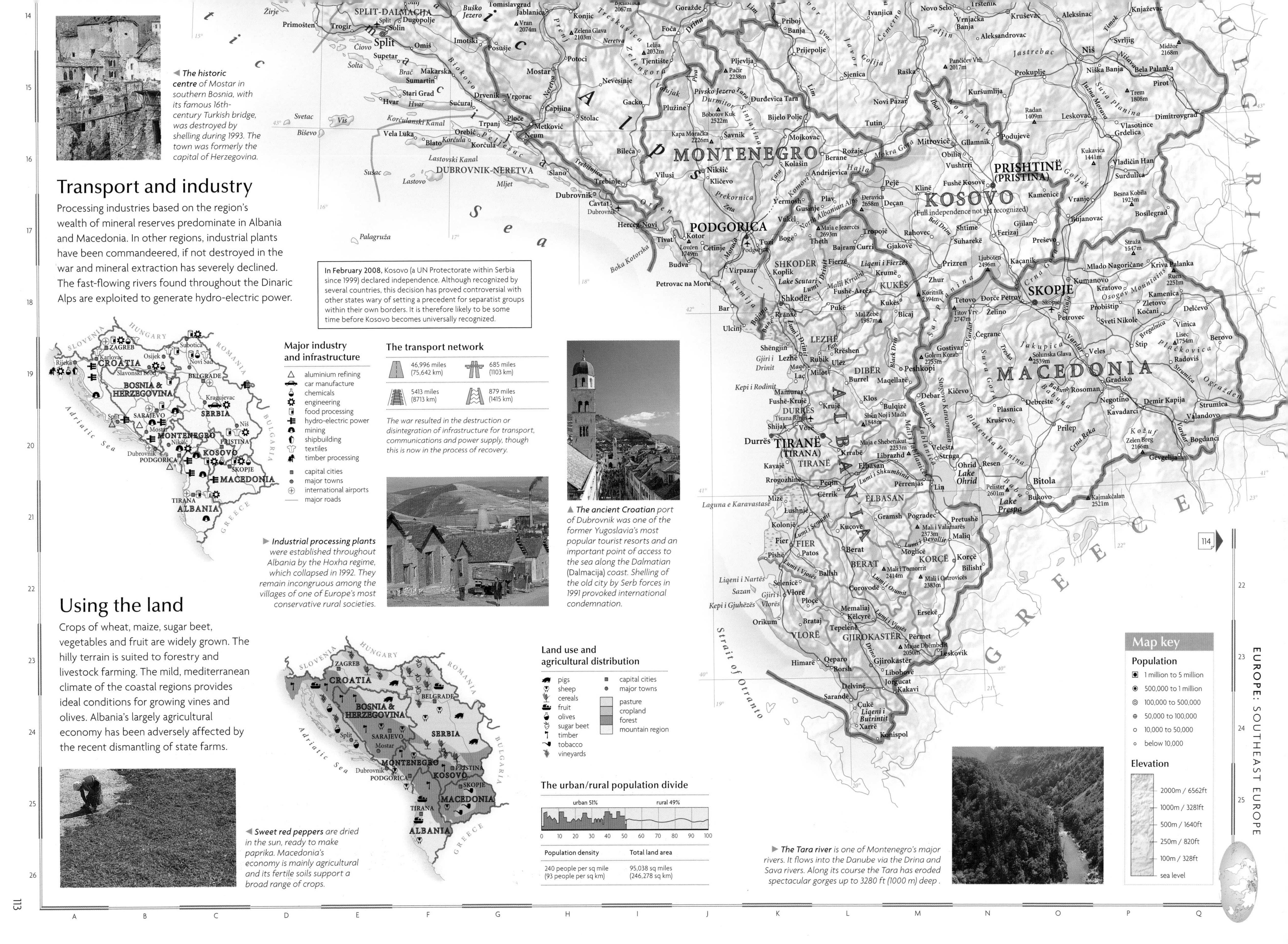
BULGARIA
MONTENEGRO
PODGORICA
KOSOVO
PRISHTINË (PRISTINA)
(Full independence not yet recognized)
MACEDONIA
SKOPJE
ALBANIA
TIRANË (TIRANA)
GREECE
Adriatic Sea
Strait of Otranto
Dinaric Alps
SPLIT-DALMACIJA
DUBROVNIK-NERETVA
Split
Dubrovnik
Mostar
Kotor
Shkodër
Durrës
Vlorë
Elbasan
Korçë
Bitola
Ohrid
Lake Ohrid
Lake Prespa
Niš
114
Map key
Population
1 million to 5 million
500,000 to 1 million
100,000 to 500,000
50,000 to 100,000
10,000 to 50,000
below 10,000
Elevation
2000m / 6562ft
1000m / 3281ft
500m / 1640ft
250m / 820ft
100m / 328ft
sea level

◀ **The historic centre** of Mostar in southern Bosnia, with its famous 16th-century Turkish bridge, was destroyed by shelling during 1993. The town was formerly the capital of Herzegovina.

Transport and industry

Processing industries based on the region's wealth of mineral reserves predominate in Albania and Macedonia. In other regions, industrial plants have been commandeered, if not destroyed in the war and mineral extraction has severely declined. The fast-flowing rivers found throughout the Dinaric Alps are exploited to generate hydro-electric power.

In February 2008, Kosovo (a UN Protectorate within Serbia since 1999) declared independence. Although recognized by several countries, this decision has proved controversial with other states wary of setting a precedent for separatist groups within their own borders. It is therefore likely to be some time before Kosovo becomes universally recognized.

HUNGARY
ROMANIA
SLOVENIA
CROATIA
ZAGREB
BOSNIA & HERZEGOVINA
SARAJEVO
SERBIA
BELGRADE
MONTENEGRO
PODGORICA
KOSOVO
PRISTINA
MACEDONIA
SKOPJE
ALBANIA
TIRANA
BULGARIA
GREECE
Adriatic Sea

Major industry and infrastructure

- aluminium refining
- car manufacture
- chemicals
- engineering
- food processing
- hydro-electric power
- mining
- shipbuilding
- textiles
- timber processing
- capital cities
- major towns
- international airports
- major roads

The transport network

46,996 miles (75,642 km)	685 miles (1103 km)
5413 miles (8713 km)	879 miles (1415 km)

The war resulted in the destruction or disintegration of infrastructure for transport, communications and power supply, though this is now in the process of recovery.

▶ ***Industrial processing plants** were established throughout Albania by the Hoxha regime, which collapsed in 1992. They remain incongruous among the villages of one of Europe's most conservative rural societies.*

▲ ***The ancient Croatian** port of Dubrovnik was one of the former Yugoslavia's most popular tourist resorts and an important point of access to the sea along the Dalmatian (Dalmacija) coast. Shelling of the old city by Serb forces in 1991 provoked international condemnation.*

Using the land

Crops of wheat, maize, sugar beet, vegetables and fruit are widely grown. The hilly terrain is suited to forestry and livestock farming. The mild, mediterranean climate of the coastal regions provides ideal conditions for growing vines and olives. Albania's largely agricultural economy has been adversely affected by the recent dismantling of state farms.

◀ ***Sweet red peppers** are dried in the sun, ready to make paprika. Macedonia's economy is mainly agricultural and its fertile soils support a broad range of crops.*

Land use and agricultural distribution

- pigs
- sheep
- cereals
- fruit
- olives
- sugar beet
- timber
- tobacco
- vineyards
- capital cities
- major towns
- pasture
- cropland
- forest
- mountain region

The urban/rural population divide

urban 51%
rural 49%
0 10 20 30 40 50 60 70 80 90 100

Population density	Total land area
240 people per sq mile (93 people per sq km)	95,038 sq miles (246,278 sq km)

▶ ***The Tara river** is one of Montenegro's major rivers. It flows into the Danube via the Drina and Sava rivers. Along its course the Tara has eroded spectacular gorges up to 3280 ft (1000 m) deep.*

Bulgaria & Greece

Including EUROPEAN TURKEY

Greece is renowned as the original hearth of western civilization. The rugged terrain and numerous islands have profoundly affected its development, creating a strong agricultural and maritime tradition. In the past 50 years, this formerly rural society has rapidly urbanized, with one third of the population now living in the capital, Athens, and in the northern city of Salonica. Bulgaria, dominated for centuries by the Ottoman Turks, became part of the eastern bloc after the Second World War, only slowly emerging from Soviet influence in 1989. Moves towards democracy led to some instability in Bulgaria and Greece, now outweighed by the challenge of integration with the European Union.

Transport and industry

Soviet investment introduced heavy industry into Bulgaria, and the processing of agricultural produce, such as tobacco, is important throughout the country. Both countries have substantial shipyards and Greece has one of the world's largest merchant fleets. Many small craft workshops, producing textiles and processed foods, are clustered around Greek cities. The service and construction sectors have profited from the successful tourist industry.

The landscape

Bulgaria's Balkan mountains divide the Danubian Plain (*Dunavska Ravnina*) and Maritsa Basin, meeting the Black Sea in the east along sandy beaches. The steep Rhodope Mountains form a natural barrier with Greece, while the younger Pindus form a rugged central spine which descends into the Aegean Sea to give a vast archipelago of over 2000 islands, the largest of which is Crete.

Mount Olympus is the mythical home of the Greek Gods and, at 9570 ft (2917 m), is the highest mountain in Greece.

Limestone rocks exposed by erosion of metamorphic rocks

Mount Olympus

Ancient metamorphic rock, formed miles below the surface

Younger limestones created in shallow seas

▲ ***Mount Olympus is** a composite of rocks formed by two major tectonic events. First the older metamorphic rocks were thrust over the limestones, then two million years ago regional warping and subsequent erosion, re-exposed the limestone.*

The Danube, Europe's second longest river, forms most of Bulgaria's northern border. The Danubian plain (*Dunavska Ravnina*), extending from the southern bank, is extremely fertile.

Balkan Mountains

Maritsa Basin

Rhodope Mountains

Pindus Mountains

The islands of Crete, Kythira, Karpathos and Rhodes are part of an arc which bends southeastwards from the Peloponnese, forming the southern boundary of the Aegean.

Kythira

Karpathos

Rhodes

Crete

Corinth Canal (*Dioryga Korinthou*)

The Peloponnese consist of several mountainous peninsulas, linked to the mainland by the Isthmus of Corinth. The Corinth Canal (*Dioryga Korinthou*), built in 1893, cuts through the isthmus, linking the Aegean and Ionian seas.

▲ ***The Arda river** cuts through the Rhodope Mountains in rugged, rocky gorges.*

▲ ***Layers of black** volcanic ash still cover the island of Santorini. This volcano last erupted 3500 years ago, but still shows signs of volcanic activity.*

112

Major industry and infrastructure

- chemicals
- engineering
- food processing
- shipbuilding
- textiles
- tourism
- capital cities
- major towns
- international airports
- major roads
- major industrial areas

The transport network

- 103,930 miles (167,630 km)
- 345 miles (557 km)
- 4346 miles (6995 km)
- 294 miles (474 km)

Bulgaria's railways require investment to revive an outdated infrastructure. In Greece, despite a developing road network, ferry-boats remain the most effective form of transport in many areas.

▲ ***A towering pinnacle** at Metéora in central Greece is home to the monastery of Roussanou. The 24 rock towers which dominate the plain of Thessaly (Thessalia) are remnants of an old plateau. Long-term weathering along fissures in the rock has worn away the rest of the plateau.*

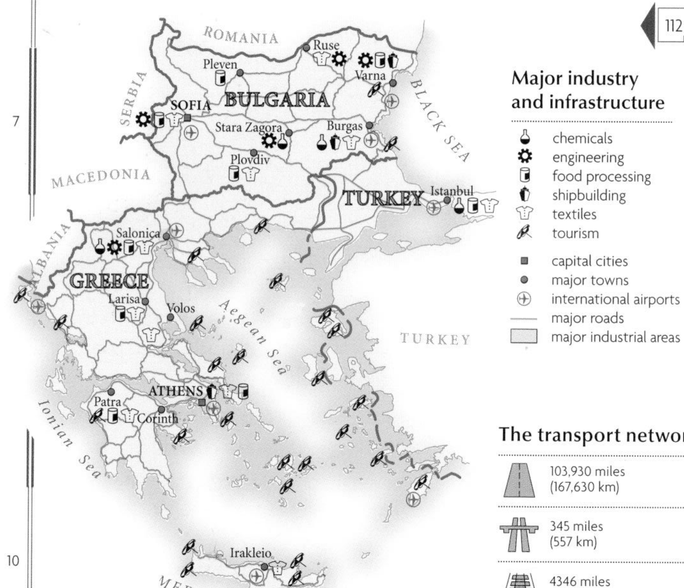

116

112

Scale 1:2,500,000

projection: Lambert Conformal Conic

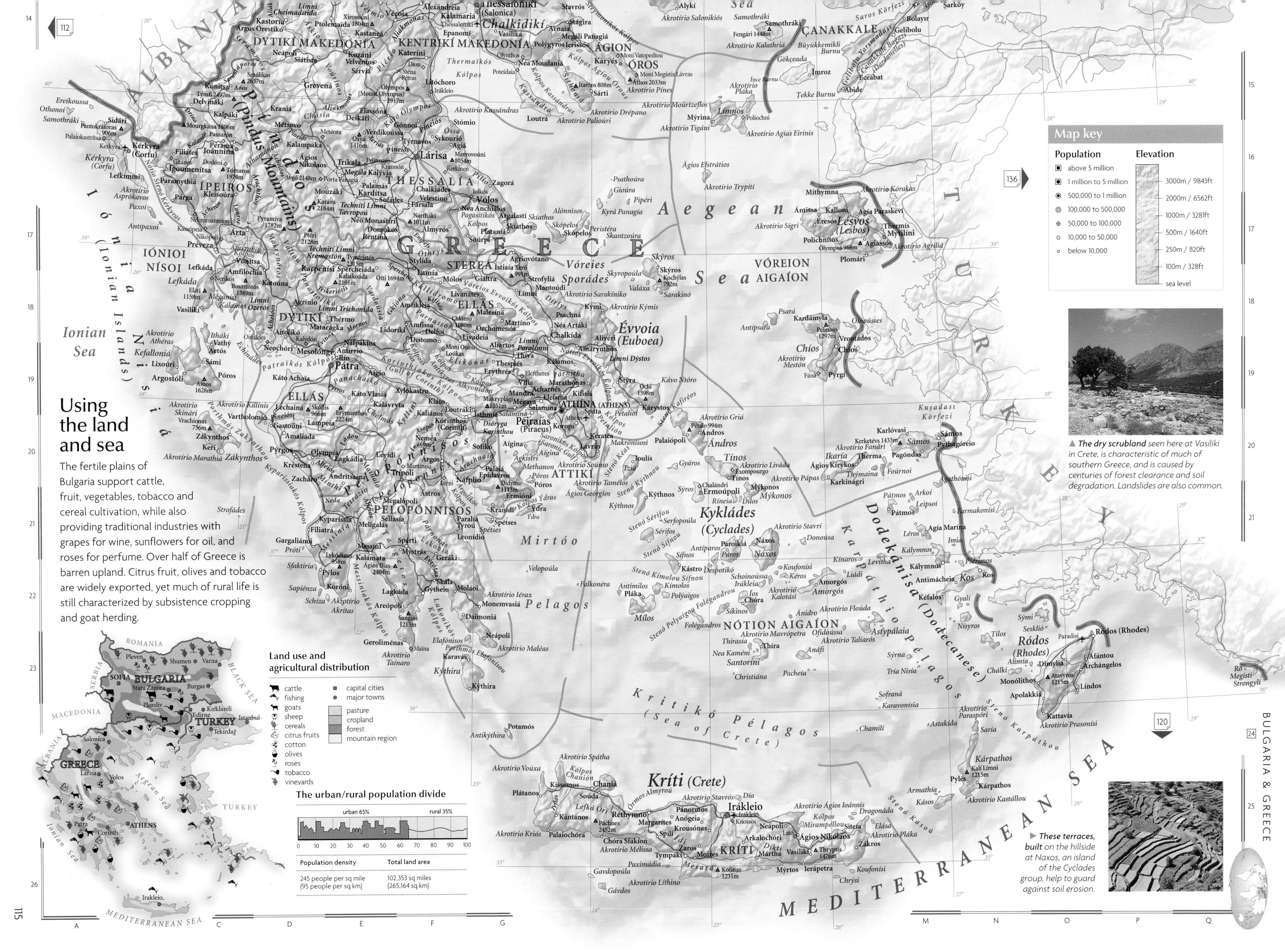

Map key
Population
above 5 million
1 million to 5 million
500,000 to 1 million
100,000 to 500,000
50,000 to 100,000
10,000 to 50,000
below 10,000
Elevation
3000m / 9843ft
2000m / 6562ft
1000m / 3281ft
500m / 1640ft
250m / 820ft
100m / 328ft
sea level
Land use and agricultural distribution
cattle
fishing
goats
sheep
cereals
citrus fruits
cotton
olives
roses
tobacco
vineyards
capital cities
major towns
pasture
cropland
forest
mountain region
The urban/rural population divide
urban 65%
rural 35%
Population density
245 people per sq mile (95 people per sq km)
Total land area
102,353 sq miles (265,164 sq km)
GREECE
TURKEY
Aegean Sea
Ionian Sea
Sea of Crete
MEDITERRANEAN SEA

Using the land and sea

The fertile plains of Bulgaria support cattle, fruit, vegetables, tobacco and cereal cultivation, while also providing traditional industries with grapes for wine, sunflowers for oil, and roses for perfume. Over half of Greece is barren upland. Citrus fruit, olives and tobacco are widely exported, yet much of rural life is still characterized by subsistence cropping and goat herding.

▲ *The dry scrubland* seen here at Vasiliki in Crete, is characteristic of much of southern Greece, and is caused by centuries of forest clearance and soil degradation. Landslides are also common.

▶ *These terraces,* built on the hillside at Naxos, an island of the Cyclades group, help to guard against soil erosion.

112 136 120 24

Romania, Moldova & Ukraine

The industrial, social and cultural make-up of Romania and the former Soviet states of Moldova and Ukraine still bear the imprint of their communist past. As part of the USSR, Ukraine was a leading agricultural, industrial and energy producer. These industries, like those in Moldova and Romania, are now being reoriented more firmly towards western markets. As a result of shifting borders, and Soviet policy actively encouraging Russian immigration into other Soviet states like Ukraine and Moldova, all three countries now contain large numbers of foreign nationals. Moldovans and Romanians are still close in terms of language and culture, although Moldova is striving to remain an independent nation.

POLAND
HUNGARY
SLOVAKIA
SERBIA
BULGARIA
ROMANIA
Pripet Marshes
Carpathian Mountains
Transylvania
L'viv
Luts'k
Rivne
Ternopil'
Ivano-Frankivs'k
Uzhhorod
Chernivtsi
Satu Mare
Baia Mare
Oradea
Cluj-Napoca
Arad
Timişoara
Sibiu
Braşov
Craiova
Piteşti
Ploieşti
Bucureşti (Bucharest)
Bacău
Iaşi
Galaţi
Brăila
Buzău
Constanţa
Danube

110

110

112

Using the land

The fertile black soils of Ukraine, often called 'the breadbasket of Europe', have enabled the cultivation of a variety of cereals and vegetables, which are widely exported. Romania and Moldova also grow cereals, sunflowers and vegetables, and are noted for the quality of their wines.

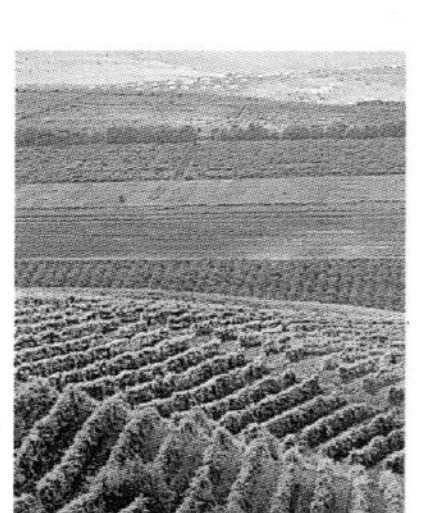

◀ *The fertile lands and tolerant climate of Moldova are ideally suited to growing grapes for wine.*

Land use and agricultural distribution

- cattle
- pigs
- poultry
- sheep
- cereals
- cotton
- sugar beet
- sunflowers
- vineyards
- capital cities
- major towns
- pasture
- cropland
- forest
- wetland

The urban/rural population divide

urban 65% — rural 35%

0 10 20 30 40 50 60 70 80 90 100

Population density	Total land area
222 people per sq mile (86 people per sq km)	334,947 sq miles (867,740 sq km)

◀ *Glacial lakes* are found *throughout the Transylvanian Alps (Carpatii Meridionali), although the mountains no longer have any permanent snow cover.*

Transport and industry

Heavy industry using local raw materials characterizes much of this region. The industrial heartland of Ukraine, specializing in metal and machine-building industries, is based around its vast mineral reserves in the Donbass region. In Moldova, food processing draws on produce from its agricultural sector. Romanian industry relies both on local raw materials and imported iron, steel and oil.

BELARUS
RUSSIAN FEDERATION
POLAND
SLOVAKIA
HUNGARY
SERBIA
BULGARIA
BLACK SEA
UKRAINE
KIEV
Luts'k
L'viv
Kharkiv
Kremenchuk
Donbass
Dnipropetrovs'k
Donets'k
Kryvyy Rih
Chernivtsi
Bălţi
MOLDOVA
CHIŞINĂU
Odesa
Simferopol'
Cluj-Napoca
Timişoara
ROMANIA
Braşov
Galaţi
BUCHAREST

Major industry and infrastructure

- car manufacture
- chemicals
- coal
- engineering
- food processing
- mining
- oil & gas
- textiles
- tourism
- capital cities
- major towns
- international airports
- major roads
- major industrial areas

The transport network

170,707 miles (274,757 km)	1170 miles (1883 km)
21,474 miles (34,563 km)	4130 miles (6647 km)

Increased industrialization has necessitated the upgrading of road and rail networks in all three countries. Modernization has tended to focus only on major cities and industrial areas.

114

▶ *During the 1960s and 1970s, many industries, like this carbon factory, developed using the mineral resources on the flanks of the Transylvanian Alps* (Carpatii Meridionali).

Scale 1:3,250,000
Km
Miles
projection: Lambert Conformal Conic
Map key
Population
1 million to 5 million
500,000 to 1 million
100,000 to 500,000
50,000 to 100,000
10,000 to 50,000
below 10,000
Elevation
2000m / 6562ft
1000m / 3281ft
500m / 1640ft
250m / 820ft
100m / 328ft
sea level
RUSSIAN FEDERATION
UKRAINE
Black Sea Lowland
Sea of Azov
BLACK SEA
Gulf of Taganrog
KYYIV (KIEV)
CHISINAU
Kharkiv
Dnipropetrovs'k
Donets'k
Odesa
Zaporizhzhya
Luhans'k
Mykolayiv
Kherson
Simferopol'
Sevastopol'
Poltava
Sumy
Chernihiv
Cherkasy
Kirovohrad
Kryvvy Rih
Mariupol'
Berdyans'k
Melitopol'
Kerch
Yalta
Zhytomyr
Bila Tserkva
Kremenchuk
Nikopol'
Tiraspol
Tulcea
Constanța
AVTONOMNA RESPUBLIKA KRYM
CHERNIHIVS'KA OBLAST'
SUMS'KA OBLAST'
KYYIVS'KA OBLAST'
POLTAVS'KA OBLAST'
KHARKIVS'KA OBLAST'
LUHANS'KA OBLAST'
DONETS'KA OBLAST'
DNIPROPETROVS'KA OBLAST'
ZAPORIZ'KA OBLAST'
KHERSONS'KA OBLAST'
MYKOLAYIVS'KA OBLAST'
ODES'KA OBLAST'
KIROVOHRADS'KA OBLAST'
CHERKAS'KA OBLAST'
Dnieper
Hora Roman-Kosh 1545m
Old glaciated valley
Water has eroded a new post-glacial valley
Uplifted and folded at the same time as the Alps, some 250 miles (400 km) of the eastern Carpathian Mountains contain ancient volcanic cones and craters.
The Apuseni Mountains (Muntii Apuseni) are rich in mineral deposits, including gold and iron ore.
Transylvanian Alps (Carpatii Meridionali)
The Danube forms a natural border between Romania and Bulgaria.
The three branches of the Danube Delta (Delta Dunării) form a triangle of wetlands covering some 1950 sq miles (5050 sq km).
At Kryms'ki Hory, three flat-topped, parallel limestone ridges run 80 miles (128 km) along the southern coast of the Crimean (Krym) Peninsula.
Anti-clockwise currents have created the sandspits which fringe the Sea of Azov.
Most of the major rivers in southeastern Europe, like the Danube, the Dniester and Dnieper flow south and east to the Black Sea.
Steppe landscape covers two-thirds of Ukraine. These flat, treeless grasslands extend from central Europe to central Asia.
The Codrii Hills dominate the landscape of central Moldova; they are intersected by deep, flat valleys and ravines.

118
122
126
120

▲ *The Swallow's Nest castle at Yalta is one of many tourist resorts on the Crimean (Krym) coast, dubbed the 'Russian Riviera'.*

▲ *Balkas are common throughout Ukraine. They are large U-shaped valleys, formed during the last Ice Age, which contain narrower, deep valleys. These were incised by a sudden flow of water, following an ice melt.*

The landscape

Vast flat lowlands and gently rolling hills cover most of southeastern Europe. In the southwest, the Carpathian Mountains form a gentle arc. To the south of the Carpathian Mountains lies the Danube Plain, across which the Danube river flows to the Black Sea. To the north and east, the hills of Moldova level out into low plains, running east to the steppes of Ukraine.

► *Divided into crystalline massifs, the southern arm of the Carpathian Mountains, the Transylvanian Alps (Carpatii Meridionali), extend 170 miles (274 km) across southwestern Romania.*

The Baltic states & Belarus

BELARUS, ESTONIA, LATVIA, LITHUANIA, Kaliningrad

Occupying Europe's main corridor to Russia, the four distinct cultures of Estonia, Latvia, Lithuania and Belarus share a history of struggle for nationhood against the interests of more powerful neighbours. As the first republics to declare their independence from the Soviet Union in 1990–91, the Baltic states of Estonia, Latvia and Lithuania sought an economic role in the EU, while reaffirming their European cultural roots through the church and a strong musical tradition. Meanwhile, Belarus has shown economic and political allegiance to Russia by joining the Commonwealth of Independent States.

▲ *The seaport of* Riga *is Latvia's capital and the centre of economic and cultural life. With a 32% Russian minority in Latvia, language and the right to national citizenship are key issues.*

Gulf of Finland
Narva Bay
Gulf of Riga
Irbe Strait
BALTIC SEA
RUSSIAN FEDERATION
RUSSIA
ESTONIA
LATVIA
LITHUANIA
TALLINN
RĪGA
Lake Peipus
Lake Pskov
Saaremaa
Hiiumaa
HARJUMAA
LÄÄNEMAA
RAPLAMAA
JÄRVAMAA
JÕGEVAMAA
PÄRNUMAA
VILJANDIMAA
TARTUMAA
PÕLVAMAA
VALGAMAA
VÕRUMAA
SAAREMAA
HIIUMAA
IDA-VIRUMAA
LÄÄNE-VIRUMAA
Vidzeme
Augšzeme
Žemaičiu Aukštumas
TELŠIAI
ŠIAULIAI
PANEVĖŽYS
UTENA
KAUNAS
TAURAGĖ
KLAIPĖDA
VITSYEBSKAYA
Tartu
Pärnu
Narva
Daugavpils
Liepāja
Ventspils
Jelgava
Šiauliai
Panevėžys
Klaipėda
Vitsyebsk
Navapolatsk
Polatsk
Suur Munamägi 318m
Gaiziņkalns 311m
Kuutsemägi 217m

Using the land

Across the four nations cattle and pig farming are widespread, together with diverse arable crops, including flax for making linen, potatoes used to produce vodka, cereals and other vegetables. Almost a third of the land is forested; demand for timber has increased the importance of forest management.

Land use and agricultural distribution

cattle
pigs
cereals
flax
potatoes
timber
capital cities
major towns
pasture
cropland
forest
wetland

The urban/rural population divide

urban 69% — rural 31%

0 10 20 30 40 50 60 70 80 90 100

Population density	Total land area
122 people per sq mile (47 people per sq km)	145,006 sq miles (375,656 sq km)

► *A pine forest in northern Belarus. Conifers in the north give way to hardwood forest further south. Timber mills are supplied with logs floated along the country's many navigable waterways.*

▲ *The Western Dvina river provides hydro-electric power and, during the summer months, access to the Baltic Sea. The lower course of the river freezes from December to April.*

Map key

Population

- 1 million to 5 million
- 500,000 to 1 million
- 100,000 to 500,000
- 50,000 to 100,000
- 10,000 to 50,000
- below 10,000

Elevation

250m / 820ft
100m / 328ft
sea level

122

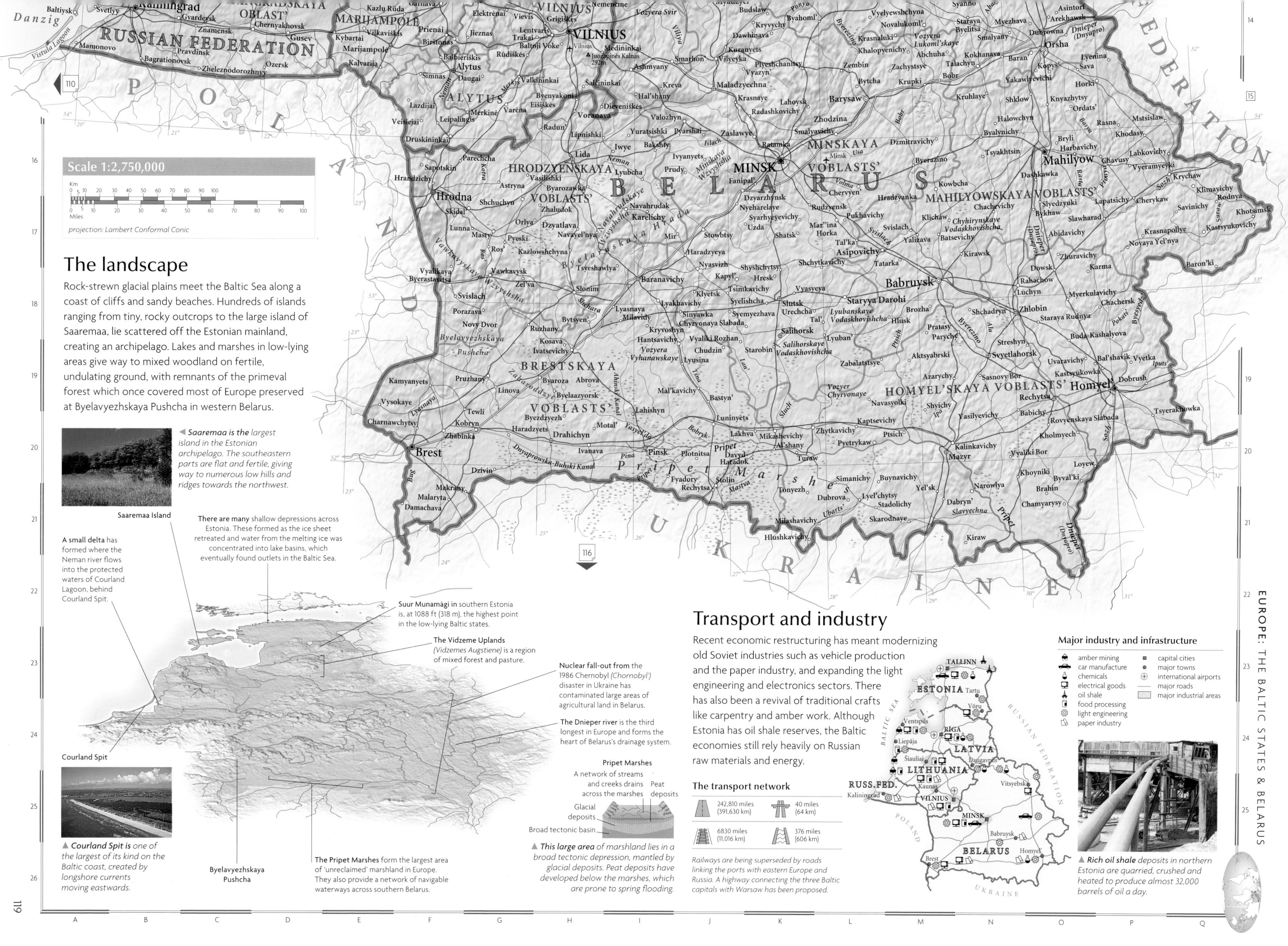
RUSSIAN FEDERATION
POLAND
UKRAINE
BELARUS
VILNIUS
MINSK
HRODZYENSKAYA VOBLASTS'
MINSKAYA VOBLASTS'
BRESTSKAYA VOBLASTS'
MAHILYOWSKAYA VOBLASTS'
HOMYEL'SKAYA VOBLASTS'
Pripet Marshes
Hrodna
Brest
Babruysk
Mahilyow
Homyel'
Scale 1:2,750,000
projection: Lambert Conformal Conic
Saaremaa Island
Courland Spit
Byelavyezhskaya Pushcha
Pripet Marshes
A network of streams and creeks drains across the marshes
Peat deposits
Glacial deposits
Broad tectonic basin
Major industry and infrastructure
amber mining
car manufacture
chemicals
electrical goods
oil shale
food processing
light engineering
paper industry
capital cities
major towns
international airports
major roads
major industrial areas
TALLINN
ESTONIA
Tartu
Võru
RIGA
LATVIA
Ventspils
Liepāja
Šiauliai
Daugavpils
LITHUANIA
Kaunas
VILNIUS
RUSS.FED.
Kaliningrad
MINSK
BELARUS
Vitsyebsk
Babruysk
Homyel
Brest
BALTIC SEA
RUSSIAN FEDERATION
POLAND
UKRAINE

The landscape

Rock-strewn glacial plains meet the Baltic Sea along a coast of cliffs and sandy beaches. Hundreds of islands ranging from tiny, rocky outcrops to the large island of Saaremaa, lie scattered off the Estonian mainland, creating an archipelago. Lakes and marshes in low-lying areas give way to mixed woodland on fertile, undulating ground, with remnants of the primeval forest which once covered most of Europe preserved at Byelavyezhskaya Pushcha in western Belarus.

◀ *Saaremaa is the largest island in the Estonian archipelago. The southeastern parts are flat and fertile, giving way to numerous low hills and ridges towards the northwest.*

There are many shallow depressions across Estonia. These formed as the ice sheet retreated and water from the melting ice was concentrated into lake basins, which eventually found outlets in the Baltic Sea.

A small delta has formed where the Neman river flows into the protected waters of Courland Lagoon, behind Courland Spit.

Suur Munamägi in southern Estonia is, at 1088 ft (318 m), the highest point in the low-lying Baltic states.

The Vidzeme Uplands *(Vidzemes Augstiene)* is a region of mixed forest and pasture.

Nuclear fall-out from the 1986 Chernobyl *(Chornobyl')* disaster in Ukraine has contaminated large areas of agricultural land in Belarus.

The Dnieper river is the third longest in Europe and forms the heart of Belarus's drainage system.

▲ *Courland Spit is one of the largest of its kind on the Baltic coast, created by longshore currents moving eastwards.*

The Pripet Marshes form the largest area of 'unreclaimed' marshland in Europe. They also provide a network of navigable waterways across southern Belarus.

▲ *This large area of marshland lies in a broad tectonic depression, mantled by glacial deposits. Peat deposits have developed below the marshes, which are prone to spring flooding.*

Transport and industry

Recent economic restructuring has meant modernizing old Soviet industries such as vehicle production and the paper industry, and expanding the light engineering and electronics sectors. There has also been a revival of traditional crafts like carpentry and amber work. Although Estonia has oil shale reserves, the Baltic economies still rely heavily on Russian raw materials and energy.

The transport network

242,810 miles (391,630 km)	40 miles (64 km)
6830 miles (11,016 km)	376 miles (606 km)

Railways are being superseded by roads linking the ports with eastern Europe and Russia. A highway connecting the three Baltic capitals with Warsaw has been proposed.

▲ *Rich oil shale deposits in northern Estonia are quarried, crushed and heated to produce almost 32,000 barrels of oil a day.*

110
116

The Mediterranean

The Mediterranean Sea stretches over 2500 miles (4000 km) east to west, separating Europe from Africa. At its most westerly point it is connected to the Atlantic Ocean through the Strait of Gibraltar. In the east, the Suez canal, opened in 1869, gives passage to the Indian Ocean. In the northeast, linked by the Sea of Marmara, lies the Black Sea. The Mediterranean is bordered by almost 30 states and territories, and more than 100 million people live on its shores and islands. Throughout history, the Mediterranean has been a focal area for many great empires and civilizations, reflected in the variety of cultures found on its shores. Since the 1960s, development along the southern coast of Europe has expanded rapidly to accommodate increasing numbers of tourists and to enable the exploitation of oil and gas reserves. This has resulted in rising levels of pollution, threatening the future of the sea.

▲ ***Monaco is just*** *one of the luxurious resorts scattered along the Riviera, which stretches along the coast from Cannes in France to La Spezia in Italy. The region's mild winters and hot summers have attracted wealthy tourists since the early 19th century.*

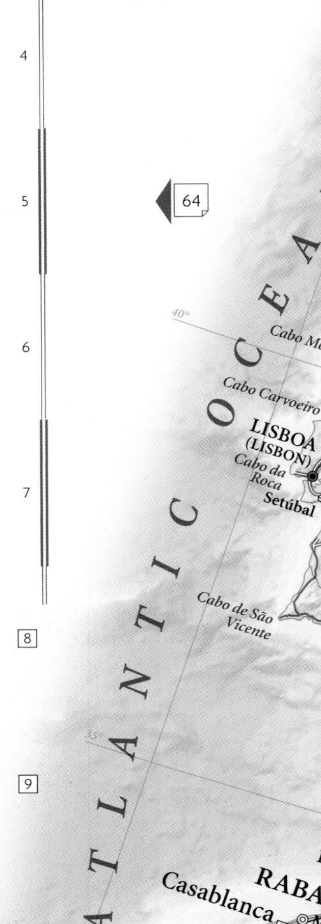
ATLANTIC OCEAN
Cabo Fisterra
A Coruña
Vigo
Porto
Vila Nova de Gaia
Cabo Mondego
Cabo Carvoeiro
LISBOA (LISBON)
Cabo da Roca
Setúbal
Cabo de São Vicente
Casablanca
Cap Beddouza
Safi

The landscape

The Mediterranean Sea is almost totally landlocked, joined to the Atlantic Ocean through the Strait of Gibraltar, which is only 8 miles (13 km) wide. Lying on an active plate margin, sea floor movements have formed a variety of basins, troughs and ridges. A submarine ridge running from Tunisia to the island of Sicily divides the Mediterranean into two distinct basins. The western basin is characterized by broad, smooth abyssal (or ocean) plains. In contrast, the eastern basin is dominated by a large ridge system, running east to west.

The narrow Strait of Gibraltar inhibits water exchange between the Mediterranean Sea and the Atlantic Ocean, producing a high degree of salinity and a low tidal range within the Mediterranean. The lack of tides has encouraged the build-up of pollutants in many semi-enclosed bays.

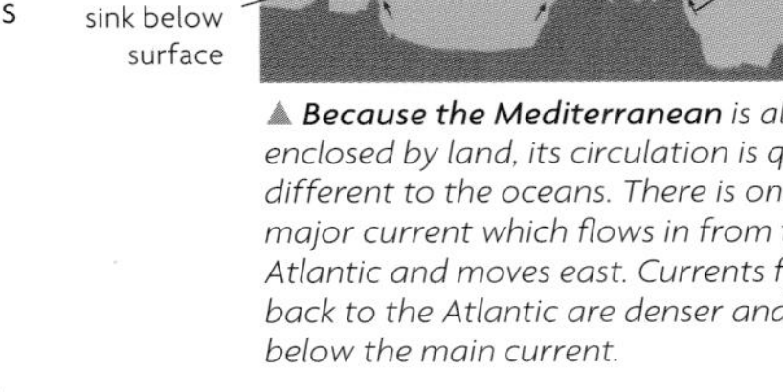
Main surface current
Dense currents sink below surface
Denser, more saline currents flow back to Atlantic

▲ ***Because the Mediterranean*** *is almost enclosed by land, its circulation is quite different to the oceans. There is one major current which flows in from the Atlantic and moves east. Currents flowing back to the Atlantic are denser and flow below the main current.*

Industrial pollution flowing from the Dnieper and Danube rivers has destroyed a large proportion of the fish population that used to inhabit the upper layers of the Black Sea.

The Ionian Basin is the deepest in the Mediterranean, reaching depths of 16,800 ft (5121 m).

The edge of the Eurasian Plate is edged by a continental shelf. In the Mediterranean Sea this is widest at the Ebro Fan where it extends 60 miles (96 km).

Oxygen in the Black Sea is dissolved only in its upper layers; at depths below 230 300 ft (70–100 m) the sea is 'dead' and can support no lifeforms other than specially-adapted bacteria.

◀ ***The Atlas Mountains*** *are a range of fold mountains which lie in Morocco and Algeria. They run parallel to the Mediterranean, forming a topographical and climatic divide between the Mediterranean coast and the western Sahara.*

An arc of active submarine, island and mainland volcanoes, including Etna and Vesuvius, lie in and around southern Italy. The area is also susceptible to earthquakes and landslides.

Nutrient flows into the eastern Mediterranean, and sediment flows to the Nile Delta have been severely lowered by the building of the Aswan Dam across the Nile in Egypt. This is causing the delta to shrink.

The Suez Canal, opened in 186 extends 100 miles (160 km) fro Port Said to the Gulf of Suez.

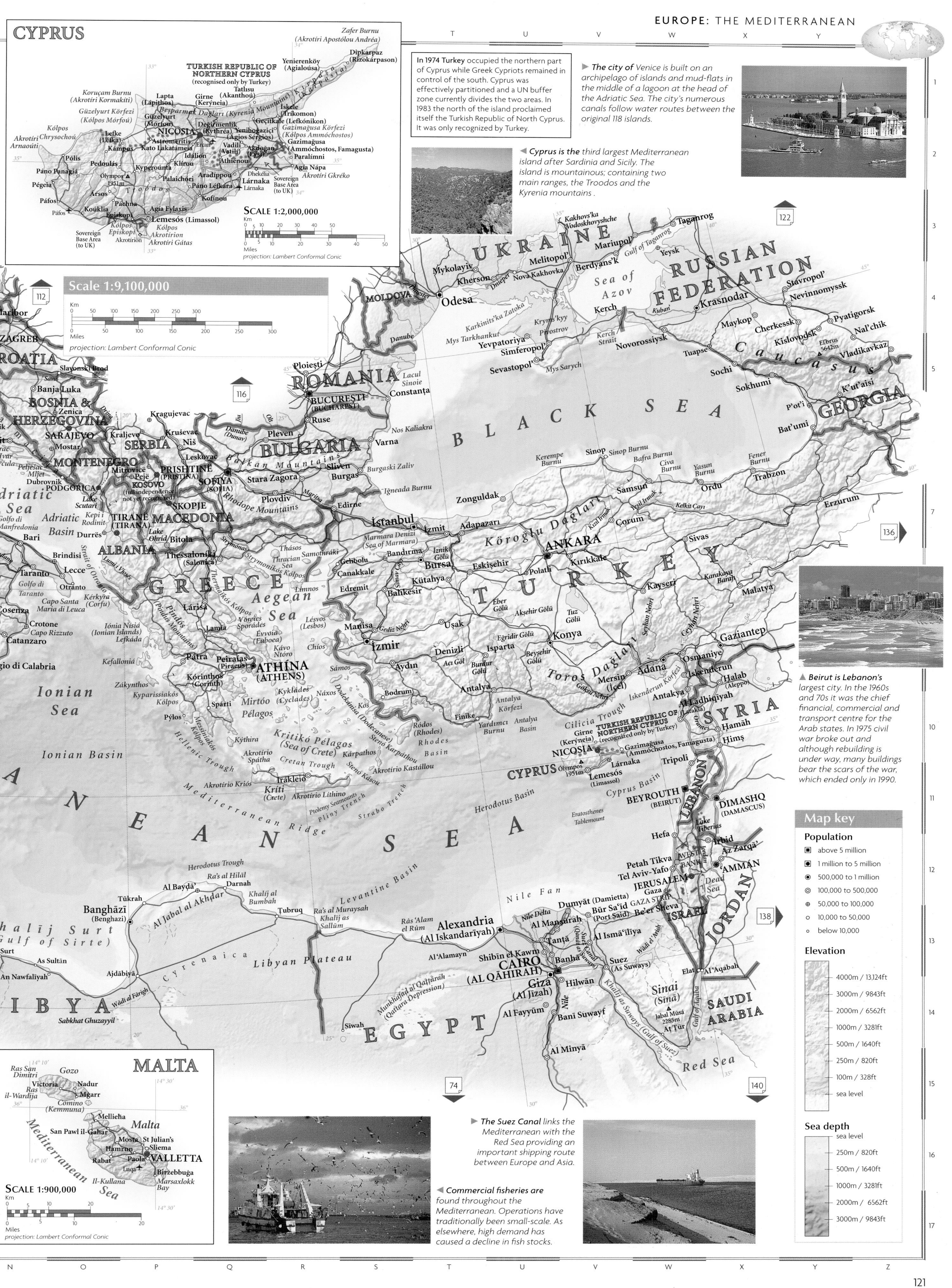
CYPRUS
TURKISH REPUBLIC OF NORTHERN CYPRUS (recognised only by Turkey)
NICOSIA
Kyrenia Mountains
Troodos
Olympos 1951m
Lemesós (Limassol)
Lárnaka
Gazimağusa (Ammóchostos, Famagusta)
Sovereign Base Area (to UK)
SCALE 1:2,000,000
projection: Lambert Conformal Conic
Scale 1:9,100,000
projection: Lambert Conformal Conic
UKRAINE
RUSSIAN FEDERATION
MOLDOVA
ROMANIA
BULGARIA
SERBIA
BOSNIA & HERZEGOVINA
MONTENEGRO
KOSOVO
MACEDONIA
ALBANIA
GREECE
TURKEY
GEORGIA
SYRIA
LEBANON
ISRAEL
JORDAN
CYPRUS
EGYPT
LIBYA
SAUDI ARABIA
BLACK SEA
Sea of Azov
Aegean Sea
Ionian Sea
Adriatic Sea
MEDITERRANEAN SEA
Red Sea
Caucasus
ANKARA
İstanbul
ATHÍNA (ATHENS)
SOFIYA (SOFIA)
BUCUREŞTI (BUCHAREST)
SKOPJE
TIRANË (TIRANA)
BEYROUTH (BEIRUT)
DIMASHQ (DAMASCUS)
JERUSALEM
'AMMĀN
CAIRO (AL QĀHIRAH)
Alexandria (Al Iskandarīyah)
Banghāzī (Benghazi)
Libyan Plateau
Sinai (Sīnā)
MALTA
VALLETTA
Gozo
SCALE 1:900,000
projection: Lambert Conformal Conic
Map key
Population
above 5 million
1 million to 5 million
500,000 to 1 million
100,000 to 500,000
50,000 to 100,000
10,000 to 50,000
below 10,000
Elevation
4000m / 13,124ft
3000m / 9843ft
2000m / 6562ft
1000m / 3281ft
500m / 1640ft
250m / 820ft
100m / 328ft
sea level
Sea depth
sea level
250m / 820ft
500m / 1640ft
1000m / 3281ft
2000m / 6562ft
3000m / 9843ft

In 1974 Turkey occupied the northern part of Cyprus while Greek Cypriots remained in control of the south. Cyprus was effectively partitioned and a UN buffer zone currently divides the two areas. In 1983 the north of the island proclaimed itself the Turkish Republic of North Cyprus. It was only recognized by Turkey.

► ***The city of*** *Venice is built on an archipelago of islands and mud-flats in the middle of a lagoon at the head of the Adriatic Sea. The city's numerous canals follow water routes between the original 118 islands.*

◄ ***Cyprus is the*** *third largest Mediterranean island after Sardinia and Sicily. The island is mountainous; containing two main ranges, the Troodos and the Kyrenia mountains.*

▲ ***Beirut is Lebanon's*** *largest city. In the 1960s and 70s it was the chief financial, commercial and transport centre for the Arab states. In 1975 civil war broke out and although rebuilding is under way, many buildings bear the scars of the war, which ended only in 1990.*

► ***The Suez Canal*** *links the Mediterranean with the Red Sea providing an important shipping route between Europe and Asia.*

◄ ***Commercial fisheries are*** *found throughout the Mediterranean. Operations have traditionally been small-scale. As elsewhere, high demand has caused a decline in fish stocks.*

The Russian Federation

The Cold War era of global relations was concluded in 1991 with the formal dissolution of the Soviet Union. The Russian Federation declared its separate sovereignty from the foundering communist empire following independence declarations from a number of former Soviet republics. As the leading member of the Commonwealth of Independent States, the Russian Federation has a central role in the development of post-Soviet Eurasia. Crossing 11 time zones, the Russian Federation is almost twice the size of the USA, and with more than 150 ethnic minorities and 21 autonomous republics, regionalist dissent within its own territory remains a danger.

▶ **Summer beds of** moss and lichen scatter a 90% surface cover of ice across the islands of Franz Josef Land (Zemlya Frantsa-Iosifa), the northernmost land in the eastern hemisphere.

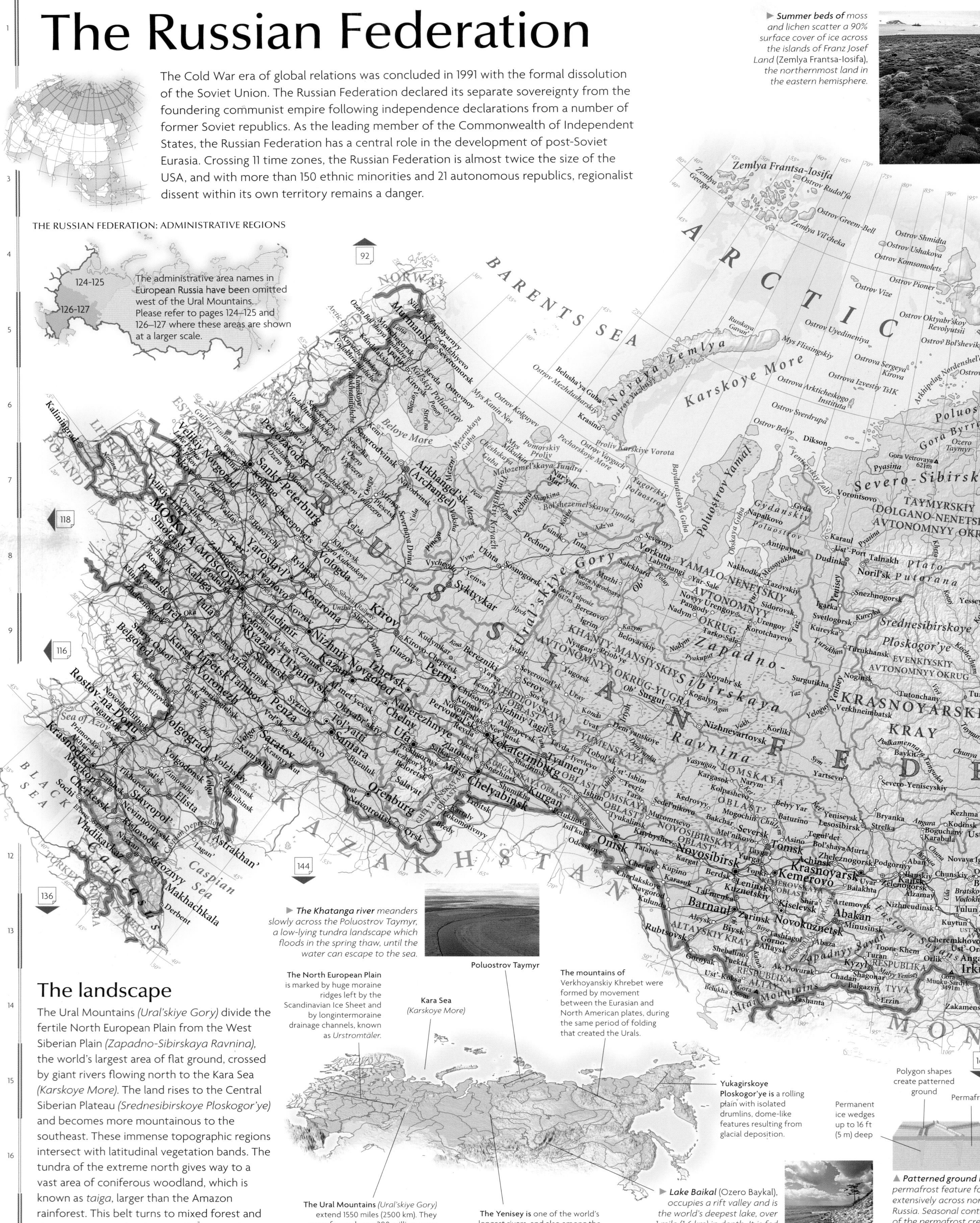

THE RUSSIAN FEDERATION: ADMINISTRATIVE REGIONS
124-125
126-127
The administrative area names in European Russia have been omitted west of the Ural Mountains. Please refer to pages 124–125 and 126–127 where these areas are shown at a larger scale.
BARENTS SEA
ARCTIC
Zemlya Frantsa-Iosifa
Novaya Zemlya
Karskoye More
Severo-Sibirskaya
TAYMYRSKIY (DOLGANO-NENETSKIY) AVTONOMNYY OKRUG
Plato Putorana
Srednesibirskoye Ploskogor'ye
EVENKIYSKIY AVTONOMNYY OKRUG
KRASNOYARSKIY KRAY
YAMALO-NENETSKIY AVTONOMNYY OKRUG
KHANTY-MANSIYSKIY AVTONOMNYY OKRUG-YUGRA
Zapadno-Sibirskaya Ravnina
Ural'skiye Gory
RUSSIAN FEDERATION
MOSKVA (MOSCOW)
Sankt-Peterburg
KAZAKHSTAN
Caspian Sea
Black Sea
Novosibirsk
Omsk
Krasnoyarsk
Irkutsk
Yekaterinburg
Chelyabinsk
Volgograd
Kaliningrad
Murmansk
Arkhangel'sk (Archangel)
Altay Mountains
Kavkaz
92
118
116
144
136
162

▶ **The Khatanga river** meanders slowly across the Poluostrov Taymyr, a low-lying tundra landscape which floods in the spring thaw, until the water can escape to the sea.

The landscape

The Ural Mountains *(Ural'skiye Gory)* divide the fertile North European Plain from the West Siberian Plain *(Zapadno-Sibirskaya Ravnina)*, the world's largest area of flat ground, crossed by giant rivers flowing north to the Kara Sea *(Karskoye More)*. The land rises to the Central Siberian Plateau *(Srednesibirskoye Ploskogor'ye)* and becomes more mountainous to the southeast. These immense topographic regions intersect with latitudinal vegetation bands. The tundra of the extreme north gives way to a vast area of coniferous woodland, which is known as *taiga*, larger than the Amazon rainforest. This belt turns to mixed forest and then steppe grasslands towards the south.

The North European Plain is marked by huge moraine ridges left by the Scandinavian Ice Sheet and by longintermoraine drainage channels, known as *Urstromtäler*.

Kara Sea *(Karskoye More)*

Poluostrov Taymyr

The mountains of Verkhoyanskiy Khrebet were formed by movement between the Eurasian and North American plates, during the same period of folding that created the Urals.

Yukagirskoye Ploskogor'ye is a rolling plain with isolated drumlins, dome-like features resulting from glacial deposition.

Polygon shapes create patterned ground

Permafrost

Permanent ice wedges up to 16 ft (5 m) deep

▲ **Patterned ground is** a permafrost feature found extensively across northern Russia. Seasonal contraction of the permafrost creates polygonal cracks, which are filled by ice wedges.

The Ural Mountains *(Ural'skiye Gory)* extend 1550 miles (2500 km). They were formed over 280 million years ago, folded as the East European and Siberian plates moved closer together.

The Yenisey is one of the world's longest rivers, and also among the most languid, dropping only 500 ft (152 m) over 1200 miles (2000 km).

▶ **Lake Baikal** (Ozero Baykal), occupies a rift valley and is the world's deepest lake, over 1 mile (1.6 km) in depth. It is fed by over 300 rivers and drained by just one, the Angara.

Transport and industry

Raw materials, particularly fossil fuels, ores and precious metals are abundant, yet often found at sites far from habitation. This inherent 'friction of distance' problem was met from the 1930s by Soviet commitment to heavy industry and the strategic location of plants east of the Urals. It has left a pattern of isolated and often vast industrial complexes, in remote areas from Vladivostok to Murmansk, in the far north and across European Russia, with lighter manufacturing concentrated in urban areas.

The transport network

- 218,683 miles (351,976 km)
- None
- 53,147 miles (85,542 km)
- 59,583 miles (95,900 km)

The recent growth of trade with China and East Asia has put pressure on Siberia's inadequate road and rail network, prompting increased use of the Amur river for freight transport.

Major industry and infrastructure

- aerospace
- car manufacture
- chemicals
- engineering
- gas
- iron & steel
- mining
- oil
- textiles
- timber processing
- capital cities
- major towns
- international airports
- major roads
- major industrial areas

▲ ***Novosibirsk was established*** *at the point where the Trans-Siberian railway crosses the Ob' river. It grew as an industrial centre under the Soviet Union and is now Siberia's largest city.*

Map key

Population

- above 5 million
- 1 million to 5 million
- 500,000 to 1 million
- 100,000 to 500,000
- 50,000 to 100,000
- 10,000 to 50,000
- below 10,000

Elevation

- 4000m / 13,124ft
- 3000m / 9843ft
- 2000m / 6562ft
- 1000m / 3281ft
- 500m / 1640ft
- 250m / 820ft
- 100m / 328ft
- sea level

▲ ***A fishing trawler*** *lies at anchor in the icy waters of Karaginskiy Zaliv, at the northern end of the Kamchatka Peninsula (Poluostrov Kamchatka) in eastern Siberia. The Russian Federation's fishing fleet is the largest in the world and operates worldwide.*

Using the land

The main agricultural regions follow the belt of rich, black *chernozem* soils between Ukraine and Novosibirsk, producing cereals, fodder, and a broad range of crops for industrial use. Small pockets of pastureland are also found in this region. Large areas of terrain are uncultivable, and the constraints of a severe climate force the Federation to be partly dependent on imported grain. The wilds of Siberia are given over to hunting and reindeer herding, and contain the world's largest timber reserves.

The urban/rural population divide

urban 76% / rural 24%

Population density	Total land area
22 people per sq mile (9 people per sq km)	65,592,800 sq miles (17,075,400 sq km)

Scale 1:18,750,000

projection: Lambert Conformal Conic

◀ *The Kamchatka Peninsula (Poluostrov Kamchatka) is a volcanic area on the margins of the Eurasian Plate, forming part of the Pacific 'Ring of Fire.' The volcano Vulkan Klyuchevskaya Sopka, at 15,585 ft (4750 m), is the highest mountain in Siberia.*

Land use and agricultural distribution

- cattle
- cereals
- root crops
- timber
- capital cities
- major towns
- pasture
- cropland
- forest
- desert
- mountain region
- barren

196
16
192
162

Northern European Russia

Reaching into the Arctic Circle, this region of lakeland, forest and tundra is historically bound to Europe by St Petersburg, the old imperial capital of Tsarist Russia and home to a third of the region's population. Communist rule from Moscow left the north politically marginalized, contributing to the present problems of outmoded industry, poor infrastructure and serious environmental neglect. However, with borders embracing Finland, Norway, the Baltic and the northern sea route to the Atlantic, the region's success in foreign trade is now of prime importance to the Russian economy.

The landscape

The ancient bedrock of the Scandinavian Shield lies exposed across the glacially scoured Khibiny Mountains of the Kola Peninsula (*Kol'skiy Poluostrov*), becoming mantled with till towards the North European Plain. The Valdai Hills *(Valdayskaya Vozvyshennost')* form an important watershed for the plain's rivers, while thick forest veils a complicated topography of moraines, lakes and ground disturbed by frost action. The Ural Mountains *(Ural'skiye Gory)* form a border with Asia in the east.

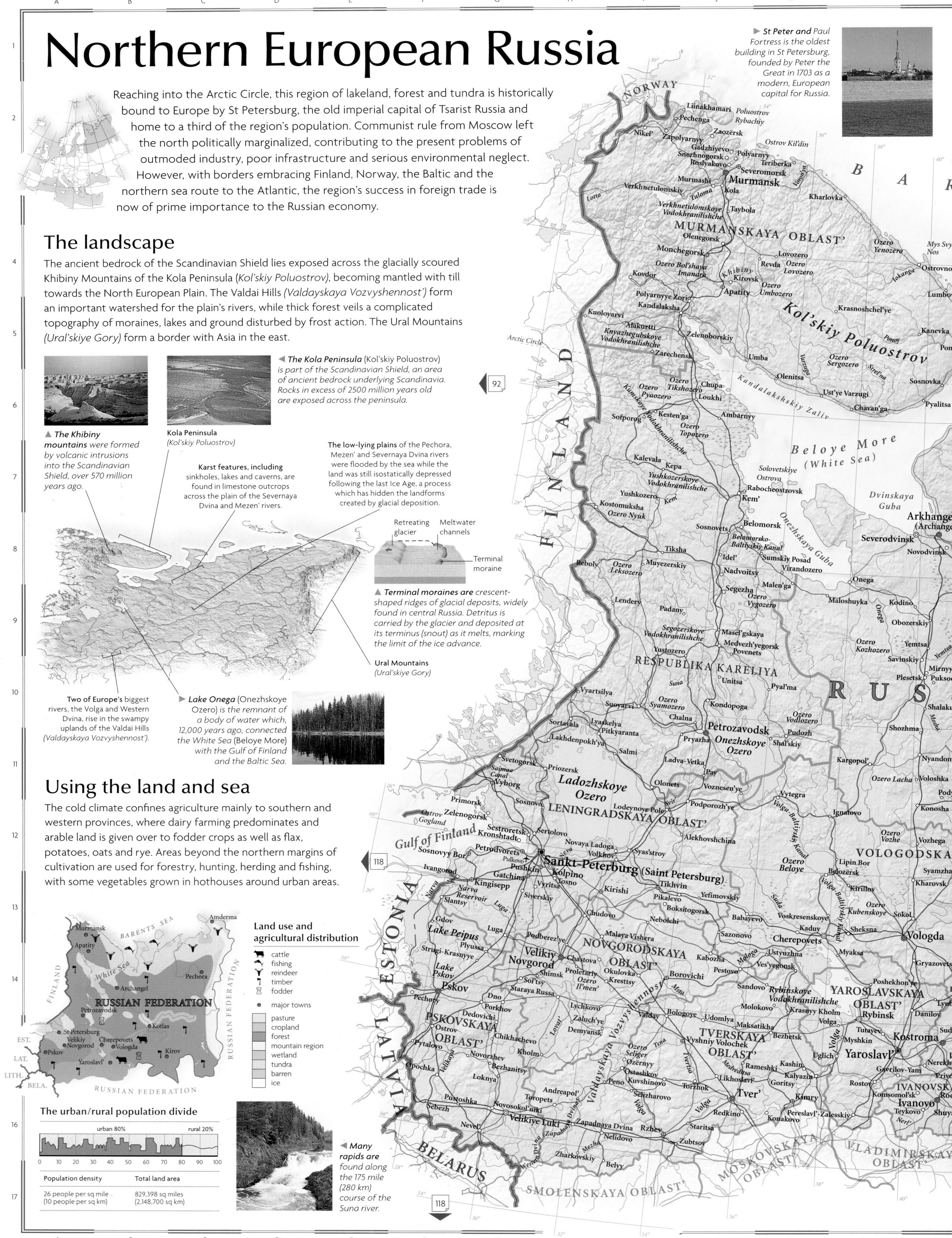

Retreating glacier
Meltwater channels
Terminal moraine
NORWAY
FINLAND
ESTONIA
LATVIA
BELARUS
Arctic Circle
Barents Sea
Beloye More (White Sea)
Kol'skiy Poluostrov
Kandalakshskiy Zaliv
Onezhskaya Guba
Dvinskaya Guba
MURMANSKAYA OBLAST'
RESPUBLIKA KARELIYA
LENINGRADSKAYA OBLAST'
NOVGORODSKAYA OBLAST'
PSKOVSKAYA OBLAST'
TVERSKAYA OBLAST'
YAROSLAVSKAYA OBLAST'
VOLOGODSKAYA
IVANOVSKAYA
VLADIMIRSKAYA OBLAST'
MOSKOVSKAYA OBLAST'
SMOLENSKAYA OBLAST'
Murmansk
Arkhangel'sk (Archangel)
Severodvinsk
Petrozavodsk
Onezhskoye Ozero
Ladozhskoye Ozero
Sankt-Peterburg (Saint Petersburg)
Gulf of Finland
Lake Peipus
Lake Pskov
Pskov
Velikiy Novgorod
Tver'
Vologda
Yaroslavl'
Kostroma
Ivanovo
Valdayskaya Vozvyshennost'
Land use and agricultural distribution
cattle
fishing
reindeer
timber
fodder
major towns
pasture
cropland
forest
mountain region
wetland
tundra
barren
ice
RUSSIAN FEDERATION
BARENTS SEA
White Sea
The urban/rural population divide
urban 80%
rural 20%
Population density
26 people per sq mile (10 people per sq km)
Total land area
829,398 sq miles (2,148,700 sq km)

▶ **St Peter and Paul** *Fortress is the oldest building in St Petersburg, founded by Peter the Great in 1703 as a modern, European capital for Russia.*

◀ **The Kola Peninsula** (Kol'skiy Poluostrov) *is part of the Scandinavian Shield, an area of ancient bedrock underlying Scandinavia. Rocks in excess of 2500 million years old are exposed across the peninsula.*

▲ **The Khibiny mountains** *were formed by volcanic intrusions into the Scandinavian Shield, over 570 million years ago.*

Kola Peninsula *(Kol'skiy Poluostrov)*

Karst features, including sinkholes, lakes and caverns, are found in limestone outcrops across the plain of the Severnaya Dvina and Mezen' rivers.

The low-lying plains of the Pechora, Mezen' and Severnaya Dvina rivers were flooded by the sea while the land was still isostatically depressed following the last Ice Age, a process which has hidden the landforms created by glacial deposition.

▲ **Terminal moraines are** *crescent-shaped ridges of glacial deposits, widely found in central Russia. Detritus is carried by the glacier and deposited at its terminus (snout) as it melts, marking the limit of the ice advance.*

Ural Mountains *(Ural'skiye Gory)*

Two of Europe's biggest rivers, the Volga and Western Dvina, rise in the swampy uplands of the Valdai Hills *(Valdayskaya Vozvyshennost')*.

▶ **Lake Onega** (Onezhskoye Ozero) *is the remnant of a body of water which, 12,000 years ago, connected the White Sea* (Beloye More) *with the Gulf of Finland and the Baltic Sea.*

Using the land and sea

The cold climate confines agriculture mainly to southern and western provinces, where dairy farming predominates and arable land is given over to fodder crops as well as flax, potatoes, oats and rye. Areas beyond the northern margins of cultivation are used for forestry, hunting, herding and fishing, with some vegetables grown in hothouses around urban areas.

◀ **Many rapids are** *found along the 175 mile (280 km) course of the Suna river.*

92
118
118

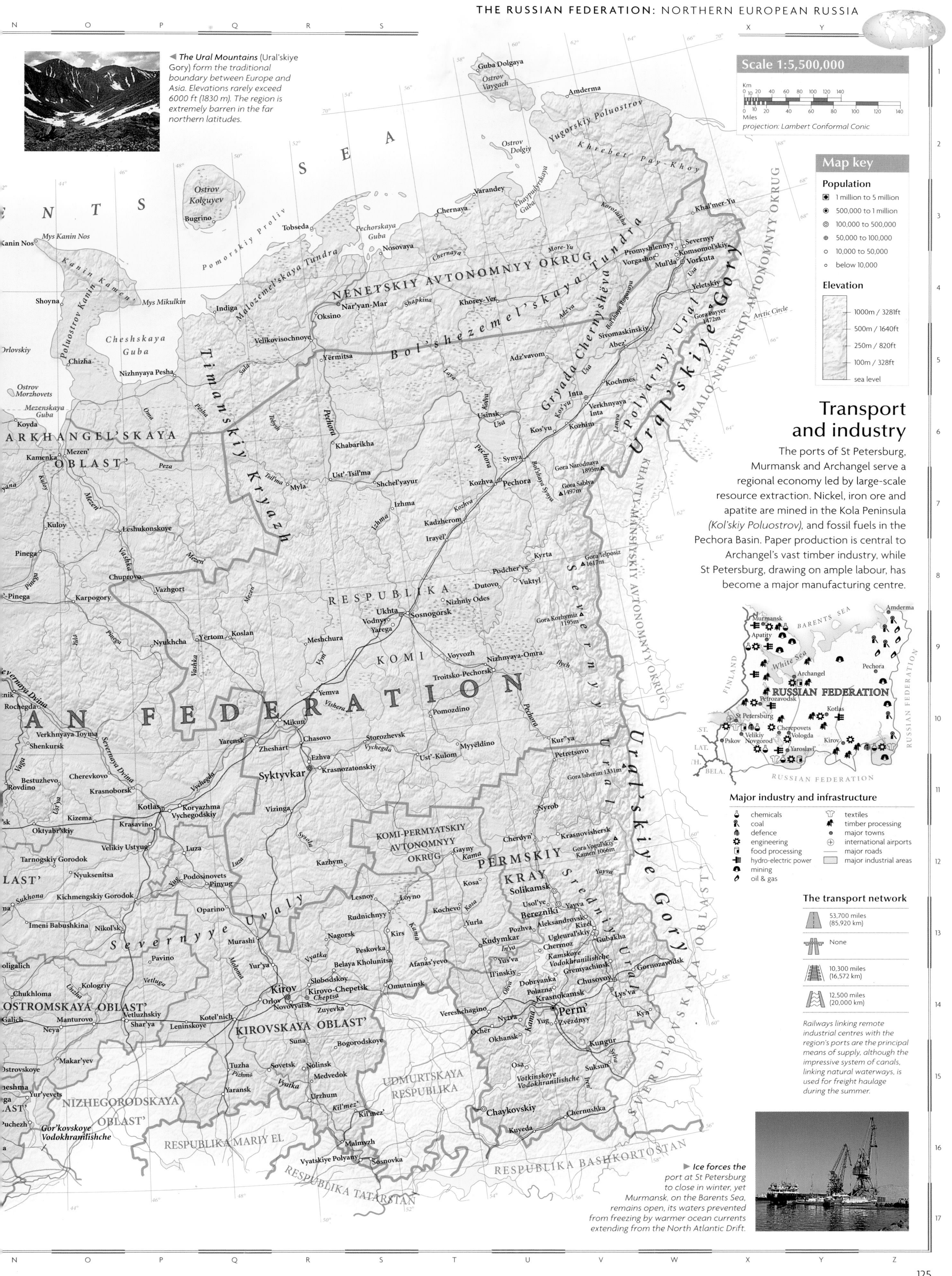
Scale 1:5,500,000
projection: Lambert Conformal Conic
Map key
Population
1 million to 5 million
500,000 to 1 million
100,000 to 500,000
50,000 to 100,000
10,000 to 50,000
below 10,000
Elevation
1000m / 3281ft
500m / 1640ft
250m / 820ft
100m / 328ft
sea level
Major industry and infrastructure
chemicals
coal
defence
engineering
food processing
hydro-electric power
mining
oil & gas
textiles
timber processing
major towns
international airports
major roads
major industrial areas
The transport network
53,700 miles (85,920 km)
None
10,300 miles (16,572 km)
12,500 miles (20,000 km)
BARENTS SEA
NENETSKIY AVTONOMNYY OKRUG
RESPUBLIKA KOMI
ARKHANGEL'SKAYA OBLAST'
KIROVSKAYA OBLAST'
PERMSKIY KRAY
KOMI-PERMYATSKIY AVTONOMNYY OKRUG
UDMURTSKAYA RESPUBLIKA
NIZHEGORODSKAYA OBLAST'
RESPUBLIKA MARIY EL
RESPUBLIKA TATARSTAN
RESPUBLIKA BASHKORTOSTAN
SVERDLOVSKAYA OBLAST'
KHANTY-MANSIYSKIY AVTONOMNYY OKRUG
YAMALO-NENETSKIY AVTONOMNYY OKRUG
Ural'skiye Gory
Timanskiy Kryazh
Syktyvkar
Kirov
Perm'
Vorkuta
Ukhta

◄ *The Ural Mountains* (Ural'skiye Gory) *form the traditional boundary between Europe and Asia. Elevations rarely exceed 6000 ft (1830 m). The region is extremely barren in the far northern latitudes.*

Transport and industry

The ports of St Petersburg, Murmansk and Archangel serve a regional economy led by large-scale resource extraction. Nickel, iron ore and apatite are mined in the Kola Peninsula *(Kol'skiy Poluostrov)*, and fossil fuels in the Pechora Basin. Paper production is central to Archangel's vast timber industry, while St Petersburg, drawing on ample labour, has become a major manufacturing centre.

Railways linking remote industrial centres with the region's ports are the principal means of supply, although the impressive system of canals, linking natural waterways, is used for freight haulage during the summer.

► *Ice forces the port at St Petersburg to close in winter, yet Murmansk, on the Barents Sea, remains open, its waters prevented from freezing by warmer ocean currents extending from the North Atlantic Drift.*

118

110

118

116

▶ *Kaliningrad has been a Russian enclave since 1945. The port is an important centre for the Russian Federation's Baltic fishing fleet.*

◀ *St Basil's Cathedral, completed in 1561, stands in Moscow's Red Square next to the Kremlin; the original fortified stronghold of the city.*

Southern European Russia

This region, divided from Asia by desert, seas and mountains, has exerted a powerful influence both east and west since the 13th century. Over 70 years of Communist rule produced a highly urbanized, industrial society dominated by Moscow, which was the capital of the Soviet Union until 1991. Almost two-thirds of the Russian Federation's population live in this core area, with a relatively high *per capita* share of its wealth. However, the rapid growth of a market economy has caused great social upheaval, with rising crime and political instability.

The landscape

Ancient folds in the deep sedimentary strata of the North European Plain have created a sequence of high and low regions. The Central Russian Upland *(Srednerusskaya Vozvyshennost')* in the west is deeply incised by rivers draining into the lowland of the Oka and Don rivers. In the east the Volga, Europe's longest river, flows south to the Caspian Sea, dividing the Volga Uplands *(Privolzhskaya Vozvyshennost')* from the foothills of the Ural Mountains *(Ural'skiye Gory)*. The Caucasus mountains and the Black Sea form a natural border to the southwest.

▲ *A plantation of* Scots pine helps *consolidate the loose sandy soils of the Meshchera Lowland* (Meshcherskaya Nizina), *which lies on the bed of an old glacial lake.*

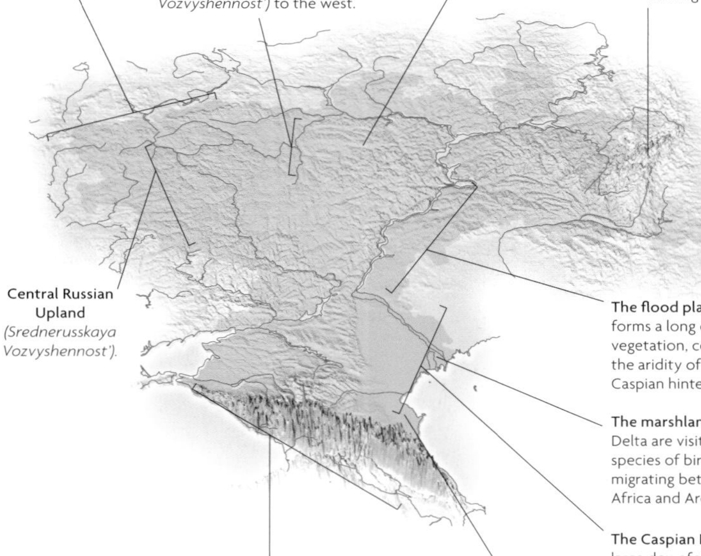

The Smolensk-Moscow Upland *(Smolensko-Moskovskaya Vozvyshennost')* is a series of terminal moraine ridges marking the southern extent of the last glaciation.

Glacial till covers the bedrock to the north of the North European Plain, giving a gentle surface relief.

The lowland of the Oka and Don rivers lies over a broad trough, between the upfolds of the Volga Uplands *(Privolzhskaya Vozvyshennost')* to the east, and the Central Russian Upland *(Srednerusskaya Vozvyshennost')* to the west.

The southern Ural Mountains *(Ural'skiye Gory)* consist of several parallel ranges of ancient fold mountains running from north to south.

Central Russian Upland *(Srednerusskaya Vozvyshennost')*.

The flood plain of the Volga forms a long oasis of verdant vegetation, contrasting with the aridity of the surrounding Caspian hinterland.

The marshlands of the Volga Delta are visited by over 260 species of bird each year, migrating between South Africa and Arctic Siberia.

The Caspian Depression is a large downfold (or syncline) which became flooded, forming the Caspian Sea. The shoreline is 98 ft (30 m) below sea level.

Drifting sand occupies large areas of the south, forming dunes up to 50 ft (15 m) high.

◀ *The Caucasus mountains run from the Black Sea to the Caspian Sea. They include El'brus which, at 18,511 ft (5642 m), is the highest point in Europe. It is still uplifting at a rate of 0.4 inches (10 mm) per year.*

Salt dome

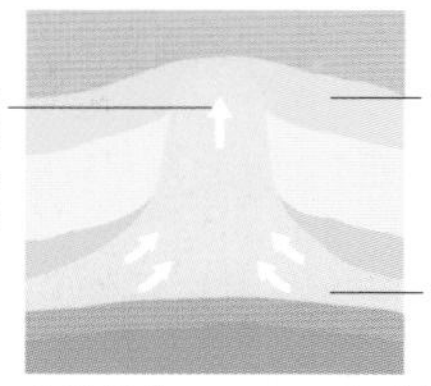

Salt dome is forced up and through the rock strata

Sedimentary strata

Salts are forced upwards by denser overlying strata

▲ *Salt domes, rounded* hills up to 500 ft (150 m) high, *are produced as less dense rock salts are displaced under the extreme pressure of denser, overlying strata and forced up towards the surface creating domes. They are widespread in the Caspian Depression.*

Scale 1:5,500,000
Km 0 10 20 40 60 80 100 120 140
Miles 0 10 20 40 60 80 100 120 140
projection: Lambert Conformal Conic
Map key
Population
above 5 million
1 million to 5 million
500,000 to 1 million
100,000 to 500,000
50,000 to 100,000
10,000 to 50,000
below 10,000
Elevation
4000m / 13,124ft
3000m / 9843ft
2000m / 6562ft
1000m / 3281ft
500m / 1640ft
250m / 820ft
100m / 328ft
sea level
RUSSIAN FEDERATION
KAZAKHSTAN
GEORGIA
AZERBAIJAN
NIZHEGORODSKAYA OBLAST'
KIROVSKAYA OBLAST'
UDMURTSKAYA RESPUBLIKA
PERMSKAYA OBLAST'
SVERDLOVSKAYA OBLAST'
CHELYABINSKAYA OBLAST'
RESPUBLIKA MARIY EL
CHUVASHSKAYA RESPUBLIKA
RESPUBLIKA TATARSTAN
RESPUBLIKA BASHKORTOSTAN
RESPUBLIKA MORDOVIYA
UL'YANOVSKAYA OBLAST'
PENZENSKAYA OBLAST'
SAMARSKAYA OBLAST'
ORENBURGSKAYA OBLAST'
SARATOVSKAYA OBLAST'
VOLGOGRADSKAYA OBLAST'
ASTRAKHANSKAYA OBLAST'
RESPUBLIKA KALMYKIYA
STAVROPOL'SKIY KRAY
CHECHENSKAYA RESPUBLIKA
RESPUBLIKA DAGESTAN
Ural'skiye Gory
Caspian Depression
Caspian Sea
Nizhniy Novgorod
Kazan'
Izhevsk
Ufa
Samara
Tol'yatti
Saratov
Volgograd
Astrakhan'
Orenburg
Penza
Ul'yanovsk
Saransk
Cheboksary
Naberezhnyye Chelny
Orsk
Elista
Groznyy
Makhachkala
Nal'chik
Vladikavkaz
136
144

Using the land

In the cold, humid north and in the southern Urals *(Ural'skiye Gory)*, small grains, potatoes and flax are commonly rotated with legumes which support livestock farming. The rich chernozem (or black earth) areas support diverse crops such as sugar beet, hemp, sunflowers, millet and vegetables. Further south, aridity restricts husbandry to extensive grazing, with intensive fruit and rice cultivation along the oasis of the Volga.

The urban/rural population divide

urban 71% | rural 29%

Population density	Total land area
119 people per sq mile (46 people per sq km)	705,916 sq miles (1,828,800 sq km)

Land use and agricultural distribution

sheep
flax
potatoes
rice
sunflowers
sugar beet
timber
capital cities
major towns
pasture
cropland
forest
wetland
mountain region
tundra
RUSSIAN FEDERATION
MOSCOW
Nizhniy Novgorod
Ufa
Samara
Voronezh
Orsk
Rostov-na-Donu
Astrakhan'
Groznyy
Sea of Azov
Caspian Sea
BLACK SEA
BELARUS
UKRAINE
KAZAKHSTAN
GEORGIA
AZERB.

Transport and industry

Manufacturing is largely based around Moscow and the Volga region, which became a major industrial area during the Second World War. Both Moscow and Nizhniy Novgorod are centres of skilled labour for light manufacturing and engineering. Most of Russia's main chemical plants are located along the Volga, and one of the world's largest car factories was recently opened in Tol'yatti. Processing and machine construction plants use oil, gas and hydro-electric power from the Volga Basin and metallic minerals from the Urals *(Ural'skiye Gory)* and Kursk.

Industrial plants are massed along the Volga. Environmental stress from decades of unbridled industrial development has prompted widespread concern about pollution levels.

The transport network

250,000 miles (402,000 km)	None
28,000 miles (44,800 km)	16,300 miles (26,080 km)

Seventy private and national flag airlines have been created from the reorganization of the state airline Aeroflot, which maintained the world's largest fleet of aircraft during the Soviet era.

Major industry and infrastructure

aerospace
car manufacture
chemicals
defence
electronics
engineering
gas
mining
oil
textiles
capital cities
major towns
international airports
major roads
major industrial areas
RUSSIAN FEDERATION
MOSCOW
Nizhniy Novgorod
Kazan'
Ufa
Ul'yanovsk
Tol'yatti
Samara
Penza
Ryazan'
Tula
Bryansk
Kursk
Voronezh
Saratov
Belgorod
Volgograd
Orsk
Rostov-na-Donu
Stavropol'
Astrakhan'
Groznyy
Sea of Azov
Caspian Sea
BLACK SEA
BELARUS
UKRAINE
KAZAKHSTAN
GEORGIA
AZERB.

Asia

Asia, the world's largest continent, covers 16,838,365 sq miles (43,608,000 sq km). It comprises 49 separate countries, including 97% of Turkey and 72% of the Russian Federation. Almost 60% of the world's population lives in Asia.

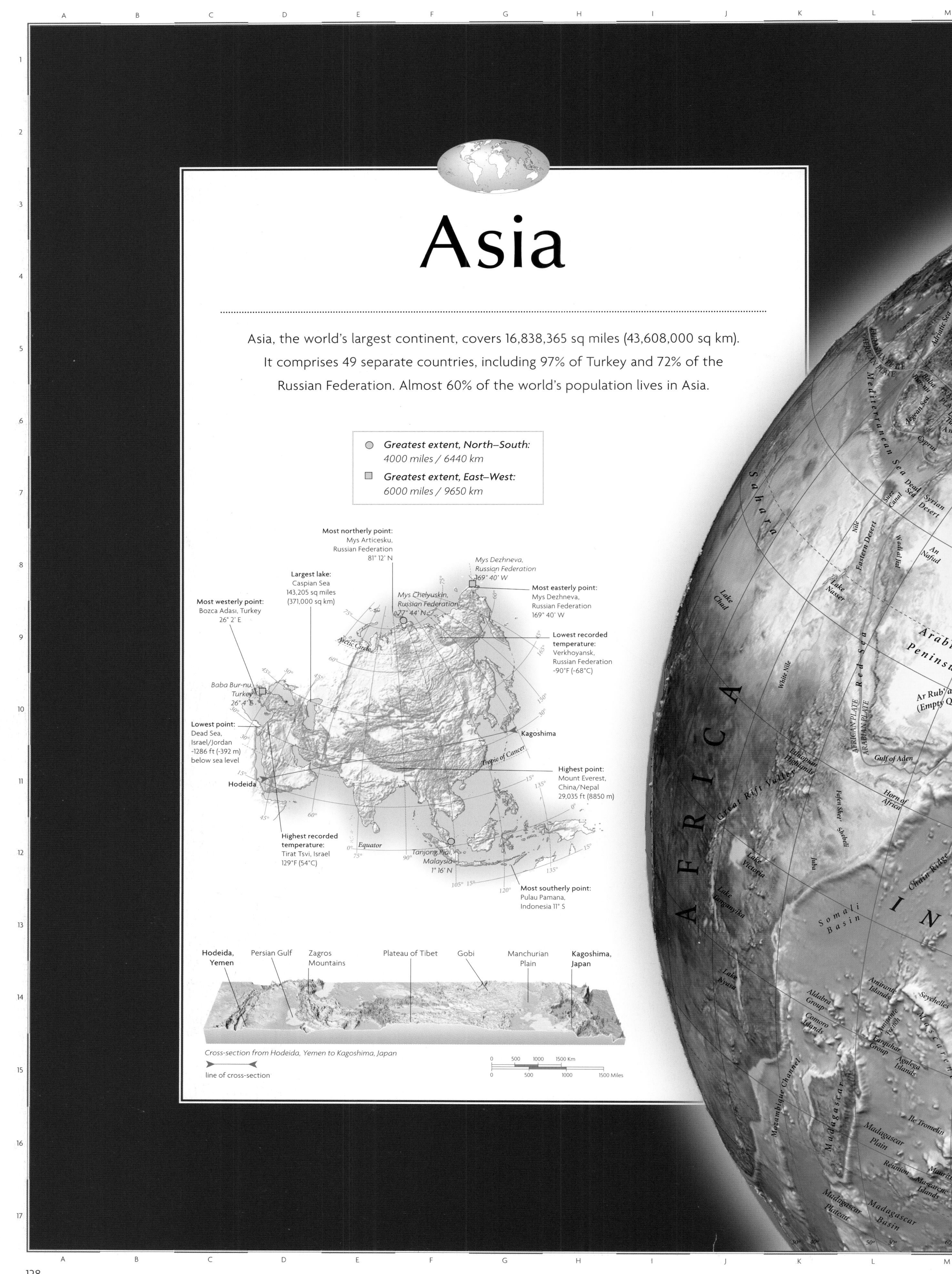

Greatest extent, North–South: 4000 miles / 6440 km
Greatest extent, East–West: 6000 miles / 9650 km
Most northerly point: Mys Articesku, Russian Federation 81° 12′ N
Largest lake: Caspian Sea 143,205 sq miles (371,000 sq km)
Most westerly point: Bozca Adası, Turkey 26° 2′ E
Mys Dezhneva, Russian Federation 169° 40′ W
Most easterly point: Mys Dezhneva, Russian Federation 169° 40′ W
Mys Chelyuskin, Russian Federation 77° 44′ N
Lowest recorded temperature: Verkhoyansk, Russian Federation -90°F (-68°C)
Arctic Circle
Baba Bur-nu, Turkey 26° 4′ E
Lowest point: Dead Sea, Israel/Jordan -1286 ft (-392 m) below sea level
Kagoshima
Tropic of Cancer
Highest point: Mount Everest, China/Nepal 29,035 ft (8850 m)
Hodeida
Highest recorded temperature: Tirat Tsvi, Israel 129°F (54°C)
Equator
Tanjong Piai, Malaysia 1° 16′ N
Most southerly point: Pulau Pamana, Indonesia 11° S
Hodeida, Yemen
Persian Gulf
Zagros Mountains
Plateau of Tibet
Gobi
Manchurian Plain
Kagoshima, Japan
Cross-section from Hodeida, Yemen to Kagoshima, Japan
line of cross-section
0 500 1000 1500 Km
0 500 1000 1500 Miles
AFRICA
Sahara
Mediterranean Sea
Red Sea
Arabian Peninsula
Gulf of Aden
Horn of Africa
Great Rift Valley
Ethiopian Highlands
Lake Chad
Lake Nasser
Lake Victoria
Lake Tanganyika
Lake Nyasa
Somali Basin
Madagascar
Mozambique Channel
Madagascar Plain
Madagascar Basin
Madagascar Plateau
Seychelles
Réunion

N O P Q R S T U V W X Y Z
ARCTIC OCEAN
North Pole
NORTH AMERICAN PLATE
EURASIAN PLATE
Franz Josef Land
Norwegian Sea
Scandinavia
North Sea
Gulf of Bothnia
Baltic Sea
Gulf of Finland
Lake Ladoga
Lake Onega
Lake Peipus
White Sea
Kola Peninsula
North Cape
Barents Sea
Novaya Zemlya
Kara Sea
Severnaya Zemlya
Mys Chelyuskin
Laptev Sea
New Siberian Islands
East Siberian Sea
Long Strait
Bering Strait
Chukot Range
Bering Sea
Koryak Range
Poluostrov Taymyr
Poluostrov Yamal
Gydanskiy Poluostrov
North Siberian Lowland
Putorana Mountains
Central Siberian Plateau
Lower Tunguska
Stony Tunguska
Khrebet Cherskogo
Kolyma Range
Verkhoyanskiy Khrebet
North European Plain
Central Russian Upland
EUROPE
Ural Mountains
West Siberian Plain
Siberia
Sea of Azov
Black Sea
Caspian Depression
Caspian Sea
Caucasus
Aral Sea
Ustyurt Plateau
Kirghiz Steppe
Lake Balkhash
Lake Zaysan
Lake Chany
Turan Lowland
Kara Kum
Lake Van
Elburz Mountains
Dasht-e Kavir
Dasht-e Lut
Great Salt Desert
Zagros Mountains
Iranian Plateau
EURASIAN PLATE
IRANIAN PLATE
Kuh-e Fuladi 5143m
Kuh-e-Baba
Hindu Kush
Karakoram Range
Pamirs
Tien Shan
Dzungaria
Altai Mountains
Sayanskiy Khrebet
Lake Baikal
Yablonovyy Khrebet
Stanovoy Khrebet
Zeya Reservoir
Sea of Okhotsk
Kamchatka
Aleutian Basin
Kurile Islands
Kurile Trench
Sakhalin
ASIA
Tarim Basin
Takla Makan Desert
Lop Nur
Gobi
Plateau of Mongolia
Great Khingan Range
Manchurian Plain
Lake Khanka
Hokkaido
Sea of Japan (East Sea)
Japan
Japan Trench
Honshu
Shikoku
Kyushu
PACIFIC OCEAN
Altun Shan
Kunlun Mountains
Plateau of Tibet
Qilian Shan
Nan Shan
Ordos Desert
Qinghai Hu
Bo Hai
Korea Bay
Yellow Sea
Cheju-do
Korea Strait
Great Plain of China
Himalayas
Annapurna 8091m
Mount Everest 8850m
Thar Desert
Punjab Plains
Sulaiman Range
Rigestan
Hamun Jaz Murian
Strait of Hormuz
Gulf of Oman
Central Makran Range
Gulf of Kachchh
Vindhya Range
Satpura Range
Gulf of Khambhat
Ajanta Range
Deccan
Western Ghats
Eastern Ghats
Malabar Coast
Coromandel Coast
Arabian Sea
Arabian Basin
Laccadive Islands
Cape Comorin
Gulf of Mannar
Sri Lanka
Maldives
Mouths of the Ganges
Khasi Hills
Patkai Range
Arakan Yoma
Bay of Bengal
East China Sea
Ryukyu Islands
Taiwan Strait
Taiwan
Hainan Strait
Gulf of Tongking
Hainan
Luzon Strait
Philippine Sea
Philippine Basin
Kyushu-Palau Ridge
Gulf of Martaban
Andaman Islands
Andaman Sea
Nicobar Islands
Isthmus of Kra
Gulf of Thailand
Tonle Sap
Mouths of the Mekong
South China Sea
South China Basin
Luzon
Mindoro
Panay
Negros
Palawan
Sulu Sea
Mindanao
Philippine Trench
Malay Peninsula
Strait of Malacca
Danau Toba
Anambas Islands
Natuna Islands
Sunda Shelf
Gunung Kinabalu 4094m
Celebes Sea
Borneo
Greater Sunda Islands
Makassar Strait
Celebes
Molucca Sea
Moluccas
Halmahera
New Guinea Trench
Tanjong Piai
Gunung Kerinci 3805m
Pulau Bangka
Sumatra
Mentawai Ridge
Selat Sunda
Java Sea
East Indies
Java
Bali
Flores Sea
Lesser Sunda Islands
Banda Sea
Timor
Timor Trough
Arafura Sea
Torres Strait
AUSTRALIA
Sunda Trough
Java Trench
Christmas Island
Cocos Islands
Investigator Ridge
Ninetyeast Ridge
Cocos Basin
Mid-Indian Basin
Ceylon Plain
Nikitin Seamount
Chagos Bank
Chagos Trench
Chagos-Laccadive Plateau
INDIAN OCEAN
INDO-AUSTRALIAN PLATE
Tropic of Cancer
Equator

Physical Asia

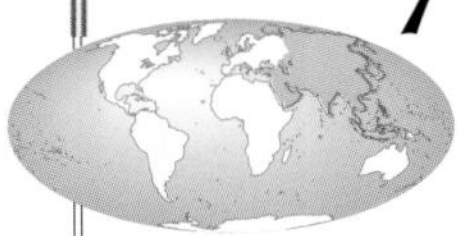

The structure of Asia can be divided into two distinct regions. The landscape of northern Asia consists of old mountain chains, shields, plateaux and basins, like the Ural Mountains in the west and the Central Siberian Plateau to the east. To the south of this region, are a series of plateaux and basins, including the vast Plateau of Tibet and the Tarim Basin. In contrast, the landscapes of southern Asia are much younger, formed by tectonic activity beginning about 65 million years ago, leading to an almost continuous mountain chain running from Europe, across much of Asia, and culminating in the mighty Himalayan mountain belt, formed when the Indo-Australian Plate collided with the Eurasian Plate. They are still being uplifted today. North of the mountains lies a belt of deserts, including the Gobi and the Takla Makan. In the far south, tectonic activity has formed narrow island arcs, extending over 4000 miles (7000 km). To the west lies the Arabian Shield, once part of the African Plate. As it was rifted apart from Africa, the Arabian Plate collided with the Eurasian Plate, uplifting the Zagros Mountains.

Coastal Lowlands and Island Arcs

The coastal plains that fringe Southeast Asia contain many large delta systems, caused by high levels of rainfall and erosion of the Himalayas, the Plateau of Tibet and relict loess deposits. To the south is an extensive island archipelago, lying on the drowned Sunda Shelf. Most of these islands are volcanic in origin, caused by the subduction of the Indo-Australian Plate beneath the Eurasian Plate.

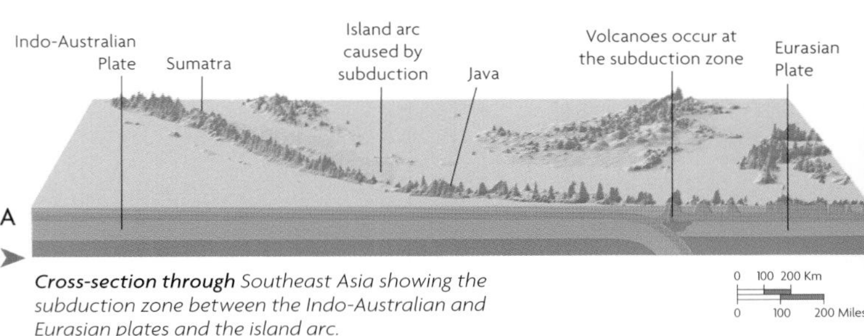
Indo-Australian Plate
Sumatra
Island arc caused by subduction
Java
Volcanoes occur at the subduction zone
Eurasian Plate
A

***Cross-section through** Southeast Asia showing the subduction zone between the Indo-Australian and Eurasian plates and the island arc.*

0 100 200 Km
0 100 200 Miles

The Indian Shield and Himalayan System

The large shield area beneath the Indian subcontinent is between 2.5 and 3.5 billion years old. As the floor of the southern Indian Ocean spread, it pushed the Indian Shield north. This was eventually driven beneath the Plateau of Tibet. This process closed up the ancient Tethys Sea and uplifted the world's highest mountain chain, the Himalayas. Much of the uplifted rock strata was from the seabed of the Tethys Sea, partly accounting for the weakness of the rocks and the high levels of erosion found in the Himalayas.

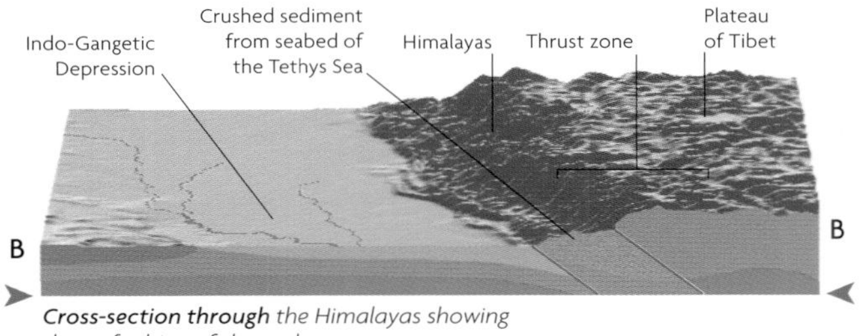

Indo-Gangetic Depression
Crushed sediment from seabed of the Tethys Sea
Himalayas
Thrust zone
Plateau of Tibet
B
B

***Cross-section through** the Himalayas showing thrust faulting of the rock strata.*

0 50 100 Km
0 50 100 Miles

East Asian Plains and Uplands

Several, small, isolated shield areas, such as the Shandong Peninsula, are found in east Asia. Between these stable shield areas, large river systems like the Yangtze and the Yellow River have deposited thick layers of sediment, forming extensive alluvial plains. The largest of these is the Great Plain of China, the relief of which does not rise above 300 ft (100 m).

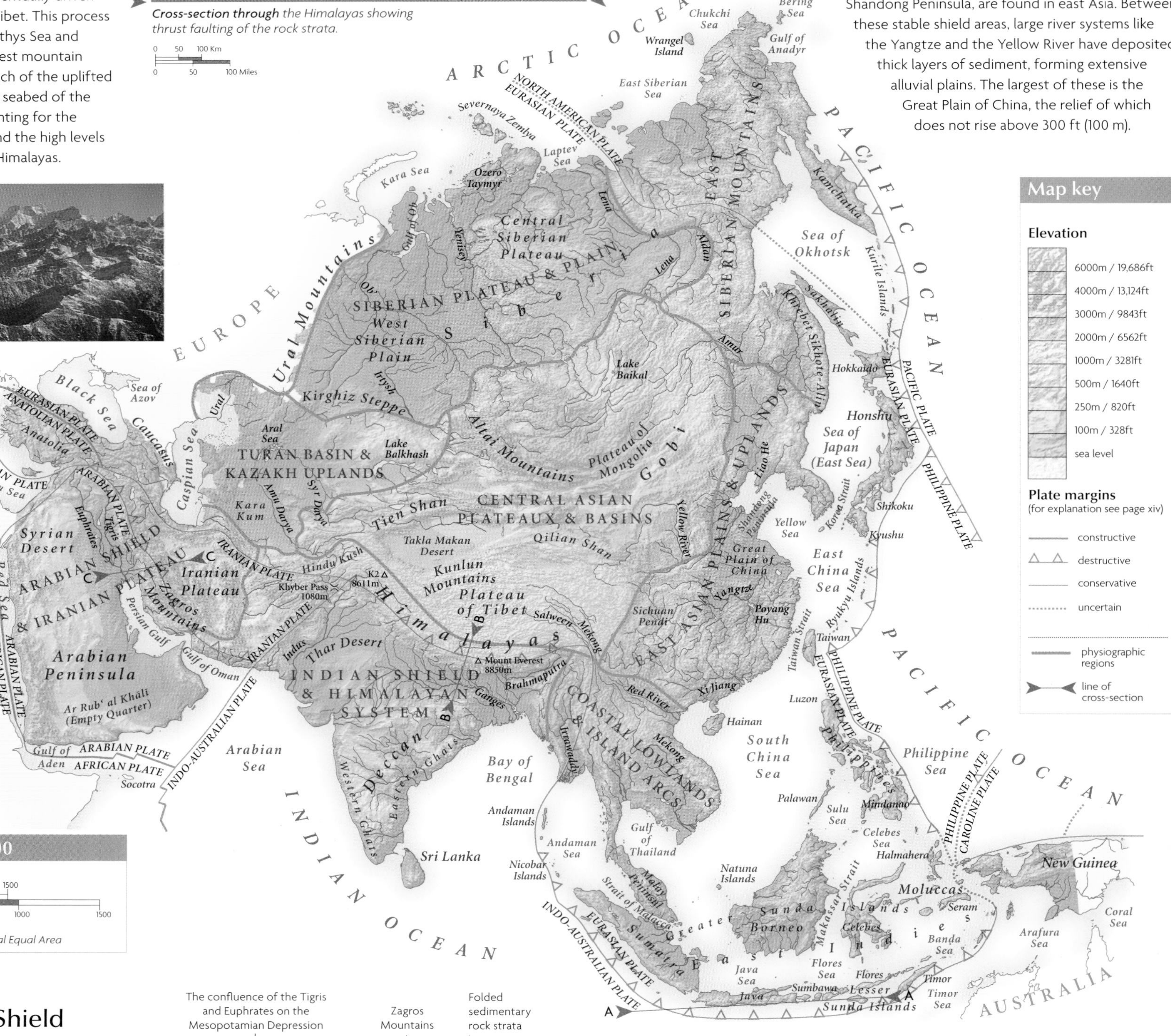

Map key

Elevation

6000m / 19,686ft
4000m / 13,124ft
3000m / 9843ft
2000m / 6562ft
1000m / 3281ft
500m / 1640ft
250m / 820ft
100m / 328ft
sea level

Plate margins
(for explanation see page xiv)

constructive
destructive
conservative
uncertain
physiographic regions
line of cross-section

Scale 1:56,750,000

Km 0 250 500 1000 1500
Miles 0 250 500 1000 1500

projection: Lambert Azimuthal Equal Area

The Arabian Shield and Iranian Plateau

Approximately five million years ago, rifting of the continental crust split the Arabian Plate from the African Plate and flooded the Red Sea. As this rift spread, the Arabian Plate collided with the Eurasian Plate, transforming part of the Tethys seabed into the Zagros Mountains which run northwest-southeast across western Iran.

The confluence of the Tigris and Euphrates on the Mesopotamian Depression
Zagros Mountains
Folded sedimentary rock strata
Iranian Plateau
C
C

***Cross-section through** southwestern Asia, showing the Mesopotamian Depression, the folded Zagros Mountains and the Iranian Plateau.*

0 50 100 Km
0 50 100 Miles

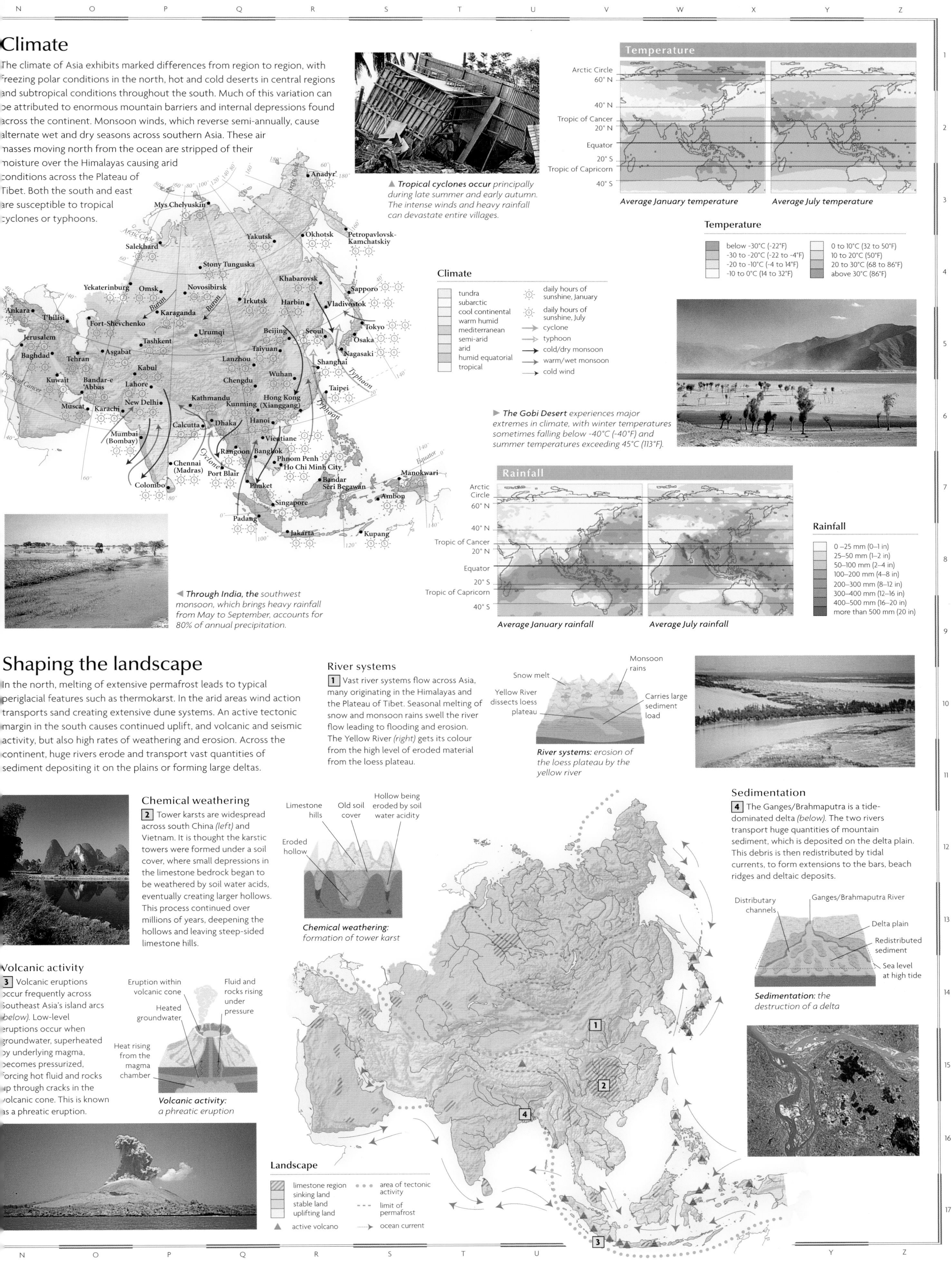
N O P Q R S T U V W X Y Z
1 2 3 4 5 6 7 8 9 10 11 12 13 14 15 16 17
Temperature
Arctic Circle 60° N
40° N
Tropic of Cancer 20° N
Equator
20° S
Tropic of Capricorn
40° S
Average January temperature
Average July temperature
Temperature
below -30°C (-22°F)
-30 to -20°C (-22 to -4°F)
-20 to -10°C (-4 to 14°F)
-10 to 0°C (14 to 32°F)
0 to 10°C (32 to 50°F)
10 to 20°C (50°F)
20 to 30°C (68 to 86°F)
above 30°C (86°F)
Climate
tundra
subarctic
cool continental
warm humid
mediterranean
semi-arid
arid
humid equatorial
tropical
daily hours of sunshine, January
daily hours of sunshine, July
cyclone
typhoon
cold/dry monsoon
warm/wet monsoon
cold wind
Rainfall
Arctic Circle 60° N
40° N
Tropic of Cancer 20° N
Equator
20° S
Tropic of Capricorn
40° S
Average January rainfall
Average July rainfall
Rainfall
0 –25 mm (0–1 in)
25–50 mm (1–2 in)
50–100 mm (2–4 in)
100–200 mm (4–8 in)
200–300 mm (8–12 in)
300–400 mm (12–16 in)
400–500 mm (16–20 in)
more than 500 mm (20 in)
Snow melt
Monsoon rains
Yellow River dissects loess plateau
Carries large sediment load
Limestone hills
Old soil cover
Hollow being eroded by soil water acidity
Eroded hollow
Eruption within volcanic cone
Fluid and rocks rising under pressure
Heated groundwater
Heat rising from the magma chamber
Distributary channels
Ganges/Brahmaputra River
Delta plain
Redistributed sediment
Sea level at high tide
Landscape
limestone region
sinking land
stable land
uplifting land
active volcano
area of tectonic activity
limit of permafrost
ocean current

Climate

The climate of Asia exhibits marked differences from region to region, with freezing polar conditions in the north, hot and cold deserts in central regions and subtropical conditions throughout the south. Much of this variation can be attributed to enormous mountain barriers and internal depressions found across the continent. Monsoon winds, which reverse semi-annually, cause alternate wet and dry seasons across southern Asia. These air masses moving north from the ocean are stripped of their moisture over the Himalayas causing arid conditions across the Plateau of Tibet. Both the south and east are susceptible to tropical cyclones or typhoons.

▲ *Tropical cyclones occur principally during late summer and early autumn. The intense winds and heavy rainfall can devastate entire villages.*

► *The Gobi Desert experiences major extremes in climate, with winter temperatures sometimes falling below -40°C (-40°F) and summer temperatures exceeding 45°C (113°F).*

◄ *Through India, the southwest monsoon, which brings heavy rainfall from May to September, accounts for 80% of annual precipitation.*

Shaping the landscape

In the north, melting of extensive permafrost leads to typical periglacial features such as thermokarst. In the arid areas wind action transports sand creating extensive dune systems. An active tectonic margin in the south causes continued uplift, and volcanic and seismic activity, but also high rates of weathering and erosion. Across the continent, huge rivers erode and transport vast quantities of sediment depositing it on the plains or forming large deltas.

River systems

1 Vast river systems flow across Asia, many originating in the Himalayas and the Plateau of Tibet. Seasonal melting of snow and monsoon rains swell the river flow leading to flooding and erosion. The Yellow River *(right)* gets its colour from the high level of eroded material from the loess plateau.

***River systems:** erosion of the loess plateau by the yellow river*

Chemical weathering

2 Tower karsts are widespread across south China *(left)* and Vietnam. It is thought the karstic towers were formed under a soil cover, where small depressions in the limestone bedrock began to be weathered by soil water acids, eventually creating larger hollows. This process continued over millions of years, deepening the hollows and leaving steep-sided limestone hills.

***Chemical weathering:** formation of tower karst*

Volcanic activity

3 Volcanic eruptions occur frequently across Southeast Asia's island arcs *(below)*. Low-level eruptions occur when groundwater, superheated by underlying magma, becomes pressurized, forcing hot fluid and rocks up through cracks in the volcanic cone. This is known as a phreatic eruption.

***Volcanic activity:** a phreatic eruption*

Sedimentation

4 The Ganges/Brahmaputra is a tide-dominated delta *(below)*. The two rivers transport huge quantities of mountain sediment, which is deposited on the delta plain. This debris is then redistributed by tidal currents, to form extensions to the bars, beach ridges and deltaic deposits.

***Sedimentation:** the destruction of a delta*

Political Asia

Asia is the world's largest continent, encompassing many different and discrete realms, from the desert Arab lands of the southwest to the subtropical archipelago of Indonesia; from the vast barren wastes of Siberia to the fertile river valleys of China and South Asia, seats of some of the world's most ancient civilizations. The collapse of the Soviet Union has fragmented the north of the continent into the Siberian portion of the Russian Federation, and the new republics of Central Asia. Strong religious traditions heavily influence the politics of South and Southwest Asia. Hindu and Muslim rivalries threaten to upset the political equilibrium in South Asia where India – in terms of population – remains the world's largest democracy. Communist China, another population giant, is reasserting its position as a world political and economic power, while on its doorstep, the dynamic Pacific Rim countries, led by Japan, continue to assert their worldwide economic force.

Population density
(people per sq km)

- below 9
- 10–49
- 50–99
- 100–249
- 250–3999
- above 4000

Population

Some of the world's most populous and least populous regions are in Asia. The plains of eastern China, the Ganges river plains in India, Japan and the Indonesian island of Java, all have very high population densities; by contrast parts of Siberia and the Plateau of Tibet are virtually uninhabited. China has the world's greatest population – 20% of the globe's total – while India, with the second largest, is likely to overtake China within 30 years.

◀ ***Kolkata's 13 million*** *inhabitants bustle through a maze of crowded, narrow streets. Population densities in India's largest city reach almost 85,000 per sq mile (33,000 per sq km).*

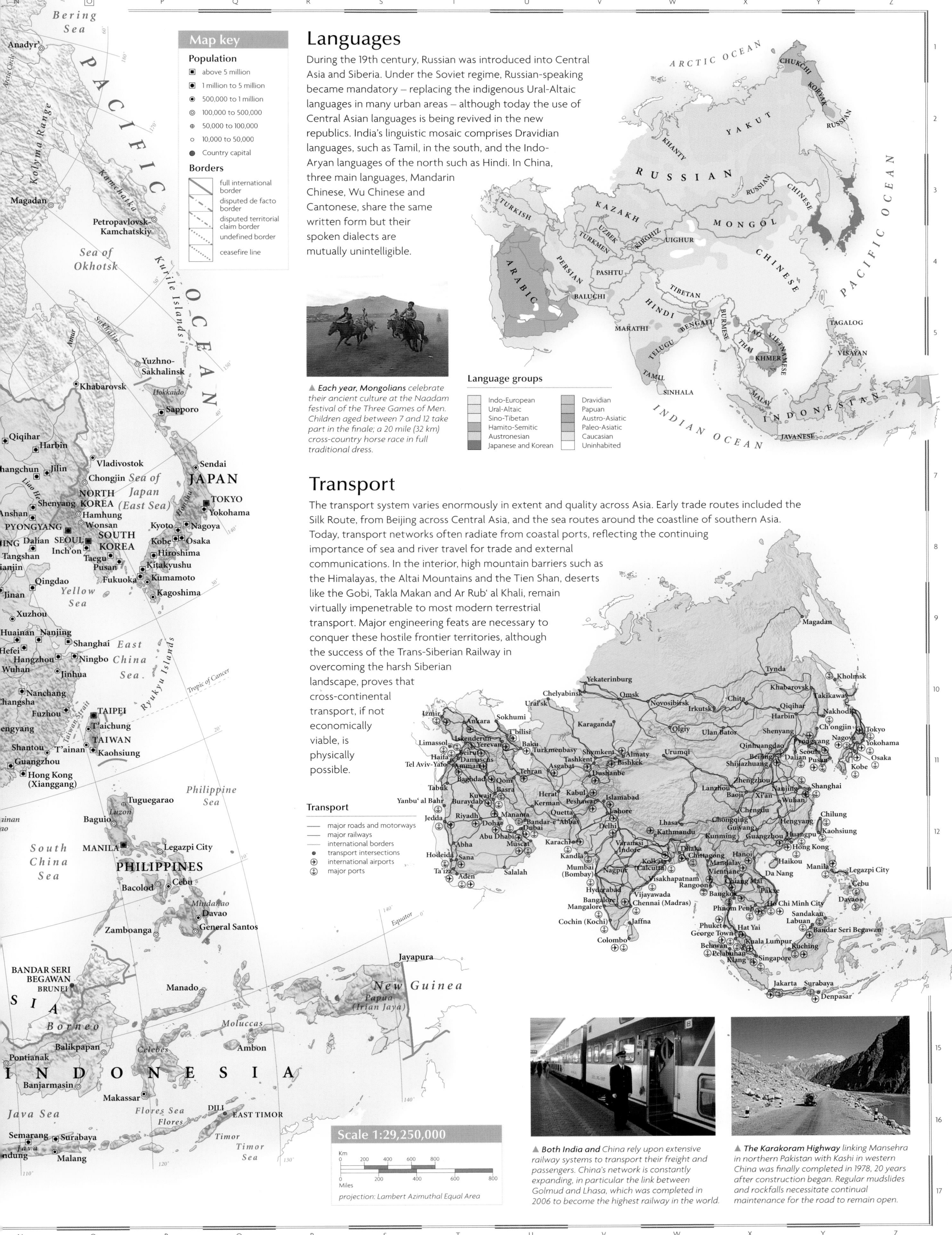

Map key
Population
above 5 million
1 million to 5 million
500,000 to 1 million
100,000 to 500,000
50,000 to 100,000
10,000 to 50,000
Country capital
Borders
full international border
disputed de facto border
disputed territorial claim border
undefined border
ceasefire line
Language groups
Indo-European
Ural-Altaic
Sino-Tibetan
Hamito-Semitic
Austronesian
Japanese and Korean
Dravidian
Papuan
Austro-Asiatic
Paleo-Asiatic
Caucasian
Uninhabited
Transport
major roads and motorways
major railways
international borders
transport intersections
international airports
major ports
Scale 1:29,250,000
projection: Lambert Azimuthal Equal Area

Languages

During the 19th century, Russian was introduced into Central Asia and Siberia. Under the Soviet regime, Russian-speaking became mandatory – replacing the indigenous Ural-Altaic languages in many urban areas – although today the use of Central Asian languages is being revived in the new republics. India's linguistic mosaic comprises Dravidian languages, such as Tamil, in the south, and the Indo-Aryan languages of the north such as Hindi. In China, three main languages, Mandarin Chinese, Wu Chinese and Cantonese, share the same written form but their spoken dialects are mutually unintelligible.

▲ *Each year, Mongolians celebrate their ancient culture at the Naadam festival of the Three Games of Men. Children aged between 7 and 12 take part in the finale; a 20 mile (32 km) cross-country horse race in full traditional dress.*

Transport

The transport system varies enormously in extent and quality across Asia. Early trade routes included the Silk Route, from Beijing across Central Asia, and the sea routes around the coastline of southern Asia. Today, transport networks often radiate from coastal ports, reflecting the continuing importance of sea and river travel for trade and external communications. In the interior, high mountain barriers such as the Himalayas, the Altai Mountains and the Tien Shan, deserts like the Gobi, Takla Makan and Ar Rub' al Khali, remain virtually impenetrable to most modern terrestrial transport. Major engineering feats are necessary to conquer these hostile frontier territories, although the success of the Trans-Siberian Railway in overcoming the harsh Siberian landscape, proves that cross-continental transport, if not economically viable, is physically possible.

▲ ***Both India and** China rely upon extensive railway systems to transport their freight and passengers. China's network is constantly expanding, in particular the link between Golmud and Lhasa, which was completed in 2006 to become the highest railway in the world.*

▲ ***The Karakoram Highway** linking Mansehra in northern Pakistan with Kashi in western China was finally completed in 1978, 20 years after construction began. Regular mudslides and rockfalls necessitate continual maintenance for the road to remain open.*

Asian resources

Although agriculture remains the economic mainstay of most Asian countries, the number of people employed in agriculture has steadily declined, as new industries have been developed during the past 30 years. China, Indonesia, Malaysia, Thailand and Turkey have all experienced far-reaching structural change in their economies, while the breakup of the Soviet Union has created a new economic challenge in the Central Asian republics. The countries of the Persian Gulf illustrate the rapid transformation from rural nomadism to modern, urban society which oil wealth has brought to parts of the continent. Asia's most economically dynamic countries, Japan, Singapore, South Korea, and Taiwan, fringe the Pacific Ocean and are known as the Pacific Rim. In contrast, other Southeast Asian countries like Laos and Cambodia remain both economically and industrially underdeveloped.

Standard of living

Despite Japan's high standards of living, and Southwest Asia's oil-derived wealth, immense disparities exist across the continent. Afghanistan remains one of the world's most underdeveloped nations, as do the mountain states of Nepal and Bhutan. Further rapid population growth is exacerbating poverty and overcrowding in many parts of India and Bangladesh.

Standard of living
(UN human development index)

low
high

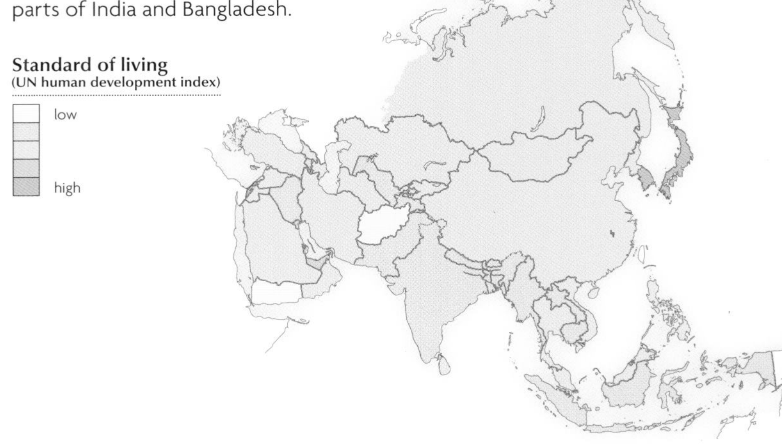

Industry

East Asian industry leads the continent in both productivity and efficiency; electronics, hi-tech industries, car manufacture and shipbuilding are important. The so-called economic 'tigers' of the Pacific Rim are Japan, South Korea and Taiwan and in recent years China has rediscovered its potential as an economic superpower. Heavy industries such as engineering, chemicals, and steel typify the industrial complexes along the corridor created by the Trans-Siberian Railway, the Fergana Valley in Central Asia, and also much of the huge industrial plain of east China. The discovery of oil in the Persian Gulf has brought immense wealth to countries that previously relied on subsistence agriculture on marginal desert land.

Industry

- aerospace
- brewing
- car/vehicle manufacture
- cement
- chemicals
- electronics
- engineering
- finance
- fish processing
- food processing
- hi-tech industry
- iron & steel
- pharmaceuticals
- printing & publishing
- shipbuilding
- sugar processing
- tea processing
- textiles
- timber processing
- tobacco processing
- coal
- oil
- gas
- industrial cities
- major industrial areas

ARCTIC OCEAN
PACIFIC OCEAN
INDIAN OCEAN
RUSSIAN FEDERATION
KAZAKHSTAN
MONGOLIA
CHINA
JAPAN
NORTH KOREA
SOUTH KOREA
TAIWAN
PHILIPPINES
VIETNAM
LAOS
THAILAND
CAMBODIA
BURMA
MALAYSIA
BRUNEI
SINGAPORE
INDONESIA
EAST TIMOR
INDIA
BANGLADESH
BHUTAN
NEPAL
SRI LANKA
PAKISTAN
AFGHANISTAN
TAJIKISTAN
KYRGYZSTAN
UZBEKISTAN
TURKMENISTAN
IRAN
IRAQ
KUWAIT
BAHRAIN
QATAR
UAE
OMAN
YEMEN
SAUDI ARABIA
JORDAN
ISRAEL
LEBANON
SYRIA
CYPRUS
TURKEY
GEORGIA
ARMENIA
AZERB.
Sea of Okhotsk
Aral Sea
Caspian Sea
Red Sea
Persian Gulf
Gulf of Oman
Gulf of Aden
Arabian Sea
South China Sea
Trans-Siberian Railway

Yekaterinburg, Chelyabinsk, Magnitogorsk, Omsk, Novosibirsk, Kemerovo, Krasnoyarsk, Novokuznetsk, Bratsk, Irkutsk, Yakutsk, Khabarovsk, Vladivostok, Karaganda, Almaty, Tashkent, Farghona, Dushanbe, Asgabat, Ulan Bator, Urumqi, Harbin, Shenyang, Beijing, Tianjin, Pyongyang, Dalian, Seoul, Tokyo, Nagoya, Kobe, Pusan, Qingdao, Jinan, Taiyuan, Zhengzhou, Lanzhou, Xi'an, Nanjing, Shanghai, Wuhan, Chengdu, Chongqing, Taipei, Guangzhou, Hong Kong, Kunming, Hanoi, Manila, Da Nang, Ho Chi Minh City, Bangkok, Rangoon, Mandalay, Chittagong, Dhaka, Kolkata (Calcutta), Kanpur, Jamshedpur, Delhi, Lahore, Rawalpindi, Karachi, Ahmadabad, Indore, Nagpur, Mumbai (Bombay), Bangalore, Chennai (Madras), Kuala Lumpur, Singapore, Jakarta, Surabaya, Istanbul, Izmir, Ankara, Tbilisi, Yerevan, Baku, Beirut, Damascus, Tel Aviv-Yafo, Amman, Kirkuk, Baghdad, Basra, Tehran, Isfahan, Kuwait, Ad Damman, Riyadh, Jedda, Abu Dhabi, Dubai

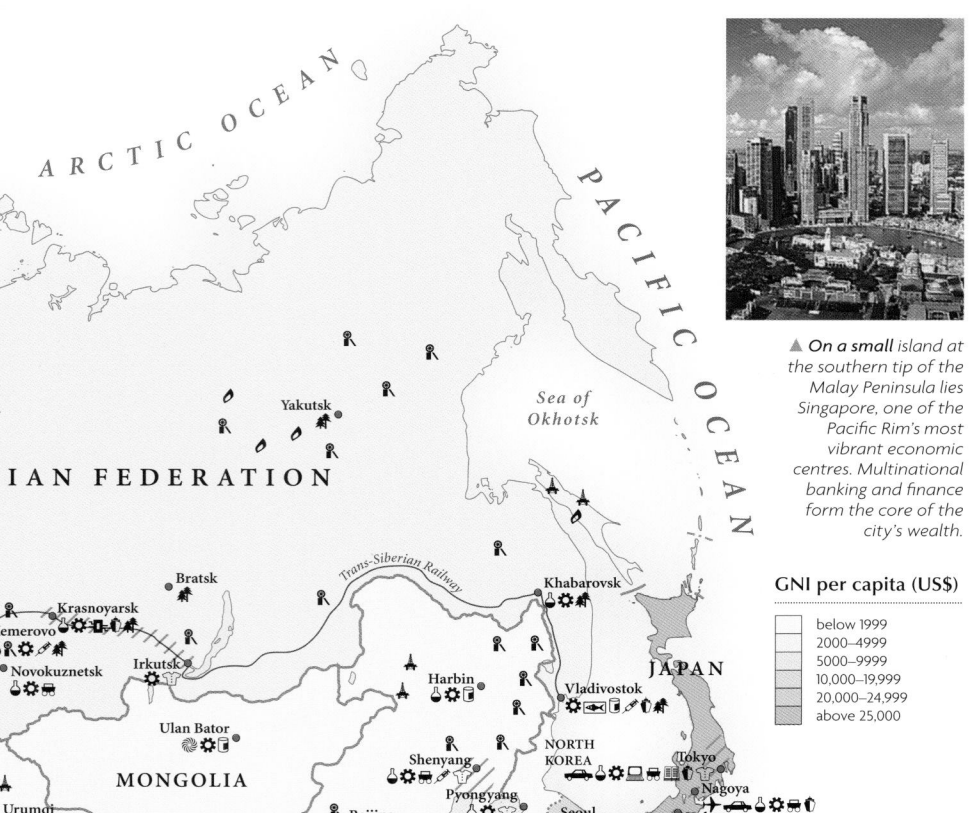

▲ *On a small island at the southern tip of the Malay Peninsula lies Singapore, one of the Pacific Rim's most vibrant economic centres. Multinational banking and finance form the core of the city's wealth.*

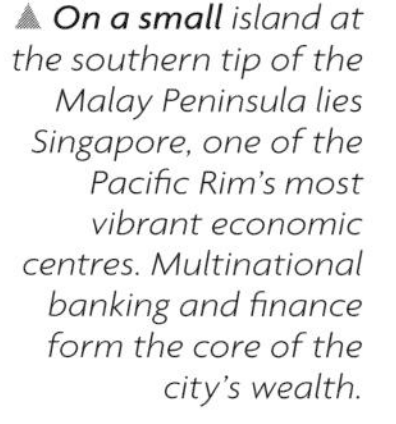

GNI per capita (US$)

- below 1999
- 2000–4999
- 5000–9999
- 10,000–19,999
- 20,000–24,999
- above 25,000

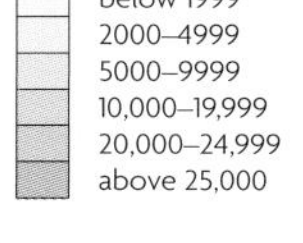

▲ *Iron and steel, engineering and shipbuilding typify the heavy industry found in eastern China's industrial cities, especially the nation's leading manufacturing centre, Shanghai.*

◀ *Traditional industries are still crucial to many rural economies across Asia. Here, on the Vietnamese coast, salt has been extracted from seawater by evaporation and is being loaded into a van to take to market.*

Environmental issues

The transformation of Uzbekistan by the former Soviet Union into the world's fifth largest producer of cotton led to the diversion of several major rivers for irrigation. Starved of this water, the Aral Sea diminished in volume by over 75% since 1960, irreversibly altering the ecology of the area. Heavy industries in eastern China have polluted coastal waters, rivers and urban air, while in Burma, Malaysia and Indonesia, ancient hardwood rainforests are felled faster than they can regenerate.

Environmental issues

- tropical forest
- forest destroyed
- desert
- desertification
- acid rain
- polluted rivers
- marine pollution
- heavy marine pollution
- radioactive contamination
- poor urban air quality

◀ ***The long-term environmental** impact of the Gulf War (1991) is still uncertain. As Iraqi troops left Kuwait, equipment was abandoned to rust and thousands of oil wells were set alight, pouring crude oil into the Persian Gulf.*

▲ ***Although Siberia remains** a quintessentially frozen, inhospitable wasteland, vast untapped mineral reserves – especially the oil and gas of the West Siberian Plain – have lured industrial development to the area since the 1950s and 1960s.*

Mineral resources

At least 60% of the world's known oil and gas deposits are found in Asia; notably the vast oil fields of the Persian Gulf, and the less-exploited oil and gas fields of the Ob' basin in west Siberia. Immense coal reserves in Siberia and China have been utilized to support large steel industries. Southeast Asia has some of the world's largest deposits of tin, found in a belt running down the Malay Peninsula to Indonesia.

Mineral resources

- oil field
- gas field
- coal field
- chromite
- copper
- gold
- iron
- lead
- nickel
- platinum
- tin
- wolfram

Using the land and sea

Vast areas of Asia remain uncultivated as a result of unsuitable climatic and soil conditions. In favourable areas such as river deltas, farming is intensive. Rice is the staple crop of most Asian countries, grown in paddy fields on waterlogged alluvial plains and terraced hillsides, and often irrigated for higher yields. Across the black earth region of the Eurasian steppe in southern Siberia and Kazakhstan, wheat farming is the dominant activity. Cash crops, like tea in Sri Lanka and dates in the Arabian Peninsula, are grown for export, and provide valuable income. The sovereignty of the rich fishing grounds in the South China Sea is disputed by China, Malaysia, Taiwan, the Philippines and Vietnam, because of potential oil reserves.

▲ ***Date palms have** been cultivated in oases throughout the Arabian Peninsula since antiquity. In addition to the fruit, palms are used for timber, fuel, rope, and for making vinegar, syrup and a liquor known as arrack.*

◀ ***Rice terraces blanket** the landscape across the small Indonesian island of Bali. The large amounts of water needed to grow rice have resulted in Balinese farmers organizing water-control co-operatives.*

Using the land and sea

- cropland
- desert
- forest
- mountain region
- pasture
- tundra
- wetland
- major conurbations
- cattle
- pigs
- goats
- sheep
- coconuts
- corn (maize)
- cotton
- dates
- fishing
- fruit
- jute
- peanuts
- rice
- rubber
- shellfish
- soya beans
- sugar beet
- sugar cane
- tea
- timber
- wheat

Turkey & the Caucasus

ARMENIA, AZERBAIJAN, GEORGIA, TURKEY

This region occupies the fragmented junction between Europe, Asia and the Russian Federation. Sunni Islam provides a common identity for the secular state of Turkey, which the revered leader Kemal Atatürk established from the remnants of the Ottoman Empire after the First World War. Turkey has a broad resource base and expanding trade links with Europe, but the east is relatively undeveloped and strife between the state and a large Kurdish minority has yet to be resolved. Georgia is similarly challenged by ethnic separatism, while the Christian state of Armenia and the mainly Muslim and oil-rich Azerbaijan are locked in conflict over the territory of Nagorno-Karabakh.

Using the land and sea

Turkey is largely self-sufficient in food. The irrigated Black Sea coastlands have the world's highest yields of hazelnuts. Tobacco, cotton, sultanas, tea and figs are the region's main cash crops and a great range of fruit and vegetables are grown. Wine grapes are among the labour-intensive crops which allow full use of limited agricultural land in the Caucasus. Sturgeon fishing is particularly important in Azerbaijan.

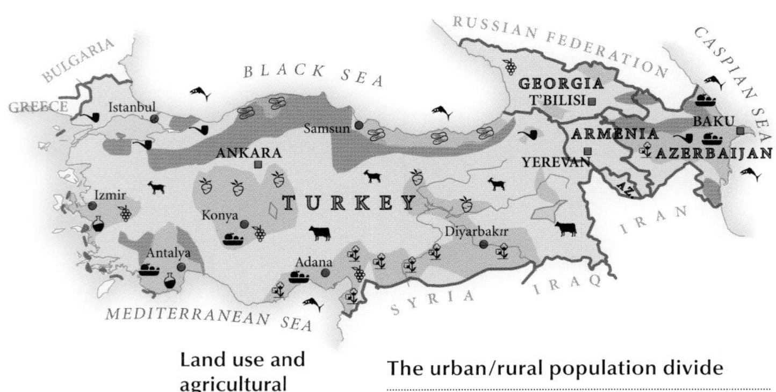

RUSSIAN FEDERATION
CASPIAN SEA
BULGARIA
GREECE
BLACK SEA
Istanbul
GEORGIA
T'BILISI
ARMENIA
BAKU
AZERBAIJAN
YEREVAN
Samsun
ANKARA
Izmir
TURKEY
Konya
Diyarbakır
IRAN
Antalya
Adana
IRAQ
SYRIA
MEDITERRANEAN SEA

Land use and agricultural distribution

- cattle
- goats
- cotton
- fishing
- fruit
- hazelnuts
- olives
- sugar beet
- tobacco
- vineyards
- capital cities
- major towns
- pasture
- cropland
- forest

The urban/rural population divide

urban 72% | rural 28%

0 10 20 30 40 50 60 70 80 90 100

Population density	Total land area
238 people per sq mile (92 people per sq km)	368,912 sq miles (955,730 sq km)

Transport and industry

Turkey leads the region's well-diversified economy. Petrochemicals, textiles, engineering and food processing are the main industries. Azerbaijan is able to export oil, while the other states rely heavily on hydro-electric power and imported fuel. Georgia produces precision machinery. War and earthquake damage have devastated Armenia's infrastructure.

▲ *Azerbaijan has substantial oil reserves, located in and around the Caspian Sea. They were some of the earliest oilfields in the world to be exploited.*

Major industry and infrastructure

- carpet weaving
- cement
- chemicals
- coal
- engineering
- food processing
- oil
- textiles
- tourism
- vehicle manufacture
- capital cities
- major towns
- international airports
- major roads
- major industrial areas

The transport network

- 114,867 miles (184,882 km)
- 5778 miles (9300 km)
- 8120 miles (13,069 km)
- 745 miles (1200 km)

Physical and political barriers have severely limited communications between Armenia, Georgia and Azerbaijan. Turkey has a relatively well-developed transport network.

▲ *For many centuries, Istanbul has held tremendous strategic importance as a crucial gateway between Europe and Asia. Founded by the Greeks as Byzantium, the city became the centre of the East Roman Empire and was known as Constantinople to the Romans. From the 15th century onwards the city became the centre of the great Ottoman Empire.*

BULGARIA
GREECE
BLACK SEA
Aegean Sea
MEDITERRANEAN SEA
Edirne
Kırklareli
Tekirdağ
İstanbul
Marmara Denizi (Sea of Marmara)
İzmit
Adapazarı
Zonguldak
Bursa
Çanakkale
Balıkesir
Eskişehir
Kütahya
Manisa
İzmir
Uşak
Afyon
Aydın
Denizli
Isparta
Burdur
Muğla
Antalya
Konya
Karaman
ANKARA
Kırıkkale
Kastamonu
Sinop
Samsun
Çorum
Amasya
Tokat
Sivas
Yozgat
Kırşehir
Nevşehir
Kayseri
Niğde
Aksaray
Adana
Mersin (İçel)
Osmaniye
Kahramanmaraş
Gaziantep
Antakya
Kilis
Tuz Gölü
Beyşehir Gölü
Eğirdir Gölü
Anadolu
Toros Dağları
Köroğlu Dağları
Küre Dağları

114
114
120

The landscape

The deeply-eroded hills and salty basins of the Anatolian Plateau are bordered by several mountain ranges along the Black Sea coast, and the limestone Taurus Mountains *(Toros Daglari)* in the south. A lowland trough divides the Caucasus and the Lesser Caucasus, which form a formidable barrier of peaks in the north.

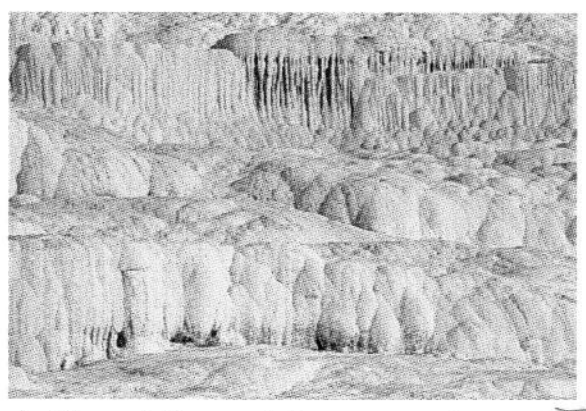

Limestone weathering in the Anatolian Plateau

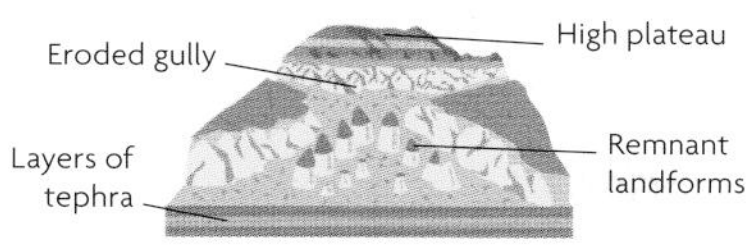

Eroded gully
High plateau
Layers of tephra
Remnant landforms

▲ ***In central Turkey,*** *rainwater has chemically weathered away numerous layers of limestone, leaving isolated outcrops and pinnacles and deep eroded gullies.*

► ***The Caucasus are*** *fold mountains, which formed around the same time as the Taurus Mountains* (Toros Daglari) *around 65 million years ago and have since been modified by volcanic eruptions.*

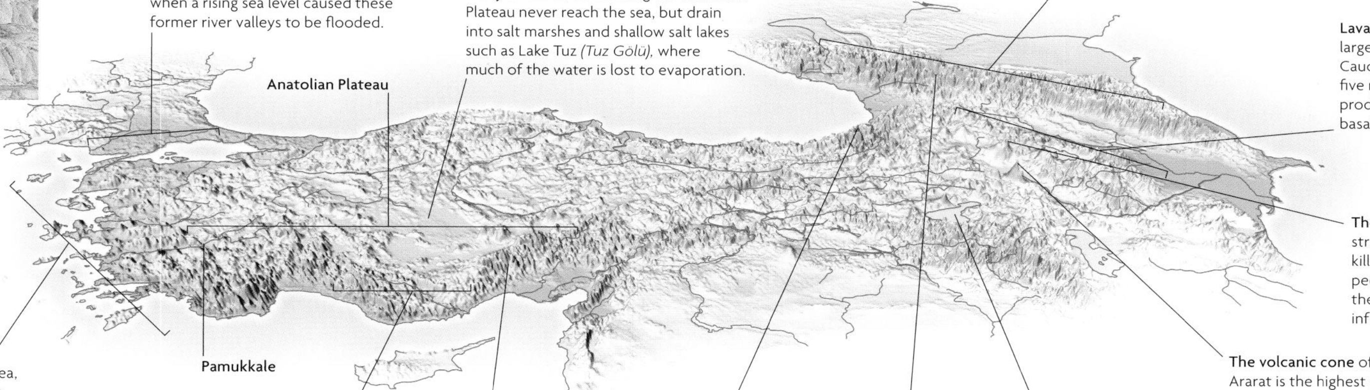

▲ ***The white rock terraces*** *at Pamukkale in western Turkey were formed when underground water, heated by volcanic activity, dissolved minerals in the rocks. When the water reached the surface and evaporated the minerals were left behind in these extraordinary formations.*

The straits of the Bosporus and the Dardanelles, respectively linking the Black and Mediterranean seas with the Sea of Marmara, formed after the last Ice Age, when a rising sea level caused these former river valleys to be flooded.

Many of the rivers crossing the Anatolian Plateau never reach the sea, but drain into salt marshes and shallow salt lakes such as Lake Tuz *(Tuz Gölü)*, where much of the water is lost to evaporation.

Anatolian Plateau

Lava has flowed over large areas of the Lesser Caucasus within the last five million years, producing extensive basalt plateaux.

The earthquake that struck Armenia in 1988 killed over 55,000 people and devastated the country's infrastructure.

Long, parallel mountain ranges run from east to west into the Aegean Sea, which has risen since the last Ice Age to form a drowned coastline of numerous islands and extended inlets.

Pamukkale

The volcanic cone of Mount Ararat is the highest peak in Turkey, with an altitude of 16,853 ft (5137 m).

The folded peaks of the Taurus Mountains *(Toros Daglari)* were formed 60–65 million years ago, at the same time as the Alps. The rock is mainly limestone, with deep caves, gorges and underground rivers.

The Cilician Gates *(Gülek Bogazi)*, a major pass through the Taurus Mountains *(Toros Daglari)*, is the point where streams flow from the interior plateau onto the lowland of Adana.

Thick, temperate forest veils the seaward slopes of the Kaçkar Daglari. The southern slopes, which lie in a rainshadow, are dry and barren.

The granite massif near Surami divides the lowlands of Georgia from the oil-rich basin of Azerbaijan's Kura river, which has built a large delta into the Caspian Sea.

The shallow, saline Lake Van *(Van Gölü)* is the largest lake in Turkey. Dry terraces mark a previous shoreline 181 ft (55 m) above the present water level.

Map key

Population

- above 5 million
- 1 million to 5 million
- 500,000 to 1 million
- 100,000 to 500,000
- 50,000 to 100,000
- 10,000 to 50,000
- below 10,000

Elevation

- 4000m / 13,124ft
- 3000m / 9843ft
- 2000m / 6562ft
- 1000m / 3281ft
- 500m / 1640ft
- 250m / 820ft
- 100m / 328ft
- sea level

► ***Since the 6th century BC,*** *the pinnacles and caves of east-central Anatolia have been utilized as dwellings. Many are still inhabited today.*

Scale 1:4,000,000

projection: Lambert Conformal Conic

▲ ***The fisheries of*** *Azerbaijan are noted for their hauls of sturgeon, and the Caspian Sea accounts for 80% of the world's total catch. However, stocks are now under serious threat due to overfishing.*

▲ ***Traditional steam baths*** *are found throughout the region, and are used for socializing as well as for bathing.*

The Near East

IRAQ, ISRAEL, JORDAN, LEBANON, SYRIA

Some of the world's oldest civilizations developed in this region – the Fertile Crescent – which is venerated by Jews, Muslims and Christians, but torn by competing religious, ethnic and national claims to the land. Turkish Ottoman rule ended with the First World War and the region was divided into areas administered by Britain and France. The UN endorsed calls for a Jewish homeland in what was then Palestine and in 1948 the state of Israel was declared. Hostility towards the Jewish state led to a series of wars with its Arab neighbours. After 2000, attempts to broker peaceful resolutions with both the Palestinian population and with adjacent Arab states were hampered by a revival of Islamic militarism and conflicting international interests in the oil-rich region. This led to an Israeli retrenchment and culminated in a US-led invasion of Iraq in 2003, which toppled the Ba'athist regime of Saddam Hussein in the name of a 'war on terror'.

Using the land and sea

Water scarcity limits cropland to the north and to areas watered principally by the Tigris, Euphrates and Jordan rivers. In Israel, new irrigation techniques are allowing cultivation in the arid Negev. Wheat is the chief grain and large areas of scrub support livestock herding. Commercial produce includes dates, tobacco, citrus fruits, olives, grapes and cotton, which is Syria's main export crop. Fishing is still important in the Mediterranean.

The urban/rural population divide

urban 70% | rural 30%

0 10 20 30 40 50 60 70 80 90 100

Population density	Total land area
217 people per sq mile (84 people per sq km)	325,460 sq miles (843,160 sq km)

Land use and agricultural distribution

- sheep
- cereals
- citrus fruits
- cotton
- dates
- fishing
- rice
- tobacco
- capital cities
- major towns
- pasture
- cropland
- wetland
- desert

Transport and industry

The petrochemical industry is well established, and central to the economies of Syria and Iraq, which was the world's second largest oil exporter before the war with Iran which began in 1980. Lebanon has traditionally been a centre for commerce, while Israel has a well-diversified economy with an expanding tourist industry, despite few natural resources.

The transport network

- 49,859 miles (80,249 km)
- 1365 miles (2197 km)
- 3826 miles (6158 km)
- 1171 miles (1885 km)

Jordan's sea port of Al 'Aqabah is connected to Damascus in Syria by road and rail. This route to the Red Sea provides for large exports of phosphate and trade with states in the Persian Gulf.

Major industry and infrastructure

- car manufacture
- cement
- chemicals
- electronics
- finance
- food processing
- iron & steel
- oil
- oil refining
- textiles
- capital cities
- major towns
- international airports
- major roads
- major industrial areas

***The Dome of the Rock** in Jerusalem is a magnificent mosque, revered by Muslims. Close by is the Wailing Wall, the city's most sacred Jewish landmark and the Church of the Holy Sepulchre, a famous Christian place of worship.*

***The city of** Petra, carved from spectacular rose-coloured limestone, lies deep within a canyon in southern Jordan. Revenues from the spice trade funded the construction of the city which was built by the Nabatean people in about 400 BC.*

***Water and wind** erosion over thousands of years have created the Canyon of the Oasis at En 'Avedat in the Negev Desert (HaNegev). Extreme diurnal temperature fluctuations, coupled with wind erosion, have caused layers of rock to crack and peel away.*

136
120
140

The landscape

The Al Jazirah plateau divides the Euphrates and Tigris rivers, which cross the Mesopotamian plain to reach their confluence in the southeast. The rocky Syrian Desert extends west to the northern extremity of the Great Rift Valley, which runs from the mountains of Lebanon to the Gulf of Aqaba. The Jordan river flows south along this trough into the Dead Sea, divided from the Mediterranean coastal plain by a steep-sided plateau.

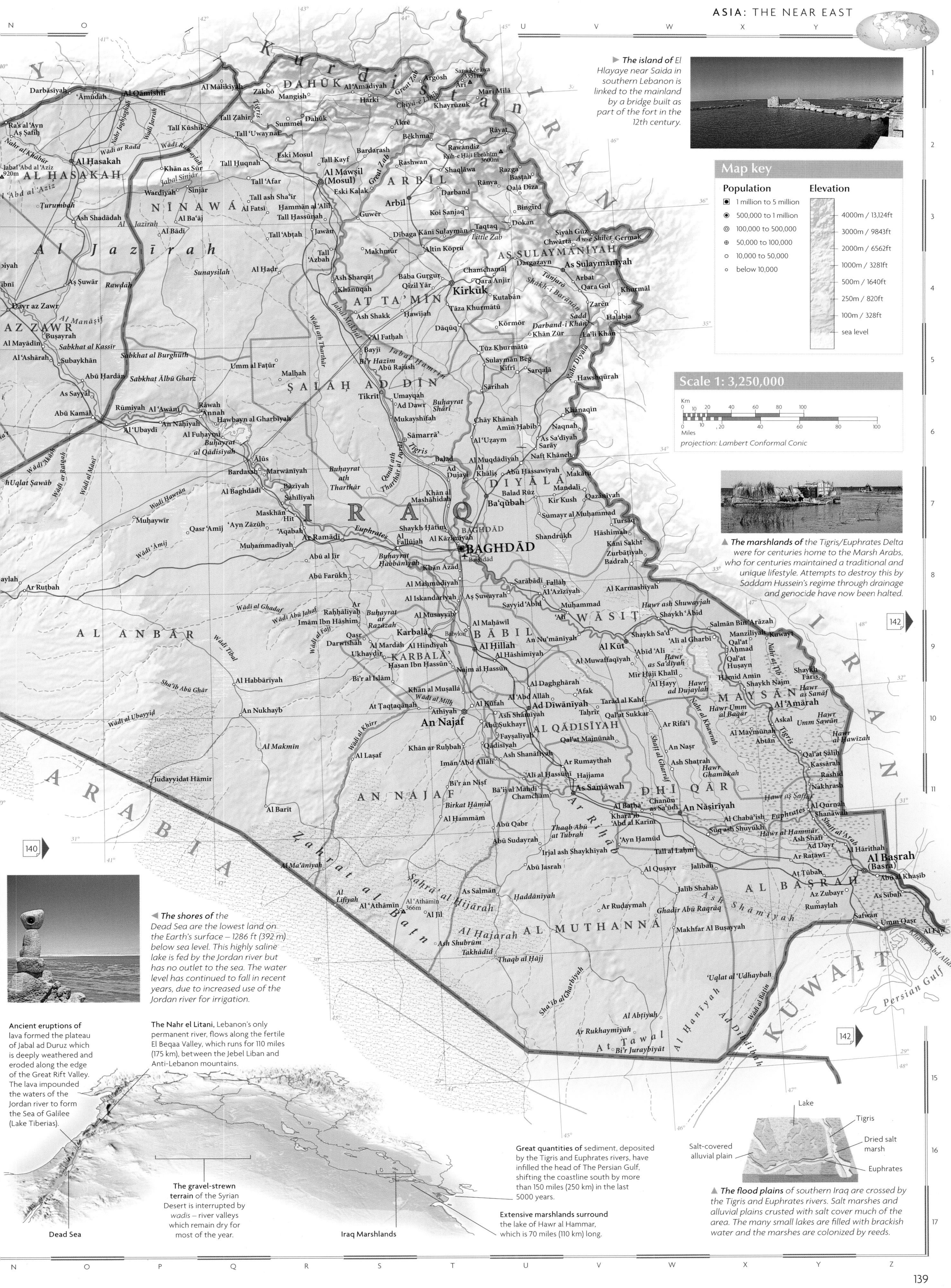

Map key
Population
1 million to 5 million
500,000 to 1 million
100,000 to 500,000
50,000 to 100,000
10,000 to 50,000
below 10,000
Elevation
4000m / 13,124ft
3000m / 9843ft
2000m / 6562ft
1000m / 3281ft
500m / 1640ft
250m / 820ft
100m / 328ft
sea level
Scale 1: 3,250,000
projection: Lambert Conformal Conic
IRAQ
BAGHDĀD
IRAN
ARABIA
KUWAIT
Persian Gulf
Al Jazīrah
Kurdistan
Lake
Tigris
Dried salt marsh
Salt-covered alluvial plain
Euphrates
Dead Sea
Iraq Marshlands

▶ **The island of** El Hlayaye near Saida in southern Lebanon is linked to the mainland by a bridge built as part of the fort in the 12th century.

▲ **The marshlands of** the Tigris/Euphrates Delta were for centuries home to the Marsh Arabs, who for centuries maintained a traditional and unique lifestyle. Attempts to destroy this by Saddam Hussein's regime through drainage and genocide have now been halted.

◀ **The shores of** the Dead Sea are the lowest land on the Earth's surface – 1286 ft (392 m) below sea level. This highly saline lake is fed by the Jordan river but has no outlet to the sea. The water level has continued to fall in recent years, due to increased use of the Jordan river for irrigation.

Ancient eruptions of lava formed the plateau of Jabal ad Duruz which is deeply weathered and eroded along the edge of the Great Rift Valley. The lava impounded the waters of the Jordan river to form the Sea of Galilee (Lake Tiberias).

The Nahr el Litani, Lebanon's only permanent river, flows along the fertile El Beqaa Valley, which runs for 110 miles (175 km), between the Jebel Liban and Anti-Lebanon mountains.

The gravel-strewn terrain of the Syrian Desert is interrupted by *wadis* – river valleys which remain dry for most of the year.

Great quantities of sediment, deposited by the Tigris and Euphrates rivers, have infilled the head of The Persian Gulf, shifting the coastline south by more than 150 miles (250 km) in the last 5000 years.

Extensive marshlands surround the lake of Hawr al Hammar, which is 70 miles (110 km) long.

▲ **The flood plains** of southern Iraq are crossed by the Tigris and Euphrates rivers. Salt marshes and alluvial plains crusted with salt cover much of the area. The many small lakes are filled with brackish water and the marshes are colonized by reeds.

The Arabian Peninsula

BAHRAIN, KUWAIT, OMAN, QATAR, SAUDI ARABIA, UNITED ARAB EMIRATES (UAE), YEMEN

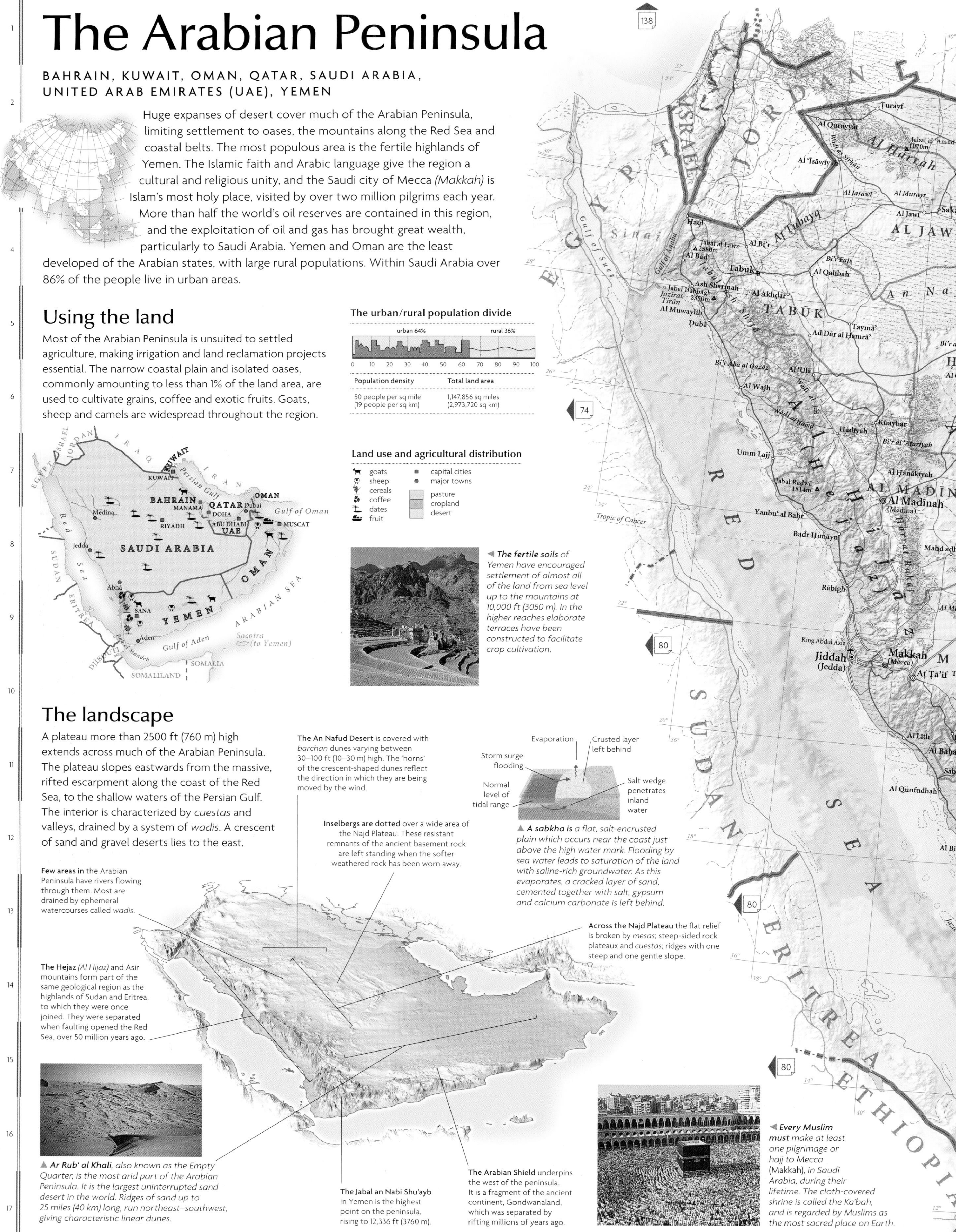

Huge expanses of desert cover much of the Arabian Peninsula, limiting settlement to oases, the mountains along the Red Sea and coastal belts. The most populous area is the fertile highlands of Yemen. The Islamic faith and Arabic language give the region a cultural and religious unity, and the Saudi city of Mecca *(Makkah)* is Islam's most holy place, visited by over two million pilgrims each year. More than half the world's oil reserves are contained in this region, and the exploitation of oil and gas has brought great wealth, particularly to Saudi Arabia. Yemen and Oman are the least developed of the Arabian states, with large rural populations. Within Saudi Arabia over 86% of the people live in urban areas.

Using the land

Most of the Arabian Peninsula is unsuited to settled agriculture, making irrigation and land reclamation projects essential. The narrow coastal plain and isolated oases, commonly amounting to less than 1% of the land area, are used to cultivate grains, coffee and exotic fruits. Goats, sheep and camels are widespread throughout the region.

The urban/rural population divide

urban 64% | rural 36%

Population density	Total land area
50 people per sq mile (19 people per sq km)	1,147,856 sq miles (2,973,720 sq km)

Land use and agricultural distribution

goats
sheep
cereals
coffee
dates
fruit
capital cities
major towns
pasture
cropland
desert
SAUDI ARABIA
KUWAIT
BAHRAIN
MANAMA
QATAR
DOHA
ABU DHABI
UAE
Dubai
OMAN
MUSCAT
YEMEN
SANA
Aden
Abhā
Medina
Jedda
RIYADH
Red Sea
Gulf of Oman
Gulf of Aden
ARABIAN SEA
Persian Gulf
IRAN
IRAQ
JORDAN
ISRAEL
EGYPT
SUDAN
ERITREA
DJIBOUTI
SOMALIA
SOMALILAND
Socotra (to Yemen)
Bab el Mandeb

The fertile soils *of Yemen have encouraged settlement of almost all of the land from sea level up to the mountains at 10,000 ft (3050 m). In the higher reaches elaborate terraces have been constructed to facilitate crop cultivation.*

The landscape

A plateau more than 2500 ft (760 m) high extends across much of the Arabian Peninsula. The plateau slopes eastwards from the massive, rifted escarpment along the coast of the Red Sea, to the shallow waters of the Persian Gulf. The interior is characterized by *cuestas* and valleys, drained by a system of *wadis*. A crescent of sand and gravel deserts lies to the east.

The An Nafud Desert is covered with *barchan* dunes varying between 30–100 ft (10–30 m) high. The 'horns' of the crescent-shaped dunes reflect the direction in which they are being moved by the wind.

Evaporation
Crusted layer left behind
Storm surge flooding
Normal level of tidal range
Salt wedge penetrates inland water

A sabkha is *a flat, salt-encrusted plain which occurs near the coast just above the high water mark. Flooding by sea water leads to saturation of the land with saline-rich groundwater. As this evaporates, a cracked layer of sand, cemented together with salt, gypsum and calcium carbonate is left behind.*

Inselbergs are dotted over a wide area of the Najd Plateau. These resistant remnants of the ancient basement rock are left standing when the softer weathered rock has been worn away.

Few areas in the Arabian Peninsula have rivers flowing through them. Most are drained by ephemeral watercourses called *wadis*.

Across the Najd Plateau the flat relief is broken by *mesas*; steep-sided rock plateaux and *cuestas*; ridges with one steep and one gentle slope.

The Hejaz *(Al Hijaz)* and Asir mountains form part of the same geological region as the highlands of Sudan and Eritrea, to which they were once joined. They were separated when faulting opened the Red Sea, over 50 million years ago.

Ar Rub' al Khali, *also known as the Empty Quarter, is the most arid part of the Arabian Peninsula. It is the largest uninterrupted sand desert in the world. Ridges of sand up to 25 miles (40 km) long, run northeast–southwest, giving characteristic linear dunes.*

The Jabal an Nabi Shu'ayb in Yemen is the highest point on the peninsula, rising to 12,336 ft (3760 m).

The Arabian Shield underpins the west of the peninsula. It is a fragment of the ancient continent, Gondwanaland, which was separated by rifting millions of years ago.

Every Muslim must *make at least one pilgrimage or hajj to Mecca* (Makkah), *in Saudi Arabia, during their lifetime. The cloth-covered shrine is called the Ka'bah, and is regarded by Muslims as the most sacred place on Earth.*

EGYPT
ISRAEL
JORDAN
Sinai
Gulf of Suez
Gulf of Aqaba
Haql
Tabūk
TABŪK
Al Qurayyāt
Turayf
Al Jawf
AL JAWF
Sakākah
Taymā'
Al 'Ulā
Al Wajh
Umm Lajj
Duba
Khaybar
Al Ḩanākiyah
AL MADĪNAH
Al Madīnah (Medina)
Yanbu' al Baḩr
Badr Ḩunayn
Rābigh
Jiddah (Jedda)
Makkah (Mecca)
Aţ Ţā'if
Al Līth
Al Qunfudhah
RED SEA
SUDAN
ERITREA
ETHIOPIA
Tropic of Cancer

138
74
80
80
80

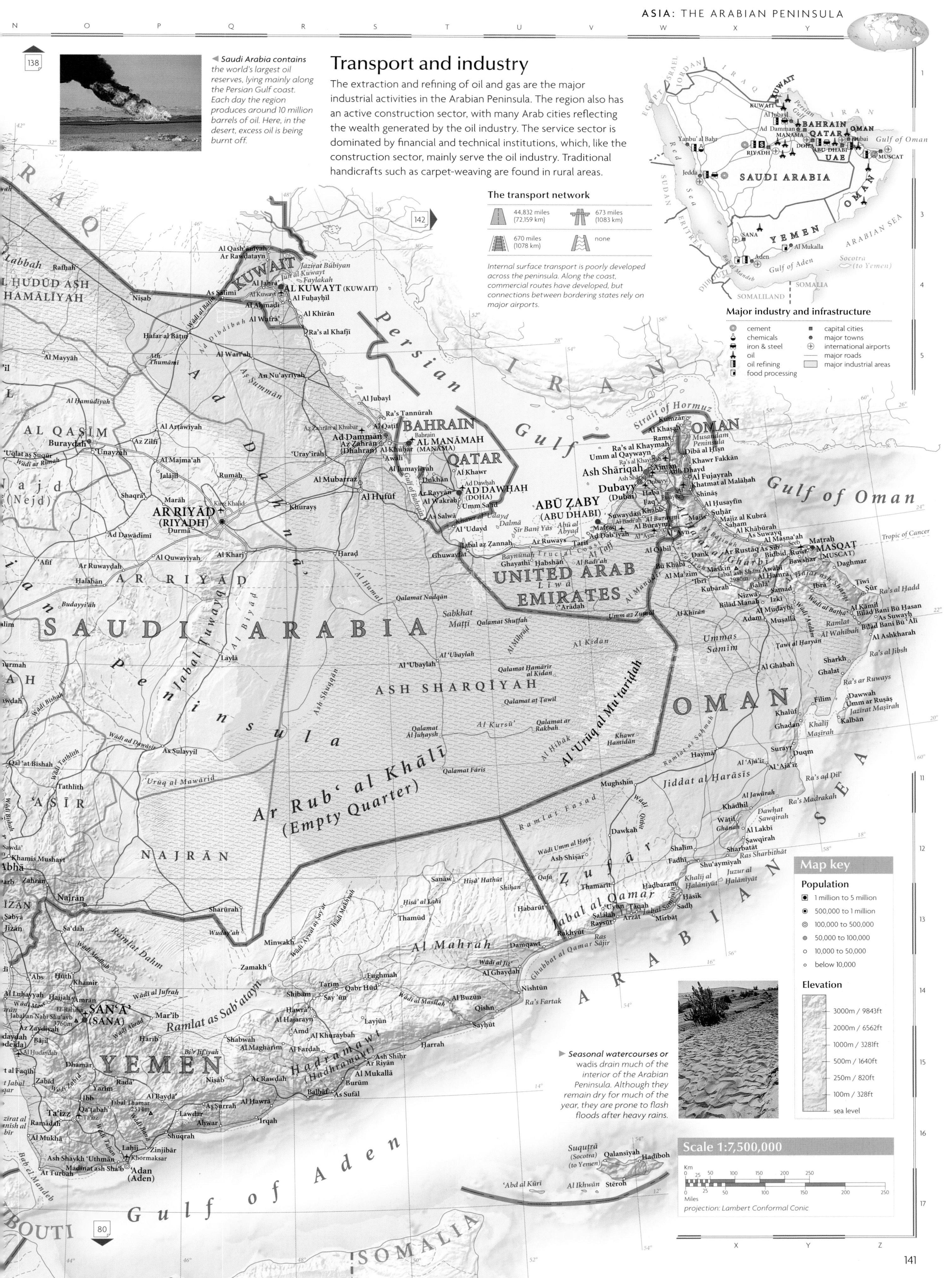

N O P Q R S T U V W X Y
138
142
80
The transport network
44,832 miles (72,159 km)
673 miles (1083 km)
670 miles (1078 km)
none
Major industry and infrastructure
cement
chemicals
iron & steel
oil
oil refining
food processing
capital cities
major towns
international airports
major roads
major industrial areas
SAUDI ARABIA
KUWAIT
BAHRAIN
QATAR
UAE
OMAN
YEMEN
IRAN
IRAQ
Persian Gulf
Gulf of Oman
Red Sea
Gulf of Aden
ARABIAN SEA
Socotra (to Yemen)
SOMALIA
SOMALILAND
Strait of Hormuz
AL KUWAYT (KUWAIT)
AL MANĀMAH (MANAMA)
AD DAWḤAH (DOHA)
ABŪ ẒABY (ABU DHABI)
AR RIYĀḌ (RIYADH)
MASQAṬ (MUSCAT)
ṢAN'Ā' (SANA)
'Adan (Aden)
UNITED ARAB EMIRATES
Ar Rub' al Khālī (Empty Quarter)
ASH SHARQĪYAH
Ad Dahnā'
Ḥaḍramawt (Hadhramaut)
Gulf of Aden
Map key
Population
1 million to 5 million
500,000 to 1 million
100,000 to 500,000
50,000 to 100,000
10,000 to 50,000
below 10,000
Elevation
3000m / 9843ft
2000m / 6562ft
1000m / 3281ft
500m / 1640ft
250m / 820ft
100m / 328ft
sea level
Scale 1:7,500,000
projection: Lambert Conformal Conic
X Y Z

◀ *Saudi Arabia contains the world's largest oil reserves, lying mainly along the Persian Gulf coast. Each day the region produces around 10 million barrels of oil. Here, in the desert, excess oil is being burnt off.*

Transport and industry

The extraction and refining of oil and gas are the major industrial activities in the Arabian Peninsula. The region also has an active construction sector, with many Arab cities reflecting the wealth generated by the oil industry. The service sector is dominated by financial and technical institutions, which, like the construction sector, mainly serve the oil industry. Traditional handicrafts such as carpet-weaving are found in rural areas.

Internal surface transport is poorly developed across the peninsula. Along the coast, commercial routes have developed, but connections between bordering states rely on major airports.

▶ ***Seasonal watercourses or*** *wadis drain much of the interior of the Arabian Peninsula. Although they remain dry for much of the year, they are prone to flash floods after heavy rains.*

Iran & the Gulf states

136

BAHRAIN, IRAN, KUWAIT, QATAR, UNITED ARAB EMIRATES (UAE)

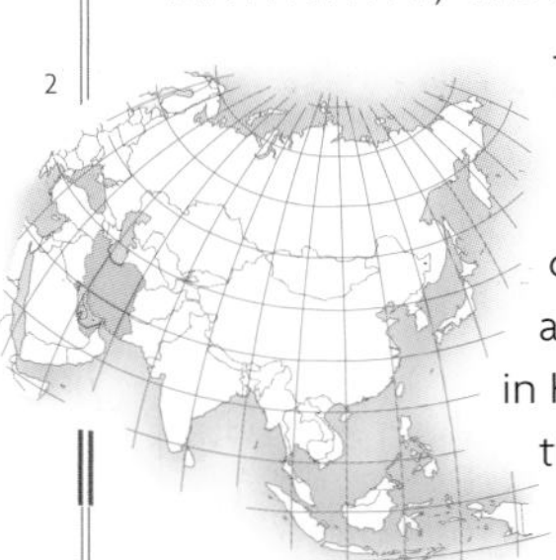

The discovery of oil in the Persian Gulf in the 1930s brought great wealth to the surrounding states. The revenue was largely used to modernize industry and infrastructure, initiating great social change in these formerly agrarian countries. Today, over 90% of the people in the Gulf states live in urban areas, and foreign nationals make up a sizeable proportion of the population in Kuwait, Qatar and the United Arab Emirates. The importance of control of the oil reserves has led to a number of territorial disputes, including most recently the Iran–Iraq War (1980-88) and the First Gulf War (1991). Islam is practised almost exclusively throughout the region and two distinct strands are found; Sunni Muslims in Qatar, Kuwait and UAE, and Shi'a Muslims in Iran and Bahrain. In 1979 Iran became the world's largest theocracy.

138

The landscape

The land rises steeply from the fragmented coastal lowlands bordering the Persian Gulf, to reach Iran's interior plateau, bounded by heavily-eroded mountain chains. An unstable plate boundary runs northwest to southeast across Iran causing frequent earthquakes. On the sandy west coast of the Persian Gulf, the relief is generally flat, with patches of salt marsh. Bahrain consists of two groups of islands, which are mostly small and rocky.

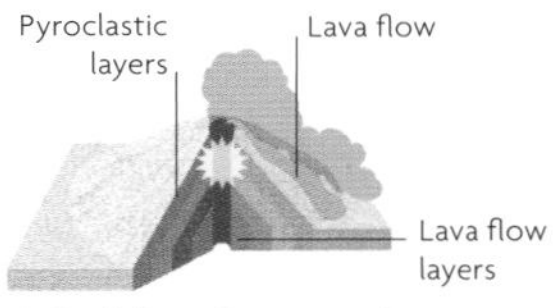

Pyroclastic layers

Lava flow

Lava flow layers

▲ **Qolleh-ye Damavand** *in the Elburz Mountains is a composite volcano. It comprises layers of lava and pyroclasts – fragmentary rocks which accumulate on the slopes of the volcano after being ejected into the air.*

▲ ***Marine sediments from** deep beneath the ancient Tethys Sea have been uplifted to form the Elburz Mountains, which stretch along the shores of the Caspian Sea, northern Iran.*

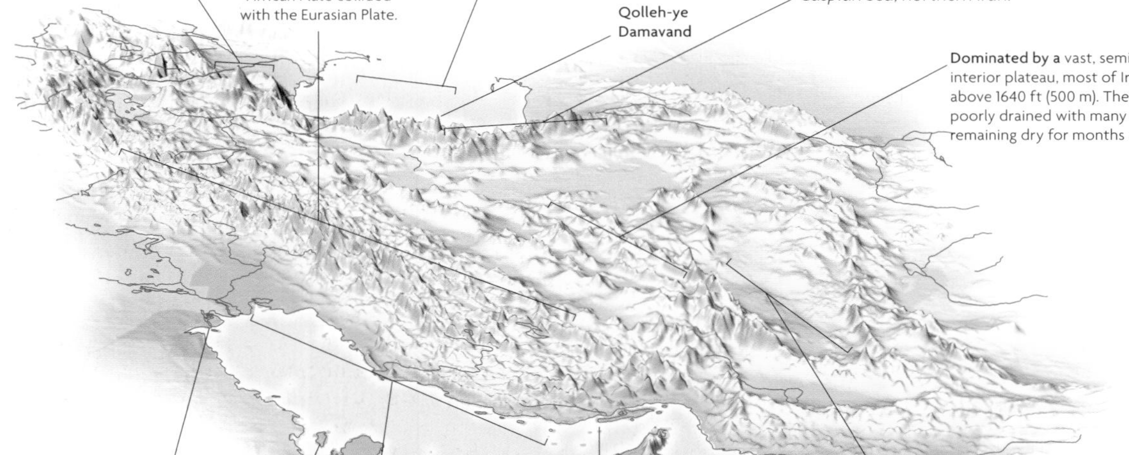

Lava and ash from previous volcanic activity covers a 200 mile (320 km) stretch from the border with Azerbaijan to the Caspian Sea.

Iran's two mountain chains, the Zagros and Elburz, were uplifted at the same time as the Alps in Europe, when the African Plate collided with the Eurasian Plate.

Caspian Sea

Qolleh-ye Damavand

Dominated by a vast, semi-arid interior plateau, most of Iran lies above 1640 ft (500 m). The region is poorly drained with many of its basins remaining dry for months at a time.

The Dasht-e Lut

The fierce Shamal wind affects much of this region. Every summer it blows dust south from the flood plains of the Tigris and Euphrates, reducing visibility to such **an extent that** Kuwait International Airport is frequently forced to close.

Autumn winds blowing across the Persian Gulf can reach speeds of up to 95 mph (150 kmph) causing severe storms, squalls and waterspouts.

Prolific springs tapping artesian water make cultivation possible across the north of Bahrain's main island. This provides a sharp contrast to the sandy plains in the south and west.

The oilfields of the Persian Gulf are formed from marine shale deposits lying in sedimentary basins at the margins of the Zagros Mountains.

Numerous islands lie along the southern coast of the Persian Gulf. Some of these are salt domes, created when less dense salts were displaced and forced up to the surface by denser, overlying strata.

◄ ***The Dasht-e Lut** covers a large portion of eastern Iran with its dry, wind-eroded plain of scattered sandstone pillars and salty depressions. During the summer, temperatures soar, making it one of the world's hottest, driest places.*

140

Using the land and sea

Along the coast of the Caspian Sea, desalinated water allows fruits and vegetables to be produced, although water shortages and desert soils still limit farming. Sheep are the most important livestock raised in Iran and commercial forests cover the northwest of the country. Shrimp stocks were decimated by pollution during the Gulf War, but fishing remains important for domestic and export markets.

◄ ***All of the** Gulf states have commercial fishing fleets. Before the discovery of oil, fishing was the region's leading industry.*

Land use and agricultural distribution

goats, sheep, cereals, citrus fruits, cotton, dates, fishing, timber

capital cities, major towns

pasture, cropland, forest, desert, wetland

The urban/rural population divide

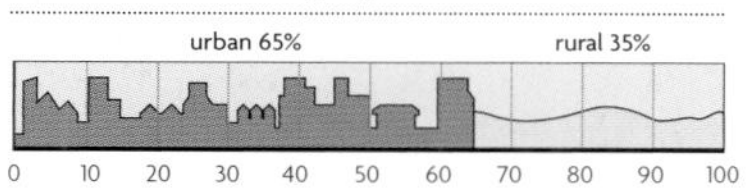

urban 65% — rural 35%

0 10 20 30 40 50 60 70 80 90 100

Population density	Total land area
112 people per sq mile (43 people per sq km)	642,883 sq miles (1,665,500 sq km)

◄ ***The Kuwait Towers** in the centre of Kuwait are symbols of the vast wealth oil has brought to the country. Before 1960, the city had only one main street and was surrounded by a mud wall.*

N O P Q R S T U V W X Y
1 2 3 4 5 6 7 8 9 10 15 16 17
146
148
148
TURKMENISTAN
AFGHANISTAN
PAKISTAN
IRAN
OMAN
QATAR
BAHRAIN
UNITED ARAB EMIRATES
Caspian Sea
Dasht-e Kavīr
Iranian Plateau
Dasht-e Lūt
Zagros Mountains
Makran Coast
Gulf of Oman
Strait of Hormuz
Trucial Coast
Tropic of Cancer
Kopet Dāgh
Kūhhā-ye Alborz (Elburz Mountains)
GOLESTĀN
KHORĀSĀN-E SHEMĀLĪ
KHORĀSĀN-E RAZAVĪ
KHORĀSĀN-E JANŪBĪ
MĀZANDARĀN
SEMNĀN
TEHRĀN
QOM
EŞFAHĀN
YAZD
KERMĀN
FĀRS
HORMOZGĀN
SĪSTĀN VA BALŪCHESTĀN
BŪSHEHR
CHAHĀR MAHALL VA BAKHTĪĀRĪ
TEHRĀN
Mashhad
Gorgān
Bojnūrd
Sārī
Semnān
Qom
Kāshān
Eşfahān
Yazd
Kermān
Shīrāz
Zāhedān
Bandar-e 'Abbās
Bandar-e Būshehr
Neyshābūr
Sabzevār
Birjand
Qeshm
Chābahār
Ra's al Khaymah
Umm al Qaywayn
'Ajmān
Ash Shāriqah
Dubayy (Dubai)
Al Fujayrah
ABŪ ZABY (ABU DHABI)
AD DAWḨAH (DOHA)
Al Khawr
Al Wakrah
Al 'Ayn
Līwā
Kūh-e Hazārān 4420m
Kūh-e Taftān 4042m
Qolleh-ye Damāvand 5671m
Scale 1:5,500,000
projection: Lambert Conformal Conic
Map key
Population
above 5 million
1 million to 5 million
500,000 to 1 million
100,000 to 500,000
50,000 to 100,000
10,000 to 50,000
below 10,000
Elevation
4000m / 13,124ft
3000m / 9843ft
2000m / 6562ft
1000m / 3281ft
500m / 1640ft
250m / 820ft
100m / 328ft
sea level
Major industry and infrastructure
carpet manufacture
chemicals
finance
food processing
oil
oil refining
textiles
capital city
major towns
international airports
major roads
major industrial areas
The transport network
63,543 miles (102,274 km)
884 miles (1423 km)
3822 miles (6151 km)
562 miles (904 km)

Many volcanoes lie in Iran's 1200 mile (1930 km) volcanic belt, including the country's highest peak, the now-extinct Qolleh-ye Damavand at 18,600 ft (5671 m).

Extensive oil and gas exploitation in the Gulf region has allowed the economic transformation of the Gulf states. Consequently, many of these states have a hugely improved per capita income compared to the 1960's.

Transport and industry

Both onshore and offshore oil reserves are exploited throughout the region. Kuwait not only extracts but also refines 80% of its oil. Bahrain has diversified its economy to become the main commercial and financial centre in the Persian Gulf. Iran produces a wide range of products: textile mills are widespread and carpet-weaving is an important export industry.

Major towns and neighbouring countries are linked by adequate road networks, although rural areas are less well served. Bahrain is linked to the mainland by a 15 mile (25 km) long causeway.

Kazakhstan

Abundant natural resources lie in the immense steppe grasslands, deserts and central plateau of the former Soviet republic of Kazakhstan. An intensive programme of industrial and agricultural development to exploit these resources during the Soviet era resulted in catastrophic industrial pollution, including fallout from nuclear testing and the shrinkage of the Aral Sea. Since independence, the government has encouraged foreign investment and liberalized the economy to promote growth. The adoption of Kazakh as the national language is intended to encourage a new sense of national identity in a state where living conditions for the majority remain harsh, both in cramped urban centres and impoverished rural areas.

Transport and industry

The single most important industry in Kazakhstan is mining, based around extensive oil deposits near the Caspian Sea, the world's largest chromium mine, and vast reserves of iron ore. Recent foreign investment has helped to develop industries including food processing and steel manufacture, and to expand the exploitation of mineral resources. The Russian space programme is still based at Baykonyr, near Kyzylorda in central Kazakhstan.

RUSSIAN FEDERATION · Petropavlovsk · Pavlodar · Rudnyy · Ural'sk · Aktobe · ASTANA · Temirtau · Karaganda · Semipalatinsk · Ust'-Kamenogorsk · KAZAKHSTAN · Atyrau · Zhezkazgan · Aral Sea · Caspian Sea · Aktau · Kyzylorda · Taldykorgan · Almaty · Taraz · Shymkent · UZBEKISTAN · TURKMENISTAN · KYRGYZSTAN · CHINA

Major industry and infrastructure

- chemicals
- engineering
- fish processing
- food processing
- iron & steel
- metallurgy
- mining
- oil
- capital cities
- major towns
- international airports
- major roads
- major industrial areas

The transport network

- 48,263 miles (77,680 km)
- none
- 8483 miles (13,660 km)
- 3900 miles (2423 km)

Industrial areas in the north and east are well-connected to Russia. Air and rail links with Germany and China have been established through foreign investment. Better access to Baltic ports is being sought.

An open-cast coal mine in Kazakhstan. Foreign investment is being actively sought by the Kazakh government in order to fully exploit the country's rich mineral reserves.

Using the land and sea

The rearing of large herds of sheep and goats on the steppe grasslands forms the core of Kazakh agriculture. Arable cultivation and cotton-growing in pasture and desert areas was encouraged during the Soviet era, but relative yields are low. The heavy use of fertilizers and the diversion of natural water sources for irrigation has degraded much of the land.

The urban/rural population divide

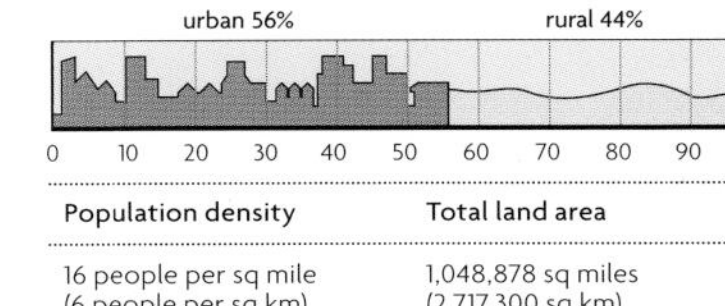
urban 56%
rural 44%
0 10 20 30 40 50 60 70 80 90 100

Population density	Total land area
16 people per sq mile (6 people per sq km)	1,048,878 sq miles (2,717,300 sq km)

Land use and agricultural distribution
cattle
goats
sheep
cotton
fishing
wheat
capital cities
major towns
pasture
cropland
forest
mountain region
desert
RUSSIAN FEDERATION
Rudnyy
Ural'sk
ASTANA
Ust'-Kamenogorsk
Semipalatinsk
Karaganda
Atyrau
KAZAKHSTAN
Aral Sea
Caspian Sea
Aktau
Kyzylorda
Taldykorgan
Almaty
Shymkent
UZBEKISTAN
TURKMENISTAN
KYRGYZSTAN
CHINA

The nomadic peoples who moved their herds around the steppe grasslands are now largely settled, although echoes of their traditional lifestyle, in particular their superb riding skills, remain.

RUSSIAN FEDERATION
Ural'sk
Kamenka
Zachagansk
Fedorovka
Burlin
Aksay
Chingirlau
ZAPADNYY KAZAKHSTAN
Dzhanibek
Kaztalovka
Zhalpaktal
Chapayev
Algabas
Ozero Shalkar
Zhympity
Lubenka
Urda
Novaya Kazanka
Ryn-Peski
Kulagino
Inderborskiy
Karabau
Caspian Depression
ATYRAU
Makhambet
Makat
Dossor
Akkystau
Ganyushkino
Atyrau
Komsomol'skiy
Koschagyl
Kul'sary
Karaton
Martuk
Aktobe (Aktyubinsk)
Khobda
Akzhar
Khromtau
Alga
Kandyagash
Zhuryn
Shubarkuduk
Emba
Miyaly
Uil
Sagiz
AKTYUBINSK
Gory Mugodzhary
Zharkamys
Shalkar
Karabutak
Komsomol'skoye
Ozero Kyzylkol'
Irgiz
Karabalyk
Fedorovka
Nadezhdinka
Ozernoye
Kostanay
Rudnyy
Lisakovsk
Tobol
Oktyabr'
Denisovka
Zhitikara
KOSTANAY
Turgayskaya Stolovaya Strana
Zhailma

Caspian Sea · Ostrov Kulaly · Mys Tyub-Karagan · Fort-Shevchenko · Mangyshlakskiy Zaliv · Zaliv Komsomolets · Sarykamys · Borankul · Sor Mertvyy Kultuk · Shebir · Tauchik · Shetpe · Zharmysh · Say-Utes · Sor Kaydak · Aktau · Plato Mangyshlak · MANGISTAU · Zhetybay · Zhanaozen · Kuryk · Beyneu · Turush · Ustyurt Plateau · Severnyy Chink Ustyurta · Plato Shagyray · Peski Bol'shiye Barsuki · Gryada Shirkala · Saksaul'skiy · Aral'sk · Zaliv Tushchybas · Aral Sea · Ostrov Vozrozhdeniya · Peski Priaral'skiye Karakumy · Ayteke Bi · Kazalinsk · Maylybas · Space Launching Centre · Dermentobe · Baykonyr · Syr Darya · Dzhusaly · KYZYLORDA · Turanskaya Nizmennost' · Uyaly · UZBEKISTAN · TURKMENISTAN

122
122
146
146

Map key

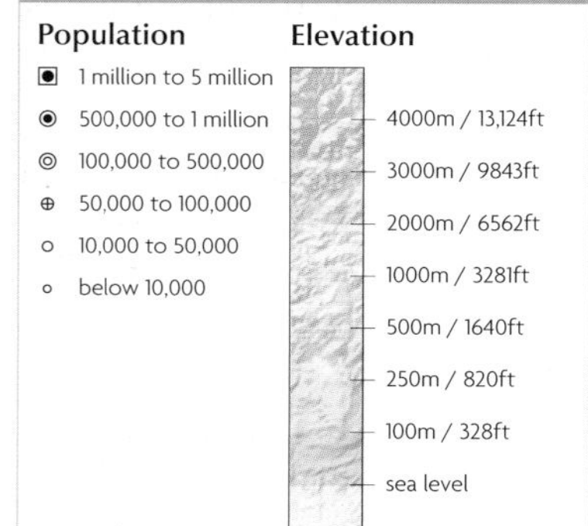
Population
1 million to 5 million
500,000 to 1 million
100,000 to 500,000
50,000 to 100,000
10,000 to 50,000
below 10,000
Elevation
4000m / 13,124ft
3000m / 9843ft
2000m / 6562ft
1000m / 3281ft
500m / 1640ft
250m / 820ft
100m / 328ft
sea level

Scale 1:6,250,000

Km 0 25 50 100 150 200 250
Miles 0 25 50 100 150 200 250

projection: Lambert Conformal Conic

The landscape

Stretching more than 1250 miles (2000 km) from the Caspian Sea in the west to China in the east, more than 40% of Kazakhstan is covered by steppe grasslands which give way to barren desert in the south. The land rises eastwards towards the mineral-rich central plateau, to form the Altai Mountains.

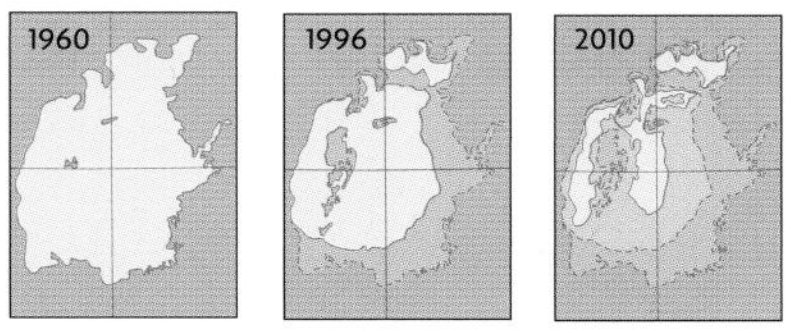

1960 1996 2010

▲ ***Since 1960, the** Aral Sea has shrunk by 90%, become extremely saline, and lost all but five of its once-abundant fish species. Factors in this ecological disaster include the excessive use of fertilizers, defoliants and the diversion of its main source rivers for the irrigation of desert lands.*

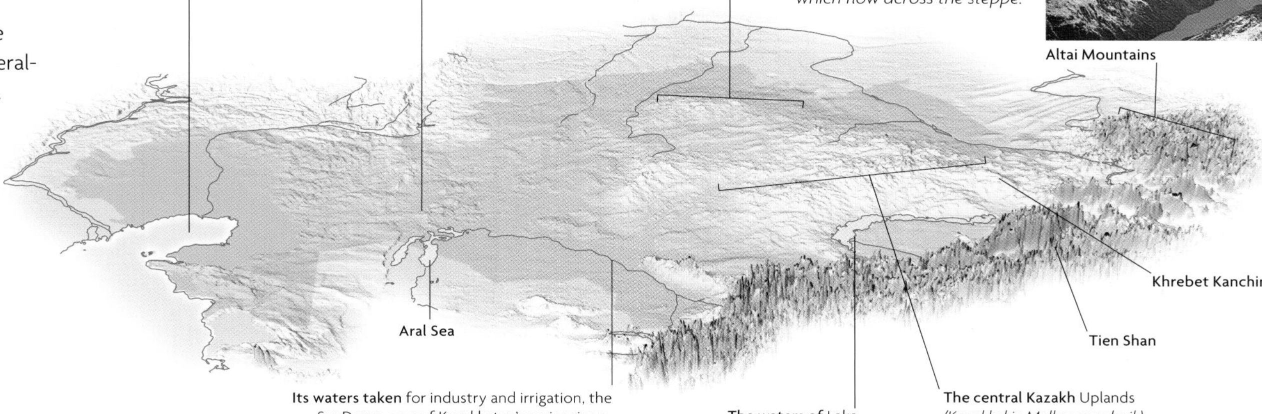

The Caspian Sea is the largest body of inland water in the world.

The desert of Peski Bol'shiye Barsuki is mainly sandy, displaying a number of classic dune formations. Groundwater supports a small amount of vegetation.

A large number of salt lakes fill depressions in the rolling uplands of central Kazakhstan.

▶ ***The Altai Mountains** lie on Kazakhstan's eastern borders with China and the Russian Federation. Cold and largely barren, they are the source of many of the rivers which flow across the steppe.*

Altai Mountains

Aral Sea

Khrebet Kanchingiz

Tien Shan

Its waters taken for industry and irrigation, the Syr Darya, one of Kazakhstan's major rivers, now barely reaches the Aral Sea which it used to fill. Like many Kazakh rivers it has been heavily polluted with chemicals and its flow has been restricted by up to 60%.

The waters of Lake Balkhash *(Ozero Balkhash)*, unlike those of the Aral Sea, are still able to support a fishing industry.

The central Kazakh Uplands *(Kazakhskiy Melkosopochnik)* contain much of the country's mineral riches. The landscape is largely flat with occasional rocky outcrops and hillocks.

▶ ***Immense stretches of** steppe grasslands characterize much of the Kazakh landscape. These lowland areas have been used for arable cultivation in recent years, although problems with irrigation have meant that much of the land is being allowed to revert to its natural vegetation and pastoral usage.*

122

122

156

146

▲ ***Rows of pine** trees edge this valley near Almaty. The snow-covered slopes in the background are used for skiing.*

Central Asia

KYRGYZSTAN, TAJIKISTAN, TURKMENISTAN, UZBEKISTAN

The four republics that declared independence in 1991 were created in the early years of the Soviet Union, promoting ethnic divisions in a region whose common focus, since the 8th century, has been Islam. Traditional rural and nomadic ways of life have survived the Soviet era, while the benefits of modern industry and grand irrigation schemes have resulted in severe pollution in the delicate, arid environment of the steppe, particularly in Uzbekistan. Many ethnic minority groups are scattered among the four republics, with isolated communities in the mountains of Kyrgyzstan.

The current Islamic revival has brought hope of greater regional unity, in spite of religious factionalism which, in 1992, plunged Tajikistan into civil war.

Aral Sea
Ustyurt Plateau
QORAQALPOG'ISTON RESPUBLIKASI
Nukus
Urganch
Daşoguz
KAZAKHSTAN
UZBEKISTAN
TURKMENISTAN
IRAN
Caspian Sea
Kyzyl Kum
Turan Lowland
Garagum
AŞGABAT
Türkmenbaşy
Balkanabat
Türkmenabat
Buxoro
Navoiy
Mary
BALKAN WELAÝATY
DAŞOGUZ WELAÝATY
AHAL WELAÝATY
LEBAP WELAÝATY
MARY WELAÝATY
NAVOIY VILOYATI
BUXORO VILOYATI
XORAZM VILOYATI
Köpetdag Gershi
Garagum Kanaly
Sarygamyş Köli
144
142
148

▲ **The southern shoreline** of the Aral Sea has retreated over 30 miles (48 km) since 1960. A major cause is the diversion of water from the Amu Darya river for irrigation via the Kara Kum Canal (Garagum Kanaly).

◀ **The desert of** the Kara Kum (Garagum) occupies over 70% of Turkmenistan; its wind-scoured surface of dune ridges and depressions severely limits human settlement.

Map key

Population

- 1 million to 5 million
- 500,000 to 1 million
- 100,000 to 500,000
- 50,000 to 100,000
- 10,000 to 50,000
- below 10,000

Elevation

- 6000m / 19,686ft
- 4000m / 13,124ft
- 3000m / 9843ft
- 2000m / 6562ft
- 1000m / 3281ft
- 500m / 1640ft
- 250m / 820ft
- 100m / 328ft
- sea level

Transport and industry

Fossil fuels are extracted and processed in all four states, with scope for further exploitation. Agriculture provides raw materials for many industries, including food and textiles processing, and the manufacture of leather goods, clothing and carpets. Farm machinery is also produced.

The transport network

73,658 miles (118,555 km)	87 miles (140 km)
4773 miles (7683 km)	1180 miles (1900 km)

The Kara Kum Canal (Garagumskiy Kanal) runs for 870 miles (1400 km) from the Amu Darya river to the Caspian Sea. The canal is principally used for irrigation but is navigable for 280 miles (450 km).

Major industry and infrastructure

- carpet weaving
- chemicals
- engineering
- food processing
- oil & gas
- textiles
- capital cities
- major towns
- international airports
- major roads
- major industrial areas

The landscape

The great Tien Shan and Pamir ranges meet in a succession of high mountain chains. These mountains encircle the fertile Fergana Valley and reach west into the desert of the Kyzyl Kum, dividing the Syr Darya and Amu Darya rivers. Sandy steppeland extends to the shores of the Caspian Sea, with the desert of the Kara Kum *(Garagum)* in the south. The Amu Darya drains into the Aral Sea in the north.

The Amu Darya is the only river in Central Asia with a sufficient volume of water to cross the desert of the Kara Kum *(Garagum)* from the Pamirs to the Aral Sea, where it forms a delta largely vegetated by scrub grasses.

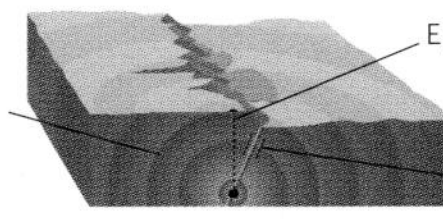

Shock waves travel through ground

Epicentre

Fault

▲ ***In the heavily-fractured** and faulted mountain region, earthquakes are common, caused by the sudden release of tension along active fault lines.*

◀ ***Bare mountains provide** a stark background to the croplands along the Naryn river in Kyrgyzstan. Irrigation is essential for cultivation in this dry region.*

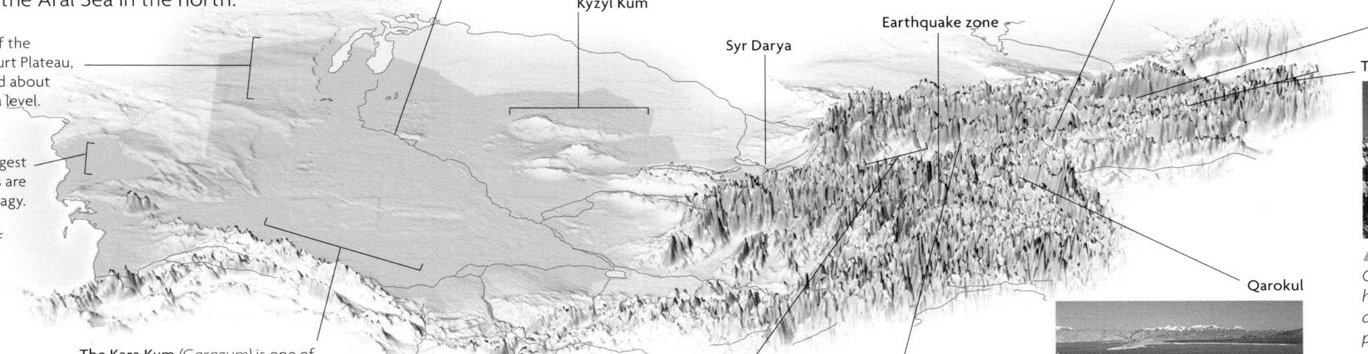

Naryn river

Ozero Issyk-Kul' lies at an altitude of 5193 ft (1584 m). The lake remains ice-free throughout the year, due to the slight salinity of the water.

Kyzyl Kum

Earthquake zone

Syr Darya

Tien Shan

Salt marshes fill many of the depressions in the Ustyurt Plateau, a barren, rocky tableland about 650 ft (200 m) above sea level.

Some of the world's largest deposits of marine salts are found in Garabogaz Aylagy. This shallow, saline gulf has an average depth of only 33 ft (10 m), and a very high evaporation rate, producing the salty deposits.

▲ ***The Tien Shan** extend from China in the east, reaching heights over 24,420 ft (7443 m) and branching into many parallel ranges in the west.*

Qarokul

The Kara Kum *(Garagum)* is one of the world's largest expanses of sand. Wind action has created a terrain of shifting, crescent-shaped sand dunes known as *barchans*.

A series of major rock faults has created the Fergana Valley, a deep depression surrounded by high mountains. Water from the Syr Darya river and from underground sources supports intensive agriculture, despite minimal rainfall.

Mount Communism *(Qullai Kommunizm)*, in the northern Pamirs, was so named for being the highest point in the former Soviet Union, rising to 24,590 ft (7495 m).

◀ ***Nestling high in** the Pamir range, and fed by glacial meltwater, Qarokul is the largest of the lakes in this region.*

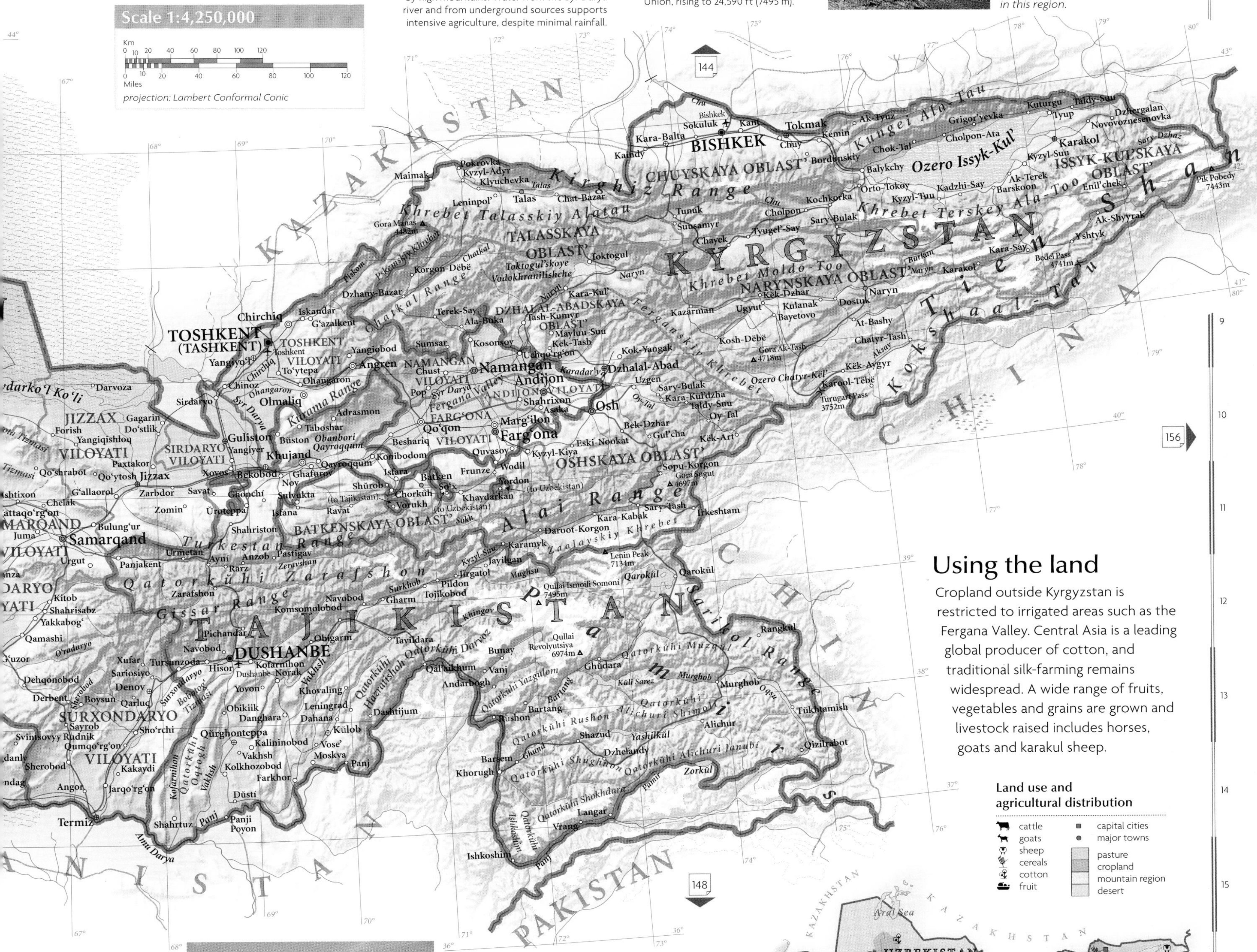

Scale 1:4,250,000

projection: Lambert Conformal Conic

144

156

148

Using the land

Cropland outside Kyrgyzstan is restricted to irrigated areas such as the Fergana Valley. Central Asia is a leading global producer of cotton, and traditional silk-farming remains widespread. A wide range of fruits, vegetables and grains are grown and livestock raised includes horses, goats and karakul sheep.

Land use and agricultural distribution

cattle, goats, sheep, cereals, cotton, fruit

capital cities, major towns

pasture, cropland, mountain region, desert

▶ ***Plentiful sunshine, rich** soils and massive irrigation schemes have made Uzbekistan the world's fifth largest cotton producer, although water shortages now prevent any further expansion of irrigated land.*

The urban/rural population divide

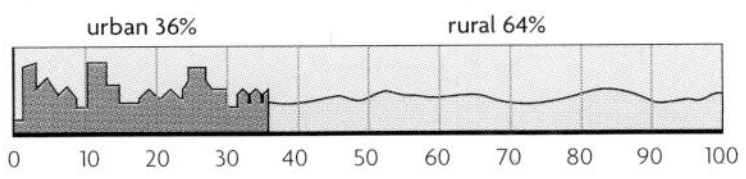

urban 36% | rural 64%

Population density	Total land area
88 people per sq mile (34 people per sq km)	492,961 sq miles (1,277,100 sq km)

Afghanistan & Pakistan

Pakistan was created by the partition of British India in 1947, becoming the western arm of a new Islamic state for Indian Muslims; the eastern sector, in Bengal, seceded to become the separate country of Bangladesh in 1971. Over half of Pakistan's 158 million people live in the Punjab, at the fertile head of the great Indus Basin. The river sustains a national economy based on irrigated agriculture, including cotton for the vital textiles industry. Afghanistan, a mountainous, landlocked country, with an ancient and independent culture, has been wracked by war since 1979. Factional strife escalated into an international conflict in late 2001, as US-led troops ousted the militant and fundamentally Islamist *taliban* regime as part of their 'war on terror'.

◀ *The town of Bamian lies high in the Hindu Kush west of Kabul. Between the 2nd and 5th centuries two huge statues of Buddha were carved into the nearby rock,the largest of which stood 125 ft (38 m) high. The statues were destroyed by the taliban regime in March 2001.*

Transport and industry

Pakistan is highly dependent on the cotton textiles industry, although diversified manufacture is expanding around cities such as Karachi and Lahore. Afghanistan's limited industry is based mainly on the processing of agricultural raw materials and includes traditional crafts such as carpet-making.

UZBEKISTAN
TAJIKISTAN
TURKMENISTAN
CHINA
IRAN
INDIA
ARABIAN SEA
AFGHANISTAN
PAKISTAN
Mazar-e Sharif
KABUL
Herat
Peshawar
ISLAMABAD
Rawalpindi
Kandahar
Lahore
Faisalabad
Quetta
Multan
Bahawalpur
Sukkur
Karachi
Hyderabad

Major industry and infrastructure

carpet weaving	capital cities
chemicals	major towns
engineering	international airports
finance	major roads
food processing	major industrial areas
iron & steel	
oil & gas	
textiles	

The transport network

96,154 miles (154,763 km)

211 miles (340 km)

4852 miles (7814 km)

745 miles (1200 km)

The Karakoram Highway was completed after 20 years of construction in 1978. It breaches the Himalayan mountain barrier providing a commercial motor route linking lowland Pakistan and China.

▶ *The Karakoram Highway is one of the highest major roads in the world. It took over 24,000 workers almost 20 years to complete.*

The landscape

Afghanistan's topography is dominated by the mountains of the Hindu Kush, which spread south and west into numerous mountain spurs. The dry plateau of southwestern Afghanistan extends into Pakistan and the hills which overlook the great Indus Basin. In northern Pakistan the Hindu Kush, Himalayan and Karakoram ranges meet to form one of the world's highest mountain regions.

◀ *The Hunza river rises in the northern Karakoram Range, running for 120 miles (193 km) before joining the Gilgit river.*

▶ *The arid Hindu Kush makes much of Afghanistan uninhabitable, with over 50% of the land lying above 6500 ft (2000 m).*

Hunza river

The plains and foothills which extend from the northern slopes of the Hindu Kush are part of the great grassy steppe lands of Central Asia.

Hindu Kush

K2 (Mount Godwin Austen), in the Karakoram Range, is the second highest mountain in the world, at an altitude of 28,251 ft (8611 m).

Frequent earthquakes mean that mountain-building processes are continuing in this region, as the Indo-Australian Plate drifts northwards, colliding with the Eurasian Plate.

Some of the largest glaciers outside the polar regions are found in the Karakoram Range, including Siachen Glacier *(Siachen Muztagh)*, which is 40 miles (72 km) long.

Himalayas

Mountain chains running southwest from the Hindu Kush into Pakistan form a barrier to the humid winds which blow from the Indian Ocean, creating arid conditions across southern Afghanistan.

The soils of the Punjab plain are nourished by enormous quantities of sediment, carried from the Himalayas by the five tributaries of the Indus river.

The Indus Basin is part of the Indus-Ganges lowland, a vast depression which has been filled with layers of sediment over the last 50 million years. These deposits are estimated to be over 16,400 ft (5000 m) deep.

The Indus Delta is prone to heavy flooding and high levels of salinity. It remains a largely uncultivated wilderness area.

Glacis covered by coarse-grained sediment

Sediments washed down from mountains accumulate on glacis slopes

Bedrock

Fine sediments deposited on salt flats are removed by wind erosion.

▲ *Glacis are gentle, debris-covered slopes which lead into salt flats or deserts. They typically occur at the base of mountains in arid regions such as Afghanistan.*

146
142
142

TURKMENISTAN
IRAN
AFGHANISTAN
Bālā Morghāb
Kārīz-e Elyās
Towraghoudī
Qarah Bāgh
Kūshk
BĀDGHĪS
Qal'eh-ye Now
Qādes
Eslām Qal'eh
Kūhestān
Dasht-e Hamdam Āb
Zendeh Jān
Ghūriān
Herāt
Selseleh-ye Sefīd Kūh
HERĀT
GHOWR
Namakzar
Farāh Rūd
Shīndand
Dak
Anār Darreh
Dasht-e Bābūs
FARĀH
Farāh
Delārām
Now Zād
Hāmūn-e Şāberī
Dasht-e Khāsh
Hāmūn-e Pūzak
NĪMRŪZ
Chakhānsūr
Shelleh-ye Pūdeh Tal
Lashkar Gāh
Gereshk
Zaranj
Dasht-e Mārgow
Darvīshān
Kūchnay Darweyshān
HELMAND
Daryā-ye Helmand
Deh Shū
Dasht-e Gowd-e Zereh
Chāgai Hills
Nok Kundi
Yakmach
Dālbandin
Dasht-i Tāhlāb
Hāmūn-i Māshkel
Kamarod
Siāhān Range
Panjgūr
Central Makran Range
Ispikān
Nihing
Mand
Nasīrābād
Kech
Hoshāb
Turbat
Dasht
Suntsar
Jiwani
Gwādar
Gwadar West Bay
Gwadar East Bay
Pasni
Khor Kalamat
Astola Island
Ormāra

Scale 1:4,500,000

projection: Lambert Conformal Conic

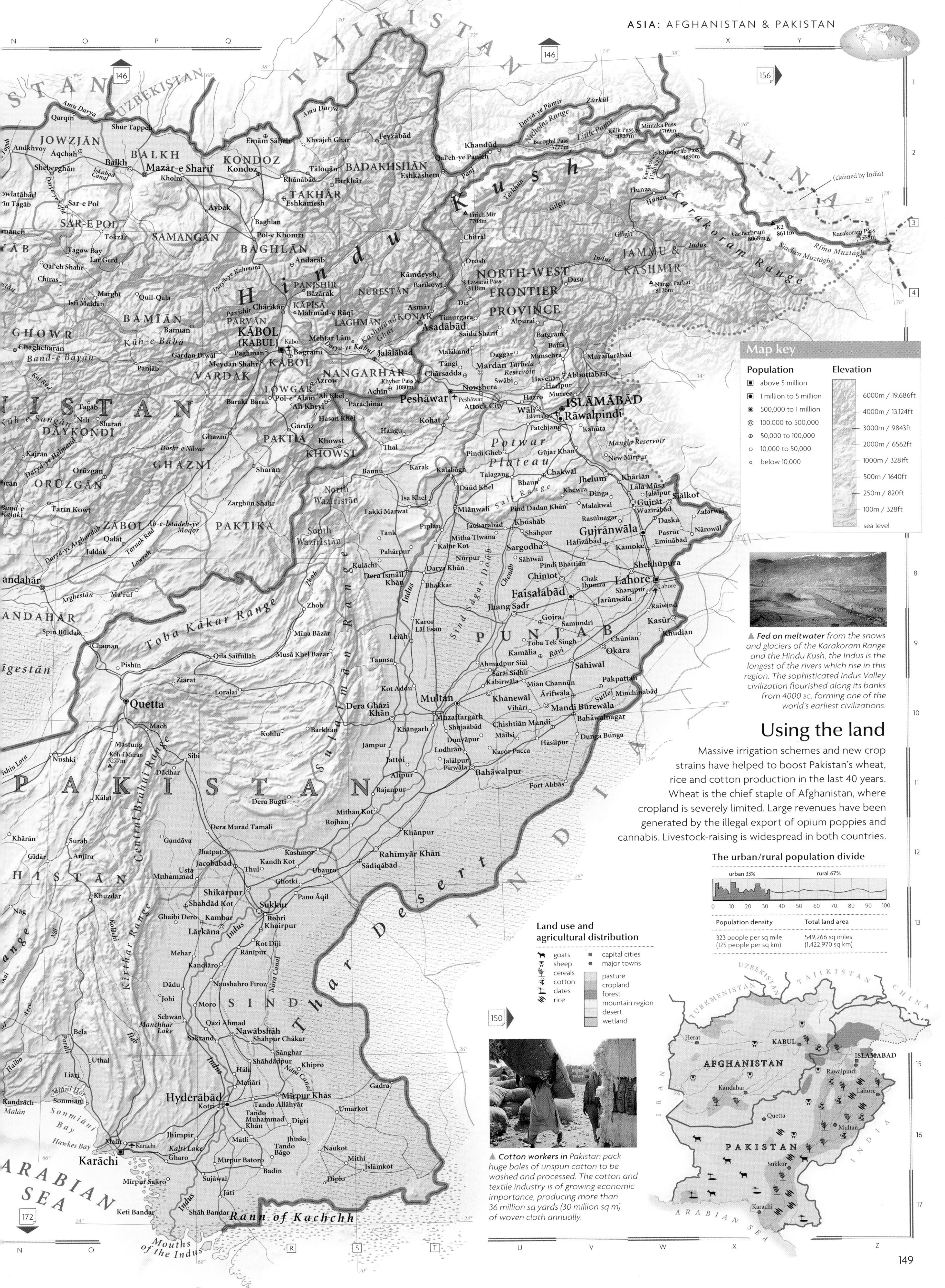

TAJIKISTAN
UZBEKISTAN
CHINA
(claimed by India)
Hindu Kush
Karakoram Range
NORTH-WEST FRONTIER PROVINCE
JAMMU & KASHMIR
ISLĀMĀBĀD
Rāwalpindi
Peshāwar
KĀBOL (KABUL)
Lahore
Faisalābād
Multān
Quetta
Hyderābād
Karāchi
Sukkur
Gujrānwāla
Potwar Plateau
Salt Range
Toba Kākar Range
Sulaimān Range
Central Brāhui Range
Kīrthar Range
Thar Desert
PUNJAB
SIND
PAKISTAN
INDIA
ARABIAN SEA
Rann of Kachchh
Mouths of the Indus
Indus
K2 8611m
Tirich Mir 7708m
Nanga Parbat 8126m
Map key
Population
above 5 million
1 million to 5 million
500,000 to 1 million
100,000 to 500,000
50,000 to 100,000
10,000 to 50,000
below 10,000
Elevation
6000m / 19,686ft
4000m / 13,124ft
3000m / 9843ft
2000m / 6562ft
1000m / 3281ft
500m / 1640ft
250m / 820ft
100m / 328ft
sea level

▲ *Fed on meltwater from the snows and glaciers of the Karakoram Range and the Hindu Kush, the Indus is the longest of the rivers which rise in this region. The sophisticated Indus Valley civilization flourished along its banks from 4000 BC, forming one of the world's earliest civilizations.*

Using the land

Massive irrigation schemes and new crop strains have helped to boost Pakistan's wheat, rice and cotton production in the last 40 years. Wheat is the chief staple of Afghanistan, where cropland is severely limited. Large revenues have been generated by the illegal export of opium poppies and cannabis. Livestock-raising is widespread in both countries.

The urban/rural population divide
urban 33%
rural 67%
0 10 20 30 40 50 60 70 80 90 100
Population density
323 people per sq mile (125 people per sq km)
Total land area
549,266 sq miles (1,422,970 sq km)
Land use and agricultural distribution
goats
sheep
cereals
cotton
dates
rice
capital cities
major towns
pasture
cropland
forest
mountain region
desert
wetland
AFGHANISTAN
PAKISTAN
KABUL
ISLAMABAD
Herat
Kandahar
Quetta
Rawalpindi
Lahore
Multan
Sukkur
Karachi

▲ *Cotton workers in Pakistan pack huge bales of unspun cotton to be washed and processed. The cotton and textile industry is of growing economic importance, producing more than 36 million sq yards (30 million sq m) of woven cloth annually.*

South Asia

BANGLADESH, BHUTAN, INDIA, MALDIVES, NEPAL, PAKISTAN, SRI LANKA

More than one-fifth of the world's population lives in the south Asian subcontinent. Great cultural diversity has come from a long succession of foreign invaders, including Hindu Aryans, Islamic Moguls and the British, whose empire incorporated the princely states of the Maharajas and extended to the borders of Nepal and Bhutan in the Himalayas. Independent since 1947, India is the world's largest democracy, and at the current rate of growth, may overtake China as the world's most populous country during the 21st century. There are points of tension in the region over claims for independence by the Sikhs in the Indian Punjab and the Tamil separatists in Sri Lanka, and the long-standing dispute with Pakistan over Jammu and Kashmir in the north.

◀ *The towering Karakoram and Hindu Kush ranges, formed at the same time as the Himalayas, dominate Pakistan's northern borders. K2 on the border of northern Pakistan is the second highest mountain on Earth, at 28,251 ft (8611 m).*

The landscape

South Asia is effectively isolated from the rest of Asia by desert along the western flank of Pakistan, and a continuous wall of mountains, dominated by the Himalayas, to the north and east. The great basins of the Indus and Ganges separate this mountain fringe from the rolling plateau of the Indian peninsula, which is bordered by a line of coastal hills, the Eastern and Western Ghats.

◀ *The Indus valley near Skardu in northern Pakistan has been partially infilled by great quantities of eroded sediment. Most of this is carried from the region's bare slopes by swollen rivers during the spring thaw and mass movement activity.*

The Himalayas are the highest and most extensive mountain system in the world. They were formed when the Indo-Australian Plate collided with the Eurasian Plate about 40 million years ago, thrusting up huge masses of land and creating a 'ripple' effect, which formed lesser mountain ranges in Tibet and Southeast Asia. Mount Everest is the world's tallest mountain at 29,035 ft (8850 m).

Almost all of Bangladesh lies in the immense delta formed by the Ganges and the Brahmaputra which merge and flow out into the Bay of Bengal.

The Indus river flows more than 1970 miles (3180 km) from southwestern Tibet to its mouth on the Arabian Sea. It has an estimated catchment area of 450,000 sq miles (1,165,500 sq km).

The coast of western Pakistan is a staircase of folded rock strata caused by successive periods of rapid uplift.

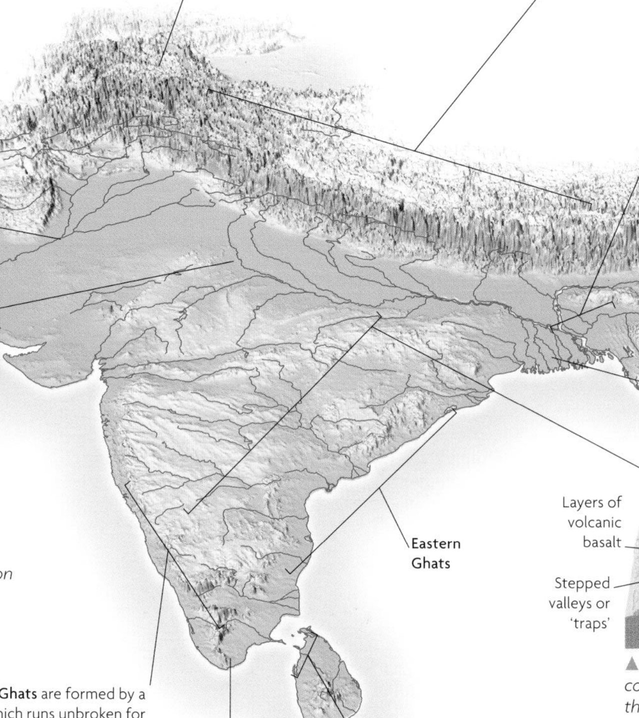

Bharatpur

Ganges delta

Deccan plateau

Eastern Ghats

▲ *Rivers flowing from the Himalayas into a broad depression in northern India have formed marshes around Bharatpur. They are now a sanctuary for numerous bird species.*

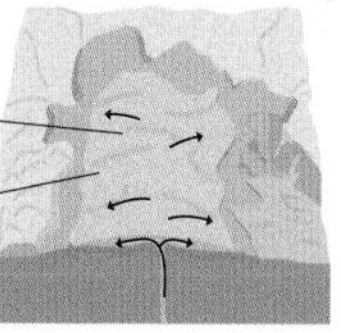

The Western Ghats are formed by a fault scarp which runs unbroken for more than 930 miles (1500 km). They reach their highest point at the southern Cardamom Hills.

Trivandrum in southern India normally receives the first of the monsoon rains, which are essential to south Asian agriculture and moderate the extreme summer heat. The monsoon then moves northwards over a period of about two months.

Coastal deposition has formed many typical features along the western coast of Sri Lanka. These include spits and bars, sometimes enclosing lagoons.

Layers of volcanic basalt

Stepped valleys or 'traps'

▲ *The Deccan plateau covers an area of more than 123,553 sq miles (320,000 sq km). It is formed of deep layers of volcanic basalt, reaching thicknesses of more than 9800 ft (3000 m) towards the coast. Distinctive stepped valleys cut in the basalt plateau by rivers are known as 'traps'.*

146 148 156 156 156 142

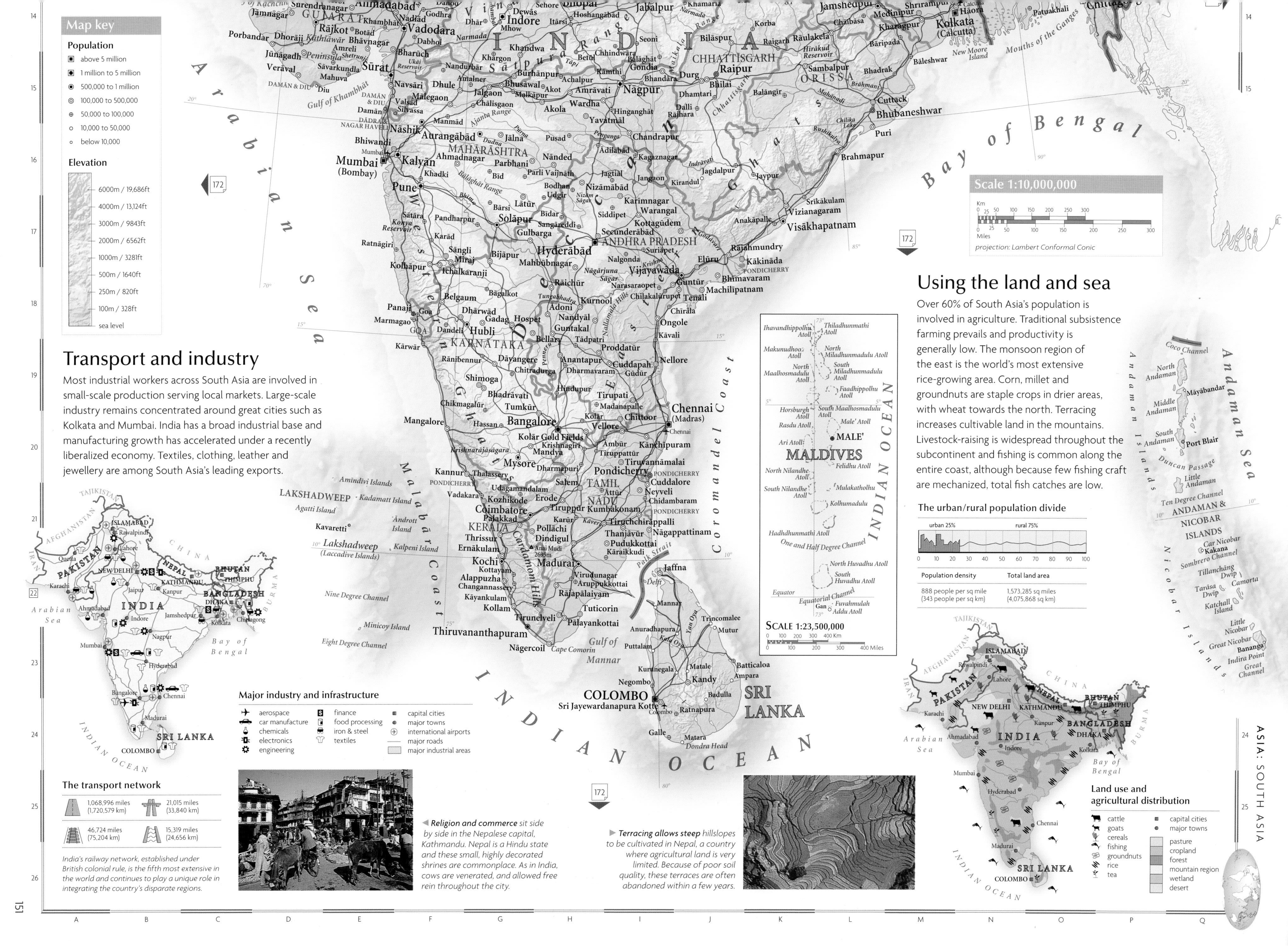
Map key
Population
above 5 million
1 million to 5 million
500,000 to 1 million
100,000 to 500,000
50,000 to 100,000
10,000 to 50,000
below 10,000
Elevation
6000m / 19,686ft
4000m / 13,124ft
3000m / 9843ft
2000m / 6562ft
1000m / 3281ft
500m / 1640ft
250m / 820ft
100m / 328ft
sea level
Scale 1:10,000,000
projection: Lambert Conformal Conic
Arabian Sea
Bay of Bengal
INDIAN OCEAN
INDIA
SRI LANKA
MALDIVES
SCALE 1:23,500,000
Mumbai (Bombay)
Kolkata (Calcutta)
Chennai (Madras)
Hyderābād
Bangalore
COLOMBO
Sri Jayewardanapura Kotte
MALE'
LAKSHADWEEP
Lakshadweep (Laccadive Islands)
ANDAMAN & NICOBAR ISLANDS
Andaman Sea
Andaman Islands
Nicobar Islands
Malabar Coast
Coromandel Coast
Western Ghats
Eastern Ghats
Cardamom Hills
Gulf of Mannar
Palk Strait
Major industry and infrastructure
aerospace
car manufacture
chemicals
electronics
engineering
finance
food processing
iron & steel
textiles
capital cities
major towns
international airports
major roads
major industrial areas
The transport network
1,068,996 miles (1,720,579 km)
21,015 miles (33,840 km)
46,724 miles (75,204 km)
15,319 miles (24,656 km)
The urban/rural population divide
urban 25%
rural 75%
Population density
888 people per sq mile (343 people per sq km)
Total land area
1,573,285 sq miles (4,075,868 sq km)
Land use and agricultural distribution
cattle
goats
cereals
fishing
groundnuts
rice
tea
capital cities
major towns
pasture
cropland
forest
mountain region
wetland
desert

Transport and industry

Most industrial workers across South Asia are involved in small-scale production serving local markets. Large-scale industry remains concentrated around great cities such as Kolkata and Mumbai. India has a broad industrial base and manufacturing growth has accelerated under a recently liberalized economy. Textiles, clothing, leather and jewellery are among South Asia's leading exports.

India's railway network, established under British colonial rule, is the fifth most extensive in the world and continues to play a unique role in integrating the country's disparate regions.

◀ ***Religion and commerce*** *sit side by side in the Nepalese capital, Kathmandu. Nepal is a Hindu state and these small, highly decorated shrines are commonplace. As in India, cows are venerated, and allowed free rein throughout the city.*

Using the land and sea

Over 60% of South Asia's population is involved in agriculture. Traditional subsistence farming prevails and productivity is generally low. The monsoon region of the east is the world's most extensive rice-growing area. Corn, millet and groundnuts are staple crops in drier areas, with wheat towards the north. Terracing increases cultivable land in the mountains. Livestock-raising is widespread throughout the subcontinent and fishing is common along the entire coast, although because few fishing craft are mechanized, total fish catches are low.

▶ ***Terracing allows steep*** *hillslopes to be cultivated in Nepal, a country where agricultural land is very limited. Because of poor soil quality, these terraces are often abandoned within a few years.*

172

Northern India & the Himalayan states

BANGLADESH, BHUTAN, NEPAL, Arunachal Pradesh, Assam, Bihar, Chandigarh, Delhi, Haryana, Himachal Pradesh, Jammu & Kashmir, Jharkhand, Manipur, Meghalaya, Mizoram, Nagaland, Punjab, Rajasthan, Sikkim, Tripura, Uttarakhand, Uttar Pradesh, West Bengal

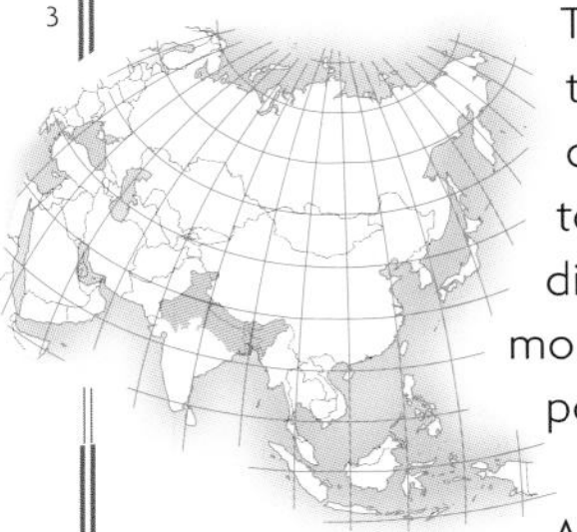

The Ganges and Brahmaputra river basins and the massive mountain barrier of the Himalayas define this region's landscape and have served to reinforce potent cultural and religious differences among its people. Hinduism pervades most aspects of national life and is a growing political force within India, a secular country which also encompasses the centre of Sikhism at Amritsar and the world's largest Muslim minority. Nepal is a crowded mountain state, which faces severe ecological problems from deforestation, while the tiny Himalayan Buddhist kingdom of Bhutan is emerging from long-term isolation, to welcome selected visitors. The Muslim state of Bangladesh, formerly East Pakistan, is one of the world's most densely populated countries and one of the poorest, with more than 145 million people living largely on the massive Ganges/Brahmaputra delta. Many Bangladeshis live under threat of repeated, catastrophic floods.

◄ ***The Golden Temple** in Amritsar, the most sacred shrine of the Sikh religion, was the scene of violent clashes between Sikh separatists and government forces in 1984.*

Scale 1:5,750,000

Km 0 10 20 40 60 80 100 120 140 160 180 200

0 10 20 40 60 80 100 120 140 160 180 200 Miles

projection: Lambert Conformal Conic

156

148

154

Map key

Population

- ■ 1 million to 5 million
- ◉ 500,000 to 1 million
- ◎ 100,000 to 500,000
- ⊕ 50,000 to 100,000
- ○ 10,000 to 50,000
- ∘ below 10,000

Elevation

- 6000m / 19,686ft
- 4000m / 13,124ft
- 3000m / 9843ft
- 2000m / 6562ft
- 1000m / 3281ft
- 500m / 1640ft
- 250m / 820ft
- 100m / 328ft
- sea level

Transport and industry

Textiles, engineering, chemicals and electronics are leading industries in north India. The plateau of Chota Nagpur provides ore for iron and steel production in the major industrial region northeast of Kolkata. Bangladesh processes jute and Nepal has a small manufacturing sector based on agricultural produce, while Bhutan's limited industry is concentrated in the southern lowland area.

Major industry and infrastructure

- adventure tourism
- car manufacture
- chemicals
- coal
- electronics
- engineering
- finance
- food processing
- iron & steel
- jute processing
- oil
- tea processing
- textiles
- capital cities
- major towns
- international airports
- major roads
- major industrial areas

The transport network

Over 60% of Bangladesh's internal trade is carried by boat. The country has a very disjointed land transport network, with no bridges over the Brahmaputra and few road crossings on the Ganges river.

The landscape

Most of the region is drained by the Ganges river, which meets the Brahmaputra in Bangladesh to form an immense delta before flowing into the Bay of Bengal. The Himalayas extend eastwards over 1500 miles (2400 km), from the parallel ranges running through Jammu and Kashmir. The Thar Desert occupies the southwest.

► *The Pir Panjal range in southwestern Kashmir rises to elevations of 12,500 ft (3810 m). Despite the freezing conditions, settlements and extensive pastures are found above the tree line.*

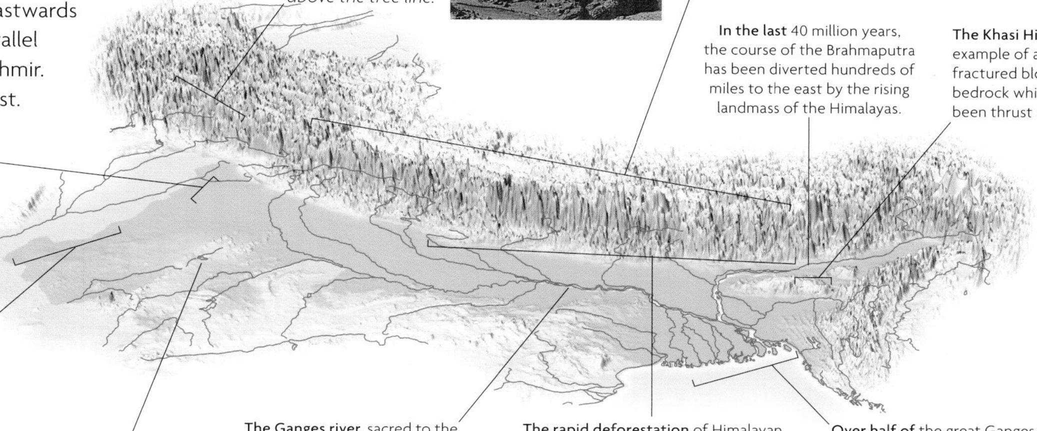

The northern ranges of the Himalayas contain the highest mountains in the world, with average heights of more than 23,000 ft (7000 m) and many peaks higher than 26,000 ft (8000 m).

In the last 40 million years, the course of the Brahmaputra has been diverted hundreds of miles to the east by the rising landmass of the Himalayas.

The Khasi Hills are an example of a *horst*, a fractured block of bedrock which has been thrust upwards.

▲ ***The summit of*** *Machhapuchhre rises to 22,942 ft (6993 m). It is also known as the 'Fish's Tail' because of its distinctive peak.*

The Indian Punjab lies mainly to the west of the Ganges watershed and its rivers flow into the Indus. Control of this water resource has been a source of great friction with neighbouring Pakistan.

The border between India and Pakistan runs through the Thar Desert, an area of sandy *seif* dunes 50–100 ft (15–30 m) in height. Fossils found in the desert indicate that the dunes, stabilized by vegetation, have been in their current position for about 3000 years.

Sambhar Salt Lake in Rajasthan is India's largest lake. Unlike most of the Himalayan lakes which are glacial in origin – formed in ice-scoured basins or as the result of depositional damming – it is an ephemeral salt lake filled periodically by flash flooding.

The Ganges river, sacred to the Hindu people, drains a vast lowland area at the base of the Himalayas. The northern plains are covered by sandy deposits, broken by mud-banks formed when the river floods.

The rapid deforestation of Himalayan valleys has led to acute soil erosion and increased rates of rainwater run-off, both cited as possible causes of the worsening floods downstream in the Ganges/Brahmaputra delta, although natural rates are high and may be the real cause.

Over half of the great Ganges/Brahmaputra delta floods each year during the monsoon as rivers, swollen by meltwater from the Himalayas and by excess rainwater, break their banks and fertilize the land with nutrient-rich sediment.

Debris slides in the middle Himalayas

Debris fans at base of slope
Soil blocks
Slide plain

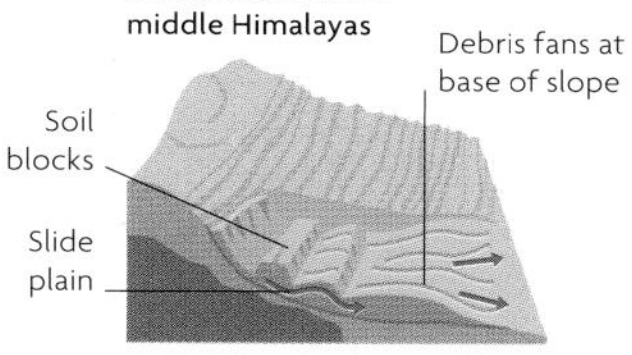

▲ ***Soil loss in*** *the middle Himalayas has largely been attributed to debris slides, where large blocks of soil are mobilized by saturation along a slide plane. Once mobile, the soil slides down the slope, gaining speed and thinning to form a fan at the base of the slope.*

Using the land

Grain production dominates land use. Rice is most widely grown in the east. Irrigation and new crop strains have dramatically increased yields in the Punjab, a major wheat-producing area. River flood plains are intensively farmed and livestock-herding is widespread, particularly in Bhutan. Regional crops include jute in Bangladesh, tea in Assam, cardamom in Sikkim and saffron in Kashmir.

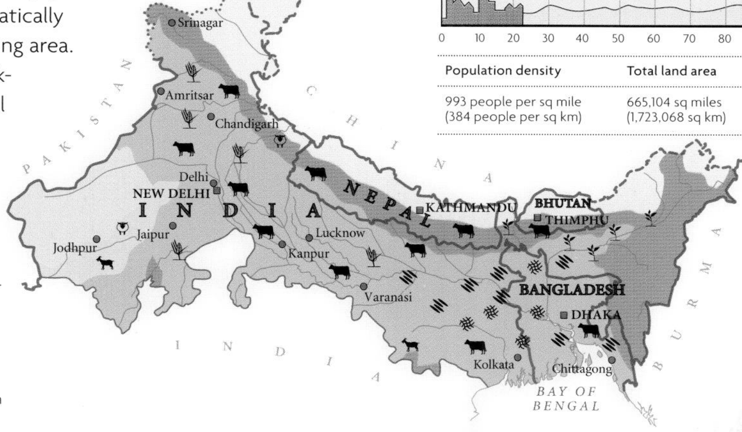

The urban/rural population divide

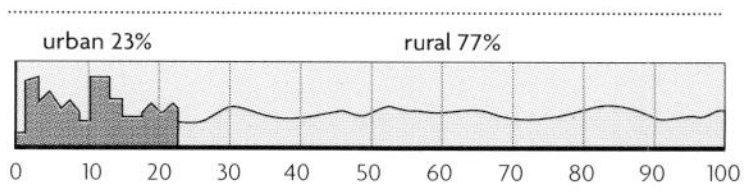

urban 23% | rural 77%

0 10 20 30 40 50 60 70 80 90 100

Population density	Total land area
993 people per sq mile (384 people per sq km)	665,104 sq miles (1,723,068 sq km)

▲ ***An adverse climate,*** *steep slopes and poor soils limit crop cultivation in Bhutan, which is a largely agrarian economy. Rice, corn and wheat are the main staples, although orchards are being established as the soil and climate suit this type of farming.*

Land use and agricultural distribution

cattle, goats, sheep, cereals, jute, rice, tea
capital cities, major towns
pasture, cropland, forest, mountain region, wetland, desert

156

166

172

▲ ***Flooded streets in*** *Dhaka, Bangladesh are a testament to the region's vulnerability to flooding. In 1988 alone, 75% of the country was flooded, leaving thousands of people dead and over 25 million homeless.*

Southern India & Sri Lanka

SRI LANKA, Andhra Pradesh, Chhattisgarh, Dadra & Nagar Haveli, Daman & Diu, Goa, Gujarat, Karnataka, Kerala, Lakshadweep, Madhya Pradesh, Maharashtra, Orissa, Pondicherry, Tamil Nadu

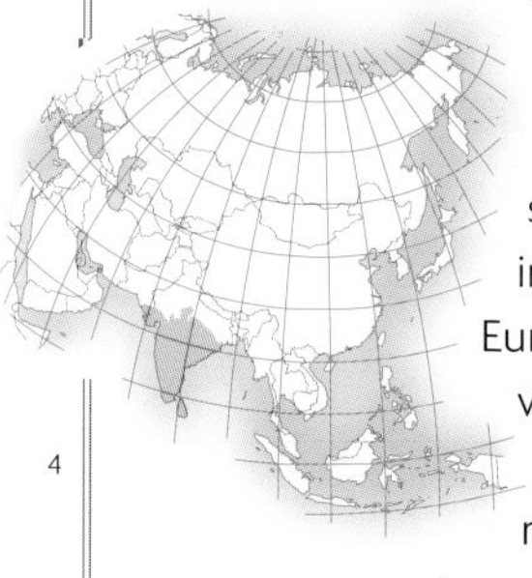

The unique and highly independent southern states reflect the diverse and decentralized nature of India, which has fourteen official languages. The southern half of the peninsula lay beyond the reach of early invaders from the north and retained the distinct and ancient culture of Dravidian peoples such as the Tamils, whose language is spoken in preference to Hindi throughout southern India. The interior plateau of southern India is less densely populated than the coastal lowlands, where the European colonial imprint is strongest. Urban and industrial growth is accelerating, but southern India's vast population remains predominantly rural. The island of Sri Lanka has two distinct cultural groups; the mainly Buddhist Sinhalese majority, and the Tamil minority whose struggle for a homeland in the northeast has led to prolonged civil war.

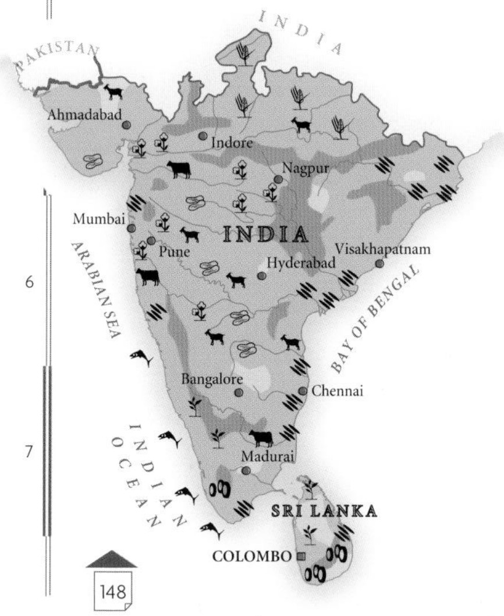

Using the land and sea

Rice is the main staple in the east, in Sri Lanka and along the humid Malabar Coast. Groundnuts are grown on the Deccan plateau, with wheat, corn and chickpeas, towards the north. Sri Lanka is a leading exporter of tea, coconuts and rubber. Cotton plantations supply local mills around Nagpur and Mumbai. Fishing supports many communities in Kerala and the Laccadive Islands.

Land use and agricultural distribution

cattle, goats, cereals, cotton, fishing, groundnuts, rice, rubber, tea, capital cities, major towns, pasture, cropland, forest, wetland

The urban/rural population divide

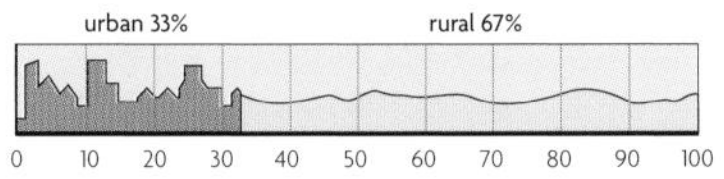

urban 33% — rural 67%

Population density	Total land area
730 people per sq mile (282 people per sq km)	698,295 sq miles (1,809,054 sq km)

The landscape

The undulating Deccan plateau underlies most of southern India; it slopes gently down towards the east and is largely enclosed by the Ghats coastal hill ranges. The Western Ghats run continuously along the Arabian Sea coast, while the Eastern Ghats are interrupted by rivers which follow the slope of the plateau and flow across broad lowlands into the Bay of Bengal. The plateaux and basins of Sri Lanka's central highlands are surrounded by a broad plain.

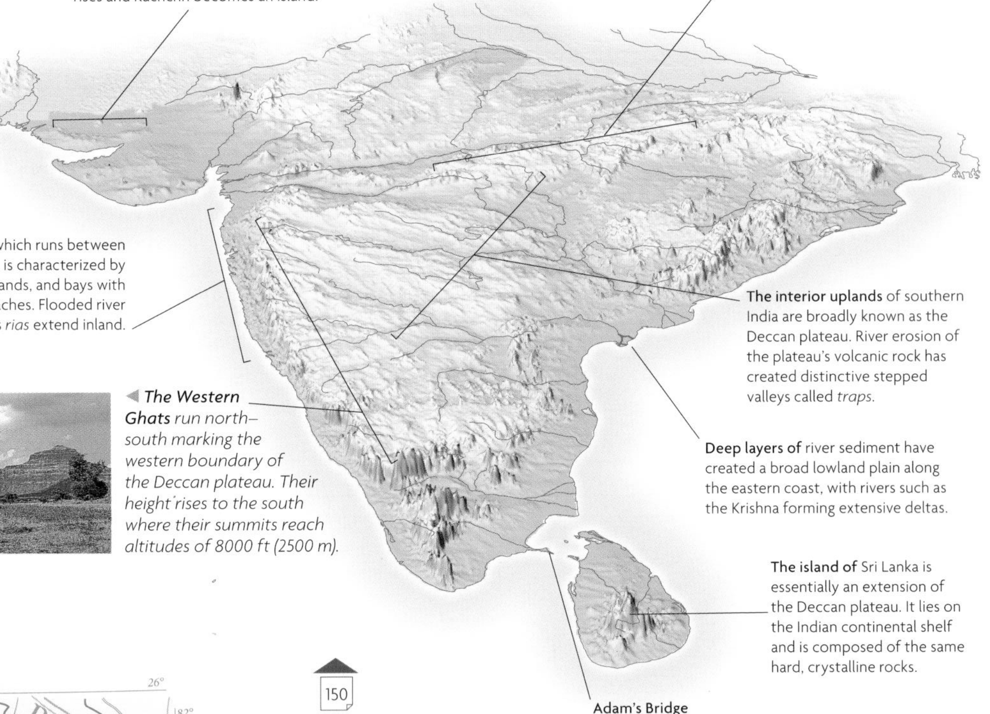

The Rann of Kachchh tidal marshes encircle the low-lying Kachchh peninsula. For several months during the rainy season the water level of the marshes rises and Kachchh becomes an island.

Along the northern boundary of the Deccan plateau, old basement rocks are interspersed with younger sedimentary strata. This creates spectacular scarplands, cut by numerous waterfalls along the softer sedimentary strata.

The Konkan coast, which runs between Daman and Goa, is characterized by rocky headlands, and bays with crescent-shaped beaches. Flooded river valleys known as *rias* extend inland.

The interior uplands of southern India are broadly known as the Deccan plateau. River erosion of the plateau's volcanic rock has created distinctive stepped valleys called *traps*.

◀ ***The Western Ghats*** *run north–south marking the western boundary of the Deccan plateau. Their height rises to the south where their summits reach altitudes of 8000 ft (2500 m).*

Deep layers of river sediment have created a broad lowland plain along the eastern coast, with rivers such as the Krishna forming extensive deltas.

The island of Sri Lanka is essentially an extension of the Deccan plateau. It lies on the Indian continental shelf and is composed of the same hard, crystalline rocks.

Adam's Bridge

Relict of ancient tombolo

Adam's Bridge

Ocean currents cause sediment build up

Sri Lanka

▲ ***Adam's Bridge (Rama's Bridge)*** *is a chain of sandy shoals lying about 4 ft (1.2 m) under the sea between India and Sri Lanka. They once formed the world's longest tombolo, or land bridge, before the sea level began to rise several thousand years ago.*

148
150
172

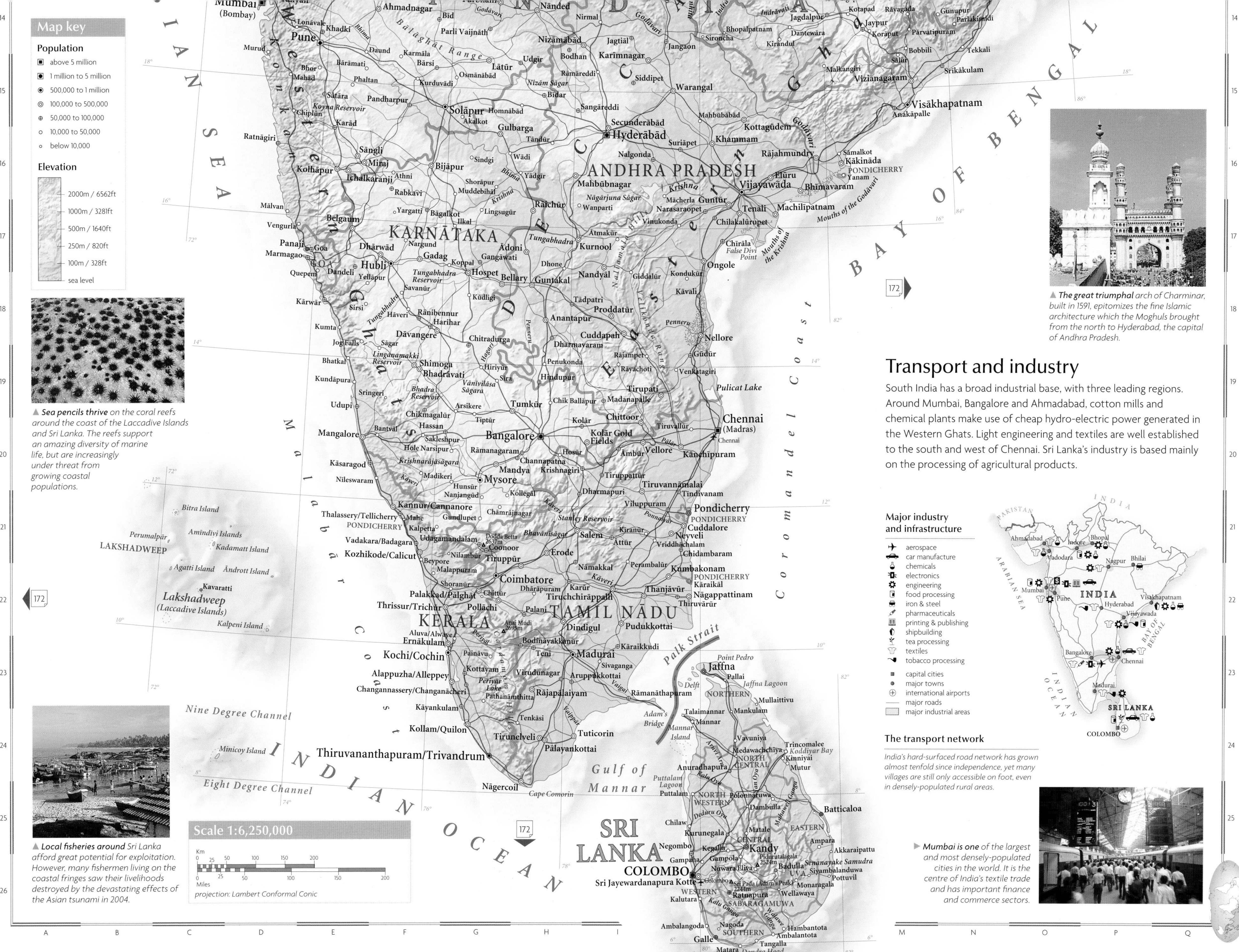
Map key
Population
above 5 million
1 million to 5 million
500,000 to 1 million
100,000 to 500,000
50,000 to 100,000
10,000 to 50,000
below 10,000
Elevation
2000m / 6562ft
1000m / 3281ft
500m / 1640ft
250m / 820ft
100m / 328ft
sea level
Scale 1:6,250,000
Km
Miles
projection: Lambert Conformal Conic
ARABIAN SEA
BAY OF BENGAL
INDIAN OCEAN
KARNATAKA
ANDHRA PRADESH
TAMIL NADU
KERALA
SRI LANKA
COLOMBO
Sri Jayewardanapura Kotte
Lakshadweep
(Laccadive Islands)
LAKSHADWEEP
Western Ghats
Eastern Ghats
Deccan
Konkan
Malabar Coast
Coromandel Coast
Gulf of Mannar
Palk Strait
Nine Degree Channel
Eight Degree Channel
Mumbai
(Bombay)
Hyderābād
Bangalore
Chennai
(Madras)
Pondicherry
172
INDIA
PAKISTAN
ARABIAN SEA
BAY OF BENGAL
INDIAN OCEAN
Ahmadabad
Vadodara
Indore
Bhopal
Nagpur
Bhilai
Mumbai
Pune
Hyderabad
Visakhapatnam
Vijayawada
Bangalore
Chennai
Madurai
SRI LANKA
COLOMBO

▲ **Sea pencils thrive** on the coral reefs around the coast of the Laccadive Islands and Sri Lanka. The reefs support an amazing diversity of marine life, but are increasingly under threat from growing coastal populations.

▲ **Local fisheries around** Sri Lanka afford great potential for exploitation. However, many fishermen living on the coastal fringes saw their livelihoods destroyed by the devastating effects of the Asian tsunami in 2004.

▲ **The great triumphal** arch of Charminar, built in 1591, epitomizes the fine Islamic architecture which the Moghuls brought from the north to Hyderabad, the capital of Andhra Pradesh.

Transport and industry

South India has a broad industrial base, with three leading regions. Around Mumbai, Bangalore and Ahmadabad, cotton mills and chemical plants make use of cheap hydro-electric power generated in the Western Ghats. Light engineering and textiles are well established to the south and west of Chennai. Sri Lanka's industry is based mainly on the processing of agricultural products.

Major industry and infrastructure

- aerospace
- car manufacture
- chemicals
- electronics
- engineering
- food processing
- iron & steel
- pharmaceuticals
- printing & publishing
- shipbuilding
- tea processing
- textiles
- tobacco processing
- capital cities
- major towns
- international airports
- major roads
- major industrial areas

The transport network

India's hard-surfaced road network has grown almost tenfold since independence, yet many villages are still only accessible on foot, even in densely-populated rural areas.

▶ **Mumbai is one** of the largest and most densely-populated cities in the world. It is the centre of India's textile trade and has important finance and commerce sectors.

Mainland East Asia

CHINA, MONGOLIA, NORTH KOREA, SOUTH KOREA, TAIWAN

China, the world's most populous nation, has an unbroken cultural history, longer than that of any other country, and is rapidly emerging as a leading world power. When Mao Zedong established Communist rule in 1949, China had become a backward feudal empire, stricken by civil war and over a century of European and Japanese incursions. The closed regime withstood the traumas of rapid industrialization, communalized farming and the brutal purges of the Cultural Revolution but, since the 1980s has introduced economic reforms, led by expanded foreign trade. China's population is heavily concentrated in the east and, despite accelerating urban growth, remains predominantly rural. One cultural group, the Han, make up over 90% of the people, while five 'Autonomous Regions' have been established in the south and west for the main ethnic minorities.

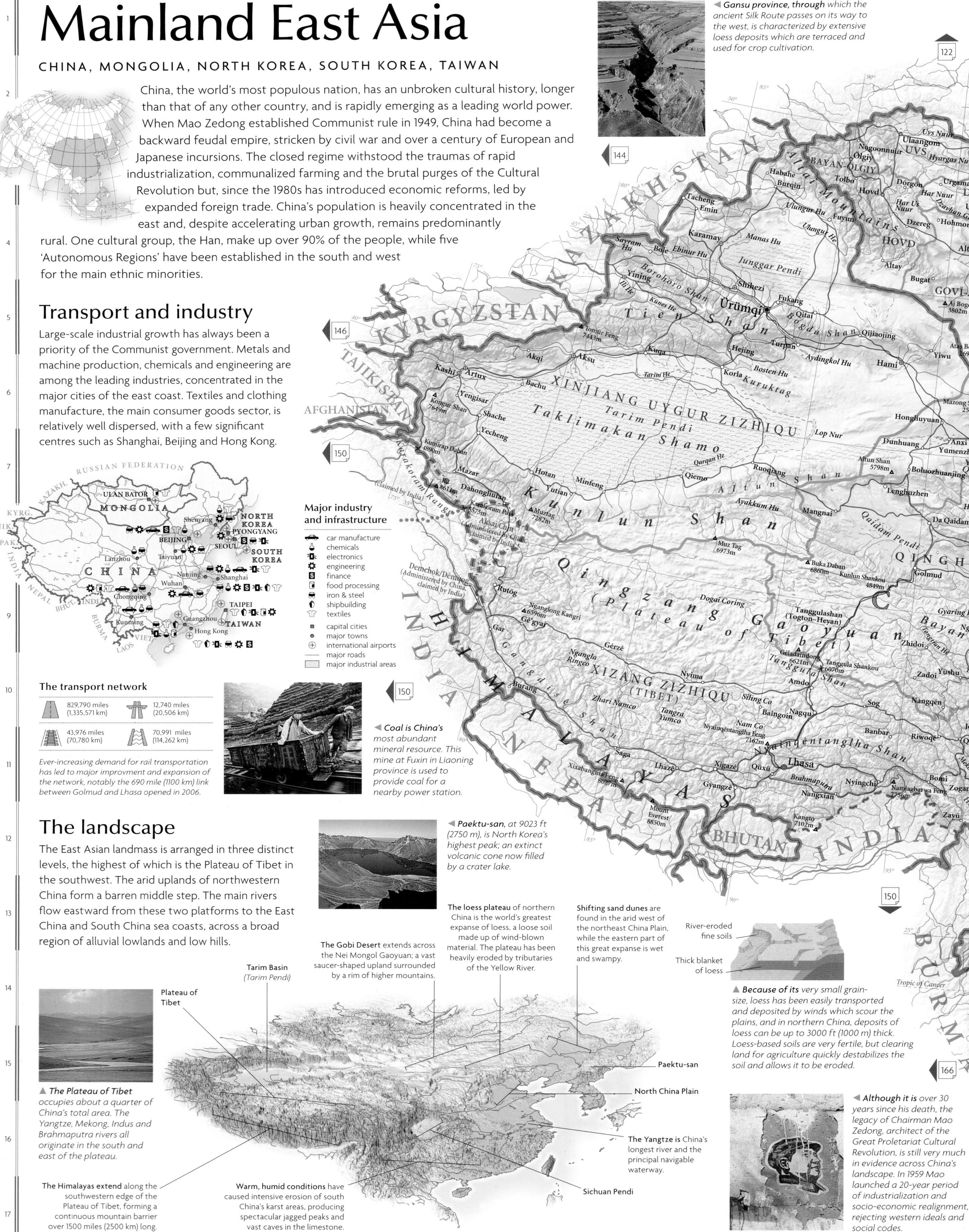

Major industry and infrastructure
car manufacture
chemicals
electronics
engineering
finance
food processing
iron & steel
shipbuilding
textiles
capital cities
major towns
international airports
major roads
major industrial areas

Transport and industry

Large-scale industrial growth has always been a priority of the Communist government. Metals and machine production, chemicals and engineering are among the leading industries, concentrated in the major cities of the east coast. Textiles and clothing manufacture, the main consumer goods sector, is relatively well dispersed, with a few significant centres such as Shanghai, Beijing and Hong Kong.

The transport network

829,790 miles (1,335,571 km)	12,740 miles (20,506 km)
43,976 miles (70,780 km)	70,991 miles (114,262 km)

Ever-increasing demand for rail transportation has led to major improvment and expansion of the network, notably the 690 mile (1100 km) link between Golmud and Lhasa opened in 2006.

◀ **Coal is China's** most abundant mineral resource. This mine at Fuxin in Liaoning province is used to provide coal for a nearby power station.

◀ **Gansu province, through** which the ancient Silk Route passes on its way to the west, is characterized by extensive loess deposits which are terraced and used for crop cultivation.

The landscape

The East Asian landmass is arranged in three distinct levels, the highest of which is the Plateau of Tibet in the southwest. The arid uplands of northwestern China form a barren middle step. The main rivers flow eastward from these two platforms to the East China and South China sea coasts, across a broad region of alluvial lowlands and low hills.

◀ **Paektu-san,** at 9023 ft (2750 m), is North Korea's highest peak; an extinct volcanic cone now filled by a crater lake.

▲ **The Plateau of Tibet** occupies about a quarter of China's total area. The Yangtze, Mekong, Indus and Brahmaputra rivers all originate in the south and east of the plateau.

Plateau of Tibet
Tarim Basin (Tarim Pendi)
Paektu-san
North China Plain
Sichuan Pendi
River-eroded fine soils
Thick blanket of loess

The Gobi Desert extends across the Nei Mongol Gaoyuan; a vast saucer-shaped upland surrounded by a rim of higher mountains.

The loess plateau of northern China is the world's greatest expanse of loess, a loose soil made up of wind-blown material. The plateau has been heavily eroded by tributaries of the Yellow River.

Shifting sand dunes are found in the arid west of the northeast China Plain, while the eastern part of this great expanse is wet and swampy.

The Yangtze is China's longest river and the principal navigable waterway.

The Himalayas extend along the southwestern edge of the Plateau of Tibet, forming a continuous mountain barrier over 1500 miles (2500 km) long.

Warm, humid conditions have caused intensive erosion of south China's karst areas, producing spectacular jagged peaks and vast caves in the limestone.

▲ **Because of its** very small grain-size, loess has been easily transported and deposited by winds which scour the plains, and in northern China, deposits of loess can be up to 3000 ft (1000 m) thick. Loess-based soils are very fertile, but clearing land for agriculture quickly destabilizes the soil and allows it to be eroded.

◀ **Although it is** over 30 years since his death, the legacy of Chairman Mao Zedong, architect of the Great Proletarian Cultural Revolution, is still very much in evidence across China's landscape. In 1959 Mao launched a 20-year period of industrialization and socio-economic realignment, rejecting western ideals and social codes.

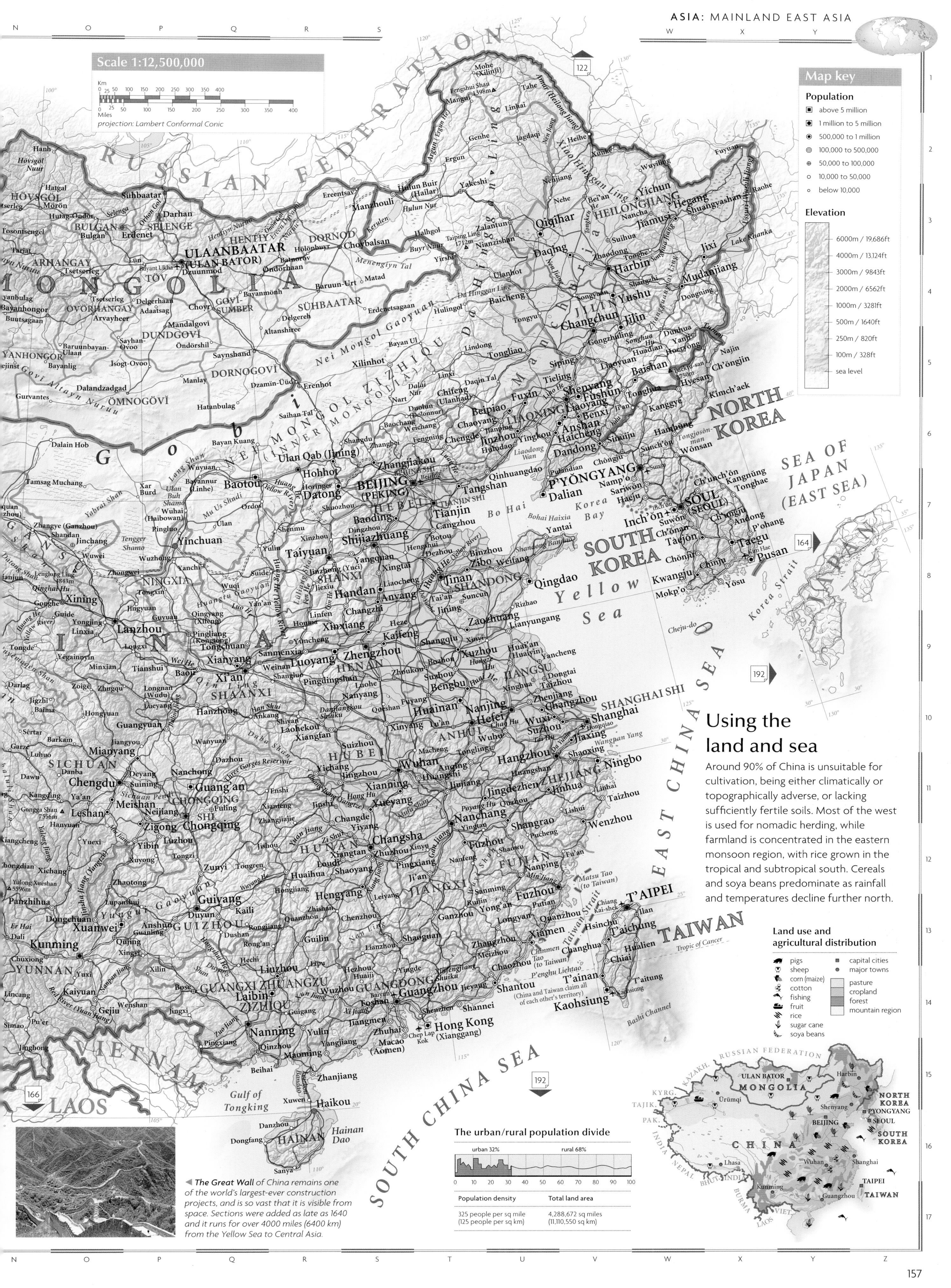
Scale 1:12,500,000
projection: Lambert Conformal Conic
Map key
Population
above 5 million
1 million to 5 million
500,000 to 1 million
100,000 to 500,000
50,000 to 100,000
10,000 to 50,000
below 10,000
Elevation
6000m / 19,686ft
4000m / 13,124ft
3000m / 9843ft
2000m / 6562ft
1000m / 3281ft
500m / 1640ft
250m / 820ft
100m / 328ft
sea level
Land use and agricultural distribution
pigs
sheep
corn (maize)
cotton
fishing
fruit
rice
sugar cane
soya beans
capital cities
major towns
pasture
cropland
forest
mountain region
The urban/rural population divide
urban 32%
rural 68%
Population density
325 people per sq mile (125 people per sq km)
Total land area
4,288,672 sq miles (11,110,550 sq km)

Using the land and sea

Around 90% of China is unsuitable for cultivation, being either climatically or topographically adverse, or lacking sufficiently fertile soils. Most of the west is used for nomadic herding, while farmland is concentrated in the eastern monsoon region, with rice grown in the tropical and subtropical south. Cereals and soya beans predominate as rainfall and temperatures decline further north.

◀ *The Great Wall of China remains one of the world's largest-ever construction projects, and is so vast that it is visible from space. Sections were added as late as 1640 and it runs for over 4000 miles (6400 km) from the Yellow Sea to Central Asia.*

Western China

Gansu, Ningxia, Qinghai, Tibet, Xinjiang

The plateaux and basins of China's dry, desolate western domain are sparsely populated and largely undeveloped, although they have rich mineral reserves; they also form a critical buffer zone for China, in a geographically important and culturally sensitive part of the Asian continent. Across most of the west, the Han Chinese are outnumbered by a range of cultural groups, including the Uygur, the largest group of the various semi-nomadic Muslim peoples from Central Asia. The remote, inhospitable Plateau of Tibet is the world's coldest and highest plateau. It has been occupied by the Chinese since 1950. Tibet is one of western China's five 'Autonomous Regions', but its reclusive Buddhist culture has been systematically undermined by the Chinese government.

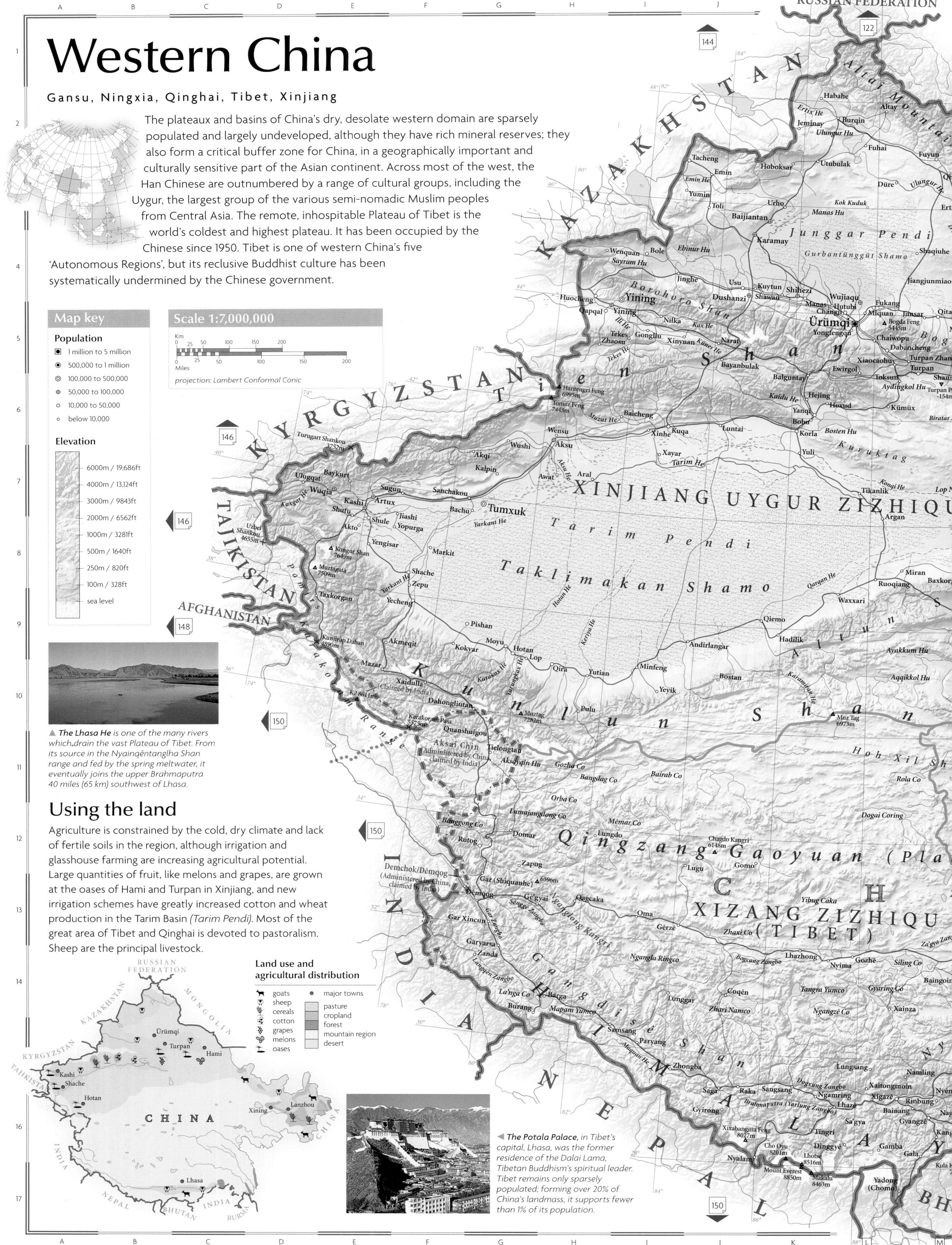

Map key
Population
1 million to 5 million
500,000 to 1 million
100,000 to 500,000
50,000 to 100,000
10,000 to 50,000
below 10,000
Elevation
6000m / 19,686ft
4000m / 13,124ft
3000m / 9843ft
2000m / 6562ft
1000m / 3281ft
500m / 1640ft
250m / 820ft
100m / 328ft
sea level
Scale 1:7,000,000
projection: Lambert Conformal Conic
RUSSIAN FEDERATION
KAZAKHSTAN
KYRGYZSTAN
TAJIKISTAN
AFGHANISTAN
INDIA
NEPAL
XINJIANG UYGUR ZIZHIQU
XIZANG ZIZHIQU (TIBET)
Tarim Pendi
Taklimakan Shamo
Junggar Pendi
Tien Shan
Kunlun Shan
Altun Shan
Qingzang Gaoyuan
Gangdisê Shan
Karakoram Range
Ürümqi
Kashi
Hotan
Mount Everest 8850m
Land use and agricultural distribution
goats
sheep
cereals
cotton
grapes
melons
oases
major towns
pasture
cropland
forest
mountain region
desert

▲ *The Lhasa He is one of the many rivers which drain the vast Plateau of Tibet. From its source in the Nyainqêntanglha Shan range and fed by the spring meltwater, it eventually joins the upper Brahmaputra 40 miles (65 km) southwest of Lhasa.*

Using the land

Agriculture is constrained by the cold, dry climate and lack of fertile soils in the region, although irrigation and glasshouse farming are increasing agricultural potential. Large quantities of fruit, like melons and grapes, are grown at the oases of Hami and Turpan in Xinjiang, and new irrigation schemes have greatly increased cotton and wheat production in the Tarim Basin *(Tarim Pendi)*. Most of the great area of Tibet and Qinghai is devoted to pastoralism. Sheep are the principal livestock.

◀ *The Potala Palace, in Tibet's capital, Lhasa, was the former residence of the Dalai Lama, Tibetan Buddhism's spiritual leader. Tibet remains only sparsely populated; forming over 20% of China's landmass, it supports fewer than 1% of its population.*

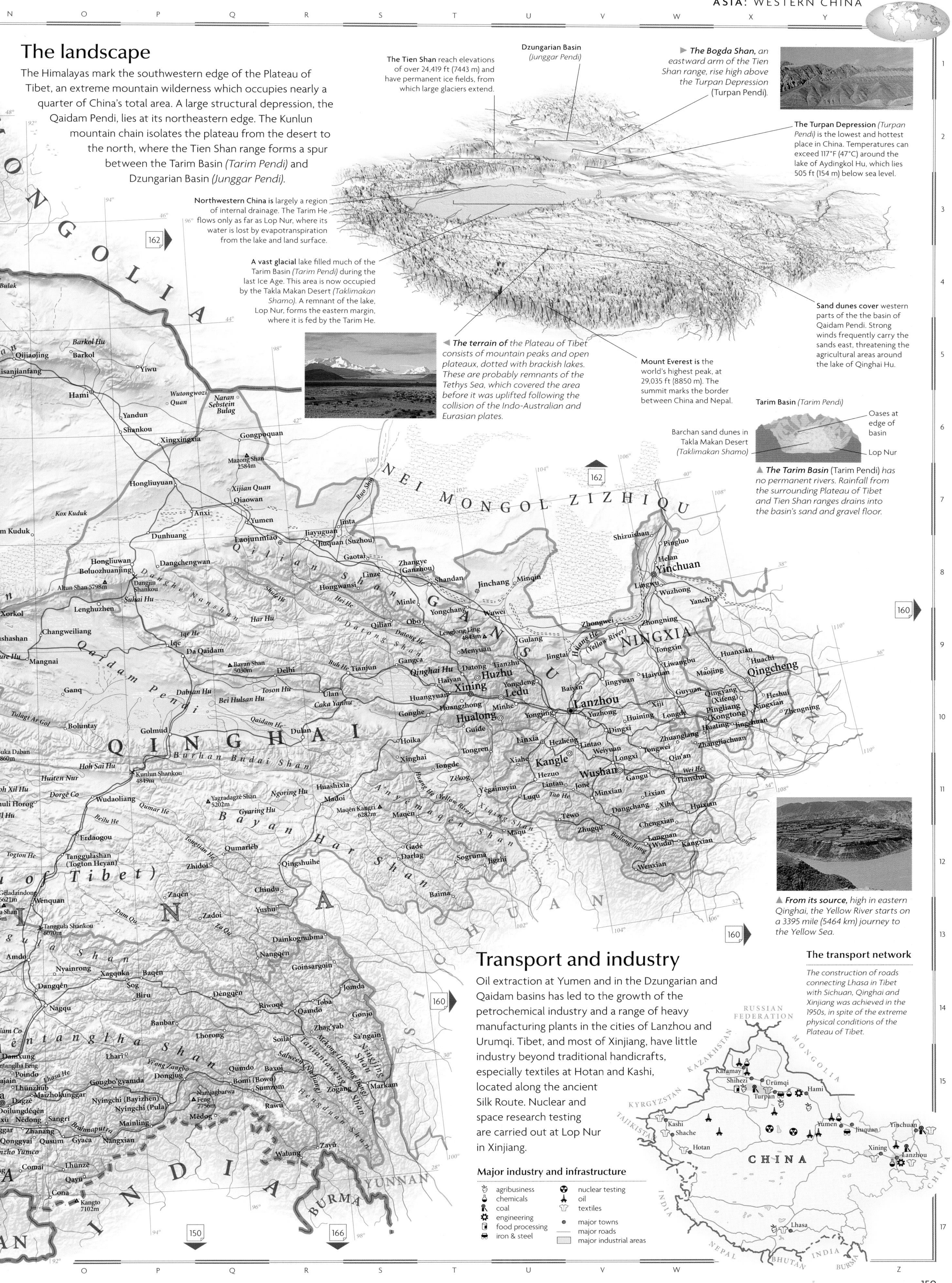

Dzungarian Basin (Junggar Pendi)
The Tien Shan reach elevations of over 24,419 ft (7443 m) and have permanent ice fields, from which large glaciers extend.
Northwestern China is largely a region of internal drainage. The Tarim He flows only as far as Lop Nur, where its water is lost by evapotranspiration from the lake and land surface.
A vast glacial lake filled much of the Tarim Basin (Tarim Pendi) during the last Ice Age. This area is now occupied by the Takla Makan Desert (Taklimakan Shamo). A remnant of the lake, Lop Nur, forms the eastern margin, where it is fed by the Tarim He.
The Turpan Depression (Turpan Pendi) is the lowest and hottest place in China. Temperatures can exceed 117°F (47°C) around the lake of Aydingkol Hu, which lies 505 ft (154 m) below sea level.
Sand dunes cover western parts of the the basin of Qaidam Pendi. Strong winds frequently carry the sands east, threatening the agricultural areas around the lake of Qinghai Hu.
Mount Everest is the world's highest peak, at 29,035 ft (8850 m). The summit marks the border between China and Nepal.
Tarim Basin (Tarim Pendi)
Oases at edge of basin
Barchan sand dunes in Takla Makan Desert (Taklimakan Shamo)
Lop Nur
MONGOLIA
NEI MONGOL ZIZHIQU
GANSU
NINGXIA
QINGHAI
SICHUAN
INDIA
BURMA
YUNNAN
Qaidam Pendi
Plateau of Tibet
Major industry and infrastructure
agribusiness
chemicals
coal
engineering
food processing
iron & steel
nuclear testing
oil
textiles
major towns
major roads
major industrial areas
RUSSIAN FEDERATION
KAZAKHSTAN
KYRGYZSTAN
TAJIKISTAN
MONGOLIA
CHINA
NEPAL
BHUTAN
INDIA
BURMA
Karamay
Shihezi
Ürümqi
Turpan
Hami
Kashi
Shache
Hotan
Yumen
Jiuquan
Yinchuan
Xining
Lanzhou
Lhasa

The landscape

The Himalayas mark the southwestern edge of the Plateau of Tibet, an extreme mountain wilderness which occupies nearly a quarter of China's total area. A large structural depression, the Qaidam Pendi, lies at its northeastern edge. The Kunlun mountain chain isolates the plateau from the desert to the north, where the Tien Shan range forms a spur between the Tarim Basin *(Tarim Pendi)* and Dzungarian Basin *(Junggar Pendi)*.

▶ *The Bogda Shan, an eastward arm of the Tien Shan range, rise high above the Turpan Depression* (Turpan Pendi).

◀ *The terrain of the Plateau of Tibet consists of mountain peaks and open plateaux, dotted with brackish lakes. These are probably remnants of the Tethys Sea, which covered the area before it was uplifted following the collision of the Indo-Australian and Eurasian plates.*

▲ *The Tarim Basin* (Tarim Pendi) *has no permanent rivers. Rainfall from the surrounding Plateau of Tibet and Tien Shan ranges drains into the basin's sand and gravel floor.*

▲ *From its source, high in eastern Qinghai, the Yellow River starts on a 3395 mile (5464 km) journey to the Yellow Sea.*

Transport and industry

Oil extraction at Yumen and in the Dzungarian and Qaidam basins has led to the growth of the petrochemical industry and a range of heavy manufacturing plants in the cities of Lanzhou and Urumqi. Tibet, and most of Xinjiang, have little industry beyond traditional handicrafts, especially textiles at Hotan and Kashi, located along the ancient Silk Route. Nuclear and space research testing are carried out at Lop Nur in Xinjiang.

The transport network

The construction of roads connecting Lhasa in Tibet with Sichuan, Qinghai and Xinjiang was achieved in the 1950s, in spite of the extreme physical conditions of the Plateau of Tibet.

Eastern China

TAIWAN, Anhui, Beijing, Chongqing, Fujian, Guangdong, Guangxi, Guizhou, Hainan, Hebei, Henan, Hubei, Hunan, Jiangsu, Jiangxi, Shaanxi, Shandong, Shanghai, Shanxi, Sichuan, Tianjin, Yunnan, Zhejiang

The east is China's heartland. Massive industrial development since 1949 has transformed much of the densely populated rural landscape, in a region still prone to flooding and drought. Over 30 cities have populations of over a million, including the giant metropolis of Shanghai and the capital Beijing, which has been China's cultural and political centre since the 13th century. The ethnically diverse southwest and the oil-rich interior provinces of Sichuan and Shaanxi have largely missed out on the remarkable economic growth occurring in designated free-trade areas along the coasts of the South and East China seas. The republic of Taiwan was established in 1949 by Chinese nationalists ousted from the mainland by the victorious Communist forces. Taiwan now has one of the strongest economies in the world but its sovereignty is not recognized by China. Hong Kong provides a major international trade link for China; a 99-year 'lease' period of British control was concluded in 1997.

Using the land and sea

This is a region of intensive cultivation. Wheat, millet, sorghum and cotton are the main crops of the Yellow River basin. South from Sichuan, rice becomes the principal crop, grown with wheat, corn and cotton along the Yangtze river. Tea is produced in the hills and sugar cane along the coast of the southeast, where flat land is limited. Pigs and poultry are raised in great numbers.

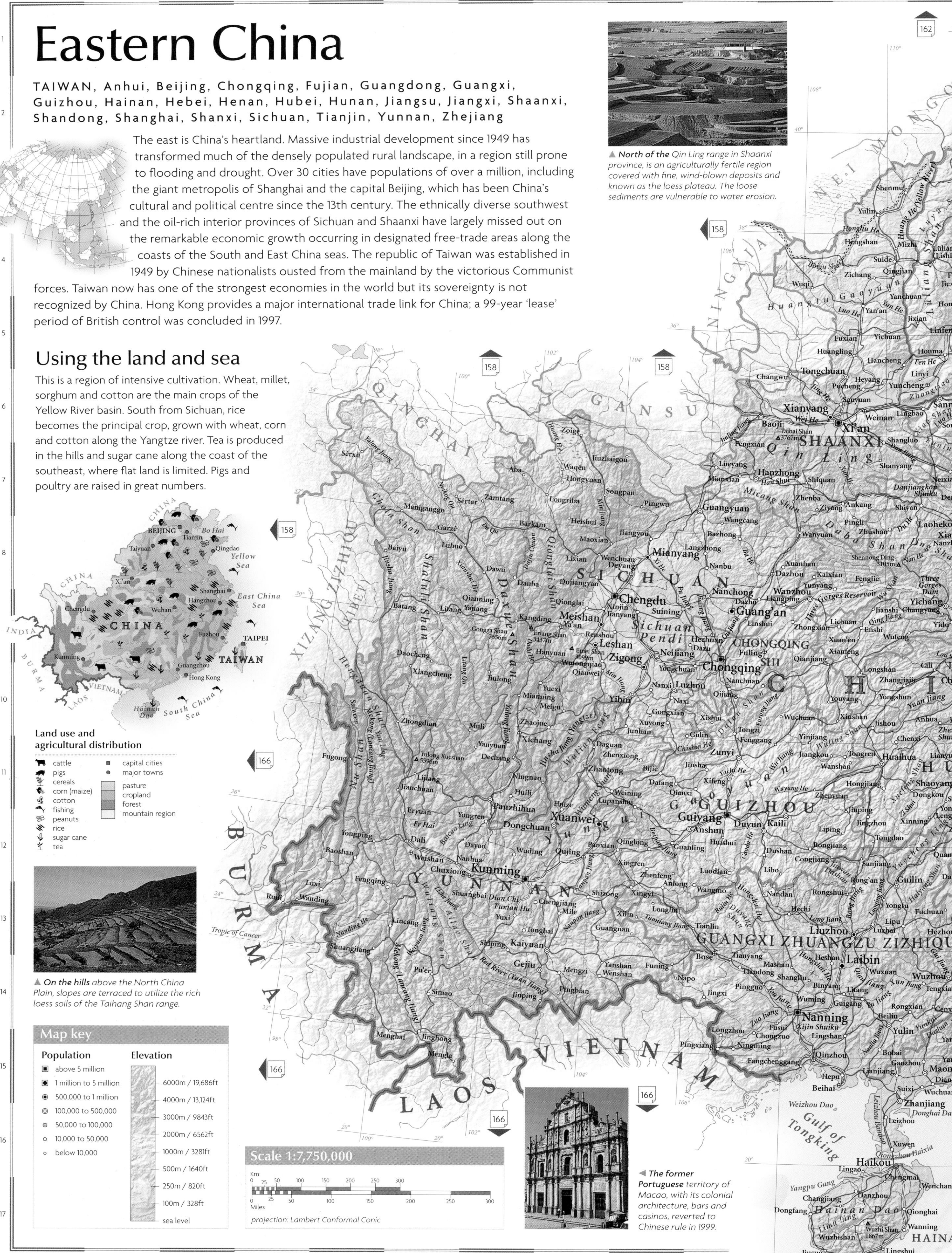

CHINA
BEIJING
Tianjin
Bo Hai
Taiyuan
Qingdao
Yellow Sea
Xi'an
Shanghai
Hangzhou
East China Sea
Chengdu
Wuhan
CHINA
INDIA
Fuzhou
TAIPEI
TAIWAN
Kunming
Guangzhou
Hong Kong
BURMA
VIETNAM
LAOS
Hainan Dao
South China Sea
Land use and agricultural distribution
cattle
pigs
cereals
corn (maize)
cotton
fishing
peanuts
rice
sugar cane
tea
capital cities
major towns
pasture
cropland
forest
mountain region
Map key
Population
above 5 million
1 million to 5 million
500,000 to 1 million
100,000 to 500,000
50,000 to 100,000
10,000 to 50,000
below 10,000
Elevation
6000m / 19,686ft
4000m / 13,124ft
3000m / 9843ft
2000m / 6562ft
1000m / 3281ft
500m / 1640ft
250m / 820ft
100m / 328ft
sea level
Scale 1:7,750,000
projection: Lambert Conformal Conic
QINGHAI
GANSU
NINGXIA
NEI MONGOL
SHAANXI
SICHUAN
CHONGQING SHI
GUIZHOU
YUNNAN
GUANGXI ZHUANGZU ZIZHIQU
XIZANG ZIZHIQU (TIBET)
BURMA
LAOS
VIETNAM
Xi'an
Chengdu
Chongqing
Kunming
Guiyang
Nanning
Haikou
Zhanjiang
Gulf of Tongking
Sichuan Pendi
Tropic of Cancer

▲ **North of the** Qin Ling range in Shaanxi province, is an agriculturally fertile region covered with fine, wind-blown deposits and known as the loess plateau. The loose sediments are vulnerable to water erosion.

▲ **On the hills** above the North China Plain, slopes are terraced to utilize the rich loess soils of the Taihang Shan range.

◀ **The former** Portuguese territory of Macao, with its colonial architecture, bars and casinos, reverted to Chinese rule in 1999.

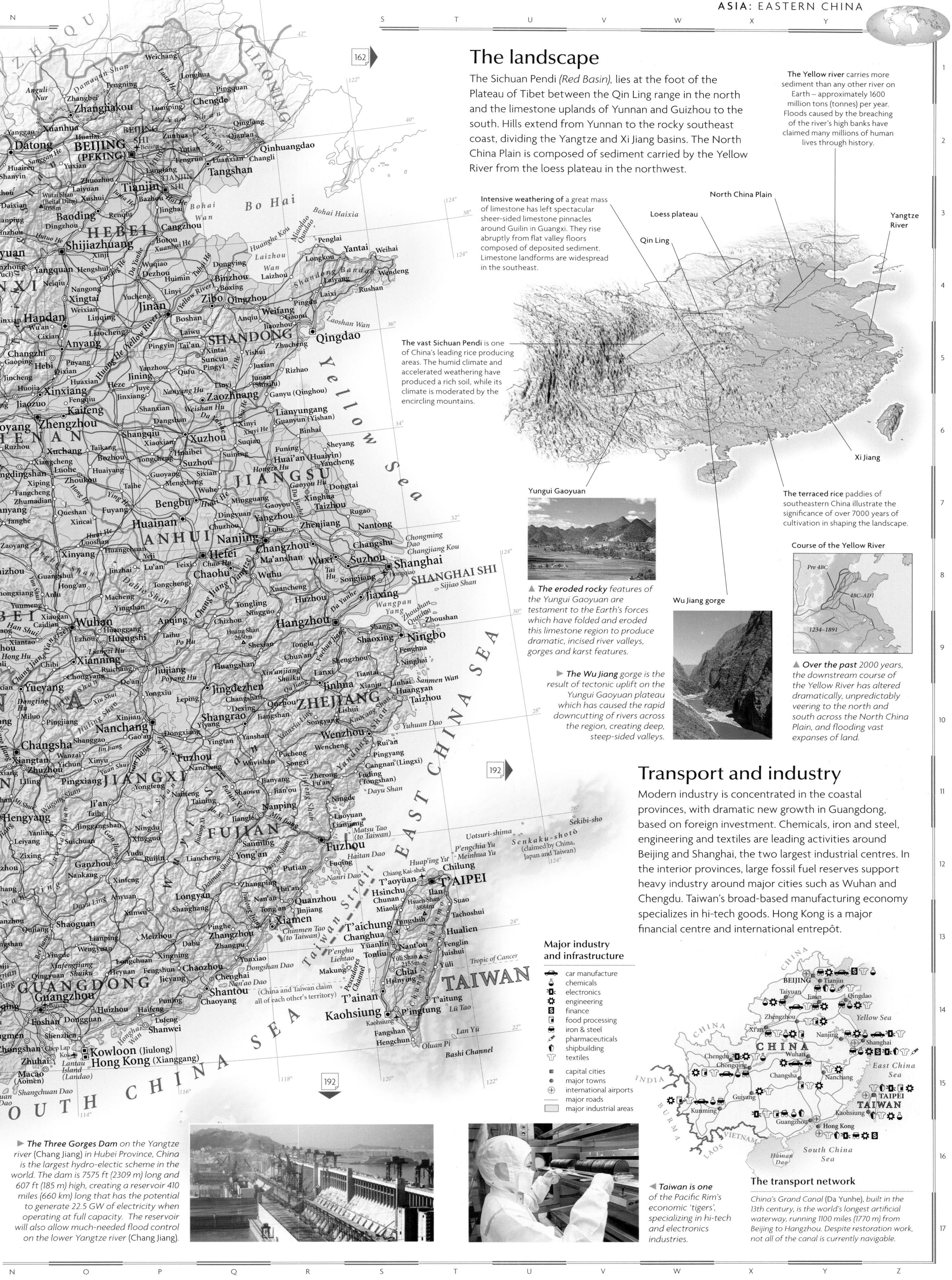

The landscape

The Sichuan Pendi *(Red Basin)*, lies at the foot of the Plateau of Tibet between the Qin Ling range in the north and the limestone uplands of Yunnan and Guizhou to the south. Hills extend from Yunnan to the rocky southeast coast, dividing the Yangtze and Xi Jiang basins. The North China Plain is composed of sediment carried by the Yellow River from the loess plateau in the northwest.

The Yellow river carries more sediment than any other river on Earth – approximately 1600 million tons (tonnes) per year. Floods caused by the breaching of the river's high banks have claimed many millions of human lives through history.

Intensive weathering of a great mass of limestone has left spectacular sheer-sided limestone pinnacles around Guilin in Guangxi. They rise abruptly from flat valley floors composed of deposited sediment. Limestone landforms are widespread in the southeast.

The vast Sichuan Pendi is one of China's leading rice producing areas. The humid climate and accelerated weathering have produced a rich soil, while its climate is moderated by the encircling mountains.

The terraced rice paddies of southeastern China illustrate the significance of over 7000 years of cultivation in shaping the landscape.

North China Plain
Loess plateau
Qin Ling
Yangtze River
Xi Jiang
Yungui Gaoyuan
Wu Jiang gorge

▲ The eroded rocky features of the Yungui Gaoyuan are testament to the Earth's forces which have folded and eroded this limestone region to produce dramatic, incised river valleys, gorges and karst features.

► The Wu Jiang gorge is the result of tectonic uplift on the Yungui Gaoyuan plateau which has caused the rapid downcutting of rivers across the region, creating deep, steep-sided valleys.

Course of the Yellow River

Pre 4BC
4BC–AD11
1234–1891

▲ Over the past 2000 years, the downstream course of the Yellow River has altered dramatically, unpredictably veering to the north and south across the North China Plain, and flooding vast expanses of land.

Transport and industry

Modern industry is concentrated in the coastal provinces, with dramatic new growth in Guangdong, based on foreign investment. Chemicals, iron and steel, engineering and textiles are leading activities around Beijing and Shanghai, the two largest industrial centres. In the interior provinces, large fossil fuel reserves support heavy industry around major cities such as Wuhan and Chengdu. Taiwan's broad-based manufacturing economy specializes in hi-tech goods. Hong Kong is a major financial centre and international entrepôt.

Major industry and infrastructure

car manufacture
chemicals
electronics
engineering
finance
food processing
iron & steel
pharmaceuticals
shipbuilding
textiles
capital cities
major towns
international airports
major roads
major industrial areas

The transport network

China's Grand Canal (Da Yunhe), built in the 13th century, is the world's longest artificial waterway, running 1100 miles (1770 m) from Beijing to Hangzhou. Despite restoration work, not all of the canal is currently navigable.

► The Three Gorges Dam on the Yangtze river (Chang Jiang) in Hubei Province, China is the largest hydro-electic scheme in the world. The dam is 7575 ft (2309 m) long and 607 ft (185 m) high, creating a reservoir 410 miles (660 km) long that has the potential to generate 22.5 GW of electricity when operating at full capacity. The reservoir will also allow much-needed flood control on the lower Yangtze river (Chang Jiang).

◄ Taiwan is one of the Pacific Rim's economic 'tigers', specializing in hi-tech and electronics industries.

162
192

Northeastern China, Mongolia & Korea

MONGOLIA, NORTH KOREA, SOUTH KOREA, Heilongjiang, Inner Mongolia, Jilin, Liaoning

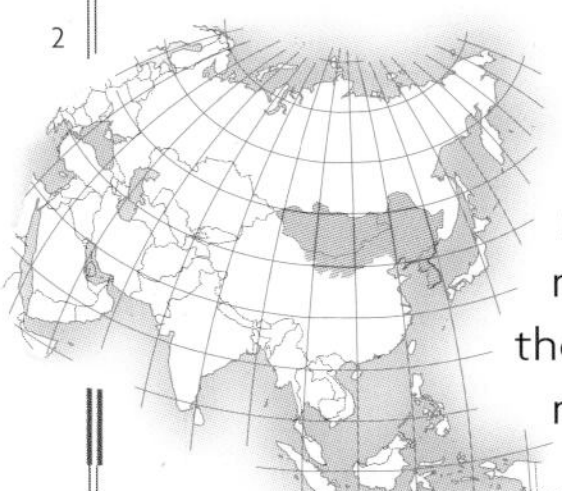

This northerly region has for centuries been a domain of shifting borders and competing colonial powers. Mongolia was the heartland of Chinghiz Khan's vast Mongol empire in the 13th century, while northeastern China was home to the Manchus, China's last ruling dynasty (1644–1911). The mineral and forest wealth of the northeast helped make this China's principal region of heavy industry, although the outdated state factories now face decline. South Korea's state-led market economy has grown dramatically and Seoul is now one of the world's largest cities. The austere communist regime of North Korea has isolated itself from the expanding markets of the Pacific Rim and faces continuing economic stagnation.

▲ *The Eurasian steppe stretches from the mouth of the Danube in Europe, to Mongolia. In Mongolia, nomadic people have lived in felt huts called yurts or gers, for thousands of years.*

Map key

Population

- above 5 million
- 1 million to 5 million
- 500,000 to 1 million
- 100,000 to 500,000
- 50,000 to 100,000
- 10,000 to 50,000
- below 10,000

Elevation

- 4000m / 13,124ft
- 3000m / 9843ft
- 2000m / 6562ft
- 1000m / 3281ft
- 500m / 1640ft
- 250m / 820ft
- 100m / 328ft
- sea level

Scale 1:7,000,000

Km 0 25 50 100 150 200

Miles 0 25 50 100 150 200

projection: Lambert Conformal Conic

The landscape

The great North China Plain is largely enclosed by mountain ranges including the Great and Lesser Khingan Ranges *(Da Hinggan Ling* and *Xiao Hinggan Ling)* in the north, and the Changbai Shan, which extend south into the rugged peninsula of Korea. The broad steppeland plateau of Nei Mongol Gaoyuan borders the southeastern edge of the great cold desert of the Gobi which extends west across the southern reaches of Mongolia. In northwest Mongolia the Altai Mountains and various lesser ranges are interspersed with lakeland basins.

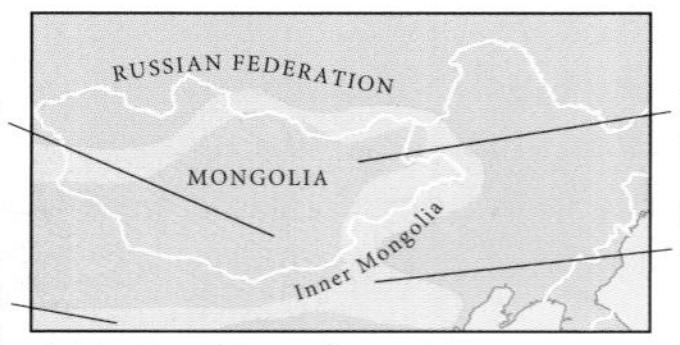

Gobi — Semi-arid zone — RUSSIAN FEDERATION — MONGOLIA — Inner Mongolia — Desert zone — Ordos Desert *(Mu Us Shadi)*

▲ *Much of Mongolia and Inner Mongolia is a vast desert area. To the south and east, a semi-arid region extends into China proper.*

▲ *The Gobi desert stretches from Central Asia, through Mongolia and into China. Bare rock surfaces, rather than sand dunes, typify the cold desert landscape of the Gobi.*

Tributaries of the Amur river follow U-shaped valleys through the Great Khingan Range *(Da Hinggan Ling)*. These were cut by ice-age glaciers between 3 and 10 million years ago.

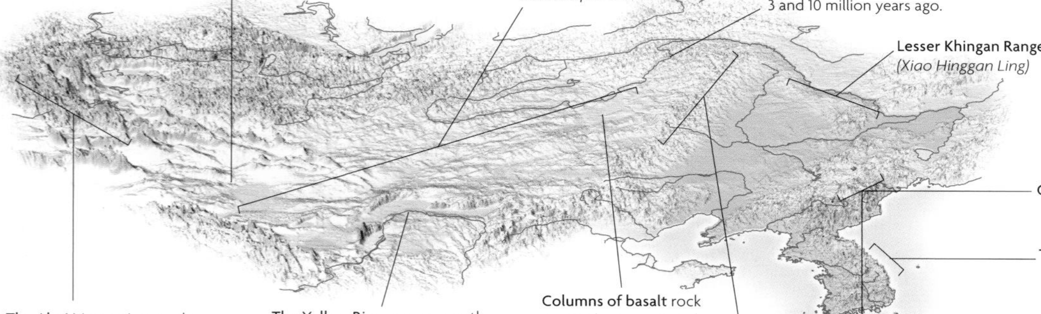

Lesser Khingan Range *(Xiao Hinggan Ling)*

Changbai Shan

T'aebaek-sanmaek

The Altai Mountains are the highest and longest of the mountain ranges which extend into Mongolia from the northwest. These mountains provide one of the last refuges for the endangered snow leopard.

The Yellow River sweeps north around the Ordos Desert *(Mu Us Shadi)*, bringing water to an otherwise barren region.

Columns of basalt rock protrude in occasional clusters from the flat surface of the eastern Gobi. Their regular, six-sided form was produced when the rock cooled and contracted from its molten state.

Great Khingan Range *(Da Hinggan Ling)*

A crater lake occupies the 9023 ft (2750 m) snowy summit of the extinct volcano Paektu-san, the highest peak in the mountains of the Changbai Shan.

◄ *The wooded mountain range of T'aebaek-sanmaek forms the backbone of the Korean peninsula, running north–south along the eastern coastline.*

Transport and industry

North Korea's centrally-planned economy is strongly oriented towards heavy industry, while South Korea has a broad manufacturing base which includes textiles, steel, electronics, and one of the world's largest shipbuilding industries. Mongolia and Inner Mongolia's great mineral resource potential is largely undeveloped. The heavy industrial region around Shenyang produces iron, steel, chemicals and cement on a massive scale.

▲ *Ulan Bator, the Mongolian capital bears many of the hallmarks of Soviet-style central planning, the result of economic and industrial assistance from the Soviet Union following Mongolian independence in 1921.*

The transport network

Liaoning has China's most comprehensive railway network, the legacy of the Japanese occupation of Manchuria in the 20th century. The railways are used primarily for freight transport.

Major industry and infrastructure

- car manufacture
- chemicals
- coal
- electronics
- engineering
- finance
- food processing
- iron & steel
- pharmaceuticals
- shipbuilding
- textiles
- capital cities
- major towns
- international airports
- major roads
- major industrial areas

▶ *While North Korea has remained politically and economically isolated from the rest of the world, South Korea has enjoyed immense economic growth. It has benefited considerably from US economic aid in the aftermath of the Korean war of 1950–1953.*

122

160

Using the land and sea

Mongolia and Inner Mongolia rely heavily on livestock farming, with only about 1% of the land area cultivated. Northeastern China produces wheat, corn, soya beans and sugar beet. The cool climate limits the range of crops and large upland areas of the northeast remain forested. Rice is the staple food of North and South Korea. The latter has become a leading ocean-fishing nation.

Land use and agricultural distribution

- goats
- pigs
- sheep
- corn (maize)
- fishing
- rice
- soya beans
- sugar beet
- wheat
- capital cities
- major towns
- pasture
- cropland
- forest
- mountain region
- desert

Japan

In the years since the end of the Second World War, Japan has become the world's most dynamic industrial nation. The country comprises a string of over 4000 islands which lie in a great northeast to southwest arc in the northwest Pacific. Four major islands: Hokkaido, Honshu, Shikoku and Kyushu are home to the great majority of Japan's population of 128 million people, although the mountainous terrain of the central region means that most cities are situated on the coast. A densely populated industrial belt stretches along much of Honshu's southern coast, including Japan's crowded capital, Tokyo. Alongside its spectacular economic growth and the increasing westernization of its cities, Japan still maintains a most singular culture, reflected in its traditional food, formal behavioural codes, unique Shinto religion and a deep reverence for the emperor.

Using the land and sea

Although only about 11% of Japan is suitable for cultivation, substantial government support, a favourable climate and intensive farming methods enable the country to be virtually self-sufficient in rice production. Northern Hokkaido, the largest and most productive farming region, has an open terrain and climate similar to that of the US Midwest, and produces over half of Japan's cereal requirements. Farmers are being encouraged to diversify by growing fruit, vegetables and wheat, as well as raising livestock.

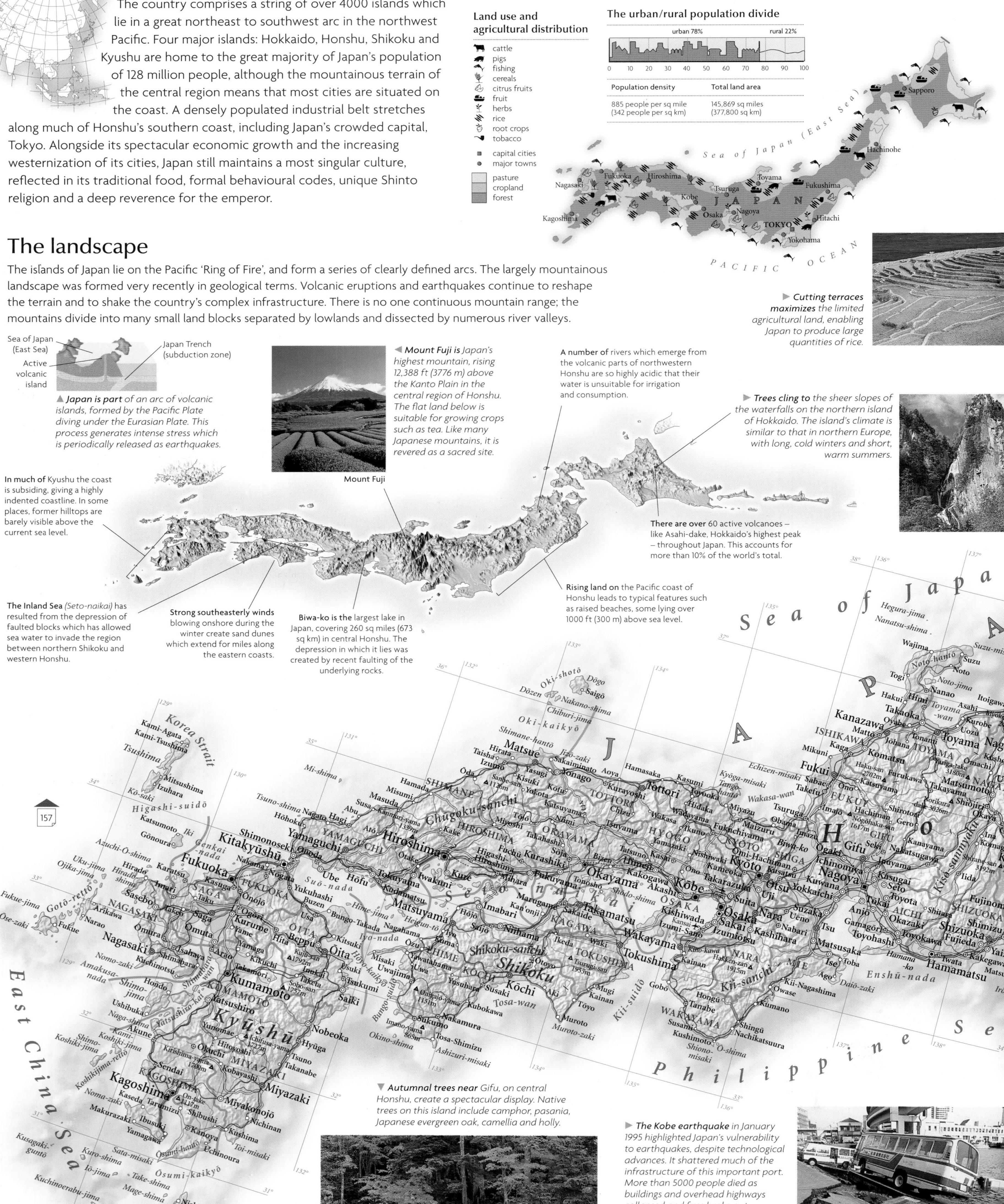

Land use and agricultural distribution
cattle
pigs
fishing
cereals
citrus fruits
fruit
herbs
rice
root crops
tobacco
capital cities
major towns
pasture
cropland
forest
The urban/rural population divide
urban 78%
rural 22%
0 10 20 30 40 50 60 70 80 90 100
Population density
885 people per sq mile (342 people per sq km)
Total land area
145,869 sq miles (377,800 sq km)
Sea of Japan (East Sea)
Pacific Ocean
Sapporo
Hachinohe
Toyama
Fukushima
Tsuruga
Hiroshima
Fukuoka
Nagasaki
Kagoshima
Kobe
Osaka
Nagoya
TOKYO
Hitachi
Yokohama
Sea of Japan (East Sea)
Active volcanic island
Japan Trench (subduction zone)
Mount Fuji
East China Sea
Philippine Sea
Kyushu
Shikoku

▶ *Cutting terraces maximizes the limited agricultural land, enabling Japan to produce large quantities of rice.*

The landscape

The islands of Japan lie on the Pacific 'Ring of Fire', and form a series of clearly defined arcs. The largely mountainous landscape was formed very recently in geological terms. Volcanic eruptions and earthquakes continue to reshape the terrain and to shake the country's complex infrastructure. There is no one continuous mountain range; the mountains divide into many small land blocks separated by lowlands and dissected by numerous river valleys.

▲ ***Japan is part** of an arc of volcanic islands, formed by the Pacific Plate diving under the Eurasian Plate. This process generates intense stress which is periodically released as earthquakes.*

◀ ***Mount Fuji is** Japan's highest mountain, rising 12,388 ft (3776 m) above the Kanto Plain in the central region of Honshu. The flat land below is suitable for growing crops such as tea. Like many Japanese mountains, it is revered as a sacred site.*

A number of rivers which emerge from the volcanic parts of northwestern Honshu are so highly acidic that their water is unsuitable for irrigation and consumption.

▶ ***Trees cling to** the sheer slopes of the waterfalls on the northern island of Hokkaido. The island's climate is similar to that in northern Europe, with long, cold winters and short, warm summers.*

In much of Kyushu the coast is subsiding, giving a highly indented coastline. In some places, former hilltops are barely visible above the current sea level.

There are over 60 active volcanoes – like Asahi-dake, Hokkaido's highest peak – throughout Japan. This accounts for more than 10% of the world's total.

Rising land on the Pacific coast of Honshu leads to typical features such as raised beaches, some lying over 1000 ft (300 m) above sea level.

The Inland Sea *(Seto-naikai)* has resulted from the depression of faulted blocks which has allowed sea water to invade the region between northern Shikoku and western Honshu.

Strong southeasterly winds blowing onshore during the winter create sand dunes which extend for miles along the eastern coasts.

Biwa-ko is the largest lake in Japan, covering 260 sq miles (673 sq km) in central Honshu. The depression in which it lies was created by recent faulting of the underlying rocks.

157

▼ ***Autumnal trees near** Gifu, on central Honshu, create a spectacular display. Native trees on this island include camphor, pasania, Japanese evergreen oak, camellia and holly.*

▶ ***The Kobe earthquake** in January 1995 highlighted Japan's vulnerability to earthquakes, despite technological advances. It shattered much of the infrastructure of this important port. More than 5000 people died as buildings and overhead highways collapsed and fires broke out.*

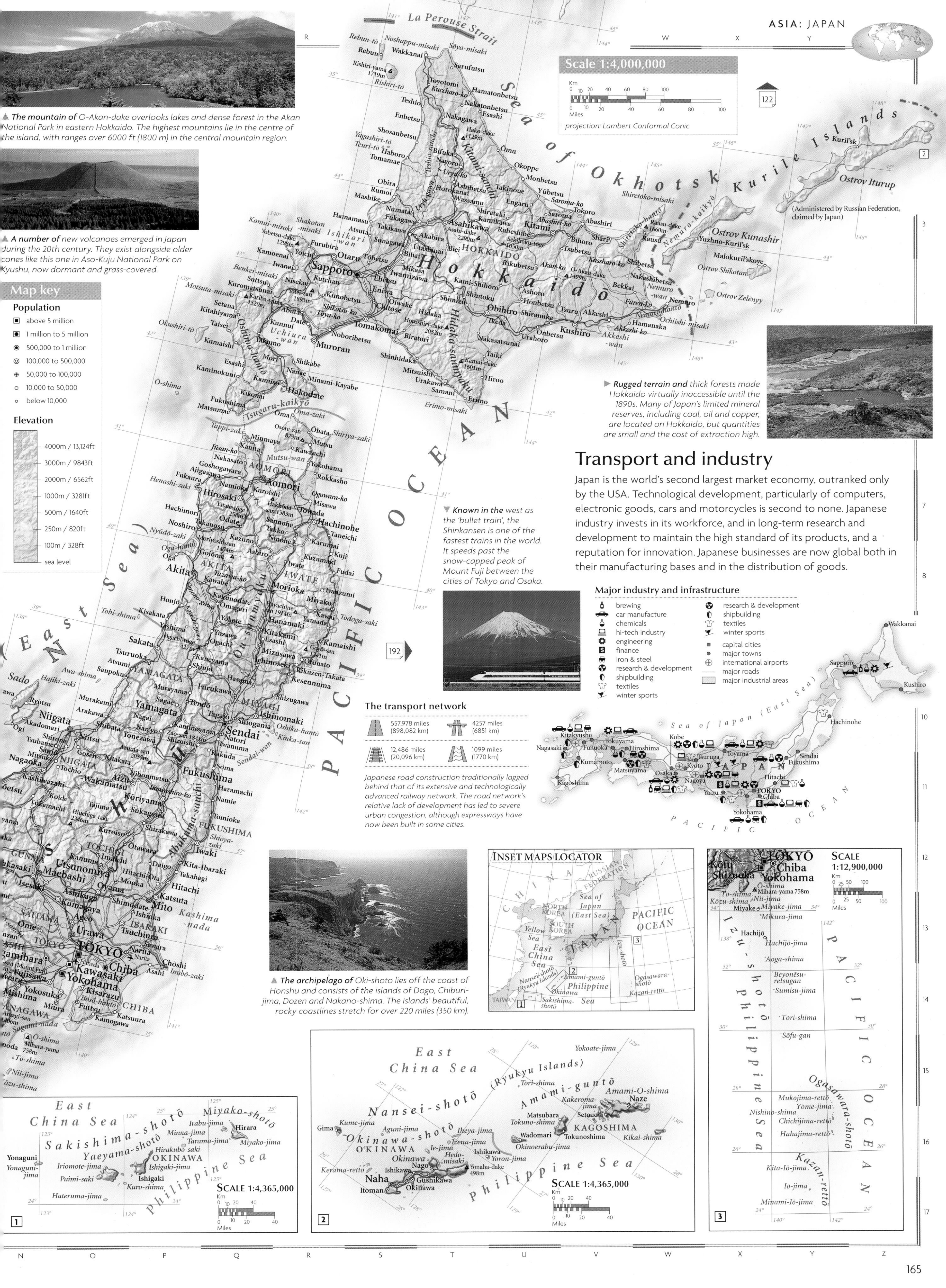
Map key
Population
above 5 million
1 million to 5 million
500,000 to 1 million
100,000 to 500,000
50,000 to 100,000
10,000 to 50,000
below 10,000
Elevation
4000m / 13,124ft
3000m / 9843ft
2000m / 6562ft
1000m / 3281ft
500m / 1640ft
250m / 820ft
100m / 328ft
sea level
Scale 1:4,000,000
projection: Lambert Conformal Conic
Major industry and infrastructure
brewing
car manufacture
chemicals
hi-tech industry
engineering
finance
iron & steel
research & development
shipbuilding
textiles
winter sports
capital cities
major towns
international airports
major roads
major industrial areas
The transport network
557,978 miles (898,082 km)
4257 miles (6851 km)
12,486 miles (20,096 km)
1099 miles (1770 km)
INSET MAPS LOCATOR
SCALE 1:4,365,000
SCALE 1:12,900,000
Sea of Okhotsk
PACIFIC OCEAN
Hokkaidō
Honshū
Kurile Islands
(Administered by Russian Federation, claimed by Japan)
East China Sea
Philippine Sea

▲ The mountain of O-Akan-dake overlooks lakes and dense forest in the Akan National Park in eastern Hokkaido. The highest mountains lie in the centre of the island, with ranges over 6000 ft (1800 m) in the central mountain region.

▲ A number of new volcanoes emerged in Japan during the 20th century. They exist alongside older cones like this one in Aso-Kuju National Park on Kyushu, now dormant and grass-covered.

► Rugged terrain and thick forests made Hokkaido virtually inaccessible until the 1890s. Many of Japan's limited mineral reserves, including coal, oil and copper, are located on Hokkaido, but quantities are small and the cost of extraction high.

Transport and industry

Japan is the world's second largest market economy, outranked only by the USA. Technological development, particularly of computers, electronic goods, cars and motorcycles is second to none. Japanese industry invests in its workforce, and in long-term research and development to maintain the high standard of its products, and a reputation for innovation. Japanese businesses are now global both in their manufacturing bases and in the distribution of goods.

▼ Known in the west as the 'bullet train', the Shinkansen is one of the fastest trains in the world. It speeds past the snow-capped peak of Mount Fuji between the cities of Tokyo and Osaka.

Japanese road construction traditionally lagged behind that of its extensive and technologically advanced railway network. The road network's relative lack of development has led to severe urban congestion, although expressways have now been built in some cities.

▲ The archipelago of Oki-shoto lies off the coast of Honshu and consists of the islands of Dogo, Chiburi-jima, Dozen and Nakano-shima. The islands' beautiful, rocky coastlines stretch for over 220 miles (350 km).

Mainland Southeast Asia

BURMA, CAMBODIA, LAOS, THAILAND, VIETNAM

Thickly forested mountains, intercut by the broad valleys of five great rivers characterize the landscape of Southeast Asia's mainland countries. Agriculture remains the main activity for much of the population, which is concentrated in the river flood plains and deltas. Linked ethnic and cultural roots give the region a distinct identity. Most people on the mainland are Theravada Buddhists, and the Philippines is the only predominantly Christian country in Southeast Asia. Foreign intervention began in the 16th century with the opening of the spice trade; Cambodia, Laos and Vietnam were French colonies until the end of the Second World War, Burma was under British control. Only Thailand was never colonized. Today, Thailand is poised to play a leading role in the economic development of the Pacific Rim, and Laos and Vietnam have begun to mend the devastation of the Vietnam War, and to develop their economies. With continuing political instability and a shattered infrastructure, Cambodia faces an uncertain future, while Burma is seeking investment and the ending of its long isolation from the world community.

▲ *The Irrawaddy river is Burma's vital central artery, watering the ricefields and providing a rich source of fish, as well as an important transport link, particularly for local traffic.*

The landscape

A series of mountain ranges runs north–south through the mainland, formed as the result of the collision between the Eurasian Plate and the Indian subcontinent, which created the Himalayas. They are interspersed by the valleys of a number of great rivers. On their passage to the sea these rivers have deposited sediment, forming huge, fertile flood plains and deltas.

The coastline of the Isthmus of Kra

Longshore drift

Eroded coastline

Spit

Lagoon

Wave attack

◀ *The east and west coasts of the Isthmus of Kra differ greatly. The tectonically uplifting west coast is exposed to the harsh south-westerly monsoon and is heavily eroded. On the east coast, longshore currents produce depositional features such as spits and lagoons.*

Hkakabo Razi is the highest point in mainland Southeast Asia. It rises 19,300 ft (5885 m) at the border between China and Burma.

Mountains dominate the Laotian landscape with more than 90% of the land lying more than 600 ft (180 m) above sea level. The mountains of the Chaîne Annamitique form the country's eastern border.

The Red River delta in northern Vietnam is fringed to the north by steep-sided, round-topped limestone hills, typical of karst scenery.

The Irrawaddy river runs virtually north–south, draining the plains of northern Burma. The Irrawaddy delta is the country's main rice-growing area.

Salween River

Isthmus of Kra

Malay Peninsula

Tonle Sap, a freshwater lake, drains into the Mekong delta via the Mekong river. It is the largest lake in Southeast Asia.

The Mekong river flows through southern China and Burma, then for much of its length forms the border between Laos and Thailand, flowing through Cambodia before terminating in a vast delta on the southern Vietnamese coast.

▲ *The coast of the Isthmus of Kra, in southeast Thailand has many small, precipitous islands like these, formed by chemical erosion on limestone, which is weathered along vertical cracks. The humidity of the climate in Southeast Asia increases the rate of weathering.*

◀ *The fast-flowing waters of the Mekong river cascade over this waterfall in Champasak province in Laos. The force of the water erodes rocks at the base of the fall.*

Using the land and sea

The fertile flood plains of rivers such as the Mekong and Salween, and the humid climate, enable the production of rice throughout the region. Cambodia, Burma and Laos still have substantial forests, producing hardwoods such as teak and rosewood. Cash crops include tropical fruits such as coconuts, bananas and pineapples, rubber, oil palm, sugar cane and the jute substitute, kenaf. Pigs and cattle are the main livestock raised. Large quantities of marine and freshwater fish are caught throughout the region.

▲ *Commercial logging – still widespread in Burma – has now been stopped in Thailand because of over-exploitation of the tropical rainforest.*

The urban/rural population divide

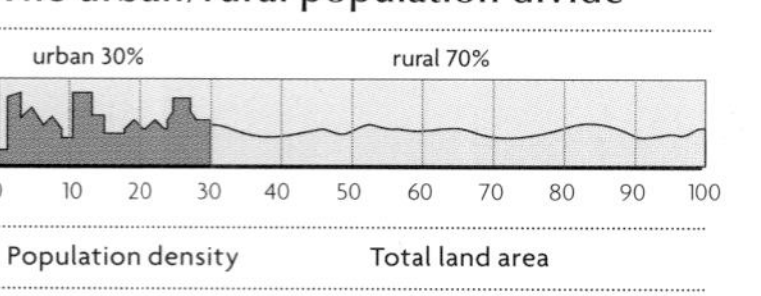
urban 30%
rural 70%
0 10 20 30 40 50 60 70 80 90 100

Population density	Total land area
345 people per sq mile (133 people per sq km)	733,828 sq miles (1,901,110 sq km)

BANGLADESH
INDIA
CHINA
Mandalay
BURMA
NAY PYI TAW
HANOI
Gulf of Tongking
Bay of Bengal
VIENTIANE
LAOS
Hue
Rangoon
THAILAND
BANGKOK
VIETNAM
CAMBODIA
Andaman Sea
PHNOM PENH
South China Sea
Gulf of Thailand
Ho Chi Minh City
MALAYSIA

Land use and agricultural distribution

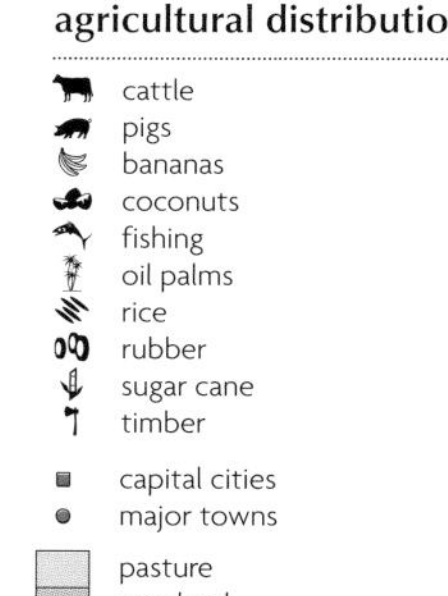
cattle
pigs
bananas
coconuts
fishing
oil palms
rice
rubber
sugar cane
timber
capital cities
major towns
pasture
cropland
forest
wetland

152
172
168

Transport and industry

Industrial manufacturing has become increasingly important in Thailand and Vietnam in recent years. The assembling of component-based electrical and electronic goods is becoming more common throughout this region, with foreign companies benefiting from low labour costs and the upgrading of technology. The economies of Burma and Cambodia are still based on agricultural produce and the processing of raw materials. Tin is the region's most important metal, and nickel, copper and chromite are also mined, although the quantities produced are not significant on a global scale. Thailand's successful tourist industry is the country's highest earner of foreign exchange.

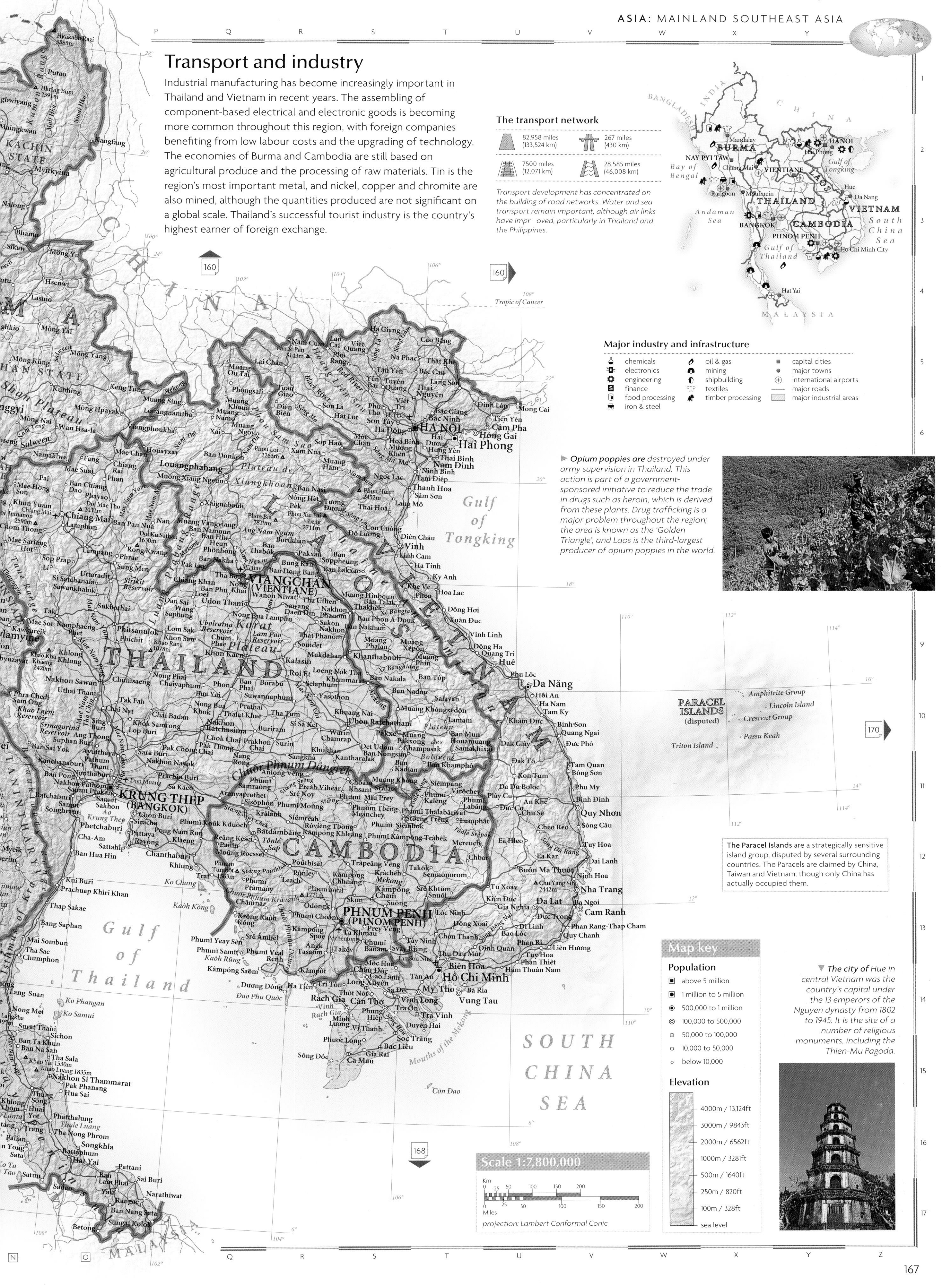

The transport network
82,958 miles (133,524 km)
267 miles (430 km)
7500 miles (12,071 km)
28,585 miles (46,008 km)
Major industry and infrastructure
chemicals
electronics
engineering
finance
food processing
iron & steel
oil & gas
mining
shipbuilding
textiles
timber processing
capital cities
major towns
international airports
major roads
major industrial areas
Map key
Population
above 5 million
1 million to 5 million
500,000 to 1 million
100,000 to 500,000
50,000 to 100,000
10,000 to 50,000
below 10,000
Elevation
4000m / 13,124ft
3000m / 9843ft
2000m / 6562ft
1000m / 3281ft
500m / 1640ft
250m / 820ft
100m / 328ft
sea level
Scale 1:7,800,000
projection: Lambert Conformal Conic
THAILAND
CAMBODIA
VIETNAM
LAOS
BURMA
CHINA
Gulf of Tongking
Gulf of Thailand
SOUTH CHINA SEA
PARACEL ISLANDS (disputed)
HÀ NÔI
VIANGCHAN (VIENTIANE)
KRUNG THEP (BANGKOK)
PHNUM PENH (PHNOM PENH)
Hô Chi Minh
Tropic of Cancer

Transport development has concentrated on the building of road networks. Water and sea transport remain important, although air links have improved, particularly in Thailand and the Philippines.

► **Opium poppies are** destroyed under army supervision in Thailand. This action is part of a government-sponsored initiative to reduce the trade in drugs such as heroin, which is derived from these plants. Drug trafficking is a major problem throughout the region; the area is known as the 'Golden Triangle', and Laos is the third-largest producer of opium poppies in the world.

The Paracel Islands are a strategically sensitive island group, disputed by several surrounding countries. The Paracels are claimed by China, Taiwan and Vietnam, though only China has actually occupied them.

▼ **The city of** Hue in central Vietnam was the country's capital under the 13 emperors of the Nguyen dynasty from 1802 to 1945. It is the site of a number of religious monuments, including the Thien-Mu Pagoda.

160 168 170

Western Maritime Southeast Asia

BRUNEI, INDONESIA, MALAYSIA, SINGAPORE

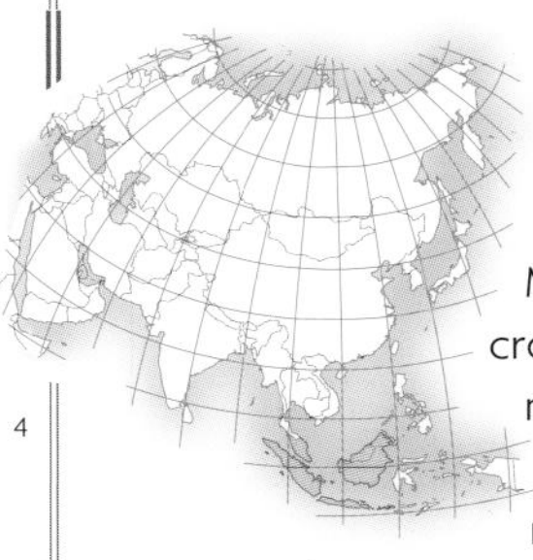

The world's largest archipelago, Indonesia's myriad islands stretch 3100 miles (5000 km) eastwards across the Pacific, from the Malay Peninsula to western New Guinea. Only about 1500 of the 13,677 islands are inhabited and the huge, predominently Muslim population is unevenly distributed, with some two-thirds crowded onto the western islands of Java, Madura and Bali. The national government is trying to resettle large numbers of people from these islands to other parts of the country to reduce population pressure there. Malaysia, split between the mainland and the east Malaysian states of Sabah and Sarawak on Borneo, has a diverse population, as well as a fast-growing economy, although the pace of its development is still far outstripped by that of Singapore. This small island nation is the financial and commercial capital of Southeast Asia. The Sultanate of Brunei in northern Borneo, one of the world's last princely states, has an extremely high standard of living, based on its oil revenues.

The landscape

Indonesia's western islands are characterized by rugged volcanic mountains cloaked with dense tropical forest, which slope down to coastal plains covered by thick alluvial swamps. The Sunda Shelf, an extension of the Eurasian Plate, lies between Java, Bali, Sumatra and Borneo. These islands' mountains rise from a base below the sea, and they were once joined together by dry land, which has since been submerged by rising sea levels.

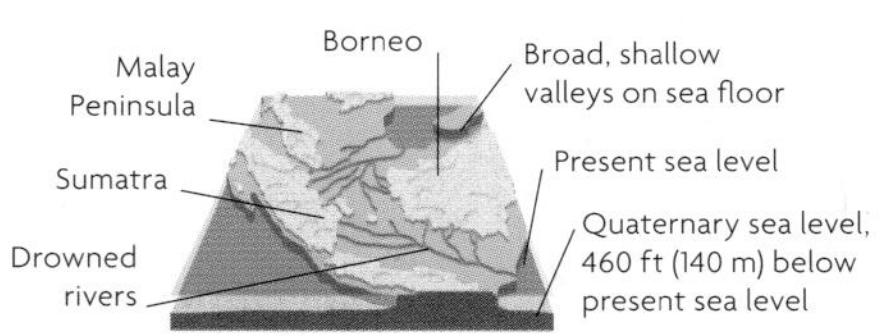
Borneo
Malay Peninsula
Broad, shallow valleys on sea floor
Sumatra
Present sea level
Drowned rivers
Quaternary sea level, 460 ft (140 m) below present sea level

▲ ***The Sunda Shelf*** *underlies this whole region. It is one of the largest submarine shelves in the world, covering an area of 714,285 sq miles (1,850,000 sq km). During the early Quaternary period, when sea levels were lower, the shelf was exposed.*

◄ ***Danau (lake) Toba*** *in Sumatra fills an enormous caldera 18 miles (30 km) wide and 62 miles (100 km) long – the largest in the world. It was formed through a combination of volcanic action and tectonic activity.*

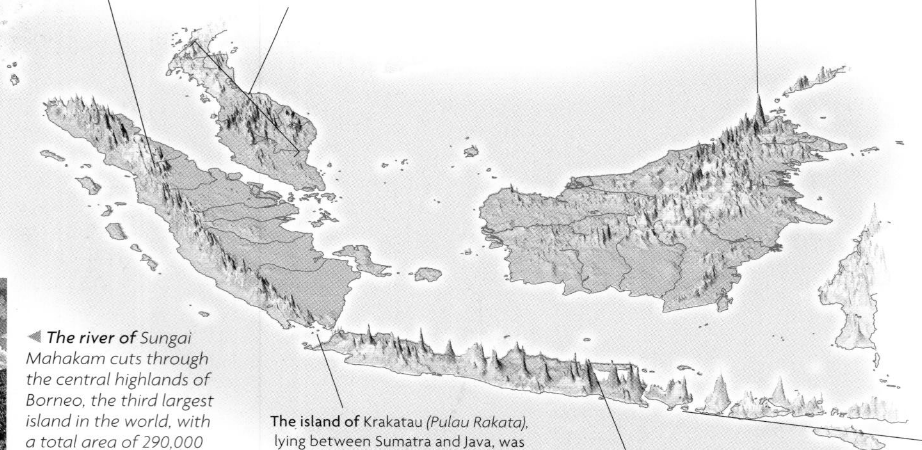

Malay Peninsula has a rugged east coast, but the west coast, fronting the Strait of Malacca, has many sheltered beaches and bays. The two coasts are divided by the Banjaran Titiwangsa, which run the length of the peninsula.

Gunung Kinabalu is the highest peak in Malaysia, rising 13,455 ft (4101 m).

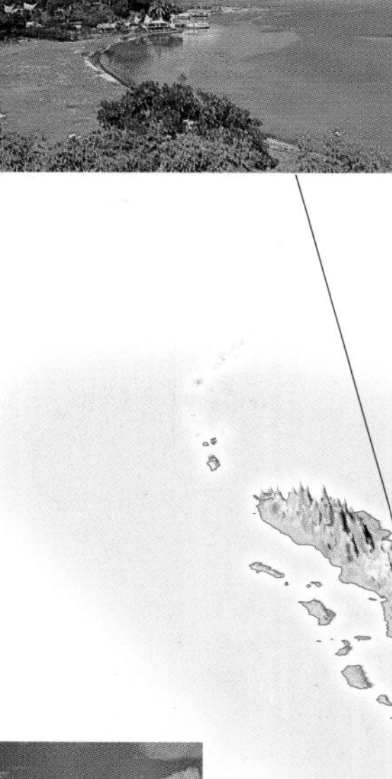

◄ ***The river of*** *Sungai Mahakam cuts through the central highlands of Borneo, the third largest island in the world, with a total area of 290,000 sq miles (757,050 sq km). Although mountainous, Borneo is one of the most stable of the Indonesian islands, with little volcanic activity.*

The island of Krakatau *(Pulau Rakata)*, lying between Sumatra and Java, was all but destroyed in 1883, when the volcano erupted. The release of gas and dust into the atmosphere disrupted cloud cover and global weather patterns for several years.

Gunung Semeru

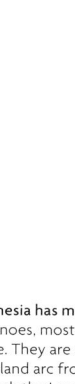

Indonesia has more than 220 volcanoes, most of which are still active. They are strung out along the island arc from Sumatra through the Lesser Sunda Islands, into the Moluccas and Celebes.

Transport and industry

Singapore has a thriving economy based on international trade and finance. Annual trade through the port is among the highest of any in the world. Indonesia's western islands still depend on natural resources, particularly petroleum, gas and wood, although the economy is rapidly diversifying with manufactured exports including garments, consumer electronics and footwear. A high-profile aircraft industry has developed in Bandung on Java. Malaysia has a fast-growing and varied manufacturing sector, although oil, gas and timber remain important resource-based industries.

► ***Ranks of gleaming*** *skyscrapers, new motorways and infrastructure construction reflect the investment which is pouring into Southeast Asian cities like the Malaysian capital, Kuala Lumpur. Traditional housing and markets still exist amidst the new developments. Many of the city's inhabitants subsist at a level far removed from the prosperity implied by its outward modernity.*

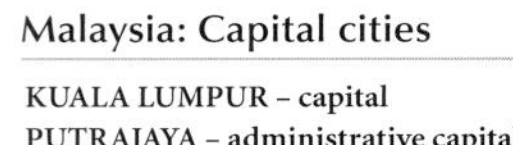

Malaysia: Capital cities
KUALA LUMPUR – capital
PUTRAJAYA – administrative capital

166

172

172

Using the land and sea

Rice is the most important arable crop in Indonesia and Malaysia, and both countries manage to meet almost all of their domestic demand. Malaysian rubber accounts for 25% of world production and is the main cash crop, grown on plantations and small farms, along with oil palms and copra. Timber is exported from both Malaysia and Indonesia. Modern agricultural techniques enable Singapore to produce fruits and vegetables despite a shortage of suitable land.

▶ *Spiral cuts in the bark of this rubber palm show where it has been tapped. Sophisticated 'cloning' techniques mean that trees which produce consistently high quantities of rubber can be easily reproduced.*

The transport network

- 165,272 miles (266,010 km)
- 958 miles (1,542 km)
- 5,061 miles (8,146 km)
- 18,070 miles (29,084 km)

Singapore's metro system, completed in 1991, is among the most efficient in the world. Malaysia has several fast, modern highways and most roads are paved. Indonesia's many islands make improvement of the shipping infrastructure a priority.

Major industry and infrastructure

- aerospace
- copra processing
- chemicals
- electronics
- engineering
- finance
- food processing
- iron & steel
- oil
- ship building
- timber processing
- textiles
- capital cities
- major towns
- international airports
- major roads
- major industrial areas

Land use and agricultural distribution

- coconuts
- fishing
- oil palms
- rice
- rubber
- shellfish
- sugar cane
- timber
- capital cities
- major towns
- pasture
- cropland
- forest
- wetland

The urban/rural population divide

urban 44% | rural 56%

0 10 20 30 40 50 60 70 80 90 100

Population density	Total land area
297 people per sq mile (115 people per sq km)	828,356 sq miles (2,146,000 sq km)

▼ *This tiny island near Kota Kinabalu, in Sabah, eastern Malaysia, is a part of a designated national park. Thickly forested, it is surrounded by broad, sandy beaches and shallow inland seas.*

▲ *The volcano of Gunung Semeru in eastern Java lies on the Pacific 'Ring of Fire'. It is part of the ancient Tennegger volcano and remains highly active.*

Scale 1:7,950,000

Km 0 25 50 100 150 200
Miles 0 25 50 100 150 200

projection: Mercator

Map key

Population

- above 5 million
- 1 million to 5 million
- 500,000 to 1 million
- 100,000 to 500,000
- 50,000 to 100,000
- 10,000 to 50,000
- below 10,000

Elevation

- 4000m / 13,124ft
- 3000m / 9843ft
- 2000m / 6562ft
- 1000m / 3281ft
- 500m / 1640ft
- 250m / 820ft
- 100m / 328ft
- sea level

166
170

Eastern Maritime Southeast Asia

EAST TIMOR, INDONESIA, PHILIPPINES

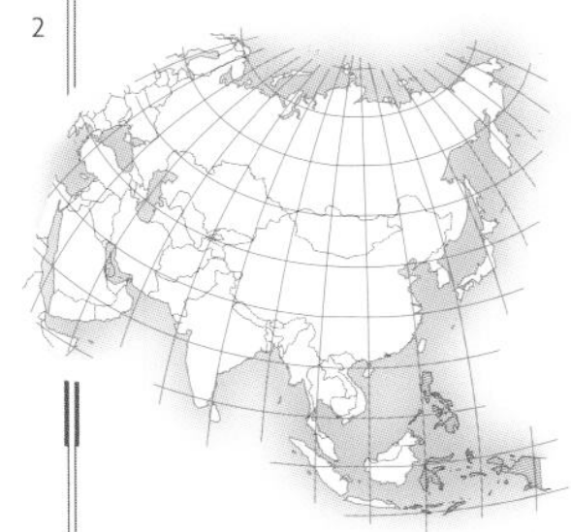

The Philippines takes its name from Philip II of Spain who was king when the islands were colonized during the 16th century. Almost 400 years of Spanish, and later US, rule have left their mark on the country's culture; English is widely spoken and over 90% of the population is Christian. The Philippines' economy is agriculturally based – inadequate infrastructure and electrical power shortages have so far hampered faster industrial growth. Indonesia's eastern islands are less economically developed than the rest of the country. Papua (Irian Jaya), which constitutes the western portion of New Guinea, is one of the world's last great wildernesses. East Timor is the newest independent state in the world, gaining full autonomy in 2002.

▲ ***The traditional boat-shaped** houses of the Toraja people in Sulawesi. Although now Christian, the Toraja still practice the animist traditions and rituals of their ancestors. They are famous for their elaborate funeral ceremonies and burial sites in cliffside caves.*

The landscape

Located on the Pacific 'Ring of Fire' the Philippines' 7100 islands are subject to frequent earthquakes and volcanic activity. Their terrain is largely mountainous, with narrow coastal plains and interior valleys and plains. Luzon and Mindanao are by far the largest islands and comprise roughly 66% of the country's area. Indonesia's eastern islands are mountainous and dotted with volcanoes, both active and dormant.

▶ ***Lake Taal on** the Philippines island of Luzon lies within the crater of an immense volcano that erupted twice in the 20th century, first in 1911 and again in 1965, causing the deaths of more than 3200 people.*

The Spratly Islands are a strategically sensitive island group, disputed by several surrounding countries. The Spratlys are claimed by China, Taiwan, Vietnam, Malaysia and the Philippines and are particularly important as they lie on oil and gas deposits.

***Mindanao has five** mountain ranges many of which have large numbers of active volcanoes. Lying just west of the Philippines Trench, which forms the boundary between the colliding Philippine and Eurasian plates, the entire island chain is subject to earthquakes and volcanic activity.*

***The 1000 islands** of the Moluccas are the fabled Spice Islands of history, whose produce attracted traders from around the globe. Most of the northern and central Moluccas have dense vegetation and rugged mountainous interiors where elevations often exceed 3000 feet (9144 m).*

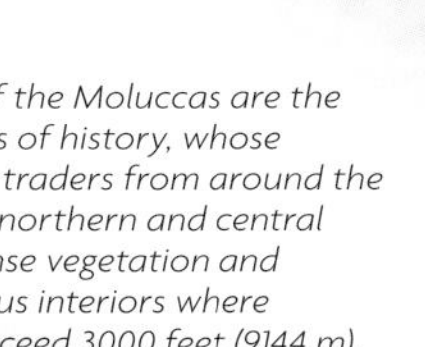

▲ ***Bohol in the** southern Philippines is famous for its so-called 'chocolate hills'. There are more than 1000 of these regular mounds on the island. The hills are limestone in origin, the smoothed remains of an earlier cycle of erosion. Their brown appearance in the dry season gives them their name.*

The four-pronged island of Celebes is the product of complex tectonic activity which ruptured and then reattached small fragments of the Earth's crust to form the island's many peninsulas.

Coral islands such as Timor in eastern Indonesia show evidence of very recent and dramatic movements of the Earth's plates. Reefs in Timor have risen by as much as 4000 ft (1300 m) in the last million years.

The Pegunungan Jayawijaya range in central Papua (Irian Jaya) contains the world's highest range of limestone mountains, some with peaks more than 16,400 ft (5000 m) high. Heavy rainfall and high temperatures, which promote rapid weathering, have led to the creation of large underground caves and river systems such as the river of Sungai Baliem.

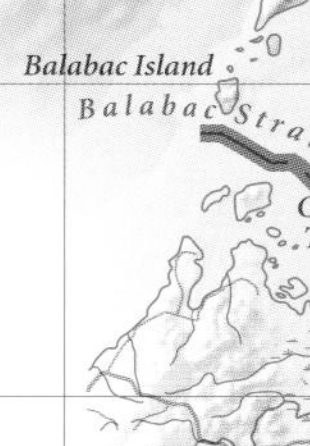

SOUTH CHINA SEA
SPRATLY ISLANDS (disputed)
MALAYSIA
KALIMANTAN TIMUR
KALIMANTAN SELATAN
Java Sea
NUSA TENGGARA
Mataram

168

Using the land and sea

Indonesia's eastern islands are less intensively cultivated than those in the west. Coconuts, coffee and spices such as cloves and nutmeg are the major commercial crops while rice, corn and soya beans are grown for local consumption. The Philippines' rich, fertile soils support year-round production of a wide range of crops. The country is one of the world's largest producers of coconuts and a major exporter of coconut products, including one-third of the world's copra. Although much of the arable land is given over to rice and corn, the main staple food crops, tropical fruits such as bananas, pineapples and mangos,and sugar cane are also grown for export.

Land use and agricultural distribution

coconuts, fishing, rice, rubber, shellfish, sugar cane

capital cities, major towns

pasture, cropland, forest, wetland

The urban/rural population divide

urban 45% — rural 55%

Population density	Total land area
258 people per sq mile (160 people per sq km)	654,771 sq miles (1,053,755 sq km)

◀ ***The terracing of** land to restrict soil erosion and create flat surfaces for agriculture is a common practice throughout Southeast Asia, particularly where land is scarce. These terraces are on Luzon in the Philippines.*

▲ ***More than two-thirds** of Papua's (Irian Jaya) land area is heavily forested and the population of around 1.5 million live mainly in isolated tribal groups using more than 80 distinct languages.*

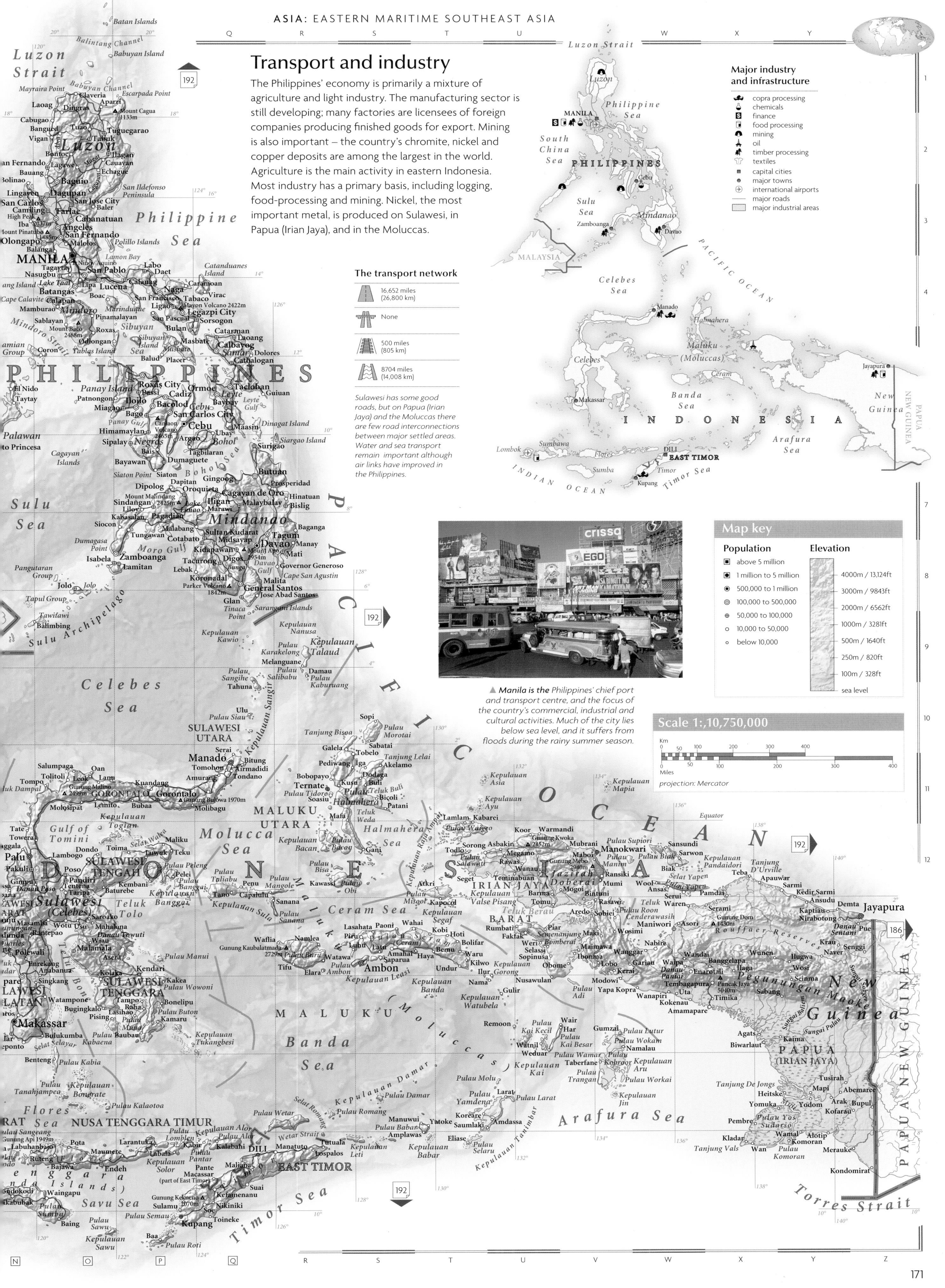

Transport and industry
The Philippines' economy is primarily a mixture of agriculture and light industry. The manufacturing sector is still developing; many factories are licensees of foreign companies producing finished goods for export. Mining is also important – the country's chromite, nickel and copper deposits are among the largest in the world. Agriculture is the main activity in eastern Indonesia. Most industry has a primary basis, including logging, food-processing and mining. Nickel, the most important metal, is produced on Sulawesi, in Papua (Irian Jaya), and in the Moluccas.
The transport network
16,652 miles (26,800 km)
None
500 miles (805 km)
8704 miles (14,008 km)
Sulawesi has some good roads, but on Papua (Irian Jaya) and the Moluccas there are few road interconnections between major settled areas. Water and sea transport remain important although air links have improved in the Philippines.
Major industry and infrastructure
copra processing
chemicals
finance
food processing
mining
oil
timber processing
textiles
capital cities
major towns
international airports
major roads
major industrial areas
Map key
Population
above 5 million
1 million to 5 million
500,000 to 1 million
100,000 to 500,000
50,000 to 100,000
10,000 to 50,000
below 10,000
Elevation
4000m / 13,124ft
3000m / 9843ft
2000m / 6562ft
1000m / 3281ft
500m / 1640ft
250m / 820ft
100m / 328ft
sea level
Scale 1:,10,750,000
projection: Mercator
PHILIPPINES
INDONESIA
PACIFIC OCEAN
Celebes Sea
Sulu Sea
Philippine Sea
Molucca Sea
Banda Sea
Arafura Sea
Timor Sea
MANILA
Luzon
Mindanao
Sulawesi (Celebes)
PAPUA (IRIAN JAYA)
New Guinea
PAPUA NEW GUINEA
EAST TIMOR
DILI

▲ Manila is the Philippines' chief port and transport centre, and the focus of the country's commercial, industrial and cultural activities. Much of the city lies below sea level, and it suffers from floods during the rainy summer season.

The Indian Ocean

Despite being the smallest of the three major oceans, the evolution of the Indian Ocean was the most complex. The ocean basin was formed during the break up of the supercontinent Gondwanaland, when the Indian subcontinent moved northeast, Africa moved west and Australia separated from Antarctica. Like the Pacific Ocean, the warm waters of the Indian Ocean are punctuated by coral atolls and islands. About one-fifth of the world's population – over 1000 million people – live on its shores. Those people living along the northern coasts are constantly threatened by flooding and typhoons caused by the monsoon winds.

The landscape

The Indian Ocean began forming about 150 million years ago, but in its present form it is relatively young, only about 36 million years old. Along the three subterranean mountain chains of its mid-ocean ridge the seafloor is still spreading. The Indian Ocean has fewer trenches than other oceans and only a narrow continental shelf around most of its surrounding land.

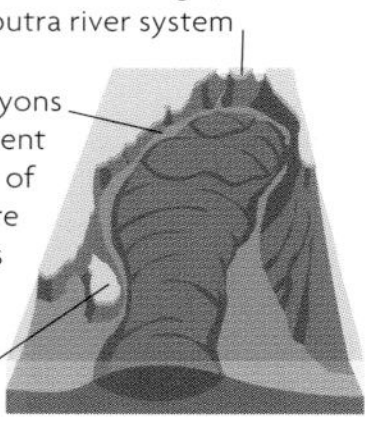

Sediments come from Ganges/Brahmaputra river system

Submarine canyons transport sediment to fan – some of these are more than 1500 miles (2500 km) long

Sri Lanka

▲ *The Ganges Fan is one of the world's largest submarine accumulations of sediment, extending far beyond Sri Lanka. It is fed by the Ganges/Brahmaputra river system, whose sediment is carried through a network of underwater canyons at the edge of the continental shelf.*

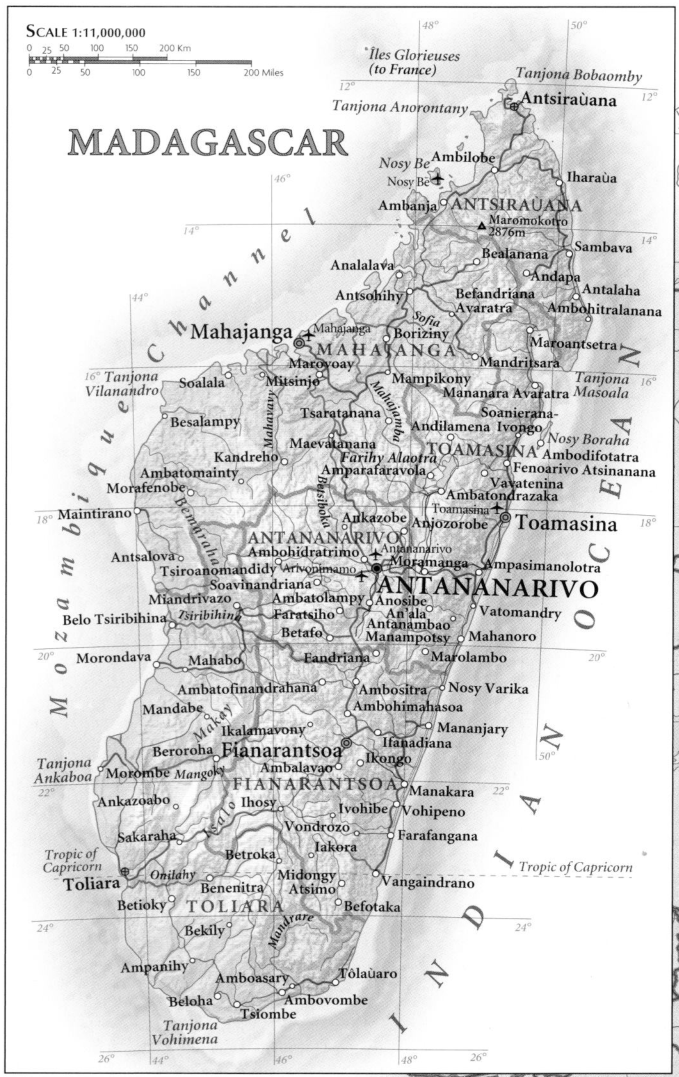

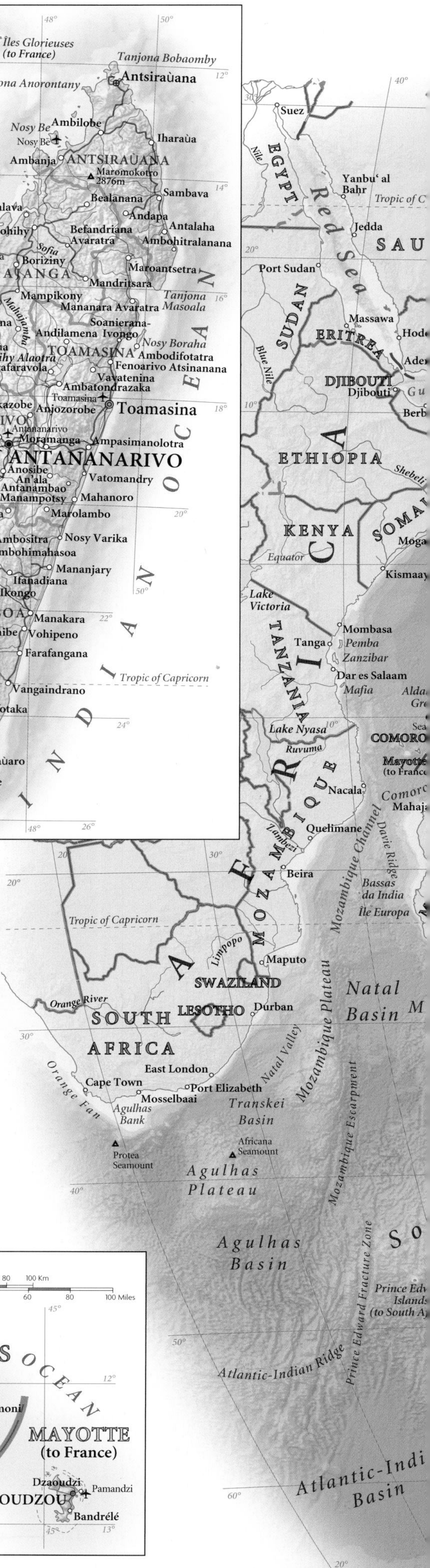

The mid-oceanic ridge runs from the Arabian Sea. It diverges east of Madagascar, one arm runs southwest to join the Mid-Atlantic Ridge, the other branches southeast, joining the Pacific-Antarctic Ridge, southeast of Tasmania.

The Ninetyeast Ridge takes its name from the line of longitude it follows. It is the world's longest and straightest under-sea ridge.

Two of the world's largest rivers flow into the Indian Ocean; the Indus and the Ganges/Brahmaputra. Both have deposited enormous fans of sediment.

Indus River

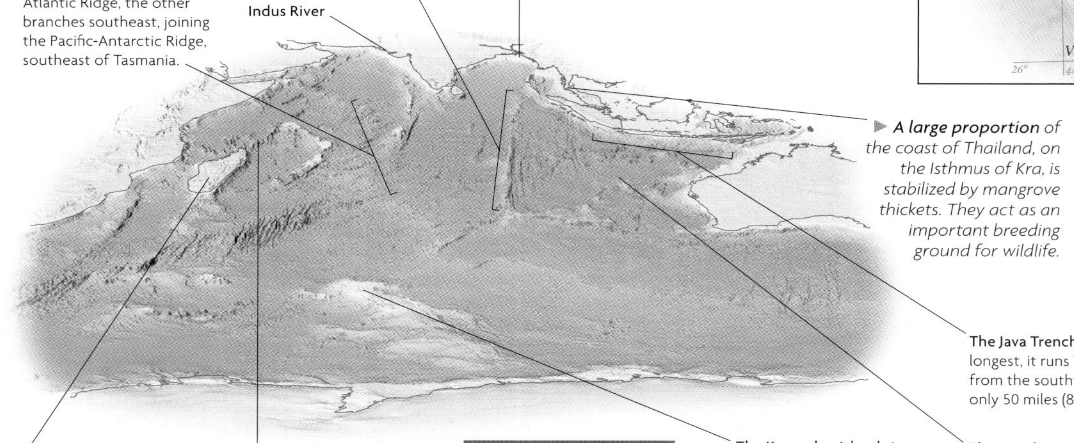

▶ *A large proportion of the coast of Thailand, on the Isthmus of Kra, is stabilized by mangrove thickets. They act as an important breeding ground for wildlife.*

The Java Trench is the world's longest, it runs 1600 miles (2570 km) from the southwest of Java, but is only 50 miles (80 km) wide.

The relief of Madagascar rises from a low-lying coastal strip in the east, to the central plateau. The plateau is also a major watershed separating Madagascar's three main river basins.

▶ *The central group of the Seychelles are mountainous, granite islands. They have a narrow coastal belt and lush, tropical vegetation cloaks the highlands.*

The Kerguelen Islands in the Southern Ocean were created by a hot spot in the Earth's crust. The islands were formed in succession as the Antarctic Plate moved slowly over the hot spot.

The circulation in the northern Indian Ocean is controlled by the monsoon winds. Biannually these winds reverse their pattern, causing a reversal in the surface currents and alternative high and low pressure conditions over Asia and Australia.

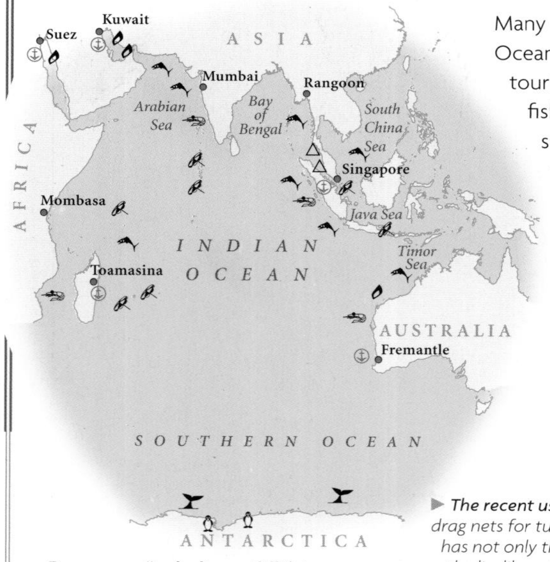

Resources

Many of the small islands in the Indian Ocean rely exclusively on tuna-fishing and tourism to maintain their economies. Most fisheries are artisanal, although large-scale tuna-fishing does take place in the Seychelles, Mauritius and the western Indian Ocean. Other resources include oil in The Gulf, pearls in the Red Sea and tin from deposits off the shores of Burma, Thailand and Indonesia.

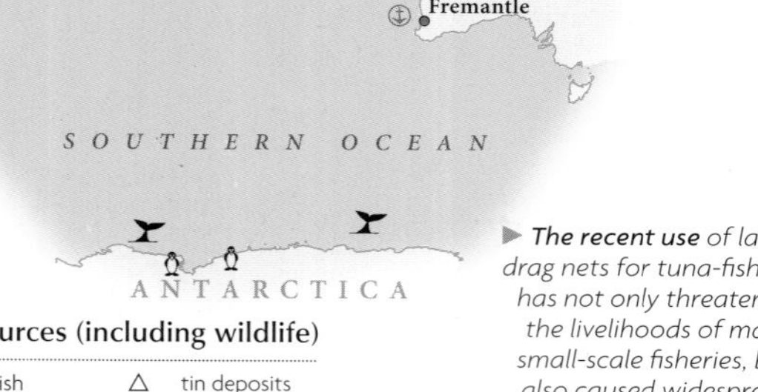

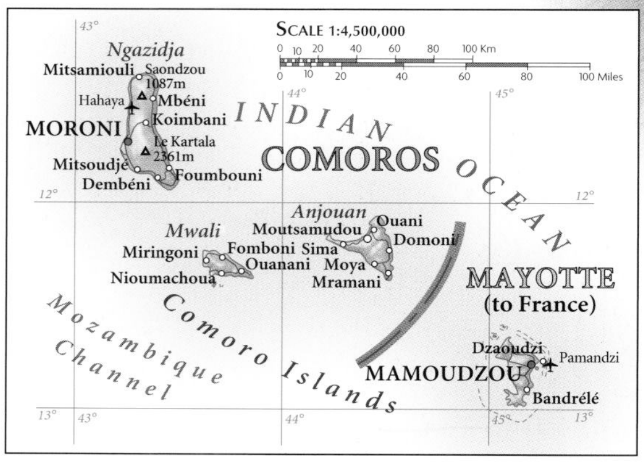

Suez
Kuwait
ASIA
Mumbai
Rangoon
Arabian Sea
Bay of Bengal
South China Sea
Singapore
AFRICA
Mombasa
Java Sea
INDIAN OCEAN
Timor Sea
Toamasina
AUSTRALIA
Fremantle
SOUTHERN OCEAN
ANTARCTICA

Resources (including wildlife)

- fish
- penguins
- shellfish
- whales
- oil & gas
- tin deposits
- tourism
- major towns
- major ports

▶ *The recent use of large drag nets for tuna-fishing has not only threatened the livelihoods of many small-scale fisheries, but also caused widespread environmental concern about the potential impact on other marine species.*

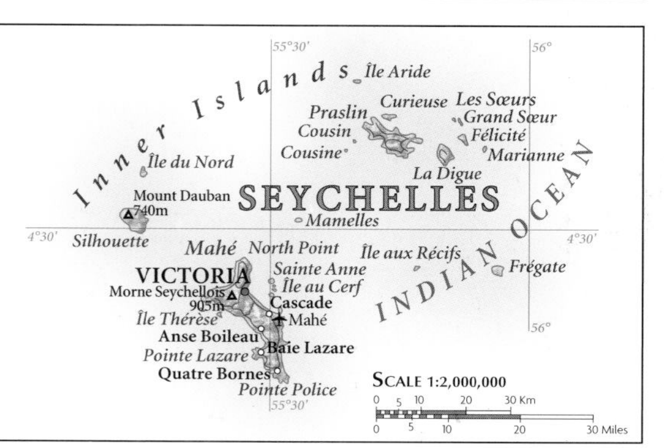

Inner Islands
Île Aride
Praslin
Curieuse
Les Sœurs
Grand Sœur
Félicité
Cousin
Cousine
Marianne
Île du Nord
La Digue
Mount Dauban 740m
SEYCHELLES
Mamelles
Silhouette
Mahé
North Point
Île aux Récifs
VICTORIA
Sainte Anne
Île au Cerf
Frégate
Morne Seychellois 905m
Cascade
Île Thérèse
Mahé
Anse Boileau
Baie Lazare
Pointe Lazare
Quatre Bornes
Pointe Police
INDIAN OCEAN
SCALE 1:2,000,000

▲ *Coral reefs support an enormous diversity of animal and plant life. Many species of tropical fish, like these squirrel fish, live and feed around the profusion of reefs and atolls in the Indian Ocean.*

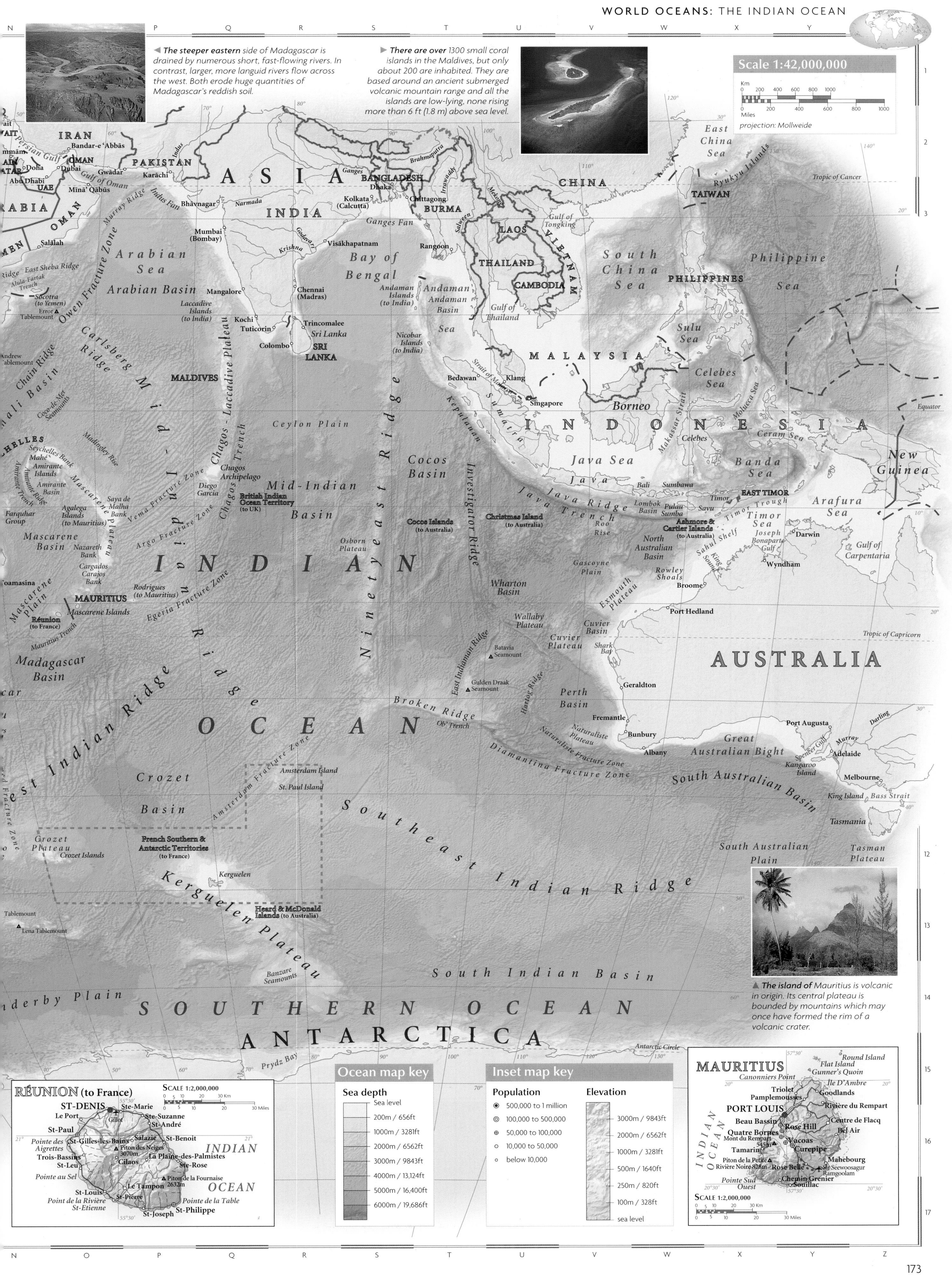

Scale 1:42,000,000
projection: Mollweide
ASIA
IRAN
PAKISTAN
INDIA
BANGLADESH
BURMA
CHINA
TAIWAN
LAOS
THAILAND
CAMBODIA
VIETNAM
MALAYSIA
PHILIPPINES
INDONESIA
EAST TIMOR
AUSTRALIA
MALDIVES
SRI LANKA
MAURITIUS
OMAN
UAE
Arabian Sea
Bay of Bengal
Andaman Sea
South China Sea
Philippine Sea
Sulu Sea
Celebes Sea
Java Sea
Banda Sea
Timor Sea
Arafura Sea
Arabian Basin
Carlsberg Ridge
Mid-Indian Ridge
Chagos-Laccadive Plateau
Ceylon Plain
Mid-Indian Basin
Ninetyeast Ridge
Cocos Basin
Investigator Ridge
Java Trench
Wharton Basin
Mascarene Basin
Madagascar Basin
INDIAN OCEAN
Southwest Indian Ridge
Crozet Basin
Broken Ridge
Southeast Indian Ridge
Kerguelen Plateau
South Australian Basin
Great Australian Bight
South Indian Basin
SOUTHERN OCEAN
ANTARCTICA
Tropic of Cancer
Equator
Tropic of Capricorn
Antarctic Circle

The steeper eastern side of Madagascar is drained by numerous short, fast-flowing rivers. In contrast, larger, more languid rivers flow across the west. Both erode huge quantities of Madagascar's reddish soil.

There are over 1300 small coral islands in the Maldives, but only about 200 are inhabited. They are based around an ancient submerged volcanic mountain range and all the islands are low-lying, none rising more than 6 ft (1.8 m) above sea level.

The island of Mauritius is volcanic in origin. Its central plateau is bounded by mountains which may once have formed the rim of a volcanic crater.

RÉUNION (to France)
SCALE 1:2,000,000
ST-DENIS
St-Paul
St-Pierre
Piton des Neiges 3070m
Piton de la Fournaise 2632m
INDIAN OCEAN
MAURITIUS
PORT LOUIS
Mahebourg
SCALE 1:2,000,000

Ocean map key

Sea depth: Sea level; 200m / 656ft; 1000m / 3281ft; 2000m / 6562ft; 3000m / 9843ft; 4000m / 13,124ft; 5000m / 16,400ft; 6000m / 19,686ft

Inset map key

Population: 500,000 to 1 million; 100,000 to 500,000; 50,000 to 100,000; 10,000 to 50,000; below 10,000

Elevation: 3000m / 9843ft; 2000m / 6562ft; 1000m / 3281ft; 500m / 1640ft; 250m / 820ft; 100m / 328ft; sea level

Australasia & Oceania

Australasia and Oceania, covering a land area of 3,285,048 sq miles (8,508,238 sq km), takes in 14 countries including the continent of Australia, New Zealand, Papua New Guinea and many island groups scattered across the Pacific Ocean.

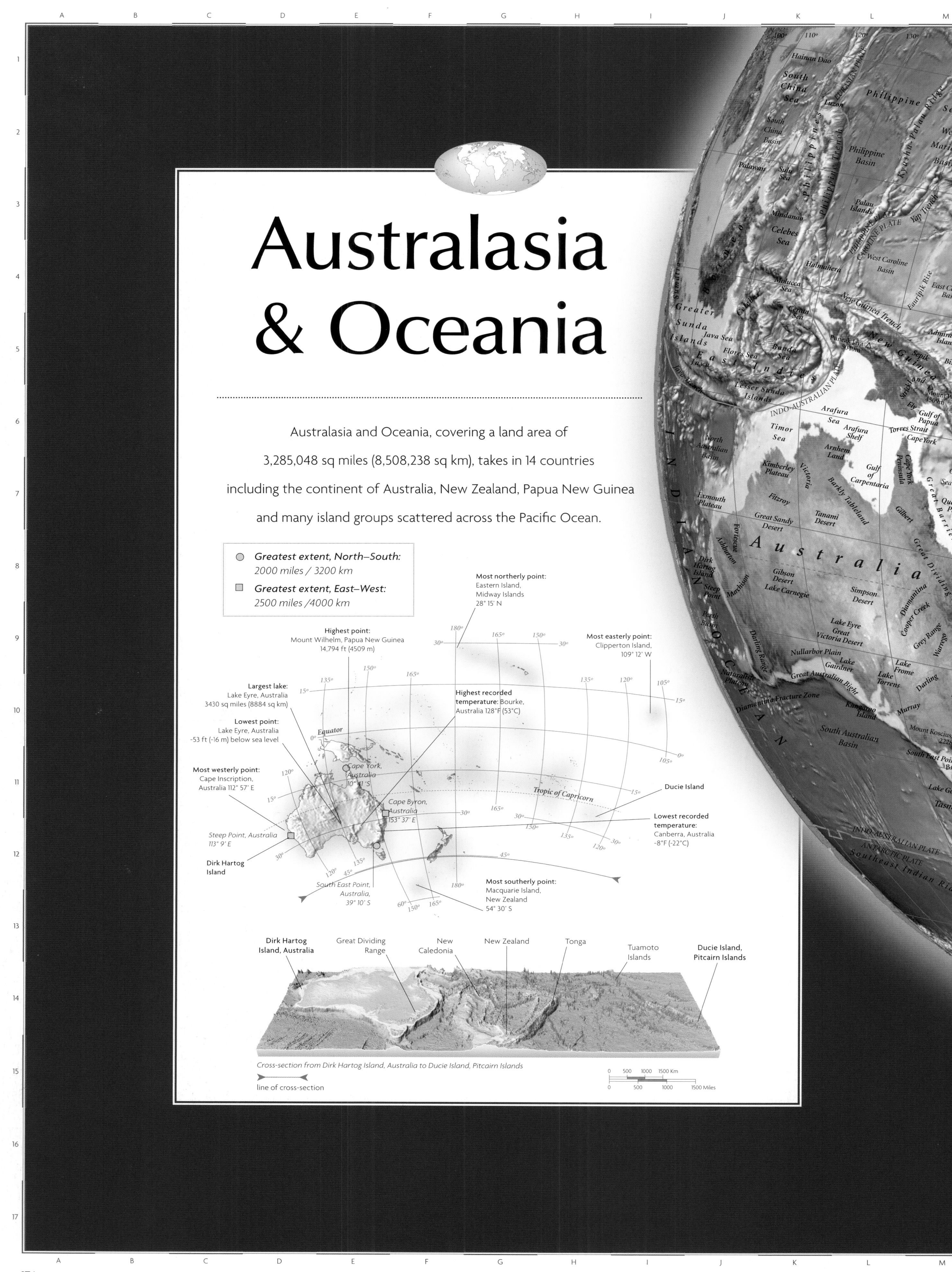

Greatest extent, North–South:
2000 miles / 3200 km
Greatest extent, East–West:
2500 miles /4000 km
Most northerly point:
Eastern Island, Midway Islands
28° 15' N
Highest point:
Mount Wilhelm, Papua New Guinea
14,794 ft (4509 m)
Most easterly point:
Clipperton Island,
109° 12' W
Largest lake:
Lake Eyre, Australia
3430 sq miles (8884 sq km)
Highest recorded temperature: Bourke, Australia 128°F (53°C)
Lowest point:
Lake Eyre, Australia
-53 ft (-16 m) below sea level
Equator
Most westerly point:
Cape Inscription, Australia 112° 57' E
Cape York, Australia 10° 41' S
Cape Byron, Australia 153° 37' E
Tropic of Capricorn
Ducie Island
Lowest recorded temperature:
Canberra, Australia
-8°F (-22°C)
Steep Point, Australia
113° 9' E
Dirk Hartog Island
South East Point, Australia, 39° 10' S
Most southerly point:
Macquarie Island, New Zealand
54° 30' S
Dirk Hartog Island, Australia
Great Dividing Range
New Caledonia
New Zealand
Tonga
Tuamoto Islands
Ducie Island, Pitcairn Islands
Cross-section from Dirk Hartog Island, Australia to Ducie Island, Pitcairn Islands
line of cross-section
0 500 1000 1500 Km
0 500 1000 1500 Miles
Hainan Dao
South China Sea
Luzon
Philippine Sea
Philippine Basin
Palawan
Sulu Sea
Mindanao
Celebes Sea
Palau Islands
Yap Trench
West Caroline Basin
Halmahera
Molucca Sea
New Guinea Trench
Greater Sunda Islands
Java Sea
Flores Sea
Banda Sea
Ceram Sea
New Guinea
Lesser Sunda Islands
INDO-AUSTRALIAN PLATE
Arafura Sea
Arafura Shelf
Gulf of Papua
Torres Strait
Cape York
Timor Sea
Arnhem Land
North Australian Basin
Kimberley Plateau
Gulf of Carpentaria
Cape York Peninsula
Exmouth Plateau
Fitzroy
Tanami Desert
Barkly Tableland
Great Sandy Desert
Australia
Dirk Hartog Island
Steep Point
Gibson Desert
Lake Carnegie
Simpson Desert
Great Dividing Range
Perth Basin
Lake Eyre
Great Victoria Desert
Nullarbor Plain
Lake Gairdner
Lake Frome
Lake Torrens
Great Australian Bight
Darling
Murray
Diamantina Fracture Zone
Kangaroo Island
South Australian Basin
INDIAN OCEAN
INDO-AUSTRALIAN PLATE
ANTARCTIC PLATE
Southeast Indian Ridge

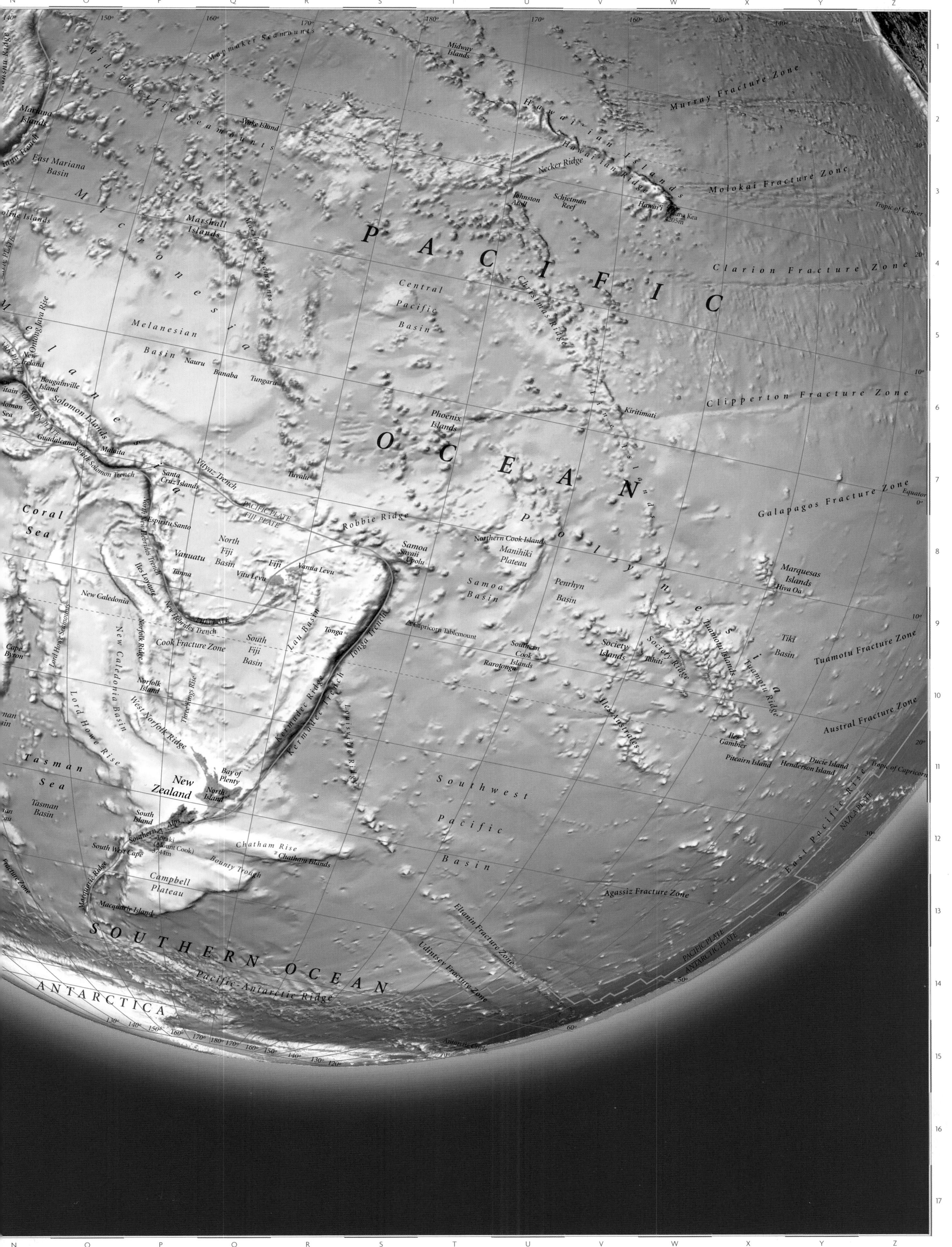
PACIFIC OCEAN
SOUTHERN OCEAN
ANTARCTICA
Mid-Pacific Seamounts
Manmaker Seamounts
Midway Islands
Hawaiian Islands
Hawaiian Ridge
Necker Ridge
Hawai'i
Mauna Kea 4205m
Johnston Atoll
Schjetman Reef
Murray Fracture Zone
Molokai Fracture Zone
Tropic of Cancer
Clarion Fracture Zone
Clipperton Fracture Zone
Galapagos Fracture Zone
Equator
Mariana Islands
East Mariana Basin
Wake Island
Marshall Islands
Micronesia
Melanesia
Melanesian Basin
Central Pacific Basin
Christmas Ridge
Line Islands
Kiritimati
Nauru
Banaba
Tungaru
Ontong Java Rise
New Ireland
Bougainville Island
Solomon Islands
Solomon Sea
Guadalcanal
Malaita
South Solomon Trench
Phoenix Islands
Santa Cruz Islands
Vityaz Trench
Tuvalu
Coral Sea
Espiritu Santo
North New Hebrides Trench
Vanuatu
Tanna
North Fiji Basin
Fiji
Vitu Levu
Vanua Levu
PACIFIC PLATE
FIJI PLATE
Robbie Ridge
Samoa
Savaii
Upolu
Northern Cook Islands
Manihiki Plateau
Samoa Basin
Penrhyn Basin
Polynesia
Marquesas Islands
Hiva Oa
Iles Loyauté
New Caledonia
New Hebrides Trench
Lau Basin
Tonga
Tonga Trench
Capricorn Tablemount
Lord Howe Seamounts
Norfolk Ridge
New Caledonia Basin
Cook Fracture Zone
South Fiji Basin
Southern Cook Islands
Rarotonga
Society Islands
Tahiti
Society Ridge
Tuamotu Islands
Tuamotu Ridge
Tiki Basin
Tuamotu Fracture Zone
Cape Byron
Norfolk Island
Three Kings Rise
West Norfolk Ridge
Lord Howe Rise
Kermadec Ridge
Kermadec Trench
Louisville Ridge
Îles Australes
Îles Gambier
Pitcairn Island
Henderson Island
Ducie Island
Austral Fracture Zone
Tropic of Capricorn
Tasman Sea
Tasman Basin
New Zealand
North Island
Bay of Plenty
South Island
Southern Alps
Aoraki (Mount Cook) 3744m
South West Cape
Chatham Rise
Chatham Islands
Bounty Trough
Campbell Plateau
Macquarie Ridge
Macquarie Island
Southwest Pacific Basin
East Pacific Rise
NAZCA PLATE
Agassiz Fracture Zone
Eltanin Fracture Zone
Udintsev Fracture Zone
PACIFIC PLATE
ANTARCTIC PLATE
Pacific-Antarctic Ridge
Antarctic Circle
N O P Q R S T U V W X Y Z
1 2 3 4 5 6 7 8 9 10 11 12 13 14 15 16 17

Political Australasia & Oceania

Vast expanses of ocean separate this geographically fragmented realm, characterized more by each country's isolation than by any political unity. Australia's and New Zealand's traditional ties with the United Kingdom, as members of the Commonwealth, are now being called into question as Australasian and Oceanian nations are increasingly looking to forge new relationships with neighbouring Asian countries like Japan. External influences have featured strongly in the politics of the Pacific Islands; the various territories of Micronesia were largely under US control until the late 1980s, and France, New Zealand, the USA and the UK still have territories under colonial rule in Polynesia. Nuclear weapons-testing by Western superpowers was widespread during the Cold War period, but has now been discontinued.

◀ *Western Australia's mineral wealth has transformed its state capital, Perth, into one of Australia's major cities. Perth is one of the world's most isolated cities – over 2500 miles (4000 km) from the population centres of the eastern seaboard.*

Scale 1:32,000,000

Km 0 200 400 600 800
Miles 0 200 400 600 800
projection: Lambert Azimuthal Equal Area

Population

Density of settlement in the region is generally low. Australia is one of the least densely populated countries on Earth with over 80% of its population living within 25 miles (40 km) of the coast – mostly in the southeast of the country. New Zealand, and the island groups of Melanesia, Micronesia and Polynesia, are much more densely populated, although many of the smaller islands remain uninhabited.

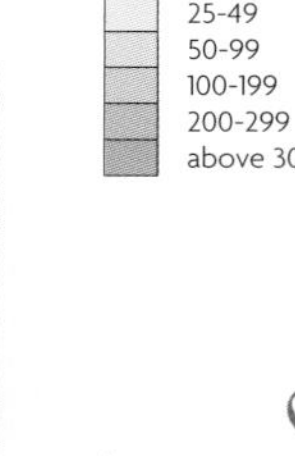

Population density
(people per sq km)

- below 4
- 5-24
- 25-49
- 50-99
- 100-199
- 200-299
- above 300

▲ *The myriad of small coral islands which are scattered across the Pacific Ocean are often uninhabited, as they offer little shelter from the weather, often no fresh water, and only limited food supplies.*

◀ *The planes of the Australian Royal Flying Doctor Service are able to cover large expanses of barren land quickly, bringing medical treatment to the most inaccessible and far-flung places.*

Philippine Sea
Northern Mariana Islands (to US)
Mariana Islands
Saipan
Guam (to US)
HAGÅTÑA
Micronesia
MICRONESIA
Caroline Islands
Yap
Chuuk
Pohnpei
PALIKIR
Kosrae
Bikini Atoll
Ralik Chain
Wake Island (to US)
MELEKEOK
Babeldaob
PALAU
Melanesia
NAURU
PAPUA NEW GUINEA
Bismarck Sea
New Ireland
New Britain
Rabaul
Wewak
Madang
New Guinea
Mount Hagen
Lae
Tapini
PORT MORESBY
Ubai
Arawa
Bougainville Island
Solomon Sea
Solomon Islands
New Georgia Islands
HONIARA
Guadalcanal
SOLOMON ISLANDS
Santa Cruz Islands
VANUATU
Espiritu Santo
Malekula
Efate
PORT-VILA
Erromango
New Caledonia (to France)
NOUMÉA
Coral Sea
Coral Sea Islands (to Australia)
Arafura Sea
Torres Strait
Timor Sea
Equator
Tropic of Capricorn
INDIAN OCEAN
Cape York Peninsula
Gulf of Carpentaria
Great Barrier Reef
Great Dividing Range
Darwin
Arnhem Land
Katherine
Joseph Bonaparte Gulf
Wyndham
Kimberley Plateau
Derby
Broome
Port Hedland
Great Sandy Desert
NORTHERN TERRITORY
Tennant Creek
Tanami Desert
Alice Springs
Simpson Desert
Cairns
Normanton
Townsville
Hughenden
Mount Isa
Mackay
Rockhampton
QUEENSLAND
Barcaldine
Charleville
Miles
Brisbane
Toowoomba
AUSTRALIA
Hamersley Range
Gibson Desert
WESTERN AUSTRALIA
Lake Eyre North
SOUTH AUSTRALIA
Lake Torrens
Flinders Ranges
Grey Range
Cunnamulla
Bourke
Darling
Barwon
Grafton
Wilcannia
NEW SOUTH WALES
Dubbo
Newcastle
Sydney
Wollongong
Campbelltown
CANBERRA
AUSTRALIAN CAPITAL TERRITORY
Carnavon
Great Victoria Desert
Lake Everard
Lake Gairdner
Port Augusta
Ceduna
Whyalla
Murray
Wagga Wagga
Mount Magnet
Kalgoorlie
Nullarbor Plain
Geraldton
Great Australian Bight
Adelaide
Kangaroo Island
Bendigo
Horsham
VICTORIA
Ballarat
Melbourne
Geelong
Mount Gambier
Perth
Esperance
Albany
Bass Strait
Launceston
TASMANIA
Tasmania
Hobart
Tasman Sea
Lord Howe Island (to Australia)
Norfolk Island (to Australia)

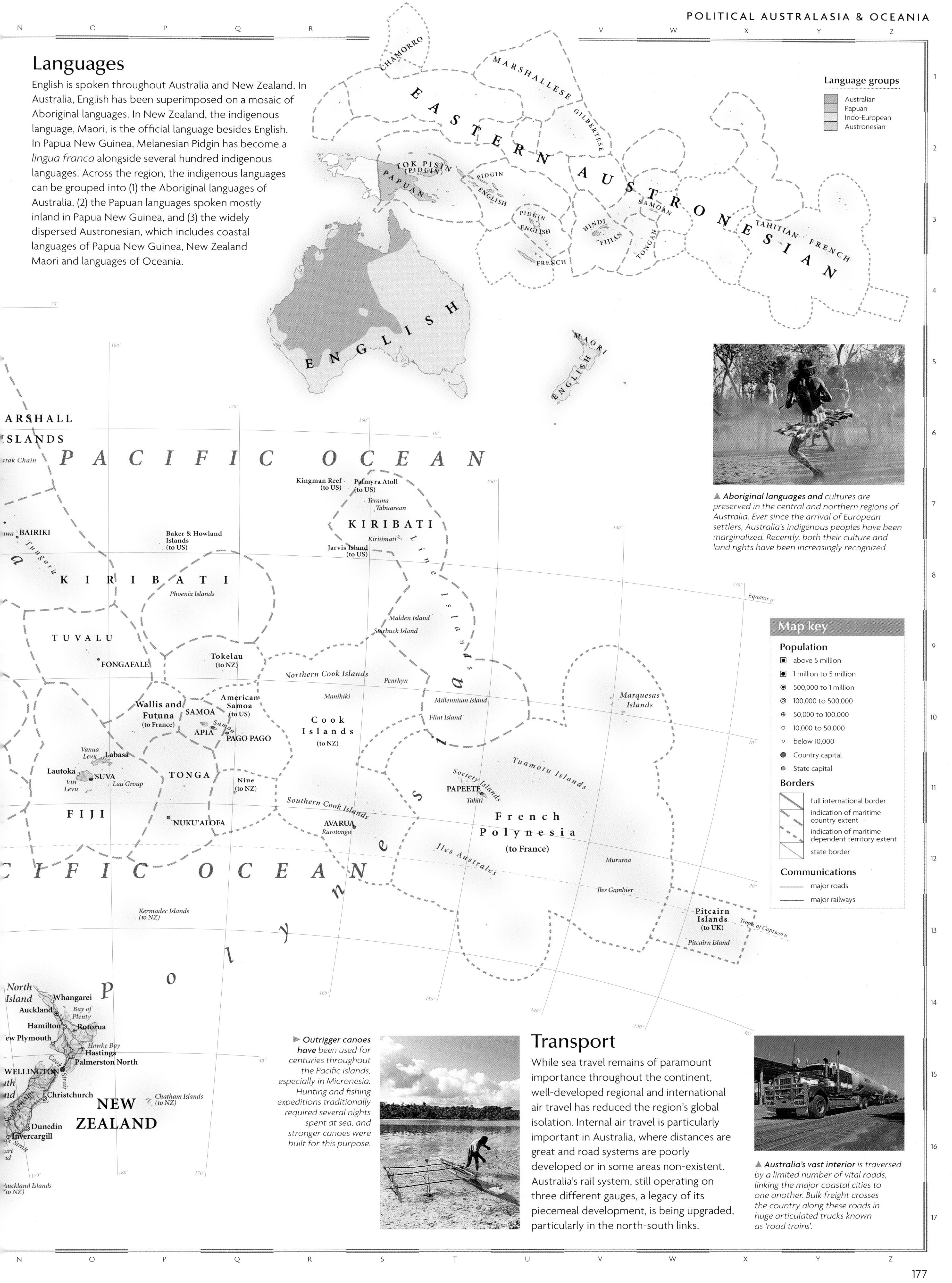

Language groups
Australian
Papuan
Indo-European
Austronesian
CHAMORRO
MARSHALLESE
GILBERTESE
EASTERN AUSTRONESIAN
TOK PISIN (PIDGIN)
PAPUAN
PIDGIN
ENGLISH
HINDI
FIJIAN
SAMOAN
TONGAN
TAHITIAN
FRENCH
ENGLISH
MAORI
PACIFIC OCEAN
KIRIBATI
TUVALU
FONGAFALE
BAIRIKI
Baker & Howland Islands (to US)
Phoenix Islands
Kingman Reef (to US)
Palmyra Atoll (to US)
Teraina
Tabuaerean
Kiritimati
Jarvis Island (to US)
Line Islands
Malden Island
Starbuck Island
Tokelau (to NZ)
Wallis and Futuna (to France)
SAMOA
American Samoa (to US)
APIA
PAGO PAGO
Northern Cook Islands
Penrhyn
Manihiki
Cook Islands (to NZ)
Millennium Island
Flint Island
Marquesas Islands
Vanua Levu
Labasa
Lautoka
SUVA
Viti Levu
Lau Group
FIJI
TONGA
Niue (to NZ)
NUKU'ALOFA
Southern Cook Islands
AVARUA
Rarotonga
Society Islands
PAPEETE
Tahiti
Tuamotu Islands
French Polynesia (to France)
Îles Australes
Mururoa
Îles Gambier
Pitcairn Islands (to UK)
Pitcairn Island
Tropic of Capricorn
Equator
Kermadec Islands (to NZ)
Polynesia
North Island
Whangarei
Auckland
Bay of Plenty
Hamilton
Rotorua
New Plymouth
Hawke Bay
Hastings
Palmerston North
WELLINGTON
Cook Strait
Christchurch
NEW ZEALAND
Chatham Islands (to NZ)
Dunedin
Invercargill
Foveaux Strait
Auckland Islands (to NZ)
Map key
Population
above 5 million
1 million to 5 million
500,000 to 1 million
100,000 to 500,000
50,000 to 100,000
10,000 to 50,000
below 10,000
Country capital
State capital
Borders
full international border
indication of maritime country extent
indication of maritime dependent territory extent
state border
Communications
major roads
major railways

Languages

English is spoken throughout Australia and New Zealand. In Australia, English has been superimposed on a mosaic of Aboriginal languages. In New Zealand, the indigenous language, Maori, is the official language besides English. In Papua New Guinea, Melanesian Pidgin has become a *lingua franca* alongside several hundred indigenous languages. Across the region, the indigenous languages can be grouped into (1) the Aboriginal languages of Australia, (2) the Papuan languages spoken mostly inland in Papua New Guinea, and (3) the widely dispersed Austronesian, which includes coastal languages of Papua New Guinea, New Zealand Maori and languages of Oceania.

▲ ***Aboriginal languages and*** *cultures are preserved in the central and northern regions of Australia. Ever since the arrival of European settlers, Australia's indigenous peoples have been marginalized. Recently, both their culture and land rights have been increasingly recognized.*

► ***Outrigger canoes have*** *been used for centuries throughout the Pacific islands, especially in Micronesia. Hunting and fishing expeditions traditionally required several nights spent at sea, and stronger canoes were built for this purpose.*

Transport

While sea travel remains of paramount importance throughout the continent, well-developed regional and international air travel has reduced the region's global isolation. Internal air travel is particularly important in Australia, where distances are great and road systems are poorly developed or in some areas non-existent. Australia's rail system, still operating on three different gauges, a legacy of its piecemeal development, is being upgraded, particularly in the north-south links.

▲ ***Australia's vast interior*** *is traversed by a limited number of vital roads, linking the major coastal cities to one another. Bulk freight crosses the country along these roads in huge articulated trucks known as 'road trains'.*

Australasian & Oceanian resources

Natural resources are of major economic importance throughout Australasia and Oceania. Australia in particular is a major world exporter of raw materials such as coal, iron ore and bauxite, while New Zealand's agricultural economy is dominated by sheep-raising. Trade with western Europe has declined significantly in the last 20 years, and the Pacific Rim countries of Southeast Asia are now the main trading partners, as well as a source of new settlers to the region. Australasia and Oceania's greatest resources are its climate and environment; tourism increasingly provides a vital source of income for the whole continent.

▲ ***The largely unpolluted** waters of the Pacific Ocean support rich and varied marine life, much of which is farmed commercially. Here, oysters are gathered for market off the coast of New Zealand's South Island.*

► ***Huge flocks of** sheep are a common sight in New Zealand, where they outnumber people by 12 to 1. New Zealand is one of the world's largest exporters of wool and frozen lamb.*

Standard of living

In marked contrast to its neighbour, Australia, with one of the world's highest life expectancies and standards of living, Papua New Guinea is one of the world's least developed countries. In addition, high population growth and urbanization rates throughout the Pacific islands contribute to overcrowding. The Aboriginal and Maori people of Australia and New Zealand have been isolated for many years. Recently, their traditional land ownership rights have begun to be legally recognized in an effort to ease their social and economic isolation, and to improve living standards.

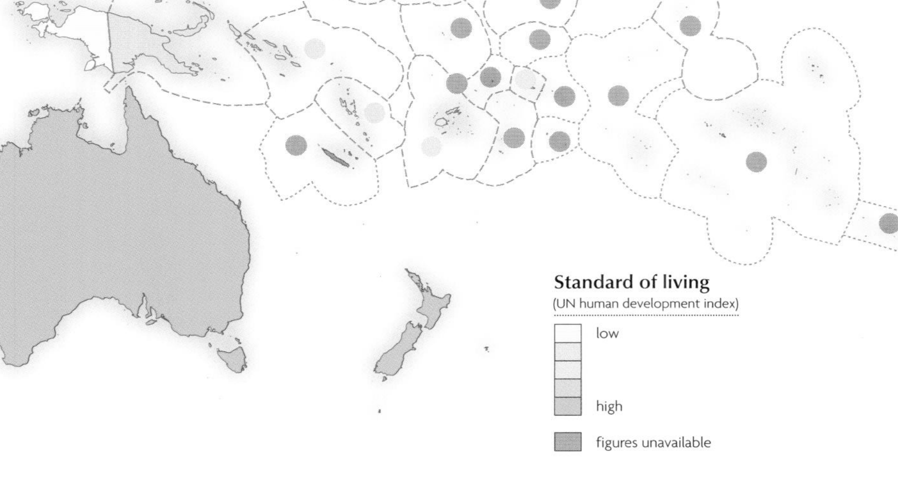
Standard of living
(UN human development index)
low
high
figures unavailable

Environmental issues

The prospect of rising sea levels poses a threat to many low-lying islands in the Pacific. Nuclear weapons-testing, once common throughout the region, was finally discontinued in 1996. Australia's ecological balance has been irreversibly altered by the introduction of alien species. Although it has the world's largest underground water reserve, the Great Artesian Basin, the availability of fresh water in Australia remains critical. Periodic droughts combined with over-grazing lead to desertification and increase the risk of devastating bush fires, and occasional flash floods.

Eniwetak Atoll
Bikini Atoll
Malden Island
Fangataufa
Coral Sea
PACIFIC OCEAN
INDIAN OCEAN
Mackenzie
Darling
Murray
Murchison
Sydney
Tasman Sea

Environmental issues

- national parks
- tropical forest
- forest destroyed
- desert
- desertification
- polluted rivers
- radioactive contamination
- marine pollution
- heavy marine pollution
- poor urban air quality

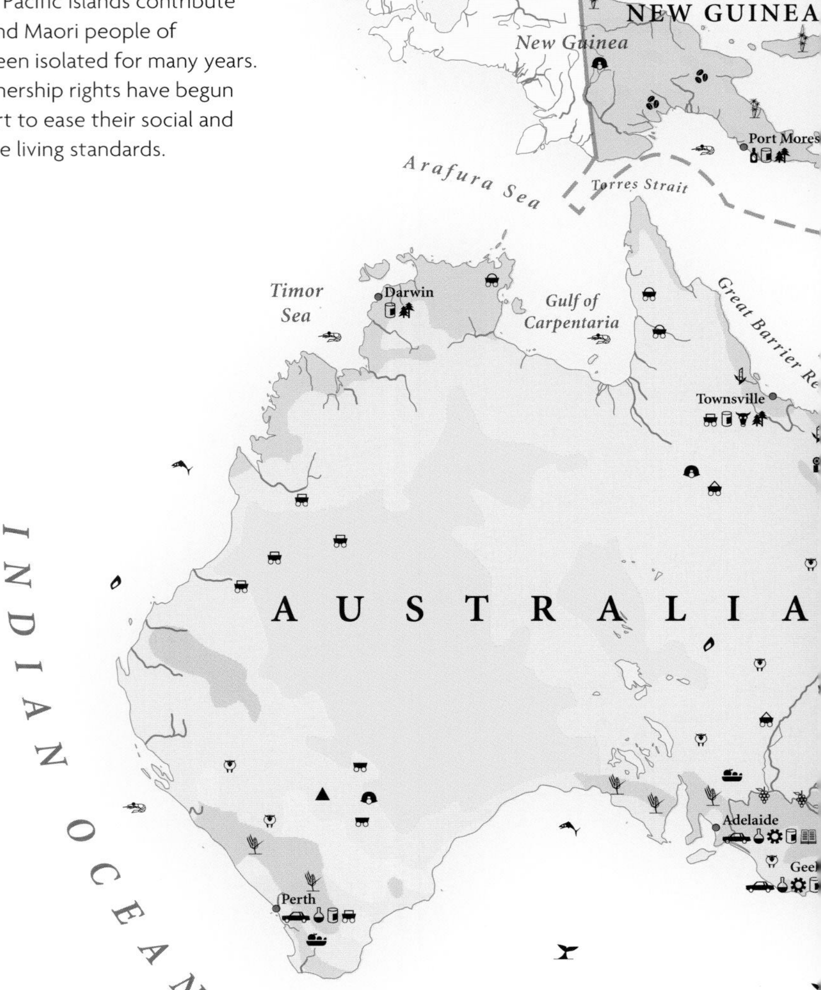
Northern Mariana Islands (to US)
Saipan
Guam (to US)
MICRO
PALAU
PAPUA NEW GUINEA
New Guinea
Arafura Sea
Torres Strait
Timor Sea
Darwin
Gulf of Carpentaria
Great Barrier Re
Townsville
AUSTRALIA
INDIAN OCEAN
Adelaide
Perth

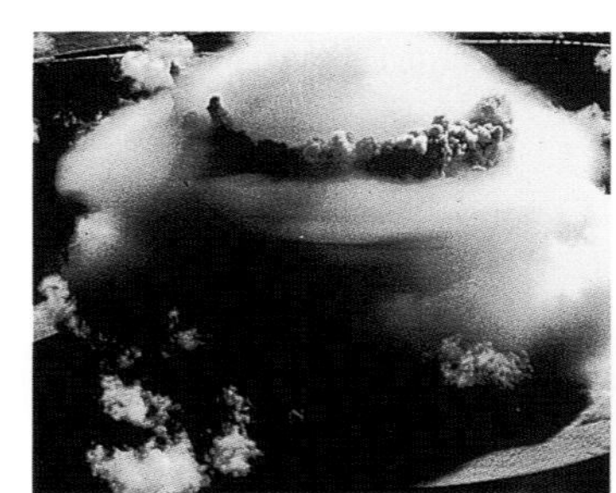

▲ ***In 1946 Bikini Atoll,** in the Marshall Islands, was chosen as the site for Operation Crossroads – investigating the effects of atomic bombs upon naval vessels. Further nuclear tests continued until the early 1990s. The long-term environmental effects are unknown.*

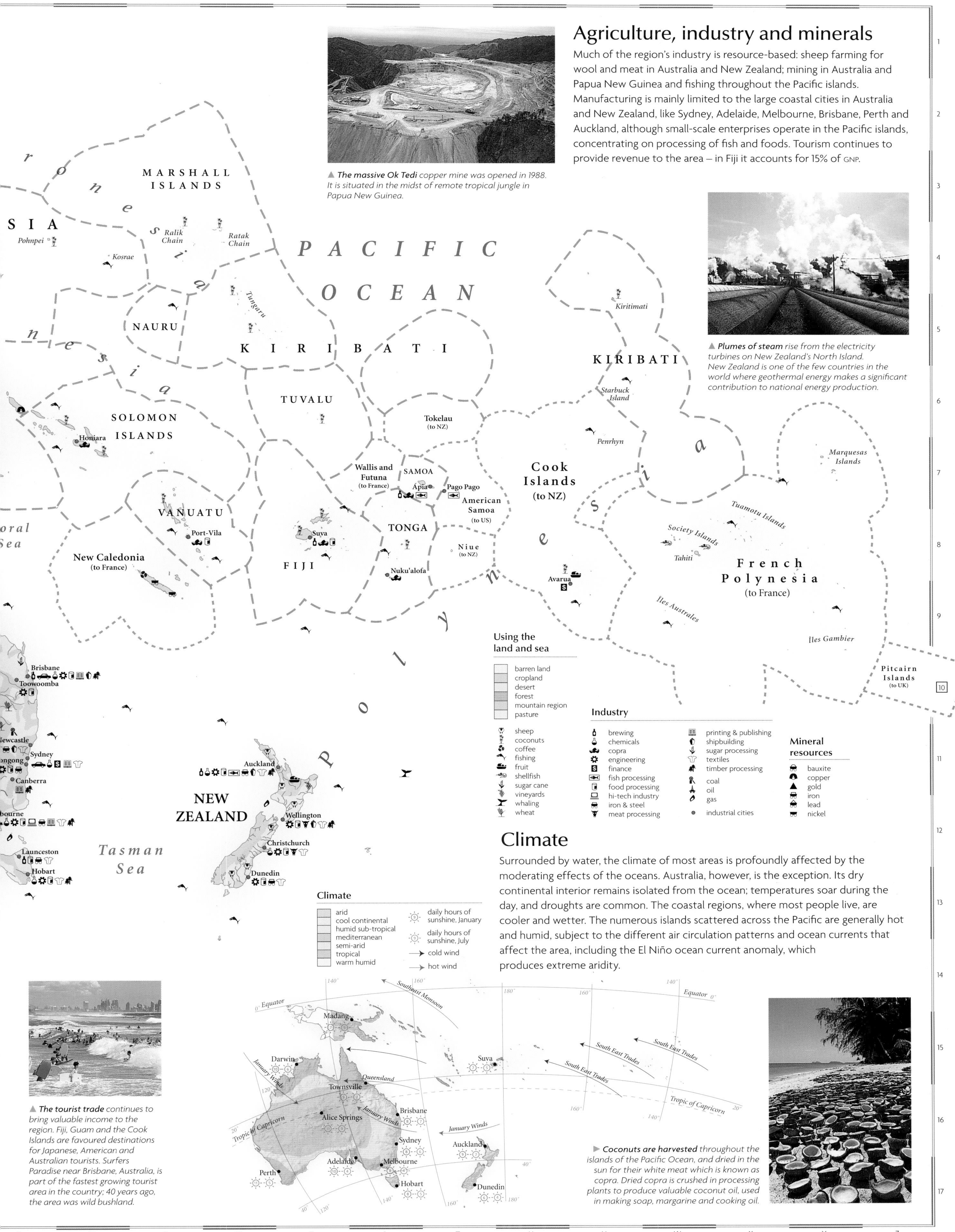

PACIFIC OCEAN
Micronesia
Polynesia
MARSHALL ISLANDS
Ralik Chain
Ratak Chain
Pohnpei
Kosrae
NAURU
KIRIBATI
Tungaru
Kiritimati
Starbuck Island
TUVALU
SOLOMON ISLANDS
Honiara
Tokelau (to NZ)
Wallis and Futuna (to France)
SAMOA
Apia
Pago Pago
American Samoa (to US)
Cook Islands (to NZ)
Penrhyn
Avarua
VANUATU
Port-Vila
New Caledonia (to France)
FIJI
Suva
TONGA
Nuku'alofa
Niue (to NZ)
Marquesas Islands
Tuamotu Islands
Society Islands
Tahiti
French Polynesia (to France)
Îles Australes
Îles Gambier
Pitcairn Islands (to UK)
Brisbane
Toowoomba
Newcastle
Sydney
Wollongong
Canberra
Melbourne
Launceston
Hobart
Tasman Sea
NEW ZEALAND
Auckland
Wellington
Christchurch
Dunedin
Coral Sea
Using the land and sea
barren land
cropland
desert
forest
mountain region
pasture
sheep
coconuts
coffee
fishing
fruit
shellfish
sugar cane
vineyards
whaling
wheat
Industry
brewing
chemicals
copra
engineering
finance
fish processing
food processing
hi-tech industry
iron & steel
meat processing
printing & publishing
shipbuilding
sugar processing
textiles
timber processing
coal
oil
gas
industrial cities
Mineral resources
bauxite
copper
gold
iron
lead
nickel
Climate
arid
cool continental
humid sub-tropical
mediterranean
semi-arid
tropical
warm humid
daily hours of sunshine, January
daily hours of sunshine, July
cold wind
hot wind
Equator
Southeast Monsoon
South East Trades
January Winds
Tropic of Capricorn
Madang
Darwin
Townsville
Queensland
Alice Springs
Perth
Adelaide
Melbourne
Hobart
Brisbane
Sydney
Auckland
Dunedin
Suva

Agriculture, industry and minerals

Much of the region's industry is resource-based: sheep farming for wool and meat in Australia and New Zealand; mining in Australia and Papua New Guinea and fishing throughout the Pacific islands. Manufacturing is mainly limited to the large coastal cities in Australia and New Zealand, like Sydney, Adelaide, Melbourne, Brisbane, Perth and Auckland, although small-scale enterprises operate in the Pacific islands, concentrating on processing of fish and foods. Tourism continues to provide revenue to the area – in Fiji it accounts for 15% of GNP.

▲ *The massive Ok Tedi copper mine was opened in 1988. It is situated in the midst of remote tropical jungle in Papua New Guinea.*

▲ *Plumes of steam rise from the electricity turbines on New Zealand's North Island. New Zealand is one of the few countries in the world where geothermal energy makes a significant contribution to national energy production.*

Climate

Surrounded by water, the climate of most areas is profoundly affected by the moderating effects of the oceans. Australia, however, is the exception. Its dry continental interior remains isolated from the ocean; temperatures soar during the day, and droughts are common. The coastal regions, where most people live, are cooler and wetter. The numerous islands scattered across the Pacific are generally hot and humid, subject to the different air circulation patterns and ocean currents that affect the area, including the El Niño ocean current anomaly, which produces extreme aridity.

▲ *The tourist trade continues to bring valuable income to the region. Fiji, Guam and the Cook Islands are favoured destinations for Japanese, American and Australian tourists. Surfers Paradise near Brisbane, Australia, is part of the fastest growing tourist area in the country; 40 years ago, the area was wild bushland.*

► *Coconuts are harvested throughout the islands of the Pacific Ocean, and dried in the sun for their white meat which is known as copra. Dried copra is crushed in processing plants to produce valuable coconut oil, used in making soap, margarine and cooking oil.*

Australia

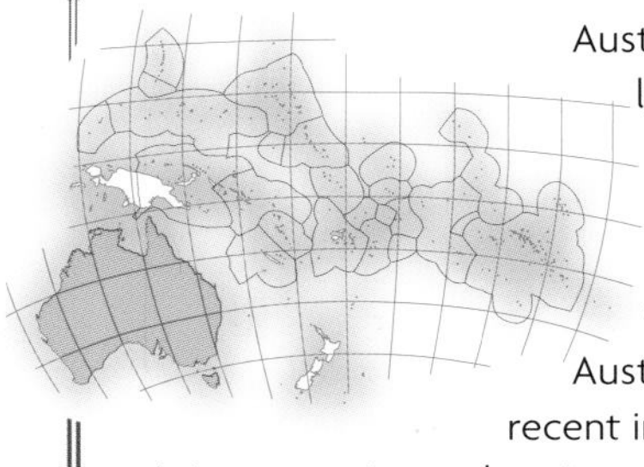

Australia is the world's smallest continent, a stable landmass lying between the Indian and Pacific oceans. Previously home to its aboriginal peoples only, since the end of the 18th century immigration has transformed the face of the country. Initially settlers came mainly from western Europe, particularly the UK, and for years Australia remained wedded to its British colonial past. More recent immigrants have come from eastern Europe, and from Asian countries such as Japan, South Korea and Indonesia. Australia is now forging strong trading links with these 'Pacific Rim' countries and its economic future seems to lie with Asia and the Americas, rather than Europe, its traditional partner.

◀ **Uluru (Ayers Rock),** *the world's largest free-standing rock, is a massive outcrop of red sandstone in Australia's desert centre. Wind and sandstorms have ground the rock into the smooth curves seen here. Uluru is revered as a sacred site by many aboriginal peoples.*

Scale 1:10,500,000

Km 0 25 50 100 150 200 250 300 350

Miles 0 25 50 100 150 200 250 300 350

projection: Lambert Conformal Conic

Map key

Population

- 1 million to 5 million
- 500,000 to 1 million
- 100,000 to 500,000
- 50,000 to 100,000
- 10,000 to 50,000
- below 10,000

Elevation

- 2000m / 6562ft
- 1000m / 3281ft
- 500m / 1640ft
- 250m / 820ft
- 100m / 328ft
- sea level

154

Using the land

Over 104 million sheep are dispersed in vast herds around the country, contributing to a major export industry. Cattle-ranching is important, particularly in the west. Wheat, and grapes for Australia's wine industry, are grown mainly in the south. Much of the country is desert, unsuitable for agriculture unless irrigation is used.

The urban/rural population divide

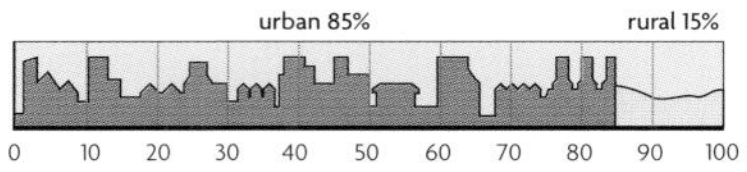

urban 85% | rural 15%

0 10 20 30 40 50 60 70 80 90 100

Population density	Total land area
6 people per sq mile (2 people per sq km)	2,967,893 sq miles (7,686,850 sq km)

Land use and agricultural distribution

- cattle
- sheep
- cereals
- sugar cane
- timber
- vineyards
- capital cities
- major towns
- pasture
- cropland
- forest
- desert
- mountain region

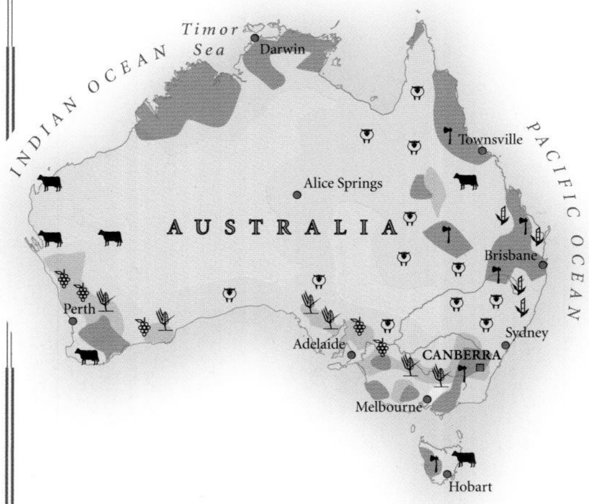

▲ ***Lines of ripening** vines stretch for miles in Barossa Valley, a major wine-growing region near Adelaide.*

The landscape

Australia consists of many eroded plateaux, lying firmly in the middle of the Indo-Australian Plate. It is the world's flattest continent, and the driest, after Antarctica. The coasts tend to be more hilly and fertile, especially in the east. The mountains of the Great Dividing Range form a natural barrier between the eastern coastal areas and the flat, dry plains and desert regions of the Australian 'outback.'

▲ ***The Great Barrier Reef** is the world's largest area of coral islands and reefs. It runs for about 1240 miles (2000 km) along the Queensland coast.*

▲ ***The Pinnacles are** a series of rugged sandstone pillars. Their strange shapes have been formed by water and wind erosion.*

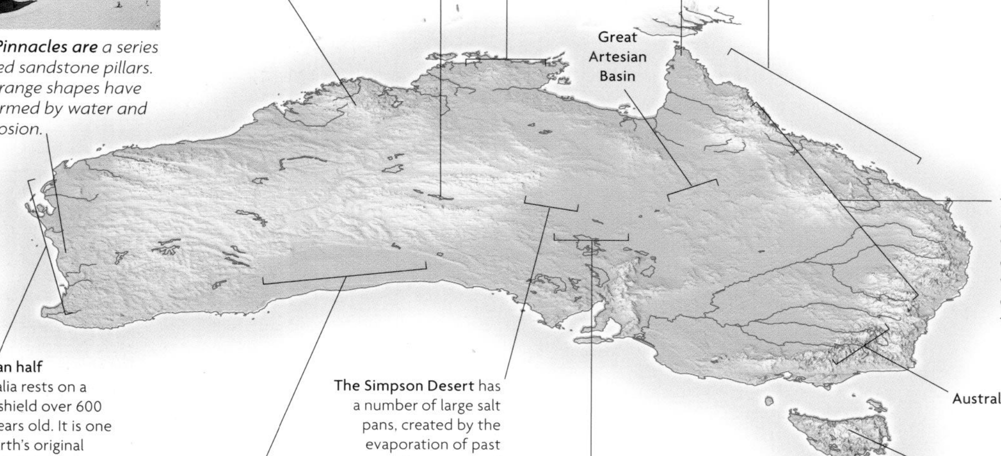

The ancient Kimberley Plateau is the source of some of Australia's richest mineral deposits, including diamonds.

Uluru (Ayers Rock)

Arnhem Land

The tropical rain forest of the Cape York Peninsula contains more than 600 different varieties of tree.

Great Artesian Basin

The Great Dividing Range forms a watershed between east- and west-flowing rivers. Erosion has created deep valleys, gorges and waterfalls where rivers tumble over escarpments on their way to the sea.

More than half of Australia rests on a uniform shield over 600 million years old. It is one of the Earth's original geological plates.

The Simpson Desert has a number of large salt pans, created by the evaporation of past rivers and now sourced by seasonal rains. Some are crusted with gypsum, but most are covered by common salt crystals.

Australian Alps

The Nullarbor Plain is a low-lying limestone plateau which is so flat that the Trans-Australian Railway runs through it in a straight line for more than 300 miles (483 km).

The Lake Eyre basin, lying 51 ft (16 m) below sea level, is one of the largest inland drainage systems in the world, covering an area of more than 500,000 sq miles (1,300,000 sq km).

Tasmania has the same geological structure as the Australian Alps. During the last period of glaciation, 18,000 years ago, sea levels were some 300 ft (100 m) lower and it was joined to the mainland.

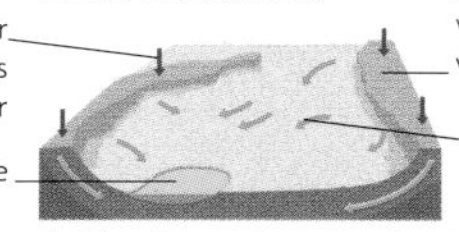

Great Artesian Basin

Rainwater replenishes aquifer

Aquifers from which artesian water is obtained

Underground water movements

Lake Eyre

▲ ***The Great Artesian Basin** underlies nearly 20% of the total area of Australia, providing a valuable store of underground water, essential to Australian agriculture. The ephemeral rivers which drain the northern part of the basin have highly braided courses and, in consequence, the area is known as 'channel country.'*

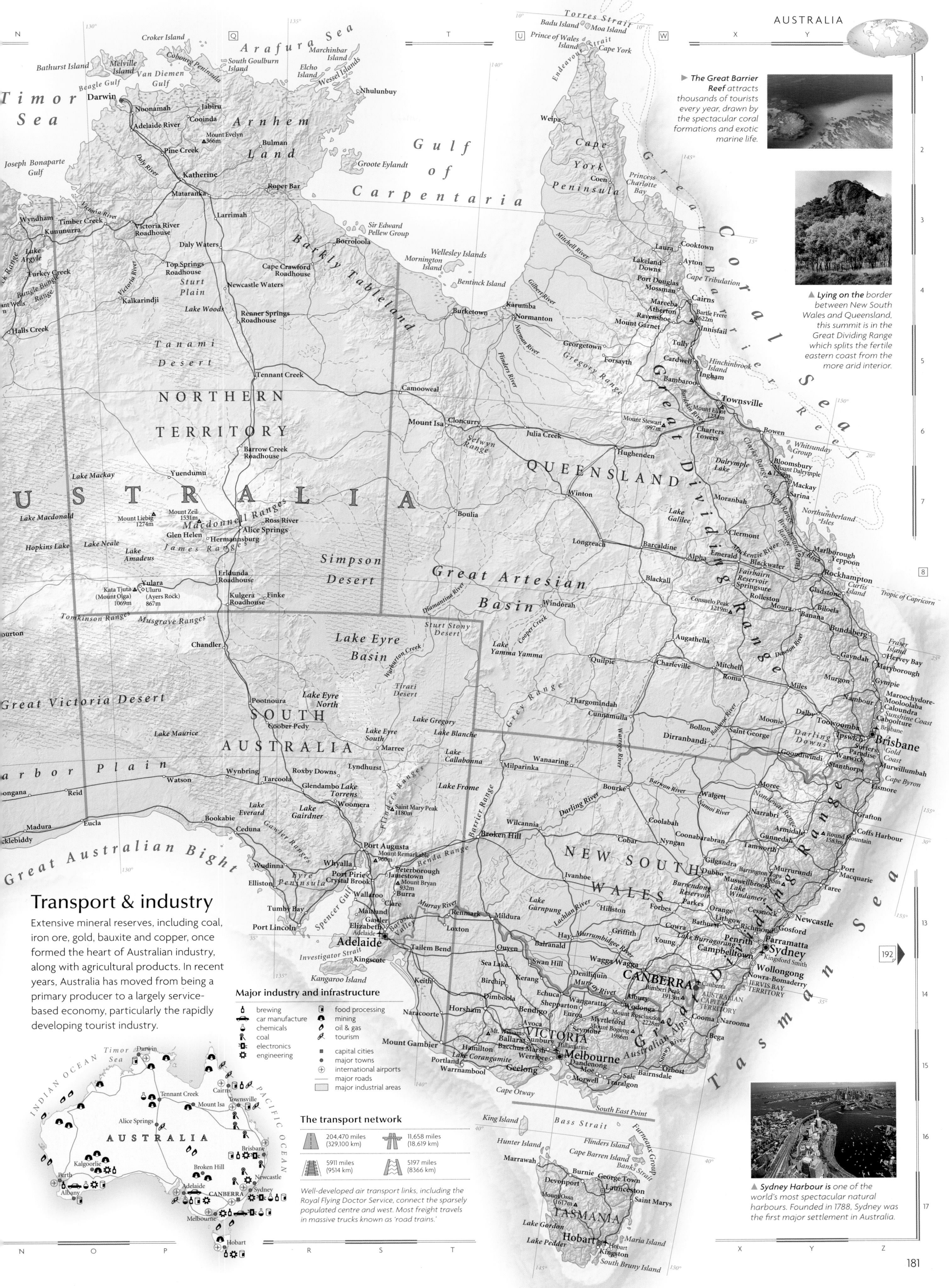
Timor Sea
Arafura Sea
Gulf of Carpentaria
Coral Sea
Great Barrier Reef
Tasman Sea
Bass Strait
Torres Strait
Great Australian Bight
Arnhem Land
Cape York Peninsula
NORTHERN TERRITORY
QUEENSLAND
SOUTH AUSTRALIA
NEW SOUTH WALES
VICTORIA
TASMANIA
AUSTRALIAN CAPITAL TERRITORY
JERVIS BAY TERRITORY
AUSTRALIA
Barkly Tableland
Tanami Desert
Simpson Desert
Great Victoria Desert
Sturt Stony Desert
Tirari Desert
Great Artesian Basin
Lake Eyre Basin
Great Dividing Range
Macdonnell Ranges
Musgrave Ranges
Flinders Ranges
Darling Downs
Nullarbor Plain
Darwin
Katherine
Tennant Creek
Alice Springs
Uluru (Ayers Rock) 867m
Kata Tjuta (Mount Olga) 1069m
Mount Isa
Cairns
Townsville
Mackay
Rockhampton
Bundaberg
Brisbane
Gold Coast
Sunshine Coast
Toowoomba
Newcastle
Sydney
Wollongong
CANBERRA
Broken Hill
Port Augusta
Whyalla
Adelaide
Mildura
Bendigo
Ballarat
Geelong
Melbourne
Launceston
Hobart
Mount Kosciuszko 2228m
Tropic of Capricorn

▲ The Great Barrier Reef attracts thousands of tourists every year, drawn by the spectacular coral formations and exotic marine life.

▲ Lying on the border between New South Wales and Queensland, this summit is in the Great Dividing Range which splits the fertile eastern coast from the more arid interior.

▲ Sydney Harbour is one of the world's most spectacular natural harbours. Founded in 1788, Sydney was the first major settlement in Australia.

Transport & industry

Extensive mineral reserves, including coal, iron ore, gold, bauxite and copper, once formed the heart of Australian industry, along with agricultural products. In recent years, Australia has moved from being a primary producer to a largely service-based economy, particularly the rapidly developing tourist industry.

Major industry and infrastructure

- brewing
- car manufacture
- chemicals
- coal
- electronics
- engineering
- food processing
- mining
- oil & gas
- tourism
- capital cities
- major towns
- international airports
- major roads
- major industrial areas

The transport network

204,470 miles (329,100 km)	11,658 miles (18,619 km)
5911 miles (9514 km)	5197 miles (8366 km)

Well-developed air transport links, including the Royal Flying Doctor Service, connect the sparsely populated centre and west. Most freight travels in massive trucks known as 'road trains.'

192

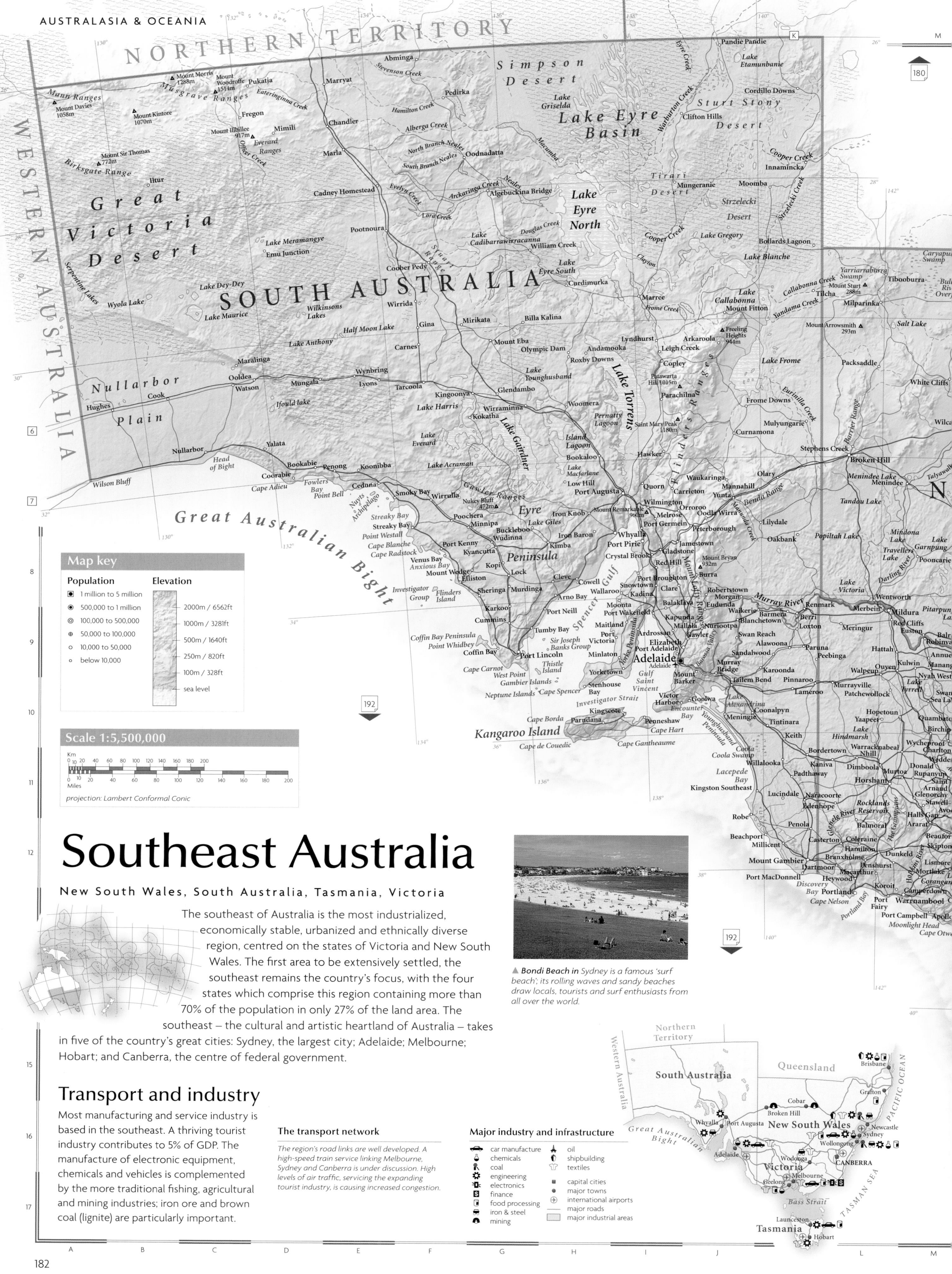
NORTHERN TERRITORY
WESTERN AUSTRALIA
SOUTH AUSTRALIA
Great Victoria Desert
Simpson Desert
Lake Eyre Basin
Sturt Stony Desert
Lake Eyre North
Lake Torrens
Flinders Ranges
Nullarbor Plain
Great Australian Bight
Eyre Peninsula
Spencer Gulf
Gulf Saint Vincent
Kangaroo Island
Adelaide
Murray River
Map key
Population
1 million to 5 million
500,000 to 1 million
100,000 to 500,000
50,000 to 100,000
10,000 to 50,000
below 10,000
Elevation
2000m / 6562ft
1000m / 3281ft
500m / 1640ft
250m / 820ft
100m / 328ft
sea level
Scale 1:5,500,000
projection: Lambert Conformal Conic

Southeast Australia

New South Wales, South Australia, Tasmania, Victoria

The southeast of Australia is the most industrialized, economically stable, urbanized and ethnically diverse region, centred on the states of Victoria and New South Wales. The first area to be extensively settled, the southeast remains the country's focus, with the four states which comprise this region containing more than 70% of the population in only 27% of the land area. The southeast – the cultural and artistic heartland of Australia – takes in five of the country's great cities: Sydney, the largest city; Adelaide; Melbourne; Hobart; and Canberra, the centre of federal government.

▲ **Bondi Beach in** *Sydney is a famous 'surf beach'; its rolling waves and sandy beaches draw locals, tourists and surf enthusiasts from all over the world.*

Transport and industry

Most manufacturing and service industry is based in the southeast. A thriving tourist industry contributes to 5% of GDP. The manufacture of electronic equipment, chemicals and vehicles is complemented by the more traditional fishing, agricultural and mining industries; iron ore and brown coal (lignite) are particularly important.

The transport network

The region's road links are well developed. A high-speed train service linking Melbourne, Sydney and Canberra is under discussion. High levels of air traffic, servicing the expanding tourist industry, is causing increased congestion.

Major industry and infrastructure

car manufacture
chemicals
coal
engineering
electronics
finance
food processing
iron & steel
mining
oil
shipbuilding
textiles
capital cities
major towns
international airports
major roads
major industrial areas
South Australia
Victoria
New South Wales
Tasmania
Queensland
CANBERRA
PACIFIC OCEAN
TASMAN SEA
Bass Strait

Using the land and sea

The western flanks of the Great Dividing Range and the northern deserts of South Australia support massive herds of sheep and cattle, while more intensive stock-rearing occurs near the cities. Sugar cane is the most important industrial crop, and cereals including wheat, maize, barley and sorghum are also grown. Grapes, citrus and orchard fruits are among the wide range of fruit and vegetables cultivated in this region. Tasmania's forestry and fishing contributes to over one-third of the state's exports.

▲ ***The fertile Darling Downs,*** *known as the 'breadbasket of Australia', support a wide range of crops including cereals, sugar cane and fruit.*

► ***The Murray River*** *has its source in the eastern uplands of the Great Dividing Range. Fed by melting snow, it runs for 1609 miles (2589 km), and has sufficient volume to reach the ocean southeast of Adelaide despite a minimal gradient for most of its lower reaches.*

The urban/rural population divide

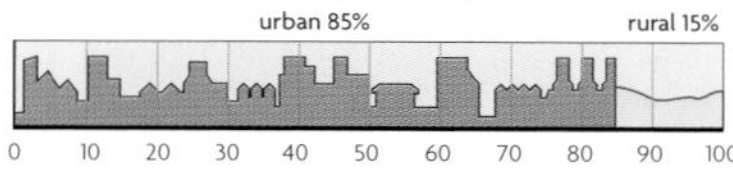

urban 85% | rural 15%

0 10 20 30 40 50 60 70 80 90 100

Population density	Total land area
18 people per sq mile (7 people per sq km)	778,022 sq miles (2,015,600 sq km)

Land use and agricultural distribution

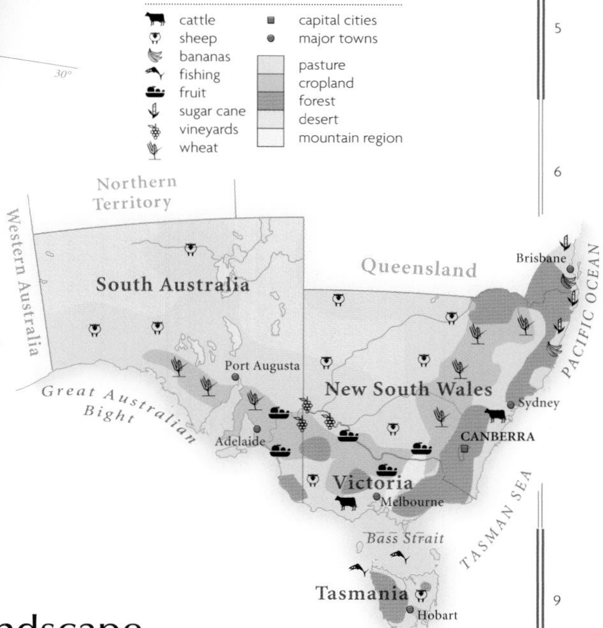

- cattle
- sheep
- bananas
- fishing
- fruit
- sugar cane
- vineyards
- wheat
- capital cities
- major towns
- pasture
- cropland
- forest
- desert
- mountain region

192

The landscape

The southern half of the Great Dividing Range runs parallel to the eastern coast of Victoria and New South Wales as far as Tasmania, which, though divided from the mainland is part of the same mountain chain. South Australia comprises the Australian shield and half of the dry, flat Nullarbor Plain. The Murray/Darling river basin is the only major river system.

◄ ***The heavily folded*** *Flinders Ranges is part of an arc of sedimentary rocks reaching northward from Kangaroo Island.*

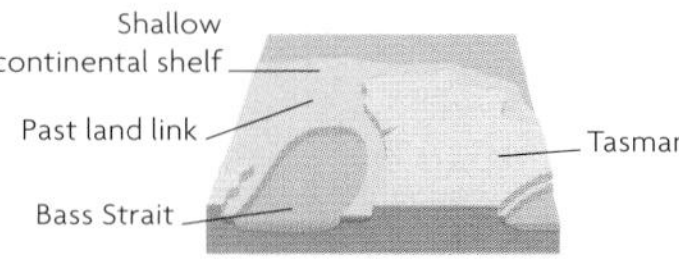

Shallow continental shelf
Past land link
Bass Strait
Tasmania

▲ ***Tasmania is part*** *of Australia's eastern highlands, separated from the mainland by 155 miles (250 km) of the Bass Strait. In the recent geological past, dry land links between Tasmania and Victoria would have been possible during periods of world-wide glaciation, when the sea level was more than 180 ft (55 m) below that of present sea levels.*

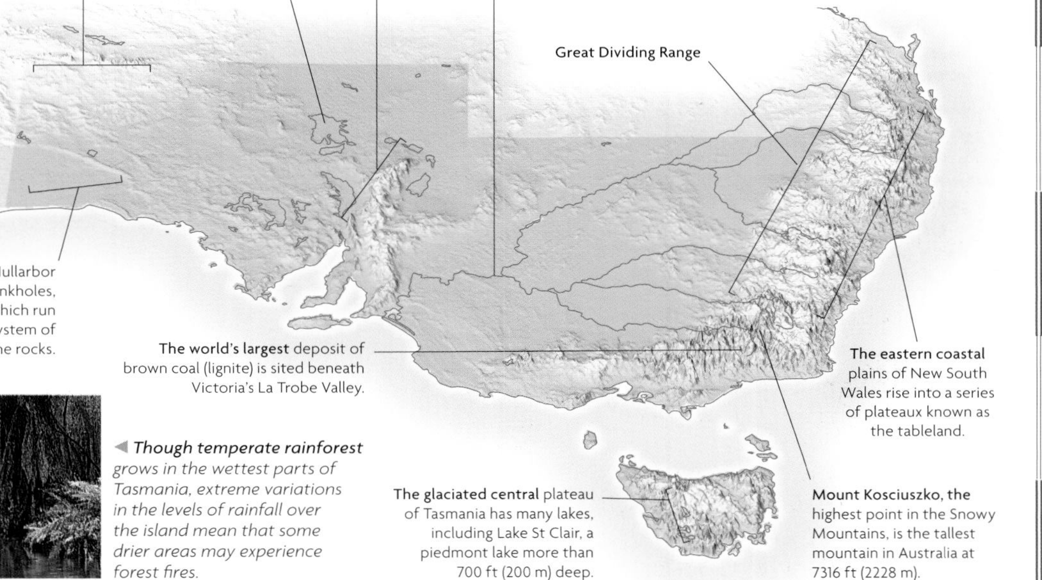

The Musgrave and Everard ranges form bare, rounded hills made up of ancient granite and gneiss.

Lake Eyre is the largest of southern Australia's dry lakes. Lying -51 ft (-16 m) below sea level, it has flooded only three times in the last century.

The Murray/Darling is Australia's longest river at 1703 miles (2739 km).

Great Dividing Range

The eastern part of the Nullarbor Plain has many sinkholes, eroded by rainwater, which run underground to form a system of long caves in the limestone rocks.

The world's largest deposit of brown coal (lignite) is sited beneath Victoria's La Trobe Valley.

The eastern coastal plains of New South Wales rise into a series of plateaux known as the tableland.

◄ ***Though temperate rainforest*** *grows in the wettest parts of Tasmania, extreme variations in the levels of rainfall over the island mean that some drier areas may experience forest fires.*

The glaciated central plateau of Tasmania has many lakes, including Lake St Clair, a piedmont lake more than 700 ft (200 m) deep.

Mount Kosciuszko, the highest point in the Snowy Mountains, is the tallest mountain in Australia at 7316 ft (2228 m).

New Zealand

Lying 1500 miles east-southeast of Australia, New Zealand was originally settled by the Maori, a people with Polynesian roots. It was one of the last major landmasses to be visited by Europeans. The islands' rugged topography means that most settlement has concentrated in coastal areas. People of European origin make up about 70% of the population of 4 million, following immigration from the 1920s onwards. Many recent settlers have come from Asia, including India and China, and a number of the Pacific islands. Although the Maori now make up a minority of less than half a million, their ancient claims to at least half of national territory are gaining increasing legal credence.

The landscape

New Zealand comprises two large islands and many scattered smaller islands. On South Island the Alpine Fault marks the boundary between the Pacific and Indo-Australian plates. Tectonic activity has strongly influenced the formation of the Southern Alps, snow-capped mountains with several peaks over 9800 ft (3000 m). North Island has a lower and less extensive mountain region, containing forested hills, a central volcanic plateau and downlands.

Mountain-building in the Southern Alps

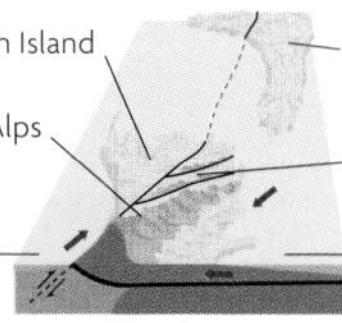

South Island
North Island
Southern Alps
Alpine Fault
Indo-Australian Plate
Pacific Plate

▲ *The Southern Alps have been formed by 'slip' faulting. The Indo-Australian and Pacific plates run in opposite directions along the Alpine Fault. Although they slide past each other, they are also being thrust over one another, causing the continental crust of the Pacific Plate to be uplifted to form the Alps.*

Northland

◀ *The Northland region is characterized by many coastal inlets. These are lined by mangrove swamps, signalling the change to a subtropical climate in the far north of the island.*

Rotorua

◀ *The Rotorua and Taupo valleys have some of the largest and most spectacular thermal springs in New Zealand. These occur when superheated groundwater rises to the surface through joints in the rocks.*

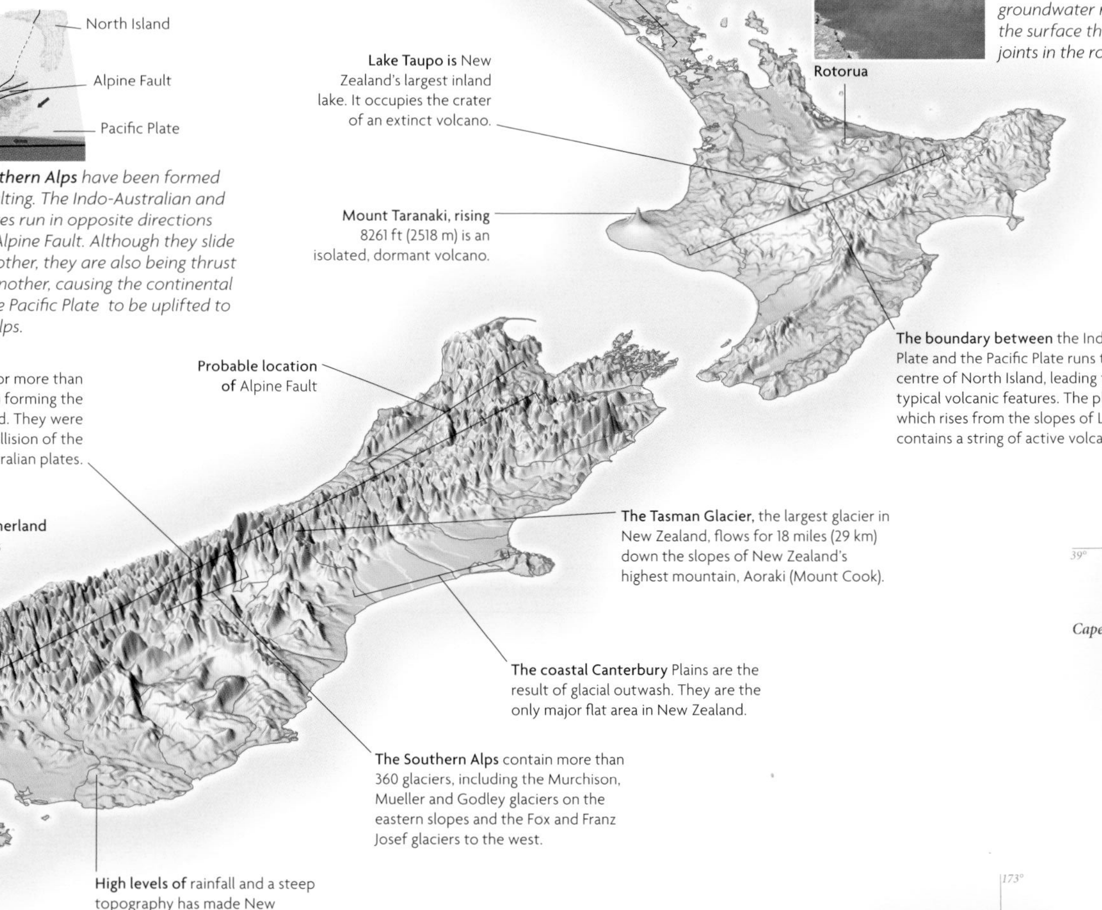

Lake Taupo is New Zealand's largest inland lake. It occupies the crater of an extinct volcano.

Mount Taranaki, rising 8261 ft (2518 m) is an isolated, dormant volcano.

The boundary between the Indo-Australian Plate and the Pacific Plate runs through the centre of North Island, leading to many typical volcanic features. The plateau which rises from the slopes of Lake Taupo contains a string of active volcanoes.

Probable location of Alpine Fault

The Southern Alps run for more than 300 miles, (483 km) forming the backbone of South Island. They were uplifted following the collision of the Pacific and Indo-Australian plates.

Fiordland, in the far south west, contains a large number of flooded glacial valleys.

Sutherland Falls

The Tasman Glacier, the largest glacier in New Zealand, flows for 18 miles (29 km) down the slopes of New Zealand's highest mountain, Aoraki (Mount Cook).

The coastal Canterbury Plains are the result of glacial outwash. They are the only major flat area in New Zealand.

The Southern Alps contain more than 360 glaciers, including the Murchison, Mueller and Godley glaciers on the eastern slopes and the Fox and Franz Josef glaciers to the west.

High levels of rainfall and a steep topography has made New Zealand's rivers swift-running. In the southern reaches of both islands, rivers such as the Mokoreta form broad, braided streams.

▶ *Clouds of steam rise from White Island, an active, offshore volcano lying in the Bay of Plenty, off the northern coast of North Island.*

Scale 1:2,750,000

projection: Lambert Conformal Conic

192

PACIFIC OCEAN

TASMAN SEA

NEW ZEALAND

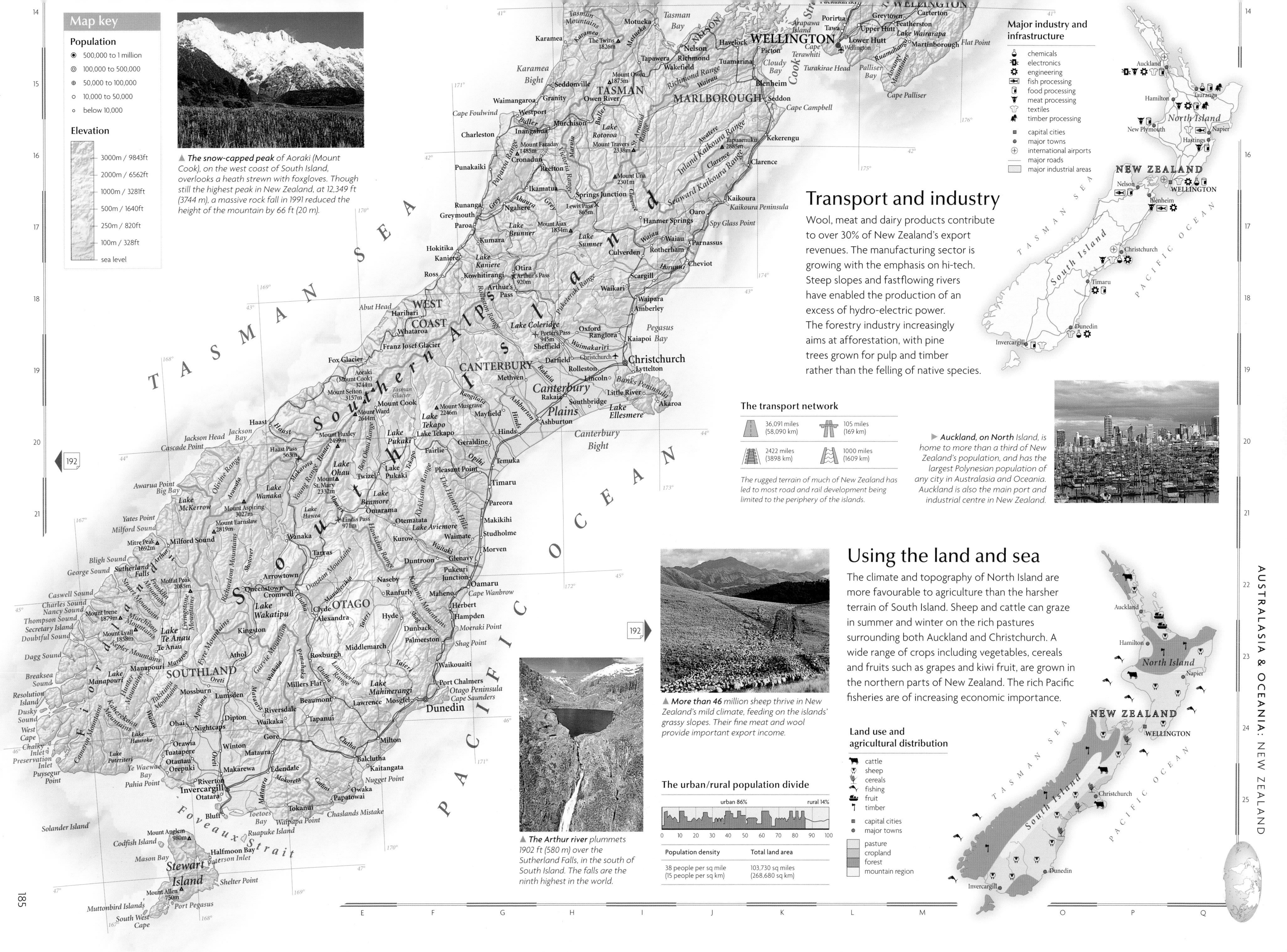
Map key
Population
500,000 to 1 million
100,000 to 500,000
50,000 to 100,000
10,000 to 50,000
below 10,000
Elevation
3000m / 9843ft
2000m / 6562ft
1000m / 3281ft
500m / 1640ft
250m / 820ft
100m / 328ft
sea level
TASMAN SEA
PACIFIC OCEAN
South Island
Southern Alps
WELLINGTON
Christchurch
Dunedin
Invercargill
CANTERBURY
OTAGO
SOUTHLAND
MARLBOROUGH
TASMAN
WEST COAST
Canterbury Plains
Foveaux Strait
Stewart Island
Major industry and infrastructure
chemicals
electronics
engineering
fish processing
food processing
meat processing
textiles
timber processing
capital cities
major towns
international airports
major roads
major industrial areas
Land use and agricultural distribution
cattle
sheep
cereals
fishing
fruit
timber
capital cities
major towns
pasture
cropland
forest
mountain region

▲ **The snow-capped peak** of Aoraki (Mount Cook), on the west coast of South Island, overlooks a heath strewn with foxgloves. Though still the highest peak in New Zealand, at 12,349 ft (3744 m), a massive rock fall in 1991 reduced the height of the mountain by 66 ft (20 m).

Transport and industry

Wool, meat and dairy products contribute to over 30% of New Zealand's export revenues. The manufacturing sector is growing with the emphasis on hi-tech. Steep slopes and fastflowing rivers have enabled the production of an excess of hydro-electric power. The forestry industry increasingly aims at afforestation, with pine trees grown for pulp and timber rather than the felling of native species.

The transport network

36,091 miles (58,090 km)		105 miles (169 km)	
2422 miles (3898 km)		1000 miles (1609 km)	

The rugged terrain of much of New Zealand has led to most road and rail development being limited to the periphery of the islands.

▶ **Auckland, on North** Island, is home to more than a third of New Zealand's population, and has the largest Polynesian population of any city in Australasia and Oceania. Auckland is also the main port and industrial centre in New Zealand.

▲ **The Arthur river** plummets 1902 ft (580 m) over the Sutherland Falls, in the south of South Island. The falls are the ninth highest in the world.

▲ **More than 46** million sheep thrive in New Zealand's mild climate, feeding on the islands' grassy slopes. Their fine meat and wool provide important export income.

Using the land and sea

The climate and topography of North Island are more favourable to agriculture than the harsher terrain of South Island. Sheep and cattle can graze in summer and winter on the rich pastures surrounding both Auckland and Christchurch. A wide range of crops including vegetables, cereals and fruits such as grapes and kiwi fruit, are grown in the northern parts of New Zealand. The rich Pacific fisheries are of increasing economic importance.

The urban/rural population divide

urban 86% / rural 14%

Population density	Total land area
38 people per sq mile (15 people per sq km)	103,730 sq miles (268,680 sq km)

192

Melanesia

FIJI, New Caledonia *(to France)*, PAPUA NEW GUINEA, SOLOMON ISLANDS, VANUATU

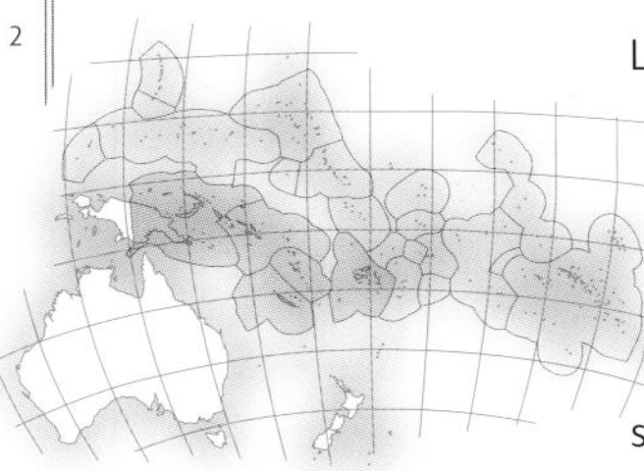

Lying in the southwest Pacific Ocean, northeast of Australia and south of the Equator, the islands of Melanesia form one of the three geographic divisions (along with Polynesia and Micronesia) of Oceania. Melanesia's name derives from the Greek melas, 'black', and nesoi, 'islands'. Most of the larger islands are volcanic in origin. The smaller islands tend to be coral atolls and are mainly uninhabited. Rugged mountains, covered by dense rainforest, take up most of the land area. Melanesian's cultivate yams, taro, and sweet potatoes for local consumption and live in small, usually dispersed, homesteads.

▲ ***Huli tribesmen from** Southern Highlands Province in Papua New Guinea parade in ceremonial dress, their powdered wigs decorated with exotic plumage and their faces and bodies painted with coloured pigments.*

Map key

Population

- 100,000 to 500,000
- 50,000 to 100,000
- 10,000 to 50,000
- below 10,000

Elevation

- 4000m / 13,124ft
- 3000m / 9843ft
- 2000m / 6562ft
- 1000m / 3281ft
- 500m / 1640ft
- 250m / 820ft
- 100m / 328ft
- sea level

192

168

180

PACIFIC OCEAN

PAPUA NEW GUINEA

◀ ***Lying close to** the banks of the Sepik river in northern Papua New Guinea, this building is known as the Spirit House. It is constructed from leaves and twigs, ornately woven and trimmed into geometric patterns. The house is decorated with a mask and topped by a carved statue.*

▲ ***On one of** Vanuatu's many islands, beach houses stand at the water's edge, surrounded by coconut palms and other tropical vegetation. The unspoilt beaches and tranquillity of its islands are drawing ever-larger numbers of tourists to Vanuatu.*

Transport and Industry

The processing of natural resources generates significant export revenue for the countries of Melanesia. The region relies mainly on copra, tuna and timber exports, with some production of cocoa and palm oil. The islands have substantial mineral resources including the world's largest copper reserves on Bougainville Island; gold, and potential oil and natural gas. Tourism has become the fastest growing sector in most of the countries' economies.

◀ ***On New Caledonia's** main island, relatively high interior plateaux descend to coastal plains. Nickel is the most important mineral resource, but the hills also harbour metallic deposits including chrome, cobalt, iron, gold, silver and copper.*

The transport network

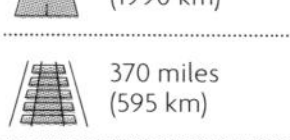

1236 miles (1990 km)	None
370 miles (595 km)	6924 miles (11,143 km)

As most of the islands of Melanesia lie off the major sea and air routes, services to and from the rest of the world are infrequent. Transport by road on rugged terrain is difficult and expensive.

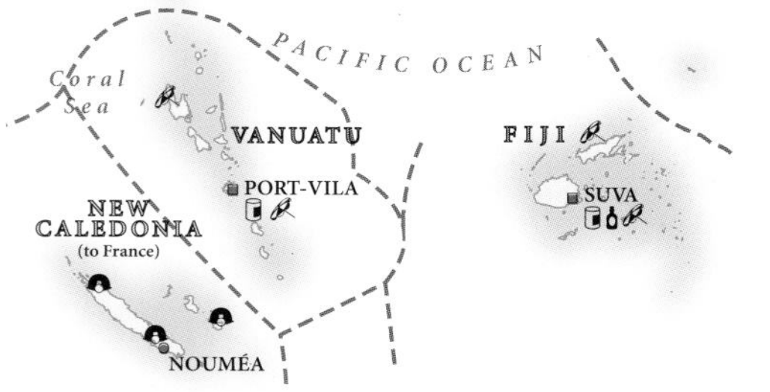

Major industry and infrastructure

- beverages
- coffee processing
- copra processing
- food processing
- mining
- textiles
- timber processing
- tourism
- capital cities
- major towns
- international airports
- major roads

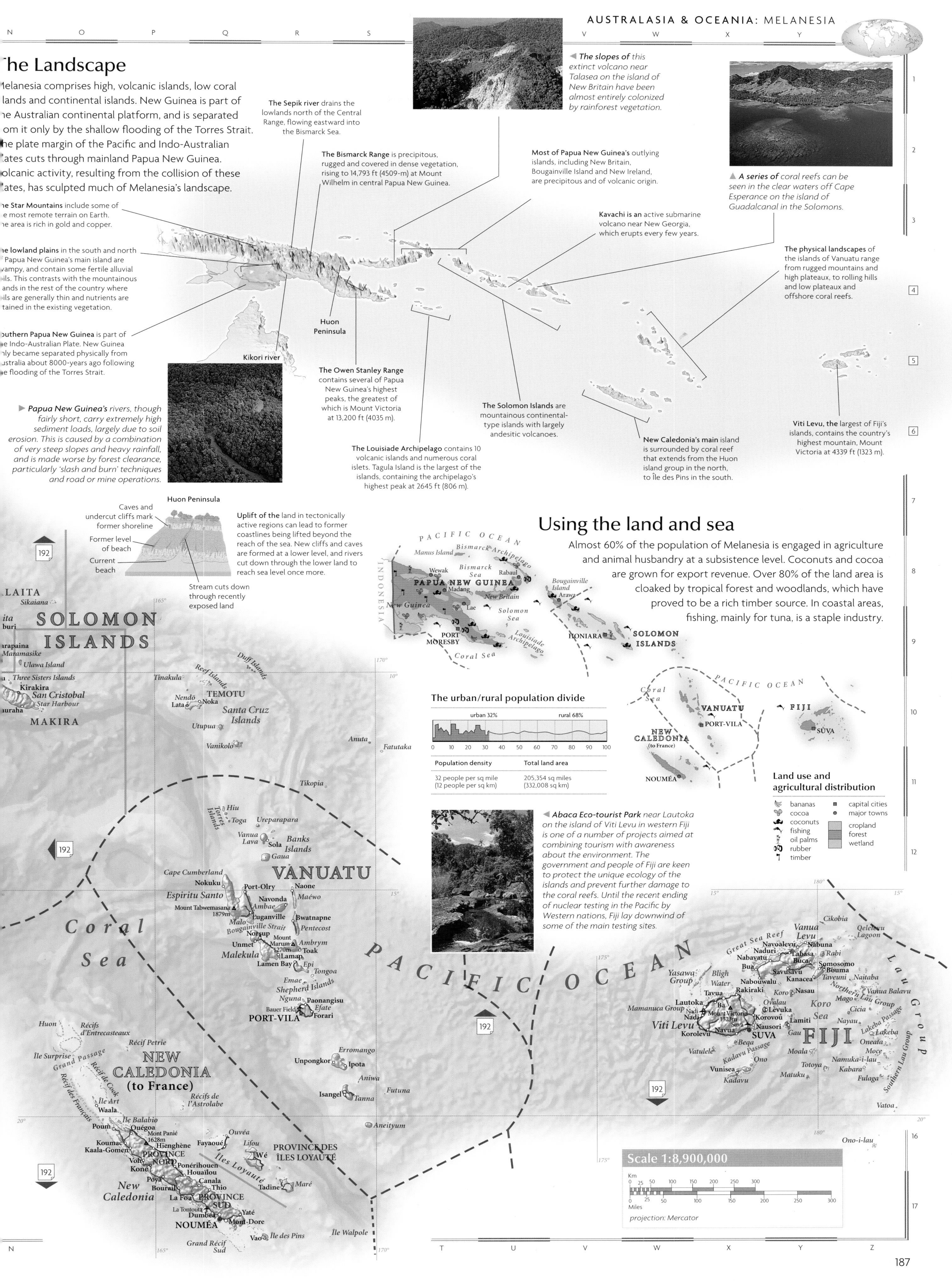
N O P Q R S
V W X Y
1 2 3 4 5 6 7 8 9 10 11 12 16 17
Huon Peninsula
Kikori river
Caves and undercut cliffs mark former shoreline
Former level of beach
Current beach
Stream cuts down through recently exposed land
192
LAITA
Sikaiana
SOLOMON ISLANDS
Ulawa Island
Three Sisters Islands
Kirakira
San Cristobal
Star Harbour
MAKIRA
Tinakula
Reef Islands
Duff Islands
Nendö
TEMOTU
Lata
Noka
Santa Cruz Islands
Utupua
Vanikolo
Anuta
Fatutaka
Tikopia
Hiu
Torres Islands
Toga
Ureparapara
Vanua Lava
Sola
Banks Islands
Gaua
VANUATU
Cape Cumberland
Nokuku
Port-Olry
Naone
Espiritu Santo
Navonda
Maéwo
Ambae
Mount Tabwemasana 1879m
Luganville
Bwatnapne
Malo
Pentecost
Bougainville Strait
Norsup
Unmet
Mount Marum 1270m
Ambrym
Malekula
Toak
Lamap
Lamen Bay
Epi
Tongoa
Emae
Shepherd Islands
Nguna
Paonangisu
Bauer Field
Efate
PORT-VILA
Forari
Erromango
Unpongkor
Ipota
Aniwa
Futuna
Isangel
Tanna
Aneityum
Coral Sea
PACIFIC OCEAN
Huon
Récifs d'Entrecasteaux
Récif Petrie
Île Surprise
Grand Passage
Récif de Cook
Récif des Français
Île Art
Waala
NEW CALEDONIA (to France)
Récifs de l'Astrolabe
Île Balabio
Poum
Ouégoa
Mont Panié 1628m
Hienghène
Koumac
Kaala-Gomen
PROVINCE NORD
Voh
Koné
Ponérihouen
Houaïlou
Poya
Canala
Bourail
Thio
La Foa
PROVINCE SUD
La Tontouta
Dumbéa
Yaté
NOUMÉA
Mont-Dore
Vao
Île des Pins
Grand Récif Sud
New Caledonia
Ouvéa
Fayaoué
Lifou
Wé
Îles Loyauté
PROVINCE DES ÎLES LOYAUTÉ
Tadine
Maré
Île Walpole
Cikobia
Vanua Levu
Qelelevu Lagoon
Great Sea Reef
Navoalevu
Nabuna
Naduri
Labasa
Rabi
Nabavatu
Buca
Somosomo
Bua
Savusavu
Bouma
Taveuni
Naitaba
Yasawa Group
Bligh Water
Nabouwalu
Kanacea
Tavua
Rakiraki
Koro
Nasau
Northern Lau Group
Vanua Balavu
Lautoka
Mago
Mamanuca Group
Nadi
Ba
Mount Victoria 1323m
Ovalau
Levuka
Koro Sea
Cicia
Viti Levu
Korovou
Lamiti
Nayau
Lakeba Passage
Korolevu
Navua
Suva
Nausori
SUVA
Gau
FIJI
Lakeba
Oneata
Vatulele
Beqa
Kadavu Passage
Ono
Moala
Moce
Vunisea
Kadavu
Totoya
Matuku
Namuka-i-lau
Kabara
Fulaga
Southern Lau Group
Lau Group
Vatoa
Ono-i-lau
Scale 1:8,900,000
Km 0 25 50 100 150 200 250 300
Miles 0 25 50 100 150 200 250 300
projection: Mercator
T U V W X Y Z
PACIFIC OCEAN
Manus Island
Bismarck Archipelago
Wewak
Bismarck Sea
Rabaul
PAPUA NEW GUINEA
Madang
Bougainville Island
Arawa
New Britain
New Guinea
Lae
Solomon Sea
INDONESIA
PORT MORESBY
Louisiade Archipelago
Coral Sea
HONIARA
SOLOMON ISLANDS
Coral Sea
VANUATU
PORT-VILA
FIJI
SUVA
NEW CALEDONIA (to France)
NOUMÉA

The Landscape

Melanesia comprises high, volcanic islands, low coral islands and continental islands. New Guinea is part of the Australian continental platform, and is separated from it only by the shallow flooding of the Torres Strait. The plate margin of the Pacific and Indo-Australian plates cuts through mainland Papua New Guinea. Volcanic activity, resulting from the collision of these plates, has sculpted much of Melanesia's landscape.

The Star Mountains include some of the most remote terrain on Earth. The area is rich in gold and copper.

The lowland plains in the south and north of Papua New Guinea's main island are swampy, and contain some fertile alluvial soils. This contrasts with the mountainous lands in the rest of the country where soils are generally thin and nutrients are retained in the existing vegetation.

Southern Papua New Guinea is part of the Indo-Australian Plate. New Guinea only became separated physically from Australia about 8000-years ago following the flooding of the Torres Strait.

The Sepik river drains the lowlands north of the Central Range, flowing eastward into the Bismarck Sea.

The Bismarck Range is precipitous, rugged and covered in dense vegetation, rising to 14,793 ft (4509-m) at Mount Wilhelm in central Papua New Guinea.

◀ *The slopes of this extinct volcano near Talasea on the island of New Britain have been almost entirely colonized by rainforest vegetation.*

Most of Papua New Guinea's outlying islands, including New Britain, Bougainville Island and New Ireland, are precipitous and of volcanic origin.

▲ *A series of coral reefs can be seen in the clear waters off Cape Esperance on the island of Guadalcanal in the Solomons.*

Kavachi is an active submarine volcano near New Georgia, which erupts every few years.

The physical landscapes of the islands of Vanuatu range from rugged mountains and high plateaux, to rolling hills and low plateaux and offshore coral reefs.

The Owen Stanley Range contains several of Papua New Guinea's highest peaks, the greatest of which is Mount Victoria at 13,200 ft (4035 m).

▶ *Papua New Guinea's rivers, though fairly short, carry extremely high sediment loads, largely due to soil erosion. This is caused by a combination of very steep slopes and heavy rainfall, and is made worse by forest clearance, particularly 'slash and burn' techniques and road or mine operations.*

The Solomon Islands are mountainous continental-type islands with largely andesitic volcanoes.

The Louisiade Archipelago contains 10 volcanic islands and numerous coral islets. Tagula Island is the largest of the islands, containing the archipelago's highest peak at 2645 ft (806 m).

New Caledonia's main island is surrounded by coral reef that extends from the Huon island group in the north, to Île des Pins in the south.

Viti Levu, the largest of Fiji's islands, contains the country's highest mountain, Mount Victoria at 4339 ft (1323 m).

Uplift of the land in tectonically active regions can lead to former coastlines being lifted beyond the reach of the sea. New cliffs and caves are formed at a lower level, and rivers cut down through the lower land to reach sea level once more.

Using the land and sea

Almost 60% of the population of Melanesia is engaged in agriculture and animal husbandry at a subsistence level. Coconuts and cocoa are grown for export revenue. Over 80% of the land area is cloaked by tropical forest and woodlands, which have proved to be a rich timber source. In coastal areas, fishing, mainly for tuna, is a staple industry.

The urban/rural population divide

urban 32% — rural 68%

0 10 20 30 40 50 60 70 80 90 100

Population density	Total land area
32 people per sq mile (12 people per sq km)	205,354 sq miles (332,008 sq km)

Land use and agricultural distribution

bananas, cocoa, coconuts, fishing, oil palms, rubber, timber; capital cities, major towns; cropland, forest, wetland

◀ *Abaca Eco-tourist Park near Lautoka on the island of Viti Levu in western Fiji is one of a number of projects aimed at combining tourism with awareness about the environment. The government and people of Fiji are keen to protect the unique ecology of the islands and prevent further damage to the coral reefs. Until the recent ending of nuclear testing in the Pacific by Western nations, Fiji lay downwind of some of the main testing sites.*

Micronesia

MARSHALL ISLANDS, MICRONESIA, NAURU, PALAU, Guam, Northern Mariana Islands, Wake Island

The Micronesian islands lie in the western reaches of the Pacific Ocean and are all part of the same volcanic zone. The Federated States of Micronesia is the largest group, with more than 600 atolls and forested volcanic islands in an area of more than 1120 sq miles (2900 sq km). Micronesia is a mixture of former colonies, overseas territories and dependencies. Most of the region still relies on aid and subsidies to sustain economies limited by resources, isolation, and an emigrating population, drawn to New Zealand and Australia by the attractions of a western lifestyle.

Palau

Palau is an archipelago of over 200 islands, only eight of which are inhabited. It was the last remaining UN trust territory in the Pacific, controlled by the USA until 1994, when it became independent. The economy operates on a subsistence level, with coconuts and cassava the principal crops. Fishing licences and tourism provide foreign currency.

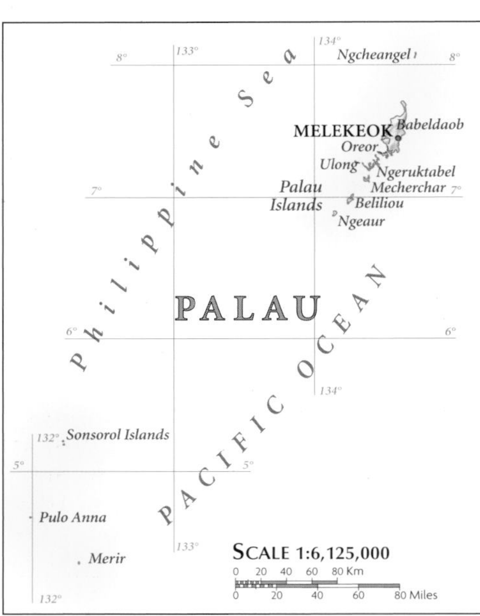

Philippine Sea
Ngcheangel
MELEKEOK
Babeldaob
Oreor
Ulong
Ngeruktabel
Mecherchar
Palau Islands
Beliliou
Ngeaur
PALAU
PACIFIC OCEAN
Sonsorol Islands
Pulo Anna
Merir
SCALE 1:6,125,000

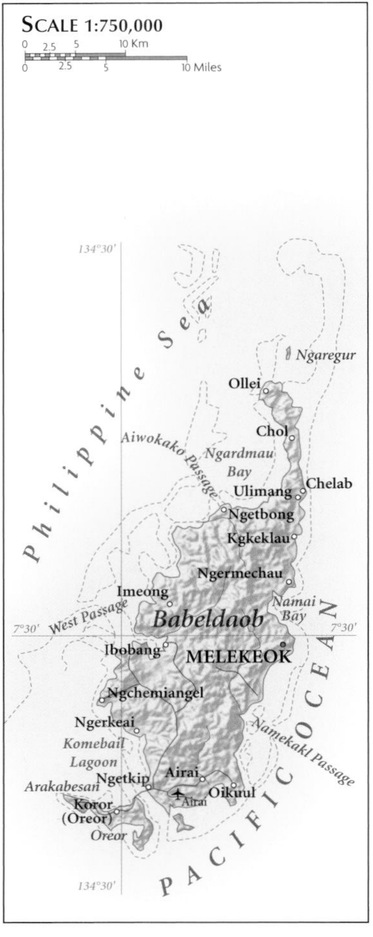

SCALE 1:750,000
Philippine Sea
Ngaregur
Ollei
Chol
Aiwokako Passage
Ngardmau Bay
Chelab
Ulimang
Ngetbong
Kgkeklau
Ngermechau
Imeong
West Passage
Babeldaob
Namai Bay
Ibobang
MELEKEOK
Ngchemiangel
Ngerkeai
Komebail Lagoon
Namekakl Passage
Arakabesan
Ngetkip
Airai
Oikuul
Koror (Oreor)
Oreor
PACIFIC OCEAN

Guam (to US)

Lying at the southern end of the Mariana Islands, Guam is an important US military base and tourist destination. Social and political life is dominated by the indigenous Chamorro, who make up just under half the population, although the increasing prevalence of western culture threatens Guam's traditional social stability.

◄ *The tranquillity of these coastal lagoons, at Inarajan in southern Guam, belies the fact that the island lies in a region where typhoons are common.*

Philippine Sea
Ritidian Point
Uruno Point
Pati Point
Andersen Air Force Base
GUAM (to US)
Yigo
Tumon Bay
Dededo
Mount Santa Rosa 252m
Agana Bay
Tamuning
Asan Point
Mongmong
Cabras Island
Piti
Asan
HAGÅTÑA (AGANA)
Apra Harbor
Sinajana
Barrigada
Orote Peninsula
Ordot
Chalan Pago
Mount Tenjo 313m
Yona
Pago Bay
Agat Bay
Apra Heights
Agat
Santa Rita
Mount Lamlam 406m
Talofofo
Facpi Point
Talofofo Bay
Cetti Bay
Mount Bolanos 379m
Umatac Bay
Mount Sasalaguan 337m
Umatac
Merizo
Inarajan
Cocos Island
Aga Point
PACIFIC OCEAN
SCALE 1:840,000

Northern Mariana Islands *(to US)*

A US Commonwealth territory, the Northern Marianas comprise the whole of the Mariana archipelago except for Guam. The islands retain their close links with the United States and continue to receive US aid. Tourism, though bringing in much-needed revenue, has speeded the decline of the traditional subsistence economy. Most of the population lives on Saipan.

Farallon de Pajaros
Supply Reef
Maug Islands
PACIFIC OCEAN
Asuncion Island
NORTHERN MARIANA ISLANDS (to US)
Agrihan
Pagan
Alamagan
Guguan
Zealandia Bank
Sarigan
Anatahan
Farallon de Medinilla
Philippine Sea
Mariana Islands
Susupe
Saipan
San Jose
Tinian
Aguijan
Rota
GUAM (to US)
HAGÅTÑA
Dededo
PACIFIC OCEAN
SCALE 1:5,000,000

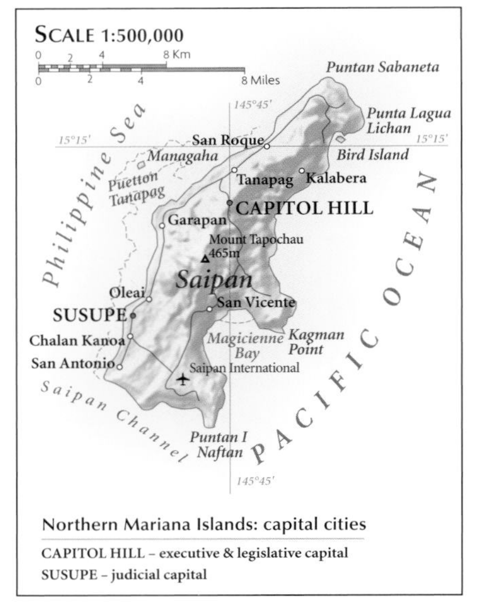

SCALE 1:500,000
Philippine Sea
Puntan Sabaneta
Punta Lagua Lichan
San Roque
Bird Island
Managaha
Puetton Tanapag
Tanapag
Kalabera
CAPITOL HILL
Garapan
Mount Tapochau 465m
Saipan
Oleai
San Vicente
SUSUPE
Chalan Kanoa
Magicienne Bay
Kagman Point
San Antonio
Saipan International
Saipan Channel
Puntan I Naftan
PACIFIC OCEAN

Northern Mariana Islands: capital cities

CAPITOL HILL – executive & legislative capital
SUSUPE – judicial capital

▲ *The Palau Islands have numerous hidden lakes and lagoons. These sustain their own ecosystems which have developed in isolation. This has produced adaptations in the animals and plants which are often unique to each lake.*

Micronesia

A mixture of high volcanic islands and low-lying coral atolls, the Federated States of Micronesia include all the Caroline Islands except Palau. Pohnpei, Kosrae, Chuuk and Yap are the four main island cluster states, each of which has its own language, with English remaining the official language. Nearly half the population is concentrated on Pohnpei, the largest island. Independent since 1986, the islands continue to receive considerable aid from the USA which supplements an economy based primarily on fishing and copra processing.

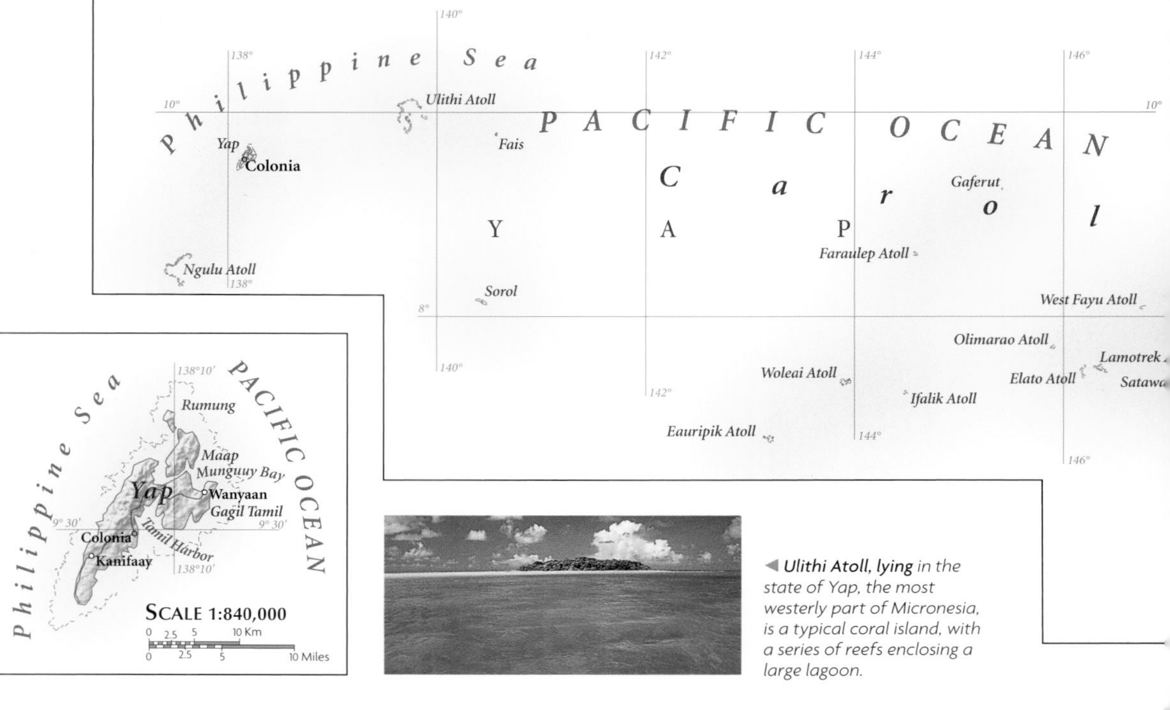

Philippine Sea
Ulithi Atoll
PACIFIC OCEAN
Yap
Colonia
Fais
Gaferut
YAP
Caroli
Ngulu Atoll
Faraulep Atoll
Sorol
West Fayu Atoll
Olimarao Atoll
Lamotrek
Woleai Atoll
Elato Atoll
Satawal
Ifalik Atoll
Eauripik Atoll

Philippine Sea
Rumung
Maap
Munguuy Bay
Yap
Wanyaan
Gagil Tamil
Colonia
Tamil Harbor
Kanifaay
PACIFIC OCEAN
SCALE 1:840,000

◄ **Ulithi Atoll, lying** *in the state of Yap, the most westerly part of Micronesia, is a typical coral island, with a series of reefs enclosing a large lagoon.*

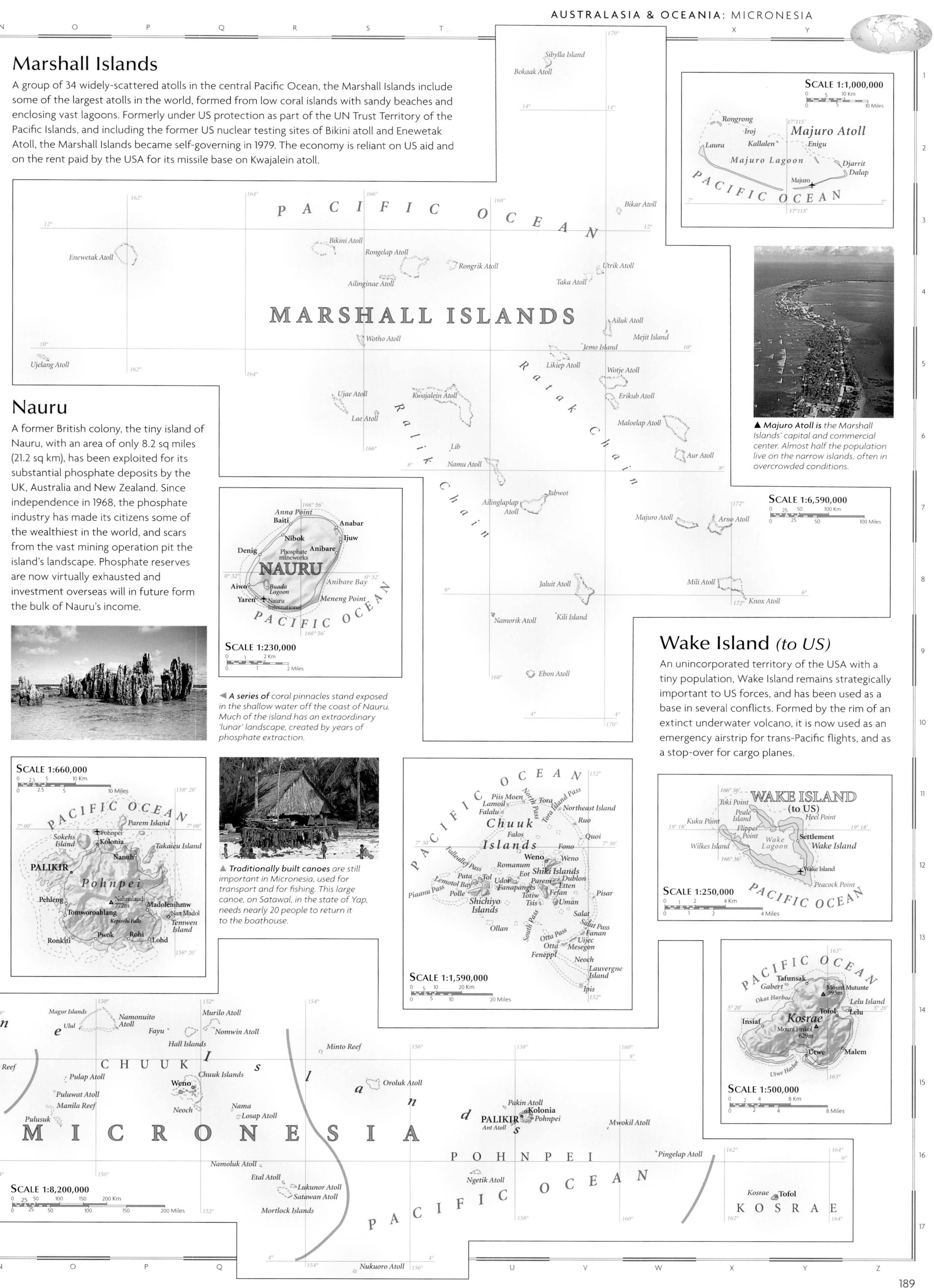

MARSHALL ISLANDS
PACIFIC OCEAN
Sibylla Island
Bokaak Atoll
Bikar Atoll
Enewetak Atoll
Bikini Atoll
Rongelap Atoll
Rongrik Atoll
Ailinginae Atoll
Utrik Atoll
Taka Atoll
Ailuk Atoll
Mejit Island
Jemo Island
Wotho Atoll
Ujelang Atoll
Likiep Atoll
Wotje Atoll
Erikub Atoll
Ratak Chain
Ralik Chain
Ujae Atoll
Lae Atoll
Kwajalein Atoll
Maloelap Atoll
Aur Atoll
Lib
Namu Atoll
Ailinglaplap Atoll
Jabwot
Majuro Atoll
Arno Atoll
Jaluit Atoll
Mili Atoll
Knox Atoll
Namorik Atoll
Kili Island
Ebon Atoll
SCALE 1:6,590,000
SCALE 1:1,000,000
Majuro Atoll
Rongrong
Iroj
Kallalen
Enigu
Laura
Majuro Lagoon
Djarrit
Dalap
Majuro
NAURU
Anna Point
Baiti
Anabar
Ijuw
Nibok
Anibare
Denig
Phosphate mineworks
Anibare Bay
Aiwo
Buada Lagoon
Yaren
Nauru International
Meneng Point
SCALE 1:230,000
SCALE 1:660,000
Parem Island
Pohnpei
Kolonia
Sokehs Island
Takaieu Island
Nanuh
PALIKIR
Nahnalaud 772m
Pehleng
Tomworoahlang
Madolenihmw
Nan Madol
Temwen Island
Ronkiti
Pwok
Rohi
Lohd
Chuuk Islands
Piis Moen
Lamoil
Falalu
Tora
Northeast Island
Ruo
Quoi
Falos
Fono
Weno
Romanum
Eot
Shiki Islands
Dublon
Etten
Pata
Tol
Udot
Fanapanges
Parem
Fefan
Totiw
Tsis
Uman
Pisar
Polle
Piaanu Pass
Shichiyo Islands
Ollan
Salat
Salat Pass
Fanan
Otta Pass
Otta
Uijec
Mesegon
Feneppi
Neoch
Lauvergne Island
Ipis
SCALE 1:1,590,000
WAKE ISLAND (to US)
Toki Point
Peale Island
Kuku Point
Heel Point
Flipper Point
Wake Lagoon
Wilkes Island
Settlement
Wake Island
Peacock Point
SCALE 1:250,000
Tafunsak
Gabert
Mount Mutunte 593m
Okat Harbor
Lelu Island
Tofol
Lelu
Insiaf
Kosrae
Mount Finkol 629m
Utwe
Malem
Utwe Harbor
SCALE 1:500,000
Magur Islands
Namonuito Atoll
Ulul
Fayu
Murilo Atoll
Nomwin Atoll
Hall Islands
CHUUK
Chuuk Islands
Pulap Atoll
Puluwat Atoll
Manila Reef
Pulusuk
Weno
Neoch
Nama
Losap Atoll
Minto Reef
Oroluk Atoll
Pakin Atoll
Kolonia
Pohnpei
PALIKIR
Ant Atoll
Mwokil Atoll
MICRONESIA
Islands
POHNPEI
Pingelap Atoll
Ngetik Atoll
Kosrae
Tofol
KOSRAE
Namoluk Atoll
Etal Atoll
Lukunor Atoll
Satawan Atoll
Mortlock Islands
Nukuoro Atoll
SCALE 1:8,200,000

Marshall Islands

A group of 34 widely-scattered atolls in the central Pacific Ocean, the Marshall Islands include some of the largest atolls in the world, formed from low coral islands with sandy beaches and enclosing vast lagoons. Formerly under US protection as part of the UN Trust Territory of the Pacific Islands, and including the former US nuclear testing sites of Bikini atoll and Enewetak Atoll, the Marshall Islands became self-governing in 1979. The economy is reliant on US aid and on the rent paid by the USA for its missile base on Kwajalein atoll.

▲ ***Majuro Atoll** is the Marshall Islands' capital and commercial center. Almost half the population live on the narrow islands, often in overcrowded conditions.*

Nauru

A former British colony, the tiny island of Nauru, with an area of only 8.2 sq miles (21.2 sq km), has been exploited for its substantial phosphate deposits by the UK, Australia and New Zealand. Since independence in 1968, the phosphate industry has made its citizens some of the wealthiest in the world, and scars from the vast mining operation pit the island's landscape. Phosphate reserves are now virtually exhausted and investment overseas will in future form the bulk of Nauru's income.

◀ ***A series of** coral pinnacles stand exposed in the shallow water off the coast of Nauru. Much of the island has an extraordinary 'lunar' landscape, created by years of phosphate extraction.*

▲ ***Traditionally built canoes** are still important in Micronesia, used for transport and for fishing. This large canoe, on Satawal, in the state of Yap, needs nearly 20 people to return it to the boathouse.*

Wake Island *(to US)*

An unincorporated territory of the USA with a tiny population, Wake Island remains strategically important to US forces, and has been used as a base in several conflicts. Formed by the rim of an extinct underwater volcano, it is now used as an emergency airstrip for trans-Pacific flights, and as a stop-over for cargo planes.

Polynesia

KIRIBATI, TUVALU, Cook Islands, Easter Island, French Polynesia, Niue, Pitcairn Islands, Tokelau, Wallis & Futuna

The numerous island groups of Polynesia lie to the east of Australia, scattered over a vast area in the south Pacific. The islands are a mixture of low-lying coral atolls, some of which enclose lagoons, and the tips of great underwater volcanoes. The populations on the islands are small, and most people are of Polynesian origin, as are the Maori of New Zealand. Local economies remain simple, relying mainly on subsistence crops, mineral deposits – many now exhausted – fishing and tourism.

Kiribati

A former British colony, Kiribati became independent in 1979. Banaba's phosphate deposits ran out in 1980, following decades of exploitation by the British. Economic development remains slow and most agriculture is at a subsistence level, though coconuts provide export income, and underwater agriculture is being developed.

PACIFIC OCEAN
Iku
Buariki
Taratai
Abaokoro
Marenanuka
Nabeina
Tabiteuea
Tarawa
Bikeman
Bonriki
Bikenebu
Betio
Eita
Tarawa
Banraeaba
BAIRIKI
SCALE 1:1,000,000

▶ **With the exception** of Banaba all the islands in Kiribati's three groups are low-lying, coral atolls. This aerial view shows the sparsely vegetated islands, intercut by many small lagoons.

Tuvalu

A chain of nine coral atolls, 360 miles (579 km) long with a land area of just over 9 sq miles (23 sq km), Tuvalu is one of the world's smallest and most isolated states. As the Ellice Islands, Tuvalu was linked to the Gilbert Islands (now part of Kiribati) as a British colony until independence in 1978. Politically and socially conservative, Tuvaluans live by fishing and subsistence farming.

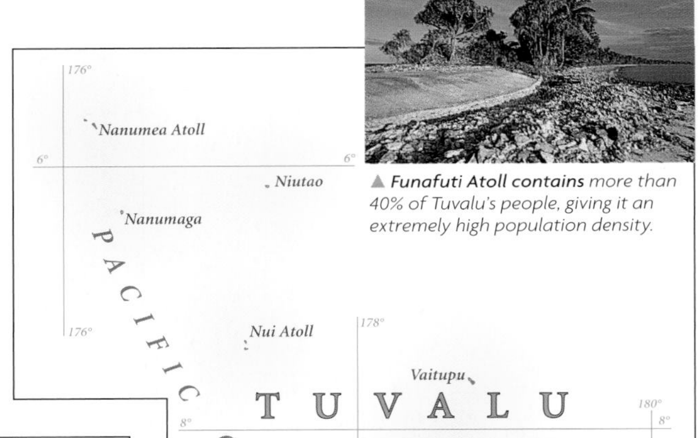
Nanumea Atoll
Niutao
Nanumaga
PACIFIC OCEAN
Nui Atoll

▲ **Funafuti Atoll contains** more than 40% of Tuvalu's people, giving it an extremely high population density.

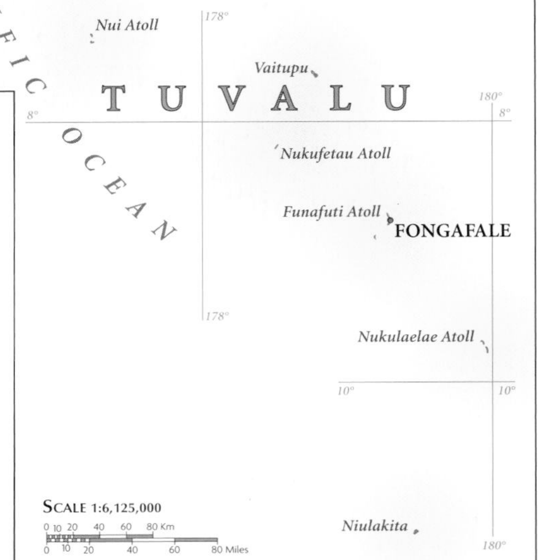
Vaitupu
TUVALU
Nukufetau Atoll
Funafuti Atoll
FONGAFALE
Nukulaelae Atoll
Niulakita
SCALE 1:6,125,000

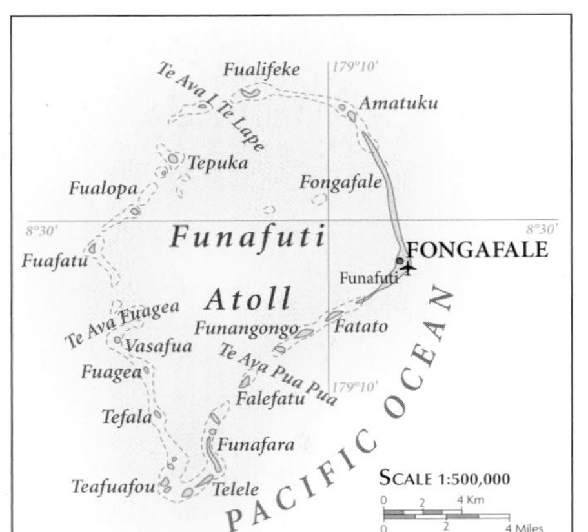
Fualifeke
Te Ava I Te Lape
Amatuku
Tepuka
Fongafale
Fualopa
Funafuti Atoll
FONGAFALE
Fuafatu
Funafuti
Te Ava Fuagea
Funangongo
Fatato
Vasafua
Te Ava Pua Pua
Fuagea
Falefatu
Tefala
Funafara
Teafuafou
Telele
PACIFIC OCEAN
SCALE 1:500,000

Tokelau *(to New Zealand)*

A low-lying coral atoll, Tokelau is a dependent territory of New Zealand with few natural resources. Although a 1990 cyclone destroyed crops and infrastructure, a tuna cannery and the sale of fishing licences have raised revenue and a catamaran link between the islands has increased their tourism potential. Tokelau's small size and economic weakness makes independence from New Zealand unlikely.

▲ **Fishermen cast their** nets to catch small fish in the shallow waters off Atafu Atoll, the most westerly island in Tokelau.

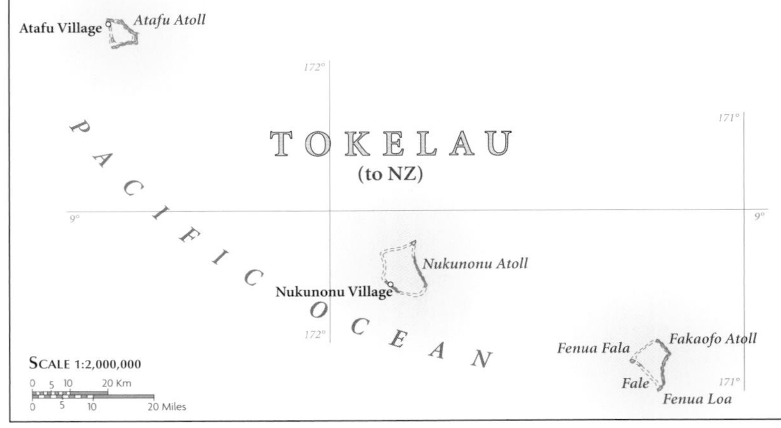
Atafu Village
Atafu Atoll
TOKELAU
(to NZ)
PACIFIC OCEAN
Nukunonu Atoll
Nukunonu Village
Fenua Fala
Fakaofo Atoll
Fale
Fenua Loa
SCALE 1:2,000,000

Wallis & Futuna *(to France)*

In contrast to other French overseas territories in the south Pacific, the inhabitants of Wallis and Futuna have shown little desire for greater autonomy. A subsistence economy produces a variety of tropical crops, while foreign currency remittances come from expatriates and from the sale of licences to Japanese and Korean fishing fleets.

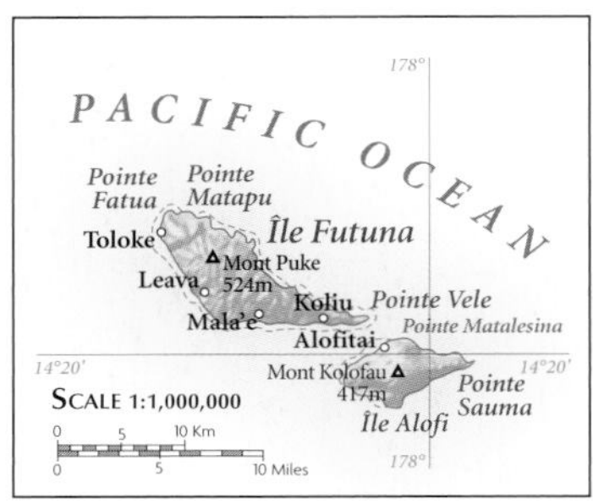
PACIFIC OCEAN
Pointe Fatua
Pointe Matapu
Île Futuna
Toloke
Mont Puke 524m
Leava
Kolia
Pointe Vele
Mala'e
Alofitai
Pointe Matalesina
Mont Kolofau 417m
Pointe Sauma
Île Alofi
SCALE 1:1,000,000

Île Wallis map: Nukuloa, Nukutapu, Hihifo, Vaitupu, Alele, Île Luaniva, MATĀ'UTU, Ahoa, Nukuhifala, Mala'etoli, Halalo, Pointe Matala'a, Nukuatea, Île Faioa, Île Fenuafo'ou, PACIFIC OCEAN, SCALE 1:1,000,000

▲ **Palm trees fringe** the white sands of a beach on Aitutaki in the Southern Cook Islands, where tourism is of increasing economic importance.

Cook Islands *(to New Zealand)*

A mixture of coral atolls and volcanic peaks, the Cook Islands achieved self-government in 1965 but exist in free association with New Zealand. A diverse economy includes pearl and giant clam farming, and an ostrich farm, plus tourism and banking. A 1991 friendship treaty with France provides for French surveillance of territorial waters.

Penrhyn
Rakahanga
Manihiki
Pukapuka
Nassau
Northern Cook Islands
Suwarrow
OCEAN
COOK ISLANDS
(to NZ)
PACIFIC
Palmerston
Southern Cook Islands
Aitutaki
Manuae
Takutea
Mitiaro
Atiu
Mauke
Rarotonga
AVARUA
Mangaia
SCALE 1:20,000,000

Niue *(to New Zealand)*

Niue, the world's largest coral island, is self-governing but exists in free association with New Zealand. Tropical fruits are grown for local consumption; tourism and the sale of postage stamps provide foreign currency. The lack of local job prospects has led more than 10,000 Niueans to emigrate to New Zealand, which has now invested heavily in Niue's economy in the hope of reversing this trend.

Hikutavake
Toi
Mutalau
Makefu
Tuapa
Makapu Point
Lakepa
Alofi Bay
ALOFI
NIUE
(to NZ)
Liku
Halagigie Point
Hanan
Tamakautoga
Avatele
Hakupu
Tepa Point
Mata Point
PACIFIC OCEAN
SCALE 1:1,000,000

▲ **Waves have cut** back the original coastline, exposing a sandy beach, near Mutalau in the northeast corner of Niue.

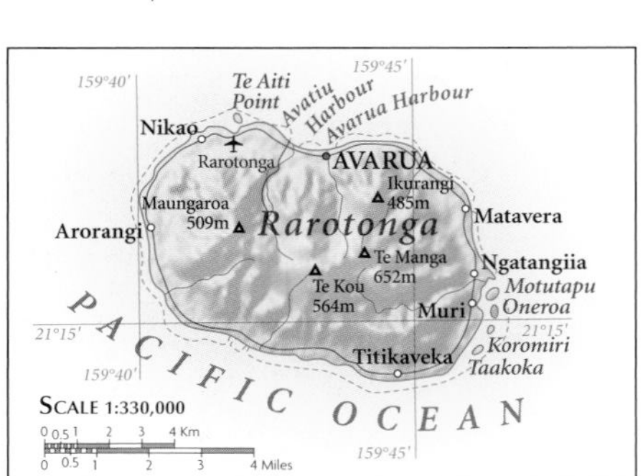
Te Aiti Point
Avatiu Harbour
Avarua Harbour
Nikao
Rarotonga
AVARUA
Ikurangi 485m
Maungaroa 509m
Matavera
Arorangi
Rarotonga
Te Manga 652m
Ngatangiia
Te Kou 564m
Motutapu
Oneroa
Muri
Koromiri
Titikaveka
Taakoka
PACIFIC OCEAN
SCALE 1:330,000

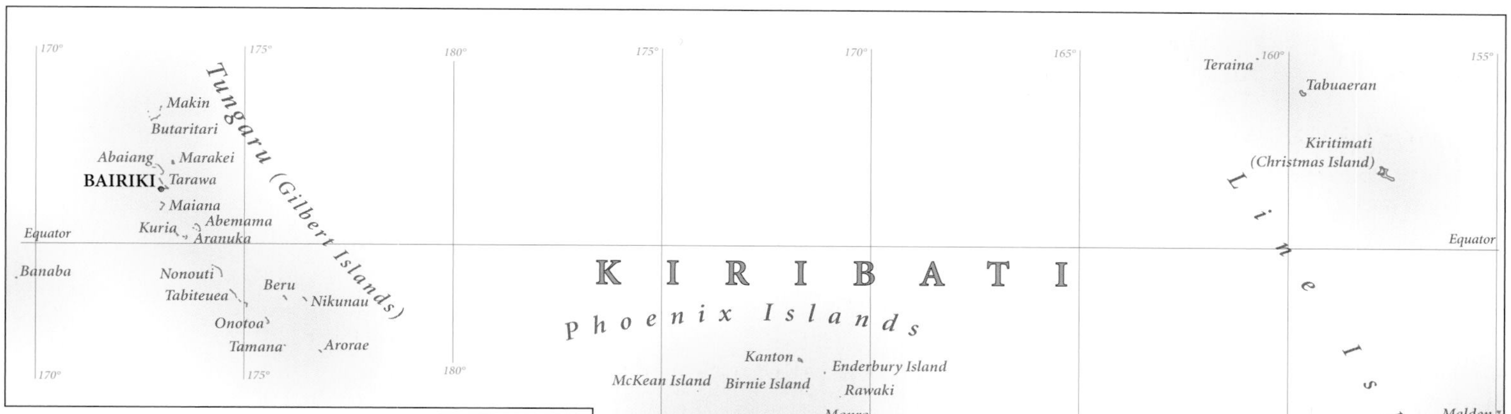

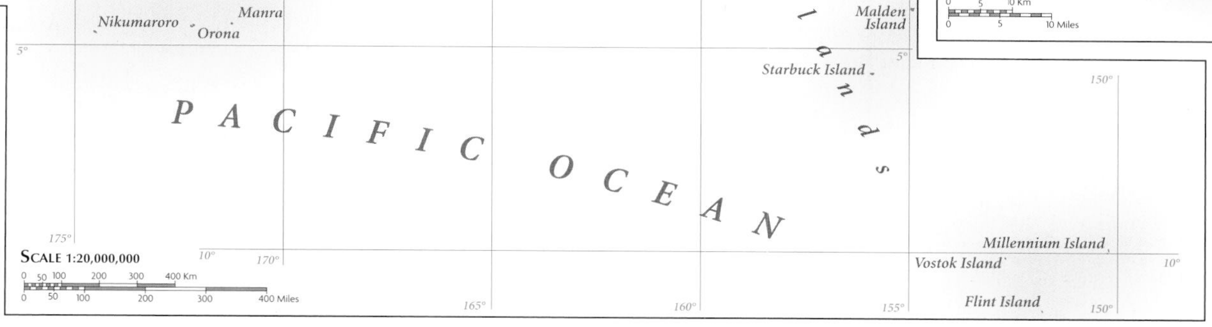

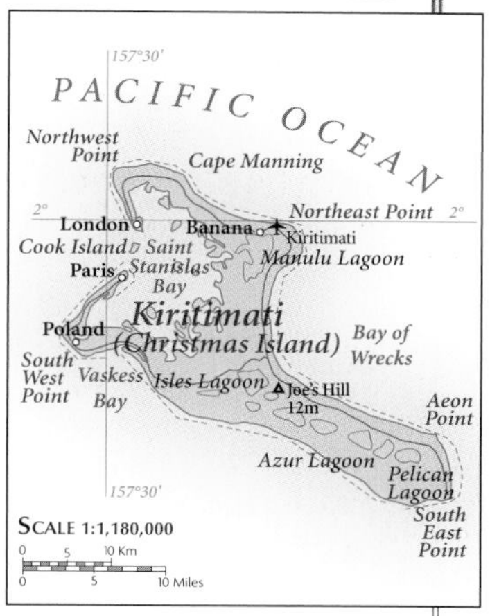

French Polynesia *(to France)*

The 130 islands of French Polynesia cover 4 million sq miles (10.5 million sq km). Nearly 75% of the people live on Tahiti. The use of Mururoa as a nuclear testing site by the French military transformed the economy, creating many jobs. The end of testing led to calls from the Polynesian majority for greater autonomy from France, the rebuilding of indigenous trade, and a reduction in tourism to stop the erosion of the islands' traditional culture.

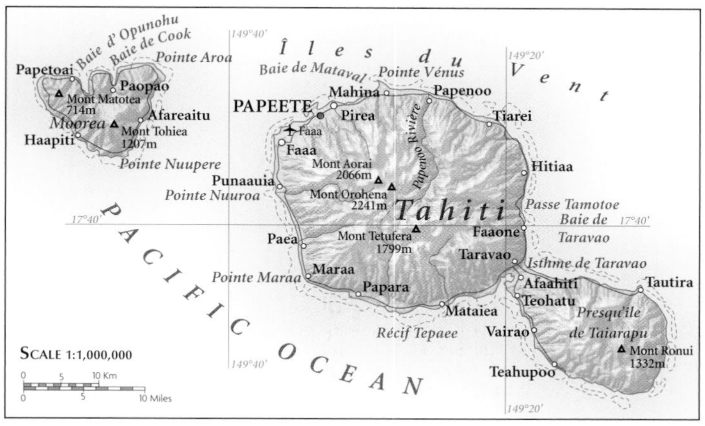

◀ *The traditional Tahitian welcome for visitors, who are greeted by parties of canoes, has become a major tourist attraction.*

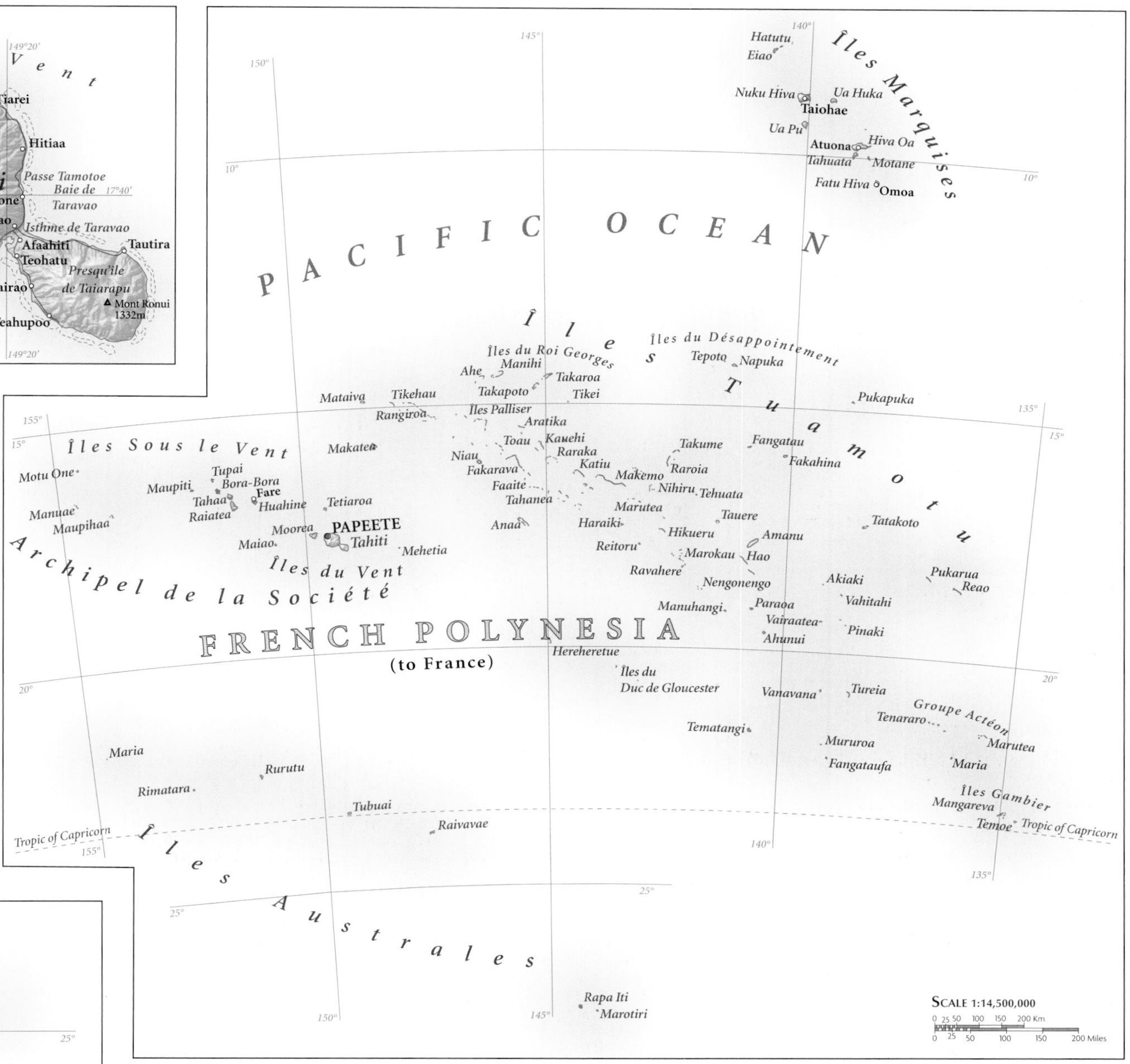

Pitcairn Islands *(to UK)*

Britain's most isolated dependency, Pitcairn Island was first populated by mutineers from the HMS *Bounty* in 1790. Emigration is further depleting the already limited gene pool of the island's inhabitants, with associated social and health problems. Barter, fishing and subsistence farming form the basis of the economy although postage stamp sales provide foreign currency earnings, and offshore mineral exploitation may boost the economy in future.

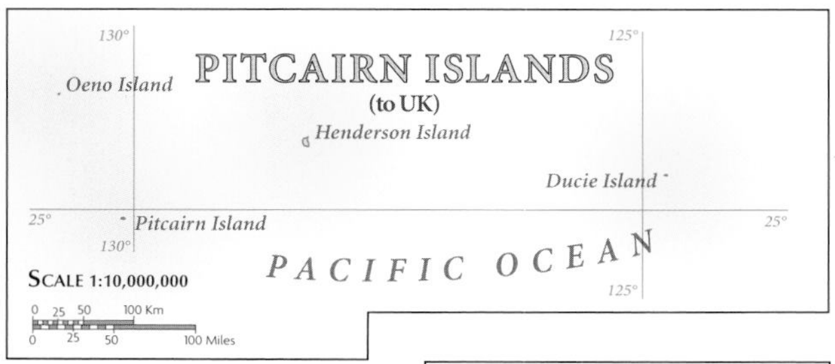

◀ *The Pitcairn Islanders rely on regular airdrops from New Zealand and periodic visits by supply vessels to provide them with basic commodities.*

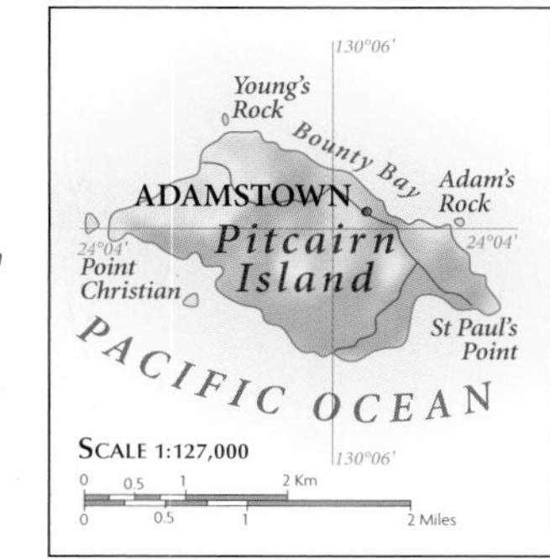
ADAMSTOWN
Pitcairn Island
Young's Rock
Bounty Bay
Adam's Rock
Point Christian
St Paul's Point
PACIFIC OCEAN
SCALE 1:127,000

Easter Island *(to Chile)*

One of the most easterly islands in Polynesia, Easter Island *(Isla de Pascua)* – also known as Rapa Nui, is part of Chile. The mainly Polynesian inhabitants support themselves by farming, which is mainly of a subsistence nature, and includes cattle rearing and crops such as sugar cane, bananas, corn, gourds and potatoes. In recent years, tourism has become the most important source of income and the island sustains a small commercial airport.

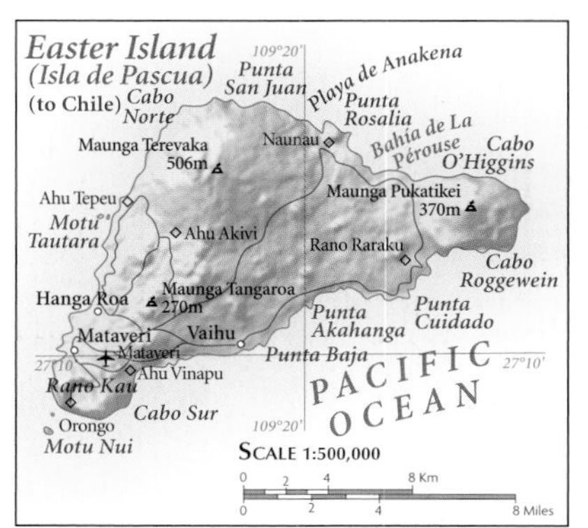
Easter Island
(Isla de Pascua)
(to Chile)
Punta San Juan
Playa de Anakena
Cabo Norte
Punta Rosalia
Bahia de La Pérouse
Cabo O'Higgins
Maunga Terevaka 506m
Nau Nau
Maunga Pukatikei 370m
Ahu Tepeu
Motu Tautara
Ahu Akivi
Rano Raraku
Cabo Roggewein
Hanga Roa
Maunga Tangaroa 270m
Punta Akahanga
Punta Cuidado
Mataveri
Vaihu
Punta Baja
Rano Kau
Ahu Vinapu
Orongo
Cabo Sur
Motu Nui
PACIFIC OCEAN
SCALE 1:500,000

▲ ***The Naunau**, a series of huge stone statues overlook Playa de Anakena, on Easter Island. Carved from a soft volcanic rock, they were erected between 400 and 900 years ago.*

The Pacific Ocean

The Pacific is the world's largest and deepest ocean. It is nearly twice the area of the Atlantic and contains almost three times as much water. The ocean is dotted with islands and surrounded by some of the world's most populous states; over half the world's population lives on its shores. The Pacific is bordered by active plate margins known as the 'Ring of Fire', causing earthquakes and tsunamis, and creating volcanic islands and subterranean mountain chains. The largest underwater mountains break the surface as island arcs. The fisheries of the Pacific are some of the most productive in the world and provide a vital resource for many of the Pacific islands. Since the Second World War there has been a shift in trading patterns, with a considerable growth in trade between the United States and the countries of the Pacific Rim.

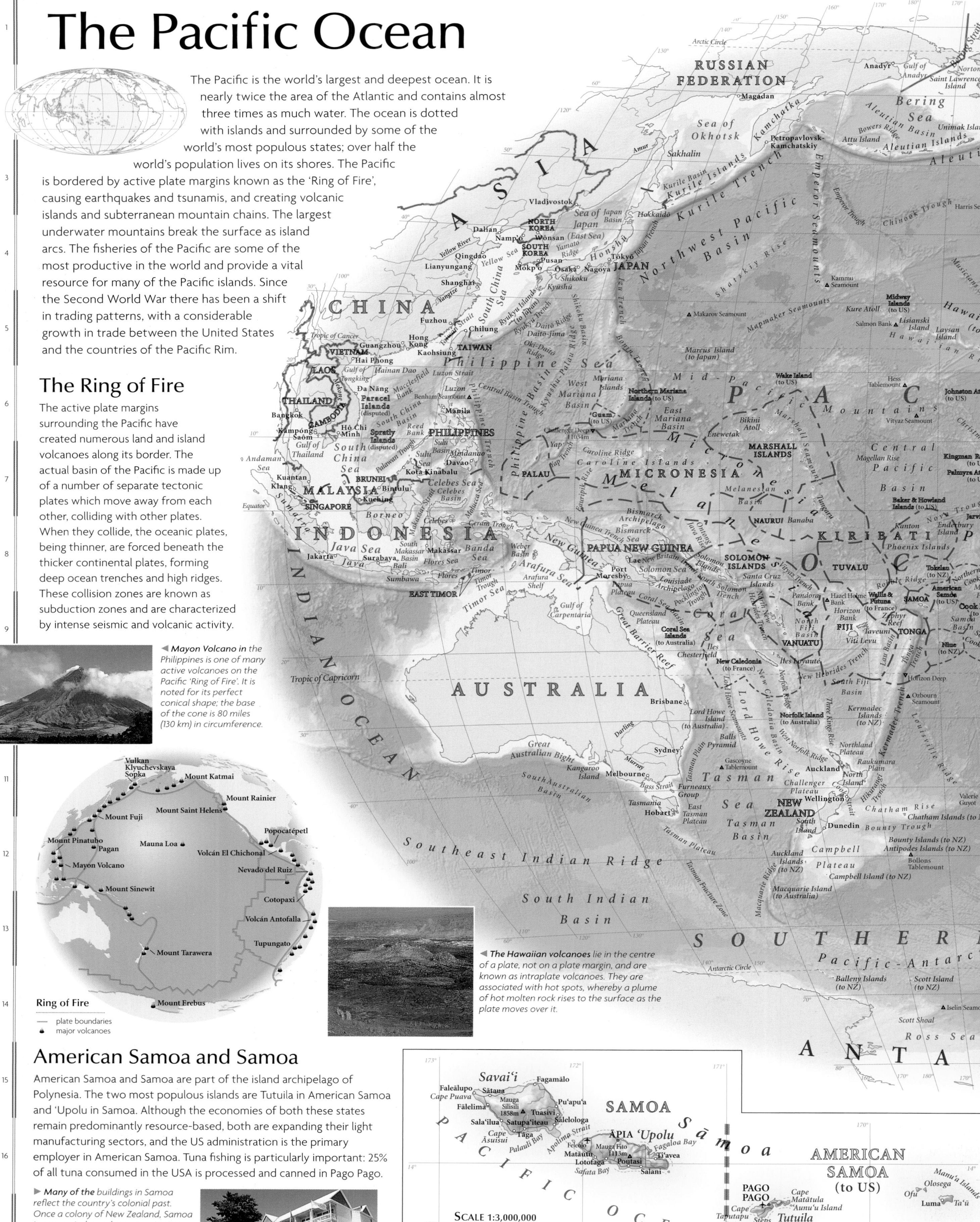

RUSSIAN FEDERATION
ASIA
CHINA
JAPAN
NORTH KOREA
SOUTH KOREA
TAIWAN
PHILIPPINES
VIETNAM
LAOS
THAILAND
CAMBODIA
MALAYSIA
SINGAPORE
BRUNEI
INDONESIA
EAST TIMOR
PAPUA NEW GUINEA
PALAU
MICRONESIA
MARSHALL ISLANDS
NAURU
KIRIBATI
SOLOMON ISLANDS
TUVALU
VANUATU
FIJI
TONGA
SAMOA
NEW ZEALAND
AUSTRALIA
INDIAN OCEAN
PACIFIC OCEAN
Sea of Okhotsk
Bering Sea
Sea of Japan
South China Sea
Philippine Sea
Coral Sea
Tasman Sea
Arafura Sea
Timor Sea
Java Sea
Banda Sea
Celebes Sea
Northwest Pacific Basin
Central Pacific Basin
Southeast Indian Ridge
South Indian Basin
Mariana Trench
Kurile Trench
Emperor Seamounts
Kermadec Trench
Tonga Trench
Mid-Pacific Mountains
Aleutian Islands
Kamchatka
Magadan
Vladivostok
Shanghai
Hong Kong
Manila
Jakarta
Brisbane
Sydney
Melbourne
Hobart
Auckland
Wellington
Dunedin
Tōkyō
SOUTHERN
Ross Sea
Arctic Circle
Antarctic Circle
Tropic of Cancer
Tropic of Capricorn
Equator

The Ring of Fire

The active plate margins surrounding the Pacific have created numerous land and island volcanoes along its border. The actual basin of the Pacific is made up of a number of separate tectonic plates which move away from each other, colliding with other plates. When they collide, the oceanic plates, being thinner, are forced beneath the thicker continental plates, forming deep ocean trenches and high ridges. These collision zones are known as subduction zones and are characterized by intense seismic and volcanic activity.

◀ *Mayon Volcano in the Philippines is one of many active volcanoes on the Pacific 'Ring of Fire'. It is noted for its perfect conical shape; the base of the cone is 80 miles (130 km) in circumference.*

Ring of Fire

plate boundaries
major volcanoes
Vulkan Klyuchevskaya Sopka
Mount Katmai
Mount Rainier
Mount Saint Helens
Mount Fuji
Mount Pinatubo
Pagan
Mayon Volcano
Mauna Loa
Popocatépetl
Volcán El Chichonal
Nevado del Ruiz
Mount Sinewit
Cotopaxi
Volcán Antofalla
Tupungato
Mount Tarawera
Mount Erebus

◀ *The Hawaiian volcanoes lie in the centre of a plate, not on a plate margin, and are known as intraplate volcanoes. They are associated with hot spots, whereby a plume of hot molten rock rises to the surface as the plate moves over it.*

American Samoa and Samoa

American Samoa and Samoa are part of the island archipelago of Polynesia. The two most populous islands are Tutuila in American Samoa and 'Upolu in Samoa. Although the economies of both these states remain predominantly resource-based, both are expanding their light manufacturing sectors, and the US administration is the primary employer in American Samoa. Tuna fishing is particularly important: 25% of all tuna consumed in the USA is processed and canned in Pago Pago.

▶ *Many of the buildings in Samoa reflect the country's colonial past. Once a colony of New Zealand, Samoa is now an independent state; American Samoa remains an unincorporated territory of the United States.*

Savai'i
SAMOA
APIA
'Upolu
Sāmoa
AMERICAN SAMOA (to US)
PAGO PAGO
Tutuila
PACIFIC OCEAN
Manu'a Islands
SCALE 1:3,000,000

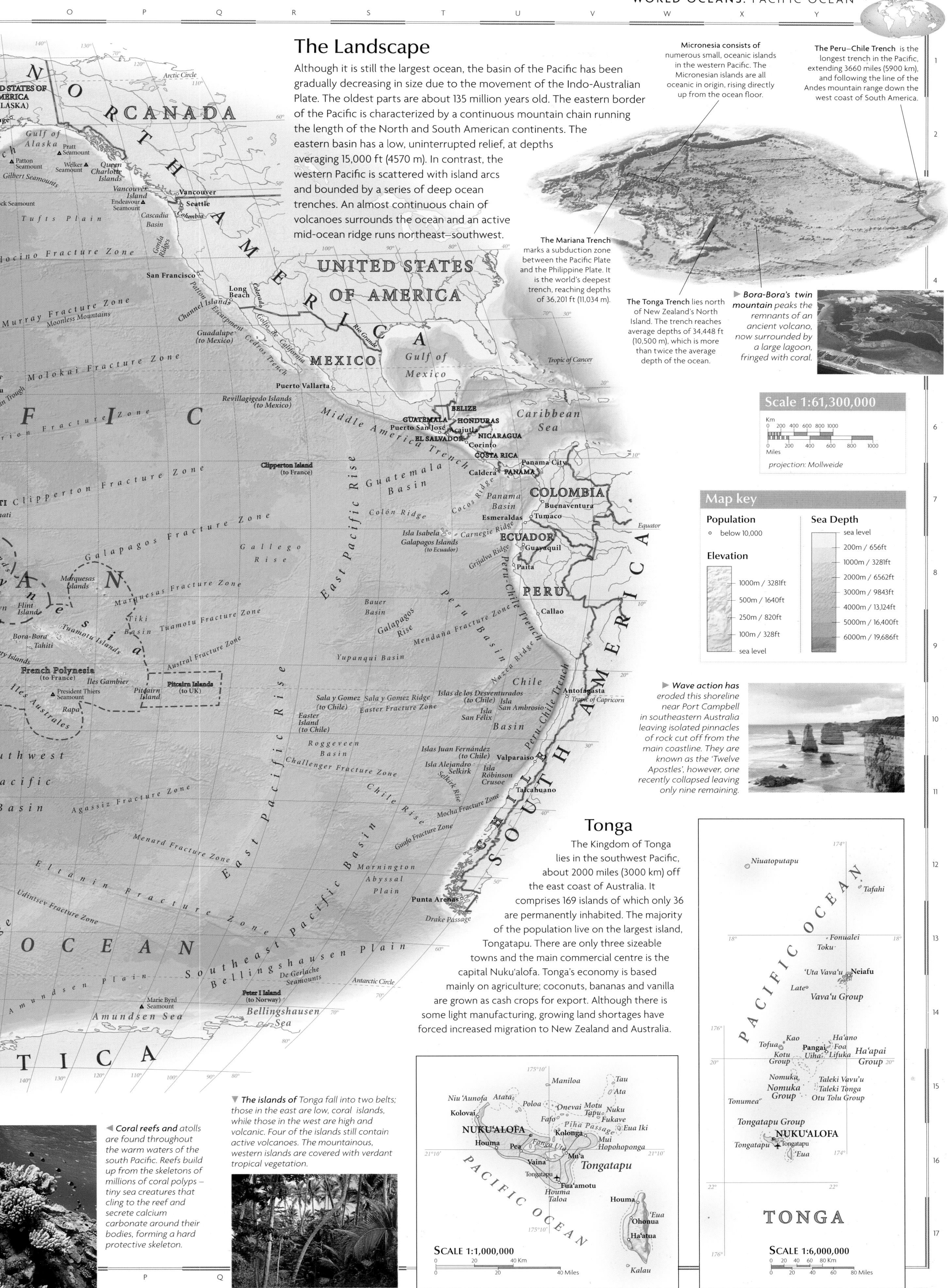
N O P Q R S T U V W X Y
NORTH AMERICA
CANADA
UNITED STATES OF AMERICA
(ALASKA)
Gulf of Alaska
Vancouver Island
Vancouver
Seattle
San Francisco
Long Beach
MEXICO
Gulf of Mexico
Puerto Vallarta
Revillagigedo Islands (to Mexico)
BELIZE
GUATEMALA
HONDURAS
EL SALVADOR
NICARAGUA
COSTA RICA
PANAMA
Caribbean Sea
Middle America Trench
Clipperton Island (to France)
Guatemala Basin
Panama Basin
COLOMBIA
Buenaventura
Esmeraldas
Tumaco
ECUADOR
Guayaquil
Isla Isabela
Galapagos Islands (to Ecuador)
Paita
PERU
Callao
Peru–Chile Trench
Peru Basin
Chile Basin
Antofagasta
Tropic of Capricorn
Isla San Ambrosio
Isla San Félix
Easter Island (to Chile)
Sala y Gomez (to Chile)
Islas Juan Fernández (to Chile)
Valparaíso
Talcahuano
Chile Rise
East Pacific Rise
SOUTH AMERICA
CHILE
Punta Arenas
Drake Passage
Mornington Abyssal Plain
Southeast Pacific Basin
Bellingshausen Plain
Peter I Island (to Norway)
Bellingshausen Sea
Amundsen Sea
Antarctic Circle
French Polynesia (to France)
Pitcairn Islands (to UK)
Marquesas Islands
Tuamotu Islands
Bora-Bora
Tahiti
Iles Australes
Rapa
Southwest Pacific Basin
OCEAN
Eltanin Fracture Zone
Clipperton Fracture Zone
Galapagos Fracture Zone
Molokai Fracture Zone
Murray Fracture Zone
Mendocino Fracture Zone
Tufts Plain
Equator
Tropic of Cancer
Arctic Circle
Micronesia consists of numerous small, oceanic islands in the western Pacific. The Micronesian islands are all oceanic in origin, rising directly up from the ocean floor.
The Peru–Chile Trench is the longest trench in the Pacific, extending 3660 miles (5900 km), and following the line of the Andes mountain range down the west coast of South America.
The Mariana Trench marks a subduction zone between the Pacific Plate and the Philippine Plate. It is the world's deepest trench, reaching depths of 36,201 ft (11,034 m).
The Tonga Trench lies north of New Zealand's North Island. The trench reaches average depths of 34,448 ft (10,500 m), which is more than twice the average depth of the ocean.
Scale 1:61,300,000
Km 0 200 400 600 800 1000
Miles 0 200 400 600 800 1000
projection: Mollweide
Map key
Population
below 10,000
Elevation
1000m / 3281ft
500m / 1640ft
250m / 820ft
100m / 328ft
sea level
Sea Depth
sea level
200m / 656ft
1000m / 3281ft
2000m / 6562ft
3000m / 9843ft
4000m / 13,124ft
5000m / 16,400ft
6000m / 19,686ft
NUKU'ALOFA
Tongatapu
'Eua
PACIFIC OCEAN
SCALE 1:1,000,000
Niuatoputapu
Tafahi
Fonualei
Toku
Neiafu
Vava'u Group
Ha'apai Group
Nomuka Group
Tongatapu Group
TONGA
SCALE 1:6,000,000

The Landscape

Although it is still the largest ocean, the basin of the Pacific has been gradually decreasing in size due to the movement of the Indo-Australian Plate. The oldest parts are about 135 million years old. The eastern border of the Pacific is characterized by a continuous mountain chain running the length of the North and South American continents. The eastern basin has a low, uninterrupted relief, at depths averaging 15,000 ft (4570 m). In contrast, the western Pacific is scattered with island arcs and bounded by a series of deep ocean trenches. An almost continuous chain of volcanoes surrounds the ocean and an active mid-ocean ridge runs northeast–southwest.

▶ *Bora-Bora's twin mountain peaks the remnants of an ancient volcano, now surrounded by a large lagoon, fringed with coral.*

▶ *Wave action has eroded this shoreline near Port Campbell in southeastern Australia leaving isolated pinnacles of rock cut off from the main coastline. They are known as the 'Twelve Apostles', however, one recently collapsed leaving only nine remaining.*

Tonga

The Kingdom of Tonga lies in the southwest Pacific, about 2000 miles (3000 km) off the east coast of Australia. It comprises 169 islands of which only 36 are permanently inhabited. The majority of the population live on the largest island, Tongatapu. There are only three sizeable towns and the main commercial centre is the capital Nuku'alofa. Tonga's economy is based mainly on agriculture; coconuts, bananas and vanilla are grown as cash crops for export. Although there is some light manufacturing, growing land shortages have forced increased migration to New Zealand and Australia.

◀ *Coral reefs and atolls are found throughout the warm waters of the south Pacific. Reefs build up from the skeletons of millions of coral polyps – tiny sea creatures that cling to the reef and secrete calcium carbonate around their bodies, forming a hard protective skeleton.*

▼ *The islands of Tonga fall into two belts; those in the east are low, coral islands, while those in the west are high and volcanic. Four of the islands still contain active volcanoes. The mountainous, western islands are covered with verdant tropical vegetation.*

Antarctica

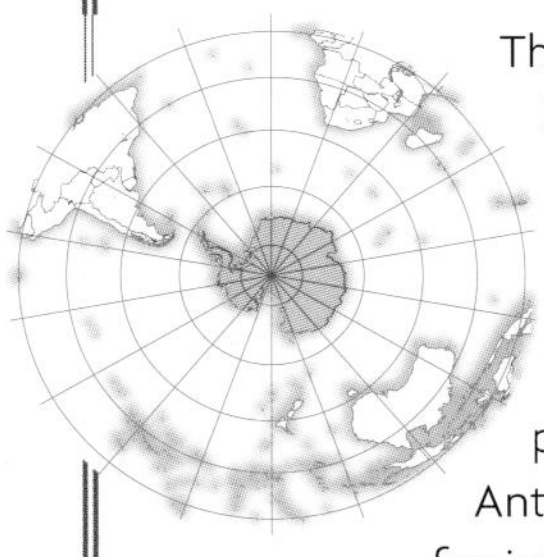

The ice-covered continent of Antarctica, which is the Earth's most southerly region, has for over 200 years drawn explorers and entrepreneurs seeking challenge and riches in its wintry lands. The extreme climate has deterred any large-scale settlement of the continent, and though commercial hunters built outposts in the past, habitation is now limited to scientific bases. The Antarctic Treaty, which came into force in 1961, provides for international governance and scientific co-operation in place of potential territorial conflict.

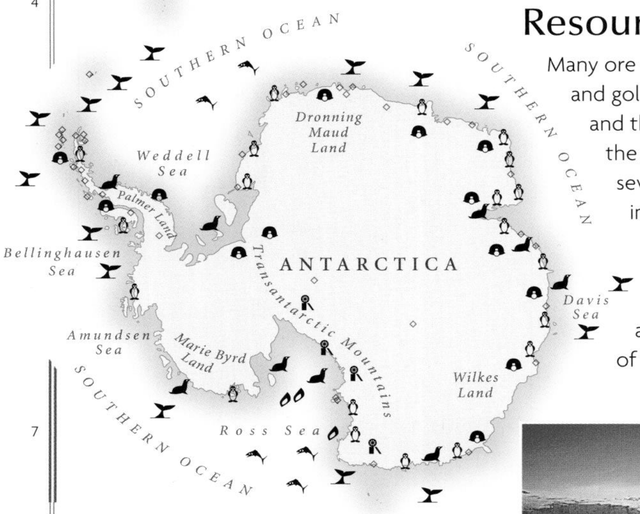

Resources

Many ore minerals, including iron and gold, are found in the Antarctic, and there are also coal reserves in the Transantarctic Mountains. The severe conditions and environmental importance of the region mean that exploitation of potential mineral resources is both uneconomic and undesirable. The unique wildlife and landscape draw a small number of tourists annually.

Resources (including wildlife)

- coal
- fish
- minerals
- oil & gas
- penguins
- seals
- whales
- polar research base

◀ *Most settlements in Antarctica are research bases such as this one at Rothera on Adelaide Island, although there is a small Chilean settlement on King George Island.*

The landscape

There are two distinct parts to Antarctica: West Antarctica, a series of ice-covered, mountainous islands, joined together by the ice; and the high plateau of East Antarctica. The Ross Sea and the Weddell Sea are outliers of the Southern Ocean – deep bays partially covered by thick ice shelves.

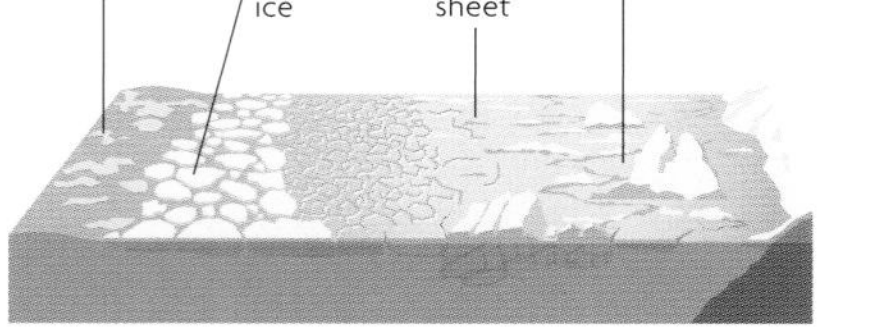

Grease ice · Pancake ice · Sea-ice sheet · Ice floe

▲ ***Pack ice forms** out at sea in freezing temperatures. At the outer limits, grease ice congeals on the surface of the ocean. This is then spun around by wind and waves into irregular 'pancakes', freezing and breaking up several times before bonding together again to form sea-ice sheets, which finally cement into enormous ice floes.*

◀ ***On Elephant Island,** the coast is edged by glaciers, although the land is not permanently covered by ice.*

Limit of winter pack ice

Limit of summer pack ice

Upper Wright Valley

Elephant Island

During the winter the seas surrounding Antarctica freeze, increasing the size of the continent by 100%.

High winds carrying snow form huge snowdrifts. The erosive power of the wind-borne snow can also sculpt the ice sheet to produce landforms known as *sastrugi* which align with the direction of the wind.

The Lambert Glacier is the largest glacier system in the world, up to 50 miles (80 km) wide at its seaward limit, and reaching 180 miles (300 km) into the interior by way of the Prince Charles Mountains.

Antarctica is the highest continent on Earth, because of the great thickness of ice which overlays the land. In places the ice alone can reach up to 15,700 ft (4800 m) thick. Much of the basement rock of west Antarctica lies below sea level, pushed down by the weight of the ice.

Many volcanoes, some of them still active, can be found in the mountains of the Antarctic Peninsula.

The mountainous Antarctic Peninsula is formed of rocks 65–225 million years old, overlain by more recent rocks and glacial deposits. It is connected to the Andes in South America by a submarine ridge.

Nearly half – 44% – of the Antarctic coastline is bounded by ice shelves, like the Ronne Ice Shelf, which float on the Ocean. These are joined to the inland ice sheet by dome-shaped ice 'rises'.

More than 30% of Antarctic ice is contained in the Ross Ice Shelf.

◀ ***The barren, flat-bottomed** Upper Wright Valley was once filled by a glacier, but is now dry, strewn with boulders and pebbles. In some dry valleys, there has been no rain for over 2 million years.*

▲ ***Large colonies of** seabirds live in the extremely harsh Antarctic climate. The Emperor penguins seen here, the smaller Adélie penguin, the Antarctic petrel and the South Polar skua are the only birds which breed exclusively on the continent.*

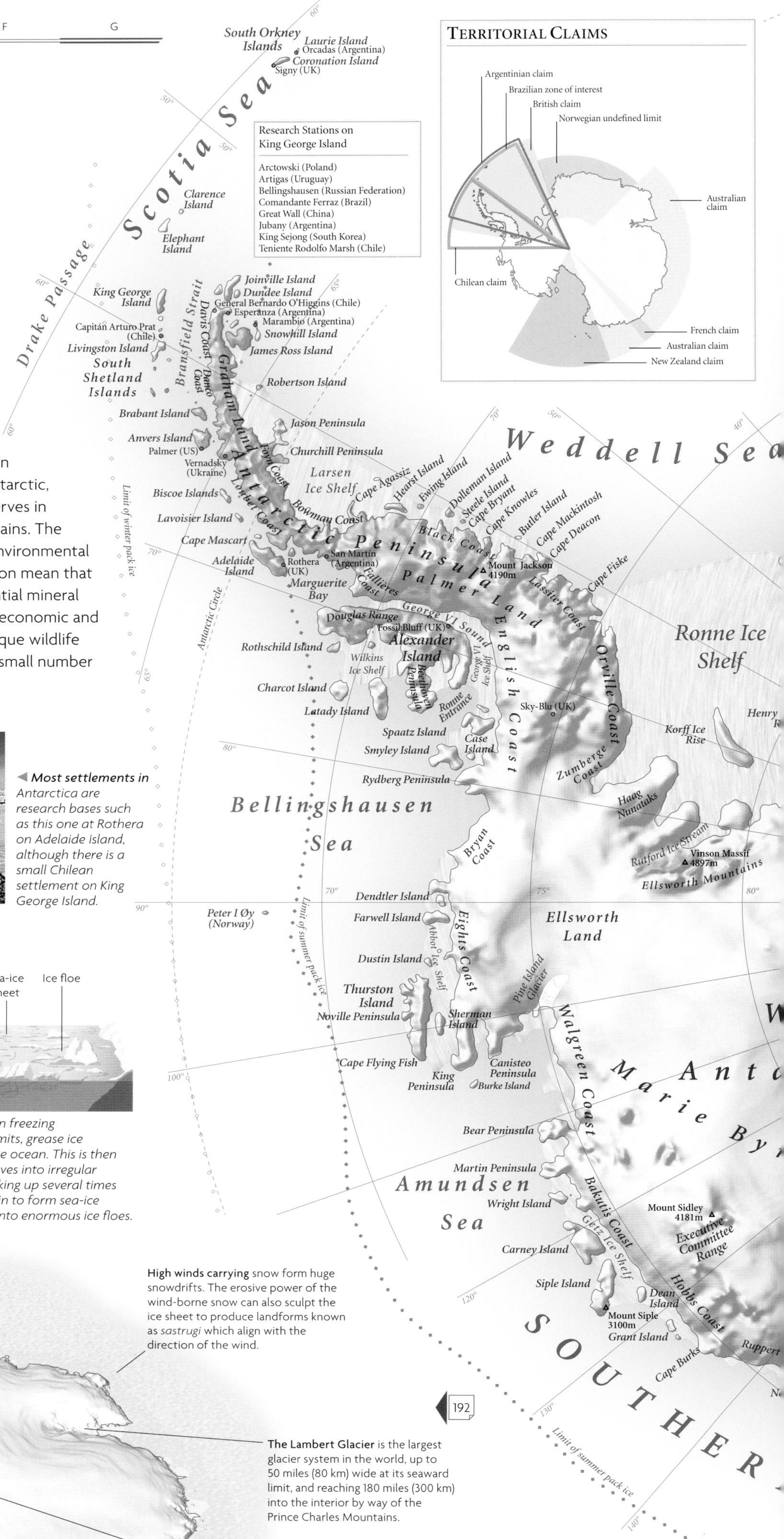

TERRITORIAL CLAIMS

Argentinian claim · Brazilian zone of interest · British claim · Norwegian undefined limit · Australian claim · Chilean claim · French claim · Australian claim · New Zealand claim

Research Stations on King George Island

- Arctowski (Poland)
- Artigas (Uruguay)
- Bellingshausen (Russian Federation)
- Comandante Ferraz (Brazil)
- Great Wall (China)
- Jubany (Argentina)
- King Sejong (South Korea)
- Teniente Rodolfo Marsh (Chile)

192

SOUTHERN OCEAN
64
172
ANTARCTICA
East Antarctica
Dronning Maud Land
Enderby Land
Kemp Land
Mac. Robertson Land
Princess Elizabeth Land
Wilhelm II Land
Wilkes Land
Terre Adélie
George V Land
Oates Land
Victoria Land
Coats Land
Transantarctic Mountains
Ross Ice Shelf
Ross Sea
Davis Sea
Dumont d'Urville Sea
Mackenzie Bay
South Pole
Amundsen-Scott (US)
Vostok (Russian Federation)
South Geomagnetic Pole
Map key
Elevation
ice cap
ice shelf
exposed land
Scale 1:14,750,000
projection: Lambert Azimuthal Equal Area

▲ **The sun sets** over the Antarctic Peninsula for more than six months during the winter. However, there are more hours of sunshine during the brief Antarctic summer than most equatorial countries experience in a whole year.

▲ **Immense, flat-topped icebergs** are formed when blocks of ice break away from the main ice sheet. Though the exposed area is enormous, the volume of ice concealed beneath the water may be many times greater.

The Arctic

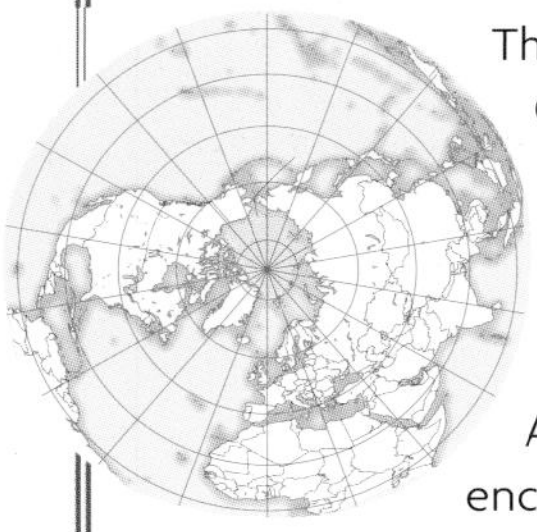

Three continents, Asia, North America and Europe, reach into the Arctic Circle at their northernmost limits, almost entirely encircling the Arctic Ocean. Despite the region's extraordinarily harsh climate, it has been inhabited for thousands of years by peoples such as the European Lapps, the Russian Nenet, and the North American Inuit, who draw a living from fishing, herding and hunting. More recently, particularly in the Russian Arctic, opportunities to exploit oil and other mineral reserves have encouraged immigration. Pollution of the Arctic's unique ecology and damage to the traditional lifestyles of many native peoples have been the unfortunate results of this activity, and international co-operation is needed to safeguard the future of the region.

Map key

Population

- above 5 million
- 1 million to 5 million
- 500,000 to 1 million
- 100,000 to 500,000
- 50,000 to 100,000
- 10,000 to 50,000
- below 10,000

Sea depth

- Sea level
- 200m / 656ft
- 1000m / 3281ft
- 2000m / 6562ft
- 3000m / 9843ft
- 4000m / 13,124ft
- 5000m / 16,400ft
- 6000m / 19,686ft

Scale 1:21,000,000

Km 0 100 200 300 400 500 600

Miles 0 100 200 300 400 500 600

projection: Lambert Azimuthal Equal Area

192

▲ *Wind-blown snow etches deep patterns in the ice sheet known as sastrugi. They align with the direction of the wind.*

Resources

Large quantities of coal, oil and natural gas are to be found in the basins of the Arctic Ocean, and in northern Canada, Alaska and the Russian Federation. The cost and difficulty of extraction and, more recently, awareness of damage to the environment, have limited exploitation to coastal regions. The unfrozen waters have stocks of fish including cod, plaice and haddock. Quotas have now been put in place to restrict the number of fish caught annually. Reindeer are herded in large numbers by many of the native Arctic peoples. Most grain and vegetables are imported from elsewhere.

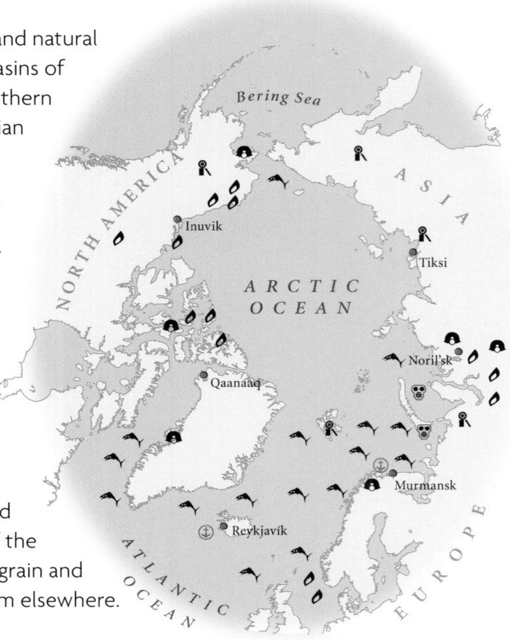

Bering Sea
ASIA
NORTH AMERICA
Inuvik
Tiksi
ARCTIC OCEAN
Noril'sk
Qaanaaq
Murmansk
Reykjavik
ATLANTIC OCEAN
EUROPE

8

▲ *Icebreakers, ships with specially strengthened hulls, designed to break a path through the ice, are used to keep important routes open during the winter, when falling temperatures cause much of the Arctic Ocean to freeze over.*

Resources

- coal
- fish
- mining
- oil & gas
- radioactive contamination
- major towns
- major ports

8

The landscape

The Arctic Ocean comprises two large ocean basins divided by three submarine ridges, the greatest of which, the Lomonosov Ridge, is a huge underwater mountain range which has an average height of more than 10,000 ft (3000 m). The lands which encircle the Arctic Ocean are underlain by great shield areas of ancient rocks, which were heavily glaciated during the last Ice Age.

◀ *Icebergs are constantly broken up and re-shaped by wind and the oceans. This flat-topped iceberg has been undercut, leaving a craggy ice cliff.*

The Canadian Shield underlies almost all of the Canadian Arctic. It is a very stable plateau of ancient rock, now covered by glacial lakes and sediment, which supports tundra vegetation.

The Arctic Ocean is the world's smallest ocean with a total area of 5,440,000 sq miles (15,100,000 sq km).

At a latitude of more than 75° N, the Arctic Ocean is almost permanently covered by pack-ice, though high winds and the movement of the seas may cause the ice to crack and break up.

In the more southerly reaches of the Arctic, like Siberia, much of the land is covered by permafrost. In the summer, higher temperatures warm the frozen ground, causing a number of typical phenomena. These include solifluction, the fast downhill movement of top soil layers; freeze/thaw activity, which patterns the ground into regular polygonal shapes, and the formation of large domes with a frozen ice core, known as pingos.

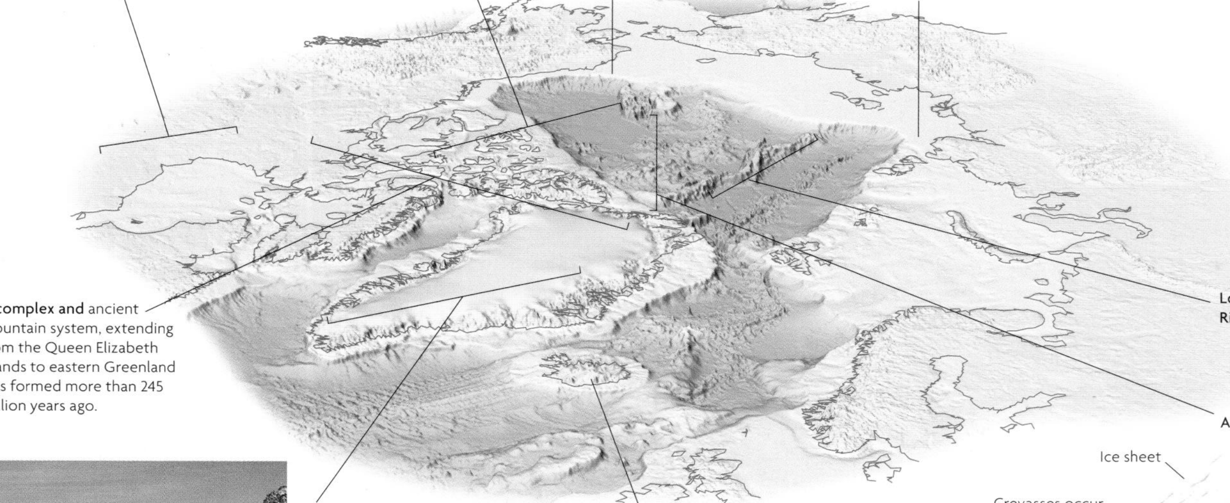

A complex and ancient mountain system, extending from the Queen Elizabeth Islands to eastern Greenland was formed more than 245 million years ago.

Lomonosov Ridge

Arctic ice shelf

◀ *Much of Greenland is covered by a massive ice sheet more than 650,000 sq miles (1,683,400 sq km) in extent. The weight of the ice has depressed the central land area to form a basin lying more than 1000 ft (300 m) below sea level. Only at the edges of the island is bare rock visible.*

Iceland has five major glaciers, sustained by heavy snowfall. Parts of the ice cap cover active volcanoes, such as Bárdharbunga, which periodically erupt causing the melted ice to form a great lake at the glacier margins.

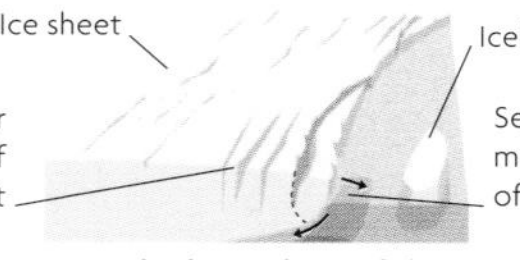

Ice sheet
Iceberg
Crevasses occur at the edge of the ice sheet
Sea water melts the edge of the ice sheet

▲ *At the boundary of the Arctic ice shelves, sea water flows under the ice causing melting and forming crevasses on the surface. This eventually weakens blocks of ice which break away as icebergs. This process is known as calving.*

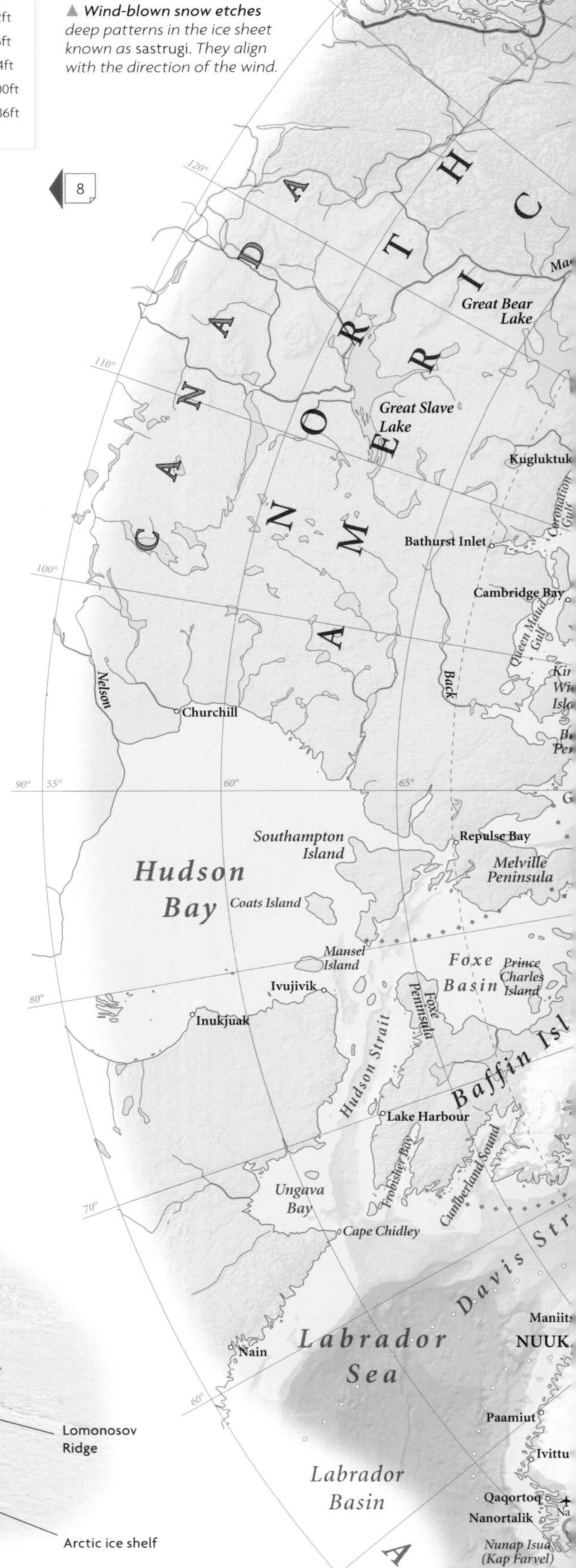

CANADA
NORTH AMERICA
Great Bear Lake
Great Slave Lake
Kugluktuk
Coronation Gulf
Bathurst Inlet
Cambridge Bay
Queen Maud Gulf
Back
Nelson
Churchill
Southampton Island
Repulse Bay
Melville Peninsula
Hudson Bay
Coats Island
Mansel Island
Foxe Basin
Prince Charles Island
Ivujivik
Foxe Peninsula
Inukjuak
Hudson Strait
Baffin Isl
Lake Harbour
Frobisher Bay
Cumberland Sound
Ungava Bay
Cape Chidley
Davis Str
Nain
Labrador Sea
Maniitsoq
NUUK
Paamiut
Ivittuut
Labrador Basin
Qaqortoq
Nanortalik
Nunap Isua (Kap Farvel)
Eirik Ridge
ATLAN

64

N
O
P
Q
R
S
T
U
V
W
X
Y
192
Limit of winter pack ice
Alaska Peninsula
Bristol Bay
Kuskokwim Bay
Kodiak Island
Nunivak Island
Saint Matthew Island
Bering Sea
Aleutian Basin
Shirshov Ridge
Komandorskaya Basin
Karaginskiy Zaliv
Poluostrov Kamchatka
Mys Olyutorskiy
Pakhachi
Sea of Okhotsk
Mys Tolstoy
Zaliv Shelikhova
Magadan
Mys Navarin
Gulf of Alaska
Cook Inlet
Kuskokwim
Yukon
Anchorage
Norton Sound
Nome
Cape Prince of Wales
Saint Lawrence Island
Provideniya
Anadyrskiy Zaliv
Anadyr'
Manily
Okhotsk
Seward Peninsula
Bering Strait
Uelen
Chukotskiy Poluostrov
Arctic Circle
UNITED STATES OF AMERICA
ALASKA
Kotzebue Sound
Vankarem
Point Hope
Chukchi Sea
Proliv Longa
Ostrov Vrangelya
Pevek
Ambarchik
Kolyma
Limit of summer pack ice
Barrow
Prudhoe Bay
Limit of permanent ice cap
East Siberian Sea
Indigirka
RUSSIAN FEDERATION
Siberia
Beaufort Sea
Inuvik
Tuktoyaktuk
Northwind Plain
Chukchi Plain
Chukchi Plateau
Mendeleyev Ridge
Proliv Dmitriya Lapteva
Yana
Ostrov Novaya Sibir'
Cape Bathurst
Canada Basin
Canada Plain
Buorkhaya Guba
Tiksi
Lena
Novosibirskiye Ostrova
Olenëk
Amundsen Gulf
Banks Island
Wrangel Plain
Laptev Sea
Ust'-Olenëk
Victoria Island
McClure Strait
Prince Patrick Island
ARCTIC OCEAN
Khatangskiy Zaliv
Melville Island
Mackenzie King Island
Poluostrov Taymyr
Khatanga
Ozero Taymyr
Prince Gustaf Adolf Sea
Ellef Ringnes Island
Bathurst Island
Viscount Melville Sound
North Geomagnetic Pole
Somerset Island
Resolute (Qausuittuq)
Queen Elizabeth Islands
Axel Heiberg Island
Alpha Cordillera
Makarov Basin
Lomonosov Ridge
Nansen Cordillera
North Pole
Pole Plain
Fram Basin
Ostrov Bol'shevik
Proliv Vil'kitskogo
Severnaya Zemlya
Ostrov Oktyabr'skoy Revolyutsii
Ostrov Komsomolets
Devon Island
Lancaster Sound
Ellesmere Island
Cape Columbia
Nansen Basin
Noril'sk
Yenisey
122
Dikson
Yeniseyskiy Zaliv
Gydanskiy Poluostrov
Kara Sea
Svyataya Anna Trough
Alert
Nares Strait
Lincoln Sea
Pond Inlet
Qaanaaq
Baffin Basin
Innaanganeq
Knud Rasmussen Land
Savissivik
Qimusseriarsuaq
Kap Morris Jesup
Wandel Sea
Independence Fjord
Barents Plain
Franz Josef Land
Novaya Zemlya
East Novaya Zemlya Trough
Ostrov Belyy
Obskaya Guba
Poluostrov Yamal
Baydaratskaya Guba
Vorkuta
Baffin Bay
AVANNAARSUA
Nord
Kullorsuaq
Upernavik
SVALBARD (to Norway)
Kong Frederik VIII Land
Longyearbyen
Spitsbergen
Kara Strait
Ural Mountains
Ob'
Uummannaq
Qeqertarsuaq
Qasigiannguit
GREENLAND (to Denmark)
Hopen
Limit of winter pack ice
Barents Sea
Nar'yan-Mar
Pechora
Ostrov Kolguyev
Cheshskaya Guba
Poluostrov Kanin
Kong Christian X Land
Petermann Bjerg 2940m
Daneborg
Greenland Plain
Bjørnøya
Barents Trough
Murmansk Rise
TUNU
Greenland Sea
Mohns Ridge
North Cape
Hammerfest
Murmansk
Kola Peninsula
Kong Oscar Fjord
Kong Christian IX Land
Mont Forel 3360m
Gunnbjørn Fjeld 3700m
Ittoqqortoormiit
Kangertittivaq
Kangikajik
JAN MAYEN (to Norway)
Jan Mayen Fracture Zone
Fugløya Bank
Tromsø
Lapland
Archangel
Northern Dvina
White Sea
Ammassalik
Denmark Strait
Kolbeinsey Ridge
Jan Mayen Ridge
Iceland Plateau
Norwegian Sea
Voring Plateau
Norwegian Basin
Reykjanes Basin
REYKJAVÍK
Akureyri
Arctic Circle
NORWAY
SWEDEN
FINLAND
EUROPE
Gulf of Bothnia
Onezhskoye Ozero
Ladozhskoye Ozero
ICELAND
Reykjanes Ridge
Faeroe-Iceland Ridge
92
FAEROE ISLANDS (to Denmark)
Faeroe-Shetland Trough
HELSINKI
Gulf of Finland
MOSCOW
Iceland Basin
Bill Baileys Bank
TALLINN
ESTONIA
Hatton Ridge
Shetland Islands
Norwegian Trench
OSLO
STOCKHOLM
Baltic Sea
RIGA
LATVIA
Orkney Islands
Skagerrak
OCEAN
X
Y
Z

▲ ***The aurora borealis*** *or Northern Lights are coloured bands of light which appear in northern latitudes. Light is emitted when dust particles from the Sun react with gases in the Earth's atmosphere.*

▲ ***Polar bears range*** *for great distances over the Arctic pack ice in search of food. They are formidable hunters who live mainly on seals. In December and January, mother bears give birth to their cubs in dens dug deep beneath the snow.*

Geographical comparisons

Largest countries

Russian Federation	6,592,735 sq miles	(17,075,200 sq km)
Canada	3,854,085 sq miles	(9,984,670 sq km)
USA	3,717,792 sq miles	(9,629,091 sq km)
China	3,705,386 sq miles	(9,596,960 sq km)
Brazil	3,286,470 sq miles	(8,511,965 sq km)
Australia	2,967,893 sq miles	(7,686,850 sq km)
India	1,269,339 sq miles	(3,287,590 sq km)
Argentina	1,068,296 sq miles	(2,766,890 sq km)
Kazakhstan	1,049,150 sq miles	(2,717,300 sq km)
Sudan	967,493 sq miles	(2,505,815 sq km)

Smallest countries

Vatican City	0.17 sq miles	(0.44 sq km)
Monaco	0.75 sq miles	(1.95 sq km)
Nauru	8.2 sq miles	(21.2 sq km)
Tuvalu	10 sq miles	(26 sq km)
San Marino	24 sq miles	(61 sq km)
Liechtenstein	62 sq miles	(160 sq km)
Marshall Islands	70 sq miles	(181 sq km)
St. Kitts & Nevis	101 sq miles	(261 sq km)
Maldives	116 sq miles	(300 sq km)
Malta	124 sq miles	(320 sq km)

Largest islands

To the nearest 1000 – or 100,000 for the largest

Greenland	849,400 sq miles	(2,200,000 sq km)
New Guinea	312,000 sq miles	(808,000 sq km)
Borneo	292,222 sq miles	(757,050 sq km)
Madagascar	229,300 sq miles	(594,000 sq km)
Sumatra	202,300 sq miles	(524,000 sq km)
Baffin Island	183,800 sq miles	(476,000 sq km)
Honshu	88,800 sq miles	(230,000 sq km)
Britain	88,700 sq miles	(229,800 sq km)
Victoria Island	81,900 sq miles	(212,000 sq km)
Ellesmere Island	75,700 sq miles	(196,000 sq km)

Richest countries

GNI per capita, in US$

Luxembourg	65,630
Norway	59,590
Switzerland	54,930
Liechtenstein	50,000
Denmark	47,390
Iceland	46,320
USA	43,740
Sweden	41,060
Ireland	40,150
Japan	38,980

Poorest countries

GNI per capita, in US$

Burundi	100
Somalia	120
Dem. Rep. Congo	120
Liberia	130
Malawi	160
Ethiopia	160
Guinea-Bissau	180
Sierra Leone	220
Eritrea	220
Afghanistan	222
Rwanda	230
Niger	240

Most populous countries

China	1,331,400,000
India	1,135,600,000
USA	303,900,000
Indonesia	228,100,000
Brazil	191,300,000
Pakistan	164,600,000
Bangladesh	147,100,000
Russian Federation	141,900,000
Nigeria	137,200,000
Japan	128,300,000

Least populous countries

Vatican City	821
Tuvalu	11,992
Nauru	13,528
Palau	20,842
San Marino	29,615
Monaco	32,671
Liechtenstein	34,247
St Kitts & Nevis	39,349
Marshall Islands	61,815
Antigua & Barbuda	69,481
Andorra	71,822
Dominica	72,386

Most densely populated countries

Monaco	43,212 people per sq mile	(16,620 per sq km)
Singapore	18,220 people per sq mile	(7049 per sq km)
Vatican City	5418 people per sq mile	(2093 per sq km)
Malta	3242 people per sq mile	(1256 per sq km)
Maldives	2836 people per sq mile	(1097 per sq km)
Bangladesh	2743 people per sq mile	(1059 per sq km)
Bahrain	2663 people per sq mile	(1030 per sq km)
China	1838 people per sq mile	(710 per sq km)
Mauritius	1671 people per sq mile	(645 per sq km)
Barbados	1627 people per sq mile	(628 per sq km)

Most sparsely populated countries

Mongolia	4 people per sq mile	(2 per sq km)
Namibia	6 people per sq mile	(2 per sq km)
Australia	7 people per sq mile	(3 per sq km)
Mauritania	8 people per sq mile	(3 per sq km)
Surinam	8 people per sq mile	(3 per sq km)
Botswana	8 people per sq mile	(3 per sq km)
Iceland	8 people per sq mile	(3 per sq km)
Canada	9 people per sq mile	(4 per sq km)
Libya	9 people per sq mile	(4 per sq km)
Guyana	10 people per sq mile	(4 per sq km)

Most widely spoken languages

1. Chinese (Mandarin)	6. Arabic
2. English	7. Bengali
3. Hindi	8. Portuguese
4. Spanish	9. Malay-Indonesian
5. Russian	10. French

Largest conurbations

	Population
Tokyo	34,200,000
Mexico City	22,800,000
Seoul	22,300,000
New York	21,900,000
São Paulo	20,200,000
Mumbai	19,850,000
Delhi	19,700,000
Shanghai	18,150,000
Los Angeles	18,000,000
Osaka	16,800,000
Jakarta	16,550,000
Kolkata	15,650,000
Cairo	15,600,000
Manila	14,950,000
Karachi	14,300,000
Moscow	13,750,000
Buenos Aires	13,450,000
Dacca	13,250,000
Rio de Janeiro	12,150,000
Beijing	12,100,000
London	12,000,000
Tehran	11,850,000
Istanbul	11,500,000
Lagos	11,100,000
Shenzhen	10,700,000

Countries with the most land borders

14: China	(Afghanistan, Bhutan, Burma, India, Kazakhstan, Kyrgyzstan, Laos, Mongolia, Nepal, North Korea, Pakistan, Russian Federation, Tajikistan, Vietnam)
14: Russian Federation	(Azerbaijan, Belarus, China, Estonia, Finland, Georgia, Kazakhstan, Latvia, Lithuania, Mongolia, North Korea, Norway, Poland, Ukraine)
10: Brazil	(Argentina, Bolivia, Colombia, French Guiana, Guyana, Paraguay, Peru, Surinam, Uruguay, Venezuela)
9: Congo, Dem. Rep.	(Angola, Burundi, Central African Republic, Congo, Rwanda, Sudan, Tanzania, Uganda, Zambia)
9: Germany	(Austria, Belgium, Czech Republic, Denmark, France, Luxembourg, Netherlands, Poland, Switzerland)
9: Sudan	(Central African Republic, Chad, Dem. Rep.Congo, Egypt, Eritrea, Ethiopia, Kenya, Libya, Uganda)
8: Austria	(Czech Republic, Germany, Hungary, Italy, Liechtenstein, Slovakia, Slovenia, Switzerland)
8: France	(Andorra, Belgium, Germany, Italy, Luxembourg, Monaco, Spain, Switzerland)
8: Tanzania	(Burundi, Dem. Rep.Congo, Kenya, Malawi, Mozambique, Rwanda, Uganda, Zambia)
8: Turkey	(Armenia, Azerbaijan, Bulgaria, Georgia, Greece, Iran, Iraq, Syria)
8: Zambia	(Angola, Botswana, Dem. Rep.Congo, Malawi, Mozambique, Namibia, Tanzania, Zimbabwe)

Longest rivers

Nile (NE Africa)	4160 miles	(6695 km)
Amazon (South America)	4049 miles	(6516 km)
Yangtze (China)	3915 miles	(6299 km)
Mississippi/Missouri (USA)	3710 miles	(5969 km)
Ob'-Irtysh (Russian Federation)	3461 miles	(5570 km)
Yellow River (China)	3395 miles	(5464 km)
Congo (Central Africa)	2900 miles	(4667 km)
Mekong (Southeast Asia)	2749 miles	(4425 km)
Lena (Russian Federation)	2734 miles	(4400 km)
Mackenzie (Canada)	2640 miles	(4250 km)
Yenisey (Russian Federation)	2541 miles	(4090km)

Highest mountains

Height above sea level

Everest	29,035 ft	(8850 m)
K2	28,253 ft	(8611 m)
Kanchenjunga I	28,210 ft	(8598 m)
Makalu I	27,767 ft	(8463 m)
Cho Oyu	26,907 ft	(8201 m)
Dhaulagiri I	26,796 ft	(8167 m)
Manaslu I	26,783 ft	(8163 m)
Nanga Parbat I	26,661 ft	(8126 m)
Annapurna I	26,547 ft	(8091 m)
Gasherbrum I	26,471 ft	(8068 m)

Largest bodies of inland water

With area and depth

Caspian Sea	143,243 sq miles (371,000 sq km)	3215 ft (980 m)
Lake Superior	31,151 sq miles (83,270 sq km)	1289 ft (393 m)
Lake Victoria	26,828 sq miles (69,484 sq km)	328 ft (100 m)
Lake Huron	23,436 sq miles (60,700 sq km)	751 ft (229 m)
Lake Michigan	22,402 sq miles (58,020 sq km)	922 ft (281 m)
Lake Tanganyika	12,703 sq miles (32,900 sq km)	4700 ft (1435 m)
Great Bear Lake	12,274 sq miles (31,790 sq km)	1047 ft (319 m)
Lake Baikal	11,776 sq miles (30,500 sq km)	5712 ft (1741 m)
Great Slave Lake	10,981 sq miles (28,440 sq km)	459 ft (140 m)
Lake Erie	9,915 sq miles (25,680 sq km)	197 ft (60 m)

Deepest ocean features

Challenger Deep, Mariana Trench (Pacific)	36,201 ft	(11,034 m)
Vityaz III Depth, Tonga Trench (Pacific)	35,704 ft	(10,882 m)
Vityaz Depth, Kurile-Kamchatka Trench (Pacific)	34,588 ft	(10,542 m)
Cape Johnson Deep, Philippine Trench (Pacific)	34,441 ft	(10,497 m)
Kermadec Trench (Pacific)	32,964 ft	(10,047 m)
Ramapo Deep, Japan Trench (Pacific)	32,758 ft	(9984 m)
Milwaukee Deep, Puerto Rico Trench (Atlantic)	30,185 ft	(9200 m)
Argo Deep, Torres Trench (Pacific)	**30,070 ft**	**(9165 m)**
Meteor Depth, South Sandwich Trench (Atlantic)	30,000 ft	(9144 m)
Planet Deep, New Britain Trench (Pacific)	29,988 ft	(9140 m)

Greatest waterfalls

Mean flow of water

Boyoma (Dem. Rep. Congo)	600,400 cu. ft/sec	(17,000 cu.m/sec)
Khône (Laos/Cambodia)	410,000 cu. ft/sec	(11,600 cu.m/sec)
Niagara (USA/Canada)	195,000 cu. ft/sec	(5500 cu.m/sec)
Grande (Uruguay)	160,000 cu. ft/sec	(4500 cu.m/sec)
Paulo Afonso (Brazil)	100,000 cu. ft/sec	(2800 cu.m/sec)
Urubupunga (Brazil)	97,000 cu. ft/sec	(2750 cu.m/sec)
Iguaçu (Argentina/Brazil)	62,000 cu. ft/sec	(1700 cu.m/sec)
Maribondo (Brazil)	53,000 cu. ft/sec	(1500 cu.m/sec)
Victoria (Zimbabwe)	39,000 cu. ft/sec	(1100 cu.m/sec)
Kabalega (Uganda)	42,000 cu. ft/sec	(1200 cu.m/sec)
Churchill (Canada)	35,000 cu. ft/sec	(1000 cu.m/sec)
Cauvery (India)	33,000 cu. ft/sec	(900 cu.m/sec)

Highest waterfalls

* Indicates that the total height is a single leap

Angel (Venezuela)	3212 ft	(979 m)
Tugela (South Africa)	3110 ft	(948 m)
Utigard (Norway)	2625 ft	(800 m)
Mongefossen (Norway)	2539 ft	(774 m)
Mtarazi (Zimbabwe)	2500 ft	(762 m)
Yosemite (USA)	2425 ft	(739 m)
Ostre Mardola Foss (Norway)	2156 ft	(657 m)
Tyssestrengane (Norway)	2119 ft	(646 m)
***Cuquenan** (Venezuela)	2001 ft	(610 m)
Sutherland (New Zealand)	1903 ft	(580 m)
***Kjellfossen** (Norway)	1841 ft	(561 m)

Largest deserts

NB – Most of Antarctica is a polar desert, with only 50mm of precipitation annually

Sahara	3,450,000 sq miles	(9,065,000 sq km)
Gobi	500,000 sq miles	(1,295,000 sq km)
Ar Rub al Khali	289,600 sq miles	(750,000 sq km)
Great Victorian	249,800 sq miles	(647,000 sq km)
Sonoran	120,000 sq miles	(311,000 sq km)
Kalahari	120,000 sq miles	(310,800 sq km)
Kara Kum	115,800 sq miles	(300,000 sq km)
Takla Makan	100,400 sq miles	(260,000 sq km)
Namib	52,100 sq miles	(135,000 sq km)
Thar	33,670 sq miles	(130,000 sq km)

Hottest inhabited places

Djibouti (Djibouti)	86° F	(30 °C)
Timbouctou (Mali)	84.7° F	(29.3 °C)
Tirunelveli (India)		
Tuticorin (India)		
Nellore (India)	84.5° F	(29.2 °C)
Santa Marta (Colombia)		
Aden (Yemen)	84° F	(28.9 °C)
Madurai (India)		
Niamey (Niger)		
Hodeida (Yemen)	83.8° F	(28.8 °C)
Ouagadougou (Burkina)		
Thanjavur (India)		
Tiruchchirappalli (India)		

Driest inhabited places

Aswân (Egypt)	0.02 in	(0.5 mm)
Luxor (Egypt)	0.03 in	(0.7 mm)
Arica (Chile)	0.04 in	(1.1 mm)
Ica (Peru)	0.1 in	(2.3 mm)
Antofagasta (Chile)	0.2 in	(4.9 mm)
El Minya (Egypt)	0.2 in	(5.1 mm)
Asyût (Egypt)	0.2 in	(5.2 mm)
Callao (Peru)	0.5 in	(12.0 mm)
Trujillo (Peru)	0.55 in	(14.0 mm)
El Faiyûm (Egypt)	0.8 in	(19.0 mm)

Wettest inhabited places

Buenaventura (Colombia)	265 in	(6743 mm)
Monrovia (Liberia)	202 in	(5131 mm)
Pago Pago (American Samoa)	196 in	(4990 mm)
Moulmein (Burma)	191 in	(4852 mm)
Lae (Papua New Guinea)	183 in	(4645 mm)
Baguio (Luzon Island, Philippines)	180 in	(4573 mm)
Sylhet (Bangladesh)	176 in	(4457 mm)
Padang (Sumatra, Indonesia)	166 in	(4225 mm)
Bogor (Java, Indonesia)	166 in	(4225 mm)
Conakry (Guinea)	171 in	(4341 mm)

The time zones

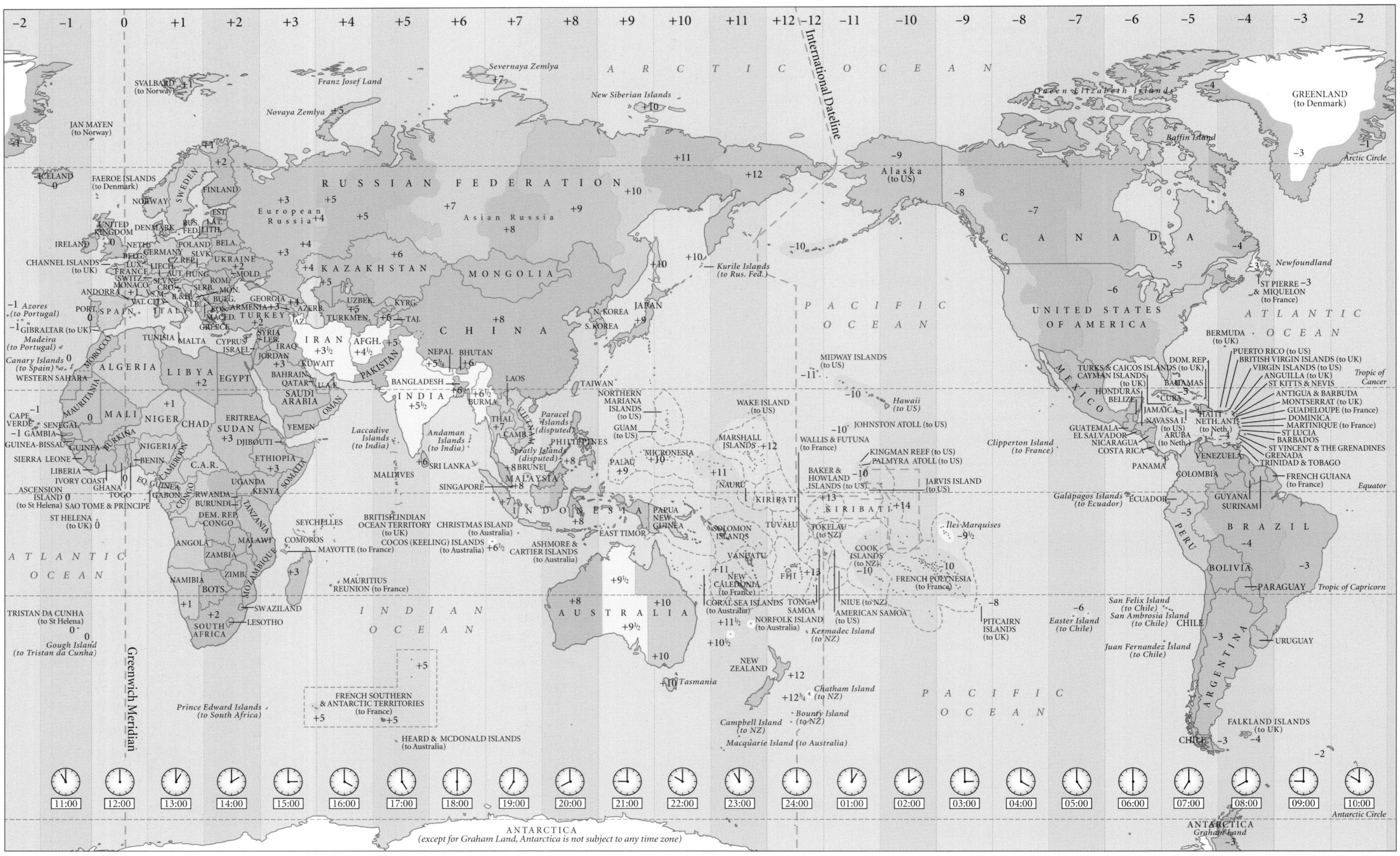

The numbers at the top of the map indicate the number of hours each time zone is ahead or behind Coordinated Universal Time (UTC). The clocks and 24-hour times given at the bottom of the map show the time in each time zone when it is 12:00 hours noon (UTC)

Time Zones

Because Earth is a rotating sphere, the Sun shines on only half of its surface at any one time. Thus, it is simultaneously morning, evening and night time in different parts of the world *(see diagram below)*. Because of these disparities, each country or part of a country adheres to a local time.

A region of Earth's surface within which a single local time is used is called a time zone. There are 24 one hour time zones around the world, arranged roughly in longitudinal bands.

Standard Time

Standard time is the official local time in a particular country or part of a country. It is defined by the time zone or zones associated with that country or region. Although time zones are arranged roughly in longitudinal bands, in many places the borders of a zone do not fall exactly on longitudinal meridians, as can be seen on the map *(above)*, but are determined by geographical factors or by borders between countries or parts of countries. Most countries have just one time zone and one standard time, but some large countries (such as the USA, Canada and Russia) are split between several time zones, so standard time varies across those countries. For example, the coterminous United States straddles four time zones and so has four standard times, called the Eastern, Central, Mountain and Pacific standard times. China is unusual in that just one standard time is used for the whole country, even though it extends across 60° of longitude from west to east.

Day and night around the world

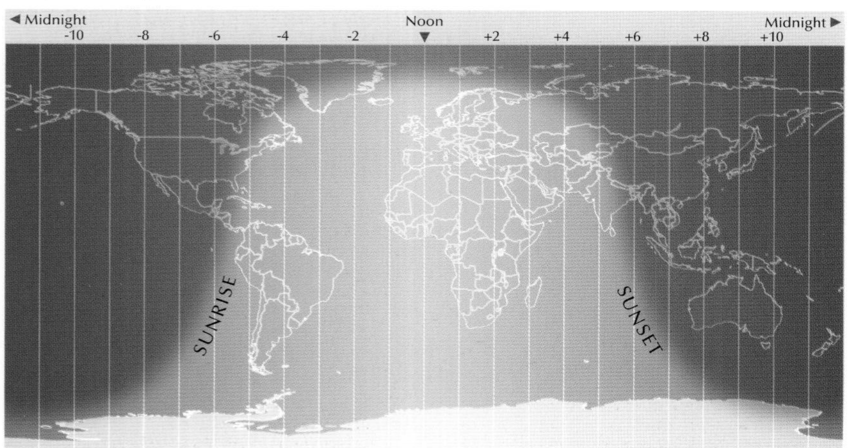
◀ Midnight
-10
-8
-6
-4
-2
Noon
+2
+4
+6
+8
Midnight ▶
+10
SUNRISE
SUNSET

Coordinated Universal Time (UTC)

Coordinated Universal Time (UTC) is a reference by which the local time in each time zone is set. For example, Australian Western Standard Time (the local time in Western Australia) is set 8 hours ahead of UTC (it is UTC+8) whereas Eastern Standard Time in the United States is set 5 hours behind UTC (it is UTC-5). UTC is a successor to, and closely approximates, Greenwich Mean Time (GMT). However, UTC is based on an atomic clock, whereas GMT is determined by the Sun's position in the sky relative to the 0° longitudinal meridian, which runs through Greenwich, UK.

The International Dateline

The International Dateline is an imaginary line from pole to pole that roughly corresponds to the 180° longitudinal meridian. It is an arbitrary marker between calendar days. The dateline is needed because of the use of local times around the world rather than a single universal time. When moving from west to east across the dateline, travellers have to set their watches back one day. Those travelling in the opposite direction, from east to west, must add a day.

Daylight Saving Time

Daylight saving is a summertime adjustment to the local time in a country or region, designed to cause a higher proportion of its citizens' waking hours to pass during daylight. To follow the system, timepieces are advanced by an hour on a pre-decided date in spring and reverted back in autumn. About half of the world's nations use daylight saving.

Countries of the World

There are currently 195 independent countries in the world – more than at any previous time – and 59 dependencies. Antarctica is the only land area on Earth that is not officially part of, and does not belong to, any single country.

In 1950, the world comprised 82 countries. In the decades following, many more states came into being as they achieved independence from their former colonial rulers. Most recent additions were caused by the breakup of the former Soviet Union in 1991, and the former Yugoslavia in 1992, which swelled the ranks of independent states. In February 2008, Kosovo became the latest country to be formed by controversially declaring independence from Serbia.

Country factfile key

Formation Date of independence / date current borders were established

Population Total population / population density – based on total *land* area / percentage of urban-based population

Languages An asterisk (*) denotes the official language(s)

Calorie consumption Average number of calories consumed daily per person

AFGHANISTAN
Central Asia

Official name The Islamic Republic of Afghanistan
Formation 1919 / 1919
Capital Kabul
Population 32.3 million / 128 people per sq mile (50 people per sq km) / 24%
Total area 250,000 sq. miles (647,500 sq. km)
Languages Pashtu*, Tajik, Dari*, Farsi, Uzbek, Turkmen
Religions Sunni Muslim 84%, Shi'a Muslim 15%, Other 1%
Ethnic mix Pashtun 38%, Tajik 25%, Hazara 19%, Uzbek and Turkmen 15%, Other 3%
Government Presidential system
Currency Afghani = 100 puls
Literacy rate 28%
Calorie consumption 1539 calories

ALBANIA
Southeast Europe

Official name Republic of Albania
Formation 1912 / 1921
Capital Tirana
Population 3.2 million / 302 people per sq mile (117 people per sq km) / 44%
Total area 11,100 sq. miles (28,748 sq. km)
Languages Albanian*, Greek
Religions Sunni Muslim 70%, Orthodox Christian 20%, Roman Catholic 10%
Ethnic mix Albanian 93%, Greek 5%, Other 2%
Government Parliamentary system
Currency Lek = 100 qindarka (qintars)
Literacy rate 99%
Calorie consumption 2848 calories

ALGERIA
North Africa

Official name People's Democratic Republic of Algeria
Formation 1962 / 1962
Capital Algiers
Population 33.9 million / 37 people per sq mile (14 people per sq km) / 59%
Total area 919,590 sq. miles (2,381,740 sq. km)
Languages Arabic*, Tamazight (Kabyle, Shawia, Tamashek), French
Religions Sunni Muslim 99%, Christian and Jewish 1%
Ethnic mix Arab 75%, Berber 24%, European and Jewish 1%
Government Presidential system
Currency Algerian dinar = 100 centimes
Literacy rate 70%
Calorie consumption 3022 calories

ANDORRA
Southwest Europe

Official name Principality of Andorra
Formation 1278 / 1278
Capital Andorra la Vella
Population 71,822 / 399 people per sq mile (154 people per sq km) / 91%
Total area 181 sq. miles (468 sq. km)
Languages Spanish, Catalan*, French, Portuguese
Religions Roman Catholic 94%, Other 6%
Ethnic mix Spanish 46%, Andorran 28%, Other 18%, French 8%
Government Parliamentary system
Currency Euro = 100 cents
Literacy rate 99%
Calorie consumption Not available

ANGOLA
Southern Africa

Official name Republic of Angola
Formation 1975 / 1975
Capital Luanda
Population 16.9 million / 35 people per sq mile (14 people per sq km) / 36%
Total area 481,351 sq. miles (1,246,700 sq. km)
Languages Portuguese*, Umbundu, Kimbundu, Kikongo
Religions Roman Catholic 50%, Other 30%, Protestant 20%
Ethnic mix Ovimbundu 37%, Other 25%, Kimbundu 25%, Bakongo 13%
Government Presidential system
Currency Readjusted kwanza = 100 lwei
Literacy rate 67%
Calorie consumption 2083 calories

ANTIGUA & BARBUDA
West Indies

Official name Antigua and Barbuda
Formation 1981 / 1981
Capital St. John's
Population 69,481 / 409 people per sq mile (158 people per sq km) / 38%
Total area 170 sq. miles (442 sq. km)
Languages English*, English patois
Religions Anglican 45%, Other Protestant 42%, Roman Catholic 10%, Other 2%, Rastafarian 1%
Ethnic mix Black African 95%, Other 5%
Government Parliamentary system
Currency Eastern Caribbean dollar = 100 cents
Literacy rate 86%
Calorie consumption 2349 calories

ARGENTINA
South America

Official name The Argentine Republic
Formation 1816 / 1816
Capital Buenos Aires
Population 39.5 million / 37 people per sq mile (14 people per sq km) / 90%
Total area 1,068,296 sq. miles (2,766,890 sq. km)
Languages Spanish*, Italian, Amerindian languages
Religions Roman Catholic 90%, Other 6%, Protestant 2%, Jewish 2%
Ethnic mix Indo-European 83%, Mestizo 14%, Jewish 2%, Amerindian 1%
Government Presidential system
Currency new Argentine peso = 100 centavos
Literacy rate 97%
Calorie consumption 2992 calories

ARMENIA
Southwest Asia

Official name Republic of Armenia
Formation 1991 / 1991
Capital Yerevan
Population 3 million / 261 people per sq mile (101 people per sq km) / 64%
Total area 11,506 sq. miles (29,800 sq. km)
Languages Armenian*, Azeri, Russian
Religions Armenian Apostolic Church (Orthodox) 88%, Other 6%, Armenian Catholic Church 6%
Ethnic mix Armenian 98%, Other 1%, Yezidi 1%
Government Parliamentary system
Currency Dram = 100 luma
Literacy rate 99%
Calorie consumption 2268 calories

AUSTRALIA
Australasia & Oceania

Official name Commonwealth of Australia
Formation 1901 / 1901
Capital Canberra
Population 20.9 million / 7 people per sq mile (3 people per sq km) / 92%
Total area 2,967,893 sq. miles (7,686,850 sq. km)
Languages English*, Italian, Cantonese, Greek, Arabic, Vietnamese, Aboriginal languages
Religions Roman Catholic 26%, Anglican 24%, Other 23%, Nonreligious 13%, United Church 8%, Other Protestant 6%
Ethnic mix European 92%, Asian 5%, Aboriginal 2%, Other 1%
Government Parliamentary system
Currency Australian dollar = 100 cents
Literacy rate 99%
Calorie consumption 3054 calories

AUSTRIA
Central Europe

Official name Republic of Austria
Formation 1918 / 1919
Capital Vienna
Population 8.2 million / 257 people per sq mile (99 people per sq km) / 66%
Total area 32,378 sq. miles (83,858 sq. km)
Languages German*, Croatian, Slovenian, Hungarian (Magyar)
Religions Roman Catholic 78%, Nonreligious 9%, Other (including Jewish and Muslim) 8%, Protestant 5%
Ethnic mix Austrian 93%, Croat, Slovene, and Hungarian 6%, Other 1%
Government Parliamentary system
Currency Euro = 100 cents
Literacy rate 99%
Calorie consumption 3673 calories

AZERBAIJAN
Southwest Asia

Official name Republic of Azerbaijan
Formation 1991 / 1991
Capital Baku
Population 8.5 million / 254 people per sq mile (98 people per sq km) / 50%
Total area 33,436 sq. miles (86,600 sq. km)
Languages Azeri*, Russian
Religions Shi'a Muslim 68%, Sunni Muslim 26%, Russian Orthodox 3%, Armenian Apostolic Church (Orthodox) 2%, Other 1%
Ethnic mix Azeri 91%, Other 3%, Lazs 2%, Armenian 2%, Russian 2%
Government Presidential system
Currency New manat = 100 gopik
Literacy rate 99%
Calorie consumption 2575 calories

BAHAMAS
West Indies

Official name Commonwealth of the Bahamas
Formation 1973 / 1973
Capital Nassau
Population 305,655 / 79 people per sq mile (31 people per sq km) / 90%
Total area 5382 sq. miles (13,940 sq. km)
Languages English*, English Creole, French Creole
Religions Baptist 32%, Anglican 20%, Roman Catholic 19%, Other 17%, Methodist 6%, Church of God 6%
Ethnic mix Black African 85%, Other 15%
Government Parliamentary system
Currency Bahamian dollar = 100 cents
Literacy rate 96%
Calorie consumption 2755 calories

BAHRAIN
Southwest Asia

Official name Kingdom of Bahrain
Formation 1971 / 1971
Capital Manama
Population 708,573 / 2596 people per sq mile (1004 people per sq km) / 90%
Total area 239 sq. miles (620 sq. km)
Languages Arabic
Religions Muslim (mainly Shi'a) 99%, Other 1%
Ethnic mix Bahraini 70%, Iranian, Indian, and Pakistani 24%, Other Arab 4%, European 2%
Government Mixed monarchical–parliamentary system
Currency Bahraini dinar = 1000 fils
Literacy rate 87%
Calorie consumption Not available

BANGLADESH
South Asia

Official name People's Republic of Bangladesh
Formation 1971 / 1971
Capital Dhaka
Population 147 million / 2845 people per sq mile (1098 people per sq km) / 25%
Total area 55,598 sq. miles (144,000 sq. km)
Languages Bengali*, Urdu, Chakma, Marma (Magh), Garo, Khasi, Santhali, Tripuri, Mro
Religions Muslim (mainly Sunni) 87%, Hindu 12%, Other 1%
Ethnic mix Bengali 98%, Other 2%
Government Transitional regime
Currency Taka = 100 poisha
Literacy rate 41%
Calorie consumption 2205 calories

BARBADOS
West Indies

Official name Barbados
Formation 1966 / 1966
Capital Bridgetown
Population 280,946 / 1692 people per sq mile (653 people per sq km) / 52%
Total area 166 sq. miles (430 sq. km)
Languages English*, Bajan (Barbadian English)
Religions Anglican 40%, Other 24%, Nonreligious 17%, Pentecostal 8%, Methodist 7%, Roman Catholic 4%
Ethnic mix Black African 92%, White 3%, Other 3%, Mixed race 2%
Government Parliamentary system
Currency Barbados dollar = 100 cents
Literacy rate 99%
Calorie consumption 3091 calories

BELARUS
Eastern Europe

Official name Republic of Belarus
Formation 1991 / 1991
Capital Minsk
Population 9.6 million / 120 people per sq mile (46 people per sq km) / 71%
Total area 80,154 sq. miles (207,600 sq. km)
Languages Belorussian*, Russian*
Religions Orthodox Christian 60%, Other 32%, Roman Catholic 8%
Ethnic mix Belorussian 81%, Russian 11%, Polish 4%, Other 2%, Ukrainian 2%
Government Presidential system
Currency Belorussian rouble = 100 kopeks
Literacy rate 99%
Calorie consumption 3000 calories

BELGIUM
Northwest Europe

Official name Kingdom of Belgium
Formation 1830 / 1919
Capital Brussels
Population 10.5 million / 829 people per sq mile (320 people per sq km) / 97%
Total area 11,780 sq. miles (30,510 sq. km)
Languages Dutch*, French*, German*
Religions Roman Catholic 88%, Other 10%, Muslim 2%
Ethnic mix Fleming 58%, Walloon 33%, Other 6%, Italian 2%, Moroccan 1%
Government Parliamentary system
Currency Euro = 100 cents
Literacy rate 99%
Calorie consumption 3584 calories

BELIZE
Central America

Official name Belize
Formation 1981 / 1981
Capital Belmopan
Population 294,385 / 33 people per sq mile (13 people per sq km) / 48%
Total area 8867 sq. miles (22,966 sq. km)
Languages English*, English Creole, Spanish, Mayan, Garifuna (Carib)
Religions Roman Catholic 62%, Other 13%, Anglican 12%, Methodist 6%, Mennonite 4%, Seventh-day Adventist 3%
Ethnic mix Mestizo 49%, Creole 25%, Maya 11%, Other 6%, Garifuna 6%, Asian Indian 3%
Government Parliamentary system
Currency Belizean dollar = 100 cents
Literacy rate 75%
Calorie consumption 2869 calories

BENIN
West Africa

Official name Republic of Benin
Formation 1960 / 1960
Capital Porto-Novo
Population 9 million / 211 people per sq mile (81 people per sq km) / 45%
Total area 43,483 sq. miles (112,620 sq. km)
Languages French*, Fon, Bariba, Yoruba, Adja, Houeda, Somba
Religions Voodoo 50%, Muslim 30%, Christian 20%
Ethnic mix Fon 41%, Other 21%, Adja 16%, Yoruba 12%, Bariba 10%
Government Presidential system
Currency CFA franc = 100 centimes
Literacy rate 35%
Calorie consumption 2548 calories

BHUTAN
South Asia

Official name Kingdom of Bhutan
Formation 1656 / 1865
Capital Thimphu
Population 2.3 million / 127 people per sq mile (49 people per sq km) / 9%
Total area 18,147 sq. miles (47,000 sq. km)
Languages Dzongkha*, Nepali, Assamese
Religions Mahayana Buddhist 70%, Hindu 24%, Other 6%
Ethnic mix Bhute 50%, Other 25%, Nepalese 25%
Government Mixed monarchical–parliamentary system
Currency Ngultrum = 100 chetrum
Literacy rate 47%
Calorie consumption Not available

BOLIVIA
South America

Official name Republic of Bolivia
Formation 1825 / 1938
Capital La Paz (administrative); Sucre (judicial)
Population 9.5 million / 23 people per sq mile (9 people per sq km) / 64%
Total area 424,162 sq. miles (1,098,580 sq. km)
Languages Aymara*, Quechua*, Spanish*
Religions Roman Catholic 93%, Other 7%
Ethnic mix Quechua 37%, Aymara 32%, Mixed race 13%, European 10%, Other 8%
Government Presidential system
Currency Boliviano = 100 centavos
Literacy rate 87%
Calorie consumption 2235 calories

BOSNIA & HERZEGOVINA
Southeast Europe

Official name Bosnia and Herzegovina
Formation 1992 / 1992
Capital Sarajevo
Population 3.9 million / 198 people per sq mile (76 people per sq km) / 45%
Total area 19,741 sq. miles (51,129 sq. km)
Languages Bosnian*, Croatian*, Serbian*
Religions Muslim (mainly Sunni) 40%, Orthodox Christian 31%, Roman Catholic 15%, Other 10%, Protestant 4%
Ethnic mix Bosniak 44%, Serb 31%, Croat 17%, Other 8%
Government Parliamentary system
Currency Marka = 100 pfeninga
Literacy rate 97%
Calorie consumption 2894 calories

BOTSWANA
Southern Africa

Official name Republic of Botswana
Formation 1966 / 1966
Capital Gaborone
Population 1.8 million / 8 people per sq mile (3 people per sq km) / 52%
Total area 231,803 sq. miles (600,370 sq. km)
Languages English*, Setswana, Shona, San, Khoikhoi, isiNdebele
Religions Traditional beliefs 50%, Christian (mainly Protestant) 30%, Other (including Muslim) 20%
Ethnic mix Tswana 98%, Other 2%
Government Presidential system
Currency Pula = 100 thebe
Literacy rate 81%
Calorie consumption 2151 calories

BRAZIL
South America

Official name Federative Republic of Brazil
Formation 1822 / 1828
Capital Brasília
Population 191 million / 59 people per sq mile (23 people per sq km) / 84%
Total area 3,286,470 sq. miles (8,511,965 sq. km)
Languages Portuguese*, German, Italian, Spanish, Polish, Japanese, Amerindian languages
Religions Roman Catholic 74%, Protestant 15%, Atheist 7%, Other 4%
Ethnic mix White 54%, Mixed race 38%, Black 6%, Other 2%
Government Presidential system
Currency Real = 100 centavos
Literacy rate 89%
Calorie consumption 3049 calories

BRUNEI
Southeast Asia

Official name Brunei Darussalam
Formation 1984 / 1984
Capital Bandar Seri Begawan
Population 374,577 / 184 people per sq mile (71 people per sq km) / 77%
Total area 2228 sq. miles (5770 sq. km)
Languages Malay*, English, Chinese
Religions Muslim (mainly Sunni) 66%, Buddhist 14%, Other 10%, Christian 10%
Ethnic mix Malay 67%, Chinese 16%, Other 11%, Indigenous 6%
Government Monarchy
Currency Brunei dollar = 100 cents
Literacy rate 93%
Calorie consumption 2855 calories

BULGARIA
Southeast Europe

Official name Republic of Bulgaria
Formation 1908 / 1947
Capital Sofia
Population 7.6 million / 178 people per sq mile (69 people per sq km) / 70%
Total area 42,822 sq. miles (110,910 sq. km)
Languages Bulgarian*, Turkish, Romani
Religions Orthodox Christian 83%, Muslim 12%, Other 4%, Roman Catholic 1%
Ethnic mix Bulgarian 84%, Turkish 9%, Roma 5%, Other 2%
Government Parliamentary system
Currency Lev = 100 stotinki
Literacy rate 98%
Calorie consumption 2848 calories

BURKINA
West Africa

Official name Burkina Faso
Formation 1960 / 1960
Capital Ouagadougou
Population 14 million / 132 people per sq mile (51 people per sq km) / 18%
Total area 105,869 sq. miles (274,200 sq. km)
Languages French*, Mossi, Fulani, Tuareg, Dyula, Songhai
Religions Muslim 55%, Traditional beliefs 35%, Roman Catholic 9%, Other Christian 1%
Ethnic mix Mossi 48%, Other 21%, Peul 10%, Lobi 7%, Bobo 7%, Mandé 7%
Government Presidential system
Currency CFA franc = 100 centimes
Literacy rate 22%
Calorie consumption 2462 calories

BURMA (MYANMAR)
Southeast Asia

Official name Union of Myanmar
Formation 1948 / 1948
Capital Nay Pyi Taw
Population 51.5 million / 203 people per sq mile (78 people per sq km) / 30%
Total area 261,969 sq. miles (678,500 sq. km)
Languages Burmese*, Shan, Karen, Rakhine, Chin, Yangbye, Kachin, Mon
Religions Buddhist 87%, Christian 6%, Muslim 4%, Other 2%, Hindu 1%
Ethnic mix Burman (Bamah) 68%, Other 13%, Shan 9%, Karen 6%, Rakhine 4%
Government Military-based regime
Currency Kyat = 100 pyas
Literacy rate 90%
Calorie consumption 2937 calories

BURUNDI
Central Africa

Official name Republic of Burundi
Formation 1962 / 1962
Capital Bujumbura
Population 8.1 million / 818 people per sq mile (316 people per sq km) / 10%
Total area 10,745 sq. miles (27,830 sq. km)
Languages Kirundi*, French*, Kiswahili
Religions Christian (mainly Roman Catholic) 60%, Traditional beliefs 39%, Muslim 1%
Ethnic mix Hutu 85%, Tutsi 14%, Twa 1%
Government Presidential system
Currency Burundian franc = 100 centimes
Literacy rate 59%
Calorie consumption 1649 calories

CAMBODIA
Southeast Asia

Official name Kingdom of Cambodia
Formation 1953 / 1953
Capital Phnom Penh
Population 14.6 million / 214 people per sq mile (83 people per sq km) / 19%
Total area 69,900 sq. miles (181,040 sq. km)
Languages Khmer*, French, Chinese, Vietnamese, Cham
Religions Buddhist 93%, Muslim 6%, Christian 1%
Ethnic mix Khmer 90%, Other 5%, Vietnamese 4%, Chinese 1%
Government Parliamentary system
Currency Riel = 100 sen
Literacy rate 74%
Calorie consumption 2046 calories

CAMEROON
Central Africa

Official name Republic of Cameroon
Formation 1960 / 1961
Capital Yaoundé
Population 16.3 million / 94 people per sq mile (36 people per sq km) / 52%
Total area 183,567 sq. miles (475,400 sq. km)
Languages English*, French*, Bamileke, Fang, Fulani
Religions Roman Catholic 35%, Traditional beliefs 25%, Muslim 22%, Protestant 18%
Ethnic mix Cameroon highlanders 31%, Other 21%, Equatorial Bantu 19%, Kirdi 11%, Fulani 10%, Northwestern Bantu 8%
Government Presidential system
Currency CFA franc = 100 centimes
Literacy rate 68%
Calorie consumption 2273 calories

CANADA
North America

Official name Canada
Formation 1867 / 1949
Capital Ottawa
Population 32.9 million / 9 people per sq mile (4 people per sq km) / 81%
Total area 3,854,085 sq. miles (9,984,670 sq. km)
Languages English*, French*, Chinese, Italian, German, Ukrainian, Portuguese, Inuktitut, Cree
Religions Roman Catholic 44%, Protestant 29%, Other and nonreligious 27%
Government Parliamentary system
Currency Canadian dollar = 100 cents
Literacy rate 99%
Calorie consumption 3589 calories

CAPE VERDE
Atlantic Ocean

Official name Republic of Cape Verde
Formation 1975 / 1975
Capital Praia
Population 423,613 / 272 people per sq mile (105 people per sq km) / 57%
Total area 1557 sq. miles (4033 sq. km)
Languages Portuguese*, Portuguese Creole
Religions Roman Catholic 97%, Other 2%, Protestant (Church of the Nazarene) 1%
Ethnic mix Mestiço 60%, African 30%, Other 10%
Government Mixed presidential–parliamentary system
Currency Cape Verde escudo = 100 centavos
Literacy rate 76%
Calorie consumption 3243 calories

CENTRAL AFRICAN REPUBLIC
Central Africa

Official name Central African Republic
Formation 1960 / 1960
Capital Bangui
Population 4.2 million / 17 people per sq mile (7 people per sq km) / 43%
Total area 240,534 sq. miles (622,984 sq. km)
Languages French*, Sango, Banda, Gbaya
Religions Traditional beliefs 60%, Christian (mainly Roman Catholic) 35%, Muslim 5%
Ethnic mix Baya 34%, Banda 27%, Mandjia 21%, Sara 10%, Other 8%
Government Presidential system
Currency CFA franc = 100 centimes
Literacy rate 49%
Calorie consumption 1980 calories

CHAD
Central Africa

Official name Republic of Chad
Formation 1960 / 1960
Capital N'Djamena
Population 10.3 million / 21 people per sq mile (8 people per sq km) / 25%
Total area 495,752 sq. miles (1,284,000 sq. km)
Languages Arabic*, French*, Sara, Maba
Religions Muslim 55%, Traditional beliefs 35%, Christian 10%
Ethnic mix Other 30%, Sara 28%, Mayo-Kebbi 12%, Arab 12%, Ouaddai 9%, Kanem-Bornou 9%
Government Presidential system
Currency CFA franc = 100 centimes
Literacy rate 26%
Calorie consumption 2114 calories

CHILE
South America

Official name Republic of Chile
Formation 1818 / 1883
Capital Santiago
Population 16.6 million / 57 people per sq mile (22 people per sq km) / 87%
Total area 292,258 sq. miles (756,950 sq. km)
Languages Spanish*, Amerindian languages
Religions Roman Catholic 80%, Other and nonreligious 20%
Ethnic mix Mixed race and European 90%, Other Amerindian 9%, Mapuche 1%
Government Presidential system
Currency Chilean peso = 100 centavos
Literacy rate 96%
Calorie consumption 2863 calories

CHINA
East Asia

Official name People's Republic of China
Formation 960 / 1999
Capital Beijing
Population 1.33 billion / 370 people per sq mile (143 people per sq km) / 40%
Total area 3,705,386 sq. miles (9,596,960 sq. km)
Languages Mandarin*, Wu, Cantonese, Hsiang, Min, Hakka, Kan
Religions Nonreligious 59%, Traditional beliefs 20%, Other 13%, Buddhist 6%, Muslim 2%
Ethnic mix Han 92%, Other 4%, Hui 1%, Miao 1%, Manchu 1%, Zhuang 1%
Government One-party state
Currency Renminbi (known as yuan) = 10 jiao = 100 fen
Literacy rate 91%
Calorie consumption 2951 calories

COLOMBIA
South America

Official name Republic of Colombia
Formation 1819 / 1903
Capital Bogotá
Population 47 million / 117 people per sq mile (45 people per sq km) / 77%
Total area 439,733 sq. miles (1,138,910 sq. km)
Languages Spanish*, Wayuu, Páez, and other Amerindian languages
Religions Roman Catholic 95%, Other 5%
Ethnic mix Mestizo 58%, White 20%, European–African 14%, African 4%, African–Amerindian 3%, Amerindian 1%
Government Presidential system
Currency Colombian peso = 100 centavos
Literacy rate 93%
Calorie consumption 2585 calories

COMOROS
Indian Ocean

Official name Union of the Comoros
Formation 1975 / 1975
Capital Moroni
Population 711,417 / 826 people per sq mile (319 people per sq km) / 36%
Total area 838 sq. miles (2170 sq. km)
Languages Arabic*, Comoran*, French*
Religions Muslim (mainly Sunni) 98%, Other 1%, Roman Catholic 1%
Ethnic mix Comoran 97%, Other 3%
Government Presidential system
Currency Comoros franc = 100 centimes
Literacy rate 56%
Calorie consumption 1754 calories

CONGO
Central Africa

Official name Republic of the Congo
Formation 1960 / 1960
Capital Brazzaville
Population 4.2 million / 32 people per sq mile (12 people per sq km) / 54%
Total area 132,046 sq. miles (342,000 sq. km)
Languages French*, Kongo, Teke, Lingala
Religions Traditional beliefs 50%, Roman Catholic 25%, Protestant 23%, Muslim 2%
Ethnic mix Bakongo 51%, Teke 17%, Other 16%, Mbochi 11%, Mbédé 5%
Government Presidential system
Currency CFA franc = 100 centimes
Literacy rate 83%
Calorie consumption 2162 calories

CONGO, DEM. REP.
Central Africa

Official name Democratic Republic of the Congo
Formation 1960 / 1960
Capital Kinshasa
Population 61.2 million / 70 people per sq mile (27 people per sq km) / 33%
Total area 905,563 sq. miles (2,345,410 sq. km)
Languages French*, Kiswahili, Tshiluba, Kikongo, Lingala
Religions Roman Catholic 50%, Protestant 20%, Traditional beliefs and other 10%, Muslim 10%, Kimbanguist 10%
Ethnic mix Other 55%, Mongo, Luba, Kongo, and Mangbetu-Azande 45%
Government Presidential system
Currency Congolese franc = 100 centimes
Literacy rate 67%
Calorie consumption 1599 calories

COSTA RICA
Central America

Official name Republic of Costa Rica
Formation 1838 / 1838
Capital San José
Population 4.5 million / 228 people per sq mile (88 people per sq km) / 61%
Total area 19,730 sq. miles (51,100 sq. km)
Languages Spanish*, English Creole, Bribri, Cabecar
Religions Roman Catholic 76%, Other (including Protestant) 24%
Ethnic mix Mestizo and European 96%, Black 2%, Chinese 1%, Amerindian 1%
Government Presidential system
Currency Costa Rican colón = 100 céntimos
Literacy rate 95%
Calorie consumption 2876 calories

CROATIA
Southeast Europe

Official name Republic of Croatia
Formation 1991 / 1991
Capital Zagreb
Population 4.6 million / 211 people per sq mile (81 people per sq km) / 59%
Total area 21,831 sq. miles (56,542 sq. km)
Languages Croatian*
Religions Roman Catholic 88%, Other 7%, Orthodox Christian 4%, Muslim 1%
Ethnic mix Croat 90%, Other 5%, Serb 5%
Government Parliamentary system
Currency Kuna = 100 lipa
Literacy rate 98%
Calorie consumption 2799 calories

CUBA
West Indies

Official name Republic of Cuba
Formation 1902 / 1902
Capital Havana
Population 11.3 million / 264 people per sq mile (102 people per sq km) / 76%
Total area 42,803 sq. miles (110,860 sq. km)
Languages Spanish
Religions Nonreligious 49%, Roman Catholic 40%, Atheist 6%, Other 4%, Protestant 1%
Ethnic mix White 66%, European–African 22%, Black 12%
Government One-party state
Currency Cuban peso = 100 centavos
Literacy rate 99%
Calorie consumption 3152 calories

CYPRUS
Southeast Europe

Official name Republic of Cyprus
Formation 1960 / 1960
Capital Nicosia
Population 788,457 / 221 people per sq mile (85 people per sq km) / 69%
Total area 3571 sq. miles (9250 sq. km)
Languages Greek*, Turkish*
Religions Orthodox Christian 78%, Muslim 18%, Other 4%
Ethnic mix Greek 81%, Turkish 11%, Other 8%
Government Presidential system
Currency Euro (Turkish lira in TRNC) = 100 cents (euro); 100 kurus (Turkish lira)
Literacy rate 97%
Calorie consumption 3255 calories

CZECH REPUBLIC
Central Europe

Official name Czech Republic
Formation 1993 / 1993
Capital Prague
Population 10.2 million / 335 people per sq mile (129 people per sq km) / 74%
Total area 30,450 sq. miles (78,866 sq. km)
Languages Czech*, Slovak, Hungarian (Magyar)
Religions Roman Catholic 39%, Atheist 38%, Other 18%, Protestant 3%, Hussite 2%
Ethnic mix Czech 90%, Other 4%, Moravian 4%, Slovak 2%
Government Parliamentary system
Currency Czech koruna = 100 haleru
Literacy rate 99%
Calorie consumption 3171 calories

DENMARK
Northern Europe

Official name Kingdom of Denmark
Formation 950 / 1944
Capital Copenhagen
Population 5.5 million / 336 people per sq mile (130 people per sq km) / 85%
Total area 16,639 sq. miles (43,094 sq. km)
Languages Danish
Religions Evangelical Lutheran 89%, Other 10%, Roman Catholic 1%
Ethnic mix Danish 96%, Other (including Scandinavian and Turkish) 3%, Faeroese and Inuit 1%
Government Parliamentary system
Currency Danish krone = 100 øre
Literacy rate 99%
Calorie consumption 3439 calories

DJIBOUTI
East Africa

Official name Republic of Djibouti
Formation 1977 / 1977
Capital Djibouti
Population 496,374 / 55 people per sq mile (21 people per sq km) / 84%
Total area 8494 sq. miles (22,000 sq. km)
Languages Arabic*, French*, Somali, Afar
Religions Muslim (mainly Sunni) 94%, Christian 6%
Ethnic mix Issa 60%, Afar 35%, Other 5%
Government Presidential system
Currency Djibouti franc = 100 centimes
Literacy rate 66%
Calorie consumption 2220 calories

DOMINICA
West Indies

Official name Commonwealth of Dominica
Formation 1978 / 1978
Capital Roseau
Population 72,386 / 250 people per sq mile (97 people per sq km) / 72%
Total area 291 sq. miles (754 sq. km)
Languages English*, French Creole
Religions Roman Catholic 77%, Protestant 15%, Other 8%
Ethnic mix Black 87%, Mixed race 9%, Carib 3%, Other 1%
Government Parliamentary system
Currency Eastern Caribbean dollar = 100 cents
Literacy rate 88%
Calorie consumption 2763 calories

DOMINICAN REPUBLIC
West Indies

Official name Dominican Republic
Formation 1865 / 1865
Capital Santo Domingo
Population 9.1 million / 487 people per sq mile (188 people per sq km) / 60%
Total area 18,679 sq. miles (48,380 sq. km)
Languages Spanish*, French Creole
Religions Roman Catholic 92%, Other and nonreligious 8%
Ethnic mix Mixed race 75%, White 15%, Black 10%
Government Presidential system
Currency Dominican Republic peso = 100 centavos
Literacy rate 87%
Calorie consumption 2347 calories

EAST TIMOR
Southeast Asia

Official name Democratic Republic of Timor-Leste
Formation 2002 / 2002
Capital Dili
Population 1.1 million / 192 people per sq mile (74 people per sq km) / 8%
Total area 5756 sq. miles (14,874 sq. km)
Languages Tetum (Portuguese/Austronesian)*, Bahasa Indonesia, and Portuguese*
Religions Roman Catholic 95%, Other (including Muslim and Protestant) 5%
Government Parliamentary system
Currency US dollar = 100 cents
Literacy rate 59%
Calorie consumption 2806 calories

ECUADOR
South America

Official name Republic of Ecuador
Formation 1830 / 1942
Capital Quito
Population 13.6 million / 127 people per sq mile (49 people per sq km) / 62%
Total area 109,483 sq. miles (283,560 sq. km)
Languages Spanish*, Quechua, other Amerindian languages
Religions Roman Catholic 93%, Protestant, Jewish, and other 7%
Ethnic mix Mestizo 55%, Amerindian 25%, White 10%, Black 10%
Government Presidential system
Currency US dollar = 100 cents
Literacy rate 91%
Calorie consumption 2754 calories

EGYPT
North Africa

Official name Arab Republic of Egypt
Formation 1936 / 1982
Capital Cairo
Population 76.9 million / 200 people per sq mile (77 people per sq km) / 42%
Total area 386,660 sq. miles (1,001,450 sq. km)
Languages Arabic*, French, English, Berber
Religions Muslim (mainly Sunni) 94%, Coptic Christian and other 6%
Ethnic mix Egyptian 99%, Nubian, Armenian, Greek, and Berber 1%
Government Presidential system
Currency Egyptian pound = 100 piastres
Literacy rate 71%
Calorie consumption 3338 calories

EL SALVADOR
Central America

Official name Republic of El Salvador
Formation 1841 / 1841
Capital San Salvador
Population 7.1 million / 888 people per sq mile (343 people per sq km) / 60%
Total area 8124 sq. miles (21,040 sq. km)
Languages Spanish
Religions Roman Catholic 80%, Evangelical 18%, Other 2%
Ethnic mix Mestizo 94%, Amerindian 5%, White 1%
Government Presidential system
Currency Salvadorean colón & US dollar = 100 centavos (colón); 100 cents (US dollar)
Literacy rate 80%
Calorie consumption 2584 calories

EQUATORIAL GUINEA
Central Africa

Official name Republic of Equatorial Guinea
Formation 1968 / 1968
Capital Malabo
Population 551,201 / 51 people per sq mile (20 people per sq km) / 49%
Total area 10,830 sq. miles (28,051 sq. km)
Languages French*, Spanish*, Fang, Bubi
Religions Roman Catholic 90%, Other 10%
Ethnic mix Fang 85%, Other 11%, Bubi 4%
Government Presidential system
Currency CFA franc = 100 centimes
Literacy rate 87%
Calorie consumption Not available

ERITREA
East Africa

Official name State of Eritrea
Formation 1993 / 2002
Capital Asmera
Population 4.7 million / 104 people per sq mile (40 people per sq km) / 20%
Total area 46,842 sq. miles (121,320 sq. km)
Languages Tigrinya*, English*, Tigre, Afar, Arabic*, Bilen, Kunama, Nara, Saho, Hadareb
Religions Christian 45%, Muslim 45%, Other 10%
Ethnic mix Tigray 50%, Tigray and Kunama 40%, Afar 4%, Other 3%, Saho 3%
Government Transitional regime
Currency Nakfa = 100 cents
Literacy rate 57%
Calorie consumption 1513 calories

ESTONIA
Northeast Europe

Official name Republic of Estonia
Formation 1991 / 1991
Capital Tallinn
Population 1.3 million / 75 people per sq mile (29 people per sq km) / 70%
Total area 17,462 sq. miles (45,226 sq. km)
Languages Estonian*, Russian
Religions Evangelical Lutheran 56%, Orthodox Christian 25%, Other 19%
Ethnic mix Estonian 68%, Russian 26%, Other 4%, Ukrainian 2%
Government Parliamentary system
Currency Kroon = 100 senti
Literacy rate 99%
Calorie consumption 3002 calories

ETHIOPIA
East Africa

Official name Federal Democratic Republic of Ethiopia
Formation 1896 / 2002
Capital Addis Ababa
Population 81.2 million / 189 people per sq mile (73 people per sq km) / 16%
Total area 435,184 sq. miles (1,127,127 sq. km)
Languages Amharic*, Tigrinya, Galla, Sidamo, Somali, English, Arabic
Religions Orthodox Christian 40%, Muslim 40%, Traditional beliefs 15%, Other 5%
Ethnic mix Oromo 32%, Amhara 30%, Other 22%, Tigrean 6%, Somali 6%, Guragie 4%
Government Parliamentary system
Currency Ethiopian birr = 100 cents
Literacy rate 42%
Calorie consumption 1857 calories

FIJI
Australasia & Oceania

Official name Republic of the Fiji Islands
Formation 1970 / 1970
Capital Suva
Population 918,675 / 130 people per sq mile (50 people per sq km) / 52%
Total area 7054 sq. miles (18,270 sq. km)
Languages Fijian, English*, Hindi, Urdu, Tamil, Telugu
Religions Hindu 38%, Methodist 37%, Roman Catholic 9%, Other 8%, Muslim 8%
Ethnic mix Melanesian 51%, Indian 44%, Other 5%
Government Transitional regime
Currency Fiji dollar = 100 cents
Literacy rate 93%
Calorie consumption 2894 calories

FINLAND
Northern Europe

Official name Republic of Finland
Formation 1917 / 1947
Capital Helsinki
Population 5.3 million / 45 people per sq mile (17 people per sq km) / 61%
Total area 130,127 sq. miles (337,030 sq. km)
Languages Finnish*, Swedish*, Sámi
Religions Evangelical Lutheran 89%, Other 9%, Orthodox Christian 1%, Roman Catholic 1%
Ethnic mix Finnish 93%, Other (including Sámi) 7%
Government Parliamentary system
Currency Euro = 100 cents
Literacy rate 99%
Calorie consumption 3100 calories

FRANCE
Western Europe

Official name French Republic
Formation 987 / 1919
Capital Paris
Population 60.9 million / 287 people per sq mile (111 people per sq km) / 76%
Total area 211,208 sq. miles (547,030 sq. km)
Languages French*, Provençal, German, Breton, Catalan, Basque
Religions Roman Catholic 88%, Muslim 8%, Protestant 2%, Buddhist 1%, Jewish 1%
Ethnic mix French 90%, North African (mainly Algerian) 6%, German (Alsace) 2%, Breton 1%, Other (including Corsicans) 1%
Government Mixed presidential–parliamentary system
Currency Euro = 100 cents
Literacy rate 99%
Calorie consumption 3654 calories

GABON
Central Africa

Official name Gabonese Republic
Formation 1960 / 1960
Capital Libreville
Population 1.4 million / 14 people per sq mile (5 people per sq km) / 84%
Total area 103,346 sq. miles (267,667 sq. km)
Languages Fang, French*, Punu, Sira, Nzebi, Mpongwe
Religions Christian (mainly Roman Catholic) 55%, Traditional beliefs 40%, Other 4%, Muslim 1%
Ethnic mix Fang 26%, Shira-punu 24%, Other 16%, Foreign residents 15%, Nzabi-duma 11%, Mbédé-Teke 8%
Government Presidential system
Currency CFA franc = 100 centimes
Literacy rate 71%
Calorie consumption 2637 calories

GAMBIA
West Africa

Official name Republic of the Gambia
Formation 1965 / 1965
Capital Banjul
Population 1.6 million / 414 people per sq mile (160 people per sq km) / 26%
Total area 4363 sq. miles (11,300 sq. km)
Languages English*, Mandinka, Fulani, Wolof, Jola, Soninke
Religions Sunni Muslim 90%, Christian 9%, Traditional beliefs 1%
Ethnic mix Mandinka 40%, Fulani 19%, Wolof 15%, Jola 11%, Serahuli 9%, Other 6%
Government Presidential system
Currency Dalasi = 100 butut
Literacy rate 38%
Calorie consumption 2273 calories

GEORGIA
Southwest Asia

Official name Georgia
Formation 1991 / 1991
Capital Tbilisi
Population 4.4 million / 164 people per sq mile (63 people per sq km) / 52%
Total area 26,911 sq. miles (69,700 sq. km)
Languages Georgian*, Russian, Azeri, Armenian, Mingrelian, Ossetian, Abkhazian* *(in Abkhazia)*
Religions Georgian Orthodox 65%, Muslim 11%, Russian Orthodox 10%, Armenian Apostolic Church (Orthodox) 8%, Other 6%
Ethnic mix Georgian 84%, Armenian 6%, Azeri 6%, Russian 2%, Other 1%, Ossetian 1%
Government Presidential system
Currency Lari = 100 tetri
Literacy rate 99%
Calorie consumption 2354 calories

GERMANY
Northern Europe

Official name Federal Republic of Germany
Formation 1871 / 1990
Capital Berlin
Population 82.7 million / 613 people per sq mile (237 people per sq km) / 88%
Total area 137,846 sq. miles (357,021 sq. km)
Languages German*, Turkish
Religions Protestant 34%, Roman Catholic 33%, Other 30%, Muslim 3%
Ethnic mix German 92%, Other European 3%, Other 3%, Turkish 2%
Government Parliamentary system
Currency Euro = 100 cents
Literacy rate 99%
Calorie consumption 3496 calories

GHANA
West Africa

Official name Republic of Ghana
Formation 1957 / 1957
Capital Accra
Population 23 million / 259 people per sq mile (100 people per sq km) / 46%
Total area 92,100 sq. miles (238,540 sq. km)
Languages English*, Twi, Fanti, Ewe, Ga, Adangbe, Gurma, Dagomba (Dagbani)
Religions Christian 69%, Muslim 16%, Traditional beliefs 9%, Other 6%
Ethnic mix Akan 49%, Mole-Dagbani 17%, Ewe 13%, Other 9%, Ga and Ga-Adangbe 8%, Guan 4%
Government Presidential system
Currency Cedi = 100 pesewas
Literacy rate 58%
Calorie consumption 2667 calories

GREECE
Southeast Europe

Official name Hellenic Republic
Formation 1829 / 1947
Capital Athens
Population 11.2 million / 222 people per sq mile (86 people per sq km) / 61%
Total area 50,942 sq. miles (131,940 sq. km)
Languages Greek*, Turkish, Macedonian, Albanian
Religions Orthodox Christian 98%, Other 1%, Muslim 1%
Ethnic mix Greek 98%, Other 2%
Government Parliamentary system
Currency Euro = 100 cents
Literacy rate 96%
Calorie consumption 3721 calories

GRENADA
West Indies

Official name Grenada
Formation 1974 / 1974
Capital St. George's
Population 89,971 / 687 people per sq mile (265 people per sq km) / 41%
Total area 131 sq. miles (340 sq. km)
Languages English*, English Creole
Religions Roman Catholic 68%, Anglican 17%, Other 15%
Ethnic mix Black African 82%, Mulatto (mixed race) 13%, East Indian 3%, Other 2%
Government Parliamentary system
Currency Eastern Caribbean dollar = 100 cents
Literacy rate 96%
Calorie consumption 2932 calories

GUATEMALA
Central America

Official name Republic of Guatemala
Formation 1838 / 1838
Capital Guatemala City
Population 13.2 million / 315 people per sq mile (122 people per sq km) / 47%
Total area 42,042 sq. miles (108,890 sq. km)
Languages Spanish*, Quiché, Mam, Cakchiquel, Kekchí
Religions Roman Catholic 65%, Protestant 33%, Other and nonreligious 2%
Ethnic mix Amerindian 60%, Mestizo 30%, Other 10%
Government Presidential system
Currency Quetzal = 100 centavos
Literacy rate 69%
Calorie consumption 2219 calories

GUINEA
West Africa

Official name Republic of Guinea
Formation 1958 / 1958
Capital Conakry
Population 9.8 million / 103 people per sq mile (40 people per sq km) / 36%
Total area 94,925 sq. miles (245,857 sq. km)
Languages French*, Pulaar, Malinke, Soussou
Religions Muslim 65%, Traditional beliefs 33%, Christian 2%
Ethnic mix Peul 39%, Malinké 23%, Other 16%, Soussou 11%, Kissi 6%, Kpellé 5%
Government Presidential system
Currency Guinea franc = 100 centimes
Literacy rate 30%
Calorie consumption 2409 calories

GUINEA-BISSAU
West Africa

Official name Republic of Guinea-Bissau
Formation 1974 / 1974
Capital Bissau
Population 1.7 million / 157 people per sq mile (60 people per sq km) / 35%
Total area 13,946 sq. miles (36,120 sq. km)
Languages Portuguese*, Portuguese Creole, Balante, Fulani, Malinke
Religions Traditional beliefs 52%, Muslim 40%, Christian 8%
Ethnic mix Balante 30%, Fulani 20%, Other 17%, Mandyako 14%, Mandinka 12%, Papel 7%
Government Presidential system
Currency CFA franc = 100 centimes
Literacy rate 40%
Calorie consumption 2024 calories

GUYANA
South America

Official name The Co-operative Republic of Guyana
Formation 1966 / 1966
Capital Georgetown
Population 769,095 / 10 people per sq mile (4 people per sq km) / 38%
Total area 83,000 sq. miles (214,970 sq. km)
Languages English*, English Creole, Hindi, Tamil, Amerindian languages
Religions Christian 57%, Hindu 33%, Muslim 9%, Other 1%
Ethnic mix East Indian 43%, Black African 30%, Mixed race 17%, Amerindian 9%, Other 1%
Government Presidential system
Currency Guyanese dollar = 100 cents
Literacy rate 97%
Calorie consumption 2692 calories

HAITI
West Indies

Official name Republic of Haiti
Formation 1804 / 1844
Capital Port-au-Prince
Population 8.8 million / 827 people per sq mile (319 people per sq km) / 38%
Total area 10,714 sq. miles (27,750 sq. km)
Languages French*, French Creole*
Religions Roman Catholic 80%, Protestant 16%, Other (including Voodoo) 3%, Nonreligious 1%
Ethnic mix Black African 95%, Mulatto (mixed race) and European 5%
Government Presidential system
Currency Gourde = 100 centimes
Literacy rate 52%
Calorie consumption 2086 calories

HONDURAS
Central America

Official name Republic of Honduras
Formation 1838 / 1838
Capital Tegucigalpa
Population 7.5 million / 174 people per sq mile (67 people per sq km) / 46%
Total area 43,278 sq. miles (112,090 sq. km)
Languages Spanish*, Garifuna (Carib), English Creole
Religions Roman Catholic 97%, Protestant 3%
Ethnic mix Mestizo 90%, Black African 5%, Amerindian 4%, White 1%
Government Presidential system
Currency Lempira = 100 centavos
Literacy rate 80%
Calorie consumption 2356 calories

HUNGARY
Central Europe

Official name Republic of Hungary
Formation 1918 / 1947
Capital Budapest
Population 10 million / 280 people per sq mile (108 people per sq km) / 66%
Total area 35,919 sq. miles (93,030 sq. km)
Languages Hungarian (Magyar)*
Religions Roman Catholic 52%, Calvinist 16%, Other 15%, Nonreligious 14%, Lutheran 3%
Ethnic mix Magyar 94%, Other 5%, Roma 1%
Government Parliamentary system
Currency Forint = 100 fillér
Literacy rate 99%
Calorie consumption 3483 calories

ICELAND
Northwest Europe

Official name Republic of Iceland
Formation 1944 / 1944
Capital Reykjavík
Population 301,931 / 8 people per sq mile (3 people per sq km) / 93%
Total area 39,768 sq. miles (103,000 sq. km)
Languages Icelandic*
Religions Evangelical Lutheran 93%, Nonreligious 6%, Other (mostly Christian) 1%
Ethnic mix Icelandic 94%, Other 5%, Danish 1%
Government Parliamentary system
Currency Icelandic króna = 100 aurar
Literacy rate 99%
Calorie consumption 3249 calories

INDIA
South Asia

Official name Republic of India
Formation 1947 / 1947
Capital New Delhi
Population 1.14 billion / 989 people per sq mile (382 people per sq km) / 29%
Total area 1,269,338 sq. miles (3,287,590 sq. km)
Languages Hindi*, English*, Urdu, Bengali, Marathi, Telugu, Tamil, Bihari, Gujarati, Kanarese
Religions Hindu 81%, Muslim 13%, Christian 2%, Sikh 2%, Other 1%, Buddhist 1%
Ethnic mix Indo-Aryan 72%, Dravidian 25%, Mongoloid and other 3%
Government Parliamentary system
Currency Indian rupee = 100 paise
Literacy rate 61%
Calorie consumption 2459 calories

INDONESIA
Southeast Asia

Official name Republic of Indonesia
Formation 1949 / 1999
Capital Jakarta
Population 228 million / 329 people per sq mile (127 people per sq km) / 47%
Total area 741,096 sq. miles (1,919,440 sq. km)
Languages Bahasa Indonesia*, Javanese, Sundanese, Madurese, Dutch
Religions Sunni Muslim 87%, Protestant 6%, Roman Catholic 3%, Hindu 2%, Other 1%, Buddhist 1%
Ethnic mix Javanese 42%, Sundanese 15%, Coastal Malays 12%, Madurese 3%, Other 28%
Government Presidential system
Currency Rupiah = 100 sen
Literacy rate 90%
Calorie consumption 2904 calories

IRAN
Southwest Asia

Official name Islamic Republic of Iran
Formation 1502 / 1990
Capital Tehran
Population 71.2 million / 113 people per sq mile (44 people per sq km) / 67%
Total area 636,293 sq. miles (1,648,000 sq. km)
Languages Farsi*, Azeri, Luri, Gilaki, Kurdish, Mazanderani, Turkmen, Arabic, Baluchi
Religions Shi'a Muslim 93%, Sunni Muslim 6%, Other 1%
Ethnic mix Persian 50%, Azari 24%, Other 10%, Kurdish 8%, Lur and Bakhtiari 8%
Government Islamic theocracy
Currency Iranian rial = 100 dinars
Literacy rate 77%
Calorie consumption 3085 calories

IRAQ
Southwest Asia

Official name Republic of Iraq
Formation 1932 / 1990
Capital Baghdad
Population 30.3 million / 179 people per sq mile (69 people per sq km) / 67%
Total area 168,753 sq. miles (437,072 sq. km)
Languages Arabic*, Kurdish*, Turkic languages, Armenian, Assyrian
Religions Shi'a Muslim 60%, Sunni Muslim 35%, Other (including Christian) 5%
Ethnic mix Arab 80%, Kurdish 15%, Turkmen 3%, Other 2%
Government Parliamentary system
Currency New Iraqi dinar = 1000 fils
Literacy rate 74%
Calorie consumption 2197 calories

IRELAND
Northwest Europe

Official name Ireland
Formation 1922 / 1922
Capital Dublin
Population 4.3 million / 162 people per sq mile (62 people per sq km) / 60%
Total area 27,135 sq. miles (70,280 sq. km)
Languages English*, Irish Gaelic*
Religions Roman Catholic 88%, Other and nonreligious 9%, Anglican 3%
Ethnic mix Irish 99%, Other 1%
Government Parliamentary system
Currency Euro = 100 cents
Literacy rate 99%
Calorie consumption 3656 calories

ISRAEL
Southwest Asia

Official name State of Israel
Formation 1948 / 1994
Capital Jerusalem (not internationally recognized)
Population 7 million / 892 people per sq mile (344 people per sq km) / 92%
Total area 8019 sq. miles (20,770 sq. km)
Languages Hebrew*, Arabic*, Yiddish, German, Russian, Polish, Romanian, Persian
Religions Jewish 76%, Muslim (mainly Sunni) 16%, Other 4%, Druze 2%, Christian 2%
Ethnic mix Jewish 76%, Other (mostly Arab) 24%
Government Parliamentary system
Currency Shekel = 100 agorot
Literacy rate 97%
Calorie consumption 3666 calories

ITALY
Southern Europe

Official name Italian Republic
Formation 1861 / 1947
Capital Rome
Population 58.2 million / 513 people per sq mile (198 people per sq km) / 67%
Total area 116,305 sq. miles (301,230 sq. km)
Languages Italian*, German, French, Rhaeto-Romanic, Sardinian
Religions Roman Catholic 85%, Other and nonreligious 13%, Muslim 2%
Ethnic mix Italian 94%, Other 4%, Sardinian 2%
Government Parliamentary system
Currency Euro = 100 cents
Literacy rate 98%
Calorie consumption 3671 calories

IVORY COAST
West Africa

Official name Republic of Côte d'Ivoire
Formation 1960 / 1960
Capital Yamoussoukro
Population 18.8 million / 153 people per sq mile (59 people per sq km) / 45%
Total area 124,502 sq. miles (322,460 sq. km)
Languages Akan, French*, Krou, Voltaique
Religions Muslim 38%, Traditional beliefs 25%, Roman Catholic 25%, Other 6%, Protestant 6%
Ethnic mix Akan 42%, Voltaique 18%, Mandé du Nord 17%, Krou 11%, Mandé du Sud 10%, Other 2%
Government Presidential system
Currency CFA franc = 100 centimes
Literacy rate 49%
Calorie consumption 2631 calories

JAMAICA
West Indies

Official name Jamaica
Formation 1962 / 1962
Capital Kingston
Population 2.7 million / 646 people per sq mile (249 people per sq km) / 52%
Total area 4243 sq. miles (10,990 sq. km)
Languages English*, English Creole
Religions Other and nonreligious 45%, Other Protestant 20%, Church of God 18%, Baptist 10%, Anglican 7%
Ethnic mix Black African 92%, Mulatto (mixed race) 6%, East Indian 1%, European and Chinese 1%
Government Parliamentary system
Currency Jamaican dollar = 100 cents
Literacy rate 80%
Calorie consumption 2685 calories

JAPAN
East Asia

Official name Japan
Formation 1590 / 1972
Capital Tokyo
Population 128 million / 883 people per sq mile (341 people per sq km) / 66%
Total area 145,882 sq. miles (377,835 sq. km)
Languages Japanese*, Korean, Chinese
Religions Shinto and Buddhist 76%, Buddhist 16%, Other (including Christian) 8%
Ethnic mix Japanese 99%, Other (mainly Korean) 1%
Government Parliamentary system
Currency Yen = 100 sen
Literacy rate 99%
Calorie consumption 2761 calories

JORDAN
Southwest Asia

Official name Hashemite Kingdom of Jordan
Formation 1946 / 1967
Capital Amman
Population 6 million / 175 people per sq mile (67 people per sq km) / 79%
Total area 35,637 sq. miles (92,300 sq. km)
Languages Arabic*
Religions Muslim (mainly Sunni) 92%, Other (mostly Christian) 8%
Ethnic mix Arab 98%, Circassian 1%, Armenian 1%
Government Monarchy
Currency Jordanian dinar = 1000 fils
Literacy rate 90%
Calorie consumption 2673 calories

KAZAKHSTAN
Central Asia

Official name Republic of Kazakhstan
Formation 1991 / 1991
Capital Astana
Population 14.8 million / 14 people per sq mile (5 people per sq km) / 56%
Total area 1,049,150 sq. miles (2,717,300 sq. km)
Languages Kazakh*, Russian, Ukrainian, German, Uzbek, Tatar, Uighur
Religions Muslim (mainly Sunni) 47%, Orthodox Christian 44%, Other 9%
Ethnic mix Kazakh 57%, Russian 27%, Other 8%, Uzbek 3%, Ukrainian 3%, German 2%
Government Presidential system
Currency Tenge = 100 tiyn
Literacy rate 99%
Calorie consumption 2677 calories

KENYA
East Africa

Official name Republic of Kenya
Formation 1963 / 1963
Capital Nairobi
Population 36 million / 164 people per sq mile (63 people per sq km) / 40%
Total area 224,961 sq. miles (582,650 sq. km)
Languages Kiswahili*, English*, Kikuyu, Luo, Kalenjin, Kamba
Religions Christian 60%, Traditional beliefs 25%, Other 9%, Muslim 6%
Ethnic mix Other 31%, Kikuyu 20%, Luhya 14%, Luo 13%, Kalenjin 11%, Kamba 11%
Government Mixed Presidential–Parliamentary system
Currency Kenya shilling = 100 cents
Literacy rate 74%
Calorie consumption 2090 calories

KIRIBATI
Australasia & Oceania

Official name Republic of Kiribati
Formation 1979 / 1979
Capital Bairiki (Tarawa Atoll)
Population 107,817 / 393 people per sq mile (152 people per sq km) / 49%
Total area 277 sq. miles (717 sq. km)
Languages English*, Kiribati
Religions Roman Catholic 53%, Kiribati Protestant Church 39%, Other 8%
Ethnic mix Micronesian 99%, Other 1%
Government Nonparty system
Currency Australian dollar = 100 cents
Literacy rate 99%
Calorie consumption 2859 calories

KOSOVO (not yet fully recognized)
Southeast Europe

Official name Republic of Kosovo
Formation 2008 / 2008
Capital Pristina
Population 2.1 million / 499 people per sq mile (193 people per sq km) / 40%
Total area 4212 sq miles (10,908 sq km)
Languages Albanian*, Serbian*, Bosniak, Gorani, Roma, Turkish
Religions Muslim 92%, Roman Catholic 4%, Orthodox Christian 4%
Ethnic mix Albanian 92%, Serb 4%, Bosniak and Gorani 2%, Turkish 1%, Roma 1%
Government Parliamentary system
Currency Euro = 100 cents
Literacy rate 92%
Calorie consumption Not available

KUWAIT
Southwest Asia

Official name State of Kuwait
Formation 1961 / 1961
Capital Kuwait City
Population 2.8 million / 407 people per sq mile (157 people per sq km) / 96%
Total area 6880 sq. miles (17,820 sq. km)
Languages Arabic*, English
Religions Sunni Muslim 45%, Shi'a Muslim 40%, Christian, Hindu, and other 15%
Ethnic mix Kuwaiti 45%, Other Arab 35%, South Asian 9%, Other 7%, Iranian 4%
Government Monarchy
Currency Kuwaiti dinar = 1000 fils
Literacy rate 93%
Calorie consumption 3010 calories

KYRGYZSTAN
Central Asia

Official name Kyrgyz Republic
Formation 1991 / 1991
Capital Bishkek
Population 5.4 million / 70 people per sq mile (27 people per sq km) / 34%
Total area 76,641 sq. miles (198,500 sq. km)
Languages Kyrgyz*, Russian*, Uzbek, Tatar, Ukrainian
Religions Muslim (mainly Sunni) 70%, Orthodox Christian 30%
Ethnic mix Kyrgyz 65%, Uzbek 14%, Russian 13%, Other 6%, Dungan 1%Ukrainian 1%
Government Presidential system
Currency Som = 100 tyiyn
Literacy rate 99%
Calorie consumption 2999 calories

LAOS
Southeast Asia

Official name Lao People's Democratic Republic
Formation 1953 / 1953
Capital Vientiane
Population 6.2 million / 70 people per sq mile (27 people per sq km) / 21%
Total area 91,428 sq. miles (236,800 sq. km)
Languages Lao*, Mon-Khmer, Yao, Vietnamese, Chinese, French
Religions Buddhist 85%, Other (including animist) 15%
Ethnic mix Lao Loum 66%, Lao Theung 30%, Other 2%, Lao Soung 2%
Government One-party state
Currency New kip = 100 at
Literacy rate 69%
Calorie consumption 2312 calories

LATVIA
Northeast Europe

Official name Republic of Latvia
Formation 1991 / 1991
Capital Riga
Population 2.3 million / 92 people per sq mile (36 people per sq km) / 66%
Total area 24,938 sq. miles (64,589 sq. km)
Languages Latvian*, Russian
Religions Lutheran 55%, Roman Catholic 24%, Other 12%, Orthodox Christian 9%
Ethnic mix Latvian 59%, Russian 29%, Belarussian 4%, Polish 3%, Ukrainian 3%, Other 2%
Government Parliamentary system
Currency Lats = 100 santimi
Literacy rate 99%
Calorie consumption 2938 calories

LEBANON
Southwest Asia

Official name The Lebanese Republic
Formation 1941 / 1941
Capital Beirut
Population 3.7 million / 937 people per sq mile (362 people per sq km) / 88%
Total area 4015 sq. miles (10,400 sq. km)
Languages Arabic*, French, Armenian, Assyrian
Religions Muslim 70%, Christian 30%
Ethnic mix Arab 94%, Armenian 4%, Other 2%
Government Parliamentary system
Currency Lebanese pound = 100 piastres
Literacy rate 86%
Calorie consumption 3196 calories

LESOTHO
Southern Africa

Official name Kingdom of Lesotho
Formation 1966 / 1966
Capital Maseru
Population 1.8 million / 154 people per sq mile (59 people per sq km) / 18%
Total area 11,720 sq. miles (30,355 sq. km)
Languages English*, Sesotho*, isiZulu
Religions Christian 90%, Traditional beliefs 10%
Ethnic mix Sotho 97%, European and Asian 3%
Government Parliamentary system
Currency Loti = 100 lisente
Literacy rate 82%
Calorie consumption 2638 calories

LIBERIA
West Africa

Official name Republic of Liberia
Formation 1847 / 1847
Capital Monrovia
Population 3.5 million / 94 people per sq mile (36 people per sq km) / 47%
Total area 43,000 sq. miles (111,370 sq. km)
Languages English*, Kpelle, Vai, Bassa, Kru, Grebo, Kissi, Gola, Loma
Religions Christian 68%, Traditional beliefs 18%, Muslim 14%
Ethnic mix Indigenous tribes (16 main groups) 95%, Americo-Liberians 5%
Government Presidential system
Currency Liberian dollar = 100 cents
Literacy rate 58%
Calorie consumption 1900 calories

LIBYA
North Africa

Official name The Great Socialist People's Libyan Arab Jamahiriyah
Formation 1951 / 1951
Capital Tripoli
Population 6.1 million / 9 people per sq mile (3 people per sq km) / 87%
Total area 679,358 sq. miles (1,759,540 sq. km)
Languages Arabic*, Tuareg
Religions Muslim (mainly Sunni) 97%, Other 3%
Ethnic mix Arab and Berber 95%, Other 5%
Government One-party state
Currency Libyan dinar = 1000 dirhams
Literacy rate 82%
Calorie consumption 3320 calories

LIECHTENSTEIN
Central Europe

Official name Principality of Liechtenstein
Formation 1719 / 1719
Capital Vaduz
Population 34,247 / 552 people per sq mile (214 people per sq km) / 22%
Total area 62 sq. miles (160 sq. km)
Languages German*, Alemannish dialect, Italian
Religions Roman Catholic 81%, Other 12%, Protestant 7%
Ethnic mix Liechtensteiner 66%, Other 12%, Swiss 10%, Austrian 6%, German 3%, Italian 3%
Government Parliamentary system
Currency Swiss franc = 100 rappen/centimes
Literacy rate 99%
Calorie consumption Not available

LITHUANIA
Northeast Europe

Official name Republic of Lithuania
Formation 1991 / 1991
Capital Vilnius
Population 3.4 million / 135 people per sq mile (52 people per sq km) / 67%
Total area 25,174 sq. miles (65,200 sq. km)
Languages Lithuanian*, Russian
Religions Roman Catholic 83%, Other 12%, Protestant 5%
Ethnic mix Lithuanian 83%, Polish 7%, Russian 6%, Other 3%, Belorussian 1%
Government Parliamentary system
Currency Litas = 100 centu
Literacy rate 99%
Calorie consumption 3324 calories

LUXEMBOURG
Northwest Europe

Official name Grand Duchy of Luxembourg
Formation 1867 / 1867
Capital Luxembourg-Ville
Population 480,222 / 481 people per sq mile (186 people per sq km) / 92%
Total area 998 sq. miles (2586 sq. km)
Languages Luxembourgish*, German*, French*
Religions Roman Catholic 97%, Protestant, Orthodox Christian, and Jewish 3%
Ethnic mix Luxembourger 62%, Foreign residents 38%
Government Parliamentary system
Currency Euro = 100 cents
Literacy rate 99%
Calorie consumption 3701 calories

MACEDONIA
Southeast Europe

Official name Republic of Macedonia
Formation 1991 / 1991
Capital Skopje
Population 2 million / 201 people per sq mile (78 people per sq km) / 60%
Total area 9781 sq. miles (25,333 sq. km)
Languages Macedonian*, Albanian*, Turkish, Romani, Serbian
Religions Orthodox Christian 59%, Muslim 26%, Other 10%, Roman Catholic 4%, Protestant 1%
Ethnic mix Macedonian 64%, Albanian 25%, Turkish 4%, Roma 3%, Other 2%, Serb 2%
Government Mixed presidential–parliamentary system
Currency Macedonian denar = 100 deni
Literacy rate 96%
Calorie consumption 2655 calories

MADAGASCAR
Indian Ocean

Official name Republic of Madagascar
Formation 1960 / 1960
Capital Antananarivo
Population 19.6 million / 87 people per sq mile (34 people per sq km) / 27%
Total area 226,656 sq. miles (587,040 sq. km)
Languages French*, Malagasy*, English*
Religions Traditional beliefs 52%, Christian (mainly Roman Catholic) 41%, Muslim 7%
Ethnic mix Other Malay 46%, Merina 26%, Betsimisaraka 15%, Betsileo 12%, Other 1%
Government Presidential system
Currency Ariary = 5 iraimbilanja
Literacy rate 71%
Calorie consumption 2005 calories

MALAWI
Southern Africa

Official name Republic of Malawi
Formation 1964 / 1964
Capital Lilongwe
Population 13.5 million / 372 people per sq mile (143 people per sq km) / 17%
Total area 45,745 sq. miles (118,480 sq. km)
Languages English*, Chewa, Lomwe, Yao, Ngoni
Religions Protestant 55%, Roman Catholic 20%, Muslim 20%, Traditional beliefs 5%
Ethnic mix Bantu 99%, Other 1%
Government Presidential system
Currency Malawi kwacha = 100 tambala
Literacy rate 64%
Calorie consumption 2155 calories

MALAYSIA
Southeast Asia

Official name Malaysia
Formation 1963 / 1965
Capital Kuala Lumpur; Putrajaya (administrative)
Population 26.2 million / 207 people per sq mile (80 people per sq km) / 64%
Total area 127,316 sq. miles (329,750 sq. km)
Languages Bahasa Malaysia*, Malay, Chinese, Tamil, English
Religions Muslim (mainly Sunni) 53%, Buddhist 19%, Chinese faiths 12%, Other 7%, Christian 7%, Traditional beliefs 2%
Ethnic mix Malay 50%, Chinese 25%, Indigenous tribes 11%, Other 7%, Indian 7%
Government Parliamentary system
Currency Ringgit = 100 sen
Literacy rate 89%
Calorie consumption 2881 calories

MALDIVES
Indian Ocean

Official name Republic of Maldives
Formation 1965 / 1965
Capital Male'
Population 369,031 / 3181 people per sq mile (1230 people per sq km) / 29%
Total area 116 sq. miles (300 sq. km)
Languages Dhivehi (Maldivian)*, Sinhala, Tamil, Arabic
Religions Sunni Muslim 100%
Ethnic mix Arab–Sinhalese–Malay 100%
Government Presidential system
Currency Rufiyaa = 100 laari
Literacy rate 96%
Calorie consumption 2548 calories

MALI
West Africa

Official name Republic of Mali
Formation 1960 / 1960
Capital Bamako
Population 14.3 million / 30 people per sq mile (12 people per sq km) / 33%
Total area 478,764 sq. miles (1,240,000 sq. km)
Languages French*, Bambara, Fulani, Senufo, Soninke
Religions Muslim (mainly Sunni) 80%, Traditional beliefs 18%, Christian 1%, Other 1%
Ethnic mix Bambara 32%, Other 26%, Fulani 14%, Senufu 12%, Soninka 9%, Tuareg 7%
Government Presidential system
Currency CFA franc = 100 centimes
Literacy rate 19%
Calorie consumption 2174 calories

MALTA
Southern Europe

Official name Republic of Malta
Formation 1964 / 1964
Capital Valletta
Population 401,880 / 3241 people per sq mile (1256 people per sq km) / 92%
Total area 122 sq. miles (316 sq. km)
Languages Maltese*, English*
Religions Roman Catholic 98%, Other and nonreligious 2%
Ethnic mix Maltese 96%, Other 4%
Government Parliamentary system
Currency Euro = 100 cents
Literacy rate 88%
Calorie consumption 3587 calories

MARSHALL ISLANDS
Australasia & Oceania

Official name Republic of the Marshall Islands
Formation 1986 / 1986
Capital Majuro
Population 61,815 / 883 people per sq mile (342 people per sq km) / 67%
Total area 70 sq. miles (181 sq. km)
Languages Marshallese*, English*, Japanese, German
Religions Protestant 90%, Roman Catholic 8%, Other 2%
Ethnic mix Micronesian 97%, Other 3%
Government Presidential system
Currency US dollar = 100 cents
Literacy rate 91%
Calorie consumption Not available

MAURITANIA
West Africa

Official name Islamic Republic of Mauritania
Formation 1960 / 1960
Capital Nouakchott
Population 3.2 million / 8 people per sq mile (3 people per sq km) / 63%
Total area 397,953 sq. miles (1,030,700 sq. km)
Languages Hassaniyah Arabic*, Wolof, French
Religions Sunni Muslim 100%
Ethnic mix Maure 81%, Wolof 7%, Tukolor 5%, Other 4%, Soninka 3%
Government Presidential system
Currency Ouguiya = 5 khoums
Literacy rate 51%
Calorie consumption 2772 calories

MAURITIUS
Indian Ocean

Official name Republic of Mauritius
Formation 1968 / 1968
Capital Port Louis
Population 1.3 million / 1811 people per sq mile (699 people per sq km) / 44%
Total area 718 sq. miles (1860 sq. km)
Languages English*, French Creole, Hindi, Urdu, Tamil, Chinese, French
Religions Hindu 52%, Roman Catholic 26%, Muslim 17%, Other 3%, Protestant 2%
Ethnic mix Indo-Mauritian 68%, Creole 27%, Sino-Mauritian 3%, Franco-Mauritian 2%
Government Parliamentary system
Currency Mauritian rupee = 100 cents
Literacy rate 84%
Calorie consumption 2955 calories

MEXICO
North America

Official name United Mexican States
Formation 1836 / 1848
Capital Mexico City
Population 110 million / 149 people per sq mile (57 people per sq km) / 76%
Total area 761,602 sq. miles (1,972,550 sq. km)
Languages Spanish*, Nahuatl, Mayan, Zapotec, Mixtec, Otomi, Totonac, Tzotzil, Tzeltal
Religions Roman Catholic 88%, Other 7%, Protestant 5%
Ethnic mix Mestizo 60%, Amerindian 30%, European 9%, Other 1%
Government Presidential system
Currency Mexican peso = 100 centavos
Literacy rate 91%
Calorie consumption 3145 calories

MICRONESIA
Australasia & Oceania

Official name Federated States of Micronesia
Formation 1986 / 1986
Capital Palikir (Pohnpei Island)
Population 107,862 / 398 people per sq mile (154 people per sq km) / 30%
Total area 271 sq. miles (702 sq. km)
Languages English*, Trukese, Pohnpeian, Mortlockese, Kosraean
Religions Roman Catholic 50%, Protestant 48%, Other 2%
Ethnic mix Chuukese 49%, Pohnpeian 24%, Other 14%, Kosraean 6%, Yapese 5%, Asian 2%
Government Nonparty system
Currency US dollar = 100 cents
Literacy rate 81%
Calorie consumption Not available

MOLDOVA
Southeast Europe

Official name Republic of Moldova
Formation 1991 / 1991
Capital Chisinau
Population 4.2 million / 323 people per sq mile (125 people per sq km) / 46%
Total area 13,067 sq. miles (33,843 sq. km)
Languages Moldovan*, Ukrainian, Russian
Religions Orthodox Christian 98%, Jewish 2%
Ethnic mix Moldovan 64%, Ukrainian 14%, Russian 13%, Gagauz 4%, Other 3%, Bulgarian 2%
Government Parliamentary system
Currency Moldovan leu = 100 bani
Literacy rate 98%
Calorie consumption 2806 calories

MONACO
Southern Europe

Official name Principality of Monaco
Formation 1861 / 1861
Capital Monaco-Ville
Population 32,671 / 43,561 people per sq mile (16,754 people per sq km) / 100%
Total area 0.75 sq. miles (1.95 sq. km)
Languages French*, Italian, Monégasque, English
Religions Roman Catholic 89%, Protestant 6%, Other 5%
Ethnic mix French 32%, Other 29%, Italian 20%, Monégasque 19%
Government Mixed monarchical–parliamentary system
Currency Euro = 100 cents
Literacy rate 99%
Calorie consumption Not available

MONGOLIA
East Asia

Official name Mongolia
Formation 1924 / 1924
Capital Ulan Bator
Population 2.7 million / 4 people per sq mile (2 people per sq km) / 57%
Total area 604,247 sq. miles (1,565,000 sq. km)
Languages Khalkha Mongolian*, Kazakh, Chinese, Russian
Religions Tibetan Buddhist 96%, Muslim 4%
Ethnic mix Khalkh 82%, Other 9%, Kazakh 4%, Dorvod 3%, Bayad 2%
Government Mixed presidential–parliamentary system
Currency Tugrik (tögrög) = 100 möngö
Literacy rate 98%
Calorie consumption 2249 calories

MONTENEGRO
Southeast Europe

Official name Republic of Montenegro
Formation 2006 / 2006
Capital Podgorica
Population 684,736 / 128 people per sq mile (50 people per sq km) / 62%
Total area 5332 sq. miles (13,812 sq. km)
Languages Montenegrin*, Serbian, Albanian, Bosniak, Croatian
Religions Orthodox Christian 74%, Muslim 18%, Other 4%Roman Catholic 4%
Ethnic mix Montenegrin 43%, Serb 32%, Other 12%, Bosniak 8%, Albanian 5%
Government Parliamentary system
Currency Euro = 100 cents
Literacy rate 98%
Calorie consumption Not available

MOROCCO
North Africa

Official name Kingdom of Morocco
Formation 1956 / 1969
Capital Rabat
Population 32.4 million / 188 people per sq mile (73 people per sq km) / 58%
Total area 172,316 sq. miles (446,300 sq. km)
Languages Arabic*, Tamazight (Berber), French, Spanish
Religions Muslim (mainly Sunni) 99%, Other (mostly Christian) 1%
Ethnic mix Arab 70%, Berber 29%, European 1%
Government Mixed monarchical–parliamentary system
Currency Moroccan dirham = 100 centimes
Literacy rate 52%
Calorie consumption 3052 calories

MOZAMBIQUE
Southern Africa

Official name Republic of Mozambique
Formation 1975 / 1975
Capital Maputo
Population 20.5 million / 68 people per sq mile (26 people per sq km) / 37%
Total area 309,494 sq. miles (801,590 sq. km)
Languages Portuguese*, Makua, Xitsonga, Sena, Lomwe
Religions Traditional beliefs 56%, Christian 30%, Muslim 14%
Ethnic mix Makua Lomwe 47%, Tsonga 23%, Malawi 12%, Shona 11%, Yao 4%, Other 3%
Government Presidential system
Currency New metical = 100 centavos
Literacy rate 46%
Calorie consumption 2079 calories

NAMIBIA
Southern Africa

Official name Republic of Namibia
Formation 1990 / 1994
Capital Windhoek
Population 2.1 million / 7 people per sq mile (3 people per sq km) / 33%
Total area 318,694 sq. miles (825,418 sq. km)
Languages English*, Ovambo, Kavango, Bergdama, German, Afrikaans
Religions Christian 90%, Traditional beliefs 10%
Ethnic mix Ovambo 50%, Other tribes 24%, Kavango 9%, Damara 8%, Herero 8%, Other 1%
Government Presidential system
Currency Namibian dollar = 100 cents
Literacy rate 85%
Calorie consumption 2278 calories

NAURU
Australasia & Oceania

Official name Republic of Nauru
Formation 1968 / 1968
Capital None
Population 13,528 / 1670 people per sq mile (644 people per sq km) /
Total area 8.1 sq. miles (21 sq. km)
Languages Nauruan*, Kiribati, Chinese, Tuvaluan, English
Religions Nauruan Congregational Church 60%, Roman Catholic 35%, Other 5%
Ethnic mix Nauruan 62%, Other Pacific islanders 27%, Asian 8%, European 3%
Government Nonparty system
Currency Australian dollar = 100 cents
Literacy rate 95%
Calorie consumption Not available

NEPAL
South Asia

Official name Nepal
Formation 1769 / 1769
Capital Kathmandu
Population 28.2 million / 534 people per sq mile (206 people per sq km) / 15%
Total area 54,363 sq. miles (140,800 sq. km)
Languages Nepali*, Maithili, Bhojpuri
Religions Hindu 90%, Buddhist 5%, Muslim 3%, Other (including Christian) 2%
Ethnic mix Other 52%, Chhetri 16%, Hill Brahman 13%, Tharu 7%, Magar 7%, Tamang 5%
Government Parliamentary system
Currency Nepalese rupee = 100 paisa
Literacy rate 49%
Calorie consumption 2453 calories

NETHERLANDS
Northwest Europe

Official name Kingdom of the Netherlands
Formation 1648 / 1839
Capital Amsterdam; The Hague (administrative)
Population 16.4 million / 1252 people per sq mile (483 people per sq km) / 66%
Total area 16,033 sq. miles (41,526 sq. km)
Languages Dutch*, Frisian
Religions Roman Catholic 36%, Other 34%, Protestant 27%, Muslim 3%
Ethnic mix Dutch 82%, Other 12%, Surinamese 2%, Turkish 2%, Moroccan 2%
Government Parliamentary system
Currency Euro = 100 cents
Literacy rate 99%
Calorie consumption 3362 calories

NEW ZEALAND
Australasia & Oceania

Official name New Zealand
Formation 1947 / 1947
Capital Wellington
Population 4.1 million / 40 people per sq mile (15 people per sq km) / 86%
Total area 103,737 sq. miles (268,680 sq. km)
Languages English*, Maori*
Religions Anglican 24%, Other 22%, Presbyterian 18%, Nonreligious 16%, Roman Catholic 15%, Methodist 5%
Ethnic mix European 75%, Maori 15%, Other 7%, Samoan 3%
Government Parliamentary system
Currency New Zealand dollar = 100 cents
Literacy rate 99%
Calorie consumption 3219 calories

NICARAGUA
Central America

Official name Republic of Nicaragua
Formation 1838 / 1838
Capital Managua
Population 5.7 million / 124 people per sq mile (48 people per sq km) / 58%
Total area 49,998 sq. miles (129,494 sq. km)
Languages Spanish*, English Creole, Miskito
Religions Roman Catholic 80%, Protestant Evangelical 17%, Other 3%
Ethnic mix Mestizo 69%, White 14%, Black 8%, Amerindian 5%, Zambo 4%
Government Presidential system
Currency Córdoba oro = 100 centavos
Literacy rate 77%
Calorie consumption 2298 calories

NIGER
West Africa

Official name Republic of Niger
Formation 1960 / 1960
Capital Niamey
Population 14.9 million / 30 people per sq mile (12 people per sq km) / 23%
Total area 489,188 sq. miles (1,267,000 sq. km)
Languages French*, Hausa, Djerma, Fulani, Tuareg, Teda
Religions Muslim 85%, Traditional beliefs 14%, Other (including Christian) 1%
Ethnic mix Hausa 55%, Djerma and Songhai 21%, Peul 9%, Tuareg 9%, Other 6%
Government Presidential system
Currency CFA franc = 100 centimes
Literacy rate 29%
Calorie consumption 2130 calories

NIGERIA
West Africa

Official name Federal Republic of Nigeria
Formation 1960 / 1961
Capital Abuja
Population 137 million / 390 people per sq mile (151 people per sq km) / 47%
Total area 356,667 sq. miles (923,768 sq. km)
Languages English*, Hausa, Yoruba, Ibo
Religions Muslim 50%, Christian 40%, Traditional beliefs 10%
Ethnic mix Other 29%, Hausa 21%, Yoruba 21%, Ibo 18%, Fulani 11%
Government Presidential system
Currency Naira = 100 kobo
Literacy rate 67%
Calorie consumption 2726 calories

NORTH KOREA
East Asia

Official name Democratic People's Republic of Korea
Formation 1948 / 1953
Capital Pyongyang
Population 22.7 million / 488 people per sq mile (189 people per sq km) / 61%
Total area 46,540 sq. miles (120,540 sq. km)
Languages Korean*
Religions Atheist 100%
Ethnic mix Korean 100%
Government One-party state
Currency North Korean won = 100 chon
Literacy rate 98%
Calorie consumption 2142 calories

NORWAY
Northern Europe

Official name Kingdom of Norway
Formation 1905 / 1905
Capital Oslo
Population 4.7 million / 40 people per sq mile (15 people per sq km) / 80%
Total area 125,181 sq. miles (324,220 sq. km)
Languages Norwegian* (Bokmål "book language" and Nynorsk "new Norsk"), Sámi
Religions Evangelical Lutheran 89%, Other and nonreligious 10%, Roman Catholic 1%
Ethnic mix Norwegian 93%, Other 6%, Sámi 1%
Government Parliamentary system
Currency Norwegian krone = 100 øre
Literacy rate 99%
Calorie consumption 3484 calories

OMAN
Southwest Asia

Official name Sultanate of Oman
Formation 1951 / 1951
Capital Muscat
Population 2.7 million / 33 people per sq mile (13 people per sq km) / 78%
Total area 82,031 sq. miles (212,460 sq. km)
Languages Arabic*, Baluchi, Farsi, Hindi, Punjabi
Religions Ibadi Muslim 75%, Other Muslim and Hindu 25%
Ethnic mix Arab 88%, Baluchi 4%, Persian 3%, Indian and Pakistani 3%, African 2%
Government Monarchy
Currency Omani rial = 1000 baisa
Literacy rate 81%
Calorie consumption Not available

PAKISTAN
South Asia

Official name Islamic Republic of Pakistan
Formation 1947 / 1971
Capital Islamabad
Population 165 million / 553 people per sq mile (214 people per sq km) / 34%
Total area 310,401 sq. miles (803,940 sq. km)
Languages Urdu*, Punjabi, Sindhi, Pashtu, Baluchi, Brahui
Religions Sunni Muslim 77%, Shi'a Muslim 20%, Hindu 2%, Christian 1%
Ethnic mix Punjabi 56%, Pathan (Pashtun) 15%, Sindhi 14%, Mohajir 7%, Other 4%, Baluchi 4%
Government Presidential system
Currency Pakistani rupee = 100 paisa
Literacy rate 50%
Calorie consumption 2419 calories

PALAU
Australasia & Oceania

Official name Republic of Palau
Formation 1994 / 1994
Capital Melekeok
Population 20,842 / 106 people per sq mile (41 people per sq km) / 68%
Total area 177 sq. miles (458 sq. km)
Languages Palauan*, English*, Japanese, Angaur, Tobi, Sonsorolese
Religions Christian 66%, Modekngei 34%
Ethnic mix Palauan 74%, Filipino 16%, Other 6%, Chinese and other Asian 4%
Government Nonparty system
Currency US dollar = 100 cents
Literacy rate 98%
Calorie consumption Not available

PANAMA
Central America

Official name Republic of Panama
Formation 1903 / 1903
Capital Panama City
Population 3.3 million / 112 people per sq mile (43 people per sq km) / 57%
Total area 30,193 sq. miles (78,200 sq. km)
Languages English Creole, Spanish*, Amerindian languages, Chibchan languages
Religions Roman Catholic 86%, Other 8%, Protestant 6%
Ethnic mix Mestizo 60%, White 14%, Black 12%, Amerindian 8%, Asian 4%, Other 2%
Government Presidential system
Currency Balboa = 100 centésimos
Literacy rate 92%
Calorie consumption 2272 calories

PAPUA NEW GUINEA
Australasia & Oceania

Official name Independent State of Papua New Guinea
Formation 1975 / 1975
Capital Port Moresby
Population 6.1 million / 35 people per sq mile (13 people per sq km) / 13%
Total area 178,703 sq. miles (462,840 sq. km)
Languages English*, Pidgin English, Papuan, Motu, 750 (est.) native languages
Religions Protestant 60%, Roman Catholic 37%, Other 3%
Ethnic mix Melanesian and mixed race 100%
Government Parliamentary system
Currency Kina = 100 toea
Literacy rate 57%
Calorie consumption 2193 calories

PARAGUAY
South America

Official name Republic of Paraguay
Formation 1811 / 1938
Capital Asunción
Population 6.4 million / 42 people per sq mile (16 people per sq km) / 58%
Total area 157,046 sq. miles (406,750 sq. km)
Languages Spanish*, Guaraní, German
Religions Roman Catholic 96%, Protestant (including Mennonite) 4%
Ethnic mix Mestizo 91%, Other 7%, Amerindian 2%
Government Presidential system
Currency Guaraní = 100 céntimos
Literacy rate 93%
Calorie consumption 2565 calories

PERU
South America

Official name Republic of Peru
Formation 1824 / 1941
Capital Lima
Population 28.8 million / 58 people per sq mile (22 people per sq km) / 74%
Total area 496,223 sq. miles (1,285,200 sq. km)
Languages Spanish*, Quechua*, Aymara
Religions Roman Catholic 95%, Other 5%
Ethnic mix Amerindian 50%, Mestizo 40%, White 7%, Other 3%
Government Presidential system
Currency New sol = 100 céntimos
Literacy rate 88%
Calorie consumption 2571 calories

PHILIPPINES
Southeast Asia

Official name Republic of the Philippines
Formation 1946 / 1946
Capital Manila
Population 85.9 million / 746 people per sq mile (288 people per sq km) / 62%
Total area 115,830 sq. miles (300,000 sq. km)
Languages English*, Filipino*, Tagalog, Cebuano, Ilocano, Hiligaynon, many other local languages
Religions Roman Catholic 83%, Protestant 9%, Muslim 5%, Other (including Buddhist) 3%
Ethnic mix Other 34%, Tagalog 28%, Cebuano 13%, Ilocano 9%, Hiligaynon 8%, Bisaya 8%
Government Presidential system
Currency Philippine peso = 100 centavos
Literacy rate 93%
Calorie consumption 2379 calories

POLAND
Northern Europe

Official name Republic of Poland
Formation 1918 / 1945
Capital Warsaw
Population 38.5 million / 328 people per sq mile (126 people per sq km) / 62%
Total area 120,728 sq. miles (312,685 sq. km)
Languages Polish*
Religions Roman Catholic 93%, Other and nonreligious 5%, Orthodox Christian 2%
Ethnic mix Polish 97%, Other 3%
Government Parliamentary system
Currency Zloty = 100 groszy
Literacy rate 99%
Calorie consumption 3374 calories

PORTUGAL
Southwest Europe

Official name The Portuguese Republic
Formation 1139 / 1640
Capital Lisbon
Population 10.6 million / 299 people per sq mile (115 people per sq km) / 55%
Total area 35,672 sq. miles (92,391 sq. km)
Languages Portuguese*
Religions Roman Catholic 97%, Other 2%, Protestant 1%
Ethnic mix Portuguese 98%, African and other 2%
Government Parliamentary system
Currency Euro = 100 cents
Literacy rate 92%
Calorie consumption 3741 calories

QATAR
Southwest Asia

Official name State of Qatar
Formation 1971 / 1971
Capital Doha
Population 907,229 / 214 people per sq mile (82 people per sq km) / 92%
Total area 4416 sq. miles (11,437 sq. km)
Languages Arabic*
Religions Muslim (mainly Sunni) 95%, Other 5%
Ethnic mix Arab 40%, Indian 18%, Pakistani 18%, Other 14%, Iranian 10%
Government Monarchy
Currency Qatar riyal = 100 dirhams
Literacy rate 89%
Calorie consumption Not available

ROMANIA
Southeast Europe

Official name Romania
Formation 1878 / 1947
Capital Bucharest
Population 21.5 million / 242 people per sq mile (93 people per sq km) / 55%
Total area 91,699 sq. miles (237,500 sq. km)
Languages Romanian*, Hungarian (Magyar), Romani, German
Religions Romanian Orthodox 87%, Roman Catholic 5%, Protestant 4%, Other 2%, Greek Orthodox 1%, Greek Catholic (Uniate) 1%
Ethnic mix Romanian 89%, Magyar 7%, Roma 2%, Other 2%
Government Presidential system
Currency New Romanian leu = 100 bani
Literacy rate 97%
Calorie consumption 3455 calories

RUSSIAN FEDERATION
Europe / Asia

Official name Russian Federation
Formation 1480 / 1991
Capital Moscow
Population 142 million / 22 people per sq mile (8 people per sq km) / 73%
Total area 6,592,735 sq. miles (17,075,200 sq. km)
Languages Russian*, Tatar, Ukrainian, Chavash, various other national languages
Religions Orthodox Christian 75%, Muslim 14%, Other 11%
Ethnic mix Russian 80%, Other 12%, Tatar 4%, Ukrainian 2%, Bashkir 1%, Chavash 1%
Government Mixed Presidential–Parliamentary system
Currency Russian rouble = 100 kopeks
Literacy rate 99%
Calorie consumption 3072 calories

RWANDA
Central Africa

Official name Republic of Rwanda
Formation 1962 / 1962
Capital Kigali
Population 9.4 million / 976 people per sq mile (377 people per sq km) / 20%
Total area 10,169 sq. miles (26,338 sq. km)
Languages Kinyarwanda*, French*, English*, Kiswahili
Religions Roman Catholic 56%, Traditional beliefs 25%, Muslim 10%, Protestant 9%
Ethnic mix Hutu 90%, Tutsi 9%, Other (including Twa) 1%
Government Presidential system
Currency Rwanda franc = 100 centimes
Literacy rate 65%
Calorie consumption 2084 calories

SAINT KITTS & NEVIS
West Indies

Official name Federation of Saint Christopher and Nevis
Formation 1983 / 1983
Capital Basseterre
Population 39,349 / 283 people per sq mile (109 people per sq km) / 32%
Total area 101 sq. miles (261 sq. km)
Languages English*, English Creole
Religions Anglican 33%, Methodist 29%, Other 22%, Moravian 9%, Roman Catholic 7%
Ethnic mix Black 95%, Mixed race 3%, White 1%, Other and Amerindian 1%
Government Parliamentary system
Currency Eastern Caribbean dollar = 100 cents
Literacy rate 98%
Calorie consumption 2609 calories

SAINT LUCIA
West Indies

Official name Saint Lucia
Formation 1979 / 1979
Capital Castries
Population 170,649 / 723 people per sq mile (280 people per sq km) / 31%
Total area 239 sq. miles (620 sq. km)
Languages English*, French Creole
Religions Roman Catholic 90%, Other 10%
Ethnic mix Black 83%, Mulatto (mixed race) 13%, Asian 3%, Other 1%
Government Parliamentary system
Currency Eastern Caribbean dollar = 100 cents
Literacy rate 95%
Calorie consumption 2988 calories

SAINT VINCENT & THE GRENADINES
West Indies

Official name Saint Vincent and the Grenadines
Formation 1979 / 1979
Capital Kingstown
Population 118,149 / 902 people per sq mile (347 people per sq km) / 59%
Total area 150 sq. miles (389 sq. km)
Languages English*, English Creole
Religions Anglican 47%, Methodist 28%, Roman Catholic 13%, Other 12%
Ethnic mix Black 77%, Mulatto (mixed race) 16%, Other 3%, Carib 3%, Asian 1%
Government Parliamentary system
Currency Eastern Caribbean dollar = 100 cents
Literacy rate 88%
Calorie consumption 2599 calories

SAMOA
Australasia & Oceania

Official name Independent State of Samoa
Formation 1962 / 1962
Capital Apia
Population 214,265 / 196 people per sq mile (76 people per sq km) / 22%
Total area 1104 sq. miles (2860 sq. km)
Languages Samoan*, English*
Religions Christian 99%, Other 1%
Ethnic mix Polynesian 90%, Euronesian 9%, Other 1%
Government Parliamentary system
Currency Tala = 100 sene
Literacy rate 99%
Calorie consumption 2945 calories

SAN MARINO
Southern Europe

Official name Republic of San Marino
Formation 1631 / 1631
Capital San Marino
Population 29,615 / 1234 people per sq mile (485 people per sq km) / 89%
Total area 23.6 sq. miles (61 sq. km)
Languages Italian*
Religions Roman Catholic 93%, Other and nonreligious 7%
Ethnic mix Sammarinese 88%, Italian 10%, Other 2%
Government Parliamentary system
Currency Euro = 100 cents
Literacy rate 99%
Calorie consumption Not available

SÃO TOMÉ & PRÍNCIPE
West Africa

Official name The Democratic Republic of Sao Tome and Principe
Formation 1975 / 1975
Capital São Tomé
Population 199,579 / 538 people per sq mile (208 people per sq km) / 38%
Total area 386 sq. miles (1001 sq. km)
Languages Portuguese*, Portuguese Creole
Religions Roman Catholic 84%, Other 16%
Ethnic mix Black 90%, Portuguese and Creole 10%
Government Presidential system
Currency Dobra = 100 céntimos
Literacy rate 83%
Calorie consumption 2460 calories

SAUDI ARABIA
Southwest Asia

Official name Kingdom of Saudi Arabia
Formation 1932 / 1932
Capital Riyadh
Population 25.8 million / 32 people per sq mile (12 people per sq km) / 88%
Total area 756,981 sq. miles (1,960,582 sq. km)
Languages Arabic*
Religions Sunni Muslim 85%, Shi'a Muslim 15%
Ethnic mix Arab 90%, Afro-Asian 10%
Government Monarchy
Currency Saudi riyal = 100 halalat
Literacy rate 79%
Calorie consumption 2844 calories

SENEGAL
West Africa

Official name Republic of Senegal
Formation 1960 / 1960
Capital Dakar
Population 12.2 million / 164 people per sq mile (63 people per sq km) / 50%
Total area 75,749 sq. miles (196,190 sq. km)
Languages French*, Wolof, Pulaar, Serer, Diola, Mandinka, Malinke, Soninke
Religions Sunni Muslim 90%, Christian (mainly Roman Catholic) 5%, Traditional beliefs 5%
Ethnic mix Wolof 43%, Serer 15%, Other 14%, Peul 14%, Toucouleur 9%, Diola 5%
Government Presidential system
Currency CFA franc = 100 centimes
Literacy rate 39%
Calorie consumption 2279 calories

SERBIA
Southeast Europe

Official name Republic of Serbia
Formation 2006 / 2008
Capital Belgrade
Population 8.1 million / 271 people per sq mile (105 people per sq km) / 52%
Total area 29,905 sq miles (77,453 sq km)
Languages Serbian*, Hungarian (Magyar)
Religions Orthodox Christian 85%, Other 6%, Roman Catholic 6%, Muslim 3%
Ethnic mix Serb 83%, Other 10%, Magyar 4%, Bosniak 2%, Roma 1%
Government Parliamentary system
Currency Dinar = 100 para
Literacy rate 96%
Calorie consumption 2678 calories

SEYCHELLES
Indian Ocean

Official name Republic of Seychelles
Formation 1976 / 1976
Capital Victoria
Population 81,895 / 787 people per sq mile (303 people per sq km) / 50%
Total area 176 sq. miles (455 sq. km)
Languages French Creole*, English*, French*
Religions Roman Catholic 90%, Anglican 8%, Other (including Muslim) 2%
Ethnic mix Creole 89%, Indian 5%, Other 4%, Chinese 2%
Government Presidential system
Currency Seychelles rupee = 100 cents
Literacy rate 92%
Calorie consumption 2465 calories

SIERRA LEONE
West Africa

Official name Republic of Sierra Leone
Formation 1961 / 1961
Capital Freetown
Population 5.8 million / 210 people per sq mile (81 people per sq km) / 40%
Total area 27,698 sq. miles (71,740 sq. km)
Languages English*, Mende, Temne, Krio
Religions Muslim 30%, Traditional beliefs 30%, Other 30%, Christian 10%
Ethnic mix Mende 35%, Temne 32%, Other 21%, Limba 8%, Kuranko 4%
Government Presidential system
Currency Leone = 100 cents
Literacy rate 35%
Calorie consumption 1936 calories

SINGAPORE
Southeast Asia

Official name Republic of Singapore
Formation 1965 / 1965
Capital Singapore
Population 4.4 million / 18644 people per sq mile (7213 people per sq km) / 100%
Total area 250 sq. miles (648 sq. km)
Languages Mandarin*, Malay*, Tamil*, English*
Religions Buddhist 55%, Taoist 22%, Muslim 16%, Hindu, Christian, and Sikh 7%
Ethnic mix Chinese 77%, Malay 14%, Indian 8%, Other 1%
Government Parliamentary system
Currency Singapore dollar = 100 cents
Literacy rate 93%
Calorie consumption Not available

SLOVAKIA
Central Europe

Official name Slovak Republic
Formation 1993 / 1993
Capital Bratislava
Population 5.4 million / 285 people per sq mile (110 people per sq km) / 58%
Total area 18,859 sq. miles (48,845 sq. km)
Languages Slovak*, Hungarian (Magyar), Czech
Religions Roman Catholic 60%, Other 18%, Atheist 10%, Protestant 8%, Orthodox Christian 4%
Ethnic mix Slovak 86%, Magyar 10%, Roma 2%, Other 1%, Czech 1%
Government Parliamentary system
Currency Euro = 100 cents
Literacy rate 99%
Calorie consumption 2889 calories

SLOVENIA
Central Europe

Official name Republic of Slovenia
Formation 1991 / 1991
Capital Ljubljana
Population 2 million / 256 people per sq mile (99 people per sq km) / 51%
Total area 7820 sq. miles (20,253 sq. km)
Languages Slovenian*
Religions Roman Catholic 96%, Other 3%, Muslim 1%
Ethnic mix Slovene 83%, Other 12%, Serb 2%, Croat 2%, Bosniak 1%
Government Parliamentary system
Currency Euro = 100 cents
Literacy rate 99%
Calorie consumption 3001 calories

SOLOMON ISLANDS
Australasia & Oceania

Official name Solomon Islands
Formation 1978 / 1978
Capital Honiara
Population 566,842 / 52 people per sq mile (20 people per sq km) / 17%
Total area 10,985 sq. miles (28,450 sq. km)
Languages English*, Pidgin English, Melanesian Pidgin
Religions Church of Melanesia (Anglican) 34%, Roman Catholic 19%, South Seas Evangelical Church 17%, Methodist 11%, Seventh-day Adventist 10%, Other 9%
Ethnic mix Melanesian 94%, Polynesian 4%, Other 2%
Government Parliamentary system
Currency Solomon Islands dollar = 100 cents
Literacy rate 77%
Calorie consumption 2265 calories

SOMALIA
East Africa

Official name The Somali Democratic Republic
Formation 1960 / 1960
Capital Mogadishu
Population 8.8 million / 36 people per sq mile (14 people per sq km) / 35%
Total area 246,199 sq. miles (637,657 sq. km)
Languages Somali*, Arabic*, English, Italian
Religions Sunni Muslim 98%, Christian 2%
Ethnic mix Somali 85%, Other 15%
Government Transitional regime
Currency Somali shilin = 100 senti
Literacy rate 24%
Calorie consumption 1628 calories

SOUTH AFRICA
Southern Africa

Official name Republic of South Africa
Formation 1934 / 1994
Capital Pretoria; Cape Town; Bloemfontein
Population 47.7 million / 101 people per sq mile (39 people per sq km) / 57%
Total area 471,008 sq. miles (1,219,912 sq. km)
Languages English, isiZulu, isiXhosa, Afrikaans, Sepedi, Setswana, Sesotho, Xitsonga, siSwati, Tshivenda, isiNdebele
Religions Christian 68%, Traditional beliefs and animist 29%, Muslim 2%, Hindu 1%
Ethnic mix Black 79%, Colored 10%, White 9%, Asian 2%
Government Presidential system
Currency Rand = 100 cents
Literacy rate 82%
Calorie consumption 2956 calories

SOUTH KOREA
East Asia

Official name Republic of Korea
Formation 1948 / 1953
Capital Seoul
Population 48.1 million / 1262 people per sq mile (487 people per sq km) / 81%
Total area 38,023 sq. miles (98,480 sq. km)
Languages Korean*
Religions Mahayana Buddhist 47%, Protestant 38%, Roman Catholic 11%, Confucianist 3%, Other 1%
Ethnic mix Korean 100%
Government Presidential system
Currency South Korean won = 100 chon
Literacy rate 98%
Calorie consumption 3058 calories

SPAIN
Southwest Europe

Official name Kingdom of Spain
Formation 1492 / 1713
Capital Madrid
Population 43.6 million / 226 people per sq mile (87 people per sq km) / 77%
Total area 194,896 sq. miles (504,782 sq. km)
Languages Spanish*, Catalan*, Galician*, Basque*
Religions Roman Catholic 96%, Other 4%
Ethnic mix Castilian Spanish 72%, Catalan 17%, Galician 6%, Basque 2%, Other 2%, Roma 1%
Government Parliamentary system
Currency Euro = 100 cents
Literacy rate 98%
Calorie consumption 3371 calories

SRI LANKA
South Asia

Official name Democratic Socialist Republic of Sri Lanka
Formation 1948 / 1948
Capital Colombo
Population 21.1 million / 844 people per sq mile (326 people per sq km) / 21%
Total area 25,332 sq. miles (65,610 sq. km)
Languages Sinhala*, Tamil*, Sinhala-Tamil, English
Religions Buddhist 69%, Hindu 15%, Muslim 8%, Christian 8%
Ethnic mix Sinhalese 82%, Tamil 9%, Moor 8%, Other 1%
Government Mixed presidential–parliamentary system
Currency Sri Lanka rupee = 100 cents
Literacy rate 91%
Calorie consumption 2385 calories

SUDAN
East Africa

Official name Republic of the Sudan
Formation 1956 / 1956
Capital Khartoum
Population 37.8 million / 39 people per sq mile (15 people per sq km) / 40%
Total area 967,493 sq. miles (2,505,810 sq. km)
Languages Arabic / Arabic, Dinka, Nuer, Nubian, Beja, Zande, Bari, Fur, Shilluk, Lotuko
Religions Muslim (mainly Sunni) 70%, Traditional beliefs 20%, Christian 9%, Other 1%
Ethnic mix Other Black 52%, Arab 40%, Dinka and Beja 7%, Other 1%
Government Presidential system
Currency new Sudanese pound or dinar = 100 piastres
Literacy rate 61%
Calorie consumption 2228 calories

SURINAM
South America

Official name Republic of Suriname
Formation 1975 / 1975
Capital Paramaribo
Population 470,784 / 8 people per sq mile (3 people per sq km) / 77%
Total area 63,039 sq. miles (163,270 sq. km)
Languages Sranan (Creole), Dutch*, Javanese, Sarnami Hindi, Saramaccan, Chinese, Carib
Religions Hindu 27%, Protestant 25%, Roman Catholic 23%, Muslim 20%, Traditional beliefs 5%
Ethnic mix Creole 34%, South Asian 34%, Javanese 18%, Black 9%, Other 5%
Government Parliamentary system
Currency Surinamese dollar = 100 cents
Literacy rate 90%
Calorie consumption 2652 calories

SWAZILAND
Southern Africa

Official name Kingdom of Swaziland
Formation 1968 / 1968
Capital Mbabane
Population 1 million / 151 people per sq mile (58 people per sq km) / 24%
Total area 6704 sq. miles (17,363 sq. km)
Languages English*, siSwati*, isiZulu, Xitsonga
Religions Christian 60%, Traditional beliefs 40%
Ethnic mix Swazi 97%, Other 3%
Government Monarchy
Currency Lilangeni = 100 cents
Literacy rate 80%
Calorie consumption 2322 calories

SWEDEN
Northern Europe

Official name Kingdom of Sweden
Formation 1523 / 1921
Capital Stockholm
Population 9.1 million / 57 people per sq mile (22 people per sq km) / 83%
Total area 173,731 sq. miles (449,964 sq. km)
Languages Swedish*, Finnish, Sámi
Religions Evangelical Lutheran 82%, Other 13%, Roman Catholic 2%, Muslim 2%, Orthodox Christian 1%
Ethnic mix Swedish 86%, Foreign-born or first-generation immigrant 12%, Finnish and Sámi 2%
Government Parliamentary system
Currency Swedish krona = 100 öre
Literacy rate 99%
Calorie consumption 3185 calories

SWITZERLAND
Central Europe

Official name Swiss Confederation
Formation 1291 / 1857
Capital Bern
Population 7.3 million / 475 people per sq mile (184 people per sq km) / 68%
Total area 15,942 sq. miles (41,290 sq. km)
Languages German*, Swiss-German, French*, Italian*, Romansch
Religions Roman Catholic 42%, Protestant 35%, Other and nonreligious 19%, Muslim 4%
Ethnic mix German 64%, French 20%, Other 9%, Italian 6%, Romansch 1%
Government Parliamentary system
Currency Swiss franc = 100 rappen/centimes
Literacy rate 99%
Calorie consumption 3526 calories

SYRIA
Southwest Asia

Official name Syrian Arab Republic
Formation 1941 / 1967
Capital Damascus
Population 20 million / 281 people per sq mile (109 people per sq km) / 50%
Total area 71,498 sq. miles (184,180 sq. km)
Languages Arabic*, French, Kurdish, Armenian, Circassian, Turkic languages, Assyrian, Aramaic
Religions Sunni Muslim 74%, Other Muslim 16%, Christian 10%
Ethnic mix Arab 89%, Kurdish 6%, Other 3%, Armenian, Turkmen, and Circassian 2%
Government One-party state
Currency Syrian pound = 100 piastres
Literacy rate 80%
Calorie consumption 3038 calories

TAIWAN
East Asia

Official name Republic of China (ROC)
Formation 1949 / 1949
Capital Taipei
Population 22.9 million / 1835 people per sq mile (709 people per sq km) / 80%
Total area 13,892 sq. miles (35,980 sq. km)
Languages Amoy Chinese, Mandarin Chinese*, Hakka Chinese
Religions Buddhist, Confucianist, and Taoist 93%, Christian 5%, Other 2%
Ethnic mix Han (pre-20th-century migration) 84%, Han (20th-century migration) 14%, Aboriginal 2%
Government Presidential system
Currency Taiwan dollar = 100 cents
Literacy rate 97%
Calorie consumption Not available

TAJIKISTAN
Central Asia

Official name Republic of Tajikistan
Formation 1991 / 1991
Capital Dushanbe
Population 6.7 million / 121 people per sq mile (47 people per sq km) / 25%
Total area 55,251 sq. miles (143,100 sq. km)
Languages Tajik*, Uzbek, Russian
Religions Sunni Muslim 80%, Other 15%, Shi'a Muslim 5%
Ethnic mix Tajik 80%, Uzbek 15%, Other 3%, Russian 1%, Kyrgyz 1%
Government Presidential system
Currency Somoni = 100 diram
Literacy rate 99%
Calorie consumption 1828 calories

TANZANIA
East Africa

Official name United Republic of Tanzania
Formation 1964 / 1964
Capital Dodoma
Population 39.7 million / 116 people per sq mile (45 people per sq km) / 36%
Total area 364,898 sq. miles (945,087 sq. km)
Languages Kiswahili*, Sukuma, Chagga, Nyamwezi, Hehe, Makonde, Yao, Sandawe, English*
Religions Muslim 33%, Christian 33%, Traditional beliefs 30%, Other 4%
Ethnic mix Native African (over 120 tribes) 99%, European, Asian, and Arab 1%
Government Presidential system
Currency Tanzanian shilling = 100 cents
Literacy rate 69%
Calorie consumption 1975 calories

THAILAND
Southeast Asia

Official name Kingdom of Thailand
Formation 1238 / 1907
Capital Bangkok
Population 68.3 million / 346 people per sq mile (134 people per sq km) / 32%
Total area 198,455 sq. miles (514,000 sq. km)
Languages Thai*, Chinese, Malay, Khmer, Mon, Karen, Miao
Religions Buddhist 95%, Muslim 4%, Other (including Christian) 1%
Ethnic mix Thai 83%, Chinese 12%, Malay 3%, Khmer and Other 2%
Government Parliamentary system
Currency Baht = 100 satang
Literacy rate 93%
Calorie consumption 2467 calories

TOGO
West Africa

Official name The Togolese Republic
Formation 1960 / 1960
Capital Lomé
Population 6.5 million / 310 people per sq mile (120 people per sq km) / 36%
Total area 21,924 sq. miles (56,785 sq. km)
Languages French*, Ewe, Kabye, Gurma
Religions Traditional beliefs 50%, Christian 35%, Muslim 15%
Ethnic mix Ewe 46%, Other African 41%, Kabye 12%, European 1%
Government Presidential system
Currency CFA franc = 100 centimes
Literacy rate 53%
Calorie consumption 2345 calories

TONGA
Australasia & Oceania

Official name Kingdom of Tonga
Formation 1970 / 1970
Capital Nuku'alofa
Population 116,921 / 421 people per sq mile (162 people per sq km) / 34%
Total area 289 sq. miles (748 sq. km)
Languages English*, Tongan*
Religions Free Wesleyan 41%, Other 17%, Roman Catholic 16%, Church of Jesus Christ of Latter-day Saints 14%, Free Church of Tonga 12%
Ethnic mix Tongan 98%, Other 2%
Government Monarchy
Currency Pa'anga (Tongan dollar) = 100 seniti
Literacy rate 99%
Calorie consumption Not available

TRINIDAD & TOBAGO
West Indies

Official name Republic of Trinidad and Tobago
Formation 1962 / 1962
Capital Port-of-Spain
Population 1.3 million / 656 people per sq mile (253 people per sq km) / 76%
Total area 1980 sq. miles (5128 sq. km)
Languages English Creole, English*, Hindi, French, Spanish
Religions Roman Catholic 32%, Hindu 24%, Protestant 14%, Anglican 14%, Other and nonreligious 9%, Muslim 7%
Ethnic mix East Indian 40%, Black 40%, Mixed race 18%, Other 1%, White and Chinese 1%
Government Parliamentary system
Currency Trinidad and Tobago dollar = 100 cents
Literacy rate 99%
Calorie consumption 2732 calories

TUNISIA
North Africa

Official name The Tunisian Republic
Formation 1956 / 1956
Capital Tunis
Population 10.3 million / 172 people per sq mile (66 people per sq km) / 64%
Total area 63,169 sq. miles (163,610 sq. km)
Languages Arabic*, French
Religions Muslim (mainly Sunni) 98%, Christian 1%, Jewish 1%
Ethnic mix Arab and Berber 98%, Jewish 1%, European 1%
Government Presidential system
Currency Tunisian dinar = 1000 millimes
Literacy rate 74%
Calorie consumption 3238 calories

TURKEY
Asia / Europe

Official name Republic of Turkey
Formation 1923 / 1939
Capital Ankara
Population 75.2 million / 253 people per sq mile (98 people per sq km) / 67%
Total area 301,382 sq. miles (780,580 sq. km)
Languages Turkish*, Kurdish, Arabic, Circassian, Armenian, Greek, Georgian, Ladino
Religions Muslim (mainly Sunni) 99%, Other 1%
Ethnic mix Turkish 70%, Kurdish 20%, Other 8%, Arab 2%
Government Parliamentary system
Currency new Turkish lira = 100 kurus
Literacy rate 98%
Calorie consumption 3357 calories

TURKMENISTAN
Central Asia

Official name Turkmenistan
Formation 1991 / 1991
Capital Ashgabat
Population 5 million / 27 people per sq mile (10 people per sq km) / 46%
Total area 188,455 sq. miles (488,100 sq. km)
Languages Turkmen*, Uzbek, Russian, Kazakh, Tatar
Religions Sunni Muslim 87%, Orthodox Christian 11%, Other 2%
Ethnic mix Turkmen 77%, Uzbek 9%, Russian 7%, Other 4%, Kazakh 2%, Tatar 1%
Government One-party state
Currency Manat = 100 tenge
Literacy rate 99%
Calorie consumption 2742 calories

TUVALU
Australasia & Oceania

Official name Tuvalu
Formation 1978 / 1978
Capital Fongafale, on Funafuti Atoll
Population 11,992 / 1199 people per sq mile (461 people per sq km) / 57%
Total area 10 sq. miles (26 sq. km)
Languages English*, Tuvaluan, Kiribati
Religions Church of Tuvalu 97%, Baha'i 1%, Seventh-day Adventist 1%, Other 1%
Ethnic mix Polynesian 92%, Other 6%, Kiribati 2%
Government Nonparty system
Currency Australian dollar and Tuvaluan dollar = 100 cents
Literacy rate 98%
Calorie consumption Not available

UGANDA
East Africa

Official name Republic of Uganda
Formation 1962 / 1962
Capital Kampala
Population 30.9 million / 401 people per sq mile (155 people per sq km) / 12%
Total area 91,135 sq. miles (236,040 sq. km)
Languages English*, Luganda, Nkole, Chiga, Lango, Acholi, Teso, Lugbara
Religions Roman Catholic 38%, Protestant 33%, Traditional beliefs 13%, Muslim (mainly Sunni) 8%, Other 8%
Ethnic mix Other 50%, Baganda 17%, Banyakole 10%, Basoga 9%, Iteso 7%, Bakiga 7%
Government Presidential system
Currency New Uganda shilling = 100 cents
Literacy rate 67%
Calorie consumption 2410 calories

UKRAINE
Eastern Europe

Official name Ukraine
Formation 1991 / 1991
Capital Kiev
Population 45.5 million / 195 people per sq mile (75 people per sq km) / 67%
Total area 233,089 sq. miles (603,700 sq. km)
Languages Ukrainian*, Russian, Tatar
Religions Christian (mainly Orthodox) 95%, Other 5%
Ethnic mix Ukrainian 78%, Russian 17%, Other 5%
Government Presidential system
Currency Hryvna = 100 kopiykas
Literacy rate 99%
Calorie consumption 3054 calories

UNITED ARAB EMIRATES
Southwest Asia

Official name United Arab Emirates
Formation 1971 / 1972
Capital Abu Dhabi
Population 4.8 million / 149 people per sq mile (57 people per sq km) / 85%
Total area 32,000 sq. miles (82,880 sq. km)
Languages Arabic*, Farsi, Indian and Pakistani languages, English
Religions Muslim (mainly Sunni) 96%, Christian, Hindu, and other 4%
Ethnic mix Asian 60%, Emirian 25%, Other Arab 12%, European 3%
Government Monarchy
Currency UAE dirham = 100 fils
Literacy rate 77%
Calorie consumption 3225 calories

UNITED KINGDOM
Northwest Europe

Official name United Kingdom of Great Britain and Northern Ireland
Formation 1707 / 1922
Capital London
Population 60 million / 643 people per sq mile (248 people per sq km) / 89%
Total area 94,525 sq. miles (244,820 sq. km)
Languages English*, Welsh* *(in Wales)*, Scottish Gaelic, Irish Gaelic
Religions Anglican 45%, Roman Catholic 9%, Presbyterian 4%, Other 42%
Ethnic mix English 80%, Scottish 9%, West Indian, Asian, and other 5%, Northern Irish 3%, Welsh 3%
Government Parliamentary system
Currency Pound sterling = 100 pence
Literacy rate 99%
Calorie consumption 3412 calories

UNITED STATES
North America

Official name United States of America
Formation 1776 / 1959
Capital Washington D.C.
Population 304 million / 86 people per sq mile (33 people per sq km) / 80%
Total area 3,717,792 sq. miles (9,626,091 sq. km)
Languages 2%, Roman Catholic 25%, Muslim 2%, Jewish 2%, Other 19%
Ethnic mix White 62%, Hispanic 13%, Black American/African 13%, Other 7%, Asian 4%, Native American 1%
Government Presidential system
Currency US dollar = 100 cents
Literacy rate 99%
Calorie consumption 3774 calories

URUGUAY
South America

Official name The Oriental Republic of Uruguay
Formation 1828 / 1828
Capital Montevideo
Population 3.5 million / 52 people per sq mile (20 people per sq km) / 93%
Total area 68,039 sq. miles (176,220 sq. km)
Languages Spanish*
Religions Roman Catholic 66%, Other and nonreligious 30%, Jewish 2%,Protestant 2%
Ethnic mix White 90%, Mestizo 6%, Black 4%
Government Presidential system
Currency Uruguayan peso = 100 centésimos
Literacy rate 98%
Calorie consumption 2828 calories

UZBEKISTAN
Central Asia

Official name Republic of Uzbekistan
Formation 1991 / 1991
Capital Tashkent
Population 27.4 million / 159 people per sq mile (61 people per sq km) / 37%
Total area 172,741 sq. miles (447,400 sq. km)
Languages Uzbek*, Russian, Tajik, Kazakh
Religions Sunni Muslim 88%, Orthodox Christian 9%, Other 3%
Ethnic mix Uzbek 80%, Other 6%, Russian 6%, Tajik 5%, Kazakh 3%
Government Presidential system
Currency Som = 100 tiyin
Literacy rate 99%
Calorie consumption 2241 calories

VANUATU
Australasia & Oceania

Official name Republic of Vanuatu
Formation 1980 / 1980
Capital Port Vila
Population 211,971 / 45 people per sq mile (17 people per sq km) / 23%
Total area 4710 sq. miles (12,200 sq. km)
Languages Bislama* (Melanesian pidgin), English*, French*, other indigenous languages
Religions Presbyterian 37%, Other 19%, Anglican 15%, Roman Catholic 15%, Traditional beliefs 8%, Seventh-day Adventist 6%
Ethnic mix Melanesian 98%, Other 1%, European 1%
Government Parliamentary system
Currency Vatu = 100 centimes
Literacy rate 74%
Calorie consumption 2587 calories

VATICAN CITY
Southern Europe

Official name The Vatican City
Formation 1929 / 1929
Capital Vatican City
Population 821 / 4829 people per sq mile (1866 people per sq km) / 100%
Total area 0.17 sq. miles (0.44 sq. km)
Languages Italian*, Latin*
Religions Roman Catholic 100%
Government Papal state
Currency Euro = 100 cents
Literacy rate 99%
Calorie consumption Not available

VENEZUELA
South America

Official name Bolivarian Republic of Venezuela
Formation 1830 / 1830
Capital Caracas
Population 27.7 million / 81 people per sq mile (31 people per sq km) / 88%
Total area 352,143 sq. miles (912,050 sq. km)
Languages Spanish*, Amerindian languages
Religions Roman Catholic 89%, Protestant and other 11%
Ethnic mix Mestizo 69%, White 20%, Black 9%, Amerindian 2%
Government Presidential system
Currency Bolívar = 100 céntimos
Literacy rate 93%
Calorie consumption 2336 calories

VIETNAM
Southeast Asia

Official name Socialist Republic of Vietnam
Formation 1976 / 1976
Capital Hanoi
Population 86.4 million / 688 people per sq mile (266 people per sq km) / 26%
Total area 127,243 sq. miles (329,560 sq. km)
Languages Vietnamese*, Chinese, Thai, Khmer, Muong, Nung, Miao, Yao, Jarai
Religions Nonreligious 81%, Buddhist 9%, Christian 7%, Other 3%
Ethnic mix Vietnamese 86%, Other 10%, Tay 2%Thai 2%
Government One-party state
Currency Dông = 10 hao = 100 xu
Literacy rate 90%
Calorie consumption 2566 calories

YEMEN
Southwest Asia

Official name Republic of Yemen
Formation 1990 / 1990
Capital Sana
Population 22.3 million / 103 people per sq mile (40 people per sq km) / 26%
Total area 203,849 sq. miles (527,970 sq. km)
Languages Arabic*
Religions Sunni Muslim 55%, Shi'a Muslim 42%, Christian, Hindu, and Jewish 3%
Ethnic mix Arab 99%, Other 1%
Government Presidential system
Currency Yemeni rial = 100 fils
Literacy rate 49%
Calorie consumption 2038 calories

ZAMBIA
Southern Africa

Official name Republic of Zambia
Formation 1964 / 1964
Capital Lusaka
Population 12.1 million / 42 people per sq mile (16 people per sq km) / 36%
Total area 290,584 sq. miles (752,614 sq. km)
Languages English*, Bemba, Tonga, Nyanja, Lozi, Lala-Bisa, Nsenga
Religions Christian 63%, Traditional beliefs 36%, Muslim and Hindu 1%
Ethnic mix Bemba 34%, Other African 26%, Tonga 16%, Nyanja 14%, Lozi 9%, European 1%
Government Presidential system
Currency Zambian kwacha = 100 ngwee
Literacy rate 68%
Calorie consumption 1927 calories

ZIMBABWE
Southern Africa

Official name Republic of Zimbabwe
Formation 1980 / 1980
Capital Harare
Population 13.2 million / 88 people per sq mile (34 people per sq km) / 35%
Total area 150,803 sq. miles (390,580 sq. km)
Languages English*, Shona, isiNdebele
Religions Syncretic (Christian/traditional beliefs) 50%, Christian 25%, Traditional beliefs 24%, Other (including Muslim) 1%
Ethnic mix Shona 71%, Ndebele 16%, Other African 11%, White 1%Asian 1%
Government Presidential system
Currency Zimbabwe dollar = 100 cents
Literacy rate 90%
Calorie consumption 1943 calories

GLOSSARY

This glossary lists all geographical, technical and foreign language terms which appear in the text, followed by a brief definition of the term. Any acronyms used in the text are also listed in full. Terms in italics are for cross-reference and indicate that the word is separately defined in the glossary.

A

Aboriginal The original (indigenous) inhabitants of a country or continent. Especially used with reference to Australia.

Abyssal plain A broad plain found in the depths of the ocean, more than 10,000 ft (3000 m) below sea level.

Acid rain Rain, sleet, snow or mist which has absorbed waste gases from fossil-fuelled power stations and vehicle exhausts, becoming more acid. It causes severe environmental damage.

Adaptation The gradual evolution of plants and animals so that they become better suited to survive and reproduce in their *environment*.

Afforestation The planting of new forest in areas which were once forested but have been cleared.

Agribusiness A term applied to activities such as the growing of crops, rearing of animals or the manufacture of farm machinery, which eventually leads to the supply of agricultural produce at market.

Air mass A huge, homogeneous mass of air, within which horizontal patterns of temperature and *humidity* are consistent. Air masses are separated by *fronts*.

Alliance An agreement between two or more states, to work together to achieve common purposes.

Alluvial fan A large fan-shaped deposit of fine sediments deposited by a river as it emerges from a narrow, mountain valley onto a broad, open *plain*.

Alluvium Material deposited by rivers. Nowadays usually only applied to finer particles of silt and clay.

Alpine Mountain *environment*, between the *treeline* and the level of permanent snow cover.

Alpine mountains Ranges of mountains formed between 30 and 65 million years ago, by *folding*, in west and central Europe.

Amerindian A term applied to people *indigenous* to North, Central and South America.

Animal husbandry The business of rearing animals.

Antarctic circle The parallel which lies at *latitude* of 66° 32' S.

Anticline A geological *fold* that forms an arch shape, curving upwards in the rock *strata*.

Anticyclone An area of relatively high atmospheric pressure.

Aquaculture Collective term for the farming of produce derived from the sea, including fish-farming, the cultivation of shellfish, and plants such as seaweed.

Aquifer A body of rock which can absorb water. Also applied to any rock strata that have sufficient porosity to yield *groundwater* through wells or springs.

Arable Land which has been ploughed and is being used, or is suitable, for growing crops.

Archipelago A group or chain of islands.

Arctic Circle The parallel which lies at a *latitude* of 66° 32' N.

Arête A thin, jagged mountain ridge which divides two adjacent *cirques*, found in regions where *glaciation* has occurred.

Arid Dry. An area of low rainfall, where the rate of *evaporation* may be greater than that of *precipitation*. Often defined as those areas that receive less than one inch (25 mm) of rain a year. In these areas only drought-resistant plants can survive.

Artesian well A naturally occurring source of underground water, stored in an *aquifer*.

Artisanal Small-scale, manual operation, such as fishing, using little or no machinery.

ASEAN Association of Southeast Asian Nations. Established in 1967 to promote economic, social and cultural co-operation. Its members include Brunei, Indonesia, Malaysia, Philippines, Singapore and Thailand.

Aseismic A region where *earthquake* activity has ceased.

Asteroid A minor planet circling the Sun, mainly between the orbits of Mars and Jupiter.

Asthenosphere A zone of hot, partially melted rock, which underlies the *lithosphere*, within the Earth's *crust*.

Atmosphere The envelope of odourless, colourless and tasteless gases surrounding the Earth, consisting of *oxygen* (23%), *nitrogen* (75%), argon (1%), *carbon dioxide* (0.03%), as well as tiny proportions of other gases.

Atmospheric pressure The pressure created by the action of gravity on the gases surrounding the Earth.

Atoll A ring-shaped island or *coral reef* often enclosing a *lagoon* of sea water.

Avalanche The rapid movement of a mass of snow and ice down a steep slope. Similar movements of other materials are described as *rock avalanches* or *landslides* and *sand avalanches*.

B

Badlands A landscape that has been heavily eroded and dissected by rainwater, and which has little or no vegetation.

Back slope The gentler windward slope of a sand *dune* or gentler slope of a *cuesta*.

Bajos An *alluvial fan* deposited by a river at the base of mountains and hills which encircle *desert* areas.

Bar, coastal An offshore strip of sand or shingle, either above or below the water. Usually parallel to the shore but sometimes crescent-shaped or at an oblique angle.

Barchan A crescent-shaped sand *dune*, formed where wind direction is very consistent. The horns of the crescent point downwind and where there is enough sand the barchan is mobile.

Barrio A Spanish term for the shanty towns – self-built settlements – which are clustered around many South and Central American cities (*see also Favela*).

Basalt Dark, fine-grained *igneous rock*. Formed near the Earth's surface from fast-cooling *lava*.

Base level The level below which flowing water cannot erode the land.

Basement rock A mass of ancient rock often of *Pre-Cambrian age*, covered by a layer of more recent *sedimentary rocks*. Commonly associated with *shield* areas.

Beach Lake or sea shore where waves break and there is an accumulation of loose material – mud, sand, shingle or pebbles.

Bedrock Solid, consolidated and relatively unweathered rock, found on the surface of the land or just below a layer of soil or *weathered* rock.

Biodiversity The quantity of animal or plant species in a given area.

Biomass The total mass of organic matter – plants and animals – in a given area. It is usually measured in kilogrammes per square metre. Plant biomass is proportionally greater than that of animals, except in cities.

Biosphere The zone just above and below the Earth's surface, where all plants and animals live.

Blizzard A severe windstorm with snow and sleet. Visibility is often severely restricted.

Bluff The steep bank of a *meander*, formed by the erosive action of a river.

Boreal forest Tracts of mainly coniferous forest found in northern *latitudes*.

Breccia A type of rock composed of sharp fragments, cemented by a fine-grained material such as clay.

Butte An isolated, flat-topped hill with steep or vertical sides, buttes are the eroded remnants of a former land surface.

C

Caatinga Portuguese (Brazilian) term for thorny woodland growing in areas of pale granitic soils.

CACM Central American Common Market. Established in 1960 to further economic ties between its members, which are Costa Rica, El Salvador, Guatemala, Honduras and Nicaragua.

Calcite Hexagonal crystals of calcium carbonate.

Caldera A huge volcanic vent, often containing a number of smaller vents, and sometimes a crater lake.

Carbon cycle The transfer of carbon to and from the *atmosphere*. This occurs on land through *photosynthesis*. In the sea, *carbon dioxide* is absorbed, some returning to the air and some taken up into the bodies of sea creatures.

Carbon dioxide A colourless, odourless gas (CO_2) which makes up 0.03% of the *atmosphere*.

Carbonation The process whereby rocks are broken down by carbonic acid. Carbon dioxide in the air dissolves in rainwater, forming carbonic acid. *Limestone* terrain can be rapidly eaten away.

Cash crop A single crop grown specifically for export sale, rather than for local use. Typical examples include coffee, tea and citrus fruits.

Cassava A type of grain meal, used to produce tapioca. A staple crop in many parts of Africa.

Castle kopje Hill or rock outcrop, especially in southern Africa, where steep sides, and a summit composed of blocks, give a castle-like appearance.

Cataracts A series of stepped waterfalls created as a river flows over a band of hard, resistant rock.

Causeway A raised route through marshland or a body of water.

CEEAC Economic Community of Central African States. Established in 1983 to promote regional co-operation and if possible, establish a common market between 16 Central African nations.

Chemical weathering The chemical reactions leading to the decomposition of rocks. Types of chemical weathering include *carbonation*, *hydrolysis* and *oxidation*.

Chernozem A fertile soil, also known as 'black earth' consisting of a layer of dark topsoil, rich in decaying vegetation, overlying a lighter chalky layer.

Cirque Armchair-shaped basin, found in mountain regions, with a steep back, or rear, wall and a raised rock lip, often containing a lake (or *tarn*). The cirque floor has been eroded by a *glacier*, while the back wall is eroded both by the *glacier* and by *weathering*.

Climate The average weather conditions in a given area over a period of years, sometimes defined as 30 years or more.

Cold War A period of hostile relations between the USA and the Soviet Union and their allies after the Second World War.

Composite volcano Also known as a strato-volcano, the volcanic cone is composed of alternating deposits of *lava* and *pyroclastic* material.

Compound A substance made up of *elements* chemically combined in a consistent way.

Condensation The process whereby a gas changes into a liquid. For example, water vapour in the *atmosphere* condenses around tiny airborne particles to form droplets of water.

Confluence The point at which two rivers meet.

Conglomerate Rock composed of large, water-worn or rounded pebbles, held together by a natural cement.

Coniferous forest A forest type containing trees which are generally, but not necessarily, *evergreen* and have slender, needle-like leaves and which reproduce by means of seeds contained in a cone.

Continental drift The theory that the continents of today are fragments of one or more prehistoric *supercontinents* which have moved across the Earth's surface, creating ocean basins. The theory has been superseded by a more sophisticated one – *plate tectonics*.

Continental shelf An area of the continental crust, below sea level, which slopes gently. It is separated from the deep ocean by a much more steeply inclined *continental slope*.

Continental slope A steep slope running from the edge of the *continental shelf* to the ocean floor.

Conurbation A vast metropolitan area created by the expansion of towns and cities into a virtually continuous urban area.

Cool continental A rainy *climate* with warm summers [warmest month below 76°F (22°C)] and often severe winters [coldest month below 32°F (0°C)].

Copra The dried, white kernel of a coconut, from which coconut oil is extracted.

Coral reef An underwater barrier created by colonies of the coral polyp. Polyps secrete a protective skeleton of calcium carbonate, and reefs develop as live polyps build on the skeletons of dead generations.

Core The centre of the Earth, consisting of a dense mass of iron and nickel. It is thought that the outer core is molten or liquid, and that the hot inner core is solid due to extremely high pressures.

Coriolis effect A deflecting force caused by the rotation of the Earth. In the northern hemisphere a body, such as an *air mass* or ocean current, is deflected to the right, and in the southern hemisphere to the left. This prevents winds from blowing straight from areas of high to low pressure.

Coulées A US / Canadian term for a ravine formed by river *erosion*.

Craton A large block of the Earth's *crust* which has remained stable for a long period of *geological time*. It is made up of ancient *shield* rocks.

Cretaceous A period of *geological time* beginning about 145 million years ago and lasting until about 65 million years ago.

Crevasse A deep crack in a *glacier*.

Crust The hard, thin outer shell of the Earth. The crust floats on the *mantle*, which is softer and more dense. Under the oceans (oceanic crust) the crust is 3.7–6.8 miles (6–11 km) thick. Continental crust averages 18–24 miles (30–40 km).

Crystalline rock Rocks formed when molten *magma* crystallizes (*igneous rocks*) or when heat or pressure cause re-crystallization (*metamorphic rocks*). Crystalline rocks are distinct from *sedimentary rocks*.

Cuesta A hill which rises into a steep slope on one side but has a gentler gradient on its other slope.

Cyclone An area of low *atmospheric pressure*, occurring where the air is warm and relatively low in density, causing low level winds to spiral. *Hurricanes* and *typhoons* are tropical cyclones.

D

De facto
1 Government or other activity that takes place, or exists in actuality if not by right.
2 A border, which exists in practice, but which is not officially recognized by all the countries it adjoins.

Deciduous forest A forest of trees which shed their leaves annually at a particular time or season. In *temperate* climates the fall of leaves occurs in the Autumn. Some *coniferous* trees, such as the larch, are deciduous. Deciduous vegetation contrasts with *evergreen*, which keeps its leaves for more than a year.

Defoliant Chemical spray used to remove foliage (leaves) from trees.

Deforestation The act of cutting down and clearing large areas of forest for human activities, such as agricultural land or urban development.

Delta Low-lying, fan-shaped area at a river mouth, formed by the *deposition* of successive layers of *sediment*. Slowing as it enters the sea, a river deposits sediment and may, as a result, split into numerous smaller channels, known as *distributaries*.

Denudation The combined effect of *weathering*, *erosion* and *mass movement*, which, over long periods, exposes underlying rocks.

Deposition The laying down of material that has accumulated:
(1) after being *eroded* and then transported by physical forces such as wind, ice or water;
(2) as organic remains, such as coal and coral;
(3) as the result of *evaporation* and chemical *precipitation*.

Depression
1 In climatic terms it is a large low pressure system.
2 A complex *fold*, producing a large valley, which incorporates both a *syncline* and an *anticline*.

Desert An *arid* region of low rainfall, with little vegetation or animal life, which is adapted to the dry conditions. The term is now applied not only to hot tropical and subtropical regions, but to arid areas of the continental interiors and to the ice deserts of the *Arctic* and *Antarctic*.

Desertification The gradual extension of *desert* conditions in *arid* or *semi-arid* regions, as a result of climatic change or human activity, such as over-grazing and *deforestation*.

Despot A ruler with absolute power. Despots are often associated with oppressive regimes.

Detritus Piles of rock deposited by an erosive agent such as a river or *glacier*.

Distributary A minor branch of a river, which does not rejoin the main stream, common at *deltas*.

Diurnal Daily, something that occurs each day. Diurnal temperature refers to the variation in temperature over the course of a full day and night.

Divide A US term describing the area of high ground separating two *drainage basins*.

Donga A steep-sided *gully*, resulting from *erosion* by a river or by floods.

Dormant A term used to describe a *volcano* which is not currently erupting. They differ from extinct volcanoes as dormant volcanoes are still considered likely to erupt in the future.

Drainage basin The area drained by a single river system, its boundary is marked by a *watershed* or *divide*.

Drought A long period of continuously low rainfall.

Drumlin A long, streamlined hillock composed of material deposited by a *glacier*. They often occur in groups known as swarms.

Dune A mound or ridge of sand, shaped, and often moved, by the wind. They are found in hot *deserts* and on low-lying coasts where onshore winds blow across sandy beaches.

Dyke A wall constructed in low-lying areas to contain floodwaters or protect from high tides.

E

Earthflow The rapid movement of soil and other loose surface material down a slope, when saturated by water. Similar to a mudflow but not as fast-flowing, due to a lower percentage of water.

Earthquake Sudden movements of the Earth's *crust*, causing the ground to shake. Frequently occurring at *tectonic plate* margins. The shock, or series of shocks, spreads out from an *epicentre*.

EC The European Community (*see* EU).

Ecosystem A system of living organisms – plants and animals – interacting with their *environment*.

ECOWAS Economic Community of West African States. Established in 1975, it incorporates 16 West African states and aims to promote closer regional and economic co-operation.

Element
1 A constituent of the *climate* – *precipitation*, *humidity*, temperature, *atmospheric pressure* or wind.
2 A substance that cannot be separated into simpler substances by chemical means.

El Niño A climatic phenomenon, the El Niño effect occurs about 14 times each century and leads to major shifts in global air circulation. It is associated with unusually warm currents off the coasts of Peru, Ecuador and Chile. The anomaly can last for up to two years.

Environment The conditions created by the surroundings (both natural and artificial) within which an organism lives. In human geography the word includes the surrounding economic, cultural and social conditions.

Eon (aeon) Traditionally a long, but indefinite, period of *geological time*.

Ephemeral A non-permanent feature, often used in connection with seasonal rivers or lakes in dry areas.

Epicentre The point on the Earth's surface directly above the underground origin – or focus – of an *earthquake*.

Equator The line of *latitude* which lies equidistant between the North and South Poles.

Erg An extensive area of sand *dunes*, particularly in the Sahara Desert.

Erosion The processes which wear away the surface of the land. *Glaciers*, wind, rivers, waves and currents all carry debris which causes *erosion*. Some definitions also include *mass movement* due to gravity as an agent of erosion.

Escarpment A steep slope at the margin of a level, upland surface. In a landscape created by *folding*, escarpments (or scarps) frequently lie behind a more gentle backward slope.

Esker A narrow, winding ridge of sand and gravel deposited by streams of water flowing beneath or at the edge of a *glacier*.

Erratic A rock transported by a *glacier* and deposited some distance from its place of origin.

Eustacy A world-wide fall or rise in ocean levels.

EU The European Union. Established in 1965, it was formerly known as the EEC (European Economic Community) and then the EC (European Community). Its members are Austria, Belgium, Denmark, Finland, France, Germany, Greece, Ireland, Italy, Luxembourg, Netherlands, Portugal, Spain, Sweden and UK. It seeks to establish an integrated European common market and eventual federation.

Evaporation The process whereby a liquid or solid is turned into a gas or vapour. Also refers to the diffusion of water vapour into the *atmosphere* from exposed water surfaces such as lakes and seas.

Evapotranspiration The loss of moisture from the Earth's surface through a combination of *evaporation*, and *transpiration* from the leaves of plants.

Evergreen Plants with long-lasting leaves, which are not shed annually or seasonally.

Exfoliation A kind of *weathering* whereby scale-like flakes of rock are peeled or broken off by the development of salt crystals in water within the rocks. *Groundwater*, which contains dissolved salts, seeps to the surface and evaporates, precipitating a film of salt crystals, which expands causing fine cracks. As these grow, flakes of rock break off.

Extrusive rock *Igneous* rock formed when molten material (*magma*) pours forth at the Earth's surface and cools rapidly. It usually has a glassy texture.

F

Factionalism The actions of one or more minority political group acting against the interests of the majority government.

Fault A fracture or crack in rock, where strains (*tectonic* movement) have caused blocks to move, vertically or laterally, relative to each other.

Fauna Collective name for the animals of a particular period of time, or region.

Favela Brazilian term for the shanty towns or self-built, temporary dwellings which have grown up around the edge of many South and Central American cities.

Ferrel cell A component in the global pattern of air circulation, which rises in the colder *latitudes* (60° N and S) and descends in warmer *latitudes* (30° N and S). The Ferrel cell forms part of the world's three-cell air circulation pattern, with the *Hadley* and Polar cells.

Fissure A deep crack in a rock or a *glacier*.

Fjord A deep, narrow inlet, created when the sea inundates the *U-shaped valley* created by a *glacier*.

Flash flood A sudden, short-lived rise in the water level of a river or stream, or surge of water down a dry river channel, or *wadi*, caused by heavy rainfall.

Flax A plant used to make linen.

Flood plain The broad, flat part of a river valley, adjacent to the river itself, formed by *sediment* deposited during flooding.

Flora The collective name for the plants of a particular period of time or region.

Flow The movement of a river within its banks, particularly in terms of the speed and volume of water.

Fold A bend in the rock *strata* of the Earth's *crust*, resulting from compression.

Fossil The remains, or traces, of a dead organism preserved in the Earth's *crust*.

Fossil dune A *dune* formed in a once-*arid* region which is now wetter. *Dunes* normally move with the wind, but in these cases vegetation makes them stable.

Fossil fuel Fuel – coal, natural gas or oil – composed of the fossilized remains of plants and animals.

Front The boundary between two *air masses*, which contrast sharply in temperature and *humidity*.

Frontal depression An area of low pressure caused by rising warm air. They are generally 600–1200 miles (1000–2000 km) in diameter. Within *depressions* there are both warm and cold fronts.

Frost shattering A form of *weathering* where water freezes in cracks, causing expansion. As temperatures fluctuate and the ice melts and refreezes, it eventually causes the rocks to shatter and fragments of rock to break off.

Gaucho South American term for a stock herder or cowboy who works on the grassy *plains* of Paraguay, Uruguay and Argentina.

Geological time-scale The chronology of the Earth's history as revealed in its rocks. Geological time is divided into a number of periods: *eon*, era, period, epoch, age and chron (the shortest). These units are not of uniform length.

Geosyncline A concave fold (*syncline*) or large depression in the Earth's *crust*, extending hundreds of kilometres. This basin contains a deep layer of sediment, especially at its centre, from the land masses around it.

Geothermal energy Heat derived from hot rocks within the Earth's *crust* and resulting in hot springs, steam or hot rocks at the surface. The energy is generated by rock movements, and from the breakdown of radioactive elements occurring under intense pressure.

GDP Gross Domestic Product. The total value of goods and services produced by a country excluding income from foreign countries.

Geyser A jet of steam and hot water that intermittently erupts from vents in the ground in areas that are, or were, *volcanic*. Some geysers occasionally reach heights of 196 ft (60 m).

Ghetto An area of a city or region occupied by an overwhelming majority of people from one racial or religious group, who may be subject to persecution or containment.

Glaciation The growth of *glaciers* and *ice sheets*, and their impact on the landscape.

Glacier A body of ice moving downslope under the influence of gravity and consisting of compacted and frozen snow. A glacier is distinct from an *ice sheet*, which is wider and less confined by features of the landscape.

Glacio-eustacy A world-wide change in the level of the oceans, caused when the formation of *ice sheets* takes up water or when their melting returns water to the ocean. The formation of ice sheets in the *Pleistocene* epoch, for example, caused sea level to drop by about 320 ft (100 m).

Glaciofluvial To do with glacial *meltwater*, the landforms it creates and its processes; *erosion*, transportation and *deposition*. Glaciofluvial effects are more powerful and rapid where they occur within or beneath the *glacier*, rather than beyond its edge.

Glacis A gentle slope or *pediment*.

Global warming An increase in the average temperature of the Earth. At present the *greenhouse effect* is thought to contribute to this.

GNP Gross National Product. The total value of goods and services produced by a country.

Gondwanaland The *supercontinent* thought to have existed over 200 million years ago in the southern hemisphere. Gondwanaland is believed to have comprised today's Africa, Madagascar, Australia, parts of South America, *Antarctica* and the Indian subcontinent.

Graben A block of rock let down between two parallel *faults*. Where the graben occurs within a valley, the structure is known as a *rift valley*.

Grease ice Slicks of ice which form in *Antarctic* seas, when ice crystals are bonded together by wind and wave action.

Greenhouse effect A change in the temperature of the *atmosphere*. Short-wave solar radiation travels through the *atmosphere* unimpeded to the Earth's surface, whereas outgoing, long-wave terrestrial radiation is absorbed by materials that re-radiate it back to the Earth. Radiation trapped in this way, by water vapour, carbon dioxide and other 'greenhouse gases', keeps the Earth warm. As more *carbon dioxide* is released into the atmosphere by the burning of *fossil fuels*, the greenhouse effect may cause a global increase in temperature.

Groundwater Water that has seeped into the pores, cavities and cracks of rocks or into soil and water held in an *aquifer*.

Gully A deep, narrow channel eroded in the landscape by *ephemeral* streams.

Guyot A small, flat-topped submarine mountain, formed as a result of subsidence which occurs during *sea-floor spreading*.

Gypsum A soft mineral *compound* (hydrated calcium sulphate), used as the basis of many forms of plaster, including plaster of Paris.

H

Hadley cell A large-scale component in the global pattern of air circulation. Warm air rises over the *Equator* and blows at high altitude towards the poles, sinking in subtropical regions (30° N and 30° S) and creating high pressure. The air then flows at the surface towards the *Equator* in the form of trade winds. There is one cell in each hemisphere. Named after G Hadley, who published his theory in 1735.

Hamada An Arabic word for a plateau of bare rock in a *desert*.

Hanging valley A tributary valley which ends suddenly, high above the bed of the main valley. The effect is found where the main valley has been more deeply eroded by a *glacier*, than has the tributary valley. A stream in a hanging valley will descend to the floor of the main valley as a waterfall or *cataract*.

Headwards The action of a river eroding back upstream, as opposed to the normal process of downstream *erosion*. Headwards erosion is often associated with *gullying*.

Hoodos Pinnacles of rock which have been worn away by *weathering* in *semi-arid* regions.

Horst A block of the Earth's *crust* which has been left upstanding by the sinking of adjoining blocks along fault lines.

Hot spot A region of the Earth's *crust* where high thermal activity occurs, often leading to volcanic eruptions. Hot spots often occur far from plate boundaries, but their movement is associated with *plate tectonics*.

Humid equatorial Rainy *climate* with no winter, where the coolest month is generally above 64°F (18°C).

Humidity The relative amount of moisture held in the Earth's *atmosphere*.

Hurricane
1 A tropical *cyclone* occurring in the Caribbean and western North Atlantic.
2 A wind of more than 65 knots (75 kmph).

Hydro-electric power Energy produced by harnessing the rapid movement of water down steep mountain slopes to drive turbines to generate electricity.

Hydrolysis The chemical breakdown of rocks in reaction with water, forming new compounds.

I

Ice Age A period in the Earth's history when surface temperatures in the temperate *latitudes* were much lower and *ice sheets* expanded considerably. There have been *ice ages* from *Pre-Cambrian* times onwards. The most recent began two million years ago and ended 10,000 years ago.

Ice cap A permanent dome of ice in highland areas. The term ice cap is often seen as distinct from *ice sheet*, which denotes a much wider covering of ice; and is also used refer to the very extensive polar and Greenland ice caps.

Ice floe A large, flat mass of ice floating free on the ocean surface. It is usually formed after the break-up of winter ice by heavy storms.

Ice sheet A continuous, very thick layer of ice and snow. The term is usually used of ice masses which are continental in extent.

Ice shelf A floating mass of ice attached to the edge of a coast. The seaward edge is usually a sheer cliff up to 100 ft (30 m) high.

Ice wedge Massive blocks of ice up to 6.5 ft (2 m) wide at the top and extending 32 ft (10 m) deep. They are found in cracks in *polygonally-patterned* ground in *periglacial* regions.

Iceberg A large mass of ice in a lake or a sea, which has broken off from a floating *ice sheet* (an *ice shelf*) or from a *glacier*.

Igneous rock Rock formed when molten material, *magma*, from the hot, lower layers of the Earth's *crust*, cools, solidifies and crystallizes, either within the Earth's *crust* (*intrusive*) or on the surface (*extrusive*).

IMF International Monetary Fund. Established in 1944 as a UN agency, it contains 182 members around the world and is concerned with world monetary stability and economic development.

Incised meander A *meander* where the river, following its original course, cuts deeply into *bedrock*. This may occur when a mature, meandering river begins to erode its bed much more vigorously after the surrounding land has been uplifted.

Indigenous People, plants or animals native to a particular region.

Infrastructure The communications and services – roads, railways and telecommunications – necessary for the functioning of a country or region.

Inselberg An isolated, steep-sided hill, rising from a low *plain* in *semi-arid* and *savannah* landscapes. Inselbergs are usually composed of a rock, such as granite, which resists *erosion*.

Interglacial A period of global *climate*, between two *ice ages*, when temperatures rise and *ice sheets* and *glaciers* retreat.

Intraplate volcano A *volcano* which lies in the centre of one of the Earth's *tectonic plates*, rather than, as is more common, at its edge. They are thought to have been formed by a *hot spot*.

Intrusion (intrusive igneous rock) Rock formed when molten material, *magma*, penetrates existing rocks below the Earth's surface before cooling and solidifying. These rocks cool more slowly than extrusive rock and therefore tend to have coarser grains.

Irrigation The artificial supply of agricultural water to dry areas, often involving the creation of canals and the diversion of natural watercourses.

Island arc A curved chain of islands. Typically, such an arc fringes an ocean trench, formed at the margin between two *tectonic plates*. As one plate overrides another, *earthquakes* and volcanic activity are common and the islands themselves are often volcanic cones.

Isostasy The state of equilibrium which the Earth's *crust* maintains as its lighter and heavier parts float on the denser underlying mantle.

Isthmus A narrow strip of land connecting two larger landmasses or islands.

J

Jet stream A narrow belt of westerly winds in the *troposphere*, at altitudes above 39,000 ft (12,000 m). Jet streams tend to blow more strongly in winter and include: the subtropical jet stream; the *polar* front jet stream in mid-*latitudes*; the *Arctic* jet stream; and the polar-night jet stream.

Joint A crack in a rock, formed where blocks of rock have not shifted relative to each other, as is the case with a *fault*. Joints are created by *folding*; by shrinkage in *igneous rock* as it cools or *sedimentary rock* as it dries out; and by the release of pressure in a rock mass when overlying materials are removed by *erosion*.

Jute A plant fibre used to make coarse ropes, sacks and matting.

K

Kame A mound of stratified sand and gravel with steep sides, deposited in a *crevasse* by *meltwater* running over a *glacier*. When the ice retreats, this forms an undulating terrain of hummocks.

Karst A barren *limestone* landscape created by carbonic acid in streams and rainwater, in areas where *limestone* is close to the surface. Typical features include caverns, tower-like hills, *sinkholes* and flat limestone pavements.

Kettle hole A round hollow formed in a glacial deposit by a detached block of glacial ice, which later melted. They can fill with water to form kettle-lakes.

L

Lagoon A shallow stretch of coastal salt-water behind a partial barrier such as a sandbank or *coral reef*. Lagoon is also used to describe the water encircled by an *atoll*.

LAIA Latin American Integration Association. Established in 1980, its members are Argentina, Bolivia, Brazil, Chile, Colombia, Ecuador, Mexico, Paraguay, Peru, Uruguay and Venezuala. It aims to promote economic co-operation between member states.

Landslide The sudden downslope movement of a mass of rock or earth on a slope, caused either by heavy rain; the impact of waves; an *earthquake* or human activity.

Laterite A hard red deposit left by *chemical weathering* in tropical conditions, and consisting mainly of oxides of iron and aluminium.

Latitude The angular distance from the *Equator*, to a given point on the Earth's surface. Imaginary lines of *latitude* running parallel to the Equator encircle the Earth, and are measured in degrees north or south of the Equator. The Equator is 0°, the poles 90° South and North respectively. Also called parallels.

Laurasia In the theory of *continental drift*, the northern part of the great *supercontinent* of *Pangaea*. Laurasia is said to consist of N America, Greenland and all of Eurasia north of the Indian subcontinent.

Lava The molten rock, *magma*, which erupts onto the Earth's surface through a *volcano*, or through a *fault* or crack in the Earth's *crust*. Lava refers to the rock both in its molten and in its later, solidified form.

Leaching The process whereby water dissolves minerals and moves them down through layers of soil or rock.

Levée A raised bank alongside the channel of a river. Levées are either human-made or formed in times of flood when the river overflows its channel, slows and deposits much of its *sediment* load.

Lichen An organism which is the symbiotic product of an algae and a fungus. Lichens form in tight crusts on stones and trees, and are resistant to extreme cold. They are often found in tundra regions.

Lignite Low-grade coal, also known as brown coal. Found in large deposits in eastern Europe.

Limestone A porous *sedimentary* rock formed from carbonate materials.

Lingua franca The language adopted as the common language between speakers whose native languages are different. This is common in former colonial states.

Lithosphere The rigid upper layer of the Earth, comprising the *crust* and the upper part of the *mantle*.

Llanos Vast grassland *plains* of northern South America.

Loess Fine-grained, yellow deposits of unstratified silts and sands. Loess is believed to be wind-carried *sediment* created in the last *Ice Age*. Some deposits may later have been redistributed by rivers. Loess-derived soils are of high quality, fertile and easy to work.

Longitude A division of the Earth which pinpoints how far east or west a given place is from the Prime Meridian (0°) which runs through the Royal Observatory at Greenwich, England (UK). Imaginary lines of longitude are drawn around the world from pole to pole. The world is divided into 360 degrees.

Longshore drift The transport of sand and silt along the coast, carried by waves hitting the beach at an angle.

M

Magma Underground, molten rock, which is very hot and highly charged with gas. It is generated at great pressure, at depths 10 miles (16 km) or more below the Earth's surface. It can issue as *lava* at the Earth's surface or, more often, solidify below the surface as *intrusive igneous rock*.

Mantle The layer of the Earth between the *crust* and the *core*. It is about 1800 miles (2900 km) thick. The uppermost layer of the mantle is the soft, 125 mile (200 km) thick *asthenosphere* on which the more rigid *lithosphere* floats.

Maquiladoras Factories on the Mexico side of the Mexico/US border, which are allowed to import raw materials and components duty-free and use low-cost labour to assemble the goods, finally exporting them for sale in the US.

Market gardening The intensive growing of fruit and vegetables close to large local markets.

Mass movement Downslope movement of weathered materials such as rock, often helped by rainfall or glacial *meltwater*. Mass movement may be a gradual process or rapid, as in a *landslide* or rockfall.

Massif A single very large mountain or an area of mountains with uniform characteristics and clearly-defined boundaries.

Meander A loop-like bend in a river, which is found typically in the lower, mature reaches of a river but can form wherever the valley is wide and the slope gentle.

Mediterranean climate A temperate *climate* of hot, dry summers and warm, damp winters. This is typical of the western fringes of the world's continents in the warm temperate regions between *latitudes* of 30° and 40° (north and south).

Meltwater Water resulting from the melting of a *glacier* or *ice sheet*.

Mesa A broad, flat-topped hill, characteristic of *arid* regions.

Mesosphere A layer of the Earth's *atmosphere*, between the *stratosphere* and the *thermosphere*. Extending from about 25–50 miles (40–80 km) above the surface of the Earth.

Mestizo A person of mixed *Amerindian* and European origin.

Metallurgy The refining and working of metals.

Metamorphic rocks Rocks which have been altered from their original form, in terms of texture, composition and structure by intense heat, pressure, or by the introduction of new chemical substances – or a combination of more than one of these.

Meteor A body of rock, metal or other material, which travels through space at great speeds. Meteors are visible as they enter the Earth's *atmosphere* as shooting stars and fireballs.

Meteorite The remains of a *meteor* that has fallen to Earth.

Meteoroid A *meteor* which is still travelling in space, outside the Earth's *atmosphere*.

Mezzogiorno A term applied to the southern portion of Italy.

Milankovitch hypothesis A theory suggesting that there are a series of cycles which slightly alter the Earth's position when rotating about the Sun. The cycles identified all affect the amount of *radiation* the Earth receives at different *latitudes*. The theory is seen as a key factor in the cause of *ice ages*.

Millet A grain-crop, forming part of the staple diet in much of Africa.

Mistral A strong, dry, cold northerly or north-westerly wind, which blows from the Massif Central of France to the Mediterranean Sea. It is common in winter and its cold blasts can cause crop damage in the Rhône Delta, in France.

Mohorovicic discontinuity (Moho) The structural divide at the margin between the Earth's *crust* and the *mantle*. On average it is 20 miles (35 km) below the continents and 6 miles (10 km) below the oceans. The different densities of the *crust* and the mantle cause *earthquake* waves to accelerate at this point.

Monarchy A form of government in which the head of state is a single hereditary monarch. The monarch may be a mere figurehead, or may retain significant authority.

Monsoon A wind which changes direction bi-annually. The change is caused by the reversal of pressure over landmasses and the adjacent oceans. Because the inflowing moist winds bring rain, the term monsoon is also used to refer to the rains themselves. The term is derived from and most commonly refers to the seasonal winds of south and east Asia.

Montaña Mountain areas along the west coast of South America.

Moraine Debris, transported and deposited by a *glacier* or *ice sheet* in unstratified, mixed, piles of rock, boulders, pebbles and clay.

Mountain-building The formation of *fold* mountains by tectonic activity. Also known as orogeny, mountain-building often occurs on the margin where two *tectonic plates* collide. The periods when most mountain-building occurred are known as orogenic phases and lasted many millions of years.

Mudflow An *avalanche* of mud which occurs when a mass of soil is drenched by rain or melting snow. It is a type of *mass movement*, faster than an *earthflow* because it is lubricated by water.

N

Nappe A mass of rocks which has been overfolded by repeated thrust *faulting*.

NAFTA The North American Free Trade Association. Established in 1994 between Canada, Mexico and the US to set up a free-trade zone.

NASA The North American Space Agency. It is a government body, established in 1958 to develop manned and unmanned space programmes.

NATO The North Atlantic Treaty Organization. Established in 1949 to promote mutual defence and co-operation between its members, which are Belgium, Canada, Czech Republic, Denmark, France, Germany, Greece, Iceland, Italy, Luxembourg, the Netherlands, Norway, Portugal, Poland, Spain, Turkey, UK, and US.

Nitrogen The odourless, colourless gas which makes up 78% of the atmosphere. Within the soil, it is a vital nutrient for plants.

Nomads (nomadic) Wandering communities who move around in search of suitable pasture for their herds of animals.

Nuclear fusion A technique used to create a new nucleus by the merging of two lighter ones, resulting in the release of large quantities of energy.

O

Oasis A fertile area in the midst of a *desert*, usually watered by an underground *aquifer*.

Oceanic ridge A mid-ocean ridge formed, according to the theory of *plate tectonics*, when plates drift apart and hot *magma* pours through to form new oceanic *crust*.

Oligarchy The government of a state by a small, exclusive group of people – such as an elite class or a family group.

Onion-skin weathering The *weathering* away or *exfoliation* of a rock or outcrop by the peeling off of surface layers.

Oriente A flatter region lying to the east of the Andes in South America.

Outwash plain *Glaciofluvial* material (typically clay, sand and gravel) carried beyond an ice sheet by *meltwater* streams, forming a broad, flat deposit.

Oxbow lake A crescent-shaped lake formed on a river *flood plain* when a river erodes the outside bend of a *meander*, making the neck of the *meander* narrower until the river cuts across the neck. The meander is cut off and is dammed off with sediment, creating an oxbow lake. Also known as a cut-off or mortlake.

Oxidation A form of *chemical weathering* where *oxygen* dissolved in water reacts with minerals in rocks – particularly iron – to form oxides. Oxidation causes brown or yellow staining on rocks, and eventually leads to the break down of the rock.

Oxygen A colourless, odourless gas which is one of the main constituents of the Earth's *atmosphere* and is essential to life on Earth.

Ozone layer A layer of enriched *oxygen* (O_3) within the stratosphere, mostly between 18–50 miles (30–80 km) above the Earth's surface. It is vital to the existence of life on Earth because it absorbs harmful shortwave ultraviolet radiation, while allowing beneficial longer wave ultraviolet radiation to penetrate to the Earth's surface.

P

Pacific Rim The name given to the economically-dynamic countries bordering the Pacific Ocean.

Pack ice Ice masses more than 10 ft (3 m) thick which form on the sea surface and are not attached to a landmass.

Pancake ice Thin discs of ice, up to 8 ft (2.4 m) wide which form when slicks of *grease ice* are tossed together by winds and stormy seas.

Pangaea In the theory of continental drift, Pangaea is the original great land mass which, about 190 million years ago, began to split into Gondwanaland in the south and Laurasia in the north, separated by the Tethys Sea.

Pastoralism Grazing of livestock– usually sheep, goats or cattle. Pastoralists in many drier areas have traditionally been *nomadic*.

Parallel *see Latitude.*

Peat Ancient, partially-decomposed vegetation found in wet, boggy conditions where there is little *oxygen*. It is the first stage in the development of coal and is often dried for use as fuel. It is also used to improve soil quality.

Pediment A gently-sloping ramp of *bedrock* below a steeper slope, often found at mountain edges in *desert* areas, but also in other climatic zones. Pediments may include depositional elements such as *alluvial fans*.

Peninsula A thin strip of land surrounded on three of its sides by water. Large examples include Florida and Korea.

Per capita Latin term meaning 'for each person'.

Periglacial Regions on the edges of *ice sheets* or *glaciers* or, more commonly, cold regions experiencing intense frost action, *permafrost* or both. Periglacial climates bring long, freezing winters and short, mild summers.

Permafrost Permanently frozen ground, typical of *Arctic* regions. Although a layer of soil above the permafrost melts in summer, the melted water does not drain through the permafrost.

Permeable rocks Rocks through which water can seep, because they are either porous or cracked.

Pharmaceuticals The manufacture of medicinal drugs.

Phreatic eruption A volcanic eruption which occurs when *lava* combines with *groundwater*, superheating the water and causing a sudden emission of steam at the surface.

Physical weathering (mechanical weathering) The breakdown of rocks by physical, as opposed to chemical, processes. Examples include: changes in pressure or temperature; the effect of windblown sand; the pressure of growing salt crystals in cracks within rock; and the expansion and contraction of water within rock as it freezes and thaws.

Pingo A dome of earth with a core of ice, found in *tundra* regions. Pingos are formed either when *groundwater* freezes and expands, pushing up the land surface, or when trapped, freezing water in a lake expands and pushes up lake *sediments* to form the pingo dome.

Placer A belt of mineral-bearing rock *strata* lying at or close to the Earth's surface, from which minerals can be easily extracted.

Plain A flat, level region of land, often relatively low-lying.

Plateau A highland tract of flat land.

Plate *see Tectonic plates.*

Plate tectonics The study of *tectonic plates*, which helps to explain *continental drift*, mountain formation and volcanic activity. The movement of tectonic plates may be explained by the currents of rock rising and falling from within the Earth's *mantle*, as it heats up and then cools. The boundaries of the plates are known as plate margins and most mountains, *earthquakes* and *volcanoes* occur at these margins. Constructive margins are moving apart; destructive margins are crunching together and conservative margins are sliding past one another.

Pleistocene A period of *geological time* spanning from about 5.2 million years ago to 1.6 million years ago.

Plutonic rock *Igneous* rocks found deep below the surface. They are coarse-grained because they cooled and solidified slowly.

Polar The zones within the *Arctic* and *Antarctic* circles.

Polje A long, broad *depression* found in *karst* (*limestone*) regions.

Polygonal patterning Typical ground patterning, found in areas where the soil is subject to severe frost action, often in *periglacial* regions.

Porosity A measure of how much water can be held within a rock or a soil. Porosity is measured as the percentage of holes or pores in a material, compared to its total volume. For example, the porosity of slate is less than 1%, whereas that of gravel is 25–35%.

Prairies Originally a French word for grassy *plains* with few or no trees.

Pre-Cambrian The earliest period of *geological time* dating from over 570 million years ago.

Precipitation The fall of moisture from the *atmosphere* onto the surface of the Earth, whether as dew, hail, rain, sleet or snow.

Pyramidal peak A steep, isolated mountain summit, formed when the back walls of three or more *cirques* are cut back and move towards each other. The cliffs around such a horned peak, or horn, are divided by sharp *arêtes*. The Matterhorn in the Swiss Alps is an example.

Pyroclasts Fragments of rock ejected during volcanic eruptions.

Q

Quaternary The current period of *geological time*, which started about 1.6 million years ago.

R

Radiation The emission of energy in the form of particles or waves. Radiation from the sun includes heat, light, ultraviolet rays, gamma rays and X-rays. Only some of the solar energy radiated into space reaches the Earth.

Rainforest Dense forests in tropical zones with high rainfall, temperature and *humidity*. Strictly, the term applies to the equatorial rainforest in tropical lowlands with constant rainfall and no seasonal change. The Congo and Amazon basins are examples. The term is applied more loosely to lush forest in other climates. Within rainforests organic life is dense and varied: at least 40% of all plant and animal species are found here and there may be as many as 100 tree species per hectare.

Rainshadow An area which experiences low rainfall, because of its position on the leeward side of a mountain range.

Reg A large area of stony *desert*, where tightly-packed gravel lies on top of clayey sand. A reg is formed where the wind blows away the finer sand.

Remote-sensing Method of obtaining information about the *environment* using unmanned equipment, such as a satellite, which relays the information to a point where it is collected and used.

Resistance The capacity of a rock to resist *denudation*, by processes such as *weathering* and *erosion*.

Ria A flooded *V-shaped river valley* or estuary, flooded by a rise in sea level (*eustacy*) or sinking land. It is shorter than a *fjord* and gets deeper as it meets the sea.

Rift valley A long, narrow depression in the Earth's *crust*, formed by the sinking of rocks between two *faults*.

River channel The trough which contains a river and is moulded by the flow of water within it.

Roche moutonée A rock found in a glaciated valley. The side facing the flow of the *glacier* has been smoothed and rounded, while the other side has been left more rugged because the *glacier*, as it flows over it, has plucked out frozen fragments and carried them away.

Runoff Water draining from a land surface by flowing across it.

S

Sabkha The floor of an isolated *depression* which occurs in an *arid environment* – usually covered by salt deposits and devoid of vegetation.

SADC Southern African Development Community. Established in 1992 to promote economic integration between its member states, which are Angola, Botswana, Lesotho, Malawi, Mauritius, Mozambique, Namibia, South Africa, Swaziland, Tanzania, Zambia and Zimbabwe.

Salt plug A rounded hill produced by the upward doming of rock *strata* caused by the movement of salt or other evaporite deposits under intense pressure.

Sastrugi Ice ridges formed by wind action. They lie parallel to the direction of the wind.

Savannah Open grassland found between the zone of *deserts*, and that of tropical *rainforests* in the tropics and subtropics. Scattered trees and shrubs are found in some kinds of savannah. A savannah *climate* usually has wet and dry seasons.

Scarp *see Escarpment.*

Scree Piles of rock fragments beneath a cliff or rock face, caused by mechanical *weathering*, especially *frost shattering*, where the expansion and contraction of freezing and thawing water within the rock, gradually breaks it up.

Sea-floor spreading The process whereby *tectonic plates* move apart, allowing hot *magma* to erupt and solidify. This forms a new sea floor and, ultimately, widens the ocean.

Seamount An isolated, submarine mountain or hill, probably of volcanic origin.

Season A period of time linked to regular changes in the weather, especially the intensity of solar *radiation*.

Sediment Grains of rock transported and deposited by rivers, sea, ice or wind.

Sedimentary rocks Rocks formed from the debris of pre-existing rocks or of organic material. They are found in many *environments* – on the ocean floor, on beaches, rivers and *deserts*. Organically-formed sedimentary rocks include coal and chalk. Other sedimentary rocks, such as flint, are formed by chemical processes. Most of these rocks contain *fossils*, which can be used to date them.

Seif A sand *dune* which lies parallel to the direction of the prevailing wind. Seifs form steep-sided ridges, sometimes extending for miles.

Seismic activity Movement within the Earth, such as an *earthquake* or *tremor*.

Selva A region of wet forest found in the Amazon Basin.

Semi-arid, semi-desert The *climate* and landscape which lies between *savannah* and *desert* or between savannah and a *mediterranean* climate. In semi-arid conditions there is a little more moisture than in a true *desert*; and more patches of drought-resistant vegetation can survive.

Shale (marine shale) A compacted *sedimentary rock*, with fine-grained particles. Marine shale is formed on the seabed. Fuel such as oil may be extracted from it.

Sheetwash Water which runs downhill in thin sheets without forming channels. It can cause *sheet erosion*.

Sheet erosion The washing away of soil by a thin film or sheet of water, known as *sheetwash*.

Shield A vast stable block of the Earth's *crust*, which has experienced little or no *mountain-building*.

Sierra The Spanish word for mountains.

Sinkhole A circular *depression* in a *limestone* region. They are formed by the collapse of an underground cave system or the *chemical weathering* of the *limestone*.

Sisal A plant-fibre used to make matting.

Slash and burn A farming technique involving the cutting down and burning of scrub forest, to create agricultural land. After a number of seasons this land is abandoned and the process is repeated. This practice is common in Africa and South America.

Slip face The steep leeward side of a sand *dune* or slope. Opposite side to a *back slope*.

Soil A thin layer of rock particles mixed with the remains of dead plants and animals. This occurs naturally on the surface of the Earth and provides a medium for plants to grow.

Soil creep The very gradual downslope movement of rock debris and soil, under the influence of gravity. This is a type of *mass movement*.

Soil erosion The wearing away of soil more quickly than it is replaced by natural processes. Soil can be carried away by wind as well as by water. Human activities, such as over-grazing and the clearing of land for farming, accelerate the process in many areas.

Solar energy Energy derived from the Sun. Solar energy is converted into other forms of energy. For example, the wind and waves, as well as the creation of plant material in photosynthesis, depend on solar energy.

Solifluction A kind of *soil creep*, where water in the surface layer has saturated the soil and rock debris which slips slowly downhill. It often happens where frozen top-layer deposits thaw, leaving frozen layers below them.

Sorghum A type of grass found in South America, similar to sugar cane. When refined it is used to make molasses.

Spit A thin linear deposit of sand or shingle extending from the sea shore. Spits are formed as angled waves shift sand along the beach, eventually extending a ridge of sand beyond a change in the angle of the coast. Spits are common where the coastline bends, especially at estuaries.

Squash A type of edible gourd.

Stack A tall, isolated pillar of rock near a coastline, created as wave action erodes away the adjacent rock.

Stalactite A tapering cylinder of mineral deposit, hanging from the roof of a cave in a *karst* area. It is formed by calcium carbonate, dissolved in water, which drips through the roof of a *limestone* cavern.

Stalagmite A cone of calcium carbonate, similar to a *stalactite*, rising from the floor of a *limestone* cavern and formed when drops of water fall from the roof of a *limestone* cave. If the water has dripped from a *stalactite* above the stalagmite, the two may join to form a continuous pillar.

Staple crop The main crop on which a country is economically and or physically reliant. For example, the major crop grown for large-scale local consumption in South Asia is rice.

Steppe Large areas of dry grassland in the northern hemisphere – particularly found in southeast Europe and central Asia.

Strata The plural of stratum, a distinct, virtually horizontal layer of deposited material, lying parallel to other layers.

Stratosphere A layer of the *atmosphere*, above the *troposphere*, extending from about 7–30 miles (11–50 km) above the Earth's surface. In the lower part of the stratosphere, the temperature is relatively stable and there is little moisture.

Strike-slip fault Occurs where plates move sideways past each other and blocks of rocks move horizontally in relation to each other, not up or down as in normal *faults*.

Subduction zone A region where two *tectonic plates* collide, forcing one beneath the other. Typically, a dense oceanic plate dips below a lighter continental plate, melting in the heat of the *asthenosphere*. This is why the zone is also called a destructive margins (*see Plate tectonics*). These zones are characterized by *earthquakes*, volcanoes, *mountain–building* and the development of oceanic trenches and *island arcs*.

Submarine canyon A steep-sided valley, which extends along the *continental shelf* to the ocean floor. Often formed by *turbidity currents*.

Submarine fan Deposits of silt and *alluvium*, carried by large rivers forming great fan-shaped deposits on the ocean floor.

Subsistence agriculture An agricultural practice, whereby enough food is produced to support the farmer and his dependents, but not providing any surplus to generate an income.

Subtropical A term applied loosely to *climates* which are nearly tropical or tropical for a part of the year – areas north or south of the *tropics* but outside the *temperate zone*.

Supercontinent A large continent that breaks up to form smaller continents or which forms when smaller continents merge. In the theory of *continental drift*, the supercontinents are *Pangaea*, *Gondwanaland* and *Laurasia*.

Sustainable development An approach to development, applied to economies across the world which exploit natural resources without destroying them or the *environment*.

Syncline A basin-shaped downfold in rock *strata*, created when the *strata* are compressed, for example where *tectonic plates* collide.

T

Tableland A highland area with a flat or gently undulating surface.

Taiga The belt of *coniferous* forest found in the north of Asia and North America. The conifers are adapted to survive low temperatures and long periods of snowfall.

Tarn A Scottish term for a small mountain lake, usually found at the head of a *glacier*.

Tectonic plates Plates, or tectonic plates, are the rigid slabs which form the Earth's outer shell, the *lithosphere*. Eight big plates and several smaller ones have been identified.

Temperate A moderate *climate* without extremes of temperature, typical of the mid-*latitudes* between the *tropics* and the *polar* circles.

Theocracy A state governed by religious laws – today Iran is the world's largest theocracy.

Thermokarst Subsidence created by the thawing of ground ice in *periglacial* areas, creating depressions.

Thermosphere A layer of the Earth's *atmosphere* which lies above the *mesophere*, about 60–300 miles (100–500 km) above the Earth

Terraces Steps cut into steep slopes to create flat surfaces for cultivating crops. They also help reduce soil *erosion* on unconsolidated slopes. They are most common in heavily-populated parts of Southeast Asia.

Till Unstratified glacial deposits or drift left by a *glacier* or *ice sheet*. Till includes mixtures of clay, sand, gravel and boulders.

Topography The typical shape and features of a given area such as land height and terrain.

Tombolo A large sand *spit* which attaches part of the mainland to an island.

Tornado A violent, spiralling windstorm, with a centre of very low pressure. Wind speeds reach 200 mph (320 kmph) and there is often thunder and heavy rain.

Transform fault In *plate tectonics*, a *fault* of continental scale, occurring where two plates slide past each other, staying close together for example, the San Andreas Fault, USA. The jerky, uneven movement creates *earthquakes* but does not destroy or add to the Earth's *crust*

Transpiration The loss of water vapour through the pores (or stomata) of plants. The process helps to return moisture to the *atmosphere*.

Trap An area of fine-grained *igneous rock* which has been extruded and cooled on the Earth's surface in stages, forming a series of steps or terraces.

Treeline The line beyond which trees cannot grow, dependent on *latitude* and altitude, as well as local factors such as soil.

Tremor A slight *earthquake*.

Trench (oceanic trench) A long, deep trough in the ocean floor, formed, according to the theory of *plate tectonics*, when two plates collide and one dives under the other, creating a *subduction zone*.

Tropics The zone between the *Tropic of Cancer* and the *Tropic of Capricorn* where the *climate* is hot. Tropical climate is also applied to areas rather further north and south of the *Equator* where the climate is similar to that of the true tropics.

Tropic of Cancer A line of *latitude* or imaginary circle round the Earth, lying at 23° 28′ N.

Tropic of Capricorn A line of *latitude* or imaginary circle round the Earth, lying at 23° 28′ S.

Troposphere The lowest layer of the Earth's *atmosphere*. From the surface, it reaches a height of between 4–10 miles (7–16 km). It is the most turbulent zone of the atmosphere and accounts for the generation of most of the world's weather. The layer above it is called the *stratosphere*.

Tsunami A huge wave created by shock waves from an *earthquake* under the sea. Reaching speeds of up to 600 mph (960 kmph), the wave may increase to heights of 50 ft (15 m) on entering coastal waters; and it can cause great damage.

Tundra The treeless *plains* of the *Arctic Circle*, found south of the *polar* region of permanent ice and snow, and north of the belt of *coniferous* forests known as *taiga*. In this region of long, very cold winters, vegetation is usually limited to mosses, *lichens*, sedges and rushes, although flowers and dwarf shrubs blossom in the brief summer.

Turbidity current An oceanic feature. A turbidity current is a mass of *sediment*-laden water which has substantial erosive power. Turbidity currents are thought to contribute to the formation of *submarine canyons*.

Typhoon A kind of *hurricane* (or tropical cyclone) bringing violent winds and heavy rain, a typhoon can do great damage. They occur in the South China Sea, especially around the Philippines.

U

U-shaped valley A river valley that has been deepened and widened by a *glacier*. They are characteristically flat-bottomed and steep-sided and generally much deeper than river valleys.

UN United Nations. Established in 1945, it contains 188 nations and aims to maintain international peace and security, and promote co-operation over economic, social, cultural and humanitarian problems.

UNICEF United Nations Children's Fund. A UN organization set up to promote family and child related programmes.

Urstromtäler A German word used to describe *meltwater* channels which flowed along the front edge of the advancing *ice sheet* during the last Ice Age, 18,000–20,000 years ago.

V

V-shaped valley A typical valley eroded by a river in its upper course.

Virgin rainforest Tropical *rainforest* in its original state, untouched by human activity such as logging, clearance for agriculture, settlement or road building.

Viticulture The cultivation of grapes for wine.

Volcano An opening or vent in the Earth's *crust* where molten rock, *magma*, erupts. Volcanoes tend to be conical but may also be a crack in the Earth's surface or a hole blasted through a mountain. The magma is accompanied by other materials such as gas, steam and fragments of rock, or *pyroclasts*. They tend to occur on destructive or constructive *tectonic plate* margins.

W-Z

Wadi The dry bed left by a torrent of water. Also classified as a *ephemeral* stream, found in *arid* and *semi-arid* regions, which are subject to sudden and often severe flash flooding.

Warm humid climate A rainy climate with warm summers and mild winters.

Water cycle The continuous circulation of water between the Earth's surface and the *atmosphere*. The processes include *evaporation* and *transpiration* of moisture into the atmosphere, and its return as *precipitation*, some of which flows into lakes and oceans.

Water table The upper level of *groundwater* saturation in permeable rock *strata*.

Watershed The dividing line between one *drainage basin* – an area where all streams flow into a single river system – and another. In the US, watershed also means the whole drainage basin of a single river system – its catchment area.

Waterspout A rotating column of water in the form of cloud, mist and spray which form on open water. Often has the appearance of a small *tornado*.

Weathering The decay and break-up of rocks at or near the Earth's surface, caused by water, wind, heat or ice, organic material or the *atmosphere*. *Physical weathering* includes the effects of frost and temperature changes. Biological weathering includes the effects of plant roots, burrowing animals and the acids produced by animals, especially as they decay after death. *Carbonation* and *hydrolysis* are among many kinds of *chemical weathering*.

Geographical names

The following glossary lists all geographical terms occurring on the maps and in main-entry names in the Index-Gazetteer. These terms may precede, follow or be run together with the proper element of the name; where they precede it the term is reversed for indexing purposes - thus Poluostrov Yamal is indexed as Yamal, Poluostrov.

Key

Geographical term
Language, Term

A

Å *Danish, Norwegian*, River
Āb *Persian*, River
Adrar *Berber*, Mountains
Agía, Ágios *Greek*, Saint
Air *Indonesian*, River
Ákra *Greek*, Cape, point
Alpen *German*, Alps
Alt- *German*, Old
Altiplanicie *Spanish*, Plateau
Älve(en) *Swedish*, River
-ån *Swedish*, River
Anse *French*, Bay
'Aqabat *Arabic*, Pass
Archipiélago *Spanish*, Archipelago
Arcipelago *Italian*, Archipelago
Arquipélago *Portuguese*, Archipelago
Arrecife(s) *Spanish*, Reef(s)
Aru *Tamil*, River
Augstiene *Latvian*, Upland
Aukštuma *Lithuanian*, Upland
Aust- *Norwegian*, Eastern
Avtonomnyy Okrug *Russian*, Autonomous district
Āw *Kurdish*, River
'Ayn *Arabic*, Spring, well
'Ayoûn *Arabic*, Wells

B

Baelt *Danish*, Strait
Bahía *Spanish*, Bay
Baḩr *Arabic*, River
Baía *Portuguese*, Bay
Baie *French*, Bay
Bañado *Spanish*, Marshy land
Bandao *Chinese*, Peninsula
Banjaran *Malay*, Mountain range
Baraji *Turkish*, Dam
Barragem *Portuguese*, Reservoir
Bassin *French*, Basin
Batang *Malay*, Stream
Beinn, Ben *Gaelic*, Mountain
-berg *Afrikaans, Norwegian*, Mountain
Besar *Indonesian, Malay*, Big
Birkat, Birket *Arabic*, Lake, well, cistern
Boğazi *Turkish*, Strait, defile
Boka *Serbo-Croatian*, Bay
Bol'sh-aya, -iye, -oy, -oye *Russian*, Big
Botigh(i) *Uzbek*, Depression basin
-bre(en) *Norwegian*, Glacier
Bredning *Danish*, Bay
Bucht *German*, Bay
Bugt(en) *Danish*, Bay
Buḩayrat *Arabic*, Lake, reservoir
Buḩeiret *Arabic*, Lake
Bukit *Malay*, Mountain
-bukta *Norwegian*, Bay
bukten *Swedish*, Bay
Bulag *Mongolian*, Spring
Bulak *Uighur*, Spring
Burnu *Turkish*, Cape, point
Buuraha *Somali*, Mountains

C

Cabo *Portuguese*, Cape
Caka *Tibetan*, Salt lake
Canal *Spanish*, Channel
Cap *French*, Cape
Capo *Italian*, Cape, headland
Cascada *Portuguese*, Waterfall
Cayo(s) *Spanish*, Islet(s), rock(s)
Cerro *Spanish*, Mountain
Chaîne *French*, Mountain range
Chapada *Portuguese*, Hills, upland
Chau *Cantonese*, Island
Chāy *Turkish*, River
Chhâk *Cambodian*, Bay
Chhu *Tibetan*, River
-chōsuji *Korean*, Reservoir
Chott *Arabic*, Depression, salt lake
Chŭli *Uzbek*, Grassland, steppe
Ch'ün-tao *Chinese*, Island group
Chuŏr Phnum *Cambodian*, Mountains
Ciudad *Spanish*, City, town
Co *Tibetan*, Lake
Colline(s) *French*, Hill(s)
Cordillera *Spanish*, Mountain range
Costa *Spanish*, Coast
Côte *French*, Coast
Coxilha *Portuguese*, Mountains
Cuchilla *Spanish*, Mountains

D

Daban *Mongolian, Uighur*, Pass
Daği *Azerbaijani, Turkish*, Mountain
Dağlari *Azerbaijani, Turkish*, Mountains
-dake *Japanese*, Peak
-dal(en) *Norwegian*, Valley
Danau *Indonesian*, Lake
Dao *Chinese*, Island
Đao *Vietnamese*, Island
Daryā *Persian*, River
Daryācheh *Persian*, Lake
Dasht *Persian*, Desert, plain
Dawḩat *Arabic*, Bay
Denizi *Turkish*, Sea
Dere *Turkish*, Stream
Desierto *Spanish*, Desert
Dili *Azerbaijani*, Spit
-do *Korean*, Island
Dooxo *Somali*, Valley
Düzü *Azerbaijani*, Steppe
-dwīp *Bengali*, Island

E

-eilanden *Dutch*, Islands
Embalse *Spanish*, Reservoir
Ensenada *Spanish*, Bay
Erg *Arabic*, Dunes
Estany *Catalan*, Lake
Estero *Spanish*, Inlet
Estrecho *Spanish*, Strait
Étang *French*, Lagoon, lake
-ey *Icelandic*, Island
Ezero *Bulgarian, Macedonian*, Lake
Ezers *Latvian*, Lake

F

Feng *Chinese*, Peak
-fjella *Norwegian*, Mountain
Fjord *Danish*, Fjord
-fjord(en) *Danish, Norwegian, Swedish*, fjord
-fjørdhur *Faeroese*, Fjord
Fleuve *French*, River
Fliegu *Maltese*, Channel
-fljór *Icelandic*, River
-flói *Icelandic*, Bay
Forêt *French*, Forest

G

-gan *Japanese*, Rock
-gang *Korean*, River
Ganga *Hindi, Nepali, Sinhala*, River
Gaoyuan *Chinese*, Plateau
Garagumy *Turkmen*, Sands
-gawa *Japanese*, River
Gebel *Arabic*, Mountain
-gebirge *German*, Mountain range
Ghadīr *Arabic*, Well
Ghubbat *Arabic*, Bay
Gjiri *Albanian*, Bay
Gol *Mongolian*, River
Golfe *French*, Gulf
Golfo *Italian, Spanish*, Gulf
Göl(ü) *Turkish*, Lake
Golyam, -a *Bulgarian*, Big
Gora *Russian, Serbo-Croatian*, Mountain
Góra *Polish*, mountain
Gory *Russian*, Mountain
Gryada *Russian*, ridge
Guba *Russian*, Bay
-gundo *Korean*, island group
Gunung *Malay*, Mountain

H

Ḩadd *Arabic*, Spit
-haehyŏp *Korean*, Strait
Haff *German*, Lagoon
Hai *Chinese*, Bay, lake, sea
Haixia *Chinese*, Strait
Ḩammādah *Arabic*, Desert
Ḩammādat *Arabic*, Rocky plateau
Hāmūn *Persian*, Lake
-hantō *Japanese*, Peninsula
Har, Haré *Hebrew*, Mountain
Ḩarrat *Arabic*, Lava-field
Hav(et) *Danish*, Swedish, Sea
Hawr *Arabic*, Lake
Hāyk' *Amharic*, Lake
He *Chinese*, River
-hegység *Hungarian*, Mountain range
Heide *German*, Heath, moorland
Helodrano *Malagasy*, Bay
Higashi- *Japanese*, East(ern)
Ḩiṣā' *Arabic*, Well
Hka *Burmese*, River
-ho *Korean*, Lake
Hô *Korean*, Reservoir
Ḩolot *Hebrew*, Dunes
Hora *Belarussian, Czech*, Mountain
Hrada *Belarussian*, Mountain, ridge
Hsi *Chinese*, River
Hu *Chinese*, Lake
Huk *Danish*, Point

I

Île(s) *French*, Island(s)
Ilha(s) *Portuguese*, Island(s)
Ilhéu(s) *Portuguese*, Islet(s)
-isen *Norwegian*, Ice shelf
Imeni *Russian*, In the name of
Inish- *Gaelic*, Island
Insel(n) *German*, Island(s)
Irmağı, Irmak *Turkish*, River
Isla(s) *Spanish*, Island(s)
Isola (Isole) *Italian*, Island(s)

J

Jabal *Arabic*, Mountain
Jāl *Arabic*, Ridge
-järv *Estonian*, Lake
-järvi *Finnish*, Lake
Jazā'ir *Arabic*, Islands
Jazīrat *Arabic*, Island
Jazīreh *Persian*, Island
Jebel *Arabic*, Mountain
Jezero *Serbo-Croatian*, Lake
Jezioro *Polish*, Lake
Jiang *Chinese*, River
-jima *Japanese*, Island
Jižní *Czech*, Southern
-jõgi *Estonian*, River
-joki *Finnish*, River
-jökull *Icelandic*, Glacier
Jūn *Arabic*, Bay
Juzur *Arabic*, Islands

K

Kaikyō *Japanese*, Strait
-kaise *Lappish*, Mountain
Kali *Nepali*, River
Kalnas *Lithuanian*, Mountain
Kalns *Latvian*, Mountain
Kang *Chinese*, Harbour
Kangri *Tibetan*, Mountain(s)
Kaôh *Cambodian*, Island
Kapp *Norwegian*, Cape
Káto *Greek*, Lower
Kavīr *Persian*, Desert
K'edi *Georgian*, Mountain range
Kediet *Arabic*, Mountain
Kepi *Albanian*, Cape, point
Kepulauan *Indonesian, Malay*, Island group
Khalig, Khalīj *Arabic*, Gulf
Khawr *Arabic*, Inlet
Khola *Nepali*, River
Khrebet *Russian*, Mountain range
Ko *Thai*, Island
-ko *Japanese*, Inlet, lake
Kólpos *Greek*, Bay
-kopf *German*, Peak
Körfäzi *Azerbaijani*, Bay
Körfezi *Turkish*, Bay
Kõrgustik *Estonian*, Upland
Kosa *Russian, Ukrainian*, Spit
Koshi *Nepali*, River
Kou *Chinese*, River-mouth
Kowtal *Persian*, Pass
Kray *Russian*, Region, territory
Kryazh *Russian*, Ridge
Kuduk *Uighur*, Well
Kūh(hā) *Persian*, Mountain(s)
-kul' *Russian*, Lake
Kŭl(i) *Tajik, Uzbek*, Lake
-kundo *Korean*, Island group
-kysten *Norwegian*, Coast
Kyun *Burmese*, Island

L

Laaq *Somali*, Watercourse
Lac *French*, Lake
Lacul *Romanian*, Lake
Lagh *Somali*, Stream
Lago *Italian, Portuguese, Spanish*, Lake
Lagoa *Portuguese*, Lagoon
Laguna *Italian, Spanish*, Lagoon, lake
Laht *Estonian*, Bay
Laut *Indonesian*, Bay
Lembalemba *Malagasy*, Plateau
Lerr *Armenian*, Mountain
Lerrnashght'a *Armenian*, Mountain range
Les *Czech*, Forest
Lich *Armenian*, Lake
Liehtao *Chinese*, Island group
Liqeni *Albanian*, Lake
Límni *Greek*, Lake
Ling *Chinese*, Mountain range
Llano *Spanish*, Plain, prairie
Lumi *Albanian*, River
Lyman *Ukrainian*, Estuary

M

Madīnat *Arabic*, City, town
Mae Nam *Thai*, River
-mägi *Estonian*, Hill
Maja *Albanian*, Mountain
Mal *Albanian*, Mountains
Mal-aya, -oye, -yy, *Russian*, Small
-man *Korean*, Bay
Mar *Spanish*, Lake
Marios *Lithuanian*, Lake
Massif *French*, Mountains
Meer *German*, Lake
-meer *Dutch*, Lake
Melkosopochnik *Russian*, Plain
-meri *Estonian*, Sea
Mifraz *Hebrew*, Bay
Minami- *Japanese*, South(ern)
-misaki *Japanese*, Cape, point
Monkhafad *Arabic*, Depression
Montagne(s) *French*, Mountain(s)
Montañas *Spanish*, Mountains
Mont(s) *French*, Mountain(s)
Monte *Italian, Portuguese*, Mountain
More *Russian*, Sea
Mörön *Mongolian*, River
Mys *Russian*, Cape, point

N

-nada *Japanese*, Open stretch of water
Nadi *Bengali*, River
Nagor'ye *Russian*, Upland
Naḩal *Hebrew*, River
Nahr *Arabic*, River
Nam *Laotian*, River
Namakzār *Persian*, Salt desert
Né-a, -on, -os *Greek*, New
Nedre- *Norwegian*, Lower
-neem *Estonian*, Cape, point
Nehri *Turkish*, River
-nes *Norwegian*, Cape, point
Nevado *Spanish*, Mountain (snow-capped)
Nieder- *German*, Lower
Nishi- *Japanese*, West(ern)
-nísi *Greek*, Island
Nisoi *Greek*, Islands
Nizhn-eye, -iy, -iye, -yaya *Russian*, Lower
Nizmennost' *Russian*, Lowland, plain
Nord *Danish, French, German*, North
Norte *Portuguese, Spanish*, North
Nos *Bulgarian*, Point, spit
Nosy *Malagasy*, Island
Nov-a, -i, *Bulgarian, Serbo-Croatian*, New
Nov-aya, -o, -oye, -yy, -yye *Russian*, New
Now-a, -e, -y *Polish*, New
Nur *Mongolian*, Lake
Nuruu *Mongolian*, Mountains
Nuur *Mongolian*, Lake
Nyzovyna *Ukrainian*, Lowland, plain

O

-ø *Danish*, Island
Ober- *German*, Upper
Oblast' *Russian*, Province
Órmos *Greek*, Bay
Orol(i) *Uzbek*, Island
Øster- *Norwegian*, Eastern
Ostrov(a) *Russian*, Island(s)
Otok *Serbo-Croatian*, Island
Oued *Arabic*, Watercourse
-oy *Faeroese*, Island
-øy(a) *Norwegian*, Island
Oya *Sinhala*, River
Ozero *Russian, Ukrainian*, Lake

P

Passo *Italian*, Pass
Pegunungan *Indonesian, Malay*, Mountain range
Pélagos *Greek*, Sea
Pendi *Chinese*, Basin
Penisola *Italian*, Peninsula
Pertuis *French*, Strait
Peski *Russian*, Sands
Phanom *Thai*, Mountain
Phou *Laotian*, Mountain
Pi *Chinese*, Point
Pic *Catalan, French*, Peak
Pico *Portuguese, Spanish*, Peak
-piggen *Danish*, Peak
Pik *Russian*, Peak
Pivostriv *Ukrainian*, Peninsula
Planalto *Portuguese*, Plateau
Planina, Planini *Bulgarian, Macedonian, Serbo-Croatian*, Mountain range
Plato *Russian*, Plateau
Ploskogor'ye *Russian*, Upland
Poluostrov *Russian*, Peninsula
Ponta *Portuguese*, Point
Porthmós *Greek*, Strait
Pótamos *Greek*, River
Presa *Spanish*, Dam
Prokhod *Bulgarian*, Pass
Proliv *Russian*, Strait
Pulau *Indonesian Malay*, Island
Pulu *Malay*, Island
Punta *Spanish*, Point
Pushcha *Belorussian*, Forest
Puszcza *Polish*, Forest

Q

Qā' *Arabic*, Depression
Qalamat *Arabic*, Well
Qatorkŭh(i) *Tajik*, Mountain
Qiuling *Chinese*, Hills
Qolleh *Persian*, Mountain
Qu *Tibetan*, Stream
Quan *Chinese*, Well
Qulla(i) *Tajik*, Peak
Qundao *Chinese*, Island group

R

Raas *Somali*, Cape
-rags *Latvian*, Cape
Ramlat *Arabic*, Sands
Ra's *Arabic*, Cape, headland, point
Ravnina *Bulgarian, Russian*, Plain
Récif *French*, Reef
Recife *Portuguese*, Reef
Reka *Bulgarian*, River
Represa (Rep.) *Portuguese, Spanish*, Reservoir
Reshteh *Persian*, Mountain range
Respublika *Russian*, Republic, first-order administrative division
Respublika(si) *Uzbek*, Republic, first-order administrative division
-retsugan *Japanese*, Chain of rocks
-rettō *Japanese*, Island chain
Riacho *Spanish*, Stream
Riban' *Malagasy*, Mountains
Rio *Portuguese*, River
Río *Spanish*, River
Riu *Catalan*, River
Rivier *Dutch*, River
Rivière *French*, River
Rowd *Pashtu*, River
Rt *Serbo-Croatian*, Point
Rūd *Persian*, River
Rūdkhāneh *Persian*, River
Rudohorie *Slovak*, Mountains
Ruisseau *French*, Stream

S

-saar *Estonian*, Island
-saari *Finnish*, Island
Sabkhat *Arabic*, Salt marsh
Sāgar(a) *Hindi*, Lake, reservoir
Şaḩrā' *Arabic*, Desert
Saint, Sainte *French*, Saint
Salar *Spanish*, Salt-pan
Salto *Portuguese, Spanish*, Waterfall
Samudra *Sinhala*, Reservoir
-san *Japanese, Korean*, Mountain
-sanchi *Japanese*, Mountains
-sandur *Icelandic*, Beach
Sankt *German, Swedish*, Saint
-sanmaek *Korean*, Mountain range
-sanmyaku *Japanese*, Mountain range
San, Santa, Santo *Italian, Portuguese, Spanish*, Saint
São *Portuguese*, Saint
Sarīr *Arabic*, Desert
Sebkha, Sebkhet *Arabic*, Depression, salt marsh
Sedlo *Czech*, Pass
See *German*, Lake
Selat *Indonesian*, Strait
Selatan *Indonesian*, Southern
-selkä *Finnish*, Lake, ridge
Selseleh *Persian*, Mountain range
Serra *Portuguese*, Mountain
Serranía *Spanish*, Mountain
-seto *Japanese*, Channel, strait
Sever-naya, -noye, -nyy, -o *Russian*, Northern
Sha'īb *Arabic*, Watercourse
Shākh *Kurdish*, Mountain
Shamo *Chinese*, Desert
Shan *Chinese*, Mountain(s)
Shankou *Chinese*, Pass
Shanmo *Chinese*, Mountain range
Shaṭṭ *Arabic*, Distributary
Shet' *Amharic*, River
Shi *Chinese*, Municipality
-shima *Japanese*, Island
Shiqqat *Arabic*, Depression
-shotō *Japanese*, Group of islands
Shuiku *Chinese*, Reservoir
Shŭrkhog(i) *Uzbek*, Salt marsh
Sierra *Spanish*, Mountains
Sint *Dutch*, Saint
-sjø(en) *Norwegian*, Lake
-sjön *Swedish*, Lake
Solonchak *Russian*, Salt lake
Solonchakovyye Vpadiny *Russian*, Salt basin, wetlands
Sơn *Vietnamese*, Mountain
Sông *Vietnamese*, River
Sør- *Norwegian*, Southern
-spitze *German*, Peak
Star-á, -é *Czech*, Old
Star-aya, -oye, -yy, -yye *Russian*, Old
Stenó *Greek*, Strait
Step' *Russian*, Steppe
Štít *Slovak*, Peak
Stœng *Cambodian*, River
Stolovaya Strana *Russian*, Plateau
Stredné *Slovak*, Middle
Střední *Czech*, Middle
Stretto *Italian*, Strait
Su Anbari *Azerbaijani*, Reservoir
-suidō *Japanese*, Channel, strait
Sund *Swedish*, Sound, strait
Sungai *Indonesian, Malay*, River
Suu *Turkish*, River

T

Tal *Mongolian*, Plain
Tandavan' *Malagasy*, Mountain range
Tangorombohitr' *Malagasy*, Mountain massif
Tanjung *Indonesian, Malay*, Cape, point
Tao *Chinese*, Island
Ţaraq *Arabic*, Hills
Tassili *Berber*, Mountain, plateau
Tau *Russian*, Mountain(s)
Taungdan *Burmese*, Mountain range
Techníti Límni *Greek*, Reservoir
Tekojärvi *Finnish*, Reservoir
Teluk *Indonesian, Malay*, Bay
Tengah *Indonesian*, Middle
Terara *Amharic*, Mountain
Timur *Indonesian*, Eastern
-tind(an) *Norwegian*, Peak
Tizma(si) *Uzbek*, Mountain range, ridge
-tō *Japanese*, island
Tog *Somali*, Valley
-tōge *Japanese*, pass
Togh(i) *Uzbek*, mountain
Tônlé *Cambodian*, Lake
Top *Dutch*, Peak
-tunturi *Finnish*, Mountain
Ţurāq *Arabic*, hills
Tur'at *Arabic*, Channel

U

Udde(n) *Swedish*, Cape, point
'Uqlat *Arabic*, Well
Utara *Indonesian*, Northern
Uul *Mongolian*, Mountains

V

Väin *Estonian*, Strait
Vallée *French*, Valley
-vatn *Icelandic*, Lake
-vatnet *Norwegian*, Lake
Velayat *Turkmen*, Province
-vesi *Finnish*, Lake
Vestre- *Norwegian*, Western
-vidda *Norwegian*, Plateau
-vík *Icelandic*, Bay
-viken *Swedish*, Bay, inlet
Vinh *Vietnamese*, Bay
Víztárloló *Hungarian*, Reservoir
Vodaskhovishcha *Belarussian*, Reservoir
Vodokhranilishche (Vdkhr.) *Russian*, Reservoir
Vodoskhovyshche (Vdskh.) *Ukrainian*, Reservoir
Volcán *Spanish*, Volcano
Vostochn-o, yy *Russian*, Eastern
Vozvyshennost' *Russian*, Upland, plateau
Vozyera *Belarussian*, Lake
Vpadina *Russian*, Depression
Vrchovina *Czech*, Mountains
Vrha *Macedonian*, Peak
Vychodné *Slovak*, Eastern
Vysochyna *Ukrainian*, Upland
Vysočina *Czech*, Upland

W

Waadi *Somali*, Watercourse
Wādī *Arabic* Watercourse
Wāḩat, Wâhat *Arabic*, Oasis
Wald *German*, Forest
Wan *Chinese*, Bay
Way *Indonesian*, River
Webi *Somali*, River
Wenz *Amharic*, River
Wiloyat(i) *Uzbek*, Province
Wyżyna *Polish*, Upland
Wzgórza *Polish*, Upland
Wzvyshsha *Belarussian*, Upland

X

Xé *Laotian*, River
Xi *Chinese*, Stream

Y

-yama *Japanese*, Mountain
Yanchi *Chinese*, Salt lake
Yang *Chinese*, Bay
Yanhu *Chinese*, Salt lake
Yarımadası *Azerbaijani, Turkish*, Peninsula
Yaylası *Turkish*, Plateau
Yazovir *Bulgarian*, Reservoir
Yoma *Burmese*, Mountains
Ytre- *Norwegian*, Outer
Yü *Chinese*, Island
Yunhe *Chinese*, Canal
Yuzhn-o, -yy *Russian*, Southern

Z

-zaki *Japanese*, Cape, point
Zaliv *Bulgarian, Russian*, Bay
-zan *Japanese*, Mountain
Zangbo *Tibetan*, River
Zapadn-aya, -o, -yy *Russian*, Western
Západné *Slovak*, Western
Západní *Czech*, Western
Zatoka *Polish, Ukrainian*, Bay
-zee *Dutch*, Sea
Zemlya *Russian*, Earth, land
Zizhiqu *Chinese*, Autonomous region

INDEX

GLOSSARY OF ABBREVIATIONS

This glossary provides a comprehensive guide to the abbreviations used in this Atlas, and in the Index.

A
abbrev. abbreviated
AD Anno Domini
Afr. Afrikaans
Alb. Albanian
Amh. Amharic
anc. ancient
approx. approximately
Ar. Arabic
Arm. Armenian
ASEAN Association of South East Asian Nations
ASSR Autonomous Soviet Socialist Republic
Aust. Australian
Az. Azerbaijani
Azerb. Azerbaijan

B
Basq. Basque
BC before Christ
Bel. Belorussian
Ben. Bengali
Ber. Berber
B-H Bosnia-Herzegovina
bn billion (one thousand million)
BP British Petroleum
Bret. Breton
Brit. British
Bul. Bulgarian
Bur. Burmese

C
C central
C. Cape
°C degrees Centigrade
CACM Central America Common Market
Cam. Cambodian
Cant. Cantonese
CAR Central African Republic
Cast. Castilian
Cat. Catalan
CEEAC Central America Common Market
Chin. Chinese
CIS Commonwealth of Independent States
cm centimetre(s)
Cro. Croat
Cz. Czech
Czech Rep. Czech Republic

D
Dan. Danish
Div. Divehi
Dom. Rep. Dominican Republic
Dut. Dutch

E
E east
EC *see* EU
EEC *see* EU
ECOWAS Economic Community of West African States
ECU European Currency Unit
EMS European Monetary System
Eng. English
est estimated
Est. Estonian
EU European Union (previously European Community [EC], European Economic Community [EEC])

F
°F degrees Fahrenheit
Faer. Faeroese
Fij. Fijian
Fin. Finnish
Fr. French
Fris. Frisian
ft foot/feet
FYROM Former Yugoslav Republic of Macedonia

G
g gram(s)
Gael. Gaelic
Gal. Galician
GDP Gross Domestic Product (the total value of goods and services produced by a country excluding income from foreign countries)
Geor. Georgian
Ger. German
Gk Greek
GNP Gross National Product (the total value of goods and services produced by a country)

H
Heb. Hebrew
HEP hydro-electric power
Hind. Hindi
hist. historical
Hung. Hungarian

I
I. Island
Icel. Icelandic
in inch(es)
In. Inuit (Eskimo)
Ind. Indonesian
Intl International
Ir. Irish
Is Islands
It. Italian

J
Jap. Japanese

K
Kaz. Kazakh
kg kilogram(s)
Kir. Kirghiz
km kilometre(s)
km² square kilometre (singular)
Kor. Korean
Kurd. Kurdish

L
L. Lake
LAIA Latin American Integration Association
Lao. Laotian
Lapp. Lappish
Lat. Latin
Latv. Latvian
Liech. Liechtenstein
Lith. Lithuanian
Lus. Lusatian
Lux. Luxembourg

M
m million/metre(s)
Mac. Macedonian
Maced. Macedonia
Mal. Malay
Malg. Malagasy
Malt. Maltese
mi. mile(s)
Mong. Mongolian
Mt. Mountain
Mts Mountains

N
N north
NAFTA North American Free Trade Agreement
Nep. Nepali
Neth. Netherlands
Nic. Nicaraguan
Nor. Norwegian
NZ New Zealand

P
Pash. Pashtu
PNG Papua New Guinea
Pol. Polish
Poly. Polynesian
Port. Portuguese
prev. previously

R
Rep. Republic
Res. Reservoir
Rmsch Romansch
Rom. Romanian
Rus. Russian
Russ. Fed. Russian Federation

S
S south
SADC Southern Africa Development Community
SCr. Serbian, Croatian
Sinh. Sinhala
Slvk Slovak
Slvn. Slovene
Som. Somali
Sp. Spanish
St., St Saint
Strs Straits
Swa. Swahili
Swe. Swedish
Switz. Switzerland

T
Taj. Tajik
Th. Thai
Thai. Thailand
Tib. Tibetan
Turk. Turkish
Turkm. Turkmenistan

U
UAE United Arab Emirates
Uigh. Uighur
UK United Kingdom
Ukr. Ukrainian
UN United Nations
Urd. Urdu
US/USA United States of America
USSR Union of Soviet Socialist Republics
Uzb. Uzbek

V
var. variant
Vdkhr. Vodokhranilishche (Russian for reservoir)
Vdskh. Vodoskhovyshche (Ukrainian for reservoir)
Vtn. Vietnamese

W
W west
Wel. Welsh

THIS INDEX LISTS all the placenames and features shown on the regional and continental maps in this Atlas. Placenames are referenced to the largest scale map on which they appear. The policy followed throughout the Atlas is to use the local spelling or local name at regional level; commonly-used English language names may occasionally be added (in parentheses) where this is an aid to identification e.g. Firenze (Florence). English names, where they exist, have been used for all international features e.g. oceans and country names; they are also used on the continental maps and in the introductory World Today section; these are then fully cross-referenced to the local names found on the regional maps. The index also contains commonly-found alternative names and variant spellings, which are also fully cross-referenced.

All main entry names are those of settlements unless otherwise indicated by the use of italicized definitions or representative symbols, which are keyed at the foot of each page.

1

10 *M16* **100 Mile House** *var.* Hundred Mile House. British Columbia, SW Canada *51°39′ °19′W*
25 de Mayo *see* Veinticinco de Mayo
137 *Y13* **26 Bakı Komissarı** *Rus.* Imeni 26 Bakinskikh Komissarov. SE Azerbaijan *39°18′N 49°13′E*
26 Baku Komissarlary Adyndaky *see* Uzboý

A

Aa *see* Gauja
95 *G24* **Aabenraa** *var.* Åbenrå, *Ger.* Apenrade. Sønderjylland, SW Denmark *55°03′N 09°26′E*
95 *G20* **Aabybro** *var.* Åbybro. Nordjylland, N Denmark *57°09′N 09°32′E*
101 *C16* **Aachen** *Dut.* Aken, *Fr.* Aix-la-Chapelle; *anc.* Aquae Grani, Aquisgranum. Nordrhein-Westfalen, W Germany *50°47′N 06°06′E*
Aaiún *see* Laâyoune
95 *M24* **Aakirkeby** *var.* Åkirkeby. Bornholm, E Denmark *55°04′N 14°56′E*
95 *G20* **Aalborg** *var.* Ålborg, Ålborg-Nørresundby; *anc.* Alburgum. Nordjylland, N Denmark *57°03′N 09°56′E*
Aalborg Bugt *see* Ålborg Bugt
101 *J21* **Aalen** Baden-Württemberg, S Germany *48°50′N 10°06′E*
95 *G21* **Aalestrup** *var.* Ålestrup. Viborg, NW Denmark *56°42′N 09°31′E*
98 *I11* **Aalsmeer** Noord-Holland, C Netherlands *52°17′N 04°43′E*
99 *F18* **Aalst** Oost-Vlaanderen, C Belgium *50°57′N 04°03′E*
99 *K18* **Aalst** *Fr.* Alost. Noord-Brabant, S Netherlands *51°23′N 05°29′E*
98 *O12* **Aalten** Gelderland, E Netherlands *51°56′N 06°35′E*
99 *D17* **Aalter** Oost-Vlaanderen, NW Belgium *51°05′N 03°28′E*
Aanaar *see* Inari
Aanaarjävri *see* Inarijärvi
93 *M17* **Äänekoski** Länsi-Suomi, W Finland *62°34′N 25°45′E*
138 *H7* **Aanjar** *var.* ʻAnjar. C Lebanon *33°45′N 35°56′E*
83 *G21* **Aansluit** Northern Cape, N South Africa *26°41′S 22°24′E*
Aar *see* Aare
108 *F7* **Aarau** Aargau, N Switzerland *47°22′N 08°00′E*
108 *D8* **Aarberg** Bern, W Switzerland *47°19′N 07°54′E*
99 *D16* **Aardenburg** Zeeland, SW Netherlands *51°16′N 03°27′E*
108 *D8* **Aare** *var.* Aar. ≈ W Switzerland
108 *F7* **Aargau** *Fr.* Argovie. ◐ *canton* N Switzerland
Aarhus *see* Århus
Aarlen *see* Arlon
95 *G21* **Aars** *var.* Års. Nordjylland, N Denmark *56°49′N 09°32′E*
99 *I17* **Aarschot** Vlaams Brabant, C Belgium *50°59′N 04°50′E*
Aassi, Nahr el *see* Orontes
Aat *see* Ath
160 *G7* **Aba** *prev.* Ngawa. Sichuan, C China *32°51′N 101°46′E*
79 *P16* **Aba** Orientale, NE Dem. Rep. Congo *03°52′N 30°14′E*
77 *V17* **Aba** Abia, S Nigeria *05°06′N 07°22′E*
140 *J6* **Abā al Qazāz, Biʼr** *well* NW Saudi Arabia
Abā as Suʻūd *see* Najrān
59 *G14* **Abacaxis, Rio** ≈ NW Brazil
Abaco Island *see* Great Abaco/Little Abaco
Abaco Island *see* Great Abaco, N Bahamas
142 *K10* **Ābādān** Khūzestān, SW Iran *30°24′N 48°18′E*
146 *F13* **Abadan** *prev.* Bezmein, Büzmeýin, *Rus.* Byuzmeyin. Ahal Welaýaty, C Turkmenistan *38°08′N 57°53′E*
143 *O10* **Ābādeh** Fārs, C Iran *31°06′N 52°40′E*
74 *H8* **Abadla** W Algeria *31°04′N 02°39′W*
59 *M20* **Abaeté** Minas Gerais, SE Brazil *19°10′S 45°24′W*
62 *P7* **Abaí** Caazapá, S Paraguay *25°58′S 55°54′W*
Abai *see* Blue Nile
191 *O2* **Abaiang** *var.* Apia; *prev.* Charlotte Island. *atoll* Tungaru, W Kiribati
Abaj *see* Abay
77 *U15* **Abaji** Federal Capital District, C Nigeria *08°35′N 06°54′E*
37 *O7* **Abajo Peak** ▲ Utah, W USA *37°51′N 109°28′W*
77 *V16* **Abakaliki** Ebonyi, SE Nigeria *06°18′N 08°07′E*
122 *K13* **Abakan** Respublika Khakasiya, S Russian Federation *53°43′N 91°25′E*
77 *S11* **Abala** Tillabéri, SW Niger *14°55′N 03°27′E*
77 *U11* **Abalak** Tahoua, C Niger *15°28′N 06°18′E*
119 *N14* **Abalyanka** *Rus.* Obolyanka. ≈ N Belarus
122 *L12* **Aban** Krasnoyarskiy Kray, S Russian Federation *56°41′N 96°04′E*
143 *P9* **Āb Anbār-e Kān Sorkh** Yazd, C Iran *31°22′N 53°38′E*
57 *G16* **Abancay** Apurímac, SE Peru *13°37′S 72°52′W*
190 *H2* **Abaokoro** *atoll* Tungaru, W Kiribati
Abariringa *see* Kanton
143 *P10* **Abarkūh** Yazd, C Iran *31°07′N 53°17′E*
165 *V3* **Abashiri** *var.* Abasiri. Hokkaidō, NE Japan *44°N 144°15′E*
165 *U3* **Abashiri-ko** ◎ Hokkaidō, NE Japan
Abasiri *see* Abashiri
41 *P10* **Abasolo** Tamaulipas, C Mexico *24°02′N 98°18′W*
186 *F9* **Abau** Central, S Papua New Guinea *10°04′S 148°34′E*
145 *R10* **Abay** *var.* Abaj. Karaganda, C Kazakhstan *49°38′N 72°50′E*
81 *I15* **Ābaya Hāykʼ** *Eng.* Lake Margherita, *It.* Abbaia. ◎ SW Ethiopia
Ābay Wenz *see* Blue Nile
122 *K13* **Abaza** Respublika Khakasiya, S Russian Federation *52°40′N 89°58′E*
Abbaia *see* Ābaya Hāykʼ
143 *Q13* **Āb Bārīk** Fārs, S Iran
107 *C18* **Abbasanta** Sardegna, Italy, C Mediterranean Sea *40°08′N 08°49′E*
Abbatis Villa *see* Abbeville
30 *M3* **Abbaye, Point** *headland* Michigan, N USA *46°58′N 88°08′W*
Abbazia *see* Opatija
Abbé, Lake *see* Abhe, Lake
103 *N2* **Abbeville** *anc.* Abbatis Villa. Somme, N France *50°06′N 01°50′E*
23 *R7* **Abbeville** Alabama, S USA *31°35′N 85°16′W*
23 *U6* **Abbeville** Georgia, SE USA *31°58′N 83°18′W*
22 *I9* **Abbeville** Louisiana, S USA *29°58′N 92°08′W*
21 *P12* **Abbeville** South Carolina, SE USA *34°10′N 82°23′W*
97 *B20* **Abbeyfeale** *Ir.* Mainistir na Féile. SW Ireland *52°24′N 09°21′W*
106 *D8* **Abbiategrasso** Lombardia, NW Italy *45°24′N 08°55′E*
93 *I14* **Abborrträsk** Norrbotten, N Sweden *65°24′N 19°33′E*
194 *J9* **Abbot Ice Shelf** *ice shelf* Antarctica
10 *M17* **Abbotsford** British Columbia, SW Canada *49°02′N 122°18′W*
30 *K6* **Abbotsford** Wisconsin, N USA *44°57′N 90°19′W*
149 *U5* **Abbottābād** North-West Frontier Province, NW Pakistan *34°12′N 73°15′E*
119 *M14* **Abchuha** *Rus.* Obchuga. Minskaya Voblastsʼ, NW Belarus *54°30′N 29°22′E*
98 *I10* **Abcoude** Utrecht, C Netherlands *52°17′N 04°59′E*
139 *N2* **ʻAbd al ʻAzīz, Jabal** ▲▲ NE Syria
141 *U17* **ʻAbd al Kūrī** *island* SE Yemen
139 *Z13* **ʻAbd Allāh, Khawr** *bay* Iraq/Kuwait
127 *U6* **Abdulino** Orenburgskaya Oblastʼ, W Russian Federation *53°37′N 53°39′E*
78 *J10* **Abéché** *var.* Abécher, Abeshr. Ouaddaï, SE Chad *13°49′N 20°49′E*
Abécher *see* Abéché
143 *S8* **Āb-e Garm va Sard** Yazd, E Iran
77 *R8* **Abeïbara** Kidal, NE Mali *19°07′N 01°52′E*
105 *P5* **Abejar** Castilla-León, N Spain *41°48′N 02°47′W*
54 *E9* **Abejorral** Antioquia, W Colombia *05°48′N 75°28′W*
Abela *see* Ávila
Abellinum *see* Avellino
92 *Q2* **Abeløya** *island* Kong Karls Land, E Svalbard
80 *I13* **Ābeltī** Oromīya, C Ethiopia *08°09′N 37°31′E*
191 *O2* **Abemama** *var.* Apamama; *prev.* Roger Simpson Island. *atoll* Tungaru, W Kiribati
171 *Y15* **Abemaree** *var.* Abermarre. Papua, E Indonesia *07°03′S 140°10′E*
77 *O16* **Abengourou** E Ivory Coast *06°42′N 03°27′W*
Åbenrå *see* Aabenraa
101 *L22* **Abens** ≈ SE Germany
77 *S16* **Abeokuta** Ogun, SW Nigeria *07°07′N 03°21′E*
97 *I20* **Aberaeron** SW Wales, United Kingdom *52°15′N 04°15′W*
Aberbrothock *see* Arbroath
Abercorn *see* Mbala
29 *R6* **Abercrombie** North Dakota, N USA *46°25′N 96°42′W*
183 *T7* **Aberdeen** New South Wales, SE Australia *32°09′S 150°55′E*
11 *T15* **Aberdeen** Saskatchewan, S Canada *52°15′N 106°19′W*
83 *H25* **Aberdeen** Eastern Cape, S South Africa *32°30′S 24°00′E*
96 *L9* **Aberdeen** *anc.* Devana. NE Scotland, United Kingdom *57°10′N 02°04′W*
21 *X2* **Aberdeen** Maryland, NE USA *39°28′N 76°09′W*
23 *N3* **Aberdeen** Mississippi, S USA *33°49′N 88°32′W*
21 *T10* **Aberdeen** North Carolina, SE USA *35°07′N 79°25′W*
29 *P8* **Aberdeen** South Dakota, N USA *45°27′N 98°29′W*
32 *F8* **Aberdeen** Washington, NW USA *46°57′N 123°48′W*
96 *K9* **Aberdeen** *cultural region* NE Scotland, United Kingdom
8 *L8* **Aberdeen Lake** ◎ Nunavut, NE Canada
96 *J10* **Aberfeldy** C Scotland, United Kingdom *56°38′N 03°49′W*
97 *K21* **Abergavenny** *anc.* Gobannium. SE Wales, United Kingdom *51°50′N 03°W*
Abergwaun *see* Fishguard
Abermarre *see* Abemaree
25 *N5* **Abernathy** Texas, SW USA *33°49′N 101°50′W*
Abersee *see* Wolfgangsee
Abertawe *see* Swansea
Aberteifi *see* Cardigan
32 *I15* **Abert, Lake** ◎ Oregon, NW USA
97 *I20* **Aberystwyth** W Wales, United Kingdom *52°25′N 04°05′W*
Abeshr *see* Abéché
Ábeskovvu *see* Abisko
106 *F10* **Abetone** Toscana, C Italy *44°09′N 10°42′E*
125 *V5* **Abezʼ** Respublika Komi, NW Russian Federation *66°32′N 61°41′E*
142 *M5* **Āb Garm** Qazvin, N Iran
141 *N12* **Abhā** ʻAsīr, SW Saudi Arabia *18°16′N 42°32′E*
142 *M5* **Abhar** Zanjān, NW Iran *36°05′N 49°18′E*
Abhé Bad/Ābhē Bid Hāykʼ *see* Abhe, Lake
80 *K12* **Abhe, Lake** *var.* Lake Abbé, *Amh.* Ābhē Bid Hāykʼ, *Som.* Abhé Bad. ◎ Djibouti/Ethiopia
77 *V17* **Abia** ◐ *state* SE Nigeria
139 *V9* **ʻAbīd ʻAlī** Wāsiṭ, E Iraq *32°20′N 45°58′E*
119 *O17* **Abidavichy** *Rus.* Obidovichi. Mahilyowskaya Voblastsʼ, E Belarus *53°20′N 30°25′E*
115 *L15* **Abide** Çanakkale, NW Turkey *40°04′N 26°13′E*
77 *N17* **Abidjan** S Ivory Coast *05°19′N 04°01′W*
Āb-i-Istāda *see* Īstādeh-ye Moqor, Āb-e-
27 *N4* **Abilene** Kansas, C USA *38°55′N 97°14′W*
25 *Q7* **Abilene** Texas, SW USA *32°27′N 99°44′W*
Abindonia *see* Abingdon
97 *M21* **Abingdon** *anc.* Abindonia. S England, United Kingdom *51°41′N 01°17′W*
30 *K12* **Abingdon** Illinois, N USA *40°48′N 90°24′W*
21 *P8* **Abingdon** Virginia, NE USA *36°42′N 81°59′W*
Abingdon *see* Pinta, Isla
18 *J15* **Abington** Pennsylvania, NE USA *40°06′N 75°05′W*
126 *K14* **Abinsk** Krasnodarskiy Kray, SW Russian Federation *44°51′N 38°12′E*
37 *R9* **Abiquiu Reservoir** ▣ New Mexico, SW USA
Āb-i-safed *see* Sefīd, Darya-ye
92 *I10* **Abisko** *Lapp.* Ábeskovvu. Norrbotten, N Sweden *68°21′N 18°50′E*
12 *G12* **Abitibi** ≈ Ontario, S Canada
12 *H12* **Abitibi, Lac** ◎ Ontario/Québec, S Canada
80 *J10* **Ābīy Ādī** Tigray, N Ethiopia *13°40′N 38°57′E*
118 *H6* **Abja-Paluoja** Viljandimaa, S Estonia *58°08′N 25°20′E*
Abkhazia *see* Apʼkhazetʼi
182 *F1* **Abminga** South Australia *26°07′S 134°49′E*
75 *W9* **Abnūb** *var.* Abnûb. C Egypt *27°18′N 31°09′E*
Abnûb *see* Abnūb
Åbo *see* Turku
152 *G9* **Abohar** Punjab, N India *30°11′N 74°14′E*
77 *O17* **Aboisso** SE Ivory Coast *05°26′N 03°13′W*
78 *H5* **Abo, Massif dʼ** ▲▲ NW Chad
77 *R16* **Abomey** S Benin *07°14′N 02°00′E*
79 *F16* **Abong Mbang** Est, SE Cameroon *03°58′N 13°10′E*
111 *L23* **Abony** Pest, C Hungary *47°10′N 20°00′E*
78 *J11* **Abou-Déïa** Salamat, SE Chad *11°30′N 19°18′E*
Aboudouhour *see* Abū aḍ Ḍuhūr
Abou Kémal *see* Abū Kamāl
Abou Simbel *see* Abū Sunbul
137 *T12* **Abovyan** C Armenia *40°16′N 44°33′E*
141 *P15* **Abrād, Wādī** *seasonal river* W Yemen
Abraham Bay *see* The Carlton
104 *G10* **Abrantes** *var.* Abrántes. Santarém, C Portugal *39°28′N 08°12′W*
62 *J4* **Abra Pampa** Jujuy, N Argentina *22°47′S 65°41′W*
Abrashlare *see* Brezovo
54 *G7* **Abrego** Norte de Santander, N Colombia *08°08′N 73°14′W*
Abrene *see* Pytalovo
40 *C7* **Abreojos, Punta** *headland* NW Mexico *26°43′N 113°36′W*
65 *J16* **Abrolhos Bank** *undersea feature* W Atlantic Ocean *18°30′S 38°45′W*
119 *H19* **Abrova** *Rus.* Obrovo. Brestskaya Voblastsʼ, SW Belarus *52°30′N 25°34′E*
116 *G11* **Abrud** *Ger.* Gross-Schlatten, *Hung.* Abrudbánya. Alba, SW Romania *46°16′N 23°05′E*
Abrudbánya *see* Abrud
118 *E6* **Abruka** *island* SW Estonia
107 *J15* **Abruzzese, Appennino** ▲▲ C Italy
107 *J14* **Abruzzo** ◐ *region* C Italy
141 *N14* **ʻAbs** *var.* Sūq ʻAbs. W Yemen *16°42′N 42°55′E*
33 *T12* **Absaroka Range** ▲▲ Montana/Wyoming, NW USA
137 *Z11* **Abşeron Yarımadası** *Rus.* Apsheronskiy Poluostrov. *peninsula* E Azerbaijan
143 *N6* **Āb Shīrīn** Eşfahān, C Iran *34°17′N 51°17′E*
139 *X10* **Abtān** Maysān, SE Iraq *31°37′N 47°06′E*
109 *R6* **Abtenau** Salzburg, NW Austria *47°33′N 13°21′E*
152 *E14* **Ābu** Rājasthān, N India *24°41′N 72°50′E*
164 *E12* **Abu** Yamaguchi, Honshū, SW Japan *34°30′N 131°26′E*
138 *I4* **Abū aḍ Ḍuhūr** *Fr.* Aboudouhour. Idlib, NW Syria *35°30′N 37°00′E*
143 *P17* **Abū al Abyaḍ** *island* C United Arab Emirates
138 *K10* **Abū al Ḥuṣayn, Khabrat** ◎ N Jordan
139 *R8* **Abū al Jīr** Al Anbār, C Iraq *33°16′N 42°55′E*
139 *Y12* **Abū al Khaṣīb** *var.* Abul Khasib. Al Başrah, SE Iraq *30°26′N 48°00′E*
139 *U12* **Abū at Tubrah, Thaqb** *well* S Iraq
Abu Balâs *see* Abu Ballās
75 *V11* **Abu Ballās** *var.* Abu Balâs. ▲ SW Egypt *24°28′N 27°36′E*
Abu Dhabi *see* Abū Ẓabī
139 *R8* **Abū Farūkh** Al Anbār, C Iraq *33°06′N 43°18′E*
80 *C12* **Abu Gabra** Southern Darfur, W Sudan *11°02′N 26°50′E*
139 *P10* **Abū Ghār, Shaʻīb** *dry watercourse* S Iraq
80 *G7* **Abu Hamed** River Nile, N Sudan *19°32′N 33°20′E*
139 *O5* **Abū Ḩardān** *var.* Hajîne. Dayr az Zawr, E Syria *34°45′N 40°49′E*
139 *T7* **Abū Ḩāssawīyah** Diyālá, E Iraq *33°52′N 44°47′E*
138 *K10* **Abū Ḩifnah, Wādī** *dry watercourse* N Jordan
77 *V15* **Abuja** ● (Nigeria) Federal Capital District, C Nigeria *09°04′N 07°28′E*
139 *R9* **Abū Jahaf, Wādī** *dry watercourse* C Iraq
56 *F12* **Abujao, Río** ≈ E Peru
139 *U12* **Abū Jasrah** Al Muthanná, S Iraq *30°43′N 44°50′E*
139 *O6* **Abū Kamāl** *Fr.* Abou Kémal. Dayr az Zawr, E Syria *34°29′N 40°56′E*
165 *P12* **Abukuma-sanchi** ▲▲ Honshū, C Japan
Abula *see* Ávila
Abul Khasib *see* Abū al Khaṣīb
79 *K16* **Abumombazi** *var.* Abumonbazi. Equateur, N Dem. Rep. Congo *03°43′N 22°06′E*
Abumonbazi *see* Abumombazi
59 *D15* **Abunã** Rondônia, W Brazil *09°41′S 65°20′W*
56 *K13* **Abunã, Rio** *var.* Río Abuná. ≈ Bolivia/Brazil
138 *G10* **Abū Nuşayr** *var.* Abu Nuseir. ʻAmmān, W Jordan *32°03′N 35°58′E*
Abu Nuseir *see* Abū Nuşayr
139 *T12* **Abū Qabr** Al Muthanná, S Iraq *31°03′N 44°34′E*
138 *K5* **Abū Raḩbah, Jabal** ▲▲ C Syria
139 *S5* **Abū Rajāsh** Şalāḩ ad Dīn, N Iraq *34°47′N 43°36′E*
139 *W13* **Abū Raqrāq, Ghadīr** *well* S Iraq
152 *E14* **Ābu Road** Rājasthān, N India *24°29′N 72°47′E*
80 *I6* **Abu Shagara, Ras** *headland* NE Sudan *18°04′N 38°31′E*
Abu Simbel *see* Abū Sunbul
139 *U12* **Abū Sudayrah** Al Muthanná, S Iraq *30°55′N 44°58′E*
139 *T10* **Abū Şukhayr** Al Qādisīyah, S Iraq *31°54′N 44°27′E*
Abū Sunbul *see* Abū Sunbul

185 E18 **Abut Head** *headland* South Island, New Zealand 43°06′S 170°16′E
80 E9 **Abu 'Urug** Northern Kordofan, C Sudan 15°52′N 30°25′E
80 K12 **Ābuyē Mēda** ▲ C Ethiopia 10°28′N 39°44′E
80 D11 **Abu Zabad** Western Kordofan, C Sudan 12°21′N 29°16′E
143 P16 **Abū Ẓabī** *var.* Abū Ẓabī, *Eng.* Abu Dhabi. ● (United Arab Emirates) Abū Ẓaby, C United Arab Emirates 24°30′N 54°20′E
Abū Ẓabī *see* Abū Ẓabī
75 X8 **Abu Zenima** E Egypt 29°01′N 33°08′E
95 N17 **Åby** Östergötland, S Sweden 58°40′N 16°10′E
Abyad, Al Baḥr al *see* White Nile
Abybro *see* Aabybro
80 D13 **Abyei** Western Kordofan, S Sudan 09°35′N 28°28′E
Abyla *see* Ávila
Abymes *see* les Abymes
Abyssinia *see* Ethiopia
Açāba *see* Assaba
54 F11 **Acacías** Meta, C Colombia 03°59′N 73°46′W
58 L13 **Açailandia** Maranhão, E Brazil 04°51′S 47°26′W
Acaill *see* Achill Island
42 E8 **Acajutla** Sonsonate, W El Salvador 13°34′N 89°50′W
79 D17 **Acalayong** SW Equatorial Guinea 01°05′N 09°34′E
41 N13 **Acámbaro** Guanajuato, C Mexico 20°01′N 100°42′W
54 C6 **Acandí** Chocó, NW Colombia 08°32′N 77°20′W
104 H4 **A Cañiza** *var.* La Cañiza. Galicia, NW Spain 42°13′N 08°16′W
40 J11 **Acaponeta** Nayarit, C Mexico 22°30′N 105°21′W
40 J11 **Acaponeta, Río de** ≈ C Mexico
41 O16 **Acapulco** *var.* Acapulco de Juárez. Guerrero, S Mexico 16°51′N 99°53′W
Acapulco de Juárez *see* Acapulco
55 T13 **Acarai Mountains** *Sp.* Serra Acaraí. ▲▲ Brazil/Guyana
Acaraí, Serra *see* Acarai Mountains
58 O13 **Acaraú** Ceará, NE Brazil 04°35′S 37°37′W
54 J6 **Acarigua** Portuguesa, N Venezuela 09°35′N 69°12′W
42 C6 **Acatenango, Volcán de** ⛰ S Guatemala 14°30′N 90°52′W
41 Q15 **Acatlán** *var.* Acatlán de Osorio. Puebla, S Mexico 18°12′N 98°02′W
Acatlán de Osorio *see* Acatlán
41 S15 **Acayucan** *var.* Acayucán. Veracruz-Llave, E Mexico 17°59′N 94°58′W
Accho *see* Akko
21 Y5 **Accomac** Virginia, NE USA 37°43′N 75°41′W
77 Q17 **Accra** ● (Ghana)SE Ghana 05°33′N 00°15′W
97 L17 **Accrington** NW England, United Kingdom 53°46′N 02°21′W
61 B19 **Acebal** Santa Fe, C Argentina 33°14′S 60°50′W
168 H8 **Aceh** *off.* Daerah Istimewa Aceh, *var.* Acheen, Achin, Atchin, Atjeh. ◈ *autonomous district* NW Indonesia
107 M18 **Acerenza** Basilicata, S Italy 40°46′N 15°51′E
107 K17 **Acerra** *anc.* Acerrae. Campania, S Italy 40°56′N 14°22′E
Acerrae *see* Acerra
57 J17 **Achacachi** La Paz, W Bolivia 16°01′S 68°44′W
54 K7 **Achaguas** Apure, C Venezuela 07°46′N 68°14′W
154 H12 **Achalpur** *prev.* Elichpur, Ellichpur. Mahārāshtra, C India 21°19′N 77°30′E
61 F18 **Achar** Tacuarembó, C Uruguay 32°20′S 56°15′W
137 R10 **Achara** *var.* Ajaria. ◈ *autonomous republic* SW Georgia
115 H19 **Acharnés** *var.* Aharnes; *prev.* Akharnaí. Attikí, C Greece 38°09′N 23°58′E
Ach'asar Lerr *see* Achkasar
Acheen *see* Aceh
99 K16 **Achel** Limburg, NE Belgium 51°15′N 05°31′E
115 D16 **Achelóos** *var.* Akhelóös, Aspropótamos; *anc.* Achelous. ≈ W Greece
Achelous *see* Achelóos
163 W8 **Acheng** Heilongjiang, NE China 45°32′N 126°56′E
109 N6 **Achenkirch** Tirol, W Austria 47°31′N 11°42′E
101 L24 **Achenpass** *pass* Austria/Germany
109 N7 **Achensee** ◎ W Austria
101 F22 **Achern** Baden-Württemberg, SW Germany 48°37′N 08°04′E
115 C16 **Acherón** ≈ W Greece
77 W11 **Achétinamou** ≈ S Niger
152 J12 **Achhnera** Uttar Pradesh, N India 27°10′N 77°45′E
42 C7 **Achiguate, Río** ≈ S Guatemala
97 A16 **Achill Head** *Ir.* Ceann Acla. *headland* W Ireland 53°58′N 10°14′W
97 A16 **Achill Island** *Ir.* Acaill. *island* W Ireland
100 H11 **Achim** Niedersachsen, NW Germany 53°01′N 09°01′E
149 S5 **Achīn** Nangarhār, E Afghanistan 34°04′N 70°41′E
Achin *see* Aceh
122 K12 **Achinsk** Krasnoyarskiy Kray, S Russian Federation 56°21′N 90°25′E
162 E5 **Achit Nuur** ◎ NW Mongolia
137 T11 **Achkasar** *Arm.* Ach'asar Lerr. ▲ Armenia/Georgia 41°09′N 43°55′E
126 K13 **Achuyevo** Krasnodarskiy Kray, SW Russian Federation 46°00′N 38°01′E
81 F16 **Achwa** *var.* Aswa. ≈ N Uganda
136 E15 **Acıgöl** *salt lake* SW Turkey
107 L24 **Acireale** Sicilia, Italy, C Mediterranean Sea 37°36′N 15°10′E
Aciris *see* Agri
25 N7 **Ackerly** Texas, SW USA 32°31′N 101°43′W
22 M4 **Ackerman** Mississippi, S USA 33°18′N 89°10′W
29 W13 **Ackley** Iowa, C USA 42°33′N 93°03′W
44 J5 **Acklins Island** *island* SE Bahamas
Acla, Ceann *see* Achill Head
62 H11 **Aconcagua, Cerro** ▲ W Argentina 32°36′S 69°53′W
Açores/Açores, Arquipélago dos/Açores, Ilhas dos *see* Azores
104 H2 **A Coruña** *Cast.* La Coruña, *Eng.* Corunna; *anc.* Caronium. Galicia, NW Spain 43°22′N 08°24′W
104 G2 **A Coruña** *Cast.* La Coruña. ◈ *province* Galicia, NW Spain
42 L10 **Acoyapa** Chontales, S Nicaragua 11°58′N 85°10′W
106 H13 **Acquapendente** Lazio, C Italy 42°44′N 11°52′E
106 J13 **Acquasanta Terme** Marche, C Italy 42°46′N 13°24′E
106 I13 **Acquasparta** Lazio, C Italy 42°41′N 12°31′E
106 C9 **Acqui Terme** Piemonte, NW Italy 44°41′N 08°28′E
Acrae *see* Palazzolo Acreide
182 F7 **Acraman, Lake** *salt lake* South Australia
59 A15 **Acre** *off.* Estado do Acre. ◈ *state* W Brazil
Acre *see* Akko
59 C16 **Acre, Rio** ≈ W Brazil
107 N20 **Acri** Calabria, SW Italy 39°30′N 16°22′E
Acte *see* Ágion Óros
191 Y12 **Actéon, Groupe** *island group* Îles Tuamotu, SE French Polynesia
15 P12 **Acton-Vale** Québec, SE Canada 45°39′N 72°31′W
41 P13 **Actopan** *var.* Actopán. Hidalgo, C Mexico 20°19′N 98°59′W
59 P14 **Açu** *var.* Assu. Rio Grande do Norte, E Brazil 05°33′S 36°55′W
Acunum Acusio *see* Montélimar
77 Q17 **Ada** SE Ghana 05°47′N 00°42′E
112 L8 **Ada** Vojvodina, N Serbia 45°48′N 20°08′E
29 R5 **Ada** Minnesota, N USA 47°18′N 96°31′W
31 R12 **Ada** Ohio, N USA 40°46′N 83°49′W
27 O12 **Ada** Oklahoma, C USA 34°47′N 96°41′W
162 L8 **Adaatsag** *var.* Tavin. Dundgovĭ, C Mongolia 46°27′N 105°43′E
Ada Bazar *see* Adapazarı
40 D3 **Adair, Bahía de** *bay* NW Mexico
104 M7 **Adaja** ≈ N Spain
38 H17 **Adak Island** *island* Aleutian Islands, Alaska, USA
Adalia *see* Antalya
Adalia, Gulf of *see* Antalya Körfezi
141 X9 **Adam** N Oman 22°22′N 57°30′E
Adama *see* Nazrēt
60 I8 **Adamantina** São Paulo, S Brazil 21°41′S 51°04′W
79 E14 **Adamaoua** *Eng.* Adamawa. ◈ *province* N Cameroon
68 F11 **Adamaoua, Massif d'** *Eng.* Adamawa Highlands. *plateau* NW Cameroon
77 Y14 **Adamawa** ◈ *state* E Nigeria
Adamawa *see* Adamaoua
Adamawa Highlands *see* Adamaoua, Massif d'
106 F6 **Adamello** ▲ N Italy 46°09′N 10°33′E
81 J14 **Ādamī Tulu** Oromīya, C Ethiopia 07°52′N 38°39′E
63 M23 **Adam, Mount** *var.* Monte Independencia. ▲ West Falkland, Falkland Islands 51°36′S 60°00′W
29 R16 **Adams** Nebraska, C USA 40°25′N 96°30′W
18 H8 **Adams** New York, NE USA 43°48′N 75°57′W
29 Q3 **Adams** North Dakota, N USA 48°23′N 98°01′W
155 I23 **Adam's Bridge** *chain of shoals* NW Sri Lanka
32 H10 **Adams, Mount** ▲ Washington, NW USA 46°12′N 121°29′W
Adam's Peak *see* Sri Pada
191 R16 **Adam's Rock** *island* Pitcairn Island, Pitcairn Islands
191 P16 **Adamstown** ○ (Pitcairn Islands)Pitcairn Island, Pitcairn Islands 25°04′S 130°05′W
20 G10 **Adamsville** Tennessee, S USA 35°14′N 88°23′W
25 S9 **Adamsville** Texas, SW USA 31°15′N 98°09′W
141 O17 **'Adan** *Eng.* Aden. SW Yemen 12°51′N 45°05′E
136 K16 **Adana** *var.* Seyhan. Adana, S Turkey 37°N 35°19′E
136 K16 **Adana** *var.* Seyhan. ◈ *province* S Turkey
Adâncata *see* Horlivka
169 V12 **Adang, Teluk** *bay* Borneo, C Indonesia
136 F11 **Adapazarı** *prev.* Ada Bazar. Sakarya, NW Turkey 40°49′N 30°24′E
80 H8 **Adarama** River Nile, NE Sudan 17°04′N 34°57′E
195 Q16 **Adare, Cape** *cape* Antarctica
Ādavānī *see* Ādoni
106 E6 **Adda** *anc.* Addua. ≈ N Italy
80 A13 **Adda** ≈ W Sudan
143 Q17 **Aḍ Ḍab'iyah** Abū Ẓaby, C United Arab Emirates 24°17′N 54°08′E
143 O18 **Aḍ Ḍafrah** *desert* S United Arab Emirates
141 Q6 **Ad Dahnā'** *desert* E Saudi Arabia
74 A11 **Ad Dakhla** *var.* Dakhla. SW Western Sahara 23°46′N 15°56′W
Ad Dalanj *see* Dilling
Ad Damar *see* Ed Damer
Ad Damazīn *see* Ed Damazin
Ad Dāmir *see* Ed Damer
173 N2 **Ad Dammām** *desert* NE Saudi Arabia
141 R6 **Ad Dammān** *var.* Dammām. Ash Sharqīyah, NE Saudi Arabia 26°23′N 50°05′E
Ad Dāmūr *see* Damoûr
140 K5 **Ad Dār al Ḥamrā'** Tabūk, NW Saudi Arabia 27°22′N 37°46′E
140 M13 **Ad Darb** Jīzān, SW Saudi Arabia 17°45′N 42°15′E
141 O8 **Ad Dawādimī** Ar Riyāḍ, C Saudi Arabia 24°32′N 44°21′E
143 N16 **Ad Dawḥah** *Eng.* Doha. ● (Qatar) C Qatar 25°15′N 51°36′E
143 N16 **Ad Dawḥah** *Eng.* Doha. ✈ C Qatar 25°11′N 51°37′E
139 S6 **Ad Dawr** Ṣalāḥ ad Dīn, N Iraq 34°30′N 43°49′E
139 Y12 **Ad Dayr** *var.* Dayr, Shahbān. Al Baṣrah, E Iraq 30°45′N 47°36′E
Addi Arkay *see* Ādī Ārk'ay
139 X15 **Ad Dibdibah** *physical region* Iraq/Kuwait
Ad Diffah *see* Libyan Plateau
Addis Ababa *see* Ādīs Ābeba
Addison *see* Webster Springs
139 U10 **Ad Dīwānīyah** *var.* Diwaniyah. C Iraq 32°00′N 44°57′E
Addoo Atoll *see* Addu Atoll
Addua *see* Adda
151 K22 **Addu Atoll** *var.* Addoo Atoll, Seenu Atoll. *atoll* S Maldives
Ad Dujail *see* Ad Dujayl
139 T7 **Ad Dujayl** *var.* Ad Dujail. Ṣalāḥ ad Dīn, N Iraq 33°49′N 44°16′E
Ad Duwaym/Ad Duwēm *see* Ed Dueim
99 D16 **Adegem** Oost-Vlaanderen, NW Belgium 51°12′N 03°31′E
23 U7 **Adel** Georgia, SE USA 31°08′N 83°25′W
29 U14 **Adel** Iowa, C USA 41°36′N 94°01′W
182 I9 **Adelaide** *state capital* South Australia 34°56′S 138°36′E
44 H2 **Adelaide** New Providence, N Bahamas 24°59′N 77°30′W
182 I9 **Adelaide** ✈ South Australia 34°55′S 138°31′E
194 H6 **Adelaide Island** *island* Antarctica
181 P2 **Adelaide River** Northern Territory, N Australia 13°12′S 131°06′E
76 M10 **'Adel Bagrou** Hodh ech Chargui, SE Mauritania 15°33′N 07°04′W
186 D6 **Adelbert Range** ▲▲ N Papua New Guinea
180 K3 **Adele Island** *island* Western Australia
107 O17 **Adelfia** Puglia, SE Italy 41°01′N 16°52′E
195 V16 **Adélie Coast** *physical region* Antarctica
195 V14 **Adélie, Terre** *physical region* Antarctica
Adelnau *see* Odolanów
Adelsberg *see* Postojna
Aden *see* Khormaksar
Aden *see* 'Adan
141 Q17 **Aden, Gulf of** *gulf* SW Arabian Sea
77 V10 **Aderbissinat** Agadez, C Niger 15°30′N 07°57′E
Adhaim *see* Al 'Uẓaym
143 R16 **Adh Dhayd** *var.* Al Dhaid. Ash Shāriqah, NE United Arab Emirates 25°19′N 55°51′E
140 M4 **'Adhfā'** *spring/well* NW Saudi Arabia 29°15′N 41°24′E
138 I13 **'Ādhriyāt, Jabāl al** ▲ S Jordan
80 I10 **Ādī Ārk'ay** *var.* Addi Arkay. Āmara, N Ethiopia 13°18′N 37°56′E
182 C7 **Adieu, Cape** *headland* South Australia 32°01′S 132°12′E
106 H8 **Adige** *Ger.* Etsch. ≈ N Italy
80 J10 **Ādīgrat** Tigray, N Ethiopia 14°17′N 39°27′E
80 J10 **'Adi Kh'eyih** C Eritrea 19°58′N 39°06′E
154 I13 **Ādilābād** *var.* Ādilābād. Andhra Pradesh, C India 19°40′N 78°31′E
35 P2 **Adin** California, W USA 41°10′N 120°57′W
171 V14 **Adi, Pulau** *island* E Indonesia
18 K8 **Adirondack Mountains** ▲▲ New York, NE USA
80 J13 **Ādīs Ābeba** *Eng.* Addis Ababa. ● (Ethiopia) Ādīs Ābeba, C Ethiopia 8°59′N 38°43′E
80 J13 **Ādīs Ābeba** ✈ Ādīs Ābeba, C Ethiopia 08°58′N 38°53′E
80 I11 **Ādīs Zemen** Āmara, N Ethiopia 12°00′N 37°43′E
Adi Ugri *see* Mendefera
137 N15 **Adıyaman** Adıyaman, SE Turkey 37°46′N 38°15′E
137 N15 **Adıyaman** ◈ *province* S Turkey
116 L11 **Adjud** Vrancea, E Romania 46°07′N 27°10′E
45 T6 **Adjuntas** C Puerto Rico 18°10′N 66°42′W
Adjuntas, Presa de las *see* Vicente Guerrero, Presa
Ādkup *see* Erikub Atoll
126 L15 **Adler** Krasnodarskiy Kray, SW Russian Federation 43°25′N 39°58′E
Adler *see* Orlice
108 G7 **Adliswil** Zürich, NW Switzerland 47°19′N 08°32′E
32 G7 **Admiralty Inlet** *inlet* Washington, NW USA
39 X13 **Admiralty Island** *island* Alexander Archipelago, Alaska, USA
186 E5 **Admiralty Islands** *island group* N Papua New Guinea
136 B14 **Adnan Menderes** ✈ (İzmir) İzmir, W Turkey 38°16′N 27°09′E
37 V6 **Adobe Creek Reservoir** ⊠ Colorado, C USA
77 T16 **Ado-Ekiti** Ekiti, SW Nigeria 07°42′N 05°13′E
Adola *see* Kibre Mengist
61 C23 **Adolfo González Chaues** Buenos Aires, E Argentina 37°57′S 60°06′W
155 H17 **Ādoni** *var.* Ādavāni. Andhra Pradesh, C India 15°38′N 77°16′E
102 K15 **Adour** *anc.* Aturus. ≈ SW France
Adowa *see* Ādwa
105 O15 **Adra** Andalucía, S Spain 36°45′N 03°01′W
107 L24 **Adrano** Sicilia, Italy, C Mediterranean Sea 37°39′N 14°49′E
74 I9 **Adrar** C Algeria 27°56′N 00°12′W
76 K7 **Adrar** ◈ *region* C Mauritania
74 L11 **Adrar** ▲▲ SE Algeria
74 A12 **Adrar Souttouf** ▲▲ SW Western Sahara
Adrasman *see* Adrasmon
147 Q10 **Adrasmon** *Rus.* Adrasman. NW Tajikistan 40°38′N 69°56′E
78 K10 **Adré** Ouaddaï, E Chad 13°26′N 22°14′E
106 H9 **Adria** *anc.* Atria, Hadria, Hatria. Veneto, NE Italy 45°03′N 12°04′E
31 R10 **Adrian** Michigan, N USA 41°54′N 84°02′W
29 S11 **Adrian** Minnesota, N USA 43°38′N 95°55′W
27 R5 **Adrian** Missouri, C USA 38°24′N 94°21′W
24 M2 **Adrian** Texas, SW USA 35°16′N 102°39′W
21 S4 **Adrian** West Virginia, NE USA 38°53′N 80°14′W
Adrianople/Adrianopolis *see* Edirne
121 P7 **Adriatic Basin** *undersea feature* Adriatic Sea, N Mediterranean Sea 42°00′N 17°30′E
Adriatico, Mare *see* Adriatic Sea
106 L13 **Adriatic Sea** *Alb.* Deti Adriatik, *It.* Mare Adriatico, *SCr.* Jadransko More, *Slvn.* Jadransko Morje. *sea* N Mediterranean Sea
Adriatik, Deti *see* Adriatic Sea
Adua *see* Ādwa
Aduana del Sásabe *see* El Sásabe
79 O17 **Adusa** Orientale, NE Dem. Rep. Congo 01°25′N 28°05′E
118 J13 **Adutiškis** Vilnius, E Lithuania 55°09′N 26°34′E
27 Y7 **Advance** Missouri, C USA 37°06′N 89°54′W
65 D25 **Adventure Sound** *bay* East Falkland, Falkland Islands
80 J10 **Ādwa** *var.* Adowa, *It.* Adua. Tigray, N Ethiopia 14°08′N 38°51′E
123 Q8 **Adycha** ≈ NE Russian Federation
126 L14 **Adygeya, Respublika** ◈ *autonomous republic* SW Russian Federation
Adzhikui *see* Ajyguýy
77 N17 **Adzopé** SE Ivory Coast 06°07′N 03°49′W
125 U4 **Adz'va** ≈ NW Russian Federation
125 U5 **Adz'vavom** Respublika Komi, NW Russian Federation 66°35′N 59°13′E
Ædua *see* Autun
115 K19 **Aegean Islands** *island group* Greece/Turkey
Aegean North *see* Vóreion Aigaíon
115 I17 **Aegean Sea** *Gk.* Aigaíon Pelagos, Aigaío Pélagos, *Turk.* Ege Denizi. *sea* NE Mediterranean Sea
Aegean South *see* Nótion Aigaíon
118 H3 **Aegviidu** *Ger.* Charlottenhof. Harjumaa, NW Estonia 59°17′N 25°37′E
Aegyptus *see* Egypt
Aelana *see* Al 'Aqabah
Aelok *see* Ailuk Atoll
Aelōninae *see* Ailinginae Atoll
Aelōnlaplap *see* Ailinglaplap Atoll
Æmilia *see* Emilia-Romagna
Æmilianum *see* Millau
Aemona *see* Ljubljana
Aenaria *see* Ischia
Aeolian Islands *see* Eolie, Isole
191 Z3 **Aeon Point** *headland* Kiritimati, NE Kiribati 01°46′N 157°11′W
Æsernia *see* Isernia
104 G3 **A Estrada** Galicia, NW Spain 42°41′N 08°29′W
115 C18 **Aetós** Itháki, Iónia Nísoi, Greece, C Mediterranean Sea 38°21′N 20°40′E
191 Q8 **Afaahiti** Tahiti, W French Polynesia 17°43′S 149°18′W
139 U10 **'Afak** Al Qādisīyah, C Iraq 32°04′N 45°17′E
Afanasjevo *see* Afanas'yevo
125 T14 **Afanas'yevo** *var.* Afanasjevo. Kirovskaya Oblast', NW Russian Federation 58°55′N 53°13′E
Afándou *see* Afántou
115 O23 **Afántou** *var.* Afándou. Ródos, Dodekánisa, Greece, Aegean Sea 36°17′N 28°10′E
80 K11 **Āfar** ◈ *region* NE Ethiopia
Afar Depression *see* Danakil Desert
191 O7 **Afareaitu** Moorea, W French Polynesia 17°33′S 149°47′W
140 L7 **'Afarīyah, Bi'r al** *well* NW Saudi Arabia
Afars et des Issas, Territoire Français des *see* Djibouti
83 D22 **Affenrücken** Karas, SW Namibia 28°05′S 15°49′E
Afghānestān, Dowlat-e Eslāmī-ye *see* Afghanistan
148 M6 **Afghanistan** *off.* Islamic Republic of Afghanistan, *Per.* Dowlat-e Eslāmī-ye Afghānestān; *prev.* Republic of Afghanistan. ◆ *islamic state* C Asia
Afgoi *see* Afgooye
81 N17 **Afgooye** *It.* Afgoi. Shabeellaha Hoose, S Somalia 02°09′N 45°07′E
141 N8 **'Afīf** Ar Riyāḍ, C Saudi Arabia 23°57′N 42°57′E
77 V17 **Afikpo** Ebonyi, S Nigeria 05°52′N 07°58′E
Afiun Karahissar *see* Afyon
Åfjord *see* Åi Åfjord
109 V6 **Aflenz Kurort** Steiermark, E Austria 47°33′N 15°14′E
74 J6 **Aflou** N Algeria 34°09′N 02°06′E
81 L18 **Afmadow** Jubbada Hoose, S Somalia 00°24′N 42°04′E
39 Q14 **Afognak Island** *island* Alaska, USA
104 J2 **A Fonsagrada** Galicia, NW Spain 43°09′N 07°03′W
186 E9 **Afore** Northern, S Papua New Guinea 09°10′S 148°30′E
59 O15 **Afrânio** Pernambuco, E Brazil 08°32′S 40°54′W
66-67 **Africa** *continent*
68 L11 **Africa, Horn of** *physical region* Ethiopia/Somalia
172 K11 **Africana Seamount** *undersea feature* SW Indian Ocean 37°10′S 29°10′E
86 A14 **African Plate** *tectonic plate*
138 I2 **'Afrīn** Ḥalab, N Syria 36°31′N 36°51′E
136 M15 **Afşin** Kahramanmaraş, C Turkey 38°14′N 36°54′E
98 J7 **Afsluitdijk** *dam* N Netherlands
29 U15 **Afton** Iowa, C USA 41°01′N 94°12′W
29 W9 **Afton** Minnesota, N USA 44°54′N 92°46′W
27 R8 **Afton** Oklahoma, C USA 36°41′N 94°57′W
136 F14 **Afyon** *prev.* Afyonkarahisar. Afyon, W Turkey 38°46′N 30°32′E
136 F14 **Afyon** *var.* Afiun Karahissar, Afyonkarahisar. ◈ *province* W Turkey
Afyonkarahisar *see* Afyon
Agadès *see* Agadez
77 V10 **Agadez** *prev.* Agadès. Agadez, C Niger 16°57′N 07°56′E
77 W8 **Agadez** ◈ *department* N Niger
74 E8 **Agadir** SW Morocco 30°30′N 09°37′W
64 M9 **Agadir Canyon** *undersea feature* SE Atlantic Ocean 32°30′N 12°50′W
145 R12 **Agadyr'** Karaganda, C Kazakhstan 48°15′N 72°55′E
173 O7 **Agalega Islands** *island group* N Mauritius
42 K6 **Agalta, Sierra de** ▲▲ E Honduras
122 I10 **Agan** ≈ C Russian Federation
Agana/Agaña *see* Hagåtña
188 B15 **Agana Bay** *bay* NW Guam
188 C15 **Aganafield** *bay* NW Guam
171 Kk13 **Agano-gawa** ≈ Honshū, C Japan
188 B17 **Aga Point** *headland* S Guam
154 G9 **Agar** Madhya Pradesh, C India 23°44′N 76°01′E
81 I14 **Āgaro** Oromīya, C Ethiopia 07°52′N 36°36′E
153 V15 **Agartala** *state capital* Tripura, NE India 23°49′N 91°15′E
194 I5 **Agassiz, Cape** *headland* Antarctica 68°29′S 62°59′W
175 V13 **Agassiz Fracture Zone** *tectonic feature* S Pacific Ocean
9 N2 **Agassiz Ice Cap** *Ice feature* Nunavut, N Canada
188 B16 **Agat** W Guam 13°20′N 144°38′E
188 B16 **Agat Bay** *bay* W Guam
145 P13 **Agat, Gory** *hill* C Kazakhstan
Agatha *see* Agde
115 M20 **Agathónisi** *island* Dodekánisa, Greece, Aegean Sea
171 X14 **Agats** Papua, E Indonesia 05°33′S 138°07′E
155 C21 **Agatti Island** *island* Lakshadweep, India, N Indian Ocean
38 D16 **Agattu Island** *island* Aleutian Islands, Alaska, USA
38 D16 **Agattu Strait** *strait* Aleutian Islands, Alaska, USA
14 B8 **Agawa** ≈ Ontario, S Canada
14 B8 **Agawa Bay** *lake bay* Ontario, S Canada
77 N17 **Agboville** SE Ivory Coast 05°55′N 04°15′W
137 V12 **Ağdam** *Rus.* Agdam. SW Azerbaijan 40°04′N 46°00′E
Agdam *see* Ağdam
103 P16 **Agde** *anc.* Agatha. Hérault, S France 43°19′N 03°29′E
103 P16 **Agde, Cap d'** *headland* S France 43°17′N 03°30′E
Agedabia *see* Ajdābiyā
102 L14 **Agen** *anc.* Aginnum. Lot-et-Garonne, SW France 44°12′N 00°37′E
Agendicum *see* Sens
165 O13 **Ageo** Saitama, Honshū, S Japan 35°58′N 139°36′E
109 R5 **Ager** ≈ N Austria
Agere Hiywet *see* Hāgere Hiywet
108 G8 **Ägerisee** ◎ W Switzerland
142 M10 **Āghā Jārī** Khūzestān, SW Iran 30°48′N 49°45′E
39 P15 **Aghiyuk Island** *island* Alaska, USA
74 B12 **Aghouinit** SE Western Sahara 22°14′N 13°10′W
Aghri Dagh *see* Büyükağrı Dağı
74 B10 **Aghzoumal, Sebkhet** *var.* Sebjet Agsumal. *salt lake* E Western Sahara
115 F15 **Agiá** *var.* Ayiá. Thessalía, C Greece 39°43′N 22°45′E
40 G7 **Agiabampo, Estero de** *estuary* NW Mexico
121 P3 **Agía Fýlaxis** *var.* Ayia Phyla. S Cyprus 34°43′N 33°02′E
Agialoúsa *see* Yenierenköy
115 M21 **Agía Marína** Léros, Dodekánisa, Greece, Aegean Sea 37°09′N 26°51′E
121 Q2 **Agía Nápa** *var.* Ayia Napa. E Cyprus 34°59′N 34°00′E
115 L16 **Agía Paraskeví** Lésvos, E Greece 39°13′N 26°19′E
115 J15 **Agías Eirínis, Akrotírio** *headland* Límnos, E Greece 39°47′N 25°21′E
Agiasós *see* Agiassós
115 L17 **Agiassós** *var.* Agiasós, Ayiásos, Ayiássos. Lésvos, E Greece 39°05′N 26°23′E
127 T3 **Agidel'** Respublika Bashkortostan, W Russian Federation 55°54′N 53°57′E
Aginnum *see* Agen
123 O14 **Aginskiy Buryatskiy Avtonomnyy Okrug** ◈ *autonomous district* S Russian Federation
123 O14 **Aginskoye** Aginskiy Buryatskiy Avtonomnyy Okrug, S Russian Federation 51°10′N 114°32′E
115 I14 **Ágion Óros** *Eng.* Mount Athos. ◈ *monastic republic* NE Greece
115 H14 **Ágion Óros** *var.* Akte, Aktí; *anc.* Acte. *peninsula* NE Greece
114 D13 **Ágios Achílleios** *religious building* Dytikí Makedonía, N Greece
115 J16 **Ágios Efstrátios** *var.* Áyios Evstrátios, Hagios Evstrátios. *island* E Greece 39°34′N 25°00′E
115 H20 **Ágios Geórgios** *island* Kykládes, Greece, Aegean Sea
Ágios Geórgios *see* Ro
115 E21 **Ágios Ilías** ▲ S Greece 36°57′N 22°19′E
115 K25 **Ágios Ioánnis, Akrotírio** *headland* Kríti, Greece, E Mediterranean Sea 35°19′N 25°46′E
115 L20 **Ágios Kírykos** *var.* Áyios Kírikos. Ikaría, Dodekánisa, Greece, Aegean Sea 37°34′N 26°15′E
115 K25 **Ágios Nikólaos** *var.* Áyios Nikólaos. Kríti, Greece, E Mediterranean Sea 35°12′N 25°43′E
115 D16 **Ágios Nikolaos** Thessalía, C Greece 39°33′N 21°21′E
115 H14 **Agíou Órous, Kólpos** *gulf* N Greece
107 K24 **Agira** *anc.* Agyrium. Sicilia, Italy, C Mediterranean Sea 37°39′N 14°32′E
115 G20 **Agkístri** *island* S Greece
114 G12 **Ágkistro** *var.* Angistro. ▲ NE Greece 41°21′N 23°29′E
103 O17 **Agly** ≈ S France
Agnetheln *see* Agnita
14 E10 **Agnew Lake** ◎ Ontario, S Canada
77 O16 **Agnibilékrou** E Ivory Coast 07°10′N 03°11′W
116 I11 **Agnita** *Ger.* Agnetheln, *Hung.* Szentágota. Sibiu, SW Romania 45°59′N 24°40′E
107 K15 **Agnone** Molise, C Italy 41°49′N 14°21′E
164 K14 **Ago** Mie, Honshū, SW Japan 34°18′N 136°50′E
106 C8 **Agogna** ≈ N Italy
Agoitz *see* Agoiz
105 R3 **Agoiz** *var.* Agoitz, Aoiz. Navarra, N Spain 42°47′N 01°23′W
77 P17 **Agona Swedru** *var.* Swedru. SE Ghana 05°31′N 00°42′W
Agordat *see* Ak'ordat
Agosta *see* Augusta
103 N15 **Agout** ≈ S France
152 J12 **Āgra** Uttar Pradesh, N India 27°09′N 78°E
Agra and Oudh, United Provinces of *see* Uttar Pradesh
Agram *see* Zagreb
105 U5 **Agramunt** Cataluña, NE Spain 41°48′N 01°07′E
105 Q5 **Agreda** Castilla-León, N Spain 41°51′N 01°55′W
137 S13 **Ağrı** *var.* Karaköse; *prev.* Karakılısse. Ağrı, NE Turkey 39°44′N 43°04′E
137 S13 **Ağrı** ◈ *province* NE Turkey
107 N19 **Agri** *anc.* Aciris. ≈ S Italy
Agri Dagi *see* Büyükağrı Dağı
107 J24 **Agrigento** *Gk.* Akragas; *prev.* Girgenti. Sicilia, Italy, C Mediterranean Sea 37°19′N 13°33′E
188 K4 **Agrihan** *island* N Northern Mariana Islands
115 L17 **Agriliá, Akrotírio** *prev.* Ákra Maléas. *cape* Lésvos, E Greece
115 D18 **Agrínio** *prev.* Agrinion. Dytikí Ellás, W Greece 38°38′N 21°25′E
Agrinion *see* Agrínio
115 G17 **Agriovótano** Évvoia, C Greece 39°00′N 23°18′E
107 L18 **Agropoli** Campania, S Italy 40°22′N 14°59′E
127 T3 **Agryz** Udmurtskaya Respublika, NW Russian Federation 56°27′N 52°58′E
137 U11 **Ağstafa** *Rus.* Akstafa. NW Azerbaijan 41°06′N 45°28′E
137 X11 **Ağsu** *Rus.* Akhsu. C Azerbaijan
Agsumal, Sebjet *see* Aghzoumal, Sebkhet
40 J11 **Agua Brava, Laguna** *lagoon* W Mexico
54 F7 **Aguachica** Cesar, N Colombia 08°16′N 73°35′W
59 J20 **Água Clara** Mato Grosso do Sul, SW Brazil 20°21′S 52°58′W
44 D5 **Aguada de Pasajeros** Cienfuegos, C Cuba 22°23′N 80°51′W
54 J5 **Aguada Grande** Lara, N Venezuela 10°38′N 69°29′W
45 S5 **Aguadilla** W Puerto Rico 18°27′N 67°08′W
43 S16 **Aguadulce** Coclé, S Panama 08°16′N 80°31′W
104 L14 **Aguadulce** Andalucía, S Spain 37°15′N 04°59′W
41 O8 **Agualeguas** Nuevo León, NE Mexico 26°17′N 99°30′W
40 L9 **Aguanaval, Río** ≈ C Mexico
42 J5 **Aguán, Río** ≈ N Honduras
25 R16 **Agua Nueva** Texas, SW USA 26°57′N 98°34′W
60 J8 **Aguapeí, Rio** ≈ S Brazil
61 E14 **Aguapey, Río** ≈ NE Argentina
40 G3 **Agua Prieta** Sonora, NW Mexico 31°16′N 109°33′W
104 G5 **A Guarda** *var.* A Guardia, Laguardia, La Guardia. Galicia, NW Spain 41°54′N 08°53′W
A Guardia *see* A Guarda
56 E6 **Aguarico, Río** ≈ Ecuador/Peru
55 O6 **Aguasay** Monagas, NE Venezuela 09°25′N 63°44′W
40 M12 **Aguascalientes** Aguascalientes, C Mexico 21°54′N 102°17′W
40 L12 **Aguascalientes** ◈ *state* C Mexico
57 I18 **Aguas Calientes, Río** ≈ S Peru
105 R7 **Aguasvivas** ≈ NE Spain
60 J7 **Água Vermelha, Represa de** ⊠ S Brazil
56 E12 **Aguaytía** Ucayali, C Peru 09°02′S 75°30′W
104 I5 **A Gudiña** *var.* La Gudiña. Galicia, NW Spain 42°04′N 07°08′W
104 G7 **Águeda** Aveiro, N Portugal 40°34′N 08°28′W
104 J8 **Águeda** ≈ Portugal/Spain
77 Q8 **Aguelhok** Kidal, NE Mali 19°18′N 00°50′E
77 V12 **Aguié** Maradi, S Niger 13°28′N 07°43′E
188 K8 **Aguijan** *island* S Northern Mariana Islands
104 M14 **Aguilar** *var.* Aguilar de la Frontera. Andalucía, S Spain 37°31′N 04°40′W
104 M3 **Aguilar de Campóo** Castilla-León, N Spain 42°47′N 04°15′W
Aguilar de la Frontera *see* Aguilar
42 F7 **Aguilares** San Salvador, C El Salvador 13°56′N 89°09′W
105 Q14 **Águilas** Murcia, SE Spain 37°24′N 01°36′W
40 L15 **Aguililla** Michoacán, SW Mexico 18°43′N 102°45′W
Agulhas *see* L'Agulhas
172 J11 **Agulhas Bank** *undersea feature* SW Indian Ocean 35°30′S 21°00′E
172 K11 **Agulhas Basin** *undersea feature* SW Indian Ocean 47°00′S 27°00′E
83 F26 **Agulhas, Cape** *Afr.* Kaap Agulhas. *headland* SW South Africa 34°51′S 19°59′E
Agulhas, Kaap *see* Agulhas, Cape
60 O9 **Agulhas Negras, Pico das** ▲ SE Brazil 22°21′S 44°39′W
172 K11 **Agulhas Plateau** *undersea feature* SW Indian Ocean 40°00′S 26°00′E
165 S16 **Aguni-jima** *island* Nansei-shotō, SW Japan
Agurain *see* Salvatierra
54 G5 **Agustín Codazzi** *var.* Codazzi. Cesar, N Colombia 10°02′N 73°15′W
Agyrium *see* Agira
74 L12 **Ahaggar** *high plateau region* SE Algeria
146 E12 **Ahal Welaýaty** *Rus.* Akhalskiy Velayat. ◈ *province* C Turkmenistan
142 K2 **Ahar** Āzarbāyjān-e Sharqī, NW Iran 38°25′N 47°07′E
Aharnes *see* Acharnés
138 J3 **Aḥaṣ, Jabal** ▲ NW Syria
138 J3 **Aḥaṣ, Jebal** ▲▲ W Syria
185 G16 **Ahaura** ≈ South Island, New Zealand
100 E13 **Ahaus** Nordrhein-Westfalen, NW Germany 52°04′N 07°01′E
191 U9 **Ahe** *atoll* Îles Tuamotu, C French Polynesia
184 N10 **Ahimanawa Range** ▲▲ North Island, New Zealand
119 I19 **Ahinski Kanal** *Rus.* Oginskiy Kanal. *canal* SW Belarus
186 G10 **Ahioma** SE Papua New Guinea 10°20′S 150°35′E
184 I2 **Ahipara** Northland, North Island, New Zealand 35°11′S 173°07′E
184 I2 **Ahipara Bay** *bay* SE Tasman Sea
Áhkká *see* Akka
39 N13 **Ahklun Mountains** ▲▲ Alaska, USA
137 R14 **Ahlat** Bitlis, E Turkey 38°45′N 42°28′E
101 F14 **Ahlen** Nordrhein-Westfalen, W Germany 51°46′N 07°53′E
154 D10 **Ahmadābād** *var.* Ahmedabad. Gujarāt, W India 23°03′N 72°40′E
143 R10 **Aḥmadābād** Kermān, C Iran 35°51′N 59°36′E
Ahmadi *see* Al Aḥmadī
Ahmad Khel *see* Ḥasan Khēl
155 F14 **Ahmadnagar** *var.* Ahmednagar. Mahārāshtra, W India 19°08′N 74°48′E
149 T9 **Ahmadpur Siāl** Punjab, E Pakistan 30°40′N 71°52′E
77 N5 **Aḥmar, 'Erg el** *desert* N Mali
80 K13 **Ahmar Mountains** ▲▲ C Ethiopia
Ahmedabad *see* Ahmadābād
Ahmednagar *see* Ahmadnagar
114 N12 **Ahmetbey** Kırklareli, NW Turkey 41°26′N 27°35′E
14 H12 **Ahmic Lake** ◎ Ontario, S Canada
190 G12 **Ahoa** Île Uvea, E Wallis and Futuna 13°17′S 176°12′W
40 G8 **Ahomé** Sinaloa, C Mexico 25°55′N 109°10′W
21 X8 **Ahoskie** North Carolina, SE USA 36°17′N 76°59′W
101 D17 **Ahr** ≈ W Germany
143 N12 **Ahram** *var.* Ahrom. Būshehr, S Iran 28°52′N 51°18′E
100 J9 **Ahrensburg** Schleswig-Holstein, N Germany 53°41′N 10°14′E
Ahrom *see* Ahram
93 L17 **Ähtäri** Länsi-Suomi, W Finland 62°34′N 24°08′E
40 K12 **Ahuacatlán** Nayarit, C Mexico 21°02′N 104°30′W
42 E7 **Ahuachapán** Ahuachapán, W El Salvador 13°55′N 89°51′W
42 A9 **Ahuachapán** ◈ *department* W El Salvador
191 V16 **Ahu Akivi** *var.* Siete Moai. *ancient monument* Easter Island, Chile, E Pacific Ocean
191 W11 **Ahunui** *atoll* Îles Tuamotu, C French Polynesia
185 E20 **Ahuriri** ≈ South Island, New Zealand
95 L22 **Åhus** Skåne, S Sweden 55°55′N 14°18′E
Ahu Tahira *see* Ahu Vinapu
191 V16 **Ahu Tepeu** *ancient monument* Easter Island, Chile, E Pacific Ocean
191 V17 **Ahu Vinapu** *var.* Ahu Tahira. *ancient monument* Easter Island, Chile, E Pacific Ocean
142 L9 **Ahvāz** *var.* Ahwāz; *prev.* Nāsiri. Khūzestān, SW Iran 31°20′N 48°38′E
Ahvenanmaa *see* Åland
154 E12 **Ahwa** Gujarāt, W India 20°44′N 73°41′E
141 Q16 **Aḥwar** SW Yemen 13°34′N 46°41′E
Ahwāz *see* Ahvāz
94 H7 **Åi Åfjord** *var.* Åfjord, Årnes. Sør-Trøndelag, C Norway 63°57′N 10°12′E
Aibak *see* Āybak
101 K22 **Aichach** Bayern, SE Germany 48°26′N 11°06′E
164 L14 **Aichi** *off.* Aichi-ken, *var.* Aiti. ◈ *prefecture* Honshū, SW Japan
Aïdin *see* Aydın
Aidussina *see* Ajdovščina
Aifir, Clochán an *see* Giant's Causeway
Aigaíon Pelagos/Aigaío Pélagos *see* Aegean Sea
109 S3 **Aigen im Mülkreis** Oberösterreich, N Austria 48°39′N 13°57′E

115 G20 **Aígina** var. Aíyina, Egina. Aígina, C Greece 37°45′N 23°26′E
115 G20 **Aígina** island S Greece
115 E18 **Aígio** var. Egio; prev. Aíyion. Dytikí Ellás, S Greece 38°15′N 22°05′E
108 C10 **Aigle** Vaud, SW Switzerland 46°20′N 06°58′E
103 P14 **Aigoual, Mont** ▲ S France 44°09′N 03°34′E
173 O16 **Aigrettes, Pointe des** headland W Réunion 21°02′S 55°14′E
61 G19 **Aiguá** var. Aigua. Maldonado, S Uruguay 34°13′S 54°46′W
103 S13 **Aigues** ~ SE France
103 N10 **Aigurande** Indre, C France 46°26′N 01°49′E
Ai-hun see Heihe
163 N10 **Aikawa** Niigata, Sado, C Japan 38°04′N 138°15′E
21 Q13 **Aiken** South Carolina, SE USA 33°34′N 81°44′W
25 N4 **Aiken** Texas, SW USA 34°06′N 101°31′W
160 F13 **Ailao Shan** ▲▲ SW China
189 R4 **Ailinginae Atoll** var. Aelōninae. atoll Ralik Chain, SW Marshall Islands
189 T7 **Ailinglaplap Atoll** var. Aelōnlaplap. atoll Ralik Chain, S Marshall Islands
Aillionn, Loch see Allen, Lough
96 H13 **Ailsa Craig** island SW Scotland, United Kingdom
189 V5 **Ailuk Atoll** var. Aelok. atoll Ratak Chain, NE Marshall Islands
123 R11 **Aim** Khabarovskiy Kray, E Russian Federation 58°45′N 134°08′E
103 R11 **Ain** ◈ department E France
103 S10 **Ain** ~ E France
118 G7 **Ainaži** Est. Heinaste, Ger. Hainasch. Limbaži, N Latvia 57°51′N 24°24′E
74 L6 **Aïn Beida** NE Algeria 35°52′N 07°25′E
76 K4 **'Aïn Ben Tili** Tiris Zemmour, N Mauritania 25°58′N 09°30′W
74 J5 **Aïn Defla** var. Aïn Eddefla. N Algeria 36°16′N 01°58′E
Aïn Eddefla see Aïn Defla
74 L5 **Ain El Bey** ✈ (Constantine) NE Algeria 36°15′N 06°36′E
115 C19 **Aínos** ▲ Kefallonía, Iónia Nísoi, Greece, C Mediterranean Sea 38°08′N 20°39′E
105 T4 **Ainsa** Aragón, NE Spain 42°25′N 00°08′E
74 I7 **Aïn Sefra** NW Algeria 32°45′N 00°32′W
29 N13 **Ainsworth** Nebraska, C USA 42°33′N 99°51′W
Aintab see Gaziantep
74 H5 **Aïn Témouchent** N Algeria 35°18′N 01°09′W
186 C6 **Aiome** Madang, N Papua New Guinea 05°08′S 144°45′E
Aïoun el Atrous/Aïoun el Atroûss see 'Ayoûn el 'Atroûs
54 E11 **Aipe** Huila, C Colombia 03°15′N 75°17′W
56 D9 **Aipena, Río** ~ N Peru
57 L19 **Aiquile** Cochabamba, C Bolivia 18°10′S 65°10′W
Aïr see Aïr, Massif de l'
188 E10 **Airai** Babeldaob, C Palau
188 E10 **Airai** ✈ (Oreor) Babeldaob, N Palau 07°22′N 134°34′E
168 I11 **Airbangis** Sumatera, NW Indonesia 0°12′N 99°22′E
11 Q16 **Airdrie** Alberta, SW Canada 51°20′N 114°00′W
96 I12 **Airdrie** S Scotland, United Kingdom 55°52′N 03°59′W
Air du Azbine see Aïr, Massif de l'
97 M17 **Aire** ~ N England, United Kingdom
102 K15 **Aire-sur-l'Adour** Landes, SW France 43°43′N 00°16′W
103 O1 **Aire-sur-la-Lys** Pas-de-Calais, N France 50°39′N 02°24′E
9 Q6 **Air Force Island** island Baffin Island, Nunavut, NE Canada
169 Q13 **Airhitam, Teluk** bay Borneo, C Indonesia
171 Q11 **Airmadidi** Sulawesi, N Indonesia 01°25′N 124°59′E
77 V8 **Aïr, Massif de l'** var. Aïr, Air du Azbine, Asben. ▲▲ NC Niger
108 G10 **Airolo** Ticino, S Switzerland 46°32′N 08°38′E
102 K9 **Airvault** Deux-Sèvres, W France 46°51′N 00°07′W
101 K19 **Aisch** ~ S Germany
63 G20 **Aisén** off. Región Aisén del General Carlos Ibañez del Campo, var. Aysen. ◈ region S Chile
10 H7 **Aishihik Lake** ◎ Yukon Territory, W Canada
103 P3 **Aisne** ◈ department N France
103 R4 **Aisne** ~ NE France
109 T4 **Aist** ~ N Austria
114 K13 **Aisými** Anatolikí Makedonía kai Thráki, NE Greece 41°00′N 25°55′E
105 S11 **Aitana** ▲ E Spain 38°39′N 00°15′W
186 B5 **Aitape** var. Eitape. Sandaun, NW Papua New Guinea 03°10′S 142°17′E
Aiti see Aichi
29 V6 **Aitkin** Minnesota, N USA 46°31′N 93°42′W
115 D18 **Aitolikó** var. Etoliko; prev. Aitolikón. Dytikí Ellás, C Greece 38°26′N 21°21′E
Aitolikón see Aitolikó
190 L15 **Aitutaki** island S Cook Islands
116 H11 **Aiud** Ger. Strassburg, Hung. Nagyenyed; prev. Engeten. Alba, SW Romania 46°19′N 23°43′E
118 I9 **Aiviekste** ~ C Latvia
189 Q8 **Aiwo** SW Nauru 0°32′S 166°54′E
188 E8 **Aiwokako Passage** passage Babeldaob, N Palau
Aix see Aix-en-Provence
103 S15 **Aix-en-Provence** var. Aix; anc. Aquae Sextiae. Bouches-du-Rhône, SE France 43°31′N 05°27′E
Aix-la-Chapelle see Aachen
103 T11 **Aix-les-Bains** Savoie, E France 45°40′N 05°55′E
186 A6 **Aiyang, Mount** ▲ NW Papua New Guinea 05°03′S 141°15′E
Aíyina see Aígina
Aíyion see Aígio
153 W15 **Āīzawl** state capital Mizoram, NE India 23°41′N 92°45′E
118 H9 **Aizkraukle** Aizkraukle, S Latvia 56°39′N 25°07′E
118 C9 **Aizpute** Liepāja, W Latvia 56°43′N 21°32′E
165 O11 **Aizu-Wakamatsu** var. Aizuwakamatu. Fukushima, Honshū, C Japan 37°30′N 139°58′E
Aizuwakamatu see Aizu-Wakamatsu
103 X15 **Ajaccio** Corse, France, C Mediterranean Sea 41°54′N 08°43′E
103 X15 **Ajaccio, Golfe d'** gulf Corse, France, C Mediterranean Sea
41 Q15 **Ajalpán** Puebla, S Mexico 18°26′N 97°20′W
154 F13 **Ajanta Range** ▲▲ C India
Ajaria see Achara
Ajastan see Armenia
93 G14 **Ajaureforsen** Västerbotten, N Sweden 65°31′N 15°44′E
185 H17 **Ajax, Mount** ▲ South Island, New Zealand 42°34′S 172°06′E
162 F9 **Aj Bogd Uul** ▲ SW Mongolia 44°49′N 95°01′E
75 R8 **Ajdābiyā** var. Agedabia, Ajdābiyah. NE Libya 30°46′N 20°14′E
Ajdābiyah see Ajdābiyā
109 S12 **Ajdovščina** Ger. Haidenschaft, It. Aidussina. W Slovenia 45°52′N 13°55′E
165 Q7 **Ajigasawa** Aomori, Honshū, C Japan 40°45′N 140°11′E
Ajjinena see El Geneina
111 H23 **Ajka** Veszprém, W Hungary 47°18′N 17°32′E
138 G9 **'Ajlūn** Irbid, N Jordan 32°20′N 35°45′E
138 H9 **'Ajlūn, Jabal** ▲▲ W Jordan
Ájluokta see Drag
143 R15 **'Ajmān** var. Ajman, 'Ujmān. 'Ajmān, NE United Arab Emirates 25°36′N 55°42′E
152 G12 **Ajmer** var. Ajmere. Rājasthān, N India 26°29′N 74°40′E
36 J15 **Ajo** Arizona, SW USA 32°22′N 112°51′W
105 N2 **Ajo, Cabo de** headland N Spain 43°31′N 03°36′W
36 J16 **Ajo Range** ▲▲ Arizona, SW USA
146 C14 **Ajyguýy** Rus. Adzhikui. Balkan Welaýaty, W Turkmenistan 39°46′N 53°57′E
Akaba see Al 'Aqabah
165 T3 **Akabira** Hokkaidō, NE Japan 43°30′N 142°04′E
165 N10 **Akadomari** Niigata, Sado, C Japan 37°54′N 138°24′E
81 E20 **Akagera** var. Kagera. ~ Rwanda/Tanzania see also Kagera
191 W16 **Akahanga, Punta** headland Easter Island, Chile, E Pacific Ocean
80 J13 **Āk'ak'i** Oromīya, C Ethiopia 08°50′N 38°51′E
155 G15 **Akalkot** Mahārāshtra, W India 17°36′N 76°10′E
Akamagaseki see Shimonoseki
165 V3 **Akan** Hokkaidō, NE Japan 44°06′N 144°03′E
165 U4 **Akan** Hokkaidō, NE Japan 43°09′N 144°08′E
165 U4 **Akan-ko** ◎ Hokkaidō, NE Japan
Akanthoú see Tatlısu
185 I19 **Akaroa** Canterbury, South Island, New Zealand 43°48′S 172°58′E
80 E6 **Akasha** Northern, N Sudan 21°03′N 30°46′E
164 I13 **Akashi** var. Akasi. Hyōgo, Honshū, SW Japan 34°39′N 135°00′E
139 N7 **'Akāsh, Wādī** var. Wādī 'Ukash. dry watercourse W Iraq
Akasi see Akashi
92 K11 **Äkäsjokisuu** Lappi, N Finland 67°28′N 23°44′E
137 S11 **Akbaba Dağı** ▲ Armenia/Turkey 41°04′N 43°28′E
Akbük Limanı see Güllük Körfezi
127 V8 **Akbulak** Orenburgskaya Oblast', W Russian Federation 51°01′N 55°35′E
137 O11 **Akçaabat** Trabzon, NE Turkey 41°00′N 39°36′E
137 N15 **Akçadağ** Malatya, C Turkey 38°21′N 37°59′E
136 G11 **Akçakoca** Düzce, NW Turkey 41°05′N 31°08′E
Akchakaya, Vpadina see Akdzhakaya, Vpadina
76 H7 **Akchâr** desert W Mauritania
145 S12 **Akchatau** Kaz. Aqshataū. Karaganda, C Kazakhstan 47°59′N 74°02′E
136 L13 **Akdağlar** ▲▲ C Turkey
136 E17 **Ak Dağları** ▲▲ SW Turkey
136 K13 **Akdağmadeni** Yozgat, C Turkey 39°40′N 35°52′E
146 G8 **Akdepe** prev. Ak-Tepe, Leninsk, Turkm. Lenin. Daşoguz Welaýat, N Turkmenistan 42°10′N 59°17′E
Ak-Dere see Byala
121 P2 **Akdoğan** Gk. Lýsi. C Cyprus 35°06′N 33°42′E
122 J14 **Ak-Dovurak** Respublika Tyva, S Russian Federation 51°09′N 90°36′E
146 F9 **Akdzhakaya, Vpadina** var. Vpadina Akchakaya. depression N Turkmenistan
171 S11 **Akelamo** Pulau Halmahera, E Indonesia 01°27′N 128°39′E
Aken see Aachen
Akermanceaster see Bath
95 P15 **Åkersberga** Stockholm, C Sweden 59°28′N 18°19′E
95 H15 **Akershus** ◈ county S Norway
79 L16 **Aketi** Orientale, N Dem. Rep. Congo 02°44′N 23°46′E
146 C10 **Akgyr Erezi** Rus. Gryada Akkyr. hill range NW Turkmenistan
Akhalskiy Velayat see Ahal Welaýaty
137 S10 **Akhalts'ikhe** SW Georgia 41°39′N 43°04′E
Akhangaran see Ohangaron
Akharnaí see Acharnés
75 R7 **Akhḑar, Al Jabal al** hill range NE Libya
Akhelóös see Achelóos
39 Q15 **Akhiok** Kodiak Island, Alaska, USA 56°57′N 154°12′W
136 C13 **Akhisar** Manisa, W Turkey 38°54′N 27°50′E
75 X10 **Akhmīm** var. Akhmîm; anc. Panopolis. C Egypt 26°35′N 31°48′E
152 H6 **Akhnūr** Jammu and Kashmir, NW India 32°53′N 74°46′E
Akhsu see Ağsu
114 N10 **Akhtopol** Burgas, E Bulgaria 42°06′N 27°57′E
127 P11 **Akhtuba** ~ SW Russian Federation
127 P11 **Akhtubinsk** Astrakhanskaya Oblast', SW Russian Federation 48°17′N 46°14′E
Akhtyrka see Okhtyrka
164 H14 **Aki** Kōchi, Shikoku, SW Japan 33°30′N 133°53′E
39 N12 **Akiachak** Alaska, USA 60°54′N 161°25′W
39 N12 **Akiak** Alaska, USA 60°54′N 161°12′W
191 X11 **Akiaki** atoll Îles Tuamotu, E French Polynesia
12 H9 **Akimiski Island** island Nunavut, C Canada
136 K17 **Akıncı Burnu** headland S Turkey 36°21′N 35°47′E
Akıncılar see Selçuk
117 U10 **Akinovka** Zaporiz'ka Oblast', S Ukraine
Åkirkeby see Aakirkeby
165 P8 **Akita** Akita, Honshū, C Japan 39°44′N 140°06′E
165 Q8 **Akita** off. Akita-ken. ◈ prefecture Honshū, C Japan
76 H8 **Akjoujt** prev. Fort-Repoux. Inchiri, W Mauritania 19°42′N 14°28′W
92 H11 **Akka** Lapp. Áhkká. ▲ N Sweden 67°33′N 17°27′E
92 H11 **Akkajaure** ◎ N Sweden
Akkala see Oqqal'a
155 L25 **Akkaraipattu** Eastern Province, E Sri Lanka 07°13′N 81°51′E
145 P13 **Akkense** Kaz. Aqkengse. Karaganda, C Kazakhstan 46°39′N 68°06′E
Akkerman see Bilhorod-Dnistrovs'kyy
127 W8 **Akkermanovka** Orenburgskaya Oblast', W Russian Federation 51°11′N 58°03′E
165 V4 **Akkeshi** Hokkaidō, NE Japan 43°03′N 144°49′E
165 V4 **Akkeshi-ko** ◎ Hokkaidō, NE Japan
165 V5 **Akkeshi-wan** bay NW Pacific Ocean
138 F8 **Akko** Eng. Acre, Fr. Saint-Jean-d'Acre, Bibl. Accho, Ptolemaïs. Northern, N Israel 32°55′N 35°04′E
145 Q8 **Akkol'** Kaz. Aqköl; prev. Alekseyevka, Kaz. Alekseevka. Akmola, C Kazakhstan 51°58′N 70°58′E
145 T14 **Akkol'** Kaz. Aqköl. Almaty, SE Kazakhstan 45°01′N 75°38′E
145 Q16 **Akkol'** Kaz. Aqköl. Zhambyl, C Kazakhstan 43°25′N 70°47′E
144 M11 **Akkol', Ozero** prev. Ozero Zhaman-Akkol. ◎ C Kazakhstan
98 L6 **Akkrum** Friesland, N Netherlands 53°01′N 05°52′E
145 U8 **Akku** Kaz. Aqqū; prev. Lebyazh'ye. Pavlodar, NE Kazakhstan 51°29′N 77°48′E
144 F12 **Akkystau** Kaz. Aqqystaū. Atyrau, SW Kazakhstan 47°17′N 51°03′E
8 G6 **Aklavik** Northwest Territories, NW Canada 68°15′N 135°02′W
118 B9 **Akmenrags** prev. Akmeņrags. headland W Latvia 56°49′N 21°03′E
Akmeņrags see Akmenrags
158 E9 **Akmeqit** Xinjiang Uygur Zizhiqu, NW China 37°10′N 76°59′E
146 J14 **Akmeydan** Mary Welaýaty, C Turkmenistan 37°50′N 62°08′E
145 P9 **Akmola** off. Akmolinskaya Oblast', Kaz. Aqmola Oblysy; prev. Tselinogradskaya Oblast. ◈ province C Kazakhstan
Akmola see Astana
Akmolinsk see Astana
Akmolinskaya Oblast' see Akmola
Aknavásár see Târgu Ocna
118 I11 **Aknīste** Jēkabpils, S Latvia 56°09′N 25°43′E
81 G14 **Akobo** Jonglei, SE Sudan 07°50′N 33°05′E
81 G14 **Akobo** var. Ākobowenz. ~ Ethiopia/Sudan
Ākobowenz see Akobo
154 H12 **Akola** Mahārāshtra, C India 20°44′N 77°00′E
80 J9 **Ak'ordat** var. Agordat, Akurdet. C Eritrea 15°33′N 38°01′E
77 Q16 **Akosombo Dam** dam SE Ghana
154 H12 **Akot** Mahārāshtra, C India 20°45′N 77°00′E
77 N16 **Akoupé** SE Ivory Coast 06°19′N 03°54′W
12 M3 **Akpatok Island** island Nunavut, E Canada
158 G7 **Akqi** Xinjiang Uygur Zizhiqu, NW China 40°51′N 78°20′E
138 I2 **Akrād, Jabal al** ▲▲ N Syria
Akragas see Agrigento
92 H3 **Akranes** Vesturland, W Iceland 64°19′N 22°01′W
139 S2 **Ākrē** Ar. 'Aqrah. Dahūk, N Iraq 36°46′N 43°52′E
95 C16 **Åkrehamn** Rogaland, S Norway 59°15′N 15°13′E
77 V9 **Akrérèb** Agadez, C Niger 17°45′N 09°01′E
115 D22 **Akrítas, Akrotírio** headland S Greece 36°43′N 21°52′E
37 V3 **Akron** Colorado, C USA 40°09′N 103°12′W
29 R12 **Akron** Iowa, C USA 42°49′N 96°33′W
31 U12 **Akron** Ohio, N USA 41°05′N 81°31′W
Akrotiri see Akrotírion
Akrotiri Bay see Akrotírion, Kólpos
121 P3 **Akrotírion** var. Akrotiri. UK air base S Cyprus 34°36′N 32°57′E
121 P3 **Akrotírion, Kólpos** var. Akrotiri Bay. bay S Cyprus
121 O3 **Akrotiri Sovereign Base Area** UK military installation S Cyprus
158 F11 **Aksai Chin** Chin. Aksayqin. disputed region China/India
Aksaj see Aksay
136 I15 **Aksaray** Aksaray, C Turkey 38°23′N 33°50′E
136 I15 **Aksaray** ◈ province C Turkey
144 G8 **Aksay** var. Aksaj, Kaz. Aqsay. Zapadnyy Kazakhstan, NW Kazakhstan 51°11′N 53°00′E
127 O11 **Aksay** Volgogradskaya Oblast', SW Russian Federation 47°59′N 43°54′E
147 W10 **Ak-say** var. Toxkan He. ~ China/Kyrgyzstan
Aksay/Aksay Kazakzu Zizhixian see Boluozhuanjing/Hongliuwan
Aksayqin see Aksai Chin
158 G11 **Aksayqin Hu** ◎ NW China
136 G14 **Akşehir** Konya, W Turkey 38°22′N 31°24′E
136 G14 **Akşehir Gölü** ◎ C Turkey
136 G16 **Akseki** Antalya, SW Turkey 37°03′N 31°46′E
123 P13 **Aksenovo-Zilovskoye** Chitinskaya Oblast', S Russian Federation 53°01′N 117°26′E
145 V11 **Akshatau, Khrebet** ▲▲ E Kazakhstan
147 Y8 **Ak-Shyyrak** Issyk-Kul'skaya Oblast', E Kyrgyzstan 41°46′N 78°34′E
Akstafa see Ağstafa
158 H7 **Aksu** Xinjiang Uygur Zizhiqu, NW China 41°17′N 80°15′E
145 R8 **Aksu** Kaz. Aqsū. Akmola, N Kazakhstan 52°31′N 72°00′E
145 W13 **Aksu** Kaz. Aqsū. Almaty, SE Kazakhstan 45°31′N 79°28′E
145 T8 **Aksu** var. Jermak, Kaz. Ermak; prev. Yermak. Pavlodar, NE Kazakhstan 52°03′N 76°55′E
145 V13 **Aksu** Kaz. Aqsū. ~ SE Kazakhstan
145 X11 **Aksuat** Kaz. Aqsūat. Vostochnyy Kazakhstan, E Kazakhstan 47°48′N 82°51′E
145 Y11 **Aksuat** Kaz. Aqsūat. Vostochnyy Kazakhstan, SE Kazakhstan 48°16′N 83°39′E
127 S4 **Aksubayevo** Respublika Tatarstan, W Russian Federation 54°52′N 50°50′E
158 H7 **Aksu He** Rus. Sary-Dzhaz. ~ China/Kyrgyzstan see also Sary-Dzhaz
80 J10 **Āksum** Tigray, N Ethiopia 14°06′N 38°42′E
145 O12 **Aktas** Kaz. Aqtas. Karaganda, C Kazakhstan 48°03′N 66°21′E
Aktash see Oqtosh
147 V9 **Ak-Tash, Gora** ▲ C Kyrgyzstan 40°53′N 74°39′E
145 R10 **Aktau** Kaz. Aqtaū. Karaganda, C Kazakhstan 50°13′N 73°06′E
144 E11 **Aktau** Kaz. Aqtaū; prev. Shevchenko. Mangistau, W Kazakhstan 43°37′N 51°14′E
Aktau, Khrebet see Oqtogh, Qatorkŭhi. SW Tajikistan
Aktau, Khrebet see Oqtov Tizmasi, C Uzbekistan
Akte see Ágion Óros
Ak-Tepe see Akdepe
147 X7 **Ak-Terek** Issyk-Kul'skaya Oblast', E Kyrgyzstan 42°14′N 77°46′E
Aktí see Ágion Óros
Aktjubinsk/Aktyubinsk see Aktobe
158 E8 **Akto** Xinjiang Uygur Zizhiqu, NW China 39°07′N 75°43′E
144 I10 **Aktobe** Kaz. Aqtöbe; prev. Aktjubinsk, Aktyubinsk. Aktyubinsk, NW Kazakhstan 50°18′N 57°10′E
145 V12 **Aktogay** Kaz. Aqtoghay. Vostochnyy Kazakhstan, E Kazakhstan 46°56′N 79°40′E
119 M18 **Aktsyabrski** Rus. Oktyabr'skiy; prev. Karpilovka. Homyel'skaya Voblasts', SE Belarus 52°38′N 28°53′E
144 H11 **Aktyubinsk** off. Aktyubinskaya Oblast', Kaz. Aqtöbe Oblysy. ◈ province W Kazakhstan
Aktyubinsk see Aktobe
147 W7 **Ak-Tyuz** var. Aktyuz. Chuyskaya Oblast', N Kyrgyzstan 42°50′N 76°05′E
79 J17 **Akula** Equateur, NW Dem. Rep. Congo 02°21′N 20°13′E
164 C15 **Akune** Kagoshima, Kyūshū, SW Japan 32°00′N 130°12′E
38 L16 **Akun Island** island Aleutian Islands, Alaska, USA
Akurdet see Ak'ordat
77 T16 **Akure** Ondo, SW Nigeria 07°18′N 05°13′E
92 J2 **Akureyri** Nordhurland Eystra, N Iceland 65°40′N 18°07′W
38 L17 **Akutan** Akutan Island, Alaska, USA 54°08′N 165°47′W
38 K17 **Akutan Island** island Aleutian Islands, Alaska, USA
77 V17 **Akwa Ibom** ◈ state SE Nigeria
Akyab see Sittwe
127 W7 **Ak"yar** Respublika Bashkortostan, W Russian Federation 51°51′N 58°13′E
144 J10 **Akzhar** prev. Novorossiyskiy, Novorossiyskoye. Aktyubinsk, NW Kazakhstan 50°14′N 57°57′E
145 Y11 **Akzhar** Kaz. Aqzhar. Vostochnyy Kazakhstan, E Kazakhstan 47°36′N 83°38′E
94 F13 **Ål** Buskerud, S Norway 60°37′N 08°33′E
119 N18 **Ala** Rus. Ola. ~ SE Belarus
23 P5 **Alabama** off. State of Alabama, also known as Camellia State, Heart of Dixie, The Cotton State, Yellowhammer State. ◈ state S USA
23 P6 **Alabama River** ~ Alabama, S USA
23 P4 **Alabaster** Alabama, S USA 33°14′N 86°49′W
139 U10 **Al 'Abd Allāh** var. Al Abdullah. Al Qādisīyah, S Iraq 32°06′N 45°08′E
139 W14 **Al Abṭīyah** well S Iraq
147 S9 **Ala-Buka** Dzhalal-Abadskaya Oblast', W Kyrgyzstan 41°22′N 71°27′E
136 J12 **Alaca** Çorum, N Turkey 40°10′N 34°52′E
136 K10 **Alaçam** Samsun, N Turkey 41°36′N 35°35′E
Alacant see Alicante
23 V9 **Alachua** Florida, SE USA 29°48′N 82°29′W
137 S13 **Aladağlar** ▲▲ W Turkey
136 K15 **Ala Dağları** ▲▲ C Turkey
162 I5 **Alag-Erdene** var. Manhan. Hövsgöl, N Mongolia 50°05′N 100°01′E
127 O16 **Alagir** Respublika Severnaya Osetiya, SW Russian Federation 43°02′N 44°10′E
106 B6 **Alagna Valsesia** Valle d'Aosta, NW Italy 45°51′N 07°50′E
103 P12 **Alagnon** ~ C France
59 P16 **Alagoas** off. Estado de Alagoas. ◈ state E Brazil
59 P17 **Alagoinhas** Bahia, E Brazil 12°09′S 38°21′W
105 R5 **Alagón** Aragón, NE Spain 41°46′N 01°07′W
104 J9 **Alagón** ~ W Spain
93 K16 **Alahärmä** Länsi-Suomi, W Finland 63°15′N 22°50′E
al Ahdar see Al Akhḑar
Álaheaieatnu see Altaelva
142 K12 **Al Aḩmadī** var. Ahmadi. E Kuwait 29°02′N 48°01′E
Al Ain see Al 'Ayn
105 Z8 **Alaior** prev. Alayor. Menorca, Spain, W Mediterranean Sea 39°56′N 04°08′E
147 T11 **Alai Range** Rus. Alayskiy Khrebet. ▲▲ Kyrgyzstan/Tajikistan
Alais see Alès
141 X11 **Al 'Ajā'iz** E Oman 19°33′N 57°12′E
141 X11 **Al 'Ajā'iz** oasis SE Oman
93 L16 **Alajärvi** Länsi-Suomi, W Finland 63°00′N 23°50′E
118 K4 **Alajõe** Ida-Virumaa, NE Estonia 59°00′N 27°26′E
42 M13 **Alajuela** Alajuela, C Costa Rica 10°00′N 84°12′W
42 L12 **Alajuela** off. Provincia de Alajuela. ◈ province N Costa Rica
43 T14 **Alajuela, Lago** ◎ C Panama
38 M11 **Alakanuk** Alaska, USA 62°41′N 164°37′W
140 K5 **Al Akhḑar** var. al Ahdar. Tabūk, NW Saudi Arabia 28°04′N 37°13′E
Alaköl see Alakol', Ozero
145 X13 **Alakol', Ozero** Kaz. Alaköl. ◎ SE Kazakhstan
124 I5 **Alakurtti** Murmanskaya Oblast', NW Russian Federation 66°57′N 30°27′E
38 F10 **Alalākeiki Channel** var. Alalakeiki Channel. channel Hawaii, USA, C Pacific Ocean
75 U8 **Al 'Alamayn** var. El 'Alamein. N Egypt 30°50′N 28°57′E
139 R1 **Al 'Amādīyah** Dahūk, N Iraq 37°09′N 43°27′E
188 K5 **Alamagan** island C Northern Mariana Islands
139 X10 **Al 'Amārah** var. Amara. Maysān, E Iraq 31°51′N 47°10′E
80 J11 **Ālamat'ā** Tigray, N Ethiopia 12°22′N 39°32′E
37 R11 **Alameda** New Mexico, SW USA 35°09′N 106°37′W
121 T13 **'Alam el Rûm, Râs** headland N Egypt 31°21′N 27°23′E
Alamícamba see Alamikamba
42 M8 **Alamikamba** var. Alamícamba. Región Autónoma Atlántico Norte, NE Nicaragua 13°26′N 84°09′W
24 K11 **Alamito Creek** ~ Texas, SW USA
40 M8 **Alamitos, Sierra de los** ▲ NE Mexico 26°15′N 102°14′W
41 Q12 **Álamo** Veracruz-Llave, C Mexico 20°55′N 97°41′W
35 X9 **Alamo** Nevada, W USA 37°21′N 115°08′W
20 F9 **Alamo** Tennessee, S USA 35°47′N 89°09′W
37 S14 **Alamogordo** New Mexico, SW USA 32°52′N 105°57′W
36 J12 **Alamo Lake** ▣ Arizona, SW USA
40 H7 **Alamos** Sonora, NW Mexico 26°59′N 108°53′W
37 S7 **Alamosa** Colorado, C USA 37°25′N 105°51′W
139 P10 **Al Anbār** ◈ governorate SW Iraq
93 J20 **Åland** var. Aland Islands, Fin. Ahvenanmaa. ◈ province SW Finland
88 K9 **Åland** var. Aland Islands, Fin. Ahvenanmaa. island group SW Finland
Aland Islands see Åland
Aland Sea see Ålands Hav
95 Q14 **Ålands Hav** var. Aland Sea. strait Baltic Sea/Gulf of Bothnia
43 P16 **Alanje** Chiriquí, SW Panama 08°26′N 82°33′W
25 O2 **Alanreed** Texas, SW USA 35°12′N 100°45′W
136 G17 **Alanya** Antalya, S Turkey 36°32′N 32°02′E
23 U7 **Alapaha River** ~ Florida/Georgia, SE USA
122 G10 **Alapayevsk** Sverdlovskaya Oblast', C Russian Federation 57°48′N 61°50′E
155 G23 **Alappuzha** var. Alleppey. Kerala, SW India 09°30′N 76°22′E see also Alleppey
138 F14 **Al 'Aqabah** var. Akaba, Aqaba, 'Aqaba; anc. Aelana, Elath. Al 'Aqabah, SW Jordan 29°32′N 35°00′E
138 G14 **Al 'Aqabah** off. Muḩāfazat Al 'Aqabah. ◈ governorate SW Jordan
Al 'Arabīyah as Su'ūdīyah see Saudi Arabia
al Araïch see Larache
105 Q10 **Alarcón** Castilla-La Mancha, C Spain 39°32′N 02°05′W
105 Q9 **Alarcón, Embalse de** ▣ C Spain
138 J2 **Al 'Arīmah** Fr. Arime. Ḩalab, N Syria 36°27′N 37°41′E
75 X7 **Al 'Arīsh** var. El 'Arîsh. NE Egypt 33°00′N 31°00′E
141 P6 **Al Arṭāwīyah** Ar Riyāḑ, N Saudi Arabia 26°34′N 45°20′E
Alasca, Golfo de see Alaska, Gulf of
136 D14 **Alaşehir** Manisa, W Turkey 38°19′N 28°30′E
139 N5 **Al 'Ashārah** var. Ashara. Dayr az Zawr, E Syria 34°51′N 40°36′E
Al Ashkhara see Al Ashkharah
141 Z9 **Al Ashkharah** var. Al Ashkhara. NE Oman 21°47′N 59°30′E
Al 'Aşimah see 'Ammān
39 P8 **Alaska** off. State of Alaska, also known as Land of the Midnight Sun, The Last Frontier, Seward's Folly; prev. Russian America. ◈ state NW USA
39 T13 **Alaska, Gulf of** var. Golfo de Alasca. gulf Canada/USA
39 O15 **Alaska Peninsula** peninsula Alaska, USA
39 Q11 **Alaska Range** ▲▲ Alaska, USA
Al-Asnam see Chlef
106 B10 **Alassio** Liguria, NW Italy 44°01′N 08°12′E
137 Y12 **Älät** Rus. Alyat; prev. Alyaty-Pristan'. SE Azerbaijan 39°57′N 49°24′E
Alat see Olot
139 S13 **Al 'Athāmīn** An Najaf, S Iraq 30°27′N 43°41′E
39 P7 **Alatna River** ~ Alaska, USA
107 J15 **Alatri** Lazio, C Italy 41°43′N 13°21′E
Alattio see Alta
127 P5 **Alatyr'** Chuvashskaya Respublika, W Russian Federation 54°50′N 46°28′E
56 C7 **Alausí** Chimborazo, C Ecuador 02°11′S 78°52′W
105 O3 **Álava** Basq. Araba. ◈ province País Vasco, N Spain
137 T11 **Alaverdi** N Armenia 41°06′N 44°37′E
Alavo see Alavus
93 N14 **Ala-Vuokki** Oulu, E Finland 64°46′N 29°29′E
93 K17 **Alavus** Swe. Alavo. Länsi-Suomi, W Finland 62°33′N 23°38′E
Al 'Awābī see Awābī
139 P6 **Al 'Awānī** Al Anbār, W Iraq 34°28′N 41°43′E
75 U12 **Al Awaynāt** SE Libya 21°46′N 24°51′E
Al Awaynāt see Al 'Uwaynāt
182 K9 **Alawoona** South Australia 34°45′S 140°28′E
Alaykel'/Alay-Kuu see Këk-Art
143 R17 **Al 'Ayn** var. Al Ain. Abū Ẕaby, E United Arab Emirates 24°13′N 55°44′E
143 R17 **Al 'Ayn** var. Al Ain. ✈ Abū Ẕaby, E United Arab Emirates 24°16′N 55°31′E
138 G12 **Al 'Aynā** Al Karak, W Jordan 30°59′N 35°43′E
Alayor see Alaior
Alayskiy Khrebet see Alai Range
123 S6 **Alazeya** ~ NE Russian Federation
139 U8 **Al 'Azīzīyah** var. Aziziya. Wāsiţ, E Iraq 32°54′N 45°05′E
120 M12 **Al 'Azīzīyah** NW Libya 32°32′N 13°01′E
138 I10 **Al Azraq al Janūbī** Az Zarqā', N Jordan 31°49′N 36°48′E
106 B9 **Alba** anc. Alba Pompeia. Piemonte, NW Italy 44°42′N 08°02′E
25 V6 **Alba** Texas, SW USA 32°47′N 95°37′W
116 G11 **Alba** ◈ county W Romania
139 P3 **Al Ba'āj** Nīnawá, N Iraq 36°02′N 41°43′E
138 J2 **Al Bāb** Ḩalab, N Syria 36°24′N 37°32′E
116 G10 **Albac** Hung. Fehérvölgy; prev. Álbák. Alba, SW Romania 46°27′N 22°58′E
105 Q11 **Albacete** Castilla-La Mancha, C Spain 39°N 01°52′W
105 P11 **Albacete** ◈ province Castilla-La Mancha, C Spain
140 I4 **Al Bad'** Tabūk, NW Saudi Arabia 28°28′N 35°00′E
104 L7 **Alba de Tormes** Castilla-León, N Spain 40°50′N 05°30′W
139 P3 **Al Bādī** Nīnawá, N Iraq 35°57′N 41°37′E
141 V8 **Al Badī'ah** ✈ (Abū Ẕaby) Abū Ẕaby, C United Arab Emirates 24°27′N 54°39′E
143 P17 **Al Badī'ah** var. Al Bedei'ah. spring/well C United Arab Emirates 23°44′N 53°50′E
95 H19 **Ålbæk** Nordjylland, N Denmark 57°33′N 10°24′E
139 Q7 **Al Baghdādī** var. Khān al Baghdādī. Al Anbār, SW Iraq 33°60′N 42°50′E
Al Bāha see Al Bāḩah
140 M11 **Al Bāḩah** var. Al Bāha. Al BāḨah, SW Saudi Arabia 20°01′N 41°29′E
140 M11 **Al Bāḩah** var. Minţaqat al Bāḩah. ◈ province W Saudi Arabia
Al Baḩrayn see Bahrain
105 S11 **Albaida** País Valenciano, E Spain 38°51′N 00°31′W
116 H11 **Alba Iulia** Ger. Weissenburg, Hung. Gyulafehérvár; prev. Bălgrad, Karlsburg, Károly-Fehérvár. Alba, W Romania 46°06′N 23°33′E
Álbák see Albac
138 G10 **Al Balqā'** off. Muḩāfaẓat al Balqā', var. Balqā'. ◈ governorate NW Jordan
14 F11 **Alban** Ontario, S Canada 46°07′N 80°37′W
103 O15 **Alban** Tarn, S France 43°52′N 02°30′E
12 K11 **Albanel, Lac** ◎ Québec, SE Canada
113 L20 **Albania** off. Republic of Albania, Alb. Republika e Shqipqërisë, Shqipëria; prev. People's Socialist Republic of Albania. ◆ republic SE Europe
Albania see Aubagne
107 H15 **Albano Laziaie** Lazio, C Italy 41°44′N 12°40′E
180 J14 **Albany** Western Australia 35°03′S 117°54′E
23 S7 **Albany** Georgia, SE USA 31°35′N 84°09′W
31 P13 **Albany** Indiana, N USA 40°18′N 85°14′W
20 L8 **Albany** Kentucky, S USA 36°42′N 85°08′W
29 U7 **Albany** Minnesota, N USA 45°39′N 94°33′W
27 R2 **Albany** Missouri, C USA 40°15′N 94°15′W
18 L10 **Albany** state capital New York, NE USA 42°39′N 73°45′W
32 G12 **Albany** Oregon, NW USA 44°38′N 123°06′W
25 Q6 **Albany** Texas, SW USA 32°44′N 99°18′W
12 F10 **Albany** ~ Ontario, S Canada
Alba Pompeia see Alba
Alba Regia see Székesfehérvár
138 J6 **Al Bāridah** var. Bāridah. Ḩimş, C Syria 34°15′N 37°39′E
139 Q11 **Al Barīt** Al Anbār, S Iraq 31°16′N 42°28′E
105 R8 **Albarracín** Aragón, NE Spain 40°24′N 01°25′W
139 Y13 **Al Başrah** ◈ governorate SE Iraq
139 Y12 **Al Başrah** Eng. Basra, hist. Busra, Bussora. Al Başrah, SE Iraq 30°30′N 47°50′E
139 V11 **Al Baţḩā'** Dhī Qār, SE Iraq 31°06′N 45°54′E
141 X8 **Al Bāţinah** var. Batinah. coastal region N Oman
0 H16 **Albatross Plateau** undersea feature E Pacific Ocean 10°00′N 103°00′W
Al Batrūn see Batroûn
121 Q12 **Al Bayḑā'** var. Beida. NE Libya 32°46′N 21°43′E
141 P16 **Al Bayḑā'** var. Al Beida. SW Yemen 13°58′N 45°38′E
Al Bedei'ah see Al Badī'ah
Al Beida see Al Bayḑā'
21 S10 **Albemarle** var. Albermarle. North Carolina, SE USA 35°21′N 80°12′W
Albemarle Island see Isabela, Isla
21 N8 **Albemarle Sound** inlet W Atlantic Ocean
106 B10 **Albenga** Liguria, NW Italy 44°04′N 08°13′E
104 L8 **Alberche** ~ C Spain
103 O17 **Albères, Chaîne des** var. les Albères, Montes Albères. ▲▲ France/Spain
Albères, Montes see Albères, Chaîne des
182 F2 **Alberga Creek** seasonal river South Australia
104 G7 **Albergaria-a-Velha** Aveiro, N Portugal 40°42′N 08°28′W
105 S10 **Alberic** País Valenciano, E Spain 39°07′N 00°31′W
Albermarle see Albemarle
107 P18 **Alberobello** Puglia, SE Italy 40°47′N 17°14′E
108 J7 **Alberschwende** Vorarlberg, W Austria 47°28′N 09°50′E
103 O3 **Albert** Somme, N France 50°N 02°38′E
11 O12 **Alberta** ◈ province SW Canada
Albert Edward Nyanza see Edward, Lake
61 C20 **Alberti** Buenos Aires, E Argentina 35°03′S 60°15′W
111 K23 **Albertirsa** Pest, C Hungary 47°15′N 19°36′E
99 I16 **Albertkanaal** canal N Belgium
79 P17 **Albert, Lake** var. Albert Nyanza, Lac Mobutu Sese Seko. ◎ Uganda/Dem. Rep. Congo
29 V11 **Albert Lea** Minnesota, N USA 43°39′N 93°22′W
81 F16 **Albert Nile** ~ NW Uganda
Albert Nyanza see Albert, Lake
103 T11 **Albertville** Savoie, E France 45°41′N 06°24′E
23 Q2 **Albertville** Alabama, S USA 34°16′N 86°12′W
Albertville see Kalemie
103 N15 **Albi** anc. Albiga. Tarn, S France 43°55′N 02°09′E
29 W15 **Albia** Iowa, C USA 41°01′N 92°48′W
Albiga see Albi
55 X9 **Albina** Marowijne, NE Surinam 05°29′N 54°08′W
83 A15 **Albina, Ponta** headland SW Angola 15°52′S 11°45′E
30 M16 **Albion** Illinois, N USA 38°22′N 88°03′W
31 P11 **Albion** Indiana, N USA 41°23′N 85°26′W
29 P14 **Albion** Nebraska, C USA 41°41′N 98°00′W
18 E9 **Albion** New York, NE USA 43°13′N 78°09′W
18 B12 **Albion** Pennsylvania, NE USA 41°52′N 80°18′W
Al Biqā' see El Beqaa
140 J4 **Al Bi'r** var. Bi'r Ibn Hirmās. Tabūk, NW Saudi Arabia 28°52′N 36°16′E
140 M12 **Al Birk** Makkah, SW Saudi Arabia 18°13′N 41°36′E
141 Q9 **Al Biyāḑ** desert C Saudi Arabia
98 H13 **Alblasserdam** Zuid-Holland, SW Netherlands 51°52′N 04°40′E
Albocácer see Albocàsser
105 T8 **Albocàsser** Cast. Albocácer. País Valenciano, E Spain 40°21′N 00°01′E
Albona see Labin
105 O17 **Alborán, Isla de** island S Spain
Alborán, Mar de see Alboran Sea
105 N17 **Alboran Sea** Sp. Mar de Alborán. sea SW Mediterranean Sea
Ålborg see Aalborg
95 H21 **Ålborg Bugt** var. Aalborg Bugt. bay N Denmark
Ålborg-Nørresundby see Aalborg
143 O5 **Alborz, Reshteh-ye Kūhhā-ye** Eng. Elburz Mountains. ▲▲ N Iran
105 Q14 **Albox** Andalucía, S Spain 37°22′N 02°08′W
101 H23 **Albstadt** Baden-Württemberg, SW Germany 48°13′N 09°01′E
104 G14 **Albufeira** Beja, S Portugal 37°05′N 08°15′W
139 P5 **Ālbū Gharz, Sabkhat** ◎ W Iraq
105 O15 **Albuñol** Andalucía, S Spain 36°48′N 03°11′W
37 Q11 **Albuquerque** New Mexico, SW USA 35°05′N 106°38′W
43 Q7 **Albuquerque, Cayos de** NW Colombia, Caribbean Sea
141 W8 **Al Buraymī** var. Buraimi. N Oman 24°16′N 55°48′E

◆ Country
● Country Capital
◇ Dependent Territory
○ Dependent Territory Capital
◈ Administrative Regions
✈ International Airport
▲ Mountain
▲▲ Mountain Range
Volcano
~ River
◎ Lake
▣ Reservoir

143 R17 **Al Buraymī** *var.* Buraimi. *spring/well* Oman/United Arab Emirates 24°27′N 55°33′E
Al Buraymī *see* Marsā al Burayqah
Alburgum *see* Aalborg
104 I10 **Alburquerque** Extremadura, W Spain 39°12′N 07°00′W
181 V14 **Albury** New South Wales, SE Australia 36°03′S 146°53′E
141 T14 **Al Buzūn** SE Yemen 15°40′N 50°53′E
93 G17 **Alby** Västernorrland, C Sweden 62°30′N 15°25′E
Albyn, Glen *see* Mor, Glen
104 G12 **Alcácer do Sal** Setúbal, W Portugal 38°22′N 08°29′W
Alcalá de Chisvert/Alcalá de Chivert *see* Alcalà de Xivert
104 K14 **Alcalá de Guadaira** Andalucía, S Spain 37°20′N 05°50′W
105 O8 **Alcalá de Henares** *Ar.* Alkal'a; *anc.* Complutum. Madrid, C Spain 40°28′N 03°22′W
104 K16 **Alcalá de los Gazules** Andalucía, S Spain 36°29′N 05°43′W
105 T8 **Alcalà de Xivert** *var.* Alcalá de Chisvert, *Cast.* Alcalá de Chivert. País Valenciano, E Spain 40°19′N 00°13′E
105 N14 **Alcalá La Real** Andalucía, S Spain 37°28′N 03°55′W
107 I23 **Alcamo** Sicilia, Italy, C Mediterranean Sea 37°58′N 12°58′E
105 T4 **Alcanadre** ⚡ NE Spain
105 T8 **Alcanar** Cataluña, NE Spain 40°33′N 00°28′E
104 J5 **Alcañices** Castilla-León, N Spain 41°41′N 06°21′W
105 T7 **Alcañiz** Aragón, NE Spain 41°03′N 00°09′W
104 J9 **Alcántara** Extremadura, W Spain 39°42′N 06°54′W
104 J9 **Alcántara, Embalse de** ⊠ W Spain
105 R13 **Alcantarilla** Murcia, SE Spain 37°59′N 01°12′W
105 P11 **Alcaraz** Castilla-La Mancha, C Spain 38°40′N 02°29′W
105 P12 **Alcaraz, Sierra de** ▲ C Spain
104 I12 **Alcarrache** ⚡ SW Spain
105 T6 **Alcarràs** Cataluña, NE Spain 41°34′N 00°31′E
105 N14 **Alcaudete** Andalucía, S Spain 37°35′N 04°05′W
Alcázar *see* Ksar-el-Kebir
105 O10 **Alcázar de San Juan** *anc.* Alce. Castilla-La Mancha, C Spain 39°24′N 03°12′W
Alcazarquivir *see* Ksar-el-Kebir
Alce *see* Alcázar de San Juan
57 B17 **Alcebo, Volcán** ⛰ Galapagos Islands, Ecuador, E Pacific Ocean 0°25′S 91°06′W
139 X12 **Al Chabā'ish** *var.* Al Kaba'ish. Dhī Qār, SE Iraq 30°58′N 47°02′E
117 Y7 **Alchevs'k** *prev.* Kommunarsk, Voroshilovsk. Luhans'ka Oblast', E Ukraine 48°29′N 38°52′E
Alcira *see* Alzira
21 N9 **Alcoa** Tennessee, S USA 35°47′N 83°58′W
104 F9 **Alcobaça** Leiria, C Portugal 39°32′N 08°59′W
105 N8 **Alcobendas** Madrid, C Spain 40°32′N 03°38′W
Alcoi *see* Alcoy
105 P7 **Alcolea del Pinar** Castilla-La Mancha, C Spain 41°02′N 02°28′W
104 I11 **Alconchel** Extremadura, W Spain 38°31′N 07°04′W
Alcora *see* L'Alcora
105 N8 **Alcorcón** Madrid, C Spain 40°20′N 03°52′W
105 S7 **Alcorisa** Aragón, NE Spain 40°53′N 00°23′W
61 B19 **Alcorta** Santa Fe, C Argentina 33°32′S 61°07′W
104 H14 **Alcoutim** Faro, S Portugal 37°28′N 07°29′W
33 W15 **Alcova** Wyoming, C USA 42°33′N 106°40′W
105 S11 **Alcoy** *Cat.* Alcoi. País Valenciano, E Spain 38°42′N 00°29′W
105 Y9 **Alcúdia** Mallorca, Spain, W Mediterranean Sea 39°51′N 03°06′E
105 Y9 **Alcúdia, Badia d'** *bay* Mallorca, Spain, W Mediterranean Sea
172 M7 **Aldabra Group** *island group* SW Seychelles
139 U10 **Al Daghghārah** Bābil, C Iraq 32°10′N 44°57′E
40 J5 **Aldama** Chihuahua, N Mexico 28°50′N 105°52′W
41 P11 **Aldama** Tamaulipas, C Mexico 22°54′N 98°05′W
123 Q11 **Aldan** Respublika Sakha (Yakutiya), NE Russian Federation 58°31′N 125°15′E
123 Q10 **Aldan** ⚡ NE Russian Federation
Aldar *see* Aldarhaan
al Dar al Baida *see* Rabat
162 G7 **Aldarhaan** *var.* Aldar. Dzavhan, W Mongolia 47°43′N 96°36′E
97 Q20 **Aldeburgh** E England, United Kingdom 52°12′N 01°36′E
105 P5 **Aldehuela de Calatañazor** Castilla-León, N Spain 41°42′N 02°46′W
Aldeia Nova *see* Aldeia Nova de São Bento
104 H13 **Aldeia Nova de São Bento** *var.* Aldeia Nova. Beja, S Portugal 37°55′N 07°24′W
29 V11 **Alden** Minnesota, N USA 43°40′N 93°34′W
184 N6 **Aldermen Islands, The** *island group* N New Zealand
97 L25 **Alderney** *island* Channel Islands
97 N22 **Aldershot** S England, United Kingdom 51°15′N 00°47′W
21 R6 **Alderson** West Virginia, NE USA 37°43′N 80°38′W
Al Dhaid *see* Adh Dhayd
30 J11 **Aledo** Illinois, N USA 41°12′N 90°45′W
76 H9 **Aleg** Brakna, SW Mauritania 17°03′N 13°53′W
64 Q10 **Alegranza** *island* Islas Canarias, Spain, NE Atlantic Ocean
37 P12 **Alegres Mountain** ▲ New Mexico, SW USA 34°09′N 108°11′W
61 F15 **Alegrete** Rio Grande do Sul, S Brazil 29°46′S 55°46′W
61 C16 **Alejandra** Santa Fe, C Argentina 29°54′S 59°50′W
193 T11 **Alejandro Selkirk, Isla** *island* Islas Juan Fernández, Chile, E Pacific Ocean
124 I12 **Alekhovshchina** Leningradskaya Oblast', NW Russian Federation 60°22′N 33°57′E
39 O13 **Aleknagik** Alaska, USA 59°16′N 158°37′W
Aleksandriya *see* Oleksandriya
Aleksandropol' *see* Gyumri
126 L3 **Aleksandrov** Vladimirskaya Oblast', W Russian Federation 56°24′N 38°42′E
113 N14 **Aleksandrovac** Serbia, C Serbia 43°28′N 21°05′E
127 R9 **Aleksandrov Gay** Saratovskaya Oblast', W Russian Federation 50°08′N 48°34′E
127 U6 **Aleksandrovka** Orenburgskaya Oblast', W Russian Federation 52°47′N 54°14′E
Aleksandrovka *see* Oleksandrivka
125 V13 **Aleksandrovsk** Permskaya Oblast', NW Russian Federation 59°12′N 57°27′E
Aleksandrovsk *see* Zaporizhzhya
127 N14 **Aleksandrovskoye** Stavropol'skiy Kray, SW Russian Federation 44°43′N 42°56′E
123 T12 **Aleksandrovsk-Sakhalinskiy** Ostrov Sakhalin, Sakhalinskaya Oblast', SE Russian Federation 50°55′N 142°12′E
110 J10 **Aleksandrów Kujawski** Kujawsko-pormorskie, C Poland 52°52′N 18°40′E
110 K12 **Aleksandrów Łódzki** Łódzkie, C Poland 51°49′N 19°19′E
Alekseevka *see* Akkol', Akmola, Kazakhstan
Alekseevka *see* Terekty
145 P7 **Alekseyevka** *Kaz.* Alekseevka. Akmola, N Kazakhstan 53°32′N 69°30′E
126 L9 **Alekseyevka** Belgorodskaya, W Russian Federation 50°35′N 38°41′E
127 S7 **Alekseyevka** Samarskaya Oblast', W Russian Federation 52°37′N 51°20′E
Alekseyevka *see* Akkol', Akmola, Kazakhstan
Alekseyevka *see* Terekty, Vostochnyy Kazakhstan, Kazakhstan
127 R4 **Alekseyevskoye** Respublika Tatarstan, W Russian Federation 55°18′N 50°11′E
126 K5 **Aleksin** Tul'skaya Oblast', W Russian Federation 54°30′N 37°08′E
113 O14 **Aleksinac** Serbia, SE Serbia 43°33′N 21°43′E
190 G11 **Alele** Île Uvea, E Wallis and Futuna 13°14′S 176°09′W
95 N20 **Älem** Kalmar, S Sweden 56°57′N 16°25′E
102 L6 **Alençon** Orne, N France 48°26′N 00°04′E
58 I12 **Alenquer** Pará, NE Brazil 01°58′S 54°45′W
38 G10 **'Alenuihaha Channel** *var.* Alenuihaha Channel. *channel* Hawai'i, USA, C Pacific Ocean
Alep/Aleppo *see* Ḥalab
103 Y15 **Aléria** Corse, France, C Mediterranean Sea 42°06′N 09°29′E
197 Q11 **Alert** Ellesmere Island, Nunavut, N Canada 82°28′N 62°13′W
103 Q14 **Alès** *prev.* Alais. Gard, S France 44°08′N 04°05′E
116 G9 **Aleșd** *Hung.* Élesd. Bihor, SW Romania 47°03′N 22°22′E
106 C9 **Alessandria** *Fr.* Alexandrie. Piemonte, N Italy 44°54′N 08°37′E
Ålestrup *see* Aalestrup
94 D9 **Ålesund** Møre og Romsdal, S Norway 62°28′N 06°11′E
108 E10 **Aletschhorn** ▲ SW Switzerland 46°33′N 08°01′E
197 S1 **Aleutian Basin** *undersea feature* Bering Sea 57°00′N 177°00′E
38 H17 **Aleutian Islands** *island group* Alaska, USA
39 P14 **Aleutian Range** ▲ Alaska, USA
0 B5 **Aleutian Trench** *undersea feature* S Bering Sea 57°00′N 177°00′W
123 T10 **Alevina, Mys** *cape* E Russian Federation
15 Q6 **Alex** ⚡ Québec, SE Canada
28 J3 **Alexander** North Dakota, N USA 47°48′N 103°38′W
39 W14 **Alexander Archipelago** *island group* Alaska, USA
Alexanderbaai *see* Alexander Bay
83 D23 **Alexander Bay** *Afr.* Alexanderbaai. Northern Cape, W South Africa 28°40′S 16°30′E
23 Q5 **Alexander City** Alabama, S USA 32°56′N 85°57′W
194 J6 **Alexander Island** *island* Antarctica
Alexander Range *see* Kirghiz Range
183 O12 **Alexandra** Victoria, SE Australia 37°12′S 145°43′E
185 D22 **Alexandra** Otago, South Island, New Zealand 45°15′S 169°25′E
115 F14 **Alexándreia** *var.* Alexándria. Kentrikí Makedonía, N Greece 40°38′N 22°27′E
Alexandretta *see* İskenderun
Alexandretta, Gulf of *see* İskenderun Körfezi
15 N13 **Alexandria** Ontario, SE Canada 45°19′N 74°37′W
121 U13 **Alexandria** *Ar.* Al Iskandarīyah. N Egypt 31°07′N 29°51′E
44 J12 **Alexandria** C Jamaica 18°18′N 77°21′W
116 J15 **Alexandria** Teleorman, S Romania 43°58′N 25°18′E
31 P13 **Alexandria** Indiana, N USA 40°15′N 85°40′W
20 M4 **Alexandria** Kentucky, S USA 38°59′N 84°22′W
22 H7 **Alexandria** Louisiana, S USA 31°19′N 92°27′W
29 T7 **Alexandria** Minnesota, N USA 45°54′N 95°22′W
29 Q11 **Alexandria** South Dakota, N USA 43°39′N 97°46′W
21 W4 **Alexandria** Virginia, NE USA 38°49′N 77°06′W
Alexándria *see* Alexándreia
18 I7 **Alexandria Bay** New York, NE USA 44°20′N 75°54′W
Alexandrie *see* Alessandria
182 J10 **Alexandrina, Lake** ◎ South Australia
114 K13 **Alexandroúpoli** *var.* Alexandroúpolis, *Turk.* Dedeagaç, Dedeagach. Anatolikí Makedonía kai Thráki, NE Greece 40°52′N 25°53′E
Alexandroúpolis *see* Alexandroúpoli
10 L15 **Alexis Creek** British Columbia, SW Canada 52°06′N 123°25′W
122 I13 **Aleysk** Altayskiy Kray, S Russian Federation 52°32′N 82°46′E
139 S8 **Al Fallūjah** *var.* Falluja. Al Anbār, C Iraq 33°21′N 43°46′E
105 R8 **Alfambra** ⚡ E Spain
Al Faqa *see* Faq'
141 R15 **Al Farḍah** C Yemen 14°51′N 48°33′E
105 Q4 **Alfaro** La Rioja, N Spain 42°13′N 01°45′W
105 U5 **Alfarràs** Cataluña, NE Spain 41°50′N 00°34′E
Al Fāshir *see* El Fasher
75 W8 **Al Fashn** *var.* El Fashn. C Egypt 28°49′N 30°54′E
114 M7 **Alfatar** Silistra, NE Bulgaria 43°56′N 27°17′E
139 S5 **Al Fatḥah** Ṣalāḥ ad Dīn, C Iraq 35°06′N 43°34′E
139 Q3 **Al Fatsī** Nīnawá, N Iraq 36°04′N 42°39′E
139 Z13 **Al Fāw** *var.* Fao. Al Baṣrah, SE Iraq 29°55′N 48°26′E
75 W8 **Al Fayyūm** *var.* El Faiyûm. N Egypt 29°19′N 30°50′E
El Faiyûm *see* Al Fayyūm
115 D20 **Alfeiós** *prev.* Alfiós; *anc.* Alpheius, Alpheus. ⚡ S Greece
100 I13 **Alfeld** Niedersachsen, C Germany 51°58′N 09°49′E
Alfiós *see* Alfeiós
Alföld *see* Great Hungarian Plain
94 C11 **Ålfotbreen** *glacier* S Norway
19 P9 **Alfred** Maine, NE USA 43°29′N 70°44′W
18 F11 **Alfred** New York, NE USA 42°15′N 77°47′W
61 K14 **Alfredo Vagner** Santa Catarina, S Brazil 27°40′S 49°22′W
94 M12 **Alfta** Gävleborg, C Sweden 61°20′N 16°05′E
140 K12 **Al Fuḥayḥīl** *var.* Fahaheel. SE Kuwait 29°01′N 48°05′E
139 Q6 **Al Fuḥaymī** Al Anbār, C Iraq 34°18′N 42°09′E
143 S16 **Al Fujayrah** *Eng.* Fujairah. Al Fujayrah, NE United Arab Emirates 25°09′N 56°18′E
143 S16 **Al Fujayrah** *Eng.* Fujairah. ✕ Al Fujayrah, NE United Arab Emirates 25°04′N 56°12′E
Al-Furāt *see* Euphrates
144 I10 **Alga** *Kaz.* Algha. Aktyubinsk, NW Kazakhstan 49°56′N 57°19′E
144 G9 **Algabas** *Kaz.* Alghabas. Zapadnyy Kazakhstan, NW Kazakhstan 50°43′N 52°09′E
95 C17 **Ålgård** Rogaland, S Norway 58°45′N 05°52′E
104 G14 **Algarve** *cultural region* S Portugal
182 G3 **Algebuckina Bridge** South Australia 28°03′S 135°48′E
104 K16 **Algeciras** Andalucía, SW Spain 36°08′N 05°27′W
105 S10 **Algemesí** País Valenciano, E Spain 39°11′N 00°27′W
Al-Genain *see* El Geneina
120 F9 **Alger** *var.* Algiers, El Djazaïr, Al Jazair. ● (Algeria) N Algeria 36°47′N 02°58′E
74 H9 **Algeria** *off.* Democratic and Popular Republic of Algeria. ◆ *republic* N Africa
Algeria, Democratic and Popular Republic of *see* Algeria
120 J8 **Algerian Basin** *var.* Balearic Plain. *undersea feature* W Mediterranean Sea
Algha *see* Alga
138 I4 **Al Ghāb** *Valley* NW Syria
141 X10 **Al Ghābah** *var.* Ghaba. C Oman 21°22′N 57°14′E
Alghabas *see* Algabas
141 U14 **Al Ghayḍah** E Yemen 16°15′N 52°13′E
140 M6 **Al Ghazālah** Ḥā'il, NW Saudi Arabia 26°55′N 41°23′E
107 B17 **Alghero** Sardegna, Italy, C Mediterranean Sea 40°34′N 08°19′E
95 M20 **Älghult** Kronoberg, S Sweden 57°00′N 15°34′E
Al Ghurdaqah *see* Hurghada
Algiers *see* Alger
105 S10 **Alginet** País Valenciano, E Spain 39°16′N 00°28′W
83 I26 **Algoa Bay** *bay* S South Africa
104 L15 **Algodonales** Andalucía, S Spain 36°54′N 05°24′W
105 N9 **Algodor** ⚡ C Spain
Al Golea *see* El Goléa
31 N6 **Algoma** Wisconsin, N USA 44°41′N 87°24′W
29 U12 **Algona** Iowa, C USA 43°04′N 94°13′W
20 L8 **Algood** Tennessee, S USA 36°12′N 85°27′W
105 O2 **Algorta** País Vasco, N Spain 43°20′N 03°00′W
61 E18 **Algorta** Río Negro, W Uruguay 32°26′S 57°18′W
Al Haba *see* Haba
139 Q10 **Al Habbārīyah** Al Anbār, S Iraq 32°16′N 42°12′E
Al Hadhar *see* Al Ḥaḍr
139 Q4 **Al Ḥaḍr** *var.* Al Hadhar; *anc.* Hatra. Nīnawýa, NW Iraq 35°34′N 42°44′E
139 T13 **Al Ḥajarah** *desert* S Iraq
141 W8 **Al Ḥajar al Gharbī** ▲ N Oman
141 Y8 **Al Ḥajar ash Sharqī** ▲ NE Oman
141 R15 **Al Ḥajarayn** C Yemen 15°29′N 48°24′E
138 L10 **Al Ḥamād** *desert* Jordan/Saudi Arabia
Al Hamad *see* Syrian Desert
75 N9 **Al Ḥamādah al Ḥamrā'** *var.* Al Ḥamrā'. *desert* NW Libya
105 N15 **Alhama de Granada** Andalucía, S Spain 37°00′N 03°59′W
105 R13 **Alhama de Murcia** Murcia, SE Spain 37°51′N 01°25′W
35 T15 **Alhambra** California, W USA 34°08′N 118°06′W
139 T12 **Al Hammām** An Najaf, S Iraq 31°09′N 44°04′E
141 X8 **Al Ḥamrā'** NE Oman 23°07′N 57°23′E
Al Ḥamrā' *see* Al Ḥamādah al Ḥamrā'
141 O6 **Al Ḥamūdīyah** *spring/well* N Saudi Arabia 27°05′N 44°24′E
140 M7 **Al Ḥanākīyah** Al Madīnah, W Saudi Arabia 24°55′N 40°31′E
139 W14 **Al Ḥanīyah** *escarpment* Iraq/Saudi Arabia
139 Y12 **Al Ḥārithah** Al Baṣrah, SE Iraq 30°43′N 47°44′E
140 L3 **Al Ḥarrah** *desert* NW Saudi Arabia
75 Q10 **Al Harūj al Aswad** *desert* C Libya
Al Hasaifin *see* Al Ḥusayfin
139 N2 **Al Ḥasakah** *var.* Al Hasijah, El Haseke, *Fr.* Hassetché. Al Ḥasakah, NE Syria 36°22′N 40°44′E
139 O2 **Al Ḥasakah** *off.* Muḥāfaẓat al Ḥasakah, *var.* Al Hasakah, Āl Hasakah, Hasakah, Hassakeh. ◆ *governorate* NE Syria
Al Hasakah *see* 'Āmūdah
Al Hasakah *see* Al Ḥasakah
139 T9 **Al Hāshimīyah** Bābil, C Iraq 32°24′N 44°39′E
138 G13 **Al Hāshimīyah** Ma'ān, S Jordan 30°31′N 35°46′E
Al Hasijah *see* Al Ḥasakah
104 M15 **Alhaurín el Grande** Andalucía, S Spain 36°39′N 04°41′W
141 Q16 **Al Ḥawrā** S Yemen 13°54′N 47°36′E
139 V10 **Al Ḥayy** *var.* Kut al Hai, Kūt al Ḥayy. Wāsiṭ, E Iraq 32°11′N 46°03′E
141 U11 **Al Ḥibāk** *desert* E Saudi Arabia
138 H8 **Al Hījānah** *var.* Hejanah, Hijanah. Dimashq, W Syria 33°23′N 36°34′E
140 K7 **Al Ḥijāz** *Eng.* Hejaz. *physical region* NW Saudi Arabia
Al Hilbeh *see* 'Ulayyānīyah, Bi'r al
139 T9 **Al Ḥillah** *var.* Hilla. Bābil, C Iraq 32°28′N 44°29′E
139 T9 **Al Hindīyah** *var.* Hindiya. Bābil, C Iraq 32°32′N 44°14′E
138 G12 **Al Ḥiṣā** Aṭ Ṭafīlah, W Jordan 30°49′N 35°58′E
74 G5 **Al-Hoceïma** *var.* al Hoceima, Al-Hoceima, Alhucemas; *prev.* Villa Sanjurjo. N Morocco 35°14′N 03°56′W
Alhucemas *see* Al-Hoceïma
105 N17 **Alhucemas, Peñon de** *island group* S Spain
141 N15 **Al Ḥudaydah** *Eng.* Hodeida. W Yemen 15°N 42°50′E
141 N15 **Al Ḥudaydah** *var.* Hodeida. ✕ W Yemen 14°45′N 43°01′E
140 M4 **Al Ḥudūd ash Shamālīyah** *var.* Minṭaqat al Ḥudūd ash Shamālīyah, *Eng.* Northern Border Region. ◆ *province* N Saudi Arabia
141 S7 **Al Hufūf** *var.* Hofuf. Ash Sharqīyah, NE Saudi Arabia 25°21′N 49°34′E
al-Hurma *see* Al Khurmah
141 X7 **Al Ḥusayfin** *var.* Al Hasaifin. N Oman 24°33′N 56°33′E
138 G9 **Al Ḥuṣn** *var.* Husn. Irbid, N Jordan 32°29′N 35°53′E
139 U9 **'Alī** Wāsiṭ, E Iraq 32°43′N 45°21′E
104 L10 **Alia** Extremadura, W Spain 39°25′N 05°12′W
143 P9 **'Alīābād** Yazd, C Iran 36°55′N 54°33′E
'Alīābad *see* Qā'emshahr
105 S7 **Aliaga** Aragón, NE Spain 40°40′N 00°42′W
136 B13 **Aliağa** İzmir, W Turkey 38°49′N 26°59′E
Aliákmon *see* Aliákmonas
115 F14 **Aliákmonas** *prev.* Aliákmon; *anc.* Haliacmon. ⚡ N Greece
139 W9 **'Alī al Gharbī** Maysān, E Iraq 32°28′N 46°42′E
139 U11 **'Alī al Ḥassūnī** Al Qādisīyah, S Iraq 31°25′N 44°50′E
115 G18 **Alíartos** Stereá Ellás, C Greece 38°23′N 23°06′E
137 Y12 **Äli-Bayramli** *Rus.* Ali-Bayramly. SE Azerbaijan 39°57′N 48°54′E
Ali-Bayramly *see* Äli-Bayramlı
114 P12 **Alibey Barajı** ⊠ NW Turkey
77 S13 **Alibori** ⚡ N Benin
112 M10 **Alibunar** Vojvodina, NE Serbia 45°06′N 20°59′E
105 S12 **Alicante** *Cat.* Alacant, *Lat.* Lucentum. País Valenciano, SE Spain 38°21′N 00°29′W
105 S12 **Alicante** ◆ *province* País Valenciano, SE Spain
105 S12 **Alicante** ✕ Murcia, E Spain 38°21′N 00°29′W
83 I25 **Alice** Eastern Cape, S South Africa 32°47′S 26°50′E
25 S14 **Alice** Texas, SW USA 27°45′N 98°06′W
83 I25 **Alicedale** Eastern Cape, S South Africa 33°19′S 26°05′E
65 B25 **Alice, Mount** *hill* West Falkland, Falkland Islands
107 P20 **Alice, Punta** *headland* S Italy 39°24′N 17°09′E
181 Q7 **Alice Springs** Northern Territory, C Australia 23°42′S 133°52′E
23 N4 **Aliceville** Alabama, S USA 33°07′N 88°09′W
147 U13 **Alichur** SE Tajikistan 37°49′N 73°45′E
147 U14 **Alichuri Janubí, Qatorkŭhi** *Rus.* Yuzhno-Alichurskiy Khrebet. ▲ SE Tajikistan
147 U13 **Alichuri Shimolí, Qatorkŭhi** *Rus.* Severo-Alichurskiy Khrebet. ▲ SE Tajikistan
107 K22 **Alicudi, Isola** *island* Isole Eolie, S Italy
Alifu Atoll *see* Ari Atoll
43 W14 **Aligandí** Kuna Yala, NE Panama 09°15′N 78°05′W
152 J11 **Alīgarh** Uttar Pradesh, N India 27°54′N 78°04′E
142 M7 **Alīgūdarz** Lorestān, W Iran 33°24′N 49°19′E
163 U5 **Alihe** *var.* Oroqen Zizhiqi. Nei Mongol Zizhiqu, N China 50°34′N 123°40′E
0 F12 **Alijos, Islas** *islets* California, SW USA
149 R6 **'Alī Kbel** *Pash.* 'Alī Khēl. Paktīkā, E Afghanistan 33°55′N 69°49′E
Ali Khel *see* 'Alī Kheyl, Paktīā, Afghanistan
'Alī Khēl *see* 'Alī Kbel, Paktīkā, Afghanistan
149 R6 **'Alī Kheyl** *var.* Ali Khel, Jajı. Paktīā, SE Afghanistan 33°55′N 69°46′E
141 V17 **Al Ikhwān** *island group* SE Yemen
Aliki *see* Alykí
79 H19 **Alima** ⚡ C Congo
Al Imārāt al 'Arabīyah al Muttaḥidah *see* United Arab Emirates
115 N23 **Alimía** *island* Dodekánisa, Greece, Aegean Sea
55 V12 **Alimimuni Piek** ▲ S Surinam 02°26′N 55°46′W
79 K15 **Alindao** Basse-Kotto, S Central African Republic 04°58′N 21°16′E
95 J18 **Alingsås** Västra Götaland, S Sweden 57°55′N 12°30′E
81 K18 **Alinjugul** *spring/well* E Kenya 0°03′S 40°31′E
153 S16 **Ālīpur** West Bengal, NE India 22°32′N 88°20′E
149 S11 **Alīpur** Punjab, E Pakistan 29°22′N 70°59′E
153 T12 **Alīpur Duār** West Bengal, NE India 26°28′N 89°25′E
18 B14 **Aliquippa** Pennsylvania, NE USA 40°36′N 80°15′W
80 L12 **'Ali Sabieh** *var.* 'Alī Sabīḥ. S Djibouti 11°07′N 42°44′E
'Alī Sabīḥ *see* 'Ali Sabieh
140 K3 **Al 'Īsāwīyah** Al Jawf, NW Saudi Arabia 30°41′N 37°58′E
104 J10 **Aliseda** Extremadura, W Spain 39°25′N 06°42′W
139 T8 **Al Iskandarīyah** Bābil, C Iraq 32°53′N 44°22′E
Al Iskandarīyah *see* Alexandria
123 T6 **Aliskerovo** Chukotskiy Avtonomnyy Okrug, NE Russian Federation 67°40′N 167°37′E
75 W7 **Al Ismā'īlīya** *var.* Ismailia, Ismâ'ilîya. N Egypt 30°32′N 32°13′E
114 H13 **Alistráti** Kentrikí Makedonía, NE Greece 41°03′N 23°58′E
39 P15 **Alitak Bay** *bay* Kodiak Island, Alaska, USA
Al Ittiḥād *see* Madīnat ash Sha'b
115 H18 **Alivéri** *var.* Alivérion. Évvoia, C Greece 38°24′N 24°02′E
Alivérion *see* Alivéri
Aliwal-Noord *see* Aliwal North
83 I24 **Aliwal North** *Afr.* Aliwal-Noord. Eastern Cape, SE South Africa 30°42′S 26°43′E
121 Q13 **Al Jabal al Akhḍar** ▲ NE Libya
138 H13 **Al Jafr** Ma'ān, S Jordan 30°18′N 36°13′E
75 T8 **Al Jaghbūb** NE Libya 29°45′N 24°31′E
142 K11 **Al Jahrā'** *var.* Al Jahrah, Jahra. C Kuwait 29°18′N 47°36′E
Al Jahrah *see* Al Jahrā'
Al Jamāhīrīyah al 'Arabīyah al Lībīyah ash Sha'bīyah al Ishtirākīy *see* Libya
140 K3 **Al Jarāwī** *spring/well* NW Saudi Arabia 30°12′N 38°48′E
141 X11 **Al Jawārah** *oasis* SE Oman
140 L3 **Al Jawf** *off.* Jauf. Al Jawf, NW Saudi Arabia 29°51′N 39°49′E
140 L4 **Al Jawf** *var.* Minṭaqat al Jawf. ◆ *province* N Saudi Arabia
Al Jawlān *see* Golan Heights
Al Jazair *see* Alger
139 N4 **Al Jazīrah** *physical region* Iraq/Syria
104 F14 **Aljezur** Faro, S Portugal 37°18′N 08°49′W
139 S13 **Al Jil** An Najaf, S Iraq 30°28′N 43°57′E
138 G11 **Al Jīzah** *var.* Jīza. 'Ammān, N Jordan 31°42′N 35°57′E
Al Jīzah *see* Giza
Al Jubail *see* Al Jubayl
141 S6 **Al Jubayl** *var.* Al Jubail. Ash Sharqīyah, NE Saudi Arabia 27°N 49°36′E
141 T10 **Āl Juḥaysh, Qalamat** *well* SE Saudi Arabia
143 N15 **Al Jumaylīyah** N Qatar 25°37′N 51°05′E
Al Junaynah *see* El Geneina
104 G13 **Aljustrel** Beja, S Portugal 37°52′N 08°10′W
Al Kaba'ish *see* Al Chabā'ish
Al-Kadhimain *see* Al Kāẓimīyah
Al Kāf *see* El Kef
Alkal'a *see* Alcalá de Henares
35 W4 **Alkali Flat** *salt flat* Nevada, W USA
35 Q1 **Alkali Lake** ◎ Nevada, W USA
141 Z9 **Al Kāmil** NE Oman 22°14′N 58°15′E
138 G11 **Al Karak** *var.* El Kerak, Karak, Kerak; *anc.* Kir Moab, Kir of Moab. Al Karak, W Jordan 31°11′N 35°42′E
138 G12 **Al Karak** *off.* Muḥāfaẓat al Karak. ◆ *governorate* W Jordan
139 W8 **Al Karmashīyah** Wāsiṭ, E Iraq 32°57′N 46°10′E
Al-Kashaniya *see* Al Qash'ānīyah
Al-Kasr al-Kebir *see* Ksar-el-Kebir
139 T8 **Al Kāẓimīyah** *var.* Al-Kadhimain, Kadhimain. Baghdād, C Iraq 33°22′N 44°20′E
99 J18 **Alken** Limburg, NE Belgium 50°52′N 05°19′E
141 X8 **Al Khābūrah** *var.* Khabura. N Oman 23°57′N 57°06′E
Al Khalil *see* Hebron
139 T7 **Al Khāliṣ** Diyālá, C Iraq 33°51′N 44°33′E
Al Khaluf *see* Khalūf
75 W10 **Al Khārijah** *var.* El Khârga. C Egypt 25°31′N 30°36′E
141 Q8 **Al Kharj** Ar Riyāḍ, C Saudi Arabia 24°12′N 47°12′E
141 W6 **Al Khaṣab** *var.* Khasab. N Oman 26°11′N 56°18′E
Al Khaur *see* Al Khawr
143 N15 **Al Khawr** *var.* Al Khaur, Al Khor. N Qatar 25°40′N 51°33′E
142 K12 **Al Khīrān** *var.* Al Khiran. SE Kuwait 28°34′N 48°21′E
141 W9 **Al Khīrān** *spring/well* NW Oman 22°31′N 55°42′E
Al Khiyām *see* El Khiyam
Al-Khobar *see* Al Khubar
Al Khor *see* Al Khawr
141 S6 **Al Khubar** *var.* Al-Khobar. Ash Sharqīyah, NE Saudi Arabia 26°00′N 50°00′E
120 M12 **Al Khums** *var.* Homs, Khoms, Khums. NW Libya 32°39′N 14°16′E
141 R15 **Al Khuraybah** C Yemen 15°05′N 48°17′E
140 M9 **Al Khurmah** *var.* al-Hurma. Makkah, W Saudi Arabia 21°59′N 42°00′E
141 V9 **Al Kidan** *desert* NE Saudi Arabia
127 V4 **Alkino-2** Respublika Bashkortostan, W Russian Federation 54°30′N 55°40′E
98 H9 **Alkmaar** Noord-Holland, NW Netherlands 52°37′N 04°45′E
139 T10 **Al Kūfah** *var.* Kufa. An Najaf, S Iraq 32°02′N 44°25′E
75 T11 **Al Kufrah** SE Libya 24°11′N 23°19′E
141 T10 **Al Kursū'** *desert* E Saudi Arabia
139 V9 **Al Kūt** *var.* Kūt al 'Amārah, Kut al Imara. Wāsiṭ, E Iraq 32°30′N 45°51′E
Al-Kuwait *see* Al Kuwayt
Al Kuwayt *see* Guwēr
142 K11 **Al Kuwayt** *var.* Al-Kuwait, *Eng.* Kuwait, Kuwait City; *prev.* Qurein. ● (Kuwait) E Kuwait 29°23′N 48°00′E
142 K11 **Al Kuwayt** ✕ C Kuwait 29°13′N 47°57′E
115 G19 **Alkyonidón, Kólpos** *gulf* C Greece
141 N4 **Al Labbah** *physical region* N Saudi Arabia
138 G4 **Al Lādhiqīyah** *Eng.* Latakia, *Fr.* Lattaquié; *anc.* Laodicea, Laodicea ad Mare. Al Lādhiqīyah, W Syria 35°31′N 35°47′E
138 H4 **Al Lādhiqīyah** *off.* Muḥāfaẓat al Lādhiqīyah, *var.* Al Lathqiyah, Latakia, Lattakia. ◆ *governorate* W Syria
19 R2 **Allagash River** ⚡ Maine, NE USA
152 M13 **Allahābād** Uttar Pradesh, N India 25°27′N 81°50′E
143 S3 **Allāh Dāgh, Reshteh-ye** ▲ NE Iran
39 Q8 **Allakaket** Alaska, USA 66°34′N 152°39′W
141 X12 **Al Lakbī** S Oman 18°27′N 56°37′E
11 T15 **Allan** Saskatchewan, S Canada 51°50′N 105°59′W
Allanmyo *see* Aunglan
83 I22 **Allanridge** Free State, C South Africa 27°45′S 26°40′E
104 H4 **Allariz** Galicia, NW Spain 42°11′N 07°48′W
139 R11 **Al Laṣaf** *var.* Al Lussuf. An Najaf, S Iraq 31°38′N 43°16′E
Al Lathqiyah *see* Al Lādhiqīyah
23 S2 **Allatoona Lake** ⊠ Georgia, SE USA
83 J19 **Alldays** Limpopo, NE South Africa 22°39′S 29°04′E
Alle *see* Łyna
31 P10 **Allegan** Michigan, N USA 42°31′N 85°51′W
18 E14 **Allegheny Mountains** ▲ NE USA
18 E12 **Allegheny Plateau** ▲ New York/Pennsylvania, NE USA
18 D11 **Allegheny Reservoir** ⊠ New York/Pennsylvania, NE USA
18 E12 **Allegheny River** ⚡ New York/Pennsylvania, NE USA
22 K9 **Allemands, Lac des** ◎ Louisiana, S USA
25 U6 **Allen** Texas, SW USA 33°06′N 96°40′W
21 R14 **Allendale** South Carolina, SE USA 33°01′N 81°19′W
41 N6 **Allende** Coahuila, NE Mexico 28°22′N 100°50′W
41 O9 **Allende** Nuevo León, NE Mexico 25°20′N 100°01′W
97 D16 **Allen, Lough** *Ir.* Loch Aillionn. ◎ NW Ireland
185 B26 **Allen, Mount** ▲ Stewart Island, Southland, SW New Zealand 47°05′S 167°49′E
109 V2 **Allensteig** Niederösterreich, N Austria 48°40′N 15°24′E
Allenstein *see* Olsztyn
18 I14 **Allentown** Pennsylvania, NE USA 40°37′N 75°30′W
155 G23 **Alleppey** *var.* Alappuzha. Kerala, SW India 09°30′N 76°22′E *see also* Alappuzha
100 J12 **Aller** ⚡ NW Germany
29 V16 **Allerton** Iowa, C USA 40°42′N 93°22′W
99 K19 **Alleur** Liège, E Belgium 50°40′N 05°33′E
101 J25 **Allgäuer Alpen** ▲ Austria/Germany
28 J13 **Alliance** Nebraska, C USA 42°08′N 102°54′W
31 U12 **Alliance** Ohio, N USA 40°55′N 81°06′W
103 O10 **Allier** ◆ *department* N France
139 R12 **Al Lifiyah** *well* An Najaf, S Iraq
44 J13 **Alligator Pond** C Jamaica 17°52′N 77°34′W
21 Y9 **Alligator River** ⚡ North Carolina, SE USA
29 W12 **Allison** Iowa, C USA 42°45′N 92°48′W
14 G14 **Alliston** Ontario, S Canada 44°09′N 79°51′W
140 L11 **Al Līth** Makkah, SW Saudi Arabia 21°N 41°E
Al Liwā' *see* Līwā
96 J12 **Alloa** C Scotland, United Kingdom 56°07′N 03°49′W
103 U14 **Allos** Alpes-de-Haute-Provence, SE France 44°16′N 06°37′E
108 D6 **Allschwil** Basel-Land, NW Switzerland 47°34′N 07°32′E
Al Lubnān *see* Lebanon
141 N14 **Al Luḥayyah** W Yemen 15°44′N 42°45′E
14 K12 **Allumettes, Île des** *island* Québec, SE Canada
Al Lussuf *see* Al Laṣaf
109 S5 **Alm** ⚡ N Austria
15 Q7 **Alma** Québec, SE Canada 48°32′N 71°41′W
27 S10 **Alma** Arkansas, C USA 35°28′N 94°13′W
23 V7 **Alma** Georgia, SE USA 31°32′N 82°27′W
27 P4 **Alma** Kansas, C USA 39°01′N 96°17′W
31 Q8 **Alma** Michigan, N USA 43°22′N 84°39′W
29 O17 **Alma** Nebraska, C USA 40°06′N 99°21′W
30 I7 **Alma** Wisconsin, N USA 44°21′N 91°54′W
139 R12 **Al Ma'ānīyah** *well* An Najaf, S Iraq
Alma-Ata *see* Almaty
Alma-Atinskaya Oblast' *see* Almaty
Almacellas *see* Almacelles
105 T5 **Almacelles** *var.* Almacellas. Cataluña, NE Spain 41°44′N 00°26′E
104 F11 **Almada** Setúbal, W Portugal 38°40′N 09°09′W
104 L11 **Almadén** Castilla-La Mancha, C Spain 38°47′N 04°50′W
66 L6 **Almadies, Pointe des** *headland* W Senegal 14°44′N 17°31′W
140 L7 **Al Madīnah** *Eng.* Medina. Al Madīnah, W Saudi Arabia 24°25′N 39°29′E
140 L7 **Al Madīnah** *off.* Minṭaqat al Madīnah. ◆ *province* W Saudi Arabia
138 H9 **Al Mafraq** *var.* Mafraq. Al Mafraq, N Jordan 32°20′N 36°12′E
138 J10 **Al Mafraq** *off.* Muḥāfaẓat al Mafraq. ◆ *governorate* NW Jordan
141 R15 **Al Maghārīm** C Yemen 15°00′N 47°49′E
105 N11 **Almagro** Castilla-La Mancha, C Spain 38°54′N 03°43′W
Al Maḥallah al Kubrá *see* El Maḥalla el Kubra
139 T9 **Al Maḥāwil** *var.* Khān al Maḥāwil. Bābil, C Iraq 32°39′N 44°28′E
Al Mahdīyah *see* Mahdia
139 T8 **Al Maḥmūdīyah** *var.* Mahmudiya. Baghdād, C Iraq 33°04′N 44°22′E
141 T14 **Al Mahrah** ▲ E Yemen
141 P7 **Al Majma'ah** Ar Riyāḍ, C Saudi Arabia 25°55′N 45°19′E
139 Q11 **Al Makmīn** *well* S Iraq
139 Q1 **Al Mālikīyah** *var.* Malkiye. Al Ḥasakah, N Syria 37°12′N 42°13′E
Almalyk *see* Olmaliq
Al Mamlakah *see* Morocco
Al Mamlaka al Urdunīya al Hashemīyah *see* Jordan
143 Q18 **Al Manādir** *var.* Al Manadir. *desert* Oman/United Arab Emirates
142 L15 **Al Manāmah** *Eng.* Manama. ● (Bahrain) N Bahrain 26°13′N 50°33′E
139 O5 **Al Manāṣif** ▲ E Syria
35 O4 **Almanor, Lake** ⊠ California, W USA
105 R11 **Almansa** Castilla-La Mancha, C Spain 38°52′N 01°06′W
75 W7 **Al Manṣūrah** *var.* Manṣûra, El Manṣûra. N Egypt 31°03′N 31°23′E
104 L3 **Almanza** Castilla-León, N Spain 42°40′N 05°01′W
104 L8 **Almanzor** ▲ W Spain 40°13′N 05°18′W
105 P14 **Almanzora** ⚡ SE Spain
139 S9 **Al Mardah** Karbalā', C Iraq 32°35′N 43°30′E
Al-Mariyya *see* Almería
75 R7 **Al Marj** *var.* Barka, *It.* Barce. NE Libya 32°30′N 20°54′E
138 L2 **Al Mashrafah** Ar Raqqah, N Syria 36°25′N 39°07′E
141 X8 **Al Maṣna'ah** *var.* Al Muṣana'a. NE Oman 23°45′N 57°38′E
Almassora *see* Almazora
Almatinskaya Oblast' *see* Almaty
145 U15 **Almaty** *var.* Alma-Ata. Almaty, SE Kazakhstan 43°19′N 76°55′E
145 S14 **Almaty** *off.* Almatinskaya Oblast', *Kaz.* Almaty Oblysy; *prev.* Alma-Atinskaya Oblast'. ◆ *province* SE Kazakhstan
145 U15 **Almaty** ✕ Almaty, SE Kazakhstan 43°15′N 76°57′E
Almaty Oblysy *see* Almaty
al-Mawailih *see* Al Muwayliḥ
139 R3 **Al Mawṣil** *Eng.* Mosul. Nīnawá, N Iraq 36°21′N 43°08′E
139 N5 **Al Mayādīn** *var.* Mayadin, *Fr.* Meyadine. Dayr az Zawr, E Syria 35°00′N 40°31′E
139 X10 **Al Maymūnah** *var.* Maimuna. Maysān, SE Iraq 31°43′N 46°55′E
141 N5 **Al Mayyāh** Ḥā'il, N Saudi Arabia 27°57′N 42°53′E
Al Ma'zam *see* Al Ma'zim
105 P6 **Almazán** Castilla-León, N Spain 41°29′N 02°31′W
141 W8 **Al Ma'zim** *var.* Al Ma'zam. NW Oman 23°22′N 56°16′E
123 N11 **Almaznyy** Respublika Sakha (Yakutiya), NE Russian Federation 62°19′N 114°14′E
105 T9 **Almazora** *Cat.* Almassora. País Valenciano, E Spain 39°55′N 00°02′W
Al Mazra' *see* Al Mazra'ah
138 G11 **Al Mazra'ah** *var.* Al Mazra', Mazra'a. Al Karak, W Jordan 31°18′N 35°32′E
101 G15 **Alme** ⚡ W Germany

◆ Country
● Country Capital
◇ Dependent Territory
○ Dependent Territory Capital
◆ Administrative Regions
✕ International Airport
▲ Mountain
▲ Mountain Range
⛰ Volcano
⚡ River
◎ Lake
⊠ Reservoir

104 *I7* **Almeida** Guarda, N Portugal *40°43´N 06°53´W*
104 *G10* **Almeirim** Santarém, C Portugal *39°12´N 08°37´W*
98 *O10* **Almelo** Overijssel, E Netherlands *52°22´N 06°42´E*
105 *S9* **Almenara** País Valenciano, E Spain *39°46´N 00°14´W*
105 *P12* **Almenaras** ▲ S Spain *38°31´N 02°27´W*
105 *P5* **Almenar de Soria** Castilla-León, N Spain *41°41´N 02°12´W*
104 *J6* **Almendra, Embalse de** ▣ Castilla-León, NW Spain
104 *J11* **Almendralejo** Extremadura, W Spain *38°41´N 06°25´W*
98 *J10* **Almere** *var.* Almere-stad. Flevoland, C Netherlands *52°22´N 05°12´E*
98 *J10* **Almere-Buiten** Flevoland, C Netherlands *52°24´N 05°15´E*
98 *J10* **Almere-Haven** Flevoland, C Netherlands *52°20´N 05°13´E*
Almere-stad *see* Almere
105 *P15* **Almería** *Ar.* Al-Mariyya; *anc.* Unci, *Lat.* Portus Magnus. Andalucía, S Spain *36°50´N 02°26´W*
105 *P14* **Almería** ◈ *province* Andalucía, S Spain
105 *P15* **Almería, Golfo de** *gulf* S Spain
127 *S5* **Al'met'yevsk** Respublika Tatarstan, W Russian Federation *54°53´N 52°20´E*
95 *L21* **Älmhult** Kronoberg, S Sweden *56°32´N 14°10´E*
141 *U9* **Al Miḩrāḑ** *desert* NE Saudi Arabia
Al Mīnā' *see* El Mina
104 *L17* **Almina, Punta** *headland* Ceuta, Spain, N Africa *35°54´N 05°16´W*
75 *W9* **Al Minyā** *var.* El Minya, Minya. C Egypt *28°06´N 30°40´E*
Al Miqdādīyah *see* Al Muqdādīyah
43 *P14* **Almirante** Bocas del Toro, NW Panama *09°20´N 82°22´W*
Almirós *see* Almyrós
140 *M9* **Al Mislaḩ** *spring/well* W Saudi Arabia *22°46´N 40°47´E*
Almissa *see* Omiš
104 *G13* **Almodôvar** *var.* Almodóvar. Beja, S Portugal *37°31´N 08°03´W*
104 *M11* **Almodóvar del Campo** Castilla-La Mancha, C Spain *38°43´N 04°10´W*
105 *Q9* **Almodóvar del Pinar** Castilla-La Mancha, C Spain *39°44´N 01°55´W*
31 *S9* **Almont** Michigan, N USA *42°53´N 83°02´W*
14 *L13* **Almonte** Ontario, SE Canada *45°13´N 76°12´W*
104 *J14* **Almonte** Andalucía, S Spain *37°16´N 06°31´W*
104 *K9* **Almonte** ≋ W Spain
152 *K9* **Almora** Uttarakhand, N India *29°36´N 79°40´E*
104 *M8* **Almorox** Castilla-La Mancha, C Spain *40°13´N 04°22´W*
141 *S7* **Al Mubarraz** Ash Sharqīyah, E Saudi Arabia *25°28´N 49°34´E*
Al Muḑaibī *see* Al Muḑaybī
138 *G15* **Al Mudawwarah** Ma'ān, SW Jordan *29°20´N 36°E*
141 *Y9* **Al Muḑaybī** *var.* Al Muḑaibī. NE Oman *22°35´N 58°08´E*
Almudébar *see* Almudévar
105 *S5* **Almudévar** *var.* Almudébar. Aragón, NE Spain *42°03´N 00°34´W*
141 *S15* **Al Mukallā** *var.* Mukalla. SE Yemen *14°36´N 49°07´E*
141 *N16* **Al Mukhā** *Eng.* Mocha. SW Yemen *13°18´N 43°17´E*
105 *N15* **Almuñécar** Andalucía, S Spain *36°44´N 03°41´W*
139 *U7* **Al Muqdādīyah** *var.* Al Miqdādīyah. Diyālá, C Iraq *33°58´N 44°58´E*
140 *L3* **Al Murayr** *spring/well* NW Saudi Arabia *30°06´N 39°54´E*
136 *M12* **Almus** Tokat, N Turkey *40°22´N 36°54´E*
Al Muşana'a *see* Al Maşna'ah
139 *T9* **Al Musayyib** *var.* Musaiyib. Bābil, C Iraq *32°47´N 44°20´E*
139 *W14* **Al Muthannā** ◈ *governorate* S Iraq
139 *V9* **Al Muwaffaqīyah** Wāsiţ, S Iraq *32°19´N 45°22´E*
138 *H10* **Al Muwaqqar** *var.* El Muwaqqar. 'Ammān, W Jordan *31°49´N 36°06´E*
140 *J5* **Al Muwayliḩ** *var.* al-Mawailih. Tabūk, NW Saudi Arabia *27°39´N 35°33´E*
115 *F17* **Almyrós** *var.* Almirós. Thessalía, C Greece *39°11´N 22°45´E*
115 *I24* **Almyroú, Órmos** *bay* Kríti, Greece, E Mediterranean Sea
Al Nūwfalīyah *see* An Nawfalīyah
96 *L13* **Alnwick** N England, United Kingdom *55°27´N 01°44´W*
Al Obayyid *see* El Obeid
Al Odaid *see* Al 'Udayd
190 *B16* **Alofi** ○ (Niue) W Niue *19°01´S 169°55´E*
190 *A16* **Alofi Bay** *bay* W Niue, C Pacific Ocean
190 *E13* **Alofi, Île** *island* S Wallis and Futuna
190 *E13* **Alofitai** Île Alofi, W Wallis and Futuna *14°21´S 178°03´W*
Aloha State *see* Hawai'i
118 *G7* **Aloja** Limbaži, N Latvia *57°47´N 24°53´E*
153 *X10* **Along** Arunāchel Pradesh, NE India *28°15´N 94°56´E*
115 *H16* **Alónnisos** *island* Vóreies Sporádes, Greece, Aegean Sea
104 *M15* **Álora** Andalucía, S Spain *36°50´N 04°43´W*
171 *Q16* **Alor, Kepulauan** *island group* E Indonesia
171 *Q16* **Alor, Pulau** *prev.* Ombai. *island* Kepulauan Alor, E Indonesia
171 *O16* **Alor, Selat** *strait* Flores Sea/Savu Sea
168 *I7* **Alor Setar** *var.* Alor Star, Alur Setar. Kedah, Peninsular Malaysia *06°06´N 100°23´E*
Alor Star *see* Alor Setar
Alost *see* Aalst
154 *F9* **Ālot** Madhya Pradesh, C India *23°56´N 75°40´E*
186 *G10* **Alotau** Milne Bay, SE Papua New Guinea *10°20´S 150°23´E*
171 *Y16* **Alotip** Papua, E Indonesia *08°07´S 140°06´E*
Al Oued *see* El Oued
35 *R12* **Alpaugh** California, W USA *35°52´N 119°29´W*
Alpen *see* Alps
31 *R6* **Alpena** Michigan, N USA *45°04´N 83°27´W*
Alpes *see* Alps
103 *S14* **Alpes-de-Haute-Provence** ◈ *department* SE France
103 *U14* **Alpes-Maritimes** ◈ *department* SE France
181 *W8* **Alpha** Queensland, E Australia *23°40´S 146°38´E*
197 *R9* **Alpha Cordillera** *var.* Alpha Ridge. *undersea feature* Arctic Ocean *85°30´N 125°00´W*
Alpha Ridge *see* Alpha Cordillera
Alpheius *see* Alfeiós
99 *I15* **Alphen** Noord-Brabant, S Netherlands *51°29´N 04°57´E*
Alphen *see* Alphen aan den Rijn
98 *H11* **Alphen aan den Rijn** *var.* Alphen. Zuid-Holland, C Netherlands *52°08´N 04°40´E*
Alpheus *see* Alfeiós
Alpi *see* Alps
104 *G10* **Alpiarça** Santarém, C Portugal *39°15´N 08°35´W*
24 *K10* **Alpine** Texas, SW USA *30°22´N 103°40´W*
108 *F8* **Alpnach** Unterwalden, W Switzerland *46°56´N 08°17´E*
108 *D11* **Alps** *Fr.* Alpes, *Ger.* Alpen, *It.* Alpi. ▲▲ C Europe
149 *U5* **Alpūrai** *var.* Alpuri. North-West Frontier Province, N Pakistan *34°54´N 72°39´E*
Alpuri *see* Alpūrai
141 *W8* **Al Qābil** *var.* Qabil. N Oman *23°55´N 55°50´E*
Al Qaḑārif *see* Gedaref
75 *P8* **Al Qaddāḩīyah** N Libya *31°21´N 15°16´E*
139 *V10* **Al Qādisīyah** ◈ *governorate* S Iraq
Al Qāhirah *see* Cairo
140 *K4* **Al Qalībah** Tabūk, NW Saudi Arabia *28°29´N 37°40´E*
139 *O1* **Al Qāmishlī** *var.* Kamishli, Qamishly. Al Ḩasakah, NE Syria *37°N 41°E*
138 *I6* **Al Qaryatayn** *var.* Qaryatayn, *Fr.* Qariateïne. Ḩimş, C Syria *34°13´N 37°13´E*
142 *K11* **Al Qash'ānīyah** *var.* Al-Kashaniya. NE Kuwait *29°59´N 47°42´E*
141 *N7* **Al Qaşīm** *var.* Minţaqat Qaşīm, Qassim. ◈ *province* C Saudi Arabia
75 *V10* **Al Qaşr** *var.* Al Qaşr *var.* El Qaşr. C Egypt *25°43´N 28°54´E*
138 *J5* **Al Qaşr** Ḩimş, C Syria *35°06´N 37°39´E*
Al Qaşr *see* Al Qaşr
Al Qaşrayn *see* Kasserine
141 *S6* **Al Qaţīf** Ash Sharqīyah, NE Saudi Arabia *26°27´N 50°01´E*
138 *G11* **Al Qaţrānah** *var.* El Qatrani, Qatrana. Al Karak, W Jordan *31°14´N 36°03´E*
75 *P11* **Al Qaţrūn** SW Libya *24°57´N 14°40´E*
Al Qayrawān *see* Kairouan
Al-Qsar al-Kbir *see* Ksar-el-Kebir
Al Qubayyāt *see* Qoubaïyât
Al Quds/Al Quds ash Sharīf *see* Jerusalem
104 *H12* **Alqueva, Barragem do** ▣ Portugal/Spain
138 *G8* **Al Qunayţirah** *var.* El Kuneitra, El Quneitra, Kuneitra, Qunaytra. Al Qunayţirah, SW Syria *33°08´N 35°49´E*
138 *G8* **Al Qunayţirah** *off.* Muḩāfaẓat al Qunayţirah, *var.* El Q'unayţirah, Qunaytirah, *Fr.* Kuneitra. ◈ *governorate* SW Syria
140 *M11* **Al Qunfudhah** Makkah, SW Saudi Arabia *19°19´N 41°03´E*
140 *K2* **Al Qurayyāt** Al Jawf, NW Saudi Arabia *31°25´N 37°26´E*
139 *Y11* **Al Qurnah** *var.* Kurna. Al Başrah, SE Iraq *31°01´N 47°27´E*
75 *Y10* **Al Quşayr** *var.* Al Quşayr *var.* Qusair, Quseir. E Egypt *26°05´N 34°16´E*
139 *V12* **Al Quşayr** Al Muthanná, S Iraq *30°36´N 45°52´E*
138 *I6* **Al Quşayr** *var.* El Quseir, Quşayr, *Fr.* Kousseir. Ḩimş, W Syria *34°36´N 36°36´E*
Al Quşayr *see* Al Quşayr
138 *H7* **Al Quţayfah** *var.* Quţayfah, Qutayfe, Quteife, *Fr.* Kouteifé. Dimashq, W Syria *33°44´N 36°33´E*
141 *P8* **Al Quwayīyah** Ar Riyāḑ, C Saudi Arabia *24°06´N 45°18´E*
Al Quwayr *see* Guwēr
138 *F14* **Al Quwayrah** *var.* El Quweira. Al 'Aqabah, SW Jordan *29°47´E 35°18´E*
Al Rayyan *see* Ar Rayyān
Al Ruweis *see* Ar Ruways
95 *G24* **Als** *Ger.* Alsen. *island* SW Denmark
103 *U5* **Alsace** *Ger.* Elsass; *anc.* Alsatia. ◈ *region* NE France
11 *R16* **Alsask** Saskatchewan, S Canada *51°24´N 109°55´W*
Alsasua *see* Altsasu
Alsatia *see* Alsace
101 *C16* **Alsdorf** Nordrhein-Westfalen, W Germany *50°52´N 06°09´E*
10 *G8* **Alsek** ≋ Canada/USA
Alsen *see* Als
101 *F19* **Alsenz** ≋ W Germany
101 *H17* **Alsfeld** Hessen, C Germany *50°45´N 09°14´E*
119 *K20* **Al'shany** *Rus.* Ol'shany. Brestskaya Voblasts', SW Belarus *52°05´N 27°21´E*
Alsókubin *see* Dolný Kubín
118 *C9* **Alsunga** Kuldīga, W Latvia *56°59´N 21°31´E*
Alt *see* Olt
92 *K9* **Alta** *Fin.* Alattio. Finnmark, N Norway *69°58´N 23°17´E*
29 *T12* **Alta** Iowa, C USA *42°40´N 95°17´W*
108 *I7* **Altach** Vorarlberg, W Austria *47°22´N 09°39´E*
92 *K9* **Altaelva** *Lapp.* Álaheaieatnu. ≋ N Norway
92 *J8* **Altafjorden** *fjord* NE Norwegian Sea
62 *K10* **Alta Gracia** Córdoba, C Argentina *31°42´S 64°25´W*
42 *K11* **Alta Gracia** Rivas, SW Nicaragua *11°35´N 85°38´W*
54 *H4* **Altagracia** Zulia, NW Venezuela *10°44´N 71°30´W*
54 *M5* **Altagracia de Orituco** Guárico, N Venezuela *09°54´N 66°24´W*
Altai *see* Altai Mountains
129 *T7* **Altai Mountains** *var.* Altai, *Chin.* Altay Shan, *Rus.* Altay. ▲▲ Asia/Europe
23 *V6* **Altamaha River** ≋ Georgia, SE USA
58 *J13* **Altamira** Pará, NE Brazil *03°13´S 52°15´W*
54 *D12* **Altamira** Huila, S Colombia *02°04´N 75°47´W*
42 *M13* **Altamira** Alajuela, N Costa Rica *10°25´N 84°21´W*
41 *Q11* **Altamira** Tamaulipas, C Mexico *22°25´N 97°55´W*
30 *L15* **Altamont** Illinois, N USA *39°03´N 88°45´W*
27 *Q7* **Altamont** Kansas, C USA *37°11´N 95°18´W*
32 *H16* **Altamont** Oregon, NW USA *42°12´N 121°44´W*
20 *K10* **Altamont** Tennessee, S USA *35°28´N 85°42´W*
23 *X11* **Altamonte Springs** Florida, SE USA *28°39´N 81°22´W*
107 *O17* **Altamura** *anc.* Lupatia. Puglia, SE Italy *40°50´N 16°33´E*
40 *H9* **Altamura, Isla** *island* C Mexico
Altan *see* Erdenehayrhan
Altanbulag *see* Bayanhayrhan
163 *Q7* **Altan Emel** *var.* Xin Barag Youqi. Nei Mongol Zizhiqu, N China *48°37´N 116°40´E*
Altan-Ovoo *see* Tsenher
163 *N9* **Altanshiree** *var.* Chamdmanī. Dornigovĭ, SE Mongolia *45°36´N 110°30´E*
Altanteel *see* Dzereg
162 *D5* **Altantsögts** *var.* Tsagaantüngi. Bayan-Ölgiy, NW Mongolia *49°06´N 90°26´E*
40 *F3* **Altar** Sonora, NW Mexico *30°41´N 111°53´W*
40 *D2* **Altar, Desierto de** *var.* Sonoran Desert. *desert* Mexico/USA *see also* Sonoran Desert
Altar, Desierto de *see* Sonoran Desert
105 *Q8* **Alta, Sierra** ▲ N Spain *40°29´N 01°36´W*
40 *H9* **Altata** Sinaloa, C Mexico *24°40´N 107°54´W*
42 *D4* **Alta Verapaz** *off.* Departamento de Alta Verapaz. ◈ *department* C Guatemala
Alta Verapaz, Departamento de *see* Alta Verapaz
107 *L18* **Altavilla Silentia** Campania, S Italy *40°32´N 15°06´E*
21 *T7* **Altavista** Virginia, NE USA *37°06´N 79°17´W*
158 *L2* **Altay** Xinjiang Uygur Zizhiqu, NW China *47°51´N 88°06´E*
162 *D6* **Altay** *var.* Chihertey. Bayan-Ölgiy, W Mongolia *48°10´N 89°35´E*
162 *G8* **Altay** *prev.* Yösönbulag. Govĭ-Altay, W Mongolia *46°23´N 96°17´E*
162 *E8* **Altay** *var.* Bor-Üdzüür. Hovd, W Mongolia *45°46´N 92°13´E*
Altay *see* Altai Mountains, Asia/Europe
Altay *see* Bayantes, Mongolia
122 *J14* **Altay, Respublika** *var.* Gornyy Altay; *prev.* Gorno-Altayskaya Respublika. ◈ *autonomous republic* S Russian Federation
Altay Shan *see* Altai Mountains
123 *I13* **Altayskiy Kray** ◈ *territory* S Russian Federation
Altbetsche *see* Bečej
101 *L20* **Altdorf** Bayern, SE Germany *49°23´N 11°22´E*
108 *G8* **Altdorf** *var.* Altorf. Uri, C Switzerland *46°53´N 08°38´E*
105 *T11* **Altea** País Valenciano, E Spain *38°37´N 00°03´W*
100 *L10* **Alte Elde** ≋ N Germany
101 *M16* **Altenburg** Thüringen, E Germany *50°59´N 12°27´E*
Altenburg *see* Bucureşti, Romania
Altenburg *see* Baia de Criş, Romania
100 *P12* **Alte Oder** ≋ NE Germany
104 *H10* **Alter do Chão** Portalegre, C Portugal *39°12´N 07°40´W*
92 *I10* **Altevatnet** *Lapp.* Álttesjávri. ◎ N Norway
27 *V12* **Altheimer** Arkansas, C USA *34°19´N 91°51´W*
109 *T9* **Althofen** Kärnten, S Austria *46°52´N 14°27´E*
114 *H7* **Altimir** Vratsa, NW Bulgaria *43°33´N 23°48´E*
136 *K11* **Altınkaya Barajī** ▣ N Turkey
139 *S3* **Altin Köprü** *var.* Altun Kupri. At Ta'mīn, N Iraq *35°50´N 44°10´E*
136 *E13* **Altıntaş** Kütahya, W Turkey *39°05´N 30°07´E*
57 *K18* **Altiplano** *physical region* W South America
Altkanischa *see* Kanjiža
103 *U7* **Altkirch** Haut-Rhin, NE France *47°37´N 07°14´E*
Altlublau *see* Stará L'ubovňa
100 *L12* **Altmark** *cultural region* N Germany
Altmoldowa *see* Moldova Veche
25 *W8* **Alto** Texas, SW USA *31°39´N 95°04´W*
104 *H11* **Alto Alentejo** *physical region* S Portugal
59 *I19* **Alto Araguaia** Mato Grosso, C Brazil *17°19´S 53°10´W*
58 *L12* **Alto Bonito** Pará, NE Brazil *01°48´S 46°18´W*
83 *O15* **Alto Molócuè** Zambézia, NE Mozambique *15°38´S 37°42´E*
30 *K15* **Alton** Illinois, N USA *38°53´N 90°10´W*
27 *W8* **Alton** Missouri, C USA *36°41´N 91°25´W*
11 *X17* **Altona** Manitoba, S Canada *49°06´N 94°35´W*
18 *E14* **Altoona** Pennsylvania, NE USA *40°32´N 78°23´W*
30 *J6* **Altoona** Wisconsin, N USA *44°49´N 91°22´W*
62 *N3* **Alto Paraguay** *off.* Departamento del Alto Paraguay. ◈ *department* N Paraguay
Alto Paraguay, Departamento del *see* Alto Paraguay
59 *L17* **Alto Paraíso de Goiás** Goiás, S Brazil *14°04´S 47°15´W*
62 *P6* **Alto Paraná** *off.* Departamento del Alto Paraná. ◈ *department* E Paraguay
Alto Paraná *see* Paraná
Alto Paraná, Departamento del *see* Alto Paraná
59 *L15* **Alto Parnaíba** Maranhão, E Brazil *09°08´S 45°56´W*
56 *H13* **Alto Purús, Río** ≋ E Peru
Altorf *see* Altdorf
63 *H19* **Alto Río Senguer** *var.* Alto Río Senguerr. Chubut, S Argentina *45°01´S 70°55´W*
Alto Río Senguerr *see* Alto Río Senguer
41 *Q13* **Altotonga** Veracruz-Llave, E Mexico *19°46´N 97°14´W*
101 *N23* **Altötting** Bayern, SE Germany *48°12´N 12°37´E*
Altpasua *see* Stara Pazova
Altraga *see* Bayandzürh
105 *P3* **Altsasu** *Cast.* Alsasua. Navarra, N Spain *42°54´N 02°10´W*
Alt-Schwanenburg *see* Gulbene
Altsohl *see* Zvolen
108 *I7* **Altstätten** Sankt Gallen, NE Switzerland *47°22´N 09°33´E*
Álttesjávri *see* Altevatnet
42 *G1* **Altun Ha** *ruins* Belize, N Belize
Altun Kupri *see* Altin Köprü
158 *D8* **Altun Shan** ▲ C China *39°19´N 93°37´E*
158 *L9* **Altun Shan** *var.* Altyn Tagh. ▲▲ NW China
35 *P2* **Alturas** California, W USA *41°28´N 120°32´W*
26 *K12* **Altus** Oklahoma, C USA *34°39´N 99°21´W*
26 *K11* **Altus Lake** ▣ Oklahoma, C USA
Altvater *see* Praděd
Altyn Tagh *see* Altun Shan
Alu *see* Shortland Island
al-'Ubaila *see* Al 'Ubaylah
139 *O6* **Al 'Ubaydī** Al Anbār, W Iraq *34°22´N 41°15´E*
141 *T9* **Al 'Ubaylah** *var.* al-'Ubaila. Ash Sharqīyah, E Saudi Arabia *22°02´N 50°57´E*
141 *T9* **Al 'Ubaylah** *spring/well* E Saudi Arabia *22°02´N 50°56´E*
Al Ubayyiḑ *see* El Obeid
141 *T7* **Al 'Udayd** *var.* Al Odaid. Abū Z̧aby, W United Arab Emirates *24°34´N 51°27´E*
118 *J8* **Alūksne** *Ger.* Marienburg. Alūksne, NE Latvia *57°26´N 27°02´E*
140 *K6* **Al 'Ulā** Al Madīnah, NW Saudi Arabia *26°39´N 37°55´E*
173 *N4* **Alula-Fartak Trench** *var.* Illaue Fartak Trench. *undersea feature* W Indian Ocean *14°04´N 51°47´E*
138 *I11* **Al 'Umarī** 'Ammān, E Jordan *37°30´N 31°30´E*
31 *S13* **Alum Creek Lake** ▣ Ohio, N USA
63 *H15* **Aluminé** Neuquén, C Argentina *39°15´S 71°00´W*
95 *O14* **Alunda** Uppsala, C Sweden *60°04´N 18°04´E*
117 *T14* **Alupka** Respublika Krym, S Ukraine *44°24´N 34°01´E*
75 *P8* **Al 'Uqaylah** N Libya *30°13´N 19°12´E*
Al Uqşur *see* Luxor
Al Urdunn *see* Jordan
168 *J9* **Alur Panal** *bay* Sumatera, W Indonesia
Alur Setar *see* Alor Setar
141 *V10* **Al 'Urūq al Mu'tariḑah** *salt lake* SE Saudi Arabia
139 *Q7* **Ālūs** Al Anbār, C Iraq *34°05´N 42°27´E*
117 *T13* **Alushta** Respublika Krym, S Ukraine *44°41´N 34°24´E*
151 *G22* **Aluva** *var.* Alwaye. Kerala, SW India *10°06´N 76°23´E* *see also* Alwaye
75 *N11* **Al 'Uwaynāt** *var.* Al Awaynāt. SW Libya *25°47´N 10°34´E*
139 *T6* **Al 'Uẓaym** *var.* Adhaim. Diyālá, E Iraq *34°12´N 44°31´E*
26 *L8* **Alva** Oklahoma, C USA *36°48´N 98°40´W*
104 *H8* **Alva** ≋ N Portugal
95 *J18* **Älvängen** Västra Götaland, S Sweden *57°56´N 12°09´E*
14 *F14* **Alvanley** Ontario, S Canada *44°33´N 81°05´W*
41 *S14* **Alvarado** Veracruz-Llave, E Mexico *18°47´N 95°45´W*
25 *T7* **Alvarado** Texas, SW USA *32°24´N 97°12´W*
58 *D13* **Alvarães** Amazonas, NW Brazil *03°13´S 64°53´W*
40 *G6* **Alvaro Obregón, Presa** ▣ W Mexico
94 *H10* **Alvdal** Hedmark, S Norway *62°07´N 10°39´E*
94 *K12* **Älvdalen** Dalarna, C Sweden *61°13´N 14°04´E*
61 *E15* **Alvear** Corrientes, NE Argentina *29°05´S 56°35´W*
104 *F10* **Alverca do Ribatejo** Lisboa, C Portugal *38°56´N 09°01´W*
95 *L20* **Alvesta** Kronoberg, S Sweden *56°52´N 14°34´E*
25 *W12* **Alvin** Texas, SW USA *29°25´N 95°14´W*
94 *O13* **Älvkarleby** Uppsala, C Sweden *60°34´N 17°30´E*
25 *S5* **Alvord** Texas, SW USA *33°22´N 97°39´W*
93 *G18* **Älvros** Jämtland, C Sweden *62°04´N 14°30´E*
92 *J13* **Älvsbyn** Norrbotten, N Sweden *65°41´N 21°00´E*
142 *K12* **Al Wafrā'** SE Kuwait *28°38´N 47°57´E*
140 *J6* **Al Wajh** Tabūk, NW Saudi Arabia *26°16´N 36°30´E*
143 *N16* **Al Wakrah** *var.* Wakra. C Qatar *25°09´N 51°36´E*
138 *M8* **al Walaj, Sha'īb** *dry watercourse* W Iraq
152 *I11* **Alwar** Rājasthān, N India *27°32´N 76°35´E*
141 *Q5* **Al Warī'ah** Ash Sharqīyah, N Saudi Arabia *27°54´N 47°23´E*
155 *G22* **Alwaye** *var.* Aluva. Kerala, SW India *10°06´N 76°23´E* *see also* Aluva
Alxa Zuoqi *see* Bayan Hot
Alx Youqi *see* Ehen Hudag
Al Yaman *see* Yemen
138 *G9* **Al Yarmūk** Irbid, N Jordan *32°41´N 35°55´E*
Alyat/Alyaty-Pristan' *see* Älät
115 *I14* **Alykí** *var.* Aliki. Thásos, N Greece *40°36´N 24°45´E*
119 *F14* **Alytus** *Pol.* Olita. Alytus, S Lithuania *54°24´N 24°02´E*
119 *F15* **Alytus** ◈ *province* S Lithuania
101 *N23* **Alz** ≋ SE Germany
33 *Y11* **Alzada** Montana, NW USA *45°00´N 104°24´W*
122 *L12* **Alzamay** Irkutskaya Oblast', S Russian Federation *55°33´N 98°36´E*
99 *M25* **Alzette** ≋ S Luxembourg
105 *S10* **Alzira** *var.* Alcira ; *anc.* Saetabicula, Suero. País Valenciano, E Spain *39°10´N 00°27´W*
Al Zubair *see* Az Zubayr
181 *O8* **Amadeus, Lake** *seasonal lake* Northern Territory, C Australia
81 *E15* **Amadi** Western Equatoria, SW Sudan *05°32´N 30°20´E*
9 *R7* **Amadjuak Lake** ◎ Baffin Island, Nunavut, N Canada
95 *J23* **Amager** *island* E Denmark
165 *N14* **Amagi-san** ▲ Honshū, S Japan *34°51´N 138°57´E*
171 *S13* **Amahai** *var.* Masohi. Palau Seram, E Indonesia *03°19´S 128°56´E*
38 *M16* **Amak Island** *island* Alaska, USA
164 *B14* **Amakusa-nada** *gulf* SW Japan
95 *J16* **Åmål** Västra Götaland, S Sweden *59°04´N 12°41´E*
54 *E8* **Amalfi** Antioquia, N Colombia *06°54´N 75°04´W*
107 *L18* **Amalfi** Campania, S Italy *40°37´N 14°35´E*
115 *D19* **Amaliáda** *var.* Amaliás. Dytikí Ellás, S Greece *37°48´N 21°21´E*
Amaliás *see* Amaliáda
154 *F12* **Amalner** Mahārāshtra, C India *21°03´N 75°04´E*
171 *W14* **Amamapare** Papua, E Indonesia *04°51´S 136°44´E*
59 *H21* **Amambaí, Serra de** *var.* Cordillera de Amambay, Serra de Amambay. ▲ Brazil/Paraguay *see also* Amambay, Cordillera de
62 *P4* **Amambay** *off.* Departamento del Amambay. ◈ *department* E Paraguay
62 *P5* **Amambay, Cordillera de** *var.* Serra de Amambaí, Serra de Amambay. ▲ Brazil/Paraguay *see also* Amambaí, Serra de
Amambay, Departamento del *see* Amambay
Amambay, Serra de *see* Amambaí, Serra de/Amambay, Cordillera de
165 *U16* **Amami-guntō** *island group* SW Japan
165 *V15* **Amami-Ō-shima** *island* S Japan
186 *A5* **Amanab** Sandaun, NW Papua New Guinea *03°38´S 141°16´E*
106 *J13* **Amandola** Marche, C Italy *42°58´N 13°22´E*
107 *N21* **Amantea** Calabria, SW Italy *39°06´N 16°05´E*
191 *W10* **Amanu** *island* Îles Tuamotu, C French Polynesia
58 *J10* **Amapá** Amapá, NE Brazil *02°00´N 50°50´W*
58 *J11* **Amapá** *off.* Estado de Amapá; *prev.* Território de Amapá. ◈ *state* NE Brazil
Amapá, Estado de *see* Amapá
42 *H8* **Amapala** Valle, S Honduras *13°16´N 87°39´W*
Amapá, Território de *see* Amapá
80 *J12* **Āmara** ◈ *federal region* N Ethiopia
Amara *see* Al 'Amārah
104 *H6* **Amarante** Porto, N Portugal *41°16´N 08°05´W*
166 *M5* **Amarapura** Mandalay, C Burma (Myanmar) *21°54´N 96°01´E*
Amardalay *see* Delgertsogt
104 *I12* **Amareleja** Beja, S Portugal *38°12´N 07°13´W*
35 *V11* **Amargosa Range** ▲▲ California, W USA
25 *N2* **Amarillo** Texas, SW USA *35°13´N 101°50´W*
Amarinthos *see* Amárynthos
107 *K15* **Amaro, Monte** ▲ C Italy *42°03´N 14°06´E*
115 *H18* **Amárynthos** *var.* Amarinthos. Évvoia, C Greece *38°24´N 23°53´E*
Amasia *see* Amasya
136 *K12* **Amasya** *anc.* Amasia. Amasya, N Turkey *40°37´N 35°50´E*
136 *K11* **Amasya** ◈ *province* N Turkey
42 *F4* **Amatique, Bahía de** *bay* Gulf of Honduras, W Caribbean Sea
42 *D6* **Amatitlán, Lago de** ◎ S Guatemala
107 *J14* **Amatrice** Lazio, C Italy *42°38´N 13°19´E*
190 *C8* **Amatuku** *atoll* C Tuvalu
99 *J20* **Amay** Liège, E Belgium *50°33´N 05°19´E*
48 *F7* **Amazon** *Sp.* Amazonas. ≋ Brazil/Peru
59 *C14* **Amazonas** *off.* Estado do Amazonas. ◈ *state* N Brazil
54 *G15* **Amazonas** *off.* Comisaria del Amazonas. ◈ *province* SE Colombia
56 *C10* **Amazonas** *off.* Departamento de Amazonas. ◈ *department* N Peru
54 *M12* **Amazonas** *off.* Territorio Amazonas. ◈ *federal territory* S Venezuela
Amazonas *see* Amazon
Amazonas, Comisaria del *see* Amazonas
Amazonas, Departamento de *see* Amazonas
Amazonas, Estado do *see* Amazonas
Amazonas, Territorio *see* Amazonas
48 *F7* **Amazon Basin** *basin* N South America
47 *V5* **Amazon Fan** *undersea feature* W Atlantic Ocean *05°00´N 47°30´W*
58 *K11* **Amazon, Mouths of the** *delta* NE Brazil
187 *R13* **Ambae** *var.* Aoba, Omba. *island* C Vanuatu
152 *I9* **Ambāla** Haryāna, NW India *30°19´N 76°49´E*
155 *J26* **Ambalangoda** Southern Province, SW Sri Lanka *06°14´N 80°03´E*
155 *K26* **Ambalantota** Southern Province, S Sri Lanka *06°07´N 81°01´E*
172 *I6* **Ambalavao** Fianarantsoa, C Madagascar *21°50´S 46°56´E*
54 *E10* **Ambalema** Tolima, C Colombia *04°49´N 74°48´W*
79 *E17* **Ambam** Sud, S Cameroon *02°23´N 11°17´E*
172 *J2* **Ambanja** Antsirañana, N Madagascar *13°40´S 48°27´E*
123 *T6* **Ambarchik** Respublika Sakha (Yakutiya), NE Russian Federation *69°33´N 162°08´E*
62 *K9* **Ambargasta, Salinas de** *salt lake* C Argentina
124 *J6* **Ambarnyy** Respublika Kareliya, NW Russian Federation *65°53´N 33°44´E*
56 *C7* **Ambato** Tungurahua, C Ecuador *01°18´S 78°39´W*
172 *I6* **Ambatofinandrahana** Fianarantsoa, SE Madagascar
172 *I5* **Ambatolampy** Antananarivo, C Madagascar *19°21´S 47°27´E*
172 *H4* **Ambatomainty** Mahajanga, W Madagascar *17°40´S 45°39´E*
172 *J4* **Ambatondrazaka** Toamasina, C Madagascar *17°49´S 48°28´E*
101 *L20* **Amberg** *var.* Amberg in der Oberpfalz. Bayern, SE Germany *49°26´N 11°52´E*
Amberg in der Oberpfalz *see* Amberg
42 *H1* **Ambergris Cay** *island* NE Belize
103 *S11* **Ambérieu-en-Bugey** Ain, E France *45°57´N 05°21´E*
185 *I18* **Amberley** Canterbury, South Island, New Zealand *43°09´S 172°43´E*
103 *P11* **Ambert** Puy-de-Dôme, C France *45°33´N 03°45´E*
Ambianum *see* Amiens
76 *J11* **Ambidédi** Kayes, SW Mali *14°37´N 11°49´W*
154 *M10* **Ambikāpur** Chhattīsgarh, C India *23°09´N 83°12´E*
172 *J2* **Ambilobe** Antsirañana, N Madagascar *13°10´S 49°03´E*
39 *O7* **Ambler** Alaska, USA *67°05´N 157°51´W*
Amblève *see* Amel
Ambo *see* Hāgere Hiywet
172 *I8* **Amboasary** Toliara, S Madagascar *25°01´S 46°23´E*
172 *J4* **Ambodifotatra** *var.* Ambodifototra. Toamasina, E Madagascar *16°59´S 49°51´E*
Amboenten *see* Ambunten
172 *I5* **Ambohidratrimo** Antananarivo, C Madagascar *18°48´S 47°26´E*
172 *I6* **Ambohimahasoa** Fianarantsoa, SE Madagascar *21°07´S 47°13´E*
172 *K3* **Ambohitralanana** Antsirañana, NE Madagascar *15°13´S 50°28´E*
Amboina *see* Ambon
102 *M8* **Amboise** Indre-et-Loire, C France *47°25´N 01°00´E*
171 *S13* **Ambon** *prev.* Amboina, Amboyna. Pulau Ambon, E Indonesia *03°41´S 128°10´E*
171 *S13* **Ambon, Pulau** *island* E Indonesia
81 *I20* **Amboseli, Lake** ◎ Kenya/Tanzania
172 *I6* **Ambositra** Fianarantsoa, SE Madagascar *20°31´S 47°15´E*
172 *I8* **Ambovombe** Toliara, S Madagascar *25°10´S 46°06´E*
35 *W14* **Amboy** California, W USA *34°33´N 115°44´W*
30 *L11* **Amboy** Illinois, N USA *41°42´N 89°19´W*
Amboyna *see* Ambon
Ambracia *see* Árta
Ambre, Cap d' *see* Bobaomby, Tanjona
18 *B14* **Ambridge** Pennsylvania, NE USA *40°33´N 80°11´W*
Ambrim *see* Ambrym
82 *A11* **Ambriz** Bengo, NW Angola *07°55´S 13°11´E*
Ambrizete *see* N'Zeto
187 *R13* **Ambrym** *var.* Ambrim. *island* C Vanuatu
169 *T16* **Ambunten** *prev.* Amboenten. Pulau Madura, E Indonesia *06°55´S 113°45´E*
186 *B6* **Ambunti** East Sepik, NW Papua New Guinea *04°12´S 142°49´E*
155 *I20* **Āmbūr** Tamil Nādu, SE India *12°48´N 78°44´E*
38 *E17* **Amchitka Island** *island* Aleutian Islands, Alaska, USA
38 *F17* **Amchitka Pass** *strait* Aleutian Islands, Alaska, USA
141 *R15* **'Amd** C Yemen *15°10´N 47°58´E*
78 *J10* **Am Dam** Ouaddaï, E Chad *12°46´N 20°29´E*
171 *U16* **Amdassa** Pulau Yamdena, E Indonesia *07°40´S 131°24´E*
125 *U1* **Amderma** Nenetskiy Avtonomnyy Okrug, NW Russian Federation *69°45´N 61°36´E*
159 *N14* **Amdo** Xizang Zizhiqu, W China *32°15´N 91°43´E*
40 *K13* **Ameca** Jalisco, SW Mexico *20°34´N 104°03´W*
41 *P14* **Amecameca** *var.* Amecameca de Juárez. México, C Mexico *19°08´N 98°48´W*
Amecameca de Juárez *see* Amecameca
61 *A20* **Ameghino** Buenos Aires, E Argentina *34°51´S 62°28´W*
99 *M21* **Amel** *Fr.* Amblève. Liège, E Belgium *50°20´N 06°13´E*
98 *K4* **Ameland** *Fris.* It Amelân. *island* Waddeneilanden, N Netherlands
Amelân, It *see* Ameland
107 *H14* **Amelia** Umbria, C Italy *42°33´N 12°26´E*
21 *V6* **Amelia Court House** Virginia, NE USA *37°20´N 77°59´W*
23 *W8* **Amelia Island** *island* Florida, SE USA
18 *L12* **Amenia** New York, NE USA *41°51´N 73°31´W*
America *see* United States of America
65 *M21* **America-Antarctica Ridge** *undersea feature* S Atlantic Ocean
America in Miniature *see* Maryland
60 *L9* **Americana** São Paulo, S Brazil *22°44´S 47°19´W*
33 *Q15* **American Falls** Idaho, NW USA *42°47´N 112°51´W*
33 *Q15* **American Falls Reservoir** ▣ Idaho, NW USA
36 *L3* **American Fork** Utah, W USA *40°24´N 111°47´W*
192 *K16* **American Samoa** ◇ *US unincorporated territory* W Polynesia
23 *S6* **Americus** Georgia, SE USA *32°04´N 84°13´W*
98 *K12* **Amerongen** Utrecht, C Netherlands *52°00´N 05°30´E*
98 *K11* **Amersfoort** Utrecht, C Netherlands *52°09´N 05°23´E*
97 *N21* **Amersham** SE England, United Kingdom *51°40´N 00°37´W*
30 *I5* **Amery** Wisconsin, N USA *45°18´N 92°20´W*
195 *W6* **Amery Ice Shelf** *ice shelf* Antarctica
29 *V13* **Ames** Iowa, C USA *42°01´N 93°37´W*
19 *P10* **Amesbury** Massachusetts, NE USA *42°51´N 70°55´W*
Amestratus *see* Mistretta
115 *F18* **Amfíkleia** *var.* Amfíklia. Stereá Ellás, C Greece *38°38´N 22°35´E*
Amfíklia *see* Amfíkleia
115 *D17* **Amfilochía** *var.* Amfilokhía. Dytikí Ellás, C Greece *38°52´N 21°09´E*
Amfilokhía *see* Amfilochía
114 *H13* **Amfípoli** *anc.* Amphipolis. *site of ancient city* Kentrikí Makedonía, NE Greece
115 *F18* **Ámfissa** Stereá Ellás, C Greece *38°32´N 22°22´E*
123 *Q10* **Amga** Respublika Sakha (Yakutiya), NE Russian Federation *60°55´N 131°45´E*
123 *Q11* **Amga** ≋ NE Russian Federation
163 *R7* **Amgalang** *var.* Xin Barag Zuoqi. Nei Mongol Zizhiqu, N China *48°12´N 118°15´E*
123 *V5* **Amguema** ≋ NE Russian Federation
123 *S12* **Amgun'** ≋ SE Russian Federation
13 *P15* **Amherst** Nova Scotia, SE Canada *45°50´N 64°14´W*
18 *M11* **Amherst** Massachusetts, NE USA *42°22´N 72°31´W*
18 *D10* **Amherst** New York, NE USA *42°57´N 78°47´W*
24 *M4* **Amherst** Texas, SW USA *33°59´N 102°24´W*
21 *U6* **Amherst** Virginia, NE USA *37°35´N 79°04´W*
Amherst *see* Kyaikkami
14 *C18* **Amherstburg** Ontario, S Canada *42°05´N 83°06´W*
21 *Q6* **Amherstdale** West Virginia, NE USA *37°46´N 81°46´W*
14 *K15* **Amherst Island** *island* Ontario, SE Canada
Amida *see* Diyarbakır
28 *J6* **Amidon** North Dakota, N USA *46°29´N 103°19´W*
103 *O3* **Amiens** *anc.* Ambianum, Samarobriva. Somme, N France *49°54´N 02°18´E*
139 *P8* **'Āmij, Wādī** *var.* Wadi 'Amīq. *dry watercourse* W Iraq
136 *L17* **Amik Ovasī** ◎ S Turkey
76 *E9* **Amilcar Cabral** ✈ Sal, NE Cape Verde
Amilḩayt, Wādī *see* Umm al Ḩayt, Wādī
Amíndaion/Amindeo *see* Amýntaio
155 *C21* **Amīndīvi Islands** *island group* Lakshadweep, India, N Indian Ocean
139 *U6* **Amīn Ḩabīb** Diyālá, E Iraq *34°17´N 45°10´E*
83 *E20* **Aminuis** Omaheke, E Namibia *23°43´S 19°21´E*
'Amīq, Wadi *see* 'Āmij, Wādī
142 *J7* **Amīrābād** Īlām, NW Iran *33°20´N 46°16´E*
Amirante Bank *see* Amirante Ridge
173 *N6* **Amirante Basin** *undersea feature* W Indian Ocean *07°00´S 54°00´E*
173 *N6* **Amirante Islands** *var.* Amirantes Group. *island group* C Seychelles
173 *N7* **Amirante Ridge** *var.* Amirante Bank. *undersea feature* W Indian Ocean *06°00´S 53°10´E*
Amirantes Group *see* Amirante Islands
173 *N7* **Amirante Trench** *undersea feature* W Indian Ocean *08°00´S 52°30´E*
11 *U13* **Amisk Lake** ◎ Saskatchewan, C Canada
Amistad, Presa de la *see* Amistad Reservoir
25 *O12* **Amistad Reservoir** *var.* Presa de la Amistad. ▣ Mexico/USA
Amisus *see* Samsun
22 *K8* **Amite** *var.* Amite City. Louisiana, S USA *30°40´N 90°30´W*
Amite City *see* Amite
27 *T12* **Amity** Arkansas, C USA *34°15´N 93°27´W*
154 *H11* **Amla** *prev.* Amulla. Madhya Pradesh, C India *21°53´N 78°10´E*
38 *I17* **Amlia Island** *island* Aleutian Islands, Alaska, USA
97 *I18* **Amlwch** NW Wales, United Kingdom *53°25´N 04°23´W*
Ammaia *see* Portalegre
138 *H10* **'Ammān** *var.* Amman; *anc.* Philadelphia, *Bibl.* Rabbah Ammon, Rabbath Ammon. ● (Jordan) 'Ammān, NW Jordan *31°57´N 35°56´E*
138 *H10* **'Ammān** *off.* Muḩāfaẓat 'Ammān; *prev.* Al 'Aşimah. ◈ *governorate* NW Jordan
'Ammān, Muḩāfaẓat *see* 'Ammān
93 *N14* **Ämmänsaari** Oulu, E Finland *64°51´N 28°58´E*

◆ Country
● Country Capital
◇ Dependent Territory
○ Dependent Territory Capital
◈ Administrative Regions
✈ International Airport
▲ Mountain
▲▲ Mountain Range
Volcano
≋ River
◎ Lake
▣ Reservoir

92 H13 **Ammarnäs** Västerbotten, N Sweden 65°58′N 16°10′E
197 O15 **Ammassalik** *var.* Angmagssalik. Tunu, S Greenland 65°51′N 37°30′W
101 K24 **Ammer** ∾ SE Germany
101 K24 **Ammersee** ◎ SE Germany
98 J13 **Ammerzoden** Gelderland, C Netherlands 51°46′N 05°07′E
Ammóchostos *see* Gazimağusa
Ammóchostos, Kólpos *see* Gazimağusa Körfezi
Amnok-kang *see* Yalu
Amoea *see* Portalegre
Amoentai *see* Amuntai
Amoerang *see* Amurang
143 O4 **Āmol** *var.* Amul. Māzandarān, N Iran 36°31′N 52°24′E
115 K21 **Amorgós** Amorgós, Kykládes, Greece, Aegean Sea 36°49′N 25°54′E
115 K22 **Amorgós** *island* Kykládes, Greece, Aegean Sea
23 N3 **Amory** Mississippi, S USA 33°58′N 88°29′W
12 I13 **Amos** Québec, SE Canada 48°34′N 78°08′W
95 G15 **Åmot** Buskerud, S Norway 59°52′N 09°55′E
95 E15 **Åmot** Telemark, S Norway 59°34′N 07°59′E
95 J15 **Åmotfors** Värmland, C Sweden 59°46′N 12°24′E
76 L10 **Amourj** Hodh ech Chargui, SE Mauritania 16°04′N 07°12′W
Amoy *see* Xiamen
172 H7 **Ampanihy** Toliara, SW Madagascar 24°40′S 44°45′E
155 L25 **Ampara** *var.* Amparai. Eastern Province, E Sri Lanka 07°17′N 81°41′E
172 J4 **Amparafaravola** Toamasina, E Madagascar 17°33′S 48°13′E
Amparai *see* Ampara
60 M9 **Amparo** São Paulo, S Brazil 22°40′S 46°49′W
172 J5 **Ampasimanolotra** Toamasina, E Madagascar 18°49′S 49°04′E
57 H17 **Ampato, Nevado** ▲ S Peru 15°52′S 71°51′W
101 L23 **Amper** ∾ SE Germany
64 M9 **Ampère Seamount** *undersea feature* E Atlantic Ocean 35°05′N 13°00′W
Amphipolis *see* Amfípoli
167 X10 **Amphitrite Group** *island group* N Paracel Islands
171 T16 **Amplawas** *var.* Emplawas. Pulau Babar, E Indonesia 08°01′S 129°42′E
105 U7 **Amposta** Cataluña, NE Spain 40°43′N 00°34′E
15 V7 **Amqui** Québec, SE Canada 48°28′N 67°27′W
141 O14 **'Amrān** W Yemen 15°39′N 43°59′E
Amraoti *see* Amrāvati
154 H12 **Amrāvati** *prev.* Amraoti. Mahārāshtra, C India 20°56′N 77°45′E
154 C11 **Amreli** Gujarāt, W India 21°36′N 71°20′E
108 H6 **Amriswil** Thurgau, NE Switzerland 47°33′N 09°18′E
138 H5 **'Amrīt** *ruins* Tarṭūs, W Syria
152 H7 **Amritsar** Punjab, N India 31°38′N 74°55′E
152 J10 **Amroha** Uttar Pradesh, N India 28°54′N 78°29′E
100 G7 **Amrum** *island* NW Germany
93 I15 **Åmsele** Västerbotten, N Sweden 64°31′N 19°24′E
98 I10 **Amstelveen** Noord-Holland, C Netherlands 52°18′N 04°50′E
98 I10 **Amsterdam** ● (Netherlands) Noord-Holland, C Netherlands 52°22′N 04°54′E
18 K10 **Amsterdam** New York, NE USA 42°56′N 74°11′W
173 Q11 **Amsterdam Fracture Zone** *tectonic feature* S Indian Ocean
173 R11 **Amsterdam Island** *island* NE French Southern and Antarctic Territories
109 U4 **Amstetten** Niederösterreich, N Austria 48°08′N 14°52′E
78 J11 **Am Timan** Salamat, SE Chad 11°02′N 20°17′E
146 L12 **Amu-Buxoro Kanali** *var.* Aral-Bukhorskiy Kanal. *canal* C Uzbekistan
139 O1 **'Āmūdah** *var.* Amude. Al Ḥasakah, N Syria 37°06′N 40°56′E
147 O15 **Amu Darya** *Rus.* Amudar'ya, *Taj.* Dar"yoi Amu, *Turkm.* Amyderya, *Uzb.* Amudaryo; *anc.* Oxus. ∾ C Asia
Amu-Dar'ya *see* Amyderya
Amudar'ya/Amudaryo/Amu, Dar"yoi *see* Amu Darya
Amude *see* 'Āmūdah
140 L3 **'Amūd, Jabal al** ▲ NW Saudi Arabia 30°59′N 39°17′E
38 J17 **Amukta Island** *island* Aleutian Islands, Alaska, USA
38 I17 **Amukta Pass** *strait* Aleutian Islands, Alaska, USA
Amul *see* Āmol
Amulla *see* Amla
Amundsen Basin *see* Fram Basin
195 X3 **Amundsen Bay** *bay* Antarctica
195 P10 **Amundsen Coast** *physical region* Antarctica
193 O14 **Amundsen Plain** *undersea feature* S Pacific Ocean
195 Q9 **Amundsen-Scott** *US research station* Antarctica 89°59′S 10°00′E
194 J11 **Amundsen Sea** *sea* S Pacific Ocean
94 M12 **Amungen** ◎ C Sweden
169 U13 **Amuntai** *prev.* Amoentai. Borneo, C Indonesia 02°24′S 115°14′E
129 W6 **Amur** *Chin.* Heilong Jiang. ∾ China/Russian Federation
171 Q11 **Amurang** *prev.* Amoerang. Sulawesi, C Indonesia 01°12′N 124°37′E
105 O3 **Amurrio** País Vasco, N Spain 43°03′N 03°00′W
123 S13 **Amursk** Khabarovskiy Kray, SE Russian Federation 50°13′N 136°34′E
123 Q12 **Amurskaya Oblast'** ◆ *province* SE Russian Federation
80 G7 **'Amur, Wadi** ∾ NE Sudan
115 C17 **Amvrakikós Kólpos** *gulf* W Greece
Amvrosiyevka *see* Amvrosiyivka
117 X8 **Amvrosiyivka** *Rus.* Amvrosiyevka. Donets'ka Oblast', SE Ukraine 47°46′N 38°30′E
146 M14 **Amyderýa** *Rus.* Amu-Dar'ya. Lebap Welaýaty, NE Turkmenistan 37°58′N 65°14′E
Amyderya *see* Amu Darya
114 E13 **Amýntaio** *var.* Amindeo; *prev.* Amíndaion. Dytikí Makedonía, N Greece 40°42′N 21°42′E
14 B6 **Amyot** Ontario, S Canada 48°28′N 84°58′W
191 U10 **Anaa** *atoll* Îles Tuamotu, C French Polynesia
Anabanoea *see* Anabanua
171 N14 **Anabanua** *prev.* Anabanoea. Sulawesi, C Indonesia 03°58′S 120°07′E
189 R8 **Anabar** NE Nauru 0°30′S 166°56′E
123 N8 **Anabar** ∾ NE Russian Federation
An Abhainn Mhór *see* Blackwater
55 O6 **Anaco** Anzoátegui, NE Venezuela 09°30′N 64°28′W
33 Q10 **Anaconda** Montana, NW USA 46°09′N 112°56′W
32 H7 **Anacortes** Washington, NW USA 48°30′N 122°36′W
26 M11 **Anadarko** Oklahoma, C USA 35°04′N 98°16′W
114 N12 **Ana Dere** ∾ NW Turkey
104 G8 **Anadia** Aveiro, N Portugal 40°26′N 08°27′W
Anadolu Dağları *see* Doğu Karadeniz Dağları
123 V6 **Anadyr'** Chukotskiy Avtonomnyy Okrug, NE Russian Federation 64°41′N 177°22′E
123 V6 **Anadyr'** ∾ NE Russian Federation
Anadyr, Gulf of *see* Anadyrskiy Zaliv
129 X4 **Anadyrskiy Khrebet** *var.* Chukot Range. ▲▲ NE Russian Federation
123 W6 **Anadyrskiy Zaliv** *Eng.* Gulf of Anadyr. *gulf* NE Russian Federation
115 K22 **Anáfi** *anc.* Anaphe. *island* Kykládes, Greece, Aegean Sea
107 J15 **Anagni** Lazio, C Italy 41°43′N 13°12′E
'Ānah *see* 'Annah
35 T15 **Anaheim** California, W USA 33°50′N 117°54′W
10 L15 **Anahim Lake** British Columbia, SW Canada 52°26′N 125°13′W
38 B8 **Anahola** Kaua'i, Hawai'i, USA, C Pacific Ocean 22°09′N 159°19′W
41 O7 **Anáhuac** Nuevo León, NE Mexico 27°13′N 100°09′W
25 X11 **Anahuac** Texas, SW USA 29°44′N 94°41′W
155 G22 **Anai Mudi** ▲ S India 10°16′N 77°08′E
Anaiza *see* 'Unayzah
155 M15 **Anakāpalle** Andhra Pradesh, E India 17°42′N 83°06′E
191 W15 **Anakena, Playa de** *beach* Easter Island, Chile, E Pacific Ocean
39 Q7 **Anaktuvuk Pass** Alaska, USA 68°08′N 151°44′W
39 Q6 **Anaktuvuk River** ∾ Alaska, USA
172 J3 **Analalava** Mahajanga, NW Madagascar 14°38′S 47°46′E
44 F6 **Ana María, Golfo de** *gulf* N Caribbean Sea
Anambas Islands *see* Anambas, Kepulauan
169 N8 **Anambas, Kepulauan** *var.* Anambas Islands. *island group* W Indonesia
77 U17 **Anambra** ◆ *state* SE Nigeria
29 N4 **Anamoose** North Dakota, N USA 47°50′N 100°14′W
29 Y13 **Anamosa** Iowa, C USA 42°06′N 91°17′W
136 H17 **Anamur** İçel, S Turkey 36°06′N 32°49′E
136 H17 **Anamur Burnu** *headland* S Turkey 36°03′N 32°49′E
154 D11 **Ānand** Gujarāt, India 22°34′N 73°01′E
154 O12 **Anandadur** Orissa, E India 21°14′N 86°10′E
155 H18 **Anantapur** Andhra Pradesh, S India 14°41′N 77°36′E
152 H5 **Anantnāg** *var.* Islamabad. Jammu and Kashmir, NW India 33°44′N 75°11′E
Ananyev *see* Anan'yiv
117 O9 **Anan'yiv** *Rus.* Ananyev. Odes'ka Oblast', SW Ukraine 47°43′N 29°51′E
126 J14 **Anapa** Krasnodarskiy Kray, SW Russian Federation 44°55′N 37°20′E
Anaphe *see* Anáfi
59 K18 **Anápolis** Goiás, C Brazil 16°19′S 48°58′W
143 R10 **Anār** Kermān, C Iran 30°49′N 55°18′E
Anār *see* Inari
143 P7 **Anārak** Eşfahān, C Iran 33°21′N 53°43′E
Anar Dara *see* Anār Darreh
148 J7 **Anār Darreh** *var.* Anar Dara. Farāh, W Afghanistan 32°45′N 61°38′E
Anárjohka *see* Inarijoki
23 X9 **Anastasia Island** *island* Florida, SE USA
188 K7 **Anatahan** *island* C Northern Mariana Islands
136 H13 **Anatolia** *plateau* C Turkey
86 F14 **Anatolian Plate** *tectonic feature* Asia/Europe
114 H13 **Anatolikí Makedonía kai Thráki** *Eng.* Macedonia East and Thrace. ◆ *region* NE Greece
Anatom *see* Aneityum
62 L8 **Añatuya** Santiago del Estero, N Argentina 28°28′S 62°52′W
An Baile Meánach *see* Ballymena
An Bhearú *see* Barrow
An Bhóinn *see* Boyne
An Blascaod Mór *see* Great Blasket Island
An Cabhán *see* Cavan
An Caisleán Nua *see* Newcastle
An Caisleán Riabhach *see* Castlerea, Ireland
An Caisleán Riabhach *see* Castlereagh
56 C13 **Ancash** *off.* Departamento de Ancash. ◆ *department* W Peru
Ancash, Departamento de *see* Ancash
An Cathair *see* Caher
102 J8 **Ancenis** Loire-Atlantique, NW France 47°23′N 01°10′W
An Chanáil Ríoga *see* Royal Canal
An Cheacha *see* Caha Mountains
39 R11 **Anchorage** Alaska, USA 61°13′N 149°52′W
39 R12 **Anchorage** ✈ Alaska, USA 61°08′N 150°00′W
39 Q13 **Anchor Point** Alaska, USA 59°46′N 151°49′W
An Chorr Chríochach *see* Cookstown
65 M24 **Anchorstock Point** *headland* W Tristan da Cunha 37°07′S 12°21′W
An Clár *see* Clare
An Clochán *see* Clifden
An Clochán Liath *see* Dunglow
23 U12 **Anclote Keys** *island group* Florida, SE USA
An Cóbh *see* Cobh
57 J17 **Ancohuma, Nevado de** ▲ W Bolivia 15°51′S 68°33′W
An Comar *see* Comber
57 D14 **Ancón** Lima, W Peru 11°45′S 77°08′W
106 J12 **Ancona** Marche, C Italy 43°38′N 13°30′E
Ancuabe *see* Ancuabi
82 Q13 **Ancuabi** *var.* Ancuabe. Cabo Delgado, NE Mozambique 13°00′S 39°50′E
63 F17 **Ancud** *prev.* San Carlos de Ancud. Los Lagos, S Chile 41°53′S 73°50′W
63 G17 **Ancud, Golfo de** *gulf* S Chile
Ancyra *see* Ankara
163 V8 **Anda** Heilongjiang, NE China 46°25′N 125°20′E
57 G16 **Andahuaylas** Apurímac, S Peru 13°39′S 73°24′W
An Daingean *see* Dingle
153 R15 **Andāl** West Bengal, NE India 23°35′N 87°14′E
94 E9 **Åndalsnes** Møre og Romsdal, S Norway 62°33′N 07°42′E
104 K13 **Andalucía** *Eng.* Andalusia. ◆ *autonomous community* S Spain
23 P7 **Andalusia** Alabama, S USA 31°18′N 86°29′W
Andalusia *see* Andalucía
151 Q21 **Andaman and Nicobar Islands** *var.* Andamans and Nicobars. ◆ *union territory* India, NE Indian Ocean
173 T4 **Andaman Basin** *undersea feature* NE Indian Ocean 10°00′N 94°00′E
151 P19 **Andaman Islands** *island group* India, NE Indian Ocean
Andamans and Nicobars *see* Andaman and Nicobar Islands
173 T4 **Andaman Sea** *sea* NE Indian Ocean
57 K19 **Andamarca** Oruro, C Bolivia 18°46′S 67°31′W
182 H5 **Andamooka** South Australia 30°26′S 137°12′E
141 Y9 **'Andām, Wādī** *seasonal river* NE Oman
172 J3 **Andapa** Antsirañana, NE Madagascar 14°39′S 49°40′E
149 R4 **Andarāb** *var.* Banow. Baghlān, NE Afghanistan 35°36′N 69°18′E
Andarbag *see* Andarbogh
147 S13 **Andarbogh** *Rus.* Andarbag, Anderbak. S Tajikistan 37°51′N 71°45′E
109 Z5 **Andau** Burgenland, E Austria 47°47′N 17°02′E
108 I10 **Andeer** Graubünden, S Switzerland 46°36′N 09°24′E
92 H9 **Andenes** Nordland, C Norway 69°18′N 16°10′E
99 J20 **Andenne** Namur, SE Belgium 50°29′N 05°06′E
77 S11 **Andéramboukane** Gao, E Mali 15°24′N 03°03′E
Anderbak *see* Andarbogh
99 G18 **Anderlecht** Brussels, C Belgium 50°50′N 04°18′E
99 G21 **Anderlues** Hainaut, S Belgium 50°24′N 04°16′E
108 G9 **Andermatt** Uri, C Switzerland 46°39′N 08°36′E
101 E17 **Andernach** *anc.* Antunnacum. Rheinland-Pfalz, SW Germany 50°26′N 07°24′E
188 D15 **Andersen Air Force Base** *air base* NE Guam 13°34′N 144°55′E
39 R9 **Anderson** Alaska, USA 64°20′N 149°11′W
35 N4 **Anderson** California, W USA 40°26′N 122°21′W
31 P13 **Anderson** Indiana, N USA 40°06′N 85°40′W
27 R8 **Anderson** Missouri, C USA 36°39′N 94°26′W
21 P11 **Anderson** South Carolina, SE USA 34°30′N 82°39′W
25 V10 **Anderson** Texas, SW USA 30°29′N 96°00′W
95 K20 **Anderstorp** Jönköping, S Sweden 57°17′N 13°38′E
54 D9 **Andes** Antioquia, W Colombia 05°40′N 75°56′W
47 P7 **Andes** ▲▲ W South America
29 P12 **Andes, Lake** ◎ South Dakota, N USA
92 H9 **Andfjorden** *fjord* E Norwegian Sea
155 H16 **Andhra Pradesh** ◆ *state* E India
98 J8 **Andijk** Noord-Holland, NW Netherlands 52°38′N 05°00′E
147 S10 **Andijon** *Rus.* Andizhan. Andijon Viloyati, E Uzbekistan 40°46′N 72°19′E
147 S10 **Andijon Viloyati** *Rus.* Andizhanskaya Oblast'. ◆ *province* E Uzbekistan
Andikíthira *see* Antikýthira
172 J4 **Andilamena** Toamasina, C Madagascar 17°00′S 48°35′E
142 L8 **Andīmeshk** *var.* Andimishk; *prev.* Salehābād. Khūzestān, SW Iran 32°30′N 48°26′E
Andimishk *see* Andīmeshk
Andipáros *see* Antíparos
Andipaxi *see* Antípaxoi
Andipsara *see* Antipsara
136 L16 **Andırın** Kahramanmaraş, S Turkey 37°33′N 36°18′E
158 J8 **Andirlangar** Xinjiang Uygur Zizhiqu, NW China 37°38′N 83°40′E
Andírrion *see* Antírrio
Ándissa *see* Ántissa
Andizhan *see* Andijon
Andizhanskaya Oblast' *see* Andijon Viloyati
149 N2 **Andkhvoy** Fāryāb, N Afghanistan 36°56′N 65°08′E
105 Q2 **Andoain** País Vasco, N Spain 43°13′N 02°02′W
163 Y15 **Andong** *Jap.* Antō. E South Korea 36°34′N 128°44′E
109 R4 **Andorf** Oberösterreich, N Austria 48°22′N 13°33′E
105 S7 **Andorra** Aragón, NE Spain 40°59′N 00°27′W
105 V4 **Andorra** *off.* Principality of Andorra, *Cat.* Valls d'Andorra, *Fr.* Vallée d'Andorre. ◆ *monarchy* SW Europe
Andorra *see* Andorra la Vella
105 V4 **Andorra la Vella** *var.* Andorra, *Fr.* Andorre la Vielle, *Sp.* Andorra la Vieja. ● (Andorra) C Andorra 42°30′N 01°30′E
Andorra la Vieja *see* Andorra la Vella
Andorra, Principality of *see* Andorra
Andorra, Valls d'/Andorra, Vallée d' *see* Andorra
Andorre la Vielle *see* Andorra la Vella
97 M22 **Andover** S England, United Kingdom 51°13′N 01°28′W
27 N6 **Andover** Kansas, C USA 37°42′N 97°08′W
92 G10 **Andøya** *island* C Norway
60 I8 **Andradina** São Paulo, S Brazil 20°54′S 51°19′W
105 X9 **Andratx** Mallorca, Spain, W Mediterranean Sea 39°35′N 02°25′E
39 N10 **Andreafsky River** ∾ Alaska, USA
38 H17 **Andreanof Islands** *island group* Aleutian Islands, Alaska, USA
124 H16 **Andreapol'** Tverskaya Oblast', W Russian Federation 56°38′N 32°17′E
Andreas, Cape *see* Zafer Burnu
Andreevka *see* Kabanbay
21 N10 **Andrews** North Carolina, SE USA 35°19′N 84°01′W
21 T13 **Andrews** South Carolina, SE USA 33°27′N 79°33′W
24 M7 **Andrews** Texas, SW USA 32°19′N 102°34′W
173 N5 **Andrew Tablemount** *var.* Gora Andryu. *undersea feature* W Indian Ocean 06°45′N 50°30′E
Andreyevka *see* Kabanbay
107 N17 **Andria** Puglia, SE Italy 41°13′N 16°17′E
113 K16 **Andrijevica** E Montenegro 42°45′N 19°45′E
115 E20 **Andrítsaina** Pelopónnisos, S Greece 37°29′N 21°52′E
An Droichead Nua *see* Newbridge
Andropov *see* Rybinsk
115 J19 **Ándros** Ándros, Kykládes, Greece, Aegean Sea 37°49′N 24°54′E
115 J20 **Ándros** *island* Kykládes, Greece, Aegean Sea
19 O7 **Androscoggin River** ∾ Maine/New Hampshire, NE USA
44 F3 **Andros Island** *island* NW Bahamas
127 R7 **Androsovka** Samarskaya Oblast', W Russian Federation 52°41′N 49°34′E
44 G3 **Andros Town** Andros Island, NW Bahamas 24°40′N 77°47′W
155 D21 **Āndrott Island** *island* Lakshadweep, India, N Indian Ocean
117 N5 **Andrushivka** Zhytomyrs'ka Oblast', N Ukraine 50°01′N 29°02′E
111 K17 **Andrychów** Małopolskie, S Poland 49°51′N 19°18′E
Andryu, Gora *see* Andrew Tablemount
92 I10 **Andselv** Troms, N Norway 69°05′N 18°30′E
79 O17 **Andudu** Orientale, NE Dem. Rep. Congo 02°26′N 28°39′E
105 N13 **Andújar** *anc.* Illiturgis. Andalucía, SW Spain 38°02′N 04°03′W
82 C12 **Andulo** Bié, W Angola 11°29′S 16°43′E
103 Q14 **Anduze** Gard, S France 44°03′N 03°59′E
An Earagail *see* Errigal Mountain
95 L19 **Aneby** Jönköping, S Sweden 57°50′N 14°45′E
Anécho *see* Aného
77 Q9 **Anéfis** Kidal, NE Mali 18°05′N 00°38′E
45 U8 **Anegada** *island* NE British Virgin Islands
61 B25 **Anegada, Bahía** *bay* E Argentina
45 U9 **Anegada Passage** *passage* Anguilla/British Virgin Islands
77 R17 **Aného** *var.* Anécho; *prev.* Petit-Popo. S Togo 06°14′N 01°36′E
197 D17 **Aneityum** *var.* Anatom; *prev.* Kéamu. *island* S Vanuatu
117 N10 **Anenii Noi** *Rus.* Novyye Aneny. C Moldova 46°52′N 29°10′E
186 F7 **Anepmete** New Britain, E Papua New Guinea 05°47′S 148°37′E
105 U4 **Aneto** ▲ NE Spain 42°36′N 00°37′E
146 F13 **Änew** *Rus.* Annau. Ahal Welaýaty, C Turkmenistan 37°51′N 58°22′E
Änewetak *see* Enewetak Atoll
77 Y8 **Aney** Agadez, NE Niger 19°22′N 13°00′E
An Fheoir *see* Nore
122 L12 **Angara** ∾ C Russian Federation
122 M13 **Angarsk** Irkutskaya Oblast', S Russian Federation 52°31′N 103°55′E
Angaur *see* Ngeaur
93 G17 **Ånge** Västernorrland, C Sweden 62°31′N 15°40′E
Angel *see* Úhlava
40 D4 **Ángel de la Guarda, Isla** *island* NW Mexico
171 O3 **Angeles** *off.* Angeles City. Luzon, N Philippines 15°16′N 120°37′E
Angeles City *see* Angeles
Angel Falls *see* Ángel, Salto
95 J22 **Ängelholm** Skåne, S Sweden 56°14′N 12°52′E
61 A17 **Angélica** Santa Fe, C Argentina 31°33′S 61°33′W
25 W8 **Angelina River** ∾ Texas, SW USA
55 Q9 **Ángel, Salto** *Eng.* Angel Falls. *waterfall* E Venezuela
95 M15 **Ängelsberg** Västmanland, C Sweden 59°57′N 16°01′E
35 P8 **Angels Camp** California, W USA 38°03′N 120°31′W
109 W7 **Anger** Steiermark, SE Austria 47°16′N 15°41′E
Angerapp *see* Ozersk
Angerburg *see* Węgorzewo
93 H15 **Ångermanälven** ∾ N Sweden
100 P11 **Angermünde** Brandenburg, NE Germany 53°02′N 13°59′E
102 K7 **Angers** *anc.* Juliomagus. Maine-et-Loire, NW France 47°30′N 00°33′W
15 W7 **Angers** ∾ Québec, SE Canada
93 J16 **Ängesön** *island* N Sweden
114 H13 **Angistis** ∾ NE Greece
167 R13 **Ângk Tasaôm** *prev.* Angtassom. Takêv, S Cambodia
185 C25 **Anglem, Mount** ▲ Stewart Island, Southland, SW New Zealand 46°44′S 167°56′E
97 I18 **Anglesey** *cultural region* NW Wales, United Kingdom
97 I18 **Anglesey** *island* NW Wales, United Kingdom
102 I15 **Anglet** Pyrénées-Atlantiques, SW France 43°29′N 01°30′W
25 W12 **Angleton** Texas, SW USA 29°10′N 95°27′W
Anglia *see* England
14 H9 **Angliers** Québec, SE Canada 47°33′N 79°17′W
Anglo-Egyptian Sudan *see* Sudan
Angmagssalik *see* Ammassalik
167 Q7 **Ang Nam Ngum** ◎ C Laos
79 N16 **Ango** Orientale, N Dem. Rep. Congo 04°01′N 25°52′E
83 Q15 **Angoche** Nampula, E Mozambique 16°10′S 39°58′E
63 G14 **Angol** Araucanía, C Chile 37°47′S 72°45′W
31 Q11 **Angola** Indiana, N USA 41°37′N 85°00′W
82 A9 **Angola** *off.* Republic of Angola; *prev.* People's Republic of Angola, Portuguese West Africa. ◆ *republic* SW Africa
65 P15 **Angola Basin** *undersea feature* E Atlantic Ocean 15°00′S 03°00′E
Angola, People's Republic of *see* Angola
Angola, Republic of *see* Angola
39 X13 **Angoon** Admiralty Island, Alaska, USA 57°33′N 134°30′W
147 O14 **Angor** Surkhondaryo Viloyati, S Uzbekistan 37°30′N 67°06′E
Angora *see* Ankara
186 C6 **Angoram** East Sepik, NW Papua New Guinea 04°04′S 144°04′E
40 H8 **Angostura** Sinaloa, C Mexico 25°18′N 108°10′W
Angostura *see* Ciudad Bolívar
41 U17 **Angostura, Presa de la** ⊠ SE Mexico
28 J11 **Angostura Reservoir** ⊠ South Dakota, N USA
102 L11 **Angoulême** *anc.* Iculisma. Charente, W France 45°39′N 00°10′E
102 K11 **Angoumois** *cultural region* W France
64 O2 **Angra do Heroísmo** Terceira, Azores, Portugal, NE Atlantic Ocean 38°40′N 27°14′W
60 O10 **Angra dos Reis** Rio de Janeiro, SE Brazil 22°59′S 44°17′W
Angra Pequena *see* Lüderitz
147 Q10 **Angren** Toshkent Viloyati, E Uzbekistan 41°05′N 70°18′E
Angtassom *see* Ângk Tasaôm
167 O10 **Ang Thong** *var.* Angthong. Ang Thong, C Thailand 14°35′N 100°25′E
Angthong *see* Ang Thong
79 M16 **Angu** Orientale, N Dem. Rep. Congo 03°38′N 24°14′E
105 S5 **Angües** Aragón, NE Spain 42°07′N 00°10′W
45 U9 **Anguilla** ◇ *UK dependent territory* E West Indies
45 V9 **Anguilla** *island* E West Indies
44 F4 **Anguilla Cays** *islets* SW Bahamas
Angul *see* Anugul
161 N1 **Anguli Nur** ◎ E China
79 O18 **Angumu** Orientale, E Dem. Rep. Congo 0°10′S 27°42′E
14 G14 **Angus** Ontario, S Canada 44°19′N 79°52′W
96 J10 **Angus** *cultural region* E Scotland, United Kingdom
59 K19 **Anhangüera** Goiás, S Brazil 18°12′S 48°19′W
99 I21 **Anhée** Namur, S Belgium 50°18′N 04°52′E
95 I21 **Anholt** *island* C Denmark
160 M11 **Anhua** *var.* Dongping. Hunan, S China 28°25′N 111°10′E
161 P8 **Anhui** *var.* Anhui Sheng, Anhwei, Wan. ◆ *province* E China
AnhuiSheng/Anhwei Wan *see* Anhui
39 O11 **Aniak** Alaska, USA 61°34′N 159°31′W
39 O12 **Aniak River** ∾ Alaska, USA
An Iarmhí *see* Westmeath
189 R8 **Anibare** E Nauru 0°31′S 166°56′E
189 R8 **Anibare Bay** *bay* E Nauru, W Pacific Ocean
Anicium *see* le Puy
115 K22 **Ánidro** *island* Kykládes, Greece, Aegean Sea
77 R15 **Anié** C Togo 07°48′N 01°12′E
77 Q15 **Anié** ∾ C Togo
102 J16 **Anie, Pic d'** ▲ SW France 42°56′N 00°44′W
127 Y7 **Anikhovka** Orenburgskaya Oblast', W Russian Federation 51°27′N 60°17′E
14 G9 **Anima Nipissing Lake** ◎ Ontario, S Canada
37 O16 **Animas** New Mexico, SW USA 31°55′N 108°49′W
37 P16 **Animas Peak** ▲ New Mexico, SW USA 31°34′N 108°46′W
37 P16 **Animas Valley** *valley* New Mexico, SW USA
116 F13 **Anina** *Ger.* Steierdorf, *Hung.* Stájerlakanina; *prev.* Ştaierdorf-Anina, Steierdorf-Anina, Steyerlak-Anina. Caraş-Severin, SW Romania 45°05′N 21°51′E
153 Y9 **Anini** Arunāchal Pradesh, NE India 28°48′N 95°54′E
29 U14 **Anita** Iowa, C USA 41°27′N 94°45′W
123 U14 **Aniva, Mys** *headland* Ostrov Sakhalin, SE Russian Federation 46°02′N 143°25′E
187 S15 **Aniwa** *island* S Vanuatu
93 M19 **Anjalankoski** Etelä-Suomi, S Finland 60°39′N 26°54′E
'Anjar *see* Aanjar
Anjiangying *see* Luanping
14 B8 **Anjigami Lake** ◎ Ontario, S Canada
149 N13 **Anjīra** Baluchistān, SW Pakistan 28°19′N 66°19′E
164 K14 **Anjō** *var.* Anzyô. Aichi, Honshū, SW Japan 34°56′N 137°05′E
102 J8 **Anjou** *cultural region* NW France
172 I13 **Anjouan** *var.* Ndzouani, Nzwani. *island* SE Comoros
172 J4 **Anjozorobe** Antananarivo, C Madagascar 18°22′S 47°52′E
163 W13 **Anju** W North Korea 39°36′N 125°44′E
98 M5 **Anjum** *Fris.* Eanjum. Friesland, N Netherlands 53°22′N 06°09′E
172 G6 **Ankaboa, Tanjona** *Fr.* Cap Saint-Vincent. *headland* W Madagascar 21°57′S 43°16′E
160 L7 **Ankang** *prev.* Xing'an. Shaanxi, C China 32°45′N 109°00′E
136 I12 **Ankara** *prev.* Angora; *anc.* Ancyra. ● (Turkey) Ankara, C Turkey 39°55′N 32°50′E
136 H12 **Ankara** ◆ *province* C Turkey
95 N19 **Ankarsrum** Kalmar, S Sweden 57°40′N 16°19′E
172 H6 **Ankazoabo** Toliara, SW Madagascar 22°18′S 44°30′E
172 I4 **Ankazobe** Antananarivo, C Madagascar 18°20′S 47°07′E
29 V14 **Ankeny** Iowa, C USA 41°43′N 93°37′W
167 V11 **An Khê** Gia Lai, C Vietnam 13°57′N 108°39′E
100 O9 **Anklam** Mecklenburg-Vorpommern, NE Germany 53°51′N 13°42′E
80 K13 **Ānkober** Āmara, N Ethiopia 09°36′N 39°44′E
77 O17 **Ankobra** ∾ S Ghana
79 N22 **Ankoro** Katanga, SE Dem. Rep. Congo 06°45′S 26°58′E
99 L24 **Anlier, Forêt d'** *forest* SE Belgium
160 I13 **Anlong** *var.* Xin'an. Guizhou, S China 25°05′N 105°29′E
An Longfort *see* Longford
167 R11 **Ânlong Vêng** Siĕmréab, NW Cambodia 14°16′N 104°08′E
An Lorgain *see* Lurgan
161 N8 **Anlu** Hubei, C China 31°15′N 113°41′E
An Mhí *see* Meath
An Mhuir Cheilteach *see* Celtic Sea
An Muileann gCearr *see* Mullingar
93 F16 **Ånn** Jämtland, C Sweden 63°19′N 12°34′E
126 M8 **Anna** Voronezhskaya Oblast', W Russian Federation 51°31′N 40°23′E
30 L17 **Anna** Illinois, N USA 37°27′N 89°15′W
25 U5 **Anna** Texas, SW USA 33°21′N 96°33′W
74 L5 **Annaba** *prev.* Bône. NE Algeria 36°55′N 07°47′E
An Nabatīyah at Taḥtā *see* Nabatîyé
101 N17 **Annaberg-Buchholz** Sachsen, E Germany 50°35′N 13°01′E
109 T9 **Annabichl** ✈ (Klagenfurt) Kärnten, S Austria 46°39′N 14°21′E
140 M5 **An Nafūd** *desert* NW Saudi Arabia
139 P6 **'Annah** *var.* 'Ānah. Al Anbār, NW Iraq 34°50′N 42°00′E
139 P6 **An Nāḥiyah** Al Anbār, W Iraq 34°24′N 41°33′E
139 S11 **An Najaf** ◆ *governorate* S Iraq
139 T10 **An Najaf** *var.* Najaf. An Najaf, S Iraq 31°59′N 44°19′E
21 V5 **Anna, Lake** ⊠ Virginia, NE USA
97 F16 **Annalee** ∾ N Ireland
167 S9 **Annamitique, Chaîne** ▲▲ C Laos
97 J14 **Annan** S Scotland, United Kingdom 55°N 03°20′W
29 U8 **Annandale** Minnesota, N USA 45°15′N 94°07′W
21 W4 **Annandale** Virginia, NE USA 38°48′N 77°10′W
189 Q7 **Anna Point** *headland* N Nauru 0°30′S 166°56′E
21 X3 **Annapolis** *state capital* Maryland, NE USA 38°59′N 76°30′W
188 A10 **Anna, Pulo** *island* S Palau
153 O10 **Annapurna** ▲ C Nepal 28°30′N 83°50′E
An Nāqūrah *see* En Nâqoûra
31 R10 **Ann Arbor** Michigan, N USA 42°17′N 83°45′W
An Nās *see* Nass
139 W12 **An Nāṣirīyah** *var.* Nasiriya. Dhī Qār, SE Iraq 31°04′N 46°17′E
139 W11 **An Naṣr** Dhī Qār, E Iraq 31°34′N 46°08′E
Annau *see* Änew
121 O13 **An Nawfalīyah** *var.* Al Nūwfalīyah. N Libya 30°46′N 17°48′E
19 P10 **Ann, Cape** *headland* Massachusetts, NE USA 42°39′N 70°35′W
180 I10 **Annean, Lake** ◎ Western Australia
Anneciacum *see* Annecy
103 T11 **Annecy** *anc.* Anneciacum. Haute-Savoie, E France 45°53′N 06°09′E
103 T11 **Annecy, Lac d'** ◎ E France
103 T10 **Annemasse** Haute-Savoie, E France 46°10′N 06°13′E
39 Z14 **Annette Island** *island* Alexander Archipelago, Alaska, USA
An Nhon *see* Binh Đinh
An Nīl al Abyaḍ *see* White Nile
An Nīl al Azraq *see* Blue Nile
23 Q3 **Anniston** Alabama, S USA 33°39′N 85°49′W
79 A19 **Annobón** *island* W Equatorial Guinea
103 R12 **Annonay** Ardèche, E France 45°15′N 04°40′E
44 K12 **Annotto Bay** C Jamaica 18°16′N 76°47′W
141 R5 **An Nu'ayrīyah** *var.* Narıya. Ash Sharqīyah, NE Saudi Arabia 27°30′N 48°30′E
182 M9 **Annuello** Victoria, SE Australia 34°54′S 142°50′E
139 Q10 **An Nukhayb** Al Anbār, S Iraq 32°02′N 42°15′E
139 U9 **An Nu'mānīyah** Wāsiţ, E Iraq 32°34′N 45°23′E
Áno Arkhánai *see* Archánes
115 J25 **Anógeia** *var.* Anogia, Anóyia. Kríti, Greece, E Mediterranean Sea 35°17′N 24°53′E
Anogia *see* Anógeia
29 V8 **Anoka** Minnesota, N USA 45°15′N 93°26′W
An Ómaigh *see* Omagh
172 I1 **Anorontany, Tanjona** *Fr.* Cap Saint-Sébastien. *headland* N Madagascar
172 J5 **Anosibe An'Ala** Toamasina, E Madagascar 19°24′S 48°11′E
Anóyia *see* Anógeia
An Pointe *see* Warrenpoint
161 P9 **Anqing** Anhui, E China 30°32′N 116°59′E
161 Q5 **Anqiu** Shandong, E China 36°25′N 119°10′E
An Ráth *see* Ráth Luirc
An Ribhéar *see* Kenmare River
An Ros *see* Rush
99 K19 **Ans** Liège, E Belgium 50°39′N 05°32′E
Anṣāb *see* Nişāb
171 W12 **Ansas** Papua, E Indonesia 01°44′S 135°52′E
101 J20 **Ansbach** Bayern, SE Germany 49°18′N 10°36′E
An Sciobairín *see* Skibbereen
An Scoil *see* Skull
An Seancheann *see* Old Head of Kinsale
45 Y5 **Anse-Bertrand** Grande Terre, N Guadeloupe 16°28′N 61°31′W
172 H17 **Anse Boileau** Mahé, NE Seychelles 04°43′S 55°29′E
45 S11 **Anse La Raye** NW Saint Lucia 13°57′N 61°01′W
54 D9 **Anserma** Caldas, W Colombia 05°15′N 75°47′W
109 T4 **Ansfelden** Oberösterreich, N Austria 48°12′N 14°17′E
163 U12 **Anshan** Liaoning, NE China 41°06′N 122°55′E
160 J12 **Anshun** Guizhou, S China 26°15′N 105°58′E
61 F17 **Ansina** Tacuarembó, C Uruguay 31°58′S 55°28′W
29 O15 **Ansley** Nebraska, C USA 41°16′N 99°22′W
25 P6 **Anson** Texas, SW USA 32°45′N 99°55′W
77 Q10 **Ansongo** Gao, E Mali 15°39′N 00°33′E
An Srath Bán *see* Strabane
21 R5 **Ansted** West Virginia, NE USA 38°08′N 81°06′W
171 Y13 **Ansudu** Papua, E Indonesia 02°09′S 139°19′E
57 G15 **Anta** Cusco, S Peru 13°30′S 72°08′W
57 G16 **Antabamba** Apurímac, C Peru 14°23′S 72°54′W
Antafalva *see* Kovačica
136 L17 **Antakya** *anc.* Antioch, Antiochia. Hatay, S Turkey 36°12′N 36°10′E
172 K3 **Antalaha** Antsirañana, NE Madagascar 14°53′S 50°16′E
136 F17 **Antalya** *prev.* Adalia; *anc.* Attaleia, *Bibl.* Attalia. Antalya, SW Turkey 36°53′N 30°42′E
136 F17 **Antalya** ◆ *province* SW Turkey
136 F16 **Antalya** ✈ Antalya, SW Turkey 36°53′N 30°45′E
121 U10 **Antalya Basin** *undersea feature* E Mediterranean Sea
Antalya, Gulf of *see* Antalya Körfezi
136 F16 **Antalya Körfezi** *var.* Gulf of Adalia, *Eng.* Gulf of Antalya. *gulf* SW Turkey
172 J5 **Antanambao Manampotsy** Toamasina, E Madagascar 19°30′S 48°36′E
172 I5 **Antananarivo** *prev.* Tananarive. ● (Madagascar) Antananarivo, C Madagascar 18°52′S 47°30′E
172 I4 **Antananarivo** ◆ *province* C Madagascar
172 J5 **Antananarivo** ✈ Antananarivo, C Madagascar 18°52′S 47°30′E
An tAonach *see* Nenagh
194-195 **Antarctica** *continent*
194 I5 **Antarctic Peninsula** *peninsula* Antarctica
174 L13 **Antarctic Plate** *tectonic feature* Africa/Antarctica/Australia/South America Atlantic Ocean/Indian Ocean/Pacific Ocean
61 J15 **Antas, Rio das** ∾ S Brazil
189 U16 **Ant Atoll** *atoll* Caroline Islands, E Micronesia
An Teampall Mór *see* Templemore
Antep *see* Gaziantep
104 M15 **Antequera** *anc.* Antikaria, Antiquaria. Andalucía, S Spain 37°01′N 04°34′W
Antequera *see* Oaxaca
37 S5 **Antero Reservoir** ⊠ Colorado, C USA
26 M7 **Anthony** Kansas, C USA 37°10′N 98°02′W
37 R16 **Anthony** New Mexico, SW USA 32°00′N 106°36′W

182 *D5* **Anthony, Lake** *salt lake* South Australia
74 *E8* **Anti-Atlas** ▲▲ SW Morocco
103 *U15* **Antibes** ***anc.*** Antipolis. Alpes-Maritimes, SE France 43°35′N 07°07′E
103 *U15* **Antibes, Cap d'** *headland* SE France 43°33′N 07°08′E
Anticaria *see* Antequera
13 *Q11* **Anticosti, Île d'** ***Eng.*** Anticosti Island. *island* Québec, E Canada
Anticosti Island *see* Anticosti, Île d'
102 *K3* **Antifer, Cap d'** *headland* N France 49°43′N 00°10′E
30 *L6* **Antigo** Wisconsin, N USA 45°10′N 89°10′W
13 *Q15* **Antigonish** Nova Scotia, SE Canada 45°39′N 62°00′W
64 *P11* **Antigua** Fuerteventura, Islas Canarias, NE Atlantic Ocean
45 *X10* **Antigua** *island* S Antigua and Barbuda, Leeward Islands
Antigua *see* Antigua Guatemala
45 *W9* **Antigua and Barbuda** ◆ *commonwealth republic* E West Indies
42 *C6* **Antigua Guatemala** ***var.*** Antigua. Sacatepéquez, SW Guatemala 14°33′N 90°42′W
41 *P11* **Antiguo Morelos** ***var.*** Antiguo-Morelos. Tamaulipas, C Mexico 22°35′N 99°08′W
115 *F19* **Antíkyras, Kólpos** *gulf* C Greece
115 *G24* **Antikýthira** ***var.*** Andikíthira. *island* S Greece
138 *I7* **Anti-Lebanon** ***var.*** Jebel esh Sharqi, ***Ar.*** Al Jabal ash Sharqī, ***Fr.*** Anti-Liban. ▲▲ Lebanon/Syria
Anti-Liban *see* Anti-Lebanon
115 *M22* **Antimácheia** Kos, Dodekánisa, Greece 47°19′N 07°54′E
115 *I22* **Antímilos** *island* Kykládes, Greece, Aegean Sea
36 *L6* **Antimony** Utah, W USA 38°07′N 112°00′W
An tInbhear Mór *see* Arklow
30 *M10* **Antioch** Illinois, N USA 42°28′N 88°06′W
Antioch *see* Antakya
102 *I10* **Antioche, Pertuis d'** *inlet* W France
Antiochia *see* Antakya
54 *D8* **Antioquia** Antioquia, C Colombia 06°36′N 75°53′W
54 *E8* **Antioquia** ***off.*** Departamento de Antioquia. ◈ *province* C Colombia
Antioquia, Departamento de *see* Antioquia
115 *J21* **Antíparos** ***var.*** Andipáros. *island* Kykládes, Greece, Aegean Sea
115 *B17* **Antípaxoi** ***var.*** Andipaxi. *island* Iónia Nísiá, Greece, C Mediterranean Sea
122 *J8* **Antipayuta** Yamalo-Nenetskiy Avtonomnyy Okrug, N Russian Federation 69°08′N 76°43′E
192 *L12* **Antipodes Islands** *island group* S New Zealand
Antipolis *see* Antibes
115 *J18* **Antípsara** ***var.*** Andípsara. *island* E Greece
Antiquaria *see* Antequera
15 *N10* **Antique, Lac** ◎ Québec, SE Canada
115 *E18* **Antírrio** ***var.*** Andírrion. Dytikí Ellás, C Greece 38°20′N 21°46′E
115 *K16* **Ántissa** ***var.*** Ándissa. Lésvos, E Greece 39°15′N 26°00′E
An tIúr *see* Newry
Antivari *see* Bar
56 *C6* **Antizana** ▲ N Ecuador 0°29′S 78°08′W
27 *Q13* **Antlers** Oklahoma, C USA 34°15′N 95°38′W
93 *J14* **Antnäs** Norrbotten, N Sweden 65°32′N 21°53′E
Antō *see* Andong
62 *G5* **Antofagasta** Antofagasta, N Chile 23°40′S 70°23′W
62 *G6* **Antofagasta** ***off.*** Región de Antofagasta. ◈ *region* N Chile
Antofagasta, Región de *see* Antofagasta
62 *I7* **Antofalla, Salar de** *salt lake* NW Argentina
99 *D20* **Antoing** Hainaut, SW Belgium 50°34′N 03°26′E
43 *S16* **Antón** Coclé, C Panama 08°23′N 80°15′W
24 *M5* **Anton** Texas, SW USA 33°48′N 102°09′W
37 *T11* **Anton Chico** New Mexico, SW USA 35°12′N 105°09′W
60 *K12* **Antonina** Paraná, S Brazil 25°28′S 48°43′W
188 *C16* **Antonio B. Won Pat International** ✈ (Agana) C Guam 13°28′N 144°48′E
103 *O5* **Antony** Hauts-de-Seine, N France 48°45′N 02°17′E
Antratsit *see* Antratsyt
117 *Y8* **Antratsyt** ***Rus.*** Antratsit. Luhans'ka Oblast', E Ukraine 48°07′N 39°05′E
97 *G15* **Antrim** ***Ir.*** Aontroim. NE Northern Ireland, United Kingdom 54°43′N 06°13′W
97 *G14* **Antrim** ***Ir.*** Aontroim. *cultural region* NE Northern Ireland, United Kingdom
97 *G14* **Antrim Mountains** ▲▲ NE Northern Ireland, United Kingdom
172 *H5* **Antsalova** Mahajanga, W Madagascar 18°40′S 44°37′E
Antserana *see* Antsirañana
An tSionainn *see* Shannon
172 *J2* **Antsirañana** ***var.*** Antserana; ***prev.*** Antsirane, Diégo-Suarez. Antsirañana, N Madagascar 12°19′S 49°17′E
172 *J2* **Antsirañana** ◈ *province* N Madagascar
Antsirane *see* Antsirañana
An tSiúir *see* Suir
118 *I7* **Antsla** ***Ger.*** Anzen. Võrumaa, SE Estonia 57°52′N 26°33′E
An tSláine *see* Slaney
172 *J3* **Antsohihy** Mahajanga, NW Madagascar 14°50′S 47°58′E
63 *G14* **Antuco, Volcán** ⋀ C Chile 37°29′S 71°25′W
169 *W10* **Antu, Gunung** ▲ Borneo, N Indonesia 0°57′N 118°51′E
An Tullach *see* Tullow
An-tung *see* Dandong
Antunnacum *see* Andernach
Antwerp *see* Antwerpen
99 *G16* **Antwerpen** ***Eng.*** Antwerp, ***Fr.*** Anvers. Antwerpen, N Belgium 51°13′N 04°25′E
99 *H16* **Antwerpen** ***Eng.*** Antwerp. ◈ *province* N Belgium
An Uaimh *see* Navan
154 *N12* **Anugul** ***var.*** Angul. Orissa, E India 20°51′N 84°59′E
152 *F9* **Anūpgarh** Rājasthān, NW India 29°10′N 73°14′E
154 *K10* **Anūppur** Madhya Pradesh, C India 23°05′N 81°45′E
155 *K24* **Anuradhapura** North Central Province, C Sri Lanka 08°20′N 80°25′E
Anvers *see* Antwerpen
194 *G4* **Anvers Island** *island* Antarctica
39 *N11* **Anvik** Alaska, USA 62°39′N 160°12′W
39 *N10* **Anvik River** ≈ Alaska, USA
38 *F17* **Anvil Peak** ▲ Semisopochnoi Island, Alaska, USA 51°59′N 179°36′E
159 *P7* **Anxi** ***var.*** Yuanquan. Gansu, N China 40°32′N 95°50′E
182 *F8* **Anxious Bay** *bay* South Australia
161 *O5* **Anyang** Henan, C China 36°11′N 114°18′E
159 *S11* **A'nyêmaqên Shan** ▲▲ C China
118 *H12* **Anykščiai** Utena, E Lithuania 55°30′N 25°34′E
161 *P13* **Anyuan** ***var.*** Xinshan. Jiangxi, S China 25°10′N 115°25′E
123 *T7* **Anyuysk** Chukotskiy Avtonomnyy Okrug, NE Russian Federation 68°22′N 161°33′E
123 *T7* **Anyuyskiy Khrebet** ▲▲ NE Russian Federation
54 *D8* **Anza** Antioquia, C Colombia 06°18′N 75°54′W
Anzen *see* Antsla
107 *I16* **Anzio** Lazio, C Italy 41°28′N 12°38′E
55 *O6* **Anzoátegui** ***off.*** Estado Anzoátegui. ◈ *state* NE Venezuela
Anzoátegui, Estado *see* Anzoátegui
147 *P12* **Anzob** W Tajikistan 39°24′N 68°55′E
Anzyô *see* Anjō
Aoba *see* Ambae
165 *X13* **Aoga-shima** *island* Izu-shotō, SE Japan
Aohan Qi *see* Xinhui
Aoiz *see* Agoiz
167 *O11* **Ao Krung Thep** ***var.*** Krung Thep Mahanakhon, ***Eng.*** Bangkok. ● (Thailand) Bangkok, C Thailand 13°44′N 100°30′E
186 *M9* **Aola** ***var.*** Tenaghau. Guadalcanal, C Solomon Islands 09°32′S 160°28′E
166 *M15* **Ao Luk Nua** Krabi, SW Thailand 08°21′N 98°43′E
Aomen *see* Macao
172 *N8* **Aomori** Aomori, Honshū, C Japan 40°50′N 140°43′E
172 *N8* **Aomori** ***off.*** Aomori-ken. ◈ *prefecture* Honshū, C Japan
Aomori-ken *see* Aomori
Aontroim *see* Antrim
115 *C15* **Aóos** ***var.*** Vijosa, Vijosë, ***Alb.*** Lumi i Vjosës. ≈ Albania/Greece *see also* Vjosës, Lumi i
Aóos *see* Vjosës, Lumi i
191 *Q7* **Aorai, Mont** ⋀ Tahiti, W French Polynesia 17°36′S 149°29′W
185 *E19* **Aoraki** ***prev.*** Aorangi, Mount Cook. ▲ South Island, New Zealand 43°38′S 170°05′E
167 *R13* **Aôral, Phnum** ***prev.*** Phnom Aural. ▲ W Cambodia 12°01′N 104°10′E
Aorangi *see* Aoraki
185 *L15* **Aorangi Mountains** ▲▲ North Island, New Zealand
184 *H13* **Aorere** ≈ South Island, New Zealand
106 *A7* **Aosta** ***anc.*** Augusta Praetoria. Valle d'Aosta, NW Italy 45°43′N 07°20′E
77 *O11* **Aougoundou, Lac** ◎ S Mali
76 *K9* **Aoukâr** ***var.*** Aouker. *plateau* C Mauritania
78 *J13* **Aouk, Bahr** ≈ Central African Republic/Chad
Aouker *see* Aoukâr
74 *B11* **Aousard** SE Western Sahara 22°42′N 14°22′W
164 *H12* **Aoya** Tottori, Honshū, SW Japan 35°31′N 134°01′E
Aoyang *see* Shanggao
78 *H5* **Aozou** Borkou-Ennedi-Tibesti, N Chad 22°01′N 17°11′E
26 *M11* **Apache** Oklahoma, C USA 34°57′N 98°21′W
36 *L14* **Apache Junction** Arizona, SW USA 33°25′N 111°33′W
24 *J9* **Apache Mountains** ▲▲ Texas, SW USA
36 *M16* **Apache Peak** ▲ Arizona, SW USA 31°50′N 110°25′W
116 *H10* **Apahida** Cluj, NW Romania 46°49′N 23°45′E
23 *T9* **Apalachee Bay** *bay* Florida, SE USA
23 *T3* **Apalachee River** ≈ Georgia, SE USA
23 *S10* **Apalachicola** Florida, SE USA 29°43′N 84°58′W
23 *S10* **Apalachicola Bay** *bay* Florida, SE USA
23 *R9* **Apalachicola River** ≈ Florida, SE USA
Apam *see* Apan
Apamama *see* Abemama
41 *P14* **Apan** ***var.*** Apam. Hidalgo, C Mexico 19°48′N 98°25′W
42 *J8* **Apanás, Lago de** ◎ NW Nicaragua
54 *H14* **Apaporis, Río** ≈ Brazil/Colombia
185 *C23* **Aparima** ≈ South Island, New Zealand
171 *O1* **Aparri** Luzon, N Philippines 18°16′N 121°42′E
112 *J9* **Apatin** Vojvodina, NW Serbia 45°40′N 19°01′E
124 *J4* **Apatity** Murmanskaya Oblast', NW Russian Federation 67°34′N 33°26′E
55 *X9* **Apatou** NW French Guiana 05°10′N 54°22′W
40 *M14* **Apatzingán** ***var.*** Apatzingán de la Constitución. Michoacán, SW Mexico 19°05′N 102°20′W
Apatzingán de la Constitución *see* Apatzingán
171 *X12* **Apauwar** Papua, E Indonesia 01°36′S 138°10′E
Apaxtla *see* Apaxtla de Castrejón
41 *O15* **Apaxtla de Castrejón** ***var.*** Apaxtla. Guerrero, S Mexico 18°06′N 99°55′W
118 *J7* **Ape** Alūksne, NE Latvia 57°32′N 26°42′E
98 *L11* **Apeldoorn** Gelderland, E Netherlands 52°13′N 05°57′E
Apennines *see* Appennino
Apenrade *see* Aabenraa
57 *L17* **Apere, Río** ≈ C Bolivia
55 *W11* **Apetina** Sipaliwini, SE Surinam 03°30′N 55°03′W
21 *U9* **Apex** North Carolina, SE USA 35°43′N 78°51′W
79 *M16* **Api** Orientale, N Dem. Rep. Congo 03°40′N 25°26′E
152 *M9* **Api** ▲ NW Nepal 30°07′N 80°57′E
192 *H16* **Āpia** ● (Samoa) Upolu, SE Samoa 13°50′S 171°47′W
Apia *see* Abaiang
60 *K11* **Apiaí** São Paulo, S Brazil 24°29′S 48°51′W
170 *M16* **Api, Gunung** ▲ Pulau Sangeang, S Indonesia 08°09′S 119°03′E
187 *N9* **Apio** Maramasike Island, N Solomon Islands 09°36′S 161°25′E
41 *O15* **Apipilulco** Guerrero, S Mexico 18°11′N 99°40′W
41 *P14* **Apizaco** Tlaxcala, S Mexico 19°26′N 98°09′W
137 *Q8* **Ap'khazet'i** ***var.*** Abkhazia. ◈ *autonomous republic* NW Georgia
104 *I4* **A Pobla de Trives** ***Cast.*** Puebla de Trives. Galicia, NW Spain 42°21′N 07°16′W
55 *U9* **Apoera** Sipaliwini, NW Surinam 05°12′N 57°13′W
115 *O23* **Apolakkiá** Ródos, Dodekánisa, Greece, Aegean Sea 36°02′N 27°48′E
101 *L16* **Apolda** Thüringen, C Germany 51°02′N 11°31′E
192 *H16* **Apolima Strait** *strait* C Pacific Ocean
182 *M13* **Apollo Bay** Victoria, SE Australia 38°40′S 143°44′E
Apollonia *see* Sozopol
57 *J16* **Apolo** La Paz, W Bolivia 14°48′S 68°31′W
57 *J16* **Apolobamba, Cordillera** ▲▲ Bolivia/Peru
171 *Q8* **Apo, Mount** ⋀ Mindanao, S Philippines 06°54′N 125°16′E
23 *W11* **Apopka** Florida, SE USA 28°40′N 81°30′W
23 *W11* **Apopka, Lake** ◎ Florida, SE USA
59 *J19* **Aporé, Rio** ≈ SW Brazil
30 *K2* **Apostle Islands** *island group* Wisconsin, N USA
Apostolas Andreas, Cape *see* Zafer Burnu
61 *F14* **Apóstoles** Misiones, NE Argentina 27°54′S 55°45′W
Apostólou Andréa, Akrotíri *see* Zafer Burnu
117 *S9* **Apostolove** ***Rus.*** Apostolovo. Dnipropetrovs'ka Oblast', E Ukraine 47°40′N 33°45′E
Apostolovo *see* Apostolove
17 *S10* **Appalachian Mountains** ▲▲ E USA
95 *K14* **Äppelbo** Dalarna, C Sweden 60°30′N 14°00′E
98 *N7* **Appelscha** ***Fris.*** Appelskea. Friesland, N Netherlands 52°57′N 06°19′E
Appelskea *see* Appelscha
106 *G11* **Appennino** ***Eng.*** Apennines. ▲▲ Italy/San Marino
107 *L17* **Appennino Campano** ▲▲ C Italy
108 *I7* **Appenzell** Appenzell, NW Switzerland 47°20′N 09°25′E
108 *H7* **Appenzell** ◈ *canton* NE Switzerland
55 *V12* **Appikalo** Sipaliwini, S Surinam 02°07′N 56°16′W
98 *O5* **Appingedam** Groningen, NE Netherlands 53°18′N 06°52′E
25 *X8* **Appleby** Texas, SW USA 31°43′N 94°36′W
97 *L15* **Appleby-in-Westmorland** Cumbria, NW England, United Kingdom 54°35′N 02°26′W
30 *K10* **Apple River** ≈ Illinois, N USA
30 *I5* **Apple River** ≈ Wisconsin, N USA
25 *W9* **Apple Springs** Texas, SW USA 31°13′N 94°57′W
29 *S8* **Appleton** Minnesota, N USA 45°12′N 96°01′W
30 *M7* **Appleton** Wisconsin, N USA 44°17′N 88°24′W
27 *S5* **Appleton City** Missouri, C USA 38°11′N 94°01′W
35 *U14* **Apple Valley** California, W USA 34°30′N 117°11′W
29 *V9* **Apple Valley** Minnesota, N USA 44°43′N 93°13′W
21 *U6* **Appomattox** Virginia, NE USA 37°21′N 78°51′W
188 *B16* **Apra Harbor** *harbour* W Guam
188 *B16* **Apra Heights** W Guam
106 *F6* **Aprica, Passo dell'** *pass* N Italy
107 *M15* **Apricena** ***anc.*** Hadria Picena. Puglia, SE Italy 41°47′N 15°27′E
114 *I9* **Apriltsi** Lovech, N Bulgaria 42°50′N 24°54′E
126 *L14* **Apsheronsk** Krasnodarskiy Kray, SW Russian Federation 44°27′N 39°45′E
Apsheronskiy Poluostrov *see* Abşeron Yarımadası
103 *S15* **Apt** ***anc.*** Apta Julia. Vaucluse, SE France 43°54′N 05°24′E
Apta Julia *see* Apt
38 *H12* **'Āpua Point** ***var.*** Apua Point. *headland* Hawai'i, USA, C Pacific Ocean 19°15′N 155°13′W
60 *I10* **Apucarana** Paraná, S Brazil 23°34′S 51°28′W
Apulia *see* Puglia
54 *K8* **Apure** ***off.*** Estado Apure. ◈ *state* C Venezuela
Apure, Estado *see* Apure
54 *J7* **Apure, Río** ≈ W Venezuela
57 *F16* **Apurímac** ***off.*** Departamento de Apurímac. ◈ *department* C Peru
Apurímac, Departamento de *see* Apurímac
57 *F15* **Apurímac, Río** ≈ S Peru
116 *G10* **Apuseni, Munții** ▲▲ W Romania
Aqaba/'Aqaba *see* Al 'Aqabah
138 *F15* **Aqaba, Gulf of** ***var.*** Gulf of Elat, ***Ar.*** Khalīj al 'Aqabah; ***anc.*** Sinus Aelaniticus. *gulf* NE Red Sea
139 *R7* **'Aqabah** Al Anbār, C Iraq 33°33′N 42°55′E
'Aqabah, Khalīj al *see* Aqaba, Gulf of
149 *O2* **Āqchah** ***var.*** Āqcheh. Jowzjān, N Afghanistan 37°N 66°07′E
Āqcheh *see* Āqchah
Aqkengse *see* Akkense
Aqköl *see* Akkol'
Aqmola *see* Astana
Aqmola Oblysy *see* Akmola
158 *L10* **Aqqikkol Hu** ◎ NW China
Aqqū *see* Akku
Aqqystaū *see* Akkystau
'Aqrah *see* Ākrē
Aqsay *see* Aksay
Aqshataū *see* Akchatau
Aqsū *see* Aksu
Aqsūat *see* Aksuat
Aqtas *see* Aktas
Aqtaū *see* Aktau
Aqtöbe *see* Aktobe
Aqtöbe Oblysy *see* Aktyubinsk
Aqtoghay *see* Aktogay
Aquae Augustae *see* Dax
Aquae Calidae *see* Bath
Aquae Flaviae *see* Chaves
Aquae Grani *see* Aachen
Aquae Panoniae *see* Baden
Aquae Sextiae *see* Aix-en-Provence
Aquae Solis *see* Bath
Aquae Tarbelicae *see* Dax
36 *J11* **Aquarius Mountains** ▲▲ Arizona, SW USA
62 *O5* **Aquidabán, Río** ≈ E Paraguay
59 *H20* **Aquidauana** Mato Grosso do Sul, S Brazil 20°27′S 55°45′W
40 *L15* **Aquila** Michoacán, S Mexico 18°36′N 103°32′W
Aquila/Aquila degli Abruzzi *see* L'Aquila
25 *T8* **Aquilla** Texas, SW USA 31°51′N 97°13′W
44 *L9* **Aquin** S Haiti 18°16′N 73°24′W
Aquisgranum *see* Aachen
102 *J13* **Aquitaine** ◈ *region* SW France
Aqzhar *see* Akzhar
153 *P13* **Āra** ***prev.*** Arrah. Bihār, N India 25°34′N 84°40′E
105 *S4* **Ara** ≈ NE Spain
23 *P2* **Arab** Alabama, S USA 34°19′N 86°30′W
Araba *see* Álava
138 *G12* **'Arabah, Wādī al** ***Heb.*** Ha'Arava. *dry watercourse* Israel/Jordan
117 *U12* **Arabats'ka Strilka, Kosa** *spit* S Ukraine
117 *U12* **Arabats'ka Zatoka** *gulf* S Ukraine
'Arab, Baḩr al *see* Arab, Bahr el
80 *C12* **Arab, Bahr el** ***var.*** Baḩr al 'Arab. ≈ S Sudan
56 *E7* **Arabela, Río** ≈ N Peru
173 *O4* **Arabian Basin** *undersea feature* N Arabian Sea 11°30′N 65°00′E
Arabian Desert *see* Sahara el Sharqîya
141 *N9* **Arabian Peninsula** *peninsula* SW Asia
85 *P15* **Arabian Plate** *tectonic feature* Africa/Asia/Europe
141 *W14* **Arabian Sea** *sea* NW Indian Ocean
Arabicus, Sinus *see* Red Sea
'Arabī, Khalīj al *see* Gulf, The
Arabistan *see* Khūzestān
'Arabīyah as Su'ūdīyah, Al Mamlakah al *see* Saudi Arabia
'Arabīyah Jumhūrīyah, Miṣr al *see* Egypt
138 *I9* **'Arab, Jabal al** ▲▲ S Syria
Arab Republic of Egypt *see* Egypt
139 *Y12* **'Arab, Shaṭṭ al** ***Eng.*** Shatt al Arab, ***Per.*** Arvand Rūd. ≈ Iran/Iraq
136 *I11* **Araç** Kastamonu, N Turkey 41°14′N 33°20′E
59 *P16* **Aracaju** *state capital* Sergipe, E Brazil 10°45′S 37°07′W
54 *F5* **Aracataca** Magdalena, N Colombia 10°38′N 74°09′W
58 *P13* **Aracati** Ceará, E Brazil 04°32′S 37°45′W
60 *J8* **Araçatuba** São Paulo, S Brazil 21°12′S 50°24′W
136 *I11* **Araç Çayı** ≈ N Turkey
104 *J13* **Aracena** Andalucía, S Spain 37°54′N 06°33′W
115 *F20* **Arachnaío** ▲▲ S Greece
115 *D16* **Árachthos** ***var.*** Arta, ***prev.*** Árakhthos; ***anc.*** Arachthus. ≈ W Greece
Arachthus *see* Árachthos
59 *N19* **Araçuaí** Minas Gerais, SE Brazil 16°52′S 42°03′W
138 *F11* **'Arad** Southern, S Israel 31°16′N 35°09′E
116 *F11* **Arad** Arad, W Romania 46°12′N 21°20′E
116 *F11* **Arad** ◈ *county* W Romania
78 *J9* **Arada** Biltine, NE Chad 15°00′N 20°38′E
143 *P18* **'Arādah** Abū Ẓaby, S United Arab Emirates 22°57′N 53°24′E
Aradhippou *see* Aradíppou
121 *Q3* **Aradíppou** ***var.*** Aradhippou. SE Cyprus 34°57′N 33°37′E
174 *K6* **Arafura Sea** ***Ind.*** Laut Arafuru. *sea* W Pacific Ocean
174 *L6* **Arafura Shelf** *undersea feature* C Arafura Sea
Arafuru, Laut *see* Arafura Sea
59 *J18* **Aragarças** Goiás, C Brazil 15°55′S 52°12′W
Aragats, Gora *see* Aragats Lerr
137 *T12* **Aragats Lerr** ***Rus.*** Gora Aragats. ▲ W Armenia 40°31′N 44°06′E
32 *E14* **Arago, Cape** *headland* Oregon, NW USA 43°17′N 124°25′W
105 *R6* **Aragón** *autonomous community* E Spain
105 *Q4* **Aragón** ≈ NE Spain
107 *I24* **Aragona** Sicilia, Italy, C Mediterranean Sea 37°25′N 13°37′E
105 *Q7* **Aragoncillo** ▲ C Spain 40°59′N 02°01′W
54 *L5* **Aragua** ***off.*** Estado Aragua. ◈ *state* N Venezuela
55 *N6* **Aragua de Barcelona** Anzoátegui, NE Venezuela 09°30′N 64°51′W
55 *O5* **Aragua de Maturín** Monagas, NE Venezuela 09°58′N 63°30′W
Aragua, Estado *see* Aragua
59 *K15* **Araguaia, Río** ***var.*** Araguaya. ≈ C Brazil
59 *K19* **Araguari** Minas Gerais, SE Brazil 18°38′S 48°13′W
58 *J11* **Araguari, Rio** ≈ SW Brazil
Araguaya *see* Araguaia, Río
104 *K14* **Arahal** Andalucía, S Spain 37°15′N 05°33′W
165 *N11* **Arai** Niigata, Honshū, C Japan 37°02′N 138°17′E
Árainn *see* Inishmore
Árainn Mhór *see* Aran Island
Ara Jovis *see* Aranjuez
74 *J11* **Arak** C Algeria 25°17′N 03°45′E
171 *Y15* **Arak** Papua, E Indonesia 07°14′S 139°40′E
142 *M7* **Arāk** ***prev.*** Sultānābād. Markazī, W Iran 34°07′N 49°39′E
188 *D10* **Arakabesan** *island* Palau Islands, N Palau
55 *S7* **Arakaka** NW Guyana 07°37′N 59°58′W
166 *K6* **Arakan State** ***var.*** Rakhine State. ◈ *state* W Burma (Myanmar)
166 *K5* **Arakan Yoma** ▲▲ W Burma (Myanmar)
165 *O10* **Arakawa** Niigata, Honshū, C Japan 38°06′N 139°25′E
Árakhthos *see* Árachthos
Araks/Arak's *see* Aras
158 *H7* **Aral** Xinjiang Uygur Zizhiqu, NW China 40°40′N 81°19′E
Aral *see* Aralsk, Kazakhstan
Aral *see* Vose', Tajikistan
Aral-Bukhorskiy Kanal *see* Amu-Buxoro Kanali
137 *T12* **Aralik** Iğdır, E Turkey 39°54′N 44°28′E
146 *H5* **Aral Sea** ***Kaz.*** Aral Tengizi, ***Rus.*** Aral'skoye More, ***Uzb.*** Orol Dengizi. *inland sea* Kazakhstan/Uzbekistan
144 *L13* **Aral'sk** ***Kaz.*** Aral. Kzylorda, SW Kazakhstan 46°48′N 61°40′E
Aral'skoye More/Aral Tengizi *see* Aral Sea
41 *O10* **Aramberri** Nuevo León, NE Mexico 24°05′N 99°52′W
186 *B8* **Aramia** ≈ SW Papua New Guinea
143 *N6* **Ārān** ***var.*** Golārā. Eşfahān, C Iran 34°03′N 51°30′E
105 *N5* **Aranda de Duero** Castilla-León, N Spain 41°40′N 03°41′W
112 *M12* **Aranđelovac** ***prev.*** Arandjelovac. Serbia, C Serbia 44°18′N 20°32′E
Arandjelovac *see* Aranđelovac
97 *J19* **Aran Fawddwy** ▲ NW Wales, United Kingdom 52°48′N 03°42′W
97 *C14* **Aran Island** ***Ir.*** Árainn Mhór. *island* NW Ireland
97 *A18* **Aran Islands** *island group* W Ireland
105 *N9* **Aranjuez** ***anc.*** Ara Jovis. Madrid, C Spain 40°02′N 03°37′W
83 *E20* **Aranos** Hardap, SE Namibia 24°10′S 19°08′E
25 *U14* **Aransas Bay** *inlet* Texas, SW USA
25 *T14* **Aransas Pass** Texas, SW USA 27°54′N 97°09′W
191 *O3* **Aranuka** ***prev.*** Nanouki. *atoll* Tungaru, W Kiribati
167 *Q11* **Aranyaprathet** Prachin Buri, S Thailand 13°42′N 102°32′E
Aranyosasztal *see* Zlatý Stôl
Aranyosgyéres *see* Câmpia Turzii
Aranyosmarót *see* Zlaté Moravce
164 *C14* **Arao** Kumamoto, Kyūshū, SW Japan 32°58′N 130°26′E
77 *O8* **Araouane** Tombouctou, N Mali 18°53′N 03°31′W
26 *L10* **Arapaho** Oklahoma, C USA 35°34′N 98°57′W
29 *N16* **Arapahoe** Nebraska, C USA 40°18′N 99°54′W
57 *I16* **Arapa, Laguna** ◎ SE Peru
185 *K14* **Arapawa Island** *island* C New Zealand
61 *E17* **Arapey Grande, Río** ≈ N Uruguay
59 *P16* **Arapiraca** Alagoas, E Brazil 09°45′S 36°40′W
140 *M3* **'Ar'ar** Al Ḩudūd ash Shamālīyah, NW Saudi Arabia 31°N 41°E
54 *G15* **Araracuara** Caquetá, S Colombia 0°36′S 72°24′W
61 *K15* **Araranguá** Santa Catarina, S Brazil 28°56′S 49°30′W
60 *L8* **Araraquara** São Paulo, S Brazil 21°46′S 48°08′W
59 *O13* **Araras** Ceará, E Brazil 04°08′S 40°30′W
58 *I14* **Araras** Pará, N Brazil 06°04′S 54°34′W
60 *L9* **Araras** São Paulo, S Brazil 22°21′S 47°21′W
60 *H11* **Araras, Serra das** ▲▲ S Brazil
137 *U12* **Ararat** S Armenia 39°49′N 44°45′E
182 *M12* **Ararat** Victoria, SE Australia 37°20′S 143°00′E
Ararat, Mount *see* Büyükağrı Dağı
140 *M3* **'Ar'ar, Wādī** *dry watercourse* Iraq/Saudi Arabia
129 *N7* **Aras** ***Arm.*** Arak's, ***Az.*** Araz Nehri, ***Per.*** Rūd-e Aras, ***Rus.*** Araks; ***prev.*** Araxes. ≈ SW Asia
Aras de Alpuente *see* Aras de los Olmos
105 *R9* **Aras de los Olmos** ***prev.*** Aras de Alpuente. País Valenciano, E Spain 39°55′N 01°09′W
137 *S13* **Aras Güneyi Dağları** ▲▲ NE Turkey
Aras, Rūd-e *see* Aras
191 *U9* **Aratika** *atoll* Îles Tuamotu, C French Polynesia
Aratürük *see* Yiwu
54 *I8* **Arauca** Arauca, NE Colombia 07°03′N 70°47′W
54 *I8* **Arauca** ***off.*** Intendencia de Arauca. ◈ *province* NE Colombia
Arauca, Intendencia de *see* Arauca
63 *G15* **Araucanía** ***off.*** Región de la Araucanía. ◈ *region* C Chile
Araucanía, Región de la *see* Araucanía
54 *L7* **Arauca, Río** ≈ Colombia/Venezuela
63 *F14* **Arauco** Bío Bío, C Chile 37°15′S 73°22′W
63 *F14* **Arauco, Golfo de** *gulf* S Chile
54 *H8* **Arauquita** Arauca, C Colombia 06°57′N 71°19′W
Arausio *see* Orange
152 *F13* **Arāvali Range** ▲▲ N India
186 *J7* **Arawa** Bougainville Island, NE Papua New Guinea 06°15′S 155°35′E
185 *C20* **Arawata** ≈ South Island, New Zealand
186 *F7* **Arawe Islands** *island group* E Papua New Guinea
59 *L20* **Araxá** Minas Gerais, SE Brazil 19°37′S 46°50′W
Araxes *see* Aras
55 *O5* **Araya** Sucre, N Venezuela 10°34′N 64°15′W
Araz Nehri *see* Aras
105 *R4* **Arba** ≈ N Spain
81 *I15* **Ārba Minch'** Southern Nationalities, S Ethiopia 06°02′N 37°34′E
139 *U4* **Arbat** As Sulaymānīyah, NE Iraq 35°26′N 45°34′E
107 *D19* **Arbatax** Sardegna, Italy, C Mediterranean Sea 39°57′N 09°42′E
Arbe *see* Rab
Arbela *see* Arbīl
139 *S3* **Arbīl** ◈ *governorate* N Iraq
139 *S3* **Arbīl** ***var.*** Erbil, Irbīl, ***Kurd.*** Hawlēr; ***anc.*** Arbela. Arbīl, N Iraq 36°12′N 44°01′E
95 *M16* **Arboga** Västmanland, C Sweden 59°24′N 15°50′E
95 *M16* **Arbogaån** ≈ C Sweden
103 *S9* **Arbois** Jura, E France 46°54′N 05°45′E
54 *D6* **Arboletes** Antioquia, NW Colombia 08°52′N 76°25′W
11 *X15* **Arborg** Manitoba, S Canada 50°52′N 97°20′W
94 *N12* **Arbrå** Gävleborg, C Sweden 61°27′N 16°21′E
96 *K10* **Arbroath** ***anc.*** Aberbrothock. E Scotland, United Kingdom 56°34′N 02°35′W
35 *N6* **Arbuckle** California, W USA 39°00′N 122°05′W
27 *N12* **Arbuckle Mountains** ▲▲ Oklahoma, C USA
162 *I5* **Arbulag** ***var.*** Mandal. Hövsgöl, N Mongolia 49°55′N 99°21′E
Arbuzinka *see* Arbuzynka
117 *Q8* **Arbuzynka** ***Rus.*** Arbuzinka. Mykolayivs'ka Oblast', S Ukraine 47°54′N 31°19′E
103 *U12* **Arc** ≈ E France
102 *J13* **Arcachon** Gironde, SW France 44°40′N 01°11′W
102 *J13* **Arcachon, Bassin d'** *inlet* SW France
18 *E10* **Arcade** New York, NE USA 42°32′N 78°19′W
23 *W14* **Arcadia** Florida, SE USA 27°13′N 81°51′W
22 *H5* **Arcadia** Louisiana, S USA 32°33′N 92°55′W
30 *J7* **Arcadia** Wisconsin, N USA 44°15′N 91°30′W
Arcae Remorum *see* Châlons-en-Champagne
44 *L9* **Arcahaie** C Haiti 18°46′N 72°32′W
34 *K3* **Arcata** California, W USA 40°51′N 124°06′W
35 *U6* **Arc Dome** ▲ Nevada, W USA 38°52′N 117°20′W
107 *J16* **Arce** Lazio, C Italy 41°35′N 13°34′E
41 *O15* **Arcelia** Guerrero, S Mexico 18°20′N 100°16′W
99 *M15* **Arcen** Limburg, SE Netherlands 51°28′N 06°10′E
115 *J25* **Archánes** ***var.*** Áno Arkhánai, Epáno Archánes; ***prev.*** Epáno Arkhánai. Kríti, Greece, E Mediterranean Sea 35°12′N 25°10′E
Archangel *see* Arkhangel'sk
Archangel Bay *see* Chëshskaya Guba
115 *O23* **Archángelos** ***var.*** Arhangelos, Arkhángelos. Ródos, Dodekánisa, Greece, Aegean Sea 36°13′N 28°07′E
114 *F7* **Archar** ≈ NW Bulgaria
31 *R11* **Archbold** Ohio, N USA 41°31′N 84°18′W
105 *R12* **Archena** Murcia, SE Spain 38°07′N 01°17′W
25 *R5* **Archer City** Texas, SW USA 33°36′N 98°37′W
104 *M14* **Archidona** Andalucía, S Spain 37°06′N 04°23′W
106 *G13* **Arcidosso** Toscana, C Italy 42°52′N 11°30′E
103 *Q5* **Arcis-sur-Aube** Aube, N France 48°32′N 04°09′E
182 *F3* **Arckaringa Creek** *seasonal river* South Australia
106 *G7* **Arco** Trentino-Alto Adige, N Italy 45°53′N 10°52′E
33 *Q14* **Arco** Idaho, NW USA 43°38′N 113°18′W
30 *M14* **Arcola** Illinois, N USA 39°39′N 88°19′W
105 *P6* **Arcos de Jalón** Castilla-León, N Spain 41°12′N 02°13′W
104 *K15* **Arcos de la Frontera** Andalucía, S Spain 36°45′N 05°49′W
104 *G5* **Arcos de Valdevez** Viana do Castelo, N Portugal 41°51′N 08°25′W
59 *P15* **Arcoverde** Pernambuco, E Brazil 08°23′S 37°W
102 *H5* **Arcovest, Pointe de l'** *headland* NW France 48°49′N 02°58′W
Arctic Mid Oceanic Ridge *see* Nansen Cordillera
197 *R8* **Arctic Ocean** *ocean*
8 *G7* **Arctic Red River** ≈ Northwest Territories/Yukon Territory, NW Canada
Arctic Red River *see* Tsiigehtchic
39 *S6* **Arctic Village** Alaska, USA 68°07′N 145°32′W
194 *H1* **Arctowski** *Polish research station* South Shetland Islands, Antarctica 61°57′S 58°23′W
114 *I12* **Arda** ***var.*** Ardhas, ***Gk.*** Ardas. ≈ Bulgaria/Greece *see also* Ardas
142 *L2* **Ardabīl** ***var.*** Ardebil. Ardabīl, NW Iran 38°15′N 48°18′E
142 *L2* **Ardabīl** ***off.*** Ostān-e Ardabīl. ◈ *province* NW Iran
Ardabīl, Ostān-e *see* Ardabīl
137 *R11* **Ardahan** Ardahan, NE Turkey 41°08′N 42°41′E
137 *S11* **Ardahan** ◈ *province* Ardahan, Turkey
143 *O10* **Ardakān** Fārs, SE Iran 30°16′N 52°01′E
143 *P8* **Ardakān** Yazd, C Iran 32°20′N 53°59′E
94 *E12* **Årdalstangen** Sogn Og Fjordane, S Norway 61°14′N 07°45′E
137 *R11* **Ardanuç** Artvin, NE Turkey 41°07′N 42°04′E
114 *L12* **Ardas** ***var.*** Ardhas, ***Bul.*** Arda. ≈ Bulgaria/Greece *see also* Arda
138 *I13* **Arḑ aş Şawwān** ***var.*** Ardh es Suwwān. *plain* S Jordan
127 *N4* **Ardatov** Nizhegorodskaya Oblast', W Russian Federation 55°14′N 43°06′E
127 *P5* **Ardatov** Respublika Mordoviya, W Russian Federation 54°49′N 46°13′E
14 *G12* **Ardbeg** Ontario, S Canada 45°38′N 80°05′W
Ardeal *see* Transylvania
Ardebil *see* Ardabīl
103 *Q13* **Ardèche** ◈ *department* E France
103 *Q13* **Ardèche** ≈ C France
97 *F17* **Ardee** ***Ir.*** Baile Átha Fhirdhia. Louth, NE Ireland 53°52′N 06°33′W
103 *Q3* **Ardennes** ◈ *department* NE France
99 *J23* **Ardennes** *physical region* Belgium/France
137 *Q11* **Ardeşen** Rize, NE Turkey 41°14′N 41°00′E
143 *O7* **Ardestān** ***var.*** Ardistan. Eşfahān, C Iran 33°29′N 52°17′E
108 *J9* **Ardez** Graubünden, SE Switzerland 46°47′N 10°09′E
Ardhas *see* Arda/Ardas
Ardh es Suwwān *see* Arḑ aş Şawwān
Ardila *see* Ardila, Ribeira de
104 *I12* **Ardila, Ribeira de** ***Sp.*** Ardilla. ≈ Portugal/Spain *see also* Ardilla
Ardila, Ribeira de *see* Ardilla
11 *T17* **Ardill** Saskatchewan, S Canada 49°56′N 105°49′W
104 *I12* **Ardilla** ***Port.*** Ribeira de Ardila. ≈ Portugal/Spain *see also* Ardila, Ribeira de
40 *M11* **Ardilla, Cerro la** ▲ C Mexico 22°15′N 102°33′W
114 *J12* **Ardino** Kŭrdzhali, S Bulgaria 41°38′N 25°22′E
Ardistan *see* Ardestān
183 *P9* **Ardlethan** New South Wales, SE Australia 34°24′S 146°52′E
Ard Mhacha *see* Armagh
23 *P1* **Ardmore** Alabama, S USA 34°59′N 86°51′W
27 *N13* **Ardmore** Oklahoma, C USA 34°11′N 97°08′W
20 *J10* **Ardmore** Tennessee, S USA 35°00′N 86°48′W
96 *G10* **Ardnamurchan, Point of** *headland* N Scotland, United Kingdom 56°42′N 06°15′W
Árdni *see* Arnøya
99 *C17* **Ardooie** West-Vlaanderen, W Belgium 50°59′N 03°10′E
182 *I9* **Ardrossan** South Australia 34°27′S 137°54′E
116 *H9* **Ardusat** ***Hung.*** Erdőszáda. Maramureş, N Romania 47°36′N 23°25′E
93 *F16* **Åre** Jämtland, C Sweden 63°25′N 13°04′E
79 *P16* **Arebi** Orientale, NE Dem. Rep. Congo 02°47′N 29°35′E
45 *T5* **Arecibo** C Puerto Rico 18°29′N 66°44′W N
171 *V13* **Aredo** Papua, E Indonesia 02°27′S 133°59′E
59 *P14* **Areia Branca** Rio Grande do Norte, E Brazil 04°53′S 37°03′W
119 *O14* **Arekhawsk** ***Rus.*** Orekhovsk. Vitsyebskaya Voblasts', N Belarus 54°42′N 30°30′E
Arel *see* Arlon
Arelas/Arelate *see* Arles
Arenal, Embalse de *see* Arenal Laguna
42 *L12* **Arenal Laguna** ***var.*** Embalse de Arenal. ◎ NW Costa Rica
42 *L13* **Arenal, Volcán** ⋀ NW Costa Rica 10°21′N 84°42′W
34 *K6* **Arena, Point** *headland* California, W USA 38°57′N 123°44′W
59 *H17* **Arenápolis** Mato Grosso, W Brazil 14°25′S 56°52′W
40 *G10* **Arena, Punta** *headland* NW Mexico 23°28′N 109°24′W
104 *L8* **Arenas de San Pedro** Castilla-León, N Spain 40°12′N 05°05′W
63 *I24* **Arenas, Punta de** *headland* S Argentina 53°10′S 68°15′W
61 *B20* **Arenaza** Buenos Aires, E Argentina 34°55′S 61°45′W
95 *F17* **Arendal** Aust-Agder, S Norway 58°27′N 08°45′E
99 *J16* **Arendonk** Antwerpen, N Belgium 51°18′N 05°06′E
43 *T15* **Arenosa** Panamá, N Panama 09°02′N 79°57′W
Arensburg *see* Kuressaare
105 *W5* **Arenys de Mar** Cataluña, NE Spain 41°35′N 02°33′E
106 *C9* **Arenzano** Liguria, NW Italy 44°25′N 08°43′E
115 *F22* **Areópoli** ***prev.*** Areópolis. Pelopónnisos, S Greece 36°40′N 22°24′E
Areópolis *see* Areópoli
57 *H18* **Arequipa** Arequipa, SE Peru 16°24′S 71°33′W
57 *G17* **Arequipa** ***off.*** Departamento de Arequipa. ◈ *department* Arequipa SW Peru
Arequipa, Departamento de *see* Arequipa
61 *B19* **Arequito** Santa Fe, C Argentina 33°09′S 61°28′W
104 *M7* **Arévalo** Castilla-León, N Spain 41°04′N 04°44′W

◆ Country ● Country Capital ◇ Dependent Territory ○ Dependent Territory Capital ◈ Administrative Regions ✈ International Airport ▲ Mountain ▲▲ Mountain Range ⋀ Volcano ≈ River ◎ Lake ▣ Reservoir

106 *H12* **Arezzo** *anc.* Arretium. Toscana, C Italy *43°28′N 11°50′E*
105 *Q4* **Arga** ≈ N Spain
Argaeus *see* Erciyes Dağı
115 *G17* **Argalastí** Thessalía, C Greece *39°13′N 23°13′E*
105 *O10* **Argamasilla de Alba** Castilla-La Mancha, C Spain *39°08′N 03°05′W*
158 *L8* **Argan** Xinjiang Uygur Zizhiqu, NW China *40°09′N 88°16′E*
105 *O8* **Arganda** Madrid, C Spain *40°19′N 03°26′W*
104 *H8* **Arganil** Coimbra, N Portugal *40°13′N 08°03′W*
171 *P6* **Argao** Cebu, C Philippines *09°52′N 123°33′E*
153 *V15* **Argartala** Tripura, NE India
123 *N9* **Arga-Sala** ≈ Respublika Sakha (Yakutiya),NE Russian Federation
103 *P17* **Argelès-sur-Mer** Pyrénées-Orientales, S France *42°33′N 03°01′E*
103 *T15* **Argens** ≈ SE France
106 *H9* **Argenta** Emilia-Romagna, N Italy *44°37′N 11°49′E*
102 *K5* **Argentan** Orne, N France *48°45′N 00°01′W*
103 *N12* **Argentat** Corrèze, C France *45°06′N 01°57′E*
106 *A9* **Argentera** Piemonte, NE Italy *44°25′N 06°57′E*
103 *N5* **Argenteuil** Val-d'Oise, N France *48°57′N 02°13′E*
62 *K13* **Argentina** *off.* Argentine Republic. ◆ *republic* S South America
Argentina Basin *see* Argentine Basin
Argentine Abyssal Plain *see* Argentine Plain
65 *I19* **Argentine Basin** *var.* Argentina Basin. *undersea feature* SW Atlantic Ocean *45°00′S 45°00′W*
65 *I20* **Argentine Plain** *var.* Argentine Abyssal Plain. *undersea feature* SW Atlantic Ocean *47°31′S 50°00′W*
Argentine Republic *see* Argentina
Argentine Rise *see* Falkland Plateau
63 *H22* **Argentino, Lago** ◎ S Argentina
102 *K8* **Argenton-Château** Deux-Sèvres, W France *46°59′N 00°22′W*
102 *M9* **Argenton-sur-Creuse** Indre, C France *46°34′N 01°32′E*
Argentoratum *see* Strasbourg
116 *I12* **Argeș** ◈ *county* S Romania
116 *K14* **Argeș** ≈ S Romania
149 *O8* **Arghandāb, Daryā-ye** ≈ SE Afghanistan
Arghastān *see* Arghestān
149 *O8* **Arghestān** *Pash.* Arghastān. ≈ SE Afghanistan
Argirocastro *see* Gjirokastër
80 *E7* **Argo** Northern, N Sudan *19°31′N 30°25′E*
173 *P7* **Argo Fracture Zone** *tectonic feature* C Indian Ocean
115 *F20* **Argolikós Kólpos** *gulf* S Greece
103 *R4* **Argonne** *physical region* NE France
115 *F20* **Árgos** Pelopónnisos, S Greece *37°38′N 22°43′E*
139 *S1* **Argōsh** Dahūk, N Iraq *37°07′N 44°13′E*
115 *D14* **Árgos Orestikó** Dytikí Makedonía, N Greece *40°27′N 21°15′E*
115 *B19* **Argostóli** *var.* Argostólion. Kefallonía, Iónia Nísiá, Greece, C Mediterranean Sea *38°13′N 20°29′E*
Argostólion *see* Argostóli
Argovie *see* Aargau
35 *O14* **Arguello, Point** *headland* California, W USA *34°34′N 120°39′W*
127 *P16* **Argun** Chechenskaya Respublika, SW Russian Federation *43°16′N 45°53′E*
157 *T2* **Argun** *Chin.* Ergun He, *Rus.* Argun'. ≈ China/Russian Federation
77 *T12* **Argungu** Kebbi, NW Nigeria *12°45′N 04°24′E*
Arguut *see* Guchin-Us
181 *N3* **Argyle, Lake** *salt lake* Western Australia
96 *G12* **Argyll** *cultural region* W Scotland, United Kingdom
Argyrokastron *see* Gjirokastër
162 *I7* **Arhangay** ◈ *province* C Mongolia
Arhangelos *see* Archángelos
95 *P14* **Arholma** Stockholm, C Sweden *59°51′N 19°01′E*
95 *G22* **Århus** *var.* Aarhus. Århus, C Denmark *56°09′N 10°11′E*
95 *G22* **Århus** ◈ *county* C Denmark
139 *T1* **Ārī** Arbīl, E Iraq *37°07′N 44°34′E*
Aria *see* Herāt
83 *F22* **Ariamsvlei** Karas, SE Namibia *28°08′S 19°50′E*
107 *L17* **Ariano Irpino** Campania, S Italy *41°08′N 15°00′E*
54 *F11* **Ariari, Río** ≈ C Colombia
151 *K19* **Ari Atoll** *var.* Alifu Atoll. *atoll* C Maldives
77 *P11* **Aribinda** N Burkina *14°12′N 00°50′W*
62 *G2* **Arica** *hist.* San Marcos de Arica. Tarapacá, N Chile *18°31′S 70°18′W*
54 *H16* **Arica** Amazonas, S Colombia *02°09′S 71°48′W*
62 *G2* **Arica** ✈ Tarapacá, N Chile *18°30′S 70°20′W*
114 *E13* **Aridaía** *var.* Aridea, Aridhaía. Dytikí Makedonía, N Greece *40°59′N 22°04′E*
Aridea *see* Aridaía
172 *I15* **Aride, Île** *island* Inner Islands, NE Seychelles
Aridhaía *see* Aridaía
103 *N17* **Ariège** ◈ *department* S France
102 *M16* **Ariège** *var.* la Riege. ≈ Andorra/France
116 *H11* **Arieș** ≈ W Romania
149 *U10* **Ārifwāla** Punjab, E Pakistan *30°15′N 73°08′E*
Ariguaní *see* El Difícil
138 *G11* **Arīhā** Al Karak, W Jordan *31°25′N 35°47′E*
138 *I3* **Arīḩā** *var.* Arīhā. Idlib, W Syria *35°50′N 36°36′E*
Arīhā *see* Arīḩā
Arīḩā *see* Jericho
37 *W4* **Arikaree River** ≈ Colorado/Nebraska, C USA
112 *L13* **Arilje** Serbia, W Serbia *43°45′N 20°06′E*
45 *U14* **Arima** Trinidad, Trinidad and Tobago *10°38′N 61°17′W*
Arime *see* Al 'Arīmah
Ariminum *see* Rimini
59 *H16* **Arinos, Rio** ≈ W Brazil
40 *M14* **Ario de Rosales** *var.* Ario de Rosáles. Michoacán, SW Mexico *19°12′N 101°42′W*
Ario de Rosáles *see* Ario de Rosales
118 *F12* **Ariogala** Kaunas, C Lithuania *55°16′N 23°30′E*
47 *T7* **Aripuanã** ≈ W Brazil
59 *E15* **Ariquemes** Rondônia, W Brazil *09°55′S 63°06′W*
121 *W13* **'Arîsh, Wâdi el** ≈ NE Egypt
54 *K6* **Arismendi** Barinas, C Venezuela *08°29′N 68°22′W*
10 *J14* **Aristazabal Island** *island* SW Canada
60 *F13* **Aristóbulo del Valle** Misiones, NE Argentina *27°09′S 54°54′W*
172 *I5* **Arivonimamo** ✈ (Antananarivo) Antananarivo, C Madagascar *19°00′S 47°11′E*
Arixang *see* Wenquan
105 *Q6* **Ariza** Aragón, NE Spain *41°19′N 02°03′W*
62 *I6* **Arizaro, Salar de** *salt lake* NW Argentina
105 *O2* **Arizgoiti** *var.* Basauri. País Vasco, N Spain *43°13′N 02°54′W*
62 *K13* **Arizona** San Luis, C Argentina *35°44′S 65°16′W*
36 *J12* **Arizona** *off.* State of Arizona, *also known as* Copper State, Grand Canyon State. ◈ *state* SW USA
40 *G4* **Arizpe** Sonora, NW Mexico *30°20′N 110°11′W*
95 *J16* **Årjäng** Värmland, C Sweden *59°24′N 12°09′E*
143 *P8* **Arjenān** Yazd, C Iran *32°19′N 53°48′E*
92 *I13* **Arjeplog** Norrbotten, N Sweden *66°04′N 18°E*
54 *E5* **Arjona** Bolívar, N Colombia *10°14′N 75°22′W*
105 *N13* **Arjona** Andalucía, S Spain *37°56′N 04°04′W*
123 *S10* **Arka** Khabarovskiy Kray, E Russian Federation *60°04′N 142°17′E*
22 *L2* **Arkabutla Lake** ⊠ Mississippi, S USA
127 *O7* **Arkadak** Saratovskaya Oblast', W Russian Federation *51°55′N 43°29′E*
27 *T13* **Arkadelphia** Arkansas, C USA *34°07′N 93°06′W*
115 *J25* **Arkalochóri** ; *prev.* Arkalokhórion. Kríti, Greece, E Mediterranean Sea *35°09′N 25°15′E*
Arkalohori/Arkalokhórion *see* Arkalochóri
145 *O10* **Arkalyk** *Kaz.* Arqalyq. Kostanay, N Kazakhstan *50°17′N 66°51′E*
27 *U10* **Arkansas** *off.* State of Arkansas, *also known as* The Land of Opportunity. ◈ *state* S USA
27 *W14* **Arkansas City** Arkansas, C USA *33°36′N 91°12′W*
27 *O7* **Arkansas City** Kansas, C USA *37°03′N 97°02′W*
16 *K11* **Arkansas River** ≈ C USA
182 *J5* **Arkaroola** South Australia *30°21′S 139°20′E*
Arkhángelos *see* Archángelos
124 *L8* **Arkhangel'sk** *Eng.* Archangel. Arkhangel'skaya Oblast', NW Russian Federation *64°32′N 40°40′E*
124 *L9* **Arkhangel'skaya Oblast'** ◈ *province* NW Russian Federation
127 *O14* **Arkhangel'skoye** Stavropol'skiy Kray, SW Russian Federation *44°37′N 44°03′E*
123 *R14* **Arkhara** Amurskaya Oblast', S Russian Federation *49°20′N 130°04′E*
97 *G19* **Arklow** *Ir.* An tInbhear Mór. SE Ireland *52°48′N 06°09′W*
115 *M20* **Arkoí** *island* Dodekánisa, Greece, Aegean Sea
27 *R11* **Arkoma** Oklahoma, C USA *35°19′N 94°27′W*
100 *O7* **Arkona, Kap** *headland* NE Germany *54°40′N 13°24′E*
95 *N17* **Arkösund** Östergötland, S Sweden *58°28′N 16°55′E*
122 *J6* **Arkticheskogo Instituta, Ostrova** *island* N Russian Federation
95 *O15* **Arlanda** ✈ (Stockholm) Stockholm, C Sweden *59°40′N 17°58′E*
146 *C11* **Arlandag** *Rus.* Gora Arlan. ▲ W Turkmenistan *39°39′N 54°28′E*
Arlan, Gora *see* Arlandag
105 *O5* **Arlanza** ≈ N Spain
105 *N5* **Arlanzón** ≈ N Spain
103 *R15* **Arles** *var.* Arles-sur-Rhône; *anc.* Arelas, Arelate. Bouches-du-Rhône, SE France *43°41′N 04°38′E*
Arles-sur-Rhône *see* Arles
103 *O17* **Arles-sur-Tech** Pyrénées-Orientales, S France *42°27′N 02°37′E*
29 *U9* **Arlington** Minnesota, N USA *44°36′N 94°04′W*
29 *R15* **Arlington** Nebraska, C USA *41°27′N 96°21′W*
32 *J11* **Arlington** Oregon, NW USA *45°43′N 120°10′W*
29 *R10* **Arlington** South Dakota, N USA *44°21′N 97°07′W*
20 *E10* **Arlington** Tennessee, S USA *35°17′N 89°40′W*
25 *T6* **Arlington** Texas, SW USA *32°44′N 97°05′W*
21 *W4* **Arlington** Virginia, NE USA *38°54′N 77°09′W*
32 *H7* **Arlington** Washington, NW USA *48°12′N 122°07′W*
30 *M10* **Arlington Heights** Illinois, N USA *42°08′N 88°03′W*
77 *U8* **Arlit** Agadez, C Niger *18°54′N 07°25′E*
99 *L24* **Arlon** *Dut.* Aarlen, *Ger.* Arel, *Lat.* Orolaunum. Luxembourg, SE Belgium *49°41′N 05°49′E*
27 *R7* **Arma** Kansas, C USA *37°32′N 94°42′W*
97 *F16* **Armagh** *Ir.* Ard Mhacha. S Northern Ireland, United Kingdom *54°15′N 06°33′W*
97 *F16* **Armagh** *cultural region* S Northern Ireland, United Kingdom
102 *K15* **Armagnac** *cultural region* S France
103 *Q7* **Armançon** ≈ C France
60 *K10* **Armando Laydner, Represa** ⊠ S Brazil
115 *M24* **Armathía** *island* SE Greece
137 *T12* **Armavir** *prev.* Hoktemberyan, *Rus.* Oktemberyan. SW Armenia *40°09′N 43°58′E*
126 *M14* **Armavir** Krasnodarskiy Kray, SW Russian Federation *44°59′N 41°07′E*
54 *E10* **Armenia** Quindío, W Colombia *04°32′N 75°40′W*
137 *T12* **Armenia** *off.* Republic of Armenia, *var.* Ajastan, *Arm.* Hayastani Hanrapetut'yun; *prev.* Armenian Soviet Socialist Republic. ◆ *republic* SW Asia
Armenian Soviet Socialist Republic *see* Armenia
Armenia, Republic of *see* Armenia
Armenierstadt *see* Gherla
103 *O1* **Armentières** Nord, N France *50°41′N 02°53′E*
40 *K14* **Armería** Colima, SW Mexico *18°55′N 103°59′W*
183 *T5* **Armidale** New South Wales, SE Australia *30°32′S 151°40′E*
29 *P11* **Armour** South Dakota, N USA *43°19′N 98°21′W*
61 *B18* **Armstrong** Santa Fe, C Argentina *32°46′S 61°39′W*
11 *N16* **Armstrong** British Columbia, SW Canada *50°27′N 119°14′W*
12 *D11* **Armstrong** Ontario, S Canada *50°20′N 89°02′W*
29 *U11* **Armstrong** Iowa, C USA *43°24′N 94°28′W*
25 *S16* **Armstrong** Texas, SW USA *26°55′N 97°47′W*
117 *S11* **Armyans'k** *Rus.* Armyansk. Respublika Krym, S Ukraine *46°05′N 33°43′E*
115 *H14* **Arnaía** *Cont.* Arnea. Kentrikí Makedonía, N Greece *40°30′N 23°36′E*
121 *N2* **Arnaoúti, Akrotíri** *var.* Arnaoútis, Cape Arnaouti. *headland* W Cyprus *35°06′N 32°16′E*
Arnaouti, Cape/Arnaoútis *see* Arnaoúti, Akrotíri
12 *L4* **Arnaud** ≈ Québec, E Canada
103 *Q8* **Arnay-le-Duc** Côte d'Or, C France *47°08′N 04°27′E*
Arnea *see* Arnaía
105 *Q4* **Arnedo** La Rioja, N Spain *42°14′N 02°05′W*
95 *I14* **Årnes** Akershus, S Norway *60°07′N 11°28′E*
Årnes *see* Åi Åfjord
26 *K9* **Arnett** Oklahoma, C USA *36°08′N 99°46′W*
98 *L12* **Arnhem** Gelderland, SE Netherlands *51°59′N 05°54′E*
181 *Q2* **Arnhem Land** *physical region* Northern Territory, N Australia
106 *F11* **Arno** ≈ C Italy
Arņo *see* Arno Atoll
189 *W7* **Arno Atoll** *var.* Arņo. *atoll* Ratak Chain, NE Marshall Islands
182 *H8* **Arno Bay** South Australia *33°55′S 136°31′E*
35 *Q8* **Arnold** California, W USA *38°15′N 120°19′W*
27 *X5* **Arnold** Missouri, C USA *38°25′N 90°22′W*
29 *N15* **Arnold** Nebraska, C USA *41°25′N 100°11′W*
109 *R10* **Arnoldstein** *Slvn.* Pod Klošter. Kärnten, S Austria *46°34′N 13°43′E*
103 *N9* **Arnon** ≈ C France
45 *P14* **Arnos Vale** ✈ (Kingstown) Saint Vincent, SE Saint Vincent and the Grenadines *13°08′N 61°13′W*
92 *I8* **Arnøya** *Lapp.* Árdni. *island* N Norway
14 *L12* **Arnprior** Ontario, SE Canada *45°31′N 76°11′W*
101 *G15* **Arnsberg** Nordrhein-Westfalen, W Germany *51°24′N 08°04′E*
101 *K16* **Arnstadt** Thüringen, C Germany *50°50′N 10°57′E*
Arnswalde *see* Choszczno
54 *K5* **Aroa** Yaracuy, N Venezuela *10°26′N 68°54′W*
83 *E21* **Aroab** Karas, SE Namibia *26°47′S 19°40′E*
Ároania *see* Chelmós
191 *O6* **Aroa, Pointe** *headland* Moorea, W French Polynesia *17°27′S 149°45′W*
Aroe Islands *see* Aru, Kepulauan
101 *H15* **Arolsen** Niedersachsen, C Germany *51°23′N 09°00′E*
106 *C7* **Arona** Piemonte, NE Italy *45°45′N 08°33′E*
19 *R3* **Aroostook River** ≈ Canada/USA
Arop Island *see* Long Island
38 *M12* **Aropuk Lake** ◎ Alaska, USA
191 *P4* **Arorae** *atoll* Tungaru, W Kiribati
190 *G16* **Arorangi** Rarotonga, S Cook Islands *21°13′S 159°49′W*
108 *I9* **Arosa** Graubünden, S Switzerland *46°48′N 09°42′E*
104 *F4* **Arousa, Ría de** *estuary* E Atlantic Ocean
184 *P8* **Arowhana** ▲ North Island, New Zealand *38°07′S 177°52′E*
137 *V12* **Arp'a** *Az.* Arpaçay. ≈ Armenia/Azerbaijan
137 *S11* **Arpaçay** Kars, NE Turkey *40°51′N 43°20′E*
Arpaçay *see* Arp'a
Arqalyq *see* Arkalyk
149 *N14* **Arra** ≈ SW Pakistan
Arrabona *see* Győr
Arrah *see* Āra
Ar Rahad *see* Er Rahad
139 *R9* **Ar Raḩḩālīyah** Al Anbār, C Iraq *32°53′N 43°21′E*
60 *Q10* **Arraial do Cabo** Rio de Janeiro, SE Brazil *22°57′S 42°00′W*
104 *H11* **Arraiolos** Évora, S Portugal *38°44′N 07°59′W*
139 *R8* **Ar Ramādī** *var.* Ramadi, Rumadiya. Al Anbār, SW Iraq *33°27′N 43°19′E*
138 *J6* **Ar Rāmī** Ḩimş, C Syria *34°32′N 37°54′E*
Ar Rams *see* Rams
138 *H9* **Ar Ramthā** *var.* Ramtha. Irbid, N Jordan *32°34′N 36°00′E*
96 *H13* **Arran, Isle of** *island* SW Scotland, United Kingdom
138 *L3* **Ar Raqqah** *var.* Rakka; *anc.* Nicephorium. Ar Raqqah, N Syria *35°57′N 39°03′E*
138 *L3* **Ar Raqqah** *off.* Muḩāfaz̧at al Raqqah, *var.* Raqqah, *Fr.* Rakka. ◈ *governorate* N Syria
103 *O2* **Arras** *anc.* Nemetocenna. Pas-de-Calais, N France *50°17′N 02°46′E*
105 *P3* **Arrasate** *Cast.* Mondragón. País Vasco, N Spain *43°04′N 02°30′W*
138 *G12* **Ar Rashādīyah** Aţ ţafilah, W Jordan *30°42′N 35°38′E*
138 *I5* **Ar Rastān** *var.* Rastâne. Ḩimş, W Syria *34°57′N 36°43′E*
139 *X12* **Ar Raţāwī** Al Başrah, E Iraq *30°37′N 47°12′E*
102 *L15* **Arrats** ≈ S France
141 *N10* **Ar Rawḑah** Makkah, S Saudi Arabia *21°19′N 42°48′E*
141 *Q15* **Ar Rawḑah** S Yemen *14°26′N 47°14′E*
142 *K11* **Ar Rawḑatayn** *var.* Raudhatain. N Kuwait *29°80′N 47°50′E*
143 *N16* **Ar Rayyān** *var.* Al Rayyan. C Qatar *25°18′N 51°29′E*
102 *L17* **Arreau** Hautes-Pyrénées, S France *42°55′N 00°21′E*
64 *Q11* **Arrecife** *var.* Arrecife de Lanzarote, Puerto Arrecife. Lanzarote, Islas Canarias, NE Atlantic Ocean *28°57′N 13°33′W*
Arrecife de Lanzarote *see* Arrecife
43 *P6* **Arrecife Edinburgh** *reef* NE Nicaragua
61 *C19* **Arrecifes** Buenos Aires, E Argentina *34°06′S 60°09′W*
102 *F6* **Arrée, Monts d'** ▲▲ NW France
Ar Refā'ī *see* Ar Rifā'ī
Arretium *see* Arezzo
Arriaca *see* Guadalajara
109 *S9* **Arriach** Kärnten, S Austria *46°43′N 13°52′E*
41 *T16* **Arriaga** Chiapas, SE Mexico *16°14′N 93°54′W*
41 *N12* **Arriaga** San Luis Potosí, C Mexico *21°55′N 101°23′W*
139 *W10* **Ar Rifā'ī** *var.* Ar Refā'ī. Dhī Qār, SE Iraq *31°47′N 46°07′E*
139 *V12* **Ar Riḩāb** *salt flat* S Iraq
104 *L2* **Arriondas** Asturias, N Spain *43°23′N 05°11′W*
141 *Q7* **Ar Riyāḑ** *Eng.* Riyadh. ● (Saudi Arabia) Ar Riyāḑ, C Saudi Arabia *24°50′N 46°50′E*
141 *O8* **Ar Riyāḑ** *off.* Minţaqat ar Riyāḑ. ◈ *province* C Saudi Arabia
141 *S15* **Ar Riyān** S Yemen *14°43′N 49°18′E*
Arrö *see* Ærø
61 *H18* **Arroio Grande** Rio Grande do Sul, S Brazil *32°15′S 53°02′W*
102 *K15* **Arros** ≈ S France
103 *Q9* **Arroux** ≈ C France
25 *R5* **Arrowhead, Lake** ⊠ Texas, SW USA
182 *L5* **Arrowsmith, Mount** *hill* New South Wales, SE Australia
185 *D21* **Arrowtown** Otago, South Island, New Zealand *44°57′S 168°51′E*
61 *D17* **Arroyo Barú** Entre Ríos, E Argentina *31°52′S 58°26′W*
104 *J10* **Arroyo de la Luz** Extremadura, W Spain *39°28′N 06°36′W*
63 *J16* **Arroyo de la Ventana** Río Negro, SE Argentina *41°41′S 66°03′W*
35 *P13* **Arroyo Grande** California, W USA *35°07′N 120°35′W*
Ar Ru'ays *see* Ar Ruways
141 *R11* **Ar Rub 'al Khālī** *Eng.* Empty Quarter, Great Sandy Desert. *desert* SW Asia
139 *V13* **Ar Ruḑaymah** Al Muthanná, S Iraq *30°20′N 45°26′E*
61 *A16* **Arrufó** Santa Fe, C Argentina *30°15′S 61°45′W*
138 *I7* **Ar Ruḩaybah** *var.* Ruhaybeh, *Fr.* Rouhaïbé. Dimashq, W Syria *33°45′N 36°40′E*
139 *V15* **Ar Rukhaymīyah** *well* S Iraq
139 *U11* **Ar Rumaythah** *var.* Rumaitha. Al Muthanná, S Iraq *31°31′N 45°15′E*
141 *X8* **Ar Rustāq** *var.* Rostak, Rustaq. N Oman *23°34′N 57°25′E*
139 *N8* **Ar Ruţbah** *var.* Rutba. Al Anbār, SW Iraq *33°03′N 40°16′E*
140 *M3* **Ar Rūthīyah** *spring/well* NW Saudi Arabia *31°18′N 41°23′E*
ar-Ruwaida *see* Ar Ruwayḑah
141 *O8* **Ar Ruwayḑah** *var.* ar-Ruwaida. Jīzān, C Saudi Arabia *23°48′N 44°44′E*
143 *N15* **Ar Ruways** *var.* Al Ruweis, Ar Ru'ays, Ruwais. N Qatar *26°08′N 51°13′E*
143 *O17* **Ar Ruways** *var.* Ar Ru'ays. Abū Z̧aby, W United Arab Emirates *24°09′N 52°57′E*
Års *see* Aars
Arsanias *see* Murat Nehri
123 *S15* **Arsen'yev** Primorskiy Kray, SE Russian Federation *44°09′N 133°28′E*
155 *G19* **Arsikere** Karnātaka, W India *13°20′N 76°13′E′N*
127 *R3* **Arsk** Respublika Tatarstan, W Russian Federation *56°07′N 49°54′E*
94 *N10* **Årskogen** Gävleborg, C Sweden *62°07′N 17°19′E*
121 *O3* **Ársos** C Cyprus *34°51′N 32°46′E*
94 *N13* **Årsunda** Gävleborg, C Sweden *60°31′N 16°45′E*
115 *C17* **Árta** *anc.* Ambracia. Ípeiros, W Greece *39°08′N 20°59′E*
105 *Y9* **Artà** Mallorca, Spain, W Mediterranean Sea *39°42′N 03°20′E*
Arta *see* Árachthos
137 *T12* **Artashat** S Armenia *39°57′N 44°34′E*
40 *M15* **Arteaga** Michoacán, SW Mexico *18°22′N 102°18′W*
123 *S15* **Artem** Primorskiy Kray, SE Russian Federation *43°24′N 132°20′E*
44 *C4* **Artemisa** La Habana, W Cuba *22°49′N 82°47′W*
117 *W7* **Artemivs'k** Donets'ka Oblast', E Ukraine *48°35′N 37°58′E*
122 *K13* **Artemovsk** Krasnoyarskiy Kray, S Russian Federation *54°22′N 93°24′E*
105 *U5* **Artesa de Segre** Cataluña, NE Spain *41°54′N 01°03′E*
37 *U14* **Artesia** New Mexico, SW USA *32°50′N 104°24′W*
25 *Q14* **Artesia Wells** Texas, SW USA *28°13′N 99°18′W*
108 *G8* **Arth** Schwyz, C Switzerland *47°05′N 08°39′E*
14 *F15* **Arthur** Ontario, S Canada *43°49′N 80°31′W*
30 *M14* **Arthur** Illinois, N USA *39°42′N 88°28′W*
28 *L14* **Arthur** Nebraska, C USA *41°35′N 101°42′W*
29 *Q5* **Arthur** North Dakota, N USA *47°03′N 97°12′W*
185 *B21* **Arthur** ≈ South Island, New Zealand
18 *B13* **Arthur, Lake** ⊠ Pennsylvania, NE USA
183 *N15* **Arthur River** ≈ Tasmania, SE Australia
185 *G18* **Arthur's Pass** Canterbury, South Island, New Zealand *42°59′S 171°33′E*
185 *G17* **Arthur's Pass** *pass* South Island, New Zealand
44 *I3* **Arthur's Town** Cat Island, C Bahamas *24°34′N 75°39′W*
44 *M9* **Artibonite, Rivière de l'** ≈ C Haiti
61 *E16* **Artigas** *prev.* San Eugenio, San Eugenio del Cuareim. Artigas, N Uruguay *30°25′S 56°28′W*
61 *E16* **Artigas** ◈ *department* N Uruguay
194 *H1* **Artigas** *Uruguayan research station* Antarctica *61°57′S 58°23′W*
137 *T11* **Art'ik** W Armenia *40°38′N 43°58′E*
187 *O16* **Art, Île** *island* Îles Belep, W New Caledonia
103 *O2* **Artois** *cultural region* N France
136 *L12* **Artova** Tokat, N Turkey *40°04′N 36°17′E*
105 *Y9* **Artrutx, Cap d'** *var.* Cabo Dartuch. *cape* Menorca, Spain, W Mediterranean Sea
Artsiz *see* Artsyz
117 *N11* **Artsyz** *Rus.* Artsiz. Odes'ka Oblast', SW Ukraine *45°59′N 29°26′E*
158 *E7* **Artux** Xinjiang Uygur Zizhiqu, NW China *39°40′N 76°10′E*
137 *R11* **Artvin** Artvin, NE Turkey *41°12′N 41°48′E*
137 *R11* **Artvin** ◈ *province* NE Turkey
146 *G14* **Artyk** Ahal Welaýaty, C Turkmenistan *37°32′N 59°16′E*
79 *Q16* **Aru** Orientale, NE Dem. Rep. Congo *02°53′N 30°50′E*
81 *E17* **Arua** NW Uganda *03°02′N 30°56′E*
104 *I4* **A Rúa de Valdeorras** *var.* La Rúa. Galicia, NW Spain *42°22′N 07°12′W*
Aruângua *see* Luangwa
45 *O15* **Aruba** *var.* Oruba. ◇ *Dutch autonomous region* S West Indies
47 *Q4* **Aruba** *island* Aruba, Lesser Antilles
Aru Islands *see* Aru, Kepulauan
171 *W15* **Aru, Kepulauan** *Eng.* Aru Islands; *prev.* Aroe Islands. *island group* E Indonesia
153 *W10* **Arunāchal Pradesh** *prev.* North East Frontier Agency, North East Frontier Agency of Assam. ◈ *state* NE India
Arun Qi *see* Naji
155 *H23* **Aruppukkottai** Tamil Nādu, SE India *09°31′N 78°03′E*
81 *I20* **Arusha** Arusha, N Tanzania *03°23′S 36°40′E*
81 *I21* **Arusha** ◈ *region* E Tanzania
81 *I20* **Arusha** ✈ Arusha, N Tanzania *03°26′S 37°07′E*
54 *C9* **Arusí, Punta** *headland* NW Colombia *05°36′N 77°30′W*
155 *J23* **Aruvi Aru** ≈ NW Sri Lanka
79 *M17* **Aruwimi** *var.* Ituri (upper course). ≈ NE Dem. Rep. Congo
Árva *see* Orava
37 *T4* **Arvada** Colorado, C USA *39°48′N 105°06′W*
Arvand Rūd *see* 'Arab, Shaţţ al
162 *J8* **Arvayheer** Övörhangay, C Mongolia *46°13′N 102°47′E*
9 *O10* **Arviat** *prev.* Eskimo Point. Nunavut, C Canada *61°10′N 94°15′W*
93 *I14* **Arvidsjaur** Norrbotten, N Sweden *65°34′N 19°12′E*
95 *J15* **Arvika** Värmland, C Sweden *59°41′N 12°38′E*
92 *J8* **Årviksand** Troms, N Norway *70°10′N 20°30′E*
35 *S13* **Arvin** California, W USA *35°12′N 118°52′W*
163 *S8* **Arxan** Nei Mongol Zizhiqu, N China *47.11N 119.58′E*
145 *P7* **Arykbalyk** *Kaz.* Aryqbalyq. Severnyy Kazakhstan, N Kazakhstan *53°00′N 68°11′E*
Aryqbalyq *see* Arykbalyk
145 *P17* **Arys'** *Kaz.* Arys. Yuzhnyy Kazakhstan, S Kazakhstan *42°26′N 68°49′E*
Arys *see* Arys'
Arys *see* Orzysz
Arys Köli *see* Arys, Ozero
145 *O14* **Arys, Ozero** *Kaz.* Arys Köli. ◎ C Kazakhstan
107 *D16* **Arzachena** Sardegna, Italy, C Mediterranean Sea *41°05′N 09°21′E*
127 *O4* **Arzamas** Nizhegorodskaya Oblast', W Russian Federation *55°25′N 43°51′E*
141 *V13* **Arzāt** S Oman *17°00′N 54°18′E*
104 *H3* **Arzúa** Galicia, NW Spain *42°55′N 08°10′W*
111 *A16* **Aš** *Ger.* Asch. Karlovarský Kraj, W Czech Republic *50°18′N 12°12′E*
95 *H15* **Ås** Akershus, S Norway *59°40′N 10°50′E*
Åsa *see* Asaa
95 *H20* **Asaa** *var.* Åsa. Nordjylland, N Denmark *57°07′N 10°24′E*
83 *E21* **Asab** Karas, S Namibia *25°29′S 17°59′E*
77 *U16* **Asaba** Delta, S Nigeria *06°10′N 06°44′E*
76 *J10* **Assaba** *var.* Açâba. ◈ *region* S Mauritania
149 *S4* **Asadābād** *var.* Asaḏābād; *prev.* Chaghasarāy. Konar, E Afghanistan *34°52′N 71°09′E*
Asaḏābād *see* Asadābād
138 *K3* **Asad, Buḩayrat al** *Eng.* Lake Assad. ◎ N Syria
63 *H20* **Asador, Pampa del** *plain* S Argentina
165 *P14* **Asahi** Chiba, Honshū, S Japan *35°43′N 140°38′E*
164 *M11* **Asahi** Toyama, Honshū, SW Japan *36°56′N 137°34′E*
165 *T13* **Asahi-dake** ▲ Hokkaidō, N Japan *43°42′N 142°50′E*
165 *T3* **Asahikawa** Hokkaidō, N Japan *43°46′N 142°23′E*
147 *S10* **Asaka** *Rus.* Assake; *prev.* Leninsk. Andijon Viloyati, E Uzbekistan *40°39′N 72°16′E*
77 *P17* **Asamankese** SE Ghana *05°47′N 00°41′W*
188 *B15* **Asan** W Guam *13°28′N 144°43′E*
188 *B15* **Asan Point** *headland* W Guam
153 *R15* **Āsānsol** West Bengal, NE India *23°40′N 86°59′E*
80 *K12* **Āsayita** Āfar, NE Ethiopia *11°35′S 41°23′E*
171 *T12* **Asbakin** Papua, E Indonesia *0°45′S 131°40′E*
Asben *see* Aïr, Massif de l'
15 *Q12* **Asbestos** Québec, SE Canada *45°46′N 71°56′W*
29 *Y13* **Asbury** Iowa, C USA *42°30′N 90°45′W*
18 *K15* **Asbury Park** New Jersey, NE USA *40°13′N 74°00′W*
41 *Z12* **Ascención, Bahiá de la** *bay* NW Caribbean Sea
40 *I3* **Ascensión** Chihuahua, N Mexico *31°07′N 107°59′W*
65 *M14* **Ascension Fracture Zone** *tectonic feature* C Atlantic Ocean
65 *G14* **Ascension Island** ◇ *dependency of St.Helena* C Atlantic Ocean
65 *N16* **Ascension Island** *island* C Atlantic Ocean
Asch *see* Aš
109 *S3* **Aschach an der Donau** Oberösterreich, N Austria *48°22′N 14°00′E*
101 *H18* **Aschaffenburg** Bayern, SW Germany *49°58′N 09°10′E*
101 *F14* **Ascheberg** Nordrhein-Westfalen, W Germany *51°46′N 07°36′E*
101 *L14* **Aschersleben** Sachsen-Anhalt, C Germany *51°46′N 11°28′E*
106 *G12* **Asciano** Toscana, C Italy *43°15′N 11°32′E*
106 *J13* **Ascoli Piceno** *anc.* Asculum Picenum. Marche, C Italy *42°51′N 13°34′E*
107 *M17* **Ascoli Satriano** *anc.* Asculub, Ausculum Apulum. Puglia, SE Italy *41°13′N 15°32′E*
108 *G11* **Ascona** Ticino, S Switzerland *46°10′N 08°45′E*
Asculub *see* Ascoli Satriano
Asculum Picenum *see* Ascoli Piceno
80 *L11* **'Aseb** *var.* Assab, *Amh.* Āseb. SE Eritrea *13°04′N 42°36′E*
95 *M20* **Åseda** Kronoberg, S Sweden *57°10′N 15°20′E*
127 *T6* **Asekeyevo** Orenburgskaya Oblast', W Russian Federation *53°36′N 52°53′E*
81 *J14* **Āsela** *var.* Asella, Aselle, Asselle. Oromīya, C Ethiopia *07°55′N 39°08′E*
93 *H15* **Åsele** Västerbotten, N Sweden *64°10′N 17°20′E*
Asella/Aselle *see* Āsela
98 *N7* **Assen** Drenthe, NE Netherlands *53°N 06°34′E*
94 *K12* **Åsen** Dalarna, C Sweden *61°18′N 13°49′E*
114 *J11* **Asenovgrad** *prev.* Stanimaka. Plovdiv, C Bulgaria *42°00′N 24°53′E*
171 *O13* **Asera** Sulawesi, C Indonesia *03°24′S 121°42′E*
95 *E17* **Åseral** Vest-Agder, S Norway *58°37′N 07°27′E*
118 *J3* **Aseri** *var.* Asserien, *Ger.* Asserin. Ida-Virumaa, NE Estonia *59°29′N 26°51′E*
40 *J10* **Aserradero** Durango, W Mexico
146 *F13* **Aşgabat** *prev.* Ashgabat, Ashkhabad, Poltoratsk. ● (Turkmenistan) Ahal Welaýaty, C Turkmenistan *37°58′N 58°22′E*
146 *F13* **Aşgabat** ✈ Ahal Welaýaty, C Turkmenistan *38°06′N 58°10′E*
95 *H16* **Åsgårdstrand** Vestfold, S Norway *59°22′N 10°27′E*
Ashara *see* Al 'Ashārah
23 *T6* **Ashburn** Georgia, SE USA *31°42′N 83°39′W*
185 *G19* **Ashburton** Canterbury, South Island, New Zealand *43°55′S 171°47′E*
185 *G19* **Ashburton** ≈ South Island, New Zealand
180 *H8* **Ashburton River** ≈ Western Australia
145 *V10* **Ashchysu** ≈ E Kazakhstan
10 *M16* **Ashcroft** British Columbia, SW Canada *50°41′N 121°17′W*
138 *E10* **Ashdod** *anc.* Azotos, *Lat.* Azotus. Central, W Israel *31°48′N 34°38′E*
27 *S14* **Ashdown** Arkansas, C USA *33°40′N 94°09′W*
21 *T9* **Asheboro** North Carolina, SE USA *35°42′N 79°50′W*
11 *X15* **Ashern** Manitoba, S Canada *51°10′N 98°22′W*
21 *P10* **Asheville** North Carolina, SE USA *35°36′N 82°33′W*
12 *E8* **Asheweig** ≈ Ontario, C Canada
27 *V9* **Ash Flat** Arkansas, C USA *36°13′N 91°36′W*
183 *T4* **Ashford** New South Wales, SE Australia *29°18′S 151°09′E*
97 *P22* **Ashford** SE England, United Kingdom *51°09′N 00°52′E*
36 *K11* **Ash Fork** Arizona, SW USA *35°12′N 112°31′W*
Ashgabat *see* Aşgabat
27 *T7* **Ash Grove** Missouri, C USA *37°19′N 93°35′W*
165 *O12* **Ashikaga** *var.* Asikaga. Tochigi, Honshū, S Japan *36°21′N 139°26′E*
165 *Q8* **Ashiro** Iwate, Honshū, C Japan *40°04′N 141°00′E*
164 *F15* **Ashizuri-misaki** Shikoku, SW Japan
138 *E10* **Ashkelon** *prev.* Ashqelon. Southern, C Israel *31°40′N 34°35′E*
143 *P9* **Ashkeẕar** Yazd, C Iran *31°56′N 54°16′E*
Ashkhabad *see* Aşgabat
23 *Q4* **Ashland** Alabama, S USA *33°16′N 85°50′W*
26 *K7* **Ashland** Kansas, C USA *37°12′N 99°47′W*
21 *P5* **Ashland** Kentucky, S USA *38°28′N 82°40′W*
19 *S2* **Ashland** Maine, NE USA *46°36′N 68°24′W*
22 *M1* **Ashland** Mississippi, S USA *34°51′N 89°10′W*
27 *U4* **Ashland** Missouri, C USA *38°46′N 92°15′W*
29 *S15* **Ashland** Nebraska, C USA *41°01′N 96°21′W*
31 *T12* **Ashland** Ohio, N USA *40°52′N 82°19′W*
32 *G15* **Ashland** Oregon, NW USA *42°11′N 122°42′W*
21 *W6* **Ashland** Virginia, NE USA *37°45′N 77°28′W*
30 *K3* **Ashland** Wisconsin, N USA *46°34′N 90°54′W*
20 *I8* **Ashland City** Tennessee, S USA *36°16′N 87°05′W*
183 *S4* **Ashley** New South Wales, SE Australia *29°21′S 149°49′E*
29 *O7* **Ashley** North Dakota, N USA *46°00′N 99°22′W*
173 *W7* **Ashmore and Cartier Islands** ◇ *Australian external territory* E Indian Ocean
119 *I14* **Ashmyany** *Rus.* Oshmyany. Hrodzyenskaya Voblasts', W Belarus *54°24′N 25°57′E*
18 *K12* **Ashokan Reservoir** ⊠ New York, NE USA
165 *U4* **Ashoro** Hokkaidō, NE Japan *43°16′N 143°33′E*
Ashqelon *see* Ashkelon
Ashraf *see* Behshahr
139 *O3* **Ash Shadādah** *var.* Ash Shaddādah, Jisr ash Shadadi, Shaddādī, Shedadi, Tell Shedadi. Al Ḩasakah, NE Syria *36°00′N 40°42′E*
Ash Shaddādah *see* Ash Shadādah
139 *Y12* **Ash Shāfī** Al Başrah, E Iraq *30°49′N 47°30′E*
139 *R4* **Ash Shakk** *var.* Shaykh. Şalāḩ ad Dīn, C Iraq *35°15′N 43°27′E*
Ash Sham/Ash Shām *see* Dimashq
139 *T10* **Ash Shāmīyah** *var.* Shamiya. Al Qādisīyah, C Iraq *31°56′N 44°37′E*
139 *Y13* **Ash Shāmīyah** *var.* Al Bādiyah al Janūbīyah. *desert* S Iraq
139 *T11* **Ash Shanāfīyah** *var.* Ash Shināfīyah. Al Qādisīyah, S Iraq *31°35′N 44°38′E*
138 *G13* **Ash Sharāh** *var.* Esh Sharā. ▲▲ W Jordan
143 *R16* **Ash Shāriqah** *Eng.* Sharjah. Ash Shāriqah, NE United Arab Emirates *25°22′N 55°28′E*
143 *R16* **Ash Shāriqah** *var.* Sharjah. ✈ Ash Shāriqah, NE United Arab Emirates *25°19′N 55°37′E*
140 *I4* **Ash Sharmah** *var.* Šarma. Tabūk, NW Saudi Arabia *28°02′N 35°16′E*
139 *R4* **Ash Sharqāţ** Nīnawýa, NW Iraq *35°31′N 43°15′E*
141 *S10* **Ash Sharqīyah** *off.* Al Minţaqah ash Sharqīyah, *Eng.* Eastern Region. ◈ *province* E Saudi Arabia
Ash Sharqīyah *see* Al 'Ubaylah
139 *W11* **Ash Shaţrah** *var.* Shatra. Dhī Qār, SE Iraq *31°26′N 46°10′E*
138 *G13* **Ash Shawbak** Ma'ān, W Jordan *30°32′N 35°34′E*
138 *L5* **Ash Shaykh Ibrāhīm** Ḩimş, C Syria *35°03′N 38°50′E*
141 *O17* **Ash Shaykh 'Uthmān** SW Yemen *12°53′N 45°00′E*
141 *S15* **Ash Shiḩr** SE Yemen *14°45′N 49°24′E*
Ash Shināfīyah *see* Ash Shanāfīyah
141 *V12* **Ash Shişar** *var.* Shisur. SW Oman *18°13′N 53°35′E*
139 *S13* **Ash Shubrūm** *well* S Iraq
141 *R10* **Ash Shuqqān** *desert* E Saudi Arabia
75 *O9* **Ash Shuwayrif** *var.* Ash Shwayrif. N Libya *29°54′N 14°16′E*
Ash Shwayrif *see* Ash Shuwayrif
31 *U10* **Ashtabula** Ohio, N USA *41°54′N 80°46′W*
29 *Q5* **Ashtabula, Lake** ⊠ North Dakota, N USA
137 *T12* **Ashtarak** W Armenia *40°18′N 44°22′E*
142 *M6* **Āshtīān** *var.* Āshtiyān. Markazī, W Iran *34°23′N 49°55′E*
Āshtiyān *see* Āshtīān
33 *R13* **Ashton** Idaho, NW USA *44°04′N 111°27′W*
13 *O10* **Ashuanipi Lake** ◎ Newfoundland and Labrador, E Canada
15 *P6* **Ashuapmushuan** ≈ Québec, SE Canada
23 *Q3* **Ashville** Alabama, S USA *33°50′N 86°15′W*
31 *S14* **Ashville** Ohio, N USA *39°43′N 82°57′W*
30 *K3* **Ashwabay, Mount** *hill* Wisconsin, N USA
128-129 **Asia** *continent*
171 *T11* **Asia, Kepulauan** *island group* E Indonesia
154 *N13* **Āsika** Orissa, E India *19°38′N 84°41′E*
Asikaga *see* Ashikaga
93 *M18* **Asikkala** *var.* Vääksy. Etelä-Suomi, S Finland *61°09′N 25°36′E*
74 *G5* **Asilah** N Morocco *35°32′N 06°04′W*
'Aşī, Nahr al *see* Orontes
107 *B16* **Asinara, Isola** *island* W Italy
122 *J12* **Asino** Tomskaya Oblast', C Russian Federation *56°56′N 86°02′E*

◆ Country
● Country Capital
◇ Dependent Territory
○ Dependent Territory Capital
◈ Administrative Regions
✈ International Airport
▲ Mountain
▲▲ Mountain Range
Volcano
≈ River
◎ Lake
⊠ Reservoir

119 O14 **Asintorf** *Rus.* Osintorf. Vitsyebskaya Voblasts', N Belarus 54°43′N 30°35′E
119 L17 **Asipovichy** *Rus.* Osipovichi. Mahilyowskaya Voblasts', C Belarus 53°18′N 28°40′E
141 N12 **'Asīr** *off.* Minṭaqat 'Asīr. ◆ *province* SW Saudi Arabia
140 M11 **'Asīr** *Eng.* Asir. ▲ SW Saudi Arabia
'Asīr, Minṭaqat *see* 'Asīr
139 X10 **Askal** Maysān, E Iraq 31°45′N 47°07′E
137 P13 **Aşkale** Erzurum, NE Turkey 39°56′N 40°39′E
117 T11 **Askaniya-Nova** Khersons'ka Oblast', S Ukraine 46°27′N 33°54′E
95 H15 **Asker** Akershus, S Norway 59°52′N 10°26′E
95 L17 **Askersund** Örebro, C Sweden 58°55′N 14°55′E
Askī Kalak *see* Eski Kaļak
95 I15 **Askim** Østfold, S Norway 59°15′N 11°10′E
127 V3 **Askino** Respublika Bashkortostan, W Russian Federation 56°07′N 56°39′E
115 D14 **Áskio** ▲ N Greece
152 L9 **Askot** Uttarakhand, N India 29°44′N 80°20′E
94 C12 **Askvoll** Sogn Og Fjordane, S Norway 61°21′N 05°04′E
136 A13 **Aslan Burnu** *headland* W Turkey 38°44′N 26°43′E
136 L16 **Aslantaş Barajı** ⊠ S Turkey
149 S4 **Asmār** *var.* Bar Kunar. Kunar, E Afghanistan 34°59′N 71°29′E
Asmara *see* Asmera
80 I9 **Asmera** *var.* Asmara. ● (Eritrea) C Eritrea 15°15′N 38°58′E
95 L21 **Åsnen** ◎ S Sweden
115 F19 **Asopós** ⤳ S Greece
171 W13 **Asori** Papua, E Indonesia 02°37′S 136°06′E
80 G12 **Āsosa** Binishangul Gumuz, W Ethiopia 10°06′N 34°27′E
32 M10 **Asotin** Washington, NW USA 46°18′N 117°03′W
Aspadana *see* Eşfahān
Aspang *see* Aspang Markt
109 X6 **Aspang Markt** *var.* Aspang. Niederösterreich, E Austria 47°34′N 16°06′E
105 S12 **Aspe** País Valenciano, E Spain 38°21′N 00°43′W
37 R5 **Aspen** Colorado, C USA 39°12′N 106°49′W
25 P6 **Aspermont** Texas, SW USA 33°08′N 100°14′W
Asphaltites, Lacus *see* Dead Sea
Aspinwall *see* Colón
185 C20 **Aspiring, Mount** ▲ South Island, New Zealand 44°21′S 168°47′E
115 B16 **Asprókavos, Akrotírio** *headland* Kérkyra, Iónia Nisiá, Greece, C Mediterranean Sea 39°22′N 20°07′E
Aspropótamos *see* Achelóos
Assab *see* 'Aseb
138 L4 **As Sabkhah** *var.* Sabkha. Ar Raqqah, NE Syria 35°30′N 35°54′E
139 U6 **As Sa'dīyah** Diyālá, E Iraq 34°11′N 45°09′E
Assad, Lake *see* Asad, Buḩayrat al
138 I8 **Aş Şafā** ▲ S Syria 33°03′N 37°07′E
138 I10 **Aş Şafāwī** Al Mafraq, N Jordan 32°12′N 32°30′E
75 W8 **Aş Şaff** *var.* El Şaff. N Egypt 29°34′N 31°16′E
139 N2 **Aş Şafīḩ** Al Ḩasakah, N Syria 36°42′N 40°12′E
Aş Şaḩrā' ash Sharqīyah *see* Sahara el Sharqîya
Assake *see* Asaka
As Salamīyah *see* Salamīyah
141 Q4 **As Sālimī** *var.* Salemy. SW Kuwait 29°07′N 46°41′E
67 W7 **'Assal, Lac** ◎ C Djibouti
139 T13 **As Salmān** Al Muthannā, S Iraq 30°29′N 44°34′E
138 G10 **As Salṭ** *var.* Salt. Al Balqā', NW Jordan 32°03′N 35°44′E
75 T7 **As Sallūm** *var.* Salûm. NW Egypt 31°31′N 25°09′E
142 M16 **As Salwā** *var.* Salwa, Salwah. S Qatar 24°44′N 50°52′E
153 V12 **Assam** ◆ *state* NE India
Assamaka *see* Assamakka
77 T8 **Assamakka** *var.* Assamaka. Agadez, NW Niger 19°24′N 05°53′E
139 U11 **As Samāwah** *var.* Samawa. Al Muthannā, S Iraq 31°17′N 45°06′E
As Saqia al Hamra *see* Saguia al Hamra
138 J4 **Aş Şā'rān** Ḩamāh, C Syria 35°15′N 37°28′E
138 G9 **Aş Şarīḩ** Irbid, N Jordan 32°31′N 35°54′E
21 Z5 **Assateague Island** *island* Maryland, NE USA
139 O6 **As Sayyāl** *var.* Sayyāl. Dayr az Zawr, E Syria 34°37′N 40°52′E
99 G18 **Asse** Vlaams Brabant, C Belgium 50°55′N 04°12′E
99 D16 **Assebroek** West-Vlaanderen, NW Belgium 51°12′N 03°16′E
Asselle *see* Āsela
107 C20 **Assemini** Sardegna, Italy, C Mediterranean Sea 39°16′N 08°58′E
99 E16 **Assenede** Oost-Vlaanderen, NW Belgium 51°15′N 03°43′E
95 G24 **Assens** Fyn, C Denmark 55°16′N 09°54′E
Asserien/Asserin *see* Aseri
99 I21 **Assesse** Namur, SE Belgium 50°22′N 05°01′E
141 Y8 **As Sib** *var.* Seeb. NE Oman 23°40′N 58°03′E
139 Z13 **As Sībah** *var.* Sibah. Al Başrah, SE Iraq 30°13′N 47°24′E
11 T17 **Assiniboia** Saskatchewan, S Canada 49°39′N 105°59′W
11 V15 **Assiniboine** ⤳ Manitoba, S Canada
11 P16 **Assiniboine, Mount** ▲ Alberta/British Columbia, SW Canada 50°54′N 115°43′W
Assiout *see* Asyūṭ
60 J9 **Assis** São Paulo, S Brazil 22°37′S 50°25′W
106 I13 **Assisi** Umbria, C Italy 43°04′N 12°36′E
Assiut *see* Asyūṭ
Assling *see* Jesenice
Assouan *see* Aswān
Assu *see* Açu
Assuan *see* Aswān
142 K12 **Aş Şubayḩīyah** *var.* Subiyah. S Kuwait 28°55′N 47°57′E
141 R16 **As Sufāl** S Yemen 14°06′N 48°42′E
138 L5 **As Sukhnah** *var.* Sukhne, *Fr.* Soukhné. Ḩimş, C Syria 34°56′N 38°52′E
139 U4 **As Sulaymānīyah** *off.* Muḩāfaẓat as Sulaymānīyah. ◆ *governorate* NE Iraq
139 U4 **As Sulaymānīyah** *var.* Sulaimaniya, *Kurd.* Slêmānî. As Sulaymānīyah, NE Iraq 35°32′N 45°27′E
141 P11 **As Sulayyil** Ar Riyāḑ, S Saudi Arabia 20°29′N 45°33′E
121 O13 **As Sulṭān** N Libya 31°01′N 17°21′E
141 Q5 **Aş Şummān** *desert* N Saudi Arabia
141 Q16 **Aş Şurrah** SW Yemen 13°56′N 46°23′E
139 N4 **Aş Şuwār** *var.* Şuwār. Dayr az Zawr, E Syria 35°31′N 40°37′E
138 H9 **As Suwaydā'** *var.* El Suweida, Es Suweida, Suweida, *Fr.* Soueida. As Suwaydā', SW Syria 32°43′N 36°33′E
138 H9 **As Suwaydā'** *off.* Muḩāfaẓat as Suwaydā', *var.* As Suwaydā, Suwaydā, Suweida. ◆ *governorate* S Syria
141 Z9 **As Suwayḩ** NE Oman 22°07′N 59°42′E
141 X8 **As Suwayq** *var.* Suwaik. N Oman 23°49′N 57°30′E
139 T8 **Aş Şuwayrah** *var.* Suwaira. Wāsiţ, E Iraq 32°57′N 44°47′E
As Suways *see* Suez
Asta Colonia *see* Asti
Astacus *see* İzmit
115 M23 **Astakída** *island* SE Greece
145 Q9 **Astana** *prev.* Akmola, Akmolinsk, Tselinograd, Aqmola. ● (Kazakhstan) Akmola, N Kazakhstan 51°13′N 71°25′E
142 M3 **Āstāneh** Gīlān, NW Iran 37°17′N 49°58′E
Asta Pompeia *see* Asti
137 Y14 **Astara** S Azerbaijan 38°28′N 48°51′E
Astarabad *see* Gorgān
99 L15 **Asten** Noord-Brabant, SE Netherlands 51°24′N 05°45′E
Asterābād *see* Gorgān
106 C8 **Asti** *anc.* Asta Colonia, Asta Pompeia, Hasta Colonia, Hasta Pompeia. Piemonte, NW Italy 44°54′N 08°11′E
Astigi *see* Ecija
Astipálaia *see* Astypálaia
148 L16 **Astola Island** *island* SW Pakistan
152 H4 **Astor** Jammu and Kashmir, NW India 35°21′N 74°52′E
104 K4 **Astorga** *anc.* Asturica Augusta. Castilla-León, N Spain 42°27′N 06°04′W
32 F10 **Astoria** Oregon, NW USA 46°12′N 123°50′W
0 F8 **Astoria Fan** *undersea feature* E Pacific Ocean 45°15′N 126°15′W
95 J22 **Åstorp** Skåne, S Sweden 56°09′N 12°57′E
Astrabad *see* Gorgān
127 Q13 **Astrakhan'** Astrakhanskaya Oblast', SW Russian Federation 46°20′N 48°01′E
Astrakhan-Bazar *see* Cälilabad
127 Q11 **Astrakhanskaya Oblast'** ◆ *province* SW Russian Federation
93 J15 **Åsträsk** Västerbotten, N Sweden 64°38′N 20°00′E
Astrida *see* Butare
65 O22 **Astrid Ridge** *undersea feature* S Atlantic Ocean
187 P15 **Astrolabe, Récifs de l'** *reef* C New Caledonia
121 P2 **Astromerítis** N Cyprus 35°09′N 33°02′E
115 F20 **Ástros** Pelopónnisos, S Greece 37°24′N 22°43′E
119 G16 **Astryna** *Rus.* Ostryna. Hrodzyenskaya Voblasts', W Belarus 53°44′N 24°33′E
104 J2 **Asturias** ◆ *autonomous community* NW Spain
Asturias *see* Oviedo
Asturica Augusta *see* Astorga
115 L22 **Astypálaia** *var.* Astipálaia, *It.* Stampalia. *island* Kykládes, Greece, Aegean Sea
192 G16 **Āsuisui, Cape** *headland* Savai'i, W Samoa 13°44′S 172°29′W
195 S2 **Asuka** *Japanese research station* Antarctica 71°49′S 23°52′E
62 O6 **Asunción** ● (Paraguay) Central, S Paraguay 25°17′S 57°36′W
62 O6 **Asunción** ✕ Central, S Paraguay 25°15′S 57°40′W
188 K3 **Asuncion Island** *island* N Northern Mariana Islands
42 E6 **Asunción Mita** Jutiapa, SE Guatemala 14°20′N 89°42′W
Asunción Nochixtlán *see* Nochixtlán
40 E3 **Asunción, Río** ⤳ NW Mexico
95 M18 **Åsunden** ◎ S Sweden
118 K11 **Asveyeya** *Rus.* Osveya. Vitsyebskaya Voblasts', N Belarus 56°00′N 28°05′E
Aswa *see* Achwa
75 X11 **Aswān** *var.* Assouan, Assuan, Aswân; *anc.* Syene. SE Egypt 24°03′N 32°59′E
Aswân *see* Aswān
Aswân Dam *see* Khazzān Aswān
75 W9 **Asyūṭ** *var.* Assiout, Assiut, Asyût, Siut; *anc.* Lycopolis. C Egypt 27°06′N 31°11′E
Asyût *see* Asyūṭ
193 W15 **Ata** *island* Tongatapu Group, SW Tonga
62 G8 **Atacama** *off.* Región de Atacama. ◆ *region* C Chile
Atacama Desert *see* Atacama, Desierto de
62 H4 **Atacama, Desierto de** *Eng.* Atacama Desert. *desert* N Chile
62 I6 **Atacama, Puna de** ▲ NW Argentina
Atacama, Región de *see* Atacama
62 I5 **Atacama, Salar de** *salt lake* N Chile
54 E11 **Ataco** Tolima, C Colombia 03°36′N 75°23′W
190 H8 **Atafu Atoll** *island* NW Tokelau
190 H8 **Atafu Village** Atafu Atoll, NW Tokelau 08°40′S 172°40′W
74 K12 **Atakor** ▲ SE Algeria
77 R14 **Atakora, Chaîne de l'** *var.* Atakora Mountains. ▲ N Benin
Atakora Mountains *see* Atakora, Chaîne de l'
77 R16 **Atakpamé** C Togo 07°32′N 01°08′E
146 F11 **Atakui** Ahal Welaýaty, C Turkmenistan 40°04′N 58°03′E
58 B13 **Atalaia do Norte** Amazonas, N Brazil 04°22′S 70°10′W
146 M14 **Atamyrat** *prev.* Kerki. Lebap Welaýaty, E Turkmenistan 37°52′N 65°06′E
76 I7 **Aṭâr** Adrar, W Mauritania 20°30′N 13°03′W
162 G10 **Atas Bogd** ▲ SW Mongolia 43°17′N 96°47′E
35 P12 **Atascadero** California, W USA 35°28′N 120°40′W
25 S13 **Atascosa River** ⤳ Texas, SW USA
145 R11 **Atasu** Karaganda, C Kazakhstan 48°42′N 71°38′E
145 R12 **Atasu** ⤳ Karaganda, C Kazakhstan
193 V15 **Atata** *island* Tongatapu Group, S Tonga
136 H10 **Atatürk** ✕ (İstanbul) İstanbul, NW Turkey 40°58′N 28°50′E
137 N16 **Atatürk Barajı** ⊠ S Turkey
115 O23 **Atavýros** *prev.* Attavyros. Ródos, Dodekánisa, Aegean Sea 36°10′N 27°50′E
115 O23 **Atavýros** *prev.* Attávyros. ▲ Ródos, Dodekánisa, Greece, Aegean Sea 36°10′N 27°50′E
Atax *see* Aude
80 G8 **Atbara** *var.* 'Aṭbārah. River Nile, NE Sudan 17°42′N 34°E
80 H8 **Atbara** *var.* Nahr 'Aṭbarah. ⤳ Eritrea/Sudan
'Aṭbārah/'Aṭbarah, Nahr *see* Atbara
145 P9 **Atbasar** Akmola, N Kazakhstan 51°49′N 68°18′E
At-Bashi *see* At-Bashy
147 W9 **At-Bashy** *var.* At-Bashi. Narynskaya Oblast', C Kyrgyzstan 41°07′N 75°48′E
22 I10 **Atchafalaya Bay** *bay* Louisiana, S USA
22 I8 **Atchafalaya River** ⤳ Louisiana, S USA
Atchin *see* Aceh
27 Q3 **Atchison** Kansas, C USA 39°31′N 95°07′W
77 P16 **Atebubu** C Ghana 07°47′N 01°00′W
105 Q6 **Ateca** Aragón, NE Spain 41°20′N 01°49′W
40 K11 **Atengo, Río** ⤳ C Mexico
Aternum *see* Pescara
107 K15 **Atessa** Abruzzo, C Italy 42°03′N 14°25′E
Ateste *see* Este
99 E19 **Ath** *var.* Aat. Hainaut, SW Belgium 50°38′N 03°47′E
11 Q13 **Athabasca** Alberta, SW Canada 54°44′N 113°15′W
11 Q12 **Athabasca** *var.* Athabaska. ⤳ Alberta, SW Canada
11 R10 **Athabasca, Lake** ◎ Alberta/ Saskatchewan, SW Canada
Athabaska *see* Athabasca
115 C16 **Athamánon** ▲ C Greece
97 F17 **Athboy** *Ir.* Baile Átha Buí. E Ireland 53°38′N 06°55′W
Athenae *see* Athína
97 C18 **Athenry** *Ir.* Baile Átha an Rí. W Ireland 53°19′N 08°49′W
23 P2 **Athens** Alabama, S USA 34°48′N 86°58′W
23 T3 **Athens** Georgia, SE USA 33°57′N 83°24′W
31 T14 **Athens** Ohio, N USA 39°20′N 82°06′W
20 M10 **Athens** Tennessee, S USA 35°27′N 84°38′W
25 V7 **Athens** Texas, SW USA 32°12′N 95°51′W
Athens *see* Athína
115 B18 **Athéras, Akrotírio** *headland* Kefallonía, Iónia Nisiá, Greece, C Mediterranean Sea 38°20′N 20°24′E
181 W4 **Atherton** Queensland, NE Australia 17°18′S 145°29′E
81 I19 **Athi** ⤳ S Kenya
121 Q2 **Athiénou** SE Cyprus 35°01′N 33°31′E
115 H19 **Athína** *Eng.* Athens, *prev.* Athínai; *anc.* Athenae. ● (Greece) Attikí, C Greece 37°59′N 23°44′E
Athínai *see* Athína
139 S10 **Athīyah** An Najaf, C Iraq 32°01′N 44°04′E
97 D18 **Athlone** *Ir.* Baile Átha Luain. C Ireland 53°25′N 07°56′W
155 F16 **Athni** Karnātaka, W India 16°43′N 75°04′E
185 C23 **Athol** Southland, South Island, New Zealand 45°30′S 168°35′E
19 N11 **Athol** Massachusetts, NE USA 42°35′N 72°11′W
115 I15 **Áthos** ▲ NE Greece 40°10′N 24°21′E
Athos, Mount *see* Ágion Óros
Ath Thawrah *see* Madīnat ath Thawrah
141 P5 **Ath Thumāmī** *spring/well* N Saudi Arabia 27°56′N 45°06′E
99 L25 **Athus** Luxembourg, SE Belgium 49°34′N 05°50′E
97 E19 **Athy** *Ir.* Baile Átha Í. C Ireland 52°59′N 06°59′W
78 I10 **Ati** Batha, C Chad 13°11′N 18°20′E
81 F16 **Atiak** NW Uganda 03°14′N 32°05′E
57 G17 **Atico** Arequipa, SW Peru 16°13′S 73°13′W
105 O6 **Atienza** Castilla-La Mancha, C Spain 41°12′N 02°52′W
39 Q6 **Atigun Pass** *pass* Alaska, USA
12 B12 **Atikokan** Ontario, S Canada 48°45′N 91°38′W
13 O9 **Atikonak Lac** ◎ Newfoundland and Labrador, E Canada
42 C6 **Atitlán, Lago de** ◎ W Guatemala
190 L16 **Atiu** *island* S Cook Islands
Atjeh *see* Aceh
123 T9 **Atka** Magadanskaya Oblast', E Russian Federation 60°45′N 151°35′E
38 H17 **Atka** Atka Island, Alaska, USA 52°12′N 174°14′W
38 H17 **Atka Island** *island* Aleutian Islands, Alaska, USA
127 O7 **Atkarsk** Saratovskaya Oblast', W Russian Federation 52°15′N 43°48′E
27 U11 **Atkins** Arkansas, C USA 35°15′N 92°56′W
29 O13 **Atkinson** Nebraska, C USA 42°31′N 98°57′W
171 T12 **Atkri** Papua, E Indonesia 01°45′S 130°04′E
41 O13 **Atlacomulco** *var.* Atlacomulco de Fabela. México, C Mexico 19°49′N 99°54′W
Atlacomulco de Fabela *see* Atlacomulco
23 S3 **Atlanta** *state capital* Georgia, SE USA 33°45′N 84°23′W
31 R6 **Atlanta** Michigan, N USA 45°01′N 84°07′W
25 X6 **Atlanta** Texas, SW USA 33°06′N 94°09′W
29 T15 **Atlantic** Iowa, C USA 41°24′N 95°00′W
21 Y10 **Atlantic** North Carolina, SE USA 34°52′N 76°20′W
23 W8 **Atlantic Beach** Florida, SE USA 30°19′N 81°24′W
18 J17 **Atlantic City** New Jersey, NE USA 39°23′N 74°27′W
172 L14 **Atlantic-Indian Basin** *undersea feature* SW Indian Ocean 60°00′S 15°00′E
172 K13 **Atlantic-Indian Ridge** *undersea feature* SW Indian Ocean 53°00′S 15°00′E
54 E4 **Atlántico** *off.* Departamento del Atlántico. ◆ *province* NW Colombia
64-65 **Atlantic Ocean** *ocean*
Atlántico, Departamento del *see* Atlántico
42 K7 **Atlántico Norte, Región Autónoma** *prev.* Zelaya Norte. ◆ *autonomous region* NE Nicaragua
42 L10 **Atlántico Sur, Región Autónoma** *prev.* Zelaya Sur. ◆ *autonomous region* SE Nicaragua
42 I5 **Atlántida** ◆ *department* N Honduras
77 Y15 **Atlantika Mountains** ▲ E Nigeria
64 J10 **Atlantis Fracture Zone** *tectonic feature* NW Atlantic Ocean
74 H7 **Atlas Mountains** ▲ NW Africa
123 V11 **Atlasova, Ostrov** *island* SE Russian Federation
123 V10 **Atlasovo** Kamchatskaya Oblast', E Russian Federation 55°42′N 159°35′E
120 G11 **Atlas Saharien** *var.* Saharan Atlas. ▲ Algeria/Morocco
Atlas, Tell *see* Atlas Tellien
120 H10 **Atlas Tellien** *Eng.* Tell Atlas. ▲ N Algeria
10 I9 **Atlin** British Columbia, W Canada 59°31′N 133°41′W
10 I9 **Atlin Lake** ◎ British Columbia, W Canada
41 P14 **Atlixco** Puebla, S Mexico 18°55′N 98°26′W
94 B11 **Atløyna** *island* S Norway
155 I17 **Ātmakūr** Andhra Pradesh, C India 15°52′N 78°42′E
23 O8 **Atmore** Alabama, S USA 31°01′N 87°29′W
101 J20 **Atmühl** ⤳ S Germany
94 H11 **Atna** ⤳ S Norway
164 E13 **Atō** Yamaguchi, Honshū, SW Japan 34°24′N 131°42′E
57 L21 **Atocha** Potosí, S Bolivia 20°55′S 66°14′W
27 P12 **Atoka** Oklahoma, C USA 34°22′N 96°08′W
27 O12 **Atoka Lake** *var.* Atoka Reservoir. ⊠ Oklahoma, C USA
Atoka Reservoir *see* Atoka Lake
33 Q14 **Atomic City** Idaho, NW USA 43°26′N 112°48′W
40 L10 **Atotonilco** Zacatecas, C Mexico 24°12′N 102°46′W
Atotonilco *see* Atotonilco el Alto
40 M13 **Atotonilco el Alto** *var.* Atotonilco. Jalisco, SW Mexico 20°35′N 102°30′W
77 N7 **Atouila, 'Erg** *desert* N Mali
41 N16 **Atoyac** *var.* Atoyac de Alvarez. Guerrero, S Mexico 17°12′N 100°28′W
Atoyac de Alvarez *see* Atoyac
41 P15 **Atoyac, Río** ⤳ S Mexico
39 O5 **Atqasuk** Alaska, USA 70°28′N 157°24′W
Atrak/Atrak, Rūd-e *see* Etrek
95 J20 **Ätran** ⤳ S Sweden
54 C7 **Atrato, Río** ⤳ NW Colombia
Atrek *see* Etrek
107 K14 **Atri** Abruzzo, C Italy 42°35′N 13°59′E
Atria *see* Adria
165 P9 **Atsumi** Yamagata, Honshū, C Japan 38°38′N 139°36′E
165 S3 **Atsuta** Hokkaidō, NE Japan 43°28′N 141°24′E
143 Q17 **Aṭ Ṭaff** *desert* C United Arab Emirates
138 G12 **Aṭ Ṭafīlah** *var.* Et Tafila, Tafila. Aṭ Ṭafīlah, W Jordan 30°52′N 35°36′E
138 G12 **Aṭ Ṭafīlah** *off.* Muḩāfaẓat aṭ Ṭafīlah. ◆ *governorate* W Jordan
140 L10 **Aṭ Ṭā'if** Makkah, W Saudi Arabia 21°50′N 40°50′E
Attaleia/Attalia *see* Antalya
23 Q3 **Attalla** Alabama, S USA 34°01′N 86°05′W
138 L2 **At Tall al Abyaḑ** *var.* Tall al Abyaḑ, Tell Abyad, *Fr.* Tell Abiad. Ar Raqqah, N Syria 36°36′N 34°00′E
139 S5 **At Ta'mīm** *off.* Muḩāfaẓat at Ta'mīm. ◆ *governorate* N Iraq
138 L7 **Aṭ Ṭanf** Ḩimş, S Syria 33°29′N 38°39′E
163 N9 **Attanshiree** Dornogovī, SE Mongolia 45°36′N 110°30′E
Attapu *see* Samakhixai
139 S10 **At Taqtaqānah** An Najaf, C Iraq 32°03′N 43°54′E
Attávyros *see* Atavýros
139 V15 **At Tawal** *desert* Iraq/Saudi Arabia
12 G9 **Attawapiskat** Ontario, C Canada 52°55′N 82°26′W
12 F9 **Attawapiskat** ⤳ Ontario, S Canada
12 D9 **Attawapiskat Lake** ◎ Ontario, C Canada
At Taybé *see* Ţayyibah
101 F16 **Attendorn** Nordrhein-Westfalen, W Germany 51°07′N 07°54′E
109 R5 **Attersee** Salzburg, NW Austria 47°55′N 13°31′E
109 R5 **Attersee** ◎ N Austria
99 L24 **Attert** Luxembourg, SE Belgium 49°45′N 05°47′E
138 M4 **At Tibnī** *var.* Tibnī. Dayr az Zawr, NE Syria 35°30′N 39°48′E
31 N13 **Attica** Indiana, N USA 40°17′N 87°15′W
18 E10 **Attica** New York, NE USA 42°51′N 78°13′W
Attica *see* Attikí
13 N7 **Attikamagen Lake** ◎ Newfoundland and Labrador, E Canada
115 H20 **Attikí** *Eng.* Attica. ◆ *region* C Greece
19 O12 **Attleboro** Massachusetts, NE USA 41°55′N 71°15′W
109 R5 **Attnang** Oberösterreich, N Austria 48°02′N 13°44′E
149 U6 **Attock City** Punjab, E Pakistan 33°52′N 72°20′E
Attopeu *see* Samakhixai
25 X8 **Attoyac River** ⤳ Texas, SW USA
38 D16 **Attu** Attu Island, Alaska, USA 52°53′N 173°18′E
139 Y12 **Aṭ Ṭūbah** Al Başrah, E Iraq 30°29′N 47°28′E
140 K4 **Aṭ Ṭubayq** *plain* Jordan/ Saudi Arabia
38 C16 **Attu Island** *island* Aleutian Islands, Alaska, USA
75 X8 **Aṭ Ṭūr** *var.* El Ṭûr. NE Egypt 28°14′N 33°36′E
155 I21 **Āttūr** Tamil Nādu, SE India 11°34′N 78°39′E
141 N17 **At Turbah** SW Yemen 12°42′N 43°31′E
62 I12 **Atuel, Río** ⤳ C Argentina
191 X7 **Atuona** Hiva Oa, NE French Polynesia 09°47′S 139°03′W
Aturus *see* Adour
95 M18 **Åtvidaberg** Östergötland, S Sweden 58°12′N 16°00′E
35 P9 **Atwater** California, W USA 37°19′N 120°33′W
29 T8 **Atwater** Minnesota, N USA 45°08′N 94°48′W
26 I2 **Atwood** Kansas, C USA 39°48′N 101°03′W
31 U12 **Atwood Lake** ⊠ Ohio, N USA
127 P5 **Atyashevo** Respublika Mordoviya, W Russian Federation 54°36′N 46°04′E
144 F12 **Atyrau** *prev.* Gur'yev. Atyrau, W Kazakhstan 47°07′N 51°56′E
144 E11 **Atyrau** *off.* Atyrauskaya Oblast', *var.* Kaz. Atyraū Oblysy; *prev.* Gur'yevskaya Oblast'. ◆ *province* W Kazakhstan
Atyraū Oblysy/ Atyrauskaya Oblast' *see* Atyrau
Atyrauskaya Oblast' *see* Atyrau
108 J7 **Au** Vorarlberg, NW Austria 47°19′N 10°01′E
186 B4 **Aua Island** *island* NW Papua New Guinea
103 S16 **Aubagne** *anc.* Albania. Bouches-du-Rhône, SE France 43°17′N 05°35′E
99 L25 **Aubange** Luxembourg, SE Belgium 49°35′N 05°49′E
103 Q6 **Aube** ◆ *department* N France
103 R6 **Aube** ⤳ N France
99 L19 **Aubel** Liège, E Belgium 50°45′N 05°49′E
103 Q13 **Aubenas** Ardèche, E France 44°37′N 04°24′E
103 O8 **Aubigny-sur-Nère** Cher, C France 47°30′N 02°27′E
103 O13 **Aubin** Aveyron, S France 44°30′N 02°18′E
103 O13 **Aubrac, Monts d'** ▲ S France
36 J10 **Aubrey Cliffs** *cliff* Arizona, SW USA
23 R5 **Auburn** Alabama, S USA 32°37′N 85°30′W
35 P6 **Auburn** California, W USA 38°53′N 121°03′W
30 K14 **Auburn** Illinois, N USA 39°35′N 89°45′W
31 Q11 **Auburn** Indiana, N USA 41°22′N 85°03′W
20 J7 **Auburn** Kentucky, S USA 36°52′N 86°42′W
19 P8 **Auburn** Maine, NE USA 44°05′N 70°15′W
19 N11 **Auburn** Massachusetts, NE USA 42°11′N 71°47′W
29 S16 **Auburn** Nebraska, C USA 40°23′N 95°50′W
18 H10 **Auburn** New York, NE USA 42°55′N 76°31′W
32 H8 **Auburn** Washington, NW USA 47°18′N 122°13′W
103 N11 **Aubusson** Creuse, C France 45°58′N 02°10′E
118 E10 **Auce** *Ger.* Autz. Dobele, SW Latvia 56°28′N 22°54′E
102 L15 **Auch** *Lat.* Augusta Auscorum, Elimberrum. Gers, S France 43°40′N 00°37′E
77 U16 **Auchi** Edo, S Nigeria 07°01′N 06°17′E
23 T9 **Aucilla River** ⤳ Florida/ Georgia, SE USA
184 L6 **Auckland** Auckland, North Island, New Zealand 36°53′S 174°46′E
184 K5 **Auckland** *off.* Auckland Region. ◆ *region* North Island, New Zealand
184 L6 **Auckland** ✕ Auckland, North Island, New Zealand 37°01′S 174°49′E
192 J12 **Auckland Islands** *island group* S New Zealand
Auckland Region *see* Auckland
103 O16 **Aude** ◆ *department* S France
103 N16 **Aude** *anc.* Atax. ⤳ S France
Audenarde *see* Oudenaarde
Audern *see* Audru
102 E6 **Audierne** Finistère, NW France 48°01′N 04°30′W
102 E6 **Audierne, Baie d'** *bay* NW France
103 U7 **Audincourt** Doubs, E France 47°29′N 06°50′E
118 G5 **Audru** *Ger.* Audern. Pärnumaa, SW Estonia 58°24′N 24°22′E
29 T14 **Audubon** Iowa, C USA 41°44′N 94°56′W
101 N17 **Aue** Sachsen, E Germany 50°35′N 12°42′E
100 H12 **Aue** ⤳ NW Germany
100 L9 **Auerbach** Bayern, SE Germany 49°41′N 11°41′E
101 M17 **Auerbach** Sachsen, E Germany 50°30′N 12°24′E
108 I10 **Auererrhein** ⤳ SW Switzerland
101 N17 **Auersberg** ▲ E Germany 50°30′N 12°42′E
181 W9 **Augathella** Queensland, E Australia 25°54′S 146°38′E
31 Q12 **Auglaize River** ⤳ Ohio, N USA
83 F22 **Augrabies Falls** *waterfall* W South Africa
31 R7 **Au Gres River** ⤳ Michigan, N USA
Augsbourg *see* Augsburg
101 K22 **Augsburg** *Fr.* Augsbourg; *anc.* Augusta Vindelicorum. Bayern, S Germany 48°22′N 10°54′E
180 I14 **Augusta** Western Australia 34°18′S 115°10′E
107 L25 **Augusta** *It.* Agosta. Sicilia, Italy, C Mediterranean Sea 37°14′N 15°14′E
27 W11 **Augusta** Arkansas, C USA 35°16′N 91°21′W
23 V3 **Augusta** Georgia, SE USA 33°29′N 81°58′W
27 O6 **Augusta** Kansas, C USA 37°40′N 96°59′W
19 Q7 **Augusta** *state capital* Maine, NE USA 44°20′N 69°44′W
33 Q8 **Augusta** Montana, NW USA 47°28′N 112°23′W
Augusta *see* London
Augusta Auscorum *see* Auch
Augusta Emerita *see* Mérida
Augusta Praetoria *see* Aosta
Augusta Suessionum *see* Soissons
Augusta Trajana *see* Stara Zagora
Augusta Treverorum *see* Trier
Augusta Vangionum *see* Worms
Augusta Vindelicorum *see* Augsburg
95 G24 **Augustenborg** *Ger.* Augustenburg. Sønderjylland, SW Denmark 54°57′N 09°53′E
Augustenburg *see* Augustenborg
39 Q13 **Augustine Island** *island* Alaska, USA
14 L9 **Augustines, Lac des** ◎ Québec, SE Canada
Augustobona Tricassium *see* Troyes
Augustodunum *see* Autun
Augustodurum *see* Bayeux
Augustoritum Lemovicensium *see* Limoges
110 O8 **Augustów** *Rus.* Avgustov. Podlaskie, NE Poland 53°52′N 22°58′E
Augustow Canal *see* Augustowski, Kanał
110 O8 **Augustowski, Kanał** *Eng.* Augustow Canal, *Rus.* Avgustovskiy Kanal. *canal* NE Poland
180 I9 **Augustus, Mount** ▲ Western Australia 24°42′S 117°42′E
186 M9 **Auki** Malaita, N Solomon Islands 08°48′S 160°45′E
21 W8 **Aulander** North Carolina, SE USA 36°15′N 77°16′W
180 L7 **Auld, Lake** *salt lake* C Western Australia
Aulie Ata/Auliye-Ata *see* Taraz
Äülīeköl *see* Auliyekol'
144 M8 **Auliyekol'** *Kaz.* Äülīeköl; *prev.* Semiozernoye. Kostanay, N Kazakhstan 52°22′N 64°06′E
106 E10 **Aulla** Toscana, C Italy 44°15′N 10°00′E
102 F6 **Aulne** ⤳ NW France
Aulong *see* Ulong
37 T3 **Ault** Colorado, C USA 40°34′N 104°43′W
95 F22 **Aulum** *var.* avlum. Ringkøbing, C Denmark 56°16′N 08°48′E
103 N3 **Aumale** Seine-Maritime, N France 49°45′N 01°43′E
Auminzatau, Gory *see* Ovminzatovo Togʻlari
77 T14 **Auna** Niger, W Nigeria 10°13′N 04°43′E
166 L6 **Aunglan** *var.* Allanmyo, Myaydo. Magway, C Burma (Myanmar) 19°25′N 95°13′E
95 H21 **Auning** Århus, C Denmark 56°26′N 10°23′E
192 K17 **'Aunu'u Island** *island* W American Samoa
83 E20 **Auob** *var.* Oup. ⤳ Namibia/South Africa
93 K19 **Aura** Länsi-Suomi, SW Finland 60°37′N 22°35′E
109 R5 **Aurach** ⤳ N Austria
Aural, Phnom *see* Aôral, Phnum
153 O14 **Aurangābād** Bihār, N India 24°46′N 84°23′E
154 F13 **Aurangābād** Mahārāshtra, C India 19°52′N 75°22′E
189 V7 **Aur Atoll** *atoll* E Marshall Islands
102 G7 **Auray** Morbihan, NW France 47°40′N 02°59′W
94 G13 **Aurdal** Oppland, S Norway 60°51′N 09°25′E
94 F8 **Aure** Møre og Romsdal, S Norway 63°16′N 08°31′E
29 T12 **Aurelia** Iowa, C USA 42°42′N 95°26′W
Aurelia Aquensis *see* Baden-Baden
Aurelianum *see* Orléans
120 J10 **Aurès, Massif de l'** ▲ NE Algeria
100 F10 **Aurich** Niedersachsen, NW Germany 53°28′N 07°28′E
103 O13 **Aurillac** Cantal, C France 44°56′N 02°26′E
Aurine, Alpi *see* Zillertaler Alpen
Aurium *see* Ourense
14 H15 **Aurora** Ontario, S Canada 44°00′N 79°26′W
55 S8 **Aurora** NW Guyana 06°46′N 59°45′W
37 T4 **Aurora** Colorado, C USA 39°42′N 104°51′W
30 M11 **Aurora** Illinois, N USA 41°46′N 88°19′W
31 Q15 **Aurora** Indiana, N USA 39°01′N 84°55′W
29 W4 **Aurora** Minnesota, N USA 47°31′N 92°14′W
27 S8 **Aurora** Missouri, C USA 36°58′N 93°43′W
29 P16 **Aurora** Nebraska, C USA 40°52′N 98°00′W
36 J5 **Aurora** Utah, W USA 38°55′N 111°55′W
Aurora *see* San Francisco, Philippines
Aurora *see* Maéwo, Vanuatu
94 F10 **Aursjøen** ◎ S Norway
94 I9 **Aursunden** ◎ S Norway
83 D21 **Aus** Karas, SW Namibia 26°38′S 16°19′E
Ausa *see* Vic
14 E16 **Ausable** ⤳ Ontario, S Canada
31 S7 **Au Sable Point** *headland* Michigan, N USA 44°19′N 83°20′W
31 O3 **Au Sable Point** *headland* Michigan, N USA 46°40′N 86°08′W
31 R6 **Au Sable River** ⤳ Michigan, N USA
57 H16 **Ausangate, Nevado** ▲ C Peru 13°47′S 71°13′W
Auschwitz *see* Oświęcim
Ausculum Apulum *see* Ascoli Satriano
105 Q4 **Ausejo** La Rioja, N Spain 42°21′N 02°10′W
Aussig *see* Ústí nad Labem
95 F17 **Aust-Agder** ◆ *county* S Norway
92 P2 **Austfonna** *glacier* NE Svalbard
31 P15 **Austin** Indiana, N USA 38°45′N 85°48′W
29 W11 **Austin** Minnesota, N USA 43°40′N 92°58′W
35 U5 **Austin** Nevada, W USA 39°30′N 117°05′W
25 S10 **Austin** *state capital* Texas, SW USA 30°16′N 97°45′W
180 J10 **Austin, Lake** *salt lake* Western Australia
31 V11 **Austintown** Ohio, N USA 41°06′N 80°45′W
25 V9 **Austonio** Texas, SW USA 31°09′N 95°39′W
Australes, Archipel des *see* Australes, Îles
Australes et Antarctiques Françaises, Terres *see* French Southern and Antarctic Territories
191 T14 **Australes, Îles** *var.* Archipel des Australes, Îles Tubuai, Tubuai Islands, *Eng.* Austral Islands. *island group* SW French Polynesia
175 Y11 **Austral Fracture Zone** *tectonic feature* S Pacific Ocean
174 M8 **Australia** *continent*
181 O7 **Australia** *off.* Commonwealth of Australia. ◆ *commonwealth republic*
Australia, Commonwealth of *see* Australia
183 Q12 **Australian Alps** ▲ SE Australia
183 R11 **Australian Capital Territory** *prev.* Federal Capital Territory. ◆ *territory* SE Australia
Australie, Bassin Nord de l' *see* North Australian Basin
Austral Islands *see* Australes, Îles
Austrava *see* Ostrov
109 T6 **Austria** *off.* Republic of Austria, *Ger.* Österreich. ◆ *republic* C Europe
Austria, Republic of *see* Austria
92 K3 **Austurland** ◆ *region* SE Iceland
92 G10 **Austvågøya** *island* C Norway
Ausuitoq *see* Grise Fiord
58 G13 **Autazes** Amazonas, N Brazil 03°37′S 59°08′W
102 M16 **Auterive** Haute-Garonne, S France 43°22′N 01°28′E
Autesiodorum *see* Auxerre
103 N2 **Authie** ⤳ N France
Autissiodorum *see* Auxerre
40 K14 **Autlán** *var.* Autlán de Navarro. Jalisco, SW Mexico 19°48′N 104°20′W
Autlán de Navarro *see* Autlán
Autricum *see* Chartres
103 Q9 **Autun** *anc.* Ædua, Augustodunum. Saône-et-Loire, C France 46°58′N 04°18′E
Autz *see* Auce
99 H20 **Auvelais** Namur, S Belgium 50°27′N 04°38′E
103 P11 **Auvergne** ◆ *region* C France
102 M12 **Auvézère** ⤳ W France
103 P7 **Auxerre** *anc.* Autesiodorum, Autissiodorum. Yonne, C France 47°48′N 03°35′E
103 N2 **Auxi-le-Château** Pas-de-Calais, N France 50°14′N 02°06′E
103 S8 **Auxonne** Côte d'Or, C France 47°12′N 05°22′E
55 P9 **Auyan Tebuy** ▲ SE Venezuela 05°48′N 62°27′W
103 O10 **Auzances** Creuse, C France 46°01′N 02°29′E
27 U8 **Ava** Missouri, C USA 36°57′N 92°39′W
142 M5 **Āvaj** Qazvīn, N Iran
95 C15 **Avaldsnes** Rogaland, S Norway 59°21′N 05°16′E
103 Q8 **Avallon** Yonne, C France 47°30′N 03°54′E
102 K6 **Avaloirs, Mont des** ▲ NW France 48°27′N 00°11′W
35 S16 **Avalon** Santa Catalina Island, California, W USA 33°20′N 118°19′W
18 J17 **Avalon** New Jersey, NE USA 39°04′N 74°42′W
13 V13 **Avalon Peninsula** *peninsula* Newfoundland and Labrador, E Canada
197 Q11 **Avannaarsua** ◆ *province* N Greenland
60 K10 **Avaré** São Paulo, S Brazil 23°06′S 48°57′W
Avaricum *see* Bourges
190 H16 **Avarua** ○ (Cook Islands) Rarotonga, S Cook Islands 21°12′S 159°46′E
190 H16 **Avarua Harbour** *harbour* Rarotonga, S Cook Islands

◆ Country ◇ Dependent Territory ◆ Administrative Regions ▲ Mountain ⩓ Volcano ◎ Lake
● Country Capital ○ Dependent Territory Capital ✕ International Airport ▲ Mountain Range ⤳ River ⊠ Reservoir

Avasfelsőfalu see Negrești-Oaș
38 L17 **Avatanak Island** island Aleutian Islands, Alaska, USA
190 B16 **Avatele** S Niue 19°06´S 169°55´E
190 H15 **Avatiu Harbour** harbour Rarotonga, S Cook Islands
Avdeyevka see Avdiyivka
114 J13 **Ávdira** Anatolikí Makedonía kai Thráki, NE Greece 40°58´N 24°58´E
117 X8 **Avdiyivka** Rus. Avdeyevka. Donets'ka Oblast', SE Ukraine 48°06´N 37°46´E
Avdzaga see Gurvanbulag
104 G6 **Ave** ≈ N Portugal
104 G7 **Aveiro** anc. Talabriga. Aveiro, W Portugal 40°38´N 08°40´W
104 G7 **Aveiro** ◐ district N Portugal
Avela see Ávila
99 D18 **Avelgem** West-Vlaanderen, W Belgium 50°46´N 03°25´E
61 D20 **Avellaneda** Buenos Aires, E Argentina 34°43´S 58°23´W
107 L17 **Avellino** anc. Abellinum. Campania, S Italy 40°54´N 14°46´E
35 Q12 **Avenal** California, W USA 36°00´N 120°07´W
Avenio see Avignon
94 E8 **Averoya** island S Norway
107 K17 **Aversa** Campania, S Italy 40°58´N 14°13´E
33 N9 **Avery** Idaho, NW USA 47°14´N 115°48´W
25 W5 **Avery** Texas, SW USA 33°33´N 94°46´W
Aves, Islas de see Las Aves, Islas
Avesnes see Avesnes-sur-Helpe
103 Q2 **Avesnes-sur-Helpe** var. Avesnes. Nord, N France 50°08´N 03°57´E
64 G12 **Aves Ridge** undersea feature SE Caribbean Sea 14°00´N 63°30´W
95 M14 **Avesta** Dalarna, C Sweden 60°09´N 16°10´E
103 O14 **Aveyron** ◐ department S France
103 N14 **Aveyron** ≈ S France
107 J15 **Avezzano** Abruzzo, C Italy 42°02´N 13°26´E
115 D16 **Avgó** ▲ C Greece 39°31´N 21°24´E
Avgustov see Augustów
Avgustovskiy Kanal see Augustowski, Kanał
96 J9 **Aviemore** N Scotland, United Kingdom 57°06´N 04°01´W
185 F21 **Aviemore, Lake** ◎ South Island, New Zealand
103 R15 **Avignon** anc. Avenio. Vaucluse, SE France 43°57´N 04°49´E
104 M7 **Ávila** var. Avila; anc. Abela, Abula, Abyla, Avela. Castilla-León, C Spain 40°39´N 04°42´W
104 L8 **Ávila** ◐ province Castilla-León, C Spain
104 K2 **Avilés** Asturias, NW Spain 43°33´N 05°55´W
118 J4 **Avinurme** Ger. Awwinorm. Ida-Virumaa, NE Estonia 58°58´N 26°53´E
104 H10 **Avis** Portalegre, C Portugal 39°03´N 07°53´W
Avlum see Aulum
182 M11 **Avoca** Victoria, SE Australia 37°09´S 143°34´E
29 T14 **Avoca** Iowa, C USA 41°27´N 95°20´W
182 M11 **Avoca River** ≈ Victoria, SE Australia
107 L25 **Avola** Sicilia, Italy, C Mediterranean Sea 36°54´N 15°08´E
18 F10 **Avon** New York, NE USA 42°53´N 77°41´W
29 P12 **Avon** South Dakota, N USA 43°00´N 98°03´W
97 M23 **Avon** ≈ S England, United Kingdom
97 L20 **Avon** ≈ C England, United Kingdom
36 K13 **Avondale** Arizona, SW USA 33°25´N 112°20´W
23 X13 **Avon Park** Florida, SE USA 27°36´N 81°30´W
102 J5 **Avranches** Manche, N France 48°42´N 01°21´W
Avveel see Ivalojoki, Finland
186 M6 **Avuavu** var. Kolotambu. Guadalcanal, C Solomon Islands 09°52´S 160°25´E
103 O3 **Avure** ≈ N France
Avveel see Ivalo, Finland
Avvil see Ivalo
77 O17 **Awaaso** var. Awaso. SW Ghana 06°10´N 02°18´W
141 X8 **Awābī** var. Al 'Awābī. NE Oman 23°20´N 57°35´E
184 L9 **Awakino** Waikato, North Island, New Zealand 38°40´S 174°37´E
142 M15 **'Awālī** C Bahrain 26°07´N 50°33´E
99 K19 **Awans** Liège, E Belgium 50°39´N 05°30´E
184 I2 **Awanui** Northland, North Island, New Zealand 35°01´S 173°16´E
148 M14 **Awārān** Baluchistān, SW Pakistan 26°31´N 65°10´E
81 K16 **Awara Plain** plain NE Kenya
80 M13 **Āwarē** Sumalē, E Ethiopia 08°12´N 44°09´E
138 M6 **'Awāriḍ, Wādī** dry watercourse E Syria
185 B20 **Awarua Point** headland South Island, New Zealand 44°15´S 168°03´E
81 J14 **Āwasa** Southern Nationalities, S Ethiopia 06°54´N 38°26´E
80 K13 **Āwash** Āfar, NE Ethiopia 08°59´N 40°16´E
80 K12 **Āwash** var. Hawash. ≈ C Ethiopia
Awaso see Awaaso
158 H7 **Awat** Xinjiang Uygur Zizhiqu, NW China 40°36´N 80°22´E
185 J15 **Awatere** ≈ South Island, New Zealand
75 O10 **Awbārī** SW Libya 26°35´N 12°46´E
75 N9 **Awbāri, Idhān** var. Edeyen d'Oubari. desert Algeria/Libya
80 M12 **Awdal** off. Gobolka Awdal. ◐ N Somalia
80 C13 **Aweil** Northern Bahr el Ghazal, SW Sudan 08°42´N 27°20´E
96 H11 **Awe, Loch** ◎ W Scotland, United Kingdom
77 U16 **Awka** Anambra, SW Nigeria 06°12´N 07°04´E
39 O6 **Awuna River** ≈ Alaska, USA
Awwinorm see Avinurme
Ax see Dax
Axarfjördhur see Öxarfjördhur
103 N17 **Axat** Aude, S France 42°47´N 02°14´E
99 F16 **Axel** Zeeland, SW Netherlands 51°16´N 03°55´E
197 P9 **Axel Heiberg Island** var. Axel Heiburg. island Nunavut, N Canada
Axel Heiburg see Axel Heiberg Island
77 O17 **Axim** S Ghana 04°53´N 02°14´W
114 F13 **Axiós** var. Vardar. ≈ Greece/FYR Macedonia see also Vardar
Axiós see Vardar
103 N17 **Ax-les-Thermes** Ariège, S France 42°43´N 01°49´E
120 D11 **Ayachi, Jbel** ▲ C Morocco 32°30´N 05°00´W
61 D22 **Ayacucho** Buenos Aires, E Argentina 37°09´S 58°30´W
57 F15 **Ayacucho** Ayacucho, S Peru 13°10´S 74°15´W
57 E16 **Ayacucho** off. Departamento de Ayacucho. ◐ department SW Peru
Ayacucho, Departamento de see Ayacucho
145 W11 **Ayagoz** var. Ayaguz, Kaz. Ayaköz; prev. Sergiopol. Vostochnyy Kazakhstan, E Kazakhstan 47°54´N 80°25´E
145 V12 **Ayagoz** var. Ayaguz, Kaz. Ayakoz. ≈ E Kazakhstan
Ayaguz see Ayagoz
Ayakagytma see Oyoqog'itma
Ayakkuduk see Oyoqquduq
158 L10 **Ayakkum Hu** ◎ NW China
Ayaköz see Ayagoz
104 H14 **Ayamonte** Andalucía, S Spain 37°13´N 07°24´W
123 S11 **Ayan** Khabarovskiy Kray, E Russian Federation 56°27´N 138°09´E
136 J10 **Ayancık** Sinop, N Turkey 41°56´N 34°35´E
55 S9 **Ayanganna Mountain** ▲ C Guyana 05°21´N 59°54´W
77 U16 **Ayangba** Kogi, C Nigeria 07°36´N 07°10´E
123 U7 **Ayanka** Koryakskiy Avtonomnyy Okrug, E Russian Federation 63°42´N 167°31´E
54 E7 **Ayapel** Córdoba, NW Colombia 08°16´N 75°10´W
136 H12 **Ayaş** Ankara, N Turkey 40°02´N 32°21´E
57 I16 **Ayaviri** Puno, S Peru 14°53´S 70°35´W
149 P3 **Āybak** var. Aibak, Haibak; prev. Samangān. Samangān, NE Afghanistan 36°16´N 68°04´E
147 N10 **Aydarko'l Ko'li** Rus. Ozero Aydarkul'. ◎ C Uzbekistan
Aydarkul', Ozero see Aydarko'l Ko'li
21 W10 **Ayden** North Carolina, SE USA 35°28´N 77°25´W
136 C15 **Aydın** var. Aïdin; anc. Tralles Aydin. Aydın, SW Turkey 37°51´N 27°51´E
136 C15 **Aydın** var. Aïdin. ◐ province SW Turkey
136 I17 **Aydıncık** İçel, S Turkey 36°08´N 33°17´E
136 C15 **Aydın Dağları** ▲▲ W Turkey
158 L6 **Aydingkol Hu** ◎ NW China
127 X7 **Aydyrlinskiy** Orenburgskaya Oblast', W Russian Federation 52°03´N 59°54´E
105 S4 **Ayerbe** Aragón, NE Spain 42°16´N 00°41´W
Ayers Rock see Uluru
Ayeyarwady see Irrawaddy
Ayiá see Agiá
Ayia Napa see Agía Nápa
Ayia Phyla see Agía Fýlaxis
Ayiásos/Ayiássos see Agiassós
Áyios Evstrátios see Ágios Efstrátios
Áyios Kírikos see Ágios Kírykos
Áyios Nikólaos see Ágios Nikólaos
80 I11 **Āykel** Āmara, N Ethiopia 12°33´N 37°01´E
123 N9 **Aykhal** Respublika Sakha (Yakutiya), NE Russian Federation 66°07´N 110°25´E
14 J12 **Aylen Lake** ◎ Ontario, SE Canada
97 N21 **Aylesbury** SE England, United Kingdom 51°50´N 00°50´W
105 O6 **Ayllón** Castilla-León, N Spain 41°25´N 03°23´W
14 F17 **Aylmer** Ontario, S Canada 42°46´N 80°57´W
14 L12 **Aylmer** Québec, SE Canada 45°23´N 75°51´W
15 R12 **Aylmer, Lac** ◎ Québec, SE Canada
8 L9 **Aylmer Lake** ◎ Northwest Territories, NW Canada
145 V14 **Aynabulak** Kaz. Aynabulaq. Almaty, SE Kazakhstan 44°37´N 77°59´E
Aynabulaq see Aynabulak
138 K2 **'Ayn al 'Arab** Ḥalab, N Syria 36°55´N 38°21´E
Aynayn see 'Aynīn
139 V12 **'Ayn Ḥamūd** Dhī Qār, S Iraq 30°51´N 45°37´E
147 P12 **Ayní** prev. Varzimanor Ayni. W Tajikistan 39°24´N 68°30´E
140 M10 **'Aynīn** var. Aynayn. spring/well SW Saudi Arabia 20°52´N 41°41´E
21 U12 **Aynor** South Carolina, SE USA 33°59´N 79°11´W
139 Q7 **'Ayn Zāzūh** Al Anbār, C Iraq 33°29´N 42°34´E
153 N12 **Ayodhya** Uttar Pradesh, N India 26°47´N 82°12´E
123 S6 **Ayon, Ostrov** island NE Russian Federation
105 R11 **Ayora** País Valenciano, E Spain 39°04´N 01°04´W
77 Q11 **Ayorou** Tillabéri, W Niger 14°45´N 00°54´E
79 E16 **Ayos** Centre, S Cameroon 03°53´N 12°31´E
76 L5 **'Ayoûn 'Abd el Mâlek** well N Mauritania
76 K10 **'Ayoûn el 'Atroûs** var. Aïoun el Atrous, Aïoun el Atroûss. Hodh el Gharbi, SE Mauritania 16°38´N 09°36´W
96 I13 **Ayr** W Scotland, United Kingdom 55°28´N 04°38´W
96 I13 **Ayr** ≈ W Scotland, United Kingdom
96 I13 **Ayrshire** cultural region SW Scotland, United Kingdom
Aysen see Aisén
80 L12 **Āysha** Sumalē, E Ethiopia 10°36´N 42°31´E
144 L14 **Ayteke Bi** Kaz. Zhangaqazaly; prev. Novokazalinsk. Kzylorda, SW Kazakhstan 45°53´N 62°10´E
146 K8 **Aytim** Navoiy Viloyati, N Uzbekistan 42°15´N 63°25´E
181 W4 **Ayton** Queensland, NE Australia 15°54´S 145°19´E
114 M9 **Aytos** Burgas, E Bulgaria 42°43´N 27°14´E
171 T11 **Ayu, Kepulauan** island group E Indonesia
A Yun Pa see Cheo Reo
169 V11 **Ayu, Tanjung** headland Borneo, N Indonesia 0°25´N 117°34´E
41 P16 **Ayutlá** var. Ayutla de los Libres. Guerrero, S Mexico 16°51´N 99°16´W
40 K13 **Ayutla** Jalisco, C Mexico 20°07´N 104°18´W
Ayutla de los Libres see Ayutlá
167 O11 **Ayutthaya** var. Phra Nakhon Si Ayutthaya. Phra Nakhon Si Ayutthaya, C Thailand 14°20´N 100°35´E
136 B13 **Ayvalık** Balıkesir, W Turkey 39°18´N 26°42´E
99 L20 **Aywaille** Liège, E Belgium 50°28´N 05°40´E
141 R13 **'Aywat aş Şay'ar, Wādī** seasonal river N Yemen
Azaffal see Azeffâl
105 T9 **Azahar, Costa del** coastal region E Spain
105 S6 **Azaila** Aragón, NE Spain 41°17´N 00°20´W
104 F10 **Azambuja** Lisboa, C Portugal 39°04´N 08°52´W
153 N13 **Āzamgarh** Uttar Pradesh, N India 26°03´N 83°10´E
77 O9 **Azaouâd** desert C Mali
77 S10 **Azaouagh, Vallée de l'** var. Azaouak. ≈ W Niger
Azaouak see Azaouagh, Vallée de l'
61 F14 **Azara** Misiones, NE Argentina 28°03´S 55°42´W
Azaran see Hashtrūd
Azärbaycan/Azärbaycan Respublikasī see Azerbaijan
Āžarbāyjān-e Bākhtarī see Āžarbāyjān-e Gharbī
142 I4 **Āžarbāyjān-e Gharbī** off. Ostān-e Āžarbāyjān-e Gharbī, Eng. West Azerbaijan; prev. Āžarbāyjān-e Bākhtarī. NW Iran
Āžarbāyjān-e Gharbī, Ostān-e see Āžarbāyjān-e Gharbī
Āžarbāyjān-e Khāvarī see Āžarbāyjān-e Sharqī
142 J3 **Āžarbāyjān-e Sharqī** off. Ostān-e Azarbāyjān-e Sharqī, Eng. East Azerbaijan; prev. Āžarbāyjān-e Khāvarī. ◐ province NW Iran
Āžarbāyjān-e Sharqī, Ostān-e see Āžarbāyjān-e Sharqī
77 W13 **Azare** Bauchi, N Nigeria 11°41´N 10°09´E
119 M19 **Azarychy** Rus. Ozarichi. Homyel'skaya Voblasts', SE Belarus 52°31´N 29°19´E
102 L8 **Azay-le-Rideau** Indre-et-Loire, C France 47°16´N 00°25´E
138 I2 **A'zāz** Ḥalab, NW Syria 36°35´N 37°03´E
76 H7 **Azeffâl** var. Azaffal. desert Mauritania/Western Sahara
137 V12 **Azerbaijan** off. Azerbaijani Republic, Az. Azärbaycan, Azärbaycan Respublikası; prev. Azerbaijan SSR. ◆ republic SE Asia
Azerbaijani Republic see Azerbaijan
Azerbaijan SSR see Azerbaijan
145 T7 **Azhbulat, Ozero** ◎ NE Kazakhstan
74 F7 **Azilal** C Morocco 31°58´N 06°53´W
Azimabad see Patna
19 O6 **Aziscohos Lake** ⊠ Maine, NE USA
Azizbekov see Vayk'
Azizie see Telish
Aziziya see Al 'Azīzīyah
127 T4 **Aznakayevo** Respublika Tatarstan, W Russian Federation 54°55´N 53°15´E
56 C8 **Azogues** Cañar, S Ecuador 02°44´S 78°48´W
64 N2 **Azores** var. Açores, Ilhas dos Açores, Port. Arquipélago dos Açores. island group Portugal, NE Atlantic Ocean
64 L8 **Azores-Biscay Rise** undersea feature E Atlantic Ocean 19°00´W 42°40´N
Azotos/Azotus see Ashdod
78 K11 **Azoum, Bahr** seasonal river SE Chad
126 L12 **Azov** Rostovskaya Oblast', SW Russian Federation 47°07´N 39°26´E
126 J13 **Azov, Sea of** Rus. Azovskoye More, Ukr. Azovs'ke More. sea NE Black Sea
Azovs'ke More/Azovskoye More see Azov, Sea of
138 I10 **Azraq, Wāḥat al** oasis N Jordan
Āzro see Āzrow
74 G6 **Azrou** C Morocco 33°30´N 05°12´W
149 R5 **Āzrow** var. Āzro. Lowgar, E Afghanistan 34°11´N 69°39´E
37 P8 **Aztec** New Mexico, SW USA 36°49´N 107°59´W
36 M13 **Aztec Peak** ▲ Arizona, SW USA 33°48´N 110°54´W
45 N9 **Azua** var. Azua de Compostela. S Dominican Republic 18°29´N 70°44´W
Azua de Compostela see Azua
104 K12 **Azuaga** Extremadura, W Spain 38°16´N 05°40´W
56 B8 **Azuay** ◐ province W Ecuador
164 C13 **Azuchi-Ō-shima** island SW Japan
105 O11 **Azuer** ≈ C Spain
43 S17 **Azuero, Península de** peninsula S Panama
62 I6 **Azufre, Volcán** var. Volcán Lastarria. ⛰ N Chile 25°16´S 68°35´W
116 J12 **Azuga** Prahova, SE Romania 45°27´N 25°34´E
61 C22 **Azul** Buenos Aires, E Argentina 36°46´S 59°50´W
62 I8 **Azul, Cerro** ▲ NW Argentina 28°28´S 68°43´W
56 E12 **Azul, Cordillera** ▲▲ C Peru
165 P11 **Azuma-san** ▲ Honshū, C Japan 37°44´N 140°05´E
103 V15 **Azur, Côte d'** coastal region SE France
191 Z3 **Azur Lagoon** ◎ Kiritimati, E Kiribati
'Azza see Gaza
Az Zāb al Kabīr see Great Zab
138 H7 **Az Zabdānī** var. Zabadani. Dimashq, W Syria 33°45´N 36°07´E
141 W8 **Aẓ Ẓāhirah** desert NW Oman
141 S6 **Aẓ Ẓahrān** Eng. Dhahran. Ash Sharqīyah, NE Saudi Arabia 26°18´N 50°02´E
141 R6 **Aẓ Ẓahrān al Khubar** var. Dhahran Al Khobar. ✈ Ash Sharqīyah, NE Saudi Arabia 26°28´N 49°42´E
75 W7 **Az Zaqāzīq** var. Az Zaqāzīq var. Zagazig. N Egypt 30°36´N 31°32´E
Az Zaqāzīq see Az Zaqāzīq
138 H10 **Az Zarqā'** var. Zarqa. Az Zarqā', NW Jordan 32°04´N 36°06´E
138 I11 **Az Zarqā'** off. Muḥāfazat az Zarqā', var. Zarqa. ◐ governorate N Jordan
75 O7 **Az Zāwiyah** var. Zawia. NW Libya 32°45´N 12°44´E
141 N15 **Az Zaydīyah** W Yemen 15°20´N 43°03´E
74 I11 **Azzel Matti, Sebkha** var. Sebkra Azz el Matti. salt flat C Algeria
141 P6 **Az Zilfī** Ar Riyāḍ, N Saudi Arabia 26°17´N 44°48´E
139 Y13 **Az Zubayr** var. Al Zubair. Al Başrah, SE Iraq 30°24´N 47°45´E
Az Zuqur see Jabal Zuqar, Jazīrat

B

187 X15 **Ba** prev. Mba. Viti Levu, W Fiji 17°35´S 177°40´E
Ba see Da Răng, Sông
171 P17 **Baa** Pulau Rote, C Indonesia 10°44´S 123°06´E
138 H7 **Baalbek** var. Ba'labakk; anc. Heliopolis. E Lebanon 34°00´N 36°15´E
108 G8 **Baar** Zug, N Switzerland 47°12´N 08°32´E
81 L17 **Baardheere** var. Bardere, It. Bardera. Gedo, SW Somalia 02°13´N 42°19´E
80 Q12 **Baargaal** Bari, NE Somalia 11°12´N 51°04´E
99 I15 **Baarle-Hertog** Antwerpen, N Belgium 51°26´N 04°56´E
99 I15 **Baarle-Nassau** Noord-Brabant, S Netherlands 51°27´N 04°56´E
98 J11 **Baarn** Utrecht, C Netherlands 52°13´N 05°16´E
162 H9 **Baatsagaan** var. Bayansayr. Bayanhongor, C Mongolia 45°36´N 99°27´E
114 D13 **Baba** var. Buševa, Gk. Varnoús. ▲▲ FYR Macedonia/Greece
76 H10 **Bababé** Brakna, W Mauritania 16°22´N 13°57´W
136 G10 **Baba Burnu** headland NW Turkey 41°18´N 31°24´E
117 N13 **Babadag** Tulcea, SE Romania 44°53´N 28°47´E
137 X10 **Babadağ Dağı** ▲ NE Azerbaijan 41°02´N 48°04´E
146 H14 **Babadaýhan** Rus. Babadaykhan; prev. Kirovsk. Ahal Welaýaty, C Turkmenistan 37°39´N 60°17´E
Babadaykhan see Babadaýhan
146 G14 **Babadurmaz** Ahal Welaýaty, C Turkmenistan 37°39´N 59°03´E
114 M12 **Babaeski** Kırklareli, NW Turkey 41°26´N 27°06´E
139 T4 **Bāba Gurgur** At Ta'mīn, N Iraq 35°34´N 44°18´E
56 B7 **Babahoyo** prev. Bodegas. Los Ríos, C Ecuador 01°53´S 79°31´W
149 P5 **Bābā, Kūh-e** ▲▲ C Afghanistan
171 N12 **Babana** Sulawesi, C Indonesia 02°03´S 119°13´E
Babao see Qilian
171 Q12 **Babar, Kepulauan** island group E Indonesia
171 T12 **Babar, Pulau** island Kepulauan Babar, E Indonesia
152 G4 **Bābāsar Pass** pass India/Pakistan
Babashy, Gory see Babaşy
146 C9 **Babaşy** Rus. Gory Babashy. ▲▲ W Turkmenistan
168 M13 **Babat** Sumatera, W Indonesia 02°45´S 104°01´E
Babatag, Khrebet see Bototog', Tizmasi
81 H21 **Babati** Manyara, NE Tanzania 04°12´S 35°45´E
124 J13 **Babayevo** Vologodskaya Oblast', NW Russian Federation 59°23´N 35°52´E
127 Q15 **Babayurt** Respublika Dagestan, SW Russian Federation 43°38´N 46°49´E
33 P6 **Babb** Montana, NW USA 48°51´N 113°26´W
29 X4 **Babbitt** Minnesota, N USA 47°42´N 91°56´W
188 E9 **Babeldaob** var. Babeldaop, Babelthuap. island N Palau
Babeldaop see Babeldaob
141 N17 **Bab el Mandeb** strait Gulf of Aden/Red Sea
Babelthuap see Babeldaob
111 K17 **Babia Góra** var. Babia Hora. ▲ Poland/Slovakia 49°33´N 19°32´E
Babia Hora see Babia Góra
Babian Jiang see Black River
Babichi see Babichy
119 N19 **Babichy** Rus. Babichi. Homyel'skaya Voblasts', SE Belarus 52°17´N 30°00´E
139 U9 **Bābil** ◐ governorate S Iraq
112 I10 **Babina Greda** Vukovar-Srijem, E Croatia 45°09´N 18°33´E
10 K13 **Babine Lake** ◎ British Columbia, SW Canada
143 O4 **Bābol** var. Babul, Balfrush, Barfrush; prev. Barfurush. Māzandarān, N Iran 36°34´N 52°39´E
143 O4 **Bābolsar** var. Babulsar; prev. Meshed-i-Sar. Māzandarān, N Iran 36°41´N 52°39´E
36 L16 **Baboquivari Peak** ▲ Arizona, SW USA 31°46´N 111°36´W
79 G15 **Baboua** Nana-Mambéré, W Central African Republic 05°46´N 14°47´E
119 M17 **Babruysk** Rus. Bobruysk. Mahilyowskaya Voblasts', E Belarus 53°07´N 29°13´E
Babu see Hezhou
Babul see Bābol
Babulsar see Bābolsar
113 O19 **Babuna** ▲▲ C FYR Macedonia
113 O19 **Babuna** ≈ C FYR Macedonia
148 K7 **Bābūs, Dasht-e** Pash. Bebas, Dasht-i. ▲▲ W Afghanistan
171 O1 **Babuyan Channel** channel N Philippines
171 O1 **Babuyan Islands** island N Philippines
139 T9 **Babylon** site of ancient city C Iraq
112 J9 **Bač** Ger. Batsch. Vojvodina, NW Serbia 45°24´N 19°17´E
58 M13 **Bacabal** Maranhão, E Brazil 04°15´S 44°45´W
41 Y14 **Bacalar** Quintana Roo, SE Mexico 18°38´N 88°17´W
41 Y14 **Bacalar Chico, Boca** strait SE Mexico
171 Q12 **Bacan, Kepulauan** island group E Indonesia
171 S12 **Bacan, Pulau** prev. Batjan. island Maluku, E Indonesia
116 L10 **Bacău** Hung. Bákó. Bacău, NE Romania 46°36´N 26°56´E
116 K11 **Bacău** ◐ county E Romania
Băc Bô, Vinh see Tongking, Gulf of
167 T5 **Băc Can** var. Bach Thong. Băc Thai, N Vietnam 22°07´N 105°50´E
103 T5 **Baccarat** Meurthe-et-Moselle, NE France 48°27´N 06°46´E
183 N12 **Bacchus Marsh** Victoria, SE Australia 37°41´S 144°30´E
40 H4 **Bacerac** Sonora, NW Mexico 30°27´N 108°55´W
116 L10 **Băcești** Vaslui, E Romania 46°50´N 27°14´E
167 T6 **Băc Giang** Ha Băc, N Vietnam 21°17´N 106°12´E
54 I5 **Bachaquero** Zulia, NW Venezuela 09°57´N 71°09´W
Bacher see Pohorje
118 M13 **Bacheykava** Rus. Bocheykovo. Vitsyebskaya Voblasts', N Belarus 55°01´N 29°09´E
40 I5 **Bachíniva** Chihuahua, N Mexico 28°41´N 107°13´W
Bach Thong see Băc Can
158 G8 **Bachu** Xinjiang Uygur Zizhiqu, NW China 39°46´N 78°30´E
9 N8 **Back** ≈ Nunavut, N Canada
112 K10 **Bačka Palanka** prev. Palanka. Serbia, NW Serbia 44°22´N 20°57´E
112 K8 **Bačka Topola** Hung. Topolya; prev. Hung. Bácstopolya. Vojvodina, N Serbia 45°48´N 19°39´E
95 J17 **Bäckefors** Västra Götaland, S Sweden 58°49´N 12°07´E
Bäckermühle Schulzenmühle see Żywiec
95 L16 **Bäckhammar** Värmland, C Sweden 59°09´N 14°13´E
112 K9 **Bački Petrovac** Hung. Petrőcz; prev. Petrovac, Petrovácz. Vojvodina, NW Serbia 45°22´N 19°34´E
101 I21 **Backnang** Baden-Württemberg, SW Germany 48°57´N 09°26´E
167 S15 **Bac Liêu** var. Vinh Loi. Minh Hai, S Vietnam 09°17´N 105°44´E
167 T6 **Băc Ninh** Ha Băc, N Vietnam 21°10´N 106°04´E
40 G4 **Bacoachi** Sonora, NW Mexico 30°36´N 110°00´W
171 P6 **Bacolod** off. Bacolod City. Negros, C Philippines 10°43´N 122°58´E
Bacolod City see Bacolod
171 O4 **Baco, Mount** ▲ Mindoro, N Philippines 12°50´N 121°08´E
111 K25 **Bácsalmás** Bács-Kiskun, S Hungary 46°07´N 19°20´E
Bácsjózseffalva see Žednik
111 J24 **Bács-Kiskun** off. Bács-Kiskun Megye. ◐ county S Hungary
Bács-Kiskun Megye see Bács-Kiskun
Bácsszenttamás see Srbobran
Bácstopolya see Bačka Topola
Bactra see Balkh
Bada see Xilin
155 F21 **Badagara** var. Vadakara. Kerala, SW India 11°36´N 75°34´E see also Vadakara
101 M24 **Bad Aibling** Bayern, SE Germany 47°52´N 12°00´E
162 I13 **Badain Jaran Shamo** desert N China
104 I11 **Badajoz** anc. Pax Augusta. Extremadura, W Spain 38°53´N 06°58´W
104 J11 **Badajoz** ◐ province Extremadura, W Spain
149 S2 **Badakhshān** ◐ province NE Afghanistan
105 W6 **Badalona** anc. Baetulo. Cataluña, E Spain 41°27´N 02°15´E
154 O11 **Bādāmapāhārh** Orissa, E India 22°04´N 86°06´E
152 K8 **Badarīnāth** ▲ N India 30°44´N 79°29´E
169 O10 **Badas, Kepulauan** island group W Indonesia
109 S6 **Bad Aussee** Salzburg, E Austria 47°35´N 13°44´E
31 S8 **Bad Axe** Michigan, N USA 43°48´N 83°00´W
101 G16 **Bad Berleburg** Nordrhein-Westfalen, W Germany 51°03´N 08°24´E
101 L17 **Bad Blankenburg** Thüringen, C Germany 50°43´N 11°19´E
Bad Borseck see Borsec
101 G18 **Bad Camberg** Hessen, W Germany 50°18´N 08°15´E
100 L8 **Bad Doberan** Mecklenburg-Vorpommern, N Germany 54°06´N 11°55´E
101 N14 **Bad Düben** Sachsen, E Germany 51°35´N 12°34´E
109 X4 **Baden** var. Baden bei Wien; anc. Aquae Panoniae, Thermae Pannonicae. Niederösterreich, NE Austria 48°01´N 16°14´E
108 F9 **Baden** Aargau, N Switzerland 47°28´N 08°19´E
101 G21 **Baden-Baden** anc. Aurelia Aquensis. Baden-Württemberg, SW Germany 48°46´N 08°14´E
Baden bei Wien see Baden
101 G22 **Baden-Württemberg** Fr. Bade-Wurtemberg. ◐ state SW Germany
112 A10 **Baderna** Istra, NW Croatia 45°12´N 13°45´E
Bade-Wurtemberg see Baden-Württemberg
101 H20 **Bad Fredrichshall** Baden-Württemberg, S Germany 49°13´N 09°15´E
100 P11 **Bad Freienwalde** Brandenburg, NE Germany 52°47´N 14°04´E
109 Q8 **Badgastein** var. Gastein. Salzburg, NW Austria 47°07´N 13°09´E
Badger State see Wisconsin
148 L4 **Bādghīs** ◐ province NW Afghanistan
109 T5 **Bad Hall** Oberösterreich, N Austria 48°03´N 14°13´E
101 J14 **Bad Harzburg** Niedersachsen, C Germany 51°52´N 10°34´E
101 I16 **Bad Hersfeld** Hessen, C Germany 50°52´N 09°42´E
98 I10 **Badhoevedorp** Noord-Holland, C Netherlands 52°21´N 04°46´E
109 Q8 **Bad Hofgastein** Salzburg, NW Austria 47°11´N 13°07´E
Bad Homburg see Bad Homburg vor der Höhe
101 G18 **Bad Homburg vor der Höhe** var. Bad Homburg. Hessen, W Germany 50°14´N 08°37´E
101 E17 **Bad Honnef** Nordrhein-Westfalen, W Germany 50°39´N 07°13´E
149 Q17 **Badīn** Sind, SE Pakistan 24°38´N 68°53´E
21 S10 **Badin Lake** ⊠ North Carolina, SE USA
40 I8 **Badiraguato** Sinaloa, C Mexico 25°21´N 107°31´W
109 R6 **Bad Ischl** Oberösterreich, N Austria 47°43´N 13°36´E
Badjawa see Bajawa
Badje-Sohppar see Övre Soppero
101 J18 **Bad Kissingen** Bayern, SE Germany 50°12´N 10°04´E
Bad Königswart see Lázně Kynžvart
101 F19 **Bad Kreuznach** Rheinland-Pfalz, SW Germany 49°51´N 07°52´E
101 F24 **Bad Krozingen** Baden-Württemberg, SW Germany 47°55´N 07°43´E
101 G16 **Bad Laasphe** Nordrhein-Westfalen, W Germany 50°57´N 08°24´E
28 J6 **Badlands** physical region North Dakota/South Dakota, N USA
101 K16 **Bad Langensalza** Thüringen, C Germany 51°05´N 10°40´E
109 T3 **Bad Leonfelden** Oberösterreich, N Austria 48°31´N 14°17´E
101 I20 **Bad Mergentheim** Baden-Württemberg, SW Germany 49°30´N 09°46´E
101 H17 **Bad Nauheim** Hessen, W Germany 50°22´N 08°45´E
101 E17 **Bad Neuenahr-Arhweiler** Rheinland-Pfalz, W Germany 50°33´N 07°07´E
Bad Neustadt see Bad Neustadt an der Saale
101 J18 **Bad Neustadt an der Saale** var. Bad Neustadt. Berlin, C Germany 50°21´N 10°13´E
Badnur see Betūl
100 H13 **Bad Oeynhausen** Nordrhein-Westfalen, NW Germany 52°12´N 08°48´E
100 J9 **Bad Oldesloe** Schleswig-Holstein, N Germany 53°49´N 10°22´E
77 Q16 **Badou** C Togo 07°37´N 00°37´E
Bad Polzin see Połczyn-Zdrój
100 H13 **Bad Pyrmont** Niedersachsen, C Germany 51°58´N 09°16´E
109 X9 **Bad Radkersburg** Steiermark, SE Austria 46°40´N 16°02´E
139 V8 **Badrah** Wāsiţ, E Iraq 33°06´N 45°58´E
Badrah see Tarialan
101 N24 **Bad Reichenhall** Bayern, SE Germany 47°43´N 12°52´E
140 K8 **Badr Ḥunayn** Al Madīnah, W Saudi Arabia 23°46´N 38°45´E
28 M10 **Bad River** ≈ South Dakota, N USA
30 K4 **Bad River** ≈ Wisconsin, N USA
100 H13 **Bad Salzuflen** Nordrhein-Westfalen, NW Germany 52°06´N 08°45´E
101 J16 **Bad Salzungen** Thüringen, C Germany 50°48´N 10°15´E
109 V8 **Bad Sankt Leonhard im Lavanttal** Kärnten, S Austria 46°55´N 14°51´E
100 K9 **Bad Schwartau** Schleswig-Holstein, N Germany 53°55´N 10°42´E
101 L24 **Bad Tölz** Bayern, SE Germany 47°44´N 11°34´E
181 U1 **Badu Island** island Queensland, NE Australia
155 K25 **Badulla** Uva Province, C Sri Lanka 06°59´N 81°03´E
109 X5 **Bad Vöslau** Niederösterreich, NE Austria 47°58´N 16°13´E
101 I24 **Bad Waldsee** Baden-Württemberg, S Germany 47°54´N 09°44´E
35 U11 **Badwater Basin** depression California, W USA
101 J20 **Bad Windsheim** Bayern, C Germany 49°30´N 10°25´E
101 J23 **Bad Wörishofen** Bayern, S Germany 48°00´N 10°36´E
100 G10 **Bad Zwischenahn** Niedersachsen, NW Germany 53°10´N 08°01´E
104 M13 **Baena** Andalucía, S Spain 36°37´N 04°20´W
Baeterrae/Baeterrae Septimanorum see Béziers
Baetic Cordillera/Baetic Mountains see Béticos, Sistemas
Baetulo see Badalona
57 K18 **Baeza** Napo, NE Ecuador 0°30´S 77°52´W
105 N13 **Baeza** Andalucía, S Spain 38°00´N 03°28´W
79 D15 **Bafang** Ouest, W Cameroon 05°10´N 10°11´E
76 H12 **Bafatá** C Guinea-Bissau 12°09´N 14°38´W
149 U5 **Baffa** North-West Frontier Province, NW Pakistan 34°30´N 73°18´E
197 O11 **Baffin Basin** undersea feature N Labrador Sea
197 N12 **Baffin Bay** bay Canada/Greenland
25 T15 **Baffin Bay** inlet Texas, SW USA
196 M12 **Baffin Island** island Nunavut, NE Canada
79 E15 **Bafia** Centre, C Cameroon 04°49´N 11°14´E
77 R14 **Bafilo** NE Togo 09°23´N 01°20´E
76 J12 **Bafing** ≈ W Africa
76 J12 **Bafoulabé** Kayes, W Mali 13°43´N 10°49´W
79 D15 **Bafoussam** Ouest, W Cameroon 05°31´N 10°25´E
143 R9 **Bāfq** Yazd, C Iran 31°35´N 55°21´E
136 L10 **Bafra** Samsun, N Turkey 41°34´N 35°56´E
136 L10 **Bafra Burnu** headland N Turkey 41°42´N 36°02´E
143 S12 **Bāft** Kermān, S Iran 29°12´N 56°36´E
79 N18 **Bafwabalinga** Orientale, NE Dem. Rep. Congo 0°52´N 26°55´E
79 N18 **Bafwaboli** Orientale, NE Dem. Rep. Congo 0°36´N 26°08´E
79 N17 **Bafwasende** Orientale, NE Dem. Rep. Congo 01°00´N 27°09´E
42 K13 **Bagaces** Guanacaste, NW Costa Rica 10°31´N 85°18´W
153 O12 **Bagaha** Bihār, N India 27°08´N 84°04´E
155 F16 **Bāgalkot** Karnātaka, W India 16°11´N 75°42´E
81 J22 **Bagamoyo** Pwani, E Tanzania 06°26´S 38°55´E
Bagan Datok see Bagan Datuk
168 J8 **Bagan Datuk** var. Bagan Datok. Perak, Peninsular Malaysia 03°58´N 100°47´E
171 R7 **Baganga** Mindanao, S Philippines 07°31´N 126°34´E
168 J9 **Bagansiapiapi** var. Pasirpangarayan. Sumatera, W Indonesia 02°06´N 100°52´E
162 M8 **Baganuur** var. Nüürst. Töv, C Mongolia 47°44´N 108°22´E
Bagaria see Bagheria
77 T11 **Bagaroua** Tahoua, W Niger 14°34´N 04°24´E
79 I20 **Bagata** Bandundu, W Dem. Rep. Congo 03°47´S 17°57´E
Bagdad see Baghdād
123 O13 **Bagdarin** Respublika Buryatiya, S Russian Federation 54°27´N 113°34´E
61 G17 **Bagé** Rio Grande do Sul, S Brazil 31°22´S 54°06´W
Bagenalstown see Muine Bheag
153 T16 **Bagerhat** var. Bagherhat. Khulna, S Bangladesh 22°40´N 89°48´E
103 P16 **Bages et de Sigean, Étang de** ◎ S France
152 K10 **Bāgeshwar** Uttarakhand, N India 29°50´N 79°46´E
33 W17 **Baggs** Wyoming, C USA 41°02´N 107°39´W
154 F11 **Bāgh** Madhya Pradesh, C India 22°22´N 74°49´E
139 T8 **Baghdād** off. Muḥāfaẓat Baghdād. ◐ governorate C Iraq
139 T8 **Baghdād** var. Bagdad, Eng. Baghdad. ● Baghdād, C Iraq 33°20´N 44°26´E
139 T8 **Baghdād** ✈ (Baghdād) Baghdād, C Iraq 33°20´N 44°26´E
Baghdad see Baghdād
Baghdād, Muḥāfaẓat see Baghdād
Bagherhat see Bagerhat
107 J23 **Bagheria** var. Bagaria. Sicilia, Italy, C Mediterranean Sea 38°05´N 13°31´E
143 S10 **Bāghīn** Kermān, C Iran 30°50´N 57°00´E
149 Q3 **Baghlān** Baghlān, NE Afghanistan 36°11´N 68°44´E
149 Q3 **Baghlān** var. Bāghlān. ◐ province NE Afghanistan
Bāghlān see Baghlān
148 M7 **Bāghrān** Helmand, S Afghanistan 32°55´N 64°57´E
29 T4 **Bagley** Minnesota, N USA 47°31´N 95°24´W
106 H10 **Bagnacavallo** Emilia-Romagna, C Italy 44°00´N 12°59´E
102 K16 **Bagnères-de-Bigorre** Hautes-Pyrénées, S France 43°04´N 00°09´E
102 L17 **Bagnères-de-Luchon** Hautes-Pyrénées, S France 42°46´N 00°34´E
106 F11 **Bagni di Lucca** Toscana, C Italy 44°01´N 10°38´E

◆ Country
● Country Capital
◇ Dependent Territory
○ Dependent Territory Capital
◐ Administrative Regions
✈ International Airport
▲ Mountain
▲▲ Mountain Range
⛰ Volcano
≈ River
◎ Lake
⊠ Reservoir

106 H11 **Bagno di Romagna** Emilia-Romagna, C Italy 43°51′N 11°57′E
103 R14 **Bagnols-sur-Cèze** Gard, S France 44°10′N 04°37′E
162 M14 **Bag Nur** ◎ N China
166 L8 **Bago** *var.* Pegu. Bago, SW Burma (Myanmar) 17°18′N 96°31′E
171 P6 **Bago** *off.* Bago City. Negros, C Philippines 10°30′N 122°49′E
166 L7 **Bago** *var.* Pegu. ⬖ *division* S Burma (Myanmar)
Bago City *see* Bago
76 M13 **Bagoé** ≈ Ivory Coast/Mali
Bagrāmē *see* Bagrāmī
149 R5 **Bagrāmī** *var.* Bagrāmē. Kâbōl, E Afghanistan 34°29′N 69°16′E
119 B14 **Bagrationovsk** *Ger.* Preussisch Eylau. Kaliningradskaya Oblast', W Russian Federation 54°24′N 20°39′E
Bagrax *see* Bohu
Bagrax Hu *see* Bosten Hu
56 C10 **Bagua** Amazonas, NE Peru 05°37′S 78°36′W
171 O2 **Baguio** *off.* Baguio City. Luzon, N Philippines 16°25′N 120°36′E
Baguio City *see* Baguio
77 V9 **Bagzane, Monts** ▲ N Niger 17°48′N 08°43′E
Bāḩah, Minṭaqat al *see* Al Bāḩah
Bahama Islands *see* Bahamas
44 H3 **Bahamas** *off.* Commonwealth of the Bahamas. ◆ *commonwealth republic* N West Indies
0 L13 **Bahamas** *var.* Bahama Islands. *island group* N West Indies
Bahamas, Commonwealth of the *see* Bahamas
153 S15 **Baharampur** *prev.* Berhampore. West Bengal, NE India 24°06′N 88°19′E
146 E12 **Baharly** *var.* Bäherden, *Rus.* Bakharden; *prev.* Bakherden. Ahal Welaýaty, C Turkmenistan 38°30′N 57°18′E
149 U10 **Bahāwalnagar** Punjab, E Pakistan 30°00′N 73°03′E
149 T11 **Bahāwalpur** Punjab, E Pakistan 29°25′N 71°40′E
136 L16 **Bahçe** Osmaniye, S Turkey 37°14′N 36°34′E
160 J8 **Ba He** ≈ C China
Bäherden *see* Baharly
59 N16 **Bahia** *off.* Estado da Bahia. ⬖ *state* E Brazil
61 B24 **Bahía Blanca** Buenos Aires, E Argentina 38°43′S 62°19′W
40 L15 **Bahía Bufadero** Michoacán, SW Mexico
63 J19 **Bahía Bustamante** Chubut, SE Argentina 45°06′S 66°30′W
40 D5 **Bahía de los Ángeles** Baja California Norte, NW Mexico
40 C6 **Bahía de Tortugas** Baja California Sur, NW Mexico 27°42′N 114°54′W
Bahia, Estado da *see* Bahia
42 J4 **Bahía, Islas de la** *Eng.* Bay Islands. *island group* N Honduras
40 E5 **Bahía Kino** Sonora, NW Mexico 28°48′N 111°55′W
40 E9 **Bahía Magdalena** *var.* Puerto Magdalena. Baja California Sur, NW Mexico 24°34′N 112°07′W
54 C8 **Bahía Solano** *var.* Ciudad Mutis, Solano. Chocó, W Colombia 06°13′N 77°27′W
80 I11 **Bahir Dar** *var.* Bahr Dar, Bahrdar Giyorgis. Āmara, N Ethiopia 11°34′N 37°23′E
141 X8 **Bahlā'** *var.* Bahlah, Bahlat. NW Oman 22°58′N 57°16′E
Bāhla *see* Bālān
Bahlah/Bahlat *see* Bahlā'
152 M11 **Bahraich** Uttar Pradesh, N India 27°35′N 81°36′E
143 M14 **Bahrain** *off.* State of Bahrain, Dawlat al Bahrayn, *Ar.* Al Baḩrayn, *prev.* Bahrein; *anc.* Tylos, Tyros. ◆ *monarchy* SW Asia
142 M14 **Bahrain** ✈ C Bahrain 26°15′N 50°39′E
142 M15 **Bahrain, Gulf of** *gulf* Persian Gulf, NW Arabian Sea
Bahrain, State of *see* Bahrain
138 I7 **Baḩrat Mallāḩah** ◎ W Syria
Bahrayn, Dawlat al *see* Bahrain
Bahr Dar/Bahrdar Giyorgis *see* Bahir Dar
Bahrein *see* Bahrain
Bahr el, Azraq *see* Blue Nile
Bahr el Gebel *see* Central Equatoria
Bahr el Jebel *see* Central Equatoria
80 E13 **Bahr ez Zaref** ≈ C Sudan
67 R8 **Bahr Kameur** ≈ N Central African Republic
Bahr Tabariya, Sea of *see* Tiberias, Lake
143 W15 **Bāhū Kalāt** Sīstān va Balūchestān, SE Iran 25°42′N 61°28′E
118 N13 **Bahushewsk** *Rus.* Bogushëvsk. Vitsyebskaya Voblasts', NE Belarus 54°51′N 30°13′E
Bai *see* Tagow Bāy
116 G13 **Baia de Aramă** Mehedinţi, SW Romania 45°00′N 22°43′E
116 G11 **Baia de Criş** *Ger.* Altenburg, *Hung.* Körösbánya. Hunedoara, SW Romania 46°10′N 22°41′E
83 A16 **Baia dos Tigres** Namibe, SW Angola 16°36′S 11°44′E
82 A13 **Baia Farta** Benguela, W Angola 12°38′S 13°12′E
116 H9 **Baia Mare** *Ger.* Frauenbach, *Hung.* Nagybánya; *prev.* Neustadt. Maramureş, NW Romania 47°40′N 23°35′E
116 H8 **Baia Sprie** *Ger.* Mittelstadt, *Hung.* Felsőbánya. Maramureş, NW Romania 47°40′N 23°42′E
78 G13 **Baïbokoum** Logone-Oriental, SW Chad 07°46′N 15°43′E
160 F12 **Baicao Ling** ▲▲ SW China
163 U9 **Baicheng** *var.* Pai-ch'eng; *prev.* T'aon-an. Jilin, NE China 45°32′N 122°51′E
158 I6 **Baicheng** *var.* Bay. Xinjiang Uygur Zizhiqu, NW China 41°49′N 81°45′E
116 J13 **Băicoi** Prahova, SE Romania 45°02′N 25°51′E
Baidoa *see* Baydhabo
15 U6 **Baie-Comeau** Québec, SE Canada 49°12′N 68°10′W
15 U6 **Baie-des-Sables** Québec, SE Canada 48°41′N 67°55′W
15 T7 **Baie-des-Bacon** Québec, SE Canada 48°31′N 69°17′W
15 S8 **Baie-des-Rochers** Québec, SE Canada 47°57′N 69°50′W
12 K11 **Baie-du-Poste** Québec, SE Canada 50°20′N 73°50′W
172 H17 **Baie Lazare** Mahé, NE Seychelles 04°45′S 55°29′E
45 Y5 **Baie-Mahault** Basse Terre, C Guadeloupe 16°16′N 61°35′W
15 R9 **Baie-St-Paul** Québec, SE Canada 47°27′N 70°30′W
15 V5 **Baie-Trinité** Québec, SE Canada 49°25′N 67°20′W
13 T11 **Baie Verte** Newfoundland and Labrador, SE Canada 49°55′N 56°12′W
Baiguan *see* Shangyu
Baihe *see* Erdaobaihe
139 U11 **Bā'ij al Mahdī** Al Muthanná, S Iraq 31°21′N 44°57′E
Baiji *see* Bayjī
158 K4 **Baijiantan** *var.* Uxin Qi. Xinjiang Uygur Zizhiqu, NW China 45°38′N 85°11′E
Baikal, Lake *see* Baykal, Ozero
154 L11 **Baikunthpur** Chhattīsgarh, SW India 23°18′N 82°32′E
Bailādila *see* Kirandul
Baile an Chaistil *see* Ballycastle
Baile an Róba *see* Ballinrobe
Baile an tSratha *see* Ballintra
Baile Átha an Rí *see* Athenry
Baile Átha Buí *see* Athboy
Baile Átha Cliath *see* Dublin
Baile Átha Fhirdhia *see* Ardee
Baile Átha Í *see* Athy
Baile Átha Luain *see* Athlone
Baile Átha Troim *see* Trim
Baile Brigín *see* Balbriggan
Baile Easa Dara *see* Ballysadare
116 I13 **Băile Govora** Vâlcea, SW Romania 45°00′N 24°08′E
116 F13 **Băile Herculane** *Ger.* Herkulesbad, *Hung.* Herkulesfürdő. Caraş-Severin, SW Romania 44°51′N 22°24′E
Baile Locha Riach *see* Loughrea
Baile Mhistéala *see* Mitchelstown
Baile Monaidh *see* Ballymoney
105 N12 **Bailén** Andalucía, S Spain 38°06′N 03°46′W
Baile na hInse *see* Ballynahinch
Baile na Lorgan *see* Castleblayney
Baile na Mainistreach *see* Newtownabbey
Baile Nua na hArda *see* Newtownards
116 I12 **Băile Olăneşti** Vâlcea, SW Romania 45°14′N 24°18′E
116 H14 **Băileşti** Dolj, SW Romania 44°01′N 23°20′E
163 N12 **Bailingmiao** *var.* Darhan Muminggan Lianheqi. Nei Mongol Zizhiqu, N China 41°41′N 110°25′E
58 K11 **Bailique, Ilha** *island* NE Brazil
103 O1 **Bailleul** Nord, N France 50°43′N 02°43′E
78 H12 **Ba Illi** Chari-Baguirmi, SW Chad 10°31′N 16°29′E
159 V12 **Bailong Jiang** ≈ C China
82 C13 **Bailundo** *Port.* Vila Teixeira da Silva. Huambo, C Angola 12°12′S 15°52′E
159 T13 **Baima** *var.* Sêraitang. Qinghai, C China 32°55′N 100°44′E
Baima *see* Baxoi
186 C8 **Baimuru** Gulf, S Papua New Guinea 07°34′S 144°49′E
158 M16 **Bainang** Xizang Zizhiqu, W China 28°57′N 89°31′E
23 S8 **Bainbridge** Georgia, SE USA 30°54′N 84°33′W
171 O17 **Baing** Pulau Sumba, SE Indonesia 10°09′S 120°34′E
158 M14 **Baingoin** *var.* Pubao. Xizang Zizhiqu, W China 31°22′N 90°00′E
104 G2 **Baio Grande** Galicia, NW Spain 43°08′N 08°58′W
104 G4 **Baiona** Galicia, NW Spain 42°06′N 08°49′W
163 V7 **Baiquan** Heilongjiang, NE China 47°37′N 126°04′E
Bā'ir *see* Bāyir
158 I11 **Bairab Co** ◎ W China
25 Q7 **Baird** Texas, SW USA 32°23′N 99°24′W
39 N7 **Baird Mountains** ▲▲ Alaska, USA
Baireuth *see* Bayreuth
190 H3 **Bairiki** ● (Kiribati) Tarawa, NW Kiribati 01°20′N 173°01′E
Bairin Youqi *see* Daban
Bairin Zuoqi *see* Lindong
145 P17 **Bairkum** *Kaz.* Bayyrqum. Yuzhnyy Kazakhstan, S Kazakhstan 41°57′N 68°05′E
183 P12 **Bairnsdale** Victoria, SE Australia 37°51′S 147°38′E
171 P6 **Bais** Negros, S Philippines 09°36′N 123°07′E
102 L15 **Baïse** *var.* Baise. ≈ S France
Baise *see* Baïse
163 W11 **Baishan** *prev.* Hunjiang. Jilin, NE China 41°57′N 126°31′E
Baishan *see* Mashan
118 F12 **Baisogala** Šiauliai, C Lithuania 55°38′N 23°44′E
189 Q7 **Baiti** N Nauru 0°30′S 166°55′E
Baitou Shan *see* Paektu-san
104 G13 **Baixo Alentejo** *physical region* S Portugal
64 P5 **Baixo, Ilhéu de** *island* Madeira, Portugal, NE Atlantic Ocean
83 E15 **Baixo Longa** Cuando Cubango, SE Angola 15°39′S 18°39′E
159 V10 **Baiyin** Gansu, C China 36°33′N 104°11′E
160 E8 **Baiyü** *var.* Jianshe. Sichuan, C China 30°37′N 97°15′E
161 N14 **Baiyun** ✈ (Guangzhou) Guangdong, S China 23°12′N 113°19′E
160 K4 **Baiyu Shan** ▲▲ C China
111 J25 **Baja** Bács-Kiskun, S Hungary 46°13′N 18°56′E
40 C4 **Baja California** *Eng.* Lower California. *peninsula* NW Mexico
40 C4 **Baja California Norte** ⬖ *state* NW Mexico
40 E9 **Baja California Sur** ⬖ *state* NW Mexico
Bājah *see* Béja
Bajan *see* Bayan
191 V16 **Baja, Punta** *headland* Easter Island, Chile, E Pacific Ocean 27°10′S 109°21′W
40 B4 **Baja, Punta** *headland* NW Mexico 29°57′N 115°48′W
55 R5 **Baja, Punta** *headland* NE Venezuela
42 D5 **Baja Verapaz** *off.* Departamento de Baja Verapaz. ⬖ *department* C Guatemala
Baja Verapaz, Departamento de *see* Baja Verapaz
171 N16 **Bajawa** *prev.* Badjawa. Flores, S Indonesia 08°46′S 120°59′E
153 S16 **Baj Baj** *prev.* Budge-Budge. West Bengal, E India 22°29′N 88°11′E
141 N15 **Bājil** W Yemen 15°05′N 43°16′E
183 U4 **Bajimba, Mount** ▲ New South Wales, SE Australia 29°19′S 152°04′E
112 K13 **Bajina Bašta** Serbia, W Serbia 43°58′N 19°33′E
153 U14 **Bajitpur** Dhaka, E Bangladesh 24°12′N 90°57′E
112 K8 **Bajmok** Vojvodina, NW Serbia 45°59′N 19°25′E
Bajo Boquete *see* Boquete
113 L17 **Bajram Curri** Kukës, N Albania 42°23′N 20°06′E
79 J14 **Bakala** Ouaka, C Central African Republic 06°03′N 20°31′E
127 T4 **Bakaly** Respublika Bashkortostan, W Russian Federation 55°10′N 53°46′E
Bakan *see* Shimonoseki
145 U14 **Bakanas** *Kaz.* Baqanas. Almaty, SE Kazakhstan 44°50′N 76°13′E
145 V12 **Bakanas** *Kaz.* Baqanas. ≈ E Kazakhstan
149 R4 **Bākārak** Panjshīr, NE Afghanistan 35°16′N 69°28′E
145 U14 **Bakbakty** *Kaz.* Baqbaqty. Almaty, SE Kazakhstan 44°36′N 76°41′E
122 J12 **Bakchar** Tomskaya Oblast', C Russian Federation 56°58′N 81°59′E
76 I11 **Bakel** E Senegal 14°54′N 12°26′W
35 W13 **Baker** California, W USA 35°15′N 116°04′W
22 J8 **Baker** Louisiana, S USA 30°35′N 91°10′W
33 Y9 **Baker** Montana, NW USA 46°22′N 104°16′W
32 L12 **Baker** Oregon, NW USA 44°46′N 117°50′W
192 L7 **Baker and Howland Islands** ◇ *US unincorporated territory* W Polynesia
36 L12 **Baker Butte** ▲ Arizona, SW USA 34°24′N 111°22′W
39 X15 **Baker Island** *island* Alexander Archipelago, Alaska, USA
9 N9 **Baker Lake** Nunavut, N Canada 64°20′N 96°10′W
9 N9 **Baker Lake** ◎ Nunavut, N Canada
32 H6 **Baker, Mount** ▲ Washington, NW USA 48°46′N 121°48′W
35 R13 **Bakersfield** California, W USA 35°22′N 119°01′W
24 M9 **Bakersfield** Texas, SW USA 30°54′N 102°21′W
21 P9 **Bakersville** North Carolina, SE USA 36°01′N 82°09′W
Bakhābī *see* Bū Khābī
Bakharden *see* Baharly
Bakhardok *see* Bokurdak
143 U5 **Bākharz, Kuhhā-ye** ▲▲ NE Iran
152 D13 **Bākhāsar** Rājasthān, NW India 24°42′N 71°11′E
Bakhchisaray *see* Bakhchysaray
117 T13 **Bakhchysaray** *Rus.* Bakhchisaray. Respublika Krym, S Ukraine 44°44′N 33°53′E
Bakherden *see* Baharly
117 R3 **Bakhmach** Chernihivs'ka Oblast', N Ukraine 51°10′N 32°48′E
Bākhtarān *see* Kermānshāh
143 Q11 **Bakhtegān, Daryācheh-ye** ◎ C Iran
145 X12 **Bakhty** Vostochnyy Kazakhstan, E Kazakhstan 46°41′N 82°45′E
137 Z11 **Bakı** *Eng.* Baku. ● (Azerbaijan) E Azerbaijan 40°24′N 49°51′E
80 M12 **Baki** Awdal, N Somalia 10°10′N 43°45′E
137 Z11 **Bakı** ✈ E Azerbaijan 40°26′N 49°55′E
136 C13 **Bakır Çayı** ≈ W Turkey
92 L1 **Bakkafjördhur** Austurland, NE Iceland 66°01′N 14°49′W
92 L1 **Bakkaflói** *sea area* W Norwegian Sea
81 I15 **Bako** Southern Nationalities, S Ethiopia 05°45′N 36°39′E
76 L15 **Bako** NW Ivory Coast 09°08′N 07°40′W
Bákó *see* Bacău
111 H23 **Bakony** *Eng.* Bakony Mountains, *Ger.* Bakonywald. ▲▲ W Hungary
Bakony Mountains/Bakonywald *see* Bakony
81 M16 **Bakool** *off.* Gobolka Bakool. ⬖ *region* W Somalia
Bakool, Gobolka *see* Bakool
79 L15 **Bakouma** Mbomou, SE Central African Republic 05°42′N 22°43′E
127 N15 **Baksan** Kabardino-Balkarskaya Respublika, SW Russian Federation 43°43′N 43°31′E
119 I16 **Bakshty** Hrodzyenskaya Voblasts', W Belarus 53°56′N 26°11′E
Baku *see* Bakı
194 K12 **Bakutis Coast** *physical region* Antarctica
Bakwanga *see* Mbuji-Mayi
145 O15 **Bakyrly** Yuzhnyy Kazakhstan, S Kazakhstan 44°30′N 67°41′E
14 H13 **Bala** Ontario, S Canada 45°01′N 79°37′W
136 I13 **Balâ** Ankara, C Turkey 39°34′N 33°07′E
97 J19 **Bala** NW Wales, United Kingdom 52°54′N 03°31′W
170 L7 **Balabac Island** *island* W Philippines
Balabac, Selat *see* Balabac Strait
169 V5 **Balabac Strait** *var.* Selat Balabac. *strait* Malaysia/Philippines
Ba'labakk *see* Baalbek
187 P16 **Balabio, Île** *island* Province Nord, W New Caledonia
116 I14 **Balaci** Teleorman, S Romania 44°21′N 24°55′E
139 S7 **Balad** Şalāḩ ad Dīn, N Iraq 34°00′N 44°07′E
139 U7 **Balad Rūz** Diyālá, E Iraq 33°42′N 45°04′E
154 J11 **Bālāghāt** Madhya Pradesh, C India 21°48′N 80°11′E
155 F14 **Bālāghāt Range** ▲▲ W India
103 X14 **Balagne** *physical region* Corse, France, C Mediterranean Sea
105 U5 **Balaguer** Cataluña, NE Spain 41°48′N 00°48′E
105 S3 **Balaïtous** *var.* Pic de Balaitous. ▲ France/Spain 42°51′N 00°17′W
Balaitous, Pic de *see* Balaïtous
Bálák *see* Ballangen
127 O3 **Balakhna** Nizhegorodskaya Oblast', W Russian Federation 56°26′N 43°43′E
122 L12 **Balakhta** Krasnoyarskiy Kray, S Russian Federation 55°22′N 91°24′E
182 I9 **Balaklava** South Australia 34°10′S 138°22′E
Balakleya *see* Balakliya
117 V6 **Balakliya** *Rus.* Balakleya. Kharkivs'ka Oblast', E Ukraine 49°27′N 36°53′E
127 Q7 **Balakovo** Saratovskaya Oblast', W Russian Federation 52°03′N 47°47′E
83 P14 **Balama** Cabo Delgado, N Mozambique 13°18′S 38°39′E
169 U6 **Balambangan, Pulau** *island* East Malaysia
148 L3 **Bālā Morghāb** Laghmān, NW Afghanistan 35°38′N 63°21′E
152 E11 **Bālān** *prev.* Bāhla. Rājasthān, NW India 27°45′N 71°32′E
116 J10 **Bălan** *Hung.* Balánbánya. Harghita, C Romania 46°39′N 25°47′E
Balánbánya *see* Bălan
171 O3 **Balanga** Luzon, N Philippines 14°40′N 120°32′E
154 M12 **Balāngīr** *prev.* Bolangir. Orissa, E India 20°41′N 83°30′E
127 N8 **Balashov** Saratovskaya Oblast', W Russian Federation 51°32′N 43°14′E
Balasore *see* Bāleshwar
111 K21 **Balassagyarmat** Nógrád, N Hungary 48°06′N 19°17′E
29 S10 **Balaton** Minnesota, N USA 44°13′N 95°52′W
111 H24 **Balaton** *var.* Lake Balaton, *Ger.* Plattensee. ◎ W Hungary
111 I23 **Balatonfüred** *var.* Füred. Veszprém, W Hungary 46°59′N 17°53′E
Balaton, Lake *see* Balaton
116 I11 **Bălăuşeri** *Ger.* Bladenmarkt, *Hung.* Balavásár. Mureş, C Romania 46°24′N 24°41′E
Balavásár *see* Bălăuşeri
105 Q11 **Balazote** Castilla-La Mancha, C Spain 38°54′N 02°09′W
Balázsfalva *see* Blaj
119 F14 **Balbieriškis** Kaunas, S Lithuania 54°29′N 23°52′E
186 J7 **Balbi, Mount** ▲ Bougainville Island, NE Papua New Guinea 05°51′S 154°58′E
58 F11 **Balbina, Represa** ⊠ NW Brazil
43 T15 **Balboa** Panamá, C Panama 08°55′N 79°36′W
97 G17 **Balbriggan** *Ir.* Baile Brigín. E Ireland 53°37′N 06°11′W
Balbunar *see* Kubrat
81 N17 **Balcad** Shabeellaha Dhexe, C Somalia 02°19′N 45°19′E
61 D23 **Balcarce** Buenos Aires, E Argentina 37°51′S 58°16′W
11 U16 **Balcarres** Saskatchewan, S Canada 50°49′N 103°31′W
114 O8 **Balchik** Dobrich, NE Bulgaria 43°25′N 28°11′E
185 E24 **Balclutha** Otago, South Island, New Zealand 46°15′S 169°45′E
25 Q12 **Balcones Escarpment** *escarpment* Texas, SW USA
18 F14 **Bald Eagle Creek** ≈ Pennsylvania, NE USA
Baldenburg *see* Biały Bór
21 V12 **Bald Head Island** *island* North Carolina, SE USA
27 W10 **Bald Knob** Arkansas, C USA 35°18′N 91°34′W
30 K17 **Bald Knob** *hill* Illinois, N USA
Baldohn *see* Baldone
118 G9 **Baldone** *Ger.* Baldohn. Rīga, W Latvia 56°46′N 24°18′E
22 I9 **Baldwin** Louisiana, S USA 29°50′N 91°32′W
31 P7 **Baldwin** Michigan, N USA 43°54′N 85°50′W
27 Q4 **Baldwin City** Kansas, C USA 38°43′N 95°12′W
39 N8 **Baldwin Peninsula** *headland* Alaska, USA 66°45′N 162°19′W
18 H9 **Baldwinsville** New York, NE USA 43°09′N 76°19′W
23 N2 **Baldwyn** Mississippi, S USA 34°30′N 88°38′W
11 W15 **Baldy Mountain** ▲ Manitoba, S Canada 51°29′N 100°46′W
33 T7 **Baldy Mountain** ▲ Montana, NW USA 48°09′N 109°39′W
37 O13 **Baldy Peak** ▲ Arizona, SW USA 33°56′N 109°37′W
Bâle *see* Basel
Balearic Plain *see* Algerian Basin
Baleares *see* Illes Baleares
105 X11 **Baleares, Islas** *Eng.* Balearic Islands. *island group* Spain, W Mediterranean Sea
Baleares Major *see* Mallorca
Balearic Islands *see* Baleares, Islas
Balearis Minor *see* Menorca
169 S9 **Baleh, Batang** ≈ East Malaysia
12 J8 **Baleine, Grande Rivière de la** ≈ Québec, E Canada
12 K7 **Baleine, Petite Rivière de la** ≈ Québec, NE Canada
12 K7 **Baleine, Petite Rivière de la** ≈ Québec, SE Canada
13 N6 **Baleine, Rivière à la** ≈ Québec, E Canada
99 J16 **Balen** Antwerpen, N Belgium 51°12′N 05°12′E
171 O3 **Baler** Luzon, N Philippines 15°47′N 121°30′E
154 P11 **Bāleshwar** *prev.* Balasore. Orissa, E India 21°31′N 86°59′E
77 S12 **Baléyara** Tillabéri, W Niger 13°48′N 02°57′E
127 T1 **Balezino** Udmurtskaya Respublika, NW Russian Federation 57°57′N 53°03′E
42 J4 **Balfate** Colón, N Honduras 15°47′N 86°24′W
11 O17 **Balfour** British Columbia, SW Canada 49°39′N 116°57′W
29 N3 **Balfour** North Dakota, N USA 47°55′N 100°34′W
Balfrush *see* Bābol
122 L14 **Balgazyn** Respublika Tyva, S Russian Federation 50°53′N 95°12′E
11 U16 **Balgonie** Saskatchewan, S Canada 50°30′N 104°12′W
Bălgrad *see* Alba Iulia
81 J19 **Balguda** *spring/well* S Kenya 01°28′S 39°50′E
158 K6 **Balguntay** Xinjiang Uygur Zizhiqu, NW China 42°45′N 86°18′E
141 R16 **Balḩāf** S Yemen 14°02′N 48°16′E
152 F13 **Bāli** Rājasthān, N India 25°10′N 73°20′E
169 U17 **Bali** ⬖ *province* S Indonesia
169 T17 **Bali** *island* C Indonesia
111 K16 **Balice** ✈ (Kraków) Małopolskie, S Poland 49°57′N 19°49′E
171 Y14 **Baliem, Sungai** ≈ Papua, E Indonesia
136 C12 **Balıkesir** Balıkesir, W Turkey 39°38′N 27°52′E
136 C12 **Balıkesir** ⬖ *province* NW Turkey
138 L3 **Balīkh, Nahr** ≈ N Syria
169 V12 **Balikpapan** Borneo, C Indonesia 01°15′S 116°50′E
Bali Laut *see* Bali Sea
171 N9 **Balimbing** Tawitawi, SW Philippines 05°10′N 120°00′E
186 B8 **Balimo** Western, SW Papua New Guinea 08°00′S 143°00′E
Bálinc *see* Balinţ
101 H23 **Balingen** Baden-Württemberg, SW Germany 48°16′N 08°51′E
116 F11 **Balinţ** *Hung.* Bálinc. Timiş, W Romania 45°48′N 21°54′E
171 O1 **Balintang Channel** *channel* N Philippines
138 K3 **Bālis** Ḩalab, N Syria 36°01′N 38°03′E
169 T16 **Bali Sea** *Ind.* Bali Laut. *sea* C Indonesia
98 K7 **Balk** Friesland, N Netherlands 52°54′N 05°34′E
146 B11 **Balkanabat** *Rus.* Nebitdag. Balkan Welaýaty, W Turkmenistan 39°33′N 54°19′E
121 R6 **Balkan Mountains** *Bul./SCr.* Stara Planina. ▲▲ Bulgaria/Serbia
Balkanskiy Welayat *see* Balkan Welaýaty
146 B9 **Balkan Welaýaty** *Rus.* Balkanskiy Velayat. ⬖ *province* W Turkmenistan
145 P8 **Balkashino** Akmola, N Kazakhstan 52°36′N 68°46′E
149 O2 **Balkh** *anc.* Bactra. Balkh, N Afghanistan 36°46′N 66°54′E
149 P2 **Balkh** ⬖ *province* N Afghanistan
145 T13 **Balkhash** *Kaz.* Balqash. Karaganda, SE Kazakhstan 46°52′N 74°55′E
Balkhash, Lake *see* Balkhash, Ozero
145 T13 **Balkhash, Ozero** *Eng.* Lake Balkhash, *Kaz.* Balqash. ◎ SE Kazakhstan
Balla Balla *see* Mbalabala
96 H10 **Ballachulish** N Scotland, United Kingdom 56°40′N 05°10′W
180 M12 **Balladonia** Western Australia 32°21′S 123°32′E
97 C16 **Ballaghaderreen** *Ir.* Bealach an Doirín. C Ireland 53°51′N 08°29′W
92 H10 **Ballangen** *Lapp.* Bálák. Nordland, NW Norway 68°18′N 16°48′E
97 H14 **Ballantrae** W Scotland, United Kingdom 55°05′N 05°W
183 N12 **Ballarat** Victoria, SE Australia 37°36′S 143°51′E
180 K11 **Ballard, Lake** *salt lake* Western Australia
Ballari *see* Bellary
76 L11 **Ballé** Koulikoro, W Mali 15°18′N 08°31′W
40 D7 **Ballenas, Bahía de** *bay* NW Mexico
40 D5 **Ballenas, Canal de** *channel* NW Mexico
195 R17 **Balleny Islands** *island group* Antarctica
40 J7 **Balleza** *var.* San Pablo Balleza. Chihuahua, N Mexico 26°55′N 106°21′W
114 M13 **Ballı** Tekirdağ, NW Turkey 40°48′N 27°03′E
153 O13 **Ballia** Uttar Pradesh, N India 25°45′N 84°09′E
183 V4 **Ballina** New South Wales, SE Australia 28°50′S 153°37′E
97 C16 **Ballina** *Ir.* Béal an Átha. W Ireland 54°07′N 09°09′W
97 D16 **Ballinamore** *Ir.* Béal an Átha Móir. NW Ireland 54°03′N 07°47′W
97 D18 **Ballinasloe** *Ir.* Béal Átha na Sluaighe. W Ireland 53°20′N 08°13′W
25 P8 **Ballinger** Texas, SW USA 31°44′N 99°57′W
97 C17 **Ballinrobe** *Ir.* Baile an Róba. W Ireland 53°37′N 09°14′W
97 A21 **Ballinskelligs Bay** *Ir.* Bá na Scealg. *inlet* SW Ireland
97 D15 **Ballintra** *Ir.* Baile an tSratha. NW Ireland 54°35′N 08°07′W
103 T7 **Ballon d'Alsace** ▲ NE France 47°50′N 06°54′E
Ballon de Guebwiller *see* Grand Ballon
113 K21 **Ballsh** *var.* Ballshi. Fier, SW Albania 40°35′N 19°45′E
Ballshi *see* Ballsh
98 K4 **Ballum** Friesland, N Netherlands 53°27′N 05°40′E
97 F16 **Ballybay** *Ir.* Béal Átha Beithe. N Ireland 54°08′N 06°54′W
97 E14 **Ballybofey** *Ir.* Bealach Féich. NW Ireland 54°49′N 07°47′W
97 G14 **Ballycastle** *Ir.* Baile an Chaistil. N Northern Ireland, United Kingdom 55°12′N 06°14′W
97 G15 **Ballyclare** *Ir.* Bealach Cláir. E Northern Ireland, United Kingdom 54°45′N 06°W
97 E16 **Ballyconnell** *Ir.* Béal Átha Conaill. N Ireland 54°07′N 07°35′W
97 C17 **Ballyhaunis** *Ir.* Beál Átha hAmhnais. W Ireland 53°45′N 08°45′W
97 G14 **Ballymena** *Ir.* An Baile Meánach. NE Northern Ireland, United Kingdom 54°52′N 06°17′W
97 F14 **Ballymoney** *Ir.* Baile Monaidh. NE Northern Ireland, United Kingdom 55°10′N 06°30′W
97 G15 **Ballynahinch** *Ir.* Baile na hInse. SE Northern Ireland, United Kingdom 54°24′N 05°54′W
97 D16 **Ballysadare** *Ir.* Baile Easa Dara. NW Ireland 54°13′N 08°30′W
97 D15 **Ballyshannon** *Ir.* Béal Átha Seanaidh. NW Ireland 54°30′N 08°11′W
63 H19 **Balmaceda** Aisén, S Chile 45°52′S 72°43′W
63 G23 **Balmaceda, Cerro** ▲ S Chile 51°27′S 73°26′W
111 N22 **Balmazújváros** Hajdú-Bihar, E Hungary 47°36′N 21°18′E
108 E10 **Balmhorn** ▲ SW Switzerland 46°27′N 07°41′E
182 L12 **Balmoral** Victoria, SE Australia 37°16′S 141°38′E
24 K9 **Balmorhea** Texas, SW USA 30°58′N 103°44′W
Balneario Claromecó *see* Claromecó
Balochistān *see* Baluchistān
82 B13 **Balombo** *Port.* Norton de Matos, Vila Norton de Matos. Benguela, W Angola 12°21′S 14°46′E
82 B13 **Balombo** ≈ W Angola
181 X10 **Balonne River** ≈ Queensland, E Australia
152 E13 **Bālotra** Rājasthān, N India 25°50′N 72°21′E
145 V14 **Balpyk Bi** *prev.* Kirovskiy, *Kaz.* Kīrov. Almaty, SE Kazakhstan 44°54′N 78°13′E
Balqā'/Balqā', Muḩāfaẓat al *see* Al Balqā'
Balqash *see* Balkhash/Balkhash, Ozero
152 M12 **Balrāmpur** Uttar Pradesh, N India 27°25′N 82°10′E
182 M9 **Balranald** New South Wales, SE Australia 34°39′S 143°33′E
116 H14 **Balş** Olt, S Romania 44°20′N 24°06′E
14 H11 **Balsam Creek** Ontario, S Canada 46°26′N 79°10′W
30 I5 **Balsam Lake** Wisconsin, N USA 45°27′N 92°28′W
14 I14 **Balsam Lake** ◎ Ontario, SE Canada
59 M14 **Balsas** Maranhão, E Brazil 07°30′S 46°W
40 M15 **Balsas, Río** *var.* Río Mexcala. ≈ S Mexico
43 W16 **Balsas, Río** ≈ SE Panama
119 O18 **Bal'shavik** *Rus.* Bol'shevik. Homyel'skaya Voblasts', SE Belarus 52°34′N 30°53′E
95 O15 **Bålsta** Uppsala, C Sweden 59°31′N 17°32′E
108 E7 **Balsthal** Solothurn, NW Switzerland 47°18′N 07°42′E
117 O8 **Balta** Odes'ka Oblast', SW Ukraine 47°58′N 29°39′E
105 N5 **Baltanás** Castilla-León, N Spain 41°56′N 04°12′W
61 E16 **Baltasar Brum** Artigas, N Uruguay 30°44′S 57°19′W
116 M9 **Bălţi** *Rus.* Bel'tsy. N Moldova 47°45′N 27°57′E
Baltic Port *see* Paldiski
118 B10 **Baltic Sea** *Ger.* Ostee, *Rus.* Baltiskoye More. *sea* N Europe
21 X3 **Baltimore** Maryland, NE USA 39°17′N 76°37′W
31 T13 **Baltimore** Ohio, N USA 39°48′N 82°33′W
21 X3 **Baltimore-Washington** ✈ Maryland, E USA 39°10′N 76°40′W
Baltischport/Baltiski *see* Paldiski
Baltiskoye More *see* Baltic Sea
119 A14 **Baltiysk** *Ger.* Pillau. Kaliningradskaya Oblast', W Russian Federation 54°39′N 19°54′E
Baltkrievija *see* Belarus
119 H14 **Baltoji Voke** Vilnius, SE Lithuania 54°35′N 25°13′E
Balūchestān va Sīstān *see* Sīstān va Balūchestān
148 M12 **Baluchistān** *var.* Balochistān, Beluchistan. ⬖ *province* SW Pakistan
171. P5 **Balud** Masbate, N Philippines 12°03′N 123°12′E
169 T9 **Balui, Batang** ≈ East Malaysia
153 S13 **Bālurghat** West Bengal, NE India 25°12′N 88°50′E
118 J8 **Balvi** Balvi, NE Latvia 57°07′N 27°14′E
147 W7 **Balykchy** *Kir.* Ysyk-Köl; *prev.* Issyk-Kul', Rybach'ye. Issyk-Kul'skaya Oblast', NE Kyrgyzstan 42°29′N 76°08′E
56 B7 **Balzar** Guayas, W Ecuador 01°25′S 79°54′W
108 I8 **Balzers** S Liechtenstein 47°04′N 09°32′E
143 T12 **Bam** Kermān, SE Iran 29°08′N 58°27′E
77 Y13 **Bama** Borno, NE Nigeria 11°28′N 13°46′E
76 L12 **Bamako** ● (Mali) Capital District, SW Mali 12°39′N 08°02′W
77 P10 **Bamba** Gao, C Mali 17°03′N 01°19′W
42 M8 **Bambana, Río** ≈ NE Nicaragua
79 J15 **Bambari** Ouaka, C Central African Republic 05°45′N 20°37′E
181 W5 **Bambaroo** Queensland, NE Australia 19°00′S 146°16′E
101 K19 **Bamberg** Bayern, SE Germany 49°54′N 10°53′E
21 R14 **Bamberg** South Carolina, SE USA 33°16′N 81°02′W
79 M16 **Bambesa** Orientale, N Dem. Rep. Congo 03°25′N 25°43′E
76 G11 **Bambey** W Senegal 14°43′N 16°26′W
79 H16 **Bambio** Sangha-Mbaéré, SW Central African Republic 03°57′N 16°54′E
83 I24 **Bamboesberge** ▲ S South Africa 31°24′S 26°10′E
79 D14 **Bamenda** Nord-Ouest, W Cameroon 05°55′N 10°09′E
10 K17 **Bamfield** Vancouver Island, British Columbia, SW Canada 48°48′N 125°05′W
Bami *see* Bamy
149 P4 **Bāmīān** *var.* Bāmiān. Bāmīān, NE Afghanistan 34°50′N 67°50′E
149 O4 **Bāmīān** ⬖ *province* C Afghanistan
79 J14 **Bamingui** Bamingui-Bangoran, C Central African Republic 07°38′N 20°06′E
78 J13 **Bamingui** ≈ N Central African Republic
78 J13 **Bamingui-Bangoran** ⬖ *prefecture* N Central African Republic
143 V13 **Bampūr** Sīstān va Balūchestān, SE Iran 27°13′N 60°28′E
186 C8 **Bamu** ≈ SW Papua New Guinea
146 E12 **Bamy** *Rus.* Bami. Ahal Welaýaty, C Turkmenistan 38°42′N 56°47′E
Bán *see* Bánovce nad Bebravou
81 N17 **Banaadir** *off.* Gobolka Banaadir. ⬖ *region* S Somalia
Banaadir, Gobolka *see* Banaadir
191 N3 **Banaba** *var.* Ocean Island. *island* Tungaru, W Kiribati
59 O14 **Banabuiú, Açude** ⊠ NE Brazil
57 O19 **Bañados del Izozog** *salt lake* SE Bolivia
97 D18 **Banagher** *Ir.* Beannchar. C Ireland 53°12′N 07°56′W
79 M17 **Banalia** Orientale, N Dem. Rep. Congo 01°33′N 25°23′E
76 L12 **Banamba** Koulikoro, W Mali 13°29′N 07°22′W
40 G4 **Banámichi** Sonora, NW Mexico 30°00′N 110°14′W
181 Y9 **Banana** Queensland, E Australia 24°33′S 150°07′E
191 Z2 **Banana** *prev.* Main Camp. Kiritimati, E Kiribati 02°00′N 157°25′W
59 K16 **Bananal, Ilha do** *island* C Brazil
23 Y12 **Banana River** *lagoon* Florida, SE USA
151 Q22 **Bananga** Andaman and Nicobar Islands, India, NE Indian Ocean 06°57′N 93°54′E
Banaras *see* Vārānasi
114 N13 **Banarlı** Tekirdağ, NW Turkey 41°04′N 27°21′E
152 H12 **Banās** ≈ N India
75 Z11 **Banās, Rās** *headland* E Egypt 23°55′N 35°47′E
112 N10 **Banatski Karlovac** Vojvodina, NE Serbia 45°03′N 21°02′E
141 P16 **Banā, Wādī** *dry watercourse* SW Yemen
136 E14 **Banaz** Uşak, W Turkey 38°47′N 29°46′E
136 E14 **Banaz Çayı** ≈ W Turkey
159 P14 **Banbar** *var.* Coka. Xizang Zizhiqu, W China 31°01′N 94°43′E
97 G15 **Banbridge** *Ir.* Droichead na Banna. SE Northern Ireland, United Kingdom 54°21′N 06°16′W
Ban Bua Yai *see* Bua Yai
97 M21 **Banbury** S England, United Kingdom 52°04′N 01°20′W
167 O7 **Ban Chiang Dao** Chiang Mai, NW Thailand 19°22′N 98°59′E
96 K9 **Banchory** NE Scotland, United Kingdom 58°05′N 00°35′W
14 J13 **Bancroft** Ontario, SE Canada 45°03′N 77°52′W
33 R15 **Bancroft** Idaho, NW USA 42°43′N 111°54′W
29 U11 **Bancroft** Iowa, C USA 43°17′N 94°13′W
154 I9 **Bānda** Madhya Pradesh, C India 24°01′N 78°59′E
152 L13 **Bānda** Uttar Pradesh, N India 25°28′N 80°20′E
168 F7 **Bandaaceh** *var.* Banda Atjeh; *prev.* Koetaradja, Kutaradja, Kutaraja. Sumatera, W Indonesia 05°30′N 95°20′E
Banda Atjeh *see* Bandaaceh
171 S14 **Banda, Kepulauan** *island group* E Indonesia
Banda, Laut *see* Banda Sea
77 N17 **Bandama** *var.* Bandama Fleuve. ≈ S Ivory Coast
77 N15 **Bandama Blanc** ≈ C Ivory Coast
Bandama Fleuve *see* Bandama
Bandar 'Abbās *see* Bandar-e 'Abbās
153 W16 **Bandarban** Chittagong, SE Bangladesh 22°13′N 92°13′E
80 Q13 **Bandarbeyla** *var.* Bender Beila, Bender Beyla. Bari, NE Somalia 09°28′N 50°48′E
143 R14 **Bandar-e 'Abbās** *var.* Bandar 'Abbās; *prev.* Gombroon. Hormozgān, S Iran 27°11′N 56°11′E
142 M3 **Bandar-e Anzalī** Gīlān, NW Iran 37°26′N 49°29′E
143 N12 **Bandar-e Būshehr** *var.* Būshehr, *Eng.* Bushire. Būshehr, S Iran 28°59′N 50°50′E
143 O13 **Bandar-e Dayyer** *var.* Deyyer. Būshehr, SE Iran 27°50′N 51°55′E

◆ Country
● Country Capital
◇ Dependent Territory
○ Dependent Territory Capital
⬖ Administrative Regions
✈ International Airport
▲ Mountain
▲▲ Mountain Range
Volcano
≈ River
◎ Lake
⊠ Reservoir

142 M11 **Bandar-e Gonāveh** *var.* Ganāveh; *prev.* Gonāveh. Būshehr, SW Iran 29°33′N 50°39′E
143 T15 **Bandar-e Jāsk** *var.* Jāsk. Hormozgān, SE Iran 25°35′N 58°06′E
143 O13 **Bandar-e Kangān** *var.* Kangān. Būshehr, S Iran 25°50′N 57°30′E
143 R14 **Bandar-e Khamīr** Hormozgān, S Iran 27°00′N 55°50′E
Bandar-e Langeh *see* Bandar-e Lengeh
143 Q14 **Bandar-e Lengeh** *var.* Bandar-e Langeh, Lingeh. Hormozgān, S Iran 26°34′N 54°52′E
142 L10 **Bandar-e Māhshahr** *var.* Māh-Shahr; *prev.* Bandar-e Ma'shūr. Khūzestān, SW Iran 30°34′N 49°10′E
Bandar-e Ma'shūr *see* Bandar-e Māhshahr
143 O14 **Bandar-e Nakhīlū** Hormozgān, S Iran
Bandar-e Shāh *see* Bandar-e Torkaman
143 P4 **Bandar-e Torkaman** *var.* Bandar-e Torkeman, Bandar-e Torkman; *prev.* Bandar-e Shāh. Golestán, N Iran 36°55′N 54°05′E
Bandar-e Torkeman/ Bandar-e Torkman *see* Bandar-e Torkaman
Bandar Kassim *see* Boosaaso
168 M15 **Bandar Lampung** *var.* Bandarlampung, Tanjungkarang-Telukbetung; *prev.* Tandjoengkarang, Tanjungkarang, Teloekbetoeng, Telukbetung. Sumatera, W Indonesia 05°28′S 105°16′E
Bandarlampung *see* Bandar Lampung
Bandar Maharani *see* Muar
Bandar Masulipatnam *see* Machilīpatnam
Bandar Penggaram *see* Batu Pahat
169 T7 **Bandar Seri Begawan** *prev.* Brunei Town. ● (Brunei) N Brunei 04°56′N 114°58′E
169 T7 **Bandar Seri Begawan** ✈ N Brunei 04°56′N 114°58′E
171 R15 **Banda Sea** *var.* Laut Banda. *sea* E Indonesia
104 H5 **Bande** Galicia, NW Spain 42°01′N 07°58′W
59 G15 **Bandeirantes** Mato Grosso, W Brazil 09°04′S 57°53′W
59 N20 **Bandeira, Pico da** ▲ SE Brazil 20°25′S 41°45′W
83 K19 **Bandelierkop** Limpopo, NE South Africa 23°21′S 29°46′E
62 L8 **Bandera** Santiago del Estero, N Argentina 28°53′S 62°15′W
25 Q11 **Bandera** Texas, SW USA 29°44′N 99°06′W
40 J13 **Banderas, Bahía de** *bay* W Mexico
77 O11 **Bandiagara** Mopti, C Mali 14°20′N 03°37′W
152 I12 **Bāndīkūi** Rājasthān, N India 27°01′N 76°33′E
136 C11 **Bandırma** *var.* Penderma. Balıkesir, NW Turkey 40°21′N 27°58′E
Bandjarmasin *see* Banjarmasin
Bandoeng *see* Bandung
97 C21 **Bandon** *Ir.* Droicheadna Bandan. SW Ireland 51°44′N 08°44′W
32 E14 **Bandon** Oregon, NW USA 43°07′N 124°24′W
167 R8 **Ban Dong Bang** Nong Khai, E Thailand 18°00′N 104°08′E
167 Q6 **Ban Donkon** Oudômxai, N Laos 20°20′N 101°37′E
172 J14 **Bandrélé** SE Mayotte
79 H20 **Bandundu** *prev.* Banningville. Bandundu, W Dem. Rep. Congo 03°19′S 17°24′E
79 I21 **Bandundu** *off.* Région de Bandundu. ◆ *region* W Dem. Rep. Congo
Bandundu, Région de *see* Bandundu
169 O16 **Bandung** *prev.* Bandoeng. Jawa, C Indonesia 06°47′S 107°28′E
116 L15 **Băneasa** Constanța, SW Romania 45°56′N 27°55′E
142 J4 **Bāneh** Kordestān, N Iran 35°58′N 45°54′E
44 I7 **Banes** Holguín, E Cuba 20°58′N 75°43′W
11 P16 **Banff** Alberta, SW Canada 51°10′N 115°34′W
96 K8 **Banff** NE Scotland, United Kingdom 57°39′N 02°33′W
96 K8 **Banff** *cultural region* NE Scotland, United Kingdom
Bánffyhunyad *see* Huedin
77 N14 **Banfora** SW Burkina 10°36′N 04°45′W
155 H19 **Bangalore** *var.* Bengalooru. *state capital* Karnātaka, S India 12°58′N 77°35′E
153 S16 **Bangaon** West Bengal, NE India 23°01′N 88°50′E
79 L15 **Bangassou** Mbomou, SE Central African Republic 04°51′N 22°55′E
186 D7 **Bangeta, Mount** ▲ C Papua New Guinea 06°11′S 147°02′E
171 P12 **Banggai, Kepulauan** *island group* C Indonesia
171 Q12 **Banggai, Pulau** *island* Kepulauan Banggai, N Indonesia
171 X13 **Banggelapa** Papua, E Indonesia 03°47′S 136°53′E
Banggi *see* Banggi, Pulau
169 V6 **Banggi, Pulau** *var.* Banggi. *island* East Malaysia
152 K5 **Banggong Co** *var.* Pangong Tso. ◎ China/India *see also* Pangong Tso
121 P13 **Banghāzī** *Eng.* Bengazi, Benghazi, *It.* Bengasi. NE Libya 32°07′N 20°04′E
Bang Hieng *see* Xé Banghiang
169 O13 **Bangka-Belitung** *off.* Propinsi Bangka-Belitung. ◆ *province* W Indonesia
169 P11 **Bangkai, Tanjung** *var.* Bankai. *headland* Borneo, N Indonesia 0°21′N 108°53′E
169 S16 **Bangkalan** Pulau Madura, C Indonesia 07°05′S 112°44′E
169 N12 **Bangka, Pulau** *island* W Indonesia
169 N13 **Bangka, Selat** *strait* Sumatera, W Indonesia
169 N13 **Bangka, Selat** *var.* Selat Likupang. *strait* Sulawesi, N Indonesia
168 J11 **Bangkinang** Sumatera, W Indonesia 0°21′N 100°52′E
168 K12 **Bangko** Sumatera, W Indonesia 02°05′S 102°20′E
Bangkok *see* Ao Krung Thep
Bangkok, Bight of *see* Krung Thep, Ao
153 T14 **Bangladesh** *off.* People's Republic of Bangladesh; *prev.* East Pakistan. ◆ *republic* S Asia
Bangladesh, People's Republic of *see* Bangladesh
167 V13 **Ba Ngoi** Khanh Hoa, S Vietnam 11°56′N 109°07′E
Bangong Co *see* Pangong Tso
97 I18 **Bangor** NW Wales, United Kingdom 53°13′N 04°08′W
97 G15 **Bangor** *Ir.* Beannchar. E Northern Ireland, United Kingdom 54°40′N 05°40′W
19 R6 **Bangor** Maine, NE USA 44°48′N 68°47′W
18 I14 **Bangor** Pennsylvania, NE USA 40°52′N 75°12′W
67 R8 **Bangoran** ≈ S Central African Republic
Bang Phra *see* Trat
Bang Pla Soi *see* Chon Buri
25 Q8 **Bangs** Texas, SW USA 31°43′N 99°07′W
167 N13 **Bang Saphan** *var.* Bang Saphan Yai. Prachuap Khiri Khan, SW Thailand 11°10′N 99°33′E
Bang Saphan Yai *see* Bang Saphan
36 I8 **Bangs, Mount** ▲ Arizona, SW USA 36°47′N 113°51′W
93 E15 **Bangsund** Nord-Trøndelag, C Norway 64°22′N 11°22′E
171 O2 **Bangued** Luzon, N Philippines 17°36′N 120°40′E
79 I15 **Bangui** ● (Central African Republic) Ombella-Mpoko, SW Central African Republic 04°21′N 18°32′E
79 I15 **Bangui** ✈ Ombella-Mpoko, SW Central African Republic 04°19′N 18°34′E
83 N16 **Bangula** Southern, S Malawi 16°38′S 35°04′E
Bangwaketse *see* Southern
82 K12 **Bangweulu, Lake** *var.* Lake Bengweulu. ◎ N Zambia
121 V13 **Banhā** *var.* Benha. N Egypt 30°28′N 31°11′E
Ban Hat Yai *see* Hat Yai
167 Q7 **Ban Hin Heup** Viangchan, C Laos 18°37′N 102°19′E
Ban Houayxay/Ban Houei Sai *see* Houayxay
167 O12 **Ban Hua Hin** *var.* Hua Hin. Prachuap Khiri Khan, SW Thailand 12°34′N 99°58′E
79 L14 **Bani** Haute-Kotto, E Central African Republic 07°06′N 22°51′E
45 O9 **Baní** S Dominican Republic 18°19′N 70°21′W
77 N12 **Bani** ≈ S Mali
Banias *see* Bāniyās
77 S11 **Bani Bangou** Tillabéri, SW Niger 15°04′N 02°40′E
76 M12 **Banifing** *var.* Ngorolaka. ≈ Burkina/Mali
Banijska Palanka *see* Glina
77 R13 **Banikoara** N Benin 11°18′N 02°26′E
75 W9 **Banī Mazār** *var.* Beni Mazâr. C Egypt 28°29′N 30°48′E
114 K8 **Baniski Lom** ≈ N Bulgaria
21 U7 **Banister River** ≈ Virginia, NE USA
121 V14 **Banī Suwayf** *var.* Beni Suef. N Egypt 29°09′N 31°04′E
75 O8 **Banī Walīd** NW Libya 31°46′N 13°59′E
138 H5 **Bāniyās** *var.* Banias, Baniyas, Paneas. Ṭarṭūs, W Syria 35°12′N 35°57′E
113 K14 **Banja** Serbia, W Serbia 43°33′N 19°35′E
Banjak, Kepulauan *see* Banyak, Kepulauan
112 J12 **Banja Koviljača** Serbia, W Serbia 44°31′N 19°11′E
112 G11 **Banja Luka** ◆ Republika Srpska, NW Bosnia and Herzegovina
169 T13 **Banjarmasin** *prev.* Bandjarmasin. Borneo, C Indonesia 03°22′S 114°33′E
76 F11 **Banjul** *prev.* Bathurst. ● (Gambia) W Gambia 13°26′N 16°43′W
76 F11 **Banjul** ✈ W Gambia 13°18′N 16°39′W
Bank *see* Bankä
137 Y13 **Bankä** *Rus.* Bank. SE Azerbaijan 39°25′N 49°13′E
167 S11 **Ban Kadian** *var.* Ban Kadiene. Champasak, S Laos 14°25′N 105°42′E
Ban Kadiene *see* Ban Kadian
Bankai *see* Bangkai, Tanjung
166 M14 **Ban Kam Phuam** Phangnga, SW Thailand 09°16′N 98°24′E
Ban Kantang *see* Kantang
77 O11 **Bankass** Mopti, S Mali 14°05′N 03°30′W
95 L19 **Bankeryd** Jönköping, S Sweden 57°51′N 14°07′E
83 K16 **Banket** Mashonaland West, N Zimbabwe 17°23′S 30°24′E
167 T11 **Ban Khamphô** Attapu, S Laos 14°35′N 106°18′E
23 O4 **Bankhead Lake** ⊠ Alabama, S USA
77 Q11 **Bankilaré** Tillabéri, SW Niger 14°34′N 00°41′E
Banks, Îles *see* Banks Islands
10 I14 **Banks Island** *island* British Columbia, SW Canada
187 R12 **Banks Islands** *Fr.* Îles Banks. *island group* N Vanuatu
23 U8 **Banks Lake** ◎ Georgia, SE USA
32 K8 **Banks Lake** ⊠ Washington, NW USA
185 I19 **Banks Peninsula** *peninsula* South Island, New Zealand
183 Q15 **Banks Strait** *strait* SW Tasman Sea
Ban Kui Nua *see* Kui Buri
153 R16 **Bānkura** West Bengal, NE India 23°14′N 87°05′E
167 S8 **Ban Lakxao** *var.* Lak Sao. Bolikhamxai, C Laos 18°10′N 104°58′E
167 O16 **Ban Lam Phai** Songkhla, SW Thailand 06°43′N 100°57′E
Ban Mae Sot *see* Mae Sot
Ban Mae Suai *see* Mae Suai
Ban Mak Khaeng *see* Udon Thani
166 M3 **Banmauk** Sagaing, N Burma (Myanmar) 24°26′N 95°54′E
Banmo *see* Bhamo
167 T10 **Ban Mun-Houamuang** S Laos 15°11′N 106°44′E
97 F14 **Bann** *var.* Lower Bann, Upper Bann. ≈ N Northern Ireland, United Kingdom
167 S10 **Ban Nadou** Salavan, S Laos 15°51′N 105°38′E
167 S9 **Ban Nakala** Savannakhét, S Laos 16°14′N 105°09′E
167 Q8 **Ban Nakha** Viangchan, C Laos 18°13′N 102°29′E
167 S9 **Ban Nakham** Khammouan, S Laos 17°10′N 105°25′E
167 P7 **Ban Namoun** Xaignabouli, N Laos 18°40′N 101°34′E
167 O17 **Ban Nang Sata** Yala, SW Thailand 06°15′N 101°13′E
167 N15 **Ban Na San** Surat Thani, SW Thailand 08°53′N 99°17′E
167 R7 **Ban Nasi** Xiangkhoang, N Laos 19°37′N 103°33′E
44 I3 **Bannerman Town** Eleuthera Island, C Bahamas 24°38′N 76°09′W
35 V15 **Banning** California, W USA 33°55′N 116°52′W
Banningville *see* Bandundu
167 S11 **Ban Nongsim** Champasak, S Laos 14°45′N 106°00′E
149 S7 **Bannu** *prev.* Edwardesabad. North-West Frontier Province, NW Pakistan 33°00′N 70°36′E
Bañolas *see* Banyoles
56 C7 **Baños** Tungurahua, C Ecuador 01°26′S 78°24′W
Bánovce *see* Bánovce nad Bebravou
111 I19 **Bánovce nad Bebravou** *var.* Bánovce, *Hung.* Bán. Trenčiansky Kraj, W Slovakia 48°43′N 18°15′E
112 I12 **Banovići** ◆ Federacija Bosna I Hercegovina, E Bosnia and Herzegovina
Banow *see* Andarāb
Ban Pak Phanang *see* Pak Phanang
167 O7 **Ban Pan Nua** Lampang, NW Thailand 18°51′N 99°57′E
167 Q9 **Ban Phai** Khon Kaen, E Thailand 16°00′N 102°42′E
167 T9 **Ban Phou A Douk** Khammouan, C Laos 17°12′N 106°07′E
167 Q8 **Ban Phu** Uthai Thani, W Thailand
167 O11 **Ban Pong** Ratchaburi, W Thailand 13°49′N 99°53′E
190 I3 **Banraeaba** Tarawa, W Kiribati 01°20′N 173°02′E
167 N10 **Ban Sai Yok** Kanchanaburi, W Thailand 14°24′N 98°54′E
Ban Sattahip/Ban Sattahipp *see* Sattahip
Ban Sichon *see* Sichon
Ban Si Racha *see* Siracha
111 J19 **Banská Bystrica** *Ger.* Neusohl, *Hung.* Besztercebánya. Banskobystricky Kraj, C Slovakia 48°46′N 19°08′E
111 K20 **Banskobystrický Kraj** ◆ *region* C Slovakia
167 R8 **Ban Sôppheung** Bolikhamxai, C Laos 18°33′N 104°18′E
Ban Sop Prap *see* Sop Prap
152 G15 **Bānswāra** Rājasthān, N India 23°32′N 74°28′E
167 N15 **Ban Ta Khun** Surat Thani, SW Thailand 08°53′N 98°52′E
Ban Takua Pa *see* Takua Pa
167 S8 **Ban Talak** Khammouan, C Laos 17°33′N 105°40′E
77 R15 **Bantè** W Benin 08°25′N 01°58′E
167 N16 **Banten** *off.* Propinsi Banten. ◆ *province* W Indonesia
Propinsi Banten *see* Banten
167 Q8 **Ban Thabôk** Bolikhamxai, C Laos 18°21′N 103°12′E
167 T9 **Ban Tôp** Savannakhét, S Laos 16°07′N 106°07′E
97 B21 **Bantry** *Ir.* Beanntraí. Cork, SW Ireland 51°41′N 09°27′W
97 A21 **Bantry Bay** *Ir.* Bá Bheanntraí. *bay* SW Ireland
155 F19 **Bantvāl** *var.* Bantwāl. Karnātaka, E India 12°57′N 75°04′E
Bantwāl *see* Bantvāl
114 N9 **Banya** Burgas, E Bulgaria 42°46′N 27°49′E
168 G10 **Banyak, Kepulauan** *prev.* Kepulauan Banjak. *island group* NW Indonesia
105 U8 **Banya, La** *headland* E Spain 40°34′N 00°37′E
79 E14 **Banyo** Adamaoua, NW Cameroon 06°47′N 11°50′E
105 X4 **Banyoles** *var.* Bañolas. Cataluña, NE Spain 42°07′N 02°46′E
167 N16 **Ban Yong Sata** Trang, SW Thailand 07°09′N 99°42′E
195 X14 **Banzare Coast** *physical region* Antarctica
173 Q14 **Banzare Seamounts** *undersea feature* S Indian Ocean
Banzart *see* Bizerte
163 Q12 **Baochang** *var.* Taibus Qi. Nei Mongol Zizhiqu, N China 41°55′N 115°22′E
161 O3 **Baoding** *var.* Pao-ting; *prev.* Tsingyuan. Hebei, E China 38°47′N 115°30′E
Baoebaoe *see* Baubau
Baoi, Oileán *see* Dursey Island
160 J6 **Baoji** *var.* Pao-chi, Paoki. Shaanxi, C China 34°23′N 107°16′E
163 U9 **Baokang** *var.* Hoqin Zuoyi Zhongji. Nei Mongol Zizhiqu, N China 44°08′N 123°18′E
186 L8 **Baolo** Santa Isabel, N Solomon Islands 07°41′S 158°47′E
167 U13 **Bao Lôc** Lâm Đông, S Vietnam 11°33′N 107°48′E
163 Z7 **Baoqing** Heilongjiang, NE China 46°15′N 132°12′E
Baoqing *see* Shaoyang
79 H15 **Baoro** Nana-Mambéré, W Central African Republic 05°40′N 16°00′E
160 E12 **Baoshan** *var.* Pao-shan. Yunnan, SW China 25°05′N 99°07′E
163 N13 **Baotou** *var.* Pao-t'ou, Paotow. Nei Mongol Zizhiqu, N China 40°38′N 109°59′E
76 L14 **Baoulé** ≈ S Mali
76 K12 **Baoulé** ≈ W Mali
Bao Yèn *see* Phô Rang
103 O2 **Bapaume** Pas-de-Calais, N France 50°06′N 02°50′E
14 J13 **Baptiste Lake** ◎ Ontario, SE Canada
Bapu *see* Meigu
Baqanas *see* Bakanas
Baqbaqty *see* Bakbakty
159 P14 **Baqên** *var.* Dartang. Xizang Zizhiqu, W China 31°50′N 94°08′E
138 F14 **Bāqir, Jabal** ▲▲ S Jordan
139 T7 **Ba'qūbah** *var.* Qubba. Diyālá, C Iraq 33°45′N 44°40′E
62 H5 **Baquedano** Antofagasta, N Chile 23°20′S 69°50′W
Baquerizo Moreno *see* Puerto Baquerizo Moreno
113 J18 **Bar** *It.* Antivari. S Montenegro 42°02′N 19°09′E
116 M6 **Bar** Vinnyts'ka Oblast', C Ukraine 49°05′N 27°40′E
80 E10 **Bara** Northern Kordofan, C Sudan 13°42′N 30°21′E
81 M18 **Baraawe** *It.* Brava. Shabeellaha Hoose, S Somalia 01°10′N 43°59′E
152 M12 **Bāra Banki** Uttar Pradesh, N India 26°56′N 81°11′E
30 L8 **Baraboo** Wisconsin, N USA 43°27′N 89°45′W
30 K8 **Baraboo Range** *hill range* Wisconsin, N USA
Baracaldo *see* San Vicente de Barakaldo
15 Y6 **Barachois** Québec, SE Canada 48°37′N 64°14′W
44 J7 **Baracoa** Guantánamo, E Cuba 20°23′N 74°31′W
61 C19 **Baradero** Buenos Aires, E Argentina 33°50′S 59°30′W
183 R6 **Baradine** New South Wales, SE Australia 30°55′S 149°03′E
Baraf Daja Islands *see* Damar, Kepulauan
154 M12 **Baragarh** *var.* Bargarh. Orissa, E India 21°25′N 83°35′E
81 I17 **Baragoi** Rift Valley, W Kenya 01°39′N 36°46′E
45 N9 **Barahona** SW Dominican Republic 18°13′N 71°07′W
153 W13 **Barail Range** ▲▲ NE India
Baraka *see* Barka
80 G10 **Barakat** Gezira, C Sudan 14°18′N 33°32′E
Barakī *see* Barakī Barak
149 Q6 **Barakī Barak** *var.* Barakī, Baraki Rajan. Lowgar, E Afghanistan 33°58′N 68°58′E
Baraki Rajan *see* Barakī Barak
154 N11 **Bārākot** Orissa, E India 21°35′N 85°00′E
55 S7 **Barama River** ≈ N Guyana
155 E14 **Bārāmati** Mahārāshtra, W India 18°12′N 74°39′E
152 H5 **Bāramūla** Jammu and Kashmir, NW India 34°15′N 74°24′E
119 N14 **Baran'** Vitsyebskaya Voblasts', NE Belarus 54°29′N 30°18′E
152 I14 **Bārān** Rājasthān, N India 25°08′N 76°32′E
139 U4 **Barānān, Shākh-i** ▲▲ E Iraq
119 I17 **Baranavichy** *Pol.* Baranowicze, *Rus.* Baranovichi. Brestskaya Voblasts', SW Belarus 53°08′N 26°02′E
75 Y11 **Baranīce** *var.* Berenice, Mînâ Baranîs. SE Egypt 23°58′N 35°29′E
123 T6 **Baranikha** Chukotskiy Avtonomnyy Okrug, NE Russian Federation 68°29′N 168°13′E
116 M4 **Baranivka** Zhytomyrs'ka Oblast', N Ukraine 50°16′N 27°40′E
39 W14 **Baranof Island** *island* Alexander Archipelago, Alaska, USA
Baranovichi/Baranowicze *see* Baranavichy
111 N15 **Baranów Sandomierski** Podkarpackie, SE Poland 50°28′N 21°31′E
111 I26 **Baranya** *off.* Baranya Megye. ◆ *county* S Hungary
Baranya Megye *see* Baranya
153 R13 **Barāri** Bihār, NE India 25°31′N 87°23′E
22 L10 **Barataria Bay** *bay* Louisiana, S USA
Barat Daya, Kepulauan *see* Damar, Kepulauan
118 L12 **Baravukha** *Rus.* Borovukha. Vitsyebskaya Voblasts', N Belarus 55°34′N 28°36′E
54 E11 **Baraya** Huila, C Colombia 03°11′N 75°04′W
59 M21 **Barbacena** Minas Gerais, SE Brazil 21°13′S 43°47′W
54 B13 **Barbacoas** Nariño, SW Colombia 01°38′N 78°08′W
54 L6 **Barbacoas** Aragua, N Venezuela 09°29′N 66°58′W
45 Z13 **Barbados** ◆ *commonwealth republic* SE West Indies
47 S3 **Barbados** *island* Barbados
105 U11 **Barbaria, Cap de** *var.* Cabo de Berberia. *headland* Formentera, E Spain 38°39′N 01°24′E
114 N13 **Barbaros** Tekirdağ, NW Turkey 40°55′N 27°28′E
74 A11 **Barbas, Cap** *headland* S Western Sahara 22°14′N 16°45′W
105 T5 **Barbastro** Aragón, NE Spain 42°02′N 00°07′E
104 K16 **Barbate** ≈ SW Spain
104 K16 **Barbate de Franco** Andalucía, S Spain 36°11′N 05°55′W
83 K21 **Barberton** Mpumalanga, NE South Africa 25°48′S 31°03′E
31 U12 **Barberton** Ohio, N USA 41°02′N 81°37′W
102 K12 **Barbezieux-St-Hilaire** Charente, W France 45°28′N 00°09′W
54 G9 **Barbosa** Boyaca, C Colombia 05°57′N 73°37′W
21 N7 **Barbourville** Kentucky, S USA 36°52′N 83°54′W
45 W9 **Barbuda** *island* N Antigua and Barbuda
181 W8 **Barcaldine** Queensland, E Australia 23°33′S 145°21′E
Barcarozsnyó *see* Râşnov
104 I11 **Barcarrota** Extremadura, W Spain 38°31′N 06°51′W
Barcău *see* Berettyó
Barce *see* Al Marj
107 L23 **Barcellona** *var.* Barcellona Pozzo di Gotto. Sicilia, Italy, C Mediterranean Sea 38°10′N 15°15′E
Barcellona Pozzo di Gotto *see* Barcellona
105 W6 **Barcelona** *anc.* Barcino, Barcinona. Cataluña, E Spain 41°25′N 02°10′E
55 N5 **Barcelona** Anzoátegui, NE Venezuela 10°08′N 64°43′W
105 S5 **Barcelona** ◆ *province* Cataluña, NE Spain
105 W6 **Barcelona** ✈ Cataluña, E Spain 41°25′N 02°10′E
103 U14 **Barcelonnette** Alpes-de-Haute-Provence, SE France 44°24′N 06°37′E
58 E12 **Barcelos** Amazonas, N Brazil 0°59′S 62°58′W
104 G5 **Barcelos** Braga, N Portugal 41°32′N 08°37′W
110 I10 **Barcin** *Ger.* Bartschin. Kujawski-pomorskie, C Poland 52°51′N 17°55′E
Barcino/Barcinona *see* Barcelona
Barcoo *see* Cooper Creek
111 H26 **Barcs** Somogy, SW Hungary 45°58′N 17°26′E
137 W11 **Bärdä** *Rus.* Barda. C Azerbaijan 40°25′N 47°07′E
Barda *see* Bärdä
78 H5 **Bardaï** Borkou-Ennedi-Tibesti, N Chad 21°21′N 16°56′E
139 R2 **Bardaṛash** Dahūk, N Iraq 36°32′N 43°36′E
139 Q7 **Bardasah** Al Anbār, SW Iraq 34°02′N 42°28′E
153 S16 **Barddhamān** West Bengal, NE India 23°10′N 88°03′E
111 N18 **Bardejov** *Ger.* Bartfeld, *Hung.* Bártfa. Presovský Kraj, E Slovakia 49°17′N 21°18′E
105 R4 **Bárdenas Reales** *physical region* N Spain
Bardera/Bardere *see* Baardheere
Bardesīr *see* Bardsīr
92 K3 **Bárdharbunga** ▲ C Iceland 64°39′N 17°30′W
Bardhë, Drini i *see* Beli Drim
106 E9 **Bardi** Emilia-Romagna, C Italy 44°39′N 09°44′E
106 A8 **Bardonecchia** Piemonte, W Italy 45°04′N 06°40′E
97 H19 **Bardsey Island** *island* NW Wales, United Kingdom
143 S11 **Bardsīr** *var.* Bardesīr, Mashīz. Kermān, C Iran 29°58′N 56°29′E
20 L6 **Bardstown** Kentucky, S USA 37°49′N 85°29′W
Barduli *see* Barletta
20 G7 **Bardwell** Kentucky, S USA 36°52′N 89°01′W
152 K11 **Bareilly** *var.* Bareli. Uttar Pradesh, N India 28°20′N 79°24′E
Bareli *see* Bareilly
Baren *see* Jiashi
98 H13 **Barendrecht** Zuid-Holland, SW Netherlands 51°52′N 04°31′E
102 M3 **Barentin** Seine-Maritime, N France 49°33′N 00°57′E
92 N3 **Barentsburg** Spitsbergen, W Svalbard 78°01′N 14°19′E
Barentsevo More/Barents Havet *see* Barents Sea
92 O3 **Barentsøya** *island* E Svalbard
197 T11 **Barents Plain** *undersea feature* N Barents Sea
125 P3 **Barents Sea** *Nor.* Barents Havet, *Rus.* Barentsevo More. *sea* Arctic Ocean
197 U14 **Barents Trough** *undersea feature* SW Barents Sea 75°00′N 29°00′E
80 I9 **Barentu** W Eritrea 15°08′N 37°35′E
102 J3 **Barfleur** Manche, N France 49°41′N 01°18′W
102 J3 **Barfleur, Pointe de** *headland* N France 49°46′N 01°09′W
Barfrush/Barfurush *see* Bābol
158 H14 **Barga** Xizang Zizhiqu, W China 30°51′N 81°20′E
Bargarh *see* Baragarh
105 N9 **Bargas** Castilla-La Mancha, C Spain 39°56′N 04°00′W
81 I15 **Bargē** Southern Nationalities, S Ethiopia 06°11′N 37°04′E
106 A9 **Barge** Piemonte, NE Italy 44°49′N 07°21′E
153 U16 **Barguna** Barisal, S Bangladesh 22°09′N 90°07′E
Bärguşad *see* Vorotan
123 N13 **Barguzin** Respublika Buryatiya, S Russian Federation 53°37′N 109°47′E
153 O13 **Barhaj** Uttar Pradesh, N India 26°16′N 83°44′E
183 N10 **Barham** New South Wales, SE Australia 35°39′S 144°09′E
152 J12 **Barhan** Uttar Pradesh, N India 27°21′N 78°11′E
19 S7 **Bar Harbor** Mount Desert Island, Maine, NE USA 44°23′N 68°14′W
153 R14 **Barharwa** Jhārkhand, NE India 24°52′N 87°47′E
153 P15 **Barhi** Jhārkhand, N India 24°19′N 85°25′E
107 O17 **Bari** *var.* Bari delle Puglie; *anc.* Barium. Puglia, SE Italy 41°06′N 16°52′E
80 P12 **Bari** *Off.* Gobolka Bari. ◆ *region* NE Somalia
167 T14 **Ba Ria** *var.* Châu Thanh. Ba Ria-Vung Tau, S Vietnam 10°30′N 107°10′E
Bāridah *see* Al Bāridah
Bari delle Puglie *see* Bari
Bari, Gobolka *see* Bari
Barikot *see* Barīkowṯ
149 T4 **Barīkowṯ** *var.* Barikot. Konar, NE Afghanistan 35°18′N 71°36′E
42 C4 **Barillas** *var.* Santa Cruz Barillas. Huehuetenango, NW Guatemala 15°50′N 91°20′W
54 J6 **Barinas** Barinas, W Venezuela 08°36′N 70°15′W
54 I7 **Barinas** *off.* Estado Barinas; *prev.* Zamora. ◆ *state* C Venezuela
Barinas, Estado *see* Barinas
54 I6 **Barinitas** Barinas, NW Venezuela 08°45′N 70°26′W
154 P11 **Bāripada** Orissa, E India 21°56′N 86°43′E
60 K9 **Bariri** São Paulo, S Brazil 22°04′S 48°46′W
75 W11 **Bārīs** *var.* Bârîs. S Egypt 24°28′N 30°39′E
152 G14 **Bari Sādri** Rājasthān, N India 24°25′N 74°28′E
153 U16 **Barisal** Barisal, S Bangladesh 22°41′N 90°20′E
153 U16 **Barisal** ◆ *division* S Bangladesh
168 I10 **Barisan, Pegunungan** ▲▲ Sumatera, W Indonesia
169 T12 **Barito, Sungai** ≈ Borneo, C Indonesia
Barium *see* Bari
Bårjås *see* Porjus
80 I9 **Barka** *var.* Baraka, *Ar.* Khawr Barakah. *seasonal river* Eritrea/Sudan
Barka *see* Al Marj
160 H8 **Barkam** Sichuan, C China 31°56′N 102°22′E
118 J9 **Barkava** Madona, C Latvia 56°43′N 26°34′E
10 M15 **Barkerville** British Columbia, SW Canada 53°06′N 121°35′W
149 R11 **Bārkhān** Baluchistān, SW Pakistan 29°54′N 69°31′E
14 J12 **Bark Lake** ◎ Ontario, SE Canada
20 H7 **Barkley, Lake** ⊠ Kentucky/ Tennessee, S USA
10 K17 **Barkley Sound** *inlet* British Columbia, W Canada
83 J24 **Barkly East** *Afr.* Barkly-Oos. Eastern Cape, SE South Africa 30°58′S 27°35′E
Barkly-Oos *see* Barkly East
181 S4 **Barkly Tableland** *plateau* Northern Territory/ Queensland, N Australia
Barkly-Wes *see* Barkly West
83 H22 **Barkly West** *Afr.* Barkly-Wes. Northern Cape, N South Africa 28°32′S 24°32′E
159 O5 **Barkol** *var.* Barkol Kazak Zizhixian. Xinjiang Uygur Zizhiqu, NW China 43°37′N 93°01′E
159 O5 **Barkol Hu** ◎ NW China
Barkol Kazak Zizhixian *see* Barkol
30 J3 **Bark Point** *headland* Wisconsin, N USA 46°53′N 91°11′W
25 P11 **Barksdale** Texas, SW USA 29°43′N 100°03′W
Bar Kunar *see* Asmār
116 L11 **Bârlad** *prev.* Bîrlad. Vaslui, E Romania 46°12′N 27°39′E
116 M11 **Bârlad** *prev.* Bîrlad. ≈ E Romania
76 D9 **Barlavento, Ilhas de** *var.* Windward Islands. *island group* N Cape Verde
103 R5 **Bar-le-Duc** *var.* Bar-sur-Ornain. Meuse, NE France 48°46′N 05°10′E
180 K11 **Barlee, Lake** ◎ Western Australia
180 H8 **Barlee Range** ▲▲ Western Australia
107 N16 **Barletta** *anc.* Barduli. Puglia, SE Italy 41°20′N 16°17′E
110 E10 **Barlinek** *Ger.* Berlinchen. Zachodnio-pomorskie, NW Poland 53°N 15°11′E
27 S11 **Barling** Arkansas, C USA 35°19′N 94°18′W
171 U12 **Barma** Papua, E Indonesia 01°55′S 132°57′E
183 Q9 **Barmedman** New South Wales, SE Australia 34°09′S 147°21′E
Barmen-Elberfeld *see* Wuppertal
152 D12 **Bārmer** Rājasthān, NW India 25°43′N 71°25′E
182 K9 **Barmera** South Australia 34°14′S 140°26′E
97 I19 **Barmouth** NW Wales, United Kingdom 52°44′N 04°04′W
154 F10 **Barnagar** Madhya Pradesh, C India 23°01′N 75°28′E
152 H9 **Barnāla** Punjab, NW India 30°26′N 75°33′E
97 L15 **Barnard Castle** N England, United Kingdom 54°35′N 01°55′W
183 O6 **Barnato** New South Wales, SE Australia 31°39′S 145°01′E
112 I13 **Barnaul** Altayskiy Kray, C Russian Federation 53°21′N 83°45′E
109 V8 **Bärnbach** Steiermark, SE Austria 47°05′N 15°07′E
18 K16 **Barnegat** New Jersey, NE USA 39°43′N 74°12′W
23 S4 **Barnesville** Georgia, SE USA 33°03′N 84°09′W
29 R6 **Barnesville** Minnesota, N USA 46°39′N 96°25′W
31 U13 **Barnesville** Ohio, N USA 39°59′N 81°10′W
98 K11 **Barneveld** *var.* Barnveld. Gelderland, C Netherlands 52°08′N 05°34′E
25 O9 **Barnhart** Texas, SW USA 31°07′N 101°09′W
27 P8 **Barnsdall** Oklahoma, C USA 36°33′N 96°09′W
97 M17 **Barnsley** N England, United Kingdom 53°34′N 01°28′W
19 Q12 **Barnstable** Massachusetts, NE USA 41°42′N 70°17′W
97 I23 **Barnstaple** SW England, United Kingdom 51°05′N 04°04′W
Barnveld *see* Barneveld
21 Q14 **Barnwell** South Carolina, SE USA 33°14′N 81°21′W
77 U15 **Baro** Niger, C Nigeria 08°35′N 06°28′E
67 U8 **Baro** *var.* Baro Wenz. ≈ Ethiopia/Sudan
Baro *see* Baro Wenz
Baroda *see* Vadodara
149 U2 **Baroghil Pass** *var.* Kowtal-e Barowghīl. *pass* Afghanistan/ Pakistan
119 Q17 **Baron'ki** *Rus.* Boron'ki. Mahilyowskaya Voblasts', E Belarus 53°09′N 32°08′E
182 J9 **Barossa Valley** *valley* South Australia
Baroui *see* Salisbury
81 H14 **Baro Wenz** *var.* Baro, Nahr Barū. ≈ Ethiopia/Sudan
Baro Wenz *see* Baro
Barowghīl, Kowtal-e *see* Baroghil Pass
153 U12 **Barpeta** Assam, NE India 26°19′N 91°05′E
31 S7 **Barques, Pointe Aux** *headland* Michigan, N USA 44°04′N 82°57′W
54 I5 **Barquisimeto** Lara, NW Venezuela 10°03′N 69°18′W
59 N16 **Barra** Bahia, E Brazil 11°06′S 43°15′W
96 E9 **Barra** *island* NW Scotland, United Kingdom
183 T5 **Barraba** New South Wales, SE Australia 30°24′S 150°37′E
60 L9 **Barra Bonita** São Paulo, S Brazil 22°30′S 48°35′W
64 J12 **Barracuda Fracture Zone** *var.* Fifteen Twenty Fracture Zone. *tectonic feature* SW Atlantic Ocean
64 G11 **Barracuda Ridge** *undersea feature* N Atlantic Ocean
43 N12 **Barra del Colorado** Limón, NE Costa Rica 10°44′N 83°35′W
43 N9 **Barra de Río Grande** Región Autónoma Atlántico Sur, E Nicaragua 12°56′N 83°30′W
82 A11 **Barra do Cuanza** Luanda, NW Angola 09°12′S 13°08′E
60 O9 **Barra do Piraí** Rio de Janeiro, SE Brazil 22°30′S 43°47′W
61 D16 **Barra do Quaraí** Rio Grande do Sul, SE Brazil 31°03′S 58°10′W
59 G14 **Barra do São Manuel** Pará, N Brazil 07°12′S 58°03′W
83 N19 **Barra Falsa, Ponta da** *headland* S Mozambique 22°57′S 35°36′E
96 E10 **Barra Head** *headland* NW Scotland, United Kingdom 56°46′N 07°37′W
60 O9 **Barra Mansa** Rio de Janeiro, SE Brazil 22°25′S 44°03′W
57 D14 **Barranca** Lima, W Peru 10°46′S 77°46′W
54 F8 **Barrancabermeja** Santander, N Colombia 07°01′N 73°51′W
54 H4 **Barrancas** La Guajira, N Colombia 10°59′N 72°46′W
54 J6 **Barrancas** Barinas, NW Venezuela 08°47′N 70°07′W
55 Q6 **Barrancas** Monagas, NE Venezuela 08°45′N 62°12′W
54 F6 **Barranco de Loba** Bolívar, N Colombia 08°56′N 74°07′W
104 I12 **Barrancos** Beja, S Portugal 38°08′N 06°59′W
62 N7 **Barranqueras** Chaco, N Argentina 27°29′S 58°54′W
54 E4 **Barranquilla** Atlántico, N Colombia 10°59′N 74°48′W
83 N20 **Barra, Ponta da** *headland* S Mozambique 23°46′S 35°33′E
105 P11 **Barrax** Castilla-La Mancha, C Spain 39°04′N 02°12′W
19 N11 **Barre** Massachusetts, NE USA 42°24′N 72°06′W
18 M7 **Barre** Vermont, NE USA 44°09′N 72°25′W
59 M17 **Barreiras** Bahia, E Brazil 12°09′S 44°58′W
104 F11 **Barreiro** Setúbal, W Portugal 38°40′N 09°05′W
20 K7 **Barren River Lake** ⊠ Kentucky, S USA
60 L7 **Barretos** São Paulo, S Brazil 20°33′S 48°33′W
11 P14 **Barrhead** Alberta, SW Canada 54°10′N 114°22′W
14 G14 **Barrie** Ontario, S Canada 44°22′N 79°42′W
11 N16 **Barrière** British Columbia, SW Canada 51°10′N 120°06′W
14 H8 **Barrière, Lac** ◎ Québec, SE Canada
182 L6 **Barrier Range** *hill range* New South Wales, SE Australia
42 G3 **Barrier Reef** *reef* E Belize
188 C16 **Barrigada** C Guam 13°27′N 144°48′E
Barrington Island *see* Santa Fe, Isla
183 T7 **Barrington Tops** ▲ New South Wales, SE Australia 32°06′S 151°18′E
183 O4 **Barringun** New South Wales, SE Australia 29°02′S 145°45′E
59 K18 **Barro Alto** Goiás, S Brazil 15°07′S 48°56′W
59 N14 **Barro Duro** Piauí, NE Brazil 05°49′S 42°30′W
30 I5 **Barron** Wisconsin, N USA 45°24′N 91°50′W
14 J12 **Barron** ≈ Ontario, SE Canada
61 H15 **Barros Cassal** Rio Grande do Sul, S Brazil 29°12′S 52°33′W
45 P14 **Barrouallie** Saint Vincent , W Saint Vincent and the Grenadines 13°14′N 61°17′W
39 O4 **Barrow** Alaska, USA 71°17′N 156°47′W
97 E20 **Barrow** *Ir.* An Bhearú. ≈ SE Ireland
181 Q6 **Barrow Creek Roadhouse** Northern Territory, N Australia 21°30′S 133°52′E
97 J16 **Barrow-in-Furness** NW England, United Kingdom 54°07′N 03°14′W
180 G7 **Barrow Island** *island* Western Australia
39 O4 **Barrow, Point** *headland* Alaska, USA 71°23′N 156°28′W
11 V14 **Barrows** Manitoba, S Canada 52°49′N 101°36′W
97 J22 **Barry** S Wales, United Kingdom 51°24′N 03°18′W
14 J12 **Barry's Bay** Ontario, SE Canada 45°30′N 77°41′W
144 K14 **Barsakel'mes, Ostrov** *island* SW Kazakhstan
Baršć Łužyca *see* Forst
147 S14 **Barsem** S Tajikistan 37°36′N 71°43′E
145 V11 **Barshatas** Vostochnyy Kazakhstan, E Kazakhstan 48°13′N 78°33′E
155 F14 **Bārsi** Mahārāshtra, W India 18°14′N 75°42′E
100 I13 **Barsinghausen** Niedersachsen, C Germany 53°19′N 09°30′E
147 X8 **Barskoon** Issyk-Kul'skaya Oblast', E Kyrgyzstan 42°07′N 77°34′E
100 F10 **Barssel** Niedersachsen, NW Germany 53°10′N 07°46′E
35 U14 **Barstow** California, W USA 34°52′N 117°00′W
24 L8 **Barstow** Texas, SW USA 31°27′N 103°23′W
103 R6 **Bar-sur-Aube** Aube, NE France 48°13′N 04°43′E
Bar-sur-Ornain *see* Bar-le-Duc
103 Q6 **Bar-sur-Seine** Aube, N France 48°06′N 04°22′E
147 S13 **Bartang** S Tajikistan 38°06′N 71°48′E
147 T13 **Bartang** ≈ SE Tajikistan

◆ Country
● Country Capital
◇ Dependent Territory
○ Dependent Territory Capital
◆ Administrative Regions
✈ International Airport
▲ Mountain
▲▲ Mountain Range
Volcano
≈ River
◎ Lake
⊠ Reservoir

Bartenstein *see* Bartoszyce
Bártfa/Bartfeld *see* Bardejov
100 *N7* **Barth** Mecklenburg-Vorpommern, NE Germany *54°21′N 12°43′E*
27 *W13* **Bartholomew, Bayou** Arkansas/Louisiana, S USA
55 *T8* **Bartica** N Guyana *06°24′N 58°36′W*
136 *H10* **Bartın** Bartın, NW Turkey *41°37′N 32°20′E*
136 *H10* **Bartın** ⬖ *province* NW Turkey
181 *W4* **Bartle Frere** ▲ Queensland, E Australia *17°15′S 145°43′E*
27 *P8* **Bartlesville** Oklahoma, C USA *36°44′N 95°59′W*
29 *P14* **Bartlett** Nebraska, C USA *41°51′N 98°32′W*
20 *E10* **Bartlett** Tennessee, S USA *35°12′N 89°52′W*
25 *T9* **Bartlett** Texas, SW USA *30°47′N 97°25′W*
36 *L13* **Bartlett Reservoir** Arizona, SW USA
19 *N6* **Barton** Vermont, NE USA *44°44′N 72°09′W*
110 *L7* **Bartoszyce** *Ger.* Bartenstein. Warmińsko-mazurskie, NE Poland *54°16′N 20°49′E*
23 *W12* **Bartow** Florida, SE USA *27°54′N 81°50′W*
Bartschin *see* Barcin
168 *J10* **Barumun, Sungai** Sumatera, W Indonesia
Barū, Nahr *see* Baro Wenz
169 *S17* **Barung, Nusa** *island* S Indonesia
168 *H9* **Barus** Sumatera, NW Indonesia *02°02′N 98°20′E*
162 *I9* **Baruunbayan-Ulaan** *var.* Höövör. Övörhangay, C Mongolia *45°10′N 101°19′E*
Baruunsuu *see* Tsogttsetsiy
163 *P8* **Baruun-Urt** Sühbaatar, E Mongolia *46°40′N 113°17′E*
43 *P15* **Barú, Volcán** *var.* Volcán de Chiriquí. W Panama *08°49′N 82°32′W*
99 *K21* **Barvaux** Luxembourg, SE Belgium *50°21′N 05°30′E*
42 *M13* **Barva, Volcán** NW Costa Rica *10°07′N 84°08′W*
117 *W6* **Barvinkove** Kharkivs'ka Oblast', E Ukraine *48°54′N 37°03′E*
154 *G11* **Barwāh** Madhya Pradesh, C India *22°17′N 76°01′E*
Bärwalde Neumark *see* Mieszkowice
154 *F11* **Barwāni** Madhya Pradesh, C India *22°02′N 74°56′E*
183 *P5* **Barwon River** New South Wales, SE Australia
119 *L15* **Barysaw** *Rus.* Borisov. Minskaya Voblasts', NE Belarus *54°14′N 28°30′E*
127 *Q6* **Barysh** Ul'yanovskaya Oblast', W Russian Federation *53°32′N 47°06′E*
117 *Q4* **Baryshivka** Kyyivs'ka Oblast', N Ukraine *50°21′N 31°21′E*
79 *J17* **Basankusu** Equateur, NW Dem. Rep. Congo *01°12′N 19°50′E*
117 *N11* **Basarabeasca** *Rus.* Bessarabka. SE Moldova *46°22′N 28°56′E*
116 *M14* **Basarabi** Constanța, SW Romania *44°10′N 28°26′E*
40 *H6* **Basaseachic** Chihuahua, NW Mexico *28°18′N 108°13′W*
Basauri *see* Arizgoiti
61 *D18* **Basavilbaso** Entre Ríos, E Argentina *32°23′S 58°55′W*
79 *F21* **Bas-Congo** *off.* Région du Bas-Congo; *prev.* Bas-Zaïre. ⬖ *region* SW Dem. Rep. Congo
108 *E6* **Basel** *Eng.* Basle, *Fr.* Bâle. Basel-Stadt, NW Switzerland *47°33′N 07°36′E*
108 *E7* **Basel** *Eng.* Basle, *Fr.* Bâle. ⬖ *canton* NW Switzerland
143 *T14* **Bashākerd, Kūhhā-ye** ▲▲ SE Iran
11 *Q15* **Bashaw** Alberta, SW Canada *52°40′N 112°53′W*
146 *K16* **Bashbedeng** Mary Welaýaty, S Turkmenistan *35°44′N 63°07′E*
161 *T15* **Bashi Channel** *Chin.* Pa-shih Hai-hsia. *channel* Philippines/Taiwan
Bashkiria *see* Bashkortostan, Respublika
122 *F11* **Bashkortostan, Respublika** *prev.* Bashkiria. ⬖ *autonomous republic* W Russian Federation
127 *N6* **Bashmakovo** Penzenskaya Oblast', W Russian Federation *53°13′N 43°00′E*
146 *J10* **Bashsakarba** Lebap Welaýaty, NE Turkmenistan *40°25′N 62°16′E*
117 *R9* **Bashtanka** Mykolayivs'ka Oblast', S Ukraine *47°24′N 32°27′E*
22 *H8* **Basile** Louisiana, S USA *30°29′N 92°36′W*
107 *M18* **Basilicata** ⬖ *region* S Italy
33 *V13* **Basin** Wyoming, C USA *44°22′N 108°02′W*
97 *N22* **Basingstoke** S England, United Kingdom *51°16′N 01°08′W*
143 *U8* **Başīrān** Khorāsān-e Janūbī, E Iran *31°57′N 59°07′E*
112 *B10* **Baška** *It.* Bescanuova. Primorje-Gorski Kotar, NW Croatia *44°58′N 14°46′E*
137 *T15* **Başkale** Van, SE Turkey *38°03′N 43°59′E*
14 *L10* **Baskatong, Réservoir** Québec, SE Canada
137 *O14* **Baskil** Elazığ, E Turkey *38°38′N 38°47′E*
Basle *see* Basel
154 *H9* **Bāsoda** Madhya Pradesh, C India *23°54′N 77°58′E*
79 *L17* **Basoko** Orientale, N Dem. Rep. Congo *01°14′N 23°26′E*
Basque Country, The *see* País Vasco
Basra *see* Al Başrah
103 *U5* **Bas-Rhin** ⬖ *department* NE France
Bassam *see* Grand-Bassam
11 *Q16* **Bassano** Alberta, SW Canada *50°48′N 112°28′W*
106 *H7* **Bassano del Grappa** Veneto, NE Italy *45°45′N 11°45′E*
77 *Q15* **Bassar** *var.* Bassari. NW Togo *09°15′N 00°47′E*
Bassari *see* Bassar
172 *L9* **Bassas da India** *island group* W Madagascar
108 *D7* **Bassecourt** Jura, W Switzerland *47°20′N 07°16′E*
Bassein *see* Pathein
79 *J15* **Basse-Kotto** ⬖ *prefecture* S Central African Republic
105 *V5* **Bassella** Cataluña, NE Spain *42°01′N 01°17′E*
102 *J5* **Basse-Normandie** *Eng.* Lower Normandy. ⬖ *region* N France
45 *Q11* **Basse-Pointe** N Martinique *14°52′N 61°07′W*
76 *H12* **Basse Santa Su** E Gambia *13°18′N 14°10′W*
Basse-Saxe *see* Niedersachsen
45 *X6* **Basse-Terre** ○ (Guadeloupe) Basse Terre, SW Guadeloupe *16°08′N 61°40′W*
45 *V10* **Basseterre** ● (Saint Kitts and Nevis) Saint Kitts, Saint Kitts and Nevis *17°16′N 62°45′W*
45 *X6* **Basse Terre** *island* W Guadeloupe
29 *O13* **Bassett** Nebraska, C USA *42°34′N 99°32′W*
21 *S7* **Bassett** Virginia, NE USA *36°45′N 79°59′W*
37 *N15* **Bassett Peak** ▲ Arizona, SW USA *32°30′N 110°16′W*
76 *M10* **Bassikounou** Hodh ech Chargui, SE Mauritania *15°55′N 05°59′W*
77 *R15* **Bassila** W Benin *08°25′N 01°58′E*
Bass, Îlots de *see* Marotiri
31 *O11* **Bass Lake** Indiana, N USA *41°12′N 86°35′W*
183 *O14* **Bass Strait** *strait* SE Australia
100 *H11* **Bassum** Niedersachsen, NW Germany *52°52′N 08°44′E*
29 *X3* **Basswood Lake** Canada/USA
95 *J21* **Båstad** Skåne, S Sweden *56°25′N 12°50′E*
139 *U2* **Basṭah** As Sulaymānīyah, E Iraq *36°20′N 45°14′E*
143 *Q14* **Bastak** Fārs, SW Iran *27°14′N 54°27′E*
153 *N12* **Basti** Uttar Pradesh, N India *26°48′N 82°44′E*
103 *X14* **Bastia** Corse, France, C Mediterranean Sea *42°42′N 09°27′E*
99 *L23* **Bastogne** Luxembourg, SE Belgium *50°N 05°43′E*
22 *I5* **Bastrop** Louisiana, S USA *32°46′N 91°54′W*
25 *T11* **Bastrop** Texas, SW USA *30°07′N 97°21′W*
93 *J15* **Bastuträsk** Västerbotten, N Sweden *64°47′N 20°05′E*
119 *J19* **Bastyn'** *Rus.* Bostyn'. Brestskaya Voblasts', SW Belarus *52°23′N 26°45′E*
Basuo *see* Dongfang
Basutoland *see* Lesotho
119 *O15* **Basya** E Belarus
117 *V8* **Basyl'kivka** Dnipropetrovs'ka Oblast', E Ukraine *48°12′N 36°00′E*
Bas-Zaïre *see* Bas-Congo
79 *D17* **Bata** NW Equatorial Guinea *01°51′N 09°48′E*
79 *D17* **Bata** ✕ S Equatorial Guinea *01°55′N 09°48′E*
Batae Coritanorum *see* Leicester
123 *Q8* **Batagay** Respublika Sakha (Yakutiya), NE Russian Federation *67°36′N 134°44′E*
123 *P8* **Batagay-Alyta** Respublika Sakha (Yakutiya), NE Russian Federation *67°48′N 130°15′E*
112 *L10* **Batajnica** Vojvodina, N Serbia *44°55′N 20°17′E*
136 *H15* **Bataklık Gölü** S Turkey
114 *H11* **Batak, Yazovir** SW Bulgaria
152 *H7* **Batāla** Punjab, N India *31°48′N 75°12′E*
104 *F9* **Batalha** Leiria, C Portugal *39°40′N 08°50′W*
79 *N17* **Batama** Orientale, NE Dem. Rep. Congo *0°54′N 26°25′E*
123 *Q10* **Batamay** Respublika Sakha (Yakutiya), NE Russian Federation *63°28′N 129°33′E*
160 *F9* **Batang** *var.* Bazhong. Sichuan, C China *30°04′N 99°10′E*
79 *I14* **Batangafo** Ouham, NW Central African Republic *07°19′N 18°22′E*
171 *P8* **Batangas** *off.* Batangas City. Luzon, N Philippines *13°47′N 121°03′E*
Batangas City *see* Batangas
Bătania *see* Battonya
171 *Q10* **Batan Islands** *island group* N Philippines
60 *L8* **Batatais** São Paulo, S Brazil *20°54′S 47°37′W*
18 *E10* **Batavia** New York, NE USA *43°00′N 78°11′W*
Batavia *see* Jakarta
173 *T9* **Batavia Seamount** *undersea feature* E Indian Ocean *27°42′S 100°36′E*
126 *L12* **Bataysk** Rostovskaya Oblast', SW Russian Federation *47°10′N 39°46′E*
14 *B9* **Batchawana** Ontario, S Canada
14 *B9* **Batchawana Bay** Ontario, S Canada *46°55′N 84°36′W*
167 *Q12* **Bătdâmbâng** *prev.* Battambang. Bătdâmbâng, NW Cambodia *13°06′N 103°13′E*
79 *G20* **Batéké, Plateaux** *plateau* S Congo
183 *S11* **Batemans Bay** New South Wales, SE Australia *35°45′S 150°09′E*
21 *Q13* **Batesburg** South Carolina, SE USA *33°54′N 81°33′W*
28 *K12* **Batesland** South Dakota, N USA *43°05′N 102°07′W*
27 *V10* **Batesville** Arkansas, C USA *35°45′N 91°39′W*
31 *Q14* **Batesville** Indiana, N USA *39°18′N 85°13′W*
22 *L2* **Batesville** Mississippi, S USA *34°18′N 89°56′W*
25 *Q13* **Batesville** Texas, SW USA *28°56′N 99°38′W*
149 *V5* **Batgrām** North-West Frontier Province, N Pakistan *34°40′N 73°03′E*
44 *L13* **Bath** E Jamaica *17°57′N 76°22′W*
97 *L22* **Bath** *hist.* Akermanceaster; *anc.* Aquae Calidae, Aquae Solis. SW England, United Kingdom *51°23′N 02°22′W*
19 *Q8* **Bath** Maine, NE USA *43°54′N 69°49′W*
18 *F11* **Bath** New York, NE USA *42°20′N 77°16′W*
Bath *see* Berkeley Springs
78 *I10* **Batha** *off.* Préfecture du Batha. ⬖ *prefecture* C Chad
78 *I10* **Batha** *seasonal river* C Chad
Batha, Préfecture du *see* Batha
141 *Y8* **Baṭḥā', Wādī al** *dry watercourse* NE Oman
152 *H9* **Bathinda** Punjab, NW India *30°14′N 74°54′E*
98 *M11* **Bathmen** Overijssel, E Netherlands *52°15′N 06°16′E*
45 *Z14* **Bathsheba** E Barbados *13°13′N 59°31′W*
183 *R8* **Bathurst** New South Wales, SE Australia *33°32′S 149°35′E*
13 *O13* **Bathurst** New Brunswick, SE Canada *47°37′N 65°40′W*
Bathurst *see* Banjul
8 *H6* **Bathurst, Cape** *headland* Northwest Territories, NW Canada *70°33′N 128°00′W*
196 *L8* **Bathurst Inlet** Nunavut, N Canada *66°23′N 107°00′W*
196 *L8* **Bathurst Inlet** *inlet* Nunavut, N Canada
181 *N1* **Bathurst Island** *island* Northern Territory, N Australia
197 *O9* **Bathurst Island** *island* Parry Islands, Nunavut, N Canada
77 *O14* **Batié** SW Burkina *09°53′N 02°53′W*
Batinah *see* Al Bāṭinah
141 *Y9* **Bāṭin, Wādī al** *dry watercourse* SW Asia
15 *P9* **Batiscan** Québec, SE Canada
136 *F16* **BatıToroslar** ▲▲ SW Turkey
Batjan *see* Bacan, Pulau
147 *R11* **Batken** Batenskaya Oblast', SW Kyrgyzstan *40°03′N 70°50′E*
Batken Oblasty *see* Batkenskaya Oblast'
147 *Q11* **Batkenskaya Oblast'** *Kir.* Batken Oblasty. ⬖ *province* SW Kyrgyzstan
Batlle y Ordóñez *see* José Batlle y Ordóñez
183 *Q10* **Batlow** New South Wales, SE Australia *35°32′S 148°09′E*
137 *Q15* **Batman** *var.* İluh. Batman, SE Turkey *37°52′N 41°06′E*
137 *Q15* **Batman** ⬖ *province* SE Turkey
74 *L6* **Batna** NE Algeria *35°34′N 06°10′E*
163 *O7* **Batnorov** *var.* Dundbürd. Hentiy, E Mongolia *47°55′N 111°37′E*
Batoe *see* Batu, Kepulauan
162 *K7* **Bat-Öldziy** *var.* Övt. Övörhangay, C Mongolia *46°50′N 102°15′E*
Bat-Öldziyt *see* Dzaamar
22 *J8* **Baton Rouge** *state capital* Louisiana, S USA *30°28′N 91°09′W*
79 *G15* **Batouri** Est, E Cameroon *04°26′N 14°27′E*
138 *G14* **Batrā', Jibāl al** ▲▲ S Jordan
138 *G6* **Batroûn** *var.* Al Batrūn. N Lebanon *34°15′N 35°42′E*
Batsch *see* Bač
Batsevichi *see* Batsevichy
119 *M17* **Batsevichy** *Rus.* Batsevichi. Mahilyowskaya Voblasts', E Belarus *53°24′N 29°14′E*
92 *M7* **Båtsfjord** Finnmark, N Norway *70°37′N 29°42′E*
Batshireet *see* Hentiy
162 *L7* **Batsümber** *var.* Mandal. Töv, C Mongolia *48°24′N 106°47′E*
Battambang *see* tBătdâmbâng
195 *X3* **Batterbee, Cape** *headland* Antarctica
155 *L24* **Batticaloa** Eastern Province, E Sri Lanka *07°44′N 81°43′E*
99 *L19* **Battice** Liège, E Belgium *50°39′N 05°50′E*
107 *L18* **Battipaglia** Campania, S Italy *40°36′N 14°59′E*
11 *R15* **Battle** Alberta/Saskatchewan, SW Canada
Battle Born State *see* Nevada
31 *Q10* **Battle Creek** Michigan, N USA *42°20′N 85°10′W*
27 *T7* **Battlefield** Missouri, C USA *37°07′N 93°22′W*
11 *S15* **Battleford** Saskatchewan, S Canada *52°45′N 108°20′W*
29 *S6* **Battle Lake** Minnesota, N USA *46°16′N 95°42′W*
35 *U3* **Battle Mountain** Nevada, W USA *40°37′N 116°55′W*
111 *M25* **Battonya** *Rom.* Bătania. Békés, SE Hungary *46°16′N 21°00′E*
162 *J7* **Battsengel** *var.* Jargalant. Arhangay, C Mongolia *47°46′N 101°56′E*
168 *D11* **Batu, Kepulauan** *prev.* Batoe. *island group* W Indonesia
137 *Q10* **Bat'umi** W Georgia *41°39′N 41°38′E*
168 *K10* **Batu Pahat** *prev.* Bandar Penggaram. Johor, Peninsular Malaysia *01°51′N 102°56′E*
171 *O12* **Baturebe** Sulawesi, N Indonesia *01°43′S 121°43′E*
122 *J12* **Baturino** Tomskaya Oblast', C Russian Federation *57°46′N 85°08′E*
117 *R3* **Baturyn** Chernihivs'ka Oblast', N Ukraine *51°20′N 32°54′E*
138 *F10* **Bat Yam** Tel Aviv, C Israel *32°01′N 34°45′E*
127 *Q4* **Batyrevo** Chuvashskaya Respublika, W Russian Federation *55°04′N 47°34′E*
Batys Qazaqstan Oblysy *see* Zapadnyy Kazakhstan
102 *F5* **Batz, Île de** *island* NW France
169 *Q10* **Bau** Sarawak, East Malaysia *01°25′N 110°10′E*
171 *N2* **Bauang** Luzon, N Philippines *16°33′N 120°19′E*
171 *P14* **Baubau** *var.* Baoebaoe. Pulau Buton, C Indonesia *05°30′S 122°37′E*
77 *W14* **Bauchi** Bauchi, NE Nigeria *10°18′N 09°46′E*
77 *W14* **Bauchi** ⬖ *state* C Nigeria
102 *H7* **Baud** Morbihan, NW France *47°52′N 02°59′W*
154 *N13* **Bauda** *var.* Baudh. Orissa, SW India *20°50′N 84°19′E*
29 *T2* **Baudette** Minnesota, N USA *48°42′N 94°36′W*
Baudh *see* Bauda
193 *S9* **Bauer Basin** *undersea feature* E Pacific Ocean *10°00′S 101°45′W*
187 *R14* **Bauer Field** *var.* Port Vila. ✕ (Port-Vila) Éfaté, C Vanuatu *17°42′S 168°21′E*
13 *T9* **Bauld, Cape** *headland* Newfoundland and Labrador, E Canada *51°35′N 55°22′W*
103 *T8* **Baume-les-Dames** Doubs, E France *47°22′N 06°20′E*
101 *I15* **Baunatal** Hessen, C Germany *51°15′N 09°25′E*
107 *D18* **Baunei** Sardegna, Italy, C Mediterranean Sea *40°04′N 09°36′E*
57 *M15* **Baures, Río** N Bolivia
60 *K9* **Bauru** São Paulo, S Brazil *22°19′S 49°07′W*
Baushar *see* Bawshar
118 *G10* **Bauska** *Ger.* Bauske. Bauska, S Latvia *56°25′N 24°11′E*
Bauske *see* Bauska
101 *Q15* **Bautzen** *Lus.* Budyšin. Sachsen, E Germany *51°11′N 14°29′E*
145 *Q16* **Bauyrzhan Momyshuly** *Kaz.* Baūyrzhan Momyshuly; *prev.* Burnoye. Zhambyl, S Kazakhstan *42°36′N 70°46′E*
Bauzanum *see* Bolzano
Bavaria *see* Bayern
109 *N7* **Bavarian Alps** *Ger.* Bayrische Alpen. ▲▲ Austria/Germany
Bavière *see* Bayern
40 *H4* **Bavispe, Río** NW Mexico
127 *T5* **Bavly** Respublika Tatarstan, W Russian Federation *54°20′N 53°21′E*
169 *P13* **Bawal, Pulau** *island* N Indonesia
169 *T12* **Bawan** Borneo, C Indonesia *01°36′S 113°55′E*
183 *O12* **Baw Baw, Mount** ▲ Victoria, SE Australia *37°49′S 146°16′E*
169 *S15* **Bawean, Pulau** *island* S Indonesia
75 *V9* **Bawīṭī** *var.* Bawîṭi. N Egypt *28°19′N 28°53′E*
Bawîṭi *see* Bawīṭī
77 *Q13* **Bawku** N Ghana *11°00′N 00°12′W*
167 *N7* **Bawlakè** Kayah State, C Burma (Myanmar) *19°10′N 97°19′E*
169 *H11* **Bawo Ofuloa** Pulau Tanahmasa, W Indonesia *0°10′S 98°24′E*
141 *Y8* **Bawshar** *var.* Baushar. NE Oman *23°32′N 58°24′E*
Baxian *see* Bazhou
Ba Xian *see* Bazhou
158 *M8* **Baxkorgan** Xinjiang Uygur Zizhiqu, W China *39°05′N 90°00′E*
23 *V6* **Baxley** Georgia, SE USA *31°46′N 82°21′W*
159 *R15* **Baxoi** *var.* Baima. Xizang Zizhiqu, W China *30°01′N 96°53′E*
29 *W14* **Baxter** Iowa, C USA *41°49′N 93°09′W*
29 *U6* **Baxter** Minnesota, N USA *46°21′N 94°18′W*
27 *R8* **Baxter Springs** Kansas, C USA *37°01′N 94°45′W*
81 *M17* **Bay** *off.* Gobolka Bay. ⬖ *region* SW Somalia
Bay *see* Baicheng
44 *H7* **Bayamo** Granma, E Cuba *20°21′N 76°38′W*
45 *U5* **Bayamón** E Puerto Rico *18°24′N 66°09′W*
163 *W8* **Bayan** Heilongjiang, NE China *46°05′N 127°24′E*
170 *L16* **Bayan** *prev.* Bajan. Pulau Lombok, C Indonesia *08°16′S 116°28′E*
162 *M8* **Bayan** *var.* Maanĭt. Töv, C Mongolia *47°14′N 107°34′E*
Bayan *see* Hölönbuyr, Dornod, Mongolia
Bayan *see* Ihhet, Dornogovĭ, Mongolia
Bayan *see* Bayan-Uul, Govĭ-Altay, Mongolia
Bayan *see* Bayanhutag, Hentiy, Mongolia
Bayan *see* Bürentogtoh, Hövsgol, Mongolia
152 *I12* **Bayāna** Rājasthān, N India *26°55′N 77°18′E*
149 *N5* **Bāyān, Band-e** ▲▲ C Afghanistan
162 *H8* **Bayanbulag** Bayanhongor, C Mongolia *46°46′N 98°07′E*
Bayanbulag *see* Ömnödelger
158 *J5* **Bayanbulak** Xinjiang Uygur Zizhiqu, W China *43°05′N 84°05′E*
162 *L7* **Bayanchandmanĭ** *var.* Ihsüüj. Töv, C Mongolia *48°12′N 106°23′E*
162 *J11* **Bayandalay** *var.* Dalay. Ömnögovĭ, S Mongolia *43°27′N 103°30′E*
163 *O9* **Bayandelger** *var.* Shireet. Sühbaatar, SE Mongolia *45°33′N 112°19′E*
162 *I5* **Bayandzürh** *var.* Altraga. Hövsgöl, N Mongolia *50°08′N 98°54′E*
Bayan Gol *see* Dengkou, China
Bayangol *see* Bugat, Mongolia
162 *I9* **Bayangovĭ** *var.* Örgön. Bayanhongor, C Mongolia *44°43′N 100°23′E*
159 *R12* **Bayan Har Shan** *var.* Bayan Khar. ▲▲ C China
162 *G6* **Bayanhayrhan** *var.* Altanbulag. Dzavhan, N Mongolia *49°16′N 96°22′E*
162 *I8* **Bayanhongor** Bayanhongor, C Mongolia *46°08′N 100°42′E*
162 *H9* **Bayanhongor** ⬖ *province* C Mongolia
162 *K14* **Bayan Hot** *var.* Alxa Zuoqi. Nei Mongol Zizhiqu, N China *38°49′N 105°40′E*
163 *O8* **Bayanhutag** *var.* Bayan. Hentiy, C Mongolia *47°13′N 110°57′E*
163 *T9* **Bayan Huxu** *var.* Horqin Zuoyi Zhongqi. Nei Mongol Zizhiqu, N China *45°02′N 121°28′E*
Bayan Khar *see* Bayan Har Shan
163 *N12* **Bayan Kuang** *prev.* Bayan Obo. Nei Mongol Zizhiqu, N China *41°45′N 109°58′E*
168 *J7* **Bayan Lepas** ✕ (George Town) Pinang, Peninsular Malaysia *05°18′N 100°15′E*
162 *I10* **Bayanlig** *var.* Hatansuudal. Bayanhongor, C Mongolia *44°34′N 100°41′E*
162 *K13* **Bayan Mod** Nei Mongol Zizhiqu, N China *40°45′N 104°29′E*
163 *N8* **Bayanmönh** *var.* Ulaan-Ereg. Hentiy, E Mongolia *46°50′N 109°39′E*
162 *L12* **Bayannur** *var.* Linhe. Nei Mongol Zizhiqu, N China *40°46′N 107°27′E*
Bayan Nuru *see* Xar Burd
162 *E5* **Bayannuur** *var.* Tsul-Ulaan. Bayan-Ölgiy, W Mongolia *48°51′N 91°13′E*
Bayan Obo *see* Bayan Kuang
43 *V15* **Bayano, Lago** E Panama
162 *C5* **Bayan-Ölgiy** ⬖ *province* NW Mongolia
162 *H9* **Bayan-Öndör** *var.* Bulgan. Bayanhongor, C Mongolia *44°48′N 98°39′E*
162 *K8* **Bayan-Öndör** *var.* Bumbat. Övörhangay, C Mongolia *46°30′N 104°08′E*
162 *L8* **Bayan-Önjüül** *var.* Ihhayrhan. Töv, C Mongolia *46°57′N 105°51′E*
163 *O7* **Bayan-Ovoo** *var.* Javhlant. Hentiy, E Mongolia *47°46′N 112°06′E*
162 *L11* **Bayan-Ovoo** *var.* Erdenetsogt. Ömnögovĭ, S Mongolia *42°54′N 106°16′E*
Bayansayr *see* Baatsagaan
159 *Q9* **Bayan Shan** ▲ C China *37°36′N 96°23′E*
162 *J9* **Bayanteeg** Övörhangay, C Mongolia *45°39′N 101°30′E*
162 *G5* **Bayantes** *var.* Altay. Dzavhan, N Mongolia *49°40′N 96°21′E*
Bayantöhöm *see* Büren
162 *M8* **Bayantsagaan** *var.* Dzogsool. Töv, C Mongolia *46°46′N 107°18′E*
163 *P7* **Bayantümen** *var.* Tsagaanders. Dornod, NE Mongolia *48°03′N 114°16′E*
Bayan-Uhaa *see* Ih-Uul
163 *R10* **Bayan Ul** *var.* Xi Ujimqin Qi. Nei Mongol Zizhiqu, N China *44°31′N 117°36′E*
Bayan-Ulaan *see* Dzüünbayan-Ulaan
163 *O7* **Bayan-Uul** *var.* Javarthushuu. Dornod, NE Mongolia *49°05′N 112°40′E*
162 *F7* **Bayan-Uul** *var.* Bayan. Govĭ-Altay, W Mongolia *47°05′N 95°13′E*
162 *M8* **Bayanuur** *var.* Tsul-Ulaan. Töv, C Mongolia *47°44′N 108°22′E*
28 *J14* **Bayard** Nebraska, C USA *41°45′N 103°19′W*
37 *P15* **Bayard** New Mexico, SW USA *32°45′N 108°07′W*
103 *T13* **Bayard, Col** *pass* SE France
Bayasgalant *see* Mönhhaan
136 *J12* **Bayat** Çorum, N Turkey *40°34′N 34°07′E*
171 *P6* **Bayawan** Negros, C Philippines *09°22′N 122°50′E*
143 *R10* **Bayāẕ** Kermān, C Iran *30°41′N 55°29′E*
171 *Q6* **Baybay** Leyte, C Philippines *10°41′N 124°49′E*
21 *X10* **Bayboro** North Carolina, SE USA *35°08′N 76°49′W*
137 *P12* **Bayburt** Bayburt, NE Turkey *40°15′N 40°16′E*
137 *P12* **Bayburt** ⬖ *province* NE Turkey
31 *R8* **Bay City** Michigan, N USA *43°35′N 83°52′W*
25 *V12* **Bay City** Texas, SW USA *28°59′N 96°00′W*
Baydarata Bay *see* Baydaratskaya Guba
122 *J7* **Baydaratskaya Guba** *var.* Baydarata Bay. *bay* N Russian Federation
81 *M16* **Baydhabo** *var.* Baydhowa, Isha Baydhabo, *It.* Baidoa. Bay, SW Somalia *03°08′N 43°39′E*
Baydhowa *see* Baydhabo
77 *U17* **Bayelsa** ⬖ *state* S Nigeria
101 *N21* **Bayerischer Wald** ▲▲ SE Germany
101 *K21* **Bayern** *Eng.* Bavaria, *Fr.* Bavière. ⬖ *state* SE Germany
147 *V9* **Bayetovo** Narynskaya Oblast', C Kyrgyzstan *41°14′N 74°55′E*
102 *K4* **Bayeux** *anc.* Augustodurum. Calvados, N France *49°16′N 00°42′W*
14 *E15* **Bayfield** Ontario, S Canada
145 *O15* **Baygekum** *Kaz.* Bäygequm. Kzylorda, S Kazakhstan *44°15′N 66°34′E*
Bäygequm *see* Baygekum
136 *C14* **Bayındır** Izmır, SW Turkey *38°12′N 27°40′E*
138 *H12* **Bāyir** *var.* Bā'ir. Ma'ān, S Jordan *30°46′N 36°40′E*
Bay Islands *see* Bahía, Islas de la
Bayizhen *see* Nyingchi
139 *R5* **Bayjī** *var.* Baiji. Şalāḥ ad Dīn, N Iraq *34°56′N 43°29′E*
Baykadam *see* Saudakent
123 *N13* **Baykal, Ozero** *Eng.* Lake Baikal. S Russian Federation
123 *M14* **Baykal'sk** Irkutskaya Oblast', S Russian Federation *51°30′N 104°03′E*
137 *R15* **Baykan** Siirt, SE Turkey *38°08′N 41°43′E*
123 *L11* **Baykit** Evenkiyskiy Avtonomnyy Okrug, C Russian Federation *61°37′N 96°23′E*
145 *N12* **Baykonur** *var.* Baykonyr. Karaganda, C Kazakhstan *47°50′N 75°33′E*
Baykonur *see* Baykonyr
144 *M14* **Baykonyr** *var.* Baykonur, *Kaz.* Bayqongyr; *prev.* Leninsk. Kyzylorda, S Kazakhstan *45°38′N 63°20′E*
Baykonyr *see* Baykonur
158 *E7* **Baykurt** Xinjiang Uygur Zizhiqu, W China *39°56′N 75°33′E*
14 *I9* **Bay, Lac** Québec, SE Canada
127 *W6* **Baymak** Respublika Bashkortostan, W Russian Federation *52°34′N 58°20′E*
23 *O8* **Bay Minette** Alabama, S USA *30°52′N 87°46′W*
143 *O17* **Baynūnah** *desert* W United Arab Emirates
184 *O8* **Bay of Plenty** *off.* Bay of Plenty Region. ⬖ *region* North Island, New Zealand
Bay of Plenty Region *see* Bay of Plenty
191 *Z3* **Bay of Wrecks** *bay* Kiritimati, E Kiribati
Bayonnaise Rocks *see* Beyonēsu-retsugan
102 *I15* **Bayonne** *anc.* Lapurdum. Pyrénées-Atlantiques, SW France *43°30′N 01°28′W*
22 *H4* **Bayou D'Arbonne Lake** Louisiana, S USA
23 *N9* **Bayou La Batre** Alabama, S USA *30°24′N 88°15′W*
Bayou State *see* Mississippi
Bayqadam *see* Saudakent
Bayqongyr *see* Baykonyr
Bayram-Ali *see* Baýramaly
146 *J14* **Baýramaly** *var.* Bayramaly; *prev.* Bayram-Ali. Mary Welaýaty, S Turkmenistan *37°33′N 62°08′E*
101 *L19* **Bayreuth** *var.* Baireuth. Bayern, SE Germany *49°57′N 11°34′E*
Bayrische Alpen *see* Bavarian Alps
Bayrūt *see* Beyrouth
22 *L9* **Bay Saint Louis** Mississippi, S USA *30°18′N 89°19′W*
Baysān *see* Beit She'an
Bayshint *see* Öndörshireet
14 *H13* **Bays, Lake of** Ontario, S Canada
22 *M6* **Bay Springs** Mississippi, S USA *31°58′N 89°17′W*
Bay State *see* Massachusetts
Baysun *see* Boysun
14 *H13* **Baysville** Ontario, S Canada *45°10′N 79°03′W*
141 *N15* **Bayt al Faqīh** W Yemen *14°30′N 43°20′E*
158 *M4* **Baytik Shan** ▲▲ China/Mongolia
Bayt Laḥm *see* Bethlehem
25 *W11* **Baytown** Texas, SW USA *29°43′N 94°59′W*
169 *V11* **Bayur, Tanjung** *headland* Borneo, N Indonesia *0°43′S 117°32′E*
121 *N14* **Bayy al Kabīr, Wādī** *dry watercourse* NW Libya
Bayyrqum *see* Bairkum
105 *P14* **Baza** Andalucía, S Spain *37°30′N 02°45′W*
137 *X10* **Bazardüzü Dağı** *Rus.* Gora Bazardyuzyu. ▲ N Azerbaijan *41°13′N 47°50′E*
Bazardyuzyu, Gora *see* Bazardüzü Dağı
Bazargic *see* Dobrich
83 *N18* **Bazaruto, Ilha do** *island* SE Mozambique
102 *K14* **Bazas** Gironde, SW France *44°27′N 00°11′W*
105 *O14* **Baza, Sierra de** ▲▲ S Spain
160 *J8* **Bazhong** *var.* Bazhou. Sichuan, C China *31°55′N 106°44′E*
Bazhong *see* Batang
161 *P3* **Bazhou** *prev.* Baxian, Ba Xian. Hebei, E China *39°05′N 116°24′E*
Bazhou *see* Bazhong
14 *M9* **Bazin** Québec, SE Canada
Bazin *see* Pezinok
139 *Q7* **Bāzīyah** Al Anbār, C Iraq *33°50′N 42°41′E*
138 *H6* **Bcharré** *var.* Bcharreh, Bsharrī, Bsherri. NE Lebanon *34°16′N 36°01′E*
Bcharreh *see* Bcharré
28 *J5* **Beach** North Dakota, N USA *46°55′N 104°00′W*
182 *K12* **Beachport** South Australia *37°29′S 140°03′E*
97 *O23* **Beachy Head** *headland* SE England, United Kingdom *50°44′N 00°16′E*
18 *K13* **Beacon** New York, NE USA *41°30′N 73°54′W*
63 *J25* **Beagle Channel** *channel* Argentina/Chile
181 *O1* **Beagle Gulf** *gulf* Northern Territory, N Australia
Bealach an Doirín *see* Ballaghaderreen
Bealach Cláir *see* Ballyclare
Bealach Féich *see* Ballybofey
172 *J3* **Bealanana** Mahajanga, NE Madagascar *14°33′S 48°44′E*
Béal an Átha *see* Ballina
Béal an Átha Móir *see* Ballinamore
Béal an Mhuirhead *see* Belmullet
Béal Átha Beithe *see* Ballybay
Béal Átha Conaill *see* Ballyconnell
Beál Átha hAmhnais *see* Ballyhaunis
Béal Átha na Sluaighe *see* Ballinasloe
Béal Átha Seanaidh *see* Ballyshannon
Bealdovuopmi *see* Peltovuoma
Béal Feirste *see* Belfast
Béal Tairbirt *see* Belturbet
Beanna Boirche *see* Mourne Mountains
Beannchar *see* Banagher, Ireland
Beannchar *see* Bangor, Northern Ireland, UK
Beanntraí *see* Bantry
Bearalváhki *see* Berlevåg
23 *N2* **Bear Creek** Alabama/Mississippi, S USA
30 *J13* **Bear Creek** Illinois, N USA
27 *U13* **Bearden** Arkansas, C USA *33°43′N 92°37′W*
195 *Q10* **Beardmore Glacier** *glacier* Antarctica
30 *K13* **Beardstown** Illinois, N USA *40°01′N 90°25′W*
28 *L14* **Bear Hill** ▲ Nebraska, C USA *41°24′N 101°49′W*
Bear Island *see* Bjørnøya
14 *H12* **Bear Lake** Ontario, S Canada *45°28′N 79°31′W*
36 *M1* **Bear Lake** Idaho/Utah, NW USA
39 *U11* **Bear, Mount** ▲ Alaska, USA *61°16′N 141°09′W*
102 *J16* **Béarn** *cultural region* SW France
194 *J11* **Bear Peninsula** *peninsula* Antarctica
152 *I7* **Beās** India/Pakistan
105 *P3* **Beasain** País Vasco, N Spain *43°03′N 02°11′W*
105 *O12* **Beas de Segura** Andalucía, S Spain *38°16′N 02°54′W*
45 *N10* **Beata, Cabo** *headland* SW Dominican Republic *17°34′N 71°25′W*
45 *N10* **Beata, Isla** *island* SW Dominican Republic
64 *F11* **Beata Ridge** *undersea feature* N Caribbean Sea *16°00′N 72°30′W*
29 *R17* **Beatrice** Nebraska, C USA *40°14′N 96°43′W*
83 *L16* **Beatrice** Mashonaland East, NE Zimbabwe *18°15′S 30°55′E*
11 *N11* **Beatton** British Columbia, W Canada
11 *N11* **Beatton River** British Columbia, W Canada *57°35′N 121°45′W*
35 *V10* **Beatty** Nevada, W USA *36°53′N 116°44′W*
21 *N6* **Beattyville** Kentucky, S USA *37°33′N 83°44′W*
173 *X16* **Beau Bassin** W Mauritius *20°13′S 57°27′E*
103 *R15* **Beaucaire** Gard, S France *43°49′N 04°37′E*
14 *I8* **Beauchastel, Lac** Québec, SE Canada
14 *I10* **Beauchêne, Lac** Québec, SE Canada
183 *V3* **Beaudesert** Queensland, E Australia *28°00′S 152°27′E*
182 *M12* **Beaufort** Victoria, SE Australia *37°27′S 143°24′E*
21 *X11* **Beaufort** North Carolina, SE USA *34°44′N 76°41′W*
21 *R15* **Beaufort** South Carolina, SE USA *32°23′N 80°40′W*
38 *M11* **Beaufort Sea** *sea* Arctic Ocean
Beaufort-Wes *see* Beaufort West
83 *G25* **Beaufort West** *Afr.* Beaufort-Wes. Western Cape, SW South Africa *32°21′S 22°35′E*
103 *N7* **Beaugency** Loiret, C France *47°46′N 01°38′E*
19 *R1* **Beau Lake** Maine, NE USA
96 *I8* **Beauly** N Scotland, United Kingdom *57°29′N 04°29′W*
99 *G21* **Beaumont** Hainaut, S Belgium *50°12′N 04°13′E*
185 *E23* **Beaumont** Otago, South Island, New Zealand *45°48′S 169°32′E*
22 *M7* **Beaumont** Mississippi, S USA *31°10′N 88°55′W*
25 *X10* **Beaumont** Texas, SW USA *30°05′N 94°06′W*
102 *M15* **Beaumont-de-Lomagne** Tarn-et-Garonne, S France *43°54′N 01°00′E*
102 *L6* **Beaumont-sur-Sarthe** Sarthe, NW France *48°15′N 00°07′E*
103 *R8* **Beaune** Côte d'Or, C France *47°02′N 04°50′E*
15 *R9* **Beaupré** Québec, SE Canada *47°03′N 70°52′W*
102 *J8* **Beaupréau** Maine-et-Loire, NW France *47°13′N 00°57′W*
99 *I22* **Beauraing** Namur, SE Belgium *50°07′N 04°57′E*
103 *R12* **Beaurepaire** Isère, E France *45°20′N 05°03′E*
11 *Y16* **Beausejour** Manitoba, S Canada *50°04′N 96°30′W*
103 *N4* **Beauvais** *anc.* Bellovacum, Caesaromagus. Oise, N France *49°27′N 02°04′E*
11 *S13* **Beauval** Saskatchewan, C Canada *55°10′N 107°37′W*
102 *I9* **Beauvoir-sur-Mer** Vendée, NW France *46°54′N 02°03′W*
39 *R8* **Beaver** Alaska, USA *66°22′N 147°31′W*
26 *J8* **Beaver** Oklahoma, C USA *36°48′N 100°32′W*
18 *B14* **Beaver** Pennsylvania, NE USA *40°39′N 80°19′W*
36 *K6* **Beaver** Utah, W USA *38°16′N 112°38′W*
10 *L9* **Beaver** British Columbia/Yukon Territory, W Canada
11 *S13* **Beaver** Saskatchewan, C Canada
29 *N17* **Beaver City** Nebraska, C USA *40°08′N 99°49′W*
10 *G6* **Beaver Creek** Yukon Territory, W Canada *62°20′N 140°45′W*
31 *R14* **Beavercreek** Ohio, N USA *39°42′N 83°58′W*
39 *S8* **Beaver Creek** Alaska, USA
26 *H3* **Beaver Creek** Kansas/Nebraska, C USA
28 *J5* **Beaver Creek** Montana/North Dakota, N USA
29 *Q14* **Beaver Creek** Nebraska, C USA
25 *Q4* **Beaver Creek** Texas, SW USA
30 *M8* **Beaver Dam** Wisconsin, N USA *43°28′N 88°49′W*
30 *M8* **Beaver Dam Lake** Wisconsin, N USA
18 *B14* **Beaver Falls** Pennsylvania, NE USA *40°45′N 80°20′W*
33 *P12* **Beaverhead Mountains** ▲▲ Idaho/Montana, NW USA
33 *Q12* **Beaverhead River** Montana, NW USA
65 *A25* **Beaver Island** *island* W Falkland Islands
31 *P5* **Beaver Island** *island* Michigan, N USA
27 *S9* **Beaver Lake** Arkansas, C USA
11 *N13* **Beaverlodge** Alberta, W Canada *55°11′N 119°29′W*
18 *I8* **Beaver River** New York, NE USA
26 *J8* **Beaver River** Oklahoma, C USA
18 *B13* **Beaver River** Pennsylvania, NE USA
65 *A25* **Beaver Settlement** Beaver Island, W Falkland Islands *51°30′S 61°15′W*
Beaver State *see* Oregon
14 *H14* **Beaverton** Ontario, S Canada *44°24′N 79°07′W*
32 *G11* **Beaverton** Oregon, NW USA *45°29′N 122°49′W*
152 *G12* **Beāwar** Rājasthān, N India *26°08′N 74°22′E*
Bebas, Dasht-i *see* Bābūs, Dasht-e
60 *L8* **Bebedouro** São Paulo, S Brazil *20°58′S 48°28′W*
101 *I16* **Bebra** Hessen, C Germany *50°59′N 09°46′E*
41 *W12* **Becal** Campeche, SE Mexico *19°49′N 90°28′W*
15 *Q11* **Bécancour** Québec, SE Canada
97 *Q19* **Beccles** E England, United Kingdom *52°27′N 01°32′E*
112 *L9* **Bečej** *Ger.* Altbetsche, *Hung.* Óbecse, Rácz-Becse; *prev.* Magyar-Becse, Stari Bečej. Vojvodina, N Serbia *45°36′N 20°02′E*

◆ Country
● Country Capital
◇ Dependent Territory
○ Dependent Territory Capital
⬖ Administrative Regions
✕ International Airport
▲ Mountain
▲▲ Mountain Range
Volcano
River
Lake
Reservoir

104 I3 **Becerréa** Galicia, NW Spain *42°51′N 07°10′W*
74 H7 **Béchar** *prev.* Colomb-Béchar. W Algeria *31°38′N 02°11′W*
39 O14 **Becharof Lake** ◎ Alaska, USA
116 H15 **Bechet** *var.* Bechetu. Dolj, SW Romania *43°45′N 23°57′E*
Bechetu *see* Bechet
21 R6 **Beckley** West Virginia, NE USA *37°46′N 81°12′W*
101 G14 **Beckum** Nordrhein-Westfalen, W Germany *51°45′N 08°03′E*
25 X7 **Beckville** Texas, SW USA *32°14′N 94°27′W*
35 X4 **Becky Peak** ▲ Nevada, W USA *39°59′N 114°33′W*
116 I9 **Beclean** *Hung.* Bethlen; *prev.* Betlen. Bistriţa-Năsăud, N Romania *47°10′N 24°11′E*
Bécs *see* Wien
111 H18 **Bečva** *Ger.* Betschau, *Pol.* Beczwa. ⟿ E Czech Republic
Beczwa *see* Bečva
103 P15 **Bédarieux** Hérault, S France *43°37′N 03°10′E*
120 B10 **Beddouza, Cap** *headland* W Morocco *32°35′N 09°16′W*
80 I13 **Bedelē** Oromīya, C Ethiopia *08°25′N 36°21′E*
147 Y8 **Bedel Pass** *Rus.* Pereval Bedel. *pass* China/Kyrgyzstan
Bedel, Pereval *see* Bedel Pass
95 H22 **Beder** Århus, C Denmark *56°03′N 10°13′E*
97 N20 **Bedford** E England, United Kingdom *52°08′N 00°29′W*
31 O15 **Bedford** Indiana, N USA *38°51′N 86°29′W*
29 U16 **Bedford** Iowa, C USA *40°40′N 94°43′W*
20 L4 **Bedford** Kentucky, S USA *38°36′N 85°18′W*
18 D15 **Bedford** Pennsylvania, NE USA *40°00′N 78°29′W*
21 T6 **Bedford** Virginia, NE USA *37°20′N 79°31′W*
97 N20 **Bedfordshire** *cultural region* E England, United Kingdom
127 N5 **Bednodem'yanovsk** Penzenskaya Oblast', W Russian Federation *53°55′N 43°14′E*
98 N5 **Bedum** Groningen, NE Netherlands *53°18′N 06°36′E*
27 V11 **Beebe** Arkansas, C USA *35°04′N 91°52′W*
Beechy Group *see* Chichijima-rettō
45 T9 **Beef Island** ✈ (Road Town) Tortola, E British Virgin Islands *18°25′N 64°31′W*
Beehive State *see* Utah
99 L18 **Beek** Limburg, SE Netherlands *50°56′N 05°47′E*
99 L18 **Beek** ✈ (Maastricht) Limburg, SE Netherlands *50°55′N 05°47′E*
99 K14 **Beek-en-Donk** Noord-Brabant, S Netherlands *51°31′N 05°37′E*
138 F13 **Be'er Menuha** *prev.* Be'ér Menuḥa. Southern, S Israel *30°22′N 35°09′E*
Be'ér Menuḥa *see* Be'er Menuha
99 D16 **Beernem** West-Vlaanderen, NW Belgium *51°09′N 03°18′E*
99 I16 **Beerse** Antwerpen, N Belgium *51°20′N 04°52′E*
Beersheba *see* Be'er Sheva
138 E11 **Be'er Sheva** *var.* Beersheba, *Ar.* Bir es Saba; *prev.* Be'ér Sheva'. Southern, S Israel *31°15′N 34°47′E*
Be'ér Sheva' *see* Be'er Sheva
98 J13 **Beesd** Gelderland, C Netherlands *51°52′N 05°12′E*
99 M16 **Beesel** Limburg, SE Netherlands *51°16′N 06°02′E*
83 J21 **Beestekraal** North-West, N South Africa *25°21′S 27°40′E*
194 J7 **Beethoven Peninsula** *peninsula* Alexander Island, Antarctica
Beetstersweach *see* Beetsterzwaag
98 M6 **Beetsterzwaag** *Fris.* Beetstersweach. Friesland, N Netherlands *53°03′N 06°04′E*
25 S13 **Beeville** Texas, SW USA *28°25′N 97°47′W*
79 J18 **Befale** Equateur, NW Dem. Rep. Congo *0°25′N 20°48′E*
Befandriana *see* Befandriana Avaratra
172 J3 **Befandriana Avaratra** *var.* Befandriana, Befandriana Nord. Mahajanga, NW Madagascar *15°14′S 48°33′E*
Befandriana Nord *see* Befandriana Avaratra
79 K18 **Befori** Equateur, N Dem. Rep. Congo *0°09′N 22°18′E*
172 I7 **Befotaka** Fianarantsoa, S Madagascar *23°49′S 47°00′E*
183 R11 **Bega** New South Wales, SE Australia *36°43′S 149°50′E*
102 G5 **Bégard** Côtes d'Armor, NW France *48°37′N 03°18′W*
112 M9 **Begejski Kanal** *canal* Vojvodina, NE Serbia
94 G13 **Begna** ⟿ S Norway
Begoml' *see* Byahoml'
Begovat *see* Bekobod
153 Q13 **Begusarai** Bihār, NE India *25°25′N 86°08′E*
143 R9 **Behābād** Yazd, C Iran *32°23′N 59°50′E*
Behagle *see* Laï
55 Z10 **Béhague, Pointe** *headland* E French Guiana *04°38′N 51°52′W*
Behar *see* Bihār
142 M10 **Behbahān** *var.* Behbehān. Khūzestān, SW Iran *30°38′N 50°07′E*
Behbehān *see* Behbahān
44 G3 **Behring Point** Andros Island, W Bahamas *24°28′N 77°44′W*
143 P4 **Behshahr** *prev.* Ashraf. Māzandarān, N Iran *36°42′N 53°36′E*
163 V6 **Bei'an** Heilongjiang, NE China *48°16′N 126°29′E*
Beibunar *see* Sredishte
Beibu Wan *see* Tongking, Gulf of
Beida *see* Al Bayḍā'
80 H13 **Beigi** Oromīya, C Ethiopia *09°13′N 34°48′E*
160 L16 **Beihai** Guangxi Zhuangzu Zizhiqu, S China *21°29′N 109°10′E*
159 Q10 **Bei Hulsan Hu** ◎ C China
161 N13 **Bei Jiang** ⟿ S China
161 O2 **Beijing** *var.* Pei-ching, *Eng.* Peking; *prev.* Pei-p'ing. ● (China) Beijing Shi, E China *39°58′N 116°23′E*
161 P2 **Beijing** ✈ Beijing Shi, N China *39°54′N 116°22′E*
Beijing *see* Beijing Shi, China
161 O2 **Beijing Shi** *var.* Beijing, Jing, Pei-ching, *Eng.* Peking; *prev.* Pei-p'ing. ◐ *municipality* E China
76 G8 **Beïla** Trarza, W Mauritania *18°07′N 15°56′W*
98 N7 **Beilen** Drenthe, NE Netherlands *52°52′N 06°27′E*
160 L15 **Beiliu** *var.* Lingcheng. Guangxi Zhuangzu Zizhiqu, S China *22°50′N 110°22′E*
159 O12 **Beilu He** ⟿ W China
Beilul *see* Beylul
163 U12 **Beining** *prev.* Beizhen. Liaoning, NE China *41°34′N 121°51′E*
96 H8 **Beinn Dearg** ▲ N Scotland, United Kingdom *57°47′N 04°52′W*
Beinn MacDuibh *see* Ben Macdui
160 I12 **Beipan Jiang** ⟿ S China
163 T12 **Beipiao** Liaoning, NE China *41°49′N 120°45′E*
83 N17 **Beira** Sofala, C Mozambique *19°45′S 34°56′E*
83 N17 **Beira** ✈ Sofala, C Mozambique *19°39′S 35°05′E*
104 I7 **Beira Alta** *former province* N Portugal
104 H9 **Beira Baixa** *former province* C Portugal
104 G8 **Beira Litoral** *former province* N Portugal
Beirut *see* Beyrouth
Beisän *see* Beit She'an
11 Q16 **Beiseker** Alberta, SW Canada *51°20′N 113°34′W*
Beitai Ding *see* Wutai Shan
83 K19 **Beitbridge** Matabeleland South, S Zimbabwe *22°10′S 30°02′E*
Beit Lekhem *see* Bethlehem
138 G9 **Beit She'an** *Ar.* Baysān, Beisān; *anc.* Scythopolis, *prev.* Bet She'an. Northern, N Israel *32°30′N 35°30′E*
116 G10 **Beiuş** *Hung.* Belényes. Bihor, NW Romania *46°40′N 22°21′E*
Beizhen *see* Beining
104 H12 **Beja** *anc.* Pax Julia. Beja, SE Portugal *38°01′N 07°52′W*
74 M5 **Béja** *var.* Bājah. N Tunisia *36°45′N 09°04′E*
104 G13 **Beja** ◐ *district* S Portugal
120 I9 **Béjaïa** *var.* Bejaïa, *Fr.* Bougie; *anc.* Saldae. NE Algeria *36°49′N 05°03′E*
Bejaïa *see* Béjaïa
104 K8 **Béjar** Castilla-León, N Spain *40°24′N 05°45′W*
Bejraburi *see* Phetchaburi
Bekaa Valley *see* El Beqaa
Bekabad *see* Bekobod
Békás *see* Bicaz
169 O15 **Bekasi** Jawa, C Indonesia *06°14′S 106°59′E*
Bek-Budi *see* Qarshi
Bekdaş/Bekdash *see* Garabogaz
147 T10 **Bek-Dzhar** Oshskaya Oblast', SW Kyrgyzstan *40°22′N 73°08′E*
111 N24 **Békés** *Rom.* Bichiş. Békés, SE Hungary *46°45′N 21°09′E*
111 M24 **Békés** *off.* Békés Megye. ◐ *county* SE Hungary
111 M24 **Békéscsaba** *Rom.* Bichiş-Ciaba. Békés, SE Hungary *46°40′N 21°05′E*
Békés Megye *see* Békés
139 S2 **Bēkhma** Arbīl, E Iraq *36°40′N 44°15′E*
172 H7 **Bekily** Toliara, S Madagascar *24°12′S 45°20′E*
165 W4 **Bekkai** *var.* Betsukai. Hokkaidō, NE Japan *43°23′N 145°07′E*
147 Q11 **Bekobod** *Rus.* Bekabad; *prev.* Begovat. Toshkent Viloyati, E Uzbekistan *40°17′N 69°11′E*
127 O7 **Bekovo** Penzenskaya Oblast', W Russian Federation *52°27′N 43°41′E*
Bel *see* Beliu
152 M13 **Bela** Uttar Pradesh, N India *25°55′N 82°00′E*
149 N15 **Bela** Baluchistān, SW Pakistan *26°12′N 66°20′E*
79 F15 **Bélabo** Est, C Cameroon *04°54′N 13°10′E*
112 N10 **Bela Crkva** *Ger.* Weisskirchen, *Hung.* Fehértemplom. Vojvodina, W Serbia *44°55′N 21°28′E*
173 Y16 **Bel Air** *var.* Rivière Sèche. E Mauritius
104 L12 **Belalcázar** Andalucía, S Spain *38°33′N 05°07′W*
113 P15 **Bela Palanka** Serbia, SE Serbia *43°13′N 22°19′E*
119 H16 **Belarus** *off.* Republic of Belarus, *var.* Belorussia, *Latv.* Baltkrievija; *prev.* Belorussian SSR, *Rus.* Belorusskaya SSR. ◆ *republic* E Europe
Belarus, Republic of *see* Belarus
Belau *see* Palau
59 H21 **Bela Vista** Mato Grosso do Sul, SW Brazil *22°04′S 56°25′W*
83 L21 **Bela Vista** Maputo, S Mozambique *26°20′S 32°40′E*
168 I8 **Belawan** Sumatera, W Indonesia *03°46′N 98°44′E*
Běla Woda *see* Weisswasser
127 U4 **Belaya** ⟿ W Russian Federation
123 R7 **Belaya Gora** Respublika Sakha (Yakutiya), NE Russian Federation *68°25′N 146°12′E*
126 M11 **Belaya Kalitiva** Rostovskaya Oblast', SW Russian Federation *48°09′N 40°43′E*
125 R14 **Belaya Kholunitsa** Kirovskaya Oblast', NW Russian Federation *58°54′N 50°52′E*
Belaya Tserkov' *see* Bila Tserkva
77 V11 **Belbédji** Zinder, S Niger *14°35′N 08°00′E*
111 K14 **Bełchatów** *var.* Belchatow. Łódzkie, C Poland *51°23′N 19°20′E*
Belchatow *see* Bełchatów
Belcher, Îles *see* Belcher Islands
12 H7 **Belcher Islands** *Fr.* Îles Belcher. *island group* Nunavut, SE Canada
105 S6 **Belchite** Aragón, NE Spain *41°18′N 00°45′W*
29 O2 **Belcourt** North Dakota, N USA *48°50′N 99°44′W*
31 P9 **Belding** Michigan, N USA *43°06′N 85°13′W*
127 U5 **Belebey** Respublika Bashkortostan, W Russian Federation *54°04′N 54°13′E*
81 N16 **Beledweyne** *var.* Belet Huen, *It.* Belet Uen. Hiiraan, C Somalia *04°39′N 45°12′E*
146 B10 **Belek** Balkan Welaýaty, W Turkmenistan *39°57′N 53°51′E*
58 L12 **Belém** *var.* Pará. *state capital* Pará, N Brazil *01°27′S 48°29′W*
65 I14 **Belém Ridge** *undersea feature* C Atlantic Ocean
62 I7 **Belén** Catamarca, NW Argentina *27°36′N 67°00′W*
54 G9 **Belén** Boyacá, C Colombia *06°01′N 72°55′W*
42 J11 **Belén** Rivas, SW Nicaragua *11°30′N 85°55′W*
62 O5 **Belén** Concepción, C Paraguay *23°25′S 57°14′W*
61 D16 **Belén** Salto, N Uruguay *30°47′S 57°47′W*
37 R12 **Belen** New Mexico, SW USA *34°37′N 106°46′W*
61 D20 **Belén de Escobar** Buenos Aires, E Argentina *34°21′S 58°47′W*
114 J7 **Belene** Pleven, N Bulgaria *43°39′N 25°09′E*
114 J7 **Belene, Ostrov** *island* N Bulgaria
43 R15 **Belén, Río** ⟿ C Panama
Belényes *see* Beiuş
Embalse de Belesar *see* Belesar, Encoro de
104 H3 **Belesar, Encoro de** *Sp.* Embalse de Belesar. ⊠ NW Spain
Belet Huen/Belet Uen *see* Beledweyne
126 J5 **Belëv** Tul'skaya Oblast', W Russian Federation *53°48′N 36°07′E*
19 R7 **Belfast** Maine, NE USA *44°25′N 69°02′W*
97 G15 **Belfast** *Ir.* Béal Feirste. ◐ E Northern Ireland, United Kingdom *54°35′N 05°55′W*
97 G15 **Belfast Aldergrove** ✈ E Northern Ireland, United Kingdom *54°37′N 06°11′W*
97 G15 **Belfast Lough** *Ir.* Loch Lao. *inlet* E Northern Ireland, United Kingdom
28 K5 **Belfield** North Dakota, N USA *46°53′N 103°12′W*
103 U7 **Belfort** Territoire-de-Belfort, E France *47°38′N 06°52′E*
Belgard *see* Białogard
155 E17 **Belgaum** Karnātaka, W India *15°52′N 74°30′E*
Belgian Congo *see* Congo (Democratic Republic of)
195 T3 **Belgicafjella** *var.* Mount Victor. ▲ Antarctica *72°49′S 33°01′E*
België/Belgique *see* Belgium
99 F20 **Belgium** *off.* Kingdom of Belgium, *Dut.* België, *Fr.* Belgique. ◆ *monarchy* NW Europe
Belgium, Kingdom of *see* Belgium
126 J8 **Belgorod** Belgorodskaya Oblast', W Russian Federation *50°38′N 36°37′E*
Belgorod-Dnestrovskiy *see* Bilhorod-Dnistrovs'kyy
126 J8 **Belgorodskaya Oblast'** ◐ *province* W Russian Federation
Belgrad *see* Beograd
29 T8 **Belgrade** Minnesota, N USA *45°27′N 94°59′W*
33 S11 **Belgrade** Montana, NW USA *45°46′N 111°10′W*
Belgrade *see* Beograd
Belgrano, Cabo *see* Meredith, Cape
195 N5 **Belgrano II** *Argentinian research station* Antarctica *77°50′S 35°25′W*
21 X9 **Belhaven** North Carolina, SE USA *35°36′N 76°50′W*
107 I23 **Belice** *anc.* Hypsas. ⟿ Sicilia, Italy, C Mediterranean Sea
Belice *see* Belize/Belize City
113 M16 **Beli Drim** *Alb.* Drini i Bardhë. ⟿ Albania/Serbia
127 R17 **Belidzhi** Respublika Dagestan, SW Russian Federation *41°53′N 48°24′E*
Beligrad *see* Berat
188 C8 **Beliliou** *prev.* Peleliu. *island* S Palau
114 L8 **Beli Lom, Yazovir** ⊠ NE Bulgaria
112 I8 **Beli Manastir** *Hung.* Pélmonostor; *prev.* Monostor. Osijek-Baranja, NE Croatia *45°46′N 16°38′E*
102 J13 **Bélin-Béliet** Gironde, SW France *44°30′N 00°48′W*
79 F17 **Bélinga** Ogooué-Ivindo, NE Gabon *01°05′N 13°12′E*
21 S4 **Belington** West Virginia, NE USA *39°01′N 79°57′W*
127 O6 **Belinskiy** Penzenskaya Oblast', W Russian Federation *52°58′N 43°25′E*
169 N12 **Belinyu** Pulau Bangka, W Indonesia *01°37′S 105°45′E*
169 O13 **Belitung, Pulau** *island* W Indonesia
116 F10 **Beliu** *Hung.* Bel. Arad, W Romania *46°31′N 21°57′E*
114 N9 **Beli Vit** ⟿ NW Bulgaria
42 G2 **Belize** *Sp.* Belice; *prev.* British Honduras, Colony of Belize. ◆ *commonwealth republic* Central America
42 F2 **Belize** *Sp.* Belice. ◐ *district* NE Belize
42 G2 **Belize** ⟿ Belize/Guatemala
Belize *see* Belize City
42 G2 **Belize City** *var.* Belize, *Sp.* Belice. Belize, NE Belize *17°29′N 88°10′W*
42 G2 **Belize City** ✈ Belize, NE Belize *17°31′N 88°15′W*
Belize, Colony of *see* Belize
Beljak *see* Villach
39 N16 **Belkofski** Alaska, USA *55°07′N 162°04′W*
123 O6 **Bel'kovskiy, Ostrov** *island* Novosibirskiye Ostrova, NE Russian Federation
14 J8 **Bell** ⟿ Québec, SE Canada
10 J15 **Bella Bella** British Columbia, SW Canada *52°04′N 128°07′W*
102 M10 **Bellac** Haute-Vienne, C France *46°07′N 01°04′E*
10 K15 **Bella Coola** British Columbia, SW Canada *52°23′N 126°46′W*
106 D6 **Bellagio** Lombardia, N Italy *45°58′N 09°15′E*
31 P6 **Bellaire** Michigan, N USA *44°59′N 85°12′W*
106 D6 **Bellano** Lombardia, N Italy *46°06′N 09°21′E*
155 G17 **Bellary** *var.* Ballari. Karnātaka, S India *15°11′N 76°54′E*
183 S5 **Bellata** New South Wales, SE Australia *29°58′S 149°49′E*
61 D16 **Bella Unión** Artigas, N Uruguay *30°18′S 57°35′W*
61 C14 **Bella Vista** Corrientes, NE Argentina *28°30′S 59°03′W*
62 J7 **Bella Vista** Tucumán, N Argentina *27°05′S 65°19′W*
62 P4 **Bella Vista** Amambay, C Paraguay *22°08′S 56°20′W*
56 B10 **Bellavista** Cajamarca, N Peru *05°43′S 78°48′W*
56 D11 **Bellavista** San Martín, N Peru *07°04′S 76°35′W*
183 U6 **Bellbrook** New South Wales, SE Australia *30°48′S 152°32′E*
27 V5 **Belle** Missouri, C USA *38°17′N 91°43′W*
21 Q5 **Belle** West Virginia, NE USA *38°13′N 81°32′W*
31 R13 **Bellefontaine** Ohio, N USA *40°22′N 83°45′W*
18 F14 **Bellefonte** Pennsylvania, NE USA *40°54′N 77°43′W*
28 J9 **Belle Fourche** South Dakota, N USA *44°40′N 103°50′W*
28 J9 **Belle Fourche Reservoir** ⊠ South Dakota, N USA
28 K9 **Belle Fourche River** ⟿ South Dakota/Wyoming, N USA
103 S10 **Bellegarde-sur-Valserine** Ain, E France *46°06′N 05°49′E*
23 Y14 **Belle Glade** Florida, SE USA *26°40′N 80°40′W*
102 G8 **Belle Île** *island* NW France
13 T9 **Belle Isle** *island* Belle Isle, Newfoundland and Labrador, E Canada
13 S10 **Belle Isle, Strait of** *strait* Newfoundland and Labrador, E Canada
Bellenz *see* Bellinzona
29 W14 **Belle Plaine** Iowa, C USA *41°54′N 92°16′W*
29 V9 **Belle Plaine** Minnesota, N USA *44°39′N 93°47′W*
14 J9 **Belleterre** Québec, SE Canada *47°24′N 78°40′W*
14 J15 **Belleville** Ontario, SE Canada *44°10′N 77°22′W*
103 R10 **Belleville** Rhône, E France *46°09′N 04°42′E*
30 K15 **Belleville** Illinois, N USA *38°31′N 89°59′W*
27 N3 **Belleville** Kansas, C USA *39°51′N 97°38′W*
29 Z13 **Bellevue** Iowa, C USA *42°15′N 90°25′W*
29 S15 **Bellevue** Nebraska, C USA *41°08′N 95°53′W*
31 S11 **Bellevue** Ohio, N USA *41°16′N 82°50′W*
25 S5 **Bellevue** Texas, SW USA *33°38′N 98°00′W*
32 H8 **Bellevue** Washington, NW USA *47°36′N 122°12′W*
55 Y11 **Bellevue de l'Inini, Montagnes** ▲▲ S French Guiana
103 S11 **Belley** Ain, E France *45°46′N 05°41′E*
Bellin *see* Kangirsuk
183 V6 **Bellingen** New South Wales, SE Australia *30°27′S 152°53′E*
97 L14 **Bellingham** N England, United Kingdom *55°09′N 02°16′W*
32 H6 **Bellingham** Washington, NW USA *48°46′N 122°29′W*
Belling Hausen Mulde *see* Southeast Pacific Basin
194 H2 **Bellingshausen** *Russian research station* South Shetland Islands, Antarctica *61°57′S 58°23′W*
Bellingshausen *see* Motu One
Bellingshausen Abyssal Plain *see* Bellingshausen Plain
196 R14 **Bellingshausen Plain** *var.* Bellingshausen Abyssal Plain. *undersea feature* SE Pacific Ocean *64°00′S 90°00′W*
194 I8 **Bellingshausen Sea** *sea* Antarctica
98 P6 **Bellingwolde** Groningen, NE Netherlands *53°07′N 07°10′E*
108 H11 **Bellinzona** *Ger.* Bellenz. Ticino, S Switzerland *46°12′N 09°02′E*
25 T8 **Bellmead** Texas, SW USA *31°36′N 97°02′W*
54 E8 **Bello** Antioquia, W Colombia *06°19′N 75°34′W*
61 B21 **Bellocq** Buenos Aires, E Argentina *35°55′S 61°32′W*
Bello Horizonte *see* Belo Horizonte
186 L10 **Bellona** *var.* Mungiki. *island* S Solomon Islands
Bellovacum *see* Beauvais
182 D7 **Bell, Point** *headland* South Australia *32°13′S 133°08′E*
20 F9 **Bells** Tennessee, S USA *35°42′N 89°05′W*
25 U5 **Bells** Texas, SW USA *33°36′N 96°24′W*
92 N3 **Bellsund** *inlet* SW Svalbard
106 H6 **Belluno** Veneto, NE Italy *46°08′N 12°13′E*
62 L11 **Bell Ville** Córdoba, C Argentina *32°35′S 62°41′W*
83 E26 **Bellville** Western Cape, SW South Africa *33°50′S 18°43′E*
25 U11 **Bellville** Texas, SW USA *29°57′N 96°15′W*
104 L12 **Belmez** Andalucía, S Spain *38°16′N 05°12′W*
29 V12 **Belmond** Iowa, C USA *42°51′N 93°36′W*
18 E11 **Belmont** New York, NE USA *42°14′N 78°02′W*
21 R10 **Belmont** North Carolina, SE USA *35°13′N 81°01′W*
59 O18 **Belmonte** Bahia, E Brazil *15°53′S 38°54′W*
104 I8 **Belmonte** Castelo Branco, C Portugal *40°21′N 07°20′W*
105 P10 **Belmonte** Castilla-La Mancha, C Spain *39°34′N 02°43′W*
42 G2 **Belmopan** ● (Belize) Cayo, C Belize *17°13′N 88°48′W*
97 B16 **Belmullet** *Ir.* Béal an Mhuirhead. Mayo, W Ireland *54°14′N 09°59′W*
99 E20 **Belœil** Hainaut, SW Belgium *50°33′N 03°45′E*
123 R13 **Belogorsk** Amurskaya Oblast', SE Russian Federation *50°53′N 128°24′E*
Belogorsk *see* Bilohirs'k
114 F7 **Belogradchik** Vidin, NW Bulgaria *43°37′N 22°42′E*
172 H8 **Beloha** Toliara, S Madagascar *25°09′S 45°04′E*
59 M20 **Belo Horizonte** *prev.* Bello Horizonte. *state capital* Minas Gerais, SE Brazil *19°54′S 43°54′W*
26 M3 **Beloit** Kansas, C USA *39°27′N 98°06′W*
30 L9 **Beloit** Wisconsin, N USA *42°31′N 89°01′W*
Belokorovichi *see* Novi Bilokorovychi
124 J8 **Belomorsk** Respublika Kareliya, NW Russian Federation *64°30′N 34°43′E*
124 J8 **Belomorsko-Baltiyskiy Kanal** *Eng.* White Sea-Baltic Canal, White Sea Canal. *canal* NW Russian Federation
153 V15 **Belonia** Tripura, NE India *23°15′N 91°25′E*
Belopol'ye *see* Bilopillya
105 O4 **Belorado** Castilla-León, N Spain *42°25′N 03°11′W*
126 L14 **Belorechensk** Krasnodarskiy Kray, SW Russian Federation *44°46′N 39°53′E*
127 W5 **Beloretsk** Respublika Bashkortostan, W Russian Federation *53°56′N 58°26′E*
Belorussia/Belorussian SSR *see* Belarus
Belorusskaya Gryada *see* Byelaruskaya Hrada
Belorusskaya SSR *see* Belarus
Beloshchel'ye *see* Nar'yan-Mar
114 N8 **Beloslav** Varna, E Bulgaria *43°13′N 27°42′E*
Belostok *see* Białystok
Belo-sur-Tsiribihina *see* Belo Tsiribihina
172 H5 **Belo Tsiribihina** *var.* Belo-sur-Tsiribihina. Toliara, W Madagascar *19°40′S 44°30′E*
Belovár *see* Bjelovar
Belovezhskaya, Pushcha *see* Białowieska, Puszcza/Byelavyezhskaya, Pushcha
114 H10 **Belovo** Pazardzhik, C Bulgaria *42°10′N 24°01′E*
Belovodsk *see* Bilovods'k
122 H9 **Beloyarskiy** Khanty-Mansiyskiy Avtonomnyy Okrug-Yugra, N Russian Federation *63°40′N 66°31′E*
124 K7 **Beloye More** *Eng.* White Sea. *sea* NW Russian Federation
124 K13 **Beloye, Ozero** ◎ NW Russian Federation
114 J10 **Belozem** Plovdiv, C Bulgaria *42°11′N 25°00′E*
124 K13 **Belozërsk** Vologodskaya Oblast', NW Russian Federation *59°59′N 37°49′E*
108 D8 **Belp** Bern, W Switzerland *46°54′N 07°31′E*
108 D8 **Belp** ✈ (Bern) Bern, C Switzerland *46°55′N 07°29′E*
107 L24 **Belpasso** Sicilia, Italy, C Mediterranean Sea *37°35′N 14°59′E*
31 U14 **Belpre** Ohio, N USA *39°14′N 81°34′W*
98 M8 **Belterwijde** ◎ N Netherlands
27 R4 **Belton** Missouri, C USA *38°48′N 94°31′W*
21 P11 **Belton** South Carolina, SE USA *34°31′N 82°29′W*
25 T9 **Belton** Texas, SW USA *31°04′N 97°30′W*
25 S9 **Belton Lake** ⊠ Texas, SW USA
Bel'tsy *see* Bălţi
97 E16 **Belturbet** *Ir.* Béal Tairbirt. Cavan, N Ireland *54°06′N 07°26′W*
Beluchistan *see* Baluchistān
145 Z9 **Belukha, Gora** ▲ Kazakhstan/Russian Federation *49°50′N 86°44′E*
107 M20 **Belvedere Marittimo** Calabria, SW Italy *39°37′N 15°52′E*
30 L10 **Belvidere** Illinois, N USA *42°15′N 88°50′W*
18 J14 **Belvidere** New Jersey, NE USA *40°50′N 75°05′W*
Bely *see* Belyy
127 V8 **Belyayevka** Orenburgskaya Oblast', W Russian Federation *51°25′N 56°26′E*
Belynichi *see* Byalynichy
124 H17 **Belyy** *var.* Bely, Beyj. Tverskaya Oblast', W Russian Federation *55°51′N 32°57′E*
126 I6 **Belyye Berega** Bryanskaya Oblast', W Russian Federation *53°11′N 34°42′E*
122 J6 **Belyy, Ostrov** *island* N Russian Federation
122 J11 **Belyy Yar** Tomskaya Oblast', C Russian Federation *58°26′N 84°57′E*
100 N13 **Belzig** Brandenburg, NE Germany *52°09′N 12°37′E*
22 K4 **Belzoni** Mississippi, S USA *33°10′N 90°29′W*
172 H4 **Bemaraha** *var.* Plateau du Bemaraha. ▲ W Madagascar
Bemaraha, Plateau du *see* Bemaraha
82 B10 **Bembe** Uíge, NW Angola *07°03′S 14°25′E*
77 S14 **Bembèrèkè** *var.* Bimbéréké. N Benin *10°10′N 02°41′E*
104 K12 **Bembézar** ⟿ SW Spain
104 J3 **Bembibre** Castilla-León, N Spain *42°37′N 06°25′W*
29 T4 **Bemidji** Minnesota, N USA *47°27′N 94°53′W*
98 L12 **Bemmel** Gelderland, SE Netherlands *51°53′N 05°54′E*
171 T13 **Bemu** Pulau Seram, E Indonesia *03°21′S 129°58′E*
Benāb *see* Bonāb
105 T5 **Benabarre** *var.* Benavarn. Aragón, NE Spain *42°06′N 00°28′E*
Benaco *see* Garda, Lago di
79 L20 **Bena-Dibele** Kasai-Oriental, C Dem. Rep. Congo *04°01′S 22°50′E*
105 R9 **Benagéber, Embalse de** ⊠ E Spain
183 O11 **Benalla** Victoria, SE Australia *36°33′S 146°00′E*
104 M14 **Benamejí** Andalucía, S Spain *37°16′N 04°33′W*
Benares *see* Vārānasi
Benavarn *see* Benabarre
104 F10 **Benavente** Santarém, C Portugal *38°59′N 08°49′W*
104 K5 **Benavente** Castilla-León, N Spain *42°00′N 05°40′W*
25 S15 **Benavides** Texas, SW USA *27°36′N 98°24′W*
96 F8 **Benbecula** *island* NW Scotland, United Kingdom
Bencovazzo *see* Benkovac
32 H13 **Bend** Oregon, NW USA *44°04′N 121°19′W*
182 K7 **Benda Range** ▲ South Australia
183 T6 **Bendemeer** New South Wales, SE Australia *30°54′S 151°12′E*
Bender *see* Tighina
Bender Beila/Bender Beyla *see* Bandarbeyla
Bender Cassim/Bender Qaasim *see* Boosaaso
Bendery *see* Tighina
183 N11 **Bendigo** Victoria, SE Australia *36°46′S 144°19′E*
118 E10 **Bēne** Dobele, SW Latvia *56°30′N 23°04′E*
98 K13 **Beneden-Leeuwen** Gelderland, C Netherlands *51°52′N 05°32′E*
101 L24 **Benediktenwand** ▲ S Germany *47°39′N 11°28′E*
Benemérita de San Cristóbal *see* San Cristóbal
77 N12 **Bénéna** Ségou, S Mali *13°04′N 04°20′W*
172 I7 **Benenitra** Toliara, S Madagascar *23°25′S 45°06′E*
Beneschau *see* Benešov
Beneški Zaliv *see* Venice, Gulf of
111 D17 **Benešov** *Ger.* Beneschau. Středočeský Kraj, W Czech Republic *49°48′N 14°41′E*
123 Q5 **Benetta, Ostrov** *island* Novosibirskiye Ostrova, NE Russian Federation
107 L17 **Benevento** *anc.* Beneventum, Malventum. Campania, S Italy *41°07′N 14°45′E*
Beneventum *see* Benevento
173 S3 **Bengal, Bay of** *bay* N Indian Ocean
Bengalooru *see* Bangalore
79 M17 **Bengamisa** Orientale, N Dem. Rep. Congo *0°58′N 25°11′E*
Bengasi *see* Banghāzī
Bengazi *see* Banghāzī
161 P7 **Bengbu** *var.* Peng-pu. Anhui, E China *32°57′N 117°17′E*
32 L9 **Benge** Washington, NW USA *46°55′N 118°01′W*
Benghazi *see* Banghāzī
168 K10 **Bengkalis** Pulau Bengkalis, W Indonesia *01°27′N 102°10′E*
168 K10 **Bengkalis, Pulau** *island* W Indonesia
169 Q10 **Bengkayang** Borneo, C Indonesia *0°45′N 109°28′E*
168 K14 **Bengkulu** *prev.* Bengkoeloe, Benkoelen, Benkulen. Sumatera, W Indonesia *03°46′S 102°16′E*
168 K13 **Bengkulu** *off.* Propinsi Bengkulu; *prev.* Bengkoeloe, Benkoelen, Benkulen. ◐ *province* W Indonesia
Bengkulu, Propinsi *see* Bengkulu
82 A11 **Bengo** ◐ *province* W Angola
95 J16 **Bengtsfors** Västra Götaland, S Sweden *59°03′N 12°14′E*
82 B13 **Benguela** *var.* Benguella. Benguela, W Angola *12°35′S 13°30′E*
83 A14 **Benguela** ◐ *province* W Angola
Benguella *see* Benguela
138 F10 **Ben Gurion** ✈ Tel Aviv, C Israel *32°04′N 34°45′E*
Bengweulu, Lake *see* Bangweulu, Lake
Benha *see* Banhā
192 F6 **Benham Seamount** *undersea feature* W Philippine Sea *15°48′N 124°15′E*
96 H6 **Ben Hope** ▲ N Scotland, United Kingdom *58°25′N 04°36′W*
79 P18 **Beni** Nord-Kivu, NE Dem. Rep. Congo *0°31′N 29°30′E*
57 L15 **Beni** *var.* El Beni. ◐ *department* N Bolivia
74 H8 **Beni Abbès** W Algeria *30°07′N 02°09′W*
105 T8 **Benicarló** País Valenciano, E Spain *40°25′N 00°25′E*
105 T9 **Benicàssim** *Cat.* Benicàssim. País Valenciano, E Spain *40°03′N 00°03′E*
Benicàssim *see* Benicàssim
105 T12 **Benidorm** País Valenciano, SE Spain *38°33′N 00°09′W*
Beni Mazâr *see* Banī Mazār
121 C11 **Beni-Mellal** C Morocco *32°20′N 06°21′W*
77 R14 **Benin** *off.* Republic of Benin; *prev.* Dahomey. ◆ *republic* W Africa
77 S17 **Benin, Bight of** *gulf* W Africa
77 U16 **Benin City** Edo, SW Nigeria *06°23′N 05°40′E*
Benin, Republic of *see* Benin
57 K16 **Beni, Río** ⟿ N Bolivia
120 F10 **Beni Saf** *var.* Beni-Saf. NW Algeria *35°19′N 01°23′W*
Beni-Saf *see* Beni Saf
105 T11 **Benissa** País Valenciano, E Spain *38°43′N 00°03′E*
Beni Suef *see* Banī Suwayf
11 V15 **Benito** Manitoba, S Canada *51°57′N 101°24′W*
Benito *see* Uolo, Río
61 C23 **Benito Juárez** Buenos Aires, E Argentina *37°43′S 59°48′W*
41 P14 **Benito Juárez Internacional** ✈ (México) México, S Mexico *19°24′N 99°02′W*
25 P5 **Benjamin** Texas, SW USA *33°35′N 99°49′W*
58 B13 **Benjamin Constant** Amazonas, N Brazil *04°22′S 70°02′W*
40 F4 **Benjamín Hill** Sonora, NW Mexico *30°13′N 111°08′W*
63 F19 **Benjamín, Isla** *island* Archipiélago de los Chonos, S Chile
164 Q4 **Benkei-misaki** *headland* Hokkaidō, NE Japan *42°49′N 140°10′E*
28 L17 **Benkelman** Nebraska, C USA *40°04′N 101°30′W*
96 I7 **Ben Klibreck** ▲ N Scotland, United Kingdom *58°15′N 04°23′W*
Benkoelen/Bengkoeloe *see* Bengkulu
112 D13 **Benkovac** *It.* Bencovazzo. Zadar, SW Croatia *44°02′N 15°36′E*
Benkulen *see* Bengkulu
96 I11 **Ben Lawers** ▲ C Scotland, United Kingdom *56°33′N 04°13′W*
96 J9 **Ben Macdui** *var.* Beinn MacDuibh. ▲ C Scotland, United Kingdom *57°02′N 03°42′W*
96 G11 **Ben More** ▲ W Scotland, United Kingdom *56°26′N 06°00′W*
96 I11 **Ben More** ▲ C Scotland, United Kingdom *56°22′N 04°31′W*
96 H7 **Ben More Assynt** ▲ N Scotland, United Kingdom *58°09′N 04°51′W*
185 E20 **Benmore, Lake** ◎ South Island, New Zealand
98 L12 **Bennekom** Gelderland, SE Netherlands *52°00′N 05°40′E*
21 T11 **Bennettsville** South Carolina, SE USA *34°36′N 79°40′W*
96 H10 **Ben Nevis** ▲ N Scotland, United Kingdom *56°80′N 05°00′W*
184 M9 **Benneydale** Waikato, North Island, New Zealand *38°31′S 175°22′E*
Bennichab *see* Bennichchâb
76 H8 **Bennichchâb** *var.* Bennichab. Inchiri, W Mauritania *19°26′N 15°21′W*
18 L10 **Bennington** Vermont, NE USA *42°51′N 73°09′W*
185 E20 **Ben Ohau Range** ▲▲ South Island, New Zealand
83 J21 **Benoni** Gauteng, NE South Africa *26°04′S 28°18′E*
172 J2 **Be, Nosy** *var.* Nossi-Bé. *island* NW Madagascar
Bénoué *see* Benue
42 F2 **Benque Viejo del Carmen** Cayo, W Belize *17°04′N 89°08′W*
101 G19 **Bensheim** Hessen, W Germany *49°41′N 08°38′E*
37 N16 **Benson** Arizona, SW USA *31°55′N 110°16′W*
29 S8 **Benson** Minnesota, N USA *45°19′N 95°36′W*
21 U10 **Benson** North Carolina, SE USA *35°22′N 78°33′W*
171 N15 **Benteng** Pulau Selayar, C Indonesia *06°07′S 120°28′E*
83 A14 **Bentiaba** Namibe, SW Angola *14°18′S 12°27′E*
181 T4 **Bentinck Island** *island* Wellesley Islands, Queensland, N Australia
80 E13 **Bentiu** Wahda, S Sudan *09°14′N 29°49′E*
138 G8 **Bent Jbaïl** *var.* Bint Jubayl. S Lebanon *33°07′N 35°26′E*
11 Q15 **Bentley** Alberta, SW Canada *52°27′N 114°02′W*
61 I15 **Bento Gonçalves** Rio Grande do Sul, S Brazil *29°12′S 51°34′W*
27 U12 **Benton** Arkansas, C USA *34°34′N 92°35′W*
30 L16 **Benton** Illinois, N USA *38°00′N 88°55′W*
20 H7 **Benton** Kentucky, S USA *36°51′N 88°21′W*
22 G5 **Benton** Louisiana, S USA *32°41′N 93°44′W*
27 Y7 **Benton** Missouri, C USA *37°05′N 89°34′W*
20 M10 **Benton** Tennessee, S USA *35°10′N 84°39′W*
31 O10 **Benton Harbor** Michigan, N USA *42°07′N 86°27′W*
27 S9 **Bentonville** Arkansas, C USA *36°23′N 94°13′W*
77 V16 **Benue** ◐ *state* SE Nigeria
78 F13 **Benue** *Fr.* Bénoué. ⟿ Cameroon/Nigeria
163 V12 **Benxi** *prev.* Pen-ch'i, Penhsihu, Penki. Liaoning, NE China *41°20′N 123°45′E*
Benyakoni *see* Byenyakoni
112 K10 **Beočin** Vojvodina, N Serbia *45°13′N 19°43′E*
Beodericsworth *see* Bury St Edmunds
112 M11 **Beograd** *Eng.* Belgrade, *Ger.* Belgrad; *anc.* Singidunum. ● (Serbia) Serbia, N Serbia *44°48′N 20°27′E*
112 L11 **Beograd** *Eng.* Belgrade. ✈ Serbia, N Serbia *44°45′N 20°21′E*
76 M16 **Béoumi** C Ivory Coast *07°40′N 05°34′W*
35 V3 **Beowawe** Nevada, W USA *40°33′N 116°31′W*
164 E14 **Beppu** Ōita, Kyūshū, SW Japan *33°18′N 131°30′E*
187 X15 **Beqa** *prev.* Mbengga. *island* W Fiji
45 Y14 **Bequia** *island* C Saint Vincent and the Grenadines
113 L16 **Berane** *prev.* Ivangrad. E Montenegro *42°51′N 19°51′E*
113 L21 **Berat** *var.* Berati, *SCr.* Beligrad. Berat, C Albania *40°43′N 19°58′E*
113 L21 **Berat** ◐ *district* C Albania
Berătău *see* Berettyó
Berati *see* Berat
Beraun *see* Berounka, Czech Republic
Beraun *see* Beroun, Czech Republic
171 U13 **Berau, Teluk** *var.* MacCluer Gulf. *bay* Papua, E Indonesia
80 G8 **Berber** River Nile, NE Sudan *18°01′N 34°00′E*
80 N12 **Berbera** Sahil, NW Somalia *10°24′N 45°02′E*
79 H16 **Berbérati** Mambéré-Kadéï, SW Central African Republic *04°14′N 15°50′E*
Berberia, Cabo de *see* Barbaria, Cap de

◆ Country
● Country Capital
◇ Dependent Territory
○ Dependent Territory Capital
◐ Administrative Regions
✈ International Airport
▲ Mountain
▲▲ Mountain Range
Volcano
⟿ River
◎ Lake
⊠ Reservoir

55 T9 **Berbice River** ≈ NE Guyana
Berchid see Berrechid
103 N2 **Berck-Plage** Pas-de-Calais, N France 50°24′N 01°35′E
25 T13 **Berclair** Texas, SW USA 28°33′N 97°32′W
117 W10 **Berda** ≈ SE Ukraine
Berdichev see Berdychiv
123 P10 **Berdigestyakh** Respublika Sakha (Yakutiya), NE Russian Federation 62°02′N 127°03′E
122 J12 **Berdsk** Novosibirskaya Oblast', C Russian Federation 54°42′N 82°56′E
117 W10 **Berdyans'k** *Rus.* Berdyansk; *prev.* Osipenko. Zaporiz'ka Oblast', SE Ukraine 46°46′N 36°49′E
117 W10 **Berdyans'ka Kosa** *spit* SE Ukraine
117 V10 **Berdyans'ka Zatoka** *gulf* S Ukraine
117 N5 **Berdychiv** *Rus.* Berdichev. Zhytomyrs'ka Oblast', N Ukraine 49°54′N 28°39′E
20 M6 **Berea** Kentucky, S USA 37°34′N 84°18′W
Beregovo/Beregszász see Berehove
116 G8 **Berehove** *Cz.* Berehovo, *Hung.* Beregszász, *Rus.* Beregovo. Zakarpats'ka Oblast', W Ukraine 48°13′N 22°39′E
Berehovo see Berehove
186 D9 **Bereina** Central, S Papua New Guinea 08°29′S 146°30′E
146 C11 **Bereket** *prev. Rus.* Gazandzhyk, Kazandzhik, *Turkm.* Gazanjyk. Balkan Welaýaty, W Turkmenistan 39°17′N 55°27′E
45 O12 **Berekua** S Dominica 15°14′N 61°19′W
77 O16 **Berekum** W Ghana 07°27′N 02°35′W
Berenice see Baranice
11 O14 **Berens** ≈ Manitoba/Ontario, C Canada
11 X14 **Berens River** Manitoba, C Canada 52°22′N 97°00′W
29 R12 **Beresford** South Dakota, N USA 43°02′N 96°45′W
116 J4 **Berestechko** Volyns'ka Oblast', NW Ukraine 50°21′N 25°06′E
116 M11 **Bereşti** Galaţi, E Romania 46°04′N 27°54′E
117 U6 **Berestova** ≈ E Ukraine
Beretău see Berettyó
111 N23 **Berettyó** *Rom.* Barcău; *prev.* Berătău, Beretău. ≈ Hungary/Romania
111 N23 **Berettyóújfalu** Hajdú-Bihar, E Hungary 47°15′N 21°33′E
Berëza/Bereza Kartuska see Byaroza
117 Q4 **Berezan'** Kyyivs'ka Oblast', N Ukraine 50°18′N 31°30′E
117 Q10 **Berezanka** Mykolayivs'ka Oblast', S Ukraine 46°51′N 31°24′E
116 J6 **Berezhany** *Pol.* Brzeżany. Ternopil's'ka Oblast', W Ukraine 49°29′N 25°00′E
Berezina see Byerezino
Berezino see Byerazino
117 P10 **Berezivka** *Rus.* Berezovka. Odes'ka Oblast', SW Ukraine 47°12′N 30°56′E
117 Q2 **Berezna** Chernihivs'ka Oblast', NE Ukraine 51°35′N 31°50′E
116 L3 **Berezne** Rivnens'ka Oblast', NW Ukraine 51°00′N 26°46′E
117 R9 **Bereznehuvate** Mykolayivs'ka Oblast', S Ukraine 47°18′N 32°52′E
125 N10 **Bereznik** Arkhangel'skaya Oblast', NW Russian Federation 62°50′N 42°40′E
125 U13 **Berezniki** Permskaya Oblast', NW Russian Federation 59°26′N 56°49′E
Berëzovka see Byarozawka, Belarus
Berezovka see Berezivka, Ukraine
122 H9 **Berezovo** Khanty-Mansiyskiy Avtonomnyy Okrug-Yugra, N Russian Federation 63°48′N 64°38′E
127 O9 **Berezovskaya** Volgogradskaya Oblast', SW Russian Federation 50°17′N 43°58′E
123 S13 **Berezovyy** Khabarovskiy Kray, E Russian Federation 51°42′N 135°39′E
83 E25 **Berg** ≈ W South Africa
Berg see Berg bei Rohrbach
105 V4 **Berga** Cataluña, NE Spain 42°06′N 01°41′E
95 N20 **Berga** Kalmar, S Sweden 57°13′N 16°03′E
136 B13 **Bergama** İzmir, W Turkey 39°08′N 27°10′E
106 E7 **Bergamo** *anc.* Bergomum. Lombardia, N Italy 45°42′N 09°40′E
105 P3 **Bergara** País Vasco, N Spain 43°05′N 02°25′W
109 S3 **Berg bei Rohrbach** *var.* Berg. Oberösterreich, N Austria 48°34′N 14°02′E
100 O6 **Bergen** Mecklenburg-Vorpommern, NE Germany 54°25′N 13°25′E
101 I11 **Bergen** Niedersachsen, NW Germany 52°49′N 09°57′E
98 H8 **Bergen** Noord-Holland, NW Netherlands 52°40′N 04°42′E
94 C13 **Bergen** Hordaland, S Norway 60°24′N 05°19′E
Bergen see Mons
55 W9 **Berg en Dal** Brokopondo, C Surinam 05°15′N 55°20′W
99 G15 **Bergen op Zoom** Noord-Brabant, S Netherlands 51°30′N 04°17′E
102 L13 **Bergerac** Dordogne, SW France 44°51′N 00°30′E
99 J16 **Bergeyk** Noord-Brabant, S Netherlands 51°19′N 05°21′E
101 D16 **Bergheim** Nordrhein-Westfalen, W Germany 50°57′N 06°39′E
55 X10 **Bergi** Sipaliwini, E Surinam 04°36′N 54°24′W
101 E16 **Bergisch Gladbach** Nordrhein-Westfalen, W Germany 50°59′N 07°09′E
101 F14 **Bergkamen** Nordrhein-Westfalen, W Germany 51°32′N 07°41′E
95 N21 **Bergkvara** Kalmar, S Sweden 56°22′N 16°04′E
Bergomum see Bergamo
98 K13 **Bergse Maas** ≈ S Netherlands
95 P15 **Bergshamra** Stockholm, C Sweden 59°37′N 18°40′E
94 N10 **Bergsjö** Gävleborg, C Sweden 62°00′N 17°10′E
93 J14 **Bergsviken** Norrbotten, N Sweden 65°16′N 21°24′E
98 L6 **Bergum** *Fris.* Burgum. Friesland, N Netherlands 53°12′N 05°59′E
98 M6 **Bergumer Meer** ◎ N Netherlands
94 N12 **Bergviken** ◎ C Sweden
168 M11 **Berhala, Selat** *strait* Sumatera, W Indonesia
Berhampore see Baharampur
99 J17 **Beringen** Limburg, NE Belgium 51°04′N 05°14′E
39 T12 **Bering Glacier** *glacier* Alaska, USA
Beringov Proliv see Bering Strait
192 L2 **Bering Sea** *sea* N Pacific Ocean
38 L9 **Bering Strait** *Rus.* Beringov Proliv. *strait* Bering Sea/Chukchi Sea
Berislav see Beryslav
105 O15 **Berja** Andalucía, S Spain 36°51′N 02°56′W
94 H9 **Berkåk** Sør-Trøndelag, S Norway 62°50′N 10°01′E
98 N11 **Berkel** ≈ Germany/Netherlands
35 N8 **Berkeley** California, W USA 37°52′N 122°16′W
65 E24 **Berkeley Sound** *sound* NE Falkland Islands
21 V2 **Berkeley Springs** *var.* Bath. West Virginia, NE USA 39°38′N 78°14′W
195 N6 **Berkner Island** *island* Antarctica
114 G8 **Berkovitsa** Montana, NW Bulgaria 43°15′N 23°05′E
97 M22 **Berkshire** *former county* S England, United Kingdom
99 H17 **Berlaar** Antwerpen, N Belgium 51°08′N 04°39′E
Berlanga see Berlanga de Duero
105 P6 **Berlanga de Duero** *var.* Berlanga. Castilla-León, N Spain 41°28′N 02°51′W
0 I16 **Berlanga Rise** *undersea feature* E Pacific Ocean 08°30′N 93°30′W
99 F17 **Berlare** Oost-Vlaanderen, NW Belgium 51°02′N 04°01′E
104 E9 **Berlenga, Ilha da** *island* C Portugal
92 M7 **Berlevåg** *Lapp.* Bearalváhki. Finnmark, N Norway 70°51′N 29°04′E
100 O12 **Berlin** ● (Germany) Berlin, NE Germany 52°31′N 13°26′E
21 Z4 **Berlin** Maryland, NE USA 38°19′N 75°13′W
19 O7 **Berlin** New Hampshire, NE USA 44°27′N 71°13′W
18 D16 **Berlin** Pennsylvania, NE USA 39°54′N 78°57′W
30 L7 **Berlin** Wisconsin, N USA 43°57′N 88°59′W
100 O12 **Berlin** ◐ *state* NE Germany
Berlinchen see Barlinek
31 U12 **Berlin Lake** ⊠ Ohio, N USA
183 R11 **Bermagui** New South Wales, SE Australia 36°26′S 150°01′E
40 L8 **Bermejillo** Durango, C Mexico 25°55′N 103°39′W
62 L5 **Bermejo, Río** ≈ N Argentina
62 I10 **Bermejo, Río** ≈ W Argentina
62 M6 **Bermejo viejo, Río** ≈ N Argentina
105 P2 **Bermeo** País Vasco, N Spain 43°25′N 02°44′W
104 K6 **Bermillo de Sayago** Castilla-León, N Spain 41°22′N 06°08′W
106 E6 **Bermina, Pizzo** *Rmsch.* Piz Bernina. ▲ Italy/Switzerland 46°22′N 09°52′E *see also* Bernina, Piz
64 A12 **Bermuda** *var.* Bermuda Islands, Bermudas; *prev.* Somers Islands. ◇ *UK crown colony* NW Atlantic Ocean
1 N11 **Bermuda** *var.* Great Bermuda, Long Island, Main Island. *island* Bermuda
Bermuda Islands see Bermuda
Bermuda-New England Seamount Arc see New England Seamounts
1 N11 **Bermuda Rise** *undersea feature* C Sargasso Sea 32°30′N 65°00′W
Bermudas see Bermuda
108 D8 **Bern** *Fr.* Berne. ● (Switzerland) Bern, W Switzerland 46°57′N 07°26′E
108 D9 **Bern** *Fr.* Berne. ◐ *canton* W Switzerland
37 R11 **Bernalillo** New Mexico, SW USA 35°18′N 106°33′W
14 H12 **Bernard Lake** ◎ Ontario, S Canada
61 B18 **Bernardo de Irigoyen** Santa Fe, NE Argentina 32°09′S 61°06′W
18 J14 **Bernardsville** New Jersey, NE USA 40°43′N 74°34′W
63 K14 **Bernasconi** La Pampa, C Argentina 37°55′S 63°44′W
100 O12 **Bernau** Brandenburg, NE Germany 52°41′N 13°36′E
102 L4 **Bernay** Eure, N France 49°05′N 00°36′E
101 L14 **Bernburg** Sachsen-Anhalt, C Germany 51°47′N 11°45′E
109 X5 **Berndorf** Niederösterreich, NE Austria 47°58′N 16°08′E
31 Q12 **Berne** Indiana, N USA 40°39′N 84°57′W
Berne see Bern
108 D10 **Berner Alpen** *var.* Berner Oberland, *Eng.* Bernese Oberland. ▲▲ SW Switzerland
Berner Oberland/Bernese Oberland see Berner Alpen
109 Y2 **Bernhardsthal** Niederösterreich, N Austria 48°40′N 16°51′E
22 H4 **Bernice** Louisiana, S USA 32°49′N 92°39′W
27 Y8 **Bernie** Missouri, C USA 36°40′N 89°58′W
180 G9 **Bernier Island** *island* Western Australia
Bernina Pass see Bernina, Passo del
108 J10 **Bernina, Passo del** *Eng.* Bernina Pass. *pass* SE Switzerland
108 J10 **Bernina, Piz** *It.* Pizzo Bernina. ▲ Italy/Switzerland 46°22′N 09°55′E *see also* Bermina, Pizzo
Bernina, Piz see Bermina, Pizzo
99 E20 **Bernissart** Hainaut, SW Belgium 50°29′N 03°37′E
101 E18 **Bernkastel-Kues** Rheinland-Pfalz, W Germany 49°55′N 07°04′E
Beroea see Ḩalab
172 H6 **Beroroha** Toliara, SW Madagascar 21°40′S 45°10′E
Béroubouay see Gbéroubouè
111 C17 **Beroun** *Ger.* Beraun. Středočeský Kraj, W Czech Republic 49°58′N 14°05′E
111 C16 **Berounka** *Ger.* Beraun. ≈ W Czech Republic
113 Q18 **Berovo** E FYR Macedonia 41°45′N 22°50′E
74 F6 **Berrechid** *var.* Berchid. W Morocco 33°16′N 07°32′W
103 R15 **Berre, Étang de** ◎ SE France
103 S15 **Berre-l'Étang** Bouches-du-Rhône, SE France 43°28′N 05°10′E
182 K9 **Berri** South Australia 34°16′S 140°35′E
31 O10 **Berrien Springs** Michigan, N USA 41°57′N 86°20′W
183 O10 **Berrigan** New South Wales, SE Australia 35°41′S 145°50′E
103 N9 **Berry** *cultural region* C France
35 N7 **Berryessa, Lake** ◎ California, W USA
44 G2 **Berry Islands** *island group* N Bahamas
27 T9 **Berryville** Arkansas, C USA 36°22′N 93°35′W
21 V3 **Berryville** Virginia, NE USA 39°08′N 77°59′W
83 D21 **Berseba** Karas, S Namibia 26°00′S 17°46′E
117 O8 **Bershad'** Vinnyts'ka Oblast', C Ukraine 48°20′N 29°30′E
28 L3 **Berthold** North Dakota, N USA 48°16′N 101°48′W
37 T3 **Berthoud** Colorado, C USA 40°18′N 105°04′W
37 S4 **Berthoud Pass** *pass* Colorado, C USA
79 F15 **Bertoua** Est, E Cameroon 04°34′N 13°42′E
25 S10 **Bertram** Texas, SW USA 30°44′N 98°03′W
63 G22 **Bertrand, Cerro** ▲ S Argentina 50°00′S 73°27′W
99 J23 **Bertrix** Luxembourg, SE Belgium 49°52′N 05°15′E
191 P3 **Beru** *var.* Peru. *atoll* Tungaru, W Kiribati
Beruni see Beruniy
146 I9 **Beruniy** *var.* Biruni, *Rus.* Beruni. Qoraqalpog'iston Respublikasi, W Uzbekistan 41°48′N 60°39′E
58 F13 **Beruri** Amazonas, NW Brazil 03°44′S 61°13′W
18 H14 **Berwick** Pennsylvania, NE USA 41°03′N 76°13′W
96 K12 **Berwick** *cultural region* SE Scotland, United Kingdom
96 L12 **Berwick-upon-Tweed** N England, United Kingdom 55°46′N 02°00′W
117 S10 **Beryslav** *Rus.* Berislav. Khersons'ka Oblast', S Ukraine 46°51′N 33°26′E
Berytus see Beyrouth
172 H4 **Besalampy** Mahajanga, W Madagascar 16°43′S 44°29′E
103 T8 **Besançon** *anc.* Besontium, Vesontio. Doubs, E France 47°14′N 06°01′E
103 P10 **Besbre** ≈ C France
Bescanuova see Baška
Besdan see Bezdan
Besed' see Byesyedz'
147 R10 **Beshariq** *Rus.* Besharyk; *prev.* Kirovo. Farg'ona Viloyati, E Uzbekistan 40°26′N 70°33′E
Besharyk see Beshariq
146 L9 **Beshbuloq** *Rus.* Beshulak. Navoiy Viloyati, N Uzbekistan 41°55′N 64°13′E
Beshenkovichi see Byeshankovichy
146 M13 **Beshkent** Qashqadaryo Viloyati, S Uzbekistan 38°47′N 65°42′E
Beshulak see Beshbuloq
112 L10 **Beška** Vojvodina, N Serbia 45°09′N 20°04′E
Beskra see Biskra
127 O16 **Beslan** Respublika Severnaya Osetiya, SW Russian Federation 43°12′N 44°33′E
113 P16 **Besna Kobila** ▲ SE Serbia 42°30′N 22°16′E
137 N16 **Besni** Adıyaman, S Turkey 37°42′N 37°53′E
Besontium see Besançon
121 Q2 **Beşparmak Dağları** *Eng.* Kyrenia Mountains. ▲▲ N Cyprus
Bessarabka see Basarabeasca
92 O2 **Bessels, Kapp** *headland* C Svalbard 78°36′N 21°43′E
23 P4 **Bessemer** Alabama, S USA 33°24′N 86°57′W
30 K3 **Bessemer** Michigan, N USA 46°28′N 90°03′W
21 Q10 **Bessemer City** North Carolina, SE USA 35°16′N 81°16′W
102 M10 **Bessines-sur-Gartempe** Haute-Vienne, C France 46°06′N 01°22′E
99 K15 **Best** Noord-Brabant, S Netherlands 51°31′N 05°24′E
25 N9 **Best** Texas, SW USA 31°13′N 101°34′W
125 O11 **Bestuzhevo** Arkhangel'skaya Oblast', NW Russian Federation 61°36′N 43°54′E
123 M11 **Bestyakh** Respublika Sakha (Yakutiya), NE Russian Federation 61°25′N 129°05′E
Beszterce see Bistriţa
Besztercebánya see Banská Bystrica
172 I5 **Betafo** Antananarivo, C Madagascar 19°50′S 46°50′E
104 H2 **Betanzos** Galicia, NW Spain 43°17′N 08°17′W
104 G2 **Betanzos, Ría de** *estuary* NW Spain
79 G15 **Bétaré Oya** Est, E Cameroon 05°34′N 14°09′E
105 S9 **Betera** País Valenciano, E Spain 39°35′N 00°28′W
77 R15 **Bétérou** C Benin 09°13′N 02°18′E
83 K21 **Bethal** Mpumalanga, NE South Africa 26°27′S 29°28′E
30 K15 **Bethalto** Illinois, N USA 38°54′N 90°02′W
83 D21 **Bethanie** *var.* Bethanien, Bethany. Karas, S Namibia 26°32′S 17°11′E
Bethanien see Bethanie
27 S2 **Bethany** Missouri, C USA 40°15′N 94°03′W
27 N10 **Bethany** Oklahoma, C USA 35°31′N 97°37′W
Bethany see Bethanie
39 N12 **Bethel** Alaska, USA 60°47′N 161°45′W
19 P7 **Bethel** Maine, NE USA 44°24′N 70°47′W
21 W9 **Bethel** North Carolina, SE USA 35°46′N 77°21′W
18 B15 **Bethel Park** Pennsylvania, NE USA 40°21′N 80°03′W
21 W3 **Bethesda** Maryland, NE USA 39°00′N 77°05′W
83 J22 **Bethlehem** Free State, C South Africa 28°12′S 28°16′E
18 I14 **Bethlehem** Pennsylvania, NE USA 40°36′N 75°22′W
138 F10 **Bethlehem** *var.* Beit Lekhem, *Ar.* Bayt Laḥm, *Heb.* Bet Leḥem. C West Bank 31°43′N 35°12′E
Bethlen see Beclean
83 I24 **Bethulie** Free State, C South Africa 30°30′S 25°59′E
103 O1 **Béthune** Pas-de-Calais, N France 50°32′N 02°38′E
102 M3 **Béthune** ≈ N France
104 M14 **Béticos, Sistemas** *var.* Sistema Penibético, *Eng.* Baetic Cordillera, Baetic Mountains. ▲▲ S Spain
54 I6 **Betijoque** Trujillo, NW Venezuela 09°25′N 70°45′W
59 M20 **Betim** Minas Gerais, SE Brazil 19°56′S 44°10′W
190 H3 **Betio** Tarawa, W Kiribati 01°21′N 172°56′E
172 H7 **Betioky** Toliara, S Madagascar 23°42′S 44°22′E
Bet Leḥem see Bethlehem
Betlen see Beclean
167 O17 **Betong** Yala, SW Thailand 05°45′N 101°05′E
79 I16 **Bétou** Likouala, N Congo 03°08′N 18°31′E
145 P14 **Betpak-Dala** *Kaz.* Betpaqdala. *plateau* S Kazakhstan
Betpaqdala see Betpak-Dala
172 H7 **Betroka** Toliara, S Madagascar 23°16′S 46°07′E
Betschau see Bečva
Bet She'an see Beit She'an
15 T6 **Betsiamites** Québec, SE Canada 48°56′N 68°40′W
15 T6 **Betsiamites** ≈ Québec, SE Canada
172 I4 **Betsiboka** ≈ N Madagascar
Betsukai see Bekkai
99 M25 **Bettembourg** Luxembourg, S Luxembourg 49°31′N 06°06′E
99 M23 **Bettendorf** Diekirch, NE Luxembourg 49°53′N 06°13′E
29 Z14 **Bettendorf** Iowa, C USA 41°31′N 90°31′W
75 R13 **Bette, Picco** *var.* Bikkū Bīttī, *It.* Picco Bette. ▲ S Libya 22°02′N 19°07′E
Bette, Picco see Bette, Picco
153 P12 **Bettiah** Bihār, N India 26°49′N 84°30′E
39 Q7 **Bettles** Alaska, USA 66°54′N 151°40′W
95 N17 **Bettna** Södermanland, C Sweden 58°52′N 16°40′E
154 H11 **Betūl** *prev.* Badnur. Madhya Pradesh, C India 21°55′N 77°54′E
154 H9 **Betwa** ≈ C India
101 F16 **Betzdorf** Rheinland-Pfalz, W Germany 50°47′N 07°50′E
82 C9 **Béu** Uíge, NW Angola 06°15′S 15°32′E
31 P6 **Beulah** Michigan, N USA 44°35′N 86°05′W
28 L5 **Beulah** North Dakota, N USA 47°16′N 101°48′W
98 M8 **Beulakerwijde** ◎ N Netherlands
98 L13 **Beuningen** Gelderland, SE Netherlands 51°52′N 05°47′E
Beuthen see Bytom
103 N7 **Beuvron** ≈ C France
99 F16 **Beveren** Oost-Vlaanderen, N Belgium 51°13′N 04°15′E
21 T9 **B. Everett Jordan Reservoir** *var.* Jordan Lake. ⊠ North Carolina, SE USA
97 N17 **Beverley** E England, United Kingdom 53°51′N 00°26′W
Beverley see Beverly
99 J17 **Beverlo** Limburg, NE Belgium 51°06′N 05°14′E
19 P11 **Beverly** Massachusetts, NE USA 42°33′N 70°49′W
32 J9 **Beverly** *var.* Beverley. Washington, NW USA 46°50′N 119°57′W
35 S15 **Beverly Hills** California, W USA 34°02′N 118°25′W
101 I14 **Beverungen** Nordrhein-Westfalen, C Germany 51°39′N 09°22′E
98 H9 **Beverwijk** Noord-Holland, W Netherlands 52°29′N 04°40′E
108 C10 **Bex** Vaud, W Switzerland 46°15′N 07°00′E
97 P23 **Bexhill** *var.* Bexhill-on-Sea. SE England, United Kingdom 50°50′N 00°28′E
Bexhill-on-Sea see Bexhill
136 E17 **Bey Dağları** ▲▲ SW Turkey
Beyj see Belyy
136 E10 **Beykoz** İstanbul, NW Turkey 41°09′N 29°06′E
76 K15 **Beyla** SE Guinea 08°43′N 08°41′W
137 X12 **Beyläqan** *prev.* Zhdanov. SW Azerbaijan 39°43′N 47°38′E
80 L10 **Beylul** *var.* Beilul. SE Eritrea 13°10′N 42°27′E
144 H14 **Beyneu** *Kaz.* Beyneū. Mangistau, SW Kazakhstan 45°20′N 55°11′E
Beyneū see Beyneu
165 X14 **Beyonēsu-retsugan** *Eng.* Bayonnaise Rocks. *island group* SE Japan
136 G12 **Beypazarı** Ankara, NW Turkey 40°10′N 31°56′E
155 F21 **Beypore** Kerala, SW India 11°10′N 75°49′E
138 G7 **Beyrouth** *var.* Bayrūt, *Eng.* Beirut; *anc.* Berytus. ● (Lebanon) W Lebanon 33°55′N 35°31′E
138 G7 **Beyrouth** ✈ W Lebanon 33°52′N 35°30′E
136 G15 **Beyşehir** Konya, SW Turkey 37°40′N 31°43′E
136 G15 **Beyşehir Gölü** ◎ C Turkey
108 J7 **Bezau** Vorarlberg, NW Austria 47°24′N 09°55′E
112 J8 **Bezdan** *Ger.* Besdan, *Hung.* Bezdán. Vojvodina, NW Serbia 45°51′N 19°00′E
Bezdezh see Byezdzyezh
124 G15 **Bezhanitsy** Pskovskaya Oblast', W Russian Federation 56°57′N 29°53′E
124 K15 **Bezhetsk** Tverskaya Oblast', W Russian Federation 57°47′N 36°42′E
103 P16 **Béziers** *anc.* Baeterrae, Baeterrae Septimanorum, Julia Beterrae. Hérault, S France 43°21′N 03°13′E
Bezmein see Abadan
Bezwada see Vijayawāda
154 P12 **Bhadrak** *var.* Bhadrakh. Orissa, E India 21°04′N 86°30′N
Bhadrakh see Bhadrak
155 F19 **Bhadra Reservoir** ⊠ SW India
155 F18 **Bhadrāvati** Karnātaka, SW India 13°52′N 75°43′E
153 R14 **Bhāgalpur** Bihār, NE India 25°14′N 86°59′E
Bhairab see Bhairab Bazar
153 U14 **Bhairab Bazar** *var.* Bhairab. Dhaka, C Bangladesh 24°04′N 91°00′E
153 O11 **Bhairahawā** Western, S Nepal 27°31′N 83°27′E
149 S8 **Bhakkar** Punjab, E Pakistan 31°40′N 71°08′E
153 P11 **Bhaktapur** Central, C Nepal 27°47′N 85°21′E
167 N3 **Bhamo** *var.* Banmo. Kachin State, N Burma (Myanmar) 24°15′N 97°15′E
Bhāmragad see Bhāmragarh
154 K13 **Bhāmragarh** *var.* Bhāmragad. Mahārāshtra, C India 19°28′N 80°39′E
154 J12 **Bhandāra** Mahārāshtra, C India 21°10′N 79°41′E
Bhārat see India
152 J12 **Bharatpur** *prev.* Bhurtpore. Rājasthān, N India 27°14′N 77°29′E
154 D11 **Bharūch** Gujarāt, W India 21°48′N 72°55′E
155 E18 **Bhatkal** Karnātaka, W India 13°59′N 74°34′E
153 O13 **Bhatni** *var.* Bhatni Junction. Uttar Pradesh, N India 26°23′N 83°56′E
Bhatni Junction see Bhatni
153 S16 **Bhātpāra** West Bengal, NE India 22°55′N 88°30′E
149 U7 **Bhaun** Punjab, E Pakistan 32°53′N 72°48′E
Bhaunagar see Bhāvnagar
154 M13 **Bhavānīpātna** *var.* Bhawanipatna. Orissa, E India 19°56′N 83°09′E
155 H21 **Bhavānīsāgar** ⊠ S India
154 D11 **Bhāvnagar** *prev.* Bhaunagar. Gujarāt, W India 21°46′N 72°14′E
Bhawanipatna see Bhavānīpātna
Bheanntraí, Bá see Bantry Bay
Bheara, Béal an see Gweebarra Bay
154 K12 **Bhilai** Chhattīsgarh, C India 21°12′N 81°26′E
152 G13 **Bhīlwāra** Rājasthān, N India 25°23′N 74°39′E
155 E14 **Bhīma** ≈ S India
155 K16 **Bhīmavaram** Andhra Pradesh, E India 16°34′N 81°35′E
154 I7 **Bhind** Madhya Pradesh, C India 26°33′N 78°47′E
152 E13 **Bhīnmāl** Rājasthān, N India 25°01′N 72°22′E
Bhir see Bīd
154 D13 **Bhiwandi** Mahārāshtra, W India 19°21′N 73°08′E
152 H10 **Bhiwāni** Haryāna, N India 28°50′N 76°10′E
152 L13 **Bhognīpur** Uttar Pradesh, N India 26°12′N 79°48′E
153 U16 **Bhola** Barisal, S Bangladesh 22°40′N 91°36′E
154 H10 **Bhopāl** *state capital* Madhya Pradesh, C India 23°17′N 77°25′E
155 J14 **Bhopālpatnam** Chhattīsgarh, C India 18°51′N 80°22′E
155 E14 **Bhor** Mahārāshtra, W India 18°10′N 73°55′E
154 O12 **Bhubaneshwar** *prev.* Bhubaneswar, Bhuvaneshwar. *state capital* Orissa, E India 20°16′N 85°51′E
Bhubaneswar see Bhubaneshwar
154 B9 **Bhuj** Gujarāt, W India 23°16′N 69°40′E
Bhuket see Phuket
Bhurtpore see Bharatpur
Bhusaval see Bhusāwal
154 G12 **Bhusāwal** *prev.* Bhusaval. Mahārāshtra, C India 21°01′N 75°50′E
153 T12 **Bhutan** *off.* Kingdom of Bhutan, *var.* Druk-yul. ◆ *monarchy* S Asia
Bhutan, Kingdom of see Bhutan
Bhuvaneshwar see Bhubaneshwar
143 T15 **Bīābān, Kūh-e** ▲▲ S Iran
77 V18 **Biafra, Bight of** *var.* Bight of Bonny. *bay* W Africa
171 W12 **Biak** Papua, E Indonesia 01°10′S 136°05′E
171 W12 **Biak, Pulau** *island* E Indonesia
110 P12 **Biała Podlaska** Lubelskie, E Poland 52°03′N 23°08′E
110 F7 **Białogard** *Ger.* Belgard. Zachodnio-pomorskie, NW Poland 54°01′N 15°59′E
110 P10 **Białowieska, Puszcza** *Bel.* Byelavyezhskaya Pushcha, *Rus.* Belovezhskaya Pushcha. *physical region* Belarus/Poland *see also* Byelavyezhskaya Pushcha
Białowieska, Puszcza see Byelavyezhskaya Pushcha
110 G8 **Biały Bór** *Ger.* Baldenburg. Zachodnio-pomorskie, NW Poland 53°53′N 16°49′E
110 P9 **Białystok** *Rus.* Belostok, Bielostok. Podlaskie, NE Poland 53°08′N 23°09′E
107 L24 **Biancavilla** *prev.* Inessa. Sicilia, Italy, C Mediterranean Sea 37°38′N 14°52′E
Bianco, Monte see Blanc, Mont
Bianjing see Xunke
76 L15 **Biankouma** W Ivory Coast 07°44′N 07°37′W
167 R7 **Bia, Phou** *var.* Pou Bia. ▲ C Laos 18°59′N 103°09′E
Bia, Pou see Bia, Phou
143 R5 **Bīārjmand** Semnān, N Iran 36°05′N 55°50′E
105 P4 **Biarra** ≈ NE Spain
102 I15 **Biarritz** Pyrénées-Atlantiques, SW France 43°25′N 01°40′W
108 H10 **Biasca** Ticino, S Switzerland 46°22′N 08°59′E
61 E17 **Biassini** Salto, N Uruguay 31°18′S 57°05′W
Biasteri see Laguardia
165 S3 **Bibai** Hokkaidō, NE Japan 43°21′N 141°53′E
83 B15 **Bibala** *Port.* Vila Arriaga. Namibe, SW Angola 14°46′S 13°21′E
104 I4 **Bibei** ≈ NW Spain
Biberach see Biberach an der Riss
101 I23 **Biberach an der Riss** *var.* Biberach, *Ger.* Biberach an der Riß. Baden-Württemberg, S Germany 48°06′N 09°48′E
108 E7 **Biberist** Solothurn, NW Switzerland 47°11′N 07°34′E
77 O16 **Bibiani** SW Ghana 06°28′N 02°20′W
112 C13 **Bibinje** Zadar, SW Croatia 44°04′N 15°17′E
Biblical Gebal see Jbail
116 I5 **Bibrka** *Pol.* Bóbrka, *Rus.* Bobrka. L'vivs'ka Oblast', NW Ukraine 49°39′N 24°16′E
117 N10 **Bic** ≈ S Moldova
113 M18 **Bicaj** Kukës, NE Albania 42°00′N 20°24′E
116 K10 **Bicaz** *Hung.* Békás. Neamţ, NE Romania 46°53′N 26°05′E
183 Q16 **Bicheno** Tasmania, SE Australia 41°56′S 148°15′E
Bichiş see Békés
Bichiş-Ciaba see Békéscsaba
Bichitra see Phichit
137 P8 **Bichvint'a** *Rus.* Pitsunda. NW Georgia 43°12′N 40°21′E
15 T7 **Bic, Île du** *island* Québec, SE Canada
32 J10 **Bickleton** Washington, NW USA 46°00′N 120°16′W
36 L6 **Bicknell** Utah, W USA 38°20′N 111°32′W
171 S11 **Bicoli** Pulau Halmahera, E Indonesia 0°34′N 128°33′E
111 J22 **Bicske** Fejér, C Hungary 47°30′N 18°36′E
155 F14 **Bīd** *prev.* Bhir. Mahārāshtra, W India 19°17′N 75°22′E
77 U15 **Bida** Niger, C Nigeria 09°06′N 06°02′E
155 H15 **Bīdar** Karnātaka, C India 17°56′N 77°35′E
141 Y8 **Bidbid** NE Oman 23°25′N 58°08′E
19 P9 **Biddeford** Maine, NE USA 43°29′N 70°27′W
98 L9 **Biddinghuizen** Flevoland, C Netherlands 52°28′N 05°41′E
33 X11 **Biddle** Montana, NW USA 45°04′N 105°21′W
97 J23 **Bideford** SW England, United Kingdom 51°01′N 04°12′W
82 D13 **Bié** ◐ *province* C Angola
35 O2 **Bieber** California, W USA 41°07′N 121°09′W
110 O10 **Biebrza** ≈ NE Poland
165 T3 **Biei** Hokkaidō, NE Japan 43°33′N 142°28′E
108 D8 **Biel** *Fr.* Bienne. Bern, W Switzerland 47°09′N 07°16′E
100 G13 **Bielefeld** Nordrhein-Westfalen, NW Germany 52°01′N 08°32′E
108 D8 **Bieler See** *Fr.* Lac de Bienne. ◎ W Switzerland
Bielitz/Bielitz-Biala see Bielsko-Biała
106 C7 **Biella** Piemonte, N Italy 45°34′N 08°04′E
Bielostok see Białystok
111 J17 **Bielsko-Biała** *Ger.* Bielitz, Bielitz-Biala. Śląskie, S Poland 49°49′N 19°01′E
110 P10 **Bielsk Podlaski** Białystok, E Poland 52°45′N 23°11′E
Bien Bien see Điện Biên
Biên Đông see South China Sea
11 V17 **Bienfait** Saskatchewan, S Canada 49°06′N 102°47′W
167 T14 **Biên Hoa** Đông Nai, S Vietnam 10°58′N 106°50′E
Bienne see Biel
Bienne, Lac de see Bieler See
12 K8 **Bienville, Lac** ◎ Québec, C Canada
82 D13 **Bié, Planalto do** *var.* Bié Plateau. *plateau* C Angola
Bié Plateau see Bié, Planalto do
108 B9 **Bière** Vaud, W Switzerland 46°32′N 06°19′E
98 O4 **Bierum** Groningen, NE Netherlands 53°25′N 06°51′E
98 I13 **Biesbos** *var.* Biesbosch. *wetland* S Netherlands
Biesbosch see Biesbos
99 H21 **Biesme** Namur, S Belgium 50°19′N 04°43′E
101 H21 **Bietigheim-Bissingen** Baden-Württemberg, SW Germany 48°57′N 09°07′E
99 I23 **Bièvre** Namur, SE Belgium 49°56′N 05°01′E
79 D18 **Bifoun** Moyen-Ogooué, NW Gabon 0°15′S 10°24′E
165 T2 **Bifuka** Hokkaidō, NE Japan 44°28′N 142°20′E
136 C11 **Biga** Çanakkale, NW Turkey 40°13′N 27°14′E
136 C13 **Bigadiç** Balıkesir, W Turkey 39°24′N 28°08′E
26 J7 **Big Basin** *basin* Kansas, C USA
185 B20 **Big Bay** *bay* South Island, New Zealand
31 O5 **Big Bay de Noc** ◎ Michigan, N USA
31 N3 **Big Bay Point** *headland* Michigan, N USA 46°51′N 87°40′W
33 R10 **Big Belt Mountains** ▲▲ Montana, NW USA
29 N10 **Big Bend Dam** *dam* South Dakota, N USA
24 K12 **Big Bend National Park** *national park* Texas, S USA
22 K5 **Big Black River** ≈ Mississippi, S USA
27 O3 **Big Blue River** ≈ Kansas/Nebraska, C USA
24 M10 **Big Canyon** ≈ Texas, SW USA
33 N12 **Big Creek** Idaho, NW USA 45°05′N 115°20′W
23 N8 **Big Creek Lake** ⊠ Alabama, S USA
23 X15 **Big Cypress Swamp** *wetland* Florida, SE USA
39 S9 **Big Delta** Alaska, USA 64°09′N 145°50′W
30 K6 **Big Eau Pleine Reservoir** ⊠ Wisconsin, N USA
19 P5 **Bigelow Mountain** ▲ Maine, NE USA 45°09′N 70°17′W
162 G9 **Biger** *var.* Jargalant. Govĭ-Altay, W Mongolia 45°39′N 97°10′E
29 U3 **Big Falls** Minnesota, N USA 48°13′N 93°48′W
33 P8 **Bigfork** Montana, NW USA 48°03′N 114°04′W
29 U3 **Big Fork River** ≈ Minnesota, N USA
11 S15 **Biggar** Saskatchewan, S Canada 52°03′N 107°59′W
180 L3 **Bigge Island** *island* Western Australia
35 O5 **Biggs** California, W USA 39°24′N 121°44′W
32 I11 **Biggs** Oregon, NW USA 45°39′N 120°49′W
14 K13 **Big Gull Lake** ◎ Ontario, SE Canada
37 P16 **Big Hachet Peak** ▲ New Mexico, SW USA 31°38′N 108°24′W
33 P11 **Big Hole River** ≈ Montana, NW USA
33 V13 **Bighorn Basin** *basin* Wyoming, C USA
33 U11 **Bighorn Lake** ◎ Montana/Wyoming, NW USA
33 W13 **Bighorn Mountains** ▲▲ Wyoming, C USA
36 J13 **Big Horn Peak** ▲ Arizona, SW USA 33°40′N 113°01′W
33 V11 **Bighorn River** ≈ Montana/Wyoming, NW USA
9 S7 **Big Island** *island* Nunavut, NE Canada
39 O16 **Big Koniuji Island** *island* Shumagin Islands, Alaska, USA
25 N9 **Big Lake** Texas, SW USA 31°12′N 101°29′W
19 T5 **Big Lake** ◎ Maine, NE USA
30 I3 **Big Manitou Falls** *waterfall* Wisconsin, N USA
35 R2 **Big Mountain** ▲ Nevada, W USA 41°18′N 119°03′W
108 G10 **Bignasco** Ticino, S Switzerland 46°21′N 08°37′E
29 R16 **Big Nemaha River** ≈ Nebraska, C USA
76 G12 **Bignona** SW Senegal 12°49′N 16°16′W
Bigorra see Tarbes
Bigosovo see Bihosava
35 S10 **Big Pine** California, W USA 37°09′N 118°18′W
35 Q14 **Big Pine Mountain** ▲ California, W USA 34°41′N 119°37′W
27 V6 **Big Piney Creek** ≈ Missouri, C USA
65 M24 **Big Point** *headland* N Tristan da Cunha 37°10′S 12°18′W
31 P8 **Big Rapids** Michigan, N USA 43°42′N 85°28′W
30 K6 **Big Rib River** ≈ Wisconsin, N USA
14 L14 **Big Rideau Lake** ◎ Ontario, SE Canada
11 T14 **Big River** Saskatchewan, C Canada 53°48′N 106°55′W
27 X5 **Big River** ≈ Missouri, C USA
31 N7 **Big Sable Point** *headland* Michigan, N USA 44°03′N 86°30′W
33 S7 **Big Sandy** Montana, NW USA 48°08′N 110°09′W
25 W6 **Big Sandy** Texas, SW USA 32°34′N 95°06′W
37 V5 **Big Sandy Creek** ≈ Colorado, C USA
29 Q16 **Big Sandy Creek** ≈ Nebraska, C USA
29 V5 **Big Sandy Lake** ◎ Minnesota, N USA
36 J11 **Big Sandy River** ≈ Arizona, SW USA
21 P5 **Big Sandy River** ≈ S USA
23 V6 **Big Satilla Creek** ≈ Georgia, SE USA
29 R12 **Big Sioux River** ≈ Iowa/South Dakota, N USA
35 U7 **Big Smoky Valley** *valley* Nevada, W USA
25 N7 **Big Spring** Texas, SW USA 32°15′N 101°30′W
19 Q5 **Big Squaw Mountain** ▲ Maine, NE USA 45°28′N 69°42′W
21 O7 **Big Stone Gap** Virginia, NE USA 36°52′N 82°45′W
29 Q8 **Big Stone Lake** ◎ Minnesota/South Dakota, N USA
22 K4 **Big Sunflower River** ≈ Mississippi, S USA
33 T11 **Big Timber** Montana, NW USA 45°50′N 109°57′W
12 D8 **Big Trout Lake** Ontario, C Canada 53°40′N 90°00′W
14 I12 **Big Trout Lake** ◎ Ontario, SE Canada
35 O2 **Big Valley Mountains** ▲▲ California, W USA
25 Q13 **Big Wells** Texas, SW USA 28°34′N 99°34′W
14 F11 **Bigwood** Ontario, S Canada 46°03′N 80°37′W
112 D11 **Bihać** ◐ Federacija Bosna I Hercegovina, NW Bosnia and Herzegovina
153 P14 **Bihār** *prev.* Behar. ◐ *state* N India
Bihār see Bihār Sharīf
81 F20 **Biharamulo** Kagera, NW Tanzania 02°37′S 31°20′E
153 R13 **Bihārīganj** Bihār, NE India 25°44′N 86°59′E
153 P14 **Bihār Sharīf** *var.* Bihār. Bihār, N India 25°13′N 85°31′E
116 F10 **Bihor** ◐ *county* NW Romania
165 V3 **Bihoro** Hokkaidō, NE Japan 43°50′N 144°05′E
118 K11 **Bihosava** *Rus.* Bigosovo. Vitsyebskaya Voblasts', NW Belarus 55°50′N 27°46′E
Bijagos Archipelago see Bijagós, Arquipélago dos
76 G13 **Bijagós, Arquipélago dos** *var.* Bijagos Archipelago. *island group* W Guinea-Bissau
155 F16 **Bijāpur** Karnātaka, C India 16°50′N 75°42′E
142 K5 **Bījār** Kordestān, W Iran 35°52′N 47°39′E

◆ Country
● Country Capital
◇ Dependent Territory
○ Dependent Territory Capital
◐ Administrative Regions
✈ International Airport
▲ Mountain
▲▲ Mountain Range
Volcano
≈ River
◎ Lake
⊠ Reservoir

112 J11 Bijeljina Republika Srpska, NE Bosnia and Herzegovina 44°46′N 19°13′E
113 K15 Bijelo Polje E Montenegro 43°03′N 19°44′E
160 I11 Bijie Guizhou, S China 27°15′N 105°16′E
152 J10 Bijnor Uttar Pradesh, N India 29°22′N 78°09′E
152 F11 Bikāner Rājasthān, NW India 28°01′N 73°22′E
189 V3 Bikar Atoll var. Pikaar. atoll Ratak Chain, N Marshall Islands
190 H3 Bikeman atoll Tungaru, W Kiribati
190 I3 Bikenebu Tarawa, W Kiribati
123 S14 Bikin Khabarovskiy Kray, SE Russian Federation 46°45′N 134°06′E
123 S14 Bikin ≈ SE Russian Federation
189 R3 Bikini Atoll var. Pikinni. atoll Ralik Chain, NW Marshall Islands
83 L17 Bikita Masvingo, E Zimbabwe 20°06′S 31°41′E
Bikkū Bīttī see Bette, Picco
79 I19 Bikoro Equateur, W Dem. Rep. Congo 0°45′S 18°09′E
141 Z9 Bilād Banī Bū 'Alī NE Oman 22°02′N 59°18′E
141 Z9 Bilād Banī Bū Ḩasan NE Oman 22°09′N 59°14′E
141 X9 Bilād Manaḩ var. Manaḩ. NE Oman 22°44′N 57°36′E
77 Q12 Bilanga C Burkina 12°35′N 00°08′W
152 F12 Bilāra Rājasthān, N India 26°10′N 73°48′E
152 K10 Bilāri Uttar Pradesh, N India 28°37′N 78°48′E
138 J5 Bil'ās, Jabal al ▲▲ C Syria
154 L11 Bilāspur Chhattīsgarh, C India 22°06′N 82°08′E
152 I8 Bilāspur Himāchal Pradesh, N India 31°18′N 76°48′E
168 J9 Bila, Sungai ≈ Sumatera, W Indonesia
137 Y13 Biläsuvar Rus. Bilyasuvar; prev. Pushkino. SE Azerbaijan 39°26′N 48°34′E
117 O5 Bila Tserkva Rus. Belaya Tserkov'. Kyyivs'ka Oblast', N Ukraine 49°49′N 30°08′E
167 N11 Bilauktaung Range var. Thanintari Taungdan. ▲▲ Burma (Myanmar)/ Thailand
105 O2 Bilbao Basq. Bilbo. País Vasco, N Spain 43°15′N 02°56′W
Bilbo see Bilbao
92 H2 Bildudalur Vestfirdhir, NW Iceland 65°40′N 23°35′W
113 I16 Bileća ◐ Republika Srpska, S Bosnia and Herzegovina
136 E12 Bilecik Bilecik, NW Turkey 39°59′N 29°54′E
136 F12 Bilecik ◐ province NW Turkey
116 E11 Biled Ger. Billed, Hung. Billéd. Timiş, W Romania 45°55′N 20°55′E
111 O15 Biłgoraj Lubelskie, E Poland 50°31′N 22°41′E
117 P11 Bilhorod-Dnistrovs'kyy Rus. Belgorod-Dnestrovskiy, Rom. Cetatea Albă, prev. Akkerman; anc. Tyras. Odes'ka Oblast', SW Ukraine 46°10′N 30°19′E
79 M16 Bili Orientale, N Dem. Rep. Congo 04°07′N 25°09′E
123 T6 Bilibino Chukotskiy Avtonomnyy Okrug, NE Russian Federation 67°56′N 166°45′E
166 M8 Bilin Mon State, S Burma (Myanmar) 17°14′N 97°12′E
113 N21 Bilisht var. Bilishti. Korçë, SE Albania 40°36′N 21°00′E
Bilishti see Bilisht
183 N10 Billabong Creek var. Moulamein Creek. seasonal river New South Wales, SE Australia
182 G4 Billa Kalina South Australia 29°57′S 136°13′E
197 Q17 Bill Baileys Bank undersea feature N Atlantic Ocean 60°35′N 10°15′W
Billed/Billéd see Biled
153 N14 Billi Uttar Pradesh, N India 24°30′N 82°59′E
97 M15 Billingham N England, United Kingdom 54°36′N 01°17′W
33 U11 Billings Montana, NW USA 45°47′N 108°32′W
95 J16 Billingsfors Västra Götaland, S Sweden 58°57′N 12°14′E
Bill of Cape Clear, The see Clear, Cape
28 L9 Billsburg South Dakota, N USA 44°22′N 101°40′W
95 F23 Billund Ribe, W Denmark 55°44′N 09°07′E
36 L11 Bill Williams Mountain ▲ Arizona, SW USA 35°12′N 112°12′W
36 I12 Bill Williams River ≈ Arizona, SW USA
77 Y8 Bilma Agadez, NE Niger 18°22′N 13°01′E
77 Y8 Bilma, Grand Erg de desert NE Niger
181 Y9 Biloela Queensland, E Australia 24°27′S 150°31′E
112 G8 Bilo Gora ▲▲ N Croatia
117 U13 Bilohirs'k Rus. Belogorsk; prev. Karasubazar. Respublika Krym, S Ukraine 45°04′N 34°35′E
Bilokurakine see Bilokurakyne
117 X5 Bilokurakyne var. Bilokurakine. Luhans'ka Oblast', E Ukraine 49°32′N 38°44′E
117 T3 Bilopillya Rus. Belopol'ye. Sums'ka Oblast', NE Ukraine 51°09′N 34°17′E
117 Y6 Bilovods'k Rus. Belovodsk. Luhans'ka Oblast', E Ukraine 49°11′N 39°34′E
22 M9 Biloxi Mississippi, S USA 30°24′N 88°53′W
117 R10 Bilozerka Khersons'ka Oblast', S Ukraine 46°36′N 32°23′E
117 W7 Bilozers'ke Donets'ka Oblast', E Ukraine 48°29′N 37°03′E
98 J11 Bilthoven Utrecht, C Netherlands 52°07′N 05°12′E
78 K9 Biltine Biltine, E Chad 14°30′N 20°53′E
78 J9 Biltine off. Préfecture de Biltine. ◐ prefecture E Chad
Biltine, Préfecture de see Biltine
Bilüü see Ulaanhus
Bilwi see Puerto Cabezas
Bilyasuvar see Biläsuvar
117 O11 Bilyayivka Odes'ka Oblast', SW Ukraine 46°28′N 30°11′E
99 K18 Bilzen Limburg, NE Belgium 50°52′N 05°31′E
Bimbéréké see Bembèrèkè
183 R10 Bimberi Peak ▲ New South Wales, SE Australia 35°42′S 148°46′E
77 Q15 Bimbila E Ghana 08°54′N 00°05′E
79 I15 Bimbo Ombella-Mpoko, SW Central African Republic 04°19′N 18°27′E
44 F2 Bimini Islands island group W Bahamas
154 I9 Bina Madhya Pradesh, C India 24°09′N 78°10′E
143 T4 Bīnālūd, Kūh-e ▲▲ NE Iran
99 F20 Binche Hainaut, S Belgium 50°25′N 04°10′E
Bindloe Island see Marchena, Isla
83 L16 Bindura Mashonaland Central, NE Zimbabwe 17°20′S 31°21′E
105 T5 Binefar Aragón, NE Spain 41°51′N 00°17′E
83 J16 Binga Matabeleland North, W Zimbabwe 17°40′S 27°22′E
183 T5 Bingara New South Wales, SE Australia 29°54′S 150°36′E
101 F18 Bingen am Rhein Rheinland-Pfalz, SW Germany 49°58′N 07°54′E
26 M11 Binger Oklahoma, C USA 35°19′N 98°19′W
Bingerau see Węgrów
Bin Ghalfān, Jazā'ir see Ḩalāniyāt, Juzur al
19 Q6 Bingham Maine, NE USA 45°01′N 69°51′W
18 H11 Binghamton New York, NE USA 42°06′N 75°55′W
Bin Ghanīmah, Jabal see Bin Ghunaymah, Jabal
75 P11 Bin Ghunaymah, Jabal var. Jabal Bin Ghanīmah. ▲▲ C Libya
139 U3 Bingird As Sulaymānīyah, NE Iraq 36°03′N 45°03′E
Bingmei see Congjiang
137 P14 Bingöl Bingöl, E Turkey 38°54′N 40°29′E
137 P14 Bingöl ◐ province E Turkey
161 R6 Binhai var. Dongkan. Jiangsu, E China 34°00′N 119°51′E
167 V11 Binh Đinh var. An Nhon. Binh Đinh, C Vietnam 13°53′N 109°07′E
167 U10 Binh Sơn var. Châu Ô. Quang Ngai, C Vietnam 15°18′N 108°45′E
Binimani see Bintimani
168 I8 Binjai Sumatera, W Indonesia 03°37′N 98°30′E
183 R6 Binnaway New South Wales, SE Australia 31°34′S 149°24′E
108 E6 Binningen Basel-Land, NW Switzerland 47°32′N 07°35′E
80 H12 Binshangul Gumuz ◐ federal region W Ethiopia
168 J8 Bintang, Banjaran ▲▲ Peninsular Malaysia
168 M10 Bintan, Pulau island Kepulauan Riau, W Indonesia
76 J14 Bintimani var. Binimani. ▲ NE Sierra Leone 09°21′N 11°09′W
Bint Jubayl see Bent Jbail
169 S9 Bintulu Sarawak, East Malaysia 03°12′N 113°01′E
169 S9 Bintuni prev. Steenkool. Papua, E Indonesia 02°03′S 133°45′E
163 W8 Binxian Heilongjiang, NE China 45°44′N 127°28′E
160 K14 Binyang var. Binzhou. Guangxi Zhuangzu Zizhiqu, S China 23°15′N 108°40′E
161 Q4 Binzhou Shandong, E China 37°23′N 118°03′E
Binzhou see Binyang
63 G14 Bío Bío var. Región del Bío Bío. ◐ region C Chile
Bío Bío, Región del see Bío Bío
63 G14 Bío Bío, Río ≈ C Chile
79 C16 Bioco, Isla de var. Bioko, Eng. Fernando Po, Sp. Fernando Póo; prev. Macías Nguema Biyogo. island NW Equatorial Guinea
112 D13 Biograd na Moru It. Zaravecchia. Zadar, SW Croatia 43°57′N 15°27′E
Bioko see Bioco, Isla de
113 F14 Biokovo ▲▲ S Croatia
Bipontium see Zweibrücken
143 W13 Bīrag, Kūh-e ▲▲ SE Iran
75 O10 Birāk var. Brak. C Libya 27°32′N 14°17′E
139 S10 Bi'r al Islām Karbalā', C Iraq 32°15′N 43°40′E
154 N11 Biramitrapur var. Birmitrapur. Orissa, E India 22°24′N 84°42′E
139 T11 Bi'r an Nişf An Najaf, S Iraq 31°22′N 44°07′E
78 L12 Birao Vakaga, NE Central African Republic 10°14′N 22°49′E
146 J10 Birata Rus. Darganata, Dargan-Ata. Lebap Welaýaty, NE Turkmenistan 40°30′N 62°09′E
158 M6 Biratar Bulak well NW China
153 R12 Birātnagar Eastern, SE Nepal 26°28′N 87°16′E
165 R5 Biratori Hokkaidō, NE Japan 42°35′N 142°07′E
39 S8 Birch Creek Alaska, USA 66°17′N 145°54′W
38 M11 Birch Creek ≈ Alaska, USA
11 T14 Birch Hills Saskatchewan, S Canada 52°58′N 105°22′W
182 M10 Birchip Victoria, SE Australia 36°01′S 142°55′E
29 X4 Birch Lake ◎ Minnesota, N USA
11 Q11 Birch Mountains ▲▲ Alberta, W Canada
11 V15 Birch River Manitoba, S Canada 52°22′N 101°03′W
44 H12 Birchs Hill hill W Jamaica
39 R11 Birchwood Alaska, USA 61°24′N 149°28′W
188 I5 Bird Island island S Northern Mariana Islands
137 N16 Birecik Şanlıurfa, S Turkey 37°03′N 37°59′E
152 M10 Birendranagar var. Surkhet. Mid Western, W Nepal 28°35′N 81°36′E
Bir es Saba see Be'er Sheva
74 A12 Bir-Gandouz SW Western Sahara 21°35′N 16°27′W
153 P12 Birganj Central, C Nepal 27°03′N 84°53′E
81 B14 Biri ≈ W Sudan
Bi'r Ibn Hirmās see Al Bi'r
143 U8 Bīrjand Khorāsān-e Janūbi, E Iran 32°54′N 59°14′E
139 T11 Birkat Ḩāmid well S Iraq
95 F18 Birkeland Aust-Agder, S Norway 58°18′N 08°13′E
101 E19 Birkenfeld Rheinland-Pfalz, SW Germany 49°39′N 07°10′E
97 K18 Birkenhead NW England, United Kingdom 53°24′N 03°02′W
109 W7 Birkfeld Steiermark, SE Austria 47°21′N 15°40′E
182 A2 Birksgate Range ▲▲ South Australia
Birlad see Bârlad
97 K20 Birmingham C England, United Kingdom 52°30′N 01°50′W
23 P4 Birmingham Alabama, S USA 33°30′N 86°47′W
97 M20 Birmingham ✈ C England, United Kingdom 52°27′N 01°46′W
Birmitrapur see Biramitrapur
Bir Moghrein see Bir Mogreïn
76 J4 Bir Mogreïn var. Bir Moghrein; prev. Fort-Trinquet. Tiris Zemmour, N Mauritania 25°10′N 11°35′W
191 S4 Birnie Island atoll Phoenix Islands, C Kiribati
77 S12 Birnin Gaouré var. Birni-Ngaouré. Dosso, SW Niger 12°59′N 03°02′E
Birni-Ngaouré see Birnin Gaouré
77 S12 Birnin Kebbi Kebbi, NW Nigeria 12°28′N 04°08′E
77 T12 Birnin Konni var. Birni-Nkonni. Tahoua, SW Niger 13°51′N 05°15′E
Birni-Nkonni see Birnin Konni
77 W13 Birnin Kudu Jigawa, N Nigeria 11°28′N 09°29′E
123 S16 Birobidzhan Yevreyskaya Avtonomnaya Oblast', SE Russian Federation 48°42′N 132°55′E
97 D18 Birr var. Parsonstown, Ir. Biorra. C Ireland 53°06′N 07°55′W
183 P4 Birrie River ≈ New South Wales/Queensland, SE Australia
108 D7 Birse ≈ NW Switzerland
Birsen see Biržai
108 E6 Birsfelden Basel-Land, NW Switzerland 47°33′N 07°37′E
127 U4 Birsk Respublika Bashkortostan, W Russian Federation 55°24′N 55°33′E
119 F14 Birštonas Kaunas, C Lithuania 54°37′N 24°00′E
159 P14 Biru Xinjiang Uygur Zizhiqu, W China 31°30′N 93°56′E
Biruni see Beruniy
122 L12 Biryusa ≈ C Russian Federation
122 L12 Biryusinsk Irkutskaya Oblast', C Russian Federation 55°52′N 97°48′E
118 G10 Biržai Ger. Birsen. Panevėžys, NE Lithuania 56°12′N 24°47′E
121 P16 Birżebbuġa SE Malta 35°50′N 14°32′E
Bisanthe see Tekirdağ
171 R12 Bisa, Pulau island Maluku, E Indonesia
37 N17 Bisbee Arizona, SW USA 31°27′N 109°55′W
29 O2 Bisbee North Dakota, N USA 48°36′N 99°21′W
Biscaia, Baía de see Biscay, Bay of
102 I13 Biscarrosse et de Parentis, Étang de ◎ SW France
104 M1 Biscay, Bay of Sp. Golfo de Vizcaya, Port. Baía de Biscaia. bay France/Spain
23 Z16 Biscayne Bay bay Florida, SE USA
64 M7 Biscay Plain undersea feature SE Bay of Biscay 07°15′W 45°00′N
107 N17 Bisceglie Puglia, SE Italy 41°14′N 16°31′E
Bischoflack see Škofja Loka
Bischofsburg see Biskupiec
109 Q7 Bischofshofen Salzburg, NW Austria 47°25′N 13°13′E
101 P15 Bischofswerda Sachsen, E Germany 51°07′N 14°13′E
103 V5 Bischwiller Bas-Rhin, NE France 48°46′N 07°52′E
21 T10 Biscoe North Carolina, SE USA 35°20′N 79°46′W
194 G5 Biscoe Islands island group Antarctica
14 E9 Biscotasi Lake ◎ Ontario, S Canada
14 E9 Biscotasing Ontario, S Canada 47°16′N 82°04′W
54 J6 Biscucuy Portuguesa, NW Venezuela 09°22′N 69°59′W
99 M24 Bissen Luxembourg, C Luxembourg 49°47′N 06°04′E
114 K11 Biser Khaskovo, S Bulgaria 41°52′N 25°59′E
113 D15 Biševo It. Busi. island SW Croatia
141 N12 Bishah, Wādī dry watercourse C Saudi Arabia
147 U7 Bishkek var. Pishpek; prev. Frunze. ● (Kyrgyzstan) Chuyskaya Oblast', N Kyrgyzstan 42°54′N 74°27′E
147 U7 Bishkek ✈ Chuyskaya Oblast', N Kyrgyzstan 42°55′N 74°37′E
153 R16 Bishnupur West Bengal, NE India 23°05′N 87°20′E
83 J25 Bisho Eastern Cape, S South Africa 32°46′S 27°21′E
35 S9 Bishop California, W USA 37°22′N 118°24′W
25 S15 Bishop Texas, SW USA 27°36′N 97°49′W
97 L15 Bishop Auckland N England, United Kingdom 54°41′N 01°41′W
Bishop's Lynn see King's Lynn
97 O21 Bishop's Stortford E England, United Kingdom 51°45′N 00°11′E
21 S12 Bishopville South Carolina, SE USA 34°18′N 80°15′W
138 M5 Bishrī, Jabal ▲▲ E Syria
163 U4 Bishui Heilongjiang, NE China 52°06′N 123°42′E
81 G17 Bisina, Lake prev. Lake Salisbury. ◎ E Uganda
Biskara see Biskra
74 L6 Biskra var. Beskra, Biskara. NE Algeria 34°51′N 05°44′E
110 M8 Biskupiec Ger. Bischofsburg. Warmińsko-Mazurskie, NE Poland 53°52′N 20°57′E
171 R7 Bislig Mindanao, S Philippines 08°10′N 126°19′E
27 X6 Bismarck Missouri, C USA 37°46′N 90°37′W
28 M5 Bismarck state capital North Dakota, N USA 46°49′N 100°47′W
186 D5 Bismarck Archipelago island group NE Papua New Guinea
129 Z16 Bismarck Plate tectonic feature W Pacific Ocean
186 D7 Bismarck Range ▲▲ N Papua New Guinea
186 E6 Bismarck Sea sea W Pacific Ocean
137 P15 Bismil Diyarbakır, SE Turkey 37°53′N 40°38′E
43 N6 Bismuna, Laguna lagoon NE Nicaragua
Bisnulok see Phitsanulok
171 R10 Bisoa, Tanjung headland Pulau Halmahera, N Indonesia 02°15′N 127°57′E
28 K7 Bison South Dakota, N USA 45°31′N 102°27′W
93 H17 Bispgården Jämtland, C Sweden 63°00′N 16°40′E
76 G13 Bissau ● (Guinea-Bissau) W Guinea-Bissau 11°52′N 15°39′W
76 G13 Bissau ✈ W Guinea-Bissau 11°53′N 15°41′W
Bissojohka see Børselv
76 G12 Bissorā W Guinea-Bissau 12°16′N 15°35′W
11 O10 Bistcho Lake ◎ Alberta, W Canada
22 G5 Bistineau, Lake ⊡ Louisiana, S USA
Bistrica see Ilirska Bistrica
116 I9 Bistriţa Ger. Bistritz, Hung. Beszterce; prev. Nösen. Bistriţa-Năsăud, N Romania 47°10′N 24°31′E
116 K10 Bistriţa Ger. Bistritz. ≈ NE Romania
116 I9 Bistriţa-Năsăud ◐ county N Romania
Bistritz see Bistriţa
Bistritz ober Pernstein see Bystřice nad Pernštejnem
152 L11 Biswān Uttar Pradesh, N India 27°30′N 81°00′E
110 M7 Bisztynek Warmińsko-Mazurskie, NE Poland 54°05′N 20°53′E
79 E17 Bitam Woleu-Ntem, N Gabon 02°05′N 11°30′E
101 D18 Bitburg Rheinland-Pfalz, SW Germany 49°58′N 06°31′E
103 U4 Bitche Moselle, NE France 49°01′N 07°27′E
78 I11 Bitkine Guéra, C Chad 11°59′N 18°13′E
137 R15 Bitlis Bitlis, SE Turkey 38°23′N 42°04′E
137 R14 Bitlis ◐ province E Turkey
Bitoeng see Bitung
113 N20 Bitola Turk. Monastir; prev. Bitolj. S FYR Macedonia 41°01′N 21°22′E
Bitolj see Bitola
107 O17 Bitonto anc. Butuntum. Puglia, SE Italy 41°07′N 16°41′E
77 Q13 Bitou var. Bittou. SE Burkina 11°19′N 00°17′W
155 C20 Bitra Island island Lakshadweep, India, N Indian Ocean
101 M14 Bitterfeld Sachsen-Anhalt, E Germany 51°37′N 12°18′E
32 O9 Bitterroot Range ▲▲ Idaho/Montana, NW USA
33 P10 Bitterroot River ≈ Montana, NW USA
107 D18 Bitti Sardegna, Italy, C Mediterranean Sea 40°30′N 09°31′E
Bittou see Bitou
171 Q11 Bitung prev. Bitoeng. Sulawesi, C Indonesia 01°28′N 125°13′E
60 I12 Bituruna Paraná, S Brazil 26°11′S 51°34′W
77 Y13 Biu Borno, E Nigeria 10°35′N 12°13′E
Biumba see Byumba
164 J13 Biwa-ko ◎ Honshū, SW Japan
171 X14 Biwarlaut Papua, E Indonesia 05°44′S 138°14′E
27 P10 Bixby Oklahoma, C USA 35°56′N 95°52′W
122 J13 Biya ≈ S Russian Federation
122 J13 Biysk Altayskiy Kray, S Russian Federation 52°34′N 85°09′E
164 H13 Bizen Okayama, Honshū, SW Japan 34°45′N 134°10′E
Bizerta see Bizerte
120 K10 Bizerte Ar. Banzart, Eng. Bizerta. N Tunisia 37°18′N 09°48′E
Bizkaia see Vizcaya
92 G2 Bjargtangar headland W Iceland 63°30′N 24°29′W
Bjärnå see Perniö
95 K22 Bjärnum Skåne, S Sweden 56°15′N 13°45′E
93 I16 Bjästa Västernorrland, C Sweden 63°12′N 18°30′E
113 I14 Bjelašnica ▲ SE Bosnia and Herzegovina 43°13′N 18°18′E
112 C10 Bjelolasica ▲ NW Croatia 45°13′N 14°56′E
112 F8 Bjelovar Hung. Belovár. Bjelovar-Bilogora, N Croatia 45°54′N 16°49′E
112 F8 Bjelovar-Bilogora off. Bjelovarsko-Bilogorska Županija. ◐ province NE Croatia
Bjelovarsko-Bilogorska Županija see Bjelovar-Bilogora
92 H10 Bjerkvik Nordland, C Norway 68°31′N 16°08′E
95 G21 Bjerringbro Viborg, NW Denmark 56°23′N 09°40′E
Bjeshkët e Namuna see North Albanian Alps
95 L14 Björbo Dalarna, C Sweden 60°28′N 14°44′E
95 I15 Bjørkelangen Akershus, S Norway 59°54′N 11°33′E
95 O14 Björklinge Uppsala, C Sweden 60°03′N 17°33′E
93 I14 Björksele Västerbotten, N Sweden 64°58′N 18°30′E
93 I16 Björna Västernorrland, C Sweden 63°34′N 18°38′E
95 C14 Bjørnafjorden fjord S Norway
95 L16 Björneborg Värmland, C Sweden 59°13′N 14°15′E
Björneborg see Pori
95 E14 Bjornesfjorden ◎ S Norway
92 M9 Bjørnevatn Finnmark, N Norway 69°40′N 29°57′E
197 T13 Bjørnøya Eng. Bear Island. island N Norway
93 I15 Bjurholm Västerbotten, N Sweden 63°57′N 19°16′E
95 J22 Bjuv Skåne, S Sweden 56°05′N 12°57′E
76 M12 Bla Ségou, W Mali 12°58′N 05°45′W
181 W8 Blackall Queensland, E Australia 24°26′S 145°32′E
29 V2 Black Bay lake bay Minnesota, N USA
27 N9 Black Bear Creek ≈ Oklahoma, C USA
97 K17 Blackburn NW England, United Kingdom 53°45′N 02°29′W
45 W10 Blackburne ✈ (Plymouth) E Montserrat 16°45′N 62°09′W
39 T11 Blackburn, Mount ▲ Alaska, USA 61°43′N 143°25′W
35 N5 Black Butte Lake ⊡ California, W USA
194 J5 Black Coast physical region Antarctica
11 Q16 Black Diamond Alberta, SW Canada 50°42′N 114°09′W
18 K11 Black Dome ▲ New York, NE USA 42°16′N 74°07′W
113 L18 Black Drin Alb. Lumi i Drinit të Zi, SCr. Crni Drim. ≈ Albania/FYR Macedonia
29 U4 Blackduck Minnesota, N USA 47°45′N 94°33′W
12 D6 Black Duck ≈ Ontario, C Canada
33 R14 Blackfoot Idaho, NW USA 43°11′N 112°20′W
33 P9 Blackfoot River ≈ Montana, NW USA
Black Forest see Schwarzwald
28 J10 Blackhawk South Dakota, N USA 44°09′N 103°18′W
28 I10 Black Hills ▲▲ South Dakota/ Wyoming, N USA
11 T10 Black Lake ◎ Saskatchewan, C Canada
22 G6 Black Lake ⊡ Louisiana, S USA
31 Q5 Black Lake ◎ Michigan, N USA
18 I7 Black Lake ◎ New York, NE USA
26 F7 Black Mesa ▲ Oklahoma, C USA 37°00′N 103°07′W
21 P10 Black Mountain North Carolina, SE USA 35°37′N 82°19′W
35 P13 Black Mountain ▲ California, W USA 35°22′N 120°21′W
37 Q2 Black Mountain ▲ Colorado, C USA 40°47′N 107°23′W
96 K1 Black Mountains ▲▲ SE Wales, United Kingdom
36 H10 Black Mountains ▲▲ Arizona, SW USA
21 O7 Black Mountains ▲ Kentucky, E USA 36°54′N 82°53′W
33 Q16 Black Pine Peak ▲ Idaho, NW USA 42°07′N 113°07′W
97 K17 Blackpool NW England, United Kingdom 53°50′N 03°03′W
37 Q14 Black Range ▲▲ New Mexico, SW USA
44 I12 Black River W Jamaica 18°02′N 77°52′W
14 J14 Black River ≈ Ontario, SE Canada
129 U12 Black River Chin. Babian Jiang, Lixian Jiang, Fr. Rivière Noire, Vtn. Sông Đa. ≈ China/Vietnam
44 I12 Black River ≈ W Jamaica
39 T7 Black River ≈ Alaska, USA
37 N13 Black River ≈ Arizona, SW USA
27 X7 Black River ≈ Arkansas/ Missouri, C USA
22 I7 Black River ≈ Louisiana, S USA
31 Q5 Black River ≈ Michigan, N USA
31 S8 Black River ≈ Michigan, N USA
18 I8 Black River ≈ New York, NE USA
21 T13 Black River ≈ South Carolina, SE USA
30 J7 Black River ≈ Wisconsin, N USA
30 J7 Black River Falls Wisconsin, N USA 44°18′N 90°51′W
35 R3 Black Rock Desert desert Nevada, W USA
Black Sand Desert see Garagum
21 S7 Blacksburg Virginia, NE USA 37°15′N 80°25′W
136 H10 Black Sea var. Euxine Sea, Bul. Cherno More, Rom. Marea Neagră, Rus. Chernoye More, Turk. Karadeniz, Ukr. Chorne More. sea Asia/ Europe
117 Q10 Black Sea Lowland Ukr. Prychornomor'ska Nyzovyna. depression SE Europe
33 S17 Blacks Fork ≈ Wyoming, C USA
23 V7 Blackshear Georgia, SE USA 31°18′N 82°14′W
23 S6 Blackshear, Lake ⊡ Georgia, SE USA
97 A16 Blacksod Bay Ir. Cuan an Fhóid Duibh. inlet W Ireland
21 V7 Blackstone Virginia, NE USA 37°04′N 78°00′W
77 O14 Black Volta var. Borongo, Mouhoun, Moun Hou, Fr. Volta Noire. ≈ W Africa
23 O5 Black Warrior River ≈ Alabama, S USA
181 X8 Blackwater Queensland, E Australia 23°34′S 148°51′E
97 D20 Blackwater Ir. An Abhainn Mhór. ≈ S Ireland
27 T4 Blackwater River ≈ Missouri, C USA
21 W7 Blackwater River ≈ Virginia, NE USA
Blackwater State see Nebraska
27 N8 Blackwell Oklahoma, C USA 36°48′N 97°16′W
25 P7 Blackwell Texas, SW USA 32°05′N 100°19′W
99 J15 Bladel Noord-Brabant, S Netherlands 51°22′N 05°13′E
Bladenmarkt see Bălăuşeri
127 O14 Blagodarnyy Stavropol'skiy Kray, SW Russian Federation 45°06′N 43°26′E
114 G11 Blagoevgrad prev. Gorna Dzhumaya. Blagoevgrad, W Bulgaria 42°01′N 23°05′E
114 G11 Blagoevgrad ◐ province SW Bulgaria
123 Q14 Blagoveshchensk Amurskaya Oblast', SE Russian Federation 50°19′N 127°30′E
127 V4 Blagoveshchensk Respublika Bashkortostan, W Russian Federation 55°03′N 56°01′E
102 I7 Blain Loire-Atlantique, NW France 47°26′N 01°47′W
29 V8 Blaine Minnesota, N USA 45°09′N 93°13′W
32 H6 Blaine Washington, NW USA 48°59′N 122°45′W
11 T15 Blaine Lake Saskatchewan, S Canada 52°49′N 106°48′W
29 S14 Blair Nebraska, C USA 41°32′N 96°07′W
96 J10 Blairgowrie C Scotland, United Kingdom 56°19′N 03°25′W
18 C15 Blairsville Pennsylvania, NE USA 40°25′N 79°12′W
116 H11 Blaj Ger. Blasendorf, Hung. Balázsfalva. Alba, SW Romania 46°10′N 23°57′E
64 F9 Blake-Bahama Ridge undersea feature W Atlantic Ocean 29°00′N 73°30′W
23 S7 Blakely Georgia, SE USA 31°22′N 84°55′W
64 E10 Blake Plateau var. Blake Terrace. undersea feature W Atlantic Ocean 31°00′N 79°00′W
30 M1 Blake Point headland Michigan, N USA 48°11′N 88°25′W
Blake Terrace see Blake Plateau
61 B24 Blanca, Bahía bay E Argentina
56 C12 Blanca, Cordillera ▲▲ W Peru
105 T12 Blanca, Costa physical region SE Spain
37 S7 Blanca Peak ▲ Colorado, C USA 37°34′N 105°29′W
24 I9 Blanca, Sierra ▲ Texas, SW USA 31°15′N 105°26′W
120 K9 Blanc, Cap headland N Tunisia 37°20′N 09°41′E
Blanc, Cap see Nouâdhibou, Râs
31 R12 Blanchard River ≈ Ohio, N USA
182 E8 Blanche, Cape headland South Australia 33°03′S 134°10′E
182 J4 Blanche, Lake ◎ South Australia
31 R14 Blanchester Ohio, N USA 39°17′N 83°59′W
182 I9 Blanchetown South Australia 34°21′S 139°36′E
45 U13 Blanchisseuse Trinidad, Trinidad and Tobago 10°47′N 61°18′W
103 T11 Blanc, Mont It. Monte Bianco. ▲ France/Italy 45°45′N 06°51′E
25 R11 Blanco Texas, SW USA 30°06′N 98°25′W
42 K14 Blanco, Cabo headland NW Costa Rica 09°34′N 85°06′W
32 D14 Blanco, Cape headland Oregon, NW USA 42°49′N 124°33′W
62 H10 Blanco, Río ≈ W Argentina
56 F10 Blanco, Río ≈ NE Peru
15 O9 Blanc, Réservoir ⊡ Québec, SE Canada
21 R7 Bland Virginia, NE USA 37°06′N 81°08′W
92 I2 Blanda ≈ N Iceland
37 O7 Blanding Utah, W USA 37°37′N 109°28′W
105 X5 Blanes Cataluña, NE Spain 41°41′N 02°48′E
103 N3 Blangy-sur-Bresle Seine-Maritime, N France 49°55′N 01°37′E
111 C18 Blanice Ger. Blanitz. ≈ SE Czech Republic
Blanitz see Blanice
99 C16 Blankenberge West-Vlaanderen, NW Belgium 51°19′N 03°08′E
101 D17 Blankenheim Nordrhein-Westfalen, W Germany 50°26′N 06°41′E
25 R8 Blanket Texas, SW USA 31°49′N 98°47′W
55 O3 Blanquilla, Isla var. La Blanquilla. island N Venezuela
Blanquilla, La see Blanquilla, Isla
61 F18 Blanquillo Durazno, C Uruguay 32°53′S 55°37′W
111 G18 Blansko Ger. Blanz. Jihomoravský Kraj, SE Czech Republic 49°22′N 16°39′E
83 N15 Blantyre var. Blantyre-Limbe. Southern, S Malawi 15°45′S 35°04′E
83 N15 Blantyre ✈ Southern, S Malawi 15°34′S 35°03′E
Blantyre-Limbe see Blantyre
Blanz see Blansko
98 J10 Blaricum Noord-Holland, C Netherlands 52°16′N 05°15′E
Blasendorf see Blaj
Blatnitsa see Durankulak
113 F15 Blato It. Blatta. Dubrovnik-Neretva, S Croatia 42°57′N 16°47′E
Blatta see Blato
108 E10 Blatten Valais, SW Switzerland 46°22′N 08°00′E
101 J20 Blaufelden Baden-Württemberg, SW Germany 49°21′N 10°01′E
95 E23 Blåvands Huk headland W Denmark 55°33′N 08°04′E
102 G6 Blavet ≈ NW France
102 J12 Blaye Gironde, SW France 45°08′N 00°40′W
183 R8 Blayney New South Wales, SE Australia 33°33′S 149°13′E
65 D25 Bleaker Island island SE Falkland Islands
109 T10 Bled Ger. Veldes. NW Slovenia 46°23′N 14°06′E
99 D20 Bléharies Hainaut, SW Belgium 50°31′N 03°25′E
109 U9 Bleiburg Slvn. Pliberk. Kärnten, S Austria 46°36′N 14°49′E
101 L17 Bleiloch-stausee ⊡ C Germany
98 H12 Bleiswijk Zuid-Holland, W Netherlands 52°01′N 04°32′E
95 L22 Blekinge ◐ county S Sweden
14 D17 Blenheim Ontario, S Canada 42°20′N 81°59′W
185 K15 Blenheim Marlborough, South Island, New Zealand 41°32′S 174°E
99 M15 Blerick Limburg, SE Netherlands 51°22′N 06°10′E
Blesae see Blois
25 V13 Blessing Texas, SW USA 28°52′N 96°12′W
14 I10 Bleu, Lac ◎ Québec, SE Canada
Blibba see Blitta
120 H10 Blida var. El Boulaida, El Boulaïda. N Algeria 36°30′N 02°50′E
95 P15 Blidö Stockholm, C Sweden 59°37′N 18°55′E
95 K18 Blidsberg Västra Götaland, S Sweden 57°55′N 13°30′E
185 A21 Bligh Sound sound South Island, New Zealand
187 X14 Bligh Water strait NW Fiji
14 D11 Blind River Ontario, S Canada 46°12′N 82°59′W
31 R11 Blissfield Michigan, N USA 41°49′N 83°51′W
77 R15 Blitta prev. Blibba. C Togo 08°19′N 00°59′E
19 O13 Block Island island Rhode Island, NE USA
19 O13 Block Island Sound sound Rhode Island, NE USA
98 H10 Bloemendaal Noord-Holland, W Netherlands 52°23′N 04°39′E
83 H23 Bloemfontein var. Mangaung. ● (South Africa-judicial capital) Free State, C South Africa 29°07′S 26°14′E
83 I22 Bloemhof North-West, NW South Africa 27°39′S 25°37′E
102 M7 Blois anc. Blesae. Loir-et-Cher, C France 47°36′N 01°20′E
98 L8 Blokzijl Overijssel, N Netherlands 52°46′N 05°58′E
95 N20 Blomstermåla Kalmar, S Sweden 56°58′N 16°19′E
92 I2 Blönduós Nordhurland Vestra, N Iceland 65°39′N 20°15′W
110 L11 Błonie Mazowieckie, C Poland 52°13′N 20°36′E
97 C14 Bloody Foreland Ir. Cnoc Fola. headland NW Ireland 55°09′N 08°18′W
31 N15 Bloomfield Indiana, N USA 39°01′N 86°58′W
29 X16 Bloomfield Iowa, C USA 40°45′N 92°24′W
27 Y8 Bloomfield Missouri, C USA 36°54′N 89°58′W
37 P9 Bloomfield New Mexico, SW USA 36°42′N 108°00′W
25 U7 Blooming Grove Texas, SW USA 32°05′N 96°43′W
29 W10 Blooming Prairie Minnesota, N USA 43°52′N 93°03′W
30 L13 Bloomington Illinois, N USA 40°28′N 88°59′W
31 O15 Bloomington Indiana, N USA 39°10′N 86°31′W
29 V9 Bloomington Minnesota, N USA 44°50′N 93°18′W
25 U13 Bloomington Texas, SW USA 28°39′N 96°53′W
18 H14 Bloomsburg Pennsylvania, NE USA 40°59′N 76°27′W
181 X7 Bloomsbury Queensland, NE Australia 20°47′S 148°35′E
169 R16 Blora Jawa, C Indonesia 06°55′S 111°29′E
18 G12 Blossburg Pennsylvania, NE USA 41°38′N 77°00′W
25 V5 Blossom Texas, SW USA 33°39′N 95°23′W
123 T5 Blossom, Mys headland Ostrov Vrangelya, NE Russian Federation 70°49′N 178°49′E
23 R8 Blountstown Florida, SE USA 30°26′N 85°03′W
21 P8 Blountville Tennessee, S USA 36°31′N 82°19′W
21 Q9 Blowing Rock North Carolina, SE USA 36°15′N 81°53′W
108 J8 Bludenz Vorarlberg, W Austria 47°10′N 09°50′E
36 L6 Blue Bell Knoll ▲ Utah, W USA 38°11′N 111°31′W
23 Y12 Blue Cypress Lake ◎ Florida, SE USA
29 U11 Blue Earth Minnesota, N USA 43°38′N 94°06′W
21 Q7 Bluefield Virginia, NE USA 37°15′N 81°16′W
21 R7 Bluefield West Virginia, NE USA 37°16′N 81°13′W
43 N10 Bluefields Región Autónoma Atlántico Sur, SE Nicaragua 12°01′N 83°47′W
43 N10 Bluefields, Bahía de bay W Caribbean Sea
29 Z14 Blue Grass Iowa, C USA 41°30′N 90°46′W
Bluegrass State see Kentucky
Blue Hen State see Delaware
19 S7 Blue Hill Maine, NE USA 44°25′N 68°36′W
29 P16 Blue Hill Nebraska, C USA 40°19′N 98°27′W
30 J5 Blue Hills hill range Wisconsin, N USA
34 L3 Blue Lake California, W USA 40°52′N 124°00′W
Blue Law State see Connecticut
37 Q6 Blue Mesa Reservoir ⊡ Colorado, C USA
27 S12 Blue Mountain ▲ Arkansas, C USA 34°42′N 94°04′W
19 O6 Blue Mountain ▲ New Hampshire, NE USA 44°48′N 71°26′W
18 K8 Blue Mountain ▲ New York, NE USA 43°52′N 74°24′W

18 H15 **Blue Mountain** *ridge* Pennsylvania, NE USA
44 H10 **Blue Mountain Peak** ▲ E Jamaica *18°02′N 76°34′W*
183 S8 **Blue Mountains** New South Wales, SE Australia
32 L11 **Blue Mountains** Oregon/ Washington, NW USA
80 G12 **Blue Nile** *state* E Sudan
80 H12 **Blue Nile** *var.* Abai, Bahr el, Azraq, *Amh.* Ābay Wenz, *Ar.* An Nīl al Azraq. Ethiopia/ Sudan
8 J7 **Bluenose Lake** Nunavut, NW Canada
27 O3 **Blue Rapids** Kansas, C USA *39°39′N 96°38′W*
23 S1 **Blue Ridge** Georgia, SE USA *34°51′N 84°19′W*
17 S11 **Blue Ridge** *var.* Blue Ridge Mountains. North Carolina/Virginia, USA
23 S1 **Blue Ridge Lake** Georgia, SE USA
Blue Ridge Mountains *see* Blue Ridge
11 N15 **Blue River** British Columbia, SW Canada *52°03′N 119°21′W*
27 O12 **Blue River** Oklahoma, C USA
27 R4 **Blue Springs** Missouri, C USA *39°01′N 94°16′W*
21 R6 **Bluestone Lake** West Virginia, NE USA
185 C25 **Bluff** Southland, South Island, New Zealand *46°36′S 168°22′E*
37 O8 **Bluff** Utah, W USA *37°15′N 109°36′W*
21 P8 **Bluff City** Tennessee, S USA *36°28′N 82°15′W*
65 E24 **Bluff Cove** East Falkland, Falkland Islands *51°45′S 58°11′W*
25 S7 **Bluff Dale** Texas, SW USA *32°18′N 98°01′W*
183 N15 **Bluff Hill Point** *headland* Tasmania, SE Australia *41°03′S 144°35′E*
31 Q12 **Bluffton** Indiana, N USA *40°44′N 85°10′W*
31 R12 **Bluffton** Ohio, N USA *40°54′N 83°53′W*
25 T7 **Blum** Texas, SW USA *32°08′N 97°24′W*
101 G24 **Blumberg** Baden-Württemberg, SW Germany *47°48′N 08°31′E*
60 K13 **Blumenau** Santa Catarina, S Brazil *26°55′S 49°07′W*
29 N9 **Blunt** South Dakota, N USA *44°30′N 99°58′E*
32 H15 **Bly** Oregon, NW USA *42°22′N 121°04′W*
39 R13 **Blying Sound** *sound* Alaska, USA
97 M14 **Blyth** N England, United Kingdom *55°07′N 01°30′W*
35 Y16 **Blythe** California, W USA *33°35′N 114°36′W*
27 Y9 **Blytheville** Arkansas, C USA *35°56′N 89°55′W*
117 V7 **Blyznyuky** Kharkivs'ka Oblast', E Ukraine *48°51′N 36°32′E*
95 G16 **Bø** Telemark, S Norway *59°24′N 09°04′E*
76 I15 **Bo** S Sierra Leone *07°58′N 11°45′W*
171 O4 **Boac** Marinduque, N Philippines *13°26′N 121°50′E*
42 K10 **Boaco** Boaco, S Nicaragua *12°28′N 85°45′W*
42 J10 **Boaco** *department* C Nicaragua
79 I15 **Boali** Ombella-Mpoko, SW Central African Republic *04°52′N 18°00′E*
Boalsert *see* Bolsward
31 V12 **Boardman** Ohio, N USA *41°01′N 80°39′W*
32 J11 **Boardman** Oregon, NW USA *45°50′N 119°42′W*
14 F13 **Boat Lake** Ontario, S Canada
58 F10 **Boa Vista** *state capital* Roraima, NW Brazil *02°51′N 60°43′W*
76 D9 **Boa Vista** *island* Ilhas de Barlavento, E Cape Verde
23 Q2 **Boaz** Alabama, S USA *34°12′N 86°10′W*
160 L15 **Bobai** Guangxi Zhuangzu Zizhiqu, S China *22°09′N 109°57′E*
172 J1 **Bobaomby, Tanjona** *Fr.* Cap d'Ambre. *headland* N Madagascar *11°58′S 49°13′E*
155 M14 **Bobbili** Andhra Pradesh, E India *18°32′N 83°29′E*
106 D9 **Bobbio** Emilia-Romagna, C Italy *44°48′N 09°27′E*
14 I14 **Bobcaygeon** Ontario, SE Canada *44°32′N 78°33′W*
Bober *see* Bóbr
103 O5 **Bobigny** Seine-St-Denis, N France *48°55′N 02°27′E*
77 N13 **Bobo-Dioulasso** SW Burkina *11°12′N 04°21′W*
110 G8 **Bobolice** *Ger.* Bublitz. Zachodnio-pomorskie, NW Poland *53°56′N 16°37′E*
83 J19 **Bobonong** Central, E Botswana *21°58′S 28°26′E*
171 R11 **Bobopayo** Pulau Halmahera, E Indonesia *01°07′N 127°26′E*
113 J15 **Bobotov Kuk** ▲ N Montenegro *43°06′N 19°00′E*
114 G10 **Bobovdol** Kyustendil, W Bulgaria *42°21′N 22°59′E*
119 M15 **Bobr** Minskaya Voblasts', NW Belarus *54°20′N 29°16′E*
119 N15 **Bobr** C Belarus
111 E14 **Bóbr** *Eng.* Bobrawa, *Ger.* Bober. SW Poland
Bobrawa *see* Bóbr
Bobrik *see* Bobryk
Bobrinets *see* Bobrynets'
Bobrka/Bóbrka *see* Bibrka
126 L8 **Bobrov** Voronezhskaya Oblast', W Russian Federation *51°10′N 40°03′E*
117 Q4 **Bobrovytsya** Chernihivs'ka Oblast', N Ukraine *50°43′N 31°24′E*
Bobruysk *see* Babruysk
119 J19 **Bobryk** *Rus.* Bobrik. SW Belarus
117 Q8 **Bobrynets'** *Rus.* Bobrinets. Kirovohrads'ka Oblast', C Ukraine *48°02′N 32°10′E*
14 K14 **Bobs Lake** Ontario, SE Canada
54 I6 **Bobures** Zulia, NW Venezuela *09°15′N 71°10′W*
42 H1 **Boca Bacalar Chico** *headland* N Belize *15°05′N 82°12′W*
112 G11 **Bočac** Republika Srpska, NW Bosnia and Herzegovina
41 R14 **Boca del Río** Veracruz-Llave, S Mexico *19°08′N 96°08′W*
55 O4 **Boca de Pozo** Nueva Esparta, NE Venezuela *11°00′N 64°23′W*
59 C15 **Boca do Acre** Amazonas, N Brazil *08°45′S 67°23′W*
55 N12 **Boca Mavaca** Amazonas, S Venezuela *02°30′N 65°11′W*
79 G14 **Bocaranga** Ouham-Pendé, W Central African Republic *07°07′N 15°40′E*
23 Z15 **Boca Raton** Florida, SE USA *26°22′N 80°05′W*
43 P14 **Bocas del Toro** Bocas del Toro, NW Panama *09°20′N 82°15′W*
43 P15 **Bocas del Toro** *off.* Provincia de Bocas del Toro. *province* NW Panama
43 P15 **Bocas del Toro, Archipiélago de** *island group* NW Panama
Bocas del Toro, Provincia de *see* Bocas del Toro
42 L7 **Bocay** Jinotega, N Nicaragua *14°19′N 85°08′W*
105 N6 **Boceguillas** Castilla-León, N Spain *41°20′N 03°39′W*
Bocheykovo *see* Bacheykava
111 L17 **Bochnia** Małopolskie, SE Poland *49°58′N 20°27′E*
99 K16 **Bocholt** Limburg, NE Belgium *51°10′N 05°37′E*
101 D14 **Bocholt** Nordrhein-Westfalen, W Germany *51°50′N 06°37′E*
101 E15 **Bochum** Nordrhein-Westfalen, W Germany *51°29′N 07°13′E*
103 Y15 **Bocognano** Corse, France, C Mediterranean Sea *42°04′N 09°03′E*
54 I6 **Boconó** Trujillo, NW Venezuela *09°17′N 70°17′W*
116 F12 **Bocşa** *Ger.* Bokschen, *Hung.* Boksánbánya. Caraş-Severin, SW Romania *45°23′N 21°47′E*
79 H15 **Boda** Lobaye, SW Central African Republic *04°17′N 17°25′E*
94 L12 **Boda** Dalarna, C Sweden *61°00′N 15°15′E*
95 O20 **Böda** Kalmar, S Sweden *57°16′N 17°04′E*
95 L19 **Bodafors** Jönköping, S Sweden *57°30′N 14°40′E*
123 O12 **Bodaybo** Irkutskaya Oblast', E Russian Federation *57°52′N 114°05′E*
22 G5 **Bodcau, Bayou** *var.* Bodcau Creek. Louisiana, S USA
Bodcau Creek *see* Bodcau, Bayou
44 D8 **Bodden Town** *var.* Boddentown. Grand Cayman, SW Cayman Islands *19°20′N 81°14′W*
Boddentown *see* Bodden Town
101 K14 **Bode** C Germany
34 L7 **Bodega Head** *headland* California, W USA *38°16′N 123°04′W*
Bodegas *see* Babahoyo
98 H11 **Bodegraven** Zuid-Holland, C Netherlands *52°05′N 04°45′E*
78 H8 **Bodélé** *depression* W Chad
92 J13 **Boden** Norrbotten, N Sweden *65°50′N 21°44′E*
Bodensee *see* Constance, Lake, C Europe
65 M15 **Bode Verde Fracture Zone** *tectonic feature* E Atlantic Ocean
155 H14 **Bodhan** Andhra Pradesh, C India *18°40′N 77°51′E*
Bodi *see* Jinst
155 H22 **Bodināyakkanūr** Tamil Nādu, SE India *10°02′N 77°18′E*
108 H10 **Bodio** Ticino, S Switzerland *46°23′N 08°55′E*
Bodjonegoro *see* Bojonegoro
97 I24 **Bodmin** SW England, United Kingdom *50°29′N 04°43′W*
97 I24 **Bodmin Moor** *moorland* SW England, United Kingdom
92 G12 **Bodø** Nordland, C Norway *67°17′N 14°22′E*
59 H20 **Bodoquena, Serra da** ▲ SW Brazil
136 B16 **Bodrum** Muğla, SW Turkey *37°01′N 27°28′E*
Bodzafordulő *see* Întorsura Buzăului
99 L14 **Boekel** Noord-Brabant, SE Netherlands *51°35′N 05°42′E*
Boeloekoemba *see* Bulukumba
103 Q11 **Boën** Loire, E France *45°45′N 04°01′E*
79 K18 **Boende** Equateur, C Dem. Rep. Congo *0°12′S 20°54′E*
25 R11 **Boerne** Texas, SW USA *29°47′N 98°44′W*
Boeroe *see* Buru, Pulau
Boetoeng *see* Buton, Pulau
22 I5 **Boeuf River** Arkansas/ Louisiana, S USA
76 H14 **Boffa** W Guinea *10°12′N 14°02′W*
Bó Finne, Inis *see* Inishbofin
Boga *see* Bogë
166 L9 **Bogale** Ayeyarwady, SW Burma (Myanmar) *16°16′N 95°21′E*
22 L8 **Bogalusa** Louisiana, S USA *30°47′N 89°51′W*
77 Q12 **Bogandé** C Burkina *13°02′N 00°08′W*
79 I15 **Bogangolo** Ombella-Mpoko, C Central African Republic *05°36′N 18°17′E*
183 Q7 **Bogan River** New South Wales, SE Australia
25 W5 **Bogata** Texas, SW USA *33°28′N 95°12′W*
111 D14 **Bogatynia** *Ger.* Reichenau. Dolnośląskie, SW Poland *50°53′N 14°55′E*
136 K13 **Boğazlıyan** Yozgat, C Turkey *39°13′N 35°17′E*
79 J17 **Bogbonga** Equateur, NW Dem. Rep. Congo *01°36′N 19°24′E*
158 J14 **Bogcang Zangbo** W China
162 I9 **Bogd** *var.* Horiult. Bayanhongor, C Mongolia *45°09′N 100°50′E*
162 J10 **Bogd** *var.* Hovd. Övörhangay, C Mongolia *44°43′N 102°08′E*
158 L5 **Bogda Feng** ▲ NW China *43°51′N 88°14′E*
114 I9 **Bogdan** ▲ C Bulgaria *42°37′N 24°28′E*
113 Q20 **Bogdanci** SE FYR Macedonia *41°12′N 22°34′E*
158 M5 **Bogda Shan** *var.* Po-ko-to Shan. ▲ NW China
113 K17 **Bogë** *var.* Boga. Shkodër, N Albania *42°25′N 19°38′E*
Bogeda'er *see* Wenquan
Bogendorf *see* Łuków
95 G23 **Bogense** Fyn, C Denmark *55°34′N 10°06′E*
183 T3 **Boggabilla** New South Wales, SE Australia *28°37′S 150°21′E*
183 S6 **Boggabri** New South Wales, SE Australia *30°44′S 150°00′E*
186 D6 **Bogia** Madang, N Papua New Guinea *04°16′S 144°56′E*
97 N23 **Bognor Regis** SE England, United Kingdom *50°47′N 00°41′W*
Bogodukhov *see* Bohodukhiv
181 V15 **Bogong, Mount** ▲ Victoria, SE Australia *36°43′S 147°19′E*
169 O16 **Bogor** *Dut.* Buitenzorg. Jawa, C Indonesia *06°34′S 106°45′E*
126 L5 **Bogoroditsk** Tul'skaya Oblast', W Russian Federation *53°46′N 38°09′E*
127 O3 **Bogorodsk** Nizhegorodskaya Oblast', W Russian Federation *56°06′N 43°29′E*
Bogorodskoje *see* Bogorodskoye
123 S12 **Bogorodskoye** Khabarovskiy Kray, SE Russian Federation *52°22′N 140°33′E*
125 R15 **Bogorodskoye** *var.* Bogorodskoje. Kirovskaya Oblast', NW Russian Federation *57°50′N 50°41′E*
54 F10 **Bogotá** *prev.* Santa Fe, Santa Fe de Bogotá. ● (Colombia) Cundinamarca, C Colombia *04°38′N 74°05′W*
153 T14 **Bogra** Rajshahi, N Bangladesh *24°52′N 89°28′E*
Bogschan *see* Boldu
122 L12 **Boguchany** Krasnoyarskiy Kray, C Russian Federation *58°20′N 97°20′E*
126 M9 **Boguchar** Voronezhskaya Oblast', W Russian Federation *49°57′N 40°34′E*
76 H10 **Bogué** Brakna, SW Mauritania *16°36′N 14°15′W*
22 K8 **Bogue Chitto** Louisiana/ Mississippi, S USA
Bogushëvsk *see* Bahushewsk
Boguslav *see* Bohuslav
44 K12 **Bog Walk** C Jamaica *18°06′N 77°01′W*
161 Q3 **Bo Hai** *var.* Gulf of Chihli. *gulf* NE China
161 R3 **Bohai Haixia** *strait* NE China
161 Q3 **Bohai Wan** *bay* NE China
111 C17 **Bohemia** *Cz.* Čechy, *Ger.* Böhmen. W Czech Republic
111 B18 **Bohemian Forest** *Cz.* Český Les, Šumava, *Ger.* Böhmerwald. C Europe
Bohemian-Moravian Highlands *see* Českomoravská Vrchovina
77 R16 **Bohicon** S Benin *07°14′N 02°04′E*
109 S11 **Bohinjska Bistrica** *Ger.* Wocheiner Feistritz. NW Slovenia *46°16′N 13°55′E*
Bohkká *see* Pokka
Böhmen *see* Bohemia
Böhmerwald *see* Bohemian Forest
Böhmisch-Krumau *see* Český Krumlov
Böhmisch-Leipa *see* Česká Lípa
Böhmisch-Mährische Höhe *see* Českomoravská Vrchovina
Böhmisch-Trübau *see* Česká Třebová
117 U5 **Bohodukhiv** *Rus.* Bogodukhov. Kharkivs'ka Oblast', E Ukraine *50°10′N 35°32′E*
171 Q6 **Bohol** *island* C Philippines
171 Q7 **Bohol Sea** *var.* Mindanao Sea. *sea* S Philippines
116 I7 **Bohorodchany** Ivano-Frankivs'ka Oblast', W Ukraine *48°46′N 24°31′E*
Böhöt *see* Öndörshil
158 K6 **Bohu** *var.* Bagrax. Xinjiang Uygur Zizhiqu, NW China *42°00′N 86°28′E*
111 I17 **Bohumín** *Ger.* Oderberg; *prev.* Neuoderberg, Nový Bohumín. Moravskoslezský Kraj, E Czech Republic *49°55′N 18°20′E*
117 P6 **Bohuslav** *Rus.* Boguslav. Kyyivs'ka Oblast', N Ukraine *49°33′N 30°53′E*
58 F11 **Boiaçu** Roraima, N Brazil *0°27′S 61°46′W*
107 K16 **Boiano** Molise, C Italy *41°28′N 14°28′E*
15 R8 **Boilleau** Québec, SE Canada *48°06′N 70°49′W*
59 O17 **Boipeba, Ilha de** *island* SE Brazil
104 G3 **Boiro** Galicia, NW Spain *42°39′N 08°53′W*
31 Q5 **Bois Blanc Island** *island* Michigan, N USA
29 R7 **Bois de Sioux River** Minnesota, N USA
33 N14 **Boise** *var.* Boise City. *state capital* Idaho, NW USA *43°39′N 116°14′W*
26 G8 **Boise City** Oklahoma, C USA *36°44′N 102°31′W*
Boise City *see* Boise
33 N14 **Boise River, Middle Fork** Idaho, NW USA
Bois, Lac des *see* Woods, Lake of the
Bois-le-Duc *see* 's-Hertogenbosch
11 W17 **Boissevain** Manitoba, S Canada *49°14′N 100°02′W*
15 T7 **Boisvert, Pointe au** *headland* Québec, SE Canada *48°34′N 69°07′W*
100 K10 **Boizenburg** Mecklenburg-Vorpommern, N Germany *53°23′N 10°43′E*
Bojador *see* Boujdour
113 K18 **Bojana** *Alb.* Bunë. Albania/Montenegro *see also* Bunë
Bojana *see* Bunë
143 S3 **Bojnūrd** *var.* Bujnurd. Khorāsān-e Shemālī, N Iran *37°31′N 57°24′E*
169 R16 **Bojonegoro** *prev.* Bodjonegoro. Jawa, C Indonesia *07°06′S 111°50′E*
189 T1 **Bokaak Atoll** *var.* Bokak, Taongi. *atoll* Ratak Chain, NE Marshall Islands
Bokak *see* Bokaak Atoll
146 K8 **Bo'kantov Tog'lari** *Rus.* Gory Bukantau. ▲ N Uzbekistan
153 Q15 **Bokāro** Jhārkhand, N India *23°46′N 85°55′E*
79 I18 **Bokatola** Equateur, NW Dem. Rep. Congo *0°37′S 18°45′E*
76 H13 **Boké** W Guinea *10°56′N 14°18′W*
Bokhara *see* Buxoro
183 Q4 **Bokharra River** New South Wales/Queensland, SE Australia
95 C16 **Boknafjorden** *fjord* S Norway
78 H11 **Bokoro** Chari-Baguirmi, W Chad *12°23′N 17°03′E*
79 K19 **Bokota** Equateur, NW Dem. Rep. Congo *0°56′S 22°24′E*
167 N13 **Bokpyin** Tanintharyi, S Burma (Myanmar) *11°16′N 98°47′E*
Boksánbánya/Bokschen *see* Bocşa
124 I13 **Boksitogorsk** Leningradskaya Oblast', NW Russian Federation *59°27′N 33°51′E*
83 F21 **Bokspits** Kgalagadi, SW Botswana *26°50′S 20°41′E*
79 K18 **Bokungu** Equateur, C Dem. Rep. Congo *0°41′S 22°19′E*
146 F12 **Bokurdak** *Rus.* Bakhardok. Ahal Welaýaty, C Turkmenistan *38°51′N 58°34′E*
78 G10 **Bol** Lac, W Chad *13°27′N 14°40′E*
76 G13 **Bolama** SW Guinea-Bissau *11°35′N 15°30′W*
Bolangir *see* Balāngīr
Bolanos *see* Bolanos, Mount, Guam
Bolaños *see* Bolaños de Calatrava, Spain
105 N11 **Bolaños de Calatrava** *var.* Bolaños. Castilla-La Mancha, C Spain *38°55′N 03°39′W*
188 B17 **Bolanos, Mount** *var.* Bolanos. ▲ S Guam *13°18′N 144°41′E*
40 L12 **Bolaños, Río** C Mexico
115 M14 **Bolayır** Çanakkale, NW Turkey *40°31′N 26°46′E*
102 L3 **Bolbec** Seine-Maritime, N France *49°34′N 00°31′E*
116 L13 **Boldu** *var.* Bogschan. Buzău, SE Romania *45°18′N 27°15′E*
146 H8 **Boldumsaz** *prev.* Kalinin, Kalininsk, Porsy. Daşoguz Welaýaty, N Turkmenistan *42°12′N 59°33′E*
158 I4 **Bole** *var.* Bortala. Xinjiang Uygur Zizhiqu, NW China *44°52′N 82°06′E*
77 O15 **Bole** NW Ghana *09°02′N 02°29′W*
79 J19 **Boleko** Equateur, W Dem. Rep. Congo *01°27′S 19°52′E*
111 E14 **Bolesławiec** *Ger.* Bunzlau. Dolnośląskie, SW Poland *51°16′N 15°34′E*
127 R4 **Bolgar** *prev.* Kuybyshev. Respublika Tatarstan, W Russian Federation *54°58′N 49°03′E*
77 P14 **Bolgatanga** N Ghana *10°45′N 00°52′W*
Bolgrad *see* Bolhrad
117 N12 **Bolhrad** *Rus.* Bolgrad. Odes'ka Oblast', SW Ukraine *45°42′N 28°35′E*
163 Y8 **Boli** Heilongjiang, NE China *45°45′N 130°32′E*
79 I19 **Bolia** Bandundu, W Dem. Rep. Congo *01°34′S 18°24′E*
93 J14 **Boliden** Västerbotten, N Sweden *64°52′N 20°20′E*
171 T13 **Bolifar** Pulau Seram, E Indonesia *03°08′S 130°34′E*
171 N2 **Bolinao** Luzon, N Philippines *16°22′N 119°52′E*
54 C12 **Bolívar** Cauca, SW Colombia *01°52′N 76°56′W*
27 T6 **Bolivar** Missouri, C USA *37°37′N 93°25′W*
20 F10 **Bolivar** Tennessee, S USA *35°17′N 88°59′W*
54 F7 **Bolívar** *off.* Departmento de Bolívar. *province* N Colombia
56 A13 **Bolívar** *province* C Ecuador
55 N9 **Bolívar** *off.* Estado Bolívar. *state* SE Venezuela
Bolívar, Departmento de *see* Bolívar
Bolívar, Estado *see* Bolívar
25 X12 **Bolivar Peninsula** *headland* Texas, SW USA *29°26′N 94°41′W*
54 I6 **Bolívar, Pico** ▲ W Venezuela *08°33′N 71°05′W*
57 K17 **Bolivia** *off.* Republic of Bolivia. ◆ *republic* W South America
Bolivia, Republic of *see* Bolivia
112 O13 **Boljevac** Serbia, E Serbia *43°50′N 21°57′E*
Bolkenhain *see* Bolków
126 J5 **Bolkhov** Orlovskaya Oblast', W Russian Federation *53°28′N 36°00′E*
111 F14 **Bolków** *Ger.* Bolkenhain. Dolnośląskie, SW Poland *50°55′N 15°49′E*
182 K3 **Bollards Lagoon** South Australia *28°58′S 140°52′E*
103 R14 **Bollène** Vaucluse, SE France *44°16′N 04°45′E*
94 N12 **Bollnäs** Gävleborg, C Sweden *61°18′N 16°27′E*
181 W10 **Bollon** Queensland, C Australia *28°07′S 147°28′E*
192 L12 **Bollons Tablemount** *undersea feature* S Pacific Ocean *49°40′S 176°10′W*
93 H17 **Bollstabruk** Västernorrland, C Sweden *63°00′N 17°41′E*
Bolluilos de Par del Condado *see* Bollulos Par del Condado
104 J14 **Bollulos Par del Condado** *var.* Bolluilos de Par del Condado. Andalucía, S Spain *37°20′N 06°32′W*
95 K21 **Bolmen** S Sweden
137 T10 **Bolnisi** S Georgia *41°28′N 44°34′E*
79 H19 **Bolobo** Bandundu, W Dem. Rep. Congo *02°10′S 16°17′E*
106 G10 **Bologna** Emilia-Romagna, N Italy *44°30′N 11°20′E*
124 I15 **Bologoye** Tverskaya Oblast', W Russian Federation *57°54′N 34°04′E*
79 J18 **Bolomba** Equateur, NW Dem. Rep. Congo *0°27′N 19°13′E*
41 X13 **Bolónchén de Rejón** *var.* Bolonchén de Rejón. Campeche, SE Mexico *20°00′N 89°34′W*
114 J13 **Boloústra, Akrotírio** *headland* NE Greece *40°56′N 24°58′E*
167 L8 **Bolovens, Plateau des** *plateau* S Laos
106 H13 **Bolsena** Lazio, C Italy *42°39′N 11°59′E*
107 G14 **Bolsena, Lago di** C Italy
126 B3 **Bol'shakovo** *Ger.* Kreuzingen; *prev.* Gross-Skaisgirren. Kaliningradskaya Oblast', W Russian Federation *54°53′N 21°38′E*
Bol'shaya Berëstovitsa *see* Vyalikaya Byerastavitsa
127 S7 **Bol'shaya Chernigovka** Samarskaya Oblast', W Russian Federation *52°07′N 50°49′E*
127 S7 **Bol'shaya Glushitsa** Samarskaya Oblast', W Russian Federation *52°22′N 50°29′E*
124 J4 **Bol'shaya Imandra, Ozero** NW Russian Federation
144 H9 **Bol'shaya Khobda** *Kaz.* Ülkenqobda. Kazakhstan/ Russian Federation
126 M12 **Bol'shaya Martynovka** Rostovskaya Oblast', SW Russian Federation *47°19′N 41°40′E*
122 K12 **Bol'shaya Murta** Krasnoyarskiy Kray, C Russian Federation *56°51′N 93°10′E*
125 V4 **Bol'shaya Rogovaya** NW Russian Federation
125 U7 **Bol'shaya Synya** NW Russian Federation
145 V9 **Bol'shaya Vladimirovka** Vostochnyy Kazakhstan, E Kazakhstan *50°53′N 79°29′E*
123 V11 **Bol'sheretsk** Kamchatskaya Oblast', E Russian Federation *52°20′N 156°24′E*
127 W3 **Bol'sheust'ikinskoye** Respublika Bashkortostan, W Russian Federation *56°00′N 58°13′E*
Bol'shevik *see* Bal'shavik
122 L5 **Bol'shevik, Ostrov** *island* Severnaya Zemlya, N Russian Federation
125 U4 **Bol'shezemel'skaya Tundra** *physical region* NW Russian Federation
144 J13 **Bol'shiye Barsuki, Peski** *desert* SW Kazakhstan
123 T7 **Bol'shoy Anyuy** NE Russian Federation
123 N7 **Bol'shoy Begichev, Ostrov** *island* NE Russian Federation
123 S15 **Bol'shoye Kamen'** Primorskiy Kray, SE Russian Federation *43°06′N 132°21′E*
127 O4 **Bol'shoye Murashkino** Nizhegorodskaya Oblast', W Russian Federation *55°46′N 44°48′E*
127 W4 **Bol'shoy Iremel'** ▲ W Russian Federation *54°31′N 58°47′E*
127 R7 **Bol'shoy Irgiz** W Russian Federation
123 Q6 **Bol'shoy Lyakhovskiy, Ostrov** *island* NE Russian Federation
123 Q11 **Bol'shoy Nimnyr** Respublika Sakha (Yakutiya), NE Russian Federation *57°55′N 125°34′E*
Bol'shoy Rozhan *see* Vyaliki Rozhan
144 E10 **Bol'shoy Uzen'** *Kaz.* Ülkenözen. Kazakhstan/ Russian Federation
40 K6 **Bolson de Mapimi** NW Mexico
98 K6 **Bolsward** *Fris.* Boalsert. Friesland, N Netherlands *53°04′N 05°31′E*
105 T4 **Boltaña** Aragón, NE Spain *42°28′N 00°02′E*
14 G15 **Bolton** Ontario, S Canada *43°52′N 79°45′W*
97 K17 **Bolton** *prev.* Bolton-le-Moors. NW England, United Kingdom *53°35′N 02°26′W*
21 V12 **Bolton** North Carolina, SE USA *34°22′N 78°26′W*
Bolton-le-Moors *see* Bolton
136 G11 **Bolu** Bolu, NW Turkey *40°45′N 31°38′E*
136 G11 **Bolu** ◆ *province* NW Turkey
186 G9 **Bolubolu** Goodenough Island, S Papua New Guinea *09°22′S 150°22′E*
92 H1 **Bolungarvík** Vestfirdhir, NW Iceland *66°09′N 23°17′W*
159 O10 **Boluntay** Qinghai, W China *36°30′N 92°11′E*
159 P8 **Boluozhuanjing**, Aksay Kazakzu Zizhixian. Gansu, N China *39°25′N 94°09′E*
136 F14 **Bolvadin** Afyon, W Turkey *38°43′N 31°02′E*
114 M10 **Bolyarovo** *prev.* Pashkeni. Yambol, E Bulgaria *42°09′N 26°49′E*
106 G6 **Bolzano** *Ger.* Bozen; *anc.* Bauzanum. Trentino-Alto Adige, N Italy *46°30′N 11°22′E*
79 F22 **Boma** Bas-Congo, W Dem. Rep. Congo *05°42′S 13°05′E*
183 R12 **Bombala** New South Wales, SE Australia *36°54′S 149°15′E*
104 F10 **Bombarral** Leiria, C Portugal *39°15′N 09°09′W*
Bombay *see* Mumbai
171 U13 **Bomberai, Semenanjung** *cape* Papua, E Indonesia
81 F18 **Bombo** S Uganda *0°36′N 32°33′E*
162 I8 **Bömbögör** *var.* Dzadgay. Bayanhongor, C Mongolia *46°12′N 99°29′E*
79 I17 **Bomboma** Equateur, NW Dem. Rep. Congo *02°23′N 19°03′E*
59 I14 **Bom Futuro** Pará, N Brazil *06°27′S 54°44′W*
159 Q15 **Bomi** *var.* Bowo, Zhamo. Xizang Zizhiqu, W China *29°43′N 96°12′E*
79 N17 **Bomili** Orientale, NE Dem. Rep. Congo *01°45′N 27°01′E*
59 N17 **Bom Jesus da Lapa** Bahia, E Brazil *13°16′S 43°23′W*
60 Q8 **Bom Jesus do Itabapoana** Rio de Janeiro, SE Brazil *21°07′S 41°43′W*
95 C15 **Bømlafjorden** *fjord* S Norway
95 B15 **Bømlo** *island* S Norway
12 Q12 **Bomnak** Amurskaya Oblast', SE Russian Federation *54°43′N 128°50′E*
79 I17 **Bomongo** Equateur, NW Dem. Rep. Congo *01°22′N 18°21′E*
61 K14 **Bom Retiro** Santa Catarina, S Brazil *27°45′S 49°31′W*
79 L15 **Bomu** *var.* Mbomou, Mbomu, M'Bomu. Central African Republic/ Dem. Rep. Congo
142 J3 **Bonāb** *var.* Benāb, Bunab. Āžarbāyjān-e Sharqī, N Iran *37°30′N 46°03′E*
45 Q16 **Bonaire** *island* E Netherlands Antilles
39 U11 **Bona, Mount** ▲ Alaska, USA *61°22′N 141°45′W*
183 Q12 **Bonang** Victoria, SE Australia *37°13′S 148°43′E*
42 L7 **Bonanza** Región Autónoma Atlántico Norte, NE Nicaragua *13°59′N 84°30′W*
37 O4 **Bonanza** Utah, W USA *40°01′N 109°12′W*
45 O9 **Bonao** C Dominican Republic *18°55′N 70°25′W*
180 L3 **Bonaparte Archipelago** *island group* Western Australia
32 K6 **Bonaparte, Mount** ▲ Washington, NW USA *48°47′N 119°07′W*
39 N11 **Bonasila Dome** ▲ Alaska, USA *62°24′N 160°28′W*
45 T15 **Bonasse** Trinidad, Trinidad and Tobago *10°02′N 61°48′W*
15 X7 **Bonaventure** Québec, SE Canada *48°03′N 65°30′W*
15 X7 **Bonaventure** Québec, SE Canada
13 V11 **Bonavista** Newfoundland, Newfoundland and Labrador, SE Canada *48°38′N 53°08′W*
13 U11 **Bonavista Bay** *inlet* NW Atlantic Ocean
79 E19 **Bonda** Ogooué-Lolo, C Gabon *0°50′S 12°28′E*
127 N6 **Bondari** Tambovskaya Oblast', W Russian Federation *52°58′N 42°02′E*
106 G9 **Bondeno** Emilia-Romagna, C Italy *44°53′N 11°24′E*
30 L4 **Bond Falls Flowage** Michigan, N USA
79 L16 **Bondo** Orientale, N Dem. Rep. Congo *03°52′N 23°41′E*
171 N17 **Bondokodi** Pulau Sumba, S Indonesia *09°36′S 119°01′E*
77 O15 **Bondoukou** E Ivory Coast *08°03′N 02°45′W*
Bondoukui/Bondoukuy *see* Boundoukui
169 T17 **Bondowoso** Jawa, C Indonesia *07°54′S 113°50′E*
33 S14 **Bondurant** Wyoming, C USA *43°14′N 110°26′W*
Bône *see* Annaba, Algeria
Bone *see* Watampone, Indonesia
30 I5 **Bone Lake** Wisconsin, N USA
171 P14 **Bonelipu** Pulau Buton, C Indonesia *04°42′S 123°09′E*
171 O15 **Bonerate, Kepulauan** *var.* Macan. *island group* C Indonesia
29 O12 **Bonesteel** South Dakota, N USA *43°01′N 98°55′W*
62 I8 **Bonete, Cerro** ▲ N Argentina *27°58′S 68°22′W*
171 O14 **Bone, Teluk** *bay* Sulawesi, C Indonesia
108 D6 **Bonfol** Jura, NW Switzerland *47°28′N 07°08′E*
153 U12 **Bongaigaon** Assam, NE India *26°30′N 90°31′E*
79 K17 **Bongandanga** Equateur, NW Dem. Rep. Congo *01°28′N 21°03′E*
78 L13 **Bongo, Massif des** *var.* Chaîne des Mongos. ▲ NE Central African Republic
78 G12 **Bongor** Mayo-Kébbi, SW Chad *10°18′N 15°20′E*
77 N16 **Bongouanou** E Ivory Coast *06°39′N 04°12′W*
167 V11 **Bông Sơn** *var.* Hoai Nhơn. Binh Dinh, C Vietnam *14°28′N 109°00′E*
25 U5 **Bonham** Texas, SW USA *33°36′N 96°12′W*
Bonhard *see* Bonyhád
103 U6 **Bonhomme, Col du** *pass* NE France
103 Y16 **Bonifacio** Corse, France, C Mediterranean Sea *41°24′N 09°09′E*
Bonifacio, Bocche de/ Bonifacio, Bouches de *see* Bonifacio, Strait of
103 Y16 **Bonifacio, Strait of** *Fr.* Bouches de Bonifacio, *It.* Bocche di Bonifacio. *strait* C Mediterranean Sea
23 Q8 **Bonifay** Florida, SE USA *30°49′N 85°42′W*
Bonin Islands *see* Ogasawara-shotō
192 H5 **Bonin Trench** *undersea feature* NW Pacific Ocean
23 W15 **Bonita Springs** Florida, SE USA *26°19′N 81°48′W*
42 I5 **Bonito, Pico** ▲ N Honduras *15°33′N 86°55′W*
101 E17 **Bonn** Nordrhein-Westfalen, W Germany *50°44′N 07°06′E*
92 H11 **Bonnåsjøen** Nordland, C Norway *67°35′N 15°39′E*
14 J12 **Bonnechere** Ontario, SE Canada *45°39′N 77°36′W*
14 J12 **Bonnechere** Ontario, SE Canada
33 N7 **Bonners Ferry** Idaho, NW USA *48°41′N 116°19′W*
27 R4 **Bonner Springs** Kansas, C USA *39°03′N 94°52′W*
102 L6 **Bonnétable** Sarthe, NW France *48°09′N 00°24′E*
27 X6 **Bonne Terre** Missouri, C USA *37°55′N 90°33′W*
10 J5 **Bonnet Plume** Yukon Territory, NW Canada
102 M6 **Bonneval** Eure-et-Loir, C France *48°12′N 01°23′E*
103 T10 **Bonneville** Haute-Savoie, E France *46°05′N 06°25′E*
36 J3 **Bonneville Salt Flats** *salt flat* Utah, W USA
77 U18 **Bonny** Rivers, S Nigeria *04°25′N 07°13′E*
Bonny, Bight of *see* Biafra, Bight of
37 W4 **Bonny Reservoir** Colorado, C USA
11 R14 **Bonnyville** Alberta, SW Canada *54°16′N 110°46′W*
107 C18 **Bono** Sardegna, Italy, C Mediterranean Sea *40°24′N 09°01′E*
Bononia *see* Vidin, Bulgaria
Bononia *see* Boulogne-sur-Mer, France
107 B18 **Bonorva** Sardegna, Italy, C Mediterranean Sea *40°27′N 08°46′E*
30 M15 **Bonpas Creek** Illinois, N USA
190 I3 **Bonriki** Tarawa, W Kiribati *01°23′N 173°09′E*
183 T4 **Bonshaw** New South Wales, SE Australia *29°06′S 151°15′E*
76 I16 **Bonthe** SW Sierra Leone *07°32′N 12°30′W*
171 N2 **Bontoc** Luzon, N Philippines *17°04′N 120°58′E*
25 Y9 **Bon Wier** Texas, SW USA *30°43′N 93°40′W*
111 J25 **Bonyhád** *Ger.* Bonhard. Tolna, S Hungary *46°20′N 18°31′E*
Bonzabaai *see* Bonza Bay
83 J25 **Bonza Bay** *Afr.* Bonzabaai. Eastern Cape, S South Africa *32°58′S 27°58′E*
182 D7 **Bookabie** South Australia *31°49′S 132°41′E*
182 H6 **Bookaloo** South Australia *31°56′S 137°21′E*
37 P5 **Book Cliffs** *cliff* Colorado/ Utah, W USA
25 P1 **Booker** Texas, SW USA *36°27′N 100°32′W*
76 K15 **Boola** SE Guinea *08°22′N 08°41′W*
183 O8 **Booligal** New South Wales, SE Australia *33°56′S 144°54′E*
99 G17 **Boom** Antwerpen, N Belgium *51°05′N 04°24′E*
43 N6 **Boom** *var.* Boon. Región Autónoma Atlántico Norte, NE Nicaragua *14°52′N 83°36′W*
183 S3 **Boomi** New South Wales, SE Australia *28°43′S 149°35′E*
Boon *see* Boom
162 H9 **Böön Tsagaan Nuur** S Mongolia
29 V13 **Boone** Iowa, C USA *42°04′N 93°52′W*
21 Q8 **Boone** North Carolina, SE USA *36°13′N 81°41′W*
27 S11 **Booneville** Arkansas, C USA *35°09′N 93°57′W*
21 N6 **Booneville** Kentucky, S USA *37°26′N 83°45′W*
23 N2 **Booneville** Mississippi, S USA *34°39′N 88°34′W*
21 V3 **Boonsboro** Maryland, NE USA *39°30′N 77°39′W*
34 L6 **Boonville** California, W USA *38°58′N 123°21′W*
31 N16 **Boonville** Indiana, N USA *38°03′N 87°16′W*
27 U4 **Boonville** Missouri, C USA *38°58′N 92°43′W*
18 I9 **Boonville** New York, NE USA *43°28′N 75°17′W*
80 M12 **Booramo** Awdal, NW Somalia *09°58′N 43°15′E*
183 O6 **Booroondarra, Mount** *hill* New South Wales, SE Australia
183 N10 **Booroorban** New South Wales, SE Australia *34°55′S 144°45′E*
183 R9 **Boorowa** New South Wales, SE Australia *34°26′S 148°42′E*
99 H17 **Boortmeerbeek** Vlaams Brabant, C Belgium *50°58′N 04°27′E*
80 P11 **Boosaaso** *var.* Bandar Kassim, Bender Qaasim, Bosaso, *It.* Bender Cassim. Bari, N Somalia *11°26′N 49°37′E*
19 Q8 **Boothbay Harbor** Maine, NE USA *43°52′N 69°35′W*
Boothia Felix *see* Boothia Peninsula
9 N6 **Boothia, Gulf of** *gulf* Nunavut, NE Canada
9 N6 **Boothia Peninsula** *prev.* Boothia Felix. *peninsula* Nunavut, NE Canada
79 E18 **Booué** Ogooué-Ivindo, NE Gabon *0°03′S 11°58′E*
101 J21 **Bopfingen** Baden-Württemberg, S Germany *48°51′N 10°21′E*
101 F18 **Boppard** Rheinland-Pfalz, W Germany *50°13′N 07°36′E*
62 M4 **Boquerón** *off.* Departamento de Boquerón. *department* W Paraguay
Boquerón, Departamento de *see* Boquerón
43 P15 **Boquete** *var.* Bajo Boquete. Chiriquí, W Panama *08°45′N 82°26′W*
40 J6 **Boquilla, Presa de la** N Mexico
40 L5 **Boquillas** *var.* Boquillas del Carmen. Coahuila, NE Mexico *29°10′N 102°55′W*
Boquillas del Carmen *see* Boquillas
127 O3 **Bor** Nizhegorodskaya Oblast', W Russian Federation *56°21′N 44°03′E*
112 P12 **Bor** Serbia, E Serbia *44°05′N 22°07′E*
81 F15 **Bor** Jonglei, S Sudan *06°12′N 31°33′E*
95 L20 **Bor** Jönköping, S Sweden *57°04′N 14°10′E*
136 J15 **Bor** Niğde, S Turkey *37°49′N 35°00′E*
191 S10 **Bora-Bora** *island* Îles Sous le Vent, W French Polynesia
167 Q9 **Borabu** Maha Sarakham, E Thailand *16°01′N 103°06′E*
172 K4 **Boraha, Nosy** *island* E Madagascar
33 P13 **Borah Peak** ▲ Idaho, NW USA *44°21′N 113°53′W*
145 U16 **Boralday** *prev.* Burunday. Almaty, SE Kazakhstan *43°21′N 76°48′E*
144 G13 **Borankul** *prev.* Opornyy. Mangistau, SW Kazakhstan *46°09′N 54°32′E*
95 J19 **Borås** Västra Götaland, S Sweden *57°44′N 12°55′E*
143 N11 **Borāzjān** *var.* Borazjān. Būshehr, S Iran *29°19′N 51°12′E*
Borazjān *see* Borāzjān
58 G13 **Borba** Amazonas, N Brazil *04°39′S 59°35′W*
104 H11 **Borba** Évora, S Portugal *38°48′N 07°28′W*

◆ Country
● Country Capital
◇ Dependent Territory
○ Dependent Territory Capital
◆ Administrative Regions
✈ International Airport
▲ Mountain
▲ Mountain Range
Volcano
River
Lake
Reservoir

Borbetomagus *see* Worms
55 *O7* **Borbón** Bolívar, E Venezuela *07°55′N 64°03′W*
59 *Q15* **Borborema, Planalto da** *plateau* NE Brazil
116 *M14* **Borcea, Braţul** ≈ S Romania
Borchalo *see* Marneuli
195 *R15* **Borchgrevink Coast** *physical region* Antarctica
137 *Q11* **Borçka** Artvin, NE Turkey *41°24′N 41°38′E*
98 *N11* **Borculo** Gelderland, E Netherlands *52°07′N 06°31′E*
182 *G10* **Borda, Cape** *headland* South Australia *35°45′S 136°34′E*
102 *K13* **Bordeaux** *anc.* Burdigala. Gironde, SW France *44°49′N 00°33′W*
11 *T15* **Borden** Saskatchewan, S Canada *52°23′N 107°10′W*
14 *D8* **Borden Lake** ◎ Ontario, S Canada
9 *N4* **Borden Peninsula** *peninsula* Baffin Island, Nunavut, NE Canada
182 *K11* **Bordertown** South Australia *36°21′S 140°48′E*
92 *H2* **Bordheyri** Vestfirdhir, NW Iceland *65°12′N 21°09′W*
95 *B18* **Bordhoy** *Dan.* Bordø. *island* NE Faeroe Islands
106 *B11* **Bordighera** Liguria, NW Italy *43°48′N 07°40′E*
74 *K5* **Bordj-Bou-Arreridj** *var.* Bordj Bou Arreridj, Bordj Bou Arréridj. N Algeria *36°02′N 04°49′E*
74 *L10* **Bordj Omar Driss** E Algeria *28°09′N 06°52′E*
143 *N13* **Bord Khūn** Hormozgān, S Iran
Bordø *see* Bordhoy
147 *V7* **Bordunskiy** Chuyskaya Oblast', N Kyrgyzstan *42°37′N 75°31′E*
95 *M17* **Borensberg** Östergötland, S Sweden *58°33′N 15°15′E*
Borgå *see* Porvoo
92 *L2* **Borgarfjördhur** Austurland, NE Iceland *65°32′N 13°46′W*
92 *H3* **Borgarnes** Vesturland, W Iceland *64°33′N 21°55′W*
93 *G14* **Børgefjelt** ▲▲ C Norway
98 *O7* **Borger** Drenthe, NE Netherlands *52°54′N 06°48′E*
25 *N2* **Borger** Texas, SW USA *35°40′N 101°24′W*
95 *N20* **Borgholm** Kalmar, S Sweden *56°50′N 16°41′E*
107 *N22* **Borgia** Calabria, SW Italy *38°48′N 16°28′E*
99 *J18* **Borgloon** Limburg, NE Belgium *50°48′N 05°21′E*
195 *P2* **Borgmassivet** ▲▲ Antarctica
22 *L9* **Borgne, Lake** ◎ Louisiana, S USA
106 *C7* **Borgomanero** Piemonte, NE Italy *45°42′N 08°33′E*
106 *G10* **Borgo Panigale** ✈ (Bologna) Emilia-Romagna, N Italy *44°33′N 11°16′E*
107 *J15* **Borgorose** Lazio, C Italy *42°10′N 13°15′E*
106 *A9* **Borgo San Dalmazzo** Piemonte, N Italy *44°19′N 07°29′E*
106 *G11* **Borgo San Lorenzo** Toscana, C Italy *43°58′N 11°22′E*
106 *C7* **Borgosesia** Piemonte, NE Italy *45°41′N 08°21′E*
106 *E9* **Borgo Val di Taro** Emilia-Romagna, C Italy *44°29′N 09°48′E*
106 *G6* **Borgo Valsugana** Trentino-Alto Adige, N Italy *46°04′N 11°31′E*
Borhoyn Tal *see* Dzamïn-Üüd
167 *R8* **Borikhan** *var.* Borikhane. Bolikhamxai, C Laos *18°36′N 103°43′E*
Borikhane *see* Borikhan
Borislav *see* Boryslav
127 *N8* **Borisoglebsk** Voronezhskaya Oblast', W Russian Federation *51°23′N 42°00′E*
Borisov *see* Barysaw
Borisovgrad *see* Pŭrvomay
Borispol' *see* Boryspil'
172 *I3* **Boriziny** *Fr.* Port-Bergé. Mahajanga, NW Madagascar *15°31′S 47°40′E*
105 *Q5* **Borja** Aragón, NE Spain *41°50′N 01°32′W*
Borjas Blancas *see* Les Borges Blanques
137 *S10* **Borjomi** *Rus.* Borzhomi. C Georgia *41°50′N 43°24′E*
118 *L12* **Borkavichy** *Rus.* Borkovichi. Vitsyebskaya Voblasts', N Belarus *55°40′N 28°20′E*
101 *H16* **Borken** Hessen, C Germany *51°01′N 09°16′E*
101 *E14* **Borken** Nordrhein-Westfalen, W Germany *51°51′N 06°51′E*
92 *H10* **Borkenes** Troms, N Norway *68°46′N 16°10′E*
78 *H7* **Borkou-Ennedi-Tibesti** *off.* Préfecture du Borkou-Ennedi-Tibesti. ◈ *prefecture* N Chad
Borkou-Ennedi-Tibesti, Préfecture du *see* Borkou-Ennedi-Tibesti
Borkovichi *see* Borkavichy
100 *E9* **Borkum** *island* NW Germany
81 *K17* **Bor, Lagh** *var.* Lak Bor. *dry watercourse* NE Kenya
Bor, Lak *see* Bor, Lagh
95 *M14* **Borlänge** Dalarna, C Sweden *60°29′N 15°25′E*
106 *C9* **Bormida** ≈ NW Italy
106 *F6* **Bormio** Lombardia, N Italy *46°27′N 10°24′E*
101 *M16* **Borna** Sachsen, E Germany *51°07′N 12°30′E*
98 *O10* **Borne** Overijssel, E Netherlands *52°18′N 06°45′E*
99 *F17* **Bornem** Antwerpen, N Belgium *51°06′N 04°14′E*
169 *S10* **Borneo** *island* Brunei/Indonesia/Malaysia
101 *E16* **Bornheim** Nordrhein-Westfalen, W Germany *50°46′N 06°58′E*
95 *L24* **Bornholm** ◈ *county* E Denmark
95 *L24* **Bornholm** *island* E Denmark
77 *Y13* **Borno** ◈ *state* NE Nigeria
104 *K15* **Bornos** Andalucía, S Spain *36°50′N 05°42′W*
162 *L7* **Bornuur** Töv, C Mongolia *48°28′N 106°15′E*
117 *O4* **Borodyanka** Kyyivs'ka Oblast', N Ukraine *50°40′N 29°54′E*
158 *I5* **Borohoro Shan** ▲▲ NW China
77 *O13* **Boromo** SW Burkina *11°47′N 02°54′W*
35 *T13* **Boron** California, W USA *35°00′N 117°42′W*
Borongo *see* Black Volta
Boron'ki *see* Baron'ki
Borosjenő *see* Ineu
Borossebes *see* Sebiş
76 *L15* **Borotou** NW Ivory Coast *08°46′N 07°30′W*
117 *W6* **Borova** Kharkivs'ka Oblast', E Ukraine *49°22′N 37°39′E*
114 *H8* **Borovan** Vratsa, NW Bulgaria *43°25′N 23°45′E*
124 *I14* **Borovichi** Novgorodskaya Oblast', W Russian Federation *58°24′N 33°56′E*
Borovlje *see* Ferlach
114 *K8* **Borovo** Ruse, N Bulgaria *43°28′N 25°46′E*
112 *J9* **Borovo** Vukovar-Srijem, NE Croatia *45°22′N 18°57′E*
145 *Q7* **Borovoye** *Kaz.* Būrabay. Akmola, N Kazakhstan *53°07′N 70°20′E*
126 *K4* **Borovsk** Kaluzhskaya Oblast', W Russian Federation *55°12′N 36°22′E*
145 *N7* **Borovskoy** Kostanay, N Kazakhstan *53°48′N 64°17′E*
Borovukha *see* Baravukha
95 *L23* **Borrby** Skåne, S Sweden *55°27′N 14°10′E*
181 *R3* **Borroloola** Northern Territory, N Australia *16°09′S 136°18′E*
116 *F9* **Borş** Bihor, NW Romania *47°07′N 21°49′E*
116 *I9* **Borşa** *Hung.* Borsa. Maramureş, N Romania *47°40′N 24°37′E*
116 *J10* **Borsec** *Ger.* Bad Borseck, *Hung.* Borszék. Harghita, C Romania *46°58′N 25°32′E*
92 *K8* **Børselv** *Lapp.* Bissojohka. Finnmark, N Norway *70°18′N 25°35′E*
113 *L23* **Borsh** *var.* Borshi. Vlorë, S Albania *40°04′N 19°51′E*
Borshchev *see* Borshchiv
116 *K7* **Borshchiv** *Pol.* Borszczów, *Rus.* Borshchev. Ternopil's'ka Oblast', W Ukraine *48°48′N 26°00′E*
Borshi *see* Borsh
111 *L20* **Borsod-Abaúj-Zemplén** *off.* Borsod-Abaúj-Zemplén Megye. ◈ *county* NE Hungary
Borsod-Abaúj-Zemplén Megye *see* Borsod-Abaúj-Zemplén
99 *E15* **Borssele** Zeeland, SW Netherlands *51°26′N 03°45′E*
Borszczów *see* Borshchiv
Borszék *see* Borsec
Bortala *see* Bole
103 *O12* **Bort-les-Orgues** Corrèze, C France *45°28′N 02°31′E*
Bor u České Lípy *see* Nový Bor
Bor-Üdzüür *see* Altay
143 *N9* **Borūjen** Chahār Maḩall va Bakhtīārī, C Iran *32°N 51°09′E*
142 *L7* **Borūjerd** *var.* Burujird. Lorestān, W Iran *33°55′N 48°46′E*
116 *H6* **Boryslav** *Pol.* Borysław, *Rus.* Borislav. L'vivs'ka Oblast', NW Ukraine *49°18′N 23°28′E*
Borysław *see* Boryslav
117 *P4* **Boryspil'** *Rus.* Borispol'. Kyyivs'ka Oblast', N Ukraine *50°21′N 30°59′E*
117 *P4* **Boryspil'** *Rus.* Borispol'. ✈ (Kyyiv) Kyyivs'ka Oblast', N Ukraine *50°21′N 30°46′E*
Borzhomi *see* Borjomi
117 *R3* **Borzna** Chernihivs'ka Oblast', NE Ukraine *51°15′N 32°25′E*
123 *O14* **Borzya** Chitinskaya Oblast', S Russian Federation *50°18′N 116°24′E*
107 *B18* **Bosa** Sardegna, Italy, C Mediterranean Sea *40°18′N 08°28′E*
112 *F10* **Bosanska Dubica** *var.* Kozarska Dubica. ◈ Republika Srpska, NW Bosnia and Herzegovina
112 *G10* **Bosanska Gradiška** *var.* Gradiška. ◈ Republika Srpska, N Bosnia and Herzegovina
112 *F10* **Bosanska Kostajnica** *var.* Srpska Kostajnica. ◈ Republika Srpska, NW Bosnia and Herzegovina
112 *E11* **Bosanska Krupa** *var.* Krupa, Krupa na Uni. ◈ Federacija Bosna I Hercegovina, NW Bosnia and Herzegovina
112 *H10* **Bosanski Brod** *var.* Srpski Brod. ◈ Republika Srpska, N Bosnia and Herzegovina
112 *E10* **Bosanski Novi** *var.* Novi Grad. Republika Srpska, NW Bosnia and Herzegovina *45°03′N 16°23′E*
112 *E11* **Bosanski Petrovac** *var.* Petrovac. Federacija Bosna I Hercegovina, NW Bosnia and Herzegovina *44°34′N 16°21′E*
112 *I10* **Bosanski Šamac** *var.* Šamac. Republika Srpska, N Bosnia and Herzegovina *45°03′N 18°27′E*
112 *E12* **Bosansko Grahovo** *var.* Grahovo, Hrvatsko Grahovi. Federacija Bosna I Hercegovina, W Bosnia and Herzegovina *44°10′N 16°22′E*
Bosaso *see* Boosaaso
186 *B7* **Bosavi, Mount** ⛰ W Papua New Guinea *06°33′S 142°50′E*
160 *J14* **Bose** Guangxi Zhuangzu Zizhiqu, S China *23°55′N 106°32′E*
161 *Q5* **Boshan** Shandong, E China *36°32′N 117°47′E*
113 *P16* **Bosilegrad** *prev.* Bosiljgrad. Serbia, SE Serbia *42°30′N 22°30′E*
Bosiljgrad *see* Bosilegrad
Bösing *see* Pezinok
98 *H12* **Boskoop** Zuid-Holland, C Netherlands *52°04′N 04°40′E*
111 *G18* **Boskovice** *Ger.* Boskowitz. Jihomoravský Kraj, SE Czech Republic *49°30′N 16°39′E*
Boskowitz *see* Boskovice
112 *I10* **Bosna** ≈ N Bosnia and Herzegovina
113 *G14* **Bosna I Hercegovina, Federacija** ◈ *republic* Bosnia and Herzegovina
112 *H12* **Bosnia and Herzegovina** *off.* Republic of Bosnia and Herzegovina. ◆ *republic* SE Europe
Bosnia and Herzegovina, Republic of *see* Bosnia and Herzegovina
79 *J16* **Bosobolo** Equateur, NW Dem. Rep. Congo *04°11′N 19°55′E*
165 *O14* **Bōsō-hantō** *peninsula* Honshū, S Japan
Bosora *see* Buşrá ash Shām
Bosphorus/Bosporus *see* İstanbul Boğazı
Bosporus Cimmerius *see* Kerch Strait
Bosporus Thracius *see* İstanbul Boğazı
Bosra *see* Buşrá ash Shām
79 *H14* **Bossangoa** Ouham, C Central African Republic *06°32′N 17°25′E*
Bossé Bangou *see* Bossey Bangou
79 *I15* **Bossembélé** Ombella-Mpoko, C Central African Republic *05°13′N 17°39′E*
79 *H15* **Bossentélé** Ouham-Pendé, W Central African Republic *05°36′N 16°37′E*
77 *R12* **Bossey Bangou** *var.* Bossé Bangou. Tillabéri, SW Niger *13°22′N 01°18′E*
22 *G5* **Bossier City** Louisiana, S USA *32°31′N 93°43′W*
83 *D20* **Bossiesvlei** Hardap, S Namibia *25°02′S 16°48′E*
77 *Y11* **Bosso** Diffa, SE Niger *13°42′N 13°18′E*
61 *F15* **Bossoroca** Rio Grande do Sul, S Brazil *28°45′S 54°54′W*
158 *J10* **Bostan** Xinjiang Uygur Zizhiqu, W China *41°20′N 83°15′E*
142 *K3* **Bostānābād** Āžarbāyjān-e Sharqī, N Iran *37°52′N 46°51′E*
158 *K6* **Bosten Hu** *var.* Bagrax Hu. ◎ NW China
97 *O18* **Boston** *prev.* St.Botolph's Town. E England, United Kingdom *52°59′N 00°01′W*
19 *O11* **Boston** *state capital* Massachusetts, NE USA *42°22′N 71°04′W*
146 *I9* **Bo'ston** *Rus.* Bustan. Qoraqalpog'iston Respublikasi, W Uzbekistan *41°49′N 60°51′E*
10 *M17* **Boston Bar** British Columbia, SW Canada *49°54′N 121°22′W*
27 *T10* **Boston Mountains** ▲▲ Arkansas, C USA
15 *P8* **Bostonnais** ≈ Québec, SE Canada
Bostyn' *see* Bastyn'
112 *J10* **Bosut** ≈ E Croatia
154 *C11* **Botād** Gujarāt, W India *22°12′N 71°44′E*
183 *T9* **Botany Bay** *inlet* New South Wales, SE Australia
83 *G18* **Boteti** *var.* Botletle. ≈ N Botswana
114 *J9* **Botev** ▲ C Bulgaria *42°45′N 24°57′E*
114 *H9* **Botevgrad** *prev.* Orkhaniye. Sofiya, W Bulgaria *42°55′N 23°47′E*
93 *J16* **Bothnia, Gulf of** *Fin.* Pohjanlahti, *Swe.* Bottniska Viken. *gulf* N Baltic Sea
183 *P17* **Bothwell** Tasmania, SE Australia *42°24′S 147°01′E*
104 *H5* **Boticas** Vila Real, N Portugal *41°41′N 07°40′W*
55 *W10* **Boti-Pasi** Sipaliwini, C Surinam *04°15′N 55°27′W*
Botletle *see* Boteti
127 *P16* **Botlikh** Chechenskaya Respublika, SW Russian Federation *42°39′N 46°12′E*
117 *N10* **Botna** ≈ E Moldova
116 *I9* **Botoşani** *Hung.* Botosány. Botoşani, NE Romania *47°44′N 26°41′E*
116 *K8* **Botoşani** ◈ *county* NE Romania
Botosány *see* Botoşani
147 *P12* **Bototog', Tizmasi** *Rus.* Khrebet Babatag. ▲▲ Tajikistan/Uzbekistan
161 *P4* **Botou** *prev.* Bozhen. Hebei, E China *38°09′N 116°37′E*
99 *M20* **Botrange** ▲ E Belgium *50°30′N 06°03′E*
107 *O21* **Botricello** Calabria, SW Italy *38°56′N 16°51′E*
83 *I23* **Botshabelo** Free State, C South Africa *29°15′S 26°51′E*
93 *J15* **Botsmark** Västerbotten, N Sweden *64°15′N 20°15′E*
83 *G19* **Botswana** *off.* Republic of Botswana. ◆ *republic* S Africa
Botswana, Republic of *see* Botswana
29 *N2* **Bottineau** North Dakota, N USA *48°50′N 100°28′W*
Bottniska Viken *see* Bothnia, Gulf of
60 *L9* **Botucatu** São Paulo, S Brazil *22°52′S 48°30′W*
76 *M16* **Bouaflé** C Ivory Coast *06°59′N 05°45′W*
77 *N16* **Bouaké** *var.* Bwake. C Ivory Coast *07°42′N 05°00′W*
79 *G14* **Bouar** Nana-Mambéré, W Central African Republic *05°58′N 15°38′E*
74 *H7* **Bouarfa** NE Morocco *32°33′N 01°54′W*
111 *B19* **Boubín** ▲ SW Czech Republic *49°00′N 13°51′E*
79 *I14* **Bouca** Ouham, W Central African Republic *06°57′N 18°18′E*
15 *T5* **Boucher** ≈ Québec, SE Canada
103 *R15* **Bouches-du-Rhône** ◈ *department* SE France
74 *C9* **Bou Craa** *var.* Bu Craa. NW Western Sahara *26°32′N 12°52′W*
77 *O9* **Boû Djébéha** *oasis* C Mali
108 *C8* **Boudry** Neuchâtel, W Switzerland *46°57′N 06°46′E*
79 *F21* **Bouenza** ◈ *province* S Congo
180 *L2* **Bougainville, Cape** *cape* Western Australia
Bougainville, Détroit de *see* Bougainville Strait
186 *J7* **Bougainville Island** *island* NE Papua New Guinea
186 *I8* **Bougainville Strait** *strait* N Solomon Islands
187 *Q13* **Bougainville Strait** *Fr.* Détroit de Bougainville. *strait* C Vanuatu
120 *I9* **Bougaroun, Cap** *headland* NE Algeria *37°07′N 06°18′E*
77 *R8* **Boughessa** Kidal, NE Mali *20°05′N 02°13′E*
Bougie *see* Béjaïa
76 *L13* **Bougouni** Sikasso, SW Mali *11°25′N 07°28′W*
99 *J24* **Bouillon** Luxembourg, SE Belgium *49°47′N 05°04′E*
74 *K5* **Bouira** *var.* Bouïra. N Algeria *36°22′N 03°55′E*
74 *D8* **Bou-Izakarn** SW Morocco *29°12′N 09°43′W*
74 *B9* **Boujdour** *var.* Bojador. W Western Sahara *26°06′N 14°29′W*
74 *G5* **Boukhalef** ✈ (Tanger) N Morocco *35°45′N 05°53′W*
Boukombé *see* Boukoumbé
77 *R14* **Boukoumbé** *var.* Boukombé. C Benin *10°13′N 01°09′E*
76 *G6* **Boû Lanouâr** Dakhlet Nouâdhibou, W Mauritania *21°17′N 16°29′W*
37 *T4* **Boulder** Colorado, C USA *40°02′N 105°18′W*
33 *R10* **Boulder** Montana, NW USA *46°14′N 112°07′W*
35 *X12* **Boulder City** Nevada, W USA *35°58′N 114°49′W*
181 *T7* **Boulia** Queensland, C Australia *23°02′S 139°58′E*
15 *N10* **Boullé** ≈ Québec, SE Canada
102 *J9* **Boulogne** ≈ NW France
Boulogne *see* Boulogne-sur-Mer
102 *L16* **Boulogne-sur-Gesse** Haute-Garonne, S France *43°18′N 00°38′E*
103 *N1* **Boulogne-sur-Mer** *var.* Boulogne; *anc.* Bononia, Gesoriacum, Gessoriacum. Pas-de-Calais, N France *50°43′N 01°36′E*
77 *Q12* **Boulsa** C Burkina *12°41′N 00°29′W*
77 *W11* **Boultoum** Zinder, C Niger *14°43′N 10°22′E*
187 *Y14* **Bouma** Taveuni, N Fiji *16°49′S 179°50′W*
79 *G16* **Boumba** ≈ SE Cameroon
76 *J9* **Boûmdeïd** *var.* Boumdeït. Assaba, S Mauritania *17°26′N 11°21′W*
Boumdeït *see* Boûmdeïd
115 *C17* **Boumistós** ▲ W Greece *38°48′N 20°59′E*
77 *O15* **Bouna** NE Ivory Coast *09°16′N 03°00′W*
19 *P4* **Boundary Bald Mountain** ▲ Maine, NE USA *45°45′N 70°10′W*
35 *S8* **Boundary Peak** ▲ Nevada, W USA *37°50′N 118°21′W*
76 *M14* **Boundiali** N Ivory Coast *09°30′N 06°31′W*
79 *G19* **Boundji** Cuvette, C Congo *01°05′S 15°18′E*
77 *O13* **Boundoukui** *var.* Bondoukui, Bondoukuy. W Burkina *11°51′N 03°47′W*
36 *L2* **Bountiful** Utah, W USA *40°53′N 111°52′W*
Bounty Basin *see* Bounty Trough
191 *Q16* **Bounty Bay** *bay* Pitcairn Island, C Pacific Ocean
192 *L12* **Bounty Islands** *island group* S New Zealand
175 *Q13* **Bounty Trough** *var.* Bounty Basin. *undersea feature* S Pacific Ocean
187 *P17* **Bourail** Province Sud, C New Caledonia *21°35′S 165°29′E*
27 *V5* **Bourbeuse River** ≈ Missouri, C USA
103 *Q9* **Bourbon-Lancy** Saône-et-Loire, C France *46°39′N 03°48′E*
31 *N11* **Bourbonnais** Illinois, N USA *41°08′N 87°52′W*
103 *O10* **Bourbonnais** *cultural region* C France
103 *S7* **Bourbonne-les-Bains** Haute-Marne, N France *48°00′N 05°43′E*
Bourbon Vendée *see* la Roche-sur-Yon
74 *M8* **Bourdj Messaouda** E Algeria *30°18′N 09°19′E*
77 *Q10* **Bourem** Gao, C Mali *16°56′N 00°21′W*
Bourg *see* Bourg-en-Bresse
103 *N11* **Bourganeuf** Creuse, C France *45°57′N 01°47′E*
Bourgas *see* Burgas
Bourge-en-Bresse *see* Bourg-en-Bresse
103 *S10* **Bourg-en-Bresse** *var.* Bourg, Bourge-en-Bresse. Ain, E France *46°12′N 05°13′E*
103 *O8* **Bourges** *anc.* Avaricum. Cher, C France *47°06′N 02°24′E*
103 *T11* **Bourget, Lac du** ◎ E France
103 *P8* **Bourgogne** *Eng.* Burgundy. ◈ *region* E France
103 *S11* **Bourgoin-Jallieu** Isère, E France *45°34′N 05°16′E*
103 *R14* **Bourg-St-Andéol** Ardèche, E France *44°24′N 04°36′E*
103 *U11* **Bourg-St-Maurice** Savoie, E France *45°37′N 06°49′E*
108 *C11* **Bourg St. Pierre** Valais, SW Switzerland *45°54′N 07°10′E*
76 *H8* **Boû Rjeimât** *well* W Mauritania
183 *P5* **Bourke** New South Wales, SE Australia *30°08′S 145°57′E*
97 *M24* **Bournemouth** S England, United Kingdom *50°43′N 01°54′W*
99 *M23* **Bourscheid** Diekirch, NE Luxembourg *49°55′N 06°04′E*
74 *K6* **Bou Saâda** *var.* Bou Saada. N Algeria *35°10′N 04°09′E*
36 *I13* **Bouse Wash** ≈ Arizona, SW USA
103 *N10* **Boussac** Creuse, C France *46°20′N 02°12′E*
102 *M16* **Boussens** Haute-Garonne, S France *43°11′N 00°58′E*
78 *H12* **Bousso** *prev.* Fort-Bretonnet. Chari-Baguirmi, S Chad *10°32′N 16°45′E*
76 *H9* **Boutilimit** Trarza, SW Mauritania *17°33′N 14°42′W*
65 *D21* **Bouvet Island** ◇ *Norwegian dependency* S Atlantic Ocean
77 *U11* **Bouza** Tahoua, SW Niger *14°25′N 06°09′E*
109 *R10* **Bovec** *Ger.* Flitsch, *It.* Plezzo. NW Slovenia *46°21′N 13°33′E*
98 *J8* **Bovenkarspel** Noord-Holland, NW Netherlands *52°33′N 05°03′E*
29 *V5* **Bovey** Minnesota, N USA *47°18′N 93°25′W*
32 *M9* **Bovill** Idaho, NW USA *46°50′N 116°24′W*
24 *L4* **Bovina** Texas, SW USA *34°30′N 102°52′W*
107 *M17* **Bovino** Puglia, SE Italy *41°14′N 15°19′E*
61 *C17* **Bovril** Entre Ríos, E Argentina *31°24′S 59°25′W*
28 *L2* **Bowbells** North Dakota, N USA *48°48′N 102°15′W*
11 *Q16* **Bow City** Alberta, SW Canada *50°27′N 112°16′W*
29 *O8* **Bowdle** South Dakota, N USA *45°27′N 99°39′W*
181 *X6* **Bowen** Queensland, NE Australia *20°S 148°10′E*
192 *L2* **Bowers Ridge** *undersea feature* S Bering Sea *50°00′N 180°00′W*
25 *S5* **Bowie** Texas, SW USA *33°33′N 97°51′W*
11 *R17* **Bow Island** Alberta, SW Canada *49°53′N 111°24′W*
Bowkān *see* Būkān
20 *J7* **Bowling Green** Kentucky, S USA *37°00′N 86°29′W*
27 *V3* **Bowling Green** Missouri, C USA *39°21′N 91°11′W*
31 *R11* **Bowling Green** Ohio, N USA *41°22′N 83°40′W*
21 *W5* **Bowling Green** Virginia, NE USA *38°02′N 77°22′W*
28 *J6* **Bowman** North Dakota, N USA *46°11′N 103°26′W*
9 *Q7* **Bowman Bay** *bay* NW Atlantic Ocean
194 *I5* **Bowman Coast** *physical region* Antarctica
28 *J7* **Bowman-Haley Lake** ⊠ North Dakota, N USA
195 *Z11* **Bowman Island** *island* Antarctica
Bowo *see* Bomi
183 *S9* **Bowral** New South Wales, SE Australia *34°28′S 150°52′E*
186 *E8* **Bowutu Mountains** ▲▲ C Papua New Guinea
83 *I16* **Bowwood** Southern, S Zambia *17°09′S 26°16′E*
28 *I12* **Box Butte Reservoir** ⊠ Nebraska, C USA
28 *J10* **Box Elder** South Dakota, N USA *44°06′N 103°04′W*
95 *M18* **Boxholm** Östergötland, S Sweden *58°12′N 15°05′E*
Bo Xian/Boxian *see* Bozhou
161 *Q4* **Boxing** Shandong, E China *37°06′N 118°05′E*
99 *L14* **Boxmeer** Noord-Brabant, SE Netherlands *51°39′N 05°57′E*
99 *J14* **Boxtel** Noord-Brabant, S Netherlands *51°36′N 05°20′E*
136 *J10* **Boyabat** Sinop, N Turkey *41°27′N 34°45′E*
54 *F9* **Boyacá** *off.* Departamento de Boyacá. ◈ *province* C Colombia
Boyacá, Departamento de *see* Boyacá
117 *O4* **Boyarka** Kyyivs'ka Oblast', N Ukraine *50°19′N 30°20′E*
22 *H7* **Boyce** Louisiana, S USA *31°23′N 92°40′W*
114 *H8* **Boychinovtsi** Montana, NW Bulgaria *43°28′N 23°20′E*
33 *U11* **Boyd** Montana, NW USA *45°27′N 109°03′W*
25 *S6* **Boyd** Texas, SW USA *33°01′N 97°33′W*
21 *V8* **Boydton** Virginia, NE USA *36°40′N 78°26′W*
Boyer Ahmadī va Kohkīlūyeh *see* Kohgīlūyeh va Būyer Aḩmad
29 *T13* **Boyer River** ≈ Iowa, C USA
21 *W8* **Boykins** Virginia, NE USA *36°35′N 77°11′W*
11 *Q13* **Boyle** Alberta, SW Canada *54°38′N 112°45′W*
97 *D16* **Boyle** *Ir.* Mainistirna Búille. C Ireland *53°58′N 08°18′W*
97 *F17* **Boyne** *Ir.* An Bhóinn. ≈ E Ireland
31 *Q5* **Boyne City** Michigan, N USA *45°13′N 85°00′W*
23 *Z14* **Boynton Beach** Florida, SE USA *26°31′N 80°04′W*
147 *O13* **Boysun** *Rus.* Baysun. Surkhondaryo Viloyati, S Uzbekistan *38°14′N 67°08′E*
Bozau *see* Întorsura Buzăului
136 *B12* **Bozcaada** *Island* Çanakkale, NW Turkey
136 *C14* **Boz Dağları** ▲▲ W Turkey
33 *S11* **Bozeman** Montana, NW USA *45°40′N 111°02′W*
Bozen *see* Bolzano
79 *J16* **Bozene** Equateur, NW Dem. Rep. Congo *02°56′N 19°15′E*
Bozhen *see* Botou
161 *P7* **Bozhou** *var.* Boxian, Bo Xian. Anhui, E China *33°46′N 115°44′E*
136 *H16* **Bozkır** Konya, S Turkey *37°10′N 32°15′E*
136 *K13* **Bozok Yaylasī** *plateau* C Turkey
79 *H14* **Bozoum** Ouham-Pendé, W Central African Republic *06°17′N 16°26′E*
137 *N16* **Bozova** Sanlıurfa, S Turkey *37°23′N 38°33′E*
Bozrah *see* Buşrá ash Shām
136 *E12* **Bozüyük** Bilecik, NW Turkey *39°55′N 30°02′E*
106 *B9* **Bra** Piemonte, NW Italy *44°42′N 07°51′E*
194 *G4* **Brabant Island** *island* Antarctica
99 *I20* **Brabant Walloon** ◈ *province* C Belgium
113 *F15* **Brač** *var.* Brach, *It.* Brazza; *anc.* Brattia. *island* S Croatia
Bracara Augusta *see* Braga
107 *H15* **Bracciano** Lazio, C Italy *42°04′N 12°12′E*
107 *H14* **Bracciano, Lago di** ◎ C Italy
14 *H13* **Bracebridge** Ontario, S Canada *45°02′N 79°19′W*
Brach *see* Brač
93 *G17* **Bräcke** Jämtland, C Sweden *62°43′N 15°30′E*
25 *P12* **Brackettville** Texas, SW USA *29°19′N 100°27′W*
97 *N22* **Bracknell** S England, United Kingdom *51°26′N 00°46′W*
61 *K14* **Braço do Norte** Santa Catarina, S Brazil *28°16′S 49°11′W*
116 *G11* **Brad** *Hung.* Brád. Hunedoara, SW Romania *45°52′N 23°00′E*
107 *N18* **Bradano** ≈ S Italy
23 *V13* **Bradenton** Florida, SE USA *27°30′N 82°34′W*
14 *H14* **Bradford** Ontario, S Canada *44°09′N 79°34′W*
97 *L17* **Bradford** N England, United Kingdom *53°48′N 01°45′W*
27 *W10* **Bradford** Arkansas, C USA *35°25′N 91°27′W*
18 *D12* **Bradford** Pennsylvania, NE USA *41°57′N 78°38′W*
27 *T15* **Bradley** Arkansas, C USA *33°06′N 93°39′W*
25 *P7* **Bradshaw** Texas, SW USA *32°06′N 99°52′W*
25 *Q9* **Brady** Texas, SW USA *31°08′N 99°22′W*
25 *Q9* **Brady Creek** ≈ Texas, SW USA
95 *G22* **Brædstrup** Vejle, C Denmark *55°58′N 09°38′E*
96 *J10* **Braemar** NE Scotland, United Kingdom *57°12′N 02°52′W*
116 *K8* **Brăeşti** Botoşani, NW Romania *47°50′N 26°26′E*
104 *G5* **Braga** *anc.* Bracara Augusta. Braga, NW Portugal *41°32′N 08°26′W*
104 *G5* **Braga** ◈ *district* N Portugal
116 *J15* **Bragadiru** Teleorman, S Romania *43°43′N 25°32′E*
61 *C20* **Bragado** Buenos Aires, E Argentina *35°10′S 60°29′W*
104 *J5* **Bragança** *Eng.* Braganza; *anc.* Julio Briga. Bragança, NE Portugal *41°47′N 06°46′W*
104 *I5* **Bragança** ◈ *district* N Portugal
60 *N9* **Bragança Paulista** São Paulo, S Brazil *22°55′S 46°30′W*
Braganza *see* Bragança
Bragin *see* Brahin
29 *V7* **Braham** Minnesota, N USA *45°43′N 93°10′W*
Brahe *see* Brda
Brahestad *see* Raahe
119 *O20* **Brahin** *Rus.* Bragin. Homyel'skaya Voblasts', SE Belarus *51°47′N 30°16′E*
153 *U15* **Brahmanbaria** Chittagong, E Bangladesh *23°58′N 91°04′E*
154 *O12* **Brāhmani** ≈ E India
154 *N13* **Brahmapur** Orissa, E India *19°21′N 84°51′E*
129 *S10* **Brahmaputra** *var.* Padma, Tsangpo, *Ben.* Jamuna, *Chin.* Yarlung Zangbo Jiang, *Ind.* Bramaputra, Dihang, Siang. ≈ S Asia
97 *H19* **Braich y Pwll** *headland* NW Wales, United Kingdom *52°47′N 04°46′W*
183 *R10* **Braidwood** New South Wales, SE Australia *35°26′S 149°48′E*
30 *M11* **Braidwood** Illinois, N USA *41°16′N 88°12′W*
116 *M13* **Brăila** Brăila, E Romania *45°17′N 27°57′E*
116 *L13* **Brăila** ◈ *county* SE Romania
99 *G19* **Braine-l'Alleud** Brabant Walloon, C Belgium *50°41′N 04°22′E*
99 *F19* **Braine-le-Comte** Hainaut, SW Belgium *50°37′N 04°08′E*
29 *U6* **Brainerd** Minnesota, N USA *46°22′N 94°10′W*
99 *J19* **Braives** Liège, E Belgium *50°37′N 05°09′E*
83 *H23* **Brak** ≈ C South Africa
Brak *see* Birāk
99 *E18* **Brakel** Oost-Vlaanderen, SW Belgium *50°50′N 03°48′E*
98 *J13* **Brakel** Gelderland, C Netherlands *51°49′N 05°05′E*
76 *H9* **Brakna** ◈ *region* S Mauritania
95 *J17* **Brålanda** Västra Götaland, S Sweden *58°32′N 12°18′E*
Bramaputra *see* Brahmaputra
95 *F23* **Bramming** Ribe, W Denmark *55°28′N 08°42′E*
14 *G15* **Brampton** Ontario, S Canada *43°42′N 79°46′W*
100 *F12* **Bramsche** Niedersachsen, NW Germany *52°25′N 07°58′E*
116 *J12* **Bran** *Ger.* Törzburg, *Hung.* Törcsvár. Braşov, S Romania *45°31′N 25°23′E*
29 *W8* **Branch** Minnesota, N USA *45°29′N 92°57′W*
21 *R14* **Branchville** South Carolina, SE USA *33°15′N 80°49′W*
47 *Y6* **Branco, Cabo** *headland* E Brazil *07°08′S 34°45′W*
58 *F11* **Branco, Rio** ≈ N Brazil
108 *J8* **Brand** Vorarlberg, W Austria *47°07′N 09°45′E*
83 *B18* **Brandberg** ▲ NW Namibia *21°20′S 14°22′E*
95 *H14* **Brandbu** Oppland, S Norway *60°24′N 10°30′E*
95 *F22* **Brande** Ringkøbing, W Denmark *55°57′N 09°08′E*
Brandebourg *see* Brandenburg
100 *M12* **Brandenburg** *var.* Brandenburg an der Havel. Brandenburg, NE Germany *52°25′N 12°34′E*
20 *K5* **Brandenburg** Kentucky, S USA *38°00′N 86°11′W*
100 *N12* **Brandenburg** *off.* Freie und Hansestadt Hamburg, *Fr.* Brandebourg. ◈ *state* NE Germany
Brandenburg an der Havel *see* Brandenburg
83 *I23* **Brandfort** Free State, C South Africa *28°42′S 26°28′E*
11 *W16* **Brandon** Manitoba, S Canada *49°50′N 99°57′W*
23 *V12* **Brandon** Florida, SE USA *27°56′N 82°17′W*
22 *L6* **Brandon** Mississippi, S USA *32°16′N 90°01′W*
97 *A20* **Brandon Mountain** *Ir.* Cnoc Bréanainn. ▲ SW Ireland *52°13′N 10°16′W*
Brandsen *see* Coronel Brandsen
95 *I14* **Brandval** Hedmark, S Norway *60°18′N 12°01′E*
83 *F24* **Brandvlei** Northern Cape, W South Africa *30°27′S 20°29′E*
23 *U9* **Branford** Florida, SE USA *29°57′N 82°54′W*
110 *K7* **Braniewo** *Ger.* Braunsberg. Warmińsko-mazurskie, N Poland *54°24′N 19°50′E*
194 *H3* **Bransfield Strait** *strait* Antarctica
37 *U8* **Branson** Colorado, C USA *37°01′N 103°52′W*
27 *T8* **Branson** Missouri, C USA *36°38′N 93°13′W*
14 *G16* **Brantford** Ontario, S Canada *43°09′N 80°17′W*
102 *L12* **Brantôme** Dordogne, SW France *45°21′N 00°37′E*
182 *L12* **Branxholme** Victoria, SE Australia *37°51′S 141°48′E*
Brasil *see* Brazil
59 *C16* **Brasiléia** Acre, W Brazil *10°59′S 48°45′W*
59 *K18* **Brasília** ● (Brazil) Distrito Federal, C Brazil *15°45′S 47°57′W*
Brasil, Repùblica Federativa do *see* Brazil
Braslav *see* Braslaw
118 *J12* **Braslaw** *Pol.* Brasław, *Rus.* Braslav. Vitsyebskaya Voblasts', N Belarus *55°38′N 27°02′E*
116 *J12* **Braşov** *Ger.* Kronstadt, *Hung.* Brassó; *prev.* Oraşul Stalin. Braşov, C Romania *45°40′N 25°35′E*
116 *I12* **Braşov** ◈ *county* C Romania
77 *U18* **Brass** Bayelsa, S Nigeria *04°19′N 06°21′E*
99 *H16* **Brasschaat** *var.* Brasschaet. Antwerpen, N Belgium *51°17′N 04°30′E*
Brasschaet *see* Brasschaat
169 *V8* **Brassey, Banjaran** *var.* Brassey Range. ▲▲ East Malaysia
Brassey Range *see* Brassey, Banjaran
Brassó *see* Braşov
23 *T1* **Brasstown Bald** ▲ Georgia, SE USA *34°52′N 83°48′W*
113 *K22* **Brataj** Vlorë, SW Albania *40°18′N 19°37′E*
114 *J10* **Bratan** *var.* Morozov. ▲ C Bulgaria *42°31′N 25°08′E*
111 *F21* **Bratislava** *Ger.* Pressburg, *Hung.* Pozsony. ● (Slovakia) Bratislavský Kraj, W Slovakia *48°10′N 17°10′E*
111 *H21* **Bratislavský Kraj** ◈ *region* W Slovakia
114 *H10* **Bratiya** ▲ C Bulgaria *42°36′N 24°08′E*
122 *M12* **Bratsk** Irkutskaya Oblast', C Russian Federation *56°20′N 101°50′E*
117 *Q8* **Brats'ke** Mykolayivs'ka Oblast', S Ukraine *47°52′N 31°34′E*
122 *M13* **Bratskoye Vodokhranilishche** *Eng.* Bratsk Reservoir. ⊠ S Russian Federation
Bratsk Reservoir *see* Bratskoye Vodokhranilishche
Brattia *see* Brač
94 *D9* **Brattvåg** Møre og Romsdal, S Norway *62°36′N 06°21′E*
112 *K12* **Bratunac** ◈ Republika Srpska, E Bosnia and Herzegovina
114 *J10* **Bratya Daskalovi** *prev.* Grozdovo. Stara Zagora, C Bulgaria *42°13′N 25°21′E*
109 *U2* **Braunau** ≈ N Austria
Braunau *see* Braunau am Inn
109 *Q4* **Braunau am Inn** *var.* Braunau. Oberösterreich, N Austria *48°16′N 13°03′E*
Braunsberg *see* Braniewo
100 *J13* **Braunschweig** *Eng./Fr.* Brunswick. Niedersachsen, N Germany *52°16′N 10°32′E*
Brava *see* Baraawe
105 *Y6* **Brava, Costa** *coastal region* NE Spain
43 *V16* **Brava, Punta** *headland* E Panama *08°21′N 78°22′W*
95 *N17* **Bråviken** *inlet* S Sweden
56 *B10* **Bravo, Cerro** ▲ N Peru *05°33′S 79°10′W*
Bravo del Norte, Río/Bravo, Río *see* Grande, Rio
35 *X17* **Brawley** California, W USA *32°58′N 115°31′W*
97 *G18* **Bray** *Ir.* Bré. E Ireland *53°12′N 06°06′W*
59 *G16* **Brazil** *off.* Federative Republic of Brazil, *Port.* Repùblica Federativa do Brasil, *Sp.* Brasil; *prev.* United States of Brazil. ◆ *federal republic* South America
65 *K15* **Brazil Basin** *var.* Brazilian Basin, Brazil'skaya Kotlovina. *undersea feature* W Atlantic Ocean *15°00′S 25°00′W*
Brazil, Federative Republic of *see* Brazil
Brazilian Basin *see* Brazil Basin
Brazilian Highlands *see* Central, Planalto
Brazil'skaya Kotlovina *see* Brazil Basin
Brazil, United States of *see* Brazil
25 *U10* **Brazos River** ≈ Texas, SW USA
Brazza *see* Brač
79 *G21* **Brazzaville** ● (Congo) Capital District, S Congo *04°14′S 15°14′E*
79 *G21* **Brazzaville** ✈ Pool, S Congo *04°15′S 15°15′E*
112 *J11* **Brčko** ◈ Republika Srpska, NE Bosnia and Herzegovina
110 *H8* **Brda** *Ger.* Brahe. ≈ N Poland
Bré *see* Bray
185 *A23* **Breaksea Sound** *sound* South Island, New Zealand
184 *L4* **Bream Bay** *bay* North Island, New Zealand
184 *L4* **Bream Head** *headland* North Island, New Zealand *35°51′S 174°35′E*
Bréanainn, Cnoc *see* Brandon Mountain
45 *S6* **Brea, Punta** *headland* W Puerto Rico *17°56′N 66°55′W*
22 *I9* **Breaux Bridge** Louisiana, S USA *30°16′N 91°54′W*
116 *J13* **Breaza** Prahova, SE Romania *45°13′N 25°38′E*
169 *P16* **Brebes** Jawa, C Indonesia *06°54′S 109°00′E*
96 *K10* **Brechin** E Scotland, United Kingdom *56°45′N 02°38′W*
99 *H15* **Brecht** Antwerpen, N Belgium *51°21′N 04°33′E*
37 *S4* **Breckenridge** Colorado, C USA *39°28′N 106°02′W*
29 *R6* **Breckenridge** Minnesota, N USA *46°15′N 96°35′W*
25 *R6* **Breckenridge** Texas, SW USA *32°45′N 98°56′W*
97 *J21* **Brecknock** *cultural region* SE Wales, United Kingdom
63 *G25* **Brecknock, Península** *headland* S Chile *54°39′S 71°48′W*
111 *G19* **Břeclav** *Ger.* Lundenburg. Jihomoravský Kraj, SE Czech Republic *49°05′N 16°51′E*
97 *J21* **Brecon** E Wales, United Kingdom *51°58′N 03°26′W*

◆ Country ● Country Capital ◇ Dependent Territory ○ Dependent Territory Capital ◈ Administrative Regions ✈ International Airport ▲ Mountain ▲▲ Mountain Range ⛰ Volcano ≈ River ◎ Lake ⊠ Reservoir

97 J21 **Brecon Beacons** ▲▲ S Wales, United Kingdom
99 I14 **Breda** Noord-Brabant, S Netherlands 51°35′N 04°46′E
95 K20 **Bredaryd** Jönköping, S Sweden 57°10′N 13°45′E
83 F26 **Bredasdorp** Western Cape, SW South Africa 34°32′S 20°02′E
93 H16 **Bredbyn** Västernorrland, N Sweden 63°28′N 18°04′E
122 F11 **Bredy** Chelyabinskaya Oblast', C Russian Federation 52°23′N 60°24′E
99 K17 **Bree** Limburg, NE Belgium 51°08′N 05°36′E
67 T15 **Breede** ≈ S South Africa
98 I7 **Breezand** Noord-Holland, NW Netherlands 52°52′N 04°47′E
113 P18 **Bregalnica** ≈ E FYR Macedonia
108 I6 **Bregenz** *anc.* Brigantium. Vorarlberg, W Austria 47°31′N 09°46′E
108 J7 **Bregenzer Wald** ▲▲ W Austria
114 F6 **Bregovo** Vidin, NW Bulgaria 44°07′N 22°40′E
102 H5 **Bréhat, Île de** *island* NW France
92 H2 **Breidhafjördhur** *bay* W Iceland
92 L3 **Breidhdalsvík** Austurland, E Iceland 64°48′N 14°02′W
108 H9 **Breil** *Ger.* Brigels. Graubünden, S Switzerland 46°46′N 09°04′E
92 I8 **Breivikbotn** Finnmark, N Norway 70°36′N 22°19′E
94 I9 **Brekken** Sør-Trøndelag, S Norway 62°39′N 11°49′E
94 G7 **Brekstad** Sør-Trøndelag, S Norway 63°42′N 09°40′E
94 B10 **Bremangerlandet** *island* S Norway
Brême *see* Bremen
100 H11 **Bremen** *Fr.* Brême. Bremen, NW Germany 53°06′N 08°48′E
23 R3 **Bremen** Georgia, SE USA 33°43′N 85°09′W
31 O11 **Bremen** Indiana, N USA 41°24′N 86°07′W
100 H10 **Bremen** *off.* Freie Hansestadt Bremen, *Fr.* Brême. ◐ *state* N Germany
100 G9 **Bremerhaven** Bremen, NW Germany 53°33′N 08°35′E
Bremersdorp *see* Manzini
32 G8 **Bremerton** Washington, NW USA 47°34′N 122°37′W
100 H10 **Bremervörde** Niedersachsen, NW Germany 53°29′N 09°06′E
25 U9 **Bremond** Texas, SW USA 31°10′N 96°40′W
25 U10 **Brenham** Texas, SW USA 30°09′N 96°24′W
108 M8 **Brenner** Tirol, W Austria 47°10′N 11°51′E
Brenner, Col du/Brennero, Passo del *see* Brenner Pass
108 M8 **Brenner Pass** *var.* Brenner Sattel, *Fr.* Col du Brenner, *Ger.* Brennerpass, *It.* Passo del Brennero. *pass* Austria/Italy
Brennerpass *see* Brenner Pass
Brenner Sattel *see* Brenner Pass
108 G10 **Brenno** ≈ SW Switzerland
106 F7 **Breno** Lombardia, N Italy 45°58′N 10°18′E
23 O5 **Brent** Alabama, S USA 32°54′N 87°10′W
106 H7 **Brenta** ≈ NE Italy
97 P21 **Brentwood** E England, United Kingdom 51°38′N 00°21′E
18 L14 **Brentwood** Long Island, New York, NE USA 40°46′N 73°12′W
106 F7 **Brescia** *anc.* Brixia. Lombardia, N Italy 45°33′N 10°13′E
99 D15 **Breskens** Zeeland, SW Netherlands 51°24′N 03°33′E
Breslau *see* Wrocław
106 H5 **Bressanone** *Ger.* Brixen. Trentino-Alto Adige, N Italy 46°44′N 11°41′E
96 M2 **Bressay** *island* NE Scotland, United Kingdom
102 K9 **Bressuire** Deux-Sèvres, W France 46°50′N 00°29′W
119 F20 **Brest** *Pol.* Brześć nad Bugiem, *Rus.* Brest-Litovsk; *prev.* Brześć Litewski. Brestskaya Voblasts', SW Belarus 52°06′N 23°42′E
102 F5 **Brest** Finistère, NW France 48°24′N 04°31′W
Brest-Litovsk *see* Brest
112 A10 **Brestova** Istra, NW Croatia 45°09′N 14°13′E
Brestskaya Oblast' *see* Brestskaya Voblasts'
119 G19 **Brestskaya Voblasts'** *prev. Rus.* Brestskaya Oblast'. ◐ *province* SW Belarus
102 G6 **Bretagne** *Eng.* Brittany, *Lat.* Britannia Minor. ◐ *region* NW France
116 G12 **Bretea-Română** *Hung.* Oláhbrettye; *prev.* Bretea-Romînă. Hunedoara, W Romania 45°39′N 23°00′E
Bretea-Romînă *see* Bretea-Română
103 O3 **Breteuil** Oise, N France 49°37′N 02°18′E
102 I10 **Breton, Pertuis** *inlet* W France
22 L10 **Breton Sound** *sound* Louisiana, S USA
184 K2 **Brett, Cape** *headland* North Island, New Zealand 35°11′S 174°21′E
101 G21 **Bretten** Baden-Württemberg, SW Germany 49°01′N 08°42′E
99 K15 **Breugel** Noord-Brabant, S Netherlands 51°30′N 05°30′E
106 B6 **Breuil-Cervinia** *It.* Cervinia. Valle d'Aosta, NW Italy 45°57′N 07°37′E
98 I11 **Breukelen** Utrecht, C Netherlands 52°11′N 05°01′E
21 P10 **Brevard** North Carolina, SE USA 35°13′N 82°46′W
38 L9 **Brevig Mission** Alaska, USA 65°19′N 166°29′W
95 G16 **Brevik** Telemark, S Norway 59°05′N 09°42′E
183 P5 **Brewarrina** New South Wales, SE Australia 30°01′S 146°50′E
19 R6 **Brewer** Maine, NE USA 44°46′N 68°44′W
29 T11 **Brewster** Minnesota, N USA 43°43′N 95°28′W
29 N14 **Brewster** Nebraska, C USA 41°57′N 99°52′W
31 U12 **Brewster** Ohio, N USA 40°42′N 81°36′W
Brewster, Kap *see* Kangikajik
183 O8 **Brewster, Lake** ◎ New South Wales, SE Australia
23 P7 **Brewton** Alabama, S USA 31°06′N 87°04′W
Brezhnev *see* Naberezhnyye Chelny
109 W12 **Brežice** *Ger.* Rann. E Slovenia 45°54′N 15°35′E
114 G9 **Breznik** Pernik, W Bulgaria 42°45′N 22°54′E
111 K19 **Brezno** *Ger.* Bries, Briesen, *Hung.* Breznóbánya; *prev.* Brezno nad Hronom. Banskobystrický Kraj, C Slovakia 48°49′N 19°40′E
Breznóbánya/Brezno nad Hronom *see* Brezno
116 I12 **Brezoi** Vâlcea, SW Romania 45°18′N 24°15′E
114 J10 **Brezovo** *prev.* Abrashlare. Plovdiv, C Bulgaria 42°19′N 25°05′E
79 K14 **Bria** Haute-Kotto, C Central African Republic 06°30′N 22°00′E
103 U13 **Briançon** *anc.* Brigantio. Hautes-Alpes, SE France 44°55′N 06°37′E
36 K7 **Brian Head** ▲ Utah, W USA 37°40′N 112°49′W
103 O7 **Briare** Loiret, C France 47°35′N 02°46′E
183 V2 **Bribie Island** *island* Queensland, E Australia
43 O14 **Bribrí** Limón, E Costa Rica 09°37′N 82°51′W
116 L8 **Briceni** *var.* Brinceni, *Rus.* Brichany. N Moldova 48°21′N 27°02′E
Bricgstow *see* Bristol
Brichany *see* Briceni
99 M24 **Bridel** Luxembourg, C Luxembourg 49°40′N 06°03′E
97 J22 **Bridgend** S Wales, United Kingdom 51°30′N 03°37′W
14 I14 **Bridgenorth** Ontario, SE Canada 44°21′N 78°22′W
23 Q1 **Bridgeport** Alabama, S USA 34°57′N 85°42′W
35 R8 **Bridgeport** California, W USA 38°14′N 119°15′W
18 L13 **Bridgeport** Connecticut, NE USA 41°10′N 73°12′W
31 N15 **Bridgeport** Illinois, N USA 38°42′N 87°45′W
28 J14 **Bridgeport** Nebraska, C USA 41°37′N 103°07′W
25 S6 **Bridgeport** Texas, SW USA 33°12′N 97°45′W
21 S3 **Bridgeport** West Virginia, NE USA 39°17′N 80°15′W
25 S5 **Bridgeport, Lake** ⊠ Texas, SW USA
33 U11 **Bridger** Montana, NW USA 45°16′N 108°55′W
18 J17 **Bridgeton** New Jersey, NE USA 39°24′N 75°10′W
180 J14 **Bridgetown** Western Australia 34°01′S 116°07′E
45 Y14 **Bridgetown** ● (Barbados) SW Barbados 13°05′N 59°36′W
183 P17 **Bridgewater** Tasmania, SE Australia 42°47′S 147°15′E
13 P16 **Bridgewater** Nova Scotia, SE Canada 44°19′N 64°30′W
19 P12 **Bridgewater** Massachusetts, NE USA 41°59′N 70°58′W
29 Q11 **Bridgewater** South Dakota, N USA 43°33′N 97°30′W
21 U5 **Bridgewater** Virginia, NE USA 38°22′N 78°58′W
19 P8 **Bridgton** Maine, NE USA 44°04′N 70°43′W
97 K23 **Bridgwater** SW England, United Kingdom 51°08′N 03°W
97 K22 **Bridgwater Bay** *bay* SW England, United Kingdom
97 O16 **Bridlington** E England, United Kingdom 54°05′N 00°12′W
97 O16 **Bridlington Bay** *bay* E England, United Kingdom
183 P15 **Bridport** Tasmania, SE Australia 41°03′S 147°26′E
97 K24 **Bridport** S England, United Kingdom 50°44′N 02°43′W
103 O5 **Brie** *cultural region* N France
Brieg *see* Brzeg
Briel *see* Brielle
98 G12 **Brielle** *var.* Briel, Bril, *Eng.* The Brill. Zuid-Holland, SW Netherlands 51°54′N 04°10′E
108 E9 **Brienz** Bern, C Switzerland 46°45′N 08°00′E
108 E9 **Brienzer See** ◎ SW Switzerland
Bries/Briesen *see* Brezno
Brietzig *see* Brzesko
103 S4 **Briey** Meurthe-et-Moselle, NE France 49°15′N 05°57′E
108 E10 **Brig** *Fr.* Brigue, *It.* Briga. Valais, SW Switzerland 46°19′N 08°E
Briga *see* Brig
101 G24 **Brigach** ≈ S Germany
18 K17 **Brigantine** New Jersey, NE USA 39°23′N 74°21′W
Brigantio *see* Briançon
Brigantium *see* Bregenz
Brigels *see* Breil
25 S9 **Briggs** Texas, SW USA 30°52′N 97°55′W
36 L1 **Brigham City** Utah, W USA 41°30′N 112°00′W
14 J15 **Brighton** Ontario, SE Canada 44°01′N 77°44′W
97 O23 **Brighton** SE England, United Kingdom 50°50′N 00°10′W
37 T4 **Brighton** Colorado, C USA 39°58′N 104°46′W
30 K15 **Brighton** Illinois, N USA 39°01′N 90°09′W
103 T16 **Brignoles** Var, W France 43°25′N 06°03′E
Brigue *see* Brig
105 O7 **Brihuega** Castilla-La Mancha, C Spain 40°45′N 02°52′W
112 A10 **Brijuni** *It.* Brioni. *island group* NW Croatia
76 G12 **Brikama** W Gambia 13°13′N 16°37′W
Bril *see* Brielle
Brill, The *see* Brielle
101 G15 **Brilon** Nordrhein-Westfalen, W Germany 51°24′N 08°34′E
Brinceni *see* Briceni
107 Q18 **Brindisi** *anc.* Brundisium, Brundusium. Puglia, SE Italy 40°39′N 17°55′E
27 W11 **Brinkley** Arkansas, C USA 34°53′N 91°11′W
Brioni *see* Brijuni
103 P12 **Brioude** *anc.* Brivas. Haute-Loire, C France 45°18′N 03°23′E
Briovera *see* St-Lô
183 U2 **Brisbane** *state capital* Queensland, E Australia 27°30′S 153°E
183 V2 **Brisbane** ✈ Queensland, E Australia 27°30′S 153°00′E
25 P2 **Briscoe** Texas, SW USA 35°34′N 100°17′W
106 H10 **Brisighella** Emilia-Romagna, C Italy 44°12′N 11°45′E
108 G11 **Brissago** Ticino, S Switzerland 46°07′N 08°40′E
97 K22 **Bristol** *anc.* Bricgstow. SW England, United Kingdom 51°27′N 02°35′W
18 M12 **Bristol** Connecticut, NE USA 41°40′N 72°56′W
23 R9 **Bristol** Florida, SE USA 30°25′N 84°58′W
19 N9 **Bristol** New Hampshire, NE USA 43°34′N 71°42′W
29 Q8 **Bristol** South Dakota, N USA 45°18′N 97°45′W
21 P8 **Bristol** Tennessee, S USA 36°36′N 82°11′W
18 M8 **Bristol** Vermont, NE USA 44°07′N 73°00′W
39 N14 **Bristol Bay** *bay* Alaska, USA
97 I22 **Bristol Channel** *inlet* England/Wales, United Kingdom
35 W14 **Bristol Lake** ◎ California, W USA
27 P10 **Bristow** Oklahoma, C USA 35°49′N 96°23′W
86 C10 **Britain** *var.* Great Britain. *island* United Kingdom
Britannia Minor *see* Bretagne
10 L12 **British Columbia** *Fr.* Colombie-Britannique. ◐ *province* SW Canada
British Guiana *see* Guyana
British Honduras *see* Belize
173 Q7 **British Indian Ocean Territory** ◇ *UK dependent territory* C Indian Ocean
86 B9 **British Isles** *island group* NW Europe
10 I1 **British Mountains** ▲▲ Yukon Territory, NW Canada
British North Borneo *see* Sabah
British Solomon Islands Protectorate *see* Solomon Islands
45 S8 **British Virgin Islands** *var.* Virgin Islands. ◇ *UK dependent territory* E West Indies
83 J21 **Brits** North-West, N South Africa 25°39′S 27°47′E
83 H24 **Britstown** Northern Cape, W South Africa 30°36′S 23°30′E
14 F12 **Britt** Ontario, S Canada 45°46′N 80°34′W
29 V12 **Britt** Iowa, C USA 43°06′N 93°48′W
Brittany *see* Bretagne
29 Q7 **Britton** South Dakota, N USA 45°47′N 97°45′W
Briva Curretia *see* Brive-la-Gaillarde
Briva Isarae *see* Pontoise
Brivas *see* Brioude
Brive *see* Brive-la-Gaillarde
102 M12 **Brive-la-Gaillarde** *prev.* Brive; *anc.* Briva Curretia. Corrèze, C France 45°09′N 01°31′E
105 O4 **Briviesca** Castilla-León, N Spain 42°33′N 03°19′W
Brixen *see* Bressanone
Brixia *see* Brescia
145 S15 **Brlik** *var.* Novotroickoje, Novotroitskoye. Zhambyl, SE Kazakhstan 43°39′N 73°45′E
Brněnský Kraj *see* Jihomoravský Kraj
111 G18 **Brno** *Ger.* Brünn. Jihomoravský Kraj, SE Czech Republic 49°11′N 16°35′E
96 G7 **Broad Bay** *bay* NW Scotland, United Kingdom
25 X8 **Broaddus** Texas, SW USA 31°18′N 94°16′W
183 O12 **Broadford** Victoria, SE Australia 37°07′S 145°04′E
96 G9 **Broadford** N Scotland, United Kingdom 57°14′N 05°54′W
96 J13 **Broad Law** ▲ S Scotland, United Kingdom 55°30′N 03°22′W
23 U3 **Broad River** ≈ Georgia, SE USA
21 N8 **Broad River** ≈ North Carolina/South Carolina, SE USA
181 Y8 **Broadsound Range** ▲▲ Queensland, E Australia
33 X11 **Broadus** Montana, NW USA 45°28′N 105°22′W
21 U4 **Broadway** Virginia, NE USA 38°36′N 78°48′W
118 E9 **Broceni** Saldus, SW Latvia 56°41′N 22°31′E
11 U11 **Brochet** Manitoba, C Canada 57°55′N 101°40′W
11 U10 **Brochet, Lac** ◎ Manitoba, C Canada
15 S5 **Brochet, Lac au** ◎ Québec, SE Canada
101 K14 **Brocken** ▲ C Germany 51°48′N 10°38′E
19 O12 **Brockton** Massachusetts, NE USA 42°04′N 71°01′W
14 L14 **Brockville** Ontario, SE Canada 44°35′N 75°44′W
18 D13 **Brockway** Pennsylvania, NE USA 41°14′N 78°45′W
Brod/Bród *see* Slavonski Brod
9 N5 **Brodeur Peninsula** *peninsula* Baffin Island, Nunavut, NE Canada
96 H13 **Brodick** W Scotland, United Kingdom 55°34′N 05°10′W
Brod na Savi *see* Slavonski Brod
110 K9 **Brodnica** *Ger.* Buddenbrock. Kujawski-pomorskie, C Poland 53°15′N 19°23′E
112 G10 **Brod-Posavina** *off.* Brodsko-Posavska Županija, *var.* Slavonski Brod-Posavina. ◐ *province* NE Croatia
Brodsko-Posavska Županija *see* Brod-Posavina
116 J5 **Brody** L'vivs'ka Oblast', NW Ukraine 50°05′N 25°08′E
98 I10 **Broek-in-Waterland** Noord-Holland, C Netherlands 52°27′N 04°59′E
32 L13 **Brogan** Oregon, NW USA 44°15′N 117°34′W
110 N10 **Brok** Mazowieckie, C Poland 52°42′N 21°53′E
27 P9 **Broken Arrow** Oklahoma, C USA 36°03′N 95°47′W
183 T9 **Broken Bay** *bay* New South Wales, SE Australia
29 N15 **Broken Bow** Nebraska, C USA 41°24′N 99°38′W
27 R13 **Broken Bow** Oklahoma, C USA 34°01′N 94°44′W
27 R12 **Broken Bow Lake** ⊠ Oklahoma, C USA
182 L6 **Broken Hill** New South Wales, SE Australia 31°58′S 141°27′E
173 S10 **Broken Ridge** *undersea feature* S Indian Ocean 31°30′S 95°00′E
186 C6 **Broken Water Bay** *bay* W Bismarck Sea
55 W10 **Brokopondo** Brokopondo, NE Surinam 05°04′N 55°00′W
55 W10 **Brokopondo** ◐ *district* C Surinam
Bromberg *see* Bydgoszcz
95 L22 **Bromölla** Skåne, S Sweden 56°04′N 14°28′E
97 L20 **Bromsgrove** W England, United Kingdom 52°20′N 02°03′W
95 G20 **Brønderslev** Nordjylland, N Denmark 57°16′N 09°58′E
106 D8 **Broni** Lombardia, N Italy 45°04′N 09°18′E
10 K11 **Bronlund Peak** ▲ British Columbia, W Canada 57°27′N 126°43′W
93 F14 **Brønnøysund** Nordland, C Norway 65°38′N 12°15′E
23 V10 **Bronson** Florida, SE USA 29°25′N 82°38′W
31 Q11 **Bronson** Michigan, N USA 41°52′N 85°11′W
25 X8 **Bronson** Texas, SW USA 31°20′N 94°00′W
107 L24 **Bronte** Sicilia, Italy, C Mediterranean Sea 37°47′N 14°50′E
25 P8 **Bronte** Texas, SW USA 31°53′N 100°17′W
25 Y9 **Brookeland** Texas, SW USA 31°05′N 93°57′W
170 M7 **Brooke's Point** Palawan, W Philippines 08°54′N 117°54′E
27 T3 **Brookfield** Missouri, C USA 39°46′N 93°04′W
22 K7 **Brookhaven** Mississippi, S USA 31°34′N 90°26′W
32 E16 **Brookings** Oregon, NW USA 42°03′N 124°16′W
29 R10 **Brookings** South Dakota, N USA 44°15′N 96°46′W
29 W14 **Brooklyn** Iowa, C USA 41°43′N 92°27′W
29 U8 **Brooklyn Park** Minnesota, N USA 45°06′N 93°18′W
21 U7 **Brookneal** Virginia, NE USA 37°03′N 78°56′W
11 R16 **Brooks** Alberta, SW Canada 50°35′N 111°54′W
25 V11 **Brookshire** Texas, SW USA 29°47′N 95°57′W
38 L8 **Brooks Mountain** ▲ Alaska, USA 65°31′N 167°24′W
38 M11 **Brooks Range** ▲▲ Alaska, USA
31 O12 **Brookston** Indiana, N USA 40°34′N 86°53′W
23 V11 **Brooksville** Florida, SE USA 28°33′N 82°23′W
23 N4 **Brooksville** Mississippi, S USA 33°13′N 88°34′W
180 J13 **Brookton** Western Australia 32°24′S 117°04′E
31 Q14 **Brookville** Indiana, N USA 39°25′N 85°00′W
18 D13 **Brookville** Pennsylvania, NE USA 41°07′N 79°05′W
31 Q14 **Brookville Lake** ⊠ Indiana, N USA
180 K5 **Broome** Western Australia 17°58′S 122°15′E
37 S4 **Broomfield** Colorado, C USA 39°55′N 105°05′W
Broos *see* Orăștie
96 J7 **Brora** N Scotland, United Kingdom 57°59′N 04°00′W
96 I7 **Brora** ≈ N Scotland, United Kingdom
95 F23 **Brørup** Ribe, W Denmark 55°29′N 09°01′E
95 L23 **Brösarp** Skåne, S Sweden 55°43′N 14°10′E
116 J9 **Broșteni** Suceava, NE Romania 47°14′N 25°43′E
102 M6 **Brou** Eure-et-Loir, C France 48°12′N 01°10′E
Broucsella *see* Brussel/Bruxelles
Broughton Bay *see* Tongjosŏn-man
Broughton Island *see* Qikiqtarjuaq
138 G7 **Broummâna** C Lebanon 33°53′N 35°39′E
22 I9 **Broussard** Louisiana, S USA 30°09′N 91°57′W
98 E13 **Brouwersdam** *dam* SW Netherlands
98 E13 **Brouwershaven** Zeeland, SW Netherlands 51°44′N 03°50′E
117 P4 **Brovary** Kyyivs'ka Oblast', N Ukraine 50°30′N 30°45′E
95 G20 **Brovst** Nordjylland, N Denmark 57°06′N 09°32′E
31 S8 **Brown City** Michigan, N USA 43°12′N 82°50′W
24 M6 **Brownfield** Texas, SW USA 33°11′N 102°16′W
33 Q7 **Browning** Montana, NW USA 48°33′N 113°00′W
36 R6 **Brown, Mount** ▲ Montana, NW USA 48°52′N 111°08′W
0 M9 **Browns Bank** *undersea feature* NW Atlantic Ocean 42°40′N 66°05′W
31 O14 **Brownsburg** Indiana, N USA 39°50′N 86°24′W
18 J16 **Browns Mills** New Jersey, NE USA 39°58′N 74°33′W
44 J12 **Browns Town** C Jamaica 18°28′N 77°22′W
31 P15 **Brownstown** Indiana, N USA 38°52′N 86°02′W
29 R8 **Browns Valley** Minnesota, N USA 45°36′N 96°49′W
20 K7 **Brownsville** Kentucky, S USA 37°10′N 86°18′W
20 F9 **Brownsville** Tennessee, S USA 35°35′N 89°15′W
25 T17 **Brownsville** Texas, SW USA 25°56′N 97°28′W
55 W10 **Brownsweg** Brokopondo, C Surinam
29 U9 **Brownton** Minnesota, N USA 44°43′N 94°21′W
19 R5 **Brownville Junction** Maine, NE USA 45°20′N 69°04′W
25 R8 **Brownwood** Texas, SW USA 31°42′N 98°59′W
25 R8 **Brownwood Lake** ⊠ Texas, SW USA
104 I9 **Brozas** Extremadura, W Spain 39°37′N 06°48′W
119 M18 **Brozha** Mahilyowskaya Voblasts', E Belarus 52°57′N 29°07′E
103 O2 **Bruay-en-Artois** Pas-de-Calais, N France 50°31′N 02°30′E
103 P2 **Bruay-sur-l'Escaut** Nord, N France 50°24′N 03°33′E
14 F13 **Bruce Peninsula** *peninsula* Ontario, S Canada
20 H9 **Bruceton** Tennessee, S USA 36°02′N 88°14′W
25 T9 **Bruceville** Texas, SW USA 31°17′N 97°15′W
101 G21 **Bruchsal** Baden-Württemberg, SW Germany 49°07′N 08°35′E
109 Q7 **Bruck** Salzburg, NW Austria 47°18′N 12°51′E
Bruck *see* Bruck an der Mur
109 Y4 **Bruck an der Leitha** Niederösterreich, NE Austria 48°02′N 16°47′E
109 V7 **Bruck an der Mur** *var.* Bruck. Steiermark, C Austria 47°25′N 15°17′E
101 M24 **Bruckmühl** Bayern, SE Germany 47°52′N 11°54′E
168 E7 **Brueuh, Pulau** *island* NW Indonesia
Bruges *see* Brugge
108 F6 **Brugg** Aargau, NW Switzerland 47°29′N 08°13′E
99 C16 **Brugge** *Fr.* Bruges. West-Vlaanderen, NW Belgium 51°13′N 03°14′E
109 R9 **Bruggen** Kärnten, S Austria 46°46′N 13°13′E
101 E16 **Brühl** Nordrhein-Westfalen, W Germany 50°50′N 06°55′E
99 F14 **Bruinisse** Zeeland, SW Netherlands 51°40′N 04°04′E
169 R9 **Bruit, Pulau** *island* East Malaysia
14 K10 **Brûlé, Lac** ◎ Québec, SE Canada
30 M4 **Brule River** ≈ Michigan/Wisconsin, N USA
99 H23 **Brûly** Namur, S Belgium 49°55′N 04°31′E
59 N17 **Brumado** Bahia, E Brazil 14°14′S 41°38′W
98 M11 **Brummen** Gelderland, E Netherlands 52°05′N 06°10′E
94 H13 **Brumunddal** Hedmark, S Norway 60°54′N 11°00′E
23 Q6 **Brundidge** Alabama, S USA 31°43′N 85°49′W
Brundisium/Brundusium *see* Brindisi
33 N15 **Bruneau River** ≈ Idaho, NW USA
Bruneck *see* Brunico
169 T8 **Brunei** *off.* Brunei Darussalam, *Mal.* Negara Brunei Darussalam. ◆ *monarchy* SE Asia
169 T7 **Brunei Bay** *var.* Teluk Brunei. *bay* N Brunei
Brunei Darussalam *see* Brunei
Brunei, Teluk *see* Brunei Bay
Brunei Town *see* Bandar Seri Begawan
106 H5 **Brunico** *Ger.* Bruneck. Trentino-Alto Adige, N Italy 46°49′N 11°57′E
Brünn *see* Brno
185 G17 **Brunner, Lake** ◎ South Island, New Zealand
99 M18 **Brunssum** Limburg, SE Netherlands 50°57′N 05°59′E
23 W7 **Brunswick** Georgia, SE USA 31°09′N 81°30′W
19 Q8 **Brunswick** Maine, NE USA 43°54′N 69°58′W
21 V3 **Brunswick** Maryland, NE USA 39°18′N 77°37′W
27 T3 **Brunswick** Missouri, C USA 39°25′N 93°07′W
31 T11 **Brunswick** Ohio, N USA 41°14′N 81°50′W
Brunswick *see* Braunschweig
63 H24 **Brunswick, Peninsula** *headland* S Chile 53°30′S 71°27′W
111 H17 **Bruntál** *Ger.* Freudenthal. Moravskoslezský Kraj, E Czech Republic 50°00′N 17°27′E
195 N3 **Brunt Ice Shelf** *ice shelf* Antarctica
Brusa *see* Bursa
114 G7 **Brusartsi** Montana, NW Bulgaria 43°39′N 23°04′E
37 U3 **Brush** Colorado, C USA 40°15′N 103°37′W
42 M5 **Brus Laguna** Gracias a Dios, E Honduras 15°46′N 84°32′W
60 K13 **Brusque** Santa Catarina, S Brazil 27°07′S 48°54′W
Brussa *see* Bursa
99 E18 **Brussel** *var.* Brussels, *Fr.* Bruxelles, *Ger.* Brüssel; *anc.* Broucsella. ● (Belgium) Brussels, C Belgium 50°52′N 04°21′E *see also* Bruxelles
Brussel *see* Bruxelles
Brüssel/Brussels *see* Brussel/Bruxelles
117 O5 **Brusyliv** Zhytomyrs'ka Oblast', N Ukraine 50°16′N 29°31′E
183 Q12 **Bruthen** Victoria, SE Australia 37°43′S 147°49′E
Bruttium *see* Calabria
Brüx *see* Most
99 E18 **Bruxelles** *var.* Brussels, *Dut.* Brussel, *Ger.* Brüssel; *anc.* Broucsella. ● Brussels, C Belgium 50°52′N 04°21′E *see also* Brussel
Bruxelles *see* Brussel
54 J7 **Bruzual** Apure, W Venezuela 07°59′N 69°18′W
31 Q11 **Bryan** Ohio, N USA 41°30′N 84°34′W
25 U10 **Bryan** Texas, SW USA 30°40′N 96°23′W
194 J4 **Bryan Coast** *physical region* Antarctica
122 L11 **Bryanka** Krasnoyarskiy Kray, C Russian Federation 59°01′N 93°13′E
117 Y7 **Bryanka** Luhans'ka Oblast', E Ukraine 48°30′N 38°45′E
182 J8 **Bryan, Mount** ▲ South Australia 33°25′S 138°59′E
126 I6 **Bryansk** Bryanskaya Oblast', W Russian Federation 53°16′N 34°07′E
126 H6 **Bryanskaya Oblast'** ◐ *province* W Russian Federation
194 J5 **Bryant, Cape** *headland* Antarctica
27 U8 **Bryant Creek** ≈ Missouri, C USA
36 K8 **Bryce Canyon** *canyon* Utah, W USA
119 O15 **Bryli** Mahilyowskaya Voblasts', E Belarus 53°54′N 30°33′E
95 C17 **Bryne** Rogaland, S Norway 58°43′N 05°40′E
25 R6 **Bryson** Texas, SW USA 33°09′N 98°23′W
21 N10 **Bryson City** North Carolina, SE USA 35°26′N 83°27′W
14 K11 **Bryson, Lac** ◎ Québec, SE Canada
126 K13 **Bryukhovetskaya** Krasnodarskiy Kray, SW Russian Federation 45°49′N 38°01′E
111 H15 **Brzeg** *Ger.* Brieg; *anc.* Civitas Altae Ripae. Opolskie, S Poland 50°52′N 17°27′E
111 G14 **Brzeg Dolny** *Ger.* Dyhernfurth. Dolnośląskie, SW Poland 51°15′N 16°40′E
Brześć Litewski/Brześć nad Bugiem *see* Brest
111 L17 **Brzesko** *Ger.* Brietzig. Małopolskie, SE Poland 49°59′N 20°34′E
Brzeżany *see* Berezhany
110 K12 **Brzeziny** Łódzkie, C Poland 51°49′N 19°41′E
Brzostowica Wielka *see* Vyalikaya Byerastavitsa
111 O17 **Brzozów** Podkarpackie, SE Poland 49°38′N 22°00′E
Bsharrī/Bsherri *see* Bcharré
187 X14 **Bua** Vanua Levu, N Fiji 16°48′S 178°36′E
95 J20 **Bua** Halland, S Sweden 57°14′N 12°07′E
82 M13 **Bua** ≈ C Malawi
Bua *see* Čiovo
81 L18 **Bu'aale** *It.* Buale. Jubbada Dhexe, SW Somalia 00°52′N 42°37′E
Buache, Mount *see* Mutunte, Mount
189 Q8 **Buada Lagoon** *lagoon* Nauru, C Pacific Ocean
186 M8 **Buala** Santa Isabel, E Solomon Islands 08°06′S 159°31′E
Buale *see* Bu'aale
190 H1 **Buariki** *atoll* Tungaru, W Kiribati
167 Q10 **Bua Yai** *var.* Ban Bua Yai. Nakhon Ratchasima, E Thailand 15°35′N 102°25′E
75 P8 **Bu'ayrāt al Ḥasūn** *var.* Buwayrat al Hasūn. C Libya 31°22′N 15°41′E
76 H13 **Buba** S Guinea-Bissau 11°36′N 14°55′W
171 P11 **Bubaa** Sulawesi, N Indonesia 00°32′N 122°27′E
81 D20 **Bubanza** NW Burundi 03°04′S 29°22′E
83 K18 **Bubi** *prev.* Bubye. ≈ S Zimbabwe
142 L11 **Būbiyan, Jazīrat** *island* E Kuwait
Bublitz *see* Bobolice
Bubye *see* Bubi
187 Y13 **Buca** *prev.* Mbutha. Vanua Levu, N Fiji 16°39′S 179°51′E
136 F16 **Bucak** Burdur, SW Turkey 37°28′N 30°37′E
54 G8 **Bucaramanga** Santander, N Colombia 07°08′N 73°10′W
107 M18 **Buccino** Campania, S Italy 40°37′N 15°25′E
116 K9 **Bucecea** Botoșani, NE Romania 47°45′N 26°30′E
116 J6 **Buchach** *Pol.* Buczacz. Ternopil's'ka Oblast', W Ukraine 49°04′N 25°23′E
183 Q12 **Buchan** Victoria, SE Australia 37°26′S 148°11′E
76 J17 **Buchanan** *prev.* Grand Bassa. SW Liberia 05°53′N 10°03′W
23 R3 **Buchanan** Georgia, SE USA 33°48′N 85°11′W
31 O11 **Buchanan** Michigan, N USA 41°49′N 86°21′W
21 T6 **Buchanan** Virginia, NE USA 37°31′N 79°40′W
25 R10 **Buchanan Dam** Texas, SW USA 30°42′N 98°24′W
25 R10 **Buchanan, Lake** ⊠ Texas, SW USA
96 L8 **Buchan Ness** *headland* NE Scotland, United Kingdom 57°28′N 01°46′W
13 T12 **Buchans** Newfoundland and Labrador, SE Canada 48°49′N 56°53′W
Bucharest *see* București
101 H20 **Buchen** Baden-Württemberg, SW Germany 49°31′N 09°18′E
100 I10 **Buchholz in der Nordheide** Niedersachsen, NW Germany 53°19′N 09°52′E
108 F7 **Buchs** Aargau, N Switzerland 47°24′N 08°04′E
108 I8 **Buchs** Sankt Gallen, NE Switzerland 47°10′N 09°28′E
100 H13 **Bückeburg** Niedersachsen, NW Germany 52°16′N 09°03′E
36 K14 **Buckeye** Arizona, SW USA 33°22′N 112°34′W
Buckeye State *see* Ohio
21 S4 **Buckhannon** West Virginia, NE USA 38°59′N 80°14′W
25 T9 **Buckholts** Texas, SW USA 30°52′N 97°07′W
96 K8 **Buckie** NE Scotland, United Kingdom 57°39′N 02°56′W
14 M12 **Buckingham** Québec, SE Canada 45°35′N 75°25′W
21 U6 **Buckingham** Virginia, NE USA 37°33′N 78°34′W
97 N21 **Buckinghamshire** *cultural region* SE England, United Kingdom
39 N8 **Buckland** Alaska, USA 65°58′N 161°07′W
182 G7 **Buckleboo** South Australia 32°55′S 136°11′E
26 K7 **Bucklin** Kansas, C USA 37°33′N 99°37′W
27 T3 **Bucklin** Missouri, C USA 39°46′N 92°53′W
36 I12 **Buckskin Mountains** ▲▲ Arizona, SW USA
19 R7 **Bucksport** Maine, NE USA 44°34′N 68°46′W
82 A9 **Buco Zau** Cabinda, NW Angola 04°45′S 12°34′E
Bu Craa *see* Bou Craa
116 K14 **București** *Eng.* Bucharest, *Ger.* Bukarest, *prev.* Altenburg; *anc.* Cetatea Damboviței. ● (Romania) București, S Romania 44°27′N 26°06′E
31 S12 **Bucyrus** Ohio, N USA 40°47′N 82°57′W
Buczacz *see* Buchach
94 E9 **Bud** Møre og Romsdal, S Norway 62°55′N 06°55′E
25 S11 **Buda** Texas, SW USA 30°05′N 97°50′W
119 O18 **Buda-Kashalyova** *Rus.* Buda-Koshelëvo. Homyel'skaya Voblasts', SE Belarus 52°43′N 30°34′E
Buda-Koshelëvo *see* Buda-Kashalyova
166 L4 **Budalin** Sagaing, C Burma (Myanmar) 22°24′N 95°08′E
111 J22 **Budapest** *off.* Budapest Főváros, *SCr.* Budimpešta. ● (Hungary) Pest, N Hungary 47°30′N 19°03′E
Budapest Főváros *see* Budapest
152 K11 **Budaun** Uttar Pradesh, N India 28°02′N 79°07′E
141 O9 **Budayyi'ah** *oasis* C Saudi Arabia
195 Y12 **Budd Coast** *physical region* Antarctica
Buddenbrock *see* Brodnica
107 C17 **Budduso** Sardegna, Italy, C Mediterranean Sea 40°37′N 09°19′E
97 I23 **Bude** SW England, United Kingdom 50°50′N 04°33′W
22 J7 **Bude** Mississippi, S USA 31°27′N 90°51′W
Budějovický Kraj *see* Jihočeský Kraj
99 K16 **Budel** Noord-Brabant, SE Netherlands 51°17′N 05°35′E
100 I8 **Büdelsdorf** Schleswig-Holstein, N Germany 54°20′N 09°40′E
127 O14 **Budënnovsk** Stavropol'skiy Kray, SW Russian Federation 44°46′N 44°07′E
116 K14 **Budești** Călărași, SE Romania 44°13′N 26°30′E
Budge-Budge *see* Baj Baj
Budgewoi *see* Budgewoi Lake
183 T8 **Budgewoi Lake** *var.* Budgewoi. New South Wales, SE Australia 33°14′S 151°34′E
92 I2 **Búdhardalur** Vesturland, W Iceland 65°07′N 21°45′W
Budimpešta *see* Budapest
79 J16 **Budjala** Equateur, NW Dem. Rep. Congo 02°39′N 19°42′E
106 G10 **Budrio** Emilia-Romagna, C Italy 44°33′N 11°34′E
Budslav *see* Budslaw
119 K14 **Budslaw** *Rus.* Budslav. Minskaya Voblasts', N Belarus 54°47′N 27°27′E
Budua *see* Budva
169 R9 **Budu, Tanjung** *headland* East Malaysia 02°51′N 111°42′E
113 J17 **Budva** *It.* Budua. W Montenegro 42°17′N 18°49′E
Budweis *see* České Budějovice
Budyšin *see* Bautzen
79 D16 **Buea** Sud-Ouest, SW Cameroon 04°09′N 09°13′E
103 S13 **Buëch** ≈ SE France
18 J17 **Buena** New Jersey, NE USA 39°30′N 74°55′W
62 K12 **Buena Esperanza** San Luis, C Argentina 34°45′S 65°15′W
54 C11 **Buenaventura** Valle del Cauca, W Colombia 03°54′N 77°02′W
40 I4 **Buenaventura** Chihuahua, N Mexico 29°50′N 107°30′W
57 M18 **Buena Vista** Santa Cruz, C Bolivia 17°28′S 63°37′W
40 G10 **Buenavista** Baja California Sur, NW Mexico 23°39′N 109°41′W
37 S5 **Buena Vista** Colorado, C USA 38°50′N 106°07′W
23 S5 **Buena Vista** Georgia, SE USA 32°19′N 84°31′W
21 T6 **Buena Vista** Virginia, NE USA 37°44′N 79°22′W
44 F5 **Buena Vista, Bahia de** *bay* N Cuba
35 R13 **Buena Vista Lake Bed** ◎ California, W USA
105 P8 **Buendía, Embalse de** ⊠ C Spain
63 F16 **Bueno, Río** ≈ S Chile
62 N12 **Buenos Aires** *hist.* Santa Maria del Buen Aire. ● (Argentina) Buenos Aires, E Argentina 34°40′S 58°30′W
43 O15 **Buenos Aires** Puntarenas, SE Costa Rica 09°10′N 83°23′W
61 C20 **Buenos Aires** *off.* Provincia de Buenos Aires. ◐ *province* E Argentina
63 H19 **Buenos Aires, Lago** *var.* Lago General Carrera. ◎ Argentina/Chile
Buenos Aires, Provincia de *see* Buenos Aires
54 C13 **Buesaco** Nariño, SW Colombia 01°22′N 77°07′W
29 U8 **Buffalo** Minnesota, N USA 45°11′N 93°50′W
26 T6 **Buffalo** Missouri, C USA 37°38′N 93°05′W
18 D10 **Buffalo** New York, NE USA 42°53′N 78°53′W
27 K8 **Buffalo** Oklahoma, C USA 36°51′N 99°38′W
28 J7 **Buffalo** South Dakota, N USA 45°25′N 103°35′W
25 V8 **Buffalo** Texas, SW USA 31°25′N 96°04′W
33 W12 **Buffalo** Wyoming, C USA 44°21′N 106°40′W
29 U11 **Buffalo Center** Iowa, C USA 43°23′N 93°57′W
24 M3 **Buffalo Lake** ⊠ Texas, SW USA
30 K7 **Buffalo Lake** ⊠ Wisconsin, N USA
11 S12 **Buffalo Narrows** Saskatchewan, C Canada 55°52′N 108°28′W
27 U9 **Buffalo River** ≈ Arkansas, C USA
29 R5 **Buffalo River** ≈ Minnesota, N USA
20 I10 **Buffalo River** ≈ Tennessee, S USA
30 J6 **Buffalo River** ≈ Wisconsin, N USA
44 L12 **Buff Bay** E Jamaica 18°18′N 76°40′W
23 T3 **Buford** Georgia, SE USA 34°07′N 84°00′W

◆ Country
● Country Capital
◇ Dependent Territory
○ Dependent Territory Capital
◐ Administrative Regions
✈ International Airport
▲ Mountain
▲▲ Mountain Range
Volcano
≈ River
◎ Lake
⊠ Reservoir

28 J3 **Buford** North Dakota, N USA *48°00′N 103°58′W*
33 Y17 **Buford** Wyoming, C USA *41°05′N 105°17′W*
116 J14 **Buftea** Ilfov, S Romania *44°34′N 25°58′E*
84 I9 **Bug** *Bel.* Zakhodni Buh, *Eng.* Western Bug, *Rus.* Zapadnyy Bug, *Ukr.* Zakhidnyy Buh. ≈ E Europe
54 D11 **Buga** Valle del Cauca, W Colombia *03°53′N 76°17′W*
Buga *see* Dörvöljin
103 O17 **Bugarach, Pic du** ▲ S France *42°52′N 02°23′E*
162 F8 **Bugat** *var.* Bayangol. Govĭ-Altay, SW Mongolia *45°33′N 94°22′E*
146 B12 **Bugdaýly** *Rus.* Bugdayly. Balkan Welaýaty, W Turkmenistan *38°42′N 54°14′E*
Bugdayly *see* Bugdaýly
Buggs Island Lake *see* John H. Kerr Reservoir
Bughotu *see* Santa Isabel
171 O14 **Bugingkalo** Sulawesi, C Indonesia *04°49′S 121°42′E*
64 P6 **Bugio** *island* Madeira, Portugal, NE Atlantic Ocean
92 M8 **Bugøynes** Finnmark, N Norway *69°57′N 29°34′E*
125 Q3 **Bugrino** Nenetskiy Avtonomnyy Okrug, NW Russian Federation *68°48′N 49°12′E*
127 T5 **Bugul'ma** Respublika Tatarstan, W Russian Federation *54°31′N 52°45′E*
Bügür *see* Luntai
127 T6 **Buguruslan** Orenburgskaya Oblast', W Russian Federation *53°38′N 52°30′E*
159 R9 **Buh He** ≈ C China
101 F22 **Bühl** Baden-Württemberg, SW Germany *48°42′N 08°07′E*
33 O15 **Buhl** Idaho, NW USA *42°36′N 114°45′W*
116 K10 **Buhuşi** Bacău, E Romania *46°41′N 26°45′E*
Buie d'Istria *see* Buje
97 J20 **Builth Wells** E Wales, United Kingdom *52°07′N 03°28′W*
186 J8 **Buin** Bougainville Island, NE Papua New Guinea *06°52′S 155°42′E*
108 J9 **Buin, Piz** ▲ Austria/Switzerland *46°51′N 10°07′E*
127 Q4 **Buinsk** Chuvashskaya Respublika, W Russian Federation *55°09′N 47°00′E*
127 Q4 **Buinsk** Respublika Tatarstan, W Russian Federation *54°58′N 48°16′E*
163 R8 **Buir Nur** *Mong.* Buyr Nuur. ◎ China/Mongolia *see also* Buyr Nuur
Buir Nur *see* Buyr Nuur
98 M5 **Buitenpost** *Fris.* Bûtenpost. Friesland, N Netherlands *53°15′N 06°09′E*
Buitenzorg *see* Bogor
83 F19 **Buitepos** Omaheke, E Namibia *22°17′S 19°59′E*
105 N7 **Buitrago del Lozoya** Madrid, C Spain *41°00′N 03°38′W*
Buj *see* Buy
104 M13 **Bujalance** Andalucía, S Spain *37°54′N 04°23′W*
113 O17 **Bujanovac** SE Serbia *42°29′N 21°44′E*
105 S6 **Bujaraloz** Aragón, NE Spain *41°29′N 00°10′W*
112 A9 **Buje** *It.* Buie d'Istria. Istra, NW Croatia *45°23′N 13°40′E*
Bujnurd *see* Bojnūrd
81 D21 **Bujumbura** *prev.* Usumbura. ● (Burundi) W Burundi *03°25′S 29°24′E*
81 D20 **Bujumbura** ✕ W Burundi *03°21′S 29°19′E*
159 N11 **Buka Daban** *var.* Bukadaban Feng. ▲ C China *36°09′N 90°52′E*
Bukadaban Feng *see* Buka Daban
186 J6 **Buka Island** *island* NE Papua New Guinea
81 F18 **Bukakata** S Uganda *0°18′S 31°57′E*
79 N24 **Bukama** Katanga, SE Dem. Rep. Congo *09°13′S 25°52′E*
142 J4 **Būkān** *var.* Bowkān. Āžarbāyjān-e Gharbī, NW Iran *36°31′N 46°10′E*
Bukantau, Gory *see* Bo'kantov Tog'lari
Bukarest *see* Bucureşti
79 O19 **Bukavu** *prev.* Costermansville. Sud-Kivu, E Dem. Rep. Congo *02°19′S 28°49′E*
81 F21 **Bukene** Tabora, NW Tanzania *04°15′S 32°51′E*
141 W8 **Bū Khābī** *var.* Bakhābī. NW Oman *23°29′N 56°06′E*
Bukhara *see* Buxoro
Bukharskaya Oblast' *see* Buxoro Viloyati
168 M14 **Bukitkemuning** Sumatera, W Indonesia *04°43′S 104°27′E*
168 I11 **Bukittinggi** *prev.* Fort de Kock. Sumatera, W Indonesia *0°18′S 100°20′E*
111 L21 **Bükk** ▲▲ NE Hungary
81 F19 **Bukoba** Kagera, NW Tanzania *01°19′S 31°49′E*
113 N20 **Bukovo** S FYR Macedonia *40°59′N 21°20′E*
108 G6 **Bülach** Zürich, NW Switzerland *47°31′N 08°30′E*
Bŭlaevo *see* Bulayevo
Bulag *see* Tünel, Hövsgöl, Mongolia
Bulag *see* Möngönmorĭt, Töv, Mongolia
Bulagiyn Denj *see* Bulgan
183 U7 **Bulahdelah** New South Wales, SE Australia *32°24′S 152°13′E*
171 P4 **Bulan** Luzon, N Philippines *12°40′N 123°55′E*
137 N11 **Bulancak** Giresun, N Turkey *40°57′N 38°14′E*
152 J10 **Bulandshahr** Uttar Pradesh, N India *28°30′N 77°49′E*
137 R14 **Bulanık** Muş, E Turkey *39°04′N 42°16′E*
127 V7 **Bulanovo** Orenburgskaya Oblast', W Russian Federation *52°27′N 55°08′E*
83 J17 **Bulawayo** *var.* Buluwayo. Bulawayo, SW Zimbabwe *20°08′S 28°37′E*
83 J17 **Bulawayo** ✕ Matabeleland North, SW Zimbabwe *20°00′S 28°36′E*
145 Q6 **Bulayevo** *Kaz.* Bülaevo. Severnyy Kazakhstan, N Kazakhstan *54°55′N 70°29′E*
136 D15 **Buldan** Denizli, SW Turkey *38°03′N 28°50′E*
154 G12 **Buldāna** Mahārāshtra, C India *20°31′N 76°18′E*
38 E16 **Buldir Island** *island* Aleutian Islands, Alaska, USA
Buldur *see* Burdur
162 I8 **Bulgan** *var.* Bulagiyn Denj. Arhangay, C Mongolia *47°14′N 100°56′E*
162 D7 **Bulgan** *var.* Jargalant. Bayan-Ölgiy, W Mongolia *46°56′N 91°07′E*
162 K6 **Bulgan** Bulgan, N Mongolia *50°31′N 101°30′E*
162 F7 **Bulgan** *var.* Bürenhayrhan. Hovd, W Mongolia *46°04′N 91°34′E*
162 J10 **Bulgan** Ömnögovĭ, S Mongolia *44°07′N 103°28′E*
162 J7 **Bulgan** ◐ *province* N Mongolia
Bulgan *see* Bayan-Öndör, Bayanhongor, C Mongolia
Bulgan *see* Darvi, Hovd, Mongolia
Bulgan *see* Tsagaan-Üür, Hövsgöl, Mongolia
114 H10 **Bulgaria** *off.* Republic of Bulgaria, *Bul.* Bŭlgariya; *prev.* People's Republic of Bulgaria. ◆ *republic* SE Europe
Bulgaria, People's Republic of *see* Bulgaria
Bulgaria, Republic of *see* Bulgaria
Bŭlgariya *see* Bulgaria
114 L9 **Bŭlgarka** ▲ E Bulgaria *42°43′N 26°19′E*
171 S11 **Buli** Pulau Halmahera, E Indonesia *0°56′N 128°17′E*
171 S11 **Buli, Teluk** *bay* Pulau Halmahera, E Indonesia
160 J13 **Buliu He** ≈ S China
Bullange *see* Büllingen
Bulla, Ostrov *see* Xără Ziră Adası
104 M11 **Bullaque** ≈ C Spain
105 Q13 **Bullas** Murcia, SE Spain *38°02′N 01°40′W*
80 M12 **Bullaxaar** Woqooyi Galbeed, NW Somalia *10°28′N 44°15′E*
108 C9 **Bulle** Fribourg, SW Switzerland *46°37′N 07°04′E*
185 G15 **Buller** ≈ South Island, New Zealand
183 P12 **Buller, Mount** ▲ Victoria, SE Australia *37°10′S 146°31′E*
36 H11 **Bullhead City** Arizona, SW USA *35°07′N 114°32′W*
99 N21 **Büllingen** *Fr.* Bullange. Liège, E Belgium *50°23′N 06°15′E*
Bullion State *see* Missouri
21 T14 **Bull Island** *island* South Carolina, SE USA
182 M4 **Bulloo River Overflow** *wetland* New South Wales, SE Australia
184 M12 **Bulls** Manawatu-Wanganui, North Island, New Zealand *40°10′S 175°22′E*
21 T14 **Bulls Bay** *bay* South Carolina, SE USA
27 U9 **Bull Shoals Lake** ⊠ Arkansas/Missouri, C USA
181 Q2 **Bulman** Northern Territory, N Australia *13°39′S 134°21′E*
162 I6 **Bulnayn Nuruu** ▲▲ N Mongolia
171 O11 **Bulowa, Gunung** ▲ Sulawesi, N Indonesia *0°33′N 123°39′E*
Bulqiza *see* Bulqizë
113 L19 **Bulqizë** *var.* Bulqiza. Dibër, C Albania *41°30′N 20°16′E*
Bulsar *see* Valsād
171 N14 **Bulukumba** *prev.* Boeloekoemba. Sulawesi, C Indonesia *05°35′S 120°13′E*
147 O11 **Bulung'ur** *Rus.* Bulungur; *prev.* Krasnogvardeysk. Samarqand Viloyati, C Uzbekistan *39°46′N 67°18′E*
79 I21 **Bulungu** Bandundu, SW Dem. Rep. Congo *04°36′S 18°34′E*
Bulungur *see* Bulung'ur
Buluwayo *see* Bulawayo
79 K17 **Bumba** Equateur, N Dem. Rep. Congo *02°14′N 22°25′E*
121 R12 **Bumbah, Khalij al** *gulf* N Libya
Bumbat *see* Bayan-Öndör
81 F19 **Bumbire Island** *island* N Tanzania
169 V8 **Bum Bun, Pulau** *island* East Malaysia
81 J17 **Buna** North Eastern, NE Kenya *02°40′N 39°34′E*
25 Y10 **Buna** Texas, SW USA *30°25′N 94°00′W*
Bunab *see* Bonāb
Bunai *see* M'bunai
147 S13 **Bunay** S Tajikistan *38°29′N 71°41′E*
180 I13 **Bunbury** Western Australia *33°24′S 115°44′E*
97 E14 **Buncrana** *Ir.* Bun Cranncha. NW Ireland *55°08′N 07°27′W*
Bun Cranncha *see* Buncrana
181 Z9 **Bundaberg** Queensland, E Australia *24°50′S 152°16′E*
183 T5 **Bundarra** New South Wales, SE Australia *30°12′S 151°06′E*
100 G13 **Bünde** Nordrhein-Westfalen, NW Germany *52°12′N 08°34′E*
152 H13 **Būndi** Rājasthān, N India *25°28′N 75°42′E*
Bun Dobhráin *see* Bundoran
97 D15 **Bundoran** *Ir.* Bun Dobhráin. NW Ireland *54°30′N 08°11′W*
113 K18 **Bunë** *SCr.* Bojana. ≈ Albania/Montenegro *see also* Bojana
Bunë *see* Bojana
171 Q8 **Bunga** ≈ Mindanao, S Philippines
168 I12 **Bungalaut, Selat** *strait* W Indonesia
167 R8 **Bung Kan** Nong Khai, E Thailand *18°19′N 103°39′E*
181 N4 **Bungle Bungle Range** ▲▲ Western Australia
82 C10 **Bungo** Uíge, NW Angola *07°30′S 15°24′E*
81 G18 **Bungoma** Western, W Kenya *0°34′N 34°34′E*
164 F15 **Bungo-suidō** *strait* SW Japan
164 E14 **Bungo-Takada** Ōita, Kyūshū, SW Japan *33°34′N 131°28′E*
100 K8 **Bungsberg** *hill* N Germany
Bungur *see* Bunyu
79 P17 **Bunia** Orientale, NE Dem. Rep. Congo *01°33′N 30°16′E*
35 U6 **Bunker Hill** ▲ Nevada, W USA *39°16′N 117°06′W*
22 I7 **Bunkie** Louisiana, S USA *30°58′N 92°12′W*
23 X10 **Bunnell** Florida, SE USA *29°28′N 81°15′W*
105 S10 **Buñol** País Valenciano, E Spain *39°25′N 00°47′W*
98 K11 **Bunschoten** Utrecht, C Netherlands *52°15′N 05°23′E*
136 K14 **Bünyan** Kayseri, C Turkey *38°51′N 35°50′E*
169 W8 **Bunyu** *var.* Bungur. Borneo, N Indonesia *03°33′N 117°50′E*
169 W8 **Bunyu, Pulau** *island* N Indonesia
Bunzlau *see* Bolesławiec
Buoddobohki *see* Patoniva
123 P7 **Buor-Khaya, Guba** *bay* N Russian Federation
123 P7 **Buor-Khaya, Guba** *bay* N Russian Federation
171 Z15 **Bupul** Papua, E Indonesia *07°24′S 140°57′E*
81 K19 **Bura** Coast, SE Kenya *01°06′S 40°01′E*
80 P12 **Buraan** Bari, N Somalia *10°03′N 49°08′E*
Būrabay *see* Borovoye
Buraida *see* Buraydah
Buraimi *see* Al Buraymī
145 Y11 **Buran** Vostochnyy Kazakhstan, E Kazakhstan *48°00′N 85°09′E*
158 G15 **Burang** Xizang Zizhiqu, W China *30°28′N 81°13′E*
Burao *see* Burco
138 H8 **Burāq** Dar'ā, S Syria *33°11′N 36°28′E*
141 O6 **Buraydah** *var.* Buraida. Al Qaşīm, N Saudi Arabia *26°50′N 44°E*
35 S15 **Burbank** California, W USA *34°10′N 118°25′W*
31 N11 **Burbank** Illinois, N USA *41°45′N 87°48′W*
183 Q8 **Burcher** New South Wales, SE Australia *33°29′S 147°16′E*
80 N13 **Burco** *var.* Burao, Bur'o. Togdheer, NW Somalia *09°29′N 45°31′E*
162 K8 **Bürd** *var.* Ongon. Övörhangay, C Mongolia *46°58′N 103°45′E*
146 L13 **Burdalyk** Lebap Welaýaty, E Turkmenistan *38°31′N 64°21′E*
181 W6 **Burdekin River** ≈ Queensland, NE Australia
27 O7 **Burden** Kansas, C USA *37°18′N 96°45′W*
Burdigala *see* Bordeaux
136 E15 **Burdur** *var.* Buldur. Burdur, SW Turkey *37°44′N 30°17′E*
136 E15 **Burdur** *var.* Buldur. ◐ *province* SW Turkey
136 E15 **Burdur Gölü** *salt lake* SW Turkey
65 H21 **Burdwood Bank** *undersea feature* SW Atlantic Ocean
80 I12 **Burē** Āmara, N Ethiopia *10°43′N 37°09′E*
80 H13 **Burē** Oromīya, C Ethiopia *08°13′N 35°09′E*
93 J15 **Bureå** Västerbotten, N Sweden *64°36′N 21°15′E*
162 K7 **Büreghangay** *var.* Darhan. Bulgan, C Mongolia *48°07′N 103°54′E*
101 G14 **Büren** Nordrhein-Westfalen, W Germany *51°34′N 08°34′E*
162 L8 **Büren** *var.* Bayantōhōm. Töv, C Mongolia *46°57′N 105°09′E*
162 L6 **Bürengiyn Nuruu** ▲▲ N Mongolia
Bürenhayrhan *see* Bulgan
162 I6 **Bürentogtoh** *var.* Bayan. Hövsgöl, C Mongolia *49°36′N 99°36′E*
Bürewāla *see* Mandi Bürewāla
92 J9 **Burfjord** Troms, N Norway *69°55′N 21°54′E*
100 L13 **Burg** *var.* Burg an der Ihle, Burg bei Magdeburg. Sachsen-Anhalt, C Germany *52°17′N 11°51′E*
Burg an der Ihle *see* Burg
114 N10 **Burgas** *var.* Bourgas. Burgas, E Bulgaria *42°31′N 27°30′E*
114 M10 **Burgas** ◐ *province* E Bulgaria
114 N9 **Burgas** ✕ Burgas, E Bulgaria *42°35′N 27°33′E*
114 N10 **Burgaski Zaliv** *gulf* E Bulgaria
114 M10 **Burgasko Ezero** *lagoon* E Bulgaria
21 V11 **Burgaw** North Carolina, SE USA *34°33′N 77°56′W*
Burg bei Magdeburg *see* Burg
108 E8 **Burgdorf** Bern, NW Switzerland *47°03′N 07°38′E*
109 Y7 **Burgenland** *off.* Land Burgenland. ◐ *state* SE Austria
13 S13 **Burgeo** Newfoundland, Newfoundland and Labrador, SE Canada *47°37′N 57°38′W*
83 I24 **Burgersdorp** Eastern Cape, SE South Africa *31°00′S 26°20′E*
83 K20 **Burgersfort** Mpumalanga, NE South Africa *24°39′S 30°18′E*
101 N23 **Burghausen** Bayern, SE Germany *48°10′N 12°48′E*
139 O5 **Burghūth, Sabkhat al** ◎ E Syria
101 M20 **Burglengenfeld** Bayern, SE Germany *49°11′N 12°01′E*
41 P9 **Burgos** Tamaulipas, C Mexico *24°55′N 98°46′W*
105 N4 **Burgos** Castilla-León, N Spain *42°21′N 03°41′W*
105 N4 **Burgos** ◐ *province* Castilla-León, N Spain
Burgstadlberg *see* Hradiště
95 P20 **Burgsvik** Gotland, SE Sweden *57°01′N 18°18′E*
Burgum *see* Bergum
Burgundy *see* Bourgogne
159 Q11 **Burhan Budai Shan** ▲▲ C China
136 B12 **Burhaniye** Balıkesir, W Turkey *39°29′N 26°59′E*
154 G12 **Burhānpur** Madhya Pradesh, C India *21°18′N 76°14′E*
127 W7 **Buribay** Respublika Bashkortostan, W Russian Federation *51°57′N 58°11′E*
43 O17 **Burica, Punta** *headland* Costa Rica/Panama *08°02′N 82°53′W*
167 Q10 **Buriram** *var.* Buri Ram, Puriramya. Buri Ram, E Thailand *15°01′N 103°06′E*
Buri Ram *see* Buriram
105 S10 **Burjassot** País Valenciano, E Spain *39°33′N 00°26′W*
81 N16 **Burka Giibi** Hiiraan, C Somalia *03°52′N 45°07′E*
147 X8 **Burkan** ≈ E Kyrgyzstan
25 R4 **Burkburnett** Texas, SW USA *34°06′N 98°34′W*
29 O12 **Burke** South Dakota, N USA *43°09′N 99°18′W*
10 K15 **Burke Channel** *channel* British Columbia, W Canada
194 J10 **Burke Island** *island* Antarctica
20 L7 **Burkesville** Kentucky, S USA *36°48′N 85°21′W*
181 T4 **Burketown** Queensland, NE Australia *17°49′S 139°28′E*
25 Q8 **Burkett** Texas, SW USA *32°01′N 99°17′W*
25 Y9 **Burkeville** Texas, SW USA *30°58′N 93°41′W*
21 V7 **Burkeville** Virginia, NE USA *37°11′N 78°12′W*
77 O12 **Burkina** *off.* Burkina Faso; *prev.* Upper Volta. ◆ *republic* W Africa
Burkina *see* Burkina
Burkina Faso *see* Burkina
194 L13 **Burks, Cape** *headland* Antarctica
14 H12 **Burk's Falls** Ontario, S Canada *45°38′N 79°25′W*
101 H23 **Burladingen** Baden-Württemberg, S Germany *48°18′N 09°05′E*
25 T7 **Burleson** Texas, SW USA *32°32′N 97°19′W*
33 P15 **Burley** Idaho, NW USA *42°32′N 113°47′W*
144 G8 **Burlin** Zapadnyy Kazakhstan, NW Kazakhstan *51°25′N 52°42′E*
14 G16 **Burlington** Ontario, S Canada *43°19′N 79°48′W*
37 W4 **Burlington** Colorado, C USA *39°17′N 102°17′W*
29 Y15 **Burlington** Iowa, C USA *40°48′N 91°05′W*
27 P5 **Burlington** Kansas, C USA *38°11′N 95°46′W*
21 T9 **Burlington** North Carolina, SE USA *36°05′N 79°27′W*
28 M3 **Burlington** North Dakota, N USA *48°16′N 101°25′W*
18 L7 **Burlington** Vermont, NE USA *44°28′N 73°14′W*
30 M9 **Burlington** Wisconsin, N USA *42°38′N 88°12′W*
27 Q1 **Burlington Junction** Missouri, C USA *40°27′N 95°04′W*
166 M4 **Burma** *off.* Union of Myanmar, Myanmar. ◆ *military dictatorship* SE Asia
10 L17 **Burnaby** British Columbia, SW Canada *49°16′N 122°58′W*
117 O12 **Burnas, Ozero** ◎ SW Ukraine
25 S10 **Burnet** Texas, SW USA *30°46′N 98°14′W*
35 O3 **Burney** California, W USA *40°52′N 121°42′W*
183 O16 **Burnie** Tasmania, SE Australia *41°07′S 145°52′E*
97 L17 **Burnley** NW England, United Kingdom *53°48′N 02°14′W*
Burnoye *see* Bauyrzhan Momyshuly
153 R15 **Burnpur** West Bengal, NE India *23°39′N 86°55′E*
32 K14 **Burns** Oregon, NW USA *43°35′N 119°03′W*
26 K11 **Burns Flat** Oklahoma, C USA *35°21′N 99°10′W*
20 M7 **Burnside** Kentucky, S USA *36°55′N 84°34′W*
8 K8 **Burnside** ≈ Nunavut, NW Canada
32 L15 **Burns Junction** Oregon, NW USA *42°46′N 117°51′W*
10 L13 **Burns Lake** British Columbia, SW Canada *54°14′N 125°45′W*
29 V9 **Burnsville** Minnesota, N USA *44°49′N 93°14′W*
21 P9 **Burnsville** North Carolina, SE USA *35°56′N 82°18′W*
21 R4 **Burnsville** West Virginia, NE USA *38°50′N 80°39′W*
14 I13 **Burnt River** ≈ Ontario, SE Canada
14 I11 **Burntroot Lake** ◎ Ontario, SE Canada
11 W12 **Burntwood** ≈ Manitoba, C Canada
Bur'o *see* Burco
158 L2 **Burqin** Xinjiang Uygur Zizhiqu, NW China *47°42′N 86°50′E*
182 J8 **Burra** South Australia *33°41′S 138°54′E*
183 S9 **Burragorang, Lake** ⊠ New South Wales, SE Australia
96 K5 **Burray** *island* NE Scotland, United Kingdom
113 L19 **Burrel** *var.* Burreli. Dibër, C Albania *41°36′N 20°00′E*
Burreli *see* Burrel
183 R8 **Burrendong Reservoir** ⊠ New South Wales, SE Australia
183 R5 **Burren Junction** New South Wales, SE Australia *30°06′S 149°01′E*
105 T9 **Burriana** País Valenciano, E Spain *39°54′N 00°05′W*
183 R10 **Burrinjuck Reservoir** ⊠ New South Wales, SE Australia
36 J12 **Burro Creek** ≈ Arizona, SW USA
40 M5 **Burro, Serranías del** ▲▲ NW Mexico
62 K7 **Burruyacú** Tucumán, N Argentina *26°30′S 64°45′W*
136 E12 **Bursa** *var.* Brussa, *prev.* Brusa; *anc.* Prusa. Bursa, NW Turkey *40°12′N 29°04′E*
136 D12 **Bursa** *var.* Brussa. ◐ *province* NW Turkey
75 Y9 **Būr Safāga** *var.* Būr Safājah. E Egypt *26°43′N 33°55′E*
Būr Safājah *see* Būr Safāga
75 W7 **Būr Sa'īd** *var.* Port Said. N Egypt *31°17′N 32°18′E*
81 O14 **Bur Tinle** Nugaal, C Somalia *07°50′N 48°01′E*
31 Q5 **Burt Lake** ◎ Michigan, N USA
118 H7 **Burtnieks** *var.* Burtnieks Ezers. ◎ N Latvia
Burtnieks Ezers *see* Burtnieks
31 Q9 **Burton** Michigan, N USA *43°00′N 83°40′W*
Burton on Trent *see* Burton upon Trent
97 M19 **Burton upon Trent** *var.* Burton on Trent, Burton-upon-Trent. C England, United Kingdom *52°48′N 01°36′W*
93 J15 **Burträsk** Västerbotten, N Sweden *64°31′N 20°40′E*
145 S14 **Burubaytal** *prev.* Burylbaytal. Zhambyl, SE Kazakhstan *44°56′N 73°59′E*
Burujird *see* Borūjerd
Burultokay *see* Fuhai
141 R15 **Burūm** SE Yemen *14°22′N 48°53′E*
Burunday *see* Boralday
81 D21 **Burundi** *off.* Republic of Burundi; *prev.* Kingdom of Burundi, Urundi. ◆ *republic* C Africa
Burundi, Kingdom of *see* Burundi
Burundi, Republic of *see* Burundi
171 R13 **Buru, Pulau** *prev.* Boeroe. *island* E Indonesia
77 T17 **Burutu** Delta, S Nigeria *05°18′N 05°32′E*
10 G7 **Burwash Landing** Yukon Territory, W Canada *61°26′N 139°12′W*
29 O14 **Burwell** Nebraska, C USA *41°46′N 99°04′W*
97 L17 **Bury** NW England, United Kingdom *53°36′N 02°17′W*
123 N13 **Buryatiya, Respublika** *prev.* Buryatskaya ASSR. ◐ *autonomous republic* S Russian Federation
Buryatskaya ASSR *see* Buryatiya, Respublika
Burylbaytal *see* Burubaytal
117 S3 **Buryn'** Sums'ka Oblast', NE Ukraine *51°13′N 33°50′E*
97 P20 **Bury St Edmunds** *hist.* Beodericsworth. E England, United Kingdom *52°15′N 00°43′E*
114 G8 **Bŭrziya** ≈ NW Bulgaria
106 D9 **Busalla** Liguria, NW Italy *44°35′N 08°55′E*
Busan *see* Pusan
139 N5 **Buşayrah** Dayr az Zawr, E Syria *35°10′N 40°25′E*
Buševa *see* Baba
143 N12 **Būshehr** *off.* Ostān-e Būshehr. ◐ *province* SW Iran
Būshehr/Bushire *see* Bandar-e Būshehr
Būshehr, Ostān-e *see* Būshehr
25 N2 **Bushland** Texas, SW USA *35°11′N 102°04′W*
30 J12 **Bushnell** Illinois, N USA *40°33′N 90°30′W*
Busi *see* Biševo
81 G18 **Busia** SE Uganda *01°20′N 34°48′E*
Busiasch *see* Buziaş
79 K16 **Businga** Equateur, NW Dem. Rep. Congo *03°20′N 20°53′E*
79 J18 **Busira** ≈ NW Dem. Rep. Congo
116 I5 **Bus'k** *Rus.* Busk. L'vivs'ka Oblast', W Ukraine *49°59′N 24°34′E*
95 E14 **Buskerud** ◐ *county* S Norway
113 F14 **Buško Jezero** ⊠ SW Bosnia and Herzegovina
111 M15 **Busko-Zdrój** Świętokrzyskie, C Poland *50°28′N 20°44′E*
Busra *see* Al Başrah, Iraq
Buşrá *see* Buşrá ash Shām, Syria
138 H9 **Buşrá ash Shām** *var.* Bosora, Bosra, Bozrah, Buşrá. Dar'ā, S Syria *32°31′N 36°29′E*
180 I13 **Busselton** Western Australia *33°43′S 115°15′E*
81 C14 **Busseri** ≈ W Sudan
106 E9 **Busseto** Emilia-Romagna, C Italy *45°00′N 10°06′E*
106 A8 **Bussoleno** Piemonte, NE Italy *45°11′N 07°07′E*
Bussora *see* Al Başrah
41 N7 **Bustamante** Nuevo León, NE Mexico *26°29′N 100°30′W*
63 I23 **Bustamante, Punta** *headland* S Argentina *51°35′S 68°58′W*
Bustan *see* Bo'ston
116 J12 **Buşteni** Prahova, SE Romania *45°23′N 25°32′E*
106 D7 **Busto Arsizio** Lombardia, N Italy *45°37′N 08°51′E*
147 Q10 **Būston** *Rus.* Buston. NW Tajikistan *40°31′N 69°21′E*
100 H8 **Büsum** Schleswig-Holstein, N Germany *54°08′N 08°52′E*
98 J10 **Bussum** Noord-Holland, C Netherlands *52°17′N 05°10′E*
79 M16 **Buta** Orientale, N Dem. Rep. Congo *02°50′N 24°41′E*
81 E20 **Butare** *prev.* Astrida. S Rwanda *02°39′S 29°44′E*
191 O2 **Butaritari** *atoll* Tungaru, W Kiribati
Butawal *see* Butwal
96 H13 **Bute** *cultural region* SW Scotland, United Kingdom
162 K6 **Büteeliyn Nuruu** ▲▲ N Mongolia
10 L16 **Bute Inlet** *fjord* British Columbia, W Canada
96 H12 **Bute, Island of** *island* SW Scotland, United Kingdom
79 P18 **Butembo** Nord-Kivu, NE Dem. Rep. Congo *0°09′N 29°17′E*
Bûtenpost *see* Buitenpost
107 K25 **Butera** Sicilia, Italy, C Mediterranean Sea *37°12′N 14°12′E*
99 M20 **Bütgenbach** Liège, E Belgium *50°25′N 06°12′E*
Butha Qi *see* Zalantun
166 J5 **Buthidaung** Rakhine State, W Burma (Myanmar) *20°50′N 92°25′E*
61 I16 **Butiá** Rio Grande do Sul, S Brazil *30°09′S 51°55′W*
81 F17 **Butiaba** NW Uganda *01°48′N 31°21′E*
23 N6 **Butler** Alabama, S USA *32°05′N 88°13′W*
23 S5 **Butler** Georgia, SE USA *32°33′N 84°14′W*
31 Q11 **Butler** Indiana, N USA *41°25′N 84°52′W*
27 R5 **Butler** Missouri, C USA *38°17′N 94°21′W*
18 B14 **Butler** Pennsylvania, NE USA *40°51′N 79°52′W*
194 K5 **Butler Island** *island* Antarctica
21 U8 **Butner** North Carolina, SE USA *36°07′N 78°45′W*
171 P14 **Buton, Pulau** *var.* Pulau Butung; *prev.* Boetoeng. *island* C Indonesia
Bütow *see* Bytów
113 L23 **Butrintit, Liqeni i** ◎ S Albania
23 N3 **Buttahatchee River** ≈ Alabama/Mississippi, S USA
33 Q10 **Butte** Montana, NW USA *46°01′N 112°33′W*
29 O12 **Butte** Nebraska, C USA *42°54′N 98°51′W*
168 J7 **Butterworth** Pinang, Peninsular Malaysia *05°24′N 100°22′E*
83 J25 **Butterworth** *var.* Gcuwa. Eastern Cape, SE South Africa *32°20′S 28°09′E*
13 O3 **Button Islands** *island group* Nunavut, NE Canada
35 R13 **Buttonwillow** California, W USA *35°24′N 119°26′W*
171 Q7 **Butuan** *off.* Butuan City. Mindanao, S Philippines *08°57′N 125°33′E*
Butuan City *see* Butuan
Butung, Pulau *see* Buton, Pulau
Butuntum *see* Bitonto
126 M8 **Buturlinovka** Voronezhskaya Oblast', W Russian Federation *50°48′N 40°33′E*
153 O11 **Butwal** *var.* Butawal. Western, C Nepal *27°41′N 83°28′E*
101 G17 **Butzbach** Hessen, W Germany *50°26′N 08°40′E*
100 L9 **Bützow** Mecklenburg-Vorpommern, N Germany *53°49′N 11°58′E*
80 N13 **Buuhoodle** Togdheer, N Somalia *08°18′N 46°15′E*
81 N16 **Buulobarde** *var.* Buulo Berde. Hiiraan, C Somalia *03°52′N 45°37′E*
Buulo Berde *see* Buulobarde
80 P12 **Buuraha Cal Miskaat** ▲▲ NE Somalia
81 L19 **Buur Gaabo** Jubbada Hoose, S Somalia *01°14′S 41°48′E*
99 M22 **Buurgplaatz** ▲ N Luxembourg *50°09′N 06°02′E*
162 H8 **Buutsagaan** *var.* Buyant. Bayanhongor, C Mongolia *46°07′N 98°45′E*
Buwayrāt al Hasūn *see* Bu'ayrāt al Ḩasūn
146 L11 **Buxoro** *var.* Bokhara, *Rus.* Bukhara. Buxoro Viloyati, C Uzbekistan *39°51′N 64°23′E*
146 J11 **Buxoro Viloyati** *Rus.* Bukharskaya Oblast'. ◐ *province* C Uzbekistan
100 I10 **Buxtehude** Niedersachsen, NW Germany *53°29′N 09°42′E*
97 L18 **Buxton** C England, United Kingdom *53°18′N 01°52′W*
124 M14 **Buy** *var.* Buj. Kostromskaya Oblast', NW Russian Federation *58°27′N 41°31′E*
Buyanbat *see* Jargalant
162 D6 **Buyant** Bayan-Ölgiy, W Mongolia *48°31′N 89°36′E*
Buyant *see* Buutsagaan, Bayanhongor, Mongolia
Buyant *see* Otgon, Dzavhan, Mongolia
Buyant *see* Galshar, Hentiy, Mongolia
163 N10 **Buyant-Uhaa** Dornogovĭ, SE Mongolia *44°52′N 110°12′E*
162 M7 **Buyant Ukha** ✕ (Ulaanbaatar) Töv, N Mongolia
127 Q16 **Buynaksk** Respublika Dagestan, SW Russian Federation *42°53′N 47°03′E*
119 L20 **Buynavichy** *Rus.* Buynovichi. Homyel'skaya Voblasts', SE Belarus *51°52′N 28°33′E*
Buynovichi *see* Buynavichy
76 L16 **Buyo** SW Ivory Coast *06°16′N 07°03′W*
76 L16 **Buyo, Lac de** ⊠ W Ivory Coast
163 R7 **Buyr Nuur** *var.* Buir Nur. ◎ China/Mongolia *see also* Buir Nur
Buyr Nuur *see* Buir Nur
137 T13 **Büyükağrı Dağı** *var.* Aghri Dagh, Agri Dagi, Koh I Noh, Masis, *Eng.* Great Ararat, Mount Ararat. ▲ E Turkey *39°43′N 44°19′E*
137 R15 **Büyük Çayı** ≈ NE Turkey
114 O13 **Büyük Çekmece** İstanbul, NW Turkey *41°02′N 28°35′E*
114 N12 **Büyükkarıştıran** Kırklareli, NW Turkey *41°17′N 27°33′E*
115 L14 **Büyükkemikli Burnu** *cape* NW Turkey
136 E15 **Büyükmenderes Nehri** ≈ SW Turkey
Büyükzap Suyu *see* Great Zab
102 M9 **Buzançais** Indre, C France *46°53′N 01°25′E*
116 K13 **Buzău** Buzău, SE Romania *45°08′N 26°51′E*
116 K13 **Buzău** ◐ *county* SE Romania
116 L12 **Buzău** ≈ E Romania
75 S11 **Buzaymah** *var.* Bzīmah. SE Libya *24°53′N 22°01′E*
164 E13 **Buzen** Fukuoka, Kyūshū, SW Japan *33°37′N 131°06′E*
116 F12 **Buziaş** *Ger.* Busiasch, *Hung.* Buziásfürdő; *prev.* Buziás. Timiş, W Romania *45°38′N 21°36′E*
Buziás *see* Buziaş
Buziásfürdő *see* Buziaş
83 M18 **Búzi, Rio** ≈ C Mozambique
117 Q10 **Buz'kyy Lyman** *bay* S Ukraine
Büzmeýin *see* Abadan
145 O8 **Buzuluk** Akmola, C Kazakhstan *51°53′N 66°09′E*
127 T6 **Buzuluk** Orenburgskaya Oblast', W Russian Federation *52°47′N 52°16′E*
127 N8 **Buzuluk** ≈ SW Russian Federation
19 P12 **Buzzards Bay** Massachusetts, NE USA *41°45′N 70°37′W*
19 P13 **Buzzards Bay** *bay* Massachusetts, NE USA
83 G16 **Bwabata** Caprivi, NE Namibia *17°52′S 22°39′E*
186 H10 **Bwagaoia** Misima Island, SE Papua New Guinea *10°39′S 152°48′E*
Bwake *see* Bouaké
187 R13 **Bwatnapne** Pentecost, C Vanuatu *15°42′S 168°07′E*
119 K14 **Byahoml'** *Rus.* Begoml'. Vitsyebskaya Voblasts', N Belarus *54°44′N 28°04′E*
114 K8 **Byala** Ruse, N Bulgaria *43°27′N 25°44′E*
114 N9 **Byala** *prev.* Ak-Dere. Varna, E Bulgaria *42°52′N 27°53′E*
Byala Reka *see* Erythropótamos
114 H8 **Byala Slatina** Vratsa, NW Bulgaria *43°28′N 23°56′E*
119 N15 **Byalynichy** *Rus.* Belynichi. Mahilyowskaya Voblasts', E Belarus *54°00′N 29°42′E*
Byan Tumen *see* Choybalsan
119 G19 **Byaroza** *Pol.* Bereza Kartuska, *Rus.* Berëza. Brestskaya Voblasts', SW Belarus *52°32′N 24°59′E*
119 H16 **Byarozawka** *Rus.* Berëzovka. Hrodzyenskaya Voblasts', W Belarus *53°45′N 25°30′E*
Bybles *see* Jbail
111 O14 **Bychawa** Lubelskie, SE Poland *51°06′N 22°34′E*
Bychikha *see* Bychykha
118 N11 **Bychykha** *Rus.* Bychikha. Vitsyebskaya Voblasts', NE Belarus *55°41′N 29°59′E*
111 I14 **Byczyna** *Ger.* Pitschen. Opolskie, S Poland *51°06′N 18°13′E*
110 I10 **Bydgoszcz** *Ger.* Bromberg. Kujawski-pomorskie, C Poland *53°06′N 18°00′E*
119 H19 **Byelaazyorsk** *Rus.* Beloozersk. Brestskaya Voblasts', SW Belarus *52°28′N 25°10′E*
119 I17 **Byelaruskaya Hrada** *Rus.* Belorusskaya Gryada. *ridge* N Belarus
119 G18 **Byelavyezhskaya Pushcha** *Pol.* Puszcza Białowieska, *Rus.* Belovezhskaya Pushcha. *forest* Belarus/Poland *see also* Białowieska, Puszcza
Byelavyezhskaya, Pushcha *see* Białowieska, Puszcza
119 H15 **Byenyakoni** *Rus.* Benyakoni. Hrodzyenskaya Voblasts', W Belarus *54°15′N 25°22′E*
119 M16 **Byerazino** *Rus.* Berezino. Minskaya Voblasts', C Belarus *53°50′N 29°00′E*
118 L13 **Byerazino** *Rus.* Berezino. Vitsyebskaya Voblasts', N Belarus *54°54′N 28°12′E*
119 L14 **Byerezino** *Rus.* Berezina. ≈ C Belarus
118 M13 **Byeshankovichy** *Rus.* Beshenkovichi. Vitsyebskaya Voblasts', N Belarus *55°03′N 29°27′E*
31 U13 **Byesville** Ohio, N USA *39°58′N 81°32′W*
119 P18 **Byesyedz'** *Rus.* Besed'. ≈ SE Belarus
119 H19 **Byezdzyezh** *Rus.* Bezdezh. Brestskaya Voblasts', SW Belarus *52°19′N 25°18′E*
93 J15 **Bygdeå** Västerbotten, N Sweden *64°03′N 20°49′E*
94 F12 **Bygdin** ◎ S Norway
93 J15 **Bygdsiljum** Västerbotten, N Sweden *64°20′N 20°31′E*
95 E17 **Bygland** Aust-Agder, S Norway *58°46′N 07°50′E*
95 E17 **Byglandsfjord** Aust-Agder, S Norway *58°42′N 07°51′E*
119 N16 **Bykhaw** *Rus.* Bykhov. Mahilyowskaya Voblasts', E Belarus *53°31′N 30°15′E*
Bykhov *see* Bykhaw
127 P9 **Bykovo** Volgogradskaya Oblast', SW Russian Federation *49°52′N 45°24′E*
123 P7 **Bykovskiy** Respublika Sakha (Yakutiya), NE Russian Federation *71°57′N 129°07′E*
195 R12 **Byrd Glacier** *glacier* Antarctica
14 K10 **Byrd, Lac** ◎ Québec, SE Canada
183 P5 **Byrock** New South Wales, SE Australia *30°40′S 146°24′E*
30 L10 **Byron** Illinois, N USA *42°06′N 89°15′W*
183 V4 **Byron Bay** New South Wales, SE Australia *28°39′S 153°34′E*
183 V4 **Byron, Cape** *headland* New South Wales, E Australia *28°37′S 153°40′E*
63 F21 **Byron, Isla** *island* S Chile
Byron Island *see* Nikunau
65 B24 **Byron Sound** *sound* NW Falkland Islands
122 M6 **Byrranga, Gora** ▲▲ N Russian Federation
93 J14 **Byske** Västerbotten, N Sweden *64°58′N 21°10′E*
111 K18 **Bystrá** ▲ N Slovakia *49°10′N 19°49′E*
111 F18 **Bystřice nad Pernštejnem** *Ger.* Bistritz ober Pernstein. Vysočina, C Czech Republic *49°32′N 16°16′E*
Bystrovka *see* Kemin
111 G16 **Bystrzyca Kłodzka** *Ger.* Habelschwerdt. Wałbrzych, SW Poland *50°19′N 16°39′E*
111 I18 **Bytča** Žilinský Kraj, N Slovakia *49°15′N 18°32′E*
119 L15 **Bytcha** Minskaya Voblasts', NE Belarus *54°19′N 28°24′E*
Byteń/Byten' *see* Bytsyen'
111 J16 **Bytom** *Ger.* Beuthen. Śląskie, S Poland *50°21′N 18°51′E*
110 H7 **Bytów** *Ger.* Bütow. Pomorskie, N Poland *54°10′N 17°30′E*
119 H18 **Bytsyen'** *Pol.* Byteń, *Rus.* Byten'. Brestskaya Voblasts', SW Belarus *52°53′N 25°30′E*
81 E19 **Byumba** *var.* Biumba. N Rwanda *01°37′S 30°05′E*
Byuzmeyin *see* Abadan
119 O20 **Byval'ki** Homyel'skaya Voblasts', SE Belarus *51°51′N 30°38′E*
95 O20 **Byxelkrok** Kalmar, S Sweden *57°18′N 17°01′E*
Byzantium *see* İstanbul
Bzīmah *see* Buzaymah

C

62 O6 **Caacupé** Cordillera, S Paraguay *25°23′S 57°05′W*
62 P6 **Caaguazú** *off.* Departamento de Caaguazú. ◐ *department* C Paraguay
Caaguazú, Departamento de *see* Caaguazú
82 C13 **Caála** *var.* Kaala, Robert Williams, *Port.* Vila Robert Williams. Huambo, C Angola *12°51′S 15°33′E*

62 P7 **Caazapá** Caazapá, S Paraguay *26°09′S 56°21′W*
62 P7 **Caazapá** *off.* Departamento de Caazapá. ◈ *department* SE Paraguay
Caazapá, Departamento de *see* Caazapá
81 P15 **Cabaad, Raas** *headland* C Somalia *06°13′N 49°01′E*
55 N10 **Cabadisocaña** Amazonas, S Venezuela *04°28′N 64°45′W*
44 F5 **Cabaiguán** Sancti Spíritus, C Cuba *22°04′N 79°32′W*
Caballeria, Cabo *see* Cavalleria, Cap de
37 Q14 **Caballo Reservoir** ⊠ New Mexico, SW USA
40 L6 **Caballos Mesteños, Llano de los** *plain* N Mexico
104 L2 **Cabañaquinta** Asturias, N Spain *43°10′N 05°37′W*
42 B9 **Cabañas** ◈ *department* E El Salvador
171 O3 **Cabanatuan** *off.* Cabanatuan City. Luzon, N Philippines *15°27′N 120°57′E*
Cabanatuan City *see* Cabanatuan
15 T8 **Cabano** Québec, SE Canada *47°40′N 68°56′W*
104 L11 **Cabeza del Buey** Extremadura, W Spain *38°44′N 05°13′W*
45 V5 **Cabezas de San Juan** *headland* E Puerto Rico *18°23′N 65°37′W*
105 N2 **Cabezón de la Sal** Cantabria, N Spain *43°19′N 04°14′W*
Cabhán *see* Cavan
61 B23 **Cabildo** Buenos Aires, E Argentina *38°28′S 61°50′W*
Cabillonum *see* Chalon-sur-Saône
54 H5 **Cabimas** Zulia, NW Venezuela *10°26′N 71°27′W*
82 A9 **Cabinda** *var.* Kabinda. Cabinda, NW Angola *05°34′S 12°12′E*
82 A9 **Cabinda** *var.* Kabinda. ◈ *province* NW Angola
33 N7 **Cabinet Mountains** ⛰ Idaho/Montana, NW USA
82 B11 **Cabiri** Bengo, NW Angola *08°50′S 13°42′E*
63 J20 **Cabo Blanco** Santa Cruz, SE Argentina *47°13′S 65°43′W*
82 P13 **Cabo Delgado** *off.* Província de Capo Delgado. ◈ *province* NE Mozambique
14 L9 **Cabonga, Réservoir** ⊠ Québec, SE Canada
27 V7 **Cabool** Missouri, C USA *37°07′N 92°06′W*
183 V2 **Caboolture** Queensland, E Australia *27°05′S 152°50′E*
Cabora Bassa, Lake *see* Cahora Bassa, Albufeira de
40 F3 **Caborca** Sonora, NW Mexico *30°44′N 112°06′W*
Cabo San Lucas *see* San Lucas
27 V11 **Cabot** Arkansas, C USA *34°58′N 92°01′W*
14 F12 **Cabot Head** *headland* Ontario, S Canada *45°13′N 81°17′W*
13 R13 **Cabot Strait** *strait* E Canada
Cabo Verde, Ilhas do *see* Cape Verde
104 M14 **Cabra** Andalucía, S Spain *37°28′N 04°28′W*
107 B19 **Cabras** Sardegna, Italy, C Mediterranean Sea *39°55′N 08°30′E*
188 A15 **Cabras Island** *island* W Guam
45 O8 **Cabrera** N Dominican Republic *19°40′N 69°54′W*
104 J4 **Cabrera** ≈ NW Spain
105 X10 **Cabrera, Illa de** *anc.* Capraria. *island* Islas Baleares, Spain, W Mediterranean Sea
105 Q15 **Cabrera, Sierra** ⛰ S Spain
11 S16 **Cabri** Saskatchewan, S Canada *50°38′N 108°28′W*
105 R10 **Cabriel** ≈ E Spain
54 M7 **Cabruta** Guárico, C Venezuela *07°39′N 66°19′W*
171 N2 **Cabugao** Luzon, N Philippines *17°55′N 120°29′E*
54 G10 **Cabuyaro** Meta, C Colombia *04°21′N 72°47′W*
60 I13 **Caçador** Santa Catarina, S Brazil *26°47′S 51°00′W*
42 G8 **Cacaguatique, Cordillera** *var.* Cordillera. ⛰ NE El Salvador
112 L13 **Čačak** Serbia, C Serbia *43°52′N 20°23′E*
55 Y10 **Cacao** NE French Guiana *04°37′N 52°29′W*
61 H16 **Caçapava do Sul** Rio Grande do Sul, S Brazil *30°28′S 53°29′W*
21 U3 **Cacapon River** ≈ West Virginia, NE USA
107 J23 **Caccamo** Sicilia, Italy, C Mediterranean Sea *37°56′N 13°40′E*
107 A17 **Caccia, Capo** *headland* Sardegna, Italy, C Mediterranean Sea *40°34′N 08°09′E*
146 H15 **Çäçe** *var.* Chäche, *Rus.* Chaacha. Ahal Welaýaty, S Turkmenistan *36°49′N 60°33′E*
59 G18 **Cáceres** Mato Grosso, W Brazil *16°05′S 57°40′W*
104 J10 **Cáceres** *Ar.* Qazris. Extremadura, W Spain *39°29′N 06°23′W*
104 J9 **Cáceres** ◈ *province* Extremadura, W Spain
Cachacrou *see* Scotts Head Village
61 C21 **Cacharí** Buenos Aires, E Argentina *36°24′S 59°32′W*
26 L12 **Cache** Oklahoma, C USA *34°37′N 98°37′W*
10 M16 **Cache Creek** British Columbia, SW Canada *50°49′N 121°20′W*
35 N6 **Cache Creek** ≈ California, W USA
37 S3 **Cache La Poudre River** ≈ Colorado, C USA
Cacheo *see* Cacheu
27 W11 **Cache River** ≈ Arkansas, C USA
30 L17 **Cache River** ≈ Illinois, N USA
76 G12 **Cacheu** *var.* Cacheo. W Guinea-Bissau *12°12′N 16°10′W*
59 I15 **Cachimbo** Pará, NE Brazil *09°21′S 54°58′W*
59 H15 **Cachimbo, Serra do** ⛰ C Brazil
82 D13 **Cachingues** Bié, C Angola *13°05′S 16°48′E*
54 G7 **Cáchira** Norte de Santander, N Colombia *07°44′N 73°07′W*
61 H16 **Cachoeira do Sul** Rio Grande do Sul, S Brazil *29°58′S 52°54′W*
59 O20 **Cachoeiro de Itapemirim** Espírito Santo, SE Brazil *20°51′S 41°07′W*
82 E12 **Cacolo** Lunda Sul, NE Angola *10°09′S 19°21′E*
83 C14 **Caconda** Huíla, C Angola *13°43′S 15°03′E*
82 A9 **Cacongo** Cabinda, NW Angola *05°13′S 12°08′E*
35 U9 **Cactus Peak** ▲ Nevada, W USA *37°42′N 116°51′W*
82 A11 **Cacuaco** Luanda, NW Angola *08°47′S 13°21′E*
83 B14 **Cacula** Huíla, SW Angola *14°33′S 14°04′E*
67 R12 **Caculuvar** ≈ SW Angola
59 O19 **Caçumba, Ilha** *island* SE Brazil
55 N10 **Cacuri** Amazonas, S Venezuela
81 N17 **Cadale** Shabeellaha Dhexe, E Somalia *02°48′N 46°19′E*
105 X4 **Cadaqués** Cataluña, NE Spain *42°17′N 03°16′E*
111 J18 **Čadca** *Hung.* Csaca. Žilinský Kraj, N Slovakia *49°27′N 18°46′E*
27 P13 **Caddo** Oklahoma, C USA *34°07′N 96°15′W*
25 R6 **Caddo** Texas, SW USA *32°42′N 98°40′W*
25 X6 **Caddo Lake** ⊠ Louisiana/Texas, SW USA
27 S12 **Caddo Mountains** ⛰ Arkansas, C USA
41 O8 **Cadereyta** Nuevo León, NE Mexico *25°35′N 99°54′W*
97 J19 **Cader Idris** ▲ NW Wales, United Kingdom *52°43′N 03°57′W*
182 F3 **Cadibarrawirracanna, Lake** *salt lake* South Australia
14 I7 **Cadillac** Québec, SE Canada *48°12′N 78°23′W*
11 T17 **Cadillac** Saskatchewan, S Canada *49°43′N 107°41′W*
102 K13 **Cadillac** Gironde, SW France *44°37′N 00°16′W*
31 P7 **Cadillac** Michigan, N USA *44°15′N 85°23′W*
105 V4 **Cadí, Torre de** ▲ NE Spain *42°16′N 01°38′E*
171 P5 **Cadiz** *off.* Cadiz City. Negros, C Philippines *10°58′N 123°18′E*
104 J15 **Cádiz** *anc.* Gades, Gadier, Gadir, Gadire. Andalucía, SW Spain *36°32′N 06°18′W*
20 H7 **Cadiz** Kentucky, S USA *36°52′N 87°50′W*
31 U13 **Cadiz** Ohio, N USA *40°16′N 81°00′W*
104 K15 **Cádiz** ◈ *province* Andalucía, SW Spain
104 I15 **Cadiz, Bahía de** *bay* SW Spain
Cadiz City *see* Cadiz
104 H15 **Cádiz, Golfo de** *Eng.* Gulf of Cadiz. *gulf* Portugal/Spain
Cadiz, Gulf of *see* Cádiz, Golfo de
35 X14 **Cadiz Lake** ◎ California, W USA
182 E2 **Cadney Homestead** South Australia *27°52′S 134°03′E*
Cadurcum *see* Cahors
Caecae *see* Xaixai
102 K4 **Caen** Calvados, N France *49°10′N 00°20′W*
Caene/Caenepolis *see* Qinā
Caerdydd *see* Cardiff
Caer Glou *see* Gloucester
Caer Gybi *see* Holyhead
Caerleon *see* Chester
Caer Luel *see* Carlisle
97 I18 **Caernarfon** *var.* Caernarvon, Carnarvon. NW Wales, United Kingdom *53°08′N 04°16′W*
97 H18 **Caernarfon Bay** *bay* NW Wales, United Kingdom
97 I19 **Caernarvon** *cultural region* NW Wales, United Kingdom
Caernarvon *see* Caernarfon
Caesaraugusta *see* Zaragoza
Caesarea Mazaca *see* Kayseri
Caesarobriga *see* Talavera de la Reina
Caesarodunum *see* Tours
Caesaromagus *see* Beauvais
Caesena *see* Cesena
59 N17 **Caetité** Bahia, E Brazil *14°04′S 42°29′W*
62 J6 **Cafayate** Salta, N Argentina *26°02′S 66°00′W*
171 O2 **Cagayan** ≈ Luzon, N Philippines
171 Q7 **Cagayan de Oro** *off.* Cagayan de Oro City. Mindanao, S Philippines *08°29′N 124°38′E*
Cagayan de Oro City *see* Cagayan de Oro
170 M8 **Cagayan de Tawi Tawi** *island* S Philippines
171 N6 **Cagayan Islands** *island group* C Philippines
31 O14 **Cagles Mill Lake** ⊠ Indiana, N USA
106 I12 **Cagli** Marche, C Italy *43°33′N 12°39′E*
107 C20 **Cagliari** *anc.* Caralis. Sardegna, Italy, C Mediterranean Sea *39°15′N 09°06′E*
107 C20 **Cagliari, Golfo di** *gulf* Sardegna, Italy, C Mediterranean Sea
103 U15 **Cagnes-sur-Mer** Alpes-Maritimes, SE France *43°40′N 07°09′E*
54 L5 **Cagua** Aragua, N Venezuela *10°09′N 67°27′W*
171 O1 **Cagua, Mount** ▲ Luzon, N Philippines *18°10′N 122°03′E*
54 F13 **Caguán, Río** ≈ SW Colombia
45 U6 **Caguas** E Puerto Rico *18°14′N 66°02′W*
146 C9 **Çagyl** *Rus.* Chagyl. Balkan Welaýaty, NW Turkmenistan *40°48′N 55°21′E*
23 P5 **Cahaba River** ≈ Alabama, S USA
42 E5 **Cahabón, Río** ≈ C Guatemala
83 B15 **Cahama** Cunene, SW Angola *16°16′S 14°23′E*
97 B21 **Caha Mountains** *Ir.* An Cheacha. ⛰ SW Ireland
97 D20 **Caher** *Ir.* An Cathair. S Ireland *52°21′N 07°58′W*
97 A21 **Caherciveen** *Ir.* Cathair Saidhbhín. SW Ireland *51°56′N 10°12′W*
30 K15 **Cahokia** Illinois, N USA *38°34′N 90°11′W*
83 L15 **Cahora Bassa, Albufeira de** *var.* Lake Cabora Bassa. ⊠ NW Mozambique
97 G20 **Cahore Point** *Ir.* Rinn Chathóir. *headland* SE Ireland *52°33′N 06°11′W*
102 M14 **Cahors** *anc.* Cadurcum. Lot, S France *44°26′N 01°27′E*
56 D9 **Cahuapanas, Río** ≈ N Peru
116 M12 **Cahul** *Rus.* Kagul. S Moldova *45°53′N 28°13′E*
Cahul, Lacul *see* Kahul, Ozero
83 N16 **Caia** Sofala, C Mozambique *17°50′S 35°21′E*
59 J19 **Caiapó, Serra do** ⛰ C Brazil
44 F5 **Caibarién** Villa Clara, C Cuba *22°31′N 79°29′W*
55 O5 **Caicara** Monagas, NE Venezuela *09°52′N 63°38′W*
54 L5 **Caicara del Orinoco** Bolívar, C Venezuela *07°38′N 66°10′W*
59 P14 **Caicó** Rio Grande do Norte, E Brazil *06°25′S 37°04′W*
44 M6 **Caicos Islands** *island group* W Turks and Caicos Islands
44 L5 **Caicos Passage** *strait* Bahamas/Turks and Caicos Islands
161 O9 **Caidian** *prev.* Hanyang. Hubei, C China *30°37′N 114°02′E*
Caiffa *see* Hefa
180 M12 **Caiguna** Western Australia *32°14′S 125°33′E*
Caillí, Ceann *see* Hag's Head
40 J11 **Caimanero, Laguna del** *var.* Laguna del Camaronero. *lagoon* E Pacific Ocean
117 N10 **Căinari** *Rus.* Kaynary. C Moldova *46°43′N 29°00′E*
57 L19 **Caine, Río** ≈ C Bolivia
Caiphas *see* Hefa
195 N4 **Caird Coast** *physical region* Antarctica
96 J9 **Cairn Gorm** ▲ C Scotland, United Kingdom *57°07′N 03°38′W*
96 J9 **Cairngorm Mountains** ⛰ C Scotland, United Kingdom
39 P12 **Cairn Mountain** ▲ Alaska, USA *61°07′N 155°23′W*
181 W4 **Cairns** Queensland, NE Australia *16°51′S 145°43′E*
121 V13 **Cairo** *var.* El Qâhira, *Ar.* Al Qāhirah. ● (Egypt) N Egypt *30°01′N 31°18′E*
23 T8 **Cairo** Georgia, SE USA *30°52′N 84°12′W*
30 L17 **Cairo** Illinois, N USA *37°00′N 89°10′W*
75 V8 **Cairo** ✈ C Egypt *30°06′N 31°36′E*
Caiseal *see* Cashel
Caisleán an Bharraigh *see* Castlebar
Caisleán na Finne *see* Castlefinn
96 J6 **Caithness** *cultural region* N Scotland, United Kingdom
83 D15 **Caiundo** Cuando Cubango, S Angola *15°41′S 17°28′E*
56 C11 **Cajamarca** *prev.* Caxamarca. Cajamarca, NW Peru *07°09′S 78°32′W*
56 B11 **Cajamarca** *off.* Departamento de Cajamarca. ◈ *department* N Peru
Cajamarca, Departamento de *see* Cajamarca
103 N14 **Cajarc** Lot, S France *44°28′N 01°51′E*
42 G6 **Cajón, Represa El** ⊠ NW Honduras
58 N12 **Caju, Ilha do** *island* NE Brazil
159 R10 **Caka Yanhu** ◎ C China
112 E7 **Čakovec** *Ger.* Csakathurn, *Hung.* Csáktornya; *prev. Ger.* Tschakathurn. Medimurje, N Croatia *46°24′N 16°29′E*
77 V17 **Calabar** Cross River, S Nigeria *04°56′N 08°25′E*
14 K13 **Calabogie** Ontario, SE Canada *45°18′N 76°46′W*
54 L6 **Calabozo** Guárico, C Venezuela *08°58′N 67°28′W*
107 N20 **Calabria** *anc.* Bruttium. ◈ *region* SW Italy
104 M16 **Calaburra, Punta de** *headland* S Spain *36°30′N 04°38′W*
116 G14 **Calafat** Dolj, SW Romania *43°59′N 22°57′E*
Calafate *see* El Calafate
105 Q4 **Calahorra** La Rioja, N Spain *42°19′N 01°58′W*
103 N1 **Calais** Pas-de-Calais, N France *51°N 01°54′E*
19 T5 **Calais** Maine, NE USA *45°09′N 67°15′W*
Calais, Pas de *see* Dover, Strait of
Calalen *see* Kallalen
62 H4 **Calama** Antofagasta, N Chile *22°26′S 68°54′W*
Calamianes *see* Calamian Group
170 M5 **Calamian Group** *var.* Calamianes. *island group* W Philippines
105 R7 **Calamocha** Aragón, NE Spain *40°54′N 01°18′W*
29 N14 **Calamus River** ≈ Nebraska, C USA
116 G12 **Călan** *Ger.* Kalan, *Hung.* Pusztakalán. Hunedoara, SW Romania *45°45′N 22°59′E*
105 S7 **Calanda** Aragón, NE Spain *40°56′N 00°15′W*
168 F9 **Calang** Sumatera, W Indonesia *04°37′N 95°37′E*
171 N4 **Calapan** Mindoro, N Philippines *13°24′N 121°08′E*
Călăras *see* Călăraşi
116 M9 **Călăraşi** *var.* Călăras, *Rus.* Kalarash. C Moldova *47°19′N 28°13′E*
116 L14 **Călăraşi** Călăraşi, SE Romania *44°18′N 26°52′E*
116 K14 **Călăraşi** ◈ *county* SE Romania
54 E10 **Calarca** Quindío, W Colombia *04°31′N 75°38′W*
105 Q12 **Calasparra** Murcia, SE Spain *38°14′N 01°41′W*
107 I23 **Calatafimi** Sicilia, Italy, C Mediterranean Sea *37°54′N 12°52′E*
105 Q6 **Calatayud** Aragón, NE Spain *41°21′N 01°39′W*
171 O4 **Calauag** Luzon, N Philippines *13°57′N 122°18′E*
35 P8 **Calaveras River** ≈ California, W USA
171 N4 **Calavite, Cape** *headland* Mindoro, N Philippines *13°25′N 120°16′E*
171 Q8 **Calbayog** *off.* Calbayog City. Samar, C Philippines *12°08′N 124°36′E*
Calbayog City *see* Calbayog
22 G9 **Calcasieu Lake** ◎ Louisiana, S USA
22 H8 **Calcasieu River** ≈ Louisiana, S USA
56 B6 **Calceta** Manabí, W Ecuador *0°51′S 80°07′W*
61 B16 **Calchaquí** Santa Fe, C Argentina *29°56′S 60°14′W*
62 J6 **Calchaquí, Río** ≈ NW Argentina
58 J10 **Calçoene** Amapá, NE Brazil *02°29′N 51°01′W*
153 S16 **Calcutta** ✈ West Bengal, N India *22°30′N 88°20′E*
Calcutta *see* Kolkata
54 E9 **Caldas** *off.* Departamento de Caldas. ◈ *province* W Colombia
104 F10 **Caldas da Rainha** Leiria, W Portugal *39°24′N 09°08′W*
Caldas, Departamento de *see* Caldas
104 G3 **Caldas de Reis** *var.* Caldas de Reyes. Galicia, NW Spain *42°36′N 08°39′W*
Caldas de Reyes *see* Caldas de Reis
58 F13 **Caldeirão** Amazonas, NW Brazil *03°18′S 60°22′W*
62 G7 **Caldera** Atacama, N Chile *27°05′S 70°48′W*
42 L14 **Caldera** Puntarenas, W Costa Rica *09°55′N 84°51′W*
105 N10 **Calderina** ▲ C Spain *39°18′N 03°49′W*
137 T13 **Çaldıran** Van, E Turkey *39°10′N 43°52′E*
32 M14 **Caldwell** Idaho, NW USA *43°39′N 116°41′W*
27 N8 **Caldwell** Kansas, C USA *37°01′N 97°36′W*
14 G15 **Caledon** Ontario, S Canada *43°51′N 79°58′W*
83 I23 **Caledon** *var.* Mohokare. ≈ Lesotho/South Africa
42 G1 **Caledonia** Corozal, N Belize *18°14′N 88°29′W*
14 G16 **Caledonia** Ontario, S Canada *43°04′N 79°57′W*
29 X11 **Caledonia** Minnesota, N USA *43°37′N 91°30′W*
105 X5 **Calella** *var.* Calella de la Costa. Cataluña, NE Spain *41°37′N 02°40′E*
Calella de la Costa *see* Calella
23 P4 **Calera** Alabama, S USA *33°06′N 86°45′W*
63 I19 **Caleta Olivia** Santa Cruz, SE Argentina *46°21′S 67°37′W*
35 X17 **Calexico** California, W USA *32°39′N 115°28′W*
97 H16 **Calf of Man** *island* SW Isle of Man
11 Q16 **Calgary** Alberta, SW Canada *51°05′N 114°05′W*
11 Q16 **Calgary** ✈ Alberta, SW Canada *51°15′N 114°03′W*
37 U5 **Calhan** Colorado, C USA *39°00′N 104°18′W*
64 O5 **Calheta** Madeira, Portugal, NE Atlantic Ocean *32°42′N 17°12′W*
23 R2 **Calhoun** Georgia, SE USA *34°30′N 84°57′W*
20 I6 **Calhoun** Kentucky, S USA *37°32′N 87°15′W*
22 M3 **Calhoun City** Mississippi, S USA *33°51′N 89°18′W*
21 P12 **Calhoun Falls** South Carolina, SE USA *34°05′N 82°36′W*
54 D11 **Cali** Valle del Cauca, W Colombia *03°24′N 76°30′W*
27 V9 **Calico Rock** Arkansas, C USA *36°07′N 92°08′W*
155 F21 **Calicut** *var.* Kozhikode. Kerala, SW India *11°17′N 75°49′E* ***see also*** Kozhikode
35 Y9 **Caliente** Nevada, W USA *37°37′N 114°30′W*
27 U5 **California** Missouri, C USA *38°39′N 92°35′W*
18 B15 **California** Pennsylvania, NE USA *40°02′N 79°52′W*
35 Q12 **California** *off.* State of California, ***also known as*** El Dorado, The Golden State. ◈ *state* W USA
35 P11 **California Aqueduct** *aqueduct* California, W USA
35 T13 **California City** California, W USA *35°06′N 117°55′W*
40 F6 **California, Golfo de** *Eng.* Gulf of California; *prev.* Sea of Cortez. *gulf* W Mexico
California, Gulf of *see* California, Golfo de
137 Y13 **Cälilabad** *Rus.* Dzhalilabad; *prev.* Astrakhan-Bazar. S Azerbaijan *39°15′N 48°30′E*
116 I12 **Călimăneşti** Vâlcea, SW Romania *45°14′N 24°20′E*
116 J9 **Călimani, Munţii** ⛰ N Romania
Calinisc *see* Cupcina
35 X17 **Calipatria** California, W USA *33°07′N 115°30′W*
Calisia *see* Kalisz
34 M7 **Calistoga** California, W USA *38°34′N 122°37′W*
83 G25 **Calitzdorp** Western Cape, SW South Africa *33°32′S 21°41′E*
41 W12 **Calkiní** Campeche, E Mexico *20°21′N 90°03′W*
182 K4 **Callabonna Creek** *var.* Tilcha Creek. *seasonal river* New South Wales/South Australia
182 J4 **Callabonna, Lake** ◎ South Australia
102 G5 **Callac** Côtes d'Armor, NW France *48°28′N 03°22′W*
35 U5 **Callaghan, Mount** ▲ Nevada, W USA *39°38′N 116°57′W*
Callain *see* Callan
97 E19 **Callan** *Ir.* Callain. S Ireland *52°33′N 07°23′W*
14 H11 **Callander** Ontario, S Canada *46°14′N 79°21′W*
96 I11 **Callander** C Scotland, United Kingdom *56°15′N 04°16′W*
98 H7 **Callantsoog** Noord-Holland, NW Netherlands *52°51′N 04°41′E*
57 D14 **Callao** Callao, W Peru *12°03′S 77°10′W*
57 D15 **Callao** *off.* Departamento del Callao. ◈ *constitutional province* W Peru
Callao, Departamento del *see* Callao
56 F11 **Callaria, Río** ≈ E Peru
Callatis *see* Mangalia
11 Q13 **Calling Lake** Alberta, W Canada *55°12′N 113°07′W*
Callosa de Ensarriá *see* Callosa d'En Sarrià
105 T11 **Callosa d'En Sarrià** *var.* Callosa de Ensarriá. País Valenciano, E Spain *38°40′N 00°08′W*
105 S12 **Callosa de Segura** País Valenciano, E Spain *38°07′N 00°53′W*
29 X11 **Calmar** Iowa, C USA *43°10′N 91°51′W*
Calmar *see* Kalmar
43 R16 **Calobre** Veraguas, C Panama *08°18′N 80°49′W*
23 X14 **Caloosahatchee River** ≈ Florida, SE USA
183 V2 **Caloundra** Queensland, E Australia *26°48′S 153°08′E*
Calp *see* Calpe
105 T11 **Calpe** *Cat.* Calp. País Valenciano, E Spain *38°39′N 00°03′E*
41 P14 **Calpulalpan** Tlaxcala, S Mexico *19°36′N 98°26′W*
107 K25 **Caltagirone** Sicilia, Italy, C Mediterranean Sea *37°14′N 14°31′E*
107 J24 **Caltanissetta** Sicilia, Italy, C Mediterranean Sea *37°30′N 14°01′E*
82 E11 **Caluango** Lunda Norte, NE Angola *08°16′S 19°36′E*
82 C12 **Calucinga** Bié, W Angola *11°18′S 16°12′E*
82 B12 **Calulo** Cuanza Sul, NW Angola *09°58′S 14°56′E*
83 B14 **Caluquembe** Huíla, W Angola *13°47′S 14°40′E*
80 Q11 **Caluula** Bari, NE Somalia *11°55′N 50°51′E*
102 K4 **Calvados** ◈ *department* N France
186 I10 **Calvados Chain, The** *island group* SE Papua New Guinea
25 U9 **Calvert** Texas, SW USA *30°58′N 96°40′W*
20 H7 **Calvert City** Kentucky, S USA *37°01′N 88°21′W*
103 X14 **Calvi** Corse, France, C Mediterranean Sea *42°34′N 08°44′E*
40 L12 **Calvillo** Aguascalientes, C Mexico *21°51′N 102°18′W*
83 F24 **Calvinia** Northern Cape, W South Africa *31°25′S 19°47′E*
104 K8 **Calvitero** ▲ W Spain *40°16′N 05°48′W*
101 G22 **Calw** Baden-Württemberg, SW Germany *48°43′N 08°43′E*
Calydon *see* Kalydón
105 N11 **Calzada de Calatrava** Castilla-La Mancha, C Spain *38°42′N 03°46′W*
Cama *see* Kama
82 C11 **Camabatela** Cuanza Norte, NW Angola *08°13′S 15°23′E*
64 Q5 **Camacha** Porto Santo, Madeira, Portugal, NE Atlantic Ocean *32°41′N 16°52′W*
14 L8 **Camachigama, Lac** ◎ Québec, SE Canada
40 M9 **Camacho** Zacatecas, C Mexico *24°23′N 102°20′W*
82 D13 **Camacupa** *var.* General Machado, *Port.* Vila General Machado. Bié, C Angola *12°S 17°31′E*
54 L7 **Camaguán** Guárico, C Venezuela *08°09′N 67°37′W*
44 G6 **Camagüey** *prev.* Puerto Príncipe. Camagüey, C Cuba *21°24′N 77°55′W*
44 G5 **Camagüey, Archipiélago de** *island group* C Cuba
40 D5 **Camalli, Sierra de** ▲ NW Mexico *28°21′N 113°26′W*
57 G18 **Camana** *var.* Camaná. Arequipa, SW Peru *16°37′S 72°42′W*
29 Z14 **Camanche** Iowa, C USA *41°47′N 90°15′W*
35 P8 **Camanche Reservoir** ⊠ California, W USA
61 I16 **Camaquã** Rio Grande do Sul, S Brazil *30°50′S 51°47′W*
61 H16 **Camaquã, Rio** ≈ S Brazil
64 P6 **Câmara de Lobos** Madeira, Portugal, NE Atlantic Ocean *32°38′N 16°59′W*
103 U16 **Camarat, Cap** *headland* SE France *43°12′N 06°42′E*
41 O8 **Camargo** Tamaulipas, C Mexico *26°16′N 98°49′W*
103 R15 **Camargue** *physical region* SE France
104 F2 **Camariñas** Galicia, NW Spain *43°07′N 09°10′W*
Camaronero, Laguna del *see* Caimanero, Laguna del
63 J18 **Camarones** Chubut, S Argentina *44°48′S 65°42′W*
63 J18 **Camarones, Bahía** *bay* S Argentina
104 J14 **Camas** Andalucía, S Spain *37°24′N 06°01′W*
167 S15 **Ca Mau** *var.* Quan Long. Minh Hai, S Vietnam *09°11′N 105°09′E*
82 E11 **Camaxilo** Lunda Norte, NE Angola *08°19′S 18°53′E*
104 G3 **Cambados** Galicia, NW Spain *42°31′N 08°49′W*
Cambay, Gulf of *see* Khambhāt, Gulf of
Camberia *see* Chambéry
97 N22 **Camberley** SE England, United Kingdom *51°21′N 00°45′W*
167 R12 **Cambodia** *off.* Kingdom of Cambodia, *var.* Democratic Kampuchea, Roat Kampuchea, *Cam.* Kampuchea; *prev.* People's Democratic Republic of Kampuchea. ◆ *republic* SE Asia
Cambodia, Kingdom of *see* Cambodia
102 I16 **Cambo-les-Bains** Pyrénées-Atlantiques, SW France *43°22′N 01°24′W*
103 P2 **Cambrai** *Flem.* Kambryk, *prev.* Cambray; *anc.* Cameracum. Nord, N France *50°10′N 03°14′E*
Cambray *see* Cambrai
104 H2 **Cambre** Galicia, NW Spain *43°18′N 08°21′W*
35 O12 **Cambria** California, W USA *35°33′N 121°04′W*
97 J20 **Cambrian Mountains** ⛰ C Wales, United Kingdom
14 G16 **Cambridge** Ontario, S Canada *43°22′N 80°20′W*
44 I12 **Cambridge** W Jamaica *18°18′N 77°54′W*
184 M8 **Cambridge** Waikato, North Island, New Zealand *37°53′S 175°28′E*
97 O20 **Cambridge** *Lat.* Cantabrigia. E England, United Kingdom *52°12′N 00°07′E*
32 M12 **Cambridge** Idaho, NW USA *44°34′N 116°42′W*
30 K11 **Cambridge** Illinois, N USA *41°18′N 90°11′W*
21 Y4 **Cambridge** Maryland, NE USA *38°34′N 76°04′W*
19 O11 **Cambridge** Massachusetts, NE USA *42°21′N 71°05′W*
29 V7 **Cambridge** Minnesota, N USA *45°34′N 93°13′W*
29 N16 **Cambridge** Nebraska, C USA *40°18′N 100°10′W*
31 U13 **Cambridge** Ohio, NE USA *40°00′N 81°34′W*
8 L7 **Cambridge Bay** *var.* Ikaluktutiak. Victoria Island, Nunavut, NW Canada *68°56′N 105°09′W*
97 O20 **Cambridgeshire** *cultural region* E England, United Kingdom
105 U6 **Cambrils de Mar** Cataluña, NE Spain *41°06′N 01°02′E*
Cambundi-Catembo *see* Nova Gaia
137 N11 **Çam Burnu** *headland* N Turkey *41°07′N 37°48′E*
183 S9 **Camden** New South Wales, SE Australia *34°04′S 150°40′E*
23 O6 **Camden** Alabama, S USA *31°59′N 87°17′W*
27 U14 **Camden** Arkansas, C USA *33°32′N 92°49′W*
21 Y3 **Camden** Delaware, NE USA *39°06′N 75°30′W*
19 R7 **Camden** Maine, NE USA *44°12′N 69°04′W*
18 I16 **Camden** New Jersey, NE USA *39°55′N 75°07′W*
18 I9 **Camden** New York, NE USA *43°21′N 75°45′W*
21 R12 **Camden** South Carolina, SE USA *34°16′N 80°36′W*
20 H8 **Camden** Tennessee, S USA *36°03′N 88°07′W*
25 X9 **Camden** Texas, SW USA *30°55′N 94°43′W*
39 S5 **Camden Bay** *bay* S Beaufort Sea
27 U6 **Camdenton** Missouri, C USA *38°01′N 92°44′W*
Camellia State *see* Alabama
18 M7 **Camels Hump** ▲ Vermont, NE USA *44°18′N 72°50′W*
117 N8 **Camenca** *Rus.* Kamenka. N Moldova *48°01′N 28°43′E*
Cameracum *see* Cambrai
22 G9 **Cameron** Louisiana, S USA *29°48′N 93°19′W*
25 T9 **Cameron** Texas, SW USA *30°51′N 96°58′W*
30 J5 **Cameron** Wisconsin, N USA *45°25′N 91°42′W*
10 M12 **Cameron** ≈ British Columbia, W Canada
185 A24 **Cameron Mountains** ⛰ South Island, New Zealand
79 D15 **Cameroon** *off.* Republic of Cameroon, *Fr.* Cameroun. ◆ *republic* W Africa
79 D15 **Cameroon Mountain** ▲ SW Cameroon *04°12′N 09°00′E*
Cameroon, Republic of *see* Cameroon
Cameroon Ridge *see* Camerounaise, Dorsale
Cameroun *see* Cameroon
79 E14 **Camerounaise, Dorsale** *Eng.* Cameroon Ridge. *ridge* NW Cameroon
136 B15 **Çamiçi Gölü** ◎ SW Turkey
171 N3 **Camiling** Luzon, N Philippines *15°41′N 120°22′E*
23 T7 **Camilla** Georgia, SE USA *31°13′N 84°12′W*
104 G5 **Caminha** Viana do Castelo, N Portugal *41°52′N 08°50′W*
35 P7 **Camino** California, W USA *38°43′N 120°39′W*
107 J24 **Cammarata** Sicilia, Italy, C Mediterranean Sea *37°36′N 13°39′E*
42 K10 **Camoapa** Boaco, S Nicaragua *12°25′N 85°30′W*
58 O13 **Camocim** Ceará, E Brazil *02°55′S 40°50′W*
106 D10 **Camogli** Liguria, NW Italy *44°21′N 09°10′E*
181 S5 **Camooweal** Queensland, C Australia *19°57′S 138°14′E*
55 Y11 **Camopi** E French Guiana *03°12′N 52°19′W*
151 Q22 **Camorta** *island* Nicobar Islands, India, NE Indian Ocean
42 I6 **Campamento** Olancho, C Honduras *14°36′N 86°38′W*
61 D19 **Campana** Buenos Aires, E Argentina *34°10′S 58°57′W*
63 F21 **Campana, Isla** *island* S Chile
104 K11 **Campanario** Extremadura, W Spain *38°52′N 05°36′W*
107 L17 **Campania** *Eng.* Champagne. ◈ *region* S Italy
27 Y8 **Campbell** Missouri, C USA *36°29′N 90°04′W*
185 K15 **Campbell, Cape** *headland* South Island, New Zealand *41°44′S 174°16′E*
14 J14 **Campbellford** Ontario, SE Canada *44°18′N 77°48′W*
31 R13 **Campbell Hill** *hill* Ohio, N USA
192 K13 **Campbell Island** *island* S New Zealand
175 P13 **Campbell Plateau** *undersea feature* SW Pacific Ocean *51°00′S 170°00′E*
10 K17 **Campbell River** Vancouver Island, British Columbia, SW Canada *49°59′N 125°18′W*
20 L6 **Campbellsville** Kentucky, S USA *37°20′N 85°21′W*
13 O13 **Campbellton** New Brunswick, SE Canada *48°00′N 66°41′W*
183 S9 **Campbelltown** New South Wales, SE Australia *34°04′S 150°46′E*
183 P16 **Campbell Town** Tasmania, SE Australia *41°57′S 147°30′E*
96 G13 **Campbeltown** W Scotland, United Kingdom *55°26′N 05°38′W*
41 W13 **Campeche** Campeche, SE Mexico *19°47′N 90°29′W*
41 W14 **Campeche** ◈ *state* SE Mexico
41 T14 **Campeche, Bahía de** *Eng.* Bay of Campeche. *bay* E Mexico
Campeche, Banco de *see* Campeche Bank
64 C11 **Campeche Bank** *Sp.* Banco de Campeche, Sonda de Campeche. *undersea feature* S Gulf of Mexico *22°00′N 90°00′W*
Campeche, Bay of *see* Campeche, Bahía de
Campeche, Sonda de *see* Campeche Bank
44 H7 **Campechuela** Granma, E Cuba *20°15′N 77°17′W*
182 M13 **Camperdown** Victoria, SE Australia *38°16′S 143°10′E*
167 U6 **Câm Pha** Quang Ninh, N Vietnam *21°04′N 107°20′E*
116 H10 **Câmpia Turzii** *Ger.* Jerischmarkt, *Hung.* Aranyosgyéres; *prev.* Cîmpia Turzii, Ghiriş, Gyéres. Cluj, NW Romania *46°33′N 23°53′E*
104 K12 **Campillo de Llerena** Extremadura, W Spain *38°30′N 05°48′W*
104 L15 **Campillos** Andalucía, S Spain *37°04′N 04°51′W*
116 J13 **Câmpina** *prev.* Cîmpina. Prahova, SE Romania *45°08′N 25°44′E*
59 Q15 **Campina Grande** Paraíba, E Brazil *07°15′S 35°50′W*
60 L9 **Campinas** São Paulo, S Brazil *22°54′S 47°06′W*
38 L10 **Camp Kulowiye** Saint Lawrence Island, Alaska, USA *63°15′N 168°45′W*
79 D17 **Campo** *var.* Kampo. Sud, SW Cameroon *02°22′N 09°50′E*
Campo *see* Ntem
59 N15 **Campo Alegre de Lourdes** Bahia, E Brazil *09°28′S 43°01′W*
107 L16 **Campobasso** Molise, C Italy *41°34′N 14°40′E*
107 H24 **Campobello di Mazara** Sicilia, Italy, C Mediterranean Sea *37°38′N 12°45′E*
Campo Criptana *see* Campo de Criptana
105 O10 **Campo de Criptana** *var.* Campo Criptana. Castilla-La Mancha, C Spain *39°25′N 03°07′W*
59 I16 **Campo de Diauarum** *var.* Pôsto Diuarum. Mato Grosso, W Brazil *11°08′S 53°16′W*
54 E5 **Campo de la Cruz** Atlántico, N Colombia *10°23′N 74°52′W*
105 P11 **Campo de Montiel** *physical region* C Spain
Campo dos Goitacazes *see* Campos
60 H12 **Campo Erê** Santa Catarina, S Brazil *26°24′S 53°04′W*
62 L7 **Campo Gallo** Santiago del Estero, N Argentina *26°32′S 62°51′W*
59 I20 **Campo Grande** *state capital* Mato Grosso do Sul, SW Brazil *20°24′S 54°35′W*
60 K12 **Campo Largo** Paraná, S Brazil *25°27′S 49°29′W*
58 N13 **Campo Maior** Piauí, E Brazil *04°50′S 42°12′W*
104 I10 **Campo Maior** Portalegre, C Portugal *39°01′N 07°04′W*
60 H10 **Campo Mourão** Paraná, S Brazil *24°01′S 52°24′W*
60 Q9 **Campos** *var.* Campo dos Goitacazes. Rio de Janeiro, SE Brazil *21°46′S 41°21′W*
59 L17 **Campos Belos** Goiás, S Brazil *13°11′S 46°47′W*
60 N9 **Campos do Jordão** São Paulo, S Brazil *22°45′S 45°36′W*
60 I13 **Campos Novos** Santa Catarina, S Brazil *27°22′S 51°11′W*
59 O14 **Campos Sales** Ceará, E Brazil *07°01′S 40°21′W*
25 Q9 **Camp San Saba** Texas, SW USA *30°57′N 99°16′W*
21 N6 **Campton** Kentucky, S USA *37°44′N 83°35′W*
116 I13 **Câmpulung** *prev.* Câmpulung-Muşcel, Cîmpulung. Argeş, S Romania *45°16′N 25°03′E*
116 J9 **Câmpulung Moldovenesc** *var.* Cîmpulung Moldovenesc, *Ger.* Kimpolung, *Hung.* Hosszúmezjő. Suceava, NE Romania *47°32′N 25°34′E*
Câmpulung-Muşcel *see* Câmpulung
Campus Stellae *see* Santiago
36 L12 **Camp Verde** Arizona, SW USA *34°33′N 111°52′W*
25 P11 **Camp Wood** Texas, SW USA *29°40′N 100°00′W*
167 V13 **Cam Ranh** Khanh Hoa, S Vietnam *11°54′N 109°14′E*
11 Q15 **Camrose** Alberta, SW Canada *53°01′N 112°48′W*
Camulodunum *see* Colchester
136 B12 **Çan** Çanakkale, NW Turkey *40°03′N 27°03′E*
18 L12 **Canaan** Connecticut, NE USA *42°00′N 73°17′W*
11 O13 **Canada** ◆ *commonwealth republic* N North America
197 P6 **Canada Basin** *undersea feature* Arctic Ocean *80°00′N 145°00′W*
61 B18 **Cañada de Gómez** Santa Fe, C Argentina *32°50′S 61°23′W*
197 P6 **Canada Plain** *undersea feature* Arctic Ocean
61 A18 **Cañada Rosquín** Santa Fe, C Argentina *32°04′S 61°35′W*
25 P1 **Canadian** Texas, SW USA *35°54′N 100°23′W*
16 K12 **Canadian River** ≈ SW USA
8 L12 **Canadian Shield** *physical region* Canada
63 I18 **Cañadón Grande, Sierra** ⛰ S Argentina
55 P9 **Canaima** Bolívar, SE Venezuela *09°41′N 72°33′W*
136 B11 **Çanakkale** *var.* Dardanelli; *prev.* Chanak, Kale Sultanie. Çanakkale, W Turkey *40°09′N 26°25′E*
136 B12 **Çanakkale** ◈ *province* NW Turkey
136 B11 **Çanakkale Boğazı** *Eng.* Dardanelles. *strait* NW Turkey
187 Q17 **Canala** Province Nord, C New Caledonia *21°31′S 165°57′E*
59 A15 **Canamari** Amazonas, W Brazil *07°37′S 72°33′W*
18 G10 **Canandaigua** New York, NE USA *42°52′N 77°14′W*

◆ Country
● Country Capital
◇ Dependent Territory
○ Dependent Territory Capital
◈ Administrative Regions
✈ International Airport
▲ Mountain
⛰ Mountain Range
∧ Volcano
≈ River
◎ Lake
⊠ Reservoir

18 F10 **Canandaigua Lake** ◎ New York, NE USA
40 G3 **Cananea** Sonora, NW Mexico 30°59′N 110°20′W
56 B8 **Cañar** ◐ province C Ecuador
64 N10 **Canarias, Islas** Eng. Canary Islands. ◐ autonomous community Spain, NE Atlantic Ocean
Canaries Basin see Canary Basin
44 C6 **Canarreos, Archipiélago de los** island group W Cuba
Canary Islands see Canarias, Islas
66 K3 **Canary Basin** var. Canaries Basin, Monaco Basin. undersea feature E Atlantic Ocean 30°00′N 25°00′W
42 L13 **Cañas** Guanacaste, NW Costa Rica 10°25′N 85°07′W
18 I10 **Canastota** New York, NE USA 43°04′N 75°45′W
40 K9 **Canatlán** Durango, C Mexico 24°33′N 104°45′W
104 J9 **Cañaveral** Extremadura, W Spain 39°47′N 06°24′W
23 Y11 **Canaveral, Cape** headland Florida, SE USA 28°27′N 80°31′W
59 O18 **Canavieiras** Bahia, E Brazil 15°44′S 38°58′W
43 R16 **Cañazas** Veraguas, W Panama 08°25′N 81°10′W
106 H6 **Canazei** Trentino-Alto Adige, N Italy 46°29′N 11°50′E
183 P6 **Canbelego** New South Wales, SE Australia 31°36′S 146°20′E
183 R10 **Canberra** ● (Australia) Australian Capital Territory, SE Australia 35°21′S 149°08′E
183 R10 **Canberra** ✈ Australian Capital Territory, SE Australia 35°19′S 149°12′E
35 P2 **Canby** California, W USA 41°27′N 120°51′W
29 S9 **Canby** Minnesota, N USA 44°42′N 96°17′W
103 N2 **Canche** ~ N France
102 L13 **Cancon** Lot-et-Garonne, SW France 44°33′N 00°37′E
41 Z11 **Cancún** Quintana Roo, SE Mexico 21°05′N 86°48′W
104 K2 **Candás** Asturias, N Spain 43°35′N 05°45′W
102 J7 **Cande** Maine-et-Loire, NW France 47°33′N 01°03′W
41 W14 **Candelaria** Campeche, SE Mexico 18°10′N 91°00′W
24 J11 **Candelaria** Texas, SW USA 30°05′N 104°40′W
41 W15 **Candelaria, Río** ~ Guatemala/Mexico
104 L8 **Candeleda** Castilla-León, N Spain 40°10′N 05°14′W
Candia see Irákleio
41 P8 **Cándido Aguilar** Tamaulipas, C Mexico 25°30′N 97°57′W
39 N8 **Candle** Alaska, USA 65°54′N 161°55′W
11 T14 **Candle Lake** Saskatchewan, C Canada 53°43′N 105°09′W
18 L13 **Candlewood, Lake** ▣ Connecticut, NE USA
29 O3 **Cando** North Dakota, N USA 48°29′N 99°12′W
Canea see Chaniá
45 O12 **Canefield** ✈ (Roseau) SW Dominica 15°20′N 61°24′W
61 F20 **Canelones** prev. Guadalupe. Canelones, S Uruguay 34°32′S 56°17′W
61 E20 **Canelones** ◐ department S Uruguay
Canendiyú see Canindeyú
63 F14 **Cañete** Bío Bío, C Chile 37°48′S 73°25′W
105 Q9 **Cañete** Castilla-La Mancha, C Spain 40°03′N 01°39′W
Cañete see San Vicente de Cañete
27 P8 **Caney** Kansas, C USA 37°00′N 95°56′W
27 P8 **Caney River** ~ Kansas/Oklahoma, C USA
105 S3 **Canfranc-Estación** Aragón, NE Spain 42°42′N 00°31′W
83 E14 **Cangamba** Port. Vila de Aljustrel. Moxico, E Angola 13°40′S 19°47′E
82 C12 **Cangandala** Malanje, NW Angola 09°47′S 16°27′E
104 G4 **Cangas** Galicia, NW Spain 42°16′N 08°46′W
104 J2 **Cangas del Narcea** Asturias, N Spain 43°10′N 06°32′W
104 L2 **Cangas de Onís** Asturias, N Spain 43°21′N 05°08′W
161 S11 **Cangnan** var. Lingxi. Zhejiang, SE China 27°29′N 120°23′E
82 C10 **Cangola** Uíge, NW Angola 07°54′S 15°57′E
83 E14 **Cangombe** Moxico, E Angola 14°27′S 20°05′E
63 H21 **Cangrejo, Cerro** ▲ S Argentina 49°19′S 72°18′W
61 H17 **Canguçu** Rio Grande do Sul, S Brazil 31°25′S 52°37′W
161 P3 **Cangzhou** Hebei, E China 38°19′N 116°54′E
12 M7 **Caniapiscau** ~ Québec, E Canada
12 M8 **Caniapiscau, Réservoir de** ▣ Québec, C Canada
107 J24 **Canicattì** Sicilia, Italy, C Mediterranean Sea 37°22′N 13°51′E
136 L11 **Canik Dağları** ▲▲ N Turkey
105 P14 **Caniles** Andalucía, S Spain 37°24′N 02°41′W
59 B16 **Canindé** Acre, W Brazil 10°55′S 69°45′W
62 P6 **Canindeyú** var. Canendiyú, Canindiyú. ◐ department E Paraguay
Canindiyú see Canindeyú
194 J10 **Canisteo Peninsula** peninsula Antarctica
18 F11 **Canisteo River** ~ New York, NE USA
40 M10 **Cañitas** var. Cañitas de Felipe Pescador. Zacatecas, C Mexico 23°35′N 102°39′W
Cañitas de Felipe Pescador see Cañitas
105 P15 **Canjáyar** Andalucía, S Spain 37°00′N 02°45′W
136 I12 **Çankırı** var. Chankiri; anc. Gangra, Germanicopolis. Çankın, N Turkey 40°36′N 33°35′E
136 I11 **Çankırı** var. Chankiri. ◐ province N Turkey
171 P6 **Canlaon Volcano** ⛰ C Philippines 10°24′N 123°05′E
11 P16 **Canmore** Alberta, SW Canada 51°07′N 115°18′W
96 F9 **Canna** island NW Scotland, United Kingdom
155 F20 **Cannanore** var. Kannur. Kerala, SW India 11°53′N 75°23′E see also Kannur
31 O17 **Cannelton** Indiana, N USA 37°54′N 86°44′W
103 U15 **Cannes** Alpes-Maritimes, SE France 43°33′N 06°59′E
39 R5 **Canning River** ~ Alaska, USA
106 C6 **Cannobio** Piemonte, NE Italy 46°04′N 08°39′E
97 L19 **Cannock** C England, United Kingdom 52°41′N 02°03′W
28 M6 **Cannonball River** ~ North Dakota, N USA
29 W9 **Cannon Falls** Minnesota, N USA 44°30′N 92°54′W
18 I11 **Cannonsville Reservoir** ▣ New York, NE USA
183 R12 **Cann River** Victoria, SE Australia 37°34′S 149°11′E
61 I16 **Canoas** Rio Grande do Sul, S Brazil 29°42′S 51°07′W
61 I14 **Canoas, Rio** ~ S Brazil
14 I12 **Canoe Lake** ◎ Ontario, SE Canada
60 J12 **Canoinhas** Santa Catarina, S Brazil 26°12′S 50°24′W
37 T6 **Canon City** Colorado, C USA 38°25′N 105°14′W
55 P8 **Caño Negro** Bolívar, SE Venezuela
173 X15 **Canonniers Point** headland N Mauritius
23 W6 **Canoochee River** ~ Georgia, SE USA
11 V15 **Canora** Saskatchewan, S Canada 51°38′N 102°28′W
45 Y14 **Canouan** island S Saint Vincent and the Grenadines
13 R15 **Canso** Nova Scotia, SE Canada 45°20′N 61°00′W
104 M3 **Cantabria** ◐ autonomous community N Spain
104 K3 **Cantábrica, Cordillera** ▲▲ N Spain
Cantabrigia see Cambridge
103 O12 **Cantal** ◐ department C France
105 N6 **Cantalejo** Castilla-León, N Spain 41°15′N 03°57′W
103 O12 **Cantal, Monts du** ▲▲ C France
104 G8 **Cantanhede** Coimbra, C Portugal 40°21′N 08°37′W
Cantaño see Cataño
55 O6 **Cantaura** Anzoátegui, NE Venezuela 09°22′N 64°24′W
116 M11 **Cantemir** Rus. Kantemir. S Moldova 46°17′N 28°12′E
97 Q22 **Canterbury** hist. Cantwaraburh; anc. Durovernum, Lat. Cantuaria. SE England, United Kingdom 51°17′N 01°05′E
185 F19 **Canterbury** off. Canterbury Region. ◐ region South Island, New Zealand
185 H20 **Canterbury Bight** bight South Island, New Zealand
185 H19 **Canterbury Plains** plain South Island, New Zealand
Canterbury Region see Canterbury
167 S14 **Cần Thơ** Cần Thơ, S Vietnam 10°03′N 105°46′E
104 K13 **Cantillana** Andalucía, S Spain 37°34′N 05°48′W
59 N15 **Canto do Buriti** Piauí, NE Brazil 08°07′S 43°00′W
23 S2 **Canton** Georgia, SE USA 34°14′N 84°29′W
30 K12 **Canton** Illinois, N USA 40°33′N 90°02′W
22 L5 **Canton** Mississippi, S USA 32°36′N 90°02′W
27 V2 **Canton** Missouri, C USA 40°07′N 91°31′W
18 J7 **Canton** New York, NE USA 44°36′N 75°10′W
21 O10 **Canton** North Carolina, SE USA 35°31′N 82°50′W
31 U12 **Canton** Ohio, N USA 40°48′N 81°23′W
26 L9 **Canton** Oklahoma, C USA 36°03′N 98°35′W
18 G12 **Canton** Pennsylvania, NE USA 41°38′N 76°49′W
29 R11 **Canton** South Dakota, N USA 43°19′N 96°33′W
25 V7 **Canton** Texas, SW USA 32°33′N 95°51′W
Canton see Guangzhou
Canton Island see Kanton
26 L9 **Canton Lake** ▣ Oklahoma, C USA
106 D7 **Cantù** Lombardia, N Italy 45°44′N 09°08′E
Cantuaria/Cantwaraburh see Canterbury
39 R10 **Cantwell** Alaska, USA 63°23′N 148°57′W
59 O16 **Canudos** Bahia, E Brazil 09°51′S 39°08′W
47 T7 **Canumã, Rio** ~ N Brazil
Canusium see Puglia, Canosa di
24 G7 **Canutillo** Texas, SW USA 31°53′N 106°34′W
25 N3 **Canyon** Texas, SW USA 34°58′N 101°56′W
33 S12 **Canyon** Wyoming, C USA 44°44′N 110°30′W
32 K13 **Canyon City** Oregon, NW USA 44°24′N 118°58′W
33 R10 **Canyon Ferry Lake** ◎ Montana, NW USA
25 S11 **Canyon Lake** ▣ Texas, SW USA
167 T5 **Cao Bằng** var. Caobang. Cao Bằng, N Vietnam 22°40′N 106°16′E
Caobang see Cao Bằng
160 J12 **Caodu He** ~ S China
Caohai see Weining
167 S14 **Cao Lanh** Đồng Tháp, S Vietnam 10°35′N 105°25′E
82 C11 **Caombo** Malanje, NW Angola 08°42′S 16°33′E
Caorach, Cuan na g see Sheep Haven
Caozhou see Heze
171 Q12 **Capalulu** Pulau Mangole, E Indonesia 01°51′S 125°53′E
54 K8 **Capanaparo, Río** ~ Colombia/Venezuela
58 L12 **Capanema** Pará, NE Brazil 01°08′S 47°07′W
60 L10 **Capão Bonito** São Paulo, S Brazil 24°01′S 48°23′W
60 I13 **Capão Doce, Morro do** ▲ S Brazil 26°37′S 51°28′W
54 I4 **Capatárida** Falcón, N Venezuela 11°11′N 70°37′W
102 I15 **Capbreton** Landes, SW France 43°40′N 01°25′W
Cap-Breton, Île du see Cape Breton Island
15 W6 **Cap-Chat** Québec, SE Canada 49°04′N 66°43′W
15 P11 **Cap-de-la-Madeleine** Québec, SE Canada 46°22′N 72°31′W
103 N13 **Capdenac** Aveyron, S France 44°35′N 02°06′E
Cap des Palmès see Palmas, Cape
183 Q15 **Cape Barren Island** island Furneaux Group, Tasmania, SE Australia
65 O18 **Cape Basin** undersea feature S Atlantic Ocean 37°00′S 07°00′E
13 R14 **Cape Breton Island** Fr. Île du Cap-Breton. island Nova Scotia, SE Canada
23 Y11 **Cape Canaveral** Florida, SE USA 28°24′N 80°36′W
21 Y6 **Cape Charles** Virginia, NE USA 37°16′N 76°01′W
77 P17 **Cape Coast** prev. Cape Coast Castle. S Ghana 05°10′N 01°13′W
Cape Coast Castle see Cape Coast
19 Q12 **Cape Cod Bay** bay Massachusetts, NE USA
23 W15 **Cape Coral** Florida, SE USA 26°33′N 81°57′W
181 R4 **Cape Crawford Roadhouse** Northern Territory, N Australia 16°39′S 135°44′E
9 Q7 **Cape Dorset** Baffin Island, Nunavut, NE Canada 76°14′N 76°32′W
21 N8 **Cape Fear River** ~ North Carolina, SE USA
27 Y7 **Cape Girardeau** Missouri, C USA 37°19′N 89°31′W
21 T14 **Cape Island** island South Carolina, SE USA
186 A6 **Capella** ▲ NW Papua New Guinea 05°00′S 141°09′E
98 H12 **Capelle aan den IJssel** Zuid-Holland, SW Netherlands 51°56′N 04°36′E
83 C15 **Capelongo** Huíla, C Angola 14°45′S 15°02′E
18 J17 **Cape May** New Jersey, NE USA 38°54′N 74°54′W
18 J17 **Cape May Court House** New Jersey, NE USA 39°03′N 74°46′W
Cape Palmas see Harper
8 I16 **Cape Parry** Northwest Territories, N Canada 70°10′N 124°33′W
65 P19 **Cape Rise** undersea feature SW Indian Ocean 42°00′S 15°00′E
Cape Saint Jacques see Vung Tau
Capesterre see Capesterre-Belle-Eau
45 Y6 **Capesterre-Belle-Eau** var. Capesterre. Basse Terre, S Guadeloupe 16°03′N 61°34′W
83 D26 **Cape Town** var. Ekapa, Afr. Kaapstad, Kapstad. ● (South Africa-legislative capital) Western Cape, SW South Africa 33°56′S 18°28′E
83 E26 **Cape Town** ✈ Western Cape, SW South Africa 31°51′S 21°06′E
76 D9 **Cape Verde** off. Republic of Cape Verde, Port. Cabo Verde, Ilhas do Cabo Verde. ◆ republic E Atlantic Ocean
64 L11 **Cape Verde Basin** undersea feature E Atlantic Ocean 15°00′N 30°00′W
66 K5 **Cape Verde Islands** island group E Atlantic Ocean
64 L10 **Cape Verde Plain** undersea feature E Atlantic Ocean 23°00′N 26°00′W
Cape Verde Plateau/Cape Verde Rise see Cape Verde Terrace
Cape Verde, Republic of see Cape Verde
64 L11 **Cape Verde Terrace** var. Cape Verde Plateau, Cape Verde Rise. undersea feature E Atlantic Ocean 18°00′N 20°00′W
181 V2 **Cape York Peninsula** peninsula Queensland, N Australia
44 M8 **Cap-Haïtien** var. Le Cap. N Haiti 19°44′N 72°12′W
43 T15 **Capira** Panamá, C Panama 08°48′N 79°51′W
14 K8 **Capitachouane** ~ Québec, SE Canada
14 L8 **Capitachouane, Lac** ◎ Québec, SE Canada
37 T13 **Capitan** New Mexico, SW USA 33°33′N 105°34′W
194 G3 **Capitán Arturo Prat** Chilean research station South Shetland Islands, Antarctica 62°24′S 59°42′W
37 S13 **Capitan Mountains** ▲▲ New Mexico, SW USA
62 M3 **Capitán Pablo Lagerenza** var. Mayor Pablo Lagerenza. Chaco, N Paraguay 19°55′S 60°46′W
37 T13 **Capitan Peak** ▲ New Mexico, SW USA 33°35′N 105°15′W
188 H5 **Capitol Hill** ● (Northern Mariana Islands-legislative capital) Saipan, S Northern Mariana Islands
60 I9 **Capivara, Represa** ▣ S Brazil
61 J16 **Capivari** Rio Grande do Sul, S Brazil 30°08′S 50°32′W
113 H15 **Čapljina** Federicija Bosna I Hercegovina, S Bosnia and Herzegovina 43°07′N 17°42′E
83 M15 **Capoche** var. Kapoche. ~ Mozambique/Zambia
Capo Delgado, Provincia de see Cabo Delgado
107 K17 **Capodichino** ✈ (Napoli) Campania, S Italy 40°53′N 14°15′E
Capodistria see Koper
106 E12 **Capraia, Isola di** island Arcipelago Toscano, C Italy
107 B16 **Caprara, Punta** var. Punta dello Scorno. headland Isola Asinara, W Italy 41°07′N 08°19′E
Capraria see Cabrera, Illa de
14 F10 **Capreol** Ontario, S Canada 46°43′N 80°56′W
107 K18 **Capri** Campania, S Italy 40°33′N 14°14′E
175 S9 **Capricorn Tablemount** undersea feature W Pacific Ocean 18°34′S 172°12′W
107 J18 **Capri, Isola di** island S Italy
83 G16 **Caprivi** ◐ district NE Namibia
Caprivi Concession see Caprivi Strip
83 F16 **Caprivi Strip** Ger. Caprivizipfel; prev. Caprivi Concession. cultural region NE Namibia
Caprivizipfel see Caprivi Strip
25 O5 **Cap Rock Escarpment** cliffs Texas, SW USA
15 R10 **Cap-Rouge** Québec, SE Canada 46°45′N 71°18′W
Cap Saint-Jacques see Vung Tau
38 F12 **Captain Cook** Hawaii, USA, C Pacific Ocean 19°30′N 155°55′W
183 R10 **Captains Flat** New South Wales, SE Australia 35°37′S 149°28′E
102 K14 **Captieux** Gironde, SW France 44°16′N 00°15′W
107 K17 **Capua** Campania, S Italy 41°06′N 14°13′E
54 F14 **Caquetá** off. Departamento del Caquetá. ◐ province S Colombia
Caquetá, Departamento del see Caquetá
54 E13 **Caquetá, Río** var. Río Japurá, Yapurá. ~ Brazil/Colombia see also Japurá, Rio
Caquetá, Río see Japurá, Rio
CAR see Central African Republic
Cara see Kara
57 I16 **Carabaya, Cordillera** ▲▲ E Peru
54 K5 **Carabobo** off. Estado Carabobo. ◐ state N Venezuela
Carabobo, Estado see Carabobo
116 I14 **Caracal** Olt, S Romania 44°07′N 24°18′E
58 F10 **Caracaraí** Rondônia, W Brazil 01°47′N 61°11′W
54 L5 **Caracas** ● (Venezuela) Distrito Federal, N Venezuela 10°29′N 66°54′W
54 I5 **Carache** Trujillo, N Venezuela 09°40′N 70°15′W
60 N10 **Caraguatatuba** São Paulo, S Brazil 23°37′S 45°24′W
48 I7 **Carajás, Serra dos** ▲▲ N Brazil
Caralis see Cagliari
54 E9 **Caramanta** Antioquia, W Colombia 05°36′N 75°38′W
171 P4 **Caramoan** Catanduanes Island, N Philippines 13°47′N 123°49′E
Caramurat see Mihail Kogălniceanu
116 F12 **Caransebes** Ger. Karansebesch, Hung. Karánsebes. Caraş-Severin, SW Romania 45°23′N 22°13′E
Carapella see Carapelle
107 M16 **Carapelle** var. Carapella. ~ SE Italy
55 O9 **Carapo** Bolívar, SE Venezuela
13 P13 **Caraquet** New Brunswick, SE Canada 47°48′N 64°59′W
Caras see Caraz
116 F12 **Caraşova** Hung. Krassóvár. Caraş-Severin, SW Romania 45°11′N 21°51′E
116 F12 **Caraş-Severin** ◐ county SW Romania
42 M5 **Caratasca, Laguna de** lagoon NE Honduras
58 C13 **Carauari** Amazonas, NW Brazil 04°55′S 66°57′W
Caravaca see Caravaca de la Cruz
105 Q12 **Caravaca de la Cruz** var. Caravaca. Murcia, SE Spain 38°06′N 01°51′W
106 E7 **Caravaggio** Lombardia, N Italy 45°31′N 09°39′E
107 C18 **Caravai, Passo di** pass Sardegna, Italy, C Mediterranean Sea
59 O19 **Caravelas** Bahia, E Brazil 17°45′S 39°15′W
56 C12 **Caraz** var. Caras. Ancash, W Peru 09°03′S 77°47′W
61 H14 **Carazinho** Rio Grande do Sul, S Brazil 28°16′S 52°46′W
42 J11 **Carazo** ◐ department SW Nicaragua
Carballiño see O Carballiño
104 G2 **Carballo** Galicia, NW Spain 43°13′N 08°41′W
11 W16 **Carberry** Manitoba, S Canada 49°52′N 99°20′W
40 F4 **Carbó** Sonora, NW Mexico 29°41′N 111°00′W
107 C20 **Carbonara, Capo** headland Sardegna, Italy, C Mediterranean Sea 39°06′N 09°31′E
37 Q5 **Carbondale** Colorado, C USA 39°24′N 107°12′W
30 L17 **Carbondale** Illinois, N USA 37°43′N 89°13′W
27 Q4 **Carbondale** Kansas, C USA 38°49′N 95°41′W
18 I13 **Carbondale** Pennsylvania, NE USA 41°34′N 75°30′W
13 V12 **Carbonear** Newfoundland, Newfoundland and Labrador, SE Canada 47°45′N 53°16′W
105 Q9 **Carboneras de Guadazaón** var. Carboneras de Guadazón. Castilla-La Mancha, C Spain 39°54′N 01°50′W
Carboneras de Guadazón see Carboneras de Guadazaón
23 O3 **Carbon Hill** Alabama, S USA 33°53′N 87°31′W
107 B20 **Carbonia** var. Carbonia Centro. Sardegna, Italy, C Mediterranean Sea 39°11′N 08°31′E
Carbonia Centro see Carbonia
105 S10 **Carcaixent** País Valenciano, E Spain 39°08′N 00°28′W
Carcaso see Carcassonne
65 B24 **Carcass Island** island NW Falkland Islands
103 O16 **Carcassonne** anc. Carcaso. Aude, S France 43°13′N 02°21′E
105 R12 **Carche** ▲ S Spain 38°24′N 01°11′W
56 A13 **Carchi** ◐ province N Ecuador
10 I8 **Carcross** Yukon Territory, W Canada 60°11′N 134°41′W
Cardamomes, Chaîne des see Krâvanh, Chuŏr Phnum
155 G22 **Cardamom Hills** ▲ SW India
Cardamom Mountains see Krâvanh, Chuŏr Phnum
104 M12 **Cardeña** Andalucía, S Spain 38°16′N 04°20′W
44 D4 **Cárdenas** Matanzas, W Cuba 23°02′N 81°12′W
41 O11 **Cárdenas** San Luis Potosí, C Mexico 22°03′N 99°30′W
41 U15 **Cárdenas** Tabasco, SE Mexico 18°00′N 93°21′W
63 H21 **Cardiel, Lago** ◎ S Argentina
97 K22 **Cardiff** Wel. Caerdydd. ◐ S Wales, United Kingdom 51°30′N 03°13′W
97 J22 **Cardiff-Wales** ✈ S Wales, United Kingdom 51°24′N 03°22′W
97 I21 **Cardigan** Wel. Aberteifi. SW Wales, United Kingdom 52°06′N 04°40′W
97 I20 **Cardigan** cultural region W Wales, United Kingdom
97 I20 **Cardigan Bay** bay W Wales, United Kingdom
19 N8 **Cardigan, Mount** ▲ New Hampshire, NE USA 43°39′N 71°52′W
14 M13 **Cardinal** Ontario, SE Canada 44°48′N 75°22′W
105 V5 **Cardona** Cataluña, NE Spain 41°55′N 01°41′E
61 E19 **Cardona** Soriano, SW Uruguay 33°53′S 57°18′W
105 V4 **Cardoner** ~ NE Spain
11 Q17 **Cardston** Alberta, SW Canada 49°14′N 113°19′W
181 W5 **Cardwell** Queensland, NE Australia 18°24′S 146°06′E
116 G8 **Carei** Ger. Gross-Karol, Karol, Hung. Nagykároly; prev. Careii-Mari. Satu Mare, NW Romania 47°40′N 22°28′E
Careii-Mari see Carei
58 F13 **Careiro** Amazonas, NW Brazil 03°40′S 60°23′W
102 J4 **Carentan** Manche, N France 49°18′N 01°15′W
104 M2 **Cares** ~ N Spain
33 P14 **Carey** Idaho, NW USA 43°17′N 113°58′W
31 S12 **Carey** Ohio, N USA 40°57′N 83°22′W
25 P4 **Carey** Texas, SW USA 34°28′N 100°18′W
180 L11 **Carey, Lake** ◎ Western Australia
173 O8 **Cargados Carajos Bank** undersea feature C Indian Ocean
102 G6 **Carhaix-Plouguer** Finistère, NW France 48°16′N 03°35′W
61 A22 **Carhué** Buenos Aires, E Argentina 37°10′S 62°45′W
55 O5 **Cariaco** Sucre, NE Venezuela 10°33′N 63°37′W
107 O20 **Cariati** Calabria, SW Italy 39°30′N 16°57′E
2 H17 **Caribbean Plate** tectonic feature
44 I11 **Caribbean Sea** sea W Atlantic Ocean
11 N15 **Cariboo Mountains** ▲▲ British Columbia, SW Canada
11 W9 **Caribou** Manitoba, C Canada 59°27′N 97°43′W
19 S2 **Caribou** Maine, NE USA 46°51′N 68°00′W
11 P10 **Caribou Mountains** ▲▲ Alberta, SW Canada
Caribrod see Dimitrovgrad
40 I6 **Carichic** Chihuahua, N Mexico 27°57′N 107°01′W
103 R3 **Carignan** Ardennes, N France 49°38′N 05°08′E
183 Q5 **Carinda** New South Wales, SE Australia 30°26′S 147°45′E
105 R6 **Cariñena** Aragón, NE Spain 41°20′N 01°13′W
107 I23 **Carini** Sicilia, Italy, C Mediterranean Sea 38°06′N 13°09′E
107 K17 **Carinola** Campania, S Italy 41°14′N 14°03′E
Carinthi see Kärnten
55 O5 **Caripe** Monagas, NE Venezuela 10°13′N 63°30′W
55 P5 **Caripito** Monagas, NE Venezuela 10°03′N 63°05′W
15 W7 **Carleton** Québec, SE Canada 48°07′N 66°07′W
31 S10 **Carleton** Michigan, N USA 42°03′N 83°23′W
13 O14 **Carleton, Mount** ▲ New Brunswick, SE Canada 47°10′N 66°54′W
14 L13 **Carleton Place** Ontario, SE Canada 45°08′N 76°09′W
35 V3 **Carlin** Nevada, W USA 40°40′N 116°09′W
30 K14 **Carlinville** Illinois, N USA 39°16′N 89°52′W
97 K14 **Carlisle** anc. Caer Luel, Luguvallium, Luguvallum. NW England, United Kingdom 54°54′N 02°55′W
27 V11 **Carlisle** Arkansas, C USA 34°46′N 91°45′W
31 N15 **Carlisle** Indiana, N USA 38°57′N 87°23′W
29 V14 **Carlisle** Iowa, C USA 41°30′N 93°29′W
21 N5 **Carlisle** Kentucky, S USA 38°19′N 84°02′W
18 F15 **Carlisle** Pennsylvania, NE USA 40°10′N 77°10′W
21 Q11 **Carlisle** South Carolina, SE USA 34°35′N 81°27′W
38 J17 **Carlisle Island** island Aleutian Islands, Alaska, USA
27 R7 **Carl Junction** Missouri, C USA 37°10′N 94°34′W
107 A20 **Carloforte** Sardegna, Italy, C Mediterranean Sea 39°10′N 08°17′E
Carlopago see Karlobag
61 B21 **Carlos Casares** Buenos Aires, E Argentina 35°39′S 61°28′W
61 E18 **Carlos Reyles** Durazno, C Uruguay 33°00′S 56°30′W
61 A21 **Carlos Tejedor** Buenos Aires, E Argentina 35°25′S 62°25′W
97 F19 **Carlow** Ir. Ceatharlach. SE Ireland 52°50′N 06°55′W
97 F19 **Carlow** Ir. Cheatharlach. cultural region SE Ireland
96 F7 **Carloway** NW Scotland, United Kingdom 58°17′N 06°48′W
35 U17 **Carlsbad** California, W USA 33°09′N 117°21′W
37 U15 **Carlsbad** New Mexico, SW USA 32°24′N 104°15′W
Carlsbad see Karlovy Vary
129 N13 **Carlsberg Ridge** undersea feature S Arabian Sea 06°00′N 61°00′E
Carlsruhe see Karlsruhe
29 W6 **Carlton** Minnesota, N USA 46°39′N 92°25′W
11 V17 **Carlyle** Saskatchewan, S Canada 49°39′N 102°18′W
30 L15 **Carlyle** Illinois, N USA 38°36′N 89°22′W
30 L15 **Carlyle Lake** ▣ Illinois, N USA
10 H7 **Carmacks** Yukon Territory, W Canada 62°04′N 136°21′W
106 B9 **Carmagnola** Piemonte, NW Italy 44°50′N 07°43′E
11 X16 **Carman** Manitoba, S Canada 49°32′N 97°59′W
Carmana/Carmania see Kermān
97 I21 **Carmarthen** SW Wales, United Kingdom 51°52′N 04°19′W
97 I21 **Carmarthen** cultural region SW Wales, United Kingdom
97 I22 **Carmarthen Bay** inlet SW Wales, United Kingdom
103 N14 **Carmaux** Tarn, S France 44°03′N 02°09′E
35 N11 **Carmel** California, W USA 36°32′N 121°54′W
31 O13 **Carmel** Indiana, N USA 39°58′N 86°07′W
18 L13 **Carmel** New York, NE USA 41°25′N 73°40′W
97 H18 **Carmel Head** headland NW Wales, United Kingdom 53°24′N 04°35′W
42 E2 **Carmelita** Petén, N Guatemala 17°33′N 90°11′W
61 D19 **Carmelo** Colonia, SW Uruguay 34°00′S 58°20′W
41 V14 **Carmen** var. Ciudad del Carmen. Campeche, SE Mexico 18°38′N 91°50′W
61 A25 **Carmen de Patagones** Buenos Aires, E Argentina 40°45′S 63°00′W
40 F8 **Carmen, Isla** island NW Mexico
40 M5 **Carmen, Sierra del** ▲▲ NW Mexico
30 M16 **Carmi** Illinois, N USA 38°05′N 88°09′W
35 O7 **Carmichael** California, W USA 38°36′N 121°21′W
Carmiel see Karmi'el
25 U11 **Carmine** Texas, SW USA 30°07′N 96°40′W
104 K14 **Carmona** Andalucía, S Spain 37°28′N 05°38′W
Carmona see Uíge
Carnaro see Kvarner
180 G9 **Carnarvon** Western Australia 24°57′S 113°38′E
14 I13 **Carnarvon** Ontario, SE Canada 45°03′N 78°41′W
83 G24 **Carnarvon** Northern Cape, W South Africa 30°59′S 22°08′E
Carnarvon see Caernarfon
180 K9 **Carnarvon Range** ▲▲ Western Australia
Carn Domhnach see Carndonagh
96 E13 **Carndonagh** Ir. Carn Domhnach. NW Ireland 55°15′N 07°15′W
11 V17 **Carnduff** Saskatchewan, S Canada 49°11′N 101°50′W
26 L11 **Carnegie** Oklahoma, C USA 35°06′N 98°36′W
180 L9 **Carnegie, Lake** salt lake Western Australia
193 U8 **Carnegie Ridge** undersea feature E Pacific Ocean 01°00′S 85°00′W
96 H9 **Carn Eige** ▲ N Scotland, United Kingdom 57°18′N 05°04′W
182 F5 **Carnes** South Australia 30°12′S 134°31′E
194 J12 **Carney Island** island Antarctica
18 H16 **Carneys Point** New Jersey, NE USA 39°38′N 75°29′W
Carniche, Alpi see Karnische Alpen
151 Q21 **Car Nicobar** island Nicobar Islands, India, NE Indian Ocean
79 H15 **Carnot** Mambéré-Kadéï, W Central African Republic 04°58′N 15°55′E
182 F10 **Carnot, Cape** headland South Australia 34°57′S 135°39′E
96 K11 **Carnoustie** E Scotland, United Kingdom 56°30′N 02°42′W
97 F20 **Carnsore Point** Ir. Ceann an Chairn. headland SE Ireland 52°10′N 06°22′W
8 H7 **Carnwath** ~ Northwest Territories, NW Canada
31 R8 **Caro** Michigan, N USA 43°29′N 83°24′W
23 Z15 **Carol City** Florida, SE USA 25°56′N 80°15′W
59 L14 **Carolina** Maranhão, E Brazil 07°20′S 47°25′W
45 U5 **Carolina** E Puerto Rico 18°22′N 65°57′W
21 V12 **Carolina Beach** North Carolina, SE USA 34°02′N 77°53′W
Caroline Island see Millennium Island
189 N15 **Caroline Islands** island group C Micronesia
129 Z14 **Caroline Plate** tectonic feature
192 H7 **Caroline Ridge** undersea feature E Philippine Sea 08°00′N 150°00′E
Carolopois see Châlons-en-Champagne
45 V14 **Caroni Arena Dam** ▣ Trinidad, Trinidad and Tobago
Caronie, Monti see Nebrodi, Monti
55 P7 **Caroní, Río** ~ E Venezuela
45 U14 **Caroni River** ~ Trinidad, Trinidad and Tobago
Caronium see A Coruña
54 J4 **Carora** Lara, N Venezuela 10°12′N 70°07′W
86 F12 **Carpathian Mountains** var. Carpathians, Cz./Pol. Karpaty, Ger. Karpaten. ▲▲ E Europe
Carpathians see Carpathian Mountains
Carpathos/Carpathus see Kárpathos
116 H12 **Carpații Meridionali** var. Alpi Transilvaniei, Carpații Sudici, Eng. South Carpathians, Transylvanian Alps, Ger. Südkarpaten, Transsylvanische Alpen, Hung. Déli-Kárpátok, Erdélyi-Havasok. ▲▲ C Romania
Carpații Sudici see Carpații Meridionali
174 L7 **Carpentaria, Gulf of** gulf N Australia
Carpentoracte see Carpentras
103 R14 **Carpentras** anc. Carpentoracte. Vaucluse, SE France 44°03′N 05°03′E
106 F9 **Carpi** Emilia-Romagna, N Italy 44°47′N 10°53′E
116 E11 **Cărpiniș** Hung. Gyertyámos. Timiș, W Romania 45°46′N 20°53′E
35 R14 **Carpinteria** California, W USA 34°24′N 119°30′W
23 S9 **Carrabelle** Florida, SE USA 29°51′N 84°39′W
Carraig Aonair see Fastnet Rock
Carraig Fhearghais see Carrickfergus
Carraig Mhachaire Rois see Carrickmacross
Carraig na Siúire see Carrick-on-Suir
Carrantual see Carrauntoohil
106 E10 **Carrara** Toscana, C Italy 44°05′N 10°07′E
61 F20 **Carrasco** ✈ (Montevideo) Canelones, S Uruguay 34°51′S 56°00′W
105 P9 **Carrascosa del Campo** Castilla-La Mancha, C Spain 40°02′N 02°35′W
54 H4 **Carrasquero** Zulia, NW Venezuela 11°00′N 72°01′W
183 O9 **Carrathool** New South Wales, SE Australia 34°25′S 145°30′E
Carrauntohil see Carrauntoohil
97 B21 **Carrauntoohil** Ir. Carrantual, Carrauntohil, Corrán Tuathail. ▲ SW Ireland 51°98′N 09°53′W
45 Y15 **Carriacou** island N Grenada
97 G15 **Carrickfergus** Ir. Carraig Fhearghais. NE Northern Ireland, United Kingdom 54°43′N 05°49′W
97 F16 **Carrickmacross** Ir. Carraig Mhachaire Rois. N Ireland 53°58′N 06°43′W
97 D16 **Carrick-on-Shannon** Ir. Cora Droma Rúisc. NW Ireland 53°37′N 08°05′W
97 E20 **Carrick-on-Suir** Ir. Carraig na Siúire. S Ireland 52°21′N 07°25′W
182 I7 **Carrieton** South Australia 32°27′S 138°33′E
40 L7 **Carrillo** Chihuahua, N Mexico 25°53′N 103°54′W
29 O4 **Carrington** North Dakota, N USA 47°27′N 99°07′W
104 M4 **Carrión** ~ N Spain
104 M4 **Carrión de los Condes** Castilla-León, N Spain 42°20′N 04°37′W
25 P13 **Carrizo Springs** Texas, SW USA 28°33′N 99°54′W
37 S13 **Carrizozo** New Mexico, SW USA 33°38′N 105°52′W
29 T13 **Carroll** Iowa, C USA 42°04′N 94°52′W
23 N4 **Carrollton** Alabama, S USA 33°13′N 88°05′W
23 R3 **Carrollton** Georgia, SE USA 33°33′N 85°04′W
30 K14 **Carrollton** Illinois, N USA 39°18′N 90°24′W
20 L4 **Carrollton** Kentucky, S USA 38°41′N 85°09′W
31 R8 **Carrollton** Michigan, N USA 43°27′N 83°55′W
27 T3 **Carrollton** Missouri, C USA 39°20′N 93°30′W
31 U12 **Carrollton** Ohio, N USA 40°34′N 81°05′W
25 T6 **Carrollton** Texas, SW USA 32°57′N 96°53′W
11 U14 **Carrot** ~ Saskatchewan, S Canada
11 U14 **Carrot River** Saskatchewan, C Canada 53°18′N 103°32′W
18 J7 **Carry Falls Reservoir** ▣ New York, NE USA
136 L11 **Çarşamba** Samsun, N Turkey 41°13′N 36°43′E
28 L6 **Carson** North Dakota, N USA 46°26′N 101°34′W
35 Q6 **Carson City** state capital Nevada, W USA 39°10′N 119°46′W
35 R6 **Carson River** ~ Nevada, W USA
35 S5 **Carson Sink** salt flat Nevada, W USA
11 Q16 **Carstairs** Alberta, SW Canada 51°35′N 114°02′W
Carstensz, Puntjak see Jaya, Puncak
54 E5 **Cartagena** var. Cartagena de los Indes. Bolívar, NW Colombia 10°24′N 75°33′W
105 R13 **Cartagena** anc. Carthago Nova. Murcia, SE Spain 37°36′N 00°59′W
54 E13 **Cartagena de Chaira** Caquetá, S Colombia 01°19′N 74°52′W
Cartagena de los Indes see Cartagena
54 D10 **Cartago** Valle del Cauca, W Colombia 04°45′N 75°55′W
43 N14 **Cartago** Cartago, C Costa Rica 09°50′N 83°54′W
42 M14 **Cartago** off. Provincia de Cartago. ◐ province C Costa Rica
Cartago, Provincia de see Cartago
25 O11 **Carta Valley** Texas, SW USA 29°46′N 100°37′W
104 F10 **Cartaxo** Santarém, C Portugal 39°10′N 08°47′W
104 I14 **Cartaya** Andalucía, S Spain 37°16′N 07°09′W
Carteret Islands see Tulun Islands
29 S15 **Carter Lake** Iowa, C USA 41°17′N 95°55′W
23 S3 **Cartersville** Georgia, SE USA 34°10′N 84°48′W
185 M14 **Carterton** Wellington, North Island, New Zealand 41°01′S 175°30′E
30 J13 **Carthage** Illinois, N USA 40°25′N 91°09′W
22 L5 **Carthage** Mississippi, S USA 32°43′N 89°31′W
27 R7 **Carthage** Missouri, C USA 37°10′N 94°20′W
18 I8 **Carthage** New York, NE USA 43°58′N 75°36′W
21 T10 **Carthage** North Carolina, SE USA 35°21′N 79°27′W
20 K8 **Carthage** Tennessee, S USA 36°14′N 85°59′W
25 X7 **Carthage** Texas, SW USA 32°10′N 94°21′W

◆ Country ◇ Dependent Territory ◐ Administrative Regions ▲ Mountain ⛰ Volcano ◎ Lake
● Country Capital ○ Dependent Territory Capital ✈ International Airport ▲▲ Mountain Range ~ River ▣ Reservoir

74 *M5* **Carthage** ✈ (Tunis) N Tunisia *36°51′N 10°12′E*
Carthago Nova *see* Cartagena
14 *E10* **Cartier** Ontario, S Canada *46°40′N 81°31′W*
13 *S8* **Cartwright** Newfoundland and Labrador, E Canada *53°40′N 57°W*
55 *P9* **Caruana de Montaña** Bolívar, SE Venezuela *05°16′N 63°12′W*
59 *Q15* **Caruaru** Pernambuco, E Brazil *08°15′S 35°55′W*
55 *P5* **Carúpano** Sucre, NE Venezuela *10°39′N 63°14′W*
Carusbur *see* Cherbourg
58 *M12* **Carutapera** Maranhão, E Brazil *01°12′S 45°57′W*
27 *Y9* **Caruthersville** Missouri, C USA *36°11′N 89°40′W*
103 *O1* **Carvin** Pas-de-Calais, N France *50°31′N 03°00′E*
58 *E12* **Carvoeiro** Amazonas, NW Brazil *01°24′S 61°59′W*
104 *E10* **Carvoeiro, Cabo** *headland* C Portugal *39°19′N 09°27′W*
21 *U9* **Cary** North Carolina, SE USA *35°47′N 78°46′W*
182 *M3* **Caryapundy Swamp** *wetland* New South Wales/ Queensland, SE Australia
74 *F6* **Casablanca** ***Ar.*** Dar-el-Beida. NW Morocco *33°39′N 07°31′W*
60 *M8* **Casa Branca** São Paulo, S Brazil *21°47′S 47°05′W*
36 *L14* **Casa Grande** Arizona, SW USA *32°52′N 111°45′W*
106 *C8* **Casale Monferrato** Piemonte, NW Italy *45°08′N 08°27′E*
106 *E8* **Casalpusterlengo** Lombardia, N Italy *45°10′N 09°37′E*
54 *H10* **Casanare** ***off.*** Intendencia de Casanare. ◈ *province* C Colombia
Casanare, Intendencia de *see* Casanare
55 *P5* **Casanay** Sucre, NE Venezuela *10°30′N 63°25′W*
24 *K11* **Casa Piedra** Texas, SW USA *29°43′N 104°03′W*
107 *Q19* **Casarano** Puglia, SE Italy *40°01′N 18°10′E*
42 *J11* **Casares** Carazo, W Nicaragua *11°37′N 86°19′W*
105 *R10* **Casas Ibáñez** Castilla-La Mancha, C Spain *39°17′N 01°28′W*
61 *I14* **Casca** Rio Grande do Sul, S Brazil *28°39′S 51°55′W*
172 *I17* **Cascade** Mahé, NE Seychelles *04°39′S 55°29′E*
33 *N13* **Cascade** Idaho, NW USA *44°31′N 116°02′W*
29 *Y13* **Cascade** Iowa, C USA *42°18′N 91°00′W*
33 *R9* **Cascade** Montana, NW USA *47°15′N 111°46′W*
185 *B20* **Cascade Point** *headland* South Island, New Zealand *44°00′S 168°23′E*
32 *G13* **Cascade Range** ▲▲ Oregon/ Washington, NW USA
33 *N12* **Cascade Reservoir** ⊠ Idaho, NW USA
0 *E8* **Cascadia Basin** *undersea feature* NE Pacific Ocean *47°00′N 127°30′W*
104 *E11* **Cascais** Lisboa, C Portugal *38°41′N 09°25′W*
15 *W7* **Cascapédia** ≈ Québec, SE Canada
59 *I22* **Cascavel** Ceará, E Brazil *04°10′S 38°15′W*
60 *G11* **Cascavel** Paraná, S Brazil *24°56′S 53°28′W*
106 *I13* **Cascia** Umbria, C Italy *42°45′N 13°01′E*
106 *F11* **Cascina** Toscana, C Italy *43°40′N 10°33′E*
19 *Q8* **Casco Bay** *bay* Maine, NE USA
194 *J7* **Case Island** *island* Antarctica
106 *B8* **Caselle** ✈ (Torino) Piemonte, NW Italy *45°06′N 07°41′E*
107 *K17* **Caserta** Campania, S Italy *41°05′N 14°20′E*
15 *N8* **Casey** Québec, SE Canada *47°50′N 74°09′W*
30 *M14* **Casey** Illinois, N USA *39°18′N 87°59′W*
195 *Y12* **Casey** *Australian research station* Antarctica *65°58′S 111°04′E*
195 *W3* **Casey Bay** *bay* Antarctica
80 *Q11* **Caseyr, Raas** *headland* NE Somalia *11°51′S 51°16′E*
97 *D20* **Cashel** ***Ir.*** Caiseal. S Ireland *52°31′N 07°53′W*
54 *G6* **Casigua** Zulia, W Venezuela *08°46′N 72°30′W*
61 *B19* **Casilda** Santa Fe, C Argentina *33°05′S 61°10′W*
Casim *see* General Toshevo
183 *V4* **Casino** New South Wales, SE Australia *28°50′S 153°02′E*
107 *J16* **Cassino** ***prev.*** San Germano; ***anc.*** Casinum. Lazio, C Italy *41°29′N 13°50′E*
Casinum *see* Cassino
111 *E17* **Čáslav** ***Ger.*** Tschaslau. Střední Čechy, C Czech Republic *49°54′N 15°23′E*
56 *C13* **Casma** Ancash, C Peru *09°30′S 78°18′W*
167 *S7* **Ca, Sông** ≈ N Vietnam
107 *K17* **Casoria** Campania, S Italy *40°54′N 14°28′E*
105 *T6* **Caspe** Aragón, NE Spain *41°14′N 00°03′W*
33 *X15* **Casper** Wyoming, C USA *42°48′N 106°22′W*
84 *M10* **Caspian Depression** ***Kaz.*** Kaspīy Mangy Oypaty, ***Rus.*** Prikaspiyskaya Nizmennost'. *depression* Kazakhstan/Russian Federation
130 *D10* **Caspian Sea** ***Az.*** Xäzär Dänizi, ***Kaz.*** Kaspiy Tengizi, ***Per.*** Baḩr-e Khazar, Daryā-ye Khazar, ***Rus.*** Kaspiyskoye More. *inland sea* Asia/Europe
83 *L14* **Cassacatiza** Tete, NW Mozambique *14°20′S 32°24′E*
Cassai *see* Kasai
82 *F13* **Cassamba** Moxico, E Angola *13°07′S 20°22′E*
107 *N20* **Cassano allo Ionio** Calabria, SE Italy *39°46′N 16°16′E*
31 *S8* **Cass City** Michigan, N USA *43°36′N 83°10′W*
Cassel *see* Kassel
14 *M13* **Casselman** Ontario, SE Canada *45°18′N 75°05′W*
29 *R5* **Casselton** North Dakota, N USA *46°53′N 97°10′W*
59 *M16* **Cássia** ***var.*** Santa Rita de Cassia. Bahia, E Brazil *11°03′S 44°16′W*
10 *J9* **Cassiar** British Columbia, W Canada *59°16′N 129°40′W*
10 *K10* **Cassiar Mountains** ▲▲ British Columbia, W Canada
83 *C15* **Cassinga** Huíla, SW Angola *15°08′S 16°05′E*
29 *T4* **Cass Lake** Minnesota, N USA *47°22′N 94°36′W*
29 *T4* **Cass Lake** ◎ Minnesota, N USA
31 *P10* **Cassopolis** Michigan, N USA *41°56′N 86°00′W*
31 *S8* **Cass River** ≈ Michigan, N USA
27 *S8* **Cassville** Missouri, C USA *36°42′N 93°52′W*
Castamoni *see* Kastamonu
58 *L12* **Castanhal** Pará, NE Brazil *01°16′S 47°55′W*
104 *G8* **Castanheira de Pêra** Leiria, C Portugal *40°01′N 08°12′W*
41 *N7* **Castaños** Coahuila, NE Mexico *26°48′N 101°26′W*
108 *I10* **Castasegna** Graubünden, SE Switzerland *46°21′N 09°30′E*
106 *D8* **Casteggio** Lombardia, N Italy *45°02′N 09°10′E*
107 *K23* **Castelbuono** Sicilia, Italy, C Mediterranean Sea *37°56′N 14°05′E*
107 *K15* **Castel di Sangro** Abruzzo, C Italy *41°46′N 14°03′E*
106 *H7* **Castelfranco Veneto** Veneto, NE Italy *45°40′N 11°55′E*
102 *K14* **Casteljaloux** Lot-et-Garonne, SW France *44°19′N 00°03′E*
107 *L18* **Castellabate** ***var.*** Santa Maria di Castellabate. Campania, S Italy *40°16′N 14°57′E*
107 *I23* **Castellammare del Golfo** Sicilia, Italy, C Mediterranean Sea *38°02′N 12°53′E*
107 *H22* **Castellammare, Golfo di** *gulf* Sicilia, Italy, C Mediterranean Sea
103 *U15* **Castellane** Alpes-de-Haute-Provence, SE France *43°49′N 06°34′E*
107 *O18* **Castellaneta** Puglia, SE Italy *40°38′N 16°57′E*
106 *E9* **Castel l'Arquato** Emilia-Romagna, C Italy *44°52′N 09°51′E*
61 *E21* **Castelli** Buenos Aires, E Argentina *36°07′S 57°47′W*
Castelló de la Plana *see* Castellón de la Plana
105 *S8* **Castellón** ◈ *province* País Valenciano, E Spain
Castellón *see* Castellón de la Plana
105 *T9* **Castellón de la Plana** ***var.*** Castellón, ***Cat.*** Castelló de la Plana. País Valenciano, E Spain *39°59′N 00°03′W*
105 *S7* **Castellote** Aragón, NE Spain *40°46′N 00°18′W*
103 *N16* **Castelnaudary** Aude, S France *43°18′N 01°57′E*
102 *L16* **Castelnau-Magnoac** Hautes-Pyrénées, S France *43°18′N 00°30′E*
106 *F10* **Castelnovo ne' Monti** Emilia-Romagna, C Italy *44°26′N 10°24′E*
Castelnuovo *see* Herceg-Novi
104 *H9* **Castelo Branco** Castelo Branco, C Portugal *39°50′N 07°30′W*
104 *H8* **Castelo Branco** ◈ *district* C Portugal
104 *I10* **Castelo de Vide** Portalegre, C Portugal *39°25′N 07°27′W*
104 *G9* **Castelo do Bode, Barragem do** ⊠ C Portugal
106 *G10* **Castel San Pietro Terme** Emilia-Romagna, C Italy *44°22′N 11°34′E*
107 *B17* **Castelsardo** Sardegna, Italy, C Mediterranean Sea *40°54′N 08°42′E*
102 *M14* **Castelsarrasin** Tarn-et-Garonne, S France *44°02′N 01°06′E*
107 *I24* **Casteltermini** Sicilia, Italy, C Mediterranean Sea *37°33′N 13°38′E*
107 *H24* **Castelvetrano** Sicilia, Italy, C Mediterranean Sea *37°40′N 12°46′E*
182 *L12* **Casterton** Victoria, SE Australia *37°37′S 141°22′E*
102 *J15* **Castets** Landes, SW France *43°55′N 01°08′W*
106 *H12* **Castiglione del Lago** Umbria, C Italy *43°07′N 12°02′E*
106 *F13* **Castiglione della Pescaia** Toscana, C Italy *42°46′N 10°53′E*
106 *F8* **Castiglione delle Stiviere** Lombardia, N Italy *45°24′N 10°31′E*
104 *M9* **Castilla-La Mancha** ◈ *autonomous community* NE Spain
104 *L5* **Castilla-León** ***var.*** Castillia y Leon. ◈ *autonomous community* NW Spain
105 *N10* **Castilla Nueva** *cultural region* C Spain
105 *N6* **Castilla Vieja** ◈ *cultural region* N Spain
Castillia y Leon *see* Castilla-León
Castillo de Locubim *see* Castillo de Locubín
105 *N14* **Castillo de Locubín** ***var.*** Castillo de Locubim. Andalucía, S Spain *37°32′N 03°56′W*
102 *K13* **Castillon-la-Bataille** Gironde, SW France *44°51′N 00°01′W*
63 *I19* **Castillo, Pampa del** *plain* S Argentina
61 *G19* **Castillos** Rocha, SE Uruguay *34°12′S 53°52′W*
97 *B16* **Castlebar** ***Ir.*** Caisleán an Bharraigh. W Ireland *53°52′N 09°17′W*
97 *F16* **Castleblayney** ***Ir.*** Baile na Lorgan. N Ireland *54°07′N 06°44′W*
45 *O11* **Castle Bruce** E Dominica *15°24′N 61°26′W*
36 *M5* **Castle Dale** Utah, W USA *39°10′N 111°02′W*
36 *I14* **Castle Dome Peak** ▲ Arizona, SW USA *33°04′N 114°08′W*
97 *J14* **Castle Douglas** S Scotland, United Kingdom *54°56′N 03°56′W*
97 *E14* **Castlefinn** ***Ir.*** Caisleán na Finne. NW Ireland *54°47′N 07°35′W*
97 *M17* **Castleford** N England, United Kingdom *53°44′N 01°21′W*
11 *O17* **Castlegar** British Columbia, SW Canada *49°18′N 117°48′W*
64 *B12* **Castle Harbour** *inlet* Bermuda, NW Atlantic Ocean
21 *V12* **Castle Hayne** North Carolina, SE USA *34°23′N 78°07′W*
97 *B20* **Castleisland** ***Ir.*** Oileán Ciarral. SW Ireland *52°12′N 09°30′W*
183 *N12* **Castlemaine** Victoria, SE Australia *37°06′S 144°13′E*
37 *R5* **Castle Peak** ▲ Colorado, C USA *39°00′N 106°51′W*
33 *O13* **Castle Peak** ▲ Idaho, NW USA *44°02′N 114°42′W*
184 *N13* **Castlepoint** Wellington, North Island, New Zealand *40°54′S 176°13′E*
97 *D17* **Castlerea** ***Ir.*** An Caisleán Riabhach. W Ireland *53°45′N 08°32′W*
97 *G15* **Castlereagh** ***Ir.*** An Caisleán Riabhach. N Northern Ireland, United Kingdom *54°33′N 05°53′W*
183 *R6* **Castlereagh River** ≈ New South Wales, SE Australia
37 *T5* **Castle Rock** Colorado, C USA *39°22′N 104°51′W*
30 *K7* **Castle Rock Lake** ⊠ Wisconsin, N USA
65 *G25* **Castle Rock Point** *headland* S Saint Helena *16°02′S 05°45′W*
97 *I16* **Castletown** SE Isle of Man *54°05′N 04°39′W*
29 *R9* **Castlewood** South Dakota, N USA *44°43′N 97°01′W*
11 *R15* **Castor** Alberta, SW Canada *52°14′N 111°54′W*
14 *M13* **Castor** ≈ Ontario, SE Canada
27 *X7* **Castor River** ≈ Missouri, C USA
Castra Albiensium *see* Castres
Castra Regina *see* Regensburg
103 *N15* **Castres** ***anc.*** Castra Albiensium. Tarn, S France *43°36′N 02°15′E*
98 *H9* **Castricum** Noord-Holland, W Netherlands *52°33′N 04°40′E*
45 *S11* **Castries** ● (Saint Lucia) N Saint Lucia *14°01′N 60°59′W*
60 *J11* **Castro** Paraná, S Brazil *24°46′S 50°03′W*
63 *F17* **Castro** Los Lagos, W Chile *42°27′S 73°48′W*
104 *H7* **Castro Daire** Viseu, N Portugal *40°54′N 07°55′W*
104 *M13* **Castro del Río** Andalucía, S Spain *37°41′N 04°29′W*
Castrogiovanni *see* Enna
104 *H14* **Castro Marim** Faro, S Portugal *37°13′N 07°26′W*
104 *J2* **Castropol** Asturias, N Spain *43°30′N 07°01′W*
105 *O2* **Castro-Urdiales** ***var.*** Castro Urdiales. Cantabria, N Spain *43°23′N 03°11′W*
104 *G13* **Castro Verde** Beja, S Portugal *37°42′N 08°05′W*
107 *N19* **Castrovillari** Calabria, SW Italy *39°48′N 16°12′E*
35 *N10* **Castroville** California, W USA *36°46′N 121°46′W*
25 *R12* **Castroville** Texas, SW USA *29°21′N 98°52′W*
104 *K11* **Castuera** Extremadura, W Spain *38°44′N 05°33′W*
61 *F19* **Casupá** Florida, S Uruguay *34°09′S 55°38′W*
185 *A22* **Caswell Sound** *sound* South Island, New Zealand
137 *Q13* **Çat** Erzurum, NE Turkey *39°40′N 41°03′E*
42 *K6* **Catacamas** Olancho, C Honduras *14°55′N 85°54′W*
56 *A10* **Catacaos** Piura, NW Peru *05°22′S 80°40′W*
22 *I7* **Catahoula Lake** ◎ Louisiana, S USA
137 *S15* **Çatak** Van, SE Turkey *38°02′N 43°05′E*
137 *S15* **Çatak Çayi** ≈ SE Turkey
114 *O12* **Çatalca** İstanbul, NW Turkey *41°09′N 28°28′E*
114 *O12* **Çatalca Yarimadasi** *physical region* NW Turkey
62 *H6* **Catalina** Antofagasta, N Chile *25°19′S 69°37′W*
Catalonia *see* Cataluña
105 *U5* **Cataluña** ***Cat.*** Catalunya, ***Eng.*** Catalonia. ◈ *autonomous community* N Spain
Catalunya *see* Cataluña
62 *I7* **Catamarca** ***off.*** Provincia de Catamarca. ◈ *province* NW Argentina
Catamarca *see* San Fernando del Valle de Catamarca
Catamarca, Provincia de *see* Catamarca
83 *M16* **Catandica** Manica, C Mozambique *18°05′S 33°10′E*
171 *P4* **Catanduanes Island** *island* N Philippines
60 *K8* **Catanduva** São Paulo, S Brazil *21°05′S 49°00′W*
107 *L24* **Catania** Sicilia, Italy, C Mediterranean Sea *37°31′N 15°04′E*
107 *M24* **Catania, Golfo di** *gulf* Sicilia, Italy, C Mediterranean Sea
45 *U5* **Cataño** ***var.*** Cantaño. E Puerto Rico *18°26′N 66°06′W*
107 *O21* **Catanzaro** Calabria, SW Italy *38°53′N 16°36′E*
107 *O22* **Catanzaro Marina** ***var.*** Marina di Catanzaro. Calabria, S Italy *38°48′N 16°33′E*
Marina di Catanzaro *see* Catanzaro Marina
25 *Q14* **Catarina** Texas, SW USA *28°19′N 99°36′W*
171 *Q5* **Catarman** Samar, C Philippines *12°29′N 124°34′E*
105 *S10* **Catarroja** País Valenciano, E Spain *39°24′N 00°24′W*
21 *R11* **Catawba River** ≈ North Carolina/South Carolina, SE USA
171 *Q5* **Catbalogan** Samar, C Philippines *11°49′N 124°55′E*
14 *I14* **Catchacoma** Ontario, SE Canada *44°43′N 78°19′W*
41 *S15* **Catemaco** Veracruz-Llave, SE Mexico *18°28′N 95°10′W*
Cathair na Mart *see* Westport
Cathair Saidhbhín *see* Caherciveen
31 *P5* **Cat Head Point** *headland* Michigan, N USA *45°11′N 85°37′W*
23 *Q2* **Cathedral Caverns** *cave* Alabama, S USA
35 *V16* **Cathedral City** California, W USA *33°45′N 116°27′W*
24 *K10* **Cathedral Mountain** ▲ Texas, SW USA *30°10′N 103°39′W*
32 *G10* **Cathlamet** Washington, NW USA *46°12′N 123°24′W*
76 *G13* **Catió** S Guinea-Bissau *11°13′N 15°10′W*
55 *O10* **Catisimiña** Bolívar, SE Venezuela *04°07′N 63°40′W*
44 *J3* **Cat Island** *island* C Bahamas
12 *B9* **Cat Lake** Ontario, S Canada *51°47′N 91°52′W*
21 *P5* **Catlettsburg** Kentucky, S USA *38°24′N 82°37′W*
185 *D24* **Catlins** ≈ South Island, New Zealand
35 *R1* **Catnip Mountain** ▲ Nevada, W USA *41°53′N 119°19′W*
41 *Z11* **Catoche, Cabo** *headland* SE Mexico *21°36′N 87°04′W*
27 *P9* **Catoosa** Oklahoma, C USA *36°11′N 95°45′W*
41 *N10* **Catorce** San Luis Potosí, C Mexico *23°42′N 100°49′W*
63 *I14* **Catriel** Río Negro, C Argentina *37°54′S 67°52′W*
62 *K13* **Catriló** La Pampa, C Argentina *36°28′S 63°20′W*
58 *F11* **Catrimani** Roraima, N Brazil *0°24′N 61°30′W*
58 *E10* **Catrimani, Rio** ≈ N Brazil
18 *K11* **Catskill** New York, NE USA *42°13′N 73°52′W*
18 *K11* **Catskill Creek** ≈ New York, NE USA
18 *J11* **Catskill Mountains** ▲▲ New York, NE USA
18 *D11* **Cattaraugus Creek** ≈ New York, NE USA
Cattaro *see* Kotor
Cattaro, Bocche di *see* Kotorska, Boka
107 *I24* **Cattolica Eraclea** Sicilia, Italy, C Mediterranean Sea *37°27′N 13°24′E*
83 *B14* **Catumbela** ≈ W Angola
83 *N14* **Catur** Niassa, N Mozambique *13°50′S 35°43′E*
82 *C10* **Cauale** ≈ NE Angola
171 *O2* **Cauayan** Luzon, N Philippines *16°55′N 121°46′E*
54 *C12* **Cauca** ***off.*** Departamento del Cauca. ◈ *province* SW Colombia
47 *P5* **Cauca** ≈ SE Venezuela
Cauca, Departamento del *see* Cauca
58 *P13* **Caucaia** Ceará, E Brazil *03°44′S 38°45′W*
54 *E7* **Cauca, Río** ≈ N Colombia
54 *E7* **Caucasia** Antioquia, NW Colombia *07°59′N 75°13′W*
137 *Q8* **Caucasus** ***Rus.*** Kavkaz. ▲▲ Georgia/Russian Federation
62 *I10* **Caucete** San Juan, W Argentina *31°38′S 68°16′W*
105 *R11* **Caudete** Castilla-La Mancha, C Spain *38°42′N 01°00′W*
103 *P2* **Caudry** Nord, N France *50°07′N 03°24′E*
82 *D11* **Caungula** Lunda Norte, NE Angola *08°22′S 18°37′E*
62 *G13* **Cauquenes** Maule, C Chile *35°58′S 72°22′W*
55 *N8* **Caura, Río** ≈ C Venezuela
15 *V7* **Causapscal** Québec, SE Canada *48°22′N 67°14′W*
117 *N10* **Căuşeni** ***Rus.*** Kaushany. E Moldova *46°37′N 29°21′E*
102 *M14* **Caussade** Tarn-et-Garonne, S France *44°10′N 01°31′E*
102 *K17* **Cauterets** Hautes-Pyrénées, S France *42°53′N 00°08′W*
10 *J15* **Caution, Cape** *headland* British Columbia, SW Canada *51°10′N 127°43′W*
44 *H7* **Cauto** ≈ E Cuba
Cauvery *see* Kāveri
102 *L3* **Caux, Pays de** *physical region* N France
107 *L18* **Cava de' Tirreni** Campania, S Italy *40°42′N 14°42′E*
104 *G6* **Cávado** ≈ N Portugal
Cavaia *see* Kavajë
103 *R15* **Cavaillon** Vaucluse, SE France *43°51′N 05°01′E*
103 *U16* **Cavalaire-sur-Mer** Var, SE France *43°10′N 06°31′E*
106 *G6* **Cavalese** ***Ger.*** Gablös. Trentino-Alto Adige, N Italy *46°18′N 11°29′E*
29 *Q2* **Cavalier** North Dakota, N USA *48°47′N 97°37′W*
76 *L17* **Cavalla** ***var.*** Cavally, Cavally Fleuve. ≈ Ivory Coast/ Liberia
105 *Y8* **Cavalleria, Cap de** ***var.*** Cabo Caballeria. *headland* Menorca, Spain, W Mediterranean Sea *40°04′N 04°06′E*
184 *K2* **Cavalli Islands** *island group* N New Zealand
Cavally/Cavally Fleuve *see* Cavalla
97 *E16* **Cavan** ***Ir.*** Cabhán. N Ireland *54°N 07°21′W*
97 *E16* **Cavan** ***Ir.*** An Cabhán. *cultural region* N Ireland
106 *H8* **Cavarzare** Veneto, NE Italy *45°08′N 12°05′E*
27 *W9* **Cave City** Arkansas, C USA *35°56′N 91°33′W*
20 *K7* **Cave City** Kentucky, S USA *37°08′N 85°57′W*
65 *M25* **Cave Point** *headland* S Tristan da Cunha
21 *N5* **Cave Run Lake** ⊠ Kentucky, S USA
58 *K11* **Caviana de Fora, Ilha** ***var.*** Ilha Caviana. *island* N Brazil
Caviana, Ilha *see* Caviana de Fora, Ilha
113 *I16* **Cavtat** ***It.*** Ragusavecchia. Dubrovnik-Neretva, SE Croatia *42°36′N 18°13′E*
Cawnpore *see* Kānpur
Caxamarca *see* Cajamarca
58 *A13* **Caxias** Amazonas, W Brazil *04°27′S 71°27′W*
58 *N13* **Caxias** Maranhão, E Brazil *04°53′S 43°20′W*
61 *I15* **Caxias do Sul** Rio Grande do Sul, S Brazil *29°14′S 51°10′W*
42 *J4* **Caxinas, Punta** *headland* N Honduras *16°01′N 86°02′W*
82 *B11* **Caxito** Bengo, NW Angola *08°34′S 13°38′E*
136 *F14* **Çay** Afyon, W Turkey *38°35′N 31°01′E*
40 *L15* **Cayacal, Punta** ***var.*** Punta Mongrove. *headland* S Mexico *17°55′N 102°09′W*
56 *C6* **Cayambe** Pichincha, N Ecuador *0°02′N 78°08′W*
56 *C6* **Cayambe** ▲ N Ecuador *0°00′S 77°58′W*
21 *R12* **Cayce** South Carolina, SE USA *33°58′N 81°04′W*
55 *Y10* **Cayenne** ○ (French Guiana) NE French Guiana *04°55′N 52°18′W*
55 *Y10* **Cayenne** ✈ NE French Guiana *04°55′N 52°18′W*
44 *K10* **Cayes** ***var.*** Les Cayes. SW Haiti *18°10′N 73°48′W*
45 *U6* **Cayey** C Puerto Rico *18°06′N 66°11′W*
45 *U6* **Cayey, Sierra de** ▲▲ E Puerto Rico
103 *N14* **Caylus** Tarn-et-Garonne, S France *44°13′N 01°42′E*
44 *E8* **Cayman Brac** *island* E Cayman Islands
44 *D8* **Cayman Islands** ◇ *UK dependent territory* W West Indies
64 *D11* **Cayman Trench** *undersea feature* NW Caribbean Sea *19°00′N 80°00′W*
47 *O3* **Cayman Trough** *undersea feature* NW Caribbean Sea *18°00′N 81°00′W*
80 *O13* **Caynabo** Sool, N Somalia *08°55′N 46°28′E*
42 *F3* **Cayo** ◈ *district* SW Belize
Cayo *see* San Ignacio
43 *N9* **Cayos Guerrero** *reef* E Nicaragua
43 *O9* **Cayos King** *reef* E Nicaragua
44 *E4* **Cay Sal** *islet* SW Bahamas
14 *G16* **Cayuga** Ontario, S Canada *42°57′N 79°49′W*
25 *V8* **Cayuga** Texas, SW USA *31°55′N 95°57′W*
18 *G10* **Cayuga Lake** ◎ New York, NE USA
104 *K13* **Cazalla de la Sierra** Andalucía, S Spain *37°56′N 05°46′W*
116 *L14* **Căzănești** Ialomița, SE Romania *44°36′N 27°03′E*
102 *M16* **Cazères** Haute-Garonne, S France *43°15′N 01°11′E*
112 *E10* **Cazin** ◈ Federacija Bosna I Hercegovina, NW Bosnia and Herzegovina
82 *G13* **Cazombo** Moxico, E Angola *11°54′S 22°56′E*
105 *O13* **Cazorla** Andalucía, S Spain *37°55′N 03°W*
Cazza *see* Sušac
104 *L4* **Cea** ≈ NW Spain
Ceadâr-Lunga *see* Ciadîr-Lunga
Ceanannas *see* Kells
Ceann Toirc *see* Kanturk
58 *O13* **Ceará** ***off.*** Estado do Ceará. ◈ *state* C Brazil
Ceará *see* Fortaleza
Ceara Abyssal Plain *see* Ceará Plain
Ceará, Estado do *see* Ceará
59 *Q14* **Ceará Mirim** Rio Grande do Norte, E Brazil *05°30′S 35°51′W*
64 *J13* **Ceará Plain** ***var.*** Ceara Abyssal Plain. *undersea feature* W Atlantic Ocean *0°00 36°30′W*
64 *I13* **Ceará Ridge** *undersea feature* C Atlantic Ocean
Ceatharlach *see* Carlow
43 *Q17* **Cébaco, Isla** *island* SW Panama
40 *K7* **Ceballos** Durango, C Mexico *26°33′N 104°07′W*
61 *G19* **Cebollatí** Rocha, E Uruguay *33°15′S 53°46′W*
61 *G19* **Cebollatí, Río** ≈ E Uruguay
105 *P5* **Cebollera** ▲ N Spain *42°01′N 02°40′W*
104 *M8* **Cebreros** Castilla-León, N Spain *40°27′N 04°28′W*
171 *P6* **Cebu** ***off.*** Cebu City. Cebu, C Philippines *10°17′N 123°46′E*
171 *P6* **Cebu** *island* C Philippines
Cebu City *see* Cebu
107 *J16* **Ceccano** Lazio, C Italy *41°34′N 13°20′E*
Čechy *see* Bohemia
106 *F12* **Cecina** Toscana, C Italy *43°19′N 10°31′E*
26 *K4* **Cedar Bluff Reservoir** ⊠ Kansas, C USA
30 *M8* **Cedarburg** Wisconsin, N USA *43°18′N 87°58′W*
36 *J7* **Cedar City** Utah, W USA *37°40′N 113°03′W*
25 *T11* **Cedar Creek** Texas, SW USA *30°04′N 97°30′W*
28 *L7* **Cedar Creek** ≈ North Dakota, N USA
25 *U7* **Cedar Creek Reservoir** ⊠ Texas, SW USA
29 *W13* **Cedar Falls** Iowa, C USA *42°31′N 92°27′W*
31 *N8* **Cedar Grove** Wisconsin, N USA *43°31′N 87°48′W*
21 *Y6* **Cedar Island** *island* Virginia, NE USA
23 *U11* **Cedar Key** Cedar Keys, Florida, SE USA *29°08′N 83°03′W*
23 *U11* **Cedar Keys** *island group* Florida, SE USA
11 *V14* **Cedar Lake** ◎ Manitoba, C Canada
14 *I11* **Cedar Lake** ◎ Ontario, SE Canada
24 *M6* **Cedar Lake** ◎ Texas, SW USA
29 *X13* **Cedar Rapids** Iowa, C USA *41°58′N 91°40′W*
29 *X14* **Cedar River** ≈ Iowa/ Minnesota, C USA
29 *O14* **Cedar River** ≈ Nebraska, C USA
31 *P8* **Cedar Springs** Michigan, N USA *43°13′N 85°33′W*
23 *R3* **Cedartown** Georgia, SE USA *34°00′N 85°16′W*
27 *O7* **Cedar Vale** Kansas, C USA *37°06′N 96°30′W*
35 *Q2* **Cedarville** California, W USA *41°30′N 120°10′W*
104 *H1* **Cedeira** Galicia, NW Spain *43°40′N 08°03′W*
42 *H8* **Cedeño** Choluteca, S Honduras *13°10′N 87°25′W*
41 *N10* **Cedral** San Luis Potosí, C Mexico *23°47′N 100°40′W*
42 *I6* **Cedros** Francisco Morazán, C Honduras *14°38′N 86°42′W*
40 *M9* **Cedros** Zacatecas, C Mexico *24°39′N 101°47′W*
40 *B5* **Cedros, Isla** *island* W Mexico
193 *R5* **Cedros Trench** *undersea feature* E Pacific Ocean *27°45′N 115°45′W*
182 *E7* **Ceduna** South Australia *32°09′S 133°43′E*
110 *D10* **Cedynia** ***Ger.*** Zehden. Zachodnio-pomorskie, W Poland *52°54′N 14°15′E*
80 *P12* **Ceelaayo** Sanaag, N Somalia *11°18′N 49°20′E*
81 *O16* **Ceel Buur** ***It.*** El Bur. Galguduud, C Somalia *04°36′N 46°33′E*
81 *N15* **Ceel Dheere** ***var.*** Ceel Dher, ***It.*** El Dere. Galguduud, C Somalia *05°18′N 46°07′E*
Ceel Dher *see* Ceel Dheere
81 *P14* **Ceel Xamure** Mudug, E Somalia *07°15′N 48°55′E*
80 *O12* **Ceerigaabo** ***var.*** Erigabo, Erigavo. Sanaag, N Somalia *10°34′N 47°22′E*
107 *J23* **Cefalù** ***anc.*** Cephaloedium. Sicilia, Italy, C Mediterranean Sea *38°02′N 14°02′E*
105 *N6* **Cega** ≈ N Spain
111 *K23* **Cegléd** ***prev.*** Czegléd. Pest, C Hungary *47°10′N 19°47′E*
113 *N18* **Čegrane** W FYR Macedonia *41°50′N 20°59′E*
105 *Q13* **Cehegín** Murcia, SE Spain *38°04′N 01°48′W*
136 *K12* **Çekerek** Yozgat, N Turkey *40°04′N 35°30′E*
146 *B13* **Çekiçler** ***Rus.*** Chekishlyar, ***Turkm.*** Chekichler. Balkan Welaýaty, W Turkmenistan *37°35′N 53°52′E*
107 *J15* **Celano** Abruzzo, C Italy *42°06′N 13°33′E*
104 *H4* **Celanova** Galicia, NW Spain *42°09′N 07°58′W*
42 *F6* **Celaque, Cordillera de** ▲▲ W Honduras
41 *N13* **Celaya** Guanajuato, C Mexico *20°32′N 100°48′W*
Celebes *see* Sulawesi
192 *F7* **Celebes Basin** *undersea feature* SE South China Sea *04°00′N 122°00′E*
192 *F7* **Celebes Sea** ***Ind.*** Laut Sulawesi. *sea* Indonesia/ Philippines
41 *W12* **Celestún** Yucatán, E Mexico *20°50′N 90°22′W*
31 *Q12* **Celina** Ohio, N USA *40°34′N 84°35′W*
20 *L8* **Celina** Tennessee, S USA *36°32′N 85°30′W*
25 *U5* **Celina** Texas, SW USA *33°19′N 96°46′W*
112 *G11* **Čelinac Donji** Republika Srpska, N Bosnia and Herzegovina *44°43′N 17°19′E*
109 *V10* **Celje** ***Ger.*** Cilli. C Slovenia *46°16′N 15°14′E*
111 *G23* **Celldömölk** Vas, W Hungary *47°16′N 17°10′E*
100 *J12* **Celle** ***var.*** Zelle. Niedersachsen, N Germany *52°38′N 10°05′E*
99 *D19* **Celles** Hainaut, SW Belgium *50°42′N 03°25′E*
104 *I7* **Celorico da Beira** Guarda, N Portugal *40°38′N 07°24′W*
Celovec *see* Klagenfurt
64 *M7* **Celtic Sea** ***Ir.*** An Mhuir Cheilteach. *sea* SW British Isles
64 *N7* **Celtic Shelf** *undersea feature* E Atlantic Ocean *07°00′W 49°15′N*
114 *L13* **Çeltik Gölu** ◎ NW Turkey
146 *J17* **Çemenibit** ***prev. Rus.*** Chemenibit. Mary Welaýaty, S Turkmenistan *35°27′N 62°19′E*
113 *M14* **Čemerno** ▲▲ C Serbia
105 *Q12* **Cenajo, Embalse del** ⊠ S Spain
171 *V13* **Cenderawasih, Teluk** ***var.*** Teluk Irian, Teluk Sarera. *bay* W Pacific Ocean
105 *P4* **Cenicero** La Rioja, N Spain *42°29′N 02°38′W*
106 *E9* **Ceno** ≈ NW Italy
102 *K13* **Cenon** Gironde, SW France *44°51′N 00°33′W*
14 *K13* **Centennial Lake** ◎ Ontario, SE Canada
Centennial State *see* Colorado
37 *S7* **Center** Colorado, C USA *37°45′N 106°06′W*
29 *Q13* **Center** Nebraska, C USA *42°33′N 97°51′W*
28 *M5* **Center** North Dakota, N USA *47°07′N 101°18′W*
25 *X8* **Center** Texas, SW USA *31°49′N 94°10′W*
29 *W8* **Center City** Minnesota, N USA *45°25′N 92°48′W*
36 *L5* **Centerfield** Utah, W USA *39°07′N 111°49′W*
20 *K9* **Center Hill Lake** ⊠ Tennessee, S USA
29 *X13* **Center Point** Iowa, C USA *42°11′N 91°47′W*
25 *R11* **Center Point** Texas, SW USA *29°56′N 99°01′W*
29 *W16* **Centerville** Iowa, C USA *40°47′N 92°51′W*
27 *W7* **Centerville** Missouri, C USA *37°27′N 91°01′W*
29 *R12* **Centerville** South Dakota, N USA *43°07′N 96°57′W*
20 *I9* **Centerville** Tennessee, S USA *35°45′N 87°29′W*
25 *V9* **Centerville** Texas, SW USA *31°17′N 95°59′W*
40 *M5* **Centinela, Picacho del** ▲ NE Mexico *29°07′N 102°40′W*
106 *G9* **Cento** Emilia-Romagna, N Italy *44°43′N 11°16′E*
Centrafricaine, République *see* Central African Republic
39 *S8* **Central** Alaska, USA *65°34′N 144°48′W*
37 *P15* **Central** New Mexico, SW USA *32°46′N 108°09′W*
83 *H18* **Central** ◈ *district* E Botswana
138 *E10* **Central** ◈ *district* C Israel
81 *I19* **Central** ◈ *province* C Kenya
82 *M13* **Central** ◈ *region* C Malawi
153 *P12* **Central** ◈ *zone* C Nepal
186 *E9* **Central** ◈ *province* S Papua New Guinea
63 *I21* **Central** ◈ *department* C Paraguay
186 *E9* **Central** ***off.*** Central Province. ◈ *province* S Solomon Islands
155 *K25* **Central** ◈ *province* C Sri Lanka
83 *J14* **Central** ◈ *province* C Zambia
117 *P11* **Central** ✈ (Odesa) Odes'ka Oblast', SW Ukraine *46°26′N 30°41′E*
Central *see* Centre
79 *H14* **Central African Republic** ***var.*** République Centrafricaine, ***abbrev.*** CAR; ***prev.*** Ubangi-Shari, Oubangui-Chari, Territoire de l'Oubangui-Chari. ◆ *republic* C Africa
192 *C6* **Central Basin Trough** *undersea feature* W Pacific Ocean *16°45′N 130°00′E*
Central Borneo *see* Kalimantan Tengah
149 *P12* **Central Brāhui Range** ▲▲ W Pakistan
Central Celebes *see* Sulawesi Tengah
29 *Y13* **Central City** Iowa, C USA *42°12′N 91°31′W*
20 *I6* **Central City** Kentucky, S USA *37°17′N 87°07′W*
29 *P15* **Central City** Nebraska, C USA *41°04′N 97°59′W*
48 *D6* **Central, Cordillera** ▲▲ W Bolivia
54 *D11* **Central, Cordillera** ▲▲ W Colombia
42 *M13* **Central, Cordillera** ▲▲ C Costa Rica
45 *N9* **Central, Cordillera** ▲▲ C Dominican Republic
43 *R16* **Central, Cordillera** ▲▲ C Panama
45 *S6* **Central, Cordillera** ▲▲ Puerto Rico
42 *H7* **Central District** ***var.*** Tegucigalpa. ◈ *district* C Honduras
81 *E16* **Central Equatoria** ***var.*** Bahr el Gebel, Bahr el Jebel. ◈ *state* S Sudan
Central Group *see* Inner Islands
30 *L15* **Centralia** Illinois, N USA *38°31′N 89°07′W*
27 *U4* **Centralia** Missouri, C USA *39°12′N 92°08′W*
32 *G9* **Centralia** Washington, NW USA *46°43′N 122°57′W*
Central Indian Ridge *see* Mid-Indian Ridge
Central Java *see* Jawa Tengah
Central Kalimantan *see* Kalimantan Tengah
148 *L14* **Central Makrān Range** ▲▲ W Pakistan
192 *K7* **Central Pacific Basin** *undersea feature* C Pacific Ocean *05°00′N 175°00′W*
59 *M19* **Central, Planalto** ***var.*** Brazilian Highlands. ▲▲ E Brazil
32 *F15* **Central Point** Oregon, NW USA *42°22′N 122°55′W*
Central Province *see* Central
Central Provinces and Berar *see* Madhya Pradesh
186 *B6* **Central Range** ▲▲ NW Papua New Guinea
Central Russian Upland *see* Srednerusskaya Vozvyshennost'
Central Siberian Plateau/ Central Siberian Uplands *see* Srednesibirskoye Ploskogor'ye
104 *K8* **Central, Sistema** ▲▲ C Spain
Central Sulawesi *see* Sulawesi Tengah
35 *N3* **Central Valley** California, W USA *40°39′N 122°21′W*
35 *P8* **Central Valley** *valley* California, W USA
23 *Q3* **Centre** Alabama, S USA *34°09′N 85°40′W*
79 *E15* **Centre** ***Eng.*** Central. ◈ *province* C Cameroon
102 *M8* **Centre** ◈ *region* N France
173 *Y16* **Centre de Flacq** E Mauritius *20°12′S 57°43′E*
55 *Y9* **Centre Spatial Guyanais** *space station* N French Guiana
23 *O5* **Centreville** Alabama, S USA *32°58′N 87°08′W*
21 *X3* **Centreville** Maryland, NE USA *39°03′N 76°04′W*
22 *J7* **Centreville** Mississippi, S USA *31°05′N 91°04′W*
Centum Cellae *see* Civitavecchia
160 *M14* **Cenxi** Guangxi Zhuangzu Zizhiqu, S China *22°58′N 111°00′E*
Ceos *see* Tziá
Cephaloedium *see* Cefalù
112 *I9* **Čepin** ***Hung.*** Csepén. Osijek-Baranja, E Croatia *45°32′N 18°33′E*
Ceram *see* Seram, Pulau
171 *R13* **Ceram Sea** ***Ind.*** Laut Seram. *sea* E Indonesia
192 *G8* **Ceram Trough** *undersea feature* W Pacific Ocean
Cerasus *see* Giresun
36 *I10* **Cerbat Mountains** ▲▲ Arizona, SW USA
103 *P17* **Cerbère, Cap** *headland* S France *42°28′N 03°15′E*
104 *F13* **Cercal do Alentejo** Setúbal, S Portugal *37°48′N 08°40′W*
111 *A18* **Čerchov** ***Ger.*** Czerkow. ▲ W Czech Republic *49°24′N 12°47′E*
103 *O13* **Cère** ≈ C France
61 *A16* **Ceres** Santa Fe, C Argentina *29°55′S 61°55′W*
59 *K18* **Ceres** Goiás, C Brazil *15°21′S 49°34′W*
Ceresio *see* Lugano, Lago di
103 *O17* **Céret** Pyrénées-Orientales, S France *42°30′N 02°44′E*
54 *E6* **Cereté** Córdoba, NW Colombia *08°54′N 75°51′W*
172 *I17* **Cerf, Île au** *island* Inner Islands, NE Seychelles
99 *G22* **Cerfontaine** Namur, S Belgium *50°08′N 04°25′E*
Cergy-Pontoise *see* Pontoise
107 *N16* **Cerignola** Puglia, SE Italy *41°17′N 15°53′E*
Cerigo *see* Kýthira
103 *O9* **Cérilly** Allier, C France *46°38′N 02°51′E*
136 *I11* **Çerkeş** Çankin, N Turkey *40°51′N 32°52′E*
136 *D10* **Çerkezköy** Tekirdağ, NW Turkey *41°17′N 28°00′E*
109 *T12* **Cerknica** ***Ger.*** Zirknitz. SW Slovenia *45°48′N 14°21′E*
109 *S11* **Cerkno** W Slovenia *46°07′N 13°58′E*
116 *F10* **Cermei** ***Hung.*** Csermő. Arad, W Romania *46°33′N 21°51′E*

◆ Country
● Country Capital
◇ Dependent Territory
○ Dependent Territory Capital
◈ Administrative Regions
✈ International Airport
▲ Mountain
▲▲ Mountain Range
Volcano
≈ River
◎ Lake
⊠ Reservoir

137 O15 **Çermik** Dıyarbakır, SE Turkey 38°09′N 39°27′E
112 I10 **Cerna** Vukovar-Srijem, E Croatia 45°10′N 18°36′E
Cernăuţi see Chernivtsi
116 M14 **Cernavodă** Constanţa, SW Romania 44°20′N 28°03′E
103 U7 **Cernay** Haut-Rhin, NE France 47°49′N 07°11′E
Černice see Schwarzach
41 O8 **Cerralvo** Nuevo León, NE Mexico 26°10′N 99°40′W
40 G9 **Cerralvo, Isla** island NW Mexico
107 L16 **Cerreto Sannita** Campania, S Italy 41°17′N 14°39′E
113 L20 **Cërrik** var. Cerriku. Elbasan, C Albania 41°01′N 19°55′E
Cerriku see Cërrik
41 O11 **Cerritos** San Luis Potosí, C Mexico 22°25′N 100°16′W
60 K11 **Cerro Azul** Paraná, S Brazil 24°48′S 49°14′W
61 F18 **Cerro Chato** Treinta y Tres, E Uruguay 33°04′S 55°08′W
61 F19 **Cerro Colorado** Florida, S Uruguay 33°52′S 55°33′W
56 E13 **Cerro de Pasco** Pasco, C Peru 10°43′S 76°15′W
61 G14 **Cêrro Largo** Rio Grande do Sul, S Brazil 28°10′S 54°43′W
61 G18 **Cerro Largo** ◐ department NE Uruguay
42 E7 **Cerrón Grande, Embalse** ⊠ N El Salvador
63 I14 **Cerros Colorados, Embalse** ◎ W Argentina
105 V5 **Cervera** Cataluña, NE Spain 41°40′N 01°16′E
104 M3 **Cervera del Pisuerga** Castilla-León, N Spain 42°51′N 04°30′W
105 Q5 **Cervera del Río Alhama** La Rioja, N Spain 42°01′N 01°58′W
107 H15 **Cerveteri** Lazio, C Italy 42°00′N 12°06′E
106 H10 **Cervia** Emilia-Romagna, N Italy 44°14′N 12°22′E
106 J7 **Cervignano del Friuli** Friuli-Venezia Giulia, NE Italy 45°49′N 13°18′E
107 L17 **Cervinara** Campania, S Italy 41°02′N 14°36′E
Cervinia see Breuil-Cervinia
106 B6 **Cervino, Monte** var. Matterhorn. ▲ Italy/Switzerland 46°00′N 07°39′E see also Matterhorn
Cervino, Monte see Matterhorn
103 Y14 **Cervione** Corse, France, C Mediterranean Sea 42°22′N 09°28′E
104 I1 **Cervo** Galicia, NW Spain 43°39′N 07°25′W
54 F5 **Cesar** off. Departamento del Cesar. ◐ province N Colombia
Cesar, Departamento del see Cesar
106 H10 **Cesena** anc. Caesena. Emilia-Romagna, N Italy 44°09′N 12°14′E
106 I10 **Cesenatico** Emilia-Romagna, N Italy 44°12′N 12°24′E
118 H8 **Cēsis** Ger. Wenden. Cēsis, C Latvia 57°19′N 25°17′E
111 D15 **Česká Lípa** Ger. Böhmisch-Leipa. Liberecký Kraj, N Czech Republic 50°43′N 14°35′E
Česká Republika see Czech Republic
111 F17 **Česká Třebová** Ger. Böhmisch-Trübau. Pardubický Kraj, C Czech Republic 49°54′N 16°27′E
111 D19 **České Budějovice** Ger. Budweis. Jihočeský Kraj, S Czech Republic 48°58′N 14°29′E
111 D19 **České Velenice** Jihočeský Kraj, S Czech Republic 48°49′N 14°57′E
111 E18 **Českomoravská Vrchovina** var. Českomoravská Vysočina, Eng. Bohemian-Moravian Highlands, Ger. Böhmisch-Mährische Höhe. ▲▲ S Czech Republic
Českomoravská Vysočina see Českomoravská Vrchovina
111 C19 **Český Krumlov** var. Böhmisch-Krumau, Ger. Krummau. Jihočeský Kraj, S Czech Republic 48°48′N 14°18′E
Český Les see Bohemian Forest
112 F8 **Česma** ≈ N Croatia
136 A14 **Çeşme** İzmir, W Turkey 38°19′N 26°20′E
Cess see Cestos
183 T8 **Cessnock** New South Wales, SE Australia 32°51′S 151°21′E
76 K17 **Cestos** var. Cess. ≈ S Liberia
118 I9 **Cesvaine** Madona, E Latvia 56°58′N 26°15′E
116 G14 **Cetate** Dolj, SW Romania 44°06′N 23°01′E
Cetatea Albă see Bilhorod-Dnistrovs'kyy
Cetatea Damboviţei see Bucureşti
113 J17 **Cetinje** It. Cettigne. S Montenegro 42°23′N 18°55′E
107 N20 **Cetraro** Calabria, S Italy 39°30′N 15°59′E
Cette see Sète
188 A17 **Cetti Bay** bay SW Guam
Cettigne see Cetinje
104 L17 **Ceuta** var. Sebta. Ceuta, Spain, N Africa 35°53′N 05°19′W
88 C16 **Ceuta** enclave Spain, N Africa
106 B9 **Ceva** Piemonte, NE Italy 44°24′N 08°01′E
103 P14 **Cévennes** ▲▲ S France
108 G10 **Cevio** Ticino, S Switzerland 46°18′N 08°36′E
136 K16 **Ceyhan** Adana, S Turkey 37°02′N 35°48′E
136 K17 **Ceyhan Nehri** ≈ S Turkey
137 P17 **Ceylanpınar** Şanlıurfa, SE Turkey 36°53′N 40°02′E
Ceylon see Sri Lanka
173 R6 **Ceylon Plain** undersea feature N Indian Ocean 04°00′S 82°00′E
Ceyre to the Caribs see Marie-Galante
103 Q14 **Cèze** ≈ S France
Chaacha see Çäçe
127 P6 **Chaadayevka** Penzenskaya Oblast', W Russian Federation 53°07′N 45°55′E
167 O12 **Cha-Am** Phetchaburi, SW Thailand 12°48′N 99°58′E
143 W15 **Chābahār** var. Chāh Bahār, Chahbar. Sīstān va Balūchestān, SE Iran 25°21′N 60°38′E
Chabaricha see Khabarikha
61 B19 **Chabas** Santa Fe, C Argentina 33°16′S 61°23′W
103 T10 **Chablais** physical region E France
61 B20 **Chacabuco** Buenos Aires, E Argentina 34°40′S 60°27′W
42 K8 **Chachagón, Cerro** ▲ N Nicaragua 13°18′N 85°39′W
56 C10 **Chachapoyas** Amazonas, NW Peru 06°13′S 77°54′W
Chäche see Çäçe
119 O18 **Chachersk** Rus. Chechersk. Homyel'skaya Voblasts', SE Belarus 52°54′N 30°54′E
119 N16 **Chachevichy** Rus. Chechevichi. Mahilyowskaya Voblasts', E Belarus 53°31′N 29°51′E
61 B14 **Chaco** off. Provincia de Chaco. ◐ province NE Argentina
Chaco see Gran Chaco
62 M6 **Chaco Austral** physical region N Argentina
62 M3 **Chaco Boreal** physical region N Paraguay
62 M6 **Chaco Central** physical region N Argentina
39 Y15 **Chacon, Cape** headland Prince of Wales Island, Alaska, USA 54°41′N 132°00′W
Chaco, Provincia de see Chaco
78 H9 **Chad** off. Republic of Chad, Fr. Tchad. ◆ republic C Africa
122 K14 **Chadan** Respublika Tyva, S Russian Federation 51°16′N 91°25′E
21 U12 **Chadbourn** North Carolina, SE USA 34°19′N 78°49′W
83 L14 **Chadiza** Eastern, E Zambia 14°04′S 32°27′E
67 Q7 **Chad, Lake** Fr. Lac Tchad. ◎ C Africa
Chad, Republic of see Chad
28 J12 **Chadron** Nebraska, C USA 42°48′N 102°57′W
Chadyr-Lunga see Ciadîr-Lunga
163 W14 **Chaeryŏng** SW North Korea 38°22′N 125°35′E
105 P17 **Chafarinas, Islas** island group S Spain
27 Y7 **Chaffee** Missouri, C USA 37°10′N 89°39′W
148 L12 **Chāgai Hills** var. Chāh Gay. ▲▲ Afghanistan/Pakistan
123 Q11 **Chagda** Respublika Sakha (Yakutiya), NE Russian Federation 58°43′N 130°38′E
Chaghasarāy see Asadābād
149 N5 **Chaghcharān** var. Chakhcharan, Cheghcheran, Qala Āhangarān. Ghowr, C Afghanistan 34°28′N 65°18′E
103 R9 **Chagny** Saône-et-Loire, C France 46°54′N 04°45′E
173 Q7 **Chagos Archipelago** var. Oil Islands. island group British Indian Ocean Territory
129 O15 **Chagos Bank** undersea feature C Indian Ocean 06°15′S 72°00′E
129 O14 **Chagos-Laccadive Plateau** undersea feature N Indian Ocean 03°00′S 73°00′E
173 Q7 **Chagos Trench** undersea feature N Indian Ocean 07°00′S 73°30′E
43 T14 **Chagres, Río** ≈ C Panama
45 U14 **Chaguanas** Trinidad, Trinidad and Tobago 10°31′N 61°25′W
54 M6 **Chaguaramas** Guárico, N Venezuela 09°23′N 66°18′W
Chagyl see Çagyl
Chahār Maḩāll and Bakhtīyārī see Chahār Maḩall va Bakhtīārī
142 M9 **Chahār Maḩall va Bakhtīārī** off. Ostān-e Chahār Maḩall va Bakhtīārī, var. Chahārmahāl and Bakhtīyārī. ◐ province SW Iran
Chahār Maḩall va Bakhtīārī, Ostān-e see Chahār Maḩall va Bakhtīārī
Chāh Bahār/Chahbar see Chābahār
143 V13 **Chāh Derāz** Sīstān va Balūchestān, SE Iran 27°07′N 60°01′E
Chāh Gay see Chāgai Hills
167 P10 **Chai Badan** Lop Buri, C Thailand 15°08′N 101°03′E
153 Q16 **Chāībāsa** Jhārkhand, N India 22°31′N 85°50′E
79 E19 **Chaillu, Massif du** ▲ C Gabon
167 O10 **Chai Nat** var. Chainat, Jainat, Jayanath. Chai Nat, C Thailand 15°10′N 100°10′E
Chainat see Chai Nat
65 M14 **Chain Fracture Zone** tectonic feature E Atlantic Ocean
173 N5 **Chain Ridge** undersea feature W Indian Ocean 06°00′N 54°00′E
Chairn, Ceann an see Carnsore Point
158 L5 **Chaiwopu** Xinjiang Uygur Zizhiqu, W China 43°32′N 87°55′E
167 Q10 **Chaiyaphum** var. Jayabum. Chaiyaphum, C Thailand 15°46′N 101°55′E
62 N10 **Chajarí** Entre Ríos, E Argentina 30°45′S 57°57′W
42 C5 **Chajul** Quiché, W Guatemala 15°28′N 91°02′W
83 K16 **Chakari** Mashonaland West, N Zimbabwe 18°05′S 29°51′E
81 K22 **Chake Chake** Pemba South, E Tanzania 05°12′S 39°44′E
148 J9 **Chakhānsūr** Nīmrūz, SW Afghanistan 31°11′N 62°06′E
Chakhānsūr see Nīmrūz
Chakhcharan see Chaghcharān
149 V8 **Chak Jhumra** var. Jhumra. Punjab, E Pakistan 31°33′N 73°14′E
146 I16 **Chaknakdysonga** Ahal Welaýaty, S Turkmenistan 35°39′N 61°24′E
153 P16 **Chakradharpur** Jhārkhand, N India 22°42′N 85°38′E
152 J8 **Chakrāta** Uttarakhand, N India 30°42′N 77°52′E
149 U7 **Chakwāl** Punjab, NE Pakistan 32°56′N 72°53′E
57 F17 **Chala** Arequipa, SW Peru 15°52′S 74°13′W
102 K12 **Chalais** Charente, W France 45°16′N 00°02′E
108 D10 **Chalais** Valais, SW Switzerland 46°18′N 07°37′E
115 J20 **Chalándri** var. Halandri; prev. Khalándrion. prehistoric site Sýros, Kykládes, Greece, Aegean Sea
188 H6 **Chalan Kanoa** Saipan, S Northern Mariana Islands 15°08′S 145°43′E
188 C16 **Chalan Pago** C Guam
Chalap Dalam/Chalap Dalan see Chehel Abdālān, Kūh-e
42 F7 **Chalatenango** Chalatenango, N El Salvador 14°04′N 88°53′W
42 A9 **Chalatenango** ◐ department NW El Salvador
83 P15 **Chalaua** Nampula, NE Mozambique 16°04′S 39°08′E
81 I16 **Chalbi Desert** desert N Kenya
42 D7 **Chalchuapa** Santa Ana, W El Salvador 13°59′N 89°41′W
Chalcidice see Chalkidikí
Chalcis see Chalkída
Chāldarān see Siāh Chashmeh
103 N6 **Châlette-sur-Loing** Loiret, C France 48°01′N 02°45′E
15 X8 **Chaleur Bay** Fr. Baie des Chaleurs. bay New Brunswick/Québec, E Canada
Chaleurs, Baie des see Chaleur Bay
57 G16 **Chalhuanca** Apurímac, S Peru 14°17′S 73°15′W
154 F12 **Chālisgaon** Mahārāshtra, C India 20°29′N 75°10′E
115 N23 **Chálki** island Dodekánisa, Greece, Aegean Sea
115 F16 **Chalkiádes** Thessalía, C Greece 39°24′N 22°25′E
115 H18 **Chalkída** var. Halkida, prev. Khalkís; anc. Chalcis. Evvoia, E Greece 38°27′N 23°38′E
115 G14 **Chalkidikí** var. Khalkidhikí; anc. Chalcidice. peninsula NE Greece
185 A24 **Chalky Inlet** inlet South Island, New Zealand
39 S7 **Chalkyitsik** Alaska, USA 66°39′N 143°43′W
102 I9 **Challans** Vendée, NW France 46°51′N 01°52′W
57 K19 **Challapata** Oruro, SW Bolivia 18°50′S 66°45′W
192 H6 **Challenger Deep** undersea feature W Pacific Ocean 11°20′N 142°12′E
Challenger Deep see Mariana Trench
193 S11 **Challenger Fracture Zone** tectonic feature SE Pacific Ocean
192 K11 **Challenger Plateau** undersea feature E Tasman Sea
33 P13 **Challis** Idaho, NW USA 44°31′N 114°14′W
22 L9 **Chalmette** Louisiana, S USA 29°56′N 89°57′W
124 J11 **Chalna** Respublika Kareliya, NW Russian Federation 61°53′N 33°59′E
103 Q5 **Châlons-en-Champagne** prev. Châlons-sur-Marne, hist. Arcae Remorum; anc. Carolopois. Marne, NE France 48°58′N 04°22′E
Châlons-sur-Marne see Châlons-en-Champagne
103 R9 **Chalon-sur-Saône** anc. Cabillonum. Saône-et-Loire, C France 46°47′N 04°51′E
Chaltel, Cerro see Fitzroy, Monte
102 M11 **Châlus** Haute-Vienne, C France 45°38′N 01°00′E
143 N4 **Chālūs** Māzandarān, N Iran 36°40′N 51°25′E
101 N20 **Cham** Bayern, SE Germany 49°13′N 12°40′E
108 F7 **Cham** Zug, N Switzerland 47°11′N 08°28′E
37 R8 **Chama** New Mexico, SW USA 36°54′N 106°34′W
Cha Mai see Thung Song
83 E22 **Chamaites** Karas, S Namibia 27°15′S 17°52′E
149 O9 **Chaman** Baluchistān, SW Pakistan 30°55′N 66°27′E
37 R9 **Chama, Rio** ≈ New Mexico, SW USA
152 I6 **Chamba** Himāchal Pradesh, N India 32°33′N 76°10′E
81 I25 **Chamba** Ruvuma, S Tanzania 11°33′S 37°01′E
150 H12 **Chambal** ≈ C India
11 U16 **Chamberlain** Saskatchewan, S Canada 50°49′N 105°29′W
29 O11 **Chamberlain** South Dakota, N USA 43°48′N 99°19′W
19 R3 **Chamberlain Lake** ◎ Maine, NE USA
39 S5 **Chamberlin, Mount** ▲ Alaska, USA 69°16′N 144°54′W
37 O11 **Chambers** Arizona, SW USA 35°11′N 109°25′W
18 F16 **Chambersburg** Pennsylvania, NE USA 39°54′N 77°39′W
31 N5 **Chambers Island** island Wisconsin, N USA
103 T11 **Chambéry** anc. Camberia. Savoie, E France 45°34′N 05°56′E
82 L12 **Chambeshi** Northern, NE Zambia 10°55′S 31°07′E
82 L12 **Chambeshi** ≈ NE Zambia
74 M6 **Chambi, Jebel** var. Jabal ash Sha'nabī. ▲ W Tunisia 35°16′N 08°39′E
15 Q7 **Chambord** Québec, SE Canada 48°25′N 72°02′W
139 U11 **Chamcham** Al Muthannā, S Iraq 31°17′N 45°05′E
139 T4 **Chamchamāl** At Ta'mīm, N Iraq 35°32′N 44°50′E
Chamdmani see Altanshiree
40 J14 **Chamela** Jalisco, SW Mexico 19°31′N 105°02′W
42 G5 **Chamelecón, Río** ≈ NW Honduras
62 J9 **Chamical** La Rioja, C Argentina 30°21′S 66°19′W
115 L23 **Chamilí** island Kykládes, Greece, Aegean Sea
167 Q13 **Châmnar** Kaôh Kông, SW Cambodia 11°45′N 103°32′E
152 K9 **Chamoli** Uttarakhand, N India 30°22′N 79°19′E
103 U11 **Chamonix-Mont-Blanc** Haute-Savoie, E France 45°55′N 06°52′E
154 L11 **Chāmpa** Chhattīsgarh, C India 22°02′N 82°42′E
10 H8 **Champagne** Yukon Territory, W Canada 60°48′N 136°22′W
103 Q5 **Champagne** cultural region N France
Champagne see Campania
103 Q5 **Champagne-Ardenne** ◐ region N France
103 S9 **Champagnole** Jura, E France 46°44′N 05°55′E
30 M13 **Champaign** Illinois, N USA 40°07′N 88°15′W
167 S10 **Champasak** Champasak, S Laos 14°50′N 105°51′E
152 L9 **Champāwat** Uttarakhand, N India 29°20′N 80°06′E
103 U6 **Champ de Feu** ▲ NE France 48°24′N 07°15′E
13 O7 **Champdoré, Lac** ◎ Québec, NE Canada
42 B6 **Champerico** Retalhuleu, SW Guatemala 14°18′N 91°54′W
108 C11 **Champéry** Valais, SW Switzerland 46°12′N 06°52′E
18 L6 **Champlain** New York, NE USA 44°58′N 73°25′W
18 L9 **Champlain Canal** canal New York, NE USA
15 P13 **Champlain, Lac** ◎ Québec, Canada/USA see also Champlain, Lake
18 L7 **Champlain, Lake** ◎ Canada/USA see also Champlain, Lac
103 S7 **Champlitte** Haute-Saône, E France 47°36′N 05°31′E
41 W13 **Champotón** Campeche, SE Mexico 19°18′N 90°43′W
155 G21 **Chāmrājnagar** var. Chamrajnagar. Karnātaka, SW India 11°58′N 76°54′E
Chamrajnagar see Chāmrājnagar
104 G10 **Chamusca** Santarém, C Portugal 39°21′N 08°29′W
119 O20 **Chamyarysy** Rus. Chemerisy. Homyel'skaya Voblasts', SE Belarus 51°42′N 30°27′E
127 P5 **Chamzinka** Respublika Mordoviya, W Russian Federation 54°22′N 45°22′E
Chanáil Mhór, An see Grand Canal
Chanak see Çanakkale
62 G7 **Chañaral** Atacama, N Chile 26°19′S 70°34′W
104 H13 **Chança, Rio** var. Chanza. ≈ Portugal/Spain
57 D14 **Chancay** Lima, W Peru 11°36′S 77°14′W
Chan-chiang/Chanchiang see Zhanjiang
62 G13 **Chanco** Maule, C Chile 35°43′S 72°35′W
39 R7 **Chandalar** Alaska, USA 67°30′N 148°29′W
39 R6 **Chandalar River** ≈ Alaska, USA
152 L10 **Chandan Chauki** Uttar Pradesh, N India 28°32′N 80°43′E
153 S16 **Chandannagar** prev. Chandernagore. West Bengal, E India 22°52′N 88°21′E
152 K10 **Chandausi** Uttar Pradesh, N India 28°27′N 78°43′E
22 M10 **Chandeleur Islands** island group Louisiana, S USA
22 M9 **Chandeleur Sound** sound N Gulf of Mexico
Chandernagore see Chandannagar
152 I8 **Chandīgarh** state capital Punjab, N India 30°41′N 76°51′E
153 Q16 **Chāndil** Jhārkhand, NE India 22°58′N 86°04′E
182 D2 **Chandler** South Australia 26°59′S 133°22′E
15 Y7 **Chandler** Québec, SE Canada 48°21′N 64°41′W
36 L14 **Chandler** Arizona, SW USA 33°18′N 111°50′W
27 O10 **Chandler** Oklahoma, C USA 35°43′N 96°54′W
25 V7 **Chandler** Texas, SW USA 32°18′N 95°28′W
39 Q6 **Chandler River** ≈ Alaska, USA
56 H13 **Chandles, Río** ≈ E Peru
162 H9 **Chandmanĭ** var. Talshand. Govĭ-Altayĭ, C Mongolia 45°21′N 98°00′E
162 E7 **Chandmanĭ** var. Urdgol. Hovd, W Mongolia 47°39′N 92°46′E
14 J13 **Chandos Lake** ◎ Ontario, SE Canada
153 U15 **Chandpur** Chittagong, C Bangladesh 23°13′N 90°43′E
154 I13 **Chandrapur** Mahārāshtra, C India 19°58′N 79°21′E
83 J15 **Changa** Southern, S Zambia 16°24′S 28°27′E
Chang'an see Rong'an, Guangxi Zhuangzu Zizhiqu, S China
Changan see Xi'an, Shaanxi, C China
155 G23 **Changanācheri** var. Changannassery. Kerala, SW India 09°26′N 76°31′E see also Changannassery
83 M19 **Changane** ≈ S Mozambique
155 G23 **Changannassery** var. Changanācheri. Kerala, SW India 09°26′N 76°31′E see also Changanācheri
83 M16 **Changara** Tete, NW Mozambique 16°54′S 33°15′E
163 X11 **Changbai** var. Changbai Chosenzu Zizhixian. Jilin, NE China 41°25′N 128°08′E
Changbai Chosenzu Zizhixian see Changbai
163 X11 **Changbai Shan** ▲▲ NE China
163 V10 **Changchun** var. Ch'angch'un, Ch'ang-ch'un; prev. Hsinking. province capital Jilin, NE China 43°53′N 125°18′E
Ch'angch'un/Ch'ang-ch'un see Changchun
160 M10 **Changde** Hunan, S China 29°04′N 111°42′E
161 S13 **Changhua** Jap. Shōka. C Taiwan 24°06′N 120°31′E
168 L10 **Changi** ✈ (Singapore) E Singapore 01°22′N 103°58′E
158 L5 **Changji** Xinjiang Uygur Zizhiqu, NW China 44°02′N 87°12′E
160 L17 **Changjiang** var. Changjiang Lizu Zizhixian, Shiliu. Hainan, S China 19°16′N 109°09′E
157 R11 **Chang Jiang** var. Yangtze Kiang, Eng. Yangtze. ≈ C China
161 S8 **Changjiang Kou** delta E China
Changjiang Lizu Zizhixian see Changjiang
Changkiakow see Zhangjiakou
167 F12 **Chang, Ko** island S Thailand
161 Q2 **Changli** Hebei, E China 39°44′N 119°13′E
163 V10 **Changling** Jilin, NE China 44°15′N 124°03′E
Changning see Xunwu
161 N11 **Changsha** var. Ch'angsha, Ch'ang-sha. province capital Hunan, S China 28°10′N 113°E
Ch'angsha/Ch'ang-sha see Changsha
161 Q10 **Changshan** Zhejiang, SE China 28°54′N 118°30′E
163 V14 **Changshan Qundao** island group NE China
161 S8 **Changshu** var. Ch'ang-shu. Jiangsu, E China 31°39′N 120°45′E
Ch'ang-shu see Changshu
163 V11 **Changtu** Liaoning, NE China 42°50′N 123°59′E
43 P14 **Changuinola** Bocas del Toro, NW Panama 09°28′N 82°31′W
159 N9 **Changweiliang** Qinghai, W China 38°24′N 92°08′E
160 K6 **Changwu** var. Zhaoren. Shaanxi, C China 35°12′N 107°46′E
163 U13 **Changxing Dao** island N China
160 M9 **Changyang** var. Longzhouping. Hubei, C China 30°45′N 111°13′E
163 W14 **Changyŏn** SW North Korea 38°19′N 125°15′E
161 N5 **Changzhi** Shanxi, C China 36°10′N 113°02′E
161 R8 **Changzhou** Jiangsu, E China 31°45′N 119°58′E
115 H24 **Chaniá** var. Hania, Khaniá, Eng. Canea; anc. Cydonia. Kriti, Greece, E Mediterranean Sea 35°31′N 24°00′E
62 J5 **Chañi, Nevado de** ▲ NW Argentina 24°09′S 65°44′W
115 H24 **Chanión, Kólpos** gulf Kriti, Greece, E Mediterranean Sea
Chankiri see Çankırı
30 M11 **Channahon** Illinois, N USA 41°25′N 88°13′W
155 H20 **Channapatna** Karnātaka, E India 12°43′N 77°14′E
97 K26 **Channel Islands** Fr. Iles Normandes. island group S English Channel
35 R16 **Channel Islands** island group California, W USA
13 S13 **Channel-Port aux Basques** Newfoundland and Labrador, SE Canada 47°35′N 59°02′W
Channel, The see English Channel
97 Q23 **Channel Tunnel** tunnel France/United Kingdom
24 M2 **Channing** Texas, SW USA 35°41′N 102°21′W
Chantabun/Chantaburi see Chanthaburi
104 H3 **Chantada** Galicia, NW Spain 42°36′N 07°46′W
167 P12 **Chanthaburi** var. Chantabun, Chantaburi. Chantaburi, S Thailand 12°35′N 102°08′E
103 O4 **Chantilly** Oise, N France 49°12′N 02°28′E
139 V12 **Chanūn as Sa'ūdī** Dhī Qār, S Iraq 31°04′N 46°00′E
27 Q6 **Chanute** Kansas, C USA 37°40′N 95°27′W
Chanza see Chança, Rio
Ch'ao-an/Chaochow see Chaozhou
161 Q8 **Chaohu** Anhui, E China 31°36′N 117°55′E
161 P8 **Chao Hu** ◎ E China
167 P11 **Chao Phraya, Mae Nam** ≈ C Thailand
Chaor He see Qulin Gol
Chaouèn see Chefchaouen
161 P14 **Chaoyang** Guangdong, S China 23°17′N 116°33′E
163 T12 **Chaoyang** Liaoning, NE China 41°34′N 120°29′E
Chaoyang see Jiayin, Heilongjiang, China
Chaoyang see Huinan, Jilin China
161 Q14 **Chaozhou** var. Chaoan, Chao'an, Ch'ao-an; prev. Chaochow. Guangdong, SE China 23°42′N 116°36′E
58 N13 **Chapadinha** Maranhão, E Brazil 03°45′S 43°23′W
12 K12 **Chapais** Québec, SE Canada 49°47′N 74°54′W
40 L13 **Chapala** Jalisco, SW Mexico 20°20′N 103°10′W
40 L13 **Chapala, Lago de** ◎ C Mexico
146 F13 **Chapan, Gora** ▲ C Turkmenistan 37°48′N 58°03′E
57 M18 **Chapare, Río** ≈ C Bolivia
54 E11 **Chaparral** Tolima, C Colombia 03°45′N 75°30′W
144 F9 **Chapayev** Zapadnyy Kazakhstan, NW Kazakhstan 50°12′N 51°09′E
123 O11 **Chapayevo** Respublika Sakha (Yakutiya), NE Russian Federation 60°03′N 117°19′E
127 R6 **Chapayevsk** Samarskaya Oblast', W Russian Federation 52°57′N 49°42′E
60 H13 **Chapecó** Santa Catarina, S Brazil 27°14′S 52°41′W
60 I13 **Chapecó, Rio** ≈ S Brazil
20 J9 **Chapel Hill** Tennessee, S USA 35°38′N 86°40′W
44 J12 **Chapelton** C Jamaica 18°05′N 77°16′W
14 C8 **Chapleau** Ontario, SE Canada 47°50′N 83°24′W
14 D7 **Chapleau** ≈ Ontario, S Canada
11 T16 **Chaplin** Saskatchewan, S Canada 50°27′N 106°37′W
126 M6 **Chaplygin** Lipetskaya Oblast', W Russian Federation 53°13′N 39°58′E
117 S11 **Chaplynka** Khersons'ka Oblast', S Ukraine 46°20′N 33°34′E
9 O6 **Chapman, Cape** headland Nunavut, NE Canada 69°15′N 89°09′W
25 T15 **Chapman Ranch** Texas, SW USA 27°32′N 97°25′W
Chapman's see Okwa
21 P5 **Chapmanville** West Virginia, NE USA 37°58′N 82°01′W
28 K15 **Chappell** Nebraska, C USA 41°05′N 102°28′W
Chapra see Chhapra
56 D9 **Chapuli, Río** ≈ N Peru
76 I6 **Châr** well N Mauritania
123 P12 **Chara** Chitinskaya Oblast', S Russian Federation 56°57′N 118°05′E
123 O11 **Chara** ≈ C Russian Federation
54 G8 **Charala** Santander, C Colombia 06°17′N 73°09′W
41 N10 **Charcas** San Luis Potosí, C Mexico 23°09′N 101°10′W
25 T13 **Charco** Texas, SW USA 28°42′N 97°35′W
194 H7 **Charcot Island** island Antarctica
64 M8 **Charcot Seamounts** undersea feature E Atlantic Ocean 11°30′W 45°00′N
Chardara see Shardara
145 P17 **Chardarinskoye Vodokhranilishche** ⊠ S Kazakhstan
31 U11 **Chardon** Ohio, N USA 41°34′N 81°12′W
44 K9 **Chardonnières** SW Haiti 18°16′N 74°10′W
Chardzhev see Türkmenabat
Chardzhevskaya Oblast see Lebap Welaýaty
Chardzhou/Chardzhui see Türkmenabat
102 L11 **Charente** ◐ department W France
102 J11 **Charente** ≈ W France
102 J10 **Charente-Maritime** ◐ department W France
137 U12 **Ch'arents'avan** C Armenia 40°23′N 44°41′E
78 I12 **Chari** var. Shari. ≈ Central African Republic/Chad
78 G11 **Chari-Baguirmi** off. Préfecture du Chari-Baguirmi. ◐ prefecture SW Chad
Chari-Baguirmi, Préfecture du see Chari-Baguirmi
149 Q4 **Chārīkār** Parvān, NE Afghanistan 35°01′N 69°11′E
29 V15 **Chariton** Iowa, C USA 41°00′N 93°18′W
27 U3 **Chariton River** ≈ Missouri, C USA
55 T7 **Charity** NW Guyana 07°22′N 58°34′W
31 R7 **Charity Island** island Michigan, N USA
Chärjew see Türkmenabat
Chärjew Oblasty see Lebap Welaýaty
Charkhlik/Charkhliq see Ruoqiang
99 G20 **Charleroi** Hainaut, S Belgium 50°25′N 04°27′E
11 V12 **Charles** Manitoba, C Canada 55°27′N 100°58′W
15 R10 **Charlesbourg** Québec, SE Canada 46°50′N 71°15′W
21 Y7 **Charles, Cape** headland Virginia, NE USA 37°09′N 75°57′W
29 W12 **Charles City** Iowa, C USA 43°04′N 92°40′W
21 W6 **Charles City** Virginia, NE USA 37°21′N 77°05′W
103 O5 **Charles de Gaulle** ✈ (Paris) Seine-et-Marne, N France 49°04′N 02°36′E
12 K1 **Charles Island** island Nunavut, NE Canada
Charles Island see Santa María, Isla
30 K9 **Charles Mound** hill Illinois, N USA
185 A22 **Charles Sound** sound South Island, New Zealand
185 G15 **Charleston** West Coast, South Island, New Zealand 41°54′S 171°25′E
27 S11 **Charleston** Arkansas, C USA 35°19′N 94°02′W
30 M14 **Charleston** Illinois, N USA 39°30′N 88°10′W
22 L3 **Charleston** Mississippi, S USA 34°00′N 90°03′W
27 Z7 **Charleston** Missouri, C USA 36°54′N 89°22′W
21 T15 **Charleston** South Carolina, SE USA 32°48′N 79°57′W
21 Q5 **Charleston** state capital West Virginia, NE USA 38°21′N 81°38′W
14 L14 **Charleston Lake** ◎ Ontario, SE Canada
35 W11 **Charleston Peak** ▲ Nevada, W USA 36°16′N 115°40′W
45 W10 **Charlestown** Nevis, Saint Kitts and Nevis 17°08′N 62°37′W
31 P16 **Charlestown** Indiana, N USA 38°27′N 85°40′W
18 M9 **Charlestown** New Hampshire, NE USA 43°14′N 72°23′W
21 V3 **Charles Town** West Virginia, NE USA 39°18′N 77°54′W
181 W9 **Charleville** Queensland, E Australia 26°25′S 146°18′E
103 R3 **Charleville-Mézières** Ardennes, N France 49°45′N 04°43′E
31 P5 **Charlevoix** Michigan, N USA 45°19′N 85°15′W
31 Q6 **Charlevoix, Lake** ◎ Michigan, N USA
39 T9 **Charley River** ≈ Alaska, USA
64 J6 **Charlie-Gibbs Fracture Zone** tectonic feature N Atlantic Ocean
103 Q10 **Charlieu** Loire, E France 46°11′N 04°10′E
31 Q9 **Charlotte** Michigan, N USA 42°33′N 84°50′W
21 R10 **Charlotte** North Carolina, SE USA 35°14′N 80°51′W
20 I8 **Charlotte** Tennessee, S USA 36°11′N 87°18′W
25 R13 **Charlotte** Texas, SW USA 28°51′N 98°42′W
21 R10 **Charlotte** ✈ North Carolina, SE USA 35°12′N 80°54′W
45 T9 **Charlotte Amalie** prev. Saint Thomas. ○ (Virgin Islands (US)) Saint Thomas, N Virgin Islands (US) 18°22′N 64°56′W
21 U7 **Charlotte Court House** Virginia, NE USA 37°04′N 78°37′W
23 W14 **Charlotte Harbor** inlet Florida, SE USA
Charlotte Island see Abaiang
95 J15 **Charlottenberg** Värmland, C Sweden 59°53′N 12°17′E
Charlottenhof see Aegviidu
21 U5 **Charlottesville** Virginia, NE USA 38°02′N 78°29′W
13 Q14 **Charlottetown** province capital Prince Edward Island, Prince Edward Island, SE Canada 46°14′N 63°09′W
Charlotte Town see Roseau, Dominica
Charlotte Town see Gouyave, Grenada
45 Z16 **Charlotteville** Tobago, Trinidad and Tobago 11°16′N 60°33′W
182 M11 **Charlton** Victoria, SE Australia 36°18′S 143°19′E
12 H10 **Charlton Island** island Northwest Territories, C Canada
103 T6 **Charmes** Vosges, NE France 48°19′N 06°19′E
119 F19 **Charnawchytsy** Rus. Chernavchitsy. Brestskaya Voblasts', SW Belarus 52°13′N 23°44′E
15 R10 **Charny** Québec, SE Canada 46°43′N 71°15′W
149 T5 **Chārsadda** North-West Frontier Province, NW Pakistan 34°12′N 71°46′E
Charshanga/Charshangngy/Charshangy see Köýtendag
Charsk see Shar
181 W6 **Charters Towers** Queensland, NE Australia 20°02′S 146°20′E
15 R12 **Chartierville** Québec, SE Canada 45°19′N 71°13′W
102 M6 **Chartres** anc. Autricum, Civitas Carnutum. Eure-et-Loir, C France 48°27′N 01°27′E
145 W15 **Charyn** Kaz. Sharyn. Almaty, SE Kazakhstan 43°48′N 79°22′E
Charyn see Sharyn
61 D21 **Chascomús** Buenos Aires, E Argentina 35°34′S 58°01′W
11 N16 **Chase** British Columbia, SW Canada 50°49′N 119°41′W
21 U7 **Chase City** Virginia, NE USA 36°48′N 78°27′W
19 S4 **Chase, Mount** ▲ Maine, NE USA 46°06′N 68°30′W
118 M13 **Chashniki** Vitsyebskaya Voblasts', N Belarus 54°52′N 29°10′E
115 D15 **Chásia** ▲▲ C Greece
29 V9 **Chaska** Minnesota, N USA 44°47′N 93°36′W
185 D25 **Chaslands Mistake** headland South Island, New Zealand 46°37′S 169°21′E
125 R11 **Chasovo** Respublika Komi, NW Russian Federation 61°58′N 50°34′E
Chasovo see Vazhgort
124 H14 **Chastova** Novgorodskaya Oblast', NW Russian Federation 58°37′N 32°05′E
143 R3 **Chāt** Golestān, N Iran 37°52′N 55°27′E
Chatak see Chhatak
Chatang see Zhanang
39 R9 **Chatanika** Alaska, USA 65°06′N 147°28′W
39 R9 **Chatanika River** ≈ Alaska, USA
147 T8 **Chat-Bazar** Talasskaya Oblast', NW Kyrgyzstan 42°29′N 72°37′E
45 Y14 **Chateaubelair** Saint Vincent, W Saint Vincent and the Grenadines 13°15′N 61°05′W
102 J7 **Châteaubriant** Loire-Atlantique, NW France 47°43′N 01°22′W
103 Q8 **Château-Chinon** Nièvre, C France 47°04′N 03°50′E
108 C10 **Château d'Oex** Vaud, W Switzerland 46°28′N 07°09′E
102 L7 **Château-du-Loir** Sarthe, NW France 47°40′N 00°25′E
102 M6 **Châteaudun** Eure-et-Loir, C France 48°04′N 01°20′E
102 K7 **Château-Gontier** Mayenne, NW France 47°49′N 00°42′W
15 O13 **Châteauguay** Québec, SE Canada 45°22′N 73°44′W
102 F6 **Châteaulin** Finistère, NW France 48°12′N 04°07′W
103 N9 **Châteaumeillant** Cher, C France 46°33′N 02°10′E
102 K11 **Châteauneuf-sur-Charente** Charente, W France 45°34′N 00°33′W
102 M7 **Château-Renault** Indre-et-Loire, C France 47°34′N 00°52′E
103 N9 **Châteauroux** prev. Indreville. Indre, C France 46°50′N 01°43′E
103 T5 **Château-Salins** Moselle, NE France 48°50′N 06°29′E
103 P4 **Château-Thierry** Aisne, N France 49°03′N 03°24′E
99 H21 **Châtelet** Hainaut, S Belgium 50°24′N 04°32′E
Châtelherault see Châtellerault
102 L9 **Châtellerault** var. Châtelherault. Vienne, W France 46°49′N 00°33′E
29 X10 **Chatfield** Minnesota, N USA 43°51′N 92°11′W
13 O14 **Chatham** New Brunswick, SE Canada 47°02′N 65°30′W
14 D17 **Chatham** Ontario, S Canada 42°24′N 82°11′W
97 P22 **Chatham** SE England, United Kingdom 51°23′N 00°31′E
30 K14 **Chatham** Illinois, N USA 39°40′N 89°42′W
21 T7 **Chatham** Virginia, NE USA 36°49′N 79°26′W
63 F22 **Chatham, Isla** island S Chile
175 R12 **Chatham Island** island Chatham Islands, New Zealand
Chatham Island see San Cristóbal, Isla
Chatham Island Rise see Chatham Rise
175 R12 **Chatham Islands** island group New Zealand, SW Pacific Ocean
175 Q12 **Chatham Rise** var. Chatham Island Rise. undersea feature S Pacific Ocean
39 X13 **Chatham Strait** strait Alaska, USA

Chathóir, Rinn see Cahore Point
102 M9 **Châtillon-sur-Indre** Indre, C France 46°58′N 01°10′E
103 Q7 **Châtillon-sur-Seine** Côte d'Or, C France 47°51′N 04°30′E
147 S8 **Chatkal** *Uzb.* Chotqol. ≈ Kyrgyzstan/Uzbekistan
147 R9 **Chatkal Range** *Rus.* Chatkal'skiy Khrebet. ▲▲ Kyrgyzstan/Uzbekistan
Chatkal'skiy Khrebet see Chatkal Range
23 N7 **Chatom** Alabama, S USA 31°28′N 88°15′W
153 P14 **Chatra** Jhārkhand, N India 24°12′N 84°52′E
Chatrapur see Chhatrapur
143 S10 **Chatrūd** Kermān, C Iran 30°39′N 56°57′E
23 S2 **Chatsworth** Georgia, SE USA 34°46′N 84°46′W
Chāttagām see Chittagong
23 S8 **Chattahoochee** Florida, SE USA 30°40′N 84°51′W
23 R8 **Chattahoochee River** ≈ SE USA
20 L10 **Chattanooga** Tennessee, SE USA 35°05′N 85°16′W
147 V10 **Chatyr-Kël', Ozero** ◎ C Kyrgyzstan
147 W9 **Chatyr-Tash** Narynskaya Oblast', C Kyrgyzstan 40°54′N 76°22′E
15 R12 **Chaudière** ≈ Québec, SE Canada
167 S14 **Châu Đôc** *var.* Chauphu, Chau Phu. An Giang, S Vietnam 10°53′N 105°07′E
152 D13 **Chauhtan** *prev.* Chohtan. Rājasthān, NW India 25°27′N 71°08′E
166 L5 **Chauk** Magway, W Burma (Myanmar) 20°52′N 94°50′E
103 R6 **Chaumont** *prev.* Chaumont-en-Bassigny. Haute-Marne, N France 48°07′N 05°08′E
Chaumont-en-Bassigny see Chaumont
123 T5 **Chaunskaya Guba** *bay* NE Russian Federation
103 P3 **Chauny** Aisne, N France 49°37′N 03°13′E
Châu Ô see Binh Sơn
Chau Phu see Châu Đôc
102 I5 **Chausey, Îles** *island group* N France
Chausy see Chavusy
18 C11 **Chautauqua Lake** ◎ New York, NE USA
ChâuThanh see Ba Ria
102 L9 **Chauvigny** Vienne, W France 46°35′N 00°37′E
124 L6 **Chavan'ga** Murmanskaya Oblast', NW Russian Federation 66°07′N 37°44′E
14 K10 **Chavannes, Lac** ◎ Québec, SE Canada
Chavantes, Represa de see Xavantes, Represa de
61 D15 **Chavarría** Corrientes, NE Argentina 28°57′S 58°35′W
Chavash Respubliki see Chuvashskaya Respublika
104 I5 **Chaves** *anc.* Aquae Flaviae. Vila Real, N Portugal 41°44′N 07°28′W
Chávez, Isla see Santa Cruz, Isla
82 G13 **Chavuma** North Western, NW Zambia 13°04′S 22°43′E
119 O16 **Chavusy** *Rus.* Chausy. Mahilyowskaya Voblasts', E Belarus 53°48′N 30°58′E
Chayan see Shayan
147 U8 **Chayek** Narynskaya Oblast', C Kyrgyzstan 41°54′N 74°28′E
139 T6 **Chāy Khānah** Diyālá, E Iraq 34°19′N 44°33′E
125 T16 **Chaykovskiy** Permskaya Oblast', NW Russian Federation 56°45′N 54°09′E
167 T12 **Chbar** Môndól Kiri, E Cambodia 12°46′N 107°10′E
23 Q4 **Cheaha Mountain** ▲ Alabama, S USA 33°29′N 85°48′W
Cheatharlach see Carlow
21 S2 **Cheat River** ≈ NE USA
111 A16 **Cheb** *Ger.* Eger. Karlovarský Kraj, W Czech Republic 50°05′N 12°23′E
127 Q3 **Cheboksary** Chuvashskaya Respublika, W Russian Federation 56°06′N 47°15′E
31 Q5 **Cheboygan** Michigan, N USA 45°40′N 84°28′W
Chechaouèn see Chefchaouen
Chechenia see Chechenskaya Respublika
127 O15 **Chechenskaya Respublika** *Eng.* Chechenia, Chechnia, *Rus.* Chechnya. ◆ *autonomous republic* SW Russian Federation
67 N4 **Chech, Erg** *desert* Algeria/Mali
Chechevichi see Chachevichy
Che-chiang see Zhejiang
Chechnia/Chechnya see Chechenskaya Respublika
163 Y15 **Chech'ŏn** *Jap.* Teisen. N South Korea 37°06′N 128°15′E
111 L15 **Chęciny** Świętokrzyskie, S Poland 50°51′N 20°31′E
27 Q10 **Checotah** Oklahoma, C USA 35°28′N 95°31′W
13 R15 **Chedabucto Bay** *inlet* Nova Scotia, E Canada
166 J7 **Cheduba Island** *island* W Burma (Myanmar)
37 T5 **Cheesman Lake** ▣ Colorado, C USA
195 S16 **Cheetham, Cape** *headland* Antarctica 70°26′S 162°40′E
74 G5 **Chefchaouen** *var.* Chaouèn, Chechaouèn, *Sp.* Xauen. N Morocco 35°10′N 05°16′W
Chefoo see Yantai
38 M12 **Chefornak** Alaska, USA 60°09′N 164°09′W
123 R13 **Chegdomyn** Khabarovskiy Kray, SE Russian Federation 51°09′N 132°58′E
76 M4 **Chegga** Tiris Zemmour, NE Mauritania 25°27′N 05°49′W
Cheghcheran see Chaghcharān
32 G9 **Chehalis** Washington, NW USA 46°39′N 122°57′W
32 G9 **Chehalis River** ≈ Washington, NW USA
148 M6 **Chehel Abdālān, Kūh-e** *var.* Chalap Dalan, *Pash.* Chalap Dalan. ▲▲ C Afghanistan
115 D14 **Cheimadítis, Límni** *var.* Límni Cheimadítis. ◎ N Greece
Cheimadítis, Límni see Cheimadítis, Límni
103 U15 **Cheiron, Mont** ▲ SE France 43°49′N 07°00′E
163 X17 **Cheju** *Jap.* Saishū. S South Korea 33°31′N 126°34′E
163 Y17 **Cheju** ✕ S South Korea 33°31′N 126°29′E
163 Y17 **Cheju-do** *Jap.* Saishū; *prev.* Quelpart. *island* S South Korea
163 Y17 **Cheju-haehyŏp** *Eng.* Cheju Strait. *strait* S South Korea
Cheju Strait see Cheju-haehyŏp
Chekiang see Zhejiang
Chekichler/Chekishlyar see Çekiçler
188 F8 **Chelab** Babeldaob, N Palau
147 N11 **Chelak** *Rus.* Chelek. Samarqand Viloyati, C Uzbekistan 39°55′N 66°45′E
32 J7 **Chelan, Lake** ▣ Washington, NW USA
Chelek see Chelak
Cheleken see Hazar
Chélif/Chéliff see Chelif, Oued
74 J5 **Chelif, Oued** *var.* Chélif, Chéliff, Chellif, Shellif. ≈ N Algeria
Chelkar see Shalkar
Chelkar Ozero see Shalkar, Ozero
Chellif see Chelif, Oued
111 P14 **Chełm** *Rus.* Kholm. Lubelskie, SE Poland 51°08′N 23°29′E
110 I9 **Chełmno** *Ger.* Culm, Kulm. Kujawski-pomorskie, C Poland 53°21′N 18°27′E
115 E19 **Chelmós** *var.* Ároania. ▲▲ S Greece
14 F10 **Chelmsford** Ontario, S Canada 46°33′N 81°16′W
97 P21 **Chelmsford** E England, United Kingdom 51°44′N 00°28′E
110 J9 **Chełmża** *Ger.* Culmsee, Kulmsee. Kujawski-pomorskie, C Poland 53°11′N 18°34′E
27 Q8 **Chelsea** Oklahoma, C USA 36°32′N 95°25′W
18 M8 **Chelsea** Vermont, NE USA 43°58′N 72°29′W
97 L21 **Cheltenham** C England, United Kingdom 51°54′N 02°04′W
105 R9 **Chelva** País Valenciano, E Spain 39°45′N 01°00′W
122 G11 **Chelyabinsk** Chelyabinskaya Oblast', C Russian Federation 55°12′N 61°25′E
122 F11 **Chelyabinskaya Oblast'** ◐ *province* C Russian Federation
123 N5 **Chelyuskin, Mys** *headland* N Russian Federation 77°42′N 104°13′E
41 Y12 **Chemax** Yucatán, SE Mexico 20°41′N 87°54′W
83 N16 **Chemba** Sofala, C Mozambique 17°11′S 34°53′E
82 J13 **Chembe** Luapula, NE Zambia 11°58′S 28°45′E
Chemenibit see Çemenibit
Chemerisy see Chamyarysy
116 K7 **Chemerivtsi** Khmel'nyts'ka Oblast', W Ukraine 49°00′N 26°21′E
102 J8 **Chemillé** Maine-et-Loire, NW France 47°15′N 00°42′W
173 X17 **Chemin Grenier** S Mauritius 20°29′S 57°28′E
101 N16 **Chemnitz** *prev.* Karl-Marx-Stadt. Sachsen, E Germany 50°50′N 12°55′E
Chemulpo see Inch'ŏn
32 H14 **Chemult** Oregon, NW USA 43°14′N 121°48′W
18 G12 **Chemung River** ≈ New York/Pennsylvania, NE USA
149 U8 **Chenāb** ≈ India/Pakistan
39 S9 **Chena Hot Springs** Alaska, USA 65°06′N 146°02′W
18 I11 **Chenango River** ≈ New York, NE USA
168 J7 **Chenderoh, Tasik** ◎ Peninsular Malaysia
15 Q11 **Chêne, Rivière du** ≈ Québec, SE Canada
32 L8 **Cheney** Washington, NW USA 47°29′N 117°34′W
26 M6 **Cheney Reservoir** ▣ Kansas, C USA
Chengchiatun see Liaoyuan
Ch'eng-chou/Chengchow see Zhengzhou
161 P1 **Chengde** *var.* Jehol. Hebei, E China 41°N 117°57′E
160 I9 **Chengdu** *var.* Chengtu, Ch'eng-tu. *province capital* Sichuan, C China 30°41′N 104°03′E
161 Q14 **Chenghai** Guangdong, S China 23°30′N 116°42′E
Chenghsien see Zhengzhou
160 H13 **Chengjiang** Yunnan, SW China 24°40′N 102°55′E
Chengjiang see Taihe
160 L17 **Chengmai** *var.* Jinjiang. Hainan, S China 19°45′N 109°56′E
Chengtu/Ch'eng-tu see Chengdu
Chengwen see Chindu
159 W12 **Chengxian** *var.* Cheng Xiang. Gansu, C China 33°42′N 105°45′E
Cheng Xiang see Chengxian
Chengyang see Juxian
Chengzhong see Ningming
Chenkiang see Zhenjiang
155 J19 **Chennai** *prev.* Madras. *state capital* Tamil Nādu, S India 13°05′N 80°18′E
155 J19 **Chennai** ✕ Tamil Nādu, S India 13°00′N 80°13′E
103 R8 **Chenôve** Côte d'Or, C France 47°16′N 05°00′E
Chenstokhov see Częstochowa
160 L11 **Chenxi** *var.* Chenyang. Hunan, S China 28°02′N 110°15′E
Chen Xian/Chenxian/Chen Xiang see Chenzhou
Chenyang see Chenxi
161 N12 **Chenzhou** *var.* Chenxian, Chen Xian, Chen Xiang. Hunan, S China 25°51′N 113°01′E
167 U12 **Cheo Reo** *var.* A Yun Pa. Gia Lai, S Vietnam 13°19′N 108°27′E
114 I11 **Chepelare** Smolyan, S Bulgaria 41°44′N 24°41′E
114 I11 **Chepelarska Reka** ≈ S Bulgaria
56 B11 **Chepén** La Libertad, C Peru 07°15′S 79°23′W
62 J10 **Chepes** La Rioja, C Argentina 31°19′S 66°40′W
161 O15 **Chep Lap Kok** ✕ S China 22°23′N 114°11′E
43 U14 **Chepo** Panamá, C Panama 09°09′N 79°03′W
Chepping Wycombe see High Wycombe
125 R14 **Cheptsa** ≈ NW Russian Federation
30 K3 **Chequamegon Point** *headland* Wisconsin, N USA 46°42′N 90°45′W
103 O8 **Cher** ◐ *department* C France
102 M8 **Cher** ≈ C France
Cherangani Hills see Cherangany Hills
81 H17 **Cherangany Hills** *var.* Cherangani Hills. ▲▲ W Kenya
21 S11 **Cheraw** South Carolina, SE USA 34°42′N 79°52′W
102 I3 **Cherbourg** *anc.* Carusbur. Manche, N France 49°40′N 01°36′W
127 R5 **Cherdakly** Ul'yanovskaya Oblast', W Russian Federation 54°21′N 48°54′E
125 U12 **Cherdyn'** Permskaya Oblast', NW Russian Federation 60°21′N 56°39′E
124 J14 **Cherekha** ≈ W Russian Federation
122 M13 **Cheremkhovo** Irkutskaya Oblast', S Russian Federation 53°16′N 102°44′E
Cheren see Keren
124 K14 **Cherepovets** Vologodskaya Oblast', NW Russian Federation 59°09′N 37°50′E
125 O11 **Cherevkovo** Arkhangel'skaya Oblast', NW Russian Federation 61°45′N 45°16′E
74 I6 **Chergui, Chott ech** *salt lake* NW Algeria
Cherikov see Cherykaw
117 P6 **Cherkas'ka Oblast'** *var.* Cherkasy, *Rus.* Cherkasskaya Oblast'. ◐ *province* C Ukraine
Cherkasskaya Oblast' see Cherkas'ka Oblast'
Cherkassy see Cherkasy
117 Q6 **Cherkasy** *Rus.* Cherkassy. Cherkas'ka Oblast', C Ukraine 49°26′N 32°05′E
Cherkasy see Cherkas'ka Oblast'
126 M15 **Cherkessk** Karachayevo-Cherkesskaya Respublika, SW Russian Federation 44°12′N 42°06′E
122 H12 **Cherlak** Omskaya Oblast', C Russian Federation 54°06′N 74°59′E
122 H12 **Cherlakskoye** Omskaya Oblast', C Russian Federation 53°42′N 74°23′E
125 U13 **Chermoz** Permskaya Oblast', NW Russian Federation 58°49′N 56°07′E
Chernavchitsy see Charnawchytsy
125 T3 **Chernaya** Nenetskiy Avtonomnyy Okrug, NW Russian Federation 68°36′N 56°34′E
125 T4 **Chernaya** ≈ NW Russian Federation
Chernigov see Chernihiv
Chernigovskaya Oblast' see Chernihivs'ka Oblast'
117 Q2 **Chernihiv** *Rus.* Chernigov. Chernihivs'ka Oblast', NE Ukraine 51°28′N 31°19′E
Chernihiv see Chernihivs'ka Oblast'
117 V9 **Chernihivka** Zaporiz'ka Oblast', SE Ukraine 47°11′N 36°10′E
117 P2 **Chernihivs'ka Oblast'** *var.* Chernihiv, *Rus.* Chernigovskaya Oblast'. ◐ *province* NE Ukraine
114 I9 **Cherni Osŭm** ≈ N Bulgaria
116 J8 **Chernivets'ka Oblast'** *var.* Chernivtsi, *Rus.* Chernovitskaya Oblast'. ◐ *province* W Ukraine
114 I9 **Cherni Vit** ≈ NW Bulgaria
114 G10 **Cherni Vrŭkh** ▲ W Bulgaria 42°33′N 23°18′E
116 K8 **Chernivtsi** *Ger.* Czernowitz, *Rom.* Cernăuţi, *Rus.* Chernovtsy. Chernivets'ka Oblast', W Ukraine 48°18′N 25°55′E
116 M7 **Chernivtsi** Vinnyts'ka Oblast', C Ukraine 48°33′N 28°06′E
Chernivtsi see Chernivets'ka Oblast'
Chernobyl' see Chornobyl'
Cherno More see Black Sea
Chernomorskoye see Chornomors'ke
145 T7 **Chernoretskoye** Pavlodar, NE Kazakhstan 52°51′N 76°37′E
Chernovitskaya Oblast' see Chernivets'ka Oblast'
Chernovtsy see Chernivtsi
145 U8 **Chernoye** Pavlodar, NE Kazakhstan 51°40′N 77°33′E
Chernoye More see Black Sea
125 U16 **Chernushka** Permskaya Oblast', NW Russian Federation 56°30′N 56°07′E
117 N4 **Chernyakhiv** *Rus.* Chernyakhov. Zhytomyrs'ka Oblast', N Ukraine 50°30′N 28°38′E
Chernyakhov see Chernyakhiv
119 C14 **Chernyakhovsk** *Ger.* Insterburg. Kaliningradskaya Oblast', W Russian Federation 54°36′N 21°49′E
126 K8 **Chernyanka** Belgorodskaya Oblast', W Russian Federation 50°59′N 37°54′E
125 V5 **Chernyshëva, Gryada** ▲▲ NW Russian Federation
144 J14 **Chernyshëva, Zaliv** *gulf* SW Kazakhstan
123 O10 **Chernyshevskiy** Respublika Sakha (Yakutiya), NE Russian Federation 62°57′N 112°29′E
127 P13 **Chernyye Zemli** *plain* SW Russian Federation
Chërnyy Irtysh see Ertix He, China/Kazakhstan
Chërnyy Irtysh see Kara Irtysh, Kazakhstan
127 V7 **Chernyy Otrog** Orenburgskaya Oblast', W Russian Federation 52°03′N 56°09′E
29 T12 **Cherokee** Iowa, C USA 42°45′N 95°33′W
26 M8 **Cherokee** Oklahoma, C USA 36°45′N 98°22′W
25 R9 **Cherokee** Texas, SW USA 30°56′N 98°42′W
21 O8 **Cherokee Lake** ▣ Tennessee, S USA
Cherokees, Lake O' The see Grand Lake O' The Cherokees
44 H1 **Cherokee Sound** Great Abaco, N Bahamas 26°16′N 77°03′W
153 V13 **Cherrapunji** Meghālaya, NE India 25°16′N 91°42′E
28 L9 **Cherry Creek** ≈ South Dakota, N USA
18 J16 **Cherry Hill** New Jersey, NE USA 39°55′N 75°01′W
27 Q7 **Cherryvale** Kansas, C USA 37°16′N 95°33′W
21 Q10 **Cherryville** North Carolina, SE USA 35°22′N 81°22′W
Cherski Range see Cherskogo, Khrebet
123 T6 **Cherskiy** Respublika Sakha (Yakutiya), NE Russian Federation 68°45′N 161°15′E
123 R8 **Cherskogo, Khrebet** *var.* Cherski Range. ▲▲ NE Russian Federation
Cherso see Cres
126 L10 **Chertkovo** Rostovskaya Oblast', SW Russian Federation 49°22′N 40°10′E
Cherven' see Chervyen'
114 H8 **Cherven Bryag** Pleven, N Bulgaria 43°16′N 24°06′E
116 M4 **Chervonoarmiys'k** Zhytomyrs'ka Oblast', N Ukraine 50°27′N 28°15′E
Chervonograd see Chervonohrad
116 I4 **Chervonohrad** *Rus.* Chervonograd. L'vivs'ka Oblast', NW Ukraine 50°25′N 24°10′E
117 W6 **Chervonooskil's'ke Vodoskhovyshche** *Rus.* Krasnooskol'skoye Vodokhranilishche. ▣ NE Ukraine
Chervonoye, Ozero see Chyrvonaye, Vozyera
117 S4 **Chervonozavods'ke** Poltavs'ka Oblast', C Ukraine 50°24′N 33°22′E
119 L16 **Chervyen'** *Rus.* Cherven'. Minskaya Voblasts', C Belarus 53°42′N 28°26′E
119 P16 **Cherykaw** *Rus.* Cherikov. Mahilyowskaya Voblasts', E Belarus 53°34′N 31°23′E
31 R9 **Chesaning** Michigan, N USA 43°10′N 84°07′W
21 X5 **Chesapeake Bay** *inlet* NE USA
Chesha Bay see Chëshskaya Guba
Cheshevlya see Tsyeshawlya
97 K18 **Cheshire** *cultural region* C England, United Kingdom
125 P5 **Chëshskaya Guba** *var.* Archangel Bay, Chesha Bay, Dvina Bay. *bay* NW Russian Federation
14 F14 **Chesley** Ontario, S Canada 44°17′N 81°06′W
21 Q10 **Chesnee** South Carolina, SE USA 35°09′N 81°51′W
97 K18 **Chester** *Wel.* Caerleon, *hist.* Legaceaster, *Lat.* Deva, Devana Castra. C England, United Kingdom 53°12′N 02°54′W
35 O4 **Chester** California, W USA 40°18′N 121°14′W
30 K16 **Chester** Illinois, N USA 37°54′N 89°49′W
33 S7 **Chester** Montana, NW USA 48°30′N 110°59′W
18 I16 **Chester** Pennsylvania, NE USA 39°51′N 75°21′W
21 R1 **Chester** South Carolina, SE USA 34°43′N 81°14′W
25 X9 **Chester** Texas, SW USA 30°55′N 94°36′W
21 W6 **Chester** Virginia, NE USA 37°22′N 77°27′W
21 R11 **Chester** West Virginia, NE USA 40°34′N 80°33′W
97 M18 **Chesterfield** C England, United Kingdom 53°15′N 01°25′W
21 S11 **Chesterfield** South Carolina, SE USA 34°44′N 80°04′W
21 W6 **Chesterfield** Virginia, NE USA 37°22′N 77°31′W
192 J9 **Chesterfield, Îles** *island group* NW New Caledonia
9 O9 **Chesterfield Inlet** Nunavut, NW Canada 63°19′N 90°57′W
9 O9 **Chesterfield Inlet** *inlet* Nunavut, N Canada
21 Y3 **Chester River** ≈ Delaware/Maryland, NE USA
21 X3 **Chestertown** Maryland, NE USA 39°13′N 76°04′W
19 R4 **Chesuncook Lake** ◎ Maine, NE USA
30 J5 **Chetek** Wisconsin, N USA 45°19′N 91°37′W
13 R14 **Chéticamp** Nova Scotia, SE Canada 46°14′N 61°19′W
27 Q8 **Chetopa** Kansas, C USA 37°02′N 95°05′W
41 Y14 **Chetumal** *var.* Payo Obispo. Quintana Roo, SE Mexico 18°32′N 88°16′W
Chetumal, Bahia/Chetumal, Bahía de see Chetumal Bay
42 G1 **Chetumal Bay** *var.* Bahia Chetumal, Bahía de Chetumal. *bay* Belize/Mexico
10 M13 **Chetwynd** British Columbia, W Canada 55°42′N 121°36′W
38 M11 **Chevak** Alaska, USA 61°31′N 165°35′W
36 M12 **Chevelon Creek** ≈ Arizona, SW USA
185 J17 **Cheviot** Canterbury, South Island, New Zealand 42°48′S 173°17′E
96 L13 **Cheviot Hills** *hill range* England/Scotland, United Kingdom
96 L13 **Cheviot, The** ▲ NE England, United Kingdom 55°28′N 02°10′W
14 M11 **Chevreuil, Lac du** ◎ Québec, SE Canada
81 I16 **Ch'ew Bahir** *var.* Lake Stefanie. ◎ Ethiopia/Kenya
32 L7 **Chewelah** Washington, NW USA 48°16′N 117°42′W
26 K10 **Cheyenne** Oklahoma, C USA 35°37′N 99°43′W
33 Z17 **Cheyenne** *state capital* Wyoming, C USA 41°08′N 104°46′W
26 L5 **Cheyenne Bottoms** ◎ Kansas, C USA
16 J8 **Cheyenne River** ≈ South Dakota/Wyoming, N USA
37 W5 **Cheyenne Wells** Colorado, C USA 38°49′N 102°21′W
108 C9 **Cheyres** Vaud, W Switzerland 46°48′N 06°48′E
Chezdi-Oşorheiu see Târgu Secuiesc
153 P13 **Chhapra** *prev.* Chapra. Bihār, N India 25°50′N 84°42′E
153 V13 **Chhatak** *var.* Chatak. Sylhet, NE Bangladesh 25°02′N 91°33′E
154 J9 **Chhatarpur** Madhya Pradesh, C India 24°54′N 79°35′E
154 N13 **Chhatrapur** *prev.* Chatrapur. Orissa, E India 19°26′N 85°02′E
154 K2 **Chhattīsgarh** ◐ *state* E India
154 L12 **Chhattīsgarh** *plain* C India
154 I11 **Chhindwāra** Madhya Pradesh, C India 22°04′N 78°58′E
153 T12 **Chhukha** SW Bhutan 27°02′N 89°36′E
161 S14 **Chiai** *var.* Chia-i, Chiayi, Kiayi, Jiayi, *Jap.* Kagi. C Taiwan 23°29′N 120°27′E
Chia-i see Chiai
Chia-mu-ssu see Jiamusi
83 B15 **Chiange** *Port.* Vila de Almoster. Huíla, SW Angola 15°44′S 13°54′E
Chiang-hsi see Jiangxi
161 S12 **Chiang Kai-shek** ✕ (T'aipei) N Taiwan 25°09′N 121°20′E
167 P8 **Chiang Khan** Loei, E Thailand 17°51′N 101°43′E
167 O7 **Chiang Mai** *var.* Chiangmai, Chiengmai, Kiangmai. Chiang Mai, NW Thailand 18°48′N 98°59′E
167 O7 **Chiang Mai** ✕ Chiang Mai, NW Thailand 18°44′N 98°53′E
Chiangmai see Chiang Mai
167 O6 **Chiang Rai** *var.* Chianpai, Chienrai, Muang Chiang Rai. Chiang Rai, NW Thailand 19°56′N 99°51′E
Chiang-su see Jiangsu
Chianning/Chian-ning see Nanjing
Chianpai see Chiang Rai
106 G12 **Chianti** *cultural region* C Italy
Chiapa see Chiapa de Corzo
41 U16 **Chiapa de Corzo** *var.* Chiapa. Chiapas, SE Mexico 16°42′N 92°59′W
41 V16 **Chiapas** ◐ *state* SE Mexico
106 J12 **Chiaravalle** Marche, C Italy 43°36′N 13°19′E
107 N22 **Chiaravalle Centrale** Calabria, SW Italy 38°40′N 16°25′E
106 E7 **Chiari** Lombardia, N Italy 45°33′N 10°00′E
108 H12 **Chiasso** Ticino, S Switzerland 45°51′N 09°02′E
137 S9 **Chiat'ura** C Georgia 42°13′N 43°11′E
41 P15 **Chiautla** *var.* Chiautla de Tapia. Puebla, S Mexico 18°16′N 98°31′W
Chiautla de Tapia see Chiautla
106 D10 **Chiavari** Liguria, NW Italy 44°19′N 09°19′E
106 E6 **Chiavenna** Lombardia, N Italy 46°19′N 09°22′E
Chiayi see Chiai
Chiazza see Piazza Armerina
165 O14 **Chiba** *var.* Tiba. Chiba, Honshū, S Japan 35°37′N 140°06′E
165 O13 **Chiba** *off.* Chiba-ken, *var.* Tiba. ◐ *prefecture* Honshū, S Japan
83 M18 **Chibabava** Sofala, C Mozambique 20°17′S 33°39′E
Chiba-ken see Chiba
161 O10 **Chibi** *prev.* Puqi. Hubei, C China 29°45′N 113°55′E
83 B15 **Chibia** *Port.* João de Almeida, Vila João de Almeida. Huíla, SW Angola 15°11′S 13°41′E
83 M18 **Chiboma** Sofala, C Mozambique 20°06′S 33°54′E
82 J12 **Chibondo** Luapula, N Zambia 10°42′S 28°42′E
82 K11 **Chibote** Luapula, NE Zambia 09°52′S 29°33′E
12 K12 **Chibougamau** Québec, SE Canada 49°56′N 74°24′W
164 H11 **Chiburi-jima** *island* Oki-shotō, SW Japan
83 M20 **Chibuto** Gaza, S Mozambique 24°40′S 33°33′E
31 N11 **Chicago** Illinois, N USA 41°51′N 87°39′W
31 N11 **Chicago Heights** Illinois, N USA 41°30′N 87°38′W
15 W6 **Chic-Chocs, Monts** *Eng.* Shickshock Mountains. ▲▲ Québec, SE Canada
39 W13 **Chichagof Island** *island* Alexander Archipelago, Alaska, USA
57 K20 **Chichas, Cordillera de** ▲▲ SW Bolivia
41 X12 **Chichén-Itzá, Ruinas** *ruins* Yucatán, SE Mexico
97 N23 **Chichester** SE England, United Kingdom 50°50′N 00°48′W
42 C5 **Chichicastenango** Quiché, W Guatemala 14°55′N 91°06′W
42 I9 **Chichigalpa** Chinandega, NW Nicaragua 12°35′N 87°04′W
Ch'i-ch'i-ha-erh see Qiqihar
165 X16 **Chichijima-rettō** *Eng.* Beechy Group. *island group* SE Japan
54 K4 **Chichiriviche** Falcón, N Venezuela 10°58′N 68°17′W
39 R11 **Chickaloon** Alaska, USA 61°48′N 148°27′W
20 L10 **Chickamauga Lake** ▣ Tennessee, S USA
23 N7 **Chickasawhay River** ≈ Mississippi, S USA
26 M11 **Chickasha** Oklahoma, C USA 35°03′N 97°57′W
39 T9 **Chicken** Alaska, USA 64°04′N 141°56′W
104 J16 **Chiclana de la Frontera** Andalucía, S Spain 36°26′N 06°09′W
56 B11 **Chiclayo** Lambayeque, NW Peru 06°47′S 79°47′W
35 N5 **Chico** California, W USA 39°42′N 121°51′W
83 L15 **Chicoa** Tete, NW Mozambique 15°45′S 32°25′E
83 M20 **Chicomo** Gaza, S Mozambique 24°29′S 34°15′E
18 M11 **Chicopee** Massachusetts, NE USA 42°08′N 72°34′W
63 I19 **Chico, Río** ≈ SE Argentina
63 I21 **Chico, Río** ≈ S Argentina
27 W14 **Chicot, Lake** ◎ Arkansas, C USA
15 R7 **Chicoutimi** Québec, SE Canada 48°24′N 71°04′W
15 Q8 **Chicoutimi** ≈ Québec, SE Canada
83 L19 **Chicualacuala** Gaza, SW Mozambique 22°06′S 31°42′E
83 B14 **Chicuma** Benguela, C Angola 13°33′S 14°41′E
155 J21 **Chidambaram** Tamil Nādu, SE India 11°25′N 79°42′E
196 K13 **Chidley, Cape** *headland* Newfoundland and Labrador, E Canada 60°25′N 64°39′W
101 N24 **Chiemsee** ◎ SE Germany
Chiengmai see Chiang Mai
Chienrai see Chiang Rai
106 B8 **Chieri** Piemonte, NW Italy 45°01′N 07°49′E
106 F8 **Chiese** ≈ N Italy
107 K14 **Chieti** *var.* Teate. Abruzzo, C Italy 42°22′N 14°10′E
99 E19 **Chièvres** Hainaut, SW Belgium 50°34′N 03°49′E
163 S12 **Chifeng** *var.* Ulanhad. Nei Mongol Zizhiqu, N China 42°17′N 118°56′E
82 F13 **Chifumage** ≈ E Angola
82 M13 **Chifunda** Eastern, NE Zambia 11°57′S 32°36′E
145 S14 **Chiganak** *var.* Čiganak, *Kaz.* Shyghanaq. Zhambyl, SE Kazakhstan 45°10′N 73°55′E
39 P15 **Chiginagak, Mount** ▲ Alaska, USA 57°10′N 157°00′W
Chigirin see Chyhyryn
41 P13 **Chignahuapan** Puebla, S Mexico 19°52′N 98°03′W
39 O15 **Chignik** Alaska, USA 56°18′N 158°24′W
83 M19 **Chigombe** ≈ S Mozambique
54 D7 **Chigorodó** Antioquia, NW Colombia 07°42′N 76°45′W
83 M19 **Chigubo** Gaza, S Mozambique 22°50′S 33°30′E
Chihertey see Altay
Chih-fu see Yantai
Chihli see Hebei
Chihli, Gulf of see Bo Hai
40 J6 **Chihuahua** Chihuahua, NW Mexico 28°40′N 106°06′W
40 I6 **Chihuahua** ◐ *state* N Mexico
145 O15 **Chiili** *Kaz.* Shieli. Kzylorda, S Kazakhstan 44°13′N 66°46′E
26 M7 **Chikaskia River** ≈ Kansas/Oklahoma, C USA
155 H19 **Chik Ballāpur** Karnātaka, W India 13°28′N 77°42′E
124 G15 **Chikhachevo** Pskovskaya Oblast', W Russian Federation 57°17′N 29°51′E
155 F19 **Chikmagalūr** Karnātaka, W India 13°20′N 75°46′E
129 V7 **Chikoy** ≈ C Russian Federation
83 J15 **Chikumbi** Lusaka, C Zambia 15°11′S 28°20′E
82 M13 **Chikwa** Eastern, NE Zambia 11°39′S 32°45′E
Chikwana see Chikwawa
83 N15 **Chikwawa** *var.* Chikwana. Southern, S Malawi 16°03′S 34°48′E
155 J16 **Chilakalūrupet** Andhra Pradesh, E India 16°09′N 80°13′E
146 L14 **Chilan** Lebap Welaýaty, E Turkmenistan 37°57′N 64°58′E
Chilapa see Chilapa de Alvarez
41 P16 **Chilapa de Alvarez** *var.* Chilapa. Guerrero, S Mexico 17°34′N 99°11′W
155 J25 **Chilaw** North Western Province, W Sri Lanka 07°34′N 79°48′E
57 D15 **Chilca** Lima, W Peru 12°35′S 76°41′W
23 Q4 **Childersburg** Alabama, S USA 33°16′N 86°21′W
25 P4 **Childress** Texas, SW USA 34°25′N 100°14′W
63 G14 **Chile** *off.* Republic of Chile. ◆ *republic* SW South America
47 R10 **Chile Basin** *undersea feature* E Pacific Ocean 33°00′S 80°00′W
63 H20 **Chile Chico** Aisén, W Chile 46°34′S 71°44′W
62 I9 **Chilecito** La Rioja, NW Argentina 29°10′S 67°30′W
62 H12 **Chilecito** Mendoza, W Argentina 33°53′S 69°03′W
83 L14 **Chilembwe** Eastern, E Zambia 13°54′S 31°38′E
Chile, Republic of see Chile
193 S11 **Chile Rise** *undersea feature* SE Pacific Ocean 40°00′S 90°00′W
117 N13 **Chilia, Braţul** ≈ SE Romania
Chilia-Nouă see Kiliya
145 V15 **Chilik** *Kaz.* Shelek. Almaty, SE Kazakhstan 43°35′N 78°12′E
145 V15 **Chilik** ≈ SE Kazakhstan
154 O13 **Chilika Lake** *var.* Chilka Lake. ◎ E India
82 J13 **Chililabombwe** Copperbelt, C Zambia 12°20′S 27°52′E
Chi-lin see Jilin
Chilka Lake see Chilika Lake
10 H9 **Chilkoot Pass** *pass* British Columbia, W Canada
Chill Ala, Cuan see Killala Bay
62 G13 **Chillán** Bío Bío, C Chile 36°37′S 72°10′W
61 C22 **Chillar** Buenos Aires, E Argentina 37°16′S 59°58′W
Chill Chiaráin, Cuan see Kilkieran Bay
30 K12 **Chillicothe** Illinois, N USA 40°55′N 89°29′W
27 S3 **Chillicothe** Missouri, C USA 39°47′N 93°33′W
31 S14 **Chillicothe** Ohio, N USA 39°20′N 83°00′W
25 Q4 **Chillicothe** Texas, SW USA 34°15′N 99°31′W
10 M17 **Chilliwack** British Columbia, SW Canada 49°09′N 121°54′W
Chill Mhantáin, Ceann see Wicklow Head
Chill Mhantáin, Sléibhte see Wicklow Mountains
108 C10 **Chillon** Vaud, W Switzerland 46°24′N 06°56′E
Chil'mamedkum, Peski/Chilmämetgum see Çilmämmetgum
63 F17 **Chiloé, Isla de** *var.* Isla Grande de Chiloé. *island* W Chile
32 H15 **Chiloquin** Oregon, NW USA 42°33′N 121°33′W
41 O16 **Chilpancingo** *var.* Chilpancingo de los Bravos. Guerrero, S Mexico 17°33′N 99°30′W
Chilpancingo de los Bravos see Chilpancingo
97 N21 **Chiltern Hills** *hill range* S England, United Kingdom
30 M7 **Chilton** Wisconsin, N USA 44°04′N 88°10′W
82 F11 **Chiluage** Lunda Sul, NE Angola 09°32′S 21°48′E
82 N12 **Chilumba** *prev.* Deep Bay. Northern, N Malawi 10°27′S 34°12′E
161 T12 **Chilung** *var.* Keelung, *Jap.* Kirun, Kirun'; *prev. Sp.* Santissima Trinidad. N Taiwan 25°10′N 121°43′E
83 N15 **Chilwa, Lake** *var.* Lago Chirua, Lake Shirwa. ◎ SE Malawi
167 R10 **Chi, Mae Nam** ≈ E Thailand
42 C6 **Chimaltenango** Chimaltenango, C Guatemala 14°40′N 90°48′W
42 A2 **Chimaltenango** *off.* Departamento de Chimaltenango. ◐ *department* S Guatemala
Chimaltenango, Departamento de see Chimaltenango
43 V15 **Chimán** Panamá, E Panama 08°42′N 78°35′W
83 M17 **Chimanimani** *prev.* Mandidzudzure, Melsetter. Manicaland, E Zimbabwe 19°48′S 32°52′E
99 G22 **Chimay** Hainaut, S Belgium 50°03′N 04°20′E
37 S10 **Chimayo** New Mexico, SW USA 36°00′N 105°55′W
Chimbay see Chimboy
56 A13 **Chimborazo** ◐ *province* C Ecuador
56 C7 **Chimborazo** Ѫ C Ecuador 01°29′S 78°50′W
56 C12 **Chimbote** Ancash, W Peru 09°04′S 78°34′W
146 H7 **Chimboy** *Rus.* Chimbay. Qoraqalpog'iston Respublikasi, NW Uzbekistan 43°03′N 59°52′E
186 D7 **Chimbu** ◐ *province* C Papua New Guinea
54 F6 **Chimichagua** Cesar, N Colombia 09°19′N 73°51′W
Chimishliya see Cimişlia
Chimkent see Shymkent
Chimkentskaya Oblast' see Yuzhnyy Kazakhstan
28 I14 **Chimney Rock** *rock* Nebraska, C USA
83 M17 **Chimoio** Manica, C Mozambique 19°08′S 33°29′E
82 K11 **Chimpembe** Northern, NE Zambia 09°31′S 29°33′E
41 O8 **China** Nuevo León, NE Mexico 25°42′N 99°15′W
156 M9 **China** *off.* People's Republic of China, *Chin.* Chung-hua Jen-min Kung-ho-kuo, Zhonghua Renmin Gongheguo; *prev.* Chinese Empire. ◆ *republic* E Asia
19 Q7 **China Lake** ◎ Maine, NE USA
42 F8 **Chinameca** San Miguel, E El Salvador 13°30′N 88°20′W*
Chi-nan/Chinan see Jinan
42 H9 **Chinandega** Chinandega, NW Nicaragua 12°37′N 87°08′W
42 H9 **Chinandega** ◐ *department* NW Nicaragua
China, People's Republic of see China
China, Republic of see Taiwan
24 J11 **Chinati Mountains** ▲▲ Texas, SW USA
Chinaz see Chinoz
57 E15 **Chincha Alta** Ica, SW Peru 13°25′S 76°07′W
11 N11 **Chinchaga** ≈ Alberta, SW Canada
Chin-chiang see Quanzhou
Chinchilla see Chinchilla de Monte Aragón
105 Q11 **Chinchilla de Monte Aragón** *var.* Chinchilla. Castilla-La Mancha, C Spain 38°56′N 01°44′W
54 D10 **Chinchiná** Caldas, W Colombia 04°59′N 75°37′W
105 O8 **Chinchón** Madrid, C Spain 40°08′N 03°26′W
41 Z14 **Chinchorro, Banco** *island* SE Mexico
Chin-chou/Chinchow see Jinzhou
21 Z5 **Chincoteague** Assateague Island, Virginia, NE USA 37°55′N 75°22′W
83 O17 **Chinde** Zambézia, NE Mozambique 18°35′S 36°28′E
163 X17 **Chin-do** *Jap.* Chin-tō. *island* SW South Korea
159 R13 **Chindu** *var.* Chengwen; *prev.* Chuqung. Qinghai, C China 33°19′N 97°08′E
Chindwin see Chindwinn
166 M2 **Chindwinn** *var.* Chindwin. ≈ N Burma (Myanmar)
Chinese Empire see China
Chinghai see Qinghai
Ch'ing Hai see Qinghai Hu, China
Chingildi see Shengeldi
144 H9 **Chingirlau** *Kaz.* Shyngghyrlaū. Zapadnyy Kazakhstan, W Kazakhstan 51°10′N 53°44′E
82 J13 **Chingola** Copperbelt, C Zambia 12°31′S 27°53′E
Ching-Tao/Ch'ing-tao see Qingdao
82 C13 **Chinguar** Huambo, C Angola 12°33′S 16°25′E
76 I7 **Chingueţţi** *var.* Chinguetti. Adrar, C Mauritania 20°25′N 12°24′W

◆ Country
● Country Capital
◇ Dependent Territory
○ Dependent Territory Capital
◐ Administrative Regions
✕ International Airport
▲ Mountain
▲▲ Mountain Range
Ѫ Volcano
≈ River
◎ Lake
▣ Reservoir

163 Z16 **Chinhae** *Jap.* Chinkai. S South Korea 35°06′N 128°48′E
166 K4 **Chin Hills** ▲▲ W Burma (Myanmar)
83 K16 **Chinhoyi** *prev.* Sinoia. Mashonaland West, N Zimbabwe 17°22′S 30°12′E
Chinhsien *see* Jinzhou
39 Q14 **Chiniak, Cape** *headland* Kodiak Island, Alaska, USA 57°37′N 152°10′W
14 G10 **Chiniguchi Lake** ◎ Ontario, S Canada
149 U8 **Chinīot** Punjab, NE Pakistan 31°40′N 73°00′E
163 Y16 **Chinju** *Jap.* Shinshū. S South Korea 35°12′N 128°06′E
Chinkai *see* Chinhae
78 M13 **Chinko** ≋ E Central African Republic
37 O9 **Chinle** Arizona, SW USA 36°09′N 109°33′W
161 R13 **Chinmen Tao** *var.* Jinmen Dao, Quemoy. *island* W Taiwan
Chinnchâr *see* Shinshār
Chinnereth *see* Tiberias, Lake
164 C12 **Chino** *var.* Tino. Nagano, Honshū, S Japan 36°00′N 138°10′E
102 L8 **Chinon** Indre-et-Loire, C France 47°10′N 00°15′E
33 T7 **Chinook** Montana, NW USA 48°35′N 109°13′W
Chinook State *see* Washington
192 L4 **Chinook Trough** *undersea feature* N Pacific Ocean
36 K11 **Chino Valley** Arizona, SW USA 34°45′N 112°27′W
147 P10 **Chinoz** *Rus.* Chinaz. Toshkent Viloyati, E Uzbekistan 40°58′N 68°46′E
82 L12 **Chinsali** Northern, NE Zambia 10°33′S 32°05′E
166 K5 **Chin State** ◐ *state* W Burma (Myanmar)
Chinsura *see* Chunchura
Chin-tō *see* Chin-do
54 E6 **Chinú** Córdoba, NW Colombia 09°07′N 75°25′W
99 K24 **Chiny, Forêt de** *forest* SE Belgium
83 M15 **Chioco** Tete, NW Mozambique 16°22′S 32°50′E
106 H8 **Chioggia** *anc.* Fossa Claudia. Veneto, NE Italy 45°14′N 12°17′E
114 H12 **Chionótrypa** ▲ NE Greece 41°16′N 24°06′E
115 L18 **Chíos** *var.* Hios, Khíos, *It.* Scio, *Turk.* Sakiz-Adasi. Chíos, E Greece 38°23′N 26°07′E
115 K18 **Chíos** *var.* Khíos. *island* E Greece
83 M14 **Chipata** *prev.* Fort Jameson. Eastern, E Zambia 13°40′S 32°42′E
83 C14 **Chipindo** Huíla, C Angola 13°53′S 15°47′E
23 R8 **Chipley** Florida, SE USA 30°46′N 85°32′W
155 D15 **Chiplūn** Mahārāshtra, W India 17°32′N 73°32′E
81 H22 **Chipogolo** Dodoma, C Tanzania 06°52′S 36°03′E
23 R8 **Chipola River** ≋ Florida, SE USA
97 L22 **Chippenham** S England, United Kingdom 51°28′N 02°07′W
30 J6 **Chippewa Falls** Wisconsin, N USA 44°56′N 91°25′W
30 J4 **Chippewa, Lake** ⊠ Wisconsin, N USA
31 Q8 **Chippewa River** ≋ Michigan, N USA
30 I6 **Chippewa River** ≋ Wisconsin, N USA
Chipping Wycombe *see* High Wycombe
114 G8 **Chiprovtsi** Montana, NW Bulgaria 43°23′N 22°53′E
19 T4 **Chiputneticook Lakes** *lakes* Canada/USA
56 D13 **Chiquián** Ancash, W Peru 10°09′S 78°08′W
41 Y11 **Chiquilá** Quintana Roo, SE Mexico 21°25′N 87°20′W
42 E6 **Chiquimula** Chiquimula, SE Guatemala 14°46′N 89°32′W
42 A3 **Chiquimula** *off.* Departamento de Chiquimula. ◐ *department* SE Guatemala
Chiquimula, Departamento de *see* Chiquimula
42 D7 **Chiquimulilla** Santa Rosa, S Guatemala 14°06′N 90°23′W
54 F9 **Chiquinquirá** Boyacá, C Colombia 05°37′N 73°51′W
155 J17 **Chīrāla** Andhra Pradesh, E India 15°49′N 80°21′E
149 N4 **Chīras** Ghowr, N Afghanistan 35°15′N 65°39′E
152 H11 **Chirāwa** Rājasthān, N India 28°12′N 75°42′E
Chirchik *see* Chirchiq
147 Q9 **Chirchiq** *Rus.* Chirchik. Toshkent Viloyati, E Uzbekistan 41°30′N 69°32′E
147 P10 **Chirchiq** ≋ E Uzbekistan
Chire *see* Shire
83 L18 **Chiredzi** Masvingo, SE Zimbabwe 21°00′S 31°38′E
25 X8 **Chireno** Texas, SW USA 31°30′N 94°21′W
77 X7 **Chirfa** Agadez, NE Niger 21°01′N 12°41′E
37 O16 **Chiricahua Mountains** ▲▲ Arizona, SW USA
37 O16 **Chiricahua Peak** ▲ Arizona, SW USA 31°51′N 109°17′W
54 F6 **Chiriguaná** Cesar, N Colombia 09°24′N 73°38′W
39 P15 **Chirikof Island** *island* Alaska, USA
43 P16 **Chiriquí** *off.* Provincia de Chiriquí. ◐ *province* SW Panama
43 P17 **Chiriquí, Golfo de** *Eng.* Chiriqui Gulf. *gulf* SW Panama
43 P15 **Chiriquí Grande** Bocas del Toro, W Panama 08°58′N 82°08′W
Chiriqui Gulf *see* Chiriquí, Golfo de
43 P15 **Chiriquí, Laguna de** *lagoon* NW Panama
Chiriquí, Provincia de *see* Chiriquí
43 O16 **Chiriquí Viejo, Río** ≋ W Panama
Chiriquí, Volcán de *see* Barú, Volcán
83 N15 **Chiromo** Southern, S Malawi 16°32′S 35°07′E
114 J10 **Chirpan** Stara Zagora, C Bulgaria 42°12′N 25°20′E
43 N14 **Chirripó Atlántico, Río** ≋ E Costa Rica
Chirripó, Cerro *see* Chirripó Grande, Cerro
Chirripó del Pacífico, Río *see* Chirripó, Río
43 N14 **Chirripó Grande, Cerro** *var.* Cerro Chirripó. ▲ SE Costa Rica 09°31′N 83°28′W
43 N13 **Chirripó, Río** *var.* Río Chirripó del Pacífico. ≋ NE Costa Rica
Chirua, Lago *see* Chilwa, Lake
83 J15 **Chirundu** Southern, S Zambia 16°03′S 28°50′E
29 W8 **Chisago City** Minnesota, N USA 45°22′N 92°53′W
83 J14 **Chisamba** Central, C Zambia 15°00′S 28°22′E
39 T10 **Chisana** Alaska, USA 62°09′N 142°07′W
82 I13 **Chisasa** North Western, NW Zambia 12°09′S 25°30′E
12 I9 **Chisasibi** *prev.* Fort George. Québec, C Canada 53°50′N 79°01′W
42 D4 **Chisec** Alta Verapaz, C Guatemala 15°50′N 90°18′W
127 U5 **Chishmy** Respublika Bashkortostan, W Russian Federation 54°33′N 55°21′E
29 V4 **Chisholm** Minnesota, N USA 47°29′N 92°52′W
149 U10 **Chishtiān Mandi** Punjab, E Pakistan 29°44′N 72°54′E
160 I11 **Chishui He** ≋ C China
Chisimaio/Chisimayu *see* Kismaayo
117 N10 **Chişinău** *Rus.* Kishinev. ● (Moldova) C Moldova 47°N 28°51′E
117 N10 **Chişinău** ✈ S Moldova 46°54′N 28°56′E
Chişinău-Criş *see* Chişineu-Criş
116 F10 **Chişineu-Criş** *Hung.* Kisjenő; *prev.* Chişinău-Criş. Arad, W Romania 46°33′N 21°30′E
83 K14 **Chisomo** Central, C Zambia 13°30′S 30°37′E
106 A8 **Chisone** ≋ NW Italy
24 K12 **Chisos Mountains** ▲▲ Texas, SW USA
39 T10 **Chistochina** Alaska, USA 62°34′N 144°39′W
127 R4 **Chistopol'** Respublika Tatarstan, W Russian Federation 55°20′N 50°39′E
145 O8 **Chistopol'ye** Severnyy Kazakhstan, N Kazakhstan 52°37′N 67°14′E
123 O13 **Chita** Chitinskaya Oblast', S Russian Federation 52°03′N 113°35′E
83 B16 **Chitado** Cunene, SW Angola 17°16′S 13°54′E
Chitaldroog/Chitaldrug *see* Chitradurga
83 C15 **Chitanda** ≋ S Angola
Chitangwiza *see* Chitungwiza
82 F10 **Chitato** Lunda Norte, NE Angola 07°23′S 20°46′E
83 C14 **Chitembo** Bié, C Angola 13°33′S 16°47′E
39 T11 **Chitina** Alaska, USA 61°31′N 144°26′W
39 T11 **Chitina River** ≋ Alaska, USA
123 O12 **Chitinskaya Oblast'** ◐ *province* S Russian Federation
82 M11 **Chitipa** Northern, NW Malawi 09°41′S 33°19′E
165 S4 **Chitose** *var.* Titose. Hokkaidō, NE Japan 42°51′N 141°40′E
155 G18 **Chitradurga** *prev.* Chitaldroog, Chitaldrug. Karnātaka, W India 14°16′N 76°23′E
149 T3 **Chitrāl** North-West Frontier Province, NW Pakistan 35°51′N 71°47′E
43 S16 **Chitré** Herrera, S Panama 07°57′N 80°26′W
153 V16 **Chittagong** *Ben.* Chāttagām. Chittagong, SE Bangladesh 22°20′N 91°48′E
153 U16 **Chittagong** ◐ *division* E Bangladesh
153 Q15 **Chittaranjan** West Bengal, NE India 23°52′N 86°40′E
152 G14 **Chittaurgarh** *var.* Chittorgarh. Rājasthān, N India 24°54′N 74°42′E
155 I19 **Chittoor** Andhra Pradesh, E India 13°13′N 79°06′E
Chittorgarh *see* Chittaurgarh
155 G21 **Chittūr** Kerala, SW India 10°42′N 76°46′E
83 K16 **Chitungwiza** *prev.* Chitangwiza. Mashonaland East, NE Zimbabwe 18°S 31°06′E
62 H4 **Chíuchíu** Antofagasta, N Chile 22°13′S 68°34′W
82 F12 **Chiumbe** *var.* Tshiumbe. ≋ Angola/Dem. Rep. Congo
83 F15 **Chiume** Moxico, E Angola 15°08′S 21°09′E
82 K13 **Chiundaponde** Northern, NE Zambia 12°14′S 30°40′E
106 H13 **Chiusi** Toscana, C Italy 43°00′N 11°56′E
54 J5 **Chivacoa** Yaracuy, N Venezuela 10°10′N 68°54′W
106 B8 **Chivasso** Piemonte, NW Italy 45°13′N 07°54′E
83 L17 **Chivhu** *prev.* Enkeldoorn. Midlands, C Zimbabwe 19°01′S 30°54′E
61 C20 **Chivilcoy** Buenos Aires, E Argentina 34°55′S 60°00′W
82 N12 **Chiweta** Northern, N Malawi 10°36′S 34°09′E
42 D4 **Chixoy, Río** *var.* Río Negro, Río Salinas. ≋ Guatemala/Mexico
82 H13 **Chizela** North Western, NW Zambia 13°11′S 24°59′E
125 O5 **Chizha** Nenetskiy Avtonomnyy Okrug, NW Russian Federation 67°04′N 44°19′E
161 Q9 **Chizhou** *var.* Guichi. Anhui, E China 30°39′N 117°29′E
164 I12 **Chizu** Tottori, Honshū, SW Japan 35°15′N 134°14′E
Chkalov *see* Orenburg
127 N3 **Chkalovsk** Nizhegorodskaya Oblast', W Russian Federation 56°45′N 43°15′E
74 J5 **Chlef** *var.* Ech Cheliff, Ech Chleff; *prev.* Al-Asnam, El Asnam, Orléansville. NW Algeria 36°11′N 01°21′E
115 G18 **Chlómo** ▲ C Greece 38°36′N 22°57′E
111 M15 **Chmielnik** Świętokrzyskie, C Poland 50°37′N 20°43′E
167 S11 **Chŏâm Khsant** Preăh Vihéar, N Cambodia 14°13′N 104°56′E
62 G10 **Choapa, Río** *var.* Choapo. ≋ C Chile
Choapas *see* Las Choapas
Choapo *see* Choapa, Río
Choarta *see* Chwārtā
67 T13 **Chobe** ≋ N Botswana
14 K8 **Chochocouane** ≋ Québec, SE Canada
110 E13 **Chocianów** *Ger.* Kotzenan. Dolnośląskie, SW Poland 51°23′N 15°55′E
54 C9 **Chocó** *off.* Departamento del Chocó. ◐ *province* W Colombia
Chocó, Departamento del *see* Chocó
35 X16 **Chocolate Mountains** ▲▲ California, W USA
21 W9 **Chocowinity** North Carolina, SE USA 35°33′N 77°03′W
27 N10 **Choctaw** Oklahoma, C USA 35°30′N 97°16′W
23 Q8 **Choctawhatchee Bay** *bay* Florida, SE USA
23 Q8 **Choctawhatchee River** ≋ Florida, SE USA
Chodau *see* Chodov
163 V14 **Ch'o-do** *island* SW North Korea
Chodorów *see* Khodoriv
111 A16 **Chodov** *Ger.* Chodau. Karlovarský Kraj, W Czech Republic 50°15′N 12°45′E
110 G10 **Chodzież** Wielkopolskie, C Poland 53°N 16°55′E
63 J15 **Choele Choel** Río Negro, C Argentina 39°19′S 65°42′W
83 L14 **Chofombo** Tete, NW Mozambique 14°43′S 31°48′E
Chohtan *see* Chauhtan
11 U14 **Choiceland** Saskatchewan, C Canada 53°28′N 104°26′W
186 K8 **Choiseul** *var.* Lauru. *island* NW Solomon Islands
63 M23 **Choiseul Sound** *sound* East Falkland, Falkland Islands
40 H7 **Choix** Sinaloa, C Mexico 26°43′N 108°20′W
110 D10 **Chojna** Zachodnio-pomorskie, W Poland 52°56′N 14°25′E
110 H8 **Chojnice** *Ger.* Konitz. Pomorskie, N Poland 53°41′N 17°34′E
111 F14 **Chojnów** *Ger.* Hainau, Haynau. Dolnośląskie, SW Poland 51°16′N 15°55′E
167 Q10 **Chok Chai** Nakhon Ratchasima, C Thailand 14°45′N 102°10′E
80 I12 **Ch'ok'ē** *var.* Choke Mountains. ▲▲ NW Ethiopia
25 R13 **Choke Canyon Lake** ⊠ Texas, SW USA
Choke Mountains *see* Ch'ok'ē
145 T15 **Chokpar** *Kaz.* Shoqpar. Zhambyl, S Kazakhstan 43°49′N 74°25′E
147 W7 **Chok-Tal** *var.* Choktal. Issyk-Kul'skaya Oblast', E Kyrgyzstan 42°37′N 76°45′E
Choktal *see* Chok-Tal
Chókué *see* Chokwè
123 R7 **Chokurdakh** Respublika Sakha (Yakutiya), NE Russian Federation 70°38′N 148°18′E
83 L20 **Chokwè** *var.* Chókué. Gaza, S Mozambique 24°27′S 32°55′E
188 F8 **Chol** Babeldaob, N Palau
160 E8 **Chola Shan** ▲▲ C China
102 J8 **Cholet** Maine-et-Loire, NW France 47°03′N 00°52′W
63 H17 **Cholila** Chubut, W Argentina 42°33′S 71°28′W
Cholo *see* Thyolo
147 V8 **Cholpon** Narynskaya Oblast', C Kyrgyzstan 42°07′N 75°25′E
147 X7 **Cholpon-Ata** Issyk-Kul'skaya Oblast', E Kyrgyzstan 42°39′N 77°05′E
41 P14 **Cholula** Puebla, S Mexico 19°03′N 98°19′W
42 I8 **Choluteca** Choluteca, S Honduras 13°15′N 87°10′W
42 H8 **Choluteca** ◐ *department* S Honduras
42 H8 **Choluteca, Río** ≋ SW Honduras
83 I15 **Choma** Southern, S Zambia 16°48′S 26°58′E
158 L17 **Chomo** *var.* Xarsingma. Xizang Zizhiqu, W China 27°31′N 88°58′E *see also* Yadong
153 T11 **Chomo Lhari** ▲ NW Bhutan 27°59′N 89°24′E
167 N7 **Chom Thong** Chiang Mai, NW Thailand 18°25′N 98°44′E
111 B15 **Chomutov** *Ger.* Komotau. Ústecký Kraj, NW Czech Republic 50°28′N 13°24′E
123 N11 **Chona** ≋ C Russian Federation
163 X15 **Ch'ŏnan** *Jap.* Tenan. W South Korea 36°51′N 127°11′E
167 P11 **Chon Buri** *prev.* Bang Pla Soi. Chon Buri, S Thailand 13°24′N 100°59′E
56 B6 **Chone** Manabí, W Ecuador 0°44′S 80°04′W
Chong'an *see* Wuyishan
163 W13 **Ch'ŏngch'ŏn-gang** ≋ W North Korea
163 Y11 **Ch'ŏngjin** NE North Korea 41°48′N 129°44′E
163 W13 **Chŏngju** W North Korea 39°44′N 125°13′E
161 S8 **Chongming Dao** *island* E China
160 J10 **Chongqing** *var.* Ch'ung-ching, Ch'ung-ch'ing, Chungking, Pahsien, Tchongking, Yuzhou. Chongqing Shi, C China 29°34′N 106°27′E
160 K10 **Chongqing Shi** ◐ *municipality* Chongqing Shi, C China
Chŏngup *see* Chŏnju
161 O10 **Chongyang** *var.* Tiancheng. Hubei, C China 29°35′N 114°03′E
160 J15 **Chongzuo** *prev.* Taiping. Guangxi Zhuangzu Zizhiqu, S China 22°18′N 107°23′E
163 Y16 **Chŏnju** *prev.* Chŏngup, *Jap.* Seiyu. SW South Korea 35°51′N 127°08′E
163 Y15 **Chŏnju** *Jap.* Zenshū. SW South Korea 35°51′N 127°08′E
Chonnacht *see* Connaught
Chonogol *see* Erdenetsagaan
63 F19 **Chonos, Archipiélago de los** *island group* S Chile
42 K10 **Chontales** ◐ *department* S Nicaragua
167 T13 **Chơn Thanh** Sông Be, S Vietnam 11°25′N 106°38′E
158 K17 **Cho Oyu** *var.* Qowowuyag. ▲ China/Nepal 28°07′N 86°37′E
116 G7 **Chop** *Cz.* Čop, *Hung.* Csap. Zakarpats'ka Oblast', W Ukraine 48°26′N 22°13′E
21 Y3 **Choptank River** ≋ Maryland, NE USA
115 J22 **Chóra** *prev.* Íos. Íos, Kykládes, Greece, Aegean Sea 36°42′N 25°16′E
115 H25 **Chóra Sfakíon** *var.* Sfákia. Kríti, Greece, E Mediterranean Sea 35°12′N 24°05′E
Chorcaí, Cuan *see* Cork Harbour
43 P15 **Chorcha, Cerro** ▲ W Panama 08°39′N 82°07′W
Chorku *see* Chorkŭh
147 R11 **Chorkŭh** *Rus.* Chorku. N Tajikistan 40°04′N 70°30′E
97 K17 **Chorley** NW England, United Kingdom 53°40′N 02°38′W
Chorne More *see* Black Sea
117 R5 **Chornobay** Cherkas'ka Oblast', C Ukraine 49°40′N 32°20′E
117 O3 **Chornobyl'** *Rus.* Chernobyl'. Kyyivs'ka Oblast', N Ukraine 51°17′N 30°15′E
117 R12 **Chornomors'ke** *Rus.* Chernomorskoye. Respublika Krym, S Ukraine 45°29′N 32°45′E
117 R4 **Chornukhy** Poltavs'ka Oblast', C Ukraine 50°15′N 32°57′E
Chorokh/Chorokhi *see* Çoruh Nehri
110 O9 **Choroszcz** Podlaskie, NE Poland 53°10′N 23°E
116 K6 **Chortkiv** *Rus.* Chortkov. Ternopil's'ka Oblast', W Ukraine 49°01′N 25°46′E
Chortkov *see* Chortkiv
Chorum *see* Çorum
110 M9 **Chorzele** Mazowieckie, C Poland 53°16′N 20°53′E
111 J16 **Chorzów** *Ger.* Königshütte; *prev.* Królewska Huta. Śląskie, S Poland 50°17′N 18°58′E
163 W12 **Ch'osan** N North Korea 40°45′N 125°52′E
Chośebuz *see* Cottbus
Chōsen-kaikyō *see* Korea Strait
164 P14 **Chōshi** *var.* Tyôsi. Chiba, Honshū, S Japan 35°44′N 140°48′E
63 H14 **Chos Malal** Neuquén, W Argentina 37°23′S 70°16′W
Chosŏn-minjujuŭi-inmin-kanghwaguk *see* North Korea
110 E9 **Choszczno** *Ger.* Arnswalde. Zachodnio-pomorskie, NW Poland 53°10′N 15°24′E
153 O15 **Chota Nāgpur** *plateau* N India
33 R8 **Choteau** Montana, NW USA 47°48′N 112°40′W
Chotqol *see* Chatkal
14 M8 **Chouart** ≋ Québec, SE Canada
76 I7 **Choûm** Adrar, C Mauritania 21°19′N 12°59′W
27 Q9 **Chouteau** Oklahoma, C USA 36°11′N 95°20′W
21 X8 **Chowan River** ≋ North Carolina, SE USA
35 Q10 **Chowchilla** California, W USA 37°06′N 120°15′W
163 P7 **Choybalsan** *prev.* Byan Tumen. Dornod, E Mongolia 48°03′N 114°32′E
163 Q7 **Choybalsan** *var.* Hulstay. Dornod, NE Mongolia 48°25′N 114°56′E
162 M9 **Choyr** Govĭ Sumber, C Mongolia 46°20′N 108°21′E
185 I19 **Christchurch** Canterbury, South Island, New Zealand 43°31′S 172°39′E
97 M24 **Christchurch** S England, United Kingdom 50°44′N 01°45′W
185 I18 **Christchurch** ✈ Canterbury, South Island, New Zealand 43°28′S 172°33′E
44 J12 **Christiana** C Jamaica 18°13′N 77°29′W
83 H22 **Christiana** Free State, C South Africa 27°55′S 25°10′E
115 J23 **Christiána** *var.* Christiani. *island* Kykládes, Greece, Aegean Sea
Christiani *see* Christiána
Christiania *see* Oslo
14 G13 **Christian Island** *island* Ontario, S Canada
191 P16 **Christian, Point** *headland* Pitcairn Island, Pitcairn Islands 25°04′S 130°08′E
38 M11 **Christian River** ≋ Alaska, USA
Christiansand *see* Kristiansand
21 S7 **Christiansburg** Virginia, NE USA 37°07′N 80°26′W
95 G23 **Christiansfeld** Sønderjylland, SW Denmark 55°21′N 09°30′E
Christianshåb *see* Qasigiannguit
39 X14 **Christian Sound** *inlet* Alaska, USA
45 T9 **Christiansted** Saint Croix, S Virgin Islands (US) 17°43′N 64°42′W
Christiansund *see* Kristiansund
25 R13 **Christine** Texas, SW USA 28°47′N 98°30′W
173 U7 **Christmas Island** ◇ *Australian external territory* E Indian Ocean
129 T17 **Christmas Island** *island* E Indian Ocean
Christmas Island *see* Kiritimati
192 M7 **Christmas Ridge** *undersea feature* C Pacific Ocean
30 L16 **Christopher** Illinois, N USA 37°58′N 89°03′W
25 P9 **Christoval** Texas, SW USA 31°09′N 100°30′W
111 F17 **Chrudim** Pardubický Kraj, C Czech Republic 49°58′N 15°49′E
115 K25 **Chrýsi** *island* SE Greece
121 N2 **Chrysochoú, Kólpos** *var.* Khrysokhou Bay. *bay* E Mediterranean Sea
114 I13 **Chrysoúpoli** *var.* Hrisoupoli; *prev.* Khrisoúpolis. Anatolikí Makedonía kai Thráki, NE Greece 40°59′N 24°42′E
111 K16 **Chrzanów** *var.* Chrzanow, *Ger.* Zaumgarten. Śląskie, S Poland 50°10′N 19°21′E
129 Q7 **Chu** *Kaz.* Shū. ≋ Kazakhstan/Kyrgyzstan
42 C5 **Chuacús, Sierra de** ▲▲ W Guatemala
153 S15 **Chuadanga** Khulna, W Bangladesh 23°38′N 88°52′E
Chuan *see* Sichuan
Ch'uan-chou *see* Quanzhou
Chuankou *see* Minhe
39 O11 **Chuathbaluk** Alaska, USA 61°36′N 159°14′W
Chubek *see* Moskva
63 I17 **Chubut** *off.* Provincia de Chubut. ◐ *province* S Argentina
Chubut, Provincia de *see* Chubut
63 I17 **Chubut, Río** ≋ SE Argentina
43 V15 **Chucanti, Cerro** ▲ E Panama 08°48′N 78°27′W
Ch'u-chiang *see* Shaoguan
43 W15 **Chucunaque, Río** ≋ E Panama
Chudin *see* Chudzin
116 M5 **Chudniv** Zhytomyrs'ka Oblast', N Ukraine 50°02′N 28°06′E
124 H13 **Chudovo** Novgorodskaya Oblast', W Russian Federation 59°07′N 31°42′E
Chudskoye Ozero *see* Peipus, Lake
119 J18 **Chudzin** *Rus.* Chudin. Brestskaya Voblasts', SW Belarus 52°44′N 26°59′E
39 Q13 **Chugach Islands** *island group* Alaska, USA
39 S11 **Chugach Mountains** ▲▲ Alaska, USA
164 G12 **Chūgoku-sanchi** ▲▲ Honshū, SW Japan
Chugqênsumdo *see* Jigzhi
Chuguyev *see* Chuhuyiv
117 V5 **Chuhuyiv** *var.* Chuguyev. Kharkivs'ka Oblast', E Ukraine 49°51′N 36°44′E
61 H19 **Chuí** Rio Grande do Sul, S Brazil 33°45′S 53°23′W
Chuí *see* Chuy
145 S15 **Chu-Iliyskiye Gory** *Kaz.* Shū-Ile Taūlary. ▲▲ S Kazakhstan
Chukai *see* Cukai
Chukchi Avtonomnyy Okrug *see* Chukotskiy Avtonomnyy Okrug
Chukchi Peninsula *see* Chukotskiy Poluostrov
197 R6 **Chukchi Plain** *undersea feature* Arctic Ocean
197 R6 **Chukchi Plateau** *undersea feature* Arctic Ocean
197 R4 **Chukchi Sea** *Rus.* Chukotskoye More. *sea* Arctic Ocean
125 N14 **Chukhloma** Kostromskaya Oblast', NW Russian Federation 58°42′N 42°39′E
Chukotka *see* Chukotskiy Avtonomnyy Okrug
Chukot Range *see* Anadyrskiy Khrebet
123 V6 **Chukotskiy Avtonomnyy Okrug** *var.* Chukchi Avtonomnyy Okrug, Chukotka. ◐ *autonomous district* NE Russian Federation
123 W5 **Chukotskiy, Mys** *headland* NE Russian Federation 64°15′N 173°03′W
123 V5 **Chukotskiy Poluostrov** *Eng.* Chukchi Peninsula. *peninsula* NE Russian Federation
Chukotskoye More *see* Chukchi Sea
Chukurkak *see* Chuqurqoq
Chulakkurgan *see* Sholakkorgan
35 U17 **Chula Vista** California, W USA 32°38′N 117°04′W
123 Q12 **Chul'man** Respublika Sakha (Yakutiya), NE Russian Federation 56°50′N 124°47′E
56 B9 **Chulucanas** Piura, NW Peru 05°08′S 80°10′W
122 J12 **Chulym** ≋ C Russian Federation
152 K6 **Chumar** Jammu and Kashmir, N India 32°38′N 78°36′E
114 K9 **Chumerna** ▲ C Bulgaria 42°45′N 25°58′E
123 R12 **Chumikan** Khabarovskiy Kray, E Russian Federation 54°41′N 135°12′E
167 Q9 **Chum Phae** Khon Kaen, C Thailand 16°31′N 102°09′E
167 N13 **Chumphon** *var.* Jumporn. Chumphon, SW Thailand 10°30′N 99°11′E
167 O9 **Chumsaeng** *var.* Chum Saeng. Nakhon Sawan, C Thailand 15°52′N 100°18′E
Chum Saeng *see* Chumsaeng
122 L12 **Chuna** ≋ C Russian Federation
161 R9 **Chun'an** *var.* Qiandaohu; *prev.* Pailing. Zhejiang, SE China 29°37′N 118°59′E
161 S13 **Chunan** N Taiwan 24°44′N 120°51′E
Chuncheng *see* Yangchun
163 Y14 **Ch'unch'ŏn** *Jap.* Shunsen. N South Korea 37°52′N 127°48′E
153 S16 **Chunchura** *prev.* Chinsura. West Bengal, NE India 22°54′N 88°20′E
145 W15 **Chundzha** *Kaz.* Shonzhy. Almaty, SE Kazakhstan 43°32′N 79°28′E
Ch'ung-ch'ing/Ch'ung-ching *see* Chongqing
Chung-hua Jen-min Kung-ho-kuo *see* China
163 Y15 **Ch'ungju** *Jap.* Chūshū. C South Korea 36°57′N 127°50′E
Chungking *see* Chongqing
161 T14 **Chungyang Shanmo** *Chin.* Taiwan Shan. ▲▲ C Taiwan
149 V9 **Chūniān** Punjab, E Pakistan 30°57′N 74°01′E
122 L12 **Chunskiy** Irkutskaya Oblast', S Russian Federation 56°10′N 99°15′E
122 M11 **Chunya** ≋ C Russian Federation
124 J6 **Chupa** Respublika Kareliya, NW Russian Federation 66°15′N 33°02′E
125 P8 **Chuprovo** Respublika Komi, NW Russian Federation 64°16′N 46°27′E
57 G17 **Chuquibamba** Arequipa, SW Peru 15°47′S 72°44′W
62 H4 **Chuquicamata** Antofagasta, N Chile 22°20′S 68°56′W
57 L21 **Chuquisaca** ◐ *department* S Bolivia
Chuquisaca *see* Sucre
Chuqung *see* Chindu
146 I8 **Chuqurqoq** *Rus.* Chukurkak. Qoraqalpog'iston Respublikasi, NW Uzbekistan 42°44′N 61°33′E
127 T2 **Chur** Udmurtskaya Respublika, NW Russian Federation 57°06′N 52°57′E
108 I9 **Chur** *Fr.* Coire, *It.* Coira, *Rmsch.* Cuera, Quera; *anc.* Curia Rhaetorum. Graubünden, E Switzerland 46°52′N 09°32′E
123 Q10 **Churapcha** Respublika Sakha (Yakutiya), NE Russian Federation 61°59′N 132°06′E
11 V16 **Churchbridge** Saskatchewan, S Canada 50°55′N 101°53′W
21 O8 **Church Hill** Tennessee, S USA 36°31′N 82°42′W
11 X9 **Churchill** Manitoba, C Canada 58°46′N 94°10′W
11 X10 **Churchill** ≋ Manitoba/Saskatchewan, C Canada
13 P9 **Churchill** ≋ Newfoundland and Labrador, E Canada
11 Y9 **Churchill, Cape** *headland* Manitoba, C Canada 58°42′N 93°12′W
13 P9 **Churchill Falls** Newfoundland and Labrador, E Canada 53°38′N 64°00′W
11 S12 **Churchill Lake** ◎ Saskatchewan, C Canada
19 Q3 **Churchill Lake** ⊠ Maine, NE USA
194 I5 **Churchill Peninsula** *peninsula* Antarctica
22 H8 **Church Point** Louisiana, S USA 30°24′N 92°13′W
29 O3 **Churchs Ferry** North Dakota, N USA 48°15′N 99°12′W
146 G12 **Churchuri** Ahal Welaýaty, C Turkmenistan 38°55′N 59°13′E
21 T5 **Churchville** Virginia, NE USA 38°13′N 79°10′W
152 G10 **Chūru** Rājasthān, NW India 28°18′N 75°00′E
54 J4 **Churuguara** Falcón, N Venezuela 10°52′N 69°35′W
167 U11 **Chư Sê** Gia Lai, C Vietnam 13°38′N 108°06′E
144 J12 **Chushkakul, Gory** ▲▲ SW Kazakhstan
Chūshū *see* Ch'ungju
37 O9 **Chuska Mountains** ▲▲ Arizona/New Mexico, SW USA
Chu, Sông *see* Sam, Nam
125 V14 **Chusovoy** Permskaya Oblast', NW Russian Federation 58°17′N 57°54′E
147 R10 **Chust** Namangan Viloyati, E Uzbekistan 40°58′N 71°12′E
Chust *see* Khust
15 U6 **Chute-aux-Outardes** Québec, SE Canada 49°07′N 68°25′W
117 U5 **Chutove** Poltavs'ka Oblast', C Ukraine 49°45′N 35°11′E
189 O15 **Chuuk** *var.* Truk. ◐ *state* C Micronesia
189 P15 **Chuuk Islands** *var.* Hogoley Islands; *prev.* Truk Islands. *island group* Caroline Islands, C Micronesia
Chuvashia *see* Chuvashskaya Respublika
Chuvashiya *see* Chuvashskaya Respublika
127 P4 **Chuvashskaya Respublika** *var.* Chuvashiya, *Eng.* Chuvashia. ◐ *autonomous republic* W Russian Federation
Chuwārtah *see* Chwārtā
Chu Xian/Chuxian *see* Chuzhou
160 G13 **Chuxiong** Yunnan, SW China 25°02′N 101°32′E
147 V7 **Chuy** Chuyskaya Oblast', N Kyrgyzstan 42°45′N 75°11′E
61 H19 **Chuy** *var.* Chuí. Rocha, E Uruguay 33°42′S 53°27′W
123 O11 **Chuya** Respublika Sakha (Yakutiya), NE Russian Federation 59°30′N 112°26′E
Chüy Oblasty *see* Chuyskaya Oblast'
147 U8 **Chuyskaya Oblast'** *Kir.* Chüy Oblasty. ◐ *province* N Kyrgyzstan
161 Q7 **Chuzhou** *var.* Chuxian, Chu Xian. Anhui, E China 32°20′N 118°18′E
139 U3 **Chwārtā** *var.* Choarta, Chuwārtah. As Sulaymānīyah, NE Iraq 35°11′N 45°59′E
119 N16 **Chyhirynskaye Vodaskhovishcha** ⊠ E Belarus
117 R6 **Chyhyryn** *Rus.* Chigirin. Cherkas'ka Oblast', N Ukraine 49°03′N 32°40′E
119 J18 **Chyrvonaya Slabada** *Rus.* Krasnaya Slabada, Krasnaya Sloboda. Minskaya Voblasts', S Belarus 52°51′N 27°10′E
119 L19 **Chyrvonaye, Vozyera** *Rus.* Ozero Chervonoye. ◎ SE Belarus
117 N11 **Ciadîr-Lunga** *var.* Ceadâr-Lunga, *Rus.* Chadyr-Lunga. S Moldova 46°03′N 28°50′E
169 P16 **Ciamis** *prev.* Tjiamis. Jawa, C Indonesia 07°20′S 108°21′E
107 I16 **Ciampino** ✈ Lazio, C Italy 41°48′N 12°36′E
169 N16 **Cianjur** *prev.* Tjiandjoer. Jawa, C Indonesia 06°50′S 107°09′E
60 H10 **Cianorte** Paraná, S Brazil 23°42′S 52°31′W
Ciarraí *see* Kerry
112 N13 **Ćićevac** Serbia, E Serbia 43°44′N 21°25′E
187 Z14 **Cicia** *prev.* Thithia. *island* Lau Group, E Fiji
105 P4 **Cidacos** ≋ N Spain
136 I10 **Cide** Kastamonu, N Turkey 41°53′N 33°01′E
110 L10 **Ciechanów** *prev.* Zichenau. Mazowieckie, C Poland 52°53′N 20°37′E
110 O10 **Ciechanowiec** *Ger.* Rudelstadt. Podlaskie, E Poland 52°43′N 22°30′E
110 J10 **Ciechocinek** Kujawskio-pomorskie, C Poland 52°53′N 18°49′E
44 F6 **Ciego de Ávila** Ciego de Ávila, C Cuba 21°50′N 78°44′W
54 F4 **Ciénaga** Magdalena, N Colombia 11°01′N 74°15′W
54 E6 **Ciénaga de Oro** Córdoba, NW Colombia 08°54′N 75°39′W
44 E5 **Cienfuegos** Cienfuegos, C Cuba 22°10′N 80°27′W
104 F4 **Cíes, Illas** *island group* NW Spain
111 P16 **Cieszanów** Podkarpackie, SE Poland 50°15′N 23°09′E
111 J17 **Cieszyn** *Cz.* Těšín, *Ger.* Teschen. Śląskie, S Poland 49°45′N 18°35′E
105 R12 **Cieza** Murcia, SE Spain 38°14′N 01°25′W
136 F13 **Çifteler** Eskişehir, W Turkey 39°25′N 31°00′E
105 P7 **Cifuentes** Castilla-La Mancha, C Spain 40°47′N 02°37′W
Čiganak *see* Chiganak
105 P9 **Cigüela** ≋ C Spain
136 H14 **Cihanbeyli** Konya, C Turkey 38°40′N 32°55′E
136 H14 **Cihanbeyli Yaylası** *plateau* C Turkey
104 L10 **Cíjara, Embalse de** ⊠ C Spain
169 P16 **Cikalong** Jawa, S Indonesia 07°46′S 108°13′E
169 N16 **Cikawung** Jawa, S Indonesia 06°49′S 105°29′E
187 Y13 **Cikobia** *prev.* Thikombia. *island* N Fiji
169 P17 **Cilacap** *prev.* Tjilatjap. Jawa, C Indonesia 07°44′S 109°E
173 O16 **Cilaos** C Réunion 21°08′S 55°28′E
137 S11 **Çıldır** Ardahan, NE Turkey 41°08′N 43°08′E
137 S11 **Çıldır Gölü** ◎ NE Turkey
160 M10 **Cili** Hunan, S China 29°24′N 110°59′E
Cilician Gates *see* Gülek Boğazı
121 V10 **Cilicia Trough** *undersea feature* E Mediterranean Sea
Cill Airne *see* Killarney
Cill Chainnigh *see* Kilkenny
Cill Chaoi *see* Kilkee
Cill Choca *see* Kilcock
Cill Dara *see* Kildare
105 N3 **Cilleruelo de Bezana** Castilla-León, N Spain 42°58′N 03°50′W
Cilli *see* Celje
Cill Mhantáin *see* Wicklow
Cill Rois *see* Kilrush
146 C11 **Çilmämmetgum** *Rus.* Peski Chil'mamedkum,, *Turkm.* Chilmämetgum. *desert* Balkan Welaýaty, W Turkmenistan
137 Z11 **Çiloy Adası** *Rus.* Ostrov Zhiloy. *island* E Azerbaijan
26 J6 **Cimarron** Kansas, C USA 37°49′N 100°20′W
37 T9 **Cimarron** New Mexico, SW USA 36°30′N 104°55′W
26 M9 **Cimarron River** ≋ Kansas/Oklahoma, C USA
117 N11 **Cimişlia** *Rus.* Chimishliya. S Moldova 46°31′N 28°45′E
Cîmpia Turzii *see* Câmpia Turzii
Cîmpina *see* Câmpina
Cîmpulung *see* Câmpulung
Cîmpulung Moldovenesc *see* Câmpulung Moldovenesc
137 P15 **Çınar** Dıyarbakır, SE Turkey 37°45′N 40°22′E
54 J8 **Cinaruco, Río** ≋ Colombia/Venezuela
Cina Selatan, Laut *see* South China Sea
105 T5 **Cinca** ≋ NE Spain
112 G13 **Cincar** ▲ SW Bosnia and Herzegovina 43°55′N 17°05′E
31 Q15 **Cincinnati** Ohio, N USA 39°04′N 84°34′W
21 M4 **Cincinnati** ✈ Kentucky, S USA 39°03′N 84°39′W
Cinco de Outubro *see* Xá-Muteba
136 C15 **Çine** Aydın, SW Turkey 37°37′N 28°03′E
99 J21 **Ciney** Namur, SE Belgium 50°17′N 05°06′E
104 H6 **Cinfães** Viseu, N Portugal 41°04′N 08°06′W
106 J12 **Cingoli** Marche, C Italy 43°25′N 13°09′E
41 U16 **Cintalapa** *var.* Cintalapa de Figueroa. Chiapas, SE Mexico 16°42′N 93°40′W
Cintalapa de Figueroa *see* Cintalapa
103 X14 **Cinto, Monte** ▲ Corse, France, C Mediterranean Sea 42°22′N 08°57′E
Cintra *see* Sintra
105 Q5 **Cintruénigo** Navarra, N Spain 42°05′N 01°50′W
Cionn tSáile *see* Kinsale
116 K13 **Ciorani** Prahova, SE Romania 44°49′N 26°25′E
113 E14 **Čiovo** *It.* Bua. *island* S Croatia
Cipiúr *see* Kippure
63 I15 **Cipolletti** Río Negro, C Argentina 38°55′S 68°W
120 L7 **Circeo, Capo** *headland* C Italy 41°15′N 13°03′E
39 S8 **Circle** *var.* Circle City. Alaska, USA 65°51′N 144°04′W
33 X8 **Circle** Montana, NW USA 47°25′N 105°32′W
Circle City *see* Circle
31 S14 **Circleville** Ohio, N USA 39°36′N 82°57′W
36 K6 **Circleville** Utah, W USA 38°10′N 112°16′W
169 P16 **Cirebon** *prev.* Tjirebon. Jawa, S Indonesia 06°46′S 108°33′E
97 L21 **Cirencester** *anc.* Corinium, Corinium Dobunorum. C England, United Kingdom 51°44′N 01°59′W
Cirkvenica *see* Crikvenica
107 O20 **Ciro** Calabria, SW Italy 39°22′N 17°02′E
107 O20 **Ciro Marino** Calabria, S Italy 39°21′N 17°07′E

◆ Country
● Country Capital
◇ Dependent Territory
○ Dependent Territory Capital
◐ Administrative Regions
✈ International Airport
▲ Mountain
▲▲ Mountain Range
△ Volcano
≋ River
◎ Lake
⊠ Reservoir

102 K14 **Ciron** ≈ SW France
Cirquenizza see Crikvenica
25 R7 **Cisco** Texas, SW USA 32°23′N 98°58′W
116 I12 **Cisnădie** Ger. Heltau, Hung. Nagydisznód. Sibiu, SW Romania 45°42′N 24°09′E
63 G18 **Cisnes, Río** ≈ S Chile
25 T11 **Cistern** Texas, SW USA 29°46′N 97°12′W
104 L3 **Cistierna** Castilla-León, N Spain 42°47′N 05°08′W
Citharista see la Ciotat
Citlaltépetl see Orizaba, Volcán Pico de
55 X10 **Citron** NW French Guiana 04°49′N 53°55′W
23 N7 **Citronelle** Alabama, S USA 31°05′N 88°13′W
35 O7 **Citrus Heights** California, W USA 38°42′N 121°18′W
106 H7 **Cittadella** Veneto, NE Italy 45°37′N 11°46′E
106 H13 **Città della Pieve** Umbria, C Italy 42°57′N 12°01′E
106 H12 **Città di Castello** Umbria, C Italy 43°27′N 12°13′E
107 I14 **Cittaducale** Lazio, C Italy 42°24′N 12°55′E
107 N22 **Cittanova** Calabria, SW Italy 38°21′N 16°05′E
Cittavecchia see Stari Grad
116 G10 **Ciucea** Hung. Csucsa. Cluj, NW Romania 46°58′N 22°50′E
116 M13 **Ciucurova** Tulcea, SE Romania 44°57′N 28°24′E
Ciudad Acuña see Villa Acuña
41 N15 **Ciudad Altamirano** Guerrero, S Mexico 18°20′N 100°40′W
42 G7 **Ciudad Barrios** San Miguel, NE El Salvador 13°46′N 88°13′W
54 I7 **Ciudad Bolívar** Barinas, NW Venezuela 08°22′N 70°37′W
55 N7 **Ciudad Bolívar** prev. Angostura. Bolívar, E Venezuela 08°08′N 63°31′W
40 K6 **Ciudad Camargo** Chihuahua, N Mexico 27°42′N 105°10′W
40 E8 **Ciudad Constitución** Baja California Sur, NW Mexico 25°09′N 111°43′W
Ciudad Cortés see Cortés
41 V17 **Ciudad Cuauhtémoc** Chiapas, SE Mexico 15°38′N 91°59′W
42 J9 **Ciudad Darío** var. Dario. Matagalpa, W Nicaragua 12°42′N 86°10′W
Ciudad de Dolores Hidalgo see Dolores Hidalgo
42 C6 **Ciudad de Guatemala** Eng. Guatemala City; prev. Santiago de los Caballeros. ● (Guatemala) Guatemala, C Guatemala 14°38′N 90°29′W
Ciudad del Carmen see Carmen
62 Q6 **Ciudad del Este** prev. Ciudad Presidente Stroessner, Presidente Stroessner, Puerto Presidente Stroessner. Alto Paraná, SE Paraguay 25°34′S 54°40′W
62 K5 **Ciudad de Libertador General San Martín** var. Libertador General San Martín. Jujuy, C Argentina 23°50′S 64°45′W
Ciudad Delicias see Delicias
41 O11 **Ciudad del Maíz** San Luis Potosí, C Mexico 22°26′N 99°36′W
Ciudad de México see México
54 J7 **Ciudad de Nutrias** Barinas, NW Venezuela 08°03′N 69°17′W
Ciudad de Panama see Panamá
55 P7 **Ciudad Guayana** prev. San Tomé de Guayana, Santo Tomé de Guayana. Bolívar, NE Venezuela 08°22′N 62°37′W
40 K14 **Ciudad Guzmán** Jalisco, SW Mexico 19°40′N 103°30′W
41 V17 **Ciudad Hidalgo** Chiapas, SE Mexico 14°40′N 92°11′W
41 N14 **Ciudad Hidalgo** Michoacán, SW Mexico 19°40′N 100°34′W
40 J3 **Ciudad Juárez** Chihuahua, N Mexico 31°39′N 106°26′W
40 L8 **Ciudad Lerdo** Durango, C Mexico 25°34′N 103°30′W
41 Q11 **Ciudad Madero** var. Villa Cecilia. Tamaulipas, C Mexico 22°18′N 97°56′W
41 P11 **Ciudad Mante** Tamaulipas, C Mexico 22°43′N 99°02′W
42 F2 **Ciudad Melchor de Mencos** var. Melchor de Mencos. Petén, NE Guatemala 17°03′N 89°12′W
41 P8 **Ciudad Miguel Alemán** Tamaulipas, C Mexico 26°20′N 98°56′W
Ciudad Mutis see Bahía Solano
40 G6 **Ciudad Obregón** Sonora, NW Mexico 27°32′N 109°53′W
54 I5 **Ciudad Ojeda** Zulia, NW Venezuela 10°12′N 71°17′W
55 P7 **Ciudad Piar** Bolívar, E Venezuela 07°25′N 63°19′W
Ciudad Porfirio Díaz see Piedras Negras
Ciudad Presidente Stroessner see Ciudad del Este
Ciudad Quesada see Quesada
105 N11 **Ciudad Real** Castilla-La Mancha, C Spain 38°59′N 03°55′W
105 N11 **Ciudad Real** ◈ province Castilla-La Mancha, C Spain
104 J7 **Ciudad-Rodrigo** Castilla-León, N Spain 40°36′N 06°33′W
42 A6 **Ciudad Tecún Umán** San Marcos, SW Guatemala 14°40′N 92°06′W
Ciudad Trujillo see Santo Domingo
41 P12 **Ciudad Valles** San Luis Potosí, C Mexico 21°59′N 99°01′W
41 O10 **Ciudad Victoria** Tamaulipas, C Mexico 23°44′N 99°07′W
42 C6 **Ciudad Vieja** Suchitepéquez, S Guatemala 14°30′N 90°46′W
116 L8 **Ciuhuru** var. Reuţel. ≈ N Moldova
105 Z8 **Ciutadella** var. Ciutadella de Menorca. Menorca, Spain, W Mediterranean Sea 40°N 03°50′E
Ciutadella Ciutadella de Menorca see Ciutadella
136 L11 **Civa Burnu** headland N Turkey 41°22′N 36°39′E
106 J7 **Cividale del Friuli** Friuli-Venezia Giulia, NE Italy 46°06′N 13°25′E
107 H14 **Civita Castellana** Lazio, C Italy 42°16′N 12°24′E
106 J12 **Civitanova Marche** Marche, C Italy 43°18′N 13°41′E
Civitas Altae Ripae see Brzeg
Civitas Carnutum see Chartres
Civitas Eburovicum see Évreux
Civitas Nemetum see Speyer
107 G15 **Civitavecchia** anc. Centum Cellae, Trajani Portus. Lazio, C Italy 42°05′N 11°47′E
102 L10 **Civray** Vienne, W France 46°10′N 00°18′E
136 E14 **Çivril** Denizli, W Turkey 38°18′N 29°43′E
161 O5 **Cixian** Hebei, E China 36°19′N 114°22′E
137 R16 **Cizre** Şırnak, SE Turkey 37°21′N 42°11′E
Clacton see Clacton-on-Sea
97 Q21 **Clacton-on-Sea** var. Clacton. E England, United Kingdom 51°48′N 01°09′E
22 H5 **Claiborne, Lake** ⊠ Louisiana, S USA
102 L10 **Clain** ≈ W France
11 Q11 **Claire, Lake** ◎ Alberta, C Canada
25 O6 **Clairemont** Texas, SW USA 33°09′N 100°45′W
34 M3 **Clair Engle Lake** ⊠ California, W USA
18 B15 **Clairton** Pennsylvania, NE USA 40°17′N 79°52′W
32 F7 **Clallam Bay** Washington, NW USA 48°13′N 124°16′W
103 P8 **Clamecy** Nièvre, C France 47°28′N 03°30′E
23 P5 **Clanton** Alabama, S USA 32°50′N 86°37′W
61 D17 **Clara** Entre Ríos, E Argentina 31°50′S 58°48′W
97 E18 **Clara** Ir. Clóirtheach. C Ireland 53°20′N 07°36′W
29 T9 **Clara City** Minnesota, N USA 44°57′N 95°22′W
61 D23 **Claraz** Buenos Aires, E Argentina 37°56′S 59°18′W
Clár Chlainne Mhuiris see Claremorris
182 I8 **Clare** South Australia 33°49′S 138°35′E
97 C19 **Clare** Ir. An Clár. cultural region W Ireland
97 C18 **Clare** ≈ W Ireland
97 A16 **Clare Island** Ir. Cliara. island W Ireland
44 J12 **Claremont** C Jamaica 18°23′N 77°11′W
29 W10 **Claremont** Minnesota, N USA 44°01′N 93°00′W
19 N9 **Claremont** New Hampshire, NE USA 43°21′N 72°18′W
27 Q9 **Claremore** Oklahoma, C USA 36°20′N 95°37′W
97 C17 **Claremorris** Ir. Clár Chlainne Mhuiris. W Ireland 53°47′N 09°W
185 J16 **Clarence** Canterbury, South Island, New Zealand 42°08′S 173°54′E
185 J16 **Clarence** ≈ South Island, New Zealand
65 F15 **Clarence Bay** bay Ascension Island, C Atlantic Ocean
63 H25 **Clarence, Isla** island S Chile
194 H2 **Clarence Island** island South Shetland Islands, Antarctica
183 V5 **Clarence River** ≈ New South Wales, SE Australia
44 J5 **Clarence Town** Long Island, C Bahamas 23°03′N 74°57′W
27 W12 **Clarendon** Arkansas, C USA 34°41′N 91°19′W
25 O3 **Clarendon** Texas, SW USA 34°57′N 100°54′W
13 U12 **Clarenville** Newfoundland, Newfoundland and Labrador, SE Canada 48°10′N 54°00′W
11 Q17 **Claresholm** Alberta, SW Canada 50°02′N 113°33′W
29 T16 **Clarinda** Iowa, C USA 40°44′N 95°02′W
55 N5 **Clarines** Anzoátegui, NE Venezuela 09°56′N 65°11′W
29 V12 **Clarion** Iowa, C USA 42°43′N 93°43′W
18 C13 **Clarion** Pennsylvania, NE USA 41°11′N 79°21′W
193 O6 **Clarion Fracture Zone** tectonic feature NE Pacific Ocean
18 D13 **Clarion River** ≈ Pennsylvania, NE USA
29 Q9 **Clark** South Dakota, N USA 44°50′N 97°44′W
36 K11 **Clarkdale** Arizona, SW USA 34°46′N 112°03′W
15 W4 **Clarke City** Québec, SE Canada 50°09′N 66°36′W
183 Q15 **Clarke Island** island Furneaux Group, Tasmania, SE Australia
181 X6 **Clarke Range** ▲▲ Queensland, E Australia
23 T2 **Clarkesville** Georgia, SE USA 34°36′N 83°31′W
29 S9 **Clarkfield** Minnesota, N USA 44°48′N 95°49′W
33 N7 **Clark Fork** Idaho, NW USA 48°06′N 116°10′W
33 N8 **Clark Fork** ≈ Idaho/Montana, NW USA
21 P13 **Clark Hill Lake** var. J.Storm Thurmond Reservoir. ⊠ Georgia/South Carolina, SE USA
39 Q12 **Clark, Lake** ◎ Alaska, USA
35 W12 **Clark Mountain** ▲ California, W USA 35°30′N 115°34′W
37 S3 **Clark Peak** ▲ Colorado, C USA 40°36′N 105°57′W
14 D14 **Clark, Point** headland Ontario, S Canada 44°04′N 81°45′W
21 S3 **Clarksburg** West Virginia, NE USA 39°16′N 80°22′W
22 K2 **Clarksdale** Mississippi, S USA 34°12′N 90°34′W
33 U12 **Clarks Fork Yellowstone River** ≈ Montana/Wyoming, NW USA
29 R14 **Clarkson** Nebraska, C USA 41°42′N 97°07′W
39 O13 **Clarks Point** Alaska, USA 58°50′N 158°33′W
18 I13 **Clarks Summit** Pennsylvania, NE USA 41°29′N 75°42′W
32 M10 **Clarkston** Washington, NW USA 46°25′N 117°02′W
44 J12 **Clark's Town** C Jamaica 18°25′N 77°32′W
27 T10 **Clarksville** Arkansas, C USA 35°29′N 93°29′W
31 P13 **Clarksville** Indiana, N USA 40°01′N 85°54′W
20 I8 **Clarksville** Tennessee, S USA 36°32′N 87°22′W
25 W5 **Clarksville** Texas, SW USA 33°37′N 95°04′W
21 U8 **Clarksville** Virginia, NE USA 36°36′N 78°36′W
21 U11 **Clarkton** North Carolina, SE USA 34°28′N 78°39′W
61 C24 **Claromecó** var. Balneario Claromecó. Buenos Aires, E Argentina 38°51′S 60°01′W
25 N3 **Claude** Texas, SW USA 35°06′N 101°22′W
Clausentum see Southampton
171 O1 **Claveria** Luzon, N Philippines 18°36′N 121°04′E
99 J20 **Clavier** Liège, E Belgium 50°27′N 05°21′E
23 W6 **Claxton** Georgia, SE USA 32°09′N 81°54′W
21 R4 **Clay** West Virginia, NE USA 38°28′N 81°17′W
27 N3 **Clay Center** Kansas, C USA 39°22′N 97°08′W
29 P16 **Clay Center** Nebraska, C USA 40°31′N 98°03′W
21 Y2 **Claymont** Delaware, NE USA 39°48′N 75°27′W
36 M14 **Claypool** Arizona, SW USA 33°24′N 110°50′W
23 R6 **Clayton** Alabama, S USA 31°52′N 85°27′W
23 T1 **Clayton** Georgia, SE USA 34°52′N 83°24′W
22 J5 **Clayton** Louisiana, S USA 31°43′N 91°32′W
27 X5 **Clayton** Missouri, C USA 38°39′N 90°21′W
37 V9 **Clayton** New Mexico, SW USA 36°27′N 103°12′W
21 V9 **Clayton** North Carolina, SE USA 35°39′N 78°27′W
27 Q12 **Clayton** Oklahoma, C USA 34°35′N 95°21′W
182 I4 **Clayton River** seasonal river South Australia
21 R7 **Claytor Lake** ⊠ Virginia, NE USA
27 P13 **Clear Boggy Creek** ≈ Oklahoma, C USA
97 B22 **Clear, Cape** var. The Bill of Cape Clear, Ir. Ceann Cléire. headland SW Ireland 51°25′N 09°31′W
36 M12 **Clear Creek** ≈ Arizona, SW USA
39 S12 **Cleare, Cape** headland Montague Island, Alaska, USA 59°46′N 147°54′W
18 E13 **Clearfield** Pennsylvania, NE USA 41°02′N 78°27′W
36 L2 **Clearfield** Utah, W USA 41°06′N 112°03′W
25 Q6 **Clear Fork Brazos River** ≈ Texas, SW USA
31 T12 **Clear Fork Reservoir** ⊠ Ohio, N USA
11 N12 **Clear Hills** ▲▲ Alberta, SW Canada
34 M6 **Clearlake** California, W USA 38°57′N 122°38′W
29 V12 **Clear Lake** Iowa, C USA 43°07′N 93°27′W
29 R9 **Clear Lake** South Dakota, N USA 44°45′N 96°40′W
34 M6 **Clear Lake** ◎ California, W USA
22 G6 **Clear Lake** ⊠ Louisiana, S USA
35 P1 **Clear Lake Reservoir** ⊠ California, W USA
11 N16 **Clearwater** British Columbia, SW Canada 51°38′N 120°02′W
23 U12 **Clearwater** Florida, SE USA 27°58′N 82°46′W
11 R12 **Clearwater** ≈ Alberta/Saskatchewan, C Canada
27 W7 **Clearwater Lake** ⊠ Missouri, C USA
33 N10 **Clearwater Mountains** ▲▲ Idaho, NW USA
33 N10 **Clearwater River** ≈ Idaho, NW USA
29 S4 **Clearwater River** ≈ Minnesota, N USA
25 T7 **Cleburne** Texas, SW USA 32°21′N 97°24′W
32 I9 **Cle Elum** Washington, NW USA 47°12′N 120°56′W
97 O17 **Cleethorpes** E England, United Kingdom 53°34′N 00°02′W
Cléire, Ceann see Clear, Cape
21 O11 **Clemson** South Carolina, SE USA 34°40′N 82°50′W
21 Q4 **Clendenin** West Virginia, NE USA 38°29′N 81°21′W
26 M9 **Cleo Springs** Oklahoma, C USA 36°25′N 98°25′W
Clerk Island see Onotoa
181 X8 **Clermont** Queensland, E Australia 22°47′S 147°41′E
15 S8 **Clermont** Québec, SE Canada 47°41′N 70°15′W
103 O4 **Clermont** Oise, N France 49°23′N 02°26′E
29 X12 **Clermont** Iowa, C USA 43°00′N 91°39′W
103 P11 **Clermont-Ferrand** Puy-de-Dôme, C France 45°47′N 03°05′E
103 Q15 **Clermont-l'Hérault** Hérault, S France 43°37′N 03°25′E
99 M22 **Clervaux** Diekirch, N Luxembourg 50°03′N 06°02′E
106 G6 **Cles** Trentino-Alto Adige, N Italy 46°22′N 11°04′E
182 H8 **Cleve** South Australia 33°43′S 136°30′E
Cleve see Kleve
23 T2 **Cleveland** Georgia, SE USA 34°36′N 83°45′W
22 K3 **Cleveland** Mississippi, S USA 33°45′N 90°43′W
31 T11 **Cleveland** Ohio, N USA 41°30′N 81°42′W
27 O9 **Cleveland** Oklahoma, C USA 36°18′N 96°27′W
20 L10 **Cleveland** Tennessee, S USA 35°10′N 84°51′W
25 W10 **Cleveland** Texas, SW USA 30°19′N 95°06′W
31 N7 **Cleveland** Wisconsin, N USA 43°58′N 87°45′W
31 O4 **Cleveland Cliffs Basin** ◎ Michigan, N USA
31 U11 **Cleveland Heights** Ohio, N USA 41°30′N 81°34′W
33 P6 **Cleveland, Mount** ▲ Montana, NW USA 48°55′N 113°51′W
Cleves see Kleve
97 B16 **Clew Bay** Ir. Cuan Mó. inlet W Ireland
23 Y14 **Clewiston** Florida, SE USA 26°45′N 80°55′W
Cliara see Clare Island
97 A17 **Clifden** Ir. An Clochán. Galway, W Ireland 53°29′N 10°14′W
37 O14 **Clifton** Arizona, SW USA 33°03′N 109°18′W
18 K14 **Clifton** New Jersey, NE USA 40°50′N 74°28′W
25 S8 **Clifton** Texas, SW USA 31°43′N 97°36′W
21 S6 **Clifton Forge** Virginia, NE USA 37°49′N 79°50′W
182 I1 **Clifton Hills** South Australia 27°03′S 138°49′E
11 S17 **Climax** Saskatchewan, S Canada 49°12′N 108°22′W
21 O8 **Clinch River** ≈ Tennessee/Virginia, S USA
25 P12 **Cline** Texas, SW USA 29°14′N 100°07′W
21 N10 **Clingmans Dome** ▲ North Carolina/Tennessee, SE USA 35°33′N 83°30′W
24 H8 **Clint** Texas, SW USA 31°35′N 106°13′W
10 M16 **Clinton** British Columbia, SW Canada 51°06′N 121°31′W
14 E15 **Clinton** Ontario, S Canada 43°36′N 81°33′W
27 U10 **Clinton** Arkansas, C USA 35°34′N 92°28′W
30 L10 **Clinton** Illinois, N USA 40°09′N 88°57′W
29 Z14 **Clinton** Iowa, C USA 41°50′N 90°11′W
20 G7 **Clinton** Kentucky, S USA 36°39′N 89°00′W
22 J8 **Clinton** Louisiana, S USA 30°52′N 91°01′W
19 N11 **Clinton** Massachusetts, NE USA 42°25′N 71°40′W
31 R10 **Clinton** Michigan, N USA 42°04′N 83°58′W
22 K5 **Clinton** Mississippi, S USA 32°22′N 90°22′W
27 S5 **Clinton** Missouri, C USA 38°22′N 93°51′W
21 V10 **Clinton** North Carolina, SE USA 35°00′N 78°19′W
26 L10 **Clinton** Oklahoma, C USA 35°31′N 98°58′W
21 Q12 **Clinton** South Carolina, SE USA 34°28′N 81°52′W
21 M9 **Clinton** Tennessee, S USA 36°07′N 84°08′W
8 L9 **Clinton-Colden Lake** ◎ Northwest Territories, NW Canada
10 H5 **Clinton Creek** Yukon Territory, NW Canada 64°24′N 140°35′W
30 L13 **Clinton Lake** ⊠ Illinois, N USA
27 Q4 **Clinton Lake** ⊠ Kansas, N USA
21 T11 **Clio** South Carolina, SE USA 34°34′N 79°33′W
193 O7 **Clipperton Fracture Zone** tectonic feature E Pacific Ocean
193 Q7 **Clipperton Island** ◇ French dependency of French Polynesia E Pacific Ocean
46 K6 **Clipperton Island** island E Pacific Ocean
0 F16 **Clipperton Seamounts** undersea feature E Pacific Ocean 08°00′N 111°00′W
102 J8 **Clisson** Loire-Atlantique, NW France 47°06′N 01°19′W
62 K7 **Clodomira** Santiago del Estero, N Argentina 27°35′S 64°14′W
Cloich na Coillte see Clonakilty
Clóirtheach see Clara
97 C21 **Clonakilty** Ir. Cloich na Coillte. SW Ireland 51°37′N 08°54′W
181 T6 **Cloncurry** Queensland, C Australia 20°45′S 140°30′E
97 F18 **Clondalkin** Ir. Cluain Dolcáin. E Ireland 53°19′N 06°24′W
97 E16 **Clones** Ir. Cluain Eois. N Ireland 54°11′N 07°14′W
97 D20 **Clonmel** Ir. Cluain Meala. S Ireland 52°21′N 07°42′W
100 G11 **Cloppenburg** Niedersachsen, NW Germany 52°51′N 08°03′E
29 W6 **Cloquet** Minnesota, N USA 46°43′N 92°27′W
37 S14 **Cloudcroft** New Mexico, SW USA 32°57′N 105°44′W
33 W12 **Cloud Peak** ▲ Wyoming, C USA 44°22′N 107°10′W
185 K14 **Cloudy Bay** inlet South Island, New Zealand
21 R10 **Clover** South Carolina, SE USA 35°06′N 81°13′W
34 M6 **Cloverdale** California, W USA 38°49′N 123°03′W
20 J5 **Cloverport** Kentucky, S USA 37°50′N 86°37′W
35 Q10 **Clovis** California, W USA 36°48′N 119°43′W
37 W12 **Clovis** New Mexico, SW USA 34°22′N 103°12′W
14 K13 **Cloyne** Ontario, SE Canada 44°48′N 77°09′W
Cluain Dolcáin see Clondalkin
Cluain Eois see Clones
Cluainín see Manorhamilton
Cluain Meala see Clonmel
116 H10 **Cluj** ◈ county NW Romania
Cluj see Cluj-Napoca
116 H10 **Cluj-Napoca** Ger. Klausenburg, Hung. Kolozsvár; prev. Cluj. Cluj, NW Romania 46°47′N 23°36′E
Clunia see Feldkirch
103 R10 **Cluny** Saône-et-Loire, C France 46°25′N 04°38′E
103 T10 **Cluses** Haute-Savoie, E France 46°04′N 06°34′E
106 E7 **Clusone** Lombardia, N Italy 45°56′N 10°00′E
25 W12 **Clute** Texas, SW USA 29°01′N 95°24′W
185 D23 **Clutha** ≈ South Island, New Zealand
97 J18 **Clwyd** cultural region NE Wales, United Kingdom
185 D22 **Clyde** Otago, South Island, New Zealand 45°12′S 169°21′E
27 N3 **Clyde** Kansas, C USA 39°35′N 97°24′W
29 P2 **Clyde** North Dakota, N USA 48°44′N 98°51′W
31 S11 **Clyde** Ohio, N USA 41°18′N 82°58′W
25 Q7 **Clyde** Texas, SW USA 32°24′N 99°29′W
14 K13 **Clyde** ≈ Ontario, SE Canada
96 J13 **Clyde** ≈ W Scotland, United Kingdom
96 H12 **Clydebank** S Scotland, United Kingdom 55°54′N 04°24′W
96 H13 **Clyde, Firth of** inlet S Scotland, United Kingdom
33 S11 **Clyde Park** Montana, NW USA 45°56′N 110°39′W
35 W16 **Coachella** California, W USA 33°38′N 116°10′W
35 W16 **Coachella Canal** canal California, W USA
40 I9 **Coacoyole** Durango, C Mexico 24°30′N 106°33′W
25 N7 **Coahoma** Texas, SW USA 32°18′N 101°18′W
10 K8 **Coal** ≈ Yukon Territory, NW Canada
40 L14 **Coalcomán** var. Coalcomán de Matamoros. Michoacán, S Mexico 18°49′N 103°13′W
Coalcomán de Matamoros see Coalcomán
39 T8 **Coal Creek** Alaska, USA 65°21′N 143°08′W
11 Q17 **Coaldale** Alberta, SW Canada 49°42′N 112°36′W
27 P12 **Coalgate** Oklahoma, C USA 34°33′N 96°15′W
35 P11 **Coalinga** California, W USA 36°08′N 120°21′W
10 L9 **Coal River** British Columbia, W Canada 59°38′N 126°45′W
21 Q6 **Coal River** ≈ West Virginia, NE USA
36 M2 **Coalville** Utah, W USA 40°56′N 111°22′W
58 E13 **Coari** Amazonas, N Brazil 04°08′S 63°07′W
104 I7 **Côa, Rio** ≈ N Portugal
59 D14 **Coari, Rio** ≈ NW Brazil
81 J20 **Coast** ◈ province SE Kenya
Coast see Pwani
10 G12 **Coast Mountains** Fr. Chaîne Côtière. ▲▲ Canada/USA
16 C7 **Coast Ranges** ▲▲ W USA
96 I12 **Coatbridge** S Scotland, United Kingdom 55°52′N 04°01′W
42 B6 **Coatepeque** Quezaltenango, SW Guatemala 14°42′N 91°50′W
18 H16 **Coatesville** Pennsylvania, NE USA 39°58′N 75°47′W
15 Q13 **Coaticook** Québec, SE Canada 45°07′N 71°46′W
9 P9 **Coats Island** island Nunavut, NE Canada
195 O4 **Coats Land** physical region Antarctica
41 T14 **Coatzacoalcos** var. Quetzalcoalco; prev. Puerto México. Veracruz-Llave, E Mexico 18°06′N 94°26′W
41 S14 **Coatzacoalcos, Río** ≈ SE Mexico
116 M15 **Cobadin** Constanţa, SW Romania 44°05′N 28°13′E
14 H9 **Cobalt** Ontario, S Canada 47°24′N 79°41′W
42 D5 **Cobán** Alta Verapaz, C Guatemala 15°28′N 90°20′W
183 O6 **Cobar** New South Wales, SE Australia 31°31′S 145°51′E
18 F12 **Cobb Hill** ▲ Pennsylvania, NE USA 41°52′N 77°52′W
0 D8 **Cobb Seamount** undersea feature E Pacific Ocean 47°00′N 131°00′W
14 K12 **Cobden** Ontario, SE Canada 45°36′N 76°54′W
97 D21 **Cobh** Ir. An Cóbh; prev. Cove of Cork, Queenstown. SW Ireland 51°51′N 08°17′W
57 J14 **Cobija** Pando, NW Bolivia 11°04′S 68°49′W
Coblence/Coblenz see Koblenz
18 J10 **Cobleskill** New York, NE USA 42°40′N 74°29′W
14 I15 **Cobourg** Ontario, SE Canada 43°57′N 78°06′W
181 P1 **Cobourg Peninsula** headland Northern Territory, N Australia 11°27′S 132°33′E
183 O10 **Cobram** Victoria, SE Australia 35°56′S 145°36′E
82 N13 **Cóbuè** Niassa, N Mozambique 12°08′S 34°46′E
101 K18 **Coburg** Bayern, SE Germany 50°16′N 10°58′E
19 Q5 **Coburn Mountain** ▲ Maine, NE USA 45°28′N 70°07′W
57 H18 **Cocachacra** Arequipa, SW Peru 17°05′S 71°45′W
59 J17 **Cocalinho** Mato Grosso, W Brazil 14°22′S 51°00′W
Cocanada see Kākināda
105 S11 **Cocentaina** País Valenciano, E Spain 38°44′N 00°27′W
57 L18 **Cochabamba** hist. Oropeza. Cochabamba, C Bolivia 17°23′S 66°10′W
57 K18 **Cochabamba** ◈ department C Bolivia
57 L18 **Cochabamba, Cordillera de** ▲▲ C Bolivia
101 E18 **Cochem** Rheinland-Pfalz, W Germany 50°09′N 07°09′E
37 R6 **Cochetopa Hills** ▲▲ Colorado, C USA
155 G22 **Cochin** var. Kochchi, Kochi. Kerala, SW India 09°56′N 76°15′E see also Kochi
44 D5 **Cochinos, Bahía de** Eng. Bay of Pigs. bay SE Cuba
37 O16 **Cochise Head** ▲ Arizona, SW USA 32°03′N 109°19′W
23 U5 **Cochran** Georgia, SE USA 32°23′N 83°21′W
11 P16 **Cochrane** Alberta, SW Canada 51°15′N 114°25′W
12 G12 **Cochrane** Ontario, S Canada 49°04′N 81°02′W
63 G20 **Cochrane** Aisén, S Chile 47°16′S 72°33′W
11 U10 **Cochrane** ≈ Manitoba/Saskatchewan, C Canada
Cochrane, Lago see Pueyrredón, Lago
Cocibolca see Nicaragua, Lago de
Cockade State see Maryland
44 M6 **Cockburn Harbour** South Caicos, S Turks and Caicos Islands 21°28′N 71°30′W
14 C11 **Cockburn Island** island Ontario, S Canada
44 J3 **Cockburn Town** San Salvador, E Bahamas 24°01′N 74°31′W
21 X2 **Cockeysville** Maryland, NE USA 39°29′N 76°34′W
181 N12 **Cocklebiddy** Western Australia 32°02′S 125°54′E
44 I12 **Cockpit Country, The** physical region W Jamaica
43 S16 **Coclé** off. Provincia de Coclé. ◈ province C Panama
43 S15 **Coclé del Norte** Colón, C Panama 09°04′N 80°32′W
Coclé, Provincia de see Coclé
23 Y12 **Cocoa** Florida, SE USA 28°23′N 80°44′W
23 Y12 **Cocoa Beach** Florida, SE USA 28°19′N 80°36′W
79 D17 **Cocobeach** Estuaire, NW Gabon 0°59′N 09°34′E
44 G5 **Coco, Cayo** island C Cuba
151 Q19 **Coco Channel** strait Andaman Sea/Bay of Bengal
173 N6 **Coco-de-Mer Seamounts** undersea feature W Indian Ocean 0°30′N 56°00′E
36 K10 **Coconino Plateau** plain Arizona, SW USA
43 N6 **Coco, Río** var. Río Wanki, Segoviao Wangkí. ≈ Honduras/Nicaragua
173 T7 **Cocos Basin** undersea feature E Indian Ocean 05°00′S 94°00′E
188 B17 **Cocos Island** island S Guam
Cocos Island Ridge see Cocos Ridge
129 S17 **Cocos Islands** island group E Indian Ocean
173 T8 **Cocos (Keeling) Islands** ◇ Australian external territory E Indian Ocean
0 G15 **Cocos Plate** tectonic feature
193 T7 **Cocos Ridge** var. Cocos Island Ridge. undersea feature E Pacific Ocean 05°30′N 86°00′W
40 K13 **Cocula** Jalisco, SW Mexico 20°22′N 103°50′W
107 D17 **Coda Cavallo, Capo** headland Sardegna, Italy, C Mediterranean Sea 40°49′N 09°43′E
58 E13 **Codajás** Amazonas, N Brazil 03°50′S 62°12′W
Codazzi see Agustín Codazzi
19 Q12 **Cod, Cape** headland Massachusetts, NE USA 41°50′N 69°56′W
185 B25 **Codfish Island** island SW New Zealand
106 H9 **Codigoro** Emilia-Romagna, N Italy 44°50′N 12°07′E
13 P5 **Cod Island** island Newfoundland and Labrador, E Canada
116 J12 **Codlea** Ger. Zeiden, Hung. Feketehalom. Braşov, C Romania 45°43′N 25°27′E
58 M13 **Codó** Maranhão, E Brazil 04°28′S 43°51′W
106 E8 **Codogno** Lombardia, N Italy 45°10′N 09°42′E
116 M10 **Codrii** hill range C Moldova
45 W9 **Codrington** Barbuda, Antigua and Barbuda 17°43′N 61°49′W
106 J7 **Codroipo** Friuli-Venezia Giulia, NE Italy 45°58′N 13°00′E
28 M12 **Cody** Nebraska, C USA 42°54′N 101°13′W
33 U12 **Cody** Wyoming, C USA 43°31′N 109°04′W
21 P7 **Coeburn** Virginia, NE USA 36°56′N 82°27′W
54 E10 **Coello** Tolima, W Colombia 04°15′N 74°52′W
Coemba see Cuemba
181 V2 **Coen** Queensland, NE Australia 14°03′S 143°16′E
101 E14 **Coesfeld** Nordrhein-Westfalen, W Germany 51°55′N 07°10′E
32 M8 **Coeur d'Alene** Idaho, NW USA 47°40′N 116°46′W
32 M8 **Coeur d'Alene Lake** ⊠ Idaho, NW USA
98 O8 **Coevorden** Drenthe, NE Netherlands 52°39′N 06°45′E
10 H6 **Coffee Creek** Yukon Territory, W Canada 62°52′N 139°05′W
30 L15 **Coffeen Lake** ⊠ Illinois, N USA
22 L3 **Coffeeville** Mississippi, S USA 33°58′N 89°40′W
27 Q8 **Coffeyville** Kansas, C USA 37°02′N 95°37′W
182 G9 **Coffin Bay** South Australia 34°39′S 135°30′E
182 F9 **Coffin Bay Peninsula** peninsula South Australia
183 V5 **Coffs Harbour** New South Wales, SE Australia 30°18′S 153°08′E
105 R10 **Cofrentes** País Valenciano, E Spain 39°14′N 01°04′W
117 N10 **Cogîlnic** Ukr. Kohyl'nyk. ≈ Moldova/Ukraine
102 K11 **Cognac** anc. Compniacum. Charente, W France 45°42′N 00°19′W
106 B7 **Cogne** Valle d'Aosta, NW Italy 45°37′N 07°27′E
103 U16 **Cogolin** Var, SE France 43°15′N 06°30′E
105 O7 **Cogolludo** Castilla-La Mancha, C Spain 40°58′N 03°05′W
Cohalm see Rupea
92 K8 **Čohkarášša** var. Cuokkarašša. ▲ N Norway 69°57′N 24°38′E
Čohkkiras see Jukkasjärvi
18 F11 **Cohocton River** ≈ New York, NE USA
18 L10 **Cohoes** New York, NE USA 42°46′N 73°42′W
183 N10 **Cohuna** Victoria, SE Australia 35°51′S 144°15′E
43 P17 **Coiba, Isla de** island SW Panama
63 H23 **Coig, Río** ≈ S Argentina
63 G19 **Coihaique** var. Coyhaique. Aisén, S Chile 45°32′S 72°00′W
155 G21 **Coimbatore** Tamil Nādu, S India 11°N 76°57′E
104 G8 **Coimbra** anc. Conimbria, Conimbriga. Coimbra, W Portugal 40°12′N 08°25′W
104 G8 **Coimbra** ◈ district N Portugal
104 L15 **Coín** Andalucía, S Spain 36°40′N 04°45′W
Coin de Mire see Gunner's Quoin
57 J20 **Coipasa, Laguna** ◎ W Bolivia
57 J20 **Coipasa, Salar de** salt lake W Bolivia
Coira/Coire see Chur
Coirib, Loch see Corrib, Lough
54 K6 **Cojedes** off. Estado Cojedes. ◈ state N Venezuela
Cojedes, Estado see Cojedes
42 F7 **Cojutepeque** Cuscatlán, C El Salvador 13°43′N 88°56′W
Coka see Banbar
33 S16 **Cokeville** Wyoming, C USA 42°03′N 110°55′W
182 M13 **Colac** Victoria, SE Australia 38°22′S 143°38′E
59 O20 **Colatina** Espírito Santo, SE Brazil 19°35′S 40°37′W
27 O13 **Colbert** Oklahoma, C USA 33°51′N 96°30′W
100 L12 **Colbitz-Letzinger Heide** heathland N Germany
26 I3 **Colby** Kansas, C USA 39°24′N 101°04′W
57 H17 **Colca, Río** ≈ SW Peru
97 P21 **Colchester** hist. Colneceaste; anc. Camulodunum. E England, United Kingdom 51°54′N 00°54′E
19 N13 **Colchester** Connecticut, NE USA 41°34′N 72°17′W
38 M16 **Cold Bay** Alaska, USA 55°11′N 162°43′W
11 R14 **Cold Lake** Alberta, SW Canada 54°26′N 110°16′W
11 R13 **Cold Lake** ◎ Alberta/Saskatchewan, S Canada
29 U8 **Cold Spring** Minnesota, N USA 45°27′N 94°25′W
25 W10 **Coldspring** Texas, SW USA 30°34′N 95°10′W
11 N17 **Coldstream** British Columbia, SW Canada 50°13′N 119°09′W
96 L13 **Coldstream** SE Scotland, United Kingdom 55°39′N 02°19′W
14 H13 **Coldwater** Ontario, S Canada 44°43′N 79°36′W
26 K7 **Coldwater** Kansas, C USA 37°16′N 99°20′W
31 Q10 **Coldwater** Michigan, N USA 41°56′N 85°00′W
25 N1 **Coldwater Creek** ≈ Oklahoma/Texas, SW USA
22 K2 **Coldwater River** ≈ Mississippi, S USA
183 O9 **Coleambally** New South Wales, SE Australia 34°48′S 145°54′E
19 O6 **Colebrook** New Hampshire, NE USA 44°52′N 71°27′W
27 T5 **Cole Camp** Missouri, C USA 38°27′N 93°12′W
39 T6 **Coleen River** ≈ Alaska, USA
11 P17 **Coleman** Alberta, SW Canada 49°36′N 114°26′W
25 Q8 **Coleman** Texas, SW USA 31°50′N 99°27′W
Çölemerik see Hakkâri
83 K22 **Colenso** KwaZulu/Natal, E South Africa 28°44′S 29°50′E
182 L12 **Coleraine** Victoria, SE Australia 37°39′S 141°42′E
97 F14 **Coleraine** Ir. Cúil Raithin. N Northern Ireland, United Kingdom 55°08′N 06°40′W
185 G18 **Coleridge, Lake** ◎ South Island, New Zealand
83 H24 **Colesberg** Northern Cape, C South Africa 30°41′S 25°08′E
22 H7 **Colfax** Louisiana, S USA 31°31′N 92°42′W
32 L9 **Colfax** Washington, NW USA 46°52′N 117°21′W
30 J6 **Colfax** Wisconsin, N USA 45°00′N 91°44′W
63 I19 **Colhué Huapí, Lago** ◎ S Argentina
45 Z6 **Colibris, Pointe des** headland Grande Terre, E Guadeloupe 16°15′N 61°10′W
106 D6 **Colico** Lombardia, N Italy 46°08′N 09°24′E
99 E14 **Colijnsplaat** Zeeland, SW Netherlands 51°36′N 03°47′E
40 L14 **Colima** Colima, S Mexico 19°13′N 103°46′W
40 K14 **Colima** ◈ state SW Mexico
40 L14 **Colima, Nevado de** ⛰ C Mexico 19°36′N 103°36′W
59 M14 **Colinas** Maranhão, E Brazil 06°02′S 44°15′W
96 F10 **Coll** island W Scotland, United Kingdom
105 N7 **Collado Villalba** var. Villalba. Madrid, C Spain 40°38′N 04°00′W
183 R4 **Collarenebri** New South Wales, SE Australia 29°31′S 148°33′E
37 P5 **Collbran** Colorado, C USA 39°14′N 107°57′W
106 G12 **Colle di Val d'Elsa** Toscana, C Italy 43°26′N 11°06′E
39 R9 **College** Alaska, USA 64°49′N 148°06′W
32 K10 **College Place** Washington, NW USA 46°03′N 118°23′W
25 U10 **College Station** Texas, SW USA 30°38′N 96°21′W
183 P4 **Collerina** New South Wales, SE Australia 29°41′S 146°36′E
180 I13 **Collie** Western Australia 33°20′S 116°06′E
180 L4 **Collier Bay** bay Western Australia
21 F10 **Collierville** Tennessee, S USA 35°02′N 89°39′W
106 F11 **Collina, Passo della** pass C Italy
14 G14 **Collingwood** Ontario, S Canada 44°30′N 80°14′W
184 I13 **Collingwood** Tasman, South Island, New Zealand 40°40′S 172°40′E
22 L7 **Collins** Mississippi, S USA 31°39′N 89°33′W
30 K15 **Collinsville** Illinois, N USA 38°40′N 89°58′W
27 P9 **Collinsville** Oklahoma, C USA 36°21′N 95°50′W
20 H10 **Collinwood** Tennessee, S USA 35°10′N 87°44′W
Collipo see Leiria
63 G14 **Collipulli** Araucanía, C Chile 37°55′S 72°30′W
97 D16 **Collooney** Ir. Cúil Mhuine. NW Ireland 54°11′N 08°29′W
29 R10 **Colman** South Dakota, N USA 43°58′N 96°48′W
103 U6 **Colmar** Ger. Kolmar. Haut-Rhin, NE France 48°05′N 07°21′E
104 M15 **Colmenar** Andalucía, S Spain 36°54′N 04°20′W
Colmenar see Colmenar de Oreja
105 O9 **Colmenar de Oreja** var. Colmenar. Madrid, C Spain 40°06′N 03°25′W

◆ Country
● Country Capital
◇ Dependent Territory
○ Dependent Territory Capital
◈ Administrative Regions
✈ International Airport
▲ Mountain
▲▲ Mountain Range
⛰ Volcano
≈ River
◎ Lake
⊠ Reservoir

105 N7 **Colmenar Viejo** Madrid, C Spain 40°39′N 03°46′W
25 X9 **Colmesneil** Texas, SW USA 30°54′N 94°25′W
Cöln *see* Köln
Colneceaste *see* Colchester
59 G15 **Colniza** Mato Grosso, W Brazil 09°16′S 59°25′W
Cologne *see* Köln
42 B6 **Colomba** Quezaltenango, SW Guatemala 14°45′N 91°39′W
Colomb-Béchar *see* Béchar
54 E11 **Colombia** Huila, C Colombia 03°24′N 74°49′W
54 G10 **Colombia** *off.* Republic of Colombia. ◆ *republic* N South America
64 E12 **Colombian Basin** *undersea feature* SW Caribbean Sea 13°00′N 76°00′W
Colombia, Republic of *see* Colombia
Colombie-Britannique *see* British Columbia
15 T6 **Colombier** Québec, SE Canada 48°51′N 68°52′W
155 J25 **Colombo** ● (Sri Lanka) Western Province, W Sri Lanka 06°55′N 79°52′E
155 J25 **Colombo** ✈ Western Province, SW Sri Lanka 06°50′N 79°59′E
29 N11 **Colome** South Dakota, N USA 43°13′N 99°42′W
61 B19 **Colón** Buenos Aires, E Argentina 33°53′S 61°06′W
61 D18 **Colon** Entre Ríos, E Argentina 32°10′S 58°16′W
44 D5 **Colón** Matanzas, C Cuba 22°43′N 80°54′W
43 T14 **Colón** *prev.* Aspinwall. Colón, C Panama 09°04′N 80°33′W
42 K5 **Colón** ◈ *department* NE Honduras
43 S15 **Colón** *off.* Provincia de Colón. ◈ *province* N Panama
57 A16 **Colón, Archipiélago de** *var.* Islas de los Galápagos, *Eng.* Galapagos Islands, Tortoise Islands. *island group* Ecuador, E Pacific Ocean
44 K5 **Colonel Hill** Crooked Island, SE Bahamas 22°43′N 74°12′W
40 C3 **Colonet** Baja California Norte, NW Mexico 31°00′N 116°1′W
40 B3 **Colonett, Cabo** *headland* NW Mexico 30°57′N 116°19′W
188 G14 **Colonia** Yap, W Micronesia 09°29′N 138°06′E
61 D19 **Colonia** ◈ *department* SW Uruguay
Colonia *see* Kolonia, Micronesia
Colonia *see* Colonia del Sacramento, Uruguay
Colonia Agrippina *see* Köln
61 D20 **Colonia del Sacramento** *var.* Colonia. Colonia, SW Uruguay 34°29′S 57°48′W
62 L8 **Colonia Dora** Santiago del Estero, N Argentina 28°34′S 62°59′W
Colonia Julia Fanestris *see* Fano
21 W5 **Colonial Beach** Virginia, NE USA 38°15′N 76°57′W
21 V6 **Colonial Heights** Virginia, NE USA 37°15′N 77°24′W
Colón, Provincia de *see* Colón
193 S7 **Colón Ridge** *undersea feature* E Pacific Ocean 02°00′N 96°00′W
96 F12 **Colonsay** *island* W Scotland, United Kingdom
57 K22 **Colorada, Laguna** ◎ SW Bolivia
37 R6 **Colorado** *off.* State of Colorado, *also known as* Centennial State, Silver State. ◈ *state* C USA
63 H22 **Colorado, Cerro** ▲ S Argentina 49°58′S 71°38′W
25 O7 **Colorado City** Texas, SW USA 32°24′N 100°51′W
36 M7 **Colorado Plateau** *plateau* W USA
61 A24 **Colorado, Río** ≈ E Argentina
43 N12 **Colorado, Río** ≈ NE Costa Rica
Colorado, Río *see* Colorado River
16 F12 **Colorado River** *var.* Río Colorado. ≈ Mexico/USA
16 K14 **Colorado River** ≈ Texas, SW USA
35 W15 **Colorado River Aqueduct** *aqueduct* California, W USA
44 A4 **Colorados, Archipiélago de los** *island group* NW Cuba
62 J9 **Colorados, Desagües de los** ◎ W Argentina
37 T5 **Colorado Springs** Colorado, C USA 38°50′N 104°47′W
40 L11 **Colotlán** Jalisco, SW Mexico 22°08′N 103°15′W
57 L19 **Colquechaca** Potosí, C Bolivia 18°40′S 66°00′W
23 S7 **Colquitt** Georgia, SE USA 31°10′N 84°43′W
29 R11 **Colton** South Dakota, N USA 43°47′N 96°55′W
32 M10 **Colton** Washington, NW USA 46°34′N 117°10′W
35 P8 **Columbia** California, W USA 38°01′N 120°22′W
30 K16 **Columbia** Illinois, N USA 38°26′N 90°12′W
20 L7 **Columbia** Kentucky, S USA 37°05′N 85°19′W
22 I6 **Columbia** Louisiana, S USA 32°05′N 92°03′W
21 W3 **Columbia** Maryland, NE USA 39°13′N 76°51′W
22 L7 **Columbia** Mississippi, S USA 31°15′N 89°50′W
27 U4 **Columbia** Missouri, C USA 38°56′N 92°19′W
21 Y9 **Columbia** North Carolina, SE USA 35°55′N 76°15′W
18 G16 **Columbia** Pennsylvania, NE USA 40°01′N 76°30′W
21 Q12 **Columbia** *state capital* South Carolina, SE USA 34°00′N 81°02′W
20 I9 **Columbia** Tennessee, S USA 35°37′N 87°02′W
0 F9 **Columbia** ≈ Canada/USA
32 K9 **Columbia Basin** *basin* Washington, NW USA
197 Q10 **Columbia, Cape** *headland* Ellesmere Island, Nunavut, NE Canada
31 Q12 **Columbia City** Indiana, N USA 41°09′N 85°29′W
21 W3 **Columbia, District of** ◈ *federal district* NE USA
33 P7 **Columbia Falls** Montana, NW USA 48°22′N 114°10′W
11 O15 **Columbia Icefield** *ice field* Alberta/British Columbia, S Canada
11 O15 **Columbia, Mount** ▲ Alberta/British Columbia, SW Canada 52°07′N 117°30′W
11 N15 **Columbia Mountains** ▲▲ British Columbia, SW Canada
23 P4 **Columbiana** Alabama, S USA 33°10′N 86°36′W
31 V12 **Columbiana** Ohio, N USA 40°53′N 80°41′W
32 M14 **Columbia Plateau** *plateau* Idaho/Oregon, NW USA
29 P7 **Columbia Road Reservoir** ⊠ South Dakota, N USA
65 K16 **Columbia Seamount** *undersea feature* C Atlantic Ocean 20°30′S 32°00′W
83 D25 **Columbine, Cape** *headland* SW South Africa 32°50′S 17°39′E
105 U9 **Columbretes, Islas** *island group* E Spain
23 R5 **Columbus** Georgia, SE USA 32°29′N 84°58′W
31 P14 **Columbus** Indiana, N USA 39°12′N 85°55′W
27 R7 **Columbus** Kansas, C USA 37°09′N 94°52′W
23 N4 **Columbus** Mississippi, S USA 33°30′N 88°25′W
33 U11 **Columbus** Montana, NW USA 45°38′N 109°15′W
29 Q15 **Columbus** Nebraska, C USA 41°25′N 97°22′W
37 Q16 **Columbus** New Mexico, SW USA 31°49′N 107°38′W
21 P10 **Columbus** North Carolina, SE USA 35°15′N 82°09′W
28 K2 **Columbus** North Dakota, N USA 48°52′N 102°47′W
31 S13 **Columbus** *state capital* Ohio, N USA 39°58′N 83°W
25 U11 **Columbus** Texas, SW USA 29°42′N 96°35′W
30 L8 **Columbus** Wisconsin, N USA 43°21′N 89°00′W
31 R12 **Columbus Grove** Ohio, N USA 40°55′N 84°03′W
29 Y15 **Columbus Junction** Iowa, C USA 41°16′N 91°21′W
44 J3 **Columbus Point** *headland* Cat Island, C Bahamas 24°07′N 75°19′W
35 T8 **Columbus Salt Marsh** *salt marsh* Nevada, W USA
35 N6 **Colusa** California, W USA 39°10′N 122°03′W
32 L7 **Colville** Washington, NW USA 48°33′N 117°54′W
184 M5 **Colville, Cape** *headland* North Island, New Zealand 36°28′S 175°20′E
184 M5 **Colville Channel** *channel* North Island, New Zealand
39 P6 **Colville River** ≈ Alaska, USA
97 J18 **Colwyn Bay** N Wales, United Kingdom 53°18′N 03°43′W
106 H9 **Comacchio** *var.* Commachio; *anc.* Comactium. Emilia-Romagna, N Italy 44°41′N 12°10′E
106 H9 **Comacchio, Valli di** *lagoon* Adriatic Sea, N Mediterranean Sea
Comactium *see* Comacchio
159 N16 **Comai** *var.* Damxoi. Xizang Zizhiqu, W China 28°29′N 91°25′E
41 V17 **Comalapa** Chiapas, SE Mexico 15°42′N 92°06′W
41 U15 **Comalcalco** Tabasco, SE Mexico 18°16′N 93°05′W
63 H16 **Comallo** Río Negro, SW Argentina 40°58′S 70°13′W
26 M12 **Comanche** Oklahoma, C USA 34°22′N 97°57′W
25 R8 **Comanche** Texas, SW USA 31°55′N 98°36′W
194 H2 **Comandante Ferraz** *Brazilian research station* Antarctica 61°57′S 58°23′W
62 N6 **Comandante Fontana** Formosa, N Argentina 25°19′S 59°42′W
63 I22 **Comandante Luis Peidra Buena** Santa Cruz, S Argentina 50°04′S 68°55′W
59 O18 **Comandatuba** Bahia, SE Brazil 15°13′S 39°00′W
116 K11 **Comănești** *Hung.* Kománfalva. Bacău, SW Romania 46°25′N 26°29′E
57 M19 **Comarapa** Santa Cruz, C Bolivia 17°53′S 64°30′W
116 J13 **Comarnic** Prahova, SE Romania 45°18′N 25°37′E
42 H6 **Comayagua** Comayagua, W Honduras 14°30′N 87°39′W
42 H6 **Comayagua** ◈ *department* W Honduras
42 I6 **Comayagua, Montañas de** ▲▲ C Honduras
21 R15 **Combahee River** ≈ South Carolina, SE USA
62 G10 **Combarbalá** Coquimbo, C Chile 31°15′S 71°03′W
103 S7 **Combeaufontaine** Haute-Saône, E France 47°43′N 05°52′E
97 G15 **Comber** *Ir.* An Comar. E Northern Ireland, United Kingdom 54°33′N 05°45′W
99 K20 **Comblain-au-Pont** Liège, E Belgium 50°29′N 05°36′E
102 I6 **Combourg** Ille-et-Vilaine, NW France 48°21′N 01°44′W
44 M9 **Comendador** *prev.* Elías Piña. W Dominican Republic 18°53′N 71°42′W
Comer See *see* Como, Lago di
25 R11 **Comfort** Texas, SW USA 29°58′N 98°54′W
153 V15 **Comilla** *Ben.* Kumillā. Chittagong, E Bangladesh 23°28′N 91°10′E
99 B18 **Comines** Hainaut, W Belgium 50°46′N 02°58′E
121 O15 **Comino** *Malt.* Kemmuna. *island* C Malta
107 D18 **Comino, Capo** *headland* Sardegna, Italy, C Mediterranean Sea 40°32′N 09°49′E
107 K25 **Comiso** Sicilia, Italy, C Mediterranean Sea 36°57′N 14°37′E
41 V16 **Comitán** *var.* Comitán de Domínguez. Chiapas, SE Mexico 16°15′N 92°06′W
Comitán de Domínguez *see* Comitán
Commachio *see* Comacchio
Commander Islands *see* Komandorskiye Ostrova
103 O10 **Commentry** Allier, C France 46°18′N 02°46′E
23 T2 **Commerce** Georgia, SE USA 34°12′N 83°27′W
27 R8 **Commerce** Oklahoma, C USA 36°55′N 94°52′W
25 V5 **Commerce** Texas, SW USA 33°16′N 95°52′W
37 T4 **Commerce City** Colorado, C USA 39°45′N 104°54′W
103 S5 **Commercy** Meuse, NE France 48°46′N 05°36′E
55 W9 **Commewijne** *var.* Commewyne. ◈ *district* NE Surinam
Commewyne *see* Commewijne
15 P8 **Commissaires, Lac des** ◎ Québec, SE Canada
64 A12 **Commissioner's Point** *headland* W Bermuda
9 O7 **Committee Bay** *bay* Nunavut, N Canada
106 D7 **Como** *anc.* Comum. Lombardia, N Italy 45°48′N 09°05′E
63 J19 **Comodoro Rivadavia** Chubut, SE Argentina 45°50′S 67°30′W
106 D6 **Como, Lago di** *var.* Lario, *Eng.* Lake Como, *Ger.* Comer See. ◎ N Italy
Como, Lake *see* Como, Lago di
40 E7 **Comondú** Baja California Sur, NW Mexico 26°01′N 111°50′W
116 F12 **Comorâște** *Hung.* Komornok. Caraș-Severin, SW Romania 45°13′N 21°34′E
Comores, République Fédérale Islamique des *see* Comoros
155 G24 **Comorin, Cape** *headland* SE India 08°00′N 77°10′E
172 M8 **Comoro Basin** *undersea feature* SW Indian Ocean 14°00′S 44°00′E
172 K14 **Comoro Islands** *island group* W Indian Ocean
172 H13 **Comoros** *off.* Federal Islamic Republic of the Comoros, *Fr.* République Fédérale Islamique des Comores. ◆ *republic* W Indian Ocean
Comoros, Federal Islamic Republic of the *see* Comoros
10 L17 **Comox** Vancouver Island, British Columbia, SW Canada 49°40′N 124°55′W
103 O4 **Compiègne** Oise, N France 49°25′N 02°50′E
Complutum *see* Alcalá de Henares
Compniacum *see* Cognac
40 K12 **Compostela** Nayarit, C Mexico 21°12′N 104°52′W
Compostella *see* Santiago
60 L11 **Comprida, Ilha** *island* S Brazil
117 N11 **Comrat** *Rus.* Komrat. S Moldova 46°18′N 28°40′E
25 O11 **Comstock** Texas, SW USA 29°39′N 101°10′W
31 P9 **Comstock Park** Michigan, N USA 43°00′N 85°40′W
193 N3 **Comstock Seamount** *undersea feature* N Pacific Ocean 48°15′N 156°55′W
Comum *see* Como
159 N17 **Cona** Xizang Zizhiqu, W China 27°59′N 91°54′E
76 H14 **Conakry** ● (Guinea) SW Guinea 09°31′N 13°43′W
76 H14 **Conakry** ✈ SW Guinea 09°37′N 13°32′W
Conamara *see* Connemara
Conca *see* Cuenca
25 Q12 **Concan** Texas, SW USA 29°27′N 99°43′W
102 F6 **Concarneau** Finistère, NW France 47°53′N 03°55′W
83 O17 **Conceição** Sofala, C Mozambique 18°47′S 36°18′E
59 K15 **Conceição do Araguaia** Pará, NE Brazil 08°15′S 49°15′W
58 F10 **Conceição do Maú** Roraima, W Brazil 03°35′N 59°52′W
61 D14 **Concepción** *var.* Concepcion. Corrientes, NE Argentina 28°25′S 57°54′W
62 J8 **Concepción** Tucumán, N Argentina 27°20′S 65°35′W
57 O17 **Concepción** Santa Cruz, E Bolivia 16°15′S 62°08′W
62 G13 **Concepción** Bío Bío, C Chile 36°47′S 73°01′W
54 E14 **Concepción** Putumayo, S Colombia 0°03′N 75°35′W
62 O5 **Concepción** *var.* Villa Concepción. Concepción, C Paraguay 23°26′S 57°24′W
62 O5 **Concepción** *off.* Departamento de Concepción. ◈ *department* E Paraguay
Concepción *see* La Concepción
Concepción de la Vega *see* La Vega
41 N9 **Concepción del Oro** Zacatecas, C Mexico 24°38′N 101°25′W
61 D18 **Concepción del Uruguay** Entre Ríos, E Argentina 32°30′S 58°15′W
Concepción, Departamento de *see* Concepción
42 K11 **Concepción, Volcán** 🌋 SW Nicaragua 11°31′N 85°37′W
44 J4 **Conception Island** *island* C Bahamas
35 P14 **Conception, Point** *headland* California, W USA 34°27′N 120°28′W
54 H6 **Concha** Zulia, W Venezuela 09°02′N 71°45′W
60 L9 **Conchas** São Paulo, S Brazil 23°00′S 47°58′W
37 U11 **Conchas Dam** New Mexico, SW USA 35°21′N 104°11′W
37 U10 **Conchas Lake** ⊠ New Mexico, SW USA
102 M5 **Conches-en-Ouche** Eure, N France 49°00′N 01°00′E
37 N12 **Concho** Arizona, SW USA 34°28′N 109°33′W
40 J5 **Conchos, Río** ≈ NW Mexico
41 O8 **Conchos, Río** ≈ C Mexico
108 C8 **Concise** Vaud, W Switzerland 46°52′N 06°40′E
35 N8 **Concord** California, W USA 37°58′N 122°01′W
19 O9 **Concord** *state capital* New Hampshire, NE USA 43°10′N 71°32′W
21 R10 **Concord** North Carolina, SE USA 35°25′N 80°34′W
61 D17 **Concordia** Entre Ríos, E Argentina 31°25′S 58°W
60 I13 **Concórdia** Santa Catarina, S Brazil 27°14′S 52°01′W
54 D9 **Concordia** Antioquia, W Colombia 06°03′N 75°57′W
40 J10 **Concordia** Sinaloa, C Mexico 23°18′N 106°02′W
57 I19 **Concordia** Tacna, SW Peru 18°12′S 70°19′W
27 N3 **Concordia** Kansas, C USA 39°35′N 97°39′W
27 S4 **Concordia** Missouri, C USA 38°58′N 93°34′W
167 S7 **Con Cuông** Nghê An, N Vietnam 19°02′N 104°54′E
167 T15 **Côn Đao** *var.* Con Son. *island* S Vietnam
Condate *see* Rennes, Ille-et-Vilaine, France
Condate *see* St-Claude, Jura, France
Condate *see* Montereau-Faut-Yonne, Seine-St-Denis, France
29 P8 **Conde** South Dakota, N USA 45°08′N 98°07′W
42 J8 **Condega** Estelí, NW Nicaragua 13°19′N 86°26′W
103 P2 **Condé-sur-l'Escaut** Nord, N France 50°27′N 03°36′E
102 K5 **Condé-sur-Noireau** Calvados, N France 48°52′N 00°31′W
Condivincum *see* Nantes
183 P8 **Condobolin** New South Wales, SE Australia 33°04′S 147°08′E
102 L15 **Condom** Gers, S France 43°56′N 00°23′E
32 J11 **Condon** Oregon, NW USA 45°15′N 120°10′W
54 D9 **Condoto** Chocó, W Colombia 05°06′N 76°37′W
23 P7 **Conecuh River** ≈ Alabama/Florida, SE USA
106 H7 **Conegliano** Veneto, NE Italy 45°53′N 12°18′E
61 C19 **Conesa** Buenos Aires, E Argentina 33°36′S 60°21′W
14 F15 **Conestogo** ≈ Ontario, S Canada
Confluentes *see* Koblenz
102 L10 **Confolens** Charente, W France 46°00′N 00°40′E
36 J4 **Confusion Range** ▲▲ Utah, W USA
62 N6 **Confuso, Río** ≈ C Paraguay
21 R12 **Congaree River** ≈ South Carolina, SE USA
Công Hoa Xa Hôi Chu Nghia Viêt Nam *see* Vietnam
160 K12 **Congjiang** *var.* Bingmei. Guizhou, S China 25°48′N 108°55′E
79 G18 **Congo** *off.* Republic of the Congo, *Fr.* Moyen-Congo; *prev.* Middle Congo. ◆ *republic* C Africa
79 K19 **Congo** *off.* Democratic Republic of Congo; *prev.* Zaire, Belgian Congo, Congo (Kinshasa). ◆ *republic* C Africa
67 T11 **Congo** *var.* Kongo, *Fr.* Zaire. ≈ C Africa
Congo *see* Zaire (province) Angola
68 G12 **Congo Basin** *drainage basin* W Dem. Rep. Congo
67 Q11 **Congo Canyon** *var.* Congo Seavalley, Congo Submarine Canyon. *undersea feature* E Atlantic Ocean 06°00′S 11°50′E
Congo Cone *see* Congo Fan
Congo/Congo (Kinshasa) *see* Congo (Democratic Republic of)
65 P15 **Congo Fan** *var.* Congo Cone. *undersea feature* E Atlantic Ocean 06°00′S 09°00′E
Congo Seavalley *see* Congo Canyon
Congo Submarine Canyon *see* Congo Canyon
Coni *see* Cuneo
63 H18 **Cónico, Cerro** ▲ SW Argentina 43°12′S 71°42′W
Conimbria/Conimbriga *see* Coimbra
Conjeeveram *see* Kānchīpuram
11 R13 **Conklin** Alberta, C Canada 55°36′N 111°06′W
24 M1 **Conlen** Texas, SW USA 36°16′N 102°10′W
Con, Loch *see* Conn, Lough
Connacht *see* Connaught
97 B17 **Connaught** *var.* Connacht, *Ir.* Chonnacht, Cúige. *cultural region* W Ireland
31 V10 **Conneaut** Ohio, N USA 41°56′N 80°32′W
18 L13 **Connecticut** *off.* State of Connecticut, *also known as* Blue Law State, Constitution State, Land of Steady Habits, Nutmeg State. ◈ *state* NE USA
19 N8 **Connecticut** ≈ Canada/USA
19 O6 **Connecticut Lakes** *lakes* New Hampshire, NE USA
32 K9 **Connell** Washington, NW USA 46°39′N 118°51′W
97 B17 **Connemara** *Ir.* Conamara. *physical region* W Ireland
31 Q14 **Connersville** Indiana, N USA 39°38′N 85°15′W
97 B16 **Conn, Lough** *Ir.* Loch Con. ◎ W Ireland
35 X6 **Connors Pass** *pass* Nevada, W USA
181 X7 **Connors Range** ▲▲ Queensland, E Australia
56 E7 **Cononaco, Río** ≈ E Ecuador
29 W13 **Conrad** Iowa, C USA 42°13′N 92°52′W
33 R7 **Conrad** Montana, NW USA 48°10′N 111°58′W
25 W10 **Conroe** Texas, SW USA 30°19′N 95°28′W
25 V10 **Conroe, Lake** ⊠ Texas, SW USA
61 C17 **Conscripto Bernardi** Entre Ríos, E Argentina 31°03′S 59°05′W
59 M20 **Conselheiro Lafaiete** Minas Gerais, SE Brazil 20°40′S 43°48′W
Consentia *see* Cosenza
97 L14 **Consett** N England, United Kingdom 54°50′N 01°53′W
44 B5 **Consolación del Sur** Pinar del Río, W Cuba 22°32′N 83°32′W
Con Son *see* Côn Đao
11 R15 **Consort** Alberta, SW Canada 51°58′N 110°44′W
Constance *see* Konstanz
108 I6 **Constance, Lake** *Ger.* Bodensee. ◎ C Europe
104 G9 **Constância** Santarém, C Portugal 39°29′N 08°22′W
117 N14 **Constanța** *var.* Küstendje, *Eng.* Constanza, *Ger.* Konstanza, *Turk.* Küstence. Constanța, SE Romania 44°09′N 28°37′E
116 L14 **Constanța** ◈ *county* SE Romania
Constantia *see* Coutances
Constantia *see* Konstanz
104 K13 **Constantina** Andalucía, S Spain 37°54′N 05°36′W
74 L5 **Constantine** *var.* Qacentina, *Ar.* Qoussantîna. NE Algeria 36°23′N 06°44′E
39 O14 **Constantine, Cape** *headland* Alaska, USA 58°23′N 158°53′W
Constantinople *see* İstanbul
Constantiola *see* Oltenița
Constanz *see* Konstanz
Constanza *see* Constanța
62 G13 **Constitución** Maule, C Chile 35°20′S 72°28′W
61 D17 **Constitución** Salto, N Uruguay 31°05′S 57°51′W
Constitution State *see* Connecticut
105 N10 **Consuegra** Castilla-La Mancha, C Spain 39°28′N 03°36′W
181 X9 **Consuelo Peak** ▲ Queensland, E Australia 24°45′S 148°01′E
56 E11 **Contamana** Loreto, N Peru 07°19′S 75°04′W
Contrasto, Colle del *see* Contrasto, Portella del
107 K23 **Contrasto, Portella del** *var.* Colle del Contrasto. *pass* Sicilia, Italy, C Mediterranean Sea
54 G8 **Contratación** Santander, C Colombia 06°18′N 73°27′W
102 M8 **Contres** Loir-et-Cher, C France 47°24′N 01°30′E
107 O17 **Conversano** Puglia, SE Italy 40°58′N 17°07′E
27 U11 **Conway** Arkansas, C USA 35°05′N 92°27′W
19 O8 **Conway** New Hampshire, NE USA 43°58′N 71°05′W
21 U13 **Conway** South Carolina, SE USA 33°51′N 79°04′W
25 N2 **Conway** Texas, SW USA 35°10′N 101°23′W
27 U11 **Conway, Lake** ⊠ Arkansas, C USA
27 N7 **Conway Springs** Kansas, C USA 37°23′N 97°38′W
97 J18 **Conwy** N Wales, United Kingdom 53°17′N 03°51′W
23 T3 **Conyers** Georgia, SE USA 33°40′N 84°01′W
Coo *see* Kos
182 F4 **Coober Pedy** South Australia 29°01′S 134°47′E
181 P2 **Cooinda** Northern Territory, N Australia 12°54′S 132°31′E
182 B6 **Cook** South Australia 30°37′S 130°26′E
29 W4 **Cook** Minnesota, N USA 47°51′N 92°41′W
191 N6 **Cook, Baie de** *bay* Moorea, W French Polynesia
10 J16 **Cook, Cape** *headland* Vancouver Island, British Columbia, SW Canada 50°04′N 127°52′W
37 Q15 **Cookes Peak** ▲ New Mexico, SW USA 32°32′N 107°43′W
20 L8 **Cookeville** Tennessee, S USA 361°00′N 85°30′W
175 P9 **Cook Fracture Zone** *tectonic feature* S Pacific Ocean
Cook, Grand Récif de *see* Cook, Récif de
39 Q12 **Cook Inlet** *inlet* Alaska, USA
191 X2 **Cook Island** *island* Line Islands, E Kiribati
190 J14 **Cook Islands** ◇ *territory in free association with New Zealand* S Pacific Ocean
Cook, Mount *see* Aoraki
187 O15 **Cook, Récif de** *var.* Grand Récif de Cook. *reef* S New Caledonia
14 G14 **Cookstown** Ontario, S Canada 44°12′N 79°39′W
97 F15 **Cookstown** *Ir.* An Chorr Chríochach. C Northern Ireland, United Kingdom 54°39′N 06°45′W
185 K14 **Cook Strait** *var.* Raukawa. *strait* New Zealand
181 W3 **Cooktown** Queensland, NE Australia 15°28′S 145°15′E
183 P6 **Coolabah** New South Wales, SE Australia 31°03′S 146°42′E
182 J11 **Coola Coola Swamp** *wetland* South Australia
183 S7 **Coolah** New South Wales, SE Australia 31°49′S 149°43′E
183 P9 **Coolamon** New South Wales, SE Australia 34°49′S 147°13′E
183 T4 **Coolatai** New South Wales, SE Australia 29°16′S 150°45′E
180 K12 **Coolgardie** Western Australia 31°01′S 121°12′E
36 L14 **Coolidge** Arizona, SW USA 32°58′N 111°29′W
25 U8 **Coolidge** Texas, SW USA 31°45′N 96°39′W
183 Q11 **Cooma** New South Wales, SE Australia 36°16′S 149°09′E
Coomassie *see* Kumasi
183 R6 **Coonabarabran** New South Wales, SE Australia 31°19′S 149°18′E
182 J10 **Coonalpyn** South Australia 35°43′S 139°50′E
183 R6 **Coonamble** New South Wales, SE Australia 30°56′S 148°22′E
Coondapoor *see* Kundāpura
155 G21 **Coonoor** Tamil Nādu, SE India 11°21′N 76°46′E
29 U14 **Coon Rapids** Iowa, C USA 41°52′N 94°40′W
29 V8 **Coon Rapids** Minnesota, N USA 45°12′N 93°18′W
25 V5 **Cooper** Texas, SW USA 33°23′N 95°42′W
181 U9 **Cooper Creek** *var.* Barcoo, Cooper's Creek. *seasonal river* Queensland/South Australia
39 R12 **Cooper Landing** Alaska, USA 60°27′N 149°59′W
21 T14 **Cooper River** ≈ South Carolina, SE USA
Cooper's Creek *see* Cooper Creek
44 H1 **Coopers Town** Great Abaco, N Bahamas 26°46′N 77°27′W
18 J10 **Cooperstown** New York, NE USA 42°43′N 74°56′W
29 P4 **Cooperstown** North Dakota, N USA 47°26′N 98°07′W
31 P9 **Coopersville** Michigan, N USA 43°03′N 85°55′W
182 D7 **Coorabie** South Australia 31°57′S 132°18′E
23 Q3 **Coosa River** ≈ Alabama/Georgia, S USA
32 E14 **Coos Bay** Oregon, NW USA 43°22′N 124°13′W
183 Q9 **Cootamundra** New South Wales, SE Australia 34°41′S 148°03′E
97 E16 **Cootehill** *Ir.* Muinchille. N Ireland 54°04′N 07°05′W
Čop *see* Chop
57 J17 **Copacabana** La Paz, W Bolivia 16°11′S 69°02′W
63 H14 **Copahué, Volcán** 🌋 C Chile 37°56′S 71°04′W
41 U16 **Copainalá** Chiapas, SE Mexico 17°04′N 93°13′W
32 F8 **Copalis Beach** Washington, NW USA 47°05′N 124°11′W
42 F6 **Copán** ◈ *department* W Honduras
Copán *see* Copán Ruinas
25 T14 **Copano Bay** *bay* NW Gulf of Mexico
42 F6 **Copán Ruinas** *var.* Copán. Copán, W Honduras 14°52′N 89°10′W
Copenhagen *see* København
107 Q19 **Copertino** Puglia, SE Italy 40°16′N 18°03′E
62 H7 **Copiapó** Atacama, N Chile 27°17′S 70°25′W
62 G8 **Copiapó, Bahía** *bay* N Chile
62 G7 **Copiapó, Río** ≈ N Chile
114 M12 **Çöpköy** Edirne, NW Turkey 41°14′N 26°51′E
182 I5 **Copley** South Australia 30°36′S 138°26′E
106 H9 **Copparo** Emilia-Romagna, C Italy 44°53′N 11°53′E
55 V10 **Coppename Rivier** *var.* Koppename. ≈ C Surinam
25 S9 **Copperas Cove** Texas, SW USA 31°07′N 97°54′W
82 J13 **Copperbelt** ◈ *province* C Zambia
39 S11 **Copper Center** Alaska, USA 61°57′N 145°21′W
8 K8 **Coppermine** ≈ Northwest Territories/Nunavut, N Canada
Coppermine *see* Kugluktuk
39 T11 **Copper River** ≈ Alaska, USA
Copper State *see* Arizona
116 I11 **Copșa Mică** *Ger.* Kleinkopisch, *Hung.* Kiskapus. Sibiu, C Romania 46°06′N 24°15′E
158 J14 **Coqên** Xizang Zizhiqu, W China 31°13′N 85°12′E
Coquilhatville *see* Mbandaka
32 E14 **Coquille** Oregon, NW USA 43°11′N 124°12′W
62 G9 **Coquimbo** Coquimbo, N Chile 30°S 71°18′W
62 G9 **Coquimbo** *off.* Región de Coquimbo. ◈ *region* C Chile
Coquimbo, Región de *see* Coquimbo
116 I15 **Corabia** Olt, S Romania 43°46′N 24°31′E
57 F17 **Coracora** Ayacucho, SW Peru 15°03′S 73°45′W
Cora Droma Rúisc *see* Carrick-on-Shannon
44 K9 **Corail** SW Haiti 18°34′N 73°53′W
183 V4 **Coraki** New South Wales, SE Australia 29°01′S 153°15′E
180 G8 **Coral Bay** Western Australia 23°02′S 113°51′E
23 Y16 **Coral Gables** Florida, SE USA 25°43′N 80°16′W
9 P8 **Coral Harbour** Southampton Island, Nunavut, NE Canada 64°10′N 83°15′W
192 I9 **Coral Sea** *sea* SW Pacific Ocean
174 M7 **Coral Sea Basin** *undersea feature* N Coral Sea
192 H9 **Coral Sea Islands** ◇ *Australian external territory* SW Pacific Ocean
182 M12 **Corangamite, Lake** ◎ Victoria, SE Australia
Corantijn Rivier *see* Courantyne River
18 B14 **Coraopolis** Pennsylvania, NE USA 40°28′N 80°08′W
107 N17 **Corato** Puglia, SE Italy 41°09′N 16°25′E
103 O17 **Corbières** ▲▲ S France
103 P8 **Corbigny** Nièvre, C France 47°15′N 03°42′E
21 N7 **Corbin** Kentucky, S USA 36°57′N 84°06′W
104 L14 **Corbones** ≈ SW Spain
Corcaigh *see* Cork
35 R11 **Corcoran** California, W USA 36°06′N 119°33′W
47 T14 **Corcovado, Golfo** *gulf* S Chile
63 G18 **Corcovado, Volcán** 🌋 S Chile 43°13′S 72°45′W
104 F3 **Corcubión** Galicia, NW Spain 42°56′N 09°12′W
Corcyra Nigra *see* Korčula
60 Q9 **Cordeiro** Rio de Janeiro, SE Brazil 22°01′S 42°20′W
23 T6 **Cordele** Georgia, SE USA 31°59′N 83°49′W
26 L11 **Cordell** Oklahoma, C USA 35°17′N 98°59′W
103 N14 **Cordes** Tarn, S France 44°03′N 01°57′E
62 O6 **Cordillera** *off.* Departamento de la Cordillera. ◈ *department* C Paraguay
Cordillera *see* Cacaguatique, Cordillera
Cordillera, Departamento de la *see* Cordillera
182 K1 **Cordillo Downs** South Australia 26°44′S 140°37′E
62 K10 **Córdoba** Córdoba, C Argentina 31°25′S 64°11′W
41 R14 **Córdoba** Veracruz-Llave, E Mexico 18°55′N 96°55′W
104 M13 **Córdoba** *var.* Cordoba, *Eng.* Cordova; *anc.* Corduba. Andalucía, SW Spain 37°53′N 04°46′W
62 K11 **Córdoba** *off.* Provincia de Córdoba. ◈ *province* C Argentina
54 D7 **Córdoba** *off.* Departamento de Córdoba. ◈ *province* NW Colombia
104 L13 **Córdoba** ◈ *province* Andalucía, S Spain
Córdoba, Departamento de *see* Córdoba
Córdoba, Provincia de *see* Córdoba
62 K10 **Córdoba, Sierras de** ▲▲ C Argentina
23 O3 **Cordova** Alabama, S USA 33°45′N 87°10′W
39 S12 **Cordova** Alaska, USA 60°32′N 145°45′W
Cordova/Cordoba *see* Córdoba
Corduba *see* Córdoba
Corentyne River *see* Courantyne River
Corfu *see* Kérkyra
104 J9 **Coria** Extremadura, W Spain 39°59′N 06°32′W
104 J14 **Coria del Río** Andalucía, S Spain 37°18′N 06°04′W
183 S8 **Coricudgy, Mount** ▲ New South Wales, SE Australia 32°49′S 150°28′E
107 N20 **Corigliano Calabro** Calabria, SW Italy 39°36′N 16°32′E
Corinium/Corinium Dobunorum *see* Cirencester
23 N1 **Corinth** Mississippi, S USA 34°56′N 88°29′W
Corinth *see* Kórinthos
Corinth Canal *see* Dióryga Korinthou
Corinth, Gulf of/ Corinthiacus Sinus *see* Korinthiakós Kólpos
Corinthus *see* Kórinthos
42 I9 **Corinto** Chinandega, NW Nicaragua 12°29′N 87°14′W
97 C21 **Cork** *Ir.* Corcaigh. S Ireland 51°54′N 07°06′W
97 C21 **Cork** *Ir.* Corcaigh. *cultural region* SW Ireland
97 C21 **Cork** ✈ Cork, SW Ireland 51°52′N 08°25′W
97 D21 **Cork Harbour** *Ir.* Cuan Chorcaí. *inlet* SW Ireland
107 I23 **Corleone** Sicilia, Italy, C Mediterranean Sea 37°49′N 13°18′E
114 N13 **Çorlu** Tekirdağ, NW Turkey 41°11′N 27°48′E
114 N12 **Çorlu Çayı** ≈ NW Turkey
Cormaiore *see* Courmayeur
11 V13 **Cormorant** Manitoba, C Canada 54°12′N 100°33′W
23 T2 **Cornelia** Georgia, SE USA 34°30′N 83°31′W
60 J10 **Cornélio Procópio** Paraná, S Brazil 23°07′S 50°40′W
55 V9 **Corneliskondre** Sipaliwini, N Surinam 05°21′N 56°10′W
30 J5 **Cornell** Wisconsin, N USA 45°09′N 91°10′W
13 S12 **Corner Brook** Newfoundland, Newfoundland and Labrador, E Canada 48°58′N 57°58′W
Corner Rise Seamounts *see* Corner Seamounts
64 I9 **Corner Seamounts** *var.* Corner Rise Seamounts. *undersea feature* NW Atlantic Ocean 35°30′N 51°30′W
116 M9 **Cornești** *Rus.* Korneshty. C Moldova 47°23′N 28°00′E
Corneto *see* Tarquinia
Cornhusker State *see* Nebraska
27 X8 **Corning** Arkansas, C USA 36°26′N 90°35′W
35 N5 **Corning** California, W USA 39°54′N 122°12′W
29 U15 **Corning** Iowa, C USA 40°58′N 94°46′W
18 G11 **Corning** New York, NE USA 42°08′N 77°03′W
Corn Islands *see* Maíz, Islas del
107 J14 **Corno Grande** ▲ C Italy 42°26′N 13°29′E
15 N13 **Cornwall** Ontario, SE Canada 45°02′N 74°45′W
97 H25 **Cornwall** *cultural region* SW England, United Kingdom
97 G25 **Cornwall, Cape** *headland* SW England, United Kingdom 50°11′N 05°39′W
54 J4 **Coro** *prev.* Santa Ana de Coro. Falcón, NW Venezuela 11°27′N 69°41′W
57 J18 **Corocoro** La Paz, W Bolivia 17°10′S 68°28′W
57 K17 **Coroico** La Paz, W Bolivia 16°09′S 67°45′W
184 M5 **Coromandel** Waikato, North Island, New Zealand 36°47′S 175°30′E
155 K20 **Coromandel Coast** *coast* E India
184 M5 **Coromandel Peninsula** *peninsula* North Island, New Zealand
184 M6 **Coromandel Range** ▲▲ North Island, New Zealand
171 N5 **Coron** Busuanga Island, W Philippines 12°02′N 120°10′E
35 T15 **Corona** California, W USA 33°52′N 117°34′W
37 T12 **Corona** New Mexico, SW USA 34°15′N 105°36′W
11 U17 **Coronach** Saskatchewan, S Canada 49°07′N 105°33′W
35 U17 **Coronado** California, W USA 32°41′N 117°10′W
43 N15 **Coronado, Bahía de** *bay* S Costa Rica
11 R15 **Coronation** Alberta, SW Canada 52°06′N 111°25′W
8 K7 **Coronation Gulf** *gulf* Nunavut, N Canada
194 I1 **Coronation Island** *island* Antarctica
39 X14 **Coronation Island** *island* Alexander Archipelago, Alaska, USA
61 B18 **Coronda** Santa Fe, C Argentina 31°58′S 60°56′W
63 F14 **Coronel** Bío Bío, C Chile 37°01′S 73°08′W
61 D20 **Coronel Brandsen** *var.* Brandsen. Buenos Aires, E Argentina 35°08′S 58°15′W
62 K4 **Coronel Cornejo** Salta, N Argentina 22°46′S 63°49′W
61 B24 **Coronel Dorrego** Buenos Aires, E Argentina 38°38′S 61°15′W
62 P6 **Coronel Oviedo** Caaguazú, SE Paraguay 25°24′S 56°30′W

◆ Country ● Country Capital ◇ Dependent Territory ○ Dependent Territory Capital ◈ Administrative Regions ✈ International Airport ▲ Mountain ▲▲ Mountain Range 🌋 Volcano ≈ River ◎ Lake ⊠ Reservoir

61 B23 **Coronel Pringles** Buenos Aires, E Argentina *37°56′S 61°25′W*
61 B23 **Coronel Suárez** Buenos Aires, E Argentina *37°30′S 61°52′W*
61 E22 **Coronel Vidal** Buenos Aires, E Argentina *37°28′S 57°45′W*
55 V9 **Coronie** ◐ *district* NW Surinam
57 G17 **Coropuna, Nevado** ▲ S Peru *15°31′S 72°31′W*
Çorovoda *see* Çorovodë
113 L22 **Çorovodë** *var.* Çorovoda. Berat, S Albania *40°29′N 20°15′E*
183 P11 **Corowa** New South Wales, SE Australia *36°01′S 146°22′E*
42 G1 **Corozal** Corozal, N Belize *18°23′N 88°23′W*
54 E6 **Corozal** Sucre, NW Colombia *09°18′N 75°19′W*
42 G1 **Corozal** ◐ *district* N Belize
25 T14 **Corpus Christi** Texas, SW USA *27°48′N 97°24′W*
25 T14 **Corpus Christi Bay** *inlet* Texas, SW USA
25 R14 **Corpus Christi, Lake** ▣ Texas, SW USA
63 F16 **Corral** Los Lagos, C Chile *39°55′S 73°30′W*
105 O9 **Corral de Almaguer** Castilla-La Mancha, C Spain *39°45′N 03°10′W*
104 K6 **Corrales** Castilla-León, N Spain *41°22′N 05°44′W*
37 R11 **Corrales** New Mexico, SW USA *35°11′N 106°37′W*
Corrán Tuathail *see* Carrauntoohil
106 F9 **Correggio** Emilia-Romagna, C Italy *44°47′N 10°46′E*
59 M16 **Corrente** Piauí, E Brazil *10°29′S 45°11′W*
59 I19 **Correntes, Rio** ≈ SW Brazil
103 N12 **Corrèze** ◐ *department* C France
97 C17 **Corrib, Lough** *Ir.* Loch Coirib. ◎ W Ireland
61 C14 **Corrientes** Corrientes, NE Argentina *27°29′S 58°42′W*
61 D15 **Corrientes** *off.* Provincia de Corrientes. ◐ *province* NE Argentina
44 A5 **Corrientes, Cabo** *headland* W Cuba *21°48′N 84°30′W*
40 I13 **Corrientes, Cabo** *headland* SW Mexico *20°25′N 105°42′W*
Corrientes, Provincia de *see* Corrientes
61 C16 **Corrientes, Río** ≈ NE Argentina
56 E8 **Corrientes, Río** ≈ Ecuador/Peru
25 W9 **Corrigan** Texas, SW USA *31°00′N 94°49′W*
55 U9 **Corriverton** E Guyana *05°55′N 57°09′W*
Corriza *see* Korçë
183 Q11 **Corryong** Victoria, SE Australia *36°14′S 147°54′E*
103 F2 **Corse** *Eng.* Corsica. ◐ *region* France, C Mediterranean Sea
101 X13 **Corse** *Eng.* Corsica. *island* France, C Mediterranean Sea
103 Y12 **Corse, Cap** *headland* Corse, France, C Mediterranean Sea *43°01′N 09°25′E*
103 X15 **Corse-du-Sud** ◐ *department* Corse, France, C Mediterranean Sea
29 P11 **Corsica** South Dakota, N USA *43°25′N 98°24′W*
Corsica *see* Corse
25 U7 **Corsicana** Texas, SW USA *32°05′N 96°27′W*
103 Y15 **Corte** Corse, France, C Mediterranean Sea *42°18′N 09°08′E*
63 G16 **Corte Alto** Los Lagos, S Chile *40°58′S 73°04′W*
104 I13 **Cortegana** Andalucía, S Spain *37°55′N 06°49′W*
43 N15 **Cortés** *var.* Ciudad Cortés. Puntarenas, SE Costa Rica *08°59′N 83°32′W*
42 G5 **Cortés** ◐ *department* NW Honduras
37 P8 **Cortez** Colorado, C USA *37°22′N 108°36′W*
Cortez, Sea of *see* California, Golfo de
106 H6 **Cortina d'Ampezzo** Veneto, NE Italy *46°33′N 12°09′E*
18 H11 **Cortland** New York, NE USA *42°34′N 76°09′W*
31 V11 **Cortland** Ohio, N USA *41°19′N 80°43′W*
106 H12 **Cortona** Toscana, C Italy *43°15′N 12°01′E*
76 H13 **Corubal, Rio** ≈ E Guinea-Bissau
104 G10 **Coruche** Santarém, C Portugal *38°58′N 08°31′W*
Çoruh *see* Rize
137 R11 **Çoruh Nehri** *Geor.* Chorokh, *Rus.* Chorokhi. ≈ Georgia/Turkey
136 K12 **Çorum** *var.* Chorum. Çorum, N Turkey *40°31′N 34°57′E*
136 J12 **Çorum** *var.* Chorum. ◐ *province* N Turkey
59 H19 **Corumbá** Mato Grosso do Sul, S Brazil *19°S 57°35′W*
14 D16 **Corunna** Ontario, S Canada *42°49′N 82°25′W*
Corunna *see* A Coruña
32 F12 **Corvallis** Oregon, NW USA *44°35′N 122°36′W*
64 M1 **Corvo** *var.* Ilha do Corvo. *island* Azores, Portugal, NE Atlantic Ocean
Corvo, Ilha do *see* Corvo
31 O16 **Corydon** Indiana, N USA *38°12′N 86°07′W*
29 V16 **Corydon** Iowa, C USA *40°45′N 93°19′W*
Cos *see* Kos
40 I9 **Cosalá** Sinaloa, C Mexico *24°25′N 106°39′W*
41 R15 **Cosamaloapan** *var.* Cosamaloapan de Carpio. Veracruz-Llave, E Mexico *18°23′N 95°50′W*
Cosamaloapan de Carpio *see* Cosamaloapan
107 N21 **Cosenza** *anc.* Consentia. Calabria, SW Italy *39°17′N 16°15′E*
31 T13 **Coshocton** Ohio, N USA *40°16′N 81°53′W*
42 H9 **Cosigüina, Punta** *headland* NW Nicaragua *12°53′N 87°42′W*
29 T9 **Cosmos** Minnesota, N USA *44°56′N 94°42′W*
103 O8 **Cosne-Cours-sur-Loire** Nièvre, C France *47°25′N 02°56′E*
108 B9 **Cossonay** Vaud, W Switzerland *46°37′N 06°28′E*
Cossyra *see* Pantelleria
47 R4 **Costa, Cordillera de la** *var.* Cordillera de Venezuela. ▲▲ N Venezuela
42 K13 **Costa Rica** *off.* Republic of Costa Rica. ◆ *republic* Central America
Costa Rica, Republic of *see* Costa Rica
43 N15 **Costeña, Fila** ▲▲ S Costa Rica
Costermansville *see* Bukavu
116 I14 **Costeşti** Argeş, SW Romania *44°40′N 24°53′E*
37 S8 **Costilla** New Mexico, SW USA *36°58′N 105°31′W*
35 O7 **Cosumnes River** ≈ California, W USA
101 O16 **Coswig** Sachsen, E Germany *51°07′N 13°36′E*
101 M14 **Coswig** Sachsen-Anhalt, E Germany *51°53′N 12°26′E*
Cosyra *see* Pantelleria
171 Q7 **Cotabato** Mindanao, S Philippines *07°13′N 124°12′E*
56 C5 **Cotacachi** ▲ N Ecuador *0°29′N 78°17′W*
57 L21 **Cotagaita** Potosí, S Bolivia *20°47′S 65°40′W*
103 V15 **Côte d'Azur** *prev.* Nice. ✈ (Nice) Alpes-Maritimes, SE France *43°40′N 07°12′E*
Côte d'Ivoire *see* Ivory Coast
Côte d'Ivoire, République de la *see* Ivory Coast
103 R7 **Côte d'Or** ◐ *department* E France
103 R8 **Côte d'Or** *cultural region* C France
Côte Française des Somalis *see* Djibouti
102 J4 **Cotentin** *peninsula* N France
102 G6 **Côtes d'Armor** *prev.* Côtes-du-Nord. ◐ *department* NW France
Côtes-du-Nord *see* Côtes d'Armor
Cöthen *see* Köthen
Côtière, Chaîne *see* Coast Mountains
40 M13 **Cotija** *var.* Cotija de la Paz. Michoacán, SW Mexico *19°49′N 102°39′W*
Cotija de la Paz *see* Cotija
77 R16 **Cotonou** *var.* Kotonu. S Benin *06°24′N 02°26′E*
77 R16 **Cotonou** ✈ S Benin *06°31′N 02°18′E*
56 B6 **Cotopaxi** *prev.* León. ◐ *province* C Ecuador
56 C6 **Cotopaxi** ⛰ N Ecuador *0°42′S 78°24′W*
Cotrone *see* Crotone
97 L21 **Cotswold Hills** *var.* Cotswolds. *hill range* S England, United Kingdom
Cotswolds *see* Cotswold Hills
32 F13 **Cottage Grove** Oregon, NW USA *43°48′N 123°03′W*
21 S14 **Cottageville** South Carolina, SE USA *32°55′N 80°28′W*
101 P14 **Cottbus** *Lus.* Chośebuz; *prev.* Kottbus. Brandenburg, E Germany *51°42′N 14°22′E*
27 U9 **Cotter** Arkansas, C USA *36°16′N 92°30′W*
106 A9 **Cottian Alps** *Fr.* Alpes Cottiennes, *It.* Alpi Cozie. ▲▲ France/Italy
Cottiennes, Alpes *see* Cottian Alps
Cotton State, The *see* Alabama
22 G4 **Cotton Valley** Louisiana, S USA *32°49′N 93°25′W*
36 L12 **Cottonwood** Arizona, SW USA *34°43′N 112°00′W*
32 M10 **Cottonwood** Idaho, NW USA *46°01′N 116°20′W*
29 S9 **Cottonwood** Minnesota, N USA *44°37′N 95°41′W*
25 Q7 **Cottonwood** Texas, SW USA *32°12′N 99°14′W*
27 O5 **Cottonwood Falls** Kansas, C USA *38°21′N 96°33′W*
36 L3 **Cottonwood Heights** Utah, W USA *40°37′N 111°48′W*
29 S10 **Cottonwood River** ≈ Minnesota, N USA
45 O9 **Cotuí** C Dominican Republic *19°04′N 70°10′W*
25 Q13 **Cotulla** Texas, SW USA *28°27′N 99°15′W*
Cotyora *see* Ordu
102 I11 **Coubre, Pointe de la** *headland* W France *45°39′N 01°23′W*
18 E12 **Coudersport** Pennsylvania, NE USA *41°45′N 78°00′W*
15 S9 **Coudres, Île aux** *island* Québec, SE Canada
182 G11 **Couedic, Cape de** *headland* South Australia *36°04′S 136°43′E*
Couentrey *see* Coventry
102 I6 **Couesnon** ≈ NW France
32 H10 **Cougar** Washington, NW USA *46°03′N 122°18′W*
102 L10 **Couhé** Vienne, W France *46°18′N 00°10′E*
32 K8 **Coulee City** Washington, NW USA *47°36′N 119°18′W*
195 Q15 **Coulman Island** *island* Antarctica
103 P5 **Coulommiers** Seine-et-Marne, N France *48°49′N 03°04′E*
14 K11 **Coulonge** ≈ Québec, SE Canada
14 K11 **Coulonge Est** ≈ Québec, SE Canada
35 Q9 **Coulterville** California, W USA *37°41′N 120°10′W*
38 M9 **Council** Alaska, USA *64°54′N 163°40′W*
32 M12 **Council** Idaho, NW USA *44°45′N 116°26′W*
29 S15 **Council Bluffs** Iowa, C USA *41°16′N 95°52′W*
27 O5 **Council Grove** Kansas, C USA *38°41′N 96°29′W*
27 O5 **Council Grove Lake** ▣ Kansas, C USA
32 G7 **Coupeville** Washington, NW USA *48°13′N 122°41′W*
55 U12 **Courantyne River** *var.* Corantijn Rivier, Corentyne River. ≈ Guyana/Surinam
99 G21 **Courcelles** Hainaut, S Belgium *50°28′N 04°23′E*
108 C7 **Courgenay** Jura, NW Switzerland *47°24′N 07°09′E*
126 B2 **Courland Lagoon** *Ger.* Kurisches Haff, *Rus.* Kurskiy Zaliv. *lagoon* Lithuania/Russian Federation
118 B12 **Courland Spit** *Lith.* Kuršių Nerija, *Rus.* Kurshskaya Kosa. *spit* Lithuania/Russian Federation
106 A6 **Courmayeur** *prev.* Cormaiore. Valle d'Aosta, NW Italy *45°48′N 07°00′E*
108 D7 **Courroux** Jura, NW Switzerland *47°22′N 07°23′E*
10 K17 **Courtenay** Vancouver Island, British Columbia, SW Canada *49°40′N 124°58′W*
21 W7 **Courtland** Virginia, NE USA *36°44′N 77°06′W*
25 V10 **Courtney** Texas, SW USA *30°16′N 96°04′W*
30 J4 **Court Oreilles, Lac** ◎ Wisconsin, N USA
Courtrai *see* Kortrijk
99 H19 **Court-Saint-Étienne** Walloon Brabant, C Belgium *50°38′N 04°34′E*
22 G6 **Coushatta** Louisiana, S USA *32°00′N 93°20′W*
172 I16 **Cousin** *island* Inner Islands, NE Seychelles
172 I16 **Cousine** *island* Inner Islands, NE Seychelles
102 J4 **Coutances** *anc.* Constantia. Manche, N France *49°04′N 01°27′W*
102 K12 **Coutras** Gironde, SW France *45°01′N 00°07′W*
45 U14 **Couva** Trinidad, Trinidad and Tobago *10°25′N 61°27′W*
108 B8 **Couvet** Neuchâtel, W Switzerland *46°57′N 06°41′E*
99 H22 **Couvin** Namur, S Belgium *50°03′N 04°30′E*
116 K12 **Covasna** *Ger.* Kowasna, *Hung.* Kovászna. Covasna, E Romania *45°51′N 26°11′E*
116 J11 **Covasna** ◐ *county* E Romania
14 E12 **Cove Island** *island* Ontario, S Canada
34 M5 **Covelo** California, W USA *39°46′N 123°16′W*
97 M20 **Coventry** *anc.* Couentrey. C England, United Kingdom *52°25′N 01°30′W*
Cove of Cork *see* Cobh
21 U5 **Covesville** Virginia, NE USA *37°52′N 78°41′W*
104 I8 **Covilhã** Castelo Branco, E Portugal *40°17′N 07°30′W*
23 T3 **Covington** Georgia, SE USA *33°34′N 83°52′W*
31 N13 **Covington** Indiana, N USA *40°08′N 87°23′W*
20 M3 **Covington** Kentucky, S USA *39°04′N 84°30′W*
22 K8 **Covington** Louisiana, S USA *30°28′N 90°06′W*
31 Q13 **Covington** Ohio, N USA *40°07′N 84°21′W*
20 F9 **Covington** Tennessee, S USA *35°32′N 89°40′W*
21 S6 **Covington** Virginia, NE USA *37°48′N 80°01′W*
183 Q8 **Cowal, Lake** *seasonal lake* New South Wales, SE Australia
11 W15 **Cowan** Manitoba, S Canada *51°59′N 100°36′W*
18 F12 **Cowanesque River** ≈ New York/Pennsylvania, NE USA
180 L12 **Cowan, Lake** ◎ Western Australia
15 P13 **Cowansville** Québec, SE Canada *45°13′N 72°44′W*
182 H8 **Cowell** South Australia *33°43′S 136°53′E*
97 M23 **Cowes** S England, United Kingdom *50°45′N 01°19′W*
27 Q10 **Coweta** Oklahoma, C USA *35°57′N 95°39′W*
0 D6 **Cowie Seamount** *undersea feature* NE Pacific Ocean *54°15′N 149°30′W*
32 G10 **Cowlitz River** ≈ Washington, NW USA
21 Q11 **Cowpens** South Carolina, SE USA *35°01′N 81°48′W*
183 R8 **Cowra** New South Wales, SE Australia *33°50′S 148°45′E*
Coxen Hole *see* Roatán
59 I19 **Coxim** Mato Grosso do Sul, S Brazil *18°28′S 54°45′W*
59 I19 **Coxim, Rio** ≈ SW Brazil
Coxin Hole *see* Roatán
153 V17 **Cox's Bazar** Chittagong, S Bangladesh *21°25′N 91°59′E*
76 H14 **Coyah** Conakry, W Guinea *09°45′N 13°26′W*
40 K5 **Coyame** Chihuahua, N Mexico *29°29′N 105°07′W*
24 L9 **Coyanosa Draw** ≈ Texas, SW USA
Coyhaique *see* Coihaique
42 C7 **Coyolate, Río** ≈ S Guatemala
Coyote State, The *see* South Dakota
40 I10 **Coyotitán** Sinaloa, C Mexico *23°48′N 106°37′W*
41 N15 **Coyuca** *var.* Coyuca de Catalán. Guerrero, S Mexico *18°21′N 100°39′W*
41 O16 **Coyuca** *var.* Coyuca de Benítez. Guerrero, S Mexico *17°01′N 100°08′W*
Coyuca de Benítez/Coyuca de Catalán *see* Coyuca
29 N15 **Cozad** Nebraska, C USA *40°52′N 99°58′W*
158 L14 **Cozhê** Xizang Zizhiqu, W China *31°53′N 87°51′E*
Cozie, Alpi *see* Cottian Alps
Cozmeni *see* Kitsman'
40 E3 **Cozón, Cerro** ▲ NW Mexico *31°16′N 112°29′W*
41 Z12 **Cozumel** Quintana Roo, E Mexico *20°29′N 86°54′W*
41 Z12 **Cozumel, Isla** *island* SE Mexico
32 K8 **Crab Creek** ≈ Washington, NW USA
44 H12 **Crab Pond Point** *headland* W Jamaica *18°07′N 78°01′W*
Cracovia/Cracow *see* Kraków
83 I25 **Cradock** Eastern Cape, S South Africa *32°07′S 25°38′E*
39 Y14 **Craig** Prince of Wales Island, Alaska, USA *55°29′N 133°04′W*
37 Q3 **Craig** Colorado, C USA *40°31′N 107°33′W*
97 F15 **Craigavon** C Northern Ireland, United Kingdom *54°28′N 06°25′W*
21 T5 **Craigsville** Virginia, NE USA *38°07′N 79°21′W*
101 J21 **Crailsheim** Baden-Württemberg, S Germany *49°07′N 10°04′E*
116 H14 **Craiova** Dolj, SW Romania *44°19′N 23°49′E*
10 K12 **Cranberry Junction** British Columbia, SW Canada *55°35′N 128°21′W*
18 J8 **Cranberry Lake** ◎ New York, NE USA
11 V13 **Cranberry Portage** Manitoba, C Canada *54°34′N 101°22′W*
11 P17 **Cranbrook** British Columbia, SW Canada *49°29′N 115°48′W*
30 M5 **Crandon** Wisconsin, N USA *45°34′N 88°54′W*
32 K14 **Crane** Oregon, NW USA *43°24′N 118°35′W*
24 M9 **Crane** Texas, SW USA *31°23′N 102°22′W*
Crane *see* The Crane
25 S8 **Cranfills Gap** Texas, SW USA *31°46′N 97°49′W*
19 O12 **Cranston** Rhode Island, NE USA *41°46′N 71°26′W*
Cranz *see* Zelenogradsk
59 L15 **Craolândia** Tocantins, E Brazil *07°17′S 47°23′W*
102 J7 **Craon** Mayenne, NW France *47°52′N 00°57′W*
195 V16 **Crary, Cape** *headland* Antarctica
Crasna *see* Kraszna
32 G14 **Crater Lake** ◎ Oregon, NW USA
33 P14 **Craters of the Moon National Monument** *national park* Idaho, NW USA
59 O14 **Crateús** Ceará, E Brazil *05°10′S 40°39′W*
Crathis *see* Crati
107 N20 **Crati** *anc.* Crathis. ≈ S Italy
11 U16 **Craven** Saskatchewan, S Canada *50°44′N 104°50′W*
54 I8 **Cravo Norte** Arauca, E Colombia *06°17′N 70°15′W*
28 J12 **Crawford** Nebraska, C USA *42°40′N 103°24′W*
25 T8 **Crawford** Texas, SW USA *31°31′N 97°26′W*
11 O17 **Crawford Bay** British Columbia, SW Canada *49°39′N 116°44′W*
65 M19 **Crawford Seamount** *undersea feature* S Atlantic Ocean *40°30′S 10°00′W*
31 O13 **Crawfordsville** Indiana, N USA *40°02′N 86°52′W*
23 S9 **Crawfordville** Florida, SE USA *30°10′N 84°22′W*
97 O23 **Crawley** SE England, United Kingdom *51°07′N 00°12′W*
33 S10 **Crazy Mountains** ▲▲ Montana, NW USA
11 T11 **Cree** ≈ Saskatchewan, C Canada
37 R7 **Creede** Colorado, C USA *37°51′N 106°55′W*
40 I6 **Creel** Chihuahua, N Mexico *27°45′N 107°36′W*
11 S11 **Cree Lake** ◎ Saskatchewan, C Canada
11 V13 **Creighton** Saskatchewan, C Canada *54°46′N 101°54′W*
29 Q13 **Creighton** Nebraska, C USA *42°28′N 97°54′W*
103 O4 **Creil** Oise, N France *49°16′N 02°29′E*
106 E8 **Crema** Lombardia, N Italy *45°22′N 09°40′E*
106 E8 **Cremona** Lombardia, N Italy *45°08′N 10°02′E*
Creole State *see* Louisiana
112 M10 **Crepaja** *Hung.* Cserépalja. Vojvodina, N Serbia *45°02′N 20°36′E*
103 O4 **Crépy-en-Valois** Oise, N France *49°13′N 02°54′E*
112 B10 **Cres** *It.* Cherso. Primorje-Gorski Kotar, NW Croatia *44°57′N 14°24′E*
112 A11 **Cres** *It.* Cherso; *anc.* Crexa. *island* W Croatia
32 H14 **Crescent** Oregon, NW USA *43°27′N 121°40′W*
34 K1 **Crescent City** California, W USA *41°45′N 124°14′W*
23 W10 **Crescent City** Florida, SE USA *29°25′N 81°30′W*
167 X10 **Crescent Group** *island group* C Paracel Islands
23 W10 **Crescent Lake** ◎ Florida, SE USA
29 X11 **Cresco** Iowa, C USA *43°22′N 92°06′W*
61 B18 **Crespo** Entre Ríos, E Argentina *32°05′S 60°20′W*
54 E5 **Crespo** ✈ (Cartagena) Bolívar, NW Colombia *10°27′N 75°31′W*
103 R13 **Crest** Drôme, E France *44°45′N 05°00′E*
37 R5 **Crested Butte** Colorado, C USA *38°52′N 106°59′W*
31 S12 **Crestline** Ohio, N USA *40°47′N 82°44′W*
11 O17 **Creston** British Columbia, SW Canada *49°05′N 116°32′W*
29 U15 **Creston** Iowa, C USA *41°03′N 94°21′W*
33 V16 **Creston** Wyoming, C USA *41°40′N 107°43′W*
37 S7 **Crestone Peak** ▲ Colorado, C USA *37°58′N 105°34′W*
23 P8 **Crestview** Florida, SE USA *30°44′N 86°34′W*
121 R10 **Cretan Trough** *undersea feature* Aegean Sea, C Mediterranean Sea
29 R16 **Crete** Nebraska, C USA *40°36′N 96°58′W*
Crete *see* Kríti
103 O5 **Créteil** Val-de-Marne, N France *48°47′N 02°28′E*
Crete, Sea of/Creticum, Mare *see* Kritikó Pélagos
105 X4 **Creus, Cap de** *headland* NE Spain *42°18′N 03°18′E*
103 N10 **Creuse** ◐ *department* C France
102 L9 **Creuse** ≈ C France
103 T4 **Creutzwald** Moselle, NE France *49°13′N 06°41′E*
105 S12 **Crevillente** País Valenciano, E Spain *38°15′N 00°48′W*
97 L18 **Crewe** C England, United Kingdom *53°05′N 02°27′W*
21 V7 **Crewe** Virginia, NE USA *37°10′N 78°07′W*
Crexa *see* Cres
43 Q15 **Cricamola, Río** ≈ NW Panama
61 K14 **Criciúma** Santa Catarina, S Brazil *28°39′S 49°23′W*
96 J11 **Crieff** C Scotland, United Kingdom *56°22′N 03°49′W*
112 B10 **Crikvenica** *It.* Cirquenizza; *prev.* Cirkvenica, Crjkvenica. Primorje-Gorski Kotar, NW Croatia *45°12′N 14°40′E*
Crimea/Crimean Oblast *see* Krym, Avtonomna Respublika
101 M16 **Crimmitschau** *var.* Krimmitschau. Sachsen, E Germany *50°48′N 12°23′E*
116 G11 **Crişcior** *Hung.* Kristyor. Hunedoara, W Romania *46°09′N 22°54′E*
21 Y5 **Crisfield** Maryland, NE USA *37°58′N 75°51′W*
31 P3 **Crisp Point** *headland* Michigan, N USA *46°45′N 85°15′W*
59 L19 **Cristalina** Goiás, C Brazil *16°43′S 47°37′W*
44 J7 **Cristal, Sierra del** ▲▲ E Cuba
43 T14 **Cristóbal** Colón, C Panama *09°18′N 79°52′W*
54 F4 **Cristóbal Colón, Pico** ▲ N Colombia *10°52′N 73°46′W*
106 C10 **Cristoforo Colombo** ✈ Liguria, NW Italy
Cristur/Cristuru Săcuiesc *see* Cristuru Secuiesc
116 I11 **Cristuru Secuiesc** *prev.* Cristur, Cristuru Săcuiesc, Sitaş Cristuru, *Ger.* Kreutz, *Hung.* Székelykeresztúr, Szitás-Keresztúr. Harghita, C Romania *46°17′N 25°02′E*
116 F10 **Crişul Alb** *var.* Weisse Kreisch, *Ger.* Weisse Körös, *Hung.* Fehér-Körös. ≈ Hungary/Romania
116 F10 **Crişul Negru** *Ger.* Schwarze Körös, *Hung.* Fekete-Körös. ≈ Hungary/Romania
116 G10 **Crişul Repede** *var.* Schnelle Kreisch, *Ger.* Schnelle Körös, *Hung.* Sebes-Körös. ≈ Hungary/Romania
117 N10 **Criuleni** *Rus.* Kriulyany. C Moldova *47°12′N 29°09′E*
Crivadia Vulcanului *see* Vulcan
Crjkvenica *see* Crikvenica
113 O17 **Crna Gora** ▲▲ FYR Macedonia/Serbia
Crna Gora *see* Montenegro
113 O20 **Crna Reka** ≈ S FYR Macedonia
Crni Drim *see* Black Drin
109 V10 **Črni vrh** ▲ NE Slovenia *46°28′N 15°14′E*
109 V13 **Črnomelj** *Ger.* Tschernembl. SE Slovenia *45°32′N 15°12′E*
97 A17 **Croagh Patrick** *Ir.* Cruach Phádraig. ▲ W Ireland *53°45′N 09°39′W*
112 D9 **Croatia** *off.* Republic of Croatia, *Ger.* Kroatien, *SCr.* Hrvatska. ◆ *republic* SE Europe
Croatia, Republic of *see* Croatia
Croce, Picco di *see* Wilde Kreuzspitze
15 P8 **Croche** ≈ Québec, SE Canada
169 V7 **Crocker, Banjaran** *var.* Crocker Range. ▲▲ East Malaysia
Crocker Range *see* Crocker, Banjaran
25 V9 **Crockett** Texas, SW USA *31°21′N 95°30′W*
67 V14 **Crocodile** *var.* Krokodil. ≈ N South Africa
Crocodile *see* Limpopo
20 I7 **Crofton** Kentucky, S USA *37°01′N 87°25′W*
29 Q12 **Crofton** Nebraska, C USA *42°43′N 97°30′W*
Croia *see* Krujë
103 R16 **Croisette, Cap** *headland* SE France *43°12′N 05°21′E*
102 G8 **Croisic, Pointe du** *headland* NW France *47°16′N 02°42′W*
103 S13 **Croix Haute, Col de la** *pass* E France
15 U5 **Croix, Pointe à la** *headland* Québec, SE Canada *49°16′N 67°46′W*
14 F13 **Croker, Cape** *headland* Ontario, S Canada *44°56′N 80°57′W*
181 P1 **Croker Island** *island* Northern Territory, N Australia
96 I8 **Cromarty** N Scotland, United Kingdom *57°40′N 04°02′W*
99 M21 **Crombach** Liège, E Belgium *50°14′N 06°07′E*
97 Q18 **Cromer** E England, United Kingdom *52°56′N 01°06′E*
185 D22 **Cromwell** Otago, South Island, New Zealand *45°03′S 169°14′E*
185 H16 **Cronadun** West Coast, South Island, New Zealand *42°03′S 171°52′E*
39 O11 **Crooked Creek** Alaska, USA *61°52′N 158°06′W*
44 K5 **Crooked Island** *island* SE Bahamas
44 J5 **Crooked Island Passage** *channel* SE Bahamas
32 I13 **Crooked River** ≈ Oregon, NW USA
29 R4 **Crookston** Minnesota, N USA *47°47′N 96°36′W*
28 I10 **Crooks Tower** ▲ South Dakota, N USA *44°09′N 103°55′W*
31 T14 **Crooksville** Ohio, N USA *39°46′N 82°05′W*
183 R9 **Crookwell** New South Wales, SE Australia *34°28′S 149°27′E*
14 L14 **Crosby** Ontario, SE Canada *44°39′N 76°13′W*
97 K17 **Crosby** *var.* Great Crosby. NW England, United Kingdom *53°30′N 03°02′W*
29 U6 **Crosby** Minnesota, N USA *46°30′N 93°58′W*
28 K2 **Crosby** North Dakota, N USA *48°54′N 103°17′W*
25 O5 **Crosbyton** Texas, SW USA *33°40′N 101°16′W*
77 V16 **Cross** ≈ Cameroon/Nigeria
23 U10 **Cross City** Florida, SE USA *29°37′N 83°08′W*
Crossen *see* Krosno Odrzańskie
27 V14 **Crossett** Arkansas, C USA *33°08′N 91°58′W*
97 K15 **Cross Fell** ▲ N England, United Kingdom *54°42′N 02°30′W*
11 P16 **Crossfield** Alberta, SW Canada *51°24′N 114°03′W*
21 Q12 **Cross Hill** South Carolina, SE USA *34°18′N 81°58′W*
19 U6 **Cross Island** *island* Maine, NE USA
11 X13 **Cross Lake** Manitoba, C Canada *54°38′N 97°35′W*
22 F5 **Cross Lake** ▣ Louisiana, S USA
36 I12 **Crossman Peak** ▲ Arizona, SW USA *34°33′N 114°09′W*
25 Q7 **Cross Plains** Texas, SW USA *32°07′N 99°10′W*
77 V17 **Cross River** ◐ *state* SE Nigeria
20 L9 **Crossville** Tennessee, S USA *35°57′N 85°02′W*
31 S8 **Croswell** Michigan, N USA *43°16′N 82°37′W*
14 K13 **Crotch Lake** ◎ Ontario, SE Canada
Croton/Crotona *see* Crotone
107 O21 **Crotone** *var.* Cotrone; *anc.* Croton, Crotona. Calabria, SW Italy *39°05′N 17°07′E*
33 V11 **Crow Agency** Montana, NW USA *45°35′N 107°28′W*
183 U7 **Crowdy Head** *headland* New South Wales, SE Australia *31°52′S 152°45′E*
25 Q4 **Crowell** Texas, SW USA *33°59′N 99°45′W*
183 O6 **Crowl Creek** *seasonal river* New South Wales, SE Australia
22 H9 **Crowley** Louisiana, S USA *30°11′N 92°21′W*
35 S9 **Crowley, Lake** ▣ California, W USA
27 X10 **Crowleys Ridge** *hill range* Arkansas, C USA
31 N11 **Crown Point** Indiana, N USA *41°25′N 87°22′W*
37 P10 **Crownpoint** New Mexico, SW USA *35°40′N 108°09′W*
33 R10 **Crow Peak** ▲ Montana, NW USA *46°17′N 111°54′W*
11 P17 **Crowsnest Pass** *pass* Alberta/British Columbia, SW Canada
29 T6 **Crow Wing River** ≈ Minnesota, N USA
97 O22 **Croydon** SE England, United Kingdom *51°21′N 00°06′W*
Crozer, Mount *see* Finkol, Mount
173 P11 **Crozet Basin** *undersea feature* S Indian Ocean *39°00′S 60°00′E*
173 O12 **Crozet Islands** *island group* French Southern and Antarctic Territories
173 N12 **Crozet Plateau** *var.* Crozet Plateaus. *undersea feature* SW Indian Ocean *46°00′S 51°00′E*
Crozet Plateaus *see* Crozet Plateau
102 E6 **Crozon** Finistère, NW France *48°14′N 04°31′W*
Cruacha Dubha, Na *see* Macgillycuddy's Reeks
Cruach Phádraig *see* Croagh Patrick
116 M14 **Crucea** Constanţa, SE Romania *44°30′N 28°18′E*
44 E5 **Cruces** Cienfuegos, C Cuba *22°20′N 80°17′W*
107 O20 **Crucoli Torretta** Calabria, SW Italy *39°26′N 17°03′E*
41 P9 **Cruillas** Tamaulipas, C Mexico *24°43′N 98°26′W*
64 K9 **Cruiser Tablemount** *undersea feature* E Atlantic Ocean *32°00′N 28°00′W*
61 G14 **Cruz Alta** Rio Grande do Sul, S Brazil *28°38′S 53°38′W*
44 G8 **Cruz, Cabo** *headland* S Cuba *19°50′N 77°43′W*
60 N9 **Cruzeiro** São Paulo, S Brazil *22°33′S 44°59′W*
60 H10 **Cruzeiro do Oeste** Paraná, S Brazil *23°45′S 53°03′W*
59 A15 **Cruzeiro do Sul** Acre, W Brazil *07°40′S 72°39′W*
23 U11 **Crystal Bay** *bay* Florida, SE USA NE Gulf of Mexico Atlantic Ocean
182 I8 **Crystal Brook** South Australia *33°24′S 138°10′E*
11 X17 **Crystal City** Manitoba, S Canada *49°07′N 98°54′W*
27 X5 **Crystal City** Missouri, C USA *38°13′N 90°22′W*
25 P13 **Crystal City** Texas, SW USA *28°43′N 99°51′W*
30 M4 **Crystal Falls** Michigan, N USA *46°06′N 88°20′W*
23 Q8 **Crystal Lake** Florida, SE USA *30°26′N 85°41′W*
31 O6 **Crystal Lake** ◎ Michigan, N USA
23 V11 **Crystal River** Florida, SE USA *28°54′N 82°35′W*
37 Q5 **Crystal River** ≈ Colorado, C USA
22 K6 **Crystal Springs** Mississippi, S USA *31°59′N 90°21′W*
Csaca *see* Čadca
Csakathurn/Csáktornya *see* Čakovec
Csap *see* Chop
Csepén *see* Čepin
Cserépalja *see* Crepaja
Csermő *see* Cermei
Csíkszereda *see* Miercurea-Ciuc
111 L24 **Csongrád** Csongrád, SE Hungary *46°42′N 20°09′E*
111 L24 **Csongrád** *off.* Csongrád Megye. ◐ *county* SE Hungary
Csongrád Megye *see* Csongrád
111 H22 **Csorna** Győr-Moson-Sopron, NW Hungary *47°37′N 17°14′E*
Csucsa *see* Ciucea
111 G25 **Csurgó** Somogy, SW Hungary *46°16′N 17°09′E*
Csurog *see* Čurug
54 L5 **Cúa** Miranda, N Venezuela *10°14′N 66°58′W*
82 C11 **Cuale** Malanje, NW Angola *08°22′S 16°10′E*
67 T12 **Cuando** *var.* Kwando. ≈ S Africa
83 E15 **Cuando Cubango** *var.* Kuando-Kubango. ◐ *province* SE Angola
83 E16 **Cuangar** Cuando Cubango, S Angola *17°34′S 18°39′E*
82 D11 **Cuango** Lunda Norte, NE Angola *09°10′S 17°59′E*
82 C10 **Cuango** Uíge, NW Angola *06°20′S 16°42′E*
82 C10 **Cuango** *var.* Kwango. ≈ Angola/Dem. Rep. Congo *see also* Kwango
Cuango *see* Kwango
Cuan, Loch *see* Strangford Lough
82 C12 **Cuanza** *var.* Kwanza. ≈ C Angola
82 B11 **Cuanza Norte** *var.* Kuanza Norte. ◐ *province* NE Angola
82 B12 **Cuanza Sul** *var.* Kuanza Sul. ◐ *province* NE Angola
61 E16 **Cuareim, Río** *var.* Río Quaraí. ≈ Brazil/Uruguay *see also* Quaraí, Rio
Cuareim, Río *see* Quaraí, Rio
83 D15 **Cuatir** ≈ S Angola
40 M7 **Cuatro Ciénegas** *var.* Cuatro Ciénegas de Carranza. Coahuila, NE Mexico *27°00′N 102°03′W*
Cuatro Ciénegas de Carranza *see* Cuatro Ciénegas
40 I6 **Cuauhtémoc** Chihuahua, N Mexico *28°22′N 106°52′W*
41 P14 **Cuautla** Morelos, S Mexico *18°48′N 98°56′W*
104 H12 **Cuba** Beja, S Portugal *38°10′N 07°54′W*
27 W6 **Cuba** Missouri, C USA *38°03′N 91°24′W*
37 R10 **Cuba** New Mexico, SW USA *36°01′N 106°57′W*
44 E6 **Cuba** *off.* Republic of Cuba. ◆ *republic* W West Indies
47 O2 **Cuba** *island* W West Indies
82 B13 **Cubal** Benguela, W Angola *12°58′S 14°16′E*
83 C15 **Cubango** *var.* Kuvango, *Port.* Vila Artur de Paiva, Vila da Ponte. Huíla, SW Angola *14°27′S 16°18′E*
83 D16 **Cubango** *var.* Kavango, Kavengo, Kubango, Okavango, Okavanggo. ≈ S Africa *see also* Okavango
Cubango *see* Okavango
54 H8 **Cubará** Boyacá, N Colombia *07°01′N 72°07′W*
Cuba, Republic of *see* Cuba
136 I12 **Çubuk** Ankara, N Turkey *40°13′N 33°02′E*
83 D14 **Cuchi** Cuando Cubango, C Angola *14°40′S 16°58′E*
42 C5 **Cuchumatanes, Sierra de los** ▲▲ W Guatemala
Cuculaya, Rio *see* Kukalaya, Rio
82 E12 **Cucumbi** *prev.* Trás-os-Montes. Lunda Sul, NE Angola *10°13′S 19°04′E*
54 G7 **Cúcuta** *var.* San José de Cúcuta. Norte de Santander, N Colombia *07°55′N 72°31′W*
31 N9 **Cudahy** Wisconsin, N USA *42°54′N 87°51′W*
155 J21 **Cuddalore** Tamil Nādu, SE India *11°43′N 79°46′E*
155 I18 **Cuddapah** Andhra Pradesh, S India *14°30′N 78°50′E*
104 M6 **Cuéllar** Castilla-León, N Spain *41°24′N 04°19′W*
82 D13 **Cuemba** *var.* Coemba. Bié, C Angola *12°09′S 18°07′E*
56 B8 **Cuenca** Azuay, S Ecuador *02°54′S 79°W*
105 Q9 **Cuenca** *anc.* Conca. Castilla-La Mancha, C Spain *40°04′N 02°07′W*
105 P9 **Cuenca** ◐ *province* Castilla-La Mancha, C Spain
40 L9 **Cuencamé** *var.* Cuencamé de Ceniceros. Durango, C Mexico *24°53′N 103°41′W*
Cuencamé de Ceniceros *see* Cuencamé
105 Q8 **Cuenca, Serrania de** ▲▲ C Spain
Cuera *see* Chur
105 P5 **Cuerda del Pozo, Embalse de la** ▣ N Spain
41 O14 **Cuernavaca** Morelos, S Mexico *18°57′N 99°15′W*
25 T12 **Cuero** Texas, SW USA *29°06′N 97°19′W*
44 I7 **Cueto** Holguín, E Cuba *20°43′N 75°54′W*
41 Q13 **Cuetzalán** *var.* Cuetzalán del Progreso. Puebla, S Mexico *20°00′N 97°27′W*
Cuetzalán del Progreso *see* Cuetzalán
105 Q14 **Cuevas de Almanzora** Andalucía, S Spain *37°19′N 01°52′W*
Cuevas de Vinromá *see* Les Coves de Vinromá
116 H12 **Cugir** *Hung.* Kudzsir. Alba, SW Romania *45°48′N 23°25′E*
59 H18 **Cuiabá** *prev.* Cuyabá. *state capital* Mato Grosso, SW Brazil *15°32′S 56°05′W*
59 H19 **Cuiabá, Rio** ≈ SW Brazil
41 R15 **Cuicatlán** *var.* San Juan Bautista Cuicatlán. Oaxaca, SE Mexico *17°49′N 96°59′W*
191 W16 **Cuidado, Punta** *headland* Easter Island, Chile, E Pacific Ocean *27°08′S 109°18′W*
Cúige *see* Connaught
Cúige Laighean *see* Leinster
Cúige Mumhan *see* Munster
Cuihua *see* Daguan
98 L13 **Cuijck** Noord-Brabant, SE Netherlands *51°41′N 05°56′E*
Cúil an tSúdaire *see* Portarlington
42 D7 **Cuilapa** Santa Rosa, S Guatemala *14°16′N 90°18′W*
42 B5 **Cuilco, Río** ≈ W Guatemala
Cúil Mhuine *see* Collooney
Cúil Raithin *see* Coleraine
83 C14 **Cuima** Huambo, C Angola *13°16′S 15°39′E*
83 E16 **Cuito** *var.* Kwito. ≈ SE Angola
83 E15 **Cuíto Cuanavale** Cuando Cubango, E Angola *15°01′S 19°07′E*
41 N14 **Cuitzeo, Lago de** ◎ C Mexico
27 W4 **Cuivre River** ≈ Missouri, C USA
Çuka *see* Çukë
168 L8 **Cukai** *var.* Chukai, Kemaman. Terengganu, Peninsular Malaysia *04°15′N 103°25′E*
113 L23 **Çukë** *var.* Çuka. Vlorë, S Albania *39°50′N 20°01′E*
Cularo *see* Grenoble
33 Y7 **Culbertson** Montana, NW USA *48°09′N 104°30′W*
28 M16 **Culbertson** Nebraska, C USA *40°13′N 100°50′W*
183 P10 **Culcairn** New South Wales, SE Australia *35°41′S 147°01′E*
45 W5 **Culebra** *var.* Dewey. E Puerto Rico *18°19′N 65°17′W*
45 W6 **Culebra, Isla de** *island* E Puerto Rico
37 T8 **Culebra Peak** ▲ Colorado, C USA *37°07′N 105°11′W*
104 J5 **Culebra, Sierra de la** ▲▲ NW Spain
98 J12 **Culemborg** Gelderland, C Netherlands *51°57′N 05°17′E*
137 V14 **Culfa** *Rus.* Dzhul'fa. SW Azerbaijan *38°58′N 45°37′E*
183 P4 **Culgoa River** ≈ New South Wales/Queensland, SE Australia

◆ Country
● Country Capital
◇ Dependent Territory
○ Dependent Territory Capital
◐ Administrative Regions
✈ International Airport
▲ Mountain
▲▲ Mountain Range
⛰ Volcano
≈ River
◎ Lake
▣ Reservoir

40 I9 **Culiacán** *var.* Culiacán Rosales, Culiacán-Rosales. Sinaloa, C Mexico 24°48′N 107°25′W
Culiacán-Rosales/Culiacán Rosales *see* Culiacán
105 P14 **Cúllar-Baza** Andalucía, S Spain 37°35′N 02°34′W
105 S10 **Cullera** País Valenciano, E Spain 39°10′N 00°15′W
23 P3 **Cullman** Alabama, S USA 34°10′N 86°50′W
108 B10 **Cully** Vaud, W Switzerland 46°58′N 06°46′E
Culm *see* Chełmno
Culmsee *see* Chełmża
21 V4 **Culpeper** Virginia, NE USA 38°28′N 78°00′W
185 I17 **Culverden** Canterbury, South Island, New Zealand 42°46′S 172°51′E
83 H18 **Cum** *var.* Xhumo. Central, C Botswana 21°13′S 24°38′E
55 N5 **Cumaná** Sucre, NE Venezuela 10°29′N 64°12′W
55 O5 **Cumanacoa** Sucre, NE Venezuela 10°17′N 63°58′W
54 C13 **Cumbal, Nevado de** *elevation* S Colombia
21 O7 **Cumberland** Kentucky, S USA 36°55′N 83°00′W
21 U2 **Cumberland** Maryland, NE USA 39°40′N 78°47′W
21 V6 **Cumberland** Virginia, NE USA 37°31′N 78°16′W
187 P12 **Cumberland, Cape** *var.* Cape Nahoi. *headland* Espiritu Santo, N Vanuatu 14°39′S 166°35′E
11 V14 **Cumberland House** Saskatchewan, C Canada 53°57′N 102°21′W
23 W8 **Cumberland Island** *island* Georgia, SE USA
20 L7 **Cumberland, Lake** ▣ Kentucky, S USA
9 R5 **Cumberland Peninsula** *peninsula* Baffin Island, Nunavut, NE Canada
2 N9 **Cumberland Plateau** *plateau* E USA
30 L1 **Cumberland Point** *headland* Michigan, N USA 47°51′N 89°14′W
21 O7 **Cumberland River** ≈ Kentucky/Tennessee, S USA
9 S6 **Cumberland Sound** *inlet* Baffin Island, Nunavut, NE Canada
96 I12 **Cumbernauld** S Scotland, United Kingdom 55°57′N 04°W
97 K15 **Cumbria** *cultural region* NW England, United Kingdom
97 K15 **Cumbrian Mountains** ▲▲ NW England, United Kingdom
23 S2 **Cumming** Georgia, SE USA 34°12′N 84°08′W
Cummin in Pommern *see* Kamień Pomorski
182 G9 **Cummins** South Australia 34°17′S 135°43′E
96 I13 **Cumnock** W Scotland, United Kingdom 55°32′N 04°28′W
40 G4 **Cumpas** Sonora, NW Mexico 30°N 109°48′W
136 H16 **Çumra** Konya, C Turkey 37°34′N 32°38′E
63 G15 **Cunco** Araucanía, C Chile 38°55′S 72°02′W
54 E9 **Cundinamarca** *off.* Departamento de Cundinamarca. ◐ *province* C Colombia
Cundinamarca, Departamento de *see* Cundinamarca
41 U15 **Cunduacán** Tabasco, SE Mexico 18°00′N 93°07′W
83 C16 **Cunene** ◐ *province* S Angola
83 A16 **Cunene** *var.* Kunene. ≈ Angola/Namibia *see also* Kunene
Cunene *see* Kunene
106 A9 **Cuneo** *Fr.* Coni. Piemonte, NW Italy 44°23′N 07°32′E
83 E15 **Cunjamba** Cuando Cubango, E Angola 15°22′S 20°07′E
181 V10 **Cunnamulla** Queensland, E Australia 28°09′S 145°44′E
Čunusavvon *see* Junosuando
Cuokkarašša *see* Čohkarášša
106 B7 **Cuorgne** Piemonte, NE Italy 45°23′N 07°34′E
96 K11 **Cupar** E Scotland, United Kingdom 56°19′N 03°01′W
116 L8 **Cupcina** *Rus.* Kupchino; *prev.* Calinisc, Kalinisk. N Moldova 48°07′N 27°22′E
54 C8 **Cupica** Chocó, W Colombia 06°43′N 77°31′W
54 C8 **Cupica, Golfo de** *gulf* W Colombia
112 N13 **Ćuprija** Serbia, E Serbia 43°57′N 21°21′E
Cura *see* Villa de Cura
45 P16 **Curaçao** *island* Netherlands Antilles
56 H13 **Curanja, Río** ≈ E Peru
56 F7 **Curaray, Rio** ≈ Ecuador/Peru
116 K14 **Curcani** Călărași, SE Romania 44°11′N 26°39′E
182 H4 **Curdimurka** South Australia 29°27′S 136°56′E
103 P7 **Cure** ≈ C France
173 Y16 **Curepipe** C Mauritius 20°19′S 57°31′E
55 R6 **Curiapo** Delta Amacuro, NE Venezuela 10°03′N 63°05′W
Curia Rhaetorum *see* Chur
62 G12 **Curicó** Maule, C Chile 35°00′S 71°15′W
Curieta *see* Krk
172 I15 **Curieuse** *island* Inner Islands, NE Seychelles
59 C16 **Curitiba** Acre, W Brazil 10°08′S 69°00′W
60 K12 **Curitiba** *prev.* Curytiba. *state capital* Paraná, S Brazil 25°25′S 49°25′W
60 J13 **Curitibanos** Santa Catarina, S Brazil 27°18′S 50°35′W
183 S6 **Curlewis** New South Wales, SE Australia 31°09′S 150°18′E
182 J6 **Curnamona** South Australia 31°39′S 139°35′E
83 A15 **Curoca** ≈ SW Angola
183 T6 **Currabubula** New South Wales, SE Australia 31°17′S 150°43′E
59 Q14 **Currais Novos** Rio Grande do Norte, E Brazil 06°12′S 36°30′W
35 W7 **Currant** Nevada, W USA 38°43′N 115°27′W
35 W6 **Currant Mountain** ▲ Nevada, W USA 38°56′N 115°19′W
44 H2 **Current** Eleuthera Island, C Bahamas 25°24′N 76°44′W
27 W8 **Current River** ≈ Arkansas/Missouri, C USA
182 M14 **Currie** Tasmania, SE Australia 39°59′S 143°51′E
21 Y8 **Currituck** North Carolina, SE USA 36°29′N 76°02′W
21 Y8 **Currituck Sound** *sound* North Carolina, SE USA
39 R11 **Curry** Alaska, USA 62°36′N 150°00′W
Curtbunar *see* Tervel
116 I13 **Curtea de Argeș** *var.* Curtea-de-Arges. Argeș, S Romania 45°06′N 24°40′E
Curtea-de-Arges *see* Curtea de Argeș
116 E10 **Curtici** *Ger.* Kurtitsch, *Hung.* Kürtös. Arad, W Romania 46°21′N 21°17′E
28 M16 **Curtis** Nebraska, C USA 40°36′N 100°27′W
104 H2 **Curtis-Estación** Galicia, NW Spain 43°09′N 08°10′W
183 O14 **Curtis Group** *island group* Tasmania, SE Australia
181 Y8 **Curtis Island** *island* Queensland, SE Australia
58 K11 **Curuá, Ilha do** *island* NE Brazil
47 U7 **Curuá, Rio** ≈ N Brazil
59 A14 **Curuçá, Rio** ≈ NW Brazil
112 L9 **Čurug** *Hung.* Csurog. Vojvodina, N Serbia 45°30′N 20°02′E
61 D16 **Curuzú Cuatiá** Corrientes, NE Argentina 29°50′S 58°05′W
59 M19 **Curvelo** Minas Gerais, SE Brazil 18°45′S 44°27′W
18 E14 **Curwensville** Pennsylvania, NE USA 40°57′N 78°29′W
30 M3 **Curwood, Mount** ▲ Michigan, N USA 46°42′N 88°14′W
Curytiba *see* Curitiba
Curzola *see* Korčula
42 A10 **Cuscatlán** ◐ *department* C El Salvador
57 H15 **Cusco** *var.* Cuzco. Cusco, C Peru 13°35′S 72°02′W
57 H15 **Cusco** *off.* Departamento de Cusco, *var.* Cuzco. ◐ *department* C Peru
Cusco, Departamento de *see* Cusco
27 O9 **Cushing** Oklahoma, C USA 36°01′N 96°46′W
25 W8 **Cushing** Texas, SW USA 31°48′N 94°50′W
40 I6 **Cusihuiriachic** Chihuahua, N Mexico 28°16′N 106°46′W
103 P10 **Cusset** Allier, C France 46°08′N 03°27′E
23 S6 **Cusseta** Georgia, SE USA 32°18′N 84°46′W
28 J10 **Custer** South Dakota, N USA 43°46′N 103°36′W
Cüstrin *see* Kostrzyn
33 Q7 **Cut Bank** Montana, NW USA 48°38′N 112°20′W
Cutch, Gulf of *see* Kachchh, Gulf of
23 S6 **Cuthbert** Georgia, SE USA 31°46′N 84°47′W
11 S15 **Cut Knife** Saskatchewan, S Canada 52°40′N 108°54′W
23 Y16 **Cutler Ridge** Florida, SE USA 25°34′N 80°21′W
22 K10 **Cut Off** Louisiana, S USA 29°32′N 90°20′W
63 I15 **Cutral-Có** Neuquén, C Argentina 38°56′S 69°13′W
107 O21 **Cutro** Calabria, SW Italy 39°01′N 16°59′E
183 O4 **Cuttaburra Channels** *seasonal river* New South Wales, SE Australia
154 O12 **Cuttack** Orissa, E India 20°28′N 85°53′E
83 C15 **Cuvelai** Cunene, SW Angola 15°40′S 15°48′E
79 G18 **Cuvette** *var.* Région de la Cuvette. ◐ *province* C Congo
79 G18 **Cuvette-Ouest** ◐ *province* C Congo
Cuvette, Région de la *see* Cuvette
173 V9 **Cuvier Basin** *undersea feature* E Indian Ocean
173 U9 **Cuvier Plateau** *undersea feature* E Indian Ocean
82 B12 **Cuvo** ≈ W Angola
100 H9 **Cuxhaven** Niedersachsen, NW Germany 53°51′N 08°43′E
Cuyabá *see* Cuiabá
Cuyuni, Río *see* Cuyuni River
55 S8 **Cuyuni River** *var.* Río Cuyuni. ≈ Guyana/Venezuela
Cuzco *see* Cusco
97 K22 **Cwmbran** *Wel.* Cwmbrân. SW Wales, United Kingdom 51°39′N 03°W
Cwmbrân *see* Cwmbran
28 K15 **C. W. McConaughy, Lake** ▣ Nebraska, C USA
81 D20 **Cyangugu** SW Rwanda 02°27′S 29°00′E
110 D11 **Cybinka** *Ger.* Ziebingen. Lubuskie, W Poland 52°11′N 14°46′E
Cyclades *see* Kykládes
Cydonia *see* Chaniá
Cymru *see* Wales
20 M5 **Cynthiana** Kentucky, S USA 38°22′N 84°18′W
11 S17 **Cypress Hills** ▲▲ Alberta/Saskatchewan, SW Canada
Cypro-Syrian Basin *see* Cyprus Basin
121 U11 **Cyprus** *off.* Republic of Cyprus, *Gk.* Kypros, *Turk.* Kıbrıs, Kıbrıs Cumhuriyeti. ◆ *republic* E Mediterranean Sea
84 L14 **Cyprus** *Gk.* Kypros, *Turk.* Kıbrıs. *island* E Mediterranean Sea
121 W11 **Cyprus Basin** *var.* Cypro-Syrian Basin. *undersea feature* E Mediterranean Sea 34°00′N 34°00′E
Cyprus, Republic of *see* Cyprus
75 S8 **Cyrenaica** ◐ *cultural region* NE Libya
Cythera *see* Kýthira
Cythnos *see* Kýthnos
110 F9 **Czaplinek** *Ger.* Tempelburg. Zachodnio-pomorskie, NW Poland 53°33′N 16°14′E
Czarna Woda *see* Wda
110 G8 **Czarne** Pomorskie, N Poland 53°40′N 17°00′E
110 G10 **Czarnków** Wielkopolskie, C Poland 52°53′N 16°32′E
111 E17 **Czech Republic** *Cz.* Česká Republika. ◆ *republic* C Europe
Czegléd *see* Cegléd
110 G12 **Czempiń** Wielkopolskie, C Poland 52°10′N 16°46′E
Czenstochau *see* Częstochowa
Czerkow *see* Čerchov
Czernowitz *see* Chernivtsi
110 I8 **Czersk** Pomorskie, N Poland 53°48′N 17°58′E
111 J15 **Częstochowa** *Ger.* Czenstochau, Tschenstochau, *Rus.* Chenstokhov. Śląskie, S Poland 50°49′N 19°07′E
110 F10 **Człopa** *Ger.* Schloppe. Zachodnio-pomorskie, NW Poland 53°05′N 16°05′E
110 H8 **Człuchów** *Ger.* Schlochau. Pomorskie, NW Poland 53°41′N 17°20′E

D

163 V9 **Da'an** *var.* Dalai. Jilin, NE China 45°28′N 124°18′E
15 S10 **Daaquam** Québec, SE Canada 46°36′N 70°03′W
Daawo, Webi *see* Dawa Wenz
54 I4 **Dabajuro** Falcón, NW Venezuela 11°00′N 70°41′W
77 N15 **Dabakala** NE Ivory Coast 08°19′N 04°24′W
163 S11 **Daban** *var.* Bairin Youqi. Nei Mongol Zizhiqu, N China 43°33′N 118°40′E
158 L5 **Dabancheng** Xinjiang Uygur Zizhiqu, W China 43°21′N 88°19′E
111 K23 **Dabas** Pest, C Hungary 47°36′N 18°22′E
160 L8 **Daba Shan** ▲▲ C China
Dabba *see* Daocheng
140 J5 **Dabbāgh, Jabal** ▲ NW Saudi Arabia 27°52′N 35°48′E
54 D8 **Dabeiba** Antioquia, NW Colombia 07°01′N 76°18′W
149 P11 **Dādhar** Baluchistān, SW Pakistan 29°28′N 67°39′E
154 E11 **Dabhoi** Gujarāt, W India 22°08′N 73°28′E
161 P8 **Dabie Shan** ▲▲ C China
76 J13 **Dabola** C Guinea 10°48′N 11°02′W
77 N17 **Dabou** S Ivory Coast 05°20′N 04°23′W
162 M15 **Dabqig** *prev.* Uxin Qi. Nei Mongol Zizhiqu, N China 38°29′N 108°48′E
110 P8 **Dąbrowa Białostocka** Podlaskie, NE Poland 53°38′N 23°18′E
111 M16 **Dąbrowa Tarnowska** Małopolskie, S Poland 50°10′N 21°E
119 M20 **Dabryn'** *Rus.* Dobryn'. Homyel'skaya Voblasts', SE Belarus 51°46′N 29°12′E
159 P10 **Dabsan Hu** ◎ C China
161 Q13 **Dabu** *var.* Huliao. Guangdong, S China 24°19′N 116°07′E
116 H15 **Dăbuleni** Dolj, SW Romania 43°48′N 24°05′E
Dacca *see* Dhaka
101 L23 **Dachau** Bayern, SE Germany 48°15′N 11°26′E
Dachuan *see* Dazhou
Dacia Bank *see* Dacia Seamount
64 M10 **Dacia Seamount** *var.* Dacia Bank. *undersea feature* E Atlantic Ocean 31°10′N 13°42′W
37 T3 **Dacono** Colorado, C USA 40°04′N 104°56′W
Đăc Tô *see* Đak Tô
Dacura *see* Dákura
23 W12 **Dade City** Florida, SE USA 28°21′N 82°12′W
152 L10 **Ḍaḍeldhurā** *var.* Dandeldhura. Far Western, W Nepal 29°12′N 80°31′E
23 Q5 **Dadeville** Alabama, S USA 32°49′N 85°45′W
Dadong *see* Donggang
103 N15 **Dadou** ≈ S France
154 D12 **Dādra and Nagar Haveli** ◐ *union territory* W India
149 P14 **Dādu** Sind, SE Pakistan 26°42′N 67°48′E
167 U11 **Da Du Bǫloc** Kon Tum, C Vietnam 14°06′N 107°40′E
160 G9 **Dadu He** ≈ C China
Daegu *see* Taegu
Daerah Istimewa Aceh *see* Aceh
171 P4 **Daet** Luzon, N Philippines 14°06′N 122°57′E
160 I11 **Dafang** Guizhou, S China 27°07′N 105°40′E
Dafeng *see* Shanglin
153 W11 **Dafla Hills** ▲▲ NE India
11 U15 **Dafoe** Saskatchewan, S Canada 51°46′N 104°11′W
76 G10 **Dagana** N Senegal 16°28′N 15°35′W
Dagana *see* Massakory, Chad
Dagana *see* Dahana, Tajikistan
Dagcagoin *see* Zoigê
118 K11 **Dagda** Krāslava, SE Latvia 56°06′N 27°36′E
Dagden *see* Hiiumaa
Dagden-Sund *see* Soela Väin
127 P16 **Dagestan, Respublika** *prev.* Dagestanskaya ASSR, *Eng.* Daghestan. ◐ *autonomous republic* SW Russian Federation
Dagestanskaya ASSR *see* Dagestan, Respublika
127 R17 **Dagestanskiye Ogni** Respublika Dagestan, SW Russian Federation 42°09′N 48°08′E
Dagezhen *see* Fengning
149 U5 **Daggar** North-West Frontier Province, N Pakistan 34°30′N 72°28′E
185 A23 **Dagg Sound** *sound* South Island, New Zealand
Daghestan *see* Dagestan, Respublika
141 Y8 **Daghmar** NE Oman 23°09′N 59°01′E
Dağliq Quarabağ *see* Nagorno-Karabakh
Dagö *see* Hiiumaa
54 D11 **Dagua** Valle del Cauca, W Colombia 03°39′N 76°40′W
160 H11 **Daguan** *var.* Cuihua. Yunnan, SW China 27°42′N 103°51′E
171 N3 **Dagupan** *off.* Dagupan City. Luzon, N Philippines 16°05′N 120°21′E
Dagupan City *see* Dagupan
159 N16 **Dagzê** *var.* Dêqên. Xizang Zizhiqu, W China 29°38′N 91°15′E
147 Q13 **Dahana** *Rus.* Dagana, Dakhana. SW Tajikistan 38°03′N 69°51′E
163 V10 **Dahei Shan** ▲▲ N China
163 T7 **Da Hinggan Ling** *Eng.* Great Khingan Range. ▲▲ NE China
Dahlac Archipelago *see* Dahlak Archipelago
80 K9 **Dahlak Archipelago** *var.* Dahlac Archipelago. *island group* E Eritrea
23 T2 **Dahlonega** Georgia, SE USA 34°31′N 83°59′W
101 O14 **Dahme** Brandenburg, E Germany 52°10′N 13°47′E
100 O13 **Dahme** ≈ E Germany
141 O14 **Dahm, Ramlat** *desert* NW Yemen
154 E10 **Dāhod** *prev.* Dohad. Gujarāt, W India 22°48′N 74°18′E
Dahomey *see* Benin
158 G10 **Dahongliutan** Xinjiang Uygur Zizhiqu, NW China 35°59′N 79°12′E
Dahra *see* Dara
Dahuaishu *see* Hongtong
139 R2 **Dahūk** *var.* Dohuk, *Kurd.* Dihōk. ◐ *governorate* N Iraq
139 R2 **Dahūk** *var.* Dohuk, *Kurd.* Dihōk. Dahūk, N Iraq 36°52′N 43°01′E
116 J15 **Daia** Giurgiu, S Romania 44°00′N 25°59′E
165 P12 **Daigo** Ibaraki, Honshū, S Japan 36°43′N 140°22′E
163 O13 **Dai Hai** ◎ N China
Daihoku *see* T'aipei
186 M8 **Dai Island** *island* N Solomon Islands
166 M8 **Daik-u** Bago, SW Burma (Myanmar) 17°46′N 96°40′E
138 H9 **Dā'īl** Dar'ā, S Syria 32°45′N 36°08′E
167 U12 **Đai Lanh** Khanh Hoa, S Vietnam 12°49′N 109°20′E
161 Q13 **Daimao Shan** ▲▲ SE China
105 N11 **Daimiel** Castilla-La Mancha, C Spain 39°04′N 03°37′W
115 F22 **Daimoniá** Pelopónnisos, S Greece 36°38′N 22°54′E
Dainan *see* T'ainan
25 W6 **Daingerfield** Texas, SW USA 33°03′N 94°42′W
Daingin, Bá an *see* Dingle Bay
159 R13 **Dainkognubma** Xizang Zizhiqu, W China 32°26′N 97°58′E
164 K14 **Daiō-zaki** *headland* Honshū, SW Japan 34°15′N 136°50′E
Dairbhre *see* Valencia Island
61 B22 **Daireaux** Buenos Aires, E Argentina 36°34′S 61°40′W
Dairen *see* Dalian
Dairûṭ *see* Dayrūṭ
25 X10 **Daisetta** Texas, SW USA 30°06′N 94°38′W
192 G5 **Daitō-jima** *island group* SW Japan
192 G5 **Daitō Ridge** *undersea feature* N Philippine Sea 25°30′N 133°00′E
161 N3 **Daixian** *var.* Dai Xian, Shangguan. Shanxi, C China 39°10′N 112°57′E
Dai Xian *see* Daixian
Daiyue *see* Shanyin
161 Q12 **Daiyun Shan** ▲▲ SE China
44 M8 **Dajabón** NW Dominican Republic 19°35′N 71°41′W
160 G8 **Dajin Chuan** ≈ C China
148 J6 **Dak** ◎ W Afghanistan
76 F11 **Dakar** ● (Senegal) W Senegal 14°44′N 17°27′W
76 F11 **Dakar** ✈ W Senegal 14°42′N 17°27′W
167 U10 **Đak Glây** Kon Tum, C Vietnam 15°05′N 107°42′E
Dakhana *see* Dahana
153 U16 **Dakhin Shahbazpur Island** *island* S Bangladesh
Dakhla *see* Ad Dakhla
76 F7 **Dakhlet Nouâdhibou** ◐ *region* NW Mauritania
Đak Lap *see* Kiên Đưc
Đak Nông *see* Gia Nghia
77 U11 **Dakoro** Maradi, S Niger 14°29′N 06°45′E
29 U12 **Dakota City** Iowa, C USA 42°42′N 94°13′W
29 R13 **Dakota City** Nebraska, C USA 42°25′N 96°25′W
Đakovica *see* Gjakovë
112 I10 **Đakovo** *var.* Djakovo, *Hung.* Diakovár. Osijek-Baranja, E Croatia 45°18′N 18°24′E
Dakshin *see* Deccan
167 U11 **Đak Tô** *var.* Đăc Tô. Kon Tum, C Vietnam 14°35′N 107°55′E
43 N7 **Dákura** *var.* Dacura. Región Autónoma Atlántico Norte, NE Nicaragua 14°22′N 83°13′W
95 I14 **Dal** Akershus, S Norway 60°19′N 11°16′E
82 E12 **Dala** Lunda Sul, E Angola 11°04′S 20°15′E
108 J8 **Dalaas** Vorarlberg, W Austria 47°08′N 10°03′E
76 I13 **Dalaba** W Guinea 10°47′N 12°12′W
Dalai *see* Da'an
162 I12 **Dalain Hob** *var.* Ejin Qi. Nei Mongol Zizhiqu, N China 41°59′N 101°04′E
Dalai Nor *see* Hulun Nur
163 Q11 **Dalai Nur** *salt lake* N China
Dala-Jarna *see* Järna
95 M14 **Dalälven** ≈ C Sweden
136 C16 **Dalaman** Muğla, SW Turkey 36°47′N 28°47′E
136 C16 **Dalaman** ✈ Muğla, SW Turkey 36°37′N 28°51′E
136 D16 **Dalaman Çayı** ≈ SW Turkey
162 K11 **Dalandzadgad** Ömnögovĭ, S Mongolia 43°35′N 104°23′E
95 D17 **Dalane** *physical region* S Norway
189 Z2 **Dalap-Uliga-Djarrit** *var.* Delap-Uliga-Darrit, D-U-D. *island group* Ratak Chain, SE Marshall Islands
94 J12 **Dalarna** *prev.* Kopparberg. ◐ *county* C Sweden
94 L13 **Dalarna** *prev. Eng.* Dalecarlia. *cultural region* C Sweden
95 P16 **Dalarö** Stockholm, C Sweden 59°07′N 18°25′E
167 U13 **Đa Lat** Lâm Đông, S Vietnam 11°56′N 108°25′E
Dalay *see* Bayandalay
148 L12 **Dālbandīn** *var.* Dāl Bandin. Baluchistān, SW Pakistan 28°48′N 64°08′E
95 J17 **Dalbosjön** *lake bay* S Sweden
181 Y10 **Dalby** Queensland, E Australia 27°11′S 151°12′E
94 D13 **Dale** Hordaland, S Norway 60°35′N 05°48′E
94 C12 **Dale** Sogn Og Fjordane, S Norway 61°22′N 05°24′E
32 K12 **Dale** Oregon, NW USA 44°58′N 118°56′W
25 T11 **Dale** Texas, SW USA 29°56′N 97°34′W
Dalecarlia *see* Dalarna
21 W4 **Dale City** Virginia, NE USA 38°38′N 77°18′W
20 L8 **Dale Hollow Lake** ▣ Kentucky/Tennessee, S USA
98 O8 **Dalen** Drenthe, NE Netherlands 52°42′N 06°45′E
95 E15 **Dalen** Telemark, S Norway 59°25′N 07°58′E
166 K14 **Daletme** Chin State, W Burma (Myanmar) 21°44′N 92°48′E
23 Q7 **Daleville** Alabama, S USA 31°18′N 85°42′W
98 M9 **Dalfsen** Overijssel, E Netherlands 52°31′N 06°16′E
24 M1 **Dalhart** Texas, SW USA 36°05′N 102°31′W
13 O13 **Dalhousie** New Brunswick, SE Canada 48°03′N 66°22′W
152 I6 **Dalhousie** Himāchal Pradesh, N India 32°32′N 76°01′E
160 F12 **Dali** *var.* Xiaguan. Yunnan, SW China 25°34′N 100°11′E
Dali *see* Idálion
163 U14 **Dalian** *var.* Dairen, Dalien, Jay Dairen, Lüda, Ta-lien, *Rus.* Dalny. Liaoning, NE China 38°53′N 121°37′E
105 O15 **Dalías** Andalucía, S Spain 36°49′N 02°50′W
Dalien *see* Dalian
Dalijan *see* Delījān
112 J9 **Dalj** *Hung.* Dalja. Osijek-Baranja, E Croatia 45°29′N 19°00′E
Dalja *see* Dalj
32 F12 **Dallas** Oregon, NW USA 44°56′N 123°20′W
25 U6 **Dallas** Texas, SW USA 32°47′N 96°48′W
25 T7 **Dallas-Fort Worth** ✈ Texas, SW USA 32°37′N 97°16′W
154 K12 **Dalli Rājhara** *var.* Dhalli Rajhara. Chhattīsgarh, C India 20°32′N 81°10′E
39 X15 **Dall Island** *island* Alexander Archipelago, Alaska, USA
38 M12 **Dall Lake** ◎ Alaska, USA
Dállogilli *see* Korpilombolo
77 S12 **Dallol Bosso** *seasonal river* W Niger
141 U7 **Dalmā** *island* W United Arab Emirates
113 E14 **Dalmacija** *Eng.* Dalmatia, *Ger.* Dalmatien, *It.* Dalmazia. *cultural region* S Croatia
Dalmatia/Dalmatien/Dalmazia *see* Dalmacija
123 S15 **Dal'negorsk** Primorskiy Kray, SE Russian Federation 44°27′N 135°30′E
Dalny *see* Dalian
76 M16 **Daloa** C Ivory Coast 06°56′N 06°28′W
160 J11 **Dalou Shan** ▲▲ S China
181 X7 **Dalrymple Lake** ◎ Queensland, E Australia
14 H14 **Dalrymple Lake** ◎ Ontario, S Canada
181 X7 **Dalrymple, Mount** ▲ Queensland, E Australia 21°01′S 148°34′E
93 K20 **Dalsbruk** *Fin.* Taalintehdas. Länsi-Suomi, W Finland 60°02′N 22°31′E
95 K19 **Dalsjöfors** Västra Götaland, S Sweden 57°43′N 13°05′E
95 J17 **Dals Långed** *var.* Långed. Västra Götaland, S Sweden 58°54′N 12°20′E
153 O15 **Dāltenganj** *prev.* Daltonganj. Jhārkhand, N India 24°02′N 84°07′E
23 R2 **Dalton** Georgia, SE USA 34°46′N 84°58′W
Daltonganj *see* Dāltenganj
195 X14 **Dalton Iceberg Tongue** *ice feature* Antarctica
92 J1 **Dalvík** Nordhurland Eystra, N Iceland 65°58′N 18°31′W
Dálvvadis *see* Jokkmokk
35 N8 **Daly City** California, W USA 37°44′N 122°27′W
181 P2 **Daly River** ≈ Northern Territory, N Australia
181 Q3 **Daly Waters** Northern Territory, N Australia 16°21′S 133°22′E
119 F20 **Damachava** *var.* Damachova, *Pol.* Domaczewo, *Rus.* Domachëvo. Brestskaya Voblasts', SW Belarus 51°45′N 23°36′E
Damachova *see* Damachava
77 W11 **Damagaram Takaya** Zinder, S Niger 14°02′N 09°28′E
154 D12 **Damān** Damān and Diu, W India 20°25′N 72°58′E
154 B12 **Damān and Diu** ◐ *union territory* W India
75 V7 **Damanhūr** *anc.* Hermopolis Parva. N Egypt 31°03′N 30°28′E
161 O1 **Damaqun Shan** ▲▲ E China
79 I15 **Damara** Ombella-Mpoko, S Central African Republic 05°00′N 18°45′E
83 D18 **Damaraland** *physical region* C Namibia
171 S15 **Damar, Kepulauan** *var.* Baraf Daja Islands, Kepulauan Barat Daya. *island group* C Indonesia
168 J8 **Damar Laut** Perak, Peninsular Malaysia 04°13′N 100°36′E
171 S15 **Damar, Pulau** *island* Maluku, E Indonesia
Damas *see* Dimashq
77 Y12 **Damasak** Borno, NE Nigeria 13°10′N 12°40′E
Damasco *see* Dimashq
21 Q8 **Damascus** Virginia, NE USA 36°37′N 81°46′W
Damascus *see* Dimashq
77 X13 **Damaturu** Yobe, NE Nigeria 11°44′N 11°58′E
171 R9 **Damau** Pulau Kaburuang, N Indonesia 03°46′N 126°49′E
143 O5 **Damāvand, Qolleh-ye** ▲ N Iran 35°56′N 52°08′E
82 B10 **Damba** Uíge, NW Angola 06°44′S 15°20′E
114 M12 **Dambaslar** Tekirdağ, NW Turkey 41°13′N 27°13′E
116 J13 **Dâmbovița** *prev.* Dîmbovița. ◐ *county* SE Romania
116 J13 **Dâmbovița** *prev.* Dîmbovița. ≈ S Romania
173 Y15 **D'Ambre, Île** *island* NE Mauritius
155 K24 **Dambulla** Central Province, C Sri Lanka 07°51′N 80°40′E
44 K9 **Dame-Marie** SW Haiti 18°36′N 74°26′W
44 J9 **Dame Marie, Cap** *headland* SW Haiti 18°37′N 74°24′W
143 Q4 **Dāmghān** Semnān, N Iran 36°13′N 54°22′E
Damietta *see* Dumyāt
138 G10 **Dāmiyā** Al Balqā', NW Jordan 32°07′N 35°33′E
146 G11 **Damla** Daşoguz Welaýaty, N Turkmenistan 40°05′N 59°15′E
Dammām *see* Ad Dammān
100 G12 **Damme** Niedersachsen, NW Germany 52°31′N 08°12′E
153 R15 **Dāmodar** ≈ NE India
154 J9 **Damoh** Madhya Pradesh, C India 23°50′N 79°30′N
77 P15 **Damongo** NW Ghana 09°05′N 01°49′W
138 G7 **Damoûr** *var.* Ad Dāmūr. W Lebanon 33°36′N 35°30′E
171 N11 **Dampal, Teluk** *bay* Sulawesi, C Indonesia
180 H7 **Dampier** Western Australia 20°40′S 116°40′E
180 H6 **Dampier Archipelago** *island group* Western Australia
141 U14 **Damqawt** *var.* Damqut. E Yemen 16°35′N 52°39′E
159 O13 **Dam Qu** ≈ C China
Damqut *see* Damqawt
167 R13 **Dâmrei, Chuŏr Phmun** *Fr.* Chaîne de l'Éléphant. ▲▲ SW Cambodia
108 C7 **Damvant** Jura, NW Switzerland 47°22′N 06°55′E
Damwâld *see* Damwoude
98 L5 **Damwoude** *Fris.* Damwâld. Friesland, N Netherlands 53°18′N 05°59′E
Damxoi *see* Comai
159 N15 **Damxung** *var.* Gongtang. Xizang Zizhiqu, W China 30°29′N 91°02′E
80 K11 **Danakil Desert** *var.* Afar Depression, Danakil Plain. *desert* E Africa
Danakil Plain *see* Danakil Desert
35 R8 **Dana, Mount** ▲ California, W USA 37°54′N 119°13′W
76 L16 **Danané** W Ivory Coast 07°16′N 08°09′W
167 U10 **Đă Năng** *prev.* Tourane. Quang Nam-Đa Năng, C Vietnam 16°04′N 108°14′E
160 G9 **Danba** *var.* Zhanggu, *Tib.* Rongzhag. Sichuan, C China 30°54′N 101°49′E
Danborg *see* Daneborg
18 L13 **Danbury** Connecticut, NE USA 41°21′N 73°27′W
25 W12 **Danbury** Texas, SW USA 29°13′N 95°20′W
35 X15 **Danby Lake** ◎ California, W USA
194 H4 **Danco Coast** *physical region* Antarctica
82 B11 **Dande** ≈ NW Angola
Dandeldhura *see* Ḍaḍeldhurā
155 E17 **Dandeli** Karnātaka, W India 15°18′N 74°42′E
183 O12 **Dandenong** Victoria, SE Australia 38°01′S 145°13′E
163 V13 **Dandong** *var.* Tan-tung; *prev.* An-tung. Liaoning, NE China 40°10′N 124°23′E
197 Q14 **Daneborg** *var.* Danborg. ◐ Tunu, N Greenland
25 V12 **Danevang** Texas, SW USA 29°03′N 96°11′W
Dänew *see* Galkynyș
Danfeng *see* Shizong
14 L12 **Danford Lake** Québec, SE Canada 45°55′N 76°12′W
19 T4 **Danforth** Maine, NE USA 45°39′N 67°54′W
37 P3 **Danforth Hills** ▲▲ Colorado, C USA
Dangara *see* Danghara
159 V12 **Dangchang** Gansu, C China 34°01′N 104°19′E
159 P8 **Dangchengwan** *var.* Subei, Subei Mongolzu Zizhixian. Gansu, N China 39°33′N 94°50′E
82 B10 **Dange** Uíge, NW Angola 07°55′S 15°01′E
Dangerous Archipelago *see* Tuamotu, Îles
83 E26 **Danger Point** *headland* SW South Africa 34°37′S 19°20′E
147 Q13 **Danghara** *Rus.* Dangara. SW Tajikistan 38°05′N 69°14′E
159 P8 **Danghe Nanshan** ▲▲ W China
80 I12 **Dangila** *var.* Dānglā. Āmara, NW Ethiopia 11°08′N 36°51′E
159 P8 **Dangjin Shankou** *pass* N China
Dangla *see* Tanggula Shan, China
Dang La *see* Tanggula Shankou, China
Dānglā *see* Dangila, Ethiopia
Dangme Chu *see* Manās
153 Y11 **Dāngori** Assam, NE India 27°40′N 95°35′E
159 N14 **Dangqên** Xizang Zizhiqu, W China 31°43′N 91°52′E
Dang Raek, Phanom/Dangrek, Chaîne des *see* Dângrêk, Chuŏr Phnum
167 S11 **Dângrêk, Chuŏr Phnum** *var.* Phanom Dang Raek, Phanom Dong Rak, *Fr.* Chaîne des Dangrek. ▲▲ Cambodia/Thailand
42 G3 **Dangriga** *prev.* Stann Creek. Stann Creek, E Belize 16°59′N 88°13′W
161 P6 **Dangshan** Anhui, E China 34°22′N 116°21′E
33 T15 **Daniel** Wyoming, C USA 42°49′N 110°04′W
83 H22 **Daniëlskuil** Northern Cape, N South Africa 28°11′S 23°33′E
19 N12 **Danielson** Connecticut, NE USA 41°48′N 71°53′W
124 M15 **Danilov** Yaroslavskaya Oblast', W Russian Federation 58°11′N 40°11′E
127 O9 **Danilovka** Volgogradskaya Oblast', SW Russian Federation 50°21′N 44°03′E
Danish West Indies *see* Virgin Islands (US)
160 L7 **Dan Jiang** ≈ C China
160 M7 **Danjiangkou Shuiku** ▣ C China
141 W8 **Ḍank** *var.* Dhank. NW Oman 23°34′N 56°16′E
152 J7 **Dankhar** Himāchal Pradesh, N India 32°08′N 78°12′E
126 L6 **Dankov** Lipetskaya Oblast', W Russian Federation 53°17′N 39°07′E
42 J7 **Danlí** El Paraíso, S Honduras 14°02′N 86°34′W
Danmark *see* Denmark
Danmarksstraedet *see* Denmark Strait
95 O14 **Dannemora** Uppsala, C Sweden 60°13′N 17°49′E
18 L6 **Dannemora** New York, NE USA 44°42′N 73°42′W
100 K11 **Dannenberg** Niedersachsen, N Germany 53°05′N 11°06′E
184 N12 **Dannevirke** Manawatu-Wanganui, North Island, New Zealand 40°14′S 176°05′E
21 U8 **Dan River** ≈ Virginia, NE USA
167 P8 **Dan Sai** Loei, C Thailand 17°15′N 101°04′E
18 F10 **Dansville** New York, NE USA 42°34′N 77°40′W
155 K14 **Dantewāra** Chhattīsgarh, E India 18°53′N 81°20′E
Dantzig *see* Gdańsk
86 E12 **Danube** *Bul.* Dunav, *Cz.* Dunaj, *Ger.* Donau, *Hung.* Duna, *Rom.* Dunărea. ≈ C Europe
Danubian Plain *see* Dunavska Ravnina
166 L8 **Danubyu** Ayeyarwady, SW Burma (Myanmar) 17°15′N 95°35′E
Danum *see* Doncaster
19 P11 **Danvers** Massachusetts, NE USA 42°34′N 70°54′W
27 T11 **Danville** Arkansas, C USA 35°03′N 93°22′W
31 N13 **Danville** Illinois, N USA 40°10′N 87°37′W
31 O14 **Danville** Indiana, N USA 39°45′N 86°31′W
29 Y15 **Danville** Iowa, C USA 40°52′N 91°18′W
20 M6 **Danville** Kentucky, S USA 37°40′N 84°49′W
18 G14 **Danville** Pennsylvania, NE USA 40°57′N 76°36′W
21 T6 **Danville** Virginia, NE USA 36°34′N 79°25′W
Danxian/Dan Xian *see* Danzhou
160 L17 **Danzhou** *prev.* Danxian, Dan Xian, Nada. Hainan, S China 19°31′N 109°31′E
Danzhou *see* Yichuan
Danzig *see* Gdańsk
Danziger Bucht *see* Danzig, Gulf of
110 J6 **Danzig, Gulf of** *var.* Gulf of Gdańsk, *Ger.* Danziger Bucht, *Pol.* Zakota Gdańska, *Rus.* Gdan'skaya Bukhta. *gulf* N Poland
160 F10 **Daocheng** *var.* Jinzhu, *Tib.* Dabba. Sichuan, C China 29°05′N 100°14′E
Daojiang *see* Daoxian
Daokou *see* Huaxian
104 H7 **Dão, Rio** ≈ N Portugal
Daosa *see* Dausa
77 Y7 **Dao Timmi** Agadez, NE Niger 20°31′N 13°34′E
160 M13 **Daoxian** *var.* Daojiang. Hunan, S China 25°30′N 111°37′E
77 Q14 **Dapaong** N Togo 10°52′N 00°12′E
23 N8 **Daphne** Alabama, S USA 30°36′N 87°54′W
171 P7 **Dapitan** Mindanao, S Philippines 08°39′N 123°26′E
159 P9 **Da Qaidam** Qinghai, C China 37°50′N 95°18′E
163 V8 **Daqing** *var.* Sartu. Heilongjiang, NE China 46°29′N 125°07′E
163 O13 **Daqing Shan** ▲▲ N China
163 T11 **Daqin Tal** *var.* Naiman Qi. Nei Mongol Zizhiqu, N China 42°51′N 120°41′E
Daqm *see* Duqm
160 G8 **Da Qu** *var.* Do Qu. ≈ C China
139 T5 **Dāqūq** *var.* Tāwūq. At Ta'mīn, N Iraq 35°08′N 44°27′E
76 G10 **Dara** *var.* Dahra. NW Senegal 15°20′N 15°28′W
138 H9 **Dar'ā** *var.* Der'a, *Fr.* Déraa. Dar'ā, SW Syria 32°37′N 36°06′E
138 H8 **Dar'ā** *off.* Muḥāfaẓat Dar'ā, *var.* Dará, Der'a, Derrá. ◐ *governorate* S Syria
143 Q12 **Dārāb** Fārs, S Iran 28°52′N 54°25′E
116 K8 **Darabani** Botoșani, NW Romania 48°10′N 26°39′E
Daraj *see* Dirj
Dar'ā, Muḥāfaẓat *see* Dar'ā
142 M8 **Dārān** Eşfahān, W Iran 33°00′N 50°27′E
167 U12 **Da Răng, Sông** *var.* Ba. ≈ S Vietnam
Daraut-Kurgan *see* Daroot-Korgon
77 W13 **Darazo** Bauchi, E Nigeria 11°01′N 10°27′E
139 S3 **Darband** Arbīl, N Iraq 36°15′N 44°17′E
139 V4 **Darband-i Khān, Sadd** *dam* NE Iraq
139 N1 **Darbāsīyah** *var.* Derbisīye. Al Ḥasakah, N Syria 37°06′N 40°42′E
118 C11 **Darbėnai** Klaipėda, NW Lithuania 56°02′N 21°16′E
153 Q13 **Darbhanga** Bihār, N India 26°10′N 85°54′E
38 M9 **Darby, Cape** *headland* Alaska, USA 64°19′N 162°46′W
112 I9 **Darda** *Hung.* Dárda. Osijek-Baranja, E Croatia 45°37′N 18°41′E
Dárda *see* Darda
27 T11 **Dardanelle** Arkansas, C USA 35°11′N 93°09′W
27 S11 **Dardanelle, Lake** ▣ Arkansas, C USA
Dardanelles *see* Çanakkale Boğazı
Dardanelli *see* Çanakkale
Dardo *see* Kangding
Dar-el-Beida *see* Casablanca
136 M14 **Darende** Malatya, C Turkey 38°34′N 37°29′E

◆ Country
● Country Capital
◇ Dependent Territory
○ Dependent Territory Capital
◐ Administrative Regions
✈ International Airport
▲ Mountain
▲▲ Mountain Range
△ Volcano
≈ River
◎ Lake
▣ Reservoir

81 J22 **Dar es Salaam** Dar es Salaam, E Tanzania 06°51′S 39°18′E
81 J22 **Dar es Salaam** ✕ Pwani, E Tanzania 06°57′S 39°17′E
185 H18 **Darfield** Canterbury, South Island, New Zealand 43°29′S 172°07′E
106 F7 **Darfo** Lombardia, N Italy 45°54′N 10°12′E
80 B10 **Darfur** *var.* Darfur Massif. *cultural region* W Sudan
Darfur Massif *see* Darfur
Darganata/Dargan-Ata *see* Birata
143 T3 **Dargaz** *var.* Darreh Gaz; *prev.* Moḩammadābād. Khorāsān-Razavī, NE Iran 37°28′N 59°08′E
139 U4 **Dargazayn** As Sulaymānīyah, NE Iraq 35°39′N 45°00′E
183 P12 **Dargo** Victoria, SE Australia 37°29′S 147°15′E
162 L6 **Darhan** Darhan Uul, N Mongolia 49°24′N 105°57′E
163 N8 **Darhan** Hentiy, C Mongolia 46°38′N 109°25′E
Darhan *see* Büreghangay
Darhan Muminggan Lianheqi *see* Bailingmiao
162 L6 **Darhan Uul** ◆ *province* N Mongolia
23 W7 **Darien** Georgia, SE USA 31°22′N 81°25′W
43 W16 **Darién** *off.* Provincia del Darién. ◆ *province* SE Panama
Darién, Golfo del *see* Darien, Gulf of
43 X14 **Darien, Gulf of** *Sp.* Golfo del Darién. *gulf* S Caribbean Sea
Darien, Isthmus of *see* Panama, Istmo de
Darién, Provincia del *see* Darién
42 K9 **Dariense, Cordillera** ▲ C Nicaragua
43 W15 **Darién, Serranía del** ▲ Colombia/Panama
163 P10 **Dariganga** *var.* Ovoot. Sühbaatar, SE Mongolia 45°08′N 113°51′E
Dario *see* Ciudad Darío
Dariorigum *see* Vannes
Dariv *see* Darvi
Darj *see* Dirj
Darjeeling *see* Dārjiling
153 S12 **Dārjiling** *prev.* Darjeeling. West Bengal, NE India 27°00′N 88°13′E
Darkehnen *see* Ozersk
159 S12 **Darlag** *var.* Gümai. Qinghai, C China 33°43′N 99°42′E
183 T3 **Darling Downs** *hill range* Queensland, E Australia
28 M2 **Darling, Lake** ⊠ North Dakota, N USA
180 I12 **Darling Range** ▲ Western Australia
182 L8 **Darling River** ~ New South Wales, SE Australia
97 M15 **Darlington** N England, United Kingdom 54°31′N 01°34′W
21 T12 **Darlington** South Carolina, SE USA 34°19′N 79°53′W
30 K9 **Darlington** Wisconsin, N USA 42°41′N 90°08′W
110 G7 **Darłowo** Zachodnio-pomorskie, NW Poland 54°24′N 16°21′E
101 G19 **Darmstadt** Hessen, SW Germany 49°52′N 08°39′E
75 S7 **Darnah** *var.* Dérna. NE Libya 32°46′N 22°39′E
103 S6 **Darney** Vosges, NE France 48°06′N 05°58′E
182 M7 **Darnick** New South Wales, SE Australia 32°52′S 143°38′E
195 Y6 **Darnley, Cape** *cape* Antarctica
105 R7 **Daroca** Aragón, NE Spain 41°07′N 01°25′W
147 S11 **Daroot-Korgon** *var.* Daraut-Kurgan. Oshskaya Oblast', SW Kyrgyzstan 39°35′N 72°13′E
61 A23 **Darragueira** *var.* Darregueira. Buenos Aires, E Argentina 37°40′S 63°12′W
Darregueira *see* Darragueira
Darreh Gaz *see* Dargaz
142 K7 **Darreh Shahr** *var.* Darreh-ye Shahr. Īlām, W Iran 33°10′N 47°18′E
Darreh-ye Shahr *see* Darreh Shahr
32 I7 **Darrington** Washington, NW USA 48°15′N 121°36′W
25 P1 **Darrouzett** Texas, SW USA 36°27′N 100°19′W
153 S15 **Darsana** *var.* Darshana. Khulna, N Bangladesh 23°32′N 88°49′E
Darshana *see* Darsana
100 M7 **Darss** *peninsula* NE Germany
100 M7 **Darsser Ort** *headland* NE Germany 54°28′N 12°31′E
97 J24 **Dart** ~ SW England, United Kingdom
Dartang *see* Baqên
97 P22 **Dartford** SE England, United Kingdom 51°27′N 00°13′E
182 L12 **Dartmoor** Victoria, SE Australia 37°56′S 141°18′E
97 I24 **Dartmoor** *moorland* SW England, United Kingdom
13 Q15 **Dartmouth** Nova Scotia, SE Canada 44°40′N 63°35′W
97 J24 **Dartmouth** SW England, United Kingdom 50°21′N 03°34′W
15 Y6 **Dartmouth** ~ Québec, SE Canada
183 Q11 **Dartmouth Reservoir** ⊚ Victoria, SE Australia
Dartuch, Cabo *see* Artrutx, Cap d'
186 C9 **Daru** Western, SW Papua New Guinea 09°05′S 143°10′E
112 G9 **Daruvar** *Hung.* Daruvár. Bjelovar-Bilogora, NE Croatia 45°34′N 17°12′E
Daruvár *see* Daruvar
Darvaza *see* Derweze, Turkmenistan
Darvaza *see* Darvoza, Uzbekistan
Darvazskiy Khrebet *see* Darvoz, Qatorkŭhi
Darvel Bay *see* Lahad Datu, Teluk
Darvel, Teluk *see* Lahad Datu, Teluk
162 F8 **Darvi** *var.* Dariv. Govĭ-Altay, W Mongolia 46°20′N 94°11′E
162 F7 **Darvi** *var.* Bulgan. Hovd, W Mongolia 46°57′N 93°40′E
148 L9 **Darvishān** *var.* Darweshan, Garmser. Helmand, S Afghanistan 31°02′N 64°12′E
147 O10 **Darvoza** *Rus.* Darvaza. Jizzax Viloyati, C Uzbekistan 40°59′N 67°19′E
147 R13 **Darvoz, Qatorkŭhi** *Rus.* Darvazskiy Khrebet. ▲ C Tajikistan
Darweshan *see* Darvishān
63 J15 **Darwin** Río Negro, S Argentina 39°13′S 65°41′W
181 O1 **Darwin** *prev.* Palmerston, Port Darwin. *territory capital* Northern Territory, N Australia 12°28′S 130°52′E
65 D24 **Darwin** *var.* Darwin Settlement. East Falkland, Falkland Islands 51°51′S 58°55′W
62 H8 **Darwin, Cordillera** ▲ N Chile
Darwin Settlement *see* Darwin
57 B17 **Darwin, Volcán** ▲ Galapagos Islands, Ecuador, E Pacific Ocean 0°12′S 91°17′W
149 S8 **Darya Khān** Punjab, E Pakistan 31°47′N 71°10′E
145 O15 **Dar'yalyktakyr, Ravnina** *plain* S Kazakhstan
143 T11 **Dārzīn** Kermān, S Iran 29°11′N 58°09′E
Dashhowuz *see* Daşoguz
Dashhowuz Welayaty *see* Daşoguz Welaýaty
162 K7 **Dashinchilen** *var.* Süüj. Bulgan, C Mongolia 47°49′N 104°06′E
119 O16 **Dashkawka** *Rus.* Dashkovka. Mahilyowskaya Voblasts', E Belarus 53°44′N 30°16′E
Dashkhovuz *see* Daşoguz Welaýaty
Dashkhovuzskiy Velayat *see* Daşoguz Welaýaty
Dashköpri *see* Daşköpri
Dashkovka *see* Dashkawka
148 J15 **Dasht** ~ SW Pakistan
Dasht-i *see* Bābūs, Dasht-e
Dashtidzhum *see* Dashtijum
147 R13 **Dashtijum** *Rus.* Dashtidzhum. SW Tajikistan 38°06′N 70°11′E
149 W7 **Daska** Punjab, NE Pakistan 32°15′N 74°23′E
146 J16 **Daşköpri** *var.* Dashköpri, *Rus.* Tashkepri. Mary Welaýaty, S Turkmenistan 36°15′N 62°37′E
146 H8 **Daşoguz** *Rus.* Dashkhovuz, *Turkm.* Dashhowuz; *prev.* Tashauz. Daşoguz Welaýaty, N Turkmenistan 41°51′N 59°53′E
146 E9 **Daşoguz Welaýaty** *var.* Dashhowuz Welayaty, *Rus.* Dashkhovuz, Dashkhovuzskiy Velayat. ◆ *province* N Turkmenistan
Da, Sông *see* Black River
77 R15 **Dassa** *var.* Dassa-Zoumé. S Benin 07°46′N 02°15′E
Dassa-Zoumé *see* Dassa
29 U8 **Dassel** Minnesota, N USA 45°06′N 94°18′W
152 H3 **Dastegil Sar** ▲ N India
149 U4 **Dasu** North-West Frontier Province, N Pakistan 35°18′N 73°2′E
136 C16 **Datça** Muğla, SW Turkey 36°46′N 27°40′E
165 R4 **Date** Hokkaidō, NE Japan 42°28′N 140°51′E
154 I8 **Datia** *prev.* Duttia. Madhya Pradesh, C India 25°41′N 78°28′E
Dātnejaevrie *see* Tunnsjøen
159 T10 **Datong** *var.* Datong Huizu Tuzu Zizhixian, Qiaotou. Qinghai, C China 37°01′N 101°33′E
161 N2 **Datong** *var.* Tatung, Ta-t'ung. Shanxi, C China 40°09′N 113°17′E
Datong *see* Tong'an
159 S8 **Datong He** ~ C China
Datong Huizu Tuzu Zizhixian *see* Datong
159 S9 **Datong Shan** ▲ C China
169 O10 **Datu, Tanjung** *headland* Indonesia/Malaysia 02°01′N 109°37′E
Datu, Teluk *see* Lahad Datu, Teluk
Daua *see* Dawa Wenz
172 H16 **Dauban, Mount** ▲ Silhouette, NE Seychelles
149 T7 **Dāūd Khel** Punjab, E Pakistan 32°52′N 71°35′E
119 G15 **Daugai** Alytus, S Lithuania 54°22′N 24°20′E
Daugava *see* Western Dvina
118 J11 **Daugavpils** *Ger.* Dünaburg; *prev. Rus.* Dvinsk. Daugvapils, SE Latvia 55°53′N 26°34′E
Dauka *see* Dawkah
Daulatabad *see* Malāyer
Daulpur *see* Dhaulpur
101 D18 **Daun** Rheinland-Pfalz, W Germany 50°13′N 06°50′E
155 E14 **Daund** *prev.* Dhond. Mahārāshtra, W India 18°28′N 74°38′E
166 M12 **Daung Kyun** *island* S Burma (Myanmar)
11 W15 **Dauphin** Manitoba, S Canada 51°09′N 100°05′W
103 S13 **Dauphiné** *cultural region* E France
23 N9 **Dauphin Island** *island* Alabama, S USA
11 X15 **Dauphin River** Manitoba, S Canada 51°55′N 98°03′W
77 V12 **Daura** Katsina, N Nigeria 13°03′N 08°18′E
152 H12 **Dausa** *prev.* Daosa. Rājasthān, N India 26°51′N 76°21′E
Dauwa *see* Dawwah
137 Y10 **Däväçi** *Rus.* Divichi. NE Azerbaijan 41°15′N 48°58′E
155 F18 **Dāvangere** Karnātaka, W India 14°30′N 75°52′E
171 Q8 **Davao** *off.* Davao City. Mindanao, S Philippines 07°06′N 125°36′E
Davao City *see* Davao
171 Q8 **Davao Gulf** *gulf* Mindanao, S Philippines
15 Q11 **Daveluyville** Québec, SE Canada 46°12′N 72°07′W
29 Z14 **Davenport** Iowa, C USA 41°31′N 90°35′W
32 L8 **Davenport** Washington, NW USA 47°39′N 118°09′W
43 P16 **David** Chiriquí, W Panama 08°26′N 82°26′W
15 O11 **David** ~ Québec, SE Canada
29 R15 **David City** Nebraska, C USA 41°15′N 97°07′W
David-Gorodok *see* Davyd-Haradok
11 T16 **Davidson** Saskatchewan, S Canada 51°15′N 105°59′W
21 R10 **Davidson** North Carolina, SE USA 35°29′N 80°49′W
26 K12 **Davidson** Oklahoma, C USA 34°15′N 99°06′W
39 S6 **Davidson Mountains** ▲ Alaska, USA
172 M8 **Davie Ridge** *undersea feature* W Indian Ocean 17°10′S 41°45′E
182 A1 **Davies, Mount** ▲ South Australia 26°14′S 129°14′E
35 O7 **Davis** California, W USA 38°33′N 121°46′W
27 N12 **Davis** Oklahoma, C USA 34°30′N 97°07′W
195 Y7 **Davis** *Australian research station* Antarctica 68°30′S 78°15′E
194 H3 **Davis Coast** *physical region* Antarctica
18 C16 **Davis, Mount** ▲ Pennsylvania, NE USA 39°47′N 79°10′W
24 K9 **Davis Mountains** ▲ Texas, SW USA
195 Z9 **Davis Sea** *sea* Antarctica
65 O20 **Davis Seamounts** *undersea feature* S Atlantic Ocean
196 M13 **Davis Strait** *strait* Baffin Bay/ Labrador Sea
127 U5 **Davlekanovo** Respublika Bashkortostan, W Russian Federation 54°13′N 55°06′E
108 J9 **Davos** *Rmsch.* Tavau. Graubünden, E Switzerland 46°48′N 09°50′E
119 J20 **Davyd-Haradok** *Pol.* Dawidgródek, *Rus.* David-Gorodok. Brestskaya Voblasts', SW Belarus 52°03′N 27°13′E
163 U12 **Dawa** Liaoning, NE China 40°55′N 122°02′E
141 O11 **Dawāsir, Wādī ad** *dry watercourse* S Saudi Arabia
81 K15 **Dawa Wenz** *var.* Daua, Webi Daawo. ~ E Africa
Dawaymah, Birkat ad *see* Umm al Baqar, Hawr
167 N10 **Dawei** *var.* Tavoy, Htawei. Tanintharyi, S Burma (Myanmar) 14°02′N 98°12′E
119 K14 **Dawhinava** *Rus.* Dolginovo. Minskaya Voblasts', N Belarus 54°39′N 27°29′E
Dawidgródek *see* Davyd-Haradok
141 V12 **Dawkah** *var.* Dauka. SW Oman 18°32′N 54°03′E
Dawlat Qaṭar *see* Qatar
24 M3 **Dawn** Texas, SW USA 34°54′N 102°10′W
Dawo *see* Maqên
140 M11 **Daws** Al Bāḩah, SW Saudi Arabia 20°19′N 41°12′E
10 H5 **Dawson** *var.* Dawson City. Yukon Territory, NW Canada 64°04′N 139°24′W
23 S6 **Dawson** Georgia, SE USA 31°46′N 84°27′W
29 S9 **Dawson** Minnesota, N USA 44°55′N 96°03′W
Dawson City *see* Dawson
11 N13 **Dawson Creek** British Columbia, W Canada 55°45′N 120°07′W
10 H7 **Dawson Range** ▲ Yukon Territory, W Canada
181 Y9 **Dawson River** ~ Queensland, E Australia
10 J15 **Dawsons Landing** British Columbia, SW Canada 51°33′N 127°38′W
20 I7 **Dawson Springs** Kentucky, S USA 37°10′N 87°41′W
23 S2 **Dawsonville** Georgia, SE USA 34°28′N 84°07′W
160 G8 **Dawu** *var.* Xianshui. Sichuan, C China 30°55′N 101°08′E
Dawu *see* Maqên
Dawukou *see* Shizuishan
141 Y10 **Dawwah** *var.* Dauwa. W Oman 20°36′N 58°52′E
102 J15 **Dax** *var.* Ax; *anc.* Aquae Augustae, Aquae Tarbelicae. Landes, SW France 43°43′N 01°03′W
Daxian *see* Dazhou
Daxiangshan *see* Gangu
Daxue *see* Wencheng
160 G9 **Daxue Shan** ▲ C China
Dayan *see* Lijiang
160 G12 **Dayao** *var.* Jinbi. Yunnan, SW China 25°41′N 101°23′E
Dayishan *see* Gaoyou
149 O6 **Dāykondī** *province* C Afghanistan
183 N12 **Daylesford** Victoria, SE Australia 37°24′S 144°07′E
35 U10 **Daylight Pass** *pass* California, W USA
61 D17 **Daymán, Río** ~ N Uruguay
Dayong *see* Zhangjiajie
Dayr *see* Ad Dayr
138 G10 **Dayr 'Allā** *var.* Deir 'Alla. Al Balqā', N Jordan 32°39′N 36°06′E
139 N4 **Dayr az Zawr** *var.* Deir ez Zor. Dayr az Zawr, E Syria 35°12′N 40°12′E
138 M5 **Dayr az Zawr** *off.* Muḩāfaẓat Dayr az Zawr, *var.* Dayr Az-Zor. ◆ *governorate* E Syria
Dayr az Zawr, Muḩāfaẓat *see* Dayr az Zawr
Dayr Az-Zor *see* Dayr az Zawr
75 W9 **Dayrūṭ** *var.* Dairûṭ. C Egypt 27°34′N 30°48′E
11 Q15 **Daysland** Alberta, SW Canada 52°53′N 112°19′W
31 R14 **Dayton** Ohio, N USA 39°46′N 84°12′W
20 L10 **Dayton** Tennessee, S USA 35°30′N 85°01′W
25 W11 **Dayton** Texas, SW USA 30°03′N 94°53′W
32 L10 **Dayton** Washington, NW USA 46°19′N 117°58′W
23 X10 **Daytona Beach** Florida, SE USA 29°12′N 81°03′W
169 U12 **Dayu** Borneo, C Indonesia 01°55′S 115°04′E
161 O13 **Dayu Ling** ▲ S China
161 R7 **Da Yunhe** *Eng.* Grand Canal. *canal* E China
161 S11 **Dayu Shan** *island* SE China
160 K8 **Dazhou** *prev.* Dachuan, Daxian. Sichuan, C China 31°16′N 107°31′E
160 J9 **Dazhu** *var.* Zhuyang. Sichuan, C China 30°45′N 107°11′E
160 J9 **Dazu** *var.* Longgang. Chongqing Shi, C China 29°47′N 106°30′E
83 H24 **De Aar** Northern Cape, C South Africa 30°40′S 24°01′E
194 K5 **Deacon, Cape** *headland* Antarctica
39 R5 **Deadhorse** Alaska, USA 70°15′N 148°28′W
33 T12 **Dead Indian Peak** ▲ Wyoming, C USA 44°36′N 109°45′W
23 R9 **Dead Lake** ⊚ Florida, SE USA
44 J4 **Deadman's Cay** Long Island, C Bahamas 23°09′N 75°06′W
138 G11 **Dead Sea** *var.* Bahret Lut, Lacus Asphaltites, *Ar.* Al Baḩr al Mayyit, Baḩrat Lūt, *Heb.* Yam HaMelaḩ. *salt lake* Israel/ Jordan
28 J9 **Deadwood** South Dakota, N USA 44°22′N 103°43′W
97 Q22 **Deal** SE England, United Kingdom 51°14′N 01°23′E
83 I22 **Dealesville** Free State, C South Africa 28°40′S 25°46′E
161 P10 **De'an** *var.* Puting. Jiangxi, S China 29°24′N 115°46′E
62 K9 **Deán Funes** Córdoba, C Argentina 30°25′S 64°22′W
194 L12 **Dean Island** *island* Antarctica
Deanuvuotna *see* Tanafjorden
31 S10 **Dearborn** Michigan, N USA 42°16′N 83°13′W
27 R3 **Dearborn** Missouri, C USA 39°31′N 94°46′W
Deargget *see* Tārendö
32 K9 **Deary** Idaho, NW USA 46°46′N 118°33′W
32 M9 **Deary** Washington, NW USA 46°42′N 116°36′W
10 J10 **Dease** ~ British Columbia, W Canada
10 J10 **Dease Lake** British Columbia, W Canada 58°28′N 130°04′W
35 U11 **Death Valley** California, W USA 36°25′N 116°50′W
35 U11 **Death Valley** *valley* California, W USA
92 M8 **Deatnu** *Fin.* Tenojoki, *Nor.* Tana. ~ Finland/Norway *see also* Tenojoki
102 L4 **Deauville** Calvados, N France 49°21′N 00°06′E
117 X7 **Debal'tseve** *Rus.* Debal'tsevo. Donets'ka Oblast', SE Ukraine 48°21′N 38°26′E
Debal'tsevo *see* Debal'tseve
113 M19 **Debar** *Ger.* Dibra, *Turk.* Debre. W FYR Macedonia 41°32′N 20°33′E
39 O9 **Debauch Mountain** ▲ Alaska, USA 64°31′N 159°52′W
De Behagle *see* Laï
25 X7 **De Berry** Texas, SW USA 32°18′N 94°09′W
127 T2 **Debessy** Udmurtskaya Respublika, NW Russian Federation 57°41′N 53°56′E
111 N16 **Dębica** Podkarpackie, SE Poland 50°04′N 21°24′E
De Bildt *see* De Bilt
98 J11 **De Bilt** *var.* De Bildt. Utrecht, C Netherlands 52°06′N 05°11′E
123 T9 **Debin** Magadanskaya Oblast', E Russian Federation 62°18′N 150°42′E
110 N13 **Dęblin** *Rus.* Ivangorod. Lubelskie, E Poland 51°34′N 21°50′E
110 D10 **Dębno** Zachodnio-pomorskie, NW Poland 52°43′N 14°42′E
39 S10 **Deborah, Mount** ▲ Alaska, USA 63°38′N 147°13′W
33 N8 **De Borgia** Montana, NW USA 47°23′N 115°24′W
Debra Birhan *see* Debre Birhan
Debra Marcos *see* Debre Mark'os
Debra Tabor *see* Debre Tabor
Debre *see* Debar
80 J13 **Debre Birhan** *var.* Debra Birhan. Āmara, N Ethiopia 09°45′N 39°40′E
111 N22 **Debrecen** *Ger.* Debreczin, *Rom.* Debreţin; *prev.* Debreczen. Hajdú-Bihar, E Hungary 47°32′N 21°38′E
Debreczen/Debreczin *see* Debrecen
80 I12 **Debre Mark'os** *var.* Debra Marcos. Āmara, N Ethiopia 10°18′N 37°48′E
113 N19 **Debrešte** SW FYR Macedonia 41°29′N 21°20′E
80 J11 **Debre Tabor** *var.* Debra Tabor. Āmara, N Ethiopia 11°46′N 38°06′E
Debreţin *see* Debrecen
80 J13 **Debre Zeyt** Oromīya, C Ethiopia 08°41′N 39°00′E
113 L16 **Deçan** *Serb.* Dečane; *prev.* Dečani. W Kosovo 42°33′N 20°18′E
Dečane *see* Deçan
Dečani *see* Deçan
23 P2 **Decatur** Alabama, S USA 34°36′N 86°58′W
23 S3 **Decatur** Georgia, SE USA 33°46′N 84°18′W
30 L13 **Decatur** Illinois, N USA 39°50′N 88°57′W
31 Q12 **Decatur** Indiana, N USA 40°50′N 84°57′W
22 M5 **Decatur** Mississippi, S USA 32°26′N 89°06′W
29 S14 **Decatur** Nebraska, C USA 42°00′N 96°19′W
25 S6 **Decatur** Texas, SW USA 33°14′N 97°35′W
20 H9 **Decaturville** Tennessee, S USA 35°35′N 88°08′W
103 O13 **Decazeville** Aveyron, S France 44°34′N 02°18′E
155 H17 **Deccan** *Hind.* Dakshin. *plateau* C India
14 J8 **Decelles, Réservoir** ⊠ Québec, SE Canada
12 K2 **Déception** Québec, NE Canada 62°06′N 74°36′W
160 G11 **Dechang** *var.* Dezhou. Sichuan, C China 27°24′N 102°09′E
111 C15 **Děčín** *Ger.* Tetschen. Ústecký Kraj, NW Czech Republic 50°48′N 14°15′E
103 P9 **Decize** Nièvre, C France 46°51′N 03°25′E
98 I6 **De Cocksdorp** Noord-Holland, NW Netherlands 53°09′N 04°52′E
29 X11 **Decorah** Iowa, C USA 43°18′N 91°47′W
Dedeagaç/Dedeagach *see* Alexandroúpoli
188 C15 **Dededo** N Guam 13°30′N 144°51′E
98 N9 **Dedemsvaart** Overijssel, E Netherlands 52°36′N 06°28′E
19 O11 **Dedham** Massachusetts, NE USA 42°14′N 71°10′W
63 H19 **Dedo, Cerro** ▲ SW Argentina 44°46′S 71°48′W
77 O13 **Dédougou** W Burkina 12°29′N 03°25′W
124 G15 **Dedovichi** Pskovskaya Oblast', W Russian Federation 57°31′N 29°53′E
Dedu *see* Wudalianchi
155 J24 **Deduru Oya** ~ W Sri Lanka
83 N14 **Dedza** Central, S Malawi 14°20′S 34°24′E
83 N14 **Dedza Mountain** ▲ C Malawi 14°22′S 34°16′E
96 K9 **Dee** ~ NE Scotland, United Kingdom
97 J19 **Dee** *Wel.* Afon Dyfrdwy. ~ England/Wales, United Kingdom
Deep Bay *see* Chilumba
21 T3 **Deep Creek Lake** ⊠ Maryland, NE USA
36 J4 **Deep Creek Range** ▲ Utah, W USA
27 P10 **Deep Fork River** ~ Oklahoma, C USA
14 J11 **Deep River** Ontario, SE Canada 46°04′N 77°29′W
21 T10 **Deep River** ~ North Carolina, SE USA
183 U4 **Deepwater** New South Wales, SE Australia 29°27′S 151°52′E
31 S14 **Deer Creek Lake** ⊚ Ohio, N USA
23 Z15 **Deerfield Beach** Florida, SE USA 26°19′N 80°06′W
39 N8 **Deering** Alaska, USA 66°04′N 162°43′W
38 M16 **Deer Island** *island* Alaska, USA
19 S7 **Deer Isle** *island* Maine, NE USA
13 S11 **Deer Lake** Newfoundland and Labrador, SE Canada 49°11′N 57°27′W
99 D18 **Deerlijk** West-Vlaanderen, W Belgium 50°52′N 03°21′E
33 Q10 **Deer Lodge** Montana, NW USA 46°24′N 112°43′W
32 L8 **Deer Park** Washington, NW USA 47°55′N 117°28′W
29 U5 **Deer River** Minnesota, N USA 47°19′N 93°47′W
Deés *see* Dej
Defeng *see* Liping
31 R11 **Defiance** Ohio, N USA 41°17′N 84°21′W
23 Q8 **De Funiak Springs** Florida, SE USA 30°43′N 86°07′W
95 L23 **Degeberga** Skåne, S Sweden 55°48′N 14°06′E
104 H12 **Degebe, Ribeira** ~ S Portugal
80 M13 **Degeh Bur** Sumalē, E Ethiopia 08°08′N 43°35′E
15 U9 **Dégelis** Québec, SE Canada 47°30′N 68°38′W
77 U17 **Degema** Rivers, S Nigeria 04°46′N 06°47′E
95 L16 **Degerfors** Örebro, C Sweden 59°14′N 14°26′E
193 R14 **De Gerlache Seamounts** *undersea feature* SE Pacific Ocean
101 N21 **Deggendorf** Bayern, SE Germany 48°50′N 12°58′E
80 I11 **Degoma** Āmara, N Ethiopia 12°22′N 37°36′E
De Gordyk *see* Gorredijk
27 T12 **De Gray Lake** ⊠ Arkansas, C USA
180 J6 **De Grey River** ~ Western Australia
126 M10 **Degtevo** Rostovskaya Oblast', SW Russian Federation 49°12′N 40°39′E
Dehbārez *see* Rūdān
Deh Bīd *see* Şafāshahr
142 M10 **Deh Dasht** Kohkīlūyeh va Būyer AḨmad, SW Iran 30°49′N 50°36′E
75 N8 **Dehibat** SE Tunisia 31°58′N 10°43′E
Dehli *see* Delhi
142 K8 **Dehlorān** Īlām, W Iran 32°41′N 47°18′E
147 N13 **Dehqonobod** *Rus.* Dekhkanabad. Qashqadaryo Viloyati, S Uzbekistan 38°24′N 66°31′E
152 J9 **Dehra Dūn** Uttaranchal, N India 30°19′N 78°04′E
153 O14 **Dehri** Bihār, N India 24°55′N 84°11′E
148 K10 **Deh Shū** *var.* Deshu. Helmand, S Afghanistan 30°28′N 63°21′E
163 W9 **Dehui** Jilin, NE China 44°23′N 125°42′E
99 D17 **Deinze** Oost-Vlaanderen, NW Belgium 50°59′N 03°32′E
Deir 'Alla *see* Dayr 'Allā
Deir ez Zor *see* Dayr az Zawr
Deirgeirt, Loch *see* Derg, Lough
116 H9 **Dej** *Hung.* Dés; *prev.* Deés. Cluj, NW Romania 47°08′N 23°55′E
95 K15 **Deje** Värmland, C Sweden 59°35′N 13°29′E
171 Y15 **De Jongs, Tanjung** *headland* Papua, SE Indonesia 06°56′S 138°32′E
De Jouwer *see* Joure
30 M10 **De Kalb** Illinois, N USA 41°55′N 88°45′W
22 M5 **De Kalb** Mississippi, S USA 32°46′N 88°39′W
25 W5 **De Kalb** Texas, SW USA 33°30′N 94°34′W
83 G18 **Dekar** *var.* D'Kar. Ghanzi, NW Botswana 21°31′S 21°55′E
Dekéleia *see* Dhekéleia
79 K20 **Dekese** Kasai-Occidental, C Dem. Rep. Congo 03°28′S 21°24′E
Dekhkanabad *see* Dehqonobod
79 I14 **Dékoa** Kémo, C Central African Republic 06°17′N 19°07′E
98 H6 **De Koog** Noord-Holland, NW Netherlands 53°06′N 04°43′E
30 M9 **Delafield** Wisconsin, N USA 43°03′N 88°22′W
61 C23 **De La Garma** Buenos Aires, E Argentina 37°58′S 60°25′W
14 K10 **Delahey, Lac** ⊚ Québec, SE Canada
80 E11 **Delami** Southern Kordofan, C Sudan 11°51′N 30°30′E
23 X11 **De Land** Florida, SE USA 29°01′N 81°18′W
35 R12 **Delano** California, W USA 35°46′N 119°15′W
29 V8 **Delano** Minnesota, N USA 45°03′N 93°46′W
36 K6 **Delano Peak** ▲ Utah, W USA 38°22′N 112°21′W
Delap-Uliga-Djarrit *see* Dalap-Uliga-Djarrit
148 L7 **Delārām** Nīmrūz, SW Afghanistan 32°11′N 63°27′E
38 F17 **Delarof Islands** *island group* Aleutian Islands, Alaska, USA
30 M9 **Delavan** Wisconsin, N USA 42°37′N 88°37′W
31 S13 **Delaware** Ohio, N USA 40°18′N 83°06′W
18 I17 **Delaware** *off.* State of Delaware, *also known as* Blue Hen State, Diamond State, First State. ◆ *state* NE USA
18 I17 **Delaware Bay** *bay* NE USA
24 J8 **Delaware Mountains** ▲ Texas, SW USA
18 I12 **Delaware River** ~ NE USA
27 Q3 **Delaware River** ~ Kansas, C USA
18 J14 **Delaware Water Gap** *valley* New Jersey/Pennsylvania, NE USA
101 G14 **Delbrück** Nordrhein-Westfalen, W Germany 51°46′N 08°34′E
11 Q15 **Delburne** Alberta, SW Canada 52°09′N 113°11′W
172 M12 **Del Cano Rise** *undersea feature* SW Indian Ocean 45°15′S 44°15′E
113 Q18 **Delčevo** NE FYR Macedonia 41°57′N 22°45′E
Delcommune, Lac *see* Nzilo, Lac
98 O10 **Delden** Overijssel, E Netherlands 52°16′N 06°41′E
183 R12 **Delegate** New South Wales, SE Australia 37°04′S 148°57′E
De Lemmer *see* Lemmer
108 D7 **Delémont** *Ger.* Delsberg. Jura, NW Switzerland 47°22′N 07°21′E
25 R7 **De Leon** Texas, SW USA 32°06′N 98°33′W
115 F18 **Delfoí** Stereá Ellás, C Greece 38°28′N 22°31′E
98 G12 **Delft** Zuid-Holland, W Netherlands 52°01′N 04°22′E
155 J23 **Delft** *island* NW Sri Lanka
98 O5 **Delfzijl** Groningen, NE Netherlands 53°20′N 06°55′E
0 E9 **Delgada Fan** *undersea feature* NE Pacific Ocean 39°15′N 126°00′W
42 F7 **Delgado** San Salvador, SW El Salvador 13°44′N 89°07′W
82 Q12 **Delgado, Cabo** *headland* N Mozambique 10°41′S 40°40′E
162 G8 **Delger** *var.* Taygan. Govĭ-Altay, C Mongolia 46°20′N 97°22′E
163 O9 **Delgereh** *var.* Hongor. Dornogovĭ, SE Mongolia 45°49′N 111°20′E
162 J8 **Delgerhaan** *var.* Hujirt. Töv, C Mongolia 46°41′N 104°40′E
162 K9 **Delgerhangay** *var.* Hashaat. Dundgovĭ, C Mongolia 45°09′N 104°51′E
162 L9 **Delgertsogt** *var.* Amardalay. Dundgovĭ, C Mongolia 46°09′N 106°24′E
80 E6 **Delgo** Northern, N Sudan 20°08′N 30°35′E
159 R10 **Delhi** *var.* Delingha. Qinghai, C China 37°19′N 97°22′E
152 I10 **Delhi** *var.* Dehli, *Hind.* Dilli, *hist.* Shahjahanabad. *union territory capital* Delhi, N India 28°40′N 77°11′E
22 J5 **Delhi** Louisiana, S USA 32°28′N 91°29′W
18 J11 **Delhi** New York, NE USA 42°16′N 74°55′W
152 I10 **Delhi** ◆ *union territory* NW India
136 J17 **Deli Burnu** *headland* S Turkey 36°43′N 34°55′E
136 J12 **Delice Çayı** ~ C Turkey
55 X10 **Délices** C French Guiana 04°45′N 53°45′W
40 J6 **Delicias** *var.* Ciudad Delicias. Chihuahua, N Mexico 28°09′N 105°22′W
143 N7 **Delījān** *var.* Dalijan, Dilijan. Markazī, W Iran 33°59′N 50°39′E
112 P12 **Deli Jovan** ▲ E Serbia
Déli-Kárpátok *see* Carpaţii Meridionali
8 I8 **Déline** *prev.* Fort Franklin. Northwest Territories, NW Canada 65°10′N 123°30′W
Delingha *see* Delhi
15 Q7 **Delisle** Québec, SE Canada 48°39′N 71°42′W
11 T15 **Delisle** Saskatchewan, S Canada 51°54′N 107°01′W
101 M15 **Delitzsch** Sachsen, E Germany 51°31′N 12°19′E
33 Q12 **Dell** Montana, NW USA 44°41′N 112°42′W
24 I7 **Dell City** Texas, SW USA 31°56′N 105°12′W
103 U7 **Delle** Territoire-de-Belfort, E France 47°30′N 07°00′E
36 J9 **Dellenbaugh, Mount** ▲ Arizona, SW USA 36°06′N 113°32′W
29 R11 **Dell Rapids** South Dakota, N USA 43°50′N 96°42′W
21 Y4 **Delmar** Maryland, NE USA 38°26′N 75°32′W
18 K11 **Delmar** New York, NE USA 42°37′N 73°49′W
100 G11 **Delmenhorst** Niedersachsen, NW Germany 53°03′N 08°38′E
112 C9 **Delnice** Primorje-Gorski Kotar, NW Croatia 45°24′N 14°49′E
37 R7 **Del Norte** Colorado, C USA 37°40′N 106°21′W
39 N6 **De Long Mountains** ▲ Alaska, USA
183 P16 **Deloraine** Tasmania, SE Australia 41°34′S 146°43′E
11 W17 **Deloraine** Manitoba, S Canada 49°12′N 100°28′W
31 O12 **Delphi** Indiana, N USA 40°35′N 86°40′W
31 Q12 **Delphos** Ohio, N USA 40°49′N 84°20′W
23 Z15 **Delray Beach** Florida, SE USA 26°27′N 80°04′W
25 O12 **Del Rio** Texas, SW USA 29°23′N 100°56′W
Delsberg *see* Delémont
94 N11 **Delsbo** Gävleborg, C Sweden 61°49′N 16°34′E
37 P6 **Delta** Colorado, C USA 38°44′N 108°04′W
36 K5 **Delta** Utah, W USA 39°21′N 112°34′W
77 T17 **Delta** ◆ *state* S Nigeria
55 Q6 **Delta Amacuro** *off.* Territorio Delta Amacuro. ◆ *federal district* NE Venezuela
Delta Amacuro, Territorio *see* Delta Amacuro
39 S9 **Delta Junction** Alaska, USA 64°02′N 145°43′W
23 X11 **Deltona** Florida, SE USA 28°54′N 81°15′W
183 T5 **Delungra** New South Wales, SE Australia 29°40′S 150°49′E
162 D6 **Delüün** *var.* Rashaant. Bayan-Ölgiy, W Mongolia 47°48′N 90°45′E
154 C12 **Delvāda** Gujarāt, W India 20°46′N 71°02′E
61 B21 **Del Valle** Buenos Aires, E Argentina 35°55′S 60°42′W
Delvina *see* Delvinë
115 C15 **Delvináki** *var.* Dhelvinákion; *prev.* Pogónion. Ípeiros, W Greece 39°57′N 20°28′E
113 L23 **Delvinë** *var.* Delvina, *It.* Delvino. Vlorë, S Albania 39°56′N 20°07′E
Delvino *see* Delvinë
116 I7 **Delyatyn** Ivano-Frankivs'ka Oblast', W Ukraine 48°32′N 24°38′E
127 U5 **Dëma** ~ W Russian Federation
105 O5 **Demanda, Sierra de la** ▲ W Spain
39 T5 **Demarcation Point** *headland* Alaska, USA 69°40′N 141°19′W
79 K21 **Demba** Kasai-Occidental, C Dem. Rep. Congo 05°24′S 22°16′E
172 H13 **Dembéni** Grande Comore, NW Comoros 11°50′S 43°25′E
79 M15 **Dembia** Mbomou, SE Central African Republic 05°08′N 24°25′E
Dembidollo *see* Dembī Dolo
80 H13 **Dembī Dolo** *var.* Dembidollo. Oromīya, C Ethiopia 08°33′N 34°49′E
152 K6 **Demchok** *var.* Dêmqog. China/India 32°30′N 79°42′E *see also* Dêmqog
152 L6 **Demchok** *var.* Dêmqog. *disputed region* China/India *see also* Dêmqog
98 I12 **De Meern** Utrecht, C Netherlands 52°06′N 05°00′E
99 I17 **Demer** ~ C Belgium
64 H12 **Demerara Plain** *undersea feature* W Atlantic Ocean 10°00′N 48°00′W
64 H12 **Demerara Plateau** *undersea feature* W Atlantic Ocean
55 T9 **Demerara River** ~ NE Guyana
126 H3 **Demidov** Smolenskaya Oblast', W Russian Federation 55°15′N 31°30′E
37 Q15 **Deming** New Mexico, SW USA 32°17′N 107°46′W
32 H6 **Deming** Washington, NW USA 48°49′N 122°13′W
58 E10 **Demini, Rio** ~ NW Brazil
136 D13 **Demirci** Manisa, W Turkey 39°03′N 28°40′E
113 P19 **Demir Kapija** *prev.* Železna Vrata. SE FYR Macedonia 41°25′N 22°15′E
114 N11 **Demirköy** Kırklareli, NW Turkey 41°48′N 27°49′E
100 N9 **Demmin** Mecklenburg-Vorpommern, NE Germany 53°53′N 13°03′E
23 O5 **Demopolis** Alabama, S USA 32°31′N 87°50′W
31 N11 **Demotte** Indiana, N USA 41°13′N 87°07′W
158 F13 **Dêmqog** *var.* Demchok. China/India 32°36′N 79°29′E *see also* Demchok
152 L6 **Dêmqog** *var.* Demchok. *disputed region* China/India *see also* Demchok
171 Y13 **Demta** Papua, E Indonesia 02°19′S 140°06′E
121 K11 **Dem'yanka** ~ C Russian Federation
124 H15 **Demyansk** Novgorodskaya Oblast', W Russian Federation 57°39′N 32°31′E
122 H10 **Dem'yanskoye** Tyumenskaya Oblast', C Russian Federation 59°39′N 69°15′E
103 P2 **Denain** Nord, N France 50°19′N 03°24′E
39 S10 **Denali** Alaska, USA 63°08′N 147°33′W
Denali *see* McKinley, Mount
81 M14 **Denan** Sumalē, E Ethiopia 06°40′N 43°31′E
Denau *see* Denov
97 J18 **Denbigh** *Wel.* Dinbych. NE Wales, United Kingdom 53°11′N 03°25′W
97 J18 **Denbigh** *cultural region* N Wales, United Kingdom
98 I6 **Den Burg** Noord-Holland, NW Netherlands 53°03′N 04°47′E
99 F18 **Dender** *Fr.* Dendre. ~ W Belgium
99 F18 **Denderleeuw** Oost-Vlaanderen, NW Belgium 50°53′N 04°05′E
99 F17 **Dendermonde** *Fr.* Termonde. Oost-Vlaanderen, NW Belgium 51°02′N 04°08′E
Dendre *see* Dender
194 I9 **Dendtler Island** *island* Antarctica
98 P10 **Denekamp** Overijssel, E Netherlands 52°23′N 07°E
77 W12 **Dengas** Zinder, S Niger 13°15′N 09°43′E
Dêngka *see* Têwo
Dêngkagoin *see* Têwo
162 L13 **Dengkou** *var.* Bayan Gol. Nei Mongol Zizhiqu, N China 40°15′N 106°59′E
159 Q14 **Dêngqên** *var.* Gyamotang. Xizang Zizhiqu, W China 31°28′N 95°28′E
Deng Xian *see* Dengzhou
160 M7 **Dengzhou** *prev.* Deng Xian. Henan, C China 32°48′N 111°59′E
Dengzhou *see* Penglai
Den Haag *see* 's-Gravenhage

◆ Country
● Country Capital
◇ Dependent Territory
○ Dependent Territory Capital
◆ Administrative Regions
✕ International Airport
▲ Mountain
▲ Mountain Range
▲ Volcano
~ River
⊚ Lake
⊠ Reservoir

180 H10 **Denham** Western Australia 25°56´S 113°35´E
98 N9 **Den Ham** Overijssel, E Netherlands 52°30´N 06°31´E
44 J12 **Denham, Mount** ▲ C Jamaica 18°13´N 77°33´W
22 J8 **Denham Springs** Louisiana, S USA 30°29´N 90°57´W
98 I7 **Den Helder** Noord-Holland, NW Netherlands 52°54´N 04°45´E
105 T11 **Dénia** País Valenciano, E Spain 38°51´N 00°07´E
189 Q8 **Denig** W Nauru
183 N10 **Deniliquin** New South Wales, SE Australia 35°33´S 144°58´E
29 T14 **Denison** Iowa, C USA 42°00´N 95°22´W
25 U5 **Denison** Texas, SW USA 33°45´N 96°32´W
144 L8 **Denisovka** *prev.* Ordzhonikidze. Kostanay, N Kazakhstan 52°27´N 61°42´E
136 D15 **Denizli** Denizli, SW Turkey 37°46´N 29°05´E
136 D15 **Denizli** ◈ *province* SW Turkey
Denjong *see* Sikkim
183 S7 **Denman** New South Wales, SE Australia 32°24´S 150°43´E
195 Y10 **Denman Glacier** *glacier* Antarctica
21 R14 **Denmark** South Carolina, SE USA 33°19´N 81°08´W
95 G23 **Denmark** *off.* Kingdom of Denmark, *Dan.* Danmark; *anc.* Hafnia. ◆ *monarchy* N Europe
Denmark, Kingdom of *see* Denmark
92 H1 **Denmark Strait** *var.* Danmarksstraedet. *strait* Greenland/Iceland
45 T11 **Dennery** E Saint Lucia 13°55´N 60°53´W
98 I7 **Den Oever** Noord-Holland, NW Netherlands 52°56´N 05°01´E
147 O13 **Denov** *Rus.* Denau. Surkhondaryo Viloyati, S Uzbekistan 38°20´N 67°48´E
169 U17 **Denpasar** *prev.* Paloe. Bali, C Indonesia 08°40´S 115°14´E
116 E12 **Denta** Timiș, W Romania 45°20´N 21°15´E
21 Y3 **Denton** Maryland, NE USA 38°53´N 75°50´W
25 T6 **Denton** Texas, SW USA 33°11´N 97°08´W
186 G9 **D'Entrecasteaux Islands** *island group* SE Papua New Guinea
37 T4 **Denver** *state capital* Colorado, C USA 39°45´N 105°W
37 T4 **Denver** ✈ Colorado, C USA 39°57´N 104°38´W
24 L6 **Denver City** Texas, SW USA 32°57´N 102°49´W
152 J9 **Deoband** Uttar Pradesh, N India 29°41´N 77°40´E
154 N12 **Deogarh** Orissa, SW India 21°32´N 84°44´E
Deoghar *see* Devghar
154 E13 **Deolāli** Mahārāshtra, W India 19°55´N 73°49´E
154 I10 **Deori** Madhya Pradesh, C India 23°09´N 78°39´E
153 O12 **Deoria** Uttar Pradesh, N India 26°31´N 83°48´E
99 A17 **De Panne** West-Vlaanderen, W Belgium 51°06´N 02°35´E
Departamento del Quindío *see* Quindío
Departamento de Narino, *see* Nariño
54 M5 **Dependencia Federal** *off.* Territorio Dependencia Federal. ◈ *federal dependency* N Venezuela
Dependencia Federal, Territorio *see* Dependencia Federal
30 M7 **De Pere** Wisconsin, N USA 44°26´N 88°03´W
18 D10 **Depew** New York, NE USA 42°54´N 78°41´W
99 E17 **De Pinte** Oost-Vlaanderen, NW Belgium 51°00´N 03°37´E
25 V5 **Deport** Texas, SW USA 33°31´N 95°19´W
123 Q8 **Deputatskiy** Respublika Sakha (Yakutiya), NE Russian Federation 69°18´N 139°48´E
Dêqên *see* Dagzê
27 S13 **De Queen** Arkansas, C USA 34°02´N 94°20´W
22 G8 **De Quincy** Louisiana, S USA 30°27´N 93°25´W
81 J20 **Dera** *spring/well* S Kenya 02°39´S 39°52´E
149 V11 **Dera Bugti** Baluchistān, SW Pakistan 28°35´N 65°25´E
Der'a/Derá/Déraa *see* Dar'ā
149 S10 **Dera Ghāzi Khān** *var.* Dera Ghāzikhān. Punjab, C Pakistan 30°01´N 70°37´E
Dera Ghāzikhān *see* Dera Ghāzi Khān
149 S8 **Dera Ismāīl Khān** North-West Frontier Province, C Pakistan 31°51´N 70°56´E
149 Q12 **Dera Murād Jamāli** Baluchistān, SW Pakistan 28°34´N 68°12´E
113 L16 **Đeravica** ▲ S Serbia 42°33´N 20°08´E
116 L6 **Derazhnya** Khmel'nyts'ka Oblast', W Ukraine 49°16´N 27°24´E
127 R17 **Derbent** Respublika Dagestan, SW Russian Federation 42°01´N 48°16´E
147 N13 **Derbent** Surkhondaryo Viloyati, S Uzbekistan 38°15´N 66°59´E
Derbisīye *see* Darbāsīyah
79 M15 **Derbissaka** Mbomou, SE Central African Republic 05°43´N 24°48´E
180 L4 **Derby** Western Australia 17°18´S 123°37´E
97 M19 **Derby** C England, United Kingdom 52°55´N 01°30´W
27 N7 **Derby** Kansas, C USA 37°33´N 97°16´W
97 L18 **Derbyshire** *cultural region* C England, United Kingdom
112 O11 **Đerdap** *physical region* E Serbia
Derelí *see* Gónnoi
162 L9 **Deren** *var.* Tsant. Dundgovĭ, C Mongolia 46°16´N 106°55´E
171 W13 **Derew** ≈ Papua, E Indonesia
127 R8 **Dergachi** Saratovskaya Oblast', W Russian Federation 51°15´N 48°58´E
Dergachi *see* Derhachi
97 C19 **Derg, Lough** *Ir.* Loch Deirgeirt. ◎ W Ireland
117 V5 **Derhachi** *Rus.* Dergachi. Kharkivs'ka Oblast', E Ukraine 50°09´N 36°11´E
22 G8 **De Ridder** Louisiana, S USA 30°51´N 93°18´W
137 P16 **Derik** Mardin, SE Turkey 37°22´N 40°16´E
83 E20 **Derm** Hardap, C Namibia 23°38´S 18°12´E
144 M14 **Dermentobe** *prev.* Dyurment'yube. Kzyl-Orda, S Kazakhstan 45°46´N 63°42´E
27 W14 **Dermott** Arkansas, C USA 33°31´N 91°26´W
Dérna *see* Darnah
Dernberg, Cape *see* Dolphin Head
22 J11 **Dernieres, Isles** *island group* Louisiana, S USA
102 I4 **Déroute, Passage de la** *strait* Channel Islands/France
Derrá *see* Dar'ā
Derry *see* Londonderry
Dertona *see* Tortona
Dertosa *see* Tortosa
80 H8 **Derudeb** Red Sea, NE Sudan 17°31´N 36°07´E
112 H10 **Derventa** Republika Srpska, N Bosnia and Herzegovina 44°57´N 17°55´E
183 O16 **Derwent Bridge** Tasmania, SE Australia 42°10´S 146°13´E
183 O17 **Derwent, River** ≈ Tasmania, SE Australia
146 F10 **Derweze** *Rus.* Darvaza. Ahal Welaýaty, C Turkmenistan 40°10´N 58°27´E
Deržavinsk *see* Derzhavinsk
145 O9 **Derzhavinsk** *var.* Deržavinsk. ◈ Akmola, C Kazakhstan
Dés *see* Dej
57 J18 **Desaguadero** Puno, S Peru 16°35´S 69°05´W
57 J18 **Desaguadero, Río** ≈ Bolivia/Peru
191 W9 **Désappointement, Îles du** *island group* Îles Tuamotu, C French Polynesia
27 W11 **Des Arc** Arkansas, C USA 34°58´N 91°30´W
14 C10 **Desbarats** Ontario, S Canada 46°20´N 83°52´W
62 H13 **Descabezado Grande, Volcán** △ C Chile 35°34´S 70°40´W
40 B2 **Descanso** Baja California Norte, NW Mexico 32°08´N 116°51´W
102 L9 **Descartes** Indre-et-Loire, C France 46°58´N 00°40´E
11 T13 **Deschambault Lake** ◎ Saskatchewan, C Canada
Deschnaer Koppe *see* Velká Deštná
32 I11 **Deschutes River** ≈ Oregon, NW USA
80 J12 **Desē** *var.* Desse, *It.* Dessie. Āmara, N Ethiopia 11°02´N 39°39´E
63 I20 **Deseado, Río** ≈ S Argentina
106 F8 **Desenzano del Garda** Lombardia, N Italy 45°28´N 10°31´E
36 K3 **Deseret Peak** ▲ Utah, W USA 40°27´N 112°37´W
64 P6 **Deserta Grande** *island* Madeira, Portugal, NE Atlantic Ocean
64 P6 **Desertas, Ilhas** *island group* Madeira, Portugal, NE Atlantic Ocean
35 X16 **Desert Center** California, W USA 33°42´N 115°22´W
35 V15 **Desert Hot Springs** California, W USA 33°57´N 116°33´W
14 K10 **Désert, Lac** ◎ Québec, SE Canada
36 J2 **Desert Peak** ▲ Utah, W USA 41°03´N 113°22´W
31 R11 **Deshler** Ohio, N USA 41°12´N 83°55´W
Deshu *see* Deh Shū
Desiderii Fanum *see* St-Dizier
106 D7 **Desio** Lombardia, N Italy 45°37´N 09°12´E
115 E15 **Deskáti** *var.* Dheskáti. Dytikí Makedonía, N Greece 39°55´N 21°49´E
28 L2 **Des Lacs River** ≈ North Dakota, N USA
27 X6 **Desloge** Missouri, C USA 37°52´N 90°31´W
11 Q12 **Desmarais** Alberta, W Canada 55°58´N 113°56´W
29 Q10 **De Smet** South Dakota, N USA 44°23´N 97°33´W
29 V14 **Des Moines** *state capital* Iowa, C USA 41°36´N 93°37´W
17 N9 **Des Moines River** ≈ C USA
117 P4 **Desna** ≈ Russian Federation/Ukraine
116 G14 **Desnățui** ≈ S Romania
63 F24 **Desolación, Isla** *island* S Chile
29 V14 **De Soto** Iowa, C USA 41°31´N 94°00´W
23 Q4 **De Soto Falls** *waterfall* Alabama, S USA
83 I25 **Despatch** Eastern Cape, S South Africa 33°48´S 25°28´E
105 N12 **Despeñaperros, Desfiladero de** *pass* S Spain
31 N10 **Des Plaines** Illinois, N USA 42°01´N 87°52´W
115 J21 **Despotikó** *island* Kykládes, Greece, Aegean Sea
112 N12 **Despotovac** Serbia, E Serbia 44°06´N 21°25´E
101 M14 **Dessau** Sachsen-Anhalt, E Germany 51°51´N 12°15´E
Desse *see* Desē
99 J16 **Dessel** Antwerpen, N Belgium 51°15´N 05°07´E
Dessie *see* Desē
Destêrro *see* Florianópolis
23 P9 **Destin** Florida, SE USA 30°23´N 86°30´W
Deštná *see* Velká Deštná
193 T10 **Desventurados, Islas de los** *island group* W Chile
103 N1 **Desvres** Pas-de-Calais, N France 50°41´N 01°48´E
116 E12 **Deta** *Ger.* Detta. Timiș, W Romania 45°24´N 21°14´E
101 H14 **Detmold** Nordrhein-Westfalen, W Germany 51°55´N 08°52´E
31 S10 **Detroit** Michigan, N USA 42°20´N 83°03´W
25 W5 **Detroit** Texas, SW USA 33°39´N 95°16´W
31 S10 **Detroit** ≈ Canada/USA
29 S6 **Detroit Lakes** Minnesota, N USA 46°49´N 95°49´W
31 S10 **Detroit Metropolitan** ✈ Michigan, N USA 42°12´N 83°16´W
Detta *see* Deta
167 S10 **Det Udom** Ubon Ratchathani, E Thailand 14°54´N 105°03´E
111 K20 **Detva** *Hung.* Gyeva. Bankobýstricky Kraj, C Slovakia 48°35´N 19°25´E
154 G13 **Deūlgaon Rāja** Mahārāshtra, C India 20°04´N 76°08´E
99 L15 **Deurne** Noord-Brabant, SE Netherlands 51°28´N 05°47´E
99 H16 **Deurne** ✈ (Antwerpen) Antwerpen, N Belgium 51°10´N 04°28´E
Deutsch-Brod *see* Havlíčkův Brod
Deutschendorf *see* Poprad
Deutsch-Eylau *see* Iława
109 Y6 **Deutschkreutz** Burgenland, E Austria 47°37´N 16°37´E
Deutsch Krone *see* Wałcz
Deutschland/Deutschland, Bundesrepublik *see* Germany
109 V9 **Deutschlandsberg** Steiermark, SE Austria 46°52´N 15°13´E
Deutsch-Südwestafrika *see* Namibia
109 Y3 **Deutsch-Wagram** Niederösterreich, E Austria 48°19´N 16°33´E
Deux-Ponts *see* Zweibrücken
14 I11 **Deux Rivieres** Ontario, SE Canada 46°13´N 78°16´W
102 K9 **Deux-Sèvres** ◈ *department* W France
116 G11 **Deva** *Ger.* Diemrich, *Hung.* Déva. Hunedoara, W Romania 45°55´N 22°55´E
Déva *see* Deva
Deva *see* Chester
Devana *see* Aberdeen
Devana Castra *see* Chester
Đevđelija *see* Gevgelija
136 L12 **Deveci Dağları** ▲▲ N Turkey
137 P15 **Devegeçidi Barajī** ▣ SE Turkey
136 K15 **Develi** Kayseri, C Turkey 38°22´N 35°28´E
98 M11 **Deventer** Overijssel, E Netherlands 52°15´N 06°10´E
15 O10 **Devenyns, Lac** ◎ Québec, SE Canada
96 K8 **Deveron** ≈ NE Scotland, United Kingdom
153 R14 **Devghar** *prev.* Deoghar. Jhārkhand, NE India
27 R10 **Devil's Den** *plateau* Arkansas, C USA
35 R7 **Devils Gate** *pass* California, W USA
30 J2 **Devils Island** *island* Apostle Islands, Wisconsin, N USA
Devil's Island *see* Diable, Île du
29 P3 **Devils Lake** North Dakota, N USA 48°08´N 98°50´W
31 R10 **Devils Lake** ◎ Michigan, N USA
29 O3 **Devils Lake** ◎ North Dakota, N USA
35 W13 **Devils Playground** *desert* California, W USA
25 O11 **Devils River** ≈ Texas, SW USA
33 Y12 **Devils Tower** ▲ Wyoming, C USA 44°33´N 104°45´W
114 I11 **Devin** *prev.* Dovlen. Smolyan, S Bulgaria 41°45´N 24°24´E
25 R12 **Devine** Texas, SW USA 29°08´N 98°54´W
152 H13 **Devli** Rājasthān, N India 25°47´N 75°23´E
Devne *see* Devnya
114 N8 **Devnya** *prev.* Devne. Varna, E Bulgaria 43°15´N 27°35´E
31 U14 **Devola** Ohio, N USA 39°28´N 81°28´W
Devoll *see* Devollit, Lumi i
113 M21 **Devollit, Lumi i** *var.* Devoll. ≈ SE Albania
11 Q14 **Devon** Alberta, SW Canada 53°21´N 113°47´W
97 I23 **Devon** *cultural region* SW England, United Kingdom
197 N10 **Devon Island** *prev.* North Devon Island. *island* Parry Islands, Nunavut, NE Canada
183 O16 **Devonport** Tasmania, SE Australia 41°14´S 146°21´E
136 H11 **Devrek** Zonguldak, N Turkey 41°14´N 31°57´E
154 G10 **Dewās** Madhya Pradesh, C India 22°59´N 76°03´E
De Westerein *see* Zwaagwesteinde
27 P8 **Dewey** Oklahoma, C USA 36°48´N 95°56´W
Dewey *see* Culebra
98 M8 **De Wijk** Drenthe, NE Netherlands 52°41´N 06°13´E
27 W12 **De Witt** Arkansas, C USA 34°17´N 91°21´W
29 Z14 **De Witt** Iowa, C USA 41°49´N 90°32´W
29 R16 **De Witt** Nebraska, C USA 40°23´N 96°55´W
97 M17 **Dewsbury** N England, United Kingdom 53°42´N 01°37´W
161 Q10 **Dexing** Jiangxi, S China 28°51´N 117°36´E
27 Y8 **Dexter** Missouri, C USA 36°48´N 89°57´W
37 U14 **Dexter** New Mexico, SW USA 33°12´N 104°25´W
160 I8 **Deyang** Sichuan, C China 31°08´N 104°23´E
182 C4 **Dey-Dey, Lake** *salt lake* South Australia
143 S7 **Deyhūk** Yazd, E Iran 33°18´N 57°30´E
Deynau *see* Galkynyș
Deyyer *see* Bandar-e Dayyer
142 L8 **Dezfūl** *var.* Dizful. Khūzestān, SW Iran 32°23´N 48°28´E
129 X4 **Dezhneva, Mys** *headland* NE Russian Federation 66°08´N 69°40´W
161 P4 **Dezhou** Shandong, E China 37°28´N 116°18´E
Dezhou *see* Dechang
Dezh Shāhpūr *see* Marīvān
Dhaalu Atoll *see* South Nilandhe Atoll
Dhahran *see* Aẓ Ẓahrān
Dhahran Al Khobar *see* Aẓ Ẓahrān al Khubar
153 U14 **Dhaka** *prev.* Dacca. ● (Bangladesh) Dhaka, C Bangladesh 23°42´N 90°22´E
153 T15 **Dhaka** ◈ *division* C Bangladesh
Dhali *see* Idálion
Dhalli Rajhara *see* Dalli Rājhara
141 O15 **Dhamār** W Yemen 14°31´N 44°25´E
154 K12 **Dhamtari** Chhattīsgarh, C India 20°43´N 81°36´E
153 Q15 **Dhanbād** Jhārkhand, NE India 23°48´N 86°27´E
152 L10 **Dhangaḍhi** *var.* Dhangarhi. Far Western, W Nepal 28°45´N 80°38´E
Dhangarhi *see* Dhangaḍhi
Dhank *see* Ḍank
153 R12 **Dhankuṭā** Eastern, E Nepal 27°06´N 87°21´E
152 I6 **Dhaola Dhār** ▲▲ NE India
154 F10 **Dhār** Madhya Pradesh, C India 22°32´N 75°24´E
153 R12 **Dharān** *var.* Dharan Bazar. Eastern, E Nepal 26°51´N 87°18´E
Dharan Bazar *see* Dharān
155 H21 **Dhārāpuram** Tamil Nādu, SE India 10°45´N 77°33´E
155 H20 **Dharmapuri** Tamil Nādu, SE India 12°11´N 78°07´E
155 H18 **Dharmavaram** Andhra Pradesh, E India 14°27´N 77°44´E
154 M11 **Dharmjaygarh** Chhattīsgarh, C India 22°27´N 83°16´E
Dharmsāla *see* Dharmshāla
152 I7 **Dharmshāla** *prev.* Dharmsāla. Himāchal Pradesh, N India 32°14´N 76°24´E
155 F17 **Dhārwād** *prev.* Dharwar. Karnātaka, SW India 15°30´N 75°04´E
Dharwar *see* Dhārwād
Dhaulagiri *see* Dhawalāgiri
152 J12 **Dhaulpur** *var.* Daulpur, Dholpur. Rājasthān, N India 26°43´N 77°54´E
153 O10 **Dhawalāgiri** *var.* Dhaulagiri. ▲ C Nepal 28°45´N 83°27´E
81 L18 **Dheere Laaq** *var.* Lak Dera, *It.* Lach Dera. *seasonal river* Kenya/Somalia
121 Q3 **Dhekeleia Sovereign Base Area** *UK military installation* E Cyprus34°59´N 33°45´E
121 Q3 **Dhekélia** *Eng.* Dhekelia, *Gk.* Dekéleia. *UK air base* SE Cyprus35°00´N 33°45´E *see* Dhekélia
Dhelvinákion *see* Delvináki
113 M22 **Dhëmbelit, Majae** ▲ S Albania 40°10´N 20°22´E
154 O12 **Dhenkānāl** Orissa, E India 20°40´N 85°36´E
Dheskáti *see* Deskáti
138 G11 **Dhībān** Ma'dabā, NW Jordan 31°30´N 35°47´E
Dhidhimótikhon *see* Didymóteicho
Dhíkti Ori *see* Díkti
153 V12 **Dhing** Assam, NE India 26°26´N 92°29´E
139 W12 **Dhī Qār** ◈ *governorate* SE Iraq
138 I12 **Dhirwah, Wādī adh** *dry watercourse* C Jordan
Dhístomon *see* Dístomo
Dhodhekánisos *see* Dodekánisa
Dhodhóni *see* Dodóni
Dhofar *see* Ẓufār
Dholpur *see* Dhaulpur
Dhomokós *see* Domokós
Dhond *see* Daund
155 H17 **Dhone** Andhra Pradesh, C India 15°25´N 77°52´E
154 B11 **Dhorāji** Gujarāt, W India 21°44´N 70°27´E
Dhráma *see* Dráma
154 C10 **Dhrāngadhra** Gujarāt, W India 22°59´N 71°32´E
Dhrepanon, Akrotírio *see* Drépano, Akrotírio
153 T13 **Dhuburi** Assam, NE India 26°06´N 89°55´E
154 F12 **Dhule** *prev.* Dhulia. Mahārāshtra, C India 20°54´N 74°47´E
Dhulia *see* Dhule
Dhún Dealgan, Cuan *see* Dundalk Bay
Dhún Droma, Cuan *see* Dundrum Bay
Dhún na nGall, Bá *see* Donegal Bay
Dhū Shaykh *see* Qazānīyah
80 Q13 **Dhuudo** Bari, NE Somalia 09°21´N 50°19´E
81 N15 **Dhuusa Marreeb** *var.* Dusa Marreb, *It.* Dusa Mareb. Galguduud, C Somalia 05°33´N 46°24´E
115 J24 **Día** *island* SE Greece
55 Y9 **Diable, Île du** *var.* Devil's Island. *island* N French Guiana
15 N12 **Diable, Rivière du** ≈ Québec, SE Canada
35 N8 **Diablo, Mount** ▲ California, W USA 37°52´N 121°57´W
35 O9 **Diablo Range** ▲▲ California, W USA
24 I8 **Diablo, Sierra** ▲▲ Texas, SW USA
45 O11 **Diablotins, Morne** ▲ N Dominica 15°30´N 61°23´W
77 N11 **Diafarabé** Mopti, C Mali 14°09´N 05°01´W
77 N11 **Diaka** ≈ SW Mali
Diakovár *see* Đakovo
76 I12 **Dialakoto** S Senegal 13°21´N 13°19´W
61 B18 **Diamante** Entre Ríos, E Argentina 32°05´S 60°40´W
62 I12 **Diamante, Río** ≈ C Argentina
59 M19 **Diamantina** Minas Gerais, SE Brazil 18°17´S 43°37´W
59 N17 **Diamantina, Chapada** ▲▲ E Brazil
173 U11 **Diamantina Fracture Zone** *tectonic feature* E Indian Ocean
181 T8 **Diamantina River** ≈ Queensland/South Australia
38 D9 **Diamond Head** *headland* O'ahu, Hawai'i, USA 21°15´N 157°48´W
37 P2 **Diamond Peak** ▲ Colorado, C USA 40°56´N 108°56´W
35 W5 **Diamond Peak** ▲ Nevada, W USA 39°34´N 115°46´W
Diamond State *see* Delaware
76 J11 **Diamou** Kayes, SW Mali 14°04´N 11°16´W
95 I23 **Dianalund** Vestsjælland, C Denmark 55°32´N 11°30´E
65 G25 **Diana's Peak** ▲ C Saint Helena
160 M16 **Dianbai** *var.* Shuidong. Guangdong, S China 21°30´N 111°05´E
160 G13 **Dian Chi** ▣ SW China
106 B10 **Diano Marina** Liguria, NW Italy 43°55´N 08°06´E
163 V11 **Diaobingshan** *var.* Tiefa. Liaoning, NE China 42°25´N 123°39´E
77 R13 **Diapaga** E Burkina 12°09´N 01°48´E
Diarbekr *see* Diyarbakır
107 J15 **Diavolo, Passo del** *pass* C Italy
61 B18 **Díaz** Santa Fe, C Argentina 32°22´S 61°05´W
141 W6 **Dibā al Ḥiṣn** *var.* Dibāh, Dibba. Ash Shāriqah, NE United Arab Emirates 25°35´N 56°16´E
139 S3 **Dībaga** Arbīl, N Iraq 35°51´N 43°49´E
Dibāh *see* Dibā al Ḥiṣn
79 L22 **Dibaya** Kasai-Occidental, S Dem. Rep. Congo 06°31´S 22°57´E
Dibba *see* Dibā al Ḥiṣn
195 W15 **Dibble Iceberg Tongue** *ice feature* Antarctica
113 L19 **Dibër** ◈ *district* E Albania
83 I20 **Dibete** Central, SE Botswana 23°45´S 26°26´E
Dibio *see* Dijon
25 W9 **Diboll** Texas, SW USA 31°11´N 94°46´W
Dibra *see* Debar
153 X11 **Dibrugarh** Assam, NE India 27°29´N 94°49´E
54 G4 **Dibulla** La Guajira, N Colombia 11°14´N 73°22´W
25 O5 **Dickens** Texas, SW USA 33°38´N 100°51´W
19 R2 **Dickey** Maine, NE USA 47°04´N 69°05´W
30 K9 **Dickeyville** Wisconsin, N USA 42°37´N 90°36´W
28 K5 **Dickinson** North Dakota, N USA 46°54´N 102°48´W
0 E6 **Dickins Seamount** *undersea feature* NE Pacific Ocean 54°30´N 137°00´W
27 O13 **Dickson** Oklahoma, C USA 34°11´N 96°58´W
20 I9 **Dickson** Tennessee, S USA 36°04´N 87°23´W
Dicle *see* Tigris
Dicsőszentmárton *see* Târnăveni
98 M12 **Didam** Gelderland, E Netherlands 51°56´N 06°08´E
163 Y8 **Didao** Heilongjiang, NE China 45°22´N 130°48´E
76 L12 **Didiéni** Koulikoro, W Mali 13°48´N 08°01´W
Didimo *see* Dídymo
Didimotiho *see* Didymóteicho
81 K17 **Didimtu** *spring/well* NE Kenya 02°58´N 40°07´E
67 U9 **Didinga Hills** ▲▲ S Sudan
11 Q16 **Didsbury** Alberta, SW Canada 51°39´N 114°09´W
152 G11 **Dīdwāna** Rājasthān, N India 27°23´N 74°36´E
115 G20 **Dídymo** *var.* Didimo. ▲ S Greece 37°28´N 23°12´E
114 L12 **Didymóteicho** *var.* Dhidhimótikhon, Didimotiho. Anatolikí Makedonía kai Thráki, NE Greece 41°22´N 26°29´E
103 S13 **Die** Drôme, E France 44°46´N 05°21´E
77 O13 **Diébougou** SW Burkina 11°00´N 03°12´W
Diedenhofen *see* Thionville
11 S16 **Diefenbaker, Lake** ▣ Saskatchewan, S Canada
62 H7 **Diego de Almagro** Atacama, N Chile 26°24´S 70°10´W
63 F23 **Diego de Almagro, Isla** *island* S Chile
61 A20 **Diego de Alvear** Santa Fe, C Argentina 34°25´S 62°10´W
173 Q7 **Diego Garcia** *island* S British Indian Ocean Territory
Diégo-Suarez *see* Antsirañana
99 M23 **Diekirch** Diekirch, C Luxembourg 49°52´N 06°10´E
99 L23 **Diekirch** ◈ *district* N Luxembourg
76 K11 **Diéma** Kayes, W Mali 14°30´N 09°12´W
101 H15 **Diemel** ≈ W Germany
98 I10 **Diemen** Noord-Holland, C Netherlands 52°21´N 04°58´E
Diemrich *see* Deva
167 R6 **Điên Biên** *var.* Bien Bien, Dien Bien Phu. Lai Châu, N Vietnam 21°23´N 103°02´E
Dien Bien Phu *see* Điên Biên
167 S7 **Diên Châu** Nghê An, N Vietnam 18°54´N 105°35´E
99 K18 **Diepenbeek** Limburg, NE Belgium 50°54´N 05°25´E
98 N11 **Diepenheim** Overijssel, E Netherlands 52°10´N 06°37´E
98 M10 **Diepenveen** Overijssel, E Netherlands 52°18´N 06°09´E
100 G12 **Diepholz** Niedersachsen, NW Germany 52°36´N 08°23´E
102 M3 **Dieppe** Seine-Maritime, N France 49°55´N 01°05´E
98 M12 **Dieren** Gelderland, E Netherlands 52°03´N 06°06´E
27 S13 **Dierks** Arkansas, C USA 34°07´N 94°01´W
99 J17 **Diest** Vlaams Brabant, C Belgium 50°58´N 05°03´E
108 F7 **Dietikon** Zürich, NW Switzerland 47°24´N 08°25´E
103 R13 **Dieulefit** Drôme, E France 44°30´N 05°01´E
103 T5 **Dieuze** Moselle, NE France 48°49´N 06°41´E
119 H15 **Dieveniškės** Vilnius, SE Lithuania 54°12´N 25°38´E
98 N7 **Diever** Drenthe, NE Netherlands 52°49´N 06°19´E
101 F17 **Diez** Rheinland-Pfalz, W Germany 50°22´N 08°01´E
77 Y12 **Diffa** Diffa, SE Niger 13°19´N 12°37´E
77 Y10 **Diffa** ◈ *department* SE Niger
99 L25 **Differdange** Luxembourg, SW Luxembourg 49°32´N 05°53´E
13 O16 **Digby** Nova Scotia, SE Canada 44°37´N 65°47´W
26 J5 **Dighton** Kansas, C USA 38°28´N 100°28´W
Dignano d'Istria *see* Vodnjan
103 T14 **Digne** *var.* Digne-les-Bains. Alpes-de-Haute-Provence, SE France 44°05´N 06°14´E
Digne-les-Bains *see* Digne
Digoel *see* Digul, Sungai
103 Q10 **Digoin** Saône-et-Loire, C France 46°30´N 04°E
171 Q8 **Digos** Mindanao, S Philippines 06°46´N 125°21´E
149 Q16 **Digri** Sind, SE Pakistan 25°11´N 69°10´E
171 Y14 **Digul Barat, Sungai** ≈ Papua, E Indonesia
171 Y15 **Digul, Sungai** *prev.* Digoel. ≈ Papua, E Indonesia
171 Z14 **Digul Timur, Sungai** ≈ Papua, E Indonesia
153 X10 **Dihāng** ≈ NE India
Dihang *see* Brahmaputra
Dihōk *see* Dahūk
81 L17 **Diinsoor** Bay, S Somalia 02°28´N 43°00´E
Dijlah *see* Tigris
99 H17 **Dijle** ≈ C Belgium
103 R8 **Dijon** *anc.* Dibio. Côte d'Or, C France 47°21´N 05°04´E
93 H14 **Dikanäs** Västerbotten, N Sweden 65°15´N 16°00´E
80 L12 **Dikhil** SW Djibouti 11°08´N 42°19´E
136 B13 **Dikili** İzmir, W Turkey 39°05´N 26°52´E
99 B17 **Diksmuide** *var.* Dixmuide, *Fr.* Dixmude. West-Vlaanderen, W Belgium 51°02´N 02°52´E
122 K7 **Dikson** Taymyrskiy (Dolgano-Nenetskiy) Avtonomnyy Okrug, N Russian Federation 73°30´N 80°35´E
115 K25 **Díkti** *var.* Dhíkti Ori. ▲▲ Kríti, Greece, E Mediterranean Sea
77 Z13 **Dikwa** Borno, NE Nigeria 12°00´N 13°57´E
81 J15 **Dīla** Southern Nationalities, S Ethiopia 06°19´N 38°16´E
99 G18 **Dilbeek** Vlaams Brabant, C Belgium 50°51´N 04°16´E
171 Q16 **Dili** *var.* Dilli, Dilly. ● (East Timor) N East Timor 08°33´S 125°34´E
77 Y11 **Dilia** *var.* Dillia. ≈ SE Niger
Dilijan *see* Delījān
167 U13 **Di Linh** Lâm Đông, S Vietnam 11°38´N 108°07´E
101 G16 **Dillenburg** Hessen, W Germany 50°45´N 08°16´E
25 Q13 **Dilley** Texas, SW USA 28°40´N 99°10´W
Dilli *see* Dili, East Timor
Dilli *see* Delhi, India
Dillia *see* Dilia
80 E11 **Dilling** *var.* Ad Dalanj. Southern Kordofan, C Sudan 12°02´N 29°41´E
101 D20 **Dillingen** Saarland, SW Germany 49°20´N 06°43´E
Dillingen *see* Dillingen an der Donau
101 J22 **Dillingen an der Donau** *var.* Dillingen. Bayern, S Germany 48°34´N 10°29´E
39 O13 **Dillingham** Alaska, USA 59°03´N 158°30´W
33 Q12 **Dillon** Montana, NW USA 45°14´N 112°38´W
21 T12 **Dillon** South Carolina, SE USA 34°25´N 79°22´W
31 T13 **Dillon Lake** ▣ Ohio, N USA
Dilly *see* Dili
Dilman *see* Salmās
79 K24 **Dilolo** Katanga, S Dem. Rep. Congo 10°42´S 22°21´E
115 J20 **Dílos** *island* Kykládes, Greece, Aegean Sea
141 Y11 **Ḍil', Ra's aḍ** *headland* E Oman 19°12´N 57°53´E
29 R5 **Dilworth** Minnesota, N USA 46°53´N 96°38´W
138 H7 **Dimashq** *var.* Ash Shām, Esh Sham, *Eng.* Damascus, *Fr.* Damas, *It.* Damasco. ● Dimashq, SW Syria 33°30´N 36°19´E
138 I8 **Dimashq** *off.* Muḥāfaẓat Dimashq, *var.* Damascus, *Ar.* Ash Sham, Ash Shām, Damasco, Esh Sham, *Fr.* Damas. ◈ *governorate* S Syria
138 I7 **Dimashq** ✈ Dimashq, S Syria 33°30´N 36°19´E
Dimashq, Muḥāfaẓat *see* Dimashq
79 L21 **Dimbelenge** Kasai-Occidental, C Dem. Rep. Congo 05°36´S 23°04´E
77 N16 **Dimbokro** E Ivory Coast 06°43´N 04°46´W
182 L11 **Dimboola** Victoria, SE Australia 36°29´S 142°03´E
Dîmbovița *see* Dâmbovița
Dimitrov *see* Dymytrov
114 K11 **Dimitrovgrad** Khaskovo, S Bulgaria 42°03´N 25°36´E
127 R5 **Dimitrovgrad** Ul'yanovskaya Oblast', W Russian Federation 54°14´N 49°37´E
113 Q15 **Dimitrovgrad** *prev.* Caribrod. Serbia, SE Serbia 43°01´N 22°46´E
Dimitrovo *see* Pernik
Dimlang *see* Vogel Peak
24 M3 **Dimmitt** Texas, SW USA 34°32´N 102°20´W
114 F7 **Dimovo** Vidin, NW Bulgaria 43°46´N 22°47´E
59 A16 **Dimpolis** Acre, W Brazil 09°52´S 71°51´W
115 O23 **Dimyliá** Ródos, Dodekánisa, Greece, Aegean Sea 36°17´N 27°59´E
171 Q6 **Dinagat Island** *island* S Philippines
153 S13 **Dinajpur** Rajshahi, NW Bangladesh 25°38´N 88°40´E
102 I6 **Dinan** Côtes d'Armor, NW France 48°27´N 02°02´W
99 I21 **Dinant** Namur, S Belgium 50°16´N 04°55´E
136 E15 **Dinar** Afyon, SW Turkey 38°05´N 30°09´E
112 F13 **Dinara** ▲ W Croatia 43°49´N 16°42´E
Dinara *see* Dinaric Alps
102 I5 **Dinard** Ille-et-Vilaine, NW France 48°38´N 02°04´W
112 F13 **Dinaric Alps** *var.* Dinara. ▲▲ Bosnia and Herzegovina/Croatia
143 N10 **Dīnār, Kūh-e** ▲ C Iran 30°51´N 51°36´E
Dinbych *see* Denbigh
155 H22 **Dindigul** Tamil Nādu, SE India 10°23´N 78°E
83 M19 **Dindiza** Gaza, S Mozambique 23°22´S 33°28´E
79 H21 **Dinga** Bandundu, SW Dem. Rep. Congo 05°00´S 16°29´E
149 V7 **Dinga** Punjab, E Pakistan 32°38´N 73°45´E
Dingchang *see* Qinxian
158 L16 **Dinggyê** *var.* Gyangkar. Xizang Zizhiqu, W China 28°18´N 88°06´E
97 A20 **Dingle** *Ir.* An Daingean. SW Ireland 52°09´N 10°16´W
97 A20 **Dingle Bay** *Ir.* Bá an Daingin. *bay* SW Ireland
18 I13 **Dingmans Ferry** Pennsylvania, NE USA 41°12´N 74°51´W
101 N22 **Dingolfing** Bayern, SE Germany 48°37´N 12°28´E
171 O1 **Dingras** Luzon, N Philippines 18°06´N 120°43´E
76 J13 **Dinguiraye** N Guinea 11°19´N 10°49´W
96 I8 **Dingwall** N Scotland, United Kingdom 57°36´N 04°26´W
159 V10 **Dingxi** Gansu, C China 35°36´N 104°33´E
Ding Xian *see* Dingzhou
161 Q7 **Dingyuan** Anhui, E China 32°30´N 117°40´E
161 O3 **Dingzhou** *prev.* Ding Xian. Hebei, E China 38°31´N 114°52´E
167 U6 **Đinh Lâp** Lang Sơn, N Vietnam 21°33´N 107°03´E
167 T13 **Đinh Quan** *var.* Tân Phu. Đông Nai, S Vietnam 11°11´N 107°20´E
100 E13 **Dinkel** ≈ Germany/Netherlands
101 J21 **Dinkelsbühl** Bayern, S Germany 49°06´N 10°18´E
101 D14 **Dinslaken** Nordrhein-Westfalen, W Germany 51°34´N 06°43´E
35 R11 **Dinuba** California, W USA 36°32´N 119°23´W
21 W7 **Dinwiddie** Virginia, NE USA 37°02´N 77°40´W
98 N13 **Dinxperlo** Gelderland, E Netherlands 51°51´N 06°30´E
Dio *see* Díon
Diófás *see* Nucet
76 M12 **Dioïla** Koulikoro, W Mali 12°28´N 06°43´W
115 F14 **Díon** *var.* Dio; *anc.* Dium. *site of ancient city* Kentrikí Makedonía, N Greece
115 G19 **Dióryga Korinthou** *Eng.* Corinth Canal. *canal* S Greece
76 G12 **Diouloulou** SW Senegal 13°00´N 16°34´W
77 N11 **Dioura** Mopti, W Mali 14°48´N 05°20´W
76 G11 **Diourbel** W Senegal 14°39´N 16°12´W
152 L10 **Dipāyal** Far Western, W Nepal 29°09´N 80°46´E
121 R1 **Dipkarpaz** *Gk.* Rizokarpaso, Rizokárpason. NE Cyprus 35°36´N 34°23´E
149 R17 **Diplo** Sind, SE Pakistan 24°29´N 69°36´E
171 P7 **Dipolog** *var.* Dipolog City. Mindanao, S Philippines 08°31´N 123°20´E
Dipolog City *see* Dipolog
185 C23 **Dipton** Southland, South Island, New Zealand 45°55´S 168°21´E
149 T4 **Dīr** North-West Frontier Province, N Pakistan 35°12´N 71°53´E
77 O10 **Diré** Tombouctou, C Mali 16°12´N 03°31´W
80 L13 **Dirē Dawa** Dirē Dawa, E Ethiopia 09°35´N 41°53´E
Dirfis *see* Dírfys
115 H18 **Dírfys** *var.* Dirfis. ▲▲ Évvioa, C Greece
75 N9 **Dirj** *var.* Daraj, Darj. W Libya 30°09´N 10°26´E
180 G10 **Dirk Hartog Island** *island* Western Australia
77 Y8 **Dirkou** Agadez, NE Niger 18°45´N 13°00´E
181 X11 **Dirranbandi** Queensland, E Australia 28°37´S 148°13´E
81 O16 **Dirri** Galguduud, C Somalia 04°15´N 46°31´E
Dirschau *see* Tczew
37 N6 **Dirty Devil River** ≈ Utah, W USA
32 E10 **Disappointment, Cape** *headland* Washington, NW USA 46°16´N 124°06´W
180 L8 **Disappointment, Lake** *salt lake* Western Australia
183 R12 **Disaster Bay** *bay* New South Wales, SE Australia
44 J11 **Discovery Bay** C Jamaica 18°27´N 77°24´W
182 K13 **Discovery Bay** *inlet* SE Australia
67 Y15 **Discovery II Fracture Zone** *tectonic feature* SW Indian Ocean
Discovery Seamount/Discovery Seamounts *see* Discovery Tablemounts
65 O19 **Discovery Tablemounts** *var.* Discovery Seamount, Discovery Seamounts. *undersea feature* SW Atlantic Ocean 42°00´S 00°10´E
108 G9 **Disentis** *Rmsch.* Mustér. Graubünden, S Switzerland 46°43´N 08°52´E
39 O10 **Dishna River** ≈ Alaska, USA
Disko Bugt *see* Qeqertarsuup Tunua
195 X4 **Dismal Mountains** ▲▲ Antarctica
28 M14 **Dismal River** ≈ Nebraska, C USA
Disna *see* Dzisna
99 L19 **Dison** Liège, E Belgium 50°37´N 05°52´E
153 V12 **Dispur** *state capital* Assam, NE India 26°03´N 91°52´E
15 R11 **Disraeli** Québec, SE Canada 45°58´N 71°21´W
115 F18 **Dístomo** *prev.* Dhístomon. Stereá Ellás, C Greece 38°25´N 22°40´E
Dístos, Límni *see* Dýstos, Límni
59 L18 **Distrito Federal** *Eng.* Federal District. ◈ *federal district* C Brazil
41 P14 **Distrito Federal** ◈ *federal district* S Mexico
54 L4 **Distrito Federal** *off.* Territorio Distrito Federal. ◈ *federal district* N Venezuela
Distrito Federal, Territorio *see* Distrito Federal
116 J10 **Ditrău** *Hung.* Ditró. Harghita, C Romania 46°49´N 25°31´E
Ditró *see* Ditrău
154 B12 **Diu** Damān and Diu, W India 20°42´N 70°59´E

◆ Country
● Country Capital
◇ Dependent Territory
○ Dependent Territory Capital
◈ Administrative Regions
✈ International Airport
▲ Mountain
▲▲ Mountain Range
△ Volcano
≈ River
◎ Lake
▣ Reservoir

Dium *see* Díon
109 *S13* **Divača** SW Slovenia *45°40′N 13°58′E*
142 *J5* **Dīvāndarreh** Kordestān, NW Iran *35°55′N 47°02′E*
102 *K5* **Dives** ≈ N France
Divichi *see* Däväçi
33 *Q11* **Divide** Montana, NW USA *45°44′N 112°47′W*
Divin *see* Dzivin
83 *N18* **Divinhe** Sofala, E Mozambique *20°41′S 34°46′E*
59 *L20* **Divinópolis** Minas Gerais, SE Brazil *20°08′S 44°55′W*
127 *N13* **Divnoye** Stavropol'skiy Kray, SW Russian Federation *45°54′N 43°18′E*
76 *M17* **Divo** S Ivory Coast *05°50′N 05°22′W*
Divodurum Mediomatricum *see* Metz
137 *N13* **Divriği** Sivas, C Turkey *39°23′N 38°06′E*
Diwaniyah *see* Ad Dīwānīyah
14 *J10* **Dix Milles, Lac** ◎ Québec, SE Canada
14 *M8* **Dix Milles, Lac des** ◎ Québec, SE Canada
Dixmude/Dixmuide *see* Diksmuide
35 *N7* **Dixon** California, W USA *38°19′N 121°49′W*
30 *L10* **Dixon** Illinois, N USA *41°51′N 89°26′W*
20 *I6* **Dixon** Kentucky, S USA *37°30′N 87°39′W*
27 *V6* **Dixon** Missouri, C USA *37°59′N 92°05′W*
37 *S9* **Dixon** New Mexico, SW USA *36°10′N 105°49′W*
39 *Y15* **Dixon Entrance** *strait* Canada/USA
18 *D14* **Dixonville** Pennsylvania, NE USA *40°43′N 79°01′W*
137 *T13* **Diyadin** Ağrı, E Turkey *39°33′N 43°41′E*
Diyālá, Nahr *see* Sīrvān, Rūdkhāneh-ye
139 *V5* **Diyālá, Sirwan Nahr** *var.* Rudkhaneh-ye Sīrvān, Sīrwān. ≈ Iran/Iraq *see also* Sīrvān, Rudkhaneh-ye
137 *P15* **Diyarbakır** *var.* Diarbekr; *anc.* Amida. Diyarbakır, SE Turkey *37°55′N 40°14′E*
137 *P15* **Diyarbakır** *var.* Diarbekr. ◈ *province* SE Turkey
Dizful *see* Dezfūl
79 *F16* **Dja** ≈ SE Cameroon
Djadié *see* Zadié
77 *X7* **Djado** Agadez, NE Niger *21°00′N 12°11′E*
77 *X6* **Djado, Plateau du** ▲▲ NE Niger
Djailolo *see* Halmahera, Pulau
Djajapura *see* Jayapura
Djakarta *see* Jakarta
Djakovo *see* Đakovo
79 *G20* **Djambala** Plateaux, C Congo *02°32′S 14°43′E*
Djambi *see* Jambi
Djambi *see* Hari, Batang
74 *M9* **Djanet** E Algeria *28°43′N 08°57′E*
74 *M11* **Djanet** *prev.* Fort Charlet. SE Algeria *24°34′N 09°33′E*
Djaul *see* Dyaul Island
Djawa *see* Jawa
Djéblé *see* Jablah
78 *I10* **Djédaa** Batha, C Chad *13°31′N 18°34′E*
74 *J6* **Djelfa** *var.* El Djelfa. N Algeria *34°43′N 03°14′E*
79 *M14* **Djéma** Haut-Mbomou, E Central African Republic *06°04′N 25°20′E*
Djember *see* Jember
Djeneponto *see* Jeneponto
77 *N12* **Djenné** *var.* Jenné. Mopti, C Mali *13°55′N 04°31′W*
Djérablous *see* Jarābulus
Djerba *see* Jerba, Île de
79 *F15* **Djérem** ≈ C Cameroon
Djevdjelija *see* Gevgelija
77 *P11* **Djibo** N Burkina *14°09′N 01°38′W*
80 *L12* **Djibouti** *var.* Jibuti. ● (Djibouti) E Djibouti *11°33′N 42°55′E*
80 *L12* **Djibouti** *off.* Republic of Djibouti, *var.* Jibuti; *prev.* French Somaliland, French Territory of the Afars and Issas, *Fr.* Côte Française des Somalis, Territoire Français des Afars et des Issas. ◆ *republic* E Africa
80 *L12* **Djibouti** ✈ C Djibouti *11°29′N 42°54′E*
Djibouti, Republic of *see* Djibouti
Djidjel/Djidjelli *see* Jijel
55 *W10* **Djoemoe** Sipaliwini, C Surinam *04°00′N 55°27′W*
Djokjakarta *see* Yogyakarta
79 *K21* **Djoku-Punda** Kasai-Occidental, S Dem. Rep. Congo *05°27′S 20°58′E*
79 *K18* **Djolu** Equateur, N Dem. Rep. Congo *0°35′N 22°30′E*
Djombang *see* Jombang
Ďjorče Petrov *see* Đorče Petrov
79 *F17* **Djoua** ≈ Congo/Gabon
77 *R14* **Djougou** W Benin *09°42′N 01°38′E*
79 *F16* **Djoum** Sud, S Cameroon *02°38′N 12°51′E*
78 *I8* **Djourab, Erg du** *desert* N Chad
79 *P17* **Djugu** Orientale, NE Dem. Rep. Congo *01°55′N 30°31′E*
Djumbir *see* Ďumbier
92 *L3* **Djúpivogur** Austurland, SE Iceland *64°40′N 14°18′W*
94 *L13* **Djura** Dalarna, C Sweden *60°37′N 15°00′E*
Djurdjevac *see* Đurđevac
D'Kar *see* Dekar
197 *U6* **Dmitriya Lapteva, Proliv** *strait* N Russian Federation
126 *J7* **Dmitriyev-L'govskiy** Kurskaya Oblast', W Russian Federation *52°08′N 35°09′E*
Dmitriyevsk *see* Makiyivka
126 *K3* **Dmitrov** Moskovskaya Oblast', W Russian Federation *56°23′N 37°30′E*
Dmitrovichi *see* Dzmitravichy
126 *J6* **Dmitrovsk-Orlovskiy** Orlovskaya Oblast', W Russian Federation *52°28′N 35°01′E*
117 *R3* **Dmytrivka** Chernihivs'ka Oblast', N Ukraine *50°56′N 32°57′E*
Dnepr *see* Dnieper
Dneprodzerzhinsk *see* Romaniv
Dneprodzerzhinskoye Vodokhranilishche *see* Dniprodzerzhyns'ke Vodoskhovyshche
Dnepropetrovsk *see* Dnipropetrovs'k
Dnepropetrovskaya Oblast' *see* Dnipropetrovs'ka Oblast'
Dneprorudnoye *see* Dniprorudne
Dneprovskiy Liman *see* Dniprovs'kyy Lyman
Dneprovsko-Bugskiy Kanal *see* Dnyaprowska-Buhski Kanal
Dnestr *see* Dniester
Dnestrovskiy Liman *see* Dnistrovs'kyy Lyman
86 *H11* **Dnieper** *Bel.* Dnyapro, *Rus.* Dnepr, *Ukr.* Dnipro. ≈ E Europe
117 *P3* **Dnieper Lowland** *Bel.* Prydnyaprowskaya Nizina, *Ukr.* Prydniprovs'ka Nyzovyna. *lowlands* Belarus/Ukraine
116 *M8* **Dniester** *Rom.* Nistru, *Rus.* Dnestr, *Ukr.* Dnister; *anc.* Tyras. ≈ Moldova/Ukraine
Dnipro *see* Dnieper
Dniprodzerzhyns'k *see* Romaniv
117 *T7* **Dniprodzerzhyns'ke Vodoskhovyshche** *Rus.* Dneprodzerzhinskoye Vodokhranilishche. ⊠ C Ukraine
117 *U7* **Dnipropetrovs'k** *Rus.* Dnepropetrovsk; *prev.* Yekaterinoslav. Dnipropetrovs'ka Oblast', E Ukraine *48°28′N 35°E*
117 *U8* **Dnipropetrovs'k** ✈ Dnipropetrovs'ka Oblast', S Ukraine *48°20′N 35°04′E*
Dnipropetrovs'k *see* Dnipropetrovs'ka Oblast'
117 *T7* **Dnipropetrovs'ka Oblast'** *var.* Dnipropetrovs'k, *Rus.* Dnepropetrovskaya Oblast'. ◈ *province* E Ukraine
117 *U9* **Dniprorudne** *Rus.* Dneprorudnoye. Zaporiz'ka Oblast', SE Ukraine *47°21′N 35°00′E*
117 *Q11* **Dniprovs'kyy Lyman** *Rus.* Dneprovskiy Liman. *bay* S Ukraine
Dnister *see* Dniester
117 *O11* **Dnistrovs'kyy Lyman** *Rus.* Dnestrovskiy Liman. *inlet* S Ukraine
124 *G14* **Dno** Pskovskaya Oblast', W Russian Federation *57°48′N 29°58′E*
Dnyapro *see* Dnieper
119 *H20* **Dnyaprowska-Buhski Kanal** *Rus.* Dneprovsko-Bugskiy Kanal. *canal* SW Belarus
13 *O14* **Doaktown** New Brunswick, SE Canada *46°34′N 66°06′W*
78 *H13* **Doba** Logone-Oriental, S Chad *08°40′N 16°50′E*
118 *E9* **Dobele** *Ger.* Doblen. Dobele, W Latvia *56°36′N 23°14′E*
101 *N16* **Döbeln** Sachsen, E Germany *51°07′N 13°07′E*
171 *U12* **Doberai, Jazirah** *Dut.* Vogelkop. *peninsula* Papua, E Indonesia
110 *F10* **Dobiegniew** *Ger.* Lubuskie, Woldenberg Neumark. Lubuskie, W Poland *52°58′N 15°43′E*
Doblen *see* Dobele
81 *K18* **Dobli** *spring/well* SW Somalia *0°24′N 41°18′E*
112 *H11* **Doboj** Republiks Srpska, N Bosnia and Herzegovina *44°45′N 18°03′E*
143 *R12* **Doborjī** *var.* Fūrg. Fārs, S Iran *28°16′N 55°13′E*
110 *L8* **Dobre Miasto** *Ger.* Guttstadt. Warmińsko-mazurskie, NE Poland *53°59′N 20°25′E*
114 *N7* **Dobrich** *Rom.* Bazargic; *prev.* Tolbukhin. Dobrich, NE Bulgaria *43°35′N 27°49′E*
114 *N7* **Dobrich** ◈ *province* NE Bulgaria
126 *M8* **Dobrinka** Lipetskaya Oblast', W Russian Federation *52°10′N 40°30′E*
126 *M7* **Dobrinka** Volgogradskaya Oblast', SW Russian Federation *50°52′N 41°48′E*
Dobrla Vas *see* Eberndorf
111 *I15* **Dobrodzień** *Ger.* Guttentag. Opolskie, S Poland *50°43′N 18°24′E*
Dobrogea *see* Dobruja
117 *W7* **Dobropillya** *Rus.* Dobropol'ye. Donets'ka Oblast', SE Ukraine *48°25′N 37°02′E*
Dobropol'ye *see* Dobropillya
117 *P8* **Dobrovelychkivka** Kirovohrads'ka Oblast', C Ukraine *48°22′N 31°12′E*
Dobrudja/Dobrudzha *see* Dobruja
114 *O7* **Dobruja** *var.* Dobrudja, *Bul.* Dobrudzha, *Rom.* Dobrogea. *physical region* Bulgaria/Romania
119 *P19* **Dobrush** Homyel'skaya Voblasts', SE Belarus *52°25′N 31°19′E*
125 *U14* **Dobryanka** Permskaya Oblast', NW Russian Federation *58°28′N 56°27′E*
117 *P2* **Dobryanka** Chernihivs'ka Oblast', N Ukraine *52°03′N 31°09′E*
Dobryn' *see* Dabryn'
21 *R8* **Dobson** North Carolina, SE USA *36°25′N 80°45′W*
59 *N20* **Doce, Rio** ≈ SE Brazil
93 *I16* **Docksta** Västernorrland, C Sweden *63°06′N 18°22′E*
41 *N10* **Doctor Arroyo** Nuevo León, NE Mexico *23°40′N 100°09′W*
62 *L4* **Doctor Pedro P. Peña** Boquerón, W Paraguay *22°22′S 62°23′W*
171 *S11* **Dodaga** Pulau Halmahera, E Indonesia *01°06′N 128°10′E*
155 *G21* **Dodda Betta** ▲ S India *11°28′N 76°44′E*
Dodecanese *see* Dodekánisa
115 *M22* **Dodekánisa** *var.* Nóties Sporádes, *Eng.* Dodecanese; *prev.* Dhodhekánisos, Dodekanisos. *island group* SE Greece
Dodekanisos *see* Dodekánisa
26 *J6* **Dodge City** Kansas, C USA *37°45′N 100°01′W*
30 *K9* **Dodgeville** Wisconsin, N USA *42°57′N 90°08′W*
97 *H25* **Dodman Point** *headland* SW England, United Kingdom *50°13′N 04°47′W*
81 *J14* **Dodola** Oromīya, C Ethiopia *07°00′N 39°15′E*
81 *H22* **Dodoma** ● (Tanzania) Dodoma, C Tanzania *06°11′S 35°45′E*
81 *H22* **Dodoma** ◈ *region* C Tanzania
115 *C16* **Dodóni** *var.* Dhodhóni. *site of ancient city* Ípeiros, W Greece
33 *U7* **Dodson** Montana, NW USA *48°25′N 108°18′W*
25 *P3* **Dodson** Texas, SW USA *34°46′N 100°01′W*
98 *M12* **Doesburg** Gelderland, E Netherlands *52°01′N 06°08′E*
98 *N12* **Doetinchem** Gelderland, E Netherlands *51°58′N 06°17′E*
158 *L12* **Dogai Coring** *var.* Lake Montcalm. ◎ W China
137 *N15* **Doğanşehir** Malatya, C Turkey *38°07′N 37°54′E*
84 *E9* **Dogger Bank** *undersea feature* C North Sea *55°00′N 03°00′E*
23 *S10* **Dog Island** *island* Florida, SE USA
14 *C7* **Dog Lake** ◎ Ontario, S Canada
106 *B9* **Dogliani** Piemonte, NE Italy *44°33′N 07°55′E*
164 *H11* **Dōgo** *island* Oki-shotō, SW Japan
143 *N10* **Do Gonbadān** *var.* Dow Gonbadān, Gonbadān. Kohkīlūyeh va Būyer AḤmad, SW Iran *30°12′N 50°48′E*
77 *S12* **Dogondoutchi** Dosso, SW Niger *13°36′N 04°03′E*
137 *T13* **Doğubayazıt** Ağrı, E Turkey *39°33′N 44°07′E*
137 *P12* **Doğu Karadeniz Dağları** *var.* Anadolu Dağları. ▲▲ NE Turkey
158 *K16* **Dogxung Zangbo** ≈ W China
Doha *see* Ad Dawḥah
Doha *see* Ad Dawḥah
Dohad *see* Dāhod
Dohuk *see* Dahūk
159 *N16* **Doilungdêqên** *var.* Namka. Xizang Zizhiqu, W China *29°41′N 90°58′E*
114 *F12* **Doïrani, Límnis** *var.* Limni Doïranis, *Bul.* Ezero Doyransko. ◎ N Greece
Doire *see* Londonderry
99 *H22* **Doische** Namur, S Belgium *50°09′N 04°43′E*
59 *P17* **Dois de Julho** ✈ (Salvador) Bahia, NE Brazil *12°04′S 38°58′W*
60 *H12* **Dois Vizinhos** Paraná, S Brazil *25°47′S 53°03′W*
80 *H10* **Doka** Gedaref, E Sudan *13°30′N 35°47′E*
Doka *see* Kéita, Bahr
139 *T3* **Dokan** *var.* Dūkān. As Sulaymānīyah, E Iraq *35°55′N 44°58′E*
94 *H13* **Dokka** Oppland, S Norway *60°49′N 10°04′E*
98 *L5* **Dokkum** Friesland, N Netherlands *53°20′N 06°E*
98 *L5* **Dokkumer Ee** ≈ N Netherlands
76 *K13* **Doko** NE Guinea *11°46′N 08°58′W*
Dokshitsy *see* Dokshytsy
118 *K13* **Dokshytsy** *Rus.* Dokshitsy. Vitsyebskaya Voblasts', N Belarus *54°54′N 27°46′E*
117 *X8* **Dokuchayevs'k** *var.* Dokuchayevsk. Donets'ka Oblast', SE Ukraine *47°43′N 37°41′E*
Dokuchayevsk *see* Dokuchayevs'k
Dolak, Pulau *see* Yos Sudarso, Pulau
29 *P9* **Doland** South Dakota, N USA *44°51′N 98°06′W*
63 *J18* **Dolavón** Chaco, S Argentina *43°16′S 65°44′W*
15 *P6* **Dolbeau** Québec, SE Canada *48°52′N 72°15′W*
102 *I5* **Dol-de-Bretagne** Ille-et-Vilaine, NW France *48°33′N 01°45′W*
64 *J13* **Doldrums Fracture Zone** *tectonic feature* W Atlantic Ocean
103 *S8* **Dôle** Jura, E France *47°05′N 05°30′E*
97 *J19* **Dolgellau** NW Wales, United Kingdom *52°45′N 03°54′W*
Dolginovo *see* Dawhinava
Dolgi, Ostrov *see* Dolgiy, Ostrov
125 *U2* **Dolgiy, Ostrov** *var.* Ostrov Dolgi. *island* NW Russian Federation
162 *J9* **Dölgöön** Övörhangay, C Mongolia *45°57′N 103°14′E*
107 *C20* **Dolianova** Sardegna, Italy, C Mediterranean Sea *39°23′N 09°08′E*
Dolina *see* Dolyna
123 *T13* **Dolinsk** Ostrov Sakhalin, Sakhalinskaya Oblast', SE Russian Federation *47°20′N 142°52′E*
Dolinskaya *see* Dolyns'ka
79 *F21* **Dolisie** *prev.* Loubomo. Niari, S Congo *04°12′S 12°41′E*
116 *G14* **Dolj** ◈ *county* SW Romania
98 *P5* **Dollard** *bay* NW Germany
194 *J5* **Dolleman Island** *island* Antarctica
114 *K8* **Dolna Oryakhovitsa** Veliko Tŭrnovo, N Bulgaria *43°09′N 25°44′E*
114 *N9* **Dolni Chiflik** Varna, E Bulgaria *42°59′N 27°43′E*
114 *I8* **Dolni Dŭbnik** Pleven, N Bulgaria *43°24′N 24°25′E*
114 *F8* **Dolni Lom** Vidin, NW Bulgaria *43°31′N 22°46′E*
Dolnja Lendava *see* Lendava
129 *F14* **Dolnośląskie** ◈ *province* SW Poland
111 *K18* **Dolný Kubín** *Hung.* Alsókubin. Žilinský Kraj, N Slovakia *49°12′N 19°17′E*
106 *H8* **Dolo** Veneto, NE Italy *45°25′N 12°06′E*
Dolomites/Dolomiti *see* Dolomitiche, Alpi
106 *H6* **Dolomitiche, Alpi** *var.* Dolomiti, *Eng.* Dolomites. ▲▲ NE Italy
Dolonnur *see* Duolun
Doloon *see* Tsogt-Ovoo
61 *E21* **Dolores** Buenos Aires, E Argentina *36°21′S 57°39′W*
42 *E3* **Dolores** Petén, N Guatemala *16°33′N 89°26′W*
171 *Q5* **Dolores** Samar, C Philippines *12°01′N 125°27′E*
105 *S12* **Dolores** País Valenciano, E Spain *38°09′N 00°45′W*
61 *D19* **Dolores** Soriano, SW Uruguay *33°34′S 58°15′W*
41 *N12* **Dolores Hidalgo** *var.* Ciudad de Dolores Hidalgo. Guanajuato, C Mexico *21°10′N 100°55′W*
8 *J7* **Dolphin and Union Strait** *strait* Northwest Territories/Nunavut, N Canada
65 *D23* **Dolphin, Cape** *headland* East Falkland, Falkland Islands *51°15′S 58°57′W*
44 *H12* **Dolphin Head** *hill* W Jamaica
83 *B21* **Dolphin Head** *var.* Cape Dernberg. *headland* SW Namibia *25°33′S 14°36′E*
110 *G12* **Dolsk** *Ger.* Dolzig. Weilkopolskie, C Poland *51°59′N 17°03′E*
167 *S8* **Đô Lương** Nghê An, N Vietnam *18°51′N 105°19′E*
116 *I6* **Dolyna** *Rus.* Dolina. Ivano-Frankivs'ka Oblast', W Ukraine *48°58′N 24°01′E*
117 *R8* **Dolyns'ka** *Rus.* Dolinskaya. Kirovohrads'ka Oblast', S Ukraine *48°06′N 32°46′E*
Dolzig *see* Dolsk
Domachëvo/Domaczewo *see* Damachava
117 *P9* **Domanivka** Mykolayivs'ka Oblast', S Ukraine *47°40′N 30°56′E*
153 *S13* **Domar** Rajshahi, N Bangladesh *26°08′N 88°57′E*
158 *G12* **Domar** *prev.* Zangkaxa. Xizang Zizhiqu, W China *33°42′N 80°21′E*
108 *I9* **Domat/Ems** Graubünden, SE Switzerland *46°50′N 09°28′E*
111 *A18* **Domažlice** *Ger.* Taus. Plzeňský Kraj, W Czech Republic *49°26′N 12°54′E*
127 *X8* **Dombarovskiy** Orenburgskaya Oblast', W Russian Federation *50°53′N 59°18′E*
94 *G10* **Dombås** Oppland, S Norway *62°04′N 09°07′E*
83 *M17* **Dombe** Manica, C Mozambique *19°59′S 33°24′E*
82 *A13* **Dombe Grande** Benguela, C Angola *12°57′S 13°07′E*
103 *R10* **Dombes** *physical region* E France
111 *I25* **Dombóvár** Tolna, S Hungary *46°24′N 18°09′E*
99 *D14* **Domburg** Zeeland, SW Netherlands *51°34′N 03°30′E*
58 *L13* **Dom Eliseu** Pará, NE Brazil *04°02′S 47°31′W*
Domel Island *see* Letsôk-aw Kyun
103 *O11* **Dôme, Puy de** ▲ C France *45°46′N 03°00′E*
36 *H13* **Dome Rock Mountains** ▲▲ Arizona, SW USA
Domesnes, Cape *see* Kolkasrags
62 *G8* **Domeyko** Atacama, N Chile *28°58′S 70°54′W*
62 *H5* **Domeyko, Cordillera** ▲▲ N Chile
102 *K5* **Domfront** Orne, N France *48°35′N 00°39′W*
171 *X13* **Dom, Gunung** ▲ Papua, E Indonesia *02°41′S 137°00′E*
45 *X11* **Dominica** *off.* Commonwealth of Dominica. ◆ *republic* E West Indies
47 *S3* **Dominica** *island* Dominica
Dominica Channel *see* Martinique Passage
Dominica, Commonwealth of *see* Dominica
43 *N15* **Dominical** Puntarenas, SE Costa Rica *09°16′N 83°52′W*
45 *Q8* **Dominican Republic** ◆ *republic* C West Indies
45 *X11* **Dominica Passage** *passage* E Caribbean Sea
99 *K14* **Dommel** ≈ S Netherlands
81 *O14* **Domo** Sumalē, E Ethiopia *07°53′N 46°55′E*
126 *L4* **Domodedovo** ✈ (Moskva) Moskovskaya Oblast', W Russian Federation *55°19′N 37°55′E*
106 *C6* **Domodossola** Piemonte, NE Italy *46°07′N 08°20′E*
115 *F17* **Domokós** *var.* Dhomokós. Stereá Ellás, C Greece *39°07′N 22°18′E*
172 *I14* **Domoni** Anjouan, SE Comoros *12°15′S 44°39′E*
61 *G16* **Dom Pedrito** Rio Grande do Sul, S Brazil *31°00′S 54°40′W*
Dompoe *see* Dompu
170 *M16* **Dompu** *prev.* Dompoe. Sumbawa, C Indonesia *08°30′S 118°28′E*
Domschale *see* Domžale
62 *H13* **Domuyo, Volcán** ⛰ W Argentina *36°36′S 70°22′W*
109 *U11* **Domžale** *Ger.* Domschale. C Slovenia *46°09′N 14°33′E*
127 *O10* **Don** *var.* Duna, Tanais. ≈ SW Russian Federation
96 *K9* **Don** ≈ NE Scotland, United Kingdom
182 *M11* **Donald** Victoria, SE Australia *36°27′S 143°03′E*
22 *J9* **Donaldsonville** Louisiana, S USA *30°06′N 90°59′W*
23 *S8* **Donalsonville** Georgia, SE USA *31°02′N 84°52′W*
Donau *see* Danube
101 *G23* **Donaueschingen** Baden-Württemberg, SW Germany *47°57′N 08°30′E*
101 *K22* **Donaumoos** *wetland* S Germany
101 *K22* **Donauwörth** Bayern, S Germany *48°43′N 10°46′E*
109 *U7* **Donawitz** Steiermark, SE Austria *47°23′N 15°00′E*
117 *X7* **Donbass** *industrial region* Russian Federation/Ukraine
104 *K11* **Don Benito** Extremadura, W Spain *38°57′N 05°52′W*
97 *M17* **Doncaster** *anc.* Danum. N England, United Kingdom *53°32′N 01°07′W*
44 *K12* **Don Christophers Point** *headland* C Jamaica *18°19′N 76°48′W*
55 *V9* **Donderkamp** Sipaliwini, NW Surinam *05°18′N 56°22′W*
82 *B12* **Dondo** Cuanza Norte, NW Angola *09°40′S 14°24′E*
171 *O12* **Dondo** Sulawesi, N Indonesia *0°54′S 121°33′E*
83 *N17* **Dondo** Sofala, C Mozambique *19°41′S 34°45′E*
155 *K26* **Dondra Head** *headland* S Sri Lanka *05°57′N 80°33′E*
Dondușani *see* Dondușeni
116 *M8* **Dondușeni** *var.* Dondușani, *Rus.* Dondyushany. N Moldova *48°13′N 27°38′E*
Dondyushany *see* Dondușeni
97 *D15* **Donegal** *Ir.* Dún na nGall. Donegal, NW Ireland *54°39′N 08°06′W*
97 *D14* **Donegal** *Ir.* Dún na nGall. *cultural region* NW Ireland
97 *C15* **Donegal Bay** *Ir.* Bá Dhún na nGall. *bay* NW Ireland
84 *K10* **Donets** ≈ Russian Federation/Ukraine
117 *X8* **Donets'k** *Rus.* Donetsk; *prev.* Stalino. Donets'ka Oblast', E Ukraine *47°58′N 37°50′E*
117 *W8* **Donets'k** ✈ Donets'ka Oblast', E Ukraine *48°03′N 37°44′E*
Donets'k *see* Donets'ka Oblast'
117 *W8* **Donets'ka Oblast'** *var.* Donets'k, *Rus.* Donetskaya Oblast'; *prev. Rus.* Stalins'kaya Oblast'. ◈ *province* SE Ukraine
Donetskaya Oblast' *see* Donets'ka Oblast'
67 *P8* **Donga** ≈ Cameroon/Nigeria
157 *O13* **Dongchuan** Yunnan, SW China *26°09′N 103°10′E*
99 *I14* **Dongen** Noord-Brabant, S Netherlands *51°38′N 04°56′E*
160 *K17* **Dongfang** *var.* Basuo. Hainan, S China *19°05′N 108°40′E*
163 *Z7* **Dongfanghong** Heilongjiang, NE China *46°13′N 133°13′E*
163 *W11* **Dongfeng** Jilin, NE China *42°39′N 125°33′E*
171 *N12* **Donggala** Sulawesi, C Indonesia *0°40′S 119°44′E*
163 *V13* **Donggang** *var.* Dadong; *prev.* Donggou. Liaoning, NE China *39°52′N 124°08′E*
Donggou *see* Donggang
161 *O14* **Dongguan** Guangdong, S China *23°03′N 113°43′E*
167 *T9* **Đông Ha** Quang Tri, C Vietnam *16°45′N 107°10′E*
Dong Hai *see* East China Sea
160 *M16* **Donghai Dao** *island* S China
162 *I12* **Dong He** *Mong.* Narin Gol. ≈ N China
Donghe *see* Wangcang
167 *T9* **Đông Hơi** Quang Binh, C Vietnam *17°32′N 106°35′E*
Donghua *see* Huating
Donghuang *see* Xishui
108 *H10* **Dongio** Ticino, S Switzerland *46°27′N 08°58′E*
159 *P15* **Dongjug** Xizang Zizhiqu, W China *29°58′N 94°51′E*
Dongkan *see* Binhai
160 *L11* **Dongkou** Hunan, S China *27°06′N 110°35′E*
Dongliao *see* Liaoyuan
Dong-nai *see* Đông Nai, Sông
167 *U13* **Đông Nai, Sông** *var.* Dong-nai, Dong Noi, Donnai. ≈ S Vietnam
161 *N14* **Dongnan Qiuling** *plateau* SE China
163 *Y9* **Dongning** Heilongjiang, NE China *44°01′N 131°03′E*
Dong Noi *see* Đông Nai, Sông
83 *C14* **Dongo** Huíla, C Angola *14°35′S 15°51′E*
80 *E7* **Dongola** *var.* Donqola, Dunqulah. Northern, N Sudan *19°10′N 30°27′E*
79 *I17* **Dongou** Likouala, NE Congo *02°05′N 18°E*
Đông Phu *see* Đông Xoai
Dongping *see* Anhua
Dong Rak, Phanom *see* Dângrêk, Chuŏr Phnum
161 *Q14* **Dongshan Dao** *island* SE China
Dongsha Qundao *see* Tungsha Tao
Dongsheng *see* Ordos
161 *R7* **Dongtai** Jiangsu, E China *32°50′N 120°22′E*
161 *N10* **Dongting Hu** *var.* Tung-t'ing Hu. ◎ S China
161 *P10* **Dongxiang** *var.* Xiaogang. Jiangxi, S China *28°16′N 116°32′E*
167 *T13* **Đông Xoai** *var.* Đông Phu. Sông Be, S Vietnam *11°31′N 106°55′E*
161 *Q4* **Dongying** Shandong, E China *37°27′N 118°01′E*
27 *X8* **Doniphan** Missouri, C USA *36°39′N 90°51′W*
Donja Łužica *see* Niederlausitz
10 *G7* **Donjek** ≈ Yukon Territory, W Canada
112 *E11* **Donji Lapac** Lika-Senj, W Croatia *44°33′N 15°58′E*
112 *H8* **Donji Miholjac** Osijek-Baranja, NE Croatia *45°45′N 18°10′E*
112 *P12* **Donji Milanovac** Serbia, E Serbia *44°27′N 22°06′E*
112 *G12* **Donji Vakuf** *var.* Srbobran. ◈ Federacija Bosna I Hercegovina, C Bosnia and Herzegovina
98 *M6* **Donkerbroek** Friesland, N Netherlands *52°58′N 05°15′E*
167 *P11* **Don Muang** ✈ (Krung Thep) Nonthaburi, C Thailand *13°51′N 100°40′E*
25 *S17* **Donna** Texas, SW USA *26°10′N 98°03′W*
15 *Q10* **Donnacona** Québec, SE Canada *46°41′N 71°46′W*
Donnai *see* Đông Nai, Sông
29 *Y16* **Donnellson** Iowa, C USA *40°38′N 91°33′W*
11 *O13* **Donnelly** Alberta, W Canada *55°42′N 117°06′W*
35 *P6* **Donner Pass** *Pass* California, W USA
101 *F19* **Donnersberg** ▲ W Germany *49°37′N 07°54′E*
Donoso *see* Miguel de la Borda
105 *P2* **Donostia-San Sebastián** País Vasco, N Spain *43°19′N 01°59′W*
115 *K21* **Donoúsa** *var.* Donoússa. *island* Kykládes, Greece, Aegean Sea
Donoússa *see* Donoúsa
35 *P8* **Don Pedro Reservoir** ⊠ California, W USA
Donqola *see* Dongola
126 *L5* **Donskoy** Tul'skaya Oblast', W Russian Federation *54°02′N 38°27′E*
81 *L16* **Doolow** Sumalē, E Ethiopia *04°10′N 42°05′E*
39 *Q7* **Doonerak, Mount** ▲ Alaska, USA *67°54′N 150°33′W*
98 *J12* **Doorn** Utrecht, C Netherlands *52°02′N 05°21′E*
Doornik *see* Tournai
31 *N6* **Door Peninsula** *peninsula* Wisconsin, N USA
80 *P13* **Dooxo Nugaaleed** *var.* Nogal Valley. *valley* E Somalia
Do Qu *see* Da Qu
106 *B7* **Dora Baltea** *anc.* Duria Major. ≈ NW Italy
180 *K7* **Dora, Lake** *salt lake* Western Australia
106 *A8* **Dora Riparia** *anc.* Duria Minor. ≈ NW Italy
Dorbiljin *see* Emin
Dorbod/Dorbod Mongolzu Zizhixian *see* Taikang
Dorbod Mongolzu Zizhixian *see* Taikang
113 *N18* **Đorče Petrov** *var.* Ďjorče Petrov, Gorče Petrov. N Macedonia *42°01′N 21°21′E*
14 *F16* **Dorchester** Ontario, S Canada *43°00′N 81°04′W*
97 *L24* **Dorchester** *anc.* Durnovaria. S England, United Kingdom *50°43′N 02°26′W*
9 *P7* **Dorchester, Cape** *headland* Baffin Island, Nunavut, NE Canada *65°25′N 77°25′W*
83 *D19* **Dordabis** Khomas, C Namibia *22°57′S 17°39′E*
102 *L12* **Dordogne** ◈ *department* SW France
103 *N12* **Dordogne** ≈ W France
98 *H13* **Dordrecht** *var.* Dordt, Dort. Zuid-Holland, SW Netherlands *51°48′N 04°40′E*
Dordt *see* Dordrecht
103 *P11* **Dore** ≈ C France
11 *S13* **Doré Lake** Saskatchewan, C Canada *54°37′N 107°36′W*
103 *O12* **Dore, Monts** ▲▲ C France
101 *M23* **Dorfen** Bayern, SE Germany *48°16′N 12°06′E*
107 *D18* **Dorgali** Sardegna, Italy, C Mediterranean Sea *40°18′N 09°34′E*
159 *N11* **Dorgê Co** *var.* Elsen Nur. ◎ C China
162 *E6* **Dörgön** *var.* Seer. Hovd, W Mongolia *48°18′N 92°37′E*
162 *F7* **Dörgön Nuur** ◎ NW Mongolia
77 *Q12* **Dori** N Burkina *14°03′N 00°02′W*
83 *E24* **Doring** ≈ S South Africa
101 *E16* **Dormagen** Nordrhein-Westfalen, W Germany *51°06′N 06°49′E*
103 *P4* **Dormans** Marne, N France *49°03′N 03°44′E*
108 *E6* **Dornach** Solothurn, NW Switzerland *47°29′N 07°37′E*
Dorna Watra *see* Vatra Dornei
108 *J7* **Dornbirn** Vorarlberg, W Austria *47°25′N 09°46′E*
96 *I7* **Dornoch** N Scotland, United Kingdom *57°52′N 04°01′W*
96 *J7* **Dornoch Firth** *inlet* N Scotland, United Kingdom
163 *P7* **Dornod** ◈ *province* E Mongolia
163 *N10* **Dornogovĭ** ◈ *province* SE Mongolia
77 *P10* **Doro** Tombouctou, S Mali *16°07′N 00°57′W*
116 *L14* **Dorobanțu** Călărași, S Romania *44°15′N 26°55′E*
111 *J22* **Dorog** Komárom-Esztergom, N Hungary *47°43′N 18°42′E*
126 *I4* **Dorogobuzh** Smolenskaya Oblast', W Russian Federation *54°56′N 33°16′E*
116 *K8* **Dorohoi** Botoșani, NE Romania *47°57′N 26°24′E*
93 *H15* **Dorotea** Västerbotten, N Sweden *64°17′N 16°30′E*
Dorpat *see* Tartu
180 *G10* **Dorre Island** *island* Western Australia
183 *U5* **Dorrigo** New South Wales, SE Australia *30°22′S 152°43′E*
35 *N1* **Dorris** California, W USA *41°58′N 121°54′W*
14 *H13* **Dorset** Ontario, SE Canada *45°12′N 78°52′W*
97 *K23* **Dorset** *cultural region* S England, United Kingdom
101 *E14* **Dorsten** Nordrhein-Westfalen, W Germany *51°38′N 06°58′E*
Dort *see* Dordrecht
101 *F15* **Dortmund** Nordrhein-Westfalen, W Germany *51°31′N 07°28′E*
100 *F12* **Dortmund-Ems-Kanal** *canal* W Germany
136 *L17* **Dörtyol** Hatay, S Turkey *36°51′N 36°11′E*
142 *L7* **Do Rūd** *var.* Dow Rūd, Durud. Lorestān, W Iran *33°28′N 49°04′E*
79 *O15* **Doruma** Orientale, N Dem. Rep. Congo *04°35′N 27°43′E*
15 *O12* **Dorval** ✈ (Montréal) Québec, SE Canada *45°27′N 73°46′W*
162 *F7* **Dörvöljin** *var.* Buga. Dzavhan, W Mongolia *47°42′N 94°53′E*
45 *T5* **Dos Bocas, Lago** ◎ C Puerto Rico
104 *K14* **Dos Hermanas** Andalucía, S Spain *37°16′N 05°55′W*
Dospad Dagh *see* Rhodope Mountains
35 *P10* **Dos Palos** California, W USA *37°00′N 120°39′W*
114 *I11* **Dospat** Smolyan, S Bulgaria *41°39′N 24°10′E*
114 *H11* **Dospat, Yazovir** ⊠ SW Bulgaria
100 *M11* **Dosse** ≈ NE Germany
77 *S12* **Dosso** Dosso, SW Niger *13°03′N 03°10′E*
77 *S12* **Dosso** ◈ *department* SW Niger
144 *G12* **Dossor** Atyrau, SW Kazakhstan *47°31′N 53°01′E*
147 *O10* **Do'stlik** Jizzax Viloyati, C Uzbekistan *40°37′N 67°59′E*
147 *V9* **Dostuk** Narynskaya Oblast', C Kyrgyzstan *41°19′N 75°40′E*
145 *X13* **Dostyk** *prev.* Druzhba. Almaty, SE Kazakhstan *45°15′N 82°29′E*
23 *R7* **Dothan** Alabama, S USA *31°13′N 85°23′W*
39 *T9* **Dot Lake** Alaska, USA *63°39′N 144°10′W*
118 *F12* **Dotnuva** Kaunas, C Lithuania *55°23′N 23°53′E*
99 *D19* **Dottignies** Hainaut, W Belgium *50°43′N 03°16′E*
103 *P2* **Douai** *prev.* Douay; *anc.* Duacum. Nord, N France *50°22′N 03°04′E*
14 *L9* **Douaire, Lac** ◎ Québec, SE Canada
79 *D16* **Douala** *var.* Duala. Littoral, W Cameroon *04°04′N 09°43′E*
79 *D16* **Douala** ✈ Littoral, W Cameroon *03°57′N 09°48′E*
102 *F6* **Douarnenez** Finistère, NW France *48°05′N 04°20′W*
102 *E6* **Douarnenez, Baie de** *bay* NW France
Douay *see* Douai
25 *O6* **Double Mountain Fork Brazos River** ≈ Texas, SW USA
23 *O3* **Double Springs** Alabama, S USA *34°09′N 87°24′W*
103 *T8* **Doubs** ◈ *department* E France
108 *C8* **Doubs** ≈ France/Switzerland
185 *A22* **Doubtful Sound** *sound* South Island, New Zealand
184 *J2* **Doubtless Bay** *bay* North Island, New Zealand
25 *X9* **Doucette** Texas, SW USA *30°48′N 94°25′W*
102 *K8* **Doué-la-Fontaine** Maine-et-Loire, NW France *47°12′N 00°16′W*
77 *O11* **Douentza** Mopti, S Mali *14°59′N 02°57′W*
97 *I16* **Douglas** ○ (Isle of Man) E Isle of Man *54°09′N 04°28′W*
83 *H23* **Douglas** Northern Cape, C South Africa *29°04′S 23°47′E*
39 *X13* **Douglas** Alexander Archipelago, Alaska, USA *58°12′N 134°18′W*
37 *O17* **Douglas** Arizona, SW USA *31°20′N 109°32′W*
23 *U7* **Douglas** Georgia, SE USA *31°30′N 82°51′W*
33 *Y15* **Douglas** Wyoming, C USA *42°48′N 105°23′W*
21 *O7* **Douglas Cape** *headland* Alaska, N USA *64°59′N 166°41′W*
10 *J14* **Douglas Channel** *channel* British Columbia, W Canada
182 *G3* **Douglas Creek** *seasonal river* South Australia
31 *P5* **Douglas Lake** ◎ Michigan, N USA
21 *O9* **Douglas Lake** ⊠ Tennessee, S USA
39 *Q13* **Douglas, Mount** ▲ Alaska, USA *58°51′N 153°31′W*
194 *I6* **Douglas Range** ▲▲ Alexander Island, Antarctica
103 *O2* **Doullens** Somme, N France *50°09′N 02°21′E*
Douma *see* Dūmā
79 *F15* **Doumé** Est, E Cameroon *04°14′N 13°27′E*
99 *E21* **Dour** Hainaut , S Belgium *50°24′N 03°47′E*
59 *K18* **Dourada, Serra** ▲▲ S Brazil
59 *I21* **Dourados** Mato Grosso do Sul, S Brazil *22°09′S 54°52′W*
103 *N5* **Dourdan** Essonne, N France *48°33′N 01°58′E*
104 *I6* **Douro** *Sp.* Duero. ≈ Portugal/Spain *see also* Duero
Douro *see* Duero
104 *G6* **Douro Litoral** *former province* N Portugal
Douvres *see* Dover
102 *K15* **Douze** ≈ SW France
183 *P17* **Dover** Tasmania, SE Australia *43°19′S 147°01′E*
97 *Q22* **Dover** *Fr.* Douvres, *Lat.* Dubris Portus. SE England, United Kingdom *51°08′N 03°E*
21 *Y3* **Dover** *state capital* Delaware, NE USA *39°09′N 75°31′W*
19 *P9* **Dover** New Hampshire, NE USA *43°10′N 70°50′W*
18 *J14* **Dover** New Jersey, NE USA *40°51′N 74°33′W*
31 *U12* **Dover** Ohio, N USA *40°31′N 81°28′W*
20 *H8* **Dover** Tennessee, S USA *36°30′N 87°50′W*
97 *Q23* **Dover, Strait of** *var.* Straits of Dover, *Fr.* Pas de Calais. *strait* England, United Kingdom/France
Dover, Straits of *see* Dover, Strait of
Dovlen *see* Devin
94 *G11* **Dovre** Oppland, S Norway *61°59′N 09°16′E*
94 *G10* **Dovrefjell** *plateau* S Norway
Dovsk *see* Dowsk
83 *M14* **Dowa** Central, C Malawi *13°40′S 33°55′E*
31 *O10* **Dowagiac** Michigan, N USA *41°58′N 86°06′W*
Dow Gonbadān *see* Do Gonbadān
148 *M2* **Dowlatābād** Fāryāb, N Afghanistan *36°30′N 64°51′E*
97 *G16* **Down** *cultural region* SE Northern Ireland, United Kingdom
33 *R16* **Downey** Idaho, NW USA *42°25′N 112°06′W*
35 *P5* **Downieville** California, W USA *39°34′N 120°49′W*
97 *G16* **Downpatrick** *Ir.* Dún Pádraig. SE Northern Ireland, United Kingdom *54°20′N 05°43′W*
26 *M3* **Downs** Kansas, C USA *39°30′N 98°33′W*
18 *J12* **Downsville** New York, NE USA *42°03′N 74°59′W*
Dow Rūd *see* Do Rūd
29 *V12* **Dows** Iowa, C USA *42°39′N 93°30′W*
119 *O17* **Dowsk** *Rus.* Dovsk. Homyel'skaya Voblasts', SE Belarus *53°09′N 30°28′E*
35 *Q4* **Doyle** California, W USA *40°00′N 120°06′W*
18 *I15* **Doylestown** Pennsylvania, NE USA *40°18′N 75°08′W*
Doyransko, Ezero *see* Doïrani, Límnis
114 *I8* **Doyrentsi** Lovech, N Bulgaria *43°13′N 24°46′E*
164 *G11* **Dōzen** *island* Oki-shotō, SW Japan
14 *K9* **Dozois, Réservoir** ⊠ Québec, SE Canada
74 *D9* **Drâa** *seasonal river* S Morocco
Drâa, Hammada du *see* Dra, Hamada du

◆ Country
● Country Capital
◇ Dependent Territory
○ Dependent Territory Capital
◈ Administrative Regions
✈ International Airport
▲ Mountain
▲▲ Mountain Range
⛰ Volcano
≈ River
◎ Lake
⊠ Reservoir

Drabble *see* José Enrique Rodó
117 Q5 **Drabiv** Cherkas'ka Oblast', C Ukraine 49°57′N 32°10′E
Drable *see* José Enrique Rodó
103 S13 **Drac** ≈ E France
Drač/Drac *see* Durrës
60 I8 **Dracena** São Paulo, S Brazil 21°27′S 51°30′W
98 M6 **Drachten** Friesland, N Netherlands 53°07′N 06°06′E
92 H11 **Drag** *Lapp.* Ájluokta. Nordland, C Norway 68°02′N 16°E
116 L14 **Dragalina** Călăraşi, SE Romania 44°26′N 27°19′E
116 I14 **Draganesti-Olt** Olt, S Romania 44°06′N 25°00′E
116 J14 **Drăgăneşti-Vlaşca** Teleorman, S Romania 44°05′N 25°39′E
116 I13 **Drăgăşani** Vâlcea, SW Romania 44°40′N 24°16′E
114 G9 **Dragoman** Sofiya, W Bulgaria 42°32′N 22°56′E
115 L25 **Dragonáda** *island* SE Greece
Dragonera, Isla *see* Sa Dragonera
45 T14 **Dragon's Mouths, The** *strait* Trinidad and Tobago/ Venezuela
95 J23 **Dragør** København, E Denmark 55°36′N 12°42′E
114 F10 **Dragovishtitsa** Kysutendil, W Bulgaria 42°22′N 22°39′E
103 U15 **Draguignan** Var, SE France 43°31′N 06°31′E
74 E9 **Dra, Hamada du** *var.* Hammada du Drâa, Haut Plateau du Dra. *plateau* W Algeria
Dra, Haut Plateau du *see* Dra, Hamada du
119 H19 **Drahichyn** *Pol.* Drohiczyn Poleski, *Rus.* Drogichin. Brestskaya Voblasts', SW Belarus 52°11′N 25°10′E
29 N4 **Drake** North Dakota, N USA 47°54′N 100°23′W
83 K23 **Drakensberg** ▲▲ Lesotho/ South Africa
194 F3 **Drake Passage** *passage* Atlantic Ocean/Pacific Ocean
114 L8 **Dralfa** Tŭrgovishte, N Bulgaria 43°17′N 26°25′E
114 I12 **Dráma** *var.* Dhráma. Anatolikí Makedonía kai Thráki, NE Greece 41°09′N 24°10′E
Dramburg *see* Drawsko Pomorskie
95 H15 **Drammen** Buskerud, S Norway 59°44′N 10°12′E
95 H15 **Drammensfjorden** *fjord* S Norway
92 H1 **Drangajökull** ▲ NW Iceland 66°13′N 22°18′W
95 F16 **Drangedal** Telemark, S Norway 59°05′N 09°05′E
92 I2 **Drangsnes** Vestfirdhir, NW Iceland 65°42′N 21°27′W
Drann *see* Dravinja
109 T10 **Drau** *var.* Drava, *Eng.* Drave, *Hung.* Dráva. ≈ C Europe *see also* Drava
Drau *see* Drava
84 I11 **Drava** *var.* Drau, *Eng.* Drave, *Hung.* Dráva. ≈ C Europe *see also* Drau
Dráva/Drave *see* Drau/ Drava
109 W10 **Dravinja** *Ger.* Drann. ≈ NE Slovenia
109 V9 **Dravograd** *Ger.* Unterdrauburg; *prev.* Spodnji Dravograd. N Slovenia 46°36′N 15°00′E
110 F10 **Drawa** ≈ NW Poland
110 F9 **Drawno** Zachodnio-pomorskie, NW Poland 53°12′N 15°44′E
110 F9 **Drawsko Pomorskie** *Ger.* Dramburg. Zachodnio-pomorskie, NW Poland 53°32′N 15°48′E
29 R3 **Drayton** North Dakota, N USA 48°34′N 97°10′W
11 P14 **Drayton Valley** Alberta, SW Canada 53°15′N 115°00′W
186 B6 **Dreikikir** East Sepik, NW Papua New Guinea 03°42′S 142°46′E
Dreikirchen *see* Teiuş
98 N7 **Drenthe** ◈ *province* NE Netherlands
115 H15 **Drépano, Akrotírio** *var.* Akrotírio Dhrepanon. *headland* N Greece 39°56′N 23°57′E
Drepanum *see* Trapani
14 D17 **Dresden** Ontario, S Canada 42°34′N 82°09′W
101 O16 **Dresden** Sachsen, E Germany 51°03′N 13°43′E
20 G8 **Dresden** Tennessee, S USA 36°17′N 88°42′W
118 M11 **Dretun'** Vitsyebskaya Voblasts', N Belarus 55°41′N 29°13′E
102 M5 **Dreux** *anc.* Drocae, Durocasses. Eure-et-Loir, C France 48°44′N 01°23′E
94 I11 **Drevsjø** Hedmark, S Norway 61°52′N 12°01′E
22 K3 **Drew** Mississippi, S USA 33°48′N 90°31′W
110 F10 **Drezdenko** *Ger.* Driesen. Lubuskie, W Poland 52°51′N 15°50′E
98 J12 **Driebergen** *var.* Driebergen-Rijsenburg. Utrecht, C Netherlands 52°03′N 05°17′E
Driebergen-Rijsenburg *see* Driebergen
Driesen *see* Drezdenko
97 N16 **Driffield** E England, United Kingdom 54°00′N 00°28′W
33 S14 **Driggs** Idaho, NW USA 43°44′N 111°06′W
Drin *see* Drinit, Lumi i
112 K12 **Drina** ≈ Bosnia and Herzegovina/Serbia
Drin, Gulf of *see* Drinit, Gjiri i
113 K18 **Drinit, Gjiri i** *var.* Pellg i Drinit, *Eng.* Gulf of Drin. *gulf* NW Albania
113 L17 **Drinit, Lumi i** *var.* Drin. ≈ NW Albania
Drinit, Pellg i *see* Drinit, Gjiri i
Drinit të Zi, Lumi i *see* Black Drin
113 L22 **Dríno** *var.* Drino, Drínos Pótamos, *Alb.* Lumi i Drinos. ≈ Albania/Greece
Drinos, Lumi i/Drínos Pótamos *see* Dríno
25 S11 **Dripping Springs** Texas, SW USA 30°11′N 98°04′W
25 S15 **Driscoll** Texas, SW USA 27°40′N 97°45′W
22 H5 **Driskill Mountain** ▲ Louisiana, S USA 32°25′N 92°54′W
Drissa *see* Drysa
94 G10 **Driva** ≈ S Norway
112 E13 **Drniš** *It.* Šibenik-Knin. Šibenik-Knin, S Croatia 43°51′N 16°10′E
95 H15 **Drøbak** Akershus, S Norway 59°40′N 10°40′E
116 G13 **Drobeta-Turnu Severin** *prev.* Turnu Severin. Mehedinţi, SW Romania 44°39′N 22°40′E
Drocae *see* Dreux
116 M8 **Drochia** *Rus.* Drokiya. N Moldova 48°02′N 27°46′E
97 F17 **Drogheda** *Ir.* Droichead Átha. NE Ireland 53°43′N 06°21′W
Drogichin *see* Drahichyn
Drogobych *see* Drohobych
Drohiczyn Poleski *see* Drahichyn
116 H6 **Drohobych** *Pol.* Drohobycz, *Rus.* Drogobych. L'vivs'ka Oblast', NW Ukraine 49°22′N 23°33′E
Drohobycz *see* Drohobych
Droichead Átha *see* Drogheda
Droicheadna Bandan *see* Bandon
Droichead na Banna *see* Banbridge
97 F18 **Droichead Nua** E Ireland 52°12′N 06°40′W
Droim Mór *see* Dromore
Drokiya *see* Drochia
103 R13 **Drôme** ◈ *department* E France
103 S13 **Drôme** ≈ E France
97 G15 **Dromore** *Ir.* Droim Mór. SE Northern Ireland, United Kingdom 54°25′N 06°09′W
106 A9 **Dronero** Piemonte, NE Italy 44°28′N 07°25′E
102 L12 **Dronne** ≈ SW France
195 Q3 **Dronning Maud Land** *physical region* Antarctica
98 K6 **Dronrijp** *Fris.* Dronryp. Friesland, N Netherlands 53°12′N 05°37′E
Dronryp *see* Dronrijp
98 L9 **Dronten** Flevoland, C Netherlands 52°31′N 05°41′E
Drontheim *see* Trondheim
102 L13 **Dropt** ≈ SW France
149 T4 **Drosh** North-West Frontier Province, NW Pakistan 35°33′N 71°48′E
Drossen *see* Ośno Lubuskie
Drug *see* Durg
Drujba *see* Pitnak
118 I12 **Drūkšiai** ◎ NE Lithuania
Druk-yul *see* Bhutan
11 Q16 **Drumheller** Alberta, SW Canada 51°28′N 112°42′W
33 Q10 **Drummond** Montana, NW USA 46°39′N 113°12′W
31 R4 **Drummond Island** *island* Michigan, N USA
Drummond Island *see* Tabiteuea
21 X7 **Drummond, Lake** ◎ Virginia, NE USA
15 P12 **Drummondville** Québec, SE Canada 45°52′N 72°28′W
39 T11 **Drum, Mount** ▲ Alaska, USA 62°11′N 144°37′W
27 O9 **Drumright** Oklahoma, C USA 35°59′N 96°36′W
99 J14 **Drunen** Noord-Brabant, S Netherlands 51°41′N 05°08′E
Druskienniki *see* Druskininkai
119 F15 **Druskininkai** *Pol.* Druskienniki. Alytus, S Lithuania 54°00′N 24°00′E
98 K13 **Druten** Gelderland, SE Netherlands 51°53′N 05°37′E
118 K11 **Druya** Vitsyebskaya Voblasts', NW Belarus 55°47′N 27°27′E
117 S2 **Druzhba** Sums'ka Oblast', NE Ukraine 52°01′N 33°56′E
Druzhba *see* Dostyk, Kazakhstan
Druzhba *see* Pitnak, Uzbekistan
123 R7 **Druzhina** Respublika Sakha (Yakutiya), NE Russian Federation 68°01′N 144°58′E
117 X7 **Druzhkivka** Donets'ka Oblast', E Ukraine 48°38′N 37°31′E
112 E12 **Drvar** Federacija Bosna I Hercegovina, W Bosnia and Herzegovina 44°21′N 16°24′E
113 G15 **Drvenik** Split-Dalmacija, SE Croatia 43°10′N 17°13′E
114 K9 **Dryanovo** Gabrovo, N Bulgaria 42°58′N 25°28′E
26 G7 **Dry Cimarron River** ≈ Kansas/Oklahoma, C USA
12 B11 **Dryden** Ontario, C Canada 49°48′N 92°48′W
24 M11 **Dryden** Texas, SW USA 30°01′N 102°06′W
195 Q14 **Drygalski Ice Tongue** *ice feature* Antarctica
118 L11 **Drysa** *Rus.* Drissa. ≈ N Belarus
23 V17 **Dry Tortugas** *island* Florida, SE USA
79 D15 **Dschang** Ouest, W Cameroon 05°28′N 10°02′E
54 J5 **Duaca** Lara, N Venezuela 10°22′N 69°08′W
Duacum *see* Douai
Duala *see* Douala
45 N9 **Duarte, Pico** ▲ C Dominican Republic 19°02′N 70°57′W
140 J5 **Ḍubā** Tabūk, NW Saudi Arabia 27°26′N 35°42′E
Dubai *see* Dubayy
117 N9 **Dubăsari** *Rus.* Dubossary. NE Moldova 47°16′N 29°07′E
117 N9 **Dubăsari Reservoir** ⊠ NE Moldova
8 M10 **Dubawnt** ≈ Nunavut, NW Canada
8 L9 **Dubawnt Lake** ◎ Northwest Territories/Nunavut, N Canada
30 L6 **Du Bay, Lake** ⊠ Wisconsin, N USA
141 U7 **Dubayy** *Eng.* Dubai. Dubayy, NE United Arab Emirates 25°11′N 55°18′E
141 W7 **Dubayy** *Eng.* Dubai. ✈ Dubayy, NE United Arab Emirates 25°15′N 55°22′E
183 R7 **Dubbo** New South Wales, SE Australia 32°16′S 148°41′E
108 G7 **Dübendorf** Zürich, NW Switzerland 47°23′N 08°37′E
97 F18 **Dublin** *Ir.* Baile Átha Cliath; *anc.* Eblana. ● (Ireland) Dublin, E Ireland 53°20′N 06°15′W
23 U5 **Dublin** Georgia, SE USA 32°32′N 82°54′W
25 R7 **Dublin** Texas, SW USA 32°05′N 98°20′W
97 G18 **Dublin** *Ir.* Baile Átha Cliath; *anc.* Eblana. *cultural region* E Ireland
97 G18 **Dublin Airport** ✈ Dublin, E Ireland 53°25′N 06°18′W
189 V12 **Dublon** *var.* Tonoas. *island* Chuuk Islands, C Micronesia
126 K2 **Dubna** Moskovskaya Oblast', W Russian Federation 56°45′N 37°09′E
111 G19 **Dubňany** *Ger.* Dubnian. Jihomoravský Kraj, SE Czech Republic 48°54′N 17°00′E
Dubnian *see* Dubňany
111 I19 **Dubnica nad Váhom** *Hung.* Máriatölgyes; *prev.* Dubnicz. Trenčiansky Kraj, W Slovakia 48°58′N 18°10′E
Dubnicz *see* Dubnica nad Váhom
116 K4 **Dubno** Rivnens'ka Oblast', NW Ukraine 50°28′N 25°40′E
33 R13 **Dubois** Idaho, NW USA 44°10′N 112°13′W
18 D13 **Du Bois** Pennsylvania, NE USA 41°07′N 78°45′W
33 T14 **Dubois** Wyoming, C USA 43°31′N 109°37′W
Dubossary *see* Dubăsari
127 O10 **Dubovka** Volgogradskaya Oblast', SW Russian Federation 49°10′N 48°49′E
76 H14 **Dubréka** SW Guinea 09°48′N 13°31′W
14 B7 **Dubreuilville** Ontario, S Canada 48°21′N 84°31′W
Dubris Portus *see* Dover
119 L20 **Dubrova** Homyel'skaya Voblasts', SE Belarus 51°47′N 28°13′E
Dubrovačko-Neretvanska Županija *see* Dubrovnik-Neretva
126 I5 **Dubrovka** Bryanskaya Oblast', W Russian Federation 53°44′N 33°27′E
113 H16 **Dubrovnik** *It.* Ragusa. Dubrovnik-Neretva, SE Croatia 42°40′N 18°06′E
113 I16 **Dubrovnik** ✈ Dubrovnik-Neretva, SE Croatia 42°34′N 18°17′E
113 F16 **Dubrovnik-Neretva** *off.* Dubrovačko-Neretvanska Županija. ◈ *province* SE Croatia
Dubrovno *see* Dubrowna
116 L2 **Dubrovytsya** Rivnens'ka Oblast', NW Ukraine 51°34′N 26°37′E
119 O14 **Dubrowna** *Rus.* Dubrovno. Vitsyebskaya Voblasts', N Belarus 54°35′N 30°41′E
29 Z13 **Dubuque** Iowa, C USA 42°30′N 90°40′W
118 E12 **Dubysa** ≈ C Lithuania
167 U11 **Đưc Cơ** Gia Lai, C Vietnam 13°48′N 107°41′E
191 V12 **Duc de Gloucester, Îles du** *Eng.* Duke of Gloucester Islands. *island group* C French Polynesia
111 C15 **Duchcov** *Ger.* Dux. Ústecký Kraj, NW Czech Republic 50°37′N 13°45′E
37 N3 **Duchesne** Utah, W USA 40°09′N 110°24′W
191 P17 **Ducie Island** *atoll* E Pitcairn Islands
11 W15 **Duck Bay** Manitoba, S Canada 52°11′N 100°08′W
23 X17 **Duck Key** *island* Florida Keys, Florida, SE USA
11 T14 **Duck Lake** Saskatchewan, S Canada 52°52′N 106°12′W
11 V15 **Duck Mountain** ▲▲ Manitoba, S Canada
20 I9 **Duck River** ≈ Tennessee, S USA
20 M10 **Ducktown** Tennessee, S USA 35°01′N 84°24′W
167 U10 **Đưc Phô** Quang Ngai, C Vietnam 14°56′N 108°55′E
Đưc Tho *see* Lin Camh
167 U13 **Đưc Trong** *var.* Liên Nghia. Lâm Đông, S Vietnam 11°45′N 108°24′E
D-U-D *see* Dalap-Uliga-Djarrit
99 M25 **Dudelange** *var.* Forge du Sud, *Ger.* Dudelingen. Luxembourg, S Luxembourg 49°28′N 06°05′E
Dudelingen *see* Dudelange
101 J15 **Duderstadt** Niedersachsen, C Germany 51°31′N 10°16′E
153 N15 **Dūdhi** Uttar Pradesh, N India 24°09′N 83°16′E
122 K8 **Dudinka** Taymyrskiy (Dolgano-Nenetskiy) Avtonomnyy Okrug, N Russian Federation 69°27′N 86°13′E
97 L20 **Dudley** C England, United Kingdom 52°30′N 02°05′W
154 G13 **Dudna** ≈ C India
76 L16 **Duékoué** W Ivory Coast 05°50′N 05°22′W
104 M5 **Dueñas** Castilla-León, N Spain 41°52′N 04°33′W
104 K4 **Duerna** ≈ NW Spain
105 O6 **Duero** *Port.* Douro. ≈ Portugal/Spain *see also* Douro
Duero *see* Douro
Duesseldorf *see* Düsseldorf
21 P12 **Due West** South Carolina, SE USA 34°19′N 82°23′W
195 P11 **Dufek Coast** *physical region* Antarctica
99 H17 **Duffel** Antwerpen, C Belgium 51°06′N 04°30′E
35 S2 **Duffer Peak** ▲ Nevada, W USA 41°40′N 118°45′W
187 Q9 **Duff Islands** *island group* E Solomon Islands
Dufour, Pizzo/Dufour, Punta *see* Dufour Spitze
108 E12 **Dufour Spitze** *It.* Pizzo Dufour, Punta Dufour. ▲ Italy/Switzerland 45°54′N 07°50′E
112 D9 **Duga Resa** Karlovac, C Croatia 45°25′N 15°30′E
22 H5 **Dugdemona River** ≈ Louisiana, S USA
154 J12 **Duggīpar** Mahārāshtra, C India 21°06′N 80°10′E
112 B13 **Dugi Otok** *var.* Isola Grossa, *It.* Isola Lunga. *island* W Croatia
113 F14 **Dugopolje** Split-Dalmacija, S Croatia 43°35′N 16°35′E
160 L8 **Du He** ≈ C China
54 M11 **Duida, Cerro** ▲ S Venezuela 03°21′N 65°45′W
Duinekerke *see* Dunkerque
101 E15 **Duisburg** *prev.* Duisburg-Hamborn. Nordrhein-Westfalen, W Germany 51°25′N 06°47′E
Duisburg-Hamborn *see* Duisburg
99 F14 **Duiveland** *island* SW Netherlands
98 M12 **Duiven** Gelderland, E Netherlands 51°57′N 06°02′E
139 W10 **Dujaylah, Hawr ad** ◎ S Iraq
160 H9 **Dujiangyan** *var.* Guanxian, Guan Xian. Sichuan, C China 31°01′N 103°40′E
81 L18 **Dujuuma** Shabeellaha Hoose, S Somalia 01°04′N 42°37′E
Dūkān *see* Dokan
39 Z14 **Duke Island** *island* Alexander Archipelago, Alaska, USA
Dukelský Priesmy/ Dukelský Průsmyk *see* Dukla Pass
Duke of Gloucester Islands *see* Duc de Gloucester, Îles du
81 F14 **Duk Faiwil** Jonglei, SE Sudan 07°30′N 31°27′E
141 T7 **Dukhān** C Qatar 25°29′N 50°48′E
Dukhan Heights *see* Dukhān, Jabal
143 N16 **Dukhān, Jabal** *var.* Dukhan Heights. *hill range* S Qatar
127 Q7 **Dukhovnitskoye** Saratovskaya Oblast', W Russian Federation 52°31′N 48°32′E
126 H4 **Dukhovshchina** Smolenskaya Oblast', W Russian Federation 55°15′N 32°22′E
Dukielska, Przełęcz *see* Dukla Pass
111 N17 **Dukla** Podkarpackie, SE Poland 49°33′N 21°40′E
Duklai Hág *see* Dukla Pass
111 N18 **Dukla Pass** *Cz.* Dukelský Průsmyk, *Ger.* Dukla-Pass, *Hung.* Duklai Hág, *Pol.* Przełęcz Dukielska, *Slvk.* Dukelský Priesmy. *pass* Poland/Slovakia
Dukla-Pass *see* Dukla Pass
Dukou *see* Panzhihua
118 I12 **Dūkštas** Utena, E Lithuania 55°32′N 26°21′E
Dulaan *see* Herlenbayan-Ulaan
159 R10 **Dulan** *var.* Qagan Us. Qinghai, C China 36°11′N 97°51′E
37 R8 **Dulce** New Mexico, SW USA 36°55′N 107°00′W
43 N16 **Dulce, Golfo** *gulf* S Costa Rica
Dulce, Golfo *see* Izabal, Lago de
42 K6 **Dulce Nombre de Culmí** Olancho, C Honduras 15°09′N 85°37′W
62 L9 **Dulce, Río** ≈ C Argentina
123 Q9 **Dulgalakh** ≈ NE Russian Federation
114 M8 **Dŭlgopol** Varna, E Bulgaria 43°05′N 27°24′E
153 V14 **Dullabchara** Assam, NE India 24°25′N 92°22′E
20 D3 **Dulles** ✈ (Washington DC)Virginia, NE USA 39°00′N 77°27′W
101 E14 **Dülmen** Nordrhein-Westfalen, W Germany 51°51′N 07°17′E
114 M7 **Dulovo** Silistra, NE Bulgaria 43°51′N 27°10′E
29 W5 **Duluth** Minnesota, N USA 46°47′N 92°06′W
138 H7 **Dūmā** *Fr.* Douma. Dimashq, SW Syria 33°33′N 36°24′E
171 O8 **Dumagasa Point** *headland* Mindanao, S Philippines 07°01′N 121°54′E
171 P6 **Dumaguete** *var.* Dumaguete City. Negros, C Philippines 09°16′N 123°17′E
Dumaguete City *see* Dumaguete
168 J10 **Dumai** Sumatera, W Indonesia 01°39′N 101°28′E
183 T4 **Dumaresq River** ≈ New South Wales/Queensland, SE Australia
27 W13 **Dumas** Arkansas, C USA 33°53′N 91°29′W
25 N1 **Dumas** Texas, SW USA 35°51′N 101°57′W
138 I7 **Ḍumayr** Dimashq, W Syria 33°36′N 36°28′E
96 I12 **Dumbarton** W Scotland, United Kingdom 55°57′N 04°35′W
96 I12 **Dumbarton** *cultural region* C Scotland, United Kingdom
187 Q17 **Dumbéa** Province Sud, S New Caledonia 22°11′S 166°27′E
111 K19 **Ďumbier** *Ger.* Djumbir, *Hung.* Gyömbér. ▲ C Slovakia 48°54′N 19°36′E
116 I11 **Dumbrăveni** *Ger.* Elisabethstedt, *Hung.* Erzsébetváros; *prev.* Ebesfalva, Eppeschdorf, Ibaşfalău. Sibiu, C Romania 46°14′N 24°34′E
116 L12 **Dumbrăveni** Vrancea, E Romania 45°31′N 27°09′E
97 J14 **Dumfries** S Scotland, United Kingdom 55°04′N 03°37′W
97 J14 **Dumfries** *cultural region* SW Scotland, United Kingdom
153 R15 **Dumka** Jhārkhand, NE India 24°17′N 87°15′E
Dümmer *see* Dümmersee
100 G12 **Dümmersee** *var.* Dümmer. ◎ NW Germany
14 J11 **Dumoine** ≈ Québec, SE Canada
14 J10 **Dumoine, Lac** ◎ Québec, SE Canada
195 V16 **Dumont d'Urville** *French research station* Antarctica 66°24′S 139°38′E
195 W15 **Dumont d'Urville Sea** *sea* S Pacific Ocean
14 K11 **Dumont, Lac** ◎ Québec, SE Canada
75 W7 **Dumyāt** *var.* Dumyât, *Eng.* Damietta. N Egypt 31°26′N 31°48′E
Duna *see* Danube, C Europe
Düna *see* Western Dvina
Duna *see* Don, Russian Federation
Dünaburg *see* Daugavpils
111 J24 **Dunaföldvár** Tolna, C Hungary 46°48′N 18°55′E
Dunaj *see* Wien, Austria
Dunaj *see* Danube, C Europe
111 L18 **Dunajec** ≈ S Poland
111 H21 **Dunajská Streda** *Hung.* Dunaszerdahely. Trnavský Kraj, W Slovakia 48°N 17°28′E
Dunapentele *see* Dunaújváros
Dunărea *see* Danube
116 M13 **Dunărea Veche, Braţul** ≈ SE Romania
117 N13 **Dunării, Delta** *delta* SE Romania
Dunaszerdahely *see* Dunajská Streda
111 J23 **Dunaújváros** *prev.* Dunapentele, Sztálinváros. Fejér, C Hungary 47°N 18°55′E
Dunav *see* Danube
114 J8 **Dunavska Ravnina** *Eng.* Danubian Plain. *lowlands* N Bulgaria
114 G7 **Dunavtsi** Vidin, NW Bulgaria 43°54′N 22°49′E
123 S15 **Dunay** Primorskiy Kray, SE Russian Federation 42°53′N 132°20′E
Dunayevtsy *see* Dunayivtsi
116 L7 **Dunayivtsi** *Rus.* Dunayevtsy. Khmel'nyts'ka Oblast', NW Ukraine 48°56′N 26°50′E
185 F22 **Dunback** Otago, South Island, New Zealand 45°22′S 170°37′E
10 L17 **Duncan** Vancouver Island, British Columbia, SW Canada 48°46′N 123°10′W
37 O15 **Duncan** Arizona, SW USA 32°43′N 109°06′W
26 M12 **Duncan** Oklahoma, C USA 34°30′N 97°57′W
Duncan Island *see* Pinzón, Isla
151 Q20 **Duncan Passage** *strait* Andaman Sea/Bay of Bengal
96 K6 **Duncansby Head** *headland* N Scotland, United Kingdom 58°37′N 03°01′W
14 G12 **Dunchurch** Ontario, S Canada 45°36′N 79°54′W
118 D7 **Dundaga** Talsi, NW Latvia 57°29′N 22°19′E
14 G14 **Dundalk** Ontario, S Canada 44°11′N 80°22′W
97 F16 **Dundalk** *Ir.* Dún Dealgan. Louth, NE Ireland 54°01′N 06°25′W
21 X3 **Dundalk** Maryland, NE USA 39°15′N 76°31′W
97 F16 **Dundalk Bay** *Ir.* Cuan Dhún Dealgan. *bay* NE Ireland
14 G16 **Dundas** Ontario, S Canada 43°16′N 79°55′W
180 L12 **Dundas, Lake** *salt lake* Western Australia
Dundbürd *see* Batnorov
Dún Dealgan *see* Dundalk
15 N13 **Dundee** Québec, SE Canada 45°01′N 74°27′W
83 K22 **Dundee** KwaZulu/Natal, E South Africa 28°09′S 30°12′E
96 K11 **Dundee** E Scotland, United Kingdom 56°28′N 03°W
31 R10 **Dundee** Michigan, N USA 41°57′N 83°39′W
25 R5 **Dundee** Texas, SW USA 33°43′N 98°52′W
194 H3 **Dundee Island** *island* Antarctica
162 L9 **Dundgovĭ** ◈ *province* C Mongolia
97 G16 **Dundrum Bay** *Ir.* Cuan Dhún Droma. *inlet* NW Irish Sea
11 T15 **Dundurn** Saskatchewan, S Canada 51°43′N 106°27′W
Dund-Us *see* Hovd
Dund-Us *see* Hovd
185 F23 **Dunedin** Otago, South Island, New Zealand 45°52′S 170°31′E
183 R7 **Dunedoo** New South Wales, SE Australia 32°04′S 149°23′E
97 D14 **Dunfanaghy** *Ir.* Dún Fionnachaidh. NW Ireland 55°11′N 07°59′W
96 J12 **Dunfermline** C Scotland, United Kingdom 56°04′N 03°29′W
Dún Fionnachaidh *see* Dunfanaghy
149 V10 **Dunga Bunga** Punjab, E Pakistan 29°51′N 73°19′E
97 F15 **Dungannon** *Ir.* Dún Geanainn. C Northern Ireland, United Kingdom 54°31′N 06°46′W
Dun Garbháin *see* Dungarvan
152 F15 **Dūngarpur** Rājasthān, N India 23°50′N 73°43′E
97 E21 **Dungarvan** *Ir.* Dun Garbháin. Waterford, S Ireland 52°05′N 07°37′W
101 N21 **Dungau** *cultural region* SE Germany
Dún Geanainn *see* Dungannon
97 P23 **Dungeness** *headland* SE England, United Kingdom 50°55′N 00°58′E
63 I23 **Dungeness, Punta** *headland* S Argentina 52°25′S 68°25′W
Dungloe *see* Dunglow
97 D14 **Dunglow** *var.* Dungloe, *Ir.* An Clochán Liath. Donegal, NW Ireland 54°57′N 08°22′W
183 T7 **Dungog** New South Wales, SE Australia 32°24′S 151°45′E
79 O16 **Dungu** Orientale, NE Dem. Rep. Congo 03°40′N 28°32′E
168 L8 **Dungun** *var.* Kuala Dungun. Terengganu, Peninsular Malaysia 04°47′N 103°26′E
80 I6 **Dungûnab** Red Sea, NE Sudan 21°10′N 37°09′E
15 P13 **Dunham** Québec, SE Canada 45°08′N 72°48′W
Dunheved *see* Launceston
Dunholme *see* Durham
163 X10 **Dunhua** Jilin, NE China 43°22′N 128°12′E
159 P8 **Dunhuang** Gansu, N China 40°10′N 94°40′E
182 L12 **Dunkeld** Victoria, SE Australia 37°41′S 142°19′E
103 O1 **Dunkerque** *Eng.* Dunkirk, *Flem.* Duinekerke; *prev.* Dunquerque. Nord, N France 51°06′N 02°34′E
97 K23 **Dunkery Beacon** ▲ SW England, United Kingdom 51°10′N 03°36′W
18 C11 **Dunkirk** New York, NE USA 42°28′N 79°19′W
Dunkirk *see* Dunkerque
77 P17 **Dunkwa** SW Ghana 05°59′N 01°45′W
97 G18 **Dún Laoghaire** *Eng.* Dunleary; *prev.* Kingstown. E Ireland 53°17′N 06°08′W
29 S14 **Dunlap** Iowa, C USA 41°51′N 95°36′W
20 L10 **Dunlap** Tennessee, S USA 35°22′N 85°23′W
Dunleary *see* Dún Laoghaire
Dún Mánmhaí *see* Dunmanway
97 B21 **Dunmanway** *Ir.* Dún Mánmhaí. Cork, SW Ireland 51°43′N 09°07′W
18 I13 **Dunmore** Pennsylvania, NE USA 41°25′N 75°37′W
21 U10 **Dunn** North Carolina, SE USA 35°18′N 78°36′W
Dún na nGall *see* Donegal
23 V11 **Dunnellon** Florida, SE USA 29°03′N 82°27′W
96 J6 **Dunnet Head** *headland* N Scotland, United Kingdom 58°40′N 03°27′W
29 N14 **Dunning** Nebraska, C USA 41°49′N 100°04′W
14 G17 **Dunnville** Ontario, S Canada 42°54′N 79°36′W
Dún Pádraig *see* Downpatrick
Dunquerque *see* Dunkerque
Dunqulah *see* Dongola
96 L12 **Duns** SE Scotland, United Kingdom 55°46′N 02°13′W
29 N2 **Dunseith** North Dakota, N USA 48°48′N 100°03′W
35 N2 **Dunsmuir** California, W USA 41°12′N 122°19′W
97 N21 **Dunstable** *Lat.* Durocobrivae. E England, United Kingdom 51°53′N 00°32′W
185 D21 **Dunstan Mountains** ▲▲ South Island, New Zealand
103 O9 **Dun-sur-Auron** Cher, C France 46°52′N 02°40′E
185 F21 **Duntroon** Canterbury, South Island, New Zealand 44°52′S 170°40′E
149 T10 **Dunyāpur** Punjab, E Pakistan 29°48′N 71°48′E
163 U5 **Duobukur He** ≈ NE China
163 R12 **Duolun** *var.* Dolonnur. Nei Mongol Zizhiqu, N China 42°11′N 116°30′E
167 R14 **Dương Đông** Kiên Giang, S Vietnam 10°15′N 103°58′E
114 G10 **Dupnitsa** *prev.* Marek, Stanke Dimitrov. Kyustendil, W Bulgaria 42°16′N 23°07′E
28 L8 **Dupree** South Dakota, N USA 45°03′N 101°36′W
33 Q7 **Dupuyer** Montana, NW USA 48°13′N 112°34′W
141 Y11 **Duqm** *var.* Daqm. E Oman 19°42′N 57°40′E
63 F23 **Duque de York, Isla** *island* S Chile
181 N4 **Durack Range** ▲▲ Western Australia
136 K10 **Durağan** Sinop, N Turkey 41°26′N 35°03′E
103 S15 **Durance** ≈ SE France
31 R9 **Durand** Michigan, N USA 42°54′N 83°58′W
30 I6 **Durand** Wisconsin, N USA 44°37′N 91°56′W
40 K10 **Durango** *var.* Victoria de Durango. Durango, W Mexico 24°03′N 104°38′W
105 P3 **Durango** País Vasco, N Spain 43°10′N 02°38′W
37 Q8 **Durango** Colorado, C USA 37°13′N 107°51′W
40 J9 **Durango** ◈ *state* C Mexico
114 O7 **Durankulak** *Rom.* Răcari; *prev.* Blatnitsa, Duranulac. Dobrich, NE Bulgaria 43°41′N 28°31′E
22 L4 **Durant** Mississippi, S USA 33°04′N 89°51′W
27 P13 **Durant** Oklahoma, C USA 33°59′N 96°24′W
Duranulac *see* Durankulak
105 N6 **Duratón** ≈ N Spain
61 E19 **Durazno** *var.* San Pedro de Durazno. Durazno, C Uruguay 33°22′S 56°31′W
61 E19 **Durazno** ◈ *department* C Uruguay
Durazzo *see* Durrës
83 K23 **Durban** *var.* Port Natal. KwaZulu/Natal, E South Africa 29°51′S 31°E
83 K23 **Durban** ✈ KwaZulu/Natal, E South Africa 29°55′S 31°01′E
118 C9 **Durbe** *Ger.* Durben. Liepāja, W Latvia 56°34′N 21°22′E
Durben *see* Durbe
99 K21 **Durbuy** Luxembourg, SE Belgium 50°21′N 05°27′E
105 N15 **Dúrcal** Andalucía, S Spain 37°00′N 03°24′W
112 F8 **Đurđevac** *Ger.* Sankt Georgen, *Hung.* Szentgyörgy; *prev.* Djurdjevac, Gjurgjevac. Koprivnica-Kri»zevci, N Croatia 46°02′N 17°03′E
113 K15 **Đurđevica Tara** N Montenegro 43°09′N 19°18′E
97 L24 **Durdle Door** *natural arch* S England, United Kingdom
158 L3 **Düre** Xinjiang Uygur Zizhiqu, W China 46°30′N 88°26′E
101 D16 **Düren** *anc.* Marcodurum. Nordrhein-Westfalen, W Germany 50°48′N 06°30′E
154 K12 **Durg** *prev.* Drug. Chhattīsgarh, C India 21°12′N 81°20′E
153 U13 **Durgapur** Dhaka, N Bangladesh 25°10′N 90°41′E
153 R15 **Durgāpur** West Bengal, NE India 23°30′N 87°20′E
14 F14 **Durham** Ontario, S Canada 44°10′N 80°48′W
97 M14 **Durham** *hist.* Dunholme. N England, United Kingdom 54°47′N 01°34′W
21 U9 **Durham** North Carolina, SE USA 36°N 78°54′W
97 L15 **Durham** *cultural region* N England, United Kingdom
168 J10 **Duri** Sumatera, W Indonesia 01°13′N 101°13′E
Duria Major *see* Dora Baltea
Duria Minor *see* Dora Riparia
Durlas *see* Thurles
141 P8 **Ḍurmā** Ar Riyāḍ, C Saudi Arabia 24°37′N 46°06′E
113 J15 **Durmitor** ▲ N Montenegro
96 H6 **Durness** N Scotland, United Kingdom 58°34′N 04°46′W
109 Y3 **Dürnkrut** Niederösterreich, E Austria 48°28′N 16°50′E
Durnovaria *see* Dorchester
Durobrivae *see* Rochester
Durocasses *see* Dreux
Durocobrivae *see* Dunstable
Durocortorum *see* Reims
Durostorum *see* Silistra
Durovernum *see* Canterbury
113 K20 **Durrës** *var.* Durrësi, Dursi, *It.* Durazzo, *SCr.* Drač, *Turk.* Draç. Durrës, W Albania 41°20′N 19°26′E
113 K19 **Durrës** ◈ *district* W Albania
Durrësi *see* Durrës
97 A21 **Dursey Island** *Ir.* Oileán Baoi. *island* SW Ireland
Dursi *see* Durrës
Duru *see* Wuchuan
Durud *see* Do Rūd
114 P12 **Durusu** İstanbul, NW Turkey 41°18′N 28°41′E
114 O12 **Durusu Gölü** ◎ NW Turkey
138 I9 **Durūz, Jabal ad** ▲ SW Syria 37°00′N 32°30′E
184 K13 **D'Urville Island** *island* C New Zealand
171 X12 **D'Urville, Tanjung** *headland* Papua, E Indonesia 01°26′S 137°52′E
146 H14 **Duşak** *Rus.* Dushak. Ahal Welaýaty, S Turkmenistan 37°15′N 59°57′E
Dusa Mareb/Dusa Marreb *see* Dhuusa Marreeb
118 I11 **Dusetos** Utena, NE Lithuania 55°44′N 25°49′E
Dushak *see* Duşak
160 K12 **Dushan** Guizhou, S China 25°50′N 107°36′E
147 P13 **Dushanbe** *var.* Dyushambe; *prev.* Stalinabad, *Taj.* Stalinobod. ● (Tajikistan) W Tajikistan 38°35′N 68°44′E
147 P13 **Dushanbe** ✈ W Tajikistan 38°31′N 68°49′E
158 J5 **Dushanzi** Xinjiang Uygur Zizhiqu, NW China 44°20′N 84°51′E
137 T9 **Dushet'i** E Georgia 42°07′N 44°44′E
18 H13 **Dushore** Pennsylvania, NE USA 41°30′N 76°23′W
185 A23 **Dusky Sound** *sound* South Island, New Zealand
101 E15 **Düsseldorf** *var.* Duesseldorf. Nordrhein-Westfalen, W Germany 51°14′N 06°49′E
147 P14 **Dŭstí** *Rus.* Dusti. SW Tajikistan 37°22′N 68°41′E
194 I9 **Dustin Island** *island* Antarctica
Dutch East Indies *see* Indonesia
Dutch Guiana *see* Surinam
38 L17 **Dutch Harbor** Unalaska Island, Alaska, USA 53°51′N 166°33′W
36 J3 **Dutch Mount** ▲ Utah, W USA 40°16′N 113°56′W
Dutch New Guinea *see* Papua
Dutch West Indies *see* Netherlands Antilles
83 H20 **Dutlwe** Kweneng, S Botswana 23°58′S 23°56′E
67 V16 **Du Toit Fracture Zone** *tectonic feature* SW Indian Ocean
125 U8 **Dutovo** Respublika Komi, NW Russian Federation 63°45′N 56°38′E
77 V13 **Dutsan Wai** *var.* Dutsen Wai. Kaduna, C Nigeria 10°49′N 08°15′E
77 W13 **Dutse** Jigawa, N Nigeria 11°43′N 09°25′E
Dutsen Wai *see* Dutsan Wai
Duttia *see* Datia
14 E17 **Dutton** Ontario, S Canada 42°40′N 81°28′W
36 L7 **Dutton, Mount** ▲ Utah, W USA 38°00′N 112°10′W
162 E7 **Duut** Hovd, W Mongolia 47°28′N 91°52′E
14 K11 **Duval, Lac** ◎ Québec, SE Canada
127 W3 **Duvan** Respublika Bashkortostan, W Russian Federation 55°42′N 57°56′E
138 L9 **Duwaykhilat Satiḥ ar Ruwayshid** *seasonal river* SE Jordan
Dux *see* Duchcov
160 J13 **Duyang Shan** ▲▲ S China
167 T14 **Duyên Hai** Tra Vinh, S Vietnam 09°39′N 106°28′E
160 K12 **Duyun** Guizhou, S China 26°16′N 107°29′E
136 G11 **Düzce** Düzce, NW Turkey 40°51′N 31°09′E
136 K14 **Düzce** ◈ *province* NW Turkey
Duzdab *see* Zāhedān
Duzenkyr, Khrebet *see* Duzkyr, Khrebet
146 I16 **Duzkyr, Khrebet** *prev.* Khrebet Duzenkyr. ▲▲ S Turkmenistan
114 K8 **Dve Mogili** Ruse, N Bulgaria 43°35′N 25°51′E
Dvina Bay *see* Chëshskaya Guba
Dvinsk *see* Daugavpils
124 L7 **Dvinskaya Guba** *bay* NW Russian Federation
112 E10 **Dvor** Sisak-Moslavina, C Croatia 45°05′N 16°22′E
117 W5 **Dvorichna** Kharkivs'ka Oblast', E Ukraine 49°52′N 37°43′E
111 F16 **Dvůr Králové nad Labem** *Ger.* Königinhof an der Elbe. Královéhradecký Kraj, N Czech Republic 50°27′N 15°50′E
154 A10 **Dwārka** Gujarāt, W India 22°14′N 68°58′E
30 M12 **Dwight** Illinois, N USA 41°05′N 88°25′W
98 N8 **Dwingeloo** Drenthe, NE Netherlands 52°49′N 06°20′E
33 N10 **Dworshak Reservoir** ⊠ Idaho, NW USA
Dyal *see* Dyaul Island
Dyanev *see* Galkynyş
Dyatlovo *see* Dzyatlava
186 G5 **Dyaul Island** *var.* Djaul, Dyal. *island* NE Papua New Guinea
20 G8 **Dyer** Tennessee, S USA 36°04′N 88°59′W
9 S5 **Dyer, Cape** *headland* Baffin Island, Nunavut, NE Canada 66°37′N 61°13′W
20 F8 **Dyersburg** Tennessee, S USA 36°02′N 89°21′W
29 Y13 **Dyersville** Iowa, C USA 42°29′N 91°07′W
97 I21 **Dyfed** *cultural region* SW Wales, United Kingdom
Dyfrdwy, Afon *see* Dee
Dyhernfurth *see* Brzeg Dolny

◆ Country
● Country Capital
◇ Dependent Territory
○ Dependent Territory Capital
◈ Administrative Regions
✈ International Airport
▲ Mountain
▲▲ Mountain Range
Volcano
≈ River
◎ Lake
⊠ Reservoir

111 E19 **Dyje** var. Thaya. ≈ Austria/Czech Republic *see also* Thaya
Dyje *see* Thaya
117 T5 **Dykan'ka** Poltavs'ka Oblast', C Ukraine 49°48'N 34°33'E
127 N16 **Dykhtau** ▲ SW Russian Federation 43°01'N 42°56'E
111 A16 **Dyleń** Ger. Tillenberg. ▲ NW Czech Republic 49°58'N 12°31'E
110 K9 **Dylewska Góra** ▲ N Poland 53°33'N 19°57'E
117 O4 **Dymer** Kyyivs'ka Oblast', N Ukraine 50°50'N 30°20'E
117 W7 **Dymytrov** Rus. Dimitrov. Donets'ka Oblast', SE Ukraine 48°18'N 37°19'E
111 O17 **Dynów** Podkarpackie, SE Poland 49°49'N 22°14'E
29 X13 **Dysart** Iowa, C USA 42°10'N 92°18'W
Dysna *see* Dzisna
115 H18 **Dýstos, Límni** var. Límni Dístos. ◎ Évvoia, C Greece
115 D18 **Dytikí Elláș** Eng. Greece West. ◐ region C Greece
115 C14 **Dytikí Makedonía** Eng. Macedonia West. ◐ region N Greece
Dyurment'yube *see* Dermentobe
127 U4 **Dyurtyuli** Respublika Bashkortostan, W Russian Federation 55°31'N 54°49'E
Dyushambe *see* Dushanbe
162 K7 **Dzaamar** var. Bat-Öldziyt. Töv, C Mongolia 48°10'N 104°49'E
Dzaanhushuu *see* Ihtamir
Dza Chu *see* Mekong
Dzadgay *see* Bömbögör
162 H8 **Dzag** Bayanhongor, C Mongolia 46°54'N 99°11'E
Dzalaa *see* Shinejinst
163 O11 **Dzamïn-Üüd** var. Borhoyn Tal. Dornogovĭ, SE Mongolia 43°43'N 111°53'E
172 J14 **Dzaoudzi** E Mayotte 12°48'S 45°18'E
Dzaudzhikau *see* Vladikavkaz
162 G7 **Dzavhan** ◐ province NW Mongolia
162 G7 **Dzavhan Gol** ≈ NW Mongolia
162 G6 **Dzavhanmandal** var. Nuga. Dzavhan, W Mongolia 48°17'N 95°07'E
Dzegstey *see* Ögiynuur
162 E7 **Dzereg** var. Altanteel. Hovd, W Mongolia 47°05'N 92°57'E
127 O3 **Dzerzhinsk** Nizhegorodskaya Oblast', W Russian Federation 56°20'N 43°22'E
Dzerzhinsk *see* Dzyarzhynsk Belarus
Dzerzhinsk *see* Dzerzhyns'k
Dzerzhinskiy *see* Nar'yan-Mar
Dzerzhinskoye *see* Tokzhaylau
Dzerzhinskoye *see* Tokzhaylau
117 X7 **Dzerzhyns'k** Rus. Dzerzhinsk. Donets'ka Oblast', SE Ukraine 48°21'N 37°50'E
116 M5 **Dzerzhyns'k** Zhytomyrs'ka Oblast', N Ukraine 50°07'N 27°56'E
Dżetygara *see* Zhitikara
Dzhailgan *see* Jayilgan
145 N14 **Dzhalagash** Kaz. Zhalaghash. Kzylorda, S Kazakhstan 45°06'N 64°40'E
147 T10 **Dzhalal-Abad** Kir. Jalal-Abad. Dzhalal-Abadskaya Oblast', W Kyrgyzstan 40°56'N 73°00'E
147 S9 **Dzhalal-Abadskaya Oblast'** Kir. Jalal-Abad Oblasty. ◐ province W Kyrgyzstan
Dzhalilabad *see* Cälilabad
Dzhambeyty *see* Zhympity
Dzhambul *see* Taraz
Dzhambulskaya Oblast' *see* Zhambyl
144 D9 **Dzhanibek** var. Dzhanybek, Kaz. Zhänibek. Zapadnyy Kazakhstan, W Kazakhstan 49°27'N 46°51'E
Dzhankel'dy *see* Jongeldi
117 T12 **Dzhankoy** Respublika Krym, S Ukraine 45°40'N 34°20'E
145 V14 **Dzhansugurov** Kaz. Zhansügirov. Almaty, SE Kazakhstan 45°23'N 79°29'E
147 R9 **Dzhany-Bazar** var. Yangibazar. Dzhalal-Abadskaya Oblast', W Kyrgyzstan 41°40'N 70°49'E
Dzhanybek *see* Dzhanibek
123 P8 **Dzhardzhan** Respublika Sakha (Yakutiya), NE Russian Federation 68°47'N 123°51'E
Dzharkurgan *see* Jarqo'rg'on
117 S11 **Dzharylhats'ka Zatoka** gulf S Ukraine
Dzhayilgan *see* Jayilgan
Dzhebel *see* Jebel
147 T14 **Dzhelandy** SE Tajikistan 37°34'N 72°35'E
147 Y7 **Dzhergalan** Kir. Jyrgalan. Issyk-Kul'skaya Oblast', NE Kyrgyzstan 42°37'N 78°56'E
Dzhetysay *see* Zhetysay
Dzhezkazgan *see* Zhezkazgan
Dzhigirbent *see* Jigerbent
Dzhirgatal' *see* Jirgatol
Dzhizak *see* Jizzax
Dzhizakskaya Oblast' *see* Jizzax Viloyati
123 P8 **Dzhugdzhur, Khrebet** ▲ E Russian Federation
Dzhul'fa *see* Culfa
Dzhuma *see* Juma
145 W14 **Dzhungarskiy Alatau** ▲ China/Kazakhstan
144 M14 **Dzhusaly** Kaz. Zhosaly. Kzylorda, SW Kazakhstan 45°29'N 64°04'E
146 J12 **Dzhynlykum, Peski** desert E Turkmenistan
110 L9 **Działdowo** Warmińsko-Mazurskie, C Poland 53°13'N 20°12'E
111 L16 **Działoszyce** Świętokrzyskie, C Poland 50°21'N 20°19'E
41 X11 **Dzidzantún** Yucatán, E Mexico
111 G15 **Dzierżoniów** Ger. Reichenbach. Dolnośląskie, SW Poland 50°43'N 16°40'E
41 X11 **Dzilam de Bravo** Yucatán, E Mexico 21°24'N 88°52'W
118 L12 **Dzisna** Rus. Disna. Vitsyebskaya Voblasts', N Belarus 55°33'N 28°13'E
118 K12 **Dzisna** Lith. Dysna, Rus. Disna. ≈ Belarus/Lithuania
119 G20 **Dzivin** Rus. Divin. Brestskaya Voblasts', SW Belarus 51°58'N 24°33'E
119 M15 **Dzmitravichy** Rus. Dmitrovichi. Minskaya Voblasts', C Belarus 53°58'N 29°14'E
Dzogsool *see* Bayantsagaan
162 I5 **Dzöölön** var. Rinchinlhumbe. Hövsgöl, N Mongolia 51°06'N 99°40'E
129 S8 **Dzungaria** var. Sungaria, Zungaria. physical region W China
Dzungarian Basin *see* Junggar Pendi
Dzür *see* Tes
162 J8 **Dzüünbayan-Ulaan** var. Bayan-Ulaan. Övörhangay, C Mongolia 46°38'N 102°30'E
Dzüünbulag *see* Matad, Dornod, Mongolia
Dzüünbulag *see* Uulbayan, Sühbaatar, Mongolia
162 L8 **Dzuunmod** Töv, C Mongolia 47°45'N 107°00'E
Dzuunmod *see* Ider
Dzüün Soyonï Nuruu *see* Eastern Sayans
Dzüyl *see* Tonhil
Dzvina *see* Western Dvina
119 J16 **Dzyarzhynsk Belarus** Rus. Dzerzhinsk; prev. Kaydanovo. Minskaya Voblasts', C Belarus 53°41'N 27°09'E
119 H17 **Dzyatlava** Pol. Zdzięcioł, Rus. Dyatlovo. Hrodzyenskaya Voblasts', W Belarus 53°27'N 25°23'E

E

E *see* Hubei
Éadan Doire *see* Edenderry
37 W6 **Eads** Colorado, C USA 38°28'N 102°46'W
37 O13 **Eagar** Arizona, SW USA 34°05'N 109°17'W
39 T8 **Eagle** Alaska, USA 64°47'N 141°12'W
13 S8 **Eagle** ≈ Newfoundland and Labrador, E Canada
10 I3 **Eagle** ≈ Yukon Territory, NW Canada
29 T7 **Eagle Bend** Minnesota, N USA 46°10'N 95°02'W
28 M8 **Eagle Butte** South Dakota, N USA 44°58'N 101°13'W
29 V12 **Eagle Grove** Iowa, C USA 42°39'N 93°54'W
19 R2 **Eagle Lake** Maine, NE USA 47°01'N 68°35'W
25 U11 **Eagle Lake** Texas, SW USA 29°35'N 96°19'W
12 A11 **Eagle Lake** ◎ Ontario, S Canada
35 P3 **Eagle Lake** ◎ California, W USA
19 R3 **Eagle Lake** ◎ Maine, NE USA
29 Y3 **Eagle Mountain** ▲ Minnesota, N USA 47°54'N 90°33'W
25 T6 **Eagle Mountain Lake** ▣ Texas, SW USA
37 S9 **Eagle Nest Lake** ▣ New Mexico, SW USA
25 P13 **Eagle Pass** Texas, SW USA 28°44'N 100°31'W
65 C25 **Eagle Passage** passage SW Atlantic Ocean
35 R8 **Eagle Peak** ▲ California, W USA 38°11'N 119°22'W
35 Q2 **Eagle Peak** ▲ California, W USA 41°16'N 120°12'W
37 P13 **Eagle Peak** ▲ New Mexico, SW USA 33°39'N 109°36'W
10 I4 **Eagle Plain** Yukon Territory, NW Canada 66°23'N 136°42'W
32 G15 **Eagle Point** Oregon, NW USA 42°28'N 122°48'W
186 P10 **Eagle Point** headland SE Papua New Guinea 10°31'S 149°53'E
39 R11 **Eagle River** Alaska, USA 61°18'N 149°38'W
30 M2 **Eagle River** Michigan, N USA 47°24'N 88°18'W
30 L4 **Eagle River** Wisconsin, N USA 45°56'N 89°15'W
21 S6 **Eagle Rock** Virginia, NE USA 37°40'N 79°46'W
36 J13 **Eagletail Mountains** ▲ Arizona, SW USA
167 U12 **Ea Hleo** Đắc Lắc, S Vietnam 13°09'N 108°14'E
167 U12 **Ea Kar** Đắc Lắc, S Vietnam 12°47'N 108°26'E
Eanjum *see* Anjum
Eanodat *see* Enontekiö
12 B10 **Ear Falls** Ontario, C Canada 50°38'N 93°13'W
27 X10 **Earle** Arkansas, C USA 35°16'N 90°28'W
35 R12 **Earlimart** California, W USA 35°52'N 119°17'W
20 I6 **Earlington** Kentucky, S USA 37°16'N 87°30'W
14 H8 **Earlton** Ontario, S Canada 47°41'N 79°46'W
29 T13 **Early** Iowa, C USA 42°27'N 95°09'W
96 J11 **Earn** ≈ N Scotland, United Kingdom
185 C21 **Earnslaw, Mount** ▲ South Island, New Zealand 44°34'S 168°26'E
24 M4 **Earth** Texas, SW USA 34°13'N 102°24'W
21 P11 **Easley** South Carolina, SE USA 34°49'N 82°36'W
East *see* Est
East Açores Fracture Zone *see* East Azores Fracture Zone
97 P19 **East Anglia** physical region E England, United Kingdom
15 Q12 **East Angus** Québec, SE Canada 45°29'N 71°39'W
195 V8 **East Antarctica** var. Greater Antarctica. physical region Antarctica
18 E10 **East Aurora** New York, NE USA 42°44'N 78°36'W
East Australian Basin *see* Tasman Basin
East Azerbaijan *see* Āzarbāyjān-e Sharqī
64 L9 **East Azores Fracture Zone** var. East Açores Fracture Zone. tectonic feature E Atlantic Ocean
22 M11 **East Bay** bay Louisiana, S USA
25 V11 **East Bernard** Texas, SW USA 29°32'N 96°04'W
29 V8 **East Bethel** Minnesota, N USA 45°24'N 93°14'W
East Borneo *see* Kalimantan Timur
97 P23 **Eastbourne** SE England, United Kingdom 50°46'N 00°16'E
15 R11 **East-Broughton** Québec, SE Canada 46°14'N 71°05'W
44 M6 **East Caicos** island E Turks and Caicos Islands
184 R7 **East Cape** headland North Island, New Zealand 37°40'S 178°31'E
174 M4 **East Caroline Basin** undersea feature SW Pacific Ocean 04°00'N 146°45'E
192 P4 **East China Sea** Chin. Dong Hai. sea W Pacific Ocean
97 P19 **East Dereham** E England, United Kingdom 52°41'N 00°55'E
30 J9 **East Dubuque** Illinois, N USA 42°29'N 90°38'W
11 S17 **Eastend** Saskatchewan, S Canada 49°29'N 108°48'W
193 S10 **Easter Fracture Zone** tectonic feature E Pacific Ocean
Easter Island *see* Pascua, Isla de
81 J18 **Eastern** ◐ province Kenya
153 Q12 **Eastern** ◐ zone E Nepal
155 K25 **Eastern** ◐ province E Sri Lanka
82 L13 **Eastern** ◐ province E Zambia
83 H24 **Eastern Cape** off. Eastern Cape Province, Afr. Oos-Kaap. ◐ province SE South Africa
Eastern Cape Province *see* Eastern Cape
Eastern Desert *see* Sahara el Sharqîya
81 F15 **Eastern Equatoria** ◐ state SE Sudan
Eastern Euphrates *see* Murat Nehri
155 J17 **Eastern Ghats** ▲ SE India
186 E7 **Eastern Highlands** ◐ province C Papua New Guinea
Eastern Region *see* Ash Sharqīyah
122 L13 **Eastern Sayans** Mong. Dzüün Soyonï Nuruu, Rus. Vostochnyy Sayan. ▲ Mongolia/Russian Federation
Eastern Scheldt *see* Oosterschelde
Eastern Sierra Madre *see* Madre Oriental, Sierra
Eastern Transvaal *see* Mpumalanga
11 W14 **Easterville** Manitoba, C Canada 53°06'N 99°53'W
Easterwâlde *see* Oosterwolde
63 M23 **East Falkland** var. Isla Soledad. island E Falkland Islands
19 P12 **East Falmouth** Massachusetts, NE USA 41°34'N 70°31'W
East Fayu *see* Fayu
East Flanders *see* Oost-Vlaanderen
39 S6 **East Fork Chandalar River** ≈ Alaska, USA
29 U12 **East Fork Des Moines River** ≈ Iowa/Minnesota, C USA
East Frisian Islands *see* Ostfriesische Inseln
18 K10 **East Glenville** New York, NE USA 42°53'N 73°55'W
29 R4 **East Grand Forks** Minnesota, N USA 47°54'N 97°59'W
97 O23 **East Grinstead** SE England, United Kingdom 51°08'N 00°00'W
18 M12 **East Hartford** Connecticut, NE USA 41°45'N 72°36'W
18 M13 **East Haven** Connecticut, NE USA 41°16'N 72°52'W
173 T9 **East Indiaman Ridge** undersea feature E Indian Ocean
129 V16 **East Indies** island group SE Asia
East Java *see* Jawa Timur
31 Q6 **East Jordan** Michigan, N USA 45°09'N 85°07'W
East Kalimantan *see* Kalimantan Timur
East Kazakhstan *see* Vostochnyy Kazakhstan
96 I12 **East Kilbride** S Scotland, United Kingdom 55°46'N 04°10'W
25 R7 **Eastland** Texas, SW USA 32°23'N 98°50'W
31 Q9 **East Lansing** Michigan, N USA 42°44'N 84°28'W
35 X11 **East Las Vegas** Nevada, W USA 36°05'N 115°02'W
97 M23 **Eastleigh** S England, United Kingdom 50°58'N 01°22'W
31 V12 **East Liverpool** Ohio, N USA 40°37'N 80°34'W
83 J25 **East London** Afr. Oos-Londen; prev. Emonti, Port Rex. Eastern Cape, S South Africa 33°S 27°54'E
96 K12 **East Lothian** cultural region SE Scotland, United Kingdom
12 I10 **Eastmain** Québec, E Canada 52°11'N 78°27'W
12 J10 **Eastmain** ≈ Québec, C Canada
15 P13 **Eastman** Québec, SE Canada 45°19'N 72°18'W
23 U6 **Eastman** Georgia, SE USA 32°12'N 83°10'W
175 O3 **East Mariana Basin** undersea feature W Pacific Ocean
30 K11 **East Moline** Illinois, N USA 41°30'N 90°26'W
186 H7 **East New Britain** ◐ province E Papua New Guinea
29 T15 **East Nishnabotna River** ≈ Iowa, C USA
197 V12 **East Novaya Zemlya Trough** var. Novaya Zemlya Trough. undersea feature W Kara Sea
East Nusa Tenggara *see* Nusa Tenggara Timur
21 X4 **Easton** Maryland, NE USA 38°46'N 76°04'W
18 I14 **Easton** Pennsylvania, NE USA 40°41'N 75°13'W
193 R16 **East Pacific Rise** undersea feature E Pacific Ocean 20°00'S 115°00'W
East Pakistan *see* Bangladesh
31 V12 **East Palestine** Ohio, N USA 40°49'N 80°32'W
30 L12 **East Peoria** Illinois, N USA 40°40'N 89°34'W
23 S3 **East Point** Georgia, SE USA 33°40'N 84°26'W
19 U6 **Eastport** Maine, NE USA 44°54'N 66°59'W
27 Z8 **East Prairie** Missouri, C USA 36°46'N 89°23'W
19 O12 **East Providence** Rhode Island, NE USA 41°48'N 71°20'W
20 L11 **East Ridge** Tennessee, S USA 35°00'N 85°15'W
97 N16 **East Riding** cultural region N England, United Kingdom
18 F9 **East Rochester** New York, NE USA 43°06'N 77°29'W
30 K15 **East Saint Louis** Illinois, N USA 38°35'N 90°07'W
65 K21 **East Scotia Basin** undersea feature SE Scotia Sea
129 Y8 **East Sea** var. Sea of Japan, Rus. Yapanskoye More. Sea NW Pacific Ocean *see also* Japan, Sea of
186 B6 **East Sepik** ◐ province NW Papua New Guinea
173 N4 **East Sheba Ridge** undersea feature W Arabian Sea 14°30'N 56°15'E
East Siberian Sea *see* Vostochno-Sibirskoye More
18 I14 **East Stroudsburg** Pennsylvania, NE USA 41°00'N 75°10'W
East Tasmanian Rise/ East Tasmania Plateau/ East Tasmania Rise *see* East Tasman Plateau
192 I12 **East Tasman Plateau** var. East Tasmanian Rise, East Tasmania Plateau, East Tasmania Rise. undersea feature SW Tasman Sea
64 L7 **East Thulean Rise** undersea feature N Atlantic Ocean
171 R16 **East Timor** var. Loro Sae; prev. Portuguese Timor, Timor Timur. ◆ country S Indonesia
21 Y6 **Eastville** Virginia, NE USA 37°22'N 75°58'W
35 R7 **East Walker River** ≈ California/Nevada, W USA
182 D1 **Eateringinna Creek** ≈ South Australia
37 T3 **Eaton** Colorado, C USA 40°31'N 104°42'W
15 Q12 **Eaton** ≈ Québec, SE Canada
11 S16 **Eatonia** Saskatchewan, S Canada 51°13'N 109°22'W
31 Q10 **Eaton Rapids** Michigan, N USA 42°30'N 84°39'W
23 U4 **Eatonton** Georgia, SE USA 33°19'N 83°23'W
32 H9 **Eatonville** Washington, NW USA 46°51'N 122°19'W
30 J6 **Eau Claire** Wisconsin, N USA 44°50'N 91°30'W
12 J7 **Eau Claire, Lac à l'** ◎ Québec, SE Canada
Eau Claire, Lac à L' *see* St. Clair, Lake
30 L6 **Eau Claire River** ≈ Wisconsin, N USA
188 J16 **Eauripik Atoll** atoll Caroline Islands, C Micronesia
192 H7 **Eauripik Rise** undersea feature W Pacific Ocean 03°00'N 142°00'E
102 K15 **Eauze** Gers, S France 43°52'N 00°06'E
41 P11 **Ébano** San Luis Potosí, C Mexico 22°16'N 98°26'W
97 K21 **Ebbw Vale** SE Wales, United Kingdom 51°48'N 03°13'W
79 E17 **Ebebiyin** NE Equatorial Guinea 02°08'N 11°15'E
95 H22 **Ebeltoft** Århus, C Denmark 56°11'N 10°42'E
109 X5 **Ebenfurth** Niederösterreich, E Austria 47°53'N 16°22'E
18 D14 **Ebensburg** Pennsylvania, NE USA 40°28'N 78°44'W
109 S5 **Ebensee** Oberösterreich, N Austria 47°48'N 13°46'E
101 H20 **Eberbach** Baden-Württemberg, SW Germany 49°28'N 08°58'E
121 U8 **Eber Gölü** salt lake C Turkey
109 U9 **Eberndorf** Slvn. Dobrla Vas. Kärnten, S Austria 46°33'N 14°35'E
109 R4 **Eberschwang** Oberösterreich, N Austria 48°09'N 13°37'E
100 O11 **Eberswalde-Finow** Brandenburg, E Germany 52°50'N 13°48'E
Ebesfalva *see* Dumbrăveni
165 T4 **Ebetsu** var. Ebetu. Hokkaidō, NE Japan 43°08'N 141°37'E
Ebetu *see* Ebetsu
Ebinayon *see* Evinayong
158 I4 **Ebinur Hu** ◎ NW China
138 I3 **Ebla** Ar. Tell Mardīkh. site of ancient city Idlib, NW Syria
Eblana *see* Dublin
108 H7 **Ebnat** Sankt Gallen, NE Switzerland 47°16'N 09°07'E
107 L18 **Eboli** Campania, S Italy 40°37'N 15°03'E
79 E16 **Ebolowa** Sud, S Cameroon 02°56'N 11°11'E
79 N21 **Ebombo** Kasai-Oriental, C Dem. Rep. Congo 05°42'S 26°07'E
189 T9 **Ebon Atoll** var. Epoon. atoll Ralik Chain, S Marshall Islands
77 U16 **Ebonyi** ◐ state SE Nigeria
Ebora *see* Évora
Eboracum *see* York
Eborodunum *see* Yverdon
101 J19 **Ebrach** Bayern, C Germany 49°49'N 10°30'E
109 X5 **Ebreichsdorf** Niederösterreich, E Austria 47°58'N 16°24'E
105 S6 **Ebro** ≈ NE Spain
105 N3 **Ebro, Embalse del** ▣ N Spain
120 G7 **Ebro Fan** undersea feature W Mediterranean Sea
Eburacum *see* York
Ebusus *see* Ibiza
Ebusus *see* Eivissa
99 F20 **Écaussinnes-d'Enghien** Hainaut, SW Belgium 50°34'N 04°10'E
Ecbatana *see* Hamadān
21 Q6 **Eccles** West Virginia, NE USA 37°46'N 81°16'W
115 L14 **Eceabat** Çanakkale, NW Turkey 40°12'N 26°22'E
171 O2 **Echague** Luzon, N Philippines 16°42'N 121°37'E
Ech Cheliff/Ech Chleff *see* Chlef
Echeng *see* Ezhou
115 C18 **Echinádes** island group W Greece
114 J12 **Echínos** var. Ehinos, Ekhínos. Anatolikí Makedonía kai Thráki, NE Greece 41°16'N 25°00'E
Echizen *see* Takefu
164 J12 **Echizen-misaki** headland Honshū, SW Japan 35°59'N 135°57'E
Echmiadzin *see* Vagharshapat
8 J8 **Echo Bay** Northwest Territories, NW Canada 66°04'N 118°W
35 Y11 **Echo Bay** Nevada, W USA 36°19'N 114°27'W
36 L9 **Echo Cliffs** cliff Arizona, SW USA
14 C10 **Echo Lake** ◎ Ontario, S Canada
35 Q7 **Echo Summit** ▲ California, W USA 38°47'N 120°06'W
14 L8 **Échouani, Lac** ◎ Québec, SE Canada
99 L17 **Echt** Limburg, SE Netherlands 51°07'N 05°52'E
101 H22 **Echterdingen** ✈ (Stuttgart) Baden-Württemberg, SW Germany 48°40'N 09°13'E
99 N24 **Echternach** Grevenmacher, E Luxembourg 49°49'N 06°25'E
183 N11 **Echuca** Victoria, SE Australia 36°10'S 144°20'E
104 L14 **Écija** anc. Astigi. Andalucía, SW Spain 37°33'N 05°04'W
Eckengraf *see* Viesīte
100 I7 **Eckernförde** Schleswig-Holstein, N Germany 54°28'N 09°49'E
100 J7 **Eckernförder Bucht** inlet N Germany
102 L7 **Écommoy** Sarthe, NW France 47°51'N 00°15'E
14 L10 **Écorce, Lac de l'** ◎ Québec, SE Canada
15 Q8 **Écorces, Rivière aux** ≈ Québec, SE Canada
56 C7 **Ecuador** off. Republic of Ecuador. ◆ republic NW South America
Ecuador, Republic of *see* Ecuador
95 I17 **Ed** Västra Götaland, S Sweden 58°55'N 11°55'E
Ed *see* 'Īdī
98 I9 **Edam** Noord-Holland, C Netherlands 52°30'N 05°02'E
96 K4 **Eday** island NE Scotland, United Kingdom
25 S17 **Edcouch** Texas, SW USA 26°17'N 97°57'W
80 C11 **Ed Da'ein** Southern Darfur, W Sudan 11°25'N 26°08'E
80 G11 **Ed Damazin** var. Ad Damazīn. Blue Nile, E Sudan 11°45'N 34°20'E
80 G8 **Ed Damer** var. Ad Dāmir, Ad Damar. River Nile, NE Sudan 17°37'N 33°59'E
80 E8 **Ed Debba** Northern, N Sudan 18°02'N 30°56'E
80 F10 **Ed Dueim** var. Ad Duwaym, Ad Duwēm. White Nile, C Sudan 13°38'N 32°36'E
183 Q16 **Eddystone Point** headland Tasmania, SE Australia 41°01'S 148°18'E
97 I25 **Eddystone Rocks** rocks SW England, United Kingdom
29 W15 **Eddyville** Iowa, C USA 41°09'N 92°37'W
20 H7 **Eddyville** Kentucky, S USA 37°03'N 88°02'W
98 L12 **Ede** Gelderland, C Netherlands 52°03'N 05°40'E
77 T16 **Ede** Osun, SW Nigeria 07°40'N 04°21'E
79 D16 **Edéa** Littoral, SW Cameroon 03°47'N 10°08'E
111 M20 **Edelény** Borsod-Abaúj-Zemplén, NE Hungary 48°18'N 20°40'E
183 R12 **Eden** New South Wales, SE Australia 37°04'S 149°51'E
21 T8 **Eden** North Carolina, SE USA 36°29'N 79°46'W
25 P9 **Eden** Texas, SW USA 31°13'N 99°51'W
97 K14 **Eden** ≈ NW England, United Kingdom
83 I23 **Edenburg** Free State, C South Africa 29°45'S 25°57'E
185 D24 **Edendale** Southland, South Island, New Zealand 46°18'S 168°48'E
97 E18 **Edenderry** Ir. Éadan Doire. Offaly, C Ireland 53°21'N 07°03'W
182 L11 **Edenhope** Victoria, SE Australia 37°04'S 141°15'E
21 X8 **Edenton** North Carolina, SE USA 36°04'N 76°39'W
101 G16 **Eder** ≈ NW Germany
101 H15 **Edersee** ◎ W Germany
114 E13 **Édessa** var. Édhessa. Kentrikí Makedonía, N Greece 40°48'N 22°03'E
Edessa *see* Şanlıurfa
Edfu *see* Idfū
29 P16 **Edgar** Nebraska, C USA 40°22'N 97°58'W
19 P13 **Edgartown** Martha's Vineyard, Massachusetts, NE USA 41°23'N 70°30'W
39 X13 **Edgecumbe, Mount** ▲ Baranof Island, Alaska, USA 57°03'N 135°45'W
21 Q13 **Edgefield** South Carolina, SE USA 33°50'N 81°57'W
29 P6 **Edgeley** North Dakota, N USA 46°19'N 98°42'W
28 I11 **Edgemont** South Dakota, N USA 43°18'N 103°49'W
92 O3 **Edgeøya** island S Svalbard
27 Q4 **Edgerton** Kansas, C USA 38°45'N 95°00'W
29 S10 **Edgerton** Minnesota, N USA 43°52'N 96°07'W
21 X3 **Edgewood** Maryland, NE USA 39°20'N 76°21'W
25 V6 **Edgewood** Texas, SW USA 32°42'N 95°53'W
Édhessa *see* Édessa
29 V9 **Edina** Minnesota, N USA 44°53'N 93°21'W
27 U2 **Edina** Missouri, C USA 40°10'N 92°10'W
25 S17 **Edinburg** Texas, SW USA 26°18'N 98°10'W
65 M24 **Edinburgh** var. Settlement of Edinburgh. ○ (Tristan da Cunha) NW Tristan da Cunha 37°03'S 12°18'W
96 J12 **Edinburgh** ● S Scotland, United Kingdom 55°57'N 03°13'W
31 P14 **Edinburgh** Indiana, N USA 39°19'N 86°00'W
96 J12 **Edinburgh** ✈ S Scotland, United Kingdom 55°57'N 03°22'W
116 L8 **Edineț** var. Edineți, Rus. Yedintsy. NW Moldova 48°10'N 27°18'E
Edineți *see* Edineț
Edingen *see* Enghien
136 B9 **Edirne** Eng. Adrianople; anc. Adrianopolis, Hadrianopolis. Edirne, NW Turkey 41°40'N 26°34'E
136 B11 **Edirne** ◐ province NW Turkey
18 K15 **Edison** New Jersey, NE USA 40°31'N 74°24'W
21 S15 **Edisto Island** South Carolina, SE USA 32°34'N 80°17'W
21 R14 **Edisto River** ≈ South Carolina, SE USA
33 S10 **Edith, Mount** ▲ Montana, NW USA 46°25'N 111°10'W
27 N10 **Edmond** Oklahoma, C USA 35°40'N 97°30'W
32 H8 **Edmonds** Washington, NW USA 47°48'N 122°22'W
11 Q14 **Edmonton** province capital Alberta, SW Canada 53°34'N 113°25'W
20 K7 **Edmonton** Kentucky, S USA 36°59'N 85°39'W
11 Q14 **Edmonton** ✈ Alberta, SW Canada 53°22'N 113°43'W
29 P3 **Edmore** North Dakota, N USA 48°22'N 98°26'W
13 N13 **Edmundston** New Brunswick, SE Canada 47°22'N 68°20'W
25 U12 **Edna** Texas, SW USA 29°00'N 96°41'W
39 X14 **Edna Bay** Kosciusko Island, Alaska, USA 55°54'N 133°40'W
77 U16 **Edo** ◐ state S Nigeria
106 F6 **Edolo** Lombardia, N Italy 46°13'N 10°20'E
64 L6 **Edoras Bank** undersea feature C Atlantic Ocean
96 G7 **Edrachillis Bay** bay NW Scotland, United Kingdom
136 B12 **Edremit** Balıkesir, NW Turkey 39°34'N 27°01'E
136 B12 **Edremit Körfezi** gulf NW Turkey
95 P14 **Edsbro** Stockholm, C Sweden 59°54'N 18°30'E
95 N18 **Edsbruk** Kalmar, S Sweden 58°01'N 16°30'E
94 M12 **Edsbyn** Gävleborg, C Sweden 61°22'N 15°45'E
11 O14 **Edson** Alberta, SW Canada 53°36'N 116°28'W
62 K13 **Eduardo Castex** La Pampa, C Argentina 35°55'S 64°18'W
58 F12 **Eduardo Gomes** ✈ (Manaus) Amazonas, NW Brazil 05°55'S 35°15'W
Edwardesabad *see* Bannu
67 U9 **Edward, Lake** var. Albert Edward Nyanza, Edward Nyanza, Lac Idi Amin, Lake Rutanzige. ◎ Uganda/Dem. Rep. Congo
Edward Nyanza *see* Edward, Lake
22 K5 **Edwards** Mississippi, S USA 32°19'N 90°36'W
25 O10 **Edwards Plateau** plain Texas, SW USA
30 J11 **Edwards River** ≈ Illinois, N USA
30 K15 **Edwardsville** Illinois, N USA 38°48'N 89°57'W
195 X4 **Edward VIII Gulf** bay Antarctica
195 O13 **Edward VII Peninsula** peninsula Antarctica
10 J11 **Edziza, Mount** ▲ British Columbia, W Canada 57°43'N 130°39'W
23 H16 **Edzo** prev. Rae-Edzo. Northwest Territories, NW Canada 62°44'N 115°55'W
39 N12 **Eek** Alaska, USA 60°13'N 162°01'W
99 D16 **Eeklo** var. Eekloo. Oost-Vlaanderen, NW Belgium 51°11'N 03°34'E
Eekloo *see* Eeklo
39 N12 **Eek River** ≈ Alaska, USA
98 N6 **Eelde** Drenthe, NE Netherlands 53°07'N 06°30'E
34 L5 **Eel River** ≈ California, W USA
31 P12 **Eel River** ≈ Indiana, N USA
Eems *see* Ems
98 O4 **Eemshaven** Groningen, NE Netherlands 53°28'N 06°50'E
98 O5 **Eems Kanaal** canal NE Netherlands
98 M11 **Eerbeek** Gelderland, E Netherlands 52°07'N 06°04'E
99 C17 **Eernegem** West-Vlaanderen, W Belgium 51°08'N 03°03'E
99 J15 **Eersel** Noord-Brabant, S Netherlands 51°22'N 05°19'E
Eesti Vabariik *see* Estonia
187 R14 **Efate** var. Efate, Fr. Vaté; prev. Sandwich Island. island C Vanuatu
Efate *see* Efate
109 S4 **Eferding** Oberösterreich, N Austria 48°18'N 14°00'E
30 M15 **Effingham** Illinois, N USA 39°07'N 88°32'W
117 N15 **Eforie-Nord** Constanța, SE Romania 44°04'N 28°37'E
117 N15 **Eforie Sud** Constanța, E Romania 44°00'N 28°38'E
Efyrnwy, Afon *see* Vyrnwy
Ega *see* Ebro
107 G23 **Egadi, Isole** island group S Italy
35 X6 **Egan Range** ▲ Nevada, W USA
14 K12 **Eganville** Ontario, SE Canada 45°33'N 77°03'W
Ege Denizi *see* Aegean Sea
39 O14 **Egegik** Alaska, USA 58°13'N 157°22'W
111 L21 **Eger** Ger. Erlau. Heves, NE Hungary 47°54'N 20°22'E
Eger *see* Cheb, Czech Republic
Eger *see* Ohre, Czech Republic/Germany
173 P8 **Egeria Fracture Zone** tectonic feature W Indian Ocean
95 C17 **Egersund** Rogaland, S Norway 58°27'N 06°01'E
108 J7 **Egg** Vorarlberg, NW Austria 47°27'N 09°55'E
101 H14 **Egge-gebirge** ▲ C Germany
109 Q4 **Eggelsberg** Oberösterreich, N Austria 48°04'N 13°00'E
109 W2 **Eggenburg** Niederösterreich, NE Austria 48°29'N 15°49'E
101 N22 **Eggenfelden** Bayern, SE Germany 48°24'N 12°45'E
18 J17 **Egg Harbor City** New Jersey, NE USA 39°31'N 74°39'W
65 G25 **Egg Island** island W Saint Helena
183 N14 **Egg Lagoon** Tasmania, SE Australia 39°42'S 143°57'E
99 I20 **Éghezèe** Namur, C Belgium 50°36'N 04°55'E
92 L2 **Egilsstadhir** Austurland, E Iceland 65°14'N 14°21'W
Egina *see* Aígina
Egindibulaq *see* Yegindybulak
Egio *see* Aígio
103 N12 **Égletons** Corrèze, C France 45°24'N 02°01'E
98 H9 **Egmond aan Zee** Noord-Holland, NW Netherlands 52°37'N 04°37'E
Egmont *see* Taranaki, Mount
184 J10 **Egmont, Cape** headland North Island, New Zealand 39°18'S 173°44'E
Egoli *see* Johannesburg
136 I15 **Eğridir Gölü** ◎ W Turkey
Eğri Palanka *see* Kriva Palanka
95 G23 **Egtved** Vejle, C Denmark 55°34'N 09°18'E
123 U5 **Egvekinot** Chukotskiy Avtonomnyy Okrug, NE Russian Federation 66°13'N 178°55'W
75 V9 **Egypt** off. Arab Republic of Egypt, Ar. Jumhūrīyah Miṣr al 'Arabīyah, prev. United Arab Republic; anc. Aegyptus. ◆ republic NE Africa
30 L17 **Egypt, Lake Of** ▣ Illinois, N USA
162 I14 **Ehen Hudag** var. Alx Youqi. Nei Mongol Zizhiqu, N China 39°12'N 101°40'E
164 F14 **Ehime** off. Ehime-ken. ◐ prefecture Shikoku, SW Japan
Ehime-ken *see* Ehime
101 I23 **Ehingen** Baden-Württemberg, S Germany 48°16'N 09°43'E
Ehinos *see* Echínos
21 R14 **Ehrhardt** South Carolina, SE USA 33°06'N 81°00'W
108 L7 **Ehrwald** Tirol, W Austria 47°24'N 10°52'E
191 W6 **Eiao** island Îles Marquises, NE French Polynesia
105 P2 **Eibar** País Vasco, N Spain 43°11'N 02°28'W
98 O11 **Eibergen** Gelderland, E Netherlands 52°06'N 06°39'E
109 V9 **Eibiswald** Steiermark, SE Austria 46°40'N 15°15'E
109 R8 **Eichham** ▲ SW Austria 47°04'N 12°24'E
101 J15 **Eichsfeld** hill range C Germany
101 K21 **Eichstätt** Bayern, SE Germany 48°53'N 11°11'E
100 H8 **Eider** ≈ N Germany
94 E13 **Eidfjord** Hordaland, S Norway 60°26'N 07°05'E
94 D13 **Eidfjorden** fjord S Norway
94 F9 **Eidsvåg** Møre og Romsdal, S Norway 62°46'N 08°00'E
95 I14 **Eidsvoll** Akershus, S Norway 60°19'N 11°14'E
92 N2 **Eidsvollfjellet** ▲ NW Svalbard 79°13'N 13°23'E
Eier-Berg *see* Suur Munamägi
101 D18 **Eifel** plateau W Germany
108 E9 **Eiger** ▲ C Switzerland 46°33'N 08°02'E
96 G10 **Eigg** island W Scotland, United Kingdom
155 D24 **Eight Degree Channel** channel India/Maldives
44 G1 **Eight Mile Rock** Grand Bahama Island, N Bahamas 26°28'N 78°43'W
194 J9 **Eights Coast** physical region Antarctica
180 K6 **Eighty Mile Beach** beach Western Australia
99 L18 **Eijsden** Limburg, SE Netherlands 50°47'N 05°41'E
95 G15 **Eikeren** ◎ S Norway
Eil *see* Eyl
Eilat *see* Elat
183 O12 **Eildon** Victoria, SE Australia 37°17'S 145°57'E
183 O12 **Eildon, Lake** ◎ Victoria, SE Australia
80 E8 **Eilei** Northern Kordofan, C Sudan 16°33'N 30°54'E
101 N15 **Eilenburg** Sachsen, E Germany 51°28'N 12°37'E
Eil Malk *see* Mecherchar
94 H13 **Eina** Oppland, S Norway 60°37'N 10°37'E
138 E12 **Ein Avdat** prev. En 'Avedat. well S Israel
101 I14 **Einbeck** Niedersachsen, C Germany 51°49'N 09°52'E
99 K15 **Eindhoven** Noord-Brabant, S Netherlands 51°26'N 05°30'E
138 F11 **Ein Gedi** prev. 'En Gedi. Southern, E Israel 31°23'N 35°21'E
108 G8 **Einsiedeln** Schwyz, NE Switzerland 47°07'N 08°45'E
Eipel *see* Ipel'
Éire *see* Ireland
Éireann, Muir *see* Irish Sea
Eirik Outer Ridge *see* Eirik Ridge
64 I6 **Eirik Ridge** var. Eirik Outer Ridge. undersea feature E Labrador Sea
92 I3 **Eiríksjökull** ▲ C Iceland 64°47'N 20°23'W
59 B14 **Eirunepé** Amazonas, N Brazil 06°38'S 69°53'W
99 L17 **Eisden** Limburg, NE Belgium 51°05'N 05°42'E
83 I18 **Eiseb** ≈ Botswana/Namibia
Eisen *see* Yŏngch'ŏn
101 J16 **Eisenach** Thüringen, C Germany 50°59'N 10°19'E
Eisenburg *see* Vasvár
109 U6 **Eisenerz** Steiermark, SE Austria 47°33'N 14°53'E
100 Q13 **Eisenhüttenstadt** Brandenburg, E Germany 52°09'N 14°36'E
109 U10 **Eisenkappel** Slvn. Železna Kapela. Kärnten, S Austria 46°27'N 14°33'E
Eisenmarkt *see* Hunedoara
109 Y5 **Eisenstadt** Burgenland, E Austria 47°50'N 16°32'E
Eishū *see* Yŏngju
119 H15 **Eišiškes** Vilnius, SE Lithuania 54°10'N 24°59'E

◆ Country
● Country Capital
◇ Dependent Territory
○ Dependent Territory Capital
◐ Administrative Regions
✈ International Airport
▲ Mountain
▲ Mountain Range
Volcano
≈ River
◎ Lake
▣ Reservoir

101 L15 **Eisleben** Sachsen-Anhalt, C Germany *51°32'N 11°33'E*
190 I3 **Eita** Tarawa, W Kiribati *01°21'N 173°05'E*
Eitape *see* Aitape
105 V11 **Eivissa** *var.* Iviza, *Cast.* Ibiza; *anc.* Ebusus. Ibiza, Spain, W Mediterranean Sea *38°54'N 01°26'E*
Eivissa *see* Ibiza
105 R4 **Ejea de los Caballeros** Aragón, NE Spain *42°07'N 01°09'W*
40 E8 **Ejido Insurgentes** Baja California Sur, NW Mexico *25°18'N 111°51'W*
Ejin Qi *see* Dalain Hob
Ejmiadzin/Ejmiatsin *see* Vagharshapat
77 P16 **Ejura** C Ghana *07°23'N 01°22'W*
41 R16 **Ejutla** *var.* Ejutla de Crespo. Oaxaca, SE Mexico *16°33'N 96°40'W*
Ejutla de Crespo *see* Ejutla
33 Y10 **Ekalaka** Montana, NW USA *45°52'N 104°32'W*
Ekapa *see* Cape Town
Ekaterinodar *see* Krasnodar
93 L20 **Ekenäs** *Fin.* Tammisaari. Etelä-Suomi, SW Finland *60°00'N 23°30'E*
146 B13 **Ekerem** *Rus.* Okarem. Balkan Welaýaty, W Turkmenistan *38°06'N 53°52'E*
184 M13 **Eketahuna** Manawatu-Wanganui, North Island, New Zealand *40°41'S 175°40'E*
Ekhínos *see* Echínos
145 T8 **Ekibastuz** Pavlodar, NE Kazakhstan *51°42'N 75°22'E*
123 R13 **Ekimchan** Amurskaya Oblast', SE Russian Federation *53°04'N 132°56'E*
77 T15 **Ekiti** ◐ *state* SW Nigeria
95 O15 **Ekoln** ◎ C Sweden
80 I7 **Ekowit** Red Sea, NE Sudan *18°46'N 37°07'E*
95 L19 **Eksjö** Jönköping, S Sweden *57°40'N 15°00'E*
93 I15 **Ekträsk** Västerbotten, N Sweden *64°28'N 19°49'E*
39 O13 **Ekuk** Alaska, USA *58°48'N 158°25'W*
123 U5 **Ekvyvatapskiy Khrebet** ▲▲ NE Russian Federation
12 F9 **Ekwan** ∿ Ontario, C Canada
39 O13 **Ekwok** Alaska, USA *59°21'N 157°28'W*
166 M6 **Ela** Mandalay, C Burma (Myanmar) *19°37'N 96°15'E*
El Aaiun *see* El Ayoun
81 N15 **Ēl Ābrēd** Sumalē, E Ethiopia *05°33'N 45°12'E*
115 F22 **Elafónisos** *island* S Greece
115 F22 **Elafonísou, Porthmós** *strait* S Greece
El-Aïoun *see* El Ayoun
El 'Alamein *see* Al 'Alamayn
41 Q12 **El Alazán** Veracruz-Llave, C Mexico *21°06'N 97°43'W*
57 J18 **El Alto** *var.* La Paz. ✈ (La Paz) La Paz, W Bolivia *16°31'S 68°07'W*
Elam *see* Īlām
El Amparo *see* El Amparo de Apure
54 I8 **El Amparo de Apure** *var.* El Amparo. Apure, C Venezuela *07°07'N 70°47'W*
171 R13 **Elara** Pulau Ambelau, E Indonesia *03°49'S 127°10'E*
El Araïch/El Araïche *see* Larache
40 D6 **El Arco** Baja California Norte, NW Mexico *28°03'N 113°25'W*
El 'Arîsh *see* Al 'Arīsh
115 L25 **Elása** *island* SE Greece
El Asnam *see* Chlef
Elassón *see* Elassóna
115 E15 **Elassóna** *prev.* Elassón. Thessalía, C Greece *39°53'N 22°10'E*
105 N2 **El Astillero** Cantabria, N Spain *43°23'N 03°45'W*
138 F14 **Elat** *var.* Eilat, Elath. Southern, S Israel *29°33'N 34°57'E*
Elat, Gulf of *see* Aqaba, Gulf of
Elath *see* Elat, Israel
Elath *see* Al 'Aqabah, Jordan
115 C17 **Eláti** ▲ Lefkáda, Iónia Nisiá, Greece, C Mediterranean Sea *38°43'N 20°38'E*
188 L16 **Elato Atoll** *atoll* Caroline Islands, C Micronesia
80 C7 **El'Atrun** Northern Darfur, NW Sudan *18°11'N 26°40'E*
74 H6 **El Ayoun** *var.* El Aaiun, El-Aïoun, La Youne. NE Morocco *34°39'N 02°29'W*
137 N14 **Elazığ** *var.* Elâzig, Elâziz. Elazığ, E Turkey *38°41'N 39°14'E*
137 O14 **Elazığ** *var.* Elâzig, Elâziz. ◐ *province* C Turkey
Elâzig/Elâziz *see* Elazığ
23 Q7 **Elba** Alabama, S USA *31°24'N 86°04'W*
106 E13 **Elba, Isola d'** *island* Archipelago Toscano, C Italy
123 S13 **El'ban** Khabarovskiy Kray, E Russian Federation *50°03'N 136°34'E*
54 F6 **El Banco** Magdalena, N Colombia *09°00'N 74°01'W*
El Barco *see* O Barco
104 L8 **El Barco de Ávila** Castilla-León, N Spain *40°21'N 05°31'W*
El Barco de Valdeorras *see* O Barco
138 H7 **El Barouk, Jabal** ▲▲ C Lebanon
113 L20 **Elbasan** *var.* Elbasani. Elbasan, C Albania *41°07'N 20°04'E*
113 L20 **Elbasan** ◐ *district* C Albania
Elbasani *see* Elbasan
54 K6 **El Baúl** Cojedes, C Venezuela *08°59'N 68°16'W*
86 D11 **Elbe** *Cz.* Labe. ∿ Czech Republic/Germany
100 L13 **Elbe-Havel-Kanal** *canal* E Germany
100 K9 **Elbe-Lübeck-Kanal** *canal* N Germany
El Beni *see* Beni
138 H7 **El Beqaa** *var.* Al Biqā', Bekaa Valley. *valley* E Lebanon
25 R6 **Elbert** Texas, SW USA *33°15'N 98°58'W*
37 R5 **Elbert, Mount** ▲ Colorado, C USA *39°07'N 106°26'W*
23 U3 **Elberton** Georgia, SE USA *34°06'N 82°52'W*
100 K11 **Elbe-Seiten-Kanal** *canal* N Germany
102 M4 **Elbeuf** Seine-Maritime, N France *49°16'N 01°01'E*
Elbing *see* Elbląg
136 M15 **Elbistan** Kahramanmaraş, S Turkey *38°14'N 37°11'E*
110 K7 **Elbląg** *var.* Elblag, *Ger.* Elbing. Warmińsko-Mazurskie, NE Poland *54°10'N 19°25'E*
43 N10 **El Bluff** Región Autónoma Atlántico Sur, SE Nicaragua *12°00'N 83°40'W*
63 H17 **El Bolsón** Río Negro, W Argentina *41°59'S 71°35'W*
105 P11 **El Bonillo** Castilla-La Mancha, C Spain *38°57'N 02°32'W*
El Bordo *see* Patía
El Boulaida/El Boulaïda *see* Blida
11 T16 **Elbow** Saskatchewan, S Canada *51°07'N 106°30'W*
29 S7 **Elbow Lake** Minnesota, N USA *45°59'N 95°58'W*
127 N16 **El'brus** *var.* Gora El'brus. ▲ SW Russian Federation *42°29'E 43°21'N*
El'brus, Gora *see* El'brus
126 M15 **El'brusskiy** Karachayevo-Cherkesskaya Respublika, SW Russian Federation *43°36'N 42°06'E*
81 D14 **El Buhayrat** *var.* Lakes State. ◐ *state* S Sudan
El Bur *see* Ceel Buur
98 L10 **Elburg** Gelderland, E Netherlands *52°27'N 05°46'E*
105 O6 **El Burgo de Osma** Castilla-León, C Spain *41°36'N 03°04'W*
Elburz Mountains *see* Alborz, Reshteh-ye Kūhhā-ye
35 V17 **El Cajon** California, W USA *32°46'N 116°52'W*
63 H22 **El Calafate** *var.* Calafate. Santa Cruz, S Argentina *50°20'S 72°13'W*
55 Q8 **El Callao** Bolívar, E Venezuela *07°18'N 61°48'W*
25 U12 **El Campo** Texas, SW USA *29°12'N 96°16'W*
54 I7 **El Cantón** Barinas, W Venezuela *07°23'N 71°10'W*
35 Q8 **El Capitan** ▲ California, W USA *37°46'N 119°39'W*
54 H5 **El Carmelo** Zulia, NW Venezuela *10°20'N 71°48'W*
62 J5 **El Carmen** Jujuy, NW Argentina *24°24'S 65°16'W*
54 E5 **El Carmen de Bolívar** Bolívar, NW Colombia *09°43'N 75°07'W*
55 O8 **El Casabe** Bolívar, SE Venezuela *06°26'N 63°35'W*
42 M12 **El Castillo de La Concepción** Río San Juan, SE Nicaragua *11°01'N 84°24'W*
El Cayo *see* San Ignacio
35 X17 **El Centro** California, W USA *32°47'N 115°33'W*
55 N6 **El Chaparro** Anzoátegui, NE Venezuela *09°12'N 65°03'W*
105 S12 **Elche** *Cat.* Elx; *anc.* Ilici, *Lat.* Illicis. País Valenciano, E Spain *38°16'N 00°41'W*
105 Q12 **Elche de la Sierra** Castilla-La Mancha, C Spain *38°27'N 02°03'W*
41 U15 **El Chichónal, Volcán** ⩘ SE Mexico *17°20'N 93°12'W*
40 C2 **El Chinero** Baja California Norte, NW Mexico
181 R1 **Elcho Island** *island* Wessel Islands, Northern Territory, N Australia
63 H18 **El Corcovado** Chubut, SW Argentina *43°31'S 71°30'W*
105 R12 **Elda** País Valenciano, E Spain *38°29'N 00°47'W*
100 M10 **Elde** ∿ NE Germany
98 L12 **Elden** Gelderland, E Netherlands *51°57'N 05°53'E*
81 J16 **El Der** *spring/well* S Ethiopia *03°55'N 39°48'E*
El Dere *see* Ceel Dheere
40 E3 **El Desemboque** Sonora, NW Mexico *30°33'N 112°59'W*
54 F5 **El Difícil** *var.* Ariguaní. Magdalena, N Colombia *09°55'N 74°12'W*
123 R10 **El'dikan** Respublika Sakha (Yakutiya), NE Russian Federation *60°46'N 135°04'E*
El Djazaïr *see* Alger
El Djelfa *see* Djelfa
29 X15 **Eldon** Iowa, C USA *40°55'N 92°13'W*
27 U5 **Eldon** Missouri, C USA *38°21'N 92°34'W*
54 E13 **El Doncello** Caquetá, S Colombia *01°43'N 75°17'W*
29 W13 **Eldora** Iowa, C USA *42°21'N 93°06'W*
60 G12 **Eldorado** Misiones, NE Argentina *26°24'S 54°38'W*
40 I9 **El Dorado** Sinaloa, C Mexico *24°19'N 107°23'W*
27 U14 **El Dorado** Arkansas, C USA *33°12'N 92°40'W*
30 M17 **Eldorado** Illinois, N USA *37°48'N 88°26'W*
27 O6 **El Dorado** Kansas, C USA *37°51'N 96°52'W*
26 K12 **Eldorado** Oklahoma, C USA *34°28'N 99°39'W*
25 O9 **Eldorado** Texas, SW USA *30°53'N 100°37'W*
55 Q8 **El Dorado** Bolívar, E Venezuela *06°45'N 61°37'W*
54 F10 **El Dorado** ✈ (Bogotá) Cundinamarca, C Colombia *01°15'N 71°52'W*
El Dorado *see* California
27 O6 **El Dorado Lake** ⊠ Kansas, C USA
27 S6 **El Dorado Springs** Missouri, C USA *37°53'N 94°01'W*
81 H18 **Eldoret** Rift Valley, W Kenya *0°31'N 35°17'E*
29 Z14 **Eldridge** Iowa, C USA *41°39'N 90°34'W*
95 J21 **Eldsberga** Halland, S Sweden *56°36'N 13°00'E*
25 R4 **Electra** Texas, SW USA *34°01'N 98°55'W*
37 Q7 **Electra Lake** ⊠ Colorado, C USA
38 B8 **'Ele'ele** *var.* Eleele. Kaua'i, Hawaii, USA, C Pacific Ocean *21°54'N 159°35'W*
Eleele *see* 'Ele'ele
Elefantes *see* Olifants
115 H19 **Elefsína** *prev.* Elevsís. Attikí, C Greece *38°02'N 23°33'E*
115 G19 **Eleftheres** *anc.* Eleutherae. *site of ancient city* Attikí/Stereá Elláda, C Greece
114 I13 **Eleftheroúpoli** *prev.* Elevtheroúpolis. Anatolikí Makedonía kai Thráki, NE Greece *40°55'N 24°15'E*
74 F10 **El Eglab** ▲▲ SW Algeria
118 F10 **Eleja** Jelgava, C Latvia *56°24'N 23°41'E*
Elek *see* Ilek
119 G14 **Elektrėnai** Vilnius, SE Lithuania *54°47'N 24°35'E*
126 L3 **Elektrostal'** Moskovskaya Oblast', W Russian Federation *55°47'N 38°24'E*
81 H15 **Elemi Triangle** *disputed region* Kenya/Sudan
114 K9 **Elena** Veliko Tŭrnovo, N Bulgaria *42°55'N 25°53'E*
54 G16 **El Encanto** Amazonas, S Colombia *01°45'S 73°12'W*
37 R14 **Elephant Butte Reservoir** ⊠ New Mexico, SW USA
Éléphant, Chaîne de l' *see* Dâmrei, Chuŏr Phnum
194 G2 **Elephant Island** *island* South Shetland Islands, Antarctica
Elephant River *see* Olifants
El Escorial *see* San Lorenzo de El Escorial
Élesd *see* Aleşd
114 F11 **Eleshnitsa** ∿ W Bulgaria
137 S13 **Eleşkirt** Ağrı, E Turkey *39°22'N 42°48'E*
42 F5 **El Estor** Izabal, E Guatemala *15°37'N 89°22'W*
Eleutherae *see* Eléftheres
44 I2 **Eleuthera Island** *island* N Bahamas
37 S5 **Elevenmile Canyon Reservoir** ⊠ Colorado, C USA
27 W8 **Eleven Point River** ∿ Arkansas/Missouri, C USA
Elevsís *see* Elefsína
Elevtheroúpolis *see* Eleftheroúpoli
80 B10 **El Fasher** *var.* Al Fāshir. Northern Darfur, W Sudan *13°37'N 25°22'E*
El Fashn *see* Al Fashn
El Ferrol/El Ferrol del Caudillo *see* Ferrol
39 W13 **Elfin Cove** Chichagof Island, Alaska, USA *58°09'N 136°16'W*
105 W4 **El Fluvià** ∿ NE Spain
40 H7 **El Fuerte** Sinaloa, W Mexico *26°28'N 108°35'W*
80 D11 **El Fula** Western Kordofan, C Sudan *11°44'N 28°20'E*
El Gedaref *see* Gedaref
80 A10 **El Geneina** *var.* Ajjinena, Al-Genain, Al Junaynah. Western Darfur, W Sudan *13°27'N 22°30'E*
96 J8 **Elgin** NE Scotland, United Kingdom *57°39'N 03°20'W*
30 M10 **Elgin** Illinois, N USA *42°02'N 88°16'W*
29 P14 **Elgin** Nebraska, C USA *41°58'N 98°04'W*
35 Y9 **Elgin** Nevada, W USA *37°19'N 114°30'W*
28 L6 **Elgin** North Dakota, N USA *46°24'N 101°51'W*
26 M12 **Elgin** Oklahoma, C USA *34°46'N 98°17'W*
25 T10 **Elgin** Texas, SW USA *30°21'N 97°22'W*
123 R9 **El'ginskiy** Respublika Sakha (Yakutiya), NE Russian Federation *64°27'N 141°57'E*
El Giza *see* Giza
74 J8 **El Goléa** *var.* Al Golea. C Algeria *30°35'N 02°59'E*
40 D2 **El Golfo de Santa Clara** Sonora, NW Mexico *31°48'N 114°40'W*
81 G18 **Elgon, Mount** ▲ E Uganda *01°07'N 34°29'E*
94 I10 **Elgpiggen** ▲ S Norway *62°13'N 11°18'E*
105 T4 **El Grado** Aragón, NE Spain *42°09'N 00°13'E*
40 L6 **El Guaje, Laguna** ⊠ NE Mexico
54 H6 **El Guayabo** Zulia, W Venezuela *08°37'N 72°20'W*
77 O6 **El Guețțâra** *oasis* N Mali
76 J6 **El Ḥammâmi** *desert* N Mauritania
76 M5 **El Ḥank** *cliff* N Mauritania
El Haseke *see* Al Ḥasakah
80 H10 **El Hawata** Gedaref, E Sudan *13°25'N 34°42'E*
El Higo *see* Higos
171 T16 **Eliase** Pulau Selaru, E Indonesia *08°16'S 130°49'E*
Elías Piña *see* Comendador
25 R6 **Eliasville** Texas, SW USA *32°55'N 98°46'W*
Elichpur *see* Achalpur
37 V13 **Elida** New Mexico, SW USA *33°57'N 103°39'W*
115 F18 **Elikónas** ▲▲ C Greece
67 T10 **Elila** ∿ W Dem. Rep. Congo
39 N9 **Elim** Alaska, USA *64°37'N 162°15'W*
Elimberrum *see* Auch
Eliocroca *see* Lorca
61 B16 **Elisa** Santa Fe, C Argentina *30°42'S 61°04'W*
Elisabethstedt *see* Dumbrăveni
Élisabethville *see* Lubumbashi
127 O13 **Elista** Respublika Kalmykiya, SW Russian Federation *46°18'N 44°09'E*
182 I9 **Elizabeth** South Australia *34°44'S 138°39'E*
21 Q3 **Elizabeth** West Virginia, NE USA *39°04'N 81°24'W*
19 Q9 **Elizabeth, Cape** *headland* Maine, NE USA *43°34'N 70°12'W*
21 Y8 **Elizabeth City** North Carolina, SE USA *36°18'N 76°16'W*
21 P8 **Elizabethton** Tennessee, S USA *36°22'N 82°15'W*
30 M17 **Elizabethtown** Illinois, N USA *37°24'N 88°21'W*
20 K6 **Elizabethtown** Kentucky, S USA *37°41'N 85°51'W*
18 L7 **Elizabethtown** New York, NE USA *44°13'N 73°38'W*
21 U11 **Elizabethtown** North Carolina, SE USA *34°36'N 78°36'W*
18 G15 **Elizabethtown** Pennsylvania, NE USA *40°08'N 76°36'W*
74 E6 **El-Jadida** *prev.* Mazagan. W Morocco *33°15'N 08°27'W*
El Jafr *see* Jafr, Qā' al
80 F11 **El Jebelein** White Nile, E Sudan *12°38'N 32°51'E*
110 N8 **Ełk** *Ger.* Lyck. Warmińsko-mazurskie, NE Poland *53°51'N 22°20'E*
110 O8 **Ełk** ∿ NE Poland
29 Y12 **Elkader** Iowa, C USA *42°51'N 91°24'W*
80 G9 **El Kamlin** Gezira, C Sudan *15°03'N 33°11'E*
33 N11 **Elk City** Idaho, NW USA *45°50'N 115°28'W*
26 K10 **Elk City** Oklahoma, C USA *35°24'N 99°24'W*
27 P7 **Elk City Lake** ⊠ Kansas, C USA
34 M5 **Elk Creek** California, W USA *39°34'N 122°34'W*
28 J10 **Elk Creek** ∿ South Dakota, N USA
74 M5 **El Kef** *var.* Al Kāf, Le Kef. NW Tunisia *36°13'N 08°44'E*
74 F7 **El Kelâa Srarhna** *var.* Kal at Sraghna. C Morocco *32°05'N 07°20'W*
El Kerak *see* Al Karak
11 P17 **Elkford** British Columbia, SW Canada *49°58'N 114°57'W*
El Khalil *see* Hebron
80 E7 **El Khandaq** Northern, N Sudan *18°34'N 30°34'E*
El Khârga *see* Al Khārijah
31 P11 **Elkhart** Indiana, N USA *41°40'N 85°58'W*
26 H7 **Elkhart** Kansas, C USA *37°00'N 101°51'W*
25 V8 **Elkhart** Texas, SW USA *31°37'N 95°34'W*
30 M7 **Elkhart Lake** ◎ Wisconsin, N USA
El Kharṭûm *see* Khartoum
37 Q3 **Elkhead Mountains** ▲▲ Colorado, C USA
18 I12 **Elk Hill** ▲ Pennsylvania, NE USA *41°42'N 75°33'W*
138 G8 **El Khiyam** *var.* Al Khiyām, Khiam. S Lebanon *33°12'N 35°42'E*
29 S15 **Elkhorn** Nebraska, C USA *41°17'N 96°13'W*
30 M9 **Elkhorn** Wisconsin, N USA *42°40'N 88°34'W*
29 R14 **Elkhorn River** ∿ Nebraska, C USA
127 O16 **El'khotovo** Respublika Severnaya Osetiya, SW Russian Federation *43°18'N 44°17'E*
114 L10 **Elkhovo** *prev.* Kizilagach. Yambol, E Bulgaria *42°10'N 26°34'E*
21 R8 **Elkin** North Carolina, SE USA *36°14'N 80°51'W*
21 S4 **Elkins** West Virginia, NE USA *38°56'N 79°53'W*
195 X3 **Elkins, Mount** ▲ Antarctica *66°25'S 53°54'E*
14 G8 **Elk Lake** Ontario, S Canada *47°44'N 80°19'W*
31 P6 **Elk Lake** ◎ Michigan, N USA
18 F12 **Elkland** Pennsylvania, NE USA *41°59'N 77°16'W*
35 W3 **Elko** Nevada, W USA *40°48'N 115°46'W*
11 R14 **Elk Point** Alberta, SW Canada *53°52'N 110°49'W*
29 R12 **Elk Point** South Dakota, N USA *42°42'N 96°37'W*
29 V8 **Elk River** Minnesota, N USA *45°18'N 93°34'W*
20 J10 **Elk River** ∿ Alabama/Tennessee, S USA
21 R4 **Elk River** ∿ West Virginia, NE USA
20 I7 **Elkton** Kentucky, S USA *36°49'N 87°11'W*
21 Y2 **Elkton** Maryland, NE USA *39°37'N 75°50'W*
29 R10 **Elkton** South Dakota, N USA *44°14'N 96°28'W*
20 I10 **Elkton** Tennessee, S USA *35°01'N 86°51'W*
21 U5 **Elkton** Virginia, NE USA *38°22'N 78°35'W*
El Kuneitra *see* Al Qunayṭirah
81 L15 **El Kure** Somali, E Ethiopia *05°37'N 42°05'E*
80 D12 **El Lagowa** Western Kordofan, C Sudan *11°23'N 29°10'E*
39 S12 **Ellamar** Alaska, USA *60°54'N 146°37'W*
Ellás *see* Greece
23 S6 **Ellaville** Georgia, SE USA *32°14'N 84°18'W*
197 P9 **Ellef Ringnes Island** *island* Nunavut, N Canada
29 V10 **Ellendale** Minnesota, N USA *43°53'N 93°19'W*
29 P7 **Ellendale** North Dakota, N USA *45°57'N 98°33'W*
36 M6 **Ellen, Mount** ▲ Utah, W USA *38°06'N 110°48'W*
32 I9 **Ellensburg** Washington, NW USA *47°00'N 124°34'W*
18 K12 **Ellenville** New York, NE USA *41°43'N 74°24'W*
Ellep *see* Lib
21 T10 **Ellerbe** North Carolina, SE USA *35°04'N 79°45'W*
197 P10 **Ellesmere Island** *island* Queen Elizabeth Islands, Nunavut, N Canada
185 H19 **Ellesmere, Lake** ◎ South Island, New Zealand
97 K18 **Ellesmere Port** C England, United Kingdom *53°17'N 02°54'W*
31 O14 **Ellettsville** Indiana, N USA *39°13'N 86°37'W*
99 E19 **Ellezelles** Hainaut, SW Belgium *50°44'N 03°40'E*
8 L7 **Ellice** ∿ Nunavut, NE Canada
Ellice Islands *see* Tuvalu
Ellichpur *see* Achalpur
21 W3 **Ellicott City** Maryland, NE USA *39°16'N 76°48'W*
23 S2 **Ellijay** Georgia, SE USA *34°42'N 84°28'W*
27 W7 **Ellington** Missouri, C USA *37°14'N 90°58'W*
26 L5 **Ellinwood** Kansas, C USA *38°21'N 98°34'W*
83 J24 **Elliot** Eastern Cape, SE South Africa *31°20'S 27°51'E*
14 D10 **Elliot Lake** Ontario, S Canada *46°24'N 82°38'W*
181 X6 **Elliot, Mount** ▲ Queensland, E Australia *19°36'S 147°02'E*
21 T5 **Elliott Knob** ▲ Virginia, NE USA *38°10'N 79°18'W*
26 K4 **Ellis** Kansas, C USA *38°56'N 99°33'W*
182 F8 **Elliston** South Australia *33°40'S 134°56'E*
22 M7 **Ellisville** Mississippi, S USA *31°36'N 89°12'W*
105 V5 **El Llobregat** ∿ NE Spain
96 L9 **Ellon** NE Scotland, United Kingdom *57°22'N 02°06'W*
Ellore *see* Elūru
21 S13 **Ellore** South Carolina, SE USA *33°34'N 80°37'W*
26 M4 **Ellsworth** Kansas, C USA *38°45'N 98°15'W*
19 S7 **Ellsworth** Maine, NE USA *44°32'N 68°25'W*
30 I6 **Ellsworth** Wisconsin, N USA *44°44'N 92°29'W*
26 M11 **Ellsworth, Lake** ⊠ Oklahoma, C USA
194 K9 **Ellsworth Land** *physical region* Antarctica
194 L9 **Ellsworth Mountains** ▲▲ Antarctica
101 J21 **Ellwangen** Baden-Württemberg, S Germany *48°58'N 10°07'E*
18 B14 **Ellwood City** Pennsylvania, NE USA *40°49'N 80°15'W*
108 H8 **Elm** Glarus, NE Switzerland *46°55'N 09°09'E*
32 G9 **Elma** Washington, NW USA *47°00'N 123°24'W*
121 V13 **El Maḥalla el Kubra** *var.* Al Maḥallah al Kubrá, Mahalla el Kubra. N Egypt *30°59'N 31°10'E*
74 E9 **El Mahbas** *var.* Mahbés. SW Western Sahara *27°26'N 09°09'W*
63 H17 **El Maitén** Chubut, W Argentina *42°03'S 71°10'W*
136 E16 **Elmalı** Antalya, SW Turkey *36°43'N 29°19'E*
80 G10 **El Manaqil** Gezira, C Sudan *14°12'N 33°01'E*
54 M12 **El Mango** Amazonas, S Venezuela *01°55'N 66°35'W*
El Manṣûra *see* Al Manṣūrah
55 P8 **El Manteco** Bolívar, E Venezuela *07°27'N 62°32'W*
29 O16 **Elm Creek** Nebraska, C USA *40°43'N 99°22'W*
El Mediyya *see* Médéa
77 V9 **Elméki** Agadez, C Niger *17°52'N 08°07'E*
108 K7 **Elmen** Tirol, W Austria *47°22'N 10°34'E*
18 I16 **Elmer** New Jersey, NE USA *39°34'N 75°09'W*
138 G6 **El Mina** *var.* Al Mīnā'. N Lebanon *34°28'N 35°49'E*
El Minya *see* Al Minyā
14 F15 **Elmira** Ontario, S Canada *43°35'N 80°34'W*
18 G11 **Elmira** New York, NE USA *42°06'N 76°50'W*
36 K13 **El Mirage** Arizona, SW USA *33°36'N 112°19'W*
29 O7 **Elm Lake** ⊠ South Dakota, N USA
El Moján *see* San Rafael
105 N7 **El Molar** Madrid, C Spain *40°43'N 03°35'W*
76 L7 **El Mrâyer** *well* C Mauritania
76 L5 **El Mreiti** *well* N Mauritania
76 L8 **El Mreyyé** *desert* E Mauritania
29 P8 **Elm River** ∿ North Dakota/South Dakota, N USA
100 I9 **Elmshorn** Schleswig-Holstein, N Germany *53°45'N 09°39'E*
80 D12 **El Muglad** Western Kordofan, C Sudan *11°02'N 27°44'E*
El Muwaqqar *see* Al Muwaqqar
14 G14 **Elmvale** Ontario, S Canada *44°34'N 79°53'W*
30 K12 **Elmwood** Illinois, N USA *40°46'N 89°58'W*
26 J8 **Elmwood** Oklahoma, C USA *36°37'N 100°31'W*
103 P17 **Elne** *anc.* Illiberis. Pyrénées-Orientales, S France *42°36'N 02°58'E*
54 F11 **El Nevado, Cerro** *elevation* C Colombia
171 N5 **El Nido** Palawan, W Philippines *11°10'N 119°25'E*
62 I12 **El Nihuil** Mendoza, W Argentina *34°58'S 68°40'W*
75 W7 **El Nouzha** ✈ (Alexandria) N Egypt *31°06'N 29°58'E*
80 E10 **El Obeid** *var.* Al Obayyid, Al Ubayyiḍ. Northern Kordofan, C Sudan *13°11'N 30°10'E*
41 O13 **El Oro** México, S Mexico *19°51'N 100°07'W*
56 B8 **El Oro** ◐ *province* SW Ecuador
61 B19 **Elortondo** Santa Fe, C Argentina *33°42'S 61°37'W*
54 J8 **Elorza** Apure, C Venezuela *07°02'N 69°30'W*
El Ouâdi *see* El Oued
74 L7 **El Oued** *var.* Al Oued, El Ouâdi, El Wad. NE Algeria *33°20'N 06°53'E*
36 L15 **Eloy** Arizona, SW USA *32°47'N 111°33'W*
55 Q7 **El Palmar** Bolívar, E Venezuela *08°01'N 61°53'W*
40 K8 **El Palmito** Durango, W Mexico *25°40'N 104°59'W*
55 P7 **El Pao** Bolívar, E Venezuela *08°03'N 62°40'W*
54 K5 **El Pao** Cojedes, N Venezuela *09°40'N 68°08'W*
42 J7 **El Paraíso** El Paraíso, S Honduras *13°51'N 86°31'W*
42 I7 **El Paraíso** ◐ *department* SE Honduras
30 L12 **El Paso** Illinois, N USA *40°44'N 89°01'W*
24 G8 **El Paso** Texas, SW USA *31°45'N 106°30'W*
24 G8 **El Paso** ✈ Texas, SW USA *31°48'N 106°24'W*
105 U7 **El Perello** Cataluña, NE Spain *40°53'N 00°43'E*
55 P5 **El Pilar** Sucre, NE Venezuela *10°31'N 63°12'W*
42 F7 **El Pital, Cerro** ▲ El Salvador/Honduras *14°19'N 89°06'W*
35 Q9 **El Portal** California, W USA *37°40'N 119°46'W*
40 J3 **El Porvenir** Chihuahua, N Mexico *31°15'N 105°48'W*
43 U14 **El Porvenir** Kuna Yala, N Panama *09°33'N 78°56'W*
105 W6 **El Prat de Llobregat** Cataluña, NE Spain *41°20'N 02°05'E*
42 H5 **El Progreso** Yoro, NW Honduras *15°25'N 87°49'W*
42 A2 **El Progreso** *off.* Departamento de El Progreso. ◐ *department* C Guatemala
El Progreso *see* Guastatoya
El Progreso, Departamento de *see* El Progreso
104 L9 **El Puente del Arzobispo** Castilla-La Mancha, C Spain *39°48'N 05°10'W*
104 J15 **El Puerto de Santa María** Andalucía, S Spain *36°36'N 06°13'W*
62 I8 **El Puesto** Catamarca, NW Argentina *27°57'S 67°37'W*
El Qâhira *see* Cairo
El Qaṣr *see* Al Qaṣr
El Qatrani *see* Al Qaṭrānah
40 I10 **El Quelite** Sinaloa, C Mexico *23°37'N 106°26'W*
62 G9 **Elqui, Río** ∿ N Chile
El Q'unaytirah *see* Al Qunayṭirah
El Quneitra *see* Al Qunayṭirah
El Quseir *see* Al Quṣayr
El Quweira *see* Al Quwayrah
141 O15 **El-Rahaba** ✈ (Ṣan'ā') W Yemen *15°28'N 44°12'E*
42 M10 **El Rama** Región Autónoma Atlántico Sur, SE Nicaragua *12°09'N 84°15'W*
43 W16 **El Real** *var.* El Real de Santa María. Darién, SE Panama *08°06'N 77°42'W*
El Real de Santa María *see* El Real
26 M10 **El Reno** Oklahoma, C USA *35°32'N 95°57'W*
40 K9 **El Rodeo** Durango, C Mexico *25°12'N 104°35'W*
104 J13 **El Ronquillo** Andalucía, S Spain *37°43'N 06°09'W*
11 S16 **Elrose** Saskatchewan, S Canada *51°07'N 107°59'W*
30 K8 **Elroy** Wisconsin, N USA *43°43'N 90°16'W*
25 S17 **Elsa** Texas, SW USA *26°17'N 97°59'W*
El Ṣaff *see* Aṣ Ṣaff
40 J10 **El Salto** Durango, C Mexico *23°47'N 105°22'W*
42 D8 **El Salvador** *off.* Republica de El Salvador. ◆ *republic* Central America
El Salvador, Republica de *see* El Salvador
54 K7 **El Samán de Apure** Apure, C Venezuela *07°54'N 68°44'W*
14 D7 **Elsas** Ontario, S Canada *48°31'N 82°53'W*
40 F3 **El Sásabe** *var.* Aduana del Sásabe. Sonora, NW Mexico *31°27'N 111°31'W*
Elsass *see* Alsace
40 J5 **El Sáuz** Chihuahua, N Mexico *29°03'N 106°15'W*
27 W4 **Elsberry** Missouri, C USA *39°10'N 90°46'W*
45 P9 **El Seibo** *var.* Santa Cruz de El Seibo, Santa Cruz del Seibo. E Dominican Republic *18°45'N 69°04'W*
42 B7 **El Semillero Barra Nahualate** Escuintla, SW Guatemala *14°01'N 91°28'W*
Elsene *see* Ixelles
Elsen Nur *see* Dorgê Co
36 L6 **Elsinore** Utah, W USA *38°40'N 112°09'W*
Elsinore *see* Helsingør
99 L18 **Elsloo** Limburg, SE Netherlands *50°57'N 05°46'E*
60 G13 **El Soberbio** Misiones, NE Argentina *27°15'S 54°05'W*
55 N6 **El Socorro** Guárico, C Venezuela *09°00'N 65°42'W*
54 L6 **El Sombrero** Guárico, N Venezuela *09°25'N 67°06'W*
98 L10 **Elspeet** Gelderland, E Netherlands *52°19'N 05°47'E*
98 L12 **Elst** Gelderland, E Netherlands *51°55'N 05°51'E*
101 O15 **Elsterwerda** Brandenburg, E Germany *51°27'N 13°32'E*
40 J4 **El Sueco** Chihuahua, N Mexico *29°53'N 106°24'W*
El Suweida *see* As Suwaydā'
El Suweis *see* Suez
54 D12 **El Tambo** Cauca, SW Colombia *02°25'N 76°50'W*
175 T13 **Eltanin Fracture Zone** *tectonic feature* SE Pacific Ocean
105 X5 **El Ter** ∿ NE Spain
184 K11 **Eltham** Taranaki, North Island, New Zealand *39°26'S 174°25'E*
55 O6 **El Tigre** Anzoátegui, NE Venezuela *08°55'N 64°15'W*
El Tigrito *see* San José de Guanipa
54 J5 **El Tocuyo** Lara, N Venezuela *09°48'N 69°51'W*
127 Q10 **El'ton** Volgogradskaya Oblast', SW Russian Federation *49°07'N 46°50'E*
32 K10 **Eltopia** Washington, NW USA *46°33'N 118°59'W*
El Toro *see* Mare de Déu del Toro
61 A18 **El Trébol** Santa Fe, C Argentina *32°12'S 61°40'W*
40 J13 **El Tuito** Jalisco, SW Mexico *20°19'N 105°22'W*
El Ṭûr *see* Aṭ Ṭūr
155 K16 **Elūru** *prev.* Ellore. Andhra Pradesh, E India *16°45'N 81°10'E*
118 H13 **Elva** *Ger.* Elwa. Tartumaa, SE Estonia *58°13'N 26°25'E*
37 R9 **El Vado Reservoir** ⊠ New Mexico, SW USA
43 S15 **El Valle** Coclé, C Panama *08°39'N 80°08'W*
104 I11 **Elvas** Portalegre, C Portugal *38°53'N 07°10'W*
54 K7 **El Venado** Apure, C Venezuela *07°25'N 68°46'W*
105 V6 **El Vendrell** Cataluña, NE Spain *41°13'N 01°32'E*
94 I13 **Elverum** Hedmark, S Norway *60°54'N 11°33'E*
42 I9 **El Viejo** Chinandega, NW Nicaragua *12°39'N 87°11'W*
54 G7 **El Viejo, Cerro** ▲ C Colombia *07°31'N 72°56'W*
54 H6 **El Vigía** Mérida, NW Venezuela *08°38'N 71°39'W*
105 Q4 **El Villar de Arnedo** La Rioja, N Spain *42°19'N 02°05'W*
59 A14 **Elvira** Amazonas, W Brazil *07°12'S 69°56'W*
Elwa *see* Elva
El Wad *see* El Oued
81 K17 **El Wak** North Eastern, NE Kenya *02°46'N 40°57'E*
33 R7 **Elwell, Lake** ⊠ Montana, NW USA
31 P13 **Elwood** Indiana, N USA *40°16'N 85°50'W*
27 R3 **Elwood** Kansas, C USA *39°43'N 94°52'W*
29 N16 **Elwood** Nebraska, C USA *40°35'N 99°51'W*
Elx *see* Elche
97 O20 **Ely** E England, United Kingdom *52°24'N 00°15'E*
29 X4 **Ely** Minnesota, N USA *47°54'N 91°52'W*
35 X6 **Ely** Nevada, W USA *39°15'N 114°53'W*
El Yopal *see* Yopal
31 T11 **Elyria** Ohio, N USA *41°22'N 82°06'W*
45 S9 **El Yunque** ▲ E Puerto Rico *18°15'N 65°46'W*
101 F23 **Elz** ∿ SW Germany
187 R14 **Emae** *island* Shepherd Islands, C Vanuatu
118 I5 **Emajõgi** *Ger.* Embach. ∿ SE Estonia
Emāmrūd *see* Shāhrūd
149 Q2 **Emām Ṣāḥeb** *var.* Emam Saheb, Hazarat Imam. Kunduz, NE Afghanistan *37°11'N 68°55'E*
Emam Saheb *see* Emām Ṣāḥeb
Emāmshahr *see* Shāhrūd
95 M20 **Emån** ∿ S Sweden
144 J11 **Emba** *Kaz.* Embi. Aktyubinsk, W Kazakhstan *48°50'N 58°10'E*
144 H12 **Emba** *Kaz.* Zhem. ∿ W Kazakhstan
Embach *see* Emajõgi
62 K5 **Embarcación** Salta, N Argentina *23°15'S 64°05'W*
30 M15 **Embarras River** ∿ Illinois, N USA
Embi *see* Emba
81 I19 **Embu** Eastern, C Kenya *0°32'N 37°28'E*
100 E10 **Emden** Niedersachsen, NW Germany *53°22'N 07°12'E*
160 H9 **Emei Shan** ▲ Sichuan, C China *29°32'N 103°21'E*
29 Q4 **Emerado** North Dakota, N USA *47°55'N 97°21'W*
181 X8 **Emerald** Queensland, E Australia *23°33'S 148°11'E*
Emerald Isle *see* Montserrat
57 J15 **Emero, Río** ∿ W Bolivia
11 Y17 **Emerson** Manitoba, S Canada *49°00'N 97°07'W*
29 T15 **Emerson** Iowa, C USA *41°00'N 95°22'W*
29 R13 **Emerson** Nebraska, C USA *42°16'N 96°43'W*
36 M5 **Emery** Utah, W USA *38°54'N 111°16'W*
Emesa *see* Ḥimṣ
136 E13 **Emet** Kütahya, W Turkey *39°22'N 29°15'E*
186 B8 **Emeti** Western, SW Papua New Guinea *07°54'S 143°18'E*
35 V3 **Emigrant Pass** *pass* Nevada, W USA
78 I6 **Emi Koussi** ▲ N Chad *19°52'N 18°34'E*
Emilia *see* Emilia-Romagna
41 V15 **Emiliano Zapata** Chiapas, SE Mexico *17°42'N 91°46'W*
106 E9 **Emilia-Romagna** *prev.* Emilia; *anc.* Æmilia. ◐ *region* N Italy
158 J3 **Emin** *var.* Dorbiljin. Xinjiang Uygur Zizhiqu, NW China *46°30'N 83°42'E*
149 W8 **Eminābād** Punjab, E Pakistan *32°02'N 73°51'E*
21 L5 **Eminence** Kentucky, S USA *38°22'N 85°10'W*
27 W7 **Eminence** Missouri, C USA *37°09'N 91°22'W*
114 N9 **Emine, Nos** *headland* E Bulgaria *42°43'N 27°53'E*
158 J3 **Emin He** ∿ NW China
186 G4 **Emirau Island** *island* N Papua New Guinea
136 F13 **Emirdağ** Afyon, W Turkey *39°01'N 31°09'E*
95 M21 **Emmaboda** Kalmar, S Sweden *56°36'N 15°30'E*
118 E5 **Emmaste** Hiiumaa, W Estonia *58°43'N 22°36'E*
18 I15 **Emmaus** Pennsylvania, NE USA *40°32'N 75°28'W*
183 U4 **Emmaville** New South Wales, SE Australia *29°26'S 151°38'E*
108 E9 **Emme** ∿ W Switzerland
98 L8 **Emmeloord** Flevoland, N Netherlands *52°43'N 05°46'E*
98 O8 **Emmen** Drenthe, NE Netherlands *52°48'N 06°57'E*
108 F8 **Emmen** Luzern, C Switzerland *47°03'N 08°14'E*
101 F23 **Emmendingen** Baden-Württemberg, SW Germany *48°07'N 07°51'E*
98 P8 **Emmer-Compascuum** Drenthe, NE Netherlands *52°47'N 07°03'E*
101 D14 **Emmerich** Nordrhein-Westfalen, W Germany *51°49'N 06°16'E*
29 U12 **Emmetsburg** Iowa, C USA *43°06'N 94°40'W*
32 M14 **Emmett** Idaho, NW USA *43°52'N 116°30'W*
38 M10 **Emmonak** Alaska, USA *62°46'N 164°31'W*
Emona *see* Ljubljana
Emonti *see* East London
24 L12 **Emory Peak** ▲ Texas, SW USA *29°15'N 103°18'W*
40 F6 **Empalme** Sonora, NW Mexico *27°57'N 110°49'W*
83 L23 **Empangeni** KwaZulu/Natal, E South Africa *28°45'S 31°54'E*
61 C14 **Empedrado** Corrientes, NE Argentina *27°59'S 58°47'W*
192 K3 **Emperor Seamounts** *undersea feature* NW Pacific Ocean *42°00'N 170°00'E*
192 L3 **Emperor Trough** *undersea feature* N Pacific Ocean
35 R4 **Empire** Nevada, W USA *40°26'N 119°21'W*
Empire State of the South *see* Georgia
Emplawas *see* Amplawas
106 F11 **Empoli** Toscana, C Italy *43°43'N 10°57'E*
27 P5 **Emporia** Kansas, C USA *38°24'N 96°10'W*
21 W7 **Emporia** Virginia, NE USA *36°42'N 77°33'W*
18 E13 **Emporium** Pennsylvania, NE USA *41°31'N 78°14'W*
Empty Quarter *see* Ar Rub 'al Khālī
100 E10 **Ems** *Dut.* Eems. ∿ NW Germany
100 F13 **Emsdetten** Nordrhein-Westfalen, NW Germany *52°11'N 07°32'E*
Ems-Hunte Canal *see* Küstenkanal
100 F10 **Ems-Jade-Kanal** *canal* NW Germany
100 F11 **Emsland** *cultural region* NW Germany
182 D3 **Emu Junction** South Australia *28°39'S 132°13'E*
163 T3 **Emur He** ∿ NE China
55 R8 **Enachu Landing** NW Guyana *06°09'N 60°02'W*
93 F16 **Enafors** Jämtland, C Sweden *63°17'N 12°24'E*
94 N11 **Enånger** Gävleborg, C Sweden *61°30'N 17°10'E*

◆ Country
● Country Capital
◇ Dependent Territory
○ Dependent Territory Capital
◐ Administrative Regions
✈ International Airport
▲ Mountain
▲▲ Mountain Range
⩘ Volcano
∿ River
◎ Lake
⊠ Reservoir

96 G7 **Enard Bay** *bay* NW Scotland, United Kingdom
Enareträsk *see* Inarijärvi
171 X14 **Enarotali** Papua, E Indonesia 03°55′S 136°21′E
En 'Avedat *see* Ein Avdat
165 T2 **Enbetsu** Hokkaidō, NE Japan 44°44′N 141°47′E
61 H16 **Encantadas, Serra das** ▲ S Brazil
40 E7 **Encantado, Cerro** ▲ NW Mexico 26°46′N 112°33′W
62 P7 **Encarnación** Itapúa, S Paraguay 27°20′S 55°50′W
40 M12 **Encarnación de Díaz** Jalisco, SW Mexico 21°33′N 102°13′W
77 O17 **Enchi** SW Ghana 05°53′N 02°48′W
25 Q14 **Encinal** Texas, SW USA 28°02′N 99°21′W
35 U17 **Encinitas** California, W USA 33°02′N 117°17′W
25 S16 **Encino** Texas, SW USA 26°58′N 98°06′W
54 H6 **Encontrados** Zulia, NW Venezuela 09°04′N 72°16′W
182 I10 **Encounter Bay** *inlet* South Australia
61 F15 **Encruzilhada** Rio Grande do Sul, S Brazil 28°58′S 55°31′W
61 H16 **Encruzilhada do Sul** Rio Grande do Sul, S Brazil 30°30′S 52°32′W
111 M20 **Encs** Borsod-Abaúj-Zemplén, NE Hungary 48°21′N 21°09′E
193 P3 **Endeavour Seamount** *undersea feature* N Pacific Ocean 48°15′N 129°04′W
181 V1 **Endeavour Strait** *strait* Queensland, NE Australia
171 O16 **Endeh** Flores, S Indonesia 08°48′S 121°37′E
95 G23 **Endelave** *island* C Denmark
191 T4 **Enderbury Island** *atoll* Phoenix Islands, C Kiribati
11 N16 **Enderby** British Columbia, SW Canada 50°34′N 119°09′W
195 W4 **Enderby Land** *physical region* Antarctica
173 N14 **Enderby Plain** *undersea feature* S Indian Ocean
29 Q6 **Enderlin** North Dakota, N USA 46°37′N 97°36′W
Endersdorf *see* Jędrzejów
28 K16 **Enders Reservoir** ⊠ Nebraska, C USA
18 H11 **Endicott** New York, NE USA 42°06′N 76°03′W
39 P7 **Endicott Mountains** ▲▲ Alaska, USA
118 I5 **Endla Raba** *wetland* C Estonia
127 X7 **Energetik** Orenburgskaya Oblast', W Russian Federation 51°37′N 58°44′E
117 T9 **Enerhodar** Zaporiz'ka Oblast', SE Ukraine 47°30′N 34°40′E
57 F14 **Ene, Río** ↝ C Peru
189 N4 **Enewetak Atoll** *var.* Ānewetak, Eniwetok. *atoll* Ralik Chain, W Marshall Islands
114 L13 **Enez** Edirne, NW Turkey 40°44′N 26°05′E
21 W8 **Enfield** North Carolina, SE USA 36°10′N 77°40′W
186 B7 **Enga** ◐ *province* W Papua New Guinea
45 Q9 **Engaño, Cabo** *headland* E Dominican Republic 18°36′N 68°19′W
164 U3 **Engaru** Hokkaidō, NE Japan 44°06′N 143°30′E
'En Gedi *see* Ein Gedi
108 F9 **Engelberg** Unterwalden, C Switzerland 46°51′N 08°25′E
21 Y9 **Engelhard** North Carolina, SE USA 35°30′N 76°00′W
127 P8 **Engel's** Saratovskaya Oblast', W Russian Federation 51°27′N 46°09′E
101 G24 **Engen** Baden-Württemberg, SW Germany 47°52′N 08°46′E
Engeten *see* Aiud
168 K15 **Enggano, Pulau** *island* W Indonesia
80 J8 **Enghershatu** ▲ N Eritrea 16°41′N 38°21′E
99 F19 **Enghien** *Dut.* Edingen. Hainaut, SW Belgium 50°42′N 04°03′E
27 V12 **England** Arkansas, C USA 34°32′N 91°58′W
97 M20 **England** *Lat.* Anglia. ◐ *national region* England, United Kingdom
14 H8 **Englehart** Ontario, S Canada 47°50′N 79°52′W
37 T4 **Englewood** Colorado, C USA 39°39′N 104°59′W
31 O16 **English** Indiana, N USA 38°20′N 86°28′W
39 Q13 **English Bay** Alaska, USA 59°21′N 151°55′W
English Bazar *see* Ingrāj Bāzār
97 N25 **English Channel** *var.* The Channel, *Fr.* la Manche. *channel* NW Europe
194 J7 **English Coast** *physical region* Antarctica
105 S11 **Enguera** País Valenciano, E Spain 38°58′N 00°42′W
118 E8 **Engure** Tukums, W Latvia 57°09′N 23°13′E
118 E8 **Engures Ezers** ◎ NW Latvia
137 R9 **Enguri** *Rus.* Inguri. ↝ NW Georgia
Engyum *see* Gangi
26 M9 **Enid** Oklahoma, C USA 36°25′N 97°53′W
22 L3 **Enid Lake** ⊠ Mississippi, S USA
189 Y2 **Enigu** *island* Ratak Chain, SE Marshall Islands
Enikale Strait *see* Kerch Strait
147 Z8 **Enil'chek** Issyk-Kul'skaya Oblast', E Kyrgyzstan 42°04′N 79°01′E
115 F17 **Enipefs** ↝ C Greece
165 S4 **Eniwa** Hokkaidō, NE Japan 42°53′N 141°14′E
Eniwetok *see* Enewetak Atoll
Enjiang *see* Yongfeng
Enkeldoorn *see* Chivhu
98 J8 **Enkhuizen** Noord-Holland, NW Netherlands 52°34′N 05°03′E
109 Q4 **Enknach** ↝ N Austria
95 N15 **Enköping** Uppsala, C Sweden 59°38′N 17°07′E
107 K24 **Enna** *var.* Castrogiovanni, Henna. Sicilia, Italy, C Mediterranean Sea 37°34′N 14°16′E
80 D11 **En Nahud** Western Kordofan, C Sudan 12°41′N 28°28′E
138 F8 **En Nâqoûra** *var.* An Nāqūrah. SW Lebanon 33°06′N 33°30′E
En Nazira *see* Natzrat
78 K8 **Ennedi** *plateau* E Chad
101 E15 **Ennepetal** Nordrhein-Westfalen, W Germany 51°18′N 07°23′E
183 P4 **Enngonia** New South Wales, SE Australia 29°19′S 145°52′E
97 C19 **Ennis** *Ir.* Inis. Clare, W Ireland 52°50′N 08°59′W
33 R11 **Ennis** Montana, NW USA 45°21′N 111°45′W
25 U7 **Ennis** Texas, SW USA 32°19′N 96°37′W
97 F20 **Enniscorthy** *Ir.* Inis Córthaidh. SE Ireland 52°30′N 06°34′W
97 E15 **Enniskillen** *var.* Inniskilling, *Ir.* Inis Ceithleann. SW Northern Ireland, United Kingdom 54°21′N 07°38′W
97 B19 **Ennistimon** *Ir.* Inis Díomáin. Clare, W Ireland 52°57′N 09°17′W
109 T4 **Enns** Oberösterreich, N Austria 48°13′N 14°28′E
109 T4 **Enns** ↝ C Austria
93 O16 **Eno** Itä-Suomi, SE Finland 62°45′N 30°15′E
24 M5 **Enochs** Texas, SW USA 33°51′N 102°46′W
93 N17 **Enonkoski** Itä-Suomi, E Finland 62°04′N 28°53′E
92 K10 **Enontekiö** *Lapp.* Eanodat. Lappi, N Finland 68°25′N 23°40′E
21 Q11 **Enoree** South Carolina, SE USA 34°39′N 81°58′W
21 P11 **Enoree River** ↝ South Carolina, SE USA
18 M6 **Enosburg Falls** Vermont, NE USA 44°54′N 72°50′W
171 N13 **Enrekang** Sulawesi, C Indonesia 03°33′S 119°46′E
45 N10 **Enriquillo** SW Dominican Republic 17°57′N 71°13′W
45 N9 **Enriquillo, Lago** ◎ SW Dominican Republic
98 L9 **Ens** Flevoland, N Netherlands 52°39′N 05°49′E
98 P11 **Enschede** Overijssel, E Netherlands 52°13′N 06°55′E
40 B2 **Ensenada** Baja California Norte, NW Mexico 31°52′N 116°32′W
101 E20 **Ensheim** ✈ (Saarbrücken) Saarland, W Germany 49°13′N 07°09′E
160 L9 **Enshi** Hubei, C China 30°16′N 109°26′E
164 L14 **Enshū-nada** *gulf* SW Japan
23 O8 **Ensley** Florida, SE USA 30°31′N 87°16′W
Enso *see* Svetogorsk
81 F18 **Entebbe** S Uganda 0°07′N 32°30′E
81 F18 **Entebbe** ✈ C Uganda 0°04′N 32°29′E
101 M18 **Entenbühl** ▲ Czech Republic/Germany 50°09′N 12°10′E
98 N10 **Enter** Overijssel, E Netherlands 52°19′N 06°34′E
23 Q7 **Enterprise** Alabama, S USA 31°19′N 85°50′W
32 L11 **Enterprise** Oregon, NW USA 45°25′N 117°18′W
36 J7 **Enterprise** Utah, W USA 37°33′N 113°42′W
32 J8 **Entiat** Washington, NW USA 47°39′N 120°15′W
105 P15 **Entinas, Punta de las** *headland* S Spain 36°40′N 02°44′W
108 F8 **Entlebuch** Luzern, W Switzerland 47°02′N 08°04′E
108 F8 **Entlebuch** *valley* C Switzerland
63 I22 **Entrada, Punta** *headland* S Argentina
103 O13 **Entraygues-sur-Truyère** Aveyron, S France 44°39′N 02°36′E
187 O14 **Entrecasteaux, Récifs d'** *reef* N New Caledonia
61 C17 **Entre Ríos** *off.* Provincia de Entre Ríos. ◐ *province* NE Argentina
42 K7 **Entre Ríos, Cordillera** ▲▲ Honduras/Nicaragua
Entre Ríos, Provincia de *see* Entre Ríos
104 G9 **Entroncamento** Santarém, C Portugal 39°28′N 08°28′W
77 V16 **Enugu** Enugu, S Nigeria 06°24′N 07°24′E
77 U16 **Enugu** ◐ *state* SE Nigeria
123 V5 **Enurmino** Chukotskiy Avtonomnyy Okrug, NE Russian Federation 66°46′N 171°40′W
54 E9 **Envigado** Antioquia, W Colombia 06°09′N 75°38′W
59 B15 **Envira** Amazonas, W Brazil 07°12′S 69°59′W
Enyélé *see* Enyellé
79 I16 **Enyellé** *var.* Enyélé. Likouala, NE Congo 02°49′N 18°02′E
101 H21 **Enz** ↝ SW Germany
165 N13 **Enzan** *var.* Kōshū. Yamanashi, Honshū, S Japan 35°44′N 138°43′E
104 I2 **Eo** ↝ NW Spain
Eochaill *see* Youghal
Eochaille, Cuan *see* Youghal Bay
107 K22 **Eolie, Isole** *var.* Isole Lipari, *Eng.* Aeolian Islands, Lipari Islands. *island group* S Italy
189 U12 **Eot** *island* Chuuk, C Micronesia
Epáno Archánes/Epáno Arkhánai *see* Archánes
115 G14 **Epanomí** Kentrikí Makedonía, N Greece 40°25′N 22°57′E
98 M10 **Epe** Gelderland, E Netherlands 52°21′N 05°59′E
77 S16 **Epe** Lagos, S Nigeria 06°37′N 04°01′E
79 I17 **Epéna** Likouala, NE Congo 01°28′N 17°29′E
Eperies/Eperjes *see* Prešov
103 Q4 **Épernay** *anc.* Sparnacum. Marne, N France 49°02′N 03°58′E
36 L5 **Ephraim** Utah, W USA 39°21′N 111°35′W
18 H15 **Ephrata** Pennsylvania, NE USA 40°09′N 76°08′W
32 J8 **Ephrata** Washington, NW USA 47°19′N 119°33′W
187 R14 **Epi** *var.* Épi. *island* C Vanuatu
Épi *see* Epi
105 R6 **Épila** Aragón, NE Spain 41°34′N 01°19′W
103 T6 **Épinal** Vosges, NE France 48°10′N 06°28′E
Epiphania *see* Ḩamāh
Epirus *see* Ípeiros
121 P3 **Episkopi** SW Cyprus 34°37′N 32°53′E
Episkopi Bay *see* Episkopí, Kólpos
121 P3 **Episkopí, Kólpos** *var.* Episkopi Bay. *bay* SE Cyprus
Epitoli *see* Tshwane
Epoon *see* Ebon Atoll
Eporedia *see* Ivrea
Eppeschdorf *see* Dumbrăveni
101 H21 **Eppingen** Baden-Württemberg, SW Germany 49°09′N 08°54′E
83 E18 **Epukiro** Omaheke, E Namibia 21°40′S 19°09′E
29 Y13 **Epworth** Iowa, C USA 42°27′N 90°55′W
143 O10 **Eqlīd** *var.* Iqlid. Fārs, C Iran 30°54′N 52°40′E
Equality State *see* Wyoming
79 J18 **Equateur** *off.* Région de l' Equateur. ◐ *region* N Dem. Rep. Congo
Equateur, Région de l' *see* Equateur
151 K22 **Equatorial Channel** *channel* S Maldives
79 B17 **Equatorial Guinea** *off.* Equatorial Guinea, Republic of. ◆ *republic* C Africa
Equatorial Guinea, Republic of *see* Equatorial Guinea
121 V11 **Eratosthenes Tablemount** *undersea feature* E Mediterranean Sea 33°48′N 32°53′E
Erautini *see* Johannesburg
136 L12 **Erbaa** Tokat, N Turkey 40°42′N 36°37′E
101 E19 **Erbeskopf** ▲ W Germany 49°43′N 07°04′E
Erbil *see* Arbīl
121 P2 **Ercan** ✈ (Nicosia) N Cyprus 35°07′N 33°30′E
Ercegnovi *see* Herceg-Novi
137 T14 **Erçek Gölü** ◎ E Turkey
137 S14 **Erciş** Van, E Turkey 39°02′N 43°21′E
136 K14 **Erciyes Dağı** *anc.* Argaeus. ▲ C Turkey 38°32′N 35°28′E
111 J22 **Érd** *Ger.* Hanselbeck. Pest, C Hungary 47°22′N 18°56′E
163 X11 **Erdaobaihe** *prev.* Baihe. Jilin, NE China 42°24′N 128°09′E
159 O12 **Erdaogou** Qinghai, W China 34°30′N 92°50′E
163 X11 **Erdao Jiang** ↝ NE China
Erdăt-Sângeorz *see* Sângeorgiu de Pădure
136 C11 **Erdek** Balıkesir, NW Turkey 40°24′N 27°47′E
Erdély *see* Transylvania
Erdélyi-Havasok *see* Carpaţii Meridionalii
136 J17 **Erdemli** İçel, S Turkey 36°35′N 34°19′E
163 O10 **Erdene** *var.* Ulaan-Uul. Dornogovĭ, SE Mongolia 44°21′N 111°06′E
162 H9 **Erdene** *var.* Sangiyn Dalay. Govĭ-Altay, C Mongolia 45°12′N 97°51′E
162 E6 **Erdenebüren** *var.* Har-Us. Hovd, W Mongolia 48°30′N 91°25′E
162 K9 **Erdenedalay** *var.* Sangiyn Dalay. Dundgovĭ, C Mongolia 45°59′N 104°58′E
162 G7 **Erdenehayrhan** *var.* Altan. Dzavhan, W Mongolia 48°05′N 95°48′E
162 J7 **Erdenemandal** *var.* Öldziyt. Arhangay, C Mongolia 48°30′N 101°25′E
162 K6 **Erdenet** Orhon, N Mongolia 49°01′N 104°07′E
163 Q9 **Erdenetsagaan** *var.* Chonogol. Sühbaatar, E Mongolia 45°55′N 115°19′E
162 I8 **Erdenetsogt** Bayanhongor, C Mongolia 46°27′N 100°53′E
Erdenetsogt *see* Bayan-Ovoo
78 K7 **Erdi** *plateau* NE Chad
78 L7 **Erdi Ma** *desert* NE Chad
101 M23 **Erding** Bayern, SE Germany 48°18′N 11°54′E
Erdőszáda *see* Ardusat
Erdőszentgyörgy *see* Sângeorgiu de Pădure
102 I7 **Erdre** ↝ NW France
195 R13 **Erebus, Mount** ▲ Ross Island, Antarctica 78°11′S 165°09′E
61 H14 **Erechim** Rio Grande do Sul, S Brazil 27°35′S 52°15′W
163 O7 **Ereen Davaanĭ Nuruu** ▲▲ NE Mongolia
163 Q6 **Ereentsav** Dornod, NE Mongolia 49°51′N 115°41′E
136 I16 **Ereğli** Konya, S Turkey 37°30′N 34°02′E
115 A15 **Ereíkoussa** *island* Iónia Nísiá, Greece, C Mediterranean Sea
163 O11 **Erenhot** *var.* Erlian. Nei Mongol Zizhiqu, NE China 43°35′N 112°E
104 M6 **Eresma** ↝ N Spain
115 K17 **Eresós** *var.* Eressós. Lésvos, E Greece 39°11′N 25°57′E
Eressós *see* Eresós
Ereymentau *see* Yereymentau
99 K21 **Érezée** Luxembourg, SE Belgium 50°16′N 05°34′E
74 G7 **Erfoud** SE Morocco 31°29′N 04°18′W
101 D16 **Erft** ↝ W Germany
101 K16 **Erfurt** Thüringen, C Germany 50°59′N 11°02′E
137 P15 **Ergani** Dıyarbakır, SE Turkey 38°17′N 39°44′E
Ergel *see* Hatanbulag
Ergene Çayi *see* Ergene Irmaği
136 C10 **Ergene Irmaği** *var.* Ergene Çayı. ↝ NW Turkey
118 I9 **Ērgļi** Madona, C Latvia 56°55′N 25°38′E
78 H11 **Erguig, Bahr** ↝ SW Chad
163 S5 **Ergun** *var.* Labudalin; *prev.* Ergun Youqi. Nei Mongol Zizhiqu, N China 50°13′N 120°09′E
Ergun He *see* Argun
Ergun Youqi *see* Ergun
Ergun Zuoqi *see* Genhe
160 F12 **Er Hai** ◎ SW China
104 K4 **Ería** ↝ NW Spain
80 H8 **Eriba** Kassala, NE Sudan 16°37′N 36°04′E
96 I6 **Eriboll, Loch** *inlet* NW Scotland, United Kingdom
65 Q18 **Erica Seamount** *undersea feature* SW Indian Ocean 38°15′S 14°30′E
107 H23 **Erice** Sicilia, Italy, C Mediterranean Sea 38°02′N 12°35′E
104 E10 **Ericeira** Lisboa, C Portugal 38°58′N 09°25′W
96 H10 **Ericht, Loch** ◎ C Scotland, United Kingdom
26 J11 **Erick** Oklahoma, C USA 35°13′N 99°52′W
18 B11 **Erie** Pennsylvania, NE USA 42°07′N 80°04′W
18 E9 **Erie Canal** *canal* New York, NE USA
Érié, Lac *see* Erie, Lake
31 T10 **Erie, Lake** *Fr.* Lac Érié. ◎ Canada/USA
Erigabo *see* Ceerigaabo
77 N8 **'Erîgât** *desert* N Mali
Erigavo *see* Ceerigaabo
92 P2 **Erik Eriksenstretet** *strait* E Svalbard
11 X15 **Eriksdale** Manitoba, S Canada 50°52′N 98°07′W
189 V6 **Erikub Atoll** *var.* Ādkup. *atoll* Ratak Chain, C Marshall Islands
102 G4 **Er, Îles d'** *island group* NW France
Erimanthos *see* Erýmanthos
165 T6 **Erimo** Hokkaidō, NE Japan 42°01′N 143°07′E
165 T6 **Erimo-misaki** *headland* Hokkaidō, NE Japan 41°57′N 143°12′E
20 H8 **Erin** Tennessee, S USA 36°19′N 87°42′W
96 E9 **Eriskay** *island* NW Scotland, United Kingdom
Erithraí *see* Erythrés
80 I9 **Eritrea** *off.* State of Eritrea, Ērtra. ◆ *transitional government* E Africa
Eritrea, State of *see* Eritrea
Erivan *see* Yerevan
101 D16 **Erkelenz** Nordrhein-Westfalen, W Germany 51°04′N 06°19′E
95 P15 **Erken** ◎ C Sweden
101 K19 **Erlangen** Bayern, S Germany 49°36′N 11°E
160 G9 **Erlang Shan** ▲ C China 29°56′N 102°24′E
Erlau *see* Eger
109 V5 **Erlauf** ↝ NE Austria
181 Q8 **Erldunda Roadhouse** Northern Territory, N Australia 25°13′S 133°13′E
Erlian *see* Erenhot
27 T15 **Erling, Lake** ⊠ Arkansas, USA
109 O8 **Erlsbach** Tirol, W Austria 46°54′N 12°15′E
Ermak *see* Aksu
98 K10 **Ermelo** Gelderland, C Netherlands 52°18′N 05°38′E
83 K21 **Ermelo** Mpumalanga, NE South Africa 26°32′S 29°59′E
136 H17 **Ermenek** Karaman, S Turkey 36°38′N 32°55′E
Érmihályfalva *see* Valea lui Mihai
115 G20 **Ermióni** Pelopónnisos, S Greece 37°24′N 23°15′E
115 J20 **Ermoúpoli** *var.* Hermoupolis; *prev.* Ermoúpolis. Sýyros, Kykládes, Greece, Aegean Sea 37°26′N 24°55′E
Ermoúpolis *see* Ermoúpoli
Ernabella *see* Pukatja
155 G22 **Ernākulam** Kerala, SW India 10°04′N 76°18′E
102 J6 **Ernée** Mayenne, NW France 48°18′N 00°54′W
61 H14 **Ernestina, Barragem** ⊠ S Brazil
54 E4 **Ernesto Cortissoz** ✈ (Barranquilla) Atlántico, N Colombia
155 H21 **Erode** Tamil Nādu, SE India 11°21′N 77°43′E
Eroj *see* Iroj
83 C19 **Erongo** ◐ *district* W Namibia
99 F21 **Erquelinnes** Hainaut, S Belgium 50°18′N 04°08′E
74 G7 **Er-Rachidia** *var.* Ksar al Soule. E Morocco 31°58′N 04°22′W
80 E11 **Er Rahad** *var.* Ar Rahad. Northern Kordofan, C Sudan 12°43′N 30°39′E
Er Ramle *see* Ramla
83 O15 **Errego** Zambézia, NE Mozambique 16°02′S 37°11′E
105 Q2 **Errenteria** *Cast.* Rentería. País Vasco, N Spain 43°17′N 01°54′W
Er Rif/Er Riff *see* Rif
97 D14 **Errigal Mountain** *Ir.* An Earagail. ▲ N Ireland 55°03′N 08°09′W
97 A15 **Erris Head** *Ir.* Ceann Iorrais. *headland* W Ireland 54°18′N 10°01′W
187 S15 **Erromango** *island* S Vanuatu
Error Guyot *see* Error Tablemount
173 O4 **Error Tablemount** *var.* Error Guyot. *undersea feature* W Indian Ocean 10°20′N 56°05′E
80 G11 **Er Roseires** Blue Nile, E Sudan 11°52′N 34°23′E
Erseka *see* Ersekë
113 M22 **Ersekë** *var.* Erseka, Kolonjë. Korçë, SE Albania 40°19′N 20°39′E
Érsekújvár *see* Nové Zámky
29 S4 **Erskine** Minnesota, N USA 47°42′N 96°00′W
103 V6 **Erstein** Bas-Rhin, NE France 48°24′N 07°39′E
108 G9 **Erstfeld** Uri, C Switzerland 46°49′N 08°41′E
158 M3 **Ertai** Xinjiang Uygur Zizhiqu, NW China 46°04′N 90°06′E
126 M7 **Ertil'** Voronezhskaya Oblast', W Russian Federation 51°51′N 40°46′E
Ertis *see* Irtysh, C Asia
Ertis *see* Irtyshsk, Kazakhstan
158 K2 **Ertix He** *Rus.* Chërnyy Irtysh. ↝ China/Kazakhstan
Ērtra *see* Eritrea
21 P9 **Erwin** North Carolina, SE USA 35°19′N 78°40′W
Erydropótamos *see* Erythropótamos
115 E19 **Erýmanthos** *var.* Erimanthos. ▲ S Greece 37°57′N 21°51′E
115 G19 **Erythrés** *prev.* Erithraí. Stereá Ellás, C Greece 38°18′N 23°20′E
114 L12 **Erythropótamos** *Bul.* Byala Reka, *var.* Erydropótamos. ↝ Bulgaria/Greece
160 F12 **Eryuan** *var.* Yuhu. Yunnan, SW China 26°09′N 100°01′E
109 U6 **Erzbach** ↝ W Austria
Erzerum *see* Erzurum
101 N17 **Erzgebirge** *Cz.* Krušné Hory, *Eng.* Ore Mountains. ▲ Czech Republic/Germany *see also* Krušné Hory
Erzgebirge *see* Krušné Hory
122 L14 **Erzin** Respublika Tyva, S Russian Federation 50°17′N 95°03′E
137 O13 **Erzincan** *var.* Erzinjan. Erzincan, E Turkey 39°44′N 39°30′E
137 N13 **Erzincan** *var.* Erzinjan. ◐ *province* NE Turkey
Erzinjan *see* Erzincan
Erzsébetváros *see* Dumbrăveni
137 Q13 **Erzurum** *prev.* Erzerum. Erzurum, NE Turkey 39°57′N 41°17′E
137 Q12 **Erzurum** *prev.* Erzerum. ◐ *province* NE Turkey
186 G9 **Esa'ala** Normanby Island, SE Papua New Guinea 09°45′S 150°47′E
165 T2 **Esashi** Hokkaidō, NE Japan 44°57′N 142°32′E
165 Q9 **Esashi** *var.* Esasi. Iwate, Honshū, C Japan 39°13′N 141°11′E
165 Q5 **Esasho** Hokkaidō, N Japan 41°52′N 140°07′E
Esasi *see* Esashi
95 F23 **Esbjerg** Ribe, W Denmark 55°28′N 08°28′E
Esbo *see* Espoo
36 L7 **Escalante** Utah, W USA 37°46′N 111°36′W
36 M7 **Escalante River** ↝ Utah, W USA
14 L12 **Escalier, Réservoir l'** ⊠ Québec, SE Canada
40 K7 **Escalón** Chihuahua, N Mexico 26°43′N 104°20′W
104 M8 **Escalona** Castilla-La Mancha, C Spain 40°10′N 04°24′W
23 O8 **Escambia River** ↝ Florida, SE USA
31 N5 **Escanaba** Michigan, N USA 45°45′N 87°03′W
31 N4 **Escanaba River** ↝ Michigan, N USA
105 R8 **Escandón, Puerto de** *pass* E Spain
41 W14 **Escárcega** Campache, SE Mexico 18°33′N 90°41′W
171 O1 **Escarpada Point** *headland* Luzon, N Philippines 18°28′N 122°10′E
23 N8 **Escatawpa River** ↝ Alabama/Mississippi, S USA
103 P2 **Escaut** ↝ N France
Escaut *see* Scheldt
99 M25 **Esch-sur-Alzette** Luxembourg, S Luxembourg 49°30′N 05°59′E
101 J15 **Eschwege** Hessen, C Germany 51°10′N 10°03′E
101 D16 **Eschweiler** Nordrhein-Westfalen, W Germany 50°49′N 06°16′E
Esclaves, Grand Lac des *see* Great Slave Lake
45 O8 **Escocesa, Bahía** *bay* N Dominican Republic
43 U15 **Escocés, Punta** *headland* NE Panama 08°50′N 77°37′W
35 U17 **Escondido** California, W USA 33°07′N 117°05′W
42 M10 **Escondido, Río** ↝ SE Nicaragua
15 S7 **Escoumins, Rivière des** ↝ Québec, SE Canada
37 O13 **Escudilla Mountain** ▲ Arizona, SW USA 33°57′N 109°07′W
40 J11 **Escuinapa** *var.* Escuinapa de Hidalgo. Sinaloa, C Mexico 22°50′N 105°46′W
Escuinapa de Hidalgo *see* Escuinapa
42 C6 **Escuintla** Escuintla, S Guatemala 14°17′N 90°46′W
41 V17 **Escuintla** Chiapas, SE Mexico 15°20′N 92°40′W
42 A2 **Escuintla** *off.* Departamento de Escuintla. ◐ *department* S Guatemala
Escuintla, Departamento de *see* Escuintla
15 W7 **Escuminac** ↝ Québec, SE Canada
79 D16 **Eséka** Centre, SW Cameroon 03°40′N 10°48′E
136 I12 **Esenboğa** ✈ (Ankara) Ankara, C Turkey 40°05′N 33°01′E
136 D17 **Eşen Çayı** ↝ SW Turkey
146 B13 **Esenguly** *Rus.* Gasan-Kuli. Balkan Welaýaty, W Turkmenistan 37°29′N 53°57′E
105 T4 **Ésera** ↝ NE Spain
143 N8 **Eşfahān** *Eng.* Isfahan; *anc.* Aspadana. Eşfahān, C Iran 32°41′N 51°41′E
143 O7 **Eşfahān** *off.* Ostān-e Eşfahān. ◐ *province* C Iran
Eşfahān, Ostān-e *see* Eşfahān
105 N5 **Esgueva** ↝ N Spain
149 Q3 **Eshkamesh** Takhār, NE Afghanistan 36°25′N 69°11′E
149 T2 **Eshkāshem** Badakhshān, NE Afghanistan 36°43′N 71°34′E
83 L23 **Eshowe** KwaZulu/Natal, E South Africa 28°53′S 31°28′E
143 T5 **'Eshqābād** Khorāsān, NE Iran 36°00′N 59°01′E
Esh Sham *see* Dimashq
Esh Sharā *see* Ash Sharāh
Esik *see* Yesik
Esil *see* Yesil'
Esil *see* Ishim, Kazakhstan/Russian Federation
183 V2 **Esk** Queensland, E Australia 27°15′S 152°23′E
184 O11 **Eskdale** Hawke's Bay, North Island, New Zealand 39°24′S 176°51′E
Eski Dzhumaya *see* Türgovishte
92 L2 **Eskifjördhur** Austurland, E Iceland 65°04′N 14°01′W
139 S3 **Eski Kaļak** *var.* Askī Kalak, Kalak. Arbīl, N Iraq 36°16′N 43°40′E
95 N16 **Eskilstuna** Södermanland, C Sweden 59°22′N 16°31′E
8 H6 **Eskimo Lakes** ◎ Northwest Territories, NW Canada
9 O10 **Eskimo Point** *headland* Nunavut, E Canada 61°19′N 93°49′W
Eskimo Point *see* Arviat
139 Q2 **Eski Mosul** Nīnawá, N Iraq 36°31′N 42°45′E
147 T10 **Eski-Nookat** *var.* Iski-Nauket. Oshskaya Oblast', SW Kyrgyzstan 40°18′N 72°29′E
136 F12 **Eskişehir** *var.* Eskishehr. Eskişehir, W Turkey 39°46′N 30°30′E
136 F13 **Eskişehir** *var.* Eski shehr. ◐ *province* NW Turkey
Eskishehr *see* Eskişehir
104 K5 **Esla** ↝ NW Spain
142 J6 **Eslāmābād** *var.* Eslāmābād-e Gharb; *prev.* Harunabad, Shāhābād. Kermānshāhān, W Iran 34°08′N 46°35′E
Eslāmābād-e Gharb *see* Eslāmābād
148 J4 **Eslām Qal'eh** *Pash.* Islam Qala. Herāt, W Afghanistan 34°41′N 61°03′E
95 K23 **Eslöv** Skåne, S Sweden 55°50′N 13°20′E
143 S12 **Esmā'īlābād** Kermān, S Iran 28°48′N 56°39′E
143 U8 **Esmā'īlābād** Khorāsān, E Iran 35°20′N 60°30′E
136 D14 **Eşme** Uşak, W Turkey 38°26′N 28°59′E
44 G6 **Esmeralda** Camagüey, E Cuba 21°51′N 78°10′W
63 F21 **Esmeralda, Isla** *island* S Chile
56 B5 **Esmeraldas** Esmeraldas, N Ecuador 0°55′N 79°40′W
56 B5 **Esmeraldas** ◐ *province* NW Ecuador
Esna *see* Isnā
14 B6 **Esnagi Lake** ◎ Ontario, S Canada
143 V14 **Espakeh** Sīstān va Balūchestān, SE Iran 26°54′N 60°09′E
103 O13 **Espalion** Aveyron, S France 44°31′N 02°45′E
España *see* Spain
14 E11 **Espanola** Ontario, S Canada 46°15′N 81°46′W
37 S10 **Espanola** New Mexico, SW USA 35°59′N 106°04′W
57 C18 **Española, Isla** *var.* Hood Island. *island* Galapagos Islands, Ecuador, E Pacific Ocean
104 M13 **Espejo** Andalucía, S Spain 37°40′N 04°34′W
94 C13 **Espeland** Hordaland, S Norway 60°22′N 05°27′E
100 G12 **Espelkamp** Nordrhein-Westfalen, NW Germany 52°22′N 08°37′E
38 M8 **Espenberg, Cape** *headland* Alaska, USA 66°33′N 163°36′W
180 L13 **Esperance** Western Australia 33°49′S 121°52′E
186 L9 **Esperance, Cape** *headland* Guadacanal, C Solomon Islands 09°09′S 159°38′E
57 P18 **Esperancita** Santa Cruz, E Bolivia
61 B17 **Esperanza** Santa Fe, C Argentina 31°29′S 61°00′W
40 G6 **Esperanza** Sonora, NW Mexico 27°37′N 109°51′W
24 H9 **Esperanza** Texas, SW USA 31°09′N 105°40′W
194 H3 **Esperanza** *Argentinian research station* Antarctica 63°29′S 56°53′W
104 E12 **Espichel, Cabo** *headland* S Portugal 38°25′N 09°15′W
54 E10 **Espinal** Tolima, C Colombia 04°08′N 74°53′W
48 K10 **Espinhaço, Serra do** ▲▲ SE Brazil
104 G6 **Espinho** Aveiro, N Portugal 41°01′N 08°38′W
59 N18 **Espinosa** Minas Gerais, SE Brazil 14°58′S 42°49′W
103 O15 **Espinouse** ▲ S France
60 Q8 **Espírito Santo** *off.* Estado do Espírito Santo. ◐ *state* E Brazil
Espírito Santo, Estado do *see* Espírito Santo
187 P13 **Espiritu Santo** *var.* Santo. *island* W Vanuatu
41 Z13 **Espíritu Santo, Bahía del** *bay* SE Mexico
40 F9 **Espíritu Santo, Isla del** *island* NW Mexico
41 Y12 **Espita** Yucatán, SE Mexico 21°00′N 88°17′W
15 Y7 **Espoir, Cap d'** *headland* Québec, SE Canada 48°24′N 64°21′W
Esponsede/Esponsende *see* Esposende
93 L20 **Espoo** *Swe.* Esbo. Etelä-Suomi, S Finland 60°10′N 24°42′E
104 G5 **Esposende** *var.* Esponsede, Esponsende. Braga, N Portugal 41°32′N 08°47′W
83 M18 **Espungabera** Manica, SW Mozambique 20°29′S 32°48′E
63 H17 **Esquel** Chubut, SW Argentina 42°55′S 71°20′W
10 L17 **Esquimalt** Vancouver Island, British Columbia, SW Canada 48°26′N 123°27′W
61 C16 **Esquina** Corrientes, NE Argentina 30°00′S 59°30′W
42 E6 **Esquipulas** Chiquimula, SE Guatemala 14°36′N 89°22′W
42 K9 **Esquipulas** Matagalpa, C Nicaragua 12°30′N 85°55′W
94 I8 **Essandjøen** ◎ S Norway
74 E7 **Essaouira** *prev.* Mogador. W Morocco 31°33′N 09°40′W
Esseg *see* Osijek
Es Semara *see* Smara
99 G15 **Essen** Antwerpen, N Belgium 51°28′N 04°28′E
101 E15 **Essen** *var.* Essen an der Ruhr. Nordrhein-Westfalen, W Germany 51°28′N 07°01′E
Essen an der Ruhr *see* Essen
74 I5 **Es Senia** ✈ (Oran) NW Algeria 35°34′N 00°42′W
55 T8 **Essequibo Islands** *island group* N Guyana
55 T11 **Essequibo River** ↝ C Guyana
14 C18 **Essex** Ontario, S Canada 42°10′N 82°50′W
29 T16 **Essex** Iowa, C USA 40°49′N 95°18′W
97 P21 **Essex** *cultural region* E England, United Kingdom
31 R8 **Essexville** Michigan, N USA 43°37′N 83°50′W
101 H22 **Esslingen** *var.* Esslingen am Neckar. Baden-Württemberg, SW Germany 48°45′N 09°19′E
Esslingen am Neckar *see* Esslingen
103 N6 **Essonne** ◐ *department* N France
Es Suweida *see* As Suwaydā'
79 F16 **Est** *Eng.* East. ◐ *province* SE Cameroon
104 I1 **Estaca de Bares, Punta da** *point* NW Spain
24 M5 **Estacado, Llano** *plain* New Mexico/Texas, SW USA
63 K25 **Estados, Isla de los** *prev. Eng.* Staten Island. *island* S Argentina
Estado Vargas *see* Vargas
143 P12 **Eşţahbān** Fārs, S Iran
14 F11 **Estaire** Ontario, S Canada 46°19′N 80°47′W
59 P16 **Estância** Sergipe, E Brazil 11°15′S 37°28′W
37 S12 **Estancia** New Mexico, SW USA 34°45′N 106°03′W
104 G7 **Estarreja** Aveiro, N Portugal 40°45′N 08°35′W
102 M17 **Estats, Pic d'** *Sp.* Pico d'Estats. ▲ France/Spain 42°39′N 01°24′E
Estats, Pico d' *see* Estats, Pic d'
83 K23 **Estcourt** KwaZulu/Natal, E South Africa 29°00′S 29°53′E
106 H8 **Este** *anc.* Ateste. Veneto, NE Italy 45°14′N 11°40′E
42 J9 **Estelí** Estelí, NW Nicaragua 13°05′N 86°21′W
42 J9 **Estelí** ◐ *department* NW Nicaragua
105 Q4 **Estella** *Bas.* Lizarra. Navarra, N Spain 42°41′N 02°02′W
29 R9 **Estelline** South Dakota, N USA 44°34′N 96°54′W
25 P4 **Estelline** Texas, SW USA 34°33′N 100°26′W
104 L14 **Estepa** Andalucía, S Spain 37°17′N 04°52′W
104 L16 **Estepona** Andalucía, S Spain 36°26′N 05°09′W
39 R9 **Ester** Alaska, USA 64°49′N 148°03′W
11 V16 **Esterhazy** Saskatchewan, S Canada 50°40′N 102°02′W
37 S3 **Estes Park** Colorado, C USA 40°22′N 105°31′W
43 Q7 **Este Sudesre, Cayos del** NW Colombia, Caribbean Sea
11 V17 **Estevan** Saskatchewan, S Canada 49°07′N 103°05′W
29 T11 **Estherville** Iowa, C USA 43°24′N 94°49′W
21 R15 **Estill** South Carolina, SE USA 32°45′N 81°14′W
103 Q6 **Estissac** Aube, N France 48°17′N 03°51′E
15 T9 **Est, Lac de l'** ◎ Québec, SE Canada
Estland *see* Estonia
11 S16 **Eston** Saskatchewan, S Canada 51°09′N 108°42′W
118 G5 **Estonia** *off.* Republic of Estonia, *Est.* Eesti Vabariik, *Ger.* Estland, *Latv.* Igaunija; *prev.* Estonian SSR, *Rus.* Estonskaya SSR. ◆ *republic* NE Europe
Estonian SSR *see* Estonia
Estonia, Republic of *see* Estonia
Estonskaya SSR *see* Estonia
104 E11 **Estoril** Lisboa, W Portugal 38°42′N 09°23′W
59 L14 **Estreito** Maranhão, E Brazil 06°34′S 47°22′W
104 I8 **Estrela, Serra da** ▲ C Portugal
40 D3 **Estrella, Punta** *headland* NW Mexico 30°53′N 114°45′W
104 F10 **Estremadura** *cultural and historical region* W Portugal
Estremadura *see* Extremadura
104 H11 **Estremoz** Évora, S Portugal 38°50′N 07°35′W
79 D18 **Estuaire** *off.* Province de l'Estuaire, *var.* L'Estuaire. ◐ *province* NW Gabon
Estuaire, Province de l' *see* Estuaire
Eszék *see* Osijek
111 I22 **Esztergom** *Ger.* Gran; *anc.* Strigonium. Komárom-Esztergom, N Hungary 47°47′N 18°44′E
152 K11 **Etah** Uttar Pradesh, N India 27°33′N 78°39′E
189 R17 **Etal Atoll** *atoll* Mortlock Islands, C Micronesia
99 K24 **Étalle** Luxembourg, SE Belgium 49°41′N 05°36′E
103 N6 **Étampes** Essonne, N France 48°26′N 02°10′E
182 J1 **Etamunbanie, Lake** *salt lake* South Australia
103 N1 **Étaples** Pas-de-Calais, N France 50°31′N 01°39′E
152 K12 **Etāwah** Uttar Pradesh, N India 26°46′N 79°01′E
15 R10 **Etchemin** ↝ Québec, SE Canada
Etchmiadzin *see* Vagharshapat
40 G7 **Etchojoa** Sonora, NW Mexico 26°54′N 109°37′W
93 L19 **Etelä-Suomi** ◐ *province* S Finland
83 B16 **Etengua** Kunene, NW Namibia 17°24′S 13°05′E
99 K25 **Éthe** Luxembourg, SE Belgium 49°34′N 05°32′E
11 W15 **Ethelbert** Manitoba, S Canada 51°30′N 100°22′W
80 H12 **Ethiopia** *off.* Federal Democratic Republic of Ethiopia; *prev.* Abyssinia, People's Democratic Republic of Ethiopia. ◆ *republic* E Africa
Ethiopia, Federal Democratic Republic of *see* Ethiopia
80 I13 **Ethiopian Highlands** *var.* Ethiopian Plateau. *plateau* N Ethiopia
Ethiopian Plateau *see* Ethiopian Highlands
Ethiopia, People's Democratic Republic of *see* Ethiopia
34 M2 **Etna** California, W USA 41°25′N 122°53′W
18 B14 **Etna** Pennsylvania, NE USA 40°29′N 79°55′W
94 G12 **Etna** ↝ S Norway
107 L24 **Etna, Monte** *Eng.* Mount Etna. ▲ Sicilia, Italy, C Mediterranean Sea 37°46′N 15°00′E
Etna, Mount *see* Etna, Monte

◆ Country ● Country Capital ◇ Dependent Territory ○ Dependent Territory Capital ◐ Administrative Regions ✈ International Airport ▲ Mountain ▲▲ Mountain Range Volcano ↝ River ◎ Lake ⊠ Reservoir

95 C15 **Etne** Hordaland, S Norway *59°40′N 05°55′E*
Etoliko *see* Aitolikó
39 Y14 **Etolin Island** *island* Alexander Archipelago, Alaska, USA
38 L12 **Etolin Strait** *strait* Alaska, USA
83 C17 **Etosha Pan** *salt lake* N Namibia
79 G18 **Etoumbi** Cuvette Ouest, NW Congo *0°01′N 14°57′E*
20 M10 **Etowah** Tennessee, S USA *35°19′N 84°31′W*
23 S2 **Etowah River** ⟿ Georgia, SE USA
146 B13 **Etrek** *var.* Gyzyletrek, *Rus.* Kizyl-Atrek. Balkan Welaýaty, W Turkmenistan *37°40′N 54°44′E*
146 C13 **Etrek** *Per.* Rūd-e Atrak, *Rus.* Atrak, Atrek. ⟿ Iran/Turkmenistan
102 L3 **Étretat** Seine-Maritime, N France *49°46′N 00°23′E*
114 H9 **Etropole** Sofiya, W Bulgaria *42°50′N 24°00′E*
Etsch *see* Adige
Et Tafila *see* Aţ Ţafilah
99 M23 **Ettelbrück** Diekirch, C Luxembourg *49°51′N 06°06′E*
189 V12 **Etten** *atoll* Chuuk Islands, C Micronesia
99 H14 **Etten-Leur** Noord-Brabant, S Netherlands *51°34′N 04°37′E*
76 G7 **Et Tîdra** *var.* Ile Tîdra. *island* Dakhlet Nouâdhibou, NW Mauritania
101 G21 **Ettlingen** Baden-Württemberg, SW Germany *48°57′N 08°25′E*
102 M2 **Eu** Seine-Maritime, N France *50°01′N 01°24′E*
193 W16 **'Eua** *prev.* Middleburg Island. *island* Tongatapu Group, SE Tonga
193 W15 **Eua Iki** *island* Tongatapu Group, S Tonga
Euboea *see* Évvoia
181 O12 **Eucla** Western Australia *31°41′S 128°51′E*
31 U11 **Euclid** Ohio, N USA *41°34′N 81°33′W*
27 W14 **Eudora** Arkansas, C USA *33°06′N 91°15′W*
27 Q4 **Eudora** Kansas, C USA *38°56′N 95°06′W*
182 J9 **Eudunda** South Australia *34°11′S 139°03′E*
23 R6 **Eufaula** Alabama, S USA *31°53′N 85°09′W*
27 Q11 **Eufaula** Oklahoma, C USA *35°16′N 95°36′W*
27 Q11 **Eufaula Lake** *var.* Eufaula Reservoir. ▣ Oklahoma, C USA
Eufaula Reservoir *see* Eufaula Lake
32 F13 **Eugene** Oregon, NW USA *44°03′N 123°05′W*
40 B6 **Eugenia, Punta** *headland* NW Mexico *27°48′N 115°03′W*
183 Q8 **Eugowra** New South Wales, SE Australia *33°28′S 148°21′E*
104 I2 **Eume** ⟿ NW Spain
104 H2 **Eume, Embalse do** ▣ NW Spain
Eumolpias *see* Plovdiv
59 O18 **Eunápolis** Bahia, SE Brazil *16°20′S 39°36′W*
22 H8 **Eunice** Louisiana, S USA *30°29′N 92°25′W*
37 W15 **Eunice** New Mexico, SW USA *32°26′N 103°09′W*
99 M19 **Eupen** Liège, E Belgium *50°38′N 06°02′E*
130 B10 **Euphrates** *Ar.* Al-Furāt, *Turk.* Firat Nehri. ⟿ SW Asia
138 L3 **Euphrates Dam** *dam* N Syria
22 M4 **Eupora** Mississippi, S USA *33°32′N 89°16′W*
93 K19 **Eura** Länsi-Suomi, SW Finland *61°07′N 22°12′E*
93 K19 **Eurajoki** Länsi-Suomi, SW Finland *61°13′N 21°45′E*
0-1 **Eurasian Plate** *tectonic feature*
102 L4 **Eure** ◐ *department* N France
102 M4 **Eure** ⟿ N France
102 M6 **Eure-et-Loir** ◐ *department* C France
34 K3 **Eureka** California, W USA *40°47′N 124°12′W*
27 P6 **Eureka** Kansas, C USA *37°51′N 96°17′W*
33 O6 **Eureka** Montana, NW USA *48°52′N 115°03′W*
35 V5 **Eureka** Nevada, W USA *39°31′N 115°58′W*
29 O7 **Eureka** South Dakota, N USA *45°46′N 99°37′W*
36 L4 **Eureka** Utah, W USA *39°57′N 112°07′W*
32 K10 **Eureka** Washington, NW USA *46°21′N 118°41′W*
27 S9 **Eureka Springs** Arkansas, C USA *36°25′N 93°45′W*
182 K6 **Eurinilla Creek** *seasonal river* South Australia
183 O11 **Euroa** Victoria, SE Australia *36°46′S 145°35′E*
172 M9 **Europa, Île** *island* W Madagascar
104 L3 **Europa, Picos de** ⛰ N Spain
104 L16 **Europa Point** *headland* S Gibraltar *36°07′N 05°20′W*
84-85 **Europe** *continent*
98 F12 **Europoort** Zuid-Holland, W Netherlands *51°59′N 04°08′E*
Euskadi *see* País Vasco
101 D17 **Euskirchen** Nordrhein-Westfalen, W Germany *50°40′N 06°47′E*
23 W11 **Eustis** Florida, SE USA *28°51′N 81°41′W*
182 M9 **Euston** New South Wales, SE Australia *34°34′S 142°45′E*
23 N5 **Eutaw** Alabama, S USA *32°50′N 87°53′W*
100 K8 **Eutin** Schleswig-Holstein, N Germany *54°08′N 10°38′E*
10 K14 **Eutsuk Lake** ▣ British Columbia, SW Canada
Euxine Sea *see* Black Sea
83 C16 **Evale** Cunene, SW Angola *16°36′S 15°46′E*
37 T3 **Evans** Colorado, C USA *40°22′N 104°41′W*
11 P14 **Evansburg** Alberta, SW Canada *53°34′N 114°57′W*
29 X13 **Evansdale** Iowa, C USA *42°28′N 92°16′W*
183 V4 **Evans Head** New South Wales, SE Australia *29°07′S 153°27′E*
12 J11 **Evans, Lac** ◎ Québec, SE Canada
37 S5 **Evans, Mount** ▲ Colorado, C USA *39°15′N 106°10′W*
9 Q6 **Evans Strait** *strait* Nunavut, N Canada
31 N10 **Evanston** Illinois, N USA *42°02′N 87°41′W*
33 S17 **Evanston** Wyoming, C USA *41°16′N 110°57′W*
14 D11 **Evansville** Manitoulin Island, Ontario, S Canada *45°48′N 82°34′W*
31 N16 **Evansville** Indiana, N USA *37°58′N 87°33′W*
30 L9 **Evansville** Wisconsin, N USA *42°46′N 89°16′W*
25 S8 **Evant** Texas, SW USA *31°28′N 98°09′W*
143 P13 **Evaz** Fārs, S Iran *27°48′N 53°58′E*
29 W4 **Eveleth** Minnesota, N USA *47°27′N 92°32′W*
182 E3 **Evelyn Creek** *seasonal river* South Australia
181 Q2 **Evelyn, Mount** ▲ Northern Territory, N Australia *13°28′S 132°50′E*
122 K10 **Evenkiyskiy Avtonomnyy Okrug** ◐ *autonomous district* Krasnoyarskiy Kray, N Russian Federation
183 R13 **Everard, Cape** *headland* Victoria, SE Australia *37°48′S 149°21′E*
182 F6 **Everard, Lake** *salt lake* South Australia
182 C2 **Everard Ranges** ⛰ South Australia
153 R11 **Everest, Mount** *Chin.* Qomolangma Feng, *Nep.* Sagarmāthā. ▲ China/Nepal *27°59′N 86°57′E*
18 E15 **Everett** Pennsylvania, NE USA *40°00′N 78°22′W*
32 H7 **Everett** Washington, NW USA *47°59′N 122°12′W*
99 E17 **Evergem** Oost-Vlaanderen, NW Belgium *51°07′N 03°43′E*
23 X16 **Everglades City** Florida, SE USA *25°51′N 81°22′W*
23 Y16 **Everglades, The** *wetland* Florida, SE USA
23 P7 **Evergreen** Alabama, S USA *31°25′N 86°55′W*
37 T4 **Evergreen** Colorado, C USA *39°37′N 105°19′W*
Evergreen State *see* Washington
97 L21 **Evesham** C England, United Kingdom *52°06′N 01°57′W*
103 T10 **Évian-les-Bains** Haute-Savoie, E France *46°22′N 06°34′E*
93 K16 **Evijärvi** Länsi-Suomi, W Finland *63°22′N 23°30′E*
79 D17 **Evinayong** *var.* Ebinayon, Evinayoung. C Equatorial Guinea *01°28′N 10°17′E*
Evinayoung *see* Evinayong
115 E18 **Évinos** ⟿ C Greece
95 E17 **Evje** Aust-Agder, S Norway *58°35′N 07°49′E*
Evmolpia *see* Plovdiv
104 H11 **Évora** *anc.* Ebora, *Lat.* Liberalitas Julia. Évora, C Portugal *38°34′N 07°54′W*
104 G11 **Évora** ◐ *district* S Portugal
102 M4 **Évreux** *anc.* Civitas Eburovicum. Eure, N France *49°02′N 01°10′E*
102 K6 **Évron** Mayenne, NW France *48°10′N 00°24′W*
114 L13 **Évros** *Bul.* Maritsa, *Turk.* Meriç; *anc.* Hebrus. ⟿ SE Europe *see also* Maritsa/Meriç
Évros *see* Meriç
Évros *see* Maritsa
115 F21 **Evrótas** ⟿ S Greece
103 O5 **Évry** Essonne, N France *48°38′N 02°34′E*
25 O8 **E. V. Spence Reservoir** ▣ Texas, SW USA
115 I18 **Évvoia** *Lat.* Euboea. *island* C Greece
38 D9 **'Ewa Beach** *var.* Ewa Beach. O'ahu, Hawaii, USA, C Pacific Ocean *21°19′N 158°00′W*
Ewa Beach *see* 'Ewa Beach
32 L9 **Ewan** Washington, NW USA *47°06′N 117°46′W*
44 K12 **Ewarton** C Jamaica *18°11′N 77°06′W*
81 J18 **Ewaso Ng'iro** *var.* Nyiro. ⟿ C Kenya
29 P13 **Ewing** Nebraska, C USA *42°13′N 98°20′W*
194 J5 **Ewing Island** *island* Antarctica
65 P17 **Ewing Seamount** *undersea feature* E Atlantic Ocean *23°20′S 08°45′E*
158 L6 **Ewirgol** Xinjiang Uygur Zizhiqu, W China *42°56′N 87°39′E*
79 G19 **Ewo** Cuvette, W Congo *0°55′S 14°49′E*
27 S3 **Excelsior Springs** Missouri, C USA *39°20′N 94°13′W*
97 J23 **Exe** ⟿ SW England, United Kingdom
194 L12 **Executive Committee Range** ⛰ Antarctica
14 E16 **Exeter** Ontario, S Canada *43°19′N 81°26′W*
97 J24 **Exeter** *anc.* Isca Damnoniorum. SW England, United Kingdom *50°43′N 03°31′W*
35 R11 **Exeter** California, W USA *36°17′N 119°08′W*
19 P10 **Exeter** New Hampshire, NE USA *42°57′N 70°55′W*
Exin *see* Kcynia
29 T14 **Exira** Iowa, C USA *41°36′N 94°55′W*
97 J23 **Exmoor** *moorland* SW England, United Kingdom
21 Y6 **Exmore** Virginia, NE USA *37°31′N 75°48′W*
180 G8 **Exmouth** Western Australia *22°01′S 114°06′E*
97 J24 **Exmouth** SW England, United Kingdom *50°36′N 03°25′W*
180 G8 **Exmouth Gulf** *gulf* Western Australia
173 V8 **Exmouth Plateau** *undersea feature* E Indian Ocean
115 J20 **Exompourgo** *ancient monument* Tínos, Kykládes, Greece, Aegean Sea
104 I10 **Extremadura** *var.* Estremadura. ◐ *autonomous community* W Spain
78 F12 **Extrême-Nord** *Eng.* Extreme North. ◐ *province* N Cameroon
Extreme North *see* Extrême-Nord
44 I3 **Exuma Cays** *islets* C Bahamas
44 I3 **Exuma Sound** *sound* C Bahamas
81 H20 **Eyasi, Lake** ◎ N Tanzania
95 F17 **Eydehavn** Aust-Agder, S Norway *58°31′N 08°53′E*
96 L12 **Eyemouth** SE Scotland, United Kingdom *55°52′N 02°07′W*
96 G7 **Eye Peninsula** *peninsula* NW Scotland, United Kingdom
80 Q13 **Eyl** *It.* Eil. Nugaal, E Somalia *08°03′N 49°49′E*
103 N11 **Eymoutiers** Haute-Vienne, C France *45°45′N 01°43′E*
Eyo (lower course) *see* Uolo, Río
29 X10 **Eyota** Minnesota, N USA *44°00′N 92°13′W*
182 H2 **Eyre Basin, Lake** *salt lake* South Australia
182 I1 **Eyre Creek** *seasonal river* Northern Territory/South Australia
174 L9 **Eyre, Lake** *salt lake* South Australia
185 C22 **Eyre Mountains** ⛰ South Island, New Zealand
182 H3 **Eyre North, Lake** *salt lake* South Australia
182 G7 **Eyre Peninsula** *peninsula* South Australia
182 H4 **Eyre South, Lake** *salt lake* South Australia
95 B18 **Eysturoy** *Dan.* Østerø. *island* N Faeroe Islands
142 J7 **Eyvān** Īlām, W Iran *33°50′N 46°18′E*
61 D20 **Ezeiza** ✈ (Buenos Aires) Buenos Aires, E Argentina *34°49′S 58°30′W*
Ezeres *see* Ezeriș
116 F12 **Ezeriș** *Hung.* Ezeres. Caraș-Severin, W Romania *45°21′N 21°55′E*
161 O9 **Ezhou** *prev.* Echeng. Hubei, C China *30°23′N 114°52′E*
125 R11 **Ezhva** Respublika Komi, NW Russian Federation *61°45′N 50°43′E*
136 B12 **Ezine** Çanakkale, NW Turkey *39°46′N 26°20′E*
Ezo *see* Hokkaidō
Ezra/Ezraa *see* Izra'

F

191 P7 **Faaa** Tahiti, W French Polynesia *17°32′S 149°36′W*
191 P7 **Faaa** ✈ (Papeete) Tahiti, W French Polynesia *17°31′S 149°36′W*
95 H24 **Faaborg** *var.* Fåborg. Fyn, C Denmark *55°06′N 10°10′E*
151 K19 **Faadhippolhu Atoll** *var.* Fadiffolu, Lhaviyani Atoll. *atoll* N Maldives
191 U10 **Faaite** *atoll* Îles Tuamotu, C French Polynesia
191 Q8 **Faaone** Tahiti, W French Polynesia *17°39′S 149°18′W*
24 H8 **Fabens** Texas, SW USA *31°30′N 106°09′W*
94 H12 **Fåberg** Oppland, S Norway *61°15′N 10°21′E*
Fåborg *see* Faaborg
106 I12 **Fabriano** Marche, C Italy *43°20′N 12°54′E*
145 U16 **Fabrichnyy** Almaty, SE Kazakhstan *43°12′N 76°19′E*
54 F10 **Facatativá** Cundinamarca, C Colombia *04°49′N 74°22′W*
77 X9 **Fachi** Agadez, C Niger *18°01′N 11°36′E*
188 B16 **Facpi Point** *headland* W Guam
18 I13 **Factoryville** Pennsylvania, NE USA *41°34′N 75°45′W*
78 K8 **Fada** Borkou-Ennedi-Tibesti, E Chad *17°14′N 21°32′E*
77 Q13 **Fada-Ngourma** E Burkina *12°05′N 00°26′E*
123 N6 **Faddeya, Zaliv** *bay* N Russian Federation
123 Q5 **Faddeyevskiy, Ostrov** *island* Novosibirskiye Ostrova, NE Russian Federation
141 W12 **Fadhī** S Oman *17°54′N 55°30′E*
Fadiffolu *see* Faadhippolhu Atoll
106 H10 **Faenza** *anc.* Faventia. Emilia-Romagna, N Italy *44°17′N 11°53′E*
64 M5 **Faeroe-Iceland Ridge** *undersea feature* NW Norwegian Sea *64°00′N 10°00′W*
64 M5 **Faeroe Islands** *Dan.* Færøerne, *Faer.* Føroyar. ◇ *Danish external territory* N Atlantic Ocean
86 C8 **Faeroe Islands** *island group* N Atlantic Ocean
Færøerne *see* Faeroe Islands
64 N6 **Faeroe-Shetland Trough** *undersea feature* NE Atlantic Ocean
104 H6 **Fafe** Braga, N Portugal *41°27′N 08°11′W*
80 K13 **Fafen Shet'** ⟿ E Ethiopia
193 V15 **Fafo** *island* Tongatapu Group, S Tonga
192 I16 **Fagaloa Bay** *bay* Upolu, E Samoa
192 H15 **Fagamālo** Savai'i, N Samoa *13°27′S 172°22′W*
116 I12 **Făgăraș** *Ger.* Fogarasch, *Hung.* Fogaras. Brașov, C Romania *45°50′N 24°59′E*
95 M20 **Fagerhult** Kalmar, S Sweden *57°07′N 15°40′E*
94 G13 **Fagernes** Oppland, S Norway *60°59′N 09°14′E*
92 I9 **Fagernes** Troms, N Norway *69°31′N 19°16′E*
95 M14 **Fagersta** Västmanland, C Sweden *59°59′N 15°49′E*
77 W13 **Faggo** *var.* Foggo. Bauchi, N Nigeria *11°22′N 09°55′E*
Faghman *see* Fughmah
Fagibina, Lake *see* Faguibine, Lac
63 J25 **Fagnano, Lago** ◎ S Argentina
99 G22 **Fagne** *hill range* S Belgium
77 N10 **Faguibine, Lac** *var.* Lake Fagibina. ◎ NW Mali
Fahaheel *see* Al Fuḩayḩīl
Fahlun *see* Falun
143 U12 **Fahraj** Kermān, SE Iran *29°00′N 59°00′E*
64 P5 **Faial** Madeira, Portugal, NE Atlantic Ocean *32°47′N 16°53′W*
64 N2 **Faial** *var.* Ilha do Faial. *island* Azores, Portugal, NE Atlantic Ocean
Faial, Ilha do *see* Faial
108 G10 **Faido** Ticino, S Switzerland *46°30′N 08°48′E*
Faifo *see* Hôi An
Failaka Island *see* Faylakah
190 G12 **Faioa, Île** *island* N Wallis and Futuna
181 W8 **Fairbairn Reservoir** ▣ Queensland, E Australia
39 R9 **Fairbanks** Alaska, USA *64°48′N 147°47′W*
21 U12 **Fair Bluff** North Carolina, SE USA *34°18′N 79°02′W*
31 R14 **Fairborn** Ohio, N USA *39°48′N 84°03′W*
23 S3 **Fairburn** Georgia, SE USA *33°34′N 84°34′W*
30 M12 **Fairbury** Illinois, N USA *40°45′N 88°30′W*
29 Q17 **Fairbury** Nebraska, C USA *40°08′N 97°10′W*
29 T9 **Fairfax** Minnesota, N USA *44°31′N 94°43′W*
27 O8 **Fairfax** Oklahoma, C USA *36°34′N 96°42′W*
21 R14 **Fairfax** South Carolina, SE USA *32°57′N 81°14′W*
35 N8 **Fairfield** California, W USA *38°14′N 122°03′W*
33 O14 **Fairfield** Idaho, NW USA *43°20′N 114°45′W*
30 M16 **Fairfield** Illinois, N USA *38°22′N 88°23′W*
29 X15 **Fairfield** Iowa, C USA *41°00′N 91°57′W*
33 R8 **Fairfield** Montana, NW USA *47°36′N 111°59′W*
31 Q14 **Fairfield** Ohio, N USA *39°21′N 84°34′W*
25 U8 **Fairfield** Texas, SW USA *31°43′N 96°10′W*
27 T7 **Fair Grove** Missouri, C USA *37°22′N 93°09′W*
19 P12 **Fairhaven** Massachusetts, NE USA *41°38′N 70°51′W*
23 N8 **Fairhope** Alabama, S USA *30°31′N 87°54′W*
96 L4 **Fair Isle** *island* NE Scotland, United Kingdom
185 F20 **Fairlie** Canterbury, South Island, New Zealand *44°06′S 170°50′E*
29 U11 **Fairmont** Minnesota, N USA *43°40′N 94°27′W*
29 Q16 **Fairmont** Nebraska, C USA *40°37′N 97°36′W*
21 S3 **Fairmont** West Virginia, NE USA *39°28′N 80°08′W*
31 P13 **Fairmount** Indiana, N USA *40°25′N 85°39′W*
18 H10 **Fairmount** New York, NE USA *43°03′N 76°14′W*
29 R7 **Fairmount** North Dakota, N USA *46°02′N 96°36′W*
37 S5 **Fairplay** Colorado, C USA *39°13′N 106°00′W*
18 F9 **Fairport** New York, NE USA *43°06′N 77°26′W*
11 O12 **Fairview** Alberta, W Canada *56°03′N 118°28′W*
26 L9 **Fairview** Oklahoma, C USA *36°16′N 98°29′W*
36 L4 **Fairview** Utah, W USA *39°37′N 111°26′W*
35 T6 **Fairview Peak** ▲ Nevada, W USA *39°13′N 118°09′W*
188 H14 **Fais** *atoll* Caroline Islands, W Micronesia
149 U8 **Faisalābād** *prev.* Lyallpur. Punjab, NE Pakistan *31°26′N 73°06′E*
Faisaliya *see* Fayşalīyah
28 L8 **Faith** South Dakota, N USA *45°01′N 102°02′W*
153 N12 **Faizābād** Uttar Pradesh, N India *26°46′N 82°08′E*
Faizabad/Faizābād *see* Feyzābād
45 S9 **Fajardo** E Puerto Rico *18°20′N 65°39′W*
139 R9 **Fajj, Wādī al** *dry watercourse* S Iraq
140 K4 **Fajr, Bi'r** *well* NW Saudi Arabia
191 W10 **Fakahina** *atoll* Îles Tuamotu, C French Polynesia
190 L10 **Fakaofo Atoll** *island* SE Tokelau
191 U10 **Fakarava** *atoll* Îles Tuamotu, C French Polynesia
127 T2 **Fakel** Udmurtskaya Respublika, NW Russian Federation *57°35′N 53°00′E*
97 P19 **Fakenham** E England, United Kingdom *52°50′N 00°51′E*
171 U13 **Fakfak** Papua, E Indonesia *02°55′S 132°17′E*
153 T12 **Fakīragrām** Assam, NE India *26°22′N 90°15′E*
114 M10 **Fakiyska Reka** ⟿ SE Bulgaria
95 J24 **Fakse** Storstrøm, SE Denmark *55°16′N 12°08′E*
95 J24 **Fakse Bugt** *bay* SE Denmark
95 J24 **Fakse Ladeplads** Storstrøm, SE Denmark *55°14′N 12°11′E*
163 V11 **Faku** Liaoning, NE China *42°30′N 123°27′E*
76 J14 **Falaba** N Sierra Leone *09°54′N 11°22′W*
102 K5 **Falaise** Calvados, N France *48°52′N 00°12′W*
114 H12 **Falakró** ⛰ NE Greece
189 T12 **Falalu** *island* Chuuk, C Micronesia
166 L4 **Falam** Chin State, W Burma (Myanmar) *22°58′N 93°45′E*
143 N8 **Falāvarjān** Eşfahān, C Iran *32°33′N 51°28′E*
116 M11 **Fălciu** Vaslui, E Romania *46°19′N 28°10′E*
54 I4 **Falcón** *off.* Estado Falcón. ◐ *state* NW Venezuela
106 J12 **Falconara Marittima** Marche, C Italy *43°37′N 13°23′E*
Falcone, Capo del *see* Falcone, Punta del
107 A16 **Falcone, Punta del** *var.* Capo del Falcone. *headland* Sardegna, Italy, C Mediterranean Sea *40°57′N 08°12′E*
Falcón, Estado *see* Falcón
11 Y16 **Falcon Lake** Manitoba, S Canada *49°44′N 95°18′W*
Falcon Lake *see* Falcón, Presa/Falcon Reservoir
41 O7 **Falcón, Presa** *var.* Falcon Lake, Falcon Reservoir. ▣ Mexico/USA *see also* Falcon Reservoir
Falcón, Presa *see* Falcon Reservoir
25 Q16 **Falcon Reservoir** *var.* Falcon Lake, Presa Falcón. ▣ Mexico/USA *see also* Falcón, Presa
Falcon Reservoir *see* Falcón, Presa
190 L10 **Fale** *island* Fakaofo Atoll, SE Tokelau
192 F15 **Faleālupo** Savai'i, NW Samoa *13°30′S 172°46′W*
190 B10 **Falefatu** *island* Funafuti Atoll, C Tuvalu
192 G15 **Fālelima** Savai'i, NW Samoa *13°30′S 172°41′W*
95 N18 **Falerum** Östergötland, S Sweden *58°07′N 16°15′E*
Faleshty *see* Fălești
116 M9 **Fălești** *Rus.* Faleshty. NW Moldova *47°33′N 27°43′E*
25 S15 **Falfurrias** Texas, SW USA *27°17′N 98°10′W*
11 O13 **Falher** Alberta, W Canada *55°45′N 117°18′W*
Falkenau an der Eger *see* Sokolov
95 J21 **Falkenberg** Halland, S Sweden *56°55′N 12°30′E*
Falkenberg *see* Niemodlin
Falkenburg in Pommern *see* Złocieniec
100 N12 **Falkensee** Brandenburg, NE Germany *52°34′N 13°04′E*
96 J12 **Falkirk** C Scotland, United Kingdom *56°N 03°48′W*
65 I20 **Falkland Escarpment** *undersea feature* SW Atlantic Ocean *50°00′S 45°00′W*
63 K24 **Falkland Islands** *var.* Falklands, Islas Malvinas. ◇ *UK dependent territory* SW Atlantic Ocean
47 W14 **Falkland Islands** *island group* SW Atlantic Ocean
65 I20 **Falkland Plateau** *var.* Argentine Rise. *undersea feature* SW Atlantic Ocean *51°00′S 50°00′W*
Falklands *see* Falkland Islands
63 M23 **Falkland Sound** *var.* Estrecho de San Carlos. *strait* C Falkland Islands
Falknov nad Ohří *see* Sokolov
115 H21 **Falkonéra** *island* S Greece
95 K18 **Falköping** Västra Götaland, S Sweden *58°10′N 13°31′E*
139 U8 **Fallāḩ** Wāsiţ, E Iraq *32°58′N 45°09′E*
35 U16 **Fallbrook** California, W USA *33°22′N 117°15′W*
189 U12 **Falleallej Pass** *passage* Chuuk Islands, C Micronesia
93 J14 **Fällfors** Västerbotten, N Sweden *65°07′N 20°46′E*
194 I6 **Fallières Coast** *physical region* Antarctica
100 I11 **Fallingbostel** Niedersachsen, NW Germany *52°52′N 09°42′E*
33 X9 **Fallon** Montana, NW USA *46°49′N 105°07′W*
35 S5 **Fallon** Nevada, W USA *39°29′N 118°47′W*
19 O12 **Fall River** Massachusetts, NE USA *41°42′N 71°09′W*
27 P6 **Fall River Lake** ▣ Kansas, C USA
35 O3 **Fall River Mills** California, W USA *41°00′N 121°28′W*
21 W4 **Falls Church** Virginia, NE USA *38°53′N 77°11′W*
29 S17 **Falls City** Nebraska, C USA *40°03′N 95°36′W*
25 S12 **Falls City** Texas, SW USA *28°58′N 98°01′W*
Falluja *see* Al Fallūjah
77 S12 **Falmey** Dosso, SW Niger *12°29′N 02°58′E*
45 W10 **Falmouth** Antigua, Antigua and Barbuda *17°02′N 61°47′W*
44 J11 **Falmouth** W Jamaica *18°28′N 77°39′W*
97 H25 **Falmouth** SW England, United Kingdom *50°08′N 05°04′W*
20 M4 **Falmouth** Kentucky, S USA *38°40′N 84°20′W*
19 P13 **Falmouth** Massachusetts, NE USA *41°31′N 70°36′W*
21 W5 **Falmouth** Virginia, NE USA *38°19′N 77°28′W*
189 U12 **Falos** *island* Chuuk, C Micronesia
83 E26 **False Bay** *Afr.* Valsbaai. *bay* SW South Africa
155 K17 **False Divi Point** *headland* E India *15°46′N 80°43′E*
38 M16 **False Pass** Unimak Island, Alaska, USA *54°52′N 163°15′W*
154 P12 **False Point** *headland* E India *20°23′N 86°52′E*
105 U6 **Falset** Cataluña, NE Spain *41°08′N 00°49′E*
95 I25 **Falster** *island* SE Denmark
116 K9 **Fălticeni** *Hung.* Falticsén. Suceava, NE Romania *47°27′N 26°20′E*
Falticsén *see* Fălticeni
94 M13 **Falun** *var.* Fahlun. Kopparberg, C Sweden *60°36′N 15°36′E*
Famagusta *see* Gazimağusa
Famagusta Bay *see* Gazimağusa Körfezi
62 I8 **Famatina** La Rioja, NW Argentina *28°58′S 67°46′W*
99 J21 **Famenne** *physical region* SE Belgium
113 D22 **Fan** *var.* Fani. ⟿ N Albania
77 X15 **Fan** ⟿ E Nigeria
76 M12 **Fana** Koulikoro, SW Mali *12°45′N 06°55′W*
115 K19 **Fána** *ancient harbour* Chíos, SE Greece
189 V13 **Fanan** *island* Chuuk, C Micronesia
189 U12 **Fanapanges** *island* Chuuk, C Micronesia
115 L20 **Fanári, Akrotírio** *headland* Ikaría, Dodekánisa, Greece, Aegean Sea *37°40′N 26°21′E*
45 Q13 **Fancy** Saint Vincent, Saint Vincent and the Grenadines *13°22′N 61°10′W*
172 I5 **Fandriana** Fianarantsoa, SE Madagascar *20°14′S 47°21′E*
167 O6 **Fang** Chiang Mai, NW Thailand *19°56′N 99°14′E*
80 E13 **Fangak** Jonglei, SE Sudan *09°05′N 30°52′E*
191 W10 **Fangatau** *atoll* Îles Tuamotu, C French Polynesia
191 X12 **Fangataufa** *island* Îles Tuamotu, SE French Polynesia
193 V15 **Fanga Uta** *bay* S Tonga
161 N7 **Fangcheng** Henan, C China *33°18′N 113°03′E*
Fangcheng *see* Fangchenggang
160 K15 **Fangchenggang** *var.* Fangcheng Gezu Zizhixian; *prev.* Fangcheng. Guangxi Zhuangzu Zizhiqu, S China *21°49′N 108°21′E*
Fangcheng Gezu Zizhixian *see* Fangchenggang
161 S15 **Fangshan** S Taiwan *22°19′N 120°41′E*
163 X8 **Fangzheng** Heilongjiang, NE China *45°50′N 128°50′E*
Fani *see* Fan
119 K16 **Fanipal'** *Rus.* Fanipol'. Minskaya Voblasts', C Belarus *53°45′N 27°20′E*
Fanipol' *see* Fanipal'
25 T13 **Fannin** Texas, SW USA *28°41′N 97°13′W*
Fanning Island *see* Tabuaeran
94 G8 **Fannrem** Sør-Trøndelag, S Norway *63°16′N 09°48′E*
106 I11 **Fano** *anc.* Colonia Julia Fanestris, Fanum Fortunae. Marche, C Italy *43°50′N 13°E*
95 E23 **Fanø** *island* W Denmark
167 R5 **Fan Si Pan** ▲ N Vietnam *22°18′N 103°36′E*
Fanum Fortunae *see* Fano
Fao *see* Al Fāw
141 W7 **Faq'** *var.* Al Faqa. Dubayy, E United Arab Emirates *24°42′N 55°37′E*
Farab *see* Farap
185 G16 **Faraday, Mount** ▲ South Island, New Zealand *42°01′S 171°37′E*
79 P16 **Faradje** Orientale, NE Dem. Rep. Congo *03°45′N 29°43′E*
Faradofay *see* Tôlañaro
172 I7 **Farafangana** Fianarantsoa, SE Madagascar *22°50′S 47°50′E*
148 J7 **Farāh** *var.* Farah, Fararud. Farāh, W Afghanistan *32°22′N 62°07′E*
148 K7 **Farāh** ◐ *province* W Afghanistan
148 J7 **Farāh Rūd** ⟿ W Afghanistan
188 K7 **Farallon de Medinilla** *island* C Northern Mariana Islands
188 J2 **Farallon de Pajaros** *var.* Uracas. *island* N Northern Mariana Islands
76 J14 **Faranah** Haute-Guinée, S Guinea *10°02′N 10°44′W*
146 K12 **Farap** *Rus.* Farab. Lebap Welaýaty, NE Turkmenistan *39°15′N 63°32′E*
Fararud *see* Farāh
140 M13 **Farasān, Jazā'ir** *island group* SW Saudi Arabia
172 I5 **Faratsiho** Antananarivo, C Madagascar *19°24′S 46°57′E*
188 K15 **Faraulep Atoll** *atoll* Caroline Islands, C Micronesia
99 H20 **Farciennes** Hainaut, S Belgium *50°26′N 04°33′E*
105 O14 **Fardes** ⟿ S Spain
191 S10 **Fare** Huahine, W French Polynesia *16°42′S 151°01′W*
97 M23 **Fareham** S England, United Kingdom *50°51′N 01°10′W*
39 P11 **Farewell** Alaska, USA *62°35′N 153°59′W*
184 H13 **Farewell, Cape** *headland* South Island, New Zealand *40°30′S 172°39′E*
Farewell, Cape *see* Nunap Isua
184 I13 **Farewell Spit** *spit* South Island, New Zealand
95 I17 **Färgelanda** Västra Götaland, S Sweden *58°34′N 11°59′E*
Farghona, Wodii/ Farghona Valley *see* Fergana Valley
Farghona Wodiysi *see* Fergana Valley
23 V8 **Fargo** Georgia, SE USA *30°42′N 82°33′W*
29 R5 **Fargo** North Dakota, N USA *46°53′N 96°47′W*
147 S10 **Farg'ona** *Rus.* Fergana; *prev.* Novyy Margilan. Farg'ona Viloyati, E Uzbekistan *40°28′N 71°44′E*
147 R10 **Farg'ona Viloyati** *Rus.* Ferganskaya Oblast'. ◐ *province* E Uzbekistan
29 V10 **Faribault** Minnesota, N USA *44°18′N 93°16′W*
152 J11 **Farīdābād** Haryāna, N India *28°26′N 77°190′E*
152 H8 **Farīdkot** Punjab, NW India *30°42′N 74°47′E*
153 T15 **Farīdpur** Dhaka, C Bangladesh *23°29′N 89°50′E*
121 P14 **Fārigh, Wādī al** ⟿ N Libya
172 I4 **Farihy Alaotra** ◎ C Madagascar
94 M11 **Färila** Gävleborg, C Sweden *61°48′N 15°55′E*
104 E9 **Farilhões** *island* C Portugal
76 G12 **Farim** NW Guinea-Bissau *12°30′N 15°09′W*
Farish *see* Forish
141 T11 **Fāris, Qalamat** *well* SE Saudi Arabia
95 N21 **Färjestaden** Kalmar, S Sweden *56°38′N 16°30′E*
149 R2 **Farkhār** Takhār, NE Afghanistan *36°39′N 69°43′E*
147 Q14 **Farkhor** *Rus.* Parkhar. SW Tajikistan *37°32′N 69°22′E*
116 F12 **Fârliug** *prev.* Fîrliug, *Hung.* Furluk. Caraș-Severin, SW Romania *45°21′N 21°55′E*
115 M21 **Farmakonísi** *island* Dodekánisa, Greece, Aegean Sea
30 M13 **Farmer City** Illinois, N USA *40°14′N 88°38′W*
31 N14 **Farmersburg** Indiana, N USA *39°14′N 87°21′W*
25 U6 **Farmersville** Texas, SW USA *33°09′N 96°21′W*
22 H5 **Farmerville** Louisiana, S USA *32°46′N 92°24′W*
29 X16 **Farmington** Iowa, C USA *40°37′N 91°43′W*
19 Q6 **Farmington** Maine, NE USA *44°40′N 70°09′W*
29 V9 **Farmington** Minnesota, N USA *44°39′N 93°09′W*
27 X6 **Farmington** Missouri, C USA *37°46′N 90°26′W*
19 O9 **Farmington** New Hampshire, NE USA *43°23′N 71°04′W*
37 P9 **Farmington** New Mexico, SW USA *36°44′N 108°13′W*
36 L2 **Farmington** Utah, W USA *40°58′N 111°53′W*
21 W9 **Farmville** North Carolina, SE USA *35°37′N 77°36′W*
21 U6 **Farmville** Virginia, NE USA *37°17′N 78°25′W*
97 N22 **Farnborough** S England, United Kingdom *51°17′N 00°46′W*
97 N22 **Farnham** S England, United Kingdom *51°13′N 00°49′W*
10 J7 **Faro** Yukon Territory, W Canada *62°15′N 133°30′W*
104 G14 **Faro** Faro, S Portugal *37°01′N 07°56′W*
95 Q18 **Fårö** Gotland, SE Sweden *57°55′N 19°10′E*
104 G14 **Faro** ◐ *district* S Portugal
78 F13 **Faro** ⟿ Cameroon/Nigeria
104 G14 **Faro** ✈ Faro, S Portugal *37°02′N 08°01′W*
Faro, Punta del *see* Peloro, Capo
95 Q18 **Fårösund** Gotland, SE Sweden *57°51′N 19°02′E*
173 N7 **Farquhar Group** *island group* S Seychelles
18 B13 **Farrell** Pennsylvania, NE USA *41°12′N 80°28′W*
152 K11 **Farrukhābād** Uttar Pradesh, N India *27°24′N 79°34′E*
143 P11 **Fārs** *off.* Ostān-e Fārs; *anc.* Persis. ◐ *province* S Iran
115 F16 **Fársala** Thessalía, C Greece *39°17′N 22°23′E*
143 R4 **Fārsīān** Golestán, N Iran
Fars, Khalīj-e *see* Gulf, The
95 G21 **Farsø** Nordjylland, N Denmark *56°47′N 09°21′E*
Fārs, Ostān-e *see* Fārs
95 D18 **Farsund** Vest-Agder, S Norway *58°05′N 06°49′E*
141 U14 **Fartak, Ra's** *headland* E Yemen *15°34′N 52°19′E*
60 H13 **Fartura, Serra da** ⛰ S Brazil
Farvel, Kap *see* Nunap Isua
24 L4 **Farwell** Texas, SW USA *34°23′N 103°03′W*
194 I9 **Farwell Island** *island* Antarctica
152 L9 **Far Western** ◐ *zone* W Nepal
148 M3 **Fāryāb** ◐ *province* N Afghanistan
143 P12 **Fasā** Fārs, S Iran *28°55′N 53°39′E*
141 U12 **Fasad, Ramlat** *desert* SW Oman
107 P17 **Fasano** Puglia, SE Italy *40°50′N 17°21′E*
92 L3 **Fáskrúdhsfjördhur** Austurland, E Iceland *64°55′N 14°01′W*
117 O5 **Fastiv** *Rus.* Fastov. Kyyivs'ka Oblast', NW Ukraine *50°08′N 29°59′E*
97 B22 **Fastnet Rock** *Ir.* Carraig Aonair. *island* SW Ireland
Fastov *see* Fastiv
190 C9 **Fatato** *island* Funafuti Atoll, C Tuvalu
152 H10 **Fatehābād** Haryāna, N India *29°31′N 75°27′E*
152 K12 **Fatehgarh** Uttar Pradesh, N India *27°22′N 79°38′E*
149 U6 **Fatehjang** Punjab, E Pakistan *33°33′N 72°43′E*
152 G11 **Fatehpur** Rājasthān, N India *27°59′N 74°58′E*
152 L13 **Fatehpur** Uttar Pradesh, N India *25°56′N 80°55′E*
126 J7 **Fatezh** Kurskaya Oblast', W Russian Federation *52°01′N 35°51′E*
76 G11 **Fatick** W Senegal *14°19′N 16°27′W*
104 G9 **Fátima** Santarém, W Portugal *39°37′N 08°39′W*
136 M11 **Fatsa** Ordu, N Turkey *41°02′N 37°31′E*
Fatshan *see* Foshan
190 D12 **Fatua, Pointe** *var.* Pointe Nord. *headland* Île Futuna, S Wallis and Futuna
191 X7 **Fatu Hiva** *island* Îles Marquises, NE French Polynesia
Fatunda *see* Fatundu
79 H21 **Fatundu** *var.* Fatunda. Bandundu, W Dem. Rep. Congo *04°08′S 17°13′E*
29 O8 **Faulkton** South Dakota, N USA *45°02′N 99°07′W*
116 L13 **Făurei** *prev.* Filimon Sîrbu. Brăila, SE Romania *45°05′N 27°15′E*
92 G12 **Fauske** Nordland, C Norway *67°15′N 15°27′E*
11 P13 **Faust** Alberta, W Canada *55°19′N 115°33′W*
99 L23 **Fauvillers** Luxembourg, SE Belgium *49°52′N 05°40′E*
107 J24 **Favara** Sicilia, Italy, C Mediterranean Sea *37°19′N 13°40′E*
Faventia *see* Faenza
107 G23 **Favignana, Isola** *island* Isole Egadi, S Italy
12 D8 **Fawn** ⟿ Ontario, SE Canada
Faxa Bay *see* Faxaflói
92 H3 **Faxaflói** *Eng.* Faxa Bay. *bay* W Iceland
78 I7 **Faya** *prev.* Faya-Largeau, Largeau. Borkou-Ennedi-Tibesti, N Chad *17°58′N 19°06′E*
Faya-Largeau *see* Faya
187 Q16 **Fayaoué** Province des Îles Loyauté, C New Caledonia *20°41′S 166°31′E*
138 M5 **Fayḑat** *hill range* E Syria
23 O3 **Fayette** Alabama, S USA *33°40′N 87°49′W*
29 X12 **Fayette** Iowa, C USA *42°50′N 91°48′W*
22 J6 **Fayette** Mississippi, S USA *31°42′N 91°03′W*
27 U4 **Fayette** Missouri, C USA *39°09′N 92°40′W*
27 S9 **Fayetteville** Arkansas, C USA *36°04′N 94°10′W*
21 U10 **Fayetteville** North Carolina, SE USA *35°03′N 78°53′W*
20 J10 **Fayetteville** Tennessee, S USA *35°08′N 86°33′W*
25 U11 **Fayetteville** Texas, SW USA *29°52′N 96°40′W*
21 R5 **Fayetteville** West Virginia, NE USA *38°03′N 81°09′W*
141 R4 **Faylakah** *var.* Failaka Island. *island* E Kuwait
139 T10 **Fayşalīyah** *var.* Faisaliya. Al Qādisīyah, S Iraq *31°48′N 44°36′E*
189 P15 **Fayu** *var.* East Fayu. *island* Hall Islands, C Micronesia
152 G8 **Fāzilka** Punjab, NW India *30°26′N 74°04′E*
Fdérick *see* Fdérik
76 I6 **Fdérik** *var.* Fdérick, *Fr.* Fort Gouraud. Tiris Zemmour, NW Mauritania *22°40′N 12°41′W*
Feabhail, Loch *see* Foyle, Lough
97 B20 **Feale** ⟿ SW Ireland
21 V12 **Fear, Cape** *headland* Bald Head Island, North Carolina, SE USA *33°50′N 77°57′W*
35 O6 **Feather River** ⟿ California, W USA
185 M14 **Featherston** Wellington, North Island, New Zealand *41°07′S 175°28′E*

◆ Country ◇ Dependent Territory ◐ Administrative Regions ▲ Mountain ▲ Volcano ◎ Lake
● Country Capital ○ Dependent Territory Capital ✈ International Airport ⛰ Mountain Range ⟿ River ▣ Reservoir

102 L3 **Fécamp** Seine-Maritime, N France 49°45´N 00°22´E
Fédala see Mohammedia
61 D17 **Federación** Entre Ríos, E Argentina 31°00´S 57°55´W
61 D17 **Federal** Entre Ríos, E Argentina 30°55´S 58°45´W
77 T15 **Federal Capital District** ◐ capital territory C Nigeria
Federal Capital Territory see Australian Capital Territory
Federal District see Distrito Federal
21 Y4 **Federalsburg** Maryland, NE USA 38°41´N 75°46´W
74 M6 **Fedjaj, Chott el** var. Chott el Fejaj, Shaṭṭ al Fijāj. salt lake C Tunisia
94 B13 **Fedje** island S Norway
144 M7 **Fedorovka** Kostanay, N Kazakhstan 51°12´N 52°00´E
127 U6 **Fedorovka** Respublika Bashkortostan, W Russian Federation 53°09´N 55°07´E
Fëdory see Fyadory
117 U11 **Fedotova Kosa** spit SE Ukraine
189 V13 **Fefan** atoll Chuuk Islands, C Micronesia
111 O21 **Fehérgyarmat** Szabolcs-Szatmár-Bereg, E Hungary 47°59´N 22°29´E
Fehér-Körös see Crişul Alb
Fehértemplom see Bela Crkva
Fehérvölgy see Albac
100 L7 **Fehmarn** island N Germany
95 H25 **Fehmarn Belt** Dan. Femern Bælt, Ger. Fehmarnbelt. strait Denmark /Germany see also Femern Bælt
Fehmarnbelt see Fehmarn Belt/Femer Bælt
109 X8 **Fehring** Steiermark, SE Austria 46°56´N 16°00´E
59 B15 **Feijó** Acre, W Brazil 08°07´S 70°27´W
184 M12 **Feilding** Manawatu-Wanganui, North Island, New Zealand 40°15´S 175°34´E
Feira see Feira de Santana
59 O17 **Feira de Santana** var. Feira. Bahia, E Brazil 12°17´S 38°53´W
109 X7 **Feistritz** ~ SE Austria
Feistritz see Ilirska Bistrica
161 P8 **Feixi** var. Shangpai; prev. Shangpaihe. Anhui, E China 31°40´N 117°08´E
Fejaj, Chott el see Fedjaj, Chott el
111 I23 **Fejér** off. Fejér Megye. ◐ county W Hungary
Fejér Megye see Fejér
95 I24 **Fejø** island SE Denmark
136 K15 **Feke** Adana, S Turkey 37°49´N 35°55´E
Feketehalom see Codlea
Fekete-Körös see Crişul Negru
105 Y9 **Felanitx** Mallorca, Spain, W Mediterranean Sea 39°28´N 03°08´E
109 T3 **Feldaist** ~ N Austria
109 W8 **Feldbach** Steiermark, SE Austria 46°58´N 15°53´E
101 F24 **Feldberg** ▲ SW Germany 47°52´N 08°01´E
116 J12 **Feldioara** Ger. Marienburg, Hung. Földvár. Braşov, C Romania 45°49´N 25°36´E
108 I7 **Feldkirch** anc. Clunia. Vorarlberg, W Austria 47°15´N 09°38´E
109 S9 **Feldkirchen in Kärnten** Slvn. Trg. Kärnten, S Austria 46°42´N 14°01´E
Félegyháza see Kiskunfélegyháza
192 H16 **Feleolo** ✈ (Āpia) Upolu, C Samoa 13°49´S 171°59´W
104 H6 **Felgueiras** Porto, N Portugal 41°22´N 08°12´W
Felicitas Julia see Lisboa
172 J16 **Félicité** island Inner Islands, NE Seychelles
151 K20 **Felidhu Atoll** atoll C Maldives
41 Y13 **Felipe Carrillo Puerto** Quintana Roo, SE Mexico 19°34´N 88°02´W
97 Q21 **Felixstowe** E England, United Kingdom 51°58´N 01°20´E
103 N11 **Felletin** Creuse, C France 45°53´N 02°12´E
Fellin see Viljandi
Felsőbánya see Baia Sprie
Felsőmuzslya see Mužlja
Felsővisó see Vişeu de Sus
35 N10 **Felton** California, W USA 37°03´N 122°04´W
106 H7 **Feltre** Veneto, NE Italy 46°01´N 11°55´E
95 H25 **Femer Bælt** Dan. Fehmarn Belt, Ger. Fehmarnbelt. strait Denmark/Germany see also Fehmarn Belt
95 I24 **Femø** island SE Denmark
94 I10 **Femunden** ◎ S Norway
104 H2 **Fene** Galicia, NW Spain 43°28´N 08°10´W
14 I14 **Fenelon Falls** Ontario, SE Canada 44°34´N 78°43´W
189 U13 **Feneppi** atoll Chuuk Islands, C Micronesia
137 O11 **Fener Burnu** headland N Turkey 41°07´N 39°26´E
Fénérive see Fenoarivo Atsinanana
115 J14 **Fengári** ▲ Samothráki, E Greece 40°27´N 25°37´E
163 V13 **Fengcheng** var. Feng-cheng, Fenghwangcheng. Liaoning, NE China 40°28´N 124°01´E
Fengcheng see Lianjiang
Feng-cheng see Fengcheng
160 K11 **Fenggang** var. Longquan. Guizhou, S China 27°57´N 107°42´E
161 S9 **Fenghua** Zhejiang, SE China 29°40´N 121°25´E
Fenghwangcheng see Fengcheng
Fengjiaba see Wangcang
160 L9 **Fengjie** var. Yong'an. Sichuan, C China 31°06´N 109°30´E
160 M14 **Fengkai** var. Jiangkou. Guangdong, S China 23°26´N 111°28´E
161 T13 **Fenglin** Jap. Hōrin. C Taiwan 23°52´N 121°30´E
161 P1 **Fengning** prev. Dagezhen. Hebei, E China 41°12´N 116°37´E
160 E13 **Fengqing** var. Fengshan. Yunnan, SW China 24°38´N 99°54´E
161 O6 **Fengqiu** Henan, C China 35°02´N 114°24´E
161 Q2 **Fengrun** Hebei, E China 39°50´N 118°10´E
Fengshan see Luoyuan, Fujian, China
Fengshan see Fengqing, Yunnan, China
163 T4 **Fengshui Shan** ▲ NE China 52°20´N 123°22´E
161 P14 **Fengshun** Guangdong, S China 23°51´N 116°11´E
Fengtien see Liaoning, China
Fengtien see Shenyang, China
160 J7 **Fengxian** var. Feng Xian; prev. Shuangshipu. Shaanxi, C China 33°50´N 106°33´E
Feng Xian see Fengxian
Fengxiang see Luobei
Fengyizhen see Maoxian
163 P13 **Fengzhen** Nei Mongol Zizhiqu, N China 40°25´N 113°09´E
160 M6 **Fen He** ~ C China
153 V15 **Feni** Chittagong, E Bangladesh 23°00´N 91°24´E
186 I6 **Feni Islands** island group NE Papua New Guinea
38 H17 **Fenimore Pass** strait Aleutian Islands, Alaska, USA
84 B9 **Feni Ridge** undersea feature N Atlantic Ocean 53°45´N 18°00´W
Fennern see Vändra
30 J9 **Fennimore** Wisconsin, N USA 42°58´N 90°39´W
172 J4 **Fenoarivo Atsinanana** Fr. Fénérive. Toamasina, E Madagascar 20°52´S 46°52´E
95 I24 **Fensmark** Storstrøm, SE Denmark 55°17´N 11°48´E
97 O19 **Fens, The** wetland E England, United Kingdom
31 R9 **Fenton** Michigan, N USA 42°48´N 83°42´W
190 K10 **Fenua Fala** island SE Tokelau
190 F12 **Fenuafo'ou, Île** island E Wallis and Futuna
190 L10 **Fenua Loa** island Fakaofo Atoll, E Tokelau
160 M4 **Fenyang** Shanxi, C China 37°14´N 111°40´E
117 U13 **Feodosiya** var. Kefe, It. Kaffa; anc. Theodosia. Respublika Krym, S Ukraine 45°03´N 35°24´E
94 I10 **Feragen** ◎ S Norway
74 L5 **Fer, Cap de** headland NE Algeria 37°05´N 07°10´E
31 O16 **Ferdinand** Indiana, N USA 38°13´N 86°51´W
Ferdinand see Montana, Bulgaria
Ferdinand see Mihail Kogălniceanu, Romania
Ferdinandsberg see Oţelu Roşu
143 T7 **Ferdows** var. Firdaus; prev. Tūn. Khorāsān-Razavī, E Iran 34°00´N 58°09´E
103 Q5 **Fère-Champenoise** Marne, N France 48°45´N 03°59´E
Ferencz-József Csúcs see Gerlachovský štít
107 J16 **Ferentino** Lazio, C Italy 41°40´N 13°16´E
114 L13 **Féres** Anatolikí Makedonía kai Thráki, NE Greece 40°54´N 26°12´E
Fergana see Farg'ona
147 S10 **Fergana Valley** var. Farghona Valley, Rus. Ferganskaya Dolina, Taj. Wodii Farghona, Uzb. Farghona Wodiysi. basin Tajikistan/Uzbekistan
Ferganskaya Dolina see Fergana Valley
Ferganskaya Oblast' see Farg'ona Viloyati
147 U9 **Ferganskiy Khrebet** ▲▲ C Kyrgyzstan
14 F15 **Fergus** Ontario, S Canada 43°42´N 80°22´W
29 S6 **Fergus Falls** Minnesota, N USA 46°15´N 96°02´W
186 G9 **Fergusson Island** var. Kaluwawa. island SE Papua New Guinea
111 K22 **Ferihegy** ✈ (Budapest) Budapest, C Hungary 47°25´N 19°13´E
113 N17 **Ferizaj** Serb. Uroševac. C Kosovo 42°23´N 21°09´E
77 N14 **Ferkessédougou** N Ivory Coast 09°36´N 05°12´W
109 T10 **Ferlach** Slvn. Borovlje. Kärnten, S Austria 46°31´N 14°18´E
97 E16 **Fermanagh** cultural region SW Northern Ireland, United Kingdom
106 J13 **Fermo** anc. Firmum Picenum. Marche, C Italy 43°09´N 13°44´E
104 J6 **Fermoselle** Castilla-León, N Spain 41°19´N 06°24´W
97 D20 **Fermoy** Ir. Mainistir Fhear Maí. SW Ireland 52°08´N 08°16´W
23 W8 **Fernandina Beach** Amelia Island, Florida, SE USA 30°40´N 81°27´W
57 A17 **Fernandina, Isla** var. Narborough Island. island Galapagos Islands, Ecuador, E Pacific Ocean
47 Y5 **Fernando de Noronha** island E Brazil
Fernando Po/Fernando Póo see Bioco, Isla de
60 J7 **Fernandópolis** São Paulo, S Brazil 20°18´S 50°13´W
104 M13 **Fernán Núñez** Andalucía, S Spain 37°40´N 04°44´W
83 Q14 **Fernão Veloso, Baia de** bay NE Mozambique
34 K3 **Ferndale** California, W USA 40°34´N 124°16´W
32 H6 **Ferndale** Washington, NW USA 48°51´N 122°35´W
11 P17 **Fernie** British Columbia, SW Canada 49°30´N 115°00´W
35 R5 **Fernley** Nevada, W USA 39°35´N 119°15´W
Ferozepore see Firozpur
107 N18 **Ferrandina** Basilicata, S Italy 40°30´N 16°25´E
106 G9 **Ferrara** anc. Forum Alieni. Emilia-Romagna, N Italy 44°50´N 11°36´E
120 F9 **Ferrat, Cap** headland NW Algeria 35°52´N 00°24´W
107 D20 **Ferrato, Capo** headland Sardegna, Italy, C Mediterranean Sea 39°18´N 09°37´E
104 G12 **Ferreira do Alentejo** Beja, S Portugal 38°04´N 08°06´W
56 B11 **Ferreñafe** Lambayeque, W Peru 06°42´S 79°45´W
108 C12 **Ferret** Valais, SW Switzerland 45°57´N 07°04´E
102 I13 **Ferret, Cap** headland W France 44°37´N 01°15´W
22 I6 **Ferriday** Louisiana, S USA 31°37´N 91°33´W
Ferro see Hierro
107 D16 **Ferro, Capo** headland Sardegna, Italy, C Mediterranean Sea 41°09´N 09°31´E
104 H2 **Ferrol** var. El Ferrol; prev. El Ferrol del Caudillo. Galicia, NW Spain 43°29´N 08°14´W
56 B12 **Ferrol, Peninsula de** peninsula W Peru
36 M5 **Ferron** Utah, W USA 39°05´N 111°07´W
21 S7 **Ferrum** Virginia, NE USA 36°54´N 80°01´W
23 O8 **Ferry Pass** Florida, SE USA 30°30´N 87°12´W
Ferryville see Menzel Bourguiba
29 S4 **Fertile** Minnesota, N USA 47°32´N 96°16´W
Fertő see Neusiedler See
98 L5 **Ferwerd** Fris. Ferwert. Friesland, N Netherlands 53°21´N 05°47´E
Ferwert see Ferwerd
74 G6 **Fès** Eng. Fez. N Morocco 34°06´N 04°57´W
79 I22 **Feshi** Bandundu, SW Dem. Rep. Congo 06°08´S 18°12´E
29 O4 **Fessenden** North Dakota, N USA 47°36´N 99°37´W
Festenberg see Twardogóra
27 X5 **Festus** Missouri, C USA 38°13´N 90°24´W
116 M14 **Feteşti** Ialomiţa, SE Romania 44°22´N 27°51´E
136 D17 **Fethiye** Muğla, SW Turkey 36°37´N 29°08´E
96 M1 **Fetlar** island NE Scotland, United Kingdom
95 I15 **Fetsund** Akershus, S Norway 59°55´N 11°03´E
12 L5 **Feuilles, Lac aux** ◎ Québec, E Canada
12 L5 **Feuilles, Rivière aux** ~ Québec, E Canada
99 M23 **Feulen** Diekirch, C Luxembourg 49°52´N 06°03´E
103 Q11 **Feurs** Loire, E France 45°44´N 04°14´E
95 F18 **Fevik** Aust-Agder, S Norway 58°22´N 08°40´E
123 R13 **Fevral'sk** Amurskaya Oblast', SE Russian Federation 52°25´N 131°06´E
149 S2 **Feyzābād** var. Faizabad, Faizābād, Feyzābād, Fyzabad. Badakhshān, NE Afghanistan 37°06´N 70°34´E
Feyzābād see Feyzābād
Fez see Fès
75 Q10 **Fezzan** ◐ cultural region C Libya
97 J19 **Ffestiniog** NW Wales, United Kingdom 52°55´N 03°54´W
Fhóid Duibh, Cuan an see Blacksod Bay
62 I8 **Fiambalá** Catamarca, NW Argentina 27°45´S 67°37´W
172 I6 **Fianarantsoa** Fianarantsoa, C Madagascar 21°27´S 47°05´E
172 H6 **Fianarantsoa** ◐ province SE Madagascar
78 G12 **Fianga** Mayo-Kébbi, SW Chad 09°57´N 15°09´E
Ficce see Fichē
80 J12 **Fichē** It. Ficce. Oromīya, C Ethiopia 09°48´N 38°43´E
101 N17 **Fichtelberg** ▲ Czech Republic/Germany 50°26´N 12°57´E
101 M18 **Fichtelgebirge** ▲▲ SE Germany
101 M19 **Fichtelnaab** ~ SE Germany
106 E9 **Fidenza** Emilia-Romagna, N Italy 44°52´N 10°04´E
113 K21 **Fier** var. Fieri. Fier, SW Albania 40°44´N 19°34´E
113 K21 **Fier** ◐ district W Albania
Fieri see Fier
Fierza see Fierzë
113 L17 **Fierzë** var. Fierza. Shkodër, N Albania 42°15´N 20°02´E
113 L17 **Fierzës, Liqeni i** ◎ N Albania
108 F10 **Fiesch** Valais, SW Switzerland 46°25´N 08°09´E
106 G11 **Fiesole** Toscana, C Italy 43°50´N 11°18´E
138 G12 **Fifah** Aţ Ţafilah, W Jordan 30°55´N 35°25´E
96 K11 **Fife** var. Kingdom of Fife. cultural region E Scotland, United Kingdom
Fife, Kingdom of see Fife
96 K11 **Fife Ness** headland E Scotland, United Kingdom 56°16´N 02°35´W
Fifteen Twenty Fracture Zone see Barracuda Fracture Zone
103 N13 **Figeac** Lot, S France 44°37´N 02°01´E
95 N19 **Figeholm** Kalmar, SE Sweden 57°12´N 16°34´E
Figig see Figuig
83 J18 **Figtree** Matabeleland South, SW Zimbabwe 20°24´S 28°21´E
104 F8 **Figueira da Foz** Coimbra, W Portugal 40°09´N 08°51´W
105 X4 **Figueres** Cataluña, E Spain 42°16´N 02°57´E
74 H7 **Figuig** var. Figig. E Morocco 32°09´N 01°13´W
Fijāj, Shaţţ al see Fedjaj, Chott el
187 Y15 **Fiji** off. Sovereign Democratic Republic of Fiji, Fij. Viti. ◆ republic SW Pacific Ocean
192 K9 **Fiji** island group SW Pacific Ocean
175 Q8 **Fiji Plate** tectonic feature
Fiji, Sovereign Democratic Republic of see Fiji
105 P14 **Filabres, Sierra de los** ▲▲ SE Spain
83 K18 **Filabusi** Matabeleland South, S Zimbabwe 20°34´S 29°20´E
42 K13 **Filadelfia** Guanacaste, W Costa Rica 10°28´N 85°33´W
111 K20 **Fil'akovo** Hung. Fülek. Banskobystrický Kraj, C Slovakia 48°15´N 19°53´E
195 N5 **Filchner Ice Shelf** ice shelf Antarctica
14 J11 **Fildegrand** ~ Québec, SE Canada
33 O15 **Filer** Idaho, NW USA 42°34´N 114°36´W
Filevo see Vŭrbitsa
116 H14 **Filiaşi** Dolj, SW Romania 44°32´N 23°31´E
115 B16 **Filiátes** Ípeiros, W Greece 39°38´N 20°16´E
115 D21 **Filiatrá** Pelopónnisos, S Greece 37°09´N 21°35´E
107 K22 **Filicudi, Isola** island Isole Eolie, S Italy
141 Y10 **Filim** E Oman 20°37´N 58°11´E
Filimon Sîrbu see Făurei
77 S11 **Filingué** Tillabéri, W Niger 14°21´N 03°22´E
Filiouri see Lissos
114 I13 **Filippoí** anc. Philippi. site of ancient city Anatolikí Makedonía kai Thráki, NE Greece
95 L15 **Filipstad** Värmland, C Sweden 59°44´N 14°10´E
108 I9 **Filisur** Graubünden, S Switzerland 46°40´N 09°43´E
94 E12 **Fillefjell** ▲ S Norway
35 R14 **Fillmore** California, W USA 34°23´N 118°56´W
36 K5 **Fillmore** Utah, W USA 38°57´N 112°19´W
14 J10 **Fils, Lac du** ◎ Québec, SE Canada
Filyos Çayı see Yenice Çayı
195 Q1 **Fimbulisen** ice shelf Antarctica
195 Q2 **Fimbutheimen** physical region Antarctica
106 G9 **Finale Emilia** Emilia-Romagna, C Italy 44°50´N 11°17´E
106 C10 **Finale Ligure** Liguria, NW Italy 44°11´N 08°22´E
105 P14 **Fiñana** Andalucía, S Spain 37°09´N 02°47´W
21 S6 **Fincastle** Virginia, NE USA 37°30´N 79°54´W
99 M25 **Findel** ✈ (Luxembourg) Luxembourg, C Luxembourg 49°39´N 06°16´E
96 J9 **Findhorn** ~ N Scotland, United Kingdom
31 R12 **Findlay** Ohio, N USA 41°02´N 83°40´W
18 G11 **Finger Lakes** ◎ New York, NE USA
83 L14 **Fingoè** Tete, NW Mozambique 15°10´S 31°51´E
136 E17 **Finike** Antalya, SW Turkey 36°18´N 30°08´E
102 F6 **Finistère** ◐ department NW France
186 D7 **Finisterre Range** ▲▲ N Papua New Guinea
181 Q8 **Finke** Northern Territory, N Australia 25°37´S 134°35´E
109 S10 **Finkenstein** Kärnten, S Austria 46°34´N 13°53´E
189 Y15 **Finkol, Mount** var. Mount Crozer. ▲ Kosrae, E Micronesia 05°18´N 163°00´E
93 L17 **Finland** off. Republic of Finland, Fin. Suomen Tasavalta, Suomi. ◆ republic N Europe
124 F12 **Finland, Gulf of** Est. Soome Laht, Fin. Suomenlahti, Ger. Finnischer Meerbusen, Rus. Finskiy Zaliv, Swe. Finska Viken. gulf E Baltic Sea
Finland, Republic of see Finland
10 L11 **Finlay** ~ British Columbia, W Canada
183 O10 **Finley** New South Wales, SE Australia 35°41´S 145°33´E
29 Q4 **Finley** North Dakota, N USA 47°30´N 97°50´W
Finnischer Meerbusen see Finland, Gulf of
92 K9 **Finnmark** ◐ county N Norway
92 K9 **Finnmarksvidda** physical region N Norway
92 I9 **Finnsnes** Troms, N Norway 69°16´N 18°00´E
186 E7 **Finschhafen** Morobe, C Papua New Guinea 06°35´S 147°51´E
94 E13 **Finse** Hordaland, S Norway 60°35´N 07°33´E
Finska Viken/Finskiy Zaliv see Finland, Gulf of
95 M17 **Finspång** Östergötland, S Sweden 58°42´N 15°45´E
108 F10 **Finsteraarhorn** ▲ Switzerland 46°33´N 08°07´E
101 O14 **Finsterwalde** Brandenburg, E Germany 51°38´N 13°43´E
185 A23 **Fiordland** physical region South Island, New Zealand
106 E9 **Fiorenzuola d'Arda** Emilia-Romagna, C Italy 44°57´N 09°53´E
Firat Nehri see Euphrates
Firdaus see Ferdows
18 M14 **Fire Island** island New York, NE USA
106 G11 **Firenze** Eng. Florence; anc. Florentia. Toscana, C Italy 43°47´N 11°15´E
106 G10 **Firenzuola** Toscana, C Italy 44°07´N 11°22´E
14 C6 **Fire River** Ontario, S Canada 48°46´N 83°34´W
Fírliug see Fârliug
61 B19 **Firmat** Santa Fe, C Argentina 33°29´S 61°29´W
103 Q12 **Firminy** Loire, E France 45°22´N 04°18´E
Firmum Picenum see Fermo
152 J12 **Fīrozābād** Uttar Pradesh, N India 27°09´N 78°24´E
152 G8 **Fīrozpur** var. Ferozepore. Punjab, NW India 30°55´N 74°38´E
First State see Delaware
143 O12 **Fīrūzābād** Fārs, S Iran 28°51´N 52°35´E
Fischamend see Fischamend Markt
109 Y4 **Fischamend Markt** var. Fischamend. Niederösterreich, NE Austria 48°08´N 16°37´E
109 W6 **Fischbacher Alpen** ▲▲ E Austria
Fischhausen see Primorsk
83 D21 **Fish** var. Vis. ~ S Namibia
83 F24 **Fish** Afr. Vis. ~ SW South Africa
11 X15 **Fisher Branch** Manitoba, S Canada 51°09´N 97°34´W
11 X15 **Fisher River** Manitoba, S Canada 51°25´N 97°23´W
19 N13 **Fishers Island** island New York, NE USA
37 U8 **Fishers Peak** ▲ Colorado, C USA 37°06´N 104°27´W
9 P9 **Fisher Strait** strait Nunavut, N Canada
97 H21 **Fishguard** Wel. Abergwaun. SW Wales, United Kingdom 51°59´N 04°49´W
19 R2 **Fish River Lake** ◎ Maine, NE USA
194 K6 **Fiske, Cape** headland Antarctica 74°27´S 60°28´W
103 P4 **Fismes** Marne, N France 49°19´N 03°41´E
104 F3 **Fisterra, Cabo** headland NW Spain 42°53´N 09°16´W
19 N11 **Fitchburg** Massachusetts, NE USA 42°34´N 71°48´W
96 L3 **Fitful Head** headland NE Scotland, United Kingdom 59°57´N 01°24´W
95 C14 **Fitjar** Hordaland, S Norway 59°55´N 05°19´E
192 H16 **Fito, Mauga** ▲ Upolu, C Samoa 13°57´S 171°42´W
23 U6 **Fitzgerald** Georgia, SE USA 31°42´N 83°15´W
180 M5 **Fitzroy Crossing** Western Australia 18°10´S 125°40´E
63 G21 **Fitzroy, Monte** var. Cerro Chaltel. ▲ S Argentina 49°18´S 73°06´W
181 Y8 **Fitzroy River** ~ Queensland, E Australia
180 L5 **Fitzroy River** ~ Western Australia
14 E12 **Fitzwilliam Island** island Ontario, S Canada
107 J15 **Fiuggi** Lazio, C Italy 41°47´N 13°16´E
Fiume see Rijeka
107 H15 **Fiumicino** Lazio, C Italy 41°46´N 12°13´E
Fiumicino see Leonardo da Vinci
106 E10 **Fivizzano** Toscana, C Italy 44°13´N 10°06´E
79 O21 **Fizi** Sud-Kivu, E Dem. Rep. Congo 04°15´S 28°57´E
Fizuli see Füzuli
92 I11 **Fjällåsen** Norrbotten, N Sweden 67°31´N 20°08´E
95 G20 **Fjerritslev** Nordjylland, N Denmark 57°06´N 09°17´E
F.J.S. see Franz Josef Strauss
95 L16 **Fjugesta** Örebro, C Sweden 59°10´N 14°50´E
Fladstrand see Frederikshavn
37 V5 **Flagler** Colorado, C USA 39°17´N 103°04´W
23 X10 **Flagler Beach** Florida, SE USA 29°28´N 81°07´W
36 L11 **Flagstaff** Arizona, SW USA 35°12´N 111°39´W
65 H24 **Flagstaff Bay** bay N Saint Helena, C Atlantic Ocean
19 P5 **Flagstaff Lake** ◎ Maine, NE USA
94 E13 **Flåm** Sogn Og Fjordane, S Norway 60°51´N 07°06´E
15 O8 **Flamand** ~ Québec, SE Canada
30 J5 **Flambeau River** ~ Wisconsin, N USA
97 O16 **Flamborough Head** headland E England, United Kingdom 54°06´N 00°03´W
100 N13 **Fläming** hill range NE Germany
16 H8 **Flaming Gorge Reservoir** ⊠ Utah/Wyoming, NW USA
99 B18 **Flanders** Dut. Vlaanderen, Fr. Flandre. cultural region Belgium/France
Flandre see Flanders
29 R10 **Flandreau** South Dakota, N USA 44°03´N 96°36´W
96 D6 **Flannan Isles** island group NW Scotland, United Kingdom
28 M6 **Flasher** North Dakota, N USA 46°25´N 101°12´W
93 G15 **Flåsjön** ◎ N Sweden
39 O11 **Flat** Alaska, USA 62°27´N 158°00´W
92 H1 **Flateyri** Vestfirdhir, NW Iceland 66°03´N 23°28´W
33 P8 **Flathead Lake** ◎ Montana, NW USA
173 Y15 **Flat Island** Fr. Île Plate. island N Mauritius
25 T11 **Flatonia** Texas, SW USA 29°41´N 97°06´W
185 M14 **Flat Point** headland North Island, New Zealand 41°12´S 176°03´E
27 X6 **Flat River** Missouri, C USA 37°51´N 90°31´W
31 P8 **Flat River** ~ Michigan, N USA
31 P14 **Flatrock River** ~ Indiana, N USA
32 E6 **Flattery, Cape** headland Washington, NW USA 48°22´N 124°43´W
64 B12 **Flatts Village** var. The Flatts Village. C Bermuda 32°19´N 64°44´W
108 H7 **Flawil** Sankt Gallen, NE Switzerland 47°25´N 09°12´E
97 N22 **Fleet** S England, United Kingdom 51°16´N 00°50´W
97 K16 **Fleetwood** NW England, United Kingdom 53°55´N 03°02´W
18 H15 **Fleetwood** Pennsylvania, NE USA 40°27´N 75°49´W
95 D18 **Flekkefjord** Vest-Agder, S Norway 58°17´N 06°40´E
21 N5 **Flemingsburg** Kentucky, S USA 38°26´N 83°43´W
18 J15 **Flemington** New Jersey, NE USA 40°30´N 74°51´W
64 I7 **Flemish Cap** undersea feature NW Atlantic Ocean 47°00´N 45°00´W
95 N16 **Flen** Södermanland, C Sweden 59°04´N 16°39´E
100 I6 **Flensburg** Schleswig-Holstein, N Germany 54°47´N 09°26´E
100 J6 **Flensburger Förde** inlet Denmark/Germany
102 K5 **Flers** Orne, N France 48°45´N 00°34´W
95 C14 **Flesland** ✈ (Bergen) Hordaland, S Norway 60°18´N 05°15´E
Flessingue see Vlissingen
21 P10 **Fletcher** North Carolina, SE USA 35°24´N 82°29´W
31 R6 **Fletcher Pond** ◎ Michigan, N USA
102 L15 **Fleurance** Gers, S France 43°50´N 00°39´E
108 B8 **Fleurier** Neuchâtel, W Switzerland 46°55´N 06°37´E
99 H20 **Fleurus** Hainaut, S Belgium 50°28´N 04°33´E
103 N7 **Fleury-les-Aubrais** Loiret, C France 47°55´N 01°55´E
98 K10 **Flevoland** ◐ province C Netherlands
Flickertail State see North Dakota
108 H9 **Flims** Glarus, NE Switzerland 46°50´N 09°16´E
182 F8 **Flinders Island** island Investigator Group, South Australia
183 P14 **Flinders Island** island Furneaux Group, Tasmania, SE Australia
182 I6 **Flinders Ranges** ▲▲ South Australia
181 U5 **Flinders River** ~ Queensland, NE Australia
11 V13 **Flin Flon** Manitoba, C Canada 54°47´N 101°51´W
97 K18 **Flint** NE Wales, United Kingdom 53°15´N 03°10´W
31 R9 **Flint** Michigan, N USA 43°01´N 83°41´W
97 J18 **Flint** cultural region NE Wales, United Kingdom
27 O7 **Flint Hills** hill range Kansas, C USA
191 Y6 **Flint Island** island Line Islands, E Kiribati
23 S4 **Flint River** ~ Georgia, SE USA
31 R9 **Flint River** ~ Michigan, N USA
189 X12 **Flipper Point** headland C Wake Island 19°18´N 166°37´E
94 I13 **Flisa** Hedmark, S Norway 60°36´N 12°02´E
94 J13 **Flisa** ~ S Norway
122 J5 **Flissingskiy, Mys** headland Novaya Zemlya, NW Russian Federation 76°43´N 69°01´E
Flitsch see Bovec
105 U6 **Flix** Cataluña, NE Spain 41°13´N 00°32´E
95 J19 **Floda** Västra Götaland, S Sweden 57°47´N 12°20´E
101 O16 **Flöha** ~ E Germany
25 O4 **Flomot** Texas, SW USA 34°13´N 100°58´W
29 V5 **Floodwood** Minnesota, N USA 46°55´N 92°55´W
30 M15 **Flora** Illinois, N USA 38°40´N 88°29´W
103 P14 **Florac** Lozère, S France 44°18´N 03°35´E
23 Q8 **Florala** Alabama, S USA 31°00´N 86°19´W
103 S4 **Florange** Moselle, NE France 49°21´N 06°06´E
Floreana, Isla see Santa María, Isla
23 O2 **Florence** Alabama, S USA 34°48´N 87°40´W
36 L14 **Florence** Arizona, SW USA 33°01´N 111°23´W
37 T6 **Florence** Colorado, C USA 38°20´N 105°06´W
27 O5 **Florence** Kansas, C USA 38°13´N 96°56´W
20 M4 **Florence** Kentucky, S USA 39°00´N 84°37´W
32 E13 **Florence** Oregon, NW USA 43°58´N 124°06´W
21 T12 **Florence** South Carolina, SE USA 34°12´N 79°44´W
25 S9 **Florence** Texas, SW USA 30°50´N 97°47´W
Florence see Firenze
54 E13 **Florencia** Caquetá, S Colombia 01°37´N 75°37´W
99 H21 **Florennes** Namur, S Belgium 50°15´N 04°36´E
Florentia see Firenze
63 J18 **Florentino Ameghino, Embalse** ⊠ S Argentina
99 J24 **Florenville** Luxembourg, SE Belgium 49°42´N 05°19´E
42 E3 **Flores** Petén, N Guatemala 16°55´N 89°56´W
61 E19 **Flores** ◐ department S Uruguay
171 O16 **Flores** island Nusa Tenggara, C Indonesia
64 M1 **Flores** island Azores, Portugal, NE Atlantic Ocean
Floreshty see Floreşti
Flores, Lago de see Petén Itzá, Lago
Flores, Laut see Flores Sea
171 N15 **Flores Sea** Ind. Laut Flores. sea C Indonesia
116 M8 **Floreşti** Rus. Floreshty. N Moldova 47°52´N 28°19´E
25 S12 **Floresville** Texas, SW USA 29°09´N 98°10´W
59 N14 **Floriano** Piauí, E Brazil 06°45´S 43°00´W
61 K14 **Florianópolis** prev. Destêrro. state capital Santa Catarina, S Brazil 27°35´S 48°32´W
44 G6 **Florida** Camagüey, C Cuba 21°32´N 78°14´W
61 F19 **Florida** Florida, S Uruguay 34°04´S 56°14´W
61 F19 **Florida** ◐ department S Uruguay
23 U9 **Florida** off. State of Florida, also known as Peninsular State, Sunshine State. ◐ state SE USA
23 Y17 **Florida Bay** bay Florida, SE USA
54 G8 **Floridablanca** Santander, N Colombia 07°04´N 73°06´W
23 Y17 **Florida Keys** island group Florida, SE USA
37 Q16 **Florida Mountains** ▲▲ New Mexico, SW USA
64 D10 **Florida, Straits of** strait Atlantic Ocean/Gulf of Mexico
114 D13 **Flórina** var. Phlórina. Dytikí Makedonía, N Greece 40°48´N 21°26´E
27 X4 **Florissant** Missouri, C USA 38°48´N 90°20´W
94 C11 **Florø** Sogn Og Fjordane, S Norway 61°36´N 05°04´E
115 L22 **Floúda, Akrotírio** headland Astypálaia, Kykládes, Greece, Aegean Sea 36°38´N 26°23´E
21 S7 **Floyd** Virginia, NE USA 36°55´N 80°22´W
25 N4 **Floydada** Texas, SW USA 33°58´N 101°20´W
Flüela Wisshorn see Weisshorn
98 K7 **Fluessen** ◎ N Netherlands
105 S5 **Flúmen** ~ NE Spain
107 C20 **Flumendosa** ~ Sardegna, Italy, C Mediterranean Sea
31 R9 **Flushing** Michigan, N USA 43°03´N 83°51´W
Flushing see Vlissingen
25 O6 **Fluvanna** Texas, SW USA 32°54´N 101°06´W
186 B8 **Fly** ~ Indonesia/Papua New Guinea
194 I10 **Flying Fish, Cape** headland Thurston Island, Antarctica 72°00´S 102°25´W
Flylân see Vlieland
193 Y15 **Foa** island Ha'apai Group, C Tonga
11 U15 **Foam Lake** Saskatchewan, S Canada 51°38´N 103°31´W
113 J14 **Foča** var. Srbinje. SE Bosnia and Herzegovina 43°32´N 18°46´E
116 L12 **Focşani** Vrancea, E Romania 45°45´N 27°13´E
Fogaras/Fogarasch see Făgăraş
107 M16 **Foggia** Puglia, SE Italy 41°28´N 15°31´E
Foggo see Faggo
76 D10 **Fogo** island Ilhas de Sotavento, SW Cape Verde
13 U11 **Fogo Island** island Newfoundland and Labrador, E Canada
109 U7 **Fohnsdorf** Steiermark, SE Austria 47°13´N 14°40´E
100 G7 **Föhr** island NW Germany
104 F14 **Fóia** ▲ S Portugal 37°19´N 08°39´W
14 I10 **Foins, Lac aux** ◎ Québec, SE Canada
103 N17 **Foix** Ariège, S France 42°58´N 01°39´E
126 I5 **Fokino** Bryanskaya Oblast', W Russian Federation 53°22´N 34°22´E
123 S15 **Fokino** Primorskiy Kray, W Russian Federation 42°58´N 132°25´E
Fola, Cnoc see Bloody Foreland
94 E13 **Folarskardnuten** ▲ S Norway 60°34´N 07°18´E
92 G11 **Folda** fjord C Norway
93 F14 **Foldereid** Nord-Trøndelag, C Norway 64°58´N 12°09´E
Földvár see Feldioara
115 J22 **Folégandros** island Kykládes, Greece, Aegean Sea
23 O9 **Foley** Alabama, S USA 30°24´N 87°40´W
29 U7 **Foley** Minnesota, N USA 45°39´N 93°54´W
14 E7 **Foleyet** Ontario, S Canada 48°15´N 82°26´W
95 D14 **Folgefonni** glacier S Norway
106 I13 **Foligno** Umbria, C Italy 42°58´N 12°40´E
97 Q23 **Folkestone** SE England, United Kingdom 51°05´N 01°11´E
23 W8 **Folkston** Georgia, SE USA 30°49´N 82°00´W
94 H10 **Folldal** Hedmark, S Norway 62°08´N 10°00´E
25 P1 **Follett** Texas, SW USA 36°25´N 100°08´W
106 F13 **Follonica** Toscana, C Italy 42°55´N 10°45´E
21 T15 **Folly Beach** South Carolina, SE USA 32°39´N 79°56´W
35 O7 **Folsom** California, W USA 38°40´N 121°11´W
116 M12 **Folteşti** Galaţi, E Romania 45°45´N 28°00´E
172 H14 **Fomboni** Mohéli, S Comoros 12°18´S 43°46´E
18 K10 **Fonda** New York, NE USA 42°57´N 74°24´W
11 S10 **Fond-du-Lac** Saskatchewan, C Canada 59°20´N 107°09´W
30 M8 **Fond du Lac** Wisconsin, N USA 43°48´N 88°27´W
11 T10 **Fond-du-Lac** ~ Saskatchewan, C Canada
190 C9 **Fongafale** var. Funafuti. ● (Tuvalu) Funafuti Atoll, SE Tuvalu 08°31´N 179°11´E
190 G8 **Fongafale** atoll C Tuvalu
107 C18 **Fonni** Sardegna, Italy, C Mediterranean Sea 40°07´N 09°17´E
189 V12 **Fono** island Chuuk, C Micronesia
54 G4 **Fonseca** La Guajira, N Colombia 10°53´N 72°51´W
Fonseca, Golfo de see Fonseca, Gulf of
42 H8 **Fonseca, Gulf of** Sp. Golfo de Fonseca. gulf C Central America
103 O6 **Fontainebleau** Seine-et-Marne, N France 48°24´N 02°42´E
63 G19 **Fontana, Lago** ◎ W Argentina
21 N10 **Fontana Lake** ⊠ North Carolina, SE USA
107 L24 **Fontanarossa** ✈ (Catania) Sicilia, Italy, C Mediterranean Sea 37°28´N 15°04´E
11 N11 **Fontas** ~ British Columbia, W Canada
58 D12 **Fonte Boa** Amazonas, N Brazil 02°32´S 66°01´W
102 J10 **Fontenay-le-Comte** Vendée, NW France 46°28´N 00°48´W
33 T16 **Fontenelle Reservoir** ⊠ Wyoming, C USA
193 Y14 **Fonualei** island Vava'u Group, N Tonga
111 H24 **Fonyód** Somogy, W Hungary 46°43´N 17°32´E
Foochow see Fuzhou
39 Q10 **Foraker, Mount** ▲ Alaska, USA 62°57´N 151°24´W
187 R14 **Forari** Éfaté, C Vanuatu 17°42´S 168°33´E
103 U4 **Forbach** Moselle, NE France 49°11´N 06°54´E
183 Q8 **Forbes** New South Wales, SE Australia 33°24´S 148°00´E
77 T17 **Forcados** Delta, S Nigeria 05°16´N 05°25´E
103 S14 **Forcalquier** Alpes-de-Haute-Provence, SE France 43°57´N 05°46´E
101 K19 **Forchheim** Bayern, SE Germany 49°43´N 11°07´E
35 R13 **Ford City** California, W USA 35°09´N 119°27´W
94 D11 **Førde** Sogn Og Fjordane, S Norway 61°27´N 05°51´E
31 N4 **Ford River** ~ Michigan, N USA
183 O4 **Fords Bridge** New South Wales, SE Australia 29°44´S 145°25´E
20 J6 **Fordsville** Kentucky, S USA 37°36´N 86°39´W
27 U13 **Fordyce** Arkansas, C USA 33°49´N 92°23´W
76 I14 **Forécariah** SW Guinea 09°28´N 13°06´W
197 O14 **Forel, Mont** ▲ SE Greenland 66°55´N 36°45´W
11 R17 **Foremost** Alberta, SW Canada 49°30´N 111°34´W
14 D16 **Forest** Ontario, S Canada 43°05´N 82°00´W
22 L5 **Forest** Mississippi, S USA 32°22´N 89°30´W
31 S12 **Forest** Ohio, N USA 40°47´N 83°26´W
29 V11 **Forest City** Iowa, C USA 43°15´N 93°38´W
21 Q10 **Forest City** North Carolina, SE USA 35°19´N 81°52´W
32 G11 **Forest Grove** Oregon, NW USA 45°31´N 123°06´W

◆ Country
● Country Capital
◇ Dependent Territory
○ Dependent Territory Capital
◐ Administrative Regions
✈ International Airport
▲ Mountain
▲▲ Mountain Range
Volcano
~ River
◎ Lake
⊠ Reservoir

183 P17 **Forestier Peninsula** *peninsula* Tasmania, SE Australia
29 V8 **Forest Lake** Minnesota, N USA 45°16′N 92°59′W
23 S3 **Forest Park** Georgia, SE USA 33°37′N 84°22′W
29 Q3 **Forest River** ⇝ North Dakota, N USA
15 T6 **Forestville** Québec, SE Canada 48°45′N 69°04′W
103 Q11 **Forez, Monts du** ▲ C France
96 K10 **Forfar** E Scotland, United Kingdom 56°38′N 02°54′W
26 J8 **Forgan** Oklahoma, C USA 36°54′N 100°32′W
Forge du Sud *see* Dudelange
101 J24 **Forggensee** ◎ S Germany
147 N10 **Forish** *Rus.* Farish. Jizzax Viloyati, C Uzbekistan 40°33′N 66°52′E
20 F9 **Forked Deer River** ⇝ Tennessee, S USA
32 F7 **Forks** Washington, NW USA 47°57′N 124°22′W
92 N2 **Forlandsundet** *sound* W Svalbard
106 H10 **Forlì** *anc.* Forum Livii. Emilia-Romagna, N Italy 44°14′N 12°02′E
29 Q7 **Forman** North Dakota, N USA 46°07′N 97°39′W
97 K17 **Formby** NW England, United Kingdom 53°34′N 03°05′W
105 V11 **Formentera** *anc.* Ophiusa, *Lat.* Frumentum. *island* Islas Baleares, Spain, W Mediterranean Sea
Formentor, Cabo de *see* Formentor, Cap de
105 Y9 **Formentor, Cap de** *var.* Cabo de Formentor, Cape Formentor. *headland* Mallorca, Spain, W Mediterranean Sea 39°57′N 03°12′E
Formentor, Cape *see* Formentor, Cap de
107 J16 **Formia** Lazio, C Italy 41°16′N 13°37′E
62 O7 **Formosa** Formosa, NE Argentina 26°07′S 58°14′W
62 M6 **Formosa** *off.* Provincia de Formosa. ◐ *province* NE Argentina
Formosa/Formo'sa *see* Taiwan
Formosa, Provincia de *see* Formosa
59 I17 **Formosa, Serra** ▲ C Brazil
Formosa Strait *see* Taiwan Strait
95 H21 **Fornæs** *headland* C Denmark 56°26′N 10°57′E
25 U6 **Forney** Texas, SW USA 32°45′N 96°28′W
106 E9 **Fornovo di Taro** Emilia-Romagna, C Italy 44°42′N 10°07′E
117 T14 **Foros** Respublika Krym, S Ukraine 44°24′N 33°47′E
Føroyar *see* Faeroe Islands
96 J8 **Forres** NE Scotland, United Kingdom 57°32′N 03°38′W
27 X11 **Forrest City** Arkansas, C USA 35°01′N 90°48′W
39 Y15 **Forrester Island** *island* Alexander Archipelago, Alaska, USA
25 N7 **Forsan** Texas, SW USA 32°06′N 101°22′W
181 V5 **Forsayth** Queensland, NE Australia 18°31′S 143°37′E
95 L19 **Forserum** Jönköping, S Sweden 57°42′N 14°28′E
95 K15 **Forshaga** Värmland, C Sweden 59°33′N 13°29′E
93 L19 **Forssa** Etelä-Suomi, S Finland 60°49′N 23°40′E
101 Q14 **Forst** *Lus.* Baršć Łužyca. Brandenburg, E Germany 51°43′N 14°38′E
183 U7 **Forster-Tuncurry** New South Wales, SE Australia 32°11′S 152°30′E
23 T4 **Forsyth** Georgia, SE USA 33°00′N 83°57′W
27 T8 **Forsyth** Missouri, C USA 36°41′N 93°07′W
33 W10 **Forsyth** Montana, NW USA 46°16′N 106°40′W
149 U11 **Fort Abbās** Punjab, E Pakistan 29°12′N 73°00′E
12 G10 **Fort Albany** Ontario, C Canada 52°15′N 81°35′W
56 L13 **Fortaleza** Pando, N Bolivia 09°48′S 65°29′W
58 P13 **Fortaleza** *prev.* Ceará. *state capital* Ceará, NE Brazil 03°45′S 38°35′W
59 D16 **Fortaleza** Rondônia, W Brazil 08°45′S 64°06′W
56 C13 **Fortaleza, Río** ⇝ W Peru
Fort-Archambault *see* Sarh
21 U3 **Fort Ashby** West Virginia, NE USA 39°30′N 78°46′W
96 I9 **Fort Augustus** N Scotland, United Kingdom 57°14′N 04°38′W
Fort-Bayard *see* Zhanjiang
33 S8 **Fort Benton** Montana, NW USA 47°49′N 110°40′W
35 Q1 **Fort Bidwell** California, W USA 41°50′N 120°07′W
34 L5 **Fort Bragg** California, W USA 39°25′N 123°48′W
31 N16 **Fort Branch** Indiana, N USA 38°15′N 87°34′W
Fort-Bretonnet *see* Bousso
33 T17 **Fort Bridger** Wyoming, C USA 41°18′N 110°19′W
Fort-Cappolani *see* Tidjikja
Fort-Carnot *see* Ikongo
Fort Charlet *see* Djanet
Fort-Chimo *see* Kuujjuaq
11 R10 **Fort Chipewyan** Alberta, C Canada 58°42′N 111°08′W
Fort Cobb Lake *see* Fort Cobb Reservoir
26 L11 **Fort Cobb Reservoir** *var.* Fort Cobb Lake. ▣ Oklahoma, C USA
37 T3 **Fort Collins** Colorado, C USA 40°35′N 105°05′W
14 K12 **Fort-Coulonge** Québec, SE Canada 45°50′N 76°45′W
Fort-Crampel *see* Kaga Bandoro
Fort-Dauphin *see* Tôlañaro
24 K10 **Fort Davis** Texas, SW USA 30°35′N 103°54′W
37 O10 **Fort Defiance** Arizona, SW USA 35°44′N 109°04′W
45 Q12 **Fort-de-France** *prev.* Fort-Royal. ○ (Martinique) W Martinique 14°36′N 61°05′W
45 P12 **Fort-de-France, Baie de** *bay* W Martinique
Fort de Kock *see* Bukittinggi
23 P6 **Fort Deposit** Alabama, S USA 31°58′N 86°34′W
29 U13 **Fort Dodge** Iowa, C USA 42°30′N 94°10′W
13 S10 **Forteau** Québec, E Canada 51°30′N 56°55′W
106 E11 **Forte dei Marmi** Toscana, C Italy 43°59′N 10°10′E
14 H17 **Fort Erie** Ontario, S Canada 42°55′N 78°56′W
180 H7 **Fortescue River** ⇝ Western Australia
19 S2 **Fort Fairfield** Maine, NE USA 46°45′N 67°51′W
Fort-Foureau *see* Kousséri
12 A11 **Fort Frances** Ontario, S Canada 48°37′N 93°23′W
Fort Franklin *see* Déljne
23 R7 **Fort Gaines** Georgia, SE USA 31°36′N 85°03′W
37 T8 **Fort Garland** Colorado, C USA 37°22′N 105°24′W
21 P5 **Fort Gay** West Virginia, NE USA 38°06′N 82°35′W
Fort George *see* La Grande Rivière
Fort George *see* Chisasibi
27 Q10 **Fort Gibson** Oklahoma, C USA 35°48′N 95°15′W
27 Q9 **Fort Gibson Lake** ▣ Oklahoma, C USA
8 H7 **Fort Good Hope** *var.* Rádeyilikóé. Northwest Territories, NW Canada 66°16′N 128°37′W
23 V4 **Fort Gordon** Georgia, SE USA 33°25′N 82°09′W
Fort Gouraud *see* Fdérik
96 I11 **Forth** ⇝ C Scotland, United Kingdom
Fort Hall *see* Murang'a
24 H8 **Fort Hancock** Texas, SW USA 31°18′N 105°49′W
Fort Hertz *see* Putao
96 K12 **Forth, Firth of** *estuary* E Scotland, United Kingdom
14 L14 **Forthton** Ontario, SE Canada 44°43′N 75°31′W
14 M8 **Fortier** ⇝ Québec, SE Canada
Fortín General Eugenio Garay *see* General Eugenio A. Garay
Fort Jameson *see* Chipata
Fort Johnston *see* Mangochi
19 R1 **Fort Kent** Maine, NE USA 47°15′N 68°33′W
Fort-Lamy *see* Ndjamena
23 Z15 **Fort Lauderdale** Florida, SE USA 26°07′N 80°09′W
21 R11 **Fort Lawn** South Carolina, SE USA 34°43′N 80°46′W
8 H10 **Fort Liard** *var.* Liard. Northwest Territories, W Canada 60°14′N 123°28′W
44 M8 **Fort-Liberté** NE Haiti 19°42′N 71°51′W
21 N9 **Fort Loudoun Lake** ▣ Tennessee, S USA
37 T3 **Fort Lupton** Colorado, C USA 40°04′N 104°48′W
11 R12 **Fort MacKay** Alberta, C Canada 57°12′N 111°41′W
11 Q17 **Fort Macleod** *var.* MacLeod. Alberta, SW Canada 49°44′N 113°24′W
29 Y16 **Fort Madison** Iowa, C USA 40°37′N 91°15′W
Fort Manning *see* Mchinji
25 P9 **Fort McKavett** Texas, SW USA 30°50′N 100°07′W
11 R12 **Fort McMurray** Alberta, C Canada 56°44′N 111°23′W
8 G7 **Fort McPherson** *var.* McPherson. Northwest Territories, NW Canada 67°29′N 134°50′W
21 R11 **Fort Mill** South Carolina, SE USA 35°00′N 80°57′W
Fort-Millot *see* Ngouri
37 U3 **Fort Morgan** Colorado, C USA 40°14′N 103°48′W
23 W14 **Fort Myers** Florida, SE USA 26°39′N 81°52′W
23 W15 **Fort Myers Beach** Florida, SE USA 26°27′N 81°57′W
10 M10 **Fort Nelson** British Columbia, W Canada 58°48′N 122°44′W
10 M10 **Fort Nelson** ⇝ British Columbia, W Canada
Fort Norman *see* Tulita
23 Q2 **Fort Payne** Alabama, S USA 34°23′N 85°43′W
33 W7 **Fort Peck** Montana, NW USA 48°00′N 106°28′W
33 V8 **Fort Peck Lake** ▣ Montana, NW USA
23 Y13 **Fort Pierce** Florida, SE USA 27°28′N 80°20′W
29 N10 **Fort Pierre** South Dakota, N USA 44°21′N 100°22′W
81 E18 **Fort Portal** SW Uganda 0°39′N 30°17′E
8 J10 **Fort Providence** *var.* Providence. Northwest Territories, W Canada 61°21′N 117°39′W
11 U16 **Fort Qu'Appelle** Saskatchewan, S Canada 50°50′N 103°52′W
Fort-Repoux *see* Akjoujt
8 K10 **Fort Resolution** *var.* Resolution. Northwest Territories, W Canada 61°10′N 113°39′W
33 T13 **Fortress Mountain** ▲ Wyoming, C USA 44°20′N 109°51′W
Fort Rosebery *see* Mansa
Fort Rousset *see* Owando
Fort-Royal *see* Fort-de-France
Fort Rupert *see* Waskaganish
8 H13 **Fort St. James** British Columbia, SW Canada 54°26′N 124°15′W
11 N12 **Fort St. John** British Columbia, W Canada 56°16′N 120°52′W
Fort Sandeman *see* Zhob
11 Q14 **Fort Saskatchewan** Alberta, SW Canada 53°42′N 113°12′W
27 R6 **Fort Scott** Kansas, C USA 37°52′N 94°43′W
12 E6 **Fort Severn** Ontario, C Canada 56°N 87°40′W
31 R12 **Fort Shawnee** Ohio, N USA 40°41′N 84°08′W
144 E14 **Fort-Shevchenko** Mangistau, W Kazakhstan 44°29′N 50°16′E
Fort-Sibut *see* Sibut
8 I10 **Fort Simpson** *var.* Simpson. Northwest Territories, W Canada 61°52′N 121°23′W
8 I10 **Fort Smith** Northwest Territories, W Canada 60°01′N 111°55′W
27 R10 **Fort Smith** Arkansas, C USA 35°23′N 94°24′W
37 T13 **Fort Stanton** New Mexico, SW USA 33°28′N 105°31′W
24 L9 **Fort Stockton** Texas, SW USA 30°54′N 102°54′W
37 U12 **Fort Sumner** New Mexico, SW USA 34°28′N 104°15′W
26 K8 **Fort Supply** Oklahoma, C USA 36°34′N 99°34′W
26 K8 **Fort Supply Lake** ▣ Oklahoma, C USA
29 O10 **Fort Thompson** South Dakota, N USA 44°01′N 99°22′W
Fort-Trinquet *see* Bir Mogreïn
105 R12 **Fortuna** Murcia, SE Spain 38°11′N 01°07′W
34 K3 **Fortuna** California, W USA 40°35′N 124°07′W
28 J2 **Fortuna** North Dakota, N USA 48°53′N 103°46′W
23 T5 **Fort Valley** Georgia, SE USA 32°33′N 83°53′W
11 P11 **Fort Vermilion** Alberta, W Canada 58°22′N 115°59′W
Fort Victoria *see* Masvingo
31 P13 **Fortville** Indiana, N USA 39°55′N 85°51′W
23 P9 **Fort Walton Beach** Florida, SE USA 30°24′N 86°37′W
31 P12 **Fort Wayne** Indiana, N USA 41°08′N 85°08′W
96 H10 **Fort William** N Scotland, United Kingdom 56°49′N 05°07′W
25 T6 **Fort Worth** Texas, SW USA 32°44′N 97°19′W
28 M7 **Fort Yates** North Dakota, N USA 46°05′N 100°37′W
39 S7 **Fort Yukon** Alaska, USA 66°35′N 145°05′W
Forum Alieni *see* Ferrara
Forum Julii *see* Fréjus
Forum Livii *see* Forlì
143 Q15 **Forūr-e Bozorg, Jazīreh-ye** *island* S Iran
94 H7 **Fosen** *physical region* S Norway
161 N14 **Foshan** *var.* Fatshan, Fo-shan, Namhoi. Guangdong, S China 23°03′N 113°08′E
Fo-shan *see* Foshan
194 J6 **Fossil Bluff** *UK research station* Antarctica 71°30′S 68°30′W
Fossa Claudia *see* Chioggia
106 B9 **Fossano** Piemonte, NW Italy 44°33′N 07°43′E
99 H21 **Fosses-la-Ville** Namur, S Belgium 50°24′N 04°42′E
32 J12 **Fossil** Oregon, NW USA 45°01′N 120°14′W
Foss Lake *see* Foss Reservoir
106 I11 **Fossombrone** Marche, C Italy 43°42′N 12°48′E
26 K10 **Foss Reservoir** *var.* Foss Lake. ▣ Oklahoma, C USA
29 S4 **Fosston** Minnesota, N USA 47°34′N 95°45′W
183 O13 **Foster** Victoria, SE Australia 38°40′S 146°15′E
11 T12 **Foster Lakes** ◎ Saskatchewan, C Canada
31 S12 **Fostoria** Ohio, N USA 41°09′N 83°25′W
79 D19 **Fougamou** Ngounié, C Gabon 01°16′S 10°30′E
102 J6 **Fougères** Ille-et-Vilaine, NW France 48°21′N 01°12′W
Fou-hsin *see* Fuxin
27 S14 **Fouke** Arkansas, C USA 33°15′N 93°53′W
96 K2 **Foula** *island* NE Scotland, United Kingdom
65 D24 **Foul Bay** *bay* East Falkland, Falkland Islands
97 P21 **Foulness Island** *island* SE England, United Kingdom
185 F15 **Foulwind, Cape** *headland* South Island, New Zealand 41°45′S 171°28′E
79 E15 **Foumban** Ouest, NW Cameroon 05°43′N 10°50′E
172 H13 **Foumbouni** Grande Comore, NW Comoros 11°49′S 43°30′E
195 N8 **Foundation Ice Stream** *glacier* Antarctica
37 T6 **Fountain** Colorado, C USA 38°40′N 104°42′W
36 L4 **Fountain Green** Utah, W USA 39°37′N 111°37′W
21 P11 **Fountain Inn** South Carolina, SE USA 34°41′N 82°12′W
27 S11 **Fourche LaFave River** ⇝ Arkansas, C USA
33 Z13 **Four Corners** Wyoming, C USA 44°04′N 104°08′W
103 Q2 **Fourmies** Nord, N France 50°01′N 04°03′E
38 J17 **Four Mountains, Islands of** *island group* Aleutian Islands, Alaska, USA
173 P17 **Fournaise, Piton de la** ⛰ SE Réunion 21°14′S 55°43′E
14 J8 **Fournière, Lac** ◎ Québec, SE Canada
115 L20 **Fournoi** *island* Dodekánisa, Greece, Aegean Sea
64 K13 **Four North Fracture Zone** *tectonic feature* W Atlantic Ocean
Fouron-Saint-Martin *see* Sint-Martens-Voeren
30 L3 **Fourteen Mile Point** *headland* Michigan, N USA 46°59′N 89°07′W
Fou-shan *see* Fushun
76 I13 **Fouta Djallon** *var.* Futa Jallon. ▲ W Guinea
185 C25 **Foveaux Strait** *strait* S New Zealand
35 Q11 **Fowler** California, W USA 36°35′N 119°40′W
37 U6 **Fowler** Colorado, C USA 38°07′N 104°01′W
31 N12 **Fowler** Indiana, N USA 40°36′N 87°20′W
182 D7 **Fowlers Bay** *bay* South Australia
25 R13 **Fowlerton** Texas, SW USA 28°27′N 98°48′W
142 M3 **Fowman** *var.* Fuman, Fumen. Gīlān, NW Iran 37°15′N 49°19′E
65 C25 **Fox Bay East** West Falkland, Falkland Islands
65 C25 **Fox Bay West** West Falkland, Falkland Islands
14 J14 **Foxboro** Ontario, SE Canada 44°16′N 77°23′W
11 O14 **Fox Creek** Alberta, W Canada 54°25′N 116°57′W
64 G5 **Foxe Basin** *sea* Nunavut, N Canada
64 G5 **Foxe Channel** *channel* Nunavut, N Canada
95 I16 **Foxen** ◎ C Sweden
9 Q7 **Foxe Peninsula** *peninsula* Baffin Island, Nunavut, NE Canada
185 E19 **Fox Glacier** West Coast, South Island, New Zealand 43°28′S 170°00′E
38 L17 **Fox Islands** *island* Aleutian Islands, Alaska, USA
30 M10 **Fox Lake** Illinois, N USA 42°24′N 88°10′W
9 V12 **Fox Mine** Manitoba, C Canada 56°36′N 101°48′W
35 R3 **Fox Mountain** ▲ Nevada, W USA 41°01′N 119°30′W
65 E25 **Fox Point** *headland* East Falkland, Falkland Islands 51°55′S 58°24′W
30 M11 **Fox River** ⇝ Illinois/ Wisconsin, N USA
30 L7 **Fox River** ⇝ Wisconsin, N USA
184 L13 **Foxton** Manawatu-Wanganui, North Island, New Zealand 40°27′S 175°18′E
11 S16 **Fox Valley** Saskatchewan, S Canada 50°29′N 109°29′W
11 W16 **Foxwarren** Manitoba, S Canada 50°30′N 101°09′W
97 E14 **Foyle, Lough** *Ir.* Loch Feabhail. *inlet* N Ireland
194 H5 **Foyn Coast** *physical region* Antarctica
104 I2 **Foz** Galicia, NW Spain 43°33′N 07°16′W
60 I12 **Foz do Areia, Represa de** ▣ S Brazil
59 A16 **Foz do Breu** Acre, W Brazil 09°21′S 72°41′W
83 A16 **Foz do Cunene** Namibe, SW Angola 17°11′S 11°52′E
60 G12 **Foz do Iguaçu** Paraná, S Brazil 25°33′S 54°31′W
58 C12 **Foz do Mamoriá** Amazonas, NW Brazil 02°28′S 66°06′W
105 T6 **Fraga** Aragón, NE Spain 41°32′N 00°21′E
44 F5 **Fragoso, Cayo** *island* C Cuba
61 G18 **Fraile Muerto** Cerro Largo, NE Uruguay 32°30′S 54°30′W
99 H21 **Fraire** Namur, S Belgium 50°16′N 04°30′E
99 L21 **Fraiture, Baraque de** *hill* SE Belgium
Frakštát *see* Hlohovec
197 S10 **Fram Basin** *var.* Amundsen Basin. *undersea feature* Arctic Ocean 88°00′N 90°00′E
99 F20 **Frameries** Hainaut, S Belgium 50°25′N 03°41′E
19 O11 **Framingham** Massachusetts, NE USA 42°15′N 71°24′W
60 L7 **Franca** São Paulo, S Brazil 20°33′S 47°27′W
187 O15 **Français, Récif des** *reef* W New Caledonia
107 K14 **Francavilla al Mare** Abruzzo, C Italy 42°25′N 14°16′E
107 P18 **Francavilla Fontana** Puglia, SE Italy 40°32′N 17°35′E
102 M8 **France** *off.* French Republic, *It./Sp.* Francia; *prev.* Gaul, Gaule, *Lat.* Gallia. ◆ *republic* W Europe
45 O8 **Francés Viejo, Cabo** *headland* NE Dominican Republic 19°39′N 69°57′W
79 F19 **Franceville** *var.* Massoukou, Masuku. Haut-Ogooué, E Gabon 01°40′S 13°31′E
79 F19 **Franceville** ✕ Haut-Ogooué, E Gabon 01°38′S 13°24′E
Francfort *see* Frankfurt am Main
103 T8 **Franche-Comté** ◐ *region* E France
Francia *see* France
29 O11 **Francis Case, Lake** ▣ South Dakota, N USA
60 H12 **Francisco Beltrão** Paraná, S Brazil 26°05′S 53°04′W
Francisco I. Madero *see* Villa Madero
61 A21 **Francisco Madero** Buenos Aires, E Argentina 35°52′S 62°03′W
42 H6 **Francisco Morazán** *prev.* Tegucigalpa. ◐ *department* C Honduras
83 J18 **Francistown** North East, NE Botswana 21°08′S 27°31′E
Franconian Forest *see* Frankenwald
Franconian Jura *see* Fränkische Alb
98 K6 **Franeker** *Fris.* Frjentsjer. Friesland, N Netherlands 53°11′N 05°33′E
Frankenalb *see* Fränkische Alb
101 H16 **Frankenberg** Hessen, C Germany 51°04′N 08°49′E
101 J20 **Frankenhöhe** *hill range* C Germany
31 R8 **Frankenmuth** Michigan, N USA 43°19′N 83°44′W
101 F20 **Frankenstein** *hill* W Germany
Frankenstein/Frankenstein in Schlesien *see* Ząbkowice Śląskie
101 G20 **Frankenthal** Rheinland-Pfalz, W Germany 49°32′N 08°22′E
101 L18 **Frankenwald** *Eng.* Franconian Forest. ▲ C Germany
44 J12 **Frankfield** C Jamaica 18°08′N 77°22′W
14 J14 **Frankford** Ontario, SE Canada 44°12′N 77°36′W
31 O13 **Frankfort** Indiana, N USA 40°16′N 86°30′W
27 O3 **Frankfort** Kansas, C USA 39°42′N 96°25′W
20 L5 **Frankfort** *state capital* Kentucky, S USA 38°12′N 84°52′W
Frankfort on the Main *see* Frankfurt am Main
Frankfurt *see* Frankfurt am Main, Germany
Frankfurt *see* Słubice, Poland
101 G18 **Frankfurt am Main** *var.* Frankfurt, *Fr.* Francfort; *prev. Eng.* Frankfort on the Main. Hessen, SW Germany 50°07′N 08°41′E
100 Q12 **Frankfurt an der Oder** Brandenburg, E Germany 52°20′N 14°32′E
101 L21 **Fränkische Alb** *var.* Frankenalb, *Eng.* Franconian Jura. ▲ S Germany
101 I18 **Fränkische Saale** ⇝ C Germany
101 L19 **Fränkische Schweiz** *hill range* C Germany
23 R4 **Franklin** Georgia, SE USA 33°15′N 85°06′W
31 P14 **Franklin** Indiana, N USA 39°29′N 86°02′W
20 J7 **Franklin** Kentucky, S USA 36°42′N 86°35′W
22 I9 **Franklin** Louisiana, S USA 29°48′N 91°30′W
29 O17 **Franklin** Nebraska, C USA 40°06′N 98°57′W
21 N10 **Franklin** North Carolina, SE USA 35°12′N 83°23′W
18 C13 **Franklin** Pennsylvania, NE USA 41°24′N 79°49′W
20 J9 **Franklin** Tennessee, S USA 35°55′N 86°52′W
25 U9 **Franklin** Texas, SW USA 31°02′N 96°30′W
21 X7 **Franklin** Virginia, NE USA 36°41′N 76°58′W
21 T4 **Franklin** West Virginia, NE USA 38°39′N 79°21′W
30 M9 **Franklin** Wisconsin, N USA 42°53′N 88°00′W
8 I6 **Franklin Bay** *inlet* Northwest Territories, N Canada
32 K7 **Franklin D. Roosevelt Lake** ▣ Washington, NW USA
35 W4 **Franklin Lake** ◎ Nevada, W USA
185 B22 **Franklin Mountains** ▲ South Island, New Zealand
39 R5 **Franklin Mountains** ▲ Alaska, USA
39 N4 **Franklin, Point** *headland* Alaska, USA 70°54′N 158°48′W
183 O17 **Franklin River** ⇝ Tasmania, SE Australia
22 K8 **Franklinton** Louisiana, S USA 30°51′N 90°09′W
21 U9 **Franklinton** North Carolina, SE USA 36°06′N 78°27′W
Frankstadt *see* Frenštát pod Radhoštěm
25 V7 **Frankston** Texas, SW USA 32°03′N 95°30′W
33 U12 **Frannie** Wyoming, C USA 44°57′N 108°37′W
15 U5 **Franquelin** Québec, SE Canada 49°17′N 67°52′W
15 U5 **Franquelin** ⇝ Québec, SE Canada
83 C18 **Fransfontein** Kunene, NW Namibia 20°12′S 15°01′E
93 H17 **Fränsta** Västernorrland, C Sweden 62°30′N 16°06′E
122 J3 **Frantsa-Iosifa, Zemlya** *Eng.* Franz Josef Land. *island group* N Russian Federation
185 E18 **Franz Josef Glacier** West Coast, South Island, New Zealand 43°22′S 170°11′E
Franz Josef Land *see* Frantsa-Iosifa, Zemlya
Franz-Josef Spitze *see* Gerlachovský štít
101 L23 **Franz Josef Strauss** *abbrev.* F.J.S.. ✕ (München) Bayern, SE Germany 48°07′N 11°43′E
107 A19 **Frasca, Capo della** *headland* Sardegna, Italy, C Mediterranean Sea 39°46′N 08°27′E
107 I15 **Frascati** Lazio, C Italy 41°48′N 12°41′E
11 N14 **Fraser** ⇝ British Columbia, SW Canada
83 G24 **Fraserburg** Western Cape, SW South Africa 31°55′S 21°31′E
96 L8 **Fraserburgh** NE Scotland, United Kingdom 57°42′N 02°20′W
181 Z9 **Fraser Island** *var.* Great Sandy Island. *island* Queensland, E Australia
10 L14 **Fraser Lake** British Columbia, SW Canada 54°00′N 124°45′W
10 L15 **Fraser Plateau** *plateau* British Columbia, SW Canada
184 P10 **Frasertown** Hawke's Bay, North Island, New Zealand 38°58′S 177°25′E
99 E19 **Frasnes-lez-Buissenal** Hainaut, SW Belgium 50°40′N 03°37′E
108 I7 **Frastanz** Vorarlberg, NW Austria 47°13′N 09°38′E
14 B8 **Frater** Ontario, S Canada 47°19′N 84°28′W
Frauenbach *see* Baia Mare
Frauenburg *see* Saldus, Latvia
Frauenburg *see* Frombork, Poland
108 H6 **Frauenfeld** Thurgau, NE Switzerland 47°34′N 08°54′E
109 Z5 **Frauenkirchen** Burgenland, E Austria 47°50′N 16°57′E
61 D19 **Fray Bentos** Río Negro, W Uruguay 33°09′S 58°14′W
61 F19 **Fray Marcos** Florida, S Uruguay 34°13′S 55°43′W
29 S6 **Frazee** Minnesota, N USA 46°42′N 95°40′W
104 M5 **Frechilla** Castilla-León, N Spain 42°08′N 04°50′W
30 I4 **Frederic** Wisconsin, N USA 45°42′N 92°30′W
95 G23 **Fredericia** Vejle, C Denmark 55°34′N 09°47′E
21 W3 **Frederick** Maryland, NE USA 39°25′N 77°25′W
26 L12 **Frederick** Oklahoma, C USA 34°24′N 99°03′W
29 P7 **Frederick** South Dakota, N USA 45°49′N 98°31′W
29 X12 **Fredericksburg** Iowa, C USA 42°58′N 92°12′W
25 R10 **Fredericksburg** Texas, SW USA 30°17′N 98°52′W
21 W5 **Fredericksburg** Virginia, NE USA 38°16′N 77°27′W
39 X13 **Frederick Sound** *sound* Alaska, USA
27 X6 **Fredericktown** Missouri, C USA 37°33′N 90°19′W
60 H13 **Frederico Westphalen** Rio Grande do Sul, S Brazil 27°22′S 53°20′W
13 O15 **Fredericton** *province capital* New Brunswick, SE Canada 45°57′N 66°40′W
95 I22 **Frederiksborg** *off.* Frederiksborgs Amt. ◐ *county* E Denmark
Frederiksborgs Amt *see* Frederiksborg
Frederikshåb *see* Paamiut
95 H19 **Frederikshavn** *prev.* Fladstrand. Nordjylland, N Denmark 57°28′N 10°33′E
95 J22 **Frederikssund** Frederiksborg, E Denmark 55°51′N 12°05′E
45 T9 **Frederiksted** Saint Croix, S Virgin Islands (US) 17°41′N 64°51′W
95 I22 **Frederiksværk** *var.* Frederiksværk og Hanehoved. Frederiksborg, E Denmark 55°58′N 12°02′E
Frederiksværk og Hanehoved *see* Frederiksværk
54 E9 **Fredonia** Antioquia, W Colombia 05°57′N 75°42′W
36 K8 **Fredonia** Arizona, SW USA 36°57′N 112°31′W
27 P7 **Fredonia** Kansas, C USA 37°32′N 95°50′W
18 C11 **Fredonia** New York, NE USA 42°26′N 79°19′W
35 P4 **Fredonyer Pass** *pass* California, W USA
93 I15 **Fredrika** Västerbotten, N Sweden 64°03′N 18°25′E
95 L14 **Fredriksberg** Dalarna, C Sweden 60°07′N 14°23′E
Fredrikshald *see* Halden
Fredrikshamn *see* Hamina
95 H16 **Fredrikstad** Østfold, S Norway 59°12′N 10°57′E
30 K16 **Freeburg** Illinois, N USA 38°25′N 89°54′W
18 K15 **Freehold** New Jersey, NE USA 40°14′N 74°14′W
18 H14 **Freeland** Pennsylvania, NE USA 41°01′N 75°54′W
182 J5 **Freeling Heights** ▲ South Australia 30°09′S 139°24′E
35 Q7 **Freel Peak** ▲ California, W USA 38°52′N 119°52′W
11 Z9 **Freels, Cape** *headland* Newfoundland and Labrador, E Canada 49°16′N 53°30′W
29 Q11 **Freeman** South Dakota, N USA 43°21′N 97°26′W
44 G1 **Freeport** Grand Bahama Island, N Bahamas 26°28′N 78°43′W
30 L10 **Freeport** Illinois, N USA 42°18′N 89°37′W
25 W12 **Freeport** Texas, SW USA 28°57′N 95°21′W
44 G1 **Freeport** ✕ Grand Bahama Island, N Bahamas 26°31′N 78°48′W
25 R14 **Freer** Texas, SW USA 27°52′N 98°37′W
83 I22 **Free State** *off.* Free State Province; *prev.* Orange Free State, *Afr.* Oranje Vrystaat. ◐ *province* C South Africa
Free State *see* Maryland
Free State Province *see* Free State
76 G15 **Freetown** ● (Sierra Leone) W Sierra Leone 08°27′N 13°16′W
172 J16 **Frégate** *island* Inner Islands, NE Seychelles
104 J12 **Fregenal de la Sierra** Extremadura, W Spain 38°10′N 06°39′W
182 C2 **Fregon** South Australia 26°44′S 132°03′E
102 H5 **Fréhel, Cap** *headland* NW France 48°41′N 02°21′W
94 F8 **Frei** Møre og Romsdal, S Norway 63°02′N 07°47′E
101 O16 **Freiberg** Sachsen, E Germany 50°55′N 13°21′E
101 O16 **Freiberger Mulde** ⇝ E Germany
Freiburg *see* Freiburg im Breisgau, Germany
Freiburg *see* Fribourg, Switzerland
101 F23 **Freiburg im Breisgau** *var.* Freiburg, *Fr.* Fribourg-en-Brisgau. Baden-Württemberg, SW Germany 48°N 07°52′E
Freiburg in Schlesien *see* Swiebodzice
Freie Hansestadt Bremen *see* Bremen
Freie und Hansestadt Hamburg *see* Brandenburg
101 L22 **Freising** Bayern, SE Germany 48°24′N 11°45′E
109 T3 **Freistadt** Oberösterreich, N Austria 48°31′N 14°31′E
Freistadtl *see* Hlohovec
101 O16 **Freital** Sachsen, E Germany 51°00′N 13°40′E
Freiwaldau *see* Jeseník
104 J6 **Freixo de Espada à Cinta** Bragança, N Portugal 41°05′N 06°49′W
103 U15 **Fréjus** *anc.* Forum Julii. Var, SE France 43°26′N 06°44′E
180 I13 **Fremantle** Western Australia 32°07′S 115°44′E
35 N9 **Fremont** California, W USA 37°34′N 122°01′W
31 Q11 **Fremont** Indiana, N USA 41°43′N 84°54′W
29 W15 **Fremont** Iowa, C USA 41°12′N 92°26′W
31 P8 **Fremont** Michigan, N USA 43°28′N 85°56′W
29 R15 **Fremont** Nebraska, C USA 41°25′N 96°30′W
31 S11 **Fremont** Ohio, N USA 41°21′N 83°08′W
33 T14 **Fremont Peak** ▲ Wyoming, C USA 43°07′N 109°37′W
36 M6 **Fremont River** ⇝ Utah, W USA
21 O9 **French Broad River** ⇝ Tennessee, S USA
21 N5 **Frenchburg** Kentucky, S USA 37°58′N 83°37′W
18 C12 **French Creek** ⇝ Pennsylvania, NE USA
32 K15 **Frenchglen** Oregon, NW USA 42°49′N 118°55′W
55 Y10 **French Guiana** *var.* Guiana, Guyane. ◇ *French overseas department* N South America
French Guinea *see* Guinea
31 O15 **French Lick** Indiana, N USA 38°33′N 86°37′W
185 J14 **French Pass** Marlborough, South Island, New Zealand 40°57′S 173°49′E
191 T11 **French Polynesia** ◇ *French overseas territory* S Pacific Ocean
French Republic *see* France
14 F11 **French River** ⇝ Ontario, S Canada
French Somaliland *see* Djibouti
173 P12 **French Southern and Antarctic Territories** *Fr.* Terres Australes et Antarctiques Françaises. ◇ *French overseas territory* S Indian Ocean
French Sudan *see* Mali
French Territory of the Afars and Issas *see* Djibouti
French Togoland *see* Togo
74 J6 **Frenda** NW Algeria 35°04′N 01°03′E
111 I18 **Frenštát pod Radhoštěm** *Ger.* Frankstadt. Moravskoslezský Kraj, E Czech Republic 49°33′N 18°10′E
76 M17 **Fresco** S Ivory Coast 05°03′N 05°31′W
195 U16 **Freshfield, Cape** *headland* Antarctica
40 L10 **Fresnillo** *var.* Fresnillo de González Echeverría. Zacatecas, C Mexico 23°11′N 102°53′W
Fresnillo de González Echeverría *see* Fresnillo
35 Q10 **Fresno** California, W USA 36°45′N 119°48′W
Freu, Cabo del *see* Freu, Cap des
105 Y9 **Freu, Cap des** *var.* Cabo del Freu. *cape* Mallorca, Spain, W Mediterranean Sea
101 G22 **Freudenstadt** Baden-Württemberg, SW Germany 48°28′N 08°25′E
Freudenthal *see* Bruntál
183 Q17 **Freycinet Peninsula** *peninsula* Tasmania, SE Australia
76 H14 **Fria** W Guinea 10°27′N 13°38′W
83 A17 **Fria, Cape** *headland* NW Namibia 18°32′S 12°00′E
35 Q10 **Friant** California, W USA 36°56′N 119°44′W
62 K8 **Frías** Catamarca, N Argentina 28°41′S 65°00′W
108 D9 **Fribourg** *Ger.* Freiburg. Fribourg, W Switzerland 46°50′N 07°10′E
108 C9 **Fribourg** *Ger.* Freiburg. ◐ *canton* W Switzerland
Fribourg-en-Brisgau *see* Freiburg im Breisgau
32 G7 **Friday Harbor** San Juan Islands, Washington, NW USA 48°31′N 123°01′W
Friedau *see* Ormož
101 K23 **Friedberg** Bayern, S Germany 48°21′N 10°58′E
101 H18 **Friedberg** Hessen, W Germany 50°19′N 08°46′E
Friedeberg Neumark *see* Strzelce Krajeńskie
Friedek-Mistek *see* Frýdek-Místek
Friedland *see* Pravdinsk
101 I24 **Friedrichshafen** Baden-Württemberg, S Germany 47°39′N 09°29′E
Friedrichstadt *see* Jaunjelgava
29 Q16 **Friend** Nebraska, C USA 40°37′N 97°16′W
Friendly Islands *see* Tonga
55 V9 **Friendship** Coronie, N Surinam 05°50′N 56°16′W
30 L7 **Friendship** Wisconsin, N USA 43°58′N 89°48′W
109 T8 **Friesach** Kärnten, S Austria 46°58′N 14°24′E
Friesche Eilanden *see* Frisian Islands
101 F22 **Friesenheim** Baden-Württemberg, SW Germany 48°27′N 07°56′E
Friesische Inseln *see* Frisian Islands
98 K6 **Friesland** ◐ *province* N Netherlands
60 Q10 **Frio, Cabo** *headland* SE Brazil 23°01′S 41°59′W
24 M3 **Friona** Texas, SW USA 34°38′N 102°43′W
42 L12 **Frío, Río** ⇝ N Costa Rica
25 R13 **Frio River** ⇝ Texas, SW USA
99 M25 **Frisange** Luxembourg, S Luxembourg 49°31′N 06°12′E
Frisches Haff *see* Vistula Lagoon
36 J6 **Frisco Peak** ▲ Utah, W USA 38°31′N 113°17′W
84 F9 **Frisian Islands** *Dut.* Friesche Eilanden, *Ger.* Friesische Inseln. *island group* N Europe
18 L12 **Frissell, Mount** ▲ Connecticut, NE USA 42°01′N 73°25′W
95 J19 **Fristad** Västra Götaland, S Sweden 57°50′N 13°01′E
25 N2 **Fritch** Texas, SW USA 35°38′N 101°36′W
95 J19 **Fritsla** Västra Götaland, S Sweden 57°33′N 12°47′E
101 H16 **Fritzlar** Hessen, C Germany 51°09′N 09°16′E
106 H6 **Friuli-Venezia Giulia** ◐ *region* NE Italy
Frjentsjer *see* Franeker
196 L13 **Frobisher Bay** *inlet* Baffin Island, Nunavut, NE Canada
Frobisher Bay *see* Iqaluit
11 S12 **Frobisher Lake** ◎ Saskatchewan, C Canada
94 G7 **Frohavet** *sound* C Norway
Frohenbruck *see* Veselí nad Lužnicí
109 V7 **Frohnleiten** Steiermark, SE Austria 47°17′N 15°20′E
99 G22 **Froidchapelle** Hainaut, S Belgium 50°10′N 04°18′E
127 O9 **Frolovo** Volgogradskaya Oblast', SW Russian Federation 49°46′N 43°38′E
110 K7 **Frombork** *Ger.* Frauenburg. Warmińsko-Mazurskie, NE Poland 54°21′N 19°40′E
97 L22 **Frome** SW England, United Kingdom 51°15′N 02°22′W
182 I4 **Frome Creek** *seasonal river* South Australia
182 J6 **Frome Downs** South Australia 31°17′S 139°48′E
182 J5 **Frome, Lake** *salt lake* South Australia
Fronicken *see* Wronki
104 H10 **Fronteira** Portalegre, C Portugal 39°03′N 07°39′W
40 M7 **Frontera** Coahuila, NE Mexico 26°55′N 101°27′W
41 U14 **Frontera** Tabasco, SE Mexico 18°32′N 92°39′W
40 G3 **Fronteras** Sonora, NW Mexico 30°51′N 109°33′W
103 Q16 **Frontignan** Hérault, S France 43°27′N 03°45′E
54 D8 **Frontino** Antioquia, NW Colombia 06°46′N 76°10′W
21 V4 **Front Royal** Virginia, NE USA 38°56′N 78°13′W
107 J16 **Frosinone** *anc.* Frusino. Lazio, C Italy 41°38′N 13°22′E
107 K16 **Frosolone** Molise, C Italy 41°34′N 14°25′E
25 U7 **Frost** Texas, SW USA 32°04′N 96°48′W

◆ Country
● Country Capital
◇ Dependent Territory
○ Dependent Territory Capital
◐ Administrative Regions
✕ International Airport
▲ Mountain
▲ Mountain Range
⛰ Volcano
⇝ River
◎ Lake
▣ Reservoir

21 *U2* **Frostburg** Maryland, NE USA *39°39′N 78°55′W*
23 *X13* **Frostproof** Florida, SE USA *27°45′N 81°31′W*
Frostviken *see* Kvarnbergsvattnet
95 *M15* **Frövi** Örebro, C Sweden *59°28′N 15°24′E*
94 *F7* **Frøya** *island* W Norway
37 *P5* **Fruita** Colorado, C USA *39°10′N 108°42′W*
28 *J9* **Fruitdale** South Dakota, N USA *44°39′N 103°38′W*
23 *W11* **Fruitland Park** Florida, SE USA *28°51′N 81°54′W*
Frumentum *see* Formentera
147 *S11* **Frunze** Batkenskaya Oblast', SW Kyrgyzstan *40°07′N 71°40′E*
Frunze *see* Bishkek
117 *O9* **Frunzivka** Odes'ka Oblast', SW Ukraine *47°19′N 29°46′E*
Frusino *see* Frosinone
108 *E9* **Frutigen** Bern, W Switzerland *46°35′N 07°38′E*
111 *I17* **Frýdek-Místek** *Ger.* Friedek-Mistek. Moravskoslezský Kraj, E Czech Republic *49°40′N 18°22′E*
193 *V16* **Fua'amotu** Tongatapu, S Tonga *21°15′S 175°08′W*
190 *A9* **Fuafatu** *island* Funafuti Atoll, C Tuvalu
190 *A9* **Fuagea** *island* Funafuti Atoll, C Tuvalu
190 *B8* **Fualifeke** *atoll* C Tuvalu
190 *A8* **Fualopa** *island* Funafuti Atoll, C Tuvalu
151 *K22* **Fuammulah** *var.* Fuammulah, Gnaviyani. *atoll* S Maldives
Fuammulah *see* Fuammulah
161 *R11* **Fu'an** Fujian, SE China *27°11′N 119°42′E*
Fu-chien *see* Fujian
Fu-chou *see* Fuzhou
164 *G13* **Fuchū** *var.* Hutyû. Hiroshima, Honshū, SW Japan *34°35′N 133°12′E*
160 *M13* **Fuchuan** *var.* Fuyang. Guangxi Zhuangzu Zizhiqu, S China *24°56′N 111°15′E*
165 *R8* **Fudai** Iwate, Honshū, C Japan *39°59′N 141°50′E*
161 *S11* **Fuding** *var.* Tongshan. Fujian, SE China *27°21′N 120°10′E*
81 *J20* **Fudua** *spring/well* S Kenya *02°13′S 39°43′E*
104 *M16* **Fuengirola** Andalucía, S Spain *36°32′N 04°38′W*
104 *J12* **Fuente de Cantos** Extremadura, W Spain *38°15′N 06°18′W*
104 *J11* **Fuente del Maestre** Extremadura, W Spain *38°31′N 06°26′W*
104 *L12* **Fuente Obejuna** Andalucía, S Spain *38°15′N 05°25′W*
104 *L6* **Fuentesaúco** Castilla-León, N Spain *41°14′N 05°30′W*
62 *O3* **Fuerte Olimpo** *var.* Olimpo. Alto Paraguay, NE Paraguay *21°02′S 57°51′W*
40 *H8* **Fuerte, Río** ~ C Mexico
64 *Q11* **Fuerteventura** *island* Islas Canarias, Spain, NE Atlantic Ocean
141 *S14* **Fughmah** *var.* Faghman, Fugma. C Yemen *16°08′N 49°23′E*
92 *M2* **Fuglehuken** *headland* W Svalbard *78°54′N 10°30′E*
Fuglø *see* Fugloy
95 *B18* **Fugloy** *Dan.* Fuglø. *island* NE Faeroe Islands
197 *T15* **Fugløya Bank** *undersea feature* E Norwegian Sea *71°00′N 19°20′E*
Fugma *see* Fughmah
160 *E11* **Fugong** Yunnan, SW China *27°00′N 98°48′E*
81 *K16* **Fugugo** *spring/well* NE Kenya *03°19′N 39°39′E*
158 *L2* **Fuhai** *var.* Burultokay. Xinjiang Uygur Zizhiqu, NW China *47°15′N 87°39′E*
161 *P10* **Fu He** ~ S China
Fuhkien *see* Fujian
100 *J9* **Fuhlsbüttel** ✈ (Hamburg) Hamburg, N Germany *53°37′N 09°57′E*
101 *L14* **Fuhne** ~ C Germany
Fu-hsin *see* Fuxin
Fujairah *see* Al Fujayrah
164 *M14* **Fuji** *var.* Huzi. Shizuoka, Honshū, S Japan *35°08′N 138°39′E*
161 *Q12* **Fujian** *var.* Fu-chien, Fuhkien, Fukien, Min, Fujian Sheng. ◈ *province* SE China
160 *I9* **Fu Jiang** ~ C China
Fujian Sheng *see* Fujian
164 *M14* **Fujieda** *var.* Huzieda. Shizuoka, Honshū, S Japan *34°54′N 138°15′E*
Fuji, Mount/Fujiyama *see* Fuji-san
163 *Y7* **Fujin** Heilongjiang, NE China *47°12′N 132°01′E*
164 *M13* **Fujinomiya** *var.* Huzinomiya. Shizuoka, Honshū, S Japan *35°16′N 138°33′E*
164 *N13* **Fuji-san** *var.* Fujiyama, *Eng.* Mount Fuji. ▲ Honshū, SE Japan *35°23′N 138°44′E*
165 *N14* **Fujisawa** *var.* Huzisawa. Kanagawa, Honshū, S Japan *35°22′N 139°29′E*
165 *T3* **Fukagawa** *var.* Hukagawa. Hokkaidō, NE Japan *43°44′N 142°03′E*
158 *L5* **Fukang** Xinjiang Uygur Zizhiqu, W China *44°07′N 87°55′E*
165 *P7* **Fukaura** Aomori, Honshū, C Japan *40°38′N 139°55′E*
193 *W15* **Fukave** *island* Tongatapu Group, S Tonga
Fukien *see* Fujian
164 *J13* **Fukuchiyama** *var.* Hukutiyama. Kyōto, Honshū, SW Japan *35°19′N 135°08′E*
164 *A14* **Fukue** *var.* Hukue. Nagasaki, Fukue-jima, SW Japan *32°41′N 128°52′E*
164 *A13* **Fukue-jima** *island* Gotō-rettō, SW Japan
164 *K12* **Fukui** *var.* Hukui. Fukui, Honshū, SW Japan *36°03′N 136°12′E*
164 *K12* **Fukui** *off.* Fukui-ken, *var.* Hukui. ◈ *prefecture* Honshū, SW Japan
Fukui-ken *see* Fukui
164 *D13* **Fukuoka** *var.* Hukuoka, *hist.* Najima. Fukuoka, Kyūshū, SW Japan *33°36′N 130°24′E*
164 *D13* **Fukuoka** *off.* Fukuoka-ken, *var.* Hukuoka. ◈ *prefecture* Kyūshū, SW Japan
Fukuoka-ken *see* Fukuoka
165 *Q6* **Fukushima** Hokkaidō, NE Japan *41°27′N 140°14′E*
165 *Q12* **Fukushima** *off.* Fukushima-ken, *var.* Hukusima. ◈ *prefecture* Honshū, C Japan
Fukushima-ken *see* Fukushima
164 *G13* **Fukuyama** *var.* Hukuyama. Hiroshima, Honshū, SW Japan *34°29′N 133°21′E*
76 *G13* **Fulacunda** C Guinea-Bissau *11°44′N 15°03′W*
129 *P8* **Fūlādī, Kūh-e** ▲ E Afghanistan *34°38′N 67°32′E*
187 *Z15* **Fulaga** *island* Lau Group, E Fiji
101 *I17* **Fulda** Hessen, C Germany *50°33′N 09°41′E*
29 *S10* **Fulda** Minnesota, N USA *43°52′N 95°36′W*
101 *I16* **Fulda** ~ C Germany
Fülek *see* Fil'akovo
Fulin *see* Hanyuan
160 *K10* **Fuling** Chongqing Shi, C China *29°45′N 107°23′E*
35 *T15* **Fullerton** California, SE USA *33°53′N 117°55′W*
29 *P15* **Fullerton** Nebraska, C USA *41°21′N 97°58′W*
108 *M8* **Fulpmes** Tirol, W Austria *47°11′N 11°22′E*
20 *G8* **Fulton** Kentucky, S USA *36°31′N 88°52′W*
23 *N2* **Fulton** Mississippi, S USA *34°16′N 88°24′W*
27 *V4* **Fulton** Missouri, C USA *38°50′N 91°57′W*
18 *H9* **Fulton** New York, NE USA *43°18′N 76°22′W*
Fuman/Fumen *see* Fowman
103 *R3* **Fumay** Ardennes, N France *49°58′N 04°42′E*
102 *M13* **Fumel** Lot-et-Garonne, SW France *44°31′N 00°58′E*
190 *B10* **Funafara** *atoll* C Tuvalu
190 *C9* **Funafuti** ✈ Funafuti Atoll, C Tuvalu *08°30′S 179°12′E*
Funafuti *see* Fongafale
190 *F8* **Funafuti Atoll** *atoll* C Tuvalu
Funan *see* Fusui
190 *B9* **Funangongo** *atoll* C Tuvalu
93 *F17* **Funäsdalen** Jämtland, C Sweden *62°33′N 12°33′E*
64 *O6* **Funchal** Madeira, Portugal, NE Atlantic Ocean *32°40′N 16°55′W*
64 *P5* **Funchal** ✈ Madeira, Portugal, NE Atlantic Ocean *32°38′N 16°53′W*
54 *F5* **Fundación** Magdalena, N Colombia *10°31′N 74°09′W*
104 *I8* **Fundão** *var.* Fundáo. Castelo Branco, C Portugal *40°08′N 07°30′W*
Fundáo *see* Fundão
13 *O16* **Fundy, Bay of** *bay* Canada/USA
Fünen *see* Fyn
54 *C13* **Fúnes** Nariño, SW Colombia *0°59′N 77°27′W*
Fünfkirchen *see* Pécs
83 *M19* **Funhalouro** Inhambane, S Mozambique *23°04′S 34°24′E*
161 *R6* **Funing** Jiangsu, E China *33°43′N 119°47′E*
160 *I14* **Funing** *var.* Xinhua. Yunnan, SW China *23°39′N 105°41′E*
160 *M7* **Funiu Shan** ▲▲ C China
77 *U13* **Funtua** Katsina, N Nigeria *11°31′N 07°19′E*
161 *R12* **Fuqing** Fujian, SE China *25°40′N 119°23′E*
83 *M14* **Furancungo** Tete, NW Mozambique *14°51′S 33°39′E*
116 *I15* **Furculești** Teleorman, S Romania *43°51′N 25°07′E*
Füred *see* Balatonfüred
165 *W4* **Füren-ko** ◎ Hokkaidō, NE Japan
Fürg *see* Doborjī
Furluk *see* Fârliug
Fūrmanov/Furmanovka *see* Moyynkum
Furmanovo *see* Zhalpaktal
59 *L20* **Furnas, Represa de** ⊠ SE Brazil
183 *Q14* **Furneaux Group** *island group* Tasmania, SE Australia
Furnes *see* Veurne
160 *J10* **Furong Jiang** ~ S China
138 *I5* **Furqlus** Ḩimş, W Syria *34°40′N 37°02′E*
100 *F12* **Fürstenau** Niedersachsen, NW Germany *52°30′N 07°40′E*
109 *X8* **Fürstenfeld** Steiermark, SE Austria *47°03′N 16°05′E*
101 *L23* **Fürstenfeldbruck** Bayern, S Germany *48°10′N 11°16′E*
100 *P12* **Fürstenwalde** Brandenburg, NE Germany *52°22′N 14°04′E*
101 *K20* **Fürth** Bayern, S Germany *49°29′N 10°59′E*
109 *W3* **Furth bei Göttweig** Niederösterreich, NW Austria *48°22′N 15°33′E*
165 *R3* **Furubira** Hokkaidō, NE Japan *43°14′N 140°38′E*
94 *L12* **Furudal** Dalarna, C Sweden *61°10′N 15°07′E*
164 *L12* **Furukawa** *var.* Hida. Gifu, Honshū, SW Japan *36°13′N 137°11′E*
165 *Q10* **Furukawa** *var.* Hurukawa, Ōsaki. Miyagi, Honshū, C Japan *38°36′N 140°57′E*
54 *F10* **Fusagasugá** Cundinamarca, C Colombia *04°22′N 74°21′W*
Fusan *see* Pusan
Fushë-Arëzi/Fushë-Arrësi *see* Fushë-Arrëz
113 *L18* **Fushë-Arrëz** *var.* Fushë-Arëzi, Fushë-Arrësi. Shkodër, N Albania *42°05′N 20°01′E*
113 *N16* **Fushë Kosovë** *Serb.* Kosovo Polje. C Kosovo *42°40′N 21°07′E*
Fushë-Kruja *see* Fushë-Krujë
113 *K19* **Fushë-Krujë** *var.* Fushë-Kruja. Durrës, C Albania *41°30′N 19°43′E*
163 *V12* **Fushun** *var.* Fou-shan, Fu-shun. Liaoning, NE China *41°50′N 123°54′E*
Fu-shun *see* Fushun
Fusin *see* Fuxin
108 *G10* **Fusio** Ticino, S Switzerland *46°27′N 08°39′E*
163 *X11* **Fusong** Jilin, NE China *42°20′N 127°17′E*
101 *K24* **Füssen** Bayern, S Germany *47°34′N 10°43′E*
160 *K15* **Fusui** *var.* Xinning; *prev.* Funan. Guangxi Zhuangzu Zizhiqu, S China *22°39′N 107°49′E*
Futa Jallon *see* Fouta Djallon
63 *G18* **Futaleufú** Los Lagos, S Chile *43°14′S 71°50′W*
112 *K10* **Futog** Vojvodina, NW Serbia *45°15′N 19°43′E*
165 *O14* **Futtsu** *var.* Huttu. Chiba, Honshū, S Japan *35°11′N 139°52′E*
187 *S15* **Futuna** *island* S Vanuatu
190 *D12* **Futuna, Île** *island* S Wallis and Futuna
161 *Q11* **Futun Xi** ~ SE China
160 *L5* **Fuxian** *var.* Fu Xian. Shaanxi, C China *36°03′N 109°19′E*
Fuxian *see* Wafangdian
Fu Xian *see* Fuxian
160 *G13* **Fuxian Hu** ⊠ SW China
163 *U12* **Fuxin** *var.* Fou-hsin, Fu-hsin, Fusin. Liaoning, NE China *41°59′N 121°40′E*
Fuxing *see* Wangmo
161 *P7* **Fuyang** Anhui, E China *32°52′N 115°51′E*
Fuyang *see* Fuchuan
161 *O4* **Fuyang He** ~ E China
163 *U7* **Fuyu** Heilongjiang, NE China *47°48′N 124°26′E*
163 *Z6* **Fuyuan** Heilongjiang, NE China *48°20′N 134°22′E*
Fuyu/Fu-yü *see* Songyuan
158 *M3* **Fuyun** *var.* Koktokay. Xinjiang Uygur Zizhiqu, NW China *46°58′N 89°30′E*
111 *L22* **Füzesabony** Heves, E Hungary *47°46′N 20°25′E*
161 *R12* **Fuzhou** *var.* Foochow, Fu-chou. *province capital* Fujian, SE China *26°09′N 119°17′E*
161 *P11* **Fuzhou** Jiangxi, S China *27°58′N 116°20′E*
137 *W13* **Füzuli** *Rus.* Fizuli. SW Azerbaijan *39°33′N 47°09′E*
119 *I20* **Fyadory** *Rus.* Fëdory. Brestskaya Voblasts', SW Belarus *51°57′N 26°24′E*
95 *G24* **Fyn** *off.* Fyns Amt, *var.* Fünen. ◈ *county* C Denmark
95 *G23* **Fyn** *Ger.* Fünen. *island* C Denmark
96 *H12* **Fyne, Loch** *inlet* W Scotland, United Kingdom
Fyns Amt *see* Fyn
95 *E16* **Fyresvatnet** ◎ S Norway
FYR Macedonia/FYROM *see* Macedonia, FYR
Fyzabad *see* Feyẕābād

G

Gaafu Alifu Atoll *see* North Huvadhu Atoll
81 *O14* **Gaalkacyo** *var.* Galka'yo, *It.* Galcaio. Mudug, C Somalia *06°42′N 47°24′E*
146 *J11* **Gabakly** *Rus.* Kabakly. Lebap Welaýaty, NE Turkmenistan *39°45′N 62°30′E*
114 *H8* **Gabare** Vratsa, NW Bulgaria *43°20′N 23°57′E*
102 *K15* **Gabas** ~ SW France
Gabasumdo *see* Tongde
35 *T7* **Gabbs** Nevada, W USA *38°51′N 117°55′W*
82 *B12* **Gabela** Cuanza Sul, W Angola *10°50′S 14°21′E*
Gaberones *see* Gaborone
189 *X14* **Gabert** *island* Caroline Islands, E Micronesia
74 *M7* **Gabès** *var.* Qābis. E Tunisia *33°53′N 10°03′E*
74 *M6* **Gabès, Golfe de** *Ar.* Khalīj Qābis. *gulf* E Tunisia
Gablonz an der Neisse *see* Jablonec nad Nisou
Gablös *see* Cavalese
79 *E18* **Gabon** *off.* Gabonese Republic. ◆ *republic* C Africa
Gabonese Republic *see* Gabon
83 *I20* **Gaborone** *prev.* Gaberones. ● (Botswana) South East, SE Botswana *24°42′S 25°50′E*
83 *I20* **Gaborone** ✈ South East, SE Botswana *24°45′S 25°49′E*
104 *K8* **Gabriel y Galán, Embalse de** ⊠ W Spain
143 *U15* **Gābrīk, Rūd-e** ~ SE Iran
114 *J9* **Gabrovo** Gabrovo, N Bulgaria *42°54′N 25°19′E*
114 *J9* **Gabrovo** ◈ *province* N Bulgaria
76 *H12* **Gabú** *prev.* Nova Lamego. E Guinea-Bissau *12°16′N 14°09′W*
29 *O6* **Gackle** North Dakota, N USA *46°34′N 99°07′W*
113 *I15* **Gacko** Repulika Srpska, S Bosnia and Herzegovina *43°08′N 18°29′E*
155 *F17* **Gadag** Karnātaka, W India *15°25′N 75°37′E*
93 *G15* **Gäddede** Jämtland, C Sweden *64°30′N 14°15′E*
159 *S12* **Gadê** *var.* Kequ; *prev.* Pagqên. Qinghai, C China *33°56′N 99°49′E*
Gades/Gadier/Gadir/Gadire *see* Cádiz
105 *P15* **Gádor, Sierra de** ▲▲ S Spain
149 *S15* **Gadra** Sind, SE Pakistan *25°39′N 70°28′E*
23 *Q3* **Gadsden** Alabama, S USA *34°00′N 86°00′W*
36 *H15* **Gadsden** Arizona, SW USA *32°33′N 114°45′W*
Gadyach *see* Hadyach
124 *J3* **Gadzhiyevo** Murmanskaya Oblast', NW Russian Federation *69°16′N 33°20′E*
79 *H15* **Gadzi** Mambéré-Kadéï, SW Central African Republic *04°46′N 16°42′E*
116 *J13* **Găești** Dâmbovița, S Romania *44°42′N 25°19′E*
107 *J17* **Gaeta** Lazio, C Italy *41°12′N 13°35′E*
107 *J17* **Gaeta, Golfo di** *var.* Gulf of Gaeta. *gulf* C Italy
Gaeta, Gulf of *see* Gaeta, Golfo di
188 *L14* **Gaferut** *atoll* Caroline Islands, W Micronesia
21 *Q10* **Gaffney** South Carolina, SE USA *35°03′N 81°40′W*
Gäfle *see* Gävle
Gäfleborg *see* Gävleborg
74 *M6* **Gafsa** *var.* Qafşah. W Tunisia *34°25′N 08°52′E*
Gafurov *see* Ghafurov
126 *J3* **Gagarin** *prev.* Gzhatsk. Smolenskaya Oblast', W Russian Federation *53°33′N 35°00′E*
147 *O10* **Gagarin** Jizzax Viloyati, C Uzbekistan *40°40′N 68°04′E*
101 *G21* **Gaggenau** Baden-Württemberg, SW Germany *48°48′N 08°19′E*
188 *F16* **Gagil Tamil** *var.* Gagil-Tomil. *island* Caroline Islands, W Micronesia
Gagil-Tomil *see* Gagil Tamil
127 *O4* **Gagino** Nizhegorodskaya Oblast', W Russian Federation *55°18′N 45°01′E*
107 *Q19* **Gagliano del Capo** Puglia, SE Italy *39°49′N 18°22′E*
94 *L13* **Gagnef** Dalarna, C Sweden *60°34′N 15°04′E*
76 *M17* **Gagnoa** C Ivory Coast *06°11′N 05°56′W*
13 *N10* **Gagnon** Québec, E Canada *51°56′N 68°16′W*
Gago Coutinho *see* Lumbala N'Guimbo
137 *P8* **Gagra** NW Georgia *43°17′N 40°18′E*
31 *S13* **Gahanna** Ohio, N USA *40°01′N 82°52′W*
143 *R13* **Gahkom** Hormozgān, S Iran *28°14′N 55°48′E*
Gahnpa *see* Ganta
57 *Q19* **Gaíba, Laguna** ◎ E Bolivia
153 *T13* **Gaibandha** *var.* Gaibanda. Rajshahi, NW Bangladesh *25°21′N 89°36′E*
Gaibhlte, Cnoc Mór na n *see* Galtymore Mountain
109 *R9* **Gail** ~ S Austria
101 *I21* **Gaildorf** Baden-Württemberg, S Germany *48°41′N 10°08′E*
103 *N15* **Gaillac** *var.* Gaillac-sur-Tarn. Tarn, S France *43°54′N 01°54′E*
Gaillac-sur-Tarn *see* Gaillac
Gaillimh *see* Galway
Gaillimhe, Cuan na *see* Galway Bay
109 *Q9* **Gailtaler Alpen** ▲▲ S Austria
63 *J17* **Gaimán** Chaco, S Argentina *43°15′S 65°30′W*
20 *K8* **Gainesboro** Tennessee, S USA *36°20′N 85°41′W*
23 *V10* **Gainesville** Florida, SE USA *29°39′N 82°19′W*
23 *T2* **Gainesville** Georgia, SE USA *34°18′N 83°49′W*
27 *U8* **Gainesville** Missouri, C USA *36°37′N 92°28′W*
25 *T5* **Gainesville** Texas, SW USA *33°39′N 97°08′W*
109 *X5* **Gainfarn** Niederösterreich, NE Austria *47°59′N 16°11′E*
97 *N18* **Gainsborough** E England, United Kingdom *53°24′N 00°48′W*
182 *G6* **Gairdner, Lake** *salt lake* South Australia
Gaissane *see* Gáissát
92 *L8* **Gáissát** *var.* Gaissane. ▲▲ N Norway
43 *T15* **Gaital, Cerro** ▲ C Panama *08°37′N 80°04′W*
21 *W3* **Gaithersburg** Maryland, NE USA *39°08′N 77°13′W*
163 *U13* **Gaizhou** Liaoning, NE China *40°24′N 122°17′E*
Gaizina Kalns *see* Gaiziņkalns
118 *H7* **Gaiziņkalns** *var.* Gaizina Kalns. ▲ E Latvia *56°51′N 25°58′E*
Gajac *see* Villeneuve-sur-Lot
39 *S10* **Gakona** Alaska, USA *62°21′N 145°16′W*
158 *M16* **Gala** Xizang Zizhiqu, China *28°17′N 89°21′E*
Galaassiya *see* Galaosiyo
Ğalāğıl *see* Jalājil
Galam, Pulau *see* Gelam, Pulau
62 *J6* **Galán, Cerro** ▲ NW Argentina *25°54′S 66°45′W*
111 *H21* **Galanta** *Hung.* Galánta. Trnavský Kraj, W Slovakia *48°12′N 17°45′E*
146 *L11* **Galaosiyo** *Rus.* Galaassiya. Buxoro Viloyati, C Uzbekistan *39°53′N 64°25′E*
57 *B17* **Galápagos** *off.* Provincia de Galápagos. ◈ *province* W Ecuador, E Pacific Ocean
193 *P8* **Galapagos Fracture Zone** *tectonic feature* E Pacific Ocean
Galapagos Islands *see* Colón, Archipiélago de
Galápagos, Islas de los *see* Colón, Archipiélago de
Galápagos, Provincia de *see* Galápagos
193 *S9* **Galapagos Rise** *undersea feature* E Pacific Ocean *15°00′S 97°00′W*
96 *K13* **Galashiels** SE Scotland, United Kingdom *55°37′N 02°49′W*
116 *M12* **Galați** *Ger.* Galatz. Galați, E Romania *45°27′N 28°00′E*
116 *L12* **Galați** ◈ *county* E Romania
107 *Q19* **Galatina** Puglia, SE Italy *40°10′N 18°10′E*
107 *Q19* **Galatone** Puglia, SE Italy *40°09′N 18°05′E*
Galatz *see* Galați
21 *R8* **Galax** Virginia, NE USA *36°40′N 88°56′W*
146 *J16* **Galaýmor** *Rus.* Kala-i-Mor. Mary Welaýaty, S Turkmenistan *35°40′N 62°28′E*
Galcaio *see* Gaalkacyo
64 *P11* **Gáldar** Gran Canaria, Islas Canarias, NE Atlantic Ocean *28°09′N 15°40′W*
94 *F11* **Galdhøpiggen** ▲ S Norway *61°30′N 08°08′E*
40 *I4* **Galeana** Chihuahua, N Mexico *30°08′N 107°38′W*
41 *O9* **Galeana** Nuevo León, NE Mexico *24°45′N 99°59′W*
60 *P9* **Galeão** ✈ (Rio de Janeiro) Rio de Janeiro, SE Brazil *22°48′S 43°16′W*
171 *R10* **Galela** Pulau Halmahera, E Indonesia *01°52′N 127°48′E*
39 *O9* **Galena** Alaska, USA *64°43′N 156°55′W*
30 *K10* **Galena** Illinois, N USA *42°25′N 90°25′W*
27 *R7* **Galena** Kansas, C USA *37°04′N 94°38′W*
27 *T8* **Galena** Missouri, C USA *36°45′N 93°30′W*
45 *V15* **Galeota Point** *headland* Trinidad, Trinidad and Tobago *10°07′N 60°59′W*
105 *P13* **Galera** Andalucía, S Spain *37°45′N 02°33′W*
45 *Y16* **Galera Point** *headland* Trinidad, Trinidad and Tobago *10°49′N 60°54′W*
56 *A5* **Galera, Punta** *headland* NW Ecuador *0°49′N 80°03′W*
30 *K12* **Galesburg** Illinois, N USA *40°57′N 90°22′W*
30 *J7* **Galesville** Wisconsin, N USA *44°04′N 91°21′W*
18 *F12* **Galeton** Pennsylvania, NE USA *41°43′N 77°38′W*
116 *H9* **Gâlgău** *Hung.* Galgó; *prev.* Gîlgău. Sălaj, NW Romania *47°17′N 23°43′E*
Galgó *see* Gâlgău
Galgóc *see* Hlohovec
81 *N15* **Galguduud** *off.* Gobolka Galguduud. ◈ *region* E Somalia
Galguduud, Gobolka *see* Galguduud
137 *Q9* **Gali** W Georgia *42°40′N 41°39′E*
125 *N14* **Galich** Kostromskaya Oblast', NW Russian Federation *58°21′N 42°21′E*
114 *H7* **Galiche** Vratsa, NW Bulgaria *43°36′N 23°53′E*
104 *H3* **Galicia** *anc.* Gallaecia. ◈ *autonomous community* NW Spain
64 *M8* **Galicia Bank** *undersea feature* E Atlantic Ocean *11°45′W 42°40′N*
Galilee *see* HaGalil
181 *W7* **Galilee, Lake** ◎ Queensland, NE Australia
Galilee, Sea of *see* Tiberias, Lake
106 *E11* **Galileo Galilei** ✈ (Pisa) Toscana, C Italy *43°40′N 10°22′E*
31 *S12* **Galion** Ohio, N USA *40°43′N 82°47′W*
Galka'yo *see* Gaalkacyo
146 *K12* **Galkynyş** *prev. Rus.* Deynau, Dyanev, *Turkm.* Dänew. Lebap Welaýaty, NE Turkmenistan *39°16′N 63°10′E*
80 *H11* **Gallabat** Gedaref, E Sudan *12°57′N 36°10′E*
Gallaecia *see* Galicia
147 *O11* **G'allaorol** Jizzax Viloyati, C Uzbekistan *40°01′N 67°30′E*
106 *C7* **Gallarate** Lombardia, NW Italy *45°39′N 08°47′E*
27 *S2* **Gallatin** Missouri, C USA *39°54′N 93°57′W*
20 *J8* **Gallatin** Tennessee, S USA *36°22′N 86°28′W*
33 *R11* **Gallatin Peak** ▲ Montana, NW USA *45°22′N 111°21′W*
33 *R12* **Gallatin River** ~ Montana/Wyoming, NW USA
155 *J26* **Galle** *prev.* Point de Galle. Southern Province, SW Sri Lanka *06°04′N 80°12′E*
105 *S5* **Gállego** ~ NE Spain
193 *Q8* **Gallego Rise** *undersea feature* E Pacific Ocean *02°00′S 115°00′W*
Gallegos *see* Río Gallegos
63 *H23* **Gallegos, Río** ~ Argentina/Chile
Gallia *see* France
22 *K10* **Galliano** Louisiana, S USA *29°26′N 90°18′W*
114 *G13* **Gallikós** ~ N Greece
37 *S12* **Gallinas Peak** ▲ New Mexico, SW USA *34°14′N 105°47′W*
54 *H3* **Gallinas, Punta** *headland* NE Colombia *12°27′N 71°44′W*
37 *T11* **Gallinas River** ~ New Mexico, SW USA
107 *Q19* **Gallipoli** Puglia, SE Italy *40°08′N 18°E*
Gallipoli *see* Gelibolu
Gallipoli Peninsula *see* Gelibolu Yarımadası
31 *T15* **Gallipolis** Ohio, N USA *38°49′N 82°14′W*
92 *J12* **Gällivare** *Lapp.* Váhtjer. Norrbotten, N Sweden *67°08′N 20°39′E*
109 *T4* **Gallneukirchen** Oberösterreich, N Austria *48°22′N 14°25′E*
93 *G17* **Gällö** Jämtland, C Sweden *62°57′N 15°15′E*
105 *Q7* **Gallo** ~ C Spain
107 *I23* **Gallo, Capo** *headland* Sicilia, Italy, C Mediterranean Sea *38°13′N 13°18′E*
37 *P13* **Gallo Mountains** ▲▲ New Mexico, SW USA
18 *G8* **Galloo Island** *island* New York, NE USA
97 *H15* **Galloway, Mull of** *headland* S Scotland, United Kingdom *54°37′N 04°54′W*
37 *P10* **Gallup** New Mexico, SW USA *35°32′N 108°45′W*
105 *R5* **Gallur** Aragón, NE Spain *41°51′N 01°21′W*
Gâlma *see* Guelma
163 *N9* **Galshar** *var.* Buyant. Hentiy, C Mongolia *46°15′N 110°50′E*
162 *I6* **Galt** *var.* Ider. Hövsgöl, C Mongolia *48°45′N 99°52′E*
35 *O8* **Galt** California, W USA *38°13′N 121°19′W*
74 *C10* **Galtat-Zemmour** C Western Sahara *25°07′N 12°21′W*
95 *G22* **Galten** Århus, C Denmark *56°09′N 09°54′E*
97 *D20* **Galtymore Mountain** *Ir.* Cnoc Mór na nGaibhlte. ▲ S Ireland *52°21′N 08°09′W*
97 *D20* **Galty Mountains** *Ir.* Na Gaibhlte. ▲▲ S Ireland
30 *K11* **Galva** Illinois, N USA *41°10′N 90°02′W*
25 *X12* **Galveston** Texas, SW USA *29°17′N 94°48′W*
25 *W11* **Galveston Bay** *inlet* Texas, SW USA
25 *W12* **Galveston Island** *island* Texas, SW USA
61 *B18* **Gálvez** Santa Fe, C Argentina *32°03′S 61°14′W*
97 *C18* **Galway** *Ir.* Gaillimh. W Ireland *53°16′N 09°03′W*
97 *B18* **Galway** *Ir.* Gaillimh. *cultural region* W Ireland
97 *B18* **Galway Bay** *Ir.* Cuan na Gaillimhe. *bay* W Ireland
83 *F18* **Gam** Otjozondjupa, NE Namibia *20°10′S 20°51′E*
164 *L14* **Gamagōri** Aichi, Honshū, SW Japan *34°49′N 137°15′E*
54 *F7* **Gamarra** Cesar, N Colombia *08°21′N 73°46′W*
Gámas *see* Kaamanen
158 *L17* **Gamba** Xizang Zizhiqu, W China *28°13′N 88°32′E*
Gamba *see* Zamtang
77 *P14* **Gambaga** NE Ghana *10°32′N 00°28′W*
80 *G13* **Gambēla** Gambēla Hizboch, W Ethiopia *08°09′N 34°15′E*
81 *H14* **Gambēla** ◈ *federal region* W Ethiopia
38 *K10* **Gambell** Saint Lawrence Island, Alaska, USA *63°44′N 171°41′W*
76 *E12* **Gambia** *off.* Republic of The Gambia, The Gambia. ◆ *republic* W Africa
76 *I12* **Gambia** *Fr.* Gambie. ~ W Africa
64 *K12* **Gambia Plain** *undersea feature* E Atlantic Ocean
Gambia, Republic of The *see* Gambia
Gambia, The *see* Gambia
Gambie *see* Gambia
31 *T13* **Gambier** Ohio, N USA *40°22′N 82°24′W*
191 *Y13* **Gambier, Îles** *island group* E French Polynesia
182 *G10* **Gambier Islands** *island group* South Australia
79 *H19* **Gamboma** Plateaux, E Congo *01°53′S 15°51′E*
79 *G16* **Gamboula** Mambéré-Kadéï, SW Central African Republic *04°09′N 15°12′E*
37 *P10* **Gamerco** New Mexico, SW USA *35°34′N 108°45′W*
137 *V12* **Gamış Dağı** ▲ W Azerbaijan *40°18′N 46°15′E*
Gamlakarleby *see* Kokkola
95 *N18* **Gamleby** Kalmar, S Sweden *57°54′N 16°25′E*
Gammelstad *see* Gammelstaden
93 *J14* **Gammelstaden** *var.* Gammelstad. Norrbotten, N Sweden *65°38′N 22°05′E*
Gammouda *see* Sidi Bouzid
155 *J25* **Gampaha** Western Province, W Sri Lanka *07°05′N 80°00′E*
155 *K25* **Gampola** Central Province, C Sri Lanka *07°10′N 80°34′E*
167 *S5* **Gâm, Sông** ~ N Vietnam
92 *L7* **Gamvik** Finnmark, N Norway *71°04′N 28°08′E*
150 *H13* **Gan** Addu Atoll, C Maldives
Gan *see* Gansu, China
Gan *see* Jiangxi, China
Ganaane *see* Juba
37 *O10* **Ganado** Arizona, SW USA *35°42′N 109°31′W*
25 *U12* **Ganado** Texas, SW USA *29°02′N 96°30′W*
14 *L14* **Gananoque** Ontario, SE Canada *44°21′N 76°11′W*
Ganāveh *see* Bandar-e Gonāveh
137 *V11* **Gäncä** *Rus.* Gyandzha; *prev.* Kirovabad, Yelisavetpol. W Azerbaijan *40°42′N 46°23′E*
Ganchi *see* Ghonchí
Gand *see* Gent
82 *B13* **Ganda** *var.* Mariano Machado, *Port.* Vila Mariano Machado. Benguela, W Angola *13°02′S 14°40′E*
79 *L22* **Gandajika** Kasai-Oriental, S Dem. Rep. Congo *06°42′S 24°01′E*
153 *O12* **Gandak** *Nep.* Nārāyāni. ~ India/Nepal
149 *P12* **Gandāva** Baluchistān, SW Pakistan *28°37′N 67°29′E*
13 *U11* **Gander** Newfoundland and Labrador, SE Canada *48°56′N 54°33′W*
13 *U11* **Gander** ✈ Newfoundland and Labrador, E Canada *49°03′N 54°49′W*
100 *G11* **Ganderkesee** Niedersachsen, NW Germany *53°01′N 08°33′E*
105 *T7* **Gandesa** Cataluña, NE Spain *41°03′N 00°26′E*
154 *B10* **Gāndhīdhām** Gujarāt, W India *23°08′N 70°05′E*
154 *D10* **Gāndhīnagar** *state capital* Gujarāt, W India *23°12′N 72°37′E*
154 *F9* **Gāndhi Sāgar** ◎ C India
105 *T11* **Gandía** País Valenciano, E Spain *38°59′N 00°11′W*
159 *O10* **Gang** Qinghai, W China
152 *G9* **Gangānagar** Rājasthān, NW India *29°54′N 73°56′E*
152 *I12* **Gangāpur** Rājasthān, N India *26°30′N 76°49′E*
153 *S17* **Ganga Sāgar** West Bengal, NE India *21°39′N 88°05′E*
Gangavathi *see* Gangāwati
155 *G17* **Gangāwati** *var.* Gangavathi. Karnātaka, C India *15°26′N 76°35′E*
159 *S9* **Gangca** *var.* Shaliuhe. Qinghai, C China *37°21′N 100°09′E*
158 *H14* **Gangdisê Shan** *Eng.* Kailas Range. ▲▲ W China
103 *Q15* **Ganges** Hérault, S France *43°57′N 03°42′E*
153 *P13* **Ganges** *Ben.* Padma. ~ Bangladesh/India *see also* Padma
Ganges *see* Padma
Ganges Cone *see* Ganges Fan
173 *S3* **Ganges Fan** *var.* Ganges Cone. *undersea feature* N Bay of Bengal *12°00′N 87°00′E*
153 *U17* **Ganges, Mouths of the** *delta* Bangladesh/India
107 *K23* **Gangi** *anc.* Engyum. Sicilia, Italy, C Mediterranean Sea *37°48′N 14°13′E*
152 *K8* **Gangotri** Uttarakhand, N India *30°56′N 79°02′E*
Gangra *see* Çankırı
153 *S11* **Gangtok** *state capital* Sikkim, N India *27°20′N 88°39′E*
159 *W11* **Gangu** *var.* Daxiangshan. Gansu, C China *34°38′N 105°18′E*
163 *U5* **Gan He** ~ NE China
171 *S12* **Gani** Pulau Halmahera, E Indonesia *0°45′S 128°13′E*
161 *O12* **Gan Jiang** ~ S China
163 *U11* **Ganjig** *var.* Horqin Zuoyi Houqi. Nei Mongol Zizhiqu, N China *42°53′N 122°22′E*
146 *H15* **Gannaly** Ahal Welaýaty, S Turkmenistan *37°02′N 60°43′E*
163 *U7* **Gannan** Heilongjiang, NE China *47°58′N 123°36′E*
103 *P10* **Gannat** Allier, C France *46°06′N 03°12′E*
33 *T14* **Gannett Peak** ▲ Wyoming, C USA *43°10′N 109°39′W*
29 *O10* **Gannvalley** South Dakota, N USA *44°01′N 98°59′W*
Ganqu *see* Lhünzhub
109 *Y3* **Gänserndorf** Niederösterreich, NE Austria *48°21′N 16°43′E*
Gansos, Lago dos *see* Goose Lake
159 *T9* **Gansu** *var.* Gan, Gansu Sheng, Kansu. ◈ *province* N China
Gansu Sheng *see* Gansu
76 *K16* **Ganta** *var.* Gahnpa. NE Liberia *07°15′N 08°59′W*
182 *H11* **Gantheaume, Cape** *headland* South Australia *36°04′S 137°28′E*
Gantsevichi *see* Hantsavichy
161 *Q6* **Ganyu** *var.* Qingkou. Jiangsu, E China *34°52′N 119°11′E*
144 *D12* **Ganyushkino** Atyrau, SW Kazakhstan *46°38′N 49°12′E*
161 *O12* **Ganzhou** Jiangxi, S China *25°51′N 114°59′E*
Ganzhou *see* Zhangye
77 *Q10* **Gao** Gao, E Mali *16°16′N 00°03′E*
77 *R10* **Gao** ◈ *region* SE Mali
161 *O10* **Gao'an** Jiangxi, S China *28°24′N 115°27′E*
Gaocheng *see* Litang
Gaoleshan *see* Xianfeng
161 *R5* **Gaomi** Shandong, C China *36°23′N 119°45′E*
161 *N5* **Gaoping** Shanxi, C China *35°51′N 112°55′E*
159 *S8* **Gaotai** Gansu, N China *39°22′N 99°44′E*
Gaoth Dobhair *see* Gweedore
77 *O14* **Gaoua** SW Burkina *10°18′N 03°12′W*
76 *I13* **Gaoual** N Guinea *11°44′N 13°14′W*
Gaoxiong *see* Kaohsiung
161 *R7* **Gaoyou** *var.* Dayishan. Jiangsu, E China *32°48′N 119°26′E*
161 *R7* **Gaoyou Hu** ◎ E China
160 *M15* **Gaozhou** Guangdong, S China *21°56′N 110°49′E*
103 *T13* **Gap** *anc.* Vapincum. Hautes-Alpes, SE France *44°33′N 06°05′E*
146 *E9* **Gaplaňgyr Platosy** *Rus.* Plato Kaplangky. *ridge* Turkmenistan/Uzbekistan
158 *G13* **Gar** Xizang Zizhiqu, W China *32°50′N 79°46′E*
Gar *see* Gar Xincun
Garabekevyul *see* Garabekewül
146 *L13* **Garabekewül** *Rus.* Garabekevyul, Karabekaul. Lebap Welaýaty, E Turkmenistan *38°31′N 64°04′E*
146 *K15* **Garabil Belentligi** *Rus.* Vozvyshennost' Karabil'. ▲▲ S Turkmenistan
146 *A8* **Garabogaz** *Rus.* Bekdash. Balkan Welaýaty, NW Turkmenistan *41°33′N 52°33′E*
146 *B9* **Garabogaz Aylagy** *Rus.* Zaliv Kara-Bogaz-Gol. *bay* NW Turkmenistan
146 *A9* **Garabogazköl** *Rus.* Kara-Bogaz-Gol. Balkan Welaýaty, NW Turkmenistan *41°03′N 52°52′E*
43 *V16* **Garachiné** Darién, SE Panama *08°03′N 78°22′W*
43 *V16* **Garachiné, Punta** *headland* SE Panama *08°05′N 78°23′W*
146 *K12* **Garagan** *Rus.* Karagan. Ahal Welaýaty, C Turkmenistan *38°16′N 57°34′E*
54 *G10* **Garagoa** Boyacá, C Colombia *05°05′N 73°20′W*
146 *A11* **Garagöl'** *Rus.* Karagel'. Balkan Welaýaty, W Turkmenistan *39°24′N 53°13′E*
146 *F12* **Garagum** *var.* Garagumy, Qara Qum, *Eng.* Black Sand Desert, Kara Kum; *prev.* Peski Karakumy. *desert* C Turkmenistan
146 *E12* **Garagum Kanaly** *var.* Kara Kum Canal, *Rus.* Karagumskiy Kanal, Karakumskiy Kanal. *canal* C Turkmenistan
Garagumy *see* Garagum
183 *S4* **Garah** New South Wales, SE Australia *29°07′S 149°37′E*
64 *O11* **Garajonay** ▲ Gomera, Islas Canarias, NE Atlantic Ocean *28°07′N 17°14′W*
114 *M8* **Gara Khitrino** Shumen, NE Bulgaria *43°26′N 26°55′E*
76 *L13* **Garalo** Sikasso, SW Mali *10°58′N 07°26′W*
Garam *see* Hron, Slovakia
146 *L14* **Garamätnyýaz** *Rus.* Karamet-Niyaz. Lebap Welaýaty, E Turkmenistan *37°45′N 64°28′E*
Garamszentkereszt *see* Žiar nad Hronom
77 *Q13* **Garango** S Burkina *11°45′N 00°30′W*
59 *Q15* **Garanhuns** Pernambuco, E Brazil *08°53′S 36°28′W*
188 *H5* **Garapan** Saipan, S Northern Mariana Islands *15°12′S 145°43′E*
Gárasavvon *see* Karesuando
Gárassavon *see* Kaaresuvanto
78 *J13* **Garba** Bamingui-Bangoran, N Central African Republic *09°09′N 20°24′E*
Garba *see* Jiulong
81 *L16* **Garbahaarrey** *It.* Garba Harre. Gedo, SW Somalia *03°14′N 42°18′E*
Garba Harre *see* Garbahaarrey
81 *J18* **Garba Tula** Eastern, C Kenya *0°31′N 38°35′E*
27 *N9* **Garber** Oklahoma, C USA *36°26′N 97°35′W*
34 *L4* **Garberville** California, W USA *40°07′N 123°48′W*
Garbo *see* Lhozhag
100 *I12* **Garbsen** Niedersachsen, N Germany *52°25′N 09°36′E*
60 *K9* **Garça** São Paulo, S Brazil *22°14′S 49°36′W*
104 *L10* **García de Solá, Embalse de** ⊠ C Spain
103 *Q14* **Gard** ◈ *department* S France
103 *Q14* **Gard** ~ S France
106 *F7* **Garda, Lago di** *var.* Benaco, *Eng.* Lake Garda, *Ger.* Gardasee. ◎ NE Italy
Garda, Lake *see* Garda, Lago di
Gardan Divāl *see* Gardan Dīwāl
149 *Q5* **Gardan Dīwāl** *var.* Gardan Divāl. Vardak, C Afghanistan *34°30′N 68°15′E*
103 *S15* **Gardanne** Bouches-du-Rhône, SE France *43°27′N 05°28′E*
Gardasee *see* Garda, Lago di
100 *L12* **Gardelegen** Sachsen-Anhalt, C Germany *52°31′N 11°25′E*

◆ Country
● Country Capital
◇ Dependent Territory
○ Dependent Territory Capital
◈ Administrative Regions
✈ International Airport
▲ Mountain
▲▲ Mountain Range
Volcano
~ River
◎ Lake
⊠ Reservoir

14 B10 **Garden** ≈ Ontario, S Canada
23 X6 **Garden City** Georgia, SE USA 32°06′N 81°09′W
26 I6 **Garden City** Kansas, C USA 37°57′N 100°54′W
27 S5 **Garden City** Missouri, C USA 38°34′N 94°12′W
25 N8 **Garden City** Texas, SW USA 31°51′N 101°30′W
23 P3 **Gardendale** Alabama, S USA 33°39′N 86°48′W
31 P5 **Garden Island** island Michigan, N USA
22 M11 **Garden Island Bay** bay Louisiana, S USA
31 O5 **Garden Peninsula** peninsula Michigan, N USA
Garden State, The see New Jersey
95 I14 **Gardermoen** Akershus, S Norway 60°10′N 11°04′E
95 I14 **Gardermoen** ✈ (Oslo) Akershus, S Norway 60°12′N 11°05′E
Gardeyz/Gardez see Gardīz
93 G14 **Gardiken** ◎ N Sweden
19 Q7 **Gardiner** Maine, NE USA 44°13′N 69°46′W
33 S12 **Gardiner** Montana, NW USA 45°02′N 110°42′W
19 N13 **Gardiners Island** island New York, NE USA
149 Q6 **Gardīz** var. Gardeyz, Gardez, Gordiaz. Paktīā, E Afghanistan 33°35′N 69°14′E
Gardner Island see Nikumaroro
19 T6 **Gardner Lake** ◎ Maine, NE USA
35 Q6 **Gardnerville** Nevada, W USA 38°55′N 119°44′W
Gardo see Qardho
106 F7 **Gardone Val Trompia** Lombardia, N Italy 45°40′N 10°11′E
Garegegasnjárga see Karigasniemi
38 F17 **Gareloi Island** island Aleutian Islands, Alaska, USA
Gares see Puente la Reina
106 B10 **Garessio** Piemonte, NE Italy 44°14′N 08°01′E
32 M9 **Garfield** Washington, NW USA 47°00′N 117°07′W
31 U11 **Garfield Heights** Ohio, N USA 41°25′N 81°36′W
Gargaliani see Gargaliánoi
115 D21 **Gargaliánoi** var. Gargaliani. Pelopónnisos, S Greece 37°04′N 21°38′E
107 N15 **Gargàno, Promontorio del** headland SE Italy 41°51′N 16°11′E
108 J8 **Gargellen** Graubünden, W Switzerland 46°57′N 09°55′E
93 I14 **Gargnäs** Västerbotten, N Sweden 65°19′N 18°00′E
118 C11 **Gargždai** Klaipėda, W Lithuania 55°42′N 21°24′E
154 J13 **Garhchiroli** Mahārāshtra, C India 20°14′N 79°58′E
153 O15 **Garhwa** Jhārkhand, N India 24°07′N 83°52′E
171 V13 **Gariau** Papua, E Indonesia 03°43′S 134°54′E
83 E24 **Garies** Northern Cape, W South Africa 30°30′S 18°00′E
107 K17 **Garigliano** ≈ C Italy
81 K19 **Garissa** Coast, E Kenya 0°27′S 39°39′E
21 V11 **Garland** North Carolina, SE USA 34°45′N 78°25′W
25 T6 **Garland** Texas, SW USA 32°50′N 96°37′W
36 L1 **Garland** Utah, W USA 41°43′N 112°07′W
106 D8 **Garlasco** Lombardia, N Italy 45°12′N 08°59′E
119 F14 **Garliava** Kaunas, S Lithuania 54°49′N 23°52′E
Garm see Gharm
142 M9 **Garm, Āb-e** var. Rūd-e Kharsān. ≈ SW Iran
101 K25 **Garmisch-Partenkirchen** Bayern, S Germany 47°30′N 11°05′E
143 O5 **Garmsār** prev. Qishlaq. Semnān, N Iran 35°18′N 52°22′E
Garmser see Darvīshān
29 V12 **Garner** Iowa, C USA 43°06′N 93°36′W
21 U9 **Garner** North Carolina, SE USA 35°42′N 78°36′W
27 Q5 **Garnett** Kansas, C USA 38°16′N 95°15′W
99 M25 **Garnich** Luxembourg, SW Luxembourg 49°37′N 05°57′E
182 M8 **Garnpung, Lake** salt lake New South Wales, SE Australia
Garoe see Garoowe
Garoet see Garut
153 U13 **Gāro Hills** hill range NE India
102 K13 **Garonne** anc. Garumna. ≈ S France
80 P13 **Garoowe** var. Garoe. Nugaal, N Somalia 08°24′N 48°29′E
78 F12 **Garoua** var. Garua. Nord, N Cameroon 09°17′N 13°22′E
79 G14 **Garoua Boulaï** Est, E Cameroon 05°54′N 14°33′E
77 O10 **Garou, Lac** ◎ C Mali
95 L16 **Garphyttan** Örebro, C Sweden 59°18′N 14°54′E
29 R11 **Garretson** South Dakota, N USA 43°43′N 96°30′W
31 Q11 **Garrett** Indiana, N USA 41°21′N 85°08′W
33 Q10 **Garrison** Montana, NW USA 46°32′N 112°46′W
28 M4 **Garrison** North Dakota, N USA 47°36′N 101°25′W
25 X8 **Garrison** Texas, SW USA 31°49′N 94°29′W
28 L4 **Garrison Dam** dam North Dakota, N USA
104 J9 **Garrovillas** Extremadura, W Spain 39°43′N 06°33′W
Garrygala see Magtymguly
8 L8 **Garry Lake** ◎ Nunavut, N Canada
Gars see Gars am Kamp
109 W3 **Gars am Kamp** var. Gars. Niederösterreich, NE Austria 48°35′N 15°40′E
81 K20 **Garsen** Coast, S Kenya 02°16′S 40°07′E
Garshy see Garşy
14 F10 **Garson** Ontario, S Canada 46°33′N 80°51′W
109 T5 **Garsten** Oberösterreich, N Austria 48°00′N 14°24′E
146 A9 **Garşy** var. Garshy, Rus. Karshi. Balkan Welaýaty, NW Turkmenistan 40°45′N 52°50′E
Gartar see Qianning
102 M10 **Gartempe** ≈ C France
Gartog see Markam
Garua see Garoua
83 D21 **Garub** Karas, SW Namibia 26°33′S 16°00′E
Garumna see Garonne
169 P16 **Garut** prev. Garoet. Jawa, C Indonesia 07°15′S 107°55′E
185 C20 **Garvie Mountains** ▲▲ South Island, New Zealand
110 N12 **Garwolin** Mazowieckie, E Poland 51°54′N 21°36′E
25 U12 **Garwood** Texas, SW USA 29°25′N 96°26′W
158 G13 **Gar Xincun** prev. Gar. Xizang Zizhiqu, W China 32°04′N 80°01′E
31 N11 **Gary** Indiana, N USA 41°36′N 87°21′W
25 X7 **Gary** Texas, SW USA 32°00′N 94°21′W
158 G13 **Garyarsa** Xizang Zizhiqu, SW China 31°44′N 80°20′E
158 G13 **Gar Zangbo** ≈ W China
160 F8 **Garzê** Sichuan, C China 31°40′N 99°58′E
54 E12 **Garzón** Huila, S Colombia 02°14′N 75°37′W
Gasan-Kuli see Esenguly
31 P13 **Gas City** Indiana, N USA 40°29′N 85°36′W
102 K15 **Gascogne** Eng. Gascony. cultural region S France
26 V5 **Gasconade River** ≈ Missouri, C USA
Gascony see Gascogne
180 H9 **Gascoyne Junction** Western Australia 25°06′S 115°10′E
173 V8 **Gascoyne Plain** undersea feature E Indian Ocean
180 H9 **Gascoyne River** ≈ Western Australia
192 J11 **Gascoyne Tablemount** undersea feature N Tasman Sea 36°30′S 156°30′E
67 U6 **Gash** var. Nahr al Qāsh. ≈ W Sudan
149 X3 **Gasherbrum** ▲ NE Pakistan 35°39′N 76°34′E
Gas Hu see Gas Hure Hu
77 X12 **Gashua** Yobe, NE Nigeria 12°55′N 11°10′E
159 N9 **Gas Hure Hu** var. Gas Hu. ◎ C China
186 G7 **Gasmata** New Britain, E Papua New Guinea 06°12′S 150°25′E
23 V14 **Gasparilla Island** island Florida, SE USA
169 O13 **Gaspar, Selat** strait W Indonesia
15 Y6 **Gaspé** Québec, SE Canada 48°50′N 64°33′W
15 Z6 **Gaspé, Cap de** headland Québec, SE Canada 48°45′N 64°10′W
15 X6 **Gaspé, Péninsule de** var. Péninsule de la Gaspésie. peninsula Québec, SE Canada
Gaspésie, Péninsule de la see Gaspé, Péninsule de
77 W15 **Gassol** Taraba, E Nigeria 08°28′N 10°24′E
Gastein see Badgastein
21 R10 **Gastonia** North Carolina, SE USA 35°14′N 81°12′W
21 V8 **Gaston, Lake** ▣ North Carolina/Virginia, SE USA
115 D19 **Gastoúni** Dytikí Elláś, S Greece 37°51′N 21°15′E
63 I17 **Gastre** Chubut, S Argentina 42°20′S 69°10′W
Gat see Ghāt
105 P15 **Gata, Cabo de** cape S Spain
Gata, Cape see Gátas, Akrotíri
105 T11 **Gata de Gorgos** País Valenciano, E Spain 38°45′N 00°06′E
116 E12 **Gătaia** Ger. Gataja, Hung. Gátalja; prev. Gáttája. Timiş, W Romania 45°24′N 21°26′E
Gataja/Gátalja see Gătaia
121 P3 **Gátas, Akrotíri** var. Cape Gata. headland S Cyprus 34°34′N 33°03′E
104 J8 **Gata, Sierra de** ▲▲ W Spain
124 G13 **Gatchina** Leningradskaya Oblast', NW Russian Federation 59°34′N 30°06′E
21 P8 **Gate City** Virginia, NE USA 36°38′N 82°37′W
97 M14 **Gateshead** NE England, United Kingdom 54°57′N 01°37′W
21 X8 **Gatesville** North Carolina, SE USA 36°24′N 76°46′W
25 S8 **Gatesville** Texas, SW USA 31°26′N 97°46′W
14 L12 **Gatineau** Québec, SE Canada 45°29′N 75°40′W
14 L11 **Gatineau** ≈ Ontario/Québec, SE Canada
21 N9 **Gatlinburg** Tennessee, S USA 35°42′N 83°30′W
Gatooma see Kadoma
Gáttája see Gătaia
43 T14 **Gatún, Lago** ▣ C Panama
59 N14 **Gaturiano** Piauí, NE Brazil 06°53′S 41°45′W
97 O22 **Gatwick** ✈ (London) SE England, United Kingdom 51°10′N 00°12′W
187 Y14 **Gau** prev. Ngau. island C Fiji
187 R12 **Gaua** var. Santa Maria. Island Banks Island, N Vanuatu
104 L16 **Gaucín** Andalucía, S Spain 36°31′N 05°19′W
Gauhāti see Guwāhāti
118 I8 **Gauja** Ger. Aa. ≈ Estonia/Latvia
118 I7 **Gaujiena** Alūksne, NE Latvia 57°31′N 26°24′E
94 H9 **Gauldalen** valley S Norway
21 R5 **Gauley River** ≈ West Virginia, NE USA
Gaul/Gaule see France
99 D19 **Gaurain-Ramecroix** Hainaut, SW Belgium 50°35′N 03°31′E
95 F15 **Gaustatoppen** ▲ S Norway 59°50′N 08°39′E
83 J21 **Gauteng** off. Gauteng Province; prev. Pretoria-Witwatersrand-Vereeniging. ⬖ province NE South Africa
Gauteng see Johannesburg, South Africa
Gauteng see Germiston, South Africa
Gauteng Province see Gauteng
137 U11 **Gavarr** prev. Kamo. C Armenia 40°21′N 45°07′E
143 P14 **Gāvbandī** Hormozgān, S Iran 27°07′N 53°21′E
115 H25 **Gavdopoúla** island SE Greece
115 H26 **Gávdos** island SE Greece
102 K16 **Gave de Pau** var. Gave-de-Pay. ≈ SW France
Gave-de-Pay see Gave de Pau
102 J16 **Gave d'Oloron** ≈ SW France
99 E18 **Gavere** Oost-Vlaanderen, NW Belgium 50°56′N 03°41′E
94 N13 **Gävle** var. Gäfle; prev. Gefle. Gävleborg, C Sweden 60°41′N 17°09′E
94 M11 **Gävleborg** var. Gäfleborg, Gefleborg. ⬖ county C Sweden
94 O13 **Gävlebukten** bay C Sweden
124 L16 **Gavrilov-Yam** Yaroslavskaya Oblast', W Russian Federation 57°19′N 39°52′E
182 I9 **Gawler** South Australia 34°38′S 138°44′E
182 G7 **Gawler Ranges** hill range South Australia
Gawso see Goaso
162 H11 **Gaxun Nur** ◎ N China
127 W7 **Gay** Orenburgskaya Oblast', W Russian Federation 51°31′N 58°31′E
153 P14 **Gaya** Bihār, N India 24°48′N 85°E
77 S13 **Gaya** Dosso, SW Niger 11°52′N 03°28′E
Gaya see Kyjov
31 Q6 **Gaylord** Michigan, N USA 45°01′N 84°40′W
29 U9 **Gaylord** Minnesota, N USA 44°33′N 94°13′W
181 Y9 **Gayndah** Queensland, E Australia 25°37′S 151°31′E
125 T12 **Gayny** Komi-Permyatskiy Avtonomnyy Okrug, NW Russian Federation 60°19′N 54°15′E
Gaysin see Haysyn
Gayvorno see Hayvoron
138 E11 **Gaza** Ar. Ghazzah, Heb. 'Azza. NE Gaza Strip 31°30′N 34°E
83 L20 **Gaza** off. Província de Gaza. ⬖ province SW Mozambique
Gaz-Achak see Gazojak
147 Q9 **G'azalkent** Rus. Gazalkent. Toshkent Viloyati, E Uzbekistan 41°30′N 69°46′E
Gazalkent see G'azalkent
Gazandzhyk/Gazanjyk see Bereket
77 V12 **Gazaoua** Maradi, S Niger 13°28′N 07°54′E
Gaza, Província de see Gaza
138 E11 **Gaza Strip** Ar. Qita Ghazzah. disputed region SW Asia
136 M16 **Gaziantep** var. Gazi Antep; prev. Aintab, Antep. Gaziantep, S Turkey 37°04′N 37°21′E
136 M17 **Gaziantep** var. Gazi Antep. ⬖ province S Turkey
Gazi Antep see Gaziantep
114 M13 **Gaziköy** Tekirdağ, NW Turkey 40°45′N 27°18′E
121 Q2 **Gazimağusa** var. Famagusta, Gk. Ammóchostos. E Cyprus 35°07′N 33°57′E
121 Q2 **Gazimağusa Körfezi** var. Famagusta Bay, Gk. Kólpos Ammóchostos. bay E Cyprus
146 K11 **Gazli** Buxoro Viloyati, C Uzbekistan 40°09′N 63°28′E
146 I9 **Gazojak** Rus. Gaz-Achak. Lebap Welaýaty, NE Turkmenistan 41°12′N 61°24′E
79 K15 **Gbadolite** Equateur, NW Dem. Rep. Congo 04°14′N 20°59′E
76 K16 **Gbanga** var. Gbarnga. N Liberia 07°02′N 09°30′W
Gbarnga see Gbanga
77 S14 **Gbéroubouè** var. Béroubouay. N Benin 10°35′N 02°47′E
77 W16 **Gboko** Benue, S Nigeria 07°21′N 08°57′E
Gcuwa see Butterworth
110 J7 **Gdańsk** Fr. Dantzig, Ger. Danzig. Pomorskie, N Poland 54°22′N 18°35′E
Gdan'skaya Bukhta/Gdańsk, Gulf of see Danzig, Gulf of
Gdańska, Zakota see Danzig, Gulf of
Gdingen see Gdynia
124 F13 **Gdov** Pskovskaya Oblast', W Russian Federation 58°43′N 27°51′E
110 I6 **Gdynia** Ger. Gdingen. Pomorskie, N Poland 54°31′N 18°30′E
26 M10 **Geary** Oklahoma, C USA 35°37′N 98°19′W
Geavvú see Kevo
76 H12 **Gêba, Rio** ≈ C Guinea-Bissau
136 E11 **Gebze** Kocaeli, NW Turkey 40°48′N 29°26′E
80 H10 **Gedaref** var. Al Qaḍārif, El Gedaref. Gedaref, E Sudan 14°03′N 35°24′E
80 H10 **Gedaref** ⬖ state E Sudan
80 B11 **Gedid Ras el Fil** Southern Darfur, W Sudan 12°45′N 25°45′E
99 I23 **Gedinne** Namur, SE Belgium 49°57′N 04°55′E
136 E13 **Gediz** Kütahya, W Turkey 39°04′N 29°25′E
136 C14 **Gediz Nehri** ≈ W Turkey
81 N14 **Gedlegubē** Sumalē, E Ethiopia 06°53′N 45°08′E
81 L17 **Gedo** off. Gobolka Gedo. ⬖ region SW Somalia
Gedo, Gobolka see Gedo
95 I25 **Gedser** Storstrøm, SE Denmark 54°34′N 11°57′E
99 I16 **Geel** var. Gheel. Antwerpen, N Belgium 51°10′N 04°59′E
183 N13 **Geelong** Victoria, SE Australia 38°10′S 144°21′E
Ge'e'mu see Golmud
99 I14 **Geertruidenberg** Noord-Brabant, S Netherlands 51°43′N 04°52′E
100 H10 **Geeste** ≈ NW Germany
100 J10 **Geesthacht** Schleswig-Holstein, N Germany 53°25′N 10°22′E
183 P17 **Geeveston** Tasmania, SE Australia 43°12′S 146°54′E
Gefle see Gävle
Gefleborg see Gävleborg
158 G13 **Gê'gyai** Xizang Zizhiqu, W China 32°29′N 81°04′E
77 X12 **Geidam** Yobe, NE Nigeria 12°52′N 11°55′E
11 T11 **Geikie** ≈ Saskatchewan, C Canada
94 F13 **Geilo** Buskerud, S Norway 60°32′N 08°13′E
94 E10 **Geiranger** Møre og Romsdal, S Norway 62°07′N 07°12′E
101 I22 **Geislingen** var. Geislingen an der Steige. Baden-Württemberg, SW Germany 48°37′N 09°50′E
Geislingen an der Steige see Geislingen
81 F20 **Geita** Mwanza, NW Tanzania 02°52′S 32°12′E
95 G15 **Geithus** Buskerud, S Norway 59°56′N 09°58′E
160 H14 **Gejiu** var. Kochiu. Yunnan, S China 23°22′N 103°07′E
Gëkdepe see Gökdepe
146 E9 **Geklengkui, Solonchak** var. Solonchak Goklenkuy. salt marsh NW Turkmenistan
81 D14 **Gel** ≈ W Sudan
107 K25 **Gela** prev. Terranova di Sicilia. Sicilia, Italy, C Mediterranean Sea 37°05′N 14°15′E
159 N13 **Gêladaindong** ▲ C China 33°24′N 91°00′E
81 N14 **Geladī** SE Ethiopia 06°58′N 46°24′E
169 P13 **Gelam, Pulau** var. Pulau Galam. island N Indonesia
Gelaozu Miaozu Zhizhixian see Wuchuan
98 L11 **Gelderland** prev. Eng. Guelders. ⬖ province E Netherlands
98 J13 **Geldermalsen** Gelderland, C Netherlands 51°53′N 05°17′E
101 D14 **Geldern** Nordrhein-Westfalen, W Germany 51°31′N 06°19′E
99 K15 **Geldrop** Noord-Brabant, SE Netherlands 51°25′N 05°34′E
99 L17 **Geleen** Limburg, SE Netherlands 50°57′N 05°49′E
126 K14 **Gelendzhik** Krasnodarskiy Kray, SW Russian Federation 44°34′N 38°06′E
Gelib see Jilib
136 B11 **Gelibolu** Eng. Gallipoli. Çanakkale, NW Turkey 40°25′N 26°41′E
115 L14 **Gelibolu Yarımadası** Eng. Gallipoli Peninsula. peninsula NW Turkey
81 O14 **Gellinsor** Mudug, C Somalia 06°25′N 46°44′E
101 H18 **Gelnhausen** Hessen, C Germany 50°12′N 09°12′E
101 E14 **Gelsenkirchen** Nordrhein-Westfalen, W Germany 51°30′N 07°05′E
83 C20 **Geluk** Hardap, SW Namibia 24°35′S 15°48′E
99 H20 **Gembloux** Namur, Belgium 50°34′N 04°42′E
79 J16 **Gemena** Equateur, NW Dem. Rep. Congo 03°13′N 19°49′E
99 L14 **Gemert** Noord-Brabant, SE Netherlands 51°33′N 05°41′E
136 E11 **Gemlik** Bursa, NW Turkey 40°26′N 29°10′E
Gem of the Mountains see Idaho
106 J6 **Gemona del Friuli** Friuli-Venezia Giulia, NE Italy 46°18′N 13°12′E
Gem State see Idaho
Genalē Wenz see Juba
169 R10 **Genali, Danau** ◎ Borneo, N Indonesia
99 G19 **Genappe** Walloon Brabant, C Belgium 50°39′N 04°27′E
137 P14 **Genç** Bingöl, E Turkey 38°44′N 40°35′E
Genck see Genk
98 M9 **Genemuiden** Overijssel, E Netherlands 52°38′N 06°03′E
63 K14 **General Acha** La Pampa, C Argentina 37°25′S 64°38′W
61 C21 **General Alvear** Buenos Aires, E Argentina 36°03′S 60°01′W
62 I12 **General Alvear** Mendoza, W Argentina 34°59′S 67°40′W
61 B20 **General Arenales** Buenos Aires, E Argentina 34°21′S 61°20′W
61 D21 **General Belgrano** Buenos Aires, E Argentina 35°47′S 58°30′W
194 H3 **General Bernardo O'Higgins** Chilean research station Antarctica 63°09′S 57°13′W
41 O8 **General Bravo** Nuevo León, NE Mexico 25°47′N 99°04′W
62 M7 **General Capdevila** Chaco, N Argentina 27°25′S 61°30′W
General Carrera, Lago see Buenos Aires, Lago
41 N9 **General Cepeda** Coahuila, NE Mexico 25°18′N 101°24′W
63 K15 **General Conesa** Río Negro, E Argentina 40°06′S 64°26′W
61 G18 **General Enrique Martínez** Treinta y Tres, E Uruguay 33°13′S 53°47′W
62 L3 **General Eugenio A. Garay** var. Fortín General Eugenio Garay; prev. Yrendagüé. Nueva Asunción, NW Paraguay 20°30′S 61°56′W
61 C18 **General Galarza** Entre Ríos, E Argentina 32°43′S 59°24′W
61 E22 **General Guido** Buenos Aires, E Argentina 36°36′S 57°45′W
General José F.Uriburu see Zárate
61 E22 **General Juan Madariaga** Buenos Aires, E Argentina 37°00′S 57°09′W
41 O16 **General Juan N Alvarez** ✈ (Acapulco) Guerrero, S Mexico 16°47′N 99°47′W
61 B22 **General La Madrid** Buenos Aires, E Argentina 37°17′S 61°20′W
61 E21 **General Lavalle** Buenos Aires, E Argentina 36°25′S 56°56′W
General Machado see Camacupa
62 I8 **General Manuel Belgrano, Cerro** ▲ W Argentina 29°05′S 67°05′W
41 O8 **General Mariano Escobero** ✈ (Monterrey) Nuevo León, NE Mexico 25°47′N 100°00′W
61 B20 **General O'Brien** Buenos Aires, E Argentina 34°54′S 60°45′W
62 K13 **General Pico** La Pampa, C Argentina 35°43′S 63°45′W
62 M7 **General Pinedo** Chaco, N Argentina 27°17′S 61°20′W
61 B20 **General Pinto** Buenos Aires, E Argentina 34°45′S 61°50′W
61 E22 **General Pirán** Buenos Aires, E Argentina 37°16′S 57°46′W
43 N15 **General, Río** ≈ S Costa Rica
63 I15 **General Roca** Río Negro, C Argentina 39°00′S 67°35′W
171 Q8 **General Santos** off. General Santos City. Mindanao, S Philippines 06°10′N 125°10′E
General Santos City see General Santos
41 O9 **General Terán** Nuevo León, NE Mexico 25°18′N 99°40′W
114 N7 **General Toshevo** Rom. I.G.Duca; prev. Casim, Kasimköj. Dobrich, NE Bulgaria 43°43′N 28°04′E
61 B20 **General Viamonte** Buenos Aires, E Argentina 35°01′S 61°00′W
61 A20 **General Villegas** Buenos Aires, E Argentina 35°02′S 63°01′W
Gênes see Genova
18 E11 **Genesee River** ≈ New York/Pennsylvania, NE USA
30 K11 **Geneseo** Illinois, N USA 41°27′N 90°08′W
18 F10 **Geneseo** New York, NE USA 42°48′N 77°46′W
57 L14 **Geneshuaya, Río** ≈ N Bolivia
23 Q8 **Geneva** Alabama, S USA 31°01′N 85°51′W
30 M10 **Geneva** Illinois, N USA 41°53′N 88°18′W
29 Q16 **Geneva** Nebraska, C USA 40°31′N 97°36′W
18 G10 **Geneva** New York, NE USA 42°52′N 76°58′W
31 U10 **Geneva** Ohio, NE USA 41°48′N 80°53′W
Geneva see Genève
108 B10 **Geneva, Lake** Fr. Lac de Genève, Lac Léman, le Léman, Ger. Genfer See. ◎ France/Switzerland
108 A10 **Genève** Eng. Geneva, Ger. Genf, It. Ginevra. Genève, SW Switzerland 46°13′N 06°09′E
108 A11 **Genève** Eng. Geneva, Ger. Genf, It. Ginevra. ⬖ canton SW Switzerland
108 A10 **Genève** var. Geneva. ✈ Vaud, SW Switzerland 46°13′N 06°06′E
Genève, Lac de see Geneva, Lake
Genf see Genève
Genfer See see Geneva, Lake
163 T5 **Genhe** prev. Ergun Zuoqi. Nei Mongol Zizhiqu, N China 50°48′N 121°30′E
163 S5 **Gen He** ≈ NE China
Genichesk see Heniches'k
104 L14 **Genil** ≈ S Spain
99 K18 **Genk** var. Genck. Limburg, NE Belgium 50°58′N 05°30′E
164 C13 **Genkai-nada** gulf Kyūshū, SW Japan
107 C19 **Gennargentu, Monti del** ▲▲ Sardegna, Italy, C Mediterranean Sea
99 M14 **Gennep** Limburg, SE Netherlands 51°43′N 05°58′E
30 M10 **Genoa** Illinois, N USA 42°06′N 88°41′W
29 Q15 **Genoa** Nebraska, C USA 41°27′N 97°43′W
Genoa see Genova
Genoa, Gulf of see Genova, Golfo di
106 D10 **Genova** Eng. Genoa; anc. Genua, Fr. Gênes. Liguria, NW Italy 44°28′N 09°E
106 D10 **Genova, Golfo di** Eng. Gulf of Genoa. gulf NW Italy
57 C17 **Genovesa, Isla** var. Tower Island. island Galapagos Islands, Ecuador, E Pacific Ocean
Genshū see Wŏnju
99 E17 **Gent** Eng. Ghent, Fr. Gand. Oost-Vlaanderen, NW Belgium 51°02′N 03°42′E
169 N16 **Genteng** Jawa, C Indonesia 07°21′S 106°20′E
100 M12 **Genthin** Sachsen-Anhalt, E Germany 52°24′N 12°10′E
27 R9 **Gentry** Arkansas, C USA 36°16′N 94°28′W
Genua see Genova
107 I15 **Genzano di Roma** Lazio, C Italy 41°42′N 12°42′E
Geokchay see Göyçay
Geok-Tepe see Gökdepe
122 I3 **Georga, Zemlya** Eng. George Land. island Zemlya Frantsa-Iosifa, N Russian Federation
83 G26 **George** Western Cape, S South Africa 33°57′S 22°28′E
29 S11 **George** Iowa, C USA 43°20′N 96°00′W
13 O5 **George** ≈ Newfoundland and Labrador/Québec, E Canada
George F L Charles see Vigie
65 C25 **George Island** island S Falkland Islands
183 R10 **George, Lake** ◎ New South Wales, SE Australia
81 E18 **George, Lake** ◎ SW Uganda
23 W10 **George, Lake** ◎ Florida, SE USA
18 L8 **George, Lake** ▣ New York, NE USA
George Land see Georga, Zemlya
Georgenburg see Jurbarkas
George River see Kangiqsualujjuaq
64 G8 **Georges Bank** undersea feature W Atlantic Ocean 41°15′N 67°30′W
185 A21 **George Sound** sound South Island, New Zealand
65 F15 **Georgetown** ○ (Ascension Island) NW Ascension Island 17°56′S 14°25′W
181 V5 **Georgetown** Queensland, NE Australia 18°17′S 143°37′E
183 P15 **George Town** Tasmania, SE Australia 41°04′S 146°48′E
44 I4 **George Town** Great Exuma Island, C Bahamas 23°28′N 75°47′W
44 D8 **George Town** var. Georgetown. ○ (Cayman Islands) Grand Cayman, SW Cayman Islands 19°16′N 81°23′W
76 H12 **Georgetown** E Gambia 13°33′N 14°49′W
55 T8 **Georgetown** ● (Guyana) N Guyana 06°46′N 58°10′W
168 J7 **George Town** var. Penang, Pinang. Pinang, Peninsular Malaysia 05°28′N 100°20′E
45 Y14 **Georgetown** Saint Vincent, Saint Vincent and the Grenadines 13°19′N 61°09′W
21 Y4 **Georgetown** Delaware, NE USA 38°39′N 75°22′W
23 R6 **Georgetown** Georgia, SE USA 31°52′N 85°04′W
20 M5 **Georgetown** Kentucky, S USA 38°13′N 84°30′W
21 T13 **Georgetown** South Carolina, SE USA 33°23′N 79°18′W
25 S10 **Georgetown** Texas, SW USA 30°39′N 97°42′W
55 T8 **Georgetown** ✈ N Guyana 06°46′N 58°10′W
Georgetown see George Town
195 U16 **George V Coast** physical region Antarctica
194 J7 **George VI Ice Shelf** ice shelf Antarctica
194 J6 **George VI Sound** sound Antarctica
195 T15 **George V Land** physical region Antarctica
25 S14 **George West** Texas, SW USA 28°21′N 98°08′W
137 R9 **Georgia** off. Republic of Georgia, Geor. Sak'art'velo, Rus. Gruzinskaya SSR, Gruziya. ◆ republic SW Asia
23 S5 **Georgia** off. State of Georgia, also known as Empire State of the South, Peach State. ⬖ state SE USA
14 F12 **Georgian Bay** lake bay Ontario, S Canada
Georgia, Republic of see Georgia
10 L17 **Georgia, Strait of** strait British Columbia, W Canada
Georgi Dimitrov see Kostenets
Georgi Dimitrov, Yazovir see Koprinka, Yazovir
114 M9 **Georgi Traykov, Yazovir** ▣ NE Bulgaria
Georgiu-Dezh see Liski
145 W10 **Georgiyevka** Vostochnyy Kazakhstan, E Kazakhstan 49°19′N 81°35′E
Georgiyevka see Korday
127 N15 **Georgiyevsk** Stavropol'skiy Kray, SW Russian Federation 44°07′N 43°22′E
100 G13 **Georgsmarienhütte** Niedersachsen, NW Germany 52°13′N 08°02′E
195 O1 **Georg von Neumayer** German research station Antarctica 70°41′S 08°18′W
101 M16 **Gera** Thüringen, E Germany 50°51′N 12°13′E
101 K16 **Gera** ≈ C Germany
99 E19 **Geraardsbergen** Oost-Vlaanderen, SW Belgium 50°47′N 03°53′E
115 F21 **Geráki** Pelopónnisos, S Greece 36°56′N 22°46′E
27 W5 **Gerald** Missouri, C USA 38°24′N 91°20′W
47 V8 **Geral de Goiás, Serra** ▲ E Brazil
185 G20 **Geraldine** Canterbury, South Island, New Zealand 44°06′S 171°14′E
180 H11 **Geraldton** Western Australia 28°48′S 114°40′E
12 E11 **Geraldton** Ontario, S Canada 49°44′N 86°59′W
60 J12 **Geral, Serra** ▲ S Brazil
103 U6 **Gérardmer** Vosges, NE France 48°05′N 06°54′E
Gerasa see Jarash
Gerdauen see Zheleznodorozhnyy
39 Q11 **Gerdine, Mount** ▲ Alaska, USA 61°40′N 152°21′W
136 H11 **Gerede** Bolu, N Turkey 40°48′N 32°13′E
136 H11 **Gerede Çayı** ≈ N Turkey
148 M8 **Gereshk** Helmand, SW Afghanistan 31°50′N 64°32′E
101 L24 **Geretsried** Bayern, S Germany 47°51′N 11°28′E
105 P14 **Gérgal** Andalucía, S Spain 37°07′N 02°34′W
28 I14 **Gering** Nebraska, C USA 41°49′N 103°39′W
35 R3 **Gerlach** Nevada, W USA 40°38′N 119°21′W
Gerlachfalvi Csúcs/Gerlachovka see Gerlachovský štít
111 L18 **Gerlachovský štít** var. Gerlachovka, Ger. Gerlsdorfer Spitze, Hung. Gerlachfalvi Csúcs; prev. Stalinov Štít, Ger. Franz-Josef Spitze, Hung. Ferencz-József Csúcs. ▲ N Slovakia 49°12′N 20°09′E
108 E8 **Gerlafingen** Solothurn, NW Switzerland 47°10′N 07°35′E
Gerlsdorfer Spitze see Gerlachovský štít
139 V3 **Germak** As Sulaymānīyah, E Iraq 35°49′N 46°09′E
German East Africa see Tanzania
Germanicopolis see Çankırı
Germanicum, Mare/German Ocean see North Sea
Germanovichi see Hyermanavichy
German Southwest Africa see Namibia
20 E10 **Germantown** Tennessee, S USA 35°06′N 89°51′W
101 I15 **Germany** off. Federal Republic of Germany, Bundesrepublik Deutschland, Ger. Deutschland. ◆ federal republic N Europe
Germany, Federal Republic of see Germany
101 L23 **Germering** Bayern, SE Germany 48°07′N 11°22′E
83 J21 **Germiston** var. Gauteng. Gauteng, NE South Africa 26°15′S 28°10′E
Gernika see Gernika-Lumo
105 P2 **Gernika-Lumo** var. Gernika, Guernica, Guernica y Lumo. País Vasco, N Spain 43°19′N 02°40′W
164 L12 **Gero** Gifu, Honshū, SW Japan 35°48′N 137°15′E
115 F22 **Geroliménas** Pelopónnisos, S Greece 36°28′N 22°25′E
Gerona see Girona
99 H21 **Gerpinnes** Hainaut, S Belgium 50°20′N 04°38′E
102 L15 **Gers** ⬖ department S France
102 L14 **Gers** ≈ S France
Gerunda see Girona
158 I13 **Gêrzê** var. Luring. Xizang Zizhiqu, W China 32°19′N 84°05′E
136 K10 **Gerze** Sinop, N Turkey 41°48′N 35°13′E
Gesoriacum see Boulogne-sur-Mer
Gessoriacum see Boulogne-sur-Mer
99 J21 **Gesves** Namur, SE Belgium 50°24′N 05°04′E
93 J20 **Geta** Åland, SW Finland 60°22′N 19°49′E
105 N8 **Getafe** Madrid, C Spain 40°18′N 03°44′W
95 J21 **Getinge** Halland, S Sweden 56°46′N 12°42′E
18 F16 **Gettysburg** Pennsylvania, NE USA 39°49′N 77°13′W
29 N8 **Gettysburg** South Dakota, N USA 45°00′N 99°57′W
194 K12 **Getz Ice Shelf** ice shelf Antarctica
137 S15 **Gevaş** Van, SE Turkey 38°16′N 43°05′E
Gevgeli see Gevgelija
113 Q20 **Gevgelija** var. Đevđelija, Djevdjelija, Turk. Gevgeli. SE Macedonia 41°09′N 22°30′E
103 T10 **Gex** Ain, E France 46°21′N 06°02′E
92 I3 **Geysir** physical region SW Iceland
136 F11 **Geyve** Sakarya, NW Turkey 40°32′N 30°18′E
80 G10 **Gezira** ⬖ state E Sudan
109 V3 **Gföhl** Niederösterreich, N Austria 48°30′N 15°27′E
83 H22 **Ghaap Plateau** Afr. Ghaapplato. plateau C South Africa
Ghaapplato see Ghaap Plateau
Ghaba see Al Ghābah
138 J8 **Ghāb, Tall** ▲ SE Syria 33°09′N 37°48′E
139 Q9 **Ghadaf, Wādī al** dry watercourse C Iraq
Ghadamès see Ghadāmis
74 M9 **Ghadāmis** var. Ghadamès, Rhadames. W Libya 30°08′N 09°30′E
141 Y10 **Ghadan** E Oman 20°20′N 57°58′E
75 O10 **Ghaddūwah** C Libya 26°36′N 14°26′E
147 Q11 **Ghafurov** Rus. Gafurov; prev. Sovetabad. NW Tajikistan 40°13′N 69°42′E
153 N12 **Ghāghara** ≈ S Asia
149 P13 **Ghaibi Dero** Sind, SE Pakistan 27°35′N 67°42′E
141 Y10 **Ghalat** E Oman 21°06′N 58°51′E
139 W11 **Ghamūkah, Hawr** ◎ S Iraq
77 P15 **Ghana** off. Republic of Ghana. ◆ republic W Africa
141 X12 **Ghānah** spring/well S Oman 18°35′N 56°34′E
Ghanongga see Ranongga
Ghansi/Ghansiland see Ghanzi
83 F18 **Ghanzi** var. Khanzi. Ghanzi, W Botswana 21°39′S 21°38′E
83 G19 **Ghanzi** var. Ghansi, Ghansiland, Khanzi. ⬖ district C Botswana
67 T14 **Ghanzi** var. Knanzi. ≈ Botswana/South Africa
Ghap'an see Kapan
138 F13 **Gharandal** Al'Aqabah, SW Jordan 30°12′N 35°18′E
139 U14 **Gharbīyah, Sha'īb al** ≈ S Iraq
Gharbt, Jabal al see Liban, Jebel
74 K7 **Ghardaïa** N Algeria 32°30′N 03°44′E
147 R12 **Gharm** Rus. Garm. C Tajikistan 39°03′N 70°25′E
149 P17 **Gharo** Sind, SE Pakistan 24°44′N 67°35′E
139 W10 **Gharrāf, Shaṭṭ al** ≈ S Iraq
Gharvān see Gharyān
75 O7 **Gharyān** var. Gharvān. NW Libya 32°10′N 13°01′E
74 M11 **Ghāt** var. Gat. SW Libya 24°58′N 10°11′E
Ghawdex see Gozo
141 U8 **Ghayathi** Abū Ẓaby, W United Arab Emirates 23°51′N 53°01′E
Ghazāl, Baḥr al see Ghazal, Bahr el
78 H9 **Ghazal, Bahr el** var. Soro. seasonal river C Chad
80 E13 **Ghazal, Bahr el** var. Baḥr al Ghazāl. ≈ S Sudan
74 H6 **Ghazaouet** NW Algeria 35°08′N 01°50′W
152 J10 **Ghāziābād** Uttar Pradesh, N India 28°42′N 77°28′E
153 O13 **Ghāzīpur** Uttar Pradesh, N India 25°36′N 83°36′E
149 Q6 **Ghaznī** var. Ghazni. Ghaznī, E Afghanistan 33°31′N 68°24′E
149 P7 **Ghaznī** ⬖ province SE Afghanistan
Ghazzah see Gaza
Gheel see Geel
Ghelīzāne see Relizane
Ghent see Gent
Gheorghe Brațul see Sfântu Gheorghe, Brațul
Gheorghe Gheorghiu-Dej see Onești
116 J10 **Gheorgheni** prev. Gheorghieni, Sîn-Miclăuș, Ger. Niklasmarkt, Hung. Gyergyószentmiklós. Harghita, C Romania 46°43′N 25°36′E
Gheorghieni see Gheorgheni
116 H10 **Gherla** Ger. Neuschliss, Hung. Szamosújvár; prev. Armenierstadt. Cluj, NW Romania 47°02′N 23°55′E
Gheweifat see Ghuwayfāt
Ghilan see Gīlān
107 C18 **Ghilarza** Sardegna, Italy, C Mediterranean Sea 40°09′N 08°50′E
Ghilizane see Relizane
Ghimbi see Gimbī
Ghiriş see Câmpia Turzii
103 Y15 **Ghisonaccia** Corse, France, C Mediterranean Sea 42°00′N 09°25′E
147 Q11 **Ghonchī** Rus. Ganchi. NW Tajikistan 39°57′N 69°10′E
Ghor see Ghowr
153 T13 **Ghoraghat** Rajshahi, NW Bangladesh 25°18′N 89°20′E
149 R13 **Ghotki** Sind, SE Pakistan 28°00′N 69°21′E
148 M5 **Ghowr** var. Ghor. ⬖ province C Afghanistan
147 T13 **Ghūdara** var. Gudara, Rus. Kudara. SE Tajikistan 38°28′N 72°39′E
153 R13 **Ghugri** ≈ N India

◆ Country ● Country Capital ◇ Dependent Territory ○ Dependent Territory Capital ⬖ Administrative Regions ✈ International Airport ▲ Mountain ▲▲ Mountain Range Volcano ≈ River ◎ Lake ▣ Reservoir

147 S14 **Ghund** *Rus.* Gunt. ≈ SE Tajikistan
Ghurābīyah, Sha'īb al *see* Gharbīyah, Sha'īb al
Ghurdaqah *see* Hurghada
148 J5 **Ghūriān** Herāt, W Afghanistan 34°20′N 61°26′E
141 T8 **Ghuwayfāt** *var.* Gheweifat. Abū Ẓaby, W United Arab Emirates 24°06′N 51°40′E
121 O14 **Ghuzayyil, Sabkhat** *salt lake* N Libya
126 J3 **Ghzatsk** Smolenskaya Oblast', W Russian Federation 55°33′N 35°00′E
115 G17 **Giáltra** Évvoia, C Greece 38°21′N 22°58′E
Giamame *see* Jamaame
167 U13 **Gia Nghia** *var.* Đak Nông. Đăc Lăc, S Vietnam 11°58′N 107°42′E
114 F13 **Giannitsá** *var.* Yiannitsá. Kentrikí Makedonía, N Greece 40°49′N 22°24′E
107 F14 **Giannutri, Isola di** *island* Archipelago Toscano, C Italy
96 F13 **Giant's Causeway** *Ir.* Clochán an Aifir. *lava flow* N Northern Ireland, United Kingdom
167 S15 **Gia Rai** Minh Hai, S Vietnam 09°14′N 105°28′E
107 L24 **Giarre** Sicilia, Italy, C Mediterranean Sea 37°44′N 15°12′E
44 I7 **Gibara** Holguín, E Cuba 21°09′N 76°11′W
29 O16 **Gibbon** Nebraska, C USA 40°45′N 98°50′W
32 K11 **Gibbon** Oregon, NW USA 45°40′N 118°22′W
33 P11 **Gibbonsville** Idaho, NW USA 45°33′N 113°55′W
64 A13 **Gibbs Hill** *hill* S Bermuda
92 I9 **Gibostad** Troms, N Norway 69°21′N 18°01′E
104 I14 **Gibraleón** Andalucía, S Spain 37°23′N 06°58′W
104 L16 **Gibraltar** ○ (Gibraltar) S Gibraltar 36°08′N 05°21′W
104 L16 **Gibraltar** ◇ *UK dependent territory* SW Europe
Gibraltar, Détroit de/ Gibraltar, Estrecho de *see* Gibraltar, Strait of
104 J17 **Gibraltar, Strait of** *Fr.* Détroit de Gibraltar, *Sp.* Estrecho de Gibraltar. *strait* Atlantic Ocean/ Mediterranean Sea
31 S11 **Gibsonburg** Ohio, N USA 41°22′N 83°19′W
30 M13 **Gibson City** Illinois, N USA 40°27′N 88°24′W
180 L8 **Gibson Desert** *desert* Western Australia
10 L17 **Gibsons** British Columbia, SW Canada 49°24′N 123°32′W
149 N12 **Gīdār** Baluchistān, SW Pakistan 28°16′N 66°00′E
155 I17 **Giddalūr** Andhra Pradesh, E India 15°24′N 78°54′E
25 U10 **Giddings** Texas, SW USA 30°12′N 96°59′W
27 Y8 **Gideon** Missouri, C USA 36°27′N 89°55′W
81 I15 **Gīdolē** Southern Nationalities, S Ethiopia 05°31′N 37°26′E
118 H13 **Giedraičiai** Utena, E Lithuania 55°05′N 25°16′E
103 O7 **Gien** Loiret, C France 47°40′N 02°37′E
101 G17 **Giessen** Hessen, W Germany 50°35′N 08°41′E
98 O6 **Gieten** Drenthe, NE Netherlands 53°00′N 06°43′E
23 Y13 **Gifford** Florida, SE USA 27°40′N 80°24′W
9 O5 **Gifford** ≈ Baffin Island, Nunavut, NE Canada
100 J12 **Gifhorn** Niedersachsen, N Germany 52°28′N 10°33′E
11 P13 **Gift Lake** Alberta, W Canada 55°49′N 115°57′W
164 L13 **Gifu** *var.* Gihu. Gifu, Honshū, SW Japan 35°24′N 136°46′E
164 K13 **Gifu** *off.* Gifu-ken, *var.* Gihu. ◐ *prefecture* Honshū, SW Japan
Gifu-ken *see* Gifu
126 M13 **Gigant** Rostovskaya Oblast', SW Russian Federation 46°29′N 41°18′E
40 E8 **Giganta, Sierra de la** ▲▲ NW Mexico
54 E12 **Gigante** Huila, S Colombia 02°24′N 75°34′W
114 I7 **Gigen** Pleven, N Bulgaria 43°40′N 24°31′E
Giggiga *see* Jijiga
96 G12 **Gigha Island** *island* SW Scotland, United Kingdom
107 E14 **Giglio, Isola del** *island* Archipelago Toscano, C Italy
Gihu *see* Gifu
146 L11 **G'ijduvon** *Rus.* Gizhduvon. Buxoro Viloyati, C Uzbekistan 40°06′N 64°38′E
104 L2 **Gijón** *var.* Xixón. Asturias, NW Spain 43°32′N 05°40′W
81 D20 **Gikongoro** SW Rwanda 02°30′S 29°32′E
36 K14 **Gila Bend** Arizona, SW USA 32°57′N 112°43′W
36 J14 **Gila Bend Mountains** ▲▲ Arizona, SW USA
37 N14 **Gila Mountains** ▲▲ Arizona, SW USA
36 I15 **Gila Mountains** ▲▲ Arizona, SW USA
142 M4 **Gīlān** *off.* Ostān-e Gīlān, *var.* Ghilan, Guilan. ◐ *province* NW Iran
Gīlān, Ostān-e *see* Gīlān
36 L14 **Gila River** ≈ Arizona, SW USA
29 W4 **Gilbert** Minnesota, N USA 47°29′N 92°27′W
Gilbert Islands *see* Tungaru
10 L16 **Gilbert, Mount** ▲ British Columbia, SW Canada 50°49′N 124°03′W
181 U4 **Gilbert River** ≈ Queensland, NE Australia
0 C6 **Gilbert Seamounts** *undersea feature* NE Pacific Ocean 52°50′N 150°10′W
33 S7 **Gildford** Montana, NW USA 48°34′N 110°21′W
83 P15 **Gilé** Zambézia, NE Mozambique 16°10′S 28°17′E
30 K4 **Gile Flowage** ◎ Wisconsin, N USA
182 G7 **Giles, Lake** *salt lake* South Australia
Gilf Kebir Plateau *see* Haḍabat al Jilf al Kabīr
183 R6 **Gilgandra** New South Wales, SE Australia 31°43′S 148°39′E
Gîlgău *see* Gâlgău
81 I19 **Gilgil** Rift Valley, SW Kenya 0°29′S 36°19′E
183 S4 **Gil Gil Creek** ≈ New South Wales, SE Australia
149 V3 **Gilgit** Jammu and Kashmir, NE Pakistan 35°54′N 74°20′E
149 V3 **Gilgit** ≈ N Pakistan
11 X11 **Gillam** Manitoba, C Canada 56°25′N 94°45′W
95 J22 **Gilleleje** Frederiksborg, E Denmark 56°05′N 12°17′E
30 K14 **Gillespie** Illinois, N USA 39°07′N 89°49′W
27 W13 **Gillett** Arkansas, C USA 34°07′N 91°22′W
33 X12 **Gillette** Wyoming, C USA 44°17′N 105°30′W
97 P22 **Gillingham** SE England, United Kingdom 51°24′N 00°33′E
195 X6 **Gillock Island** *island* Antarctica
173 O16 **Gillot** ✕ (St-Denis) N Réunion 20°53′S 55°31′E
65 H25 **Gill Point** *headland* E Saint Helena 15°59′S 05°38′W
30 M12 **Gilman** Illinois, N USA 40°44′N 87°58′W
25 W6 **Gilmer** Texas, SW USA 32°44′N 94°58′W
Gilolo *see* Halmahera, Pulau
81 G14 **Gīlo Wenz** ≈ SW Ethiopia
35 O10 **Gilroy** California, W USA 37°00′N 121°34′W
123 Q12 **Gilyuy** ≈ SE Russian Federation
99 I14 **Gilze** Noord-Brabant, S Netherlands 51°33′N 04°56′E
165 R16 **Gima** Okinawa, Kume-jima, SW Japan
80 H13 **Gīmbī** *It.* Ghimbi. Oromīya, C Ethiopia 09°13′N 35°39′E
45 T12 **Gimie, Mount** ▲ C Saint Lucia 13°51′N 61°00′W
11 X16 **Gimli** Manitoba, S Canada 50°39′N 97°00′W
Gimma *see* Jīma
95 O14 **Gimo** Uppsala, C Sweden 60°11′N 18°12′E
102 L15 **Gimone** ≈ S France
Gimpoe *see* Gimpu
171 N12 **Gimpu** *prev.* Gimpoe. Sulawesi, C Indonesia 01°38′S 120°00′E
182 F5 **Gina** South Australia 29°56′S 134°33′E
Ginevra *see* Genève
99 J19 **Gingelom** Limburg, NE Belgium 50°46′N 05°09′E
180 I12 **Gingin** Western Australia 31°22′S 115°51′E
171 Q7 **Gingoog** Mindanao, S Philippines 08°47′N 125°05′E
81 K14 **Gīnīr** Oromīya, C Ethiopia 07°12′N 40°43′E
Giohar *see* Jawhar
107 O17 **Gióia del Colle** Puglia, SE Italy 40°47′N 16°56′E
107 M22 **Gioia, Golfo di** *gulf* S Italy
Giona *see* Gkióna
115 I16 **Gioúra** *island* Vóreies Sporádes, Greece, Aegean Sea
107 O17 **Giovinazzo** Puglia, SE Italy 41°11′N 16°40′E
Gipeswic *see* Ipswich
Gipuzkoa *see* Guipúzcoa
Giran *see* Ilan
30 K14 **Girard** Illinois, N USA 39°27′N 89°46′W
27 R7 **Girard** Kansas, C USA 37°30′N 94°50′W
25 O6 **Girard** Texas, SW USA 33°18′N 100°38′W
54 E10 **Girardot** Cundinamarca, C Colombia 04°19′N 74°47′W
172 M7 **Giraud Seamount** *undersea feature* SW Indian Ocean 09°57′S 46°55′E
83 A15 **Giraul** ≈ SW Angola
96 L9 **Girdle Ness** *headland* NE Scotland, United Kingdom 57°09′N 02°04′W
137 N11 **Giresun** *var.* Kerasunt; *anc.* Cerasus, Pharnacia. Giresun, NE Turkey 40°55′N 38°35′E
137 N12 **Giresun** *var.* Kerasunt. ◐ *province* NE Turkey
137 N12 **Giresun Dağları** ▲▲ N Turkey
Girga *see* Jirjā
Girgeh *see* Jirjā
Girgenti *see* Agrigento
153 Q15 **Girīdīh** Jhārkhand, NE India 24°10′N 86°20′E
183 P6 **Girilambone** New South Wales, SE Australia 31°19′S 146°57′E
Girin *see* Jilin
121 W10 **Girne** *Gk.* Kerýneia, Kyrenia. N Cyprus 35°20′N 33°20′E
Giron *see* Kiruna
105 X5 **Girona** *var.* Gerona; *anc.* Gerunda. Cataluña, NE Spain 41°59′N 02°49′E
105 W5 **Girona** *var.* Gerona. ◐ *province* Cataluña, NE Spain
102 J12 **Gironde** ◐ *department* SW France
102 J11 **Gironde** *estuary* SW France
105 V5 **Gironella** Cataluña, NE Spain 42°02′N 01°53′E
103 N15 **Girou** ≈ S France
97 H14 **Girvan** W Scotland, United Kingdom 55°14′N 04°53′W
24 M9 **Girvin** Texas, SW USA 31°05′N 102°24′W
184 Q9 **Gisborne** Gisborne, North Island, New Zealand 38°41′S 178°01′E
184 P9 **Gisborne** *off.* Gisborne District. ◐ *unitary authority* North Island, New Zealand
Gisborne District *see* Gisborne
Giseifu *see* Ŭijŏngbu
Gisenye *see* Gisenyi
81 D19 **Gisenyi** *var.* Gisenye. NW Rwanda 01°42′S 29°18′E
95 K20 **Gislaved** Jönköping, S Sweden 57°19′N 13°30′E
103 N4 **Gisors** Eure, N France 49°18′N 01°46′E
Gissar *see* Hisor
147 P12 **Gissar Range** *Rus.* Gissarskiy Khrebet. ▲▲ Tajikistan/Uzbekistan
Gissarskiy Khrebet *see* Gissar Range
99 B16 **Gistel** West-Vlaanderen, W Belgium 51°09′N 02°58′E
108 F9 **Giswil** Unterwalden, C Switzerland 46°49′N 08°11′E
115 B16 **Gitánes** *ancient monument* Ípeiros, W Greece
81 E20 **Gitarama** C Rwanda 02°05′S 29°45′E
81 E20 **Gitega** C Burundi 03°20′S 29°56′E
Githio *see* Gýtheio
108 H11 **Giubiasco** Ticino, S Switzerland 46°11′N 09°01′E
106 K13 **Giulianova** Abruzzi, C Italy 42°45′N 13°58′E
Giulie, Alpi *see* Julian Alps
Giumri *see* Gyumri
116 M13 **Giurgeni** Ialomiţa, SE Romania 44°45′N 27°48′E
116 J15 **Giurgiu** Giurgiu, S Romania 43°54′N 25°58′E
116 J14 **Giurgiu** ◐ *county* SE Romania
95 F22 **Give** Vejle, C Denmark 55°51′N 09°15′E
103 R2 **Givet** Ardennes, N France 50°08′N 04°50′E
103 R11 **Givors** Rhône, E France 45°35′N 04°47′E
83 K19 **Giyani** Limpopo, NE South Africa 23°20′S 30°37′E
80 I13 **Giyon** Oromīya, C Ethiopia 08°31′N 37°56′E
75 W8 **Gîza** *var.* Al Jīzah, El Gîza, Gizeh. N Egypt 30°01′N 31°13′E
75 V8 **Giza, Pyramids of** *ancient monument* N Egypt
Gizhduvon *see* G'ijduvon
123 U8 **Gizhiga** Magadanskaya Oblast', E Russian Federation 61°58′N 160°16′E
123 T9 **Gizhiginskaya Guba** *bay* E Russian Federation
186 K8 **Gizo** Gizo, NW Solomon Islands 08°03′S 156°49′E
110 N7 **Giżycko** *Ger.* Lötzen. Warmińsko-Mazurskie, NE Poland 54°03′N 21°48′E
Gízymałów *see* Hrymayliv
113 M17 **Gjakovë** *Serb.* Đakovica. W Kosovo 42°22′N 20°30′E
94 F12 **Gjende** ◎ S Norway
95 F17 **Gjerstad** Aust-Agder, S Norway 58°54′N 09°03′E
113 O17 **Gjilan** *Serb.* Gnjilane. E Kosovo 42°27′N 21°28′E
Gjinokastër *see* Gjirokastër
113 L23 **Gjirokastër** *var.* Gjirokastra; *prev.* Gjinokastër, *Gk.* Argyrokastron, *It.* Argirocastro. Gjirokastër, S Albania 40°04′N 20°09′E
113 L22 **Gjirokastër** ◐ *district* S Albania
Gjirokastra *see* Gjirokastër
9 N7 **Gjoa Haven** *var.* Uqsuqtuuq. King William Island, Nunavut, NW Canada 68°38′N 95°57′W
94 H13 **Gjøvik** Oppland, S Norway 60°47′N 10°40′E
113 J22 **Gjuhëzës, Kepi i** *headland* SW Albania 40°25′N 19°19′E
Gjurgjevac *see* Đurđevac
115 E18 **Gkióna** *var.* Giona. ▲▲ C Greece
121 R3 **Gkréko, Akrotíri** *var.* Cape Greco, Pidálion. *cape* E Cyprus
99 I18 **Glabbeek-Zuurbemde** Vlaams Brabant, C Belgium 50°54′N 04°58′E
13 R14 **Glace Bay** Cape Breton Island, Nova Scotia, SE Canada 46°12′N 59°57′W
11 O16 **Glacier** British Columbia, SW Canada 51°12′N 117°33′W
39 W12 **Glacier Bay** *inlet* Alaska, USA
32 I7 **Glacier Peak** ▲ Washington, NW USA 48°06′N 121°06′W
21 Q7 **Glade Spring** Virginia, NE USA 36°47′N 81°46′W
43 W7 **Gladewater** Texas, SW USA 32°32′N 94°57′W
181 Y8 **Gladstone** Queensland, E Australia 23°52′S 151°16′E
182 I8 **Gladstone** South Australia 33°16′S 138°21′E
11 X16 **Gladstone** Manitoba, S Canada 50°12′N 98°56′W
31 O5 **Gladstone** Michigan, N USA 45°51′N 87°01′W
27 R4 **Gladstone** Missouri, C USA 39°12′N 94°33′W
31 Q7 **Gladwin** Michigan, N USA 43°58′N 84°29′W
95 J15 **Glafsfjorden** ◎ C Sweden
92 H2 **Gláma** *physical region* NW Iceland
94 I12 **Gláma** *var.* Glommen. ≈ S Norway
112 F13 **Glamoč** Federacija Bosna I Hercegovina, NE Boznia and Herzegovina 44°01′N 16°51′E
97 J22 **Glamorgan** *cultural region* S Wales, United Kingdom
95 G24 **Glamsbjerg** Fyn, C Denmark 55°17′N 10°07′E
171 Q8 **Glan** Mindanao, S Philippines 05°49′N 125°11′E
109 T9 **Glan** ≈ SE Austria
101 F19 **Glan** ≈ W Germany
95 M17 **Glan** ◎ S Sweden
Glaris *see* Glarus
108 H9 **Glarner Alpen** *Eng.* Glarus Alps. ▲▲ E Switzerland
108 H8 **Glarus** Glarus, E Switzerland 47°03′N 09°04′E
108 H9 **Glarus** *Fr.* Glaris. ◐ *canton* C Switzerland
Glarus Alps *see* Glarner Alpen
27 N3 **Glasco** Kansas, C USA 39°21′N 97°50′W
96 I12 **Glasgow** S Scotland, United Kingdom 55°53′N 04°15′W
20 K7 **Glasgow** Kentucky, S USA 37°00′N 85°54′W
27 T4 **Glasgow** Missouri, C USA 39°13′N 92°51′W
33 W7 **Glasgow** Montana, NW USA 48°12′N 106°37′W
21 T6 **Glasgow** Virginia, NE USA 37°37′N 79°27′W
96 I12 **Glasgow** ✕ W Scotland, United Kingdom 55°52′N 04°27′W
11 S14 **Glaslyn** Saskatchewan, S Canada 53°20′N 108°18′W
18 I16 **Glassboro** New Jersey, NE USA 39°40′N 75°05′W
24 L10 **Glass Mountains** ▲▲ Texas, SW USA
97 K23 **Glastonbury** SW England, United Kingdom 51°09′N 02°43′W
Glatz *see* Kłodzko
101 N16 **Glauchau** Sachsen, E Germany 50°48′N 12°32′E
114 M7 **Glavinitsa** Silistra, NE Bulgaria 43°55′N 26°50′E
Glavn'a Morava *see* Velika Morava
Glavnik *see* Gllamnik
127 T1 **Glazov** Udmurtskaya Respublika, NW Russian Federation 58°06′N 52°38′E
Głda *see* Gwda
109 U8 **Gleinalpe** ▲▲ SE Austria
109 W8 **Gleisdorf** Steiermark, SE Austria 47°07′N 15°43′E
Gleiwitz *see* Gliwice
39 S11 **Glenallen** Alaska, USA 62°06′N 145°33′W
102 F7 **Glénan, Îles** *island group* NW France
185 G21 **Glenavy** Canterbury, South Island, New Zealand 44°53′S 171°04′E
10 H5 **Glenboyle** Yukon Territory, NW Canada 63°55′N 138°43′W
21 X3 **Glen Burnie** Maryland, NE USA 39°09′N 76°37′W
36 L8 **Glen Canyon** *canyon* Utah, W USA
36 L8 **Glen Canyon Dam** *dam* Arizona, SW USA
30 K15 **Glen Carbon** Illinois, N USA 38°45′N 89°58′W
14 E17 **Glencoe** Ontario, S Canada 42°44′N 81°42′W
83 K22 **Glencoe** KwaZulu/Natal, E South Africa 28°10′S 30°15′E
29 U9 **Glencoe** Minnesota, N USA 44°46′N 94°09′W
96 H10 **Glen Coe** *valley* N Scotland, United Kingdom
36 K13 **Glendale** Arizona, SW USA 33°32′N 112°11′W
35 S15 **Glendale** California, W USA 34°09′N 118°20′W
182 G5 **Glendambo** South Australia 30°59′S 135°45′E
33 Y8 **Glendive** Montana, NW USA 47°08′N 104°42′W
33 Y15 **Glendo** Wyoming, C USA 42°27′N 105°01′W
55 S10 **Glendor Mountains** C Guyana
182 K12 **Glenelg River** ≈ South Australia/Victoria, SE Australia
29 P4 **Glenfield** North Dakota, N USA 47°25′N 98°33′W
25 V12 **Glen Flora** Texas, SW USA 29°22′N 96°12′W
181 P7 **Glen Helen** Northern Territory, N Australia 23°45′S 132°46′E
183 U5 **Glen Innes** New South Wales, SE Australia 29°42′S 151°45′E
31 P6 **Glen Lake** ◎ Michigan, N USA
10 I7 **Glenlyon Peak** ▲ Yukon Territory, W Canada 62°32′N 134°51′W
37 N16 **Glenn, Mount** ▲ Arizona, SW USA 31°55′N 110°00′W
33 N15 **Glenns Ferry** Idaho, NW USA 42°57′N 115°18′W
23 W6 **Glennville** Georgia, SE USA 31°56′N 81°55′W
10 J10 **Glenora** British Columbia, W Canada 57°52′N 131°16′W
182 M11 **Glenorchy** Victoria, SE Australia 36°56′S 142°39′E
183 V5 **Glenreagh** New South Wales, SE Australia 30°04′S 153°00′E
33 X15 **Glenrock** Wyoming, C USA 42°51′N 105°52′W
96 K11 **Glenrothes** E Scotland, United Kingdom 56°11′N 03°09′W
18 L9 **Glens Falls** New York, NE USA 43°18′N 73°38′W
97 D14 **Glenties** *Ir.* Na Gleannta. Donegal, NW Ireland 54°47′N 08°17′W
28 L5 **Glen Ullin** North Dakota, N USA 46°49′N 101°49′W
21 R4 **Glenville** West Virginia, NE USA 38°57′N 80°51′W
27 T12 **Glenwood** Arkansas, C USA 34°19′N 93°33′W
29 S15 **Glenwood** Iowa, C USA 41°03′N 95°44′W
29 T7 **Glenwood** Minnesota, N USA 45°39′N 95°23′W
36 L5 **Glenwood** Utah, W USA 38°45′N 111°59′W
30 I5 **Glenwood City** Wisconsin, N USA 45°04′N 92°11′W
37 Q4 **Glenwood Springs** Colorado, C USA 39°33′N 107°21′W
108 F10 **Gletsch** Valais, S Switzerland 46°34′N 08°21′E
Glevum *see* Gloucester
29 U14 **Glidden** Iowa, C USA 42°03′N 94°43′W
112 E9 **Glina** *var.* Banijska Palanka. Sisak-Moslavina, NE Croatia 45°19′N 16°07′E
94 F11 **Glittertind** ▲ S Norway 61°24′N 08°19′E
111 J16 **Gliwice** *Ger.* Gleiwitz. Śląskie, S Poland 50°19′N 18°49′E
113 N16 **Gllamnik** *Serb.* Glavnik. N Kosovo 42°53′N 21°10′E
36 M14 **Globe** Arizona, SW USA 33°24′N 110°47′W
Globino *see* Hlobyne
108 L9 **Glockturm** ▲ SW Austria 46°54′N 10°42′E
116 L9 **Glodeni** *Rus.* Glodyany. N Moldova 47°47′N 27°33′E
109 S9 **Glödnitz** Kärnten, S Austria 46°57′N 14°03′E
Glodyany *see* Glodeni
Glogau *see* Głogów
109 W6 **Gloggnitz** Niederösterreich, E Austria 47°41′N 15°57′E
110 F13 **Głogów** *Ger.* Glogau, Glogow. Dolnośląskie, SW Poland 51°40′N 16°04′E
Glogow *see* Głogów
111 I16 **Głogówek** *Ger.* Oberglogau. Opolskie, S Poland 50°21′N 17°51′E
92 G12 **Glomfjord** Nordland, C Norway 66°49′N 14°00′E
Glomma *see* Gláma
Glommen *see* Gláma
93 I14 **Glommersträsk** Norrbotten, N Sweden 65°17′N 19°40′E
172 I1 **Glorieuses, Îles** *Eng.* Glorioso Islands. *island* (to France) N Madagascar
Glorioso Islands *see* Glorieuses, Îles
38 J12 **Glory of Russia Cape** *headland* Saint Matthew Island, Alaska, USA 60°36′N 172°57′W
22 J7 **Gloster** Mississippi, S USA 31°12′N 91°01′W
183 U7 **Gloucester** New South Wales, SE Australia 32°01′S 152°00′E
186 F7 **Gloucester** New Britain, E Papua New Guinea 05°30′S 148°30′E
97 L21 **Gloucester** *hist.* Caer Glou, *Lat.* Glevum. C England, United Kingdom 51°53′N 02°14′W
19 P10 **Gloucester** Massachusetts, NE USA 42°36′N 70°36′W
21 X6 **Gloucester** Virginia, NE USA 37°26′N 76°33′W
97 K21 **Gloucestershire** *cultural region* C England, United Kingdom
31 T14 **Glouster** Ohio, N USA 39°30′N 82°04′W
42 H3 **Glovers Reef** *reef* E Belize
18 K10 **Gloversville** New York, NE USA 43°03′N 74°20′W
110 K12 **Głowno** Łódź, C Poland 51°58′N 19°43′E
111 H16 **Głubczyce** *Ger.* Leobschütz. Opolskie, S Poland 50°13′N 17°50′E
126 L11 **Glubokiy** Rostovskaya Oblast', SW Russian Federation 48°34′N 40°16′E
145 W9 **Glubokoye** Vostochnyy Kazakhstan, E Kazakhstan 50°08′N 82°16′E
Glubokoye *see* Hlybokaye
111 H16 **Głuchołazy** *Ger.* Ziegenhais. Opolskie, S Poland 50°20′N 17°23′E
100 I9 **Glückstadt** Schleswig-Holstein, N Germany 53°47′N 09°26′E
Glukhov *see* Hlukhiv
Glushkevichi *see* Hlushkavichy
Glusk/Glussk *see* Hlusk
Glybokaya *see* Hlyboka
95 F21 **Glyngøre** Viborg, NW Denmark 56°45′N 08°55′E
127 Q9 **Gmelinka** Volgogradskaya Oblast', SW Russian Federation 50°50′N 46°51′E
109 R8 **Gmünd** Kärnten, S Austria 46°56′N 13°32′E
109 U2 **Gmünd** Niederösterreich, N Austria 48°47′N 14°59′E
Gmünd *see* Schwäbisch Gmünd
109 S5 **Gmunden** Oberösterreich, N Austria 47°56′N 13°48′E
Gmundner See *see* Traunsee
94 N10 **Gnarp** Gävleborg, C Sweden 62°03′N 17°19′E
109 W8 **Gnas** Steiermark, SE Austria 46°53′N 15°48′E
Gnaviyani *see* Fuammulah
Gnesen *see* Gniezno
95 O16 **Gnesta** Södermanland, C Sweden 59°05′N 17°20′E
110 H11 **Gniezno** *Ger.* Gnesen. Weilkopolskie, C Poland 52°33′N 17°35′E
Gnjilane *see* Gjilan
95 K20 **Gnosjö** Jönköping, S Sweden 57°22′N 13°44′E
155 E17 **Goa** *prev.* Old Goa, Vela Goa, Velha Goa. Goa, W India 15°31′N 73°56′E
155 E17 **Goa** *var.* Old Goa. ◐ *state* W India
Goabddális *see* Kåbdalis
153 U12 **Goalpārā** Assam, NE India 26°11′N 90°37′E
42 H7 **Goascorán, Río** ≈ El Salvador/Honduras
77 O16 **Goaso** *var.* Gawso. W Ghana 06°49′N 02°27′W
81 K14 **Goba** *It.* Oromo. Bīnishangul Gumuz, C Ethiopia 07°02′N 39°58′E
83 C20 **Gobabed** Erongo, W Namibia 23°36′S 15°03′E
83 E19 **Gobabis** Omaheke, E Namibia 22°25′S 18°58′E
Gobannium *see* Abergavenny
64 M7 **Goban Spur** *undersea feature* NW Atlantic Ocean
63 H21 **Gobernador Gregores** Santa Cruz, S Argentina 48°43′S 70°21′W
61 F14 **Gobernador Ingeniero Virasoro** Corrientes, NE Argentina 28°06′S 56°00′W
162 L12 **Gobi** *desert* China/Mongolia
164 I14 **Gobō** Wakayama, Honshū, SW Japan 33°52′N 135°09′E
Gobolka Awdal *see* Awdal
Gobolka Sahil *see* Sahil
Gobolka Sool *see* Sool
101 D14 **Goch** Nordrhein-Westfalen, W Germany 51°41′N 06°10′E
83 E20 **Gochas** Hardap, S Namibia 24°54′S 18°43′E
155 I14 **Godāvari** *var.* Godavari. ≈ C India
Godavari *see* Godāvari
155 L16 **Godāvari, Mouths of the** *delta* E India
15 V5 **Godbout** Québec, SE Canada 49°19′N 67°37′W
15 U5 **Godbout** ≈ Québec, SE Canada
15 U5 **Godbout Est** ≈ Québec, SE Canada
153 R14 **Godda** Jharkhand, India 24°50′N 87°13′E
27 N6 **Goddard** Kansas, C USA 37°39′N 97°34′W
14 E15 **Goderich** Ontario, S Canada 43°43′N 81°43′W
Godhavn *see* Qeqertarsuaq
154 E10 **Godhra** Gujarāt, W India 22°49′N 73°40′E
Göding *see* Hodonín
111 K22 **Gödöllő** Pest, N Hungary 47°36′N 19°20′E
62 H11 **Godoy Cruz** Mendoza, W Argentina 32°59′S 68°49′W
11 Y11 **Gods** ≈ Manitoba, C Canada
11 Y13 **Gods Lake** Manitoba, C Canada 54°29′N 94°21′W
11 X13 **Gods Lake** ◎ Manitoba, C Canada
Godthaab/Godthåb *see* Nuuk
Godwin Austen, Mount *see* K2
Goede Hoop, Kaap de *see* Good Hope, Cape of
Goedgegun *see* Nhlangano
Goeie Hoop, Kaap die *see* Good Hope, Cape of
13 O7 **Goélands, Lac aux** ◎ Québec, SE Canada
98 E13 **Goeree** *island* SW Netherlands
99 F15 **Goes** Zeeland, SW Netherlands 51°30′N 03°55′E
Goettingen *see* Göttingen
19 O10 **Goffstown** New Hampshire, NE USA 43°01′N 71°34′W
14 E8 **Gogama** Ontario, S Canada 47°42′N 81°44′W
30 L3 **Gogebic, Lake** ◎ Michigan, N USA
30 K3 **Gogebic Range** *hill range* Michigan/Wisconsin, N USA
Gogi Lerr *see* Gogi, Mount
137 V13 **Gogi, Mount** *Arm.* Gogi Lerr, *Az.* Küküdağ. ▲ Armenia/Azerbaijan 39°33′N 45°35′E
124 F12 **Gogland, Ostrov** *island* NW Russian Federation
111 I15 **Gogolin** Opolskie, S Poland 50°28′N 18°04′E
Gogonou *see* Gogounou
77 S14 **Gogounou** *var.* Gogonou. N Benin 10°50′N 02°50′E
152 I10 **Gohāna** Haryāna, N India 29°06′N 76°43′E
59 K18 **Goianésia** Goiás, C Brazil 15°21′S 49°02′W
59 K18 **Goiânia** *prev.* Goyania. *state capital* Goiás, C Brazil 16°43′S 49°18′W
59 K18 **Goiás** Goiás, C Brazil 15°57′S 50°07′W
59 J18 **Goiás** *off.* Estado de Goiás; *prev.* Goiaz, Goyaz. ◐ *state* C Brazil
Goiás, Estado de *see* Goiás
Goiaz *see* Goiás
Goidhoo Atoll *see* Horsburgh Atoll
159 R14 **Goinsargoin** Xizang Zizhiqu, W China 31°56′N 98°04′E
60 H10 **Goio-Erê** Paraná, SW Brazil 24°08′S 53°07′W
99 I15 **Goirle** Noord-Brabant, S Netherlands 51°31′N 05°04′E
104 H8 **Góis** Coimbra, N Portugal 40°10′N 08°06′W
165 Q8 **Gojōme** Akita, Honshū, NW Japan 39°55′N 140°07′E
149 U9 **Gojra** Punjab, E Pakistan 31°10′N 72°43′E
136 A11 **Gökçeada** *var.* Imroz Adasī, *Gk.* Imbros. *island* NW Turkey
Gökçeada *see* İmroz
146 F13 **Gökdepe** *Rus.* Gëkdepe, Geok-Tepe. Ahal Welaýaty, C Turkmenistan 38°05′N 58°08′E
136 I10 **Gökırmak** ≈ N Turkey
Goklenkuy, Solonchak *see* Geklengkui, Solonchak
136 C16 **Gökova Körfezi** *gulf* SW Turkey
136 K15 **Göksu** ≈ S Turkey
136 L15 **Göksun** Kahramanmaraş, C Turkey 38°03′N 36°30′E
136 I17 **Göksu Nehri** ≈ S Turkey
83 J16 **Gokwe** Midlands, NW Zimbabwe 18°13′S 28°55′E
94 F13 **Gol** Buskerud, S Norway 60°42′N 08°57′E
153 X12 **Golāghāt** Assam, NE India 26°31′N 93°54′E
110 H10 **Gołańcz** Wielkopolskie, C Poland 52°57′N 17°17′E
138 G8 **Golan Heights** *Ar.* Al Jawlān, *Heb.* HaGolan. ▲▲ SW Syria
Golārā *see* Ārān
Golaya Pristan *see* Hola Prystan'
143 T11 **Golbāf** Kermān, C Iran 29°51′N 57°44′E
136 M15 **Gölbaşı** Adıyaman, S Turkey 37°46′N 37°40′E
109 P9 **Gölbner** ▲ SW Austria 46°51′N 12°31′E
30 M17 **Golconda** Illinois, N USA 37°20′N 88°29′W
35 T3 **Golconda** Nevada, W USA 40°56′N 117°29′W
136 E11 **Gölcük** Kocaeli, NW Turkey 40°44′N 29°50′E
108 I7 **Goldach** Sankt Gallen, NE Switzerland 47°28′N 09°28′E
110 N7 **Gołdap** *Ger.* Goldap. Warmińsko-Mazurskie, NE Poland 54°19′N 22°23′E
32 E15 **Gold Beach** Oregon, NW USA 42°25′N 124°27′W
Goldberg *see* Złotoryja
183 V3 **Gold Coast** *cultural region* Queensland, E Australia
68 D12 **Gold Coast** *coastal region* S Ghana
39 R10 **Gold Creek** Alaska, USA 62°48′N 149°40′W
11 O16 **Golden** British Columbia, SW Canada 51°19′N 116°58′W
37 T4 **Golden** Colorado, C USA 39°40′N 105°12′W
184 I13 **Golden Bay** *bay* South Island, New Zealand
27 R7 **Golden City** Missouri, C USA 37°23′N 94°05′W
32 I11 **Goldendale** Washington, NW USA 45°49′N 120°49′W
Goldener Tisch *see* Zlatý Stôl
44 L13 **Golden Grove** E Jamaica 17°56′N 76°17′W
14 J12 **Golden Lake** ◎ Ontario, SE Canada
22 K10 **Golden Meadow** Louisiana, S USA 29°22′N 90°15′W
45 V10 **Golden Rock** ✕ (Basseterre) Saint Kitts, Saint Kitts and Nevis 17°16′N 62°43′W
Golden State, The *see* California
83 K16 **Golden Valley** Mashonaland West, N Zimbabwe 18°11′S 29°50′E
35 U9 **Goldfield** Nevada, W USA 37°42′N 117°15′W
Goldingen *see* Kuldīga
Goldmarkt *see* Zlatna
10 K17 **Gold River** Vancouver Island, British Columbia, SW Canada 49°41′N 126°05′W
21 V10 **Goldsboro** North Carolina, SE USA 35°23′N 78°00′W
24 M8 **Goldsmith** Texas, SW USA 31°58′N 102°36′W
25 R8 **Goldthwaite** Texas, SW USA 31°28′N 98°35′W
137 R11 **Göle** Ardahan, NE Turkey 40°47′N 42°36′E
Golema Ada *see* Ostrovo
114 H9 **Golema Planina** ▲▲ W Bulgaria
114 F9 **Golemi Vrŭkh** ▲ W Bulgaria 42°41′N 22°38′E
110 D8 **Goleniów** *Ger.* Gollnow. Zachodnio-pomorskie, NW Poland 53°34′N 14°48′E
143 R3 **Golestān** ◐ *province* N Iran
35 Q14 **Goleta** California, W USA 34°26′N 119°50′W
43 O16 **Golfito** Puntarenas, SE Costa Rica 08°42′N 83°10′W
25 T13 **Goliad** Texas, SW USA 28°40′N 97°26′W
113 L14 **Golija** ▲▲ SW Serbia
Golinka *see* Gongbo'gyamda
113 O16 **Goljak** ▲▲ SE Serbia
136 M12 **Gölköy** Ordu, N Turkey 40°42′N 37°37′E
Gollel *see* Lavumisa
109 X3 **Göllersbach** ≈ NE Austria
Gollnow *see* Goleniów
Golmo *see* Golmud
159 P10 **Golmud** *var.* Ge'e'mu, Golmo, *Chin.* Ko-erh-mu. Qinghai, C China 36°23′N 94°56′E
103 Y14 **Golo** ≈ Corse, France, C Mediterranean Sea
Golovanevsk *see* Holovanivs'k
Golovchin *see* Halowchyn
39 N9 **Golovin** Alaska, USA 64°33′N 162°54′W
142 M7 **Golpāyegān** *var.* Gulpaigan. Eşfahān, W Iran 33°23′N 50°18′E
Golshan *see* Ţabas
Gol'shany *see* Hal'shany
96 J7 **Golspie** N Scotland, United Kingdom 57°59′N 03°56′W
112 O11 **Golubac** Serbia, NE Serbia 44°38′N 21°36′E
110 J9 **Golub-Dobrzyń** Kujawski-pomorskie, C Poland 53°07′N 19°03′E
145 S7 **Golubovka** Pavlodar, N Kazakhstan 53°07′N 74°11′E
82 B11 **Golungo Alto** Cuanza Norte, NW Angola 09°10′S 14°45′E
114 M8 **Golyama Kamchiya** ≈ E Bulgaria
114 L8 **Golyama Reka** ≈ N Bulgaria
114 H11 **Golyama Syutkya** ▲ SW Bulgaria 41°55′N 24°03′E
114 I12 **Golyam Perelik** ▲ S Bulgaria 41°37′N 24°34′E
114 I11 **Golyam Persenk** ▲ S Bulgaria 41°50′N 24°33′E
79 P19 **Goma** Nord-Kivu, NE Dem. Rep. Congo 01°36′S 29°08′E
153 N13 **Gomati** *var.* Gumti. ≈ N India
77 X14 **Gombe** Gombe, E Nigeria 10°19′N 11°02′E
67 U10 **Gombe** *var.* Igombe. ≈ E Tanzania
77 Y14 **Gombi** Adamawa, E Nigeria 10°07′N 12°45′E
Gombroon *see* Bandar-e 'Abbās
Gomel' *see* Homyel'
Gomel'skaya Oblast' *see* Homyel'skaya Voblasts'
64 N11 **Gomera** *island* Islas Canarias, Spain, NE Atlantic Ocean
40 I5 **Gómez Farias** Chihuahua, N Mexico 29°25′N 107°46′W
40 L8 **Gómez Palacio** Durango, C Mexico 25°39′N 103°30′W
158 J13 **Gomo** Xizang Zizhiqu, W China 33°37′N 86°40′E
143 T6 **Gonābād** *var.* Gunabad. Khorāsān-Razavī, NE Iran 36°30′N 59°18′E
44 L8 **Gonaïves** *var.* Les Gonaïves. N Haiti 19°26′N 72°41′W
123 Q12 **Gonam** ≈ NE Russian Federation
44 L9 **Gonâve, Canal de la** *var.* Canal de Sud. *channel* N Caribbean Sea
44 K9 **Gonâve, Golfe de la** *gulf* N Caribbean Sea
Gonāveh *see* Bandar-e Gonāveh
44 K9 **Gonâve, Île de la** *island* C Haiti
Gonbadān *see* Do Gonbadān
143 Q3 **Gonbad-e Kāvūs** *var.* Gunbad-i-Qawus. Golestán, N Iran 37°15′N 55°11′E
152 M12 **Gonda** Uttar Pradesh, N India 27°08′N 81°58′E
Gondar *see* Gonder
80 I11 **Gonder** *var.* Gondar. Āmara, NW Ethiopia 12°36′N 37°27′E
78 J13 **Gondey** Moyen-Chari, S Chad 09°07′N 19°10′E
154 J12 **Gondia** Mahārāshtra, C India 21°27′N 80°12′E
104 G6 **Gondomar** Porto, NW Portugal 41°10′N 08°35′W
136 C12 **Gönen** Balıkesir, W Turkey 40°06′N 27°39′E
136 C12 **Gönen Çayı** ≈ NW Turkey
159 O15 **Gongbo'gyamda** *var.* Golinka. Xizang Zizhiqu, W China 30°03′N 93°10′E
Gongchang *see* Longxi
159 N16 **Gonggar** *var.* Gyixong. Xizang Zizhiqu, W China 29°18′N 90°56′E
160 G9 **Gongga Shan** ▲ C China 29°50′N 101°55′E
159 T10 **Gonghe** *var.* Qabqa. Qinghai, C China 36°20′N 100°46′E
Gongjiang *see* Yudu
158 I5 **Gongliu** *var.* Tokkuztara. Xinjiang Uygur Zizhiqu, NW China 43°29′N 82°16′E
77 W14 **Gongola** ≈ E Nigeria
Gongoleh State *see* Jonglei
183 P5 **Gongolgon** New South Wales, SE Australia 30°19′S 146°57′E
159 Q6 **Gongpoquan** Gansu, N China 41°45′N 100°27′E
Gongquan *see* Gongxian
Gongtang *see* Damxung
160 I10 **Gongxian** *var.* Gongquan, Gong Xian. Sichuan, C China 28°25′N 104°51′E
Gong Xian *see* Gongxian
157 V10 **Gongzhuling** *prev.* Huaide. Jilin, NE China 43°30′N 124°48′E
159 S14 **Gonjo** Xizang Zizhiqu, W China 30°51′N 98°16′E
107 B20 **Gonnesa** Sardegna, Italy, C Mediterranean Sea 39°15′N 08°27′E
Gonni/Gónnos *see* Gónnoi
115 F15 **Gónnoi** *var.* Gonni, Gónnos; *prev.* Derelí. Thessalía, C Greece 39°52′N 22°27′E
164 C13 **Gōnoura** Nagasaki, Iki, SW Japan 33°44′N 129°41′E
35 O11 **Gonzales** California, W USA 36°30′N 121°26′W
22 J9 **Gonzales** Louisiana, S USA 30°14′N 90°55′W
25 T12 **Gonzales** Texas, SW USA 29°31′N 97°29′W
41 P11 **González** Tamaulipas, C Mexico 22°50′N 98°25′W
21 V6 **Goochland** Virginia, NE USA 37°42′N 77°54′W
195 X14 **Goodenough, Cape** *headland* Antarctica 66°15′S 126°35′E
186 F9 **Goodenough Island** *var.* Morata. *island* SE Papua New Guinea
39 N8 **Goodhope Bay** *bay* Alaska, USA

◆ Country
● Country Capital
◇ Dependent Territory
○ Dependent Territory Capital
◐ Administrative Regions
✕ International Airport
▲ Mountain
▲▲ Mountain Range
Volcano
≈ River
◎ Lake
Reservoir

83 D26 **Good Hope, Cape of** *Afr.* Kaap de Goede Hoop, Kaap die Goeie Hoop. *headland* SW South Africa 34°19′S 18°25′E
10 K10 **Good Hope Lake** British Columbia, W Canada 59°15′N 129°18′W
83 E23 **Goodhouse** Northern Cape, W South Africa 28°54′S 18°13′E
33 O15 **Gooding** Idaho, NW USA 42°56′N 114°42′W
26 H3 **Goodland** Kansas, C USA 39°20′N 101°43′W
173 Y15 **Goodlands** NW Mauritius 20°02′S 57°39′E
20 J8 **Goodlettsville** Tennessee, S USA 36°19′N 86°42′W
39 N13 **Goodnews** Alaska, USA 59°07′N 161°35′W
25 O3 **Goodnight** Texas, SW USA 35°00′N 101°07′W
183 Q4 **Goodooga** New South Wales, SE Australia 29°09′S 147°30′E
29 N4 **Goodrich** North Dakota, N USA 47°24′N 100°07′W
25 W10 **Goodrich** Texas, SW USA 30°36′N 94°57′W
29 X10 **Goodview** Minnesota, N USA 44°04′N 91°42′W
26 H8 **Goodwell** Oklahoma, C USA 36°36′N 101°38′W
97 N17 **Goole** E England, United Kingdom 53°43′N 00°46′W
183 O8 **Goolgowi** New South Wales, SE Australia 34°00′S 145°43′E
182 I10 **Goolwa** South Australia 35°31′S 138°43′E
181 Y11 **Goondiwindi** Queensland, E Australia 28°33′S 150°22′E
98 O11 **Goor** Overijssel, E Netherlands 52°13′N 06°33′E
Goose Bay *see* Happy Valley-Goose Bay
33 V13 **Gooseberry Creek** ≈ Wyoming, C USA
21 S14 **Goose Creek** South Carolina, SE USA 32°58′N 80°01′W
63 M23 **Goose Green** *var.* Prado del Ganso. East Falkland, Falkland Islands 51°52′S 59°W
16 D8 **Goose Lake** *var.* Lago dos Gansos. ◎ California/Oregon, W USA
29 Q4 **Goose River** ≈ North Dakota, N USA
153 T16 **Gopalganj** Dhaka, S Bangladesh 23°00′N 89°48′E
153 O12 **Gopālganj** Bihār, N India 26°28′N 84°26′E
Gopher State *see* Minnesota
101 I22 **Göppingen** Baden-Württemberg, SW Germany 48°42′N 09°39′E
110 G13 **Góra** *Ger.* Guhrau. Dolnośląskie, SW Poland 51°40′N 16°03′E
110 M12 **Góra Kalwaria** Mazowieckie, C Poland 52°00′N 21°14′E
153 O12 **Gorakhpur** Uttar Pradesh, N India 26°45′N 83°23′E
Gora Kyuren *see* Kürendag
Gorany *see* Harany
113 J14 **Goražde** Federacija Bosna I Hercegovina, SE Bosnia and Herzegovina 43°39′N 18°58′E
Gorbovichi *see* Harbavichy
Gorče Petrov *see* Đorče Petrov
0 E9 **Gorda Ridges** *undersea feature* NE Pacific Ocean 41°30′N 128°00′W
Gordiaz *see* Gardīz
78 K12 **Gordil** Vakaga, N Central African Republic 09°37′N 21°42′E
23 U5 **Gordon** Georgia, SE USA 32°52′N 83°19′W
28 K12 **Gordon** Nebraska, C USA 42°48′N 102°12′W
25 R7 **Gordon** Texas, SW USA 32°32′N 98°21′W
28 L13 **Gordon Creek** ≈ Nebraska, C USA
63 I25 **Gordon, Isla** *island* S Chile
183 O17 **Gordon, Lake** ◎ Tasmania, SE Australia
183 O17 **Gordon River** ≈ Tasmania, SE Australia
21 V5 **Gordonsville** Virginia, NE USA 38°08′N 78°11′W
78 H13 **Goré** Logone-Oriental, S Chad 07°55′N 16°38′E
80 H13 **Gorē** Oromīya, C Ethiopia 08°08′N 35°33′E
185 D24 **Gore** Southland, South Island, New Zealand 46°06′S 168°58′E
14 D11 **Gore Bay** Manitoulin Island, Ontario, S Canada 45°54′N 82°28′W
25 Q5 **Goree** Texas, SW USA 33°28′N 99°31′W
137 O11 **Görele** Giresun, NE Turkey 41°00′N 39°00′E
19 N6 **Gore Mountain** ▲ Vermont, NE USA 44°55′N 71°47′W
39 R13 **Gore Point** *headland* Alaska, USA 59°12′N 150°57′W
37 R4 **Gore Range** ▲▲ Colorado, C USA
97 F19 **Gorey** *Ir.* Guaire. Wexford, SE Ireland 52°40′N 06°18′W
143 R12 **Gorgāb** Kermān, S Iran
143 Q4 **Gorgān** *var.* Astarabad, Astrabad, Gurgan, *prev.* Asterābād; *anc.* Hyrcania. Golestān, N Iran 36°53′N 54°28′E
143 Q4 **Gorgān, Rūd-e** ≈ N Iran
76 I10 **Gorgol** ◈ *region* S Mauritania
106 D12 **Gorgona, Isola di** *island* Archipelago Toscano, C Italy
19 P8 **Gorham** Maine, NE USA 43°41′N 70°27′W
137 T10 **Gori** C Georgia 42°00′N 44°07′E
98 I13 **Gorinchem** *var.* Gorkum. Zuid-Holland, C Netherlands 51°50′N 04°59′E
137 V13 **Goris** SE Armenia 39°31′N 46°20′E
124 K16 **Goritsy** Tverskaya Oblast', W Russian Federation 57°09′N 36°44′E
106 J7 **Gorizia** *Ger.* Görz. Friuli-Venezia Giulia, NE Italy 45°57′N 13°37′E
116 G13 **Gorj** ◈ *county* SW Romania
109 W12 **Gorjanci** *var.* Uskočke Planine, Žumberak, Žumberačko Gorje, *Ger.* Uskokengebirge; *prev.* Sichelburger Gerbirge. ▲ Croatia/Slovenia Europe *see also* Žumberačko Gorje
Görkau *see* Jirkov
Gorki *see* Horki
Gor'kiy *see* Nizhniy Novgorod
127 O11 **Gor'kovskiy** Volgogradskaya Oblast', SW Russian Federation 48°41′N 44°20′E
Gorkum *see* Gorinchem
95 I23 **Gørlev** Vestsjælland, E Denmark 55°33′N 11°14′E
111 M17 **Gorlice** Małopolskie, S Poland 49°40′N 21°09′E
101 Q15 **Görlitz** Sachsen, E Germany 51°09′N 14°58′E
Görlitz *see* Zgorzelec
Gorlovka *see* Horlivka
25 R7 **Gorman** Texas, SW USA 32°12′N 98°40′W
21 T3 **Gormania** West Virginia, NE USA 39°16′N 79°18′W
Gorna Dzhumaya *see* Blagoevgrad
114 K8 **Gorna Oryakhovitsa** Veliko Tŭrnovo, N Bulgaria 43°07′N 25°40′E
114 J8 **Gorna Studena** Veliko Tŭrnovo, N Bulgaria 43°26′N 25°21′E
Gornja Mužlja *see* Mužlja
109 X9 **Gornja Radgona** *Ger.* Oberradkersburg. NE Slovenia 46°39′N 16°00′E
112 M13 **Gornji Milanovac** Serbia, C Serbia 44°01′N 20°26′E
112 G13 **Gornji Vakuf** *var.* Uskoplje. Federacija Bosna I Hercegovina, SW Bosnia and Herzegovina 43°55′N 17°34′E
122 J13 **Gorno-Altaysk** Respublika Altay, S Russian Federation 51°59′N 85°56′E
Gorno-Altayskaya Respublika *see* Altay, Respublika
123 N12 **Gorno-Chuyskiy** Irkutskaya Oblast', C Russian Federation 57°33′N 111°38′E
125 V14 **Gornozavodsk** Permskaya Oblast', NW Russian Federation 58°21′N 58°24′E
125 V14 **Gornozavodsk** Ostrov Sakhalin, Sakhalinskaya Oblast', SE Russian Federation 46°34′N 141°52′E
122 I13 **Gornyak** Altayskiy Kray, S Russian Federation 50°58′N 81°24′E
123 O14 **Gornyy** Chitinskaya Oblast', S Russian Federation 51°42′N 114°16′E
127 R8 **Gornyy** Saratovskaya Oblast', W Russian Federation 51°42′N 48°26′E
Gornyy Altay *see* Altay, Respublika
127 O10 **Gornyy Balykley** Volgogradskaya Oblast', SW Russian Federation 49°37′N 45°03′E
80 I13 **Goroch'an** ▲ W Ethiopia 09°09′N 37°16′E
116 J7 **Gorodenka** *var.* Horodenka. Ivano-Frankivs'ka Oblast', W Ukraine 48°41′N 25°28′E
127 O3 **Gorodets** Nizhegorodskaya Oblast', W Russian Federation 56°36′N 43°27′E
Gorodets *see* Haradzyets
Gorodeya *see* Haradzyeya
127 P6 **Gorodishche** Penzenskaya Oblast', W Russian Federation 53°17′N 45°39′E
Gorodishche *see* Horodyshche
Gorodnya *see* Horodnya
Gorodok *see* Haradok
Gorodok/Gorodok Yagellonski *see* Horodok
126 M13 **Gorodovikovsk** Respublika Kalmykiya, SW Russian Federation 46°07′N 41°56′E
186 D7 **Goroka** Eastern Highlands, C Papua New Guinea 06°02′S 145°22′E
Gorokhov *see* Horokhiv
127 N3 **Gorokhovets** Vladimirskaya Oblast', W Russian Federation 56°12′N 42°40′E
77 Q11 **Gorom-Gorom** NE Burkina 14°27′N 00°14′W
171 U13 **Gorong, Kepulauan** *island group* E Indonesia
83 M17 **Gorongosa** Sofala, C Mozambique 18°40′S 34°03′E
171 P11 **Gorontalo** Sulawesi, C Indonesia 0°33′N 123°05′E
171 O11 **Gorontalo** *off.* Propinsi Gorontalo. ◈ *province* N Indonesia
Propinsi Gorontalo *see* Gorontalo
Gorontalo, Teluk *see* Tomini, Gulf of
110 L7 **Górowo Iławeckie** *Ger.* Landsberg. Warmińsko-Mazurskie, NE Poland 54°18′N 20°30′E
98 M7 **Gorredijk** *Fris.* De Gordyk. Friesland, N Netherlands 53°00′N 06°04′E
84 C14 **Gorringe Ridge** *undersea feature* E Atlantic Ocean 36°40′N 11°35′W
98 M11 **Gorssel** Gelderland, E Netherlands 52°12′N 06°13′E
109 T8 **Görtschitz** ≈ S Austria
Görz *see* Gorizia
110 E10 **Gorzów Wielkopolski** *Ger.* Landsberg, Landsberg an der Warthe. Lubuskie, W Poland 52°44′N 15°12′E
146 B10 **Goşabo** *var.* Goshoba, *Rus.* Koshoba. Balkan Welaýaty, NW Turkmenistan 40°28′N 54°11′E
108 G9 **Göschenen** Uri, C Switzerland 46°40′N 08°36′E
165 O11 **Gosen** Niigata, Honshū, C Japan 37°45′N 139°11′E
183 T8 **Gosford** New South Wales, SE Australia 33°25′S 151°18′E
31 P11 **Goshen** Indiana, N USA 41°34′N 85°49′W
18 K13 **Goshen** New York, NE USA 41°24′N 74°17′W
Goshoba *see* Goşabo
Goshoba *see* Goşoba
165 Q7 **Goshogawara** *var.* Gosyogawara. Aomori, Honshū, C Japan 40°47′N 140°24′E
Goshquduq Qum *see* Tosquduq Qumlari
101 J14 **Goslar** Niedersachsen, C Germany 51°55′N 10°25′E
27 Y9 **Gosnell** Arkansas, C USA 35°57′N 89°58′W
146 B10 **Goşoba** *var.* Goshoba, *Rus.* Koshoba. Balkanskiy Velayat, NW Turkmenistan 40°28′N 54°11′E
112 C11 **Gospić** Lika-Senj, C Croatia 44°32′N 15°21′E
97 N23 **Gosport** S England, United Kingdom 50°48′N 01°08′W
94 D9 **Gossa** *island* S Norway
108 H7 **Gossau** Sankt Gallen, NE Switzerland 47°25′N 09°16′E
99 G20 **Gosselies** *var.* Goss'lies. Hainaut, S Belgium 50°28′N 04°26′E
77 P10 **Gossi** Tombouctou, C Mali 15°44′N 01°19′W
Goss'lies *see* Gosselies
113 N18 **Gostivar** W FYR Macedonia 41°48′N 20°55′E
Gostomel' *see* Hostomel'
110 G12 **Gostyń** *var.* Gostyn. Wielkopolskie, C Poland 51°52′N 17°00′E
Gostyn *see* Gostyń
110 K11 **Gostynin** Mazowieckie, C Poland 52°25′N 19°27′E
Gosyogawara *see* Goshogawara
95 J18 **Göta Älv** ≈ S Sweden
95 N17 **Göta kanal** *canal* S Sweden
95 K18 **Götaland** *cultural region* S Sweden
95 H17 **Göteborg** *Eng.* Gothenburg. Västra Götaland, S Sweden 57°43′N 11°58′E
77 X16 **Gotel Mountains** ▲▲ E Nigeria
95 K17 **Götene** Västra Götaland, S Sweden 58°32′N 13°29′E
Gotera *see* San Francisco
101 K16 **Gotha** Thüringen, C Germany 50°57′N 10°43′E
29 N15 **Gothenburg** Nebraska, C USA 40°57′N 100°09′W
Gothenburg *see* Göteborg
77 R12 **Gothèye** Tillabéri, SW Niger 13°52′N 01°27′E
Gothland *see* Gotland
95 P19 **Gotland** *var.* Gothland, Gottland. ◈ *county* SE Sweden
95 O18 **Gotland** *island* SE Sweden
164 B13 **Gotō-rettō** *island group* SW Japan
114 H12 **Gotse Delchev** *prev.* Nevrokop. Blagoevgrad, SW Bulgaria 41°33′N 23°42′E
95 P17 **Gotska Sandön** *island* SE Sweden
101 I15 **Göttingen** *var.* Goettingen. Niedersachsen, C Germany 51°33′N 09°55′E
Gottland *see* Gotland
93 I16 **Gottne** Västernorrland, C Sweden 63°27′N 18°25′E
Gottschee *see* Kočevje
Gottwaldov *see* Zlín
146 B11 **Goturdepe** *Rus.* Koturdepe. Balkan Welaýaty, W Turkmenistan 39°32′N 53°39′E
108 I7 **Götzis** Vorarlberg, NW Austria 47°21′N 09°40′E
98 H12 **Gouda** Zuid-Holland, C Netherlands 52°01′N 04°42′E
76 I11 **Goudiri** *var.* Goudiry. E Senegal 14°12′N 12°41′W
Goudiry *see* Goudiri
77 X12 **Goudoumaria** Diffa, S Niger 13°28′N 11°15′E
15 R9 **Gouffre, Rivière du** ≈ Québec, SE Canada
65 M19 **Gough Fracture Zone** *tectonic feature* S Atlantic Ocean
65 M19 **Gough Island** *island* Tristan da Cunha, S Atlantic Ocean
15 N8 **Gouin, Réservoir** ⊠ Québec, SE Canada
14 B10 **Goulais River** Ontario, S Canada 46°41′N 84°22′W
183 R9 **Goulburn** New South Wales, SE Australia 34°45′S 149°44′E
183 O11 **Goulburn River** ≈ Victoria, SE Australia
195 O10 **Gould Coast** *physical region* Antarctica
Goulimime *see* Guelmime
114 F13 **Gouménissa** Kentrikí Makedonía, N Greece 40°56′N 22°27′E
77 O10 **Goundam** Tombouctou, NW Mali 16°27′N 03°39′W
78 H12 **Goundi** Moyen-Chari, S Chad 09°22′N 17°21′E
78 G12 **Gounou-Gaya** Mayo-Kébbi, SW Chad 09°37′N 15°30′E
Gourci *see* Goursi
Gourcy *see* Goursi
102 M13 **Gourdon** Lot, S France 44°45′N 01°22′E
77 W11 **Gouré** Zinder, SE Niger 13°59′N 10°16′E
102 G6 **Gourin** Morbihan, NW France 48°07′N 03°37′W
77 P10 **Gourma-Rharous** Tombouctou, C Mali 16°54′N 01°55′W
103 N4 **Gournay-en-Bray** Seine-Maritime, N France 49°29′N 01°42′E
78 J6 **Gouro** Borkou-Ennedi-Tibesti, N Chad 19°26′N 19°36′E
77 O12 **Goursi** *var.* Gourci, Gourcy. NW Burkina 13°13′N 02°20′W
104 H8 **Gouveia** Guarda, N Portugal 40°29′N 07°35′W
18 I7 **Gouverneur** New York, NE USA 44°20′N 75°27′W
99 L21 **Gouvy** Luxembourg, E Belgium 50°10′N 05°55′E
45 R14 **Gouyave** *var.* Charlotte Town. NW Grenada 12°10′N 61°44′W
Goverla, Gora *see* Hoverla, Hora
59 N20 **Governador Valadares** Minas Gerais, SE Brazil 18°51′S 41°57′W
171 R8 **Governor Generoso** Mindanao, S Philippines 06°36′N 126°06′E
44 I2 **Governor's Harbour** Eleuthera Island, C Bahamas 25°11′N 76°15′W
162 F9 **Govĭ-Altay** ◈ *province* SW Mongolia
162 I10 **Govĭ Altayn Nuruu** ▲▲ S Mongolia
154 L9 **Govind Ballabh Pant Sāgar** ⊠ C India
152 I7 **Govind Sāgar** ⊠ NE India
162 M8 **Govĭ-Sumber** ◈ *province* C Mongolia
Govurdak *see* Magdanly
18 D11 **Gowanda** New York, NE USA 42°25′N 78°55′W
148 J10 **Gowd-e Zereh, Dasht-e** *var.* Guad-i-Zirreh. *marsh* SW Afghanistan
14 F8 **Gowganda** Ontario, S Canada 47°41′N 80°46′W
14 G8 **Gowganda Lake** ◎ Ontario, S Canada
29 U13 **Gowrie** Iowa, C USA 42°16′N 94°17′W
Gowurdak *see* Magdanly
61 C15 **Goya** Corrientes, NE Argentina 29°10′S 59°15′W
Goyania *see* Goiânia
Goyaz *see* Goiás
137 X11 **Göyçay** *Rus.* Geokchay. C Azerbaijan 40°38′N 47°44′E
146 D10 **Goymat** *Rus.* Koymat. Balkan Welaýaty, NW Turkmenistan 40°23′N 55°45′E
146 D10 **Goymatdag, Gory** *Rus.* Gory Koymatdag. *hill range* Balkan Welaýaty, NW Turkmenistan
136 F12 **Göynük** Bolu, NW Turkey 40°24′N 30°45′E
165 R9 **Goyō-san** ▲ Honshū, C Japan 39°12′N 141°40′E
78 K11 **Goz Beïda** Ouaddaï, SE Chad 12°06′N 21°22′E
146 M10 **Gozgon** *Rus.* Gazgan. Navoiy Viloyati, C Uzbekistan 40°36′N 65°29′E
158 H11 **Gozha Co** ◎ W China
121 O15 **Gozo** *var.* Ghawdex. *island* N Malta
80 H9 **Göz Regeb** Kassala, NE Sudan 16°03′N 35°33′E
83 H25 **Graaff-Reinet** Eastern Cape, S South Africa 32°15′S 24°32′E
Graasten *see* Gråsten
76 L17 **Grabo** SW Ivory Coast 04°57′N 07°30′W
112 P11 **Grabovica** Serbia, E Serbia 44°30′N 22°29′E
110 I13 **Grabów nad Prosną** Wielkopolskie, C Poland 51°30′N 18°06′E
108 I8 **Grabs** Sankt Gallen, NE Switzerland 47°10′N 09°27′E
112 D12 **Gračac** Zadar, SW Croatia 44°18′N 15°52′E
112 I11 **Gračanica** Federacija Bosna I Hercegovina, NE Bosnia and Herzegovina 44°41′N 18°20′E
14 L11 **Gracefield** Québec, SE Canada 46°06′N 76°03′W
99 K19 **Grâce-Hollogne** Liège, E Belgium 50°38′N 05°30′E
23 R8 **Graceville** Florida, SE USA 30°57′N 85°31′W
29 R8 **Graceville** Minnesota, N USA 45°34′N 96°25′W
42 G6 **Gracias** Lempira, W Honduras 14°35′N 88°35′W
Gracias *see* Lempira
42 L5 **Gracias a Dios** ◈ *department* E Honduras
43 O6 **Gracias a Dios, Cabo de** *headland* Honduras/Nicaragua 15°00′N 83°10′W
64 O2 **Graciosa** *var.* Ilha Graciosa. *island* Azores, Portugal, NE Atlantic Ocean
64 Q11 **Graciosa** *island* Islas Canarias, Spain, NE Atlantic Ocean
Graciosa, Ilha *see* Graciosa
112 I11 **Gradačac** Federacija Bosna I Hercegovina, N Bosnia and Herzegovina 44°51′N 18°24′E
59 J15 **Gradaús, Serra dos** ▲▲ C Brazil
104 L3 **Gradefes** Castilla-León, N Spain 42°37′N 05°14′W
Gradiška *see* Bosanska Gradiška
Gradizhsk *see* Hradyz'k
106 J7 **Grado** Friuli-Venezia Giulia, NE Italy 45°41′N 13°24′E
104 K2 **Grado** Asturias, N Spain 43°23′N 06°04′W
113 P19 **Gradsko** C FYR Macedonia 41°34′N 21°56′E
37 V11 **Grady** New Mexico, SW USA 34°49′N 103°19′W
Grad Zagreb *see* Zagreb
29 T12 **Graettinger** Iowa, C USA 43°14′N 94°45′W
101 M23 **Grafing** Bayern, SE Germany 48°01′N 11°57′E
25 S6 **Graford** Texas, SW USA 32°56′N 98°15′W
183 V5 **Grafton** New South Wales, SE Australia 29°41′S 152°55′E
29 Q3 **Grafton** North Dakota, N USA 48°24′N 97°24′W
21 S3 **Grafton** West Virginia, NE USA 39°21′N 80°03′W
21 T9 **Graham** North Carolina, SE USA 36°05′N 79°25′W
25 R6 **Graham** Texas, SW USA 33°07′N 98°36′W
Graham Bell Island *see* Greem-Bell, Ostrov
10 I13 **Graham Island** *island* Queen Charlotte Islands, British Columbia, SW Canada
19 S6 **Graham Lake** ◎ Maine, NE USA
194 H4 **Graham Land** *physical region* Antarctica
37 N15 **Graham, Mount** ▲ Arizona, SW USA 32°42′N 109°52′W
Grahamstad *see* Grahamstown
83 I25 **Grahamstown** *Afr.* Grahamstad. Eastern Cape, S South Africa 33°18′S 26°32′E
Grahovo *see* Bosansko Grahovo
68 C12 **Grain Coast** *coastal region* S Liberia
169 S17 **Grajagan, Teluk** *bay* Jawa, S Indonesia
58 L14 **Grajaú** Maranhão, E Brazil 05°50′S 46°12′W
58 M13 **Grajaú, Rio** ≈ NE Brazil
110 O8 **Grajewo** Podlaskie, NE Poland 53°38′N 22°26′E
95 F24 **Gram** Sønderjylland, SW Denmark 55°18′N 09°03′E
103 N13 **Gramat** Lot, S France 44°45′N 01°45′E
22 H5 **Grambling** Louisiana, S USA 32°31′N 92°43′W
115 C14 **Grámmos** ▲ Albania/Greece
96 I9 **Grampian Mountains** ▲▲ C Scotland, United Kingdom
182 L12 **Grampians, The** ▲▲ Victoria, SE Australia
98 O9 **Gramsbergen** Overijssel, E Netherlands 52°37′N 06°39′E
113 L21 **Gramsh** *var.* Gramshi. Elbasan, C Albania 40°52′N 20°12′E
Gramshi *see* Gramsh
Gran *see* Esztergom, Hungary
Gran *see* Hron
54 F11 **Granada** Meta, C Colombia 03°33′N 73°44′W
42 J10 **Granada** Granada, SW Nicaragua 11°55′N 85°58′W
105 N14 **Granada** Andalucía, S Spain 37°13′N 03°41′W
37 W6 **Granada** Colorado, C USA 38°00′N 102°18′W
42 J11 **Granada** ◈ *department* SW Nicaragua
105 N14 **Granada** ◈ *province* Andalucía, S Spain
63 I21 **Gran Antiplanicie Central** *plain* S Argentina
97 E17 **Granard** *Ir.* Gránard. C Ireland 53°47′N 07°30′W
Gránard *see* Granard
63 J20 **Gran Bajo** *basin* S Argentina
63 J15 **Gran Bajo del Gualicho** *basin* E Argentina
63 I21 **Gran Bajo de San Julián** *basin* SE Argentina
25 S7 **Granbury** Texas, SW USA 32°27′N 97°47′W
15 P12 **Granby** Québec, SE Canada 45°23′N 72°44′W
27 S8 **Granby** Missouri, C USA 36°55′N 94°14′W
37 S3 **Granby, Lake** ⊠ Colorado, C USA
64 O12 **Gran Canaria** *var.* Grand Canary. *island* Islas Canarias, Spain, NE Atlantic Ocean
47 T11 **Gran Chaco** *var.* Chaco. *lowland plain* South America
45 R14 **Grand Anse** SW Grenada 12°01′N 61°45′W
Grand-Anse *see* Portsmouth
44 G1 **Grand Bahama Island** *island* N Bahamas
Grand Balé *see* Tui
103 U7 **Grand Ballon** *Ger.* Ballon de Guebwiller. ▲ NE France 47°53′N 07°06′E
13 T13 **Grand Bank** Newfoundland, Newfoundland and Labrador, SE Canada 47°06′N 55°48′W
64 I7 **Grand Banks of Newfoundland** *undersea feature* NW Atlantic Ocean 45°00′N 40°00′W
Grand Bassa *see* Buchanan
77 N17 **Grand-Bassam** *var.* Bassam. SE Ivory Coast 05°14′N 03°45′W
14 E16 **Grand Bend** Ontario, S Canada 43°17′N 81°46′W
76 L17 **Grand-Bérébi** *var.* Grand-Béréby. SW Ivory Coast 04°38′N 06°55′W
Grand-Béréby *see* Grand-Bérébi
45 X11 **Grand-Bourg** Marie-Galante, SE Guadeloupe 15°53′N 61°19′W
44 M6 **Grand Caicos** *var.* Middle Caicos. *island* C Turks and Caicos Islands
14 K12 **Grand Calumet, Île du** *island* Québec, SE Canada
97 E18 **Grand Canal** *Ir.* An Chanáil Mhór. *canal* C Ireland
Grand Canal *see* Da Yunhe
Grand Canary *see* Gran Canaria
36 K10 **Grand Canyon** Arizona, SW USA 36°01′N 112°10′W
36 J9 **Grand Canyon** *canyon* Arizona, SW USA
Grand Canyon State *see* Arizona
44 D8 **Grand Cayman** *island* SW Cayman Islands
11 R14 **Grand Centre** Alberta, SW Canada 54°25′N 110°13′W
76 L17 **Grand Cess** SE Liberia 04°36′N 08°12′W
108 D12 **Grand Combin** ▲ S Switzerland 45°58′N 07°27′E
32 K8 **Grand Coulee** Washington, NW USA 47°56′N 119°00′W
32 J8 **Grand Coulee** *valley* Washington, NW USA
45 X5 **Grand Cul-de-Sac Marin** *bay* N Guadeloupe
Grand Duchy of Luxembourg *see* Luxembourg
63 I22 **Grande, Bahía** *bay* S Argentina
11 N14 **Grande Cache** Alberta, W Canada 53°53′N 119°07′W
103 U12 **Grande Casse** ▲ E France 45°22′N 06°50′E
Grande-Comore *see* Ngazidja
61 G18 **Grande, Cuchilla** *hill range* E Uruguay
45 S5 **Grande de Añasco, Río** ≈ W Puerto Rico
Grande de Chiloé, Isla *see* Chiloé, Isla de
58 J12 **Grande de Gurupá, Ilha** *river island* NE Brazil
57 K21 **Grande de Lipez, Río** ≈ SW Bolivia
45 U6 **Grande de Loíza, Río** ≈ E Puerto Rico
45 T5 **Grande de Manatí, Río** ≈ C Puerto Rico
42 L9 **Grande de Matagalpa, Río** ≈ C Nicaragua
40 K12 **Grande de Santiago, Río** *var.* Santiago. ≈ C Mexico
43 O15 **Grande de Térraba, Río** *var.* Río Térraba. ≈ SE Costa Rica
12 J9 **Grande Deux, Réservoir la** ⊠ Québec, E Canada
60 O10 **Grande, Ilha** *island* SE Brazil
11 O13 **Grande Prairie** Alberta, W Canada 55°10′N 118°52′W
74 I8 **Grand Erg Occidental** *desert* W Algeria
74 L9 **Grand Erg Oriental** *desert* Algeria/Tunisia
57 M18 **Grande, Río** ≈ C Bolivia
59 J20 **Grande, Rio** ≈ S Brazil
2 F15 **Grande, Rio** *var.* Río Bravo, *Sp.* Río Bravo del Norte, Bravo del Norte. ≈ Mexico/USA
15 Y7 **Grande-Rivière** Québec, SE Canada 48°27′N 64°37′W
15 Y6 **Grande Rivière** ≈ Québec, SE Canada
44 M8 **Grande-Rivière-du-Nord** N Haiti 19°36′N 72°10′W
62 K9 **Grande, Salina** *var.* Gran Salitral. *salt lake* C Argentina
15 S7 **Grandes-Bergeronnes** Québec, SE Canada 48°16′N 69°32′W
47 W6 **Grande, Serra** ▲▲ W Brazil
40 K4 **Grande, Sierra** ▲▲ N Mexico
103 S12 **Grandes Rousses** ▲▲ E France
63 K17 **Grandes, Salinas** *salt lake* E Argentina
45 Y5 **Grande Terre** *island* E West Indies
15 X5 **Grande-Vallée** Québec, SE Canada 49°14′N 65°08′W
45 Y5 **Grande Vigie, Pointe de la** *headland* Grande Terre, N Guadeloupe 16°31′N 61°27′W
13 N14 **Grand Falls** New Brunswick, SE Canada 47°02′N 67°46′W
13 T11 **Grand Falls** Newfoundland, Newfoundland and Labrador, SE Canada 48°57′N 55°48′W
24 L9 **Grandfalls** Texas, SW USA 31°20′N 102°51′W
21 P9 **Grandfather Mountain** ▲ North Carolina, SE USA 36°06′N 81°48′W
26 L13 **Grandfield** Oklahoma, C USA 34°15′N 98°40′W
11 N17 **Grand Forks** British Columbia, SW Canada 49°02′N 118°30′W
29 R4 **Grand Forks** North Dakota, N USA 47°54′N 97°03′W
31 O9 **Grand Haven** Michigan, N USA 43°03′N 86°13′W
Grandichi *see* Hrandzichy
29 P15 **Grand Island** Nebraska, C USA 40°55′N 98°20′W
31 O3 **Grand Island** *island* Michigan, N USA
22 K10 **Grand Isle** Louisiana, S USA 29°12′N 90°00′W
65 A23 **Grand Jason** *island* Jason Islands, NW Falkland Islands
37 P5 **Grand Junction** Colorado, C USA 39°03′N 108°33′W
20 F10 **Grand Junction** Tennessee, S USA 35°03′N 89°11′W
14 J9 **Grand-Lac-Victoria** Québec, SE Canada 47°33′N 77°28′W
14 J9 **Grand lac Victoria** ◎ Québec, SE Canada
77 N17 **Grand-Lahou** *var.* Grand Lahu. S Ivory Coast 05°09′N 05°01′W
Grand Lahu *see* Grand-Lahou
37 S3 **Grand Lake** Colorado, C USA 40°15′N 105°49′W
13 S11 **Grand Lake** ◎ Newfoundland and Labrador, E Canada
22 G9 **Grand Lake** ◎ Louisiana, S USA
31 R5 **Grand Lake** ◎ Michigan, N USA
31 Q13 **Grand Lake** ⊠ Ohio, N USA
27 R9 **Grand Lake O' The Cherokees** *var.* Lake O' The Cherokees. ⊠ Oklahoma, C USA
31 Q9 **Grand Ledge** Michigan, N USA 42°45′N 84°45′W
102 I8 **Grand-Lieu, Lac de** ◎ NW France
19 U6 **Grand Manan Channel** *channel* Canada/USA
13 O15 **Grand Manan Island** *island* New Brunswick, SE Canada
29 Y4 **Grand Marais** Minnesota, N USA 47°45′N 90°19′W
15 P10 **Grand-Mère** Québec, SE Canada 46°36′N 72°41′W
37 P5 **Grand Mesa** ▲ Colorado, C USA
108 C10 **Grand Muveran** ▲ W Switzerland 46°16′N 07°12′E
104 G12 **Grândola** Setúbal, S Portugal 38°10′N 08°34′W
Grand Paradis *see* Gran Paradiso
187 O15 **Grand Passage** *passage* N New Caledonia
77 R16 **Grand-Popo** S Benin 06°19′N 01°50′E
29 Z3 **Grand Portage** Minnesota, N USA 48°00′N 89°36′W
25 T6 **Grand Prairie** Texas, SW USA 32°45′N 97°00′W
11 W14 **Grand Rapids** Manitoba, C Canada 53°12′N 99°19′W
31 P9 **Grand Rapids** Michigan, N USA 42°57′N 86°40′W
29 V5 **Grand Rapids** Minnesota, N USA 47°14′N 93°31′W
14 L10 **Grand-Remous** Québec, SE Canada 46°36′N 75°53′W
14 F15 **Grand River** ≈ Ontario, S Canada
31 P9 **Grand River** ≈ Michigan, N USA
27 T3 **Grand River** ≈ Missouri, C USA
28 M7 **Grand River** ≈ South Dakota, N USA
45 Q11 **Grand' Rivière** N Martinique 14°52′N 61°11′W
32 F11 **Grand Ronde** Oregon, NW USA 45°03′N 123°43′W
32 L11 **Grand Ronde River** ≈ Oregon/Washington, NW USA
Grand-Saint-Bernard, Col du *see* Great Saint Bernard Pass
25 V6 **Grand Saline** Texas, SW USA 32°40′N 95°42′W
55 X10 **Grand-Santi** W French Guiana 04°19′N 54°24′W
Grandsee *see* Grandson
172 J16 **Grand Sœur** *island* Les Sœurs, NE Seychelles
108 B9 **Grandson** *prev.* Grandsee. Vaud, W Switzerland 46°49′N 06°39′E
33 S14 **Grand Teton** ▲ Wyoming, C USA 43°44′N 110°48′W
31 P5 **Grand Traverse Bay** *lake bay* Michigan, N USA
45 N6 **Grand Turk** ○ (Turks and Caicos Islands) Grand Turk Island, S Turks and Caicos Islands 21°24′N 71°08′W
45 N6 **Grand Turk Island** *island* SE Turks and Caicos Islands
103 S13 **Grand Veymont** ▲ E France 44°51′N 05°32′E
11 W15 **Grandview** Manitoba, S Canada 51°11′N 100°41′W
27 R4 **Grandview** Missouri, C USA 38°53′N 94°31′W
36 I10 **Grand Wash Cliffs** *cliff* Arizona, SW USA
14 J8 **Granet, Lac** ◎ Québec, SE Canada
95 L14 **Grangärde** Dalarna, C Sweden 60°15′N 15°00′E
44 H12 **Grange Hill** W Jamaica 18°19′N 78°11′W
96 J12 **Grangemouth** C Scotland, United Kingdom 56°01′N 03°44′W
25 T10 **Granger** Texas, SW USA 30°43′N 97°26′W
32 J10 **Granger** Washington, NW USA 46°20′N 120°11′W
33 T17 **Granger** Wyoming, C USA 41°37′N 109°58′W
Granges *see* Grenchen
95 L14 **Grängesberg** Dalarna, C Sweden 60°06′N 15°00′E
33 N11 **Grangeville** Idaho, NW USA 45°55′N 116°07′W
10 K13 **Granisle** British Columbia, SW Canada 54°55′N 126°14′W
30 K15 **Granite City** Illinois, N USA 38°42′N 90°09′W
29 S9 **Granite Falls** Minnesota, N USA 44°48′N 95°33′W
21 Q9 **Granite Falls** North Carolina, SE USA 35°48′N 81°25′W
36 K12 **Granite Mountain** ▲ Arizona, SW USA 34°38′N 112°34′W
33 T12 **Granite Peak** ▲ Montana, NW USA 45°09′N 109°48′W
35 T2 **Granite Peak** ▲ Nevada, W USA 41°40′N 117°35′W
36 J3 **Granite Peak** ▲ Utah, W USA 40°09′N 113°18′W
Granite State *see* New Hampshire
107 H24 **Granitola, Capo** *headland* Sicilia, Italy, C Mediterranean Sea 37°33′N 12°39′E
185 H15 **Granity** West Coast, South Island, New Zealand 41°37′S 171°53′E
Gran Lago *see* Nicaragua, Lago de
63 J18 **Gran Laguna Salada** ◎ S Argentina
Gran Malvina *see* West Falkland
95 L18 **Gränna** Jönköping, S Sweden 58°02′N 14°30′E
105 W5 **Granollers** *var.* Granollérs. Cataluña, NE Spain 41°37′N 02°18′E
Granollérs *see* Granollers
106 A7 **Gran Paradiso** *Fr.* Grand Paradis. ▲ NW Italy 45°31′N 07°13′E
Gran Pilastro *see* Hochfeiler
Gran Salitral *see* Grande, Salina
Gran San Bernardo, Passo di *see* Great Saint Bernard Pass
Gran Santiago *see* Santiago
107 J14 **Gran Sasso d'Italia** ▲▲ C Italy
100 N11 **Gransee** Brandenburg, NE Germany 53°00′N 13°10′E
28 L15 **Grant** Nebraska, C USA 40°50′N 101°43′W
27 R1 **Grant City** Missouri, C USA 40°29′N 94°25′W
97 N19 **Grantham** E England, United Kingdom 52°55′N 00°39′W
194 K13 **Grant Island** *island* Antarctica
45 Z14 **Grantley Adams** ✈ (Bridgetown) SE Barbados 13°04′N 59°29′W
35 S7 **Grant, Mount** ▲ Nevada, W USA 38°34′N 118°47′W
96 J9 **Grantown-on-Spey** N Scotland, United Kingdom 57°11′N 03°53′W
35 W8 **Grant Range** ▲▲ Nevada, W USA
37 Q11 **Grants** New Mexico, SW USA 35°09′N 107°50′W
30 I4 **Grantsburg** Wisconsin, N USA 45°47′N 92°40′W
32 F15 **Grants Pass** Oregon, NW USA 42°26′N 123°20′W
36 K3 **Grantsville** Utah, W USA 40°36′N 112°27′W
21 R4 **Grantsville** West Virginia, NE USA 38°55′N 81°07′W
102 I5 **Granville** Manche, N France 48°50′N 01°35′W
11 V12 **Granville Lake** ◎ Manitoba, C Canada
25 V8 **Grapeland** Texas, SW USA 31°29′N 95°28′W
25 T6 **Grapevine** Texas, SW USA 32°55′N 97°04′W
83 K20 **Graskop** Mpumalanga, NE South Africa 24°58′S 30°49′E
95 P14 **Gräsö** Uppsala, C Sweden 60°22′N 18°30′E
93 I19 **Gräsö** *island* C Sweden
103 U15 **Grasse** Alpes-Maritimes, SE France 43°42′N 06°52′E
18 E14 **Grassflat** Pennsylvania, NE USA 41°00′N 78°04′W
33 U9 **Grassrange** Montana, NW USA 47°02′N 108°48′W
18 J6 **Grass River** ≈ New York, NE USA
35 P6 **Grass Valley** California, W USA 39°12′N 121°04′W
183 N14 **Grassy** Tasmania, SE Australia 40°03′S 144°04′E
28 K4 **Grassy Butte** North Dakota, N USA 47°20′N 103°13′W
21 R5 **Grassy Knob** ▲ West Virginia, NE USA 38°04′N 80°31′W
95 G24 **Gråsten** *var.* Graasten. Sønderjylland, SW Denmark 54°55′N 09°37′E
95 J18 **Grästorp** Västra Götaland, S Sweden 58°20′N 12°40′E
Gratianopolis *see* Grenoble
109 V8 **Gratwein** Steiermark, SE Austria 47°08′N 15°20′E
Gratz *see* Graz
108 I9 **Graubünden** *Fr.* Grisons, *It.* Grigioni. ◈ *canton* SE Switzerland
Graudenz *see* Grudziądz
103 N15 **Graulhet** Tarn, S France 43°45′N 01°58′E
105 T4 **Graus** Aragón, NE Spain 42°11′N 00°21′E
61 I16 **Gravataí** Rio Grande do Sul, S Brazil 29°55′S 51°00′W
98 L13 **Grave** Noord-Brabant, SE Netherlands 51°45′N 05°45′E
11 T17 **Gravelbourg** Saskatchewan, S Canada 49°53′N 106°33′W
103 N1 **Gravelines** Nord, N France 51°00′N 02°07′E
Graven *see* Grez-Doiceau
14 H13 **Gravenhurst** Ontario, S Canada 44°55′N 79°22′W
33 O10 **Grave Peak** ▲ Idaho, NW USA 46°24′N 114°43′W
102 I11 **Grave, Pointe de** *headland* W France 45°33′N 01°24′W
183 S4 **Gravesend** New South Wales, SE Australia 29°37′S 150°15′E
97 P22 **Gravesend** SE England, United Kingdom 51°27′N 00°24′E
107 N17 **Gravina in Puglia** Puglia, SE Italy 40°48′N 16°25′E
103 S8 **Gray** Haute-Saône, E France 47°28′N 05°34′E
23 T4 **Gray** Georgia, SE USA 33°00′N 83°31′W
195 V16 **Gray, Cape** *headland* Antarctica 67°30′S 143°30′E
32 F9 **Grayland** Washington, NW USA 46°46′N 124°07′W

◆ Country
● Country Capital
◇ Dependent Territory
○ Dependent Territory Capital
◈ Administrative Regions
✈ International Airport
▲ Mountain
▲▲ Mountain Range
Volcano
≈ River
◎ Lake
⊠ Reservoir

39 N10 **Grayling** Alaska, USA 62°55′N 160°07′W
31 Q6 **Grayling** Michigan, N USA 44°40′N 84°43′W
32 F9 **Grays Harbor** *inlet* Washington, NW USA
21 O5 **Grayson** Kentucky, S USA 38°21′N 82°59′W
37 S4 **Grays Peak** ▲ Colorado, C USA 39°37′N 105°49′W
30 M16 **Grayville** Illinois, N USA 38°15′N 87°59′W
109 V8 **Graz** *prev.* Gratz. Steiermark, SE Austria 47°05′N 15°23′E
104 L15 **Grazalema** Andalucía, S Spain 36°46′N 05°23′W
113 P15 **Grdelica** Serbia, SE Serbia 42°54′N 22°05′E
44 H1 **Great Abaco** *var.* Abaco Island. *island* N Bahamas
Great Admiralty Island *see* Manus Island
Great Alfold *see* Great Hungarian Plain
Great Ararat *see* Büyükağrı Dağı
181 U8 **Great Artesian Basin** *lowlands* Queensland, C Australia
181 O12 **Great Australian Bight** *bight* S Australia
64 E11 **Great Bahama Bank** *undersea feature* E Gulf of Mexico 23°15′N 78°00′W
184 M4 **Great Barrier Island** *island* N New Zealand
181 X4 **Great Barrier Reef** *reef* Queensland, NE Australia
18 L11 **Great Barrington** Massachusetts, NE USA 42°11′N 73°20′W
0 F10 **Great Basin** *basin* W USA
8 I8 **Great Bear Lake** *Fr.* Grand Lac de l'Ours. ◎ Northwest Territories, NW Canada
Great Belt *see* Storebælt
26 L5 **Great Bend** Kansas, C USA 38°22′N 98°47′W
Great Bermuda *see* Bermuda
97 A20 **Great Blasket Island** *Ir.* An Blascaod Mór. *island* SW Ireland
Great Britain *see* Britain
151 Q23 **Great Channel** *channel* Andaman Sea/Indian Ocean
166 J10 **Great Coco Island** *island* SW Burma (Myanmar)
Great Crosby *see* Crosby
21 X7 **Great Dismal Swamp** *wetland* North Carolina/Virginia, SE USA
33 V16 **Great Divide Basin** *basin* Wyoming, C USA
181 W7 **Great Dividing Range** ▲▲ NE Australia
14 D12 **Great Duck Island** *island* Ontario, S Canada
Great Elder Reservoir *see* Waconda Lake
44 G8 **Greater Antilles** *island group* West Indies
129 V16 **Greater Sunda Islands** *var.* Sunda Islands. *island group* Indonesia
184 I1 **Great Exhibition Bay** *inlet* North Island, New Zealand
44 H4 **Great Exuma Island** *island* C Bahamas
33 R8 **Great Falls** Montana, NW USA 47°30′N 111°18′W
21 R11 **Great Falls** South Carolina, SE USA 34°34′N 80°54′W
84 F9 **Great Fisher Bank** *undersea feature* C North Sea 57°00′N 04°00′E
Great Glen *see* Mor, Glen
Great Grimsby *see* Grimsby
44 I4 **Great Guana Cay** *island* C Bahamas
64 I5 **Great Hellefiske Bank** *undersea feature* N Atlantic Ocean
111 L24 **Great Hungarian Plain** *var.* Great Alfold, Plain of Hungary, *Hung.* Alföld. *plain* SE Europe
44 L7 **Great Inagua** *var.* Inagua Islands. *island* S Bahamas
Great Indian Desert *see* Thar Desert
83 G25 **Great Karoo** *var.* Great Karroo, High Veld, *Afr.* Groot Karoo, Hoë Karoo. *plateau region* S South Africa
Great Karroo *see* Great Karoo
Great Kei *see* Nciba
Great Khingan Range *see* Da Hinggan Ling
14 E11 **Great La Cloche Island** *island* Ontario, S Canada
183 P16 **Great Lake** ◎ Tasmania, SE Australia
Great Lake *see* Tônlé Sap
11 R15 **Great Lakes** *lakes* Ontario, Canada/USA
Great Lakes State *see* Michigan
97 L20 **Great Malvern** W England, United Kingdom 52°07′N 02°19′W
184 M5 **Great Mercury Island** *island* N New Zealand
Great Meteor Seamount *see* Great Meteor Tablemount
64 K10 **Great Meteor Tablemount** *var.* Great Meteor Seamount. *undersea feature* E Atlantic Ocean 30°00′N 28°30′W
31 Q14 **Great Miami River** ≈ Ohio, N USA
151 Q24 **Great Nicobar** *island* Nicobar Islands, India, NE Indian Ocean
97 O19 **Great Ouse** *var.* Ouse. ≈ E England, United Kingdom
183 Q17 **Great Oyster Bay** *bay* Tasmania, SE Australia
44 I13 **Great Pedro Bluff** *headland* W Jamaica 17°51′N 77°44′W
21 T12 **Great Pee Dee River** ≈ North Carolina/South Carolina, SE USA
129 W9 **Great Plain of China** *plain* E China
0 F12 **Great Plains** *var.* High Plains. *plains* Canada/USA
37 W6 **Great Plains Reservoirs** ▣ Colorado, C USA
19 Q13 **Great Point** *headland* Nantucket Island, Massachusetts, NE USA 41°23′N 70°03′W
68 I13 **Great Rift Valley** *var.* Rift Valley. *depression* Asia/Africa
81 I23 **Great Ruaha** ≈ S Tanzania
18 K10 **Great Sacandaga Lake** ▣ New York, NE USA
108 C12 **Great Saint Bernard Pass** *Fr.* Col du Grand-Saint-Bernard, *It.* Passo del Gran San Bernardo. *pass* Italy/Switzerland
44 F1 **Great Sale Cay** *island* N Bahamas
Great Salt Desert *see* Kavīr, Dasht-e
36 K1 **Great Salt Lake** *salt lake* Utah, W USA
36 J3 **Great Salt Lake Desert** *plain* Utah, W USA
26 M8 **Great Salt Plains Lake** ▣ Oklahoma, C USA
75 T9 **Great Sand Sea** *desert* Egypt/Libya
180 L6 **Great Sandy Desert** *desert* Western Australia
Great Sandy Desert *see* Ar Rub 'al Khālī
Great Sandy Island *see* Fraser Island
187 Y13 **Great Sea Reef** *reef* Vanua Levu, N Fiji
38 H17 **Great Sitkin Island** *island* Aleutian Islands, Alaska, USA
8 J10 **Great Slave Lake** *Fr.* Grand Lac des Esclaves. ◎ Northwest Territories, NW Canada
21 O10 **Great Smoky Mountains** ▲▲ North Carolina/Tennessee, SE USA
10 L11 **Great Snow Mountain** ▲ British Columbia, W Canada 57°22′N 124°08′W
Great Socialist People's Libyan Arab Jamahiriya *see* Libya
64 A12 **Great Sound** *sound* Bermuda, NW Atlantic Ocean
180 M10 **Great Victoria Desert** *desert* South Australia/Western Australia
194 H2 **Great Wall** *Chinese research station* South Shetland Islands, Antarctica 61°57′S 58°23′W
19 T7 **Great Wass Island** *island* Maine, NE USA
97 Q19 **Great Yarmouth** *var.* Yarmouth. E England, United Kingdom 52°37′N 01°44′E
139 S1 **Great Zab** *Ar.* Az Zāb al Kabīr, *Kurd.* Zē-i Bādīnān, *Turk.* Büyükzap Suyu. ≈ Iraq/Turkey
95 I17 **Grebbestad** Västra Götaland, S Sweden 58°42′N 11°15′E
Grebenka *see* Hrebinka
42 M13 **Grecia** Alajuela, C Costa Rica 10°04′N 84°19′W
61 E18 **Greco** Río Negro, W Uruguay 32°49′S 57°03′W
Greco, Cape *see* Gkréko, Akrotíri
104 L8 **Gredos, Sierra de** ▲▲ W Spain
18 F9 **Greece** New York, NE USA 43°12′N 77°41′W
115 E17 **Greece** *off.* Hellenic Republic, *Gk.* Ellás; *anc.* Hellas. ◆ *republic* SE Europe
Greece Central *see* Stereá Elláa
Greece West *see* Dytikí Elláa
37 T3 **Greeley** Colorado, C USA 40°21′N 104°41′W
29 P14 **Greeley** Nebraska, C USA 41°33′N 98°31′W
122 K3 **Greem-Bell, Ostrov** *Eng.* Graham Bell Island. *island* Zemlya Frantsa-Iosifa, N Russian Federation
30 M6 **Green Bay** Wisconsin, N USA 44°32′N 88°00′W
31 N6 **Green Bay** *lake bay* Michigan/Wisconsin, N USA
21 S5 **Greenbrier River** ≈ West Virginia, NE USA
29 S2 **Greenbush** Minnesota, N USA 48°42′N 96°10′W
183 R12 **Green Cape** *headland* New South Wales, SE Australia 37°15′S 150°03′E
31 O14 **Greencastle** Indiana, N USA 39°38′N 86°51′W
18 F16 **Greencastle** Pennsylvania, NE USA 39°47′N 77°43′W
27 T2 **Green City** Missouri, C USA 40°16′N 92°57′W
21 O9 **Greeneville** Tennessee, S USA 36°10′N 82°50′W
35 O11 **Greenfield** California, W USA 36°19′N 121°15′W
31 P14 **Greenfield** Indiana, N USA 39°47′N 85°46′W
29 U15 **Greenfield** Iowa, C USA 41°18′N 94°27′W
18 M11 **Greenfield** Massachusetts, NE USA 42°33′N 72°34′W
27 S7 **Greenfield** Missouri, C USA 37°25′N 93°50′W
31 S14 **Greenfield** Ohio, N USA 39°21′N 83°22′W
20 G8 **Greenfield** Tennessee, S USA 36°09′N 88°48′W
30 M9 **Greenfield** Wisconsin, N USA 42°55′N 87°59′W
27 T9 **Green Forest** Arkansas, C USA 36°19′N 93°24′W
37 T7 **Greenhorn Mountain** ▲ Colorado, C USA 37°50′N 104°59′W
Green Island *see* Lü Tao
186 I6 **Green Islands** *var.* Nissan Islands. *island group* NE Papua New Guinea
11 S14 **Green Lake** Saskatchewan, C Canada 54°15′N 107°51′W
30 L8 **Green Lake** ◎ Wisconsin, N USA
197 O14 **Greenland** *Dan.* Grønland, *Inuit* Kalaallit Nunaat. ◇ *Danish external territory* NE North America
84 D4 **Greenland** *island* NE North America
197 R13 **Greenland Plain** *undersea feature* N Greenland Sea
197 R14 **Greenland Sea** *sea* Arctic Ocean
37 R4 **Green Mountain Reservoir** ▣ Colorado, C USA
18 M8 **Green Mountains** ▲▲ Vermont, NE USA
Green Mountain State *see* Vermont
96 H12 **Greenock** W Scotland, United Kingdom 55°57′N 04°45′W
39 T5 **Greenough, Mount** ▲ Alaska, USA 69°15′N 141°37′W
186 A6 **Green River** Sandaun, NW Papua New Guinea 03°54′S 141°08′E
37 N5 **Green River** Utah, W USA 39°00′N 110°07′W
33 U17 **Green River** Wyoming, C USA 41°33′N 109°27′W
16 H9 **Green River** ≈ W USA
30 K11 **Green River** ≈ Illinois, N USA
20 J7 **Green River** ≈ Kentucky, C USA
28 K5 **Green River** ≈ North Dakota, N USA
37 N6 **Green River** ≈ Utah, W USA
33 T16 **Green River** ≈ Wyoming, C USA
20 L7 **Green River Lake** ▣ Kentucky, S USA
23 O5 **Greensboro** Alabama, S USA 32°42′N 87°36′W
23 U3 **Greensboro** Georgia, SE USA 33°34′N 83°10′W
21 T9 **Greensboro** North Carolina, SE USA 36°04′N 79°48′W
31 P14 **Greensburg** Indiana, N USA 39°20′N 85°28′W
26 K6 **Greensburg** Kansas, C USA 37°36′N 99°17′W
20 L7 **Greensburg** Kentucky, S USA 37°14′N 85°30′W
18 C15 **Greensburg** Pennsylvania, NE USA 40°18′N 79°32′W
37 O13 **Greens Peak** ▲ Arizona, SW USA 34°06′N 109°34′W
21 V12 **Green Swamp** *wetland* North Carolina, SE USA
21 O4 **Greenup** Kentucky, S USA 38°34′N 82°49′W
36 M16 **Green Valley** Arizona, SW USA 31°49′N 111°00′W
76 K17 **Greenville** *var.* Sino, Sinoe. SE Liberia 05°01′N 09°03′W
23 P6 **Greenville** Alabama, S USA 31°49′N 86°37′W
23 T8 **Greenville** Florida, SE USA 30°28′N 83°37′W
23 S5 **Greenville** Georgia, SE USA 33°03′N 84°42′W
30 L15 **Greenville** Illinois, N USA 38°53′N 89°24′W
20 I7 **Greenville** Kentucky, S USA 37°11′N 87°11′W
19 Q5 **Greenville** Maine, NE USA 45°26′N 69°36′W
31 P9 **Greenville** Michigan, N USA 43°10′N 85°15′W
22 J4 **Greenville** Mississippi, S USA 33°24′N 91°03′W
21 W9 **Greenville** North Carolina, SE USA 35°36′N 77°23′W
31 Q13 **Greenville** Ohio, N USA 40°06′N 84°37′W
19 O12 **Greenville** Rhode Island, NE USA 41°52′N 71°33′W
21 P11 **Greenville** South Carolina, SE USA 34°51′N 82°24′W
25 U6 **Greenville** Texas, SW USA 33°09′N 96°07′W
31 T12 **Greenwich** Ohio, N USA 41°01′N 82°31′W
27 S11 **Greenwood** Arkansas, C USA 35°13′N 94°15′W
31 O14 **Greenwood** Indiana, N USA 39°38′N 86°06′W
22 K4 **Greenwood** Mississippi, S USA 33°30′N 90°11′W
21 P12 **Greenwood** South Carolina, SE USA 34°11′N 82°10′W
21 Q12 **Greenwood, Lake** ▣ South Carolina, SE USA
21 P11 **Greer** South Carolina, SE USA 34°56′N 82°13′W
27 V10 **Greers Ferry Lake** ▣ Arkansas, C USA
27 S13 **Greeson, Lake** ▣ Arkansas, C USA
29 O12 **Gregory** South Dakota, N USA 43°11′N 99°26′W
182 J3 **Gregory, Lake** *salt lake* South Australia
180 J9 **Gregory Lake** ◎ Western Australia
181 V5 **Gregory Range** ▲▲ Queensland, E Australia
Greifenberg/Greifenberg in Pommern *see* Gryfice
Greifenhagen *see* Gryfino
100 O8 **Greifswald** Mecklenburg-Vorpommern, NE Germany 54°04′N 13°24′E
100 O8 **Greifswalder Bodden** *bay* NE Germany
109 U4 **Grein** Oberösterreich, N Austria 48°14′N 14°50′E
101 M17 **Greiz** Thüringen, C Germany 50°40′N 12°11′E
125 V14 **Gremyachinsk** Permskaya Oblast', NW Russian Federation 58°33′N 57°52′E
Grenå *see* Grenaa
95 H21 **Grenaa** *var.* Grenå. Århus, C Denmark 56°25′N 10°53′E
22 L3 **Grenada** Mississippi, S USA 33°46′N 89°48′W
45 W15 **Grenada** ◆ *commonwealth republic* SE West Indies
47 S4 **Grenada** *island* Grenada
47 R4 **Grenada Basin** *undersea feature* W Atlantic Ocean 13°30′N 62°00′W
22 L3 **Grenada Lake** ▣ Mississippi, S USA
45 Y14 **Grenadines, The** *island group* Grenada/St Vincent and the Grenadines
108 D7 **Grenchen** *Fr.* Granges. Solothurn, NW Switzerland 47°13′N 07°24′E
183 Q9 **Grenfell** New South Wales, SE Australia 33°54′S 148°09′E
11 V16 **Grenfell** Saskatchewan, S Canada 50°24′N 102°56′W
92 J1 **Grenivík** Nordhurland Eystra, N Iceland 65°57′N 18°10′W
103 S12 **Grenoble** *anc.* Cularo, Gratianopolis. Isère, E France 45°11′N 05°42′E
28 J2 **Grenora** North Dakota, N USA 48°36′N 103°57′W
92 N8 **Grense-Jakobselv** Finnmark, N Norway 69°46′N 30°39′E
45 S14 **Grenville** E Grenada 12°07′N 61°37′W
32 G11 **Gresham** Oregon, NW USA 45°30′N 122°25′W
Gresk *see* Hresk
106 B7 **Gressoney-St-Jean** Valle d'Aosta, NW Italy 45°48′N 07°49′E
22 K9 **Gretna** Louisiana, S USA 29°54′N 90°03′W
21 T7 **Gretna** Virginia, NE USA 36°57′N 79°21′W
98 F13 **Grevelingen** *inlet* S North Sea
100 F13 **Greven** Nordrhein-Westfalen, NW Germany 52°07′N 07°38′E
115 D15 **Grevená** Dytikí Makedonía, N Greece 40°05′N 21°26′E
101 D16 **Grevenbroich** Nordrhein-Westfalen, W Germany 51°06′N 06°34′E
99 N24 **Grevenmacher** Grevenmacher, E Luxembourg 49°41′N 06°27′E
99 M24 **Grevenmacher** ◐ *district* E Luxembourg
100 K9 **Grevesmühlen** Mecklenburg-Vorpommern, N Germany 53°52′N 11°12′E
185 H16 **Grey** ≈ South Island, New Zealand
33 V12 **Greybull** Wyoming, C USA 44°29′N 108°03′W
33 U13 **Greybull River** ≈ Wyoming, C USA
65 A24 **Grey Channel** *sound* Falkland Islands
Greyerzer See *see* Gruyère, Lac de la
13 T10 **Grey Islands** *island group* Newfoundland and Labrador, E Canada
18 L10 **Greylock, Mount** ▲ Massachusetts, NE USA 42°38′N 73°09′W
185 G17 **Greymouth** West Coast, South Island, New Zealand 42°29′S 171°14′E
181 U10 **Grey Range** ▲▲ New South Wales/Queensland, E Australia
97 G18 **Greystones** *Ir.* Na Clocha Liatha. E Ireland 53°08′N 06°05′W
185 M14 **Greytown** Wellington, North Island, New Zealand 41°04′S 175°29′E
83 K23 **Greytown** KwaZulu/Natal, E South Africa 29°04′S 30°35′E
Greytown *see* San Juan del Norte
99 H19 **Grez-Doiceau** *Dut.* Graven. Walloon Brabant, C Belgium 50°43′N 04°41′E
115 J19 **Griá, Akrotírio** *headland* Ándros, Kykládes, Greece, Aegean Sea 37°54′N 24°57′E
127 N8 **Gribanovskiy** Voronezhskaya Oblast', W Russian Federation 51°27′N 41°53′E
78 I13 **Gribingui** ≈ N Central African Republic
35 O6 **Gridley** California, W USA 39°21′N 121°41′W
83 G23 **Griekwastad** Northern Cape, C South Africa 28°50′S 23°16′E
23 S4 **Griffin** Georgia, SE USA 33°15′N 84°17′W
183 O9 **Griffith** New South Wales, SE Australia 34°18′S 146°04′E
14 F13 **Griffith Island** *island* Ontario, S Canada
21 W10 **Grifton** North Carolina, SE USA 35°22′N 77°26′W
Grigioni *see* Graubünden
119 H14 **Grigiškes** Vilnius, SE Lithuania 54°42′N 25°00′E
117 N10 **Grigoriopol** C Moldova 47°09′N 29°18′E
147 X7 **Grigor'yevka** Issyk-Kul'skaya Oblast', E Kyrgyzstan 42°43′N 77°27′E
193 U8 **Grijalva Ridge** *undersea feature* E Pacific Ocean
41 U15 **Grijalva, Río** *var.* Tabasco. ≈ Guatemala/Mexico
98 N5 **Grijpskerk** Groningen, NE Netherlands 53°15′N 06°18′E
83 C22 **Grillenthal** Karas, SW Namibia 26°55′S 15°24′E
79 J15 **Grimari** Ouaka, C Central African Republic 05°44′N 20°02′E
Grimaylov *see* Hrymayliv
99 G18 **Grimbergen** Vlaams Brabant, C Belgium 50°56′N 04°22′E
183 N15 **Grim, Cape** *headland* Tasmania, SE Australia 40°42′S 144°42′E
100 N8 **Grimmen** Mecklenburg-Vorpommern, NE Germany 54°06′N 13°03′E
14 G16 **Grimsby** Ontario, S Canada 43°12′N 79°35′W
97 O17 **Grimsby** *prev.* Great Grimsby. E England, United Kingdom 53°35′N 00°05′W
92 J1 **Grímsey** *var.* Grimsey. *island* N Iceland
Grimsey *see* Grímsey
11 O12 **Grimshaw** Alberta, W Canada 56°11′N 117°37′W
95 F18 **Grimstad** Aust-Agder, S Norway 58°20′N 08°35′E
92 H4 **Grindavík** Reykjanes, W Iceland 65°57′N 18°10′W
108 F9 **Grindelwald** Bern, S Switzerland 46°37′N 08°04′E
95 F23 **Grindsted** Ribe, W Denmark 55°46′N 08°56′E
29 W14 **Grinnell** Iowa, C USA 41°44′N 92°43′W
109 U10 **Grintovec** ▲ N Slovenia 46°21′N 14°31′E
9 N4 **Grise Fiord** *var.* Ausuittuq. Northwest Territories, Ellesmere Island, N Canada 76°10′N 83°15′W
182 H1 **Griselda, Lake** *salt lake* South Australia
Grisons *see* Graubünden
95 P14 **Grisslehamn** Stockholm, C Sweden 60°04′N 18°50′E
29 T15 **Griswold** Iowa, C USA 41°14′N 95°08′W
102 M1 **Griz Nez, Cap** *headland* N France 50°51′N 01°34′E
112 P13 **Grljan** Serbia, E Serbia 43°52′N 22°18′E
112 E11 **Grmeč** ▲▲ NW Bosnia and Herzegovina
99 H16 **Grobbendonk** Antwerpen, N Belgium 51°12′N 04°41′E
Grobin *see* Grobiņa
118 C10 **Grobiņa** *Ger.* Grobin. Liepāja, W Latvia 56°32′N 21°12′E
83 K20 **Groblersdal** Mpumalanga, NE South Africa 25°15′S 29°25′E
83 G23 **Groblershoop** Northern Cape, W South Africa 28°51′S 22°01′E
Gródek Jagielloński *see* Horodok
109 Q6 **Grödig** Salzburg, W Austria 47°42′N 13°06′E
111 H15 **Grodków** Opolskie, S Poland 50°42′N 17°23′E
Grodnenskaya Oblast' *see* Hrodzyenskaya Voblasts'
Grodno *see* Hrodna
110 L12 **Grodzisk Mazowiecki** Mazowieckie, C Poland 52°09′N 20°38′E
110 F12 **Grodzisk Wielkopolski** Wielkopolskie, C Poland 52°13′N 16°21′E
Grodzyanka *see* Hradzyanka
98 O12 **Groenlo** Gelderland, E Netherlands 52°02′N 06°36′E
83 E22 **Groenrivier** Karas, SE Namibia 27°27′S 18°52′E
25 U8 **Groesbeck** Texas, SW USA 31°31′N 96°35′W
98 L13 **Groesbeek** Gelderland, SE Netherlands 51°47′N 05°56′E
102 G7 **Groix, Îles de** *island group* NW France
110 M12 **Grójec** Mazowieckie, C Poland 51°51′N 20°52′E
65 K15 **Gröll Seamount** *undersea feature* C Atlantic Ocean 12°54′S 33°24′W
100 E13 **Gronau** *var.* Gronau in Westfalen. Nordrhein-Westfalen, NW Germany 52°13′N 07°02′E
Gronau in Westfalen *see* Gronau
93 F15 **Grong** Nord-Trøndelag, C Norway 64°29′N 12°19′E
95 N22 **Grönhögen** Kalmar, S Sweden 56°16′N 16°09′E
98 N5 **Groningen** Groningen, NE Netherlands 53°13′N 06°35′E
55 W9 **Groningen** Saramacca, N Surinam 05°45′N 55°31′W
98 N5 **Groningen** ◐ *province* NE Netherlands
Gronland *see* Greenland
108 H11 **Grono** Graubünden, S Switzerland 46°15′N 09°07′E
95 M20 **Grönskåra** Kalmar, S Sweden 57°04′N 15°45′E
25 O2 **Groom** Texas, SW USA 35°12′N 101°06′W
35 W9 **Groom Lake** ◎ Nevada, W USA
83 H25 **Groot** ≈ S South Africa
181 S2 **Groote Eylandt** *island* Northern Territory, N Australia
98 M6 **Grootegast** Groningen, NE Netherlands 53°11′N 06°12′E
83 D17 **Grootfontein** Otjozondjupa, N Namibia 19°32′S 18°05′E
83 E22 **Groot Karasberge** ▲▲ S Namibia
Groot Karoo *see* Great Karoo
Groot-Kei *see* Nciba
15 V6 **Grosses-Roches** Québec, SE Canada 48°55′N 67°06′W
109 V2 **Gross-Siegharts** Niederösterreich, N Austria 48°48′N 15°25′E
45 T10 **Gros Islet** N Saint Lucia 14°04′N 60°57′W
44 L8 **Gros-Morne** NW Haiti 19°45′N 72°46′W
13 S11 **Gros Morne** ▲ Newfoundland, Newfoundland and Labrador, E Canada 49°38′N 57°45′W
103 R9 **Grosne** ≈ C France
45 S12 **Gros Piton** ▲ SW Saint Lucia 13°48′N 61°04′W
Grossa, Isola *see* Dugi Otok
Grossbetschkerek *see* Zrenjanin
Grosse Isper *see* Grosse Ysper
Grosse Kokel *see* Târnava Mare
101 M21 **Grosse Laaber** *var.* Grosse Laber. ≈ SE Germany
Grosse Laber *see* Grosse Laaber
Grosse Morava *see* Velika Morava
101 O15 **Grossenhain** Sachsen, E Germany 51°18′N 13°31′E
109 Y4 **Grossenzersdorf** Niederösterreich, NE Austria 48°12′N 16°33′E
101 O21 **Grosser Arber** ▲ SE Germany 49°07′N 13°10′E
101 K17 **Grosser Beerberg** ▲ C Germany 50°39′N 10°45′E
101 G18 **Grosser Feldberg** ▲ W Germany 50°13′N 08°28′E
109 O8 **Grosser Löffler** *It.* Monte Lovello. ▲ Austria/Italy 47°02′N 11°56′E
109 N8 **Grosser Möseler** *var.* Mesule. ▲ Austria/Italy 47°01′N 11°52′E
100 J8 **Grosser Plöner See** ◎ N Germany
101 O21 **Grosser Rachel** ▲ SE Germany 48°59′N 13°23′E
Grosser Sund *see* Suur Väin
109 P8 **Grosses Wiesbachhorn** *var.* Wiesbachhorn. ▲ W Austria 47°09′N 12°44′E
106 F13 **Grosseto** Toscana, C Italy 42°45′N 11°07′E
101 M22 **Grosse Vils** ≈ SE Germany
109 U4 **Grosse Ysper** *var.* Grosse Isper. ≈ N Austria
101 G19 **Gross-Gerau** Hessen, W Germany 49°55′N 08°28′E
109 U3 **Gross Gerungs** Niederösterreich, N Austria 48°33′N 14°58′E
109 P8 **Grossglockner** ▲ W Austria 47°05′N 12°39′E
Grosskanizsa *see* Nagykanizsa
Gross-Karol *see* Carei
Grosskikinda *see* Kikinda
109 W9 **Grossklein** Steiermark, SE Austria 46°43′N 15°24′E
Grosskoppe *see* Velká Deštná
Grossmeseritsch *see* Velké Meziříčí
Grossmichel *see* Michalovce
110 H19 **Grossostheim** Bayern, C Germany 49°54′N 09°03′E
109 X7 **Grosspetersdorf** Burgenland, SE Austria 47°15′N 16°19′E
109 T5 **Grossraming** Oberösterreich, C Austria 47°54′N 14°34′E
101 P14 **Grossräschen** Brandenburg, E Germany 51°34′N 14°00′E
Grossrauschenbach *see* Revúca
Gross-Sankt-Johannis *see* Suure-Jaani
Gross-Schlatten *see* Abrud
Gross-Skaisgirren *see* Bol'shakovo
Gross-Steffelsdorf *see* Rimavská Sobota
Gross Strehlitz *see* Strzelce Opolskie
109 O8 **Grossvenediger** ▲ W Austria 47°07′N 12°19′E
Grosswardein *see* Oradea
Gross Wartenberg *see* Syców
109 U11 **Grosuplje** C Slovenia 46°00′N 14°36′E
99 H17 **Grote Nete** ≈ N Belgium
94 E10 **Grotli** Oppland, S Norway 62°02′N 07°36′E
19 N13 **Groton** Connecticut, NE USA 41°20′N 72°03′W
29 P8 **Groton** South Dakota, N USA 45°27′N 98°06′W
107 P18 **Grottaglie** Puglia, SE Italy 40°32′N 17°26′E
107 L17 **Grottaminarda** Campania, S Italy 41°04′N 15°02′E
106 K13 **Grottammare** Marche, C Italy 43°00′N 13°52′E
21 U5 **Grottoes** Virginia, NE USA 38°16′N 78°49′W
Grou *see* Grouw
13 N10 **Groulx, Monts** ▲▲ Québec, E Canada
14 E7 **Groundhog** ≈ Ontario, S Canada
36 J1 **Grouse Creek** Utah, W USA 41°41′N 113°52′W
36 J1 **Grouse Creek Mountains** ▲▲ Utah, W USA
98 L6 **Grouw** *Fris.* Grou. Friesland, N Netherlands 53°07′N 05°51′E
27 R8 **Grove** Oklahoma, C USA 36°35′N 94°46′W
31 S13 **Grove City** Ohio, N USA 39°52′N 83°05′W
18 B13 **Grove City** Pennsylvania, NE USA 41°09′N 80°02′W
23 O6 **Grove Hill** Alabama, S USA 31°42′N 87°46′W
33 S15 **Grover** Wyoming, C USA 42°48′N 110°57′W
35 P13 **Grover City** California, W USA 35°08′N 120°37′W
25 Y11 **Groves** Texas, SW USA 29°57′N 93°55′W
19 O7 **Groveton** New Hampshire, NE USA 44°35′N 71°28′W
25 W9 **Groveton** Texas, SW USA 31°04′N 95°08′W
36 J15 **Growler Mountains** ▲▲ Arizona, SW USA
Grozdovo *see* Bratya Daskalovi
127 P16 **Groznyy** Chechenskaya Respublika, SW Russian Federation 43°20′N 45°43′E
Grubeshov *see* Hrubieszów
112 G9 **Grubišno Polje** Bjelovar-Bilogora, NE Croatia 45°42′N 17°09′E
Grudovo *see* Sredets
110 J9 **Grudziądz** *Ger.* Graudenz. Kujawsko-pomorskie, C Poland 53°29′N 18°45′E
25 R17 **Grulla** *var.* La Grulla. Texas, SW USA 26°15′N 98°37′W
40 K14 **Grullo** Jalisco, SW Mexico 19°45′N 104°15′W
67 V10 **Grumeti** ≈ N Tanzania
95 K16 **Grums** Värmland, C Sweden 59°22′N 13°11′E
109 S5 **Grünau im Almtal** Oberösterreich, N Austria 47°51′N 13°56′E
101 H17 **Grünberg** Hessen, W Germany 50°36′N 08°57′E
Grünberg/Grünberg in Schlesien *see* Zielona Góra
92 H3 **Grundarfjördhur** Vestfirdhir, W Iceland 64°55′N 23°15′W
21 P7 **Grundy** Virginia, NE USA 37°17′N 82°06′W
29 W13 **Grundy Center** Iowa, C USA 42°21′N 92°46′W
Grüneberg *see* Zielona Góra
25 N1 **Gruver** Texas, SW USA 36°16′N 101°24′W
108 C9 **Gruyère, Lac de la** *Ger.* Greyerzer See. ◎ SW Switzerland
108 C9 **Gruyères** Fribourg, W Switzerland 46°34′N 07°04′E
118 E11 **Gruzdžiai** Šiauliai, N Lithuania 56°06′N 23°15′E
Gruzinskaya SSR/Gruziya *see* Georgia
Gryada Akkyr *see* Akgyr Erezi
126 L7 **Gryazi** Lipetskaya Oblast', W Russian Federation 52°27′N 39°56′E
124 M14 **Gryazovets** Vologodskaya Oblast', NW Russian Federation 58°52′N 40°12′E
111 M17 **Grybów** Małopolskie, SE Poland 49°35′N 20°54′E
94 M13 **Grycksbo** Dalarna, C Sweden 60°40′N 15°30′E
110 E8 **Gryfice** *Ger.* Greifenberg, Greifenberg in Pommern. Zachodnio-pomorskie, NW Poland 53°55′N 15°11′E
110 D9 **Gryfino** *Ger.* Greifenhagen. Zachodnio-pomorskie, NW Poland 53°15′N 14°30′E
92 H9 **Gryllefjord** Troms, N Norway 69°21′N 17°07′E
95 L15 **Grythyttan** Örebro, C Sweden 59°52′N 14°31′E
108 D10 **Gstaad** Bern, W Switzerland 46°30′N 07°16′E
43 P14 **Guabito** Bocas del Toro, NW Panama 09°30′N 82°35′W
44 G7 **Guacanayabo, Golfo de** *gulf* S Cuba
40 I7 **Guachochi** Chihuahua, N Mexico
104 J11 **Guadajira** ≈ SW Spain
104 M13 **Guadajoz** ≈ S Spain
40 L13 **Guadalajara** Jalisco, C Mexico 20°43′N 103°24′W
105 O8 **Guadalajara** *Ar.* Wad Al-Hajarah; *anc.* Arriaca. Castilla-La Mancha, C Spain 40°37′N 03°10′W
105 O7 **Guadalajara** ◐ *province* Castilla-La Mancha, C Spain
104 K12 **Guadalcanal** Andalucía, S Spain 38°06′N 05°49′W
186 L10 **Guadalcanal** *off.* Guadalcanal Province. ◐ *province* C Solomon Islands
186 M9 **Guadalcanal** *island* C Solomon Islands
Guadalcanal Province *see* Guadalcanal
105 O12 **Guadalén** ≈ S Spain
105 R13 **Guadalentín** ≈ SE Spain
104 K15 **Guadalete** ≈ SW Spain
105 O13 **Guadalimar** ≈ S Spain
105 P12 **Guadalmena** ≈ S Spain
104 L11 **Guadalmez** ≈ W Spain
105 S7 **Guadalope** ≈ E Spain
104 K13 **Guadalquivir** ≈ W Spain
104 J14 **Guadalquivir, Marismas del** *var.* Las Marismas. *wetland* SW Spain
40 M11 **Guadalupe** Zacatecas, C Mexico 22°47′N 102°30′W
57 E16 **Guadalupe** Ica, W Peru 13°59′S 75°49′W
104 L10 **Guadalupe** Extremadura, W Spain 39°26′N 05°18′W
36 L14 **Guadalupe** Arizona, SW USA 33°20′N 111°57′W
35 P13 **Guadalupe** California, W USA 34°55′N 120°34′W
Guadalupe *see* Canelones
40 J3 **Guadalupe Bravos** Chihuahua, N Mexico 31°22′N 106°04′W
40 A4 **Guadalupe, Isla** *island* NW Mexico
37 U15 **Guadalupe Mountains** ▲▲ New Mexico/Texas, SW USA
24 J8 **Guadalupe Peak** ▲ Texas, SW USA 31°53′N 104°51′W
25 R11 **Guadalupe River** ≈ SW USA
104 K10 **Guadalupe, Sierra de** ▲▲ W Spain
40 K9 **Guadalupe Victoria** Durango, C Mexico 24°30′N 104°08′W
40 I8 **Guadalupe y Calvo** Chihuahua, N Mexico 26°04′N 106°58′W
105 N7 **Guadarrama** Madrid, C Spain 40°40′N 04°06′W
105 N7 **Guadarrama** ≈ C Spain
104 M7 **Guadarrama, Puerto de** *pass* C Spain
105 N9 **Guadarrama, Sierra de** ▲▲ C Spain
105 Q9 **Guadazaón** ≈ C Spain
45 X10 **Guadeloupe** ◇ *French overseas department* E West Indies
47 S3 **Guadeloupe** *island group* E West Indies
45 W10 **Guadeloupe Passage** *passage* E Caribbean Sea
104 H13 **Guadiana** ≈ Portugal/Spain
105 O13 **Guadiana Menor** ≈ S Spain
105 Q8 **Guadiela** ≈ C Spain
105 O14 **Guadix** Andalucía, S Spain 37°19′N 03°08′W
Guad-i-Zirreh *see* Gowd-e Zereh, Dasht-e
193 T12 **Guafo Fracture Zone** *tectonic feature* SE Pacific Ocean
63 F18 **Guafo, Isla** *island* S Chile
42 I6 **Guaimaca** Francisco Morazán, C Honduras 14°34′N 86°49′W
54 J12 **Guainía** *off.* Comisaría del Guainía. ◐ *province* E Colombia
Guainía, Comisaría del *see* Guainía
54 K12 **Guainía, Río** ≈ Colombia/Venezuela
55 O9 **Guaiquinima, Cerro** *elevation* SE Venezuela
60 G10 **Guaira** Paraná, S Brazil 24°05′S 54°15′W
60 L7 **Guaíra** São Paulo, S Brazil 20°17′S 48°21′W
62 O7 **Guairá** *off.* Departamento del Guairá. ◐ *department* S Paraguay
Guairá, Departamento del *see* Guairá
Guaire *see* Gorey
63 F18 **Guaiteca, Isla** *island* S Chile
44 G6 **Guajaba, Cayo** *headland* C Cuba 21°50′N 77°33′W
59 D16 **Guajará-Mirim** Rondônia, W Brazil 10°50′S 65°21′W
Guajira *see* La Guajira
Guajira, Departamento de La *see* La Guajira
54 H3 **Guajira, Península de la** *peninsula* N Colombia
42 J6 **Gualaco** Olancho, C Honduras 15°00′N 86°03′W
34 L7 **Gualala** California, W USA 38°45′N 123°33′W
42 E5 **Gualán** Zacapa, C Guatemala 15°06′N 89°22′W
61 C19 **Gualeguay** Entre Ríos, E Argentina 33°09′S 59°20′W
61 D18 **Gualeguaychú** Entre Ríos, E Argentina 33°03′S 58°31′W
61 C18 **Gualeguay, Río** ≈ E Argentina
63 K16 **Gualicho, Salina del** *salt lake* E Argentina
188 B15 **Guam** ◇ *US unincorporated territory* W Pacific Ocean
63 F19 **Guamblin, Isla** *island* Archipiélago de los Chonos, S Chile
61 A22 **Guaminí** Buenos Aires, E Argentina 37°01′S 62°28′W
40 H8 **Guamúchil** Sinaloa, C Mexico 25°23′N 108°01′W
54 H4 **Guana** *var.* Misión de Guana. Zulia, NW Venezuela 11°07′N 72°17′W
44 C4 **Guanabacoa** La Habana, W Cuba 23°02′N 82°12′W
42 K13 **Guanacaste** *off.* Provincia de Guanacaste. ◐ *province* NW Costa Rica
42 K12 **Guanacaste, Cordillera de** ▲▲ NW Costa Rica
Guanacaste, Provincia de *see* Guanacaste
40 J8 **Guanaceví** Durango, C Mexico 25°55′N 105°51′W
44 A5 **Guanahacabibes, Golfo de** *gulf* W Cuba
42 K4 **Guanaja, Isla de** *island* Islas de la Bahía, N Honduras
44 C4 **Guanajay** La Habana, W Cuba 22°56′N 82°42′W
41 N12 **Guanajuato** Guanajuato, C Mexico 21°N 101°19′W
40 M12 **Guanajuato** ◐ *state* C Mexico
54 J6 **Guanare** Portuguesa, N Venezuela 09°04′N 69°45′W
54 K7 **Guanare, Río** ≈ W Venezuela
54 J6 **Guanarito** Portuguesa, NW Venezuela 08°43′N 69°12′W
160 M3 **Guancen Shan** ▲▲ C China
62 I9 **Guandacol** La Rioja, W Argentina 29°32′S 68°37′W
44 A5 **Guane** Pinar del Río, W Cuba 22°12′N 84°05′W
160 J9 **Guang'an** Sichuan, C China 30°28′N 106°22′E
161 N14 **Guangdong** *var.* Guangdong Sheng, Kuang-tung, Kwangtung, Yue. ◐ *province* S China
Guangdong Sheng *see* Guangdong
Guanghua *see* Laohekou
Guangju *see* Kwangju
160 I13 **Guangnan** *var.* Liancheng. Yunnan, SW China 24°07′N 104°54′E
161 N8 **Guangshui** *prev.* Yingshan. Hubei, C China 31°41′N 113°53′E

◆ Country
● Country Capital
◇ Dependent Territory
○ Dependent Territory Capital
◐ Administrative Regions
✈ International Airport
▲ Mountain
▲▲ Mountain Range
Volcano
≈ River
◎ Lake
▣ Reservoir

Guangxi *see* Guangxi Zhuangzu Zizhiqu
160 *K14* **Guangxi Zhuangzu Zizhiqu** *var.* Guangxi, Gui, Kuang-hsi, Kwangsi, *Eng.* Kwangsi Chuang Autonomous Region. ◐ *autonomous region* S China
160 *J8* **Guangyuan** *var.* Kuang-yuan, Kwangyuan. Sichuan, C China *32°27′N 105°49′E*
161 *N14* **Guangzhou** *var.* Kuang-chou, Kwangchow, *Eng.* Canton. *province capital* Guangdong, S China *23°11′N 113°19′E*
59 *N19* **Guanhães** Minas Gerais, SE Brazil *18°46′S 42°58′W*
160 *I12* **Guanling** *var.* Guanling Bouyeizu Miaozu Zizhixian. Guizhou, S China *26°00′N 105°40′E*
Guanling Bouyeizu Miaozu Zizhixian *see* Guanling
55 *N5* **Guanta** Anzoátegui, NE Venezuela *10°15′N 64°38′W*
44 *J8* **Guantánamo** Guantánamo, SE Cuba *20°06′N 75°16′W*
44 *J8* **Guantánamo, Bahía de** *Eng.* Guantanamo Bay. *US military base* SE Cuba*20°06′N 75°16′W*
Guantanamo Bay *see* Guantánamo, Bahía de
Guanxian/Guan Xian *see* Dujiangyan
161 *Q6* **Guanyun** *var.* Yishan. Jiangsu, E China *34°18′N 119°14′E*
54 *C12* **Guapi** Cauca, SW Colombia *02°36′N 77°54′W*
43 *N13* **Guápiles** Limón, NE Costa Rica *10°15′N 83°46′W*
61 *I15* **Guaporé** Rio Grande do Sul, S Brazil *28°55′S 51°53′W*
47 *S8* **Guaporé, Río** *var.* Río Iténez. ∼ Bolivia/Brazil *see also* Río Iténez
Guaporé, Rio *see* Iténez, Río
56 *B7* **Guaranda** Bolívar, C Ecuador *01°35′S 78°59′W*
60 *H11* **Guaraniaçu** Paraná, S Brazil *25°05′S 52°52′W*
59 *O20* **Guarapari** Espírito Santo, SE Brazil *20°39′S 40°31′W*
60 *I12* **Guarapuava** Paraná, S Brazil *25°22′S 51°28′W*
60 *J8* **Guararapes** São Paulo, S Brazil *21°16′S 50°37′W*
105 *S4* **Guara, Sierra de** ▲ NE Spain
60 *N10* **Guaratinguetá** São Paulo, S Brazil *22°44′S 45°16′W*
104 *I7* **Guarda** Guarda, N Portugal *40°32′N 07°17′W*
104 *I7* **Guarda** ◐ *district* N Portugal
Guardak *see* Magdanly
104 *M3* **Guardo** Castilla-León, N Spain *42°48′N 04°50′W*
104 *K11* **Guareña** Extremadura, W Spain *38°51′N 06°06′W*
60 *J11* **Guaricana, Pico** ▲ S Brazil *25°13′S 48°50′W*
54 *L6* **Guárico** *off.* Estado Guárico. ◐ *state* N Venezuela
Guárico, Estado *see* Guárico
44 *J7* **Guarico, Punta** *headland* E Cuba *20°36′N 74°43′W*
54 *L7* **Guárico, Río** ∼ C Venezuela
60 *M10* **Guarujá** São Paulo, SE Brazil *23°50′S 46°27′W*
61 *L22* **Guarulhos** ✈ (São Paulo) São Paulo, S Brazil *23°23′S 46°32′W*
43 *R17* **Guarumal** Veraguas, S Panama *07°48′N 81°15′W*
Guasapa *see* Guasopa
40 *H8* **Guasave** Sinaloa, C Mexico *25°33′N 108°29′W*
54 *I8* **Guasdualito** Apure, C Venezuela *07°15′N 70°40′W*
55 *Q7* **Guasipati** Bolívar, E Venezuela *07°28′N 61°58′W*
186 *I9* **Guasopa** *var.* Guasapa. Woodlark Island, SE Papua New Guinea *09°12′S 152°58′E*
106 *F9* **Guastalla** Emilia-Romagna, C Italy *44°54′N 10°38′E*
42 *D6* **Guastatoya** *var.* El Progreso. El Progreso, C Guatemala *14°51′N 90°01′W*
42 *D5* **Guatemala** *off.* Republic of Guatemala. ◆ *republic* Central America
42 *A2* **Guatemala** *off.* Departamento de Guatemala. ◐ *department* S Guatemala
193 *S7* **Guatemala Basin** *undersea feature* E Pacific Ocean *11°00′N 95°00′W*
Guatemala City *see* Ciudad de Guatemala
Guatemala, Departamento de *see* Guatemala
Guatemala, Republic of *see* Guatemala
45 *V14* **Guatuaro Point** *headland* Trinidad, Trinidad and Tobago *10°19′N 60°58′W*
186 *B8* **Guavi** ∼ SW Papua New Guinea
54 *G13* **Guaviare** *off.* Comisaría Guaviare. ◐ *province* S Colombia
Guaviare, Comisaría *see* Guaviare
54 *J11* **Guaviare, Río** ∼ E Colombia
61 *E15* **Guaviravi** Corrientes, NE Argentina *29°20′S 56°50′W*
54 *F11* **Guayabero, Río** ∼ SW Colombia
45 *U6* **Guayama** E Puerto Rico *17°59′N 66°07′W*
42 *J7* **Guayambre, Río** ∼ S Honduras
Guayanas, Macizo de las *see* Guiana Highlands
45 *V6* **Guayanés, Punta** *headland* E Puerto Rico *18°03′N 65°48′W*
42 *J6* **Guayape, Río** ∼ C Honduras
56 *B7* **Guayaquil** *var.* Santiago de Guayaquil. Guayas, SW Ecuador *02°13′S 79°54′W*
Guayaquil *see* Simon Bolivar
56 *A8* **Guayaquil, Golfo de** *var.* Gulf of Guayaquil. *gulf* SW Ecuador
Guayaquil, Gulf of *see* Guayaquil, Golfo de
56 *A7* **Guayas** ◐ *province* W Ecuador
62 *N7* **Guaycurú, Río** ∼ NE Argentina
40 *F6* **Guaymas** Sonora, NW Mexico *27°56′N 110°54′W*
45 *U5* **Guaynabo** E Puerto Rico *18°19′N 66°05′W*
80 *H12* **Guba** Binishangul Gumuz, W Ethiopia *11°11′N 35°21′E*
146 *H8* **Gubadag** *Turkm.* Tel'man; *prev.* Tel'mansk. Daşoguz Welaýaty, N Turkmenistan *42°07′N 59°55′E*
125 *T1* **Guba Dolgaya** Nenetskiy Avtonomnyy Okrug, NW Russian Federation *70°16′N 58°45′E*
125 *V13* **Gubakha** Permskaya Oblast', NW Russian Federation *58°52′N 57°35′E*
106 *I12* **Gubbio** Umbria, C Italy *43°27′N 12°34′E*
100 *Q13* **Guben** *var.* Wilhelm-Pieck-Stadt. Brandenburg, E Germany *51°59′N 14°42′E*
Guben *see* Gubin
110 *D12* **Gubin** *Ger.* Guben. Lubuskie, W Poland *51°59′N 14°43′E*
126 *K8* **Gubkin** Belgorodskaya Oblast', W Russian Federation *51°16′N 37°32′E*
162 *J9* **Guchin-Us** *var.* Arguut. Övörhangay, C Mongolia *45°27′N 102°25′E*
Gudara *see* Ghŭdara
105 *S8* **Gúdar, Sierra de** ▲ E Spain
137 *P8* **Gudaut'a** NW Georgia *43°07′N 40°35′E*
94 *G12* **Gudbrandsdalen** *valley* S Norway
95 *G21* **Gudenå** *var.* Gudenaa. ∼ C Denmark
Gudenaa *see* Gudenå
127 *P16* **Gudermes** Chechenskaya Respublika, SW Russian Federation *43°23′N 46°06′E*
155 *J18* **Gūdūr** Andhra Pradesh, E India *14°10′N 79°51′E*
146 *B13* **Gudurolum** Balkan Welaýaty, W Turkmenistan *37°28′N 54°30′E*
94 *D13* **Gudvangen** Sogn Og Fjordane, S Norway *60°54′N 06°49′E*
103 *U7* **Guebwiller** Haut-Rhin, NE France *47°55′N 07°13′E*
Guéckédou *see* Guékédou
14 *K8* **Guéguen, Lac** ◎ Québec, SE Canada
76 *J15* **Guékédou** *var.* Guéckédou. Guinée-Forestière, S Guinea *08°33′N 10°08′W*
41 *R16* **Guelatao** Oaxaca, SE Mexico
Guelders *see* Gelderland
78 *G11* **Guélengdeng** Mayo-Kébbi, W Chad *10°55′N 15°31′E*
74 *L5* **Guelma** *var.* Gâlma. NE Algeria *36°29′N 07°25′E*
74 *D8* **Guelmime** *var.* Goulimime. SW Morocco *28°59′N 10°10′W*
14 *G15* **Guelph** Ontario, S Canada *43°34′N 80°16′W*
102 *I7* **Gueméné-Penfao** Loire-Atlantique, NW France *47°37′N 01°49′W*
102 *I7* **Guer** Morbihan, NW France *47°54′N 02°07′W*
78 *I11* **Guéra** *off.* Préfecture du Guéra. ◐ *prefecture* S Chad
102 *H8* **Guérande** Loire-Atlantique, NW France *47°20′N 02°25′W*
Guéra, Préfecture du *see* Guéra
78 *K9* **Guéréda** Biltine, E Chad *14°30′N 22°05′E*
103 *N10* **Guéret** Creuse, C France *46°10′N 01°52′E*
Guernica/Guernica y Lumo *see* Gernika-Lumo
33 *Z15* **Guernsey** Wyoming, C USA *42°16′N 104°44′W*
97 *K25* **Guernsey** *island* Channel Islands, NW Europe
76 *J10* **Guérou** Assaba, S Mauritania *16°48′N 11°40′W*
25 *R16* **Guerra** Texas, SW USA *26°54′N 98°53′W*
41 *O15* **Guerrero** ◐ *state* S Mexico
40 *D6* **Guerrero Negro** Baja California Sur, NW Mexico *27°56′N 114°04′W*
103 *P9* **Gueugnon** Saône-et-Loire, C France *46°36′N 04°03′E*
76 *M17* **Guéyo** S Ivory Coast *05°25′N 06°04′W*
107 *L15* **Guglionesi** Molise, C Italy *41°54′N 14°54′E*
188 *K5* **Guguan** *island* C Northern Mariana Islands
Guhrau *see* Góra
Gui *see* Guangxi Zhuangzu Zizhiqu
Guiana *see* French Guiana
47 *V4* **Guiana Basin** *undersea feature* W Atlantic Ocean *11°00′N 52°00′W*
48 *G6* **Guiana Highlands** *var.* Macizo de las Guayanas. ▲ N South America
Guiba *see* Juba
102 *I7* **Guichen** Ille-et-Vilaine, NW France *47°57′N 01°47′W*
Guicheng *see* Chizhou
61 *E18* **Guichón** Paysandú, W Uruguay *32°30′S 57°13′W*
77 *U12* **Guidan-Roumji** Maradi, S Niger *13°40′N 06°41′E*
Guidder *see* Guider
159 *T10* **Guide** *var.* Heyin. Qinghai, C China *36°06′N 101°25′E*
78 *F12* **Guider** *var.* Guidder. Nord, N Cameroon *09°55′N 13°59′E*
76 *I11* **Guidimaka** ◐ *region* S Mauritania
77 *W12* **Guidimouni** Zinder, S Niger *13°40′N 09°31′E*
76 *G10* **Guier, Lac de** *var.* Lac de Guiers. ◎ N Senegal
Guiers, Lac de *see* Guier, Lac de
160 *L14* **Guigang** *var.* Guixian, Gui Xian. Guangxi Zhuangzu Zizhiqu, S China *23°06′N 109°36′E*
76 *L16* **Guiglo** W Ivory Coast *06°33′N 07°29′W*
54 *L5* **Güigüe** Carabobo, N Venezuela *10°05′N 67°48′W*
83 *M20* **Guijá** Gaza, S Mozambique *24°31′S 33°02′E*
42 *E7* **Güija, Lago de** ◎ El Salvador/Guatemala
160 *L14* **Gui Jiang** *var.* Gui Shui. ∼ S China
104 *K8* **Guijuelo** Castilla-León, N Spain *40°34′N 05°40′W*
Guilan *see* Gīlān
97 *N22* **Guildford** SE England, United Kingdom *51°14′N 00°35′W*
19 *R5* **Guildford** Maine, NE USA *45°10′N 69°22′W*
19 *O7* **Guildhall** Vermont, NE USA *44°34′N 71°36′W*
103 *R13* **Guilherand** Ardèche, E France *44°57′N 04°49′E*
160 *L13* **Guilin** *var.* Kuei-lin, Kweilin. Guangxi Zhuangzu Zizhiqu, S China *25°15′N 110°16′E*
12 *J6* **Guillaume-Delisle, Lac** ◎ Québec, NE Canada
103 *U13* **Guillestre** Hautes-Alpes, SE France *44°41′N 06°39′E*
104 *H6* **Guimarães** *var.* Guimaráes. Braga, N Portugal *41°26′N 08°19′W*
Guimaráes *see* Guimarães
58 *D11* **Guimarães Rosas, Pico** ▲ NW Brazil
23 *N3* **Guin** Alabama, S USA *33°58′N 87°54′W*
Güina *see* Wina
76 *I14* **Guinea** *off.* Republic of Guinea, *var.* Guinée; *prev.* French Guinea, People's Revolutionary Republic of Guinea. ◆ *republic* W Africa
64 *N13* **Guinea Basin** *undersea feature* E Atlantic Ocean *0°00′N 05°00′W*
76 *E12* **Guinea-Bissau** *off.* Republic of Guinea-Bissau, *Fr.* Guinée-Bissau, *Port.* Guiné-Bissau; *prev.* Portuguese Guinea. ◆ *republic* W Africa
Guinea-Bissau, Republic of *see* Guinea-Bissau
66 *K7* **Guinea Fracture Zone** *tectonic feature* E Atlantic Ocean
64 *O13* **Guinea, Gulf of** *Fr.* Golfe de Guinée. *gulf* E Atlantic Ocean
Guinea, People's Revolutionary Republic of *see* Guinea
Guinea, Republic of *see* Guinea
Guiné-Bissau *see* Guinea-Bissau
Guinée *see* Guinea
Guinée-Bissau *see* Guinea-Bissau
Guinée, Golfe de *see* Guinea, Gulf of
44 *C4* **Güines** La Habana, W Cuba *22°50′N 82°02′W*
102 *G5* **Guingamp** Côtes d'Armor, NW France *48°34′N 03°09′W*
105 *P3* **Guipúzcoa** *Basq.* Gipuzkoa. ◐ *province* País Vasco, N Spain
44 *C5* **Güira de Melena** La Habana, W Cuba *22°47′N 82°33′W*
74 *G8* **Guir, Hamada du** *desert* Algeria/Morocco
55 *P5* **Güiria** Sucre, NE Venezuela *10°37′N 62°21′W*
Gui Shui *see* Gui Jiang
104 *H2* **Guitiriz** Galicia, NW Spain *43°10′N 07°52′W*
77 *N17* **Guitri** S Ivory Coast *05°31′N 05°14′W*
171 *Q5* **Guiuan** Samar, C Philippines *11°02′N 125°45′E*
Gui Xian/Guixian *see* Guigang
160 *J12* **Guiyang** *var.* Kuei-Yang, Kuei-yang, Kueyang, Kweiyang; *prev.* Kweichu. *province capital* Guizhou, S China *26°33′N 106°45′E*
160 *J12* **Guizhou** *var.* Guizhou Sheng, Kuei-chou, Kweichow, Qian. ◐ *province* S China
Guizhou Sheng *see* Guizhou
102 *J13* **Gujan-Mestras** Gironde, SW France *44°39′N 01°04′W*
154 *B10* **Gujarāt** *var.* Gujerat. ◐ *state* W India
149 *V6* **Gujar Khān** Punjab, E Pakistan *33°19′N 73°23′E*
Gujerat *see* Gujarāt
149 *V7* **Gujrānwāla** Punjab, NE Pakistan *32°11′N 74°09′E*
149 *V7* **Gujrāt** Punjab, E Pakistan *32°34′N 74°04′E*
146 *B8* **Gulandag** *Rus.* Gory Kulandag. ▲ Balkan Welaýaty, W Turkmenistan
159 *U9* **Gulang** Gansu, C China *37°31′N 102°55′E*
183 *R6* **Gulargambone** New South Wales, SE Australia *31°19′S 148°31′E*
155 *G15* **Gulbarga** Karnātaka, C India *17°22′N 76°47′E*
118 *J8* **Gulbene** *Ger.* Alt-Schwanenburg. Gulbene, NE Latvia *57°10′N 26°44′E*
147 *U10* **Gul'cha** *Kir.* Gülchö. Oshskaya Oblast', SW Kyrgyzstan *40°16′N 73°27′E*
Gülchö *see* Gul'cha
173 *T10* **Gulden Draak Seamount** *undersea feature* E Indian Ocean *33°45′S 101°00′E*
136 *J16* **Gülek Boğazı** *var.* Cilician Gates. *pass* S Turkey
186 *D8* **Gulf** ◐ *province* S Papua New Guinea
23 *O9* **Gulf Breeze** Florida, SE USA *30°21′N 87°09′W*
Gulf of Liaotung *see* Liaodong Wan
23 *V13* **Gulfport** Florida, SE USA *27°45′N 82°42′W*
22 *M9* **Gulfport** Mississippi, S USA *30°22′N 89°06′W*
23 *O9* **Gulf Shores** Alabama, S USA *30°15′N 87°40′W*
141 *T5* **Gulf, The** *var.* Persian Gulf, *Ar.* Khalīj al 'Arabī, *Per.* Khalīj-e Fars. *gulf* SW Asia *see also* Persian Gulf
183 *R7* **Gulgong** New South Wales, SE Australia *32°22′S 149°31′E*
160 *I11* **Gulin** Sichuan, C China *28°06′N 105°47′E*
171 *U14* **Gulir** Pulau Kasiui, E Indonesia *04°27′S 131°41′E*
Gulistan *see* Guliston
147 *P10* **Guliston** *Rus.* Gulistan. Sirdaryo Viloyati, E Uzbekistan *40°29′N 68°46′E*
163 *T6* **Guliya Shan** ▲ NE China *49°42′N 122°22′E*
Gulja *see* Yining
39 *S11* **Gulkana** Alaska, USA *62°17′N 145°25′W*
11 *S17* **Gull Lake** Saskatchewan, S Canada *50°05′N 108°30′W*
31 *P10* **Gull Lake** ◎ Michigan, N USA
29 *T6* **Gull Lake** ◎ Minnesota, N USA
95 *L16* **Gullspång** Västra Götaland, S Sweden *58°58′N 14°04′E*
136 *B15* **Güllük Körfezi** *prev.* Akbük Limanı. *bay* W Turkey
152 *H5* **Gulmarg** Jammu and Kashmir, NW India *34°04′N 74°25′E*
Gulpaigan *see* Golpāyegān
99 *L18* **Gulpen** Limburg, SE Netherlands *50°48′N 05°53′E*
Gul'shad *see* Gul'shat
145 *S13* **Gul'shat** *var.* Gul'shad. Karaganda, E Kazakhstan *46°37′N 74°22′E*
81 *F17* **Gulu** N Uganda *02°46′N 32°21′E*
114 *K10* **Gŭlŭbovo** Stara Zagora, C Bulgaria *42°08′N 25°51′E*
114 *I7* **Gulyantsi** Pleven, N Bulgaria *43°37′N 24°40′E*
Gulyaypole *see* Hulyaypole
Guma *see* Pishan
Gümai *see* Darlag
79 *K16* **Gumba** Equateur, NW Dem. Rep. Congo *02°58′N 21°23′E*
Gumbinnen *see* Gusev
81 *H24* **Gumbiro** Ruvuma, S Tanzania *10°19′S 35°40′E*
146 *B11* **Gumdag** *prev.* Kum-Dag. Balkan Welaýaty, W Turkmenistan *39°13′N 54°35′E*
77 *W12* **Gumel** Jigawa, N Nigeria *12°37′N 09°23′E*
105 *N5* **Gumiel de Hizán** Castilla-León, N Spain *41°46′N 03°42′W*
153 *P16* **Gumla** Jharkhand, N India *23°03′N 84°36′E*
Gumma *see* Gunma
101 *F16* **Gummersbach** Nordrhein-Westfalen, W Germany *51°01′N 07°34′E*
77 *T13* **Gummi** Zamfara, NW Nigeria *12°07′N 05°07′E*
Gumpolds *see* Humpolec
Gumti *see* Gomati
Gümülcine/Gümüljina *see* Komotiní
Gümüşane *see* Gümüşhane
137 *O12* **Gümüşhane** *var.* Gümüşane, Gumushkhane. Gümüşhane, NE Turkey *40°31′N 39°27′E*
137 *O12* **Gümüşhane** *var.* Gümüşane, Gumushkhane. ◐ *province* NE Turkey
Gumushkhane *see* Gümüşhane
171 *V14* **Gumzai** Pulau Kola, E Indonesia *05°27′S 134°38′E*
154 *H9* **Guna** Madhya Pradesh, C India *24°39′N 77°18′E*
Gunabad *see* Gonābād
Gunan *see* Qijiang
Gunbad-i-Qawus *see* Gonbad-e Kāvūs
183 *O9* **Gunbar** New South Wales, SE Australia *34°03′S 145°32′E*
183 *O9* **Gun Creek** *seasonal river* New South Wales, SE Australia
183 *Q10* **Gundagai** New South Wales, SE Australia *35°06′S 148°03′E*
79 *K17* **Gundji** Equateur, N Dem. Rep. Congo *02°03′N 21°31′E*
155 *G20* **Gundlupet** Karnātaka, W India *11°48′N 76°42′E*
136 *G16* **Gündoğmuş** Antalya, S Turkey *36°50′N 32°07′E*
137 *O14* **Güney Doğu Toroslar** ▲ SE Turkey
79 *J21* **Gungu** Bandundu, SW Dem. Rep. Congo *05°43′S 19°20′E*
127 *P17* **Gunib** Respublika Dagestan, SW Russian Federation *42°24′N 46°55′E*
112 *J11* **Gunja** Vukovar-Srijem, E Croatia *44°53′N 18°51′E*
31 *P9* **Gun Lake** ◎ Michigan, N USA
165 *N12* **Gunma** *off.* Gunma-ken, *var.* Gumma. ◐ *prefecture* Honshū, S Japan
Gunma-ken *see* Gunma
197 *P15* **Gunnbjørn Fjeld** *var.* Gunnbjörns Bjerge. ▲ C Greenland *69°03′N 29°36′W*
Gunnbjörns Bjerge *see* Gunnbjørn Fjeld
183 *S6* **Gunnedah** New South Wales, SE Australia *30°59′S 150°15′E*
173 *Y15* **Gunner's Quoin** *var.* Coin de Mire. *island* N Mauritius
37 *R6* **Gunnison** Colorado, C USA *38°33′N 106°55′W*
36 *L5* **Gunnison** Utah, W USA *39°09′N 111°49′W*
37 *P5* **Gunnison River** ∼ Colorado, C USA
21 *X2* **Gunpowder River** ∼ Maryland, NE USA
Güns *see* Kőszeg
Gunsan *see* Kunsan
109 *S4* **Gunskirchen** Oberösterreich, N Austria *48°07′N 13°54′E*
Gunt *see* Ghund
155 *H17* **Guntakal** Andhra Pradesh, C India *15°11′N 77°24′E*
23 *Q2* **Guntersville** Alabama, S USA *34°21′N 86°17′W*
23 *Q2* **Guntersville Lake** ⊡ Alabama, S USA
109 *X4* **Guntramsdorf** Niederösterreich, E Austria *48°03′N 16°19′E*
155 *J16* **Guntūr** *var.* Guntur. Andhra Pradesh, SE India *16°20′N 80°27′E*
168 *H10* **Gunungsitoli** Pulau Nias, W Indonesia *01°11′N 97°35′E*
155 *M14* **Gunupur** Orissa, E India *19°04′N 83°52′E*
101 *J23* **Günz** ∼ S Germany
Gunzan *see* Kunsan
101 *J22* **Günzburg** Bayern, S Germany *48°26′N 10°18′E*
101 *K21* **Gunzenhausen** Bayern, S Germany *49°07′N 10°45′E*
Guoliezhen *see* Lingbao
Guovdageaidnu *see* Kautokeino
161 *P7* **Guoyang** Anhui, E China *33°30′N 116°12′E*
116 *G11* **Gurahonț** *Hung.* Honctő. Arad, W Romania *46°16′N 22°21′E*
Gurahumora *see* Gura Humorului
116 *K9* **Gura Humorului** *Ger.* Gurahumora. Suceava, NE Romania *47°31′N 26°00′E*
146 *H8* **Gurbansoltan Eje** *prev.* Ýylanly, *Rus.* Il'yaly. Daşoguz Welaýaty, N Turkmenistan *41°57′N 59°42′E*
158 *K4* **Gurbantünggüt Shamo** *desert* W China
152 *H7* **Gurdāspur** Punjab, N India *32°04′N 75°28′E*
27 *T13* **Gurdon** Arkansas, C USA *33°55′N 93°09′W*
Gurdzhaani *see* Gurjaani
Gurgan *see* Gorgān
152 *I10* **Gurgaon** Haryāna, N India *28°27′N 77°01′E*
59 *M15* **Gurguéia, Rio** ∼ NE Brazil
55 *Q7* **Guri, Embalse de** ⊡ E Venezuela
137 *V10* **Gurjaani** *Rus.* Gurdzhaani. E Georgia *41°42′N 45°47′E*
109 *T8* **Gurk** Kärnten, S Austria *46°52′N 14°17′E*
109 *T9* **Gurk** *Slvn.* Krka. ∼ S Austria
Gurkfeld *see* Krško
114 *K9* **Gurkovo** *prev.* Kolupchii. Stara Zagora, C Bulgaria *42°42′N 25°46′E*
109 *S9* **Gurktaler Alpen** ▲ S Austria
146 *H8* **Gurlan** *Rus.* Gurlen. Xorazm Viloyati, W Uzbekistan *41°54′N 60°18′E*
Gurlen *see* Gurlan
83 *M16* **Guro** Manica, C Mozambique *17°28′S 33°18′E*
136 *M14* **Gürün** Sivas, C Turkey *38°44′N 37°15′E*
59 *K16* **Gurupi** Tocantins, C Brazil *11°44′S 49°01′W*
58 *L12* **Gurupi, Rio** ∼ NE Brazil
152 *E14* **Guru Sikhar** ▲ NW India *24°45′N 72°51′E*
162 *H8* **Gurvanbulag** *var.* Höviyn Am. Bayanhongor, C Mongolia *47°08′N 98°41′E*
162 *K7* **Gurvanbulag** *var.* Avdzaga. Bulgan, C Mongolia *47°43′N 103°30′E*
162 *I11* **Gurvantes** *var.* Urt. Ömnögovĭ, S Mongolia *43°16′N 101°00′E*
Gur'yev/Gur'yevskaya Oblast' *see* Atyrau
77 *U13* **Gusau** Zamfara, NW Nigeria *12°18′N 06°27′E*
126 *C3* **Gusev** *Ger.* Gumbinnen. Kaliningradskaya Oblast', W Russian Federation *54°36′N 22°14′E*
146 *J17* **Gushgy** *Rus.* Kushka. ∼ Mary Welaýaty, S Turkmenistan
Gushiago *see* Gushiegu
77 *Q14* **Gushiegu** *var.* Gushiago. NE Ghana *09°54′N 00°12′W*
165 *S17* **Gushikawa** Okinawa, Okinawa, SW Japan *26°21′N 127°50′E*
113 *L16* **Gusinje** E Montenegro *42°34′N 19°51′E*
126 *M4* **Gus'-Khrustal'nyy** Vladimirskaya Oblast', W Russian Federation *55°39′N 40°42′E*
107 *B19* **Guspini** Sardegna, Italy, C Mediterranean Sea *39°33′N 08°39′E*
109 *X8* **Güssing** Burgenland, SE Austria *47°03′N 16°19′E*
109 *V6* **Gusswerk** Steiermark, E Austria *47°43′N 15°18′E*
92 *O2* **Gustav Adolf Land** *physical region* NE Svalbard
195 *X5* **Gustav Bull Mountains** ▲ Antarctica
39 *W13* **Gustavus** Alaska, USA *58°24′N 135°44′W*
92 *O1* **Gustav V Land** *physical region* NE Svalbard
35 *P9* **Gustine** California, W USA *37°14′N 121°00′W*
25 *R8* **Gustine** Texas, SW USA *31°51′N 98°24′W*
100 *M9* **Güstrow** Mecklenburg-Vorpommern, NE Germany *53°48′N 12°12′E*
95 *N18* **Gusum** Östergötland, S Sweden *58°15′N 16°30′E*
Guta/Gúta *see* Kolárovo
Gutenstein *see* Ravne na Koroškem
101 *G14* **Gütersloh** Nordrhein-Westfalen, W Germany *51°54′N 08°23′E*
27 *N10* **Guthrie** Oklahoma, C USA *35°53′N 97°26′W*
25 *P5* **Guthrie** Texas, SW USA *33°38′N 100°21′W*
29 *U14* **Guthrie Center** Iowa, C USA *41°40′N 94°30′W*
41 *Q13* **Gutiérrez Zamora** Veracruz-Llave, E Mexico *20°29′N 97°07′W*
Gutta *see* Kolárovo
29 *Y12* **Guttenberg** Iowa, C USA *42°47′N 91°06′W*
Guttentag *see* Dobrodzień
Guttstadt *see* Dobre Miasto
162 *G8* **Guulin** Govĭ-Altay, C Mongolia *46°33′N 97°21′E*
153 *V12* **Guwāhāti** *prev.* Gauhāti. Assam, NE India *26°09′N 91°42′E*
139 *R3* **Guwēr** *var.* Al Kuwayr, Al Quwayr, Quwair. Arbīl, N Iraq *36°03′N 43°30′E*
146 *A10* **Guwlumaýak** *Rus.* Kuuli-Mayak. Balkan Welaýaty, NW Turkmenistan *40°14′N 52°43′E*
55 *R9* **Guyana** *off.* Co-operative Republic of Guyana; *prev.* British Guiana. ◆ *republic* N South America
Guyana, Co-operative Republic of *see* Guyana
21 *P5* **Guyandotte River** ∼ West Virginia, NE USA
Guyane *see* French Guiana
Guyi *see* Sanjiang
26 *H8* **Guymon** Oklahoma, C USA *36°42′N 101°30′W*
146 *K12* **Guynuk** Lebap Welaýaty, NE Turkmenistan *39°18′N 63°00′E*
Guyong *see* Jiangle
21 *O9* **Guyot, Mount** ▲ North Carolina/Tennessee, SE USA *35°42′N 83°15′W*
183 *U5* **Guyra** New South Wales, SE Australia *30°13′S 151°42′E*
159 *W10* **Guyuan** Ningxia, N China *35°57′N 106°13′E*
Guzar *see* G'uzor
121 *P2* **Güzelyurt** *Gk.* Kólpos Mórfu, Morphou. W Cyprus *35°12′N 33°E*
121 *N2* **Güzelyurt Körfezi** *var.* Morfou Bay, Mórfou Bay, Morphou Bay, *Gk.* Kólpos Mórfou. *bay* W Cyprus
Guzhou *see* Rongjiang
40 *I3* **Guzmán** Chihuahua, N Mexico *31°13′N 107°27′W*
147 *N13* **G'uzor** *Rus.* Guzar. Qashqadaryo Viloyati, S Uzbekistan *38°41′N 66°12′E*
119 *B14* **Gvardeysk** *Ger.* Tapaiu. Kaliningradskaya Oblast', W Russian Federation *54°39′N 21°02′E*
Gvardeyskoye *see* Hvardiys'ke
183 *R5* **Gwabegar** New South Wales, SE Australia *30°34′S 148°58′E*
148 *J16* **Gwādar** *var.* Gwadur. Baluchistān, SW Pakistan *25°09′N 62°21′E*
148 *J16* **Gwādar East Bay** *bay* SW Pakistan
148 *J16* **Gwādar West Bay** *bay* SW Pakistan
Gwadur *see* Gwādar
83 *J17* **Gwai** Matabeleland North, W Zimbabwe *19°17′S 27°37′E*
154 *I7* **Gwalior** Madhya Pradesh, C India *26°16′N 78°12′E*
83 *J18* **Gwanda** Matabeleland South, SW Zimbabwe *20°56′S 29°E*
79 *N15* **Gwane** Orientale, N Dem. Rep. Congo *04°40′N 25°51′E*
83 *I17* **Gwayi** ∼ W Zimbabwe
110 *G8* **Gwda** *var.* Głda, *Ger.* Küddow. ∼ NW Poland
97 *C14* **Gweebarra Bay** *Ir.* Béal an Bheara. *inlet* W Ireland
97 *D14* **Gweedore** *Ir.* Gaoth Dobhair. Donegal, NW Ireland *55°03′N 08°14′W*
Gwelo *see* Gweru
97 *K21* **Gwent** *cultural region* S Wales, United Kingdom
83 *K17* **Gweru** *prev.* Gwelo. Midlands, C Zimbabwe *19°27′S 29°49′E*
29 *Q7* **Gwinner** North Dakota, N USA *46°10′N 97°42′W*
77 *Y13* **Gwoza** Borno, NE Nigeria *11°07′N 13°40′E*
Gwy *see* Wye
183 *R4* **Gwydir River** ∼ New South Wales, SE Australia
97 *I19* **Gwynedd** *var.* Gwyneth. *cultural region* NW Wales, United Kingdom
Gwyneth *see* Gwynedd
159 *O16* **Gyaca** *var.* Ngarrab. Xizang Zizhiqu, W China *29°06′N 92°37′E*
Gya'gya *see* Saga
Gyaijêpozhanggê *see* Zhidoi
Gyaisi *see* Jiulong
115 *M22* **Gyalí** *var.* Yialí. *island* Dodekánisa, Greece, Aegean Sea
Gyamotang *see* Dêngqên
Gyandzha *see* Gäncä
Gyangkar *see* Dinggyê
158 *M16* **Gyangzê** Xizang Zizhiqu, W China *28°50′N 89°38′E*
158 *L14* **Gyaring Co** ◎ W China
159 *Q12* **Gyaring Hu** ◎ C China
115 *I20* **Gyáros** *var.* Yioúra. *island* Kykládes, Greece, Aegean Sea
122 *J7* **Gyda** Yamalo-Nenetskiy Avtonomnyy Okrug, N Russian Federation *70°55′N 78°34′E*
122 *J7* **Gydanskiy Poluostrov** *Eng.* Gyda Peninsula. *peninsula* N Russian Federation
Gyda Peninsula *see* Gydanskiy Poluostrov
Gyêgu *see* Yushu
Gyéres *see* Câmpia Turzii
Gyergyószentmiklós *see* Gheorgheni
Gyergyótölgyes *see* Tulgheş
Gyertyámos *see* Cărpiniş
Gyeva *see* Detva
Gyigang *see* Zayü
158 *J16* **Gyirong** Xizang Zizhiqu, W China *28°55′N 85°16′E*
Gyixong *see* Gonggar
95 *I23* **Gyldenløveshøy** *hill range* C Denmark
181 *Z10* **Gympie** Queensland, E Australia *26°05′S 152°40′E*
166 *L7* **Gyobingauk** Bago, SW Burma (Myanmar) *18°14′N 95°39′E*
111 *M23* **Gyomaendrőd** Békés, SE Hungary *46°56′N 20°50′E*
Gyömbér *see* Ďumbier
111 *L22* **Gyöngyös** Heves, NE Hungary *47°44′N 19°49′E*
111 *H22* **Győr** *Ger.* Raab, *Lat.* Arrabona. Győr-Moson-Sopron, NW Hungary *47°41′N 17°40′E*
111 *G22* **Győr-Moson-Sopron** *off.* Győr-Moson-Sopron Megye. ◐ *county* NW Hungary
Győr-Moson-Sopron Megye *see* Győr-Moson-Sopron
11 *X15* **Gypsumville** Manitoba, S Canada *51°47′N 98°38′W*
12 *M4* **Gyrfalcon Islands** *island group* Northwest Territories, NE Canada
95 *N14* **Gysinge** Gävleborg, C Sweden *60°16′N 16°55′E*
115 *F22* **Gýtheio** *var.* Githio; *prev.* Yíthion. Pelopónnisos, S Greece *36°46′N 22°34′E*
146 *L13* **Gyuichbirleshik** Lebap Welaýaty, E Turkmenistan *38°10′N 64°33′E*
111 *N24* **Gyula** *Rom.* Jula. Békés, SE Hungary *46°39′N 21°17′E*
Gyulafehérvár *see* Alba Iulia
Gyulovo *see* Roza
137 *T11* **Gyumri** *var.* Giumri, *Rus.* Kumayri; *prev.* Aleksandropol', Leninakan. W Armenia *40°48′N 43°51′E*
146 *D13* **Gyunuzyndag, Gora** ▲ Balkan Welaýaty, W Turkmenistan *38°15′N 56°25′E*
146 *J15* **Gyzylbaydak** *Rus.* Krasnoye Znamya. Mary Welaýaty, S Turkmenistan *36°51′N 62°24′E*
Gyzyletrek *see* Etrek
146 *D10* **Gyzylgaýa** *Rus.* Kizyl-Kaya. Balkan Welaýaty, NW Turkmenistan *40°37′N 55°15′E*
146 *A10* **Gyzylsuw** *Rus.* Kizyl-Su. Balkan Welaýaty, W Turkmenistan *39°49′N 53°00′E*
Gyzyrlabat *see* Serdar
Gzhatsk *see* Gagarin

H

153 *T12* **Ha** W Bhutan *27°17′N 89°22′E*
Haabai *see* Ha'apai Group
99 *H17* **Haacht** Vlaams Brabant, C Belgium *50°58′N 04°38′E*
109 *T4* **Haag** Niederösterreich, NE Austria *48°07′N 14°32′E*
194 *L8* **Haag Nunataks** ▲ Antarctica
92 *N2* **Haakon VII Land** *physical region* NW Svalbard
98 *O11* **Haaksbergen** Overijssel, E Netherlands *52°09′N 06°45′E*
99 *E14* **Haamstede** Zeeland, SW Netherlands *51°43′N 03°45′E*
193 *Y15* **Ha'ano** *island* Ha'apai Group, C Tonga
193 *Y15* **Ha'apai Group** *var.* Haabai. *island group* C Tonga
93 *L15* **Haapajärvi** Oulu, C Finland *63°45′N 25°20′E*
93 *L17* **Haapamäki** Länsi-Suomi, C Finland *62°11′N 24°32′E*
93 *L15* **Haapavesi** Oulu, C Finland *64°09′N 25°25′E*
191 *N7* **Haapiti** Moorea, W French Polynesia *17°33′S 149°52′W*
118 *F4* **Haapsalu** *Ger.* Hapsal. Läänemaa, W Estonia *58°58′N 23°32′E*
Ha'Arava *see* 'Arabah, Wādī al
95 *G24* **Haarby** *var.* Hårby. Fyn, C Denmark *55°13′N 10°07′E*
98 *H10* **Haarlem** *prev.* Harlem. Noord-Holland, W Netherlands *52°23′N 04°39′E*
185 *D19* **Haast** West Coast, South Island, New Zealand *43°53′S 169°02′E*
185 *C20* **Haast** ∼ South Island, New Zealand
185 *D20* **Haast Pass** *pass* South Island, New Zealand
193 *W16* **Ha'atua** 'Eau, E Tonga *21°23′S 174°57′W*
149 *P15* **Hab** ∼ SW Pakistan
141 *W7* **Haba** *var.* Al Haba. Dubayy, NE United Arab Emirates *25°01′N 55°37′E*
158 *K2* **Habahe** *var.* Kaba. Xinjiang Uygur Zizhiqu, NW China *48°04′N 86°20′E*
141 *U13* **Ḩabarūt** *var.* Habrut. SW Oman *17°19′N 52°45′E*
81 *J18* **Habaswein** North Eastern, NE Kenya *01°01′N 39°27′E*
99 *L24* **Habay-la-Neuve** Luxembourg, SE Belgium *49°43′N 05°38′E*
139 *S8* **Ḩabbānīyah, Buḩayrat** ◎ C Iraq
Habelschwerdt *see* Bystrzyca Kłodzka
153 *V14* **Habiganj** Sylhet, NE Bangladesh *24°23′N 91°25′E*
163 *Q12* **Habirag** Nei Mongol Zizhiqu, N China *42°18′N 115°40′E*
95 *L19* **Habo** Västra Götaland, S Sweden *57°55′N 14°05′E*
123 *V14* **Habomai Islands** *island group* Kuril'skiye Ostrova, SE Russian Federation
165 *S2* **Haboro** Hokkaidō, NE Japan *44°19′N 141°42′E*
153 *S16* **Habra** West Bengal, NE India *22°39′N 88°17′E*
Habrut *see* Ḩabarūt
143 *P17* **Ḩabshān** Abū Zaby, C United Arab Emirates *23°51′N 53°34′E*
54 *E14* **Hacha** Putumayo, S Colombia *0°02′S 75°30′W*
165 *X13* **Hachijō** Tōkyō, Hachijō-jima, SE Japan *33°40′N 139°20′E*
165 *X13* **Hachijō-jima** *island* Izu-shotō, SE Japan
165 *P7* **Hachimori** Akita, Honshū, C Japan *40°22′N 139°59′E*
165 *R7* **Hachinohe** Aomori, Honshū, C Japan *40°30′N 141°29′E*
93 *G17* **Hackås** Jämtland, C Sweden *62°55′N 14°31′E*
18 *K14* **Hackensack** New Jersey, NE USA *40°51′N 73°57′W*
75 *U12* **Ḩaḑabat al Jilf al Kabīr** *var.* Gilf Kebir Plateau. *plateau* SW Egypt
Hadama *see* Nazrēt
141 *W13* **Ḩadbaram** S Oman *17°27′N 55°13′E*
139 *U13* **Ḩaddānīyah** *well* S Iraq
96 *K12* **Haddington** SE Scotland, United Kingdom *55°59′N 02°46′W*
141 *Z8* **Ḩadd, Ra's al** *headland* NE Oman *22°28′N 59°58′E*
Haded *see* Xadeed
77 *W12* **Hadejia** Jigawa, N Nigeria *12°22′N 10°02′E*
77 *W12* **Hadejia** ∼ N Nigeria
138 *F9* **Hadera** *var.* Khadera; *prev.* Ḩadera. Haifa, C Israel *32°26′N 34°55′E*
Ḩadera *see* Hadera
Hadersleben *see* Haderslev
95 *G24* **Haderslev** *Ger.* Hadersleben. Sønderjylland, SW Denmark *55°15′N 09°30′E*
151 *J21* **Hadhdhunmathi Atoll** *atoll* S Maldives
141 *W17* **Ḩadīboh** Suquṭrā, SE Yemen *12°38′N 54°05′E*
158 *K9* **Hadilik** Xinjiang Uygur Zizhiqu, W China *37°51′N 86°10′E*
136 *H16* **Hadım** Konya, S Turkey *36°58′N 32°27′E*
140 *K7* **Ḩadīyah** Al Madīnah, W Saudi Arabia *25°36′N 38°31′E*
8 *L5* **Hadley Bay** *bay* Victoria Island, Nunavut, N Canada
167 *S6* **Ha Đông** *var.* Hadong. Ha Tây, N Vietnam *20°58′N 105°46′E*
Hadong *see* Ha Đông
Hadramaut *see* Ḩaḑramawt
141 *R15* **Ḩaḑramawt** *Eng.* Hadramaut. ▲ S Yemen
Hadria *see* Adria
Hadrianopolis *see* Edirne
Hadria Picena *see* Apricena
95 *G22* **Hadsten** Århus, C Denmark *56°19′N 10°03′E*
95 *G21* **Hadsund** Nordjylland, N Denmark *56°43′N 10°08′E*
117 *S4* **Hadyach** *Rus.* Gadyach. Poltavs'ka Oblast', NE Ukraine *50°21′N 34°00′E*
112 *I13* **Hadžići** Federacija Bosna I Hercegovina, SE Bosnia and Herzegovina *43°49′N 18°12′E*
163 *W14* **Haeju** S North Korea *38°04′N 125°40′E*
Haerbin/Haerhpin/Ha-erh-pin *see* Harbin
141 *P5* **Ḩafar al Bāṭin** Ash Sharqīyah, N Saudi Arabia *28°25′N 45°59′E*
11 *T15* **Hafford** Saskatchewan, S Canada *52°43′N 107°19′W*
136 *M13* **Hafik** Sivas, N Turkey *39°53′N 37°24′E*
149 *V8* **Ḩāfizābād** Punjab, E Pakistan *32°03′N 73°42′E*
153 *W13* **Hāflong** Assam, NE India *25°10′N 93°01′E*
92 *H4* **Hafnarfjördhur** Reykjanes, W Iceland *64°03′N 21°57′W*
Hafnia *see* Denmark
Hafnia *see* København

◆ Country ● Country Capital ◇ Dependent Territory ○ Dependent Territory Capital ◐ Administrative Regions ✈ International Airport ▲ Mountain ▲ Mountain Range ▲ Volcano ∼ River ◎ Lake ⊡ Reservoir

Hafren see Severn
Hafun see Xaafuun
Hafun, Ras see Xaafuun, Raas
80 G10 **Hag 'Abdullah** Sinnar, E Sudan 13°59′N 33°35′E
81 K18 **Hagadera** North Eastern, E Kenya 0°06′N 40°23′E
138 G8 **HaGalil** *Eng.* Galilee. ▲ N Israel
14 G10 **Hagar** Ontario, S Canada 46°27′N 80°22′W
155 G18 **Hagari** *var.* Vedāvati. ~ W India
188 B16 **Hagåtña** , *var.* Agaña. ○ (Guam) NW Guam 13°27′N 144°45′E
100 M13 **Hagelberg** *hill* NE Germany
39 N14 **Hagemeister Island** *island* Alaska, USA
101 F15 **Hagen** Nordrhein-Westfalen, W Germany 51°22′N 07°27′E
100 K10 **Hagenow** Mecklenburg-Vorpommern, N Germany 53°27′N 11°10′E
10 K15 **Hagensborg** British Columbia, SW Canada 52°24′N 126°24′W
80 I13 **Hägere Hiywet** *var.* Agere Hiywet, Ambo. Oromīya, C Ethiopia 09°00′N 37°55′E
33 O15 **Hagerman** Idaho, NW USA 42°48′N 114°53′W
37 U14 **Hagerman** New Mexico, SW USA 33°07′N 104°19′W
21 V2 **Hagerstown** Maryland, NE USA 39°39′N 77°44′W
14 G16 **Hagersville** Ontario, S Canada 42°58′N 80°03′W
102 J15 **Hagetmau** Landes, SW France 43°40′N 00°36′W
95 K14 **Hagfors** Värmland, C Sweden 60°03′N 13°45′E
93 G16 **Häggenås** Jämtland, C Sweden 63°24′N 14°53′E
164 E12 **Hagi** Yamaguchi, Honshū, SW Japan 34°25′N 131°22′E
167 S5 **Ha Giang** Ha Giang, N Vietnam 22°50′N 104°58′E
Hagios Evstrátios see Ágios Efstrátios
HaGolan see Golan Heights
103 T4 **Hagondange** Moselle, NE France 49°16′N 06°06′E
97 B18 **Hag's Head** *Ir.* Ceann Caillí. *headland* W Ireland 52°56′N 09°29′W
102 I3 **Hague, Cap de la** *headland* N France 49°43′N 01°56′W
103 V5 **Haguenau** Bas-Rhin, NE France 48°49′N 07°47′E
165 X16 **Hahajima-rettō** *island group* SE Japan
15 R8 **Há Há, Lac** ◎ Québec, SE Canada
172 H13 **Hahaya** ✈ (Moroni) Grande Comore, NW Comoros
22 K9 **Hahnville** Louisiana, S USA 29°58′N 90°24′W
83 E22 **Haib** Karas, S Namibia 28°12′S 18°19′E
Haibak see Āybak
149 N15 **Haibo** ~ SW Pakistan
Haibowan see Wuhai
163 U12 **Haicheng** Liaoning, NE China 40°53′N 122°45′E
Haicheng see Haifeng
Haicheng see Haiyuan
Haida see Nový Bor
Haidarabad see Hyderābād
Haidenschaft see Ajdovščina
167 T6 **Hai Dương** Hai Hưng, N Vietnam 20°56′N 106°21′E
138 F9 **Haifa** ◐ *district* NW Israel
Haifa see Hefa
Haifa, Bay of see Mifrats Hefa
161 P14 **Haifeng** *var.* Haicheng. Guangdong, S China 22°56′N 115°19′E
Haifong see Hai Phong
161 P3 **Hai He** ~ E China
Haikang see Leizhou
160 L17 **Haikou** *var.* Hai-k'ou, Hoihow, *Fr.* Hoï-Hao. *province capital* Hainan, S China 20°N 110°17′E
Hai-k'ou see Haikou
140 M6 **Ḩā'il** Ḩā'il, NW Saudi Arabia 27°N 42°50′E
141 N5 **Ḩā'il** *off.* Minţaqah Ḩā'il. ◐ *province* N Saudi Arabia
163 S6 **Hailar He** ~ NE China
33 P14 **Hailey** Idaho, NW USA 43°31′N 114°18′W
14 H9 **Haileybury** Ontario, S Canada 47°27′N 79°39′W
163 X9 **Hailin** Heilongjiang, NE China 44°37′N 129°24′E
Ḩā'il, Minţaqah see Ḩā'il
Hailong see Meihekou
93 K14 **Hailuoto** *Swe.* Karlö. *island* W Finland
Haima see Haymā'
Haimen see Taizhou
160 M17 **Hainan** *var.* Hainan Sheng, Qiong. ◐ *province* S China
160 K17 **Hainan Dao** *island* S China
Hainan Sheng see Hainan
Hainan Strait see Qiongzhou Haixia
Hainasch see Ainaži
Hainau see Chojnów
99 E20 **Hainaut** ◐ *province* SW Belgium
Hainburg see Hainburg an der Donau
109 Z4 **Hainburg an der Donau** *var.* Hainburg. Niederösterreich, NE Austria 48°09′N 16°57′E
39 W12 **Haines** Alaska, USA 59°13′N 135°27′W
32 L12 **Haines** Oregon, NW USA 44°53′N 117°56′W
23 W12 **Haines City** Florida, SE USA 28°06′N 81°37′W
10 H8 **Haines Junction** Yukon Territory, W Canada 60°45′N 137°30′W
109 W4 **Hainfeld** Niederösterreich, NE Austria 48°03′N 15°47′E
101 N16 **Hainichen** Sachsen, E Germany 50°58′N 13°08′E
Hai Ninh see Mong Cai
167 T6 **Hai Phong** *var.* Haifong, Haiphong. N Vietnam 20°50′N 106°41′E
Haiphong see Hai Phong
161 S12 **Haitan Dao** *island* SE China
44 K8 **Haiti** *off.* Republic of Haiti. ◆ *republic* C West Indies
Haiti, Republic of see Haiti
35 T11 **Haiwee Reservoir** ⊠ California, W USA
80 I7 **Haiya** Red Sea, NE Sudan 18°17′N 36°21′E
159 T10 **Haiyan** *var.* Sanjiaocheng. Qinghai, W China 36°55′N 100°54′E
160 M13 **Haiyang Shan** ▲▲ S China
159 V10 **Haiyuan** Ningxia, N China 36°32′N 105°31′E
Hajda see Nový Bor
111 M22 **Hajdú-Bihar** *off.* Hajdú-Bihar Megye. ◐ *county* E Hungary
Hajdú-Bihar Megye see Hajdú-Bihar
111 N22 **Hajdúböszörmény** Hajdú-Bihar, E Hungary 47°39′N 21°32′E
111 N22 **Hajdúhadház** Hajdú-Bihar, E Hungary 47°40′N 21°40′E
111 N21 **Hajdúnánás** Hajdú-Bihar, E Hungary 47°50′N 21°26′E
111 N22 **Hajdúszoboszló** Hajdú-Bihar, E Hungary 47°27′N 21°24′E
142 I3 **Ḩājī Ebrāhīm, Kūh-e** ▲ Iran/Iraq 36°53′N 44°56′E
165 O9 **Hajiki-zaki** *headland* Sado, C Japan 38°19′N 138°28′E
Hajine see Abū Ḩardān
153 P13 **Hājīpur** Bihār, N India 25°41′N 85°13′E
141 N14 **Ḩajjah** W Yemen 15°43′N 43°33′E
139 U11 **Ḩajjama** Al Muthannā, S Iraq 31°24′N 45°20′E
143 Q13 **Ḩājjīābād** Fārs, S Iran 28°21′N 54°27′E
143 R12 **Ḩājjīābād** Hormozgān, C Iran
139 U14 **Ḩājj, Thaqb al** *well* S Iraq
113 L16 **Hajla** ▲ E Montenegro
110 P10 **Hajnówka** *Ger.* Hermhausen. Podlaskie, NE Poland 52°45′N 23°32′E
Haka see Hakha
Hakapehi see Punaauia
Hakâri see Hakkâri
138 F12 **HaKatan, HaMakhtesh** *prev.* HaMakhtesh HaQatan. ▲ S Israel
166 K4 **Hakha** *var.* Haka. Chin State, W Burma (Myanmar) 22°42′N 93°41′E
137 T16 **Hakkâri** *var.* Çölemerik, Hakâri. Hakkâri, SE Turkey 37°36′N 43°45′E
137 T16 **Hakkâri** *var.* Hakkari. ◐ *province* SE Turkey
Hakkari see Hakkâri
92 J12 **Hakkas** Norrbotten, N Sweden 66°53′N 21°36′E
164 J14 **Hakken-zan** ▲ Honshū, SW Japan 34°11′N 135°57′E
165 R7 **Hakkōda-san** ▲ Honshū, C Japan 40°40′N 140°49′E
165 T2 **Hako-dake** ▲ Hokkaidō, NE Japan 44°40′N 142°22′E
165 R5 **Hakodate** Hokkaidō, NE Japan 41°46′N 140°43′E
164 L11 **Hakui** Ishikawa, Honshū, SW Japan 36°55′N 136°46′E
190 B16 **Hakupu** SE Niue 19°06′S 169°50′E
164 L12 **Haku-san** ▲ Honshū, SW Japan 36°07′N 136°45′E
Hakusan see Mattō
Hal see Halle
149 Q15 **Hāla** Sind, SE Pakistan 25°47′N 68°28′E
138 I3 **Ḩalab** *Eng.* Aleppo, *Fr.* Alep; *anc.* Beroea. Ḩalab, NW Syria 36°14′N 37°10′E
138 J3 **Ḩalab** *off.* Muḩāfaẓat Ḩalab, *var.* Aleppo, Halab. ◐ *governorate* NW Syria
138 J3 **Ḩalab** ✈ Ḩalab, NW Syria 36°12′N 37°10′E
Halab see Ḩalab
141 O8 **Ḩalabān** *var.* Halibān. Ar Riyāḑ, C Saudi Arabia 23°29′N 44°20′E
139 V4 **Ḩalabja** As Sulaymānīyah, NE Iraq 35°11′N 45°59′E
Ḩalab, Muḩāfaẓat see Ḩalab
146 L13 **Halaç** *Rus.* Khalach. Lebap Welaýaty, E Turkmenistan 38°05′N 64°46′E
190 A16 **Halagigie Point** *headland* W Niue
75 Z11 **Halaib** SE Egypt 22°10′N 36°33′E
190 G12 **Halalo** Île Uvea, N Wallis and Futuna 13°21′S 176°11′W
Halandri see Chalándri
141 X13 **Ḩalānīyāt, Juzur al** *var.* Jazā'ir Bin Ghalfān, *Eng.* Kuria Muria Islands. *island group* S Oman
141 W13 **Ḩalānīyāt, Khalīj al** *Eng.* Kuria Muria Bay. *bay* S Oman
Halas see Kiskunhalas
38 G11 **Hālawa** *var.* Halawa. Hawaii, USA, C Pacific Ocean 20°13′N 155°46′W
Halawa see Hālawa
38 F9 **Hālawa, Cape** *var.* Cape Halawa. *headland* Moloka'i, Hawai'i, USA 21°09′N 156°43′W
Cape Halawa see Hālawa, Cape
Halban see Tsetserleg
101 K14 **Halberstadt** Sachsen-Anhalt, C Germany 51°54′N 11°04′E
184 M12 **Halcombe** Manawatu-Wanganui, North Island, New Zealand 40°09′S 175°30′E
95 I16 **Halden** *prev.* Fredrikshald. Østfold, S Norway 59°08′N 11°20′E
100 L13 **Haldensleben** Sachsen-Anhalt, C Germany 52°18′N 11°25′E
Háldi see Halti
153 S17 **Haldia** West Bengal, NE India 22°04′N 88°02′E
152 K10 **Haldwāni** Uttarakhand, N India 29°13′N 79°31′E
163 P9 **Haldzan** Sühbaatar, E Mongolia 46°10′N 112°57′E
163 P9 **Haldzan** *var.* Hatavch. Sühbaatar, E Mongolia 46°10′N 112°57′E
38 F10 **Haleakalā** *var.* Haleakala. *crater* Maui, Hawai'i, USA
Haleakala see Haleakalā
25 N4 **Hale Center** Texas, SW USA 34°03′N 101°50′W
99 J18 **Halen** Limburg, NE Belgium 50°35′N 05°08′E
23 O2 **Haleyville** Alabama, S USA 34°13′N 87°37′W
77 O17 **Half Assini** SW Ghana 05°03′N 02°57′W
35 R8 **Half Dome** ▲ California, W USA 37°46′N 119°27′W
185 C25 **Halfmoon Bay** *var.* Oban. Stewart Island, Southland, New Zealand 46°53′S 168°08′E
182 E5 **Half Moon Lake** *salt lake* South Australia
163 R7 **Halhgol** Dornod, E Mongolia 47°57′N 118°07′E
163 S8 **Halhgol** *var.* Tsagaannuur. Dornod, E Mongolia 47°30′N 118°45′E
Haliacmon see Aliákmonas
Halibān see Ḩalabān
14 I13 **Haliburton** Ontario, SE Canada 45°03′N 78°20′W
14 I12 **Haliburton Highlands** *var.* Madawaska Highlands. *hill range* Ontario, SE Canada
13 Q15 **Halifax** *province capital* Nova Scotia, SE Canada 44°38′N 63°35′W
97 L17 **Halifax** N England, United Kingdom 53°44′N 01°52′W
21 W8 **Halifax** North Carolina, SE USA 36°19′N 77°37′W
21 U7 **Halifax** Virginia, NE USA 36°46′N 78°55′W
13 Q15 **Halifax** ✈ Nova Scotia, SE Canada 44°33′N 63°48′W
143 T13 **Halīl Rūd** *seasonal river* SE Iran
138 I6 **Ḩalīmah** ▲ Lebanon/Syria 34°12′N 36°37′E
162 G8 **Haliun** Govĭ-Altay, W Mongolia 45°55′N 96°06′E
118 I3 **Haljala** *Ger.* Halljal. Lääne-Virumaa, N Estonia 59°25′N 26°18′E
39 Q4 **Halkett, Cape** *headland* Alaska, USA 70°48′N 152°11′W
Halkida see Chalkída
96 J6 **Halkirk** N Scotland, United Kingdom 58°30′N 03°29′W
15 X7 **Hall** ~ Québec, SE Canada
Hall see Schwäbisch Hall
93 H15 **Hälla** Västerbotten, N Sweden 63°56′N 17°20′E
96 J6 **Halladale** ~ N Scotland, United Kingdom
95 J21 **Halland** ◐ *county* S Sweden
23 Z15 **Hallandale** Florida, SE USA 25°58′N 80°09′W
95 K22 **Hallandsås** *physical region* S Sweden
9 P6 **Hall Beach** Nunavut, N Canada 68°10′N 81°56′W
99 G19 **Halle** *Fr.* Hal. Vlaams Brabant, C Belgium 50°44′N 04°14′E
101 M15 **Halle** *var.* Halle an der Saale. Sachsen-Anhalt, C Germany 51°28′N 11°58′E
Halle an der Saale see Halle
35 W3 **Halleck** Nevada, W USA 40°57′N 115°27′W
95 L15 **Hällefors** Örebro, C Sweden 59°46′N 14°30′E
95 N16 **Hälleforsnäs** Södermanland, C Sweden 59°10′N 16°30′E
109 Q6 **Hallein** Salzburg, N Austria 47°41′N 13°06′E
101 L15 **Halle-Neustadt** Sachsen-Anhalt, C Germany 51°29′N 11°54′E
25 U12 **Hallettsville** Texas, SW USA 29°27′N 96°57′W
195 N4 **Halley** *UK research station* Antarctica 75°42′S 26°30′W
28 L4 **Halliday** North Dakota, N USA 47°19′N 102°19′W
37 S2 **Halligan Reservoir** ⊠ Colorado, C USA
100 G7 **Halligen** *island group* N Germany
94 G13 **Hallingdal** *valley* S Norway
38 J12 **Hall Island** *island* Alaska, USA
Hall Island see Maiana
189 P15 **Hall Islands** *island group* C Micronesia
118 H6 **Halliste** ~ S Estonia
Halljal see Haljala
93 I15 **Hällnäs** Västerbotten, N Sweden 64°20′N 19°41′E
29 R2 **Hallock** Minnesota, N USA 48°47′N 96°56′W
9 S6 **Hall Peninsula** *peninsula* Baffin Island, Nunavut, NE Canada
20 F9 **Halls** Tennessee, S USA 35°52′N 89°24′W
95 M16 **Hallsberg** Örebro, C Sweden 59°05′N 15°07′E
181 N5 **Halls Creek** Western Australia 18°17′S 127°39′E
182 L12 **Halls Gap** Victoria, SE Australia 37°09′S 142°30′E
95 N15 **Hallstahammar** Västmanland, C Sweden 59°37′N 16°13′E
109 R6 **Hallstatt** Salzburg, W Austria 47°32′N 13°39′E
109 R6 **Hallstätter See** ◎ C Austria
95 P14 **Hallstavik** Stockholm, C Sweden 60°12′N 18°45′E
25 X7 **Hallsville** Texas, SW USA 32°31′N 94°30′W
103 P1 **Halluin** Nord, N France 50°46′N 03°07′E
Halmahera, Laut see Halmahera Sea
171 R11 **Halmahera, Pulau** *prev.* Djailolo, Gilolo, Jailolo. *island* E Indonesia
171 S12 **Halmahera Sea** *Ind.* Laut Halmahera. *sea* E Indonesia
95 J21 **Halmstad** Halland, S Sweden 56°41′N 12°49′E
119 N15 **Halowchyn** *Rus.* Golovchin. Mahilyowskaya Voblasts', E Belarus 54°04′N 29°55′E
95 H20 **Hals** Nordjylland, N Denmark 57°00′N 10°19′E
94 F8 **Halsa** Møre og Romsdal, S Norway 63°04′N 08°13′E
119 I15 **Hal'shany** *Rus.* Gol'shany. Hrodzyenskaya Voblasts', W Belarus 54°15′N 26°01′E
Hälsingborg see Helsingborg
29 R5 **Halstad** Minnesota, N USA 47°21′N 96°49′W
27 N6 **Halstead** Kansas, C USA 38°00′N 97°30′W
99 G15 **Halsteren** Noord-Brabant, S Netherlands 51°32′N 04°16′E
93 L16 **Halsua** Länsi-Suomi, W Finland 63°28′N 24°10′E
101 E14 **Haltern** Nordrhein-Westfalen, W Germany 51°45′N 07°10′E
92 J9 **Halti** *var.* Haltiatunturi, *Lapp.* Háldi. ▲ Finland/Norway 69°18′N 21°19′E
Haltiatunturi see Halti
116 J6 **Halych** Ivano-Frankivs'ka Oblast', W Ukraine 49°08′N 24°44′E
Halycus see Platani
103 P3 **Ham** Somme, N France 49°46′N 03°03′E
Hama see Ḩamāh
164 F12 **Hamada** Shimane, Honshū, SW Japan 34°54′N 132°07′E
142 L6 **Hamadān** *anc.* Ecbatana. Hamadān, W Iran 34°51′N 48°31′E
142 L6 **Hamadān** *off.* Ostān-e Hamadān. ◐ *province* W Iran
Hamadān, Ostān-e see Hamadān
138 I5 **Ḩamāh** *var.* Hama; *anc.* Epiphania, *Bibl.* Hamath. Ḩamāh, W Syria 35°09′N 36°44′E
138 I5 **Ḩamāh** *off.* Muḩāfaẓat Ḩamāh, *var.* Hama. ◐ *governorate* C Syria
Ḩamāh, Muḩāfaẓat see Ḩamāh
1665 S3 **Hamamasu** Hokkaidō, NE Japan 43°37′N 141°24′E
164 L14 **Hamamatsu** *var.* Hamamatu. Shizuoka, Honshū, S Japan 34°43′N 137°46′E
Hamamatu see Hamamatsu
165 W14 **Hamanaka** Hokkaidō, NE Japan 43°05′N 145°05′E
164 L14 **Hamana-ko** ◎ Honshū, S Japan
94 I13 **Hamar** *prev.* Storhammer. Hedmark, S Norway 60°57′N 10°55′E
141 U10 **Ḩamārīr al Kidan, Qalamat** *well* E Saudi Arabia
164 I12 **Hamasaka** Hyōgo, Honshū, SW Japan 35°37′N 134°27′E
Hamath see Ḩamāh
165 T1 **Hamatonbetsu** Hokkaidō, NE Japan 45°07′N 142°21′E
155 K26 **Hambantota** Southern Province, SE Sri Lanka 06°07′N 81°07′E
Hambourg see Hamburg
100 J9 **Hamburg** Hamburg, N Germany 53°33′N 10°03′E
27 V14 **Hamburg** Arkansas, C USA 33°13′N 91°50′W
29 S16 **Hamburg** Iowa, C USA 40°36′N 95°39′W
18 D10 **Hamburg** New York, NE USA 42°40′N 78°49′W
100 I10 **Hamburg** *Fr.* Hambourg. ◐ *state* N Germany
148 K5 **Hamdam Āb, Dasht-e** *Pash.* Dasht-i Hamdamab. ▲▲ W Afghanistan
Hamdamab, Dasht-i see Hamdam Āb, Dasht-e
18 M13 **Hamden** Connecticut, NE USA 41°23′N 72°55′W
140 K6 **Ḩamḑ, Wādī al** *dry watercourse* W Saudi Arabia
93 K18 **Hämeenkyrö** Länsi-Suomi, W Finland 61°39′N 23°10′E
93 L19 **Hämeenlinna** *Swe.* Tavastehus. Etelä-Suomi, S Finland 61°N 24°25′E
HaMelaḩ, Yam see Dead Sea
Hamelin see Hameln
100 I13 **Hameln** *Eng.* Hamelin. Niedersachsen, N Germany 52°07′N 09°22′E
180 I8 **Hamersley Range** ▲▲ Western Australia
163 Y12 **Hamgyŏng-sanmaek** ▲▲ N North Korea
163 X13 **Hamhŭng** C North Korea 39°53′N 127°31′E
159 O6 **Hami** *var.* Ha-mi, *Uigh.* Kumul, Qomul. Xinjiang Uygur Zizhiqu, NW China 42°48′N 93°27′E
Ha-mi see Hami
139 X10 **Ḩāmid Amīn** Maysān, E Iraq 32°06′N 46°53′E
141 W11 **Hamīdān, Khawr** *oasis* SE Saudi Arabia
138 H5 **Ḩamīdīyah** *var.* Hamīdīyé. Ţarţūs, W Syria 34°43′N 35°58′E
114 L12 **Hamidiye** Edirne, NW Turkey 41°09′N 26°40′E
Hamīdīyé see Ḩamīdīyah
182 L12 **Hamilton** Victoria, SE Australia 37°45′S 142°04′E
64 B12 **Hamilton** ○ (Bermuda) C Bermuda 32°18′N 64°48′W
14 G16 **Hamilton** Ontario, S Canada 43°15′N 79°50′W
184 M7 **Hamilton** Waikato, North Island, New Zealand 37°49′S 175°16′E
96 I12 **Hamilton** S Scotland, United Kingdom 55°47′N 04°03′W
23 N3 **Hamilton** Alabama, S USA 34°08′N 87°59′W
38 M10 **Hamilton** Alaska, USA 62°54′N 163°53′W
30 I13 **Hamilton** Illinois, N USA 40°24′N 91°20′W
27 S3 **Hamilton** Missouri, C USA 39°44′N 94°00′W
33 P10 **Hamilton** Montana, NW USA 46°15′N 114°09′W
25 S8 **Hamilton** Texas, SW USA 31°42′N 98°08′W
14 G16 **Hamilton** ✈ Ontario, SE Canada 43°12′N 79°54′W
64 I6 **Hamilton Bank** *undersea feature* SE Labrador Sea
182 E1 **Hamilton Creek** *seasonal river* South Australia
13 R8 **Hamilton Inlet** *inlet* Newfoundland and Labrador, E Canada
27 T12 **Hamilton, Lake** ⊠ Arkansas, C USA
35 W6 **Hamilton, Mount** ▲ Nevada, W USA 39°15′N 115°30′W
75 S8 **Ḩamīm, Wādī al** ~ NE Libya
93 N19 **Hamina** *Swe.* Fredrikshamn. Kymi, S Finland 60°33′N 27°15′E
11 W16 **Hamiota** Manitoba, S Canada 50°13′N 100°37′W
152 L13 **Hamīrpur** Uttar Pradesh, N India 25°57′N 80°08′E
Hamis Musait see Khamīs Mushayt
21 T11 **Hamlet** North Carolina, SE USA 34°52′N 79°41′W
25 P6 **Hamlin** Texas, SW USA 32°52′N 100°07′W
21 P5 **Hamlin** West Virginia, NE USA 38°16′N 82°07′W
31 O7 **Hamlin Lake** ◎ Michigan, N USA
101 F14 **Hamm** *var.* Hamm in Westfalen. Nordrhein-Westfalen, W Germany 51°39′N 07°49′E
Ḩammāmāt, Khalīj al see Hammamet, Golfe de
75 N5 **Hammamet, Golfe de** *Ar.* Khalīj al Ḩammāmāt. *gulf* NE Tunisia
139 R3 **Ḩammām al 'Alīl** Nīnawé, N Iraq 36°07′N 43°15′E
139 Y12 **Ḩammār, Hawr al** ◎ SE Iraq
93 J20 **Hammarland** Åland, SW Finland 60°13′N 19°45′E
93 H16 **Hammarstrand** Jämtland, C Sweden 63°07′N 16°27′E
93 O17 **Hammaslahti** Itä-Suomi, SE Finland 62°26′N 29°58′E
99 F17 **Hamme** Oost-Vlaanderen, NW Belgium 51°06′N 04°08′E
100 H10 **Hamme** ~ NW Germany
95 G22 **Hammel** Århus, C Denmark 56°15′N 09°53′E
101 I18 **Hammelburg** Bayern, C Germany 50°06′N 09°50′E
99 H18 **Hamme-Mille** Walloon Brabant, C Belgium 50°48′N 04°42′E
100 H10 **Hamme-Oste-Kanal** *canal* NW Germany
93 G16 **Hammerdal** Jämtland, C Sweden 63°34′N 15°19′E
92 K8 **Hammerfest** Finnmark, N Norway 70°40′N 23°44′E
101 D14 **Hamminkeln** Nordrhein-Westfalen, W Germany 51°43′N 06°36′E
Hamm in Westfalen see Hamm
26 K10 **Hammon** Oklahoma, C USA 35°37′N 99°22′W
31 N11 **Hammond** Indiana, N USA 41°35′N 87°30′W
22 K8 **Hammond** Louisiana, S USA 30°30′N 90°27′W
99 K20 **Hamoir** Liège, E Belgium 50°28′N 05°35′E
99 J21 **Hamois** Namur, SE Belgium 50°21′N 05°09′E
99 K16 **Hamont** Limburg, NE Belgium 51°15′N 05°33′E
185 F22 **Hampden** Otago, South Island, New Zealand 45°18′S 170°49′E
19 R6 **Hampden** Maine, NE USA 44°44′N 68°51′W
97 M23 **Hampshire** *cultural region* S England, United Kingdom
13 O15 **Hampton** New Brunswick, SE Canada 45°30′N 65°50′W
27 U14 **Hampton** Arkansas, C USA 33°33′N 92°28′W
29 V12 **Hampton** Iowa, C USA 42°44′N 93°12′W
19 P10 **Hampton** New Hampshire, NE USA 42°55′N 70°48′W
21 R14 **Hampton** South Carolina, SE USA 32°52′N 81°06′W
21 P8 **Hampton** Tennessee, S USA 36°16′N 82°10′W
21 X7 **Hampton** Virginia, NE USA 37°02′N 76°23′W
94 L11 **Hamra** Gävleborg, C Sweden 61°40′N 15°00′E
80 D10 **Hamrat esh Sheikh** Northern Kordofan, C Sudan 14°38′N 27°56′E
139 S5 **Ḩamrīn, Jabal** ▲ N Iraq
121 P16 **Ḩamrun** C Malta 35°53′N 14°28′E
167 U14 **Ham Thuận Nam** Bình Thuận, S Vietnam 10°49′N 107°49′E
Hāmūn, Daryācheh-ye see Şāberī, Hāmūn-e/Sīstān, Daryācheh-ye
Hamwih see Southampton
38 G10 **Hāna** *var.* Hana. Maui, Hawaii, USA, C Pacific Ocean 20°45′N 155°59′W
Hana see Hāna
21 S14 **Hanahan** South Carolina, SE USA 32°55′N 80°01′W
38 B8 **Hanalei** Kaua'i, Hawaii, USA, C Pacific Ocean 22°12′N 159°30′W
167 U10 **Ha Nam** Quang Nam-Đa Nẵng, C Vietnam 15°42′N 108°24′E
165 Q9 **Hanamaki** Iwate, Honshū, C Japan 39°25′N 141°04′E
38 F10 **Hanamanioa, Cape** *headland* Maui, Hawai'i, USA 20°34′N 156°22′W
190 B16 **Hanan** ✈ (Alofi) SW Niue
101 H18 **Hanau** Hessen, W Germany 50°06′N 08°56′E
162 M11 **Hanbogd** *var.* Ih Bulag. Ömnögovĭ, S Mongolia 43°04′N 107°42′E
8 L9 **Hanbury** ~ Northwest Territories, NW Canada
Hâncești see Hîncești
10 M15 **Hanceville** British Columbia, SW Canada 51°54′N 122°56′W
23 P3 **Hanceville** Alabama, S USA 34°03′N 86°46′W
Hancewicze see Hantsavichy
160 L6 **Hancheng** Shaanxi, C China 35°22′N 110°27′E
21 V2 **Hancock** Maryland, NE USA 39°42′N 78°10′W
30 M3 **Hancock** Michigan, N USA 47°07′N 88°34′W
29 S8 **Hancock** Minnesota, N USA 45°30′N 95°47′W
18 I12 **Hancock** New York, NE USA 41°57′N 75°15′W
80 Q12 **Handa** Bari, NE Somalia 10°35′N 51°09′E
161 O5 **Handan** *var.* Han-tan. Hebei, E China 36°35′N 114°28′E
95 P16 **Handen** Stockholm, C Sweden 59°12′N 18°09′E
81 J22 **Handeni** Tanga, E Tanzania 05°25′S 38°04′E
37 Q7 **Handies Peak** ▲ Colorado, C USA 37°54′N 107°30′W
111 J19 **Handlová** *Ger.* Krickerhäu, *Hung.* Nyitrabánya; *prev.* Kriegerhaj. Trenčiansky Kraj, C Slovakia 48°45′N 18°45′E
165 O13 **Haneda** ✈ (Tōkyō) Tōkyō, Honshū, S Japan 35°33′N 139°45′E
138 F13 **HaNegev** *Eng.* Negev. *desert* S Israel
Hanfeng see Kaixian
35 Q11 **Hanford** California, W USA 36°19′N 119°39′W
191 V16 **Hanga Roa** Easter Island, Chile, E Pacific Ocean 27°09′S 109°26′W
162 I7 **Hangay** *var.* Hunt. Arhangay, C Mongolia 47°49′N 99°24′E
162 H7 **Hangayn Nuruu** ▲▲ C Mongolia
Hang-chou/Hangchow see Hangzhou
95 K20 **Hånger** Jönköping, S Sweden 57°06′N 13°58′E
Hangö see Hanko
149 T6 **Hangu** North-West Frontier Province, NW Pakistan 33°32′N 71°04′E
161 R9 **Hangzhou** *var.* Hang-chou, Hangchow. *province capital* Zhejiang, SE China 30°18′N 120°07′E
162 J4 **Hanh** *var.* Turt. Hövsgöl, N Mongolia 51°30′N 100°40′E
162 F5 **Hanhöhiy Uul** ▲▲ NW Mongolia
162 K10 **Hanhongor** *var.* Ögöömör. Ömnögovĭ, S Mongolia 43°47′N 104°31′E
146 I14 **Hanhowuz** *Rus.* Khauz-Khan. Ahal Welaýaty, S Turkmenistan 37°15′N 61°12′E
146 I14 **Hanhowuz Suw Howdany** *Rus.* Khauzkhanskoye Vodoranilishche. ⊠ S Turkmenistan
137 P15 **Hani** Diyarbakır, SE Turkey 38°26′N 40°23′E
Hania see Chaniá
141 R11 **Ḩanīsh al Kabīr, Jazīrat al** *island* SW Yemen
Hanka, Lake see Khanka, Lake
93 M17 **Hankasalmi** Länsi-Suomi, C Finland 62°25′N 26°27′E
29 R7 **Hankinson** North Dakota, N USA 46°04′N 96°54′W
93 K20 **Hanko** *Swe.* Hangö. Etelä-Suomi, SW Finland 59°50′N 23°E
Han-kou/Han-k'ou/Hankow see Wuhan
36 M6 **Hanksville** Utah, W USA 38°21′N 110°43′W
152 K6 **Hanle** Jammu and Kashmir, NW India 32°46′N 79°01′E
185 I17 **Hanmer Springs** Canterbury, South Island, New Zealand 42°31′S 172°49′E
11 R16 **Hanna** Alberta, SW Canada 51°38′N 111°56′W
27 V3 **Hannibal** Missouri, C USA 39°42′N 91°23′W
180 M3 **Hann, Mount** ▲ Western Australia 15°53′S 125°46′E
100 I12 **Hannover** *Eng.* Hanover. Niedersachsen, NW Germany 52°23′N 09°43′E
99 J19 **Hannut** Liège, C Belgium 50°40′N 05°05′E
95 L22 **Hanöbukten** *bay* S Sweden
167 T6 **Ha Nôi** *Eng.* Hanoi, *Fr.* Hanoï. ● (Vietnam) N Vietnam 21°01′N 105°52′E
14 F14 **Hanover** Ontario, S Canada 44°10′N 81°03′W
31 P15 **Hanover** Indiana, N USA 38°42′N 85°28′W
18 G16 **Hanover** Pennsylvania, NE USA 39°46′N 76°57′W
21 W6 **Hanover** Virginia, NE USA 37°44′N 77°21′W
Hanover see Hannover
63 G23 **Hanover, Isla** *island* S Chile
Hanselbeck see Érd
195 X5 **Hansen Mountains** ▲▲ Antarctica
160 M8 **Han Shui** ~ C China
152 H10 **Hānsi** Haryāna, NW India 29°06′N 76°01′E
95 F20 **Hanstholm** Viborg, NW Denmark 57°05′N 08°39′E
Han-tan see Handan
158 H6 **Hantengri Feng** *var.* Pik Khan-Tengri. ▲ China/Kazakhstan 42°17′N 80°11′E *see also* Khan-Tengri, Pik
119 I18 **Hantsavichy** *Pol.* Hancewicze, *Rus.* Gantsevichi. Brestskaya Voblasts', SW Belarus 52°45′N 26°27′E
9 Q6 **Hantzsch** ~ Baffin Island, Nunavut, NE Canada
152 G9 **Hanumāngarh** Rājasthān, NW India 29°33′N 74°21′E
183 O9 **Hanwood** New South Wales, SE Australia 34°19′S 146°03′E
Hanyang see Wuhan
Hanyang see Caidian
160 H10 **Hanyuan** *var.* Fulin. Sichuan, C China 29°29′N 102°45′E
Hanyuan see Xihe
160 J7 **Hanzhong** Shaanxi, C China 33°12′N 107°E
191 W11 **Hao** *atoll* Îles Tuamotu, C French Polynesia
153 S16 **Hāora** *prev.* Howrah. West Bengal, NE India 22°35′N 88°20′E
78 K8 **Haouach, Ouadi** *dry watercourse* E Chad
92 K13 **Haparanda** Norrbotten, N Sweden 65°49′N 24°05′E
25 N3 **Happy** Texas, SW USA 34°44′N 101°51′W
34 M1 **Happy Camp** California, W USA 41°48′N 123°24′W
13 Q9 **Happy Valley-Goose Bay** *prev.* Goose Bay. Newfoundland and Labrador, E Canada 53°19′N 60°24′W
Hapsal see Haapsalu
152 J10 **Hāpur** Uttar Pradesh, N India 28°43′N 77°47′E
HaQatan, HaMakhtesh see HaKatan, HaMakhtesh
140 I4 **Ḩaql** Tabūk, NW Saudi Arabia 29°18′N 34°58′E
171 U14 **Har** Pulau Kai Besar, E Indonesia 05°21′S 133°09′E
Haraat see Tsagaandelger
141 R8 **Ḩaraḑ** *var.* Haradh. Ash Sharqīyah, E Saudi Arabia 24°08′N 49°02′E
Haradh see Ḩaraḑ
118 N12 **Haradok** *Rus.* Gorodok. Vitsyebskaya Voblasts', N Belarus 55°28′N 30°00′E
92 J13 **Harads** Norrbotten, N Sweden 66°04′N 21°04′E
119 G19 **Haradzyets** *Rus.* Gorodets. Brestskaya Voblasts', SW Belarus 52°12′N 24°40′E
119 J17 **Haradzyeya** *Rus.* Gorodeya. Minskaya Voblasts', C Belarus 53°19′N 26°32′E
191 V10 **Haraiki** *atoll* Îles Tuamotu, C French Polynesia
165 Q11 **Haramachi** Fukushima, Honshū, E Japan 37°40′N 140°55′E
118 M12 **Harany** *Rus.* Gorany. Vitsyebskaya Voblasts', N Belarus 55°25′N 29°03′E
83 L16 **Harare** *prev.* Salisbury. ● (Zimbabwe) Mashonaland East, NE Zimbabwe 17°47′S 31°04′E
83 L16 **Harare** ✈ Mashonaland East, NE Zimbabwe 17°51′S 31°06′E
78 J10 **Haraz-Djombo** Batha, C Chad 14°10′N 19°35′E
119 O16 **Harbavichy** *Rus.* Gorbovichi. Mahilyowskaya Voblasts', E Belarus 53°49′N 30°42′E
76 J16 **Harbel** W Liberia 06°19′N 10°20′W
163 W8 **Harbin** *var.* Haerbin, Ha-erh-pin, Kharbin; *prev.* Haerhpin, Pingkiang, Pinkiang. *province capital* Heilongjiang, NE China 45°45′N 126°41′E
31 S7 **Harbor Beach** Michigan, N USA 43°50′N 82°39′W
13 T13 **Harbour Breton** Newfoundland, Newfoundland and Labrador, E Canada 47°29′N 55°50′W
65 D25 **Harbours, Bay of** *bay* East Falkland, Falkland Islands
Hårby see Haarby
36 I13 **Harcuvar Mountains** ▲▲ Arizona, SW USA
108 I7 **Hard** Vorarlberg, NW Austria 47°29′N 09°42′E
154 H11 **Harda Khas** Madhya Pradesh, C India 22°22′N 77°06′E
95 D14 **Hardanger** *physical region* S Norway
95 D14 **Hardangerfjorden** *fjord* S Norway
94 E13 **Hardangerjøkulen** *glacier* S Norway
95 E14 **Hardangervidda** *plateau* S Norway
83 D20 **Hardap** ◐ *district* S Namibia
21 R15 **Hardeeville** South Carolina, SE USA 32°18′N 81°04′W
98 L5 **Hardegarijp** *Fris.* Hurdegaryp. Friesland, N Netherlands 53°13′N 05°57′E
98 O9 **Hardenberg** Overijssel, E Netherlands 52°34′N 06°38′E
183 Q9 **Harden-Murrumburrah** New South Wales, SE Australia 34°33′S 148°22′E
98 K10 **Harderwijk** Gelderland, C Netherlands 52°21′N 05°37′E
30 J14 **Hardin** Illinois, N USA 39°10′N 90°38′W
33 V11 **Hardin** Montana, NW USA 45°44′N 107°35′W
23 R5 **Harding, Lake** ⊠ Alabama/Georgia, SE USA
20 J6 **Hardinsburg** Kentucky, S USA 37°46′N 86°29′W
98 I13 **Hardinxveld-Giessendam** Zuid-Holland, C Netherlands 51°52′N 04°49′E
11 R15 **Hardisty** Alberta, SW Canada 52°42′N 111°22′W
152 L12 **Hardoi** Uttar Pradesh, N India 27°23′N 80°06′E
Hardwar see Haridwār
23 U4 **Hardwick** Georgia, SE USA 33°03′N 83°13′W
27 W9 **Hardy** Arkansas, C USA 36°19′N 91°29′W
94 D10 **Hareid** Møre og Romsdal, S Norway 62°22′N 06°02′E
8 H7 **Hare Indian** ~ Northwest Territories, NW Canada
99 D18 **Harelbeke** *var.* Harlebeke. West-Vlaanderen, W Belgium 50°51′N 03°19′E
Harem see Ḩārim
100 E11 **Haren** Niedersachsen, NW Germany 52°47′N 07°16′E
98 N6 **Haren** Groningen, NE Netherlands 53°10′N 06°37′E
80 L13 **Hārer** E Ethiopia 09°17′N 42°19′E
95 P14 **Harg** Uppsala, C Sweden 60°13′N 18°25′E
Hargeisa see Hargeysa
80 M13 **Hargeysa** *var.* Hargeisa. Woqooyi Galbeed, NW Somalia 09°32′N 44°07′E
116 J10 **Harghita** ◐ *county* NE Romania
25 S17 **Hargill** Texas, SW USA 26°26′N 98°00′W
162 J8 **Harhorin** Övörhangay, C Mongolia 47°13′N 102°48′E
159 Q9 **Har Hu** ◎ C China
Hariana see Haryāna
141 P15 **Ḩarīb** W Yemen 15°08′N 45°35′E
168 M12 **Hari, Batang** *prev.* Djambi. ~ Sumatera, W Indonesia
152 J9 **Haridwār** *prev.* Hardwar. Uttarakhand, N India 29°58′N 78°09′E
155 F18 **Harihar** Karnātaka, W India 14°33′N 75°44′E
185 F18 **Harihari** West Coast, South Island, New Zealand 43°09′S 170°35′E
138 I3 **Ḩārim** *var.* Harem. Idlib, W Syria 36°30′N 36°30′E
98 F13 **Haringvliet** *channel* SW Netherlands
98 F13 **Haringvlietdam** *dam* SW Netherlands
149 U5 **Harīpur** North-West Frontier Province, NW Pakistan 34°00′N 73°01′E
148 J4 **Harīrūd** *var.* Tedzhen, *Turkm.* Tejen. ~ Afghanistan/Iran *see also* Tejen
Harīrūd see Tejen
94 J11 **Härjahågnen** *Swe.* Härjahågnen, *var.* Härjehågna. ▲ Norway/Sweden 61°43′N 12°07′E
Härjahågnen see Østrehogna
Härjahågnen see Härjahågnen
93 K18 **Harjavalta** Länsi-Suomi, W Finland 61°19′N 22°10′E
Härjehågna see Østrehogna
Härjehågna see Härjahågnen
118 G4 **Harjumaa** *var.* Harju Maakond. ◐ *province* NW Estonia
Harju Maakond see Harjumaa
21 X11 **Harkers Island** North Carolina, SE USA 34°42′N 76°33′W
139 S1 **Harkī** Dahūk, N Iraq 37°03′N 43°39′E
29 T14 **Harlan** Iowa, C USA 41°40′N 95°19′W
21 O7 **Harlan** Kentucky, S USA 36°50′N 83°19′W
29 N17 **Harlan County Lake** ⊠ Nebraska, C USA
116 L9 **Hârlău** *var.* Hîrlău. Iaşi, NE Romania 47°26′N 26°54′E
Harlebeke see Harelbeke
33 U7 **Harlem** Montana, NW USA 48°31′N 108°46′W
Harlem see Haarlem
95 G22 **Harlev** Århus, C Denmark 56°08′N 10°00′E
98 K6 **Harlingen** *Fris.* Harns. Friesland, N Netherlands 53°10′N 05°25′E
25 T17 **Harlingen** Texas, SW USA 26°12′N 97°43′W
97 O21 **Harlow** E England, United Kingdom 51°47′N 00°07′E
33 T10 **Harlowton** Montana, NW USA 46°26′N 109°49′W
94 N11 **Harmånger** Gävleborg, C Sweden 61°55′N 17°19′E
98 I11 **Harmelen** Utrecht, C Netherlands 52°06′N 04°58′E
29 X11 **Harmony** Minnesota, N USA 43°33′N 92°00′W

◆ Country
● Country Capital
◇ Dependent Territory
○ Dependent Territory Capital
◐ Administrative Regions
✈ International Airport
▲ Mountain
▲▲ Mountain Range
Volcano
~ River
◎ Lake
⊠ Reservoir

32 J14 **Harney Basin** basin Oregon, NW USA
32 J14 **Harney Lake** ◎ Oregon, NW USA
28 J10 **Harney Peak** ▲ South Dakota, N USA 43°52′N 103°31′W
93 H17 **Härnösand** var. Hernösand. Västernorrland, C Sweden 62°37′N 17°55′E
Harns see Harlingen
162 F6 **Har Nuur** ◎ NW Mongolia
105 P4 **Haro** La Rioja, N Spain 42°34′N 02°52′W
40 F6 **Haro, Cabo** headland NW Mexico 27°50′N 110°55′W
94 D9 **Harøy** island S Norway
97 N21 **Harpenden** E England, United Kingdom 51°49′N 00°22′W
76 L18 **Harper** var. Cape Palmas. NE Liberia 04°25′N 07°43′W
26 M7 **Harper** Kansas, C USA 37°17′N 98°01′W
32 L13 **Harper** Oregon, NW USA 43°51′N 117°37′W
25 Q10 **Harper** Texas, SW USA 30°18′N 99°18′W
35 U13 **Harper Lake** salt flat California, W USA
39 T9 **Harper, Mount** ▲ Alaska, USA 64°18′N 143°54′W
95 J21 **Harplinge** Halland, S Sweden 56°45′N 12°45′E
36 J13 **Harquahala Mountains** ▲ Arizona, SW USA
141 T15 **Ḩarrah** SE Yemen 15°02′N 50°23′E
12 H11 **Harricana** ↝ Québec, SE Canada
20 M9 **Harriman** Tennessee, S USA 35°57′N 84°33′W
13 R11 **Harrington Harbour** Québec, E Canada 50°34′N 59°29′W
64 B12 **Harrington Sound** bay Bermuda, NW Atlantic Ocean
96 F8 **Harris** physical region NW Scotland, United Kingdom
27 X10 **Harrisburg** Arkansas, C USA 35°33′N 90°43′W
30 M17 **Harrisburg** Illinois, N USA 37°44′N 88°32′W
28 I14 **Harrisburg** Nebraska, C USA 41°33′N 103°46′W
32 F12 **Harrisburg** Oregon, NW USA 44°16′N 123°10′W
18 G15 **Harrisburg** state capital Pennsylvania, NE USA 40°16′N 76°53′W
182 F6 **Harris, Lake** ◎ South Australia
23 W11 **Harris, Lake** ◎ Florida, SE USA
83 J22 **Harrismith** Free State, E South Africa 28°16′S 29°08′E
27 T9 **Harrison** Arkansas, C USA 36°13′N 93°07′W
31 Q7 **Harrison** Michigan, N USA 44°02′N 84°46′W
28 I12 **Harrison** Nebraska, C USA 42°42′N 103°53′W
39 Q5 **Harrison Bay** inlet Alaska, USA
22 I6 **Harrisonburg** Louisiana, S USA 31°44′N 91°51′W
21 U4 **Harrisonburg** Virginia, NE USA 38°27′N 78°54′W
13 R7 **Harrison, Cape** headland Newfoundland and Labrador, E Canada 54°55′N 57°48′W
27 R5 **Harrisonville** Missouri, C USA 38°40′N 94°21′W
Harris Ridge see Lomonosov Ridge
192 M3 **Harris Seamount** undersea feature N Pacific Ocean 46°09′N 161°25′W
96 F8 **Harris, Sound of** strait NW Scotland, United Kingdom
31 R6 **Harrisville** Michigan, N USA 44°41′N 83°19′W
21 R3 **Harrisville** West Virginia, NE USA 39°13′N 81°04′W
20 M6 **Harrodsburg** Kentucky, S USA 37°45′N 84°51′W
97 M16 **Harrogate** N England, United Kingdom 54°N 01°33′W
25 Q4 **Harrold** Texas, SW USA 34°05′N 99°02′W
27 S5 **Harry S. Truman Reservoir** ⊡ Missouri, C USA
100 G13 **Harsewinkel** Nordrhein-Westfalen, W Germany 51°58′N 08°13′E
116 M14 **Hârşova** prev. Hîrşova. Constanţa, SE Romania 44°41′N 27°56′E
92 H10 **Harstad** Troms, N Norway 68°48′N 16°31′E
31 O8 **Hart** Michigan, N USA 43°43′N 86°22′W
24 M4 **Hart** Texas, SW USA 34°23′N 102°07′W
10 I5 **Hart** ↝ Yukon Territory, NW Canada
83 F23 **Hartbees** ↝ C South Africa
109 X7 **Hartberg** Steiermark, SE Austria 47°18′N 15°58′E
182 I10 **Hart, Cape** headland South Australia 35°54′S 138°01′E
95 E14 **Hårteigen** ▲ S Norway 60°11′N 07°01′E
23 Q7 **Hartford** Alabama, S USA 31°06′N 85°42′W
27 R11 **Hartford** Arkansas, C USA 35°01′N 94°22′W
18 M12 **Hartford** state capital Connecticut, NE USA 41°46′N 72°41′W
20 J6 **Hartford** Kentucky, S USA 37°26′N 86°57′W
31 P10 **Hartford** Michigan, N USA 42°12′N 85°54′W
29 R11 **Hartford** South Dakota, N USA 43°37′N 96°56′W
30 M8 **Hartford** Wisconsin, N USA 43°19′N 88°25′W
31 P13 **Hartford City** Indiana, N USA 40°27′N 85°22′W
29 Q13 **Hartington** Nebraska, C USA 42°37′N 97°15′W
13 N14 **Hartland** New Brunswick, SE Canada 46°18′N 67°31′W
97 H23 **Hartland Point** headland SW England, United Kingdom 51°01′N 04°33′W
97 M15 **Hartlepool** N England, United Kingdom 54°41′N 01°13′W
29 T12 **Hartley** Iowa, C USA 43°10′N 95°28′W
24 M1 **Hartley** Texas, SW USA 35°52′N 102°24′W
32 J15 **Hart Mountain** ▲ Oregon, NW USA 42°24′N 119°46′W
173 U10 **Hartog Ridge** undersea feature W Indian Ocean
93 M18 **Hartola** Etelä-Suomi, S Finland 61°34′N 26°04′E
67 U14 **Harts** var. Hartz. ↝ N South Africa
23 P2 **Hartselle** Alabama, S USA 34°26′N 86°56′W
23 S3 **Hartsfield Atlanta** ✈ Georgia, SE USA 33°38′N 84°24′W
27 Q11 **Hartshorne** Oklahoma, C USA 34°51′N 95°33′W
21 S12 **Hartsville** South Carolina, SE USA 34°22′N 80°04′W
20 K8 **Hartsville** Tennessee, S USA 36°23′N 86°11′W
27 U7 **Hartville** Missouri, C USA 37°15′N 92°30′W
23 U2 **Hartwell** Georgia, SE USA 34°21′N 82°55′W
21 O11 **Hartwell Lake** ⊡ Georgia/South Carolina, SE USA
Hartz see Harts
Harunabad see Eslāmābād
Har-Us see Erdenebüren
162 F6 **Har Us Gol** ◎ Hovd, W Mongolia
162 E6 **Har Us Nuur** ◎ NW Mongolia
30 M10 **Harvard** Illinois, N USA 42°25′N 88°36′W
29 P16 **Harvard** Nebraska, C USA 40°37′N 98°06′W
37 R5 **Harvard, Mount** ▲ Colorado, C USA 38°55′N 106°19′W
31 N11 **Harvey** Illinois, N USA 41°36′N 87°39′W
29 N4 **Harvey** North Dakota, N USA 47°43′N 99°55′W
97 Q21 **Harwich** E England, United Kingdom 51°56′N 01°16′E
152 H10 **Haryāna** var. Hariana. ◆ state N India
141 Y9 **Ḩaryān, Ţawī al** spring/well NE Oman 21°56′N 58°33′E
101 J14 **Harz** ▲ C Germany
Hasakah, Muḩāfaẓat al see Al Ḩasakah
165 Q9 **Hasama** Miyagi, Honshū, C Japan 38°42′N 141°09′E
136 J15 **Hasan Dağı** ▲ C Turkey 38°09′N 34°15′E
139 T9 **Ḩasan Ibn Ḩassūn** An Najaf, C Iraq 32°24′N 44°13′E
149 R6 **Ḩasan Khēl** var. Ahmad Khel. Paktiā, SE Afghanistan 33°46′N 69°37′E
100 F12 **Hase** ↝ NW Germany
Haselberg see Krasnoznamensk
100 F12 **Haselünne** Niedersachsen, NW Germany 52°40′N 07°28′E
Hashaat see Delgerhangay
Hashemite Kingdom of Jordan see Jordan
139 V8 **Hāshimah** Wāsiţ, E Iraq 33°22′N 45°56′E
142 K3 **Hashtrūd** var. Azaran. Āžarbāyjān-e Khāvarī, N Iran 37°34′N 47°10′E
141 W13 **Ḩāsik** S Oman 17°22′N 55°18′E
149 U10 **Hāsilpur** Punjab, E Pakistan 29°42′N 72°40′E
27 Q10 **Haskell** Oklahoma, C USA 35°49′N 95°40′W
25 Q6 **Haskell** Texas, SW USA 33°10′N 99°45′W
114 M11 **Hasköy** Edirne, NW Turkey 41°37′N 26°51′E
95 L24 **Hasle** Bornholm, E Denmark 55°12′N 14°43′E
97 N23 **Haslemere** SE England, United Kingdom 51°06′N 00°45′W
102 I16 **Hasparren** Pyrénées-Atlantiques, SW France 43°23′N 01°18′W
Hassakeh see Al Ḩasakah
155 G19 **Hassan** Karnātaka, W India 13°01′N 76°03′E
36 J13 **Hassayampa River** ↝ Arizona, SW USA
101 J18 **Hassberge** hill range C Germany
94 N10 **Hassela** Gävleborg, C Sweden 62°06′N 16°45′E
99 J18 **Hasselt** Limburg, NE Belgium 50°56′N 05°20′E
98 M9 **Hasselt** Overijssel, E Netherlands 52°36′N 06°06′E
Hassetché see Al Ḩasakah
101 J18 **Hassfurt** Bayern, C Germany 50°02′N 10°32′E
74 L9 **Hassi Bel Guebbour** E Algeria 28°41′N 06°29′E
74 L8 **Hassi Messaoud** E Algeria 31°41′N 06°10′E
95 K22 **Hässleholm** Skåne, S Sweden 56°09′N 13°45′E
Hasta Colonia/Hasta Pompeia see Asti
183 O13 **Hastings** Victoria, SE Australia 38°18′S 145°12′E
184 O11 **Hastings** Hawke's Bay, North Island, New Zealand 39°39′S 176°51′E
97 P23 **Hastings** SE England, United Kingdom 50°51′N 00°36′E
31 P9 **Hastings** Michigan, N USA 42°38′N 85°17′W
29 W9 **Hastings** Minnesota, N USA 44°44′N 92°51′W
29 P16 **Hastings** Nebraska, C USA 40°35′N 98°23′W
95 K22 **Hästveda** Skåne, S Sweden 56°16′N 13°55′E
92 J8 **Hasvik** Finnmark, N Norway 70°29′N 22°08′E
37 V6 **Haswell** Colorado, C USA 38°27′N 103°09′W
163 N11 **Hatanbulag** var. Ergel. Dornogovĭ, SE Mongolia 43°10′N 109°13′E
Hatansuudal see Bayanlig
Hatavch see Haldzan
136 K17 **Hatay** ◆ province S Turkey
37 R15 **Hatch** New Mexico, SW USA 32°40′N 107°10′W
36 K7 **Hatch** Utah, W USA 37°39′N 112°25′W
20 F9 **Hatchie River** ↝ Tennessee, S USA
116 G12 **Haţeg** Ger. Wallenthal, Hung. Hátszeg; prev. Hatzeg, Hötzing. Hunedoara, SW Romania 45°35′N 22°57′E
165 O17 **Hateruma-jima** island Yaeyama-shotō, SW Japan
183 N8 **Hatfield** New South Wales, SE Australia 33°54′S 143°43′E
162 I5 **Hatgal** Hövsgöl, N Mongolia 50°24′N 100°12′E
153 V16 **Hathazari** Chittagong, SE Bangladesh 22°30′N 91°46′E
141 T13 **Hathūt, Hiṣā'** oasis NE Yemen
167 R14 **Ha Tiên** Kiên Giang, S Vietnam 10°24′N 104°30′E
167 T8 **Ha Tinh** Ha Tinh, N Vietnam 18°21′N 105°55′E
Ḩatira, Haré see Hatira, Harei
138 F12 **Hatira, Harei** prev. Haré Ḩatira. hill range S Israel
167 R6 **Hat Lot** var. Mai Son. Son La, N Vietnam 21°07′N 104°10′E
45 P16 **Hato Airport** ✈ (Willemstad) Curaçao, SW Netherlands Antilles 12°10′N 68°56′W
54 H9 **Hato Corozal** Casanare, C Colombia 06°08′N 71°45′W
Hato del Volcán see Volcán
45 P9 **Hato Mayor** E Dominican Republic 18°49′N 69°16′W
Hatra see Al Ḩaḑr
Hatria see Adria
Hátszeg see Haţeg
143 R16 **Ḩattā** Dubayy, NE United Arab Emirates 24°50′N 56°06′E
182 L9 **Hattah** Victoria, SE Australia 34°49′S 142°18′E
98 M9 **Hattem** Gelderland, E Netherlands 52°29′N 06°04′E
21 Z10 **Hatteras** Hatteras Island, North Carolina, SE USA 35°13′N 75°39′W
21 Rr10 **Hatteras, Cape** headland North Carolina, SE USA 35°29′N 75°33′W
21 Z9 **Hatteras Island** island North Carolina, SE USA
64 F10 **Hatteras Plain** undersea feature W Atlantic Ocean 31°00′N 71°00′W
93 G14 **Hattfjelldal** Troms, N Norway 65°37′N 13°58′E
22 M7 **Hattiesburg** Mississippi, S USA 31°20′N 89°17′W
29 Q4 **Hatton** North Dakota, N USA 47°38′N 97°27′W
Hatton Bank see Hatton Ridge
64 L6 **Hatton Ridge** var. Hatton Bank. undersea feature N Atlantic Ocean 59°00′N 17°30′W
191 W6 **Hatutu** island Îles Marquises, NE French Polynesia
111 K22 **Hatvan** Heves, NE Hungary 47°40′N 19°39′E
167 O16 **Hat Yai** var. Ban Hat Yai. Songkhla, SW Thailand 07°01′N 100°27′E
Hatzeg see Haţeg
Hatzfeld see Jimbolia
80 N13 **Haud** plateau Ethiopia/Somalia
95 D18 **Hauge** Rogaland, S Norway 58°20′N 06°17′E
95 C15 **Haugesund** Rogaland, S Norway 59°24′N 05°17′E
109 X2 **Haugsdorf** Niederösterreich, NE Austria 48°41′N 16°04′E
184 M9 **Hauhungaroa Range** ▲ North Island, New Zealand
95 E15 **Haukeligrend** Telemark, S Norway 59°45′N 07°33′E
93 L14 **Haukipudas** Oulu, C Finland 65°11′N 25°21′E
93 M17 **Haukivesi** ◎ SE Finland
93 M17 **Haukivuori** Itä-Suomi, E Finland 62°02′N 27°11′E
Hauptkanal see Havelländ Grosse
187 N10 **Hauraha** San Cristobal, SE Solomon Islands 10°47′S 162°00′E
184 L5 **Hauraki Gulf** gulf North Island, N New Zealand
185 B24 **Hauroko, Lake** ◎ South Island, New Zealand
167 S14 **Hâu, Sông** ↝ S Vietnam
92 N12 **Hautajärvi** Lappi, NE Finland 66°30′N 29°01′E
74 F7 **Haut Atlas** Eng. High Atlas. ▲ C Morocco
79 M17 **Haut-Congo** off. Région du Haut-Congo; prev. Haut-Zaïre. ◆ region NE Dem. Rep. Congo
103 Y14 **Haute-Corse** ◆ department Corse, France, C Mediterranean Sea
102 L16 **Haute-Garonne** ◆ department S France
79 K14 **Haute-Kotto** ◆ prefecture E Central African Republic
103 P12 **Haute-Loire** ◆ department C France
103 R6 **Haute-Marne** ◆ department N France
102 M3 **Haute-Normandie** ◆ region N France
15 U6 **Hauterive** Québec, SE Canada 49°11′N 68°16′W
103 T13 **Hautes-Alpes** ◆ department SE France
103 S7 **Haute-Saône** ◆ department E France
103 T10 **Haute-Savoie** ◆ department E France
99 M20 **Hautes Fagnes** Ger. Hohes Venn. ▲ E Belgium
102 K16 **Hautes-Pyrénées** ◆ department S France
99 L23 **Haute Sûre, Lac de la** ⊡ NW Luxembourg
102 M11 **Haute-Vienne** ◆ department C France
19 S8 **Haut, Isle au** island Maine, NE USA
79 M14 **Haut-Mbomou** ◆ prefecture SE Central African Republic
103 Q2 **Hautmont** Nord, N France 50°15′N 03°55′E
79 F19 **Haut-Ogooué** off. Province du Haut-Ogooué, var. Le Haut-Ogooué. ◆ province SE Gabon
Haut-Ogooué, Le see Haut-Ogooué
Haut-Ogooué, Province du see Haut-Ogooué
103 U7 **Haut-Rhin** ◆ department NE France
74 I6 **Hauts Plateaux** plateau Algeria/Morocco
Haut-Zaïre see Haut-Congo
38 D9 **Hau'ula** var. Hauula. O'ahu, Hawaii, USA, C Pacific Ocean 21°36′N 157°54′W
Hauula see Hau'ula
101 O22 **Hauzenberg** Bayern, SE Germany 48°39′N 13°37′E
30 K13 **Havana** Illinois, N USA 40°18′N 90°03′W
Havana see La Habana
97 N23 **Havant** S England, United Kingdom 50°51′N 00°59′W
35 Y14 **Havasu, Lake** ⊡ Arizona/California, W USA
95 J23 **Havdrup** Roskilde, E Denmark 55°33′N 12°08′E
100 N10 **Havel** ↝ NE Germany
99 J21 **Havelange** Namur, SE Belgium 50°23′N 05°14′E
100 M11 **Havelberg** Sachsen-Anhalt, NE Germany 52°49′N 12°05′E
149 U5 **Haveliān** North-West Frontier Province, NW Pakistan 34°05′N 73°14′E
100 N12 **Havelländ Grosse** var. Hauptkanal. canal NE Germany
14 J14 **Havelock** Ontario, SE Canada 44°22′N 77°57′W
185 J14 **Havelock** Marlborough, South Island, New Zealand 41°17′S 173°46′E
21 X11 **Havelock** North Carolina, SE USA 34°52′N 76°54′W
184 O11 **Havelock North** Hawke's Bay, North Island, New Zealand 39°40′S 176°53′E
98 M8 **Havelte** Drenthe, NE Netherlands 52°46′N 06°14′E
27 N6 **Haven** Kansas, C USA 37°54′N 97°46′W
97 H21 **Haverfordwest** SW Wales, United Kingdom 51°50′N 04°57′W
97 P20 **Haverhill** E England, United Kingdom 52°05′N 00°26′E
19 O10 **Haverhill** Massachusetts, NE USA 42°46′N 71°02′W
155 F18 **Hāveri** Karnātaka, SW India 14°47′N 75°24′E
93 G17 **Haverö** Västernorrland, C Sweden 62°25′N 15°04′E
111 I17 **Havířov** Moravskoslezský Kraj, E Czech Republic 49°47′N 18°30′E
111 E17 **Havlíčkův Brod** Ger. Deutsch-Brod; prev. Německý Brod. Vysočina, C Czech Republic 49°38′N 15°46′E
92 K7 **Havøysund** Finnmark, N Norway 70°59′N 24°39′E
99 F20 **Havré** Hainaut, S Belgium 50°29′N 04°03′E
33 T7 **Havre** Montana, NW USA 48°33′N 109°41′W
Havre see le Havre
13 P11 **Havre-St-Pierre** Québec, E Canada 50°16′N 63°36′W
136 B10 **Havsa** Edirne, NW Turkey 41°32′N 26°49′E
38 D8 **Hawai'i** off. State of Hawai'i, also known as Aloha State, Paradise of the Pacific, var. Hawaii. ◆ state USA, C Pacific Ocean
38 G12 **Hawai'i** var. Hawaii. island Hawaiian Islands, USA, C Pacific Ocean
192 M5 **Hawaiian Islands** prev. Sandwich Islands. island group Hawaii, USA
192 L5 **Hawaiian Ridge** undersea feature N Pacific Ocean 24°00′N 165°00′W
193 N6 **Hawaiian Trough** undersea feature N Pacific Ocean
29 R12 **Hawarden** Iowa, C USA 43°00′N 96°29′W
Hawash see Āwash
139 P6 **Ḩawbayn al Gharbiyah** Al Anbār, C Iraq 34°24′N 42°06′E
185 D21 **Hawea, Lake** ◎ South Island, New Zealand
184 K11 **Hawera** Taranaki, North Island, New Zealand 39°36′S 174°16′E
20 J5 **Hawesville** Kentucky, S USA 37°53′N 86°47′W
38 G11 **Hawi** Hawaii, USA, C Pacific Ocean 20°14′N 155°50′W
38 G11 **Hāwī** var. Hawi. Hawaii, USA, C Pacific Ocean 20°13′N 155°49′W
Hawi see Hāwī
96 K13 **Hawick** SE Scotland, United Kingdom 55°24′N 02°49′W
139 S4 **Ḩawījah** At Ta'mīn, C Iraq 35°15′N 43°54′E
139 Y10 **Ḩawīzah, Hawr al** ◎ S Iraq
185 E21 **Hawkdun Range** ▲ South Island, New Zealand
184 P10 **Hawke Bay** bay North Island, New Zealand
182 I6 **Hawker** South Australia 31°54′S 138°25′E
184 N11 **Hawke's Bay** off. Hawkes Bay Region. ◆ region North Island, New Zealand
149 O16 **Hawkes Bay** bay SE Pakistan
Hawkes Bay Region see Hawke's Bay
15 N12 **Hawkesbury** Ontario, SE Canada 45°36′N 74°38′W
Hawkeye State see Iowa
23 T5 **Hawkinsville** Georgia, SE USA 32°16′N 83°28′W
14 B7 **Hawk Junction** Ontario, S Canada 48°05′N 84°34′W
21 N10 **Haw Knob** ▲ North Carolina/Tennessee, SE USA 35°18′N 84°01′W
21 Q9 **Hawksbill Mountain** ▲ North Carolina, SE USA 35°54′N 81°53′W
33 Z16 **Hawk Springs** Wyoming, C USA 41°48′N 104°17′W
Hawler see Arbil
29 S5 **Hawley** Minnesota, N USA 46°53′N 96°18′W
25 P7 **Hawley** Texas, SW USA 32°36′N 99°47′W
141 R14 **Ḩawrā'** C Yemen 15°39′N 48°21′E
139 P7 **Ḩawrān, Wadi** dry watercourse W Iraq
21 T9 **Haw River** ↝ North Carolina, SE USA
139 U5 **Ḩawshqūrah** Diyālá, E Iraq 34°34′N 45°33′E
35 S7 **Hawthorne** Nevada, W USA 38°30′N 118°38′W
37 W3 **Haxtun** Colorado, C USA 40°36′N 102°38′W
183 N9 **Hay** New South Wales, SE Australia 34°31′S 144°51′E
11 O10 **Hay** ↝ W Canada
171 S13 **Haya** Pulau Seram, E Indonesia 03°22′S 129°31′E
165 R9 **Hayachine-san** ▲ Honshū, C Japan 39°31′N 141°28′E
103 S4 **Hayange** Moselle, NE France 49°19′N 06°04′E
HaYarden see Jordan
Hayastani Hanrapetut'yun see Armenia
Hayasui-seto see Hōyo-kaikyō
39 N9 **Haycock** Alaska, USA 65°12′N 161°10′W
36 M14 **Hayden** Arizona, SW USA 33°00′N 110°46′W
37 Q3 **Hayden** Colorado, C USA 40°29′N 107°15′W
28 M10 **Hayes** South Dakota, N USA 44°20′N 101°01′W
9 X13 **Hayes** ↝ Manitoba, C Canada
11 P12 **Hayes** ↝ Nunavut, NE Canada
28 M16 **Hayes Center** Nebraska, C USA 40°30′N 101°02′W
39 S10 **Hayes, Mount** ▲ Alaska, USA 63°37′N 146°43′W
21 N11 **Hayesville** North Carolina, SE USA 35°03′N 83°49′W
35 X10 **Hayford Peak** ▲ Nevada, W USA 36°40′N 115°10′W
34 M3 **Hayfork** California, W USA 40°33′N 123°10′W
Hayir, Qasr al see Ḩayr al Gharbī, Qaşr al
Haylaastay see Sühbaatar
14 I12 **Hay Lake** ◎ Ontario, SE Canada
141 X11 **Haymā'** var. Haima. C Oman 19°59′N 56°20′E
136 H13 **Haymana** Ankara, C Turkey 39°26′N 32°30′E
138 J7 **Ḩaymūr, Jabal** ▲ W Syria
Haynau see Chojnów
22 G4 **Haynesville** Louisiana, S USA 32°57′N 93°08′W
23 P6 **Hayneville** Alabama, S USA 32°13′N 86°34′W
114 M12 **Hayrabolu** Tekirdağ, NW Turkey 41°14′N 27°04′E
136 C10 **Hayrabolu Deresi** ↝ NW Turkey
138 J6 **Ḩayr al Gharbī, Qaşr al** var. Qasr al Hayir, Qasr al Hir al Gharbi. ruins Ḩimş, C Syria
138 L5 **Ḩayr ash Sharqī, Qaşr al** var. Qasr al Hir Ash Sharqī. ruins Ḩimş, C Syria
162 J7 **Hayrhan** var. Uubulan. Arhangay, C Mongolia 48°37′N 101°58′E
162 J9 **Hayrhandulaan** var. Mardzad. Övörhangay, C Mongolia 45°58′N 102°06′E
8 J10 **Hay River** Northwest Territories, W Canada 60°51′N 115°42′W
26 K4 **Hays** Kansas, C USA 38°53′N 99°20′W
28 K12 **Hay Springs** Nebraska, C USA 42°40′N 102°41′W
65 H25 **Haystack, The** ▲ NE Saint Helena 15°55′S 05°40′W
27 N7 **Haysville** Kansas, C USA 37°34′N 97°21′W
117 O7 **Haysyn** Rus. Gaysin. Vinnyts'ka Oblast', C Ukraine 48°50′N 29°29′E
27 Y9 **Hayti** Missouri, C USA 36°13′N 89°45′W
29 Q9 **Hayti** South Dakota, N USA 44°40′N 97°22′W
117 O8 **Hayvoron** Rus. Gayvorno. Kirovohrads'ka Oblast', C Ukraine 48°20′N 29°52′E
35 N9 **Hayward** California, W USA 37°40′N 122°07′W
30 J4 **Hayward** Wisconsin, N USA 46°02′N 91°26′W
97 O23 **Haywards Heath** SE England, United Kingdom 51°N 00°06′W
146 A11 **Hazar** prev. Rus. Cheleken. Balkan Welaýaty, W Turkmenistan 39°26′N 53°07′E
143 S11 **Hazārān, Kūh-e** var. Kūh-e ā Hazr. ▲ SE Iran 29°26′N 57°15′E
Hazarat Imam see Emām Şāḩeb
21 O7 **Hazard** Kentucky, S USA 37°14′N 83°11′W
137 O15 **Hazar Gölü** ◎ C Turkey
153 P15 **Hazārībāg** var. Hazāribāgh. Jhārkhand, N India 24°00′N 85°23′E
Hazāribāgh see Hazārībāg
103 O1 **Hazebrouck** Nord, N France 50°43′N 02°33′E
30 K9 **Hazel Green** Wisconsin, N USA 42°33′N 90°26′W
192 K9 **Hazel Holme Bank** undersea feature S Pacific Ocean 12°49′S 174°30′E
10 K13 **Hazelton** British Columbia, SW Canada 55°15′N 127°38′W
29 N6 **Hazelton** North Dakota, N USA 46°27′N 100°17′W
35 R5 **Hazen** Nevada, W USA 39°33′N 119°02′W
28 L5 **Hazen** North Dakota, N USA 47°18′N 101°37′W
38 L12 **Hazen Bay** bay E Bering Sea
9 N1 **Hazen, Lake** ◎ Nunavut, N Canada
139 S5 **Hazīm, Bi'r** well C Iraq
23 V6 **Hazlehurst** Georgia, SE USA 31°51′N 82°35′W
22 K6 **Hazlehurst** Mississippi, S USA 31°51′N 90°24′W
18 K15 **Hazlet** New Jersey, NE USA 40°24′N 74°10′W
146 I9 **Hazorasp** Rus. Khazarosp. Xorazm Viloyati, W Uzbekistan 41°21′N 61°01′E
147 R13 **Hazratishoh, Qatorkŭhi** var. Khrebet Khazretishi, Rus. Khrebet Khozretishi. ▲ S Tajikistan
Hazr, Kūh-e ā see Hazārān, Kūh-e
149 U6 **Hazro** Punjab, E Pakistan 33°55′N 72°33′E
23 R7 **Headland** Alabama, S USA 31°21′N 85°20′W
182 C6 **Head of Bight** headland South Australia 31°33′S 131°05′E
33 N10 **Headquarters** Idaho, NW USA 46°38′N 115°52′W
34 M7 **Healdsburg** California, W USA 38°36′N 122°52′W
27 N13 **Healdton** Oklahoma, C USA 34°13′N 97°29′W
183 O12 **Healesville** Victoria, SE Australia 37°41′S 145°31′E
39 R10 **Healy** Alaska, USA 63°51′N 148°58′W
173 R13 **Heard and McDonald Islands** ◇ Australian external territory S Indian Ocean
173 R13 **Heard Island** island Heard and McDonald Islands, S Indian Ocean
25 U9 **Hearne** Texas, SW USA 30°52′N 96°35′W
12 F12 **Hearst** Ontario, S Canada 49°42′N 83°40′W
194 J5 **Hearst Island** island Antarctica
Heart of Dixie see Alabama
28 L5 **Heart River** ↝ North Dakota, N USA
31 T13 **Heath** Ohio, N USA 40°01′N 82°26′W
183 N11 **Heathcote** Victoria, SE Australia 36°57′S 144°43′E
97 N22 **Heathrow** ✈ (London) SE England, United Kingdom 51°28′N 00°27′W
21 X5 **Heathsville** Virginia, NE USA 37°55′N 76°29′W
27 R11 **Heavener** Oklahoma, C USA 34°53′N 94°36′W
25 R15 **Hebbronville** Texas, SW USA 27°19′N 98°41′W
163 Q13 **Hebei** var. Hebei Sheng, Hopeh, Hopei, Ji; prev. Chihli. ◆ province E China
Hebei Sheng see Hebei
36 M3 **Heber City** Utah, W USA 40°31′N 111°25′W
27 V10 **Heber Springs** Arkansas, C USA 35°30′N 92°01′W
161 N5 **Hebi** Henan, C China 35°57′N 114°08′E
32 F11 **Hebo** Oregon, NW USA 45°10′N 123°55′W
96 F9 **Hebrides, Sea of the** sea NW Scotland, United Kingdom
13 P5 **Hebron** Newfoundland and Labrador, E Canada 58°15′N 62°45′W
31 N11 **Hebron** Indiana, N USA 41°19′N 87°12′W
29 Q17 **Hebron** Nebraska, C USA 40°10′N 97°35′W
28 L5 **Hebron** North Dakota, N USA 46°54′N 102°03′W
138 F11 **Hebron** var. Al Khalil, El Khalil, Heb. Hevron; anc. Kiriath-Arba. S West Bank 31°30′N 35°E
Hebrus see Évros/Maritsa/Meriç
95 N14 **Heby** Västmanland, C Sweden 59°56′N 16°53′E
10 I14 **Hecate Strait** strait British Columbia, W Canada
41 W12 **Hecelchakán** Campeche, SE Mexico 20°09′N 90°04′W
160 K13 **Hechi** var. Jinchengjiang. Guangxi Zhuangzu Zizhiqu, S China 24°39′N 108°02′E
101 H23 **Hechingen** Baden-Württemberg, S Germany 48°20′N 08°58′E
99 K17 **Hechtel** Limburg, NE Belgium 51°07′N 05°24′E
160 J9 **Hechuan** var. Heyang. Chongqing Shi, C China 30°02′N 106°15′E
29 P7 **Hecla** South Dakota, N USA 45°52′N 98°09′W
9 N1 **Hecla, Cape** headland Nunavut, N Canada 82°00′N 64°00′W
29 T9 **Hector** Minnesota, N USA 44°44′N 94°43′W
93 F17 **Hede** Jämtland, C Sweden 62°25′N 13°33′E
Hede see Sheyang
95 M14 **Hedemora** Dalarna, C Sweden 60°18′N 15°58′E
92 K13 **Hedenäset** Norrbotten, N Sweden 66°12′N 23°40′E
95 G23 **Hedensted** Vejle, C Denmark 55°47′N 09°43′E
95 N14 **Hedesunda** Gävleborg, C Sweden 60°25′N 17°00′E
95 N14 **Hedesundafjord** ◎ C Sweden
25 O3 **Hedley** Texas, SW USA 34°52′N 100°39′W
94 I12 **Hedmark** ◆ county S Norway
165 T16 **Hedo-misaki** headland Okinawa, SW Japan 26°55′N 128°15′E
29 X15 **Hedrick** Iowa, C USA 41°10′N 92°18′W
99 L16 **Heel** Limburg, SE Netherlands 51°12′N 06°01′E
189 Y12 **Heel Point** point Wake Island
98 H9 **Heemskerk** Noord-Holland, W Netherlands 52°31′N 04°40′E
98 M10 **Heerde** Gelderland, E Netherlands 52°24′N 06°02′E
98 L7 **Heerenveen** Fris. It Hearrenfean. Friesland, N Netherlands 52°57′N 05°55′E
98 I8 **Heerhugowaard** Noord-Holland, NW Netherlands 52°40′N 04°50′E
92 O3 **Heer Land** physical region C Svalbard
99 M18 **Heerlen** Limburg, SE Netherlands 50°55′N 06°E
99 J19 **Heers** Limburg, NE Belgium 50°46′N 05°17′E
Heerwegen see Polkowice
98 K13 **Heesch** Noord-Brabant, S Netherlands 51°44′N 05°32′E
99 K15 **Heeze** Noord-Brabant, SE Netherlands 51°23′N 05°35′E
138 F8 **Hefa** var. Haifa, hist. Caiffa, Caiphas; anc. Sycaminum. Haifa, N Israel 32°49′N 34°59′E
Ḩefa, Mifraz see Mifrats Hefa
161 Q8 **Hefei** var. Hofei, hist. Luchow. province capital Anhui, E China 31°51′N 117°20′E
23 R3 **Heflin** Alabama, S USA 33°39′N 85°35′W
163 X7 **Hegang** Heilongjiang, NE China 47°18′N 130°16′E
164 L10 **Hegura-jima** island SW Japan
Heguri-jima see Heigun-tō
Hei see Heilongjiang
100 H8 **Heide** Schleswig-Holstein, N Germany 54°12′N 09°06′E
101 G20 **Heidelberg** Baden-Württemberg, SW Germany 49°24′N 08°41′E
83 J21 **Heidelberg** Gauteng, NE South Africa 26°31′S 28°21′E
22 M6 **Heidelberg** Mississippi, S USA 31°53′N 88°58′W
Heidenheim see Heidenheim an der Brenz
101 J22 **Heidenheim an der Brenz** var. Heidenheim. Baden-Württemberg, S Germany 48°41′N 10°09′E
109 U2 **Heidenreichstein** Niederösterreich, N Austria 48°53′N 15°07′E
164 F14 **Heigun-tō** var. Heguri-jima. island SW Japan
163 W5 **Heihe** prev. Ai-hun. Heilongjiang, NE China 50°13′N 127°29′E
162 S8 **Hei He** ↝ C China
Hei-ho see Nagqu
83 J22 **Heilbron** Free State, N South Africa 27°17′S 27°58′E
101 H21 **Heilbronn** Baden-Württemberg, SW Germany 49°09′N 09°13′E
Heiligenbeil see Mamonovo
109 Q8 **Heiligenblut** Tirol, W Austria 47°04′N 12°50′E
100 K7 **Heiligenhafen** Schleswig-Holstein, N Germany 54°22′N 10°57′E
Heiligenkreuz see Žiar nad Hronom
101 J15 **Heiligenstadt** Thüringen, C Germany 51°22′N 10°09′E
163 W8 **Heilongjiang** var. Hei, Heilongjiang Sheng, Hei-lung-chiang, Heilungkiang. ◆ province NE China
Heilong Jiang see Amur
Heilongjiang Sheng see Heilongjiang
98 H9 **Heiloo** Noord-Holland, NW Netherlands 52°36′N 04°43′E
Heilsberg see Lidzbark Warmiński
Hei-lung-chiang/Heilungkiang see Heilongjiang
Heimaæy see Heimaey
92 I4 **Heimaey** var. Heimaæy. island S Iceland
94 H8 **Heimdal** Sør-Trøndelag, S Norway 63°21′N 10°23′E
Heinaste see Ainaži
93 N17 **Heinävesi** Itä-Suomi, E Finland 62°22′N 28°42′E
99 M22 **Heinerscheid** Diekirch, N Luxembourg 50°06′N 06°05′E
98 M10 **Heino** Overijssel, E Netherlands 52°26′N 06°13′E
93 M18 **Heinola** Etelä-Suomi, S Finland 61°13′N 26°05′E
101 C16 **Heinsberg** Nordrhein-Westfalen, W Germany 51°02′N 06°01′E
163 U12 **Heishan** Liaoning, NE China 41°43′N 122°12′E
160 H8 **Heishui** var. Luhua. Sichuan, C China 32°08′N 102°54′E
99 H17 **Heist-op-den-Berg** Antwerpen, C Belgium 51°04′N 04°43′E
Heitō see P'ingtung
171 X15 **Heitske** Papua, E Indonesia 07°02′S 138°45′E
Hejanah see Al Hījānah
Hejaz see Al Ḩijāz
160 M14 **He Jiang** ↝ S China
Hejiayan see Lüeyang
158 K6 **Hejing** Xinjiang Uygur Zizhiqu, NW China 42°21′N 86°19′E
Héjjasfalva see Vânători
Heka see Hoika
137 N14 **Hekimhan** Malatya, C Turkey 38°50′N 37°56′E
92 J4 **Hekla** ▲ S Iceland 63°56′N 19°42′W
Hekou see Yanshan, Jiangxi, China
Hekou see Yajiang, Sichuan, China
110 J6 **Hel** Ger. Hela. Pomorskie, N Poland 54°35′N 18°48′E
Hela see Hel
93 F17 **Helagsfjället** ▲ C Sweden 62°57′N 12°31′E
159 W8 **Helan** var. Xigang. Ningxia, N China 38°33′N 106°21′E
162 K14 **Helan Shan** ▲ N China
99 M16 **Helden** Limburg, SE Netherlands 51°20′N 06°00′E
27 X12 **Helena** Arkansas, C USA 34°32′N 90°34′W
33 R10 **Helena** state capital Montana, NW USA 46°36′N 112°02′W
96 H12 **Helensburgh** W Scotland, United Kingdom 56°00′N 04°45′W
184 K5 **Helensville** Auckland, North Island, New Zealand 36°42′S 174°26′E
95 L20 **Helgasjön** ◎ S Sweden
100 G8 **Helgoland** Eng. Heligoland. island NW Germany
Helgoland Bay see Helgoländer Bucht
100 G8 **Helgoländer Bucht** var. Helgoland Bay, Heligoland Bight. bay NW Germany
Heligoland see Helgoland
Heligoland Bight see Helgoländer Bucht
Heliopolis see Baalbek
92 I4 **Hella** Sudhurland, SW Iceland 63°51′N 20°24′W
Hellas see Greece
143 N11 **Ḩelleh, Rūd-e** ↝ S Iran
98 N10 **Hellendoorn** Overijssel, E Netherlands 52°22′N 06°27′E
Hellenic Republic see Greece
121 Q10 **Hellenic Trough** undersea feature Aegean Sea, C Mediterranean Sea 22°00′E 35°30′N
94 E10 **Hellesylt** Møre og Romsdal, S Norway 62°06′N 06°51′E
98 F13 **Hellevoetsluis** Zuid-Holland, SW Netherlands 51°49′N 04°08′E
105 Q12 **Hellín** Castilla-La Mancha, C Spain 38°31′N 01°43′W
115 H19 **Hellinikon** ✈ (Athína) Attikí, C Greece 37°53′N 23°43′E
32 M12 **Hells Canyon** valley Idaho/Oregon, NW USA
148 L9 **Helmand** ◆ province S Afghanistan
148 K10 **Helmand, Daryā-ye** var. Rūd-e Hirmand. ↝ Afghanistan/Iran see also Hirmand, Rūd-e
Helmand, Daryā-ye see Hirmand, Rūd-e
Helmantica see Salamanca
101 K15 **Helme** ↝ C Germany
99 L15 **Helmond** Noord-Brabant, S Netherlands 51°29′N 05°41′E
96 J7 **Helmsdale** N Scotland, United Kingdom 58°06′N 03°36′W
100 K13 **Helmstedt** Niedersachsen, N Germany 52°14′N 11°01′E
163 Y10 **Helong** Jilin, NE China 42°38′N 129°01′E
36 M4 **Helper** Utah, W USA 39°40′N 110°52′W
100 O10 **Helpter Berge** hill NE Germany
95 J22 **Helsingborg** prev. Hälsingborg. Skåne, S Sweden 56°N 12°48′E
Helsingfors see Helsinki
95 J22 **Helsingør** Eng. Elsinore. Frederiksborg, E Denmark 56°03′N 12°38′E
93 M20 **Helsinki** Swe. Helsingfors. ● (Finland) Etelä-Suomi, S Finland 60°18′N 24°58′E
97 H25 **Helston** SW England, United Kingdom 50°04′N 05°17′W
Heltau see Cisnădie
61 C17 **Helvecia** Santa Fe, C Argentina 31°09′S 60°09′W

97 K15 **Helvellyn** ▲ NW England, United Kingdom 54°31′N 03°00′W
Helvetia *see* Switzerland
Helwân *see* Hilwān
97 N21 **Hemel Hempstead** E England, United Kingdom 51°46′N 00°28′W
35 U16 **Hemet** California, W USA 33°45′N 116°58′W
28 J13 **Hemingford** Nebraska, C USA 42°18′N 103°02′W
21 T13 **Hemingway** South Carolina, SE USA 33°45′N 79°25′W
92 G13 **Hemnesberget** Nordland, C Norway 66°14′N 13°40′E
25 Y8 **Hemphill** Texas, SW USA 31°21′N 93°50′W
25 V11 **Hempstead** Texas, SW USA 30°06′N 96°06′W
95 P20 **Hemse** Gotland, SE Sweden 57°12′N 18°22′E
94 F13 **Hemsedal** *valley* S Norway
161 N6 **Henan** *var.* Henan Sheng, Honan, Yu. ◆ *province* C China
184 L4 **Hen and Chickens** *island group* N New Zealand
Henan Mongolzu Zizhixian/Henan Sheng *see* Yêgainnyin
105 O7 **Henares** ≈ C Spain
165 P7 **Henashi-zaki** *headland* Honshū, C Japan 40°37′N 139°51′E
102 I16 **Hendaye** Pyrénées-Atlantiques, SW France 43°22′N 01°46′W
136 F11 **Hendek** Sakarya, NW Turkey 40°47′N 30°45′E
61 B21 **Henderson** Buenos Aires, E Argentina 36°18′S 61°43′W
20 I5 **Henderson** Kentucky, S USA 37°50′N 87°35′W
35 X11 **Henderson** Nevada, W USA 36°02′N 114°58′W
21 V8 **Henderson** North Carolina, SE USA 36°20′N 78°26′W
20 G10 **Henderson** Tennessee, S USA 35°27′N 88°40′W
25 W7 **Henderson** Texas, SW USA 32°11′N 94°48′W
30 J12 **Henderson Creek** ≈ Illinois, N USA
186 M9 **Henderson Field** ✈ (Honiara) Guadalcanal, C Solomon Islands 09°28′S 160°02′E
191 O17 **Henderson Island** *atoll* N Pitcairn Islands
21 O10 **Hendersonville** North Carolina, SE USA 35°19′N 82°28′W
20 J8 **Hendersonville** Tennessee, S USA 36°18′N 86°37′W
143 O14 **Hendorābī, Jazīreh-ye** *island* S Iran
55 V10 **Hendrik Top** *var.* Hendriktop. *elevation* C Surinam
Hendriktop *see* Hendrik Top
Hendû Kosh *see* Hindu Kush
14 L12 **Heney, Lac** ◎ Québec, SE Canada
Hengchow *see* Hengyang
161 S15 **Hengchun** S Taiwan 22°09′N 120°43′E
159 R16 **Hengduan Shan** ▲▲ SW China
98 N12 **Hengelo** Gelderland, E Netherlands 52°03′N 06°19′E
98 O10 **Hengelo** Overijssel, E Netherlands 52°16′N 06°46′E
Hengnan *see* Hengyang
161 N11 **Hengshan** Hunan, S China 27°17′N 112°51′E
160 L4 **Hengshan** Shaanxi, C China 37°57′N 109°17′E
161 O4 **Hengshui** Hebei, E China 37°42′N 115°39′E
161 N12 **Hengyang** *var.* Hengnan, Heng-yang; *prev.* Hengchow. Hunan, S China 26°55′N 112°34′E
Heng-yang *see* Hengyang
117 U11 **Heniches'k** *Rus.* Genichesk. Khersons'ka Oblast', S Ukraine 46°10′N 34°49′E
21 Z4 **Henlopen, Cape** *headland* Delaware, NE USA 38°48′N 75°06′W
Henna *see* Enna
94 M10 **Hennan** Gävleborg, C Sweden 62°01′N 15°55′E
102 G7 **Hennebont** Morbihan, NW France 47°48′N 03°17′W
30 L11 **Hennepin** Illinois, N USA 41°14′N 89°21′W
26 M9 **Hennessey** Oklahoma, C USA 36°06′N 97°54′W
100 N12 **Hennigsdorf** *var.* Hennigsdorf bei Berlin. Brandenburg, NE Germany 52°37′N 13°13′E
Hennigsdorf bei Berlin *see* Hennigsdorf
19 N9 **Henniker** New Hampshire, NE USA 43°10′N 71°47′W
25 S5 **Henrietta** Texas, SW USA 33°49′N 98°13′W
Henrique de Carvalho *see* Saurimo
30 L12 **Henry** Illinois, N USA 41°06′N 89°21′W
21 Y7 **Henry, Cape** *headland* Virginia, NE USA 36°55′N 76°01′W
27 P10 **Henryetta** Oklahoma, C USA 35°26′N 95°58′W
194 M7 **Henry Ice Rise** *ice cap* Antarctica
9 R5 **Henry Kater, Cape** *headland* Baffin Island, Nunavut, NE Canada 69°09′N 66°45′W
33 R13 **Henrys Fork** ≈ Idaho, NW USA
14 E15 **Hensall** Ontario, S Canada 43°25′N 81°28′W
100 J9 **Henstedt-Ulzburg** Schleswig-Holstein, N Germany 53°45′N 09°59′E
163 N7 **Hentiy** *var.* Batshireet, Eg. ◆ *province* N Mongolia
162 M7 **Hentiyn Nuruu** ▲▲ N Mongolia
183 P10 **Henty** New South Wales, SE Australia 35°33′S 147°03′E
Henzada *see* Hinthada
Heping *see* Huishui
101 G19 **Heppenheim** Hessen, W Germany 49°39′N 08°38′E
32 J11 **Heppner** Oregon, NW USA 45°21′N 119°32′W
160 L15 **Hepu** *var.* Lianzhou. Guangxi Zhuangzu Zizhiqu, S China 21°40′N 109°12′E
Heracleum *see* Irákleio
92 J2 **Heradhsvötn** ≈ C Iceland
Herakleion *see* Irákleio
148 K5 **Herāt** *var.* Herat; *anc.* Aria. Herāt, W Afghanistan 34°23′N 62°11′E
148 J5 **Herāt** ◆ *province* W Afghanistan
103 P14 **Hérault** ◆ *department* S France
103 P15 **Hérault** ≈ S France
11 T16 **Herbert** Saskatchewan, S Canada 50°27′N 107°09′W
185 F22 **Herbert** Otago, South Island, New Zealand 45°14′S 170°48′E
38 J17 **Herbert Island** *island* Aleutian Islands, Alaska, USA
Herbertshöhe *see* Kokopo
15 Q7 **Hérbertville** Québec, SE Canada 48°23′N 71°42′W
101 G17 **Herborn** Hessen, W Germany 50°40′N 08°18′E
113 I17 **Herceg-Novi** *It.* Castelnuovo; *prev.* Ercegnovi. SW Montenegro 42°28′N 18°35′E
11 X10 **Herchmer** Manitoba, C Canada 57°25′N 94°12′W
186 E8 **Hercules Bay** *bay* E Papua New Guinea
92 K2 **Herdhubreidh** ▲ C Iceland 65°12′N 16°26′W
42 M13 **Heredia** Heredia, C Costa Rica 10°N 84°06′W
42 M12 **Heredia** *off.* Provincia de Heredia. ◆ *province* N Costa Rica
Heredia, Provincia de *see* Heredia
97 K21 **Hereford** W England, United Kingdom 52°04′N 02°43′W
24 M3 **Hereford** Texas, SW USA 34°49′N 102°25′W
15 Q13 **Hereford, Mont** ▲ Québec, SE Canada 45°04′N 71°38′W
97 K21 **Herefordshire** *cultural region* W England, United Kingdom
191 U11 **Hereheretue** *atoll* Îles Tuamotu, C French Polynesia
105 N10 **Herencia** Castilla-La Mancha, C Spain 39°22′N 03°12′W
99 H18 **Herent** Vlaams Brabant, C Belgium 50°54′N 04°40′E
99 I16 **Herentals** *var.* Herenthals. Antwerpen, N Belgium 51°11′N 04°50′E
Herenthals *see* Herentals
99 H17 **Herenthout** Antwerpen, N Belgium 51°09′N 04°45′E
95 J23 **Herfølge** Roskilde, E Denmark 55°25′N 12°09′E
100 G13 **Herford** Nordrhein-Westfalen, NW Germany 52°07′N 08°41′E
27 O5 **Herington** Kansas, C USA 38°37′N 96°55′W
108 H7 **Herisau** *Fr.* Hérisau. Appenzell Ausser Rhoden, NE Switzerland 47°23′N 09°17′E
Hérisau *see* Herisau
Héristal *see* Herstal
99 J18 **Herk-de-Stad** Limburg, NE Belgium 50°57′N 05°12′E
Herkulesbad/Herkulesfürdő *see* Băile Herculane
162 M8 **Herlenbayan-Ulaan** *var.* Dulaan. Hentiy, C Mongolia 47°09′N 108°48′E
Herlen Gol/Herlen He *see* Kerulen
35 Q4 **Herlong** California, W USA 40°07′N 120°06′W
97 L26 **Herm** *island* Channel Islands
109 R9 **Hermagor** *Slvn.* Šmohor. Kärnten, S Austria 46°37′N 13°24′E
29 S7 **Herman** Minnesota, N USA 45°49′N 96°08′W
96 L1 **Herma Ness** *headland* NE Scotland, United Kingdom 60°51′N 00°55′W
27 V4 **Hermann** Missouri, C USA 38°43′N 91°26′W
181 Q8 **Hermannsburg** Northern Territory, N Australia 23°59′S 132°55′E
Hermannstadt *see* Sibiu
94 E12 **Hermansverk** Sogn Og Fjordane, S Norway 61°11′N 06°52′E
138 H6 **Hermel** *var.* Hirmil. NE Lebanon 34°23′N 36°19′E
Hermhausen *see* Hajnówka
183 P6 **Hermidale** New South Wales, SE Australia 31°36′S 146°42′E
55 X9 **Herminadorp** Sipaliwini, NE Surinam 05°05′N 54°22′W
32 K11 **Hermiston** Oregon, NW USA 45°50′N 119°17′W
27 T6 **Hermitage** Missouri, C USA 37°57′N 93°21′W
186 D4 **Hermit Islands** *island group* N Papua New Guinea
25 O7 **Hermleigh** Texas, SW USA 32°37′N 100°44′W
138 G7 **Hermon, Mount** *Ar.* Jabal ash Shaykh. ▲ S Syria 35°30′N 33°30′E
Hermopolis Parva *see* Damanhûr
28 J10 **Hermosa** South Dakota, N USA 43°49′N 103°12′W
40 F5 **Hermosillo** Sonora, NW Mexico 28°59′N 110°53′W
Hermoupolis *see* Ermoúpoli
111 N20 **Hernád** *var.* Hornád, *Ger.* Kundert. ≈ Hungary/Slovakia
61 C18 **Hernández** Entre Ríos, E Argentina 32°21′S 60°02′W
23 V11 **Hernando** Florida, SE USA 28°54′N 82°22′W
22 L1 **Hernando** Mississippi, S USA 34°49′N 89°59′W
105 Q2 **Hernani** País Vasco, N Spain 43°16′N 01°59′W
99 F19 **Herne** Vlaams Brabant, C Belgium 50°45′N 04°03′E
101 E14 **Herne** Nordrhein-Westfalen, W Germany 51°32′N 07°12′E
95 F22 **Herning** Ringkøbing, W Denmark 56°08′N 08°59′E
Hernösand *see* Härnösand
121 U11 **Herodotus Basin** *undersea feature* E Mediterranean Sea
121 Q12 **Herodotus Trough** *undersea feature* C Mediterranean Sea
29 T11 **Heron Lake** Minnesota, N USA 43°48′N 95°18′W
Herowābād *see* Khalkhāl
95 G16 **Herre** Telemark, S Norway 59°06′N 09°34′E
29 N7 **Herreid** South Dakota, N USA 45°49′N 100°04′W
101 H22 **Herrenberg** Baden-Württemberg, S Germany 48°36′N 08°52′E
104 L14 **Herrera** Andalucía, S Spain 37°22′N 04°50′W
43 R17 **Herrera** *off.* Provincia de Herrera. ◆ *province* S Panama
104 L10 **Herrera del Duque** Extremadura, W Spain 39°10′N 05°03′W
104 M4 **Herrera de Pisuerga** Castilla-León, N Spain 42°35′N 04°20′W
Herrera, Provincia de *see* Herrera
41 Z13 **Herrero, Punta** *headland* SE Mexico 19°15′N 87°28′W
183 P16 **Herrick** Tasmania, SE Australia 41°07′S 147°53′E
30 L17 **Herrin** Illinois, N USA 37°48′N 89°01′W
20 M6 **Herrington Lake** ⊠ Kentucky, S USA
95 K18 **Herrljunga** Västra Götaland, S Sweden 58°05′N 13°02′E
103 N16 **Hers** ≈ S France
10 I1 **Herschel Island** *island* Yukon Territory, NW Canada
99 I17 **Herselt** Antwerpen, C Belgium 51°04′N 04°53′E
18 G15 **Hershey** Pennsylvania, NE USA 40°17′N 76°39′W
99 K19 **Herstal** *Fr.* Héristal. Liège, E Belgium 50°40′N 05°38′E
97 O21 **Hertford** E England, United Kingdom 51°48′N 00°05′W
21 X8 **Hertford** North Carolina, SE USA 36°11′N 76°30′W
97 O21 **Hertfordshire** *cultural region* E England, United Kingdom
181 Z9 **Hervey Bay** Queensland, E Australia 25°17′S 152°48′E
101 O14 **Herzberg** Brandenburg, E Germany 51°42′N 13°15′E
99 E18 **Herzele** Oost-Vlaanderen, NW Belgium 50°52′N 03°52′E
101 K20 **Herzogenaurach** Bayern, SE Germany 49°34′N 10°52′E
109 W4 **Herzogenburg** Niederösterreich, NE Austria 48°18′N 15°43′E
Herzogenbusch *see* 's-Hertogenbosch
103 N2 **Hesdin** Pas-de-Calais, N France 50°21′N 02°00′E
160 K14 **Heshan** Guangxi Zhuangzu Zizhiqu, S China 23°45′N 108°58′E
159 X10 **Heshui** *var.* Xihuachi. Gansu, C China 35°42′N 108°06′E
99 M25 **Hespérange** Luxembourg, SE Luxembourg 49°34′N 06°10′E
35 U14 **Hesperia** California, W USA 34°25′N 117°17′W
37 P7 **Hesperus Mountain** ▲ Colorado, C USA 37°27′N 108°05′W
10 J6 **Hess** ≈ Yukon Territory, NW Canada
Hesse *see* Hessen
101 J21 **Hesselberg** ▲ S Germany 49°04′N 10°32′E
95 I22 **Hesselø** *island* E Denmark
101 H17 **Hessen** *Eng./Fr.* Hesse. ◆ *state* C Germany
192 L6 **Hess Tablemount** *undersea feature* C Pacific Ocean 17°49′N 174°15′W
27 N6 **Hesston** Kansas, C USA 38°08′N 97°25′W
93 G15 **Hestkjøltoppen** ▲ C Norway 64°21′N 13°57′E
97 K18 **Heswall** NW England, United Kingdom 53°20′N 03°06′W
153 P12 **Hetauda** Central, C Nepal
Hétfalu *see* Săcele
28 K7 **Hettinger** North Dakota, N USA 46°00′N 102°38′W
101 L14 **Hettstedt** Sachsen-Anhalt, C Germany 51°39′N 11°31′E
92 P3 **Heuglin, Kapp** *headland* SE Svalbard 78°15′N 22°49′E
187 N10 **Heuru** San Cristobal, SE Solomon Islands 10°13′S 161°25′E
99 J17 **Heusden** Limburg, NE Belgium 51°02′N 05°17′E
98 J13 **Heusden** Noord-Brabant, S Netherlands 51°43′N 05°05′E
102 K3 **Hève, Cap de la** *headland* N France 49°28′N 00°13′W
99 H18 **Heverlee** Vlaams Brabant, C Belgium 50°52′N 04°41′E
111 L22 **Heves** Heves, NE Hungary 47°36′N 20°17′E
111 L22 **Heves** *off.* Heves Megye. ◆ *county* NE Hungary
Heves Megye *see* Heves
Hevron *see* Hebron
45 Y13 **Hewanorra** ✈ (Saint Lucia) S Saint Lucia 13°44′N 60°57′W
Hexian *see* Hezhou
160 L6 **Heyang** Shaanxi, C China 35°14′N 110°02′E
Heyang *see* Hechuan
Heydebrech *see* Kędzierzyn-Kozle
Heydekrug *see* Šilutė
Heyin *see* Guide
97 K16 **Heysham** NW England, United Kingdom 54°02′N 02°54′W
161 O14 **Heyuan** *var.* Yuancheng. Guangdong, S China 23°41′N 114°45′E
182 L12 **Heywood** Victoria, SE Australia 38°09′S 141°38′E
180 K3 **Heywood Islands** *island group* Western Australia
161 O6 **Heze** *var.* Caozhou. Shandong, E China 35°16′N 115°27′E
159 U11 **Hezheng** Gansu, C China 35°29′N 103°36′E
160 M13 **Hezhou** *var.* Babu; *prev.* Hexian. Guangxi Zhuangzu Zizhiqu, S China 24°33′N 111°30′E
159 U11 **Hezuo** Gansu, C China 34°55′N 102°49′E
23 Z16 **Hialeah** Florida, SE USA 25°51′N 80°16′W
27 Q3 **Hiawatha** Kansas, C USA 39°51′N 95°34′W
36 M4 **Hiawatha** Utah, W USA 39°28′N 111°00′W
29 V4 **Hibbing** Minnesota, N USA 47°24′N 92°55′W
183 N17 **Hibbs, Point** *headland* Tasmania, SE Australia 42°37′S 145°15′E
Hibernia *see* Ireland
20 F8 **Hickman** Kentucky, S USA 36°33′N 89°11′W
21 Q9 **Hickory** North Carolina, SE USA 35°44′N 81°20′W
21 Q9 **Hickory, Lake** ◎ North Carolina, SE USA
184 Q7 **Hicks Bay** Gisborne, North Island, New Zealand 37°36′S 178°18′E
25 S8 **Hico** Texas, SW USA 31°58′N 98°01′W
Hida *see* Furukawa
165 T4 **Hidaka** Hokkaidō, NE Japan 42°53′N 142°24′E
164 I12 **Hidaka** Hyōgo, Honshū, SW Japan 35°27′N 134°43′E
165 T5 **Hidaka-sanmyaku** ▲▲ Hokkaidō, NE Japan
41 O6 **Hidalgo** *var.* Villa Hidalgo. Coahuila, NE Mexico 27°46′N 99°54′W
41 N8 **Hidalgo** Nuevo León, NE Mexico 29°59′N 100°27′W
41 O10 **Hidalgo** Tamaulipas, C Mexico 24°16′N 99°28′W
41 O13 **Hidalgo** ◆ *state* C Mexico
40 J7 **Hidalgo del Parral** *var.* Parral. Chihuahua, N Mexico 26°58′N 105°40′W
100 N7 **Hiddensee** *island* NE Germany
80 G6 **Hidiglib, Wadi** ≈ NE Sudan
109 U6 **Hieflau** Salzburg, E Austria 47°36′N 14°34′E
187 P16 **Hienghène** Province Nord, C New Caledonia 20°43′S 164°54′E
Hierosolyma *see* Jerusalem
64 N12 **Hierro** *var.* Ferro. *island* Islas Canarias, Spain, NE Atlantic Ocean
164 G13 **Higashi-Hiroshima** *var.* Higasihiroshima. Hiroshima, Honshū, SW Japan 34°27′N 132°43′E
164 C12 **Higashi-suidō** *strait* SW Japan
Higasihiroshima *see* Higashi-Hiroshima
25 P1 **Higgins** Texas, SW USA 36°06′N 100°01′W
31 P7 **Higgins Lake** ◎ Michigan, N USA
27 S4 **Higginsville** Missouri, C USA 39°04′N 93°43′W
High Atlas *see* Haut Atlas
30 M5 **High Falls Reservoir** ⊠ Wisconsin, N USA
44 K12 **Highgate** C Jamaica 18°16′N 76°53′W
25 X11 **High Island** Texas, SW USA 29°35′N 94°24′W
31 O5 **High Island** *island* Michigan, N USA
30 K15 **Highland** Illinois, N USA 38°44′N 89°40′W
31 N10 **Highland Park** Illinois, N USA 42°10′N 87°48′W
21 O10 **Highlands** North Carolina, SE USA 35°04′N 83°10′W
11 O11 **High Level** Alberta, W Canada 58°31′N 117°08′W
29 O9 **Highmore** South Dakota, N USA 44°29′N 99°26′W
171 N3 **High Peak** ▲ Luzon, N Philippines 15°28′N 120°07′E
High Plains *see* Great Plains
21 S9 **High Point** North Carolina, SE USA 35°58′N 80°00′W
18 J13 **High Point** *hill* New Jersey, NE USA
11 P13 **High Prairie** Alberta, W Canada 55°27′N 116°28′W
11 Q16 **High River** Alberta, SW Canada 50°35′N 113°50′W
21 S9 **High Rock Lake** ⊠ North Carolina, SE USA
23 V9 **High Springs** Florida, SE USA 29°49′N 82°36′W
High Veld *see* Great Karoo
97 J24 **High Willhays** ▲ SW England, United Kingdom 50°39′N 03°58′W
97 N22 **High Wycombe** *prev.* Chepping Wycombe, Chipping Wycombe. SE England, United Kingdom 51°38′N 00°46′W
41 P12 **Higos** *var.* El Higo. Veracruz-Llave, E Mexico 21°48′N 98°25′W
102 I16 **Higuer, Cap** *headland* NE Spain 43°23′N 01°46′W
45 R5 **Higüero, Punta** *headland* W Puerto Rico 18°21′N 67°15′W
45 P9 **Higüey** *var.* Salvaleón de Higüey. E Dominican Republic 18°40′N 68°43′W
190 G11 **Hihifo** ✈ (Matā'utu) Île Uvea, N Wallis and Futuna
81 N16 **Hiiraan** *off.* Gobolka Hiiraan. ◆ *region* C Somalia
Hiiraan, Gobolka *see* Hiiraan
118 E4 **Hiiumaa** *var.* Hiiumaa Maakond. ◆ *province* W Estonia
118 D4 **Hiiumaa** *Ger.* Dagden, *Swe.* Dagö. *island* W Estonia
Hiiumaa Maakond *see* Hiiumaa
Hijanah *see* Al Hījānah
105 S6 **Híjar** Aragón, NE Spain 41°10′N 00°27′W
191 V10 **Hikueru** *atoll* Îles Tuamotu, C French Polynesia
184 K3 **Hikurangi** Northland, North Island, New Zealand 35°37′S 174°16′E
184 Q8 **Hikurangi** ▲ North Island, New Zealand 37°55′S 177°59′E
192 L11 **Hikurangi Trench** *var.* Hikurangi Trough. *undersea feature* SW Pacific Ocean
Hikurangi Trough *see* Hikurangi Trench
190 B15 **Hikutavake** NW Niue
121 Q12 **Hilāl, Ra's al** *headland* N Libya 32°55′N 22°09′E
61 A24 **Hilario Ascasubi** Buenos Aires, E Argentina 39°22′S 62°39′W
101 K17 **Hildburghausen** Thüringen, C Germany 50°26′N 10°44′E
101 E15 **Hilden** Nordrhein-Westfalen, W Germany 51°12′N 06°56′E
100 I13 **Hildesheim** Niedersachsen, N Germany 52°09′N 09°57′E
33 T9 **Hilger** Montana, NW USA 47°15′N 109°18′W
153 S13 **Hili** *var.* Hilli. Rajshahi, NW Bangladesh 25°16′N 89°04′E
Hilla *see* Al Ḩillah
45 O14 **Hillaby, Mount** ▲ N Barbados 13°12′N 59°34′W
95 K19 **Hillared** Västra Götaland, S Sweden 57°37′N 13°10′E
195 R12 **Hillary Coast** *physical region* Antarctica
42 G2 **Hill Bank** Orange Walk, N Belize 17°36′N 88°43′W
33 O14 **Hill City** Idaho, NW USA 43°18′N 115°03′W
26 K3 **Hill City** Kansas, C USA 39°23′N 99°51′W
29 V5 **Hill City** Minnesota, N USA 46°59′N 93°36′W
28 J10 **Hill City** South Dakota, N USA 43°54′N 103°33′W
98 H10 **Hillegom** Zuid-Holland, W Netherlands 52°18′N 04°35′E
95 J22 **Hillerød** Frederiksborg, E Denmark 55°56′N 12°19′E
36 M7 **Hillers, Mount** ▲ Utah, W USA 37°53′N 110°42′W
Hilli *see* Hili
29 R11 **Hills** Minnesota, N USA 43°31′N 96°21′W
30 L14 **Hillsboro** Illinois, N USA 39°09′N 89°29′W
27 N5 **Hillsboro** Kansas, C USA 38°21′N 97°12′W
27 X5 **Hillsboro** Missouri, C USA 38°13′N 90°33′W
19 N10 **Hillsboro** New Hampshire, NE USA 43°06′N 71°52′W
37 Q14 **Hillsboro** New Mexico, SW USA 32°55′N 107°33′W
29 R4 **Hillsboro** North Dakota, N USA 47°25′N 97°03′W
31 R14 **Hillsboro** Ohio, N USA 39°12′N 83°36′W
32 G11 **Hillsboro** Oregon, NW USA 45°32′N 122°59′W
25 T8 **Hillsboro** Texas, SW USA 32°01′N 97°08′W
30 K8 **Hillsboro** Wisconsin, N USA 43°40′N 90°21′W
23 Y14 **Hillsboro Canal** *canal* Florida, SE USA
45 Y15 **Hillsborough** Carriacou, N Grenada 12°28′N 61°28′W
97 G15 **Hillsborough** E Northern Ireland, United Kingdom 54°27′N 06°06′W
21 U9 **Hillsborough** North Carolina, SE USA 36°04′N 79°06′W
31 Q10 **Hillsdale** Michigan, N USA 41°55′N 84°37′W
183 O8 **Hillston** New South Wales, SE Australia 33°30′S 145°33′E
21 R7 **Hillsville** Virginia, NE USA 36°46′N 80°44′W
96 L2 **Hillswick** NE Scotland, United Kingdom 60°28′N 01°37′W
Hill Tippera *see* Tripura
38 H11 **Hilo** Hawaii, USA, C Pacific Ocean 19°42′N 155°04′W
18 F9 **Hilton** New York, NE USA 43°17′N 77°47′W
14 C10 **Hilton Beach** Ontario, S Canada 46°14′N 83°51′W
21 R16 **Hilton Head Island** South Carolina, SE USA 32°13′N 80°45′W
21 R16 **Hilton Head Island** *island* South Carolina, SE USA
99 J15 **Hilvarenbeek** Noord-Brabant, S Netherlands 51°29′N 05°08′E
98 J11 **Hilversum** Noord-Holland, C Netherlands 52°14′N 05°10′E
75 W8 **Hilwān** *var.* Helwân, Hulwan, Hulwân. N Egypt 29°51′N 31°20′E
Hilwân *see* Hilwān
152 J7 **Himāchal Pradesh** ◆ *state* NW India
Himalaya/Himalaya Shan *see* Himalayas
152 M9 **Himalayas** *var.* Himalaya, *Chin.* Himalaya Shan. ▲▲ S Asia
171 P6 **Himamaylan** Negros, C Philippines 10°04′N 122°52′E
93 K15 **Himanka** Länsi-Suomi, W Finland 64°04′N 23°40′E
Himara *see* Himarë
113 L23 **Himarë** *var.* Himara. Vlorë, S Albania 40°06′N 19°45′E
138 M2 **Ḩimār, Wādī al** *dry watercourse* N Syria
154 D9 **Himatnagar** Gujarāt, W India 23°38′N 73°02′E
109 Y4 **Himberg** Niederösterreich, E Austria 48°05′N 16°27′E
164 I13 **Himeji** *var.* Himezi. Hyōgo, Honshū, SW Japan 34°47′N 134°32′E
164 E14 **Hime-jima** *island* SW Japan
Himezi *see* Himeji
164 L13 **Himi** Toyama, Honshū, SW Japan 36°54′N 136°59′E
109 S9 **Himmelberg** Kärnten, S Austria 46°45′N 14°01′E
138 I5 **Ḩimş** *var.* Homs; *anc.* Emesa. Ḩimş, C Syria 34°44′N 36°43′E
138 K6 **Ḩimş** *off.* Muḩāfazat Hims, *var.* Homs. ◆ *governorate* C Syria
138 I5 **Ḩimş, Buḩayrat** *var.* Buhayrat Qattinah. ◎ W Syria
171 R7 **Hinatuan** Mindanao, S Philippines 08°21′N 126°19′E
117 N10 **Hînceşti** *var.* Hânceşti; *prev.* Kotovsk. C Moldova 46°48′N 28°33′E
44 M9 **Hinche** C Haiti 19°07′N 72°00′W
181 X5 **Hinchinbrook Island** *island* Queensland, NE Australia
39 S12 **Hinchinbrook Island** *island* Alaska, USA
97 M19 **Hinckley** C England, United Kingdom 52°33′N 01°21′W
29 V7 **Hinckley** Minnesota, N USA 46°01′N 92°57′W
36 K5 **Hinckley** Utah, W USA 39°21′N 112°39′W
18 J9 **Hinckley Reservoir** ⊠ New York, NE USA
152 I12 **Hindaun** Rājasthān, N India 26°44′N 77°02′E
Hindenburg/Hindenburg in Oberschlesien *see* Zabrze
Hindiya *see* Al Hindīyah
21 O6 **Hindman** Kentucky, S USA 37°20′N 82°58′W
182 L10 **Hindmarsh, Lake** ◎ Victoria, SE Australia
185 G19 **Hinds** Canterbury, South Island, New Zealand 44°01′S 171°33′E
185 G19 **Hinds** ≈ South Island, New Zealand
95 H23 **Hindsholm** *island* C Denmark
149 S4 **Hindu Kush** *Per.* Hendû Kosh. ▲▲ Afghanistan/Pakistan
155 H19 **Hindupur** Andhra Pradesh, E India 13°46′N 77°33′E
11 O12 **Hines Creek** Alberta, W Canada 56°14′N 118°36′W
23 W6 **Hinesville** Georgia, SE USA 31°51′N 81°36′W
154 I12 **Hinganghāt** Mahārāshtra, C India 20°32′N 78°52′E
149 N15 **Hingol** ≈ SW Pakistan
154 H13 **Hingoli** Mahārāshtra, C India 19°45′N 77°08′E
137 R13 **Hınıs** Erzurum, E Turkey 39°22′N 41°44′E
92 O2 **Hinlopenstretet** *strait* N Svalbard
92 G10 **Hinnøya** *Lapp.* Iinnasuolu. *island* C Norway
108 H10 **Hinterrhein** ≈ SW Switzerland
166 L8 **Hinthada** *var.* Henzada. Ayeyarwady, SW Burma (Myanmar) 17°36′N 95°26′E
11 O14 **Hinton** Alberta, SW Canada 53°24′N 117°35′W
26 M10 **Hinton** Oklahoma, C USA 35°28′N 98°21′W
21 R6 **Hinton** West Virginia, NE USA 37°42′N 80°54′W
Hios *see* Chíos
41 N8 **Hipolito** Coahuila, NE Mexico 25°42′N 101°22′W
Hipponium *see* Vibo Valentia
164 B13 **Hirado** Nagasaki, Hirado-shima, SW Japan 33°22′N 129°31′E
164 B13 **Hirado-shima** *island* SW Japan
165 P16 **Hirakubo-saki** *headland* Ishigaki-jima, SW Japan 24°36′N 124°19′E
154 M11 **Hīrākud Reservoir** ⊠ E India
Hir al Gharbi, Qasr al *see* Ḩayr al Gharbī, Qaşr al
165 Q16 **Hirara** Okinawa, Miyako-jima, SW Japan 24°48′N 125°17′E
Hir Ash Sharqī, Qasr al *see* Ḩayr ash Sharqī, Qaşr al
164 G12 **Hirata** Shimane, Honshū, SW Japan 35°25′N 132°45′E
136 J13 **Hirfanlı Barajı** ⊠ C Turkey
155 G18 **Hiriyūr** Karnātaka, W India 13°58′N 76°33′E
Hîrlău *see* Hârlău
148 K10 **Hirmand, Rūd-e** *var.* Daryā-ye Helmand. ≈ Afghanistan/Iran *see also* Helmand, Daryā-ye
Hīrmand, Rūd-e *see* Helmand, Daryā-ye
Hirmil *see* Hermel
165 T5 **Hiroo** Hokkaidō, NE Japan 42°16′N 143°16′E
165 Q7 **Hirosaki** Aomori, Honshū, C Japan 40°34′N 140°28′E
164 G13 **Hiroshima** *var.* Hirosima. Hiroshima, Honshū, SW Japan 34°23′N 132°26′E
164 F13 **Hiroshima** *off.* Hiroshima-ken, *var.* Hirosima. ◆ *prefecture* Honshū, SW Japan
Hiroshima-ken *see* Hiroshima
Hirosima *see* Hiroshima
Hirschberg/Hirschberg im Riesengebirge/Hirschberg in Schlesien *see* Jelenia Góra
103 Q3 **Hirson** Aisne, N France 49°56′N 04°05′E
Hirşova *see* Hârşova
95 G19 **Hirtshals** Nordjylland, N Denmark 57°34′N 09°58′E
152 H10 **Hisār** Haryāna, NW India 29°10′N 75°45′E
162 K7 **Hishig Öndör** *var.* Maanit. Bulgan, C Mongolia 48°17′N 103°29′E
186 E9 **Hisiu** Central, SW Papua New Guinea 09°20′S 146°48′E
147 P13 **Hisor** *Rus.* Gissar. W Tajikistan 38°34′N 68°29′E
Hispalis *see* Sevilla
Hispana/Hispania *see* Spain
44 M7 **Hispaniola** *island* Dominion Republic/Haiti
64 F11 **Hispaniola Basin** *var.* Hispaniola Trough. *undersea feature* SW Atlantic Ocean
Hispaniola Trough *see* Hispaniola Basin
Histonium *see* Vasto
139 R7 **Hīt** Al Anbār, SW Iraq 33°38′N 42°50′E
165 P14 **Hita** Ōita, Kyūshū, SW Japan 33°19′N 130°55′E
165 P12 **Hitachi** *var.* Hitati. Ibaraki, Honshū, S Japan 36°40′N 140°42′E
165 P12 **Hitachi-Ōta** *var.* Hitatiôta. Ibaraki, Honshū, S Japan 36°32′N 140°31′E
Hitati *see* Hitachi
Hitatiôta *see* Hitachi-Ōta
97 O21 **Hitchin** E England, United Kingdom 51°57′N 00°17′W
191 Q7 **Hitiaa** Tahiti, W French Polynesia 17°35′S 149°17′W
164 D15 **Hitoyoshi** *var.* Hitoyosi. Kumamoto, Kyūshū, SW Japan 32°12′N 130°48′E
Hitoyosi *see* Hitoyoshi
94 F7 **Hitra** *prev.* Hitteren. *island* S Norway
Hitteren *see* Hitra
187 Q11 **Hiu** *island* Torres Islands, N Vanuatu
165 O11 **Hiuchiga-take** ▲ Honshū, C Japan 36°57′N 139°18′E
191 X7 **Hiva Oa** *island* Îles Marquises, N French Polynesia
20 M10 **Hiwassee Lake** ⊠ North Carolina, SE USA
20 M10 **Hiwassee River** ≈ SE USA
95 H20 **Hjallerup** Nordjylland, N Denmark 57°10′N 10°10′E
95 M16 **Hjälmaren** *Eng.* Lake Hjalmar. ◎ C Sweden
Hjalmar, Lake *see* Hjälmaren
95 C14 **Hjellestad** Hordaland, S Norway 60°15′N 05°13′E
95 D16 **Hjelmeland** Rogaland, S Norway 59°12′N 06°07′E
94 G10 **Hjerkinn** Oppland, S Norway 62°13′N 09°37′E
95 L18 **Hjo** Västra Götaland, S Sweden 58°18′N 14°17′E
95 G19 **Hjørring** Nordjylland, N Denmark 57°28′N 09°59′E
167 O1 **Hkakabo Razi** ▲ Burma (Myanmar)/China 28°17′N 97°28′E
167 N1 **Hkring Bum** ▲ N Burma (Myanmar) 27°05′N 97°16′E
83 L21 **Hlathikulu** *var.* Hlatikulu. S Swaziland 26°58′S 31°19′E
Hlatikulu *see* Hlathikulu
Hliboka *see* Hlyboka
111 F17 **Hlinsko** *var.* Hlinsko v Čechách. Pardubický Kraj, C Czech Republic 49°46′N 15°54′E
Hlinsko v Čechách *see* Hlinsko
117 S6 **Hlobyne** *Rus.* Globino. Poltavs'ka Oblast', NE Ukraine 49°24′N 33°16′E
111 H20 **Hlohovec** *Ger.* Freistadtl, *Hung.* Galgóc; *prev.* Frakštát. Trnavský Kraj, W Slovakia 48°26′N 17°49′E
83 J23 **Hlotse** *var.* Leribe. NW Lesotho 28°55′S 28°01′E
111 I17 **Hlučín** *Ger.* Hultschin, *Pol.* Hulczyn. Moravskoslezský Kraj, E Czech Republic 49°54′N 18°11′E
117 S2 **Hlukhiv** *Rus.* Glukhov. Sums'ka Oblast', NE Ukraine 51°40′N 33°53′E
119 K21 **Hlushkavichy** *Rus.* Glushkevichi. Homyel'skaya Voblasts', SE Belarus 51°34′N 27°47′E
119 L18 **Hlusk** *Rus.* Glusk, Glussk. Mahilyowskaya Voblasts', E Belarus 52°54′N 28°41′E
116 K8 **Hlyboka** *Ger.* Hliboka, *Rus.* Glybokaya. Chernivets'ka Oblast', W Ukraine 48°04′N 25°56′E
118 K13 **Hlybokaye** *Rus.* Glubokoye. Vitsyebskaya Voblasts', N Belarus 55°08′N 27°41′E
77 Q16 **Ho** SE Ghana 06°36′N 00°28′E
167 S6 **Hoa Binh** Hoa Binh, N Vietnam 20°49′N 105°20′E
83 E20 **Hoachanas** Hardap, C Namibia 23°55′S 18°04′E
Hoai Nhơn *see* Bông Sơn
167 T8 **Hoa Lac** Quang Binh, C Vietnam 17°54′N 106°24′E
167 S5 **Hoang Liên Sơn** ▲▲ N Vietnam
83 B17 **Hoanib** ≈ NW Namibia
33 S15 **Hoback Peak** ▲ Wyoming, C USA 43°04′N 110°34′W
183 P17 **Hobart** *prev.* Hobarton, Hobart Town. *state capital* Tasmania, SE Australia 42°54′S 147°18′E
26 L11 **Hobart** Oklahoma, C USA 35°03′N 99°04′W
183 P17 **Hobart** ✈ Tasmania, SE Australia 42°52′S 147°28′E
Hobarton/Hobart Town *see* Hobart
37 W14 **Hobbs** New Mexico, SW USA 32°42′N 103°08′W
194 L12 **Hobbs Coast** *physical region* Antarctica
23 Z14 **Hobe Sound** Florida, SE USA 27°03′N 80°08′W
Hobicaurikány *see* Uricani
54 E12 **Hobo** Huila, S Colombia 02°34′N 75°28′W
99 G16 **Hoboken** Antwerpen, N Belgium 51°12′N 04°22′E
158 K3 **Hoboksar** *var.* Hoboksar Mongol Zizhixian. Xinjiang Uygur Zizhiqu, NW China 46°48′N 85°42′E
Hoboksar Mongol Zizhixian *see* Hoboksar
95 G21 **Hobro** Nordjylland, N Denmark 56°39′N 09°51′E
21 X10 **Hobucken** North Carolina, SE USA 35°15′N 76°31′W
95 O20 **Hoburgen** *headland* SE Sweden 56°54′N 18°07′E
81 P15 **Hobyo** *It.* Obbia. Mudug, E Somalia 05°16′N 48°24′E
109 R8 **Hochalmspitze** ▲ SW Austria 47°00′N 13°19′E
109 Q4 **Hochburg** Oberösterreich, N Austria 48°10′N 12°57′E
108 F8 **Hochdorf** Luzern, N Switzerland 47°10′N 08°16′E
109 N8 **Hochfeiler** *It.* Gran Pilastro. ▲ Austria/Italy 46°59′N 11°42′E
167 T14 **Hô Chi Minh** *var.* Ho Chi Minh City; *prev.* Saigon. S Vietnam 10°46′N 106°43′E
Ho Chi Minh City *see* Hô Chi Minh
108 I7 **Höchst** Vorarlberg, NW Austria 47°28′N 09°40′E
Höchstadt *see* Höchstadt an der Aisch
101 K19 **Höchstadt an der Aisch** *var.* Höchstadt. Bayern, C Germany 49°43′N 10°48′E
108 L9 **Hochwilde** *It.* L'Altissima. ▲ Austria/Italy 46°45′N 11°00′E
109 S7 **Hochwildstelle** ▲ C Austria 47°21′N 13°53′E
31 T14 **Hocking River** ≈ Ohio, N USA
Hocûm *see* Hoctún
41 X12 **Hoctún** *var.* Hocûm. Yucatán, E Mexico 20°48′N 89°14′W
Hodeida *see* Al Ḩudaydah
20 K6 **Hodgenville** Kentucky, S USA 37°34′N 85°45′W
11 T17 **Hodgeville** Saskatchewan, S Canada 50°06′N 106°55′W
76 L9 **Hodh ech Chargui** ◆ *region* E Mauritania
Hodh el Garbi *see* Hodh el Gharbi
76 J10 **Hodh el Gharbi** *var.* Hodh el Garbi. ◆ *region* S Mauritania
111 L25 **Hódmezővásárhely** Csongrád, SE Hungary 46°27′N 20°18′E
74 J6 **Hodna, Chott El** *var.* Chott el-Hodna, *Ar.* Shatt al-Hodna. *salt lake* N Algeria
Hodna, Chott el-/Hodna, Shatt al- *see* Hodna, Chott El
111 G19 **Hodonín** *Ger.* Göding. Jihomoravský Kraj, SE Czech Republic 48°52′N 17°07′E
Hödrögö *see* Nömrög
Hodság/Hodschag *see* Odžaci
39 R7 **Hodzana River** ≈ Alaska, USA
Hoei *see* Huy
99 H19 **Hoeilaart** Vlaams Brabant, C Belgium 50°46′N 04°28′E
Hoë Karoo *see* Great Karoo
98 F12 **Hoek van Holland** *Eng.* Hook of Holland. Zuid-Holland, W Netherlands 52°00′N 04°07′E
98 L11 **Hoenderloo** Gelderland, E Netherlands 52°08′N 05°46′E
99 L18 **Hoensbroek** Limburg, SE Netherlands 50°55′N 05°55′E
163 Y11 **Hoeryŏng** NE North Korea 42°23′N 129°46′E
99 K18 **Hoeselt** Limburg, NE Belgium 50°50′N 05°30′E
98 K11 **Hoevelaken** Gelderland, C Netherlands 52°10′N 05°27′E
Hoey *see* Huy
101 M18 **Hof** Bayern, SE Germany 50°19′N 11°55′E
Höfdhakaupstadhur *see* Skagaströnd
Hofei *see* Hefei
101 G18 **Hofheim am Taunus** Hessen, W Germany 50°04′N 08°27′E
Hofmarkt *see* Odorheiu Secuiesc

◆ Country
● Country Capital
◇ Dependent Territory
○ Dependent Territory Capital
◆ Administrative Regions
✈ International Airport
▲ Mountain
▲▲ Mountain Range
Volcano
≈ River
◎ Lake
⊠ Reservoir

92 *L3* **Höfn** Austurland, SE Iceland *64°14′N 15°17′W*
94 *N13* **Hofors** Gävleborg, C Sweden *60°33′N 16°21′E*
92 *J6* **Hofsjökull** *glacier* C Iceland
92 *J1* **Hofsós** Nordhurland Vestra, N Iceland *65°54′N 19°25′W*
164 *E13* **Hōfu** Yamaguchi, Honshū, SW Japan *34°01′N 131°34′E*
Hofuf *see* Al Hufūf
95 *J22* **Höganäs** Skåne, S Sweden *56°11′N 12°39′E*
183 *P14* **Hogan Group** *island group* Tasmania, SE Australia
23 *R4* **Hogansville** Georgia, SE USA *33°10′N 84°55′W*
39 *P8* **Hogatza River** ≈ Alaska, USA
28 *I14* **Hogback Mountain** ▲ Nebraska, C USA *41°40′N 103°44′W*
95 *G14* **Høgevarde** ▲ S Norway *60°19′N 09°27′E*
Högfors *see* Karkkila
31 *P5* **Hog Island** *island* Michigan, N USA
21 *Y6* **Hog Island** *island* Virginia, NE USA
Hogoley Islands *see* Chuuk Islands
95 *N20* **Högsby** Kalmar, S Sweden *57°10′N 16°03′E*
36 *K1* **Hogup Mountains** ▲▲ Utah, W USA
101 *E17* **Hohe Acht** ▲ W Germany *50°23′N 07°00′E*
Hohenelbe *see* Vrchlabí
108 *I7* **Hohenems** Vorarlberg, W Austria *47°23′N 09°43′E*
Hohenmauth *see* Vysoké Mýto
Hohensalza *see* Inowrocław
Hohenstadt *see* Zábřeh
Hohenstein in Ostpreussen *see* Olsztynek
20 *I9* **Hohenwald** Tennessee, S USA *35°33′N 87°31′W*
101 *L17* **Hohenwarte-Stausee** ▣ C Germany
Hohes Venn *see* Hautes Fagnes
109 *Q8* **Hohe Tauern** ▲▲ W Austria
163 *O13* **Hohhot** *var.* Huhehot, Huhohaote, ***Mong.*** Kukukhoto; ***prev.*** Kweisui, Kwesui. Nei Mongol Zizhiqu, N China *40°49′N 111°37′E*
162 *F7* **Hohmorït** *var.* Sayn-Ust. Govĭ-Altay, W Mongolia *47°23′N 94°19′E*
103 *U6* **Hohneck** ▲ NE France *48°04′N 07°01′E*
77 *Q16* **Hohoe** E Ghana *07°08′N 00°32′E*
164 *E12* **Hōhoku** Yamaguchi, Honshū, SW Japan *34°15′N 130°56′E*
159 *O11* **Hoh Sai Hu** ◎ C China
159 *N11* **Hoh Xil Hu** ◎ C China
158 *L11* **Hoh Xil Shan** ▲▲ W China
167 *U10* **Hôi An** ***prev.*** Faifo. Quang Nam-Đa Năng, C Vietnam *15°54′N 108°19′E*
Hoï-Hao/Hoihow *see* Haikou
159 *S11* **Hoika** ***prev.*** Heka. Qinghai, W China *35°49′N 99°50′E*
81 *F17* **Hoima** W Uganda *01°25′N 31°22′E*
26 *L5* **Hoisington** Kansas, C USA *38°31′N 98°46′W*
146 *D12* **Hojagala** ***Rus.*** Khodzhakala. Balkan Welaýaty, W Turkmenistan *38°46′N 56°14′E*
146 *M13* **Hojambaz** ***Rus.*** Khodzhambas. Lebap Welaýaty, E Turkmenistan *38°11′N 64°33′E*
95 *H23* **Højby** Fyn, C Denmark *55°20′N 10°27′E*
95 *F24* **Højer** Sønderjylland, SW Denmark *54°57′N 08°43′E*
164 *E14* **Hōjō** *var.* Hôzyô. Ehime, Shikoku, SW Japan *33°58′N 132°47′E*
184 *J3* **Hokianga Harbour** *inlet* SE Tasman Sea
185 *F17* **Hokitika** West Coast, South Island, New Zealand *42°44′S 170°58′E*
165 *U4* **Hokkai-dō** ⬖ *territory* Hokkaidō, NE Japan
165 *T3* **Hokkaidō** ***prev.*** Ezo, Yeso, Yezo. *island* NE Japan
95 *G15* **Hokksund** Buskerud, S Norway *59°45′N 09°55′E*
143 *S4* **Hokmābād** Khorāsān-Razavī, N Iran *36°37′N 57°34′E*
Hokō *see* P'ohang
Hoko-guntō/Hoko-shotō *see* P'enghu Liehtao
Hoktemberyan *see* Armavir
94 *F13* **Hol** Buskerud, S Norway *60°36′N 08°18′E*
117 *R11* **Hola Prystan'** ***Rus.*** Golaya Pristan. Khersons'ka Oblast', S Ukraine *46°31′N 32°31′E*
95 *I23* **Holbæk** Vestsjælland, E Denmark *55°42′N 11°42′E*
Holboo *see* Santmargats
183 *P10* **Holbrook** New South Wales, SE Australia *35°45′S 147°18′E*
37 *N11* **Holbrook** Arizona, SW USA *34°54′N 110°09′W*
27 *S5* **Holden** Missouri, C USA *38°42′N 93°59′W*
36 *K5* **Holden** Utah, W USA *39°06′N 112°16′W*
27 *O11* **Holdenville** Oklahoma, C USA *35°05′N 96°25′W*
29 *O16* **Holdrege** Nebraska, C USA *40°28′N 99°28′W*
35 *X3* **Hole in the Mountain Peak** ▲ Nevada, W USA *40°54′N 115°06′W*
155 *G20* **Hole Narsipur** Karnātaka, W India *12°46′N 76°14′E*
111 *H18* **Holešov** ***Ger.*** Holleschau. Zlínský Kraj, E Czech Republic *49°20′N 17°35′E*
45 *N14* **Holetown** ***prev.*** Jamestown. W Barbados *13°11′N 59°38′W*
31 *Q12* **Holgate** Ohio, N USA *41°12′N 84°06′W*
44 *I7* **Holguín** Holguín, SE Cuba *20°51′N 76°16′W*
23 *V12* **Holiday** Florida, SE USA *28°11′N 82°44′W*
39 *O12* **Holitna River** ≈ Alaska, USA
94 *J13* **Höljes** Värmland, C Sweden *60°54′N 12°34′E*
109 *X3* **Hollabrunn** Niederösterreich, NE Austria *48°33′N 16°06′E*
36 *L3* **Holladay** Utah, W USA *40°39′N 111°49′W*
11 *X16* **Holland** Manitoba, S Canada *49°36′N 98°52′W*
31 *O9* **Holland** Michigan, N USA *42°47′N 86°06′W*
25 *T9* **Holland** Texas, SW USA *30°52′N 97°24′W*
Holland *see* Netherlands
22 *K4* **Hollandale** Mississippi, S USA *33°10′N 90°51′W*
Hollandia *see* Jayapura
Hollandsch Diep *see* Hollands Diep
99 *H14* **Hollands Diep** *var.* Hollandsch Diep. *channel* SW Netherlands
Holleschau *see* Holešov
25 *R5* **Holliday** Texas, SW USA *33°49′N 98°41′W*
18 *E15* **Hollidaysburg** Pennsylvania, NE USA *40°24′N 78°22′W*
21 *S6* **Hollins** Virginia, NE USA *37°20′N 79°56′W*
26 *J12* **Hollis** Oklahoma, C USA *34°42′N 99°56′W*
35 *O10* **Hollister** California, W USA *36°51′N 121°25′W*
27 *T8* **Hollister** Missouri, C USA *36°37′N 93°13′W*
93 *M19* **Hollola** Etelä-Suomi, S Finland *61°N 25°32′E*
98 *K4* **Hollum** Friesland, N Netherlands *53°27′N 05°38′E*
95 *J23* **Höllviksnäs** Skåne, S Sweden *55°25′N 12°57′E*
37 *W6* **Holly** Colorado, C USA *38°03′N 102°07′W*
31 *R9* **Holly** Michigan, N USA *42°47′N 83°37′W*
21 *S14* **Holly Hill** South Carolina, SE USA *33°19′N 80°24′W*
21 *W11* **Holly Ridge** North Carolina, SE USA *34°31′N 77°31′W*
22 *L1* **Holly Springs** Mississippi, S USA *34°47′N 89°25′W*
23 *Z15* **Hollywood** Florida, SE USA *26°00′N 80°09′W*
8 *J6* **Holman** Victoria Island, Northwest Territories, N Canada *70°42′N 117°45′W*
92 *I2* **Hólmavík** Vestfirdhir, NW Iceland *65°42′N 21°43′W*
30 *J7* **Holmen** Wisconsin, N USA *43°57′N 91°14′W*
23 *R8* **Holmes Creek** ≈ Alabama/Florida, SE USA
95 *H16* **Holmestrand** Vestfold, S Norway *59°29′N 10°20′E*
93 *J16* **Holmön** *island* N Sweden
95 *E22* **Holmsland Klit** *beach* W Denmark
93 *J16* **Holmsund** Västerbotten, N Sweden *63°42′N 20°26′E*
95 *Q18* **Holmudden** *headland* SE Sweden *57°59′N 19°14′E*
138 *F10* **Holon** *var.* Kholon; ***prev.*** Holon. Tel Aviv, C Israel *32°01′N 34°46′E*
Holon *see* Holon
163 *P7* **Hölönbuyr** *var.* Bayan. Dornod, E Mongolia *47°56′N 112°58′E*
117 *P8* **Holovanivs'k** ***Rus.*** Golovanevsk. Kirovohrads'ka Oblast', C Ukraine *48°21′N 30°26′E*
95 *F21* **Holstebro** Ringkøbing, W Denmark *56°22′N 08°38′E*
95 *F23* **Holsted** Ribe, W Denmark *55°30′N 08°54′E*
29 *T13* **Holstein** Iowa, C USA *42°29′N 95°32′W*
Holsteinborg/Holsteinsborg/Holstenborg/Holstensborg *see* Sisimiut
21 *O8* **Holston River** ≈ Tennessee, S USA
31 *Q9* **Holt** Michigan, N USA *42°38′N 84°31′W*
98 *N10* **Holten** Overijssel, E Netherlands *52°16′N 06°25′E*
27 *P3* **Holton** Kansas, C USA *39°27′N 95°44′W*
27 *U5* **Holts Summit** Missouri, C USA *38°38′N 92°07′W*
35 *X17* **Holtville** California, W USA *32°48′N 115°22′W*
98 *L5* **Holwerd** ***Fris.*** Holwert. Friesland, N Netherlands *53°22′N 05°51′E*
Holwert *see* Holwerd
39 *O11* **Holy Cross** Alaska, USA *62°12′N 159°46′W*
37 *R4* **Holy Cross, Mount Of The** ▲ Colorado, C USA *39°28′N 106°28′W*
97 *I18* **Holyhead** ***Wel.*** Caer Gybi. NW Wales, United Kingdom *53°19′N 04°38′W*
97 *H18* **Holy Island** *island* NW Wales, United Kingdom
96 *L12* **Holy Island** *island* NE England, United Kingdom
37 *W3* **Holyoke** Colorado, C USA *40°31′N 102°18′W*
18 *M11* **Holyoke** Massachusetts, NE USA *42°12′N 72°37′W*
101 *I14* **Holzminden** Niedersachsen, C Germany *51°49′N 09°27′E*
81 *G19* **Homa Bay** Nyanza, W Kenya *0°31′S 34°30′E*
Homāyūnshahr *see* Khomeynīshahr
77 *P11* **Hombori** Mopti, S Mali *15°13′N 01°39′W*
101 *E20* **Homburg** Saarland, SW Germany *49°20′N 07°20′E*
9 *R5* **Home Bay** *bay* Baffin Bay, Nunavut, NE Canada
Homenau *see* Humenné
39 *Q13* **Homer** Alaska, USA *59°38′N 151°33′W*
22 *H4* **Homer** Louisiana, S USA *32°47′N 93°03′W*
18 *H10* **Homer** New York, NE USA *42°38′N 76°10′W*
23 *V7* **Homerville** Georgia, SE USA *31°02′N 82°45′W*
23 *Y16* **Homestead** Florida, SE USA *25°28′N 80°28′W*
27 *O9* **Hominy** Oklahoma, C USA *36°24′N 96°24′W*
94 *H8* **Hommelvik** Sør-Trøndelag, S Norway *63°24′N 10°48′E*
95 *C16* **Hommersåk** Rogaland, S Norway *58°55′N 05°51′E*
155 *H15* **Homnābād** Karnātaka, C India *17°46′N 77°08′E*
22 *J7* **Homochitto River** ≈ Mississippi, S USA
83 *N20* **Homoíne** Inhambane, SE Mozambique *23°51′S 35°04′E*
112 *O12* **Homoljske Planine** ▲▲ E Serbia
Homonna *see* Humenné
Homs *see* Al Khums, Libya
Homs *see* Ḥimṣ
119 *P19* **Homyel'** ***Rus.*** Gomel'. Homyel'skaya Voblasts', SE Belarus *52°25′N 31°E*
118 *L12* **Homyel'** Vitsyebskaya Voblasts', N Belarus *55°20′N 28°52′E*
119 *L19* **Homyel'skaya Voblasts'** ***prev. Rus.*** Gomel'skaya Oblast'. ⬖ *province* SE Belarus
Honan *see* Luoyang, China
Honan *see* Henan, China
164 *U4* **Honbetsu** Hokkaidō, NE Japan *43°09′N 143°46′E*
Honctő *see* Gurahonț
54 *E9* **Honda** Tolima, C Colombia *05°12′N 74°45′W*
83 *D24* **Hondeklip** ***Afr.*** Hondeklipbaai. Northern Cape, W South Africa *30°15′S 17°17′E*
Hondeklipbaai *see* Hondeklip
11 *Q13* **Hondo** Alberta, W Canada *54°43′N 113°14′W*
164 *C15* **Hondo** Kumamoto, Shimo-jima, SW Japan *32°28′N 130°12′E*
25 *Q12* **Hondo** Texas, SW USA *29°21′N 99°09′W*
42 *G1* **Hondo** ≈ Central America
Hondo *see* Honshū
42 *G6* **Honduras** ***off.*** Republic of Honduras. ◆ *republic* Central America
Honduras, Golfo de *see* Honduras, Gulf of
42 *H4* **Honduras, Gulf of** ***Sp.*** Golfo de Honduras. *gulf* W Caribbean Sea
Honduras, Republic of *see* Honduras
11 *V12* **Hone** Manitoba, C Canada *56°13′N 101°12′W*
21 *P12* **Honea Path** South Carolina, SE USA *34°27′N 82°23′W*
95 *H14* **Hønefoss** Buskerud, S Norway *60°10′N 10°15′E*
31 *S12* **Honey Creek** ≈ Ohio, N USA
25 *V5* **Honey Grove** Texas, SW USA *33°34′N 95°54′W*
35 *Q4* **Honey Lake** ◎ California, W USA
102 *L4* **Honfleur** Calvados, N France *49°25′N 00°14′E*
Hon Gai *see* Hông Gai
161 *O8* **Hong'an** ***prev.*** Huang'an. Hubei, C China *31°20′N 114°43′E*
Hongay *see* Hông Gai
167 *T6* **Hông Gai** *var.* Hon Gai, Hongay. Quang Ninh, N Vietnam *20°57′N 107°06′E*
161 *O15* **Honghai Wan** *bay* N South China Sea
Hông Hà, Sông *see* Red River
161 *O7* **Hong He** ≈ C China
161 *N9* **Hong Hu** ◎ C China
160 *L11* **Hongjiang** Hunan, S China *27°09′N 109°58′E*
Hongjiang *see* Wangcang
161 *O15* **Hong Kong** ***Chin.*** Xianggang. Hong Kong, S China *22°17′N 114°09′E*
160 *L4* **Hongliu He** ≈ C China
160 *L4* **Hongliu He** ≈ C China
159 *P8* **Hongliuwan** *var.* Aksay, Aksay Kazakzu Zizhixian. Gansu, N China *39°25′N 94°09′E*
159 *P7* **Hongliuyuan** Gansu, N China *41°02′N 95°24′E*
Hongor *see* Delgereh
161 *S8* **Hongqiao** ✈ (Shanghai) Shanghai Shi, E China *31°28′N 121°08′E*
Hongshui *see* Minle
160 *K14* **Hongshui He** ≈ S China
160 *M5* **Hongtong** *var.* Dahuaishu. Shanxi, C China *36°30′N 111°42′E*
164 *J15* **Hongū** Wakayama, Honshū, SW Japan *33°50′N 135°42′E*
Honguedo, Détroit d' *see* Honguedo Passage
15 *Y5* **Honguedo Passage** *var.* Honguedo Strait, ***Fr.*** Détroit d'Honguedo. *strait* Québec, E Canada
Honguedo Strait *see* Honguedo Passage
Hongwan *see* Hongwansi
159 *S8* **Hongwansi** *var.* Sunan, Sunan Yugurzu Zizhixian; ***prev.*** Hongwan. Gansu, N China *38°55′N 99°29′E*
163 *X13* **Hongwŏn** E North Korea *40°03′N 127°54′E*
160 *H7* **Hongyuan** *var.* Qiongxi; ***prev.*** Hurama. Sichuan, C China *32°49′N 102°40′E*
161 *Q7* **Hongze Hu** *var.* Hung-tse Hu. ◎ E China
186 *L9* **Honiara** ● (Solomon Islands) Guadalcanal, C Solomon Islands *09°27′S 159°56′E*
165 *P8* **Honjō** *var.* Honzyô, Yurihonjō. Akita, Honshū, C Japan *39°23′N 140°03′E*
93 *K18* **Honkajoki** Länsi-Suomi, SW Finland *62°00′N 22°15′E*
92 *K7* **Honningsvåg** Finnmark, N Norway *70°58′N 25°59′E*
95 *I19* **Hönö** Västra Götaland, S Sweden *57°42′N 11°39′E*
38 *G11* **Honoka'a** Hawaii, USA, C Pacific Ocean *20°04′N 155°27′W*
38 *G11* **Honoka'a** *var.* Honokaa. Hawaii, USA, C Pacific Ocean *20°04′N 155°27′W*
Honokaa *see* Honoka'a
38 *D9* **Honolulu** *state capital* O'ahu, Hawaii, USA, C Pacific Ocean *21°18′N 157°52′W*
38 *H11* **Honomú** *var.* Honomu. Hawaii, USA, C Pacific Ocean *19°51′N 155°06′W*
105 *P10* **Honrubia** Castilla-La Mancha, C Spain *39°36′N 02°17′W*
164 *M12* **Honshū** *var.* Hondo, Honsyû. *island* SW Japan
Honsyû *see* Honshū
Honte *see* Westerschelde
Honzyô *see* Honjō
8 *K8* **Hood** ≈ Nunavut, NW Canada
Hood Island *see* Española, Isla
32 *H11* **Hood, Mount** ▲ Oregon, NW USA *45°22′N 121°41′W*
32 *H11* **Hood River** Oregon, NW USA *45°44′N 121°31′W*
98 *H10* **Hoofddorp** Noord-Holland, W Netherlands *52°18′N 04°41′E*
99 *G15* **Hoogerheide** Noord-Brabant, S Netherlands *51°25′N 04°19′E*
98 *N8* **Hoogeveen** Drenthe, NE Netherlands *52°44′N 06°30′E*
98 *O6* **Hoogezand-Sappemeer** Groningen, NE Netherlands *53°10′N 06°47′E*
98 *J8* **Hoogkarspel** Noord-Holland, NW Netherlands *52°42′N 04°59′E*
98 *N5* **Hoogkerk** Groningen, NE Netherlands *53°13′N 06°30′E*
98 *G13* **Hoogvliet** Zuid-Holland, SW Netherlands *51°51′N 04°23′E*
26 *I8* **Hooker** Oklahoma, C USA *36°51′N 101°12′W*
97 *E21* **Hook Head** ***Ir.*** Rinn Duáin. *headland* SE Ireland *52°07′N 06°55′W*
Hook of Holland *see* Hoek van Holland
Hoolt *see* Tögrög
39 *W13* **Hoonah** Chichagof Island, Alaska, USA *58°05′N 135°21′W*
38 *L11* **Hooper Bay** Alaska, USA *61°31′N 166°06′W*
31 *N13* **Hoopeston** Illinois, N USA *40°28′N 87°40′W*
95 *K22* **Höör** Skåne, S Sweden *55°55′N 13°33′E*
98 *I9* **Hoorn** Noord-Holland, NW Netherlands *52°38′N 05°04′E*
18 *L10* **Hoosic River** ≈ New York, NE USA
Hoosier State *see* Indiana
35 *Y11* **Hoover Dam** *dam* Arizona/Nevada, W USA
Höövör *see* Baruunbayan-Ulaan
137 *Q11* **Hopa** Artvin, NE Turkey *41°23′N 41°28′E*
18 *J14* **Hopatcong** New Jersey, NE USA *40°55′N 74°39′W*
10 *M17* **Hope** British Columbia, SW Canada *49°21′N 121°28′W*
39 *R12* **Hope** Alaska, USA *60°55′N 149°38′W*
27 *T14* **Hope** Arkansas, C USA *33°40′N 93°36′W*
31 *P14* **Hope** Indiana, N USA *39°18′N 85°46′W*
29 *Q5* **Hope** North Dakota, N USA *47°18′N 97°42′W*
13 *Q7* **Hopedale** Newfoundland and Labrador, NE Canada *55°26′N 60°14′W*
Hopeh/Hopei *see* Hebei
180 *K13* **Hope, Lake** *salt lake* Western Australia
41 *X13* **Hopelchén** Campeche, SE Mexico *19°46′N 89°50′W*
21 *U11* **Hope Mills** North Carolina, SE USA *34°58′N 78°57′W*
183 *O7* **Hope, Mount** New South Wales, SE Australia *32°49′S 145°55′E*
92 *P4* **Hopen** *island* SE Svalbard
197 *Q4* **Hope, Point** *headland* Alaska, USA
12 *M3* **Hopes Advance, Cap** *cape* Québec, NE Canada
182 *L10* **Hopetoun** Victoria, SE Australia *35°46′S 142°23′E*
83 *H23* **Hopetown** Northern Cape, W South Africa *29°37′S 24°05′E*
21 *W6* **Hopewell** Virginia, NE USA *37°16′N 77°15′W*
109 *O7* **Hopfgarten im Brixental** Tirol, W Austria *47°28′N 12°14′E*
181 *N8* **Hopkins Lake** *salt lake* Western Australia
182 *M12* **Hopkins River** ≈ Victoria, SE Australia
20 *I7* **Hopkinsville** Kentucky, S USA *36°50′N 87°30′W*
34 *M6* **Hopland** California, W USA *38°58′N 123°09′W*
95 *G24* **Hoptrup** Sønderjylland, SW Denmark *55°09′N 09°27′E*
Hoqin Zuoyi Zhongji *see* Baokang
32 *F9* **Hoquiam** Washington, NW USA *46°58′N 123°53′W*
29 *R6* **Horace** North Dakota, N USA *46°44′N 96°54′W*
117 *T14* **Hora Roman-Kash** ▲ S Ukraine *44°37′N 34°13′E*
137 *R12* **Horasan** Erzurum, NE Turkey *40°03′N 42°10′E*
101 *G22* **Horb am Neckar** Baden-Württemberg, S Germany *48°27′N 08°42′E*
95 *K23* **Hörby** Skåne, S Sweden *55°51′N 13°42′E*
43 *P16* **Horconcitos** Chiriquí, W Panama *08°20′N 82°10′W*
95 *C14* **Hordaland** ⬖ *county* S Norway
116 *H13* **Horezu** Vâlcea, SW Romania *45°06′N 24°00′E*
108 *G7* **Horgen** Zürich, N Switzerland *47°16′N 08°36′E*
Horgo *see* Tariat
Hōrin *see* Fenglin
163 *O13* **Horinger** Nei Mongol Zizhiqu, N China *40°23′N 111°48′E*
Horiult *see* Bogd
11 *U17* **Horizon** Saskatchewan, S Canada *49°33′N 105°05′W*
192 *K9* **Horizon Bank** *undersea feature* S Pacific Ocean
192 *L10* **Horizon Deep** *undersea feature* W Pacific Ocean
95 *L14* **Hörken** Örebro, S Sweden *60°03′N 14°55′E*
119 *O15* **Horki** ***Rus.*** Gorki. Mahilyowskaya Voblasts', E Belarus *54°18′N 31°E*
195 *O10* **Horlick Mountains** ▲▲ Antarctica
117 *X7* **Horlivka** ***Rom.*** Adâncata, ***Rus.*** Gorlovka. Donets'ka Oblast', E Ukraine *48°19′N 38°04′E*
143 *V11* **Ḩormak** Sīstān va Balūchestān, SE Iran *30°00′N 60°50′E*
143 *R13* **Hormozgān** ***off.*** Ostān-e Hormozgān. ⬖ *province* S Iran
Hormozgān, Ostān-e *see* Hormozgān
Hormoz, Tangeh-ye *see* Hormuz, Strait of
141 *W6* **Hormuz, Strait of** *var.* Strait of Ormuz, ***Per.*** Tangeh-ye Hormoz. *strait* Iran/Oman
109 *W2* **Horn** Niederösterreich, NE Austria *48°40′N 15°40′E*
95 *M18* **Horn** Östergötland, S Sweden *57°54′N 15°49′E*
8 *J9* **Horn** ≈ Northwest Territories, NW Canada
Hornád *see* Hernád
8 *I6* **Hornaday** ≈ Northwest Territories, NW Canada
92 *H13* **Hornavan** ◎ N Sweden
65 *C24* **Hornby Mountains** *hill range* West Falkland, Falkland Islands
Horn, Cape *see* Hornos, Cabo de
97 *O18* **Horncastle** E England, United Kingdom *53°12′N 00°07′W*
95 *N14* **Horndal** Dalarna, C Sweden *60°16′N 16°25′E*
93 *I16* **Hörnefors** Västerbotten, N Sweden *63°37′N 19°54′E*
18 *F11* **Hornell** New York, NE USA *42°19′N 77°38′W*
Horné Nové Mesto *see* Kysucké Nové Mesto
12 *F12* **Hornepayne** Ontario, S Canada *49°14′N 84°48′W*
94 *D10* **Hornindalsvatnet** ◎ S Norway
101 *G22* **Hornisgrinde** ▲ SW Germany *48°37′N 08°13′E*
22 *M9* **Horn Island** *island* Mississippi, S USA
Hornja Łužica *see* Oberlausitz
63 *J26* **Hornos, Cabo de** ***Eng.*** Cape Horn. *headland* S Chile *55°52′S 67°00′W*
117 *S10* **Hornostayivka** Khersons'ka Oblast', S Ukraine *47°00′N 33°42′E*
183 *T9* **Hornsby** New South Wales, SE Australia *33°44′S 151°08′E*
97 *O16* **Hornsea** E England, United Kingdom *53°54′N 00°10′W*
94 *O11* **Hornslandet** *peninsula* C Sweden
95 *H22* **Hornslet** Århus, C Denmark *56°19′N 10°20′E*
92 *O4* **Hornsundtind** ▲ S Svalbard *76°54′N 16°07′E*
Horochów *see* Horokhiv
Horodenka *see* Gorodenka
117 *Q2* **Horodnya** ***Rus.*** Gorodnya. Chernihivs'ka Oblast', NE Ukraine *51°54′N 31°30′E*
116 *K6* **Horodok** Khmel'nyts'ka Oblast', W Ukraine *49°10′N 26°34′E*
116 *H5* **Horodok** ***Pol.*** Gródek Jagielloński, ***Rus.*** Gorodok, Gorodok Yagellonski. L'vivs'ka Oblast', NW Ukraine *49°48′N 23°39′E*
117 *Q6* **Horodyshche** ***Rus.*** Gorodishche. Cherkas'ka Oblast', C Ukraine *49°19′N 31°27′E*
165 *T3* **Horokanai** Hokkaidō, NE Japan *44°02′N 142°08′E*
116 *J4* **Horokhiv** ***Pol.*** Horochów, ***Rus.*** Gorokhov. Volyns'ka Oblast', NW Ukraine *50°31′N 24°50′E*
165 *T4* **Horoshiri-dake** *var.* Horosiri Dake. ▲ Hokkaidō, N Japan *42°43′N 142°41′E*
Horosiri Dake *see* Horoshiri-dake
111 *C17* **Hořovice** ***Ger.*** Horowitz. Střední Čechy, W Czech Republic *49°49′N 13°53′E*
Horowitz *see* Hořovice
Horqin Zuoyi Houqi *see* Ganjig
Horqin Zuoyi Zhongqi *see* Bayan Huxu
62 *O5* **Horqueta** Concepción, C Paraguay *23°24′S 56°53′W*
55 *O12* **Horqueta Minas** Amazonas, S Venezuela *02°20′N 63°32′W*
95 *J20* **Horred** Västra Götaland, S Sweden *57°22′N 12°25′E*
151 *J19* **Horsburgh Atoll** *var.* Goidhoo Atoll. *atoll* N Maldives
20 *K7* **Horse Cave** Kentucky, S USA *37°10′N 85°54′W*
37 *V6* **Horse Creek** ≈ Colorado, C USA
27 *S6* **Horse Creek** ≈ Missouri, C USA
18 *G11* **Horseheads** New York, NE USA *42°10′N 76°49′W*
37 *P13* **Horse Mount** ▲ New Mexico, SW USA *33°58′N 108°10′W*
95 *G22* **Horsens** Vejle, C Denmark *55°53′N 09°53′E*
65 *F25* **Horse Pasture Point** *headland* W Saint Helena *15°57′S 05°46′W*
33 *N13* **Horseshoe Bend** Idaho, NW USA *43°55′N 116°11′W*
36 *L13* **Horseshoe Reservoir** ▣ Arizona, SW USA
64 *M9* **Horseshoe Seamounts** *undersea feature* E Atlantic Ocean *36°30′N 15°00′W*
182 *L11* **Horsham** Victoria, SE Australia *36°44′S 142°13′E*
97 *O23* **Horsham** SE England, United Kingdom *51°01′N 00°21′W*
99 *M15* **Horst** Limburg, SE Netherlands *51°30′N 06°05′E*
64 *N2* **Horta** Faial, Azores, Portugal, NE Atlantic Ocean *38°32′N 28°39′W*
95 *H16* **Horten** Vestfold, S Norway *59°25′N 10°25′E*
111 *M23* **Hortobágy-Berettyó** ≈ E Hungary
27 *Q3* **Horton** Kansas, C USA *39°39′N 95°31′W*
8 *I7* **Horton** ≈ Northwest Territories, NW Canada
95 *I23* **Hørve** Vestsjælland, E Denmark *55°46′N 11°28′E*
95 *L22* **Hörvik** Blekinge, S Sweden *56°01′N 14°45′E*
Horvot Haluza *see* Horvot Halutsa
14 *E7* **Horwood Lake** ◎ Ontario, S Canada
116 *K4* **Horyn'** ***Rus.*** Goryn. ≈ NW Ukraine
81 *I14* **Hosa'ina** *var.* Hosseina, ***It.*** Hosanna. Southern Nationalities, S Ethiopia *07°38′N 37°58′E*
Hosanna *see* Hosa'ina
101 *H18* **Hösbach** Bayern, C Germany *50°00′N 09°12′E*
Hose Mountains *see* Hose, Pegunungan
169 *T9* **Hose, Pegunungan** *var.* Hose Mountains. ▲▲ East Malaysia
148 *L15* **Hoshāb** Baluchistān, SW Pakistan *26°01′N 63°51′E*
154 *H10* **Hoshangābād** Madhya Pradesh, C India *22°44′N 77°45′E*
116 *L4* **Hoshcha** Rivnens'ka Oblast', NW Ukraine *50°37′N 26°38′E*
152 *I7* **Hoshiārpur** Punjab, NW India *31°30′N 75°59′E*
Höshööt *see* Öldziyt
99 *M23* **Hosingen** Diekirch, NE Luxembourg *50°01′N 06°05′E*
186 *G7* **Hoskins** New Britain, E Papua New Guinea *05°28′S 150°25′E*
155 *G17* **Hospet** Karnātaka, C India *15°16′N 76°20′E*
104 *K4* **Hospital de Orbigo** Castilla-León, N Spain *42°27′N 05°53′W*
Hospitalet *see* L'Hospitalet de Llobregat
92 *N13* **Hossa** Oulu, E Finland *65°28′N 29°36′E*
Hosseina *see* Hosa'ina
Hosszúmezjő *see* Câmpulung Moldovenesc
63 *I25* **Hoste, Isla** *island* S Chile
117 *O4* **Hostomel'** ***Rus.*** Gostomel'. Kyyivs'ka Oblast', N Ukraine *50°41′N 30°15′E*
155 *H20* **Hosūr** Tamil Nādu, SE India *12°45′N 77°51′E*
167 *N8* **Hot** Chiang Mai, NW Thailand *18°07′N 98°34′E*
158 *G10* **Hotan** *var.* Khotan, ***Chin.*** Ho-t'ien. Xinjiang Uygur Zizhiqu, NW China *37°10′N 79°51′E*
158 *H9* **Hotan He** ≈ NW China
83 *G22* **Hotazel** Northern Cape, N South Africa *27°12′S 22°58′E*
37 *Q5* **Hotchkiss** Colorado, C USA *38°47′N 107°43′W*
35 *V7* **Hot Creek Range** ▲▲ Nevada, W USA
Hote *see* Hoti
171 *T13* **Hoti** *var.* Hote. Pulau Seram, E Indonesia *02°58′S 130°19′E*
Ho-t'ien *see* Hotan
Hotin *see* Khotyn
93 *H15* **Hoting** Jämtland, C Sweden *64°07′N 16°14′E*
162 *L14* **Hotong Qagan Nur** ◎ N China
162 *J8* **Hotont** Arhangay, C Mongolia *47°21′N 102°27′E*
27 *T12* **Hot Springs** Arkansas, C USA *34°31′N 93°03′W*
28 *J11* **Hot Springs** South Dakota, N USA *43°26′N 103°29′W*
21 *S5* **Hot Springs** Virginia, NE USA *38°00′N 79°50′W*
35 *Q4* **Hot Springs Peak** ▲ California, W USA *40°23′N 120°06′W*
27 *T12* **Hot Springs Village** Arkansas, C USA *34°39′N 93°03′W*
Hotspur Bank *see* Hotspur Seamount
65 *J16* **Hotspur Seamount** *var.* Hotspur Bank. *undersea feature* C Atlantic Ocean *18°00′S 35°00′W*
8 *J8* **Hottah Lake** ◎ Northwest Territories, NW Canada
44 *K9* **Hotte, Massif de la** ▲▲ SW Haiti
99 *K21* **Hotton** Luxembourg, SE Belgium *50°18′N 05°25′E*
Hötzing *see* Hațeg
187 *P17* **Houaïlou** Province Nord, C New Caledonia *21°17′S 165°37′E*
74 *K5* **Houari Boumediène** ✈ (Alger) N Algeria *36°38′N 03°15′E*
167 *P6* **Houayxay** *var.* Ban Houayxay. Bokèo, N Laos *20°17′N 100°27′E*
103 *N5* **Houdan** Yvelines, N France *48°48′N 01°36′E*
99 *F20* **Houdeng-Goegnies** *var.* Houdeng-Gœgnies. Hainaut, S Belgium *50°29′N 04°10′E*
102 *K14* **Houeillès** Lot-et-Garonne, SW France *44°15′N 00°02′E*
99 *L22* **Houffalize** Luxembourg, SE Belgium *50°08′N 05°47′E*
30 *M3* **Houghton** Michigan, N USA *47°07′N 88°34′W*
31 *Q7* **Houghton Lake** Michigan, N USA *44°18′N 84°45′W*
31 *Q7* **Houghton Lake** ◎ Michigan, N USA
19 *T3* **Houlton** Maine, NE USA *46°09′N 67°50′W*
160 *M5* **Houma** Shanxi, C China *35°36′N 11°23′E*
193 *U16* **Houma** Tongatapu, S Tonga *21°18′S 174°55′W*
22 *J10* **Houma** Louisiana, S USA *29°35′N 90°44′W*
196 *V16* **Houma Taloa** *headland* Tongatapu, S Tonga *21°16′S 175°08′W*
77 *O13* **Houndé** SW Burkina *11°34′N 03°31′W*
102 *J12* **Hourtin-Carcans, Lac d'** ◎ SW France
36 *J5* **House Range** ▲▲ Utah, W USA
10 *K13* **Houston** British Columbia, SW Canada *54°24′N 126°39′W*
39 *R11* **Houston** Alaska, USA *61°37′N 149°50′W*
29 *X10* **Houston** Minnesota, N USA *43°45′N 91°34′W*
22 *M3* **Houston** Mississippi, S USA *33°54′N 89°00′W*
27 *V7* **Houston** Missouri, C USA *37°19′N 91°59′W*
25 *W11* **Houston** Texas, SW USA *29°46′N 95°22′W*
25 *W11* **Houston** ✈ Texas, SW USA *30°03′N 95°18′W*
98 *J12* **Houten** Utrecht, C Netherlands *52°02′N 05°10′E*
99 *K17* **Houthalen** Limburg, NE Belgium *51°02′N 05°22′E*
99 *I22* **Houyet** Namur, SE Belgium *50°10′N 05°00′E*
95 *H22* **Hov** Århus, C Denmark *55°54′N 10°13′E*
95 *L17* **Hova** Västra Götaland, S Sweden *58°52′N 14°13′E*
162 *E6* **Hovd** *var.* Khovd, Kobdo; ***prev.*** Jirgalanta. Hovd, W Mongolia *47°59′N 91°41′E*
162 *J10* **Hovd** *var.* Dund-Us. Hovd, W Mongolia *48°06′N 91°22′E*
162 *E6* **Hovd** *var.* Dund-Us. Hovd, W Mongolia *48°06′N 91°22′E*
162 *E7* **Hovd** ⬖ *province* W Mongolia
Hovd *see* Bogd
162 *C5* **Hovd Gol** ≈ NW Mongolia
97 *O23* **Hove** SE England, United Kingdom *50°49′N 00°11′W*
29 *N8* **Hoven** South Dakota, N USA *45°12′N 99°47′W*
116 *I8* **Hoverla, Hora** ***Rus.*** Gora Goverla. ▲ W Ukraine *48°09′N 24°30′E*
Höviyn Am *see* Gurvanbulag
95 *M21* **Hovmantorp** Kronoberg, S Sweden *56°47′N 15°08′E*
163 *N11* **Hövsgöl** Dornogovĭ, SE Mongolia *43°35′N 109°40′E*
162 *I5* **Hövsgöl** ⬖ *province* N Mongolia
Hovsgol, Lake *see* Hövsgöl Nuur
162 *J5* **Hövsgöl Nuur** *var.* Lake Hovsgol. ◎ N Mongolia
78 *L9* **Howa, Ouadi** *var.* Wādi Howar. ≈ Chad/Sudan ***see also*** Howar, Wādi
Howa, Ouadi *see* Howar, Wādi
27 *P7* **Howard** Kansas, C USA *37°27′N 96°16′W*
29 *Q10* **Howard** South Dakota, N USA *43°58′N 97°31′W*
25 *N10* **Howard Draw** *valley* Texas, SW USA
29 *U8* **Howard Lake** Minnesota, N USA *45°03′N 94°03′W*
80 *B8* **Howar, Wādi** *var.* Ouadi Howa. ≈ Chad/Sudan ***see also*** Howa, Ouadi
Howar, Wādi *see* Howa, Ouadi
25 *U5* **Howe** Texas, SW USA *33°29′N 96°38′W*
183 *R12* **Howe, Cape** *headland* New South Wales/Victoria, SE Australia *37°30′S 149°58′E*
31 *R9* **Howell** Michigan, N USA *42°36′N 83°55′W*
28 *L9* **Howes** South Dakota, N USA *44°34′N 102°03′W*
83 *K23* **Howick** KwaZulu/Natal, E South Africa *29°29′S 30°13′E*
Howrah *see* Hāora
27 *W9* **Hoxie** Arkansas, C USA *36°03′N 90°58′W*
26 *J3* **Hoxie** Kansas, C USA *39°21′N 100°27′W*
101 *I14* **Höxter** Nordrhein-Westfalen, W Germany *51°46′N 09°22′E*
158 *K6* **Hoxud** *var.* Tewulike. Xinjiang Uygur Zizhiqu, NW China *42°18′N 86°51′E*
96 *J5* **Hoy** *island* N Scotland, United Kingdom
43 *S17* **Hoya, Cerro** ▲ S Panama *07°22′N 80°38′W*
94 *D12* **Høyanger** Sogn Og Fjordane, S Norway *61°13′N 06°05′E*
101 *P15* **Hoyerswerda** ***Lus.*** Wojerecy. Sachsen, E Germany *51°27′N 14°18′E*
164 *R14* **Hōyo-kaikyō** *var.* Hayasui-seto. *strait* SW Japan
104 *J8* **Hoyos** Extremadura, W Spain *40°10′N 06°43′W*
29 *W4* **Hoyt Lakes** Minnesota, N USA *47°31′N 92°08′W*
87 *V2* **Hoyvík** Streymoy, N Faeroe Islands
137 *O14* **Hozat** Tunceli, E Turkey *39°09′N 39°13′E*
Hôzyô *see* Hōjō
167 *N8* **Hpa-an** *var.* Pa-an. Kayin State, S Burma (Myanmar) *16°51′N 97°37′E*
Hpyu *see* Phyu
111 *F16* **Hradec Králové** ***Ger.*** Königgrätz. Královéhradecký Kraj, N Czech Republic *50°13′N 15°50′E*
Hradecký Kraj *see* Královehradecký Kraj
111 *B16* **Hradiště** ***Ger.*** Burgstadlberg. ▲ NW Czech Republic *50°12′N 13°04′E*
117 *R6* **Hradyz'k** ***Rus.*** Gradizhsk. Poltavs'ka Oblast', NE Ukraine *49°14′N 33°07′E*
119 *M16* **Hradzyanka** ***Rus.*** Grodzyanka. Mahilyowskaya Voblasts', E Belarus *53°33′N 28°45′E*
119 *F16* **Hrandzichy** ***Rus.*** Grandichi. Hrodzyenskaya Voblasts', W Belarus *53°43′N 23°49′E*
111 *H18* **Hranice** ***Ger.*** Mährisch-Weisskirchen. Olomoucký Kraj, E Czech Republic *49°34′N 17°45′E*
112 *I13* **Hrasnica** Federacija Bosna I Hercegovinia, SE Bosnia and Herzegovina *43°48′N 18°19′E*
109 *V11* **Hrastnik** C Slovenia *46°09′N 15°08′E*
137 *U12* **Hrazdan** ***Rus.*** Razdan. C Armenia *40°30′N 44°50′E*
137 *T12* **Hrazdan** *var.* Zanga, ***Rus.*** Razdan. ≈ C Armenia
117 *R5* **Hrebinka** ***Rus.*** Grebenka. Poltavs'ka Oblast', NE Ukraine *50°08′N 32°27′E*
119 *K17* **Hresk** ***Rus.*** Gresk. Minskaya Voblasts', C Belarus *53°10′N 27°29′E*
Hrisoupoli *see* Chrysoúpoli
119 *F16* **Hrodna** ***Pol.*** Grodno. Hrodzyenskaya Voblasts', W Belarus *53°40′N 23°50′E*
119 *F16* **Hrodzyenskaya Voblasts'** ***prev. Rus.*** Grodnenskaya Oblast'. ⬖ *province* W Belarus
111 *J21* **Hron** ***Ger.*** Gran, ***Hung.*** Garam. ≈ C Slovakia
111 *Q14* **Hrubieszów** ***Rus.*** Grubeshov. Lubelskie, E Poland *50°49′N 23°53′E*
112 *F13* **Hrvace** Split-Dalmacija, SE Croatia *43°46′N 16°35′E*
Hrvatska *see* Croatia
112 *F10* **Hrvatska Kostanjnica** *var.* Kostajnica. Sisak-Moslavina, C Croatia *45°14′N 16°35′E*
Hrvatsko Grahovi *see* Bosansko Grahovo
116 *K6* **Hrymayliv** ***Pol.*** Gízymałów, ***Rus.*** Grimaylov. Ternopil's'ka Oblast', W Ukraine *49°18′N 26°02′E*
167 *N4* **Hsenwi** Shan State, E Burma (Myanmar) *23°20′N 97°59′E*
Hsia-men *see* Xiamen
Hsiang-t'an *see* Xiangtan
Hsi Chiang *see* Xi Jiang
167 *N6* **Hsihseng** Shan State, C Burma (Myanmar) *20°07′N 97°17′E*
161 *S13* **Hsinchu** N Taiwan *24°48′N 120°59′E*
Hsing-K'ai Hu *see* Khanka, Lake
Hsi-ning/Hsining *see* Xining
Hsinking *see* Changchun
Hsin-yang *see* Xinyang
161 *S14* **Hsinying** *var.* Sinying, ***Jap.*** Shinei. C Taiwan *23°12′N 120°15′E*
167 *N4* **Hsipaw** Shan State, C Burma (Myanmar) *22°32′N 97°12′E*
Hsu-chou *see* Xuzhou
161 *S13* **Hsüeh Shan** ▲ N Taiwan

◆ Country
● Country Capital
◇ Dependent Territory
○ Dependent Territory Capital
⬖ Administrative Regions
✈ International Airport
▲ Mountain
▲▲ Mountain Range
Volcano
≈ River
◎ Lake
▣ Reservoir

Htawei *see* Dawei
Hu *see* Shanghai Shi
83 *B18* **Huab** W Namibia
57 *M21* **Huacaya** Chuquisaca, S Bolivia *20°45′S 63°42′W*
57 *J19* **Huachacalla** Oruro, SW Bolivia *18°47′S 68°23′W*
159 *X9* **Huachi** *var.* Rouyuan, Rouyuanchengzi. Gansu, C China *36°24′N 107°58′E*
57 *N16* **Huachi, Laguna** N Bolivia
57 *D14* **Huacho** Lima, W Peru *11°05′S 77°36′W*
163 *Y7* **Huachuan** Heilongjiang, NE China *46°57′S 130°48′E*
163 *P12* **Huade** Nei Mongol Zizhiqu, N China *41°52′N 113°58′E*
163 *W10* **Huadian** Jilin, NE China *42°59′N 126°38′E*
56 *E13* **Huagaruncho, Cordillera** ▲▲ C Peru
Hua Hin *see* Ban Hua Hin
191 *S10* **Huahine** *island* Îles Sous le Vent, W French Polynesia
Huahua, Rio *see* Wawa, Río
167 *R8* **Huai** E Thailand
161 *Q7* **Huai'an** *var.* Qingjiang; *prev.* Huaiyin. Jiangsu, E China *33°33′N 119°03′E*
161 *P6* **Huaibei** Anhui, E China *34°00′N 116°48′E*
Huaide *see* Gongzhuling
157 *T10* **Huai He** C China
160 *L11* **Huaihua** Hunan, S China *27°36′N 109°57′E*
161 *N14* **Huaiji** Guangdong, S China *23°54′N 112°12′E*
161 *O2* **Huailai** *var.* Shacheng. Hebei, E China *40°22′N 115°34′E*
161 *P7* **Huainan** *var.* Huai-nan, Hwainan. Anhui, E China *32°37′N 116°57′E*
Huai-nan *see* Huainan
161 *N2* **Huairen** *var.* Yunzhong. Shanxi, C China *35°28′N 110°29′E*
161 *O7* **Huaiyang** Henan, C China *33°44′N 114°55′E*
161 *Q7* **Huaiyin** Jiangsu, E China *33°31′N 119°03′E*
Huaiyin *see* Huai'an
167 *N16* **Huai Yot** Trang, SW Thailand *07°45′N 99°36′E*
41 *Q15* **Huajuapan** *var.* Huajuapan de León. Oaxaca, SE Mexico *17°50′N 97°48′W*
Huajuapan de León *see* Huajuapan
41 *O9* **Hualahuises** Nuevo León, NE Mexico *24°56′N 99°42′W*
36 *I11* **Hualapai Mountains** ▲▲ Arizona, SW USA
36 *I11* **Hualapai Peak** ▲ Arizona, SW USA *35°04′N 113°54′W*
62 *J7* **Hualfín** Catamarca, N Argentina *27°15′S 66°53′W*
161 *T13* **Hualien** *var.* Hwalien, *Jap.* Karen. C Taiwan *23°58′N 121°35′E*
56 *E10* **Huallaga, Río** N Peru
159 *U10* **Hualong** Qinghai, C China *36°06′N 102°16′E*
56 *C11* **Huamachuco** La Libertad, C Peru *07°50′S 78°01′W*
41 *Q14* **Huamantla** Tlaxcala, S Mexico *19°18′N 97°57′W*
82 *C13* **Huambo** *Port.* Nova Lisboa. Huambo, C Angola *12°48′S 15°45′E*
82 *B13* **Huambo** ◐ *province* C Angola
41 *P15* **Huamuxtitlán** Guerrero, S Mexico *17°49′N 98°34′W*
163 *Y8* **Huanan** Heilongjiang, NE China *46°21′N 130°43′E*
63 *H17* **Huancache, Sierra** ▲▲ SW Argentina
57 *I17* **Huancané** Puno, SE Peru *15°10′S 69°44′W*
57 *F16* **Huancapi** Ayacucho, C Peru *13°40′S 74°05′W*
57 *E15* **Huancavelica** Huancavelica, SW Peru *12°45′S 75°03′W*
57 *E15* **Huancavelica** *off.* Departamento de Huancavelica. ◐ *department* W Peru
Huancavelica, Departamento de *see* Huancavelica
57 *E14* **Huancayo** Junín, C Peru *12°03′S 75°14′W*
57 *K20* **Huanchaca, Cerro** ▲ S Bolivia *20°12′S 66°35′W*
Huancheng *see* Huanxian
56 *C12* **Huandoy, Nevado** ▲ W Peru *08°48′S 77°33′W*
Huang'an *see* Hong'an
161 *O8* **Huangchuan** Henan, C China *32°00′N 115°02′E*
161 *O9* **Huanggang** Hubei, C China *30°27′N 114°48′E*
Huang Hai *see* Yellow Sea
157 *Q8* **Huang He** *var.* Yellow River. C China
Huanghe *see* Madoi
161 *Q4* **Huanghe Kou** *delta* E China
Huangheyan *see* Madoi
160 *L5* **Huangling** Shaanxi, C China *35°40′N 109°14′E*
161 *O9* **Huangpi** Hubei, C China *30°53′N 114°22′E*
163 *P13* **Huangqi Hai** N China
161 *Q9* **Huangshan** *var.* Tunxi. Anhui, E China *29°43′N 118°20′E*
161 *Q9* **Huangshan** ▲ Anhui, China *30°06′N 118°04′E*
161 *O9* **Huangshi** *var.* Huang-shih, Hwangshih. Hubei, C China *30°14′N 115°E*
Huang-shih *see* Huangshi
160 *L5* **Huangtu Gaoyuan** *plateau* C China
61 *B22* **Huanguelén** Buenos Aires, E Argentina *37°02′S 61°57′W*
161 *S10* **Huangyan** Zhejiang, SE China *28°39′N 121°19′E*
159 *T10* **Huangyuan** Qinghai, C China *36°40′N 101°12′E*
159 *T10* **Huangzhong** *var.* Lushar. Qinghai, C China *36°31′N 101°32′E*
163 *W12* **Huanren** *var.* Huanren Manzu Zizhixian. Liaoning, NE China *41°16′N 125°25′E*
Huanren Manzu Zizhixian *see* Huanren
57 *F15* **Huanta** Ayacucho, C Peru *12°54′S 74°13′W*
56 *E13* **Huánuco** Huánuco, C Peru *09°58′S 76°16′W*
56 *D13* **Huánuco** *off.* Departamento de Huánuco. ◐ *department* C Peru
Huánuco, Departamento de *see* Huánuco
57 *K19* **Huanuni** Oruro, W Bolivia *18°15′S 66°48′W*
159 *X9* **Huanxian** *var.* Huancheng. Gansu, C China *36°30′N 107°20′E*
161 *S12* **Huap'ing Yu** *island* N Taiwan
62 *H3* **Huara** Tarapacá, N Chile *19°59′S 69°42′W*
57 *D14* **Huaral** Lima, W Peru *11°31′S 77°10′W*
Huarás *see* Huaraz
56 *D13* **Huaraz** *var.* Huarás. Ancash, W Peru *09°31′S 77°32′W*
57 *I16* **Huari Huari, Río** S Peru
56 *C13* **Huarmey** Ancash, W Peru *10°03′S 78°08′W*
40 *H4* **Huásabas** Sonora, NW Mexico *29°47′N 109°18′W*
56 *D8* **Huasaga, Río** Ecuador/Peru
167 *O15* **Hua Sai** Nakhon Si Thammarat, SW Thailand *08°02′N 100°18′E*
56 *D12* **Huascarán, Nevado** ▲ W Peru *09°01′S 77°27′W*
62 *G8* **Huasco** Atacama, N Chile *28°30′S 71°15′W*
62 *G8* **Huasco, Río** C Chile
159 *S11* **Huashikia** Qinghai, W China
40 *G7* **Huatabampo** Sonora, NW Mexico *26°49′N 109°40′W*
159 *W10* **Huating** *var.* Donghua. Gansu, C China *35°13′N 106°39′E*
167 *S7* **Huatt, Phou** ▲ N Vietnam *19°45′N 104°48′E*
41 *Q14* **Huatusco** *var.* Huatusco de Chicuellar. Veracruz-Llave, C Mexico *19°13′N 96°57′W*
Huatusco de Chicuellar *see* Huatusco
41 *P13* **Huauchinango** Puebla, S Mexico *20°11′N 98°04′W*
Huaunta *see* Wounta
41 *R15* **Huautla** *var.* Huautla de Jiménez. Oaxaca, SE Mexico *18°10′N 96°51′W*
Huautla de Jiménez *see* Huautla
161 *O5* **Huaxian** *var.* Daokou, Hua Xian. Henan, C China *35°33′N 114°30′E*
Hua Xian *see* Huaxian
Huazangsi *see* Tianzhu
29 *V13* **Hubbard** Iowa, C USA *42°18′N 93°18′W*
25 *U8* **Hubbard** Texas, SW USA *31°52′N 96°43′W*
25 *Q6* **Hubbard Creek Lake** Texas, SW USA
31 *R6* **Hubbard Lake** Michigan, N USA
160 *M9* **Hubei** *var.* E, Hubei Sheng, Hupeh, Hupei. ◐ *province* C China
Hubei Sheng *see* Hubei
109 *P8* **Huben** Tirol, W Austria *46°55′N 12°35′E*
31 *R13* **Huber Heights** Ohio, N USA *39°50′N 84°07′W*
155 *F17* **Hubli** Karnātaka, SW India *15°20′N 75°14′E*
163 *X12* **Huch'ang** N North Korea *41°25′N 127°04′E*
97 *M18* **Hucknall** C England, United Kingdom *53°02′N 01°11′W*
97 *L17* **Huddersfield** N England, United Kingdom *53°39′N 01°47′W*
95 *O16* **Huddinge** Stockholm, C Sweden *59°15′N 17°57′E*
94 *N11* **Hudiksvall** Gävleborg, C Sweden *61°45′N 17°12′E*
29 *W13* **Hudson** Iowa, C USA *42°24′N 92°27′W*
19 *O11* **Hudson** Massachusetts, NE USA *42°24′N 71°34′W*
31 *Q11* **Hudson** Michigan, N USA *41°51′N 84°21′W*
30 *H6* **Hudson** Wisconsin, N USA *44°59′N 92°43′W*
11 *V14* **Hudson Bay** Saskatchewan, S Canada *52°51′N 102°23′W*
12 *G6* **Hudson Bay** *bay* NE Canada
195 *T16* **Hudson, Cape** *headland* Antarctica *68°15′S 154°00′E*
Hudson, Détroit d' *see* Hudson Strait
27 *Q9* **Hudson, Lake** Oklahoma, C USA
18 *K9* **Hudson River** New Jersey/New York, NE USA
10 *M12* **Hudson's Hope** British Columbia, W Canada *56°03′N 121°59′W*
12 *L2* **Hudson Strait** *Fr.* Détroit d'Hudson. *strait* Northwest Territories/Québec, NE Canada
Ḥudūd ash Shamālīyah, Minṭaqat al *see* Al Ḥudūd ash Shamālīyah
Hudur *see* Xuddur
167 *U9* **Huê** Th,a Thiên-Huê, C Vietnam *16°28′N 107°35′E*
104 *J7* **Huebra** W Spain
24 *H8* **Hueco Mountains** ▲▲ Texas, SW USA
116 *G10* **Huedin** *Hung.* Bánffyhunyad. Cluj, NW Romania *46°52′N 23°02′E*
40 *J10* **Huehuento, Cerro** ▲ C Mexico *24°04′N 105°42′W*
42 *B5* **Huehuetenango** Huehuetenango, W Guatemala *15°19′N 91°26′W*
42 *B4* **Huehuetenango** *off.* Departamento de Huehuetenango. ◐ *department* W Guatemala
Huehuetenango, Departamento de *see* Huehuetenango
40 *L11* **Huejuquilla** Jalisco, SW Mexico *22°40′N 103°52′W*
41 *P12* **Huejutla** *var.* Huejutla de Reyes. Hidalgo, C Mexico *21°10′N 98°25′W*
Huejutla de Reyes *see* Huejutla
102 *G6* **Huelgoat** Finistère, NW France *48°22′N 03°45′W*
105 *O13* **Huelma** Andalucía, S Spain *37°39′N 03°28′W*
104 *I14* **Huelva** *anc.* Onuba. Andalucía, SW Spain *37°15′N 06°56′W*
104 *I13* **Huelva** ◐ *province* Andalucía, SW Spain
104 *J13* **Huelva** SW Spain
105 *Q14* **Huercal-Overa** Andalucía, S Spain *37°23′N 01°56′W*
37 *Q9* **Huerfano Mountain** ▲ New Mexico, SW USA *36°25′N 107°50′W*
37 *T7* **Huerfano River** Colorado, C USA
105 *S12* **Huertas, Cabo** *headland* SE Spain *38°21′N 00°25′W*
105 *R6* **Huerva** N Spain
105 *S4* **Huesca** *anc.* Osca. Aragón, NE Spain *42°08′N 00°25′W*
105 *T4* **Huesca** ◐ *province* Aragón, NE Spain
105 *P13* **Huéscar** Andalucía, S Spain *37°39′N 02°32′W*
41 *N15* **Huetamo** *var.* Huetamo de Núñez. Michoacán, SW Mexico *18°36′N 100°54′W*
Huetamo de Núñez *see* Huetamo
105 *P8* **Huete** Castilla-La Mancha, C Spain *40°09′N 02°42′W*
23 *P4* **Hueytown** Alabama, S USA *33°27′N 87°00′W*
28 *L16* **Hugh Butler Lake** Nebraska, C USA
181 *V6* **Hughenden** Queensland, NE Australia *20°57′S 144°16′E*
182 *A6* **Hughes** South Australia *30°41′S 129°31′E*
39 *P8* **Hughes** Alaska, USA *66°03′N 154°15′W*
27 *X11* **Hughes** Arkansas, C USA *34°57′N 90°28′W*
25 *W6* **Hughes Springs** Texas, SW USA *33°00′N 94°37′W*
153 *S17* **Hugli** N India
37 *V5* **Hugo** Colorado, C USA *39°08′N 103°28′W*
27 *Q13* **Hugo** Oklahoma, C USA *34°01′N 95°31′W*
27 *Q13* **Hugo Lake** Oklahoma, C USA
26 *H7* **Hugoton** Kansas, C USA *37°11′N 101°22′W*
Huhehot/Huhohaote *see* Hohhot
Huhttán *see* Kvikkjokk
161 *R13* **Hui'an** *var.* Luocheng. Fujian, SE China *25°06′N 118°45′E*
184 *O9* **Huiarau Range** ▲▲ North Island, New Zealand
83 *D22* **Huib-Hoch Plateau** *plateau* S Namibia
41 *O13* **Huichapán** Hidalgo, C Mexico *20°24′N 99°40′W*
Huicheng *see* Shexian
163 *W13* **Hŭich'ŏn** C North Korea *40°09′N 126°17′E*
83 *B15* **Huíla** ◐ *province* SW Angola
54 *E12* **Huila** *off.* Departamento del Huila. ◐ *province* S Colombia
Huila, Departamento del *see* Huila
54 *D11* **Huila, Nevado del** *elevation* C Colombia
83 *B15* **Huíla Plateau** *plateau* S Angola
160 *G12* **Huili** Sichuan, C China *26°39′N 102°13′E*
161 *P4* **Huimin** Shandong, E China *37°29′N 117°30′E*
163 *W11* **Huinan** *var.* Chaoyang. Jilin, NE China *42°40′N 126°03′E*
62 *K12* **Huinca Renancó** Córdoba, C Argentina *34°51′S 64°22′W*
159 *V10* **Huining** *var.* Huishi. Gansu, C China *35°42′N 105°01′E*
Huishi *see* Huining
160 *J12* **Huishui** *var.* Heping. Guizhou, S China *26°07′N 106°39′E*
102 *L6* **Huisne** NW France
98 *L12* **Huissen** Gelderland, SE Netherlands *51°57′N 05°57′E*
159 *N11* **Huiten Nur** C China
93 *K19* **Huittinen** Länsi-Suomi, SW Finland *61°11′N 22°40′E*
41 *O15* **Huitzuco** *var.* Huitzuco de los Figueroa. Guerrero, S Mexico *18°18′N 99°22′W*
Huitzuco de los Figueroa *see* Huitzuco
159 *W11* **Huixian** *var.* Hui Xian. Gansu, C China *33°48′N 106°02′E*
Hui Xian *see* Huixian
41 *V17* **Huixtla** Chiapas, SE Mexico *15°09′N 92°30′W*
160 *H12* **Huize** *var.* Zhongping. Yunnan, SW China *26°28′N 103°18′E*
98 *J10* **Huizen** Noord-Holland, C Netherlands *52°17′N 05°15′E*
161 *O14* **Huizhou** Guangdong, S China *23°02′N 114°28′E*
162 *J6* **Hujirt** Arhangay, C Mongolia *48°49′N 101°20′E*
Hujirt *see* Tsetserleg, Övörhangay, Mongolia
Hujirt *see* Delgerhaan, Töv, Mongolia
Hukagawa *see* Fukagawa
163 *W17* **Hŭksan-chedo** *var.* Hŭksan-chedo. *island group* SW South Korea
Hŭksan-chedo *see* Hŭksan-chedo
Hukue *see* Fukue
Hukui *see* Fukui
83 *G20* **Hukuntsi** Kgalagadi, SW Botswana *23°59′S 21°44′E*
Hukuoka *see* Fukuoka
Hukusima *see* Fukushima
Hukutiyama *see* Fukuchiyama
Hukuyama *see* Fukuyama
163 *W8* **Hulan** Heilongjiang, NE China *45°59′N 126°37′E*
163 *W8* **Hulan He** NE China
31 *Q4* **Hulbert Lake** Michigan, N USA
Hulczyn *see* Hlučín
Huliao *see* Dabu
163 *Z8* **Hulin** Heilongjiang, NE China *45°48′N 133°06′E*
163 *S9* **Hulingol** *prev.* Huolin Gol. Nei Mongol Zizhiqu, N China *45°36′N 119°54′E*
14 *L12* **Hull** Québec, SE Canada *45°26′N 75°45′W*
29 *S12* **Hull** Iowa, C USA *43°11′N 96°07′W*
Hull *see* Kingston upon Hull
Hull Island *see* Orona
99 *F16* **Hulst** Zeeland, SW Netherlands *51°17′N 04°03′E*
Hulstay *see* Choybalsan
Hultschin *see* Hlučín
95 *M19* **Hultsfred** Kalmar, S Sweden *57°30′N 15°50′E*
163 *T13* **Huludao** *prev.* Jinxi, Lianshan. Liaoning, NE China *40°46′N 120°47′E*
Hulun *see* Hulun Buir
163 *S6* **Hulun Buir** *var.* Hailar; *prev.* Hulun. Nei Mongol Zizhiqu, N China *49°15′N 119°41′E*
Hu-lun Ch'ih *see* Hulun Nur
163 *Q6* **Hulun Nur** *var.* Hu-lun Ch'ih; *prev.* Dalai Nor. NE China
Hulwan/Hulwân *see* Hilwān
117 *V8* **Hulyaypole** *Rus.* Gulyaypole. Zaporiz'ka Oblast', SE Ukraine *47°41′N 36°10′E*
163 *V4* **Huma** Heilongjiang, NE China *51°40′N 126°38′E*
45 *V6* **Humacao** E Puerto Rico *18°09′N 65°50′W*
163 *U4* **Huma He** NE China
62 *J5* **Humahuaca** Jujuy, N Argentina *23°13′S 65°20′W*
59 *E14* **Humaitá** Amazonas, N Brazil *07°33′S 63°01′W*
62 *N7* **Humaitá** Ñeembucú, S Paraguay *27°02′S 58°31′W*
83 *H26* **Humansdorp** Eastern Cape, S South Africa *34°01′S 24°45′E*
27 *S6* **Humansville** Missouri, C USA *37°47′N 93°34′W*
40 *I8* **Humaya, Río** C Mexico
83 *C16* **Humbe** Cunene, SW Angola *16°37′S 14°52′E*
97 *N17* **Humber** *estuary* E England, United Kingdom
97 *N17* **Humberside** *cultural region* E England, United Kingdom
Humberto *see* Umberto
25 *W11* **Humble** Texas, SW USA *29°58′N 95°15′W*
11 *U15* **Humboldt** Saskatchewan, S Canada *52°13′N 105°09′W*
29 *U12* **Humboldt** Iowa, C USA *42°42′N 94°13′W*
27 *Q6* **Humboldt** Kansas, C USA *37°48′N 95°26′W*
29 *S17* **Humboldt** Nebraska, C USA *40°09′N 95°56′W*
35 *S3* **Humboldt** Nevada, W USA *40°36′N 118°15′W*
20 *G9* **Humboldt** Tennessee, S USA *35°49′N 88°55′W*
34 *K3* **Humboldt Bay** *bay* California, W USA
35 *S4* **Humboldt Lake** Nevada, W USA
35 *S4* **Humboldt River** Nevada, W USA
35 *T5* **Humboldt Salt Marsh** *wetland* Nevada, W USA
183 *P11* **Hume, Lake** New South Wales/Victoria, SE Australia
111 *N19* **Humenné** *Ger.* Homenau, *Hung.* Homonna. Prešovský Kraj, E Slovakia *48°57′N 21°54′E*
29 *V15* **Humeston** Iowa, C USA *40°51′N 93°30′W*
54 *J5* **Humocaro Bajo** Lara, N Venezuela *09°41′N 70°00′W*
29 *Q14* **Humphrey** Nebraska, C USA *41°38′N 97°29′W*
35 *S9* **Humphreys, Mount** ▲ California, W USA *37°11′N 118°39′W*
36 *L11* **Humphreys Peak** ▲ Arizona, SW USA *35°18′N 111°40′W*
111 *E17* **Humpolec** *Ger.* Gumpolds, Humpoletz. Vysočina, C Czech Republic *49°33′N 15°23′E*
Humpoletz *see* Humpolec
93 *K19* **Humppila** Etelä-Suomi, S Finland *60°54′N 23°21′E*
32 *F8* **Humptulips** Washington, NW USA *47°13′N 123°57′W*
42 *H7* **Humuya, Río** W Honduras
75 *P9* **Hūn** N Libya *29°06′N 15°56′E*
92 *I1* **Húnaflói** *bay* NW Iceland
160 *M11* **Hunan** *var.* Hunan Sheng, Xiang. ◐ *province* S China
Hunan Sheng *see* Hunan
163 *Y10* **Hunchun** Jilin, NE China *42°51′N 130°21′E*
95 *I22* **Hundested** Frederiksborg, E Denmark *55°58′N 11°53′E*
Hundred Mile House *see* 100 Mile House
116 *G12* **Hunedoara** *Ger.* Eisenmarkt, *Hung.* Vajdahunyad. Hunedoara, SW Romania *45°45′N 22°54′E*
116 *G12* **Hunedoara** ◐ *county* W Romania
101 *I17* **Hünfeld** Hessen, C Germany *50°41′N 09°46′E*
Hungarian People's Republic *see* Hungary
111 *H23* **Hungary** *off.* Republic of Hungary, *Ger.* Ungarn, *Hung.* Magyarország, *Rom.* Ungaria, *SCr.* Mađarska, *Ukr.* Uhorshchyna; *prev.* Hungarian People's Republic. ◆ *republic* C Europe
Hungary, Plain of *see* Great Hungarian Plain
Hungary, Republic of *see* Hungary
Hungiy *see* Urgamal
163 *X13* **Hŭngnam** E North Korea *39°50′N 127°36′E*
33 *P8* **Hungry Horse Reservoir** Montana, NW USA
Hungt'ou *see* Lan Yü
Hung-tse Hu *see* Hongze Hu
167 *T6* **Hưng Yên** Hai Hưng, N Vietnam *20°38′N 106°05′E*
Hunjiang *see* Baishan
95 *I18* **Hunnebostrand** Västra Götaland, S Sweden *58°26′N 11°19′E*
101 *E19* **Hunsrück** ▲▲ W Germany
97 *P18* **Hunstanton** E England, United Kingdom *52°57′N 00°27′E*
155 *G20* **Hunsūr** Karnātaka, E India *12°18′N 76°15′E*
Hunt *see* Hangay
100 *G12* **Hunte** NW Germany
29 *Q5* **Hunter** North Dakota, N USA *47°10′N 97°11′W*
25 *S11* **Hunter** Texas, SW USA *29°47′N 98°01′W*
185 *D20* **Hunter** South Island, New Zealand
183 *N15* **Hunter Island** *island* Tasmania, SE Australia
18 *K11* **Hunter Mountain** ▲ New York, NE USA *42°10′N 74°13′W*
185 *B23* **Hunter Mountains** ▲▲ South Island, New Zealand
183 *S7* **Hunter River** New South Wales, SE Australia
32 *L7* **Hunters** Washington, NW USA *48°07′N 118°13′W*
185 *F20* **Hunters Hills, The** *hill range* South Island, New Zealand
184 *M12* **Hunterville** Manawatu-Wanganui, North Island, New Zealand *39°55′S 175°34′E*
31 *N16* **Huntingburg** Indiana, N USA *38°18′N 86°57′W*
97 *O20* **Huntingdon** E England, United Kingdom *52°20′N 00°12′W*
18 *E15* **Huntingdon** Pennsylvania, NE USA *40°28′N 78°00′W*
20 *G9* **Huntingdon** Tennessee, S USA *36°00′N 88°25′W*
97 *O20* **Huntingdonshire** *cultural region* C England, United Kingdom
31 *P12* **Huntington** Indiana, N USA *40°52′N 85°30′W*
32 *L13* **Huntington** Oregon, NW USA *44°22′N 117°18′W*
25 *X9* **Huntington** Texas, SW USA *31°16′N 94°34′W*
36 *M5* **Huntington** Utah, W USA *39°19′N 110°57′W*
21 *P5* **Huntington** West Virginia, NE USA *38°25′N 82°27′W*
35 *T16* **Huntington Beach** California, W USA *33°39′N 118°00′W*
35 *W4* **Huntington Creek** Nevada, W USA
184 *L7* **Huntly** Waikato, North Island, New Zealand *37°34′S 175°09′E*
96 *K8* **Huntly** NE Scotland, United Kingdom *57°25′N 02°48′W*
10 *K8* **Hunt, Mount** ▲ Yukon Territory, NW Canada *61°29′N 129°10′W*
14 *H12* **Huntsville** Ontario, S Canada *45°20′N 79°14′W*
23 *P2* **Huntsville** Alabama, S USA *34°44′N 86°35′W*
27 *S9* **Huntsville** Arkansas, C USA *36°04′N 93°46′W*
27 *U3* **Huntsville** Missouri, C USA *39°27′N 92°31′W*
20 *M8* **Huntsville** Tennessee, S USA *36°25′N 84°30′W*
25 *V10* **Huntsville** Texas, SW USA *30°43′N 95°34′W*
36 *L2* **Huntsville** Utah, W USA *41°16′N 111°47′W*
41 *W12* **Hunucmá** Yucatán, SE Mexico *20°59′N 89°55′W*
149 *W3* **Hunza** *var.* Karīmābād. Jammu and Kashmir, NE Pakistan *36°23′N 74°43′E*
149 *W3* **Hunza** NE Pakistan
Hunze *see* Oostermoers Vaart
158 *H4* **Huocheng** *var.* Shuiding. Xinjiang Uygur Zizhiqu, NW China *44°03′N 80°49′E*
161 *N6* **Huojia** Henan, C China *35°14′N 113°38′E*
Huolin Gol *see* Hulingol
186 *N14* **Huon** *reef* N New Caledonia
186 *E7* **Huon Peninsula** *headland* C Papua New Guinea *06°24′S 147°50′E*
Huoshao Dao *see* Lü Tao
Huoshao Tao *see* Lan Yü
Hupeh/Hupei *see* Hubei
Hurama *see* Hongyuan
95 *H14* **Hurdalssjøen** S Norway
14 *E13* **Hurd, Cape** *headland* Ontario, S Canada *45°12′N 81°43′W*
Hurdegaryp *see* Hardegarijp
29 *N4* **Hurdsfield** North Dakota, N USA *47°24′N 99°55′W*
Hüremt *see* Sayhan, Bulgan, Mongolia
Hüremt *see* Taragt, Övörhangay, Mongolia
75 *X9* **Hurghada** *var.* Al Ghurdaqah, Ghurdaqah. E Egypt *27°17′N 33°47′E*
67 *V9* **Huri Hills** ▲▲ NW Kenya
37 *P15* **Hurley** New Mexico, SW USA *32°42′N 108°07′W*
30 *K4* **Hurley** Wisconsin, N USA *46°25′N 90°15′W*
21 *Y4* **Hurlock** Maryland, NE USA *38°37′N 75°51′W*
162 *K11* **Hürmen** *var.* Tsoohor. Ömnögovĭ, S Mongolia *43°15′N 104°04′E*
29 *P10* **Huron** South Dakota, N USA *44°19′N 98°13′W*
31 *S6* **Huron, Lake** Canada/USA
31 *N3* **Huron Mountains** *hill range* Michigan, N USA
36 *J8* **Hurricane** Utah, W USA *37°10′N 113°18′W*
21 *P5* **Hurricane** West Virginia, NE USA *38°25′N 82°01′W*
36 *J8* **Hurricane Cliffs** *cliff* Arizona, SW USA
23 *V6* **Hurricane Creek** Georgia, SE USA
94 *E12* **Hurrungane** ▲ S Norway *61°25′N 07°48′E*
101 *E16* **Hürth** Nordrhein-Westfalen, W Germany *50°52′N 06°49′E*
Hurukawa *see* Furukawa
185 *I17* **Hurunui** South Island, New Zealand
95 *F21* **Hurup** Viborg, NW Denmark *56°46′N 08°26′E*
117 *T14* **Hurzuf** Respublika Krym, S Ukraine *44°33′N 34°18′E*
Huș *see* Huși
95 *B19* **Húsavík** *Dan.* Husevig. Sandoy, C Faeroe Islands *65°24′N 06°38′W*
92 *K1* **Húsavík** Nordhurland Eystra, NE Iceland *66°03′N 17°20′W*
Husevig *see* Húsavík
116 *M10* **Huși** *var.* Huș. Vaslui, E Romania *46°40′N 28°05′E*
95 *L19* **Huskvarna** Jönköping, S Sweden *57°47′N 14°15′E*
39 *P8* **Huslia** Alaska, USA *65°42′N 156°24′W*
Husn *see* Al Ḥuṣn
95 *C15* **Husnes** Hordaland, S Norway *59°52′N 05°46′E*
94 *D8* **Hustadvika** *sea area* S Norway
Husté *see* Khust
100 *H7* **Husum** Schleswig-Holstein, N Germany *54°29′N 09°04′E*
93 *I16* **Husum** Västernorrland, C Sweden *63°21′N 19°12′E*
116 *K6* **Husyatyn** Ternopil's'ka Oblast', W Ukraine *49°04′N 26°10′E*
Huszt *see* Khust
Hutag *see* Hutag-Öndör
162 *K6* **Hutag-Öndör** *var.* Hutag. Bulgan, N Mongolia *49°22′N 102°50′E*
26 *M6* **Hutchinson** Kansas, C USA *38°03′N 97°56′W*
29 *U9* **Hutchinson** Minnesota, N USA *44°53′N 94°22′W*
23 *Y13* **Hutchinson Island** *island* Florida, SE USA
36 *L11* **Hutch Mountain** ▲ Arizona, SW USA *34°49′N 111°22′W*
141 *O14* **Ḥūth** NW Yemen *16°14′N 44°E*
186 *I7* **Hutjena** Buka Island, NE Papua New Guinea *05°19′S 154°40′E*
109 *T8* **Hüttenberg** Kärnten, S Austria *46°58′N 14°33′E*
25 *T10* **Hutto** Texas, SW USA *30°32′N 97°33′W*
Huttu *see* Futtsu
108 *E8* **Huttwil** Bern, W Switzerland *47°06′N 07°48′E*
158 *K5* **Hutubi** Xinjiang Uygur Zizhiqu, NW China *44°10′N 86°51′E*
161 *N4* **Hutuo He** C China
Hutyû *see* Fuchū
185 *E20* **Huxley, Mount** ▲ South Island, New Zealand *44°02′S 169°42′E*
99 *J20* **Huy** *Dut.* Hoei, Hoey. Liège, E Belgium *50°32′N 05°14′E*
161 *R8* **Huzhou** *var.* Wuxing. Zhejiang, SE China *30°54′N 120°05′E*
159 *T10* **Huzhu** Qinghai, China *36°40′N 101°58′E*
Huzi *see* Fuji
Huzieda *see* Fujieda
Huzinomiya *see* Fujinomiya
Huzisawa *see* Fujisawa
92 *I2* **Hvammstangi** Nordhurland Vestra, N Iceland *65°22′N 20°54′W*
92 *K4* **Hvannadalshnúkur** S Iceland *64°01′N 16°39′W*
113 *E15* **Hvar** *It.* Lesina. Split-Dalmacija, S Croatia *43°10′N 16°27′E*
113 *F15* **Hvar** *It.* Lesina; *anc.* Pharus. *island* S Croatia
117 *T13* **Hvardiys'ke** *Rus.* Gvardeyskoye. Respublika Krym, S Ukraine *45°08′N 34°01′E*
92 *I4* **Hveragerdhi** Sudhurland, SW Iceland *64°00′N 21°13′W*
95 *E22* **Hvide Sande** Ringkøbing, W Denmark *56°00′N 08°08′E*
92 *I3* **Hvitá** C Iceland
95 *G15* **Hvittingfoss** Buskerud, S Norway *59°28′N 10°00′E*
92 *I4* **Hvolsvöllur** Sudhurland, SW Iceland *63°44′N 20°12′W*
Hwach'ŏn-chŏsuji *see* P'aro-ho
Hwainan *see* Huainan
Hwalien *see* Hualien
83 *I16* **Hwange** *prev.* Wankie. Matabeleland North, W Zimbabwe *18°18′S 26°31′E*
Hwang-Hae *see* Yellow Sea
Hwangshih *see* Huangshi
83 *L17* **Hwedza** Mashonaland East, E Zimbabwe *18°35′S 31°35′E*
63 *G20* **Hyades, Cerro** ▲ S Chile *46°57′S 73°09′W*
162 *K6* **Hyalganat** *var.* Selenge. Bulgan, N Mongolia *49°34′N 104°18′E*
19 *Q12* **Hyannis** Massachusetts, NE USA *41°38′N 70°15′W*
28 *L13* **Hyannis** Nebraska, C USA *42°00′N 101°45′W*
162 *F6* **Hyargas Nuur** NW Mongolia
Hybla/Hybla Major *see* Paternò
39 *Y14* **Hydaburg** Prince of Wales Island, Alaska, USA *55°10′N 132°44′W*
185 *F22* **Hyde** Otago, South Island, New Zealand *45°17′S 170°17′E*
21 *O7* **Hyden** Kentucky, S USA *37°08′N 83°23′W*
18 *K12* **Hyde Park** New York, NE USA *41°46′N 73°52′W*
39 *Z14* **Hyder** Alaska, USA *55°55′N 130°01′W*
155 *I15* **Hyderābād** *var.* Haidarabad. *state capital* Andhra Pradesh, C India *17°22′N 78°26′E*
149 *Q16* **Hyderābād** *var.* Haidarabad. Sind, SE Pakistan *25°26′N 68°22′E*
103 *T16* **Hyères** Var, SE France *43°07′N 06°08′E*
103 *T16* **Hyères, Îles d'** *island group* S France
118 *K12* **Hyermanavichy** *Rus.* Germanovichi. Vitsyebskaya Voblasts', N Belarus *55°24′N 27°48′E*
163 *X12* **Hyesan** NE North Korea *41°18′N 128°13′E*
10 *K8* **Hyland** Yukon Territory, NW Canada
95 *K20* **Hyltebruk** Halland, S Sweden *57°N 13°14′E*
18 *D16* **Hyndman** Pennsylvania, NE USA *39°49′N 78°42′W*
33 *P14* **Hyndman Peak** ▲ Idaho, NW USA *43°45′N 114°07′W*
164 *I13* **Hyōgo** *off.* Hyōgo-ken. ◐ *prefecture* Honshū, SW Japan
Hyōgo-ken *see* Hyōgo
Hypsas *see* Belice
Hyrcania *see* Gorgān
36 *L1* **Hyrum** Utah, W USA *41°37′N 111°51′W*
93 *N14* **Hyrynsalmi** Oulu, C Finland *64°41′N 28°30′E*
33 *V10* **Hysham** Montana, NW USA *46°16′N 107°14′W*
11 *N13* **Hythe** Alberta, W Canada *55°18′N 119°44′W*
97 *Q23* **Hythe** SE England, United Kingdom *51°05′N 01°04′E*
Hyvinge *see* Hyvinkää
93 *L19* **Hyvinkää** *Swe.* Hyvinge. Etelä-Suomi, S Finland *60°37′N 24°50′E*

I

116 *J9* **Iacobeni** *Ger.* Jakobeny. Suceava, NE Romania *47°24′N 25°20′E*
Iader *see* Zadar
172 *I7* **Iakora** Fianarantsoa, SE Madagascar *23°04′S 46°40′E*
116 *K14* **Ialomița** *var.* Jalomitsa. ◐ *county* SE Romania
116 *K14* **Ialomița** SE Romania
117 *N10* **Ialoveni** *Rus.* Yaloveny. C Moldova *46°57′N 28°47′E*
117 *N11* **Ialpug** *var.* Ialpugul Mare, *Rus.* Yalpug. Moldova/Ukraine
Ialpugul Mare *see* Ialpug
23 *T8* **Iamonia, Lake** Florida, SE USA
116 *L13* **Ianca** Brăila, SE Romania *45°06′N 27°29′E*
116 *M10* **Iași** *Ger.* Jassy. Iași, NE Romania *47°08′N 27°38′E*
116 *L9* **Iași** *Ger.* Jassy, Yassy. ◐ *county* NE Romania
114 *J13* **Íasmos** Anatolikí Makedonía kai Thráki, NE Greece *41°07′N 25°12′E*
22 *H6* **Iatt, Lake** Louisiana, S USA
58 *B11* **Iauretê** Amazonas, NW Brazil *0°37′N 69°10′W*
171 *N3* **Iba** Luzon, N Philippines *15°25′N 119°55′E*
77 *S16* **Ibadan** Oyo, SW Nigeria *07°22′N 04°01′E*
54 *E10* **Ibagué** Tolima, C Colombia *04°27′N 75°14′W*
60 *J10* **Ibaiti** Paraná, S Brazil *23°49′S 50°15′W*
36 *J4* **Ibapah Peak** ▲ Utah, W USA *39°51′N 113°55′W*
113 *M15* **Ibar** *Alb.* Ibër. C Serbia
165 *P13* **Ibaraki** *off.* Ibaraki-ken. ◐ *prefecture* Honshū, S Japan
Ibaraki-ken *see* Ibaraki
56 *C5* **Ibarra** *var.* San Miguel de Ibarra. Imbabura, N Ecuador *0°23′S 78°08′W*
Ibașfalău *see* Dumbrăveni
141 *O16* **Ibb** W Yemen *13°55′N 44°10′E*
100 *F13* **Ibbenbüren** Nordrhein-Westfalen, NW Germany *52°17′N 07°43′E*
79 *H16* **Ibenga** N Congo
Ibër *see* Ibar
57 *I14* **Iberia** Madre de Dios, E Peru *11°21′S 69°36′W*
Iberia *see* Spain
66 *M1* **Iberian Basin** *undersea feature* E Atlantic Ocean *39°00′N 16°00′W*
Iberian Mountains *see* Ibérico, Sistema
84 *D12* **Iberian Peninsula** *physical region* Portugal/Spain
64 *M8* **Iberian Plain** *undersea feature* E Atlantic Ocean *13°30′W 43°45′N*
Ibérica, Cordillera *see* Ibérico, Sistema
105 *P6* **Ibérico, Sistema** *var.* Cordillera Ibérica, *Eng.* Iberian Mountains. ▲▲ NE Spain
12 *K7* **Iberville Lac d'** Québec, NE Canada
77 *T14* **Ibeto** Niger, W Nigeria *10°30′N 05°07′E*
77 *W15* **Ibi** Taraba, C Nigeria *08°13′N 09°46′E*
105 *S11* **Ibi** País Valenciano, E Spain *38°38′N 00°35′W*
59 *L20* **Ibiá** Minas Gerais, SE Brazil *19°30′S 46°31′W*
61 *F15* **Ibicuí, Rio** S Brazil
61 *C19* **Ibicuy** Entre Ríos, E Argentina *33°44′S 59°10′W*
61 *F16* **Ibirapuitã** S Brazil
105 *V10* **Ibiza** *var.* Iviza, *Cast.* Eivissa; *anc.* Ebusus. *island* Islas Baleares, Spain, W Mediterranean Sea
Ibiza *see* Eivissa
138 *J4* **Ibn Wardān, Qaṣr** *ruins* Ḥamāh, C Syria
Ibo *see* Sassandra
188 *E9* **Ibobang** Babeldaob, N Palau
171 *V13* **Ibonma** Papua, E Indonesia *03°27′S 133°30′E*
59 *N17* **Ibotirama** Bahia, E Brazil *12°13′S 43°12′W*
141 *Y8* **Ibrā** NE Oman *22°45′N 58°30′E*
127 *Q4* **Ibresi** Chuvashskaya Respublika, W Russian Federation *55°22′N 47°04′E*
141 *X8* **'Ibrī** NW Oman *23°12′N 56°28′E*
164 *C16* **Ibusuki** Kagoshima, Kyūshū, SW Japan *31°15′N 130°40′E*
57 *E16* **Ica** Ica, SW Peru *14°02′S 75°48′W*
57 *E16* **Ica** *off.* Departamento de Ica. ◐ *department* SW Peru
Ica, Departamento de *see* Ica
58 *C11* **Içana** Amazonas, NW Brazil *0°22′N 67°25′W*
Icaria *see* Ikaría
58 *B13* **Içá, Rio** *var.* Río Putumayo. NW South America *see also* Putumayo, Río
Içá, Rio *see* Putumayo, Río
136 *I17* **İçel** *prev.* Ichili; *prev.* Mersin. ◐ *province* S Turkey
İçel *see* Mersin
92 *I3* **Iceland** *off.* Republic of Iceland, *Dan.* Island, *Icel.* Ísland. ◆ *republic* N Atlantic Ocean
86 *B6* **Iceland** *island* N Atlantic Ocean
64 *L5* **Iceland Basin** *undersea feature* N Atlantic Ocean *61°00′N 19°00′W*
Icelandic Plateau *see* Iceland Plateau
197 *Q15* **Iceland Plateau** *var.* Icelandic Plateau. *undersea feature* S Greenland Sea *12°00′W 69°30′N*
Iceland, Republic of *see* Iceland
155 *E16* **Ichalkaranji** Mahārāshtra, W India *16°42′N 74°28′E*
164 *D15* **Ichifusa-yama** ▲ Kyūshū, SW Japan *32°18′N 131°05′E*
Ichili *see* İçel
164 *K13* **Ichinomiya** *var.* Itinomiya. Aichi, Honshū, SW Japan *35°18′N 136°48′E*
165 *Q9* **Ichinoseki** *var.* Itinoseki. Iwate, Honshū, C Japan *38°56′N 141°08′E*
117 *R3* **Ichnya** Chernihivs'ka Oblast', NE Ukraine *50°52′N 32°24′E*
57 *L17* **Ichoa, Río** C Bolivia
Iconium *see* Konya
Iculisma *see* Angoulême
39 *U12* **Icy Bay** *inlet* Alaska, USA
39 *N5* **Icy Cape** *headland* Alaska, USA *70°19′N 161°52′W*
39 *W13* **Icy Strait** *strait* Alaska, USA
27 *R13* **Idabel** Oklahoma, C USA *33°54′N 94°50′W*
29 *T13* **Ida Grove** Iowa, C USA *42°21′N 95°28′W*
77 *U16* **Idah** Kogi, S Nigeria *07°06′N 06°45′E*
33 *N13* **Idaho** *off.* State of Idaho, *also known as* Gem of the Mountains, Gem State. ◐ *state* NW USA
33 *N14* **Idaho City** Idaho, NW USA *43°48′N 115°51′W*
33 *R14* **Idaho Falls** Idaho, NW USA *43°28′N 112°01′W*
121 *P2* **Idálion** *var.* Dali, Dhali. C Cyprus *35°00′N 33°25′E*
25 *N5* **Idalou** Texas, SW USA *33°40′N 101°40′W*
104 *I9* **Idanha-a-Nova** Castelo Branco, C Portugal *39°55′N 07°15′W*
101 *E19* **Idar-Oberstein** Rheinland-Pfalz, SW Germany *49°43′N 07°19′E*
118 *J3* **Ida-Virumaa** *var.* Ida-Viru Maakond. ◐ *province* NE Estonia
Ida-Viru Maakond *see* Ida-Virumaa
124 *J8* **Idel'** Respublika Kareliya, NW Russian Federation *64°08′N 34°12′E*
79 *C15* **Idenao** Sud-Ouest, SW Cameroon *04°04′N 09°01′E*
Idensalmi *see* Iisalmi
162 *I6* **Ider** *var.* Dzuunmod. Hövsgöl, C Mongolia *48°09′N 97°22′E*

◆ Country
● Country Capital
◇ Dependent Territory
○ Dependent Territory Capital
◐ Administrative Regions
✈ International Airport
▲ Mountain
▲▲ Mountain Range
Volcano
River
Lake
Reservoir

Ider *see* Galt
75 *X10* **Idfū** *var.* Edfu. SE Egypt *24°55′N 32°52′E*
Ídhi Óros *see* Ídi
Ídhra *see* Ýdra
80 *L10* **ʻĪdi** *var.* Ed. SE Eritrea *13°54′N 41°39′E*
168 *H7* **Idi** Sumatera, W Indonesia *05°00′N 98°00′E*
115 *I25* **Ídi** *var.* Ídhi Óros. ▲▲ Kríti, Greece, E Mediterranean Sea
Idi Amin, Lac *see* Edward, Lake
106 *G10* **Idice** ≋ N Italy
76 *G9* **Idîni** Trarza, W Mauritania *17°58′N 15°40′W*
79 *J21* **Idiofa** Bandundu, SW Dem. Rep. Congo *05°00′S 19°38′E*
39 *O10* **Iditarod River** ≋ Alaska, USA
95 *M14* **Idkerberget** Dalarna, C Sweden *60°22′N 15°15′E*
138 *I3* **Idlib** Idlib, NW Syria *35°57′N 36°38′E*
138 *I4* **Idlib** *off.* Muḩāfaẓat Idlib. ⬖ *governorate* NW Syria
Idlib, Muḩāfaẓat *see* Idlib
Idra *see* Ýdra
94 *J11* **Idre** Dalarna, C Sweden *61°52′N 12°45′E*
Idria *see* Idrija
109 *S11* **Idrija** *It.* Idria. W Slovenia *46°00′N 14°59′E*
101 *G18* **Idstein** Hessen, W Germany *50°10′N 08°16′E*
83 *J25* **Idutywa** Eastern Cape, SE South Africa *32°06′S 28°20′E*
Idzhevan *see* Ijevan
118 *G9* **Iecava** Bauska, S Latvia *56°36′N 24°10′E*
165 *T16* **Ie-jima** *var.* Ii-shima. *island* Nansei-shotō, SW Japan
99 *B18* **Ieper** *Fr.* Ypres. West-Vlaanderen, W Belgium *50°51′N 02°53′E*
115 *K25* **Ierápetra** Kríti, Greece, E Mediterranean Sea *35°00′N 25°45′E*
115 *G22* **Iérax, Akrotírio** *headland* S Greece *36°45′N 23°06′E*
Ierisós *see* Ierissós
115 *H14* **Ierissós** *var.* Ierisós. Kentrikí Makedonía, N Greece *40°24′N 23°53′E*
116 *I11* **Iernut** *Hung.* Radnót. Mureş, C Romania *46°27′N 24°15′E*
106 *J12* **Iesi** *var.* Jesi. Marche, C Italy *43°33′N 13°16′E*
92 *K9* **Iešjávri** ◎ N Norway
Iesolo *see* Jesolo
188 *K16* **Ifalik Atoll** *atoll* Caroline Islands, C Micronesia
172 *I6* **Ifanadiana** Fianarantsoa, SE Madagascar *21°19′S 47°39′E*
77 *T16* **Ife** Osun, SW Nigeria *07°25′N 04°31′E*
77 *V8* **Iferouâne** Agadez, N Niger *19°05′N 08°24′E*
Iferten *see* Yverdon
92 *L8* **Ifjord** Finnmark, N Norway *70°27′N 27°06′E*
77 *R8* **Ifôghas, Adrar des** *var.* Adrar des Iforas. ▲▲ NE Mali
Iforas, Adrar des *see* Ifôghas, Adrar des
182 *D6* **Ifould lake** *salt lake* South Australia
74 *G6* **Ifrane** C Morocco *33°31′N 05°09′W*
171 *S11* **Iga** Pulau Halmahera, E Indonesia *01°23′N 128°17′E*
81 *G18* **Iganga** SE Uganda *0°34′N 33°27′E*
60 *L7* **Igarapava** São Paulo, S Brazil *20°01′S 47°46′W*
122 *K9* **Igarka** Krasnoyarskiy Kray, N Russian Federation *67°31′N 86°33′E*
Igaunija *see* Estonia
137 *T12* **Iğdır** E Turkey *39°50′N 44°00′E*
I.G.Duca *see* General Toshevo
Igel *see* Jihlava
94 *N11* **Iggesund** Gävleborg, C Sweden *61°38′N 17°04′E*
39 *P7* **Igikpak, Mount** ▲ Alaska, USA *67°28′N 154°55′W*
39 *P13* **Igiugig** Alaska, USA *59°19′N 155°53′W*
Iglau/Iglawa/Igława *see* Jihlava
107 *B20* **Iglesias** Sardegna, Italy, C Mediterranean Sea *39°20′N 08°34′E*
127 *V4* **Iglino** Respublika Bashkortostan, W Russian Federation *54°51′N 56°29′E*
Igló *see* Spišská Nová Ves
9 *O6* **Igloolik** Nunavut, N Canada *69°24′N 81°55′W*
12 *B11* **Ignace** Ontario, S Canada *49°26′N 91°40′W*
118 *I12* **Ignalina** Utena, E Lithuania *55°20′N 26°10′E*
127 *Q5* **Ignatovka** Ul'yanovskaya Oblast', W Russian Federation *53°56′N 47°40′E*
124 *K12* **Ignatovo** Vologodskaya Oblast', NW Russian Federation *60°47′N 37°51′E*
114 *N11* **İğneada** Kırklareli, NW Turkey *41°54′N 27°58′E*
121 *S7* **İğneada Burnu** *headland* NW Turkey *41°54′N 28°03′E*
Igombe *see* Gombe
115 *B16* **Igoumenítsa** Ípeiros, W Greece *39°30′N 20°16′E*
127 *T2* **Igra** Udmurtskaya Respublika, NW Russian Federation *57°30′N 53°01′E*
122 *H9* **Igrim** Khanty-Mansiyskiy Avtonomnyy Okrug-Yugra, N Russian Federation *63°09′N 64°33′E*
60 *G12* **Iguaçu, Rio** *Sp.* Río Iguazú. ≋ Argentina/Brazil *see also* Iguazú, Río
Iguaçu, Rio *see* Iguazú, Río
59 *I22* **Iguaçu, Salto do** *Sp.* Cataratas del Iguazú; *prev.* Victoria Falls. *waterfall* Argentina/Brazil *see also* Iguazú, Cataratas del
Iguaçu, Salto do *see* Iguazú, Cataratas del
41 *O15* **Iguala** *var.* Iguala de la Independencia. Guerrero, S Mexico *18°21′N 99°31′W*
105 *V5* **Igualada** Cataluña, NE Spain *41°35′N 01°37′E*
Iguala de la Independencia *see* Iguala
60 *G12* **Iguazú, Cataratas del** *Port.* Salto do Iguaçu; *prev.* Victoria Falls. *waterfall* Argentina/Brazil *see also* Iguaçu, Salto do
Iguazú, Cataratas del *see* Iguaçu, Salto do
62 *Q6* **Iguazú, Río** *var.* Río Iguaçu. ≋ Argentina/Brazil *see also* Iguaçu, Rio
Iguazú, Río *see* Iguaçu, Rio
79 *D19* **Iguéla** Ogooué-Maritime, SW Gabon *02°00′S 09°23′E*
Iguid, Erg *see* Iguîdi, 'Erg
67 *M5* **Iguîdi, 'Erg** *var.* Erg Iguid. *desert* Algeria/Mauritania
172 *K2* **Iharaña** *prev.* Vohémar. Antsiranana, NE Madagascar *13°22′S 50°00′E*
151 *K18* **Ihavandhippolhu Atoll** *var.* Ihavandiffulu Atoll. *atoll* N Maldives
Ihavandiffulu Atoll *see* Ihavandhippolhu Atoll
Ih Bulag *see* Hanbogd
165 *T16* **Iheya-jima** *island* Nansei-shotō, SW Japan
Ihhayrhan *see* Bayan-Önjüül
163 *N9* **Ihhet** *var.* Bayan. Dornogovĭ, SE Mongolia *46°15′N 110°16′E*
172 *I6* **Ihosy** Fianarantsoa, S Madagascar *22°23′S 46°09′E*
Ihsüüj *see* Bayanchandmanĭ
162 *I7* **Ihtamir** *var.* Dzaanhushuu. Arhangay, C Mongolia *47°36′N 101°06′E*
162 *H6* **Ih-Uul** *var.* Bayan-Uhaa. Dzavhan, C Mongolia *48°41′N 98°46′E*
162 *J6* **Ih-Uul** *var.* Selenge. Hövsgöl, N Mongolia *49°25′N 101°30′E*
93 *L14* **Ii** Oulu, C Finland *65°18′N 25°23′E*
164 *M13* **Iida** Nagano, Honshū, S Japan *35°32′N 137°48′E*
93 *M14* **Iijoki** ≋ C Finland
Iinnasuolu *see* Hinnøya
118 *J4* **Iisaku** *Ger.* Isaak. Ida-Virumaa, NE Estonia *59°06′N 27°19′E*
93 *M16* **Iisalmi** *var.* Idensalmi. Itä-Suomi, C Finland *63°32′N 27°10′E*
Ii-shima *see* Ie-jima
165 *N11* **Iiyama** Nagano, Honshū, S Japan *36°52′N 138°22′E*
77 *S16* **Ijebu-Ode** Ogun, SW Nigeria *06°46′N 03°57′E*
137 *U11* **Ijevan** *Rus.* Idzhevan. N Armenia *40°53′N 45°07′E*
98 *H9* **IJmuiden** Noord-Holland, W Netherlands *52°28′N 04°38′E*
98 *M12* **IJssel** *var.* Yssel. ≋ Netherlands
98 *J8* **IJsselmeer** *prev.* Zuider Zee. ◎ N Netherlands
98 *L9* **IJsselmuiden** Overijssel, E Netherlands *52°34′N 05°55′E*
98 *I12* **IJsselstein** Utrecht, C Netherlands *52°01′N 05°02′E*
61 *G14* **Ijuí** Rio Grande do Sul, S Brazil *28°23′S 53°55′W*
61 *G14* **Ijuí, Rio** ≋ S Brazil
189 *R8* **Ijuw** NE Nauru *0°30′S 166°57′E*
99 *E16* **IJzendijke** Zeeland, SW Netherlands *51°20′N 03°36′E*
99 *A18* **Ijzer** ≋ W Belgium
Ikaahuk *see* Sachs Harbour
93 *K18* **Ikaalinen** Länsi-Suomi, W Finland *61°46′N 23°05′E*
172 *I6* **Ikalamavony** Fianarantsoa, SE Madagascar *21°10′S 46°35′E*
Ikaluktutiak *see* Cambridge Bay
185 *G16* **Ikamatua** West Coast, South Island, New Zealand *42°16′S 171°42′E*
77 *U16* **Ikare** Ondo, SW Nigeria *07°36′N 05°52′E*
115 *L20* **Ikaría** *var.* Kariot, Nicaria, Nikaria; *anc.* Icaria. *island* Dodekánisa, Greece, Aegean Sea
95 *F22* **Ikast** Ringkøbing, W Denmark *56°09′N 09°10′E*
184 *O9* **Ikawhenua Range** ▲▲ North Island, New Zealand
165 *U4* **Ikeda** Hokkaidō, NE Japan *42°54′N 143°25′E*
164 *H14* **Ikeda** Tokushima, Shikoku, SW Japan *34°00′N 133°47′E*
77 *S16* **Ikeja** Lagos, SW Nigeria *06°36′N 03°16′E*
79 *L19* **Ikela** Equateur, C Dem. Rep. Congo *01°11′S 23°16′E*
114 *H10* **Ikhtiman** Sofiya, W Bulgaria *42°26′N 23°49′E*
164 *C13* **Iki** *island* SW Japan
127 *O13* **Iki Burul** Respublika Kalmykiya, SW Russian Federation *45°48′N 44°44′E*
137 *P11* **İkizdere** Rize, NE Turkey *40°47′N 40°34′E*
39 *P14* **Ikolik, Cape** *headland* Kodiak Island, Alaska, USA *57°12′N 154°46′W*
77 *V17* **Ikom** Cross River, SE Nigeria *05°57′N 08°43′E*
172 *I6* **Ikongo** *prev.* Fort-Carnot. Fianarantsoa, SE Madagascar *21°52′S 47°27′E*
39 *P5* **Ikpikpuk River** ≋ Alaska, USA
190 *H1* **Iku** *prev.* Lone Tree Islet. *atoll* Tungaru, W Kiribati
164 *I12* **Ikuno** Hyōgo, Honshū, SW Japan *35°13′N 134°48′E*
190 *H16* **Ikurangi** ▲ Rarotonga, S Cook Islands *21°12′S 159°45′W*
171 *X14* **Ilaga** Papua, E Indonesia *03°54′S 137°30′E*
171 *O2* **Ilagan** Luzon, N Philippines *17°08′N 121°54′E*
142 *J7* **Īlām** *var.* Elam. Īlām, W Iran *33°37′N 46°27′E*
153 *R12* **Ilām** Eastern, E Nepal *26°52′N 87°58′E*
142 *J8* **Īlām** *off.* Ostān-e Īlām. ⬖ *province* W Iran
Īlām, Ostān-e *see* Īlām
161 *T13* **Ilan** *Jap.* Giran. N Taiwan *24°45′N 121°44′E*
146 *G9* **Ilanly Obvodnitel'nyy Kanal** *canal* N Turkmenistan
122 *L12* **Ilanskiy** Krasnoyarskiy Kray, S Russian Federation *56°16′N 95°59′E*
108 *H9* **Ilanz** Graubünden, S Switzerland *46°46′N 09°10′E*
77 *S16* **Ilaro** Ogun, SW Nigeria *06°52′N 03°01′E*
57 *I17* **Ilave** Puno, S Peru *16°07′S 69°40′W*
110 *K8* **Iława** *Ger.* Deutsch-Eylau. Warmińsko-Mazurskie, NE Poland *53°36′N 19°35′E*
123 *P10* **Il'benge** Respublika Sakha (Yakutiya), NE Russian Federation *62°52′N 124°13′E*
129 *R7* **Ile** *var.* Ili, *Chin.* Ili He, *Rus.* Reka Ili. ≋ China/Kazakhstan *see also* Ili He
Ile *see* Ili He
11 *S13* **Ile-à-la-Crosse** Saskatchewan, C Canada *55°29′N 108°00′W*
79 *J21* **Ilebo** *prev.* Port-Francqui. Kasai-Occidental, W Dem. Rep. Congo *04°19′S 20°32′E*
103 *N5* **Île-de-France** ⬖ *region* N France
144 *I9* **Ilek** *Kaz.* Elek. ≋ Kazakhstan/Russian Federation
Ilerda *see* Lleida
77 *T16* **Ilesha** Osun, SW Nigeria *07°35′N 04°49′E*
187 *Q16* **Îles Loyauté, Province des** ⬖ *province* E New Caledonia
11 *X12* **Ilford** Manitoba, C Canada *56°02′N 95°48′W*
116 *K14* **Ilfov** ⬖ *county* S Romania
97 *I23* **Ilfracombe** SW England, United Kingdom *51°12′N 04°10′W*
136 *I11* **Ilgaz Dağları** ▲▲ N Turkey
136 *G15* **Ilgın** Konya, W Turkey *38°16′N 31°57′E*
60 *I7* **Ilha Solteira** São Paulo, S Brazil *20°28′S 51°19′W*
104 *G7* **Ílhavo** Aveiro, N Portugal *40°36′N 08°40′W*
59 *O18* **Ilhéus** Bahia, E Brazil *14°50′S 39°06′W*
Ili *see* Ile/Ili He
116 *G11* **Ilia** *Hung.* Marosillye. Hunedoara, SW Romania *45°57′N 22°40′E*
39 *P13* **Iliamna** Alaska, USA *59°42′N 154°49′W*
39 *P13* **Iliamna Lake** ◎ Alaska, USA
137 *N13* **Iliç** Erzincan, C Turkey *39°27′N 38°34′E*
Il'ichevsk *see* Şärur, Azerbaijan
Il'ichevsk *see* Illichivs'k, Ukraine
Ilici *see* Elche
37 *V2* **Iliff** Colorado, C USA *40°46′N 103°04′W*
171 *Q7* **Iligan** *off.* Iligan City. Mindanao, S Philippines *08°12′N 124°16′E*
171 *Q7* **Iligan Bay** *bay* S Philippines
Iligan City *see* Iligan
158 *I5* **Ili He** *var.* Ili, *Kaz.* Ile, *Rus.* Reka Ili. ≋ China/Kazakhstan *see also* Ile
Ili He *see* Ile
56 *C6* **Iliniza** ▲ N Ecuador *0°37′S 78°41′W*
Ilinski *see* Il'inskiy
125 *U14* **Il'inskiy** *var.* Ilinski. Permskaya Oblast', NW Russian Federation *58°33′N 55°31′E*
125 *U14* **Il'inskiy** Ostrov Sakhalin, Sakhalinskaya Oblast', SE Russian Federation *47°59′N 142°14′E*
18 *I10* **Ilion** New York, NE USA *43°01′N 75°02′W*
38 *E9* **ʻIlio Point** *var.* Ilio Point. *headland* Molokaʻi, Hawaiʻi, USA *21°13′N 157°15′W*
Ilio Point *see* ʻIlio Point
109 *T13* **Ilirska Bistrica** *prev.* Bistrica, *Ger.* Feistritz, Illyrisch-Feistritz, *It.* Villa del Nevoso. SW Slovenia *45°34′N 14°12′E*
137 *Q16* **Ilisu Barajı** ⊡ SE Turkey
155 *G17* **Ilkal** Karnātaka, C India *15°59′N 76°08′E*
97 *M19* **Ilkeston** C England, United Kingdom *52°59′N 01°18′W*
121 *O16* **Il-Kullana** *headland* SW Malta *35°49′N 14°26′E*
108 *J8* **Ill** ≋ W Austria
103 *U6* **Ill** ≋ NE France
62 *G10* **Illapel** Coquimbo, C Chile *31°40′S 71°13′W*
Illaue Fartak Trench *see* Alula-Fartak Trench
182 *C2* **Illbillee, Mount** ▲ South Australia *27°01′S 132°13′E*
102 *I6* **Ille-et-Vilaine** ⬖ *department* NW France
77 *T11* **Illéla** Tahoua, SW Niger *14°25′N 05°10′E*
101 *J24* **Iller** ≋ S Germany
101 *J23* **Illertissen** Bayern, S Germany *48°13′N 10°08′E*
105 *X9* **Illes Baleares** ⬖ *autonomous community* E Spain
105 *N8* **Illescas** Castilla-La Mancha, C Spain *40°08′N 03°51′W*
Ille-sur-la-Têt *see* Ille-sur-Têt
103 *O17* **Ille-sur-Têt** *var.* Ille-sur-la-Têt. Pyrénées-Orientales, S France *42°40′N 02°37′E*
Illiberis *see* Elne
117 *P11* **Illichivs'k** *Rus.* Il'ichevsk. Odes'ka Oblast', SW Ukraine *46°18′N 30°36′E*
Illicis *see* Elche
102 *M6* **Illiers-Combray** Eure-et-Loir, C France *48°18′N 01°15′E*
30 *K12* **Illinois** *off.* State of Illinois, *also known as* Prairie State, Sucker State. ⬖ *state* C USA
30 *J13* **Illinois River** ≋ Illinois, N USA
117 *N6* **Illintsi** Vinnyts'ka Oblast', C Ukraine *49°07′N 29°13′E*
Illiturgis *see* Andújar
74 *M10* **Illizi** SE Algeria *26°30′N 08°28′E*
27 *Y7* **Illmo** Missouri, C USA *37°13′N 89°30′W*
Illurco *see* Lorca
Illuro *see* Mataró
Illyrisch-Feistritz *see* Ilirska Bistrica
101 *K16* **Ilm** ≋ C Germany
101 *K17* **Ilmenau** Thüringen, C Germany *50°40′N 10°55′E*
124 *H14* **Il'men', Ozero** ◎ NW Russian Federation
57 *H18* **Ilo** Moquegua, SW Peru *17°42′S 71°20′W*
171 *O6* **Iloilo** *off.* Iloilo City. Panay Island, C Philippines *10°42′N 122°34′E*
Iloilo City *see* Iloilo
112 *K10* **Ilok** *Hung.* Újlak. Vojvodina, NW Serbia *45°12′N 19°22′E*
93 *O16* **Ilomantsi** Itä-Suomi, SE Finland *62°40′N 30°55′E*
42 *F8* **Ilopango, Lago de** *volcanic lake* C El Salvador
77 *T15* **Ilorin** Kwara, W Nigeria *08°32′N 04°35′E*
117 *X8* **Ilovays'k** *Rus.* Ilovaysk. Donets'ka Oblast', SE Ukraine *47°55′N 38°14′E*
Ilovaysk *see* Ilovays'k
127 *O10* **Ilovlya** Volgogradskaya Oblast', SW Russian Federation *49°45′N 44°19′E*
127 *O10* **Ilovlya** ≋ SW Russian Federation
126 *K14* **Il'skiy** Krasnodarskiy Kray, SW Russian Federation *44°52′N 38°26′E*
182 *B2* **Iltur** South Australia *27°33′S 130°31′E*
171 *Y13* **Ilugwa** Papua, E Indonesia *03°42′S 139°09′E*
İluh *see* Batman
118 *I11* **Ilūkste** Daugvapils, SE Latvia *55°58′N 26°21′E*
171 *Y13* **Ilur** Pulau Gorong, E Indonesia *04°00′S 131°25′E*
32 *F10* **Ilwaco** Washington, NW USA *46°19′N 124°03′W*
Il'yaly *see* Gurbansoltan Eje
İlyasbaba Burnu *see* Tekke Burnu
125 *U9* **Ilych** ≋ NW Russian Federation
101 *O21* **Ilz** ≋ SE Germany
111 *M14* **Iłża** Radom, SE Poland *51°09′N 21°15′E*
164 *G13* **Imabari** *var.* Imaharu. Ehime, Shikoku, SW Japan *34°04′N 132°59′E*
Imaharu *see* Imabari
165 *O12* **Imaichi** *var.* Imaiti. Tochigi, Honshū, S Japan *36°43′N 139°41′E*
Imaiti *see* Imaichi
164 *K12* **Imajō** Fukui, Honshū, SW Japan *35°45′N 136°10′E*
139 *R9* **Imām Ibn Hāshim** Karbalā', C Iraq *32°46′N 43°21′E*
139 *T11* **Imān 'Abd Allāh** Al Qādisīyah, S Iraq *31°36′N 44°34′E*
164 *F15* **Imano-yama** ▲ Shikoku, SW Japan *32°51′N 132°48′E*
164 *C13* **Imari** Saga, Kyūshū, SW Japan *33°18′N 129°51′E*
Imarssuak Mid-Ocean Seachannel *see* Imarssuak Seachannel
64 *J6* **Imarssuak Seachannel** *var.* Imarssuak Mid-Ocean Seachannel. *channel* N Atlantic Ocean
93 *N18* **Imatra** Etelä-Suomi, SE Finland *61°14′N 28°50′E*
164 *K13* **Imazu** Shiga, Honshū, SW Japan *35°25′N 136°00′E*
56 *C6* **Imbabura** ⬖ *province* N Ecuador
55 *R9* **Imbaimadai** W Guyana *05°44′N 60°23′W*
61 *K14* **Imbituba** Santa Catarina, S Brazil *28°15′S 48°44′W*
27 *W9* **Imboden** Arkansas, C USA *36°12′N 91°10′W*
Imbros *see* Gökçeada
Imeni 26 Bakinskikh Komissarov *see* 26 Bakı Komissarı
Imeni 26 Bakinskikh Komissarov *see* Uzboý
125 *N13* **Imeni Babushkina** Vologodskaya Oblast', NW Russian Federation *59°40′N 43°04′E*
126 *J7* **Imeni Karla Libknekhta** Kurskaya Oblast', W Russian Federation *51°36′N 35°28′E*
Imeni Mollanepesa *see* Mollanepes Adyndaky
Imeni S. A. Niyazova *see* S. A.Nyýazow Adyndaky
Imeni Sverdlova Rudnik *see* Sverdlovs'k
188 *E9* **Imeong** Babeldaob, N Palau
81 *L14* **Īmī** Sumalē, E Ethiopia *06°27′N 42°10′E*
115 *M21* **Imia** *Turk.* Kardak. *island* Dodekánisa, Greece, Aegean Sea
Imishli *see* İmişli
137 *X12* **İmişli** *Rus.* Imishli. C Azerbaijan *39°54′N 48°04′E*
163 *X14* **Imjin-gang** ≋ North Korea/South Korea
35 *S3* **Imlay** Nevada, W USA *40°39′N 118°10′W*
31 *S9* **Imlay City** Michigan, N USA *43°01′N 83°04′W*
23 *X15* **Immokalee** Florida, SE USA *26°24′N 81°25′W*
77 *U17* **Imo** ⬖ *state* SE Nigeria
106 *G10* **Imola** Emilia-Romagna, N Italy *44°22′N 11°43′E*
186 *A5* **Imonda** Sandaun, NW Papua New Guinea *03°21′S 141°10′E*
Imoschi *see* Imotski
113 *G14* **Imotski** *It.* Imoschi. Split-Dalmacija, SE Croatia *43°28′N 17°13′E*
59 *L14* **Imperatriz** Maranhão, NE Brazil *05°32′S 47°28′W*
106 *B10* **Imperia** Liguria, NW Italy *43°53′N 08°03′E*
57 *E15* **Imperial** Lima, W Peru *13°04′S 76°21′W*
35 *X17* **Imperial** California, W USA *32°51′N 115°34′W*
28 *L16* **Imperial** Nebraska, C USA *40°30′N 101°37′W*
24 *M9* **Imperial** Texas, SW USA *31°15′N 102°40′W*
35 *Y17* **Imperial Dam** *dam* California, W USA
79 *I17* **Impfondo** Likouala, NE Congo *01°37′N 18°04′E*
153 *X14* **Imphāl** *state capital* Manipur, NE India *24°47′N 93°55′E*
103 *P9* **Imphy** Nièvre, C France *46°55′N 03°16′E*
106 *G11* **Impruneta** Toscana, C Italy *43°42′N 11°16′E*
115 *K15* **İmroz** *var.* Gökçeada. Çanakkale, NW Turkey *40°06′N 25°50′E*
Imroz Adası *see* Gökçeada
108 *L7* **Imst** Tirol, W Austria *47°14′N 10°45′E*
40 *F3* **Imuris** Sonora, NW Mexico *30°48′N 110°52′W*
164 *M13* **Ina** Nagano, Honshū, S Japan *35°52′N 137°58′E*
65 *M18* **Inaccessible Island** *island* W Tristan da Cunha
115 *F20* **Ínachos** ≋ S Greece
188 *H6* **I Naftan, Puntan** *headland* Saipan, S Northern Mariana Islands
Inagua Islands *see* Great Inagua
Inagua Islands *see* Little Inagua
185 *H15* **Inangahua** West Coast, South Island, New Zealand *41°51′S 171°58′E*
57 *I14* **Iñapari** Madre de Dios, E Peru *11°00′S 69°34′W*
188 *B17* **Inarajan** SE Guam *13°16′N 144°45′E*
92 *L10* **Inari** *Lapp.* Anár, Aanaar. Lappi, N Finland *68°54′N 27°06′E*
92 *L10* **Inarijärvi** *Lapp.* Aanaarjävri, *Swe.* Enareträsk. ◎ N Finland
92 *L9* **Inarijoki** *Lapp.* Anárjohka. ≋ Finland/Norway
Inău *see* Ineu
165 *P11* **Inawashiro-ko** *var.* Inawasiro Ko. ◎ Honshū, C Japan
Inawasiro Ko *see* Inawashiro-ko
105 *X9* **Inca** Mallorca, Spain, W Mediterranean Sea *39°43′N 02°54′E*
62 *H7* **Inca de Oro** Atacama, N Chile *26°45′S 69°54′W*
115 *J15* **İnce Burnu** *cape* NW Turkey
136 *K9* **İnce Burnu** *headland* N Turkey *42°06′N 34°57′E*
136 *I17* **İncekum Burnu** *headland* S Turkey *36°13′N 33°57′E*
76 *G7* **Inchiri** ⬖ *region* NW Mauritania
163 *X15* **Inch'ŏn** *off.* Inch'ŏn-gwangyŏksi, *Jap.* Jinsen; *prev.* Chemulpo. NW South Korea *37°27′N 126°41′E*
161 *X15* **Inch'on** ✈ (Sŏul) NW South Korea *37°37′N 126°42′E*
Inch'ŏn-gwangyŏksi *see* Inch'ŏn
83 *M17* **Inchope** Manica, C Mozambique *19°09′S 33°54′E*
Incoronata *see* Kornat
103 *Y15* **Incudine, Monte** ▲ Corse, France, C Mediterranean Sea *41°52′N 09°13′E*
60 *M10* **Indaiatuba** São Paulo, S Brazil *23°03′S 47°14′W*
93 *H17* **Indal** Västernorrland, C Sweden *62°36′N 17°06′E*
93 *H17* **Indalsälven** ≋ C Sweden
40 *K8* **Inde** Durango, C Mexico *25°55′N 105°10′W*
Indefatigable Island *see* Santa Cruz, Isla
35 *S10* **Independence** California, W USA *36°48′N 118°14′W*
29 *X13* **Independence** Iowa, C USA *42°28′N 91°42′W*
27 *P7* **Independence** Kansas, C USA *37°13′N 95°43′W*
20 *M4* **Independence** Kentucky, S USA *38°56′N 84°32′W*
27 *R4* **Independence** Missouri, C USA *39°04′N 94°27′W*
21 *R8* **Independence** Virginia, NE USA *36°38′N 81°11′W*
30 *J7* **Independence** Wisconsin, N USA *44°21′N 91°25′W*
197 *R12* **Independence Fjord** *fjord* N Greenland
Independence Island *see* Malden Island
35 *W2* **Independence Mountains** ▲▲ Nevada, W USA
57 *K18* **Independencia** Cochabamba, C Bolivia *17°08′S 66°52′W*
57 *E16* **Independencia, Bahía de la** *bay* W Peru
Independencia, Monte *see* Adam, Mount
116 *M12* **Independenţa** Galaţi, SE Romania *45°29′N 27°45′E*
Inderagiri *see* Indragiri, Sungai
Inderbor *see* Inderborskiy
144 *F11* **Inderborskiy** *Kaz.* Inderbor. Atyrau, W Kazakhstan *48°35′N 51°45′E*
151 *I14* **India** *off.* Republic of India, *var.* Indian Union, Union of India, *Hind.* Bhārat. ◆ *republic* S Asia
India *see* Inđija
18 *D14* **Indiana** Pennsylvania, NE USA *40°37′N 79°09′W*
31 *N13* **Indiana** *off.* State of Indiana, *also known as* Hoosier State. ⬖ *state* N USA
31 *O14* **Indianapolis** *state capital* Indiana, N USA *39°46′N 86°09′W*
11 *O10* **Indian Cabins** Alberta, W Canada *59°51′N 117°06′W*
42 *G1* **Indian Church** Orange Walk, N Belize *17°47′N 88°39′W*
Indian Desert *see* Thar Desert
11 *U16* **Indian Head** Saskatchewan, S Canada *50°32′N 103°41′W*
31 *O4* **Indian Lake** ◎ Michigan, N USA
18 *K9* **Indian Lake** ◎ New York, NE USA
31 *R13* **Indian Lake** ⊡ Ohio, N USA
172-173 **Indian Ocean** *ocean*
29 *V15* **Indianola** Iowa, C USA *41°21′N 93°33′W*
22 *K4* **Indianola** Mississippi, S USA *33°27′N 90°39′W*
36 *J6* **Indian Peak** ▲ Utah, W USA *38°18′N 113°52′W*
23 *Y13* **Indian River** *lagoon* Florida, SE USA
35 *W10* **Indian Springs** Nevada, W USA *36°33′N 115°40′W*
23 *Y14* **Indiantown** Florida, SE USA *27°01′N 80°29′W*
Indian Union *see* India
59 *K19* **Indiara** Goiás, S Brazil *17°12′S 50°09′W*
India, Republic of *see* India
India, Union of *see* India
125 *Q4* **Indiga** Nenetskiy Avtonomnyy Okrug, NW Russian Federation *67°40′N 49°01′E*
123 *R9* **Indigirka** ≋ NE Russian Federation
112 *L10* **Inđija** *Hung.* India; *prev.* Indjija. Vojvodina, N Serbia *45°03′N 20°04′E*
35 *V16* **Indio** California, W USA *33°42′N 116°13′W*
42 *M12* **Indio, Río** ≋ SE Nicaragua
152 *I10* **Indira Gandhi** ✈ (Delhi) Delhi, N India
151 *Q23* **Indira Point** *headland* Andaman and Nicobar Island, India, NE Indian Ocean *6°54′N 93°54′E*
Indjija *see* Inđija
129 *Q13* **Indo-Australian Plate** *tectonic feature*
173 *N11* **Indomed Fracture Zone** *tectonic feature* SW Indian Ocean
170 *L12* **Indonesia** *off.* Republic of Indonesia, *Ind.* Republik Indonesia; *prev.* Dutch East Indies, Netherlands East Indies, United States of Indonesia. ◆ *republic* SE Asia
Indonesian Borneo *see* Kalimantan
Indonesia, Republic of *see* Indonesia
Indonesia, Republik *see* Indonesia
Indonesia, United States of *see* Indonesia
154 *G10* **Indore** Madhya Pradesh, C India *22°42′N 75°51′E*
168 *L11* **Indragiri, Sungai** *var.* Batang Kuantan, Inderagiri. ≋ Sumatera, W Indonesia
Indramajoe/Indramaju *see* Indramayu
169 *P15* **Indramayu** *prev.* Indramajoe, Indramaju. Jawa, C Indonesia *06°22′S 108°20′E*
155 *K14* **Indrāvati** ≋ S India
103 *N9* **Indre** ⬖ *department* C France
102 *M8* **Indre** ≋ C France
94 *D13* **Indre Ålvik** Hordaland, S Norway *60°26′N 06°27′E*
102 *L8* **Indre-et-Loire** ⬖ *department* C France
Indreville *see* Châteauroux
152 *G3* **Indus** *Chin.* Yindu He; *prev.* Yin-tu Ho. ≋ S Asia
Indus Cone *see* Indus Fan
173 *P3* **Indus Fan** *var.* Indus Cone. *undersea feature* N Arabian Sea *16°00′N 66°30′E*
149 *P17* **Indus, Mouths of the** *delta* S Pakistan
83 *I24* **Indwe** Eastern Cape, SE South Africa *31°28′S 27°20′E*
136 *I10* **İnebolu** Kastamonu, N Turkey *41°57′N 33°45′E*
77 *P8* **I-n-Échaï** *oasis* C Mali
114 *M13* **İnecik** Tekirdağ, NW Turkey *40°55′N 27°16′E*
136 *E12* **İnegöl** Bursa, NW Turkey *40°06′N 29°31′E*
Inessa *see* Biancavilla
116 *F10* **Ineu** *Hung.* Borosjenő; *prev.* Inău. Arad, W Romania *46°26′N 21°51′E*
Ineul/Ineu, Vîrful *see* Ineu, Vârful
116 *J9* **Ineu, Vârful** *var.* Ineul; *prev.* Vîrful Ineu. ▲ N Romania *47°31′N 24°52′E*
21 *P6* **Inez** Kentucky, S USA *37°53′N 82°33′W*
74 *E8* **Inezgane** ✈ (Agadir) W Morocco *30°35′N 09°27′W*
41 *T17* **Inferior, Laguna** *lagoon* S Mexico
40 *M15* **Infiernillo, Presa del** ⊡ S Mexico
104 *L2* **Infiesto** Asturias, N Spain *43°21′N 05°21′W*
93 *L20* **Ingå** *Fin.* Inkoo. Etelä-Suomi, S Finland *60°01′N 24°05′E*
77 *U10* **Ingal** *var.* I-n-Gall. Agadez, C Niger *16°52′N 06°57′E*
I-n-Gall *see* Ingal
99 *C18* **Ingelmunster** West-Vlaanderen, W Belgium *50°12′N 03°15′E*
79 *I18* **Ingende** Equateur, W Dem. Rep. Congo *0°15′S 18°58′E*
62 *L5* **Ingeniero Guillermo Nueva Juárez** Formosa, N Argentina *23°55′S 61°50′W*
63 *H16* **Ingeniero Jacobacci** Río Negro, C Argentina *41°18′S 69°35′W*
14 *F16* **Ingersoll** Ontario, S Canada *43°03′N 80°53′W*
Ingettolgoy *see* Selenge
181 *W5* **Ingham** Queensland, NE Australia *18°35′S 146°12′E*
146 *M11* **Ingichka** Samarqand Viloyati, C Uzbekistan *39°46′N 65°56′E*
97 *L16* **Ingleborough** ▲ N England, United Kingdom *54°07′N 02°22′W*
25 *T14* **Ingleside** Texas, SW USA *27°52′N 97°12′W*
184 *K10* **Inglewood** Taranaki, North Island, New Zealand *39°07′S 174°13′E*
35 *S15* **Inglewood** California, W USA *33°57′N 118°21′W*
101 *L21* **Ingolstadt** Bayern, S Germany *48°46′N 11°26′E*
33 *V9* **Ingomar** Montana, NW USA *46°34′N 107°21′W*
13 *R14* **Ingonish Beach** Cape Breton Island, Nova Scotia, SE Canada *46°42′N 60°22′W*
153 *S14* **Ingrāj Bāzār** *prev.* English Bazar. West Bengal, NE India *25°00′N 88°10′E*
25 *Q11* **Ingram** Texas, SW USA *30°04′N 99°14′W*
195 *X7* **Ingrid Christensen Coast** *physical region* Antarctica
74 *K14* **I-n-Guezzam** S Algeria *19°35′N 05°49′E*
Ingulets *see* Inhulets'
Inguri *see* Enguri
Ingushetia/Ingushetiya, Respublika *see* Ingushetiya, Respublika
127 *O15* **Ingushetiya, Respublika** *var.* Respublika Ingushetiya, *Eng.* Ingushetia. ⬖ *autonomous republic* SW Russian Federation
83 *N20* **Inhambane** Inhambane, SE Mozambique *23°52′S 35°31′E*
83 *M20* **Inhambane** *off.* Província de Inhambane. ⬖ *province* S Mozambique
Inhambane, Província de *see* Inhambane
83 *N17* **Inhaminga** Sofala, C Mozambique *18°24′S 35°00′E*
83 *N20* **Inharrime** Inhambane, SE Mozambique *24°29′S 35°01′E*
83 *M18* **Inhassoro** Inhambane, E Mozambique *21°32′S 35°13′E*
117 *S9* **Inhulets'** *Rus.* Ingulets. Dnipropetrovs'ka Oblast', E Ukraine *47°43′N 33°16′E*
117 *R10* **Inhulets'** *Rus.* Ingulets. ≋ S Ukraine
105 *Q10* **Iniesta** Castilla-La Mancha, C Spain *39°27′N 01°45′W*
I-ning *see* Yining
54 *K11* **Inírida, Río** ≋ E Colombia
Inis *see* Ennis
Inis Ceithleann *see* Enniskillen
Inis Córthaidh *see* Enniscorthy
Inis Díomáin *see* Ennistimon
97 *A17* **Inishbofin** *Ir.* Inis Bó Finne. *island* W Ireland
97 *B18* **Inisheer** *var.* Inishere, *Ir.* Inis Oírr. *island* W Ireland
Inishere *see* Inisheer
97 *B18* **Inishmaan** *Ir.* Inis Meáin. *island* W Ireland
97 *A18* **Inishmore** *Ir.* Árainn. *island* W Ireland
96 *E13* **Inishtrahull** *Ir.* Inis Trá Tholl. *island* NW Ireland
97 *A17* **Inishturk** *Ir.* Inis Toirc. *island* W Ireland
Inkoo *see* Ingå
185 *J16* **Inland Kaikoura Range** ▲▲ South Island, New Zealand
Inland Sea *see* Seto-naikai
21 *P11* **Inman** South Carolina, SE USA *35°03′N 82°05′W*
108 *L7* **Inn** ≋ C Europe
197 *O11* **Innaanganeq** *var.* Kap York. *headland* NW Greenland *75°54′N 66°27′W*
182 *K2* **Innamincka** South Australia *27°47′S 140°45′E*
92 *G12* **Inndyr** Nordland, C Norway *67°01′N 14°00′E*
42 *G3* **Inner Channel** *inlet* SE Belize
96 *F11* **Inner Hebrides** *island group* W Scotland, United Kingdom
172 *H15* **Inner Islands** *var.* Central Group. *island group* NE Seychelles
Inner Mongolia/Inner Mongolian Autonomous Region *see* Nei Mongol Zizhiqu
96 *G8* **Inner Sound** *strait* NW Scotland, United Kingdom
100 *J13* **Innerste** ≋ C Germany
181 *W5* **Innisfail** Queensland, NE Australia *17°29′S 146°03′E*
11 *Q15* **Innisfail** Alberta, SW Canada *52°01′N 113°59′W*
Inniskilling *see* Enniskillen
39 *O11* **Innoko River** ≋ Alaska, USA
Innsbruch *see* Innsbruck
108 *M7* **Innsbruck** *var.* Innsbruch. Tirol, W Austria *47°17′N 11°25′E*
79 *I19* **Inongo** Bandundu, W Dem. Rep. Congo *01°55′S 18°20′E*
Inoucdjouac *see* Inukjuak
Inowrazlaw *see* Inowrocław
110 *I10* **Inowrocław** *Ger.* Hohensalza; *prev.* Inowrazlaw. Kujawski-pomorskie, C Poland *52°47′N 18°15′E*
57 *K18* **Inquisivi** La Paz, W Bolivia *16°55′S 67°10′W*
Inrin *see* Yüanlin
77 *O8* **I-n-Sâkâne, 'Erg** *desert* N Mali
77 *O8* **I-n-Sâkâne, 'Erg** *desert* N Mali
74 *J10* **I-n-Salah** *var.* In Salah. C Algeria *27°11′N 02°31′E*
127 *O5* **Insar** Respublika Mordoviya, W Russian Federation *53°52′N 44°26′E*
189 *X15* **Insiaf** Kosrae, E Micronesia
94 *L13* **Insjön** Dalarna, C Sweden *60°40′N 15°05′E*
Insterburg *see* Chernyakhovsk
Insula *see* Lille
116 *L13* **Însurăţei** Brăila, SE Romania *44°55′N 27°40′E*
125 *V6* **Inta** Respublika Komi, NW Russian Federation *66°00′N 60°10′E*
77 *R9* **I-n-Tebezas** Kidal, E Mali *17°58′N 01°51′E*
Interamna *see* Teramo
Interamna Nahars *see* Terni
28 *L11* **Interior** South Dakota, N USA *43°42′N 101°57′W*
108 *E9* **Interlaken** Bern, SW Switzerland *46°41′N 07°51′E*
29 *V2* **International Falls** Minnesota, N USA *48°38′N 93°26′W*
167 *O7* **Inthanon, Doi** ▲ NW Thailand *18°33′N 98°29′E*
42 *G7* **Intibucá** ⬖ *department* SW Honduras
42 *G8* **Intipucá** La Unión, SE El Salvador *13°10′N 88°03′W*
61 *B15* **Intiyaco** Santa Fe, C Argentina *28°43′S 60°04′W*
116 *K12* **Întorsura Buzăului** *Ger.* Bozau, *Hung.* Bodzafordulő. Covasna, E Romania *45°40′N 26°02′E*
22 *H9* **Intracoastal Waterway** *inland waterway system* Louisiana, S USA
25 *V13* **Intracoastal Waterway** *inland waterway system* Texas, SW USA
108 *G11* **Intragna** Ticino, S Switzerland *46°12′N 08°42′E*
165 *P14* **Inubō-zaki** *headland* Honshū, S Japan *35°42′N 140°51′E*
164 *E14* **Inukai** Ōita, Kyūshū, SW Japan *33°05′N 131°37′E*
12 *I5* **Inukjuak** *var.* Inoucdjouac; *prev.* Port Harrison. Québec, NE Canada *58°28′N 77°58′W*
63 *I24* **Inútil, Bahía** *bay* S Chile
Inuuvik *see* Inuvik
11 *R8* **Inuvik** *var.* Inuuvik. Northwest Territories, NW Canada *68°25′N 133°35′W*
164 *L13* **Inuyama** Aichi, Honshū, SW Japan *35°23′N 136°56′E*
56 *G13* **Inuya, Río** ≋ E Peru
125 *U13* **In'va** ≋ NW Russian Federation
96 *H11* **Inveraray** W Scotland, United Kingdom *56°13′N 05°05′W*
185 *C24* **Invercargill** Southland, South Island, New Zealand *46°25′S 168°22′E*
183 *T5* **Inverell** New South Wales, SE Australia *29°46′S 151°10′E*
96 *I8* **Invergordon** N Scotland, United Kingdom *57°42′N 04°02′W*
11 *P16* **Invermere** British Columbia, SW Canada *50°30′N 116°00′W*
13 *R14* **Inverness** Cape Breton Island, Nova Scotia, SE Canada *46°14′N 61°19′W*
96 *I8* **Inverness** N Scotland, United Kingdom *57°27′N 04°15′W*
23 *V11* **Inverness** Florida, SE USA *28°50′N 82°19′W*
96 *I9* **Inverness** *cultural region* NW Scotland, United Kingdom
96 *K9* **Inverurie** NE Scotland, United Kingdom *57°14′N 02°14′W*
182 *F8* **Investigator Group** *island group* South Australia
173 *T7* **Investigator Ridge** *undersea feature* E Indian Ocean *11°30′S 98°10′E*

◆ Country
● Country Capital
◇ Dependent Territory
○ Dependent Territory Capital
⬖ Administrative Regions
✈ International Airport
▲ Mountain
▲▲ Mountain Range
Volcano
≋ River
◎ Lake
⊡ Reservoir

182 H10 **Investigator Strait** *strait* South Australia
29 R11 **Inwood** Iowa, C USA *43°16′N 96°25′W*
123 S10 **Inya** ≈ E Russian Federation
Inyanga *see* Nyanga
83 M16 **Inyangani** ▲ NE Zimbabwe *18°22′S 32°57′E*
83 J17 **Inyathi** Matabeleland North, SW Zimbabwe *19°39′S 28°54′E*
35 T12 **Inyokern** California, W USA *35°37′N 117°48′W*
35 T10 **Inyo Mountains** ▲▲ California, W USA
127 P6 **Inza** Ul'yanovskaya Oblast', W Russian Federation *53°51′N 46°21′E*
127 W5 **Inzer** Respublika Bashkortostan, W Russian Federation *54°11′N 57°37′E*
127 N7 **Inzhavino** Tambovskaya Oblast', W Russian Federation *52°18′N 42°28′E*
115 C16 **Ioánnina** *var.* Janina, Yannina. Ípeiros, W Greece *39°39′N 20°52′E*
164 B17 **Iō-jima** *var.* Iwojima. *island* Nansei-shotō, SW Japan
124 L4 **Iokan'ga** ≈ NW Russian Federation
27 Q6 **Iola** Kansas, C USA *37°55′N 95°24′W*
Iolcus *see* Iolkós
115 G16 **Iolkós** *anc.* Iolcus. *site of ancient city* Thessalía, C Greece
Iolotan' *see* Ýolöten
83 A16 **Iona** Namibe, SW Angola *16°54′S 12°39′E*
96 F11 **Iona** *island* W Scotland, United Kingdom
116 M15 **Ion Corvin** Constanţa, SE Romania *44°07′N 27°50′E*
35 P7 **Ione** California, W USA *38°21′N 120°55′W*
116 I13 **Ioneşti** Vâlcea, SW Romania *44°52′N 24°12′E*
31 Q9 **Ionia** Michigan, N USA *42°59′N 85°04′W*
Ionia Basin *see* Ionian Basin
121 O10 **Ionian Basin** *var.* Ionia Basin. *undersea feature* Ionian Sea, C Mediterranean Sea *36°00′N 20°00′E*
115 B17 **Iónia Nisiá** *var.* Iónioi Nísoi, *Eng.* Ionian Islands. *island group* W Greece
Ionian Islands *see* Iónia Nisiá/Iónioi Nísoi
121 O10 **Ionian Sea** *Gk.* Iónio Pélagos, *It.* Mar Ionio. *sea* C Mediterranean Sea
115 B17 **Iónioi Nísoi** *Eng.* Ionian Islands. ◐ *region* W Greece
Iónioi Nísoi *see* Iónia Nisiá
Ionio, Mar/Iónio Pélagos *see* Ionian Sea
Iordan *see* Yordon
137 U10 **Iori** *var.* Qabırrı. ≈ Azerbaijan/Georgia
Iorrais, Ceann *see* Erris Head
115 J22 **Íos** *var.* Nio. *island* Kykládes, Greece, Aegean Sea
Íos *see* Chóra
115 I20 **Ioulís** *prev.* Kéa. Tziá, Kykládes, Greece, Aegean Sea *37°40′N 24°19′E*
22 G9 **Iowa** Louisiana, S USA *30°12′N 93°00′W*
29 V13 **Iowa** *off.* State of Iowa, *also known as* Hawkeye State. ◐ *state* C USA
29 Y14 **Iowa City** Iowa, C USA *41°40′N 91°32′W*
29 V13 **Iowa Falls** Iowa, C USA *42°31′N 93°15′W*
25 R4 **Iowa Park** Texas, SW USA *33°57′N 98°40′W*
29 Y14 **Iowa River** ≈ Iowa, C USA
119 M19 **Ipa** *Rus.* Ipa. ≈ SE Belaeus
Ipa *see* Ipa
59 N20 **Ipatinga** Minas Gerais, SE Brazil *19°32′S 42°30′W*
127 N13 **Ipatovo** Stavropol'skiy Kray, SW Russian Federation *45°40′N 42°51′E*
115 C16 **Ípeiros** *Eng.* Epirus. ◐ *region* W Greece
111 J21 **Ipel'** *var.* Ipoly, *Ger.* Eipel. ≈ Hungary/Slovakia
54 C13 **Ipiales** Nariño, SW Colombia *0°52′N 77°38′W*
189 V14 **Ipis** *atoll* Chuuk Islands, C Micronesia
59 A14 **Ipixuna** Amazonas, W Brazil *06°57′S 71°42′W*
168 J8 **Ipoh** Perak, Peninsular Malaysia *04°36′N 101°02′E*
Ipoly *see* Ipel'
187 S15 **Ipota** Erromango, S Vanuatu *18°54′S 169°19′E*
79 K14 **Ippy** Ouaka, C Central African Republic *06°17′N 21°13′E*
114 L13 **İpsala** Edirne, NW Turkey *40°56′N 26°23′E*
Ipsario *see* Ypsário
183 V3 **Ipswich** Queensland, E Australia *27°28′S 152°40′E*
97 Q20 **Ipswich** *hist.* Gipeswic. E England, United Kingdom *52°05′N 01°08′E*
29 O8 **Ipswich** South Dakota, N USA *45°24′N 99°00′W*
Iput' *see* Iputs'
119 P18 **Iputs'** *Rus.* Iput'. ≈ Belarus/Russian Federation
9 R7 **Iqaluit** *prev.* Frobisher Bay. *province capital* Baffin Island, Nunavut, NE Canada *63°44′N 68°28′W*
159 P9 **Iqe** Qinghai, W China *38°03′N 94°45′E*
159 P9 **Iqe He** ≈ C China
Iqlid *see* Eqlīd
62 G3 **Iquique** Tarapacá, N Chile *20°15′S 70°08′W*
56 G8 **Iquitos** Loreto, N Peru *03°51′S 73°13′W*
25 N9 **Iraan** Texas, SW USA *30°52′N 101°52′W*
79 K14 **Ira Banda** Haute-Kotto, E Central African Republic *05°57′N 22°05′E*
165 P16 **Irabu-jima** *island* Miyako-shotō, SW Japan
55 Y9 **Iracoubo** N French Guiana *05°28′N 53°15′W*
60 H13 **Iraí** Rio Grande do Sul, S Brazil *27°15′S 53°17′W*
114 G12 **Irákleia** Kentrikí Makedonía, N Greece *41°09′N 23°16′E*
115 J21 **Irákleia** *island* Kykládes, Greece, Aegean Sea
115 J25 **Irákleio** *var.* Herakleion, *Eng.* Candia; *prev.* Iráklion. Kríti, Greece, E Mediterranean Sea *35°20′N 25°08′E*
115 F15 **Irákleio** *anc.* Heracleum. *castle* Kentrikí Makedonía, N Greece
115 J25 **Irákleio** ✈ Kríti, Greece, E Mediterranean Sea *35°20′N 25°10′E*
Iráklion *see* Irákleio
143 O7 **Iran** *off.* Islamic Republic of Iran; *prev.* Persia. ◆ *republic* SW Asia
58 F13 **Iranduba** Amazonas, NW Brazil *03°19′S 60°09′W*
85 P13 **Iranian Plate** *tectonic feature*
143 Q9 **Iranian Plateau** *var.* Plateau of Iran. *plateau* N Iran
Iran, Islamic Republic of *see* Iran
Iran Mountains *see* Iran, Pegunungan
169 U9 **Iran, Pegunungan** *var.* Iran Mountains. ▲▲ Indonesia/Malaysia
Iran, Plateau of *see* Iranian Plateau
143 W13 **Īrānshahr** Sīstān va Balūchestān, SE Iran *27°14′N 60°40′E*
55 P5 **Irapa** Sucre, NE Venezuela *10°37′N 62°35′W*
41 N13 **Irapuato** Guanajuato, C Mexico *20°40′N 101°23′W*
139 R7 **Iraq** *off.* Republic of Iraq, *Ar.* 'Irāq. ◆ *republic* SW Asia
'Irāq *see* Iraq
Iraq, Republic of *see* Iraq
60 J12 **Irati** Paraná, S Brazil *25°25′S 50°38′W*
105 R3 **Irati** ≈ N Spain
125 T8 **Irayël'** Respublika Komi, NW Russian Federation *64°28′N 55°20′E*
43 N13 **Irazú, Volcán** Ѧ C Costa Rica *09°57′N 83°52′W*
Irbenskiy Zaliv/Irbes Šaurums *see* Irbe Strait
118 D7 **Irbe Strait** *Est.* Kura Kurk, *Latv.* Irbes Šaurums, Irbenskiy Zaliv; *prev. Est.* Irbe Väin. *strait* Estonia/Latvia
Irbe Väin *see* Irbe Strait
138 G9 **Irbid** Irbid, N Jordan *32°33′N 35°51′E*
138 G9 **Irbid** *off.* Muḩāfaẓat Irbid. ◐ *governorate* N Jordan
Irbid, Muḩāfaẓat *see* Irbid
Irbīl *see* Arbīl
109 S6 **Irdning** Steiermark, SE Austria *47°29′N 14°04′E*
79 I18 **Irebu** Equateur, W Dem. Rep. Congo *0°32′S 17°44′E*
97 D17 **Ireland** *off.* Republic of Ireland, *Ir.* Éire. ◆ *republic* NW Europe
84 C9 **Ireland** *Lat.* Hibernia. *island* Ireland/United Kingdom
64 A12 **Ireland Island North** *island* W Bermuda
64 A12 **Ireland Island South** *island* W Bermuda
Ireland, Republic of *see* Ireland
125 V15 **Iren'** ≈ NW Russian Federation
185 A22 **Irene, Mount** ▲ South Island, New Zealand *45°04′S 167°24′E*
Irgalem *see* Yirga 'Alem
144 L11 **Irgiz** *Kaz.* Yrghyz. Aktyubinsk, C Kazakhstan *48°36′N 61°14′E*
Irian *see* New Guinea
Irian Barat *see* Papua
Irian Jaya *see* Papua
Irian, Teluk *see* Cenderawasih, Teluk
78 K9 **Iriba** Biltine, NE Chad *15°10′N 22°11′E*
127 X7 **Iriklinskoye Vodokhranilishche** ⊠ W Russian Federation
81 H23 **Iringa** Iringa, C Tanzania *07°49′S 35°39′E*
81 H23 **Iringa** ◐ *region* S Tanzania
165 O16 **Iriomote-jima** *island* Sakishima-shotō, SW Japan
42 L4 **Iriona** Colón, NE Honduras *15°55′N 85°10′W*
47 U7 **Iriri** ≈ N Brazil
58 I13 **Iriri, Rio** ≈ C Brazil
Iris *see* Yeşilırmak
35 W9 **Irish, Mount** ▲ Nevada, W USA *37°39′N 115°22′W*
97 H17 **Irish Sea** *Ir.* Muir Éireann. *sea* C British Isles
139 U12 **Irjal ash Shaykhīyah** Al Muthanná, S Iraq *30°49′N 44°58′E*
147 U11 **Irkeshtam** Oshskaya Oblast', SW Kyrgyzstan *39°39′N 73°49′E*
122 M13 **Irkutsk** Irkutskaya Oblast', S Russian Federation *52°18′N 104°15′E*
122 M12 **Irkutskaya Oblast'** ◐ *province* S Russian Federation
Irlir, Gora *see* Irlir Tog'i
146 K8 **Irlir Tog'i** *var.* Gora Irlir. ▲ N Uzbekistan *42°43′N 63°24′E*
Irminger Basin *see* Reykjanes Basin
21 R12 **Irmo** South Carolina, SE USA *34°05′N 81°10′W*
102 E6 **Iroise** *sea* NW France
189 X2 **Iroj** *var.* Eroj. *island* Ratak Chain, SE Marshall Islands
182 H7 **Iron Baron** South Australia *33°01′S 137°13′E*
14 C10 **Iron Bridge** Ontario, S Canada *46°16′N 83°12′W*
20 H10 **Iron City** Tennessee, S USA *35°01′N 87°34′W*
14 I13 **Irondale** ≈ Ontario, SE Canada
182 H7 **Iron Knob** South Australia *32°46′S 137°08′E*
30 M5 **Iron Mountain** Michigan, N USA *45°51′N 88°03′W*
30 M4 **Iron River** Michigan, N USA *46°05′N 88°38′W*
30 J3 **Iron River** Wisconsin, N USA *46°34′N 91°22′W*
27 X6 **Ironton** Missouri, C USA *37°37′N 90°40′W*
31 S15 **Ironton** Ohio, N USA *38°32′N 82°40′W*
30 K4 **Ironwood** Michigan, N USA *46°27′N 90°10′W*
12 H12 **Iroquois Falls** Ontario, S Canada *48°47′N 80°41′W*
31 N12 **Iroquois River** ≈ Illinois/Indiana, N USA
164 M15 **Irō-zaki** *headland* Honshū, S Japan *34°36′N 138°49′E*
Irpen' *see* Irpin'
117 O4 **Irpin'** *Rus.* Irpen'. Kyyivs'ka Oblast', N Ukraine *50°31′N 30°16′E*
117 O4 **Irpin'** *Rus.* Irpen'. ≈ N Ukraine
141 Q16 **'Irqah** SW Yemen *13°42′N 47°21′E*
166 K8 **Irrawaddy** *var.* Ayeyarwady. ◐ *division* SW Burma (Myanmar)
166 L6 **Irrawaddy** *var.* Ayeyarwady. ≈ W Burma (Myanmar)
166 K8 **Irrawaddy, Mouths of the** *delta* SW Burma (Myanmar)
117 N4 **Irsha** ≈ N Ukraine
116 H7 **Irshava** Zakarpats'ka Oblast', W Ukraine *48°19′N 23°03′E*
107 N18 **Irsina** Basilicata, S Italy *40°42′N 16°18′E*
Irtish *see* Irtysh
129 R5 **Irtysh** *var.* Irtish, *Kaz.* Ertis. ≈ C Asia
145 S7 **Irtyshsk** *Kaz.* Ertis. Pavlodar, NE Kazakhstan *53°21′N 75°27′E*
79 P17 **Irumu** Orientale, E Dem. Rep. Congo *01°27′N 29°52′E*
105 Q2 **Irun** *Cast.* Irún. País Vasco, N Spain *43°20′N 01°48′W*
Irún *see* Irun
Iruña *see* Pamplona
105 Q3 **Irurtzun** Navarra, N Spain *42°55′N 01°50′W*
96 I13 **Irvine** W Scotland, United Kingdom *55°37′N 04°40′W*
21 N6 **Irvine** Kentucky, S USA *37°42′N 83°59′W*
25 T6 **Irving** Texas, SW USA *32°47′N 96°57′W*
20 K5 **Irvington** Kentucky, S USA *37°52′N 86°16′W*
Isaak *see* Iisaku
28 L8 **Isabel** South Dakota, N USA *45°21′N 101°25′W*
186 L8 **Isabel** *off.* Isabel Province. ◐ *province* N Solomon Islands
171 O8 **Isabela** Basilan Island, SW Philippines *06°41′N 122°00′E*
45 S5 **Isabela** W Puerto Rico *18°30′N 67°02′W*
45 N8 **Isabela, Cabo** *headland* NW Dominican Republic *19°54′N 71°03′W*
57 A18 **Isabela, Isla** *var.* Albemarle Island. *island* Galapagos Islands, Ecuador, E Pacific Ocean
40 I12 **Isabela, Isla** *island* C Mexico
42 K9 **Isabella, Cordillera** ▲▲ NW Nicaragua
35 S12 **Isabella Lake** ⊠ California, W USA
31 N2 **Isabelle, Point** *headland* Michigan, N USA *47°20′N 87°56′W*
Isabel Province *see* Isabel
Isabel Segunda *see* Vieques
116 M13 **Isaccea** Tulcea, E Romania *45°16′N 28°28′E*
92 H1 **Ísafjarðardjúp** *inlet* NW Iceland
92 H1 **Ísafjördhur** Vestfirdhir, NW Iceland *66°04′N 23°09′W*
164 C14 **Isahaya** Nagasaki, Kyūshū, SW Japan *32°51′N 130°02′E*
149 S7 **Īsa Khel** Punjab, E Pakistan *32°39′N 71°20′E*
172 H7 **Isalo** *var.* Massif de L'Isalo. ▲▲ SW Madagascar
79 K20 **Isandja** Kasai-Occidental, C Dem. Rep. Congo *03°03′S 21°57′E*
187 R15 **Isangel** Tanna, S Vanuatu *19°34′S 169°17′E*
79 M18 **Isangi** Orientale, C Dem. Rep. Congo *0°46′N 24°15′E*
101 L24 **Isar** ≈ Austria/Germany
101 M23 **Isar-Kanal** *canal* SE Germany
Isbarta *see* Isparta
Isca Damnoniorum *see* Exeter
107 K18 **Ischia** *var.* Isola d'Ischia; *anc.* Aenaria. Campania, S Italy *40°44′N 13°57′E*
107 J18 **Ischia, Isola d'** *island* S Italy
54 B12 **Iscuandé** *var.* Santa Bárbara. Nariño, SW Colombia *02°32′N 78°00′W*
164 K14 **Ise** Mie, Honshū, SW Japan *34°29′N 136°43′E*
100 J12 **Ise** ≈ N Germany
95 I23 **Isefjord** *fjord* E Denmark
Iseghem *see* Izegem
192 M14 **Iselin Seamount** *undersea feature* S Pacific Ocean *72°30′S 179°00′W*
Isenhof *see* Püssi
106 E7 **Iseo** Lombardia, N Italy *45°40′N 10°03′E*
103 U12 **Iseran, Col de l'** *pass* E France
103 S11 **Isère** ◐ *department* E France
103 S12 **Isère** ≈ E France
101 F15 **Iserlohn** Nordrhein-Westfalen, W Germany *51°23′N 07°42′E*
107 K16 **Isernia** *var.* Æsernia. Molise, C Italy *41°35′N 14°14′E*
165 N12 **Isesaki** Gunma, Honshū, S Japan *36°19′N 139°11′E*
129 Q5 **Iset'** ≈ C Russian Federation
77 S15 **Iseyin** Oyo, W Nigeria *07°56′N 03°33′E*
Isfahan *see* Eşfahān
147 Q11 **Isfana** Batkenskaya Oblast', SW Kyrgyzstan *39°51′N 69°31′E*
147 R11 **Isfara** N Tajikistan *40°06′N 70°34′E*
149 O4 **Isfi Maidān** Ghowr, N Afghanistan *35°09′N 66°16′E*
92 O3 **Isfjorden** *fjord* W Svalbard
Isgender *see* Kul'mach
Isha Baydhabo *see* Baydhabo
125 V11 **Isherim, Gora** ▲ NW Russian Federation *61°06′N 59°09′E*
127 Q5 **Isheyevka** Ul'yanovskaya Oblast', W Russian Federation *54°27′N 48°18′E*
165 P16 **Ishigaki** Okinawa, Ishigaki-jima, SW Japan *24°20′N 124°09′E*
165 P16 **Ishigaki-jima** *island* Sakishima-shotō, SW Japan
165 R3 **Ishikari-wan** *bay* Hokkaidō, NE Japan
165 S16 **Ishikawa** *var.* Isikawa. Okinawa, Okinawa, SW Japan *26°25′N 127°47′E*
164 K11 **Ishikawa** *off.* Ishikawa-ken, *var.* Isikawa. ◐ *prefecture* Honshū, SW Japan
Ishikawa-ken *see* Ishikawa
122 H11 **Ishim** Tyumenskaya Oblast', C Russian Federation *56°13′N 69°25′E*
129 R6 **Ishim** *Kaz.* Esil. ≈ Kazakhstan/Russian Federation
127 V6 **Ishimbay** Respublika Bashkortostan, W Russian Federation *53°21′N 56°03′E*
145 O9 **Ishimskoye** Akmola, C Kazakhstan *51°23′N 67°07′E*
165 Q10 **Ishinomaki** *var.* Isinomaki. Miyagi, Honshū, C Japan *38°26′N 141°17′E*
165 P13 **Ishioka** *var.* Isioka. Ibaraki, Honshū, S Japan *36°11′N 140°16′E*
Ishkashim *see* Ishkoshim
Ishkashimskiy Khrebet *see* Ishkoshim, Qatorkŭhi
147 S15 **Ishkoshim** *Rus.* Ishkashim. S Tajikistan *36°46′N 71°35′E*
147 S15 **Ishkoshim, Qatorkŭhi** *Rus.* Ishkashimskiy Khrebet. ▲▲ SE Tajikistan
31 N4 **Ishpeming** Michigan, N USA *46°29′N 87°40′W*
147 N11 **Ishtixon** *Rus.* Ishtykhan. Samarqand Viloyati, C Uzbekistan *39°59′N 66°28′E*
Ishtykhan *see* Ishtixon
Ishurdi *see* Iswardi
61 G17 **Isidoro Noblia** Cerro Largo, NE Uruguay *31°58′S 54°09′W*
102 J4 **Isigny-sur-Mer** Calvados, N France *49°20′N 01°06′W*
Isikawa *see* Ishikawa
136 C11 **Işıklar Dağı** ▲▲ NW Turkey
107 C19 **Isili** Sardegna, Italy, C Mediterranean Sea *39°46′N 09°06′E*
122 H12 **Isil'kul'** Omskaya Oblast', C Russian Federation *54°52′N 71°07′E*
Isinomaki *see* Ishinomaki
Isioka *see* Ishioka
81 I18 **Isiolo** Eastern, C Kenya *0°20′N 37°36′E*
79 O16 **Isiro** Orientale, NE Dem. Rep. Congo *02°51′N 27°47′E*
92 P2 **Isispynten** *headland* NE Svalbard *79°51′N 26°44′E*
123 P11 **Isit** Respublika Sakha (Yakutiya), NE Russian Federation *60°53′N 125°32′E*
149 O2 **Iskabad Canal** *canal* N Afghanistan
147 Q9 **Iskandar** *Rus.* Iskander. Toshkent Viloyati, E Uzbekistan *41°32′N 69°46′E*
Iskander *see* Iskandar
Iskăr *see* Iskŭr
121 Q2 **İskele** *var.* Trikomo, *Gk.* Tríkomon. E Cyprus *35°16′N 33°54′E*
136 K17 **İskenderun** *Eng.* Alexandretta. Hatay, S Turkey *36°34′N 36°10′E*
138 H2 **İskenderun Körfezi** *Eng.* Gulf of Alexandretta. *gulf* S Turkey
136 J11 **İskilip** Çorum, N Turkey *40°45′N 34°28′E*
Iski-Nauket *see* Eski-Nookat
114 J11 **Iskra** *prev.* Popovo. Khaskovo, S Bulgaria *41°55′N 25°12′E*
114 G10 **Iskŭr** *var.* Iskăr. ≈ NW Bulgaria
114 H10 **Iskŭr, Yazovir** *prev.* Yazovir Stalin. ⊠ W Bulgaria
41 S15 **Isla** Veracruz-Llave, SE Mexico *18°01′N 95°30′W*
119 J15 **Islach** *Rus.* Isloch'. ≈ C Belarus
104 H14 **Isla Cristina** Andalucía, S Spain *37°12′N 07°20′W*
Isla de León *see* San Fernando
149 U6 **Islāmābād** ● (Pakistan) Federal Capital Territory Islāmābād, NE Pakistan *33°40′N 73°08′E*
149 V6 **Islāmābād** ✈ Federal Capital Territory Islāmābād, NE Pakistan *33°40′N 73°08′E*
Islamabad *see* Anantnāg
149 R17 **Islāmkot** Sind, SE Pakistan *24°37′N 70°04′E*
23 Y17 **Islamorada** Florida Keys, Florida, SE USA *24°55′N 80°37′W*
153 P14 **Islāmpur** Bihār, N India *25°09′N 85°13′E*
Islam Qala *see* Eslām Qal'eh
18 K16 **Island Beach** *spit* New Jersey, NE USA
19 S4 **Island Falls** Maine, NE USA *45°59′N 68°16′W*
Island/Ísland *see* Iceland
182 H6 **Island Lagoon** ◎ South Australia
11 Y13 **Island Lake** ◎ Manitoba, C Canada
29 W5 **Island Lake Reservoir** ⊠ Minnesota, N USA
33 R13 **Island Park** Idaho, NW USA *44°27′N 111°21′W*
19 N6 **Island Pond** Vermont, NE USA *44°48′N 71°51′W*
184 K2 **Islands, Bay of** *inlet* North Island, New Zealand
103 R7 **Is-sur-Tille** Côte d'Or, C France *47°34′N 05°03′E*
42 J3 **Islas de la Bahía** ◐ *department* N Honduras
65 L20 **Islas Orcadas Rise** *undersea feature* S Atlantic Ocean
96 F12 **Islay** *island* SW Scotland, United Kingdom
116 I15 **Islaz** Teleorman, S Romania *43°44′N 24°45′E*
29 V7 **Isle** Minnesota, N USA *46°08′N 93°28′W*
102 M12 **Isle** ≈ W France
97 I16 **Isle of Man** ◇ *UK crown dependency* NW Europe
21 X7 **Isle of Wight** Virginia, NE USA *36°54′N 76°41′W*
97 M24 **Isle of Wight** *cultural region* S England, United Kingdom
191 Y3 **Isles Lagoon** ◎ Kiritimati, E Kiribati
37 R11 **Isleta Pueblo** New Mexico, SW USA *34°54′N 106°40′W*
Isloch' *see* Islach
61 E19 **Ismael Cortinas** Flores, S Uruguay *33°57′S 57°05′W*
Ismailia *see* Al Ismā'īlīya
Ismâ'ilîya *see* Al Ismā'īlīya
Ismailly *see* İsmayıllı
137 X11 **İsmayıllı** *Rus.* Ismailly. N Azerbaijan *40°47′N 48°09′E*
Ismid *see* İzmit
147 S12 **Ismoili Somoní, Qullai** *prev.* Qullai Kommunizm. ▲ E Tajikistan
75 X10 **Isnā** *var.* Esna. SE Egypt *25°16′N 32°30′E*
93 K18 **Isojoki** Länsi-Suomi, W Finland *62°07′N 22°00′E*
82 M12 **Isoka** Northern, NE Zambia *10°08′S 32°43′E*
Isola d'Ischia *see* Ischia
Isola d'Istria *see* Izola
Isonzo *see* Soča
15 U4 **Isoukustouc** ≈ Québec, SE Canada
136 F15 **İsparta** *var.* Isbarta. Isparta, SW Turkey *37°46′N 30°32′E*
136 F15 **İsparta** *var.* Isbarta. ◐ *province* SW Turkey
114 M7 **Isperikh** *prev.* Kemanlar. Razgrad, N Bulgaria *43°43′N 26°49′E*
107 L26 **Ispica** Sicilia, Italy, C Mediterranean Sea *36°47′N 14°55′E*
148 J14 **Ispikān** Baluchistān, SW Pakistan *26°21′N 62°15′E*
137 Q12 **İspir** Erzurum, NE Turkey *40°29′N 41°02′E*
138 E12 **Israel** *off.* State of Israel, *var.* Medinat Israel, *Heb.* Yisrael, Yisra'el. ◆ *republic* SW Asia
Israel, State of *see* Israel
Issa *see* Vis
55 S9 **Issano** C Guyana *05°49′N 59°28′W*
76 M16 **Issia** SW Ivory Coast *06°33′N 06°33′W*
Issiq Köl *see* Issyk-Kul', Ozero
103 P11 **Issoire** Puy-de-Dôme, C France *45°33′N 03°15′E*
103 N9 **Issoudun** *anc.* Uxellodunum. Indre, C France *46°57′N 01°59′E*
81 H22 **Issuna** Singida, C Tanzania *05°24′S 34°48′E*
Issyk *see* Yesik
Issyk-Kul' *see* Balykchy
147 X7 **Issyk-Kul', Ozero** *var.* Issiq Köl, *Kir.* Ysyk-Köl. ◎ E Kyrgyzstan
147 X7 **Issyk-Kul'skaya Oblast'** *Kir.* Ysyk-Köl Oblasty. ◐ *province* E Kyrgyzstan
149 Q7 **Īstādeh-ye Moqor, Āb-e-** *var.* Āb-i-Istāda. ◎ SE Afghanistan
136 D11 **İstanbul** *Bul.* Tsarigrad, *Eng.* Istanbul, *prev.* Constantinople; *anc.* Byzantium. Istanbul, NW Turkey *41°02′N 28°57′E*
114 P12 **İstanbul** ◐ *province* NW Turkey
114 P12 **İstanbul Boğazı** *var.* Bosporus Thracius, *Eng.* Bosphorus, Bosporus, *Turk.* Karadeniz Boğazi. *strait* NW Turkey
Istarska Županija *see* Istra
115 G19 **Isthmía** Pelopónnisos, S Greece *37°55′N 23°02′E*
115 G17 **Istiaía** Évvoia, C Greece *38°57′N 23°09′E*
54 D9 **Istmina** Chocó, W Colombia *05°09′N 76°42′W*
23 W13 **Istokpoga, Lake** ◎ Florida, SE USA
112 A9 **Istra** *off.* Istarska Županija. ◐ *province* NW Croatia
112 I10 **Istra** *Eng.* Istria, *Ger.* Istrien. *cultural region* NW Croatia
103 R15 **Istres** Bouches-du-Rhône, SE France *43°30′N 04°59′E*
Istria/Istrien *see* Istra
153 T15 **Iswardi** *var.* Ishurdi. Rajshahi, W Bangladesh *24°10′N 89°04′E*
127 V7 **Isyangulovo** Respublika Bashkortostan, W Russian Federation *52°10′N 56°38′E*
62 O6 **Itá** Central, S Paraguay *25°29′S 57°21′W*
59 O17 **Itaberaba** Bahia, E Brazil *12°34′S 40°21′W*
59 M20 **Itabira** *prev.* Presidente Vargas. Minas Gerais, SE Brazil *19°39′S 43°14′W*
59 O18 **Itabuna** Bahia, E Brazil *14°48′S 39°18′W*
59 J18 **Itacaiu** Mato Grosso, S Brazil *14°49′S 51°21′W*
58 G12 **Itacoatiara** Amazonas, N Brazil *03°06′S 58°22′W*
54 D9 **Itagüí** Antioquia, W Colombia *06°12′N 75°40′W*
60 D13 **Itá Ibaté** Corrientes, NE Argentina *27°27′S 57°24′W*
60 G11 **Itaipú, Represa de** ⊠ Brazil/Paraguay
58 H13 **Itaituba** Pará, NE Brazil *04°15′S 55°56′W*
60 K13 **Itajaí** Santa Catarina, S Brazil *26°50′S 48°39′W*
Italia/Italiana, Republica/Italian Republic, The *see* Italy
Italian Somaliland *see* Somalia
25 T7 **Italy** Texas, SW USA *32°10′N 96°52′W*
106 G12 **Italy** *off.* The Italian Republic, *It.* Italia, Repubblica Italiana. ◆ *republic* S Europe
59 O19 **Itamaraju** Bahia, E Brazil *16°58′S 39°32′W*
59 C14 **Itamarati** Amazonas, W Brazil *06°13′S 68°17′W*
59 M19 **Itambé, Pico de** ▲ SE Brazil *18°23′S 43°21′W*
164 J13 **Itami** ✈ (Ōsaka) Ōsaka, Honshū, SW Japan *34°47′N 135°24′E*
115 H15 **Ítamos** ▲ N Greece *40°06′N 23°51′E*
153 W11 **Itānagar** *state capital* Arunāchal Pradesh, NE India *27°02′N 93°38′E*
Itany *see* Litani
59 N19 **Itaobim** Minas Gerais, SE Brazil *16°34′S 41°27′W*
59 P15 **Itaparica, Represa de** ⊠ E Brazil
58 M13 **Itapecuru-Mirim** Maranhão, E Brazil *03°24′S 44°20′W*
60 Q8 **Itaperuna** Rio de Janeiro, SE Brazil *21°14′S 41°51′W*
59 O18 **Itapetinga** Bahia, E Brazil *15°17′S 40°16′W*
60 L10 **Itapetininga** São Paulo, S Brazil *23°36′S 48°07′W*
60 K10 **Itapeva** São Paulo, S Brazil *23°58′S 48°54′W*
47 W6 **Itapicuru, Rio** ≈ NE Brazil
58 O13 **Itapipoca** Ceará, E Brazil *03°29′S 39°35′W*
60 M9 **Itapira** São Paulo, S Brazil *22°25′S 46°46′W*
60 K8 **Itápolis** São Paulo, S Brazil *21°36′S 48°43′W*
60 K10 **Itaporanga** São Paulo, S Brazil *23°43′S 49°28′W*
62 P7 **Itapúa** *off.* Departamento de Itapúa. ◐ *department* SE Paraguay
Itapúa, Departamento de *see* Itapúa
59 E15 **Itapuã do Oeste** Rondônia, W Brazil *09°21′S 63°07′W*
61 E15 **Itaqui** Rio Grande do Sul, S Brazil *29°10′S 56°28′W*
60 K10 **Itararé** São Paulo, S Brazil *24°07′S 49°16′W*
60 K10 **Itararé, Rio** ≈ S Brazil
154 H11 **Itārsi** Madhya Pradesh, C India *22°39′N 77°48′E*
25 T7 **Itasca** Texas, SW USA *32°09′N 97°09′W*
Itassi *see* Vieille Case
93 N17 **Itä-Suomi** ◐ *province* E Finland
60 D13 **Itatí** Corrientes, NE Argentina *27°16′S 58°15′W*
60 K10 **Itatinga** São Paulo, S Brazil *23°08′S 48°36′W*
115 F18 **Itéas, Kólpos** *gulf* C Greece
57 N15 **Iténez, Río** *var.* Rio Guaporé. ≈ Bolivia/Brazil *see also* Rio Guaporé
Iténez, Río *see* Guaporé, Rio
54 H11 **Iteviate, Río** ≈ C Colombia
100 I13 **Ith** *hill range* C Germany
31 Q8 **Ithaca** Michigan, N USA *43°17′N 84°36′W*
18 H11 **Ithaca** New York, NE USA *42°26′N 76°30′W*
115 C18 **Itháki** *island* Iónia Nísiá, Greece, C Mediterranean Sea
Itháki *see* Vathy
It Hearrenfean *see* Heerenveen
79 L17 **Itimbiri** ≈ N Dem. Rep. Congo
Itinomiya *see* Ichinomiya
Itinoseki *see* Ichinoseki
39 Q5 **Itkilik River** ≈ Alaska, USA
164 M11 **Itoigawa** Niigata, Honshū, C Japan *37°02′N 137°53′E*
15 R6 **Itomamo, Lac** ◎ Québec, SE Canada
165 S17 **Itoman** Okinawa, SW Japan *26°05′N 127°40′E*
102 M5 **Iton** ≈ N France
57 M16 **Itonamas Río** ≈ NE Bolivia
Itoupé, Mont *see* Sommet Tabulaire
Itseqqortoormiit *see* Ittoqqortoormiit
22 K4 **Itta Bena** Mississippi, S USA *33°30′N 90°19′W*
107 B17 **Ittiri** Sardegna, Italy, C Mediterranean Sea *40°36′N 08°34′E*
197 Q14 **Ittoqqortoormiit** *var.* Itseqqortoormiit, *Dan.* Scoresbysund, *Eng.* Scoresby Sound. Tunu, C Greenland *70°33′N 21°52′W*
60 M10 **Itu** São Paulo, S Brazil *23°17′S 47°16′W*
54 D8 **Ituango** Antioquia, NW Colombia *07°07′N 75°46′W*
59 A14 **Ituí, Rio** ≈ NW Brazil
79 O20 **Itula** Sud-Kivu, E Dem. Rep. Congo *03°30′S 27°50′E*
59 K19 **Itumbiara** Goiás, C Brazil *18°25′S 49°15′W*
55 T9 **Ituni** E Guyana *05°24′N 58°18′W*
41 X13 **Iturbide** Campeche, SE Mexico *19°41′N 89°29′W*
Ituri *see* Aruwimi
123 V13 **Iturup, Ostrov** *island* Kuril'skiye Ostrova, SE Russian Federation
60 L7 **Ituverava** São Paulo, S Brazil *20°22′S 47°48′W*
59 C15 **Ituxi, Rio** ≈ W Brazil
61 E14 **Ituzaingó** Corrientes, NE Argentina *27°34′S 56°44′W*
101 K18 **Itz** ≈ C Germany
100 I9 **Itzehoe** Schleswig-Holstein, N Germany *53°56′N 09°31′E*
23 N2 **Iuka** Mississippi, S USA *34°48′N 88°11′W*
60 I11 **Ivaiporã** Paraná, S Brazil *24°16′S 51°46′W*
60 I11 **Ivaí, Rio** ≈ S Brazil
92 L10 **Ivalo** *Lapp.* Avveel, Avvil. Lappi, N Finland *68°34′N 27°29′E*
92 L10 **Ivalojoki** *Lapp.* Avveel. ≈ N Finland
119 H20 **Ivanava** *Pol.* Janów, Janów Poleski, *Rus.* Ivanovo. Brestskaya Voblasts', SW Belarus *52°09′N 25°32′E*
124 F13 **Ivangorod** *Est.* Jaanilinn. Leningradskaya Oblast', NW Russian Federation *59°22′N 28°14′E*
Ivangorod *see* Dęblin
Ivangrad *see* Berane
183 N7 **Ivanhoe** New South Wales, SE Australia *32°55′S 144°21′E*
29 S9 **Ivanhoe** Minnesota, N USA *44°27′N 96°15′W*
14 D8 **Ivanhoe** ≈ Ontario, S Canada
112 E8 **Ivanić-Grad** Sisak-Moslavina, N Croatia *45°43′N 16°23′E*
117 T10 **Ivanivka** Khersons'ka Oblast', S Ukraine *46°43′N 34°28′E*
117 P10 **Ivanivka** Odes'ka Oblast', SW Ukraine *46°57′N 30°26′E*
113 L14 **Ivanjica** Serbia, C Serbia *43°36′N 20°14′E*
112 G11 **Ivanjska** *var.* Potkozarje. Republika Srpska, NW Bosnia and Herzegovina *44°54′N 17°04′E*
111 H21 **Ivanka** ✈ (Bratislava) Bratislavský Kraj, W Slovakia *48°10′N 17°13′E*
117 O3 **Ivankiv** *Rus.* Ivankov. Kyyivs'ka Oblast', N Ukraine *50°55′N 29°53′E*
Ivankov *see* Ivankiv
39 O15 **Ivanof Bay** Alaska, USA *55°55′N 159°28′W*
116 J7 **Ivano-Frankivs'k** *Ger.* Stanislau, *Pol.* Stanisławów, *Rus.* Ivano-Frankovsk; *prev.* Stanislav. Ivano-Frankivs'ka Oblast', W Ukraine *48°55′N 24°45′E*
Ivano-Frankivs'k *see* Ivano-Frankivs'ka Oblast'
116 I7 **Ivano-Frankivs'ka Oblast'** *var.* Ivano-Frankivs'k, *Rus.* Ivano-Frankovskaya Oblast'; *prev.* Stanislavskaya Oblast'. ◐ *province* W Ukraine
Ivano-Frankovsk *see* Ivano-Frankivs'k
Ivano-Frankovskaya Oblast' *see* Ivano-Frankivs'ka Oblast'
124 M16 **Ivanovo** Ivanovskaya Oblast', W Russian Federation *57°02′N 40°58′E*
Ivanovo *see* Ivanava
124 M16 **Ivanovskaya Oblast'** ◐ *province* W Russian Federation
35 X12 **Ivanpah Lake** ◎ California, W USA
112 E7 **Ivanščica** ▲▲ NE Croatia
127 R7 **Ivanteyevka** Saratovskaya Oblast', W Russian Federation *52°13′N 49°06′E*
Ivantsevichi/Ivatsevichi *see* Ivatsevichy
116 I4 **Ivanychi** Volyns'ka Oblast', NW Ukraine *50°37′N 24°22′E*
119 H18 **Ivatsevichy** *Pol.* Iwacewicze, *Rus.* Ivantsevichi, Ivatsevichi. Brestskaya Voblasts', SW Belarus *52°43′N 25°21′E*
114 L12 **Ivaylovgrad** Khaskovo, S Bulgaria *41°32′N 26°06′E*
114 K11 **Ivaylovgrad, Yazovir** ⊠ S Bulgaria
122 G9 **Ivdel'** Sverdlovskaya Oblast', C Russian Federation *60°42′N 60°07′E*
Ivenets *see* Ivyanyets
116 L12 **Iveşti** Galaţi, E Romania *45°27′N 28°00′E*
Ivgovuotna *see* Lyngen
Ivigtut *see* Ivittuut
79 F18 **Ivindo** ≈ Congo/Gabon
59 I21 **Ivinheima** Mato Grosso do Sul, SW Brazil *22°16′S 53°52′W*
196 M15 **Ivittuut** *var.* Ivigtut. Kitaa, S Greenland *61°28′N 48°33′W*
Iviza *see* Eivissa\Ibiza
172 I6 **Ivohibe** Fianarantsoa, SE Madagascar *22°28′S 46°53′E*
Ivoire, Côte d' *see* Ivory Coast
76 L15 **Ivory Coast** *off.* Republic of the Ivory Coast, *Fr.* Côte d'Ivoire, République de la Côte d'Ivoire. ◆ *republic* W Africa
68 C12 **Ivory Coast** *Fr.* Côte d'Ivoire. *coastal region* S Ivory Coast
Ivory Coast, Republic of the *see* Ivory Coast
95 L22 **Ivösjön** ◎ S Sweden
106 B7 **Ivrea** *anc.* Eporedia. Piemonte, NW Italy *45°28′N 07°52′E*
12 J2 **Ivujivik** Québec, NE Canada *62°26′N 77°49′W*
119 J16 **Ivyanyets** *Rus.* Ivenets. Minskaya Voblasts', C Belarus *53°53′N 26°45′E*
Iv'ye *see* Iwye
Iwacewicze *see* Ivatsevichy
165 R8 **Iwaizumi** Iwate, Honshū, NE Japan *39°48′N 141°46′E*
165 P12 **Iwaki** Fukushima, Honshū, N Japan *37°01′N 140°52′E*
164 F13 **Iwakuni** Yamaguchi, Honshū, SW Japan *34°08′N 132°06′E*
165 S4 **Iwamizawa** Hokkaidō, NE Japan *43°12′N 141°47′E*
165 R4 **Iwanai** Hokkaidō, NE Japan *42°51′N 140°21′E*
165 Q10 **Iwanuma** Miyagi, Honshū, C Japan *38°06′N 140°51′E*
164 L14 **Iwata** Shizuoka, Honshū, S Japan *34°42′N 137°51′E*
165 R8 **Iwate** Iwate, Honshū, N Japan *40°03′N 141°12′E*
165 R8 **Iwate** *off.* Iwate-ken. ◐ *prefecture* Honshū, C Japan
Iwate-ken *see* Iwate
77 S16 **Iwo** Oyo, SW Nigeria *07°21′N 03°58′E*
Iwojima *see* Iō-jima
119 I16 **Iwye** *Pol.* Iwje, *Rus.* Iv'ye. Hrodzyenskaya Voblasts', W Belarus *53°56′N 25°46′E*
42 C4 **Ixcán, Río** ≈ Guatemala/Mexico
99 G18 **Ixelles** *Dut.* Elsene. Brussels, C Belgium *50°49′N 04°21′E*
57 J16 **Ixiamas** La Paz, NW Bolivia *13°45′S 68°10′W*
41 O13 **Ixmiquilpan** *var.* Ixmiquilpán. Hidalgo, C Mexico *20°30′N 99°15′W*
Ixmiquilpán *see* Ixmiquilpan
83 K23 **Ixopo** KwaZulu/Natal, E South Africa *30°10′S 30°05′E*
Ixtaccíhuatal, Volcán *see* Iztaccíhuati, Volcán
40 M16 **Ixtapa** Guerrero, S Mexico *17°38′N 101°29′W*
41 S16 **Ixtepec** Oaxaca, SE Mexico *16°32′N 95°03′W*
40 K12 **Ixtlán** *var.* Ixtlán del Río. Nayarit, C Mexico *21°02′N 104°21′W*
Ixtlán del Río *see* Ixtlán
122 H11 **Iyevlevo** Tyumenskaya Oblast', C Russian Federation *57°36′N 67°20′E*
164 F14 **Iyo** Ehime, Shikoku, SW Japan *33°43′N 132°42′E*
164 E14 **Iyo-nada** *sea* S Japan
42 E4 **Izabal** *off.* Departamento de Izabal. ◐ *department* E Guatemala
Izabal, Departamento de *see* Izabal
42 F5 **Izabal, Lago de** *prev.* Golfo Dulce. ◎ E Guatemala
143 O9 **Īzad Khvāst** Fārs, C Iran *31°31′N 52°09′E*
41 X12 **Izamal** Yucatán, SE Mexico *20°58′N 89°00′W*
127 Q16 **Izberbash** Respublika Dagestan, SW Russian Federation *42°32′N 47°51′E*
99 C18 **Izegem** *prev.* Iseghem. West-Vlaanderen, W Belgium *50°55′N 03°13′E*
142 M9 **Īzeh** Khūzestān, SW Iran *31°48′N 49°49′E*
165 T16 **Izena-jima** *island* Nansei-shotō, SW Japan
114 N10 **Izgrev** Burgas, E Bulgaria *42°09′N 27°49′E*
127 T2 **Izhevsk** *prev.* Ustinov. Udmurtskaya Respublika, NW Russian Federation *56°48′N 53°12′E*
125 S7 **Izhma** Respublika Komi, NW Russian Federation *64°56′N 53°52′E*
125 S7 **Izhma** ≈ NW Russian Federation
141 X8 **Izkī** NE Oman *22°45′N 57°36′E*
Izmail *see* Izmayil
117 N13 **Izmayil** *Rus.* Izmail. Odes'ka Oblast', SW Ukraine *45°19′N 28°49′E*
136 B14 **İzmir** *prev.* Smyrna. İzmir, W Turkey *38°25′N 27°10′E*
136 C14 **İzmir** *prev.* Smyrna. ◐ *province* W Turkey
136 E11 **İzmit** *var.* Ismid; *anc.* Astacus. Kocaeli, NW Turkey *40°47′N 29°55′E*
104 M14 **Iznájar** Andalucía, S Spain *37°17′N 04°16′W*
104 M14 **Iznajar, Embalse de** ⊠ S Spain
105 N14 **Iznalloz** Andalucía, S Spain *37°23′N 03°31′W*
136 E11 **İznik** Bursa, NW Turkey *40°27′N 29°43′E*
136 E12 **İznik Gölü** ◎ NW Turkey
126 M14 **Izobil'nyy** Stavropol'skiy Kray, SW Russian Federation *45°22′N 41°40′E*

◆ Country
● Country Capital
◇ Dependent Territory
○ Dependent Territory Capital
◐ Administrative Regions
✈ International Airport
▲ Mountain
▲▲ Mountain Range
Ѧ Volcano
≈ River
◎ Lake
⊠ Reservoir

109 S13 **Izola** *It.* Isola d'Istria. SW Slovenia 45°31′N 13°40′E
138 H9 **Izra'** *var.* Ezra, Ezraa. Dar'ā, S Syria 32°52′N 36°15′E
41 P14 **Iztaccíhuatl, Volcán** *var.* Volcán Ixtaccíhuatal. S Mexico 19°07′N 98°37′W
42 C7 **Iztapa** Escuintla, SE Guatemala 13°58′N 90°42′W
Izúcar de Matamoros *see* Matamoros
165 N14 **Izu-hantō** *peninsula* Honshū, S Japan
164 C12 **Izuhara** Nagasaki, Tsushima, SW Japan 34°11′N 129°16′E
164 J14 **Izumiōtsu** Ōsaka, Honshū, SW Japan 34°29′N 135°25′E
164 I14 **Izumi-Sano** Ōsaka, Honshū, SW Japan 34°23′N 135°18′E
164 G12 **Izumo** Shimane, Honshū, SW Japan 35°22′N 132°46′E
192 H5 **Izu Trench** *undersea feature* NW Pacific Ocean
122 K6 **Izvestiy TsIK, Ostrova** *island* N Russian Federation
114 G10 **Izvor** Pernik, W Bulgaria 42°27′N 22°53′E
116 L5 **Izyaslav** Khmel'nyts'ka Oblast', W Ukraine 50°08′N 26°53′E
117 W6 **Izyum** Kharkivs'ka Oblast', E Ukraine 49°12′N 37°19′E

J

93 M18 **Jaala** Etelä-Suomi, S Finland 61°04′N 26°30′E
Jaaniinn *see* Ivangorod
140 J5 **Jabal ash Shifā** *desert* NW Saudi Arabia
141 U8 **Jabal az Zannah** *var.* Jebel Dhanna. Abū Zaby, W United Arab Emirates 24°10′N 52°36′E
138 E11 **Jabalīya** *var.* Jabāliyah. NE Gaza Strip 31°32′N 34°29′E
Jabāliyah *see* Jabalīya
105 N11 **Jabalón** C Spain
154 J10 **Jabalpur** *prev.* Jubbulpore. Madhya Pradesh, C India 23°10′N 79°59′E
141 N15 **Jabal Zuqar, Jazīrat** *var.* Az Zuqur. *island* SW Yemen
Jabat *see* Jabwot
138 J3 **Jabbūl, Sabkhat al** *sabkha* NW Syria
181 P1 **Jabiru** Northern Territory, N Australia 12°44′S 132°48′E
138 H4 **Jablah** *var.* Jeble, *Fr.* Djéblé. Al Lādhiqīyah, W Syria 35°00′N 36°00′E
112 C11 **Jablanac** Lika-Senj, W Croatia 44°43′N 14°54′E
113 H14 **Jablanica** Federacija Bosna I Hercegovina, SW Bosnia and Herzegovina 43°39′N 17°43′E
113 M20 **Jablanica** *Alb.* Mali i Jablanicës, *var.* Malet e Jablanicës. Albania/ FYR Macedonia *see also* Jablanicës, Mali i
Jablanicës, Malet e *see* Jablanica/Jablanicës, Mali i
113 M20 **Jablanicës, Mali i**, *Mac.* Jablanica. Albania/ FYR Macedonia *see also* Jablanica
111 E15 **Jablonec nad Nisou** *Ger.* Gablonz an der Neisse. Liberecký Kraj, N Czech Republic 50°44′N 15°10′E
Jablonków/Jablunkau *see* Jablunkov
110 J9 **Jabłonowo Pomorskie** Kujawski-pomorskie, C Poland 53°24′N 19°08′E
111 J17 **Jablunkov** *Ger.* Jablunkau, *Pol.* Jabłonków. Moravskoslezský Kraj, E Czech Republic 49°35′N 18°46′E
59 Q15 **Jaboatão** Pernambuco, E Brazil 08°05′S 35°W
60 L8 **Jaboticabal** São Paulo, S Brazil 21°15′S 48°17′W
189 U7 **Jabwot** *var.* Jabat, Jebat, Jōwat. *island* Ralik Chain, S Marshall Islands
105 S4 **Jaca** Aragón, NE Spain 42°34′N 00°33′W
42 B4 **Jacaltenango** Huehuetenango, W Guatemala 15°39′N 91°46′W
59 G14 **Jacaré-a-Canga** Pará, NE Brazil 05°59′S 57°32′W
60 N10 **Jacareí** São Paulo, S Brazil 23°18′S 45°55′W
59 I18 **Jaciara** Mato Grosso, W Brazil 15°59′S 54°57′W
59 E15 **Jaciparaná** Rondônia, W Brazil 09°20′S 64°28′W
19 P5 **Jackman** Maine, NE USA 45°35′N 70°14′W
35 X1 **Jackpot** Nevada, W USA 41°57′N 114°41′W
20 M8 **Jacksboro** Tennessee, S USA 36°19′N 84°11′W
25 S6 **Jacksboro** Texas, SW USA 33°13′N 98°11′W
23 N7 **Jackson** Alabama, S USA 31°30′N 87°53′W
35 P7 **Jackson** California, W USA 38°19′N 120°46′W
23 T4 **Jackson** Georgia, SE USA 33°17′N 83°58′W
21 O6 **Jackson** Kentucky, S USA 37°32′N 83°24′W
22 J8 **Jackson** Louisiana, S USA 30°50′N 91°13′W
31 Q10 **Jackson** Michigan, N USA 42°15′N 84°24′W
29 T11 **Jackson** Minnesota, N USA 43°38′N 95°00′W
22 K5 **Jackson** *state capital* Mississippi, S USA 32°19′N 90°12′W
27 Y7 **Jackson** Missouri, C USA 37°23′N 89°40′W
21 W8 **Jackson** North Carolina, SE USA 36°24′N 77°25′W
31 T15 **Jackson** Ohio, NE USA 39°03′N 82°40′W
20 G9 **Jackson** Tennessee, S USA 35°37′N 88°50′W
33 S14 **Jackson** Wyoming, C USA 43°28′N 110°45′W
185 C19 **Jackson Bay** *bay* South Island, New Zealand
186 E9 **Jackson Field** ✕ (Port Moresby) National Capital District, S Papua New Guinea 09°28′S 147°12′E
185 C20 **Jackson Head** *headland* South Island, New Zealand 43°57′S 168°38′E
23 S8 **Jackson, Lake** Florida, SE USA
33 S13 **Jackson Lake** Wyoming, C USA
194 J6 **Jackson, Mount** Antarctica 71°43′S 63°45′W
37 U3 **Jackson Reservoir** Colorado, C USA
23 Q3 **Jacksonville** Alabama, S USA 33°48′N 85°45′W
27 V11 **Jacksonville** Arkansas, C USA 34°52′N 92°08′W
23 W8 **Jacksonville** Florida, SE USA 30°20′N 81°39′W
30 K14 **Jacksonville** Illinois, N USA 39°43′N 90°13′W
21 W11 **Jacksonville** North Carolina, SE USA 34°45′N 77°26′W
25 W7 **Jacksonville** Texas, SW USA 31°57′N 95°16′W
23 X9 **Jacksonville Beach** Florida, SE USA 30°17′N 81°23′W
44 L9 **Jacmel** *var.* Jaquemel. S Haiti 18°13′N 72°33′W
Jacob *see* Nkayi
149 Q12 **Jacobābād** Sind, SE Pakistan 28°16′N 68°30′E
55 T11 **Jacobs Ladder Falls** *waterfall* S Guyana
45 O11 **Jaco, Pointe** *headland* N Dominica 15°38′N 61°25′W
15 Q9 **Jacques-Cartier** Québec, SE Canada
13 P11 **Jacques-Cartier, Détroit de** *var.* Jacques-Cartier Passage. *strait* Gulf of St. Lawrence/St. Lawrence River, Canada
15 W6 **Jacques-Cartier, Mont** Québec, SE Canada 48°58′N 66°00′W
Jacques-Cartier Passage *see* Jacques-Cartier, Détroit de
61 H16 **Jacuí, Rio** S Brazil
60 L11 **Jacupiranga** São Paulo, S Brazil 24°42′S 48°00′W
100 G10 **Jade** NW Germany
100 G10 **Jadebusen** *bay* NW Germany
Jadotville *see* Likasi
Jadransko More/Jadransko Morje *see* Adriatic Sea
105 O7 **Jadraque** Castilla-La Mancha, C Spain 40°55′N 02°55′W
95 I22 **Jægerspris** Frederiksborg, E Denmark 55°52′N 11°59′E
56 C10 **Jaén** Cajamarca, N Peru 05°45′S 78°51′W
105 N13 **Jaén** Andalucía, SW Spain 37°46′N 03°48′W
105 N13 **Jaén** ◈ *province* Andalucía, S Spain
95 C17 **Jæren** *physical region* S Norway
155 J23 **Jaffna** Northern Province, N Sri Lanka 09°42′N 80°03′E
155 K23 **Jaffna Lagoon** *lagoon* N Sri Lanka
19 N10 **Jaffrey** New Hampshire, NE USA 42°46′N 72°00′W
138 H13 **Jafr, Qā' al** *var.* El Jafr. *salt pan* S Jordan
152 J9 **Jagādhri** Haryāna, N India 30°11′N 77°18′E
118 H4 **Jägala** *var.* Jägala Jõgi, *Ger.* Jaggowal. NW Estonia
Jägala Jõgi *see* Jägala
Jagannath *see* Puri
154 P13 **Jagatsinghapur** Orissa, E India 20°15′N 86°10′E
155 L14 **Jagdalpur** Chhattisgarh, C India 19°07′N 82°04′E
163 U5 **Jagdaqi** Nei Mongol Zizhiqu, N China 50°26′N 124°03′E
Jägerndorf *see* Krnov
Jaggowal *see* Jägala
139 O2 **Jaghjaghah, Nahr** N Syria
112 N13 **Jagodina** *prev.* Svetozarevo. Serbia, C Serbia 43°59′N 21°15′E
112 K12 **Jagodnja** W Serbia
101 I20 **Jagst** SW Germany
155 I14 **Jagtial** Andhra Pradesh, C India 18°49′N 78°53′E
61 H18 **Jaguarão** Rio Grande do Sul, S Brazil 32°30′S 53°25′W
61 H18 **Jaguarão, Rio** *var.* Río Yaguarón. Brazil/ Uruguay
60 K11 **Jaguariaíva** Paraná, S Brazil 24°15′S 49°44′W
44 D5 **Jagüey Grande** Matanzas, W Cuba 22°31′N 81°07′W
153 P14 **Jahānābād** Bihār, N India 25°13′N 84°59′E
Jahra *see* Al Jahrā'
143 P12 **Jahrom** *var.* Jahrum. Fārs, S Iran 28°35′N 53°32′E
Jahrum *see* Jahrom
Jailolo *see* Halmahera, Pulau
Jainat *see* Chai Nat
Jainti *see* Jayanti
152 H12 **Jaipur** *prev.* Jeypore. *state capital* Rājasthān, N India 26°54′N 75°47′E
153 T14 **Jaipurhat** *var.* Joypurhat. Rajshahi, NW Bangladesh 25°04′N 89°06′E
152 D11 **Jaisalmer** Rājasthān, NW India 26°55′N 70°56′E
154 O12 **Jājapur** *var.* Jajpur, Panikoilli. Orissa, E India 18°54′N 82°36′E
143 R4 **Jājarm** Khorāsān-e Shemālī, NE Iran 36°58′N 56°26′E
112 G12 **Jajce** Federacija Bosna I Hercegovina, W Bosnia and Herzegovina 44°20′N 17°16′E
Jaji *see* 'Alī Kheyl
Jajpur *see* Jājapur
83 D17 **Jakalsberg** Otjozondjupa, N Namibia 19°23′S 17°28′E
169 O15 **Jakarta** *prev.* Djakarta, *Dut.* Batavia. ● (Indonesia) Jawa, C Indonesia 06°08′S 106°45′E
10 I8 **Jakes Corner** Yukon Territory, W Canada 60°18′N 134°00′W
152 H9 **Jākhal** Haryāna, NW India 29°46′N 75°51′E
Jakobeny *see* Iacobeni
93 K16 **Jakobstad** *Fin.* Pietarsaari. Länsi-Suomi, W Finland 63°41′N 22°40′E
Jakobstadt *see* Jēkabpils
113 O18 **Jakupica** C FYR Macedonia
37 W15 **Jal** New Mexico, SW USA 32°07′N 103°10′W
141 P7 **Jalājil** *var.* Ĝalāĝil. Ar Riyāḑ, C Saudi Arabia 25°43′N 45°22′E
149 S5 **Jalālābād** *var.* Jalalabad, Jelalabad. Nangarhār, E Afghanistan 34°26′N 70°28′E
Jalal-Abad *see* Dzhalal-Abad, Dzhalal-Abadskaya Oblast', Kyrgyzstan
Jalal-Abad Oblasty *see* Dzhalal-Abadskaya Oblast'
149 V7 **Jalālpur** Punjab, E Pakistan 32°39′N 74°11′E
149 T11 **Jalālpur Pīrwāla** Punjab, E Pakistan 29°30′N 71°20′E
152 H8 **Jalandhar** *prev.* Jullundur. Punjab, N India 31°20′N 75°37′E
42 J7 **Jalán, Río** S Honduras
42 E6 **Jalapa** Jalapa, C Guatemala 14°39′N 89°59′W
42 J7 **Jalapa** Nueva Segovia, NW Nicaragua 13°56′N 86°11′W
42 A3 **Jalapa** *off.* Departamento de Jalapa. ◈ *department* SE Guatemala
Jalapa, Departamento de *see* Jalapa
42 E6 **Jalapa, Río** SE Guatemala
143 X13 **Jālaq** Sīstān va Balūchestān, SE Iran
93 K17 **Jalasjärvi** Länsi-Suomi, W Finland 62°30′N 22°50′E
149 O8 **Jaldak** Zābol, SE Afghanistan 32°00′N 66°45′E
60 J7 **Jales** São Paulo, S Brazil 20°15′S 50°34′W
154 P11 **Jaleshwar** *var.* Jaleswar. Orissa, NE India 21°51′N 87°15′E
Jaleswar *see* Jaleshwar
154 F12 **Jalgaon** Mahārāshtra, C India 21°01′N 75°34′E
139 W12 **Jalībah** Dhī Qār, S Iraq 30°37′N 46°31′E
139 W13 **Jalīb Shahāb** Al Muthannā, S Iraq 30°26′N 46°09′E
77 X15 **Jalingo** Taraba, E Nigeria 08°54′N 11°22′E
40 K13 **Jalisco** ◈ *state* SW Mexico
154 G13 **Jālna** Mahārāshtra, W India 19°50′N 75°53′N
Jalomitsa *see* Ialomiţa
105 R5 **Jalón** N Spain
152 E13 **Jālor** Rājasthān, N India 25°21′N 72°43′E
112 K11 **Jalovik** Serbia, W Serbia 44°37′N 19°48′E
40 L12 **Jalpa** Zacatecas, C Mexico 21°40′N 103°W
153 S12 **Jalpāiguri** West Bengal, NE India 26°43′N 88°24′E
41 O12 **Jalpán** *var.* Jalpan. Querétaro de Arteaga, C Mexico 21°13′N 99°28′W
Jalpan *see* Jalpán
67 P2 **Jalta** *island* N Tunisia
75 S9 **Jālū** *var.* Jūlā. NE Libya 29°02′N 21°33′E
189 U8 **Jaluit Atoll** *var.* Jālwōj. *atoll* Ralik Chain, S Marshall Islands
Jālwōj *see* Jaluit Atoll
81 L18 **Jamaame** *It.* Giamame; *prev.* Margherita. Jubbada Hoose, S Somalia 0°00′N 42°43′E
77 W13 **Jamaare** NE Nigeria
44 G9 **Jamaica** ◆ *commonwealth republic* W West Indies
47 P3 **Jamaica** *island* W West Indies
44 I9 **Jamaica Channel** *channel* Haiti/Jamaica
153 T14 **Jamalpur** Dhaka, N Bangladesh 24°54′N 89°57′E
153 Q14 **Jamālpur** Bihār, NE India 25°19′N 86°30′E
168 L9 **Jamaluang** *var.* Jemaluang. Johor, Peninsular Malaysia 02°15′N 103°50′E
59 I14 **Jamanxim, Rio** C Brazil
56 B8 **Jambeli, Canal de** *channel* S Ecuador
99 I20 **Jambes** Namur, SE Belgium 50°26′N 04°51′E
168 L12 **Jambi** *var.* Telanaipura; *prev.* Djambi. Sumatera, W Indonesia 01°34′S 103°37′E
168 K12 **Jambi** *off.* Propinsi Jambi, *var.* Djambi. ◈ *province* W Indonesia
Jambi, Propinsi *see* Jambi
Jamdena *see* Yamdena, Pulau
12 H8 **James Bay** *bay* Ontario/ Québec, E Canada
63 F19 **James, Isla** *island* Archipiélago de los Chonos, S Chile
181 Q8 **James Ranges** Northern Territory, C Australia
29 P8 **James River** North Dakota/South Dakota, N USA
21 X7 **James River** Virginia, NE USA
194 H4 **James Ross Island** *island* Antarctica
182 I8 **Jamestown** South Australia 33°13′S 138°36′E
65 G25 **Jamestown** ○ (Saint Helena) NW Saint Helena 15°56′S 05°44′W
35 P8 **Jamestown** California, W USA 37°57′N 120°25′W
20 L7 **Jamestown** Kentucky, S USA 36°58′N 85°03′W
18 D11 **Jamestown** New York, NE USA 42°05′N 79°15′W
29 P5 **Jamestown** North Dakota, N USA 46°54′N 98°42′W
20 L8 **Jamestown** Tennessee, S USA 36°24′N 84°58′W
Jamestown *see* Holetown
15 N10 **Jamet** Québec, SE Canada
41 Q17 **Jamiltepec** *var.* Santiago Jamiltepec. Oaxaca, SE Mexico 16°18′N 97°51′W
95 F20 **Jammerbugten** *bay* Skagerrak, E North Sea
152 H6 **Jammu** *prev.* Jummoo. *state capital* Jammu and Kashmir, NW India 32°43′N 74°54′E
152 I5 **Jammu and Kashmir** *var.* Jammu-Kashmir, Kashmir. ◈ *state* NW India
149 V4 **Jammu and Kashmir** *disputed region* India/Pakistan
Jammu-Kashmir *see* Jammu and Kashmir
154 B10 **Jāmnagar** *prev.* Navanagar. Gujarāt, W India 22°28′N 70°06′E
149 S11 **Jāmpur** Punjab, E Pakistan 29°38′N 70°40′E
93 L18 **Jämsä** Länsi-Suomi, C Finland 61°51′N 25°10′E
93 L18 **Jämsänkoski** Länsi-Suomi, C Finland 61°54′N 25°10′E
153 Q16 **Jamshedpur** Jhārkhand, NE India 22°47′N 86°12′E
94 K9 **Jämtland** ◈ *county* C Sweden
153 Q14 **Jamūi** Bihār, NE India 24°57′N 86°14′E
Jamuna *see* Brahmaputra
153 T14 **Jamuna Nadi** N Bangladesh
Jamundá *see* Nhamundá, Rio
54 D11 **Jamundí** Valle del Cauca, SW Colombia 03°16′N 76°31′W
153 Q12 **Janakpur** Central, C Nepal 26°45′N 85°55′E
59 N18 **Janaúba** Minas Gerais, SE Brazil 15°47′S 43°16′W
58 K11 **Janaucu, Ilha** *island* NE Brazil
143 Q7 **Jandaq** Eşfahān, C Iran 34°04′N 54°26′E
64 Q11 **Jandia, Punta de** *headland* Fuerteventura, Islas Canarias, Spain, NE Atlantic Ocean 28°03′N 14°32′W
59 B14 **Jandiatuba, Rio** NW Brazil
105 N12 **Jándula** S Spain
29 V10 **Janesville** Minnesota, N USA 44°07′N 93°43′W
30 L9 **Janesville** Wisconsin, N USA 42°42′N 89°02′W
83 N20 **Jangamo** Inhambane, SE Mozambique 24°04′S 35°25′E
155 J14 **Jangaon** Andhra Pradesh, C India 18°47′N 79°25′E
153 S14 **Jangipur** West Bengal, NE India 24°31′N 88°03′E
Janina *see* Ioánnina
Janischken *see* Joniškis
112 J11 **Janja** NE Bosnia and Herzegovina 44°40′N 19°15′E
154 L12 **Jānjgīr** Chhattīsgarh, SW India 22°02′N 82°30′E
Jankovac *see* Jánoshalma
197 Q15 **Jan Mayen** ◈ *Norwegian dependency* N Atlantic Ocean
84 D5 **Jan Mayen** *island* N Atlantic Ocean
197 R15 **Jan Mayen Fracture Zone** *tectonic feature* Greenland Sea/Norwegian Sea
197 R15 **Jan Mayen Ridge** *undersea feature* Greenland Sea/Norwegian Sea 69°00′N 08°00′W
40 H3 **Janos** Chihuahua, N Mexico 30°50′N 108°10′W
111 K25 **Jánoshalma** *SCr.* Jankovac. Bács-Kiskun, S Hungary 46°19′N 19°16′E
Janów *see* Ivanava, Belarus
110 H10 **Janowiec Wielkopolski** *Ger.* Janowitz. Kujawski-pomorskie, C Poland 52°47′N 17°30′E
Janowitz *see* Janowiec Wielkopolski
Janów/Janów *see* Jonava, Lithuania
111 O15 **Janów Lubelski** Lubelski, E Poland 50°42′N 22°24′E
Janów Poleski *see* Ivanava
83 H25 **Jansenville** Eastern Cape, S South Africa 32°56′S 24°40′E
59 M18 **Januária** Minas Gerais, SE Brazil 15°28′S 44°23′W
Janūbīyah, Al Bādiyah al *see* Ash Shāmīyah
102 I7 **Janzé** Ille-et-Vilaine, NW France 47°55′N 01°28′W
154 F10 **Jaora** Madhya Pradesh, C India 23°40′N 75°10′E
131 Y9 **Japan** *var.* Nippon, *Jap.* Nihon. ◆ *monarchy* E Asia
129 Y9 **Japan** *island group* E Asia
192 H4 **Japan Basin** *undersea feature* N Sea of Japan 40°00′N 135°00′E
129 Y8 **Japan, Sea of** *var.* East Sea, *Rus.* Yapanskoye More. *sea* NW Pacific Ocean *see also* East Sea
192 H4 **Japan Trench** *undersea feature* NW Pacific Ocean 37°00′N 143°00′E
Japen *see* Yapen, Pulau
59 A15 **Japiim** *var.* Máncio Lima. Acre, W Brazil 08°00′S 73°39′W
58 D12 **Japurá** Amazonas, N Brazil 01°43′S 66°14′W
58 C12 **Japurá, Rio** *var.* Río Caquetá, Yapurá. Brazil/ Colombia *see also* Caquetá, Río
Japurá, Rio *see* Caquetá, Río
43 W17 **Jaqué** Darién, SE Panama 07°31′N 78°09′W
Jaquemel *see* Jacmel
Jarablos *see* Jarābulus
138 K2 **Jarābulus** *var.* Jarablos, Jerablus, *Fr.* Djérablous. Ḩalab, N Syria 36°51′N 38°02′E
60 K13 **Jaraguá do Sul** Santa Catarina, S Brazil 26°29′S 49°07′W
104 K9 **Jaraicejo** Extremadura, W Spain 39°40′N 05°49′W
104 K9 **Jaráiz de la Vera** Extremadura, W Spain 40°04′N 05°45′W
105 O7 **Jarama** C Spain
63 J20 **Jaramillo** Santa Cruz, SE Argentina 47°10′S 67°07′W
Jarandilla de la Vega *see* Jarandilla de la Vera
104 K8 **Jarandilla de la Vera** *var.* Jarandilla de la Vega. Extremadura, W Spain 40°08′N 05°39′W
149 V9 **Jarānwāla** Punjab, E Pakistan 31°20′N 73°26′E
138 G9 **Jarash** *var.* Jerash; *anc.* Gerasa. Irbid, NW Jordan 32°17′N 35°54′E
Jarbah, Jazīrat *see* Jerba, Île de
94 N13 **Järbo** Gävleborg, C Sweden 60°43′N 16°40′E
Jardan *see* Yordon
44 F7 **Jardines de la Reina, Archipiélago de los** *island group* C Cuba
162 I8 **Jargalant** Bayanhongor, C Mongolia 47°14′N 99°43′E
162 K6 **Jargalant** Bulgan, N Mongolia 49°09′N 104°19′E
162 G7 **Jargalant** *var.* Buyanbat. Govĭ-Altay, W Mongolia 47°00′N 95°57′E
162 I6 **Jargalant** *var.* Orgil. Hövsgöl, C Mongolia 48°31′N 99°19′E
Jargalant *see* Battsengel
Jargalant *see* Bulgan, Bayan-Ölgiy, Mongolia
Jargalant *see* Biger, Govĭ-Altay, Mongolia
Jarīd, Shaţţ al *see* Jerid, Chott el
58 I11 **Jari, Rio** *var.* Jary. N Brazil
141 N7 **Jarīr, Wādī al** *dry watercourse* C Saudi Arabia
Jarja *see* Yur'ya
94 L13 **Järna** *var.* Dala-Jarna. Dalarna, C Sweden 60°31′N 14°22′E
95 O16 **Järna** Stockholm, C Sweden 59°05′N 17°35′E
102 K11 **Jarnac** Charente, W France 45°41′N 00°10′W
110 H12 **Jarocin** Wielkopolskie, C Poland 51°59′N 17°30′E
111 F16 **Jaroměř** *Ger.* Jermer. Královéhradecký Kraj, N Czech Republic 50°22′N 15°55′E
Jaroslau *see* Jarosław
111 O16 **Jarosław** *Ger.* Jaroslau, *Rus.* Yaroslav. Podkarpackie, SE Poland 50°01′N 22°41′E
93 F16 **Järpen** Jämtland, C Sweden 63°21′N 13°30′E
147 O14 **Jarqo'rg'on** *Rus.* Dzharkurgan. Surkhondaryo Viloyati, S Uzbekistan 37°31′N 67°20′E
139 P2 **Jarrāh, Wadi** *dry watercourse* NE Syria
Jars, Plain of *see* Xiangkhoang, Plateau de
162 K14 **Jartai Yanchi** N China
59 E16 **Jaru** Rondônia, W Brazil 10°24′S 62°45′W
Jarud Qi *see* Lubei
118 I4 **Järva-Jaani** *Ger.* Sankt-Johannis. Järvamaa, N Estonia 59°03′N 25°54′E
118 G5 **Järvakandi** *Ger.* Jerwakant. Raplamaa, NW Estonia 58°45′N 24°49′E
118 H4 **Järvamaa** *var.* Järva Maakond. ◈ *province* N Estonia
Järva Maakond *see* Järvamaa
93 L19 **Järvenpää** Etelä-Suomi, S Finland 60°29′N 25°06′E
14 G17 **Jarvis** Ontario, S Canada 42°53′N 80°06′W
177 R8 **Jarvis Island** ◇ *US unincorporated territory* C Pacific Ocean
94 M11 **Järvsö** Gävleborg, C Sweden 61°43′N 16°25′E
Jary *see* Jari, Rio
112 M9 **Jaša Tomić** Vojvodina, NE Serbia 45°27′N 20°51′E
112 D12 **Jasenice** Zadar, SW Croatia 44°15′N 15°33′E
154 L12 **Jashpurnagar** Chhattīsgarh, SW India 22°53′N 84°09′E
138 I11 **Jashshat al 'Adlah, Wādī al** *dry watercourse* C Jordan
77 Q16 **Jasikan** E Ghana 07°24′N 00°28′E
Jāsk *see* Bandar-e Jāsk
146 F6 **Jasliq** *Rus.* Zhaslyk. Qoraqalpog'iston Respublikasi, NW Uzbekistan 43°57′N 57°30′E
111 N17 **Jasło** Podkarpackie, SE Poland 49°45′N 21°28′E
11 U16 **Jasmin** Saskatchewan, S Canada 51°11′N 103°34′W
65 A23 **Jason Islands** *island group* NW Falkland Islands
194 I4 **Jason Peninsula** *peninsula* Antarctica
31 N15 **Jasonville** Indiana, N USA 39°09′N 87°12′W
11 O15 **Jasper** Alberta, SW Canada 52°55′N 118°05′W
14 L13 **Jasper** Ontario, SE Canada 44°50′N 75°57′W
23 O3 **Jasper** Alabama, S USA 33°49′N 87°16′W
27 T9 **Jasper** Arkansas, C USA 36°00′N 93°11′W
23 U8 **Jasper** Florida, SE USA 30°31′N 82°57′W
31 N16 **Jasper** Indiana, N USA 38°22′N 86°57′W
29 R11 **Jasper** Minnesota, N USA 43°51′N 96°24′W
27 S7 **Jasper** Missouri, C USA 37°20′N 94°18′W
20 K10 **Jasper** Tennessee, S USA 35°04′N 85°36′W
25 Y9 **Jasper** Texas, SW USA 30°55′N 94°00′W
11 O15 **Jasper National Park** *national park* Alberta/British Columbia, SW Canada
Jassy *see* Iaşi
113 N14 **Jastrebac** SE Serbia
112 D9 **Jastrebarsko** Zagreb, N Croatia 45°40′N 15°40′E
Jastrow *see* Jastrowie
110 G9 **Jastrowie** *Ger.* Jastrow. Wielkopolskie, C Poland 53°25′N 16°48′E
111 J17 **Jastrzębie-Zdrój** Śląskie, S Poland 49°58′N 18°34′E
111 L22 **Jászapáti** Jász-Nagykun-Szolnok, E Hungary 47°30′N 20°10′E
111 L22 **Jászberény** Jász-Nagykun-Szolnok, E Hungary 47°30′N 19°56′E
111 L23 **Jász-Nagykun-Szolnok** *off.* Jász-Nagykun-Szolnok Megye. ◈ *county* E Hungary
Jász-Nagykun-Szolnok Megye *see* Jász-Nagykun-Szolnok
59 J19 **Jataí** Goiás, C Brazil 17°58′S 51°45′W
58 G12 **Jatapu, Serra do** N Brazil
41 W16 **Jatate, Río** SE Mexico
149 P17 **Jāti** Sind, SE Pakistan 24°20′N 68°18′E
44 F6 **Jatibonico** Sancti Spíritus, C Cuba 21°56′N 79°11′W
169 O16 **Jatiluhur, Danau** Jawa, S Indonesia
Jativa *see* Xàtiva
149 S11 **Jattoi** Punjab, E Pakistan 29°29′N 70°58′E
60 L9 **Jaú** São Paulo, S Brazil 22°11′S 48°35′W
58 F11 **Jauaperi, Rio** N Brazil
99 I19 **Jauche** Walloon Brabant, C Belgium 50°42′N 04°55′E
Jauer *see* Jawor
Jauf *see* Al Jawf
149 U7 **Jauharābād** Punjab, E Pakistan 32°16′N 72°17′E
57 E14 **Jauja** Junín, C Peru 11°48′S 75°30′W
41 O10 **Jaumave** Tamaulipas, C Mexico 23°28′N 99°22′W
118 H10 **Jaunjelgava** *Ger.* Friedrichstadt. Aizkraukle, S Latvia 56°38′N 25°03′E
Jaunlatgale *see* Pytalovo
118 J8 **Jaunpiebalga** Gulbene, NE Latvia 57°10′N 26°02′E
118 E9 **Jaunpils** Tukums, C Latvia 56°45′N 23°03′E
153 N13 **Jaunpur** Uttar Pradesh, N India 25°44′N 82°41′E
29 N8 **Java** South Dakota, N USA 45°29′N 99°54′W
Java *see* Jawa
105 R9 **Javalambre** E Spain 40°02′N 01°06′W
173 V7 **Java Ridge** *undersea feature* E Indian Ocean
59 A14 **Javari, Rio** *var.* Yavarí. Brazil/Peru
Javarthushuu *see* Bayan-Uul
169 Q15 **Java Sea** *Ind.* Laut Jawa. *sea* W Indonesia
173 U7 **Java Trench** *var.* Sunda Trench. *undersea feature* E Indian Ocean
143 Q10 **Javazm** *var.* Jowzam. Kermān, C Iran 30°31′N 55°01′E
105 T11 **Jávea** *Cat.* Xàbia. País Valenciano, E Spain 38°48′N 00°10′E
Javhlant *see* Bayan-Ovoo
63 G20 **Javier, Isla** *island* S Chile
113 L14 **Javor** Bosnia and Herzegovina/Serbia
111 K20 **Javorie** *Hung.* Jávoros. S Slovakia 48°26′N 19°16′E
Jávoros *see* Javorie
93 J14 **Jävre** Norrbotten, N Sweden 65°07′N 21°31′E
192 E8 **Jawa** *Eng.* Java; *prev.* Djawa. *island* C Indonesia
169 O16 **Jawa Barat** *off.* Propinsi Jawa Barat, *Eng.* West Java. ◈ *province* S Indonesia
Jawa Barat, Propinsi *see* Jawa Barat
Jawa, Laut *see* Java Sea
139 R3 **Jawān** Nīnawýa, NW Iraq 35°57′N 43°03′E
169 P16 **Jawa Tengah** *off.* Propinsi Jawa Tengah, *Eng.* Central Java. ◈ *province* S Indonesia
Jawa Tengah, Propinsi *see* Jawa Tengah
169 R16 **Jawa Timur** *off.* Propinsi Jawa Timur, *Eng.* East Java. ◈ *province* S Indonesia
Jawa Timur, Propinsi *see* Jawa Timur
81 N17 **Jawhar** *var.* Jowhar, *It.* Giohar. Shabeellaha Dhexe, S Somalia 02°37′N 45°30′E
111 F14 **Jawor** *Ger.* Jauer. Dolnośląskie, SW Poland 51°01′N 16°11′E
Jaworów *see* Yavoriv
111 J16 **Jaworzno** Śląskie, S Poland 50°13′N 19°11′E
Jaxartes *see* Syr Darya
27 R9 **Jay** Oklahoma, C USA 36°25′N 94°49′W
Jayabum *see* Chaiyaphum
Jayanath *see* Chai Nat
153 T12 **Jayanti** *prev.* Jainti. West Bengal, NE India 26°45′N 89°40′E
171 X14 **Jaya, Puncak** *prev.* Puntjak Carstensz, Puntjak Sukarno. Papua, E Indonesia 04°00′S 137°10′E
171 Z13 **Jayapura** *var.* Djajapura, *Dut.* Hollandia; *prev.* Kotabaru, Sukarnapura. Papua, E Indonesia 02°37′S 140°39′E
Jay Dairen *see* Dalian
Jayhawker State *see* Kansas
147 S12 **Jayilgan** *Rus.* Dzhailgan, Dzhayilgan. C Tajikistan 39°17′N 71°32′E
155 L14 **Jaypur** *var.* Jeypore, Jeypur. Orissa, E India 18°54′N 82°36′E
25 O6 **Jayton** Texas, SW USA 33°16′N 100°35′W
143 U13 **Jaz Mūriān, Hāmūn-e** SE Iran
138 M4 **Jazrah** Ar Raqqah, C Syria 35°56′N 39°02′E
138 G6 **Jbaïl** *var.* Jebeil, Jubayl, Jubeil; *anc.* Biblical Gebal, Bybles. W Lebanon 34°00′N 35°45′E
25 O7 **J. B. Thomas, Lake** Texas, SW USA
Jdaïdé *see* Judaydah
35 X12 **Jean** Nevada, W USA 35°45′N 115°20′W
22 I9 **Jeanerette** Louisiana, S USA 29°54′N 91°39′W
44 L8 **Jean-Rabel** NW Haiti 19°48′N 73°05′W
143 T12 **Jebāl Bārez, Kūh-e** SE Iran
Jebat *see* Jabwot
Jebeil *see* Jbaïl
77 T15 **Jebba** Kwara, W Nigeria 09°04′N 04°50′E
116 E12 **Jebel** *Hung.* Széphely; *prev.* Hung. Zsebely. Timiş, W Romania 45°33′N 21°14′E
146 B11 **Jebel** *Rus.* Dzhebel. Balkan Welaýaty, W Turkmenistan 39°42′N 54°10′E
Jebel, Bahr el *see* White Nile
Jebel Dhanna *see* Jabal az Zannah
Jeble *see* Jablah
96 K13 **Jedburgh** SE Scotland, United Kingdom 55°29′N 02°34′W
Jedda *see* Jiddah
111 L15 **Jędrzejów** *Ger.* Endersdorf. Świętokrzyskie, C Poland 50°39′N 20°18′E
100 K12 **Jeetze** *var.* Jeetzel. C Germany
Jeetzel *see* Jeetze
29 U14 **Jefferson** Iowa, C USA 42°01′N 94°22′W
21 Q8 **Jefferson** North Carolina, SE USA 36°24′N 81°33′W
25 X6 **Jefferson** Texas, SW USA 32°45′N 94°21′W
30 M9 **Jefferson** Wisconsin, N USA 43°01′N 88°48′W
27 U5 **Jefferson City** *state capital* Missouri, C USA 38°33′N 92°13′W
33 R10 **Jefferson City** Montana, NW USA 46°24′N 112°01′W
21 N9 **Jefferson City** Tennessee, S USA 36°07′N 83°29′W
35 U7 **Jefferson, Mount** Nevada, W USA 38°49′N 116°54′W
32 H12 **Jefferson, Mount** Oregon, NW USA 44°40′N 121°48′W
20 L5 **Jeffersontown** Kentucky, S USA 38°11′N 85°33′W
31 P16 **Jeffersonville** Indiana, N USA 38°16′N 85°45′W
33 V15 **Jeffrey City** Wyoming, C USA 42°29′N 107°49′W
77 T13 **Jega** Kebbi, NW Nigeria 12°15′N 04°21′E
Jehol *see* Chengde
62 P5 **Jejui-Guazú, Río** E Paraguay
118 I10 **Jēkabpils** *Ger.* Jakobstadt. Jēkabpils, S Latvia 56°30′N 25°56′E
23 W7 **Jekyll Island** *island* Georgia, SE USA
169 R13 **Jelai, Sungai** Borneo, N Indonesia
Jelalabad *see* Jalālābād
111 H14 **Jelcz-Laskowice** Dolnośląskie, SW Poland 51°01′N 17°24′E
111 E14 **Jelenia Góra** *Ger.* Hirschberg, Hirschberg im Riesengebirge, Hirschberg im Riesengebirge, Hirschberg in Schlesien. Dolnośląskie, SW Poland 50°54′N 15°48′E
153 S11 **Jelep La** *pass* N India
118 F9 **Jelgava** *Ger.* Mitau. Jelgava, C Latvia 56°38′N 23°47′E
112 L13 **Jelica** C Serbia
20 M8 **Jellico** Tennessee, S USA 36°33′N 84°06′W
95 G23 **Jelling** Vejle, C Denmark 55°45′N 09°24′E
169 N9 **Jemaja, Pulau** *island* W Indonesia
Jemaluang *see* Jamaluang
99 E20 **Jemappes** Hainaut, S Belgium 50°27′N 03°53′E
169 S17 **Jember** *prev.* Djember. Jawa, C Indonesia 08°07′S 113°45′E
99 I20 **Jemeppe-sur-Sambre** Namur, S Belgium 50°27′N 04°41′E
37 R10 **Jemez Pueblo** New Mexico, SW USA 35°36′N 106°43′W
158 K2 **Jeminay** *var.* Tuotiereke. Xinjiang Uygur Zizhiqu, NW China 47°28′N 85°49′E
189 U5 **Jemo Island** *atoll* Ratak Chain, C Marshall Islands
169 U11 **Jempang, Danau** Borneo, N Indonesia
101 L16 **Jena** Thüringen, C Germany 50°56′N 11°35′E
22 I6 **Jena** Louisiana, S USA 31°40′N 92°07′W
108 I8 **Jenaz** Graubünden, SE Switzerland 46°56′N 09°43′E
109 N7 **Jenbach** Tirol, W Austria 47°24′N 11°47′E
171 N15 **Jeneponto** *prev.* Djeneponto. Sulawesi, C Indonesia 05°41′S 119°42′E
138 F9 **Jenin** N West Bank 32°28′N 35°17′E
21 P7 **Jenkins** Kentucky, S USA 37°10′N 82°37′W
27 P9 **Jenks** Oklahoma, C USA 36°01′N 95°58′W
Jenné *see* Djenné
109 X8 **Jennersdorf** Burgenland, SE Austria 46°57′N 16°08′E
22 H9 **Jennings** Louisiana, S USA 30°13′N 92°39′W
11 N7 **Jenny Lind Island** *island* Nunavut, N Canada
23 Y13 **Jensen Beach** Florida, SE USA 27°15′N 80°13′W
9 P6 **Jens Munk Island** *island* Nunavut, NE Canada
59 O17 **Jequié** Bahia, E Brazil 13°52′S 40°06′W
59 O18 **Jequitinhonha, Rio** E Brazil
Jerablus *see* Jarābulus
74 H6 **Jerada** NE Morocco 34°16′N 02°07′W
Jerash *see* Jarash
75 N7 **Jerba, Île de** *var.* Djerba, Jazīrat Jarbah. *island* E Tunisia
44 K9 **Jérémie** SW Haiti 18°39′N 74°11′W
Jeréz *see* Jerez de García Salinas, Mexico
Jerez *see* Jeréz de la Frontera, Spain
40 L11 **Jerez de García Salinas** *var.* Jeréz. Zacatecas, C Mexico 22°40′N 103°00′W
104 J15 **Jeréz de la Frontera** *var.* Jerez; *prev.* Xeres. Andalucía, SW Spain 36°41′N 06°08′W
104 I12 **Jeréz de los Caballeros** Extremadura, W Spain 38°20′N 06°45′W
Jergucati *see* Jorgucat
138 G10 **Jericho** *Ar.* Arīḩā, *Heb.* Yeriḩo. E West Bank 31°51′N 35°27′E
74 M7 **Jerid, Chott el** *var.* Shaţţ al Jarīd. *salt lake* SW Tunisia
183 O10 **Jerilderie** New South Wales, SE Australia 35°24′S 145°43′E
Jerischmarkt *see* Câmpia Turzii
92 K11 **Jerisjärvi** NW Finland
Jermak *see* Aksu
Jermentau *see* Yereymentau
Jermer *see* Jaroměř
36 K11 **Jerome** Arizona, SW USA 34°45′N 112°06′W
33 O15 **Jerome** Idaho, NW USA 42°43′N 114°31′W
97 L26 **Jersey** *island* NW Europe
18 K14 **Jersey City** New Jersey, NE USA 40°42′N 74°01′W
18 F13 **Jersey Shore** Pennsylvania, NE USA 41°12′N 77°13′W
30 K14 **Jerseyville** Illinois, N USA 39°07′N 90°19′W
104 K8 **Jerte** W Spain
138 F10 **Jerusalem** *Ar.* Al Quds, Al Quds ash Sharif, *Heb.* Yerushalayim; *anc.* Hierosolyma. ● (Israel) Jerusalem, NE Israel 31°47′N 35°13′E
138 G10 **Jerusalem** ◈ *district* E Israel
183 S10 **Jervis Bay** New South Wales, SE Australia 35°09′S 150°42′E
183 S10 **Jervis Bay Territory** ◈ *territory* SE Australia
Jerwakant *see* Järvakandi
109 S10 **Jesenice** *Ger.* Assling. NW Slovenia 46°26′N 14°01′E
111 H16 **Jeseník** *Ger.* Freiwaldau. Olomoucký Kraj, E Czech Republic 50°14′N 17°12′E
Jesi *see* Iesi
106 I8 **Jesolo** *var.* Iesolo. Veneto, NE Italy 45°32′N 12°37′E
Jesselton *see* Kota Kinabalu
95 I14 **Jessheim** Akershus, S Norway 60°07′N 11°10′E
153 T15 **Jessore** Khulna, W Bangladesh 23°10′N 89°12′E
23 W6 **Jesup** Georgia, SE USA 31°36′N 81°54′W
41 S15 **Jesús Carranza** Veracruz-Llave, SE Mexico 17°30′N 95°01′W
62 K10 **Jesús María** Córdoba, C Argentina 30°59′S 64°05′W
26 K6 **Jetmore** Kansas, C USA 38°05′N 99°55′W
103 Q2 **Jeumont** Nord, N France 50°18′N 04°06′E
95 H14 **Jevnaker** Oppland, S Norway 60°15′N 10°25′E
Jewe *see* Jõhvi
25 V9 **Jewett** Texas, SW USA 31°21′N 96°08′W
19 N12 **Jewett City** Connecticut, NE USA 41°36′N 71°58′W
Jeypore *see* Jaipur, Rājasthān, India
Jeypore/Jeypur *see* Jaypur, Orissa, India
113 L17 **Jezercës, Maja e** N Albania 42°27′N 19°49′E
111 B18 **Jezerní Hora** SW Czech Republic 49°10′N 13°11′E
154 F10 **Jhābua** Madhya Pradesh, C India 22°44′N 74°37′E
152 H10 **Jhajjar** Haryāna, N India 28°35′N 76°39′E
152 H14 **Jhālāwār** Rājasthān, N India 24°37′N 76°12′E
Jhang/Jhang Sadar *see* Jhang Sadr

◆ Country ● Country Capital ◇ Dependent Territory ○ Dependent Territory Capital ◈ Administrative Regions ✕ International Airport ▲ Mountain ▲ Mountain Range Volcano River Lake Reservoir

149 U9 **Jhang Sadr** var. Jhang, Jhang Sadar. Punjab, NE Pakistan 31°16′N 72°19′E
152 J13 **Jhānsi** Uttar Pradesh, N India 25°27′N 78°34′E
153 O16 **Jhārkhand** ◈ state NE India
154 M11 **Jhārsuguda** Orissa, E India 21°56′N 84°04′E
149 Q12 **Jhatpat** Baluchistān, SW Pakistan 28°22′N 68°21′E
149 V7 **Jhelum** Punjab, NE Pakistan 32°55′N 73°42′E
129 P9 **Jhelum** ≈ E Pakistan
Jhenaida see Jhenaidaha
153 T15 **Jhenaidaha** var. Jhenaida, Jhenida. Khulna, Bangladesh 23°32′N 89°09′E
Jhenaidaha see Jhenida
153 T15 **Jhenida** var. Jhenaidaha. Dhaka, W Bangladesh 23°34′N 89°39′E
jhenida see Jhenaidaha
149 P16 **Jhimpīr** Sind, SE Pakistan 25°00′N 68°01′E
Jhind see Jīnd
149 R16 **Jhudo** Sind, SE Pakistan 24°58′N 69°18′E
Jhumra see Chak Jhumra
152 H11 **Jhunjhunūn** Rājasthān, N India 28°05′N 75°30′E
Ji see Hebei, China
Ji see Jilin, China
Jiading see Xinfeng
153 S14 **Jiāganj** West Bengal, NE India 24°18′N 88°07′E
Jiaji see Qionghai
160 J7 **Jialing Jiang** ≈ C China
163 Y7 **Jiamusi** var. Chia-mu-ssu, Kiamusze. Heilongjiang, NE China 46°46′N 130°19′E
161 O11 **Ji'an** Jiangxi, S China 27°08′N 115°00′E
163 W12 **Ji'an** Jilin, NE China 41°04′N 126°07′E
163 T13 **Jianchang** Liaoning, NE China 40°48′N 119°51′E
Jianchang see Nancheng
Jiancheng see Jianyang
160 F11 **Jianchuan** var. Jinhuan. Yunnan, SW China 26°28′N 99°49′E
158 M4 **Jiangjunmiao** Xinjiang Uygur Zizhiqu, W China 44°42′N 90°06′E
160 K11 **Jiangkou** var. Shuangjiang. Guizhou, S China 27°46′N 108°53′E
Jiangkou see Fengkai
161 Q12 **Jiangle** var. Guyong. Fujian, SE China 26°44′N 117°26′E
161 N15 **Jiangmen** Guangdong, S China 22°35′N 113°02′E
Jiangna see Yanshan
161 Q10 **Jiangshan** Zhejiang, SE China 28°41′N 118°33′E
161 Q7 **Jiangsu** var. Chiang-su, Jiangsu Sheng, Kiangsu, Su. ◈ province E China
Jiangsu see Nanjing
Jiangsu Sheng see Jiangsu
161 O11 **Jiangxi** var. Chiang-hsi, Gan, Jiangxi Sheng, Kiangsi. ◈ province S China
Jiangxi Sheng see Jiangxi
160 I8 **Jiangyou** prev. Zhongba. Sichuan, C China 31°52′N 104°52′E
161 N9 **Jianli** var. Rongcheng. Hubei, C China 29°51′N 112°50′E
161 Q11 **Jian'ou** Fujian, SE China 27°04′N 118°20′E
163 S12 **Jianping** var. Yebaishou. Liaoning, NE China 41°13′N 119°37′E
Jianshe see Baiyü
160 L9 **Jianshi** var. Yezhou. Hubei, C China 30°37′N 109°42′E
129 V11 **Jian Xi** ≈ SE China
161 Q11 **Jianyang** Fujian, SE China 27°20′N 118°01′E
160 I9 **Jianyang** var. Jiancheng. Sichuan, C China 30°22′N 104°31′E
163 X10 **Jiaohe** Jilin, NE China 43°41′N 127°20′E
Jiaojiang see Taizhou
Jiaoxian see Jiaozhou
161 R5 **Jiaozhou** prev. Jiaoxian. Shandong, E China 36°17′N 120°00′E
161 N6 **Jiaozuo** Henan, C China 35°14′N 113°13′E
Jiashan see Mingguang
158 F8 **Jiashi** var. Baren, Payzawat. Xinjiang Uygur Zizhiqu, NW China 39°27′N 76°45′E
154 L9 **Jiāwān** Madhya Pradesh, C India 24°20′N 82°17′E
161 S9 **Jiaxing** Zhejiang, SE China 30°44′N 120°46′E
Jiayi see Chiai
163 X6 **Jiayin** var. Chaoyang. Heilongjiang, NE China 48°51′N 130°24′E
159 R8 **Jiayuguan** Gansu, N China 39°47′N 98°14′E
Jibhalanta see Uliastay
138 M4 **Jibli** Ar Raqqah, C Syria 35°49′N 39°23′E
116 H9 **Jibou** Hung. Zsibó. Sălaj, NW Romania 47°15′N 23°17′E
141 Z9 **Jibsh, Ra's al** headland E Oman 21°20′N 59°23′E
Jibuti see Djibouti
Jichang see Jixian
111 E15 **Jičín** Ger. Jitschin. Královéhradecký Kraj, N Czech Republic 50°27′N 15°20′E
140 K10 **Jiddah** Eng. Jedda. (Saudi Arabia) Makkah, W Saudi Arabia 21°34′N 39°13′E
141 W11 **Jiddat al Ḩarāsīs** desert C Oman
Jiesjavrre see Iešjávri
160 M4 **Jiexiu** Shanxi, C China 37°00′N 111°50′E
161 P14 **Jieyang** Guangdong, S China 23°32′N 116°20′E
119 F14 **Jieznas** Kaunas, S Lithuania 54°37′N 24°10′E
Jīfa', Bi'r see Jif'īyah, Bi'r
141 P15 **Jif'īyah, Bi'r** var. Bi'r Jīfa'. well C Yemen
77 W13 **Jigawa** ◈ state N Nigeria
146 J10 **Jigerbent** Rus. Dzhigirbent. Lebap Welaýaty, NE Turkmenistan 40°44′N 61°56′E
44 I7 **Jiguaní** Granma, E Cuba 20°24′N 76°26′W
159 T12 **Jigzhi** var. Chugqênsumdo. Qinghai, C China 33°23′N 101°25′E
Jih-k'a-tse see Xigazê
111 E18 **Jihlava** Ger. Iglau, Pol. Igława. Vysocina, S Czech Republic 49°22′N 15°36′E
111 E18 **Jihlava** var. Igel, Ger. Iglawa. ≈ Vysočina, C Czech Republic
Jihlavský Kraj see Vysočina
111 C18 **Jihočeský Kraj** prev. Budějovický Kraj. ◈ region Czech Republic
111 G19 **Jihomoravský Kraj** prev. Brněnský Kraj. ◈ region SE Czech Republic
74 L5 **Jijel** var. Djidjel; prev. Djidjelli. NE Algeria 36°50′N 05°43′E
116 L9 **Jijia** ≈ N Romania
80 L13 **Jijiga** It. Giggiga. Sumalē, E Ethiopia 09°21′N 42°53′E
105 S12 **Jijona** var. Xixona. País Valenciano, E Spain 38°34′N 00°29′W
81 L18 **Jilib** It. Gelib. Jubbada Dhexe, S Somalia 0°18′N 42°48′E
163 W10 **Jilin** var. Chi-lin, Girin, Kirin; prev. Yungki, Yunki. Jilin, NE China 43°46′N 126°32′E
163 W10 **Jilin** var. Chi-lin, Girin, Ji, Jilin Sheng, Kirin. ◈ province NE China
163 W11 **Jilin Hada Ling** ▲▲ NE China
Jilin Sheng see Jilin
163 S4 **Jiliu He** ≈ NE China
105 Q6 **Jiloca** ≈ N Spain
81 I14 **Jīma** var. Jimma, It. Gimma. Oromīya, C Ethiopia 07°42′N 36°51′E
44 M9 **Jimaní** W Dominican Republic 18°29′N 71°49′W
116 E11 **Jimbolia** Ger. Hatzfeld, Hung. Zsombolya. Timiș, W Romania 45°47′N 20°43′E
104 K16 **Jimena de la Frontera** Andalucía, S Spain 36°27′N 05°28′W
40 K7 **Jiménez** Chihuahua, N Mexico 27°09′N 104°54′W
41 N5 **Jiménez** Coahuila, NE Mexico 29°05′N 100°40′W
41 P9 **Jiménez** var. Santander Jiménez. Tamaulipas, C Mexico 24°11′N 98°29′W
40 L10 **Jiménez del Teul** Zacatecas, C Mexico 23°13′N 103°46′W
77 Y14 **Jimeta** Adamawa, E Nigeria 09°16′N 12°25′E
Jimma see Jīma
158 M5 **Jimsar** Xinjiang Uygur Zizhiqu, NW China 44°05′N 88°48′E
18 I14 **Jim Thorpe** Pennsylvania, NE USA 40°51′N 75°43′W
Jin see Shanxi
Jin see Tianjin Shi
161 P5 **Jinan** var. Chinan, Chi-nan, Tsinan. province capital Shandong, E China 36°43′N 116°58′E
Jin'an see Songpan
Jinbi see Dayao
159 T8 **Jinchang** Gansu, N China 38°31′N 102°07′E
161 N5 **Jincheng** Shanxi, C China 35°30′N 112°52′E
Jincheng see Wuding
Jinchengjiang see Hechi
152 I9 **Jīnd** prev. Jhind. Haryāna, NW India 29°29′N 76°22′E
183 Q11 **Jindabyne** New South Wales, SE Australia 36°28′S 148°36′E
111 O18 **Jindřichův Hradec** Ger. Neuhaus. Jihočeský Kraj, S Czech Republic 49°09′N 15°01′E
Jing see Beijing Shi
Jing see Jinghe, China
159 X10 **Jingchuan** Gansu, C China 35°20′N 107°45′E
161 Q10 **Jingdezhen** Jiangxi, S China 29°18′N 117°18′E
161 O12 **Jinggangshan** Jiangxi, S China 26°36′N 114°11′E
161 P3 **Jinghai** Tianjin Shi, E China 38°53′N 116°45′E
158 I4 **Jinghe** var. Jing. Xinjiang Uygur Zizhiqu, NW China 44°35′N 82°55′E
160 K6 **Jing He** ≈ C China
160 F15 **Jinghong** var. Yunjinghong. Yunnan, SW China 22°03′N 100°56′E
160 M9 **Jingmen** Hubei, C China 30°58′N 112°09′E
163 X10 **Jingpo Hu** ◎ NE China
160 M8 **Jing Shan** ▲▲ C China
159 V9 **Jingtai** var. Yitiaoshan. Gansu, C China 37°12′N 104°06′E
160 J14 **Jingxi** var. Xinjing. Guangxi Zhuangzu Zizhiqu, S China 23°10′N 106°22′E
Jing Xian see Jingzhou, Hunan, China
163 W11 **Jingyu** Jilin, NE China 42°23′N 126°48′E
159 V10 **Jingyuan** var. Wulan. Gansu, C China 36°35′N 104°40′E
160 M9 **Jingzhou** prev. Shashi, Shashih, Shasi. Hubei, C China 30°21′N 112°09′E
160 L12 **Jingzhou** var. Jing Xian, Jingzhou Miaouzu Dongzu Zizhixian, Quyang. Hunan, S China 26°35′N 109°40′E
Jingzhou Miaouzu Dongzu Zizhixian see Jingzhou
Jinhe see Jinping
161 R10 **Jinhua** Zhejiang, SE China 29°15′N 119°36′E
Jinhuan see Jianchuan
161 P5 **Jining** Shandong, E China 35°25′N 116°35′E
Jining see Ulan Qab
81 G18 **Jinja** S Uganda 0°27′N 33°14′E
161 R13 **Jinjiang** var. Qingyang. Fujian, SE China 24°53′N 118°36′E
161 O11 **Jin Jiang** ≈ S China
Jinjiang see Chengmai
171 V15 **Jin, Kepulauan** island group E Indonesia
Jinmen Dao see Chinmen Tao
42 J9 **Jinotega** Jinotega, NW Nicaragua 13°03′N 85°59′W
42 K7 **Jinotega** ◈ department N Nicaragua
42 J11 **Jinotepe** Carazo, SW Nicaragua 11°50′N 86°10′W
160 L13 **Jinping** var. Sanjiang. Guizhou, S China 26°42′N 109°13′E
160 H14 **Jinping** var. Jinhe. Yunnan, SW China 22°47′N 103°12′E
Jinsen see Inch'ŏn
160 J11 **Jinsha** Guizhou, S China 27°24′N 106°16′E
157 N12 **Jinsha Jiang** Eng. Yangtze. ≈ SW China
160 M10 **Jinshi** Hunan, S China 29°42′N 111°46′E
Jinshi see Xinning
162 I9 **Jinst** var. Bodī. Bayanhongor, C Mongolia 45°25′N 100°33′E
159 R7 **Jinta** Gansu, N China 40°01′N 98°57′E
161 Q12 **Jin Xi** ≈ SE China
Jinxi see Huludao
Jinxian see Jinzhou
161 P6 **Jinxiang** Shandong, E China 35°08′N 116°19′E
161 P8 **Jinzhai** var. Meishan. Anhui, E China 31°42′N 115°47′E
161 N4 **Jinzhong** var. Yuci. Shanxi, C China 37°34′N 112°45′E
163 U14 **Jinzhou** prev. Jinxian. Liaoning, NE China 39°04′N 121°45′E
163 T12 **Jinzhou** var. Chin-chou, Chinchow; prev. Chinhsien. Liaoning, NE China 41°07′N 121°06′E
Jinzhu see Daocheng
138 H12 **Jinz, Qā' al** ◎ C Jordan
47 S8 **Jiparaná, Rio** ≈ W Brazil
56 A7 **Jipijapa** Manabí, W Ecuador 01°23′S 80°35′W
42 F8 **Jiquilisco** Usulután, S El Salvador 13°19′N 88°35′W
Jirgalanta see Hovd
147 S12 **Jirgatol** Rus. Dzhirgatal'. C Tajikistan 39°13′N 71°09′E
75 X10 **Jirjā** var. Girga, Jirjā, Girgeh. C Egypt 26°17′N 31°58′E
Jirjā see Jirjā
111 B15 **Jirkov** Ger. Görkau. Ústecký Kraj, NW Czech Republic 50°30′N 13°27′E
143 T12 **Jīroft** var. Sabzvārān. Kermān, SE Iran 28°40′N 57°40′E
160 L11 **Jishou** Hunan, S China 28°20′N 109°43′E
Jisr ash Shadadi see Ash Shadādah
116 I14 **Jitaru** Olt, S Romania 44°27′N 24°32′E
Jitschin see Jičín
116 H14 **Jiu** Ger. Schil, Schyl, Hung. Zsil, Zsily. ≈ S Romania
161 R11 **Jiufeng Shan** ▲▲ SE China
161 P9 **Jiujiang** Jiangxi, S China 29°45′N 115°59′E
161 O10 **Jiuling Shan** ▲▲ S China
160 G10 **Jiulong** var. Garba, Tib. Gyaisi. Sichuan, C China 29°00′N 101°30′E
161 Q13 **Jiulong Jiang** ≈ SE China
161 Q12 **Jiulong Xi** ≈ SE China
159 R8 **Jiuquan** var. Suzhou. Gansu, N China 39°47′N 98°30′E
160 K17 **Jiusuo** Hainan, S China 18°25′N 109°55′E
163 W10 **Jiutai** Jilin, NE China 44°01′N 125°51′E
160 K13 **Jiuwan Dashan** ▲▲ S China
160 I7 **Jiuzhaigou** prev. Nanping. Sichuan, C China 33°25′N 104°05′E
148 I16 **Jīwani** Baluchistān, SW Pakistan 25°05′N 61°46′E
163 Y8 **Jixi** Heilongjiang, NE China 45°17′N 131°01′E
163 Y7 **Jixian** var. Jichang. Heilongjiang, NE China 46°43′N 131°10′E
160 M5 **Jixian** var. Ji Xian. Shanxi, C China 36°15′N 110°41′E
Ji Xian see Jixian
Jiza see Al Jīzah
141 N13 **Jīzān** var. Qīzān. Jīzān, SW Saudi Arabia 17°50′N 42°50′E
141 N13 **Jīzān** var. Minṭaqat Jīzān. ◈ province SW Saudi Arabia
Jīzān, Minṭaqat see Jīzān
140 K6 **Jizl, Wādī al** dry watercourse W Saudi Arabia
164 H12 **Jizō-zaki** headland Honshū, SW Japan 35°34′N 133°16′E
141 U14 **Jiz', Wādī al** dry watercourse E Yemen
147 O11 **Jizzax** Rus. Dzhizak. Jizzax Viloyati, C Uzbekistan 40°08′N 67°47′E
147 N10 **Jizzax Viloyati** Rus. Dzhizakskaya Oblast'. ◈ province C Uzbekistan
60 I13 **Joaçaba** Santa Catarina, S Brazil 27°08′S 51°30′W
Joal see Joal-Fadiout
76 F11 **Joal-Fadiout** prev. Joal. W Senegal 14°09′N 16°50′W
76 E10 **João Barrosa** Boa Vista, E Cape Verde 16°01′N 22°44′W
João Belo see Xai-Xai
João de Almeida see Chibia
59 Q15 **João Pessoa** prev. Paraíba. state capital Paraíba, E Brazil 07°06′S 34°53′W
25 X7 **Joaquin** Texas, SW USA 31°58′N 94°03′W
62 K6 **Joaquín V. González** Salta, N Argentina 25°06′S 64°07′W
Joazeiro see Juazeiro
Job'urg see Johannesburg
109 O7 **Jochberger Ache** ≈ W Austria
Jo-ch'iang see Ruoqiang
92 K12 **Jock** Norrbotten, N Sweden 66°40′N 22°45′E
42 I5 **Jocón** Yoro, N Honduras 15°17′N 86°55′W
105 O13 **Jódar** Andalucía, S Spain 37°51′N 03°18′W
152 F12 **Jodhpur** Rājasthān, NW India 26°17′N 73°02′E
99 I19 **Jodoigne** Walloon Brabant, C Belgium 50°43′N 04°52′E
93 O16 **Joensuu** Itä-Suomi, SE Finland 62°36′N 29°45′E
37 W4 **Joes** Colorado, C USA 39°36′N 102°40′W
191 Z3 **Joe's Hill** hill Kiritimati, NE Kiribati
165 N11 **Jōetsu** var. Zyôetu. Niigata, Honshū, C Japan 37°09′N 138°13′E
83 M18 **Jofane** Inhambane, S Mozambique 21°16′S 34°21′E
153 R12 **Jogbani** Bihār, NE India 26°23′N 87°16′E
118 I5 **Jõgeva** Ger. Laisholm. Jõgevamaa, E Estonia 58°48′N 26°28′E
118 I4 **Jõgevamaa** off. Jõgeva Maakond. ◈ province E Estonia
Jõgeva Maakond see Jõgevamaa
155 E18 **Jog Falls** Waterfall Karnātaka, W India
143 S4 **Joghatāy** Khorāsān, NE Iran 36°34′N 57°00′E
153 U12 **Jogīghopa** Assam, NE India 26°14′N 90°35′E
152 I7 **Jogindarnagar** Himāchal Pradesh, N India 31°51′N 76°47′E
Jogjakarta see Yogyakarta
164 L11 **Jōhana** Toyama, Honshū, SW Japan 36°30′N 136°53′E
83 J21 **Johannesburg** var. Egoli, Erautini, Gauteng, abbrev. Job'urg. Gauteng, NE South Africa 26°10′S 28°02′E
35 T13 **Johannesburg** California, W USA 35°20′N 117°37′W
Johannisburg see Pisz
149 P14 **Johi** Sind, SE Pakistan 26°46′N 67°28′E
55 T13 **Johi Village** S Guyana 01°48′N 58°33′W
32 K13 **John Day** Oregon, NW USA 44°25′N 118°57′W
32 I11 **John Day River** ≈ Oregon, NW USA
18 L14 **John F Kennedy** ✈ (New York) Long Island, New York, NE USA 40°39′N 73°45′W
21 V8 **John H. Kerr Reservoir** var. Buggs Island Lake, Kerr Lake. ⊠ North Carolina/Virginia, SE USA
37 V6 **John Martin Reservoir** ⊠ Colorado, C USA
96 K6 **John o'Groats** N Scotland, United Kingdom 58°38′N 03°03′W
27 P5 **John Redmond Reservoir** ⊠ Kansas, C USA
39 Q7 **John River** ≈ Alaska, USA
26 H6 **Johnson** Kansas, C USA 37°33′N 101°46′W
18 M7 **Johnson** Vermont, NE USA 44°39′N 72°40′W
18 D13 **Johnsonburg** Pennsylvania, NE USA 41°28′N 78°37′W
18 H11 **Johnson City** New York, NE USA 42°06′N 75°54′W
21 P8 **Johnson City** Tennessee, S USA 36°18′N 82°21′W
25 R10 **Johnson City** Texas, SW USA 30°17′N 98°27′W
35 S12 **Johnsondale** California, W USA 35°58′N 118°32′W
10 I8 **Johnsons Crossing** Yukon Territory, W Canada 60°30′N 133°15′W
21 T13 **Johnsonville** South Carolina, SE USA 33°50′N 79°26′W
21 Q13 **Johnston** South Carolina, SE USA 33°49′N 81°48′W
192 M6 **Johnston Atoll** ◇ US unincorporated territory C Pacific Ocean
175 Q3 **Johnston Atoll** atoll C Pacific Ocean
30 L17 **Johnston City** Illinois, N USA 37°49′N 88°55′W
180 K12 **Johnston, Lake** salt lake Western Australia
31 S13 **Johnstown** Ohio, N USA 40°08′N 82°39′W
18 D15 **Johnstown** Pennsylvania, NE USA 40°20′N 78°56′W
168 L10 **Johor** var. Johore. ◈ state Peninsular Malaysia
Johor Baharu see Johor Bahru
168 K10 **Johor Bahru** var. Johor Baharu, Johore Bahru. Johor, Peninsular Malaysia 01°29′N 103°44′E
Johore see Johor
Johore Bahru see Johor Bahru
118 K3 **Jõhvi** Ger. Jewe. Ida-Virumaa, NE Estonia 59°21′N 27°25′E
103 P7 **Joigny** Yonne, C France 47°58′N 03°24′E
Joinvile see Joinville
60 K12 **Joinville** var. Joinvile. Santa Catarina, S Brazil 26°20′S 48°55′W
103 R6 **Joinville** Haute-Marne, N France 48°26′N 05°07′E
194 H3 **Joinville Island** island Antarctica
41 O15 **Jojutla** var. Jojutla de Juárez. Morelos, S Mexico 18°38′N 99°10′W
Jojutla de Juárez see Jojutla
92 I12 **Jokkmokk** Lapp. Dálvvadis. Norrbotten, N Sweden 66°35′N 19°57′E
92 L2 **Jökulsá á Dal** ≈ E Iceland
92 K2 **Jökulsá á Fjöllum** ≈ NE Iceland
Jokyakarta see Yogyakarta
30 M11 **Joliet** Illinois, N USA 41°33′N 88°05′W
15 O11 **Joliette** Québec, SE Canada 46°02′N 73°27′W
171 O8 **Jolo** Jolo Island, SW Philippines 06°02′N 121°00′E
94 D11 **Jølstervatnet** ◎ S Norway
169 S16 **Jombang** prev. Djombang. Jawa, S Indonesia 07°33′S 112°14′E
159 R14 **Jomda** Xizang Zizhiqu, W China 31°26′N 98°09′E
118 G13 **Jonava** Ger. Janow, Pol. Janów. Kaunas, C Lithuania 55°05′N 24°19′E
146 L11 **Jondor** Rus. Zhondor. Buxoro Viloyati, C Uzbekistan 39°46′N 64°11′E
159 V11 **Jonê** var. Liulin. Gansu, C China 34°36′N 103°39′E
27 X9 **Jonesboro** Arkansas, C USA 35°50′N 90°42′W
23 S4 **Jonesboro** Georgia, SE USA 33°31′N 84°21′W
30 L17 **Jonesboro** Illinois, N USA 37°25′N 89°19′W
22 H5 **Jonesboro** Louisiana, S USA 32°14′N 92°43′W
21 P8 **Jonesboro** Tennessee, S USA 36°17′N 82°28′W
19 T6 **Jonesport** Maine, NE USA 44°33′N 67°35′W
0 J4 **Jones Sound** channel Nunavut, N Canada
22 I6 **Jonesville** Louisiana, S USA 31°37′N 91°49′W
31 Q10 **Jonesville** Michigan, N USA 41°58′N 84°39′W
21 Q11 **Jonesville** South Carolina, SE USA 34°49′N 81°38′W
146 K10 **Jongeldi** Rus. Dzhankel'dy. Buxoro Viloyati, C Uzbekistan 40°50′N 63°16′E
81 F14 **Jonglei** Jonglei, SE Sudan 06°54′N 31°19′E
81 F14 **Jonglei** var. Gongoleh State. ◈ state SE Sudan
81 F14 **Jonglei Canal** canal S Sudan
118 F11 **Joniškėlis** Panevėžys, N Lithuania 56°02′N 24°10′E
118 F10 **Joniškis** Ger. Janischken. Šiaulai, N Lithuania 56°15′N 23°36′E
95 L19 **Jönköping** Jönköping, S Sweden 57°45′N 14°10′E
95 K20 **Jönköping** ◈ county S Sweden
15 Q7 **Jonquière** Québec, SE Canada 48°25′N 71°16′W
41 V15 **Jonuta** Tabasco, SE Mexico 18°04′N 92°03′W
102 K12 **Jonzac** Charente-Maritime, W France 45°26′N 00°25′W
27 R7 **Joplin** Missouri, C USA 37°04′N 94°31′W
33 W8 **Jordan** Montana, NW USA 47°18′N 106°54′W
138 H12 **Jordan** off. Hashemite Kingdom of Jordan, Ar. Al Mamlaka al Urdunīya al Hashemīyah, Al Urdunn; prev. Transjordan. ◆ monarchy SW Asia
138 G9 **Jordan** Ar. Urdunn, Heb. HaYarden. ≈ SW Asia
Jordan Lake see B. Everett Jordan Reservoir
111 K17 **Jordanów** Małopolskie, S Poland 49°39′N 19°51′E
32 M15 **Jordan Valley** Oregon, NW USA 42°59′N 117°03′W
138 G9 **Jordan Valley** valley N Israel
57 D15 **Jorge Chávez International** var. Lima. ✈ (Lima) Lima, W Peru 12°07′S 77°01′W
113 L23 **Jorgucat** var. Jergucati, Jorgucati. Gjirokastër, S Albania 39°57′N 20°14′E
Jorgucati see Jorgucat
153 X12 **Jorhāt** Assam, NE India 26°45′N 94°09′E
93 J14 **Jörn** Västerbotten, N Sweden 65°03′N 20°04′E
37 R14 **Jornada Del Muerto** valley New Mexico, SW USA
93 N17 **Joroinen** Itä-Suomi, E Finland 62°11′N 27°50′E
95 C16 **Jørpeland** Rogaland, S Norway 59°01′N 06°04′E
77 W14 **Jos** Plateau, C Nigeria 09°59′N 08°57′E
171 Q8 **Jose Abad Santos** var. Trinidad. Mindanao, S Philippines 05°51′N 125°35′E
61 F19 **José Batlle y Ordóñez** var. Batlle y Ordóñez. Florida, C Uruguay 33°28′S 55°08′W
63 H18 **José de San Martín** Chubut, S Argentina 44°04′S 70°29′W
61 E19 **José Enrique Rodó** var. Rodó, José E.Rodo; prev. Drabble, Drable. Soriano, SW Uruguay 33°43′S 57°33′W
José E.Rodo see José Enrique Rodó
Josefsdorf see Žabalj
44 C4 **José Martí** ✈ (La Habana) Cuidad de La Habana, N Cuba 23°03′N 82°22′W
61 F19 **José Pedro Varela** var. José P.Varela. Lavalleja, S Uruguay 33°30′S 54°28′W
181 N2 **Joseph Bonaparte Gulf** gulf N Australia
37 N11 **Joseph City** Arizona, SW USA 34°56′N 110°18′W
13 O9 **Joseph, Lake** ◎ Newfoundland and Labrador, E Canada
14 G13 **Joseph, Lake** ◎ Ontario, S Canada
186 C6 **Josephstaal** Madang, N Papua New Guinea 04°42′S 144°55′E
José P.Varela see José Pedro Varela
59 J14 **José Rodrigues** Pará, N Brazil 05°45′S 51°20′W
152 K9 **Joshīmath** Uttarakhand, N India 30°33′N 79°35′E
25 T7 **Joshua** Texas, SW USA 32°27′N 97°23′W
35 V15 **Joshua Tree** California, W USA 34°07′N 116°18′W
77 V14 **Jos Plateau** plateau C Nigeria
102 H6 **Josselin** Morbihan, NW France 47°57′N 02°35′W
Jos Sudarso see Yos Sudarso, Pulau
94 E11 **Jostedalsbreen** glacier S Norway
94 F12 **Jotunheimen** ▲▲ S Norway
138 G7 **Joûnié** var. Junīyah. W Lebanon 33°54′N 33°36′E
25 R13 **Jourdanton** Texas, SW USA 28°55′N 98°34′W
98 L7 **Joure** Fris. De Jouwer. Friesland, N Netherlands 52°58′N 05°48′E
93 M18 **Joutsa** Länsi-Suomi, C Finland 61°46′N 26°09′E
93 N18 **Joutseno** Etelä-Suomi, SE Finland 61°06′N 28°30′E
92 M12 **Joutsijärvi** Lappi, NE Finland 66°40′N 28°00′E
108 A9 **Joux, Lac de** ◎ W Switzerland
143 O12 **Jovakān** Fārs, S Iran
44 D5 **Jovellanos** Matanzas, W Cuba 22°49′N 81°11′W
153 V13 **Jowai** Meghālaya, NE India 25°25′N 92°21′E
Jōwat see Jabwot
Jowhar see Jawhar
Jowzam see Javazm
149 N2 **Jowzjān** ◈ province N Afghanistan
Joypurhat see Jaipurhat
Józseffalva see Žabalj
J.Storm Thurmond Reservoir see Clark Hill Lake
45 T6 **Juana Díaz** C Puerto Rico 18°03′N 66°30′W
40 L9 **Juan Aldama** Zacatecas, C Mexico 24°20′N 103°23′W
0 E9 **Juan de Fuca Plate** tectonic feature
32 F7 **Juan de Fuca, Strait of** strait Canada/USA
Juan Fernandez Islands see Juan Fernández, Islas
193 S11 **Juan Fernández, Islas** Eng. Juan Fernandez Islands. island group W Chile
55 O4 **Juangriego** Nueva Esparta, NE Venezuela 11°06′N 63°59′W
56 D11 **Juanjuí** var. Juanjuy. San Martín, N Peru 07°10′S 76°44′W
Juanjuy see Juanjuí
93 N16 **Juankoski** Itä-Suomi, C Finland 63°01′N 28°24′E
Juan Lacaze see Juan L. Lacaze
61 E20 **Juan L. Lacaze** var. Juan Lacaze, Puerto Sauce; prev. Sauce. Colonia, SW Uruguay 34°26′S 57°25′W
62 L5 **Juan Solá** Salta, N Argentina 23°30′S 62°42′W
63 F21 **Juan Stuven, Isla** island S Chile
59 H16 **Juará** Mato Grosso, W Brazil 11°10′S 57°28′W
41 N7 **Juárez** var. Villa Juárez. Coahuila, NE Mexico 27°39′N 100°43′W
40 C2 **Juárez, Sierra de** ▲▲ NW Mexico
59 O15 **Juazeiro** prev. Joazeiro. Bahia, E Brazil 09°25′S 40°30′W
59 P14 **Juazeiro do Norte** Ceará, E Brazil 07°10′S 39°18′W
81 F15 **Juba** var. Jūbā. Bahr el Gabel, S Sudan 04°50′N 31°35′E
81 L17 **Juba** Amh. Genalē Wenz, It. Guiba, Som. Ganaane, Webi Jubba. ≈ Ethiopia/Somalia
194 H2 **Jubany** Argentinian research station Antarctica 61°57′S 58°23′W
Jubayl see Jbaïl
81 L18 **Jubbada Dhexe** off. Gobolka Jubbada Dhexe. ◈ region SW Somalia
Jubbada Dhexe, Gobolka see Jubbada Dhexe
81 K18 **Jubbada Hoose** ◈ region SW Somalia
Jubba, Webi see Juba
Jubbulpore see Jabalpur
Jubeil see Jbaïl
74 B9 **Juby, Cap** headland SW Morocco 27°58′N 12°56′W
105 R10 **Júcar** var. Jucar. ≈ C Spain
40 L12 **Juchipila** Zacatecas, C Mexico 21°25′N 103°06′W
41 S16 **Juchitán** var. Juchitán de Zaragosa. Oaxaca, SE Mexico 16°27′N 95°W
Juchitán de Zaragosa see Juchitán
138 G11 **Judaea** cultural region Israel/West Bank
138 F11 **Judaean Hills** Heb. Haré Yehuda. hill range E Israel
138 H8 **Judaydah** Fr. Jdaïdé. Dimashq, W Syria 33°17′N 36°15′E
139 P11 **Judayyidat Hāmir** Al Anbār, S Iraq 31°50′N 41°50′E
109 U8 **Judenburg** Steiermark, C Austria 47°09′N 14°43′E
33 T8 **Judith River** ≈ Montana, NW USA
27 V11 **Judsonia** Arkansas, C USA 35°16′N 91°38′W
141 P14 **Jufrah, Wādī al** dry watercourse NW Yemen
Jugar see Sêrxü
Jugoslavija see Serbia
42 K10 **Juigalpa** Chontales, S Nicaragua 12°04′N 85°21′W
161 T13 **Juishui** C Taiwan 23°43′N 121°28′E
100 E9 **Juist** island NW Germany
59 M21 **Juiz de Fora** Minas Gerais, SE Brazil 21°47′S 43°23′W
62 J5 **Jujuy** off. Provincia de Jujuy. ◈ province N Argentina
Jujuy see San Salvador de Jujuy
Jujuy, Provincia de see Jujuy
92 J11 **Jukkasjärvi** Lapp. Čohkkiras. Norrbotten, N Sweden 67°52′N 20°39′E
Jula see Gyula, Hungary
Jūlā see Jālū, Libya
37 W2 **Julesburg** Colorado, C USA 40°59′N 102°15′W
Julia Beterrae see Béziers
57 I17 **Juliaca** Puno, SE Peru 15°32′S 70°10′W
181 U6 **Julia Creek** Queensland, C Australia 20°40′S 141°49′E
35 V17 **Julian** California, W USA 33°04′N 116°36′W
98 H7 **Julianadorp** Noord-Holland, NW Netherlands 52°53′N 04°43′E
109 S11 **Julian Alps** Ger. Julische Alpen, It. Alpi Giulie, Slvn. Julijske Alpe. ▲▲ Italy/Slovenia
55 V11 **Juliana Top** ▲ C Surinam 03°39′N 56°36′W
Julianehåb see Qaqortoq
Julijske Alpe see Julian Alps
40 J6 **Julimes** Chihuahua, N Mexico 28°29′N 105°21′W
Julio Briga see Bragança
Juliobriga see Logroño
61 G15 **Júlio de Castilhos** Rio Grande do Sul, S Brazil 29°14′S 53°42′W
Juliomagus see Angers
Julische Alpen see Julian Alps
Jullundur see Jalandhar
147 N11 **Juma** Rus. Dzhuma. Samarqand Viloyati, C Uzbekistan 39°43′N 66°37′E
161 O3 **Juma He** ≈ E China
81 L18 **Jumboo** Jubbada Hoose, S Somalia 0°12′S 42°34′E
35 Y11 **Jumbo Peak** ▲ Nevada, W USA 36°12′N 114°09′W
105 R12 **Jumilla** Murcia, SE Spain 38°28′N 01°19′W
153 N10 **Jumla** Mid Western, NW Nepal 29°22′N 82°13′E
Jummoo see Jammu
Jumna see Yamuna
Jumporn see Chumphon
30 K5 **Jump River** ≈ Wisconsin, N USA
154 B11 **Jūnāgadh** var. Junagarh. Gujarāt, W India 21°32′N 70°32′E
Junagarh see Jūnāgadh
161 Q6 **Junan** var. Shizilu. Shandong, E China 35°11′N 118°47′E
62 G11 **Juncal, Cerro** ▲ C Chile 33°03′S 70°02′W
25 Q10 **Junction** Texas, SW USA 30°31′N 99°48′W
36 K6 **Junction** Utah, W USA 38°14′N 112°13′W
27 O4 **Junction City** Kansas, C USA 39°02′N 96°51′W
32 F13 **Junction City** Oregon, NW USA 44°13′N 123°12′W
60 M10 **Jundiaí** São Paulo, S Brazil 23°10′S 46°54′W
39 X12 **Juneau** state capital Alaska, USA 58°13′N 134°11′W
30 M8 **Juneau** Wisconsin, N USA 43°23′N 88°42′W
105 U6 **Juneda** Cataluña, NE Spain 41°33′N 00°49′E
183 Q9 **Junee** New South Wales, SE Australia 34°51′S 147°33′E
35 R8 **June Lake** California, W USA 37°46′N 119°04′W
Jungbunzlau see Mladá Boleslav
158 L4 **Junggar Pendi** Eng. Dzungarian Basin. basin NW China
99 N24 **Junglinster** Grevenmacher, C Luxembourg 49°43′N 06°15′E
18 F14 **Juniata River** ≈ Pennsylvania, NE USA
61 B20 **Junín** Buenos Aires, E Argentina 34°36′S 61°02′W
57 E14 **Junín** Junín, C Peru 11°11′S 76°00′W
57 F14 **Junín** off. Departamento de Junín. ◈ department C Peru
63 H15 **Junín de los Andes** Neuquén, W Argentina 39°57′S 71°05′W
Junín, Departamento de see Junín
57 D14 **Junín, Lago de** ◎ C Peru
Junīyah see Joûnié
Junkseylon see Phuket
160 I11 **Junlian** Sichuan, C China 28°11′N 104°31′E
25 O11 **Juno** Texas, SW USA 30°09′N 101°07′W
92 J11 **Junosuando** Lapp. Čunusavvon. Norrbotten, N Sweden 67°25′N 22°28′E
93 H16 **Junsele** Västernorrland, C Sweden 63°42′N 16°54′E
Junten see Sunch'ŏn
32 L14 **Juntura** Oregon, NW USA 43°43′N 118°05′W
93 N14 **Juntusranta** Oulu, E Finland 65°12′N 29°30′E
118 H11 **Juodupė** Panevėžys, NE Lithuania 56°07′N 25°37′E
119 H14 **Juozapinės Kalnas** ▲ SE Lithuania 54°29′N 25°27′E
99 K19 **Juprelle** Liège, E Belgium 50°43′N 05°31′E
80 D13 **Jur** ≈ C Sudan
103 S9 **Jura** ◈ department E France
108 C7 **Jura** ◈ canton NW Switzerland
108 B8 **Jura** var. Jura Mountains. ▲▲ France/Switzerland
96 G12 **Jura** island SW Scotland, United Kingdom
Juraciszki see Yuratsishki
54 C8 **Juradó** Chocó, NW Colombia 07°07′N 77°45′W
Jura Mountains see Jura
96 G12 **Jura, Sound of** strait W Scotland, United Kingdom
139 V15 **Juraybīyāt, Bi'r** well S Iraq
118 E13 **Jurbarkas** Ger. Georgenburg, Jurburg. Tauragė, W Lithuania 55°04′N 22°45′E
99 F20 **Jurbise** Hainaut, SW Belgium 50°33′N 03°54′E
Jurburg see Jurbarkas
118 F9 **Jūrmala** Rīga, C Latvia 56°57′N 23°42′E
58 D13 **Juruá** Amazonas, NW Brazil 03°08′S 65°59′W
48 F7 **Juruá, Rio** var. Río Yuruá. ≈ Brazil/Peru
59 G16 **Juruena** Mato Grosso, W Brazil 10°32′S 58°38′W
59 G16 **Juruena, Rio** ≈ W Brazil
165 Q6 **Jūsan-ko** ◎ Honshū, C Japan
25 O6 **Justiceburg** Texas, SW USA 32°57′N 101°07′W
Justinianopolis see Kirşehir
62 K11 **Justo Daract** San Luis, C Argentina 33°52′S 65°12′W
59 C14 **Jutaí** Amazonas, W Brazil 05°10′S 68°45′W
58 C13 **Jutaí, Rio** ≈ NW Brazil
100 N13 **Jüterbog** Brandenburg, E Germany 51°58′N 13°06′E
42 E6 **Jutiapa** Jutiapa, S Guatemala 14°18′N 89°52′W
42 A3 **Jutiapa** off. Departamento de Jutiapa. ◈ department SE Guatemala
Jutiapa, Departamento de see Jutiapa
42 J6 **Juticalpa** Olancho, C Honduras 14°39′N 86°12′W
82 I13 **Jutila** North Western, NW Zambia 12°33′S 26°09′E
Jutland see Jylland
84 F8 **Jutland Bank** undersea feature SE North Sea 56°50′N 07°20′E
93 N16 **Juuka** Itä-Suomi, E Finland 63°12′N 29°17′E
93 N17 **Juva** Itä-Suomi, E Finland 61°55′N 27°54′E
Juvavum see Salzburg
44 A6 **Juventud, Isla de la** var. Isla de Pinos, Eng. Isle of Youth; prev. The Isle of the Pines. island W Cuba
161 Q5 **Juxian** var. Chengyang, Ju Xian. Shandong, E China 35°33′N 118°45′E
Ju Xian see Juxian
161 P6 **Juye** Shandong, E China 35°26′N 116°04′E
113 O15 **Južna Morava** Ger. Südliche Morava. ≈ SE Serbia
83 H20 **Jwaneng** Southern, S Botswana 24°35′N 24°45′E
95 I23 **Jyderup** Vestsjælland, E Denmark 55°40′N 11°25′E
95 F22 **Jylland** Eng. Jutland. peninsula W Denmark
Jyrgalan see Dzhergalan
93 M17 **Jyväskylä** Länsi-Suomi, C Finland 62°08′N 25°47′E

K

38 D9 **Ka'a'awa** var. Kaaawa. O'ahu, Hawaii, USA, C Pacific Ocean 21°33′N 157°47′W
Kaaawa see Ka'a'awa
81 G16 **Kaabong** NE Uganda 03°30′N 34°08′E
Kaaden see Kadaň
Kaafu Atoll see Male' Atoll
55 V9 **Kaaimanston** Sipaliwini, N Surinam 05°06′N 56°04′W
Kaakhka see Kaka
Kaala see Caála
187 O16 **Kaala-Gomen** Province Nord, W New Caledonia 20°40′S 164°24′E
92 L9 **Kaamanen** Lapp. Gámas. Lappi, N Finland 69°05′N 27°16′E
Kaapstad see Cape Town
Kaarasjoki see Karasjok
Kaaresuanto see Karesuando
92 J10 **Kaaresuvanto** Lapp. Gárassavon. Lappi, N Finland 68°28′N 22°29′E
93 K19 **Kaarina** Länsi-Suomi, SW Finland 60°24′N 22°25′E
99 I14 **Kaatsheuvel** Noord-Brabant, S Netherlands 51°39′N 05°02′E
93 N16 **Kaavi** Itä-Suomi, C Finland 62°58′N 28°30′E
Kaba see Habahe
171 O14 **Kabaena, Pulau** island C Indonesia
Kabakly see Gabakly
76 J14 **Kabala** N Sierra Leone 09°40′N 11°36′W
81 E19 **Kabale** SW Uganda 01°15′S 29°58′E
55 U10 **Kabalebo Rivier** ≈ W Surinam

◆ Country
● Country Capital
◇ Dependent Territory
○ Dependent Territory Capital
◈ Administrative Regions
✈ International Airport
▲ Mountain
▲▲ Mountain Range
Volcano
≈ River
◎ Lake
⊠ Reservoir

79 N22 **Kabalo** Katanga, SE Dem. Rep. Congo 06°02′S 26°55′E
79 O21 **Kabambare** Maniema, E Dem. Rep. Congo 04°40′S 27°41′E
145 W13 **Kabanbay** *Kaz.* Qabanbay; *prev.* Andreyevka, *Kaz.* Andreevka. Almaty, SE Kazakhstan 45°50′N 80°34′E
187 Y15 **Kabara** *prev.* Kambara. *island* Lau Group, E Fiji
Kabardino-Balkaria *see* Kabardino-Balkarskaya Respublika
126 M15 **Kabardino-Balkarskaya Respublika** *Eng.* Kabardino-Balkaria. ◈ *autonomous republic* SW Russian Federation
79 O19 **Kabare** Sud-Kivu, E Dem. Rep. Congo 02°13′S 28°40′E
171 T11 **Kabarei** Papua, E Indonesia 0°01′S 130°58′E
171 P7 **Kabasalan** Mindanao, S Philippines 07°46′N 122°49′E
77 U15 **Kabba** Kogi, S Nigeria 07°48′N 06°07′E
92 I13 **Kåbdalis** *Lapp.* Goabddális. Norrbotten, N Sweden 66°08′N 20°03′E
138 M6 **Kabd aş Şārim** *hill range* E Syria
14 B7 **Kabenung Lake** ◎ Ontario, S Canada
29 W3 **Kabetogama Lake** ◎ Minnesota, N USA
Kabia, Pulau *see* Kabin, Pulau
79 M22 **Kabinda** Kasai-Oriental, SE Dem. Rep. Congo 06°09′S 24°29′E
Kabinda *see* Cabinda
171 O15 **Kabin, Pulau** *var.* Pulau Kabia. *island* W Indonesia
171 P16 **Kabir** Pulau Pantar, S Indonesia 08°15′S 124°12′E
149 T10 **Kabīrwāla** Punjab, E Pakistan 30°24′N 71°51′E
114 M9 **Kableshkovo** Burgas, E Bulgaria 42°65′N 27°34′E
78 I13 **Kabo** Ouham, NW Central African Republic 07°43′N 18°38′E
149 Q5 **Kābol** *var.* Kabul, *Pash.* Kābul. ● (Afghanistan) Kābul, E Afghanistan 34°34′N 69°08′E
149 Q5 **Kābol** *Eng.* Kabul, *Pash.* Kābul. ◈ *province* E Afghanistan
149 Q5 **Kābol** ✈ Kābul, E Afghanistan 34°31′N 69°11′E
83 H14 **Kabompo** North Western, W Zambia 13°36′S 24°10′E
83 H14 **Kabompo** ≈ W Zambia
79 M22 **Kabongo** Katanga, SE Dem. Rep. Congo 07°20′S 25°34′E
120 K11 **Kaboudia, Rass** *headland* E Tunisia 35°13′N 11°09′E
124 J14 **Kabozha** Novgorodskaya Oblast′, W Russian Federation 58°48′N 35°00′E
Kabūd Gonbad *see* Kalāt
142 L5 **Kabūd Rāhang** Hamadān, W Iran 35°12′N 48°44′E
82 L12 **Kabuko** Northern, NE Zambia 11°31′S 31°16′E
149 R5 **Kabul** *var.* Daryā-ye Kābul. ≈ Afghanistan/Pakistan *see also* Kābul, Daryā-ye
Kābul *see* Kābol
Kabul *see* Kābul, Daryā-ye
149 S5 **Kābul, Daryā-ye** *var.* Kabul. ≈ Afghanistan/Pakistan *see also* Kabul
Kābul, Daryā-ye *see* Kabul
79 O25 **Kabunda** Katanga, SE Dem. Rep. Congo 12°21′S 29°14′E
171 R9 **Kaburuang, Pulau** *island* Kepulauan Talaud, N Indonesia
80 G8 **Kabushiya** River Nile, NE Sudan 16°54′N 33°41′E
83 J14 **Kabwe** Central, C Zambia 14°29′S 28°25′E
186 E7 **Kabwum** Morobe, C Papua New Guinea 06°04′S 147°09′E
113 N17 **Kaçanik** *Serb.* Kačanik. S Kosovo 42°13′N 21°16′E
Kačanik *see* Kaçanik
118 F13 **Kačerginė** Kaunas, C Lithuania 54°55′N 23°40′E
117 S13 **Kacha** Respublika Krym, S Ukraine 44°46′N 33°33′E
154 A10 **Kachchh, Gulf of** *var.* Gulf of Cutch, Gulf of Kutch. *gulf* W India
154 I11 **Kachchhīdhāna** Madhya Pradesh, C India 21°33′N 78°54′E
149 Q11 **Kachchh, Rann of** *var.* Rann of Kachh, Rann of Kutch. *salt marsh* India/Pakistan
39 Q13 **Kachemak Bay** *bay* Alaska, USA
Kachh, Rann of *see* Kachchh, Rann of
77 V14 **Kachia** Kaduna, C Nigeria 09°52′N 08°00′E
167 N2 **Kachin State** ◈ *state* N Burma (Myanmar)
145 T7 **Kachiry** Pavlodar, NE Kazakhstan 53°07′N 76°08′E
137 Q11 **Kaçkar Dağları** ▲▲ NE Turkey
155 C21 **Kadamatt Island** *island* Lakshadweep, India, N Indian Ocean
111 B15 **Kadaň** *Ger.* Kaaden. Ústecký Kraj, NW Czech Republic 50°24′N 13°16′E
1667 N11 **Kadan Kyun** *prev.* King Island. *island* Mergui Archipelago, S Burma (Myanmar)
187 X15 **Kadavu** *prev.* Kandavu. *island* S Fiji
187 X15 **Kadavu Passage** *channel* S Fiji
79 G16 **Kadéï** ≈ Cameroon/Central African Republic
Kadhimain *see* Al Kāẓimīyah
Kadijica *see* Kadiytsa
114 M13 **Kadıköy Barajı** ⊠ NW Turkey
182 I8 **Kadina** South Australia 33°59′S 137°43′E
136 H15 **Kadınhanı** Konya, C Turkey 38°15′N 32°14′E
76 M14 **Kadiolo** Sikasso, S Mali 10°30′N 05°43′W
136 L16 **Kadirli** Osmaniye, S Turkey 37°22′N 36°05′E
114 G11 **Kadiytsa** *Mac.* Kadijica. ▲ Bulgaria/FYR Macedonia 41°48′N 22°58′E
28 L10 **Kadoka** South Dakota, N USA 43°49′N 101°30′W
127 N5 **Kadom** Ryazanskaya Oblast′, W Russian Federation 54°35′N 42°27′E
83 K16 **Kadoma** *prev.* Gatooma. Mashonaland West, C Zimbabwe !8°22′S 29°55′E
80 E12 **Kadugli** Southern Kordofan, S Sudan 11°N 29°44′E
77 V14 **Kaduna** Kaduna, C Nigeria 10°32′N 07°26′E
77 V14 **Kaduna** ◈ *state* C Nigeria
77 V15 **Kaduna** ≈ N Nigeria
124 K14 **Kaduy** Vologodskaya Oblast′, NW Russian Federation 59°10′N 37°11′E
154 E13 **Kadwa** ≈ W India
123 S9 **Kadykchan** Magadanskaya Oblast′, E Russian Federation 62°54′N 146°53′E
Kadzharan *see* K′ajaran
125 T7 **Kadzherom** Respublika Komi, NW Russian Federation 64°42′N 55°51′E
147 X8 **Kadzhi-Say** *Kir.* Kajisay. Issyk-Kul′skaya Oblast′, NE Kyrgyzstan 42°07′N 77°11′E
76 I10 **Kaédi** Gorgol, S Mauritania 16°12′N 13°32′W
78 G12 **Kaélé** Extrême-Nord, N Cameroon 10°05′N 14°28′E
38 C9 **Ka'ena Point** *var.* Kaena Point. *headland* O'ahu, Hawai'i, USA 21°34′N 158°16′W
184 J2 **Kaeo** Northland, North Island, New Zealand 35°03′S 173°40′E
163 X14 **Kaesŏng** *var.* Kaesŏng-si. S North Korea 37°58′N 126°31′E
Kaesŏng-si *see* Kaesŏng
Kaewieng *see* Kavieng
79 L24 **Kafakumba** Shaba, S Dem. Rep. Congo 09°39′S 23°43′E
Kafan *see* Kapan
77 V14 **Kafanchan** Kaduna, C Nigeria 09°32′N 08°18′E
Kaffa *see* Feodosiya
76 G11 **Kaffrine** C Senegal 14°07′N 15°27′W
Kafiréas, Akrotírio *see* Ntóro, Kávo
115 I19 **Kafiréos, Stenó** *strait* Évvoia/Kykládes, Greece, Aegean Sea
Kafirnigan *see* Kofarnihon
Kafo *see* Kafu
75 W7 **Kafr ash Shaykh** *var.* Kafrel Sheik, Kafr el Sheikh. N Egypt 31°07′N 30°56′E
Kafr el Sheikh *see* Kafr ash Shaykh
81 F17 **Kafu** *var.* Kafo. ≈ W Uganda
83 J15 **Kafue** Lusaka, SE Zambia 15°44′S 28°10′E
83 I14 **Kafue** ≈ C Zambia
67 T13 **Kafue Flats** *plain* C Zambia
164 K12 **Kaga** Ishikawa, Honshū, SW Japan 36°18′N 136°19′E
79 J14 **Kaga Bandoro** *prev.* Fort-Crampel. Nana-Grébizi, C Central African Republic 06°54′N 19°10′E
81 E18 **Kagadi** W Uganda 0°57′N 30°52′E
38 H17 **Kagalaska Island** *island* Aleutian Islands, Alaska, USA
Kagan *see* Kogon
Kaganovichabad *see* Kolkhozobod
Kagarlyk *see* Kaharlyk
164 H14 **Kagawa** *off.* Kagawa-ken. ◈ *prefecture* Shikoku, SW Japan
Kagawa-ken *see* Kagawa
154 J13 **Kagaznagar** Andhra Pradesh, C India 19°25′N 79°30′E
93 J14 **Kåge** Västerbotten, N Sweden 64°49′N 21°00′E
81 E19 **Kagera** *var.* Ziwa Magharibi, *Eng.* West Lake. ◈ *region* NW Tanzania
81 E19 **Kagera** *var.* Akagera. ≈ Rwanda/Tanzania *see also* Akagera
76 L5 **Kâgheṭ** *var.* Karet. *physical region* N Mauritania
Kagi *see* Chiai
137 S12 **Kağızman** Kars, NE Turkey 40°08′N 43°07′E
188 I6 **Kagman Point** *headland* Saipan, S Northern Mariana Islands
164 C16 **Kagoshima** *var.* Kagosima. Kagoshima, Kyūshū, SW Japan 31°37′N 130°33′E
164 C16 **Kagoshima** *off.* Kagoshima-ken, *var.* Kagosima. ◈ *prefecture* Kyūshū, SW Japan
Kagoshima-ken *see* Kagoshima
Kagosima *see* Kagoshima
Kagul *see* Cahul
Kagul, Ozero *see* Kahul, Ozero
38 B8 **Kahala Point** *headland* Kaua'i, Hawai'i, USA 22°08′N 159°17′W
81 F21 **Kahama** Shinyanga, NW Tanzania 03°48′S 32°36′E
117 P5 **Kaharlyk** *Rus.* Kagarlyk. Kyyivs′ka Oblast′, N Ukraine 49°50′N 30°50′E
169 T13 **Kahayan, Sungai** ≈ Borneo, C Indonesia
79 I22 **Kahemba** Bandundu, SW Dem. Rep. Congo 07°20′S 19°00′E
185 A23 **Kaherekoau Mountains** ▲▲ South Island, New Zealand
143 W14 **Kahīrī** *var.* Kūhīrī. Sīstān va Balūchestān, SE Iran 26°55′N 61°04′E
101 L16 **Kahla** Thüringen, C Germany 50°49′N 11°33′E
101 G15 **Kahler Asten** ▲ W Germany 51°11′N 08°32′E
149 Q4 **Kahmard, Daryā-ye** *prev.* Darya-i-surkhab. ≈ NE Afghanistan
143 T13 **Kahnūj** Kermān, SE Iran 28°N 57°41′E
27 V1 **Kahoka** Missouri, C USA 40°24′N 91°44′W
38 E10 **Kaho'olawe** *var.* Kahoolawe. *island* Hawai'i, USA, C Pacific Ocean
Kahoolawe *see* Kaho'olawe
136 M16 **Kahramanmaraş** *var.* Kahraman Maraş, Maraş, Marash. Kahramanmaraş, S Turkey 37°34′N 36°54′E
136 L15 **Kahramanmaraş** *var.* Kahraman Maraş, Maraş, Marash. ◈ *province* C Turkey
Kahraman Maraş *see* Kahramanmaraş
Kahror/Kahror Pakka *see* Karor Pacca
137 N15 **Kâhta** Adıyaman, S Turkey 37°48′N 38°35′E
38 D8 **Kahuku** O'ahu, Hawaii, USA, C Pacific Ocean 21°40′N 157°57′W
38 D8 **Kahuku Point** *headland* O'ahu, Hawai'i, USA 21°42′N 157°59′W
116 M12 **Kahul, Ozero** *var.* Lacul Cahul, *Rus.* Ozero Kagul. ◎ Moldova/Ukraine
143 V11 **Kahūrak** Sīstān va Balūchestān, SE Iran 29°25′N 59°38′E
184 G13 **Kahurangi Point** *headland* South Island, New Zealand 40°41′S 171°57′E
149 V6 **Kahūta** Punjab, E Pakistan 33°38′N 73°27′E
77 S14 **Kaiama** Kwara, W Nigeria 09°37′N 03°58′E
186 D7 **Kaiapit** Morobe, C Papua New Guinea 06°12′S 146°09′E
185 I18 **Kaiapoi** Canterbury, South Island, New Zealand 43°23′S 172°40′E
36 K9 **Kaibab Plateau** *plain* Arizona, SW USA
171 U14 **Kai Besar, Pulau** *island* Kepulauan Kai, E Indonesia
36 L9 **Kaibito Plateau** *plain* Arizona, SW USA
158 K6 **Kaidu He** *var.* Karaxahar. ≈ NW China
55 S10 **Kaieteur Falls** *waterfall* C Guyana
161 O6 **Kaifeng** Henan, C China 34°47′N 114°20′E
184 J3 **Kaihu** Northland, North Island, New Zealand 35°47′S 173°39′E
Kaihua *see* Wenshan
171 U14 **Kai Kecil, Pulau** *island* Kepulauan Kai, E Indonesia
169 U16 **Kai, Kepulauan** *prev.* Kei Islands. *island group* Maluku, SE Indonesia
184 J3 **Kaikohe** Northland, North Island, New Zealand 35°25′S 173°48′E
185 J16 **Kaikoura** Canterbury, South Island, New Zealand 42°22′S 173°40′E
185 J16 **Kaikoura Peninsula** *peninsula* South Island, New Zealand
Kailas Range *see* Gangdisê Shan
160 K12 **Kaili** Guizhou, S China 26°34′N 107°58′E
38 F10 **Kailua** Maui, Hawaii, USA, C Pacific Ocean 20°53′N 156°13′W
Kailua *see* Kalaoa
38 G11 **Kailua-Kona** *var.* Kona. Hawaii, USA, C Pacific Ocean 19°43′N 155°58′W
186 B7 **Kaim** ≈ W Papua New Guinea
171 X14 **Kaima** Papua, E Indonesia 05°36′S 138°39′E
184 M7 **Kaimai Range** ▲▲ North Island, New Zealand
114 E13 **Kaïmaktsalán** *var.* Kajmakčalan. ▲ Greece/FYR Macedonia 40°57′N 21°48′E *see also* Kajmakčalan
Kaïmaktsalán *see* Kajmakčalan
185 C20 **Kaimanawa Mountains** ▲▲ North Island, New Zealand
118 E4 **Käina** *Ger.* Keinis; *prev.* Keina. Hiiumaa, W Estonia 58°50′N 22°49′E
109 V7 **Kainach** ≈ SE Austria
164 I14 **Kainan** Tokushima, Shikoku, SW Japan 33°36′N 134°20′E
164 H15 **Kainan** Wakayama, Honshū, SW Japan 34°09′N 135°12′E
147 U7 **Kaindy** *Kir.* Kayyngdy. Chuyskaya Oblast′, N Kyrgyzstan 42°48′N 73°39′E
77 T14 **Kainji Dam** *dam* W Nigeria
Kainji Lake *see* Kainji Reservoir
77 T14 **Kainji Reservoir** *var.* Kainji Lake. ⊠ W Nigeria
186 D8 **Kaintiba** *var.* Kamina. Gulf, S Papua New Guinea 07°29′S 146°04′E
92 K12 **Kainulasjärvi** Norrbotten, N Sweden 67°00′N 22°31′E
184 K5 **Kaipara Harbour** *harbour* North Island, New Zealand
152 I10 **Kairāna** Uttar Pradesh, N India 29°24′N 77°10′E
74 M6 **Kairouan** *var.* Al Qayrawān. E Tunisia 35°46′N 10°11′E
Kaisaria *see* Kayseri
101 F20 **Kaiserslautern** Rheinland-Pfalz, SW Germany 49°27′N 07°46′E
118 G13 **Kaišiadorys** Kaunas, S Lithuania 54°51′N 24°27′E
184 I2 **Kaitaia** Northland, North Island, New Zealand 35°07′S 173°13′E
185 E24 **Kaitangata** Otago, South Island, New Zealand 46°18′S 169°52′E
152 I9 **Kaithal** Haryāna, NW India 29°47′N 76°26′E
Kaitong *see* Tongyu
169 N13 **Kait, Tanjung** *headland* Sumatera, W Indonesia 03°13′S 106°03′E
38 E9 **Kaiwi Channel** *channel* Hawai'i, USA, C Pacific Ocean
160 K9 **Kaixian** *var.* Hanfeng. Sichuan, C China 31°13′N 108°25′E
163 V11 **Kaiyuan** *var.* K'ai-yüan. Liaoning, NE China 42°33′N 124°04′E
160 H14 **Kaiyuan** Yunnan, SW China 23°42′N 103°14′E
K'ai-yüan *see* Kaiyuan
39 O9 **Kaiyuh Mountains** ▲▲ Alaska, USA
93 M15 **Kajaani** *Swe.* Kajana. Oulu, C Finland 64°17′N 27°46′E
149 N7 **Kajakī, Band-e** ◎ C Afghanistan
Kajan *see* Kayan, Sungai
Kajana *see* Kajaani
137 V13 **K'ajaran** *Rus.* Kadzharan. SE Armenia 39°10′N 46°09′E
Kajisay *see* Kadzhi-Say
113 O20 **Kajmakčalan** *var.* Kaïmaktsalán. ▲ S FYR Macedonia 40°57′N 21°48′E *see also* Kaïmaktsalán
Kajmakčalan *see* Kaïmaktsalán
Kajnar *see* Kaynar
149 N6 **Kajrān** Dāykondī, C Afghanistan 33°12′N 65°28′E
149 N5 **Kaj Rūd** ≈ C Afghanistan
146 G14 **Kaka** *Rus.* Kaakhka. Ahal Welaýaty, S Turkmenistan 37°20′N 59°37′E
12 C12 **Kakabeka Falls** Ontario, S Canada 48°24′N 89°40′W
83 F23 **Kakamas** Northern Cape, W South Africa 28°45′S 20°33′E
81 H18 **Kakamega** Western, W Kenya 0°17′N 34°47′E
155 Q22 **Kakana** Andaman and Nicobar Islands, SE India 09°08′N 92°48′E
112 H13 **Kakanj** Federacija Bosna I Hercegovina, C Bosnia and Herzegovina 44°06′N 18°07′E
185 F22 **Kakanui Mountains** ▲▲ South Island, New Zealand
184 K11 **Kakaramea** Taranaki, North Island, New Zealand 39°42′S 174°27′E
76 J16 **Kakata** C Liberia 06°35′N 10°19′W
184 M11 **Kakatahi** Manawatu-Wanganui, North Island, New Zealand 39°40′S 175°20′E
113 M23 **Kakavi** Gjirokastër, S Albania 39°55′N 20°19′E
147 O14 **Kakaydi** Surkhondaryo Viloyati, S Uzbekistan 37°37′N 67°30′E
164 F13 **Kake** Hiroshima, Honshū, SW Japan 34°37′N 132°17′E
39 X13 **Kake** Kupreanof Island, Alaska, USA 56°58′N 133°57′W
171 P14 **Kakea** Pulau Wowoni, C Indonesia 04°09′S 123°06′E
164 M14 **Kakegawa** Shizuoka, Honshū, S Japan 34°47′N 138°02′E
165 V16 **Kakeroma-jima** Kagoshima, SW Japan
143 T6 **Kākhak** Khorāsān, E Iran
118 L11 **Kakhanavichy** *Rus.* Kokhanovichi. Vitsyebskaya Voblasts′, N Belarus 55°52′N 28°08′E
39 P13 **Kakhonak** Alaska, USA 59°26′N 154°48′W
117 S10 **Kakhovka** Khersons′ka Oblast′, S Ukraine 46°40′N 33°30′E
117 U9 **Kakhovs'ke Vodoskhovyshche** *Rus.* Kakhovskoye Vodokhranilishche. ⊠ SE Ukraine
Kakhovskoye Vodokhranilishche *see* Kakhovs'ke Vodoskhovyshche
117 T11 **Kakhovs'kyy Kanal** *canal* S Ukraine
Kakia *see* Khakhea
155 L16 **Kākināda** *prev.* Cocanada. Andhra Pradesh, E India 16°56′N 82°13′E
Käkisalmi *see* Priozersk
164 I13 **Kakogawa** Hyōgo, Honshū, SW Japan 34°49′N 134°52′E
81 F18 **Kakoge** C Uganda 01°03′N 32°30′E
145 O7 **Kak, Ozero** ◎ N Kazakhstan
Ka-Krem *see* Malyy Yenisey
Kakshaal-Too, Khrebet *see* Kokshaal-Tau
39 S5 **Kaktovik** Alaska, USA 70°08′N 143°37′W
165 Q11 **Kakuda** Miyagi, Honshū, C Japan 37°59′N 140°48′E
165 Q8 **Kakunodate** Akita, Honshū, C Japan 39°37′N 140°35′E
Kalaallit Nunaat *see* Greenland
149 T7 **Kālābāgh** Punjab, E Pakistan 33°00′N 71°35′E
171 Q16 **Kalabahi** Pulau Alor, S Indonesia 08°14′S 124°32′E
188 I5 **Kalabera** Saipan, S Northern Mariana Islands
83 G14 **Kalabo** Western, W Zambia 15°00′S 22°37′E
126 M9 **Kalach** Voronezhskaya Oblast′, W Russian Federation 50°24′N 41°00′E
127 N10 **Kalach-na-Donu** Volgogradskaya Oblast′, SW Russian Federation 48°45′N 43°29′E
166 K5 **Kaladan** ≈ W Burma (Myanmar)
14 K14 **Kaladar** Ontario, SE Canada 44°38′N 77°06′W
38 G13 **Ka Lae** *var.* South Cape, South Point. *headland* Hawai'i, USA, C Pacific Ocean 18°54′N 155°40′W
83 G19 **Kalahari Desert** *desert* Southern Africa
38 B8 **Kalāheo** *var.* Kalaheo. Kaua'i, Hawaii, USA, C Pacific Ocean 21°55′N 159°31′W
Kalaheo *see* Kalāheo
Kalaikhum *see* Qal'aikhum
Kala-i-Mor *see* Galaýmor
93 K15 **Kalajoki** Oulu, W Finland 64°15′N 24°E
Kalak *see* Eski Kaļak
Kal al Sraghna *see* El Kelâa Srarhna
32 G10 **Kalama** Washington, NW USA 46°00′N 122°50′W
Kalámai *see* Kalámata
115 G14 **Kalamariá** Kentrikí Makedonía, N Greece 40°37′N 22°58′E
115 C15 **Kalamás** *var.* Thiamis; *prev.* Thýamis. ≈ W Greece
115 E21 **Kalámata** *prev.* Kalámai. Pelopónnisos, S Greece 37°02′N 22°07′E
148 L16 **Kalamat, Khor** *Eng.* Kalmat Lagoon. *lagoon* SW Pakistan
148 L16 **Kalamat, Khor** *Eng.* Kalmat Lagoon. *lagoon* SW Pakistan
31 P10 **Kalamazoo** Michigan, N USA 42°17′N 85°35′W
31 P9 **Kalamazoo River** ≈ Michigan, N USA
Kalambaka *see* Kalampáka
117 S13 **Kalamits'ka Zatoka** *Rus.* Kalamitskiy Zaliv. *gulf* S Ukraine
Kalamitskiy Zaliv *see* Kalamits'ka Zatoka
115 H18 **Kálamos** Attikí, C Greece 38°16′N 23°51′E
115 C18 **Kálamos** *island* Iónioi Nísia, Greece, C Mediterranean Sea
115 D15 **Kalampáka** *var.* Kalambaka. Thessalía, C Greece 39°43′N 21°36′E
Kalan *see* Călan, Romania
Kalan *see* Tunceli, Turkey
117 S11 **Kalanchak** Khersons'ka Oblast′, S Ukraine 46°14′N 33°19′E
38 G11 **Kalaoa** *var.* Kailua. Hawaii, USA, C Pacific Ocean 19°43′N 155°59′W
171 O15 **Kalaotoa, Pulau** *island* W Indonesia
155 J24 **Kala Oya** ≈ NW Sri Lanka
Kalarash *see* Călăraşi
93 H17 **Kälarne** Jämtland, C Sweden 63°00′N 16°10′E
143 V15 **Kalar Rūd** ≈ SE Iran
169 R9 **Kalasin** *var.* Muang Kalasin. Kalasin, E Thailand 16°29′N 103°31′E
143 U4 **Kalāt** *var.* Kabūd Gonbad. Khorāsān, NE Iran 37°02′N 59°46′E
149 O11 **Kālat** *var.* Kelat, Khelat. Baluchistān, SW Pakistan 29°01′N 66°38′E
Kalāt *see* Qalāt
115 J14 **Kalathriá, Ákrotirio** *headland* Samothráki, NE Greece 40°24′N 25°34′E
193 W14 **Kalau** *island* Tongatapu Group, SE Tonga
38 E9 **Kalaupapa** Moloka'i, Hawaii, USA, C Pacific Ocean 21°11′N 156°59′W
127 N13 **Kalaus** ≈ SW Russian Federation
Kalávrita *see* Kalávryta
115 E19 **Kalávryta** *var.* Kalávrita. Dytikí Ellás, S Greece 38°02′N 22°06′E
141 Y10 **Kalbān** W Oman 20°19′N 58°40′E
180 H11 **Kalbarri** Western Australia 27°43′S 114°08′E
145 X10 **Kalbinskiy Khrebet** *Kaz.* Qalba Zhotasy. ▲▲ E Kazakhstan
144 G10 **Kaldygayty** ≈ W Kazakhstan
136 I12 **Kalecik** Ankara, N Turkey 40°08′N 33°27′E
79 O19 **Kalehe** Sud-Kivu, E Dem. Rep. Congo 02°05′S 28°52′E
79 P22 **Kalemie** *prev.* Albertville. Katanga, SE Dem. Rep. Congo 05°55′S 29°09′E
166 L4 **Kalemyo** Sagaing, W Burma (Myanmar) 23°11′N 94°03′E
82 H12 **Kalene Hill** North Western, NW Zambia 11°10′S 24°12′E
Kale Sultanie *see* Çanakkale
124 I7 **Kalevala** Respublika Kareliya, NW Russian Federation 65°12′N 31°16′E
166 L4 **Kalewa** Sagaing, C Burma (Myanmar) 23°15′N 94°19′E
Kalgan *see* Zhangjiakou
39 Q12 **Kalgin Island** *island* Alaska, USA
180 L12 **Kalgoorlie** Western Australia 30°51′S 121°27′E
Kali *see* Sārda
115 E17 **Kaliakoúda** ▲ C Greece 38°47′N 21°42′E
114 O8 **Kaliakra, Nos** *headland* NE Bulgaria 43°22′N 28°28′E
115 F19 **Kaliánoi** Pelopónnisos, S Greece 37°55′N 22°28′E
115 N24 **Kalí Límni** ▲ Kárpathos, SE Greece 35°34′N 27°08′E
79 N20 **Kalima** Maniema, E Dem. Rep. Congo 02°34′S 26°27′E
169 S11 **Kalimantan** *Eng.* Indonesian Borneo. ◈ *geopolitical region* Borneo, C Indonesia
169 Q11 **Kalimantan Barat** *off.* Propinsi Kalimantan Berat, *Eng.* West Borneo, West Kalimantan. ◈ *province* N Indonesia
Kalimantan Barat, Propinsi *see* Kalimantan Barat
169 T13 **Kalimantan Selatan** *off.* Propinsi Kalimantan Selatan, *Eng.* South Borneo, South Kalimantan. ◈ *province* N Indonesia
Kalimantan Selatan, Propinsi *see* Kalimantan Selatan
169 R12 **Kalimantan Tengah** *off.* Propinsi Kalimantan Tengah, *Eng.* Central Borneo, Central Kalimantan. ◈ *province* N Indonesia
Kalimantan Tengah, Propinsi *see* Kalimantan Tengah
169 U10 **Kalimantan Timur** *off.* Propinsi Kalimantan Timur, *Eng.* East Borneo, East Kalimantan. ◈ *province* N Indonesia
Kalimantan Timur, Propinsi *see* Kalimantan Timur
Kálimnos *see* Kálymnos
153 S12 **Kālimpang** West Bengal, NE India 27°02′N 88°34′E
Kalinin *see* Tver'
Kalinin *see* Boldumsaz
Kalininabad *see* Kalininobod
126 B3 **Kaliningrad** Kaliningradskaya Oblast′, W Russian Federation 54°48′N 21°33′E
Kaliningrad *see* Kaliningradskaya Oblast'
126 A3 **Kaliningradskaya Oblast'** *var.* Kaliningrad. ◈ *province and enclave* W Russian Federation
Kalinino *see* Tashir
147 P14 **Kalininobod** *Rus.* Kalininabad. SW Tajikistan 37°49′N 68°55′E
127 O8 **Kalininsk** Saratovskaya Oblast′, W Russian Federation 51°31′N 44°25′E
Kalininsk *see* Boldumsaz
Kalinisk *see* Cupcina
119 M19 **Kalinkavichy** *Rus.* Kalinkovichi. Homyel'skaya Voblasts′, SE Belarus 52°08′N 29°19′E
Kalinkovichi *see* Kalinkavichy
81 G18 **Kaliro** SE Uganda 0°54′N 33°30′E
Kalisch/Kalish *see* Kalisz
33 O7 **Kalispell** Montana, NW USA 48°12′N 114°18′W
110 I13 **Kalisz** *Ger.* Kalisch, *Rus.* Kalish; *anc.* Calisia. Wielkopolskie, C Poland 51°46′N 18°04′E
110 F9 **Kalisz Pomorski** *Ger.* Kallies. Zachodnio-pomorskie, NW Poland 53°55′N 15°55′E
126 M10 **Kalitva** ≈ SW Russian Federation
81 F21 **Kaliua** Tabora, C Tanzania 05°03′S 31°48′E
92 K13 **Kalix** Norrbotten, N Sweden 65°51′N 23°14′E
92 K12 **Kalixälven** ≈ N Sweden
92 J11 **Kalixfors** Norrbotten, N Sweden 67°45′N 20°20′E
145 T8 **Kalkaman** *Kaz.* Qalqaman. Pavlodar, NE Kazakhstan 51°57′N 75°58′E
Kalkandelen *see* Tetovo
181 O4 **Kalkarindji** Northern Territory, N Australia 17°32′S 130°40′E
31 P6 **Kalkaska** Michigan, N USA 44°44′N 85°11′W
93 F16 **Kall** Jämtland, C Sweden 63°31′N 13°16′E
189 X2 **Kallalen** *var.* Calalen. *island* Ratak Chain, SE Marshall Islands
118 J5 **Kallaste** *Ger.* Krasnogor. Tartumaa, SE Estonia 58°40′N 27°12′E
93 N16 **Kallavesi** ◎ SE Finland
115 F17 **Kallídromo** ▲▲ C Greece
Kallies *see* Kalisz Pomorski
95 M22 **Kallinge** Blekinge, S Sweden 56°14′N 15°17′E
115 L16 **Kalloní** Lésvos, E Greece 39°14′N 26°16′E
93 F16 **Kallsjön** ◎ C Sweden
95 N21 **Kalmar** *var.* Calmar. Kalmar, S Sweden 56°40′N 16°22′E
95 M19 **Kalmar** *var.* Calmar. ◈ *county* S Sweden
95 N20 **Kalmarsund** *strait* S Sweden
Kalmat Lagoon *see* Kalamat, Khor
117 X9 **Kal'mius** ≈ E Ukraine
99 H15 **Kalmthout** Antwerpen, N Belgium 51°24′N 04°27′E
Kalmykia/Kalmykiya-Khal'mg Tangch, Respublika *see* Kalmykiya, Respublika
127 O12 **Kalmykiya, Respublika** *var.* Respublika Kalmykiya-Khal'mg Tangch, *Eng.* Kalmykia; *prev.* Kalmytskaya ASSR. ◈ *autonomous republic* SW Russian Federation
Kalmytskaya ASSR *see* Kalmykiya, Respublika
118 F9 **Kalnciems** Jelgava, C Latvia 56°46′N 23°37′E
114 L10 **Kalnitsa** ≈ SE Bulgaria
111 J24 **Kalocsa** Bács-Kiskun, S Hungary 46°31′N 19°00′E
114 J9 **Kalofer** Plovdiv, C Bulgaria 42°36′N 25°00′E
38 E10 **Kalohi Channel** *channel* C Pacific Ocean
83 I16 **Kalomo** Southern, S Zambia 17°02′S 26°29′E
29 X14 **Kalona** Iowa, C USA 41°28′N 91°42′W
115 K22 **Kalotási, Akrotírio** *cape* Amorgós, Kykládes, Greece, Aegean Sea
152 J8 **Kalpa** Himāchal Pradesh, N India 31°33′N 78°16′E
115 C15 **Kalpáki** Ípeiros, W Greece 39°53′N 20°38′E
155 C22 **Kalpeni Island** *island* Lakshadweep, India, N Indian Ocean
155 F21 **Kalpetta** Kerala, SW India 11°36′N 76°05′E
152 K13 **Kālpi** Uttar Pradesh, N India 26°07′N 79°44′E
158 G7 **Kalpin** Xinjiang Uygur Zizhiqu, NW China 40°35′N 78°52′E
149 P16 **Kalri Lake** ◎ SE Pakistan
143 R5 **Kāl Shūr** ≈ N Iran
39 N11 **Kalskag** Alaska, USA 61°32′N 160°15′W
Kalsø *see* Kalsoy
95 B18 **Kalsoy** *Dan.* Kalsø. *island* N Faeroe Islands
39 O9 **Kaltag** Alaska, USA 64°19′N 158°43′W
108 H7 **Kaltbrunn** Sankt Gallen, NE Switzerland 47°11′N 09°00′E
Kaltdorf *see* Pruszków
77 X14 **Kaltungo** Gombe, E Nigeria 09°49′N 11°22′E
126 K4 **Kaluga** Kaluzhskaya Oblast′, W Russian Federation 54°31′N 36°16′E
155 J26 **Kalu Ganga** ≈ S Sri Lanka
82 J13 **Kalulushi** Copperbelt, C Zambia 12°50′S 28°03′E
180 M2 **Kalumburu** Western Australia 14°11′S 126°40′E
95 H23 **Kalundborg** Vestsjælland, E Denmark 55°42′N 11°06′E
82 K11 **Kalungwishi** ≈ N Zambia
149 T8 **Kalūr Kot** Punjab, E Pakistan 32°08′N 71°20′E
116 I6 **Kalush** *Pol.* Kałusz. Ivano-Frankivs'ka Oblast′, W Ukraine 49°02′N 24°20′E
Kałusz *see* Kalush
110 N11 **Kałuszyn** Mazowieckie, C Poland 52°12′N 21°43′E
155 J26 **Kalutara** Western Province, SW Sri Lanka 06°35′N 79°59′E
Kaluwawa *see* Fergusson Island
126 I5 **Kaluzhskaya Oblast'** ◈ *province* W Russian Federation
119 E14 **Kalvarija** *Pol.* Kalwaria. Marijampolė, S Lithuania 54°25′N 23°13′E
93 K15 **Kälviä** Länsi-Suomi, W Finland 63°53′N 23°30′E
109 U6 **Kalwang** Steiermark, E Austria 47°25′N 14°48′E
Kalwaria *see* Kalvarija
154 D13 **Kalyān** Mahārāshtra, W India 19°17′N 73°11′E
124 K16 **Kalyazin** Tverskaya Oblast′, W Russian Federation 57°15′N 37°53′E
115 D18 **Kalydón** *anc.* Calydon. *site of ancient city* Dytikí Ellás, C Greece
115 M21 **Kálymnos** *var.* Kálimnos. Kálymnos, Dodekánisa, Greece, Aegean Sea 36°57′N 26°59′E
115 M21 **Kálymnos** *var.* Kálimnos. *island* Dodekánisa, Greece, Aegean Sea
117 O5 **Kalynivka** Kyyivs'ka Oblast′, N Ukraine 50°14′N 30°16′E
117 N6 **Kalynivka** Vinnyts'ka Oblast′, C Ukraine 49°27′N 28°32′E
42 M10 **Kama** *var.* Cama. Región Autónoma Atlántico Sur, SE Nicaragua 12°06′N 83°55′W
165 R9 **Kamaishi** *var.* Kamaisi. Iwate, Honshū, C Japan 39°18′N 141°52′E
Kamaisi *see* Kamaishi
118 H11 **Kamajai** Panevėžys, NE Lithuania 55°16′N 25°30′E
118 H13 **Kamajai** Utena, E Lithuania 55°49′N 25°30′E
149 U9 **Kamālia** Punjab, NE Pakistan 30°44′N 72°39′E
83 I14 **Kamalondo** North Western, NW Zambia 13°42′S 25°38′E
136 I13 **Kaman** Kirşehir, C Turkey 39°22′N 33°43′E
79 O20 **Kamanyola** Sud-Kivu, E Dem. Rep. Congo 02°54′S 29°04′E
141 N14 **Kamarān** *island* W Yemen
55 R9 **Kamarang** W Guyana 05°49′N 60°38′W
Kāmāreddi/Kamareddy *see* Rāmāreddi
Kama Reservoir *see* Kamskoye Vodokhranilishche
148 K13 **Kamarod** Baluchistān, SW Pakistan 27°34′N 63°36′E
171 P14 **Kamaru** Pulau Buton, C Indonesia 05°10′S 123°03′E
77 S13 **Kamba** Kebbi, NW Nigeria 11°50′N 03°44′E
Kambaeng Petch *see* Kamphaeng Phet
180 L12 **Kambalda** Western Australia 31°15′S 121°33′E
149 P13 **Kambar** *var.* Qambar. Sind, SE Pakistan 27°35′N 68°03′E
Kambara *see* Kabara
127 U3 **Kambarka** Udmurtskaya Respublika, NW Russian Federation 56°16′N 54°15′E
76 I14 **Kambia** W Sierra Leone 09°09′N 12°53′W
Kambos *see* Kámpos
79 N25 **Kambove** Katanga, SE Dem. Rep. Congo 10°50′S 26°39′E
Kambryk *see* Cambrai
123 V10 **Kamchatka** ≈ E Russian Federation
Kamchatka *see* Kamchatka, Poluostrov
Kamchatka Basin *see* Komandorskaya Basin
123 U10 **Kamchatka, Poluostrov** *Eng.* Kamchatka. *peninsula* E Russian Federation
123 V10 **Kamchatskaya Oblast'** ◈ *province* E Russian Federation
123 V10 **Kamchatskiy Zaliv** *gulf* E Russian Federation
114 N9 **Kamchiya** ≈ E Bulgaria
114 L9 **Kamchiya, Yazovir** ◎ E Bulgaria
Kamdesh *see* Kāmdeysh
149 T4 **Kāmdeysh** *var.* Kamdesh. Nūrestān, E Afghanistan 35°25′N 71°26′E
118 M13 **Kamen'** Vitsyebskaya Voblasts′, N Belarus 55°01′N 28°53′E
Kamenets *see* Kamyanyets
Kamenets-Podol'skaya Oblast' *see* Khmel'nyts'ka Oblast'
Kamenets-Podol'skiy *see* Kam"yanets'-Podil's'kyy
113 Q18 **Kamenica** NE Macedonia 42°03′N 22°34′E
Kamenica *see* Kamenicë
113 O16 **Kamenicë** *Serb.* Kamenica; *prev.* Kosovska Kamenica. E Kosovo 42°37′N 21°33′E
112 A11 **Kamenjak, Rt** *headland* NW Croatia
144 F8 **Kamenka** Zapadnyy Kazakhstan, NW Kazakhstan 51°06′N 51°16′E
125 O6 **Kamenka** Arkhangel'skaya Oblast′, NW Russian Federation 65°55′N 44°01′E
126 6 **Kamenka** Penzenskaya Oblast′, W Russian Federation 53°12′N 44°00′E
127 L8 **Kamenka** Voronezhskaya Oblast′, W Russian Federation 50°44′N 39°31′E
Kamenka *see* Camenca
Kamenka *see* Kam"yanka
Kamenka-Bugskaya *see* Kam"yanka-Buz'ka
Kamenka Dneprovskaya *see* Kam"yanka-Dniprovs'ka
Kamen Kashirskiy *see* Kamin'-Kashyrs'kyy
126 L15 **Kamennomostskiy** Respublika Adygeya, SW Russian Federation 44°13′N 40°12′E
126 L11 **Kamenolomni** Rostovskaya Oblast′, SW Russian Federation 47°36′N 40°18′E
127 P8 **Kamenskiy** Saratovskaya Oblast′, W Russian Federation 50°56′N 45°32′E
Kamenskoye *see* Romaniv
126 L11 **Kamensk-Shakhtinskiy** Rostovskaya Oblast′, SW Russian Federation 48°18′N 40°16′E
101 P15 **Kamenz** Sachsen, E Germany 51°15′N 14°06′E
164 J13 **Kameoka** Kyōto, Honshū, SW Japan 35°02′N 135°35′E
126 M3 **Kameshkovo** Vladimirskaya Oblast′, W Russian Federation 56°21′N 41°01′E
164 C11 **Kami-Agata** Nagasaki, Tsushima, SW Japan 34°40′N 129°27′E
33 N10 **Kamiah** Idaho, NW USA 46°13′N 116°01′W
Kamień Koszyrski *see* Kamin'-Kashyrs'kyy
110 H9 **Kamień Krajeński** *Ger.* Kamin in Westpreussen. Kujawski-pomorskie, C Poland 53°31′N 17°31′E
111 F15 **Kamienna Góra** *Ger.* Landeshut, Landeshut in Schlesien. Dolnośląskie, SW Poland 50°48′N 16°00′E
110 D8 **Kamień Pomorski** *Ger.* Cummin in Pommern. Zachodnio-pomorskie, NW Poland 53°57′N 14°44′E
165 R5 **Kamiiso** Hokkaidō, NE Japan 41°50′N 140°38′E
79 L22 **Kamiji** Kasai-Oriental, S Dem. Rep. Congo 06°39′S 23°27′E
165 T3 **Kamikawa** Hokkaidō, NE Japan 43°51′N 142°47′E
164 B15 **Kami-Koshiki-jima** *island* SW Japan
79 M23 **Kamina** Katanga, S Dem. Rep. Congo 08°42′S 25°01′E
Kamina *see* Kaintiba
42 C6 **Kaminaljuyú** *ruins* Guatemala, C Guatemala
Kamin in Westpreussen *see* Kamień Krajeński
116 J2 **Kamin'-Kashyrs'kyy** *Pol.* Kamień Koszyrski, *Rus.* Kamen Kashirskiy. Volyns'ka Oblast′, NW Ukraine 51°39′N 24°59′E
165 Q5 **Kaminokuni** Hokkaidō, NE Japan 41°48′N 140°05′E

◆ Country ◇ Dependent Territory ◈ Administrative Regions ▲ Mountain Ѫ Volcano ◎ Lake
● Country Capital ○ Dependent Territory Capital ✈ International Airport ▲▲ Mountain Range ≈ River ⊠ Reservoir

165 P10 **Kaminoyama** Yamagata, Honshū, C Japan 38°10′N 140°16′E
39 Q13 **Kamishak Bay** bay Alaska, USA
165 U4 **Kami-Shihoro** Hokkaidō, NE Japan 43°14′N 143°18′E
Kamishli see Al Qāmishlī
Kamissar see Kamsar
164 C11 **Kami-Tsushima** Nagasaki, Tsushima, SW Japan 34°40′N 129°27′E
79 O20 **Kamituga** Sud-Kivu, E Dem. Rep. Congo 03°07′S 28°10′E
164 B17 **Kamiyaku** Kagoshima, Yaku-shima, SW Japan 30°24′N 130°32′E
11 N16 **Kamloops** British Columbia, SW Canada 50°39′N 120°24′W
107 G25 **Kamma** Sicilia, Italy, C Mediterranean Sea 36°46′N 12°03′E
192 K4 **Kammu Seamount** undersea feature N Pacific Ocean 32°09′N 173°00′E
109 U11 **Kamnik** Ger. Stein. C Slovenia 46°13′N 14°34′E
Kamniške Alpe see Kamniško-Savinjske Alpe
109 T10 **Kamniško-Savinjske Alpe** var. Kamniške Alpe, Sanntaler Alpen, Ger. Steiner Alpen. ▲▲ N Slovenia
Kamo see Gavarr
165 R3 **Kamoenai** var. Kamuenai. Hokkaidō, NE Japan 43°07′N 140°25′E
165 O14 **Kamogawa** Chiba, Honshū, S Japan 35°05′N 140°04′E
149 W8 **Kāmoke** Punjab, E Pakistan 31°58′N 74°15′E
82 L13 **Kamoto** Eastern, E Zambia 13°16′S 32°04′E
109 V3 **Kamp** ≈ N Austria
81 F18 **Kampala** ● (Uganda) S Uganda 0°20′N 32°28′E
168 K11 **Kampar, Sungai** ≈ Sumatera, W Indonesia
98 L9 **Kampen** Overijssel, E Netherlands 52°33′N 05°55′E
79 N20 **Kampene** Maniema, E Dem. Rep. Congo 03°35′S 26°40′E
29 Q9 **Kampeska, Lake** ◎ South Dakota, N USA
167 O9 **Kamphaeng Phet** var. Kambaeng Petch. Kamphaeng Phet, W Thailand 16°28′N 99°31′E
Kampo see Campo, Cameroon
Kampo see Ntem, Cameroon/Equatorial Guinea
167 S12 **Kâmpóng Cham** prev. Kompong Cham. Kâmpóng Cham, C Cambodia 12°N 105°27′E
167 R12 **Kâmpóng Chhnăng** prev. Kompong. Kâmpóng Chhnăng, C Cambodia 12°15′N 104°40′E
167 R12 **Kâmpóng Khleăng** prev. Kompong Kleang. Siĕmréab, NW Cambodia 13°04′N 104°07′E
167 Q14 **Kâmpóng Saôm** prev. Kompong Som, Sihanoukville. Kâmpóng Saôm, SW Cambodia 10°38′N 103°30′E
167 R13 **Kâmpóng Spoe** prev. Kompong Speu. Kâmpóng Spœ, S Cambodia 11°28′N 104°29′E
121 O2 **Kámpos** var. Kambos. NW Cyprus 35°03′N 32°44′E
167 R14 **Kâmpôt** Kâmpôt, SW Cambodia 10°37′N 104°11′E
Kamptee see Kāmthi
77 O14 **Kampti** SW Burkina 10°07′N 03°22′W
Kampuchea see Cambodia
Kampuchea, Democratic see Cambodia
Kampuchea, People's Democratic Republic of see Cambodia
169 Q9 **Kampung Sirik** Sarawak, East Malaysia 02°42′N 111°28′E
11 V15 **Kamsack** Saskatchewan, S Canada 51°34′N 101°51′W
76 H13 **Kamsar** var. Kamissar. Guinée-Maritime, W Guinea 10°33′N 14°34′W
127 R4 **Kamskoye Ust'ye** Respublika Tatarstan, W Russian Federation 55°13′N 49°11′E
125 U14 **Kamskoye Vodokhranilishche** var. Kama Reservoir. ⊠ NW Russian Federation
154 I12 **Kāmthi** prev. Kamptee. Mahārāshtra, C India 21°19′N 79°11′E
Kamuela see Waimea
Kamuenai see Kamoenai
165 T5 **Kamui-dake** ▲ Hokkaidō, NE Japan 42°24′N 142°57′E
165 R3 **Kamui-misaki** headland Hokkaidō, NE Japan 43°20′N 140°20′E
43 O15 **Kámuk, Cerro** ▲ SE Costa Rica 09°15′N 83°01′W
116 K7 **Kam"yanets'-Podil's'kyy** Rus. Kamenets-Podol'skiy. Khmel'nyts'ka Oblast', W Ukraine 48°43′N 26°36′E
117 Q6 **Kam"yanka** Rus. Kamenka. Cherkas'ka Oblast', C Ukraine 49°03′N 32°06′E
116 I5 **Kam"yanka-Buz'ka** Rus. Kamenka-Bugskaya. L'vivs'ka Oblast', NW Ukraine 50°04′N 24°21′E
117 T9 **Kam"yanka-Dniprovs'ka** Rus. Kamenka Dneprovskaya. Zaporiz'ka Oblast', SE Ukraine 47°28′N 34°24′E
119 F19 **Kamyanyets** Rus. Kamenets. Brestskaya Voblasts', SW Belarus 52°24′N 23°49′E
127 P9 **Kamyshin** Volgogradskaya Oblast', SW Russian Federation 50°07′N 45°20′E
127 Q13 **Kamyzyak** Astrakhanskaya Oblast', SW Russian Federation 46°07′N 48°03′E
12 K8 **Kanaaupscow** ≈ Québec, C Canada
36 K8 **Kanab** Utah, W USA 37°03′N 112°31′W
36 K9 **Kanab Creek** ≈ Arizona/Utah, SW USA
187 Y14 **Kanacea** prev. Kanathea. Taveuni, N Fiji 16°59′S 179°54′E
38 G17 **Kanaga Island** island Aleutian Islands, Alaska, USA
38 G17 **Kanaga Volcano** ▲ Kanaga Island, Alaska, USA 51°55′N 177°09′W
164 N14 **Kanagawa** off. Kanagawa-ken. ◐ prefecture Honshū, S Japan
Kanagawa-ken see Kanagawa
13 Q8 **Kanairiktok** ≈ Newfoundland and Labrador, E Canada
Kanaky see New Caledonia
79 K22 **Kananga** prev. Luluabourg. Kasai-Occidental, S Dem. Rep. Congo 05°51′S 22°22′E
Kanara see Karnātaka
36 J7 **Kanarraville** Utah, W USA 37°32′N 113°10′W
127 Q4 **Kanash** Chuvashskaya Respublika, W Russian Federation 55°30′N 47°27′E
Kanathea see Kanacea
21 Q4 **Kanawha River** ≈ West Virginia, NE USA
164 L13 **Kanayama** Gifu, Honshū, SW Japan 35°46′N 137°15′E
164 L11 **Kanazawa** Ishikawa, Honshū, SW Japan 36°35′N 136°40′E
166 M4 **Kanbalu** Sagaing, C Burma (Myanmar) 23°10′N 95°31′E
166 L8 **Kanbe** Yangon, SW Burma (Myanmar) 16°40′N 96°01′E
167 O11 **Kanchanaburi** Kanchanaburi, W Thailand 14°02′N 99°32′E
Kanchanjańghā/Kānchenjunga see Kangchenjunga
145 V11 **Kanchingiz, Khrebet** ▲▲ E Kazakhstan
155 J19 **Kānchipuram** prev. Conjeeveram. Tamil Nādu, SE India 12°50′N 79°44′E
149 N8 **Kandahār** Per. Qandahār. Kandahār, S Afghanistan 31°36′N 65°48′E
149 N9 **Kandahār** Per. Qandahār. ◐ province SE Afghanistan
Kandalakša see Kandalaksha
124 I5 **Kandalaksha** var. Kandalakša, Fin. Kantalahti. Murmanskaya Oblast', NW Russian Federation 67°09′N 32°14′E
Kandalaksha Gulf/Kandalakshskaya Guba see Kandalakshskiy Zaliv
124 K6 **Kandalakshskiy Zaliv** var. Kandalakshskaya Guba, Eng. Kandalaksha Gulf. bay NW Russian Federation
83 G17 **Kandalengoti** var. Kandalengoti. Ngamiland, NW Botswana 19°25′S 22°12′E
Kandalengoti see Kandalengoti
169 U13 **Kandangan** Borneo, C Indonesia 02°50′S 115°15′E
Kandau see Kandava
118 E8 **Kandava** Ger. Kandau. Tukums, W Latvia 57°02′N 22°48′E
Kandavu see Kadavu
77 R14 **Kandé** var. Kanté. NE Togo 09°55′N 01°01′E
101 F23 **Kandel** ▲ SW Germany 48°03′N 08°00′E
186 C7 **Kandep** Enga, W Papua New Guinea 05°54′S 143°34′E
149 R12 **Kandh Kot** Sind, SE Pakistan 28°15′N 69°18′E
77 S13 **Kandi** N Benin 11°05′N 02°59′E
149 P14 **Kandiāro** Sind, SE Pakistan 27°02′N 68°16′E
136 F11 **Kandıra** Kocaeli, NW Turkey 41°05′N 30°08′E
183 S8 **Kandos** New South Wales, SE Australia 32°52′S 149°58′E
148 M16 **Kandrāch** var. Kanrach. Baluchistān, SW Pakistan 25°26′N 65°28′E
172 I4 **Kandreho** Mahajanga, C Madagascar 17°27′S 46°06′E
186 F7 **Kandrian** New Britain, E Papua New Guinea 06°14′S 149°32′E
Kandukur see Kondukūr
155 K25 **Kandy** Central Province, C Sri Lanka 07°17′N 80°40′E
144 I10 **Kandyagash** Kaz. Qandyaghash; prev. Oktyab'rsk. Aktyubinsk, W Kazakhstan 49°25′N 57°24′E
18 D12 **Kane** Pennsylvania, NE USA 41°39′N 78°47′W
64 I11 **Kane Fracture Zone** tectonic feature NW Atlantic Ocean
Kanëka see Kanëvka
78 G9 **Kanem** off. Préfecture du Kanem. ◐ prefecture W Chad
Kanem, Préfecture du see Kanem
38 D9 **Kāne'ohe** var. Kaneohe. O'ahu, Hawaii, USA, C Pacific Ocean 21°25′N 157°48′W
Kanestron, Akrotírio see Palioúri, Akrotírio
Kanëv see Kaniv
124 M5 **Kanëvka** var. Kanëka. Murmanskaya Oblast', NW Russian Federation 67°07′N 39°43′E
126 K13 **Kanevskaya** Krasnodarskiy Kray, SW Russian Federation 46°07′N 38°57′E
Kanevskoye Vodokhranilishche see Kanivs'ke Vodoskhovyshche
165 P9 **Kaneyama** Yamagata, Honshū, C Japan 38°54′N 140°20′E
83 G20 **Kang** Kgalagadi, C Botswana 23°41′S 22°50′E
76 L13 **Kangaba** Koulikoro, SW Mali 11°57′N 08°24′W
136 M13 **Kangal** Sivas, C Turkey 39°15′N 37°23′E
143 S15 **Kangān** Hormozgān, SE Iran 27°49′N 52°04′E
Kangān see Bandar-e Kangān
168 J6 **Kangar** Perlis, Peninsular Malaysia 06°28′N 100°10′E
76 L13 **Kangaré** Sikasso, S Mali 11°39′N 08°10′W
182 F10 **Kangaroo Island** island South Australia
93 M17 **Kangasniemi** Itä-Suomi, E Finland 61°58′N 26°37′E
142 K6 **Kangāvar** var. Kangāwar. Kermānshāhān, W Iran 34°29′N 47°55′E
Kangāwar see Kangāvar
153 S11 **Kangchenjunga** var. Kānchenjunga, Nep. Kanchanjańghā. ▲ NE India 27°36′N 88°06′E
160 G9 **Kangding** var. Lucheng, Tib. Dardo. Sichuan, C China 30°03′N 101°56′E
169 U16 **Kangean, Kepulauan** island group S Indonesia
169 T16 **Kangean, Pulau** island Kepulauan Kangean, S Indonesia
67 U8 **Kangen** var. Kengen. ≈ SE Sudan
197 N14 **Kangerlussuaq** Dan. Søndre Strømfjord. ✈ Kitaa, W Greenland 66°59′N 50°28′E
197 Q15 **Kangertittivaq** Dan. Scoresby Sund. fjord E Greenland
167 O2 **Kangfang** Kachin State, N Burma (Myanmar) 26°09′N 98°36′E
163 X12 **Kanggye** N North Korea 40°58′N 126°37′E
197 P15 **Kangikajik** var. Kap Brewster. headland E Greenland 70°10′N 22°00′W
13 N5 **Kangiqsualujjuaq** prev. George River, Port-Nouveau-Québec. Québec, E Canada 58°35′N 65°59′W
12 L2 **Kangiqsujuaq** prev. Maricourt, Wakeham Bay. Québec, NE Canada 61°35′N 72°00′W
12 M4 **Kangirsuk** prev. Bellin, Payne. Québec, E Canada 60°00′N 70°01′W
159 V11 **Kangle** Gansu, C China 35°22′N 103°42′E
Kangle see Wanzai
158 M16 **Kangmar** Xizang Zizhiqu, W China 28°34′N 89°40′E
163 Y14 **Kangnŭng** Jap. Kōryō. NE South Korea 37°47′N 128°51′E
79 D18 **Kango** Estuaire, NW Gabon 0°17′N 10°00′E
152 I7 **Kāngra** Himāchal Pradesh, NW India 32°04′N 76°16′E
153 Q16 **Kangsabati Reservoir** ⊠ N India
159 O17 **Kangto** ▲ China/India 27°54′N 92°33′E
159 W12 **Kangxian** var. Kang Xian, Zuitai, Zuitaizi. Gansu, C China 33°21′N 105°40′E
Kang Xian see Kangxian
76 M15 **Kani** NW Ivory Coast 08°29′N 06°36′W
166 L4 **Kani** Sagaing, C Burma (Myanmar) 22°24′N 94°55′E
79 M23 **Kaniama** Katanga, S Dem. Rep. Congo 07°32′S 24°11′E
Kanibadam see Konibodom
169 V6 **Kanibongan** Sabah, East Malaysia 06°40′N 117°12′E
185 F17 **Kaniere** West Coast, South Island, New Zealand 42°45′S 171°00′E
185 G17 **Kaniere, Lake** ◎ South Island, New Zealand
188 E17 **Kanifaay** Yap, W Micronesia
125 O4 **Kanin Kamen'** ▲▲ NW Russian Federation
125 N3 **Kanin Nos** Nenetskiy Avtonomnyy Okrug, NW Russian Federation 68°38′N 43°19′E
125 N3 **Kanin Nos, Mys** cape NW Russian Federation
125 O5 **Kanin, Poluostrov** peninsula NW Russian Federation
139 V8 **Kānī Sakht** Wāsiṭ, E Iraq 33°19′N 46°04′E
139 T3 **Kānī Sulaymān** Arbīl, N Iraq 35°54′N 44°35′E
165 Q6 **Kanita** Aomori, Honshū, C Japan 41°04′N 140°36′E
117 Q5 **Kaniv** Rus. Kanëv. Cherkas'ka Oblast', C Ukraine 49°46′N 31°28′E
182 K11 **Kaniva** Victoria, SE Australia 36°25′S 141°13′E
117 Q5 **Kanivs'ke Vodoskhovyshche** Rus. Kanevskoye Vodokhranilishche. ⊠ C Ukraine
112 L8 **Kanjiža** Ger. Altkanischa, Hung. Magyarkanizsa, Okanizsa; prev. Stara Kanjiža. Vojvodina, N Serbia 46°03′N 20°03′E
93 K18 **Kankaanpää** Länsi-Suomi, SW Finland 61°47′N 22°25′E
30 M12 **Kankakee** Illinois, N USA 41°07′N 87°51′W
31 O11 **Kankakee River** ≈ Illinois/Indiana, N USA
76 K14 **Kankan** E Guinea 10°25′N 09°19′W
154 K13 **Kānker** Chhattīsgarh, C India 20°19′N 81°29′E
76 J10 **Kankossa** Assaba, S Mauritania 15°54′N 11°31′W
169 N12 **Kanmaw Kyun** var. Kisseraing, Kithareng. island Mergui Archipelago, S Burma (Myanmar)
164 F12 **Kanmuri-yama** ▲ Kyūshū, SW Japan 34°28′N 132°03′E
21 R10 **Kannapolis** North Carolina, SE USA 35°30′N 80°36′W
93 L16 **Kannonkoski** Länsi-Suomi, C Finland 62°59′N 25°20′E
155 F20 **Kannur** var. Cannanore. Kerala, SW India 11°53′N 75°23′E see also Cannanore
93 K15 **Kannus** Länsi-Suomi, W Finland 63°55′N 23°55′E
77 V13 **Kano** Kano, N Nigeria 11°56′N 08°31′E
77 V13 **Kano** ◐ state N Nigeria
77 V13 **Kano** ✈ Kano, N Nigeria 11°56′N 08°26′E
164 G14 **Kan'onji** var. Kanonzi. Kagawa, Shikoku, SW Japan 34°08′N 133°38′E
Kanonzi see Kan'onji
26 M5 **Kanopolis Lake** ⊠ Kansas, C USA
36 K5 **Kanosh** Utah, W USA 38°48′N 112°26′W
169 R9 **Kanowit** Sarawak, East Malaysia 02°03′N 112°15′E
164 C16 **Kanoya** Kagoshima, Kyūshū, SW Japan 31°22′N 130°50′E
152 L13 **Kānpur** Eng. Cawnpore. Uttar Pradesh, N India 26°28′N 80°21′E
Kanrach see Kandrāch
164 I14 **Kansai** ✈ (Ōsaka) Ōsaka, Honshū, SW Japan 34°25′N 135°13′E
27 R9 **Kansas** Oklahoma, C USA 36°14′N 94°46′W
26 L5 **Kansas** off. State of Kansas, also known as Jayhawker State, Sunflower State. ◐ state C USA
27 R4 **Kansas City** Kansas, C USA 39°07′N 94°38′W
27 R4 **Kansas City** Missouri, C USA 39°06′N 94°35′W
27 R3 **Kansas City** ✈ Missouri, C USA 39°18′N 94°45′W
27 P4 **Kansas River** ≈ Kansas, C USA
122 L14 **Kansk** Krasnoyarskiy Kray, S Russian Federation 56°11′N 95°32′E
Kansu see Gansu
147 V7 **Kant** Chuyskaya Oblast', N Kyrgyzstan 42°54′N 74°47′E
Kantalahti see Kandalaksha
167 N16 **Kantang** var. Ban Kantang. Trang, SW Thailand 07°25′N 99°30′E
115 H25 **Kántanos** Kríti, Greece, E Mediterranean Sea 35°20′N 23°42′E
77 R12 **Kantchari** E Burkina 12°47′N 01°37′E
Kanté see Kandé
Kantemir see Cantemir
126 L9 **Kantemirovka** Voronezhskaya Oblast', W Russian Federation 49°44′N 39°53′E
167 R11 **Kantharalak** Si Sa Ket, E Thailand 14°32′N 104°37′E
Kantipur see Kathmandu
39 Q9 **Kantishna River** ≈ Alaska, USA
191 S3 **Kanton** var. Abariringa, Canton Island; prev. Mary Island. atoll Phoenix Islands, C Kiribati
97 C20 **Kanturk** Ir. Ceann Toirc. Cork, SW Ireland 52°12′N 08°54′W
55 T11 **Kanuku Mountains** ▲▲ S Guyana
165 O12 **Kanuma** Tochigi, Honshū, S Japan 36°34′N 139°44′E
83 H20 **Kanye** Southern, SE Botswana 24°55′S 25°14′E
83 H17 **Kanyu** North-West, C Botswana 20°04′S 24°36′E
166 M7 **Kanyutkwin** Bago, C Burma (Myanmar) 18°19′N 96°30′E
79 M24 **Kanzenze** Katanga, SE Dem. Rep. Congo 10°33′S 25°28′E
193 Y15 **Kao** island Kotu Group, W Tonga
161 S14 **Kaohsiung** var. Gaoxiong, Jap. Takao, Takow. S Taiwan 22°36′N 120°17′E
161 S14 **Kaohsiung** ✈ S Taiwan 22°26′N 120°32′E
Kaokaona see Kirakira
83 B17 **Kaoko Veld** ▲▲ N Namibia
76 G11 **Kaolack** var. Kaolak. W Senegal 14°09′N 16°08′W
Kaolak see Kaolack
Kaolan see Lanzhou
114 M7 **Kaolinovo** Shumen, NE Bulgaria 43°36′N 27°04′E
186 M8 **Kaolo** San Jorge, N Solomon Islands 08°24′S 159°35′E
83 H14 **Kaoma** Western, W Zambia 14°50′S 24°48′E
38 B8 **Kapa'a** var. Kapaa. Kaua'i, Hawaii, USA, C Pacific Ocean 22°04′N 159°19′W
Kapaa see Kapa'a
113 J16 **Kapa Moračka** ▲ C Montenegro 42°53′N 19°01′E
137 V13 **Kapan** Rus. Kafan; prev. Ghap'an. SE Armenia 39°13′N 46°25′E
82 L13 **Kapandashila** Northern, NE Zambia 12°43′S 31°00′E
79 L23 **Kapanga** Katanga, S Dem. Rep. Congo 08°22′S 22°37′E
145 U15 **Kapchagay** Kaz. Qapshaghay. Almaty, SE Kazakhstan 43°52′N 77°05′E
145 V15 **Kapchagayskoye Vodokhranilishche** Kaz. Qapshagay Böyeni. ⊠ SE Kazakhstan
99 F15 **Kapelle** Zeeland, SW Netherlands 51°29′N 03°58′E
99 G16 **Kapellen** Antwerpen, N Belgium 51°19′N 04°25′E
95 P15 **Kapellskär** Stockholm, C Sweden 59°43′N 19°03′E
81 H18 **Kapenguria** Rift Valley, W Kenya 01°14′N 35°08′E
109 V6 **Kapfenberg** Steiermark, C Austria 47°27′N 15°18′E
83 J14 **Kapiri Mposhi** Central, C Zambia 13°59′S 28°40′E
149 R4 **Kāpīsā** ◐ province E Afghanistan
12 G10 **Kapiskau** ≈ Ontario, C Canada
184 K13 **Kapiti Island** island C New Zealand
78 K9 **Kapka, Massif du** ▲▲ E Chad
Kaplamada see Kaubalatmada, Gunung
22 H9 **Kaplan** Louisiana, S USA 30°00′N 92°16′W
Kaplangky, Plato see Gaplaňgyr Platosy
111 D19 **Kaplice** Ger. Kaplitz. Jihočeský Kraj, S Czech Republic 48°42′N 14°27′E
Kaplitz see Kaplice
Kapoche see Capoche
171 T12 **Kapocol** Papua, E Indonesia 01°59′S 130°11′E
167 N14 **Kapoe** Ranong, SW Thailand 09°33′N 98°37′E
Kapoeas see Kapuas, Sungai
81 G15 **Kapoeta** Eastern Equatoria, SE Sudan 04°50′N 33°35′E
111 I25 **Kapos** ≈ S Hungary
111 H25 **Kaposvár** Somogy, SW Hungary 46°23′N 17°54′E
94 H13 **Kapp** Oppland, S Norway 60°42′N 10°49′E
100 I7 **Kappeln** Schleswig-Holstein, N Germany 54°41′N 09°56′E
Kaproncza see Koprivnica
109 P7 **Kaprun** Salzburg, C Austria 47°15′N 12°48′E
Kapstad see Cape Town
Kapsukas see Marijampolė
171 Y13 **Kaptiau** Papua, E Indonesia 02°23′S 139°51′E
119 L19 **Kaptsevichy** Rus. Koptsevichi. Homyel'skaya Voblasts', SE Belarus 52°14′N 28°19′E
Kapuas Hulu, Banjaran/Kapuas Hulu, Pegunungan see Kapuas Mountains
169 S10 **Kapuas Mountains** Ind. Banjaran Kapuas Hulu, Pegunungan Kapuas Hulu. ▲▲ Indonesia/Malaysia
169 P11 **Kapuas, Sungai** ≈ Borneo, N Indonesia
169 T13 **Kapuas, Sungai** prev. Kapoeas. ≈ Borneo, C Indonesia
182 J9 **Kapunda** South Australia 34°23′S 138°51′E
152 H8 **Kapūrthala** Punjab, N India 31°20′N 75°26′E
12 G12 **Kapuskasing** Ontario, S Canada 49°25′N 82°26′W
14 D6 **Kapuskasing** ≈ Ontario, S Canada
127 P11 **Kapustin Yar** Astrakhanskaya Oblast', SW Russian Federation 48°36′N 45°49′E
82 K11 **Kaputa** Northern, NE Zambia 08°28′S 29°41′E
111 G22 **Kapuvár** Győr-Moson-Sopron, NW Hungary 47°35′N 17°01′E
Kapydzhik, Gora see Qazangödağ
119 J17 **Kapyl'** Rus. Kopyl'. Minskaya Voblasts', C Belarus 53°09′N 27°05′E
43 N9 **Kara** var. Cara. Región Autónoma Atlántico Sur, E Nicaragua 12°50′N 83°35′W
77 R14 **Kara** var. Lama-Kara. NE Togo 09°33′N 01°12′E
77 Q14 **Kara** ≈ N Togo
147 U7 **Kara-Balta** Chuyskaya Oblast', N Kyrgyzstan 42°51′N 73°51′E
144 L7 **Karabalyk** var. Komsomolets, Kaz. Komsomol. Kostanay, N Kazakhstan 53°47′N 61°58′E
144 G11 **Karabau** Kaz. Qarabaū. Atyrau, W Kazakhstan 48°29′N 53°05′E
146 E7 **Karabaur', Uval** Kaz. Korabavur Pastligi, Uzb. Qorabowur Kirlari. physical region Kazakhstan/Uzbekistan
Karabekaul see Garabekewül
Karabil', Vozvyshennost' see Garabil Belentligi
Kara-Bogaz-Gol see Garabogazköl
Kara-Bogaz-Gol, Zaliv see Garabogaz Aylagy
145 R15 **Karaboget** Kaz. Qaraböget. Zhambyl, S Kazakhstan 44°36′N 72°03′E
136 H11 **Karabük** Karabük, NW Turkey 41°12′N 32°36′E
136 H11 **Karabük** ◐ province NW Turkey
122 L12 **Karabula** Krasnoyarskiy Kray, C Russian Federation 58°01′N 97°17′E
145 V14 **Karabulak** Kaz. Qarabulaq. Taldykorgan, SE Kazakhstan 44°53′N 78°29′E
145 Y11 **Karabulak** Kaz. Qarabulaq. Vostochnyy Kazakhstan, E Kazakhstan 47°34′N 84°40′E
145 Q17 **Karabulak** Kaz. Qarabulaq. Yuzhnyy Kazakhstan, S Kazakhstan 42°31′N 69°47′E
Karabura see Yumin
136 C17 **Kara Burnu** headland SW Turkey 36°34′N 28°00′E
144 K10 **Karabutak** Kaz. Qarabutaq. Aktyubinsk, W Kazakhstan 49°55′N 60°05′E
136 D12 **Karacabey** Bursa, NW Turkey 40°14′N 28°22′E
114 O12 **Karacaköy** İstanbul, NW Turkey 41°24′N 28°21′E
114 M12 **Karacaoğlan** Kırklareli, NW Turkey 41°30′N 27°06′E
Karachay-Cherkessia see Karachayevo-Cherkesskaya Respublika
126 L15 **Karachayevo-Cherkesskaya Respublika** Eng. Karachay-Cherkessia. ◐ autonomous republic SW Russian Federation
126 M15 **Karachayevsk** Karachayevo-Cherkesskaya Respublika, SW Russian Federation 43°43′N 41°53′E
126 J6 **Karachev** Bryanskaya Oblast', W Russian Federation 53°07′N 35°56′E
149 O16 **Karāchi** Sind, SE Pakistan 24°51′N 67°02′E
149 O16 **Karāchi** ✈ Sind, S Pakistan 24°51′N 67°02′E
Karácsonkő see Piatra-Neamţ
155 E15 **Karād** Mahārāshtra, W India 17°19′N 74°15′E
136 H16 **Karadağ** ▲ S Turkey 37°00′N 33°00′E
147 T10 **Karadar'ya** Uzb. Qoradaryo. ≈ Kyrgyzstan/Uzbekistan
Karadeniz see Black Sea
Karadeniz Boğazi see İstanbul Boğazi
146 B13 **Karadepe** Balkan Welaýaty, W Turkmenistan 38°04′N 54°01′E
Karadzhar see Qorajar
Karaferiye see Véroia
Karagan see Garagan
145 R10 **Karaganda** Kaz. Qaraghandy. Karaganda, C Kazakhstan 49°53′N 73°07′E
145 R10 **Karaganda** off. Karagandinskaya Oblast', Kaz. Qaraghandy Oblysy. ◐ province C Kazakhstan
Karagandinskaya Oblast' see Karaganda
145 T10 **Karagayly** Kaz. Qaraghayly. Karaganda, C Kazakhstan 49°25′N 75°31′E
Karagel' see Garagöl'
123 U9 **Karaginskiy, Ostrov** island E Russian Federation
197 T1 **Karaginskiy Zaliv** bay E Russian Federation
137 P13 **Karagöl Dağları** ▲▲ NE Turkey
Karagumskiy Kanal see Garagum Kanaly
114 L13 **Karahisar** Edirne, NW Turkey 40°47′N 26°34′E
127 V3 **Karaidel'** Respublika Bashkortostan, W Russian Federation 55°50′N 56°55′E
114 L13 **Karaidemir Barajı** ⊠ NW Turkey
155 J21 **Kāraikāl** Pondicherry, SE India 10°58′N 79°50′E
155 I22 **Kāraikkudi** Tamil Nādu, SE India 10°04′N 78°46′E
145 Y11 **Kara Irtysh** Rus. Chërnyy Irtysh. ≈ NE Kazakhstan
143 N5 **Karaj** Tehrān, N Iran 35°44′N 51°26′E
168 K8 **Karak** Pahang, Peninsular Malaysia 03°24′N 101°59′E
149 T7 **Karak** North-West Frontier Province, N Pakistan 33°07′N 71°06′E
Karak see Al Karak
147 T11 **Kara-Kabak** Oshskaya Oblast', SW Kyrgyzstan 39°40′N 72°45′E
Kara-Kala see Magtymguly
Karakala see Oqqal'a
Karakalpakstan, Respublika see Qoraqalpog'iston Respublikasi
Karakalpakya see Qoraqalpog'iston
Karakax see Moyu
158 G10 **Karakax He** ≈ NW China
121 X8 **Karakaya Barajı** ⊠ C Turkey
171 Q9 **Karakelong, Pulau** island N Indonesia
Karakılısse see Ağrı
Karak, Muḥāfaẓat al see Al Karak
147 X8 **Karakol** var. Karakolka. Issyk-Kul'skaya Oblast', NE Kyrgyzstan 41°30′N 77°18′E
147 Y7 **Karakol** prev. Przheval'sk. Issyk-Kul'skaya Oblast', NE Kyrgyzstan 42°32′N 78°21′E
Kara-Köl see Kara-Kul'
Karakolka see Karakol
149 W2 **Karakoram Highway** road China/Pakistan
149 Z3 **Karakoram Pass** Chin. Karakoram Shankou. pass C Asia
152 I3 **Karakoram Range** ▲▲ C Asia
Karakoram Shankou see Karakoram Pass
Karaköse see Ağrı
145 P14 **Karakoyyn, Ozero** Kaz. Qaraqoyyn. ◎ C Kazakhstan
83 F19 **Karakubis** Ghanzi, W Botswana 22°03′S 20°36′E
147 T9 **Kara-Kul'** Kir. Kara-Köl. Dzhalal-Abadskaya Oblast', W Kyrgyzstan 40°35′N 73°36′E
Karakul' see Qarokŭl, Tajikistan
Karakul' see Qorako'l, Uzbekistan
147 U10 **Kara-Kul'dzha** Oshskaya Oblast', SW Kyrgyzstan 40°32′N 73°50′E
127 T3 **Karakulino** Udmurtskaya Respublika, NW Russian Federation 56°02′N 53°45′E
Karakul', Ozero see Qarokŭl
Kara Kum see Garagum
Kara Kum Canal/Karakumskiy Kanal see Garagum Kanaly
Karakumy, Peski see Garagum
83 E17 **Karakuwisa** Okavango, NE Namibia 18°56′S 19°40′E
122 M13 **Karam** Irkutskaya Oblast', S Russian Federation 55°07′N 107°21′E
Karamai see Karamay
169 T14 **Karamain, Pulau** island N Indonesia
136 I16 **Karaman** Karaman, S Turkey 37°11′N 33°13′E
136 H16 **Karaman** ◐ province S Turkey
114 M8 **Karamandere** ≈ NE Bulgaria
158 J4 **Karamay** var. Karamai, Kelamayi; prev. Chin. K'o-la-ma-i. Xinjiang Uygur Zizhiqu, NW China 45°33′N 84°45′E
169 U14 **Karambu** Borneo, N Indonesia 03°48′S 116°06′E
185 H14 **Karamea** West Coast, South Island, New Zealand 41°15′S 172°07′E
185 H14 **Karamea** ≈ South Island, New Zealand
185 G15 **Karamea Bight** gulf South Island, New Zealand
Karamet-Niyaz see Garamätnyýaz
158 K10 **Karamiran He** ≈ NW China
147 S11 **Karamyk** Oshskaya Oblast', SW Kyrgyzstan 39°28′N 71°45′E
169 U17 **Karangasem** Bali, S Indonesia 08°24′S 115°40′E
154 H12 **Kāranja** Mahārāshtra, C India 20°30′N 77°26′E
Karanpur see Karanpura
152 F9 **Karanpura** var. Karanpur. Rājasthān, NW India 29°46′N 73°30′E
Karánsebes/Karansebesch see Caransebeş
145 T14 **Karaoy** Kaz. Qaraoy. Almaty, SE Kazakhstan 45°52′N 74°44′E
114 N7 **Karapelit** Rom. Stejarul. Dobrich, NE Bulgaria 43°40′N 27°33′E
136 I15 **Karapınar** Konya, C Turkey 37°43′N 33°34′E
83 D22 **Karas** ◐ district S Namibia
147 Y8 **Kara-Say** Issyk-Kul'skaya Oblast', NE Kyrgyzstan 41°34′N 77°56′E
83 E22 **Karasburg** Karas, S Namibia 27°59′S 18°46′E
Kara Sea see Karskoye More
92 K9 **Kárášjohka** var. Karašjokka. ≈ N Norway
Kárášjohka see Karasjok
92 L9 **Karasjok** Fin. Kaarasjoki, Lapp. Kárášjohka. Finnmark, N Norway 69°27′N 25°28′E
Karašjokka see Kárášjohka
Kara Strait see Karskiye Vorota, Proliv
145 N8 **Karasu** Kaz. Qarasū. Kostanay, N Kazakhstan 52°44′N 65°29′E
136 F11 **Karasu** Sakarya, NW Turkey 41°07′N 30°37′E
Kara Su see Mesta/Néstos
Karasubazar see Bilohirs'k
122 I12 **Karasuk** Novosibirskaya Oblast', C Russian Federation 53°41′N 78°04′E
145 U13 **Karatal** Kaz. Qaratal. ≈ SE Kazakhstan
136 K17 **Karataş** Adana, S Turkey 36°32′N 35°22′E
145 Q16 **Karatau** Kaz. Qarataū. Zhambyl, S Kazakhstan 43°09′N 70°28′E
Karatau see Karatau, Khrebet
145 P16 **Karatau, Khrebet** var. Karatau, Kaz. Qarataū. ▲▲ S Kazakhstan
144 G13 **Karaton** Kaz. Qaraton. Atyrau, W Kazakhstan 46°33′N 53°31′E
164 C13 **Karatsu** var. Karatu. Saga, Kyūshū, SW Japan 33°28′N 129°48′E
Karatu see Karatsu
122 K8 **Karaul** Taymyrskiy (Dolgano-Nenetskiy) Avtonomnyy Okrug, N Russian Federation 70°07′N 83°12′E
Karaulbazar see Qorowulbozor
152 I13 **Karauli** Rājasthān, N India 26°29′N 77°01′E
Karauzyak see Qorao'zak
115 D16 **Karáva** ▲ C Greece 39°19′N 21°33′E
Karavanke see Karawanken
115 F22 **Karavás** Kýthira, S Greece 36°21′N 22°57′E
113 J20 **Karavastasë, Laguna e** var. Kënet' e Karavastas, Kravasta Lagoon. lagoon W Albania
Karavastas, Kënet' e see Karavastasë, Laguna e
118 I5 **Käravere** Tartumaa, E Estonia 58°25′N 26°29′E
115 L23 **Karavonísia** island Kykládes, Greece, Aegean Sea
169 O15 **Karawang** prev. Krawang. Jawa, C Indonesia 06°13′S 107°16′E
109 T10 **Karawanken** Slvn. Karavanke. ▲▲ Austria/Serbia
Karaxahar see Kaidu He
137 R13 **Karayazı** Erzurum, NE Turkey 39°40′N 42°09′E
145 Q12 **Karazhal** Kaz. Qarazhal. Karaganda, C Kazakhstan 48°00′N 70°52′E
139 T10 **Karbalā'** ◐ governorate S Iraq
139 S9 **Karbalā'** var. Kerbala, Kerbela. Karbalā', S Iraq 32°37′N 44°03′E
94 L11 **Kårböle** Gävleborg, C Sweden 61°59′N 15°16′E
111 M23 **Karcag** Jász-Nagykun-Szolnok, E Hungary 47°22′N 20°51′E
Kardak see Imia
114 N7 **Kardam** Dobrich, NE Bulgaria 43°45′N 28°06′E
Kardamila see Kardámyla
115 L18 **Kardámyla** var. Kardamila, Kardhámila. Chíos, E Greece 38°33′N 26°04′E
Kardeljevo see Ploče
Kardh see Qardho
Kardhámila see Kardámyla
Kardhítsa see Kardítsa
115 E16 **Kardítsa** var. Kardhítsa. Thessalía, C Greece 39°22′N 21°56′E
118 E4 **Kärdla** Ger. Kertel. Hiiumaa, W Estonia 59°00′N 22°42′E
Karelia see Kareliya, Respublika
119 I16 **Karelichy** Pol. Korelicze, Rus. Korelichi. Hrodzyenskaya Voblasts', W Belarus 53°34′N 26°08′E
124 I10 **Kareliya, Respublika** prev. Karel'skaya ASSR, Eng. Karelia. ◐ autonomous republic NW Russian Federation
Karel'skaya ASSR see Kareliya, Respublika
81 E22 **Karema** Rukwa, W Tanzania 06°50′S 30°25′E
Karen see Hualien
83 I14 **Karenda** Central, C Zambia 14°42′S 26°52′E
167 N8 **Karen State** var. Kawthule State, Kayin State. ◐ state S Burma (Myanmar)
92 J10 **Karesuando** Fin. Kaaresuanto, Lapp. Gárasavvon. Norrbotten, N Sweden 68°25′N 22°28′E
Karet see Kâgheț
Kareyz-e-Elyās/Kārez Iliās see Kārīz-e Elyās
122 J11 **Kargasok** Tomskaya Oblast', C Russian Federation 59°01′N 80°34′E
122 I12 **Kargat** Novosibirskaya Oblast', C Russian Federation 55°07′N 80°19′E
136 J11 **Kargı** Çorum, N Turkey 41°09′N 34°32′E
152 I5 **Kargil** Jammu and Kashmir, NW India 34°34′N 76°06′E
Kargilik see Yecheng
124 L11 **Kargopol'** Arkhangel'skaya Oblast', NW Russian Federation 61°30′N 38°53′E
110 F12 **Kargowa** Ger. Unruhstadt. Lubuskie, W Poland 52°05′N 15°50′E
77 X13 **Kari** Bauchi, E Nigeria 11°13′N 10°34′E
83 J15 **Kariba** Mashonaland West, N Zimbabwe 16°29′S 28°48′E
83 J16 **Kariba, Lake** ⊠ Zambia/Zimbabwe
165 Q4 **Kariba-yama** ▲ Hokkaidō, NE Japan 42°36′N 139°55′E
83 C19 **Karibib** Erongo, C Namibia 21°56′S 15°51′E
Karies see Karyés
92 L9 **Karigasniemi** Lapp. Garegegasnjárga. Lappi, N Finland 69°24′N 25°52′E
184 J2 **Karikari, Cape** headland North Island, New Zealand 34°47′S 173°24′E
Karimābād see Hunza
169 P12 **Karimata, Kepulauan** island group N Indonesia
169 P12 **Karimata, Pulau** island Kepulauan Karimata, N Indonesia
169 O11 **Karimata, Selat** strait W Indonesia
155 I14 **Karīmnagar** Andhra Pradesh, C India 18°28′N 79°09′E
186 C7 **Karimui** Chimbu, C Papua New Guinea 06°19′S 144°48′E
169 Q15 **Karimunjawa, Pulau** island S Indonesia
80 N12 **Karin** Sahil, N Somalia 10°48′N 45°46′E
Kariot see Ikaría
93 L20 **Karis** Fin. Karjaa. Etelä-Suomi, SW Finland 60°05′N 23°39′E
Káristos see Kárystos
148 J4 **Kārīz-e Elyās** var. Kareyz-e-Elyās, Kārez Iliās. Herāt, NW Afghanistan 35°26′N 61°24′E
Karjaa see Karis
145 T10 **Karkaralinsk** Kaz. Qarqaraly. Karaganda, E Kazakhstan 49°31′N 75°53′E
186 D6 **Karkar Island** island N Papua New Guinea
142 M7 **Karkas, Kūh-e** ▲ C Iran
142 K8 **Karkheh, Rūd-e** ≈ SW Iran
115 L20 **Karkinágri** var. Karkinagrio. Ikaría, Dodekánisa, Greece, Aegean Sea 37°31′N 26°01′E
Karkinagrio see Karkinágri
117 R12 **Karkinits'ka Zatoka** Rus. Karkinitskiy Zaliv. gulf S Ukraine

◆ Country ● Country Capital ◇ Dependent Territory ○ Dependent Territory Capital ◐ Administrative Regions ✈ International Airport ▲ Mountain ▲▲ Mountain Range ▲ Volcano ≈ River ◎ Lake ⊠ Reservoir

Karkinitskiy Zaliv *see* Karkinits'ka Zatoka
93 L19 **Karkkila** *Swe.* Högfors. Uusimaa, S Finland 60°32′N 24°10′E
93 M19 **Kärkölä** Etelä-Suomi, S Finland 60°52′N 25°17′E
182 G9 **Karkoo** South Australia 34°03′S 135°45′E
Karkūk *see* Kirkūk
118 D5 **Kärla** *Ger.* Kergel. Saaremaa, W Estonia 58°20′N 22°15′E
Karleby *see* Kokkola
110 F7 **Karlino** *Ger.* Körlin an der Persante. Zachodinio-pomorskie, NW Poland 54°02′N 15°52′E
137 Q13 **Karlıova** Bingöl, E Turkey 39°16′N 41°01′E
117 U6 **Karlivka** Poltavs'ka Oblast', C Ukraine 49°27′N 35°08′E
Karl-Marx-Stadt *see* Chemnitz
Karlö *see* Hailuoto
112 C11 **Karlobag** *It.* Carlopago. Lika-Senj, W Croatia 44°31′N 15°06′E
112 D9 **Karlovac** *Ger.* Karlstadt, *Hung.* Károlyváros. Karlovac, C Croatia 45°29′N 15°31′E
112 C10 **Karlovac** *off.* Karlovačka Županija. ⬖ *province* C Croatia
Karlovačka Županija *see* Karlovac
111 A16 **Karlovarský Kraj** ⬖ W Czech Republic
115 M19 **Karlovási** *var.* Néon Karlovásion, Néon Karlovasi. Sámos, Dodekánisa, Greece, Aegean Sea 37°47′N 26°40′E
114 J9 **Karlovo** *prev.* Levskigrad. Plovdiv, C Bulgaria 42°38′N 24°49′E
111 A16 **Karlovy Vary** *Ger.* Karlsbad; *prev. Eng.* Carlsbad. Karlovarský Kraj, W Czech Republic 50°13′N 12°51′E
Karlsbad *see* Karlovy Vary
95 L17 **Karlsborg** Västra Götaland, S Sweden 58°32′N 14°32′E
Karlsburg *see* Alba Iulia
95 L22 **Karlshamn** Blekinge, S Sweden 56°10′N 14°50′E
95 L16 **Karlskoga** Örebro, C Sweden 59°19′N 14°33′E
95 M22 **Karlskrona** Blekinge, S Sweden 56°11′N 15°39′E
101 G21 **Karlsruhe** *var.* Carlsruhe. Baden-Württemberg, SW Germany 49°01′N 08°24′E
95 K16 **Karlstad** Värmland, C Sweden 59°22′N 13°36′E
29 R3 **Karlstad** Minnesota, N USA 48°34′N 96°31′W
101 I18 **Karlstadt** Bayern, C Germany 49°58′N 09°46′E
Karlstadt *see* Karlovac
39 Q14 **Karluk** Kodiak Island, Alaska, USA 57°34′N 154°27′W
Karluk *see* Qarluq
119 O17 **Karma** *Rus.* Korma. Homyel'skaya Voblasts', SE Belarus 53°07′N 30°48′E
155 F14 **Karmāla** Mahārāshtra, W India 18°26′N 75°08′E
146 M11 **Karmana** Navoiy Viloyati, C Uzbekistan 40°09′N 65°18′E
138 G8 **Karmi'el** *var.* Carmiel. Northern, N Israel 32°55′N 35°18′E
95 B16 **Karmøy** *island* S Norway
152 I9 **Karnāl** Haryāna, N India 29°41′N 76°58′E
153 W15 **Karnaphuli Reservoir** ⊠ NE India
155 F17 **Karnātaka** *var.* Kanara; *prev.* Maisur, Mysore. ⬖ *state* W India
25 S13 **Karnes City** Texas, SW USA 28°54′N 97°55′W
109 P9 **Karnische Alpen** *It.* Alpi Carniche. ▲▲ Austria/Italy
114 M9 **Karnobat** Burgas, E Bulgaria 42°39′N 26°59′E
109 Q9 **Kärnten** *off.* Land Kärten, *Eng.* Carinthi, *Slvn.* Koroška. ⬖ *state* S Austria
Karnul *see* Kurnool
83 K16 **Karoi** Mashonaland West, N Zimbabwe 16°50′S 29°40′E
Karol *see* Carei
Károly-Fehérvár *see* Alba Iulia
Károlyváros *see* Karlovac
82 M12 **Karonga** Northern, N Malawi 09°54′S 33°55′E
147 W10 **Karool-Tëbë** Narynskaya Oblast', C Kyrgyzstan 40°33′N 75°52′E
182 J9 **Karoonda** South Australia 35°04′S 139°58′E
149 S9 **Karor Lāl Esan** Punjab, E Pakistan 31°15′N 70°58′E
149 T11 **Karor Pacca** *var.* Kahror, Kahror Pakka. Punjab, E Pakistan 29°38′N 71°59′E
Karosa *see* Karossa
171 N12 **Karossa** *var.* Karosa. Sulawesi, C Indonesia 01°38′S 119°21′E
Karpaten *see* Carpathian Mountains
115 L22 **Karpáthio Pélagos** *sea* Dodekánisa, Greece, Aegean Sea
115 N24 **Kárpathos** Kárpathos, SE Greece 35°30′N 27°13′E
115 N24 **Kárpathos** *It.* Scarpanto; *anc.* Carpathos, Carpathus. *island* SE Greece
Karpathos Strait *see* Karpathou, Stenó
115 N24 **Karpathou, Stenó** *var.* Karpathos Strait, Scarpanto Strait. *strait* Dodekánisa, Greece, Aegean Sea
Karpaty *see* Carpathian Mountains
115 E17 **Karpenísi** *prev.* Karpenísion. Stereá Ellás, C Greece 38°55′N 21°46′E
Karpenísion *see* Karpenísi
Karpilovka *see* Aktsyabrski
125 O8 **Karpogory** Arkhangel'skaya Oblast', NW Russian Federation 64°01′N 44°22′E
180 I7 **Karratha** Western Australia 20°44′S 116°52′E
137 S12 **Kars** *var.* Qars. Kars, NE Turkey 40°35′N 43°05′E
137 S12 **Kars** *var.* Qars. ⬖ *province* NE Turkey
145 O12 **Karsakpay** *Kaz.* Qarsaqbay. Karaganda, C Kazakhstan 47°51′N 66°42′E
93 L15 **Kärsämäki** Oulu, C Finland 63°58′N 25°49′E
Karsau *see* Kārsava
118 K9 **Kārsava** *Ger.* Karsau; *prev. Rus.* Korsovka. Ludza, E Latvia 56°46′N 27°39′E
Karshi *see* Garşy, Turkmenistan
Karshi *see* Qarshi, Uzbekistan
Karshinskaya Step *see* Qarshi Cho'li
Karshinskiy Kanal *see* Qarshi Kanali
84 I5 **Karskiye Vorota, Proliv** *Eng.* Kara Strait. *strait* N Russian Federation
122 J6 **Karskoye More** *Eng.* Kara Sea. *sea* Arctic Ocean
93 L17 **Karstula** Länsi-Suomi, C Finland 62°52′N 24°48′E
127 Q5 **Karsun** Ul'yanovskaya Oblast', W Russian Federation 54°12′N 47°00′E
122 F11 **Kartaly** Chelyabinskaya Oblast', C Russian Federation 53°02′N 60°42′E
18 E13 **Karthaus** Pennsylvania, NE USA 41°06′N 78°03′W
110 I7 **Kartuzy** Pomorskie, NW Poland 54°21′N 18°11′E
165 R8 **Karumai** Iwate, Honshū, C Japan 40°19′N 141°27′E
181 U4 **Karumba** Queensland, NE Australia 17°31′S 140°51′E
142 L10 **Kārūn** *var.* Rūd-e Kārūn. ≈ SW Iran
92 K13 **Karungi** Norrbotten, N Sweden 66°03′N 23°55′E
92 K13 **Karunki** Lappi, N Finland 66°01′N 24°06′E
Kārūn, Rūd-e *see* Kārūn
155 H21 **Karūr** Tamil Nādu, SE India 10°58′N 78°03′E
93 K17 **Karvia** Länsi-Suomi, SW Finland 62°07′N 22°34′E
111 J17 **Karviná** *Ger.* Karwin, *Pol.* Karwina; *prev.* Nová Karvinná. Moravskoslezský Krajj, E Czech Republic 49°50′N 18°30′E
155 E17 **Kārwār** Karnātaka, W India 14°50′N 74°09′E
108 M7 **Karwendelgebirge** ▲▲ Austria/Germany
Karwin/Karwina *see* Karviná
115 I14 **Karyés** *var.* Karies. Ágion Óros, N Greece 40°15′N 24°15′E
115 I19 **Kárystos** *var.* Káristos. Évvoia, C Greece 38°01′N 24°25′E
136 E17 **Kaş** Antalya, SW Turkey 36°12′N 29°38′E
39 Y14 **Kasaan** Prince of Wales Island, Alaska, USA 55°32′N 132°24′W
164 I13 **Kasai** Hyōgo, Honshū, SW Japan 34°56′N 134°49′E
79 K21 **Kasai** *var.* Cassai, Kassai. ≈ Angola/Dem. Rep. Congo
79 K22 **Kasai-Occidental** *off.* Région Kasai Occidental. ⬖ *region* S Dem. Rep. Congo
Kasai Occidental, Région *see* Kasai-Occidental
79 L21 **Kasai-Oriental** *off.* Région Kasai Oriental. ⬖ *region* C Dem. Rep. Congo
Kasai Oriental, Région *see* Kasai-Oriental
79 L24 **Kasaji** Katanga, S Dem. Rep. Congo 10°22′S 23°29′E
82 L12 **Kasama** Northern, N Zambia 10°14′S 31°12′E
Kasan *see* Koson
83 H16 **Kasane** North-West, NE Botswana 17°48′S 20°06′E
81 E23 **Kasanga** Rukwa, W Tanzania 08°27′S 31°10′E
79 G21 **Kasangulu** Bas-Congo, W Dem. Rep. Congo 04°33′S 15°12′E
Kasansay *see* Kosonsoy
155 E20 **Kāsaragod** Kerala, SW India 12°30′N 74°59′E
Kasargen *see* Kasari
118 P13 **Kasari** *var.* Kasari Jōgi, *Ger.* Kasargen. ≈ W Estonia
Kasari Jōgi *see* Kasari
8 L11 **Kasba Lake** ◎ Northwest Territories, Nunavut N Canada
Kaschau *see* Košice
164 B16 **Kaseda** *var.* Minami-Satsuma. Kagoshima, Kyūshū, SW Japan 31°25′N 130°17′E
83 I14 **Kasempa** North Western, NW Zambia 13°27′S 25°49′E
79 O24 **Kasenga** Katanga, SE Dem. Rep. Congo 10°22′S 28°37′E
79 P17 **Kasenye** *var.* Kasenyi. Orientale, NE Dem. Rep. Congo 01°23′N 30°25′E
Kasenyi *see* Kasenye
79 O19 **Kasese** Maniema, E Dem. Rep. Congo 01°36′S 27°31′E
81 E18 **Kasese** SW Uganda 0°10′N 30°06′E
152 J11 **Kāsganj** Uttar Pradesh, N India 27°48′N 78°38′E
143 U4 **Kashaf Rūd** ≈ NE Iran
143 N7 **Kāshān** Eşfahān, C Iran 33°57′N 51°31′E
126 M10 **Kashary** Rostovskaya Oblast', SW Russian Federation 49°02′N 40°58′E
39 O12 **Kashegelok** Alaska, USA 60°57′N 157°46′W
Kashgar *see* Kashi
158 E7 **Kashi** *Chin.* Kaxgar, K'o-shih, *Uigh.* Kashgar. Xinjiang Uygur Zizhiqu, NW China 39°32′N 75°58′E
164 J14 **Kashihara** *var.* Kasihara. Nara, Honshū, SW Japan 34°28′N 135°46′E
165 P13 **Kashima-nada** *gulf* S Japan
124 K15 **Kashin** Tverskaya Oblast', W Russian Federation 57°20′N 37°34′E
152 K10 **Kāshīpur** Uttarakhand, N India 29°13′N 78°58′E
126 L4 **Kashira** Moskovskaya Oblast', W Russian Federation 54°53′N 38°13′E
165 N11 **Kashiwazaki** *var.* Kasiwazaki. Niigata, Honshū, C Japan 37°22′N 138°33′E
Kashkadar'inskaya Oblast' *see* Qashqadaryo Viloyati
143 T5 **Kāshmar** *var.* Turshiz; *prev.* Solţānābād, Torshiz. Khorāsān, NE Iran 35°13′N 58°25′E
Kashmir *see* Jammu and Kashmir
149 R12 **Kashmor** Sind, SE Pakistan 28°24′N 69°42′E
149 S5 **Kashmūnd Ghar** *Eng.* Kashmund Range. ▲▲ E Afghanistan
Kashmund Range *see* Kashmūnd Ghar
Kasi *see* Vārānasi
153 O12 **Kasia** Uttar Pradesh, N India 26°45′N 83°55′E
39 N12 **Kasigluk** Alaska, USA 60°54′N 162°31′W
Kasihara *see* Kashihara
39 R12 **Kasilof** Alaska, USA 60°20′N 151°16′W
Kasimköj *see* General Toshevo
126 M4 **Kasimov** Ryazanskaya Oblast', W Russian Federation 54°59′N 41°22′E
79 P18 **Kasindi** Nord-Kivu, E Dem. Rep. Congo 0°03′N 29°43′E
82 M12 **Kasitu** ≈ N Malawi
Kasiwazaki *see* Kashiwazaki
30 L14 **Kaskaskia River** ≈ Illinois, N USA
93 J17 **Kaskinen** *Swe.* Kaskö. Länsi-Suomi, W Finland 62°23′N 21°10′E
Kaskö *see* Kaskinen
Kas Kong *see* Kŏng, Kaôh
11 O17 **Kaslo** British Columbia, SW Canada 49°54′N 116°57′W
Käsmark *see* Kežmarok
169 T12 **Kasongan** Borneo, C Indonesia 02°01′S 113°21′E
79 N21 **Kasongo** Maniema, E Dem. Rep. Congo 04°22′S 26°42′E
79 H22 **Kasongo-Lunda** Bandundu, SW Dem. Rep. Congo 06°30′S 16°51′E
115 M24 **Kásos** *island* S Greece
Kasos Strait *see* Kasou, Stenó
115 M25 **Kasou, Stenó** *var.* Kasos Strait. *strait* Dodekánisos/Kríti, Greece, Aegean Sea
137 T10 **Kaspi** C Georgia 41°54′N 44°25′E
114 M8 **Kaspichan** Shumen, NE Bulgaria 43°18′N 27°09′E
Kaspīy Mangy Oypaty *see* Caspian Depression
127 Q16 **Kaspiysk** Respublika Dagestan, SW Russian Federation 42°52′N 47°40′E
Kaspiyskiy *see* Lagan'
Kaspiyskoye More/Kaspiy Tengizi *see* Caspian Sea
Kassa *see* Košice
Kassai *see* Kasai
80 I9 **Kassala** Kassala, E Sudan 15°24′N 36°25′E
80 H9 **Kassala** ⬖ *state* NE Sudan
115 G15 **Kassándra** *prev.* Pallíni; *anc.* Pallene. *peninsula* NE Greece
115 G15 **Kassándra** *headland* N Greece 39°58′N 23°22′E
115 H15 **Kassándras, Kólpos** *var.* Kólpos Toronaíos. *gulf* N Greece
139 Y11 **Kassārah** Maysān, E Iraq 31°21′N 47°25′E
101 I15 **Kassel** *prev.* Cassel. Hessen, C Germany 51°19′N 09°30′E
74 M6 **Kasserine** *var.* Al Qaşrayn. W Tunisia 35°15′N 08°52′E
14 J14 **Kasshabog Lake** ◎ Ontario, SE Canada
139 O5 **Kassīr, Sabkhat al** ◎ E Syria
29 W10 **Kasson** Minnesota, N USA 44°00′N 92°42′W
115 C17 **Kassópeia** *Var.* Kassópi. *site of ancient city* Ípeiros, W Greece
Kassópi *see* Kassópeia
115 N24 **Kastállou, Akrotírio** *headland* Kárpathos, SE Greece 35°24′N 27°08′E
136 I11 **Kastamonu** *var.* Castamoni, Kastamuni. Kastamonu, N Turkey 41°22′N 33°47′E
136 I10 **Kastamonu** *var.* Kastamuni. ⬖ *province* N Turkey
Kastamuni *see* Kastamonu
115 E14 **Kastaneá** Kentrikí Makedonía, N Greece 40°25′N 22°09′E
Kastélli *see* Kíssamos
Kastellórizon *see* Megísti
95 N21 **Kastlösa** Kalmar, S Sweden 56°25′N 16°25′E
115 D14 **Kastoría** Dytikí Makedonía, N Greece 40°33′N 21°15′E
126 K7 **Kastornoye** Kurskaya Oblast', W Russian Federation 51°49′N 38°07′E
115 I21 **Kástro** Sífnos, Kykládes, Greece, Aegean Sea 36°58′N 24°45′E
95 J23 **Kastrup** ✈ (København) København, E Denmark 55°36′N 12°39′E
119 Q17 **Kastsyukovichy** *Rus.* Kostyukovichi. Mahilyowskaya Voblasts', E Belarus 53°20′N 32°03′E
119 O18 **Kastsyukowka** *Rus.* Kostyukovka. Homyel'skaya Voblasts', SE Belarus 52°32′N 30°54′E
164 D13 **Kasuga** Fukuoka, Kyūshū, SW Japan 33°31′N 130° 27′E
164 L13 **Kasugai** Aichi, Honshū, SW Japan 35°15′N 136°57′E
81 E21 **Kasulu** Kigoma, W Tanzania 04°33′S 30°06′E
164 I12 **Kasumi** Hyōgo, Honshū, SW Japan 35°36′N 134°37′E
127 R17 **Kasumkent** Respublika Dagestan, SW Russian Federation 41°39′N 48°09′E
82 M13 **Kasungu** Central, C Malawi 13°04′S 33°29′E
149 W9 **Kasūr** Punjab, E Pakistan 31°07′N 74°30′E
83 G15 **Kataba** Western, W Zambia 15°28′S 23°25′E
19 R4 **Katahdin, Mount** ▲ Maine, NE USA 45°55′N 68°52′W
79 M20 **Katako-Kombe** Kasai-Oriental, C Dem. Rep. Congo 03°24′S 24°25′E
39 T12 **Katalla** Alaska, USA 60°12′N 144°31′W
Katana *see* Qaţanā
79 L24 **Katanga** *off.* Région du Katanga; *prev.* Shaba. ⬖ *region* SE Dem. Rep. Congo
122 M11 **Katanga** ≈ C Russian Federation
Katanga, Région du *see* Katanga
154 J11 **Katāngi** Madhya Pradesh, C India 21°46′N 79°50′E
180 J13 **Katanning** Western Australia 33°45′S 117°33′E
181 P8 **Kata Tjuta** *var.* Mount Olga. ▲ Northern Territory, C Australia 25°20′S 130°47′E
Katawaz *see* Zarghūn Shahr
151 Q22 **Katchall Island** *island* Nicobar Islands, India, NE Indian Ocean
115 F14 **Kateríni** Kentrikí Makedonía, N Greece 40°15′N 22°30′E
117 P7 **Katerynopil'** Cherkas'ka Oblast', C Ukraine 49°00′N 30°59′E
166 M3 **Katha** Sagaing, N Burma (Myanmar) 24°11′N 96°20′E
181 P2 **Katherine** Northern Territory, N Australia 14°29′S 132°20′E
154 B11 **Kāthiāwār Peninsula** *peninsula* W India
153 P11 **Kathmandu** *prev.* Kantipur. ● (Nepal) Central, C Nepal 27°46′N 85°17′E
152 H7 **Kathua** Jammu and Kashmir, NW India 32°23′N 75°34′E
76 L12 **Kati** Koulikoro, SW Mali 12°41′N 08°04′W
153 R13 **Katihār** Bihār, NE India 25°33′N 87°34′E
184 N7 **Katikati** Bay of Plenty, North Island, New Zealand 37°34′S 175°55′E
83 H16 **Katima Mulilo** Caprivi, NE Namibia 17°31′S 24°20′E
77 N15 **Katiola** C Ivory Coast 08°11′N 05°04′W
191 V10 **Katiu** *atoll* Îles Tuamotu, C French Polynesia
117 N12 **Katlabukh, Ozero** ◎ SW Ukraine
39 P14 **Katmai, Mount** ▲ Alaska, USA 58°16′N 154°57′W
154 J9 **Katni** Madhya Pradesh, C India 23°47′N 80°29′E
115 D19 **Káto Achaïa** *var.* Kato Ahaia, Káto Akhaía. Dytikí Ellás, S Greece 38°08′N 21°33′E
Kato Ahaia/Káto Akhaía *see* Káto Achaïa
121 P2 **Kato Lakatámeia** *var.* Kato Lakatamia. C Cyprus 35°07′N 33°20′E
Kato Lakatamia *see* Kato Lakatámeia
79 N22 **Katompi** Katanga, SE Dem. Rep. Congo 06°10′S 26°19′E
83 K14 **Katondwe** Lusaka, C Zambia 15°08′S 30°10′E
114 H12 **Káto Nevrokópi** *prev.* Káto Nevrokópion. Anatolikí Makedonía kai Thráki, NE Greece 41°21′N 23°51′E
Káto Nevrokópion *see* Káto Nevrokópi
81 E18 **Katonga** ≈ S Uganda
115 F15 **Káto Ólympos** ▲▲ C Greece
115 D17 **Katoúna** Dytikí Ellás, C Greece 38°47′N 21°07′E
115 E19 **Káto Vlasiá** Dytikí Makedonía, S Greece 38°02′N 21°54′E
111 J16 **Katowice** *Ger.* Kattowitz. Śląskie, S Poland 50°15′N 19°01′E
153 S15 **Kātoya** West Bengal, NE India 23°39′N 88°11′E
136 E16 **Katrançik Daği** ▲▲ SW Turkey
95 N16 **Katrineholm** Södermanland, C Sweden 58°59′N 16°15′E
96 I11 **Katrine, Loch** ◎ C Scotland, United Kingdom
77 V12 **Katsina** Katsina, N Nigeria 12°59′N 07°33′E
77 U12 **Katsina** ⬖ *state* N Nigeria
67 P8 **Katsina Ala** ≈ S Nigeria
164 C13 **Katsumoto** Nagasaki, Iki, SW Japan 33°49′N 129°42′E
165 P13 **Katsuta** *var.* Katuta. Ibaraki, Honshū, S Japan 36°24′N 140°32′E
165 O14 **Katsuura** *var.* Katuura. Chiba, Honshū, S Japan 35°09′N 140°16′E
164 K12 **Katsuyama** *var.* Katuyama. Fukui, Honshū, SW Japan 36°00′N 136°30′E
164 H12 **Katsuyama** Okayama, Honshū, SW Japan 35°06′N 133°43′E
Kattakurgan *see* Kattaqo'rg'on
147 N11 **Kattaqo'rg'on** *Rus.* Kattakurgan. Samarqand Viloyati, C Uzbekistan 39°56′N 66°11′E
115 O23 **Kattavía** Ródos, Dodekánisa, Greece, Aegean Sea 35°56′N 27°47′E
95 I21 **Kattegat** *Dan.* Kattegatt. *strait* N Europe
Kattegatt *see* Kattegat
95 P19 **Katthammarsvik** Gotland, SE Sweden 57°27′N 18°54′E
Kattowitz *see* Katowice
122 J13 **Katun'** ≈ S Russian Federation
Katuta *see* Katsuta
Katuura *see* Katsuura
Katuyama *see* Katsuyama
Katwijk *see* Katwijk aan Zee
98 G11 **Katwijk aan Zee** *var.* Katwijk. Zuid-Holland, W Netherlands 59°12′N 04°24′E
38 B8 **Kaua'i** *var.* Kauai. *island* Hawaiian Islands, Hawai'i, USA, C Pacific Ocean
Kauai *see* Kaua'i
38 C8 **Kaua'i Channel** *var.* Kauai Channel. *channel* Hawai'i, USA, C Pacific Ocean
Kauai Channel *see* Kaua'i Channel
171 R13 **Kaubalatmada, Gunung** *var.* Kaplamada. ▲ Pulau Buru, E Indonesia 03°16′S 126°17′E
191 U10 **Kauehi** *atoll* Îles Tuamotu, C French Polynesia
Kauen *see* Kaunas
101 K24 **Kaufbeuren** Bayern, S Germany 47°53′N 10°37′E
25 U7 **Kaufman** Texas, SW USA 32°35′N 96°18′W
101 I15 **Kaufungen** Hessen, C Germany 51°16′N 09°39′E
93 K17 **Kauhajoki** Länsi-Suomi, W Finland 62°26′N 22°10′E
93 K16 **Kauhava** Länsi-Suomi, W Finland 63°06′N 23°08′E
30 M7 **Kaukauna** Wisconsin, N USA 44°18′N 88°18′W
92 L11 **Kaukonen** Lappi, N Finland 67°28′N 24°49′E
38 A8 **Kaulakahi Channel** *channel* Hawai'i, USA, C Pacific Ocean
38 E9 **Kaunakakai** Moloka'i, Hawaii, USA, C Pacific Ocean 21°05′N 157°01′W
38 F12 **Kaunā Point** *var.* Kauna Point. *headland* Hawai'i, USA, C Pacific Ocean 19°02′N 155°52′W
Kauna Point *see* Kaunā Point
118 F13 **Kaunas** *Ger.* Kauen, *Pol.* Kowno; *prev. Rus.* Kovno. Kaunas, C Lithuania 54°54′N 23°57′E
118 F13 **Kaunas** ⬖ *province* C Lithuania
186 C6 **Kaup** East Sepik, NW Papua New Guinea 03°50′S 144°01′E
77 U12 **Kaura Namoda** Zamfara, NW Nigeria 12°43′N 06°17′E
Kaushany *see* Căuşeni
93 K16 **Kaustinen** Länsi-Suomi, W Finland 63°33′N 23°40′E
99 M23 **Kautenbach** Diekirch, NE Luxembourg 49°57′N 06°01′E
92 K10 **Kautokeino** *Lapp.* Guovdageaidnu. Finnmark, N Norway 69°N 23°01′E
Kavadar *see* Kavadarci
113 P19 **Kavadarci** *Turk.* Kavadar. C Macedonia 41°25′N 22°00′E
Kavaja *see* Kavajë
113 K20 **Kavajë** *It.* Cavaia, Kavaja. Tiranë, W Albania 41°11′N 19°33′E
114 M13 **Kavak Çayı** ≈ NW Turkey
Kavakli *see* Topolovgrad
114 I13 **Kavála** *prev.* Kavalla. Anatolikí Makedonía kai Thráki, NE Greece 40°57′N 24°26′E
114 I13 **Kaválas, Kólpos** *gulf* Aegean Sea, NE Mediterranean Sea
155 J17 **Kāvali** Andhra Pradesh, E India 15°05′N 80°02′E
Kavalla *see* Kavála
Kavango *see* Cubango/Okavango
155 C21 **Kavaratti** Lakshadweep, SW India 10°33′N 72°38′E
114 O8 **Kavarna** Dobrich, NE Bulgaria 43°27′N 28°21′E
118 G12 **Kavarskas** Utena, E Lithuania 55°27′N 24°55′E
76 I13 **Kavendou** ▲ C Guinea 10°49′N 12°14′W
Kavengo *see* Cubango/Okavango
155 F20 **Kāveri** *var.* Cauvery. ≈ S India
186 G5 **Kavieng** *var.* Kaewieng. New Ireland, NE Papua New Guinea 04°13′S 152°11′E
83 H16 **Kavimba** North-West, NE Botswana 18°02′S 24°38′E
83 I15 **Kavingu** Southern, S Zambia 15°39′S 26°03′E
143 Q6 **Kavīr, Dasht-e** *var.* Great Salt Desert. *salt pan* N Iran
Kavirondo Gulf *see* Winam Gulf
Kavkaz *see* Caucasus
95 K23 **Kävlinge** Skåne, S Sweden 55°47′N 13°05′E
82 G12 **Kavungo** Moxico, E Angola 11°31′S 22°59′E
165 Q8 **Kawabe** Akita, Honshū, C Japan 39°39′N 140°14′E
165 R9 **Kawai** Iwate, Honshū, C Japan 39°36′N 141°40′E
38 A8 **Kawaihoa Point** *headland* Ni'ihau, Hawai'i, USA, C Pacific Ocean 21°47′N 160°12′W
184 K3 **Kawakawa** Northland, North Island, New Zealand 35°23′S 174°06′E
82 I13 **Kawama** North Western, NW Zambia 13°04′S 25°59′E
82 K11 **Kawambwa** Luapula, N Zambia 09°45′S 29°10′E
154 K11 **Kawardha** Chhattīsgarh, C India 21°59′N 81°12′E
14 I14 **Kawartha Lakes** ◎ Ontario, SE Canada
165 O13 **Kawasaki** Kanagawa, Honshū, S Japan 35°32′N 139°41′E
171 R12 **Kawassi** Pulau Obi, E Indonesia 01°32′S 127°25′E
165 R6 **Kawauchi** Aomori, Honshū, C Japan 41°11′N 141°00′E
184 L5 **Kawau Island** *island* N New Zealand
184 N10 **Kaweka Range** ▲▲ North Island, New Zealand
Kawelecht *see* Puhja
184 O8 **Kawerau** Bay of Plenty, North Island, New Zealand 38°06′S 176°43′E
184 L8 **Kawhia** Waikato, North Island, New Zealand 38°04′S 174°49′E
184 K8 **Kawhia Harbour** *inlet* North Island, New Zealand
35 V8 **Kawich Peak** ▲ Nevada, W USA 38°00′N 116°27′W
35 V9 **Kawich Range** ▲▲ Nevada, W USA
14 G12 **Kawigamog Lake** ◎ Ontario, S Canada
171 P9 **Kawio, Kepulauan** *island group* N Indonesia
167 N9 **Kawkareik** Kayin State, S Burma (Myanmar) 16°33′N 98°18′E
27 O8 **Kaw Lake** ⊠ Oklahoma, C USA
166 M3 **Kawlin** Sagaing, N Burma (Myanmar) 23°48′N 95°41′E
Kawm Umbū *see* Kom Ombo
Kawthule State *see* Karen State
Kaxgar *see* Kashi
158 D7 **Kaxgar He** ≈ NW China
158 J5 **Kax He** ≈ NW China
77 P12 **Kaya** C Burkina 13°04′N 01°09′W
167 N6 **Kayah State** ⬖ *state* C Burma (Myanmar)
39 T12 **Kayak Island** *island* Alaska, USA
114 M11 **Kayalıköy Barajı** ⊠ NW Turkey
166 M8 **Kayan** Yangon, SW Burma (Myanmar) 16°54′N 96°35′E
Kayangel Islands *see* Ngcheangel
155 G23 **Kāyankulam** Kerala, SW India 09°10′N 76°31′E
169 V9 **Kayan, Sungai** *prev.* Kajan. ≈ Borneo, C Indonesia
144 F14 **Kaydak, Sor** *salt flat* SW Kazakhstan
Kaydanovo *see* Dzyarzhynsk Belarus
37 N9 **Kayenta** Arizona, SW USA 36°43′N 110°15′W
76 J11 **Kayes** Kayes, W Mali 14°26′N 11°22′W
76 J11 **Kayes** ⬖ *region* SW Mali
Kayin State *see* Karen State
145 U10 **Kaynar** *Kaz.* Qaynar, *var.* Kajnar. Vostochnyy Kazakhstan, E Kazakhstan 49°13′N 77°27′E
Kaynary *see* Căinari
83 H15 **Kayoya** Western, W Zambia 16°13′S 24°09′E
Kayrakkum *see* Qayroqqum
Kayrakkumskoye Vodokhranilishche *see* Qayroqqum, Obanbori
136 K14 **Kayseri** *var.* Kaisaria; *anc.* Caesarea Mazaca, Mazaca. Kayseri, C Turkey 38°42′N 35°28′E
136 K14 **Kayseri** *var.* Kaisaria. ⬖ *province* C Turkey
36 L2 **Kaysville** Utah, W USA 41°10′N 111°55′W
Kayyngdy *see* Kaindy
14 L11 **Kazabazua** Québec, SE Canada 45°58′N 76°00′W
14 L12 **Kazabazua** ≈ Québec, SE Canada
123 Q7 **Kazach'ye** Respublika Sakha (Yakutiya), NE Russian Federation 70°38′N 135°54′E
Kazakdar'ya *see* Qozoqdaryo
146 E9 **Kazakhlyshor, Solonchak** *var.* Solonchak Shorkazakhly. *salt marsh* NW Turkmenistan
Kazakhskaya SSR/Kazakh Soviet Socialist Republic *see* Kazakhstan
145 R9 **Kazakhskiy Melkosopochnik** *Eng.* Kazakh Uplands, Kirghiz Steppe, *Kaz.* Saryarqa. *uplands* C Kazakhstan
144 L12 **Kazakhstan** *off.* Republic of Kazakhstan, *var.* Kazakstan, *Kaz.* Qazaqstan, Qazaqstan Respublikasy; *prev.* Kazakh Soviet Socialist Republic, *Rus.* Kazakhskaya SSR. ◆ *republic* C Asia
Kazakhstan, Republic of *see* Kazakhstan
Kazakh Uplands *see* Kazakhskiy Melkosopochnik
Kazakstan *see* Kazakhstan
144 L14 **Kazalinsk** Kzyl-Orda, S Kazakhstan 45°45′N 62°01′E
127 R4 **Kazan'** Respublika Tatarstan, W Russian Federation 55°43′N 49°07′E
8 M10 **Kazan** ≈ Nunavut, NW Canada
127 R4 **Kazan'** ✈ Respublika Tatarstan, W Russian Federation 55°46′N 49°21′E
Kazandzhik *see* Bereket
117 R8 **Kazanka** Mykolayivs'ka Oblast', S Ukraine 47°49′N 32°50′E
Kazanketken *see* Qozonketkan
Kazanlik *see* Kazanlŭk
114 J9 **Kazanlŭk** *prev.* Kazanlik. Stara Zagora, C Bulgaria 42°38′N 25°24′E
165 Y16 **Kazan-rettō** *Eng.* Volcano Islands. *island group* SE Japan
117 V12 **Kazantip, Mys** *headland* S Ukraine 45°27′N 35°50′E
147 U9 **Kazarman** Narynskaya Oblast', C Kyrgyzstan 41°21′N 74°03′E
Kazatin *see* Kozyatyn
Kazbegi *see* Qazbegi
Kazbegi *see* Kazbek
137 T9 **Kazbek** *var.* Kazbegi, *Geor.* Mqinvartsveri. ▲ N Georgia 42°43′N 44°28′E
82 M13 **Kazembe** Eastern, NE Zambia 12°06′S 32°45′E
143 N11 **Kāzerūn** Fārs, S Iran 29°41′N 51°38′E
125 R12 **Kazhym** Respublika Komi, NW Russian Federation 60°19′N 51°26′E
Kazi Ahmad *see* Qāzi Ahmad
Kazi Magomed *see* Qazimämmäd
136 H16 **Kazımkarabekir** Karaman, S Turkey 37°13′N 32°58′E
111 M20 **Kazincbarcika** Borsod-Abaúj-Zemplén, NE Hungary 48°15′N 20°40′E
119 H17 **Kazlowshchyna** *Pol.* Kozlowszczyzna, *Rus.* Kozlovshchina. Hrodzyenskaya Voblasts', W Belarus 53°19′N 25°18′E
119 E14 **Kazlų Rūda** Marijampolė, S Lithuania 54°45′N 23°28′E
144 E9 **Kaztalovka** Zapadnyy Kazakhstan, W Kazakhstan 49°45′N 48°42′E
79 K22 **Kazumba** Kasai-Occidental, S Dem. Rep. Congo 06°25′S 22°02′E
165 Q8 **Kazuno** Akita, Honshū, C Japan 40°14′N 140°48′E
Kazvin *see* Qazvīn
118 J12 **Kaz'yany** *Rus.* Koz'yany. Vitsyebskaya Voblasts', NW Belarus 55°18′N 26°52′E
122 H9 **Kazym** ≈ N Russian Federation
110 H10 **Kcynia** *Ger.* Exin. Kujawsko-pomorskie, C Poland 53°00′N 17°29′E
Kéa *see* Tziá
Kéa *see* Ioulís
38 H11 **Kea'au** *var.* Keaau. Hawaii, USA, C Pacific Ocean 19°36′N 155°01′W
Keaau *see* Kea'au
38 F11 **Keāhole Point** *var.* Keahole Point. *headland* Hawai'i, USA, C Pacific Ocean 19°43′N 156°03′W
38 G12 **Kealakekua** Hawaii, USA, C Pacific Ocean 19°31′N 155°56′W
38 H11 **Kea, Mauna** ▲ Hawai'i, USA 19°50′N 155°30′W
37 N10 **Keams** Arizona, SW USA 35°47′N 110°09′W
Kéamu *see* Aneityum
29 O16 **Kearney** Nebraska, C USA 40°42′N 99°06′W
36 L3 **Kearns** Utah, W USA 40°39′N 112°00′W
115 H20 **Kéas, Stenó** *strait* SE Greece
137 O14 **Keban Barajı** *dam* C Turkey
137 O14 **Keban Barajı** ⊠ C Turkey
77 S13 **Kebbi** ⬖ *state* NW Nigeria
76 G10 **Kébémèr** NW Senegal 15°24′N 16°25′W
74 M7 **Kebili** *var.* Qibilī. C Tunisia 33°42′N 09°06′E
138 H4 **Kebir, Nahr el** ≈ NW Syria
80 A10 **Kebkabiya** Northern Darfur, W Sudan 13°39′N 24°05′E
92 I11 **Kebnekaise** ▲ N Sweden 68°01′N 18°24′E
81 M14 **K'ebrī Dehar** Sumalē, E Ethiopia 06°43′N 44°15′E
148 K15 **Kech** ≈ SW Pakistan
10 K10 **Kechika** ≈ British Columbia, W Canada
111 K23 **Kecskemét** Bács-Kiskun, C Hungary 46°54′N 19°42′E
168 J6 **Kedah** ⬖ *state* Peninsular Malaysia
118 F12 **Kėdainiai** Kaunas, C Lithuania 55°19′N 24°00′E
152 K8 **Kedārnāth** Uttarakhand, N India 30°44′N 79°03′E
Kedder *see* Kehra
13 N13 **Kedgwick** New Brunswick, SE Canada 47°38′N 67°21′W
169 R16 **Kediri** Jawa, C Indonesia 07°45′S 112°01′E
171 Y13 **Kedir Sarmi** Papua, E Indonesia 02°00′S 139°01′E
163 V7 **Kedong** Heilongjiang, NE China 48°00′N 126°15′E
76 I12 **Kédougou** SE Senegal 12°35′N 12°09′W
122 I11 **Kedrovyy** Tomskaya Oblast', C Russian Federation 57°31′N 79°45′E
111 H16 **Kędzierzyn-Kozle** *Ger.* Heydebrech. Opolskie, S Poland 50°20′N 18°12′E
8 H8 **Keele** ≈ Northwest Territories, NW Canada
10 K6 **Keele Peak** ▲ Yukon Territory, NW Canada 63°31′N 130°21′W
Keelung *see* Chilung
19 N10 **Keene** New Hampshire, NE USA 42°56′N 72°14′W
99 H17 **Keerbergen** Vlaams Brabant, C Belgium 51°01′N 04°39′E
83 E21 **Keetmanshoop** Karas, S Namibia 26°36′S 18°08′E
12 A11 **Keewatin** Ontario, S Canada 49°47′N 94°30′W
29 V4 **Keewatin** Minnesota, N USA 47°24′N 93°04′W
Kefallinía *see* Kefallonía
115 B18 **Kefallonía** *var.* Kefallinía. *island* Iónia Nisiá, Greece, C Mediterranean Sea
115 M22 **Kéfalos** Kos, Dodekánisa, Greece, Aegean Sea 36°44′N 26°58′E
171 Q17 **Kefamenanu** Timor, C Indonesia 09°31′S 124°29′E
Kefar Sava *see* Kfar Sava
Kefe *see* Feodosiya
77 V15 **Keffi** Nassarawa, C Nigeria 08°52′N 07°54′E
92 H4 **Keflavík** Reykjanes, W Iceland 64°01′N 22°35′W
92 H4 **Keflavik** ✈ (Reykjavík) Reykjanes, W Iceland 63°58′N 22°37′W
Kegalee *see* Kegalla
155 J25 **Kegalla** *var.* Kegalee, Kegalle. Sabaragamuwa Province, C Sri Lanka 07°14′N 80°21′E
Kegalle *see* Kegalla
Kegayli *see* Kegeyli
Kegel *see* Keila
145 W16 **Kegen** Almaty, SE Kazakhstan 42°58′N 79°12′E
146 H7 **Kegeyli** *prev.* Kegayli. Qoraqalpog'iston Respublikasi, W Uzbekistan 42°46′N 59°49′E
101 F22 **Kehl** Baden-Württemberg, SW Germany 48°34′N 07°49′E
118 H3 **Kehra** *Ger.* Kedder. Harjumaa, NW Estonia 59°19′N 25°21′E
117 U6 **Kehychivka** Kharkivs'ka Oblast', E Ukraine 49°18′N 35°46′E
97 L17 **Keighley** N England, United Kingdom 53°51′N 01°58′W
Kei Islands *see* Kai, Kepulauan
Keijō *see* Sŏul
118 G3 **Keila** *Ger.* Kegel. Harjumaa, NW Estonia 59°18′N 24°29′E
Keilberg *see* Klínovec
83 F23 **Keimoes** Northern Cape, W South Africa 28°41′S 20°59′E
Keina/Keinis *see* Käina
Keishū *see* Kyŏngju
77 T11 **Keïta** Tahoua, C Niger 14°45′N 05°40′E
78 J12 **Kéita, Bahr** *var.* Doka. ≈ S Chad
182 K10 **Keith** South Australia 36°01′S 140°22′E
96 K8 **Keith** NE Scotland, United Kingdom 57°33′N 02°57′W
26 K3 **Keith Sebelius Lake** ⊠ Kansas, C USA
32 G11 **Keizer** Oregon, NW USA 44°59′N 123°01′W
38 A8 **Kekaha** Kaua'i, Hawaii, USA, C Pacific Ocean 21°58′N 159°43′W
147 U10 **Këk-Art** *prev.* Alaykel', Alay-Kuu. Oshskaya Oblast', SW Kyrgyzstan 40°16′N 74°21′E
147 W10 **Këk-Aygyr** *var.* Keyaygyr. Narynskaya Oblast', C Kyrgyzstan 40°42′N 75°37′E
147 V9 **Këk-Dzhar** Narynskaya Oblast', C Kyrgyzstan 41°28′N 74°48′E
14 L8 **Kekek** ≈ Québec, SE Canada
185 K15 **Kekerengu** Canterbury, South Island, New Zealand 41°55′S 174°05′E
111 L21 **Kékes** ▲ N Hungary 47°53′N 19°59′E
171 P17 **Kekneno, Gunung** ▲ Timor, S Indonesia
147 S9 **Këk-Tash** *Kir.* Kök-Tash. Dzhalal-Abadskaya Oblast', W Kyrgyzstan 41°08′N 72°25′E
81 M15 **K'elafo** Sumalē, E Ethiopia 05°36′N 44°12′E
169 U10 **Kelai, Sungai** ≈ Borneo, N Indonesia
Kelamayi *see* Karamay
Kelang *see* Klang
168 K7 **Kelantan** ⬖ *state* Peninsular Malaysia
Kelantan *see* Kelantan, Sungai
168 K7 **Kelantan, Sungai** *var.* Kelantan. ≈ Peninsular Malaysia
Kelat *see* Kālat
Këlcyra *see* Këlcyrë
113 L22 **Këlcyrë** *var.* Këlcyra. Gjirokastër, S Albania 40°19′N 20°10′E
Kelifskiy Uzboy *see* Kelif Uzboýy
146 L14 **Kelif Uzboýy** *Rus.* Kelifskiy Uzboy. *salt marsh* E Turkmenistan
137 O12 **Kelkit** Gümüşhane, NE Turkey 40°07′N 39°28′E
136 M12 **Kelkit Çayı** ≈ N Turkey
79 G18 **Kéllé** Cuvette-Quest, W Congo 0°04′S 14°33′E
77 W11 **Kellé** Zinder, S Niger 14°10′N 10°10′E
145 P7 **Kellerovka** Severnyy Kazakhstan, N Kazakhstan 53°51′N 69°15′E
8 I5 **Kellett, Cape** *headland* Banks Island, Northwest Territories, NW Canada 71°57′N 125°55′W

◆ Country
● Country Capital
◇ Dependent Territory
○ Dependent Territory Capital
⬖ Administrative Regions
✈ International Airport
▲ Mountain
▲▲ Mountain Range
Ѫ Volcano
≈ River
◎ Lake
⊠ Reservoir

31 S11 Kelleys Island island Ohio, N USA
33 N8 Kellogg Idaho, NW USA 47°30′N 116°07′W
92 M12 Kelloselkä Lappi, N Finland 66°56′N 28°52′E
97 F17 Kells Ir. Ceanannas. Meath, E Ireland 53°44′N 06°53′W
118 E12 Kelmė Šiauliai, C Lithuania 55°39′N 22°57′E
99 M19 Kelmis var. La Calamine. Liège, E Belgium 50°43′N 06°01′E
78 H12 Kélo Tandjilé, SW Chad 09°21′N 15°50′E
83 I14 Kelongwa North Western, NW Zambia 13°41′S 26°19′E
11 N17 Kelowna British Columbia, SW Canada 49°50′N 119°29′W
11 X12 Kelsey Manitoba, C Canada 56°02′N 96°31′W
34 M6 Kelseyville California, W USA 38°58′N 122°51′W
96 K13 Kelso SE Scotland, United Kingdom 55°36′N 02°27′W
32 G10 Kelso Washington, NW USA 46°09′N 122°54′W
195 W15 Keltie, Cape headland Antarctica
Keltsy see Kielce
168 L9 Keluang var. Kluang. Johor, Peninsular Malaysia 02°01′N 103°18′E
168 M11 Kelume Pulau Lingga, W Indonesia 0°12′S 104°27′E
11 U15 Kelvington Saskatchewan, S Canada 52°10′N 103°30′W
124 J7 Kem' Respublika Kareliya, NW Russian Federation 64°55′N 34°18′E
124 I7 Kem' NW Russian Federation
137 O13 Kemah Erzincan, E Turkey 39°35′N 39°02′E
137 N13 Kemaliye Erzincan, C Turkey 39°16′N 38°29′E
Kemaman see Cukai
Kemanlar see Isperikh
10 K14 Kemano British Columbia, SW Canada 53°39′N 127°58′W
Kemarat see Khemmarat
171 P12 Kembani Pulau Peleng, N Indonesia 01°32′S 122°57′E
136 F17 Kemer Antalya, SW Turkey 36°39′N 30°33′E
122 J12 Kemerovo prev. Shcheglovsk. Kemerovskaya Oblast', C Russian Federation 55°25′N 86°05′E
122 K12 Kemerovskaya Oblast' ◆ province S Russian Federation
92 L13 Kemi Lappi, NW Finland 65°46′N 24°34′E
92 M12 Kemijärvi Swe. Kemiträsk. Lappi, N Finland 66°41′N 27°24′E
92 M12 Kemijärvi ◎ N Finland
92 L13 Kemijoki NW Finland
147 V7 Kemin prev. Bystrovka. Chuyskaya Oblast', N Kyrgyzstan
92 L13 Keminmaa Lappi, NW Finland 65°49′N 24°34′E
Kemins Island see Nikumaroro
Kemiö see Kimito
Kemiträsk see Kemijärvi
127 P5 Kemlya Respublika Mordoviya, W Russian Federation 54°42′N 45°16′E
99 B18 Kemmel West-Vlaanderen, W Belgium 50°42′N 02°51′E
33 S16 Kemmerer Wyoming, C USA 41°47′N 110°32′W
Kemmuna see Comino
79 I14 Kémo ◆ prefecture S Central African Republic
25 U7 Kemp Texas, SW USA 32°26′N 96°13′W
93 L14 Kempele Oulu, C Finland 64°56′N 25°26′E
101 D15 Kempen Nordrhein-Westfalen, W Germany 51°22′N 06°25′E
25 Q5 Kemp, Lake ◎ Texas, SW USA
195 W5 Kemp Land physical region Antarctica
25 S9 Kempner Texas, SW USA 31°03′N 98°01′W
44 H3 Kemp's Bay Andros Island, W Bahamas 24°02′N 77°32′W
183 U6 Kempsey New South Wales, SE Australia 31°05′S 152°50′E
101 J24 Kempten Bayern, S Germany 47°44′N 10°19′E
15 N9 Kempt, Lac ◎ Québec, SE Canada
183 P17 Kempton Tasmania, SE Australia 42°34′S 147°13′E
154 J9 Ken C India
39 R12 Kenai Alaska, USA 60°33′N 151°15′W
0 D5 Kenai Mountains ▲ Alaska, USA
39 R12 Kenai Peninsula peninsula Alaska, USA
21 V11 Kenansville North Carolina, SE USA 34°57′N 77°54′W
146 A10 Kenar prev. Rus. Ufra. Balkan Welaýaty, NW Turkmenistan 40°00′N 53°05′E
121 U13 Kenâyis, Râs el- headland N Egypt 31°13′N 27°53′E
97 K16 Kendal NW England, United Kingdom 54°20′N 02°45′W
23 Y16 Kendall Florida, SE USA 25°39′N 80°18′W
9 O8 Kendall, Cape headland Nunavut, E Canada 63°31′N 87°09′W
18 J15 Kendall Park New Jersey, NE USA 40°25′N 74°33′W
31 Q11 Kendallville Indiana, N USA 41°24′N 85°10′W
171 P14 Kendari Sulawesi, C Indonesia 03°57′S 122°36′E
169 Q13 Kendawangan Borneo, C Indonesia 02°32′S 110°13′E
154 O12 Kendrāpāra var. Kendrāparha. Orissa, E India 20°29′N 86°25′E
Kendrāparha see Kendrāpāra
154 O11 Kendujhargarh prev. Keonjihargarh. Orissa, E India 21°38′N 85°40′E
25 S13 Kenedy Texas, SW USA 28°49′N 97°51′W
76 J15 Kenema SE Sierra Leone 07°55′N 11°12′W
29 P16 Kenesaw Nebraska, C USA 40°37′N 98°39′W
Këneurgench see Köneürgenç
79 H21 Kenge Bandundu, SW Dem. Rep. Congo 04°52′S 16°59′E
Kengen see Kangen
167 O5 Keng Tung var. Kentung. Shan State, E Burma (Myanmar) 21°18′N 99°36′E
83 F23 Kenhardt Northern Cape, W South Africa 29°19′S 21°08′E
76 J12 Kéniéba Kayes, W Mali 12°47′N 11°16′W
Kenimekh see Konimex
169 U7 Keningau Sabah, East Malaysia 05°21′N 116°11′E
74 F6 Kénitra prev. Port-Lyautey. NW Morocco 34°20′N 06°29′W
21 V9 Kenly North Carolina, SE USA 35°39′N 78°16′W
97 B21 Kenmare Ir. Neidín. S Ireland 51°53′N 09°35′W
28 L2 Kenmare North Dakota, N USA 48°40′N 102°04′W
97 A21 Kenmare River Ir. An Ribhéar. inlet NE Atlantic Ocean
18 D10 Kenmore New York, NE USA 42°58′N 78°52′W
25 W8 Kennard Texas, SW USA 31°21′N 95°10′W
29 N10 Kennebec South Dakota, N USA 43°53′N 99°51′W
19 Q7 Kennebec River Maine, NE USA
19 P9 Kennebunk Maine, NE USA 43°22′N 70°33′W
39 R13 Kennedy Entrance strait Alaska, USA
166 L3 Kennedy Peak ▲ W Burma (Myanmar) 23°18′N 93°52′E
22 K9 Kenner Louisiana, S USA 29°57′N 90°15′W
180 I8 Kenneth Range ▲ Western Australia
27 Y9 Kennett Missouri, C USA 36°15′N 90°04′W
18 I16 Kennett Square Pennsylvania, NE USA 39°50′N 75°40′W
32 K10 Kennewick Washington, NW USA 46°12′N 119°08′W
12 E11 Kenogami Ontario, S Canada
15 Q7 Kénogami, Lac ◎ Québec, SE Canada
14 G8 Kenogami Lake Ontario, S Canada 48°04′N 80°10′W
14 F7 Kenogamissi Lake ◎ Ontario, S Canada
10 I6 Keno Hill Yukon Territory, NW Canada 63°54′N 135°18′W
12 A11 Kenora Ontario, S Canada 49°47′N 94°26′W
31 N9 Kenosha Wisconsin, N USA 42°34′N 87°50′W
13 P14 Kensington Prince Edward Island, SE Canada 46°26′N 63°39′W
26 L3 Kensington Kansas, C USA 39°46′N 99°01′W
32 I11 Kent Oregon, NW USA 45°14′N 120°43′W
24 J9 Kent Texas, SW USA 31°03′N 104°13′W
32 H8 Kent Washington, NW USA 47°22′N 122°13′W
97 P22 Kent cultural region SE England, United Kingdom
145 P16 Kentau Yuzhnyy Kazakhstan, S Kazakhstan 43°28′N 68°41′E
183 P14 Kent Group island group Tasmania, SE Australia
31 N12 Kentland Indiana, N USA 40°46′N 87°26′W
31 R12 Kenton Ohio, N USA 40°39′N 83°36′W
8 K7 Kent Peninsula peninsula Nunavut, N Canada
115 F14 Kentrikí Makedonía Eng. Macedonia Central. ◆ region N Greece
20 J6 Kentucky off. Commonwealth of Kentucky, also known as Bluegrass State. ◆ state C USA
20 H8 Kentucky Lake ▣ Kentucky/Tennessee, S USA
Kentung see Keng Tung
13 P15 Kentville Nova Scotia, SE Canada 45°04′N 64°30′W
22 K8 Kentwood Louisiana, S USA 30°56′N 90°30′W
31 P9 Kentwood Michigan, N USA 42°52′N 85°33′W
81 H17 Kenya off. Republic of Kenya. ◆ republic E Africa
Kenya, Mount see Kirinyaga
Kenya, Republic of see Kenya
168 L7 Kenyir, Tasik var. Tasek Kenyir. ◎ Peninsular Malaysia
29 W10 Kenyon Minnesota, N USA 44°16′N 92°59′W
29 Y16 Keokuk Iowa, C USA 40°24′N 91°22′W
Keonjihargarh see Kendujhargarh
Kéos see Tziá
29 X16 Keosauqua Iowa, C USA 40°43′N 91°58′W
29 X15 Keota Iowa, C USA 41°21′N 91°57′W
21 O11 Keowee, Lake ▣ South Carolina, SE USA
124 I7 Kepa var. Kepe. Respublika Kareliya, NW Russian Federation 65°09′N 32°15′E
Kepe see Kepa
189 O13 Kepirohi Falls waterfall Pohnpei, E Micronesia
185 B22 Kepler Mountains ▲ South Island, New Zealand
111 I14 Kępno Wielkopolskie, C Poland 51°17′N 17°57′E
65 C24 Keppel Island island N Falkland Islands
Keppel Island see Niuatoputapu
65 C23 Keppel Sound sound N Falkland Islands
136 D12 Kepsut Balıkesir, NW Turkey 39°41′N 28°09′E
168 M11 Kepulauan Riau off. Propinsi Kepulauan Riau. ◆ province NW Indonesia
Kequ see Gadê
171 V13 Kerai Papua, E Indonesia 03°53′S 134°30′E
Kerak see Al Karak
155 F22 Kerala ◆ state S India
175 R16 Kerama-rettō island group SW Japan
183 N10 Kerang Victoria, SE Australia 35°46′S 144°01′E
Kerasunt see Giresun
115 H19 Keratéa var. Keratea. Attikí, C Greece 37°48′N 23°58′E
Keratea see Keratéa
93 M19 Kerava Swe. Kervo. Etelä-Suomi, S Finland 60°25′N 25°10′E
Kerbala/Kerbela see Karbalā'
32 F15 Kerby Oregon, NW USA 42°10′N 123°39′W
117 W12 Kerch Rus. Kerch'. Respublika Krym, SE Ukraine 45°22′N 36°30′E
Kerch' see Kerch
Kerchens'ka Protska/Kerchenskiy Proliv see Kerch Strait
117 V13 Kerchens'kyy Pivostriv peninsula S Ukraine
121 V4 Kerch Strait var. Bosporus Cimmerius, Enikale Strait, Rus. Kerchenskiy Proliv, Ukr. Kerchens'ka Protska. strait Black Sea/Sea of Azov
Kerdilio see Kerdýlio
114 H13 Kerdýlio var. Kerdilio. ▲ N Greece 40°46′N 23°37′E
186 D8 Kerema Gulf, S Papua New Guinea 07°59′S 145°46′E
Keremitlik see Lyulyakovo
136 I9 Kerempe Burnu headland N Turkey 42°01′N 33°20′E
80 J9 Keren var. Cheren. C Eritrea 15°45′N 38°22′E
25 U7 Kerens Texas, SW USA 32°07′N 96°13′W
184 M6 Kerepehi Waikato, North Island, New Zealand 37°18′S 175°33′E
145 P10 Kerey, Ozero ◎ C Kazakhstan
Kergel see Kärla
173 Q12 Kerguelen island C French Southern and Antarctic Territories
173 Q13 Kerguelen Plateau undersea feature S Indian Ocean
115 C20 Kerí Zákynthos, Iónia Nisiá, Greece, C Mediterranean Sea 37°40′N 20°48′E
81 H19 Kericho Rift Valley, W Kenya 0°22′S 35°19′E
184 K2 Kerikeri Northland, North Island, New Zealand 35°14′S 173°58′E
93 O17 Kerimäki Itä-Suomi, E Finland 61°56′N 29°18′E
168 K12 Kerinci, Gunung ▲ Sumatera, W Indonesia 02°00′S 101°40′E
Keriya see Yutian
158 H9 Keriya He NW China
98 I9 Kerkbuurt Noord-Holland, C Netherlands 52°29′N 05°08′E
98 J13 Kerkdriel Gelderland, C Netherlands 51°46′N 05°21′E
75 N6 Kerkenah, Îles de var. Kerkenna Islands, Ar. Juzur Qarqannah. island group E Tunisia
Kerkenna Islands see Kerkenah, Îles de
115 M20 Kerketévs ▲ Sámos, Dodekánisa, Greece, Aegean Sea 37°44′N 26°39′E
29 T8 Kerkhoven Minnesota, N USA 45°12′N 95°18′W
Kerki see Atamyrat
Kerkichi see Kerkiçi
146 M14 Kerkiçi Rus. Kerkichi. Lebap Welaýaty, E Turkmenistan 37°46′N 65°18′E
115 F16 Kerkíneo prehistoric site Thessalía, C Greece
114 G12 Kerkíni, Límni var. Límni Kerkinitis. ◎ N Greece
Kerkinitis Límni see Kerkíni, Límni
Kérkira see Kérkyra
99 M18 Kerkrade Limburg, SE Netherlands 50°53′N 06°04′E
Kerkuk see Kirkūk
115 B16 Kérkyra var. Kérkira, Eng. Corfu. Kérkyra, Iónia Nisiá, Greece, C Mediterranean Sea 39°37′N 19°56′E
115 B16 Kérkyra ✈ Kérkyra, Iónia Nisiá, Greece, C Mediterranean Sea 39°36′N 19°55′E
115 A16 Kérkyra var. Kérkira, Eng. Corfu. island Iónia Nisiá, Greece, C Mediterranean Sea
192 K10 Kermadec Islands island group New Zealand, SW Pacific Ocean
175 R10 Kermadec Ridge undersea feature SW Pacific Ocean 30°30′S 178°30′W
175 R11 Kermadec Trench undersea feature SW Pacific Ocean
143 S10 Kermān var. Kirman; anc. Carmana. Kermān, C Iran 30°18′N 57°05′E
143 R11 Kermān off. Ostān-e Kermān, var. Kirman; anc. Carmania. ◆ province SE Iran
143 U12 Kermān, Bīābān-e desert SE Iran
Kermān, Ostān-e see Kermān
142 K6 Kermānshāh var. Qahremānshahr; prev. Bākhtarān. Kermānshāhān, W Iran 34°19′N 47°04′E
143 Q9 Kermānshāh Yazd, C Iran 34°19′N 47°04′E
142 J6 Kermānshāh off. Ostān-e Kermānshāhān; prev. Bākhtarān. ◆ province W Iran
Kermānshāhān, Ostān-e see Kermānshāh
114 L10 Kermen Sliven, C Bulgaria 42°30′N 26°12′E
24 L8 Kermit Texas, SW USA 31°49′N 103°07′W
21 P6 Kermit West Virginia, NE USA 37°51′N 82°24′W
21 S9 Kernersville North Carolina, SE USA 36°12′N 80°13′W
35 S12 Kern River California, W USA
35 S12 Kernville California, W USA 35°44′N 118°25′W
115 K21 Kéros island Kykládes, Greece, Aegean Sea
76 K14 Kérouané SE Guinea 09°16′N 09°00′W
101 D16 Kerpen Nordrhein-Westfalen, W Germany 50°51′N 06°40′E
146 I11 Kerpichli Lebap Welaýaty, NE Turkmenistan 40°12′N 61°09′E
24 M1 Kerrick Texas, SW USA 36°29′N 102°14′W
Kerr Lake see John H. Kerr Reservoir
11 S15 Kerrobert Saskatchewan, S Canada 51°56′N 109°09′W
25 Q11 Kerrville Texas, SW USA 30°03′N 99°09′W
97 B20 Kerry Ir. Ciarraí. cultural region SW Ireland
21 S11 Kershaw South Carolina, SE USA 34°33′N 80°34′W
Kertel see Kärdla
95 H23 Kerteminde Fyn, C Denmark 55°27′N 10°40′E
163 Q7 Kerulen Chin. Herlen He, Mong. Herlen Gol. China/Mongolia
Kervo see Kerava
Kerýneia see Girne
12 H11 Kesagami Lake ◎ Ontario, SE Canada
93 O17 Kesälahti Itä-Suomi, SE Finland 61°54′N 29°49′E
136 B11 Keşan Edirne, NW Turkey 40°52′N 26°37′E
165 R9 Kesennuma Miyagi, Honshū, C Japan 38°55′N 141°35′E
163 V7 Keshan Heilongjiang, NE China 48°00′N 125°46′E
30 M6 Keshena Wisconsin, N USA 44°54′N 88°37′W
136 I13 Keskin Kırıkkale, C Turkey 39°41′N 33°36′E
Késmárk see Kežmarok
124 I6 Kesten'ga var. Kest Enga. Respublika Kareliya, NW Russian Federation 65°53′N 31°47′E
Kest Enga see Kesten'ga
98 K12 Kesteren Gelderland, C Netherlands 51°55′N 05°34′E
14 H14 Keswick Ontario, S Canada 44°15′N 79°26′W
97 K15 Keswick NW England, United Kingdom 54°30′N 03°04′W
111 H24 Keszthely Zala, SW Hungary 46°47′N 17°16′E
122 K11 Ket' C Russian Federation
77 R17 Keta SE Ghana 05°55′N 00°59′E
169 Q12 Ketapang Borneo, C Indonesia 01°50′S 109°59′E
127 O12 Ketchenery prev. Sovetskoye. Respublika Kalmykiya, SW Russian Federation 47°18′N 44°31′E
39 Y14 Ketchikan Revillagigedo Island, Alaska, USA 55°21′N 131°39′W
33 O14 Ketchum Idaho, NW USA 43°40′N 114°24′W
Kete/Kete Krakye see Kete-Krachi
77 Q15 Kete-Krachi var. Kete, Kete Krakye. E Ghana 07°50′N 00°03′W
98 L9 Ketelmeer channel E Netherlands
149 P17 Keti Bandar Sind, SE Pakistan 23°55′N 67°31′E
145 W16 Ketmen', Khrebet ▲ SE Kazakhstan
77 S16 Kétou SE Benin 07°25′N 02°36′E
110 M7 Kętrzyn Ger. Rastenburg. Warmińsko-Mazurskie, NE Poland 54°05′N 21°24′E
97 N20 Kettering C England, United Kingdom 52°24′N 00°44′W
31 R14 Kettering Ohio, N USA 39°41′N 84°10′W
18 F13 Kettle Creek Pennsylvania, NE USA
32 L7 Kettle Falls Washington, NW USA 48°36′N 118°03′W
14 D16 Kettle Point headland Ontario, S Canada 43°12′N 82°01′W
29 V6 Kettle River Minnesota, N USA
186 B7 Ketu W Papua New Guinea
18 G10 Keuka Lake ◎ New York, NE USA
Keupriya see Primorsko
93 L17 Keuruu Länsi-Suomi, C Finland 62°15′N 24°34′E
Kevevára see Kovin
92 L9 Kevo Lapp. Geavvú. Lappi, N Finland 69°42′N 27°08′E
44 M6 Kew North Caicos, N Turks and Caicos Islands 21°52′N 71°57′W
30 K11 Kewanee Illinois, N USA 41°15′N 89°55′W
31 N7 Kewaunee Wisconsin, N USA 44°27′N 87°31′W
30 M3 Keweenaw Bay ◎ Michigan, N USA
31 N2 Keweenaw Peninsula peninsula Michigan, N USA
31 N2 Keweenaw Point peninsula Michigan, N USA
29 N12 Keya Paha River Nebraska/South Dakota, N USA
Keyaygyr see Këk-Aygyr
23 Z16 Key Biscayne Florida, SE USA 25°41′N 80°09′W
26 G8 Keyes Oklahoma, C USA 36°48′N 102°15′W
23 Y17 Key Largo Key Largo, Florida, SE USA 25°06′N 80°25′W
21 U3 Keyser West Virginia, NE USA 39°25′N 78°59′W
27 O9 Keystone Lake ▣ Oklahoma, C USA
36 L16 Keystone Peak ▲ Arizona, SW USA 31°52′N 111°12′W
Keystone State see Pennsylvania
21 U7 Keysville Virginia, NE USA 37°02′N 78°28′W
27 T3 Keytesville Missouri, C USA 39°25′N 92°56′W
23 W17 Key West Florida Keys, Florida, SE USA 24°34′N 81°48′W
127 T1 Kez Udmurtskaya Respublika, NW Russian Federation 57°55′N 53°42′E
Kezdivásárhely see Târgu Secuiesc
122 M12 Kezhma Krasnoyarskiy Kray, C Russian Federation 58°57′N 101°00′E
111 L18 Kežmarok Ger. Käsmark, Hung. Késmárk. Prešovský Kraj, E Slovakia 49°09′N 20°25′E
Kfar Saba see Kfar Sava
138 F10 Kfar Sava var. Kfar Saba; prev. Kefar Sava. Central, C Israel 32°11′N 34°58′E
83 F20 Kgalagadi ◆ district SW Botswana
83 I20 Kgatleng ◆ district SE Botswana
188 F8 Kgkeklau Babeldaob, N Palau
125 R6 Khabarikha var. Chabaricha. Respublika Komi, NW Russian Federation 65°52′N 52°19′E
123 S14 Khabarovsk Khabarovskiy Kray, SE Russian Federation 48°32′N 135°08′E
123 R11 Khabarovskiy Kray ◆ territory E Russian Federation
141 W7 Khabb Abū Ẓaby, E United Arab Emirates 24°39′N 55°43′E
Khabour, Nahr al see Khābūr, Nahr al
Khabura see Al Khābūrah
139 N2 Khābūr, Nahr al var. Nahr al Khabour. Syria/Turkey
Khachmas see Xaçmaz
80 B12 Khadari W Sudan
Khadera see Hadera
141 X12 Khādhil var. Khudal. SE Oman 18°48′N 56°48′E
155 E14 Khadki prev. Kirkee. Mahārāshtra, W India 18°34′N 73°52′E
126 L14 Khadyzhensk Krasnodarskiy Kray, SW Russian Federation 44°26′N 39°31′E
114 N9 Khadzhiyska Reka E Bulgaria
117 P10 Khadzhybeys'kyy Lyman ◎ SW Ukraine
138 K3 Khafsah Ḥalab, N Syria 36°16′N 38°03′E
152 M13 Khāga Uttar Pradesh, N India 25°47′N 81°05′E
153 Q13 Khagaria Bihār, NE India 25°31′N 86°27′E
149 Q13 Khairpur Sind, SE Pakistan 27°30′N 68°50′E
122 K13 Khakasiya, Respublika prev. Khakasskaya Avtonomnaya Oblast', Eng. Khakassia. ◆ autonomous republic C Russian Federation
Khakassia/Khakasskaya Avtonomnaya Oblast' see Khakasiya, Respublika
167 N9 Kha Khaeng, Khao ▲ W Thailand 16°13′N 99°03′E
83 G20 Khakhea var. Kakia. Southern, S Botswana 24°41′S 23°29′E
Khalach see Halaç
Khalándrion see Chalándri
75 T7 Khalīj as Sallūm Ar. Gulf of Salūm. gulf Egypt/Libya
75 X8 Khalīj as Suways var. Suez, Gulf of. gulf NE Egypt
127 W7 Khalilovo Orenburgskaya Oblast', W Russian Federation 51°25′N 58°13′E
Khalkabad see Xalqobod
142 L3 Khalkhāl prev. Herowābād. Ardabīl, NW Iran 37°36′N 48°36′E
Khalkidhikí see Chalkidikí
Khalkís see Chalkída
125 W3 Khal'mer-Yu Respublika Komi, NW Russian Federation 68°00′N 64°45′E
119 M14 Khalopyenichy Rus. Kholopenichi. Minskaya Voblasts', NE Belarus 54°31′N 28°58′E
Khalturin see Orlov
141 Y10 Khalūf var. Al Khaluf. E Oman 20°27′N 57°59′E
154 K10 Khamaria Madhya Pradesh, C India 23°07′N 80°54′E
154 D11 Khambhāt Gujarāt, W India 22°19′N 72°39′E
154 C12 Khambhāt, Gulf of Eng. Gulf of Cambay. gulf W India
167 U10 Khâm Đưc var. Phươc Sơn. Quang Nam-Đa Năng, C Vietnam 15°28′N 107°49′E
154 G12 Khāmgaon Mahārāshtra, C India 20°41′N 76°34′E
141 O14 Khamir var. Khamr. W Yemen 16°N 43°56′E
141 N12 Khamis Mushayt var. Hamīs Musait. 'Asīr, SW Saudi Arabia 18°19′N 42°41′E
155 I18 Khammam Andhra Pradesh, India 17°16′N 80°13′E
123 P10 Khampa Respublika Sakha (Yakutiya), NE Russian Federation 63°43′N 123°02′E
Khamr see Khamir
83 C19 Khan W Namibia
149 Q2 Khānābād Kunduz, NE Afghanistan 36°42′N 69°08′E
Khân Abou Châmâte/Khan Abou Ech Cham see Khān Abū Shāmāt
138 I7 Khān Abū Shāmāt var. Khân Abou Châmâte, Khan Abou Ech Cham. Dimashq, W Syria 33°43′N 36°56′E
Khān al Baghdādī see Al Baghdādī
Khān al Maḥāwīl see Al Maḥāwīl
139 T7 Khān al Mashāhidah Baghdād, C Iraq 33°40′N 44°15′E
139 T10 Khān al Muṣallá An Najaf, S Iraq 32°09′N 44°20′E
139 U6 Khānaqīn Diyālá, E Iraq 34°22′N 45°22′E
139 T11 Khān ar Ruḥbah An Najaf, S Iraq 31°42′N 44°18′E
139 P2 Khān as Sūr Nīnawá, N Iraq 36°28′N 41°36′E
139 T8 Khān Āzād Baghdād, C Iraq 33°08′N 44°21′E
154 N13 Khandaparha prev. Khandpara. Orissa, E India 20°15′N 85°11′E
Khandpara see Khandaparha
149 T2 Khandūd var. Khandud, Wakhan. Badakhshān, NE Afghanistan 36°57′N 72°19′E
Khandud see Khandūd
154 G11 Khandwa Madhya Pradesh, C India 21°49′N 76°23′E
123 R10 Khandyga Respublika Sakha (Yakutiya), NE Russian Federation 62°39′N 135°30′E
149 T10 Khānewāl Punjab, NE Pakistan 30°18′N 71°56′E
149 S10 Khāngarh Punjab, E Pakistan 29°57′N 71°14′E
Khanh Hung see Soc Trăng
Khaniá see Chaniá
Khanka see Xonqa
163 Z8 Khanka, Lake var. Hsing-K'ai Hu, Lake Hanka, Chin. Xingkai Hu, Rus. Ozero Khanka. ◎ China/Russian Federation
Khanka, Ozero see Khanka, Lake
Khankendi see Xankändi
Khanlar see Xanlar
123 O9 Khannya NE Russian Federation
149 S12 Khānpur Punjab, E Pakistan 28°31′N 70°30′E
138 I4 Khān Shaykhūn var. Khan Sheikhun. Idlib, NW Syria 35°27′N 36°38′E
Khan Sheikhun see Khān Shaykhūn
145 S15 Khantau Zhambyl, S Kazakhstan 44°13′N 73°47′E
145 W16 Khan Tengri, Pik ▲ SE Kazakhstan 42°17′N 80°11′E
Khan-Tengri, Pik see Hantengri Feng
167 S9 Khanthabouli prev. Savannakhét. Savannakhét, S Laos 16°38′N 104°49′E
127 V8 Khanty-Mansiysk prev. Ostyako-Voguls'k. Khanty-Mansiyskiy Avtonomnyy Okrug-Yugra, C Russian Federation 61°01′N 69°E
125 V8 Khanty-Mansiyskiy Avtonomnyy Okrug-Yugra ◆ autonomous district C Russian Federation
139 R4 Khānūqah Nīnawýé, C Iraq 35°25′N 43°15′E
138 E11 Khān Yūnis var. Khān Yūnus. S Gaza Strip 31°21′N 34°18′E
Khān Yūnus see Khān Yūnis
Khanzi see Ghanzi
139 U5 Khān Zūr As Sulaymānīyah, E Iraq 35°03′N 45°08′E
167 N10 Khao Laem Reservoir ▣ W Thailand
123 O14 Khapcheranga Chitinskaya Oblast', S Russian Federation 49°46′N 112°21′E
127 Q12 Kharabali Astrakhanskaya Oblast', SW Russian Federation 47°28′N 47°14′E
153 R16 Kharagpur West Bengal, NE India 22°30′N 87°19′E
139 V11 Kharā'ib 'Abd al Karīm Al Muthannā, S Iraq 31°07′N 45°33′E
149 N12 Khārān Baluchistān, SW Pakistan 28°35′N 65°25′E
143 Q8 Kharānaq Yazd, C Iran 31°54′N 54°21′E
Kharbin see Harbin
Kharchi see Mārwār
146 H13 Khardzhagaz Ahal Welaýaty, C Turkmenistan 37°54′N 60°10′E
154 F11 Khargon Madhya Pradesh, C India 21°49′N 75°39′E
149 V7 Khāriān Punjab, NE Pakistan 32°52′N 73°52′E
117 X8 Kharisyz'k Donets'ka Oblast', E Ukraine 48°01′N 38°10′E
117 V5 Kharkiv Rus. Khar'kov. Kharkivs'ka Oblast', NE Ukraine 50°N 36°14′E
117 V5 Kharkiv ✈ Kharkivs'ka Oblast', E Ukraine 49°54′N 36°20′E
Kharkiv see Kharkivs'ka Oblast'
117 U5 Kharkivs'ka Oblast' var. Kharkiv, Rus. Khar'kovskaya Oblast'. ◆ province E Ukraine
Khar'kov see Kharkiv
Khar'kovskaya Oblast' see Kharkivs'ka Oblast'
124 L3 Kharlovka Murmanskaya Oblast', NW Russian Federation 68°47′N 37°09′E
114 K11 Kharmanli Khaskovo, S Bulgaria 41°56′N 25°54′E
114 K11 Kharmanliyska Reka S Bulgaria
124 M13 Kharovsk Vologodskaya Oblast', NW Russian Federation 59°57′N 40°05′E
80 F9 Khartoum var. El Khartûm, Khartum. ● (Sudan) Khartoum, C Sudan 15°33′N 32°32′E
80 F9 Khartoum ◆ state NE Sudan
80 F9 Khartoum ✈ Khartoum, C Sudan 15°36′N 32°37′E
80 F9 Khartoum North Khartoum, C Sudan 15°38′N 32°33′E
117 X8 Khartsyz'k Rus. Khartsyzsk. Donets'ka Oblast', SE Ukraine 48°01′N 38°10′E
Khartsyzsk see Khartsyz'k
Khartum see Khartoum
154 G12 Khās Madhya Pradesh, C India 22°12′N 77°30′E
Khasab see Al Khaṣab
123 S15 Khasan Primorskiy Kray, SE Russian Federation 42°24′N 130°45′E
127 P16 Khasavyurt Respublika Dagestan, SW Russian Federation 43°16′N 46°33′E
143 W12 Khāsh prev. Vāsht. Sīstān va Balūchestān, SE Iran 28°15′N 61°11′E
148 K8 Khāsh, Dasht-e Eng. Khash Desert. desert SW Afghanistan
Khash Desert see Khāsh, Dasht-e
Khashim Al Qirba/Khashm al Qirbah see Khashm el Girba
80 H9 Khashm el Girba var. Khashim Al Qirba, Khashm al Qirbah. Kassala, E Sudan 15°00′N 35°59′E
138 G14 Khashsh, Jabal al ▲ S Jordan
137 S10 Khashuri C Georgia 41°59′N 43°36′E
153 V13 Khāsi Hills hill range NE India
114 K11 Khaskovo Khaskovo, S Bulgaria 41°56′N 25°35′E
114 K11 Khaskovo ◆ province S Bulgaria
122 M7 Khatanga N Russian Federation
Khatanga, Gulf of see Khatangskiy Zaliv
123 N7 Khatangskiy Zaliv var. Gulf of Khatanga. bay N Russian Federation
141 W7 Khatmat al Malāḥah N Oman 24°58′N 56°22′E
143 S16 Khaṭmat al Malāḥah Ash Shāriqah, E United Arab Emirates
123 V7 Khatyrka Chukotskiy Avtonomnyy Okrug, NE Russian Federation 62°03′N 175°09′E
Khauz-Khan see Hanhowuz
Khauzkhanskoye Vodoranilishche see Hanhowuz Suw Howdany
Khavaling see Khovaling
Khavast see Xovos
139 W10 Khawrah, Nahr al S Iraq
141 W7 Khawr Fakkān var. Khor Fakkan. Ash Shāriqah, NE United Arab Emirates 25°22′N 56°19′E
140 L6 Khaybar Al Madīnah, NW Saudi Arabia 25°53′N 39°16′E
Khaybar, Kowtal-e see Khyber Pass
147 S11 Khaydarkan var. Khaydarken. Batkenskaya Oblast', SW Kyrgyzstan 39°56′N 71°17′E
Khaydarken see Khaydarkan
125 U2 Khaypudyrskaya Guba bay NW Russian Federation
139 S1 Khayrūzuk Arbīl, E Iraq 36°58′N 44°19′E
Khazar, Baḥr-e/Khazar, Daryā-ye see Caspian Sea
Khazarosp see Hazorasp
Khazretishi, Khrebet see Hazratishoh, Qatorkŭhi
75 X11 Khazzān Aswān var. Aswān Dam. dam SE Egypt
Khelat see Kālat
74 F6 Khemisset NW Morocco 33°52′N 06°04′W
167 R10 Khemmarat var. Kemarat. Ubon Ratchathani, E Thailand 16°03′N 105°11′E
74 L6 Khenchela var. Khenchla. NE Algeria 35°22′N 07°09′E
Khenchla see Khenchela
74 G7 Khénifra C Morocco 32°59′N 05°37′W
152 L12 Kheri Uttar Pradesh, N India 27°54′N 80°47′E
Khersān, Rūd-e see Garm, Āb-e
117 R10 Kherson Khersons'ka Oblast', S Ukraine 46°39′N 32°38′E
Kherson see Khersons'ka Oblast'
117 S14 Khersones, Mys Rus. Mys Khersonesskiy. headland S Ukraine 44°34′N 33°24′E
Khersonesskiy, Mys see Khersones, Mys
117 R10 Khersons'ka Oblast' var. Kherson, Rus. Khersonskaya Oblast'. ◆ province S Ukraine
Khersonskaya Oblast' see Khersons'ka Oblast'
122 L8 Kheta N Russian Federation
167 S8 Khe Ve Quang Binh, C Vietnam 17°52′N 105°49′E
149 U7 Khewra Punjab, E Pakistan 32°41′N 73°04′E
Khiam see El Khiyam
124 J4 Khibiny ▲ NW Russian Federation
126 K3 Khimki Moskovskaya Oblast', W Russian Federation 55°57′N 37°48′E
147 S12 Khingov Rus. Obi-Khingou. C Tajikistan
Khíos see Chíos
149 R15 Khipro Sind, SE Pakistan 25°50′N 69°24′E
139 S10 Khirr, Wādī al dry watercourse S Iraq
114 I10 Khisarya Plovdiv, C Bulgaria 42°33′N 24°43′E
Khiva/Khiwa see Xiva
167 N9 Khlong Khlung Kamphaeng Phet, W Thailand 16°15′N 99°41′E
167 N15 Khlong Thom Krabi, SW Thailand 07°55′N 99°09′E
167 P12 Khlung Chantaburi, S Thailand 12°25′N 102°12′E
Khmel'nik see Khmil'nyk
Khmel'nitskaya Oblast' see Khmel'nyts'ka Oblast'
Khmel'nitskiy see Khmel'nyts'kyy
116 K5 Khmel'nyts'ka Oblast' var. Khmel'nyts'kyy, Rus. Khmel'nitskaya Oblast'; prev. Kamenets-Podol'skaya Oblast'. ◆ province NW Ukraine
116 L6 Khmel 'nyts'kyy Rus. Khmel'nitskiy; prev. Proskurov. Khmel'nyts'ka Oblast', W Ukraine 49°24′N 26°59′E
Khmel'nyts'kyy see Khmel'nyts'ka Oblast'
116 M6 Khmil'nyk Rus. Khmel'nik. Vinnyts'ka Oblast', C Ukraine 49°36′N 27°59′E
144 I10 Khobda prev. Novoalekseyevka. Aktyubinsk, W Kazakhstan 50°09′N 55°39′E
137 R9 Khobi W Georgia 42°20′N 41°54′E
119 P15 Khodasy Rus. Khodosy. Mahilyowskaya Voblasts', E Belarus 53°56′N 31°29′E
116 I6 Khodoriv Pol. Chodorów, Rus. Khodorov. L'vivs'ka Oblast', NW Ukraine 49°20′N 24°19′E
Khodorov see Khodoriv
Khodosy see Khodasy
Khodzhakala see Hojagala
Khodzhambas see Hojambaz
Khodzhent see Khujand
Khodzheyli see Xo'jayli
Khoi see Khvoy
Khojend see Khujand
Khokand see Qo'qon
126 L8 Khokhol'skiy Voronezhskaya Oblast', W Russian Federation 51°33′N 38°43′E
167 P10 Khok Samrong Lop Buri, C Thailand 15°03′N 100°44′E
149 P2 Kholm var. Tashqurghan, Pash. Khulm. Balkh, N Afghanistan 36°42′N 67°41′E
124 H15 Kholm Novgorodskaya Oblast', W Russian Federation 57°10′N 31°06′E
Kholm see Chełm
Kholmech' see Kholmyech
123 T13 Kholmsk Ostrov Sakhalin, Sakhalinskaya Oblast', SE Russian Federation 46°57′N 142°10′E
119 O19 Kholmyech Rus. Kholmech'. Homyel'skaya Voblasts', SE Belarus 52°09′N 30°37′E
Kholon see Holon
Kholopenichi see Khalopyenichy
83 D19 Khomas ◆ district C Namibia
83 D19 Khomas Hochland var. Khomasplato. plateau C Namibia
Khomasplato see Khomas Hochland
Khomein see Khomeyn
142 M7 Khomeyn var. Khomein, Khumain. Markazī, W Iran 33°38′N 50°03′E
143 N8 Khomeynīshahr prev. Homāyūnshahr. Eşfahān, C Iran 32°42′N 51°28′E
Khoms see Al Khums
Khong Sedone see Muang Khôngxédôn

◆ Country
● Country Capital
◇ Dependent Territory
○ Dependent Territory Capital
◆ Administrative Regions
✈ International Airport
▲ Mountain
▲ Mountain Range
Volcano
River
◎ Lake
▣ Reservoir

167 Q9 Khon Kaen var. Muang Khon Kaen. Khon Kaen, E Thailand 16°25´N 102°50´E
Khonqa see Xonqa
153 Y11 Khonsa Arunāchal Pradesh, NE India 27°01´N 95°95´E
167 Q9 Khon San Khon Kaen, E Thailand 16°40´N 101°51´E
123 R8 Khonuu Respublika Sakha (Yakutiya), NE Russian Federation 66°24´N 143°15´E
127 N8 Khopër var. Khoper. SW Russian Federation
Khoper see Khopër
123 S14 Khor Khabarovskiy Kray, SE Russian Federation 47°44´N 134°48´E
143 U9 Khorāsān-e Janūbī off. Ostan-e Khorāsān-e Janūbī. ◆ province E Iran
143 U5 Khorāsān-e Razavī off. Ostān-e Khorāsān, var. Khorassan, Khurasan. ◆ province NE Iran
143 S3 Khorāsān-e Shemālī off. Ostan-e Khorāsān-e Shemālī. ◆ province NE Iran
Khorāsān, Ostān-e see Khorāsān-e Razavī
Khorassan see Khorāsān-e Razavī
Khorat see Nakhon Ratchasima
154 O13 Khordha prev. Khurda. Orissa, E India 20°10´N 85°42´E
125 U4 Khorey-Ver Nenetskiy Avtonomnyy Okrug, NW Russian Federation 67°25´N 58°05´E
Khorezmskaya Oblast' see Xorazm Viloyati
Khor Fakkan see Khawr Fakkān
145 W15 Khorgos Almaty, SE Kazakhstan 44°13´N 80°22´E
123 N13 Khorinsk Respublika Buryatiya, S Russian Federation 52°13´N 109°52´E
83 C18 Khorixas Kunene, NW Namibia 20°23´S 14°55´E
141 O17 Khormaksar var. Aden. ✕ ('Adan) SW Yemen 12°56´N 45°00´E
Khormal see Khurmāl
Khormuj see Khvormūj
Khorog see Khorugh
117 S5 Khorol Poltavs'ka Oblast', NE Ukraine 49°49´N 33°17´E
142 L7 Khorramābād var. Khurramabad. Lorestān, W Iran 33°29´N 48°21´E
143 R9 Khorramdasht Kermān, C Iran 31°41´N 56°10´E
142 K10 Khorramshahr var. Khurramshahr, Muhammerah; prev. Mohammerah. Khūzestān, SW Iran 30°30´N 48°09´E
147 S14 Khorugh Rus. Khorog. S Tajikistan 37°30´N 71°31´E
Khorvot Khalutsa see Horvot Haluza
127 Q12 Khosheutovo Astrakhanskaya Oblast', SW Russian Federation 47°04´N 47°49´E
Khotan see Hotan
Khotimsk see Khotsimsk
Khotin see Khotyn
119 R16 Khotsimsk Rus. Khotimsk. Mahilyowskaya Voblasts', E Belarus 53°24´N 32°35´E
116 K7 Khotyn Rom. Hotin, Rus. Khotin. Chernivets'ka Oblast', W Ukraine 48°29´N 26°30´E
74 F7 Khouribga C Morocco 32°55´N 06°51´W
147 Q13 Khovaling Rus. Khavaling. SW Tajikistan 38°22´N 69°54´E
Khovd see Hovd
149 R6 Khowst Khowst, E Afghanistan 33°22´N 69°57´E
149 S6 Khowst ◆ province E Afghanistan
Khoy see Khvoy
119 N20 Khoyniki Homyel'skaya Voblasts', SE Belarus 51°54´N 29°58´E
Khozretishi, Khrebet see Hazratishoh, Qatorkŭhi
Khrisoúpolis see Chrysoúpoli
144 J10 Khromtau Kaz. Khromtaū. Aktyubinsk, W Kazakhstan 50°14´N 58°22´E
Khromtaū see Khromtau
Khrysokhou Bay see Chrysochoú, Kólpos
117 O7 Khrystynivka Cherkas'ka Oblast', C Ukraine 48°49´N 29°55´E
167 R10 Khuang Nai Ubon Ratchathani, E Thailand 15°22´N 104°33´E
Khudal see Khādhil
Khudat see Xudat
149 W9 Khudiān Punjab, E Pakistan 30°59´N 74°19´E
Khudzhand see Khujand
83 G21 Khuis Kgalagadi, SW Botswana 26°37´S 21°50´E
147 Q11 Khujand var. Khodzhent, Khojend, Rus. Khudzhand; prev. Leninabad, Taj. Leninobod. N Tajikistan 40°17´N 69°37´E
167 R11 Khukhan Si Sa Ket, E Thailand 14°38´N 104°12´E
Khulm see Kholm
153 T16 Khulna Khulna, SW Bangladesh 22°48´N 89°32´E
153 T16 Khulna ◆ division SW Bangladesh
Khumain see Khomeyn
Khums see Al Khums
149 W2 Khunjerāb Pass pass China/Pakistan
Khūnjerāb Pass see Kunjirap Daban
153 P16 Khunti Jhārkhand, N India 23°02´N 85°19´E
167 N7 Khun Yuam Mae Hong Son, NW Thailand 18°54´N 97°54´E
Khurais see Khurayş
Khurasan see Khorāsān-e Razavī
141 R7 Khurayş var. Khurais. Ash Sharqiyah, C Saudi Arabia 25°06´N 48°03´E
Khurda see Khordha
152 J11 Khurja Uttar Pradesh, N India 28°15´N 77°51´E
139 V4 Khurmāl var. Khormal. As Sulaymānīyah, NE Iraq 35°19´N 46°06´E
Khurramabad see Khorramābād
Khurramshahr see Khorramshahr
149 U7 Khushāb Punjab, NE Pakistan 32°16´N 72°18´E
116 H8 Khust var. Husté, Cz. Chust, Hung. Huszt. Zakarpats'ka Oblast', W Ukraine 48°11´N 23°19´E
80 D11 Khuwei Western Kordofan, C Sudan 13°02´N 29°13´E
149 O13 Khuzdār Baluchistān, SW Pakistan 27°49´N 66°39´E
142 L9 Khūzestān off. Ostān-e Khūzestān, var. Khuzistan, prev. Arabistan; anc. Susiana. ◆ province SW Iran
Khūzestān, Ostān-e see Khūzestān
149 R2 Khvājeh Ghār var. Khwajaghar, Khwaja-i-Ghar. Takhār, NE Afghanistan 37°08´N 69°24´E
127 Q7 Khvalynsk Saratovskaya Oblast', W Russian Federation 52°30´N 48°06´E
143 N12 Khvormūj var. Khormuj. Būshehr, S Iran 28°32´N 51°22´E
142 I2 Khvoy var. Khoi, Khoy. Āžarbāyjān-e Bākhtarī, NW Iran 38°36´N 45°04´E
Khwajaghar/Khwaja-i-Ghar see Khvājeh Ghār
149 S5 Khyber Pass var. Kowtal-e Khaybar. pass Afghanistan/Pakistan
186 L8 Kia Santa Isabel, N Solomon Islands 07°34´S 158°31´E
183 S10 Kiama New South Wales, SE Australia 34°41´S 150°49´E
79 O22 Kiambi Katanga, SE Dem. Rep. Congo 07°15´S 28°01´E
27 Q12 Kiamichi Mountains ▲▲ Oklahoma, C USA
27 Q12 Kiamichi River Oklahoma, C USA
14 M10 Kiamika, Réservoir ⊠ Québec, SE Canada
Kiamusze see Jiamusi
39 N7 Kiana Alaska, USA 66°58´N 160°25´W
Kiangmai see Chiang Mai
Kiang-ning see Nanjing
Kiangsi see Jiangxi
Kiangsu see Jiangsu
93 M14 Kiantajärvi ◎ E Finland
115 F19 Kiáto prev. Kiáton. Pelopónnisos, S Greece 38°01´N 22°45´E
Kiáton see Kiáto
Kiayi see Chiai
95 F22 Kibæk Ringkøbing, W Denmark 56°03´N 08°52´E
67 T9 Kibali var. Uele (upper course). NE Dem. Rep. Congo
79 E20 Kibangou Niari, SW Congo 03°27´S 12°21´E
Kibarty see Kybartai
92 M8 Kiberg Finnmark, N Norway 70°17´N 30°47´E
79 N20 Kibombo Maniema, E Dem. Rep. Congo 03°52´S 25°59´E
81 E20 Kibondo Kigoma, NW Tanzania 03°34´S 30°41´E
81 J15 Kibre Mengist var. Adola. Oromiya, C Ethiopia 05°50´N 39°06´E
Kıbrıs see Cyprus
Kıbrıs/Kıbrıs Cumhuriyeti see Cyprus
81 E20 Kibungo var. Kibungu. SE Rwanda 02°09´S 30°30´E
Kibungu see Kibungo
113 N19 Kičevo SW FYR Macedonia 41°31´N 20°57´E
125 P13 Kichmengskiy Gorodok Vologodskaya Oblast', NW Russian Federation 60°00´N 45°52´E
30 J8 Kickapoo River Wisconsin, N USA
11 P16 Kicking Horse Pass pass Alberta/British Columbia, SW Canada
77 R9 Kidal Kidal, C Mali 18°22´N 01°21´E
77 Q8 Kidal ◆ region NE Mali
171 Q7 Kidapawan Mindanao, S Philippines 07°02´N 125°04´E
97 L20 Kidderminster C England, United Kingdom 52°23´N 02°14´W
76 I11 Kidira E Senegal 14°28´N 12°13´W
184 O11 Kidnappers, Cape headland North Island, New Zealand 41°13´S 175°15´E
100 J8 Kiel Schleswig-Holstein, N Germany 54°21´N 10°05´E
111 L15 Kielce Rus. Keltsy. Świętokrzyskie, C Poland 50°53´N 20°39´E
100 K7 Kieler Bucht bay N Germany
100 J7 Kieler Förde inlet N Germany
167 U13 Kiên Đưc var. Đak Lap. Đắc Lắc, S Vietnam 11°59´N 107°30´E
79 N24 Kienge Katanga, SE Dem. Rep. Congo 10°33´S 27°33´E
100 Q12 Kietz Brandenburg, NE Germany 52°33´N 14°36´E
Kiev see Kyyiv
Kiev Reservoir see Kyyivs'ke Vodoskhovyshche
76 J10 Kiffa Assaba, S Mauritania 16°38´N 11°23´W
115 H19 Kifisiá Attikí, C Greece 38°04´N 23°49´E
115 F18 Kifisós C Greece
139 U5 Kifrī At Ta'mīn, N Iraq 34°44´N 44°58´E
81 D20 Kigali ● (Rwanda) C Rwanda 01°59´S 30°02´E
81 E20 Kigali ✕ C Rwanda 01°43´S 30°01´E
137 P13 Kiğı Bingöl, E Turkey 39°19´N 40°20´E
81 E21 Kigoma Kigoma, W Tanzania 04°52´S 29°36´E
81 E21 Kigoma ◆ region W Tanzania
38 F10 Kihei var. Kihei. Maui, Hawaii, USA, C Pacific Ocean 20°47´N 156°28´W
93 K17 Kihniö Länsi-Suomi, W Finland 62°11´N 23°10´E
118 F6 Kihnu var. Kihnu Saar, Ger. Kühnö. island SW Estonia
Kihnu Saar see Kihnu
38 A8 Kii Landing Ni'ihau, Hawaii, USA, C Pacific Ocean 21°58´N 160°03´W
93 L14 Kiiminki Oulu, C Finland 65°05´N 25°47´E
164 J14 Kii-Nagashima var. Nagashima. Mie, Honshū, SW Japan 34°10´N 136°18´E
164 J14 Kii-sanchi ▲▲ Honshū, SW Japan
92 L11 Kiistala Lappi, N Finland 67°52´N 25°19´E
164 I15 Kii-suidō strait S Japan
165 V16 Kikai-shima island Nansei-shotō, SW Japan
112 M8 Kikinda Ger. Grosskikinda, Hung. Nagykikinda; prev. Velika Kikinda. Vojvodina, N Serbia 45°48´N 20°29´E
Kikládhes see Kykládes
165 Q5 Kikonai Hokkaidō, NE Japan 41°40´N 140°25´E
186 C8 Kikori Gulf, S Papua New Guinea 07°25´S 144°13´E
186 C8 Kikori W Papua New Guinea
165 O14 Kikuchi var. Kikuti. Kumamoto, Kyūshū, SW Japan 33°00´N 130°49´E
Kikuti see Kikuchi
127 N8 Kikvidze Volgogradskaya Oblast', SW Russian Federation 50°47´N 42°58´E
14 I10 Kikwissi, Lac ◎ Québec, SE Canada
79 I21 Kikwit Bandundu, W Dem. Rep. Congo 05°S 18°53´E
95 K15 Kil Värmland, C Sweden 59°30´N 13°20´E
94 N12 Kilafors Gävleborg, C Sweden 61°13´N 16°34´E
38 B8 Kilauea Kaua'i, Hawaii, USA, C Pacific Ocean 22°12´N 159°24´W
38 H12 Kilauea Caldera var. Kilauea Caldera. crater Hawai'i, USA, C Pacific Ocean 19°25´N 155°17´W
Kilauea Caldera see Kilauea Caldera
109 V4 Kilb Niederösterreich, C Austria 48°06´N 15°21´E
39 O12 Kilbuck Mountains ▲▲ Alaska, USA
163 Y12 Kilchu NE North Korea 40°58´N 129°22´E
97 F18 Kilcock Ir. Cill Choca. Kildare, E Ireland 53°25´N 06°40´W
183 V2 Kilcoy Queensland, E Australia 26°58´S 152°30´E
97 F18 Kildare Ir. Cill Dara. E Ireland 53°10´N 06°55´W
97 F18 Kildare Ir. Cill Dara. cultural region E Ireland
124 K2 Kil'din, Ostrov island NW Russian Federation
25 W7 Kilgore Texas, SW USA 32°23´N 94°52´W
Kilien Mountains see Qilian Shan
114 K9 Kilifarevo Veliko Tŭrnovo, N Bulgaria 43°00´N 25°36´E
81 K20 Kilifi Coast, SE Kenya 03°37´S 39°50´E
189 U9 Kili Island var. Kōle. island Ralik Chain, S Marshall Islands
149 V2 Kilik Pass pass Afghanistan/China
Kilimane see Quelimane
81 I21 Kilimanjaro ◆ region E Tanzania
81 I20 Kilimanjaro var. Uhuru Peak. NE Tanzania 03°01´S 37°14´E
Kilimbangara see Kolombangara
Kilinailau Islands see Tulun Islands
81 K23 Kilindoni Pwani, E Tanzania 07°56´S 39°40´E
118 H6 Kilingi-Nõmme Ger. Kurkund. Pärnumaa, SW Estonia 58°07´N 24°00´E
136 M17 Kilis Kilis, S Turkey 36°43´N 37°07´E
136 M16 Kilis ◆ province S Turkey
117 N12 Kiliya Rom. Chilia-Nouă. Odes'ka Oblast', SW Ukraine 45°30´N 29°16´E
97 B19 Kilkee Ir. Cill Chaoi. Clare, W Ireland 52°41´N 09°38´W
97 E19 Kilkenny Ir. Cill Chainnigh. Kilkenny, S Ireland 52°39´N 07°15´W
97 E19 Kilkenny Ir. Cill Chainnigh. cultural region S Ireland
97 B18 Kilkieran Bay Ir. Cuan Chill Chiaráin. bay W Ireland
114 G13 Kilkís Kentrikí Makedonía, N Greece 40°59´N 22°55´E
97 C15 Killala Bay Ir. Cuan Chill Ala. inlet NW Ireland
11 R15 Killam Alberta, SW Canada 52°45´N 111°46´W
183 U3 Killarney Queensland, E Australia 28°18´S 152°15´E
11 W17 Killarney Manitoba, S Canada 49°12´N 99°40´W
14 E11 Killarney Ontario, S Canada 45°58´N 81°27´W
97 B20 Killarney Ir. Cill Airne. Kerry, SW Ireland 52°03´N 09°30´W
28 K4 Killdeer North Dakota, N USA 47°21´N 102°45´W
28 J4 Killdeer Mountains ▲▲ North Dakota, N USA
45 V15 Killdeer River Trinidad, Trinidad and Tobago
25 S9 Killeen Texas, SW USA 31°07´N 97°44´W
39 P6 Killik River Alaska, USA
11 T7 Killinek Island island Nunavut, NE Canada
Killini see Kyllíni
115 C19 Killínis, Akrotírio headland S Greece 37°55´N 21°07´E
97 D15 Killybegs Ir. Na Cealla Beaga. NW Ireland 54°38´N 08°27´W
Kilmain see Quelimane
96 I13 Kilmarnock W Scotland, United Kingdom 55°37´N 04°30´W
21 X6 Kilmarnock Virginia, NE USA 37°42´N 76°22´W
125 S16 Kil'mez' Kirovskaya Oblast', NW Russian Federation 56°55´N 51°03´E
127 S2 Kil'mez' Udmurtskaya Respublika, NW Russian Federation 57°04´N 51°22´E
125 R16 Kil'mez' NW Russian Federation
67 V11 Kilombero S Tanzania
92 J10 Kilpisjärvi Lappi, N Finland 69°03´N 20°50´E
97 B19 Kilrush Ir. Cill Rois. Clare, W Ireland 52°39´N 09°29´W
79 O24 Kilwa Katanga, SE Dem. Rep. Congo 09°22´S 28°19´E
Kilwa see Kilwa Kivinje
81 J24 Kilwa Kivinje var. Kilwa. Lindi, SE Tanzania 08°45´S 39°21´E
81 J24 Kilwa Masoko Lindi, SE Tanzania 08°55´S 39°31´E
171 T13 Kilwo Pulau Seram, E Indonesia 03°36´S 130°48´E
114 P12 Kilyos İstanbul, NW Turkey 41°15´N 29°01´E
37 V8 Kim Colorado, C USA 37°12´N 103°22´W
169 U7 Kimanis, Teluk bay Sabah, East Malaysia
182 H8 Kimba South Australia 33°09´S 136°26´E
28 I15 Kimball Nebraska, C USA 41°16´N 103°40´W
29 O11 Kimball South Dakota, N USA 43°45´N 98°57´W
79 I21 Kimbao Bandundu, SW Dem. Rep. Congo 05°27´S 17°40´E
186 F7 Kimbe New Britain, E Papua New Guinea 05°36´S 150°10´E
186 G7 Kimbe Bay inlet New Britain, E Papua New Guinea
11 P17 Kimberley British Columbia, SW Canada 49°40´N 115°58´W
83 H23 Kimberley Northern Cape, C South Africa 28°45´S 24°46´E
180 M4 Kimberley Plateau plateau Western Australia
33 P15 Kimberly Idaho, NW USA 42°31´N 114°21´W
163 Y12 Kimch'aek prev. Sŏngjin. E North Korea 40°42´N 129°13´E
163 Y15 Kimch'ŏn C South Korea 36°08´N 128°06´E
163 Z16 Kim Hae var. Pusan. ✕ (Pusan) SE South Korea 35°10´N 128°57´E
Kími see Kými
93 K20 Kimito Swe. Kemiö. Länsi-Suomi, SW Finland 60°10´N 22°45´E
9 R7 Kimmirut prev. Lake Harbour. Baffin Island, Nunavut, NE Canada 62°48´N 69°49´W
165 R4 Kimobetsu Hokkaidō, NE Japan 42°47´N 140°55´E
115 I21 Kímolos island Kykládes, Greece, Aegean Sea
115 I21 Kímolou Sífnou, Stenó strait Kykládes, Greece, Aegean Sea
126 L5 Kimovsk Tul'skaya Oblast', W Russian Federation 53°59´N 38°34´E
Kimpolung see Câmpulung Moldovenesc
124 K16 Kimry Tverskaya Oblast', W Russian Federation 56°52´N 37°21´E
79 H21 Kimvula Bas-Congo, SW Dem. Rep. Congo 05°44´S 15°58´E
169 U6 Kinabalu, Gunung ▲ East Malaysia 05°52´N 116°08´E
Kinabatangan see Kinabatangan, Sungai
169 V7 Kinabatangan, Sungai var. Kinabatangan. East Malaysia
115 L21 Kínaros island Kykládes, Greece, Aegean Sea
11 O15 Kinbasket Lake ⊠ British Columbia, SW Canada
96 I7 Kinbrace N Scotland, United Kingdom 58°16´N 02°59´W
14 E14 Kincardine Ontario, S Canada 44°11´N 81°38´W
96 K10 Kincardine cultural region E Scotland, United Kingdom
79 K21 Kinda Kasai-Occidental, SE Dem. Rep. Congo 04°48´S 21°50´E
79 M24 Kinda Katanga, SE Dem. Rep. Congo 09°20´S 25°06´E
166 L4 Kindat Sagaing, N Burma (Myanmar) 23°42´N 94°29´E
109 V6 Kindberg Steiermark, C Austria 47°31´N 15°27´E
22 H8 Kinder Louisiana, S USA 30°29´N 92°51´W
98 H13 Kinderdijk Zuid-Holland, SW Netherlands 51°52´N 04°37´E
97 M17 Kinder Scout ▲ C England, United Kingdom 53°25´N 01°52´W
11 S16 Kindersley Saskatchewan, S Canada 51°29´N 109°08´W
76 I14 Kindia Guinée-Maritime, SW Guinea 10°12´N 12°26´W
64 B11 Kindley Field air base E Bermuda
29 R6 Kindred North Dakota, N USA 46°39´N 97°01´W
79 N20 Kindu prev. Kindu-Port-Empain. Maniema, C Dem. Rep. Congo 02°57´S 25°54´E
Kindu-Port-Empain see Kindu
127 S6 Kinel' Samarskaya Oblast', W Russian Federation 53°14´N 50°40´E
125 N15 Kineshma Ivanovskaya Oblast', W Russian Federation 57°28´N 42°08´E
King see King William's Town
140 K10 King Abdul Aziz ✕ (Makkah) Makkah, W Saudi Arabia 21°44´N 39°08´E
21 X6 King and Queen Court House Virginia, NE USA 37°40´N 76°49´W
King Charles Islands see Kong Karls Land
King Christian IX Land see Kong Christian IX Land
King Christian X Land see Kong Christian X Land
35 O11 King City California, W USA 36°12´N 121°09´W
27 R2 King City Missouri, C USA 40°03´N 94°31´W
38 M16 King Cove Alaska, USA 55°03´N 162°19´W
26 M10 Kingfisher Oklahoma, C USA 35°53´N 97°56´W
King Frederik VI Coast see Kong Frederik VI Kyst
King Frederik VIII Land see Kong Frederik VIII Land
65 B24 King George Bay bay West Falkland, Falkland Islands
194 G3 King George Island var. King George Land. island South Shetland Islands, Antarctica
12 I6 King George Islands island group Northwest Territories, C Canada
King George Land see King George Island
124 G13 Kingisepp Leningradskaya Oblast', NW Russian Federation 59°23´N 28°37´E
183 N14 King Island island Tasmania, SE Australia
10 J15 King Island island British Columbia, SW Canada
King Island see Kadan Kyun
Kingissepp see Kuressaare
141 Q7 King Khalid ✕ (Ar Riyāḍ) Ar Riyāḍ, C Saudi Arabia 25°00´N 46°40´E
35 S2 King Lear Peak ▲ Nevada, W USA 41°13´N 118°30´W
195 Y8 King Leopold and Queen Astrid Land physical region Antarctica
180 M4 King Leopold Ranges ▲▲ Western Australia
36 I11 Kingman Arizona, SW USA 35°12´N 114°02´W
26 M6 Kingman Kansas, C USA 37°39´N 98°07´W
192 L7 Kingman Reef ◇ US territory C Pacific Ocean
79 N20 Kingombe Maniema, E Dem. Rep. Congo 02°37´S 26°39´E
182 F5 Kingoonya South Australia 30°56´S 135°20´E
194 J10 King Peninsula peninsula Antarctica
39 P13 King Salmon Alaska, USA 58°41´N 156°39´W
35 Q6 Kings Beach California, W USA 39°13´N 120°02´W
35 R11 Kingsburg California, W USA 36°30´N 119°33´W
182 I10 Kingscote South Australia 35°41´S 137°36´E
King's County see Offaly
194 H2 King Sejong South Korean research station Antarctica 61°57´S 58°23´W
183 T9 Kingsford Smith ✕ (Sydney) New South Wales, SE Australia 33°58´S 151°09´E
11 P17 Kingsgate British Columbia, SW Canada 48°58´N 116°09´W
23 W8 Kingsland Georgia, SE USA 30°48´N 81°41´W
29 S13 Kingsley Iowa, C USA 42°35´N 95°58´W
97 O19 King's Lynn var. Bishop's Lynn, Kings Lynn, Lynn, Lynn Regis. E England, United Kingdom 52°45´N 00°24´E
Kings Lynn see King's Lynn
21 Q10 Kings Mountain North Carolina, SE USA 35°15´N 81°20´W
180 K4 King Sound sound Western Australia
37 N2 Kings Peak ▲ Utah, W USA 40°43´N 110°27´W
21 O8 Kingsport Tennessee, S USA 36°32´N 82°33´W
35 R11 Kings River California, W USA
183 P17 Kingston Tasmania, SE Australia 42°57´S 147°18´E
14 K14 Kingston Ontario, SE Canada 44°14´N 76°30´W
44 K13 Kingston ● (Jamaica) E Jamaica 17°58´N 76°48´W
185 C22 Kingston Otago, South Island, New Zealand 45°20´S 168°45´E
19 P12 Kingston Massachusetts, NE USA 41°59´N 70°43´W
27 S3 Kingston Missouri, C USA 39°36´N 94°02´W
18 K12 Kingston New York, NE USA 41°55´N 74°00´W
31 S14 Kingston Ohio, N USA 39°28´N 82°54´W
19 O13 Kingston Rhode Island, NE USA 41°28´N 71°31´W
20 M9 Kingston Tennessee, S USA 35°52´N 84°30´W
35 W12 Kingston Peak ▲ California, W USA 35°43´N 115°54´W
182 J11 Kingston Southeast South Australia 36°51´S 139°53´E
97 N17 Kingston upon Hull var. Hull. E England, United Kingdom 53°45´N 00°20´W
97 N22 Kingston upon Thames SE England, United Kingdom 51°26´N 00°18´W
45 P14 Kingstown ● (Saint Vincent and the Grenadines) Saint Vincent, Saint Vincent and the Grenadines 13°09´N 61°14´W
Kingstown see Dún Laoghaire
21 T13 Kingstree South Carolina, SE USA 33°40´N 79°50´W
64 L8 Kings Trough undersea feature E Atlantic Ocean 22°00´W 43°48´N
14 C18 Kingsville Ontario, S Canada 42°03´N 82°43´W
25 S15 Kingsville Texas, SW USA 27°32´N 97°53´W
21 W6 King William Virginia, NE USA 37°42´N 77°03´W
9 N7 King William Island island Nunavut, N Canada
83 I25 King William's Town var. King, Kingwilliamstown. Eastern Cape, S South Africa 32°53´S 27°24´E
Kingwilliamstown see King William's Town
21 T3 Kingwood West Virginia, NE USA 39°27´N 79°43´W
136 C13 Kınık İzmir, W Turkey 39°05´N 27°25´E
79 G21 Kinkala Pool, S Congo 04°18´S 14°49´E
165 R10 Kinka-san headland Honshū, C Japan 38°17´N 141°34´E
184 M8 Kinleith Waikato, North Island, New Zealand 38°16´S 175°53´E
95 J19 Kinna Västra Götaland, S Sweden 57°32´N 12°42´E
96 L8 Kinnaird Head var. Kinnairds Head. headland NE Scotland, United Kingdom 58°39´N 03°22´W
Kinnairds Head see Kinnaird Head
95 K20 Kinnared Halland, S Sweden 57°01´N 13°04´E
Kinneret, Yam see Tiberias, Lake
155 K24 Kinniyai Eastern Province, NE Sri Lanka 08°30´N 81°11´E
93 L16 Kinnula Länsi-Suomi, C Finland 63°24´N 25°E
14 I8 Kinojévis Québec, SE Canada
164 I14 Kino-kawa Honshū, SW Japan
11 U11 Kinoosao Saskatchewan, C Canada 57°06´N 101°02´W
99 L17 Kinrooi Limburg, NE Belgium 51°09´N 05°48´E
96 J11 Kinross C Scotland, United Kingdom 56°14´N 03°27´W
96 J11 Kinross cultural region C Scotland, United Kingdom
97 C21 Kinsale Ir. Cionn tSáile. Cork, SW Ireland 51°42´N 08°32´W
95 D14 Kinsarvik Hordaland, S Norway 60°22´N 06°43´E
79 G21 Kinshasa prev. Léopoldville. ● Kinshasa, W Dem. Rep. Congo 04°21´S 15°16´E
79 G21 Kinshasa off. Ville de Kinshasa, var. Kinshasa City. ◆ region (Dem. Rep. Congo) SW Dem. Rep. Congo
79 G21 Kinshasa ✕ Kinshasa, SW Dem. Rep. Congo 04°23´S 15°30´E
Kinshasa City see Kinshasa
117 U9 Kins'ka SE Ukraine
26 K6 Kinsley Kansas, C USA 37°55´N 99°26´W
21 W10 Kinston North Carolina, SE USA 35°16´N 77°35´W
77 P15 Kintampo W Ghana 08°06´N 01°40´W
182 B1 Kintore, Mount ▲ South Australia 26°30´S 130°24´E
96 G13 Kintyre peninsula W Scotland, United Kingdom
96 G13 Kintyre, Mull of headland W Scotland, United Kingdom 55°16´N 05°46´W
166 M4 Kin-u Sagaing, C Burma (Myanmar) 22°47´N 95°36´E
12 G8 Kinushseo Ontario, C Canada
11 P13 Kinuso Alberta, W Canada 55°19´N 115°23´W
154 I13 Kinwat Mahārāshtra, C India 19°37´N 78°12´E
81 F16 Kinyeti ▲ S Sudan 03°56´N 32°52´E
101 I17 Kinzig SW Germany
Kioga, Lake see Kyoga, Lake
26 M8 Kiowa Kansas, C USA 37°01´N 98°29´W
27 P12 Kiowa Oklahoma, C USA 34°43´N 95°54´W
Kiparissía see Kyparissía
14 H10 Kipawa, Lac ◎ Québec, SE Canada
81 G24 Kipengere Range ▲▲ SW Tanzania
81 E23 Kipili Rukwa, W Tanzania 07°30´S 30°39´E
81 K20 Kipini Coast, SE Kenya 02°30´S 40°30´E
11 V16 Kipling Saskatchewan, S Canada 50°04´N 102°45´W
38 M13 Kipnuk Alaska, USA 59°56´N 164°02´W
97 F18 Kippure Ir. Cipiúr. ▲ E Ireland 53°10´N 06°22´W
79 N25 Kipushi Katanga, SE Dem. Rep. Congo 11°45´S 27°20´E
187 N10 Kirakira var. Kaokaona. San Cristobal, SE Solomon Islands 10°28´S 161°54´E
155 K14 Kirandul var. Bailādila. Chhattīsgarh, C India 18°46´N 81°18´E
155 I21 Kiranūr Tamil Nādu, SE India 11°37´N 79°10´E
119 N21 Kiraw Rus. Kirovo. Homyel'skaya Voblasts', SE Belarus 51°30´N 29°25´E
119 M17 Kirawsk Rus. Kirovsk; prev. Startsy. Mahilyowskaya Voblasts', E Belarus 53°16´N 29°29´E
118 F5 Kirbla Läänemaa, W Estonia 58°45´N 23°57´E
25 Y9 Kirbyville Texas, SW USA 30°39´N 93°53´W
114 M12 Kırcasalih Edirne, NW Turkey 41°24´N 26°48´E
109 W8 Kirchbach var. Kirchbach in Steiermark. Steiermark, SE Austria 46°55´N 15°40´E
Kirchbach in Steiermark see Kirchbach
108 H7 Kirchberg Sankt Gallen, NE Switzerland 47°24´N 09°03´E
109 S5 Kirchdorf an der Krems Oberösterreich, N Austria 47°55´N 14°08´E
Kirchheim see Kirchheim unter Teck
101 I22 Kirchheim unter Teck var. Kirchheim. Baden-Württemberg, SW Germany 48°39´N 09°28´E
Kirdzhali see Kŭrdzhali
123 N13 Kirenga S Russian Federation
123 N12 Kirensk Irkutskaya Oblast', C Russian Federation 57°37´N 107°54´E
Kirghizia see Kyrgyzstan
145 S16 Kirghiz Range Rus. Kirgizskiy Khrebet; prev. Alexander Range. ▲▲ Kazakhstan/Kyrgyzstan
Kirghiz SSR see Kyrgyzstan
Kirghiz Steppe see Kazakhskiy Melkosopochnik
Kirgizskaya SSR see Kyrgyzstan
Kirgizskiy Khrebet see Kirghiz Range
79 I19 Kiri Bandundu, W Dem. Rep. Congo 01°29´S 19°00´E
Kiriath-Arba see Hebron
191 R3 Kiribati off. Republic of Kiribati. ◆ republic C Pacific Ocean
Kiribati, Republic of see Kiribati
136 L17 Kırıkhan Hatay, S Turkey 36°30´N 36°20´E
136 I13 Kırıkkale Kırıkkale, C Turkey 39°50´N 33°31´E
136 C10 Kırıkkale ◆ province C Turkey
124 L13 Kirillov Vologodskaya Oblast', NW Russian Federation 59°52´N 38°24´E
Kirin see Jilin
81 I18 Kirinyaga prev. Mount Kenya. ▲ C Kenya 0°02´S 37°19´E
124 H13 Kirishi var. Kirisi. Leningradskaya Oblast', NW Russian Federation 59°28´N 32°02´E
164 C16 Kirishima-yama ▲ Kyūshū, SW Japan 31°58´N 130°51´E
Kirisi see Kirishi
191 Y2 Kiritimati ✕ Kiritimati, E Kiribati 02°00´N 157°30´W
191 Y2 Kiritimati prev. Christmas Island. atoll Line Islands, E Kiribati
186 G9 Kiriwina Island Eng. Trobriand Island. island SE Papua New Guinea
186 G9 Kiriwina Islands var. Trobriand Islands. island group S Papua New Guinea
96 K12 Kirkcaldy E Scotland, United Kingdom 56°07´N 03°10´W
97 I14 Kirkcudbright S Scotland, United Kingdom 54°50´N 04°03´W
97 I14 Kirkcudbright cultural region S Scotland, United Kingdom
Kirkee see Khadki
95 I14 Kirkenær Hedmark, S Norway 60°27´N 12°04´E
92 M8 Kirkenes Fin. Kirkkoniemi. Finnmark, N Norway 69°43´N 30°02´E
92 J4 Kirkjubæjarklaustur Sudhurland, S Iceland 63°46´N 18°03´W
Kirk-Kilissa see Kırklareli
Kirkkoniemi see Kirkenes
93 L20 Kirkkonummi Swe. Kyrkslätt. Uusimaa, S Finland 60°06´N 24°20´E
14 G7 Kirkland Lake Ontario, S Canada 48°10´N 80°02´W
136 C9 Kırklareli prev. Kirk-Kilissa. Kırklareli, NW Turkey 41°45´N 27°12´E
136 I13 Kırklareli ◆ province NW Turkey
185 F20 Kirkliston Range ▲▲ South Island, New Zealand
14 D10 Kirkpatrick Lake ◎ Ontario, S Canada
195 Q11 Kirkpatrick, Mount ▲ Antarctica 84°37´S 164°36´E
27 U2 Kirksville Missouri, C USA 40°12´N 92°35´W
139 T4 Kirkūk var. Karkūk, Kerkuk. At Ta'mīn, N Iraq 35°28´N 44°26´E
139 U7 Kir Kush Diyālá, E Iraq 33°42´N 45°15´E
96 K5 Kirkwall NE Scotland, United Kingdom 58°59´N 02°58´W
83 H25 Kirkwood Eastern Cape, S South Africa 33°23´S 25°19´E
27 X5 Kirkwood Missouri, C USA 38°35´N 90°24´W
Kirman see Kermān
Kir Moab/Kir of Moab see Al Karak
126 I5 Kirov Kaluzhskaya Oblast', W Russian Federation 54°02´N 34°17´E
125 R14 Kirov prev. Vyatka. Kirovskaya Oblast', NW Russian Federation 58°35´N 49°39´E
Kirov see Balpyk Bi/Ust'yevoye
Kirovabad see Gäncä
Kirovabad see Panj, Tajikistan
Kirovakan see Vanadzor
Kirov/Kirova see Kopbirlik, Kazakhstan
Kirovo see Kiraw, Belarus
Kirovo see Beshariq, Uzbekistan
125 R14 Kirovo-Chepetsk Kirovskaya Oblast', NW Russian Federation 58°33´N 50°06´E
Kirovogradskaya Oblast'/Kirovohrad see Kirovohrads'ka Oblast'
117 R7 Kirovohrad Rus. Kirovograd; prev. Kirovo, Yelizavetgrad, Zinov'yevsk. Kirovohrads'ka Oblast', C Ukraine 48°30´N 31°17´E
117 P7 Kirovohrads'ka Oblast' var. Kirovohrad, Rus. Kirovogradskaya Oblast'. ◆ province C Ukraine
Kirovo/Kirovograd see Kirovohrad
124 J4 Kirovsk Murmanskaya Oblast', NW Russian Federation 67°37´N 33°38´E
117 X7 Kirovs'k Luhans'ka Oblast', E Ukraine 48°40´N 38°39´E
Kirovsk see Kirawsk, Belarus
Kirovsk see Babadaýhan, Turkmenistan
122 E9 Kirovskaya Oblast' ◆ province NW Russian Federation
117 X8 Kirov'ske Donets'ka Oblast', E Ukraine 48°12´N 38°20´E
117 U13 Kirovs'ke Rus. Kirovskoye. Respublika Krym, S Ukraine 45°13´N 35°12´E
Kirovskiy see Balpyk Bi
Kirovskiy see Ust'yevoye
Kirovskoye see Kyzyl-Adyr
Kirovskoye see Kirovs'ke
146 E11 Kirpili Ahal Welaýaty, C Turkmenistan 39°31´N 57°13´E
96 K10 Kirriemuir E Scotland, United Kingdom 56°38´N 03°01´W
125 S13 Kirs Kirovskaya Oblast', NW Russian Federation 59°22´N 52°20´E
127 N7 Kirsanov Tambovskaya Oblast', W Russian Federation 52°40´N 42°48´E
136 J14 Kırşehir anc. Justinianopolis. Kırşehir, C Turkey 39°09´N 34°08´E
136 I13 Kırşehir ◆ province C Turkey
149 P4 Kirthar Range ▲▲ S Pakistan
37 P9 Kirtland New Mexico, SW USA 36°43´N 108°21´W
92 J11 Kiruna Lapp. Giron. Norrbotten, N Sweden 67°50´N 20°16´E
79 M18 Kirundu Orientale, NE Dem. Rep. Congo 0°45´S 25°28´E
Kirun/Kirun' see Chilung
26 L3 Kirwin Reservoir ⊠ Kansas, C USA
127 Q4 Kirya Chuvashskaya Respublika, W Russian Federation 55°04´N 46°50´E
138 G8 Kiryat Shmona prev. Qiryat Shemona. Northern, N Israel 33°13´N 35°35´E
95 M18 Kisa Östergötland, S Sweden 58°N 15°39´E
165 P9 Kisakata Akita, Honshū, C Japan 39°12´N 139°55´E
Kisalföld see Little Alföld
79 L18 Kisangani prev. Stanleyville. Orientale, NE Dem. Rep. Congo 0°30´N 25°14´E
39 N12 Kisaralik River Alaska, USA
165 O14 Kisarazu Chiba, Honshū, S Japan 35°23´N 139°57´E
111 I22 Kisbér Komárom-Esztergom, NW Hungary 47°30´N 18°00´E
11 V17 Kisbey Saskatchewan, S Canada 49°41´N 102°39´W
122 J13 Kiselevsk Kemerovskaya Oblast', S Russian Federation 54°00´N 86°38´E
153 R13 Kishanganj Bihār, NE India 26°06´N 87°57´E
152 G12 Kishangarh Rājasthān, N India 26°33´N 74°52´E

◆ Country
● Country Capital
◇ Dependent Territory
○ Dependent Territory Capital
◆ Administrative Regions
✕ International Airport
▲ Mountain
▲▲ Mountain Range
Volcano
River
◎ Lake
⊠ Reservoir

Kishegyes see Mali Iđoš
77 S15 **Kishi** Oyo, W Nigeria 09°01′N 03°53′E
Kishinev see Chişinău
Kishiözen see Malyy Uzen'
164 I14 **Kishiwada** var. Kisiwada. Ōsaka, Honshū, SW Japan 34°28′N 135°22′E
143 P14 **Kīsh, Jazīreh-ye** var. Qey. island S Iran
145 R7 **Kishkenekol'** prev. Kzyltu, Kaz. Qyzyltū. Kokshetau, N Kazakhstan 53°39′N 72°22′E
138 G9 **Kishon, Nahal** prev. Naḫal Qishon. 〰 N Israel
152 I6 **Kishtwār** Jammu and Kashmir, NW India 33°20′N 75°49′E
81 H19 **Kisii** Nyanza, SW Kenya 0°40′S 34°47′E
81 J23 **Kisiju** Pwani, E Tanzania 07°25′S 39°20′E
Kisiwada see Kishiwada
Kisjenő see Chişineu-Criş
38 E17 **Kiska Island** island Aleutian Islands, Alaska, USA
Kiskapus see Copşa Mică
111 M22 **Kiskörei-víztároló** ⊠ E Hungary
Kis-Küküllo see Târnava Mică
111 L24 **Kiskunfélegyháza** var. Félegyháza. Bács-Kiskun, C Hungary 46°42′N 19°52′E
111 K25 **Kiskunhalas** var. Halas. Bács-Kiskun, S Hungary 46°26′N 19°29′E
111 K24 **Kiskunmajsa** Bács-Kiskun, S Hungary 46°30′N 19°46′E
127 N15 **Kislovodsk** Stavropol'skiy Kray, SW Russian Federation 43°55′N 42°45′E
81 L18 **Kismaayo** var. Chisimayu, Kismayu, It. Chisimaio. Jubbada Hoose, S Somalia 0°05′S 42°35′E
Kismayu see Kismaayo
164 M13 **Kiso-sanmyaku** ▲▲ Honshū, S Japan
115 H24 **Kíssamos** prev. Kastélli. Kríti, Greece, E Mediterranean Sea 35°30′N 23°39′E
Kisseraing see Kanmaw Kyun
76 K14 **Kissidougou** Guinée-Forestière, S Guinea 09°15′N 10°08′W
23 X12 **Kissimmee** Florida, SE USA 28°17′N 81°24′W
23 X12 **Kissimmee, Lake** ◎ Florida, SE USA
23 X13 **Kissimmee River** 〰 Florida, SE USA
11 V13 **Kississing Lake** ◎ Manitoba, C Canada
111 L24 **Kistelek** Csongrád, SE Hungary 46°27′N 19°58′E
Kistna see Krishna
111 M23 **Kisújszállás** Jász-Nagykun-Szolnok, E Hungary 47°14′N 20°45′E
164 G12 **Kisuki** var. Unnan. Shimane, Honshū, SW Japan 35°25′N 133°15′E
81 H18 **Kisumu** prev. Port Florence. Nyanza, W Kenya 0°02′N 34°42′E
Kisutzaneustadtl see Kysucké Nové Mesto
111 O20 **Kisvárda** Ger. Kleinwardein. Szabolcs-Szatmár-Bereg, E Hungary 48°13′N 22°03′E
81 J24 **Kiswere** Lindi, SE Tanzania 09°24′S 39°37′E
Kiszucaújhely see Kysucké Nové Mesto
76 K12 **Kita** Kayes, W Mali 13°00′N 09°28′W
197 N14 **Kitaa** ◈ province W Greenland
Kita-Akita see Takanosu
Kitab see Kitob
165 Q4 **Kitahiyama** Hokkaidō, NE Japan 42°25′N 139°55′E
165 P12 **Kita-Ibaraki** Ibaraki, Honshū, S Japan 36°46′N 140°45′E
165 X16 **Kita-Iō-jima** Eng. San Alessandro. island SE Japan
165 Q9 **Kitakami** Iwate, Honshū, C Japan 39°18′N 141°05′E
165 P11 **Kitakata** Fukushima, Honshū, C Japan 37°38′N 139°52′E
164 D13 **Kitakyūshū** var. Kitakyûsyû. Fukuoka, Kyūshū, SW Japan 33°51′N 130°49′E
Kitakyûsyû see Kitakyūshū
81 H18 **Kitale** Rift Valley, W Kenya 01°01′N 35°01′E
165 U3 **Kitami** Hokkaidō, NE Japan 43°52′N 143°51′E
165 T2 **Kitami-sanchi** ▲▲ Hokkaidō, NE Japan
37 W5 **Kit Carson** Colorado, C USA 38°45′N 102°47′W
180 M12 **Kitchener** Western Australia 31°03′S 124°00′E
14 F16 **Kitchener** Ontario, S Canada 43°28′N 80°27′W
93 O17 **Kitee** Itä-Suomi, SE Finland 62°06′N 30°09′E
81 G16 **Kitgum** N Uganda 03°17′N 32°54′E
Kithareng see Kanmaw Kyun
Kíthira see Kýthira
Kíthnos see Kýthnos
10 J13 **Kitimat** British Columbia, SW Canada 54°05′N 128°38′W
92 L11 **Kitinen** 〰 N Finland
147 N12 **Kitob** Rus. Kitab. Qashqadaryo Viloyati, S Uzbekistan 39°06′N 66°47′E
116 K7 **Kitsman'** Ger. Kotzman, Rom. Cozmeni, Rus. Kitsman. Chernivets'ka Oblast', W Ukraine 48°30′N 25°50′E
164 E14 **Kitsuki** var. Kituki. Ōita, Kyūshū, SW Japan 33°24′N 131°36′E
18 C14 **Kittanning** Pennsylvania, NE USA 40°48′N 79°28′W
19 P10 **Kittery** Maine, NE USA 43°05′N 70°44′W
92 L11 **Kittilä** Lappi, N Finland 67°39′N 24°53′E
109 Z4 **Kittsee** Burgenland, E Austria 48°06′N 17°03′E
81 J19 **Kitui** Eastern, S Kenya 01°25′S 38°00′E
Kituki see Kitsuki
81 G22 **Kitunda** Tabora, C Tanzania 06°47′S 33°13′E
10 K13 **Kitwanga** British Columbia, SW Canada 55°07′N 128°03′W
82 J13 **Kitwe** var. Kitwe-Nkana. Copperbelt, C Zambia 12°48′S 28°13′E
Kitwe-Nkana see Kitwe
109 O7 **Kitzbühel** Tirol, W Austria 47°27′N 12°23′E
109 O7 **Kitzbüheler Alpen** ▲▲ W Austria
101 J19 **Kitzingen** Bayern, SE Germany 49°45′N 10°11′E
153 Q14 **Kiul** Bihār, NE India 25°10′N 86°06′E
186 A7 **Kiunga** Western, SW Papua New Guinea 06°10′S 141°15′E
93 M16 **Kiuruvesi** Itä-Suomi, C Finland 63°38′N 26°40′E
38 M7 **Kivalina** Alaska, USA 67°44′N 164°32′W
92 L13 **Kivalo** ridge C Finland
116 J3 **Kivertsi** Pol. Kiwerce, Rus. Kivertsy. Volyns'ka Oblast', NW Ukraine 50°50′N 25°31′E
Kivertsy see Kivertsi
93 L16 **Kivijärvi** Länsi-Suomi, C Finland 63°09′N 25°04′E
95 L23 **Kivik** Skåne, S Sweden 55°40′N 14°15′E
118 J3 **Kiviõli** Ida-Virumaa, NE Estonia 59°20′N 27°00′E
Kivu, Lac see Kivu, Lake
67 U10 **Kivu, Lake** Fr. Lac Kivu. ◎ Rwanda/Dem. Rep. Congo
186 C9 **Kiwai Island** island SW Papua New Guinea
39 N8 **Kiwalik** Alaska, USA 66°01′N 161°50′W
Kiwerce see Kivertsi
Kiyev see Kyyiv
145 R10 **Kiyevka** Karaganda, C Kazakhstan 50°15′N 71°33′E
Kiyevskaya Oblast' see Kyyivs'ka Oblast'
Kiyevskoye Vodokhranilishche see Kyyivs'ke Vodoskhovyshche
136 D10 **Kıyıköy** Kırklareli, NW Turkey 41°37′N 28°07′E
145 O9 **Kiyma** Akmola, C Kazakhstan 51°37′N 67°31′E
125 V13 **Kizel** Permskaya Oblast', NW Russian Federation 58°59′N 57°37′E
125 O12 **Kizema** var. Kizëma. Arkhangel'skaya Oblast', NW Russian Federation 61°06′N 44°51′E
Kizëma see Kizema
Kizilagach see Elkhovo
136 H12 **Kızılcahamam** Ankara, N Turkey 40°28′N 32°37′E
136 J10 **Kızıl Irmak** 〰 C Turkey
Kizil Kum see Kyzyl Kum
137 P16 **Kızıltepe** Mardin, SE Turkey 37°12′N 40°36′E
Ki Zil Uzen see Qezel Owzan, Rūd-e
127 Q16 **Kizilyurt** Respublika Dagestan, SW Russian Federation 43°13′N 46°54′E
127 Q15 **Kizlyar** Respublika Dagestan, SW Russian Federation 43°51′N 46°39′E
127 S3 **Kizner** Udmurtskaya Respublika, NW Russian Federation 56°19′N 51°37′E
Kizyl-Arvat see Serdar
Kizyl-Atrek see Etrek
Kizyl-Kaya see Gyzylgaýa
Kizyl-Su see Gyzylsuw
95 H16 **Kjerkøy** island S Norway
Kjølen see Kölen
92 L7 **Kjøllefjord** Finnmark, N Norway 70°55′N 27°19′E
92 H11 **Kjøpsvik** Nordland, C Norway 68°06′N 16°21′E
169 N12 **Klabat, Teluk** bay Pulau Bangka, W Indonesia
112 I12 **Kladanj** ◈ Fedederacijia Bosna I Hercegovina, E Bosnia and Herzegovina
171 X16 **Kladar** Papua, E Indonesia 08°14′S 137°46′E
111 C16 **Kladno** Středočeský, NW Czech Republic 50°10′N 14°05′E
112 P11 **Kladovo** Serbia, E Serbia 44°37′N 22°36′E
167 P12 **Klaeng** Rayong, S Thailand 12°48′N 101°41′E
109 T9 **Klagenfurt** Slvn. Celovec. Kärnten, S Austria 46°38′N 14°20′E
118 B11 **Klaipėda** Ger. Memel. Klaipeda, NW Lithuania 55°42′N 21°09′E
118 C11 **Klaipėda** ◈ province W Lithuania
Klaksvig see Klaksvík
95 B18 **Klaksvík** Dan. Klaksvig. Faeroe Islands 62°13′N 06°34′W
34 L2 **Klamath** California, W USA 41°31′N 124°02′W
32 H16 **Klamath Falls** Oregon, NW USA 42°14′N 121°47′W
34 M1 **Klamath Mountains** ▲▲ California/Oregon, W USA
34 L2 **Klamath River** 〰 California/Oregon, W USA
168 K9 **Klang** var. Kelang; prev. Port Swettenham. Selangor, Peninsular Malaysia 03°02′N 101°27′E
94 J13 **Klarälven** 〰 Norway/Sweden
111 B15 **Klášterec nad Ohří** Ger. Klösterle an der Eger. Ústecky Kraj, NW Czech Republic 50°24′N 13°10′E
111 B18 **Klatovy** Ger. Klattau. Plzeňský Kraj, W Czech Republic 49°24′N 13°16′E
Klattau see Klatovy
Klausenburg see Cluj-Napoca
39 Y14 **Klawock** Prince of Wales Island, Alaska, USA 55°33′N 133°06′W
98 P8 **Klazienaveen** Drenthe, NE Netherlands 52°43′N 07°E
Kleck see Klyetsk
110 H11 **Kłecko** Weilkopolskie, C Poland 52°37′N 17°27′E
110 I11 **Kleczew** Wielkopolskie, C Poland 52°22′N 18°12′E
10 L15 **Kleena Kleene** British Columbia, SW Canada 51°55′N 124°54′W
83 D20 **Klein Aub** Hardap, C Namibia 23°48′S 16°39′E
Kleine Donau see Mosoni-Duna
101 O14 **Kleine Elster** 〰 E Germany
Kleine Kokel see Târnava Mică
99 I16 **Kleine Nete** 〰 N Belgium
Kleines Ungarisches Tiefland see Little Alföld
83 E22 **Klein Karas** Karas, S Namibia 27°36′S 18°05′E
Kleinkopisch see Copşa Mică
Klein-Marien see Väike-Maarja
Kleinschlatten see Zlatna
83 D23 **Kleinsee** Northern Cape, W South Africa 29°43′S 17°03′E
Kleinwardein see Kisvárda
115 C16 **Kleisoúra** Ípeiros, W Greece 39°21′N 20°52′E
95 C17 **Klepp** Rogaland, S Norway 58°46′N 05°39′E
83 I22 **Klerksdorp** North-West, N South Africa 26°52′S 26°39′E
126 I5 **Kletnya** Bryanskaya Oblast', W Russian Federation 53°25′N 32°58′E
Kletsk see Klyetsk
101 D14 **Kleve** Eng. Cleves, Fr. Clèves; prev. Cleve. Nordrhein-Westfalen, W Germany 51°47′N 06°11′E
113 J16 **Kličevo** C Montenegro 42°45′N 18°58′E
119 M16 **Klichaw** Rus. Klichev. Mahilyowskaya Voblasts', E Belarus 53°29′N 29°21′E
Klichev see Klichaw
119 Q16 **Klimavichy** Rus. Klimovichi. Mahilyowskaya Voblasts', E Belarus 53°37′N 31°58′E
114 M7 **Kliment** Shumen, NE Bulgaria 43°37′N 27°00′E
Klimovichi see Klimavichy
93 G14 **Klimpfjäll** Västerbotten, N Sweden 65°05′N 14°50′E
126 K3 **Klin** Moskovskaya Oblast', W Russian Federation 56°19′N 36°45′E
Klina see Klinë
113 M16 **Klinë** Serb. Klina. W Kosovo 42°38′N 20°35′E
111 B15 **Klínovec** Ger. Keilberg. ▲ NW Czech Republic 50°23′N 12°57′E
95 P19 **Klintehamn** Gotland, SE Sweden 57°22′N 18°15′E
127 R8 **Klintsovka** Saratovskaya Oblast', W Russian Federation 51°42′N 49°17′E
126 H6 **Klintsy** Bryanskaya Oblast', W Russian Federation 52°46′N 32°21′E
95 K22 **Klippan** Skåne, S Sweden 56°08′N 13°10′E
92 G13 **Klippen** Västerbotten, N Sweden 65°50′N 15°07′E
121 P2 **Klírou** W Cyprus 35°01′N 33°11′E
114 I9 **Klisura** Plovdiv, C Bulgaria 42°40′N 24°28′E
95 F20 **Klitmøller** Viborg, NW Denmark 57°01′N 08°29′E
112 F11 **Ključ** Federacija Bosna I Hercegovina, NW Bosnia and Herzegovina 44°32′N 16°46′E
111 J14 **Kłobuck** Śląskie, S Poland 50°56′N 18°55′E
110 J11 **Kłodawa** Wielkopolskie, C Poland 52°14′N 18°55′E
111 G16 **Kłodzko** Ger. Glatz. Dolnośląskie, SW Poland 50°27′N 16°37′E
95 I14 **Kløfta** Akershus, S Norway 60°04′N 11°06′E
112 P12 **Klokočevac** Serbia, E Serbia 44°19′N 22°11′E
118 G3 **Klooga** Ger. Lodensee. Harjumaa, NW Estonia 59°18′N 24°10′E
99 F15 **Kloosterzande** Zeeland, SW Netherlands 51°22′N 04°01′E
113 L19 **Klos** var. Klosi. Dibër, C Albania 41°30′N 20°07′E
Klosi see Klos
Klösterle an der Eger see Klášterec nad Ohří
109 X3 **Klosterneuburg** Niederösterreich, NE Austria 48°19′N 16°20′E
108 J9 **Klosters** Graubünden, SE Switzerland 46°54′N 09°52′E
108 G7 **Kloten** Zürich, N Switzerland 47°27′N 08°35′E
108 G7 **Kloten** ✈ (Zürich) Zürich, N Switzerland 47°25′N 08°36′E
100 K12 **Klötze** Sachsen-Anhalt, C Germany 52°37′N 11°09′E
12 K3 **Klotz, Lac** ◎ Québec, NE Canada
101 O15 **Klotzsche** ✈ (Dresden) Sachsen, E Germany 51°06′N 13°44′E
10 H7 **Kluane Lake** ◎ Yukon Territory, W Canada
Kluang see Keluang
111 I14 **Kluczbork** Ger. Kreuzburg, Kreuzburg in Oberschlesien. Opolskie, S Poland 50°59′N 18°13′E
39 W12 **Klukwan** Alaska, USA 59°24′N 135°49′W
Klyastitsy see Klyastsitsy
118 L11 **Klyastsitsy** Rus. Klyastitsy. Vitsyebskaya Voblasts', N Belarus 55°53′N 28°36′E
127 T5 **Klyavlino** Samarskaya Oblast', W Russian Federation 54°21′N 52°12′E
84 K9 **Klyaz'in** 〰 W Russian Federation
127 N3 **Klyaz'ma** 〰 W Russian Federation
119 J17 **Klyetsk** Pol. Kleck, Rus. Kletsk. Minskaya Voblasts', SW Belarus 53°04′N 26°38′E
147 S8 **Klyuchevka** Talasskaya Oblast', NW Kyrgyzstan 42°34′N 71°45′E
123 V10 **Klyuchevskaya Sopka, Vulkan** ⛰ E Russian Federation 56°03′N 160°38′E
95 D17 **Knaben** Vest-Agder, S Norway 58°46′N 07°04′E
95 K21 **Knäred** Halland, S Sweden 56°30′N 13°21′E
97 M16 **Knaresborough** N England, United Kingdom 54°01′N 01°35′W
114 H8 **Knezha** Vratsa, NW Bulgaria 43°29′N 24°04′E
25 O9 **Knickerbocker** Texas, SW USA 31°18′N 100°35′W
28 K5 **Knife River** 〰 North Dakota, N USA
10 K16 **Knight Inlet** inlet British Columbia, W Canada
39 S12 **Knight Island** island Alaska, USA
97 K20 **Knighton** E Wales, United Kingdom 52°20′N 03°01′W
35 O7 **Knights Landing** California, W USA 38°47′N 121°43′W
112 E13 **Knin** Šibenik-Knin, S Croatia 44°03′N 16°12′E
25 Q12 **Knippal** Texas, SW USA
109 U7 **Knittelfeld** Steiermark, C Austria 47°14′N 14°50′E
95 O15 **Knivsta** Uppsala, C Sweden 59°43′N 17°49′E
113 P14 **Knjaževac** Serbia, E Serbia 43°34′N 22°16′E
27 S4 **Knob Noster** Missouri, C USA 38°47′N 93°33′W
99 D15 **Knokke-Heist** West-Vlaanderen, NW Belgium 51°21′N 03°19′E
95 H20 **Knøsen** hill N Denmark
Knosós see Knossos
115 J25 **Knossos** Gk. Knosós. prehistoric site Kríti, Greece, E Mediterranean Sea
25 N7 **Knott** Texas, SW USA 32°21′N 101°35′W
194 K5 **Knowles, Cape** headland Antarctica 71°45′S 60°20′W
31 O11 **Knox** Indiana, N USA 41°17′N 86°37′W
29 O3 **Knox** North Dakota, N USA 48°19′N 99°43′W
18 C13 **Knox** Pennsylvania, NE USA 41°13′N 79°33′W
189 X8 **Knox Atoll** var. Ṇadikdik, Narikrik. atoll Ratak Chain, SE Marshall Islands
10 H13 **Knox, Cape** headland Graham Island, British Columbia, SW Canada 54°05′N 133°02′W
25 P5 **Knox City** Texas, SW USA 33°25′N 99°49′W
195 Y11 **Knox Coast** physical region Antarctica
31 T12 **Knox Lake** ⊠ Ohio, N USA
23 T5 **Knoxville** Georgia, SE USA 32°44′N 83°58′W
30 K12 **Knoxville** Illinois, N USA 40°54′N 90°16′W
29 W15 **Knoxville** Iowa, C USA 41°19′N 93°06′W
21 N9 **Knoxville** Tennessee, S USA 35°58′N 83°55′W
197 P11 **Knud Rasmussen Land** physical region N Greenland
Knüll see Knüllgebirge
101 I16 **Knüllgebirge** var. Knüll. ▲▲ C Germany
124 I5 **Knyazhegubskoye Vodokhranilishche** ◎ NW Russian Federation
Knyazhevo see Sredishte
Knyazhitsy see Knyazhytsy
119 O15 **Knyazhytsy** Rus. Knyazhitsy. Mahilyowskaya Voblasts', E Belarus 54°10′N 30°28′E
83 G26 **Knysna** Western Cape, SW South Africa 34°03′S 23°03′E
Koartac see Quaqtaq
81 J23 **Koani** Zanzibar South, E Tanzania 06°08′S 39°18′E
169 N13 **Koba** Pulau Bangka, W Indonesia 02°30′S 106°26′E
164 D16 **Kobayashi** var. Kobayasi. Miyazaki, Kyūshū, SW Japan 32°00′N 130°58′E
Kobayasi see Kobayashi
Kobdo see Hovd
164 I13 **Kōbe** Hyōgo, Honshū, SW Japan 34°40′N 135°10′E
Kobelyaki see Kobelyaky
117 T6 **Kobelyaky** Rus. Kobelyaki. Poltavs'ka Oblast', NE Ukraine 49°10′N 34°13′E
95 J22 **København** Eng. Copenhagen; anc. Hafnia. ● (Denmark) Sjælland, København, E Denmark 55°43′N 12°34′E
95 J23 **København** off. Københavns Amt. ◈ county E Denmark
Københavns Amt see København
76 K10 **Kobenni** Hodh el Gharbi, S Mauritania 15°58′N 09°24′W
171 T13 **Kobi** Pulau Seram, E Indonesia 02°56′S 129°53′E
101 F17 **Koblenz** prev. Coblenz, Fr. Coblence; anc. Confluentes. Rheinland-Pfalz, W Germany 50°21′N 07°36′E
108 F6 **Koblenz** Aargau, N Switzerland 47°34′N 08°16′E
Kobrin see Kobryn
171 V15 **Kobroor, Pulau** island Kepulauan Aru, E Indonesia
119 G19 **Kobryn** Rus. Kobrin. Brestskaya Voblasts', SW Belarus 52°13′N 24°21′E
39 O7 **Kobuk** Alaska, USA 66°54′N 156°52′W
39 O7 **Kobuk River** 〰 Alaska, USA
137 Q10 **K'obulet'i** W Georgia 41°47′N 41°47′E
123 P10 **Kobyay** Respublika Sakha (Yakutiya), NE Russian Federation 63°36′N 126°33′E
136 E11 **Kocaeli** ◈ province NW Turkey
113 P18 **Kočani** NE FYR Macedonia 41°55′N 22°25′E
112 K12 **Koceljevo** Serbia, W Serbia 44°28′N 19°49′E
109 U12 **Kočevje** Ger. Gottschee. S Slovenia 45°41′N 14°48′E
153 T12 **Koch Bihār** West Bengal, NE India 26°19′N 89°26′E
Kochchi see Cochin/Kochi
122 M9 **Kochechum** 〰 N Russian Federation
101 I20 **Kocher** 〰 SW Germany
125 T13 **Kochevo** Komi-Permyatskiy Avtonomnyy Okrug, NW Russian Federation 59°37′N 54°16′E
155 G22 **Kochi** var. Cochin, Kochchi. Kerala, SW India 09°56′N 76°15′E see also Cochin
164 G14 **Kōchi** var. Kôti. Kōchi, Shikoku, SW Japan 33°31′N 133°30′E
164 G14 **Kōchi** off. Kōchi-ken, var. Kôti. ◈ prefecture Shikoku, SW Japan
Kōchi-ken see Kōchi
Kochiu see Gejiu
Kochkor see Kochkorka
147 V8 **Kochkorka** Kir. Kochkor. Narynskaya Oblast', C Kyrgyzstan 42°09′N 75°42′E
125 V5 **Kochmes** Respublika Komi, NW Russian Federation 66°10′N 60°46′E
127 P15 **Kochubey** Respublika Dagestan, SW Russian Federation 44°25′N 46°33′E
115 I17 **Kochýlas** ▲ Skńyros, Vóreies Sporádes, Greece, Aegean Sea 38°50′N 24°35′E
110 O13 **Kock** Lubelskie, E Poland 51°39′N 22°26′E
81 J19 **Kodacho** spring/well S Kenya 01°52′S 39°22′E
153 Q14 **Kodarma** Jharkhand, N India 24°26′N 85°31′E
155 K24 **Koddiyar Bay** bay NE Sri Lanka
39 Q14 **Kodiak** Kodiak Island, Alaska, USA 57°47′N 152°24′W
39 Q14 **Kodiak Island** island Alaska, USA
154 B12 **Kodīnār** Gujarāt, W India 20°44′N 70°46′E
124 M9 **Kodino** Arkhangel'skaya Oblast', NW Russian Federation 63°36′N 39°54′E
122 M12 **Kodinsk** Krasnoyarskiy Kray, C Russian Federation 58°37′N 99°18′E
80 F12 **Kodok** Upper Nile, SE Sudan 09°51′N 32°07′E
117 N8 **Kodyma** Odes'ka Oblast', SW Ukraine 48°05′N 29°09′E
Koedoes see Kudus
99 B17 **Koekelare** West-Vlaanderen, W Belgium 51°07′N 02°58′E
Koeln see Köln
Koepang see Kupang
Ko-erh-mu see Golmud
99 J17 **Koersel** Limburg, NE Belgium 51°04′N 05°17′E
83 E21 **Koës** Karas, SE Namibia 25°59′S 19°08′E
Koetai see Mahakam, Sungai
Koetaradja see Bandaaceh
36 I14 **Kofa Mountains** ▲▲ Arizona, SW USA
171 Y15 **Kofarau** Papua, E Indonesia 07°29′S 140°28′E
147 P13 **Kofarnihon** Rus. Kofarnikhon; prev. Ordzhonikidzeabad, Taj. Orjonikidzeobod, Yangi-Bazar. W Tajikistan 38°32′N 68°56′E
147 P14 **Kofarnihon** Rus. Kafirnigan. 〰 SW Tajikistan
Kofarnikhon see Kofarnihon
114 M11 **Kofçaz** Kırklareli, NW Turkey 41°58′N 27°12′E
115 J25 **Kófinas** ▲ Kríti, Greece, E Mediterranean Sea 34°58′N 25°03′E
121 P3 **Kofínou** var. Kophinou. S Cyprus 34°49′N 33°24′E
109 V8 **Köflach** Steiermark, SE Austria 47°04′N 15°04′E
77 Q17 **Koforidua** SE Ghana 06°01′N 00°12′W
164 H12 **Kōfu** Tottori, Honshū, SW Japan 35°16′N 133°31′E
164 M13 **Kōfu** var. Kôhu. Yamanashi, Honshū, S Japan 35°41′N 138°33′E
81 F22 **Koga** Tabora, C Tanzania 06°08′S 32°20′E
Kogălniceanu see Mihail Kogălniceanu
13 P6 **Kogaluk** 〰 Newfoundland and Labrador, E Canada
12 J4 **Kogaluk** 〰 Québec, NE Canada
122 I10 **Kogalym** Khanty-Mansiyskiy Avtonomnyy Okrug-Yugra, C Russian Federation 62°13′N 74°34′E
95 J23 **Køge** Roskilde, E Denmark 55°28′N 12°12′E
95 J23 **Køge Bugt** bay E Denmark
77 U16 **Kogi** ◈ state C Nigeria
146 L11 **Kogon** Rus. Kagan. Buxoro Viloyati, C Uzbekistan 39°47′N 64°29′E
163 Y17 **Kŏgŭm-do** island S South Korea
Kőhalom see Rupea
149 T6 **Kohāt** North-West Frontier Province, NW Pakistan 33°37′N 71°30′E
142 L10 **Kohgīlūyeh va Būyer Aḥmad** off. Ostān-e Kohkīlūyeh va Būyer Aḥmadī, var. Boyer Ahmadī va Kohkīlūyeh. ◈ province SW Iran
118 G4 **Kohila** Ger. Koil. Raplamaa, NW Estonia 59°09′N 24°45′E
153 X13 **Kohīma** state capital Nāgāland, E India 25°40′N 94°08′E
Koh I Noh see Büyükağrı Dağı
Kohkīlūyeh va Būyer Aḥmadī, Ostān-e see Kohgīlūyeh va Būyer Aḥmad
149 R10 **Kohlu** Baluchistān, SW Pakistan 29°54′N 69°15′E
Kohsān see Kūhestān
118 J3 **Kohtla-Järve** Ida-Virumaa, NE Estonia 59°22′N 27°21′E
Kôhu see Kōfu
Kohyl'nyk see Cogîlnic
165 N11 **Koide** Niigata, Honshū, C Japan 37°13′N 138°58′E
10 G7 **Koidern** Yukon Territory, W Canada 61°55′N 140°22′W
76 J15 **Koidu** E Sierra Leone 08°40′N 11°01′W
118 I4 **Koigi** Järvamaa, C Estonia 58°51′N 25°45′E
Koil see Kohila
172 H13 **Koimbani** Grande Comore, NW Comoros 11°37′S 43°23′E
139 T3 **Koi Sanjaq** var. Koysanjaq, Kūysanjaq. Arbīl, N Iraq 36°05′N 44°38′E
93 O16 **Koitere** ◎ E Finland
Koivisto see Primorsk
163 Z16 **Kŏje-do** Jap. Kyōsai-tō. island S South Korea
80 J13 **K'ok'a Hāyk'** ◎ C Ethiopia
Kokand see Qo'qon
182 F6 **Kokatha** South Australia 31°17′S 135°16′E
146 M10 **Ko'kcha** Rus. Kokcha. Buxoro Viloyati, C Uzbekistan 40°30′N 64°58′E
Kokcha see Ko'kcha
Kokchetav see Kokshetau
93 K18 **Kokemäenjoki** 〰 SW Finland
171 W14 **Kokenau** var. Kokonau. Papua, E Indonesia 04°38′S 136°24′E
83 E22 **Kokerboom** Karas, SE Namibia 28°11′S 19°25′E
119 N14 **Kokhanava** Rus. Kokhanovo. Vitsyebskaya Voblasts', NE Belarus 54°28′N 29°59′E
Kokhanovichi see Kakhanavichy
Kokhanovo see Kokhanava
Kök-Janggak see Kok-Yangak
93 K16 **Kokkola** Swe. Karleby; prev. Swe. Gamlakarleby. Länsi-Suomi, W Finland 63°50′N 23°10′E
158 L3 **Kok Kuduk** spring/well N China 46°03′N 87°34′E
118 H9 **Koknese** Aizkraukle, C Latvia 56°38′N 25°27′E
77 T13 **Koko** Kebbi, W Nigeria 11°25′N 04°33′E
186 E9 **Kokoda** Northern, S Papua New Guinea 08°52′S 147°44′E
76 K12 **Kokofata** Kayes, W Mali 12°48′N 09°56′W
39 N6 **Kokolik River** 〰 Alaska, USA
31 O13 **Kokomo** Indiana, N USA 40°29′N 86°07′W
Kokonau see Kokenau
Koko Nor see Qinghai Hu, China
Koko Nor see Qinghai, China
186 H6 **Kokopo** var. Kopopo; prev. Herbertshöhe. New Britain, E Papua New Guinea 04°18′S 152°17′E
145 X10 **Kokpekti** Kaz. Kökpekti. Vostochnyy Kazakhstan, E Kazakhstan 48°47′N 82°28′E
145 X11 **Kokpekti** 〰 E Kazakhstan
Kökpekti see Kokpekti
153 T12 **Kokrajhar** Assam, NE India 26°24′N 90°16′E
39 P9 **Kokrines** Alaska, USA 64°58′N 154°42′W
39 P9 **Kokrines Hills** ▲▲ Alaska, USA
145 P17 **Koksaray** Yuzhnyy Kazakhstan, S Kazakhstan 42°34′N 68°06′E
147 X9 **Kokshaal-Tau** Rus. Khrebet Kakshaal-Too. ▲▲ China/Kyrgyzstan
145 P7 **Kokshetau** Kaz. Kökshetaū; prev. Kokchetav. Kokshetau, N Kazakhstan 53°18′N 69°25′E
Kökshetaū see Kokshetau
99 A17 **Koksijde** West-Vlaanderen, W Belgium 51°07′N 02°40′E
12 M5 **Koksoak** 〰 Québec, E Canada
83 K24 **Kokstad** KwaZulu/Natal, E South Africa 30°23′S 29°23′E
145 V14 **Koksu** Kaz. Rūdnīchnyy. Almaty, SE Kazakhstan 44°39′N 78°57′E
145 W15 **Koktal** Kaz. Köktal. Almaty, SE Kazakhstan 44°05′N 79°44′E
145 Q12 **Koktas** 〰 C Kazakhstan
Kök-Tash see Këk-Tash
Koktokay see Fuyun
147 T9 **Kok-Yangak** Kir. Kök-Janggak. Dzhalal-Abadskaya Oblast', W Kyrgyzstan 41°02′N 73°11′E
158 F9 **Kokyar** Xinjiang Uygur Zizhiqu, W China 37°24′N 77°15′E
124 J3 **Kola** Murmanskaya Oblast', NW Russian Federation 68°52′N 33°03′E
149 O13 **Kolāchi** var. Kulachi. 〰 SW Pakistan
76 J15 **Kolahun** N Liberia 08°24′N 10°02′W
171 O14 **Kolaka** Sulawesi, C Indonesia 04°04′S 121°38′E
K'o-la-ma-i see Karamay
Kola Peninsula see Kol'skiy Poluostrov
155 H19 **Kolār** Karnātaka, E India 13°10′N 78°10′E
155 H19 **Kolār Gold Fields** Karnātaka, E India 12°56′N 78°16′E
92 K11 **Kolari** Lappi, NW Finland 67°20′N 23°51′E
111 I21 **Kolárovo** Ger. Gutta; prev. Guta, Hung. Gúta. Nitriansky Kraj, SW Slovakia 47°54′N 18°01′E
113 K16 **Kolašin** E Montenegro 42°49′N 19°32′E
152 F11 **Kolāyat** Rājasthān, NW India 27°56′N 73°02′E
95 N15 **Kolbäck** Västmanland, C Sweden 59°33′N 16°15′E
Kolbcha see Kowbcha
197 Q15 **Kolbeinsey Ridge** undersea feature Denmark Strait/Norwegian Sea 69°00′N 17°30′W
Kolberg see Kołobrzeg
95 H15 **Kolbotn** Akershus, S Norway 62°15′N 10°24′E
111 N16 **Kolbuszowa** Podkarpackie, SE Poland 50°12′N 22°07′E
126 L3 **Kol'chugino** Vladimirskaya Oblast', W Russian Federation 56°19′N 39°24′E
76 H12 **Kolda** S Senegal 12°58′N 14°58′W
95 G23 **Kolding** Vejle, C Denmark 55°29′N 09°30′E
79 K20 **Kole** Kasai-Oriental, SW Dem. Rep. Congo 03°30′S 22°28′E
79 M17 **Kole** Orientale, N Dem. Rep. Congo 02°08′N 25°25′E
Kōle see Kili Island
84 F6 **Kölen** Nor. Kjølen. ▲▲ Norway/Sweden
Kolepom, Pulau see Yos Sudarso, Pulau
118 H3 **Kolga Laht** Ger. Kolko-Wiek. bay N Estonia
125 Q3 **Kolguyev, Ostrov** island NW Russian Federation
155 E16 **Kolhāpur** Mahārāshtra, SW India 16°42′N 74°13′E
151 K21 **Kolhumadulu** var. Thaa Atoll. atoll S Maldives
93 O16 **Koli** var. Kolinkylä. Itä-Suomi, E Finland 63°06′N 29°46′E
39 O13 **Koliganek** Alaska, USA 59°43′N 157°16′W
111 E16 **Kolín** Ger. Kolin. Střední Čechy, C Czech Republic 50°02′N 15°10′E
Kolinkylä see Koli
190 E12 **Koliu** Île Futuna, W Wallis and Futuna
118 E7 **Kolka** Talsi, NW Latvia 57°44′N 22°34′E
118 E7 **Kolkasrags** prev. Eng. Cape Domesnes. headland NW Latvia 57°45′N 22°35′E
153 S16 **Kolkata** prev. Calcutta. state capital West Bengal, NE India 22°30′N 88°20′E
Kolkhozabad see Kolkhozobod
147 P14 **Kolkhozobod** Rus. Kolkhozabad; prev. Kaganovichabad, Tugalan. SW Tajikistan 37°33′N 68°34′E
Kolki/Kołki see Kolky
Kolko-Wiek see Kolga Laht
116 K3 **Kolky** Pol. Kołki, Rus. Kolki. Volyns'ka Oblast', NW Ukraine 51°05′N 25°40′E
155 G23 **Kollam** var. Quilon. Kerala, SW India 08°57′N 76°37′E see also Quilon
155 G20 **Kollegāl** Karnātaka, W India 12°08′N 77°06′E
98 M5 **Kollum** Friesland, N Netherlands 53°17′N 06°09′E
Kolmar see Colmar
101 E16 **Köln** var. Koeln, Eng./Fr. Cologne, prev. Cöln; anc. Colonia Agrippina, Oppidum Ubiorum. Nordrhein-Westfalen, W Germany 50°57′N 06°57′E
110 N9 **Kolno** Podlaskie, NE Poland 53°24′N 21°57′E
110 J12 **Koło** Wielkopolskie, C Poland 52°11′N 18°39′E
38 B8 **Kōloa** var. Koloa. Kaua'i, Hawaii, USA, C Pacific Ocean 21°54′N 159°28′W
Koloa see Kōloa
110 E7 **Kołobrzeg** Ger. Kolberg. Zachodnio-pomorskie, NW Poland 54°11′N 15°34′E
126 H4 **Kolodnya** Smolenskaya Oblast', W Russian Federation 54°57′N 32°22′E
190 E13 **Kolofau, Mont** ⛰ Île Alofi, S Wallis and Futuna 14°21′S 178°02′W
125 O14 **Kologriv** Kostromskaya Oblast', NW Russian Federation 58°49′N 44°22′E
76 L12 **Kolokani** Koulikoro, W Mali 13°35′N 08°01′W
77 N13 **Koloko** W Burkina 11°06′N 05°18′W
186 K8 **Kolombangara** var. Kilimbangara, Nduke. island New Georgia Islands, NW Solomon Islands
Kolomea see Kolomyya
126 L4 **Kolomna** Moskovskaya Oblast', W Russian Federation 55°03′N 38°52′E
116 J7 **Kolomyya** Ger. Kolomea. Ivano-Frankivs'ka Oblast', W Ukraine 48°31′N 25°00′E
76 M13 **Kolondiéba** Sikasso, SW Mali 11°04′N 06°55′W
193 V15 **Kolonga** Tongatapu, S Tonga 21°07′S 175°05′W
189 U16 **Kolonia** var. Colonia. Pohnpei, E Micronesia 06°57′N 158°12′E
Kolonja see Kolonjë
113 K21 **Kolonjë** var. Kolonja. Fier, C Albania 40°49′N 19°37′E
Kolonjë see Ersekë
Kolosjoki see Nikel'
Kolotambu see Avuavu
193 U15 **Kolovai** Tongatapu, S Tonga 21°05′S 175°20′W
Kolozsvár see Cluj-Napoca
112 C9 **Kolpa** Ger. Kulpa, SCr. Kupa. 〰 Croatia/Slovenia
122 J11 **Kolpashevo** Tomskaya Oblast', C Russian Federation 58°21′N 82°44′E
124 H13 **Kolpino** Leningradskaya Oblast', NW Russian Federation 59°44′N 30°39′E
100 M10 **Kölpinsee** ◎ NE Germany
Kólpos Mórfu see Güzelyurt
146 K8 **Ko'lquduq** Rus. Kulkuduk. Navoiy Viloyati, N Uzbekistan 42°36′N 63°24′E
124 K5 **Kol'skiy Poluostrov** Eng. Kola Peninsula. peninsula NW Russian Federation
127 T6 **Koltubanovskiy** Orenburgskaya Oblast', W Russian Federation 53°00′N 52°00′E
112 L11 **Kolubara** 〰 C Serbia
Kolupchii see Gurkovo
110 K13 **Koluszki** Łódźskie, C Poland 51°44′N 19°50′E
125 T6 **Kolva** 〰 NW Russian Federation
93 E14 **Kolvereid** Nord-Trøndelag, W Norway 64°47′N 11°22′E
79 M24 **Kolwezi** Katanga, S Dem. Rep. Congo 10°43′S 25°29′E
123 S7 **Kolyma** 〰 NE Russian Federation
Kolyma Lowland see Kolymskaya Nizmennost'
Kolyma Range/Kolymskiy, Khrebet see Kolymskoye Nagor'ye
123 S7 **Kolymskaya Nizmennost'** Eng. Kolyma Lowland. lowlands NE Russian Federation
123 S7 **Kolymskoye** Respublika Sakha (Yakutiya), NE Russian Federation 68°42′N 158°46′E
123 U8 **Kolymskoye Nagor'ye** var. Khrebet Kolymskiy, Eng. Kolyma Range. ▲▲ E Russian Federation
123 V5 **Kolyuchinskaya Guba** bay NE Russian Federation
145 W15 **Kol'zhat** Kaz. Qalzhat. Almaty, SE Kazakhstan 43°29′N 80°37′E
114 G8 **Kom** ▲ NW Bulgaria 43°10′N 23°02′E
80 I13 **Koma** Oromīya, C Ethiopia 08°19′N 36°48′E
77 X12 **Komadugu Gana** 〰 NE Nigeria
164 M13 **Komagane** Nagano, Honshū, S Japan 35°44′N 137°54′E
79 P17 **Komanda** Orientale, NE Dem. Rep. Congo 01°25′N 29°43′E
197 U1 **Komandorskaya Basin** var. Kamchatka Basin. undersea feature SW Bering Sea 57°00′N 168°00′E
125 Pp9 **Komandorskiye Ostrova** Eng. Commander Islands. island group E Russian Federation
Kománfalva see Comăneşti
111 I22 **Komárno** Ger. Komorn, Hung. Komárom. Nitriansky Kraj, SW Slovakia 47°46′N 18°07′E
111 I22 **Komárom** Komárom-Esztergom, NW Hungary 47°43′N 18°06′E
Komárom see Komárno
111 I22 **Komárom-Esztergom** off. Komárom-Esztergom Megye. ◈ county N Hungary
Komárom-Esztergom Megye see Komárom-Esztergom
164 K11 **Komatsu** var. Komatu. Ishikawa, Honshū, SW Japan 36°25′N 136°27′E
Komatu see Komatsu
83 D17 **Kombat** Otjozondjupa, N Namibia 19°42′S 17°45′E
Kombissiguiri see Kombissiri
77 P13 **Kombissiri** var. Kombissiguiri. C Burkina 12°01′N 01°27′W
188 E10 **Komebail Lagoon** lagoon N Palau
81 F20 **Kome Island** island N Tanzania
Komeyo see Wandai
117 P10 **Kominternivs'ke** Odes'ka Oblast', SW Ukraine 46°52′N 30°56′E
125 S12 **Komi-Permyatskiy Avtonomnyy Okrug** ◈ autonomous district Permskiy Kray, W Russian Federation

◆ Country
● Country Capital
◇ Dependent Territory
○ Dependent Territory Capital
◈ Administrative Regions
✈ International Airport
▲ Mountain
▲▲ Mountain Range
⛰ Volcano
〰 River
◎ Lake
⊠ Reservoir

125 R8 **Komi, Respublika** ◈ *autonomous republic* NW Russian Federation
111 I25 **Komló** Baranya, SW Hungary 46°11′N 18°15′E
Kommunarsk *see* Alchevs'k
Kommunizm, Qullai *see* Ismoili Somoní, Qullai
186 B7 **Komo** Southern Highlands, W Papua New Guinea 06°06′S 142°52′E
170 M16 **Komodo, Pulau** *island* Nusa Tenggara, S Indonesia
77 N15 **Komoé** *var.* Komoé Fleuve. ≈ E Ivory Coast
Komoé Fleuve *see* Komoé
75 X11 **Kom Ombo** *var.* Kôm Ombo, Kawm Umbū. SE Egypt 24°26′N 32°57′E
79 F20 **Komono** Lékoumou, SW Congo 03°15′S 13°14′E
171 Y16 **Komoran** Papua, E Indonesia 08°14′S 138°51′E
171 Y16 **Komoran, Pulau** *island* E Indonesia
Komorn *see* Komárno
Komornok *see* Comorâşte
Komosolabad *see* Komsomolobod
Komotau *see* Chomutov
114 K13 **Komotiní** *var.* Gümüljina, *Turk.* Gümülcine. Anatolikí Makedonía kai Thráki, NE Greece 41°07′N 25°27′E
113 K16 **Komovi** ▲▲ E Montenegro
117 R8 **Kompaniyivka** Kirovohrads'ka Oblast', C Ukraine 48°16′N 32°12′E
Kompong *see* Kâmpóng Chhnăng
Kompong Cham *see* Kâmpóng Cham
Kompong Kleang *see* Kâmpóng Khleăng
Kompong Som *see* Kâmpóng Saôm
Kompong Speu *see* Kâmpóng Spoe
Komrat *see* Comrat
Komsomol *see* Komsomol'skiy
122 K14 **Komsomolets, Ostrov** *island* Severnaya Zemlya, N Russian Federation
144 F13 **Komsomolets, Zaliv** *lake gulf* SW Kazakhstan
Komsomol/Komsomolets *see* Karabalyk, Kostanay, Kazakhstan
147 Q12 **Komsomolobod** *Rus.* Komosolabad. C Tajikistan 38°51′N 69°54′E
124 M16 **Komsomol'sk** Ivanovskaya Oblast', W Russian Federation 56°58′N 40°15′E
117 S6 **Komsomol's'k** Poltavs'ka Oblast', C Ukraine 49°01′N 33°37′E
146 M11 **Komsomol'sk** Navoiy Viloyati, N Uzbekistan 40°14′N 65°10′E
144 G12 **Komsomol'skiy** *Kaz.* Komsomol. Atyrau, W Kazakhstan 47°18′N 53°37′E
127 P5 **Komsomol'skiy** Respublika Mordoviya, W Russian Federation 54°26′N 45°50′E
125 W4 **Komsomol'skiy** Respublika Komi, NW Russian Federation 67°33′N 64°00′E
123 S13 **Komsomol'sk-na-Amure** Khabarovskiy Kray, SE Russian Federation 50°32′N 136°59′E
Komsomol'sk-na-Ustyurte *see* Kubla-Ustyurt
144 K10 **Komsomol'skoye** Aktyubinsk, NW Kazakhstan
127 Q8 **Komsomol'skoye** Saratovskaya Oblast', W Russian Federation 50°45′N 47°00′E
145 P10 **Kon** ≈ C Kazakhstan
Kona *see* Kailua-Kona
124 K16 **Konakovo** Tverskaya Oblast', W Russian Federation 56°42′N 36°44′E
149 S4 **Konar** *Per.* Konarhā, *Pash.* Kunar. ◈ *province* E Afghanistan
143 V15 **Konārak** Sīstān va Balūchestān, SE Iran 25°26′N 60°23′E
Konarhā *see* Konar
27 O11 **Konawa** Oklahoma, C USA 34°57′N 96°45′W
122 H10 **Konda** ≈ C Russian Federation
154 L13 **Kondagaon** Chhattīsgarh, C India 19°38′N 81°41′E
14 K10 **Kondiaronk, Lac** ◎ Québec, SE Canada
180 J13 **Kondinin** Western Australia 32°31′S 118°15′E
81 H21 **Kondoa** Dodoma, C Tanzania 04°54′S 35°46′E
127 P6 **Kondol'** Penzenskaya Oblast', W Russian Federation 52°49′N 45°03′E
114 N10 **Kondolovo** Burgas, E Bulgaria 42°07′N 27°43′E
171 Z16 **Kondomirat** Papua, E Indonesia 08°57′S 140°55′E
124 J10 **Kondopoga** Respublika Kareliya, NW Russian Federation 62°13′N 34°17′E
149 Q2 **Kondoz** *var.* Kondūz, Qondūz, *Pash.* Kunduz, Kundūz. Kunduz, NE Afghanistan 36°49′N 68°50′E
149 Q2 **Kondoz** *Pash.* Kunduz. ◈ *province* NE Afghanistan
155 J17 **Kondukūr** *var.* Kandukur. Andhra Pradesh, E India 15°17′N 79°49′E
Kondūz *see* Kondoz
187 P16 **Koné** Province Nord, W New Caledonia 21°04′S 164°51′E
Konechnaya *see* Kurchatov
146 E13 **Könekesir** Balkan Welaýaty, W Turkmenistan 38°16′N 56°51′E
146 G8 **Köneürgenç** *var.* Köneürgench, *Rus.* Këneurgench; *prev.* Kunya-Urgench. Daşoguz Welaýaty, N Turkmenistan 42°21′N 59°09′E
77 N15 **Kong** N Ivory Coast 09°10′N 04°33′W
39 S5 **Kongakut River** ≈ Alaska, USA
197 O14 **Kong Christian IX Land** *Eng.* King Christian IX Land. *physical region* SE Greenland
197 P13 **Kong Christian X Land** *Eng.* King Christian X Land. *physical region* E Greenland
197 N13 **Kong Frederik IX Land** *physical region* SW Greenland
197 Q12 **Kong Frederik VIII Land** *Eng.* King Frederik VIII Land. *physical region* NE Greenland
197 N15 **Kong Frederik VI Kyst** *Eng.* King Frederik VI Coast. *physical region* SE Greenland
167 P13 **Kŏng, Kaôh** *prev.* Kas Kong. *island* SW Cambodia
92 P2 **Kong Karls Land** *Eng.* King Charles Islands. *island group* SE Svalbard
81 G14 **Kong Kong** ≈ SE Sudan
Kongo *see* Congo (river)
83 G16 **Kongola** Caprivi, NE Namibia 17°47′S 23°24′E
79 N21 **Kongolo** Katanga, E Dem. Rep. Congo 05°20′S 26°58′E
81 F14 **Kongor** Jonglei, SE Sudan 07°09′N 31°44′E
197 Q14 **Kong Oscar Fjord** *fjord* E Greenland
77 P12 **Kongoussi** N Burkina 13°19′N 01°31′W
95 G15 **Kongsberg** Buskerud, S Norway 59°39′N 09°38′E
92 Q2 **Kongsøya** *island* Kong Karls Land, E Svalbard
95 I14 **Kongsvinger** Hedmark, S Norway 60°10′N 12°00′E
Kongtong *see* Pingliang
167 T11 **Kông, Tônle** *var.* Xê Kong. ≈ Cambodia/Laos
158 E8 **Kongur Shan** ▲ NW China 38°39′N 75°21′E
81 I22 **Kongwa** Dodoma, C Tanzania 06°13′S 36°28′E
Kong, Xê *see* Kông, Tônle
Konia *see* Konya
147 R11 **Konibodom** *Rus.* Kanibadam. N Tajikistan 40°16′N 70°20′E
111 K15 **Koniecpol nad Pilicą** Śląskie, S Poland 50°47′N 19°45′E
Konieh *see* Konya
Königgrätz *see* Hradec Králové
Königinhof an der Elbe *see* Dvůr Králové nad Labem
101 K23 **Königsbrunn** Bayern, S Germany 48°16′N 10°52′E
101 O24 **Königssee** ◎ SE Germany
Königshütte *see* Chorzów
109 S8 **Königstuhl** ▲ S Austria 46°57′N 13°47′E
109 U3 **Königswiesen** Oberösterreich, N Austria 48°25′N 14°48′E
101 E17 **Königswinter** Nordrhein-Westfalen, W Germany 50°40′N 07°12′E
146 M11 **Konimex** *Rus.* Kenimekh. Navoiy Viloyati, N Uzbekistan 40°14′N 65°10′E
110 I12 **Konin** *Ger.* Kuhnau. Weilkopolskie, C Poland 52°13′N 18°17′E
Koninkrijk der Nederlanden *see* Netherlands
113 L24 **Konispol** *var.* Konispoli. Vlorë, S Albania 39°40′N 20°10′E
Konispoli *see* Konispol
115 C15 **Kónitsa** Ípeiros, W Greece 40°04′N 20°48′E
Konitz *see* Chojnice
108 D8 **Köniz** Bern, W Switzerland 46°56′N 07°25′E
113 H14 **Konjic** ◈ Federacija Bosna I Hercegovina, S Bosnia and Herzegovina
92 J10 **Könkämäälven** ≈ Finland/Sweden
155 D14 **Konkan** *plain* W India
83 D22 **Konkiep** ≈ S Namibia
76 I14 **Konkouré** ≈ W Guinea
77 O11 **Konna** Mopti, S Mali 14°58′N 03°49′W
186 H6 **Konogaiang, Mount** ▲ New Ireland, NE Papua New Guinea 04°05′S 152°43′E
186 H5 **Konogogo** New Ireland, NE Papua New Guinea 03°25′S 152°09′E
108 E9 **Konolfingen** Bern, W Switzerland 46°53′N 07°36′E
77 P16 **Konongo** C Ghana 06°39′N 01°06′W
186 H5 **Konos** New Ireland, NE Papua New Guinea 03°09′S 151°47′E
124 M12 **Konosha** Arkhangel'skaya Oblast', NW Russian Federation 60°58′N 40°09′E
117 R3 **Konotop** Sums'ka Oblast', NE Ukraine 51°15′N 33°14′E
158 L7 **Konqi He** ≈ NW China
111 L14 **Końskie** Śiętokrzyskie, C Poland 51°12′N 20°23′E
Konstantinovka *see* Kostyantynivka
126 M11 **Konstantinovsk** Rostovskaya Oblast', SW Russian Federation 47°37′N 41°07′E
101 H24 **Konstanz** *var.* Constanz, *Eng.* Constance, *hist.* Kostnitz; *anc.* Constantia. Baden-Württemberg, S Germany 47°40′N 09°10′E
Konstanza *see* Constanţa
77 T14 **Kontagora** Niger, W Nigeria 10°25′N 05°29′E
78 E13 **Kontcha** Nord, N Cameroon 08°00′N 12°13′E
99 G17 **Kontich** Antwerpen, N Belgium 51°08′N 04°27′E
93 O16 **Kontiolahti** Itä-Suomi, SE Finland 62°46′N 29°51′E
93 M15 **Kontiomäki** Oulu, C Finland 64°20′N 28°09′E
167 U11 **Kon Tum** *var.* Kontum. Kon Tum, C Vietnam 14°23′N 108°00′E
Kontum *see* Kon Tum
Konur *see* Sulakyurt
136 H15 **Konya** *var.* Konieh, *prev.* Konia; *anc.* Iconium. Konya, C Turkey 37°51′N 32°30′E
136 H15 **Konya** *var.* Konia, Konieh. ◈ *province* C Turkey
151 E15 **Konya Reservoir** *var.* Shivāji Sāgar. ⊠ W India
145 T13 **Konyrat** *var.* Kounradskiy, *Kaz.* Qongyrat. Karaganda, SE Kazakhstan 46°57′N 75°01′E
145 W15 **Konyrolen** Almaty, SE Kazakhstan 44°16′N 79°18′E
81 I19 **Konza** Eastern, S Kenya 01°44′S 37°07′E
98 I9 **Koog aan den Zaan** Noord-Holland, C Netherlands 52°28′N 04°49′E
182 E7 **Koonibba** South Australia 31°55′S 133°23′E
31 O11 **Koontz Lake** Indiana, N USA 41°25′N 86°24′W
171 U12 **Koor** Papua, E Indonesia 0°21′S 132°28′E
183 R9 **Koorawatha** New South Wales, SE Australia 34°03′S 148°33′E
118 J5 **Koosa** Tartumaa, E Estonia 58°31′N 27°06′E
33 N7 **Kootenai** *var.* Kootenay. ≈ Canada/USA *see also* Kootenay
Kootenai *see* Kootenay
11 P17 **Kootenay** *var.* Kootenai. ≈ Canada/USA *see also* Kootenai
Kootenay *see* Kootenai
83 F24 **Kootjieskolk** Northern Cape, W South Africa 31°16′S 20°21′E
Kopal *see* Koppal
113 M15 **Kopaonik** ▲▲ S Serbia
Kopar *see* Koper
92 K1 **Kópasker** Nordhurland Eystra, N Iceland 66°15′N 16°23′W
92 H4 **Kópavogur** Reykjanes, W Iceland 64°06′N 21°47′W
145 U13 **Kopbirlik** *prev.* Kīrov, Kirova. Almaty, SE Kazakhstan 46°24′N 77°16′E
109 S13 **Koper** *It.* Capodistria; *prev.* Kopar. SW Slovenia 45°32′N 13°43′E
95 C16 **Kopervik** Rogaland, S Norway 59°17′N 05°20′E
Köpetdag Gershi/Kopetdag, Khrebet *see* Koppeh Dāgh
Kophinou *see* Kofínou
182 G8 **Kopi** South Australia 33°24′S 135°40′E
153 W12 **Kopili** ≈ NE India
95 M15 **Köping** Västmanland, C Sweden 59°31′N 16°00′E
113 K17 **Koplik** *var.* Kopliku. Shkodër, NW Albania 42°12′N 19°26′E
Kopliku *see* Koplik
Kopopo *see* Kokopo
155 G18 **Koppal** *var.* Kopal. Karnātaka, SW India 14°20′N 76°09′E
94 I11 **Koppang** Hedmark, S Norway 61°34′N 11°04′E
Kopparberg *see* Dalarna
143 S3 **Koppeh Dāgh** *Rus.* Khrebet Kopetdag, *Turkm.* Köpetdag Gershi. ▲▲ Iran/Turkmenistan
Koppename *see* Coppename Rivier
95 J15 **Koppom** Värmland, C Sweden 59°42′N 12°07′E
Kopreinitz *see* Koprivnica
114 K9 **Koprinka, Yazovir** *prev.* Yazovir Georgi Dimitrov. ⊠ C Bulgaria
112 F7 **Koprivnica** *Ger.* Kopreinitz, *Hung.* Kaproncza. Koprivnica-Križevci, N Croatia 46°10′N 16°49′E
112 F8 **Koprivnica-Križevci** *off.* Koprivničko-Križevačka Županija. ◈ *province* N Croatia
111 I17 **Kopřivnice** *Ger.* Nesselsdorf. Moravskoslezský Kraj, E Czech Republic 49°36′N 18°09′E
Koprivničko-Križevačka Županija *see* Koprivnica-Križevci
Köprülü *see* Veles
Koptsevichi *see* Kaptsevichy
Kopyl' *see* Kapyl'
119 O14 **Kopys'** Vitsyebskaya Voblasts', NE Belarus 54°19′N 30°18′E
113 M18 **Korab** ▲ Albania/FYR Macedonia 41°48′N 20°33′E
Korabavur Pastligi *see* Karabaur', Uval
81 M14 **K'orahē** Sumalē, E Ethiopia 06°36′N 44°21′E
115 L16 **Kórakas, Akrotírio** *cape* Lésvos, E Greece
112 D9 **Korana** ≈ C Croatia
155 L14 **Korāput** Orissa, E India 18°48′N 82°41′E
Korat *see* Nakhon Ratchasima
167 Q9 **Korat Plateau** *plateau* E Thailand
139 T1 **Kōrāwa, Sar-i** ▲ NE Iraq 37°08′N 44°39′E
154 L11 **Korba** Chhattīsgarh, C India 22°25′N 82°43′E
101 H15 **Korbach** Hessen, C Germany 51°16′N 08°52′E
Korça *see* Korçë
113 M21 **Korçë** *var.* Korça, *Gk.* Korytsa, *It.* Corriza; *prev.* Koritsa. Korçë, SE Albania 40°38′N 20°47′E
113 M21 **Korçë** ◈ *district* SE Albania
113 G15 **Korčula** *It.* Curzola. Dubrovnik-Neretva, S Croatia 42°57′N 17°08′E
113 F15 **Korčula** *It.* Curzola; *anc.* Corcyra Nigra. *island* S Croatia
113 F15 **Korčulanski Kanal** *channel* S Croatia
145 T6 **Korday** *prev.* Georgiyevka. Zhambyl, SE Kazakhstan 43°03′N 74°43′E
142 J5 **Kordestān** *off.* Ostān-e Kordestān, *var.* Kurdestan. ◈ *province* W Iran
Kordestān, Ostān-e *see* Kordestān
143 P4 **Kord Kūy** *var.* Kurd Kui. Golestán, N Iran 36°49′N 54°05′E
163 V13 **Korea Bay** *bay* China/North Korea
Korea, Democratic People's Republic of *see* North Korea
171 T15 **Koreare** Pulau Yamdena, E Indonesia 07°33′S 131°13′E
Korea, Republic of *see* South Korea
163 Z17 **Korea Strait** *Jap.* Chōsen-kaikyō, *Kor.* Taehan-haehyŏp. *channel* Japan/South Korea
Korelichi/Korelicze *see* Karelichy
80 J11 **Korem** Tigrai, N Ethiopia 12°32′N 39°29′E
77 U11 **Korén Adoua** ≈ C Niger
126 I7 **Korenevo** Kurskaya Oblast', W Russian Federation 51°21′N 34°53′E
126 L13 **Korenovsk** Krasnodarskiy Kray, SW Russian Federation 45°28′N 39°25′E
116 L4 **Korets'** *Pol.* Korzec, *Rus.* Korets. Rivnens'ka Oblast', NW Ukraine 50°38′N 27°12′E
Korets *see* Korets'
194 L7 **Korff Ice Rise** *ice cap* Antarctica
145 Q10 **Korgalzhyn** *var.* Kurgal'dzhino, Kurgal'dzhinsky, *Kaz.* Qorghalzhyn. Akmola, C Kazakhstan 50°33′N 69°58′E
92 G13 **Korgen** Troms, N Norway 66°04′N 13°51′E
147 R9 **Korgon-Dĕbē** Dzhalal-Abadskaya Oblast', W Kyrgyzstan 41°51′N 70°52′E
76 M14 **Korhogo** N Ivory Coast 09°29′N 05°39′W
115 F19 **Korinthiakós Kólpos** *Eng.* Gulf of Corinth; *anc.* Corinthiacus Sinus. *gulf* C Greece
115 F19 **Kórinthos** *anc.* Corinthus *Eng.* Corinth. Pelopónnisos, S Greece 37°56′N 22°55′E
113 M18 **Koritnik** ▲ S Serbia 42°06′N 20°34′E
Koritsa *see* Korçë
165 P11 **Kōriyama** Fukushima, Honshū, C Japan 37°25′N 140°20′E
136 E16 **Korkuteli** Antalya, SW Turkey 37°07′N 30°11′E
158 K6 **Korla** *Chin.* K'u-erh-lo. Xinjiang Uygur Zizhiqu, NW China 41°48′N 86°10′E
122 J10 **Korliki** Khanty-Mansiyskiy Avtonomnyy Okrug-Yugra, C Russian Federation 61°28′N 82°12′E
Körlin an der Persante *see* Karlino
Korma *see* Karma
14 D8 **Kormak** Ontario, S Canada 47°38′N 83°00′W
Kormakíti, Akrotíri/Kormakiti, Cape/Kormakítis *see* Koruçam Burnu
111 G23 **Körmend** Vas, W Hungary 47°02′N 16°35′E
139 T5 **Kōrmōr** Şalāḩ ad Dīn, E Iraq 35°06′N 44°47′E
112 C13 **Kornat** *It.* Incoronata. *island* W Croatia
Korneshty *see* Corneşti
109 X3 **Korneuburg** Niederösterreich, NE Austria 48°22′N 16°20′E
145 P7 **Korneyevka** Severnyy Kazakhstan, N Kazakhstan 54°01′N 68°30′E
95 I17 **Kornsjø** Østfold, S Norway 58°55′N 11°40′E
77 O11 **Koro** Mopti, S Mali 14°05′N 03°06′W
1873 Y14 **Koro** *island* C Fiji
186 B7 **Koroba** Southern Highlands, W Papua New Guinea 05°46′S 142°48′E
126 K8 **Korocha** Belgorodskaya Oblast', W Russian Federation 50°49′N 37°08′E
136 H12 **Köroğlu Dağları** ▲▲ C Turkey
183 V6 **Korogoro Point** *headland* New South Wales, SE Australia 31°03′S 153°04′E
81 J21 **Korogwe** Tanga, E Tanzania 05°10′S 38°30′E
182 L13 **Koroit** Victoria, SE Australia 38°17′S 142°22′E
187 X15 **Korolevu** Viti Levu, W Fiji 18°12′S 177°44′E
190 I17 **Koromiri** *island* S Cook Islands
171 Q8 **Koronadal** Mindanao, S Philippines 06°23′N 124°54′E
114 G13 **Koróneia, Límni** *var.* Límni Korónia. ◎ N Greece
115 E22 **Koróni** Pelopónnisos, S Greece 36°47′N 21°57′E
Korónia, Límni *see* Koróneia, Límni
110 I9 **Koronowo** *Ger.* Krone an der Brahe. Kujawski-pomorskie, C Poland 53°18′N 17°56′E
117 R2 **Korop** Chernihivs'ka Oblast', N Ukraine 51°35′N 32°57′E
115 H19 **Koropí** Attikí, C Greece 37°54′N 23°52′E
188 C8 **Koror** (Palau) Oreor, N Palau 07°21′N 134°28′E
Koror *see* Oreor
111 L23 **Körös** ≈ E Hungary
Kőrös *see* Križevci
Körösbánya *see* Baia de Criş
187 Y14 **Koro Sea** *sea* C Fiji
Koroška *see* Kärnten
117 N3 **Korosten'** Zhytomyrs'ka Oblast', NW Ukraine 50°56′N 28°39′E
Korostyshev *see* Korostyshiv
117 N4 **Korostyshiv** *Rus.* Korostyshev. Zhytomyrs'ka Oblast', N Ukraine 50°18′N 29°05′E
125 V3 **Korotaikha** ≈ NW Russian Federation
122 J9 **Korotchayevo** Yamalo-Nenetskiy Avtonomnyy Okrug, N Russian Federation 66°00′N 78°11′E
78 I8 **Koro Toro** Borkou-Ennedi-Tibesti, N Chad 16°01′N 18°27′E
39 N16 **Korovin Island** *island* Shumagin Islands, Alaska, USA
187 X14 **Korovou** Viti Levu, W Fiji 17°48′S 178°32′E
93 M17 **Korpilahti** Länsi-Suomi, C Finland 62°02′N 25°34′E
92 K12 **Korpilombolo** *Lapp.* Dállogilli. Norrbotten, N Sweden 66°51′N 23°00′E
123 T13 **Korsakov** Ostrov Sakhalin, Sakhalinskaya Oblast', SE Russian Federation 46°41′N 142°45′E
93 J16 **Korsholm** *Fin.* Mustasaari. Länsi-Suomi, W Finland 63°05′N 21°43′E
95 I23 **Korsør** Vestsjælland, E Denmark 55°19′N 11°09′E
Korsovka *see* Kārsava
117 P6 **Korsun'-Shevchenkivs'kyy** *Rus.* Korsun'-Shevchenkovskiy. Cherkas'ka Oblast', C Ukraine 49°26′N 31°15′E
Korsun'-Shevchenkovskiy *see* Korsun'-Shevchenkivs'kyy
99 C17 **Kortemark** West-Vlaanderen, W Belgium 51°03′N 03°03′E
99 H18 **Kortenberg** Vlaams Brabant, C Belgium 50°53′N 04°33′E
99 K18 **Kortessem** Limburg, NE Belgium 50°52′N 05°22′E
99 E14 **Kortgene** Zeeland, SW Netherlands 51°34′N 03°48′E
80 F8 **Korti** Northern, N Sudan 18°06′N 31°33′E
99 C18 **Kortrijk** *Fr.* Courtrai. West-Vlaanderen, W Belgium 50°50′N 03°17′E
121 O2 **Koruçam Burnu** *var.* Cape Kormakiti, Kormakítis, *Gk.* Akrotíri Kormakíti. *headland* N Cyprus 35°24′N 32°55′E
183 O13 **Korumburra** Victoria, SE Australia 38°27′S 145°48′E
Koryak Range *see* Koryakskoye Nagor'ye
123 V8 **Koryakskiy Avtonomnyy Okrug** ◈ *autonomous district* E Russian Federation
Koryakskiy Khrebet *see* Koryakskoye Nagor'ye
123 V7 **Koryakskoye Nagor'ye** *var.* Koryakskiy Khrebet, *Eng.* Koryak Range. ▲▲ NE Russian Federation
125 P11 **Koryazhma** Arkhangel'skaya Oblast', NW Russian Federation 61°16′N 47°07′E
Kōryō *see* Kangnŭng
Korytsa *see* Korçë
117 Q2 **Koryukivka** Chernihivs'ka Oblast', N Ukraine 51°45′N 32°16′E
Korzec *see* Korets'
115 N21 **Kos** Kos, Dodekánisa, Greece, Aegean Sea 36°53′N 27°19′E
115 M21 **Kos** *It.* Coo; *anc.* Cos. *island* Dodekánisa, Greece, Aegean Sea
125 T12 **Kosa** Komi-Permyatskiy Avtonomnyy Okrug, NW Russian Federation 59°55′N 54°54′E
125 T13 **Kosa** ≈ NW Russian Federation
164 B12 **Kō-saki** *headland* Nagasaki, Tsushima, SW Japan 34°06′N 129°13′E
163 X13 **Kosan** SE North Korea 38°50′N 127°26′E
119 H18 **Kosava** *Rus.* Kosovo. Brestskaya Voblasts', SW Belarus 52°45′N 25°16′E
Kosch *see* Kose
144 G12 **Koschagyl** *Kaz.* Qosshaghyl. Atyrau, W Kazakhstan 46°52′N 53°46′E
110 G12 **Kościan** *Ger.* Kosten. Wielkopolskie, C Poland 52°05′N 16°38′E
110 I7 **Kościerzyna** Pomorskie, NW Poland 54°07′N 17°55′E
22 L4 **Kosciusko** Mississippi, S USA 33°03′N 89°35′W
Kosciusko, Mount *see* Kosciuszko, Mount
183 R11 **Kosciuszko, Mount** *prev.* Mount Kosciusko. ▲ New South Wales, SE Australia 36°28′S 148°15′E
118 H4 **Kose** *Ger.* Kosch. Harjumaa, NW Estonia 59°11′N 25°10′E
25 U9 **Kosse** Texas, SW USA 31°16′N 96°38′W
114 G6 **Koshava** Vidin, NW Bulgaria 44°03′N 23°00′E
147 U9 **Kosh-Dĕbē** *var.* Koshtebë. Narynskaya Oblast', C Kyrgyzstan 41°03′N 74°08′E
K'o-shih *see* Kashi
164 B12 **Koshikijima-rettō** *var.* Kosikizima Rettô. *island group* SW Japan
145 W13 **Koshkarkol', Ozero** ◎ SE Kazakhstan
30 L9 **Koshkonong, Lake** ◎ Wisconsin, N USA
Koshoba *see* Goşabo
Koshoba *see* Goşoba
164 M12 **Kōshoku** *var.* Kôsyoku. Nagano, Honshū, S Japan 36°33′N 138°09′E
Koshtebë *see* Kosh-Dĕbē
Kōshū *see* Enzan
Kōshū *see* Kwangju
111 N19 **Košice** *Ger.* Kaschau, *Hung.* Kassa. Košický Kraj, E Slovakia 48°44′N 21°15′E
111 M20 **Košický Kraj** ◈ *region* E Slovakia
Kosikizima Rettô *see* Koshikijima-rettō
153 R12 **Kosi Reservoir** ⊠ E Nepal
116 J8 **Kosiv** Ivano-Frankivs'ka Oblast', W Ukraine 48°19′N 25°04′E
145 O11 **Koskol'** *Kaz.* Qosköl. Karaganda, C Kazakhstan 49°32′N 67°08′E
125 Q9 **Koslan** Respublika Komi, NW Russian Federation 63°27′N 48°52′E
Köslin *see* Koszalin
146 M12 **Koson** *Rus.* Kasan. Qashqadaryo Viloyati, S Uzbekistan 39°04′N 65°35′E
163 Y13 **Kosŏng** SE North Korea 38°41′N 128°14′E
147 S9 **Kosonsoy** *Rus.* Kasansay. Namangan Viloyati, E Uzbekistan 41°15′N 71°28′E
113 M16 **Kosovo** *prev.* Autonomous Province of Kosovo and Metohija. ◆ *republic* SE Europe
Kosovo *see* Kosava
Kosovo and Metohija, Autonomous Province of *see* Kosovo
Kosovo Polje *see* Fushë Kosovë
Kosovska Kamenica *see* Kamenicë
Kosovska Mitrovica *see* Mitrovicë
189 X17 **Kosrae** ◈ *state* E Micronesia
189 Y14 **Kosrae** *prev.* Kusaie. *island* Caroline Islands, E Micronesia
109 P6 **Kössen** Tirol, W Austria 47°40′N 12°24′E
76 M16 **Kossou, Lac de** ◎ C Ivory Coast
Kossukavak *see* Krumovgrad
Kostajnica *see* Hrvatska Kostanjnica
Kostamus *see* Kostomuksha
144 M7 **Kostanay** *var.* Kustanay, *Kaz.* Qostanay. Kostanay, N Kazakhstan 53°16′N 63°34′E
144 L8 **Kostanay** *var.* Kostanayskaya Oblast', *Kaz.* Qostanay Oblysy. ◈ *province* N Kazakhstan
Kostanayskaya Oblast' *see* Kostanay
Kosten *see* Kościan
114 H10 **Kostenets** *prev.* Georgi Dimitrov. Sofiya, W Bulgaria 42°15′N 23°48′E
80 F10 **Kosti** White Nile, C Sudan 13°11′N 32°38′E
Kostnitz *see* Konstanz
124 H7 **Kostomuksha** *Fin.* Kostamus. Respublika Kareliya, NW Russian Federation 64°33′N 30°28′E
116 K3 **Kostopil'** *Rus.* Kostopol'. Rivnens'ka Oblast', NW Ukraine 50°20′N 26°29′E
Kostopol' *see* Kostopil'
124 M15 **Kostroma** Kostromskaya Oblast', NW Russian Federation 57°46′N 41°E
125 N14 **Kostroma** ≈ NW Russian Federation
125 N14 **Kostromskaya Oblast'** ◈ *province* NW Russian Federation
110 D11 **Kostrzyn** *Ger.* Cüstrin, Küstrin. Lubuskie, W Poland 52°35′N 14°40′E
110 H11 **Kostrzyn** Wielkopolskie, C Poland 52°23′N 17°13′E
117 X7 **Kostyantynivka** *Rus.* Konstantinovka. Donets'ka Oblast', SE Ukraine
Kostyukovichi *see* Kastsyukovichy
Kostyukovka *see* Kastsyukowka
Kôsyoku *see* Kōshoku
125 U6 **Kos'yu** Respublika Komi, NW Russian Federation 65°39′N 59°01′E
125 U6 **Kos'yu** ≈ NW Russian Federation
110 F7 **Koszalin** *Ger.* Köslin. Zachodnio-pomorskie, NW Poland 54°12′N 16°10′E
111 F22 **Kőszeg** *Ger.* Güns. Vas, W Hungary 47°23′N 16°33′E
152 H13 **Kota** *prev.* Kotah. Rājasthān, N India 25°14′N 75°52′E
Kota Baharu *see* Kota Bharu
Kota Bahru *see* Kota Bharu
169 U13 **Kotabaru** Pulau Laut, C Indonesia 03°15′S 116°15′E
168 K12 **Kota Baru** Sumatera, W Indonesia 01°07′S 101°43′E
Kotabaru *see* Jayapura
168 K6 **Kota Bharu** *var.* Kota Baharu, Kota Bahru. Kelantan, Peninsular Malaysia 06°07′N 102°15′E
Kotaboemi *see* Kotabumi
168 M14 **Kotabumi** *prev.* Kotaboemi. Sumatera, W Indonesia 04°50′S 104°54′E
149 S10 **Kot Addu** Punjab, E Pakistan 30°28′N 70°58′E
Kotah *see* Kota
169 U7 **Kota Kinabalu** *prev.* Jesselton. Sabah, East Malaysia 05°59′N 116°04′E
169 U7 **Kota Kinabalu** ✕ Sabah, East Malaysia 05°59′N 116°04′E
92 M12 **Kotala** Lappi, N Finland 67°01′N 29°00′E
Kotamobagoe *see* Kotamobagu
171 Q11 **Kotamobagu** *prev.* Kotamobagoe. Sulawesi, C Indonesia 0°46′N 124°21′E
155 L14 **Kotapad** *var.* Kotapārh. Orissa, E India 19°10′N 82°23′E
Kotapārh *see* Kotapad
166 N17 **Ko Ta Ru Tao** *island* SW Thailand
169 R13 **Kotawaringin, Teluk** *bay* Borneo, C Indonesia
149 Q13 **Kot Dīji** Sind, SE Pakistan 27°16′N 68°44′E
152 K9 **Kotdwāra** Uttarakhand, N India 29°44′N 78°33′E
125 Q14 **Kotel'nich** Kirovskaya Oblast', NW Russian Federation 58°19′N 48°12′E
127 N12 **Kotel'nikovo** Volgogradskaya Oblast', SW Russian Federation 47°37′N 43°07′E
123 Q6 **Kotel'nyy, Ostrov** *island* Novosibirskiye Ostrova, N Russian Federation
117 T5 **Kotel'va** Poltavs'ka Oblast', C Ukraine 50°04′N 34°46′E
101 M14 **Köthen** *var.* Cöthen. Sachsen-Anhalt, C Germany 51°46′N 11°59′E
Kôti *see* Kōchi
81 G17 **Kotido** NE Uganda 03°03′N 34°07′E
93 N19 **Kotka** Etelä-Suomi, S Finland 60°28′N 26°55′E
125 P11 **Kotlas** Arkhangel'skaya Oblast', NW Russian Federation 61°14′N 46°43′E
38 M10 **Kotlik** Alaska, USA 63°01′N 163°33′W
77 Q17 **Kotoka** ✕ (Accra) S Ghana 05°41′N 00°10′W
Kotonu *see* Cotonou
113 J17 **Kotor** *It.* Cattaro. SW Montenegro 42°25′N 18°47′E
Kotor *see* Kotoriba
112 F7 **Kotoriba** *Hung.* Kotor. Medimurje, N Croatia 46°20′N 16°47′E
113 I17 **Kotorska, Boka** *It.* Bocche di Cattaro. *bay* SW Montenegro
112 H11 **Kotorsko** ◈ Republika Srpska, N Bosnia and Herzegovina
112 G11 **Kotor Varoš** ◈ Republika Srpska, N Bosnia and Herzegovina
Koto Sho/Kotosho *see* Lan Yü
126 M7 **Kotovsk** Tambovskaya Oblast', W Russian Federation 52°39′N 41°31′E
117 O9 **Kotovs'k** *Rus.* Kotovsk. Odes'ka Oblast', SW Ukraine 47°42′N 29°30′E
Kotovsk *see* Hînceşti
119 G16 **Kotra** ≈ W Belarus
149 P16 **Kotri** Sind, SE Pakistan 25°22′N 68°18′E
109 Q9 **Kötschach** Kärnten, S Austria 46°41′N 12°57′E
155 K15 **Kottagūdem** Andhra Pradesh, E India 17°36′N 80°40′E
155 F21 **Kottappadi** Kerala, SW India 11°38′N 76°03′E
155 G23 **Kottayam** Kerala, SW India 09°34′N 76°31′E
Kottbus *see* Cottbus
79 K15 **Kotto** ≈ Central African Republic/Dem. Rep. Congo
193 X15 **Kotu Group** *island group* W Tonga
Koturdepe *see* Goturdepe
122 M9 **Kotuy** ≈ N Russian Federation
83 M16 **Kotwa** Mashonaland East, NE Zimbabwe 16°58′S 32°46′E
39 N7 **Kotzebue** Alaska, USA 66°54′N 162°36′W
38 M7 **Kotzebue Sound** *inlet* Alaska, USA
Kotzenan *see* Chocianów
Kotzman *see* Kitsman'
77 R14 **Kouandé** NW Benin 10°20′N 01°42′E
79 J15 **Kouango** Ouaka, S Central African Republic 05°00′N 20°01′E
77 O13 **Koudougou** C Burkina 12°15′N 02°23′W
98 K7 **Koudum** Friesland, N Netherlands 52°55′N 05°26′E
115 L25 **Koufonísi** *island* SE Greece
115 K21 **Koufonísi** *island* Kykládes, Greece, Aegean Sea
38 M8 **Kougarok Mountain** ▲ Alaska, USA 65°41′N 165°29′W
79 E21 **Kouilou** ◈ *province* SW Congo
79 E20 **Kouilou** ≈ S Congo
121 O3 **Koúklia** SW Cyprus 34°42′N 32°35′E
79 E19 **Koulamoutou** Ogooué-Lolo, C Gabon 01°07′S 12°27′E
76 L12 **Koulikoro** Koulikoro, SW Mali 12°55′N 07°31′W
76 L11 **Koulikoro** ◈ *region* SW Mali
187 P16 **Koumac** Province Nord, W New Caledonia 20°34′S 164°18′E
165 N12 **Koumi** Nagano, Honshū, S Japan 36°06′N 138°27′E
78 I13 **Koumra** Moyen-Chari, S Chad 08°56′N 17°32′E
Kounadougou *see* Koundougou
76 M15 **Kounahiri** C Ivory Coast 07°47′N 05°51′W
76 I12 **Koundâra** Moyenne-Guinée, NW Guinea 12°28′N 13°15′W
77 N13 **Koundougou** *var.* Kounadougou. C Burkina 11°43′N 04°40′W
76 H11 **Koungheul** C Senegal 14°00′N 14°48′W
Kounradskiy *see* Konyrat
25 X10 **Kountze** Texas, SW USA 30°22′N 94°20′W
77 Q13 **Koupéla** C Burkina 12°07′N 00°21′W
77 N13 **Kouri** Sikasso, SW Mali 12°09′N 04°46′W
55 Y9 **Kourou** N French Guiana 05°08′N 52°37′W
114 J12 **Kouroú** ≈ NE Greece
76 K14 **Kouroussa** C Guinea 10°40′N 09°50′W
Kousseir *see* Al Quşayr
78 G11 **Kousséri** *prev.* Fort-Foureau. Extrême-Nord, NE Cameroon 12°05′N 14°56′E
Kouteifé *see* Al Quţayfah
76 M13 **Koutiala** Sikasso, S Mali 12°20′N 05°23′W
76 M14 **Kouto** NW Ivory Coast 09°51′N 06°25′W
93 M19 **Kouvola** Etelä-Suomi, S Finland 60°50′N 26°48′E
79 G18 **Kouyou** ≈ C Congo
112 M10 **Kovačica** *Hung.* Antafalva; *prev.* Kovacsicza. Vojvodina, N Serbia 45°08′N 20°36′E
Kovacsicza *see* Kovačica
Kővárhosszúfalu *see* Satulung
Kovászna *see* Covasna
124 I4 **Kovdor** Murmanskaya Oblast', NW Russian Federation 67°32′N 30°27′E
116 J3 **Kovel'** *Pol.* Kowel. Volyns'ka Oblast', NW Ukraine 51°14′N 24°43′E
112 M11 **Kovin** *Hung.* Kevevára; *prev.* Temes-Kubin. Vojvodina, NE Serbia 44°45′N 20°59′E
Kovno *see* Kaunas
127 N3 **Kovrov** Vladimirskaya Oblast', W Russian Federation 56°24′N 41°21′E
127 O5 **Kovylkino** Respublika Mordoviya, W Russian Federation 54°03′N 43°52′E
110 J11 **Kowal** Kujawsko-pomorskie, C Poland 52°31′N 19°09′E
110 J9 **Kowalewo Pomorskie** *Ger.* Schönsee. Kujawsko-pomorskie, N Poland 53°07′N 18°48′E
Kowasna *see* Covasna
119 M16 **Kowbcha** *Rus.* Kolbcha. Mahilyowskaya Voblasts', E Belarus 53°39′N 29°14′E
Koweit *see* Kuwait
Kowel *see* Kovel'
185 F17 **Kowhitirangi** West Coast, South Island, New Zealand 42°54′S 171°01′E
161 O15 **Kowloon** Hong Kong, S China
Kowno *see* Kaunas
159 N7 **Kox Kuduk** *well* NW China
136 D16 **Köyceğiz** Muğla, SW Turkey 36°57′N 28°40′E
125 N6 **Koyda** Arkhangel'skaya Oblast', NW Russian Federation 66°22′N 42°42′E
Koymat *see* Goymat
Koymatdag, Gory *see* Goymatdag, Gory
151 E15 **Koyna Reservoir** ⊠ W India
165 P9 **Koyoshi-gawa** ≈ Honshū, C Japan
Koysanjaq *see* Koi Sanjaq
Koytash *see* Qo'ytosh
146 M14 **Köýtendag** *prev. Rus.* Charshanga, Charshangy, *Turkm.* Charshangngy. Lebap Welaýaty, E Turkmenistan 37°31′N 65°58′E
39 N9 **Koyuk** Alaska, USA 64°55′N 161°09′W
39 N9 **Koyuk River** ≈ Alaska, USA
39 O9 **Koyukuk** Alaska, USA 64°52′N 157°42′W
39 O9 **Koyukuk River** ≈ Alaska, USA
136 J13 **Kozaklı** Nevşehir, C Turkey 39°12′N 34°48′E
136 K16 **Kozan** Adana, S Turkey 37°27′N 35°47′E
115 E14 **Kozáni** Dytikí Makedonía, N Greece 40°19′N 21°48′E
112 F10 **Kozara** ▲▲ NW Bosnia and Herzegovina
Kozarska Dubica *see* Bosanska Dubica
117 P3 **Kozelets'** *Rus.* Kozelets. Chernihivs'ka Oblast', NE Ukraine 50°54′N 31°09′E
Kozelets *see* Kozelets'
117 S6 **Kozel'shchyna** Poltavs'ka Oblast', C Ukraine 49°13′N 33°49′E
126 J5 **Kozel'sk** Kaluzhskaya Oblast', W Russian Federation 54°04′N 35°51′E
151 F21 **Kozhikode** *var.* Calicut. Kerala, SW India 11°17′N 75°49′E *see also* Calicut

◆ Country
● Country Capital
◇ Dependent Territory
○ Dependent Territory Capital
◈ Administrative Regions
✕ International Airport
▲ Mountain
▲▲ Mountain Range
Volcano
≈ River
◎ Lake
⊠ Reservoir

125 U6 **Kozhim** Respublika Komi, NW Russian Federation 65°43´N 59°25´E
124 L9 **Kozhozero, Ozero** ◎ NW Russian Federation
125 T7 **Kozhva** Respublika Komi, NW Russian Federation 65°06´N 57°00´E
125 T7 **Kozhva** ~ NW Russian Federation
125 V9 **Kozhymiz, Gora** ▲ NW Russian Federation 63°13´N 58°54´E
110 N13 **Kozienice** Mazowieckie, C Poland 51°35´N 21°31´E
109 S13 **Kozina** SW Slovenia 45°36´N 13°56´E
114 H7 **Kozloduy** Vratsa, NW Bulgaria 43°48´N 23°42´E
127 Q3 **Kozlovka** Chuvashskaya Respublika, W Russian Federation 55°53´N 48°07´E
Kozlovshchina/ Kozlowszczyzna *see* Kazlowshchyna
127 P3 **Koz'modem'yansk** Respublika Mariy El, W Russian Federation 56°19´N 46°33´E
116 J6 **Kozova** Ternopil's'ka Oblast', W Ukraine 49°25´N 25°09´E
113 P20 **Kožuf** ▲▲ Greece/Macedonia
165 N15 **Kōzu-shima** *island* E Japan
Koz'yany *see* Kaz'yany
117 N5 **Kozyatyn** *Rus.* Kazatin. Vinnyts'ka Oblast', C Ukraine 49°41´N 28°49´E
77 Q16 **Kpalimé** *var.* Palimé. SW Togo 06°54´N 00°38´E
77 Q16 **Kpandu** E Ghana 07°00´N 00°18´E
99 F15 **Krabbendijke** Zeeland, SW Netherlands 51°25´N 04°07´E
167 N15 **Krabi** *var.* Muang Krabi. Krabi, SW Thailand 08°04´N 98°52´E
167 N13 **Kra Buri** Ranong, SW Thailand 10°25´N 98°48´E
167 S12 **Krâchéh** *prev.* Kratie. Krâchéh, E Cambodia 12°29´N 106°01´E
95 G17 **Kragerø** Telemark, S Norway 58°54´N 09°25´E
112 M13 **Kragujevac** Serbia, C Serbia 44°01´N 20°55´E
Krainburg *see* Kranj
166 N13 **Kra, Isthmus of** *isthmus* Malaysia/Thailand
112 D12 **Krajina** *cultural region* SW Croatia
Krakatau, Pulau *see* Rakata, Pulau
Krakau *see* Kraków
111 L16 **Kraków** *Eng.* Cracow, *Ger.* Krakau; *anc.* Cracovia. Małopolskie, S Poland 50°03´N 19°58´E
100 L9 **Krakower See** ◎ NE Germany
167 Q11 **Krâlănh** Siĕmréab, NW Cambodia 13°35´N 103°27´E
45 Q16 **Kralendijk** Bonaire, E Netherlands Antilles 12°07´N 68°13´W
112 B10 **Kraljevica** *It.* Porto Re. Primorje-Gorski Kotar, NW Croatia 45°15´N 14°36´E
112 M13 **Kraljevo** *prev.* Rankovićevo. Serbia, C Serbia 43°44´N 20°40´E
111 E16 **Královehradecký Kraj** *prev.* Hradecký Kraj. ◈ *region* N Czech Republic
Kralup an der Moldau *see* Kralupy nad Vltavou
111 C16 **Kralupy nad Vltavou** *Ger.* Kralup an der Moldau. Středočeský Kraj, NW Czech Republic 50°15´N 14°20´E
117 W7 **Kramators'k** *Rus.* Kramatorsk. Donets'ka Oblast', SE Ukraine 48°43´N 37°34´E
Kramatorsk *see* Kramators'k
93 H17 **Kramfors** Västernorrland, C Sweden 62°55´N 17°50´E
Kranéa *see* Kraniá
108 M7 **Kranebitten** ✈ (Innsbruck) Tirol, W Austria 47°18´N 11°21´E
115 D15 **Kraniá** *var.* Kranéa. Dytikí Makedonía, N Greece 39°54´N 21°21´E
115 G20 **Kranídi** Pelopónnisos, S Greece 37°21´N 23°09´E
109 T11 **Kranj** *Ger.* Krainburg. NW Slovenia 46°17´N 14°16´E
115 F16 **Krannón** *battleground* Thessalía, C Greece
Kranz *see* Zelenogradsk
112 D7 **Krapina** Krapina-Zagorje, N Croatia 46°12´N 15°52´E
112 E8 **Krapina** ~ N Croatia
112 D8 **Krapina-Zagorje** *off.* Krapinsko-Zagorska Županija. ◈ *province* N Croatia
114 L7 **Krapinets** ~ NE Bulgaria
Krapinsko-Zagorska Županija *see* Krapina-Zagorje
111 I15 **Krapkowice** *Ger.* Krappitz. Opolskie, SW Poland 50°29´N 17°56´E
Krappitz *see* Krapkowice
125 O12 **Krasavino** Vologodskaya Oblast', NW Russian Federation 60°56´N 46°27´E
122 H6 **Krasino** Novaya Zemlya, Arkhangel'skaya Oblast', N Russian Federation 70°45´N 54°16´E
123 S15 **Kraskino** Primorskiy Kray, SE Russian Federation 42°40´N 130°51´E
118 J11 **Krāslava** Krāslava, SE Latvia 55°56´N 27°08´E
119 M14 **Krasnaluki** *Rus.* Krasnoluki. Vitsyebskaya Voblasts', N Belarus 54°37´N 28°50´E
119 P17 **Krasnapollye** *Rus.* Krasnopol'ye. Mahilyowskaya Voblasts', E Belarus 53°20´N 31°24´E
126 L15 **Krasnaya Polyana** Krasnodarskiy Kray, SW Russian Federation 43°40´N 40°13´E
Krasnaya Slabada / Krasnaya Sloboda *see* Chyrvonaya Slabada
119 J15 **Krasnaye** *Rus.* Krasnoye. Minskaya Voblasts', C Belarus 54°14´N 27°05´E
111 O14 **Kraśnik** *Ger.* Kratznick. Lubelskie, E Poland 50°56´N 22°14´E
117 O9 **Krasni Okny** Odes'ka Oblast', SW Ukraine 47°33´N 29°28´E
127 P8 **Krasnoarmeysk** Saratovskaya Oblast', W Russian Federation 51°02´N 45°42´E
Krasnoarmeysk *see* Tayynsha
Krasnoarmeysk *see* Krasnoarmiys'k/Tayynsha
123 T6 **Krasnoarmeyskiy** Chukotskiy Avtonomnyy Okrug, NE Russian Federation 69°30´N 171°44´E
117 W7 **Krasnoarmiys'k** *Rus.* Krasnoarmeysk. Donets'ka Oblast', SE Ukraine 48°17´N 37°14´E
125 P11 **Krasnoborsk** Arkhangel'skaya Oblast', NW Russian Federation 61°31´N 45°57´E
126 K14 **Krasnodar** *prev.* Ekaterinodar, Yekaterinodar. Krasnodarskiy Kray, SW Russian Federation 45°06´N 39°01´E
126 K13 **Krasnodarskiy Kray** ◈ *territory* SW Russian Federation
117 Z7 **Krasnodon** Luhans'ka Oblast', E Ukraine 48°17´N 39°44´E
Krasnogor *see* Kallaste
127 T2 **Krasnogorskoye** *Latv.* Sarkaņi. Udmurtskaya Respublika, NW Russian Federation 57°42´N 52°29´E
Krasnograd *see* Krasnohrad
Krasnogvardeysk *see* Bulungh'ur
126 M13 **Krasnogvardeyskoye** Stavropol'skiy Kray, SW Russian Federation 45°49´N 41°31´E
Krasnogvardeyskoye *see* Krasnohvardiys'ke
117 U6 **Krasnohrad** *Rus.* Krasnograd. Kharkivs'ka Oblast', E Ukraine 49°22´N 35°28´E
117 S12 **Krasnohvardiys'ke** *Rus.* Krasnogvardeyskoye. Respublika Krym, S Ukraine 45°30´N 34°19´E
123 P14 **Krasnokamensk** Chitinskaya Oblast', S Russian Federation 50°03´N 118°01´E
125 U14 **Krasnokamsk** Permskaya Oblast', W Russian Federation 58°08´N 55°48´E
127 U8 **Krasnokholm** Orenburgskaya Oblast', W Russian Federation 51°34´N 54°11´E
117 U5 **Krasnokuts'k** *Rus.* Krasnokutsk. Kharkivs'ka Oblast', E Ukraine 50°01´N 35°03´E
Krasnokutsk *see* Krasnokuts'k
126 L7 **Krasnolesnyy** Voronezhskaya Oblast', W Russian Federation 51°53´N 39°37´E
Krasnoluki *see* Krasnaluki
Krasnoosol'skoye Vodokhranilishche *see* Chervonooskil's'ke Vodoskhovyshche
117 S11 **Krasnoperekops'k** *Rus.* Krasnoperekopsk. Respublika Krym, S Ukraine 45°56´N 33°47´E
Krasnoperekopsk *see* Krasnoperekops'k
117 U4 **Krasnopillya** Sums'ka Oblast', NE Ukraine 50°46´N 35°17´E
Krasnopol'ye *see* Krasnapollye
124 L5 **Krasnoshchel'ye** Murmanskaya Oblast', NW Russian Federation 67°22´N 37°03´E
127 O5 **Krasnoslobodsk** Respublika Mordoviya, W Russian Federation 54°24´N 43°51´E
127 T2 **Krasnoslobodsk** Volgogradskaya Oblast', SW Russian Federation 48°41´N 44°34´E
Krasnostav *see* Krasnystaw
127 V5 **Krasnousol'skiy** Respublika Bashkortostan, W Russian Federation 53°55´N 56°22´E
125 U12 **Krasnovishersk** Permskaya Oblast', NW Russian Federation 60°22´N 57°04´E
Krasnovodsk *see* Türkmenbaşy
Krasnovodskiy Zaliv *see* Türkmenbasy Aylagy
146 B10 **Krasnovodskoye Plato** *Turkm.* Krasnowodsk Platosy. *plateau* NW Turkmenistan
Krasnowodsk Aylagy *see* Türkmenbasy Aylagy
Krasnowodsk Platosy *see* Krasnovodskoye Plato
122 K12 **Krasnoyarsk** Krasnoyarskiy Kray, S Russian Federation 56°05´N 92°46´E
127 X7 **Krasnoyarskiy** Orenburgskaya Oblast', W Russian Federation 51°56´N 59°54´E
122 K11 **Krasnoyarskiy Kray** ◈ *territory* C Russian Federation
Krasnoye *see* Krasnaye
Krasnoye Znamya *see* Gyzylbaydak
125 R11 **Krasnozatonskiy** Respublika Komi, NW Russian Federation 61°39´N 51°00´E
118 D13 **Krasnoznamensk** *prev.* Lasdehnen, *Ger.* Haselberg. Kaliningradskaya Oblast', W Russian Federation 54°57´N 22°28´E
126 K3 **Krasnoznamensk** Moskovskaya Oblast', W Russian Federation 55°40´N 37°05´E
117 R11 **Krasnoznam"yans'kyy Kanal** *canal* S Ukraine
111 P14 **Krasnystaw** *Rus.* Krasnostav. Lubelskie, SE Poland 51°N 23°10´E
126 H4 **Krasnyy** Smolenskaya Oblast', W Russian Federation 54°36´N 31°27´E
127 P2 **Krasnyye Baki** Nizhegorodskaya Oblast', W Russian Federation 57°07´N 45°12´E
127 Q13 **Krasnyye Barrikady** Astrakhanskaya Oblast', SW Russian Federation 46°14´N 47°48´E
124 K15 **Krasnyy Kholm** Tverskaya Oblast', W Russian Federation 58°04´N 37°05´E
127 Q8 **Krasnyy Kut** Saratovskaya Oblast', W Russian Federation 50°54´N 46°58´E
Krasnyy Liman *see* Krasnyy Lyman
117 Y7 **Krasnyy Luch** *prev.* Krindachevka. Luhans'ka Oblast', E Ukraine 48°09´N 38°52´E
117 X6 **Krasnyy Lyman** *Rus.* Krasnyy Liman. Donets'ka Oblast', SE Ukraine 49°00´N 37°50´E
127 R3 **Krasnyy Steklovar** Respublika Mariy El, W Russian Federation 56°14´N 48°49´E
127 P8 **Krasnyy Tekstil'shchik** Saratovskaya Oblast', W Russian Federation 51°35´N 45°49´E
127 R13 **Krasnyy Yar** Astrakhanskaya Oblast', SW Russian Federation 46°33´N 48°21´E
Krassóvár *see* Caraşova
116 L5 **Krasyliv** Khmel'nyts'ka Oblast', W Ukraine 49°38´N 26°59´E
111 O21 **Kraszna** *Rom.* Crasna. ~ Hungary/Romania
Kratie *see* Krâchéh
113 P17 **Kratovo** NE FYR Macedonia 42°04´N 22°08´E
Kratznick *see* Kraśnik
171 Y13 **Krau** Papua, E Indonesia 03°15´S 140°07´E
167 Q13 **Krâvanh, Chuŏr Phnum** *Eng.* Cardamom Mountains, *Fr.* Chaîne des Cardamomes. ▲▲ W Cambodia
Kravasta Lagoon *see* Karavastasë, Laguna e
Krawang *see* Karawang
127 Q15 **Kraynovka** Respublika Dagestan, SW Russian Federation 43°58´N 47°24´E
118 D12 **Kražiai** Šiaulai, C Lithuania 55°36´N 22°41´E
27 P11 **Krebs** Oklahoma, C USA 34°55´N 95°43´W
101 D15 **Krefeld** Nordrhein-Westfalen, W Germany 51°20´N 06°34´E
Kreisstadt *see* Krosno Odrzańskie
115 D17 **Kremastón, Technití Límni** ⊠ C Greece
Kremenchug *see* Kremenchuk
Kremenchugskoye Vodokhranilishche/ Kremenchuk Reservoir *see* Kremenchuts'ke Vodoskhovyshche
117 S6 **Kremenchuk** *Rus.* Kremenchug. Poltavs'ka Oblast', NE Ukraine 49°04´N 33°27´E
117 R6 **Kremenchuts'ke Vodoskhovyshche** *Eng.* Kremenchuk Reservoir, *Rus.* Kremenchugskoye Vodokhranilishche. ⊠ C Ukraine
116 K5 **Kremenets'** *Pol.* Krzemieniec, *Rus.* Kremenets. Ternopil's'ka Oblast', W Ukraine 50°06´N 25°43´E
Kremennaya *see* Kreminna
117 X6 **Kreminna** *Rus.* Kremennaya. Luhans'ka Oblast', E Ukraine 49°03´N 38°15´E
37 R4 **Kremmling** Colorado, C USA 40°03´N 106°23´W
109 V3 **Krems** ~ NE Austria
Krems *see* Krems an der Donau
109 W3 **Krems an der Donau** *var.* Krems. Niederösterreich, N Austria 48°25´N 15°36´E
Kremsier *see* Kroměříž
109 S4 **Kremsmünster** Oberösterreich, N Austria 48°04´N 14°08´E
38 M17 **Krenitzin Islands** *island* Aleutian Islands, Alaska, USA
Kresena *see* Kresna
114 G11 **Kresna** *var.* Kresena. Blagoevgrad, SW Bulgaria 41°43´N 23°10´E
112 O12 **Krespoljin** Serbia, E Serbia 44°22´N 21°36´E
25 N4 **Kress** Texas, SW USA 34°21´N 101°43´W
123 V6 **Kresta, Zaliv** *bay* E Russian Federation
115 D20 **Kréstena** *prev.* Selinoús. Dytikí Ellás, S Greece 37°36´N 21°36´E
124 H14 **Kresttsy** Novgorodskaya Oblast', W Russian Federation 58°15´N 32°28´E
Kretikon Delagos *see* Kritikó Pélagos
118 C11 **Kretinga** *Ger.* Krottingen. Klaipėda, NW Lithuania 55°53´N 21°13´E
Kreutz *see* Cristuru Secuiesc
Kreuz *see* Križevci, Croatia
Kreuz *see* Risti, Estonia
Kreuzburg/Kreuzburg in Oberschlesien *see* Kluczbork
Kreuzingen *see* Bol'shakovo
108 H6 **Kreuzlingen** Thurgau, NE Switzerland 47°38´N 09°12´E
101 K25 **Kreuzspitze** ▲ S Germany 47°30´N 10°55´E
101 F16 **Kreuztal** Nordrhein-Westfalen, W Germany 50°58´N 08°00´E
119 I15 **Kreva** *Rus.* Krevo. Hrodzyenskaya Voblasts', W Belarus 54°19´N 26°17´E
Krevo *see* Kreva
Kría Vrísi *see* Krýa Vrýsi
79 D16 **Kribi** Sud, SW Cameroon 02°53´N 09°57´E
Krichëv *see* Krychaw
Krickerhäu/Kriegerhaj *see* Handlová
109 W6 **Krieglach** Steiermark, E Austria 47°33´N 15°37´E
108 F8 **Kriens** Luzern, W Switzerland 47°03´N 08°17´E
Krievija *see* Russian Federation
Krimmitschau *see* Crimmitschau
98 H12 **Krimpen aan den IJssel** Zuid-Holland, SW Netherlands 51°56´N 04°39´E
Krindachevka *see* Krasnyy Luch
115 G25 **Kríos, Akrotírio** *headland* Kríti, Greece, E Mediterranean Sea 35°17´N 23°31´E
155 J16 **Krishna** *prev.* Kistna. ~ C India
155 H20 **Krishnagiri** Tamil Nādu, SE India 12°33´N 78°11´E
155 K17 **Krishna, Mouths of the** *delta* SE India
153 S15 **Krishnanagar** West Bengal, N India 23°22´N 88°32´E
155 G20 **Krishnarājāsāgara Reservoir** ⊠ W India
95 N19 **Kristdala** Kalmar, S Sweden 57°24´N 16°12´E
Kristiania *see* Oslo
95 E18 **Kristiansand** *var.* Christiansand. Vest-Agder, S Norway 58°08´N 07°52´E
95 L22 **Kristianstad** Skåne, S Sweden 56°02´N 14°10´E
94 F8 **Kristiansund** *var.* Christiansund. Møre og Romsdal, S Norway 63°07´N 07°45´E
Kristiinankaupunki *see* Kristinestad
93 I14 **Kristineberg** Västerbotten, N Sweden 65°07´N 18°36´E
95 L16 **Kristinehamn** Värmland, C Sweden 59°17´N 14°09´E
93 J17 **Kristinestad** *Fin.* Kristiinankaupunki. Länsi-Suomi, W Finland 62°15´N 21°24´E
Kristyor *see* Crişcior
115 J25 **Kríti** *Eng.* Crete. ◈ *region* Greece, Aegean Sea
115 J24 **Kríti** *Eng.* Crete. *island* Greece, Aegean Sea
115 J23 **Kritikó Pélagos** *var.* Kretikon Delagos, *Eng.* Sea of Crete; *anc.* Mare Creticum. *sea* Greece, Aegean Sea
Kriulyany *see* Criuleni
112 I12 **Krivaja** ~ NE Bosnia and Herzegovina
Krivaja *see* Mali Iđoš
113 P17 **Kriva Palanka** *Turk.* Eğri Palanka. NE Macedonia 42°13´N 22°19´E
Krivichi *see* Kryvychy
114 H8 **Krivodol** Vratsa, NW Bulgaria 43°23´N 23°30´E
126 M10 **Krivorozh'ye** Rostovskaya Oblast', SW Russian Federation 48°51´N 40°49´E
Krivoshin *see* Kryvoshyn
Krivoy Rog *see* Kryvyy Rih
112 F7 **Križevci** *Ger.* Kreuz, *Hung.* Kőrös. Varaždin, NE Croatia 46°02´N 16°32´E
112 B10 **Krk** *It.* Veglia. Primorje-Gorski Kotar, NW Croatia 45°01´N 14°36´E
112 B10 **Krk** *It.* Veglia; *anc.* Curieta. *island* NW Croatia
109 V12 **Krka** ~ SE Slovenia
Krka *see* Gurk
109 R11 **Krn** ▲ NW Slovenia 46°15´N 13°37´E
111 H16 **Krnov** *Ger.* Jägerndorf. Moravskoslezský Kraj, E Czech Republic 50°05´N 17°40´E
Kroatien *see* Croatia
95 G14 **Krøderen** Buskerud, S Norway 60°06´N 09°48´E
95 G14 **Krøderen** ◎ S Norway
Kroi *see* Krui
95 N17 **Krokek** Östergötland, S Sweden 58°40´N 16°25´E
Krokodil *see* Crocodile
93 G16 **Krokom** Jämtland, C Sweden 63°20´N 14°30´E
117 S2 **Krolevets'** *Rus.* Krolevets. Sums'ka Oblast', NE Ukraine 51°34´N 33°24´E
Krolevets *see* Krolevets'
Królewska Huta *see* Chorzów
111 H18 **Kroměříž** *Ger.* Kremsier. Zlínský Kraj, E Czech Republic 49°18´N 17°24´E
98 I9 **Krommenie** Noord-Holland, C Netherlands 52°30´N 04°46´E
126 J6 **Kromy** Orlovskaya Oblast', W Russian Federation 52°41´N 35°45´E
101 L18 **Kronach** Bayern, E Germany 50°14´N 11°19´E
Krone an der Brahe *see* Koronowo
167 Q13 **Krŏng Kaôh Kŏng** Kaôh Kông, SW Cambodia 11°37´N 102°59´E
95 K21 **Kronoberg** ◈ *county* S Sweden
123 V10 **Kronotskiy Zaliv** *bay* E Russian Federation
195 O2 **Kronprinsesse Märtha Kyst** *physical region* Antarctica
195 V3 **Kronprins Olav Kyst** *physical region* Antarctica
124 G12 **Kronshtadt** Leningradskaya Oblast', NW Russian Federation 60°01´N 29°42´E
Kronstadt *see* Braşov
83 I22 **Kroonstad** Free State, C South Africa 27°40´S 27°15´E
123 O12 **Kropotkin** Irkutskaya Oblast', C Russian Federation 58°30´N 115°21´E
126 L14 **Kropotkin** Krasnodarskiy Kray, SW Russian Federation 45°29´N 40°31´E
110 J11 **Krośniewice** Łódzskie, C Poland 52°14´N 19°10´E
111 N17 **Krosno** *Ger.* Krossen. Podkarpackie, SE Poland 49°40´N 21°46´E
110 E12 **Krosno Odrzańskie** *Ger.* Crossen, Kreisstadt. Lubuskie, W Poland 52°02´N 15°06´E
Krossen *see* Krosno
Krotoschin *see* Krotoszyn
110 H13 **Krotoszyn** *Ger.* Krotoschin. Wielkopolskie, C Poland 51°43´N 17°24´E
Krottingen *see* Kretinga
Krousón *see* Krousónas
115 J25 **Krousónas** *prev.* Krousón, Kroussón. Kríti, Greece, E Mediterranean Sea 35°14´N 24°59´E
Kroussón *see* Krousónas
Krraba *see* Krrabë
113 L20 **Krrabë** *var.* Krraba. Tiranë, C Albania 41°15´N 19°56´E
113 L17 **Krrabit, Mali i** ▲▲ N Albania
109 W12 **Krško** *Ger.* Gurkfeld; *prev.* Videm-Krško. E Slovenia 45°57´N 15°31´E
83 K19 **Kruger National Park** *national park* Northern, N South Africa
83 J21 **Krugersdorp** Gauteng, NE South Africa 26°06´S 27°46´E
38 D16 **Krugloi Point** *headland* Agattu Island, Alaska, USA 52°30´N 173°46´E
Krugloye *see* Kruhlaye
119 N15 **Kruhlaye** *Rus.* Krugloye. Mahilyowskaya Voblasts', E Belarus 54°15´N 29°48´E
168 L15 **Krui** *var.* Kroi. Sumatera, SW Indonesia 05°11´S 103°55´E
99 G16 **Kruibeke** Oost-Vlaanderen, N Belgium 51°10´N 04°18´E
83 G25 **Kruidfontein** Western Cape, SW South Africa 32°50´S 21°59´E
99 F15 **Kruiningen** Zeeland, SW Netherlands 51°28´N 04°01´E
Kruja *see* Krujë
113 L19 **Krujë** *var.* Kruja, *It.* Croia. Durrës, C Albania 41°30´N 19°48´E
Krulevshchina/ Krulewshchyna *see* Krulyewshchyna
118 K13 **Krulyewshchyna** *Rus.* Krulevshchina, Krulewshchyna. Vitsyebskaya Voblasts', N Belarus 55°02´N 27°45´E
25 T6 **Krum** Texas, SW USA 33°15´N 97°14´W
101 J23 **Krumbach** Bayern, S Germany 48°12´N 10°21´E
113 M17 **Krumë** Kukës, NE Albania 42°11´N 20°25´E
Krummau *see* Český Krumlov
114 K12 **Krumovgrad** *prev.* Kossukavak. Yambol, E Bulgaria 41°27´N 25°40´E
114 K12 **Krumovitsa** ~ S Bulgaria
114 L10 **Krumovo** Yambol, E Bulgaria 42°16´N 26°25´E
167 O11 **Krung Thep, Ao** *var.* Bight of Bangkok. *bay* S Thailand
Krung Thep Mahanakhon *see* Ao Krung Thep
Krupa/Krupa na Uni *see* Bosanska Krupa
119 M15 **Krupki** Minskaya Voblasts', C Belarus 54°19´N 29°08´E
95 G24 **Kruså** *var.* Krusaa. Sønderjylland, SW Denmark 54°50´N 09°25´E
Krusaa *see* Kruså
113 N14 **Kruševac** Serbia, C Serbia 43°37´N 21°20´E
113 N19 **Kruševo** SW FYR Macedonia 41°22´N 21°15´E
111 A15 **Krušné Hory** *Eng.* Ore Mountains, *Ger.* Erzgebirge. ▲ Czech Republic/Germany *see also* Erzgebirge
Krušné Hory *see* Erzgebirge
39 W13 **Kruzof Island** *island* Alexander Archipelago, Alaska, USA
114 F13 **Krýa Vrýsi** *var.* Kría Vrísi. Kentrikí Makedonía, N Greece 40°41´N 22°18´E
119 P16 **Krychaw** *Rus.* Krichëv. Mahilyowskaya Voblasts', E Belarus 53°42´N 31°43´E
64 K11 **Krylov Seamount** *undersea feature* E Atlantic Ocean 17°35´N 30°07´W
Krym *see* Krym, Avtonomna Respublika
117 S13 **Krym, Avtonomna Respublika** *var.* Krym, *Eng.* Crimea, Crimean Oblast; *prev. Rus.* Krymskaya ASSR, Krymskaya Oblast'. ◈ *province* SE Ukraine
126 K14 **Krymsk** Krasnodarskiy Kray, SW Russian Federation 44°56´N 38°02´E
Krymskaya ASSR/ Krymskaya Oblast' *see* Krym, Avtonomna Respublika
117 T13 **Kryms'ki Hory** ▲▲ S Ukraine
117 T13 **Kryms'kyy Pivostriv** *peninsula* S Ukraine
111 M18 **Krynica** *Ger.* Tannenhof. Małopolskie, S Poland 49°25´N 20°56´E
117 P8 **Kryve Ozero** Odes'ka Oblast', SW Ukraine 47°54´N 30°19´E
119 I18 **Kryvoshyn** *Rus.* Krivoshin. Brestskaya Voblasts', SW Belarus 52°52´N 26°08´E
119 K14 **Kryvychy** *Rus.* Krivichi. Minskaya Voblasts', C Belarus 54°43´N 27°17´E
117 S8 **Kryvyy Rih** *Rus.* Krivoy Rog. Dnipropetrovs'ka Oblast', SE Ukraine 47°53´N 33°24´E
117 N8 **Kryzhopil'** Vinnyts'ka Oblast', C Ukraine 48°22´N 28°51´E
Krzemieniec *see* Kremenets'
111 J14 **Krzepice** Śląskie, S Poland 50°58´N 18°42´E
110 F10 **Krzyż Wielkopolskie** Wielkopolskie, W Poland 52°52´N 16°03´E
Ksar al Kabir *see* Ksar-el-Kebir
Ksar al Soule *see* Er-Rachidia
74 J5 **Ksar El Boukhari** N Algeria 35°55´N 02°47´E
74 G5 **Ksar-el-Kebir** *var.* Alcázar, Ksar al Kabir, Ksar-el-Kébir, *Ar.* Al-Kasr al-Kebir, Al-Qsar al-Kbir, *Sp.* Alcazarquivir. NW Morocco 35°04´N 05°56´W
Ksar-el-Kébir *see* Ksar-el-Kebir
110 H12 **Książ Wielkopolski** *Ger.* Xions. Weilkopolskie, W Poland 52°03´N 17°10´E
127 O3 **Kstovo** Nizhegorodskaya Oblast', W Russian Federation 56°07´N 44°12´E
169 T8 **Kuala Belait** W Brunei 04°48´N 114°12´E
Kuala Dungun *see* Dungun
169 S10 **Kualakeriau** Borneo, C Indonesia
169 S12 **Kualakuayan** Borneo, C Indonesia 02°01´S 112°35´E
168 K8 **Kuala Lipis** Pahang, Peninsular Malaysia 04°11´N 102°00´E
168 K9 **Kuala Lumpur** ● (Malaysia) Kuala Lumpur, Peninsular Malaysia 03°08´N 101°42´E
168 K9 **Kuala Lumpur International** ✈ Selangor, Peninsular Malaysia 02°51´N 101°45´E
Kuala Pelabohan Kelang *see* Pelabuhan Klang
169 U7 **Kuala Penyu** Sabah, East Malaysia 05°37´N 115°36´E
38 E9 **Kualapu'u** *var.* Kualapuu. Moloka'i, Hawaii, USA, C Pacific Ocean 21°09´N 157°02´W
Kualapuu *see* Kualapu'u
168 L7 **Kuala Terengganu** *var.* Kuala Trengganu. Terengganu, Peninsular Malaysia 05°20´N 103°07´E
168 L11 **Kualatungkal** Sumatera, W Indonesia 0°49´S 103°22´E
171 P11 **Kuandang** Sulawesi, N Indonesia 0°50´N 122°55´E
163 V12 **Kuandian** *var.* Kuandian Manzu Zizhixian. Liaoning, NE China 40°41´N 124°46´E
Kuandian Manzu Zizhixian *see* Kuandian
Kuando-Kubango *see* Cuando Cubango
Kuang-chou *see* Guangzhou
Kuang-hsi *see* Guangxi Zhuangzu Zizhiqu
Kuang-tung *see* Guangdong
Kuang-yuan *see* Guangyuan
Kuantan, Batang *see* Indragiri, Sungai
Kuanza Norte *see* Cuanza Norte
Kuanza Sul *see* Cuanza Sul
Kuanzhou *see* Qingjian
Kuba *see* Quba
Kubango *see* Cubango/ Okavango
141 X8 **Kubārah** NW Oman 23°03´N 56°52´E
93 H16 **Kubbe** Västernorrland, C Sweden 63°31´N 18°04´E
80 A11 **Kubbum** Southern Darfur, W Sudan 11°47´N 23°47´E
124 L13 **Kubenskoye, Ozero** ◎ NW Russian Federation
146 G6 **Kubla-Ustyurt** *Rus.* Komsomol'sk-na-Ustyurte. Qoraqalpog'iston Respublikasi, NW Uzbekistan 44°06´N 58°14´E
164 G15 **Kubokawa** Kōchi, Shikoku, SW Japan 33°22´N 133°14´E
114 L7 **Kubrat** *prev.* Balbunar. Razgrad, N Bulgaria 43°48´N 26°31´E
112 O13 **Kučajske Planine** ▲▲ E Serbia
165 T1 **Kuccharo-ko** ◎ Hokkaidō, N Japan
112 O11 **Kučevo** Serbia, NE Serbia 44°29´N 21°42´E
Kuchan *see* Qūchān
169 Q10 **Kuching** *prev.* Sarawak. Sarawak, East Malaysia 01°32´N 110°20´E
169 Q10 **Kuching** ✈ Sarawak, East Malaysia 01°32´N 110°20´E
164 B17 **Kuchinoerabu-jima** *island* Nansei-shotō, SW Japan
164 C14 **Kuchinotsu** Nagasaki, Kyūshū, SW Japan 32°36´N 130°11´E
109 Q6 **Kuchl** Salzburg, NW Austria 47°37´N 13°12´E
148 L9 **Kūchnay Darweyshān** Helmand, S Afghanistan 31°02´N 64°10´E
Kuchurgan *see* Kuchurhan
117 O9 **Kuchurhan** *Rus.* Kuchurgan. ~ NE Ukraine
Kuçova *see* Kuçovë
113 L21 **Kuçovë** *var.* Kuçova; *prev.* Qyteti Stalin. Berat, C Albania 40°48´N 19°55´E
136 D11 **Küçük Çekmece** İstanbul, NW Turkey 41°01´N 28°47´E
164 F14 **Kudamatsu** *var.* Kudamatu. Yamaguchi, Honshū, SW Japan 34°00´N 131°53´E
Kudamatu *see* Kudamatsu
Kudara *see* Ghŭdara
169 V6 **Kudat** Sabah, East Malaysia 06°54´N 116°47´E
Küddow *see* Gwda
155 G17 **Kūdligi** Karnātaka, W India 14°58´N 76°24´E
Kudowa *see* Kudowa-Zdrój
111 F16 **Kudowa-Zdrój** *Ger.* Kudowa. Wałbrzych, SW Poland 50°27´N 16°20´E
117 P9 **Kudryavtsivka** Mykolayivs'ka Oblast', S Ukraine 47°18´N 31°02´E
169 R16 **Kudus** *prev.* Koedoes. Jawa, C Indonesia 06°46´S 110°48´E
125 T13 **Kudymkar** Komi-Permyatskiy Avtonomnyy Okrug, NW Russian Federation 59°01´N 54°40´E
Kudzsir *see* Cugir
Kuei-chou *see* Guizhou
Kuei-lin *see* Guilin
Kuei-Yang/Kuei-yang *see* Guiyang
K'u-erh-lo *see* Korla
Kueyang *see* Guiyang
Kufa *see* Al Kūfah
136 E14 **Küfiçayı** ~ C Turkey
109 O6 **Kufstein** Tirol, W Austria 47°36´N 12°10´E
9 N7 **Kugaaruk** *prev.* Pelly Bay. Nunavut, N Canada 68°38´N 89°45´W
145 V14 **Kugaly** *Kaz.* Qoghaly. Almaty, SE Kazakhstan 44°30´N 78°40´E
8 K8 **Kugluktuk** *var.* Qurlurtuuq; *prev.* Coppermine. Nunavut, NW Canada 67°49´N 115°12´W
143 Y13 **Kūhak** Sīstān va Balūchestān, SE Iran 27°10´N 63°15´E
143 R9 **Kūhbonān** Kermān, C Iran 31°23´N 56°16´E
148 J5 **Kūhestān** *var.* Kohsān. Herāt, W Afghanistan 34°40´N 61°11´E
Kūhīrī *see* Kahīrī
93 N15 **Kuhmo** Oulu, E Finland 64°04´N 29°34´E
93 L18 **Kuhmoinen** Länsi-Suomi, C Finland 61°32´N 25°09´E
Kuhnau *see* Konin
Kühnö *see* Kihnu
143 O8 **Kūhpāyeh** Eşfahān, C Iran 32°42´N 52°25´E
167 O12 **Kui Buri** *var.* Ban Kui Nua. Prachuap Khiri Khan, SW Thailand 12°10´N 99°49´E
Kuibyshev *see* Kuybyshevskoye Vodokhranilishche
82 D13 **Kuito** *Port.* Silva Porto. Bié, C Angola 12°21´S 16°55´E
39 X14 **Kuiu Island** *island* Alexander Archipelago, Alaska, USA
92 L13 **Kuivaniemi** Oulu, C Finland 65°34´N 25°13´E
77 V14 **Kujama** Kaduna, C Nigeria 10°27´N 07°39´E
110 I10 **Kujawsko-pomorskie** ◈ *province* C Poland
165 R8 **Kuji** *var.* Kuzi. Iwate, Honshū, C Japan 40°12´N 141°47´E
Kujto, Ozero *see* Yushkozerskoye Vodokhranilishche
Kujū-renzan *see* Kujū-san
164 D14 **Kujū-san** *var.* Kujū-renzan. ▲ Kyūshū, SW Japan 33°07´N 131°13´E
43 N7 **Kukalaya, Rio** *var.* Rio Cuculaya, Rio Kukulaya. ~ NE Nicaragua
113 O16 **Kukavica** *var.* Vlajna. ▲ SE Serbia 42°46´N 21°58´E
113 M18 **Kukës** *var.* Kukësi. Kukës, NE Albania 42°03´N 20°25´E
113 L18 **Kukës** ◈ *district* NE Albania
Kukësi *see* Kukës
186 D8 **Kukipi** Gulf, S Papua New Guinea 08°11´S 146°09´E
127 S3 **Kukmor** Respublika Tatarstan, W Russian Federation 56°11´N 50°56´E
Kukong *see* Shaoguan
39 N6 **Kukpowruk River** ~ Alaska, USA
38 M6 **Kukpuk River** ~ Alaska, USA
Küküdağ *see* Gogi, Mount
Kukukhoto *see* Hohhot
Kukulaya, Rio *see* Kukalaya, Rio
189 W12 **Kuku Point** *headland* NW Wake Island 19°19´N 166°36´E
146 G11 **Kukurtli** Ahal Welaýaty, C Turkmenistan 39°58´N 58°47´E
Kül *see* Kūl, Rūd-e
114 F7 **Kula** Vidin, NW Bulgaria 43°55´N 22°32´E
112 K9 **Kula** Vojvodina, NW Serbia 45°37´N 19°31´E
136 D14 **Kula** Manisa, W Turkey 38°33´N 28°38´E
149 S8 **Kulāchi** North-West Frontier Province, NW Pakistan 31°58´N 70°30´E
Kulachi *see* Kolāchi
144 F11 **Kulagino** *Kaz.* Kūlagīno. Atyrau, W Kazakhstan 48°30´N 51°33´E
Kūlagīno *see* Kulagino
168 L10 **Kulai** Johor, Peninsular Malaysia 01°41´N 103°33´E
114 M7 **Kulak** ~ NE Bulgaria
153 T11 **Kula Kangri** *var.* Kulhakangri. ▲ Bhutan/ China 28°06´N 90°19´E
144 E13 **Kulaly, Ostrov** *island* SW Kazakhstan
145 S16 **Kulan** *Kaz.* Qulan; *prev.* Lugovoy, Lugovoye. Zhambyl, S Kazakhstan 42°54´N 72°45´E
147 V9 **Kulanak** Narynskaya Oblast', C Kyrgyzstan 41°18´N 75°38´E
Gory Kulandag *see* Gulandag
153 V14 **Kulaura** Sylhet, NE Bangladesh 24°32´N 92°02´E
118 D9 **Kuldīga** *Ger.* Goldingen. Kuldīga, W Latvia 56°57´N 21°59´E
Kuldja *see* Yining
Kul'dzhuktau, Gory *see* QuljuqtovTog'lari
127 N4 **Kulebaki** Nizhegorodskaya Oblast', W Russian Federation 55°25´N 42°31´E
112 E11 **Kulen Vakuf** *var.* Spasovo. ◈ Federacija Bosna I Hercegovina, NW Bosnia and Herzegovina
181 Q9 **Kulgera Roadhouse** Northern Territory, N Australia 25°49´S 133°30´E
Kulhakangri *see* Kula Kangri
127 T1 **Kuliga** Udmurtskaya Respublika, NW Russian Federation 58°14´N 53°49´E
Kulkuduk *see* Ko'lquduq
118 G4 **Kullamaa** Läänemaa, W Estonia 58°52´N 24°05´E
197 O12 **Kullorsuaq** *var.* Kuvdlorssuak. ◈ Kitaa, C Greenland
29 O6 **Kulm** North Dakota, N USA 46°18´N 98°57´W
Kulm *see* Chełmno
146 D12 **Kul'mach** *prev. Turkm.* Isgender. Balkan Welaýaty, W Turkmenistan 39°04´N 55°49´E
101 L18 **Kulmbach** Bayern, SE Germany 50°07´N 11°27´E
Kulmsee *see* Chełmża
147 Q14 **Kŭlob** *Rus.* Kulyab. SW Tajikistan 37°55´N 68°46´E
92 M13 **Kuloharju** Lappi, N Finland 65°51´N 28°10´E
125 N7 **Kuloy** Arkhangel'skaya Oblast', NW Russian Federation 64°55´N 43°35´E
125 N7 **Kuloy** ~ NW Russian Federation
137 Q14 **Kulp** Dıyarbakır, SE Turkey 38°32´N 41°01´E
Kulpa *see* Kolpa
77 P14 **Kulpawn** ~ N Ghana
143 R13 **Kūl, Rūd-e** *var.* Kül. ~ S Iran
144 G12 **Kul'sary** *Kaz.* Qulsary. Atyrau, W Kazakhstan 46°59´N 54°02´E
153 R15 **Kulti** West Bengal, NE India 23°45´N 86°50´E
93 G14 **Kultsjön** ◎ N Sweden
136 I14 **Kulu** Konya, W Turkey 39°06´N 33°02´E
123 S9 **Kulu** ~ E Russian Federation
122 I13 **Kulunda** Altayskiy Kray, S Russian Federation 52°33´N 79°04´E
145 T7 **Kulunda Steppe** *Kaz.* Qulyndy Zhazyghy, *Rus.* Kulundinskaya Ravnina. *grassland* Kazakhstan/Russian Federation
Kulundinskaya Ravnina *see* Kulunda Steppe
182 M9 **Kulwin** Victoria, SE Australia 35°04´S 142°37´E
Kulyab *see* Kŭlob
117 Q3 **Kulykivka** Chernihivs'ka Oblast', N Ukraine 51°23´N 31°39´E
Kum *see* Qom
164 F14 **Kuma** Ehime, Shikoku, SW Japan 33°36´N 132°53´E
127 P14 **Kuma** ~ SW Russian Federation
165 O12 **Kumagaya** Saitama, Honshū, S Japan 36°09´N 139°22´E
165 Q5 **Kumaishi** Hokkaidō, NE Japan 42°08´N 139°57´E
169 R13 **Kumai, Teluk** *bay* Borneo, C Indonesia
127 Y7 **Kumak** Orenburgskaya Oblast', W Russian Federation 51°16´N 60°06´E
164 C14 **Kumamoto** Kumamoto, Kyūshū, SW Japan 32°49´N 130°41´E

◆ Country
● Country Capital
◇ Dependent Territory
○ Dependent Territory Capital
◈ Administrative Regions
✈ International Airport
▲ Mountain
▲▲ Mountain Range
Volcano
~ River
◎ Lake
⊠ Reservoir

164 *D15* **Kumamoto** *off.* Kumamoto-ken. ⬖ *prefecture* Kyūshū, SW Japan
Kumamoto-ken *see* Kumamoto
164 *J15* **Kumano** Mie, Honshū, SW Japan *33°54′N 136°08′E*
Kumanova *see* Kumanovo
113 *O17* **Kumanovo** *Turk.* Kumanova. N Macedonia *42°08′N 21°43′E*
185 *G17* **Kumara** West Coast, South Island, New Zealand *42°39′S 171°12′E*
180 *J8* **Kumarina Roadhouse** Western Australia *24°46′S 119°39′E*
153 *T15* **Kumarkhali** Khulna, W Bangladesh *23°54′N 89°16′E*
77 *P16* **Kumasi** *prev.* Coomassie. C Ghana *06°41′N 01°40′W*
Kumayri *see* Gyumri
79 *D15* **Kumba** Sud-Ouest, W Cameroon *04°39′N 09°26′E*
114 *N13* **Kumbağ** Tekirdağ, NW Turkey *40°51′N 27°26′E*
155 *J21* **Kumbakonam** Tamil Nādu, SE India *10°59′N 79°24′E*
Kum-Dag *see* Gumdag
165 *R16* **Kume-jima** *island* Nansei-shotō, SW Japan
127 *V6* **Kumertau** Respublika Bashkortostan, W Russian Federation *52°48′N 55°48′E*
Kumillā *see* Comilla
35 *R4* **Kumiva Peak** ▲ Nevada, W USA *40°24′N 119°16′W*
159 *N7* **Kum Kuduk** Xinjiang Uygur Zizhiqu, W China *40°15′N 91°55′E*
159 *N8* **Kum Kuduk** *well* NW China
Kumkurgan *see* Qumqo'rg'on
95 *M16* **Kumla** Örebro, C Sweden *59°08′N 15°09′E*
136 *E17* **Kumluca** Antalya, SW Turkey *36°23′N 30°17′E*
100 *N9* **Kummerower See** ◎ NE Germany
77 *X14* **Kumo** Gombe, E Nigeria *10°03′N 11°14′E*
145 *O13* **Kumola** ≈ C Kazakhstan
167 *N1* **Kumon Range** ⛰ N Burma (Myanmar)
83 *F22* **Kums** Karas, SE Namibia *28°07′S 19°40′E*
124 *I7* **Kumskoye Vodokhranilishche** ⊠ NW Russian Federation
155 *E18* **Kumta** Karnātaka, W India *14°25′N 74°24′E*
158 *L6* **Kümük** Xinjiang Uygur Zizhiqu, W China
38 *H12* **Kumukahi, Cape** *headland* Hawai'i, USA, C Pacific Ocean *19°31′N 154°48′W*
127 *Q17* **Kumukh** Respublika Dagestan, SW Russian Federation *42°10′N 47°07′E*
Kumul *see* Hami
127 *N9* **Kumylzhenskaya** Volgogradskaya Oblast', SW Russian Federation *49°54′N 42°35′E*
141 *W6* **Kumzār** N Oman *26°19′N 56°26′E*
43 *W15* **Kuna de Madungandí** ⬖ *special territory* NE Panama
Kunar *see* Konar
Kunashiri *see* Kunashir, Ostrov
123 *U14* **Kunashir, Ostrov** *var.* Kunashiri. *island* Kuril'skiye Ostrova, SE Russian Federation
43 *V14* **Kuna Yala** *prev.* San Blas. ⬖ *special territory* NE Panama
118 *I3* **Kunda** Lääne-Virumaa, NE Estonia *59°31′N 26°33′E*
152 *M13* **Kunda** Uttar Pradesh, N India *25°43′N 81°31′E*
155 *E19* **Kundāpura** *var.* Coondapoor. Karnātaka, W India *13°39′N 74°41′E*
79 *O24* **Kundelungu, Monts** ⛰ S Dem. Rep. Congo
Kundert *see* Hernád
186 *D7* **Kundiawa** Chimbu, W Papua New Guinea *06°00′S 144°57′E*
Kundla *see* Sāvarkundla
Kunduk, Ozero *see* Sasyk, Ozero
168 *L10* **Kundur, Pulau** *island* W Indonesia
Kunduz *see* Kondoz
Kunduz/Kundūz *see* Kondoz
Kuneitra *see* Al Qunayṭirah
83 *B18* **Kunene** ⬖ *district* NE Namibia
83 *A16* **Kunene** *var.* Cunene. ≈ Angola/Namibia *see also* Cunene
Kunene *see* Cunene
Künes *see* Xinyuan
158 *J5* **Künes He** ≈ NW China
95 *I19* **Kungälv** Västra Götaland, S Sweden *57°54′N 12°00′E*
147 *W7* **Kungei Ala-Tau** *Rus.* Khrebet Kyungëy Ala-Too, *Kir.* Küngöy Ala-Too. ⛰ Kazakhstan/Kyrgyzstan
Küngöy Ala-Too *see* Kungei Ala-Tau
Kungrad *see* Qo'ng'irot
95 *J19* **Kungsbacka** Halland, S Sweden *57°30′N 12°05′E*
95 *I18* **Kungshamn** Västra Götaland, S Sweden *58°21′N 11°15′E*
95 *M16* **Kungsör** Västmanland, C Sweden *59°25′N 16°05′E*
79 *J16* **Kungu** Equateur, NW Dem. Rep. Congo *02°47′N 19°12′E*
125 *V15* **Kungur** Permskaya Oblast', NW Russian Federation *57°24′N 56°56′E*
166 *L9* **Kungyangon** Yangon, SW Burma (Myanmar) *16°27′N 96°00′E*
111 *M22* **Kunhegyes** Jász-Nagykun-Szolnok, E Hungary *47°22′N 20°36′E*
167 *O5* **Kunhing** Shan State, E Burma (Myanmar) *21°17′N 98°26′E*
158 *D9* **Kunjirap Daban** *var.* Khūnjerāb Pass. *pass* China/Pakistan *see also* Khūnjerāb Pass
Kunjirap Daban *see* Khunjerāb Pass
Kunlun Mountains *see* Kunlun Shan
158 *H10* **Kunlun Shan** *Eng.* Kunlun Mountains. ⛰ NW China
159 *P11* **Kunlun Shankou** *pass* C China
160 *G13* **Kunming** *var.* K'un-ming; *prev.* Yunnan. *province capital* Yunnan, SW China *25°04′N 102°41′E*
K'un-ming *see* Kunming
Kunø *see* Kunoy
95 *B18* **Kunoy** *Dan.* Kunø. *island* N Faeroe Islands
163 *X16* **Kunsan** *var.* Gunsan, *Jap.* Gunzan. W South Korea *35°58′N 126°42′E*
111 *L24* **Kunszentmárton** Jász-Nagykun-Szolnok, E Hungary *46°50′N 20°19′E*
111 *J23* **Kunszentmiklós** Bács-Kiskun, C Hungary *47°00′N 19°07′E*
181 *N3* **Kununurra** Western Australia *15°50′S 128°44′E*
Kunyang *see* Pingyang
Kunya-Urgench *see* Köneürgenç
Kunyé *see* Pins, Île des
169 *T11* **Kunyi** Borneo, C Indonesia *03°23′S 119°20′E*
101 *I20* **Künzelsau** Baden-Württemberg, S Germany *49°22′N 09°43′E*
161 *S10* **Kuocang Shan** ⛰ SE China
Kuolajärvi *see* Kuoloyarvi
124 *H5* **Kuoloyarvi** *Finn.* Kuolajärvi, *var.* Luolajarvi. Murmanskaya Oblast', NW Russian Federation *66°58′N 29°13′E*
93 *N16* **Kuopio** Itä-Suomi, C Finland *62°54′N 27°41′E*
93 *K17* **Kuortane** Länsi-Suomi, W Finland *62°48′N 23°30′E*
93 *M18* **Kuortti** Itä-Suomi, E Finland *61°25′N 26°25′E*
112 *E9* **Kupa** ≈ Croatia/Slovenia
Kupa *see* Kolpa
171 *P17* **Kupang** *prev.* Koepang. Timor, C Indonesia *10°13′S 123°38′E*
39 *Q5* **Kuparuk River** ≈ Alaska, USA
Kupchino *see* Cupcina
186 *E9* **Kupiano** Central, S Papua New Guinea *10°06′S 148°12′E*
180 *M4* **Kupingarri** Western Australia *16°46′S 125°57′E*
122 *I12* **Kupino** Novosibirskaya Oblast', C Russian Federation *54°22′N 77°09′E*
118 *H11* **Kupiškis** Panevėžys, NE Lithuania *55°51′N 24°58′E*
114 *L13* **Küplü** Edirne, NW Turkey *41°06′N 26°23′E*
39 *X13* **Kupreanof Island** *island* Alexander Archipelago, Alaska, USA
39 *O16* **Kupreanof Point** *headland* Alaska, USA *55°34′N 159°36′W*
112 *G13* **Kupres** ⬖ Federacija Bosna I Hercegovina, SW Bosnia and Herzegovina
117 *W5* **Kup"yans'k** *Rus.* Kupyansk. Kharkivs'ka Oblast', E Ukraine *49°42′N 37°36′E*
Kupyansk *see* Kup"yans'k
117 *W5* **Kup"yans'k-Vuzlovyy** Kharkivs'ka Oblast', E Ukraine *49°40′N 37°41′E*
158 *I6* **Kuqa** Xinjiang Uygur Zizhiqu, NW China *41°43′N 82°58′E*
Kür *see* Kura
137 *W11* **Kura** *Az.* Kür, *Geor.* Mtkvari, *Turk.* Kura Nehri. ≈ SW Asia
55 *R8* **Kuracki** NW Guyana *06°52′N 60°13′W*
Kura Kurk *see* Irbe Strait
147 *Q10* **Kurama Range** *Rus.* Kuraminskiy Khrebet. ⛰ Tajikistan/Uzbekistan
Kuraminskiy Khrebet *see* Kurama Range
Kura Nehri *see* Kura
119 *J14* **Kuranyets** *Rus.* Kurenets. Minskaya Voblasts', C Belarus *54°33′N 26°57′E*
164 *H13* **Kurashiki** *var.* Kurasiki. Okayama, Honshū, SW Japan *34°35′N 133°44′E*
154 *L10* **Kurasia** Chhattīsgarh, C India *23°11′N 82°16′E*
Kurasiki *see* Kurashiki
164 *H12* **Kurayoshi** *var.* Kurayosi. Tottori, Honshū, SW Japan *35°27′N 133°52′E*
Kurayosi *see* Kurayoshi
163 *X6* **Kurbin He** ≈ NE China
145 *U9* **Kurchatov** *prev.* Konechnaya. Pavlodar, NE Kazakhstan *50°45′N 78°32′E*
145 *X10* **Kurchum** *Kaz.* Kürshim. Vostochnyy Kazakhstan, E Kazakhstan *48°35′N 83°37′E*
145 *Y10* **Kurchum** ≈ E Kazakhstan
137 *X11* **Kürdämir** *Rus.* Kyurdamir. C Azerbaijan *40°21′N 48°08′E*
Kurdestan *see* Kordestān
139 *S1* **Kurdistan** *cultural region* SW Asia
Kurd Kui *see* Kord Kūy
155 *F15* **Kurduvādi** Mahārāshtra, W India *18°06′N 75°31′E*
114 *J11* **Kŭrdzhali** *var.* Kirdzhali. Kŭrdzhali, S Bulgaria *41°39′N 25°23′E*
114 *K11* **Kŭrdzhali** ⬖ *province* S Bulgaria
114 *J11* **Kŭrdzhali, Yazovir** ⊠ S Bulgaria
164 *F13* **Kure** Hiroshima, Honshū, SW Japan *34°15′N 132°33′E*
192 *K5* **Kure Atoll** *var.* Ocean Island. *atoll* Hawaiian Islands, Hawaii, USA
136 *J10* **Küre Dağları** ⛰ N Turkey
146 *C11* **Kürendag** *Rus.* Gora Kyuren. ▲ W Turkmenistan *39°05′N 55°09′E*
Kurenets *see* Kuranyets
118 *E6* **Kuressaare** *Ger.* Arensburg; *prev.* Kingissepp. Saaremaa, W Estonia *58°17′N 22°29′E*
122 *K9* **Kureyka** Krasnoyarskiy Kray, N Russian Federation *66°22′N 87°21′E*
122 *K9* **Kureyka** ≈ N Russian Federation
Kurgal'dzhino/Kurgal'dzhinsky *see* Korgalzhyn
122 *G11* **Kurgan** Kurganskaya Oblast', C Russian Federation *55°30′N 65°20′E*
126 *L14* **Kurganinsk** Krasnodarskiy Kray, SW Russian Federation *44°55′N 40°45′E*
122 *G11* **Kurganskaya Oblast'** ⬖ *province* C Russian Federation
Kurgan-Tyube *see* Qŭrghonteppa
191 *O2* **Kuria** *prev.* Woodle Island. *island* Tungaru, W Kiribati
Kuria Muria Bay *see* Ḥalāniyāt, Khalīj al
Kuria Muria Islands *see* Ḥalāniyāt, Juzur al
153 *T13* **Kurigram** Rajshahi, N Bangladesh *25°49′N 89°39′E*
93 *K17* **Kurikka** Länsi-Suomi, W Finland *62°36′N 22°25′E*
192 *I3* **Kurile Basin** *undersea feature* NW Pacific Ocean *47°00′N 150°00′E*
Kurile Islands *see* Kuril'skiye Ostrova
Kurile-Kamchatka Depression *see* Kurile Trench
192 *J3* **Kurile Trench** *var.* Kurile-Kamchatka Depression. *undersea feature* NW Pacific Ocean *47°00′N 155°00′E*
127 *Q9* **Kurilovka** Saratovskaya Oblast', W Russian Federation *50°39′N 48°02′E*
123 *U13* **Kuril'sk** *Jap.* Shana. Kuril'skiye Ostrova, Sakhalinskaya Oblats', SE Russian Federation *45°10′N 147°51′E*
122 *G11* **Kuril'skiye Ostrova** *Eng.* Kurile Islands. *island group* SE Russian Federation
42 *M9* **Kurinwas, Río** ≈ E Nicaragua
Kurisches Haff *see* Courland Lagoon
Kurkund *see* Kilingi-Nõmme
126 *M4* **Kurlovskiy** Vladimirskaya Oblast', W Russian Federation *55°25′N 40°39′E*
80 *G12* **Kurmuk** Blue Nile, SE Sudan *10°36′N 34°16′E*
Kurna *see* Al Qurnah
155 *H17* **Kurnool** *var.* Karnul. Andhra Pradesh, S India *15°51′N 78°01′E*
164 *M11* **Kurobe** Toyama, Honshū, SW Japan *36°55′N 137°24′E*
165 *Q7* **Kuroishi** *var.* Kuroisi. Aomori, Honshū, C Japan *40°37′N 140°34′E*
Kuroisi *see* Kuroishi
165 *O12* **Kuroiso** Tochigi, Honshū, S Japan *36°58′N 140°02′E*
165 *Q4* **Kuromatsunai** Hokkaidō, NE Japan *42°40′N 140°18′E*
164 *B17* **Kuro-shima** *island* SW Japan
185 *F21* **Kurow** Canterbury, South Island, New Zealand *44°44′S 170°29′E*
127 *N15* **Kursavka** Stavropol'skiy Kray, SW Russian Federation *44°28′N 42°31′E*
118 *E11* **Kuršėnai** Šiauliai, N Lithuania *56°00′N 22°56′E*
Kürshim *see* Kurchum
Kurshskaya Kosa/Kuršių Nerija *see* Courland Spit
126 *J7* **Kursk** Kurskaya Oblast', W Russian Federation *51°44′N 36°47′E*
126 *I7* **Kurskaya Oblast'** ⬖ *province* W Russian Federation
Kurskiy Zaliv *see* Courland Lagoon
113 *N15* **Kuršumlija** Serbia, S Serbia *43°09′N 21°16′E*
137 *R15* **Kurtalan** Siirt, SE Turkey *37°58′N 41°36′E*
Kurtbunar *see* Tervel
Kurt-Dere *see* Vŭlchidol
Kurtitsch/Kürtös *see* Curtici
145 *U15* **Kurtty** ≈ SE Kazakhstan
93 *L18* **Kuru** Länsi-Suomi, W Finland *61°51′N 23°46′E*
80 *C13* **Kuru** ≈ W Sudan
114 *M13* **Kuru Dağı** ⛰ NW Turkey
158 *L7* **Kuruktag** ⛰ NW China
83 *G22* **Kuruman** Northern Cape, N South Africa *27°28′S 23°27′E*
67 *T14* **Kuruman** ≈ W South Africa
164 *D14* **Kurume** Fukuoka, Kyūshū, SW Japan *33°15′N 130°27′E*
123 *N13* **Kurumkan** Respublika Buryatiya, S Russian Federation *54°13′N 110°21′E*
155 *J25* **Kurunegala** North Western Province, C Sri Lanka *07°28′N 80°23′E*
55 *T10* **Kurupukari** C Guyana *04°39′N 58°39′W*
125 *U10* **Kur"ya** Respublika Komi, NW Russian Federation *61°38′N 57°12′E*
144 *E15* **Kuryk** *var.* Yeraliyev, *Kaz.* Quryq. Mangistau, SW Kazakhstan *43°12′N 51°43′E*
136 *B15* **Kuşadası** Aydın, SW Turkey *37°50′N 27°16′E*
115 *M19* **Kuşadası Körfezi** *gulf* SW Turkey
164 *A17* **Kusagaki-guntō** *island* SW Japan
Kusaie *see* Kosrae
145 *T12* **Kusak** ≈ C Kazakhstan
Kusary *see* Qusar
167 *P7* **Ku Sathan, Doi** ▲ NW Thailand *18°22′N 100°31′E*
164 *J13* **Kusatsu** *var.* Kusatu. Shiga, Honshū, SW Japan *35°02′N 136°00′E*
Kusatu *see* Kusatsu
138 *F11* **Kuseifa** Southern, C Israel *31°15′N 35°01′E*
136 *C12* **Kuş Gölü** ◎ NW Turkey
126 *L12* **Kushchevskaya** Krasnodarskiy Kray, SW Russian Federation *46°35′N 39°40′E*
164 *D16* **Kushima** *var.* Kusima. Miyazaki, Kyūshū, SW Japan *31°28′N 131°14′E*
164 *I15* **Kushimoto** Wakayama, Honshū, SW Japan *33°28′N 135°45′E*
165 *V4* **Kushiro** *var.* Kusiro. Hokkaidō, NE Japan *42°58′N 144°24′E*
148 *K4* **Kūshk** Herāt, W Afghanistan *34°55′N 62°20′E*
Kushka *see* Serhetabat
Kushka *see* Gushgy/Serhetabat
145 *N8* **Kushmurun** *Kaz.* Qusmuryn. Kostanay, N Kazakhstan *52°27′N 64°31′E*
145 *N8* **Kushmurun, Ozero** *Kaz.* Qusmuryn. ◎ N Kazakhstan
127 *U4* **Kushnarenkovo** Respublika Bashkortostan, W Russian Federation *55°07′N 55°24′E*
Kushrabat *see* Qo'shrabot
Kushtia *see* Kustia
Kusima *see* Kushima
Kusiro *see* Kushiro
38 *M13* **Kuskokwim Bay** *bay* Alaska, USA
39 *P11* **Kuskokwim Mountains** ⛰ Alaska, USA
39 *N12* **Kuskokwim River** ≈ Alaska, USA
108 *G7* **Küsnacht** Zürich, N Switzerland *47°19′N 08°34′E*
165 *V4* **Kussharo-ko** *var.* Kussyaro. ◎ Hokkaidō, NE Japan
Küssnacht *see* Küssnacht am Rigi
108 *F8* **Küssnacht am Rigi** *var.* Küssnacht. Schwyz, C Switzerland *47°03′N 08°25′E*
Kussyaro *see* Kussharo-ko
Kustanay *see* Kostanay
Küstence/Küstendje *see* Constanța
100 *F11* **Küstenkanal** *var.* Ems-Hunte Canal. *canal* NW Germany
153 *T15* **Kustia** *var.* Kushtia. Khulna, W Bangladesh *23°54′N 89°07′E*
Küstrin *see* Kostrzyn
171 *R11* **Kusu** Pulau Halmahera, E Indonesia *0°51′N 127°41′E*
170 *L16* **Kuta** Pulau Lombok, S Indonesia *08°53′S 116°15′E*
139 *T4* **Kutabān** At Ta'mīn, N Iraq *35°21′N 44°45′E*
136 *E13* **Kütahya** *prev.* Kutaia. Kütahya, W Turkey *39°25′N 29°56′E*
136 *E13* **Kütahya** *var.* Kutaia. ⬖ *province* W Turkey
Kutai *see* Mahakam, Sungai
Kutaia *see* Kütahya
137 *R9* **K'ut'aisi** W Georgia *42°16′N 42°42′E*
Kūt al 'Amārah *see* Al Kūt
Kut al Hai/Kūt al Ḥayy *see* Al Ḥayy
Kut al Imara *see* Al Kūt
123 *Q11* **Kutana** Respublika Sakha (Yakutiya), NE Russian Federation *59°05′N 131°43′E*
Kutaradja/Kutaraja *see* Bandaaceh
165 *R4* **Kutchan** Hokkaidō, NE Japan *42°54′N 140°46′E*
Kutch, Gulf of *see* Kachchh, Gulf of
Kutch, Rann of *see* Kachchh, Rann of
112 *F9* **Kutina** Sisak-Moslavina, NE Croatia *45°29′N 16°45′E*
112 *H9* **Kutjevo** Požega-Slavonija, NE Croatia *45°26′N 17°54′E*
111 *E17* **Kutná Hora** *Ger.* Kuttenberg. Střední Čechy, C Czech Republic *49°58′N 15°18′E*
110 *K12* **Kutno** Łódzkie, C Poland *52°14′N 19°23′E*
Kuttenberg *see* Kutná Hora
79 *I20* **Kutu** Bandundu, W Dem. Rep. Congo *02°42′S 18°10′E*
153 *V17* **Kutubdia Island** *island* SE Bangladesh
80 *B10* **Kutum** Northern Darfur, W Sudan *14°10′N 24°40′E*
147 *Y7* **Kuturgu** Issyk-Kul'skaya Oblast', E Kyrgyzstan *42°45′N 78°04′E*
12 *M5* **Kuujjuaq** *prev.* Fort-Chimo. Québec, E Canada *58°10′N 68°15′W*
12 *I7* **Kuujjuarapik** Québec, C Canada *55°07′N 78°09′W*
Kuuli-Mayak *see* Guwlumaýak
118 *I6* **Kuulsemägi** ▲ S Estonia
92 *N13* **Kuusamo** Oulu, E Finland *65°57′N 29°15′E*
93 *M19* **Kuusankoski** Etelä-Suomi, S Finland *60°51′N 26°40′E*
127 *W7* **Kuvandyk** Orenburgskaya Oblast', W Russian Federation *51°27′N 57°18′E*
Kuvango *see* Cubango
Kuvasay *see* Quvasoy
Kuvdlorssuak *see* Kullorsuaq
124 *I16* **Kuvshinovo** Tverskaya Oblast', W Russian Federation *57°03′N 34°09′E*
141 *Q4* **Kuwait** *off.* State of Kuwait, *var.* Dawlat al Kuwait, Koweit, Kuweit. ◆ *monarchy* SW Asia
Kuwait *see* Al Kuwayt
Kuwait Bay *see* Kuwayt, Jūn al
Kuwait City *see* Al Kuwayt
Kuwait, Dawlat al *see* Kuwait
Kuwait, State of *see* Kuwait
Kuwajleen *see* Kwajalein Atoll
164 *K13* **Kuwana** Mie, Honshū, SW Japan *35°04′N 136°40′E*
139 *X9* **Kuwayt** Maysān, E Iraq *32°26′N 47°12′E*
142 *K11* **Kuwayt, Jūn al** *var.* Kuwait Bay. *bay* E Kuwait
Kuweit *see* Kuwait
117 *P10* **Kuyal'nyts'kyy Lyman** ◎ SW Ukraine
122 *I12* **Kuybyshev** Novosibirskaya Oblast', C Russian Federation *55°28′N 77°55′E*
Kuybyshev *see* Bolgar, Respublika Tatarstan, Russian Federation
Kuybyshev *see* Samara
117 *W9* **Kuybysheve** *Rus.* Kuybyshevo. Zaporiz'ka Oblast', SE Ukraine *47°20′N 36°41′E*
Kuybyshevo *see* Kuybysheve
Kuybyshev Reservoir *see* Kuybyshevskoye Vodokhranilishche
Kuybyshevskaya Oblast' *see* Samarskaya Oblast'
Kuybyshevskiy *see* Novoishimskiy
127 *R4* **Kuybyshevskoye Vodokhranilishche** *var.* Kuibyshev, *Eng.* Kuybyshev Reservoir. ⊠ W Russian Federation
123 *S9* **Kuydusun** Respublika Sakha (Yakutiya), NE Russian Federation *63°15′N 143°10′E*
125 *U16* **Kuyeda** Permskaya Oblast', NW Russian Federation *56°23′N 55°19′E*
Kūysanjaq *see* Koi Sanjaq
158 *J4* **Kuytun** Xinjiang Uygur Zizhiqu, NW China *44°25′N 84°55′E*
122 *M13* **Kuytun** Irkutskaya Oblast', S Russian Federation *54°18′N 101°28′E*
55 *S12* **Kuyuwini Landing** S Guyana *02°06′N 59°14′W*
Kuzi *see* Kuji
38 *M9* **Kuzitrin River** ≈ Alaska, USA
127 *P6* **Kuznetsk** Penzenskaya Oblast', W Russian Federation *53°06′N 46°27′E*
116 *K3* **Kuznetsovs'k** Rivnens'ka Oblast', NW Ukraine *51°21′N 25°51′E*
165 *R8* **Kuzumaki** Iwate, Honshū, C Japan *40°04′N 141°26′E*
95 *H24* **Kværndrup** Fyn, C Denmark *55°10′N 10°31′E*
92 *H9* **Kvaløya** *island* N Norway
92 *K8* **Kvalsund** Finnmark, N Norway *70°30′N 23°56′E*
94 *G11* **Kvam** Oppland, S Norway *61°42′N 09°43′E*
127 *X7* **Kvarkeno** Orenburgskaya Oblast', W Russian Federation *52°09′N 59°44′E*
93 *G15* **Kvarnbergsvattnet** *var.* Frostviken. ◎ N Sweden
112 *A11* **Kvarner** *var.* Carnaro, *It.* Quarnero. *gulf* W Croatia
112 *B11* **Kvarnerić** *channel* W Croatia
39 *O14* **Kvichak Bay** *bay* Alaska, USA
92 *H12* **Kvikkjokk** *Lapp.* Huhttán. Norrbotten, N Sweden *66°58′N 17°45′E*
95 *D17* **Kvina** ≈ S Norway
92 *Q1* **Kvitøya** *island* NE Svalbard
95 *F16* **Kvitseid** Telemark, S Norway *59°23′N 08°31′E*
79 *H20* **Kwa** ≈ W Dem. Rep. Congo
77 *Q15* **Kwadwokurom** C Ghana *07°49′N 00°15′W*
186 *M8* **Kwailibesi** Malaita, N Solomon Islands *08°25′S 160°48′E*
189 *S6* **Kwajalein Atoll** *var.* Kuwajleen. *atoll* Ralik Chain, C Marshall Islands
55 *W9* **Kwakoegron** Brokopondo, N Surinam *05°14′N 55°20′W*
81 *J21* **Kwale** Coast, S Kenya *04°10′S 39°27′E*
77 *U17* **Kwale** Delta, S Nigeria *05°51′N 06°29′E*
79 *H20* **Kwamouth** Bandundu, W Dem. Rep. Congo *03°11′S 16°16′E*
Kwando *see* Cuando
Kwangchow *see* Guangzhou
Kwangchu *see* Kwangju
163 *X16* **Kwangju** *off.* Kwangju-gwangyŏksi, *var.* Guangju, Kwangchu, *Jap.* Kōshū. SW South Korea *35°09′N 126°53′E*
Kwangju-gwangyŏksi *see* Kwangju
79 *H20* **Kwango** *Port.* Cuango. ≈ Angola/Dem. Rep. Congo *see also* Cuango
Kwango *see* Cuango
Kwangsi/Kwangsi Chuang Autonomous Region *see* Guangxi Zhuangzu Zizhiqu
Kwangtung *see* Guangdong
Kwangyuan *see* Guangyuan
81 *F17* **Kwania, Lake** ◎ C Uganda
Kwanza *see* Cuanza
77 *S15* **Kwara** ⬖ *state* SW Nigeria
83 *K22* **KwaZulu/Natal** *off.* KwaZulu/Natal Province; *prev.* Natal. ⬖ *province* E South Africa
KwaZulu/Natal Province *see* KwaZulu/Natal
Kweichow *see* Guizhou
Kweichu *see* Guiyang
Kweilin *see* Guilin
Kweisui *see* Hohhot
Kweiyang *see* Guiyang
83 *K17* **Kwekwe** *prev.* Que Que. Midlands, C Zimbabwe *18°56′S 29°49′E*
83 *G20* **Kweneng** ⬖ *district* S Botswana
Kwesui *see* Hohhot
39 *N12* **Kwethluk** Alaska, USA *60°48′N 161°26′W*
39 *N12* **Kwethluk River** ≈ Alaska, USA
110 *J8* **Kwidzyń** *Ger.* Marienwerder. Pomorskie, N Poland *53°44′N 18°55′E*
38 *M13* **Kwigillingok** Alaska, USA *59°52′N 163°08′W*
186 *E9* **Kwikila** Central, S Papua New Guinea *09°51′S 147°43′E*
79 *I20* **Kwilu** ≈ W Dem. Rep. Congo
Kwito *see* Cuito
171 *U12* **Kwoka, Gunung** ▲ Papua, E Indonesia *0°34′S 132°25′E*
78 *I12* **Kyabé** Moyen-Chari, S Chad *09°28′N 18°54′E*
183 *O11* **Kyabram** Victoria, SE Australia *36°21′S 145°05′E*
166 *M9* **Kyaikkami** *prev.* Amherst. Mon State, S Burma (Myanmar) *16°03′N 97°36′E*
166 *L9* **Kyaiklat** Ayeyarwady, SW Burma (Myanmar) *16°25′N 95°42′E*
166 *M8* **Kyaikto** Mon State, S Burma (Myanmar) *17°16′N 97°01′E*
123 *N14* **Kyakhta** Respublika Buryatiya, S Russian Federation *50°25′N 106°13′E*
182 *G8* **Kyancutta** South Australia *33°10′S 135°33′E*
167 *T8* **Ky Anh** Ha Tinh, N Vietnam *18°05′N 106°16′E*
166 *L5* **Kyaukpadaung** Mandalay, C Burma (Myanmar) *20°50′N 95°08′E*
166 *J6* **Kyaukpyu** Rakhine State, W Burma (Myanmar) *19°27′N 93°33′E*
166 *M5* **Kyaukse** Mandalay, C Burma (Myanmar) *21°33′N 96°06′E*
166 *L8* **Kyaunggon** Ayeyarwady, SW Burma (Myanmar) *17°04′N 95°12′E*
119 *E14* **Kybartai** *Pol.* Kibarty. Marijampolė, S Lithuania *54°37′N 22°44′E*
152 *I7* **Kyelang** Himāchal Pradesh, NW India *32°33′N 77°03′E*
111 *G19* **Kyjov** *Ger.* Gaya. Jihomoravský Kraj, SE Czech Republic *49°00′N 17°07′E*
115 *J21* **Kykládes** *var.* Kikládhes, *Eng.* Cyclades. *island group* SE Greece
25 *S11* **Kyle** Texas, SW USA *29°59′N 97°52′W*
96 *G9* **Kyle of Lochalsh** N Scotland, United Kingdom *57°18′N 05°39′W*
101 *D18* **Kyll** ≈ W Germany
115 *F19* **Kyllíni** *var.* Killini. ⛰ S Greece
115 *H18* **Kými** *prev.* Kími. Évvoia, C Greece *38°38′N 24°06′E*
93 *M19* **Kymijoki** ≈ S Finland
115 *H18* **Kýmis, Akrotírio** *headland* Évvoia, C Greece *38°39′N 24°08′E*
125 *W14* **Kyn** Permskaya Oblast', NW Russian Federation *57°48′N 58°38′E*
183 *N12* **Kyneton** Victoria, SE Australia *37°14′S 144°28′E*
81 *G17* **Kyoga, Lake** *var.* Lake Kioga. ◎ C Uganda
164 *J12* **Kyōga-misaki** *headland* Honshū, SW Japan *35°46′N 135°13′E*
183 *V4* **Kyogle** New South Wales, SE Australia *28°37′S 153°00′E*
163 *W15* **Kyŏnggi-man** *bay* NW South Korea
163 *Z16* **Kyŏngju** *Jap.* Keishū. SE South Korea *35°49′N 129°09′E*
Kyŏngsŏng *see* Sŏul
Kyōsai-tō *see* Kŏje-do
81 *F19* **Kyotera** S Uganda *0°38′S 31°34′E*
164 *J13* **Kyōto** Kyōto, Honshū, SW Japan *35°01′N 135°46′E*
164 *J13* **Kyōto** *off.* Kyōto-fu, *var.* Kyōto Hu. ⬖ *urban prefecture* Honshū, SW Japan
Kyōto-fu/Kyōto Hu *see* Kyōto
115 *D21* **Kyparissía** *var.* Kiparissía. Pelopónnisos, S Greece *37°15′N 21°40′E*
115 *D20* **Kyparissiakós Kólpos** *gulf* S Greece
Kyperounda *see* Kyperoúnta
121 *P3* **Kyperoúnta** *var.* Kyperounda. C Cyprus *34°57′N 33°02′E*
Kypros *see* Cyprus
115 *H16* **Kyrá Panagía** *island* Vóreies Sporádes, Greece, Aegean Sea
Kyrenia *see* Girne
Kyrenia Mountains *see* Beşparmak Dağları
Kyrgyz Republic *see* Kyrgyzstan
147 *U9* **Kyrgyzstan** *off.* Kyrgyz Republic, *var.* Kirghizia; *prev.* Kirgizskaya SSR, Kirghiz SSR, Republic of Kyrgyzstan. ◆ *republic* C Asia
Kyrgyzstan, Republic of *see* Kyrgyzstan
138 *F11* **Kyriat Gat** *prev.* Qiryat Gat. Southern, C Israel *31°37′N 34°47′E*
100 *M11* **Kyritz** Brandenburg, NE Germany *52°56′N 12°24′E*
94 *G8* **Kyrkseterøra** Sør-Trøndelag, S Norway *63°17′N 09°06′E*
Kyrkslätt *see* Kirkkonummi
125 *U8* **Kyrta** Respublika Komi, NW Russian Federation *64°03′N 57°41′E*
111 *J18* **Kysucké Nové Mesto** *prev.* Horné Nové Mesto, *Ger.* Kisutzaneustadtl, Oberneustadtl, *Hung.* Kiszucaújhely. Žilinský Kraj, N Slovakia *49°18′N 18°48′E*
117 *N12* **Kytay, Ozero** ◎ SW Ukraine
115 *F23* **Kýthira** *var.* Kíthira, *It.* Cerigo, *Lat.* Cythera. Kńythira, S Greece *41°39′N 26°30′E*
115 *F23* **Kýthira** *var.* Kíthira, *It.* Cerigo, *Lat.* Cythera. *island* S Greece
115 *I20* **Kýthnos** Kńythnos, Kykládes, Greece, Aegean Sea *37°24′N 24°28′E*
115 *I20* **Kýthnos** *var.* Kíthnos, Thermiá, *It.* Termia; *anc.* Cythnos. *island* Kykládes, Greece, Aegean Sea
115 *I20* **Kýthnou, Stenó** *strait* Kykládes, Greece, Aegean Sea
Kyungëy Ala-Too, Khrebet *see* Kungei Ala-Tau
Kyurdamir *see* Kürdämir
164 *D15* **Kyūshū** *var.* Kyûsyû. *island* SW Japan
192 *H6* **Kyushu-Palau Ridge** *var.* Kyusyu-Palau Ridge. *undersea feature* W Pacific Ocean *20°00′N 136°00′E*
114 *F10* **Kyustendil** *anc.* Pautalia. Kyustendil, W Bulgaria *42°17′N 22°42′E*
114 *G11* **Kyustendil** ⬖ *province* W Bulgaria
Kyûsyû *see* Kyūshū
Kyusyu-Palau Ridge *see* Kyushu-Palau Ridge
123 *P8* **Kyusyur** Respublika Sakha (Yakutiya), NE Russian Federation *70°36′N 127°19′E*
183 *P10* **Kywong** New South Wales, SE Australia *34°59′S 146°42′E*
117 *P4* **Kyyiv** *Eng.* Kiev, *Rus.* Kiyev. ● (Ukraine) Kyyivs'ka Oblast', N Ukraine *50°26′N 30°32′E*
Kyyiv *see* Kyyivs'ka Oblast'
117 *O4* **Kyyivs'ka Oblast'** *var.* Kyyiv, *Rus.* Kiyevskaya Oblast'. ⬖ *province* N Ukraine
117 *P3* **Kyyivs'ke Vodoskhovyshche** *Eng.* Kiev Reservoir, *Rus.* Kiyevskoye Vodokhranilishche. ⊠ N Ukraine
93 *L16* **Kyyjärvi** Länsi-Suomi, C Finland *63°02′N 24°34′E*
122 *K14* **Kyzyl** Respublika Tyva, C Russian Federation *51°45′N 94°28′E*
147 *S8* **Kyzyl-Adyr** *var.* Kirovskoye. Talasskaya Oblast', NW Kyrgyzstan *42°37′N 71°34′E*
145 *V14* **Kyzylagash** *Kaz.* Qyzylaghash. Almaty, SE Kazakhstan *45°20′N 78°45′E*
146 *C13* **Kyzylbair** Balkan Welaýaty, W Turkmenistan *38°13′N 55°38′E*
Kyzyl-Dzhiik, Pereval *see* Uzbel Shankou
145 *S7* **Kyzylkak, Ozero** ◎ NE Kazakhstan
145 *X11* **Kyzylkesek** Vostochnyy Kazakhstan, E Kazakhstan *47°56′N 82°02′E*
147 *S10* **Kyzyl-Kiya** *Kir.* Kyzyl-Kyya. Batkenskaya Oblast', SW Kyrgyzstan *40°15′N 72°07′E*
144 *L11* **Kyzylkol', Ozero** ◎ C Kazakhstan
122 *K14* **Kyzyl Kum** *var.* Kizil Kum, Qizil Qum, *Uzb.* Qizilqum. *desert* Kazakhstan/Uzbekistan
Kyzyl-Kyya *see* Kyzyl-Kiya
144 *L14* **Kyzylorda** *off.* Kyzylordinskaya Oblast', *Kaz.* Qyzylorda Oblysy. ⬖ *province* S Kazakhstan
Kyzylordinskaya Oblast' *see* Kyzylorda
Kyzylrabat *see* Qizilravote
Kyzylrabot *see* Qizilrabot
Kyzylsu *see* Kyzyl-Suu
147 *X7* **Kyzyl-Suu** *prev.* Pokrovka. Issyk-Kul'skaya Oblast', NE Kyrgyzstan *42°20′N 77°55′E*
147 *S12* **Kyzyl-Suu** *var.* Kyzylsu. ≈ Kyrgyzstan/Tajikistan
147 *X8* **Kyzyl-Tuu** Issyk-Kul'skaya Oblast', E Kyrgyzstan *42°06′N 76°54′E*
145 *Q12* **Kyzylzhar** *Kaz.* Qyzylzhar. Karaganda, C Kazakhstan *48°22′N 70°00′E*
145 *N15* **Kzylorda** *var.* Kzyl-Orda, Qizil Orda, Qyzylorda; *prev.* Perovsk. Kyzylorda, S Kazakhstan *44°54′N 65°31′E*
Kzyl-Orda *see* Kzylorda
Kzyltu *see* Kishkenekol'

L

109 *X2* **Laa an der Thaya** Niederösterreich, NE Austria *48°44′N 16°23′E*
63 *K15* **La Adela** La Pampa, SE Argentina *38°57′S 64°02′W*
Laagen *see* Numedalslågen
109 *S5* **Laakirchen** Oberösterreich, N Austria *47°59′N 13°49′E*
Laaland *see* Lolland
104 *I11* **La Albuera** Extremadura, W Spain *38°43′N 06°49′W*
105 *O7* **La Alcarria** *physical region* C Spain
104 *K14* **La Algaba** Andalucía, S Spain *37°27′N 06°01′W*
105 *P9* **La Almarcha** Castilla-La Mancha, C Spain *39°41′N 02°23′W*
105 *R6* **La Almunia de Doña Godina** Aragón, NE Spain *41°28′N 01°23′W*
41 *N5* **La Amistad, Presa** ⊠ NW Mexico
118 *F4* **Läänemaa** *var.* Lääne Maakond. ⬖ *province* NW Estonia
Lääne Maakond *see* Läänemaa
118 *I3* **Lääne-Virumaa** *off.* Lääne-Viru Maakond. ⬖ *province* NE Estonia
Lääne-Viru Maakond *see* Lääne-Virumaa
62 *J9* **La Antigua, Salina** *salt lake* W Argentina
99 *E17* **Laarne** Oost-Vlaanderen, NW Belgium *51°03′N 03°50′E*
80 *O13* **Laas Caanood** Sool, N Somalia *08°33′N 47°44′E*
41 *O9* **La Ascensión** Nuevo León, NE Mexico *24°15′N 99°53′W*
80 *N12* **Laas Dhaareed** Sanaag, N Somalia *10°12′N 46°09′E*
55 *O4* **La Asunción** Nueva Esparta, NE Venezuela *11°06′N 63°53′W*
Laatokka *see* Ladozhskoye, Ozero
100 *I13* **Laatzen** Niedersachsen, NW Germany *52°19′N 09°46′E*
38 *E9* **La'au Point** *var.* Laau Point. *headland* Moloka'i, Hawai'i, USA *21°06′N 157°18′W*
Laau Point *see* La'au Point
42 *D6* **La Aurora** ✈ (Ciudad de Guatemala) Guatemala, C Guatemala *14°33′N 90°30′W*
74 *C9* **Laâyoune** *var.* Aaiún. ● (Western Sahara) NW Western Sahara *27°10′N 13°11′W*
126 *L14* **Laba** ≈ SW Russian Federation
40 *M6* **La Babia** Coahuila, NE Mexico *28°39′N 102°00′W*
15 *R7* **La Baie** Québec, SE Canada *48°20′N 70°54′W*
171 *P16* **Labala** Pulau Lomblen, S Indonesia *08°30′S 123°27′E*
62 *K8* **La Banda** Santiago del Estero, N Argentina *27°44′S 64°14′W*
La Banda Oriental *see* Uruguay
104 *K4* **La Bañeza** Castilla-León, N Spain *42°18′N 05°54′W*
40 *M13* **La Barca** Jalisco, SW Mexico *20°20′N 102°33′W*
40 *K14* **La Barra de Navidad** Jalisco, C Mexico *19°12′N 104°38′W*
187 *Y13* **Labasa** *prev.* Lambasa. Vanua Levu, N Fiji *16°25′S 179°24′E*
102 *H8* **la Baule-Escoublac** Loire-Atlantique, NW France *47°17′N 02°24′W*
76 *I13* **Labé** NW Guinea *11°19′N 12°17′W*
Labe *see* Elbe
15 *N11* **Labelle** Québec, SE Canada *46°15′N 74°43′W*
23 *X14* **La Belle** Florida, SE USA *26°45′N 81°26′W*
10 *H7* **Laberge, Lake** ◎ Yukon Territory, W Canada
Labes *see* Łobez
Labiau *see* Polessk
112 *A10* **Labin** *It.* Albona. Istra, NW Croatia *45°05′N 14°10′E*
126 *L14* **Labinsk** Krasnodarskiy Kray, SW Russian Federation *44°39′N 40°43′E*
105 *X5* **La Bisbal d'Empordà** Cataluña, NE Spain *41°58′N 03°02′E*
119 *P16* **Labkovichy** *Rus.* Lobkovichi. Mahilyowskaya Voblasts', E Belarus *53°50′N 31°45′E*
15 *S4* **La Blache, Lac de** ◎ Québec, SE Canada
171 *P4* **Labo** Luzon, N Philippines *14°10′N 122°47′E*
Laboehanbadjo *see* Labuhanbajo
Laborca *see* Laborec
111 *N18* **Laborec** *Hung.* Laborca. ≈ E Slovakia
108 *D11* **La Borgne** ≈ S Switzerland
45 *T12* **Laborie** SW Saint Lucia *13°45′N 61°00′W*
102 *J14* **Labouheyre** Landes, SW France *44°12′N 00°55′W*
62 *L12* **Laboulaye** Córdoba, C Argentina *34°05′S 63°20′W*
13 *Q7* **Labrador** *cultural region* Newfoundland and Labrador, SW Canada
64 *I6* **Labrador Basin** *var.* Labrador Sea Basin. *undersea feature* Labrador Sea *53°00′N 48°00′W*
13 *N9* **Labrador City** Newfoundland and Labrador, E Canada *52°56′N 66°52′W*

13 Q5 **Labrador Sea** *sea* NW Atlantic Ocean
Labrador Sea Basin *see* Labrador Basin
Labrang *see* Xiahe
54 G9 **Labranzagrande** Boyacá, C Colombia 05°34′N 72°34′W
59 D14 **Lábrea** Amazonas, N Brazil 07°20′S 64°46′W
45 U15 **La Brea** Trinidad, Trinidad and Tobago 10°14′N 61°37′W
15 S6 **Labrieville** Québec, SE Canada 49°15′N 69°31′W
102 K14 **Labrit** Landes, SW France 44°03′N 00°29′W
108 C9 **La Broye** ≈ SW Switzerland
103 N15 **Labruguière** Tarn, S France 43°32′N 02°15′E
168 M11 **Labu** Pulau Singkep, W Indonesia 0°34′S 104°24′E
169 T7 **Labuan** *var.* Victoria. Labuan, East Malaysia 05°20′N 115°14′E
169 T7 **Labuan** ◈ *federal territory* East Malaysia
Labuan *see* Labuan, Pulau
169 T7 **Labuan, Pulau** *var.* Labuan. *island* East Malaysia
Labudalin *see* Ergun
171 N16 **Labuhanbajo** *prev.* Laboehanbadjo. Flores, S Indonesia 08°33′S 119°55′E
168 J9 **Labuhanbilik** Sumatera, N Indonesia 02°30′N 100°10′E
168 G8 **Labuhanhaji** Sumatera, W Indonesia 03°31′N 97°00′E
Labuk *see* Labuk, Sungai
Labuk Bay *see* Labuk, Teluk
169 V7 **Labuk, Sungai** *var.* Labuk. ≈ East Malaysia
169 W6 **Labuk, Teluk** *var.* Labuk Bay, Telukan Labuk. *bay* S Sulu Sea
Labuk, Telukan *see* Labuk, Teluk
166 K9 **Labutta** Ayeyarwady, SW Burma (Myanmar) 16°08′N 94°45′E
122 I8 **Labytnangi** Yamalo-Nenetskiy Avtonomnyy Okrug, N Russian Federation 66°39′N 66°26′E
113 K19 **Laç** *var.* Laci. Lezhë, C Albania 41°37′N 19°37′E
78 F10 **Lac** *off.* Préfecture du Lac. ◈ *prefecture* W Chad
57 K19 **Lacajahuira, Rio** ≈ W Bolivia
La Calamine *see* Kelmis
62 G11 **La Calera** Valparaíso, C Chile 32°47′S 71°16′W
13 P11 **Lac-Allard** Québec, E Canada 50°37′N 63°26′W
104 L13 **La Campana** Andalucía, S Spain 37°35′N 05°24′W
102 J12 **Lacanau** Gironde, SW France 44°59′N 01°04′W
42 C2 **Lacandón, Sierra del** ▲▲ Guatemala/Mexico
La Cañiza *see* A Cañiza
41 W16 **Lacantún, Río** ≈ SE Mexico
103 Q3 **la Capelle** Aisne, N France 49°58′N 03°55′E
112 K10 **Laćarak** Vojvodina, NW Serbia 45°00′N 19°34′E
62 L11 **La Carlota** Córdoba, C Argentina 33°30′S 63°15′W
104 L13 **La Carlota** Andalucía, S Spain 37°40′N 04°56′W
105 N12 **La Carolina** Andalucía, S Spain 38°15′N 03°37′W
103 O15 **Lacaune** Tarn, S France 43°42′N 02°42′E
15 P7 **Lac-Bouchette** Québec, SE Canada 48°14′N 72°11′W
Laccadive Islands/ Laccadive Minicoy and Amindivi Islands, the *see* Lakshadweep
11 Y16 **Lac du Bonnet** Manitoba, S Canada 50°13′N 96°04′W
30 L4 **Lac du Flambeau** Wisconsin, N USA 45°58′N 89°51′W
15 P8 **Lac-Édouard** Québec, SE Canada 47°39′N 72°16′W
42 I4 **La Ceiba** Atlántida, N Honduras 15°45′N 86°29′W
54 E9 **La Ceja** Antioquia, W Colombia 06°02′N 75°30′W
182 J11 **Lacepede Bay** *bay* South Australia
32 G9 **Lacey** Washington, NW USA 47°01′N 122°49′W
103 P12 **la Chaise-Dieu** Haute-Loire, C France 45°19′N 03°41′E
114 G13 **Lachanás** Kentrikí Makedonía, N Greece 40°57′N 23°15′E
124 L11 **Lacha, Ozero** ◎ NW Russian Federation
103 O8 **la Charité-sur-Loire** Nièvre, C France 47°10′N 02°59′E
103 N9 **la Châtre** Indre, C France 46°35′N 01°59′E
108 C8 **La Chaux-de-Fonds** Neuchâtel, W Switzerland 47°07′N 06°51′E
Lach Dera *see* Dheere Laaq
108 G8 **Lachen** Schwyz, C Switzerland 47°12′N 08°51′E
183 Q8 **Lachlan River** ≈ New South Wales, SE Australia
43 T15 **La Chorrera** Panamá, C Panama 08°51′N 79°46′W
15 V7 **Lac-Humqui** Québec, SE Canada 48°21′N 67°32′W
15 N12 **Lachute** Québec, SE Canada 45°39′N 74°21′W
Lachyn *see* Laçın
Laci *see* Laç
137 W13 **Laçın** *Rus.* Lachyn. SW Azerbaijan 39°36′N 46°34′E
103 S16 **la Ciotat** *anc.* Citharista. Bouches-du-Rhône, SE France 43°10′N 05°36′E
18 D10 **Lackawanna** New York, NE USA 42°49′N 78°49′W
11 Q13 **Lac La Biche** Alberta, SW Canada 54°46′N 111°59′W
Lac la Martre *see* Wha Ti
15 R12 **Lac-Mégantic** *var.* Mégantic. Québec, SE Canada 45°35′N 70°53′W
Lacobriga *see* Lagos
40 G5 **La Colorada** Sonora, NW Mexico 28°49′N 110°32′W
11 Q15 **Lacombe** Alberta, SW Canada 52°30′N 113°42′W
30 L12 **Lacon** Illinois, N USA 41°01′N 89°24′W
43 P16 **La Concepción** *var.* Concepción. Chiriquí, W Panama 08°31′N 82°39′W
54 H5 **La Concepción** Zulia, NW Venezuela 10°48′N 71°46′W
107 C19 **Laconi** Sardegna, Italy, C Mediterranean Sea 39°52′N 09°02′E
19 O9 **Laconia** New Hampshire, NE USA 43°32′N 71°29′W
61 H19 **La Coronilla** Rocha, E Uruguay 33°44′S 53°31′W
La Coruña *see* A Coruña
103 O11 **la Courtine** Creuse, C France 45°42′N 02°18′E
Lac, Préfecture du *see* Lac
102 J16 **Lacq** Pyrénées-Atlantiques, SW France 43°25′N 00°37′W
15 P9 **La Croche** Québec, SE Canada 47°38′N 72°42′W
29 X3 **la Croix, Lac** ◎ Canada/USA
26 K5 **La Crosse** Kansas, C USA 38°32′N 99°19′W
21 V7 **La Crosse** Virginia, NE USA 36°41′N 78°03′W
32 L9 **La Crosse** Washington, NW USA 46°48′N 117°51′W
30 J7 **La Crosse** Wisconsin, N USA 43°46′N 91°12′W
54 C13 **La Cruz** Nariño, SW Colombia 01°33′N 76°58′W
42 K12 **La Cruz** Guanacaste, NW Costa Rica 11°05′N 85°39′W
40 I10 **La Cruz** Sinaloa, W Mexico 23°53′N 106°53′W
61 F19 **La Cruz** Florida, S Uruguay 33°54′S 56°11′W
42 M9 **La Cruz de Río Grande** Región Autónoma Atlántico Sur, E Nicaragua 13°04′N 84°12′W
54 J4 **La Cruz de Taratara** Falcón, N Venezuela 11°03′N 69°44′W
15 Q10 **Lac-St-Charles** Québec, SE Canada 46°56′N 71°24′W
40 M6 **La Cuesta** Coahuila, NE Mexico 28°45′N 102°26′W
57 A17 **La Cumbra, Volcán** ⛰ Galapagos Islands, Ecuador, E Pacific Ocean 0°21′S 91°30′W
152 J5 **Ladākh Range** ▲▲ NE India
26 I5 **Ladder Creek** ≈ Kansas, C USA
45 X10 **la Désirade** *atoll* E Guadeloupe
Lādhiqīyah, Muḩāfaz̧at al *see* Al Lādhiqīyah
172 J16 **La Digue** *island* Inner Islands, NE Seychelles
83 F25 **Ladismith** Western Cape, SW South Africa 33°30′S 12°15′E
152 G11 **Lādnūn** Rājasthān, NW India 27°36′N 74°26′E
Ladoga, Lake *see* Ladozhskoye, Ozero
115 E19 **Ládon** ≈ S Greece
54 E9 **La Dorada** Caldas, C Colombia 05°28′N 74°41′W
124 H11 **Ladozhskoye, Ozero** *Eng.* Lake Ladoga, *Fin.* Laatokka. ◎ NW Russian Federation
37 R12 **Ladron Peak** ▲ New Mexico, SW USA 34°25′N 107°04′W
124 J11 **Ladva-Vetka** Respublika Kareliya, NW Russian Federation 61°18′N 34°24′E
183 Q15 **Lady Barron** Tasmania, SE Australia 40°12′S 148°12′E
14 G9 **Lady Evelyn Lake** ◎ Ontario, S Canada
23 W11 **Lady Lake** Florida, SE USA 28°55′N 81°55′W
10 L17 **Ladysmith** Vancouver Island, British Columbia, SW Canada 48°55′N 123°45′W
83 J22 **Ladysmith** KwaZulu/Natal, E South Africa 28°34′S 29°47′E
30 J5 **Ladysmith** Wisconsin, N USA 45°27′N 91°07′W
145 P9 **Ladyzhenka** Akmola, C Kazakhstan 50°58′N 68°44′E
186 E7 **Lae** Morobe, W Papua New Guinea 06°45′S 147°00′E
189 R6 **Lae Atoll** *atoll* Ralik Chain, W Marshall Islands
40 C3 **La Encantada, Cerro de** ▲ NW Mexico 31°03′N 115°25′W
55 N11 **La Esmeralda** Amazonas, S Venezuela 03°11′N 65°33′W
42 G7 **La Esperanza** Intibucá, SW Honduras 14°19′N 88°09′W
30 K8 **La Farge** Wisconsin, N USA 43°36′N 90°39′W
23 R5 **Lafayette** Alabama, S USA 32°54′N 85°24′W
37 T4 **Lafayette** Colorado, C USA 39°59′N 105°06′W
23 R2 **La Fayette** Georgia, SE USA 34°42′N 85°16′W
31 O13 **Lafayette** Indiana, N USA 40°25′N 86°52′W
22 I9 **Lafayette** Louisiana, S USA 30°13′N 92°01′W
20 K8 **Lafayette** Tennessee, S USA 36°31′N 86°01′W
19 N7 **Lafayette, Mount** ▲ New Hampshire, NE USA 44°09′N 71°37′W
La Fe *see* Santa Fé
103 P3 **la Fère** Aisne, N France 49°41′N 03°20′E
102 L6 **la Ferté-Bernard** Sarthe, NW France 48°13′N 00°40′E
102 K5 **la Ferté-Macé** Orne, N France 48°35′N 00°21′W
103 N7 **la Ferté-St-Aubin** Loiret, C France 47°42′N 01°57′E
103 P5 **la Ferté-sous-Jouarre** Seine-et-Marne, N France 48°57′N 03°08′E
77 V15 **Lafia** Nassarawa, C Nigeria 08°29′N 08°34′E
77 T15 **Lafiagi** Kwara, W Nigeria 08°52′N 05°25′E
11 T17 **Lafleche** Saskatchewan, S Canada 49°40′N 106°28′W
102 K7 **la Flèche** Sarthe, NW France 47°42′N 00°04′W
109 X7 **Lafnitz** *Hung.* Lapines. ≈ Austria/Hungary
187 P17 **La Foa** Province Sud, S New Caledonia 21°46′S 165°49′E
20 M8 **La Follette** Tennessee, S USA 36°22′N 84°07′W
15 N12 **Lafontaine** Québec, SE Canada 45°52′N 74°01′W
22 K10 **Lafourche, Bayou** ≈ Louisiana, S USA
62 K6 **La Fragua** Santiago del Estero, N Argentina 26°06′S 64°06′W
54 H7 **La Fría** Táchira, NW Venezuela 08°13′N 72°15′W
104 J7 **La Fuente de San Esteban** Castilla-León, N Spain 40°48′N 06°14′W
186 C7 **Lagaip** ≈ W Papua New Guinea
61 B15 **La Gallareta** Santa Fe, C Argentina 29°34′S 60°23′W
127 Q14 **Lagan'** *prev.* Kaspiyskiy. Respublika Kalmykiya, SW Russian Federation 45°25′N 47°19′E
95 L20 **Lagan** Kronoberg, S Sweden 56°55′N 14°01′E
95 K21 **Lågan** ≈ S Sweden
92 L2 **Lagarfljót** *var.* Lögurinn. ◎ E Iceland
37 R7 **La Garita Mountains** ▲▲ Colorado, C USA
171 O2 **Lagawe** Luzon, N Philippines 16°46′N 121°06′E
78 F13 **Lagdo** Nord, N Cameroon 09°12′N 13°43′E
78 F13 **Lagdo, Lac de** ◎ N Cameroon
100 H13 **Lage** Nordrhein-Westfalen, W Germany 52°00′N 08°48′E
94 H12 **Lågen** ≈ S Norway
61 J14 **Lages** Santa Catarina, S Brazil 27°45′S 50°16′W
Lágesvuotna *see* Laksefjorden
149 R4 **Laghmān** ◈ *province* E Afghanistan
74 J6 **Laghouat** N Algeria 33°49′N 02°59′E
105 Q10 **La Gineta** Castilla-La Mancha, C Spain 39°08′N 02°00′W
115 E21 **Lagkáda** *var.* Langada. Pelopónnisos, S Greece 36°49′N 22°19′E
114 G13 **Lagkadás** *var.* Langades, Langadhás. Kentrikí Makedonía, N Greece 40°45′N 23°04′E
115 E20 **Lagkádia** *var.* Langádhia, *cont.* Langadia. Pelopónnisos, S Greece 37°40′N 22°01′E
54 F6 **La Gloria** Cesar, N Colombia 08°37′N 73°51′W
41 O7 **La Gloria** Nuevo León, NE Mexico
92 N3 **Lågneset** *headland* W Svalbard 77°46′N 13°44′E
104 G14 **Lagoa** Faro, S Portugal 37°07′N 08°27′W
La Goagira *see* La Guajira
Lago Agrio *see* Nueva Loja
61 I14 **Lagoa Vermelha** Rio Grande do Sul, S Brazil 28°13′S 51°32′W
137 V10 **Lagodekhi** SE Georgia 41°49′N 46°15′E
42 C7 **La Gomera** Escuintla, S Guatemala 14°05′N 91°03′W
Lagone *see* Logone
107 M19 **Lagonegro** Basilicata, S Italy 40°06′N 15°42′E
63 G16 **Lago Ranco** Los Lagos, S Chile 40°21′S 72°29′W
77 S16 **Lagos** Lagos, SW Nigeria 06°24′N 03°17′E
104 F14 **Lagos** *anc.* Lacobriga. Faro, S Portugal 37°05′N 08°40′W
77 S16 **Lagos** ◈ *state* SW Nigeria
40 M12 **Lagos de Moreno** Jalisco, SW Mexico 21°21′N 101°55′W
Lagosta *see* Lastovo
74 A12 **Lagouira** SW Western Sahara 20°55′N 17°05′W
92 O1 **Lågøya** *island* N Svalbard
32 L11 **La Grande** Oregon, NW USA 45°21′N 118°05′W
103 Q14 **la Grande-Combe** Gard, S France 44°13′N 04°01′E
12 K9 **La Grande Rivière** *var.* Fort George. ≈ Québec, SE Canada
23 R4 **La Grange** Georgia, SE USA 33°02′N 85°02′W
31 P11 **Lagrange** Indiana, N USA 41°38′N 85°25′W
20 L5 **La Grange** Kentucky, S USA 38°24′N 85°23′W
27 V2 **La Grange** Missouri, C USA 40°00′N 91°31′W
21 V10 **La Grange** North Carolina, SE USA 35°18′N 77°47′W
25 U11 **La Grange** Texas, SW USA 29°55′N 96°54′W
105 N7 **La Granja** Castilla-León, N Spain 40°53′N 04°01′W
55 Q9 **La Gran Sabana** *grassland* E Venezuela
54 H7 **La Grita** Táchira, NW Venezuela 08°09′N 71°58′W
La Grulla *see* Grulla
15 R11 **La Guadeloupe** Québec, SE Canada 45°57′N 70°56′W
65 L6 **La Guaira** Distrito Federal, N Venezuela 10°35′N 66°52′W
54 G4 **La Guajira** *off.* Departamento de La Guajira, *var.* Guajira, La Goagira. ◈ *province* NE Colombia
188 I4 **Lagua Lichan, Punta** *headland* Saipan, S Northern Mariana Islands
105 P4 **Laguardia** *Basq.* Biasteri. País Vasco, N Spain 42°32′N 02°31′W
18 K14 **La Guardia** ✈ (New York) Long Island, New York, NE USA 40°44′N 73°51′W
La Guardia/Laguardia *see* A Guarda
La Gudiña *see* A Gudiña
103 O9 **la Guerche-sur-l'Aubois** Cher, C France 46°55′N 03°00′E
103 O13 **Laguiole** Aveyron, S France 44°42′N 02°51′E
83 F26 **L'Agulhas** *var.* Agulhas. Western Cape, SW South Africa 34°49′S 20°01′E
61 K14 **Laguna** Santa Catarina, S Brazil 28°29′S 48°45′W
37 Q11 **Laguna** New Mexico, SW USA 35°03′N 107°30′W
35 T16 **Laguna Beach** California, W USA 33°32′N 117°46′W
35 Y17 **Laguna Dam** *dam* Arizona/ California, W USA
40 L7 **Laguna El Rey** Coahuila, N Mexico
35 V17 **Laguna Mountains** ▲▲ California, W USA
61 B17 **Laguna Paiva** Santa Fe, C Argentina 31°21′S 60°40′W
62 H3 **Lagunas** Tarapacá, N Chile 21°01′S 69°36′W
56 E9 **Lagunas** Loreto, N Peru 05°15′S 75°24′W
57 M20 **Lagunillas** Santa Cruz, SE Bolivia 19°38′S 63°39′W
54 H6 **Lagunillas** Mérida, NW Venezuela 08°31′N 71°24′W
44 C4 **La Habana** *var.* Havana. ● (Cuba) Ciudad de La Habana, W Cuba 23°07′N 82°25′W
169 W7 **Lahad Datu** Sabah, East Malaysia 05°01′N 118°20′E
169 W7 **Lahad Datu, Teluk** *var.* Telukan Lahad Datu, Teluk Darvel, Teluk Datu; *prev.* Darvel Bay. *bay* Sabah, East Malaysia, C Pacific Ocean
Lahad Datu, Telukan *see* Lahad Datu, Teluk
38 F10 **Lahaina** Maui, Hawaii, USA, C Pacific Ocean 20°52′N 156°40′W
168 L14 **Lahat** Sumatera, W Indonesia 03°46′S 103°32′E
La Haye *see* 's-Gravenhage
Lahej *see* Laḩij
62 G9 **La Higuera** Coquimbo, N Chile 29°33′S 71°15′W
141 S13 **Lahī, Ḩisā' al** *spring/well* NE Yemen 17°28′N 50°05′E
141 O16 **Laḩij** *var.* Laḩj, *Eng.* Lahej. SW Yemen 13°04′N 44°55′E
142 M3 **Lāhījān** Gīlān, NW Iran 37°12′N 50°00′E
119 I19 **Lahishyn** *Pol.* Lohiszyn, *Rus.* Logishin. Brestskaya Voblasts', SW Belarus 52°20′N 25°59′E
Laḩj *see* Laḩij
101 F18 **Lahn** ≈ W Germany
Lähn *see* Wleń
95 J21 **Laholm** Halland, S Sweden 56°30′N 13°05′E
95 J21 **Laholmsbukten** *bay* S Sweden
35 R6 **Lahontan Reservoir** ⊠ Nevada, W USA
149 W8 **Lahore** Punjab, NE Pakistan 31°36′N 74°18′E
149 W8 **Lahore** ✈ Punjab, E Pakistan 31°34′N 74°22′E
55 Q6 **La Horqueta** Delta Amacuro, NE Venezuela 09°13′N 62°02′W
119 K15 **Lahoysk** *Rus.* Logoysk. Minskaya Voblasts', C Belarus 54°12′N 27°53′E
101 F22 **Lahr** Baden-Württemberg, S Germany 48°21′N 07°52′E
93 M19 **Lahti** *Swe.* Lahtis. Etelä-Suomi, S Finland 61°N 25°40′E
Lahtis *see* Lahti
40 M14 **La Huacana** Michoacán, SW Mexico 18°56′N 101°52′W
40 K14 **La Huerta** Jalisco, SW Mexico 19°29′N 104°40′W
78 H12 **Laï** *prev.* Behagle, De Behagle. Tandjilé, S Chad 09°22′N 16°14′E
Laibach *see* Ljubljana
160 K14 **Laibin** Guangxi Zhuangzu Zizhiqu, China 23°26′N 109°09′E
167 Q5 **Lai Châu** Lai Châu, N Vietnam 22°04′N 103°10′E
Laichow Bay *see* Laizhou Wan
38 D9 **Lā'ie** *var.* Laie. O'ahu, Hawaii, USA, C Pacific Ocean 21°39′N 157°55′W
Laie *see* Lā'ie
102 L5 **l'Aigle** Orne, N France 48°46′N 00°37′E
103 Q7 **Laignes** Côte d'Or, C France 47°51′N 04°24′E
93 K17 **Laihia** Länsi-Suomi, W Finland 62°58′N 22°00′E
Laila *see* Laylā
83 F25 **Laingsburg** Western Cape, SW South Africa 33°12′S 20°51′E
109 U2 **Lainsitz** *Cz.* Lužnice. ≈ Austria/Czech Republic
96 I7 **Lairg** N Scotland, United Kingdom 58°02′N 04°23′W
81 I17 **Laisamis** Eastern, N Kenya 01°35′N 37°49′E
Laisberg *see* Leisi
127 R4 **Laishevo** Respublika Tatarstan, W Russian Federation 55°26′N 49°27′E
Laisholm *see* Jõgeva
92 H13 **Laisvall** Norrbotten, N Sweden 66°07′N 17°10′E
93 K19 **Laitila** Länsi-Suomi, SW Finland 60°52′N 21°40′E
161 P5 **Laiwu** Shandong, E China 36°14′N 117°40′E
161 R4 **Laixi** *var.* Shuiji. Shandong, E China 36°50′N 120°40′E
161 R4 **Laiyang** Shandong, E China 36°58′N 120°40′E
161 O3 **Laiyuan** Hebei, E China 39°19′N 114°44′E
161 R4 **Laizhou** *var.* Ye Xian. Shandong, E China 37°12′N 120°01′E
161 Q4 **Laizhou Wan** *var.* Laichow Bay. *bay* E China
37 S8 **La Jara** Colorado, C USA 37°16′N 105°57′W
61 I15 **Lajeado** Rio Grande do Sul, S Brazil 29°28′S 52°00′W
112 L12 **Lajkovac** Serbia, C Serbia 44°22′N 20°12′E
111 K23 **Lajosmizse** Bács-Kiskun, C Hungary 47°02′N 19°31′E
Lajta *see* Leitha
40 I6 **La Junta** Chihuahua, N Mexico 28°30′N 107°20′W
37 V7 **La Junta** Colorado, C USA 37°59′N 103°34′W
92 J13 **Lakaträsk** Norrbotten, N Sweden 66°16′N 21°10′E
Lak Dera *see* Dheere Laaq
Lakeamu *see* Lakekamu
29 P12 **Lake Andes** South Dakota, N USA 43°08′N 98°33′W
22 H9 **Lake Arthur** Louisiana, S USA 30°04′N 92°40′W
187 Z15 **Lakeba** *prev.* Lakemba. *island* Lau Group, E Fiji
187 Z14 **Lakeba Passage** *channel* E Fiji
29 S10 **Lake Benton** Minnesota, N USA 44°15′N 96°17′W
23 V9 **Lake Butler** Florida, SE USA 30°01′N 82°20′W
183 P8 **Lake Cargelligo** New South Wales, SE Australia 33°21′S 146°25′E
22 G9 **Lake Charles** Louisiana, S USA 30°14′N 93°13′W
27 X9 **Lake City** Arkansas, C USA 35°50′N 90°28′W
37 Q7 **Lake City** Colorado, C USA 38°01′N 107°18′W
23 V9 **Lake City** Florida, SE USA 30°12′N 82°39′W
29 U13 **Lake City** Iowa, C USA 42°16′N 94°43′W
31 P7 **Lake City** Michigan, N USA 44°22′N 85°12′W
29 W9 **Lake City** Minnesota, N USA 44°27′N 92°16′W
21 T13 **Lake City** South Carolina, SE USA 33°52′N 79°45′W
29 Q7 **Lake City** South Dakota, N USA 45°42′N 97°22′W
20 M8 **Lake City** Tennessee, S USA 36°13′N 84°09′W
10 L17 **Lake Cowichan** Vancouver Island, British Columbia, SW Canada 48°50′N 124°04′W
29 U10 **Lake Crystal** Minnesota, N USA 44°07′N 94°13′W
25 T6 **Lake Dallas** Texas, SW USA 33°06′N 97°01′W
97 K15 **Lake District** *physical region* NW England, United Kingdom
18 D10 **Lake Erie Beach** New York, NE USA 42°37′N 79°04′W
29 T11 **Lakefield** Minnesota, N USA 43°40′N 95°10′W
25 V6 **Lake Fork Reservoir** ◎ Texas, SW USA
30 M9 **Lake Geneva** Wisconsin, N USA 42°36′N 88°25′W
18 L9 **Lake George** New York, NE USA 43°25′N 73°45′W
Lake Harbour *see* Kimmirut
36 I12 **Lake Havasu City** Arizona, SW USA 34°26′N 114°20′W
25 W12 **Lake Jackson** Texas, SW USA 29°01′N 95°25′W
186 D8 **Lakekamu** *var.* Lakeamu. ≈ S Papua New Guinea
180 K13 **Lake King** Western Australia 33°09′S 119°46′E
23 V12 **Lakeland** Florida, SE USA 28°03′N 81°57′W
23 U7 **Lakeland** Georgia, SE USA 31°02′N 83°04′W
181 W4 **Lakeland Downs** Queensland, NE Australia 15°54′S 144°54′E
11 P16 **Lake Louise** Alberta, SW Canada 51°26′N 116°10′W
Lakemba *see* Lakeba
29 V11 **Lake Mills** Iowa, C USA 43°25′N 93°31′W
39 Q10 **Lake Minchumina** Alaska, USA 63°55′N 152°25′W
Lakemti *see* Nek'emtē
186 A7 **Lake Murray** Western, SW Papua New Guinea 06°35′S 141°28′E
31 R9 **Lake Orion** Michigan, N USA 42°46′N 83°14′W
190 B16 **Lakepa** NE Niue 18°59′S 169°48′E
29 T11 **Lake Park** Iowa, C USA 43°27′N 95°19′W
18 K7 **Lake Placid** New York, NE USA 44°16′N 73°57′W
18 K9 **Lake Pleasant** New York, NE USA 43°27′N 74°24′W
34 M6 **Lakeport** California, W USA 39°04′N 122°56′W
29 Q10 **Lake Preston** South Dakota, N USA 44°21′N 97°22′W
22 J5 **Lake Providence** Louisiana, S USA 32°48′N 91°10′W
185 E20 **Lake Pukaki** Canterbury, South Island, New Zealand 44°12′S 170°10′E
183 Q12 **Lakes Entrance** Victoria, SE Australia 37°52′S 147°58′E
37 N12 **Lakeside** Arizona, SW USA 34°09′N 109°58′W
35 V17 **Lakeside** California, W USA 32°50′N 116°55′W
23 S9 **Lakeside** Florida, SE USA 30°22′N 84°18′W
28 K13 **Lakeside** Nebraska, C USA 42°01′N 102°27′W
32 E13 **Lakeside** Oregon, NW USA 43°34′N 124°10′W
21 W6 **Lakeside** Virginia, NE USA 37°36′N 77°28′W
Lakes State *see* El Buhayrat
Lake State *see* Michigan
185 F20 **Lake Tekapo** Canterbury, South Island, New Zealand 44°01′S 170°29′E
21 O10 **Lake Toxaway** North Carolina, SE USA 35°06′N 82°57′W
29 T13 **Lake View** Iowa, C USA 42°18′N 95°04′W
32 I16 **Lakeview** Oregon, NW USA 42°13′N 120°21′W
25 O3 **Lakeview** Texas, SW USA 34°38′N 100°36′W
27 W14 **Lake Village** Arkansas, C USA 33°20′N 91°19′W
23 W12 **Lake Wales** Florida, SE USA 27°54′N 81°35′W
37 T4 **Lakewood** Colorado, C USA 39°38′N 105°07′W
18 K15 **Lakewood** New Jersey, NE USA 40°04′N 74°11′W
18 C11 **Lakewood** New York, NE USA 42°03′N 79°19′W
31 T11 **Lakewood** Ohio, N USA 41°28′N 81°48′W
23 Y13 **Lakewood Park** Florida, SE USA 27°32′N 80°24′W
23 Z14 **Lake Worth** Florida, SE USA 26°37′N 80°03′W
124 H11 **Lakhdenpokh'ya** Respublika Kareliya, NW Russian Federation 61°25′N 30°05′E
152 L11 **Lakhīmpur** Uttar Pradesh, N India 27°57′N 80°47′E
154 J11 **Lakhnādon** Madhya Pradesh, C India 22°34′N 79° 38′E
Lakhnau *see* Lucknow
154 A9 **Lakhpat** Gujarāt, W India 23°49′N 68°54′E
119 K19 **Lakhva** Brestskaya Voblasts', SW Belarus 52°13′N 27°06′E
26 I6 **Lakin** Kansas, C USA 37°57′N 101°16′W
149 S7 **Lakki Marwat** North-West Frontier Province, NW Pakistan 32°35′N 70°58′E
115 F21 **Lakonía** *historical region* S Greece
115 F22 **Lakonikós Kólpos** *gulf* S Greece
76 M17 **Lakota** S Ivory Coast 05°50′N 05°40′W
29 U11 **Lakota** Iowa, C USA 43°22′N 94°04′W
29 P3 **Lakota** North Dakota, N USA 48°02′N 98°20′W
Lak Sao *see* Ban Lakxao
92 L8 **Laksefjorden** *Lapp.* Lágesvuotna. *fjord* N Norway
92 K8 **Lakselv** *Lapp.* Leavdnja. Finnmark, N Norway 70°02′N 24°57′E
155 B21 **Lakshadweep** *prev.* the Laccadive Minicoy and Amindivi Islands. ◈ *union territory* India, N Indian Ocean
155 C22 **Lakshadweep** *Eng.* Laccadive Islands. *island group* India, N Indian Ocean
153 S17 **Lakshmikāntapur** West Bengal, NE India 22°05′N 88°19′E
112 G11 **Laktaši** ◈ Republika Srpska, N Bosnia and Herzegovina
149 V7 **Lāla Mūsa** Punjab, NE Pakistan 32°41′N 74°01′E
la Laon *see* Laon
114 M11 **Lalapaşa** Edirne, NW Turkey 41°52′N 26°44′E
83 P14 **Lalaua** Nampula, N Mozambique 14°21′S 38°16′E
105 S9 **L'Alcora** *var.* Alcora. País Valenciano, E Spain 40°05′N 00°14′W
105 S10 **L'Alcúdia** *var.* L'Alcudia. País Valenciano, E Spain 39°10′N 00°30′W
80 J11 **Lalibela** Āmara, Ethiopia 12°01′N 39°05′E
42 E8 **La Libertad** La Libertad, SW El Salvador 13°28′N 89°20′W*
42 E3 **La Libertad** Petén, N Guatemala 16°49′N 90°08′W
42 H6 **La Libertad** Comayagua, SW Honduras 14°43′N 87°36′W
40 E4 **La Libertad** *var.* Puerto Libertad. Sonora, NW Mexico 29°52′N 112°39′W
42 K10 **La Libertad** Chontales, S Nicaragua 12°12′N 85°10′W
42 A9 **La Libertad** ◈ *department* SW El Salvador
56 B11 **La Libertad** *off.* Departamento de La Libertad. ◈ *department* W Peru
La Libertad, Departamento de *see* La Libertad
62 G11 **La Ligua** Valparaíso, C Chile 31°30′S 71°16′W
139 U5 **La'lī Khān** As Sulaymānīyah, E Iraq 34°58′N 45°36′E
104 H3 **Lalín** Galicia, NW Spain 42°40′N 08°06′W
102 L13 **Lalinde** Dordogne, SW France 44°52′N 00°42′E
104 K16 **La Línea** *var.* La Línea de la Concepción. Andalucía, S Spain 36°10′N 05°21′W
La Línea de la Concepción *see* La Línea
152 J14 **Lalitpur** Uttar Pradesh, N India 24°42′N 78°24′E
153 P11 **Lalitpur** Central, C Nepal 27°45′N 85°18′E
152 K10 **Lālkua** Uttarachal, N India 29°04′N 79°31′E
153 T12 **Lalmanirhat** Rājshāhi, N Bangladesh 25°51′N 89°34′E
11 R12 **La Loche** Saskatchewan, C Canada 56°31′N 109°27′W
102 M6 **la Loupe** Eure-et-Loir, C France 48°30′N 01°04′E
99 G20 **La Louvière** Hainaut, S Belgium 50°29′N 04°15′E
L'Altissima *see* Hochwilde
104 L14 **La Luisiana** Andalucía, S Spain 37°30′N 05°14′W
37 S14 **La Luz** New Mexico, SW USA 32°58′N 105°56′W
107 D16 **la Maddalena** Sardegna, Italy, C Mediterranean Sea 41°13′N 09°25′E
62 J7 **La Madrid** Tucumán, N Argentina 27°37′S 65°16′W
Lama-Kara *see* Kara
15 S8 **La Malbaie** Québec, SE Canada 47°39′N 70°11′W
167 T10 **Lamam** Xékong, S Laos 15°22′N 106°40′E
105 P10 **La Mancha** *physical region* C Spain
la Manche *see* English Channel
187 R13 **Lamap** Malekula, C Vanuatu 16°26′S 167°47′E
37 W6 **Lamar** Colorado, C USA 38°40′N 102°37′W
27 S7 **Lamar** Missouri, C USA 37°30′N 94°18′W
21 S12 **Lamar** South Carolina, SE USA 34°10′N 80°03′W
Lamard *see* Lāmerd
107 C19 **La Marmora, Punta** ▲ Sardegna, Italy, C Mediterranean Sea 39°58′N 09°20′E
8 I9 **La Martre, Lac** ◎ Northwest Territories, NW Canada
56 D10 **Lamas** San Martín, N Peru 06°28′S 76°31′W
42 I5 **La Masica** Atlántida, NW Honduras 15°38′N 87°08′W
103 R12 **Lamastre** Ardèche, E France 45°00′N 04°32′E
La Matepec *see* Santa Ana, Volcán de
44 I7 **La Maya** Santiago de Cuba, E Cuba 20°11′N 75°40′W
109 S5 **Lambach** Oberösterreich, N Austria 48°06′N 13°52′E
168 I11 **Lambak** Pulau Pini, W Indonesia 0°08′N 98°36′E
102 H5 **Lamballe** Côtes d'Armor, NW France 48°28′N 02°31′W
79 D18 **Lambaréné** Moyen-Ogooué, W Gabon 0°41′S 10°13′E
Lambasa *see* Labasa
56 B11 **Lambayeque** Lambayeque, W Peru 06°42′S 79°55′W
56 A10 **Lambayeque** *off.* Departamento de Lambayeque. ◈ *department* NW Peru
Lambayeque, Departamento de *see* Lambayeque
97 G17 **Lambay Island** *Ir.* Reachrainn. *island* E Ireland
186 G6 **Lambert, Cape** *headland* New Britain, E Papua New Guinea 04°15′S 151°31′E
195 W6 **Lambert Glacier** *glacier* Antarctica
29 T10 **Lamberton** Minnesota, N USA 44°14′N 95°15′W
27 X4 **Lambert-Saint Louis** ✈ Missouri, C USA 38°43′N 90°19′W
31 R11 **Lambertville** Michigan, N USA 41°46′N 83°37′W
18 J15 **Lambertville** New Jersey, NE USA 40°20′N 74°55′W
171 N12 **Lambogo** Sulawesi, N Indonesia 0°57′S 120°23′E
106 D8 **Lambro** ≈ N Italy
33 W11 **Lame Deer** Montana, NW USA 45°37′N 106°37′W
104 H6 **Lamego** Viseu, N Portugal 41°05′N 07°49′W
187 Q14 **Lamen Bay** Épi, C Vanuatu 16°36′S 168°10′E
45 X6 **Lamentin** Basse Terre, N Guadeloupe 16°16′N 61°38′W
Lamentin *see* le Lamentin
143 P14 **Lāmerd** *var.* Lamard. Fārs, S Iran 27°22′N 53°08′E
182 K10 **Lameroo** South Australia 35°22′S 140°30′E
54 F10 **La Mesa** Cundinamarca, C Colombia 04°37′N 74°30′W
35 U17 **La Mesa** California, W USA 32°44′N 117°00′W
37 R16 **La Mesa** New Mexico, SW USA 32°03′N 106°41′W
25 N6 **Lamesa** Texas, SW USA 32°43′N 101°57′W
107 N21 **Lamezia Terme** Calabria, SE Italy 38°54′N 16°13′E
115 F17 **Lamía** Stereá Ellás, C Greece 38°54′N 22°27′E
171 O8 **Lamitan** Basilan Island, SW Philippines 06°40′N 122°07′E
187 Y14 **Lamiti** Gau, C Fiji 18°00′S 179°20′E
171 T11 **Lamlam** Papua, E Indonesia 0°03′S 130°46′E
188 B16 **Lamlam, Mount** ▲ SW Guam 13°20′N 144°40′E
109 Q6 **Lammer** ≈ E Austria
185 E23 **Lammerlaw Range** ▲▲ South Island, New Zealand
95 L20 **Lammhult** Kronoberg, S Sweden 57°09′N 14°35′E
93 L18 **Lammi** Etelä-Suomi, S Finland 61°06′N 25°00′E
189 U11 **Lamoil** *island* Chuuk, C Micronesia
35 W3 **Lamoille** Nevada, W USA 40°47′N 115°37′W
18 M7 **Lamoille River** ≈ Vermont, NE USA
30 J13 **La Moine River** ≈ Illinois, N USA
171 P4 **Lamon Bay** *bay* Luzon, N Philippines
29 V16 **Lamoni** Iowa, C USA 40°37′N 93°56′W
35 R13 **Lamont** California, W USA 35°15′N 118°54′W
27 N8 **Lamont** Oklahoma, C USA 36°41′N 97°33′W
54 E13 **La Montañita** *var.* Montañita. Caquetá, S Colombia 01°22′N 75°25′W
43 N8 **La Mosquitia** *var.* Miskito Coast, *Eng.* Mosquito Coast. *coastal region* E Nicaragua
102 I9 **la Mothe-Achard** Vendée, NW France 46°37′N 01°37′W
188 L15 **Lamotrek Atoll** *atoll* Caroline Islands, C Micronesia
29 P6 **La Moure** North Dakota, N USA 46°21′N 98°17′W
167 O8 **Lampang** *var.* Muang Lampang. Lampang, NW Thailand 18°16′N 99°30′E
167 R9 **Lam Pao Reservoir** ⊠ E Thailand
25 S9 **Lampasas** Texas, SW USA 31°04′N 98°12′W
25 S9 **Lampasas River** ≈ Texas, SW USA
41 N7 **Lampazos** *var.* Lampazos de Naranjo. Nuevo León, NE Mexico 27°00′N 100°28′W
Lampazos de Naranjo *see* Lampazos
115 E19 **Lámpeia** Dytikí Ellás, S Greece 37°51′N 21°48′E
101 G19 **Lampertheim** Hessen, W Germany 49°36′N 08°28′E
97 I20 **Lampeter** SW Wales, United Kingdom 52°08′N 04°04′W
167 O7 **Lamphun** *var.* Lampun, Muang Lamphun. Lamphun, NW Thailand 18°36′N 99°02′E
11 X10 **Lamprey** Manitoba, C Canada 58°18′N 94°06′W
Lampun *see* Lamphun
168 M15 **Lampung** *off.* Propinsi Lampung. ◈ *province* SW Indonesia
Lampung, Propinsi *see* Lampung
126 K6 **Lamskoye** Lipetskaya Oblast', W Russian Federation 52°57′N 38°04′E
81 K20 **Lamu** Coast, SE Kenya 02°17′S 40°54′E
43 N14 **La Muerte, Cerro** ▲ C Costa Rica 09°33′N 83°47′W
103 S13 **la Mure** Isère, E France 44°54′N 05°48′E
37 S10 **Lamy** New Mexico, SW USA 35°27′N 105°52′W
119 J18 **Lan'** *Rus.* Lan'. ≈ C Belarus
38 E10 **Lāna'i** *var.* Lanai. *island* Hawai'i, USA, C Pacific Ocean
38 E10 **Lāna'i City** *var.* Lanai City. Lanai, Hawaii, USA, C Pacific Ocean 20°49′N 156°55′W
Lanai City *see* Lāna'i City
99 L18 **Lanaken** Limburg, NE Belgium 50°53′N 05°39′E
171 Q7 **Lanao, Lake** *var.* Lake Sultan Alonto. ◎ Mindanao, S Philippines
96 J12 **Lanark** S Scotland, United Kingdom 55°38′N 04°25′W
96 I13 **Lanark** *cultural region* C Scotland, United Kingdom
104 L9 **La Nava de Ricomalillo** Castilla-La Mancha, C Spain 39°40′N 04°59′W
166 M13 **Lanbi Kyun** *prev.* Sullivan Island. *island* Mergui Archipelago, S Burma (Myanmar)
Lancang Jiang *see* Mekong
97 K17 **Lancashire** *cultural region* N England, United Kingdom
15 N13 **Lancaster** Ontario, SE Canada 45°10′N 74°31′W
97 K16 **Lancaster** NW England, United Kingdom 54°03′N 02°48′W
35 T14 **Lancaster** California, W USA 34°42′N 118°08′W
20 M6 **Lancaster** Kentucky, S USA 37°35′N 84°34′W
27 U1 **Lancaster** Missouri, C USA 40°32′N 92°31′W
19 O7 **Lancaster** New Hampshire, NE USA 44°29′N 71°34′W
18 D10 **Lancaster** New York, NE USA 42°54′N 78°40′W
31 T14 **Lancaster** Ohio, N USA 39°42′N 82°36′W
18 H16 **Lancaster** Pennsylvania, NE USA 40°03′N 76°18′W
21 R11 **Lancaster** South Carolina, SE USA 34°43′N 80°47′W
25 U7 **Lancaster** Texas, SW USA 32°35′N 96°45′W
21 X5 **Lancaster** Virginia, NE USA 37°48′N 76°30′W
30 J9 **Lancaster** Wisconsin, N USA 42°52′N 90°43′W
197 N10 **Lancaster Sound** *sound* Nunavut, N Canada
Lan-chou/Lan-chow/ Lanchow *see* Lanzhou
107 K14 **Lanciano** Abruzzo, C Italy 42°13′N 14°23′E
111 O16 **Łańcut** Podkarpackie, SE Poland 50°04′N 22°14′E
169 Q11 **Landak, Sungai** ≈ Borneo, N Indonesia
Landao *see* Lantau Island
Landau *see* Landau an der Isar
Landau *see* Landau in der Pfalz
101 N22 **Landau an der Isar** *var.* Landau. Bayern, SE Germany 48°40′N 12°41′E
101 F20 **Landau in der Pfalz** *var.* Landau. Rheinland-Pfalz, SW Germany 49°12′N 08°07′E
Land Burgenland *see* Burgenland
108 K8 **Landeck** Tirol, W Austria 47°09′N 10°35′E
99 J19 **Landen** Vlaams Brabant, C Belgium 50°45′N 05°05′E

◆ Country
● Country Capital
◇ Dependent Territory
○ Dependent Territory Capital
◈ Administrative Regions
✈ International Airport
▲ Mountain
▲▲ Mountain Range
⛰ Volcano
≈ River
◎ Lake
⊠ Reservoir

33 U15 **Lander** Wyoming, C USA 42°49′N 108°43′W
102 F5 **Landerneau** Finistère, NW France 48°27′N 04°16′W
95 K20 **Landeryd** Halland, S Sweden 57°04′N 13°15′E
102 J15 **Landes** ⬖ department SW France
Landeshut/Landeshut in Schlesien see Kamienna Góra
105 R9 **Landete** Castilla-La Mancha, C Spain 39°54′N 01°22′W
99 M18 **Landgraaf** Limburg, SE Netherlands 50°55′N 06°04′E
102 F5 **Landivisiau** Finistère, NW France 48°31′N 04°03′W
Land Kärten see Kärnten
Land of Enchantment see New Mexico
The Land of Opportunity see Arkansas
Land of Steady Habits see Connecticut
Land of the Midnight Sun see Alaska
108 I8 **Landquart** Graubünden, SE Switzerland 46°58′N 09°35′E
108 J9 **Landquart** ≈ Austria/Switzerland
21 P10 **Landrum** South Carolina, SE USA 35°10′N 82°11′W
Landsberg see Gorzów Wielkopolski, Lubuskie, Poland
Landsberg see Górowo Iławeckie, Warmińsko-Mazurskie, NE Poland
101 K23 **Landsberg am Lech** Bayern, S Germany 48°03′N 10°52′E
Landsberg an der Warthe see Gorzów Wielkopolski
97 G25 **Land's End** headland SW England, United Kingdom 50°02′N 05°41′W
101 M22 **Landshut** Bayern, SE Germany 48°32′N 12°09′E
Landskron see Lanškroun
95 J22 **Landskrona** Skåne, S Sweden 55°52′N 12°52′E
98 I10 **Landsmeer** Noord-Holland, C Netherlands 52°26′N 04°55′E
95 J19 **Landvetter** ✈ (Göteborg) Västra Götaland, S Sweden 57°39′N 12°22′E
Landwarów see Lentvaris
23 R5 **Lanett** Alabama, S USA 32°52′N 85°11′W
108 C8 **La Neuveville** var. Neuveville, Ger. Neuenstadt. Neuchâtel, W Switzerland 47°05′N 07°03′E
95 G21 **Langå** var. Langaa. Århus, C Denmark 56°23′N 09°55′E
Langaa see Langå
158 G14 **La'nga Co** ◎ W China
Langada see Lagkáda
Langades/Langadhás see Lagkadás
Langádhia/ see Lagkádia
147 T14 **Langar** Rus. Lyangar. SE Tajikistan 37°04′N 72°39′E
146 M10 **Langar** Rus. Lyangar. Navoiy Viloyati, C Uzbekistan 40°27′N 65°54′E
142 M3 **Langarūd** Gīlān, NW Iran 37°10′N 50°09′E
11 V16 **Langbank** Saskatchewan, S Canada 50°01′N 102°16′W
29 P2 **Langdon** North Dakota, N USA 48°45′N 98°22′W
103 P12 **Langeac** Haute-Loire, C France 45°06′N 03°31′E
102 L8 **Langeais** Indre-et-Loire, C France 47°22′N 00°27′E
80 I8 **Langeb, Wadi** ≈ NE Sudan
Långed see Dals Långed
95 G25 **Langeland** island S Denmark
99 B18 **Langemark** West-Vlaanderen, W Belgium 50°55′N 02°55′E
101 G18 **Langen** Hessen, W Germany 49°58′N 08°40′E
101 J22 **Langenau** Baden-Württemberg, S Germany 48°30′N 10°08′E
11 V16 **Langenburg** Saskatchewan, S Canada 50°50′N 101°43′W
108 L8 **Längenfeld** Tirol, W Austria 47°04′N 10°59′E
101 E16 **Langenfeld** Nordrhein-Westfalen, W Germany 51°06′N 06°57′E
100 I12 **Langenhagen** Niedersachsen, N Germany 52°26′N 09°45′E
100 I12 **Langenhagen** ✈ (Hannover) Niedersachsen, NW Germany 52°28′N 09°40′E
109 W3 **Langenlois** Niederösterreich, NE Austria 48°29′N 15°42′E
108 E7 **Langenthal** Bern, NW Switzerland 47°13′N 07°48′E
109 W6 **Langenwang** Steiermark, E Austria 47°34′N 15°39′E
109 X3 **Langenzersdorf** Niederösterreich, E Austria 48°20′N 16°22′E
100 F9 **Langeoog** island NW Germany
95 H23 **Langeskov** Fyn, C Denmark 55°22′N 10°36′E
95 G16 **Langesund** Telemark, S Norway 59°00′N 09°43′E
95 G17 **Langesundsfjorden** fjord S Norway
94 D10 **Langevågen** Møre og Romsdal, S Norway 62°26′N 06°15′E
161 P3 **Langfang** Hebei, E China 39°30′N 116°39′E
94 E9 **Langfjorden** fjord S Norway
29 Q8 **Langford** South Dakota, N USA 45°36′N 97°48′W
168 I10 **Langgapayung** Sumatera, W Indonesia 01°42′N 99°57′E
106 E9 **Langhirano** Emilia-Romagna, C Italy 44°37′N 10°16′E
97 K14 **Langholm** S Scotland, United Kingdom 55°14′N 03°11′W
92 I3 **Langjökull** glacier C Iceland
168 I6 **Langkawi, Pulau** island Peninsular Malaysia
166 M14 **Langkha Tuk, Khao** ▲ SW Thailand 09°19′N 98°39′E
14 L8 **Langlade** Québec, SE Canada 48°13′N 75°58′W
10 M17 **Langley** British Columbia, SW Canada 49°07′N 122°39′W
167 S7 **Lang Mô** Thanh Hoa, N Vietnam 19°36′N 105°30′E
Langnau see Langnau im Emmental
108 E8 **Langnau im Emmental** var. Langnau. Bern, W Switzerland 46°57′N 07°47′E
103 Q13 **Langogne** Lozère, S France 44°40′N 03°52′E
102 K13 **Langon** Gironde, SW France 44°33′N 00°14′W
La Ngounié see Ngounié
92 G10 **Langøya** island C Norway
158 G14 **Langqên Zangbo** ≈ China/India
104 K2 **Langreo** var. Sama de Langreo. Asturias, N Spain 43°18′N 05°40′W
103 S7 **Langres** Haute-Marne, N France 47°53′N 05°20′E
103 R8 **Langres, Plateau de** plateau C France
168 H8 **Langsa** Sumatera, W Indonesia 04°30′N 97°53′E
93 H16 **Långsele** Västernorrland, C Sweden 63°11′N 17°05′E
162 L12 **Lang Shan** ▲▲ N China
95 M14 **Långshyttan** Dalarna, C Sweden 60°26′N 16°02′E
167 T5 **Lang Sơn** var. Langson. Lang Sơn, N Vietnam 21°50′N 106°45′E
Langson see Lang Sơn
167 N14 **Lang Suan** Chumphon, SW Thailand 09°55′N 99°07′E
93 J14 **Långträsk** Norrbotten, N Sweden 65°22′N 20°19′E
25 N11 **Langtry** Texas, SW USA 29°46′N 101°25′W
103 P16 **Languedoc** cultural region S France
103 P15 **Languedoc-Roussillon** ⬖ region S France
27 X10 **L'Anguille River** ≈ Arkansas, C USA
93 I16 **Långviksmon** Västernorrland, N Sweden 63°39′N 18°45′E
101 K22 **Langweid** Bayern, S Germany 48°29′N 10°50′E
160 J8 **Langzhong** Sichuan, C China 31°46′N 105°55′E
Lan Hsü see Lan Yü
11 U15 **Lanigan** Saskatchewan, S Canada 51°50′N 105°01′W
116 K5 **Lanivtsi** Ternopil's'ka Oblast', W Ukraine 49°52′N 26°05′E
137 Y13 **Länkäran** Rus. Lenkoran'. S Azerbaijan 38°46′N 48°51′E
102 L16 **Lannemezan** Hautes-Pyrénées, S France 43°08′N 00°22′E
102 G5 **Lannion** Côtes d'Armor, NW France 48°44′N 03°27′W
14 M11 **L'Annonciation** Québec, SE Canada 46°22′N 74°51′W
105 V5 **L'Anoia** ≈ NE Spain
18 I15 **Lansdale** Pennsylvania, NE USA 40°14′N 75°13′W
14 L14 **Lansdowne** Ontario, SE Canada 44°25′N 76°00′W
152 K9 **Lansdowne** Uttarakhand, N India 29°50′N 78°42′E
30 M3 **L'Anse** Michigan, N USA 46°45′N 88°27′W
15 S7 **L'Anse-St-Jean** Québec, SE Canada 48°14′N 70°13′W
29 Y11 **Lansing** Iowa, C USA 43°22′N 91°11′W
27 R4 **Lansing** Kansas, C USA 39°15′N 94°54′W
31 Q9 **Lansing** state capital Michigan, N USA 42°44′N 84°33′W
93 K18 **Länsi-Suomi** ⬖ province W Finland
92 J12 **Lansjärv** Norrbotten, N Sweden 66°39′N 22°10′E
111 G17 **Lanškroun** Ger. Landskron. Pardubický Kraj, E Czech Republic 49°55′N 16°38′E
167 N16 **Lanta, Ko** island S Thailand
161 O15 **Lantau Island** Cant. Tai Yue Shan, Chin. Landao. island Hong Kong, S China
Lantian see Lianyuan
Lan-ts'ang Chiang see Mekong
Lantung, Gulf of see Liaodong Wan
171 O11 **Lanu** Sulawesi, N Indonesia 01°00′N 121°33′E
107 D19 **Lanusei** Sardegna, Italy, C Mediterranean Sea 39°55′N 09°31′E
102 H7 **Lanvaux, Landes de** physical region NW France
163 W8 **Lanxi** Heilongjiang, NE China 46°18′N 126°15′E
161 R10 **Lanxi** Zhejiang, SE China 29°12′N 119°27′E
La Nyanga see Nyanga
161 T15 **Lan Yü** var. Huoshao Tao, Hungt'ou, Lan Hsü, Lanyü, Eng. Orchid Island; prev. Kotosho, Koto Sho. island SE Taiwan
Lanyü see Lan Yü
64 P11 **Lanzarote** island Islas Canarias, Spain, NE Atlantic Ocean
159 V10 **Lanzhou** var. Lan-chou, Lanchow, Lan-chow; prev. Kaolan. province capital Gansu, C China 36°01′N 103°52′E
106 B8 **Lanzo Torinese** Piemonte, NE Italy 45°18′N 07°26′E
171 O11 **Laoag** Luzon, N Philippines 18°11′N 120°34′E
171 Q5 **Laoang** Samar, C Philippines 12°29′N 125°01′E
167 R5 **Lao Cai** Lao Cai, N Vietnam 22°29′N 104°00′E
Laodicea/Laodicea ad Mare see Al Lādhiqīyah
Laoet see Laut, Pulau
163 T11 **Laoha He** ≈ NE China
160 M8 **Laohekou** var. Guanghua. Hubei, C China 32°20′N 111°42′E
Laoi, An see Lee
97 E19 **Laois** prev. Leix, Queen's County. cultural region C Ireland
159 R8 **Laojunmiao** prev. Yumen. Gansu, N China 39°49′N 97°47′E
163 W12 **Lao Ling** ▲▲ N China
64 Q11 **La Oliva** var. Oliva. Fuerteventura, Islas Canarias, Spain, NE Atlantic Ocean 28°36′N 13°53′W
Lao, Loch see Belfast Lough
Laolong see Longchuan
Lao Mangnai see Mangnai
103 P3 **Laon** var. la Laon; anc. Laudunum. Aisne, N France 49°34′N 03°37′E
Lao People's Democratic Republic see Laos
54 M3 **La Orchila, Isla** island N Venezuela
64 O11 **La Orotava** Tenerife, Islas Canarias, Spain, NE Atlantic Ocean 28°23′N 16°32′W
57 E14 **La Oroya** Junín, C Peru 11°36′S 75°54′W
167 Q7 **Laos** off. Lao People's Democratic Republic. ◆ republic SE Asia
161 R5 **Laoshan Wan** bay E China
163 Y10 **Laoye Ling** ▲▲ NE China
60 J12 **Lapa** Paraná, S Brazil 25°46′S 49°44′W
103 P10 **Lapalisse** Allier, C France 46°13′N 03°39′E
54 F9 **La Palma** Cundinamarca, C Colombia 05°23′N 74°24′W
42 F7 **La Palma** Chalatenango, N El Salvador 14°19′N 89°10′W
43 W16 **La Palma** Darién, SE Panama 08°24′N 78°09′W
64 N11 **La Palma** island Islas Canarias, Spain, NE Atlantic Ocean
104 J14 **La Palma del Condado** Andalucía, S Spain 37°23′N 06°33′W
61 F18 **La Paloma** Durazno, C Uruguay 32°54′S 55°36′W
61 G20 **La Paloma** Rocha, E Uruguay 34°37′S 54°08′W
61 A21 **La Pampa** off. Provincia de La Pampa. ⬖ province C Argentina
La Pampa, Provincia de see La Pampa
55 P8 **La Paragua** Bolívar, E Venezuela 06°53′N 63°16′W
119 O16 **Lapatsichy** Rus. Lopatichi. Mahilyowskaya Voblasts', E Belarus 53°34′N 30°53′E
61 C16 **La Paz** Entre Ríos, E Argentina 30°45′S 59°36′W
62 I11 **La Paz** Mendoza, C Argentina 33°30′S 67°36′W
57 J18 **La Paz** var. La Paz de Ayacucho. ● (Bolivia-legislative and administrative capital) La Paz, W Bolivia 16°30′S 68°13′W
42 H6 **La Paz** La Paz, SW Honduras 14°20′N 87°40′W
40 F9 **La Paz** Baja California Sur, NW Mexico 24°07′N 110°18′W
61 F20 **La Paz** Canelones, S Uruguay 34°46′S 56°13′W
57 J16 **La Paz** ⬖ department W Bolivia
42 B9 **La Paz** ⬖ department S El Salvador
42 G7 **La Paz** ⬖ department SW Honduras
La Paz see El Alto, Bolivia
La Paz see Robles, Colombia
La Paz see La Paz Centro
40 F9 **La Paz, Bahía de** bay NW Mexico
42 I10 **La Paz Centro** var. La Paz. León, W Nicaragua 12°20′N 86°41′W
La Paz de Ayacucho see La Paz
54 J15 **La Pedrera** Amazonas, SE Colombia 01°19′S 69°31′W
31 S9 **Lapeer** Michigan, N USA 43°03′N 83°19′W
40 K6 **La Perla** Chihuahua, N Mexico 28°18′N 104°34′W
165 T1 **La Perouse Strait** Jap. Sōya-kaikyō, Rus. Proliv Laperuza. strait Japan/Russian Federation
63 I14 **La Perra, Salitral de** salt lake C Argentina
Laperuza, Proliv see La Perouse Strait
41 Q10 **La Pesca** Tamaulipas, C Mexico 23°49′N 97°45′W
40 M13 **La Piedad Cavadas** Michoacán, C Mexico 20°20′N 102°01′W
Lapines see Lafnitz
93 M16 **Lapinlahti** Itä-Suomi, C Finland 63°21′N 27°25′E
Lápithos see Lapta
22 K9 **Laplace** Louisiana, S USA 30°04′N 90°28′W
45 X12 **La Plaine** SE Dominica 15°20′N 61°15′W
173 P16 **La Plaine-des-Palmistes** C Réunion
92 K11 **Lapland** Fin. Lappi, Swe. Lappland. cultural region N Europe
28 M8 **La Plant** South Dakota, N USA 45°06′N 100°40′W
61 D20 **La Plata** Buenos Aires, E Argentina 34°56′S 57°55′W
54 D12 **La Plata** Huila, SW Colombia 02°33′N 75°55′W
21 W4 **La Plata** Maryland, NE USA 38°32′N 76°59′W
La Plata see Sucre
45 U6 **la Plata, Río de** ≈ C Puerto Rico
105 W4 **La Pobla de Lillet** Cataluña, NE Spain 42°15′N 01°57′E
105 U4 **La Pobla de Segur** Cataluña, NE Spain 42°15′N 00°58′E
15 S9 **La Pocatière** Québec, SE Canada 47°21′N 70°04′W
104 L3 **La Pola de Gordón** Castilla-León, N Spain 42°50′N 05°38′W
31 O11 **La Porte** Indiana, N USA 41°36′N 86°43′W
18 H13 **Laporte** Pennsylvania, NE USA 41°25′N 76°29′W
29 X13 **La Porte City** Iowa, C USA 42°19′N 92°11′W
62 J8 **La Posta** Catamarca, C Argentina 27°59′S 65°32′W
40 E8 **La Poza Grande** Baja California Sur, NW Mexico 25°50′N 112°00′W
93 K16 **Lappajärvi** Länsi-Suomi, W Finland 63°13′N 23°40′E
93 L16 **Lappajärvi** ◎ W Finland
93 N18 **Lappeenranta** Swe. Villmanstrand. Etelä-Suomi, SE Finland 61°04′N 28°15′E
93 J17 **Lappfjärd** Fin. Lapväärtti. Länsi-Suomi, W Finland 62°14′N 21°30′E
92 L12 **Lappi** Swe. Lappland. ⬖ province N Finland
Lappi/Lappland see Lapland
Lappo see Lapua
61 C23 **Laprida** Buenos Aires, E Argentina 37°34′S 60°45′W
25 P13 **La Pryor** Texas, SW USA 28°56′N 99°51′W
136 B11 **Lâpseki** Çanakkale, NW Turkey 40°22′N 26°42′E
121 P2 **Lapta** Gk. Lápithos. NW Cyprus 35°20′N 33°11′E
Laptev Sea see Laptevykh, More
122 N6 **Laptevykh, More** Eng. Laptev Sea. sea Arctic Ocean
93 K16 **Lapua** Swe. Lappo. Länsi-Suomi, W Finland 62°57′N 23°E
105 P3 **La Puebla de Arganzón** País Vasco, N Spain 42°45′N 02°49′W
104 L14 **La Puebla de Cazalla** Andalucía, S Spain 37°14′N 05°18′W
104 M9 **La Puebla de Montalbán** Castilla-La Mancha, C Spain 39°52′N 04°22′W
54 I6 **La Puerta** Trujillo, NW Venezuela 09°08′N 70°46′W
Lapurdum see Bayonne
40 E7 **La Purísima** Baja California Sur, NW Mexico 26°10′N 112°05′W
Lapväärtti see Lappfjärd
110 O10 **Łapy** Podlaskie, NE Poland 53°N 22°54′E
80 D6 **Laqiya Arba'in** Northern, NW Sudan 20°01′N 28°01′E
62 J4 **La Quiaca** Jujuy, N Argentina 22°12′S 65°36′W
107 J14 **L'Aquila** var. Aquila, Aquila degli Abruzzi. Abruzzo, C Italy 42°21′N 13°24′E
143 Q13 **Lār** Fārs, S Iran 27°42′N 54°19′E
54 J5 **Lara** off. Estado Lara. ⬖ state NW Venezuela
104 G2 **Laracha** Galicia, NW Spain 43°14′N 08°34′W
74 G5 **Larache** var. al Araïch, El Araïch, prev. El Araïche; anc. Lixus. NW Morocco 35°12′N 06°10′W
Lara, Estado see Lara
103 T14 **Laragne-Montéglin** Hautes-Alpes, SE France 44°21′N 05°46′E
104 M13 **La Rambla** Andalucía, S Spain 37°37′N 04°44′W
33 Y17 **Laramie** Wyoming, C USA 41°18′N 105°35′W
33 X15 **Laramie Mountains** ▲▲ Wyoming, C USA
33 Y16 **Laramie River** ≈ Wyoming, C USA
Larang see Zhongdian
60 H12 **Laranjeiras do Sul** Paraná, S Brazil 25°23′S 52°23′W
Larantoeka see Larantuka
171 P16 **Larantuka** prev. Larantoeka. Flores, C Indonesia 08°20′S 123°00′E
171 U15 **Larat** Pulau Larat, E Indonesia 07°07′S 131°46′E
171 U15 **Larat, Pulau** island Kepulauan Tanimbar, E Indonesia
95 P19 **Lärbro** Gotland, SE Sweden 57°46′N 18°49′E
106 A9 **Larche, Col de** pass France/Italy
14 H8 **Larder Lake** Ontario, S Canada 48°06′N 79°44′W
105 O2 **Laredo** Cantabria, N Spain 43°23′N 03°22′W
25 Q15 **Laredo** Texas, SW USA 27°30′N 99°30′W
40 H9 **La Reforma** Sinaloa, W Mexico 25°05′N 108°03′W
98 N11 **Laren** Gelderland, E Netherlands 52°12′N 06°22′E
98 J11 **Laren** Noord-Holland, C Netherlands 52°15′N 05°13′E
102 K13 **la Réole** Gironde, SW France 44°34′N 00°00′W
La Réunion see Réunion
Largeau see Faya
103 U13 **l'Argentière-la-Bessée** Hautes-Alpes, SE France 44°49′N 06°34′E
149 O4 **Lar Gerd** var. Largird. Balkh, N Afghanistan 35°36′N 66°48′E
Largird see Lar Gerd
23 V12 **Largo** Florida, SE USA 27°55′N 82°47′W
37 Q9 **Largo, Canon** valley New Mexico, SW USA
44 D6 **Largo, Cayo** island W Cuba
23 Z17 **Largo, Key** island Florida Keys, Florida, SE USA
96 H12 **Largs** W Scotland, United Kingdom 55°48′N 04°50′W
102 I16 **la Rhune** var. Larrún. ▲ France/Spain 43°19′N 01°36′W see also Larrún
la Rhune see Larrún
la Riege see Ariège
29 Q4 **Larimore** North Dakota, N USA 47°54′N 97°37′W
107 L15 **Larino** Molise, C Italy 41°46′N 14°50′E
Lario see Como, Lago di
62 J9 **La Rioja** La Rioja, NW Argentina 29°26′S 66°50′W
62 I9 **La Rioja** off. Provincia de La Rioja. ⬖ province NW Argentina
105 O4 **La Rioja** ⬖ autonomous community N Spain
La Rioja, Provincia de see La Rioja
115 F16 **Lárisa** var. Larissa. Thessalía, C Greece 39°38′N 22°27′E
Larissa see Lárisa
149 Q13 **Lārkāna** var. Larkhana. Sind, SE Pakistan 27°32′N 68°18′E
Larkhana see Lārkāna
Larnaca see Lárnaka
121 Q3 **Lárnaka** var. Larnaca, Larnax. SE Cyprus 34°55′N 33°39′E
121 Q3 **Lárnaka** ✈ SE Cyprus 34°52′N 33°38′E
Larnax see Lárnaka
97 G14 **Larne** Ir. Latharna. E Northern Ireland, United Kingdom 54°51′N 05°49′W
26 L5 **Larned** Kansas, C USA 38°12′N 99°05′W
104 L3 **La Robla** Castilla-León, N Spain 42°48′N 05°37′W
104 J10 **La Roca de la Sierra** Extremadura, W Spain 39°06′N 06°41′W
99 K22 **La Roche-en-Ardenne** Luxembourg, SE Belgium 50°11′N 05°35′E
102 L11 **la Rochefoucauld** Charente, W France 45°43′N 00°23′E
102 J10 **la Rochelle** anc. Rupella. Charente-Maritime, W France 46°09′N 01°07′W
102 I9 **la Roche-sur-Yon** prev. Bourbon Vendée, Napoléon-Vendée. Vendée, NW France 46°40′N 01°26′W
105 Q10 **La Roda** Castilla-La Mancha, C Spain 39°13′N 02°10′W
104 L14 **La Roda de Andalucía** Andalucía, S Spain 37°12′N 04°45′W
45 P9 **La Romana** E Dominican Republic 18°25′N 69°00′W
11 T13 **La Ronge** Saskatchewan, C Canada 55°07′N 105°18′W
11 U13 **La Ronge, Lac** ◎ Saskatchewan, C Canada
22 K10 **Larose** Louisiana, S USA 29°34′N 90°22′W
42 M7 **La Rosita** Región Autónoma Atlántico Norte, NE Nicaragua 13°55′N 84°23′W
181 Q3 **Larrimah** Northern Territory, N Australia 15°30′S 133°12′E
62 N11 **Larroque** Entre Ríos, E Argentina 33°05′S 59°06′W
105 Q2 **Larrún** Fr. la Rhune. ▲ France/Spain 43°18′N 01°35′W see also la Rhune
Larrún see la Rhune
195 X6 **Lars Christensen Coast** physical region Antarctica
39 Q14 **Larsen Bay** Kodiak Island, Alaska, USA 57°32′N 153°58′W
194 I5 **Larsen Ice Shelf** ice shelf Antarctica
8 M6 **Larsen Sound** sound Nunavut, N Canada
La Rúa see A Rúa de Valdeorras
102 K16 **Laruns** Pyrénées-Atlantiques, SW France 43°00′N 00°25′W
95 G16 **Larvik** Vestfold, S Norway 59°04′N 10°02′E
La-sa see Lhasa
171 S13 **Lasahata** Pulau Seram, E Indonesia 02°52′S 128°27′E
Lasahau see Lasihao
37 O6 **La Sal** Utah, W USA 38°19′N 109°14′W
14 C17 **La Salle** Ontario, S Canada 42°13′N 83°05′W
30 L11 **La Salle** Illinois, N USA 41°19′N 89°06′W
45 O9 **Las Americas** ✈ (Santo Domingo) S Dominican Republic 18°24′N 69°38′W
37 V6 **Las Animas** Colorado, C USA 38°04′N 103°13′W
108 D10 **La Sarine** var. Sarine. ≈ SW Switzerland
108 B9 **La Sarraz** Vaud, W Switzerland 46°40′N 06°32′E
12 H12 **La Sarre** Québec, SE Canada 48°49′N 79°12′W
54 L3 **Las Aves, Islas** var. Islas de Aves. island group N Venezuela
55 N7 **Las Bonitas** Bolívar, C Venezuela 07°50′N 65°40′W
104 K15 **Las Cabezas de San Juan** Andalucía, S Spain 36°59′N 05°56′W
61 G19 **Lascano** Rocha, E Uruguay 33°40′S 54°12′W
62 I5 **Lascar, Volcán** △ N Chile 23°22′S 67°33′W
41 T15 **Las Choapas** var. Choapas. Veracruz-Llave, SE Mexico 17°51′N 94°00′W
37 R15 **Las Cruces** New Mexico, SW USA 32°19′N 106°49′W
Lasdehnen see Krasnoznamensk
105 V4 **La See d'Urgel** var. La Seu d'Urgell, Seo de Urgel. Cataluña, NE Spain 42°22′N 01°27′E
La Selle see Selle, Pic de la
62 G9 **La Serena** Coquimbo, C Chile 29°54′S 71°18′W
104 K11 **La Serena** physical region W Spain
La Seu d'Urgell see La See d'Urgel
103 T16 **la Seyne-sur-Mer** Var, SE France 43°07′N 05°53′E
61 D21 **Las Flores** Buenos Aires, E Argentina 36°03′S 59°08′W
62 H9 **Las Flores** San Juan, W Argentina 30°14′S 69°10′W
11 S14 **Lashburn** Saskatchewan, S Canada 53°09′N 109°37′W
62 I11 **Las Heras** Mendoza, W Argentina 32°48′S 68°50′W
148 M8 **Lashkar Gāh** var. Lash-Kar-Gar'. Helmand, S Afghanistan 31°35′N 64°21′E
Lash-Kar-Gar' see Lashkar Gāh
171 P14 **Lasihao** var. Lasahau. Pulau Muna, C Indonesia 05°01′S 122°23′E
107 N21 **La Sila** ▲▲ SW Italy
63 H23 **La Silueta, Cerro** ▲ S Chile 52°22′S 72°09′W
42 L9 **La Sirena** Región Autónoma Atlántico Sur, E Nicaragua 12°59′N 84°35′W
110 J13 **Łask** Łódzkie, C Poland 51°36′N 19°06′E
109 V11 **Laško** Ger. Tüffer. C Slovenia 46°08′N 15°13′E
63 H14 **Las Lajas** Neuquén, W Argentina 38°31′S 70°22′W
63 H15 **Las Lajas, Cerro** ▲ W Argentina 38°49′S 70°42′W
62 M6 **Las Lomitas** Formosa, N Argentina 24°45′S 60°35′W
41 V16 **Las Margaritas** Chiapas, SE Mexico 16°15′N 91°58′W
Las Marismas see Guadalquivir, Marismas del
54 M6 **Las Mercedes** Guárico, N Venezuela 09°08′N 66°27′W
42 F6 **Las Minas, Cerro** ▲ W Honduras 14°33′N 88°41′W
105 O11 **La Solana** Castilla-La Mancha, C Spain 38°56′N 03°14′W
45 Q14 **La Soufrière** △ Saint Vincent, Saint Vincent and the Grenadines 13°20′N 61°11′W
102 M10 **la Souterraine** Creuse, C France 46°15′N 01°28′E
62 N7 **Las Palmas** Chaco, N Argentina 27°08′S 58°45′W
43 Q16 **Las Palmas** Veraguas, W Panama 08°09′N 81°28′W
64 P12 **Las Palmas** var. Las Palmas de Gran Canaria. Gran Canaria, Islas Canarias, Spain, NE Atlantic Ocean 28°08′N 15°27′W
64 P12 **Las Palmas** ⬖ province Islas Canarias, Spain, NE Atlantic Ocean
64 Q12 **Las Palmas** ✈ Gran Canaria, Islas Canarias, Spain, NE Atlantic Ocean
Las Palmas de Gran Canaria see Las Palmas
40 D6 **Las Palomas** Baja California Norte, W Mexico 31°44′N 107°37′W
105 P10 **Las Pedroñeras** Castilla-La Mancha, C Spain 39°27′N 02°41′W
106 E10 **La Spezia** Liguria, NW Italy 44°08′N 09°50′E
61 F20 **Las Piedras** Canelones, S Uruguay 34°42′S 56°14′W
63 J18 **Las Plumas** Chubut, S Argentina 43°46′S 67°15′W
61 B18 **Las Rosas** Santa Fe, C Argentina 32°27′S 61°30′W
Lassa see Lhasa
35 O4 **Lassen Peak** ▲ California, W USA 40°27′N 121°28′W
194 K6 **Lassiter Coast** physical region Antarctica
109 V9 **Lassnitz** ≈ SE Austria
15 O12 **L'Assomption** Québec, SE Canada 45°48′N 73°27′W
15 N11 **L'Assomption** ≈ Québec, SE Canada
43 S17 **Las Tablas** Los Santos, S Panama 07°45′N 80°17′W
Lastarria, Volcán see Azufre, Volcán
37 V4 **Last Chance** Colorado, C USA 39°41′N 103°34′W
Last Frontier, The see Alaska
11 U16 **Last Mountain Lake** ◎ Saskatchewan, S Canada
62 H9 **Las Tórtolas, Cerro** ▲ W Argentina 29°57′S 69°49′W
61 C14 **Las Toscas** Santa Fe, C Argentina 28°22′S 59°20′W
79 F19 **Lastoursville** Ogooué-Lolo, E Gabon 0°50′S 12°43′E
113 F16 **Lastovo** It. Lagosta. island SW Croatia
113 F16 **Lastovski Kanal** channel SW Croatia
40 E6 **Las Tres Vírgenes, Volcán** △ NW Mexico 27°27′N 112°34′W
40 F4 **Las Trincheras** Sonora, NW Mexico 30°21′N 111°27′W
55 N8 **Las Trincheras** Bolívar, E Venezuela 06°57′N 64°49′W
44 H7 **Las Tunas** var. Victoria de las Tunas. Las Tunas, E Cuba 20°58′N 76°59′W
La Suisse see Switzerland
40 I5 **Las Varas** Chihuahua, N Mexico 29°35′N 108°01′W
40 J12 **Las Varas** Nayarit, C Mexico 21°12′N 105°10′W
62 L10 **Las Varillas** Córdoba, E Argentina 31°54′S 62°45′W
35 X11 **Las Vegas** Nevada, W USA 36°09′N 115°10′W
37 T10 **Las Vegas** New Mexico, SW USA 35°35′N 105°15′W
187 P10 **Lata** Nendö, Solomon Islands 10°45′S 165°43′E
13 R10 **La Tabatière** Québec, E Canada 50°51′N 58°59′W
56 C6 **Latacunga** Cotopaxi, C Ecuador 0°58′S 78°36′W
194 I7 **Latady Island** island Antarctica
54 E14 **La Tagua** Putumayo, S Colombia 0°05′S 74°39′W
Latakia see Al Lādhiqīyah
92 J10 **Lätäseno** ≈ NW Finland
14 H9 **Latchford** Ontario, S Canada 47°20′N 79°45′W
14 J13 **Latchford Bridge** Ontario, SE Canada 45°16′N 77°29′W
193 Y14 **Late** island Vava'u Group, N Tonga
153 P15 **Lātehār** Jhārkhand, N India 23°48′N 84°28′E
15 R7 **Laterrière** Québec, SE Canada 48°17′N 71°10′W
102 J13 **la Teste** Gironde, SW France 44°38′N 01°04′W
25 V8 **Latexo** Texas, SW USA 31°24′N 95°28′W
18 L10 **Latham** New York, NE USA 42°45′N 73°45′W
Latharna see Larne
108 B9 **La Thielle** var. Thièle. ≈ W Switzerland
27 R3 **Lathrop** Missouri, C USA 39°33′N 94°19′W
107 I16 **Latina** prev. Littoria. Lazio, C Italy 41°28′N 12°53′E
41 R14 **La Tinaja** Veracruz-Llave, S Mexico
106 J7 **Latisana** Friuli-Venezia Giulia, NE Italy 45°47′N 13°01′E
Latium see Lazio
115 K25 **Lató** site of ancient city Kríti, Greece, E Mediterranean Sea
187 Q17 **La Tontouta** ✈ (Noumea) Province Sud, S New Caledonia 22°06′S 166°12′E
55 N4 **La Tortuga, Isla** var. Isla Tortuga. island N Venezuela
108 C10 **La Tour-de-Peilz** var. La Tour de Peilz. Vaud, SW Switzerland 46°28′N 06°52′E
La Tour de Peilz see La Tour-de-Peilz
103 S11 **la Tour-du-Pin** Isère, E France 45°34′N 05°25′E
102 J11 **la Tremblade** Charente-Maritime, W France 45°45′N 01°07′W
102 L10 **la Trimouille** Vienne, W France 46°27′N 01°02′E
42 J9 **La Trinidad** Estelí, NW Nicaragua 12°57′N 86°15′W
41 V16 **La Trinitaria** Chiapas, SE Mexico 16°02′N 92°00′W
45 Q11 **la Trinité** E Martinique 14°44′N 60°58′W
15 U7 **La Trinité-des-Monts** Québec, SE Canada 48°07′N 68°31′W
18 C15 **Latrobe** Pennsylvania, NE USA 40°18′N 79°19′W
183 P13 **La Trobe River** ≈ Victoria, SE Australia
Lattakia/Lattaquié see Al Lādhiqīyah
171 S13 **Latu** Pulau Seram, E Indonesia 03°24′S 128°37′E
15 P9 **La Tuque** Québec, SE Canada 47°26′N 72°47′W
155 G14 **Lātūr** Mahārāshtra, C India 18°24′N 76°34′E
118 G8 **Latvia** off. Republic of Latvia, Ger. Lettland, Latv. Latvija, Latvijas Republika; prev. Latvian SSR, Rus. Latviyskaya SSR. ◆ republic NE Europe
Latvian SSR/Latvija/Latvijas Republika/Latviyskaya SSR see Latvia
Latvia, Republic of see Latvia
186 H7 **Lau** New Britain, E Papua New Guinea 05°46′S 151°21′E
175 R9 **Lau Basin** undersea feature S Pacific Ocean
101 O15 **Lauchhammer** Brandenburg, E Germany 51°30′N 13°48′E
Laudunum see Laon
Laudus see St-Lô
Lauenburg/Lauenburg in Pommern see Lębork
101 L20 **Lauf an der Pegnitz** Bayern, SE Germany 49°31′N 11°16′E
108 D7 **Laufen** Basel, NW Switzerland 47°26′N 07°31′E
109 P5 **Lauffen** Salzburg, NW Austria 47°54′N 12°57′E
92 I2 **Laugarbakki** Nordhurland Vestra, N Iceland 65°18′N 20°51′W
92 I4 **Laugarvatn** Sudhurland, SW Iceland 64°09′N 20°43′W
31 O3 **Laughing Fish Point** headland Michigan, N USA 46°31′N 87°01′W
187 Z14 **Lau Group** island group E Fiji
Lauis see Lugano
93 M17 **Laukaa** Länsi-Suomi, C Finland 62°27′N 25°58′E
118 D12 **Laukuva** Tauragė, W Lithuania 55°37′N 22°12′E
Laun see Louny
183 P16 **Launceston** Tasmania, SE Australia 41°25′S 147°07′E
97 I24 **Launceston** anc. Dunheved. SW England, United Kingdom 50°38′N 04°21′W
54 C13 **La Unión** Nariño, SW Colombia 01°35′N 77°09′W
42 H8 **La Unión** La Unión, SE El Salvador 13°20′N 87°50′W
42 I6 **La Unión** Olancho, C Honduras 15°02′N 86°40′W
40 M15 **La Unión** Guerrero, S Mexico 17°58′N 101°49′W
41 Y14 **La Unión** Quintana Roo, E Mexico 18°00′N 101°48′W
105 S13 **La Unión** Murcia, SE Spain 37°37′N 00°54′W
54 L7 **La Unión** Barinas, C Venezuela 08°15′N 67°46′W
42 B10 **La Unión** ⬖ department E El Salvador
38 H11 **Laupāhoehoe** var. Laupahoehoe. Hawaii, USA, C Pacific Ocean 20°00′N 155°15′W
Laupahoehoe see Laupāhoehoe
101 I23 **Laupheim** Baden-Württemberg, S Germany 48°13′N 09°54′E
181 W3 **Laura** Queensland, NE Australia 15°37′S 144°34′E
189 X2 **Laura** atoll Majuro Atoll, SE Marshall Islands
Laurana see Lovran
54 L8 **La Urbana** Bolívar, C Venezuela 07°05′N 66°58′W
21 Y4 **Laurel** Delaware, NE USA 38°33′N 75°34′W
23 V14 **Laurel** Florida, SE USA 27°07′N 82°27′W
21 W3 **Laurel** Maryland, NE USA 39°06′N 76°51′W
22 M6 **Laurel** Mississippi, S USA 31°41′N 89°10′W
33 U11 **Laurel** Montana, NW USA 45°40′N 108°46′W
29 R13 **Laurel** Nebraska, C USA 42°25′N 97°04′W
18 H15 **Laureldale** Pennsylvania, NE USA 40°24′N 75°52′W
18 C16 **Laurel Hill** ridge Pennsylvania, NE USA
29 T12 **Laurens** Iowa, C USA 42°51′N 94°51′W
21 P11 **Laurens** South Carolina, SE USA 34°29′N 82°01′W
Laurentian Highlands see Laurentian Mountains
15 P10 **Laurentian Mountains** var. Laurentian Highlands, Fr. Les Laurentides. plateau Newfoundland and Labrador/Québec, Canada
15 O12 **Laurentides** Québec, SE Canada 45°51′N 73°49′W
Laurentides, Les see Laurentian Mountains
107 M19 **Lauria** Basilicata, S Italy 40°03′N 15°50′E
194 I1 **Laurie Island** island Antarctica
21 T11 **Laurinburg** North Carolina, SE USA 34°46′N 79°29′W
30 M2 **Laurium** Michigan, N USA 47°14′N 88°26′W
Lauru see Choiseul
108 B9 **Lausanne** It. Losanna. Vaud, SW Switzerland 46°32′N 06°39′E
101 Q16 **Lausche** var. Luže. ▲ Czech Republic/Germany 50°52′N 14°39′E see also Luže
Lausche see Luže
101 Q16 **Lausitzer Bergland** var. Lausitzer Gebirge, Cz. Gory Lužycke, Lužické Hory', Eng. Lusatian Mountains. ▲▲ E Germany
Lausitzer Gebirge see Lausitzer Bergland
Lausitzer Neisse see Neisse
103 T12 **Lautaret, Col du** pass SE France
63 G15 **Lautaro** Araucanía, C Chile 38°30′S 71°30′W
101 F21 **Lauter** ≈ W Germany
108 I7 **Lauterach** Vorarlberg, NW Austria 47°29′N 09°44′E
101 I17 **Lauterbach** Hessen, C Germany 50°37′N 09°24′E
108 E9 **Lauterbrunnen** Bern, C Switzerland 46°36′N 07°52′E
169 U14 **Laut Kecil, Kepulauan** island group N Indonesia
187 X14 **Lautoka** Viti Levu, W Fiji 17°36′S 177°28′E
169 O8 **Laut, Pulau** prev. Laoet. island Borneo, C Indonesia
169 V14 **Laut, Pulau** island Kepulauan Natuna, W Indonesia
169 U13 **Laut, Selat** strait Borneo, C Indonesia
168 H8 **Laut Tawar, Danau** ◎ Sumatera, NW Indonesia
189 V14 **Lauvergne Island** island Antarctica
98 M5 **Lauwers Meer** ◎ N Netherlands
98 M4 **Lauwersoog** Groningen, NE Netherlands 53°25′N 06°14′E
102 M14 **Lauzerte** Tarn-et-Garonne, S France 44°15′N 01°08′E
25 U13 **Lavaca Bay** bay Texas, SW USA
25 U12 **Lavaca River** ≈ Texas, SW USA
15 O12 **Laval** Québec, SE Canada 45°32′N 73°44′W
102 J6 **Laval** Mayenne, NW France 48°04′N 00°46′W
15 T6 **Laval** ≈ Québec, SE Canada
105 S9 **La Vall d'Uixó** var. Vall D'Uxó. País Valenciano, E Spain 39°49′N 00°15′W

61 F19 **Lavalleja** *department* S Uruguay
15 O12 **Lavaltrie** Québec, SE Canada 45°56′N 73°14′W
186 M10 **Lavanggu** Rennell, S Solomon Islands 11°39′S 160°13′E
143 O14 **Lāvān, Jazīreh-ye** *island* S Iran
109 U8 **Lavant** S Austria
118 G5 **Lavassaare** *Ger.* Lawassaar. Pärnumaa, SW Estonia 58°29′N 24°22′E
104 L3 **La Vecilla de Curueño** Castilla-León, N Spain 42°51′N 05°24′W
45 N8 **La Vega** *var.* Concepción de la Vega. C Dominican Republic 19°15′N 70°33′W
La Vela *see* La Vela de Coro
54 J4 **La Vela de Coro** *var.* La Vela. Falcón, N Venezuela 11°30′N 69°33′W
103 N17 **Lavelanet** Ariège, S France 42°56′N 01°50′E
107 M17 **Lavello** Basilicata, S Italy 41°03′N 15°48′E
36 J8 **La Verkin** Utah, W USA 37°12′N 113°16′W
26 J8 **Laverne** Oklahoma, C USA 36°42′N 99°53′W
25 S12 **La Vernia** Texas, SW USA 29°19′N 98°07′W
93 K18 **Lavia** Länsi-Suomi, SW Finland 61°36′N 22°34′E
14 I12 **Lavieille, Lake** Ontario, SE Canada
94 C12 **Lavik** Sogn Og Fjordane, S Norway 61°06′N 05°25′E
La Vila Joíosa *see* Villajoyosa
33 U10 **Lavina** Montana, NW USA 46°18′N 108°55′W
194 H5 **Lavoisier Island** *island* Antarctica
23 U2 **Lavonia** Georgia, SE USA 34°26′N 83°06′W
103 R13 **la Voulte-sur-Rhône** Ardèche, E France 44°49′N 04°46′E
123 W5 **Lavrentiya** Chukotskiy Avtonomnyy Okrug, NE Russian Federation 65°33′N 171°12′W
115 H20 **Lávrio** *prev.* Lávrion. Attikí, C Greece 37°43′N 24°03′E
Lávrion *see* Lávrio
83 L22 **Lavumisa** *prev.* Gollel. SE Swaziland 27°18′S 31°55′E
149 T4 **Lawarai Pass** *pass* N Pakistan
Lawassaar *see* Lavassaare
141 P16 **Lawdar** SW Yemen 13°49′N 45°55′E
25 Q7 **Lawn** Texas, SW USA 32°07′N 99°45′W
195 Y4 **Law Promontory** *headland* Antarctica
77 O14 **Lawra** NW Ghana 10°40′N 02°49′W
185 E23 **Lawrence** Otago, South Island, New Zealand 45°53′S 169°43′E
31 P14 **Lawrence** Indiana, N USA 39°49′N 86°01′W
27 Q4 **Lawrence** Kansas, C USA 38°58′N 95°15′W
19 O10 **Lawrence** Massachusetts, NE USA 42°42′N 71°09′W
20 L5 **Lawrenceburg** Kentucky, S USA 38°02′N 84°53′W
20 I10 **Lawrenceburg** Tennessee, S USA 35°16′N 87°20′W
23 T3 **Lawrenceville** Georgia, SE USA 33°57′N 83°59′W
31 N15 **Lawrenceville** Illinois, N USA 38°43′N 87°40′W
21 V7 **Lawrenceville** Virginia, NE USA 36°45′N 77°50′W
27 S3 **Lawson** Missouri, C USA 39°26′N 94°12′W
26 L12 **Lawton** Oklahoma, C USA 34°35′N 98°20′W
140 I4 **Lawz, Jabal al** NW Saudi Arabia 28°45′N 35°20′E
95 L16 **Laxå** Örebro, C Sweden 59°00′N 14°37′E
125 T5 **Laya** NW Russian Federation
57 I19 **La Yarada** Tacna, SW Peru 18°14′S 70°30′W
141 S15 **Layjūn** C Yemen 15°27′N 49°16′E
141 Q9 **Laylā** *var.* Laila. Ar Riyāḍ, C Saudi Arabia 22°14′N 46°40′E
23 P4 **Lay Lake** Alabama, S USA
45 P14 **Layou** Saint Vincent, Saint Vincent and the Grenadines 13°11′N 61°16′W
La Youne *see* El Ayoun
192 L5 **Laysan Island** *island* Hawaiian Islands, Hawai'i, USA
36 L2 **Layton** Utah, W USA 41°03′N 112°00′W
34 L5 **Laytonville** California, W USA 39°39′N 123°30′W
172 H17 **Lazare, Pointe** *headland* Mahé, NE Seychelles 04°46′S 55°28′E
123 T12 **Lazarev** Khabarovskiy Kray, SE Russian Federation 52°11′N 141°18′E
112 L12 **Lazarevac** Serbia, C Serbia 44°25′N 20°17′E
65 N22 **Lazarev Sea** *sea* Antarctica
40 M15 **Lázaro Cárdenas** Michoacán, SW Mexico 17°56′N 102°13′W
119 F15 **Lazdijai** Alytus, S Lithuania 54°13′N 23°33′E
107 H15 **Lazio** *anc.* Latium. *region* C Italy
111 A16 **Lázně Kynžvart** *Ger.* Bad Königswart. Karlovarský Kraj, W Czech Republic 50°00′N 12°40′E
Lazovsk *see* Sîngerei
167 R12 **Leach** Poŭthĭsăt, W Cambodia 12°19′N 103°45′E
27 X9 **Leachville** Arkansas, C USA 35°56′N 90°15′W
28 I9 **Lead** South Dakota, N USA 44°21′N 103°45′W
11 S16 **Leader** Saskatchewan, S Canada 50°55′N 109°31′W
19 S6 **Lead Mountain** Maine, NE USA 44°53′N 68°07′W
37 R5 **Leadville** Colorado, C USA 39°15′N 106°17′W
11 V12 **Leaf Rapids** Manitoba, C Canada 56°30′N 100°02′W
22 M7 **Leaf River** Mississippi, S USA
25 W11 **League City** Texas, SW USA 29°30′N 95°05′W
92 K8 **Leaibevuotna** *Nor.* Olderfjord. Finnmark, N Norway 70°29′N 24°58′E
23 N7 **Leakesville** Mississippi, S USA 31°09′N 88°33′W
25 Q11 **Leakey** Texas, SW USA 29°44′N 99°48′W
Leal *see* Lihula
83 G15 **Lealui** Western, W Zambia 15°12′S 22°59′E
Leamhcán *see* Lucan
14 C18 **Leamington** Ontario, S Canada 42°03′N 82°35′W
Leamington/Leamington Spa *see* Royal Leamington Spa
Leammi *see* Lemmenjoki
25 S10 **Leander** Texas, SW USA 30°34′N 97°51′W
60 F13 **Leandro N. Alem** Misiones, NE Argentina 27°34′S 55°15′W
97 A20 **Leane, Lough** *Ir.* Loch Léin. SW Ireland
180 G8 **Learmouth** Western Australia 22°17′S 114°03′E
Leau *see* Zoutleeuw
L'Eau d'Heure *see* Plate Taille, Lac de la
190 D12 **Leava** Île Futuna, S Wallis and Futuna
Leavdnja *see* Lakselv
27 R3 **Leavenworth** Kansas, C USA 39°19′N 94°55′W
32 I8 **Leavenworth** Washington, NW USA 47°36′N 120°39′W
92 L8 **Leavvajohka** *var.* Levajok. Finnmark, N Norway 69°57′N 26°18′E
27 R4 **Leawood** Kansas, C USA 38°57′N 94°37′W
110 H6 **Łeba** *Ger.* Leba. Pomorskie, N Poland 54°45′N 17°32′E
110 I6 **Łeba** *Ger.* Leba. N Poland
Leba *see* Łeba
101 D20 **Lebach** Saarland, SW Germany 49°25′N 06°54′E
Łeba, Jezioro *see* Łebsko, Jezioro
171 P8 **Lebak** Mindanao, S Philippines 06°28′N 124°03′E
Lebanese Republic *see* Lebanon
31 O13 **Lebanon** Indiana, N USA 40°03′N 86°28′W
20 L6 **Lebanon** Kentucky, S USA 37°33′N 85°15′W
27 U6 **Lebanon** Missouri, C USA 37°40′N 92°40′W
19 N9 **Lebanon** New Hampshire, NE USA 43°40′N 72°15′W
32 G12 **Lebanon** Oregon, NW USA 44°32′N 122°54′W
18 H15 **Lebanon** Pennsylvania, NE USA 40°20′N 76°24′W
20 J8 **Lebanon** Tennessee, S USA 36°11′N 86°19′W
21 P7 **Lebanon** Virginia, NE USA 36°52′N 82°07′W
138 G6 **Lebanon** *off.* Lebanese Republic, *Ar.* Al Lubnān, *Fr.* Liban. ◆ *republic* SW Asia
20 K6 **Lebanon Junction** Kentucky, S USA 37°49′N 85°43′W
Lebanon, Mount *see* Liban, Jebel
146 J10 **Lebap** Lebapskiy Velayat, NE Turkmenistan 41°04′N 61°49′E
Lebapskiy Velayat *see* Lebap Welaýaty
146 J11 **Lebap Welaýaty** *Rus.* Lebapskiy Velayat; *prev. Rus.* Chardzhevskaya Oblast, *Turkm.* Chärjew Oblasty. *province* E Turkmenistan
Lebasee *see* Łebsko, Jezioro
99 F17 **Lebbeke** Oost-Vlaanderen, NW Belgium 51°00′N 04°08′E
35 S14 **Lebec** California, W USA 34°51′N 118°52′W
Lebedin *see* Lebedyn
123 Q11 **Lebedinyy** Respublika Sakha (Yakutiya), NE Russian Federation 58°23′N 125°24′E
126 L6 **Lebedyan'** Lipetskaya Oblast', W Russian Federation 53°00′N 39°11′E
117 T4 **Lebedyn** *Rus.* Lebedin. Sums'ka Oblast', NE Ukraine 50°36′N 34°30′E
12 I12 **Lebel-sur-Quévillon** Québec, SE Canada 49°01′N 76°56′W
92 L8 **Lebesby** Finnmark, N Norway 70°31′N 27°00′E
102 M9 **le Blanc** Indre, C France 46°38′N 01°04′E
79 L15 **Lebo** Orientale, N Dem. Rep. Congo 04°30′N 23°58′E
27 P5 **Lebo** Kansas, C USA 38°22′N 95°50′W
110 H6 **Lębork** *var.* Lębórk, *Ger.* Lauenburg, Lauenburg in Pommern. Pomorskie, N Poland 54°32′N 17°43′E
103 O17 **le Boulou** Pyrénées-Orientales, S France 42°32′N 02°50′E
108 A9 **Le Brassus** Vaud, W Switzerland 46°35′N 06°14′E
104 J15 **Lebrija** Andalucía, S Spain 36°55′N 06°04′W
110 G6 **Łebsko, Jezioro** *Ger.* Lebasee; *prev.* Jezioro Łeba. N Poland
63 F14 **Lebu** Bío Bío, C Chile 37°38′S 73°43′W
Lebyazh'ye *see* Akku
104 F6 **Leça da Palmeira** Porto, N Portugal 41°12′N 08°43′W
103 U15 **le Cannet** Alpes-Maritimes, SE France 43°35′N 07°E
Le Cap *see* Cap-Haïtien
103 P2 **le Cateau-Cambrésis** Nord, N France 50°05′N 03°32′E
107 Q18 **Lecce** Puglia, SE Italy 40°23′N 18°11′E
106 D7 **Lecco** Lombardia, N Italy 45°51′N 09°23′E
29 V10 **Le Center** Minnesota, N USA 44°23′N 93°43′W
108 J7 **Lech** Vorarlberg, W Austria 47°14′N 10°10′E
101 K22 **Lech** Austria/Germany
115 D19 **Lechainá** *var.* Lehena, Lekhainá. Dytikí Ellás, S Greece 37°57′N 21°16′E
102 J11 **le Château d'Oléron** Charente-Maritime, W France 45°53′N 01°12′W
103 R3 **le Chesne** Ardennes, N France 49°33′N 04°42′E
103 R13 **le Cheylard** Ardèche, E France 44°55′N 04°27′E
108 K7 **Lechtaler Alpen** W Austria
100 H6 **Leck** Schleswig-Holstein, N Germany 54°45′N 09°00′E
14 L9 **Lecointre, Lac** Québec, SE Canada
22 H7 **Lecompte** Louisiana, S USA 31°05′N 92°24′W
103 Q9 **le Creusot** Saône-et-Loire, C France 46°48′N 04°27′E
Lecumberri *see* Lekunberri
110 P13 **Łęczna** Lubelskie, E Poland 51°20′N 22°52′E
110 J12 **Łęczyca** *Ger.* Lentschiza, *Rus.* Lenchitsa. Łódzkie, C Poland 52°04′N 19°10′E
100 F10 **Leda** NW Germany
109 Y9 **Ledava** NE Slovenia
99 F17 **Lede** Oost-Vlaanderen, NW Belgium 50°58′N 03°59′E
104 K6 **Ledesma** Castilla-León, N Spain 41°05′N 06°00′W
45 Q12 **le Diamant** SW Martinique 14°29′N 61°02′W
172 J16 **Le Digue** *island* Inner Islands, NE Seychelles
103 Q10 **le Donjon** Allier, C France 46°19′N 03°50′E
102 M10 **le Dorat** Haute-Vienne, C France 46°14′N 01°05′E
Ledo Salinarius *see* Lons-le-Saunier
159 U10 **Ledu** Qinghai, China 36°18′N 102°13′E
11 Q14 **Leduc** Alberta, SW Canada 53°17′N 113°30′W
123 V7 **Ledyanaya, Gora** E Russian Federation 61°51′N 171°03′E
97 C21 **Lee** *Ir.* An Laoi. SW Ireland
29 U5 **Leech Lake** Minnesota, N USA
26 K10 **Leedey** Oklahoma, C USA 35°54′N 99°21′W
97 M17 **Leeds** N England, United Kingdom 53°50′N 01°35′W
23 P4 **Leeds** Alabama, S USA 33°33′N 86°32′W
29 O3 **Leeds** North Dakota, N USA 48°19′N 99°43′W
98 N6 **Leek** Groningen, NE Netherlands 53°10′N 06°24′E
99 K15 **Leende** Noord-Brabant, SE Netherlands 51°21′N 05°34′E
100 F10 **Leer** Niedersachsen, NW Germany 53°14′N 07°26′E
98 J13 **Leerdam** Zuid-Holland, C Netherlands 51°54′N 05°06′E
98 K12 **Leersum** Utrecht, C Netherlands 52°01′N 05°26′E
23 W11 **Leesburg** Florida, SE USA 28°48′N 81°52′W
21 V3 **Leesburg** Virginia, NE USA 39°09′N 77°34′W
27 R4 **Lees Summit** Missouri, C USA 38°55′N 94°21′W
22 G7 **Leesville** Louisiana, S USA 31°08′N 93°15′W
25 S12 **Leesville** Texas, SW USA 29°22′N 97°45′W
31 U13 **Leesville Lake** Ohio, N USA
Leesville Lake *see* Smith Mountain Lake
183 P9 **Leeton** New South Wales, SE Australia 34°33′S 146°24′E
98 L6 **Leeuwarden** *Fris.* Ljouwert. Friesland, N Netherlands 53°15′N 05°48′E
180 I14 **Leeuwin, Cape** *headland* Western Australia 34°18′S 115°03′E
35 R8 **Lee Vining** California, W USA 37°57′N 119°07′W
45 V8 **Leeward Islands** *island group* E West Indies
Leeward Islands *see* Sotavento, Ilhas de
Leeward Islands *see* Vent, Îles Sous le
79 G20 **Léfini** SE Congo
115 C17 **Lefkáda** *prev.* Levkás. Lefkáda, Iónia Nisiá, Greece, C Mediterranean Sea 38°50′N 20°42′E
115 B17 **Lefkáda** *It.* Santa Maura, *prev.* Levkás; *anc.* Leucas. *island* Iónia Nisiá, Greece, C Mediterranean Sea
115 H25 **Lefká Óri** Kríti, Greece, E Mediterranean Sea
115 B16 **Lefkímmi** *var.* Levkímmi. Kérkyra, Iónia Nisiá, Greece, C Mediterranean Sea 39°26′N 20°05′E
Lefkosía/Lefkoşa *see* Nicosia
25 O2 **Lefors** Texas, SW USA 35°26′N 100°48′W
45 R12 **le François** E Martinique 14°36′N 60°59′W
180 L12 **Lefroy, Lake** *salt lake* Western Australia
Legaceaster *see* Chester
105 N8 **Leganés** Madrid, C Spain 40°20′N 03°46′W
Legaspi *see* Legazpi City
Leghorn *see* Livorno
110 M11 **Legionowo** Mazowieckie, C Poland 52°25′N 20°56′E
99 K24 **Léglise** Luxembourg, SE Belgium 49°48′N 05°31′E
106 G8 **Legnago** Lombardia, NE Italy 45°13′N 11°18′E
106 D7 **Legnano** Veneto, NE Italy 45°36′N 08°54′E
111 F14 **Legnica** *Ger.* Liegnitz. Dolnośląskie, SW Poland 51°12′N 16°11′E
35 Q9 **Le Grand** California, W USA 37°12′N 120°15′W
103 Q15 **le Grau-du-Roi** Gard, S France 43°32′N 04°10′E
183 U3 **Legume** New South Wales, SE Australia 28°24′S 152°20′E
102 L4 **le Havre** *Eng.* Havre; *prev.* le Havre-de-Grâce. Seine-Maritime, N France 49°30′N 00°06′E
le Havre-de-Grâce *see* le Havre
Lehena *see* Lechainá
36 L3 **Lehi** Utah, W USA 40°23′N 111°51′W
18 I14 **Lehighton** Pennsylvania, NE USA 40°49′N 75°42′W
29 O6 **Lehr** North Dakota, N USA 46°15′N 99°21′W
38 A8 **Lehua Island** *island* Hawaiian Islands, Hawai'i, USA
149 S9 **Leiāh** Punjab, NE Pakistan 30°59′N 70°58′E
109 W9 **Leibnitz** Steiermark, SE Austria 46°48′N 15°33′E
97 M19 **Leicester** *Lat.* Batae Coritanorum. C England, United Kingdom 52°38′N 01°05′W
97 M19 **Leicestershire** *cultural region* C England, United Kingdom
Leicheng *see* Leizhou
98 H11 **Leiden** *prev.* Leyden; *anc.* Lugdunum Batavorum. Zuid-Holland, W Netherlands 52°09′N 04°30′E
98 H11 **Leiderdorp** Zuid-Holland, W Netherlands 52°08′N 04°32′E
98 G11 **Leidschendam** Zuid-Holland, W Netherlands 52°05′N 04°24′E
99 D18 **Leie** *Fr.* Lys. Belgium/France
Leifear *see* Lifford
184 L4 **Leigh** Auckland, North Island, New Zealand 36°17′S 174°48′E
97 K17 **Leigh** NW England, United Kingdom 53°30′N 02°33′W
182 I5 **Leigh Creek** South Australia 30°27′S 138°23′E
23 O2 **Leighton** Alabama, S USA 34°42′N 87°31′W
97 M21 **Leighton Buzzard** E England, United Kingdom 51°55′N 00°41′W
Léim an Bhradáin *see* Leixlip
Léim An Mhadaidh *see* Limavady
Léime, Ceann *see* Loop Head, Ireland
Léime, Ceann *see* Slyne Head, Ireland
101 G20 **Leimen** Baden-Württemberg, SW Germany 49°21′N 08°40′E
100 I13 **Leine** NW Germany
101 J15 **Leinefelde** Thüringen, C Germany 51°22′N 10°19′E
Léin, Loch *see* Leane, Lough
97 D19 **Leinster** *Ir.* Cúige Laighean. *cultural region* E Ireland
97 F19 **Leinster, Mount** *Ir.* Stua Laighean. SE Ireland 52°36′N 06°45′W
119 F15 **Leipalingis** Alytus, S Lithuania 54°05′N 23°52′E
92 J12 **Leipojärvi** Norrbotten, N Sweden 67°03′N 21°15′E
31 R12 **Leipsic** Ohio, N USA 41°06′N 83°58′W
Leipsic *see* Leipzig
115 M20 **Leipsoí** *island* Dodekánisa, Greece, Aegean Sea
101 M15 **Leipzig** *Pol.* Lipsk, *hist.* Leipsic; *anc.* Lipsia. Sachsen, E Germany 51°19′N 12°24′E
101 M15 **Leipzig Halle** Sachsen, E Germany 51°26′N 12°14′E
104 G9 **Leiria** *anc.* Collipo. Leiria, C Portugal 39°45′N 08°49′W
104 F9 **Leiria** *district* C Portugal
95 C15 **Leirvik** Hordaland, S Norway 59°49′N 05°27′E
118 E5 **Leisi** *Ger.* Laisberg. Saaremaa, W Estonia 58°33′N 22°41′E
104 J3 **Leitariegos, Puerto de** *pass* NW Spain
20 J6 **Leitchfield** Kentucky, S USA 37°28′N 86°19′W
109 Y5 **Leitha** *Hung.* Lajta. Austria/Hungary
Leitir Ceanainn *see* Letterkenny
Leitmeritz *see* Litoměřice
Leitomischl *see* Litomyšl
97 D16 **Leitrim** *Ir.* Liatroim. *cultural region* NW Ireland
Leix *see* Laois
97 F18 **Leixlip** *Eng.* Salmon Leap, *Ir.* Léim an Bhradáin. Kildare, E Ireland 53°23′N 06°32′W
64 N8 **Leixões** Porto, N Portugal 41°11′N 08°41′W
161 N12 **Leiyang** Hunan, S China 26°23′N 112°49′E
160 L16 **Leizhou** *var.* Haikang, Leicheng. Guangdong, S China 20°54′N 110°05′E
160 L16 **Leizhou Bandao** *var.* Luichow Peninsula. *peninsula* S China
98 H13 **Lek** SW Netherlands
114 I13 **Lekánis** NE Greece
172 H13 **Le Kartala** Grande Comore, NW Comoros
Le Kef *see* El Kef
79 G20 **Lékéti, Monts de la** S Congo
Lekhainá *see* Lechainá
92 G11 **Leknes** Nordland, C Norway 68°07′N 13°36′E
79 F20 **Lékoumou** *province* SW Congo
94 L13 **Leksand** Dalarna, C Sweden 60°44′N 15°E
124 H8 **Leksozero, Ozero** NW Russian Federation
105 Q3 **Lekunberri** *var.* Lecumberri. Navarra, N Spain 43°00′N 01°54′W
171 S11 **Lelai, Tanjung** *headland* Pulau Halmahera, N Indonesia 01°32′N 128°43′E
45 Q12 **le Lamentin** *var.* Lamentin. C Martinique 14°37′N 61°01′W
45 Q12 **le Lamentin** (Fort-de-France) C Martinique 14°34′N 61°00′W
31 P6 **Leland** Michigan, N USA 45°01′N 85°44′W
22 J4 **Leland** Mississippi, S USA 33°24′N 90°54′W
95 J16 **Lelång** *var.* Lelången. S Sweden
Lelången *see* Lelång
Lel'chytsy *see* Lyel'chytsy
le Léman *see* Geneva, Lake
Leli *see* Tianlin
25 O3 **Lelia Lake** Texas, SW USA 34°52′N 100°42′W
113 I14 **Lelija** SE Bosnia and Herzegovina 43°25′N 18°31′E
108 C8 **Le Locle** Neuchâtel, W Switzerland 47°04′N 06°45′E
189 Y14 **Lelu** Kosrae, E Micronesia
Lelu *see* Lelu Island
189 Y14 **Lelu Island** *var.* Lelu. *island* Kosrae, E Micronesia
55 W9 **Lelydorp** Wanica, N Surinam 05°36′N 55°04′W
98 K9 **Lelystad** Flevoland, C Netherlands 52°30′N 05°26′E
63 K25 **Le Maire, Estrecho de** *strait* S Argentina
168 L10 **Lemang** Pulau Rangsang, W Indonesia 01°04′N 102°44′E
186 I7 **Lemankoa** Buka Island, NE Papua New Guinea 05°06′S 154°23′E
Léman, Lac *see* Geneva, Lake
102 L6 **le Mans** Sarthe, NW France 48°N 00°12′E
29 S12 **Le Mars** Iowa, C USA 42°47′N 96°10′W
109 S3 **Lembach im Mühlkreis** Oberösterreich, N Austria 48°28′N 13°53′E
101 G23 **Lemberg** SW Germany 48°09′N 08°47′E
Lemberg *see* L'viv
Lemdiyya *see* Médéa
121 P3 **Lemesós** *var.* Limassol. SW Cyprus 34°41′N 33°02′E
100 H13 **Lemgo** Nordrhein-Westfalen, W Germany 52°02′N 08°54′E
33 P13 **Lemhi Range** Idaho, NW USA
9 S6 **Lemieux Islands** *island group* Nunavut, NE Canada
171 O11 **Lemito** Sulawesi, N Indonesia 0°34′N 121°31′E
92 L10 **Lemmenjoki** *Lapp.* Leammi. NE Finland
98 L7 **Lemmer** *Fris.* De Lemmer. Friesland, N Netherlands 52°50′N 05°43′E
28 L7 **Lemmon** South Dakota, N USA 45°54′N 102°08′W
36 M15 **Lemmon, Mount** Arizona, SW USA 32°26′N 110°47′W
Lemnos *see* Límnos
31 O14 **Lemon, Lake** Indiana, N USA
102 J5 **le Mont St-Michel** *castle* Manche, N France
35 Q11 **Lemoore** California, W USA 36°16′N 119°48′W
189 T13 **Lemotol Bay** *bay* Chuuk Islands, C Micronesia
45 Y5 **le Moule** *var.* Moule. Grande Terre, NE Guadeloupe 16°20′N 61°21′W
Lemovices *see* Limoges
Le Moyen-Ogooué *see* Moyen-Ogooué
12 M6 **le Moyne, Lac** Québec, E Canada
93 L18 **Lempäälä** Länsi-Suomi, W Finland 61°14′N 23°47′E
42 E7 **Lempa, Río** Central America
42 F7 **Lempira** *prev.* Gracias. *department* SW Honduras
Lemsalu *see* Limbaži
107 N17 **Le Murge** SE Italy
125 V6 **Lemva** NW Russian Federation
95 F21 **Lemvig** Ringkøbing, W Denmark 56°31′N 08°19′E
166 K8 **Lemyethna** Ayeyarwady, SW Burma (Myanmar) 17°36′N 95°08′E
30 K10 **Lena** Illinois, N USA 42°22′N 89°49′W
129 V4 **Lena** NE Russian Federation
173 N13 **Lena Tablemount** *undersea feature* S Indian Ocean 51°06′S 56°54′E
Lenchitsa *see* Łęczyca
59 N17 **Lençóis** Bahia, E Brazil 12°36′S 41°24′W
60 K9 **Lençóis Paulista** São Paulo, S Brazil 22°35′S 48°51′W
109 Y9 **Lendava** *Hung.* Lendva, *Ger.* Unterlimbach; *prev.* Dolnja Lendava. NE Slovenia 46°33′N 16°27′E
83 F20 **Lendepas** Hardap, SE Namibia 24°41′S 19°58′E
124 H9 **Lendery** *Finn.* Lentiira. Respublika Kareliya, NW Russian Federation 63°20′N 31°18′E
Lendum *see* Lens
Lendva *see* Lendava
27 R4 **Lenexa** Kansas, C USA 38°57′N 94°43′W
109 Q5 **Lengau** Oberösterreich, N Austria 48°01′N 13°17′E
145 Q17 **Lenger** Yuzhnyy Kazakhstan, S Kazakhstan 42°10′N 69°54′E
Lenghu *see* Lenghuzhen
159 O9 **Lenghuzhen** *var.* Lenghu. Qinghai, C China 38°50′N 93°25′E
159 T9 **Lenglong Ling** N China 37°40′N 102°13′E
108 D7 **Lengnau** Bern, W Switzerland 47°12′N 07°23′E
Lengshuitan *see* Yongzhou
95 M20 **Lenhovda** Kronoberg, S Sweden 57°00′N 15°16′E
Lenin *see* Uzynkol', Kazakhstan
Lenin *see* Akdepe, Turkmenistan
Leninabad *see* Khujand
Leninakan *see* Gyumri
Lenina, Pik *see* Lenin Peak
117 V12 **Lenine** *Rus.* Lenino. Respublika Krym, S Ukraine 45°18′N 35°47′E
Leningor *see* Ridder
147 Q13 **Leningrad** *Rus.* Leningradskiy; *prev.* Mü'minobod, *Rus.* Muminabad. SW Tajikistan 38°03′N 69°50′E
Leningrad *see* Sankt-Peterburg
126 L13 **Leningradskaya** Krasnodarskiy Kray, SW Russian Federation 46°19′N 39°23′E
195 S16 **Leningradskaya** *Russian research station* Antarctica 69°30′S 159°51′E
124 H12 **Leningradskaya Oblast'** *province* NW Russian Federation
Leningradskiy *see* Leningrad
Lenino *see* Lyenina, Belarus
Lenino *see* Lenine, Ukraine
Leninobod *see* Khujand
127 T5 **Leninogorsk** Respublika Tatarstan, W Russian Federation 54°34′N 52°27′E
147 T12 **Lenin Peak** *Rus.* Pik Lenina, *Taj.* Qullai Lenin. Kyrgyzstan/Tajikistan 39°20′N 72°50′E
147 S8 **Leninpol'** Talasskaya Oblast', NW Kyrgyzstan 42°29′N 71°54′E
Lenin, Qullai *see* Lenin Peak
127 P11 **Leninsk** Volgogradskaya Oblast', SW Russian Federation 48°41′N 45°18′E
Leninsk *see* Baykonyr, Kazakhstan
Leninsk *see* Akdepe, Turkmenistan
Leninsk *see* Asaka, Uzbekistan
145 T8 **Leninskiy** Pavlodar, E Kazakhstan 52°13′N 76°50′E
122 I13 **Leninsk-Kuznetskiy** Kemerovskaya Oblast', S Russian Federation 54°42′N 86°16′E
125 P15 **Leninskoje** Kirovskaya Oblast', NW Russian Federation 58°19′N 47°03′E
Leninskoye *see* Uzynkol'
Lenin-Turkmenski *see* Türkmenabat
Leninváros *see* Tiszaújváros
Lenkoran' *see* Länkäran
101 F15 **Lenne** W Germany
101 G16 **Lennestadt** Nordrhein-Westfalen, W Germany 51°07′N 08°04′E
29 R11 **Lennox** South Dakota, N USA 43°21′N 96°53′W
63 J25 **Lennox, Isla** *Eng.* Lennox Island. *island* S Chile
Lennox Island *see* Lennox, Isla
21 Q9 **Lenoir** North Carolina, SE USA 35°56′N 81°31′W
20 M9 **Lenoir City** Tennessee, S USA 35°48′N 84°15′W
108 C7 **Le Noirmont** Jura, NW Switzerland 47°14′N 06°57′E
14 L9 **Lenôtre, Lac** Québec, SE Canada
29 U15 **Lenox** Iowa, C USA 40°52′N 94°33′W
103 O2 **Lens** *anc.* Lendum, Lentium. Pas-de-Calais, N France 50°26′N 02°50′E
123 O11 **Lensk** Respublika Sakha (Yakutiya), NE Russian Federation 60°43′N 115°16′E
111 F24 **Lenti** Zala, SW Hungary 46°38′N 16°30′E
Lentia *see* Linz
93 N14 **Lentiira** Oulu, E Finland 64°22′N 29°52′E
Lentiira *see* Lendery
107 L25 **Lentini** *anc.* Leontini. Sicilia, Italy, C Mediterranean Sea 37°17′N 15°00′E
Lentium *see* Lens
Lentschiza *see* Łęczyca
93 N15 **Lentua** E Finland
119 H14 **Lentvaris** *Pol.* Landwarów. Vilnius, SE Lithuania 24°39′N 24°58′E
108 F7 **Lenzburg** Aargau, N Switzerland 47°23′N 08°11′E
109 R5 **Lenzing** Oberösterreich, N Austria 47°58′N 13°34′E
77 P13 **Léo** SW Burkina 11°07′N 02°08′W
109 V7 **Leoben** Steiermark, C Austria 47°23′N 15°06′E
Leobschütz *see* Głubczyce
44 L9 **Léogâne** S Haiti 18°32′N 72°37′W
171 O11 **Leok** Sulawesi, N Indonesia 01°10′N 121°20′E
29 O7 **Leola** South Dakota, N USA 45°41′N 98°58′W
97 K20 **Leominster** W England, United Kingdom 52°09′N 02°18′W
19 N11 **Leominster** Massachusetts, NE USA 42°29′N 71°43′W
102 I15 **Léon** Landes, SW France 43°54′N 01°17′W
40 M12 **León** *var.* León de los Aldamas. Guanajuato, C Mexico 21°05′N 101°43′W
42 I10 **León** León, NW Nicaragua 12°24′N 86°52′W
104 L4 **León** Castilla-León, NW Spain 42°34′N 05°34′W
29 V16 **Leon** Iowa, C USA 40°44′N 93°45′W
42 I9 **León** *department* W Nicaragua
104 K4 **León** *province* Castilla-León, NW Spain
León *see* Cotopaxi
25 V9 **Leona** Texas, SW USA 31°09′N 95°58′W
180 K11 **Leonara** Western Australia 28°52′S 121°16′E
25 U5 **Leonard** Texas, SW USA 33°22′N 96°15′W
107 H15 **Leonardo da Vinci** *prev.* Fiumicino. (Roma) Lazio, C Italy 41°48′N 12°15′E
21 X5 **Leonardtown** Maryland, NE USA 38°17′N 76°35′W
25 Q13 **Leona River** Texas, SW USA
41 Z11 **Leona Vicario** Quintana Roo, SE Mexico 20°57′N 87°06′W
101 H21 **Leonberg** Baden-Württemberg, SW Germany 48°48′N 09°01′E
62 M3 **León, Cerro** NW Paraguay 20°21′S 60°16′W
León de los Aldamas *see* León
109 T4 **Leonding** Oberösterreich, N Austria 48°17′N 14°15′E
107 I14 **Leonessa** Lazio, C Italy 42°36′N 12°56′E
107 K24 **Leonforte** Sicilia, Italy, C Mediterranean Sea 37°38′N 14°23′E
183 O13 **Leongatha** Victoria, SE Australia 38°30′S 145°56′E
Leonídi *see* Leonídio
115 F21 **Leonídio** *var.* Leonídi. Pelopónnisos, S Greece 37°11′N 22°50′E
104 J4 **León, Montes de** NW Spain
25 S8 **Leon River** Texas, SW USA
Leontini *see* Lentini
Léopold II, Lac *see* Mai-Ndombe, Lac
99 J17 **Leopoldsburg** Limburg, NE Belgium 51°07′N 05°16′E
Léopoldville *see* Kinshasa
26 I5 **Leoti** Kansas, C USA 38°28′N 101°22′W
116 M11 **Leova** *Rus.* Leovo. SW Moldova 46°31′N 28°16′E
Leovo *see* Leova
102 G8 **le Palais** Morbihan, NW France 47°20′N 03°08′W
27 X10 **Lepanto** Arkansas, C USA 35°34′N 90°21′W
169 N13 **Lepar, Pulau** *island* W Indonesia
104 I14 **Lepe** Andalucía, S Spain 37°15′N 07°12′W
Lepel' *see* Lyepyel'
83 I20 **Lephepe** *var.* Lephephe. Kweneng, SE Botswana 23°20′S 25°50′E
Lephephe *see* Lephepe
161 Q10 **Leping** Jiangxi, S China 28°57′N 117°07′E
Lépontiennes, Alpes/Lepontine, Alpi *see* Lepontine Alps
108 G10 **Lepontine Alps** *Fr.* Alpes Lépontiennes, *It.* Alpi Lepontine. Italy/Switzerland
79 G20 **Le Pool** *province* S Congo
173 O16 **Le Port** NW Réunion
103 N1 **le Portel** Pas-de-Calais, N France 50°42′N 01°35′E
93 N17 **Leppävirta** Itä-Suomi, C Finland 62°30′N 27°50′E
45 Q11 **le Prêcheur** NW Martinique 14°48′N 61°14′W
Lepsi *see* Lepsy
145 V13 **Lepsy** *Kaz.* Lepsi. Taldykorgan, SE Kazakhstan 46°14′N 78°56′E
145 V13 **Lepsy** *Kaz.* Lepsi. SE Kazakhstan
Le Puglie *see* Puglia
103 Q12 **le Puy** *prev.* le Puy-en-Velay, *hist.* Anicium, Podium Anicensis. Haute-Loire, C France 45°03′N 03°53′E
le Puy-en-Velay *see* le Puy
45 X11 **le Raizet** *var.* le Raizet. (Pointe-à-Pitre) Grande Terre, C Guadeloupe 16°16′N 61°31′W
107 J24 **Lercara Friddi** Sicilia, Italy, C Mediterranean Sea 37°45′N 13°37′E
78 G12 **Léré** Mayo-Kébbi, SW Chad 09°41′N 14°17′E
Leribe *see* Hlotse
106 E10 **Lerici** Liguria, NW Italy 44°06′N 09°53′E
54 I14 **Lérida** Vaupés, SE Colombia 0°01′S 70°28′W
105 U5 **Lérida** *province* Cataluña, NE Spain
Lérida *see* Lleida
105 N5 **Lerma** Castilla-León, N Spain 42°02′N 03°46′W
40 M13 **Lerma, Río** C Mexico
Lerna *see* Lérni
115 F20 **Lérni** *var.* Lerna. *prehistoric site* Pelopónnisos, S Greece
45 R11 **le Robert** E Martinique 14°41′N 60°57′W
115 M21 **Léros** *island* Dodekánisa, Greece, Aegean Sea
30 L13 **Le Roy** Illinois, N USA 40°21′N 88°45′W
27 Q6 **Le Roy** Kansas, C USA 38°04′N 95°37′W
29 W11 **Le Roy** Minnesota, N USA 43°30′N 92°30′W
18 E10 **Le Roy** New York, NE USA 42°58′N 77°58′W
Lerrnayin Gharabakh *see* Nagorno-Karabakh
95 J19 **Lerum** Västra Götaland, S Sweden 57°46′N 12°12′E
96 M2 **Lerwick** NE Scotland, United Kingdom 60°09′N 01°09′W
45 Y6 **les Abymes** *var.* Abymes. Grande Terre, C Guadeloupe 16°16′N 61°31′W
les Albères *see* Albères, Chaîne des
102 M4 **les Andelys** Eure, N France 49°15′N 01°26′E
45 Q12 **les Anses-d'Arlets** SW Martinique 14°29′N 61°05′W
105 U6 **Les Borges Blanques** *var.* Borjas Blancas. Cataluña, NE Spain 41°31′N 00°52′E
Lesbos *see* Lésvos
Les Cayes *see* Cayes
31 Q4 **Les Cheneaux Islands** *island* Michigan, N USA
105 T8 **Les Coves de Vinromá** *Cast.* Cuevas de Vinromá. País Valenciano, E Spain 40°18′N 00°07′E
103 T12 **les Écrins** E France 44°54′N 06°25′E
108 C10 **Le Sépey** Vaud, W Switzerland 46°21′N 07°04′E
15 T7 **Les Escoumins** Québec, SE Canada 48°21′N 69°26′W
Les Gonaïves *see* Gonaïves
160 H9 **Leshan** Sichuan, C China 29°42′N 103°43′E
108 D11 **Les Haudères** Valais, SW Switzerland 46°02′N 07°27′E
102 J9 **les Herbiers** Vendée, NW France 46°52′N 01°01′W
Lesh/Leshi *see* Lezhë
125 O8 **Leshukonskoye** Arkhangel'skaya Oblast', NW Russian Federation 64°54′N 45°48′E
Lesina *see* Hvar
107 M15 **Lesina, Lago di** SE Italy
114 K13 **Lesítse** NE Greece
94 G10 **Lesja** Oppland, S Norway 62°07′N 08°56′E
95 L15 **Lesjöfors** Värmland, C Sweden 59°57′N 14°12′E
111 O18 **Lesko** Podkarpackie, SE Poland 49°28′N 22°19′E
113 O15 **Leskovac** Serbia, SE Serbia 43°00′N 21°58′E
113 M22 **Leskovik** *var.* Leskoviku. Korçë, S Albania 40°09′N 20°39′E
Leskoviku *see* Leskovik
33 P14 **Leslie** Idaho, NW USA 43°51′N 113°28′W
31 Q10 **Leslie** Michigan, N USA 42°27′N 84°25′W
Lesna/Lesnaya *see* Lyasnaya
Lesnaya *see* Lyasnaya
102 F5 **Lesneven** Finistère, NW France 48°35′N 04°19′W
112 J11 **Lešnica** Serbia, W Serbia 44°40′N 19°18′E
125 S13 **Lesnoy** Kirovskaya Oblast', NW Russian Federation 59°49′N 52°07′E
122 G10 **Lesnoy** Sverdlovskaya Oblast', C Russian Federation 58°40′N 59°48′E
122 K12 **Lesosibirsk** Krasnoyarskiy Kray, C Russian Federation 58°13′N 92°23′E
83 J23 **Lesotho** *off.* Kingdom of Lesotho; *prev.* Basutoland. ◆ *monarchy* S Africa
Lesotho, Kingdom of *see* Lesotho
102 J12 **Lesparre-Médoc** Gironde, SW France 45°18′N 00°57′W
108 C8 **Les Ponts-de-Martel** Neuchâtel, W Switzerland 47°00′N 06°45′E
103 P1 **Lesquin** Nord, N France 50°34′N 03°07′E
102 I9 **les Sables-d'Olonne** Vendée, NW France 46°30′N 01°47′W
109 S7 **Lessach** *var.* Lessachbach. E Austria
Lessachbach *see* Lessach
45 W11 **les Saintes** *var.* Îles des Saintes. *island group* S Guadeloupe
74 L5 **Les Salines** (Annaba) NE Algeria 36°45′N 07°57′E
99 J22 **Lesse** SE Belgium
95 M21 **Lessebo** Kronoberg, S Sweden 56°45′N 15°19′E
Lesser Antarctica *see* West Antarctica
45 P15 **Lesser Antilles** *island group* E West Indies
137 T10 **Lesser Caucasus** *Rus.* Malyy Kavkaz. SW Asia
Lesser Khingan Range *see* Xiao Hinggan Ling
11 P13 **Lesser Slave Lake** Alberta, W Canada
99 E19 **Lessines** Hainaut, SW Belgium 50°43′N 03°50′E
172 J16 **Les Sœurs** *island* Les Sœurs, NE Seychelles
103 R16 **les Stes-Maries-de-la-Mer** Bouches-du-Rhône, SE France 43°27′N 04°26′E

◆ Country
● Country Capital
◇ Dependent Territory
○ Dependent Territory Capital
Administrative Regions
International Airport
Mountain
Mountain Range
Volcano
River
Lake
Reservoir

14 G15 **Lester B. Pearson** var. Toronto. ✈ (Toronto) Ontario, S Canada 43°59′N 81°30′W
29 U9 **Lester Prairie** Minnesota, N USA 44°52′N 94°02′W
93 L16 **Lestijärvi** Länsi-Suomi, W Finland 63°29′N 24°41′E
L'Estuaire see Estuaire
29 U9 **Le Sueur** Minnesota, N USA 44°27′N 93°53′W
108 B8 **Les Verrières** Neuchâtel, W Switzerland 46°54′N 06°29′E
115 L17 **Lésvos** anc. Lesbos. island E Greece
110 G12 **Leszno** Ger. Lissa. Wielkopolskie, C Poland 51°51′N 16°35′E
83 L20 **Letaba** Northern, NE South Africa 23°44′S 31°29′E
173 P17 **Le Tampon** SW Réunion
97 O21 **Letchworth** E England, United Kingdom 51°58′N 00°14′W
111 G25 **Letenye** Zala, SW Hungary 46°25′N 16°44′E
11 Q17 **Lethbridge** Alberta, SW Canada 49°43′N 112°48′W
55 S11 **Lethem** S Guyana 03°24′N 59°45′W
83 H18 **Letiahau** ≈ W Botswana
54 J18 **Leticia** Amazonas, S Colombia 04°09′N 69°57′W
171 S16 **Leti, Kepulauan** island group E Indonesia
83 I18 **Letlhakane** Central, C Botswana 21°26′S 25°36′E
83 H20 **Letlhakeng** Kweneng, SE Botswana 24°05′S 25°03′E
114 J8 **Letnitsa** Lovech, N Bulgaria 43°19′N 25°02′E
103 N1 **le Touquet-Paris-Plage** Pas-de-Calais, N France 50°31′N 01°36′E
166 L8 **Letpadan** Bago, SW Burma (Myanmar) 17°46′N 94°45′E
166 K6 **Letpan** Rakhine State, W Burma (Myanmar) 19°22′N 94°11′E
102 M2 **le Tréport** Seine-Maritime, N France 50°03′N 01°21′E
166 M12 **Letsôk-aw Kyun** var. Letsutan Island; prev. Domel Island. island Mergui Archipelago, S Burma (Myanmar)
Letsutan Island see Letsôk-aw Kyun
97 E14 **Letterkenny** Ir. Leitir Ceanainn. Donegal, NW Ireland 54°57′N 07°44′W
Lettland see Latvia
116 M6 **Letychiv** Khmel'nyts'ka Oblast', W Ukraine 49°24′N 27°39′E
Lëtzebuerg see Luxembourg
116 H14 **Leu** Dolj, SW Romania 44°10′N 24°01′E
Leucas see Lefkáda
103 P17 **Leucate** Aude, S France 42°55′N 03°03′E
103 P17 **Leucate, Étang de** ◎ S France
108 E10 **Leuk** Valais, SW Switzerland 46°18′N 07°46′E
108 E10 **Leukerbad** Valais, SW Switzerland 46°22′N 07°47′E
Leusden see Leusden-Centrum
98 K11 **Leusden-Centrum** var. Leusden. Utrecht, C Netherlands 52°08′N 05°25′E
Leutensdorf see Litvínov
Leutschau see Levoča
99 H18 **Leuven** Fr. Louvain, Ger. Löwen. Vlaams Brabant, C Belgium 50°53′N 04°42′E
99 I20 **Leuze** Namur, C Belgium 50°33′N 04°55′E
Leuze see Leuze-en-Hainaut
99 E19 **Leuze-en-Hainaut** var. Leuze. Hainaut, SW Belgium 50°36′N 03°37′E
Léva see Levice
Levádia see Livádeia
Levajok see Leavvajohka
36 L4 **Levan** Utah, W USA 39°33′N 111°51′W
93 E16 **Levanger** Nord-Trøndelag, C Norway 63°45′N 11°18′E
106 D10 **Levanto** Liguria, W Italy 44°12′N 09°33′E
107 H23 **Levanzo, Isola di** island Isole Egadi, S Italy
127 Q17 **Levashi** Respublika Dagestan, SW Russian Federation 42°27′N 47°19′E
24 M5 **Levelland** Texas, SW USA 33°35′N 102°23′W
39 P13 **Levelock** Alaska, USA 59°07′N 156°51′W
101 E16 **Leverkusen** Nordrhein-Westfalen, W Germany 51°02′N 07°E
111 J21 **Levice** Ger. Lewentz, Hung. Léva, Lewenz. Nitriansky Kraj, SW Slovakia 48°14′N 18°38′E
106 G6 **Levico Terme** Trentino-Alto Adige, N Italy 46°02′N 11°19′E
115 E20 **Levídi** Pelopónnisos, S Greece 37°39′N 22°13′E
103 P14 **le Vigan** Gard, S France 43°00′N 03°36′E
184 L13 **Levin** Manawatu-Wanganui, North Island, New Zealand 40°38′S 175°17′E
15 R10 **Lévis** var. Levis. Québec, SE Canada 46°47′N 71°12′W
Levis see Lévis
21 P6 **Levisa Fork** ≈ Kentucky/Virginia, S USA
115 L21 **Levítha** island Kykládes, Greece, Aegean Sea
18 L14 **Levittown** Long Island, New York, NE USA 40°42′N 73°29′W
18 J15 **Levittown** Pennsylvania, NE USA 40°09′N 74°50′W
Levkás see Lefkáda
Levkímmi see Lefkímmi
111 L19 **Levoča** Ger. Leutschau, Hung. Locse. Prešovský Kraj, E Slovakia 49°01′N 20°34′E
Lévrier, Baie du see Nouâdhibou, Dakhlet
103 N9 **Levroux** Indre, C France 47°00′N 01°37′E
114 J8 **Levski** Pleven, N Bulgaria 43°21′N 25°11′E
Levskigrad see Karlovo
126 L6 **Lev Tolstoy** Lipetskaya Oblast', W Russian Federation 53°12′N 39°28′E
187 X14 **Levuka** Ovalau, C Fiji 17°42′S 178°50′E
166 L6 **Lewe** Mandalay, C Burma (Myanmar) 19°40′N 96°04′E
Lewentz/Lewenz see Levice
97 O23 **Lewes** SE England, United Kingdom 50°52′N 00°01′E
21 Z4 **Lewes** Delaware, NE USA 38°46′N 75°08′W
29 Q12 **Lewis And Clark Lake** ⊠ Nebraska/South Dakota, N USA
18 G14 **Lewisburg** Pennsylvania, NE USA 40°57′N 76°52′W
20 J10 **Lewisburg** Tennessee, S USA 35°29′N 86°49′W
21 S6 **Lewisburg** West Virginia, NE USA 37°49′N 80°28′W
96 F6 **Lewis, Butt of** headland NW Scotland, United Kingdom 58°31′N 06°18′W
96 F7 **Lewis, Isle of** island NW Scotland, United Kingdom
35 U4 **Lewis, Mount** ▲ Nevada, W USA 40°22′N 116°50′W
185 H16 **Lewis Pass** pass South Island, New Zealand
33 P7 **Lewis Range** ▲▲ Montana, NW USA
23 O3 **Lewis Smith Lake** ⊠ Alabama, S USA
32 M10 **Lewiston** Idaho, NW USA 46°25′N 117°01′W
19 P7 **Lewiston** Maine, NE USA 44°08′N 70°14′W
29 X10 **Lewiston** Minnesota, N USA 43°58′N 91°52′W
18 D9 **Lewiston** New York, NE USA 43°10′N 79°02′W
36 L1 **Lewiston** Utah, W USA 41°58′N 111°52′W
30 K13 **Lewistown** Illinois, N USA 40°23′N 90°09′W
33 T9 **Lewistown** Montana, NW USA 47°04′N 109°26′W
27 T14 **Lewisville** Arkansas, C USA 33°21′N 93°38′W
25 T6 **Lewisville** Texas, SW USA 33°00′N 96°57′W
25 T6 **Lewisville, Lake** ⊠ Texas, SW USA
Le Woleu-Ntem see Woleu-Ntem
23 U3 **Lexington** Georgia, SE USA 33°51′N 83°04′W
20 M5 **Lexington** Kentucky, S USA 38°03′N 84°30′W
22 L4 **Lexington** Mississippi, S USA 33°06′N 90°03′W
27 S4 **Lexington** Missouri, C USA 39°11′N 93°52′W
29 N16 **Lexington** Nebraska, C USA 40°46′N 99°44′W
20 S9 **Lexington** North Carolina, SE USA 35°49′N 80°15′W
27 N11 **Lexington** Oklahoma, C USA 35°00′N 97°20′W
21 R12 **Lexington** South Carolina, SE USA 33°59′N 81°15′W
20 G9 **Lexington** Tennessee, S USA 35°39′N 88°24′W
25 T10 **Lexington** Texas, SW USA 30°25′N 97°00′W
21 T6 **Lexington** Virginia, NE USA 37°47′N 79°27′W
21 X5 **Lexington Park** Maryland, NE USA 38°16′N 76°27′W
Leyden see Leiden
102 J14 **Leyre** ≈ SW France
171 Q5 **Leyte** island C Philippines
171 Q6 **Leyte Gulf** gulf E Philippines
111 O16 **Leżajsk** Podkarpackie, SE Poland 50°15′N 22°25′E
Lezha see Lezhë
113 K18 **Lezhë** var. Lezha; prev. Lesh, Leshi. Lezhë, NW Albania 41°46′N 19°40′E
113 K18 **Lezhë** ◐ district NW Albania
103 O16 **Lézignan-Corbières** Aude, S France 43°12′N 02°46′E
126 J7 **L'gov** Kurskaya Oblast', W Russian Federation 51°38′N 35°17′E
159 P15 **Lhari** Xizang Zizhiqu, W China 30°34′N 93°40′E
159 N16 **Lhasa** var. La-sa, Lassa. Xizang Zizhiqu, W China 29°41′N 91°10′E
159 O15 **Lhasa He** ≈ W China
Lhaviyani Atoll see Faadhippolhu Atoll
158 K16 **Lhazê** var. Quxar. Xizang Zizhiqu, W China 29°07′N 87°32′E
158 K14 **Lhazhong** Xizang Zizhiqu, W China 31°58′N 86°43′E
168 H7 **Lhoksukon** Sumatera, W Indonesia 05°04′N 97°19′E
159 Q15 **Lhorong** var. Zito. Xizang Zizhiqu, W China 30°51′N 95°41′E
105 W6 **L'Hospitalet de Llobregat** var. Hospitalet. Cataluña, NE Spain 41°21′N 02°06′E
153 R11 **Lhotse** ▲ China/Nepal 28°00′N 86°55′E
159 N17 **Lhozhag** var. Garbo. Xizang Zizhiqu, W China 28°21′N 90°47′E
159 O16 **Lhünzê** var. Xingba. Xizang Zizhiqu, W China 28°25′N 92°30′E
159 N15 **Lhünzhub** var. Ganqu. Xizang Zizhiqu, W China 30°14′N 91°20′E
167 N8 **Li** Lamphun, NW Thailand 17°46′N 98°54′E
115 L21 **Liádi** var. Livádi. island Kykládes, Greece, Aegean Sea
Liancheng see Lianjiang, Guangdong, China
Liancheng see Qinglong, Guizhou, China
Liancheng see Guangnan, Yunnan, China
Lianfeng see Liangcheng
161 P12 **Liangcheng** var. Lianfeng. Fujian, SE China 25°47′N 116°42′E
160 K9 **Liangping** var. Liangshan. Sichuan, C China 30°40′N 107°46′E
Liangshan see Liangping
Liangzhou see Wuwei
161 O9 **Liangzi Hu** ⊠ C China
161 R12 **Lianjiang** var. Fengcheng. Fujian, SE China 26°14′N 119°33′E
160 L15 **Lianjiang** var. Liancheng. Guangdong, S China 21°41′N 110°12′E
Lianjiang see Xingguo
161 O13 **Lianping** var. Yuanshan. Guangdong, S China 24°18′N 114°27′E
Lianshan see Huludao
Lian Xian see Lianzhou
160 M11 **Lianyuan** prev. Lantian. Hunan, S China 27°51′N 111°44′E
161 Q6 **Lianyungang** var. Xinpu. Jiangsu, E China 34°38′N 119°12′E
161 N13 **Lianzhou** var. Linxian; prev. Lian Xian. Guangdong, S China 24°48′N 112°26′E
Lianzhou see Hepu
Liao see Liaoning
161 P5 **Liaocheng** Shandong, E China 36°31′N 115°59′E
163 U13 **Liaodong Bandao** var. Liaotung Peninsula. peninsula NE China
163 T13 **Liaodong Wan** Eng. Gulf of Lantung, Gulf of Liaotung. gulf NE China
163 U11 **Liao He** ≈ NE China
163 U12 **Liaoning** var. Liao, Liaoning Sheng, Shengking, hist. Fengtien, Shenking. ◐ province NE China
Liaoning Sheng see Liaoning
Liaotung Peninsula see Liaodong Bandao
163 V12 **Liaoyang** var. Liao-yang. Liaoning, NE China 41°16′N 123°12′E
Liao-yang see Liaoyang
163 V11 **Liaoyuan** var. Dongliao, Shuang-liao, Jap. Chengchiatun. Jilin, NE China 42°52′N 125°09′E
163 U12 **Liaozhong** Liaoning, NE China 41°33′N 122°54′E
Liaqatabad see Piplān
10 M10 **Liard** ≈ W Canada
Liard see Fort Liard
10 L10 **Liard River** British Columbia, W Canada 59°23′N 126°05′W
149 O15 **Liāri** Baluchistān, SW Pakistan 25°43′N 66°28′E
Liatroim see Leitrim
189 S6 **Lib** var. Ellep. island Ralik Chain, C Marshall Islands
Liban see Lebanon
138 H6 **Liban, Jebel** Ar. Jabal al Gharbt, Jabal Lubnān, Eng. Mount Lebanon. ▲▲ C Lebanon
Libau see Liepāja
33 N7 **Libby** Montana, NW USA 48°25′N 115°33′W
79 I16 **Libenge** Equateur, NW Dem. Rep. Congo 03°39′N 18°39′E
26 I7 **Liberal** Kansas, C USA 37°03′N 100°56′W
27 R7 **Liberal** Missouri, C USA 37°33′N 94°31′W
Liberalitas Julia see Évora
111 D15 **Liberec** Ger. Reichenberg. Liberecký Kraj, N Czech Republic 50°45′N 15°05′E
111 D15 **Liberecky Kraj** ◐ region N Czech Republic
42 K12 **Liberia** Guanacaste, NW Costa Rica 10°36′N 85°26′W
76 K17 **Liberia** off. Republic of Liberia. ◆ republic W Africa
Liberia, Republic of see Liberia
61 D16 **Libertad** Corrientes, NE Argentina 30°01′S 57°51′W
61 E20 **Libertad** San José, S Uruguay 34°38′S 56°39′W
54 I7 **Libertad** Barinas, NW Venezuela 08°21′N 69°39′W
54 K6 **Libertad** Cojedes, N Venezuela 09°15′N 68°30′W
62 G12 **Libertador** off. Región del Libertador General Bernardo O'Higgins. ◐ region C Chile
Libertador General Bernardo O'Higgins, Región del see Libertador
Libertador General San Martín see Ciudad de Libertador General San Martín
20 L6 **Liberty** Kentucky, S USA 37°19′N 84°58′W
22 J7 **Liberty** Mississippi, S USA 31°09′N 90°49′W
27 R4 **Liberty** Missouri, C USA 39°15′N 94°22′W
18 J12 **Liberty** New York, NE USA 41°48′N 74°45′W
21 T9 **Liberty** North Carolina, SE USA 35°49′N 79°34′W
Libian Desert see Libyan Desert
99 J23 **Libin** Luxembourg, SE Belgium 50°01′N 05°13′E
Lībīyah, Aş Şahrā' al see Libyan Desert
160 K13 **Libo** var. Yuping. Guizhou, S China 25°28′N 107°52′E
Libohova see Libohovë
113 L23 **Libohovë** var. Libohova. Gjirokastër, S Albania 40°03′N 20°13′E
81 K18 **Liboi** North Eastern, E Kenya 0°23′N 40°55′E
102 K13 **Libourne** Gironde, SW France 44°55′N 00°14′W
99 K23 **Libramont** Luxembourg, SE Belgium 49°55′N 05°21′E
113 M20 **Librazhd** var. Librazhdi. Elbasan, E Albania 41°10′N 20°22′E
Librazhdi see Librazhd
79 C18 **Libreville** ● (Gabon) Estuaire, NW Gabon 0°25′N 09°29′E
75 P10 **Libya** off. Great Socialist People's Libyan Arab Jamahiriya, Ar. Al Jamāhīrīyah al 'Arabīyah al Lībīyah ash Sha'bīyah al Ishtirākīy; prev. Libyan Arab Republic. ◆ Islamic state N Africa
Libyan Arab Republic see Libya
75 T11 **Libyan Desert** var. Libian Desert, Ar. Aş Şahrā' al Lībīyah. desert N Africa
75 T8 **Libyan Plateau** var. Aḑ Ḑiffah. plateau Egypt/Libya
62 G12 **Licantén** Maule, C Chile 35°00′S 72°00′W
107 J25 **Licata** anc. Phintias. Sicilia, Italy, C Mediterranean Sea 37°07′N 13°57′E
137 P14 **Lice** Dıyarbakır, SE Turkey 38°29′N 40°39′E
Licheng see Lipu
97 L19 **Lichfield** C England, United Kingdom 52°42′N 01°48′W
83 N14 **Lichinga** Niassa, N Mozambique 13°19′S 35°13′E
109 V3 **Lichtenau** Niederösterreich, N Austria 48°29′N 15°24′E
83 I21 **Lichtenburg** North-West, N South Africa 26°09′S 26°11′E
101 K18 **Lichtenfels** Bayern, SE Germany 50°09′N 11°04′E
98 O12 **Lichtenvoorde** Gelderland, E Netherlands 51°59′N 06°34′E
Lichtenwald see Sevnica
99 C17 **Lichtervelde** West-Vlaanderen, W Belgium 51°02′N 03°09′E
160 L9 **Lichuan** Hubei, C China 30°20′N 108°56′E
27 V7 **Licking** Missouri, C USA 37°30′N 91°51′W
20 M4 **Licking River** ≈ Kentucky, S USA
112 C11 **Lički Osik** Lika-Senj, C Croatia 44°36′N 15°24′E
Ličko-Senjska Županija see Lika-Senj
107 K19 **Licosa, Punta** headland S Italy 40°15′N 14°54′E
119 H16 **Lida** Hrodzyenskaya Voblasts', W Belarus 53°53′N 25°20′E
93 H17 **Liden** Västernorrland, C Sweden 62°43′N 16°49′E
29 R7 **Lidgerwood** North Dakota, N USA 46°04′N 97°09′W
Lidhorikíon see Lidoríki
95 K21 **Lidhult** Kronoberg, S Sweden 56°49′N 13°25′E
95 P16 **Lidingö** Stockholm, C Sweden 59°22′N 18°10′E
95 K17 **Lidköping** Västra Götaland, S Sweden 58°30′N 13°10′E
Lido di Iesolo see Lido di Jesolo
106 I8 **Lido di Jesolo** var. Lido di Iesolo. Veneto, NE Italy 45°30′N 12°37′E
107 H15 **Lido di Ostia** Lazio, C Italy 41°42′N 12°19′E
Lidokhorikion see Lidoríki
115 E18 **Lidoríki** prev. Lidhorikíon, Lidokhorikion. Stereá Ellás, C Greece 38°32′N 22°12′E
110 K9 **Lidzbark** Warmińsko-Mazurskie, NE Poland 53°15′N 19°49′E
110 L7 **Lidzbark Warmiński** Ger. Heilsberg. Olsztyn, N Poland 54°08′N 20°35′E
109 U3 **Liebenau** Oberösterreich, N Austria 48°33′N 14°48′E
181 P7 **Liebig, Mount** ▲ Northern Territory, C Australia 23°19′S 131°30′E
109 V8 **Lieboch** Steiermark, SE Austria 47°00′N 15°21′E
108 I8 **Liechtenstein** off. Principality of Liechtenstein. ◆ principality C Europe
Liechtenstein, Principality of see Liechtenstein
99 F18 **Liedekerke** Vlaams Brabant, C Belgium 50°51′N 04°05′E
99 K19 **Liège** Dut. Luik, Ger. Lüttich. Liège, E Belgium 50°38′N 05°35′E
99 K20 **Liège** Dut. Luik. ◐ province E Belgium
Liegnitz see Legnica
93 O16 **Lieksa** Itä-Suomi, E Finland 63°20′N 30°E
118 F10 **Lielupe** ≈ Latvia/Lithuania
118 G9 **Lielvārde** Ogre, C Latvia 56°45′N 24°48′E
167 U13 **Liên Hương** var. Tuy Phong. Binh Thuận, S Vietnam 11°13′N 108°40′E
Liên Nghia see Đưc Trong
109 P9 **Lienz** Tirol, W Austria 46°50′N 12°45′E
118 B10 **Liepāja** Ger. Libau. Liepāja, W Latvia 56°32′N 21°02′E
99 H17 **Lier** Fr. Lierre. Antwerpen, N Belgium 51°08′N 04°35′E
95 H15 **Lierbyen** Buskerud, S Norway 59°57′N 10°14′E
99 L21 **Lierneux** Liège, E Belgium 50°12′N 05°51′E
Lierre see Lier
101 D18 **Lieser** ≈ W Germany
109 U7 **Liesing** ≈ E Austria
108 E6 **Liestal** Basel-Land, N Switzerland 47°29′N 07°43′E
Lietuva see Lithuania
Lievenhof see Līvāni
103 O2 **Liévin** Pas-de-Calais, N France 50°25′N 02°48′E
14 M9 **Lièvre, Rivière du** ≈ Québec, SE Canada
109 T6 **Liezen** Steiermark, C Austria 47°34′N 14°12′E
97 E14 **Lifford** Ir. Leifear. Donegal, NW Ireland 54°50′N 07°29′W
187 Q16 **Lifou** island Îles Loyauté, E New Caledonia
193 Y15 **Lifuka** island Ha'apai Group, C Tonga
171 P4 **Ligao** Luzon, N Philippines 13°16′N 123°30′E
Liger see Loire
42 H2 **Lighthouse Reef** reef E Belize
183 Q4 **Lightning Ridge** New South Wales, SE Australia 29°29′S 148°00′E
103 N9 **Lignières** Cher, C France 46°45′N 02°10′E
103 S5 **Ligny-en-Barrois** Meuse, NE France 48°42′N 05°22′E
83 P15 **Ligonha** ≈ NE Mozambique
31 P11 **Ligonier** Indiana, N USA 41°25′N 85°33′W
81 I25 **Ligunga** Ruvuma, S Tanzania 10°51′S 37°10′E
106 D9 **Ligure, Appennino** Eng. Ligurian Mountains. ▲▲ NW Italy
Ligure, Mar see Ligurian Sea
106 C9 **Liguria** ◐ region NW Italy
Ligurian Mountains see Ligure, Appennino
120 K6 **Ligurian Sea** Fr. Mer Ligurienne, It. Mar Ligure. sea N Mediterranean Sea
Ligurienne, Mer see Ligurian Sea
186 H5 **Lihir Group** island group NE Papua New Guinea
38 B8 **Līhu'e** var. Lihue. Kaua'i, Hawaii, USA 21°59′N 159°23′W
Lihue see Līhu'e
118 F5 **Lihula** Ger. Leal. Läänemaa, W Estonia 58°44′N 23°49′E
124 I2 **Liinakhamari** var. Linacmamari. Murmanskaya Oblast', NW Russian Federation 69°40′N 31°27′E
Liivi Laht see Riga, Gulf of
160 F11 **Lijiang** var. Dayan, Lijiang Naxizu Zizhixian. Yunnan, SW China 26°52′N 100°10′E
Lijiang Naxizu Zizhixian see Lijiang
112 C11 **Lika-Senj** off. Ličko-Senjska Županija. ◐ province W Croatia
79 N25 **Likasi** prev. Jadotville. Shaba, SE Dem. Rep. Congo 11°02′S 26°51′E
79 L16 **Likati** Orientale, N Dem. Rep. Congo 03°28′N 23°45′E
10 M15 **Likely** British Columbia, SW Canada 52°40′N 121°34′W
153 Y11 **Likhapāni** Assam, NE India 27°19′N 95°54′E
124 J16 **Likhoslavl'** Tverskaya Oblast', W Russian Federation 57°08′N 35°27′E
189 U5 **Likiep Atoll** atoll Ratak Chain, C Marshall Islands
95 D18 **Liknes** Vest-Agder, S Norway 58°20′N 06°58′E
79 H16 **Likouala** ◐ province NE Congo
79 H18 **Likouala** ≈ N Congo
79 H18 **Likouala aux Herbes** ≈ E Congo
190 B16 **Liku** E Niue 19°02′S 169°47′E
Likupang, Selat see Bangka, Selat
27 Y8 **Lilbourn** Missouri, C USA 36°35′N 89°37′W
103 X14 **l'Île-Rousse** Corse, France, C Mediterranean Sea 42°39′N 08°59′E
109 W5 **Lilienfeld** Niederösterreich, NE Austria 48°01′N 15°36′E
161 N11 **Liling** Hunan, S China 27°42′N 113°49′E
95 J18 **Lilla Edet** Västra Götaland, S Sweden 58°08′N 12°08′E
103 P1 **Lille** var. l'Isle, Dut. Rijssel, Flem. Ryssel, prev. Lisle; anc. Insula. Nord, N France 50°38′N 03°04′E
95 G24 **Lillebælt** var. Lille Bælt, Eng. Little Belt. strait S Denmark
Lille Bælt see Lillebælt
102 L3 **Lillebonne** Seine-Maritime, N France 49°30′N 00°34′E
94 H12 **Lillehammer** Oppland, S Norway 61°07′N 10°28′E
103 O1 **Lillers** Pas-de-Calais, N France 50°34′N 02°26′E
95 F18 **Lillesand** Aust-Agder, S Norway 58°15′N 08°23′E
95 I15 **Lillestrøm** Akershus, S Norway 59°58′N 11°05′E
93 F18 **Lillhärdal** Jämtland, C Sweden 61°51′N 14°04′E
21 U10 **Lillington** North Carolina, SE USA 35°25′N 78°50′W
105 O9 **Lillo** Castilla-La Mancha, C Spain 39°43′N 03°19′W
10 M16 **Lillooet** British Columbia, SW Canada 50°41′N 121°59′W
83 M14 **Lilongwe** ● (Malawi) Central, W Malawi 13°58′S 33°48′E
83 M14 **Lilongwe** ✈ Central, W Malawi 13°46′S 33°44′E
83 M14 **Lilongwe** ≈ W Malawi
171 P7 **Liloy** Mindanao, S Philippines 08°04′N 122°42′E
Lilybaeum see Marsala
182 J7 **Lilydale** South Australia 32°57′S 140°00′E
183 P16 **Lilydale** Tasmania, SE Australia 41°17′S 147°13′E
113 J14 **Lim** ≈ SE Europe
57 D15 **Lima** ● (Peru) Lima, W Peru 12°06′S 78°W
94 K13 **Lima** Dalarna, C Sweden 60°55′N 13°19′E
31 R12 **Lima** Ohio, NE USA 40°43′N 84°06′W
57 D14 **Lima** ◐ department W Peru
Lima see Jorge Chávez International
127 R13 **Liman** Astrakhanskaya Oblast', SW Russian Federation 45°48′N 47°17′E
111 L17 **Limanowa** Małopolskie, S Poland 49°43′N 20°25′E
104 G5 **Lima, Rio** Sp. Limia. ≈ Portugal/Spain see also Limia
Lima, Rio see Limia
168 M11 **Limas** Pulau Sebangka, W Indonesia 0°09′N 104°31′E
Limassol see Lemesós
97 F14 **Limavady** Ir. Léim An Mhadaidh. NW Northern Ireland, United Kingdom 55°03′N 06°57′W
63 J14 **Limay Mahuida** La Pampa, C Argentina 37°09′S 66°40′W
63 H15 **Limay, Río** ≈ W Argentina
101 N16 **Limbach-Oberfrohna** Sachsen, E Germany 50°52′N 12°46′E
81 F22 **Limba Limba** ≈ C Tanzania
107 C17 **Limbara, Monte** ▲ Sardegna, Italy, C Mediterranean Sea 40°50′N 09°10′E
118 G7 **Limbaži** Est. Lemsalu. Limbaži, N Latvia 57°33′N 24°46′E
44 M8 **Limbé** N Haiti 19°44′N 72°25′W
99 L19 **Limbourg** Liège, E Belgium 50°37′N 05°56′E
99 K17 **Limburg** ◐ province NE Belgium
99 L16 **Limburg** ◐ province SE Netherlands
101 F17 **Limburg an der Lahn** Hessen, W Germany 50°22′N 08°04′E
94 K13 **Limedsforsen** Dalarna, C Sweden 60°52′N 13°25′E
60 L9 **Limeira** São Paulo, S Brazil 22°34′S 47°25′W
97 C19 **Limerick** Ir. Luimneach. Limerick, SW Ireland 52°40′N 08°38′W
97 C20 **Limerick** Ir. Luimneach. cultural region SW Ireland
19 S2 **Limestone** Maine, NE USA 46°52′N 67°49′W
25 U9 **Limestone, Lake** ◎ Texas, SW USA
39 P12 **Lime Village** Alaska, USA 61°21′N 155°26′W
95 F20 **Limfjorden** fjord N Denmark
95 J23 **Limhamn** Skåne, S Sweden 55°34′N 12°57′E
104 H5 **Limia** Port. Rio Lima. ≈ Portugal/Spain see also Lima, Rio
Limia see Lima, Rio
93 L14 **Liminka** Oulu, C Finland 64°48′N 25°19′E
Limín Vathéos see Sámos
115 G17 **Límni** Évvoia, C Greece 38°46′N 23°20′E
115 J15 **Límnos** anc. Lemnos. island E Greece
102 M11 **Limoges** anc. Augustoritum Lemovicensium, Lemovices. Haute-Vienne, C France 45°51′N 01°16′E
43 O13 **Limón** var. Puerto Limón. Limón, E Costa Rica 09°59′N 83°02′W
42 K4 **Limón** Colón, NE Honduras 15°50′N 85°31′W
37 U5 **Limon** Colorado, C USA 39°15′N 103°41′W
43 N13 **Limón** off. Provincia de Limón. ◐ province E Costa Rica
106 A10 **Limone Piemonte** Piemonte, NE Italy 44°12′N 07°37′E
Limones see Valdéz
Limón, Provincia de see Limón
Limonum see Poitiers
103 N11 **Limousin** ◐ region C France
103 N16 **Limoux** Aude, S France 43°03′N 02°13′E
83 J20 **Limpopo** off. Limpopo Province; prev. Northern, Northern Transvaal. ◐ province NE South Africa
83 L19 **Limpopo** var. Crocodile. ≈ S Africa
Limpopo Province see Limpopo
160 K17 **Limu Ling** ▲▲ S China
113 M20 **Lin** var. Lini. Elbasan, E Albania 41°03′N 20°37′E
Linacmamari see Liinakhamari
62 G13 **Linares** Maule, C Chile 35°50′S 71°37′W
54 C13 **Linares** Nariño, SW Colombia 01°24′N 77°30′W
41 O9 **Linares** Nuevo León, NE Mexico 24°54′N 99°38′W
105 N12 **Linares** Andalucía, S Spain 38°05′N 03°38′W
107 G15 **Linaro, Capo** headland C Italy 42°01′N 11°49′E
106 D8 **Linate** ✈ (Milano) Lombardia, N Italy 45°27′N 09°18′E
167 T8 **Lin Camh** prev. Đưc Tho. Ha Tinh, N Vietnam 18°30′N 105°36′E
160 F13 **Lincang** Yunnan, SW China 23°55′N 100°03′E
Lincheng see Lingao
61 B20 **Lincoln** Buenos Aires, E Argentina 34°54′S 61°30′W
185 H19 **Lincoln** Canterbury, South Island, New Zealand 43°37′S 172°30′E
97 N18 **Lincoln** anc. Lindum, Lindum Colonia. E England, United Kingdom 53°14′N 00°33′W
35 O6 **Lincoln** California, W USA 38°52′N 121°18′W
30 L13 **Lincoln** Illinois, N USA 40°09′N 89°21′W
26 M4 **Lincoln** Kansas, C USA 39°03′N 98°09′W
19 S5 **Lincoln** Maine, NE USA 45°22′N 68°30′W
27 T5 **Lincoln** Missouri, C USA 38°23′N 93°19′W
29 R16 **Lincoln** state capital Nebraska, C USA 40°46′N 96°43′W
32 F11 **Lincoln City** Oregon, NW USA 44°57′N 124°01′W
167 X10 **Lincoln Island** island E Paracel Islands
197 Q11 **Lincoln Sea** sea Arctic Ocean
97 N18 **Lincolnshire** cultural region E England, United Kingdom
21 R10 **Lincolnton** North Carolina, SE USA 35°27′N 81°16′W
25 V7 **Lindale** Texas, SW USA 32°31′N 95°24′W
101 I25 **Lindau** var. Lindau am Bodensee. Bayern, S Germany 47°33′N 09°41′E
Lindau am Bodensee see Lindau
123 P9 **Linde** ≈ NE Russian Federation
55 T9 **Linden** E Guyana 05°58′N 58°12′W
23 O6 **Linden** Alabama, S USA 32°18′N 87°48′W
20 H9 **Linden** Tennessee, S USA 35°38′N 87°50′W
25 X6 **Linden** Texas, SW USA 33°01′N 94°22′W
18 J16 **Lindenwold** New Jersey, NE USA 39°47′N 74°58′W
95 M15 **Lindesberg** Örebro, C Sweden 59°36′N 15°15′E
95 D18 **Lindesnes** headland S Norway 57°58′N 07°03′E
Líndhos see Líndos
81 K24 **Lindi** Lindi, SE Tanzania 10°S 39°41′E
81 J24 **Lindi** ◐ region SE Tanzania
79 N17 **Lindi** ≈ NE Dem. Rep. Congo
163 V7 **Lindian** Heilongjiang, NE China 47°15′N 124°51′E
185 E21 **Lindis Pass** pass South Island, New Zealand
83 J22 **Lindley** Free State, C South Africa 27°52′S 27°55′E
95 J19 **Lindome** Västra Götaland, S Sweden 57°34′N 12°05′E
163 S10 **Lindong** var. Bairin Zuoqi. Nei Mongol Zizhiqu, N China 43°59′N 119°24′E
115 O23 **Líndos** var. Líndhos. Ródos, Dodekánisa, Greece, Aegean Sea 36°05′N 28°05′E
14 I14 **Lindsay** Ontario, SE Canada 44°21′N 78°44′W
35 R11 **Lindsay** California, W USA 36°11′N 119°06′W
33 X8 **Lindsay** Montana, NW USA 47°13′N 105°10′W
27 N11 **Lindsay** Oklahoma, C USA 34°50′N 97°37′W
27 N5 **Lindsborg** Kansas, C USA 38°34′N 97°39′W
95 N21 **Lindsdal** Kalmar, S Sweden 56°44′N 16°18′E
Lindum/Lindum Colonia see Lincoln
191 W3 **Line Islands** island group E Kiribati
Linëvo see Linova
160 M5 **Linfen** var. Lin-fen. Shanxi, C China 36°08′N 111°34′E
Lin-fen see Linfen
155 F18 **Linganamakki Reservoir** ⊠ SW India
160 L17 **Lingao** var. Lincheng. Hainan, S China 19°44′N 109°23′E
171 N3 **Lingayen** Luzon, N Philippines 16°00′N 120°12′E
160 M6 **Lingbao** var. Guolüezhen. Henan, C China 34°34′N 110°50′E
94 N12 **Lingbo** Gävleborg, C Sweden 61°04′N 16°45′E
Lingcheng see Beiliu,Guangxi, China
Lingcheng see Lingshan, Guangxi, China
Lingeh see Bandar-e Lengeh
100 E12 **Lingen** var. Lingen an der Ems. Niedersachsen, NW Germany 52°31′N 07°19′E
Lingen an der Ems see Lingen
168 M11 **Lingga, Kepulauan** island group W Indonesia
168 L11 **Lingga, Pulau** island Kepulauan Lingga, W Indonesia
14 J14 **Lingham Lake** ◎ Ontario, SE Canada
94 M13 **Linghed** Dalarna, C Sweden 60°48′N 15°55′E
33 Z15 **Lingle** Wyoming, C USA 42°07′N 104°21′W
18 G15 **Linglestown** Pennsylvania, NE USA 40°20′N 76°46′W
79 K18 **Lingomo 11** Equateur, NW Dem. Rep. Congo 0°42′N 21°59′E
160 L15 **Lingshan** var. Lingcheng. Guangxi Zhuangzu Zizhiqu, S China 22°28′N 109°19′E
160 L17 **Lingshui** var. Lingshui Lizu Zizhixian. Hainan, S China 18°35′N 110°03′E
Lingshui Lizu Zizhixian see Lingshui
155 G16 **Lingsugūr** Karnātaka, C India 16°13′N 76°33′E
107 L23 **Linguaglossa** Sicilia, Italy, C Mediterranean Sea 37°51′N 15°06′E
76 H10 **Linguère** N Senegal 15°24′N 15°06′W
159 W8 **Lingwu** Ningxia, N China 38°04′N 106°21′E
Lingxi see Yongshun, Hunan, China
Lingxi see Cangnan, Zhejiang, China
Lingxian/Ling Xian see Yanling
163 S12 **Lingyuan** Liaoning, NE China 41°09′N 119°24′E
163 U4 **Linhai** Heilongjiang, NE China 51°30′N 124°18′E
161 S10 **Linhai** var. Taizhou. Zhejiang, SE China 28°54′N 121°08′E
59 O20 **Linhares** Espírito Santo, SE Brazil 19°22′S 40°04′W
Linhe see Bayannur
Lini see Lin
139 S1 **Līnik, Chiyā-ē** ▲▲ N Iraq
Linjiang see Shanghang
95 M18 **Linköping** Östergötland, S Sweden 58°25′N 15°37′E
163 Y8 **Linkou** Heilongjiang, NE China 45°18′N 130°17′E
118 F11 **Linkuva** Šiaulai, N Lithuania 56°06′N 23°58′E
27 V5 **Linn** Missouri, C USA 38°29′N 91°51′W
25 S16 **Linn** Texas, SW USA 26°32′N 98°06′W
27 T2 **Linneus** Missouri, C USA 39°53′N 93°10′W
96 H10 **Linnhe, Loch** inlet W Scotland, United Kingdom
119 G19 **Linova** Rus. Linëvo. Brestskaya Voblasts', SW Belarus 52°29′N 24°30′E
161 O5 **Linqing** Shandong, E China 36°51′N 115°42′E
60 K8 **Lins** São Paulo, S Brazil 21°40′S 49°44′W
93 F17 **Linsell** Jämtland, C Sweden 62°10′N 14°E
160 J9 **Linshui** Sichuan, C China 30°24′N 106°54′E
44 K12 **Linstead** C Jamaica 18°08′N 77°02′W
159 U11 **Lintan** Gansu, N China 34°43′N 101°27′E
159 V11 **Lintao** var. Taoyang. Gansu, C China 35°23′N 103°54′E
15 S12 **Lintère** ≈ Québec, SE Canada
108 H8 **Linth** ≈ NW Switzerland
108 H8 **Linthal** Glarus, NE Switzerland 46°59′N 08°57′E
31 N15 **Linton** Indiana, N USA 39°01′N 87°10′W
29 N6 **Linton** North Dakota, N USA 46°16′N 100°13′W
163 R11 **Linxi** Nei Mongol Zizhiqu, N China 43°29′N 117°59′E
159 U11 **Linxia** var. Linxia Huizu Zizhizhou. Gansu, C China 35°34′N 103°08′E
Linxia Huizu Zizhizhou see Linxia
Linxian see Lianzhou
161 Q6 **Linyi** Shandong, S China 37°06′N 118°18′E
161 P4 **Linyi** var. Yishi. Shandong, E China 37°12′N 116°54′E
160 M6 **Linyi** Shanxi, C China 35°10′N 118°18′E
109 T4 **Linz** anc. Lentia. Oberösterreich, N Austria 48°19′N 14°18′E
159 S8 **Linze** var. Shahe; prev. Shahepu. Gansu, N China 39°06′N 100°03′E
44 J13 **Lionel Town** C Jamaica 17°49′N 77°14′W
103 Q16 **Lion, Golfe du** Eng. Gulf of Lion, Gulf of Lions; anc. Sinus Gallicus. gulf S France
Lion, Gulf of/Lions, Gulf of see Lion, Golfe du
83 K16 **Lions Den** Mashonaland West, N Zimbabwe 17°16′S 30°00′E
14 F13 **Lion's Head** Ontario, S Canada 44°59′N 81°16′W
Lios Ceannúir, Bá see Liscannor Bay
Lios Mór see Lismore
Lios na gCearrbhach see Lisburn
Lios Tuathail see Listowel
79 G17 **Liouesso** Sangha, N Congo 01°02′N 15°43′E
Liozno see Lyozna
171 O4 **Lipa** off. Lipa City. Luzon, N Philippines 13°57′N 121°10′E
Lipa City see Lipa
25 S7 **Lipan** Texas, SW USA 32°31′N 98°03′W
Lipari Islands/Lipari, Isole see Eolie, Isole
107 L22 **Lipari, Isola** island Isole Eolie, S Italy
116 L8 **Lipcani** Rus. Lipkany. N Moldova 48°16′N 26°47′E
93 N17 **Liperi** Itä-Suomi, SE Finland 62°33′N 29°29′E
126 L7 **Lipetsk** Lipetskaya Oblast', W Russian Federation 52°37′N 39°38′E
126 K6 **Lipetskaya Oblast'** ◐ province W Russian Federation
57 K22 **Lipez, Cordillera de** ▲▲ SW Bolivia
110 E10 **Lipiany** Ger. Lippehne. Zachodnio-pomorskie, W Poland 53°00′N 14°58′E
112 G9 **Lipik** Požega-Slavonija, NE Croatia 45°24′N 17°08′E
124 L12 **Lipin Bor** Vologodskaya Oblast', NW Russian Federation 60°12′N 38°04′E

◆ Country
● Country Capital
◇ Dependent Territory
○ Dependent Territory Capital
◐ Administrative Regions
✈ International Airport
▲ Mountain
▲▲ Mountain Range
Volcano
≈ River
◎ Lake
⊠ Reservoir

160 L12 **Liping** var. Defeng. Guizhou, S China 26°16′N 109°08′E
Lipkany see Lipcani
119 H15 **Lipnishki** Hrodzyenskaya Voblasts', W Belarus 54°00′N 25°37′E
110 J10 **Lipno** Kujawsko-pomorskie, C Poland 52°52′N 19°11′E
116 F11 **Lipova** Hung. Lippa. Arad, W Romania 46°05′N 21°42′E
Lipovets see Lypovets'
Lippa see Lipova
101 E14 **Lippe** W Germany
Lippehne see Lipiany
101 G14 **Lippstadt** Nordrhein-Westfalen, W Germany 51°41′N 08°20′E
25 P1 **Lipscomb** Texas, SW USA 36°14′N 100°16′W
Lipsia/Lipsk see Leipzig
Liptau-Sankt-Nikolaus/Liptószentmiklós see Liptovský Mikuláš
111 K19 **Liptovský Mikuláš** Ger. Liptau-Sankt-Nikolaus, Hung. Liptószentmiklós. Žilinský Kraj, N Slovakia 49°06′N 19°36′E
183 O13 **Liptrap, Cape** headland Victoria, SE Australia 38°55′S 145°58′E
160 L13 **Lipu** var. Licheng. Guangxi Zhuangzu Zizhiqu, S China 24°25′N 110°15′E
81 G17 **Lira** N Uganda 02°15′N 32°55′E
57 F15 **Lircay** Huancavelica, C Peru 12°59′S 74°44′W
107 K17 **Liri** C Italy
144 M8 **Lisakovsk** Kostanay, NW Kazakhstan 52°32′N 62°32′E
79 K17 **Lisala** Equateur, N Dem. Rep. Congo 02°10′N 21°29′E
104 F11 **Lisboa** Eng. Lisbon; anc. Felicitas Julia, Olisipo. ● (Portugal) Lisboa, W Portugal 38°44′N 09°08′W
104 F10 **Lisboa** Eng. Lisbon. ◐ district C Portugal
19 N7 **Lisbon** New Hampshire, NE USA 44°11′N 71°52′W
29 Q6 **Lisbon** North Dakota, N USA 46°27′N 97°42′W
Lisbon see Lisboa
19 Q8 **Lisbon Falls** Maine, NE USA 44°00′N 70°03′W
97 G15 **Lisburn** Ir. Lios na gCearrbhach. E Northern Ireland, United Kingdom 54°31′N 06°03′W
38 L6 **Lisburne, Cape** headland Alaska, USA 68°52′N 166°13′W
97 B19 **Liscannor Bay** Ir. Bá Lios Ceannúir. inlet W Ireland
113 Q18 **Lisec** ▲ E FYR Macedonia 41°46′N 22°30′E
160 F13 **Lishe Jiang** SW China
Lishi see Lüliang
163 V10 **Lishu** Jilin, NE China 43°25′N 124°19′E
161 R10 **Lishui** Zhejiang, SE China 28°27′N 119°25′E
192 L5 **Lisianski Island** island Hawaiian Islands, Hawai'i, USA
Lisichansk see Lysychans'k
102 L4 **Lisieux** anc. Noviomagus. Calvados, N France 49°09′N 00°13′E
126 L8 **Liski** prev. Georgiu-Dezh. Voronezhskaya Oblast', W Russian Federation 51°00′N 39°36′E
103 N4 **l'Isle-Adam** Val-d'Oise, N France 49°07′N 02°13′E
Lisle/l'Isle see Lille
103 R15 **l'Isle-sur-la-Sorgue** Vaucluse, SE France 43°55′N 05°03′E
15 S9 **L'Islet** Québec, SE Canada 47°07′N 70°18′W
183 V4 **Lismore** New South Wales, SE Australia 28°48′S 153°12′E
182 M12 **Lismore** Victoria, SE Australia 37°59′S 143°18′E
97 D20 **Lismore** Ir. Lios Mór. S Ireland 52°10′N 07°10′W
Lissa see Vis, Croatia
Lissa see Leszno, Poland
98 H11 **Lisse** Zuid-Holland, W Netherlands 52°15′N 04°33′E
114 K13 **Líssos** var. Filiouri. NE Greece
95 D18 **Lista** peninsula S Norway
95 D18 **Listafjorden** fjord S Norway
195 R13 **Lister, Mount** ▲ Antarctica 78°12′S 161°46′E
126 M8 **Listopadovka** Voronezhskaya Oblast', W Russian Federation 51°54′N 41°08′E
14 F15 **Listowel** Ontario, S Canada 43°44′N 80°57′W
97 B20 **Listowel** Ir. Lios Tuathail. Kerry, SW Ireland 52°27′N 09°29′W
160 L14 **Litang** Guangxi Zhuangzu Zizhiqu, S China 23°09′N 109°08′E
160 F9 **Litang** var. Gaocheng. Sichuan, C China 30°03′N 100°12′E
160 F10 **Litang Qu** C China
55 X12 **Litani** var. Itany. French Guiana/Surinam
138 G8 **Lītani, Nahr el** var. Nahr al Litant. C Lebanon
Litant, Nahr al see Lītani, Nahr el
Litauen see Lithuania
30 K14 **Litchfield** Illinois, N USA 39°17′N 89°52′W
29 U8 **Litchfield** Minnesota, N USA 45°09′N 94°31′W
36 K13 **Litchfield Park** Arizona, SW USA 33°29′N 112°21′W
183 S8 **Lithgow** New South Wales, SE Australia 33°30′S 150°09′E
115 I26 **Líthino, Akrotírio** headland Kríti, Greece, E Mediterranean Sea 34°55′N 24°43′E
118 D12 **Lithuania** off. Republic of Lithuania, Ger. Litauen, Lith. Lietuva, Pol. Litwa, Rus. Litva; prev. Lithuanian SSR, Rus. Litovskaya SSR. ◆ republic NE Europe
Lithuanian SSR see Lithuania
Lithuania, Republic of see Lithuania
109 U11 **Litija** Ger. Littai. C Slovenia 46°03′N 14°50′E
18 H15 **Lititz** Pennsylvania, NE USA 40°09′N 76°18′W
115 F15 **Litóchoro** var. Litohoro, Litókhoron. Kentrikí Makedonía, N Greece 40°06′N 22°30′E
Litohoro/Litókhoron see Litóchoro
111 C15 **Litoměřice** Ger. Leitmeritz. Ústecký Kraj, NW Czech Republic 50°33′N 14°10′E
111 F17 **Litomyšl** Ger. Leitomischl. Pardubický Kraj, C Czech Republic 49°54′N 16°18′E
111 G17 **Litovel** Ger. Littau. Olomoucký Kraj, E Czech Republic 49°42′N 17°05′E
123 S13 **Litovko** Khabarovskiy Kray, SE Russian Federation 49°22′N 135°10′E
Litovskaya SSR see Lithuania
Littai see Litija
Littau see Litovel
44 G1 **Little Abaco** var. Abaco Island. island N Bahamas
111 I21 **Little Alföld** Ger. Kleines Ungarisches Tiefland, Hung. Kisalföld, Slvk. Podunajská Rovina. plain Hungary/Slovakia
151 Q20 **Little Andaman** island Andaman Islands, India, NE Indian Ocean
26 M5 **Little Arkansas River** Kansas, C USA
184 L4 **Little Barrier Island** island N New Zealand
Little Belt see Lillebælt
38 M11 **Little Black River** Alaska, USA
27 O2 **Little Blue River** Kansas/Nebraska, C USA
44 D8 **Little Cayman** island E Cayman Islands
11 X11 **Little Churchill** Manitoba, C Canada
166 J10 **Little Coco Island** island SW Burma (Myanmar)
36 L10 **Little Colorado River** Arizona, SW USA
14 E11 **Little Current** Manitoulin Island, Ontario, S Canada 45°57′N 81°56′W
12 E11 **Little Current** Ontario, S Canada
38 L8 **Little Diomede Island** island Alaska, USA
44 I4 **Little Exuma** island C Bahamas
29 U7 **Little Falls** Minnesota, N USA 45°59′N 94°21′W
18 J10 **Little Falls** New York, NE USA 43°02′N 74°51′W
24 M5 **Littlefield** Texas, SW USA 33°56′N 102°20′W
29 V3 **Littlefork** Minnesota, N USA 48°24′N 93°33′W
29 V3 **Little Fork River** Minnesota, N USA
11 N16 **Little Fort** British Columbia, SW Canada 51°27′N 120°15′W
11 Y14 **Little Grand Rapids** Manitoba, C Canada 52°06′N 95°29′W
97 N23 **Littlehampton** SE England, United Kingdom 50°48′N 00°33′W
35 T2 **Little Humboldt River** Nevada, W USA
44 K6 **Little Inagua** var. Inagua Islands. island S Bahamas
21 Q4 **Little Kanawha River** West Virginia, NE USA
83 F25 **Little Karoo** plateau S South Africa
39 O16 **Little Koniuji Island** island Shumagin Islands, Alaska, USA
44 H12 **Little London** W Jamaica 18°15′N 78°13′W
13 R10 **Little Mecatina** Fr. Rivière du Petit Mécatina. Newfoundland and Labrador/Québec, E Canada
96 F8 **Little Minch, The** strait NW Scotland, United Kingdom
27 T13 **Little Missouri River** Arkansas, USA
28 J7 **Little Missouri River** NW USA
28 J3 **Little Muddy River** North Dakota, N USA
151 Q22 **Little Nicobar** island Nicobar Islands, India, NE Indian Ocean
27 R6 **Little Osage River** Missouri, C USA
97 P20 **Little Ouse** E England, United Kingdom
149 V2 **Little Pamir** Pash. Pāmīr-e Khord, Rus. Malyy Pamir. ▲▲ Afghanistan/Tajikistan
21 U12 **Little Pee Dee River** North Carolina/South Carolina, SE USA
27 V10 **Little Red River** Arkansas, C USA
Little Rhody see Rhode Island
185 I19 **Little River** Canterbury, South Island, New Zealand 43°45′S 172°49′E
21 U12 **Little River** South Carolina, SE USA 33°52′N 78°36′W
27 Y9 **Little River** Arkansas/Missouri, C USA
27 R13 **Little River** Arkansas/Oklahoma, USA
23 T7 **Little River** Georgia, SE USA
22 H6 **Little River** Louisiana, S USA
25 T10 **Little River** Texas, SW USA
27 V12 **Little Rock** state capital Arkansas, C USA 34°45′N 92°17′W
31 N8 **Little Sable Point** headland Michigan, N USA 43°38′N 86°32′W
103 U11 **Little Saint Bernard Pass** Fr. Col du Petit St-Bernard, It. Colle del Piccolo San Bernardo. pass France/Italy
36 K7 **Little Salt Lake** Utah, W USA
180 K8 **Little Sandy Desert** desert Western Australia
29 S13 **Little Sioux River** Iowa, C USA
38 E17 **Little Sitkin Island** island Aleutian Islands, Alaska, USA
11 O13 **Little Smoky** Alberta, W Canada 54°35′N 117°06′W
11 O14 **Little Smoky** Alberta, W Canada
37 P3 **Little Snake River** Colorado, C USA
64 A12 **Little Sound** bay Bermuda, NW Atlantic Ocean
37 T4 **Littleton** Colorado, C USA 39°36′N 105°01′W
19 N7 **Littleton** New Hampshire, NE USA 44°18′N 71°46′W
18 D11 **Little Valley** New York, NE USA 42°15′N 78°47′W
30 M15 **Little Wabash River** Illinois, N USA
14 D10 **Little White River** Ontario, S Canada
28 M12 **Little White River** South Dakota, N USA
25 R5 **Little Wichita River** Texas, SW USA
142 I4 **Little Zab** Ar. Nahraz Zāb aş Şaghīr, Kurd. Zē-i Kōya, Per. Rūdkhāneh-ye Zāb-e Kūchek. Iran/Iraq
79 D15 **Littoral** ◐ province W Cameroon
Littoria see Latina
Litva/Litwa see Lithuania
111 B15 **Litvínov** Ger. Leutensdorf. Ústecký Kraj, NW Czech Republic 50°38′N 13°30′E
116 M6 **Lityn** Vinnyts'ka Oblast', C Ukraine 49°19′N 28°06′E
Liu-chou/Liuchow see Liuzhou
163 W11 **Liuhe** Jilin, NE China 42°15′N 125°49′E
Liujiaxia see Yongjing
Liulin see Jonê
83 Q15 **Liúpo** Nampula, NE Mozambique 15°36′S 39°57′E
83 G14 **Liuwa Plain** plain W Zambia
160 L13 **Liuzhou** var. Liu-chou, Liuchow. Guangxi Zhuangzu Zizhiqu, S China 24°09′N 108°55′E
116 H8 **Livada** Hung. Sárköz. Satu Mare, NW Romania 47°52′N 23°04′E
115 J20 **Liváda, Akrotírio** headland Tínos, Kykládes, Greece, Aegean Sea 37°36′N 25°15′E
115 F18 **Livádeia** prev. Levádia. Stereá Ellás, C Greece 38°24′N 22°51′E
Livádi see Liádi
Livanátai see Livanátes
115 G18 **Livanátes** prev. Livanátai. Stereá Ellás, C Greece 38°43′N 23°03′E
118 I10 **Līvāni** Ger. Lievenhof. Preiļi, SE Latvia 56°22′N 26°12′E
65 E25 **Lively Island** island SE Falkland Islands
65 D25 **Lively Sound** sound SE Falkland Islands
39 R8 **Livengood** Alaska, USA 65°31′N 148°32′W
106 I7 **Livenza** NE Italy
35 O6 **Live Oak** California, W USA 39°17′N 121°41′W
23 U9 **Live Oak** Florida, SE USA 30°18′N 82°59′W
35 O9 **Livermore** California, W USA 37°40′N 121°46′W
20 I6 **Livermore** Kentucky, S USA 37°31′N 87°08′W
19 Q7 **Livermore Falls** Maine, NE USA 44°30′N 70°09′W
24 J10 **Livermore, Mount** ▲ Texas, SW USA 30°37′N 104°10′W
13 P16 **Liverpool** Nova Scotia, SE Canada 44°03′N 64°43′W
97 K17 **Liverpool** NW England, United Kingdom 53°25′N 02°55′W
183 S7 **Liverpool Range** ▲▲ New South Wales, SE Australia
42 F4 **Lívingston** Izabal, E Guatemala 15°50′N 88°44′W
96 J12 **Livingston** C Scotland, United Kingdom 55°51′N 03°31′W
23 N5 **Livingston** Alabama, S USA 32°35′N 88°12′W
35 P9 **Livingston** California, W USA 37°22′N 120°45′W
22 J8 **Livingston** Louisiana, S USA 30°30′N 90°45′W
33 S11 **Livingston** Montana, NW USA 45°40′N 110°33′W
20 L8 **Livingston** Tennessee, S USA 36°22′N 85°20′W
25 W9 **Livingston** Texas, SW USA 30°42′N 94°58′W
83 I16 **Livingstone** var. Maramba. Southern, S Zambia 17°51′S 25°48′E
185 B22 **Livingstone Mountains** ▲▲ South Island, New Zealand
80 K13 **Livingstone Mountains** ▲▲ S Tanzania
82 N12 **Livingstonia** Northern, N Malawi 10°29′S 34°06′E
194 G4 **Livingston Island** island Antarctica
25 W9 **Livingston, Lake** Texas, SW USA
112 F13 **Livno** ◐ Federicija Bosna I Hercegovina, SW Bosnia and Herzegovina
126 K7 **Livny** Orlovskaya Oblast', W Russian Federation 52°25′N 37°42′E
93 M14 **Livojoki** C Finland
31 R10 **Livonia** Michigan, N USA 42°22′N 83°22′W
106 E11 **Livorno** Eng. Leghorn. Toscana, C Italy 43°32′N 10°18′E
Livramento see Santana do Livramento
141 U8 **Līwā** var. Al Liwā'. oasis region S United Arab Emirates
81 I24 **Liwale** Lindi, SE Tanzania 09°46′S 37°56′E
159 W9 **Liwangbu** Ningxia, N China 36°42′N 106°05′E
83 N15 **Liwonde** Southern, S Malawi 15°01′S 35°15′E
159 V11 **Lixian** var. Li Xian. Gansu, C China 34°15′N 105°07′E
160 H8 **Lixian** var. Li Xian, Zagunao. Sichuan, C China 31°27′N 103°06′E
Li Xian see Lixian
Lixian Jiang see Black River
115 B18 **Lixoúri** prev. Lixoúrion. Kefallinía, Iónia Nisiá, Greece, C Mediterranean Sea 38°14′N 20°24′E
Lixoúrion see Lixoúri
Lixus see Larache
33 U15 **Lizard Head Peak** ▲ Wyoming, C USA 42°47′N 109°12′W
97 H25 **Lizard Point** headland SW England, United Kingdom 49°57′N 05°12′W
Lizarra see Estella
112 L12 **Ljig** Serbia, C Serbia 44°14′N 20°16′E
Ljouwert see Leeuwarden
Ljubelj see Loibl Pass
109 U11 **Ljubljana** Ger. Laibach, It. Lubiana; anc. Aemona, Emona. ● (Slovenia) C Slovenia 46°03′N 14°29′E
109 T11 **Ljubljana** C Slovenia 46°14′N 14°26′E
113 N17 **Ljuboten** ▲ S Serbia 42°12′N 21°06′E
95 P19 **Ljugarn** Gotland, SE Sweden 57°23′N 18°45′E
84 G7 **Ljungan** N Sweden
93 F17 **Ljungan** C Sweden
95 K21 **Ljungby** Kronoberg, S Sweden 56°49′N 13°55′E
95 M17 **Ljungsbro** Östergötland, S Sweden 58°31′N 15°30′E
95 I18 **Ljungskile** Västra Götaland, S Sweden 58°14′N 11°55′E
94 M11 **Ljusdal** Gävleborg, C Sweden 61°50′N 16°10′E
94 M11 **Ljusnan** C Sweden
94 N12 **Ljusne** Gävleborg, C Sweden 61°11′N 17°07′E
95 P15 **Ljusterö** Stockholm, C Sweden 59°31′N 18°40′E
109 X9 **Ljutomer** Ger. Luttenberg. NE Slovenia 46°31′N 16°12′E
63 G15 **Llaima, Volcán** S Chile 39°01′S 71°38′W
105 X4 **Llançà** var. Llansá. Cataluña, NE Spain 42°23′N 03°08′E
97 J21 **Llandovery** C Wales, United Kingdom 52°01′N 03°47′W
97 J20 **Llandrindod Wells** E Wales, United Kingdom 52°15′N 03°23′W
97 J18 **Llandudno** N Wales, United Kingdom 53°19′N 03°49′W
97 I21 **Llanelli** prev. Llanelly. SW Wales, United Kingdom 51°41′N 04°12′W
Llanelly see Llanelli
104 M2 **Llanes** Asturias, N Spain 43°25′N 04°46′W
97 K19 **Llangollen** NE Wales, United Kingdom 52°58′N 03°10′W
25 R10 **Llano** Texas, SW USA 30°49′N 98°42′W
25 Q10 **Llano River** Texas, SW USA
54 I9 **Llanos** physical region Colombia/Venezuela
63 G16 **Llanquihue, Lago** S Chile
Llansá see Llançà
105 U5 **Lleida** Cast. Lérida; anc. Ilerda. Cataluña, NE Spain 41°38′N 00°35′E
104 K12 **Llerena** Extremadura, W Spain 38°13′N 06°00′W
105 S9 **Llíria** País Valenciano, E Spain 39°38′N 00°36′W
105 W4 **Llivia** Cataluña, NE Spain 42°27′N 02°00′E
105 O3 **Llodio** País Vasco, N Spain 43°08′N 02°59′W
105 X5 **Lloret de Mar** Cataluña, NE Spain 41°42′N 02°51′E
Llorri see Tossal de l'Orri
10 L11 **Lloyd George, Mount** ▲ British Columbia, W Canada 57°46′N 124°57′W
11 R14 **Lloydminster** Alberta/Saskatchewan, SW Canada 53°18′N 110°00′W
105 X9 **Llucmajor** Mallorca, Spain, W Mediterranean Sea 39°29′N 02°53′E
36 L6 **Loa** Utah, W USA 38°24′N 111°38′W
169 S8 **Loagan Bunut** East Malaysia
38 G12 **Loa, Mauna** ▲ Hawai'i, USA 19°28′N 155°39′W
Loanda see Luanda
79 J22 **Loange** S Dem. Rep. Congo
79 E21 **Loango** Kouilou, S Congo 04°38′S 11°50′E
106 B10 **Loano** Liguria, NW Italy 44°07′N 08°15′E
62 H4 **Loa, Río** N Chile
83 I20 **Lobatse** var. Lobatsi. Kgatleng, SE Botswana 25°11′S 25°40′E
Lobatsi see Lobatse
101 Q15 **Löbau** Sachsen, E Germany 51°07′N 14°40′E
79 H16 **Lobaye** ◐ prefecture SW Central African Republic
79 I16 **Lobaye** SW Central African Republic
99 G21 **Lobbes** Hainaut, S Belgium 50°21′N 04°16′E
61 D23 **Lobería** Buenos Aires, E Argentina 38°08′S 58°48′W
110 F8 **Łobez** Ger. Labes. Zacodniopomorskie, NW Poland 53°38′N 15°39′E
82 A13 **Lobito** Benguela, W Angola 12°20′S 13°34′E
Lobkovichi see Labkovichy
Lob Nor see Lop Nur
171 V13 **Lobo** Papua, E Indonesia 03°41′S 134°06′E
104 J11 **Lobón** Extremadura, W Spain 38°51′N 06°38′W
61 D20 **Lobos** Buenos Aires, E Argentina 35°11′S 59°08′W
40 E4 **Lobos, Cabo** headland NW Mexico 29°53′N 112°43′W
40 F6 **Lobos, Isla** island NW Mexico
Lobositz see Lovosice
Lobsens see Łobżenica
Loburi see Lop Buri
110 H9 **Łobżenica** Ger. Lobsens. Wielkopolskie, C Poland 53°19′N 17°11′E
108 G11 **Locarno** Ger. Luggarus. Ticino, S Switzerland 46°11′N 08°48′E
96 E9 **Lochboisdale** NW Scotland, United Kingdom 57°08′N 07°17′W
98 N11 **Lochem** Gelderland, E Netherlands 52°10′N 06°25′E
102 M8 **Loches** Indre-et-Loire, C France 47°08′N 01°00′E
Loch Garman see Wexford
96 H12 **Lochgilphead** W Scotland, United Kingdom 56°02′N 05°27′W
96 H7 **Lochinver** N Scotland, United Kingdom 58°10′N 05°15′W
96 F8 **Lochmaddy** NW Scotland, United Kingdom 57°35′N 07°10′W
96 J10 **Lochnagar** ▲ C Scotland, United Kingdom 56°58′N 03°09′W
99 E17 **Lochristi** Oost-Vlaanderen, NW Belgium 51°07′N 03°49′E
96 H9 **Lochy, Loch** N Scotland, United Kingdom
182 G8 **Lock** South Australia 33°37′S 135°45′E
97 J14 **Lockerbie** S Scotland, United Kingdom 55°11′N 03°27′W
27 S13 **Lockesburg** Arkansas, C USA 33°58′N 94°10′W
183 P10 **Lockhart** New South Wales, SE Australia 35°15′S 146°43′E
25 S11 **Lockhart** Texas, SW USA 29°54′N 97°41′W
18 F13 **Lock Haven** Pennsylvania, NE USA 41°08′N 77°27′W
25 N4 **Lockney** Texas, SW USA 34°06′N 101°27′W
100 O12 **Löcknitz** NE Germany
18 E9 **Lockport** New York, NE USA 43°09′N 78°40′W
167 T13 **Lôc Ninh** Sông Be, S Vietnam 11°51′N 106°35′E
107 N23 **Locri** Calabria, SW Italy 38°16′N 16°16′E
Locse see Levoča
27 T2 **Locust Creek** Missouri, C USA
23 P3 **Locust Fork** Alabama, S USA
27 Q9 **Locust Grove** Oklahoma, C USA 36°12′N 95°10′W
94 E11 **Lodalskåpa** ▲ S Norway 61°47′N 07°10′E
183 N10 **Loddon River** Victoria, SE Australia
Lodensee see Klooga
103 P15 **Lodève** anc. Luteva. Hérault, S France 43°44′N 03°19′E
124 I12 **Lodeynoye Pole** Leningradskaya Oblast', NW Russian Federation 60°41′N 33°29′E
33 V11 **Lodge Grass** Montana, NW USA 45°19′N 107°20′W
28 J15 **Lodgepole Creek** Nebraska/Wyoming, C USA
149 T11 **Lodhrān** Punjab, E Pakistan 29°32′N 71°40′E
106 D8 **Lodi** Lombardia, NW Italy 45°19′N 09°30′E
35 O8 **Lodi** California, W USA 38°07′N 121°17′W
31 T12 **Lodi** Ohio, N USA 41°00′N 82°01′W
92 H10 **Lødingen** Nordland, C Norway 68°25′N 16°00′E
79 L20 **Lodja** Kasai-Oriental, C Dem. Rep. Congo 03°29′S 23°25′E
37 O3 **Lodore, Canyon of** canyon Colorado, C USA
105 Q4 **Lodosa** Navarra, N Spain 42°26′N 02°05′W
81 H16 **Lodwar** Rift Valley, NW Kenya 03°06′N 35°38′E
110 K13 **Łódź** Rus. Lodz. Łódź, C Poland 51°51′N 19°26′E
110 E12 **Łódzskie** ◐ province C Poland
167 P8 **Loei** var. Loey, Muang Loei. Loei, C Thailand 17°32′N 101°40′E
98 I11 **Loenen** Utrecht, C Netherlands 52°13′N 05°01′E
167 R9 **Loeng Nok Tha** Yasothon, E Thailand 16°12′N 104°31′E
83 F24 **Loeriesfontein** Northern Cape, W South Africa 30°59′S 19°29′E
Loewoek see Luwuk
Loey see Loei
76 J16 **Lofa** N Liberia
109 P6 **Lofer** Salzburg, C Austria 47°37′N 12°42′E
92 F11 **Lofoten** var. Lofoten Islands. island group C Norway
Lofoten Islands see Lofoten
95 N18 **Loftahammar** Kalmar, S Sweden 57°55′N 16°45′E
127 O10 **Log** Volgogradskaya Oblast', SW Russian Federation 49°32′N 43°52′E
77 S12 **Loga** Dosso, SW Niger 13°40′N 03°15′E
29 S14 **Logan** Iowa, C USA 41°38′N 95°47′W
26 K3 **Logan** Kansas, C USA 39°39′N 99°34′W
31 T14 **Logan** Ohio, N USA 39°32′N 82°24′W
36 L1 **Logan** Utah, W USA 41°45′N 111°50′W
21 P6 **Logan** West Virginia, NE USA 37°52′N 82°00′W
35 Y10 **Logandale** Nevada, W USA 36°36′N 114°28′W
19 O11 **Logan International** (Boston) Massachusetts, NE USA 42°22′N 71°00′W
11 N16 **Logan Lake** British Columbia, SW Canada 50°28′N 120°42′W
23 Q4 **Logan Martin Lake** Alabama, S USA
10 G8 **Logan, Mount** ▲ Yukon Territory, W Canada 60°32′N 140°34′W
32 I7 **Logan, Mount** ▲ Washington, NW USA 48°32′N 120°57′W
33 P7 **Logan Pass** pass Montana, NW USA
31 O12 **Logansport** Indiana, N USA 40°44′N 86°25′W
22 F6 **Logansport** Louisiana, S USA 31°58′N 94°00′W
Logar see Lowgar
67 R11 **Loge** NW Angola
Logishin see Lahishyn
Log na Coille see Lugnaquillia Mountain
78 G11 **Logone** var. Lagone. Cameroon/Chad
78 G13 **Logone-Occidental** off. Préfecture du Logone-Occidental. ◐ prefecture SW Chad
78 H13 **Logone Occidental** SW Chad
Logone-Occidental, Préfecture du see Logone-Occidental
78 G13 **Logone-Oriental** off. Préfecture du Logone-Oriental. ◐ prefecture SW Chad
78 H13 **Logone Oriental** SW Chad
Logone Oriental see Pendé
Logone-Oriental, Préfecture du see Logone-Oriental
L'Ogooué-Ivindo see Ogooué-Ivindo
L'Ogooué-Lolo see Ogooué-Lolo
L'Ogooué-Maritime see Ogooué-Maritime
Logoysk see Lahoysk
105 P4 **Logroño** anc. Vareia, Lat. Juliobriga. La Rioja, N Spain 42°28′N 02°26′W
104 L10 **Logrosán** Extremadura, W Spain 39°21′N 05°29′W
95 G20 **Løgstør** Nordjylland, N Denmark 56°57′N 09°19′E
95 H22 **Løgten** Århus, C Denmark 56°17′N 10°20′E
95 F24 **Løgumkloster** Sønderjylland, SW Denmark 55°04′N 08°58′E
Lögurinn see Lagarfljót
153 P15 **Lohārdaga** Jhārkhand, N India 23°27′N 84°42′E
152 H10 **Lohāru** Haryāna, N India 28°28′N 75°50′E
101 D15 **Lohausen** (Düsseldorf) Nordrhein-Westfalen, W Germany 51°18′N 06°51′E
189 O14 **Lohd** Pohnpei, E Micronesia
92 L12 **Lohiniva** Lappi, N Finland 67°09′N 25°04′E
Lohiszyn see Lahishyn
93 L20 **Lohja** var. Lojo. Etelä-Suomi, S Finland 60°14′N 24°07′E
169 V11 **Lohjanan** Borneo, C Indonesia
25 Q9 **Lohn** Texas, SW USA 31°15′N 99°22′W
100 G12 **Lohne** Niedersachsen, NW Germany 52°40′N 08°13′E
Lohr see Lohr am Main
101 I18 **Lohr am Main** var. Lohr. Bayern, C Germany 50°00′N 09°30′E
109 T10 **Loibl Pass** Ger. Loiblpass, Slvn. Ljubelj. pass Austria/Slovenia
Loiblpass see Loibl Pass
167 N6 **Loikaw** Kayah State, C Burma (Myanmar) 19°40′N 97°17′E
93 K19 **Loimaa** Länsi-Suomi, SW Finland 60°51′N 23°03′E
103 O6 **Loing** C France
167 R6 **Loi, Phou** ▲ N Laos 20°18′N 103°14′E
102 L7 **Loir** C France
103 Q11 **Loire** ◐ department E France
102 M7 **Loire** var. Liger. C France
102 I7 **Loire-Atlantique** ◐ department NW France
103 O7 **Loiret** ◐ department C France
102 M8 **Loir-et-Cher** ◐ department C France
101 L24 **Loisach** SE Germany
56 B9 **Loja** Loja, S Ecuador 03°59′S 79°16′W
104 M14 **Loja** Andalucía, S Spain 37°10′N 04°09′W
56 B9 **Loja** ◐ province S Ecuador
Lojo see Lohja
116 J4 **Lokachi** Volyns'ka Oblast', NW Ukraine 50°44′N 24°39′E
79 M20 **Lokandu** Maniema, C Dem. Rep. Congo 02°34′S 25°44′E
92 M11 **Lokan Tekojärvi** NE Finland
137 Z11 **Lökbatan** Rus. Lokbatan. E Azerbaijan 40°21′N 49°43′E
Lokbatan see Lökbatan
99 F17 **Lokeren** Oost-Vlaanderen, NW Belgium 51°06′N 03°59′E
Lokhvitsa see Lokhvytsya
117 S4 **Lokhvytsya** Rus. Lokhvitsa. Poltavs'ka Oblast', NE Ukraine 50°22′N 33°16′E
81 H17 **Lokichar** Rift Valley, NW Kenya 02°23′N 35°40′E
81 G16 **Lokichokio** Rift Valley, NW Kenya 04°16′N 34°22′E
81 H16 **Lokitaung** Rift Valley, NW Kenya 04°15′N 35°45′E
92 M11 **Lokka** Lappi, N Finland 67°48′N 27°41′E
94 G8 **Løkken Verk** Sør-Trøndelag, S Norway 63°06′N 09°43′E
124 G16 **Loknya** Pskovskaya Oblast', W Russian Federation 56°48′N 30°08′E
77 V15 **Loko** Nassarawa, C Nigeria 08°00′N 07°48′E
77 U15 **Lokoja** Kogi, C Nigeria 07°48′N 06°45′E
81 H17 **Lokori** Rift Valley, W Kenya 01°56′N 36°03′E
77 R16 **Lokossa** S Benin 06°38′N 01°43′E
118 I3 **Loksa** Ger. Loxa. Harjumaa, NW Estonia 59°32′N 25°42′E
9 T7 **Loks Land** island Nunavut, NE Canada
80 C13 **Lol** S Sudan
76 K15 **Lola** SE Guinea 07°52′N 08°29′W
35 Q5 **Lola, Mount** ▲ California, W USA 39°27′N 120°20′W
81 H20 **Loliondo** Arusha, NE Tanzania 02°03′S 35°46′E
95 H25 **Lolland** prev. Laaland. island S Denmark
186 G6 **Lolobau Island** island E Papua New Guinea
79 E16 **Lolodorf** Sud, SW Cameroon 03°17′N 10°50′E
114 G7 **Lom** prev. Lom-Palanka. Montana, NW Bulgaria 43°49′N 23°16′E
114 G7 **Lom** NW Bulgaria
79 M19 **Lomami** C Dem. Rep. Congo
57 F17 **Lomas** Arequipa, SW Peru 15°29′S 74°54′W
63 I23 **Lomas, Bahía** bay S Chile
61 D20 **Lomas de Zamora** Buenos Aires, E Argentina 34°53′S 58°26′W
61 D20 **Loma Verde** Buenos Aires, E Argentina 35°16′S 58°24′W
180 K4 **Lombadina** Western Australia 16°39′S 122°54′E
106 E6 **Lombardia** Eng. Lombardy. ◐ region N Italy
Lombardy see Lombardia
102 M15 **Lombez** Gers, S France 43°29′N 00°54′E
171 Q16 **Lomblen, Pulau** island Nusa Tenggara, S Indonesia
173 W7 **Lombok Basin** undersea feature E Indian Ocean 09°50′S 116°00′E
170 L16 **Lombok, Pulau** island Nusa Tenggara, C Indonesia
77 Q16 **Lomé** ● (Togo) S Togo 06°08′N 01°13′E
77 Q16 **Lomé** S Togo 06°08′N 01°13′E
79 L19 **Lomela** Kasai-Oriental, C Dem. Rep. Congo 02°19′S 23°15′E
25 R9 **Lometa** Texas, SW USA 31°13′N 98°23′W
79 F16 **Lomié** Est, SE Cameroon 03°09′N 13°35′E
30 M8 **Lomira** Wisconsin, N USA 43°36′N 88°26′W
95 K23 **Lomma** Skåne, S Sweden 55°41′N 13°05′E
99 J16 **Lommel** Limburg, N Belgium 51°14′N 05°19′E
96 I11 **Lomond, Loch** C Scotland, United Kingdom
197 R9 **Lomonosov Ridge** var. Harris Ridge, Rus. Khrebet Homonsova. undersea feature Arctic Ocean 88°00′N 140°00′E
Lomonsova, Khrebet see Lomonosov Ridge
Lom-Palanka see Lom
Lomphat see Lumphăt
35 P14 **Lompoc** California, W USA 34°39′N 120°29′W
167 P9 **Lom Sak** var. Muang Lom Sak. Phetchabun, C Thailand 16°45′N 101°12′E
110 N9 **Łomża** Rus. Lomzha. Podlaskie, NE Poland 53°11′N 22°04′E
Lomzha see Łomża
Lonaula see Lonāvale
155 D14 **Lonāvale** prev. Lonaula. Mahārāshtra, W India 18°45′N 73°27′E
63 G15 **Loncoche** Araucanía, C Chile 39°22′S 72°34′W
63 H14 **Loncopue** Neuquén, W Argentina 38°04′S 70°43′W
99 G17 **Londerzeel** Vlaams Brabant, C Belgium 51°00′N 04°19′E
Londinium see London
14 E16 **London** Ontario, S Canada 42°59′N 81°13′W
191 Y2 **London** Kiritimati, E Kiribati 02°00′N 157°28′W
97 O22 **London** anc. Augusta, Lat. Londinium. ● (United Kingdom) SE England, United Kingdom 51°30′N 00°10′W
21 N7 **London** Kentucky, S USA 37°07′N 84°05′W
31 S13 **London** Ohio, NE USA 39°52′N 83°27′W
25 Q10 **London** Texas, SW USA 30°40′N 99°33′W
97 O22 **London City** SE England, United Kingdom 51°31′N 00°07′E
97 E14 **Londonderry** var. Derry, Ir. Doire. NW Northern Ireland, United Kingdom 55°N 07°19′W
97 F14 **Londonderry** cultural region NW Northern Ireland, United Kingdom
180 M2 **Londonderry, Cape** cape Western Australia
63 H25 **Londonderry, Isla** island S Chile
43 O7 **Londres, Cayos** reef NE Nicaragua
60 I10 **Londrina** Paraná, S Brazil 23°18′S 51°13′W
27 N13 **Lone Grove** Oklahoma, C USA 34°11′N 97°15′W
14 E12 **Lonely Island** island Ontario, S Canada
35 T8 **Lone Mountain** ▲ Nevada, W USA 38°01′N 117°28′W
25 V6 **Lone Oak** Texas, SW USA 33°02′N 95°58′W
35 T11 **Lone Pine** California, W USA 36°36′N 118°04′W
Lone Star State see Texas
Lone Tree Islet see Iku
83 D14 **Longa** Cuando Cubango, C Angola 14°44′S 18°36′E
82 B12 **Longa** W Angola
83 E15 **Longa** SE Angola
Long'an see Pingwu
163 W11 **Longang Shan** ▲▲ NE China
197 S4 **Longa, Proliv** Eng. Long Strait. strait NE Russian Federation
44 J13 **Long Bay** bay W Jamaica
21 V13 **Long Bay** bay North Carolina/South Carolina, E USA
35 T16 **Long Beach** California, W USA 33°46′N 118°11′W
22 M9 **Long Beach** Mississippi, S USA 30°21′N 89°09′W
18 L14 **Long Beach** Long Island, New York, NE USA 40°34′N 73°38′W
32 F9 **Long Beach** Washington, NW USA 46°21′N 124°03′W
18 K16 **Long Beach Island** island New Jersey, NE USA
65 M25 **Longbluff** headland SW Tristan da Cunha
23 U13 **Longboat Key** island Florida, SE USA
18 K15 **Long Branch** New Jersey, NE USA 40°18′N 73°59′W
44 J5 **Long Cay** island SE Bahamas
Longcheng see Xiaoxian
161 P14 **Longchuan** var. Laolong. Guangdong, S China 24°07′N 115°10′E
Longchuan see Nanhua
Longchuan Jiang see Shweli
32 K12 **Long Creek** Oregon, NW USA 44°40′N 119°07′W
159 W10 **Longde** Ningxia, N China 35°37′N 106°07′E
183 P16 **Longford** Tasmania, SE Australia 41°41′S 147°03′E
97 D17 **Longford** Ir. An Longfort. Longford, C Ireland 53°45′N 07°50′W
97 E17 **Longford** Ir. An Longfort. cultural region C Ireland
Longgang see Dazu
161 P1 **Longhua** Hebei, E China 41°18′N 117°44′E
169 U11 **Longiram** Borneo, C Indonesia 0°02′S 115°36′E
44 J4 **Long Island** island C Bahamas
12 H8 **Long Island** island Nunavut, C Canada
186 D7 **Long Island** var. Arop Island. island N Papua New Guinea
18 L14 **Long Island** island New York, NE USA
Long Island see Bermuda
18 M14 **Long Island Sound** sound NE USA
163 U7 **Longjiang** Heilongjiang, NE China 47°20′N 123°09′E
160 K13 **Long Jiang** S China
163 Y10 **Longjing** var. Yanji. Jilin, NE China 42°48′N 129°26′E
161 R4 **Longkou** Shandong, E China 37°40′N 120°21′E
12 E11 **Longlac** Ontario, S Canada 49°47′N 86°34′W
19 S1 **Long Lake** Maine, NE USA
31 R5 **Long Lake** Michigan, N USA
31 O6 **Long Lake** Michigan, N USA
29 N6 **Long Lake** North Dakota, N USA
30 J4 **Long Lake** Wisconsin, N USA
99 K23 **Longlier** Luxembourg, SE Belgium 49°51′N 05°27′E
160 I13 **Longlin** var. Longlin Gezu Zizhixian, Xinzhou. Guangxi Zhuangzu Zizhiqu, S China 24°46′N 105°19′E
Longlin Gezu Zizhixian see Longlin
37 T3 **Longmont** Colorado, C USA 40°09′N 105°07′W
157 P10 **Longnan** var. Wudu. Gansu, C China 33°27′N 104°57′E
29 N13 **Long Pine** Nebraska, C USA 42°32′N 99°42′W
Longping see Luodian

◆ Country
● Country Capital
◇ Dependent Territory
○ Dependent Territory Capital
◐ Administrative Regions
International Airport
▲ Mountain
▲▲ Mountain Range
Volcano
River
Lake
Reservoir

14 F17 **Long Point** headland Ontario, S Canada 42°33′N 80°15′W
14 K15 **Long Point** headland Ontario, SE Canada 43°56′N 76°53′W
184 P10 **Long Point** headland North Island, New Zealand 39°07′S 177°41′E
30 L2 **Long Point** headland Michigan, N USA 47°50′N 89°09′W
14 G17 **Long Point Bay** lake bay Ontario, S Canada
29 T7 **Long Prairie** Minnesota, N USA 45°58′N 94°52′W
Longquan see Fenggang
Longquan see Yanggao
13 S11 **Long Range Mountains** hill range Newfoundland and Labrador, E Canada
65 H25 **Long Range Point** headland SE Saint Helena 16°00′S 05°41′W
181 V8 **Longreach** Queensland, E Australia 23°31′S 144°18′E
160 H7 **Longriba** Sichuan, C China 32°32′N 102°20′E
160 L10 **Longshan** var. Min'an. Hunan, S China 29°25′N 109°28′E
37 S3 **Longs Peak** ▲ Colorado, C USA 40°15′N 105°37′W
Long Strait see Longa, Proliv
102 K8 **Longué** Maine-et-Loire, NW France 47°23′N 00°07′W
13 P11 **Longue-Pointe** Québec, E Canada 50°20′N 64°13′W
103 S4 **Longuyon** Meurthe-et-Moselle, NE France 49°25′N 05°37′E
25 W7 **Longview** Texas, SW USA 32°30′N 94°45′W
32 G10 **Longview** Washington, NW USA 46°08′N 122°56′W
65 H25 **Longwood** C Saint Helena
25 P7 **Longworth** Texas, SW USA 32°37′N 100°20′W
103 S3 **Longwy** Meurthe-et-Moselle, NE France 49°31′N 05°46′E
159 V11 **Longxi** var. Gongchang. Gansu, C China 35°00′N 104°34′E
Longxian see Wengyuan
167 S14 **Long Xuyên** var. Longxuyen. An Giang, S Vietnam 10°23′N 105°25′E
Longxuyen see Long Xuyên
161 Q13 **Longyan** Fujian, SE China 25°06′N 117°02′E
92 O3 **Longyearbyen** ○ (Svalbard) Spitsbergen, W Svalbard 78°12′N 15°39′E
160 J15 **Longzhou** Guangxi Zhuangzu Zizhiqu, S China 22°22′N 106°46′E
Longzhouping see Changyang
100 F12 **Löningen** Niedersachsen, NW Germany 52°43′N 07°42′E
27 V11 **Lonoke** Arkansas, C USA 34°46′N 91°56′W
95 L21 **Lönsboda** Skåne, S Sweden 56°24′N 14°19′E
103 S9 **Lons-le-Saunier** anc. Ledo Salinarius. Jura, E France 46°41′N 05°32′E
31 O15 **Loogootee** Indiana, N USA 38°40′N 86°54′W
31 Q9 **Looking Glass River** ≈ Michigan, N USA
21 X11 **Lookout, Cape** headland North Carolina, SE USA 34°36′N 76°31′W
39 O6 **Lookout Ridge** ridge Alaska, USA
Lookransar see Lūnkaransar
181 N11 **Loongana** Western Australia 30°53′S 127°15′E
99 I14 **Loon op Zand** Noord-Brabant, S Netherlands 51°38′N 05°05′E
97 A19 **Loop Head** Ir. Ceann Léime. promontory W Ireland
109 V4 **Loosdorf** Niederösterreich, NE Austria 48°13′N 15°25′E
158 G10 **Lop** Xinjiang Uygur Zizhiqu, NW China 37°06′N 80°12′E
112 J11 **Lopare** ◈ Republika Srpska, NE Bosnia and Herzegovina
Lopatichi see Lapatsichy
127 P7 **Lopatino** Penzenskaya Oblast', W Russian Federation 52°38′N 45°46′E
167 P10 **Lop Buri** var. Loburi. Lop Buri, C Thailand 14°49′N 100°37′E
25 R16 **Lopeno** Texas, SW USA 26°42′N 99°06′W
79 C18 **Lopez, Cap** headland W Gabon 00°39′S 08°44′E
98 I12 **Lopik** Utrecht, C Netherlands 51°58′N 04°57′E
Lop Nor see Lop Nur
158 M7 **Lop Nur** var. Lob Nor, Lop Nor, Lo-pu Po. seasonal lake NW China
Lopnur see Yuli
79 K17 **Lopori** ≈ NW Dem. Rep. Congo
98 O5 **Loppersum** Groningen, NE Netherlands 53°20′N 06°45′E
92 I8 **Lopphavet** sound N Norway
Lo-pu Po see Lop Nur
Lora see Lowrah
182 F3 **Lora Creek** seasonal river South Australia
104 K13 **Lora del Río** Andalucía, S Spain 37°39′N 05°32′W
148 M11 **Lora, Hāmūn-i** wetland SW Pakistan
31 T11 **Lorain** Ohio, N USA 41°27′N 82°10′W
25 O7 **Loraine** Texas, SW USA 32°24′N 100°42′W
149 Q10 **Loralai** Baluchistān, SW Pakistan 30°22′N 68°36′E
31 R13 **Loramie, Lake** ⊠ Ohio, N USA
105 Q13 **Lorca** Ar. Lurka; anc. Eliocroca, Lat. Illurco. Murcia, S Spain 37°40′N 01°41′W
143 N11 **Lordegān** Chahār Mahall va Bakhtiārī, C Iran 31°31′N 50°48′E
192 I10 **Lord Howe Island** island E Australia
Lord Howe Island see Ontong Java Atoll
175 O10 **Lord Howe Rise** undersea feature SW Pacific Ocean
192 J10 **Lord Howe Seamounts** undersea feature W Pacific Ocean
37 P15 **Lordsburg** New Mexico, SW USA 32°19′N 108°42′W
186 E5 **Lorengau** var. Lorungau. Manus Island, N Papua New Guinea 02°01′S 147°15′E
25 N5 **Lorenzo** Texas, SW USA 33°40′N 101°31′W
142 K7 **Lorestān** off. Ostān-e Lorestān, var. Luristan. ◈ province W Iran
Lorestān, Ostān-e see Lorestān
57 M17 **Loreto** Beni, N Bolivia 15°13′S 64°44′W
106 J12 **Loreto** Marche, C Italy 43°25′N 13°37′E
40 F8 **Loreto** Baja California Sur, NW Mexico 25°59′N 111°22′W
40 M11 **Loreto** Zacatecas, C Mexico 22°15′N 102°00′W
56 E9 **Loreto** off. Departamento de Loreto. ◈ department NE Peru
Loreto, Departamento de see Loreto
81 K18 **Lorian Swamp** swamp E Kenya
54 E6 **Lorica** Córdoba, NW Colombia 09°14′N 75°50′W
102 G7 **Lorient** prev. l'Orient. Morbihan, NW France 47°45′N 03°22′W
l'Orient see Lorient
111 K22 **Lőrinci** Heves, NE Hungary 47°46′N 19°40′E
14 G11 **Loring** Ontario, S Canada 45°55′N 79°59′W
33 V6 **Loring** Montana, NW USA 48°49′N 107°48′W
103 R13 **Loriol-sur-Drôme** Drôme, E France 44°46′N 04°51′E
21 U12 **Loris** South Carolina, SE USA 34°03′N 78°53′W
57 I18 **Loriscota, Laguna** ◎ S Peru
183 N13 **Lorne** Victoria, SE Australia 38°33′S 143°57′E
96 G11 **Lorn, Firth of** inlet W Scotland, United Kingdom
Loro Sae see East Timor
101 F24 **Lörrach** Baden-Württemberg, S Germany 47°38′N 07°40′E
103 T5 **Lorraine** ◈ region NE France
Lorungau see Lorengau
94 L11 **Los** Gävleborg, C Sweden 61°43′N 15°15′E
35 P14 **Los Alamos** California, W USA 34°44′N 120°16′W
37 S10 **Los Alamos** New Mexico, SW USA 35°52′N 106°17′W
42 F5 **Los Amates** Izabal, E Guatemala 15°14′N 89°06′W
63 G14 **Los Ángeles** Bío Bío, C Chile 37°30′S 72°18′W
35 S15 **Los Angeles** California, W USA 34°03′N 118°15′W
35 S15 **Los Angeles** ✕ California, W USA 33°54′N 118°24′W
35 T13 **Los Angeles Aqueduct** aqueduct California, W USA
Losanna see Lausanne
63 H20 **Los Antiguos** Santa Cruz, SW Argentina 46°36′S 71°31′W
189 Q16 **Losap Atoll** atoll C Micronesia
35 P10 **Los Banos** California, W USA 37°00′N 120°39′W
104 K16 **Los Barrios** Andalucía, S Spain 36°11′N 05°30′W
62 L5 **Los Blancos** Salta, N Argentina 23°36′S 62°35′W
42 L12 **Los Chiles** Alajuela, NW Costa Rica 11°00′N 84°42′W
105 O2 **Los Corrales de Buelna** Cantabria, N Spain 43°15′N 04°04′W
25 T17 **Los Fresnos** Texas, SW USA 26°03′N 97°28′W
35 N9 **Los Gatos** California, W USA 37°13′N 121°58′W
127 P10 **Loshchina** Volgogradskaya Oblast', SW Russian Federation 48°58′N 46°14′E
110 O11 **Łosice** Mazowieckie, C Poland 52°13′N 22°42′E
112 B11 **Lošinj** Ger. Lussin, It. Lussino. island W Croatia
Los Jardines see Ngetik Atoll
63 G15 **Los Lagos** Los Lagos, C Chile 39°50′S 72°50′W
63 F17 **Los Lagos** off. Región de los Lagos. ◈ region C Chile
los Lagos, Región de see Los Lagos
Loslau see Wodzisław Śląski
64 N11 **Los Llanos de Aridane** var. Los Llanos de Aridane. La Palma, Islas Canarias, Spain, NE Atlantic Ocean 28°39′N 17°54′W
Los Llanos de Aridane see Los Llanos de Aridane
37 R11 **Los Lunas** New Mexico, SW USA 34°48′N 106°43′W
63 I16 **Los Menucos** Río Negro, C Argentina 40°52′S 68°07′W
40 H8 **Los Mochis** Sinaloa, C Mexico 25°48′N 108°58′W
35 N4 **Los Molinos** California, W USA 40°00′N 122°05′W
104 M9 **Los Navalmorales** Castilla-La Mancha, C Spain 39°43′N 04°38′W
25 S15 **Los Olmos Creek** ≈ Texas, SW USA
Losonc/Losontz see Lučenec
167 S5 **Lô, Sông** var. Panlong Jiang. ≈ China/Vietnam
44 B5 **Los Palacios** Pinar del Río, W Cuba 22°35′N 83°16′W
104 K14 **Los Palacios y Villafranca** Andalucía, S Spain 37°10′N 05°55′W
37 R12 **Los Pinos Mountains** ▲ New Mexico, SW USA
37 R11 **Los Ranchos de Albuquerque** New Mexico, SW USA 35°09′N 106°37′W
40 M14 **Los Reyes** Michoacán, SW Mexico 19°36′N 102°29′W
56 B7 **Los Ríos** ◈ province C Ecuador
64 O11 **Los Rodeos** ✕ (Santa Cruz de Tenerife) Tenerife, Islas Canarias, Spain, NE Atlantic Ocean 28°27′N 16°20′W
54 L4 **Los Roques, Islas** island group N Venezuela
43 S17 **Los Santos** Los Santos, S Panama 07°56′N 80°23′W
43 S17 **Los Santos** off. Provincia de Los Santos. ◈ province S Panama
Los Santos see Los Santos de Maimona
104 J12 **Los Santos de Maimona** var. Los Santos. Extremadura, W Spain 38°27′N 06°22′W
Los Santos, Provincia de see Los Santos
98 P10 **Losser** Overijssel, E Netherlands 52°16′N 06°25′E
96 J8 **Lossiemouth** NE Scotland, United Kingdom 57°43′N 03°18′W
61 B14 **Los Tábanos** Santa Fe, C Argentina 28°27′S 59°57′W
54 J4 **Los Taques** Falcón, N Venezuela 11°50′N 70°16′W
14 G11 **Lost Channel** Ontario, S Canada 45°54′N 80°20′W
54 L5 **Los Teques** Miranda, N Venezuela 10°25′N 67°01′W
35 Q12 **Lost Hills** California, W USA 35°35′N 119°40′W
36 I7 **Lost Peak** ▲ Utah, W USA 37°30′N 113°57′W
33 P11 **Lost Trail Pass** pass Montana, NW USA
186 G9 **Losuia** Kiriwina Island, SE Papua New Guinea 08°29′S 151°03′E
62 G10 **Los Vilos** Coquimbo, C Chile 31°56′S 71°35′W
105 N10 **Los Yébenes** Castilla-La Mancha, C Spain 39°35′N 03°52′W
103 N13 **Lot** ◈ department S France
103 N13 **Lot** ≈ S France
63 F14 **Lota** Bío Bío, C Chile 37°07′S 73°10′W
81 G15 **Lotagipi Swamp** wetland Kenya/Sudan
102 K14 **Lot-et-Garonne** ◈ department SW France
83 K21 **Lothair** Mpumalanga, NE South Africa 26°23′S 30°26′E
33 R7 **Lothair** Montana, NW USA 48°28′N 111°15′W
79 L20 **Loto** Kasai-Oriental, C Dem. Rep. Congo 02°48′S 22°30′E
108 E10 **Lötschbergtunnel** tunnel Valais, SW Switzerland
25 T9 **Lott** Texas, SW USA 31°12′N 97°02′W
124 H3 **Lotta** var. Lutto. ≈ Finland/Russian Federation
184 Q7 **Lottin Point** headland North Island, New Zealand 37°26′S 178°07′E
Lötzen see Giżycko
Loualaba see Lualaba
167 P6 **Louangnamtha** var. Luong Nam Tha. Louang Namtha, N Laos 20°55′N 101°24′E
167 Q7 **Louangphabang** var. Louangphrabang, Luang Prabang. Louangphabang, N Laos 19°51′N 102°08′E
Louangphrabang see Louangphabang
194 H5 **Loubet Coast** physical region Antarctica
Loubomo see Dolisie
Louch see Loukhi
102 H6 **Loudéac** Côtes d'Armor, NW France 48°11′N 02°45′W
160 M11 **Loudi** Hunan, S China 27°51′N 111°59′E
79 F21 **Loudima** Bouenza, S Congo 04°06′S 13°05′E
20 M9 **Loudon** Tennessee, S USA 35°43′N 84°19′W
31 T12 **Loudonville** Ohio, N USA 40°38′N 82°13′W
102 L8 **Loudun** Vienne, W France 47°01′N 00°05′E
102 K7 **Loué** Sarthe, NW France 48°00′N 00°14′W
76 G10 **Louga** NW Senegal 15°36′N 16°15′W
97 M19 **Loughborough** C England, United Kingdom 52°47′N 01°11′W
97 C18 **Loughrea** Ir. Baile Locha Riach. Galway, W Ireland 53°12′N 08°34′W
103 S9 **Louhans** Saône-et-Loire, C France 46°38′N 05°12′E
21 P5 **Louisa** Kentucky, S USA 38°06′N 82°37′W
21 V5 **Louisa** Virginia, NE USA 38°02′N 78°00′W
21 V9 **Louisburg** North Carolina, SE USA 36°05′N 78°18′W
25 U12 **Louise** Texas, SW USA 29°07′N 96°22′W
15 P11 **Louiseville** Québec, SE Canada 46°15′N 72°54′W
27 W3 **Louisiana** Missouri, C USA 39°25′N 91°03′W
22 G8 **Louisiana** off. State of Louisiana, also known as Creole State, Pelican State. ◈ state S USA
Louis Trichardt see Makhado
23 V4 **Louisville** Georgia, SE USA 33°00′N 82°24′W
30 M15 **Louisville** Illinois, N USA 38°46′N 88°32′W
20 K5 **Louisville** Kentucky, S USA 38°15′N 85°46′W
22 M4 **Louisville** Mississippi, S USA 33°07′N 89°03′W
29 S15 **Louisville** Nebraska, C USA 41°00′N 96°09′W
192 L11 **Louisville Ridge** undersea feature S Pacific Ocean
124 J6 **Loukhi** var. Louch. Respublika Kareliya, NW Russian Federation 66°05′N 33°04′E
79 H19 **Loukoléla** Cuvette, E Congo 01°04′S 17°10′E
104 G14 **Loulé** Faro, S Portugal 37°08′N 08°02′W
111 C16 **Louny** Ger. Laun. Ústecký Kraj, NW Czech Republic 50°22′N 13°50′E
29 O15 **Loup City** Nebraska, C USA 41°16′N 98°58′W
29 P15 **Loup River** ≈ Nebraska, C USA
15 S9 **Loup, Rivière du** ≈ Québec, SE Canada
12 K7 **Loups Marins, Lacs des** ◎ Québec, NE Canada
102 K16 **Lourdes** Hautes-Pyrénées, S France 43°06′N 00°03′W
Lourenço Marques see Maputo
104 F11 **Loures** Lisboa, C Portugal 38°50′N 09°10′W
104 F10 **Lourinhã** Lisboa, C Portugal 39°14′N 09°19′W
115 C16 **Loúros** ≈ W Greece
104 G8 **Lousã** Coimbra, N Portugal 40°07′N 08°15′W
Loushanguan see Tongzi
160 M10 **Lou Shui** ≈ C China
183 O5 **Louth** New South Wales, SE Australia 30°34′S 145°07′E
97 O18 **Louth** E England, United Kingdom 53°19′N 00°00′E
97 F17 **Louth** Ir. Lú. cultural region NE Ireland
115 H15 **Loutrá** Kentrikí Makedonía, N Greece 39°55′N 23°37′E
115 G19 **Loutráki** Pelopónnisos, S Greece 37°55′N 22°55′E
Louvain see Leuven
99 H19 **Louvain-la Neuve** Walloon Brabant, C Belgium 50°39′N 04°36′E
14 J8 **Louvicourt** Québec, SE Canada 48°04′N 77°22′W
102 M4 **Louviers** Eure, N France 49°13′N 01°11′E
30 K14 **Lou Yaeger, Lake** ⊠ Illinois, N USA
93 J15 **Lövånger** Västerbotten, N Sweden 64°22′N 21°19′E
124 J14 **Lovat'** ≈ NW Russian Federation
113 J17 **Lovćen** ▲ SW Montenegro 42°22′N 18°49′E
114 I8 **Lovech** Lovech, N Bulgaria 43°08′N 24°45′E
114 I9 **Lovech** ◈ province N Bulgaria
25 V9 **Lovelady** Texas, SW USA 31°07′N 95°27′W
37 T3 **Loveland** Colorado, C USA 40°24′N 105°04′W
33 U12 **Lovell** Wyoming, C USA 44°50′N 108°23′W
Lovello, Monte see Grosser Löffler
35 S4 **Lovelock** Nevada, W USA 40°11′N 118°30′W
106 E7 **Lovere** Lombardia, N Italy 45°51′N 10°06′E
30 L10 **Loves Park** Illinois, N USA 42°19′N 89°03′W
26 M2 **Lovewell Reservoir** ⊠ Kansas, C USA
93 M19 **Loviisa** Swe. Lovisa. Etelä-Suomi, S Finland 60°27′N 26°15′E
37 V15 **Loving** New Mexico, SW USA 32°17′N 104°06′W
21 U6 **Lovingston** Virginia, NE USA 37°46′N 78°54′W
37 V14 **Lovington** New Mexico, SW USA 32°56′N 103°21′W
Lovisa see Loviisa
111 C15 **Lovosice** Ger. Lobositz. Ústecký Kraj, NW Czech Republic 50°30′N 14°02′E
124 K4 **Lovozero** Murmanskaya Oblast', NW Russian Federation 68°00′N 35°03′E
124 K4 **Lovozero, Ozero** ◎ NW Russian Federation
112 B9 **Lovran** It. Laurana. Primorje-Gorski Kotar, NW Croatia 45°16′N 14°15′E
116 E11 **Lovrin** Ger. Lowrin. Timiș, W Romania 45°58′N 20°49′E
82 E10 **Lóvua** Lunda Norte, NE Angola 07°21′S 20°09′E
82 G12 **Lóvua** Moxico, E Angola 11°33′S 23°35′E
65 D25 **Low Bay** bay East Falkland, Falkland Islands
9 P9 **Low, Cape** headland Nunavut, E Canada 63°05′N 85°27′W
33 N10 **Lowell** Idaho, NW USA 46°07′N 115°36′W
19 O10 **Lowell** Massachusetts, NE USA 42°38′N 71°19′W
Löwen see Leuven
Löwenberg in Schlesien see Lwówek Śląski
Lower Austria see Niederösterreich
Lower Bann see Bann
Lower California see Baja California
Lower Danube see Niederösterreich
185 L14 **Lower Hutt** Wellington, North Island, New Zealand 41°13′S 174°51′E
39 N11 **Lower Kalskag** Alaska, USA 61°30′N 160°28′W
35 O1 **Lower Klamath Lake** ◎ California, W USA
35 Q2 **Lower Lake** ◎ California/Nevada, W USA
97 E15 **Lower Lough Erne** ◎ SW Northern Ireland, United Kingdom
Lower Lusatia see Niederlausitz
Lower Normandy see Basse-Normandie
10 K9 **Lower Post** British Columbia, W Canada 59°53′N 128°19′W
29 T4 **Lower Red Lake** ◎ Minnesota, N USA
Lower Rhine see Neder Rijn
Lower Saxony see Niedersachsen
97 Q19 **Lowestoft** E England, United Kingdom 52°29′N 01°45′E
149 Q5 **Lowgar** var. Logar. ◈ province E Afghanistan
182 H7 **Low Hill** South Australia 32°17′S 136°46′E
110 K12 **Łowicz** Łódzkie, C Poland 52°06′N 19°55′E
33 N13 **Lowman** Idaho, NW USA 44°04′N 115°37′W
149 P8 **Lowrah** var. Lora. ≈ SE Afghanistan
Lowrin see Lovrin
183 N17 **Low Rocky Point** headland Tasmania, SE Australia 42°59′S 145°28′E
18 I8 **Lowville** New York, NE USA 43°47′N 75°29′W
Loxa see Loksa
182 K9 **Loxton** South Australia 34°30′S 140°36′E
81 G21 **Loya** Tabora, C Tanzania 04°57′S 33°53′E
30 K6 **Loyal** Wisconsin, N USA 44°45′N 90°30′W
18 G13 **Loyalsock Creek** ≈ Pennsylvania, NE USA
35 Q5 **Loyalton** California, W USA 39°39′N 120°16′W
Lo-yang see Luoyang
187 Q16 **Loyauté, Îles** island group S New Caledonia
Loyev see Loyew
119 O20 **Loyew** Rus. Loyev. Homyel'skaya Voblasts', SE Belarus 51°56′N 30°48′E
125 S13 **Loyno** Kirovskaya Oblast', NW Russian Federation 59°44′N 52°42′E
103 P13 **Lozère** ◈ department S France
103 Q14 **Lozère, Mont** ▲ S France 44°27′N 03°44′E
112 J11 **Loznica** Serbia, W Serbia 44°32′N 19°13′E
114 L8 **Loznitsa** Razgrad, N Bulgaria 43°22′N 26°36′E
117 V7 **Lozova** Rus. Lozovaya. Kharkivs'ka Oblast', E Ukraine 48°54′N 36°23′E
Lozovaya see Lozova
105 N7 **Lozoyuela** Madrid, C Spain 40°55′N 03°36′W
Lu see Shandong, China
Lú see Louth, Ireland
82 F12 **Luacano** Moxico, E Angola 11°19′S 21°30′E
79 N21 **Lualaba** Fr. Loualaba. ≈ SE Dem. Rep. Congo
83 H14 **Luampa** Western, NW Zambia 15°02′S 24°27′E
83 H15 **Luampa Kuta** Western, W Zambia 15°22′S 24°40′E
161 P8 **Lu'an** Anhui, E China 31°46′N 116°31′E
104 K2 **Luanco** Asturias, N Spain 43°36′N 05°48′W
82 A11 **Luanda** var. Loanda, Port. São Paulo de Loanda. ● Luanda, NW Angola 08°48′S 13°17′E
82 A11 **Luanda** ◈ province (Angola) NW Angola
82 A11 **Luanda** ✕ Luanda, NW Angola 08°49′S 13°16′E
82 D12 **Luando** ≈ C Angola
Luang see Tapi, Mae Nam
83 G14 **Luanginga** var. Luanguinga. ≈ Angola/Zambia
167 N15 **Luang, Khao** ▲ SW Thailand 08°21′N 99°46′E
Luang Prabang see Louangphabang
167 P8 **Luang Prabang Range** Th. Thiukhaoluang Phrahang. ▲ Laos/Thailand
167 N16 **Luang, Thale** lagoon S Thailand
Luangua, Rio see Luangwa
82 E11 **Luangue** ≈ NE Angola
Luanguinga see Luanginga
83 K15 **Luangwa** var. Aruângua. Lusaka, C Zambia 15°36′S 30°27′E
83 K14 **Luangwa** var. Aruângua, Rio Luangua. ≈ Mozambique/Zambia
161 Q2 **Luan He** ≈ E China
190 G11 **Luaniva, Île** island E Wallis and Futuna
161 P2 **Luanping** var. Anjiangying. Hebei, E China 40°55′N 117°19′E
82 J13 **Luanshya** Copperbelt, C Zambia 13°09′S 28°24′E
62 K13 **Luan Toro** La Pampa, C Argentina 36°14′S 64°15′W
161 Q2 **Luanxian** var. Luan Xian. Hebei, E China 39°46′N 118°46′E
Luan Xian see Luanxian
82 J12 **Luapula** ◈ province N Zambia
79 O25 **Luapula** ≈ Dem. Rep. Congo/Zambia
104 J2 **Luarca** Asturias, N Spain 43°33′N 06°31′W
169 R10 **Luar, Danau** ◎ Borneo, N Indonesia
79 L25 **Luashi** Katanga, S Dem. Rep. Congo 10°54′S 23°55′E
82 G12 **Luau** Port. Vila Teixeira de Sousa. Moxico, NE Angola 10°42′S 22°12′E
79 C16 **Luba** prev. San Carlos. Isla de Bioco, NW Equatorial Guinea 03°26′N 08°36′E
42 F4 **Lubaantun** ruins Toledo, S Belize
111 P16 **Lubaczów** var. Lúbaczów. Podkarpackie, SE Poland 50°10′N 23°08′E
Lubale see Lubalo
82 E11 **Lubalo** Lunda Norte, NE Angola 09°02′S 19°11′E
82 E11 **Lubalo** var. Lubale. ≈ Angola/Dem. Rep. Congo
118 J9 **Lubāna** Madona, E Latvia 56°55′N 26°43′E
Lubānas Ezers see Lubāns
171 N4 **Lubang Island** island N Philippines
83 B15 **Lubango** Port. Sá da Bandeira. Huíla, SW Angola 14°55′S 13°33′E
118 J9 **Lubāns** var. Lubānas Ezers. ◎ E Latvia
79 M21 **Lubao** Kasai-Oriental, C Dem. Rep. Congo 05°21′S 25°42′E
110 O13 **Lubartów** Ger. Qumälisch. Lublin, E Poland 51°29′N 22°38′E
100 G13 **Lübbecke** Nordrhein-Westfalen, NW Germany 52°18′N 08°37′E
100 O13 **Lübben** Brandenburg, E Germany 51°56′N 13°52′E
101 P14 **Lübbenau** Brandenburg, E Germany 51°52′N 13°57′E
25 N5 **Lubbock** Texas, SW USA 33°35′N 101°51′W
Lubcz see Lyubcha
19 U6 **Lubec** Maine, NE USA 44°49′N 67°00′W
100 K9 **Lübeck** Schleswig-Holstein, N Germany 53°52′N 10°41′E
100 K8 **Lübecker Bucht** bay N Germany
79 M21 **Lubefu** Kasai-Oriental, C Dem. Rep. Congo 04°43′S 24°25′E
163 T10 **Lubei** var. Jarud Qi. Nei Mongol Zizhiqu, N China 44°25′N 121°12′E
111 O14 **Lubelska, Wyżyna** plateau SE Poland
110 O13 **Lubelskie** ◈ province E Poland
Lubembe see Luembe
Lüben see Lubin
144 H9 **Lubenka** Zapadnyy Kazakhstan, W Kazakhstan 50°27′N 54°07′E
79 P18 **Lubero** Nord-Kivu, E Dem. Rep. Congo 0°10′S 29°12′E
79 L22 **Lubi** ≈ S Dem. Rep. Congo
Lubiana see Ljubljana
110 J11 **Lubień Kujawski** Kujawsko-pomorskie, C Poland 52°25′N 19°10′E
67 T11 **Lubilandji** ≈ S Dem. Rep. Congo
110 F13 **Lubin** Ger. Lüben. Dolnośląskie, SW Poland 51°23′N 16°12′E
111 O14 **Lublin** Rus. Lyublin. Lubelskie, E Poland 51°15′N 22°33′E
111 J15 **Lubliniec** Śląskie, S Poland 50°41′N 18°41′E
Lubnān, Jabal see Liban, Jebel
117 R5 **Lubny** Poltavs'ka Oblast', NE Ukraine 50°00′N 33°00′E
Luboml see Lyuboml'
110 G11 **Luboń** Ger. Peterhof. Wielkolpolskie, C Poland 52°23′N 16°54′E
110 D12 **Lubsko** Ger. Sommerfeld. Lubuskie, W Poland 51°47′N 14°57′E
79 N24 **Lubudi** Katanga, SE Dem. Rep. Congo 09°57′S 25°59′E
168 L13 **Lubuklinggau** Sumatera, W Indonesia 03°10′S 102°52′E
79 N25 **Lubumbashi** prev. Élisabethville. Shaba, SE Dem. Rep. Congo 11°40′S 27°31′E
83 I14 **Lubungu** Central, C Zambia 14°28′S 26°30′E
110 E12 **Lubuskie** ◈ province W Poland
Lubuskie see Dobiegniew
79 N18 **Lubutu** Maniema, E Dem. Rep. Congo 0°48′S 26°39′E
Luca see Lucca
82 C11 **Lucala** ≈ W Angola
14 E16 **Lucan** Ontario, S Canada 43°10′N 81°22′W
97 F18 **Lucan** Ir. Leamhcán. Dublin, E Ireland 53°22′N 06°27′W
Lucanian Mountains see Lucano, Appennino
107 M18 **Lucano, Appennino** Eng. Lucanian Mountains. ▲ S Italy
82 F11 **Lucapa** var. Lukapa. Lunda Norte, NE Angola 08°24′S 20°42′E
29 V15 **Lucas** Iowa, C USA 41°01′N 93°26′W
61 C18 **Lucas González** Entre Ríos, E Argentina 32°25′S 59°33′W
31 S15 **Lucasville** Ohio, N USA 38°52′N 83°00′W
106 F11 **Lucca** anc. Luca. Toscana, C Italy 43°50′N 10°30′E
44 H12 **Lucea** W Jamaica 18°26′N 78°11′W
97 H15 **Luce Bay** inlet SW Scotland, United Kingdom
22 M8 **Lucedale** Mississippi, S USA 30°55′N 88°35′W
171 O4 **Lucena** off. Lucena City. Luzon, N Philippines 13°57′N 121°38′E
104 M14 **Lucena** Andalucía, S Spain 37°25′N 04°29′W
Lucena City see Lucena
105 S8 **Lucena del Cid** País Valenciano, E Spain 40°07′N 00°15′W
111 D15 **Lučenec** Ger. Losontz, Hung. Losonc. Banskobystrický Kraj, C Slovakia 48°21′N 19°37′E
Lucentum see Alicante
107 M16 **Lucera** Puglia, SE Italy 41°30′N 15°19′E
Lucerna/Lucerne see Luzern
Lucerne, Lake of see Vierwaldstätter See
40 J4 **Lucero** Chihuahua, N Mexico 30°50′N 106°30′W
123 S14 **Luchegorsk** Primorskiy Kray, SE Russian Federation 46°26′N 134°10′E
105 Q13 **Luchena** ≈ SE Spain
Lucheng see Kangding
82 N13 **Lucheringo** var. Luchulingo. ≈ N Mozambique
Luchesa see Luchosa
Luchin see Lyachyn
118 N13 **Luchosa** Rus. Luchesa. ≈ N Belarus
100 K11 **Lüchow** Mecklenburg-Vorpommern, N Germany 52°57′N 11°10′E
Luchow see Hefei
Luchulingo see Lucheringo
119 N17 **Luchyn** Rus. Luchin. Homyel'skaya Voblasts', SE Belarus 53°01′N 30°01′E
55 U11 **Lucie Rivier** ≈ W Surinam
182 K11 **Lucindale** South Australia 36°57′S 140°20′E
83 A14 **Lucira** Namibe, SW Angola 13°51′S 12°35′E
Łuck see Luts'k
101 O14 **Luckau** Brandenburg, E Germany 51°50′N 13°42′E
100 N13 **Luckenwalde** Brandenburg, E Germany 52°05′N 13°11′E
14 E15 **Lucknow** Ontario, S Canada 43°58′N 81°30′W
152 L12 **Lucknow** var. Lakhnau. state capital Uttar Pradesh, N India 26°50′N 80°54′E
102 J10 **Luçon** Vendée, NW France 46°27′N 01°10′W
44 I7 **Lucrecia, Cabo** headland E Cuba 21°00′N 75°34′W
82 F13 **Lucusse** Moxico, E Angola 12°32′S 20°46′E
Lüda see Dalian
114 M9 **Luda Kamchiya** ≈ E Bulgaria
Ludasch see Luduş
114 I10 **Luda Yana** ≈ C Bulgaria
112 F7 **Ludbreg** Varaždin, N Croatia 46°15′N 16°36′E
29 P7 **Ludden** North Dakota, N USA 45°58′N 98°07′W
101 F15 **Lüdenscheid** Nordrhein-Westfalen, W Germany 51°13′N 07°38′E
83 C21 **Lüderitz** prev. Angra Pequena. Karas, SW Namibia 26°38′S 15°10′E
152 H8 **Ludhiāna** Punjab, N India 30°56′N 75°52′E
31 O7 **Ludington** Michigan, N USA 43°58′N 86°27′W
97 K20 **Ludlow** W England, United Kingdom 52°20′N 02°28′W
35 W14 **Ludlow** California, W USA 34°43′N 116°07′W
28 J7 **Ludlow** South Dakota, N USA 45°48′N 103°21′W
18 M9 **Ludlow** Vermont, NE USA 43°24′N 72°39′W
114 L7 **Ludogorie** physical region NE Bulgaria
23 W6 **Ludowici** Georgia, SE USA 31°42′N 81°44′W
Ludsan see Ludza
116 I10 **Luduş** Ger. Ludasch, Hung. Marosludas. Mureş, C Romania 46°28′N 24°05′E
95 M14 **Ludvika** Dalarna, C Sweden 60°08′N 15°14′E
101 H21 **Ludwigsburg** Baden-Württemberg, SW Germany 48°54′N 09°12′E
100 O13 **Ludwigsfelde** Brandenburg, NE Germany 52°17′N 13°15′E
101 G20 **Ludwigshafen** var. Ludwigshafen am Rhein. Rheinland-Pfalz, W Germany 49°29′N 08°24′E
Ludwigshafen am Rhein see Ludwigshafen
101 L20 **Ludwigskanal** canal SE Germany
100 L10 **Ludwigslust** Mecklenburg-Vorpommern, N Germany 53°19′N 11°29′E
118 K10 **Ludza** Ger. Ludsan. Ludza, E Latvia 56°32′N 27°41′E
79 K21 **Luebo** Kasai-Occidental, SW Dem. Rep. Congo 05°19′S 21°21′E
25 Q6 **Lueders** Texas, SW USA 32°46′N 99°38′W
79 N20 **Lueki** Maniema, C Dem. Rep. Congo 03°25′S 25°50′E
82 F10 **Luembe** var. Lubembe. ≈ Angola/Dem. Rep. Congo
82 E13 **Luena** var. Lwena, Port. Luso. Moxico, E Angola 11°47′S 19°52′E
79 M24 **Luena** Katanga, SE Dem. Rep. Congo 09°28′S 25°45′E
82 K12 **Luena** Northern, NE Zambia 10°40′S 30°21′E
82 F13 **Luena** ≈ E Angola
83 F16 **Luengue** ≈ SE Angola
67 V13 **Luenha** ≈ W Mozambique
83 G15 **Lueti** ≈ Angola/Zambia
160 J7 **Lüeyang** var. Hejiayan. Shaanxi, C China 33°12′N 106°31′E
161 P14 **Lufeng** Guangdong, S China 22°59′N 115°40′E
79 N24 **Lufira** ≈ SE Dem. Rep. Congo
79 N25 **Lufira, Lac de Retenue de la** var. Lac Tshangalele. ◎ SE Dem. Rep. Congo
25 W8 **Lufkin** Texas, SW USA 31°21′N 94°47′W
82 L11 **Lufubu** ≈ N Zambia
124 G14 **Luga** Leningradskaya Oblast', NW Russian Federation 58°43′N 29°46′E
124 G13 **Luga** ≈ NW Russian Federation
Luganer See see Lugano, Lago di
108 H11 **Lugano** Ger. Lauis. Ticino, S Switzerland 46°01′N 08°57′E
108 H12 **Lugano, Lago di** var. Ceresio, Ger. Luganer See. ◎ S Switzerland
Lugansk see Luhans'k
187 Q13 **Luganville** Espiritu Santo, C Vanuatu 15°31′S 167°12′E
Lugdunum see Lyon
Lugdunum Batavorum see Leiden
83 O15 **Lugela** Zambézia, NE Mozambique 16°27′S 36°47′E
83 O16 **Lugela** ≈ C Mozambique
82 P13 **Lugenda, Rio** ≈ N Mozambique
Luggarus see Locarno
Lugh Ganana see Luuq
97 G19 **Lugnaquillia Mountain** Ir. Log na Coille. ▲ E Ireland 52°58′N 06°27′W
106 H10 **Lugo** Emilia-Romagna, N Italy 44°25′N 11°53′E
104 I3 **Lugo** anc. Lugus Augusti. Galicia, NW Spain 43°N 07°33′W
104 I3 **Lugo** ◈ province Galicia, NW Spain
21 R12 **Lugoff** South Carolina, SE USA 34°13′N 80°41′W
116 F12 **Lugoj** Ger. Lugosch, Hung. Lugos. Timiș, W Romania 45°41′N 21°56′E
Lugos/Lugosch see Lugoj
Lugovoy/Lugovoye see Kulan
158 I13 **Lugu** Xizang Zizhiqu, W China 33°26′N 84°10′E
Lugus Augusti see Lugo
Luguvallium/Luguvallum see Carlisle
117 Y7 **Luhans'k** Rus. Lugansk; prev. Voroshilovgrad. Luhans'ka Oblast', E Ukraine 48°32′N 39°21′E
117 Y7 **Luhans'k** ✕ Luhans'ka Oblast', E Ukraine 48°25′N 39°24′E
Luhans'k see Luhans'ka Oblast'
117 X6 **Luhans'ka Oblast'** var. Luhans'k; prev. Voroshilovgrad, Rus. Voroshilovgradskaya Oblast'. ◈ province E Ukraine
161 Q7 **Luhe** Jiangsu, E China 32°20′N 118°52′E
171 S13 **Luhu** Pulau Seram, E Indonesia 03°20′S 127°58′E
Luhua see Heishui
160 G8 **Luhuo** var. Xindu, Tib. Zhaggo. Sichuan, C China 31°18′N 100°39′E
116 M3 **Luhyny** Zhytomyrs'ka Oblast', N Ukraine 51°06′N 28°24′E
83 G15 **Lui** ≈ W Zambia
83 G16 **Luiana** ≈ SE Angola
83 L15 **Luia, Rio** var. Ruya. ≈ Mozambique/Zimbabwe
Luichow Peninsula see Leizhou Bandao
Luik see Liège
82 C13 **Luimbale** Huambo, C Angola 12°15′S 15°19′E
Luimneach see Limerick
106 D6 **Luino** Lombardia, N Italy 46°00′N 08°45′E
82 E13 **Luio** ≈ E Angola
92 L11 **Luiro** ≈ NE Finland
79 N25 **Luishia** Katanga, SE Dem. Rep. Congo 11°18′S 27°08′E
59 M19 **Luislândia do Oeste** Minas Gerais, SE Brazil 17°59′S 45°35′W
40 K5 **Luis L. León, Presa** ⊠ N Mexico
Luis Muñoz Marin see San Juan
195 N5 **Luitpold Coast** physical region Antarctica
79 K22 **Luiza** Kasai-Occidental, S Dem. Rep. Congo 07°11′S 22°27′E
61 D20 **Luján** Buenos Aires, E Argentina 34°34′S 59°07′W
79 N24 **Lukafu** Katanga, SE Dem. Rep. Congo 10°28′S 27°32′E
Lukapa see Lucapa
112 I11 **Lukavac** ◈ Federacija Bosna I Hercegovina, NE Bosnia and Herzegovina
79 I20 **Lukenie** ≈ C Dem. Rep. Congo
114 J11 **Lŭki** Plovdiv, C Bulgaria 41°50′N 24°49′E
79 H19 **Lukolela** Equateur, W Dem. Rep. Congo 01°10′S 17°11′E
119 M14 **Lukoml'skaye, Vozyera** Rus. Ozero Lukoml'skoye. ◎ N Belarus
Lukoml'skoye, Ozero see Lukoml'skaye, Vozyera
114 I8 **Lukovit** Lovech, N Bulgaria 43°11′N 24°10′E
110 O12 **Łuków** Ger. Bogendorf. Lubelskie, E Poland 51°57′N 22°22′E
127 O4 **Lukoyanov** Nizhegorodskaya Oblast', W Russian Federation 55°02′N 44°26′E
Lukransar see Lūnkaransar

◆ Country ● Country Capital ◇ Dependent Territory ○ Dependent Territory Capital ◈ Administrative Regions ✕ International Airport ▲ Mountain ▲ Mountain Range Volcano ≈ River ◎ Lake ⊠ Reservoir

79 N22 **Lukuga** SE Dem. Rep. Congo
79 F21 **Lukula** Bas-Congo, SW Dem. Rep. Congo 05°23′S 12°57′E
83 G14 **Lukulu** Western, NW Zambia 14°24′S 23°12′E
189 R17 **Lukunor Atoll** *atoll* Mortlock Islands, C Micronesia
82 J12 **Lukwesa** Luapula, NE Zambia 10°03′S 28°42′E
93 K14 **Luleå** Norrbotten, N Sweden 65°35′N 22°10′E
92 J13 **Luleälven** N Sweden
136 C10 **Lüleburgaz** Kırklareli, NW Turkey 41°25′N 27°22′E
160 M4 **Lüliang** *var.* Lishi. Shanxi, C China 37°27′N 111°05′E
160 M4 **Lüliang Shan** ▲ C China
79 O21 **Lulimba** Maniema, E Dem. Rep. Congo 04°42′S 28°38′E
22 K9 **Luling** Louisiana, S USA 29°55′N 90°22′W
25 T11 **Luling** Texas, SW USA 29°40′N 97°39′W
79 I18 **Lulonga** NW Dem. Rep. Congo
79 K22 **Lulua** S Dem. Rep. Congo
Luluabourg *see* Kananga
192 L17 **Luma** Ta'ū, E American Samoa 14°15′S 169°30′W
169 S17 **Lumajang** Jawa, C Indonesia 08°06′S 113°13′E
158 G12 **Lumajangdong Co** ◎ W China
82 G13 **Lumbala Kaquengue** Moxico, E Angola 12°40′S 22°34′E
83 F14 **Lumbala N'Guimbo** *var.* Nguimbo, Gago Coutinho, *Port.* Vila Gago Coutinho. Moxico, E Angola 14°08′S 21°25′E
21 T11 **Lumber River** North Carolina/South Carolina, SE USA
Lumber State *see* Maine
22 L8 **Lumberton** Mississippi, S USA 31°00′N 89°27′W
21 U11 **Lumberton** North Carolina, SE USA 34°37′N 79°00′W
105 R4 **Lumbier** Navarra, N Spain 42°39′N 01°19′W
83 Q15 **Lumbo** Nampula, NE Mozambique 15°S 40°40′E
124 M4 **Lumbovka** Murmanskaya Oblast', NW Russian Federation 67°41′N 40°31′E
104 J7 **Lumbrales** Castilla-León, N Spain 40°57′N 06°43′W
153 W13 **Lumding** Assam, NE India 25°46′N 93°10′E
82 F12 **Lumege** *var.* Lumeje. Moxico, E Angola 11°30′S 20°57′E
Lumeje *see* Lumege
99 J17 **Lummen** Limburg, NE Belgium 50°58′N 05°12′E
93 J20 **Lumparland** Åland, SW Finland 60°06′N 20°15′E
167 T11 **Lumphăt** *prev.* Lomphat. Rôtânôkiri, NE Cambodia 13°30′N
11 U16 **Lumsden** Saskatchewan, S Canada 50°39′N 104°52′W
185 C23 **Lumsden** Southland, South Island, New Zealand 45°43′S 168°26′E
169 N14 **Lumut, Tanjung** *headland* Sumatera, W Indonesia 03°47′S 105°55′E
157 P4 **Lün** Töv, C Mongolia 47°51′N 105°11′E
116 I13 **Lunca Corbului** Argeş, S Romania 44°41′N 24°46′E
95 K23 **Lund** Skåne, S Sweden 55°42′N 13°10′E
35 X6 **Lund** Nevada, W USA 38°50′N 115°00′W
82 D11 **Lunda Norte** ◈ *province* NE Angola
82 E12 **Lunda Sul** ◈ *province* NE Angola
82 M13 **Lundazi** Eastern, NE Zambia 12°19′S 33°11′E
95 G16 **Lunde** Telemark, S Norway 61°31′N 06°38′E
Lundenburg *see* Břeclav
95 C17 **Lundevatnet** ◎ S Norway
Lundi *see* Runde
97 I23 **Lundy** *island* SW England, United Kingdom
100 J10 **Lüneburg** Niedersachsen, N Germany 53°15′N 10°25′E
100 J11 **Lüneburger Heide** *heathland* NW Germany
103 Q15 **Lunel** Hérault, S France 43°40′N 04°08′E
101 F14 **Lünen** Nordrhein-Westfalen, W Germany 51°37′N 07°31′E
13 P16 **Lunenburg** Nova Scotia, SE Canada 44°23′N 64°21′W
21 V7 **Lunenburg** Virginia, NE USA 36°56′N 78°15′W
103 T5 **Lunéville** Meurthe-et-Moselle, NE France 48°35′N 06°30′E
83 I14 **Lunga** C Zambia
Lunga, Isola *see* Dugi Otok
158 H12 **Lungdo** Xizang Zizhiqu, W China 33°45′N 82°09′E
158 I14 **Lunggar** Xizang Zizhiqu, W China 31°10′N 84°01′E
76 I15 **Lungi** ✈ (Freetown) W Sierra Leone 08°36′N 13°10′W
Lungkiang *see* Qiqihar
Lungleh *see* Lunglei
153 W15 **Lunglei** *prev.* Lungleh. Mizoram, NE India 22°55′N 92°49′E
158 L15 **Lungsang** Xizang Zizhiqu, W China 29°50′N 88°27′E
82 E13 **Lungué-Bungo** *var.* Lungwebungu. Angola/Zambia *see also* Lungwebungu
Lungué-Bungo *see* Lungwebungu
83 G14 **Lungwebungu** *var.* Lungué-Bungo. Angola/Zambia *see also* Lungué-Bungo
Lungwebungu *see* Lungué-Bungo
152 F12 **Lūni** Rājasthān, N India 26°03′N 73°00′E
152 F12 **Lūni** N India
Luninets *see* Luninyets
35 S7 **Luning** Nevada, W USA 38°29′N 118°10′W
Łuniniec *see* Luninyets
127 P6 **Lunino** Penzenskaya Oblast', W Russian Federation 53°35′N 45°12′E
119 J19 **Luninyets** *Pol.* Łuniniec, *Rus.* Luninets. Brestskaya Voblasts', SW Belarus 52°15′N 26°48′E
152 F10 **Lūnkaransar** *var.* Lookransar, Lukransar. Rājasthān, NW India 28°32′N 73°50′E
119 G17 **Lunna** *Pol.* Łunna. Hrodzyenskaya Voblasts', W Belarus 53°27′N 24°16′E
76 I15 **Lunsar** W Sierra Leone 08°41′N 12°32′W
83 K14 **Lunsemfwa** C Zambia
158 J6 **Luntai** *var.* Bügür. Xinjiang Uygur Zizhiqu, NW China 41°48′N 84°14′E
98 K11 **Lunteren** Gelderland, C Netherlands 52°05′N 05°38′E
109 U5 **Lunz am See** Niederösterreich, C Austria 47°54′N 15°01′E
163 Y7 **Luobei** *var.* Fengxiang. Heilongjiang, NE China 47°35′N 130°51′E
Luocheng *see* Hui'an, Fujian, China
Luocheng *see* Luoding, Guangdong, China
160 J13 **Luodian** *var.* Longping. Guizhou, S China 25°25′N 106°49′E
160 M15 **Luoding** *var.* Luocheng. Guangdong, S China 22°44′N 111°28′E
161 N7 **Luohe** Henan, C China 33°37′N 114°00′E
160 M6 **Luo He** C China
160 L5 **Luo He** C China
Luolajarvi *see* Kuoloyarvi
Luong Nam Tha *see* Louangnamtha
160 L13 **Luoqing Jiang** S China
161 O8 **Luoshan** Henan, C China 32°12′N 114°30′E
161 O12 **Luoxiao Shan** ▲ S China
161 N6 **Luoyang** *var.* Honan, Lo-yang. Henan, C China 34°41′N 112°25′E
161 R12 **Luoyuan** *var.* Fengshan. Fujian, SE China 26°29′N 119°32′E
79 F21 **Luozi** Bas-Congo, W Dem. Rep. Congo 04°57′S 14°08′E
83 J17 **Lupane** Matabeleland North, W Zimbabwe 18°54′S 27°44′E
160 I12 **Lupanshui** *prev.* Shuicheng. Guizhou, S China 26°38′N 104°49′E
169 R10 **Lupar, Batang** East Malaysia
Lupatia *see* Altamura
116 G12 **Lupeni** *Hung.* Lupény. Hunedoara, SW Romania 45°20′N 23°10′E
Lupény *see* Lupeni
82 N13 **Lupiliche** Niassa, N Mozambique 11°36′S 35°15′E
83 E14 **Lupire** Cuando Cubango, E Angola 14°39′S 19°39′E
79 L22 **Luputa** Kasai-Oriental, S Dem. Rep. Congo 07°07′S 23°43′E
121 P16 **Luqa** ✈ (Valletta) S Malta 35°53′N 14°27′E
159 U11 **Luqu** *var.* Ma'ai. Gansu, C China 34°34′N 102°27′E
45 U5 **Luquillo, Sierra de** ▲ E Puerto Rico
26 L4 **Luray** Kansas, C USA 39°06′N 98°41′W
21 U4 **Luray** Virginia, NE USA 38°40′N 78°28′W
103 T7 **Lure** Haute-Saône, E France 47°42′N 06°30′E
82 D11 **Luremo** Lunda Norte, NE Angola 08°32′S 17°55′E
97 F15 **Lurgan** *Ir.* An Lorgain. S Northern Ireland, United Kingdom 54°28′N 06°20′W
57 K18 **Luribay** La Paz, W Bolivia 17°05′S 67°37′W
Luring *see* Gêrzê
83 Q14 **Lúrio** Nampula, NE Mozambique 13°32′S 40°34′E
83 P14 **Lúrio, Rio** NE Mozambique
Luristan *see* Lorestān
Lurka *see* Lorca
83 J15 **Lusaka** ● (Zambia) Lusaka, SE Zambia 15°24′S 28°17′E
83 J15 **Lusaka** ◈ *province* C Zambia
83 J15 **Lusaka** ✈ Lusaka, C Zambia 15°10′S 28°22′E
79 L21 **Lusambo** Kasai-Oriental, C Dem. Rep. Congo 04°59′S 23°26′E
186 F8 **Lusancay Islands and Reefs** *island group* SE Papua New Guinea
79 I21 **Lusanga** Bandundu, SW Dem. Rep. Congo 04°55′S 18°40′E
79 N21 **Lusangi** Maniema, E Dem. Rep. Congo 04°39′S 27°10′E
Lusatian Mountains *see* Lausitzer Bergland
Lushar *see* Huangzhong
Lushnja *see* Lushnjë
113 K21 **Lushnjë** *var.* Lushnja. Fier, C Albania 40°54′N 19°43′E
81 J21 **Lushoto** Tanga, E Tanzania 04°48′S 38°20′E
102 L10 **Lusignan** Vienne, W France 46°25′N 00°06′E
33 Z15 **Lusk** Wyoming, C USA 42°45′N 104°27′W
Luso *see* Luena
102 L10 **Lussac-les-Châteaux** Vienne, W France 46°23′N 00°44′E
Lussin/Lussino *see* Lošinj
Lussinpiccolo *see* Mali Lošinj
108 I7 **Lustenau** Vorarlberg, W Austria 47°26′N 09°42′E
161 T14 **Lü Tao** *var.* Huoshao Dao, Lütao, *Eng.* Green Island. *island* SE Taiwan
Lütao *see* Lü Tao
Lūt, Baḩrat/Lut, Bahret *see* Dead Sea
22 K9 **Lutcher** Louisiana, S USA 30°02′N 90°42′W
143 T9 **Lūt, Dasht-e** *var.* Kavīr-e Lūt. *desert* E Iran
83 F14 **Lutembo** Moxico, E Angola 13°30′S 21°21′E
Lutetia/Lutetia Parisiorum *see* Paris
Luteva *see* Lodève
14 G15 **Luther Lake** ◎ Ontario, S Canada
186 K8 **Luti** Choiseul Island, NW Solomon Islands 07°13′S 157°01′E
Lūt, Kavīr-e *see* Lūt, Dasht-e
97 N21 **Luton** E England, United Kingdom 51°53′N 00°25′W
97 N21 **Luton** ✈ (London) SE England, United Kingdom 51°54′N 00°24′W
108 B10 **Lutry** Vaud, SW Switzerland 46°31′N 06°32′E
8 K10 **Łutselk'e** *prev.* Snowdrift. Northwest Territories, W Canada 62°24′N 110°42′W
29 Y4 **Lutsen** Minnesota, N USA 47°39′N 90°37′W
116 J4 **Luts'k** *Pol.* Łuck, *Rus.* Lutsk. Volyns'ka Oblast', NW Ukraine 50°45′N 25°23′E
Lutsk *see* Luts'k
Luttenberg *see* Ljutomer
Lüttich *see* Liège
83 G25 **Luttig** Western Cape, SW South Africa 32°33′S 22°13′E
Lutto *see* Lotta
82 E13 **Lutuai** Moxico, E Angola 12°38′S 20°06′E
117 Y7 **Lutuhyne** Luhans'ka Oblast', E Ukraine 48°24′N 39°12′E
171 V14 **Lutur, Pulau** *island* Kepulauan Aru, E Indonesia
23 V12 **Lutz** Florida, SE USA 28°09′N 82°27′W
Lutzow-Holm Bay *see* Lützow Holmbukta
195 V2 **Lützow Holmbukta** *var.* Lutzow-Holm Bay. *bay* Antarctica
81 L16 **Luuq** *It.* Lugh Ganana. Gedo, SW Somalia 03°42′N 42°34′E
92 M12 **Luusua** Lappi, NE Finland 66°28′N 27°16′E
23 Q6 **Luverne** Alabama, S USA 31°43′N 86°15′W
29 S11 **Luverne** Minnesota, N USA 43°39′N 96°12′W
79 O22 **Luvua** SE Dem. Rep. Congo
82 F13 **Luvuei** Moxico, E Angola 13°08′S 21°09′E
81 H24 **Luwego** S Tanzania
82 K12 **Luwingu** Northern, NE Zambia 10°13′S 29°58′E
171 P12 **Luwuk** *prev.* Loewoek. Sulawesi, C Indonesia 0°56′S 122°47′E
23 N3 **Luxapallila Creek** Alabama/Mississippi, S USA
99 M25 **Luxembourg** ● (Luxembourg) Luxembourg, S Luxembourg 49°37′N 06°08′E
99 M25 **Luxembourg** *off.* Grand Duchy of Luxembourg, *var.* Lëtzebuerg, Luxemburg. ◆ *monarchy* NW Europe
99 J23 **Luxembourg** ◈ *province* SE Belgium
99 L24 **Luxembourg** ◈ *district* S Luxembourg
31 N6 **Luxemburg** Wisconsin, N USA 44°32′N 87°42′W
Luxemburg *see* Luxembourg
103 U7 **Luxeuil-les-Bains** Haute-Saône, E France 47°49′N 06°22′E
160 E13 **Luxi** *prev.* Mangshi. Yunnan, SW China 24°27′N 98°31′E
82 E10 **Luxico** Angola/Dem. Rep. Congo
75 X10 **Luxor** *Ar.* Al Uqşur. E Egypt 25°39′N 32°39′E
75 X10 **Luxor** ✈ C Egypt 25°39′N 32°48′E
160 M4 **Luya Shan** ▲ C China
102 J15 **Luy de Béarn** SW France
102 J15 **Luy de France** SW France
125 P12 **Luza** Kirovskaya Oblast', NW Russian Federation 60°38′N 47°13′E
125 Q12 **Luza** NW Russian Federation
104 I16 **Luz, Costa de la** *coastal region* SW Spain
111 K20 **Luže** *var.* Lausche. ▲ Czech Republic/Germany 50°51′N 14°40′E *see also* Lausche
Luže *see* Lausche
108 F8 **Luzern** *Fr.* Lucerne, *It.* Lucerna. Luzern, C Switzerland 47°03′N 08°17′E
108 E8 **Luzern** *Fr.* Lucerne. ◈ *canton* C Switzerland
160 L13 **Luzhai** Guangxi Zhuangzu Zizhiqu, S China 24°31′N 109°46′E
118 K12 **Luzhki** Vitsyebskaya Voblasts', N Belarus 55°21′N 27°52′E
160 I10 **Luzhou** Sichuan, C China 28°55′N 105°25′E
Lužická Nisa *see* Neisse
Lužické Hory' *see* Lausitzer Bergland
Lužnice *see* Lainsitz
171 O2 **Luzon** *island* N Philippines
171 N1 **Luzon Strait** *strait* Philippines/Taiwan
Lużyckie, Gory *see* Lausitzer Bergland
116 I5 **L'viv** *Ger.* Lemberg, *Pol.* Lwów, *Rus.* L'vov. L'vivs'ka Oblast', W Ukraine 49°49′N 24°05′E
L'viv *see* L'vivs'ka Oblast'
116 I4 **L'vivs'ka Oblast'** *var.* L'viv, *Rus.* L'vovskaya Oblast'. ◈ *province* NW Ukraine
L'vov *see* L'viv
L'vovskaya Oblast' *see* L'vivs'ka Oblast'
Lwena *see* Luena
Lwów *see* L'viv
110 F11 **Lwówek** *Ger.* Neustadt bei Pinne. Wielkopolskie, C Poland 52°27′N 16°10′E
111 E14 **Lwówek Śląski** *Ger.* Löwenberg in Schlesien. Jelenia Góra, SW Poland 51°06′N 15°35′E
119 I18 **Lyakhavichy** *Rus.* Lyakhovichi. Brestskaya Voblasts', SW Belarus 53°02′N 26°16′E
Lyakhovichi *see* Lyakhavichy
185 B22 **Lyall, Mount** ▲ South Island, New Zealand 45°14′S 167°31′E
Lyallpur *see* Faisalābād
Lyangar *see* Langar
124 H11 **Lyaskelya** Respublika Kareliya, NW Russian Federation 61°42′N 31°06′E
119 I18 **Lyasnaya** *Rus.* Lesnaya. Brestskaya Voblasts', SW Belarus 52°59′N 25°46′E
119 F19 **Lyasnaya** *Pol.* Leśna, *Rus.* Lesnaya. SW Belarus
124 H15 **Lychkovo** Novgorodskaya Oblast', W Russian Federation 57°55′N 32°24′E
Lyck *see* Ełk
93 I15 **Lycksele** Västerbotten, N Sweden 64°34′N 18°40′E
18 G13 **Lycoming Creek** Pennsylvania, NE USA
Lycopolis *see* Asyūţ
195 N3 **Lyddan Island** *island* Antarctica
83 K20 **Lydenburg** Mpumalanga, NE South Africa 25°10′S 30°29′E
119 L20 **Lyel'chytsy** *Rus.* Lel'chitsy. Homyel'skaya Voblasts', SE Belarus 51°47′N 28°20′E
119 P14 **Lyenina** *Rus.* Lenino. Mahilyowskaya Voblasts', E Belarus 54°25′N 31°08′E
118 L13 **Lyepyel'** *Rus.* Lepel'. Vitsyebskaya Voblasts', N Belarus 54°54′N 28°44′E
25 S17 **Lyford** Texas, SW USA 26°24′N 97°47′W
95 E17 **Lygna** S Norway
18 G14 **Lykens** Pennsylvania, NE USA 40°33′N 76°42′W
115 E21 **Lykódimo** ▲ S Greece 36°56′N 21°49′E
97 K24 **Lyme Bay** *bay* S England, United Kingdom
97 K24 **Lyme Regis** S England, United Kingdom 50°44′N 02°56′W
110 L7 **Łyna** *Ger.* Alle. N Poland
29 P12 **Lynch** Nebraska, C USA 42°49′N 98°27′W
20 J10 **Lynchburg** Tennessee, S USA 35°17′N 86°22′W
21 T6 **Lynchburg** Virginia, NE USA 37°24′N 79°09′W
21 T12 **Lynches River** South Carolina, SE USA
32 H6 **Lynden** Washington, NW USA 48°57′N 122°27′W
182 I5 **Lyndhurst** South Australia 30°19′S 138°20′E
27 Q5 **Lyndon** Kansas, C USA 38°37′N 95°40′W
19 N7 **Lyndonville** Vermont, NE USA 44°31′N 71°58′W
95 D18 **Lyngdal** Vest-Agder, S Norway 58°10′N 07°08′E
92 I9 **Lyngen** *Lapp.* Ivgovuotna. *inlet* Arctic Ocean
95 G17 **Lyngør** Aust-Agder, S Norway 58°38′N 09°05′E
92 I9 **Lyngseidet** Troms, N Norway 69°36′N 20°07′E
19 P11 **Lynn** Massachusetts, NE USA 42°28′N 70°57′W
Lynn *see* King's Lynn
23 R9 **Lynn Haven** Florida, SE USA 30°15′N 85°39′W
11 V11 **Lynn Lake** Manitoba, C Canada 56°51′N 101°01′W
Lynn Regis *see* King's Lynn
118 I13 **Lyntupy** Vitsyebskaya Voblasts', NW Belarus 55°03′N 26°19′E
103 R11 **Lyon** *Eng.* Lyons; *anc.* Lugdunum. Rhône, E France 45°46′N 04°50′E
8 I6 **Lyon, Cape** *headland* Northwest Territories, NW Canada 69°47′N 123°10′W
18 K6 **Lyon Mountain** ▲ New York, NE USA 44°42′N 73°52′W
103 Q11 **Lyonnais, Monts du** ▲ C France
65 N25 **Lyon Point** *headland* SE Tristan da Cunha 37°06′S 12°13′W
182 E5 **Lyons** South Australia 30°40′S 133°50′E
37 T3 **Lyons** Colorado, C USA 40°13′N 105°16′W
23 V6 **Lyons** Georgia, SE USA 32°12′N 82°19′W
26 M5 **Lyons** Kansas, C USA 38°22′N 98°13′W
29 R14 **Lyons** Nebraska, C USA 41°56′N 96°28′W
18 G10 **Lyons** New York, NE USA 43°03′N 76°58′W
Lyons *see* Lyon
118 O13 **Lyozna** *Rus.* Liozno. Vitsyebskaya Voblasts', NE Belarus 55°02′N 30°48′E
117 S4 **Lypova Dolyna** Sums'ka Oblast', NE Ukraine 50°36′N 33°50′E
117 N6 **Lypovets'** *Rus.* Lipovets. Vinnyts'ka Oblast', C Ukraine 49°13′N 29°06′E
Lys *see* Leie
111 I18 **Lysá Hora** ▲ E Czech Republic 49°31′N 18°27′E
95 D16 **Lysefjorden** *fjord* S Norway
95 I18 **Lysekil** Västra Götaland, S Sweden 58°16′N 11°26′E
Lýsi *see* Akdoğan
33 V14 **Lysite** Wyoming, C USA 43°16′N 107°42′W
127 P3 **Lyskovo** Nizhegorodskaya Oblast', W Russian Federation 56°04′N 45°01′E
108 D8 **Lyss** Bern, W Switzerland 47°04′N 07°19′E
95 H22 **Lystrup** Århus, C Denmark 56°14′N 10°14′E
125 V14 **Lys'va** Permskaya Oblast', NW Russian Federation 58°04′N 57°48′E
117 P6 **Lysyanka** Cherkas'ka Oblast', C Ukraine 49°15′N 30°50′E
117 X6 **Lysychans'k** *Rus.* Lisichansk. Luhans'ka Oblast', E Ukraine 48°52′N 38°27′E
97 K17 **Lytham St Anne's** NW England, United Kingdom 53°45′N 03°01′W
185 I19 **Lyttelton** South Island, New Zealand 43°35′S 172°44′E
10 M17 **Lytton** British Columbia, SW Canada 50°12′N 121°34′W
119 L18 **Lyuban'** Minskaya Voblasts', S Belarus 52°48′N 28°00′E
119 L18 **Lyubanskaye Vodaskhovishcha** ▣ C Belarus
116 M5 **Lyubar** Zhytomyrs'ka Oblast', N Ukraine 49°54′N 27°48′E
Lyubashëvka *see* Lyubashivka
117 O8 **Lyubashivka** *Rus.* Lyubashëvka. Odes'ka Oblast', SW Ukraine 47°49′N 30°18′E
119 I16 **Lyubcha** *Pol.* Lubcz. Hrodzyenskaya Voblasts', W Belarus 53°45′N 26°04′E
126 L4 **Lyubertsy** Moskovskaya Oblast', W Russian Federation 55°37′N 38°02′E
116 K2 **Lyubeshiv** Volyns'ka Oblast', NW Ukraine 51°46′N 25°33′E
124 M14 **Lyubim** Yaroslavskaya Oblast', NW Russian Federation 58°21′N 40°46′E
114 K11 **Lyubimets** Khaskovo, S Bulgaria 41°51′N 26°03′E
Lyublin *see* Lublin
116 I3 **Lyuboml'** *Pol.* Luboml. Volyns'ka Oblast', NW Ukraine 51°12′N 24°01′E
Lyubotin *see* Lyubotyn
117 U5 **Lyubotyn** *Rus.* Lyubotin. Kharkivs'ka Oblast', E Ukraine 49°57′N 35°57′E
126 I5 **Lyudinovo** Kaluzhskaya Oblast', W Russian Federation 53°52′N 34°28′E
127 T2 **Lyuk** Udmurtskaya Respublika, NW Russian Federation 56°55′N 52°45′E
114 M9 **Lyulyakovo** *prev.* Keremitlik. Burgas, E Bulgaria 42°53′N 27°05′E
119 I18 **Lyusina** *Rus.* Lyusino. Brestskaya Voblasts', SW Belarus 52°38′N 26°31′E
Lyusino *see* Lyusina

M

138 G9 **Ma'ād** Irbid, N Jordan 32°37′N 35°36′E
Ma'ai *see* Luqu
Maalahti *see* Malax
Maale *see* Male'
138 G13 **Ma'ān** Ma'ān, SW Jordan 30°11′N 35°45′E
138 H13 **Ma'ān** *off.* Muḩāfaẓat Ma'ān, *var.* Ma'an, Ma'ān. ◈ *governorate* S Jordan
93 M16 **Maaninka** Itä-Suomi, C Finland 63°10′N 27°19′E
Maanĭt *see* Bayan, Töv, Mongolia
Maanĭt *see* Hishig Öndör, Bulgan, Mongolia
Ma'ān, Muḩāfaẓat *see* Ma'ān
93 N15 **Maanselkä** Oulu, C Finland 63°54′N 28°28′E
161 Q8 **Ma'anshan** Anhui, E China 31°45′N 118°32′E
188 F16 **Maap** *island* Caroline Islands, W Micronesia
118 H3 **Maardu** *Ger.* Maart. Harjumaa, NW Estonia 59°28′N 24°56′E
Ma'aret-en-Nu'man *see* Ma'arrat an Nu'mān
99 K16 **Maarheeze** Noord-Brabant, SE Netherlands 51°19′N 05°37′E
Maarianhamina *see* Mariehamn
138 I4 **Ma'arrat an Nu'mān** *var.* Ma'aret-en-Nu'man, *Fr.* Maarret enn Naamâne. Idlib, NW Syria 35°40′N 36°40′E
Maarret enn Naamâne *see* Ma'arrat an Nu'mān
98 I11 **Maarssen** Utrecht, C Netherlands 52°08′N 05°03′E
Maart *see* Maardu
99 L17 **Maas** *Fr.* Meuse. W Europe *see also* Meuse
Maas *see* Meuse
99 M15 **Maasbree** Limburg, SE Netherlands 51°22′N 06°03′E
99 L17 **Maaseik** *prev.* Maeseyck. Limburg, NE Belgium 51°05′N 05°48′E
171 Q6 **Maasin** Leyte, C Philippines 10°10′N 124°55′E
99 L17 **Maasmechelen** Limburg, NE Belgium 50°58′N 05°42′E
98 G12 **Maassluis** Zuid-Holland, SW Netherlands 51°55′N 04°15′E
99 L18 **Maastricht** *var.* Maestricht; *anc.* Traiectum ad Mosam, Traiectum Tungorum. Limburg, SE Netherlands 50°51′N 05°42′E
183 N18 **Maatsuyker Group** *island group* Tasmania, SE Australia
Maba *see* Qujiang
83 L20 **Mabalane** Gaza, S Mozambique 23°43′S 32°37′E
25 V7 **Mabank** Texas, SW USA 32°22′N 96°06′W
97 O18 **Mablethorpe** E England, United Kingdom 53°21′N 00°14′E
171 V12 **Maboi** Papua, E Indonesia 01°00′S 134°02′E
83 M19 **Mabote** Inhambane, S Mozambique 22°03′S 34°09′E
32 J10 **Mabton** Washington, NW USA 46°13′N 120°00′W
83 H20 **Mabutsane** Southern, S Botswana 24°24′S 23°34′E
63 G19 **Macá, Cerro** ▲ S Chile 45°07′S 73°11′W
60 Q9 **Macaé** Rio de Janeiro, SE Brazil 22°21′S 41°48′W
82 N13 **Macaloge** Niassa, N Mozambique 12°27′S 35°25′E
Macan *see* Bonerate, Kepulauan
161 N15 **Macao** *Chin.* Aomen, *Port.* Macau. Guangdong, SE China 22°06′N 113°30′E
104 H9 **Mação** Santarém, C Portugal 39°33′N 08°00′W
58 J11 **Macapá** *state capital* Amapá, N Brazil 0°04′N 51°04′W
43 S17 **Macaracas** Los Santos, S Panama 07°46′N 80°31′W
55 P6 **Macare, Caño** NE Venezuela
55 Q6 **Macareo, Caño** NE Venezuela
Macarsca *see* Makarska
182 L12 **Macarthur** Victoria, SE Australia 38°04′S 142°02′E
MacArthur *see* Ormoc
56 C7 **Macas** Morona Santiago, SE Ecuador 02°22′S 78°08′W
Macassar *see* Makassar
59 Q14 **Macau** Rio Grande do Norte, E Brazil 05°05′S 36°37′W
Macău *see* Makó, Hungary
Macau *see* Macao
65 E24 **Macbride Head** *headland* East Falkland, Falkland Islands 51°25′S 57°55′W
23 V9 **Macclenny** Florida, SE USA 30°16′N 82°07′W
97 L18 **Macclesfield** C England, United Kingdom 53°16′N 02°07′W
192 F6 **Macclesfield Bank** *undersea feature* N South China Sea 15°50′N 114°20′E
MacCluer Gulf *see* Berau, Teluk
181 N7 **Macdonald, Lake** *salt lake* Western Australia
181 Q7 **Macdonnell Ranges** ▲ Northern Territory, C Australia
96 K8 **Macduff** NE Scotland, United Kingdom 57°40′N 02°29′W
104 I6 **Macedo de Cavaleiros** Bragança, N Portugal 41°31′N 06°57′W
Macedonia *see* Macedonia, FYR
Macedonia Central *see* Kentrikí Makedonía
Macedonia East and Thrace *see* Anatolikí Makedonía kai Thráki
113 O19 **Macedonia, FYR** *off.* the Former Yugoslav Republic of Macedonia, *var.* Macedonia, *Mac.* Makedonija, *abbrev.* FYR Macedonia, FYROM. ◆ *republic* SE Europe
Macedonia, the Former Yugoslav Republic of *see* Macedonia, FYR
Macedonia West *see* Dytikí Makedonía
59 Q16 **Maceió** *state capital* Alagoas, E Brazil 09°40′S 35°44′W
76 K15 **Macenta** SE Guinea 08°31′N 09°32′W
106 J12 **Macerata** Marche, C Italy 43°18′N 13°27′E
11 S11 **MacFarlane** Saskatchewan, C Canada
182 H7 **Macfarlane, Lake** *var.* Lake Mcfarlane. ◎ South Australia
Macgillicuddy's Reeks Mountains *see* Macgillycuddy's Reeks
97 B21 **Macgillycuddy's Reeks** *var.* Macgillicuddy's Reeks Mountains, *Ir.* Na Cruacha Dubha. ▲ SW Ireland
11 X16 **MacGregor** Manitoba, S Canada 49°58′N 98°49′W
149 O10 **Mach** Baluchistān, SW Pakistan 29°52′N 67°20′E
56 C6 **Machachi** Pichincha, C Ecuador 0°33′S 78°34′W
83 M19 **Machaila** Gaza, S Mozambique 22°15′S 32°57′E
Machaire Fíolta *see* Magherafelt
Machaire Rátha *see* Maghera
81 I19 **Machakos** Eastern, S Kenya 01°31′S 37°16′E
56 B8 **Machala** El Oro, SW Ecuador 03°20′S 79°57′W
83 J19 **Machaneng** Central, SE Botswana 23°12′S 27°30′E
83 M18 **Machanga** Sofala, E Mozambique 20°56′S 35°04′E
80 G13 **Machar Marshes** *wetland* SE Sudan
102 I8 **Machecoul** Loire-Atlantique, NW France 46°59′N 01°51′W
161 O8 **Macheng** Hubei, C China 31°10′N 115°00′E
155 J16 **Mācherla** Andhra Pradesh, C India 16°29′N 79°25′E
153 O11 **Māchhāpuchhre** ▲ C Nepal 28°30′N 83°57′E
19 T6 **Machias** Maine, NE USA 44°44′N 67°28′W
19 R3 **Machias River** Maine, NE USA
19 T6 **Machias River** Maine, NE USA
64 P5 **Machico** Madeira, Portugal, NE Atlantic Ocean 32°43′N 16°47′W
155 K16 **Machilīpatnam** *var.* Bandar Masulipatnam. Andhra Pradesh, E India 16°12′N 81°11′E
54 G5 **Machiques** Zulia, NW Venezuela 10°04′N 72°37′W
57 G15 **Machu Picchu** Cusco, C Peru 13°08′S 72°30′W
83 M20 **Macia** *var.* Vila de Macia. Gaza, S Mozambique 25°02′S 33°08′E
Macías Nguema Biyogo *see* Bioco, Isla de
116 M13 **Măcin** Tulcea, SE Romania 45°15′N 28°09′E
183 T4 **Macintyre River** New South Wales/Queensland, SE Australia
181 Y7 **Mackay** Queensland, NE Australia 21°10′S 149°10′E
181 O7 **Mackay, Lake** *salt lake* Northern Territory/Western Australia
10 M13 **Mackenzie** British Columbia, W Canada 55°18′N 123°09′W
8 I9 **Mackenzie** Northwest Territories, NW Canada
195 Y6 **Mackenzie Bay** *bay* Antarctica
10 J1 **Mackenzie Bay** *bay* NW Canada
2 D9 **Mackenzie Delta** *delta* Northwest Territories, NW Canada
197 P8 **Mackenzie King Island** *island* Queen Elizabeth Islands, Northwest Territories, N Canada
8 H8 **Mackenzie Mountains** ▲ Northwest Territories, NW Canada
31 Q5 **Mackinac, Straits of** ◎ Michigan, N USA
194 K5 **Mackintosh, Cape** *headland* Antarctica 72°52′S 60°00′W
11 R15 **Macklin** Saskatchewan, S Canada 52°19′N 109°51′W
183 V6 **Macksville** New South Wales, SE Australia 30°39′S 152°54′E
183 V5 **Maclean** New South Wales, SE Australia 29°30′S 153°15′E
83 J24 **Maclear** Eastern Cape, SE South Africa 31°05′S 28°22′E
183 U6 **Macleay River** New South Wales, SE Australia
MacLeod *see* Fort Macleod
180 G9 **Macleod, Lake** ◎ Western Australia
10 I6 **Macmillan** Yukon Territory, NW Canada
30 J12 **Macomb** Illinois, N USA 40°27′N 90°40′W
107 B18 **Macomer** Sardegna, Italy, C Mediterranean Sea 40°15′N 08°47′E
82 Q13 **Macomia** Cabo Delgado, NE Mozambique 12°15′S 40°06′E
103 R10 **Mâcon** *anc.* Matisco, Matisco Ædourum. Saône-et-Loire, C France 46°19′N 04°49′E
23 T5 **Macon** Georgia, SE USA 32°49′N 83°41′W
23 N4 **Macon** Mississippi, S USA 33°06′N 88°33′W
27 U3 **Macon** Missouri, C USA 39°44′N 92°27′W
22 J6 **Macon, Bayou** Arkansas/Louisiana, S USA
82 G13 **Macondo** Moxico, E Angola 12°31′S 23°45′E
83 M16 **Macossa** Manica, C Mozambique 17°51′S 33°54′E
11 T12 **Macoun Lake** ◎ Saskatchewan, C Canada
30 K14 **Macoupin Creek** Illinois, N USA
Macouria *see* Tonate
83 N18 **Macovane** Inhambane, SE Mozambique 21°30′S 35°07′E
183 N17 **Macquarie Harbour** *inlet* Tasmania, SE Australia
192 J13 **Macquarie Island** *island* New Zealand, SW Pacific Ocean
183 T8 **Macquarie, Lake** *lagoon* New South Wales, SE Australia
183 Q6 **Macquarie Marshes** *wetland* New South Wales, SE Australia
175 O13 **Macquarie Ridge** *undersea feature* SW Pacific Ocean 57°00′S 159°00′E
183 Q6 **Macquarie River** New South Wales, SE Australia
183 P17 **Macquarie River** Tasmania, SE Australia
195 V5 **Mac. Robertson Land** *physical region* Antarctica
97 C21 **Macroom** *Ir.* Maigh Chromtha. Cork, SW Ireland 51°54′N 08°57′W
42 G5 **Macuelizo** Santa Bárbara, NW Honduras 15°21′N 88°31′W
182 G2 **Macumba River** South Australia
57 I16 **Macusani** Puno, S Peru 14°05′S 70°24′W
56 E8 **Macusari, Río** N Peru
41 U15 **Macuspana** Tabasco, SE Mexico 17°43′N 92°36′W
138 G10 **Ma'dabā** *var.* Mādabā, Madeba; *anc.* Medeba. Ma'dabā, NW Jordan 31°44′N 35°48′E
138 G11 **Ma'dabā** *off.* Muḩāfaẓat Ma'dabā. ◈ *governorate* C Jordan
Mādabā *see* Ma'dabā
172 G2 **Madagascar** *off.* Democratic Republic of Madagascar, *Malg.* Madagasikara; *prev.* Malagasy Republic. ◆ *republic* W Indian Ocean
172 I5 **Madagascar** *island* W Indian Ocean
128 L17 **Madagascar Basin** *undersea feature* W Indian Ocean 27°00′S 53°00′E
Madagascar, Democratic Republic of *see* Madagascar
128 L16 **Madagascar Plain** *undersea feature* W Indian Ocean 19°00′S 52°00′E
67 Y14 **Madagascar Plateau** *var.* Madagascar Ridge, Madagascar Rise, *Rus.* Madagaskarskiy Khrebet. *undersea feature* W Indian Ocean 30°00′S 45°00′E
Madagascar Rise/Madagascar Ridge *see* Madagascar Plateau
Madagasikara *see* Madagascar
Madagaskarskiy Khrebet *see* Madagascar Plateau
64 N2 **Madalena** Pico, Azores, Portugal, NE Atlantic Ocean 38°32′N 28°15′W
77 Y6 **Madama** Agadez, NE Niger 21°54′N 13°43′E
114 J12 **Madan** Smolyan, S Bulgaria 41°29′N 24°56′E
155 I19 **Madanapalle** Andhra Pradesh, E India 13°33′N 78°31′E
186 D7 **Madang** Madang, N Papua New Guinea 05°14′S 145°45′E
186 C6 **Madang** ◈ *province* N Papua New Guinea
146 G7 **Madaniyat** *Rus.* Madeniyet. Qoraqalpog'iston Respublikasi, W Uzbekistan 42°48′N 59°00′E
Madanīyīn *see* Médenine
77 U11 **Madaoua** Tahoua, SW Niger 14°06′N 06°01′E
Madaras *see* Vtáčnik
153 U15 **Madaripur** Dhaka, C Bangladesh 23°09′N 90°11′E
77 U12 **Madarounfa** Maradi, S Niger 13°16′N 07°07′E
Mađarska *see* Hungary
146 B13 **Madau** Balkan Welaýaty, W Turkmenistan 38°11′N 54°46′E
186 H9 **Madau Island** *island* SE Papua New Guinea
19 S1 **Madawaska** Maine, NE USA 47°19′N 68°19′W
14 J13 **Madawaska** Ontario, SE Canada
Madawaska Highlands *see* Haliburton Highlands
166 M4 **Madaya** Mandalay, C Burma (Myanmar) 22°12′N 96°05′E
107 K17 **Maddaloni** Campania, S Italy 41°03′N 14°23′E
29 O3 **Maddock** North Dakota, N USA 47°57′N 99°31′W
99 I14 **Made** Noord-Brabant, S Netherlands 51°41′N 04°48′E
Madeba *see* Ma'dabā
64 L9 **Madeira** *var.* Ilha de Madeira. *island* Madeira, Portugal, NE Atlantic Ocean
Madeira, Ilha de *see* Madeira
64 O5 **Madeira Islands** *Port.* Região Autoónoma da Madeira. ◈ *autonomous region* Madeira, Portugal, NE Atlantic Ocean
64 L9 **Madeira Plain** *undersea feature* E Atlantic Ocean
Madeira, Região Autoónoma da *see* Madeira Islands
64 L9 **Madeira Ridge** *undersea feature* E Atlantic Ocean 35°30′N 15°45′W
59 F14 **Madeira, Rio** *var.* Río Madera. Bolivia/Brazil *see also* Madera, Río
Madeira, Rio *see* Madera, Río
101 J25 **Mädelegabel** ▲ Austria/Germany 47°18′N 10°19′E
15 X6 **Madeleine** Québec, SE Canada
15 X5 **Madeleine, Cap de la** *headland* Québec, SE Canada 49°13′N 65°20′W
13 Q13 **Madeleine, Îles de la** *Eng.* Magdalen Islands. *island group* Québec, E Canada
29 U10 **Madelia** Minnesota, N USA 44°03′N 94°26′W
35 P3 **Madeline** California, W USA 41°02′N 120°28′W
30 K3 **Madeline Island** *island* Apostle Islands, Wisconsin, N USA
137 O15 **Maden** Elazığ, SE Turkey 38°24′N 39°42′E
145 V12 **Madeniyet** Vostochnyy Kazakhstan, E Kazakhstan 47°51′N 78°37′E

◆ Country
● Country Capital
◇ Dependent Territory
○ Dependent Territory Capital
◈ Administrative Regions
✈ International Airport
▲ Mountain
▲ Mountain Range
Volcano
River
◎ Lake
▣ Reservoir

Madeniyet *see* Madaniyat
40 H5 **Madera** Chihuahua, N Mexico 29°10′N 108°10′W
35 Q10 **Madera** California, W USA 36°57′N 120°02′W
56 L13 **Madera, Río** *Port.* Rio Madeira. ≈ Bolivia/Brazil *see also* Madeira, Rio
Madera, Río *see* Madeira, Rio
106 D6 **Madesimo** Lombardia, N Italy 46°20′N 09°26′E
141 O14 **Madhāb, Wādī** *dry watercourse* NW Yemen
153 R13 **Madhepura** *prev.* Madhipure. Bihār, NE India 25°56′N 86°48′E
Madhipure *see* Madhepura
153 Q13 **Madhubani** Bihār, N India 26°21′N 86°05′E
153 Q15 **Madhupur** Jhārkhand, NE India 24°17′N 86°38′E
154 I10 **Madhya Pradesh** *prev.* Central Provinces and Berar. ◐ *state* C India
57 K15 **Madidi, Río** ≈ W Bolivia
155 F20 **Madikeri** *prev.* Mercara. Karnātaka, W India 12°29′N 75°40′E
27 O13 **Madill** Oklahoma, C USA 34°06′N 96°46′W
79 G21 **Madimba** Bas-Congo, SW Dem. Rep. Congo 04°58′S 15°08′E
138 M4 **Ma'din** Ar Raqqah, C Syria 35°45′N 39°36′E
Madīnah, Minṭaqat al *see* Al Madīnah
76 M14 **Madinani** NW Ivory Coast 09°37′N 06°57′W
141 O17 **Madīnat ash Sha'b** *prev.* Al Ittiḥād. SW Yemen 12°52′N 44°55′E
138 K3 **Madīnat ath Thawrah** *var.* Ath Thawrah. Ar Raqqah, N Syria 35°36′N 39°00′E
173 O6 **Madingley Rise** *undersea feature* W Indian Ocean
79 E21 **Madingo-Kayes** Kouilou, S Congo 04°27′S 11°43′E
79 F21 **Madingou** Bouenza, S Congo 04°10′S 13°33′E
Madioen *see* Madiun
23 U8 **Madison** Florida, SE USA 30°27′N 83°24′W
23 T3 **Madison** Georgia, SE USA 33°37′N 83°28′W
31 P15 **Madison** Indiana, N USA 38°44′N 85°22′W
27 P6 **Madison** Kansas, C USA 45′01′N 96°11′W
19 Q6 **Madison** Maine, NE USA 44°48′N 69°52′W
29 S9 **Madison** Minnesota, N USA 45°00′N 96°12′W
22 K5 **Madison** Mississippi, S USA 32°27′N 90°07′W
29 Q14 **Madison** Nebraska, C USA 41°49′N 97°27′W
29 R10 **Madison** South Dakota, N USA 44°00′N 97°06′W
21 V5 **Madison** Virginia, NE USA 38°23′N 78°16′W
21 Q5 **Madison** West Virginia, NE USA 38°03′N 81°50′W
30 L9 **Madison** *state capital* Wisconsin, N USA 43°04′N 89°22′W
21 T6 **Madison Heights** Virginia, NE USA 37°25′N 79°07′W
20 I6 **Madisonville** Kentucky, S USA 37°20′N 87°30′W
20 M10 **Madisonville** Tennessee, S USA 35°31′N 84°21′W
25 V9 **Madisonville** Texas, SW USA 30°58′N 95°56′W
Madisonville *see* Taiohae
169 R16 **Madiun** *prev.* Madioen. Jawa, C Indonesia 07°37′S 111°33′E
Madjene *see* Majene
14 J14 **Madoc** Ontario, SE Canada 44°31′N 77°27′W
Madoera *see* Madura, Pulau
81 J18 **Mado Gashi** North Eastern, E Kenya 0°40′N 39°09′E
159 R11 **Madoi** *var.* Huanghe; *prev.* Huangheyan. Qinghai, C China 34°53′N 98°07′E
189 O13 **Madolenihmw** Pohnpei, E Micronesia
118 I9 **Madona** *Ger.* Modohn. Madona, E Latvia 56°51′N 26°10′E
107 J23 **Madonie** ▲▲ Sicilia, Italy, C Mediterranean Sea
141 Y11 **Madrakah, Ra's** *headland* E Oman 18°56′N 57°54′E
32 I12 **Madras** Oregon, NW USA 44°39′N 121°08′W
Madras *see* Tamil Nādu
Madras *see* Chennai
57 H14 **Madre de Dios** *off.* Departamento de Madre de Dios. ◐ *department* E Peru
Madre de Dios, Departamento de *see* Madre de Dios
63 F22 **Madre de Dios, Isla** *island* S Chile
57 J14 **Madre de Dios, Río** ≈ Bolivia/Peru
0 H15 **Madre del Sur, Sierra** ▲▲ S Mexico
41 Q9 **Madre, Laguna** *lagoon* NE Mexico
25 T16 **Madre, Laguna** *lagoon* Texas, SW USA
37 Q12 **Madre Mount** ▲ New Mexico, SW USA 34°18′N 107°54′W
0 H13 **Madre Occidental, Sierra** *var.* Western Sierra Madre. ▲▲ C Mexico
0 H13 **Madre Oriental, Sierra** *var.* Eastern Sierra Madre. ▲▲ C Mexico
41 U17 **Madre, Sierra** *var.* Sierra de Soconusco. ▲▲ Guatemala/Mexico
37 R2 **Madre, Sierra** ▲▲ Colorado/Wyoming, C USA
105 N8 **Madrid** ● (Spain) Madrid, C Spain 40°25′N 03°43′W
29 V14 **Madrid** Iowa, C USA 41°52′N 93°49′W
105 N7 **Madrid** ◐ *autonomous community* C Spain
105 N10 **Madridejos** Castilla-La Mancha, C Spain 39°29′N 03°32′W
104 L7 **Madrigal de las Altas Torres** Castilla-León, N Spain 41°05′N 05°00′W
104 K10 **Madrigalejo** Extremadura, W Spain 39°08′N 05°36′W
34 L3 **Mad River** ≈ California, W USA
42 J8 **Madriz** ◐ *department* NW Nicaragua
104 K10 **Madroñera** Extremadura, W Spain 39°25′N 05°46′W
181 N12 **Madura** Western Australia 31°52′S 127°01′E
Madura *see* Madurai
155 H22 **Madurai** *prev.* Madura, Mathurai. Tamil Nādu, S India 09°55′N 78°07′E
169 S16 **Madura, Pulau** *prev.* Madoera. *island* C Indonesia
169 S16 **Madura, Selat** *strait* C Indonesia
127 Q17 **Madzhalis** Respublika Dagestan, SW Russian Federation 42°12′N 47°46′E
114 K12 **Madzharovo** Khaskovo, S Bulgaria 41°36′N 25°52′E
83 M14 **Madzimoyo** Eastern, E Zambia 13°42′S 32°34′E
165 O12 **Maebashi** *var.* Maebasi, Mayebashi. Gunma, Honshū, S Japan 36°24′N 139°02′E
Maebasi *see* Maebashi
167 O6 **Mae Chan** Chiang Rai, NW Thailand 20°13′N 99°52′E
167 N7 **Mae Hong Son** *var.* Maehongson, Muai To. Mae Hong Son, NW Thailand 19°16′N 97°56′E
Maehongson *see* Mae Hong Son
Mae Nam Khong *see* Mekong
167 Q7 **Mae Nam Nan** ≈ NW Thailand
167 O10 **Mae Nam Tha Chin** ≈ W Thailand
167 P7 **Mae Nam Yom** ≈ W Thailand
37 O3 **Maeser** Utah, W USA 40°28′N 109°35′W
Maeseyck *see* Maaseik
167 N9 **Mae Sot** *var.* Ban Mae Sot. Tak, W Thailand 16°44′N 98°32′E
44 H8 **Maestra, Sierra** ▲▲ E Cuba
Maestricht *see* Maastricht
167 O7 **Mae Suai** *var.* Ban Mae Suai. Chiang Rai, NW Thailand 19°43′N 99°30′E
167 O7 **Mae Tho, Doi** ▲ NW Thailand 18°56′N 99°20′E
172 I4 **Maevatanana** Mahajanga, C Madagascar 16°57′S 46°50′E
187 R13 **Maéwo** *prev.* Aurora. *island* C Vanuatu
171 S11 **Mafa** Pulau Halmahera, E Indonesia 0°01′N 127°50′E
83 I23 **Mafeteng** W Lesotho 29°48′S 27°15′E
99 J21 **Maffe** Namur, SE Belgium 50°21′N 05°19′E
183 P12 **Maffra** Victoria, SE Australia 37°59′S 147°03′E
81 K23 **Mafia** *island* E Tanzania
81 J23 **Mafia Channel** *sea waterway* E Tanzania
83 I21 **Mafikeng** North-West, N South Africa 25°53′S 25°39′E
60 J12 **Mafra** Santa Catarina, S Brazil 26°08′S 49°47′W
104 F10 **Mafra** Lisboa, C Portugal 38°57′N 09°19′W
143 Q17 **Mafraq** Abū Ẓaby, C United Arab Emirates 24°21′N 54°33′E
Mafraq/Muḥāfaẓat al Mafraq *see* Al Mafraq
123 T10 **Magadan** Magadanskaya Oblast', E Russian Federation 59°38′N 150°50′E
123 T9 **Magadanskaya Oblast'** ◐ *province* E Russian Federation
108 G11 **Magadino** Ticino, S Switzerland 46°09′N 08°50′E
63 G23 **Magallanes** *var.* Región de Magallanes y de la Antártica Chilena. ◐ *region* S Chile
Magallanes *see* Punta Arenas
Magallanes, Estrecho de *see* Magellan, Strait of
Magallanes y de la Antártica Chilena, Región de *see* Magallanes
14 I10 **Maganasipi, Lac** ◎ Québec, SE Canada
54 F6 **Magangué** Bolívar, N Colombia 09°14′N 74°46′W
Magareva *see* Mangareva
77 V12 **Magaria** Zinder, S Niger 13°00′N 08°55′E
186 F10 **Magarida** Central, SW Papua New Guinea 10°10′S 149°21′E
171 O2 **Magat** ≈ Luzon, N Philippines
27 T11 **Magazine Mountain** ▲ Arkansas, C USA 35°10′N 93°38′W
76 I15 **Magburaka** C Sierra Leone 08°44′N 11°57′W
123 Q13 **Magdagachi** Amurskaya Oblast', SE Russian Federation 53°25′N 125°41′E
62 O12 **Magdalena** Buenos Aires, E Argentina 35°05′S 57°30′W
57 M15 **Magdalena** Beni, N Bolivia 13°22′S 64°07′W
40 F4 **Magdalena** Sonora, NW Mexico 30°38′N 110°59′W
37 Q13 **Magdalena** New Mexico, SW USA 34°07′N 107°14′W
54 F5 **Magdalena** *off.* Departamento del Magdalena. ◐ *province* N Colombia
40 E9 **Magdalena, Bahía** *bay* W Mexico
Magdalena, Departamento del *see* Magdalena
63 G19 **Magdalena, Isla** *island* Archipiélago de los Chonos, S Chile
40 D8 **Magdalena, Isla** *island* NW Mexico
47 P6 **Magdalena, Río** ≈ C Colombia
40 F4 **Magdalena, Río** ≈ NW Mexico
Magdalen Islands *see* Madeleine, Îles de la
147 N14 **Magdanly** *Rus.* Govurdak; *prev.* gowurdak, Guardak. Lebap Welaýaty, E Turkmenistan 37°50′N 66°06′E
100 L13 **Magdeburg** Sachsen-Anhalt, C Germany 52°08′N 11°39′E
22 L6 **Magee** Mississippi, S USA 31°52′N 89°43′W
169 Q16 **Magelang** Jawa, C Indonesia 07°28′S 110°11′E
192 K7 **Magellan Rise** *undersea feature* C Pacific Ocean
63 H24 **Magellan, Strait of** *Sp.* Estrecho de Magallanes. *strait* Argentina/Chile
106 D7 **Magenta** Lombardia, NW Italy 45°28′N 08°52′E
Magerøy *see* Magerøya
92 K7 **Magerøya** *var.* Magerøy, *Lapp.* Máhkarávju. *island* N Norway
164 C17 **Mage-shima** *island* Nansei-shotō, SW Japan
108 G11 **Maggia** Ticino, S Switzerland 46°15′N 08°42′E
108 G10 **Maggia** ≈ SW Switzerland
Maggiore, Lago *see* Maggiore, Lake
106 C6 **Maggiore, Lake** *It.* Lago Maggiore. ◎ Italy/Switzerland
44 I12 **Maggotty** W Jamaica 18°09′N 77°46′W
76 I10 **Maghama** Gorgol, S Mauritania 15°31′N 12°50′W
97 F14 **Maghera** *Ir.* Machaire Rátha. C Northern Ireland, United Kingdom 54°51′N 06°40′W
97 F15 **Magherafelt** *Ir.* Machaire Fíolta. C Northern Ireland, United Kingdom 54°45′N 06°36′W
188 H6 **Magicienne Bay** *bay* Saipan, S Northern Mariana Islands
105 O13 **Magina** ▲ S Spain 37°43′N 03°24′W
81 H24 **Magingo** Ruvuma, S Tanzania 09°57′S 35°23′E
112 H11 **Maglaj** ◐ Federacija Bosna I Hercegovina, N Bosnia and Herzegovina
107 Q19 **Maglie** Puglia, SE Italy 40°07′N 18°18′E
36 L2 **Magna** Utah, W USA 40°42′N 112°06′W
Magnesia *see* Manisa
14 G12 **Magnetawan** ≈ Ontario, S Canada
27 T14 **Magnolia** Arkansas, C USA 33°17′N 93°16′W
22 K7 **Magnolia** Mississippi, S USA 31°08′N 90°27′W
25 V10 **Magnolia** Texas, SW USA 30°12′N 95°46′W
Magnolia State *see* Mississippi
95 J15 **Magnor** Hedmark, S Norway 59°57′N 12°14′E
187 Y14 **Mago** *prev.* Mango. *island* Lau Group, E Fiji
83 L15 **Màgoé** Tete, NW Mozambique 15°50′S 31°42′E
15 Q13 **Magog** Québec, SE Canada 45°16′N 72°09′W
83 J15 **Magoye** Southern, S Zambia 16°00′S 27°34′E
41 Q12 **Magozal** Veracruz-Llave, C Mexico 21°33′N 97°57′W
14 B7 **Magpie** ≈ Ontario, S Canada
11 Q17 **Magrath** Alberta, SW Canada 49°27′N 112°52′W
105 R10 **Magre** ≈ E Spain
76 I9 **Magṭa' Laḥjar** *var.* Magta Lahjar, Magta' Lahjar, Magtá Lahjar. Brakna, SW Mauritania 17°27′N 13°07′W
146 D12 **Magtymguly** *prev.* Garrygala, *Rus.* Kara-Kala. Balkan Welaýaty, W Turkmenistan 38°27′N 56°15′E
83 L20 **Magude** Maputo, S Mozambique 25°02′S 32°40′E
77 Y12 **Magumeri** Borno, NE Nigeria 12°07′N 12°48′E
189 O14 **Magur Islands** *island group* Caroline Islands, C Micronesia
166 L6 **Magway** *var.* Magwe. Magway, W Burma (Myanmar) 20°08′N 94°55′E
Magway *see* Magwe
166 L6 **Magwe** *var.* Magway. ◐ *division* C Burma (Myanmar)
Magyar-Becse *see* Bečej
Magyarkanizsa *see* Kanjiža
Magyarország *see* Hungary
Magyarzsombor *see* Zimbor
142 J4 **Mahābād** *var.* Mehabad; *prev.* Sāūjbulāgh. Āẕarbāyjān-e Gharbī, NW Iran 36°44′N 45°44′E
172 H5 **Mahabo** Toliara, W Madagascar 20°22′S 44°39′E
Maha Chai *see* Samut Sakhon
155 D14 **Mahād** Mahārāshtra, W India 18°04′N 73°21′E
81 N17 **Mahadday Weyne** Shabeellaha Dhexe, C Somalia 02°55′N 45°30′E
79 Q17 **Mahagi** Orientale, NE Dem. Rep. Congo 02°16′N 30°59′E
Mahāil *see* Muhāyil
172 I4 **Mahajamba** *seasonal river* NW Madagascar
152 G10 **Mahājan** Rājasthān, NW India 28°47′N 73°50′E
172 I3 **Mahajanga** *var.* Majunga. Mahajanga, NW Madagascar 15°40′S 46°20′E
172 I3 **Mahajanga** ◐ *province* W Madagascar
172 I3 **Mahajanga** ✈ Mahajanga, NW Madagascar 15°40′S 46°20′E
169 U10 **Mahakam, Sungai** *var.* Koetai, Kutai. ≈ Borneo, C Indonesia
83 I19 **Mahalapye** *var.* Mahalatswe. Central, SE Botswana 23°02′S 26°53′E
Mahalatswe *see* Mahalapye
Mahalla el Kubra *see* El Maḥalla el Kubra
171 O13 **Mahalona** Sulawesi, C Indonesia 02°37′S 121°26′E
Mahameru *see* Semeru, Gunung
143 S11 **Māhān** Kermān, E Iran 30°00′N 57°00′E
154 N12 **Mahanādi** ≈ E India
172 J5 **Mahanoro** Toamasina, E Madagascar 19°53′S 48°48′E
153 P13 **Mahārājganj** Bihār, N India 26°07′N 84°31′E
153 O12 **Mahārājganj** Uttar Pradesh, N India 27°08′N 83°34′E
154 G13 **Mahārāshtra** ◐ *state* W India
154 L13 **Mahāsamund** Chhattīsgarh, SW India 21°06′N 82°06′E
172 I4 **Mahavavy** *seasonal river* N Madagascar
155 K24 **Mahaweli Ganga** ≈ C Sri Lanka
Mahbés *see* El Mahbas
155 J15 **Mahbūbābād** Andhra Pradesh, E India 17°35′N 80°00′E
155 H16 **Mahbūbnagar** Andhra Pradesh, C India 16°46′N 78°01′E
140 M8 **Mahd adh Dhahab** Al Madīnah, W Saudi Arabia 23°33′N 40°56′E
55 S9 **Mahdia** C Guyana 05°16′N 59°08′W
75 N6 **Mahdia** *var.* Al Mahdīyah, Mehdia. NE Tunisia 35°14′N 11°06′E
155 F20 **Mahe** *Fr.* Mahé; *prev.* Mayyali. Pondicherry, SW India 11°41′N 75°31′E
172 I16 **Mahé** ✈ Mahé, NE Seychelles 04°37′S 55°27′E
172 H16 **Mahé** *island* Inner Islands, NE Seychelles
Mahé *see* Mahe
173 Y17 **Mahebourg** SE Mauritius 20°24′S 57°42′E
152 L10 **Mahendranagar** Far Western, W Nepal 28°58′N 80°13′E
81 I23 **Mahenge** Morogoro, SE Tanzania 08°41′S 36°41′E
185 F22 **Maheno** Otago, South Island, New Zealand 45°10′S 170°51′E
154 D9 **Mahesāna** Gujarāt, W India 23°37′N 72°28′E
154 F11 **Maheshwar** Madhya Pradesh, C India 22°11′N 75°40′E
153 V17 **Maheskhali Island** *var.* Maiskhal Island. *island* SE Bangladesh
151 F14 **Mahi** ≈ N India
184 Q10 **Mahia Peninsula** *peninsula* North Island, New Zealand
119 O16 **Mahilyow** *Rus.* Mogilëv. Mahilyowskaya Voblasts', E Belarus 53°55′N 30°23′E
119 M16 **Mahilyowskaya Voblasts'** *prev. Rus.* Mogilëvskaya Oblast'. ◐ *province* E Belarus
191 P7 **Mahina** Tahiti, W French Polynesia 17°29′S 149°27′W
185 E23 **Mahinerangi, Lake** ◎ South Island, New Zealand
Máhkarávju *see* Magerøya
83 L22 **Mahlabatini** KwaZulu/Natal, E South Africa 28°15′S 31°28′E
166 L5 **Mahlaing** Mandalay, C Burma (Myanmar) 21°03′N 95°44′E
109 X8 **Mahldorf** Steiermark, SE Austria 46°54′N 15°55′E
Mahmūd-e 'Erāqī *see* Maḥmūd-e Rāqī
149 R4 **Maḥmūd-e Rāqī** *var.* Mahmūd-e 'Erāqī. Kāpīsā, NE Afghanistan 35°01′N 69°20′E
Mahmudiya *see* Al Maḥmūdīyah
29 S5 **Mahnomen** Minnesota, N USA 47°19′N 95°58′W
152 K14 **Mahoba** Uttar Pradesh, N India 25°18′N 79°53′E
105 Z9 **Mahón** *Cat.* Maó, *Eng.* Port Mahon; *anc.* Portus Magonis. Menorca, Spain, W Mediterranean Sea 39°54′N 04°15′E
81 J23 **Mahonda** Zanzibar North, E Tanzania 6°00′S 39°14′E
18 D14 **Mahoning Creek Lake** ⊠ Pennsylvania, NE USA
105 Q10 **Mahora** Castilla-La Mancha, C Spain 39°13′N 01°44′W
Mähren *see* Moravia
Mährisch-Budwitz *see* Moravské Budějovice
Mährisch-Kromau *see* Moravský Krumlov
Mährisch-Neustadt *see* Uničov
Mährisch-Schönberg *see* Šumperk
Mährisch-Trübau *see* Moravská Třebová
Mährisch-Weisskirchen *see* Hranice
Māh-Shahr *see* Bandar-e Māhshahr
79 N19 **Mahulu** Maniema, E Dem. Rep. Congo 01°04′S 27°10′E
154 C12 **Mahuva** Gujarāt, W India 21°06′N 71°46′E
114 N11 **Mahya Dağı** ▲ NW Turkey 41°47′N 27°34′E
105 T6 **Maials** *var.* Mayals. Cataluña, NE Spain 41°22′N 00°30′E
191 O2 **Maiana** *prev.* Hall Island. *atoll* Tungaru, W Kiribati
191 S11 **Maiao** *var.* Tapuaemanu, Tubuai-Manu. *island* Îles du Vent, W French Polynesia
54 H4 **Maicao** La Guajira, N Colombia 11°23′N 72°16′W
Mai Ceu/Mai Chio *see* Maych'ew
103 U8 **Maîche** Doubs, E France 47°15′N 06°43′E
97 N22 **Maidenhead** S England, United Kingdom 51°32′N 00°44′W
11 S15 **Maidstone** Saskatchewan, S Canada 53°06′N 109°21′W
97 P22 **Maidstone** SE England, United Kingdom 51°17′N 00°31′E
77 Y13 **Maiduguri** Borno, NE Nigeria 11°51′N 13°10′E
108 I8 **Maienfeld** Sankt Gallen, NE Switzerland 47°01′N 09°30′E
116 J12 **Măieruș** *Hung.* Szászmagyarós. Brașov, C Romania 45°55′N 25°30′E
Maigh Chromtha *see* Macroom
Maigh Eo *see* Mayo
55 N9 **Maigualida, Sierra** ▲▲ S Venezuela
154 K9 **Maihar** Madhya Pradesh, C India 24°18′N 80°46′E
154 K11 **Maikala Range** ▲▲ C India
67 T10 **Maiko** ≈ W Dem. Rep. Congo
Mailand *see* Milano
152 L11 **Mailāni** Uttar Pradesh, N India 28°17′N 80°20′E
149 U10 **Māilsi** Punjab, E Pakistan 29°46′N 72°15′E
147 R8 **Maimak** Talasskaya Oblast', NW Kyrgyzstan 42°40′N 71°12′E
Maimāna *see* Meymaneh
171 V13 **Maimawa** Papua, E Indonesia 03°21′S 133°36′E
Maimuna *see* Al Maymūnah
101 G18 **Main** ≈ C Germany
115 F22 **Maïna** *ancient monument* Pelopónnisos, S Greece
115 E20 **Maínalo** ▲▲ S Greece
101 L22 **Mainburg** Bayern, SE Germany 48°40′N 11°48′E
Main Camp *see* Banana
14 E12 **Main Channel** *lake channel* Ontario, S Canada
79 I20 **Mai-Ndombe, Lac** *prev.* Lac Léopold II. ◎ W Dem. Rep. Congo
101 K20 **Main-Donau-Kanal** *canal* SE Germany
19 R6 **Maine** *off.* State of Maine, *also known as* Lumber State, Pine Tree State. ◐ *state* NE USA
102 K6 **Maine** *cultural region* NW France
102 J7 **Maine-et-Loire** ◐ *department* NW France
19 Q9 **Maine, Gulf of** *gulf* NE USA
77 X12 **Maïné-Soroa** Diffa, SE Niger 13°14′N 12°00′E
167 N2 **Maingkwan** *var.* Mungkawn. Kachin State, N Burma (Myanmar) 26°20′N 96°37′E
Main Island *see* Bermuda
Mainistir Fhear Maí *see* Fermoy
Mainistirna Búille *see* Boyle
Mainistir na Corann *see* Midleton
Mainistir na Féile *see* Abbeyfeale
96 J5 **Mainland** *island* N Scotland, United Kingdom
96 L2 **Mainland** *island* NE Scotland, United Kingdom
159 P16 **Mainling** *var.* Tungdor. Xizang Zizhiqu, W China 29°12′N 94°06′E
152 K12 **Mainpuri** Uttar Pradesh, N India 27°14′N 79°01′E
103 N5 **Maintenon** Eure-et-Loir, C France 48°35′N 01°34′E
172 H4 **Maintirano** Mahajanga, W Madagascar 18°01′S 44°03′E
93 M15 **Mainua** Oulu, C Finland 64°05′N 27°28′E
101 G18 **Mainz** *Fr.* Mayence. Rheinland-Pfalz, SW Germany 50°00′N 08°16′E
76 I9 **Maio** *var.* Vila do Maio. Maio, S Cape Verde 15°07′N 23°12′W
76 E10 **Maio** *var.* Mayo. *island* Ilhas de Sotavento, SE Cape Verde
62 G12 **Maipo, Río** ≈ C Chile
62 H12 **Maipo, Volcán** ⛰ W Argentina 34°09′S 69°51′W
61 E22 **Maipú** Buenos Aires, E Argentina 36°52′S 57°52′W
62 I11 **Maipú** Mendoza, E Argentina 33°00′S 68°46′W
62 H11 **Maipú** Santiago, C Chile 33°30′S 70°52′W
106 A9 **Maira** ≈ NW Italy
108 I10 **Maira** *It.* Mera. ≈ Italy/Switzerland
153 V12 **Mairābari** Assam, NE India 26°28′N 92°22′E
44 K7 **Maisí** Guantánamo, E Cuba 20°13′N 74°08′W
118 H13 **Maišiagala** Vilnius, SE Lithuania 54°52′N 25°03′E
Maiskhal Island *see* Maheskhali Island
167 N13 **Mai Sombun** Chumphon, SW Thailand 10°49′N 99°13′E
Mai Son *see* Hat Lot
Maisur *see* Karnātaka, India
Maisur *see* Mysore, India
183 T8 **Maitland** New South Wales, SE Australia 32°33′S 151°33′E
182 I9 **Maitland** South Australia 34°21′S 137°42′E
14 F15 **Maitland** ≈ Ontario, S Canada
195 R1 **Maitri** *Indian research station* Antarctica 70°03′S 08°59′E
159 N15 **Maizhokunggar** Xizang Zizhiqu, W China 29°50′N 91°40′E
43 O10 **Maíz, Islas del** *var.* Corn Islands. *island group* SE Nicaragua
164 J12 **Maizuru** Kyōto, Honshū, SW Japan 35°30′N 135°20′E
54 F6 **Majagual** Sucre, N Colombia 08°36′N 74°39′W
41 Z13 **Majahual** Quintana Roo, E Mexico 18°43′N 87°43′W
Mājeej *see* Mejit Island
171 N13 **Majene** *prev.* Madjene. Sulawesi, C Indonesia 03°33′S 118°59′E
43 V15 **Majé, Serranía de** ▲▲ E Panama
112 I11 **Majevica** ▲▲ NE Bosnia and Herzegovina
81 H15 **Majī** Southern Nationalities, S Ethiopia 06°11′N 35°32′E
141 X7 **Majīs** NW Oman 24°25′N 56°34′E
Majorca *see* Mallorca
105 X9 **Major, Puig** ▲ Mallorca, Spain, W Mediterranean Sea 39°50′N 2°50′E
Mājro *see* Majuro Atoll
Majunga *see* Mahajanga
189 Y3 **Majuro** ✈ Majuro Atoll, SE Marshall Islands 07°05′N 171°08′E
189 Y2 **Majuro Atoll** *var.* Mājro. *atoll* Ratak Chain, SE Marshall Islands
189 X2 **Majuro Lagoon** *lagoon* Majuro Atoll, SE Marshall Islands
76 H11 **Maka** C Senegal 13°40′N 14°12′W
79 F20 **Makabana** Niari, SW Congo 03°28′S 12°36′E
38 D9 **Mākaha** *var.* Makaha. O'ahu, Hawaii, USA, C Pacific Ocean 21°28′N 158°13′W
38 B8 **Makahū'ena Point** *var.* Makahuena Point. *headland* Kaua'i, Hawai'i, USA 21°52′N 159°28′W
38 D9 **Makakilo City** O'ahu, Hawaii, USA, C Pacific Ocean 21°21′N 158°05′W
83 H18 **Makalamabedi** Central, C Botswana 20°19′S 23°51′E
Makale *see* Mek'elē
158 K17 **Makalu** *Chin.* Makaru Shan. ▲ China/Nepal 27°53′N 87°09′E
81 G23 **Makampi** Mbeya, S Tanzania 08°00′S 33°17′E
145 X12 **Makanchi** *Kaz.* Maqanshy. Vostochnyy Kazakhstan, E Kazakhstan 46°47′N 82°00′E
42 M8 **Makantaka** Región Autónoma Atlántico Norte, NE Nicaragua 13°13′N 84°04′W
190 B16 **Makapu Point** *headland* W Niue 18°59′S 169°56′E
185 C24 **Makarewa** Southland, South Island, New Zealand 46°17′S 168°16′E
117 O4 **Makariv** Kyyivs'ka Oblast', N Ukraine 50°28′N 29°49′E
185 D20 **Makarora** ≈ South Island, New Zealand
123 T13 **Makarov** Ostrov Sakhalin, Sakhalinskaya Oblast', SE Russian Federation 48°24′N 142°37′E
197 R9 **Makarov Basin** *undersea feature* Arctic Ocean
192 I5 **Makarov Seamount** *undersea feature* W Pacific Ocean 29°30′N 153°30′E
113 F15 **Makarska** *It.* Macarsca. Split-Dalmacija, SE Croatia 43°18′N 17°00′E
Makaru Shan *see* Makalu
125 O15 **Makar'yev** Kostromskaya Oblast', NW Russian Federation 57°52′N 43°46′E
82 L11 **Makasa** Northern, NE Zambia 09°42′S 31°54′E
Makasar *see* Makassar
Makasar, Selat *see* Makassar Straits
170 M14 **Makassar** *var.* Macassar, Makasar; *prev.* Ujungpandang. Sulawesi, C Indonesia 05°09′S 119°28′E
192 F7 **Makassar Straits** *Ind.* Makasar Selat. *strait* C Indonesia
144 G12 **Makat** *Kaz.* Maqat. Atyrau, SW Kazakhstan 47°40′N 53°28′E
191 T10 **Makatea** *island* Îles Tuamotu, C French Polynesia
139 U7 **Makātū** Diyālá, E Iraq 33°55′N 45°25′E
172 H6 **Makay** *var.* Massif du Makay. ▲▲ SW Madagascar
Makay, Massif du *see* Makay
114 J12 **Makaza** *pass* Bulgaria/Greece
Makedonija *see* Macedonia, FYR
190 B16 **Makefu** W Niue 18°59′S 169°55′W
191 V10 **Makemo** *atoll* Îles Tuamotu, C French Polynesia
76 I15 **Makeni** C Sierra Leone 08°57′N 12°02′W
Makenzen *see* Orlyak
Makeyevka *see* Makiyivka
127 Q16 **Makhachkala** *prev.* Petrovsk-Port. Respublika Dagestan, SW Russian Federation 42°58′N 47°30′E
83 K19 **Makhado** *prev.* Louis Trichardt. Northern, NE South Africa 23°01′S 29°43′E
144 F11 **Makhambet** Atyrau, W Kazakhstan 47°35′N 51°35′E
Makharadze *see* Ozurget'i
139 W13 **Makhfar Al Buṣayyah** Al Muthanná, S Iraq 30°09′N 46°09′E
139 R4 **Makhmūr** Arbīl, N Iraq 35°47′N 43°32′E
138 I11 **Makhrūq, Wadi al** *dry watercourse* E Jordan
139 R4 **Makḥūl, Jabal** ▲▲ C Iraq
141 R13 **Makhyah, Wādī** *dry watercourse* N Yemen
171 V13 **Maki** Papua, E Indonesia 03°00′S 134°10′E
185 G21 **Makikihi** Canterbury, South Island, New Zealand 44°36′S 171°09′E
191 O2 **Makin** *prev.* Pitt Island. *atoll* Tungaru, W Kiribati
81 I20 **Makindu** Eastern, S Kenya 02°15′S 37°49′E
145 Q8 **Makinsk** Akmola, N Kazakhstan 52°40′N 70°28′E
187 N10 **Makira** *off.* Makira Province. ◐ *province* SE Solomon Islands
Makira *see* San Cristobal
Makira Province *see* Makira
117 X8 **Makiyivka** *Rus.* Makeyevka; *prev.* Dmitriyevsk. Donets'ka Oblast', E Ukraine 47°57′N 37°47′E
140 L10 **Makkah** *Eng.* Mecca. Makkah, W Saudi Arabia 21°28′N 39°50′E
140 M10 **Makkah** *var.* Minṭaqat Makkah. ◐ *province* W Saudi Arabia
Makkah, Minṭaqat *see* Makkah
13 R7 **Makkovik** Newfoundland and Labrador, NE Canada 55°06′N 59°07′W
98 K6 **Makkum** Friesland, N Netherlands 53°03′N 05°25′E
111 M25 **Makó** *Rom.* Macău. Csongrád, SE Hungary 46°14′N 20°28′E
Mako *see* Makung
14 G9 **Makobe Lake** ◎ Ontario, S Canada
79 F18 **Makokou** Ogooué-Ivindo, NE Gabon 0°38′N 12°47′E
81 G23 **Makongolosi** Mbeya, S Tanzania 08°24′S 33°09′E
81 E19 **Makota** SW Uganda 0°37′S 30°12′E
79 G18 **Makoua** Cuvette, C Congo 0°01′S 15°40′E
110 M10 **Maków Mazowiecki** Mazowieckie, C Poland 52°51′N 21°06′E
111 K17 **Maków Podhalański** Małopolskie, S Poland 49°43′N 19°40′E
143 V14 **Makran** *cultural region* Iran/Pakistan
152 G12 **Makrāna** Rājasthān, N India 27°02′N 74°44′E
143 U15 **Makran Coast** *coastal region* SE Iran
119 F20 **Makrany** *Rus.* Mokrany. Brestskaya Voblasts', SW Belarus 51°50′N 24°15′E
Makrinoros *see* Makrynóros
115 H20 **Makrónisosi** *island* Kykládes, Greece, Aegean Sea
115 D17 **Makrynóros** *var.* Makrinoros. ▲▲ C Greece
115 G19 **Makryplági** ▲ C Greece 38°00′N 23°06′E
Maksamaa *see* Maxmo
Maksatha *see* Maksatikha
Maksaticha *see* Maksatikha
124 J15 **Maksatikha** *var.* Maksatha, Maksaticha. Tverskaya Oblast', W Russian Federation 57°49′N 35°46′E
154 G10 **Maksi** Madhya Pradesh, C India 23°20′N 76°36′E
142 I1 **Mākū** Āẕarbāyjān-e Gharbī, NW Iran 39°20′N 44°50′E
153 Y11 **Mākum** Assam, NE India 27°28′N 95°28′E
Makun *see* Makung
161 R14 **Makung** *prev.* Mako, Makun. W Taiwan 23°35′N 119°35′E
164 B16 **Makurazaki** Kagoshima, Kyūshū, SW Japan 31°16′N 130°18′E
77 V15 **Makurdi** Benue, C Nigeria 07°42′N 08°36′E
38 L17 **Makushin Volcano** ▲ Unalaska Island, Alaska, USA 53°53′N 166°55′W
83 K16 **Makwiro** Mashonaland West, N Zimbabwe 17°58′S 30°25′E
57 D15 **Mala** Lima, W Peru 12°40′S 76°36′W
93 I14 **Malå** Västerbotten, N Sweden 65°12′N 18°45′E
Mala *see* Mallow, Ireland
Mala *see* Malaita, Solomon Islands
171 P8 **Malabang** Mindanao, S Philippines
155 E21 **Malabār Coast** *coast* SW India
79 C16 **Malabo** *prev.* Santa Isabel. ● (Equatorial Guinea) Isla de Bioco, NW Equatorial Guinea 03°43′N 08°52′E
79 C16 **Malabo** ✈ Isla de Bioco, N Equatorial Guinea 03°44′N 08°51′E
Malaca *see* Málaga
Malacca *see* Melaka
168 I7 **Malacca, Strait of** *Ind.* Selat Malaka. *strait* Indonesia/Malaysia
Malacka *see* Malacky
111 G20 **Malacky** *Hung.* Malacka. Bratislavský Kraj, W Slovakia 48°26′N 17°01′E
33 R16 **Malad City** Idaho, NW USA 42°10′N 112°16′W
117 Q4 **Mala Divytsya** Chernihivs'ka Oblast', N Ukraine 50°40′N 32°13′E
119 J15 **Maladzyechna** *Pol.* Molodeczno, *Rus.* Molodechno. Minskaya Voblasts', C Belarus 54°19′N 26°51′E
190 D12 **Malaee** Île Futuna, N Wallis and Futuna
190 G12 **Mala'etoli** Île Uvea, E Wallis and Futuna
54 G8 **Málaga** Santander, C Colombia 06°44′N 72°45′W
104 M15 **Málaga** *anc.* Malaca. Andalucía, S Spain 36°43′N 04°25′W
37 V15 **Malaga** New Mexico, SW USA 32°10′N 104°04′W
104 L15 **Málaga** ◐ *province* Andalucía, S Spain
104 M15 **Málaga** ✈ Andalucía, S Spain 36°38′N 04°36′W
Malagasy Republic *see* Madagascar
105 N10 **Malagón** Castilla-La Mancha, C Spain 39°10′N 03°51′W
97 G18 **Malahide** *Ir.* Mullach Íde. Dublin, E Ireland 53°27′N 06°09′W
187 N9 **Malaita** *off.* Malaita Province. ◐ *province* N Solomon Islands
187 N8 **Malaita** *var.* Mala. *island* N Solomon Islands
Malaita Province *see* Malaita
80 F13 **Malakal** Upper Nile, S Sudan 09°31′N 31°40′E
Malakanagiri *see* Malkangiri
149 T5 **Malākand** North-West Frontier Province, N Pakistan 34°34′N 71°56′E
112 C10 **Mala Kapela** ▲▲ NW Croatia
25 V7 **Malakoff** Texas, SW USA 32°10′N 96°00′W
Malakula *see* Malekula
149 V7 **Malakwāl** *var.* Mālikwāla. Punjab, E Pakistan 32°32′N 73°18′E
186 E7 **Malalamai** Madang, W Papua New Guinea 05°49′S 146°44′E
171 O13 **Malamala** Sulawesi, C Indonesia 03°21′S 120°58′E
169 S17 **Malang** Jawa, C Indonesia 07°59′S 112°45′E
83 O14 **Malanga** Niassa, N Mozambique 13°27′S 36°05′E
Malange *see* Malanje
92 I9 **Malangen** *sound* N Norway
82 C11 **Malanje** *var.* Malange. Malanje, NW Angola 09°34′S 16°25′E
82 C11 **Malanje** *var.* Malange. ◐ *province* N Angola
148 M16 **Malān, Rās** *cape* SW Pakistan
77 S13 **Malanville** NE Benin 11°50′N 03°23′E
Malapane *see* Ozimek
155 F21 **Malappuram** Kerala, SW India 11°00′N 76°02′E
43 T17 **Mala, Punta** *headland* S Panama 07°28′N 79°58′W
148 L15 **Malar** Baluchistān, SW Pakistan 26°19′N 64°55′E
95 N16 **Mälaren** ◎ C Sweden
62 H13 **Malargüe** Mendoza, W Argentina 35°32′S 69°35′W
14 J8 **Malartic** Québec, SE Canada 48°09′N 78°09′W
119 F20 **Malaryta** *Pol.* Maloryta, *Rus.* Malorita. Brestskaya Voblasts', SW Belarus 51°47′N 24°05′E
63 J19 **Malaspina** Chubut, SE Argentina 44°56′S 66°52′W
39 U12 **Malaspina Glacier** *glacier* Alaska, USA
137 N15 **Malatya** *anc.* Melitene. Malatya, SE Turkey 38°22′N 38°18′E
136 M14 **Malatya** ◐ *province* C Turkey
Malavate *see* Pédima
117 Q7 **Mala Vyska** *Rus.* Malaya Viska. Kirovohrads'ka Oblast', S Ukraine 48°37′N 31°36′E
83 M14 **Malawi** *off.* Republic of Malaŵi; *prev.* Nyasaland, Nyasaland Protectorate. ◆ *republic* S Africa
Malawi, Lake *see* Nyasa, Lake
Malaŵi, Republic of *see* Malawi
93 J17 **Malax** *Fin.* Maalahti. Länsi-Suomi, W Finland 62°55′N 21°30′E
124 H14 **Malaya Vishera** Novgorodskaya Oblast', W Russian Federation 58°52′N 32°12′E
Malaya Viska *see* Mala Vyska
171 Q7 **Malaybalay** Mindanao, S Philippines 08°10′N 125°08′E
142 L6 **Malāyer** *prev.* Daulatabad. Hamadān, W Iran 34°20′N 48°47′E

◆ Country ● Country Capital ◇ Dependent Territory ○ Dependent Territory Capital ◐ Administrative Regions ✈ International Airport ▲ Mountain ▲▲ Mountain Range ⛰ Volcano ≈ River ◎ Lake ⊠ Reservoir

168 J7 **Malay Peninsula** *peninsula* Malaysia/Thailand
168 L7 **Malaysia** *off.* Malaysia, *var.* Federation of Malaysia; *prev.* the separate territories of Federation of Malaya, Sarawak and Sabah (North Borneo) and Singapore. ◆ *monarchy* SE Asia
Malaysia, Federation of *see* Malaysia
137 R14 **Malazgirt** Muş, E Turkey 39°09′N 42°30′E
15 R8 **Malbaie** ≈ Québec, SE Canada
77 T12 **Malbaza** Tahoua, S Niger 13°57′N 05°32′E
110 J7 **Malbork** *Ger.* Marienburg, Marienburg in Westpreussen. Pomorskie, N Poland 54°01′N 19°03′E
100 N9 **Malchin** Mecklenburg-Vorpommern, N Germany 53°43′N 12°46′E
100 M9 **Malchiner See** ◎ NE Germany
99 D16 **Maldegem** Oost-Vlaanderen, NW Belgium 51°12′N 03°27′E
98 L13 **Malden** Gelderland, SE Netherlands 51°47′N 05°51′E
19 O11 **Malden** Massachusetts, NE USA 42°25′N 71°04′W
27 Y8 **Malden** Missouri, C USA 36°33′N 89°58′W
191 X4 **Malden Island** *prev.* Independence Island. *atoll* E Kiribati
173 Q6 **Maldives** *off.* Maldivian Divehi, Republic of Maldives. ◆ *republic* N Indian Ocean
Maldives, Republic of *see* Maldives
Maldivian Divehi *see* Maldives
97 P21 **Maldon** E England, United Kingdom 51°44′N 00°40′E
61 G20 **Maldonado** Maldonado, S Uruguay 34°57′S 54°59′W
61 G20 **Maldonado** ◐ *department* S Uruguay
41 P17 **Maldonado, Punta** *headland* S Mexico 16°18′N 98°31′W
106 G6 **Malè** Trentino-Alto Adige, N Italy 46°21′N 10°51′E
151 K19 **Male'** *Div.* Maale. ● (Maldives) Male' Atoll, C Maldives 04°10′N 73°29′E
76 K13 **Maléa** *var.* Maléya. NE Guinea 11°46′N 09°43′W
Maléas, Ákra *see* Agriliá, Akrotírio
115 G22 **Maléas, Akrotírio** *headland* S Greece 36°25′N 23°11′E
151 K19 **Male' Atoll** *var.* Kaafu Atoll. *atoll* C Maldives
Malebo, Pool *see* Stanley Pool
154 E12 **Mālegaon** Mahārāshtra, W India 20°33′N 74°32′E
81 F15 **Malek** Jonglei, S Sudan 06°04′N 31°36′E
187 Q13 **Malekula** *var.* Malakula; *prev.* Mallicolo. *island* W Vanuatu
189 Y15 **Malem** Kosrae, E Micronesia 05°16′N 163°01′E
83 O15 **Malema** Nampula, N Mozambique 14°57′S 37°28′E
79 N23 **Malemba-Nkulu** Katanga, SE Dem. Rep. Congo 08°01′S 26°48′E
124 K9 **Malen'ga** Respublika Kareliya, NW Russian Federation 63°50′N 36°21′E
95 M20 **Målerås** Kalmar, S Sweden 56°55′N 15°34′E
103 O6 **Malesherbes** Loiret, C France 48°18′N 02°25′E
115 G18 **Malesína** Stereá Ellás, E Greece 38°37′N 23°15′E
Maléya *see* Maléa
127 O15 **Malgobek** Respublika Ingushetiya, SW Russian Federation 43°34′N 44°34′E
105 X5 **Malgrat de Mar** Cataluña, NE Spain 41°39′N 02°45′E
80 C9 **Malha** Northern Darfur, W Sudan 15°07′N 26°00′E
139 Q5 **Malḥah** *var.* Malḥāt. Ṣalāḥ ad Dīn, C Iraq 34°44′N 42°41′E
Malḥāt *see* Malḥah
32 K14 **Malheur Lake** ◎ Oregon, NW USA
32 L14 **Malheur River** ≈ Oregon, NW USA
76 I13 **Mali** NW Guinea 12°08′N 12°29′W
77 O9 **Mali** *off.* Republic of Mali, *Fr.* République du Mali; *prev.* French Sudan, Sudanese Republic. ◆ *republic* W Africa
171 Q16 **Maliana** W East Timor 08°57′S 125°25′E
167 O2 **Mali Hka** ≈ N Burma (Myanmar)
Mali Idjoš *see* Mali Iđoš
112 K8 **Mali Iđoš** *var.* Mali Idjoš, *Hung.* Kishegyes; *prev.* Krivaja. Vojvodina, N Serbia 45°43′N 19°40′E
112 K9 **Mali Kanal** *canal* N Serbia
171 P12 **Maliku** Sulawesi, N Indonesia 0°36′S 123°13′E
Malik, Wadi al *see* Milk, Wadi el
Mālikwāla *see* Malakwāl
167 N11 **Mali Kyun** *var.* Tavoy Island. *island* Mergui Archipelago, S Burma (Myanmar)
95 M19 **Målilla** Kalmar, S Sweden 57°24′N 15°49′E
112 B11 **Mali Lošinj** *It.* Lussinpiccolo. Primorje-Gorski Kotar, W Croatia 44°31′N 14°28′E
Malin *see* Malyn
171 P7 **Malindang, Mount** ▲ Mindanao, S Philippines 08°12′N 123°37′E
81 K20 **Malindi** Coast, SE Kenya 03°14′S 40°05′E
Malines *see* Mechelen
96 E13 **Malin Head** *Ir.* Cionn Mhálanna. *headland* NW Ireland 55°37′N 07°37′W
171 O11 **Malino, Gunung** ▲ Sulawesi, N Indonesia 0°44′N 120°45′E
113 M21 **Maliq** *var.* Maliqi. Korçë, SE Albania 40°45′N 20°45′E
Maliqi *see* Maliq
149 O16 **Malīr** Sind, SE Pakistan 24°52′N 67°11′E
Mali, Republic of *see* Mali
Mali, République du *see* Mali
171 Q8 **Malita** Mindanao, S Philippines 06°13′N 125°39′E
155 L15 **Malkangiri** *var.* Malakanagiri. Orissa, E India 18°21′N 81°53′E
154 G12 **Malkāpur** Mahārāshtra, C India 20°52′N 76°18′E
136 B10 **Malkara** Tekirdağ, NW Turkey 40°54′N 26°54′E
119 J19 **Mal'kavichy** *Rus.* Mal'kovichi. Brestskaya Voblasts', SW Belarus 52°31′N 26°36′E
Malkiye *see* Al Mālikīyah
114 L11 **Malko Sharkovo, Yazovir** ▣ SE Bulgaria
114 N11 **Malko Tŭrnovo** Burgas, E Bulgaria 42°00′N 27°33′E
Mal'kovichi *see* Mal'kavichy
183 R12 **Mallacoota** Victoria, SE Australia 37°34′S 149°45′E
96 G10 **Mallaig** N Scotland, United Kingdom 57°04′N 05°48′W
182 I9 **Mallala** South Australia 34°29′S 138°30′E
75 W9 **Mallawī** *var.* Mallawi. C Egypt 27°44′N 30°50′E
Mallawi *see* Mallawī
105 R5 **Mallén** Aragón, NE Spain 41°53′N 01°25′W
106 F5 **Malles Venosta** *Ger.* Mals im Vinschgau. Trentino-Alto Adige, N Italy 46°40′N 10°37′E
Mallicolo *see* Malekula
109 Q8 **Mallnitz** Salzburg, S Austria 46°58′N 13°09′E
105 W9 **Mallorca** *Eng.* Majorca; *anc.* Baleares Major. *island* Islas Baleares, Spain, W Mediterranean Sea
97 C20 **Mallow** *Ir.* Mala. SW Ireland 52°08′N 08°39′W
93 E15 **Malm** Nord-Trøndelag, C Norway 64°04′N 11°12′E
95 L19 **Malmbäck** Jönköping, S Sweden 57°34′N 14°30′E
92 J12 **Malmberget** *Lapp.* Malmivaara. Norrbotten, N Sweden 67°09′N 20°39′E
99 M20 **Malmédy** Liège, E Belgium 50°26′N 06°02′E
83 E25 **Malmesbury** Western Cape, SW South Africa 33°28′S 18°43′E
Malmivaara *see* Malmberget
95 N16 **Malmköping** Södermanland, C Sweden 59°08′N 16°49′E
95 K23 **Malmö** Skåne, S Sweden 55°36′N 13°E
95 K23 **Malmo** ✕ Skåne, S Sweden 55°33′N 13°23′E
45 Q16 **Malmok** *headland* Bonaire, S Netherlands Antilles 12°16′N 68°21′W
95 M18 **Malmslätt** Östergötland, S Sweden 58°25′N 15°30′E
125 R16 **Malmyzh** Kirovskaya Oblast', NW Russian Federation 56°30′N 50°37′E
187 Q13 **Malo** *island* W Vanuatu
126 J7 **Maloarkhangel'sk** Orlovskaya Oblast', W Russian Federation 52°25′N 36°37′E
Maļoeļap *see* Maloelap Atoll
189 V6 **Maloelap Atoll** *var.* Maļoeļap. *atoll* E Marshall Islands
Maloenda *see* Malunda
108 I10 **Maloja** Graubünden, S Switzerland 46°25′N 09°42′E
82 L12 **Malole** Northern, NE Zambia 10°05′S 31°37′E
171 O3 **Malolos** Luzon, N Philippines 14°51′N 120°49′E
18 K6 **Malone** New York, NE USA 44°51′N 74°18′W
79 K25 **Malonga** Katanga, S Dem. Rep. Congo 10°26′S 23°10′E
111 L17 **Małopolskie** ◐ *province* SE Poland
Malorita/Maloryta *see* Malaryta
124 K9 **Maloshuyka** Arkhangel'skaya Oblast', NW Russian Federation 63°43′N 37°20′E
114 G10 **Mal'ovitsa** ▲ W Bulgaria 42°12′N 23°19′E
145 V15 **Malovodnoye** Almaty, SE Kazakhstan 43°31′N 77°42′E
94 C10 **Måløy** Sogn Og Fjordane, S Norway 61°57′N 05°06′E
126 K4 **Maloyaroslavets** Kaluzhskaya Oblast', W Russian Federation 55°03′N 36°31′E
122 G7 **Malozemel'skaya Tundra** *physical region* NW Russian Federation
104 J10 **Malpartida de Cáceres** Extremadura, W Spain 39°26′N 06°30′W
104 K9 **Malpartida de Plasencia** Extremadura, W Spain 39°59′N 06°03′W
106 C7 **Malpensa** ✕ (Milano) Lombardia, N Italy 45°41′N 08°40′E
76 J6 **Malqteïr** *desert* N Mauritania
Mals im Vinschgau *see* Malles Venosta
118 J10 **Malta** Rēzekne, SE Latvia 56°19′N 27°11′E
33 V7 **Malta** Montana, NW USA 48°21′N 107°52′W
120 M11 **Malta** *off.* Republic of Malta. ◆ *republic* C Mediterranean Sea
109 R8 **Malta** *var.* Maltabach. ≈ S Austria
120 M11 **Malta** *island* Malta, C Mediterranean Sea
Maltabach *see* Malta
Malta, Canale di *see* Malta Channel
120 M11 **Malta Channel** *It.* Canale di Malta. *strait* Italy/Malta
83 D20 **Maltahöhe** Hardap, SW Namibia 24°50′S 17°00′E
Malta, Republic of *see* Malta
97 N16 **Malton** N England, United Kingdom 54°07′N 00°50′W
171 R13 **Maluku** *off.* Propinsi Maluku, *Dut.* Molukken, *Eng.* Moluccas. ◐ *province* E Indonesia
171 R13 **Maluku** *Dut.* Molukken, *Eng.* Moluccas; *prev.* Spice Islands. *island group* E Indonesia
Maluku, Laut *see* Molucca Sea
Maluku, Propinsi *see* Maluku
171 R11 **Maluku Utara** *off.* Propinsi Maluku Utara. ◐ *province* E Indonesia
Maluku Utara, Propinsi *see* Maluku Utara
77 V13 **Malumfashi** Katsina, N Nigeria 11°51′N 07°39′E
171 N13 **Malunda** *prev.* Maloenda. Sulawesi, C Indonesia 02°58′S 118°52′E
94 K13 **Malung** Dalarna, C Sweden 60°40′N 13°45′E
94 K13 **Malungsfors** Dalarna, C Sweden 60°43′N 13°34′E
186 M8 **Maluu** *var.* Malu'u. Malaita, N Solomon Islands 08°22′S 160°39′E
Malu'u *see* Maluu
155 D16 **Mālvan** Mahārāshtra, W India 16°05′N 73°28′E
Malventum *see* Benevento
27 U12 **Malvern** Arkansas, C USA 34°21′N 92°50′W
29 S15 **Malvern** Iowa, C USA 40°59′N 95°36′W
44 I13 **Malvern** ▲ W Jamaica 17°59′N 77°42′W
Malvina, Isla Gran *see* West Falkland
Malvinas, Islas *see* Falkland Islands
117 N4 **Malyn** *Rus.* Malin. Zhytomyrs'ka Oblast', N Ukraine 50°46′N 29°14′E
127 O11 **Malyye Derbety** Respublika Kalmykiya, SW Russian Federation 47°57′N 44°39′E
Malyy Kavkaz *see* Lesser Caucasus
123 Q6 **Malyy Lyakhovskiy, Ostrov** *island* NE Russian Federation
Malyy Pamir *see* Little Pamir
122 N5 **Malyy Taymyr, Ostrov** *island* Severnaya Zemlya, N Russian Federation
144 E10 **Malyy Uzen'** *Kaz.* Kishiözen. ≈ Kazakhstan/Russian Federation
122 L14 **Malyy Yenisey** *var.* Ka-Krem. ≈ S Russian Federation
127 S3 **Mamadysh** Respublika Tatarstan, W Russian Federation 55°46′N 51°22′E
117 N14 **Mamaia** Constanţa, E Romania 44°13′N 28°37′E
187 W14 **Mamanuca Group** *island group* Yasawa Group, W Fiji
146 L13 **Mamash** Lebap Welaýaty, E Turkmenistan 38°24′N 64°12′E
79 O17 **Mambasa** Orientale, NE Dem. Rep. Congo 01°20′N 29°05′E
171 X13 **Mamberamo, Sungai** ≈ Papua, E Indonesia
79 G15 **Mambéré** ≈ SW Central African Republic
79 G15 **Mambéré-Kadéï** ◐ *prefecture* SW Central African Republic
Mambij *see* Manbij
79 H18 **Mambili** ≈ W Congo
83 N18 **Mambone** *var.* Nova Mambone. Inhambane, E Mozambique 20°59′S 35°04′E
171 O4 **Mamburao** Mindoro, N Philippines 13°16′N 120°36′E
172 I16 **Mamelles** *island* Inner Islands, NE Seychelles
99 M25 **Mamer** Luxembourg, SW Luxembourg 49°37′N 06°01′E
102 L6 **Mamers** Sarthe, NW France 48°21′N 00°22′E
79 D15 **Mamfe** Sud-Ouest, W Cameroon 05°46′N 09°18′E
145 P6 **Mamlyutka** Severnyy Kazakhstan, N Kazakhstan 54°54′N 68°36′E
36 M15 **Mammoth** Arizona, SW USA 32°43′N 110°38′W
33 S12 **Mammoth Hot Springs** Wyoming, C USA 44°57′N 110°40′W
Mamoedjoe *see* Mamuju
119 A14 **Mamonovo** *Ger.* Heiligenbeil. Kaliningradskaya Oblast', W Russian Federation 54°28′N 19°57′E
57 L14 **Mamoré, Rio** ≈ Bolivia/Brazil
76 I14 **Mamou** W Guinea 10°24′N 12°05′W
22 H8 **Mamou** Louisiana, S USA 30°37′N 92°25′W
172 I14 **Mamoudzou** ○ (Mayotte) C Mayotte 12°48′S 45°E
172 I3 **Mampikony** Mahajanga, N Madagascar 16°03′S 47°39′E
77 P16 **Mampong** C Ghana 07°06′N 01°20′W
110 M7 **Mamry, Jezioro** *Ger.* Mauersee. ◎ NE Poland
171 N13 **Mamuju** *prev.* Mamoedjoe. Sulawesi, S Indonesia 02°41′S 118°55′E
83 F19 **Mamuno** Ghanzi, W Botswana 22°15′S 20°02′E
113 K19 **Mamuras** *var.* Mamurasi, Mamurras. Lezhë, C Albania 41°34′N 19°42′E
Mamurasi/Mamurras *see* Mamuras
76 L16 **Man** W Ivory Coast 07°24′N 07°33′W
55 X9 **Mana** NW French Guiana 05°40′N 53°49′W
56 A6 **Manabí** ◐ *province* W Ecuador
42 G4 **Manabique, Punta** *var.* Cabo Tres Puntas. *headland* E Guatemala 15°57′N 88°37′W
54 G11 **Manacacías, Río** ≈ C Colombia
58 F13 **Manacapuru** Amazonas, N Brazil 03°16′S 60°37′W
105 Y9 **Manacor** Mallorca, Spain, W Mediterranean Sea 39°35′N 03°12′E
171 Q11 **Manado** *prev.* Menado. Sulawesi, C Indonesia 01°32′N 124°55′E
188 H5 **Managaha** *island* S Northern Mariana Islands
99 G20 **Manage** Hainaut, S Belgium 50°30′N 04°14′E
42 J10 **Managua** ● (Nicaragua) Managua, W Nicaragua 12°08′N 86°15′W
42 J10 **Managua** ◐ *department* W Nicaragua
42 J10 **Managua** ✕ Managua, W Nicaragua 12°07′N 86°11′W
42 J10 **Managua, Lago de** *var.* Xolotlán. ◎ W Nicaragua
Manaḥ *see* Bilād Manaḥ
18 K16 **Manahawkin** New Jersey, NE USA 39°39′N 74°12′W
184 K11 **Manaia** Taranaki, North Island, New Zealand 39°33′S 174°07′E
172 J6 **Manakara** Fianarantsoa, SE Madagascar 22°09′S 48°E
152 J7 **Manāli** Himāchal Pradesh, NW India 32°12′N 77°06′E
Ma, Nam *see* Sông Ma
Manama *see* Al Manāmah
186 D6 **Manam Island** *island* N Papua New Guinea
67 Y13 **Mananara Avaratra** ≈ SE Madagascar
182 M9 **Manangatang** Victoria, SE Australia 35°04′S 142°53′E
172 J6 **Mananjary** Fianarantsoa, SE Madagascar 21°13′S 48°20′E
76 L14 **Manankoro** Sikasso, SW Mali 10°33′N 07°25′W
76 J12 **Manantali, Lac de** ▣ W Mali
Manáos *see* Manaus
185 B23 **Manapouri** Southland, South Island, New Zealand 45°33′S 167°38′E
185 B23 **Manapouri, Lake** ◎ South Island, New Zealand
58 F13 **Manaquiri** Amazonas, NW Brazil 03°27′S 60°37′W
Manar *see* Mannar
158 K5 **Manas** Xinjiang Uygur Zizhiqu, NW China 44°16′N 86°12′E
153 U12 **Manās** *var.* Dangme Chu. ≈ Bhutan/India
153 P10 **Manāsalu** *var.* Manaslu. ▲ C Nepal 28°33′N 84°33′E
147 R8 **Manas, Gora** ▲ Kyrgyzstan/Uzbekistan 42°17′N 71°04′E
158 K3 **Manas Hu** ◎ NW China
Manaslu *see* Manāsalu
37 S8 **Manassa** Colorado, C USA 37°10′N 105°56′W
21 W4 **Manassas** Virginia, NE USA 38°45′N 77°28′W
45 T5 **Manatí** C Puerto Rico 18°26′N 66°29′W
186 E8 **Manau** Northern, S Papua New Guinea 08°02′S 148°00′E
54 H4 **Manaure** La Guajira, N Colombia 11°46′N 72°28′W
58 F12 **Manaus** *prev.* Manáos. *state capital* Amazonas, NW Brazil 03°06′S 60°W
136 G17 **Manavgat** Antalya, SW Turkey 36°47′N 31°28′E
184 M13 **Manawatu** ≈ North Island, New Zealand
184 L11 **Manawatu-Wanganui** *off.* Manawatu-Wanganui Region. ◐ *region* North Island, New Zealand
Manawatu-Wanganui Region *see* Manawatu-Wanganui
171 R7 **Manay** Mindanao, S Philippines 07°12′N 126°29′E
138 K2 **Manbij** *var.* Mambij, *Fr.* Membidj. Ḥalab, N Syria 36°32′N 37°55′E
105 N13 **Mancha Real** Andalucía, S Spain 37°47′N 03°37′W
102 I4 **Manche** ◐ *department* N France
97 L17 **Manchester** *Lat.* Mancunium. NW England, United Kingdom 53°30′N 02°15′W
23 S5 **Manchester** Georgia, SE USA 32°51′N 84°37′W
29 Y13 **Manchester** Iowa, C USA 42°28′N 91°27′W
21 N7 **Manchester** Kentucky, S USA 37°09′N 83°46′W
19 O10 **Manchester** New Hampshire, NE USA 42°59′N 71°26′W
20 K10 **Manchester** Tennessee, S USA 35°28′N 86°05′W
18 M9 **Manchester** Vermont, NE USA 43°09′N 73°03′W
97 L18 **Manchester** ✕ NW England, United Kingdom 53°21′N 02°16′W
149 P15 **Manchhar Lake** ◎ SE Pakistan
Man-chou-li *see* Manzhouli
129 X7 **Manchurian Plain** *plain* NE China
Máncio Lima *see* Japiim
Mancunium *see* Manchester
148 J15 **Mand** Baluchistān, SW Pakistan 26°06′N 61°58′E
Mand *see* Mand, Rūd-e
81 H25 **Manda** Iringa, SW Tanzania 10°30′S 34°37′E
172 H6 **Mandabe** Toliara, W Madagascar 21°02′S 44°56′E
162 M10 **Mandah** *var.* Töhöm. Dornogovĭ, SE Mongolia 44°25′N 108°18′E
95 E18 **Mandal** Vest-Agder, S Norway 58°02′N 07°30′E
Mandal *see* Arbulag, Hövsgöl, Mongolia
Mandal *see* Batsümber, Töv, Mongolia
166 L5 **Mandalay** Mandalay, C Burma (Myanmar) 21°57′N 96°04′E
166 M6 **Mandalay** ◐ *division* C Burma (Myanmar)
162 L9 **Mandalgovĭ** Dundgovĭ, C Mongolia 45°47′N 106°18′E
139 V7 **Mandalī** Diyālá, E Iraq 33°43′N 45°33′E
162 K10 **Mandal-Ovoo** *var.* Sharhulsan. Ömnögovĭ, S Mongolia 44°43′N 104°06′E
95 E18 **Mandalselva** ≈ S Norway
163 P11 **Mandalt** *var.* Sonid Zuoqi. Nei Mongol Zizhiqu, N China 43°49′N 113°36′E
28 M5 **Mandan** North Dakota, N USA 46°49′N 100°53′W
Mandargiri Hill *see* Mandār Hill
153 R14 **Mandār Hill** *prev.* Mandargiri Hill. Bihār, NE India 24°51′N 87°03′E
170 M13 **Mandar, Teluk** *bay* Sulawesi, C Indonesia
107 C19 **Mandas** Sardegna, Italy, C Mediterranean Sea 39°40′N 09°07′E
Mandasor *see* Mandsaur
81 L16 **Mandera** North Eastern, NE Kenya 03°56′N 41°53′E
33 V13 **Manderson** Wyoming, C USA 44°13′N 107°55′W
44 J12 **Mandeville** C Jamaica 18°02′N 77°31′W
22 K9 **Mandeville** Louisiana, S USA 30°21′N 90°04′W
152 I7 **Mandi** Himāchal Pradesh, NW India 31°40′N 76°59′E
76 K14 **Mandiana** E Guinea 10°37′N 08°39′W
149 U10 **Mandi Būrewāla** *var.* Būrewāla. Punjab, E Pakistan 30°05′N 72°47′E
152 G9 **Mandi Dabwāli** Haryāna, NW India 29°56′N 74°40′E
Mandidzudzure *see* Chimanimani
83 M15 **Mandié** Manica, NW Mozambique 16°27′S 33°28′E
83 N14 **Mandimba** Niassa, N Mozambique 14°21′S 35°40′E
57 Q19 **Mandioré, Laguna** ◎ E Bolivia
154 J10 **Mandla** Madhya Pradesh, C India 22°36′N 80°23′E
83 M20 **Mandlakazi** *var.* Manjacaze. Gaza, S Mozambique 24°47′S 33°50′E
95 E24 **Mandø** *var.* Manø. *island* W Denmark
Mandoúdhion/Mandoudi *see* Mantoúdi
115 G19 **Mándra** Attikí, C Greece 38°04′N 23°30′E
172 I7 **Mandrare** ≈ S Madagascar
114 M10 **Mandra, Yazovir** *salt lake* SE Bulgaria
107 L23 **Mandrazzi, Portella** *pass* Sicilia, Italy, C Mediterranean Sea
172 J3 **Mandritsara** Mahajanga, N Madagascar 15°49′S 48°50′E
143 O13 **Mand, Rūd-e** *var.* Mand. ≈ S Iran
154 F9 **Mandsaur** *prev.* Mandasor. Madhya Pradesh, C India 24°03′N 75°10′E
154 F11 **Māndu** Madhya Pradesh, C India 22°22′N 75°24′E
169 W8 **Mandul, Pulau** *island* N Indonesia
83 G15 **Mandundu** Western, W Zambia 16°34′S 22°18′E
180 I13 **Mandurah** Western Australia 32°31′S 115°41′E
107 P18 **Manduria** Puglia, SE Italy 40°24′N 17°38′E
155 G20 **Mandya** Karnātaka, C India 12°34′N 76°55′E
77 P12 **Mané** C Burkina 12°59′N 01°21′W
106 E8 **Manerbio** Lombardia, NW Italy 45°22′N 10°09′E
Manevichi *see* Manevychi
116 K3 **Manevychi** *Pol.* Maniewicze, *Rus.* Manevichi. Volyns'ka Oblast', NW Ukraine 51°18′N 25°29′E
107 N16 **Manfredonia** Puglia, SE Italy 41°38′N 15°54′E
107 N16 **Manfredonia, Golfo di** *gulf* Adriatic Sea, N Mediterranean Sea
77 P13 **Manga** C Burkina 11°41′N 01°04′W
59 L16 **Mangabeiras, Chapada das** ▲▲ E Brazil
79 J20 **Mangai** Bandundu, W Dem. Rep. Congo 03°58′S 19°32′E
190 L17 **Mangaia** *island group* S Cook Islands
184 M9 **Mangakino** Waikato, North Island, New Zealand 38°23′S 175°47′E
153 V12 **Mangaldai** Assam, NE India 26°26′N 92°02′E
116 M15 **Mangalia** *anc.* Callatis. Constanţa, SE Romania 43°48′N 28°35′E
78 J11 **Mangalmé** Guéra, SE Chad 12°26′N 19°37′E
155 E19 **Mangalore** Karnātaka, W India 12°54′N 74°51′E
191 Y13 **Mangareva** *var.* Magareva. *island* Îles Tuamotu, SE French Polynesia
83 I23 **Mangaung** Free State, C South Africa 29°10′S 26°19′E
Mangaung *see* Bloemfontein
154 K9 **Mangawān** Madhya Pradesh, C India 24°39′N 81°33′E
184 M11 **Mangaweka** Manawatu-Wanganui, North Island, New Zealand 39°49′S 175°47′E
184 N11 **Mangaweka** ▲ North Island, New Zealand 39°51′S 176°06′E
79 P17 **Mangbwalu** Orientale, NE Dem. Rep. Congo 02°06′N 30°04′E
101 L24 **Mangfall** ≈ SE Germany
169 P13 **Manggar** Pulau Belitung, W Indonesia 02°52′S 108°13′E
166 M2 **Mangin Range** ▲▲ N Burma (Myanmar)
139 R1 **Mangish** Dahūk, N Iraq 37°03′N 43°04′E
144 F15 **Mangistau** *Kaz.* Mangqystaū Oblysy; *prev.* Mangyshlaskaya. ◐ *province* SW Kazakhstan
146 H8 **Mang'it** *Rus.* Mangit. Qoraqalpog'iston Respublikasi, W Uzbekistan 42°06′N 60°02′E
Mangit *see* Mang'it
54 A13 **Manglares, Cabo** *headland* SW Colombia 01°36′N 79°02′W
149 V6 **Mangla Reservoir** ▣ NE Pakistan
159 N9 **Mangnai** *var.* Lao Mangnai. Qinghai, C China 37°52′N 91°45′E
Mango *see* Mago, Fiji
Mango *see* Sansanné-Mango, Togo
Mangoche *see* Mangochi
83 N14 **Mangochi** *var.* Mangoche; *prev.* Fort Johnston. Southern, SE Malawi 14°30′S 35°15′E
77 N14 **Mangodara** SW Burkina 09°49′N 04°22′W
172 H6 **Mangoky** ≈ W Madagascar
171 Q12 **Mangole, Pulau** *island* Kepulauan Sula, E Indonesia
184 J2 **Mangonui** Northland, North Island, New Zealand 35°00′S 173°30′E
Mangqystaū Oblysy *see* Mangistau
Mangqystaū Shyghanaghy *see* Mangyshlakskiy Zaliv
Mangshi *see* Luxi
104 H7 **Mangualde** Viseu, N Portugal 40°36′N 07°46′W
61 H18 **Mangueira, Lagoa** ◎ S Brazil
77 X6 **Manguéni, Plateau du** ▲▲ NE Niger
163 T4 **Mangui** Nei Mongol Zizhiqu, N China 52°02′N 122°13′E
26 K11 **Mangum** Oklahoma, C USA 34°52′N 99°30′W
79 O18 **Manguredjipa** Nord-Kivu, E Dem. Rep. Congo 0°28′N 28°33′E
83 L16 **Mangwendi** Mashonaland East, E Zimbabwe 18°22′S 31°24′E
144 F15 **Mangyshlak, Plato** *plateau* SW Kazakhstan
144 E14 **Mangyshlakskiy Zaliv** *Kaz.* Mangqystaū Shyghanaghy. *gulf* SW Kazakhstan
Mangyshlaskaya *see* Mangistau
162 E7 **Manhan** *var.* Tögrög. Hovd, W Mongolia 47°24′N 92°06′E
Manhan *see* Alag-Erdene
27 O4 **Manhattan** Kansas, C USA 39°11′N 96°35′W
99 L21 **Manhay** Luxembourg, SE Belgium 50°13′N 05°43′E
83 L21 **Manhiça** *prev.* Vila de Manhiça. Maputo, S Mozambique 25°25′S 32°49′E
83 L21 **Manhoca** Maputo, S Mozambique 26°49′S 32°36′E
59 N20 **Manhuaçu** Minas Gerais, SE Brazil 20°16′S 42°01′W
117 W9 **Manhush** *prev.* Pershotravneve. Donets'ka Oblast', E Ukraine 47°03′N 37°20′E
54 H10 **Maní** Casanare, C Colombia 04°50′N 72°15′W
143 R11 **Mānī** Kermān, C Iran
83 M17 **Manica** *var.* Vila de Manica. Manica, W Mozambique 18°56′S 32°52′E
83 M17 **Manica** *off.* Província de Manica. ◐ *province* W Mozambique
83 L17 **Manicaland** ◐ *province* E Zimbabwe
Manica, Província de *see* Manica
15 U5 **Manic Deux, Réservoir** ▣ Québec, SE Canada
Manich *see* Manych
59 F14 **Manicoré** Amazonas, N Brazil 05°48′S 61°16′W
13 N11 **Manicouagan** Québec, SE Canada 50°40′N 68°46′W
13 N11 **Manicouagan** ≈ Québec, SE Canada
15 U6 **Manicouagan, Péninsule de** *peninsula* Québec, SE Canada
13 N11 **Manicouagan, Réservoir** ◎ Québec, E Canada
15 T4 **Manic Trois, Réservoir** ▣ Québec, SE Canada
79 M20 **Maniema** *off.* Région du Maniema. ◐ *region* E Dem. Rep. Congo
Maniema, Région du *see* Maniema
Maniewicze *see* Manevychi
160 F8 **Maniganggo** Sichuan, C China 32°01′N 99°04′E
11 Y15 **Manigotagan** Manitoba, S Canada 51°06′N 96°18′W
153 R13 **Manihāri** Bihār, N India 25°21′N 87°37′E
191 U9 **Manihi** *island* Îles Tuamotu, C French Polynesia
190 L13 **Manihiki** *atoll* N Cook Islands
175 U8 **Manihiki Plateau** *undersea feature* C Pacific Ocean
196 M14 **Maniitsoq** *var.* Manîtsoq, *Dan.* Sukkertoppen. ◐ Kitaa, S Greenland
153 T15 **Manikganj** Dhaka, C Bangladesh 23°52′N 90°00′E
152 M14 **Mānikpur** Uttar Pradesh, N India 25°04′N 81°06′E
171 N4 **Manila** *off.* City of Manila. ● (Philippines) Luzon, N Philippines 14°34′N 120°59′E
27 Y9 **Manila** Arkansas, C USA 35°52′N 90°10′W
Manila, City of *see* Manila
189 N16 **Manila Reef** *reef* W Micronesia
183 T6 **Manilla** New South Wales, SE Australia 30°44′S 150°43′E
192 P6 **Maniloa** *island* Tongatapu Group, S Tonga
123 U8 **Manily** Koryakskiy Avtonomnyy Okrug, E Russian Federation 62°33′N 165°03′E
171 V12 **Manim, Pulau** *island* E Indonesia
168 I11 **Maninjau, Danau** ◎ Sumatera, W Indonesia
153 W13 **Manipur** ◐ *state* NE India
153 X14 **Manipur Hills** *hill range* E India
136 C14 **Manisa** *var.* Manissa, *prev.* Saruhan; *anc.* Magnesia. Manisa, W Turkey 38°36′N 27°29′E
136 C13 **Manisa** *var.* Manissa. ◐ *province* W Turkey
Manissa *see* Manisa
31 O7 **Manistee** Michigan, N USA 44°14′N 86°19′W
31 P7 **Manistee River** ≈ Michigan, N USA
31 O4 **Manistique** Michigan, N USA 45°57′N 86°15′W
31 P4 **Manistique Lake** ◎ Michigan, N USA
11 W13 **Manitoba** ◐ *province* S Canada
11 X16 **Manitoba, Lake** ◎ Manitoba, S Canada
11 X17 **Manitou** Manitoba, S Canada 49°12′N 98°28′W
31 N2 **Manitou Island** *island* Michigan, N USA
14 H11 **Manitou Lake** ◎ Ontario, SE Canada
12 G15 **Manitoulin Island** *island* Ontario, S Canada
37 T5 **Manitou Springs** Colorado, C USA 38°51′N 104°56′W
14 G12 **Manitouwabing Lake** ◎ Ontario, S Canada
12 E12 **Manitouwadge** Ontario, S Canada 49°14′N 85°51′W
12 G15 **Manitowaning** Manitoulin Island, Ontario, S Canada 45°44′N 81°50′W
14 B7 **Manitowik Lake** ◎ Ontario, S Canada
31 N7 **Manitowoc** Wisconsin, N USA 44°04′N 87°40′W
Manîtsoq *see* Maniitsoq
139 O7 **Mānī', Wādī al** *dry watercourse* W Iraq
12 J14 **Maniwaki** Québec, SE Canada 46°22′N 75°58′W
171 W13 **Maniwori** Papua, E Indonesia 02°49′S 136°00′E
54 E10 **Manizales** Caldas, W Colombia 05°03′N 73°52′W
112 F11 **Manjača** ▲▲ NW Bosnia and Herzegovina
Manjacaze *see* Mandlakazi
180 J14 **Manjimup** Western Australia 34°18′S 116°14′E
109 V4 **Mank** Niederösterreich, C Austria 48°06′N 15°13′E
79 I17 **Mankanza** Equateur, NW Dem. Rep. Congo 01°40′N 19°08′E
153 N12 **Mankāpur** Uttar Pradesh, N India 27°03′N 82°12′E
26 M3 **Mankato** Kansas, C USA 39°48′N 98°13′W
29 U10 **Mankato** Minnesota, N USA 44°10′N 94°00′W
117 O7 **Man'kivka** Cherkas'ka Oblast', C Ukraine 48°58′N 30°10′E
76 M15 **Mankono** C Ivory Coast 08°01′N 06°09′W
11 T17 **Mankota** Saskatchewan, S Canada 49°25′N 107°05′W
155 K23 **Mankulam** Northern Province, N Sri Lanka 09°07′N 80°27′E
162 L10 **Manlay** *var.* Üydzen. Ömnögovĭ, S Mongolia 44°08′N 106°48′E
39 Q9 **Manley Hot Springs** Alaska, USA 65°00′N 150°37′W
18 H10 **Manlius** New York, NE USA 43°00′N 75°58′W
105 W5 **Manlleu** Cataluña, NE Spain 41°59′N 02°17′E
29 V11 **Manly** Iowa, C USA 43°17′N 93°12′W
154 E13 **Manmād** Mahārāshtra, W India 20°15′N 74°29′E
182 J7 **Mannahill** South Australia 32°29′S 139°58′E
155 J23 **Mannar** *var.* Manar. Northern Province, NW Sri Lanka 09°01′N 79°53′E
155 I24 **Mannar, Gulf of** *gulf* India/Sri Lanka
155 J23 **Mannar Island** *island* N Sri Lanka
Mannersdorf *see* Mannersdorf am Leithagebirge
109 Y5 **Mannersdorf am Leithagebirge** *var.* Mannersdorf. Niederösterreich, E Austria 47°59′N 16°36′E
109 Y6 **Mannersdorf an der Rabnitz** Burgenland, E Austria 47°25′N 16°32′E
101 G20 **Mannheim** Baden-Württemberg, SW Germany 49°29′N 08°29′E
11 O12 **Manning** Alberta, W Canada 56°53′N 117°39′W
29 T14 **Manning** Iowa, C USA 41°54′N 95°03′W
28 K5 **Manning** North Dakota, N USA 47°15′N 102°48′W
21 S13 **Manning** South Carolina, SE USA 33°42′N 80°12′W
191 Y2 **Manning, Cape** *headland* Kiritimati, NE Kiribati 02°02′N 157°26′W
21 S3 **Mannington** West Virginia, NE USA 39°31′N 80°20′W
182 A1 **Mann Ranges** ▲▲ South Australia
107 C19 **Mannu** ≈ Sardegna, Italy, C Mediterranean Sea
11 R14 **Mannville** Alberta, SW Canada 53°19′N 111°08′W
76 J15 **Mano** ≈ Liberia/Sierra Leone
Manø *see* Mandø
39 O13 **Manokotak** Alaska, USA 59°00′N 158°58′W
171 V12 **Manokwari** Papua, E Indonesia 0°53′S 134°05′S
79 N22 **Manono** Shaba, SE Dem. Rep. Congo 07°18′S 27°25′E
25 T10 **Manor** Texas, SW USA 30°20′N 97°33′W
97 D16 **Manorhamilton** *Ir.* Cluainín. Leitrim, NW Ireland 54°18′N 08°10′W
103 S15 **Manosque** Alpes-de-Haute-Provence, SE France 43°50′N 05°47′E
12 L11 **Manouane, Lac** ◎ Québec, SE Canada
163 W12 **Manp'o** *var.* Manp'ojin. NW North Korea 41°10′N 126°24′E
Manp'ojin *see* Manp'o
191 T4 **Manra** *prev.* Sydney Island. *atoll* Phoenix Islands, C Kiribati
105 V5 **Manresa** Cataluña, NE Spain 41°43′N 01°50′E
152 H9 **Mānsa** Punjab, NW India 30°00′N 75°25′E
82 J12 **Mansa** *prev.* Fort Rosebery. Luapula, N Zambia 11°14′S 28°55′E
76 G12 **Mansa Konko** C Gambia 13°26′N 15°29′W
15 Q11 **Manseau** Québec, SE Canada 46°23′N 71°59′W
149 U5 **Mānsehra** North-West Frontier Province, NW Pakistan 34°23′N 73°18′E
9 Q9 **Mansel Island** *island* Nunavut, NE Canada
183 O12 **Mansfield** Victoria, SE Australia 37°04′S 146°06′E
97 M18 **Mansfield** C England, United Kingdom 53°09′N 01°11′W
27 S11 **Mansfield** Arkansas, C USA 35°03′N 94°15′W
22 G6 **Mansfield** Louisiana, S USA 32°02′N 93°42′W
19 O12 **Mansfield** Massachusetts, NE USA 42°00′N 71°11′W
31 T12 **Mansfield** Ohio, N USA 40°45′N 82°31′W
18 G12 **Mansfield** Pennsylvania, NE USA 41°46′N 77°02′W
18 M7 **Mansfield, Mount** ▲ Vermont, NE USA 44°31′N 72°49′W
59 M16 **Mansidão** Bahia, E Brazil 10°46′S 44°04′W
102 L11 **Mansle** Charente, W France 45°52′N 00°11′E
76 G12 **Mansôa** C Guinea-Bissau 12°08′N 15°18′W
47 V8 **Manso, Rio** ≈ C Brazil
Manṣûra *see* Al Manṣūrah
Mansurabad *see* Mehrān, Rūd-e
56 A6 **Manta** Manabí, W Ecuador 0°59′S 80°44′W
56 A6 **Manta, Bahía de** *bay* W Ecuador
57 F14 **Mantaro, Río** ≈ C Peru
35 O8 **Manteca** California, W USA 37°48′N 121°13′W
54 J7 **Mantecal** Apure, C Venezuela 07°34′N 69°07′W
31 N11 **Manteno** Illinois, N USA 41°15′N 87°49′W
21 Y9 **Manteo** Roanoke Island, North Carolina, SE USA 35°54′N 75°42′W
Mantes-Gassicourt *see* Mantes-la-Jolie
103 N5 **Mantes-la-Jolie** *prev.* Mantes-Gassicourt, Mantes-sur-Seine; *anc.* Medunta. Yvelines, N France 48°59′N 01°43′E
Mantes-sur-Seine *see* Mantes-la-Jolie
36 L5 **Manti** Utah, W USA 39°16′N 111°38′W
Mantinea *see* Mantíneia
115 F20 **Mantíneia** *anc.* Mantinea. *site of ancient city* Pelopónnisos, S Greece
59 M21 **Mantiqueira, Serra da** ▲▲ S Brazil
29 W10 **Mantorville** Minnesota, N USA 44°04′N 92°45′W

◆ Country
● Country Capital
◇ Dependent Territory
○ Dependent Territory Capital
◐ Administrative Regions
✕ International Airport
▲ Mountain
▲▲ Mountain Range
Volcano
≈ River
◎ Lake
▣ Reservoir

115 G17 **Mantoúdi** var. Mandoudi; prev. Mandoúdhion. Évvoia, C Greece 38°47'N 23°29'E
Mantoue see Mantova
106 F8 **Mantova** Eng. Mantua, Fr. Mantoue. Lombardia, NW Italy 45°10'N 10°47'E
93 M19 **Mäntsälä** Etelä-Suomi, S Finland 60°38'N 25°21'E
93 L17 **Mänttä** Länsi-Suomi, W Finland 62°00'N 24°36'E
Mantua see Mantova
125 O14 **Manturovo** Kostromskaya Oblast', NW Russian Federation 58°19'N 44°42'E
93 M18 **Mäntyharju** Itä-Suomi, SE Finland 61°25'N 26°53'E
92 M13 **Mäntyjärvi** Lappi, N Finland 66°00'N 27°35'E
190 L16 **Manuae** island S Cook Islands
191 Q10 **Manuae** atoll Îles Sous le Vent, W French Polynesia
192 L16 **Manu'a Islands** island group E American Samoa
40 L5 **Manuel Benavides** Chihuahua, N Mexico 29°07'N 103°52'W
61 D21 **Manuel J. Cobo** Buenos Aires, E Argentina 35°49'S 57°54'W
58 M12 **Manuel Luís, Recife** reef E Brazil
61 F15 **Manuel Viana** Rio Grande do Sul, S Brazil 29°33'S 55°28'W
59 I14 **Manuel Zinho** Pará, N Brazil 07°21'S 54°47'W
191 V11 **Manuhangi** atoll Îles Tuamotu, C French Polynesia
185 E22 **Manuherikia** ≈ South Island, New Zealand
171 P13 **Manui, Pulau** island N Indonesia
Manukau see Manurewa
184 L6 **Manukau Harbour** harbour North Island, New Zealand
191 Z2 **Manulu Lagoon** ◎ Kiritimati, E Kiribati
182 J7 **Manunda Creek** seasonal river South Australia
57 K15 **Manupari, Río** ≈ N Bolivia
184 L6 **Manurewa** var. Manukau. Auckland, North Island, New Zealand 37°01'S 174°55'E
57 K15 **Manurimi, Río** ≈ NW Bolivia
186 D5 **Manus** ◈ province N Papua New Guinea
186 D5 **Manus Island** var. Great Admiralty Island. island N Papua New Guinea
171 T16 **Manuwui** Pulau Babar, E Indonesia 07°47'S 129°39'E
29 Q3 **Manvel** North Dakota, N USA 48°07'N 97°15'W
33 Z14 **Manville** Wyoming, C USA 42°45'N 104°38'W
22 G6 **Many** Louisiana, S USA 31°34'N 93°28'W
81 I22 **Manyara** ◈ NE Tanzania
81 H21 **Manyara, Lake** ◎ NE Tanzania
126 L12 **Manych** var. Manich. ≈ SW Russian Federation
83 H14 **Manyinga** North Western, NW Zambia 13°28'S 24°18'E
105 O11 **Manzanares** Castilla-La Mancha, C Spain 39°N 03°23'W
44 H7 **Manzanillo** Granma, E Cuba 20°21'N 77°07'W
40 K14 **Manzanillo** Colima, SW Mexico 19°00'N 104°19'W
40 K14 **Manzanillo, Bahía** bay SW Mexico
37 S11 **Manzano Mountains** ▲▲ New Mexico, SW USA
37 R12 **Manzano Peak** ▲ New Mexico, SW USA 34°35'N 106°27'W
163 R6 **Manzhouli** var. Man-chou-li. Nei Mongol Zizhiqu, N China 49°36'N 117°28'E
Manzil Bū Ruqaybah see Menzel Bourguiba
139 X9 **Manzilīyah** Maysān, E Iraq 32°26'N 47°01'E
83 L21 **Manzini** prev. Bremersdorp. C Swaziland 26°30'S 31°22'E
83 L21 **Manzini** ✈ (Mbabane) C Swaziland 26°36'S 31°25'E
78 G10 **Mao** Kanem, W Chad 14°06'N 15°17'E
45 N8 **Mao** NW Dominican Republic 19°37'N 71°04'W
Maó see Mahón
Maoemere see Maumere
159 W9 **Maojing** Gansu, N China 36°26'N 106°36'E
171 Y14 **Maoke, Pegunungan** Dut. Sneeuw-gebergte, Eng. Snow Mountains. ▲▲ Papua, E Indonesia
Maol Réidh, Caoc see Mweelrea
160 M15 **Maoming** Guangdong, S China 21°46'N 110°51'E
160 H8 **Maoxian** var. Mao Xian; prev. Fengyizhen. Sichuan, C China 31°42'N 103°48'E
Mao Xian see Maoxian
83 L19 **Mapai** Gaza, SW Mozambique 22°52'S 32°00'E
158 H15 **Mapam Yumco** ◎ W China
83 I15 **Mapanza** Southern, S Zambia 16°16'S 26°54'E
54 J4 **Mapararí** Falcón, N Venezuela 10°52'N 69°27'W
41 U17 **Mapastepec** Chiapas, SE Mexico 15°28'N 93°00'W
169 V9 **Mapat, Pulau** island N Indonesia
171 Y15 **Mapi** Papua, E Indonesia 07°02'S 139°24'E
171 V11 **Mapia, Kepulauan** island group E Indonesia
40 L8 **Mapimí** Durango, C Mexico 25°50'N 103°50'W
83 N19 **Mapinhane** Inhambane, SE Mozambique 22°14'S 35°07'E
55 N7 **Mapire** Monagas, NE Venezuela 07°48'N 64°40'W
11 S17 **Maple Creek** Saskatchewan, S Canada 49°55'N 109°28'W
31 Q9 **Maple River** ≈ Michigan, N USA
29 P7 **Maple River** ≈ North Dakota/South Dakota, N USA
29 S13 **Mapleton** Iowa, C USA 42°10'N 95°47'W
29 U10 **Mapleton** Minnesota, N USA 43°55'N 93°57'W
29 R5 **Mapleton** North Dakota, N USA 46°51'N 97°04'W
32 F13 **Mapleton** Oregon, NW USA 44°01'N 123°56'W
36 L3 **Mapleton** Utah, W USA 40°07'N 111°37'W
192 K5 **Mapmaker Seamounts** undersea feature N Pacific Ocean 25°00'N 165°00'E
186 B6 **Maprik** East Sepik, NW Papua New Guinea 03°38'S 143°02'E
83 L21 **Maputo** prev. Lourenço Marques. ● (Mozambique) Maputo, S Mozambique 25°58'S 32°35'E
83 L21 **Maputo** ◈ province S Mozambique
67 V14 **Maputo** ≈ S Mozambique
83 L21 **Maputo** ✈ Maputo, S Mozambique 25°47'S 32°36'E
Maqanshy see Makanchi
Maqat see Makat
113 K19 **Maqë** ≈ NW Albania
113 M19 **Maqellarë** Dibër, C Albania 41°36'N 20°29'E
159 S12 **Maqên** var. Dawo; prev. Dawu. Qinghai, C China 34°32'N 100°17'E
159 S11 **Maqên Kangri** ▲ C China 34°44'N 99°25'E
141 X7 **Maqiz al Kurbā** N Oman 24°13'N 56°48'E
159 U12 **Maqu** var. Nyinma. Gansu, C China 34°02'N 102°00'E
104 M9 **Maqueda** Castilla-La Mancha, C Spain 40°04'N 04°22'W
82 B9 **Maquela do Zombo** Uíge, NW Angola 06°06'S 15°12'E
63 I16 **Maquinchao** Río Negro, C Argentina 41°19'S 68°47'W
29 Z13 **Maquoketa** Iowa, C USA 42°03'N 90°42'W
29 Y13 **Maquoketa River** ≈ Iowa, C USA
14 F13 **Mar** Ontario, S Canada 44°48'N 81°12'W
95 F14 **Mår** ◎ S Norway
81 G19 **Mara** ◈ region N Tanzania
58 D12 **Maraã** Amazonas, NW Brazil 01°48'S 65°21'W
191 P8 **Maraa** Tahiti, W French Polynesia 17°44'S 149°34'W
191 O8 **Maraa, Pointe** headland Tahiti, W French Polynesia 17°44'S 149°34'W
59 K14 **Marabá** Pará, NE Brazil 05°23'S 49°10'W
54 H5 **Maracaibo** Zulia, NW Venezuela 10°40'N 71°39'W
Maracaibo, Gulf of see Venezuela, Golfo de
54 H5 **Maracaibo, Lago de** var. Lake Maracaibo. inlet NW Venezuela
Maracaibo, Lake see Maracaibo, Lago de
58 K10 **Maracá, Ilha de** island NE Brazil
59 H20 **Maracaju, Serra de** ▲▲ S Brazil
58 I11 **Maracanaquará, Planalto** ▲ NE Brazil
54 L5 **Maracay** Aragua, N Venezuela 10°15'N 67°36'W
Marada see Marādah
75 R9 **Marādah** var. Marada. N Libya 29°16'N 19°29'E
77 U12 **Maradi** Maradi, S Niger 13°30'N 07°05'E
77 U11 **Maradi** ◈ department S Niger
81 E21 **Maragarazi** var. Muragarazi. ≈ Burundi/Tanzania
Maragha see Marāgheh
142 J3 **Marāgheh** var. Maragha. Āžarbāyjān-e Khāvarī, NW Iran 37°21'N 46°14'E
141 P7 **Marāh** var. Marrāt. Ar Riyāḍ, C Saudi Arabia 25°04'N 45°30'E
55 N11 **Marahuaca, Cerro** ▲ S Venezuela 03°37'N 65°25'W
27 R5 **Marais des Cygnes River** ≈ Kansas/Missouri, C USA
58 L11 **Marajó, Baía de** bay N Brazil
59 K12 **Marajó, Ilha de** island N Brazil
191 O2 **Marakei** atoll Tungaru, W Kiribati
Marakesh see Marrakech
81 I18 **Maralal** Rift Valley, C Kenya 01°05'N 36°42'E
83 G21 **Maralaleng** Kgalagadi, S Botswana 25°42'S 22°39'E
145 U8 **Maraldy, Ozero** ◎ NE Kazakhstan
182 C5 **Maralinga** South Australia 30°16'S 131°35'E
Máramarossziget see Sighetu Marmaţiei
187 N9 **Maramasike** var. Small Malaita. island N Solomon Islands
Maramba see Livingstone
194 H3 **Marambio** Argentinian research station Antarctica 64°22'S 57°18'W
116 H9 **Maramureş** ◈ county NW Romania
36 L15 **Marana** Arizona, SW USA 32°24'N 111°12'W
105 P7 **Maranchón** Castilla-La Mancha, C Spain 41°02'N 02°11'W
142 J2 **Marand** var. Merend. Āžarbāyjān-e Sharqī, NW Iran 38°25'N 45°40'E
Marandellas see Marondera
58 L13 **Maranhão** off. Estado do Maranhão. ◈ state E Brazil
104 H10 **Maranhão, Barragem do** ⊡ C Portugal
Maranhão, Estado do see Maranhão
149 O11 **Mārān, Koh-i** ▲ SW Pakistan 29°24'N 66°50'E
106 J7 **Marano, Laguna di** lagoon NE Italy
56 E9 **Marañón, Río** ≈ N Peru
102 J10 **Marans** Charente-Maritime, W France 46°19'N 00°58'W
83 M20 **Marão** Inhambane, S Mozambique 24°15'S 34°09'E
185 B23 **Mararoa** ≈ South Island, New Zealand
Maraş/Marash see Kahramanmaraş
107 M19 **Maratea** Basilicata, S Italy 39°57'N 15°44'E
104 G11 **Marateca** Setúbal, S Portugal 38°34'N 08°40'W
115 B20 **Marathiá, Akrotírio** headland Zákynthos, Iónia Nisiá, Greece, C Mediterranean Sea 37°39'N 20°49'E
12 E12 **Marathon** Ontario, S Canada 48°44'N 86°23'W
23 Y17 **Marathon** Florida Keys, Florida, SE USA 24°42'N 81°05'W
24 L10 **Marathon** Texas, SW USA 30°10'N 103°14'W
Marathón see Marathónas
115 H19 **Marathónas** prev. Marathón. Attikí, C Greece 38°09'N 23°57'E
169 W9 **Maratua, Pulau** island N Indonesia
59 O18 **Maraú** Bahia, SE Brazil 14°07'S 39°02'W
143 R3 **Marāveh Tappeh** Golestán, N Iran 37°53'N 55°57'E
24 L11 **Maravillas Creek** ≈ Texas, SW USA
186 D8 **Marawaka** Eastern Highlands, C Papua New Guinea 06°56'S 145°54'E
171 Q7 **Marawi** Mindanao, S Philippines 07°59'N 124°16'E
137 Y11 **Märäzä** Rus. Maraza. E Azerbaijan 40°32'N 48°56'E
Maraza see Märäzä
Marbat see Mirbāṭ
104 L16 **Marbella** Andalucía, S Spain 36°31'N 04°50'W
180 J7 **Marble Bar** Western Australia 21°13'S 119°48'E
36 L9 **Marble Canyon** canyon Arizona, SW USA
25 S10 **Marble Falls** Texas, SW USA 30°34'N 98°16'W
27 Y7 **Marble Hill** Missouri, C USA 37°18'N 89°58'W
33 T15 **Marbleton** Wyoming, C USA 42°31'N 110°06'W
Marburg see Marburg an der Lahn, Germany
Marburg see Maribor, Slovenia
101 H16 **Marburg an der Lahn** hist. Marburg. Hessen, W Germany 50°49'N 08°46'E
111 H23 **Marcal** ≈ W Hungary
42 G7 **Marcala** La Paz, SW Honduras 14°11'N 88°00'W
111 H24 **Marcali** Somogy, SW Hungary 46°33'N 17°29'E
83 A16 **Marca, Ponta da** headland SW Angola 16°31'S 11°42'E
59 I16 **Marcelândia** Mato Grosso, W Brazil 11°18'S 54°49'W
27 T3 **Marceline** Missouri, C USA 39°42'N 92°57'W
60 I13 **Marcelino Ramos** Rio Grande do Sul, S Brazil 27°31'S 51°57'W
55 Y12 **Marcel, Mont** ▲ S French Guiana 02°32'N 53°00'W
97 O19 **March** E England, United Kingdom 52°37'N 00°13'E
109 Z3 **March** var. Morava. ≈ C Europe see also Morava
March see Morava
106 I12 **Marche** Eng. Marches. ◈ region C Italy
103 N11 **Marche** cultural region C France
99 J21 **Marche-en-Famenne** Luxembourg, SE Belgium 50°13'N 05°21'E
104 K14 **Marchena** Andalucía, S Spain 37°20'N 05°24'W
57 B17 **Marchena, Isla** var. Bindloe Island. island Galapagos Islands, Ecuador, E Pacific Ocean
Marches see Marche
99 J20 **Marchin** Liège, E Belgium 50°30'N 05°17'E
181 S1 **Marchinbar Island** island Wessel Islands, Northern Territory, N Australia
62 L9 **Mar Chiquita, Laguna** ◎ C Argentina
103 Q10 **Marcigny** Saône-et-Loire, C France 46°16'N 04°04'E
23 W16 **Marco** Florida, SE USA 25°56'N 81°43'W
Marcodurum see Düren
59 O15 **Marcolândia** Pernambuco, E Brazil 07°21'S 40°40'W
106 I8 **Marco Polo** ✈ (Venezia) Veneto, NE Italy 45°30'N 12°21'E
Marcounda see Markounda
Marcq see Mark
116 M8 **Mărculeşti** Rus. Markulesty. N Moldova 47°54'N 28°14'E
29 S12 **Marcus** Iowa, C USA 42°49'N 95°48'W
39 S11 **Marcus Baker, Mount** ▲ Alaska, USA 61°26'N 147°45'W
192 I5 **Marcus Island** var. Minami Tori Shima. island E Japan
18 K8 **Marcy, Mount** ▲ New York, NE USA 44°06'N 73°55'W
149 T5 **Mardān** North-West Frontier Province, N Pakistan 34°14'N 71°59'E
63 N14 **Mar del Plata** Buenos Aires, E Argentina 38°S 57°32'W
137 Q16 **Mardin** Mardin, SE Turkey 37°19'N 40°43'E
137 Q16 **Mardin** ◈ province SE Turkey
137 Q16 **Mardin Dağları** ▲▲ SE Turkey
Mardzad see Hayrhandulaan
187 R17 **Maré** island Îles Loyauté, E New Caledonia
Marea Neagră see Black Sea
105 Z8 **Mare de Déu del Toro** var. El Toro. ▲ Menorca, Spain, W Mediterranean Sea 39°59'N 04°06'E
181 W4 **Mareeba** Queensland, NE Australia 17°03'S 145°30'E
96 G8 **Maree, Loch** ◎ N Scotland, United Kingdom
Mareeq see Mereeg
Marek see Dupnitsa
76 J11 **Maréna** Kayes, W Mali 14°36'N 10°57'W
190 I2 **Marenanuka** atoll Tungaru, W Kiribati
29 X14 **Marengo** Iowa, C USA 41°48'N 92°04'W
102 J11 **Marennes** Charente-Maritime, W France 45°47'N 01°04'W
107 G23 **Marettimo, Isola** island Isole Egadi, S Italy
24 K10 **Marfa** Texas, SW USA 30°19'N 104°03'W
57 P17 **Marfil, Laguna** ◎ E Bolivia
Marganets see Marhanets'
25 Q4 **Margaret** Texas, SW USA 34°00'N 99°38'W
180 I14 **Margaret River** Western Australia 33°58'S 115°10'E
186 C7 **Margarima** Southern Highlands, W Papua New Guinea 06°00'S 143°23'E
55 N4 **Margarita, Isla de** island N Venezuela
115 I25 **Margarites** Kríti, Greece, E Mediterranean Sea 35°19'N 24°40'E
97 Q22 **Margate** prev. Mergate. SE England, United Kingdom 51°24'N 01°24'E
23 Z15 **Margate** Florida, SE USA 26°14'N 80°12'W
Margelan see Marg'ilon
103 P13 **Margeride, Montagnes de la** ▲▲ C France
Margherita see Jamaame
107 N16 **Margherita di Savoia** Puglia, SE Italy 41°23'N 16°09'E
Margherita, Lake see Ābaya Hāyk'
81 E18 **Margherita Peak** Fr. Pic Marguerite. ▲ Uganda/Dem. Rep. Congo 0°28'N 29°58'E
149 O4 **Marghī** Bāmīān, N Afghanistan 35°10'N 66°26'E
116 G9 **Marghita** Hung. Margitta. Bihor, NW Romania 47°20'N 22°20'E
Margilan see Marg'ilon
147 S10 **Marg'ilon** var. Margelan, Rus. Margilan. Farg'ona Viloyati, E Uzbekistan 40°29'N 71°43'E
116 K8 **Marginea** Suceava, NE Romania 47°49'N 25°47'E
Margitta see Marghita
148 K9 **Mārgow, Dasht-e** desert SW Afghanistan
99 L18 **Margraten** Limburg, SE Netherlands 50°49'N 05°49'E
10 M15 **Marguerite** British Columbia, SW Canada 52°17'N 122°10'W
15 V3 **Marguerite** ≈ Québec, SE Canada
194 I6 **Marguerite Bay** bay Antarctica
Marguerite, Pic see Margherita Peak
117 T9 **Marhanets'** Rus. Marganets. Dnipropetrovs'ka Oblast', E Ukraine 47°35'N 34°37'E
186 B9 **Mari** Western, SW Papua New Guinea 09°10'S 141°39'E
191 Y12 **Maria** atoll Groupe Actéon, SE French Polynesia
191 R12 **Maria** island Îles Australes, SW French Polynesia
40 I12 **María Cleofas, Isla** island C Mexico
62 H4 **María Elena** var. Oficina María Elena. Antofagasta, N Chile 22°18'S 69°40'W
95 G21 **Mariager** Århus, C Denmark 56°39'N 09°59'E
61 C22 **María Ignacia** Buenos Aires, E Argentina 37°24'S 59°30'W
183 P17 **Maria Island** island Tasmania, SE Australia
40 H12 **María Madre, Isla** island C Mexico
40 I12 **María Magdalena, Isla** island C Mexico
192 H6 **Mariana Islands** island group Guam/Northern Mariana Islands
175 N3 **Mariana Trench** var. Challenger Deep. undersea feature W Pacific Ocean 15°00'N 147°30'E
153 X12 **Mariāni** Assam, NE India 26°39'N 94°18'E
27 X11 **Marianna** Arkansas, C USA 34°46'N 90°49'W
23 R8 **Marianna** Florida, SE USA 30°46'N 85°13'W
172 J16 **Marianne** island Inner Islands, NE Seychelles
95 M19 **Mariannelund** Jönköping, S Sweden 57°37'N 15°33'E
61 D15 **Mariano I. Loza** Corrientes, NE Argentina 29°22'S 58°12'W
Mariano Machado see Ganda
111 A16 **Mariánské Lázně** Ger. Marienbad. Karlovarský Kraj, W Czech Republic 49°57'N 12°43'E
Máriaradna see Radna
33 S7 **Marias River** ≈ Montana, NW USA
Maria-Theresiopel see Subotica
Máriatölgyes see Dubnica nad Váhom
184 H1 **Maria van Diemen, Cape** headland North Island, New Zealand 34°27'S 172°38'E
109 V5 **Mariazell** Steiermark, E Austria 47°47'N 15°20'E
141 P15 **Mar'ib** W Yemen 15°28'N 45°25'E
95 I25 **Maribo** Storstrøm, S Denmark 54°47'N 11°30'E
109 W9 **Maribor** Ger. Marburg. NE Slovenia 46°34'N 15°40'E
Marica see Maritsa
35 R13 **Maricopa** California, W USA 35°03'N 119°24'W
Maricourt see Kangiqsujuaq
81 D15 **Maridi** Western Equatoria, SW Sudan 04°55'N 29°30'E
194 M11 **Marie Byrd Land** physical region Antarctica
193 P14 **Marie Byrd Seamount** undersea feature N Amundsen Sea 70°00'S 118°00'W
45 X11 **Marie-Galante** var. Ceyre to the Caribs. island SE Guadeloupe
45 Y6 **Marie-Galante, Canal de** channel S Guadeloupe
93 J20 **Mariehamn** Fin. Maarianhamina. Åland, SW Finland 60°05'N 19°55'E
44 C4 **Mariel** La Habana, W Cuba 23°02'N 82°44'W
99 H22 **Mariembourg** Namur, S Belgium 50°07'N 04°30'E
Marienbad see Mariánské Lázně
Marienburg see Alūksne, Latvia
Marienburg see Malbork, Poland
Marienburg see Feldioara, Romania
Marienburg in Westpreussen see Malbork
Marienhausen see Viļaka
83 D20 **Mariental** Hardap, SW Namibia 24°35'S 17°56'E
18 D13 **Marienville** Pennsylvania, NE USA 41°27'N 79°07'W
Marienwerder see Kwidzyń
58 C12 **Marié, Rio** ≈ NW Brazil
95 K17 **Mariestad** Västra Götaland, S Sweden 58°42'N 13°50'E
23 S3 **Marietta** Georgia, SE USA 33°57'N 84°34'W
31 U14 **Marietta** Ohio, N USA 39°25'N 81°27'W
27 N13 **Marietta** Oklahoma, C USA 33°57'N 97°08'W
81 H18 **Marigat** Rift Valley, W Kenya 0°29'S 35°59'E
103 S16 **Marignane** Bouches-du-Rhône, SE France 43°25'N 05°12'E
Marignano see Melegnano
45 O11 **Marigot** NE Dominica 15°32'N 61°18'W
122 K12 **Mariinsk** Kemerovskaya Oblast', S Russian Federation 56°13'N 87°27'E
127 Q3 **Mariinskiy Posad** Respublika Mariy El, W Russian Federation 56°07'N 47°44'E
119 E14 **Marijampolė** prev. Kapsukas. Marijampolė, S Lithuania 54°33'N 23°21'E
114 G12 **Marikostinovo** Blagoevgrad, SW Bulgaria 41°25'N 23°21'E
60 J9 **Marília** São Paulo, S Brazil 22°13'S 49°58'W
82 D11 **Marimba** Malanje, NW Angola 08°18'S 16°58'E
139 T1 **Marī Mīlā** Arbīl, E Iraq 36°58'N 44°42'E
104 G4 **Marín** Galicia, NW Spain 42°23'N 08°43'W
35 N10 **Marina** California, W USA 36°40'N 121°48'W
Mar"ina Gorka see Mar"ina Horka
119 L17 **Mar"ina Horka** Rus. Mar'ina Gorka. Minskaya Voblasts', C Belarus 53°31'N 28°09'E
171 O4 **Marinduque** island C Philippines
31 S9 **Marine City** Michigan, N USA 42°43'N 82°29'W
31 N6 **Marinette** Wisconsin, N USA 45°06'N 87°38'W
60 I10 **Maringá** Paraná, S Brazil 23°26'S 51°55'W
83 N16 **Maringuè** Sofala, C Mozambique 17°57'S 34°23'E
104 F9 **Marinha Grande** Leiria, C Portugal 39°45'N 08°55'W
107 I15 **Marino** Lazio, C Italy 41°46'N 12°40'E
59 A15 **Mário Lobão** Acre, W Brazil 08°21'S 72°58'W
23 O5 **Marion** Alabama, S USA 32°37'N 87°19'W
27 Y11 **Marion** Arkansas, C USA 35°12'N 90°12'W
30 L17 **Marion** Illinois, N USA 37°43'N 88°55'W
31 P13 **Marion** Indiana, N USA 40°32'N 85°40'W
29 X13 **Marion** Iowa, C USA 42°01'N 91°36'W
27 O5 **Marion** Kansas, C USA 38°22'N 97°02'W
20 H6 **Marion** Kentucky, S USA 37°19'N 88°06'W
21 P9 **Marion** North Carolina, SE USA 35°43'N 82°00'W
31 S12 **Marion** Ohio, N USA 40°35'N 83°08'W
21 T12 **Marion** South Carolina, SE USA 34°11'N 79°23'W
21 Q7 **Marion** Virginia, NE USA 36°51'N 81°30'W
27 O5 **Marion Lake** ⊡ Kansas, C USA
21 S13 **Marion, Lake** ⊡ South Carolina, SE USA
27 S8 **Marionville** Missouri, C USA 37°00'N 93°38'W
55 N7 **Maripa** Bolívar, E Venezuela 07°27'N 65°10'W
55 X11 **Maripasoula** W French Guiana 03°43'N 54°04'W
35 Q9 **Mariposa** California, W USA 37°28'N 119°59'W
61 G19 **Mariscala** Lavalleja, S Uruguay 34°03'S 54°47'W
62 M4 **Mariscal Estigarribia** Boquerón, NW Paraguay 22°03'S 60°39'W
56 C6 **Mariscal Sucre** var. Quito. ✈ (Quito) Pichincha, C Ecuador 0°21'S 78°37'W
30 K16 **Marissa** Illinois, N USA 38°15'N 89°45'W
103 U14 **Maritime Alps** Fr. Alpes Maritimes, It. Alpi Marittime. ▲▲ France/Italy
Maritimes, Alpes see Maritime Alps
Maritime Territory see Primorskiy Kray
114 K11 **Maritsa** var. Marica, Gk. Évros, Turk. Meriç; anc. Hebrus. ≈ SW Europe see also Évros/Meriç
Maritsa see Simeonovgrad, Bulgaria
Marittime, Alpi see Maritime Alps
Maritzburg see Pietermaritzburg
117 X9 **Mariupol'** prev. Zhdanov. Donets'ka Oblast', SE Ukraine 47°06'N 37°34'E
55 Q6 **Mariusa, Caño** ≈ NE Venezuela
142 J5 **Marīvān** prev. Dezh Shāhpūr. Kordestān, W Iran 35°30'N 46°09'E
127 R3 **Mariyets** Respublika Mariy El, W Russian Federation 56°31'N 49°48'E
118 G4 **Märjamaa** Ger. Merjama. Raplamaa, NW Estonia 58°54'N 24°21'E
99 I15 **Mark** Fr. Marcq. ≈ Belgium/Netherlands
81 N17 **Marka** var. Merca. Shabeellaha Hoose, S Somalia 01°43'N 44°45'E
145 Z10 **Markakol', Ozero** Kaz. Marqaköl. ◎ E Kazakhstan
76 M12 **Markala** Ségou, W Mali 13°38'N 06°07'W
159 S15 **Markam** var. Gartog. Xizang Zizhiqu, W China 29°40'N 98°33'E
95 K21 **Markaryd** Kronoberg, S Sweden 56°26'N 13°35'E
142 L7 **Markazī** off. Ostān-e Markazī. ◈ province W Iran
Markazī, Ostān-e see Markazī
14 F14 **Markdale** Ontario, S Canada 44°19'N 80°37'W
27 X10 **Marked Tree** Arkansas, C USA 35°31'N 90°25'W
98 N11 **Markelo** Overijssel, E Netherlands 52°15'N 06°30'E
98 J9 **Markermeer** ◎ C Netherlands
97 N20 **Market Harborough** C England, United Kingdom 52°30'N 00°57'W
97 N18 **Market Rasen** E England, United Kingdom 53°23'N 00°21'W
123 O10 **Markha** ≈ NE Russian Federation
12 H16 **Markham** Ontario, S Canada 43°54'N 79°16'W
25 V12 **Markham** Texas, SW USA 28°57'N 96°04'W
186 E7 **Markham** ≈ C Papua New Guinea
195 Q11 **Markham, Mount** ▲ Antarctica 82°58'S 163°30'E
110 M11 **Marki** Mazowieckie, C Poland 52°20'N 21°07'E
158 F8 **Markit** Xinjiang Uygur Zizhiqu, NW China 38°55'N 77°40'E
117 Y5 **Markivka** Rus. Markovka. Luhans'ka Oblast', E Ukraine 49°34'N 39°35'E
35 Q7 **Markleeville** California, W USA 38°41'N 119°46'W
98 L8 **Marknesse** Flevoland, N Netherlands 52°44'N 05°54'E
79 H14 **Markounda** var. Marcounda. Ouham, NW Central African Republic 07°38'N 17°00'E
Markovka see Markivka
123 U7 **Markovo** Chukotskiy Avtonomnyy Okrug, NE Russian Federation 64°43'N 170°13'E
127 P8 **Marks** Saratovskaya Oblast', W Russian Federation 51°40'N 46°44'E
22 K2 **Marks** Mississippi, S USA 34°15'N 90°16'W
22 I7 **Marksville** Louisiana, S USA 31°07'N 92°04'W
101 I19 **Marktheidenfeld** Bayern, C Germany 49°50'N 09°36'E
101 J24 **Marktoberdorf** Bayern, S Germany 47°45'N 10°36'E
101 M18 **Marktredwitz** Bayern, E Germany 50°N 12°04'E
Markt-Übelbach see Übelbach
27 V3 **Mark Twain Lake** ⊡ Missouri, C USA
Markuleshty see Mărculeşti
101 E14 **Marl** Nordrhein-Westfalen, W Germany 51°38'N 07°06'E
182 E2 **Marla** South Australia 27°19'S 133°35'E
181 Y8 **Marlborough** Queensland, E Australia 22°55'S 150°07'E
97 M22 **Marlborough** S England, United Kingdom 51°25'N 01°45'W
185 I15 **Marlborough** off. Marlborough District. ◈ unitary authority South Island, New Zealand
Marlborough District see Marlborough
103 P3 **Marle** Aisne, N France 49°44'N 03°47'E
31 S8 **Marlette** Michigan, N USA 43°20'N 83°05'W
25 T9 **Marlin** Texas, SW USA 31°20'N 96°55'W
21 S5 **Marlinton** West Virginia, NE USA 38°14'N 80°06'W
26 M12 **Marlow** Oklahoma, C USA 34°39'N 97°57'W
155 E17 **Marmagao** Goa, W India 15°26'N 73°50'E
Marmanda see Marmande
102 L13 **Marmande** anc. Marmanda. Lot-et-Garonne, SW France 44°30'N 00°10'E
136 C11 **Marmara** Balıkesir, NW Turkey 40°36'N 27°34'E
136 D11 **Marmara Denizi** Eng. Sea of Marmara. sea NW Turkey
114 N13 **Marmaraereğlisi** Tekirdağ, NW Turkey 40°59'N 27°57'E
Marmara, Sea of see Marmara Denizi
136 C16 **Marmaris** Muğla, SW Turkey 36°52'N 28°17'E
28 J6 **Marmarth** North Dakota, N USA 46°17'N 103°55'W
21 Q5 **Marmet** West Virginia, NE USA 38°12'N 81°31'W
106 H5 **Marmolada, Monte** ▲ N Italy 46°36'N 11°58'E
104 M13 **Marmolejo** Andalucía, S Spain 38°03'N 04°10'W
14 J14 **Marmora** Ontario, SE Canada 44°29'N 77°40'W
39 Q14 **Marmot Bay** bay Alaska, USA
103 Q4 **Marne** ◈ department N France
103 Q4 **Marne** ≈ N France
137 U10 **Marneuli** prev. Borchalo, Sarvani. S Georgia 41°28'N 44°45'E
78 I13 **Maro** Moyen-Chari, S Chad 08°25'N 18°46'E
54 L12 **Maroa** Amazonas, S Venezuela 02°40'N 67°33'W
172 J3 **Maroantsetra** Toamasina, NE Madagascar 15°23'S 49°44'E
191 W11 **Marokau** atoll Îles Tuamotu, C French Polynesia
172 J5 **Marolambo** Toamasina, E Madagascar 20°03'S 48°08'E
172 J2 **Maromokotro** ▲ N Madagascar
83 L16 **Marondera** prev. Marandellas. Mashonaland East, NE Zimbabwe 18°11'S 31°33'E
55 X9 **Maroni** Dut. Marowijne. ≈ French Guiana/Surinam
183 V2 **Maroochydore-Mooloolaba** Queensland, E Australia 26°36'S 153°04'E
171 N14 **Maros** Sulawesi, C Indonesia 04°59'S 119°35'E
116 H11 **Maros** var. Mureş, Mureşul, Ger. Marosch, Mieresch. ≈ Hungary/Romania see also Mureş
Marosch see Maros/Mureş
Marosheviz see Toplița
Marosillye see Ilia
Marosludas see Luduş
Marosújvár/Marosújvárakna see Ocna Mureş
Marosvásárhely see Târgu Mureş
191 V14 **Marotiri** var. Îlots de Bass, Morotiri. island group Îles Australes, SW French Polynesia
78 G12 **Maroua** Extrême-Nord, N Cameroon 10°35'N 14°20'E
55 X12 **Marouini Rivier** ≈ SE Surinam
172 I3 **Marovoay** Mahajanga, NW Madagascar 16°05'S 46°40'E
55 W9 **Marowijne** ◈ district NE Surinam
Marowijne see Maroni
Marqaköl see Markakol', Ozero
193 P8 **Marquesas Fracture Zone** tectonic feature E Pacific Ocean
Marquesas Islands see Marquises, Îles
23 W17 **Marquesas Keys** island group Florida, SE USA
29 Y12 **Marquette** Iowa, C USA 43°02'N 91°10'W
31 N3 **Marquette** Michigan, N USA 46°32'N 87°24'W
103 N1 **Marquise** Pas-de-Calais, N France 50°49'N 01°42'E
191 X7 **Marquises, Îles** Eng. Marquesas Islands. island group N French Polynesia
183 Q6 **Marra Creek** ≈ New South Wales, SE Australia
80 B10 **Marra Hills** plateau W Sudan
80 B11 **Marra, Jebel** ▲ W Sudan 12°59'N 24°16'E
74 E7 **Marrakech** var. Marakesh, Eng. Marrakesh; prev. Morocco. W Morocco 31°39'N 07°58'W
Marrakesh see Marrakech
Marrāt see Marāh
183 N15 **Marrawah** Tasmania, SE Australia 40°56'S 144°41'E
182 I4 **Marree** South Australia 29°40'S 138°06'E
81 L17 **Marrehan** ▲▲ SW Somalia
83 N17 **Marromeu** Sofala, C Mozambique 18°18'S 35°58'E
104 J17 **Marroquí, Punta** headland SW Spain 36°01'N 05°39'W
183 N8 **Marrowie Creek** seasonal river New South Wales, SE Australia
83 O14 **Marrupa** Niassa, N Mozambique 13°10'S 37°30'E
182 D1 **Marryat** South Australia 26°22'S 133°22'E
75 Y10 **Marsā al 'Alam** var. Marsa 'Alam. SE Egypt 25°03'N 33°44'E
Marsa 'Alam see Marsā al 'Alam
75 R8 **Marsá al Burayqah** var. Al Burayqah. N Libya 30°21'N 19°37'E
81 J17 **Marsabit** Eastern, N Kenya 02°20'N 37°59'E
107 H23 **Marsala** anc. Lilybaeum. Sicilia, Italy, C Mediterranean Sea 37°48'N 12°26'E
121 P16 **Marsaxlokk Bay** bay SE Malta
65 G15 **Mars Bay** bay Ascension Island, C Atlantic Ocean
101 H15 **Marsberg** Nordrhein-Westfalen, W Germany 51°28'N 08°51'E
11 R15 **Marsden** Saskatchewan, S Canada 52°50'N 109°45'W
98 H7 **Marsdiep** strait NW Netherlands
103 R16 **Marseille** Eng. Marseilles; anc. Massilia. Bouches-du-Rhône, SE France 43°19'N 05°22'E
Marseille-Marignane see Provence
30 M11 **Marseilles** Illinois, N USA 41°19'N 88°42'W
Marseilles see Marseille
76 J16 **Marshall** W Liberia 06°10'N 10°23'W
39 N11 **Marshall** Alaska, USA 61°52'N 162°04'W
27 U9 **Marshall** Arkansas, C USA 35°54'N 92°40'W
31 N14 **Marshall** Illinois, N USA 39°23'N 87°41'W
31 Q10 **Marshall** Michigan, N USA 42°16'N 84°57'W
29 S9 **Marshall** Minnesota, N USA 44°26'N 95°48'W
27 T4 **Marshall** Missouri, C USA 39°07'N 93°12'W
21 O9 **Marshall** North Carolina, SE USA 35°48'N 82°43'W
25 X6 **Marshall** Texas, SW USA 32°33'N 94°22'W
189 S4 **Marshall Islands** off. Republic of the Marshall Islands. ◆ republic W Pacific Ocean
175 Q3 **Marshall Islands** island group W Pacific Ocean
Marshall Islands, Republic of the see Marshall Islands
192 K6 **Marshall Seamounts** undersea feature SW Pacific Ocean 10°00'N 165°00'E
29 W13 **Marshalltown** Iowa, C USA 42°01'N 92°54'W
19 P12 **Marshfield** Massachusetts, NE USA 42°04'N 70°40'W
27 T7 **Marshfield** Missouri, C USA 37°20'N 92°55'W
30 K6 **Marshfield** Wisconsin, N USA 44°41'N 90°12'W
44 H1 **Marsh Harbour** Great Abaco, W Bahamas 26°31'N 77°03'W
19 S3 **Mars Hill** Maine, NE USA 46°31'N 67°51'W
21 P9 **Mars Hill** North Carolina, SE USA 35°49'N 82°33'W
22 H10 **Marsh Island** island Louisiana, S USA
21 S11 **Marshville** North Carolina, SE USA 34°59'N 80°22'W
15 W5 **Marsoui** Québec, SE Canada 49°12'N 65°58'W
15 R8 **Mars, Rivière à** ≈ Québec, SE Canada
95 O15 **Märsta** Stockholm, C Sweden 59°37'N 17°52'E
95 H24 **Marstal** Fyn, C Denmark 54°52'N 10°32'E
95 I19 **Marstrand** Västra Götaland, S Sweden 57°54'N 11°31'E
25 U8 **Mart** Texas, SW USA 31°32'N 96°49'W
166 M9 **Martaban** var. Moktama. Mon State, S Burma (Myanmar) 16°32'N 97°35'E
166 L9 **Martaban, Gulf of** gulf S Burma (Myanmar)
107 Q19 **Martano** Puglia, SE Italy 40°12'N 18°19'E
Martapoera see Martapura
169 T13 **Martapura** prev. Martapoera. Borneo, C Indonesia 03°25'S 114°51'E
99 L23 **Martelange** Luxembourg, SE Belgium 49°50'N 05°43'E
114 L7 **Marten** Ruse, N Bulgaria 43°57'N 26°08'E
14 H10 **Marten River** Ontario, S Canada 46°43'N 79°45'W
11 T15 **Martensville** Saskatchewan, S Canada 52°15'N 106°42'W
Marteskirch see Târnăveni
Martes Tolosane see Martres-Tolosane
115 K25 **Mártha** Kríti, Greece, E Mediterranean Sea 35°03'N 25°22'E
183 Q6 **Marthaguy Creek** ≈ New South Wales, SE Australia

◆ Country
● Country Capital
◇ Dependent Territory
○ Dependent Territory Capital
◈ Administrative Regions
✈ International Airport
▲ Mountain
▲▲ Mountain Range
⛰ Volcano
≈ River
◎ Lake
⊡ Reservoir

19 P13 **Martha's Vineyard** *island* Massachusetts, NE USA
108 C11 **Martigny** Valais, SW Switzerland 46°06′N 07°04′E
103 R16 **Martigues** Bouches-du-Rhône, SE France 43°24′N 05°03′E
111 J19 **Martin** *Ger.* Sankt Martin, *Hung.* Turócszentmárton; *prev.* Turčianský Svätý Martin. Žilinský Kraj, N Slovakia 49°03′N 18°54′E
28 L11 **Martin** South Dakota, N USA 43°10′N 101°43′W
20 G8 **Martin** Tennessee, S USA 36°20′N 88°51′W
105 S7 **Martín** ≋ E Spain
107 P18 **Martina Franca** Puglia, SE Italy 40°42′N 17°20′E
185 M14 **Martinborough** Wellington, North Island, New Zealand 41°12′S 175°28′E
25 S11 **Martindale** Texas, SW USA 29°49′N 97°49′W
35 N8 **Martinez** California, W USA 38°00′N 122°12′W
23 V3 **Martinez** Georgia, SE USA 33°31′N 82°04′W
41 Q13 **Martínez de La Torre** Veracruz-Llave, E Mexico 20°05′N 97°02′W
45 Y12 **Martinique** ◇ *French overseas department* E West Indies
1 O15 **Martinique** *island* E West Indies
Martinique Channel *see* Martinique Passage
45 X12 **Martinique Passage** *var.* Dominica Channel, Martinique Channel. *channel* Dominica/Martinique
23 Q5 **Martin Lake** ⊠ Alabama, S USA
115 G18 **Martíno** *prev.* Martínon. Stereá Ellás, C Greece 38°34′N 23°13′E
Martínon *see* Martíno
194 J11 **Martin Peninsula** *peninsula* Antarctica
39 S5 **Martin Point** *headland* Alaska, USA 70°06′N 143°04′W
109 V3 **Martinsberg** Niederösterreich, NE Austria 48°23′N 15°09′E
21 V3 **Martinsburg** West Virginia, NE USA 39°28′N 77°59′W
31 V13 **Martins Ferry** Ohio, N USA 40°06′N 80°43′W
Martinskirch *see* Târnăveni
31 O14 **Martinsville** Indiana, N USA 39°25′N 86°25′W
21 S8 **Martinsville** Virginia, NE USA 36°43′N 79°53′W
65 K16 **Martin Vaz, Ilhas** *island group* E Brazil
Martök *see* Martuk
184 M12 **Marton** Manawatu-Wanganui, North Island, New Zealand 40°05′S 175°22′E
105 N13 **Martos** Andalucía, S Spain 37°44′N 03°58′W
102 M16 **Martres-Tolosane** *var.* Martes Tolosane. Haute-Garonne, S France 43°13′N 01°00′E
92 M11 **Martti** Lappi, NE Finland 67°28′N 28°20′E
144 I9 **Martuk** *Kaz.* Martök. Aktyubinsk, NW Kazakhstan 50°45′N 56°30′E
137 U12 **Martuni** E Armenia 40°07′N 45°20′E
58 L11 **Marudá** Pará, E Brazil 05°25′S 49°04′W
169 V6 **Marudu, Teluk** *bay* East Malaysia
149 O8 **Ma'rūf** Kandahār, SE Afghanistan 31°34′N 67°06′E
164 H13 **Marugame** Kagawa, Shikoku, SW Japan 34°17′N 133°46′E
185 H16 **Maruia** ≋ South Island, New Zealand
98 M6 **Marum** Groningen, NE Netherlands 53°07′N 06°16′E
187 R13 **Marum, Mount** ▲ Ambrym, C Vanuatu 16°15′S 168°07′E
79 P23 **Marungu** ▲▲ SE Dem. Rep. Congo
191 Y12 **Marutea** *atoll* Groupe Actéon, C French Polynesia
143 O11 **Marv Dasht** *var.* Mervdasht. Fārs, S Iran 29°50′N 52°40′E
103 P13 **Marvejols** Lozère, S France 44°35′N 03°16′E
27 X12 **Marvell** Arkansas, C USA 34°33′N 90°52′W
36 L6 **Marvine, Mount** ▲ Utah, W USA 38°40′N 111°38′W
139 Q7 **Marwānīyah** Al Anbār, C Iraq 33°58′N 42°31′E
152 F13 **Mārwār** *var.* Kharchi, Marwar Junction. Rājasthān, N India 25°41′N 73°42′E
Marwar Junction *see* Mārwār
11 R14 **Marwayne** Alberta, SW Canada 53°30′N 110°25′W
146 I14 **Mary** *prev.* Merv. Mary Welaýaty, S Turkmenistan 37°25′N 61°48′E
Mary *see* Mary Welaýaty
181 Z9 **Maryborough** Queensland, E Australia 25°32′S 152°36′E
182 M11 **Maryborough** Victoria, SE Australia 37°05′S 143°47′E
Maryborough *see* Port Laoise
83 G23 **Marydale** Northern Cape, W South Africa 29°25′S 22°06′E
117 W8 **Mar"yinka** Donets'ka Oblast', E Ukraine 47°57′N 37°27′E
Mary Island *see* Kanton
21 W4 **Maryland** *off.* State of Maryland, *also known as* America in Miniature, Cockade State, Free State, Old Line State. ◐ *state* NE USA
Maryland, State of *see* Maryland
25 P7 **Maryneal** Texas, SW USA 32°12′N 100°25′W
97 J15 **Maryport** NW England, United Kingdom 54°45′N 03°28′W
13 U13 **Marystown** Newfoundland, Newfoundland and Labrador, SE Canada 47°10′N 55°10′W
36 K6 **Marysvale** Utah, W USA 38°26′N 112°14′W
35 O6 **Marysville** California, W USA 39°07′N 121°35′W
27 O3 **Marysville** Kansas, C USA 39°48′N 96°37′W
31 S13 **Marysville** Michigan, N USA 42°54′N 82°29′W
31 S9 **Marysville** Ohio, NE USA 40°13′N 83°22′W
32 H7 **Marysville** Washington, NW USA 48°03′N 122°10′W
27 R2 **Maryville** Missouri, C USA 40°20′N 94°53′W
21 N9 **Maryville** Tennessee, S USA 35°45′N 83°59′W
146 I15 **Mary Welaýaty** *var.* Mary, *Rus.* Maryyskiy Velayat. ◐ *province* S Turkmenistan
Maryyskiy Velayat *see* Mary Welaýaty
Marzūq *see* Murzuq
42 J11 **Masachapa** *var.* Puerto Masachapa. Managua, W Nicaragua 11°47′N 86°31′W
81 G19 **Masai Mara National Reserve** *reserve* C Kenya
81 I21 **Masai Steppe** *grassland* NW Tanzania
81 F19 **Masaka** SW Uganda 0°20′S 31°46′E
169 T15 **Masalembo Besar, Pulau** *island* S Indonesia
137 Y13 **Masallı** *Rus.* Masally. S Azerbaijan 39°03′N 48°39′E
Masally *see* Masallı
171 N13 **Masamba** Sulawesi, C Indonesia 02°33′S 120°20′E
Masampo *see* Masan
163 Y16 **Masan** *prev.* Masampo. S South Korea 35°11′N 128°36′E
Masandam Peninsula *see* Musandam Peninsula
81 J25 **Masasi** Mtwara, SE Tanzania 10°43′S 38°48′E
Masawa/Massawa *see* Mits'iwa
42 J10 **Masaya** Masaya, W Nicaragua 11°59′N 86°06′W
42 J10 **Masaya** ◐ *department* W Nicaragua
171 P5 **Masbate** Masbate, N Philippines 12°21′N 123°34′E
171 P5 **Masbate** *island* C Philippines
74 I6 **Mascara** *var.* Mouaskar. NW Algeria 35°20′N 00°09′E
173 O7 **Mascarene Basin** *undersea feature* W Indian Ocean 15°00′S 56°00′E
173 O9 **Mascarene Islands** *island group* W Indian Ocean
173 N9 **Mascarene Plain** *undersea feature* W Indian Ocean 19°00′S 52°00′E
173 O7 **Mascarene Plateau** *undersea feature* W Indian Ocean 10°00′S 60°00′E
194 H5 **Mascart, Cape** *headland* Adelaide Island, Antarctica
62 J10 **Mascasín, Salinas de** *salt lake* C Argentina
40 K13 **Mascota** Jalisco, C Mexico 20°31′N 104°46′W
15 O12 **Mascouche** Québec, SE Canada 45°46′N 73°37′W
124 J9 **Masel'gskaya** Respublika Kareliya, NW Russian Federation 63°09′N 34°22′E
83 J23 **Maseru** ● (Lesotho) W Lesotho 29°21′S 27°35′E
83 J23 **Maseru** ✈ W Lesotho 29°27′S 27°37′E
Mashaba *see* Mashava
160 K14 **Mashan** *var.* Baishan. Guangxi Zhuangzu Zizhiqu, S China 23°40′N 108°10′E
83 K17 **Mashava** *prev.* Mashaba. Masvingo, SE Zimbabwe 20°03′S 30°29′E
143 U4 **Mashhad** *var.* Meshed. Khorāsān-Razavī, NE Iran 36°16′N 59°34′E
165 S3 **Mashike** Hokkaidō, NE Japan 43°51′N 141°30′E
Mashīz *see* Bardsīr
149 N14 **Mashkai** ≋ SW Pakistan
143 X13 **Māshkel** *var.* Rūd-i Māshkel, Rūd-e Māshkīd. ≋ Iran/Pakistan
148 K12 **Māshkel, Hāmūn-i** *salt marsh* SW Pakistan
Māshkel, Rūd-i/Māshkīd, Rūd-e *see* Māshkel
83 K15 **Mashonaland Central** ◐ *province* N Zimbabwe
83 K16 **Mashonaland East** ◐ *province* NE Zimbabwe
83 J16 **Mashonaland West** ◐ *province* NW Zimbabwe
Mashtagi *see* Maştağa
141 S14 **Masīlah, Wādī al** *dry watercourse* SE Yemen
79 I21 **Masi-Manimba** Bandundu, SW Dem. Rep. Congo 04°47′S 17°54′E
81 F17 **Masindi** W Uganda 01°41′N 31°45′E
81 I19 **Masinga Reservoir** ⊠ S Kenya
Masīra *see* Maşīrah, Jazīrat
Masira, Gulf of *see* Maşīrah, Khalīj
141 Y10 **Maşīrah, Jazīrat** *var.* Masīra. *island* E Oman
141 Y10 **Maşīrah, Khalīj** *var.* Gulf of Masira. *bay* E Oman
Masis *see* Büyükağrı Dağı
79 O19 **Masisi** Nord-Kivu, E Dem. Rep. Congo 01°25′S 28°50′E
Masjed-e Soleymān *see* Masjed Soleymān
142 L9 **Masjed Soleymān** *var.* Masjed-e Soleymān, Masjid-i Sulaiman. Khūzestān, SW Iran 31°59′N 49°18′E
Masjid-i Sulaiman *see* Masjed Soleymān
Maskat *see* Masqaţ
139 Q7 **Maskhān** Al Anbār, C Iraq 33°41′N 42°46′E
141 X8 **Maskin** *var.* Miskin. NW Oman 23°28′N 56°46′E
97 B17 **Mask, Lough** *Ir.* Loch Measca. ◎ W Ireland
114 N10 **Maslen Nos** *headland* E Bulgaria 42°19′N 27°47′E
172 K3 **Masoala, Tanjona** *headland* NE Madagascar 15°59′N 50°13′E
Masohi *see* Amahai
31 Q9 **Mason** Michigan, N USA 42°33′N 84°25′W
31 R14 **Mason** Ohio, N USA 39°21′N 84°18′W
25 Q10 **Mason** Texas, SW USA 30°45′N 99°15′W
21 P4 **Mason** West Virginia, NE USA 39°01′N 82°01′W
185 B25 **Mason Bay** *bay* Stewart Island, New Zealand
30 K13 **Mason City** Illinois, N USA 40°12′N 89°42′W
29 V12 **Mason City** Iowa, C USA 43°09′N 93°12′W
18 B16 **Masontown** Pennsylvania, NE USA 39°49′N 79°53′W
141 Y8 **Masqaţ** *var.* Maskat, *Eng.* Muscat. ● (Oman) NE Oman 23°35′N 58°36′E
106 E10 **Massa** Toscana, C Italy 44°02′N 10°07′E
18 M11 **Massachusetts** *off.* Commonwealth of Massachusetts, *also known as* Bay State, Old Bay State, Old Colony State. ◐ *state* NE USA
19 P11 **Massachusetts Bay** *bay* Massachusetts, NE USA
35 R2 **Massacre Lake** ◎ Nevada, W USA
107 O18 **Massafra** Puglia, SE Italy 40°35′N 17°08′E
108 G11 **Massagno** Ticino, S Switzerland 46°01′N 08°55′E
78 G11 **Massaguet** Chari-Baguirmi, W Chad 12°28′N 15°26′E
Massakori *see* Massakory
78 G10 **Massakory** *var.* Massakori; *prev.* Dagana. Chari-Baguirmi, W Chad 13°02′N 15°43′E
78 H11 **Massalassef** Chari-Baguirmi, SW Chad 11°37′N 17°09′E
106 F13 **Massa Marittima** Toscana, C Italy 43°03′N 10°55′E
82 B11 **Massangano** Cuanza Norte, NW Angola 09°40′S 14°13′E
83 M18 **Massangena** Gaza, S Mozambique 21°34′S 32°57′E
80 K9 **Massawa Channel** *channel* E Eritrea
18 J6 **Massena** New York, NE USA 44°55′N 74°53′W
78 H11 **Massenya** Chari-Baguirmi, SW Chad 11°21′N 16°09′E
10 I13 **Masset** Graham Island, British Columbia, SW Canada 54°00′N 132°09′W
102 L16 **Masseube** Gers, S France 43°26′N 00°33′E
14 E11 **Massey** Ontario, S Canada 46°13′N 82°06′W
103 P12 **Massiac** Cantal, C France 45°16′N 03°13′E
103 P12 **Massif Central** *plateau* C France
Massif de L'Isalo *see* Isalo
Massilia *see* Marseille
31 U12 **Massillon** Ohio, N USA 40°48′N 81°31′W
77 N12 **Massina** Ségou, W Mali 13°58′N 05°24′W
83 N19 **Massinga** Inhambane, SE Mozambique 23°20′S 35°25′E
83 L20 **Massingir** Gaza, SW Mozambique 23°51′S 31°58′E
195 Z10 **Masson Island** *island* Antarctica
Massoukou *see* Franceville
137 Z11 **Maştağa** *Rus.* Mashtagi, Mastaga. E Azerbaijan 40°31′N 50°01′E
Mastanli *see* Momchilgrad
184 M13 **Masterton** Wellington, North Island, New Zealand 40°56′S 175°40′E
18 M14 **Mastic** Long Island, New York, NE USA 40°48′N 72°50′W
149 O10 **Mastung** Baluchistān, SW Pakistan 29°44′N 66°56′E
119 J20 **Mastva** *Rus.* Mostva. ≋ SW Belarus
119 G17 **Masty** *Rus.* Mosty. Hrodzyenskaya Voblasts', W Belarus 53°25′N 24°32′E
164 F12 **Masuda** Shimane, Honshū, SW Japan 34°40′N 131°50′E
92 J11 **Masugnsbyn** Norrbotten, N Sweden 67°28′N 22°01′E
Masuku *see* Franceville
83 K17 **Masvingo** *prev.* Fort Victoria, Nyanda, Victoria. Masvingo, SE Zimbabwe 20°05′S 30°50′E
83 K18 **Masvingo** *prev.* Victoria. ◐ *province* SE Zimbabwe
138 H5 **Maşyāf** *Fr.* Misiaf. Ḩamāh, C Syria 35°04′N 36°21′E
110 E9 **Maszewo** Zachodniopomorskie, NW Poland 53°29′N 15°01′E
83 I17 **Matabeleland North** ◐ *province* W Zimbabwe
83 J18 **Matabeleland South** ◐ *province* S Zimbabwe
82 O13 **Mataca** Niassa, N Mozambique 12°27′S 36°13′E
14 G8 **Matachewan** Ontario, S Canada 47°58′N 80°37′W
163 Q8 **Matad** *var.* Dzüünbulag. Dornod, E Mongolia 46°48′N 115°21′E
79 F22 **Matadi** Bas-Congo, W Dem. Rep. Congo 05°49′S 13°31′E
25 O4 **Matador** Texas, SW USA 34°01′N 100°50′W
42 J9 **Matagalpa** Matagalpa, C Nicaragua 12°53′N 85°56′W
42 K9 **Matagalpa** ◐ *department* W Nicaragua
12 I12 **Matagami** Québec, S Canada 49°47′N 77°38′W
25 U13 **Matagorda** Texas, SW USA 28°40′N 96°57′W
25 U13 **Matagorda Bay** *inlet* Texas, SW USA
25 U14 **Matagorda Island** *island* Texas, SW USA
25 V13 **Matagorda Peninsula** *headland* Texas, SW USA 28°34′N 96°01′W
191 Q8 **Mataiea** Tahiti, W French Polynesia 17°46′S 149°25′W
191 T9 **Mataiva** *atoll* Îles Tuamotu, C French Polynesia
183 O7 **Matakana** New South Wales, SE Australia 32°59′S 145°53′E
184 N7 **Matakana Island** *island* NE New Zealand
83 C15 **Matala** Huíla, SW Angola 14°45′S 15°02′E
190 G12 **Matala'a Pointe** *headland* Île Uvea, N Wallis and Futuna 13°20′S 176°08′W
155 K25 **Matale** Central Province, C Sri Lanka 07°29′N 80°38′E
190 E12 **Matalesina, Pointe** *headland* Île Alofi, W Wallis and Futuna
76 I10 **Matam** NE Senegal 15°40′N 13°18′W
184 M8 **Matamata** Waikato, North Island, New Zealand 37°49′S 175°45′E
77 V12 **Matamey** Zinder, S Niger 13°27′N 08°27′E
40 L8 **Matamoros** Coahuila, NE Mexico 25°34′N 103°13′W
41 P15 **Matamoros** *var.* Izúcar de Matamoros. Puebla, S Mexico 18°38′N 98°30′W
41 Q8 **Matamoros** Tamaulipas, C Mexico 25°50′N 97°31′W
75 S13 **Ma'ţan as Sārah** SE Libya 21°45′N 21°55′E
82 J12 **Matanda** Luapula, N Zambia 11°24′S 28°25′E
81 J24 **Matandu** ≋ S Tanzania
15 V6 **Matane** Québec, SE Canada 48°50′N 67°31′W
15 V6 **Matane** ≋ Québec, SE Canada
77 S12 **Matankari** Dosso, SW Niger 13°39′N 04°03′E
39 R11 **Matanuska River** ≋ Alaska, USA
54 G7 **Matanza** Santander, N Colombia 07°22′N 73°02′W
44 D4 **Matanzas** Matanzas, NW Cuba 23°N 81°32′W
15 V7 **Matapédia** ≋ Québec, SE Canada
15 V6 **Matapédia, Lac** ◎ Québec, SE Canada
190 B17 **Mata Point** *headland* SE Niue 19°07′S 169°51′E
190 D12 **Matapu, Pointe** *headland* Île Futuna, W Wallis and Futuna
62 G12 **Mataquito, Río** ≋ C Chile
155 K26 **Matara** Southern Province, S Sri Lanka 05°58′N 80°33′E
115 D18 **Matarágka** *var.* Mataránga. Dytikí Ellás, C Greece 38°32′N 21°28′E
171 K16 **Mataram** Pulau Lombok, C Indonesia 08°36′S 116°07′E
Mataránga *see* Matarágka
181 Q3 **Mataranka** Northern Territory, N Australia 14°55′S 133°03′E
105 W6 **Mataró** *anc.* Illuro. Cataluña, E Spain 41°32′N 02°27′E
184 O8 **Matata** Bay of Plenty, North Island, New Zealand 37°54′S 176°45′E
192 K16 **Matātula, Cape** *headland* Tutuila, W American Samoa 14°15′S 170°35′W
185 D24 **Mataura** Southland, South Island, New Zealand 46°12′S 168°53′E
185 D24 **Mataura** ≋ South Island, New Zealand
Mata Uta *see* Matā'utu
192 H16 **Matāutu** Upolu, C Samoa 13°57′S 171°55′W
190 G11 **Matā'utu** *var.* Mata Uta. ○ (Wallis and Futuna) Île Uvea, Wallis and Futuna 13°22′S 176°12′W
190 G12 **Matā'utu, Baie de** *bay* Île Uvea, Wallis and Futuna
191 P7 **Mataval, Baie de** *bay* Tahiti, W French Polynesia
190 I16 **Matavera** Rarotonga, S Cook Islands 21°13′S 159°44′W
191 V16 **Mataveri** Easter Island, Chile, E Pacific Ocean 27°10′S 109°27′W
191 V17 **Mataveri** ✈ (Easter Island) Easter Island, Chile, E Pacific Ocean 27°10′S 109°27′W
184 P9 **Matawai** Gisborne, North Island, New Zealand 38°23′S 177°31′E
15 O10 **Matawin** ≋ Québec, SE Canada
145 V13 **Matay** Almaty, SE Kazakhstan 45°53′N 78°45′E
14 K8 **Matchi-Manitou, Lac** ◎ Québec, SE Canada
41 O10 **Matehuala** San Luis Potosí, C Mexico 23°40′N 100°40′W
45 V13 **Matelot** Trinidad, Trinidad and Tobago 10°48′N 61°06′W
83 M15 **Matenge** Tete, NW Mozambique 15°22′S 33°47′E
107 O18 **Matera** Basilicata, S Italy 40°39′N 16°35′E
111 O21 **Mátészalka** Szabolcs-Szatmár-Bereg, E Hungary 47°58′N 22°17′E
93 H17 **Matfors** Västernorrland, C Sweden 62°21′N 17°02′E
102 K11 **Matha** Charente-Maritime, W France 45°50′N 00°13′W
0 F15 **Mathematicians Seamounts** *undersea feature* E Pacific Ocean 15°00′N 111°00′W
21 X6 **Mathews** Virginia, NE USA 37°26′N 76°20′W
25 S14 **Mathis** Texas, SW USA 28°05′N 97°49′W
152 J11 **Mathura** *prev.* Muttra. Uttar Pradesh, N India 27°30′N 77°42′E
Mathurai *see* Madurai
171 R7 **Mati** Mindanao, S Philippines 06°58′N 126°11′E
Matianus *see* Orūmīyeh, Daryācheh-ye
Matiara *see* Matiāri
149 Q15 **Matiāri** *var.* Matiara. Sind, SE Pakistan 25°38′N 68°29′E
41 S16 **Matías Romero** Oaxaca, SE Mexico 16°53′N 95°02′W
43 O13 **Matina** Limón, E Costa Rica 10°06′N 83°18′W
14 D10 **Matinenda Lake** ◎ Ontario, S Canada
19 R8 **Matinicus Island** *island* Maine, NE USA
Matisco/Matisco Ædourum *see* Mâcon
190 G12 **Mati'utu, Baie de** E Wallis and Futuna
149 Q16 **Mātli** Sind, SE Pakistan 25°06′N 68°37′E
97 M18 **Matlock** C England, United Kingdom 53°08′N 01°32′W
59 F18 **Mato Grosso** *prev.* Vila Bela da Santissima Trindade. Mato Grosso, W Brazil 14°53′S 59°58′W
59 G17 **Mato Grosso** *off.* Estado de Mato Grosso; *prev.* Matto Grosso. ◐ *state* W Brazil
60 H8 **Mato Grosso do Sul** *off.* Estado de Mato Grosso do Sul. ◐ *state* S Brazil
Mato Grosso do Sul, Estado de *see* Mato Grosso do Sul
Mato Grosso, Estado de *see* Mato Grosso
59 I18 **Mato Grosso, Planalto de** *plateau* C Brazil
83 L21 **Matola** Maputo, S Mozambique 25°57′S 32°27′E
104 G6 **Matosinhos** *prev.* Matozinhos. Porto, NW Portugal 41°11′N 08°42′W
191 O7 **Matotea, Mont** ▲ Moorea, W French Polynesia 17°31′S 149°52′W
Matou *see* Pingguo
55 Z10 **Matoury** NE French Guiana 04°49′N 52°17′W
Matozinhos *see* Matosinhos
111 L21 **Mátra** ▲▲ N Hungary
141 Y8 **Maţraḩ** *var.* Mutrah. NE Oman 23°35′N 58°31′E
116 L12 **Mătrăşeşti** Vrancea, E Romania 45°53′N 27°14′E
108 M8 **Matrei am Brenner** Tirol, W Austria 47°09′N 11°28′E
109 P8 **Matrei in Osttirol** Tirol, W Austria 47°04′N 12°31′E
76 I15 **Matru** SW Sierra Leone 07°37′N 12°08′W
Maţrûḩ *see* Mersá Maţrûḩ
165 U16 **Matsubara** *var.* Matubara. Kagoshima, Tokuno-shima, SW Japan 32°58′N 129°56′E
164 G12 **Matsue** *var.* Matsuye, Matue. Shimane, Honshū, SW Japan 35°27′N 133°04′E
165 Q6 **Matsumae** Hokkaidō, NE Japan 41°27′N 140°04′E
164 M12 **Matsumoto** *var.* Matumoto. Nagano, Honshū, S Japan 36°18′N 137°58′E
164 K14 **Matsusaka** *var.* Matsuzaka, Matusaka. Mie, Honshū, SW Japan 34°33′N 136°31′E
161 S12 **Matsu Tao** *Chin.* Mazu Dao. *island* NW Taiwan
Matsutō *see* Mattō
164 F14 **Matsuyama** *var.* Matuyama. Ehime, Shikoku, SW Japan 33°50′N 132°47′E
Matsuye *see* Matsue
Matsuzaka *see* Matsusaka
164 M14 **Matsuzaki** Shizuoka, Honshū, S Japan 34°43′N 138°45′E
14 F8 **Mattagami** ≋ Ontario, S Canada
14 F8 **Mattagami Lake** ◎ Ontario, S Canada
62 K12 **Mattaldi** Córdoba, C Argentina 34°26′S 64°14′W
21 Y9 **Mattamuskeet, Lake** ◎ North Carolina, SE USA
21 W6 **Mattaponi River** ≋ Virginia, NE USA
14 I11 **Mattawa** Ontario, SE Canada 46°19′N 78°42′W
14 I11 **Mattawa** ≋ Ontario, SE Canada
19 S5 **Mattawamkeag** Maine, NE USA 45°30′N 68°20′W
19 S4 **Mattawamkeag Lake** ◎ Maine, NE USA
108 D11 **Matterhorn** *It.* Monte Cervino. ▲ Italy/Switzerland 45°58′N 07°36′E *see also* Cervino, Monte
32 L12 **Matterhorn** *var.* Sacajawea Peak. ▲ Oregon, NW USA 45°12′N 117°18′W
35 W1 **Matterhorn** ▲ Nevada, W USA 41°48′N 115°22′W
Matterhorn *see* Cervino, Monte
35 R8 **Matterhorn Peak** ▲ California, W USA 38°06′N 119°19′W
109 Y5 **Mattersburg** Burgenland, E Austria 47°45′N 16°24′E
108 E11 **Matter Vispa** ≋ S Switzerland
55 R7 **Matthews Ridge** N Guyana 07°30′N 60°07′W
44 K7 **Matthew Town** Great Inagua, S Bahamas 20°56′N 73°41′W
109 Q4 **Mattighofen** Oberösterreich, NW Austria 48°07′N 13°09′E
107 N16 **Mattinata** Puglia, SE Italy 41°41′N 16°01′E
141 T9 **Maţţī, Sabkhat** *salt flat* Saudi Arabia/United Arab Emirates
18 M14 **Mattituck** Long Island, New York, NE USA 40°59′N 72°31′W
164 L11 **Mattō** *var.* Hakusan, Matsutō. Ishikawa, Honshū, SW Japan 36°31′N 136°34′E
Matto Grosso *see* Mato Grosso
30 M14 **Mattoon** Illinois, N USA 39°28′N 88°22′W
57 L16 **Mattos, Río** ≋ C Bolivia
Mattu *see* Metu
169 R9 **Matu** Sarawak, East Malaysia 02°39′N 111°31′E
Matubara *see* Matsubara
57 E14 **Matucana** Lima, W Peru 11°54′S 76°25′W
Matue *see* Matsue
187 Y15 **Matuku** *island* S Fiji
112 B9 **Matulji** Primorje-Gorski Kotar, NW Croatia 45°21′N 14°18′E
Matumoto *see* Matsumoto
55 P5 **Maturín** Monagas, NE Venezuela 09°45′N 63°10′W
Matusaka *see* Matsusaka
Matuyama *see* Matsuyama
126 K11 **Matveyev Kurgan** Rostovskaya Oblast', SW Russian Federation 47°31′N 38°55′E
127 O8 **Matyshevo** Volgogradskaya Oblast', SW Russian Federation 50°53′N 44°09′E
153 O13 **Mau** *var.* Maunāth Bhanjan. Uttar Pradesh, N India 25°57′N 83°33′E
83 O14 **Maúa** Niassa, N Mozambique 13°53′S 37°10′E
102 M17 **Maubermé, Pic de** *var.* Tuc de Moubermé, *Sp.* Pico Mauberme; *prev.* Tuc de Maubermé. ▲ France/Spain 42°48′N 00°54′E *see also* Moubermé, Tuc de
Maubermé, Pic de *see* Moubermé, Tuc de
Mauberme, Pico *see* Maubermé, Pic de/Moubermé, Tuc de
Maubermé, Tuc de *see* Maubermé, Pic de/Moubermé, Tuc de
103 Q2 **Maubeuge** Nord, N France 50°16′N 04°00′E
166 L8 **Maubin** Ayeyarwady, SW Burma (Myanmar) 16°44′N 95°37′E
152 L13 **Maudaha** Uttar Pradesh, N India 25°41′N 80°07′E
183 N9 **Maude** New South Wales, SE Australia 34°30′S 144°20′E
195 P3 **Maudheimvidda** *physical region* Antarctica
65 N22 **Maud Rise** *undersea feature* S Atlantic Ocean
109 Q4 **Mauerkirchen** Oberösterreich, NW Austria 48°11′N 13°08′E
Mauersee *see* Mamry, Jezioro
188 K2 **Maug Islands** *island group* N Northern Mariana Islands
103 Q15 **Mauguio** Hérault, S France 43°37′N 04°01′E
193 N5 **Maui** *island* Hawai'i, USA, C Pacific Ocean
190 M16 **Mauke** *atoll* S Cook Islands
62 G13 **Maule** *var.* Región del Maule. ◐ *region* C Chile
102 J9 **Mauléon** Deux-Sèvres, W France 46°55′N 00°45′W
102 J16 **Mauléon-Licharre** Pyrénées-Atlantiques, SW France 43°14′N 00°51′W
Maule, Región del *see* Maule
62 G13 **Maule, Río** ≋ C Chile
63 G17 **Maullín** Los Lagos, S Chile 41°38′S 73°35′W
31 R11 **Maumee** Ohio, N USA 41°34′N 83°40′W
31 Q12 **Maumee River** ≋ Indiana/Ohio, N USA
27 U11 **Maumelle** Arkansas, C USA 34°51′N 92°24′W
27 T11 **Maumelle, Lake** ⊠ Arkansas, C USA
171 O16 **Maumere** *prev.* Maoemere. Flores, S Indonesia 08°35′S 122°13′E
83 G17 **Maun** North-West, C Botswana 20°01′S 23°28′E
Maunāth Bhanjan *see* Mau
Maunawai *see* Waimea
190 H16 **Maungaroa** ▲ Rarotonga, S Cook Islands 21°13′S 159°48′W
184 K3 **Maungatapere** Northland, North Island, New Zealand 35°46′S 174°10′E
184 K4 **Maungaturoto** Northland, North Island, New Zealand 36°06′S 174°21′E
191 R10 **Maupiti** *var.* Maurua. *island* Îles Sous le Vent, W French Polynesia
152 K14 **Mau Rānīpur** Uttar Pradesh, N India 25°14′N 79°07′E
22 K9 **Maurepas, Lake** ◎ Louisiana, S USA
103 T16 **Maures** ▲▲ SE France
103 O12 **Mauriac** Cantal, C France 45°13′N 02°21′E
Maurice *see* Mauritius
65 J20 **Maurice Ewing Bank** *undersea feature* SW Atlantic Ocean 51°00′S 43°00′W
182 C4 **Maurice, Lake** *salt lake* South Australia
18 I17 **Maurice River** ≋ New Jersey, NE USA
25 Y10 **Mauriceville** Texas, SW USA 30°13′N 93°52′W
98 K12 **Maurik** Gelderland, C Netherlands 51°57′N 05°25′E
76 H8 **Mauritania** *off.* Islamic Republic of Mauritania, *Ar.* Mūrītānīyah. ◆ *republic* W Africa
Mauritania, Islamic Republic of *see* Mauritania
173 W15 **Mauritius** *off.* Republic of Mauritius, *Fr.* Maurice. ◆ *republic* W Indian Ocean
128 M17 **Mauritius** *island* W Indian Ocean
Mauritius, Republic of *see* Mauritius
173 N9 **Mauritius Trench** *undersea feature* W Indian Ocean
102 H6 **Mauron** Morbihan, NW France 48°06′N 02°16′W
103 N13 **Maurs** Cantal, C France 44°45′N 02°12′E
Maurua *see* Maupiti
Maury Mid-Ocean Channel *see* Maury Seachannel
64 L6 **Maury Seachannel** *var.* Maury Mid-Ocean Channel. *undersea feature* N Atlantic Ocean 56°33′N 24°00′W
30 K8 **Mauston** Wisconsin, N USA 43°46′N 90°06′W
109 R8 **Mauterndorf** Salzburg, NW Austria 47°09′N 13°39′E
109 T4 **Mauthausen** Oberösterreich, N Austria 48°13′N 14°30′E
109 Q9 **Mauthen** Kärnten, S Austria 46°39′N 12°58′E
83 F15 **Mavinga** Cuando Cubango, SE Angola 15°44′S 20°21′E
83 M17 **Mavita** Manica, W Mozambique 19°31′S 33°09′E
115 K22 **Mavrópetra, Akrotírio** *headland* Santoríni, Kykládes, Greece, Aegean Sea 36°28′N 25°22′E
115 F16 **Mavrovoúni** ▲ C Greece 39°37′N 22°45′E
184 Q8 **Mawhai Point** *headland* North Island, New Zealand 38°08′S 178°24′E
166 L3 **Mawlaik** Sagaing, C Burma (Myanmar) 23°40′N 94°26′E
Mawlamyaing *see* Mawlamyine
166 M9 **Mawlamyine** *var.* Mawlamyaing, Moulmein. Mon State, S Burma (Myanmar) 16°30′N 97°39′E
141 N14 **Mawr, Wādī** *dry watercourse* NW Yemen
195 X5 **Mawson** *Australian research station* Antarctica 67°24′S 63°16′E
195 X5 **Mawson Coast** *physical region* Antarctica
28 M4 **Max** North Dakota, N USA 47°48′N 101°18′W
41 W12 **Maxcanú** Yucatán, SE Mexico 20°35′N 90°00′W
Maxesibebi *see* Mount Ayliff
109 Q5 **Maxglan** ✈ (Salzburg) Salzburg, W Austria 47°46′N 13°00′E
93 K16 **Maxmo** *Fin.* Maksamaa. Länsi-Suomi, W Finland 63°13′N 22°04′E
21 T11 **Maxton** North Carolina, SE USA 34°47′N 79°34′W
25 R8 **May** Texas, SW USA 31°58′N 98°54′W
186 B6 **May** ≋ NW Papua New Guinea
123 R10 **Maya** ≋ E Russian Federation
151 Q19 **Māyābandar** Andaman and Nicobar Islands, India, E Indian Ocean 12°43′N 92°52′E
Mayadin *see* Al Mayādīn
44 L5 **Mayaguana** *island* SE Bahamas
44 L5 **Mayaguana Passage** *passage* SE Bahamas
45 S6 **Mayagüez** W Puerto Rico 18°12′N 67°08′W
45 R6 **Mayagüez, Bahía de** *bay* W Puerto Rico
Mayals *see* Maials
79 G20 **Mayama** Pool, SE Congo 03°50′S 14°52′E
37 V8 **Maya, Mesa De** ▲ Colorado, C USA 37°06′N 103°30′W
143 R4 **Mayamey** Semnān, N Iran 36°50′N 55°50′E
42 F3 **Maya Mountains** *Sp.* Montañas Mayas. ▲▲ Belize/Guatemala
44 I7 **Mayarí** Holguín, E Cuba 20°41′N 75°42′W
Mayas, Montañas *see* Maya Mountains
18 I17 **May, Cape** *headland* New Jersey, NE USA 38°55′N 74°57′W
80 J11 **Maych'ew** *var.* Mai Chio, *It.* Mai Ceu. Tigray, N Ethiopia 12°55′N 39°30′E
138 I2 **Maydān Ikbiz** Ḩalab, N Syria 36°51′N 36°40′E
Maydān Shahr *see* Meydān Shahr
80 O12 **Maydh** Sanaag, N Somalia 10°57′N 47°07′E
Maydī *see* Mīdī
Mayebashi *see* Maebashi
Mayence *see* Mainz
102 K6 **Mayenne** Mayenne, NW France 48°18′N 00°37′W
102 J6 **Mayenne** ◐ *department* NW France
102 J7 **Mayenne** ≋ N France
36 K12 **Mayer** Arizona, SW USA 34°25′N 112°15′W
22 J4 **Mayersville** Mississippi, S USA 32°54′N 91°04′W
11 P14 **Mayerthorpe** Alberta, SW Canada 53°59′N 115°06′W
21 S12 **Mayesville** South Carolina, SE USA 34°00′N 80°10′W
185 G19 **Mayfield** Canterbury, South Island, New Zealand 43°50′S 171°24′E
33 N14 **Mayfield** Idaho, NW USA 43°24′N 115°56′W
20 G7 **Mayfield** Kentucky, S USA 36°45′N 88°40′W
36 L5 **Mayfield** Utah, W USA 39°06′N 111°42′W
Mayhan *see* Sant
37 T14 **Mayhill** New Mexico, SW USA 32°52′N 105°28′W
145 T9 **Maykain** *Kaz.* Mayqayyng. Pavlodar, NE Kazakhstan 51°27′N 75°52′E
126 L14 **Maykop** Respublika Adygeya, SW Russian Federation 44°36′N 40°07′E
Maylibash *see* Maylybas
Mayli-Say *see* Mayluu-Suu
147 T9 **Mayluu-Suu** *prev.* Mayli-Say, *Kir.* Mayly-Say. Dzhalal-Abadskaya Oblast', W Kyrgyzstan 41°16′N 72°27′E
144 L14 **Maylybas** *prev.* Maylibash. Kzylorda, S Kazakhstan 45°51′N 62°37′E
Mayly-Say *see* Mayluu-Suu
Maymana *see* Meymaneh
Maymyo *see* Pyin-Oo-Lwin
123 V7 **Mayn** ≋ NE Russian Federation
127 Q5 **Mayna** Ul'yanovskaya Oblast', W Russian Federation 54°04′N 47°20′E
21 N8 **Maynardville** Tennessee, S USA 36°15′N 83°48′W
14 J13 **Maynooth** Ontario, SE Canada 45°14′N 77°54′W
10 I6 **Mayo** Yukon Territory, NW Canada 63°37′N 135°48′W
23 U9 **Mayo** Florida, SE USA 30°03′N 83°10′W
97 B16 **Mayo** *Ir.* Maigh Eo. *cultural region* W Ireland
Mayo *see* Maio
78 G12 **Mayo-Kébbi** *off.* Préfecture du Mayo-Kébbu, *var.* Mayo-Kébi. ◐ *prefecture* SW Chad
Mayo-Kébbu, Préfecture du *see* Mayo-Kébbi
Mayo-Kébi *see* Mayo-Kébbi
79 F19 **Mayoko** Niari, SW Congo 02°19′S 12°47′E
171 P4 **Mayon Volcano** 🌋 Luzon, N Philippines 13°15′N 123°41′E
61 A24 **Mayor Buratovich** Buenos Aires, E Argentina 39°15′S 62°35′W
104 L4 **Mayorga** Castilla-León, N Spain 42°10′N 05°16′W
184 N6 **Mayor Island** *island* NE New Zealand
Mayor Pablo Lagerenza *see* Capitán Pablo Lagerenza
173 I14 **Mayotte** ◇ *French territorial collectivity* E Africa
Mayoumba *see* Mayumba
44 J13 **May Pen** C Jamaica 17°58′N 77°15′W
Mayqayyng *see* Maykain
171 O1 **Mayraira Point** *headland* Luzon, N Philippines 18°36′N 120°47′E
109 N8 **Mayrhofen** Tirol, W Austria 47°09′N 11°52′E
186 A6 **May River** East Sepik, NW Papua New Guinea 04°24′S 141°52′E
139 X10 **Maysān** ◐ *governorate* SE Iraq
123 R13 **Mayskiy** Amurskaya Oblast', SE Russian Federation 52°13′N 129°30′E
127 O15 **Mayskiy** Kabardino-Balkarskaya Respublika, SW Russian Federation 43°37′N 44°04′E
145 U9 **Mayskoye** Pavlodar, NE Kazakhstan 50°55′N 78°11′E
18 J17 **Mays Landing** New Jersey, NE USA 39°27′N 74°44′W
21 N4 **Maysville** Kentucky, S USA 38°38′N 83°46′W
27 R2 **Maysville** Missouri, C USA 39°53′N 94°21′W
79 D20 **Mayumba** *var.* Mayoumba. Nyanga, S Gabon 03°23′S 10°38′E
31 S8 **Mayville** Michigan, N USA 43°18′N 83°16′W
18 C11 **Mayville** New York, NE USA 42°15′N 79°32′W
29 Q4 **Mayville** North Dakota, N USA 47°27′N 97°17′W
Mayyali *see* Mahe
Mayyit, Al Baḩr al *see* Dead Sea
83 J15 **Mazabuka** Southern, S Zambia 15°52′S 27°46′E
Mazaca *see* Kayseri
Mazagan *see* El-Jadida
32 J7 **Mazama** Washington, NW USA 48°34′N 120°26′W
103 O15 **Mazamet** Tarn, S France 43°30′N 02°21′E
143 O4 **Māzandarān** *off.* Ostān-e Māzandarān. ◐ *province* N Iran
Māzandarān, Ostān-e *see* Māzandarān
156 F7 **Mazar** Xinjiang Uygur Zizhiqu, NW China 36°28′N 77°00′E
107 H24 **Mazara del Vallo** Sicilia, Italy, C Mediterranean Sea 37°39′N 12°36′E
149 O2 **Mazār-e Sharīf** *var.* Mazār-i Sharif. Balkh, N Afghanistan 36°44′N 67°06′E
Mazār-i Sharif *see* Mazār-e Sharīf
105 R13 **Mazarrón** Murcia, SE Spain 37°36′N 01°19′W

◆ Country
● Country Capital
◇ Dependent Territory
○ Dependent Territory Capital
◐ Administrative Regions
✈ International Airport
▲ Mountain
▲▲ Mountain Range
🌋 Volcano
≋ River
◎ Lake
⊠ Reservoir

105 R14 **Mazarrón, Golfo de** *gulf* SE Spain
55 S9 **Mazaruni River** ≈ N Guyana
42 B6 **Mazatenango** Suchitepéquez, SW Guatemala 14°31′N 91°30′W
40 I10 **Mazatlán** Sinaloa, C Mexico 23°15′N 106°24′W
36 L12 **Mazatzal Mountains** ▲▲ Arizona, SW USA
118 D10 **Mažeikiai** Telšiai, NW Lithuania 56°19′N 22°22′E
118 D7 **Mazirbe** Talsi, NW Latvia 57°39′N 22°16′E
40 G5 **Mazocahui** Sonora, NW Mexico 29°32′N 110°09′W
57 I18 **Mazocruz** Puno, S Peru 16°41′S 69°42′W
Mazoe, Rio *see* Mazowe
79 N21 **Mazomeno** Maniema, E Dem. Rep. Congo 04°54′S 27°13′E
159 Q6 **Mazong Shan** ▲ N China 41°40′N 97°10′E
83 L16 **Mazowe** *var.* Rio Mazoe. ≈ Mozambique/Zimbabwe
110 M11 **Mazowieckie** ◐ *province* C Poland
Mazra'a *see* Al Mazra'ah
138 G6 **Mazraat Kfar Debiâne** C Lebanon 34°00′N 35°51′E
118 H7 **Mazsalaca** *Est.* Väike-Salatsi, *Ger.* Salisburg. Valmiera, N Latvia 57°52′N 25°03′E
Mazu Dao *see* Matsu Tao
110 L9 **Mazury** *physical region* NE Poland
119 M20 **Mazyr** *Rus.* Mozyr'. Homyel'skaya Voblasts', SE Belarus 52°04′N 29°15′E
107 K25 **Mazzarino** Sicilia, Italy, C Mediterranean Sea 37°18′N 14°13′E
Mba *see* Ba
83 L21 **Mbabane** ● (Swaziland) NW Swaziland 26°24′S 31°13′E
Mbacké *see* Mbaké
77 N16 **Mbahiakro** E Ivory Coast 07°33′N 04°19′W
79 I16 **Mbaïki** *var.* M'Baiki. Lobaye, SW Central African Republic 03°52′N 17°58′E
M'Baiki *see* Mbaïki
79 F14 **Mbakaou, Lac de** ⊚ C Cameroon
76 G11 **Mbaké** *var.* Mbacké. W Senegal 14°47′N 15°54′W
82 L11 **Mbala** *prev.* Abercorn. Northern, NE Zambia 08°50′S 31°23′E
83 J18 **Mbalabala** *prev.* Balla Balla. Matabeleland South, SW Zimbabwe 20°27′S 29°03′E
81 G18 **Mbale** E Uganda 01°04′N 34°12′E
79 E16 **Mbalmayo** *var.* M'Balmayo. Centre, S Cameroon 03°30′N 11°31′E
M'Balmayo *see* Mbalmayo
81 H25 **Mbamba Bay** Ruvuma, S Tanzania 11°15′S 34°44′E
79 I18 **Mbandaka** *prev.* Coquilhatville. Equateur, NW Dem. Rep. Congo 0°07′N 18°12′E
82 B9 **M'Banza Congo** *var.* Mbanza Congo; *prev.* São Salvador, São Salvador do Congo. Dem. Rep. Congo, NW Angola 06°11′S 14°16′E
79 G21 **Mbanza-Ngungu** Bas-Congo, W Dem. Rep. Congo 05°19′S 14°45′E
67 V11 **Mbarangandu** ≈ E Tanzania
81 E19 **Mbarara** SW Uganda 0°36′S 30°40′E
79 L15 **Mbari** ≈ SE Central African Republic
81 I24 **Mbarika Mountains** ▲▲ S Tanzania
78 F13 **Mbé** Nord, N Cameroon 07°51′N 13°36′E
81 J24 **Mbemkuru** *var.* Mbwemkuru. ≈ S Tanzania
Mbengga *see* Beqa
172 H13 **Mbéni** Grande Comore, NW Comoros
83 K18 **Mberengwa** Midlands, S Zimbabwe 20°29′S 29°55′E
81 G24 **Mbeya** Mbeya, SW Tanzania 08°54′S 33°29′E
81 G23 **Mbeya** ◐ *region* S Tanzania
83 J24 **Mbhashe** *prev.* Mbashe. ≈ S South Africa
79 E19 **Mbigou** Ngounié, C Gabon 01°54′S 12°00′E
Mbilua *see* Vella Lavella
79 F19 **Mbinda** Niari, SW Congo 02°07′S 12°52′E
79 D17 **Mbini** W Equatorial Guinea 01°34′N 09°39′E
Mbini *see* Uolo, Río
83 L18 **Mbizi** Masvingo, SE Zimbabwe 21°23′S 30°54′E
81 G23 **Mbogo** Mbeya, W Tanzania 07°24′S 33°26′E
79 N15 **Mboki** Haut-Mbomou, SE Central African Republic 05°18′N 25°52′E
79 G18 **Mbomo** Cuvette, NW Congo 0°25′N 14°42′E
79 L15 **Mbomou** ◐ *prefecture* SE Central African Republic
Mbomou/M'Bomu/ Mbomu *see* Bomu
76 F11 **Mbour** W Senegal 14°22′N 16°54′W
76 I10 **Mbout** Gorgol, S Mauritania 16°02′N 12°38′W
79 J14 **Mbrès** *var.* Mbrés. Nana-Grébizi, C Central African Republic 06°40′N 19°46′E
Mbrés *see* Mbrès
79 L22 **Mbuji-Mayi** *prev.* Bakwanga. Kasai-Oriental, S Dem. Rep. Congo 06°05′S 23°30′E
81 H21 **Mbulu** Manyara, N Tanzania 03°45′S 35°33′E
186 E5 **M'bunai** *var.* Bunai. Manus Island, N Papua New Guinea 02°08′S 147°13′E
62 N8 **Mburucuyá** Corrientes, NE Argentina 28°03′S 58°15′W
Mbutha *see* Buca
Mbwemkuru *see* Mbemkuru
81 G21 **Mbwikwe** Singida, C Tanzania 05°19′S 34°09′E
13 O15 **McAdam** New Brunswick, SE Canada 45°34′N 67°20′W
25 O5 **McAdoo** Texas, SW USA 33°41′N 100°58′W
35 V2 **McAfee Peak** ▲ Nevada, W USA 41°31′N 115°57′W
27 P11 **McAlester** Oklahoma, C USA 34°56′N 95°46′W
25 S17 **McAllen** Texas, SW USA 26°12′N 98°14′W
21 S11 **McBee** South Carolina, SE USA 34°30′N 80°12′W
11 N14 **McBride** British Columbia, SW Canada 53°21′N 120°19′W
24 M9 **McCamey** Texas, SW USA 31°08′N 102°13′W
33 R15 **McCammon** Idaho, NW USA 42°38′N 112°10′W
35 X11 **McCarran** ✈ (Las Vegas) Nevada, W USA 36°04′N 115°07′W
39 T11 **McCarthy** Alaska, USA 61°25′N 142°55′W
30 M5 **McCaslin Mountain** *hill* Wisconsin, N USA
25 O2 **McClellan Creek** ≈ Texas, SW USA
21 T14 **McClellanville** South Carolina, SE USA 33°07′N 79°27′W
8 L6 **McClintock Channel** *channel* Nunavut, N Canada
195 R12 **McClintock, Mount** ▲ Antarctica 80°09′S 156°42′E
35 N2 **McCloud** California, W USA 41°15′N 122°09′W
35 N3 **McCloud River** ≈ California, W USA
35 Q9 **McClure, Lake** ⊠ California, W USA
197 O8 **McClure Strait** *strait* Northwest Territories, N Canada
29 N4 **McClusky** North Dakota, N USA 47°27′N 100°25′W
21 T11 **McColl** South Carolina, SE USA 34°40′N 79°33′W
22 K7 **McComb** Mississippi, S USA 31°14′N 90°27′W
18 E16 **McConnellsburg** Pennsylvania, NE USA 39°56′N 78°00′W
31 T14 **McConnelsville** Ohio, N USA 39°39′N 81°51′W
28 M17 **McCook** Nebraska, C USA 40°12′N 100°38′W
21 P13 **McCormick** South Carolina, SE USA 33°55′N 82°19′W
11 W16 **McCreary** Manitoba, S Canada 50°48′N 99°34′W
27 W11 **McCrory** Arkansas, C USA 35°15′N 91°12′W
25 T10 **McDade** Texas, SW USA 30°15′N 97°15′W
23 O8 **McDavid** Florida, SE USA 30°51′N 87°18′W
35 T1 **McDermitt** Nevada, W USA 41°57′N 117°43′W
23 S4 **McDonough** Georgia, SE USA 33°27′N 84°09′W
36 L12 **McDowell Mountains** ▲▲ Arizona, SW USA
20 H8 **McEwen** Tennessee, S USA 36°06′N 87°37′W
35 R12 **McFarland** California, W USA 35°41′N 119°14′W
Mcfarlane, Lake *see* Macfarlane, Lake
27 P12 **McGee Creek Lake** ⊠ Oklahoma, C USA
27 W13 **McGehee** Arkansas, C USA 33°37′N 91°24′W
35 X5 **Mcgill** Nevada, W USA 39°24′N 114°46′W
14 K11 **McGillivray, Lac** ⊚ Québec, SE Canada
39 P10 **McGrath** Alaska, USA 62°57′N 155°36′W
25 T8 **McGregor** Texas, SW USA 31°26′N 97°24′W
33 O12 **McGuire, Mount** ▲ Idaho, NW USA 45°10′N 114°36′W
83 M14 **Mchinji** *prev.* Fort Manning. Central, W Malawi 13°48′S 32°55′E
28 M7 **McIntosh** South Dakota, N USA 45°56′N 101°21′W
9 S7 **McKeand** ≈ Baffin Island, Nunavut, NE Canada
191 R4 **McKean Island** *island* Phoenix Islands, C Kiribati
30 J13 **McKee Creek** ≈ Illinois, N USA
18 C15 **McKeesport** Pennsylvania, NE USA 40°18′N 79°48′W
21 V7 **McKenney** Virginia, NE USA 36°57′N 77°42′W
20 G8 **McKenzie** Tennessee, S USA 36°07′N 88°31′W
185 B20 **McKerrow, Lake** ⊚ South Island, New Zealand
39 Q10 **McKinley, Mount** *var.* Denali. ▲ Alaska, USA 63°04′N 151°00′W
39 R10 **McKinley Park** Alaska, USA 63°42′N 149°01′W
34 K3 **McKinleyville** California, W USA 40°56′N 124°06′W
25 U6 **McKinney** Texas, SW USA 33°14′N 96°37′W
26 I5 **McKinney, Lake** ⊚ Kansas, C USA
28 M7 **McLaughlin** South Dakota, N USA 45°48′N 100°48′W
25 O2 **McLean** Texas, SW USA 35°13′N 100°36′W
30 M16 **Mcleansboro** Illinois, N USA 38°05′N 88°32′W
11 O13 **McLennan** Alberta, W Canada 55°42′N 116°50′W
14 L9 **McLennan, Lac** ⊚ Québec, SE Canada
10 M13 **McLeod Lake** British Columbia, W Canada 55°03′N 123°02′W
27 N10 **McLoud** Oklahoma, C USA 35°26′N 97°05′W
32 G15 **McLoughlin, Mount** ▲ Oregon, NW USA 42°27′N 122°18′W
37 U15 **McMillan, Lake** ⊠ New Mexico, SW USA
32 G11 **McMinnville** Oregon, NW USA 45°14′N 123°12′W
20 K9 **McMinnville** Tennessee, S USA 35°40′N 85°49′W
195 R13 **McMurdo** *US research station* Antarctica 77°40′S 167°16′E
37 N13 **Mcnary** Arizona, SW USA 34°04′N 109°51′W
24 H9 **McNary** Texas, SW USA 31°15′N 105°46′W
27 N5 **McPherson** Kansas, C USA 38°22′N 97°41′W
McPherson *see* Fort McPherson
23 U6 **McRae** Georgia, SE USA 32°04′N 82°54′W
29 P4 **McVille** North Dakota, N USA 47°45′N 98°10′W
83 J25 **Mdantsane** Eastern Cape, SE South Africa 32°55′S 27°39′E
167 T6 **Me** Ninh Binh, N Vietnam 20°21′N 105°49′E
26 J7 **Meade** Kansas, C USA 37°17′N 100°21′W
39 O5 **Meade River** ≈ Alaska, USA
35 Y11 **Mead, Lake** ⊠ Arizona/Nevada, W USA
24 M5 **Meadow** Texas, SW USA 33°20′N 102°12′W
11 S14 **Meadow Lake** Saskatchewan, C Canada 54°90′N 108°30′W
35 Y10 **Meadow Valley Wash** ≈ Nevada, W USA
22 J7 **Meadville** Mississippi, S USA 31°28′N 90°51′W
18 B12 **Meadville** Pennsylvania, NE USA 41°38′N 80°09′W
14 F14 **Meaford** Ontario, S Canada 44°35′N 80°35′W
Meáin, Inis *see* Inishmaan
104 G8 **Mealhada** Aveiro, N Portugal 40°22′N 08°27′W
13 R8 **Mealy Mountains** ▲▲ Newfoundland and Labrador, E Canada
11 O10 **Meander River** Alberta, W Canada 59°02′N 117°42′W
32 E11 **Meares, Cape** *headland* Oregon, NW USA 45°29′N 123°59′W
47 V6 **Mearim, Rio** ≈ NE Brazil
Measca, Loch *see* Mask, Lough
97 F17 **Meath** *Ir.* An Mhí. *cultural region* E Ireland
11 T14 **Meath Park** Saskatchewan, S Canada 53°25′N 105°18′W
103 O5 **Meaux** Seine-et-Marne, N France 48°47′N 02°54′E
21 T9 **Mebane** North Carolina, SE USA 36°06′N 79°16′W
171 U12 **Mebo, Gunung** ▲ Papua, E Indonesia 01°10′S 133°53′E
94 I8 **Mebonden** Sør-Trøndelag, S Norway 63°13′N 11°00′E
82 A10 **Mebridege** ≈ NW Angola
35 W16 **Mecca** California, W USA 33°34′N 116°04′W
Mecca *see* Makkah
29 Y14 **Mechanicsville** Iowa, C USA 41°54′N 91°15′W
18 L10 **Mechanicville** New York, NE USA 42°54′N 73°41′W
99 H17 **Mechelen** *Eng.* Mechlin, *Fr.* Malines. Antwerpen, C Belgium 51°02′N 04°29′E
188 C8 **Mecherchar** *var.* Eil Malk. *island* Palau Islands, Palau
101 D17 **Mechernich** Nordrhein-Westfalen, W Germany 50°36′N 06°39′E
126 L12 **Mechetinskaya** Rostovskaya Oblast', SW Russian Federation 46°46′N 40°30′E
114 J11 **Mechka** ≈ S Bulgaria
Mechlin *see* Mechelen
61 D23 **Mechongué** Buenos Aires, E Argentina 38°09′S 58°13′W
115 L14 **Mecidiye** Edirne, NW Turkey 40°39′N 26°33′E
101 I24 **Meckenbeuren** Baden-Württemberg, S Germany 47°42′N 09°34′E
100 L8 **Mecklenburger Bucht** *bay* N Germany
100 M10 **Mecklenburgische Seenplatte** *wetland* NE Germany
100 L9 **Mecklenburg-Vorpommern** ◐ *state* NE Germany
83 Q15 **Meconta** Nampula, NE Mozambique 15°01′S 39°52′E
111 I25 **Mecsek** ▲▲ SW Hungary
83 P14 **Mecubúri** ≈ N Mozambique
83 Q14 **Mecúfi** Cabo Delgado, NE Mozambique 13°20′S 40°32′E
82 O13 **Mecula** Niassa, N Mozambique 12°03′S 37°37′E
168 I8 **Medan** Sumatera, E Indonesia 03°35′N 98°39′E
61 A24 **Médanos** *var.* Medanos. Buenos Aires, E Argentina 38°52′S 62°45′W
61 C19 **Médanos** Entre Ríos, E Argentina 33°28′S 59°07′W
155 K24 **Medawachchiya** North Central Province, N Sri Lanka 08°32′N 80°30′E
106 C8 **Mede** Lombardia, N Italy 45°06′N 08°43′E
74 J5 **Médéa** *var.* El Mediyya, Lemdiyya. N Algeria 36°15′N 02°48′E
Medeba *see* Ma'dabā
54 E8 **Medellín** Antioquia, NW Colombia 06°15′N 75°36′W
100 H9 **Medem** ≈ NW Germany
98 J8 **Medemblik** Noord-Holland, NW Netherlands 52°47′N 05°06′E
75 N7 **Médenine** *var.* Madanīyīn. SE Tunisia 33°23′N 10°30′E
76 G9 **Mederdra** Trarza, SW Mauritania 16°56′N 15°40′W
Medeshamstede *see* Peterborough
42 F4 **Medesto Mendez** Izabal, NE Guatemala 15°54′N 89°13′W
19 O11 **Medford** Massachusetts, NE USA 42°25′N 71°08′W
27 N8 **Medford** Oklahoma, C USA 36°48′N 97°45′W
32 G15 **Medford** Oregon, NW USA 42°20′N 122°52′W
30 K6 **Medford** Wisconsin, N USA 45°08′N 90°22′W
39 P10 **Medfra** Alaska, USA 63°06′N 154°42′W
116 M14 **Medgidia** Constanța, SE Romania 44°15′N 28°16′E
Medgyes *see* Mediaș
43 O5 **Media Luna, Arrecifes de la** *reef* E Honduras
60 G11 **Medianeira** Paraná, S Brazil 25°15′S 54°07′W
29 Y15 **Mediapolis** Iowa, C USA 41°00′N 91°09′W
116 I11 **Mediaș** *Ger.* Mediasch, *Hung.* Medgyes. Sibiu, C Romania 46°10′N 24°20′E
41 S15 **Medias Aguas** Veracruz-Llave, SE Mexico 17°40′N 95°02′W
Mediasch *see* Mediaș
106 G10 **Medicina** Emilia-Romagna, C Italy 44°29′N 11°41′E
33 X16 **Medicine Bow** Wyoming, C USA 41°52′N 106°11′W
37 S2 **Medicine Bow Mountains** ▲▲ Colorado/Wyoming, C USA
33 X16 **Medicine Bow River** ≈ Wyoming, C USA
11 R17 **Medicine Hat** Alberta, SW Canada 50°03′N 110°41′W
26 L7 **Medicine Lodge** Kansas, C USA 37°18′N 98°35′W
26 L7 **Medicine Lodge River** ≈ Kansas/Oklahoma, C USA
112 E7 **Međimurje** *off.* Međimurska Županija. ◐ *province* N Croatia
Međimurska Županija *see* Međimurje
54 G10 **Medina** Cundinamarca, C Colombia 04°31′N 73°21′W
18 E9 **Medina** New York, NE USA 43°13′N 78°23′W
29 O5 **Medina** North Dakota, N USA 46°53′N 99°18′W
31 T11 **Medina** Ohio, N USA 41°08′N 81°51′W
25 Q11 **Medina** Texas, SW USA 29°46′N 99°14′W
Medina *see* Al Madīnah
105 P6 **Medinaceli** Castilla-León, N Spain 41°10′N 02°26′W
104 L6 **Medina del Campo** Castilla-León, N Spain 41°18′N 04°55′W
104 L5 **Medina de Ríoseco** Castilla-León, N Spain 41°53′N 05°03′W
Médina Gonassé *see* Médina Gounas
76 H12 **Médina Gounas** *var.* Médina Gonassé. S Senegal 13°06′N 13°49′W
25 S12 **Medina River** ≈ Texas, SW USA
104 K16 **Medina Sidonia** Andalucía, S Spain 36°28′N 05°55′W
Medinat Israel *see* Israel
119 H14 **Medininkai** Vilnius, SE Lithuania 54°32′N 25°40′E
153 R16 **Medinīpur** West Bengal, NE India 22°25′N 87°24′E
Mediolanum *see* Saintes, France
Mediolanum *see* Milano, Italy
Mediomatrica *see* Metz
121 Q11 **Mediterranean Ridge** *undersea feature* C Mediterranean Sea 34°00′N 23°00′E
121 O16 **Mediterranean Sea** *Fr.* Mer Méditerranée. *sea* Africa/Asia/Europe
Méditerranée, Mer *see* Mediterranean Sea
79 N17 **Medje** Orientale, NE Dem. Rep. Congo 02°27′N 27°14′E
Medjerda, Oued *see* Mejerda
114 G7 **Medkovets** Montana, NW Bulgaria 43°39′N 23°22′E
93 J15 **Medle** Västerbotten, N Sweden 64°45′N 20°45′E
127 W7 **Mednogorsk** Orenburgskaya Oblast', W Russian Federation 51°24′N 57°37′E
123 W9 **Mednyy, Ostrov** *island* E Russian Federation
102 J12 **Médoc** *cultural region* SW France
159 Q16 **Mêdog** Xizang Zizhiqu, W China 29°26′N 95°26′E
28 J5 **Medora** North Dakota, N USA 46°56′N 103°40′W
79 E17 **Médouneu** Woleu-Ntem, N Gabon 0°58′N 10°50′E
106 J7 **Meduna** ≈ NE Italy
Medunta *see* Mantes-la-Jolie
127 P3 **Medvedevo** Respublika Mariy El, W Russian Federation 56°38′N 47°48′E
Medvedica *see* Medveditsa
124 J16 **Medveditsa** *var.* Medvedica. ≈ W Russian Federation
127 O9 **Medveditsa** ≈ SW Russian Federation
112 E8 **Medvednica** ▲▲ NE Croatia
125 R15 **Medvedok** Kirovskaya Oblast', NW Russian Federation 57°23′N 50°01′E
123 S6 **Medvezh'i, Ostrova** *island group* NE Russian Federation
124 J9 **Medvezh'yegorsk** Respublika Kareliya, NW Russian Federation 62°56′N 34°26′E
109 T11 **Medvode** *Ger.* Zwischenwässern. NW Slovenia 46°09′N 14°21′E
126 J4 **Medyn'** Kaluzhskaya Oblast', W Russian Federation 54°59′N 35°52′E
180 J10 **Meekatharra** Western Australia 26°37′S 118°35′E
37 Q4 **Meeker** Colorado, C USA 40°02′N 107°54′W
13 T12 **Meelpaeg Lake** ⊚ Newfoundland, Newfoundland and Labrador, E Canada
Meemu Atoll *see* Mulakatholhu
Meenen *see* Menen
101 M16 **Meerane** Sachsen, E Germany 50°50′N 12°28′E
101 D15 **Meerbusch** Nordrhein-Westfalen, W Germany 51°19′N 06°43′E
98 I12 **Meerkerk** Zuid-Holland, C Netherlands 51°55′N 05°00′E
99 L18 **Meerssen** *var.* Mersen. Limburg, SE Netherlands 50°53′N 05°45′E
152 J10 **Meerut** Uttar Pradesh, N India 29°01′N 77°41′E
33 U13 **Meeteetse** Wyoming, C USA 44°10′N 108°53′W
99 K17 **Meeuwen** Limburg, NE Belgium 51°04′N 05°36′E
81 J16 **Mēga** Oromīya, C Ethiopia 04°03′N 38°15′E
81 J16 **Mēga Escarpment** *escarpment* S Ethiopia
Megála Kalívia *see* Megála Kalývia
115 E16 **Megála Kalývia** *var.* Megála Kalívia. Thessalía, C Greece 39°30′N 21°48′E
115 H14 **Megáli Panagiá** *var.* Megáli Panayía. Kentrikí Makedonía, N Greece 40°24′N 23°42′E
Megáli Panayía *see* Megáli Panagiá
Megáli Préspa, Límni *see* Prespa, Lake
114 K12 **Megálo Livádi** ▲ Bulgaria/Greece 41°18′N 25°51′E
115 E20 **Megalópoli** *prev.* Megalópolis. Pelopónnisos, S Greece 37°24′N 22°08′E
Megalópolis *see* Megalópoli
171 U12 **Megamo** Papua, E Indonesia 0°55′S 131°46′E
115 C18 **Meganísi** *island* Iónia Nisiá, Greece, C Mediterranean Sea
Meganom, Mys *see* Mehanom, Mys
Mégantic *see* Lac-Mégantic
15 R12 **Mégantic, Mont** ▲ Québec, SE Canada 45°27′N 71°09′W
115 G19 **Mégara** Attikí, C Greece 38°00′N 23°20′E
25 R5 **Megargel** Texas, SW USA 33°27′N 98°55′W
98 K13 **Megen** Noord-Brabant, S Netherlands 51°49′N 05°34′E
153 U13 **Meghālaya** ◐ *state* NE India
153 U16 **Meghna Nadi** ≈ S Bangladesh
137 V14 **Meghri** *Rus.* Megri. SE Armenia 38°57′N 46°15′E
115 Q23 **Megísti** *var.* Kastellórizon. *island* SE Greece
Megri *see* Meghri
Mehabad *see* Mahābād
116 F13 **Mehadia** *Hung.* Mehádia. Caraș-Severin, SW Romania 44°53′N 22°20′E
Mehádia *see* Mehadia
92 L7 **Mehamn** Finnmark, N Norway 71°01′N 27°46′E
117 U13 **Mehanom, Mys** *Rus.* Mys Meganom. *headland* S Ukraine 44°48′N 35°04′E
149 P14 **Mehar** Sind, SE Pakistan 27°12′N 67°51′E
180 J8 **Meharry, Mount** ▲ Western Australia 23°17′S 118°48′E
Mehdia *see* Mahdia
116 G14 **Mehedinți** ◐ *county* SW Romania
153 S15 **Meherpur** Khulna, W Bangladesh 23°47′N 88°40′E
21 W8 **Meherrin River** ≈ North Carolina/Virginia, SE USA
Meheso *see* Mi'ëso
191 T11 **Mehetia** *island* Îles du Vent, W French Polynesia
118 K6 **Mehikoorma** Tartumaa, E Estonia 58°14′N 27°29′E
Me Hka *see* Nmai Hka
143 N5 **Mehrabad** ✈ (Tehrān) Tehrān, N Iran 35°46′N 51°07′E
142 J7 **Mehrān** Īlām, W Iran 33°07′N 46°10′E
143 Q14 **Mehrān, Rūd-e** *prev.* Mansurabad. ≈ W Iran
143 Q9 **Mehrīz** Yazd, C Iran 31°32′N 54°28′E
149 R5 **Mehtar Lām** *var.* Mehtarlām, Meterlam, Metharlam, Metharlam. Laghmān, E Afghanistan 34°39′N 70°10′E
Mehtarlām *see* Mehtar Lām
103 N8 **Mehun-sur-Yèvre** Cher, C France 47°09′N 02°15′E
79 G14 **Meiganga** Adamaoua, NE Cameroon 06°31′N 14°07′E
160 H10 **Meigu** *var.* Bapu. Sichuan, C China 28°16′N 103°20′E
163 W11 **Meihekou** *var.* Hailong. Jilin, NE China 42°31′N 125°40′E
99 L15 **Meijel** Limburg, SE Netherlands 51°22′N 05°52′E
Meijiang *see* Ningdu
166 M5 **Meiktila** Mandalay, C Burma (Myanmar) 20°53′N 95°54′E
Meilbhe, Loch *see* Melvin, Lough
108 G7 **Meilen** Zürich, N Switzerland 47°17′N 08°39′E
Meilu *see* Wuchuan
161 T12 **Meinhua Yu** *island* N Taiwan
101 J17 **Meiningen** Thüringen, C Germany 50°34′N 10°25′E
108 F9 **Meiringen** Bern, S Switzerland 46°42′N 08°13′E
160 H9 **Meishan** Sichuan, C China 30°02′N 103°29′E
Meishan *see* Jinzhai
101 O15 **Meissen** *Ger.* Meißen. Sachsen, E Germany 51°10′N 13°28′E
Meißen *see* Meissen
101 I15 **Meissner** ▲ C Germany 51°13′N 09°52′E
99 K25 **Meix-devant-Virton** Luxembourg, SE Belgium 49°36′N 05°27′E
Meixian *see* Meizhou
Meixing *see* Xinjin
161 P13 **Meizhou** *var.* Meixian, Mei Xian. Guangdong, S China 24°21′N 116°05′E
67 P2 **Mejerda** *var.* Oued Medjerda, Wādī Majardah. ≈ Algeria/Tunisia *see also* Medjerda, Oued
42 F7 **Mejicanos** San Salvador, C El Salvador 13°50′N 89°13′W
Méjico *see* Mexico
62 G5 **Mejillones** Antofagasta, N Chile 23°03′S 70°25′W
189 V5 **Mejit Island** *var.* Mājeej. *island* Ratak Chain, NE Marshall Islands
79 F17 **Mékambo** Ogooué-Ivindo, NE Gabon 01°03′N 13°50′E
80 J10 **Mek'elē** *var.* Makale. Tigray, N Ethiopia 13°36′N 39°29′E
74 I10 **Mekerrhane, Sebkha** *var.* Sebkha Meqerghane, Sebkra Mekerrhane. *salt flat* C Algeria
Mekerrhane, Sebkra *see* Mekerrhane, Sebkha
76 G10 **Mékhé** NW Senegal 15°02′N 16°40′W
146 G14 **Mekhinli** Ahal Welaýaty, C Turkmenistan 37°28′N 59°20′E
15 P9 **Mékinac, Lac** ⊚ Québec, SE Canada
Meklong *see* Samut Songhram
74 G6 **Meknès** N Morocco 33°54′N 05°27′W
129 U12 **Mekong** *var.* Lan-ts'ang Chiang, *Cam.* Mékôngk, *Chin.* Lancang Jiang, *Lao.* Mènam Khong, *Th.* Mae Nam Khong, *Tib.* Dza Chu, *Vtn.* Sông Tiên Giang. ≈ SE Asia
Mékôngk *see* Mekong
167 T15 **Mekong, Mouths of the** *delta* S Vietnam
38 L12 **Mekoryuk** Nunivak Island, Alaska, USA 60°23′N 166°11′W
77 R14 **Mékrou** ≈ N Benin
168 K9 **Melaka** *var.* Malacca. Melaka, Peninsular Malaysia 02°14′N 102°14′E
168 L9 **Melaka** *var.* Malacca. ◐ *state* Peninsular Malaysia
Melaka, Selat *see* Malacca, Strait of
175 O6 **Melanesia** *island group* W Pacific Ocean
175 P5 **Melanesian Basin** *undersea feature* W Pacific Ocean 0°05′N 160°35′E
171 R9 **Melanguane** Pulau Karakelang, N Indonesia 04°02′N 126°43′E
169 R11 **Melawi, Sungai** ≈ Borneo, N Indonesia
183 N12 **Melbourne** *state capital* Victoria, SE Australia 37°51′S 144°56′E
27 V9 **Melbourne** Arkansas, C USA 36°04′N 91°54′W
23 Y12 **Melbourne** Florida, SE USA 28°04′N 80°36′W
29 W14 **Melbourne** Iowa, C USA 41°57′N 93°07′W
92 G10 **Melbu** Nordland, C Norway 68°31′N 14°50′E
Melchor de Mencos *see* Ciudad Melchor de Mencos
63 F19 **Melchor, Isla** *island* Archipiélago de los Chonos, S Chile
40 M9 **Melchor Ocampo** Zacatecas, C Mexico 24°45′N 101°38′W
14 C11 **Meldrum Bay** Manitoulin Island, Ontario, S Canada 45°55′N 83°06′W
Meleda *see* Mljet
106 D8 **Melegnano** *prev.* Marignano. Lombardia, N Italy 45°22′N 09°19′E
Melekeiok *see* Melekeok
188 F9 **Melekeok** *var.* Melekeiok. ● Babeldaob, N Palau 07°30′N 134°39′E
112 L9 **Melenci** *Hung.* Melencze. Vojvodina, N Serbia 45°32′N 20°18′E
Melencze *see* Melenci
127 N4 **Melenki** Vladimirskaya Oblast', W Russian Federation 55°21′N 41°37′E
127 V6 **Meleuz** Respublika Bashkortostan, W Russian Federation 52°55′N 55°54′E
12 L6 **Mélèzes, Rivière aux** ≈ Québec, C Canada
78 I11 **Melfi** Guéra, S Chad 11°05′N 17°57′E
107 M17 **Melfi** Basilicata, S Italy 41°00′N 15°33′E
11 U14 **Melfort** Saskatchewan, S Canada 52°52′N 104°38′W
104 H4 **Melgaço** Viana do Castelo, N Portugal 42°07′N 08°15′W
105 N4 **Melgar de Fernamental** Castilla-León, N Spain 42°24′N 04°15′W
74 L6 **Melghir, Chott** *var.* Chott Melrhir. *salt lake* E Algeria
94 H8 **Melhus** Sør-Trøndelag, S Norway 63°17′N 10°18′E
104 H3 **Melide** Galicia, NW Spain 42°54′N 08°01′W
Meligalá *see* Meligalás
115 E21 **Meligalás** *prev.* Meligalá. Pelopónnisos, S Greece 37°13′N 21°58′E
60 L12 **Mel, Ilha do** *island* S Brazil
120 E10 **Melilla** *anc.* Rusaddir, Russadir. Melilla, Spain, N Africa 35°18′N 02°56′W
71 N1 **Melilla** *enclave* Spain, N Africa
63 G18 **Melimoyu, Monte** ▲ S Chile 44°06′S 72°49′W
169 V11 **Melintang, Danau** ⊚ Borneo, N Indonesia
117 U7 **Melioratyvne** Dnipropetrovs'ka Oblast', E Ukraine 48°35′N 35°18′E
62 G11 **Melipilla** Santiago, C Chile 33°42′S 71°15′W
115 I25 **Mélissa, Akrotírio** *headland* Kríti, Greece, E Mediterranean Sea 35°06′N 24°33′E
11 W17 **Melita** Manitoba, S Canada 49°16′N 100°59′W
Melita *see* Mljet
Melitene *see* Malatya
107 M23 **Melito di Porto Salvo** Calabria, SW Italy 37°55′N 15°48′E
117 U10 **Melitopol'** Zaporiz'ka Oblast', SE Ukraine 46°49′N 35°23′E
109 V4 **Melk** Niederösterreich, NE Austria 48°14′N 15°21′E
95 K15 **Mellan-Fryken** ⊚ C Sweden
99 E17 **Melle** Oost-Vlaanderen, NW Belgium 51°N 03°48′E
100 G13 **Melle** Niedersachsen, NW Germany 52°12′N 08°19′E
95 J17 **Mellerud** Västra Götaland, S Sweden 58°42′N 12°27′E
102 K10 **Melle-sur-Bretonne** Deux-Sèvres, W France 46°13′N 00°07′W
29 P8 **Mellette** South Dakota, N USA 45°07′N 98°29′W
121 O15 **Mellieħa** E Malta 35°58′N 14°21′E
80 B10 **Mellit** Northern Darfur, W Sudan 14°07′N 25°34′E
75 N7 **Mellita** ✈ SE Tunisia 33°47′N 10°51′E
63 G21 **Mellizo Sur, Cerro** ▲ S Chile 48°27′S 73°10′W
100 G9 **Mellum** *island* NW Germany
83 L22 **Melmoth** KwaZulu/Natal, E South Africa 28°35′S 31°25′E
111 D16 **Mělník** *Ger.* Melnik. Středočeský Kraj, NW Czech Republic 50°21′N 14°30′E
122 J12 **Mel'nikovo** Tomskaya Oblast', C Russian Federation 56°35′N 84°11′E
61 G18 **Melo** Cerro Largo, NE Uruguay 32°22′S 54°10′W
Melodunum *see* Melun
Melrhir, Chott *see* Melghir, Chott
183 P7 **Melrose** New South Wales, SE Australia 32°41′S 146°58′E
182 I7 **Melrose** South Australia 32°52′S 138°16′E
29 T7 **Melrose** Minnesota, N USA 45°40′N 94°46′W
33 Q11 **Melrose** Montana, NW USA 45°33′N 112°41′W
37 V12 **Melrose** New Mexico, SW USA 34°25′N 103°37′W
108 I8 **Mels** Sankt Gallen, NE Switzerland 47°03′N 09°26′E
Melsetter *see* Chimanimani
33 V9 **Melstone** Montana, NW USA 46°37′N 107°49′W
101 I16 **Melsungen** Hessen, C Germany 51°08′N 09°33′E
92 L12 **Meltaus** Lappi, NW Finland 66°54′N 25°18′E
97 N19 **Melton Mowbray** C England, United Kingdom 52°46′N 01°04′W
82 Q13 **Meluco** Cabo Delgado, NE Mozambique 12°31′S 39°39′E
103 O5 **Melun** *anc.* Melodunum. Seine-et-Marne, N France 48°32′N 02°40′E
80 F12 **Melut** Upper Nile, SE Sudan 10°27′N 32°13′E
27 P5 **Melvern Lake** ⊠ Kansas, C USA
11 V16 **Melville** Saskatchewan, S Canada 50°57′N 102°49′W
Melville Bay/Melville Bugt *see* Qimusseriarsuaq
45 O11 **Melville Hall** ✈ (Dominica) NE Dominica 15°33′N 61°19′W
181 O1 **Melville Island** *island* Northern Territory, N Australia
197 O8 **Melville Island** *island* Parry Islands, Northwest Territories, NW Canada
11 W9 **Melville, Lake** ⊚ Newfoundland and Labrador, E Canada
9 O7 **Melville Peninsula** *peninsula* Nunavut, NE Canada
Melville Sound *see* Viscount Melville Sound
25 Q9 **Melvin** Texas, SW USA 31°12′N 99°34′W
97 D15 **Melvin, Lough** *Ir.* Loch Meilbhe. ⊚ S Northern Ireland, United Kingdom/Ireland
169 S12 **Memala** Borneo, C Indonesia 01°44′S 112°36′E
113 L22 **Memaliaj** Gjirokastër, S Albania 40°21′N 19°56′E
83 Q14 **Memba** Nampula, NE Mozambique 14°07′S 40°33′E
83 Q14 **Memba, Baia de** *inlet* NE Mozambique
Membidj *see* Manbij
Memel *see* Neman, NE Europe
Memel *see* Klaipeda, Lithuania
101 J23 **Memmingen** Bayern, S Germany 47°59′N 10°11′E
27 U1 **Memphis** Missouri, C USA 40°28′N 92°11′W
20 E10 **Memphis** Tennessee, S USA 35°09′N 90°03′W
25 P3 **Memphis** Texas, SW USA 34°43′N 100°34′W
20 E10 **Memphis** ✈ Tennessee, S USA 35°02′N 89°57′W
15 Q13 **Memphrémagog, Lac** *var.* Lake Memphremagog. ⊚ Canada/USA *see also* Lake Memphremagog
19 N6 **Memphremagog, Lake** *var.* Lac Memphrémagog. ⊚ Canada/USA *see also* Memphrémagog, Lac
117 Q2 **Mena** Chernihivs'ka Oblast', NE Ukraine 51°30′N 32°15′E
27 S12 **Mena** Arkansas, C USA 34°40′N 94°15′W
Menaam *see* Menaldum
Menado *see* Manado
106 D6 **Menaggio** Lombardia, N Italy 46°03′N 09°14′E
29 T6 **Menahga** Minnesota, N USA 46°45′N 95°06′W
77 R10 **Ménaka** Goa, E Mali 15°55′N 02°25′E
98 K5 **Menaldum** *Fris.* Menaam. Friesland, N Netherlands 53°14′N 05°38′E
Mènam Khong *see* Mekong
74 E7 **Menara** ✈ (Marrakech) C Morocco 31°36′N 08°00′W
25 Q9 **Menard** Texas, SW USA 30°56′N 99°48′W
193 Q12 **Menard Fracture Zone** *tectonic feature* E Pacific Ocean
30 M7 **Menasha** Wisconsin, N USA 44°13′N 88°25′W
Mencezi Garagum *see* Merkezi Garagumy
193 U9 **Mendaña Fracture Zone** *tectonic feature* E Pacific Ocean
169 S13 **Mendawai, Sungai** ≈ Borneo, C Indonesia
103 P13 **Mende** *anc.* Mimatum. Lozère, S France 44°32′N 03°30′E
81 J14 **Mendebo** ▲▲ C Ethiopia
80 J9 **Mendefera** *prev.* Adi Ugri. S Eritrea 14°53′N 38°51′E
197 S7 **Mendeleyev Ridge** *undersea feature* Arctic Ocean
127 T3 **Mendeleyevsk** Respublika Tatarstan, W Russian Federation 55°54′N 52°19′E
101 F15 **Menden** Nordrhein-Westfalen, W Germany 51°26′N 07°47′E
22 L6 **Mendenhall** Mississippi, S USA 31°57′N 89°52′W
38 L13 **Mendenhall, Cape** *headland* Nunivak Island, Alaska, USA 59°45′N 166°10′W
41 P9 **Méndez** *var.* Villa de Méndez. Tamaulipas, C Mexico 25°06′N 98°32′W
80 H13 **Mendī** Oromīya C Ethiopia 09°43′N 35°07′E
186 C7 **Mendi** Southern Highlands, W Papua New Guinea 06°13′S 143°39′E
97 K22 **Mendip Hills** *var.* Mendips. *hill range* S England, United Kingdom
Mendips *see* Mendip Hills
34 L6 **Mendocino** California, W USA 39°18′N 123°48′W
34 J3 **Mendocino, Cape** *headland* California, W USA 40°26′N 124°24′W
0 B8 **Mendocino Fracture Zone** *tectonic feature* NE Pacific Ocean
35 P10 **Mendota** California, W USA 36°44′N 120°24′W
30 L11 **Mendota** Illinois, N USA 41°32′N 89°04′W
30 K8 **Mendota, Lake** ⊚ Wisconsin, N USA
62 I11 **Mendoza** Mendoza, W Argentina 33°00′S 68°47′W
62 I12 **Mendoza** *off.* Provincia de Mendoza. ◐ *province* W Argentina
Mendoza, Provincia de *see* Mendoza
108 H12 **Mendrisio** Ticino, S Switzerland 45°53′N 08°59′E
168 L10 **Mendung** Pulau Mendol, W Indonesia 0°33′N 103°09′E
54 I5 **Mene de Mauroa** Falcón, NW Venezuela 10°39′N 71°04′W
54 I5 **Mene Grande** Zulia, NW Venezuela 09°51′N 70°57′W
136 B14 **Menemen** İzmir, W Turkey 38°34′N 27°03′E
99 C18 **Menen** *var.* Meenen, *Fr.* Menin. West-Vlaanderen, W Belgium 50°48′N 03°07′E
163 Q8 **Menengiyn Tal** *plain* E Mongolia
189 R9 **Meneng Point** *headland* SW Nauru 0°33′S 166°57′E
92 L10 **Menesjärvi** *Lapp.* Menesjávri. Lappi, N Finland 68°39′N 26°22′E

Menešjávri *see* Menesjärvi
107 *I24* **Menfi** Sicilia, Italy, C Mediterranean Sea *37°36′N 12°59′E*
161 *P7* **Mengcheng** Anhui, E China *33°15′N 116°33′E*
160 *F15* **Menghai** Yunnan, SW China *22°02′N 100°18′E*
160 *F15* **Mengla** Yunnan, SW China *21°30′N 101°33′E*
160 *M13* **Mengzhu Ling** ▲▲ S China
160 *H14* **Mengzi** Yunnan, SW China *23°20′N 103°32′E*
114 *H13* **Meníkio** *var.* Menoíkio. ▲ NE Greece *40°50′N 12°40′E*
Menin *see* Menen
182 *L7* **Menindee** New South Wales, SE Australia *32°24′S 142°25′E*
182 *L7* **Menindee Lake** ◎ New South Wales, SE Australia
182 *J10* **Meningie** South Australia *35°43′S 139°20′E*
103 *O5* **Mennecy** Essonne, N France *48°34′N 02°25′E*
29 *Q12* **Menno** South Dakota, N USA *43°14′N 97°34′W*
114 *H13* **Menoíkio** ▲▲ NE Greece
Menoíkio *see* Meníkio
31 *N5* **Menominee** Michigan, N USA *45°06′N 87°36′W*
30 *M5* **Menominee River** Michigan/Wisconsin, N USA
30 *M8* **Menomonee Falls** Wisconsin, N USA *43°11′N 88°09′W*
30 *I6* **Menomonie** Wisconsin, N USA *44°52′N 91°55′W*
83 *D14* **Menongue** *var.* Vila Serpa Pinto, *Port.* Serpa Pinto. Cuando Cubango, C Angola *14°38′S 17°39′E*
120 *H8* **Menorca** *Eng.* Minorca; *anc.* Balearis Minor. *island* Islas Baleares, Spain, W Mediterranean Sea
105 *S13* **Menor, Mar** *lagoon* SE Spain
39 *S10* **Mentasta Lake** ◎ Alaska, USA
39 *S10* **Mentasta Mountains** ▲▲ Alaska, USA
168 *I13* **Mentawai, Kepulauan** *island group* W Indonesia
168 *I12* **Mentawai, Selat** *strait* W Indonesia
168 *M12* **Mentok** Pulau Bangka, W Indonesia *02°01′S 105°10′E*
103 *V15* **Menton** *It.* Mentone. Alpes-Maritimes, SE France *43°47′N 07°30′E*
24 *K8* **Mentone** Texas, SW USA *31°42′N 103°36′W*
Mentone *see* Menton
31 *U11* **Mentor** Ohio, N USA *41°40′N 81°20′W*
169 *U10* **Menyapa, Gunung** ▲ Borneo, N Indonesia *01°04′N 116°01′E*
159 *T9* **Menyuan** *var.* Menyuan Huizu Zizhixian. Qinghai, C China *37°27′N 101°33′E*
Menyuan Huizu Zizhixian *see* Menyuan
74 *M5* **Menzel Bourguiba** *var.* Manzil Bū Ruqaybah; *prev.* Ferryville. N Tunisia *37°09′N 09°51′E*
136 *M15* **Menzelet Barajı** ▣ C Turkey
127 *T4* **Menzelinsk** Respublika Tatarstan, W Russian Federation *55°44′N 53°00′E*
180 *K11* **Menzies** Western Australia *29°42′S 121°04′E*
195 *V6* **Menzies, Mount** ▲ Antarctica *73°32′S 61°02′E*
40 *J6* **Meoqui** Chihuahua, N Mexico *28°18′N 105°30′W*
83 *N14* **Meponda** Niassa, NE Mozambique *13°20′S 34°53′E*
98 *M8* **Meppel** Drenthe, NE Netherlands *52°42′N 06°12′E*
100 *E12* **Meppen** Niedersachsen, NW Germany *52°42′N 07°18′E*
Meqerghane, Sebkha *see* Mekerrhane, Sebkha
105 *T6* **Mequinenza, Embalse de** ▣ NE Spain
30 *M8* **Mequon** Wisconsin, N USA *43°13′N 87°57′W*
Mera *see* Maira
182 *D3* **Meramangye, Lake** *salt lake* South Australia
27 *W5* **Meramec River** Missouri, C USA
Meran *see* Merano
168 *K13* **Merangin** Sumatera, W Indonesia
106 *G5* **Merano** *Ger.* Meran. Trentino-Alto Adige, N Italy *46°40′N 11°10′E*
168 *K8* **Merapuh Lama** Pahang, Peninsular Malaysia *04°37′N 101°58′E*
106 *D7* **Merate** Lombardia, N Italy *45°42′N 09°26′E*
169 *U13* **Meratus, Pegunungan** ▲▲ Borneo, N Indonesia
171 *Y16* **Merauke, Sungai** Papua, E Indonesia
182 *L9* **Merbein** Victoria, SE Australia *34°11′S 142°03′E*
99 *F21* **Merbes-le-Château** Hainaut, S Belgium *50°19′N 04°09′E*
Merca *see* Marka
54 *C13* **Mercaderes** Cauca, SW Colombia *01°46′N 77°09′W*
Mercara *see* Madikeri
35 *P9* **Merced** California, W USA *37°17′N 120°30′W*
61 *C20* **Mercedes** Buenos Aires, E Argentina *34°42′S 59°30′W*
61 *D15* **Mercedes** Corrientes, NE Argentina *29°09′S 58°05′W*
61 *D19* **Mercedes** Soriano, SW Uruguay *33°16′S 58°01′W*
25 *S17* **Mercedes** Texas, SW USA *26°09′N 97°54′W*
Mercedes *see* Villa Mercedes
35 *R9* **Merced Peak** ▲ California, W USA *37°34′N 119°30′W*
35 *P9* **Merced River** California, W USA
18 *B13* **Mercer** Pennsylvania, NE USA *41°14′N 80°14′W*
99 *G18* **Merchtem** Vlaams Brabant, C Belgium *50°57′N 04°14′E*
15 *O13* **Mercier** Québec, SE Canada *45°15′N 73°45′W*
25 *Q9* **Mercury** Texas, SW USA *31°23′N 99°09′W*
184 *M5* **Mercury Islands** *island group* N New Zealand
19 *O9* **Meredith** New Hampshire, NE USA *43°36′N 71°28′W*
65 *B25* **Meredith, Cape** *var.* Cabo Belgrano. *headland* West Falkland, Falkland Islands *52°15′S 60°40′W*
37 *V6* **Meredith, Lake** ◎ Colorado, C USA
25 *N2* **Meredith, Lake** ▣ Texas, SW USA
81 *O16* **Mereeg** *var.* Mareeq, *It.* Meregh. Galguduud, E Somalia *03°47′N 47°19′E*
117 *V5* **Merefa** Kharkivs'ka Oblast', E Ukraine *49°49′N 36°05′E*
Meregh *see* Mereeg
99 *E17* **Merelbeke** Oost-Vlaanderen, NW Belgium *51°00′N 03°45′E*
Merend *see* Marand
167 *T12* **Mereuch** Môndól Kiri, E Cambodia *13°01′N 107°26′E*
Mergate *see* Margate
Mergui *see* Myeik
166 *M12* **Mergui Archipelago** *island group* S Burma (Myanmar)
114 *L12* **Meriç** Edirne, NW Turkey *41°12′N 26°24′E*
114 *L12* **Meriç** *Bul.* Maritsa, *Gk.* Évros; *anc.* Hebrus. SE Europe *see also* Évros/Maritsa
41 *X12* **Mérida** Yucatán, SW Mexico *20°58′N 89°35′W*
104 *J11* **Mérida** *anc.* Augusta Emerita. Extremadura, W Spain *38°55′N 06°20′W*
54 *I6* **Mérida** Mérida, W Venezuela *08°36′N 71°08′W*
54 *H7* **Mérida** *off.* Estado Mérida. ◐ *state* W Venezuela
Mérida, Estado *see* Mérida
18 *M13* **Meriden** Connecticut, NE USA *41°32′N 72°48′W*
22 *M5* **Meridian** Mississippi, S USA *32°24′N 88°43′W*
25 *S8* **Meridian** Texas, SW USA *31°56′N 97°40′W*
102 *J13* **Mérignac** Gironde, SW France *44°50′N 00°40′W*
102 *J13* **Mérignac** ✕ (Bordeaux) Gironde, SW France *44°51′N 00°44′W*
93 *J18* **Merikarvia** Länsi-Suomi, SW Finland *61°51′N 21°30′E*
183 *R12* **Merimbula** New South Wales, SE Australia *36°52′S 149°51′E*
182 *L9* **Meringur** Victoria, SE Australia *34°26′S 141°19′E*
Merín, Laguna *see* Mirim Lagoon
97 *I19* **Merioneth** *cultural region* W Wales, United Kingdom
188 *A11* **Merir** *island* Palau Islands, N Palau
188 *B17* **Merizo** SW Guam *13°15′N 144°40′E*
Merjama *see* Märjamaa
145 *S16* **Merke** Zhambyl, S Kazakhstan *42°48′N 73°10′E*
25 *P7* **Merkel** Texas, SW USA *32°28′N 100°00′W*
146 *E12* **Merkezi Garagumy** *var.* Mencezi Garagum, *Rus.* Tsentral'nyye Nizmennyye Garagumy. *desert* C Turkmenistan
119 *F15* **Merkinė** Alytus, S Lithuania *54°09′N 24°11′E*
99 *G16* **Merksem** Antwerpen, N Belgium *51°17′N 04°26′E*
99 *I15* **Merksplas** Antwerpen, N Belgium *51°22′N 04°54′E*
Merkulovichi *see* Myerkulavichy
119 *G15* **Merkys** S Lithuania
32 *F15* **Merlin** Oregon, NW USA *42°34′N 123°23′W*
61 *C20* **Merlo** Buenos Aires, E Argentina *34°39′S 58°45′W*
138 *G8* **Meron, Harei** *prev.* Haré Meron. ▲ N Israel *35°06′N 33°00′E*
74 *K6* **Merouane, Chott** *salt lake* NE Algeria
80 *F7* **Merowe** Northern, N Sudan *18°29′N 31°49′E*
180 *J12* **Merredin** Western Australia *31°31′S 118°18′E*
97 *I14* **Merrick** ▲ S Scotland, United Kingdom *55°09′N 04°28′W*
32 *H16* **Merrill** Oregon, NW USA *42°00′N 121°37′W*
30 *L5* **Merrill** Wisconsin, N USA *45°12′N 89°43′W*
31 *N11* **Merrillville** Indiana, N USA *41°28′N 87°19′W*
19 *O10* **Merrimack River** Massachusetts/New Hampshire, NE USA
28 *L12* **Merriman** Nebraska, C USA *42°54′N 101°42′W*
11 *N17* **Merritt** British Columbia, SW Canada *50°09′N 120°49′W*
23 *Y12* **Merritt Island** Florida, SE USA *28°21′N 80°42′W*
23 *Y11* **Merritt Island** *island* Florida, SE USA
28 *M12* **Merritt Reservoir** ▣ Nebraska, C USA
183 *S7* **Merriwa** New South Wales, SE Australia *32°09′S 150°24′E*
183 *O8* **Merriwagga** New South Wales, SE Australia *33°51′S 145°38′E*
22 *G8* **Merryville** Louisiana, S USA *30°45′N 93°32′W*
80 *K9* **Mersa Fat'ma** E Eritrea *14°52′N 40°16′E*
102 *M7* **Mer St-Aubin** Loir-et-Cher, C France *47°42′N 01°31′E*
75 *U7* **Mersá Maṭrûḥ** *var.* Maṭrûḥ; *anc.* Paraetonium. NW Egypt *31°21′N 27°15′E*
99 *M24* **Mersch** Luxembourg, C Luxembourg *49°45′N 06°06′E*
101 *M15* **Merseburg** Sachsen-Anhalt, C Germany *51°22′N 12°00′E*
Mersen *see* Meerssen
97 *K18* **Mersey** NW England, United Kingdom
136 *J17* **Mersin** *var.* İçel. İçel, S Turkey *36°50′N 34°39′E*
Mersin *see* İçel
168 *L9* **Mersing** Johor, Peninsular Malaysia *02°25′N 103°50′E*
118 *E8* **Mērsrags** Talsi, NW Latvia *57°21′N 23°05′E*
152 *G12* **Merta** *var.* Merta City. Rājasthān, N India *26°40′N 74°04′E*
Merta City *see* Merta
152 *F12* **Merta Road** Rājasthān, N India *26°42′N 73°54′E*
97 *J21* **Merthyr Tydfil** S Wales, United Kingdom *51°46′N 03°23′W*
104 *H13* **Mértola** Beja, S Portugal *37°38′N 07°40′W*
144 *G14* **Mertvyy Kultuk, Sor** *salt flat* SW Kazakhstan
195 *V16* **Mertz Glacier** *glacier* Antarctica
99 *M24* **Mertzig** Diekirch, C Luxembourg *49°50′N 06°00′E*
25 *O9* **Mertzon** Texas, SW USA *31°16′N 100°50′W*
103 *N4* **Méru** Oise, N France *49°15′N 02°07′E*
81 *I18* **Meru** Eastern, C Kenya *0°03′N 37°38′E*
81 *I20* **Meru, Mount** ▲ NE Tanzania *03°12′S 36°45′E*
Merv *see* Mary
Mervdasht *see* Marv Dasht
136 *K11* **Merzifon** Amasya, N Turkey *40°52′N 35°28′E*
101 *D20* **Merzig** Saarland, SW Germany *49°27′N 06°39′E*
36 *L14* **Mesa** Arizona, SW USA *33°25′N 111°49′W*
29 *V4* **Mesabi Range** ▲▲ Minnesota, N USA
54 *H6* **Mesa Bolívar** Mérida, NW Venezuela *08°30′N 71°38′W*
107 *Q18* **Mesagne** Puglia, SE Italy *40°33′N 17°49′E*
39 *P12* **Mesa Mountain** ▲ Alaska, USA *60°26′N 155°14′W*
115 *J25* **Mesará** *lowland* Kríti, Greece, E Mediterranean Sea
37 *S14* **Mescalero** New Mexico, SW USA *33°09′N 105°46′W*
101 *G15* **Meschede** Nordrhein-Westfalen, W Germany *51°21′N 08°16′E*
137 *Q12* **Mescit Dağları** ▲▲ NE Turkey
189 *V13* **Mesegon** *island* Chuuk, C Micronesia
Meseritz *see* Międzyrzecz
54 *F11* **Mesetas** Meta, C Colombia *03°14′N 74°09′W*
Meshchera Lowland *see* Meshcherskaya Nizmennost'
Meshcherskaya Nizina *see* Meshcherskaya Nizmennost'
126 *M4* **Meshcherskaya Nizmennost'** *var.* Meshcherskaya Nizina, *Eng.* Meshchera Lowland. *basin* W Russian Federation
126 *J5* **Meshchovsk** Kaluzhskaya Oblast', W Russian Federation *54°21′N 35°23′E*
125 *R9* **Meshchura** Respublika Komi, NW Russian Federation *63°18′N 50°56′E*
Meshed *see* Mashhad
Meshed-i-Sar *see* Bābolsar
80 *E13* **Meshra'er Req** Warab, S Sudan *08°30′N 29°27′E*
37 *R15* **Mesilla** New Mexico, SW USA *32°15′N 106°49′W*
108 *H10* **Mesocco** *Ger.* Misox. Ticino, S Switzerland *46°18′N 09°13′E*
115 *D18* **Mesolóngi** *prev.* Mesolóngion. Dytikí Ellás, W Greece *38°21′N 21°26′E*
Mesolóngion *see* Mesolóngi
14 *E8* **Mesomikenda Lake** ◎ Ontario, S Canada
61 *D15* **Mesopotamia** *var.* Mesopotamia Argentina. *physical region* NE Argentina
Mesopotamia Argentina *see* Mesopotamia
35 *Y10* **Mesquite** Nevada, W USA *36°47′N 114°04′W*
82 *Q13* **Messalo, Rio** *var.* Mualo. NE Mozambique
Messana/Messene *see* Messina
99 *L25* **Messancy** Luxembourg, SE Belgium *49°36′N 05°49′E*
107 *M23* **Messina** *var.* Messana, Messene; *anc.* Zancle. Sicilia, Italy, C Mediterranean Sea *38°12′N 15°33′E*
Messina *see* Musina
Messina, Strait of *see* Messina, Stretto di
107 *M23* **Messina, Stretto di** *Eng.* Strait of Messina. *strait* SW Italy
115 *E21* **Messíni** Pelopónnisos, S Greece *37°03′N 22°00′E*
115 *E21* **Messinía** *peninsula* S Greece
115 *E22* **Messiniakós Kólpos** *gulf* S Greece
122 *J8* **Messoyakha** N Russian Federation
114 *H11* **Mesta** *Gk.* Néstos, *Turk.* Kara Su. Bulgaria/Greece *see also* Néstos
Mesta *see* Néstos
Mestghanem *see* Mostaganem
137 *R8* **Mestia** *var.* Mestiya. N Georgia *43°03′N 42°50′E*
Mestiya *see* Mestia
115 *K18* **Mestón, Akrotírio** *cape* Chíos, E Greece
106 *H8* **Mestre** Veneto, NE Italy *45°30′N 12°14′E*
59 *M16* **Mestre, Espigão** ▲▲ E Brazil
169 *N14* **Mesuji** Sumatera, W Indonesia
Mesule *see* Grosser Möseler
10 *J10* **Meszah Peak** ▲ British Columbia, W Canada *58°31′N 131°28′W*
54 *G11* **Meta** *off.* Departamento del Meta. ◐ *province* C Colombia
15 *Q8* **Metabetchouane** Québec, SE Canada
Meta, Departamento del *see* Meta
9 *S7* **Meta Incognita Peninsula** *peninsula* Baffin Island, Nunavut, NE Canada
22 *K9* **Metairie** Louisiana, S USA *29°58′N 90°09′W*
32 *M6* **Metaline Falls** Washington, NW USA *48°51′N 117°21′W*
62 *K6* **Metán** Salta, N Argentina *25°29′S 64°57′W*
82 *N13* **Metangula** Niassa, N Mozambique *12°41′S 34°50′E*
42 *E7* **Metapán** Santa Ana, NW El Salvador *14°20′N 89°28′W*
54 *K9* **Meta, Río** Colombia/Venezuela
106 *I11* **Metauro** C Italy
80 *H11* **Metema** Āmara, N Ethiopia *12°53′N 36°10′E*
115 *D15* **Metéora** *religious building* Thessalía, C Greece
65 *O20* **Meteor Rise** *undersea feature* SW Indian Ocean *46°00′S 05°30′E*
186 *G5* **Meteran** New Hanover, NE Papua New Guinea *02°40′S 150°12′E*
Meterlam *see* Mehtar Lām
115 *G20* **Methanon** *peninsula* S Greece
Methariam/Metharlam *see* Mehtar Lām
32 *J6* **Methow River** Washington, NW USA
19 *O10* **Methuen** Massachusetts, NE USA *42°43′N 71°10′W*
185 *G19* **Methven** Canterbury, South Island, New Zealand *43°37′S 171°38′E*
Metis *see* Metz
113 *G15* **Metković** Dubrovnik-Neretva, SE Croatia *43°02′N 17°37′E*
39 *Y14* **Metlakatla** Annette Island, Alaska, USA *55°07′N 131°34′W*
109 *V13* **Metlika** *Ger.* Möttling. SE Slovenia *45°38′N 15°18′E*
109 *T8* **Metnitz** Kärnten, S Austria *46°58′N 14°09′E*
27 *W12* **Meto, Bayou** Arkansas, C USA
168 *M15* **Metro** Sumatera, W Indonesia *05°05′S 105°20′E*
30 *M17* **Metropolis** Illinois, N USA *37°09′N 88°43′W*
Metropolitan *see* Santiago
35 *N8* **Metropolitan Oakland** ✕ California, W USA *37°42′N 122°13′W*
115 *D15* **Métsovo** *prev.* Métsovon. Ípeiros, C Greece *39°47′N 21°12′E*
Métsovon *see* Métsovo
23 *V5* **Metter** Georgia, SE USA *32°24′N 82°03′W*
99 *H21* **Mettet** Namur, S Belgium *50°19′N 04°43′E*
101 *D20* **Mettlach** Saarland, SW Germany *49°28′N 06°37′E*
Mettu *see* Metu
80 *H13* **Metu** *var.* Mattu, Mettu. Oromīya, C Ethiopia *08°18′N 35°39′E*
138 *G8* **Metula** *prev.* Metulla. Northern, N Israel *33°16′N 35°35′E*
169 *T10* **Metulang** Borneo, N Indonesia *01°28′N 114°40′E*
Metulla *see* Metula
103 *T4* **Metz** *anc.* Divodurum Mediomatricum, Mediomatrica, Metis. Moselle, NE France *49°07′N 06°09′E*
101 *H22* **Metzingen** Baden-Württemberg, S Germany *48°31′N 09°16′E*
168 *G8* **Meulaboh** Sumatera, W Indonesia *04°10′N 96°09′E*
99 *D18* **Meulebeke** West-Vlaanderen, W Belgium *50°57′N 03°18′E*
103 *U6* **Meurthe** NE France
103 *S5* **Meurthe-et-Moselle** ◐ *department* NE France
103 *S4* **Meuse** ◐ *department* NE France
84 *F10* **Meuse** *Dut.* Maas. W Europe *see also* Maas
Meuse *see* Maas
Mexcala, Río *see* Balsas, Río
25 *U8* **Mexia** Texas, SW USA *31°40′N 96°28′W*
58 *K11* **Mexiana, Ilha** *island* NE Brazil
40 *C1* **Mexicali** Baja California Norte, NW Mexico *32°34′N 115°26′W*
Mexicanos, Estados Unidos *see* Mexico
41 *O14* **México** *var.* Ciudad de México, *Eng.* Mexico City. ● (Mexico) México, C Mexico *19°26′N 99°08′W*
27 *V4* **Mexico** Missouri, C USA *19°10′N 99°04′W*
18 *H9* **Mexico** New York, NE USA *43°27′N 76°14′W*
40 *L7* **Mexico** *off.* United Mexican States, *var.* Méjico, México, *Sp.* Estados Unidos Mexicanos. ◆ *federal republic* N Central America
41 *O13* **México** ◐ *state* S Mexico
México *see* Mexico
0 *J13* **Mexico Basin** *var.* Sigsbee Deep. *undersea feature* C Gulf of Mexico *25°00′N 92°00′W*
Mexico City *see* México
México, Golfo de *see* Mexico, Gulf of
44 *B4* **Mexico, Gulf of** *Sp.* Golfo de México. *gulf* W Atlantic Ocean
Meyadine *see* Al Mayādīn
143 *Q9* **Meybod** Yazd, C Iran *32°16′N 53°59′E*
149 *Q5* **Meydān Shahr** *var.* Maydān Shahr. Vardak, E Afghanistan *34°27′N 68°48′E*
39 *Y14* **Meyers Chuck** Etolin Island, Alaska, USA *55°44′N 132°15′W*
148 *M3* **Meymaneh** *var.* Maimāna, Maymana. Fāryāb, NW Afghanistan *35°57′N 64°48′E*
143 *N7* **Meymeh** Eşfahān, C Iran *33°29′N 51°09′E*
123 *V7* **Meynypil'gyno** Chukotskiy Avtonomnyy Okrug, NE Russian Federation *62°33′N 177°00′E*
108 *A10* **Meyrin** Genève, SW Switzerland *46°14′N 06°05′E*
166 *L7* **Mezaligon** Ayeyarwady, SW Burma (Myanmar) *17°53′N 95°12′E*
41 *O15* **Mezcala** Guerrero, S Mexico *17°55′N 99°34′W*
114 *H8* **Mezdra** Vratsa, NW Bulgaria *43°08′N 23°42′E*
103 *P16* **Mèze** Hérault, S France *43°26′N 03°37′E*
125 *O6* **Mezen'** Arkhangel'skaya Oblast', NW Russian Federation *65°54′N 44°10′E*
125 *P8* **Mezen'** NW Russian Federation
Mezen, Bay of *see* Mezenskaya Guba
103 *Q13* **Mézenc, Mont** ▲ C France *44°57′N 04°15′E*
125 *O8* **Mezenskaya Guba** *var.* Bay of Mezen. *bay* NW Russian Federation
Mezha *see* Myazha
122 *H6* **Mezhdusharskiy, Ostrov** *island* Novaya Zemlya, N Russian Federation
Mezhëvo *see* Myezhava
Mezhgor'ye *see* Mizhhir"ya
117 *V8* **Mezhova** Dnipropetrovs'ka Oblast', E Ukraine *48°15′N 36°44′E*
10 *J12* **Meziadin Junction** British Columbia, W Canada *56°06′N 129°15′W*
111 *G16* **Mezileské Sedlo** *var.* Przełęcz Międzyleska. *pass* Czech Republic/Poland
102 *L14* **Mézin** Lot-et-Garonne, SW France *44°03′N 00°16′E*
111 *M24* **Mezőberény** Békés, SE Hungary *46°49′N 21°00′E*
111 *M25* **Mezőhegyes** Békés, SE Hungary *46°20′N 20°48′E*
111 *M25* **Mezőkovácsháza** Békés, SE Hungary *46°24′N 20°52′E*
111 *M21* **Mezőkövesd** Borsod-Abaúj-Zemplén, NE Hungary *47°49′N 20°32′E*
Mezőtelegd *see* Tileagd
111 *M23* **Mezőtúr** Jász-Nagykun-Szolnok, E Hungary *47°N 20°37′E*
40 *K10* **Mezquital** Durango, C Mexico *23°31′N 104°19′W*
106 *G6* **Mezzolombardo** Trentino-Alto Adige, N Italy *46°13′N 11°08′E*
82 *L13* **Mfuwe** Northern, N Zambia *13°00′S 31°45′E*
121 *O15* **Mġarr** Gozo, N Malta *36°01′N 14°18′E*
126 *H6* **Mglin** Bryanskaya Oblast', W Russian Federation *53°01′N 32°54′E*
Mhálanna, Cionn *see* Malin Head
154 *G10* **Mhow** Madhya Pradesh, C India *22°32′N 75°49′E*
Miadzioł Nowy *see* Myadzyel
171 *O6* **Miagao** Panay Island, C Philippines *10°40′N 122°15′E*
41 *R17* **Miahuatlán** *var.* Miahuatlán de Porfirio Díaz. Oaxaca, SE Mexico *16°21′N 96°36′W*
Miahuatlán de Porfirio Díaz *see* Miahuatlán
104 *K10* **Miajadas** Extremadura, W Spain *39°10′N 05°54′W*
Miajlar *see* Myājlār
36 *M14* **Miami** Arizona, SW USA *33°23′N 110°53′W*
23 *Z16* **Miami** Florida, SE USA *25°46′N 80°12′W*
27 *R8* **Miami** Oklahoma, C USA *36°53′N 94°54′W*
25 *O2* **Miami** Texas, SW USA *35°42′N 100°37′W*
23 *Z16* **Miami** ✕ Florida, SE USA *25°47′N 80°16′W*
23 *Z16* **Miami Beach** Florida, SE USA *25°47′N 80°08′W*
23 *Y15* **Miami Canal** *canal* Florida, SE USA
31 *R14* **Miamisburg** Ohio, N USA *39°38′N 84°17′W*
149 *U10* **Miān Channūn** Punjab, E Pakistan *30°24′N 72°27′E*
142 *J4* **Mīāndowāb** *var.* Mianduab, Miyāndoāb. Āzarbāyjān-e Gharbī, NW Iran *36°57′N 46°06′E*
172 *H5* **Miandrivazo** Toliara, C Madagascar *19°31′S 45°29′E*
Mianduab *see* Mīāndowāb
142 *K3* **Mīāneh** *var.* Miyāneh. Āzarbāyjān-e Sharqī, NW Iran *37°23′N 47°45′E*
149 *O16* **Miāni Hōr** *lagoon* S Pakistan
160 *G10* **Mianning** Sichuan, C China *28°34′N 102°12′E*
149 *T7* **Miānwāli** Punjab, NE Pakistan *32°32′N 71°33′E*
160 *J7* **Mianxian** *var.* Mian Xian. Shaanxi, C China *33°12′N 106°36′E*
Mian Xian *see* Mianxian
160 *I8* **Mianyang** Sichuan, C China *31°29′N 104°43′E*
Mianyang *see* Xiantao
161 *R3* **Miaodao Qundao** *island group* E China
161 *S13* **Miaoli** N Taiwan *24°33′N 120°48′E*
122 *F11* **Miass** Chelyabinskaya Oblast', C Russian Federation *55°00′N 59°55′E*
110 *G8* **Miastko** *Ger.* Rummelsburg in Pommern. Pomorskie, N Poland *54°N 16°58′E*
Miava *see* Myjava
11 *O15* **Mica Creek** British Columbia, SW Canada *51°58′N 118°29′W*
160 *J7* **Micang Shan** ▲▲ C China
Mi Chai *see* Nong Khai
111 *O19* **Michalovce** *Ger.* Grossmichel, *Hung.* Nagymihály. Košický Kraj, E Slovakia *48°46′N 21°55′E*
99 *M20* **Michel, Baraque** *hill* E Belgium
39 *S5* **Michelson, Mount** ▲ Alaska, USA *69°19′N 144°16′W*
45 *P9* **Miches** E Dominican Republic *18°59′N 69°03′W*
30 *M4* **Michigamme, Lake** ◎ Michigan, N USA
30 *M4* **Michigamme Reservoir** ▣ Michigan, N USA
31 *N4* **Michigamme River** Michigan, N USA
31 *O7* **Michigan** *off.* State of Michigan, *also known as* Great Lakes State, Lake State, Wolverine State. ◐ *state* N USA
31 *O11* **Michigan City** Indiana, N USA *41°43′N 86°52′W*
31 *O8* **Michigan, Lake** ◎ N USA
31 *P2* **Michipicoten Bay** *lake bay* Ontario, N Canada
14 *A8* **Michipicoten Island** *island* Ontario, S Canada
14 *B7* **Michipicoten River** Ontario, S Canada *47°56′N 84°48′W*
Michurin *see* Tsarevo
126 *M6* **Michurinsk** Tambovskaya Oblast', W Russian Federation *52°56′N 40°31′E*
Mico, Punta/Mico, Punto *see* Monkey Point
42 *L10* **Mico, Río** SE Nicaragua
45 *T12* **Micoud** SE Saint Lucia *13°49′N 60°54′W*
189 *N16* **Micronesia** *off.* Federated States of Micronesia. ◆ *federation* W Pacific Ocean
175 *P4* **Micronesia** *island group* W Pacific Ocean
Micronesia, Federated States of *see* Micronesia
169 *O9* **Midai, Pulau** *island* Kepulauan Natuna, W Indonesia
Mid-Atlantic Cordillera *see* Mid-Atlantic Ridge
65 *M17* **Mid-Atlantic Ridge** *var.* Mid-Atlantic Cordillera, Mid-Atlantic Rise, Mid-Atlantic Swell. *undersea feature* Atlantic Ocean *0°00′N 20°00′W*
Mid-Atlantic Rise/Mid-Atlantic Swell *see* Mid-Atlantic Ridge
99 *E15* **Middelburg** Zeeland, SW Netherlands *51°30′N 03°36′E*
83 *H24* **Middelburg** Eastern Cape, S South Africa *31°28′S 25°01′E*
83 *K21* **Middelburg** Mpumalanga, NE South Africa *25°47′S 29°28′E*
95 *G23* **Middelfart** Fyn, C Denmark *55°30′N 09°44′E*
98 *G13* **Middelharnis** Zuid-Holland, SW Netherlands *51°45′N 04°10′E*
99 *B16* **Middelkerke** West-Vlaanderen, W Belgium *51°12′N 02°51′E*
98 *I9* **Middenbeemster** Noord-Holland, C Netherlands *52°33′N 04°55′E*
98 *I8* **Middenmeer** Noord-Holland, NW Netherlands *52°48′N 04°58′E*
35 *Q2* **Middle Alkali Lake** ◎ California, W USA
193 *S6* **Middle America Trench** *undersea feature* E Pacific Ocean *15°00′N 95°00′W*
151 *P19* **Middle Andaman** *island* Andaman Islands, India, NE Indian Ocean
Middle Atlas *see* Moyen Atlas
21 *R3* **Middlebourne** West Virginia, NE USA *39°30′N 80°53′W*
23 *W9* **Middleburg** Florida, SE USA *30°03′N 81°55′W*
Middleburg Island *see* 'Eua
Middle Caicos *see* Grand Caicos
25 *N8* **Middle Concho River** Texas, SW USA
Middle Congo *see* Congo (Republic of)
39 *R6* **Middle Fork Chandalar River** Alaska, USA
39 *Q7* **Middle Fork Koyukuk River** Alaska, USA
33 *O12* **Middle Fork Salmon River** Idaho, NW USA
11 *T15* **Middle Lake** Saskatchewan, S Canada *52°31′N 105°16′W*
28 *L13* **Middle Loup River** Nebraska, C USA
185 *E22* **Middlemarch** Otago, South Island, New Zealand *45°30′S 170°07′E*
31 *T15* **Middleport** Ohio, N USA *39°00′N 82°03′W*
29 *U14* **Middle Raccoon River** Iowa, C USA
29 *R3* **Middle River** Minnesota, N USA
21 *N8* **Middlesboro** Kentucky, S USA *36°37′N 83°42′W*
97 *M15* **Middlesbrough** N England, United Kingdom *54°35′N 01°14′W*
42 *G3* **Middlesex** Stann Creek, C Belize *17°00′N 88°31′W*
97 *N22* **Middlesex** *cultural region* SE England, United Kingdom
13 *P15* **Middleton** Nova Scotia, SE Canada *44°56′N 65°04′W*
20 *F10* **Middleton** Tennessee, S USA *35°05′N 88°57′W*
30 *L9* **Middleton** Wisconsin, N USA *43°06′N 89°30′W*
39 *S13* **Middleton Island** *island* Alaska, USA
34 *M7* **Middletown** California, W USA *38°44′N 122°39′W*
21 *Y2* **Middletown** Delaware, NE USA *39°25′N 75°39′W*
18 *K15* **Middletown** New Jersey, NE USA *40°23′N 74°08′W*
18 *K13* **Middletown** New York, NE USA *41°27′N 74°25′W*
31 *R14* **Middletown** Ohio, N USA *39°33′N 84°19′W*
18 *G15* **Middletown** Pennsylvania, NE USA *40°11′N 76°42′W*
141 *N14* **Mīdī** *var.* Maydī. NW Yemen *16°18′N 42°51′E*
103 *O16* **Midi, Canal du** *canal* S France
102 *K17* **Midi de Bigorre, Pic du** ▲ S France *42°57′N 00°08′E*
102 *K17* **Midi d'Ossau, Pic du** ▲ SW France *42°51′N 00°27′W*
173 *R7* **Mid-Indian Basin** *undersea feature* N Indian Ocean *10°00′S 80°00′E*
173 *P7* **Mid-Indian Ridge** *var.* Central Indian Ridge. *undersea feature* C Indian Ocean *12°00′S 66°00′E*
103 *N14* **Midi-Pyrénées** ◐ *region* S France
25 *N8* **Midkiff** Texas, SW USA *31°35′N 101°51′W*
14 *G13* **Midland** Ontario, S Canada *44°45′N 79°53′W*
31 *R8* **Midland** Michigan, N USA *43°37′N 84°15′W*
28 *M10* **Midland** South Dakota, N USA *44°04′N 101°07′W*
24 *M8* **Midland** Texas, SW USA *32°N 102°05′W*
83 *K17* **Midlands** ◐ *province* C Zimbabwe
97 *D21* **Midleton** *Ir.* Mainistir na Corann. SW Ireland *51°55′N 08°10′W*
25 *T7* **Midlothian** Texas, SW USA *32°28′N 96°59′W*
96 *K12* **Midlothian** *cultural region* S Scotland, United Kingdom
172 *I7* **Midongy Atsimo** Fianarantsoa, S Madagascar *21°58′S 47°47′E*
102 *K15* **Midou** SW France
192 *J6* **Mid-Pacific Mountains** *var.* Mid-Pacific Seamounts. *undersea feature* NW Pacific Ocean *20°00′N 178°00′W*
Mid-Pacific Seamounts *see* Mid-Pacific Mountains
171 *Q7* **Midsayap** Mindanao, S Philippines *07°12′N 124°31′E*
36 *L3* **Midway** Utah, W USA *40°30′N 111°28′W*
192 *L5* **Midway Islands** ◇ *US territory* C Pacific Ocean
33 *X14* **Midwest** Wyoming, C USA *43°24′N 106°15′W*
27 *N10* **Midwest City** Oklahoma, C USA *35°28′N 98°24′W*
152 *M10* **Mid Western** ◐ *zone* W Nepal
98 *P5* **Midwolda** Groningen, NE Netherlands *53°12′N 07°00′E*
137 *Q16* **Midyat** Mardin, SE Turkey *37°25′N 41°20′E*
114 *F8* **Midzhur** *SCr.* Midžor. ▲ Bulgaria/Serbia *43°24′N 22°41′E* *see also* Midžor
Midzhur *see* Midžor
113 *Q14* **Midžor** *Bul.* Midzhur. ▲ Bulgaria/Serbia *43°24′N 22°40′E* *see also* Midzhur
Midžor *see* Midzhur
164 *K14* **Mie** *off.* Mie-ken. ◐ *prefecture* Honshū, SW Japan
111 *L16* **Miechów** Małopolskie, S Poland *50°21′N 20°01′E*
110 *F11* **Międzychód** *Ger.* Mitteldorf. Wielkopolskie, C Poland *52°36′N 15°53′E*
Międzyleska, Przełęcz *see* Mezileské Sedlo
110 *O12* **Międzyrzec Podlaski** Lubelskie, E Poland *52°N 22°47′E*
110 *E11* **Międzyrzecz** *Ger.* Meseritz. Lubuskie, W Poland *52°26′N 15°33′E*
Mie-ken *see* Mie
102 *L16* **Miélan** Gers, S France *43°26′N 00°19′E*
111 *N16* **Mielec** Podkarpackie, SE Poland *50°18′N 21°27′E*
95 *L21* **Mien** ◎ S Sweden
41 *O8* **Mier** Tamaulipas, C Mexico *26°28′N 99°10′W*
116 *J11* **Miercurea-Ciuc** *Ger.* Szeklerburg, *Hung.* Csíkszereda. Harghita, C Romania *46°24′N 25°48′E*
Mieresch *see* Maros/Mureş
Mieres del Camín *see* Mieres del Camino
104 *K2* **Mieres del Camino** *var.* Mieres del Camín. Asturias, NW Spain *43°15′N 05°46′W*
99 *K15* **Mierlo** Noord-Brabant, SE Netherlands *51°27′N 05°37′E*
41 *O10* **Mier y Noriega** Nuevo León, NE Mexico *23°24′N 100°06′W*
Mies *see* Stříbro
80 *K13* **Mī'ēso** *var.* Meheso, Miesso. Oromīya, C Ethiopia *09°13′N 40°47′E*
Miesso *see* Mī'ēso
110 *D10* **Mieszkowice** *Ger.* Bärwalde Neumark. Zachodnio-pomorskie, W Poland *52°45′N 14°24′E*
18 *G14* **Mifflinburg** Pennsylvania, NE USA *40°55′N 77°03′W*
18 *F14* **Mifflintown** Pennsylvania, NE USA *40°34′N 77°24′W*
138 *F8* **Mifrats Hefa** *Eng.* Bay of Haifa; *prev.* MifrazHefa. *bay* N Israel
41 *R15* **Miguel Alemán, Presa** ▣ SE Mexico
40 *L9* **Miguel Asua** *var.* Miguel Auza. Zacatecas, C Mexico *24°17′N 103°29′W*
Miguel Auza *see* Miguel Asua
43 *S15* **Miguel de la Borda** *var.* Donoso. Colón, C Panama *09°09′N 80°20′W*
41 *N13* **Miguel Hidalgo** ✕ (Guadalajara) Jalisco, SW Mexico *20°52′N 101°09′W*
40 *H7* **Miguel Hidalgo, Presa** ▣ W Mexico
116 *J14* **Mihăileşti** Giurgiu, S Romania *44°20′N 25°54′E*
116 *M14* **Mihail Kogălniceanu** *var.* Kogălniceanu; *prev.* Caramurat, Ferdinand. Constanţa, SE Romania *44°22′N 28°27′E*
117 *N14* **Mihai Viteazu** Constanţa, SE Romania *44°37′N 28°41′E*
136 *G12* **Mihalıççık** Eskişehir, NW Turkey *39°52′N 31°30′E*
164 *G13* **Mihara** Hiroshima, Honshū, SW Japan *34°24′N 133°04′E*
165 *N14* **Mihara-yama** Miyako-jima, SE Japan *34°43′N 139°23′E*
105 *S8* **Mijares** E Spain
98 *I11* **Mijdrecht** Utrecht, C Netherlands *52°12′N 04°52′E*
165 *S4* **Mikasa** Hokkaidō, NE Japan *43°15′N 141°57′E*
Mikashevichi *see* Mikashevichy
119 *K19* **Mikashevichy** *Pol.* Mikaszewicze, *Rus.* Mikashevichi. Brestskaya Voblasts', SW Belarus *52°13′N 27°28′E*
Mikaszewicze *see* Mikashevichy
126 *L5* **Mikhaylov** Ryazanskaya Oblast', W Russian Federation *54°12′N 39°03′E*
Mikhaylovgrad *see* Montana
195 *Z8* **Mikhaylov Island** *island* Antarctica
145 *T6* **Mikhaylovka** Pavlodar, N Kazakhstan *53°49′N 76°31′E*
127 *N9* **Mikhaylovka** Volgogradskaya Oblast', SW Russian Federation *50°06′N 43°17′E*
Mikhaylovka *see* Mykhaylivka
81 *K24* **Mikindani** Mtwara, SE Tanzania *10°16′S 40°05′E*
93 *N18* **Mikkeli** *Swe.* Sankt Michel. Itä-Suomi, SE Finland *61°41′N 27°14′E*
110 *M8* **Mikołajki** *Ger.* Nikolaiken. Warmińsko-Mazurskie, NE Poland *53°49′N 21°31′E*
Míkonos *see* Mýkonos
114 *I9* **Mikre** Lovech, N Bulgaria *43°01′N 24°31′E*
114 *C13* **Mikrí Préspa, Límni** ◎ N Greece
125 *P4* **Mikulkin, Mys** *headland* NW Russian Federation *67°50′N 46°36′E*
81 *I23* **Mikumi** Morogoro, SE Tanzania *07°22′S 37°00′E*
125 *R10* **Mikun'** Respublika Komi, NW Russian Federation *62°20′N 50°02′E*
164 *K13* **Mikuni** Fukui, Honshū, SW Japan *36°12′N 136°09′E*
165 *X13* **Mikura-jima** *island* E Japan
29 *V7* **Milaca** Minnesota, N USA *45°45′N 93°40′W*
62 *J10* **Milagro** La Rioja, C Argentina *31°00′S 66°01′W*
56 *B7* **Milagro** Guayas, SW Ecuador *02°11′S 79°36′W*
31 *P4* **Milakokia Lake** ◎ Michigan, N USA
30 *J1* **Milan** Illinois, N USA *41°27′N 90°33′W*
31 *R10* **Milan** Michigan, N USA *42°05′N 83°40′W*
27 *T2* **Milan** Missouri, C USA *40°12′N 93°08′W*
37 *Q11* **Milan** New Mexico, SW USA *35°10′N 107°53′W*
20 *G9* **Milan** Tennessee, S USA *35°55′N 88°45′W*
Milan *see* Milano
95 *F15* **Miland** Telemark, S Norway *59°57′N 08°48′E*
83 *N15* **Milange** Zambézia, NE Mozambique *16°09′S 35°44′E*

◆ Country
● Country Capital
◇ Dependent Territory
○ Dependent Territory Capital
◐ Administrative Regions
✕ International Airport
▲ Mountain
▲▲ Mountain Range
Volcano
River
◎ Lake
▣ Reservoir

106 D8 **Milano** Eng. Milan, Ger. Mailand; anc. Mediolanum. Lombardia, N Italy 45°28´N 09°10´E
25 U10 **Milano** Texas, SW USA 30°42´N 96°51´W
136 C15 **Milas** Muğla, SW Turkey 37°17´N 27°46´E
119 K21 **Milashavichy** Rus. Milashevichi. Homyel'skaya Voblasts', SE Belarus 51°39´N 27°56´E
Milashevichi see Milashavichy
119 I18 **Milavidy** Rus. Milovidy. Brestskaya Voblasts', SW Belarus 52°54´N 25°51´E
107 L23 **Milazzo** anc. Mylae. Sicilia, Italy, C Mediterranean Sea 38°13´N 15°15´E
29 R8 **Milbank** South Dakota, N USA 45°12´N 96°36´W
19 T7 **Milbridge** Maine, NE USA 44°31´N 67°55´W
100 L11 **Milde** ≈ C Germany
14 F14 **Mildmay** Ontario, S Canada 44°03´N 81°07´W
182 L9 **Mildura** Victoria, SE Australia 34°13´S 142°09´E
137 X12 **Mil Düzü** Rus. Mil'skaya Ravnina, Mil'skaya Step'. physical region C Azerbaijan
160 H13 **Mile** var. Miyang. Yunnan, SW China 24°28´N 103°26´E
Mile see Mili Atoll
181 Y10 **Miles** Queensland, E Australia 26°41´S 150°15´E
25 P8 **Miles** Texas, SW USA 31°36´N 100°10´W
33 X9 **Miles City** Montana, NW USA 46°24´N 105°48´W
11 U17 **Milestone** Saskatchewan, S Canada 50°00´N 104°24´W
107 N22 **Mileto** Calabria, SW Italy 38°35´N 16°03´E
107 K16 **Miletto, Monte** ▲ C Italy 41°28´N 14°21´E
18 M13 **Milford** Connecticut, NE USA 41°12´N 73°01´W
21 Y3 **Milford** var. Milford City. Delaware, NE USA 38°54´N 75°25´W
29 T11 **Milford** Iowa, C USA 43°19´N 95°09´W
19 S6 **Milford** Maine, NE USA 44°57´N 68°37´W
29 R16 **Milford** Nebraska, C USA 40°46´N 97°03´W
19 O10 **Milford** New Hampshire, NE USA 42°49´N 71°38´W
18 J13 **Milford** Pennsylvania, NE USA 41°20´N 74°48´W
25 T7 **Milford** Texas, SW USA 32°07´N 96°57´W
36 K6 **Milford** Utah, W USA 38°22´N 112°57´W
Milford see Milford Haven
Milford City see Milford
97 H21 **Milford Haven** prev. Milford. SW Wales, United Kingdom 51°44´N 05°02´W
27 O4 **Milford Lake** ⊠ Kansas, C USA
185 B21 **Milford Sound** Southland, South Island, New Zealand 44°41´S 167°57´E
185 B21 **Milford Sound** inlet South Island, New Zealand
Milhau see Millau
Milḩ, Baḩr al see Razāzah, Buḩayrat ar
139 T10 **Milḩ, Wādī al** dry watercourse S Iraq
189 W8 **Mili Atoll** var. Mile. atoll Ratak Chain, SE Marshall Islands
110 H13 **Milicz** Dolnośląskie, SW Poland 51°32´N 17°15´E
107 L25 **Militello in Val di Catania** Sicilia, Italy, C Mediterranean Sea 37°17´N 14°47´E
11 R17 **Milk River** Alberta, SW Canada 49°10´N 112°06´W
44 J13 **Milk River** ≈ C Jamaica
33 W7 **Milk River** ≈ Montana, NW USA
80 D9 **Milk, Wadi el** var. Wadi al Malik. ≈ C Sudan
99 L14 **Mill** Noord-Brabant, SE Netherlands 51°42´N 05°46´E
103 P14 **Millau** var. Milhau; anc. Æmilianum. Aveyron, S France 44°06´N 03°05´E
14 I14 **Millbrook** Ontario, SE Canada 44°09´N 78°26´W
23 U4 **Milledgeville** Georgia, SE USA 33°04´N 83°13´W
12 C12 **Mille Lacs, Lac des** ◎ Ontario, S Canada
29 V6 **Mille Lacs Lake** ◎ Minnesota, N USA
23 V4 **Millen** Georgia, SE USA 32°50´N 81°56´W
191 Y5 **Millennium Island** prev. Caroline Island, Thornton Island. atoll Line Islands, E Kiribati
29 O9 **Miller** South Dakota, N USA 44°31´N 98°59´W
30 K5 **Miller Dam Flowage** ◎ Wisconsin, N USA
39 U12 **Miller, Mount** ▲ Alaska, USA 60°29´N 142°16´W
126 L10 **Millerovo** Rostovskaya Oblast', SW Russian Federation 48°57´N 40°26´E
37 N17 **Miller Peak** ▲ Arizona, SW USA 31°23´N 110°17´W
31 T12 **Millersburg** Ohio, N USA 40°33´N 81°55´W
18 G15 **Millersburg** Pennsylvania, NE USA 40°31´N 76°56´W
185 D23 **Millers Flat** Otago, South Island, New Zealand 45°42´S 169°25´E
25 Q8 **Millersview** Texas, SW USA 31°26´N 99°44´W
106 B10 **Millesimo** Piemonte, NE Italy 44°24´N 08°09´E
12 C12 **Milles Lacs, Lac des** ◎ Ontario, SW Canada
25 Q13 **Millett** Texas, SW USA 28°33´N 99°10´W
103 N11 **Millevaches, Plateau de** plateau C France
182 K12 **Millicent** South Australia 37°29´S 140°01´E
98 M13 **Millingen aan den Rijn** Gelderland, SE Netherlands 51°52´N 06°02´E
20 E10 **Millington** Tennessee, S USA 35°20´N 89°54´W
19 R4 **Millinocket** Maine, NE USA 45°38´N 68°45´W
19 R4 **Millinocket Lake** ◎ Maine, NE USA
195 Z11 **Mill Island** island Antarctica
183 T3 **Millmerran** Queensland, E Australia 27°53´S 151°15´E
109 R9 **Millstatt** Kärnten, S Austria 46°45´N 13°36´E
97 B19 **Milltown Malbay** Ir. Sráid na Cathrach. W Ireland 52°51´N 09°23´W
18 J17 **Millville** New Jersey, NE USA 39°24´N 75°01´W
27 S13 **Millwood Lake** ⊠ Arkansas, C USA
Milne Bank see Milne Seamounts
186 G10 **Milne Bay** ◈ province SE Papua New Guinea
64 J8 **Milne Seamounts** var. Milne Bank. undersea feature N Atlantic Ocean
29 Q6 **Milnor** North Dakota, N USA 46°15´N 97°27´W
19 R5 **Milo** Maine, NE USA 45°15´N 69°01´W
115 I22 **Mílos** island Kykládes, Greece, Aegean Sea
Mílos see Pláka
110 H11 **Miłosław** Wielkopolskie, C Poland 52°13´N 17°28´E
113 K19 **Milot** var. Miloti. Lezhë, C Albania 41°42´N 19°43´E
Miloti see Milot
117 Z5 **Milove** Luhans'ka Oblast', E Ukraine 49°22´N 40°09´E
Milovidy see Milavidy
182 L4 **Milparinka** New South Wales, SE Australia 29°48´S 141°57´E
35 N9 **Milpitas** California, W USA 37°25´N 121°54´W
Mil'skaya Ravnina/ Mil'skaya Step' see Mil Düzü
14 G15 **Milton** Ontario, S Canada 43°31´N 79°53´W
185 E24 **Milton** Otago, South Island, New Zealand 46°08´S 169°59´E
21 Y4 **Milton** Delaware, NE USA 38°48´N 75°21´W
23 P8 **Milton** Florida, SE USA 30°37´N 87°02´W
18 G14 **Milton** Pennsylvania, NE USA 41°01´N 76°49´W
18 L7 **Milton** Vermont, NE USA 44°37´N 73°04´W
32 K11 **Milton-Freewater** Oregon, NW USA 45°54´N 118°24´W
97 N21 **Milton Keynes** SE England, United Kingdom 52°N 00°43´W
27 N3 **Miltonvale** Kansas, C USA 39°21´N 97°27´W
161 N10 **Miluo** Hunan, S China 28°52´N 113°00´E
30 M9 **Milwaukee** Wisconsin, N USA 43°03´N 87°56´W
Milyang see Miryang
Mimatum see Mende
37 Q15 **Mimbres Mountains** ▲▲ New Mexico, SW USA
182 D2 **Mimili** South Australia 27°01´S 132°33´E
102 J14 **Mimizan** Landes, SW France 44°12´N 01°12´W
Mimmaya see Minmaya
79 E19 **Mimongo** Ngounié, C Gabon 01°36´S 11°44´E
Min see Fujian
35 T7 **Mina** Nevada, W USA 38°23´N 118°07´W
143 S14 **Mīnāb** Hormozgān, SE Iran 27°08´N 57°02´E
Mînâ Baranîs see Baranīce
149 R9 **Mīna Bāzār** Baluchistān, SW Pakistan 30°58´N 69°11´E
Minami-Awaji see Nandan
165 X17 **Minami-Iō-jima** Eng. San Augustine. island SE Japan
165 R5 **Minami-Kayabe** Hokkaidō, NE Japan 41°54´N 140°58´E
Minami-Satsuma see Kaseda
164 C17 **Minamitane** Kagoshima, Tanega-shima, SW Japan 30°23´N 130°54´E
Minami Tori Shima see Marcus Island
Min'an see Longshan
62 J4 **Mina Pirquitas** Jujuy, NW Argentina 22°48´S 66°24´W
173 O3 **Mīnā' Qābūs** NE Oman
61 F19 **Minas** Lavalleja, S Uruguay 34°20´S 55°15´W
13 P15 **Minas Basin** bay Nova Scotia, SE Canada
61 F17 **Minas de Corrales** Rivera, NE Uruguay 31°35´S 55°20´W
44 A5 **Minas de Matahambre** Pinar del Río, W Cuba 22°34´N 83°57´W
104 J13 **Minas de Ríotinto** Andalucía, S Spain 37°40´N 06°36´W
60 K7 **Minas Gerais** off. Estado de Minas Gerais. ◈ state E Brazil
Minas Gerais, Estado de see Minas Gerais
42 E5 **Minas, Sierra de las** ▲▲ E Guatemala
41 T15 **Minatitlán** Veracruz-Llave, E Mexico 17°59´N 94°32´W
166 L6 **Minbu** Magway, W Burma (Myanmar) 20°09´N 94°52´E
149 V10 **Minchinābād** Punjab, E Pakistan 30°10´N 73°40´E
63 G17 **Minchinmávida, Volcán** ⛰ S Chile 42°51´S 72°23´W
96 G7 **Minch, The** var. North Minch. strait NW Scotland, United Kingdom
106 F8 **Mincio** anc. Mincius. ≈ N Italy
Mincius see Mincio
26 M11 **Minco** Oklahoma, C USA 35°18´N 97°56´W
171 Q7 **Mindanao** island S Philippines
Mindanao Sea see Bohol Sea
101 J23 **Mindel** ≈ S Germany
101 J23 **Mindelheim** Bayern, S Germany 48°03´N 10°30´E
Mindello see Mindelo
76 C9 **Mindelo** var. Mindello; prev. Porto Grande. São Vicente, N Cape Verde 16°54´N 25°01´W
14 I13 **Minden** Ontario, SE Canada 44°54´N 78°41´W
100 H13 **Minden** anc. Minthun. Nordrhein-Westfalen, NW Germany 52°18´N 08°55´E
22 G5 **Minden** Louisiana, S USA 32°37´N 93°17´W
29 O16 **Minden** Nebraska, C USA 40°30´N 98°57´W
35 Q6 **Minden** Nevada, W USA 38°58´N 119°47´W
182 L8 **Mindona Lake** seasonal lake New South Wales, SE Australia
171 O4 **Mindoro** island N Philippines
171 N5 **Mindoro Strait** strait W Philippines
159 S9 **Mine** Gansu, N China
97 J23 **Minehead** SW England, United Kingdom 51°13´N 03°29´W
97 E21 **Mine Head** Ir. Mionn Ard. headland S Ireland 51°58´N 07°36´W
59 J19 **Mineiros** Goiás, C Brazil 17°34´S 52°33´W
25 V6 **Mineola** Texas, SW USA 32°39´N 95°29´W
25 S13 **Mineral** Texas, SW USA 28°32´N 97°54´W
127 N15 **Mineral'nyye Vody** Stavropol'skiy Kray, SW Russian Federation 44°13´N 43°06´E
30 K9 **Mineral Point** Wisconsin, N USA 42°54´N 90°09´W
25 S6 **Mineral Wells** Texas, SW USA 32°48´N 98°06´W
36 K6 **Minersville** Utah, W USA 38°12´N 112°56´W
31 U12 **Minerva** Ohio, N USA 40°43´N 81°06´W
107 N17 **Minervino Murge** Puglia, SE Italy 41°06´N 16°05´E
103 O16 **Minervois** physical region S France
158 I10 **Minfeng** var. Niya. Xinjiang Uygur Zizhiqu, NW China 37°07´N 82°43´E
79 O25 **Minga** Katanga, SE Dem. Rep. Congo 11°06´S 27°57´E
137 W11 **Mingäçevir** Rus. Mingechaur, Mingechevir. C Azerbaijan 40°46´N 47°02´E
137 W11 **Mingäçevir Su Anbarı** Rus. Mingechaurskoye Vodokhranilishche, Mingechevirskoye Vodokhranilishche. ⊠ NW Azerbaijan
166 L8 **Mingaladon** ✈ (Yangon) Yangon, SW Burma (Myanmar) 16°55´N 96°11´E
13 P11 **Mingan** Québec, E Canada 50°19´N 64°02´W
146 K8 **Mingbuloq** Rus. Mynbulak. Navoiy Viloyati, N Uzbekistan 42°18´N 62°53´E
146 K9 **Mingbuloq Botig'I** Rus. Vpadina Mynbulak. depression N Uzbekistan
Mingechaur/Mingechevir see Mingäçevir
Mingechaurskoye Vodokhranilishche/ Mingechevirskoye Vodokhranilishche see Mingäçevir Su Anbarı
161 Q7 **Mingguang** prev. Jiashan. Anhui, SE China 32°45´N 117°59´E
166 L4 **Mingin** Sagaing, C Burma (Myanmar) 22°51´N 94°30´E
105 Q10 **Minglanilla** Castilla-La Mancha, C Spain 39°32´N 01°36´W
31 V13 **Mingo Junction** Ohio, N USA 40°19´N 80°36´W
Mingora see Saidu Sharif
163 V7 **Mingshui** Heilongjiang, NE China 47°10´N 125°53´E
Mingtekl Daban see Mintaka Pass
Mingu see Zhenfeng
83 Q14 **Minguri** Nampula, NE Mozambique 14°30´S 40°37´E
Mingzhou see Suide
159 U10 **Minhe** var. Chuankou; prev. Minhe Huizu Tuzu Zizhixian, Shangchuankou. Qinghai, C China 36°21´N 102°40´E
Minhe Huizu Tuzu Zizhixian see Minhe
166 L6 **Minhla** Magway, W Burma (Myanmar) 19°58´N 95°03´E
167 S14 **Minh Lương** Kiên Giang, S Vietnam 09°52´N 105°10´E
104 G5 **Minho** former province N Portugal
104 G5 **Minho, Rio** Sp. Miño. ≈ Portugal/Spain see also Miño
Minho, Rio see Miño
155 C24 **Minicoy Island** island SW India
33 P15 **Minidoka** Idaho, NW USA 42°45´N 113°29´W
118 C11 **Minija** ≈ W Lithuania
180 G9 **Minilya** Western Australia 23°45´S 114°03´E
14 E8 **Minisinakwa Lake** ◎ Ontario, S Canada
45 T12 **Ministre Point** headland S Saint Lucia 13°42´N 60°57´W
11 V15 **Minitonas** Manitoba, S Canada 52°07´N 101°02´W
Minius see Miño
161 R12 **Min Jiang** ≈ SE China
160 H10 **Min Jiang** ≈ C China
182 H9 **Minlaton** South Australia 34°52´S 137°33´E
159 S9 **Minle** var. Hongshui. Gansu, N China 38°15´N 100°36´E
165 Q6 **Minmaya** var. Mimmaya. Aomori, Honshū, C Japan 41°10´N 140°24´E
77 U14 **Minna** Niger, C Nigeria 09°33´N 06°33´E
165 P16 **Minna-jima** island Sakishima-shotō, SW Japan
27 N4 **Minneapolis** Kansas, C USA 39°08´N 97°43´W
29 U9 **Minneapolis** Minnesota, N USA 44°59´N 93°16´W
29 V8 **Minneapolis-Saint Paul** ✈ Minnesota, N USA 44°53´N 93°13´W
11 W16 **Minnedosa** Manitoba, S Canada 50°14´N 99°50´W
26 J7 **Minneola** Kansas, C USA 37°26´N 100°00´W
29 S7 **Minnesota** off. State of Minnesota, also known as Gopher State, New England of the West, North Star State. ◈ state N USA
29 S9 **Minnesota River** ≈ Minnesota/South Dakota, N USA
29 V9 **Minnetonka** Minnesota, N USA 44°55´N 93°28´W
29 O3 **Minnewaukan** North Dakota, N USA 48°04´N 99°14´W
182 F7 **Minnipa** South Australia 32°52´S 135°07´E
104 H2 **Miño** Galicia, NW Spain 43°21´N 08°12´W
104 G5 **Miño** var. Mino, Minius, Port. Rio Minho. ≈ Portugal/Spain see also Minho, Rio
Miño see Minho, Rio
30 L4 **Minocqua** Wisconsin, N USA 45°53´N 89°42´W
30 L12 **Minonk** Illinois, N USA 40°54´N 89°01´W
Minorca see Menorca
28 M3 **Minot** North Dakota, N USA 48°15´N 101°19´W
159 U8 **Minqin** Gansu, N China 38°35´N 103°07´E
119 J16 **Minsk** ● (Belarus) Minskaya Voblasts', C Belarus 53°52´N 27°34´E
119 L16 **Minsk** ✈ Minskaya Voblasts', C Belarus 53°52´N 27°58´E
Minskaya Oblast' see Minskaya Voblasts'
119 K16 **Minskaya Voblasts'** prev. Rus. Minskaya Oblast'. ◈ province C Belarus
119 J16 **Minskaya Wzvyshsha** ▲▲ C Belarus
110 N12 **Mińsk Mazowiecki** var. Nowo-Minsk. Mazowieckie, C Poland 52°10´N 21°31´E
31 Q13 **Minster** Ohio, N USA 40°23´N 84°22´W
79 F15 **Minta** Centre, C Cameroon 04°34´N 12°54´E
149 W2 **Mintaka Pass** Chin. Mingtekl Daban. pass China/ Pakistan
115 D20 **Mínthi** ▲▲ S Greece
Minthun see Minden
13 O14 **Minto** New Brunswick, SE Canada 46°05´N 66°05´W
10 H6 **Minto** Yukon Territory, W Canada 62°33´N 136°45´W
39 R9 **Minto** Alaska, USA 65°07´N 149°22´W
29 Q3 **Minto** North Dakota, N USA 48°17´N 97°22´W
12 K6 **Minto, Lac** ◎ Québec, C Canada
195 R16 **Minto, Mount** ▲ Antarctica 71°38´S 169°11´E
11 U17 **Minton** Saskatchewan, S Canada 49°12´N 104°33´W
189 R15 **Minto Reef** atoll Caroline Islands, C Micronesia
37 R4 **Minturn** Colorado, C USA 39°34´N 106°21´W
107 J16 **Minturno** Lazio, C Italy 41°15´N 13°47´E
122 K13 **Minusinsk** Krasnoyarskiy Kray, S Russian Federation 53°37´N 91°49´E
108 G11 **Minusio** Ticino, S Switzerland 46°11´N 08°47´E
79 E17 **Minvoul** Woleu-Ntem, N Gabon 02°08´N 12°12´E
141 R13 **Minwakh** N Yemen 16°55´N 48°04´E
159 V11 **Minxian** var. Min Xian, Minyang. Gansu, C China 34°20´N 104°09´E
Min Xian see Minxian
Minya see Al Minyā
Minyang see Minxian
31 R6 **Mio** Michigan, N USA 44°40´N 84°09´W
Mionn Ard see Mine Head
158 L5 **Miquan** Xinjiang Uygur Zizhiqu, NW China 44°04´N 87°40´E
119 I17 **Mir** Hrodzyenskaya Voblasts', W Belarus 53°25´N 26°28´E
106 H8 **Mira** Veneto, NE Italy 45°25´N 12°07´E
12 K15 **Mirabel** var. Montreal. ✈ (Montréal) Québec, SE Canada 45°27´N 73°47´W
60 Q8 **Miracema** Rio de Janeiro, SE Brazil 21°24´S 42°10´W
54 G9 **Miraflores** Boyacá, C Colombia 05°07´N 73°09´W
40 G10 **Miraflores** Baja California Sur, NW Mexico 23°24´N 109°45´W
44 L9 **Miragoâne** S Haiti 18°25´N 73°07´W
155 E16 **Miraj** Mahārāshtra, W India 16°51´N 74°42´E
61 E23 **Miramar** Buenos Aires, E Argentina 38°15´S 57°50´W
103 R15 **Miramas** Bouches-du-Rhône, SE France 43°33´N 05°02´E
102 K12 **Mirambeau** Charente-Maritime, W France 45°23´N 00°33´W
102 L13 **Miramont-de-Guyenne** Lot-et-Garonne, SW France 44°34´N 00°20´E
115 L25 **Mirampéllou Kólpos** gulf Kríti, Greece, E Mediterranean Sea
158 L8 **Miran** Xinjiang Uygur Zizhiqu, NW China 39°13´N 88°58´E
54 M5 **Miranda** off. Estado Miranda. ◈ state N Venezuela
Miranda de Corvo see Miranda do Corvo
105 O3 **Miranda de Ebro** La Rioja, N Spain 42°41´N 02°57´W
104 G8 **Miranda do Corvo** var. Miranda de Corvo. Coimbra, N Portugal 40°05´N 08°20´W
104 J6 **Miranda do Douro** Bragança, N Portugal 41°30´N 06°16´W
Miranda, Estado see Miranda
102 L15 **Mirande** Gers, S France 43°31´N 00°25´E
104 I6 **Mirandela** Bragança, N Portugal 41°28´N 07°10´W
25 R15 **Mirando City** Texas, SW USA 27°24´N 99°00´W
106 G9 **Mirandola** Emilia-Romagna, N Italy 44°52´N 11°04´E
60 I8 **Mirandópolis** São Paulo, S Brazil 21°10´S 51°03´W
104 G13 **Mira, Rio** ≈ S Portugal
60 K8 **Mirassol** São Paulo, S Brazil 20°50´S 49°30´W
104 J3 **Miravalles** ▲ NW Spain 42°52´N 06°45´W
42 L12 **Miravalles, Volcán** ⛰ NW Costa Rica 10°43´N 85°07´W
141 W13 **Mirbāṭ** var. Marbat. S Oman 17°03´N 54°44´E
44 M9 **Mirebalais** C Haiti 18°51´N 72°08´W
103 T6 **Mirecourt** Vosges, NE France 48°19´N 06°04´E
103 N16 **Mirepoix** Ariège, S France 43°05´N 01°51´E
Mirgorod see Myrhorod
139 W10 **Mīr Ḩājī Khalīl** Wāsiţ, E Iraq 32°11´N 46°19´E
169 T8 **Miri** Sarawak, East Malaysia 04°23´N 113°59´E
77 W12 **Miria** Zinder, S Niger 13°39´N 09°15´E
182 F5 **Mirikata** South Australia 29°56´S 135°13´E
54 K4 **Mirimire** Falcón, N Venezuela 11°14´N 68°39´W
61 H18 **Mirim Lagoon** var. Lake Mirim, Sp. Laguna Merín. lagoon Brazil/Uruguay
Mirim, Lake see Mirim Lagoon
Mírina see Mýrina
172 H14 **Miringoni** Mohéli, S Comoros 12°17´S 93°39´E
143 W11 **Mīrjāveh** Sīstān va Balūchestān, SE Iran 29°04´N 61°24´E
195 Z9 **Mirny** Russian research station Antarctica 66°25´S 93°09´E
124 M10 **Mirnyy** Arkhangel'skaya Oblast', NW Russian Federation 62°50´N 40°20´E
123 O10 **Mirnyy** Respublika Sakha (Yakutiya), NE Russian Federation 62°30´N 113°58´E
Mironovka see Myronivka
110 F9 **Mirosławiec** Zachodnio-pomorskie, NW Poland 53°21´N 16°04´E
Mirovo see Vrattsa
100 N10 **Mirow** Mecklenburg-Vorpommern, N Germany 53°16´N 12°48´E
152 G6 **Mīrpur** Jammu and Kashmir, NW India 33°06´N 73°49´E
Mīrpur see New Mīrpur
149 P17 **Mīrpur Batoro** Sind, SE Pakistan 24°40´N 68°15´E
149 Q16 **Mīrpur Khās** Sind, SE Pakistan 25°31´N 69°01´E
149 P17 **Mīrpur Sakro** Sind, SE Pakistan 24°32´N 67°38´E
143 T14 **Mīr Shahdād** Hormozgān, S Iran 26°15´N 58°29´E
Mirtoan Sea see Mirtóo Pélagos
115 G21 **Mirtóo Pélagos** Eng. Mirtoan Sea; anc. Myrtoum Mare. sea S Greece
163 Z16 **Miryang** var. Milyang, Jap. Mitsuō. SE South Korea 35°30´N 128°46´E
Mirzachirla see Murzechirla
164 E14 **Misaki** Ehime, Shikoku, SW Japan 33°22´N 132°04´E
41 Q13 **Misantla** Veracruz-Llave, E Mexico 19°54´N 96°51´W
165 R7 **Misawa** Aomori, Honshū, C Japan 40°42´N 141°26´E
57 G14 **Mishagua, Río** ≈ C Peru
163 Z8 **Mishan** Heilongjiang, NE China 45°30´N 131°53´E
31 O11 **Mishawaka** Indiana, N USA 41°40´N 86°10´W
39 N6 **Misheguk Mountain** ▲ Alaska, USA 68°13´N 161°11´W
165 N14 **Mishima** var. Misima. Shizuoka, Honshū, S Japan 35°08´N 138°54´E
164 E12 **Mi-shima** island SW Japan
127 V4 **Mishkino** Respublika Bashkortostan, W Russian Federation 55°31´N 55°57´E
153 Y10 **Mishmi Hills** hill range NE India
161 N11 **Mi Shui** ≈ S China
Misiaf see Maşyāf
107 J23 **Misilmeri** Sicilia, Italy, C Mediterranean Sea 38°03´N 13°27´E
Misima see Mishima
14 C7 **Missinaibi Lake** ◎ Ontario, S Canada
Misión de Guana see Guana
60 F13 **Misiones** off. Provincia de Misiones. ◈ province NE Argentina
62 P8 **Misiones** off. Departamento de las Misiones. ◈ department S Paraguay
Misiones, Departamento de las see Misiones
Misiones, Provincia de see Misiones
Misión San Fernando see San Fernando
Miskin see Maskin
Miskito Coast see La Mosquitia
43 O7 **Miskitos, Cayos** island group NE Nicaragua
111 M21 **Miskolc** Borsod-Abaúj-Zemplén, NE Hungary 48°05´N 20°46´E
171 T12 **Misool, Pulau** island Maluku, E Indonesia
Misox see Mesocco
29 Y3 **Misquah Hills** hill range Minnesota, N USA
75 P7 **Mişrātah** var. Misurata. NW Libya 32°23´N 15°06´E
75 P7 **Mişrātah, Râs** headland N Libya 32°22´N 15°16´E
14 C7 **Missanabie** Ontario, S Canada 48°18´N 84°04´W
58 E10 **Missão Catrimani** Roraima, N Brazil 01°26´N 62°05´W
14 D6 **Missinaibi** ≈ Ontario, S Canada
11 T13 **Missinipe** Saskatchewan, C Canada 55°36´N 104°45´W
28 M11 **Mission** South Dakota, N USA 43°16´N 100°38´W
25 S17 **Mission** Texas, SW USA 26°13´N 98°19´W
12 F10 **Missisa Lake** ◎ Ontario, C Canada
18 M6 **Missisquoi Bay** lake bay Canada/USA
14 C10 **Mississagi** ≈ Ontario, S Canada
14 G15 **Mississauga** Ontario, S Canada 43°38´N 79°36´W
31 P12 **Mississinewa Lake** ⊠ Indiana, N USA
31 P12 **Mississinewa River** ≈ Indiana/Ohio, N USA
22 K4 **Mississippi** off. State of Mississippi, also known as Bayou State, Magnolia State. ◈ state SE USA
14 K13 **Mississippi** ≈ Ontario, SE Canada
47 N1 **Mississippi Fan** undersea feature N Gulf of Mexico 26°45´N 88°30´W
14 L13 **Mississippi Lake** ◎ Ontario, SE Canada
22 M10 **Mississippi Delta** delta Louisiana, S USA
0 J11 **Mississippi River** ≈ C USA
22 M9 **Mississippi Sound** sound Alabama/Mississippi, S USA
33 P9 **Missoula** Montana, NW USA 46°54´N 114°03´W
27 T5 **Missouri** off. State of Missouri, also known as Bullion State, Show Me State. ◈ state C USA
25 V11 **Missouri City** Texas, SW USA 29°37´N 95°32´W
0 J10 **Missouri River** ≈ C USA
15 Q6 **Mistassibi** ≈ Québec, SE Canada
15 P6 **Mistassini** ≈ Québec, SE Canada
15 P6 **Mistassini** Québec, SE Canada 48°54´N 72°13´W
12 J11 **Mistassini, Lac** ◎ Québec, SE Canada
109 Y3 **Mistelbach an der Zaya** Niederösterreich, NE Austria 48°34´N 16°33´E
107 L24 **Misterbianco** Sicilia, Italy, C Mediterranean Sea 37°31´N 15°01´E
95 N19 **Misterhult** Kalmar, S Sweden 57°28´N 16°34´E
57 H17 **Misti, Volcán** ⛰ S Peru 16°20´S 71°22´W
Mistras see Mystrás
107 K23 **Mistretta** anc. Amestratus. Sicilia, Italy, C Mediterranean Sea 37°56´N 14°22´E
164 F12 **Misumi** Shimane, Honshū, SW Japan 34°47´N 132°00´E
Misurata see Mişrātah
83 O14 **Mitande** Niassa, N Mozambique 14°06´S 36°03´E
40 J13 **Mita, Punta de** headland C Mexico 20°46´N 105°31´W
55 W12 **Mitaraka, Massif du** ▲ NE South America 02°18´N 54°31´W
Mitau see Jelgava
181 X9 **Mitchell** Queensland, E Australia 26°29´S 148°00´E
14 E15 **Mitchell** Ontario, S Canada 43°28´N 81°11´W
28 I13 **Mitchell** Nebraska, C USA 41°56´N 103°48´W
32 J12 **Mitchell** Oregon, NW USA 44°34´N 120°09´W
29 P11 **Mitchell** South Dakota, N USA 43°42´N 98°01´W
23 P5 **Mitchell Lake** ⊠ Alabama, S USA
31 P7 **Mitchell, Lake** ◎ Michigan, N USA
21 P9 **Mitchell, Mount** ▲ North Carolina, SE USA 35°46´N 82°16´W
181 V3 **Mitchell River** ≈ Queensland, NE Australia
97 D20 **Mitchelstown** Ir. Baile Mhistéala. SW Ireland 52°20´N 08°16´W
14 M9 **Mitchinamécus, Lac** ◎ Québec, SE Canada
Mitèmboni see Mitemele, Río
79 D17 **Mitemele, Río** var. Mitèmboni, Temboni, Utamboni. ≈ S Equatorial Guinea
149 S12 **Mithān Kot** Punjab, E Pakistan 28°53´N 70°25´E
149 T7 **Mitha Tiwāna** Punjab, E Pakistan 32°18´N 72°08´E
149 R17 **Mithi** Sind, SE Pakistan 24°43´N 69°53´E
Míthimna see Míthymna
Mi Tho see My Tho
115 L16 **Míthymna** var. Míthimna. Lésvos, E Greece 39°20´N 26°12´E
190 L16 **Mitiaro** island S Cook Islands
Mitilíni see Mytilíni
15 U7 **Mitis** ≈ Québec, SE Canada
41 R16 **Mitla** Oaxaca, SE Mexico 16°56´N 96°19´W
165 P13 **Mito** Ibaraki, Honshū, S Japan 36°21´N 140°26´E
92 N2 **Mitra, Kapp** headland W Svalbard 79°07´N 11°11´E
184 M13 **Mitre** ▲ North Island, New Zealand 40°46´S 175°27´E
185 B21 **Mitre Peak** ▲ South Island, New Zealand 44°37´S 167°45´E
39 O15 **Mitrofania Island** island Alaska, USA
Mitrovica/Mitrovicë see Kosovska Mitrovica, Serbia
Mitrovica/Mitrowitz see Sremska Mitrovica, Serbia
113 M16 **Mitrovicë** Serb. Mitrovica, Kosovska Mitrovica, Titova Mitrovica. N Kosovo 42°54´N 20°52´E
172 H12 **Mitsamiouli** Grande Comore, NW Comoros 11°22´S 43°19´E
172 I3 **Mitsinjo** Mahajanga, NW Madagascar 16°00´S 45°52´E
80 J9 **Mīts'īwa** var. Masawa, Massawa. E Eritrea 15°37´N 39°27´E
172 H13 **Mitsoudjé** Grande Comore, NW Comoros
138 F12 **Mitspe Ramon** prev. Miẕpe Ramon. Southern, S Israel 30°38´N 34°47´E
165 T5 **Mitsuishi** Hokkaidō, NE Japan 42°12´N 142°40´E
165 O11 **Mitsuke** var. Mituke. Niigata, Honshū, C Japan 37°30´N 138°54´E
Mitsuō see Miryang
164 C12 **Mitsushima** Nagasaki, Tsushima, SW Japan 34°16´N 129°18´E
100 G12 **Mittelandkanal** canal NW Germany
108 J7 **Mittelberg** Vorarlberg, NW Austria 47°19´N 10°09´E
Mitteldorf see Międzychód
Mittelstadt see Baia Sprie
Mitterburg see Pazin
109 P7 **Mittersill** Salzburg, NW Austria 47°16´N 12°27´E
101 N16 **Mittweida** Sachsen, E Germany 50°59´N 12°57´E
54 J13 **Mitú** Vaupés, SE Colombia 01°07´N 70°05´W
Mituke see Mitsuke
Mitumba, Chaîne des/ Mitumba Range see Mitumba, Monts
79 O22 **Mitumba, Monts** var. Chaîne des Mitumba, Mitumba Range. ▲▲ E Dem. Rep. Congo
79 N23 **Mitwaba** Katanga, SE Dem. Rep. Congo 08°37´S 27°20´E
79 E18 **Mitzic** Woleu-Ntem, N Gabon 0°48´N 11°30´E
82 K11 **Miueru Wantipa, Lake** ◎ N Zambia
165 N14 **Miura** Kanagawa, Honshū, S Japan 35°08´N 139°37´E
165 Q10 **Miyagi** off. Miyagi-ken. ◈ prefecture Honshū, C Japan
Miyagi-ken see Miyagi
138 M7 **Miyāh, Wādī al** dry watercourse E Syria
165 X13 **Miyake** Tōkyō, Miyako-jima, SE Japan 34°35´N 135°33´E
165 Q16 **Miyake-jima** island Sakishima-shotō, SW Japan
165 R8 **Miyako** Iwate, Honshū, C Japan 39°39´N 141°57´E
164 D16 **Miyakonojō** var. Miyakonzyô. Miyazaki, Kyūshū, SW Japan 31°42´N 131°04´E
Miyakonzyô see Miyakonojō
165 Q16 **Miyako-shotō** island group SW Japan
144 G11 **Miyaly** Atyrau, W Kazakhstan 48°52´N 53°55´E
Miyāndoāb see Mīāndowāb
Miyāneh see Mīāneh
Miyang see Mile
164 D16 **Miyazaki** Miyazaki, Kyūshū, SW Japan 31°55´N 131°24´E
164 D16 **Miyazaki** off. Miyazaki-ken. ◈ prefecture Kyūshū, SW Japan
Miyazaki-ken see Miyazaki
164 J12 **Miyazu** Kyōto, Honshū, SW Japan 35°33´N 135°12´E
Miyory see Myory
164 G12 **Miyoshi** var. Miyosi. Hiroshima, Honshū, SW Japan 34°48´N 132°51´E
Miyosi see Miyoshi
Miza see Mizë
81 H14 **Mīzan Teferī** Southern Nationalities, S Ethiopia 06°57´N 35°30´E
Mizda see Mizdah
75 O8 **Mizdah** var. Mizda. NW Libya 31°26´N 12°59´E
113 K20 **Mizë** var. Miza. Fier, W Albania 40°58´N 19°32´E
97 A22 **Mizen Head** Ir. Carn Uí Néid. headland SW Ireland 51°26´N 09°50´W
116 H7 **Mizhhir"ya** Rus. Mezhgor'ye. Zakarpats'ka Oblast', W Ukraine 48°30´N 23°30´E
160 L4 **Mizhi** Shaanxi, C China 37°50´N 110°03´E
116 K13 **Mizil** Prahova, SE Romania 45°00´N 26°29´E
114 H7 **Miziya** Vratsa, NW Bulgaria 43°42´N 23°52´E
153 W15 **Mizo Hills** hill range E India
153 W15 **Mizoram** ◈ state NE India
Miẕpe Ramon see Mitspe Ramon
57 L19 **Mizque** Cochabamba, C Bolivia 17°57´S 65°10´W
57 M19 **Mizque, Río** ≈ C Bolivia
165 Q9 **Mizusawa** var. Ōshū. Iwate, Honshū, C Japan 39°10´N 141°07´E
95 M18 **Mjölby** Östergötland, S Sweden 58°19´N 15°10´E
95 G15 **Mjøndalen** Buskerud, S Norway 59°45´N 09°58´E
95 J19 **Mjörn** ◎ S Sweden
94 I13 **Mjøsa** var. Mjøsen. ◎ S Norway
Mjøsen see Mjøsa
81 G21 **Mkalama** Singida, C Tanzania 04°09´S 34°35´E
80 K13 **Mkata** ≈ C Tanzania
83 K14 **Mkushi** Central, C Zambia 13°40´S 29°26´E
83 L22 **Mkuze** KwaZulu/Natal, E South Africa 27°37´S 32°03´E
81 J22 **Mkwaja** Tanga, E Tanzania 05°42´S 38°48´E
111 D16 **Mladá Boleslav** Ger. Jungbunzlau. Středočeský Kraj, N Czech Republic 50°26´N 14°55´E
112 M12 **Mladenovac** Serbia, C Serbia 44°27´N 20°42´E
114 L11 **Mladinovo** Khaskovo, S Bulgaria 41°57´N 26°13´E
113 O17 **Mlado Nagoričane** N FYR Macedonia 42°11´N 21°49´E
Mlanje see Mulanje
112 N12 **Mlava** ≈ E Serbia
110 L9 **Mława** Mazowieckie, C Poland 53°07´N 20°23´E
113 G16 **Mljet** It. Meleda; anc. Melita. island S Croatia
116 K4 **Mlyniv** Rivnens'ka Oblast', NW Ukraine 50°31´N 25°36´E
83 I21 **Mmabatho** North-West, N South Africa 25°51´S 25°37´E
83 I19 **Mmashoro** Central, E Botswana 21°56´S 26°39´E
44 J7 **Moa** Holguín, E Cuba 20°42´N 74°57´W
76 J15 **Moa** ≈ Guinea/Sierra Leone
37 O6 **Moab** Utah, W USA 38°35´N 109°34´W
181 V1 **Moa Island** island Queensland, NE Australia
187 Y15 **Moala** island S Fiji
83 L21 **Moamba** Maputo, SW Mozambique 25°35´S 32°13´E
79 F19 **Moanda** var. Mouanda. Haut-Ogooué, SE Gabon 01°31´S 13°07´E
83 M15 **Moatize** Tete, NW Mozambique 16°04´S 33°43´E
79 P22 **Moba** Katanga, E Dem. Rep. Congo 07°03´S 29°52´E
Mobay see Montego Bay
79 K15 **Mobaye** Basse-Kotto, S Central African Republic 04°19´N 21°17´E
79 K15 **Mobayi-Mbongo** Equateur, NW Dem. Rep. Congo 04°21´N 21°10´E
25 P2 **Mobeetie** Texas, SW USA 35°33´N 100°25´W
27 U3 **Moberly** Missouri, C USA 39°25´N 92°26´W
23 N8 **Mobile** Alabama, S USA 30°42´N 88°03´W
23 N9 **Mobile Bay** bay Alabama, S USA
23 N8 **Mobile River** ≈ Alabama, S USA
29 N8 **Mobridge** South Dakota, N USA 45°32´N 100°25´W
Mobutu Sese Seko, Lac see Albert, Lake
45 N8 **Moca** N Dominican Republic 19°26´N 70°33´W
83 Q15 **Moçambique** Nampula, NE Mozambique 15°00´S 40°44´E
Moçâmedes see Namibe
167 S6 **Môc Châu** Sơn La, N Vietnam 20°49´N 104°38´E
187 Z15 **Moce** island Lau Group, E Fiji
Mocha see Al Mukhā
193 T11 **Mocha Fracture Zone** tectonic feature SE Pacific Ocean
63 F14 **Mocha, Isla** island C Chile
56 C12 **Moche, Río** ≈ W Peru
167 S14 **Môc Hoa** Long An, S Vietnam 10°46´N 105°56´E
83 I20 **Mochudi** Kgatleng, SE Botswana 24°25´S 26°07´E
82 Q13 **Mocímboa da Praia** var. Vila de Mocímboa da Praia. Cabo Delgado, N Mozambique 11°17´S 40°21´E
94 L13 **Mockfjärd** Dalarna, C Sweden 60°30´N 14°57´E
21 R9 **Mocksville** North Carolina, SE USA 35°53´N 80°33´W

◆ Country
● Country Capital
◇ Dependent Territory
○ Dependent Territory Capital
◈ Administrative Regions
✈ International Airport
▲ Mountain
▲▲ Mountain Range
⛰ Volcano
≈ River
◎ Lake
⊠ Reservoir

32 F8 **Moclips** Washington, NW USA 47°11′N 124°13′W
82 C13 **Môco** var. Morro de Môco. ▲ W Angola 12°36′S 15°09′E
54 D13 **Mocoa** Putumayo, SW Colombia 01°07′N 76°38′W
60 M8 **Mococa** São Paulo, S Brazil 21°30′S 47°00′W
Môco, Morro de see Môco
40 H8 **Mocorito** Sinaloa, C Mexico 25°24′N 107°55′W
40 J4 **Moctezuma** Chihuahua, N Mexico 30°10′N 106°28′W
41 N11 **Moctezuma** San Luis Potosí, C Mexico 22°46′N 101°06′W
40 G4 **Moctezuma** Sonora, NW Mexico 29°50′N 109°40′W
41 P12 **Moctezuma, Río** ↝ C Mexico
Mó, Cuan see Clew Bay
83 O16 **Mocuba** Zambézia, NE Mozambique 16°50′S 37°02′E
103 U12 **Modane** Savoie, E France 45°14′N 06°41′E
106 F9 **Modena** anc. Mutina. Emilia-Romagna, N Italy 44°39′N 10°55′E
36 I7 **Modena** Utah, W USA 37°46′N 113°54′W
35 O9 **Modesto** California, W USA 37°38′N 121°02′W
107 L25 **Modica** anc. Motyca. Sicilia, Italy, C Mediterranean Sea 36°52′N 14°45′E
83 J20 **Modimolle** prev. Nylstroom. Limpopo, NE South Africa 24°39′N 28°23′E
79 K17 **Modjamboli** Equateur, N Dem. Rep. Congo 02°27′N 22°03′E
109 X4 **Mödling** Niederösterreich, NE Austria 48°06′N 16°18′E
Modohn see Madona
Modot see Tsenhermandal
171 V14 **Modowi** Papua, E Indonesia 04°05′S 134°39′E
112 I12 **Modračko Jezero** ⊠ NE Bosnia and Herzegovina
112 I10 **Modriča** Republika Srpska, N Bosnia and Herzegovina 44°57′N 18°17′E
183 O13 **Moe** Victoria, SE Australia 38°11′S 146°18′E
Moearatewe see Muaratewe
Moei, Mae Nam see Thaungyin
94 H13 **Moelv** Hedmark, S Norway 60°55′N 10°47′E
92 I10 **Moen** Troms, N Norway 69°08′N 18°35′E
Möen see Møn, Denmark
Moen see Weno, Micronesia
Moena see Muna, Pulau
36 M10 **Moenkopi Wash** ↝ Arizona, SW USA
185 F22 **Moeraki Point** headland South Island, New Zealand 45°23′S 170°52′E
99 F16 **Moerbeke** Oost-Vlaanderen, NW Belgium 51°11′N 03°57′E
99 H14 **Moerdijk** Noord-Brabant, S Netherlands 51°42′N 04°37′E
Moero, Lac see Mweru, Lake
101 D15 **Moers** var. Mörs. Nordrhein-Westfalen, W Germany 51°27′N 06°36′E
Moesi see Musi, Air
Moeskroen see Mouscron
96 J13 **Moffat** S Scotland, United Kingdom 55°29′N 03°36′W
185 C22 **Moffat Peak** ▲ South Island, New Zealand 44°57′S 168°10′E
79 N19 **Moga** Sud-Kivu, E Dem. Rep. Congo 02°16′S 26°54′E
152 H8 **Moga** Punjab, N India 30°49′N 75°13′E
Mogadiscio/Mogadishu see Muqdisho
Mogador see Essaouira
104 J6 **Mogadouro** Bragança, N Portugal 41°20′N 06°43′W
167 N2 **Mogaung** Kachin State, N Burma (Myanmar) 25°20′N 96°54′E
110 L13 **Mogielnica** Mazowieckie, C Poland 51°40′N 20°42′E
Mogilëv see Mahilyow
Mogilev-Podol'skiy see Mohyliv-Podil's'kyy
Mogilëvskaya Oblast' see Mahilyowskaya Voblasts'
110 I11 **Mogilno** Kujawsko-pomorskie, C Poland 52°39′N 17°58′E
60 L9 **Mogi-Mirim** var. Moji-Mirim. São Paulo, S Brazil 22°26′S 46°55′W
83 Q15 **Mogincual** Nampula, NE Mozambique 15°33′S 40°28′E
114 E13 **Moglenitsas** ↝ N Greece
106 H8 **Mogliano Veneto** Veneto, NE Italy 45°34′N 12°14′E
113 M21 **Mogliçë** Korçë, SE Albania 40°43′N 20°22′E
123 O13 **Mogocha** Chitinskaya Oblast', S Russian Federation 53°39′N 119°47′E
122 J11 **Mogochin** Tomskaya Oblast', C Russian Federation 57°42′N 83°24′E
80 F13 **Mogogh** Jonglei, SE Sudan 08°26′N 31°19′E
171 U12 **Mogoi** Papua, E Indonesia 01°44′S 133°13′E
166 M4 **Mogok** Mandalay, C Burma (Myanmar) 22°55′N 96°29′E
37 P14 **Mogollon Mountains** ▲▲ New Mexico, SW USA
36 M12 **Mogollon Rim** cliff Arizona, SW USA
61 E23 **Mogotes, Punta** headland E Argentina 38°03′S 57°31′W
42 J8 **Mogotón** ▲ NW Nicaragua 13°45′N 86°22′W
104 I14 **Moguer** Andalucía, S Spain 37°15′N 06°52′W
111 J26 **Mohács** Baranya, SW Hungary 46°N 18°40′E
185 C20 **Mohaka** ↝ North Island, New Zealand
28 M2 **Mohall** North Dakota, N USA 48°45′N 101°30′W
Moḥammadābād see Dargaz
143 U12 **Moḥammadābād-e Rigān** Kermān, SE Iran 28°39′N 59°01′E
74 F6 **Mohammedia** prev. Fédala. NW Morocco 33°46′N 07°16′W
74 F6 **Mohammed V** ✕ (Casablanca) W Morocco 33°07′N 08°28′W
Mohammerah see Khorramshahr
36 H10 **Mohave, Lake** ⊠ Arizona/Nevada, W USA
36 I12 **Mohave Mountains** ▲▲ Arizona, SW USA
36 I15 **Mohawk Mountains** ▲▲ Arizona, SW USA
18 J10 **Mohawk River** ↝ New York, NE USA
163 T3 **Mohe** var. Xilinji. Heilongjiang, NE China 53°00′N 122°34′E
95 L20 **Moheda** Kronoberg, S Sweden 57°00′N 14°34′E
Mohéli see Mwali
152 I11 **Mohendergarh** Haryāna, N India 28°17′N 76°14′E
38 K12 **Mohican, Cape** headland Nunivak Island, Alaska, USA 60°12′N 167°25′W
Mohn see Muhu
101 G15 **Möhne** ↝ W Germany
101 G15 **Möhne-Stausee** ⊠ W Germany
92 P2 **Mohn, Kapp** headland NW Svalbard 79°26′N 25°44′E
197 S14 **Mohns Ridge** undersea feature Greenland Sea/Norwegian Sea 72°30′N 05°00′E
57 I17 **Moho** Puno, SE Peru 15°21′S 69°32′W
Mohokare see Caledon
95 L17 **Moholm** Västra Götaland, S Sweden 58°37′N 14°04′E
36 J11 **Mohon Peak** ▲ Arizona, SW USA 34°55′N 113°07′W
81 J23 **Mohoro** Pwani, E Tanzania 08°09′S 39°10′E
Mohra see Moravice
Mohrungen see Morąg
116 M7 **Mohyliv-Podil's'kyy** Rus. Mogilev-Podol'skiy. Vinnyts'ka Oblast', C Ukraine 48°29′N 27°49′E
95 D17 **Moi** Rogaland, S Norway 58°27′N 06°32′E
Moili see Mwali
116 K11 **Moinești** Hung. Mojnest. Bacău, E Romania 46°27′N 26°31′E
Móinteach Mílic see Mountmellick
14 J14 **Moira** ↝ Ontario, SE Canada
92 G13 **Mo i Rana** Nordland, C Norway 66°19′N 14°10′E
153 X14 **Moirāng** Manipur, NE India 24°29′N 93°45′E
115 J25 **Moíres** Kríti, Greece, E Mediterranean Sea 35°03′N 24°51′E
118 H6 **Mõisaküla** Ger. Moiseküll. Viljandimaa, S Estonia 58°05′N 25°12′E
Moiseküll see Mõisaküla
15 W4 **Moisie** Québec, E Canada 50°12′N 66°06′W
15 W3 **Moisie** ↝ Québec, SE Canada
102 M14 **Moissac** Tarn-et-Garonne, S France 44°07′N 01°05′E
78 I13 **Moïssala** Moyen-Chari, S Chad 08°21′N 17°46′E
55 O7 **Moitaco** Bolívar, E Venezuela 08°00′N 64°22′W
95 P15 **Möja** Stockholm, C Sweden 59°25′N 18°55′E
105 Q14 **Mojácar** Andalucía, S Spain 37°09′N 01°50′W
35 T13 **Mojave** California, W USA 35°03′N 118°10′W
35 V13 **Mojave Desert** plain California, W USA
35 V13 **Mojave River** ↝ California, W USA
Moji-Mirim see Mogi-Mirim
113 K15 **Mojkovac** E Montenegro 42°57′N 19°34′E
Mojnest see Moinești
Mōka see Mooka
153 Q13 **Mokāma** prev. Mokameh, Mukama. Bihār, N India 25°24′N 85°55′E
79 O25 **Mokambo** Katanga, SE Dem. Rep. Congo 12°23′S 28°21′E
Mokameh see Mokāma
38 D9 **Mōkapu Point** var. Mokapu Point. headland O'ahu, Hawai'i, USA 21°27′N 157°43′W
184 L9 **Mokau** Waikato, North Island, New Zealand 38°42′S 174°37′E
184 L9 **Mokau** ↝ North Island, New Zealand
35 P7 **Mokelumne River** ↝ California, W USA
83 J23 **Mokhotlong** NE Lesotho 29°19′S 29°06′E
Mokil Atoll see Mwokil Atoll
95 N14 **Möklinta** Västmanland, C Sweden 60°04′N 16°34′E
184 L4 **Mokohinau Islands** island group N New Zealand
153 X12 **Mokokchūng** Nāgāland, NE India 26°20′N 94°30′E
78 F12 **Mokolo** Extrême-Nord, N Cameroon 10°49′N 13°54′E
83 J20 **Mokopane** prev. Potgietersrus. Limpopo, NE South Africa 24°09′S 28°58′E
185 D24 **Mokoreta** ↝ South Island, New Zealand
163 X17 **Mokp'o** Jap. Moppo. SW South Korea 34°50′N 126°26′E
113 L16 **Mokra Gora** ▲▲ S Serbia
Mokrany see Makrany
127 O5 **Moksha** ↝ W Russian Federation
127 O6 **Mokshan** Penzenskaya Oblast', W Russian Federation 53°26′N 44°38′E
143 X12 **Mok Sukhteh-ye Pāyīn** Sīstān va Balūchestān, SE Iran
Moktama see Martaban
77 T14 **Mokwa** Niger, W Nigeria 09°19′N 05°01′E
99 J16 **Mol** prev. Moll. Antwerpen, N Belgium 51°11′N 05°07′E
107 O17 **Mola di Bari** Puglia, SE Italy 41°03′N 17°05′E
Molai see Moláoi
41 P13 **Molango** Hidalgo, C Mexico 20°48′N 98°44′W
115 F22 **Moláoi** var. Molai. Pelopónnisos, S Greece 36°48′N 22°51′E
41 Z12 **Molas del Norte, Punta** var. Punta Molas. headland SE Mexico 20°34′N 86°43′W
Molas, Punta see Molas del Norte, Punta
105 R11 **Molatón** ▲ C Spain 38°58′N 01°19′W
97 K18 **Mold** NE Wales, United Kingdom 53°10′N 03°08′W
Moldau see Vltava, Czech Republic
Moldau see Moldova
Moldavia see Moldova
Moldavian SSR/Moldavskaya SSR see Moldova
94 E9 **Molde** Møre og Romsdal, S Norway 62°44′N 07°08′E
Moldotau, Khrebet see Moldo-Too, Khrebet
147 V9 **Moldo-Too, Khrebet** prev. Khrebet Moldotau. ▲▲ C Kyrgyzstan
116 L9 **Moldova** off. Republic of Moldova, var. Moldavia; prev. Moldavian SSR, Rus. Moldavskaya SSR. ◆ republic SE Europe
116 K9 **Moldova** Eng. Moldavia, Ger. Moldau. former province NE Romania
116 K9 **Moldova** ↝ N Romania
116 F13 **Moldova Nouă** Ger. Neumoldowa, Hung. Újmoldova. Caraș-Severin, SW Romania 44°45′N 21°39′E
Moldova, Republic of see Moldova
116 F13 **Moldova Veche** Ger. Altmoldowa, Hung. Ómoldova. Caraș-Severin, SW Romania 44°45′N 21°13′E
Moldoveanul see Vârful Moldoveanu
83 I20 **Molepolole** Kweneng, SE Botswana 24°25′S 25°30′E
44 L8 **Môle-St-Nicolas** NW Haiti 19°46′N 73°19′W
118 H13 **Molėtai** Utena, E Lithuania 55°14′N 25°25′E
107 O17 **Molfetta** Puglia, SE Italy 41°12′N 16°35′E
171 P11 **Molibagu** Sulawesi, N Indonesia 0°25′N 123°57′E
62 G12 **Molina** Maule, C Chile 35°06′S 71°18′W
105 Q7 **Molina de Aragón** Castilla-La Mancha, C Spain 40°50′N 01°54′W
105 R13 **Molina de Segura** Murcia, SE Spain 38°03′N 01°11′W
30 J11 **Moline** Illinois, N USA 41°30′N 90°31′W
27 P7 **Moline** Kansas, C USA 37°21′N 96°18′W
79 P23 **Moliro** Katanga, SE Dem. Rep. Congo 08°11′S 30°31′E
107 K16 **Molise** ◈ region S Italy
95 K15 **Molkom** Värmland, C Sweden 59°36′N 13°43′E
109 Q9 **Möll** ↝ S Austria
Moll see Mol
146 I14 **Mollanepes Adyndaky** Rus. Imeni Mollanepesa. Mary Welaýaty, S Turkmenistan 37°36′N 61°54′E
95 J22 **Mölle** Skåne, S Sweden 56°15′N 12°19′E
57 H18 **Mollendo** Arequipa, SW Peru 17°02′S 72°01′W
105 U5 **Mollerussa** Cataluña, NE Spain 41°37′N 00°53′E
108 H8 **Mollis** Glarus, NE Switzerland 47°05′N 09°03′E
95 J19 **Mölndal** Västra Götaland, S Sweden 57°39′N 12°05′E
95 J19 **Mölnlycke** Västra Götaland, S Sweden 57°39′N 12°09′E
117 U9 **Molochans'k** Rus. Molochansk. Zaporiz'ka Oblast', SE Ukraine 47°10′N 35°38′E
117 U10 **Molochna** Rus. Molochnaya. ↝ S Ukraine
Molochnaya see Molochna
117 U10 **Molochnyy Lyman** bay N Black Sea
Molodechno/Molodeczno see Maladzyechna
195 V3 **Molodezhnaya** Russian research station Antarctica 67°33′S 46°12′E
124 J14 **Mologa** ↝ NW Russian Federation
38 E9 **Moloka'i** var. Molokai. island Hawaiian Islands, Hawai'i, USA
175 X3 **Molokai Fracture Zone** tectonic feature NE Pacific Ocean
124 K15 **Molokovo** Tverskaya Oblast', W Russian Federation 58°10′N 36°43′E
125 Q14 **Moloma** ↝ NW Russian Federation
183 R8 **Molong** New South Wales, SE Australia 33°07′S 148°52′E
83 H21 **Molopo** seasonal river Botswana/South Africa
115 F17 **Mólos** Stereá Elláda, C Greece 38°48′N 22°39′E
171 O11 **Molosipat** Sulawesi, N Indonesia 0°28′N 121°08′E
Molotov see Severodvinsk, Arkhangel'skaya Oblast', Russian Federation
Molotov see Perm', Permskaya Oblast', Russian Federation
79 G17 **Moloundou** Est, SE Cameroon 02°03′N 15°14′E
103 U5 **Molsheim** Bas-Rhin, NE France 48°33′N 07°30′E
11 X13 **Molson Lake** ◎ Manitoba, C Canada
Moluccas see Maluku
171 Q12 **Molucca Sea** Ind. Laut Maluku. sea E Indonesia
Molukken see Maluku
83 O15 **Molumbo** Zambézia, N Mozambique 15°33′S 36°19′E
171 T15 **Molu, Pulau** island Maluku, E Indonesia
83 P16 **Moma** Nampula, NE Mozambique 16°42′S 39°12′E
171 X14 **Momats** ↝ Papua, E Indonesia
42 J11 **Mombacho, Volcán** ⛰ SW Nicaragua 11°49′N 85°58′W
81 K21 **Mombasa** Coast, SE Kenya 04°04′N 39°40′E
81 J21 **Mombasa** ✕ Coast, SE Kenya 04°01′S 39°31′E
Mombetsu see Monbetsu
114 J12 **Momchilgrad** prev. Mastanli. Kŭrdzhali, S Bulgaria 41°33′N 25°25′E
99 F23 **Momignies** Hainaut, S Belgium 50°02′N 04°10′E
54 E6 **Momil** Córdoba, NW Colombia 09°15′N 75°40′W
42 I10 **Momotombo, Volcán** ⛰ W Nicaragua 12°25′N 86°33′W
56 B5 **Mompiche, Ensenada de** bay NW Ecuador
79 K18 **Mompono** Equateur, NW Dem. Rep. Congo 0°11′N 21°31′E
54 F6 **Mompós** Bolívar, NW Colombia 09°15′N 74°29′W
95 J24 **Møn** prev. Möen. island SE Denmark
153 Y12 **Mon** Nāgāland, NE India 26°43′N 95°01′E
36 L4 **Mona** Utah, W USA 39°49′N 111°52′W
Mona, Canal de la see Mona Passage
96 E8 **Monach Islands** island group NW Scotland, United Kingdom
103 V14 **Monaco** var. Monaco-Ville; anc. Monoecus. ● (Monaco) S Monaco 43°46′N 07°23′E
103 V14 **Monaco** off. Principality of Monaco. ◆ monarchy W Europe
Monaco see München
Monaco Basin see Canary Basin
Monaco, Principality of see Monaco
Monaco-Ville see Monaco
96 I9 **Monadhliath Mountains** ▲▲ N Scotland, United Kingdom
55 O6 **Monagas** off. Estado Monagas. ◈ state NE Venezuela
Monagas, Estado see Monagas
97 F16 **Monaghan** Ir. Muineachán. Monaghan, N Ireland 54°15′N 06°58′W
97 E16 **Monaghan** Ir. Muineachán. cultural region N Ireland
43 S16 **Monagrillo** Herrera, S Panama 08°00′N 80°28′W
24 L8 **Monahans** Texas, SW USA 31°35′N 102°54′W
45 Q9 **Mona, Isla** island W Puerto Rico
45 Q9 **Mona Passage** Sp. Canal de la Mona. channel Dominican Republic/Puerto Rico
43 O14 **Mona, Punta** headland E Costa Rica 09°44′N 82°48′W
155 K25 **Monaragala** Uva Province, SE Sri Lanka 06°52′N 81°22′E
33 S9 **Monarch** Montana, NW USA 47°04′N 110°51′W
10 H14 **Monarch Mountain** ▲ British Columbia, SW Canada 51°59′N 125°56′W
Monasterio see Monesterio
Monasterzyska see Monastyrys'ka
Monastir see Bitola
Monastyriska see Monastyrys'ka
117 O7 **Monastyryshche** Cherkas'ka Oblast', C Ukraine 48°59′N 29°47′E
116 J6 **Monastyrys'ka** Pol. Monasterzyska, Rus. Monastyriska. Ternopil's'ka Oblast', W Ukraine 49°05′N 25°10′E
79 E15 **Monatélé** Centre, SW Cameroon 04°16′N 11°12′E
165 U2 **Monbetsu** var. Mombetsu, Monbetu. Hokkaidō, NE Japan 44°23′N 143°22′E
Monbetu see Monbetsu
106 B8 **Moncalieri** Piemonte, NW Italy 45°00′N 07°41′E
104 G4 **Monção** Viana do Castelo, N Portugal 42°03′N 08°29′W
105 Q5 **Moncayo** ▲ N Spain 41°43′N 01°51′W
105 Q5 **Moncayo, Sierra del** ▲▲ N Spain
124 J4 **Monchegorsk** Murmanskaya Oblast', NW Russian Federation 67°56′N 32°47′E
101 D15 **Mönchengladbach** prev. München-Gladbach. Nordrhein-Westfalen, W Germany 51°12′N 06°35′E
104 F14 **Monchique** Faro, S Portugal 37°19′N 08°33′W
104 G14 **Monchique, Serra de** ▲▲ S Portugal
21 S14 **Moncks Corner** South Carolina, SE USA 33°12′N 80°00′W
41 N7 **Monclova** Coahuila, NE Mexico 26°55′N 101°25′W
Moncorvo see Torre de Moncorvo
13 P14 **Moncton** New Brunswick, SE Canada 46°04′N 64°50′W
104 F8 **Mondego, Cabo** headland N Portugal 40°10′N 08°58′W
104 G8 **Mondego, Rio** ↝ N Portugal
104 I2 **Mondoñedo** Galicia, NW Spain 43°25′N 07°22′W
99 N25 **Mondorf-les-Bains** Grevenmacher, SE Luxembourg 49°30′N 06°16′E
102 M7 **Mondoubleau** Loir-et-Cher, C France 48°00′N 00°49′E
106 B9 **Mondovì** Piemonte, NW Italy 44°23′N 07°56′E
30 J6 **Mondovi** Wisconsin, N USA 44°34′N 91°40′W
Mondragón see Arrasate
107 J17 **Mondragone** Campania, S Italy 41°07′N 13°53′E
109 R5 **Mondsee** ◎ N Austria
115 G22 **Monemvasiá** var. Monemvasia. Pelopónnisos, S Greece 36°22′N 23°03′E
18 B15 **Monessen** Pennsylvania, NE USA 40°07′N 79°51′W
104 J12 **Monesterio** var. Monasterio. Extremadura, W Spain 38°05′N 06°16′W
14 L8 **Monet** Québec, SE Canada 48°09′N 75°37′W
27 S8 **Monett** Missouri, C USA 36°55′N 93°55′W
27 X9 **Monette** Arkansas, C USA 35°53′N 90°20′W
14 G11 **Monetville** Ontario, S Canada 46°08′N 80°24′W
106 J7 **Monfalcone** Friuli-Venezia Giulia, NE Italy 45°49′N 13°32′E
104 H10 **Monforte** Portalegre, C Portugal 39°03′N 07°26′W
104 I4 **Monforte de Lemos** Galicia, NW Spain 42°32′N 07°30′W
79 L16 **Monga** Orientale, N Dem. Rep. Congo 04°12′N 22°49′E
81 I24 **Monga** Lindi, SE Tanzania 09°05′S 37°51′E
81 F15 **Mongalla** Bahr el Gabel, S Sudan 05°12′N 31°42′E
153 U11 **Mongar** E Bhutan 27°16′N 91°07′E
167 U6 **Mong Cai** var. Hai Ninh. Quang Ninh, N Vietnam 21°33′N 107°56′E
180 I11 **Mongers Lake** salt lake Western Australia
186 K8 **Mongga** Kolombangara, NW Solomon Islands 07°51′S 157°00′E
167 O6 **Möng Hpayak** Shan State, E Burma (Myanmar) 20°56′N 100°00′E
Monghyr see Munger
106 B10 **Mongioie** ▲ NW Italy 44°13′N 07°46′E
153 T16 **Mongla** var. Mungla. Khulna, S Bangladesh 22°18′N 89°34′E
188 C15 **Mongmong** C Guam
167 N6 **Möng Nai** Shan State, E Burma (Myanmar) 20°28′N 97°51′E
78 I11 **Mongo** Guéra, C Chad 12°12′N 18°40′E
76 I14 **Mongo** ↝ N Sierra Leone
163 I8 **Mongolia** Mong. Mongol Uls. ◆ republic E Asia
129 V8 **Mongolia, Plateau of** plateau E Mongolia
Mongolküre see Zhaosu
Mongol Uls see Mongolia
79 E17 **Mongomo** E Equatorial Guinea 01°39′N 11°18′E
162 M7 **Möngönmorit** var. Bulag. Töv, C Mongolia 48°09′N 108°33′E
77 Y12 **Mongonu** var. Monguno. Borno, NE Nigeria 12°42′N 13°37′E
Mongora see Saidu Sharif
78 K11 **Mongororo** Ouaddaï, SE Chad 12°03′N 22°26′E
Mongos, Chaîne des see Bongo, Massif des
79 I16 **Mongoumba** Lobaye, SW Central African Republic 03°39′N 18°30′E
Mongrove, Punta see Cayacal, Punta
83 G15 **Mongu** Western, W Zambia 15°13′S 23°09′E
76 I10 **Mônguel** Gorgol, SW Mauritania 16°25′N 13°08′W
Monguno see Mongonu
167 N4 **Möng Yai** Shan State, E Burma (Myanmar) 22°25′N 98°02′E
167 O5 **Möng Yang** Shan State, E Burma (Myanmar) 21°52′N 99°31′E
167 N3 **Möng Yu** Shan State, E Burma (Myanmar) 24°00′N 97°57′E
Mönhbulag see Yösöndzüyl
163 O8 **Mönhhaan** var. Bayasgalant. Sühbaatar, E Mongolia 46°55′N 112°11′E
162 E7 **Mönhhayrhan** var. Tsenher. Hovd, W Mongolia 47°07′N 92°04′E
Mönh Sarīdag see Munku-Sardyk, Gora
186 P9 **Moni** ↝ S Papau New Guinea
115 I15 **Moní Megístis Lávras** monastery Kentrikí Makedonía, N Greece
115 F18 **Moní Osíou Loúkas** monastery Stereá Elláda, C Greece
54 F9 **Moniquirá** Boyacá, C Colombia 05°54′N 73°35′W
103 Q12 **Monistrol-sur-Loire** Haute-Loire, C France 45°19′N 04°12′E
35 V7 **Monitor Range** ▲▲ Nevada, W USA
115 I14 **Moní Vatopedíou** monastery Kentrikí Makedonía, N Greece
Monkchester see Newcastle upon Tyne
83 N14 **Monkey Bay** Southern, SE Malawi 14°09′S 34°53′E
43 N11 **Monkey Point** var. Punta Mico, Punte Mono, Punto Mico. headland SE Nicaragua 11°37′N 83°39′W
Monkey River see Monkey River Town
42 G3 **Monkey River Town** var. Monkey River. Toledo, SE Belize 16°22′N 88°29′W
14 M13 **Monkland** Ontario, SE Canada 45°11′N 74°51′W
79 J19 **Monkoto** Equateur, NW Dem. Rep. Congo 01°39′S 20°41′E
97 K21 **Monmouth** Wel. Trefynwy. SE Wales, United Kingdom 51°50′N 02°43′W
30 J12 **Monmouth** Illinois, N USA 40°54′N 90°39′W
32 F12 **Monmouth** Oregon, NW USA 44°51′N 123°13′W
97 K21 **Monmouth** cultural region SE Wales, United Kingdom
98 I10 **Monnickendam** Noord-Holland, C Netherlands 52°28′N 05°02′E
77 R15 **Mono** ↝ C Togo
Monoecus see Monaco
35 R8 **Mono Lake** ◎ California, W USA
115 O23 **Monólithos** Ródos, Dodekánisa, Greece, Aegean Sea 36°08′N 27°45′E
19 Q12 **Monomoy Island** island Massachusetts, NE USA
31 O12 **Monon** Indiana, N USA 40°52′N 86°54′W
29 Y12 **Monona** Iowa, C USA 43°03′N 91°23′W
30 L9 **Monona** Wisconsin, N USA 43°03′N 89°18′W
18 B15 **Monongahela** Pennsylvania, NE USA 40°10′N 79°54′W
18 B16 **Monongahela River** ↝ NE USA
107 P17 **Monopoli** Puglia, SE Italy 40°57′N 17°18′E
Mono, Punte see Monkey Point
111 K23 **Monor** Pest, C Hungary 47°21′N 19°27′E
Monostor see Beli Manastir
78 K8 **Monou** Borkou-Ennedi-Tibesti, NE Chad 16°22′N 22°15′E
105 S12 **Monovar** Cat. Monover. País Valenciano, E Spain 38°26′N 00°50′W
Monover see Monovar
105 R7 **Monreal del Campo** Aragón, NE Spain 40°47′N 01°20′W
107 I23 **Monreale** Sicilia, Italy, C Mediterranean Sea 38°05′N 13°17′E
23 T3 **Monroe** Georgia, SE USA 33°47′N 83°42′W
29 W14 **Monroe** Iowa, C USA 41°31′N 93°06′W
22 I5 **Monroe** Louisiana, S USA 32°32′N 92°06′W
31 S10 **Monroe** Michigan, N USA 41°55′N 83°24′W
18 K13 **Monroe** New York, NE USA 41°18′N 74°09′W
21 S11 **Monroe** North Carolina, SE USA 35°00′N 80°35′W
36 L6 **Monroe** Utah, W USA 38°37′N 112°07′W
32 H7 **Monroe** Washington, NW USA 47°51′N 121°58′W
30 L9 **Monroe** Wisconsin, N USA 42°35′N 89°39′W
27 V3 **Monroe City** Missouri, C USA 39°39′N 91°43′W
31 O15 **Monroe Lake** ⊠ Indiana, N USA
23 O7 **Monroeville** Alabama, S USA 31°31′N 87°19′W
18 C15 **Monroeville** Pennsylvania, NE USA 40°24′N 79°44′W
76 J16 **Monrovia** ● (Liberia) W Liberia 06°18′N 10°48′W
76 J16 **Monrovia** ✕ W Liberia 06°22′N 10°50′W
105 T7 **Monroyo** Aragón, NE Spain 40°47′N 00°03′W
99 F20 **Mons** Dut. Bergen. Hainaut, S Belgium 50°28′N 03°58′E
104 I8 **Monsanto** Castelo Branco, C Portugal 40°02′N 07°07′W
106 H8 **Monselice** Veneto, NE Italy 45°15′N 11°47′E
166 M9 **Mon State** ◈ state S Burma (Myanmar)
98 G12 **Monster** Zuid-Holland, W Netherlands 52°01′N 04°10′E
95 N20 **Mönsterås** Kalmar, S Sweden 57°03′N 16°27′E
101 F17 **Montabaur** Rheinland-Pfalz, W Germany 50°25′N 07°48′E
106 G8 **Montagnana** Veneto, NE Italy 45°14′N 11°31′E
35 N1 **Montague** California, W USA 41°43′N 122°31′W
25 S5 **Montague** Texas, SW USA 33°40′N 97°44′W
183 S11 **Montague Island** island New South Wales, SE Australia
39 S12 **Montague Island** island Alaska, USA
39 S13 **Montague Strait** strait N Gulf of Alaska
102 J8 **Montaigu** Vendée, NW France 46°58′N 01°18′W
Montaigu see Scherpenheuvel
105 S7 **Montalbán** Aragón, NE Spain 40°49′N 00°48′W
106 G13 **Montalcino** Toscana, C Italy 43°01′N 11°34′E
104 H5 **Montalegre** Vila Real, N Portugal 41°49′N 07°48′W
114 G8 **Montana** prev. Ferdinand, Mikhaylovgrad. Montana, NW Bulgaria 43°25′N 23°14′E
108 D10 **Montana** Valais, SW Switzerland 46°23′N 07°29′E
39 R11 **Montana** Alaska, USA 62°06′N 150°03′W
114 G8 **Montana** ◈ province NW Bulgaria
33 T9 **Montana** off. State of Montana, also known as Mountain State, Treasure State. ◈ state NW USA
104 J10 **Montánchez** Extremadura, W Spain 39°15′N 06°07′W
Montañita see La Montañita
15 Q8 **Mont-Apica** Québec, SE Canada 47°57′N 71°24′W
104 G10 **Montargil** Portalegre, C Portugal 39°05′N 08°10′W
104 G10 **Montargil, Barragem de** ⊠ C Portugal
103 O7 **Montargis** Loiret, C France 48°N 02°44′E
103 O4 **Montataire** Oise, N France 49°16′N 02°24′E
102 M14 **Montauban** Tarn-et-Garonne, S France 44°01′N 01°20′E
19 N14 **Montauk** Long Island, New York, NE USA 41°01′N 71°58′W
19 N14 **Montauk Point** headland Long Island, New York, NE USA 41°04′N 71°51′W
103 Q7 **Montbard** Côte d'Or, C France 47°35′N 04°25′E
103 U7 **Montbéliard** Doubs, E France 47°31′N 06°49′E
25 W11 **Mont Belvieu** Texas, SW USA 29°51′N 94°53′W
105 U6 **Montblanc** var. Montblanch. Cataluña, NE Spain 41°23′N 01°10′E
Montblanch see Montblanc
103 Q11 **Montbrison** Loire, E France 45°37′N 04°04′E
Montcalm, Lake see Dogai Coring
103 Q9 **Montceau-les-Mines** Saône-et-Loire, C France 46°40′N 04°19′E
103 U12 **Mont Cenis, Col du** pass E France
102 K15 **Mont-de-Marsan** Landes, SW France 43°54′N 00°30′W
103 O3 **Montdidier** Somme, N France 49°39′N 02°35′E
187 Q17 **Mont-Dore** Province Sud, S New Caledonia 22°18′S 166°34′E
20 K10 **Monteagle** Tennessee, S USA 35°15′N 85°47′W
57 M20 **Monteagudo** Chuquisaca, S Bolivia 19°48′S 63°57′W
41 R16 **Monte Albán** ruins Oaxaca, S Mexico
105 R11 **Montealegre del Castillo** Castilla-La Mancha, C Spain 38°48′N 01°18′W
59 N18 **Monte Azul** Minas Gerais, SE Brazil 15°13′S 42°53′W
14 M12 **Montebello** Québec, SE Canada 45°40′N 74°56′W
106 H7 **Montebelluna** Veneto, NE Italy 45°46′N 12°03′E
60 G13 **Montecarlo** Misiones, NE Argentina 26°38′S 54°45′W
61 D16 **Monte Caseros** Corrientes, NE Argentina 30°15′S 57°39′W
60 J13 **Monte Castelo** Santa Catarina, S Brazil 26°34′S 50°12′W
106 F11 **Montecatini Terme** Toscana, C Italy 43°53′N 10°46′E
42 H7 **Montecillos, Cordillera de** ▲▲ W Honduras
62 I12 **Monte Comén** Mendoza, W Argentina 34°35′S 67°53′W
44 M8 **Monte Cristi** var. San Fernando de Monte Cristi. NW Dominican Republic 19°52′N 71°39′W
58 C13 **Monte Cristo** Amazonas, W Brazil 03°14′S 68°00′W
107 E14 **Montecristo, Isola di** island Archipelago Toscano, C Italy
Monte Croce Carnico, Passo di see Plöcken Pass
58 J12 **Monte Dourado** Pará, NE Brazil 0°48′S 52°32′W
40 L11 **Monte Escobedo** Zacatecas, C Mexico 22°19′N 103°30′W
106 I13 **Montefalco** Umbria, C Italy 42°54′N 12°40′E
107 H14 **Montefiascone** Lazio, C Italy 42°33′N 12°01′E
105 N14 **Montefrío** Andalucía, S Spain 37°19′N 04°00′W
44 I11 **Montego Bay** var. Mobay. W Jamaica 18°28′N 77°55′W
Montego Bay see Sangster
104 J8 **Montehermoso** Extremadura, W Spain 40°05′N 06°20′W
104 F10 **Montejunto, Serra de** ▲ C Portugal 39°10′N 09°01′W
Monteleone di Calabria see Vibo Valentia
54 E7 **Montelíbano** Córdoba, NW Colombia 08°02′N 75°29′W
103 R13 **Montélimar** anc. Acunum Acusio, Montilium Adhemari. Drôme, E France 44°33′N 04°45′E
104 K15 **Montellano** Andalucía, S Spain 37°00′N 05°34′W
35 Y2 **Montello** Nevada, W USA 41°18′N 114°10′W
30 L8 **Montello** Wisconsin, N USA 43°47′N 89°20′W
63 J18 **Montemayor, Meseta de** plain SE Argentina
41 O9 **Montemorelos** Nuevo León, NE Mexico 25°10′N 99°52′W
104 G11 **Montemor-o-Novo** Évora, S Portugal 38°38′N 08°13′W
104 G8 **Montemor-o-Velho** var. Montemor-o-Vélho. Coimbra, N Portugal 40°11′N 08°41′W
Montemor-o-Vélho see Montemor-o-Velho
104 H7 **Montemuro, Serra de** ▲ N Portugal 40°59′N 07°59′W
102 K12 **Montendre** Charente-Maritime, W France 45°17′N 00°24′W
61 I15 **Montenegro** Rio Grande do Sul, S Brazil 29°40′S 51°32′W
113 J16 **Montenegro** Serb. Crna Gora. ◆ republic SW Europe
62 G10 **Monte Patria** Coquimbo, N Chile 30°40′S 71°00′W
45 O9 **Monte Plata** E Dominican Republic 18°50′N 69°47′W
83 P14 **Montepuez** Cabo Delgado, N Mozambique 13°09′S 39°00′E
83 P14 **Montepuez** ↝ N Mozambique
106 G13 **Montepulciano** Toscana, C Italy 43°02′N 11°51′E
62 L6 **Monte Quemado** Santiago del Estero, N Argentina 25°48′S 62°52′W
103 O6 **Montereau-Faut-Yonne** anc. Condate. Seine-St-Denis, N France 48°23′N 02°57′E
35 N11 **Monterey** California, W USA 36°36′N 121°53′W
20 L9 **Monterey** Tennessee, S USA 36°09′N 85°16′W
21 T5 **Monterey** Virginia, NE USA 38°24′N 79°36′W
Monterey see Monterrey
35 N10 **Monterey Bay** bay California, W USA
54 D6 **Montería** Córdoba, NW Colombia 08°45′N 75°54′W
57 N18 **Montero** Santa Cruz, C Bolivia 17°20′S 63°15′W
62 J7 **Monteros** Tucumán, C Argentina 27°12′S 65°30′W
104 I5 **Monterrei** Galicia, NW Spain 41°56′N 07°27′W
41 O8 **Monterrey** var. Monterey. Nuevo León, NE Mexico 25°41′N 100°16′W
32 F9 **Montesano** Washington, NW USA 46°58′N 123°37′W
107 M19 **Montesano sulla Marcellana** Campania, S Italy 40°15′N 15°41′E
107 N16 **Monte Sant' Angelo** Puglia, SE Italy 41°43′N 15°58′E
59 O16 **Monte Santo** Bahia, E Brazil 10°25′S 39°18′W
107 D18 **Monte Santu, Capo di** headland Sardegna, Italy, C Mediterranean Sea 40°05′N 09°43′E
59 M19 **Montes Claros** Minas Gerais, SE Brazil 16°45′S 43°52′W
107 K14 **Montesilvano Marina** Abruzzo, C Italy 42°28′N 14°07′E
23 P4 **Montevallo** Alabama, S USA 33°06′N 86°51′W
106 G12 **Montevarchi** Toscana, C Italy 43°32′N 11°34′E
61 F20 **Montevideo** ● (Uruguay) Montevideo, S Uruguay 34°55′S 56°10′W
29 S9 **Montevideo** Minnesota, N USA 44°56′N 95°43′W
37 S7 **Monte Vista** Colorado, C USA 37°33′N 106°08′W
23 T5 **Montezuma** Georgia, SE USA 32°18′N 84°01′W
29 W14 **Montezuma** Iowa, C USA 41°35′N 92°31′W
26 J6 **Montezuma** Kansas, C USA 37°33′N 100°25′W
103 U12 **Montgenèvre, Col de** pass France/Italy
97 K20 **Montgomery** E Wales, United Kingdom 52°38′N 03°05′W
23 Q5 **Montgomery** state capital Alabama, S USA 32°22′N 86°18′W
29 V9 **Montgomery** Minnesota, N USA 44°26′N 93°34′W
18 G13 **Montgomery** Pennsylvania, NE USA 41°08′N 76°52′W
21 Q5 **Montgomery** West Virginia, NE USA 38°07′N 81°19′W
97 K19 **Montgomery** cultural region E Wales, United Kingdom
Montgomery see Sāhīwāl
27 V4 **Montgomery City** Missouri, C USA 38°57′N 91°27′W
35 S8 **Montgomery Pass** pass Nevada, W USA
102 K12 **Montguyon** Charente-Maritime, W France 45°12′N 00°13′W
108 C10 **Monthey** Valais, SW Switzerland 46°15′N 06°56′E
27 V13 **Monticello** Arkansas, C USA 33°38′N 91°49′W
23 T4 **Monticello** Florida, SE USA 30°33′N 83°52′W
23 T8 **Monticello** Georgia, SE USA 33°18′N 83°40′W
30 M13 **Monticello** Illinois, N USA 40°01′N 88°34′W
31 O12 **Monticello** Indiana, N USA 40°45′N 86°46′W

29 Y13 **Monticello** Iowa, C USA 42°14′N 91°11′W
20 L7 **Monticello** Kentucky, S USA 36°50′N 84°50′W
29 V8 **Monticello** Minnesota, N USA 45°19′N 93°45′W
22 K7 **Monticello** Mississippi, S USA 31°33′N 90°06′W
27 V2 **Monticello** Missouri, C USA 40°07′N 91°42′W
18 J12 **Monticello** New York, NE USA 41°39′N 74°41′W
37 O7 **Monticello** Utah, W USA 37°52′N 109°20′W
106 F8 **Montichiari** Lombardia, N Italy 45°24′N 10°27′E
102 M12 **Montignac** Dordogne, SW France 45°24′N 00°54′E
99 G21 **Montignies-le-Tilleul** *var.* Montigny-le-Tilleul. Hainaut, S Belgium 50°22′N 04°23′E
14 J8 **Montigny, Lac de** ◎ Québec, SE Canada
103 S6 **Montigny-le-Roi** Haute-Marne, N France 48°02′N 05°28′E
Montigny-le-Tilleul *see* Montignies-le-Tilleul
43 R16 **Montijo** Veraguas, S Panama 07°59′N 80°58′W
104 F11 **Montijo** Setúbal, W Portugal 38°42′N 08°59′W
104 J11 **Montijo** Extremadura, W Spain 38°55′N 06°38′W
Montilium Adhemari *see* Montélimar
104 M13 **Montilla** Andalucía, S Spain 37°36′N 04°39′W
102 L3 **Montivilliers** Seine-Maritime, N France 49°31′N 00°10′E
15 U7 **Mont-Joli** Québec, SE Canada 48°36′N 68°14′W
14 M10 **Mont-Laurier** Québec, SE Canada 46°33′N 75°31′W
15 X5 **Mont-Louis** Québec, SE Canada 49°15′N 65°46′W
103 N17 **Mont-Louis** *var.* Mont Louis. Pyrénées-Orientales, S France 42°30′N 02°08′E
103 O10 **Montluçon** Allier, C France 46°21′N 02°37′E
15 R10 **Montmagny** Québec, SE Canada 47°00′N 70°31′W
103 S3 **Montmédy** Meuse, NE France 49°31′N 05°21′E
103 P5 **Montmirail** Marne, N France 48°53′N 03°31′E
15 R9 **Montmorency** ≈ Québec, SE Canada
102 M10 **Montmorillon** Vienne, W France 46°26′N 00°52′E
107 J14 **Montorio al Vomano** Abruzzo, C Italy 42°31′N 13°39′E
104 M13 **Montoro** Andalucía, S Spain 38°00′N 04°21′W
33 S16 **Montpelier** Idaho, NW USA 42°19′N 111°18′W
29 P6 **Montpelier** North Dakota, N USA 46°40′N 98°34′W
18 M7 **Montpelier** *state capital* Vermont, NE USA 44°16′N 72°32′W
103 Q15 **Montpellier** Hérault, S France 43°37′N 03°52′E
102 L12 **Montpon-Ménestérol** Dordogne, SW France 45°01′N 00°10′E
12 K15 **Montréal** *Eng.* Montreal. Québec, SE Canada 45°30′N 73°36′W
14 G8 **Montreal** ≈ Ontario, S Canada
Montreal *see* Mirabel
11 T14 **Montreal Lake** ◎ Saskatchewan, C Canada
14 B9 **Montreal River** Ontario, S Canada 47°13′N 84°36′W
103 N2 **Montreuil** Pas-de-Calais, N France 50°28′N 01°46′E
102 K8 **Montreuil-Bellay** Maine-et-Loire, NW France 47°07′N 00°10′W
108 C10 **Montreux** Vaud, SW Switzerland 46°27′N 06°55′E
108 B9 **Montricher** Vaud, W Switzerland 46°37′N 06°24′E
96 K10 **Montrose** E Scotland, United Kingdom 56°43′N 02°29′W
27 W14 **Montrose** Arkansas, C USA 33°18′N 91°29′W
37 Q6 **Montrose** Colorado, C USA 38°29′N 107°53′W
29 Y16 **Montrose** Iowa, C USA 40°31′N 91°24′W
18 H12 **Montrose** Pennsylvania, NE USA 41°49′N 75°53′W
21 X5 **Montross** Virginia, NE USA 38°04′N 76°51′W
15 O12 **Mont-St-Hilaire** Québec, SE Canada 45°34′N 73°10′W
103 S3 **Mont-St-Martin** Meurthe-et-Moselle, NE France 49°31′N 05°51′E
45 V10 **Montserrat** *var.* Emerald Isle. ◇ *UK dependent territory* E West Indies
105 V5 **Montserrat** ▲ NE Spain 41°39′N 01°44′E
104 M7 **Montuenga** Castilla-León, N Spain 41°04′N 04°38′W
99 M19 **Montzen** Liège, E Belgium 50°42′N 05°59′E
37 N8 **Monument Valley** *valley* Arizona/Utah, SW USA
166 L4 **Monywa** Sagaing, C Burma (Myanmar) 22°05′N 95°12′E
106 D7 **Monza** Lombardia, N Italy 45°35′N 09°16′E
83 J15 **Monze** Southern, S Zambia 16°20′S 27°29′E
105 T5 **Monzón** Aragón, NE Spain 41°54′N 00°12′E
25 T9 **Moody** Texas, SW USA 31°18′N 97°21′W
98 L13 **Mook** Limburg, SE Netherlands 51°45′N 05°52′E
165 O12 **Mooka** *var.* Mōka. Tochigi, Honshū, S Japan 36°27′N 139°59′E
182 K3 **Moomba** South Australia 28°07′S 140°12′E
14 G13 **Moon** ≈ Ontario, S Canada
Moon *see* Muhu
181 Y10 **Moonie** Queensland, E Australia 27°46′S 150°22′E
193 O5 **Moonless Mountains** *undersea feature* E Pacific Ocean 30°40′N 140°00′W
182 L13 **Moonlight Head** *headland* Victoria, SE Australia 38°47′S 143°12′E
Moon-Sund *see* Väinameri
182 H8 **Moonta** South Australia 34°03′S 137°36′E
Moor *see* Mór
180 I12 **Moora** Western Australia 30°23′S 116°05′E
98 H12 **Moordrecht** Zuid-Holland, C Netherlands 51°59′N 04°40′E
33 T9 **Moore** Montana, NW USA 47°00′N 109°40′W
27 N11 **Moore** Oklahoma, C USA 35°21′N 97°30′W
25 R12 **Moore** Texas, SW USA 29°03′N 99°01′W
191 S10 **Moorea** *island* Îles du Vent, W French Polynesia
21 U3 **Moorefield** West Virginia, NE USA 39°04′N 78°59′W
23 X14 **Moore Haven** Florida, SE USA 26°49′N 81°05′W
180 J11 **Moore, Lake** ◎ Western Australia
19 N7 **Moore Reservoir** ⊠ New Hampshire/Vermont, NE USA
44 G1 **Moores Island** *island* N Bahamas
21 R10 **Mooresville** North Carolina, SE USA 35°34′N 80°48′W
29 R5 **Moorhead** Minnesota, N USA 46°51′N 96°44′W
22 K4 **Moorhead** Mississippi, S USA 33°27′N 90°30′W
99 F18 **Moorsel** Oost-Vlaanderen, C Belgium 50°58′N 04°06′E
99 C18 **Moorslede** West-Vlaanderen, W Belgium 50°53′N 03°03′E
18 L8 **Moosalamoo, Mount** ▲ Vermont, NE USA 43°55′N 73°03′W
101 M22 **Moosburg in der Isar** Bayern, SE Germany 48°28′N 11°55′E
33 S14 **Moose** Wyoming, C USA 43°38′N 110°42′W
12 H11 **Moose** ≈ Ontario, S Canada
12 H10 **Moose Factory** Ontario, S Canada 51°16′N 80°32′W
19 Q4 **Moosehead Lake** ◎ Maine, NE USA
11 U16 **Moose Jaw** Saskatchewan, S Canada 50°23′N 105°35′W
11 V14 **Moose Lake** Manitoba, C Canada 53°42′N 100°22′W
29 W6 **Moose Lake** Minnesota, N USA 46°28′N 92°46′W
19 P6 **Mooselookmeguntic Lake** ◎ Maine, NE USA
39 R12 **Moose Pass** Alaska, USA 60°28′N 149°21′W
19 P5 **Moose River** ≈ Maine, NE USA
18 J9 **Moose River** ≈ New York, NE USA
11 V16 **Moosomin** Saskatchewan, S Canada 50°09′N 101°41′W
12 H10 **Moosonee** Ontario, SE Canada 51°18′N 80°40′W
19 N12 **Moosup** Connecticut, NE USA 41°42′N 71°51′W
83 N16 **Mopeia** Zambézia, NE Mozambique 17°59′S 35°43′E
83 H18 **Mopipi** Central, C Botswana 21°07′S 24°55′E
Moppo *see* Mokp'o
77 N11 **Mopti** Mopti, C Mali 14°30′N 04°15′W
77 O11 **Mopti** ◈ *region* S Mali
57 H18 **Moquegua** Moquegua, SE Peru 17°07′S 70°55′W
57 H18 **Moquegua** *off.* Departamento de Moquegua. ◈ *department* S Peru
Moquegua, Departamento de *see* Moquegua
111 I23 **Mór** *Ger.* Moor. Fejér, C Hungary 47°21′N 18°12′E
78 G11 **Mora** Extrême-Nord, N Cameroon 11°02′N 14°07′E
104 G11 **Mora** Évora, S Portugal 38°56′N 08°10′W
105 N9 **Mora** Castilla-La Mancha, C Spain 39°40′N 03°46′W
94 L12 **Mora** Dalarna, C Sweden 61°N 14°30′E
29 V7 **Mora** Minnesota, N USA 45°52′N 93°18′W
37 T10 **Mora** New Mexico, SW USA 35°56′N 105°16′W
113 J17 **Morača** ≈ S Montenegro
152 K10 **Morādābād** Uttar Pradesh, N India 28°50′N 78°45′E
105 U6 **Móra d'Ebre** *var.* Mora de Ebro. Cataluña, NE Spain 41°05′N 00°38′E
Mora de Ebro *see* Móra d'Ebre
105 S8 **Mora de Rubielos** Aragón, NE Spain 40°15′N 00°45′W
172 H4 **Morafenobe** Mahajanga, W Madagascar 17°49′S 44°54′E
110 K8 **Morąg** *Ger.* Mohrungen. Warmińsko-Mazurskie, N Poland 53°55′N 19°56′E
111 L25 **Mórahalom** Csongrád, S Hungary 46°14′N 19°52′E
105 N11 **Moral de Calatrava** Castilla-La Mancha, C Spain 38°50′N 03°34′W
63 G19 **Moraleda, Canal** *strait* SE Pacific Ocean
54 J3 **Morales** Bolívar, N Colombia 08°17′N 73°52′W
54 D12 **Morales** Cauca, SW Colombia 02°46′N 76°44′W
42 F5 **Morales** Izabal, E Guatemala 15°28′N 88°46′W
172 J5 **Moramanga** Toamasina, E Madagascar 18°57′S 48°13′E
27 Q6 **Moran** Kansas, C USA 37°55′N 95°10′W
25 Q7 **Moran** Texas, SW USA 32°33′N 99°10′W
181 X7 **Moranbah** Queensland, NE Australia 22°01′S 148°08′E
44 L13 **Morant Bay** E Jamaica 17°53′N 76°25′W
96 G10 **Morar, Loch** ◎ N Scotland, United Kingdom
Morata *see* Goodenough Island
105 Q12 **Moratalla** Murcia, SE Spain 38°11′N 01°53′W
108 C8 **Morat, Lac de** *Ger.* Murtensee. ◎ W Switzerland
84 I11 **Morava** *var.* March. ≈ C Europe *see also* March
Morava *see* Moravia, Czech Republic
Morava *see* Velika Morava, Serbia
29 W15 **Moravia** Iowa, C USA 40°53′N 92°49′W
111 F18 **Moravia** *Cz.* Morava, *Ger.* Mähren. *cultural region* E Czech Republic
111 H17 **Moravice** *Ger.* Mohra. ≈ NE Czech Republic
116 E12 **Moravița** Timiș, SW Romania 45°15′N 21°17′E
111 G17 **Moravská Třebová** *Ger.* Mährisch-Trübau. Pardubický Kraj, C Czech Republic 49°47′N 16°40′E
111 E19 **Moravské Budějovice** *Ger.* Mährisch-Budwitz. Vysočina, C Czech Republic 49°03′N 15°48′E
111 H17 **Moravskoslezský Kraj** *prev.* Ostravský Kraj. ◈ *region* E Czech Republic
111 F19 **Moravský Krumlov** *Ger.* Mährisch-Kromau. Jihomoravský Kraj, SE Czech Republic 48°58′N 16°30′E
96 J8 **Moray** *cultural region* N Scotland, United Kingdom
96 J8 **Moray Firth** *inlet* N Scotland, United Kingdom
42 B10 **Morazán** ◈ *department* NE El Salvador
154 C10 **Morbi** Gujarāt, W India 22°51′N 70°49′E
102 G7 **Morbihan** ◈ *department* NW France
Mörbisch *see* Mörbisch am See
109 Y5 **Mörbisch am See** *var.* Mörbisch. Burgenland, E Austria 47°43′N 16°40′E
95 N21 **Mörbylånga** Kalmar, S Sweden 56°31′N 16°25′E
102 J14 **Morcenx** Landes, SW France 44°04′N 00°55′W
Morcheh Khort *see* Mūrcheh Khvort
163 T5 **Mordaga** Nei Mongol Zizhiqu, N China 51°15′N 120°47′E
11 X17 **Morden** Manitoba, S Canada 49°12′N 98°05′W
Mordovia *see* Mordoviya, Respublika
127 N5 **Mordoviya, Respublika** *prev.* Mordovskaya ASSR, *Eng.* Mordovia, Mordvinia. ◈ *autonomous republic* W Russian Federation
126 M7 **Mordovo** Tambovskaya Oblast', W Russian Federation 52°05′N 40°49′E
Mordovskaya ASSR/ Mordvinia *see* Mordoviya, Respublika
Morea *see* Pelopónnisos
28 K8 **Moreau River** ≈ South Dakota, N USA
97 K16 **Morecambe** NW England, United Kingdom 54°04′N 02°53′W
97 K16 **Morecambe Bay** *inlet* NW England, United Kingdom
183 S4 **Moree** New South Wales, SE Australia 29°29′S 149°53′E
21 N5 **Morehead** Kentucky, S USA 38°11′N 83°27′W
21 X11 **Morehead City** North Carolina, SE USA 34°43′N 76°43′W
27 Y8 **Morehouse** Missouri, C USA 36°51′N 89°41′W
108 E10 **Mörel** Valais, SW Switzerland 46°22′N 08°03′E
54 D13 **Morelia** Caquetá, S Colombia 01°30′N 75°43′W
41 N14 **Morelia** Michoacán, S Mexico 19°40′N 101°11′W
105 T7 **Morella** País Valenciano, E Spain 40°37′N 00°06′W
40 I7 **Morelos** Chihuahua, N Mexico 26°37′N 107°37′W
41 O15 **Morelos** ◈ *state* S Mexico
154 H7 **Morena** Madhya Pradesh, C India 26°30′N 78°04′E
104 L12 **Morena, Sierra** ▲ S Spain
37 O14 **Morenci** Arizona, SW USA 33°05′N 109°21′W
31 R11 **Morenci** Michigan, N USA 41°43′N 84°13′W
116 J13 **Moreni** Dâmbovița, S Romania 44°59′N 25°39′E
94 D9 **Møre og Romsdal** ◈ *county* S Norway
10 I14 **Moresby Island** *island* Queen Charlotte Islands, British Columbia, SW Canada
183 W2 **Moreton Island** *island* Queensland, E Australia
103 O3 **Moreuil** Somme, N France 49°47′N 02°28′E
35 V7 **Morey Peak** ▲ Nevada, W USA 38°40′N 116°16′W
125 U4 **More-Yu** ≈ NW Russian Federation
103 T9 **Morez** Jura, E France 46°33′N 06°01′E
Morfou Bay/Mórfou, Kólpos *see* Güzelyurt Körfezi
182 J8 **Morgan** South Australia 34°02′S 139°39′E
23 S7 **Morgan** Georgia, SE USA 31°31′N 84°34′W
25 S8 **Morgan** Texas, SW USA 32°01′N 97°36′W
22 J10 **Morgan City** Louisiana, S USA 29°42′N 91°12′W
20 H6 **Morganfield** Kentucky, S USA 37°41′N 87°55′W
35 O10 **Morgan Hill** California, W USA 37°05′N 121°38′W
21 Q9 **Morganton** North Carolina, SE USA 35°44′N 81°43′W
20 J7 **Morgantown** Kentucky, S USA 37°12′N 86°42′W
21 S2 **Morgantown** West Virginia, NE USA 39°38′N 79°57′W
108 B10 **Morges** Vaud, SW Switzerland 46°31′N 06°30′E
148 M4 **Morghāb, Daryā-ye** *Rus.* Murgab, Murghab, *Turk.* Murgap, Deryasy Murgap. ≈ Afghanistan/ Turkmenistan *see also* Murgap
Morghāb, Daryā-ye *see* Murgap
96 I9 **Mor, Glen** *var.* Glen Albyn, Great Glen. *valley* N Scotland, United Kingdom
103 T5 **Morhange** Moselle, NE France 48°56′N 06°37′E
158 M5 **Mori** *var.* Mori Kazak Zizhixian. Xinjiang Uygur Zizhiqu, NW China 43°48′N 90°21′E
165 R5 **Mori** Hokkaidō, NE Japan 42°04′N 140°36′E
35 Y6 **Moriah, Mount** ▲ Nevada, W USA 39°16′N 114°10′W
37 S11 **Moriarty** New Mexico, SW USA 34°59′N 106°03′W
54 J12 **Morichal** Guaviare, E Colombia 02°09′N 70°35′W
Mori Kazak Zizhixian *see* Mori
Morin Dawa Daurzu Zizhiqi *see* Nirji
11 Q14 **Morinville** Alberta, SW Canada 53°48′N 113°38′W
165 R8 **Morioka** Iwate, Honshū, C Japan 39°42′N 141°08′E
183 T8 **Morisset** New South Wales, SE Australia 33°07′S 151°32′E
165 Q8 **Moriyoshi-zan** ▲ Honshū, C Japan 39°58′N 140°32′E
92 K13 **Morjärv** Norrbotten, N Sweden 66°03′N 22°45′E
127 R3 **Morki** Respublika Mariy El, W Russian Federation 56°27′N 49°01′E
123 N10 **Morkoka** ≈ NE Russian Federation
102 F5 **Morlaix** Finistère, NW France 48°35′N 03°50′W
95 M20 **Mörlunda** Kalmar, S Sweden 57°19′N 15°52′E
107 N19 **Mormanno** Calabria, SW Italy 39°54′N 15°58′E
36 L11 **Mormon Lake** ◎ Arizona, SW USA
35 Y10 **Mormon Peak** ▲ Nevada, W USA 36°59′N 114°25′W
Mormon State *see* Utah
45 Y5 **Morne-à-l'Eau** Grande Terre, N Guadeloupe 16°20′N 61°31′W
29 Y15 **Morning Sun** Iowa, C USA 41°06′N 91°15′W
193 S12 **Mornington Abyssal Plain** *undersea feature* SE Pacific Ocean 50°00′S 90°00′W
63 F22 **Mornington, Isla** *island* S Chile
181 T4 **Mornington Island** *island* Wellesley Islands, Queensland, N Australia
115 E18 **Mórnos** ≈ C Greece
149 P14 **Moro** Sind, SE Pakistan 26°36′N 67°59′E
32 I11 **Moro** Oregon, NW USA 45°30′N 120°46′W
186 E8 **Morobe** Morobe, C Papua New Guinea 07°46′S 147°35′E
186 E8 **Morobe** ◈ *province* C Papua New Guinea
31 N12 **Morocco** Indiana, N USA 40°57′N 87°27′W
74 E8 **Morocco** *off.* Kingdom of Morocco, *Ar.* Al Mamlakah. ◆ *monarchy* N Africa
Morocco *see* Marrakech
Morocco, Kingdom of *see* Morocco
81 I22 **Morogoro** Morogoro, E Tanzania 06°49′S 37°40′E
81 H24 **Morogoro** ◈ *region* SE Tanzania
171 Q7 **Moro Gulf** *gulf* S Philippines
41 N13 **Moroleón** Guanajuato, C Mexico 20°00′N 101°13′W
172 H6 **Morombe** Toliara, W Madagascar 21°47′S 43°21′E
44 G5 **Morón** Ciego de Ávila, C Cuba 22°08′N 78°39′W
163 N8 **Mörön** Hentiy, C Mongolia 47°21′N 110°21′E
162 I6 **Mörön** Hövsgöl, N Mongolia 49°39′N 100°08′E
54 K5 **Morón** Carabobo, N Venezuela 10°29′N 68°11′W
Morón *see* Morón de la Frontera
56 D8 **Morona, Río** ≈ N Peru
56 C8 **Morona Santiago** ◈ *province* E Ecuador
172 H5 **Morondava** Toliara, W Madagascar 20°19′S 44°17′E
104 K14 **Morón de la Frontera** *var.* Morón. Andalucía, S Spain 37°07′N 05°27′W
172 G13 **Moroni** ● (Comoros) Grande Comore, NW Comoros 11°41′S 43°16′E
171 S10 **Morotai, Pulau** *island* Maluku, E Indonesia
Morotiri *see* Marotiri
81 H17 **Moroto** NE Uganda 02°32′N 34°41′E
Morozov *see* Bratan
126 M11 **Morozovsk** Rostovskaya Oblast', SW Russian Federation 48°21′N 41°54′E
97 L14 **Morpeth** N England, United Kingdom 55°10′N 01°41′W
Morphou *see* Güzelyurt
Morphou Bay *see* Güzelyurt Körfezi
28 I13 **Morrill** Nebraska, C USA 41°57′N 103°55′W
27 U11 **Morrilton** Arkansas, C USA 35°09′N 92°45′W
11 Q16 **Morrin** Alberta, SW Canada 51°40′N 112°45′W
184 M7 **Morrinsville** Waikato, North Island, New Zealand 37°41′S 175°32′E
11 X16 **Morris** Manitoba, S Canada 49°22′N 97°21′W
30 M11 **Morris** Illinois, N USA 41°21′N 88°25′W
29 S8 **Morris** Minnesota, N USA 45°32′N 95°53′W
14 M13 **Morrisburg** Ontario, SE Canada 44°55′N 75°07′W
197 R11 **Morris Jesup, Kap** *headland* N Greenland 83°33′N 32°40′W
182 B1 **Morris, Mount** ▲ South Australia 26°04′S 131°03′E
30 K10 **Morrison** Illinois, N USA 41°48′N 89°58′W
36 K13 **Morristown** Arizona, SW USA 33°48′N 112°34′W
18 J14 **Morristown** New Jersey, NE USA 40°48′N 74°29′W
21 O8 **Morristown** Tennessee, S USA 36°13′N 83°18′W
42 L11 **Morrito** Río San Juan, SW Nicaragua 11°37′N 85°05′W
35 P13 **Morro Bay** California, W USA 35°21′N 120°51′W
95 L22 **Mörrum** Blekinge, S Sweden 56°11′N 14°45′E
83 N16 **Morrumbala** Zambézia, NE Mozambique 17°17′S 35°35′E
83 N20 **Morrumbene** Inhambane, SE Mozambique 23°41′S 35°25′E
95 F21 **Mors** *island* NW Denmark
Mörs *see* Moers
25 N1 **Morse** Texas, SW USA 36°03′N 101°28′W
127 N6 **Morshansk** Tambovskaya Oblast', W Russian Federation 53°27′N 41°46′E
102 L5 **Mortagne-au-Perche** Orne, N France 48°32′N 00°31′E
102 J8 **Mortagne-sur-Sèvre** Vendée, NW France 47°00′N 00°57′W
104 G8 **Mortágua** Viseu, N Portugal 40°24′N 08°14′W
102 J5 **Mortain** Manche, N France 48°39′N 00°51′W
106 C8 **Mortara** Lombardia, N Italy 45°15′N 08°44′E
59 J17 **Mortes, Rio das** ≈ C Brazil
182 M12 **Mortlake** Victoria, SE Australia 38°06′S 142°48′E
Mortlock Group *see* Takuu Islands
189 Q17 **Mortlock Islands** *prev.* Nomoi Islands. *island group* C Micronesia
29 T9 **Morton** Minnesota, N USA 44°33′N 94°58′W
22 L5 **Morton** Mississippi, S USA 32°21′N 89°39′W
24 M5 **Morton** Texas, SW USA 33°40′N 102°45′W
32 H9 **Morton** Washington, NW USA 46°33′N 122°16′W
0 D7 **Morton Seamount** *undersea feature* NE Pacific Ocean 50°15′N 142°45′W
45 U15 **Moruga** Trinidad, Trinidad and Tobago 10°04′N 61°16′W
183 P9 **Morundah** New South Wales, SE Australia 34°57′S 146°18′E
Moruroa *see* Mururoa
183 S11 **Moruya** New South Wales, SE Australia 35°55′S 150°04′E
103 Q8 **Morvan** *physical region* C France
185 G21 **Morven** Canterbury, South Island, New Zealand 44°51′S 171°07′E
183 O13 **Morwell** Victoria, SE Australia 38°14′S 146°25′E
125 N6 **Morzhovets, Ostrov** *island* NW Russian Federation
126 J4 **Mosal'sk** Kaluzhskaya Oblast', W Russian Federation 54°30′N 34°55′E
101 H20 **Mosbach** Baden-Württemberg, SW Germany 49°21′N 09°06′E
95 E18 **Mosby** Vest-Agder, S Norway 58°12′N 07°55′E
33 V9 **Mosby** Montana, NW USA 46°58′N 107°53′W
32 M9 **Moscow** Idaho, NW USA 46°43′N 117°00′W
20 F10 **Moscow** Tennessee, S USA 35°04′N 89°27′W
Moscow *see* Moskva
101 D19 **Mosel** *Fr.* Moselle. ≈ W Europe *see also* Moselle
Mosel *see* Moselle
103 T4 **Moselle** ◈ *department* NE France
103 T6 **Moselle** *Ger.* Mosel. ≈ W Europe *see also* Mosel
Moselle *see* Mosel
32 K9 **Moses Lake** ◎ Washington, NW USA
83 I18 **Mosetse** Central, E Botswana 20°40′S 26°38′E
92 H4 **Mosfellsbær** Sudhurland, SW Iceland 65°09′N 21°43′W
183 N8 **Mossgiel** New South Wales, SE Australia 33°16′S 144°34′E
185 F23 **Mossgiel** Otago, South Island, New Zealand 45°51′S 170°22′E
124 M11 **Mosha** ≈ NW Russian Federation
81 I20 **Moshi** Kilimanjaro, NE Tanzania 03°21′S 37°19′E
110 G12 **Mosina** Wielkolpolskie, C Poland 52°15′N 16°50′E
30 L6 **Mosinee** Wisconsin, N USA 44°45′N 89°39′W
92 F13 **Mosjøen** Nordland, C Norway 65°49′N 13°12′E
123 S12 **Moskal'vo** Ostrov Sakhalin, Sakhalinskaya Oblast', SE Russian Federation 53°36′N 142°31′E
92 I13 **Moskosel** Norrbotten, N Sweden 65°52′N 19°30′E
126 K4 **Moskovskaya Oblast'** ◈ *province* W Russian Federation
Moskovskiy *see* Moskva
126 J3 **Moskva** *Eng.* Moscow. ● (Russian Federation) Gorod Moskva, W Russian Federation 55°45′N 37°42′E
147 Q14 **Moskva** *Rus.* Moskovskiy; *prev.* Chubek. SW Tajikistan 37°41′N 69°33′E
126 L4 **Moskva** ≈ W Russian Federation
83 I20 **Mosomane** Kgatleng, SE Botswana 24°04′S 26°15′E
Moson and Magyaróvár *see* Mosonmagyaróvár
111 H21 **Mosoni-Duna** *Ger.* Kleine Donau. ≈ NW Hungary
111 H21 **Mosonmagyaróvár** *Ger.* Wieselburg-Ungarisch-Altenburg; *prev.* Moson and Magyaróvár, *Ger.* Wieselburg and Ungarisch-Altenburg. Győr-Moson-Sopron, NW Hungary 47°52′N 17°15′E
Mospino *see* Mospyne
117 X8 **Mospyne** *Rus.* Mospino. Donets'ka Oblast', E Ukraine 47°53′N 38°03′E
54 B12 **Mosquera** Nariño, SW Colombia 02°32′N 78°24′W
37 U10 **Mosquero** New Mexico, SW USA 35°46′N 103°57′W
Mosquito Coast *see* La Mosquitia
31 U11 **Mosquito Creek Lake** ⊠ Ohio, N USA
Mosquito Gulf *see* Mosquitos, Golfo de los
23 X11 **Mosquito Lagoon** *wetland* Florida, SE USA
43 N10 **Mosquito, Punta** *headland* E Nicaragua 12°18′N 83°38′W
43 W14 **Mosquito, Punta** *headland* NE Panama 09°06′N 77°52′W
43 Q15 **Mosquitos, Golfo de los** *Eng.* Mosquito Gulf. *gulf* N Panama
95 H16 **Moss** Østfold, S Norway 59°25′N 10°40′E
Mossâmedes *see* Namibe
22 G8 **Moss Bluff** Louisiana, S USA 30°18′N 93°11′W
185 C23 **Mossburn** Southland, South Island, New Zealand 45°40′S 168°15′E
83 G26 **Mosselbaai** *var.* Mosselbai, *Eng.* Mossel Bay. Western Cape, SW South Africa 34°11′S 22°08′E
Mosselbai/Mossel Bay *see* Mosselbaai
79 F20 **Mossendjo** Niari, SW Congo 02°57′S 12°40′E
101 H22 **Mössingen** Baden-Württemberg, S Germany 48°22′N 09°01′E
181 W4 **Mossman** Queensland, NE Australia 16°34′S 145°27′E
59 P14 **Mossoró** Rio Grande do Norte, NE Brazil 05°11′S 37°20′W
23 N9 **Moss Point** Mississippi, S USA 30°24′N 88°31′W
183 S9 **Moss Vale** New South Wales, SE Australia 34°33′S 150°20′E
32 G9 **Mossyrock** Washington, NW USA 46°32′N 122°30′W
111 B15 **Most** *Ger.* Brüx. Ústecký Kraj, NW Czech Republic 50°30′N 13°37′E
162 E7 **Möst** *var.* Ulaantolgoy. Hovd, W Mongolia 46°39′N 92°50′E
121 P16 **Mosta** *var.* Musta. C Malta 35°54′N 14°25′E
74 I5 **Mostaganem** *var.* Mestghanem. NW Algeria 35°54′N 00°05′E
113 H14 **Mostar** Federacija Bosna I Hercegovina, S Bosnia and Herzegovina 43°21′N 17°47′E
61 J17 **Mostardas** Rio Grande do Sul, S Brazil 31°02′S 50°51′W
116 K14 **Mostiștea** ≈ S Romania
Mostva *see* Mastva
116 H5 **Mostys'ka** L'vivs'ka Oblast', W Ukraine 49°47′N 23°09′E
Mosul *see* Al Mawșil
95 F15 **Møsvatnet** ◎ S Norway
80 J12 **Mot'a** Āmara, N Ethiopia 11°03′N 38°03′E
79 H16 **Motaba** ≈ N Congo
105 O10 **Mota del Cuervo** Castilla-La Mancha, C Spain 39°30′N 02°52′W
104 L5 **Mota del Marqués** Castilla-León, N Spain 41°38′N 05°11′W
42 F5 **Motagua, Río** ≈ Guatemala/Honduras
119 H19 **Motal'** Brestskaya Voblasts', SW Belarus 52°13′N 25°34′E
95 L17 **Motala** Östergötland, S Sweden 58°34′N 15°05′E
191 X7 **Motane** *island* Îles Marquises, NE French Polynesia
152 K13 **Moth** Uttar Pradesh, N India 25°44′N 78°56′E
Mother of Presidents/ Mother of States *see* Virginia
96 I12 **Motherwell** C Scotland, United Kingdom 55°48′N 04°00′W
153 P12 **Motīhāri** Bihār, N India 26°40′N 84°55′E
105 Q10 **Motilla del Palancar** Castilla-La Mancha, C Spain 39°34′N 01°55′W
184 N7 **Motiti Island** *island* NE New Zealand
83 J19 **Motloutse** ≈ E Botswana
41 V17 **Motozintla de Mendoza** Chiapas, SE Mexico 15°21′N 92°14′W
105 N15 **Motril** Andalucía, S Spain 36°45′N 03°30′W
116 G13 **Motru** Gorj, SW Romania 44°49′N 22°56′E
165 Q4 **Motsuta-misaki** *headland* Hokkaidō, NE Japan 42°36′N 139°48′E
28 L6 **Mott** North Dakota, N USA 46°21′N 102°17′W
Möttling *see* Metlika
107 O18 **Mottola** Puglia, SE Italy 40°38′N 17°02′E
184 P8 **Motu** ≈ North Island, New Zealand
185 I14 **Motueka** Tasman, South Island, New Zealand 41°08′S 173°00′E
185 I14 **Motueka** ≈ South Island, New Zealand
Motu Iti *see* Tupai
41 X12 **Motul** *var.* Motul de Felipe Carrillo Puerto. Yucatán, SE Mexico 21°06′N 89°17′W
Motul de Felipe Carrillo Puerto *see* Motul
191 U17 **Motu Nui** *island* Easter Island, Chile, E Pacific Ocean
191 Q10 **Motu One** *var.* Bellingshausen. *atoll* Îles Sous le Vent, W French Polynesia
190 I16 **Motutapu** *island* E Cook Islands
193 V15 **Motu Tapu** *island* Tongatapu Group, S Tonga
184 L5 **Motutapu Island** *island* N New Zealand
Motyca *see* Modica
Mouanda *see* Moanda
Mouaskar *see* Mascara
105 U3 **Moubermé, Tuc de** *Fr.* Pic de Maubermé, *Sp.* Pico Mauberme; *prev.* Tuc de Maubermé. ▲ France/ Spain 42°48′N 00°57′E *see also* Maubermé, Pic de
Moubermé, Tuc de *see* Maubermé, Pic de
45 N7 **Mouchoir Passage** *passage* SE Turks and Caicos Islands
76 I9 **Moudjéria** Tagant, SW Mauritania 17°52′N 12°20′W
108 C9 **Moudon** Vaud, W Switzerland 46°41′N 06°49′E
Mouhoun *see* Black Volta
79 E19 **Mouila** Ngounié, C Gabon 01°50′S 11°02′E
79 K14 **Mouka** Haute-Kotto, C Central African Republic 07°12′N 21°52′E
Moukden *see* Shenyang
183 N10 **Moulamein** New South Wales, SE Australia 35°06′S 144°03′E
Moulamein Creek *see* Billabong Creek
74 F6 **Moulay-Bousselham** NW Morocco 35°00′N 06°22′W
Moule *see* le Moule
80 M11 **Moulhoulé** N Djibouti 12°34′N 43°06′E
103 P9 **Moulins** Allier, C France 46°34′N 03°20′E
Moulmein *see* Mawlamyine
166 L8 **Moulmeingyun** Ayeyarwady, SW Burma (Myanmar) 16°24′N 95°15′E
74 G6 **Moulouya** *var.* Mulucha, Muluya, Mulwiya. *seasonal river* NE Morocco
23 O2 **Moulton** Alabama, S USA 34°28′N 87°18′W
29 W16 **Moulton** Iowa, C USA 40°41′N 92°40′W
25 T11 **Moulton** Texas, SW USA 29°34′N 97°08′W
23 T7 **Moultrie** Georgia, SE USA 31°10′N 83°47′W
21 S14 **Moultrie, Lake** ⊠ South Carolina, SE USA
22 K3 **Mound Bayou** Mississippi, S USA 33°52′N 90°43′W
30 L17 **Mound City** Illinois, N USA 37°06′N 89°09′W
27 R6 **Mound City** Kansas, C USA 38°07′N 94°49′W
27 Q2 **Mound City** Missouri, C USA 40°07′N 95°13′W
29 N7 **Mound City** South Dakota, N USA 45°44′N 100°03′W
78 H13 **Moundou** Logone-Occidental, SW Chad 08°35′N 16°01′E
27 P10 **Mounds** Oklahoma, C USA 35°52′N 96°03′W
21 R2 **Moundsville** West Virginia, NE USA 39°54′N 80°44′W
167 Q12 **Moŭng Roessei** Bătdâmbâng, W Cambodia 12°47′N 103°28′E
Moun Hou *see* Black Volta
8 H8 **Mountain** ≈ Northwest Territories, NW Canada
37 S12 **Mountainair** New Mexico, SW USA 34°31′N 106°14′W
35 V1 **Mountain City** Nevada, W USA 41°48′N 115°58′W
21 Q8 **Mountain City** Tennessee, S USA 36°28′N 81°48′W
27 U7 **Mountain Grove** Missouri, C USA 37°07′N 92°15′W
27 U9 **Mountain Home** Arkansas, C USA 36°19′N 92°24′W
33 N15 **Mountain Home** Idaho, NW USA 43°07′N 115°42′W
25 Q11 **Mountain Home** Texas, SW USA 30°11′N 99°19′W
29 W4 **Mountain Iron** Minnesota, N USA 47°31′N 92°37′W
29 T10 **Mountain Lake** Minnesota, N USA 43°57′N 94°54′W
23 S3 **Mountain Park** Georgia, SE USA 34°04′N 84°24′W
35 W12 **Mountain Pass** *pass* California, W USA
27 T12 **Mountain Pine** Arkansas, C USA 34°34′N 93°10′W
39 Y14 **Mountain Point** Annette Island, Alaska, USA 55°17′N 131°31′W
Mountain State *see* Montana
Mountain State *see* West Virginia
27 V7 **Mountain View** Arkansas, C USA 35°52′N 92°07′W
38 H12 **Mountain View** Hawaii, USA, C Pacific Ocean 19°32′N 155°03′W
27 V10 **Mountain View** Missouri, C USA 37°00′N 91°42′W
38 M11 **Mountain Village** Alaska, USA 62°06′N 163°42′W
21 R8 **Mount Airy** North Carolina, SE USA 36°30′N 80°36′W
83 K24 **Mount Ayliff** *Xh.* Maxesibebi. Eastern Cape, SE South Africa 30°48′S 29°23′E
29 U16 **Mount Ayr** Iowa, C USA 40°42′N 94°14′W
182 I9 **Mount Barker** South Australia 35°06′S 138°52′E
180 J14 **Mount Barker** Western Australia 34°42′S 117°40′E
183 P11 **Mount Beauty** Victoria, SE Australia 36°47′S 147°12′E
14 E16 **Mount Brydges** Ontario, S Canada 42°54′N 81°29′W
31 N16 **Mount Carmel** Illinois, N USA 38°23′N 87°46′W
30 K10 **Mount Carroll** Illinois, N USA 42°05′N 89°59′W
31 S9 **Mount Clemens** Michigan, N USA 42°36′N 82°52′W
185 E19 **Mount Cook** Canterbury, South Island, New Zealand 43°47′S 170°06′E
83 L16 **Mount Darwin** Mashonaland Central, NE Zimbabwe 16°45′S 31°39′E
19 S7 **Mount Desert Island** *island* Maine, NE USA
23 W11 **Mount Dora** Florida, SE USA 28°48′N 81°38′W
182 G5 **Mount Eba** South Australia 30°11′S 135°40′E
25 W8 **Mount Enterprise** Texas, SW USA 31°53′N 94°40′W
182 J4 **Mount Fitton** South Australia 29°55′S 139°26′E
83 J24 **Mount Fletcher** Eastern Cape, SE South Africa 30°41′S 28°30′E
14 F15 **Mount Forest** Ontario, S Canada 43°58′N 80°44′W
182 K12 **Mount Gambier** South Australia 37°47′S 140°49′E
181 W5 **Mount Garnet** Queensland, NE Australia 17°41′S 145°07′E
21 P6 **Mount Gay** West Virginia, NE USA 37°49′N 82°00′W
31 S12 **Mount Gilead** Ohio, N USA 40°33′N 82°49′W
186 C7 **Mount Hagen** Western Highlands, C Papua New Guinea 05°54′S 144°13′E
18 J16 **Mount Holly** New Jersey, NE USA 39°59′N 74°46′W
21 R10 **Mount Holly** North Carolina, SE USA 35°18′N 81°01′W
27 T12 **Mount Ida** Arkansas, C USA 34°32′N 93°38′W
181 T6 **Mount Isa** Queensland, C Australia 20°48′S 139°32′E
21 U4 **Mount Jackson** Virginia, NE USA 38°45′N 78°38′W
18 D12 **Mount Jewett** Pennsylvania, NE USA 41°43′N 78°37′W
18 L13 **Mount Kisco** New York, NE USA 41°12′N 73°42′W
18 B15 **Mount Lebanon** Pennsylvania, NE USA 40°21′N 80°03′W
182 J8 **Mount Lofty Ranges** ▲ South Australia
180 J10 **Mount Magnet** Western Australia 28°09′S 117°52′E
184 N7 **Mount Maunganui** Bay of Plenty, North Island, New Zealand 37°39′S 176°11′E
97 E18 **Mountmellick** *Ir.* Móinteach Mílic. Laois, C Ireland 53°07′N 07°20′W
30 L10 **Mount Morris** Illinois, N USA 42°03′N 89°25′W
31 R9 **Mount Morris** Michigan, N USA 43°07′N 83°42′W
18 F10 **Mount Morris** New York, NE USA 42°43′N 77°51′W
18 B16 **Mount Morris** Pennsylvania, NE USA 39°43′N 80°06′W
30 K15 **Mount Olive** Illinois, N USA 39°04′N 89°43′W
21 V10 **Mount Olive** North Carolina, SE USA 35°12′N 78°03′W
21 N4 **Mount Olivet** Kentucky, S USA 38°32′N 84°01′W
29 Y15 **Mount Pleasant** Iowa, C USA 40°57′N 91°33′W
31 Q8 **Mount Pleasant** Michigan, N USA 43°36′N 84°46′W
18 C15 **Mount Pleasant** Pennsylvania, NE USA 40°07′N 79°33′W
21 T14 **Mount Pleasant** South Carolina, SE USA 32°47′N 79°51′W
20 I9 **Mount Pleasant** Tennessee, S USA 35°32′N 87°11′W
25 W6 **Mount Pleasant** Texas, SW USA 33°10′N 94°49′W
36 L4 **Mount Pleasant** Utah, W USA 39°33′N 111°27′W

◆ Country
● Country Capital
◇ Dependent Territory
○ Dependent Territory Capital
◈ Administrative Regions
✈ International Airport
▲ Mountain
▲ Mountain Range
Volcano
≈ River
◎ Lake
⊠ Reservoir

63 N23 **Mount Pleasant** ✈ (Stanley) East Falkland, Falkland Islands
97 G25 **Mount's Bay** *inlet* SW England, United Kingdom
35 N2 **Mount Shasta** California, W USA 41°18′N 122°19′W
30 J13 **Mount Sterling** Illinois, N USA 39°59′N 90°44′W
21 N5 **Mount Sterling** Kentucky, S USA 38°03′N 83°56′W
18 E15 **Mount Union** Pennsylvania, NE USA 40°21′N 77°51′W
23 V6 **Mount Vernon** Georgia, SE USA 32°10′N 82°35′W
30 L16 **Mount Vernon** Illinois, N USA 38°19′N 88°54′W
20 M6 **Mount Vernon** Kentucky, S USA 37°20′N 84°20′W
27 S7 **Mount Vernon** Missouri, C USA 37°05′N 93°49′W
31 T13 **Mount Vernon** Ohio, N USA 40°23′N 82°29′W
32 K13 **Mount Vernon** Oregon, NW USA 44°22′N 119°07′W
25 W6 **Mount Vernon** Texas, SW USA 33°11′N 95°13′W
32 H7 **Mount Vernon** Washington, NW USA 48°25′N 122°19′W
20 L5 **Mount Washington** Kentucky, S USA 38°03′N 85°33′W
182 F8 **Mount Wedge** South Australia 33°29′S 135°08′E
30 L14 **Mount Zion** Illinois, N USA 39°46′N 88°52′W
181 Y9 **Moura** Queensland, NE Australia 24°34′S 149°57′E
58 F12 **Moura** Amazonas, NW Brazil 01°32′S 61°43′W
104 H12 **Moura** Beja, S Portugal 38°08′N 07°27′W
104 I12 **Mourão** Évora, S Portugal 38°22′N 07°20′W
76 L11 **Mourdiah** Koulikoro, W Mali 14°28′N 07°31′W
78 K7 **Mourdi, Dépression du** *desert lowland* Chad/Sudan
102 J16 **Mourenx** Pyrénées-Atlantiques, SW France 43°24′N 00°37′W
Mourgana *see* Mourgkána
115 C15 **Mourgkána** *var.* Mourgana. ⛰ Albania/Greece 39°48′N 20°24′E
97 G16 **Mourne Mountains** *Ir.* Beanna Boirche. ⛰ SE Northern Ireland, United Kingdom
115 I15 **Moúrtzeflos, Akrotírio** *headland* Límnos, E Greece 40°00′N 25°02′E
99 C19 **Mouscron** *Dut.* Moeskroen. Hainaut, W Belgium 50°44′N 03°14′E
Mouse River *see* Souris River
78 H10 **Moussoro** Kanem, W Chad 13°41′N 16°31′E
103 T11 **Moûtiers** Savoie, E France 45°28′N 06°31′E
172 J14 **Moutsamudou** *var.* Mutsamudu. Anjouan, SE Comoros 12°10′S 44°25′E
74 K11 **Mouydir, Monts de** ⛰ S Algeria
79 F20 **Mouyondzi** Bouenza, S Congo 03°58′S 13°57′E
115 E16 **Mouzáki** *prev.* Mouzákion. Thessalía, C Greece 39°25′N 21°40′E
Mouzákion *see* Mouzáki
29 S13 **Moville** Iowa, C USA 42°30′N 96°04′W
82 E13 **Moxico** ◐ *province* E Angola
172 I14 **Moya** Anjouan, SE Comoros 12°18′S 44°27′E
40 L12 **Moyahua** Zacatecas, C Mexico 21°18′N 103°09′W
81 J16 **Moyalē** Oromīya, C Ethiopia 03°34′N 38°58′E
76 I15 **Moyamba** W Sierra Leone 08°04′N 12°30′W
74 G7 **Moyen Atlas** *Eng.* Middle Atlas. ⛰ N Morocco
78 H13 **Moyen-Chari** *off.* Préfecture du Moyen-Chari. ◐ *prefecture* S Chad
Moyen-Chari, Préfecture du *see* Moyen-Chari
Moyen-Congo *see* Congo (Republic of)
83 J24 **Moyeni** *var.* Quthing. SW Lesotho 30°25′S 27°43′E
79 D18 **Moyen-Ogooué** *off.* Province du Moyen-Ogooué, *var.* Le Moyen-Ogooué. ◐ *province* C Gabon
Moyen-Ogooué, Province du *see* Moyen-Ogooué
103 S4 **Moyeuvre-Grande** Moselle, NE France 49°15′N 06°03′E
33 N7 **Moyie Springs** Idaho, NW USA 48°43′N 116°15′W
146 G6 **Mo'ynoq** *Rus.* Muynak. Qoraqalpog'iston Respublikasi, NW Uzbekistan 43°45′N 59°03′E
81 F16 **Moyo** NW Uganda 03°38′N 31°43′E
56 D10 **Moyobamba** San Martín, NW Peru 06°04′S 76°56′W
78 H10 **Moyto** Chari-Baguirmi, W Chad 12°35′N 16°33′E
158 G9 **Moyu** *var.* Karakax. Xinjiang Uygur Zizhiqu, NW China 37°16′N 79°39′E
122 M9 **Moyyero** ≈ N Russian Federation
145 S15 **Moyynkum** *var.* Furmanovka, *Kaz.* Fūrmanov. Zhambyl, S Kazakhstan 44°15′N 72°55′E
145 Q15 **Moyynkum, Peski** *Kaz.* Moyynqum. *desert* S Kazakhstan
Moyynqum *see* Moyynkum, Peski
145 S12 **Moyynty** Karaganda, C Kazakhstan 47°10′N 73°24′E
145 S12 **Moyynty** ≈ Karaganda, C Kazakhstan
Mozambika, Lakandranon' i *see* Mozambique Channel
83 M18 **Mozambique** *off.* Republic of Mozambique; *prev.* People's Republic of Mozambique, Portuguese East Africa. ◆ *republic* S Africa
Mozambique Basin *see* Natal Basin
Mozambique, Canal de *see* Mozambique Channel
83 P17 **Mozambique Channel** *Fr.* Canal de Mozambique, *Mal.* Lakandranon' i Mozambika. *strait* W Indian Ocean
172 L11 **Mozambique Escarpment** *var.* Mozambique Scarp. *undersea feature* SW Indian Ocean 33°00′S 36°30′E
Mozambique, People's Republic of *see* Mozambique
172 L10 **Mozambique Plateau** *var.* Mozambique Rise. *undersea feature* SW Indian Ocean 32°00′S 35°00′E
Mozambique, Republic of *see* Mozambique
Mozambique Rise *see* Mozambique Plateau
Mozambique Scarp *see* Mozambique Escarpment
127 O15 **Mozdok** Respublika Severnaya Osetiya, SW Russian Federation 43°48′N 44°42′E
57 K17 **Mozetenes, Serranías de** ⛰ C Bolivia
126 J4 **Mozhaysk** Moskovskaya Oblast', W Russian Federation 55°31′N 36°01′E
127 T3 **Mozhga** Udmurtskaya Respublika, NW Russian Federation 56°24′N 52°13′E
Mozyr' *see* Mazyr
79 P22 **Mpala** Katanga, E Dem. Rep. Congo 06°43′S 29°28′E
79 G19 **Mpama** ≈ C Congo
81 E22 **Mpanda** Rukwa, W Tanzania 06°21′S 31°01′E
82 L11 **Mpande** Northern, NE Zambia 09°13′S 31°42′E
83 J18 **Mphoengs** Matabeleland South, SW Zimbabwe 21°04′S 27°56′E
81 F18 **Mpigi** S Uganda 0°14′N 32°19′E
82 L13 **Mpika** Northern, NE Zambia 11°50′S 31°30′E
83 J14 **Mpima** Central, C Zambia 14°25′S 28°34′E
83 J14 **Mpongwe** Copperbelt, C Zambia 13°25′S 28°13′E
82 K11 **Mporokoso** Northern, N Zambia 09°22′S 30°06′E
79 H20 **Mpouya** Plateaux, SE Congo 02°38′S 16°13′E
77 P16 **Mpraeso** C Ghana 06°36′N 00°43′W
82 L11 **Mpulungu** Northern, N Zambia 08°50′S 31°06′E
83 K21 **Mpumalanga** *prev.* Eastern Transvaal, *Afr.* Oos-Transvaal. ◐ *province* NE South Africa
83 D16 **Mpungu** Okavango, N Namibia 17°36′S 18°16′E
81 I22 **Mpwapwa** Dodoma, C Tanzania 06°21′S 36°29′E
Mqinvartsveri *see* Kazbek
110 M8 **Mrągowo** *Ger.* Sensburg. Warmińsko-Mazurskie, NE Poland 53°53′N 21°19′E
127 V6 **Mrakovo** Respublika Bashkortostan, W Russian Federation 52°43′N 56°36′E
172 I13 **Mramani** Anjouan, E Comoros 12°18′N 44°39′E
166 K5 **Mrauk-oo** *var.* Mrauk U, Myohaung. Rakhine State, W Burma (Myanmar) 20°35′N 93°12′E
Mrauk U *see* Mrauk-oo
112 F12 **Mrkonjić Grad** ◐ Republika Srpska, W Bosnia and Herzegovina
110 H9 **Mrocza** Kujawsko-pomorskie, C Poland 53°15′N 17°38′E
124 I14 **Msta** ≈ NW Russian Federation
Mstislavl' *see* Mstsislaw
119 P15 **Mstsislaw** *Rus.* Mstislavl'. Mahilyowskaya Voblasts', E Belarus 54°01′N 31°43′E
Mtkvari *see* Kura
Mtoko *see* Mutoko
126 K6 **Mtsensk** Orlovskaya Oblast', W Russian Federation 53°17′N 36°34′E
81 K24 **Mtwara** Mtwara, SE Tanzania 10°17′S 40°11′E
81 J25 **Mtwara** ◐ *region* SE Tanzania
104 G14 **Mu** ▲ S Portugal 37°24′N 08°04′W
193 V15 **Mu'a** Tongatapu, S Tonga 21°11′S 175°07′W
Muai To *see* Mae Hong Son
83 P16 **Mualama** Zambézia, NE Mozambique 16°51′S 38°21′E
Mualo *see* Messalo, Rio
79 E22 **Muanda** Bas-Congo, SW Dem. Rep. Congo 05°53′S 12°17′E
Muang Chiang Rai *see* Chiang Rai
167 R6 **Muang Ham** Houaphan, N Laos 20°19′N 104°00′E
167 S8 **Muang Hinboun** Khammouan, C Laos 17°37′N 104°37′E
Muang Kalasin *see* Kalasin
Muang Khammouan *see* Thakhèk
167 S11 **Muang Không** Champasak, S Laos 14°08′N 105°48′E
167 S10 **Muang Khôngxédôn** *var.* Khong Sedone. Salavan, S Laos 15°34′N 105°46′E
Muang Khon Kaen *see* Khon Kaen
167 Q6 **Muang Khoua** Phôngsali, N Laos 21°07′N 102°31′E
Muang Krabi *see* Krabi
Muang Lampang *see* Lampang
Muang Lamphun *see* Lamphun
Muang Loei *see* Loei
Muang Lom Sak *see* Lom Sak
Muang Nakhon Sawan *see* Nakhon Sawan
167 Q6 **Muang Namo** Oudômxai, N Laos 20°58′N 101°46′E
Muang Nan *see* Nan
167 Q6 **Muang Ngoy** Louangphabang, N Laos 20°43′N 102°42′E
167 Q5 **Muang Ou Tai** Phôngsali, N Laos 22°06′N 101°59′E
Muang Pak Lay *see* Pak Lay
Muang Pakxan *see* Pakxan
167 T10 **Muang Pakxong** Champasak, S Laos 15°10′N 106°17′E
167 S9 **Muang Phalan** *var.* Muang Phalane. Savannakhét, S Laos 16°40′N 105°33′E
Muang Phalane *see* Muang Phalan
Muang Phan *see* Phan
Muang Phayao *see* Phayao
Muang Phichit *see* Phichit
167 T9 **Muang Phin** Savannakhét, S Laos 16°31′N 106°01′E
Muang Phitsanulok *see* Phitsanulok
Muang Phrae *see* Phrae
Muang Roi Et *see* Roi Et
Muang Sakon Nakhon *see* Sakon Nakhon
Muang Samut Prakan *see* Samut Prakan
167 P6 **Muang Sing** Louang Namtha, N Laos 21°12′N 101°09′E
Muang Ubon *see* Ubon Ratchathani
Muang Uthai Thani *see* Uthai Thani
167 P7 **Muang Vangviang** Viangchan, C Laos 18°53′N 102°27′E
Muang Xaignabouri *see* Xaignabouli
Muang Xay *see* Xai
167 S9 **Muang Xépôn** *var.* Sepone. Savannakhét, S Laos 16°40′N 106°15′E
168 K10 **Muar** *var.* Bandar Maharani. Johor, Peninsular Malaysia 02°01′N 102°35′E
168 J9 **Muara** Sumatera, W Indonesia 02°18′N 98°54′E
168 L13 **Muarabeliti** Sumatera, W Indonesia 03°13′S 103°00′E
168 K12 **Muarabungo** Sumatera, W Indonesia 01°28′S 102°06′E
168 L13 **Muaraenim** Sumatera, W Indonesia 03°40′S 103°48′E
169 T11 **Muarajuloi** Borneo, C Indonesia 0°12′S 114°03′E
169 U12 **Muarakaman** Borneo, C Indonesia 0°09′S 116°43′E
168 H12 **Muarasigep** Pulau Siberut, W Indonesia 01°01′S 98°48′E
168 L12 **Muaratembesi** Sumatera, W Indonesia 01°40′S 103°08′E
169 T12 **Muaratewe** *var.* Muarateweh; *prev.* Moearatewe. Borneo, C Indonesia 0°58′S 114°52′E
Muarateweh *see* Muaratewe
169 U10 **Muarawahau** Borneo, N Indonesia 01°03′N 116°48′E
138 G13 **Mubārak, Jabal** ▲ S Jordan 29°19′N 35°13′E
153 N13 **Mubārakpur** Uttar Pradesh, N India 26°05′N 83°19′E
Mubarek *see* Muborak
81 F18 **Mubende** SW Uganda 0°35′N 31°24′E
77 Y14 **Mubi** Adamawa, NE Nigeria 10°15′N 13°18′E
146 M12 **Muborak** *Rus.* Mubarek. Qashqadaryo Viloyati, S Uzbekistan 39°17′N 65°10′E
171 U12 **Mubrani** Papua, E Indonesia 0°42′S 133°25′E
67 U12 **Muchinga Escarpment** *escarpment* NE Zambia
127 N7 **Muchkapskiy** Tambovskaya Oblast', W Russian Federation 51°51′N 42°25′E
96 G10 **Muck** *island* W Scotland, United Kingdom
82 Q13 **Mucojo** Cabo Delgado, N Mozambique 12°05′S 40°30′E
82 F12 **Muconda** Lunda Sul, NE Angola 10°37′S 21°19′E
54 I10 **Muco, Río** ≈ E Colombia
83 O16 **Mucubela** Zambézia, NE Mozambique 16°51′S 37°48′E
42 J5 **Mucupina, Monte** ▲ N Honduras 15°07′N 86°36′W
136 J14 **Mucur** Kirşehir, C Turkey 39°05′N 34°25′E
143 U8 **Mūd** Khorāsān-e Janūbī, E Iran 32°41′N 59°30′E
163 Y9 **Mudanjiang** *var.* Mu-tan-chiang. Heilongjiang, NE China 44°33′N 129°40′E
163 Y9 **Mudan Jiang** ≈ NE China
136 D11 **Mudanya** Bursa, NW Turkey 40°23′N 28°53′E
28 K8 **Mud Butte** South Dakota, N USA 45°00′N 102°51′W
155 G16 **Muddebihāl** Karnātaka, C India 16°26′N 76°07′E
27 P12 **Muddy Boggy Creek** ≈ Oklahoma, C USA
36 M6 **Muddy Creek** ≈ Utah, W USA
37 V7 **Muddy Creek Reservoir** ⊡ Colorado, C USA
33 W15 **Muddy Gap** Wyoming, C USA 42°21′N 107°27′W
35 Y11 **Muddy Peak** ▲ Nevada, W USA 36°17′N 114°40′W
183 R7 **Mudgee** New South Wales, SE Australia 32°37′S 149°36′E
29 S3 **Mud Lake** ◎ Minnesota, N USA
29 P7 **Mud Lake Reservoir** ⊡ South Dakota, N USA
167 N9 **Mudon** Mon State, S Burma (Myanmar) 16°17′N 97°40′E
81 O14 **Mudug** *off.* Gobolka Mudug. ◐ *region* NE Somalia
81 O14 **Mudug** *var.* Mudugh. *plain* N Somalia
Mudug, Gobolka *see* Mudug
Mudugh *see* Mudug
83 Q15 **Muecate** Nampula, NE Mozambique 14°56′S 39°38′E
82 Q13 **Mueda** Cabo Delgado, NE Mozambique 11°40′S 39°31′E
42 L10 **Muelle de los Bueyes** Región Autónoma Atlántico Sur, SE Nicaragua 12°03′N 84°34′W
Muenchen *see* München
83 M14 **Muende** Tete, NW Mozambique 14°22′S 33°00′E
25 T5 **Muenster** Texas, SW USA 33°39′N 97°22′W
Muenster *see* Münster
43 O6 **Muerto, Cayo** *reef* NE Nicaragua
41 T17 **Muerto, Mar** *lagoon* SE Mexico
64 F11 **Muertos Trough** *undersea feature* N Caribbean Sea
83 H14 **Mufaya Kuta** Western, NW Zambia 14°30′S 24°18′E
82 J13 **Mufulira** Copperbelt, C Zambia 12°33′S 28°16′E
161 O10 **Mufu Shan** ⛰ C China
Mugalzhar Taūlary *see* Mugodzhary, Gory
137 Y12 **Muğan Düzü** *Rus.* Muganskaya Ravnina, Muganskaya Step'. *physical region* S Azerbaijan
Muganskaya Ravnina/Muganskaya Step' *see* Muğan Düzü
106 K8 **Múggia** Friuli-Venezia Giulia, NE Italy 45°36′N 13°48′E
153 N14 **Mughal Sarāi** Uttar Pradesh, N India 25°18′N 83°07′E
Mughla *see* Muğla
141 W11 **Mughshin** *var.* Muqshin. S Oman 19°26′N 54°38′E
147 S12 **Mughsu** *Rus.* Muksu. ≈ C Tajikistan
164 H14 **Mugi** Tokushima, Shikoku, SW Japan 33°39′N 134°24′E
136 C16 **Muğla** *var.* Mughla. Muğla, SW Turkey 37°13′N 28°22′E
136 C16 **Muğla** *var.* Mughla. ◐ *province* SW Turkey
114 K10 **Mŭglizh** Stara Zagora, C Bulgaria 42°36′N 25°32′E
144 J11 **Mugodzhary, Gory** *Kaz.* Mugalzhar Taūlary. ⛰ W Kazakhstan
83 O15 **Mugulama** Zambézia, NE Mozambique 16°01′S 37°33′E
Muḩāfazat Hims *see* Ḩimş
Muḩāfazat Ma'dabā *see* Ma'dabā
139 U9 **Muḩammad** Wāsiţ, E Iraq 32°46′N 45°14′E
139 R8 **Muḩammadīyah** Al Anbār, C Iraq 33°22′N 42°48′E
80 I6 **Muhammad Qol** Red Sea, NE Sudan 20°53′N 37°09′E
75 Y9 **Muhammad, Râs** *headland* E Egypt 27°45′N 34°18′E
Muhammerah *see* Khorramshahr
Muḩāfazat Al 'Aqabah *see* Al 'Aqabah
140 M12 **Muḩāyil** *var.* Mahāil. 'Asīr, SW Saudi Arabia 18°34′N 42°01′E
139 O7 **Muḩaywīr** Al Anbār, W Iraq 33°35′N 41°06′E
101 H21 **Mühlacker** Baden-Württemberg, SW Germany 48°57′N 08°51′E
Mühlbach *see* Sebeş
Mühldorf *see* Mühldorf am Inn
101 N23 **Mühldorf am Inn** *var.* Mühldorf. Bayern, SE Germany 48°14′N 12°32′E
101 J15 **Mühlhausen** *var.* Mühlhausen in Thüringen. Thüringen, C Germany 51°13′N 10°28′E
Mühlhausen in Thüringen *see* Mühlhausen
195 Q2 **Mühlig-Hofmanfjella** ⛰ Antarctica
93 L14 **Muhos** Oulu, C Finland 64°48′N 26°00′E
138 K6 **Muḩ, Sabkhat al** ◎ C Syria
118 E5 **Muhu** *Ger.* Mohn, Moon. *island* W Estonia
81 F19 **Muhutwe** Kagera, NW Tanzania 01°31′S 31°41′E
Muhu Väin *see* Väinameri
98 J10 **Muiden** Noord-Holland, C Netherlands 52°19′N 05°04′E
193 W15 **Mui Hopohoponga** *headland* Tongatapu, S Tonga 21°09′S 175°02′W
Muinchille *see* Cootehill
Muineachán *see* Monaghan
97 F19 **Muine Bheag** *Eng.* Bagenalstown. Carlow, SE Ireland 52°42′N 06°57′W
56 B5 **Muisne** Esmeraldas, NW Ecuador 0°35′N 79°58′W
83 P14 **Muite** Nampula, NE Mozambique 14°02′S 39°06′E
41 Z11 **Mujeres, Isla** *island* E Mexico
116 G7 **Mukacheve** *Hung.* Munkács, *Rus.* Mukachevo. Zakarpats'ka Oblast', W Ukraine 48°27′N 22°45′E
Mukachevo *see* Mukacheve
169 R9 **Mukah** Sarawak, East Malaysia 02°56′N 112°02′E
Mukalla *see* Al Mukallā
Mukama *see* Mokāma
Mukāshafa/Mukashshafah *see* Mukayshīfah
139 S6 **Mukayshīfah** *var.* Mukāshafa, Mukashshafah. Şalāḩ ad Dīn, N Iraq 34°24′N 43°44′E
167 R9 **Mukdahan** Mukdahan, E Thailand 16°31′N 104°43′E
Mukden *see* Shenyang
165 Y15 **Mukojima-rettō** *Eng.* Parry group. *island group* SE Japan
146 M14 **Mukry** Lebap Welaýaty, E Turkmenistan 37°39′N 65°37′E
Muksu *see* Mughsu
Muktagacha *see* Muktagachha
153 U14 **Muktagachha** *var.* Muktagacha. Dhaka, N Bangladesh 24°46′N 90°16′E
82 K13 **Mukuku** Central, C Zambia 12°10′S 29°50′E
82 K11 **Mukupa Kaoma** Northern, NE Zambia 09°55′S 30°19′E
81 I18 **Mukutan** Rift Valley, W Kenya 01°06′N 36°16′E
83 F16 **Mukwe** Caprivi, NE Namibia 18°01′S 21°24′E
105 R13 **Mula** Murcia, SE Spain 38°02′N 01°29′W
151 K20 **Mulakatholhu** *var.* Meemu Atoll, Mulaku Atoll. *atoll* C Maldives
Mulaku Atoll *see* Mulakatholhu
83 J15 **Mulalika** Lusaka, C Zambia 15°37′S 28°48′E
163 X8 **Mulan** Heilongjiang, NE China 45°57′N 128°00′E
83 N15 **Mulanje** *var.* Mlanje. Southern, S Malawi 16°05′S 35°29′E
40 H5 **Mulatos** Sonora, NW Mexico 28°42′N 108°44′W
23 P3 **Mulberry Fork** ≈ Alabama, S USA
39 P12 **Mulchatna River** ≈ Alaska, USA
125 W4 **Mul'da** Respublika Komi, NW Russian Federation 67°29′N 63°55′E
101 M14 **Mulde** ≈ E Germany
27 R10 **Muldrow** Oklahoma, C USA 35°25′N 94°34′W
40 E7 **Mulegé** Baja California Sur, NW Mexico 26°54′N 112°00′W
108 I10 **Mulegns** Graubünden, S Switzerland 46°30′N 09°36′E
79 M21 **Mulenda** Kasai-Oriental, C Dem. Rep. Congo 04°19′S 24°55′E
24 M4 **Muleshoe** Texas, SW USA 34°13′N 102°43′W
83 O15 **Mulevala** Zambézia, NE Mozambique 16°25′S 37°35′E
183 P5 **Mulgoa Creek** *seasonal river* New South Wales, SE Australia
105 O15 **Mulhacén** *var.* Cerro de Mulhacén. ▲ S Spain 37°07′N 03°11′W
Mulhacén, Cerro de *see* Mulhacén
Mülhausen *see* Mulhouse
101 E24 **Müllheim** Baden-Württemberg, SW Germany 47°50′N 07°37′E
101 E15 **Mülheim** *var.* Mulheim an der Ruhr. Nordrhein-Westfalen, W Germany 51°25′N 06°50′E
Mulheim an der Ruhr *see* Mülheim
103 U7 **Mulhouse** *Ger.* Mülhausen. Haut-Rhin, NE France 47°45′N 07°20′E
160 G11 **Muli** *var.* Qiaowa, Muli Zangzu Zizhixian. Sichuan, C China 27°49′N 101°10′E
171 X15 **Muli** *channel* Papua, E Indonesia
163 Y9 **Muling** Heilongjiang, NE China 44°54′N 130°35′E
Muli Zangzu Zizhixian *see* Muli
Mullach Íde *see* Malahide
Mullaitivu *see* Mullaittivu
155 K23 **Mullaittivu** *var.* Mullaitivu. Northern Province, N Sri Lanka 09°15′N 80°48′E
33 N8 **Mullan** Idaho, NW USA 47°28′N 115°48′W
28 M13 **Mullen** Nebraska, C USA 42°02′N 101°01′W
183 Q6 **Mullengudgery** New South Wales, SE Australia 31°42′S 147°24′E
21 Q6 **Mullens** West Virginia, NE USA 37°34′N 81°22′W
Müller-gerbergte *see* Muller, Pegunungan
169 T10 **Muller, Pegunungan** *Dut.* Müller-gerbergte. ⛰ Borneo, C Indonesia
31 Q5 **Mullett Lake** ◎ Michigan, N USA
18 J16 **Mullica River** ≈ New Jersey, NE USA
25 R8 **Mullin** Texas, SW USA 31°33′N 98°40′W
97 E17 **Mullingar** *Ir.* An Muileann gCearr. C Ireland 53°32′N 07°20′W
21 T12 **Mullins** South Carolina, SE USA 34°12′N 79°15′W
96 G11 **Mull, Isle of** *island* W Scotland, United Kingdom
127 R5 **Mullovka** Ul'yanovskaya Oblast', W Russian Federation 54°13′N 49°19′E
95 K19 **Mullsjö** Västra Götaland, S Sweden 57°56′N 13°55′E
183 V4 **Mullumbimby** New South Wales, SE Australia 28°34′S 153°28′E
83 H15 **Mulobezi** Western, SW Zambia 16°48′S 25°11′E
83 C15 **Mulondo** Huíla, SW Angola 15°41′S 15°09′E
83 G15 **Mulonga Plain** *plain* W Zambia
79 N23 **Mulongo** Katanga, SE Dem. Rep. Congo 07°44′S 26°57′E
149 T10 **Multān** Punjab, E Pakistan 30°12′N 71°30′E
93 L17 **Multia** Länsi-Suomi, C Finland 62°27′N 24°49′E
Mulucha *see* Moulouya
83 J14 **Mulungushi** Central, C Zambia 14°15′S 28°27′E
83 K14 **Mulungwe** Central, C Zambia 13°57′S 29°51′E
Muluya *see* Moulouya
27 N7 **Mulvane** Kansas, C USA 37°28′N 97°14′W
183 O10 **Mulwala** New South Wales, SE Australia 35°59′S 146°00′E
182 K6 **Mulyungarie** South Australia 31°29′S 140°45′E
154 D13 **Mumbai** *prev.* Bombay. *state capital* Mahārāshtra, W India 18°56′N 72°51′E
154 D13 **Mumbai** ✈ Mahārāshtra, W India 19°10′N 72°51′E
83 D14 **Mumbué** Bié, C Angola 13°52′S 17°15′E
186 E8 **Mumeng** Morobe, C Papua New Guinea 06°57′S 146°34′E
171 V12 **Mumi** Papua, E Indonesia 01°33′S 134°09′E
Muminabad/Mŭ'minobod *see* Leningrad
127 Q13 **Mumra** Astrakhanskaya Oblast', SW Russian Federation 45°46′N 47°46′E
41 X12 **Muna** Yucatán, SE Mexico 20°29′N 89°41′W
123 O9 **Muna** ≈ NE Russian Federation
152 C12 **Munābāo** Rājasthān, NW India 25°46′N 70°19′E
Munamägi *see* Suur Munamägi
171 O14 **Muna, Pulau** *prev.* Moena. *island* C Indonesia
101 L18 **Münchberg** Bayern, E Germany 50°10′N 11°50′E
101 L23 **München** *var.* Muenchen, *Eng.* Munich, *It.* Monaco. Bayern, SE Germany 48°09′N 11°34′E
München-Gladbach *see* Mönchengladbach
108 E6 **Münchenstein** Basel-Land, NW Switzerland 47°31′N 07°38′E
10 L11 **Muncho Lake** British Columbia, W Canada 58°52′N 125°40′W
31 P13 **Muncie** Indiana, N USA 40°11′N 85°22′W
18 G13 **Muncy** Pennsylvania, NE USA 41°10′N 76°46′W
11 Q14 **Mundare** Alberta, SW Canada 53°34′N 112°20′W
25 Q5 **Munday** Texas, SW USA 33°27′N 99°37′W
31 N10 **Mundelein** Illinois, N USA 42°15′N 88°00′W
101 I15 **Münden** Niedersachsen, C Germany 52°16′N 08°54′E
105 Q12 **Mundo** ≈ S Spain
82 B12 **Munenga** Cuanza Sul, NW Angola 10°03′S 14°40′E
105 P11 **Munera** Castilla-La Mancha, C Spain 39°03′N 02°29′W
20 E9 **Munford** Tennessee, S USA 35°27′N 89°49′W
20 K7 **Munfordville** Kentucky, S USA 37°17′N 85°55′W
182 D5 **Mungala** South Australia 30°36′S 132°57′E
83 M16 **Mungári** Manica, C Mozambique 17°09′S 33°33′E
79 O16 **Mungbere** Orientale, NE Dem. Rep. Congo 02°38′N 28°30′E
153 Q13 **Munger** *prev.* Monghyr. Bihār, NE India 25°23′N 86°28′E
182 I2 **Mungeranie** South Australia 28°02′S 138°42′E
Mu Nggava *see* Rennell
169 O10 **Mungguresak, Tanjung** *headland* Borneo, N Indonesia 01°57′N 109°19′E
Mungiki *see* Bellona
183 R4 **Mungindi** New South Wales, SE Australia 28°59′S 149°00′E
Mungkawn *see* Maingkwan
Mungla *see* Mongla
82 C13 **Mungo** Huambo, W Angola 11°49′S 16°16′E
188 F16 **Munguy Bay** *bay* Yap, W Micronesia
82 E13 **Munhango** Bié, C Angola 12°12′S 18°34′E
Munich *see* München
105 S7 **Muniesa** Aragón, NE Spain 41°02′N 00°49′W
31 O4 **Munising** Michigan, N USA 46°24′N 86°39′W
Munkács *see* Mukacheve
95 I17 **Munkedal** Västra Götaland, S Sweden 58°28′N 11°38′E
95 K15 **Munkfors** Värmland, C Sweden 59°50′N 13°35′E
122 M14 **Munku-Sardyk, Gora** *var.* Mönh Sarĭdag. ▲ Mongolia/Russian Federation 51°45′N 100°22′E
99 E18 **Munkzwalm** Oost-Vlaanderen, NW Belgium 50°53′N 03°44′E
167 R10 **Mun, Mae Nam** ≈ E Thailand
153 U15 **Munshiganj** Dhaka, C Bangladesh 23°32′N 90°32′E
108 D8 **Münsingen** Bern, W Switzerland 46°53′N 07°34′E
103 U6 **Munster** Haut-Rhin, NE France 48°03′N 07°09′E
100 J11 **Munster** Niedersachsen, NW Germany 52°59′N 10°07′E
100 F13 **Münster** *var.* Muenster, Münster in Westfalen. Nordrhein-Westfalen, W Germany 51°58′N 07°38′E
108 F10 **Münster** Valais, S Switzerland 46°31′N 08°18′E
97 B20 **Munster** *Ir.* Cúige Mumhan. *cultural region* S Ireland
Münsterberg in Schlesien *see* Ziębice
Münster in Westfalen *see* Münster
100 E13 **Münsterland** *cultural region* NW Germany
100 F13 **Münster-Osnabruck** ✈ Nordrhein-Westfalen, NW Germany 52°08′N 07°41′E
31 R4 **Munuscong Lake** ◎ Michigan, N USA
83 K17 **Munyati** ≈ C Zimbabwe
109 R3 **Münzkirchen** Oberösterreich, N Austria 48°29′N 13°37′E
92 K11 **Muodoslompolo** Norrbotten, N Sweden 67°57′N 23°31′E
92 M13 **Muojärvi** ◎ NE Finland
167 S6 **Muong Khên** Hoa Binh, N Vietnam 20°34′N 105°18′E
Muong Sai *see* Xai
167 Q7 **Muong Xiang Ngeun** *var.* Xieng Ngeun. Louangphabang, N Laos 19°43′N 102°09′E
92 K11 **Muonio** Lappi, N Finland 67°58′N 23°40′E
Muonioälv/Muoniojoki *see* Muonionjoki
92 K11 **Muonionjoki** *var.* Muoniojoki, *Swe.* Muonioälv. ≈ Finland/Sweden
83 N17 **Mupa** ≈ C Mozambique
83 E16 **Mupini** Okavango, NE Namibia 17°55′S 19°34′E
80 F8 **Muqaddam, Wadi** ≈ N Sudan
138 K9 **Muqāţ** Al Mafraq, E Jordan 32°28′N 38°04′E
81 N17 **Muqdisho** *Eng.* Mogadishu, *It.* Mogadiscio. ● (Somalia) Banaadir, S Somalia 02°06′N 45°27′E
81 N17 **Muqdisho** ✈ Banaadir, E Somalia 01°58′N 45°18′E
Muqshin *see* Mughshin
109 T8 **Mur** *SCr.* Mura. ≈ C Europe
109 X9 **Mura** ≈ NE Slovenia
Mura *see* Mur
137 T14 **Muradiye** Van, E Turkey 39°N 43°44′E
Muragarazi *see* Maragarazi
165 O10 **Murakami** Niigata, Honshū, C Japan 38°13′N 139°28′E
63 G22 **Murallón, Cerro** ▲ S Argentina 49°49′S 73°25′W
81 E20 **Muramvya** C Burundi 03°18′S 29°41′E
81 I19 **Murang'a** *prev.* Fort Hall. Central, SW Kenya 0°43′S 37°10′E
81 H16 **Murangering** Rift Valley, NW Kenya 03°48′N 35°29′E
Murapara *see* Murupara
140 M5 **Murār, Bi'r al** *well* NW Saudi Arabia
125 Q13 **Murashi** Kirovskaya Oblast', NW Russian Federation 59°27′N 48°02′E
103 O12 **Murat** Cantal, C France 45°07′N 02°52′E
114 N12 **Muratlı** Tekirdağ, NW Turkey 41°12′N 27°30′E
137 R14 **Murat Nehri** *var.* Eastern Euphrates; *anc.* Arsanias. ≈ NE Turkey
107 D20 **Muravera** Sardegna, Italy, C Mediterranean Sea 39°24′N 09°34′E
165 P10 **Murayama** Yamagata, Honshū, C Japan 38°29′N 140°21′E
121 R13 **Muraysah, Ra's al** *headland* N Libya 31°58′N 25°00′E
104 I6 **Murça** Vila Real, N Portugal 41°24′N 07°28′W
80 Q11 **Murcanyo** Bari, NE Somalia 11°39′N 50°27′E
143 N8 **Mūrcheh Khvort** *var.* Morcheh Khort. Eşfahān, C Iran 33°07′N 51°26′E
185 H15 **Murchison** Tasman, South Island, New Zealand 41°48′S 172°19′E
185 B22 **Murchison Mountains** ⛰ South Island, New Zealand
180 I10 **Murchison River** ≈ Western Australia
105 R13 **Murcia** Murcia, SE Spain 37°59′N 01°08′W
105 Q13 **Murcia** ◐ *autonomous community* SE Spain
103 O13 **Mur-de-Barrez** Aveyron, S France 44°48′N 02°39′E
182 G8 **Murdinga** South Australia 33°46′S 135°46′E
28 M10 **Murdo** South Dakota, N USA 43°53′N 100°42′W
15 X6 **Murdochville** Québec, SE Canada 48°57′N 65°30′W
109 W9 **Mureck** Steiermark, SE Austria 46°42′N 15°46′E
114 M13 **Mürefte** Tekirdağ, NW Turkey 40°40′N 27°15′E
116 I10 **Mureş** ◐ *county* N Romania
84 J11 **Mureş** ≈ Hungary/Romania
Mureş *see* Maros
Mureşul *see* Maros/Mureş
102 M16 **Muret** Haute-Garonne, S France 43°28′N 01°19′E
27 T13 **Murfreesboro** Arkansas, C USA 34°04′N 93°42′W
21 W8 **Murfreesboro** North Carolina, SE USA 36°26′N 77°06′W
20 J9 **Murfreesboro** Tennessee, S USA 35°50′N 86°25′W
Murgab *see* Morghāb, Daryā-ye/Murgap
Murgab *see* Murghob
146 I14 **Murgap** Mary Welaýaty, S Turkmenistan 37°19′N 61°48′E
146 J16 **Murgap** *var.* Deryasy Murgap, Murghab, *Pash.* Daryā-ye Morghāb, *Rus.* Murgab. ≈ Afghanistan/Turkmenistan *see also* Morghāb, Daryā-ye
Murgap *see* Morghāb, Daryā-ye
Murgap, Deryasy *see* Morghāb, Daryā-ye/Murgap
114 H9 **Murgash** ▲ W Bulgaria 42°51′N 23°58′E
Murghab *see* Morghāb, Daryā-ye/Murgap
147 U13 **Murghob** *Rus.* Murgab. SE Tajikistan 38°11′N 74°E
147 U13 **Murghob** *Rus.* Murgab. ≈ SE Tajikistan
181 Z10 **Murgon** Queensland, E Australia 26°08′S 152°04′E
190 I16 **Muri** Rarotonga, S Cook Islands 21°15′S 159°44′W
108 F7 **Muri** Aargau, W Switzerland 47°16′N 08°21′E
108 D8 **Muri** *var.* Muri bei Bern. Bern, W Switzerland 46°55′N 07°30′E
104 K3 **Murias de Paredes** Castilla-León, N Spain 42°51′N 06°11′W
Muri bei Bern *see* Muri
82 F11 **Muriege** Lunda Sul, NE Angola 09°55′S 21°12′E
189 P14 **Murilo Atoll** *atoll* Hall Islands, C Micronesia
Mūrītānīyah *see* Mauritania
100 N10 **Müritz** *var.* Müritzee. ◎ NE Germany
Müritzee *see* Müritz
100 L10 **Müritz-Elde-Kanal** *canal* N Germany
184 K6 **Muriwai Beach** Auckland, North Island, New Zealand 36°56′S 174°28′E
92 J13 **Murjek** Norrbotten, N Sweden 66°27′N 20°54′E
124 J3 **Murmansk** Murmanskaya Oblast', NW Russian Federation 68°59′N 33°08′E
124 I4 **Murmanskaya Oblast'** ◐ *province* NW Russian Federation
197 V14 **Murmansk Rise** *undersea feature* SW Barents Sea 71°00′N 37°00′E
124 J3 **Murmashi** Murmanskaya Oblast', NW Russian Federation 68°49′N 32°43′E
126 M5 **Murmino** Ryazanskaya Oblast', W Russian Federation 54°31′N 40°01′E
101 K24 **Murnau** Bayern, SE Germany 47°41′N 11°12′E
103 X16 **Muro, Capo di** *headland* Corse, France, C Mediterranean Sea 41°45′N 08°40′E
107 M18 **Muro Lucano** Basilicata, S Italy 40°48′N 15°33′E
127 N4 **Murom** Vladimirskaya Oblast', W Russian Federation 55°33′N 42°03′E
122 I11 **Muromtsevo** Omskaya Oblast', C Russian Federation 56°18′N 75°15′E
165 R5 **Muroran** Hokkaidō, NE Japan 42°20′N 140°58′E
104 G3 **Muros** Galicia, NW Spain 42°47′N 09°04′W
104 F3 **Muros e Noia, Ría de** *estuary* NW Spain
164 H15 **Muroto** Kōchi, Shikoku, SW Japan 33°16′N 134°10′E
164 H15 **Muroto-zaki** Shikoku, SW Japan
116 L7 **Murovani Kurylivtsi** Vinnyts'ka Oblast', C Ukraine 48°43′N 27°31′E
110 G11 **Murowana Goślina** Wielkolpolskie, W Poland 52°33′N 16°59′E
32 M14 **Murphy** Idaho, NW USA 43°14′N 116°36′W
21 N10 **Murphy** North Carolina, SE USA 35°05′N 84°02′W
35 P8 **Murphys** California, W USA 38°07′N 120°27′W
30 L17 **Murphysboro** Illinois, N USA 37°45′N 89°20′W
29 V15 **Murray** Iowa, C USA 41°03′N 93°56′W
20 H8 **Murray** Kentucky, S USA 36°35′N 88°20′W
182 J10 **Murray Bridge** South Australia 35°10′S 139°17′E
175 X2 **Murray Fracture Zone** *tectonic feature* NE Pacific Ocean
192 H11 **Murray, Lake** ◎ SW Papua New Guinea
21 P12 **Murray, Lake** ⊡ South Carolina, SE USA
10 K8 **Murray, Mount** ▲ Yukon Territory, NW Canada 60°49′N 128°57′W
Murray Range *see* Murray Ridge
173 O3 **Murray Ridge** *var.* Murray Range. *undersea feature* N Arabian Sea 21°45′N 61°50′E
183 N10 **Murray River** ≈ SE Australia
182 K10 **Murrayville** Victoria, SE Australia 35°17′S 141°12′E
149 U5 **Murree** Punjab, E Pakistan 33°55′N 73°26′E
101 I21 **Murrhardt** Baden-Württemberg, S Germany 49°00′N 09°34′E
183 O9 **Murrumbidgee River** ≈ New South Wales, SE Australia
83 P15 **Murrupula** Nampula, NE Mozambique 15°26′S 38°46′E

◆ Country ● Country Capital ◇ Dependent Territory ○ Dependent Territory Capital ◐ Administrative Regions ✈ International Airport ▲ Mountain ⛰ Mountain Range Volcano ≈ River ◎ Lake ⊡ Reservoir

183 T7 **Murrurundi** New South Wales, SE Australia 31°47′S 150°51′E
109 X9 **Murska Sobota** *Ger.* Olsnitz. NE Slovenia 46°41′N 16°09′E
154 G12 **Murtajāpur** *prev.* Murtazapur. Mahārāshtra, C India 20°43′N 77°28′E
77 S16 **Murtala Muhammed** ✈ (Lagos) Ogun, SW Nigeria 06°31′N 03°12′E
Murtazapur *see* Murtajāpur
108 C8 **Murten** Neuchâtel, W Switzerland 46°55′N 07°06′E
Murtensee *see* Morat, Lac de
182 L11 **Murtoa** Victoria, SE Australia 36°39′S 142°27′E
92 N13 **Murtovaara** Oulu, E Finland 65°40′N 29°25′E
Murua Island *see* Woodlark Island
155 D14 **Murud** Mahārāshtra, W India 18°27′N 72°56′E
184 O9 **Murupara** *var.* Murapara. Bay of Plenty, North Island, New Zealand 38°27′S 176°41′E
191 X12 **Mururoa** *var.* Moruroa. *atoll* Îles Tuamotu, SE French Polynesia
Murviedro *see* Sagunto
154 J9 **Murwāra** Madhya Pradesh, N India 23°50′N 80°23′E
183 V4 **Murwillumbah** New South Wales, SE Australia 28°20′S 153°24′E
146 H11 **Murzechirla** *prev.* Mirzachirla. Ahal Welaýaty, C Turkmenistan 39°33′N 60°02′E
Murzuk *see* Murzuq
75 O11 **Murzuq** *var.* Marzūq, Murzuk. SW Libya 25°55′N 13°55′E
Murzuq, Edeyin *see* Murzuq, Idhān
75 N11 **Murzuq, Ḥammādat** *plateau* W Libya
75 O11 **Murzuq, Idhān** *var.* Edeyin Murzuq. *desert* SW Libya
109 W6 **Mürzzuschlag** Steiermark, E Austria 47°35′N 15°41′E
137 Q14 **Muş** *var.* Mush. Muş, E Turkey 38°45′N 41°30′E
137 Q14 **Muş** *var.* Mush. ◐ *province* E Turkey
118 G11 **Mūša** ∽ Latvia/Lithuania
186 F9 **Musa** ∽ S Papua New Guinea
Mûsa, Gebel *see* Mūsá, Jabal
Musaiyib *see* Al Musayyib
75 X8 **Mūsá, Jabal** *var.* Gebel Mûsa. ▲ NE Egypt 28°33′N 33°51′E
Musa Khel *see* Mūsa Khel Bāzār
149 R9 **Mūsa Khel Bāzār** *var.* Musa Khel. Baluchistān, SW Pakistan 30°53′N 69°52′E
114 H10 **Musala** ▲ W Bulgaria 42°12′N 23°36′E
168 H10 **Musala, Pulau** *island* W Indonesia
83 I15 **Musale** Southern, S Zambia 15°27′S 26°50′E
141 Y9 **Muşalla** NE Oman 22°20′N 58°03′E
141 W6 **Musandam Peninsula** *Ar.* Masandam Peninsula. *peninsula* N Oman
Musay'id *see* Umm Sa'id
Muscat *see* Masqaṭ
Muscat and Oman *see* Oman
29 Y14 **Muscatine** Iowa, C USA 41°25′N 91°03′W
Muscat Sib Airport *see* Seeb
31 O15 **Muscatuck River** ∽ Indiana, N USA
30 K8 **Muscoda** Wisconsin, N USA 43°11′N 90°27′W
185 F19 **Musgrave, Mount** ▲ South Island, New Zealand 43°48′S 170°43′E
181 P9 **Musgrave Ranges** ▲▲ South Australia
Mush *see* Muş
138 H12 **Mushayyish, Qaṣr al** *castle* Ma'ān, C Jordan
79 H20 **Mushie** Bandundu, W Dem. Rep. Congo 03°00′S 16°55′E
168 M13 **Musi, Air** *prev.* Moesi. ∽ Sumatera, W Indonesia
192 M4 **Musicians Seamounts** *undersea feature* N Pacific Ocean
83 K19 **Musina** *prev.* Messina. Limpopo, NE South Africa 22°18′S 30°02′E
54 D8 **Musinga, Alto** ▲ NW Colombia 06°49′N 76°24′W
29 T2 **Muskeg Bay** *lake bay* Minnesota, N USA
31 O8 **Muskegon** Michigan, N USA 43°13′N 86°15′W
31 O8 **Muskegon Heights** Michigan, N USA 43°12′N 86°14′W
31 P8 **Muskegon River** ∽ Michigan, N USA
31 T14 **Muskingum River** ∽ Ohio, N USA
95 P16 **Muskö** Stockholm, C Sweden 58°58′N 18°10′E
Muskogean *see* Tallahassee
27 Q10 **Muskogee** Oklahoma, C USA 35°45′N 95°21′W
14 H13 **Muskoka, Lake** ◎ Ontario, S Canada
80 H8 **Musmar** Red Sea, NE Sudan 18°13′N 35°40′E
83 K14 **Musofu** Central, C Zambia 13°31′S 29°02′E
81 G19 **Musoma** Mara, N Tanzania 01°31′S 33°49′E
82 L13 **Musoro** Central, C Zambia 13°21′S 31°04′E
186 F4 **Mussau Island** *island* NE Papua New Guinea
98 P7 **Musselkanaal** Groningen, NE Netherlands 52°55′N 07°01′E
33 V9 **Musselshell River** ∽ Montana, NW USA
82 C12 **Mussende** Cuanza Sul, NW Angola 10°33′S 16°02′E
102 L12 **Mussidan** Dordogne, SW France 45°03′N 00°22′E
99 L25 **Musson** Luxembourg, SE Belgium 49°33′N 05°42′E
152 J9 **Mussoorie** Uttarakhand, N India 30°26′N 78°04′E
Musta *see* Mosta
152 M13 **Mustafābād** Uttar Pradesh, N India 25°54′N 81°17′E
136 D12 **Mustafakemalpaşa** Bursa, NW Turkey 40°03′N 28°25′E
Mustafa-Pasha *see* Svilengrad
81 M15 **Mustahīl** Sumalē, E Ethiopia 05°18′N 44°34′E
24 M7 **Mustang Draw** *valley* Texas, SW USA
25 T14 **Mustang Island** *island* Texas, SW USA
Mustasaari *see* Korsholm
Mustér *see* Disentis
63 I19 **Musters, Lago** ◎ S Argentina
45 Y14 **Mustique** *island* C Saint Vincent and the Grenadines
118 I6 **Mustla** Viljandimaa, S Estonia 58°12′N 25°50′E
118 J4 **Mustvee** *Ger.* Tschorna. Jõgevamaa, E Estonia 58°51′N 26°59′E
42 L9 **Musún, Cerro** ▲ NE Nicaragua 13°01′N 85°02′W
183 T7 **Muswellbrook** New South Wales, SE Australia 32°17′S 150°55′E
111 M18 **Muszyna** Małopolskie, SE Poland 49°21′N 20°54′E
75 V10 **Mūṭ** *var.* Mut. C Egypt 25°28′N 28°58′E
136 I17 **Mut** İçel, S Turkey 36°38′N 33°27′E
109 V9 **Muta** N Slovenia 46°37′N 15°09′E
190 B15 **Mutalau** N Niue 18°56′S 169°50′E
Mu-tan-chiang *see* Mudanjiang
82 I13 **Mutanda** North Western, NW Zambia 12°24′S 26°13′E
59 O17 **Mutá, Ponta do** *headland* E Brazil 13°54′S 38°54′W
83 L17 **Mutare** *var.* Mutari; *prev.* Umtali. Manicaland, E Zimbabwe 18°55′S 32°36′E
Mutari *see* Mutare
54 D8 **Mutatá** Antioquia, NW Colombia 07°16′N 76°32′W
Mutina *see* Modena
83 L16 **Mutoko** *prev.* Mtoko. Mashonaland East, NE Zimbabwe 17°24′S 32°13′E
81 J20 **Mutomo** Eastern, S Kenya 01°50′S 38°13′E
Mutrah *see* Maṭraḥ
Mutsamudu *see* Moutsamoudou
79 M24 **Mutshatsha** Katanga, S Dem. Rep. Congo 10°40′S 24°26′E
165 R6 **Mutsu** *var.* Mutu. Aomori, Honshū, N Japan 41°18′N 141°11′E
165 R6 **Mutsu-wan** *bay* N Japan
108 E6 **Muttenz** Basel-Land, NW Switzerland 47°31′N 07°39′E
185 A26 **Muttonbird Islands** *island group* SW New Zealand
Muttra *see* Mathura
Mutu *see* Mutsu
83 O15 **Mutuáli** Nampula, N Mozambique 14°51′S 37°01′E
82 D13 **Mutumbo** Bié, C Angola 13°10′S 17°22′E
189 Y14 **Mutunte, Mount** *var.* Mount Buache. ▲ Kosrae, E Micronesia 05°21′N 163°00′E
155 K24 **Mutur** Eastern Province, E Sri Lanka 08°27′N 81°15′E
92 L13 **Muurola** Lappi, NW Finland 66°22′N 25°20′E
162 M14 **Mu Us Shadi** *var.* Ordos Desert; *prev.* Mu Us Shamo. *desert* N China
Mu Us Shamo *see* Mu Us Shadi
82 B11 **Muxima** Bengo, NW Angola 09°33′S 13°58′E
124 I8 **Muyezerskiy** Respublika Kareliya, NW Russian Federation 63°54′N 32°00′E
81 E20 **Muyinga** NE Burundi 02°54′S 30°19′E
42 K9 **Muy Muy** Matagalpa, C Nicaragua 12°43′N 85°35′W
Muynak *see* Mo'ynoq
79 N22 **Muyumba** Katanga, SE Dem. Rep. Congo 07°13′S 27°02′E
149 V5 **Muzaffarābād** Jammu and Kashmir, NE Pakistan 34°23′N 73°34′E
149 S10 **Muzaffargarh** Punjab, E Pakistan 30°04′N 71°15′E
152 J9 **Muzaffarnagar** Uttar Pradesh, N India 29°28′N 77°42′E
153 P13 **Muzaffarpur** Bihār, N India 26°07′N 85°23′E
158 H6 **Muzat He** ∽ W China
83 L15 **Muze** Tete, NW Mozambique 15°05′S 31°16′E
122 H8 **Muzhi** Yamalo-Nenetskiy Avtonomnyy Okrug, N Russian Federation 65°25′N 64°28′E
102 H7 **Muzillac** Morbihan, NW France 47°34′N 02°30′W
Muzkol, Khrebet *see* Muzqul, Qatorkŭhi
112 L9 **Mužlja** *Hung.* Felsőmuzslya; *prev.* Gornja Mužlja. Vojvodina, N Serbia 45°21′N 20°25′E
54 F9 **Muzo** Boyacá, C Colombia 05°34′N 74°07′W
83 A15 **Muzoka** Southern, S Zambia 16°39′S 27°18′E
39 Y15 **Muzon, Cape** *headland* Dall Island, Alaska, USA 54°39′N 132°41′W
40 M6 **Múzquiz** Coahuila, NE Mexico 27°54′N 101°30′W
147 U13 **Muzqŭl, Qatorkŭhi** *Rus.* Khrebet Muzkol. ▲▲ SE Tajikistan
158 G10 **Muz Tag** ▲ NW China 36°02′N 80°13′E
158 K10 **Muztag** ▲ W China 36°26′N 87°15′E
158 D8 **Muztagata** ▲ NW China 38°16′N 75°03′E
83 K17 **Mvuma** *prev.* Umvuma. Midlands, C Zimbabwe 19°17′S 30°32′E
172 H13 **Mwali** *var.* Moili, *Fr.* Mohéli. *island* S Comoros
82 L13 **Mwanya** Eastern, E Zambia 12°40′S 32°15′E
79 N23 **Mwanza** Katanga, SE Dem. Rep. Congo 07°49′S 26°49′E
81 G20 **Mwanza** Mwanza, NW Tanzania 02°31′S 32°56′E
81 F20 **Mwanza** ◐ *region* N Tanzania
82 M13 **Mwase Lundazi** Eastern, E Zambia 12°26′S 33°20′E
97 B17 **Mweelrea** *Ir.* Caoc Maol Réidh. ▲ W Ireland 53°37′N 09°47′W
79 K21 **Mweka** Kasai-Occidental, C Dem. Rep. Congo 04°52′S 21°38′E
82 K12 **Mwenda** Luapula, N Zambia 10°30′S 30°21′E
79 L22 **Mwene-Ditu** Kasai-Oriental, S Dem. Rep. Congo 07°06′S 23°34′E
83 L18 **Mwenezi** ∽ S Zimbabwe
79 O20 **Mwenga** Sud-Kivu, E Dem. Rep. Congo 03°00′S 28°28′E
82 K11 **Mweru, Lake** *var.* Lac Moero. ◎ Dem. Rep. Congo/Zambia
82 H13 **Mwinilunga** North Western, NW Zambia 11°44′S 24°24′E
189 V16 **Mwokil Atoll** *prev.* Mokil Atoll. *atoll* Caroline Islands, E Micronesia
Myadel' *see* Myadzyel
118 J13 **Myadzyel** *Pol.* Miadzioł Nowy, *Rus.* Myadel'. Minskaya Voblasts', N Belarus 54°51′N 26°51′E
152 C12 **Myājlār** *var.* Miajlar. Rājasthān, NW India 26°16′N 70°21′E
123 T9 **Myakit** Magadanskaya Oblast', E Russian Federation 61°23′N 151°58′E
23 W13 **Myakka River** ∽ Florida, SE USA
124 L14 **Myaksa** Vologodskaya Oblast', NW Russian Federation 58°54′N 38°15′E
183 U8 **Myall Lake** ◎ New South Wales, SE Australia
166 L7 **Myanaung** Ayeyarwady, SW Burma (Myanmar) 18°17′N 95°19′E
Myanmar *see* Burma
166 K8 **Myaungmya** Ayeyarwady, SW Burma (Myanmar) 16°33′N 94°55′E
Myaydo *see* Aunglan
118 N11 **Myazha** *Rus.* Mezha. Vitsyebskaya Voblasts', NE Belarus 55°41′N 30°25′E
167 N12 **Myeik** *var.* Mergui. Tanintharyi, S Burma (Myanmar) 12°26′N 98°34′E
119 O18 **Myerkulavichy** *Rus.* Merkulovichi. Homyel'skaya Voblasts', SE Belarus 52°58′N 30°36′E
119 N14 **Myezhava** *Rus.* Mezhëvo. Vitsyebskaya Voblasts', NE Belarus 54°38′N 30°20′E
Myggenaes *see* Mykines
166 L5 **Myingyan** Mandalay, C Burma (Myanmar) 21°25′N 95°20′E
167 N12 **Myitkyina** Kachin State, N Burma (Myanmar) 25°24′N 97°25′E
166 M5 **Myittha** Mandalay, C Burma (Myanmar) 21°21′N 96°06′E
111 H19 **Myjava** *Hung.* Miava. Trenčiansky Kraj, W Slovakia 48°45′N 17°35′E
Myjeldino *see* Myyëldino
117 U9 **Mykhaylivka** *Rus.* Mikhaylovka. Zaporiz'ka Oblast', SE Ukraine 47°16′N 35°14′E
95 A18 **Mykines** *Dan.* Myggenaes. *island* W Faeroe Islands
116 I5 **Mykolayiv** L'vivs'ka Oblast', W Ukraine 49°34′N 23°58′E
117 Q10 **Mykolayiv** *Rus.* Nikolayev. Mykolayivs'ka Oblast', S Ukraine 46°58′N 31°59′E
117 Q10 **Mykolayiv** ✈ Mykolayivs'ka Oblast', S Ukraine 47°02′N 31°54′E
Mykolayiv *see* Mykolayivs'ka Oblast'
117 P9 **Mykolayivka** Odes'ka Oblast', SW Ukraine 47°34′N 30°48′E
117 S13 **Mykolayivka** Respublika Krym, S Ukraine 44°58′N 33°37′E
117 P9 **Mykolayivs'ka Oblast'** *var.* Mykolayiv, *Rus.* Nikolayevskaya Oblast'. ◐ *province* S Ukraine
115 J20 **Mýkonos** Mýkonos, Kykládes, Greece, Aegean Sea 37°27′N 25°20′E
115 K20 **Mýkonos** *var.* Míkonos. *island* Kykládes, Greece, Aegean Sea
125 R7 **Myla** Respublika Komi, NW Russian Federation 65°24′N 50°51′E
Mylae *see* Milazzo
93 M19 **Myllykoski** Etelä-Suomi, S Finland 60°45′N 26°52′E
153 U14 **Mymensing** *var.* Mymensingh. Dhaka, N Bangladesh 24°45′N 90°23′E
Mymensingh *see* Mymensing
93 K19 **Mynämäki** Länsi-Suomi, SW Finland 60°41′N 22°00′E
145 S14 **Mynaral** *Kaz.* Myngaral. Zhambyl, S Kazakhstan 45°25′N 73°37′E
Mynbulak *see* Mingbuloq
Mynbulak, Vpadina *see* Mingbuloq Botig'I
Myngaral *see* Mynaral
Myohaung *see* Mrauk-oo
163 W13 **Myohyang-sanmaek** ▲▲ C North Korea
164 M11 **Myōkō-san** ▲ Honshū, S Japan 36°54′N 138°05′E
83 J15 **Myooye** Central, C Zambia 15°11′S 27°10′E
118 K12 **Myory** *prev.* Miyory. Vitsyebskaya Voblasts', N Belarus 55°39′N 27°39′E
92 J4 **Mýrdalsjökull** *glacier* S Iceland
92 G10 **Myre** Nordland, C Norway 68°54′N 15°04′E
117 S5 **Myrhorod** *Rus.* Mirgorod. Poltavs'ka Oblast', NE Ukraine 49°58′N 33°37′E
115 J15 **Mýrina** *var.* Mírina. Límnos, SE Greece 39°52′N 25°04′E
117 P5 **Myronivka** *Rus.* Mironovka. Kyyivs'ka Oblast', N Ukraine 49°40′N 30°59′E
21 U13 **Myrtle Beach** South Carolina, SE USA 33°41′N 78°53′W
32 F14 **Myrtle Creek** Oregon, NW USA 43°01′N 123°19′W
183 P11 **Myrtleford** Victoria, SE Australia 36°34′S 146°45′E
32 E14 **Myrtle Point** Oregon, NW USA 43°04′N 124°08′W
115 K25 **Mýrtos** Kríti, Greece, E Mediterranean Sea 35°00′N 25°34′E
Myrtoum Mare *see* Mirtóo Pélagos
93 G17 **Myrviken** Jämtland, C Sweden 62°59′N 14°19′E
95 I15 **Mysen** Østfold, S Norway 59°33′N 11°20′E
124 L15 **Myshkin** Yaroslavskaya Oblast', NW Russian Federation 57°47′N 38°28′E
111 K17 **Myślenice** Małopolskie, S Poland 49°50′N 19°55′E
110 D10 **Myślibórz** Zachodnio-pomorskie, NW Poland 52°55′N 14°51′E
155 G20 **Mysore** *var.* Maisur. Karnātaka, W India 12°18′N 76°37′E
Mysore *see* Karnātaka
115 F21 **Mystrás** *var.* Mistras. Pelopónnisos, S Greece 37°03′N 22°22′E
111 K15 **Myszków** Śląskie, S Poland 50°36′N 19°20′E
167 T14 **My Tho** *var.* Mi Tho. Tiên Giang, S Vietnam 10°21′N 106°21′E
Mytilene *see* Mytilíni
115 L17 **Mytilíni** *var.* Mitilíni; *anc.* Mytilene. Lésvos, E Greece 39°06′N 26°33′E
126 K3 **Mytishchi** Moskovskaya Oblast', W Russian Federation 56°00′N 37°51′E
37 N3 **Myton** Utah, W USA 40°11′N 110°03′W
92 K2 **Mývatn** ◎ C Iceland
125 T11 **Myyëldino** *var.* Myjeldino. Respublika Komi, NW Russian Federation 61°46′N 54°48′E
82 M13 **Mzimba** Northern, NW Malawi 11°56′S 33°36′E
82 M12 **Mzuzu** Northern, N Malawi 11°23′S 34°03′E

N

101 M19 **Naab** ∽ SE Germany
98 G12 **Naaldwijk** Zuid-Holland, W Netherlands 52°00′N 04°13′E
38 G12 **Nā'ālehu** *var.* Naalehu. Hawaii, USA, C Pacific Ocean 19°04′N 155°36′W
93 K19 **Naantali** *Swe.* Nådendal. Länsi-Suomi, SW Finland 60°28′N 22°05′E
98 J10 **Naarden** Noord-Holland, C Netherlands 52°18′N 05°10′E
109 U4 **Naarn** ∽ N Austria
97 F18 **Naas** *Ir.* An Nás, Nás na Ríogh. Kildare, C Ireland 53°13′N 06°39′W
92 M9 **Näätämöjoki** *Lapp.* Njávdám. ∽ NE Finland
83 E23 **Nababeep** *var.* Nababiep. Northern Cape, W South Africa 29°36′S 17°46′E
Nababiep *see* Nababeep
Nabadwip *see* Navadwīp
155 L14 **Nabarangapur** *var.* Nowrangapur. Orissa, E India 19°13′N 82°33′E
164 J14 **Nabari** Mie, Honshū, SW Japan 34°37′N 136°05′E
Nabatié *see* Nabatîyé
138 G8 **Nabatîyé** *var.* An Nabatīyah at Taḥtā, Nabatié, Nabatiyet et Tahta. SW Lebanon 33°18′N 35°36′E
Nabatiyet et Tahta *see* Nabatîyé
187 X14 **Nabavatu** Vanua Levu, N Fiji 16°35′S 178°55′E
190 I2 **Nabeina** *island* Tungaru, W Kiribati
127 T4 **Naberezhnyye Chelny** *prev.* Brezhnev. Respublika Tatarstan, W Russian Federation 55°43′N 52°21′E
39 T10 **Nabesna** Alaska, USA 62°22′N 143°00′W
39 T10 **Nabesna River** ∽ Alaska, USA
75 N5 **Nabeul** *var.* Nābul. NE Tunisia 36°32′N 10°45′E
152 I9 **Nābha** Punjab, NW India 30°22′N 76°12′E
171 W13 **Nabire** Papua, E Indonesia 03°23′S 135°31′E
141 O15 **Nabī Shu'ayb, Jabal an** ▲ W Yemen 15°24′N 44°04′E
138 F10 **Nablus** *var.* Nābulus, *Heb.* Shekhem; *anc.* Neapolis, *Bibl.* Shechem. N West Bank 32°13′N 35°16′E
187 X14 **Nabouwalu** Vanua Levu, N Fiji 17°00′S 178°43′E
Nābul *see* Nabeul
Nābulus *see* Nablus
187 Y13 **Nabuna** Vanua Levu, N Fiji 16°13′S 179°46′E
83 Q14 **Nacala** Nampula, NE Mozambique 14°30′S 40°37′E
42 H8 **Nacaome** Valle, S Honduras 13°30′N 87°31′W
Na Cealla Beaga *see* Killybegs
Na-Ch'ii *see* Nagqu
164 J15 **Nachikatsuura** *var.* Nachi-Katsuura. Wakayama, Honshū, SE Japan 33°37′N 135°54′E
Nachi-Katsuura *see* Nachikatsuura
81 J24 **Nachingwea** Lindi, SE Tanzania 10°21′S 38°46′E
111 F16 **Náchod** Královéhradecký Kraj, N Czech Republic 50°26′N 16°10′E
Na Clocha Liatha *see* Greystones
40 G3 **Naco** Sonora, NW Mexico 31°16′N 109°56′W
25 X8 **Nacogdoches** Texas, SW USA 31°36′N 94°40′W
40 G4 **Nacozari de García** Sonora, NW Mexico 30°27′N 109°43′W
Nada *see* Danzhou
77 O14 **Nadawli** NW Ghana 10°30′N 02°40′W
104 I3 **Nadela** Galicia, NW Spain 42°58′N 07°33′W
Nådendal *see* Naantali
144 M7 **Nadezhdinka** *prev.* Nadezhdinskiy. Kostanay, N Kazakhstan 53°46′N 63°44′E
Nadezhdinskiy *see* Nadezhdinka
Nadgan *see* Nadqān, Qalamat
187 W14 **Nadi** *prev.* Nandi. Viti Levu, W Fiji 17°47′S 177°28′E
187 X14 **Nadi** *prev.* Nandi. ✈ Viti Levu, W Fiji 17°46′S 177°28′E
154 D10 **Nadiād** Gujarāt, W India 22°42′N 72°55′E
Nadikdik *see* Knox Atoll
116 E11 **Nădlac** *Ger.* Nadlak, *Hung.* Nagylak. Arad, W Romania 46°10′N 20°47′E
Nadlak *see* Nădlac
74 H6 **Nador** *prev.* Villa Nador. NE Morocco 35°10′N 05°22′W
141 S9 **Nadqān, Qalamat** *var.* Nadgan. *well* E Saudi Arabia
111 N22 **Nádudvar** Hajdú-Bihar, E Hungary 47°36′N 21°09′E
121 O15 **Nadur** Gozo, N Malta 36°03′N 14°18′E
187 X13 **Naduri** *prev.* Nanduri. Vanua Levu, N Fiji 16°26′S 179°08′E
116 I7 **Nadvirna** *Pol.* Nadwórna, *Rus.* Nadvornaya. Ivano-Frankivs'ka Oblast', W Ukraine 48°27′N 24°30′E
124 J8 **Nadvoitsy** Respublika Kareliya, NW Russian Federation 63°53′N 34°17′E
Nadvornaya/Nadwórna *see* Nadvirna
122 I9 **Nadym** Yamalo-Nenetskiy Avtonomnyy Okrug, N Russian Federation 65°25′N 72°40′E
122 I9 **Nadym** ∽ C Russian Federation
186 E7 **Nadzab** Morobe, C Papua New Guinea 06°36′S 146°46′E
95 C17 **Nærbø** Rogaland, S Norway 58°40′N 05°39′E
95 I24 **Næstved** Storstrøm, SE Denmark 55°12′N 11°47′E
77 X13 **Nafada** Gombe, E Nigeria 11°02′N 11°18′E
108 H8 **Näfels** Glarus, NE Switzerland 47°06′N 09°04′E
115 E18 **Náfpaktos** *var.* Návpaktos. Dytikí Ellás, C Greece 38°23′N 21°50′E
115 F20 **Náfplio** *prev.* Návplion. Pelopónnisos, S Greece 37°34′N 22°50′E
139 U6 **Naft Khāneh** Diyālá, E Iraq 34°01′N 45°26′E
149 N13 **Nāg** Baluchistān, SW Pakistan 27°43′N 65°31′E
171 P4 **Naga** *off.* Naga City; *prev.* Nueva Caceres. Luzon, N Philippines 13°36′N 123°10′E
Nagaarzê *see* Nagarzê
Naga City *see* Naga
12 F11 **Nagagami** ∽ Ontario, S Canada
164 F14 **Nagahama** Ehime, Shikoku, SW Japan 33°36′N 132°29′E
153 X12 **Nāga Hills** ▲▲ NE India
165 P10 **Nagai** Yamagata, Honshū, C Japan 38°08′N 140°00′E
Na Gaibhlte *see* Galty Mountains
39 N16 **Nagai Island** *island* Shumagin Islands, Alaska, USA
153 X12 **Nāgāland** ◐ *state* NE India
164 M11 **Nagano** Nagano, Honshū, S Japan 36°39′N 138°11′E
164 M12 **Nagano** *off.* Nagano-ken. ◐ *prefecture* Honshū, S Japan
Nagano-ken *see* Nagano
165 N11 **Nagaoka** Niigata, Honshū, C Japan 37°26′N 138°48′E
153 W12 **Nagaon** *prev.* Nowgong. Assam, NE India 26°21′N 92°41′E
155 J21 **Nāgappattinam** *var.* Negapatam, Negapattinam. Tamil Nādu, SE India 10°45′N 79°50′E
Nagara Nayok *see* Nakhon Nayok
Nagara Panom *see* Nakhon Phanom
Nagara Pathom *see* Nakhon Pathom
Nagara Sridharmaraj *see* Nakhon Si Thammarat
Nagara Svarga *see* Nakhon Sawan
155 H16 **Nāgārjuna Sāgar** ⊠ E India
42 I10 **Nagarote** León, SW Nicaragua 12°15′N 86°35′W
158 M16 **Nagarzê** *var.* Nagaarzê. Xizang Zizhiqu, W China 28°57′N 90°26′E
164 C14 **Nagasaki** Nagasaki, Kyūshū, SW Japan 32°45′N 129°52′E
164 C14 **Nagasaki** *off.* Nagasaki-ken. ◐ *prefecture* Kyūshū, SW Japan
Nagasaki-ken *see* Nagasaki
Nagashima *see* Kii-Nagashima
164 E12 **Nagato** Yamaguchi, Honshū, SW Japan 34°22′N 131°10′E
152 F11 **Nāgaur** Rājasthān, NW India 27°12′N 73°48′E
154 F10 **Nāgda** Madhya Pradesh, C India 23°30′N 75°29′E
98 L8 **Nagele** Flevoland, N Netherlands 52°39′N 05°43′E
155 H24 **Nāgercoil** Tamil Nādu, SE India 08°11′N 77°30′E
153 X12 **Nāginimāra** Nāgāland, NE India 26°44′N 94°51′E
Na Gleannta *see* Glenties
165 T16 **Nago** Okinawa, Okinawa, SW Japan 26°36′N 127°59′E
154 K9 **Nāgod** Madhya Pradesh, C India 24°34′N 80°34′E
155 J26 **Nagoda** Southern Province, S Sri Lanka 06°13′N 80°13′E
101 G22 **Nagold** Baden-Württemberg, SW Germany 48°33′N 08°43′E
137 V12 **Nagorno-Karabakh** *var.* Nagorno- Karabakhskaya Avtonomnaya Oblast, *Arm.* Lerrnayin Gharabakh, *Az.* Dağliq Quarabağ, *Rus.* Nagornyy Karabakh. *former autonomous region* SW Azerbaijan
Nagorno- Karabakhskaya Avtonomnaya Oblast *see* Nagorno-Karabakh
123 Q12 **Nagornyy** Respublika Sakha (Yakutiya), NE Russian Federation 55°53′N 124°58′E
Nagornyy Karabakh *see* Nagorno-Karabakh
125 R13 **Nagorsk** Kirovskaya Oblast', NW Russian Federation 59°18′N 50°49′E
164 K13 **Nagoya** Aichi, Honshū, SW Japan 35°10′N 136°53′E
154 I12 **Nāgpur** Mahārāshtra, C India 21°09′N 79°06′E
156 K10 **Nagqu** *Chin.* Na-Ch'ii; *prev.* Hei-ho. Xizang Zizhiqu, W China 31°30′N 91°57′E
152 J8 **Nāg Tibba Range** ▲▲ N India
45 O8 **Nagua** NE Dominican Republic 19°25′N 69°49′W
111 H25 **Nagyatád** Somogy, SW Hungary 46°15′N 17°25′E
Nagybánya *see* Baia Mare
Nagybecskerek *see* Zrenjanin
Nagydisznód *see* Cisnădie
Nagyenyed *see* Aiud
111 N21 **Nagykálló** Szabolcs-Szatmár-Bereg, E Hungary 47°50′N 21°47′E
111 G25 **Nagykanizsa** *Ger.* Grosskanizsa. Zala, SW Hungary 46°27′N 17°E
Nagykároly *see* Carei
111 K22 **Nagykáta** Pest, C Hungary 47°25′N 19°45′E
Nagykikinda *see* Kikinda
111 K23 **Nagykőrös** Pest, C Hungary 47°01′N 19°46′E
Nagy-Küküllő *see* Târnava Mare
Nagylak *see* Nădlac
Nagymihály *see* Michalovce
Nagyrőce *see* Revúca
Nagysomkút *see* Şomcuta Mare
Nagysurány *see* Šurany
Nagyszalonta *see* Salonta
Nagyszeben *see* Sibiu
Nagyszentmiklós *see* Sânnicolau Mare
Nagyszöllös *see* Vynohradiv
Nagyszombat *see* Trnava
Nagytapolcsány *see* Topoľčany
Nagyvárad *see* Oradea
165 S17 **Naha** Okinawa, Okinawa, SW Japan 26°10′N 127°40′E
152 J8 **Nāhan** Himāchal Pradesh, NW India 30°33′N 77°18′E
Nahang, Rūd-e *see* Nihing
138 F8 **Nahariya** *prev.* Nahariyya. Northern, N Israel 33°01′N 35°05′E
Nahariyya *see* Nahariya
142 L6 **Nahāvand** *var.* Nehavend. Hamadān, W Iran 34°13′N 48°21′E
101 F19 **Nahe** ∽ SW Germany
Na H-Iarmhidhe *see* Westmeath
189 O13 **Nahnalaud** ▲ Pohnpei, E Micronesia
Nahoi, Cape *see* Cumberland, Cape
Nahtavárr *see* Nattavaara
63 H16 **Nahuel Huapí, Lago** ◎ W Argentina
23 W7 **Nahunta** Georgia, SE USA 31°11′N 81°58′W
40 J6 **Naica** Chihuahua, N Mexico 27°53′N 105°30′W
11 U15 **Naicam** Saskatchewan, S Canada 52°26′N 104°30′W
Naiman Qi *see* Daqin Tal
158 M4 **Naimin Bulak** *spring* NW China
13 P6 **Nain** Newfoundland and Labrador, NE Canada 56°33′N 61°46′W
143 P8 **Nā'īn** Eşfahān, C Iran 32°52′N 53°05′E
152 K10 **Naini Tāl** Uttarakhand, N India 29°22′N 79°26′E
154 J11 **Nainpur** Madhya Pradesh, C India 22°26′N 80°10′E
96 J8 **Nairn** N Scotland, United Kingdom 57°36′N 03°51′W
96 J8 **Nairn** *cultural region* NE Scotland, United Kingdom
81 I19 **Nairobi** ● (Kenya) Nairobi Area, S Kenya 01°17′S 36°50′E
81 I19 **Nairobi** ✈ Nairobi Area, S Kenya 01°21′S 37°01′E
82 P13 **Nairoto** Cabo Delgado, NE Mozambique 12°22′S 39°05′E
118 G3 **Naissaar** *island* N Estonia
Naissus *see* Niš
187 Z14 **Naitaba** *var.* Naitauba; *prev.* Naitamba. *island* Lau Group, E Fiji
Naitamba/Naitauba *see* Naitaba
81 I19 **Naivasha** Rift Valley, SW Kenya 0°44′S 36°26′E
81 H19 **Naivasha, Lake** ◎ SW Kenya
Najaf *see* An Najaf
143 N8 **Najafābād** *var.* Nejafabad. Eşfahān, C Iran 32°38′N 51°23′E
141 N7 **Najd** *var.* Nejd. *cultural region* C Saudi Arabia
105 O4 **Nájera** La Rioja, N Spain 42°25′N 02°45′W
105 P4 **Najerilla** ∽ N Spain
163 U7 **Naji** *var.* Arun Qi. Nei Mongol Zizhiqu, N China 48°05′N 123°28′E
152 J9 **Najībābād** Uttar Pradesh, N India 29°37′N 78°19′E
Najima *see* Fukuoka
163 Y11 **Najin** NE North Korea 42°13′N 130°16′E
139 T9 **Najm al Ḥassūn** Bābil, C Iraq 32°24′N 44°13′E
141 O13 **Najrān** *var.* Abā as Su'ūd. Najrān, S Saudi Arabia 17°31′N 44°09′E
141 P12 **Najrān** *var.* Minṭaqat al Najrān. ◐ *province* S Saudi Arabia
Najrān, Minṭaqat al *see* Najrān
165 T2 **Nakagawa** Hokkaidō, NE Japan 44°49′N 142°04′E
38 F9 **Nākālele Point** *var.* Nakalele Point. *headland* Maui, Hawai'i, USA 21°01′N 156°35′W
164 D13 **Nakama** Fukuoka, Kyūshū, SW Japan 33°53′N 130°48′E
Nakambé *see* White Volta
Nakamti *see* Nek'emtē
164 F15 **Nakamura** *var.* Shimanto. Kōchi, Shikoku, SW Japan 33°00′N 132°55′E
186 H7 **Nakanai Mountains** ▲▲ New Britain, E Papua New Guinea
164 H11 **Nakano-shima** *island* Oki-shotō, SW Japan
165 Q6 **Nakasato** Aomori, Honshū, C Japan 40°58′N 140°26′E
165 T5 **Nakasatsunai** Hokkaidō, NE Japan 42°42′N 143°09′E
165 W4 **Nakashibetsu** Hokkaidō, NE Japan 43°31′N 144°58′E
81 F18 **Nakasongola** C Uganda 01°19′N 32°28′E
165 T1 **Nakatonbetsu** Hokkaidō, NE Japan 44°58′N 142°18′E
164 L13 **Nakatsugawa** *var.* Nakatugawa. Gifu, Honshū, SW Japan 35°30′N 137°29′E
Nakatugawa *see* Nakatsugawa
Nakdong *see* Naktong-gang
Nakel *see* Nakło nad Notecią
Nakfa *see* Nakh'fa
80 J8 **Nakh'fa** *var.* Nakfa. N Eritrea 16°38′N 38°26′E
Nakhichevan' *see* Naxçıvan
123 S15 **Nakhodka** Primorskiy Kray, SE Russian Federation 42°46′N 132°48′E
122 J8 **Nakhodka** Yamalo-Nenetskiy Avtonomnyy Okrug, N Russian Federation 67°48′N 77°48′E
Nakhon Navok *see* Nakhon Nayok
167 P11 **Nakhon Nayok** *var.* Nagara Nayok, Nakhon Navok. Nakhon Nayok, C Thailand 14°15′N 101°12′E
167 O11 **Nakhon Pathom** *var.* Nagara Pathom, Nakorn Pathom. Nakhon Pathom, W Thailand 13°49′N 100°06′E
167 R8 **Nakhon Phanom** *var.* Nagara Panom. Nakhon Phanom, E Thailand 17°22′N 104°46′E
167 Q10 **Nakhon Ratchasima** *var.* Khorat, Korat. Nakhon Ratchasima, E Thailand 15°N 102°06′E
167 O9 **Nakhon Sawan** *var.* Muang Nakhon Sawan, Nagara Svarga. Nakhon Sawan, W Thailand 15°42′N 100°06′E
167 N15 **Nakhon Si Thammarat** *var.* Nagara Sridharmaraj, Nakhon Sithamnaraj. Nakhon Si Thammarat, SW Thailand 08°24′N 99°58′E
Nakhon Sithamnaraj *see* Nakhon Si Thammarat
139 Y11 **Nakhrash** Al Başrah, SE Iraq 31°13′N 47°24′E
10 I9 **Nakina** British Columbia, W Canada 59°12′N 132°48′W
110 H9 **Nakło nad Notecią** *Ger.* Nakel. Kujawsko-pomorskie, C Poland 53°08′N 17°35′E
39 P13 **Naknek** Alaska, USA 58°45′N 157°01′W
152 H8 **Nakodar** Punjab, NW India 31°06′N 75°31′E
82 M11 **Nakonde** Northern, NE Zambia 09°22′S 42°47′E
Nakorn Pathom *see* Nakhon Pathom
95 H24 **Nakskov** Storstrøm, SE Denmark 54°50′N 11°10′E
163 Y15 **Naktong-gang** *var.* Nakdong, *Jap.* Rakutō-kō. ∽ C South Korea
81 H18 **Nakuru** Rift Valley, SW Kenya 0°16′S 36°04′E
81 H19 **Nakuru, Lake** ◎ Rift Valley, C Kenya
11 O17 **Nakusp** British Columbia, SW Canada 50°14′N 117°48′W
149 N15 **Nāl** ∽ W Pakistan
162 M7 **Nalayh** Töv, C Mongolia 47°48′N 107°17′E
153 V12 **Nalbāri** Assam, NE India 26°36′N 91°49′E
63 G19 **Nalcayec, Isla** *island* Archipiélago de los Chonos, S Chile
127 N15 **Nal'chik** Kabardino-Balkarskaya Respublika, SW Russian Federation 43°30′N 43°39′E
155 I16 **Nalgonda** Andhra Pradesh, C India 17°04′N 79°15′E
153 S14 **Nalhāti** West Bengal, NE India 24°19′N 87°53′E
153 U14 **Nalitabari** Dhaka, N Bangladesh 25°06′N 90°11′E
155 I17 **Nallamala Hills** ▲▲ E India
136 G12 **Nallıhan** Ankara, NW Turkey 40°12′N 31°22′E
104 K2 **Nalón** ∽ NW Spain
167 N3 **Nalong** Kachin State, N Burma (Myanmar) 24°42′N 97°27′E
75 N8 **Nālūt** NW Libya 31°52′N 10°59′E
171 T14 **Nama** Pulau Manawoka, E Indonesia 04°07′S 131°22′E
189 Q16 **Nama** *island* C Micronesia
83 O16 **Namacurra** Zambézia, NE Mozambique 17°31′S 37°03′E
188 F9 **Namai Bay** *bay* Babeldaob, N Palau
Namakal *see* Nāmakkal
29 W2 **Namakan Lake** ◎ Canada/USA
143 O6 **Namak, Daryācheh-ye** *marsh* N Iran
155 H22 **Nāmakkal** *var.* Namakal. Tamil Nādu, SE India 11°13′N 78°13′E
143 T6 **Namak, Kavīr-e** *salt pan* NE Iran
167 O6 **Namaklwe** Shan State, E Burma (Myanmar) 19°45′N 99°01′E
Namaksār, Kowl-e/Namakzār, Daryācheh-ye *see* Namakzar
148 J5 **Namakzar** *Pash.* Daryācheh-ye Namakzār, Kowl-e Namaksār. *marsh* Afghanistan/Iran
171 V15 **Namalau** Pulau Jursian, E Indonesia 05°50′S 134°43′E
81 I20 **Namanga** Rift Valley, S Kenya 02°33′S 36°48′E
147 S10 **Namangan** Namangan Viloyati, E Uzbekistan 40°59′N 71°34′E
Namanganskaya Oblast' *see* Namangan Viloyati
147 R10 **Namangan Viloyati** *Rus.* Namanganskaya Oblast'. ◐ *province* E Uzbekistan
83 Q14 **Namapa** Nampula, NE Mozambique 13°43′S 39°48′E
83 C21 **Namaqualand** *physical region* S Namibia
81 G18 **Namasagali** C Uganda 01°02′N 32°58′E
186 H6 **Namatanai** New Ireland, NE Papua New Guinea 03°40′S 152°26′E
83 I14 **Nambala** Central, C Zambia 15°04′S 26°56′E
81 J23 **Nambanje** Lindi, SE Tanzania 08°37′S 38°21′E
183 V2 **Nambour** Queensland, E Australia 26°40′S 152°52′E
183 V6 **Nambucca Heads** New South Wales, SE Australia 30°37′S 153°00′E
159 N15 **Nam Co** ◎ W China
167 R5 **Nam Cum** Lai Châu, N Vietnam 22°37′N 103°12′E
Namdik *see* Namorik Atoll
167 T6 **Nam Định** Nam Ha, N Vietnam 20°25′N 106°12′E
99 I20 **Namêche** Namur, SE Belgium 50°29′N 05°02′E
30 J4 **Namekagon Lake** ◎ Wisconsin, N USA
188 F10 **Namekakl Passage** *passage* Babeldaob, N Palau
Namen *see* Namur
83 P15 **Nametil** Nampula, NE Mozambique 15°46′S 39°21′E
163 X14 **Nam-gang** ∽ C North Korea
163 Y16 **Nam-gang** ∽ S South Korea
163 Y17 **Namhae-do** *Jap.* Nankai-tō. *island* S South Korea

◆ Country ◇ Dependent Territory ◐ Administrative Regions ▲ Mountain Volcano ◎ Lake
● Country Capital ○ Dependent Territory Capital ✈ International Airport ▲▲ Mountain Range ∽ River ⊠ Reservoir

Namhoi see Foshan
83 C19 **Namib Desert** *desert* W Namibia
83 A15 **Namibe** *Port.* Moçâmedes, Mossâmedes. Namibe, SW Angola *15°10′S 12°09′E*
83 A15 **Namibe** ◆ *province* SE Angola
83 C18 **Namibia** *off.* Republic of Namibia, *var.* South West Africa, *Afr.* Suidwes-Afrika, *Ger.* Deutsch-Südwestafrika; *prev.* German Southwest Africa, South-West Africa. ◆ *republic* S Africa
65 O17 **Namibia Plain** *undersea feature* S Atlantic Ocean
Namibia, Republic of see Namibia
165 Q11 **Namie** Fukushima, Honshū, C Japan *37°29′N 140°58′E*
165 Q7 **Namioka** Aomori, Honshū, C Japan *40°43′N 140°34′E*
40 I5 **Namiquipa** Chihuahua, N Mexico *29°15′N 107°25′W*
159 P15 **Namjagbarwa Feng** ▲ W China *29°39′N 95°00′E*
Namka see Doilungdêqên
171 R13 **Namlea** Pulau Buru, E Indonesia *03°12′S 127°06′E*
158 L16 **Namling** Xizang Zizhiqu, W China *29°40′N 88°58′E*
Namnetes see Nantes
167 R8 **Nam Ngum** ⤳ C Laos
Namo see Namu Atoll
183 R5 **Namoi River** ⤳ New South Wales, SE Australia
189 Q17 **Namoluk Atoll** *atoll* Mortlock Islands, C Micronesia
189 O15 **Namonuito Atoll** *atoll* Caroline Islands, C Micronesia
189 T9 **Namorik Atoll** *var.* Namdik. *atoll* Ralik Chain, S Marshall Islands
167 Q6 **Nam Ou** ⤳ N Laos
32 M14 **Nampa** Idaho, NW USA *43°32′N 116°33′W*
77 M11 **Nampala** Ségou, W Mali *15°21′N 05°32′W*
163 W14 **Namp'o** SW North Korea *38°46′N 125°25′E*
83 P15 **Nampula** Nampula, NE Mozambique *15°09′S 39°14′E*
83 P15 **Nampula** *off.* Província de Nampula. ◆ *province* NE Mozambique
Nampula, Província de see Nampula
163 W13 **Namsan-ni** NW North Korea *40°25′N 125°01′E*
Namslau see Namysłów
93 E15 **Namsos** Nord-Trøndelag, C Norway *64°28′N 11°31′E*
93 F14 **Namsskogan** Nord-Trøndelag, C Norway *64°57′N 13°04′E*
167 O6 **Nam Teng** ⤳ E Burma (Myanmar)
167 P6 **Nam Tha** ⤳ N Laos
123 Q10 **Namtsy** Respublika Sakha (Yakutiya), NE Russian Federation *62°42′N 129°30′E*
167 N4 **Namtu** Shan State, E Burma (Myanmar) *23°04′N 97°26′E*
10 J15 **Namu** British Columbia, SW Canada *51°46′N 127°49′W*
189 T7 **Namu Atoll** *var.* Namo. *atoll* Ralik Chain, C Marshall Islands
187 Y15 **Namuka-i-lau** *island* Lau Group, E Fiji
83 O15 **Namuli, Mont** ▲ NE Mozambique *15°15′S 37°33′E*
83 P14 **Namuno** Cabo Delgado, N Mozambique *13°39′S 38°50′E*
99 I20 **Namur** *Dut.* Namen. Namur, SE Belgium *50°28′N 04°52′E*
99 H21 **Namur** *Dut.* Namen. ◆ *province* S Belgium
83 D17 **Namutoni** Kunene, N Namibia *18°49′S 16°55′E*
163 Y16 **Namwŏn** *Jap.* Nangen. S South Korea *35°24′N 127°20′E*
111 H14 **Namysłów** *Ger.* Namslau. Opole, SW Poland *51°03′N 17°41′E*
167 P7 **Nan** *var.* Muang Nan. Nan, NW Thailand *18°47′N 100°50′E*
79 G15 **Nana** ⤳ W Central African Republic
165 R5 **Nanae** Hokkaidō, NE Japan *41°55′N 140°40′E*
79 I14 **Nana-Grébizi** ◆ *prefecture* N Central African Republic
10 L17 **Nanaimo** Vancouver Island, British Columbia, SW Canada *49°08′N 123°58′W*
38 C9 **Nānākuli** *var.* Nanakuli. O'ahu, Hawaii, USA, C Pacific Ocean *21°23′N 158°09′W*
79 G15 **Nana-Mambéré** ◆ *prefecture* W Central African Republic
161 R13 **Nan'an** Fujian, SE China *24°57′N 118°22′E*
183 U2 **Nanango** Queensland, E Australia *26°42′S 151°58′E*
164 L11 **Nanao** Ishikawa, Honshū, SW Japan *37°03′N 136°58′E*
161 Q14 **Nan'ao Dao** *island* S China
164 L10 **Nanatsu-shima** *island* SW Japan
56 F8 **Nanay, Río** ⤳ NE Peru
160 J8 **Nanbu** Sichuan, C China *31°19′N 106°02′E*
163 X7 **Nancha** Heilongjiang, NE China *47°09′N 129°17′E*
161 P10 **Nanchang** *var.* Nan-ch'ang, Nanch'ang-hsien. *province capital* Jiangxi, S China *28°38′N 115°58′E*
Nan-ch'ang see Nanchang
Nanch'ang-hsien see Nanchang
161 P11 **Nancheng** *var.* Jianchang. Jiangxi, S China *27°37′N 116°37′E*
Nan-ching see Nanjing
160 J9 **Nanchong** Sichuan, C China *30°47′N 106°03′E*
160 J10 **Nanchuan** Chongqing Shi, C China *29°06′N 107°13′E*
103 T5 **Nancy** Meurthe-et-Moselle, NE France *48°40′N 06°11′E*
185 A22 **Nancy Sound** *sound* South Island, New Zealand
152 L9 **Nanda Devi** ▲ NW India *30°27′N 80°00′E*
42 J11 **Nandaime** Granada, SW Nicaragua *11°45′N 86°02′W*
160 K13 **Nandan** *var.* Minami-Awaji. Guangxi Zhuangzu Zizhiqu, S China *25°03′N 107°31′E*
155 H14 **Nānded** Mahārāshtra, C India *19°11′N 77°21′E*
183 S5 **Nandewar Range** ▲ New South Wales, SE Australia
Nandi see Nadi
160 E13 **Nanding He** ⤳ China/Vietnam
Nándorhgy see Oţelu Roşu
154 E11 **Nandurbār** Mahārāshtra, W India *21°22′N 74°18′E*
Nanduri see Naduri
155 I17 **Nandyāl** Andhra Pradesh, E India *15°30′N 78°28′E*
161 P11 **Nanfeng** *var.* Qincheng. Jiangxi, S China *27°15′N 116°16′E*
Nang see Nangxian
79 E15 **Nanga Eboko** Centre, C Cameroon *04°38′N 12°21′E*
Nangah Serawai see Nangaserawai
149 W4 **Nanga Parbat** ▲ India/Pakistan *35°15′N 74°36′E*
169 R11 **Nangapinoh** Borneo, C Indonesia *00°21′S 111°44′E*
149 R5 **Nangarhār** ◆ *province* E Afghanistan
169 S11 **Nangaserawai** *var.* Nangah Serawai. Borneo, C Indonesia *00°20′S 112°26′E*
169 Q12 **Nangatayap** Borneo, C Indonesia *01°30′S 110°33′E*
Nangen see Namwŏn
103 P5 **Nangis** Seine-et-Marne, N France *48°36′N 03°02′E*
163 X13 **Nangnim-sanmaek** ▲ C North Korea
161 O4 **Nangong** Hebei, E China *37°22′N 115°20′E*
159 Q14 **Nangqên** *var.* Xangda. Qinghai, C China *32°05′N 96°28′E*
167 Q10 **Nang Rong** Buri Ram, E Thailand *14°37′N 102°48′E*
159 O16 **Nangxian** *var.* Nang. Xizang Zizhiqu, W China *29°04′N 93°03′E*
Nan Hai see South China Sea
160 L8 **Nan He** ⤳ C China
160 F12 **Nanhua** *var.* Longchuan. Yunnan, SW China *25°15′N 101°15′E*
Naniwa see Ōsaka
155 G20 **Nanjangūd** Karnātaka, W India *12°07′N 76°40′E*
161 Q8 **Nanjing** *var.* Nan-ching, Nanking; *prev.* Chianning, Chian-ning, Kiang-ning, Jiangsu. *province capital* Jiangsu, E China *32°03′N 118°47′E*
Nankai-tō see Namhae-do
161 O12 **Nankang** *var.* Rongjiang. Jiangxi, S China *25°42′N 114°45′E*
Nanking see Nanjing
161 N13 **Nan Ling** ▲ S China
160 L15 **Nanliu Jiang** ⤳ S China
189 P13 **Nan Madol** *ruins* Temwen Island, E Micronesia
160 K15 **Nanning** *var.* Nan-ning; *prev.* Yung-ning. Guangxi Zhuangzu Zizhiqu, S China *22°50′N 108°19′E*
Nan-ning see Nanning
196 M15 **Nanortalik** Kitaa, S Greenland *60°12′N 44°53′W*
Nanouki see Aranuka
160 H13 **Nanpan Jiang** ⤳ S China
152 M11 **Nānpāra** Uttar Pradesh, N India *27°51′N 81°30′E*
161 Q12 **Nanping** *var.* Nan-p'ing; *prev.* Yenping. Fujian, SE China *26°40′N 118°07′E*
Nan-p'ing see Nanping
Nanping see Jiuzhaigou
Nanpu see Pucheng
161 R12 **Nanri Dao** *island* SE China
165 S16 **Nansei-shotō** *Eng.* Ryukyu Islands. *island group* SW Japan
Nansei Syotō Trench see Ryukyu Trench
197 T10 **Nansen Basin** *undersea feature* Arctic Ocean
197 T10 **Nansen Cordillera** *var.* Arctic Mid Oceanic Ridge, Nansen Ridge. *undersea feature* Arctic Ocean *87°00′N 90°00′E*
Nansen Ridge see Nansen Cordillera
129 T9 **Nan Shan** ▲ C China
Nansha Qundao see Spratly Islands
12 K3 **Nantais, Lac** ◎ Québec, NE Canada
103 N5 **Nanterre** Hauts-de-Seine, N France *48°53′N 02°13′E*
102 I8 **Nantes** *Bret.* Naoned; *anc.* Condivincum, Namnetes. Loire-Atlantique, NW France *47°12′N 01°32′W*
14 G17 **Nanticoke** Ontario, S Canada *42°49′N 80°04′W*
18 H13 **Nanticoke** Pennsylvania, NE USA *41°12′N 76°00′W*
21 Y4 **Nanticoke River** ⤳ Delaware/Maryland, NE USA
11 Q17 **Nanton** Alberta, SW Canada *50°21′N 113°47′W*
161 S8 **Nantong** Jiangsu, E China *32°00′N 120°52′E*
161 S13 **Nant'ou** W Taiwan *23°54′N 120°51′E*
103 S10 **Nantua** Ain, E France *46°10′N 05°34′E*
19 Q13 **Nantucket** Nantucket Island, Massachusetts, NE USA *41°15′N 70°05′W*
19 Q13 **Nantucket Island** *island* Massachusetts, NE USA
19 Q13 **Nantucket Sound** *sound* Massachusetts, NE USA
82 P13 **Nantulo** Cabo Delgado, N Mozambique *12°30′S 39°03′E*
189 O12 **Nanuh** Pohnpei, E Micronesia
190 D6 **Nanumaga** *var.* Nanumanga. *atoll* NW Tuvalu
Nanumanga see Nanumaga
190 D5 **Nanumea Atoll** *atoll* NW Tuvalu
59 O19 **Nanuque** Minas Gerais, SE Brazil *17°49′S 40°21′W*
171 R10 **Nanusa, Kepulauan** *island group* N Indonesia
163 U4 **Nanweng He** ⤳ NE China
160 I10 **Nanxi** Sichuan, C China *28°54′N 104°59′E*
161 N10 **Nanxian** *var.* Nan Xian, Nanzhou. Hunan, S China *29°23′N 112°18′E*
Nan Xian see Nanxian
161 N7 **Nanyang** *var.* Nan-yang. Henan, C China *32°59′N 112°29′E*
Nan-yang see Nanyang
161 P6 **Nanyang Hu** ◎ E China
165 P10 **Nan'yō** Yamagata, Honshū, C Japan *38°04′N 140°06′E*
81 I18 **Nanyuki** Central, C Kenya *0°01′N 37°05′E*
160 M8 **Nanzhang** Hubei, C China *31°47′N 111°48′E*
Nanzhou see Nanxian
105 T11 **Nao, Cabo de La** *headland* E Spain *38°43′N 00°13′E*
12 M9 **Naococane, Lac** ◎ Québec, E Canada
153 S14 **Naogaon** Rajshahi, NW Bangladesh *24°49′N 88°59′E*
Naokot see Naukot
187 R13 **Naone** Maewo, C Vanuatu *15°03′S 168°06′E*
Naoned see Nantes
115 E14 **Náousa** Kentrikí Makedonía, N Greece *40°38′N 22°04′E*
35 N8 **Napa** California, W USA *38°15′N 122°17′W*
39 O11 **Napaimiut** Alaska, USA *61°32′N 158°46′W*
39 N12 **Napakiak** Alaska, USA *60°42′N 161°57′W*
122 J7 **Napalkovo** Yamalo-Nenetskiy Avtonomnyy Okrug, N Russian Federation *70°06′N 73°43′E*
12 J16 **Napanee** Ontario, SE Canada *44°13′N 76°57′W*
39 N12 **Napaskiak** Alaska, USA *60°42′N 161°46′W*
167 S5 **Na Phac** Cao Bằng, N Vietnam *22°24′N 105°54′E*
184 O11 **Napier** Hawke's Bay, North Island, New Zealand *39°30′S 176°55′E*
195 X3 **Napier Mountains** ▲ Antarctica
15 O13 **Napierville** Québec, SE Canada *45°12′N 73°25′W*
23 W15 **Naples** Florida, SE USA *26°08′N 81°48′W*
25 W5 **Naples** Texas, SW USA *33°12′N 94°40′W*
Naples see Napoli
160 I14 **Napo** Guangxi Zhuangzu Zizhiqu, S China *23°21′N 105°47′E*
56 C6 **Napo** ◆ *province* NE Ecuador
29 O6 **Napoleon** North Dakota, N USA *46°30′N 99°46′W*
31 R11 **Napoleon** Ohio, N USA *41°23′N 84°07′W*
Napoléon-Vendée see La Roche-sur-Yon
22 J9 **Napoleonville** Louisiana, S USA *29°55′N 91°01′W*
107 K17 **Napoli** *Eng.* Naples, *Ger.* Neapel; *anc.* Neapolis. Campania, S Italy *40°52′N 14°15′E*
107 J18 **Napoli, Golfo di** *gulf* S Italy
57 F7 **Napo, Río** ⤳ Ecuador/Peru
191 W9 **Napuka** *island* Îles Tuamotu, C French Polynesia
142 J3 **Naqadeh** Āžarbāyjān-e Bākhtarī, NW Iran *36°57′N 45°24′E*
139 U6 **Naqnah** Diyālá, E Iraq *34°13′N 45°33′E*
Nar see Nera
164 J14 **Nara** Nara, Honshū, SW Japan *34°41′N 135°49′E*
76 L11 **Nara** Koulikoro, W Mali *15°04′N 07°19′W*
149 R14 **Nāra Canal** *irrigation canal* S Pakistan
182 K11 **Naracoorte** South Australia *37°02′S 140°45′E*
183 P8 **Naradhan** New South Wales, SE Australia *33°37′S 146°19′E*
Naradhivas see Narathiwat
56 B8 **Naranjal** Guayas, W Ecuador *02°43′S 79°38′W*
57 Q19 **Naranjos** Santa Cruz, E Bolivia
41 Q12 **Naranjos** Veracruz-Llave, E Mexico *21°21′N 97°41′W*
159 Q6 **Naran Sebstein Bulag** *spring* NW China
164 B14 **Narao** Nagasaki, Nakadōri-jima, SW Japan *32°40′N 129°03′E*
155 J16 **Narasaraopet** Andhra Pradesh, E India *16°16′N 80°06′E*
158 J5 **Narat** Xinjiang Uygur Zizhiqu, W China *43°20′N 84°02′E*
167 P17 **Narathiwat** *var.* Naradhivas. Narathiwat, SW Thailand *06°25′N 101°48′E*
37 V10 **Nara Visa** New Mexico, SW USA *35°35′N 103°06′W*
Nārāyāni see Gandak
Narbada see Narmada
Narbo Martius see Narbonne
103 P16 **Narbonne** *anc.* Narbo Martius. Aude, S France *43°11′N 03°E*
Narborough Island see Fernandina, Isla
104 J2 **Narcea** ⤳ NW Spain
152 J9 **Narendranagar** Uttarakhand, N India *30°10′N 78°21′E*
Nares Abyssal Plain see Nares Plain
64 G11 **Nares Plain** *var.* Nares Abyssal Plain. *undersea feature* NW Atlantic Ocean *23°30′N 63°00′W*
Nares Stræde see Nares Strait
197 P10 **Nares Strait** *Dan.* Nares Stræde. *strait* Canada/Greenland
110 O9 **Narew** ⤳ E Poland
155 F17 **Nargund** Karnātaka, W India *15°43′N 75°23′E*
83 D20 **Narib** Hardap, S Namibia *24°11′S 17°46′E*
Narikrik see Knox Atoll
Narin Gol see Dong He
54 B13 **Nariño** *off.* Departamento de Nariño. ◆ *province* SW Colombia
165 P13 **Narita** Chiba, Honshū, S Japan *35°46′N 140°20′E*
165 P13 **Narita** ✈ (Tōkyō) Chiba, Honshū, S Japan *35°45′N 140°23′E*
Nariya see An Nu'ayrīyah
162 F5 **Nariyn Gol** ⤳ Mongolia/Russian Federation
162 J8 **Narīynteel** *var.* Tsagaan-Ovoo. Övörhangay, C Mongolia *45°57′N 101°25′E*
152 J8 **Narkanda** Himāchal Pradesh, NW India *31°14′N 77°27′E*
92 L13 **Narkaus** Lappi, NW Finland *66°13′N 26°09′E*
154 E11 **Narmada** *var.* Narbada. ⤳ C India
152 H11 **Narnaul** *var.* Nārnaul. Haryāna, N India *28°04′N 76°10′E*
107 I14 **Narni** Umbria, C Italy *42°31′N 12°31′E*
107 J24 **Naro** Sicilia, Italy, C Mediterranean Sea *37°18′N 13°48′E*
Narodichi see Narodychi
125 V7 **Narodnaya, Gora** ▲ NW Russian Federation *65°04′N 60°12′E*
117 N3 **Narodychi** *Rus.* Narodichi. Zhytomyrs'ka Oblast', N Ukraine *51°11′N 29°01′E*
126 J4 **Naro-Fominsk** Moskovskaya Oblast', W Russian Federation *55°25′N 36°41′E*
81 H19 **Narok** Rift Valley, SW Kenya *01°04′S 35°54′E*
104 H2 **Narón** Galicia, NW Spain *43°31′N 08°08′W*
183 S11 **Narooma** New South Wales, SE Australia *36°16′S 150°08′E*
Narova see Narva
Narovlya see Narowlya
149 W8 **Nārowāl** Punjab, E Pakistan *32°04′N 74°54′E*
119 N20 **Narowlya** *Rus.* Narovlya. Homyel'skaya Voblasts', SE Belarus *51°48′N 29°30′E*
93 J17 **Närpes** *Fin.* Närpiö. Länsi-Suomi, W Finland *62°28′N 21°19′E*
Närpiö see Närpes
183 S5 **Narrabri** New South Wales, SE Australia *30°21′S 149°48′E*
183 P9 **Narrandera** New South Wales, SE Australia *34°46′S 146°32′E*
183 Q4 **Narran Lake** ◎ New South Wales, SE Australia
183 Q4 **Narran River** ⤳ New South Wales/Queensland, SE Australia
180 J13 **Narrogin** Western Australia *32°53′S 117°17′E*
183 Q7 **Narromine** New South Wales, SE Australia *32°16′S 148°15′E*
21 R6 **Narrows** Virginia, NE USA *37°19′N 80°48′W*
196 M15 **Narsarsuaq** ✈ Kitaa, S Greenland *61°07′N 45°03′W*
154 I10 **Narsimhapur** Madhya Pradesh, C India *22°58′N 79°15′E*
153 U15 **Narsingdi** *var.* Narsinghdi. Dhaka, C Bangladesh *23°56′N 90°40′E*
Narsinghdi see Narsingdi
154 H9 **Narsinghgarh** Madhya Pradesh, C India *23°42′N 77°08′E*
163 Q11 **Nart** Nei Mongol Zizhiqu, N China *42°54′N 115°55′E*
Nartës, Gjol i/Nartës, Laguna e see Nartës, Liqeni i
113 J22 **Nartës, Liqeni i** *var.* Gjol i Nartës, Laguna e Nartës. ◎ SW Albania
115 F17 **Narthákí** ▲ C Greece *39°12′N 22°24′E*
127 O15 **Nartkala** Kabardino-Balkarskaya Respublika, SW Russian Federation *43°34′N 43°55′E*
118 K3 **Narva** Ida-Virumaa, NE Estonia *59°23′N 28°12′E*
118 K4 **Narva** *prev.* Narova. ⤳ Estonia/Russian Federation
118 J3 **Narva Bay** *Est.* Narva Laht, *Ger.* Narwa-Bucht, *Rus.* Narvskiy Zaliv. *bay* Estonia/Russian Federation
Narva Laht see Narva Bay
124 F13 **Narva Reservoir** *Est.* Narva Veehoidla, *Rus.* Narvskoye Vodokhranilishche. ⊠ Estonia/Russian Federation
Narva Veehoidla see Narva Reservoir
92 H10 **Narvik** Nordland, C Norway *68°26′N 17°24′E*
Narvskiy Zaliv see Narva Bay
Narvskoye Vodokhranilishche see Narva Reservoir
Narwa-Bucht see Narva Bay
152 I9 **Narwāna** Haryāna, NW India *29°36′N 76°11′E*
125 R4 **Nar'yan-Mar** *prev.* Beloshchel'ye, Dzerzhinskiy. Nenetskiy Avtonomnyy Okrug, NW Russian Federation *67°38′N 53°E*
122 J12 **Narym** Tomskaya Oblast', C Russian Federation *58°59′N 81°20′E*
145 Y10 **Narymskiy Khrebet** *Kaz.* Naryn Zhotasy. ▲ E Kazakhstan
147 W9 **Naryn** Narynskaya Oblast', C Kyrgyzstan *41°24′N 76°E*
147 U8 **Naryn** ⤳ Kyrgyzstan/Uzbekistan
145 W16 **Narynkol** *Kaz.* Naryngol. Almaty, SE Kazakhstan *42°45′N 80°12′E*
Naryn Oblasty see Narynskaya Oblast'
Narynqol see Narynkol
147 V9 **Narynskaya Oblast'** *Kir.* Naryn Oblasty. ◆ *province* C Kyrgyzstan
Naryn Zhotasy see Narymskiy Khrebet
126 J6 **Naryshkino** Orlovskaya Oblast', W Russian Federation *53°00′N 35°41′E*
95 L14 **Nås** Dalarna, C Sweden *60°28′N 14°30′E*
10 J11 **Nass** ⤳ British Columbia, SW Canada
92 G13 **Nasafjellet** *Lapp.* Násávárre. ▲ C Norway *66°29′N 15°23′E*
93 H16 **Näsåker** Västernorrland, C Sweden *63°27′N 16°55′E*
44 H2 **Nassau** ● (Bahamas) New Providence, N Bahamas *25°03′N 77°21′W*
187 Y14 **Nasau** Koro, C Fiji *17°20′S 179°26′E*
44 H2 **Nassau** ✈ New Providence, C Bahamas *25°00′N 77°26′W*
190 J13 **Nassau** *island* N Cook Islands
116 I9 **Năsăud** *Ger.* Nussdorf, *Hung.* Naszód. Bistriţa-Năsăud, N Romania *47°16′N 24°24′E*
Násávárre see Nasafjellet
103 P13 **Nasbinals** Lozère, S France *44°40′N 03°03′E*
Na Sceirí see Skerries
Nase see Naze
185 E22 **Naseby** Otago, South Island, New Zealand *45°02′S 170°09′E*
143 R10 **Nāşerīyeh** Kermān, C Iran
25 X5 **Nash** Texas, SW USA *33°26′N 94°04′W*
154 E13 **Nāshik** *prev.* Nāsik. Mahārāshtra, W India *20°05′N 73°48′E*
56 E7 **Nashiño, Río** ⤳ Ecuador/Peru
29 W12 **Nashua** Iowa, C USA *42°57′N 92°32′W*
33 W7 **Nashua** Montana, NW USA *48°06′N 106°16′W*
19 O10 **Nashua** New Hampshire, NE USA *42°45′N 71°26′W*
27 S13 **Nashville** Arkansas, C USA *33°57′N 93°50′W*
23 U7 **Nashville** Georgia, SE USA *31°12′N 83°15′W*
30 L16 **Nashville** Illinois, N USA *38°20′N 89°22′W*
31 O14 **Nashville** Indiana, N USA *39°13′N 86°15′W*
21 V9 **Nashville** North Carolina, SE USA *35°58′N 78°00′W*
20 J8 **Nashville** *state capital* Tennessee, S USA *36°11′N 86°48′W*
20 J9 **Nashville** ✈ Tennessee, S USA *36°06′N 86°44′W*
64 H10 **Nashville Seamount** *undersea feature* NW Atlantic Ocean *30°00′N 57°20′W*
112 H9 **Našice** Osijek-Baranja, E Croatia *45°29′N 18°05′E*
110 M11 **Nasielsk** Mazowieckie, C Poland *52°33′N 20°46′E*
93 K18 **Näsijärvi** ◎ SW Finland
Nāsik see Nāshik
80 G13 **Nasir** Upper Nile, SE Sudan *08°37′N 33°06′E*
148 K15 **Nasīrābād** Baluchistān, SW Pakistan *26°15′N 62°32′E*
Nasir, Buhayrat/Nâşir, Buḩeiret see Nasser, Lake
Nāsiri see Ahvāz
Nasiriya see An Nāşirīyah
Nás na Ríogh see Naas
107 L23 **Naso** Sicilia, Italy, C Mediterranean Sea *38°07′N 14°46′E*
Nasratabad see Zābol
77 V15 **Nassarawa** Nassarawa, C Nigeria *08°33′N 07°42′E*
23 W8 **Nassau Sound** *sound* Florida, SE USA
108 L7 **Nassereith** Tirol, W Austria *47°19′N 10°51′E*
80 F5 **Nasser, Lake** *var.* Buhayrat Nasir, Buḩayrat Nāşir, Buḩeiret Nâşir. ◎ Egypt/Sudan
95 L19 **Nässjö** Jönköping, S Sweden *57°39′N 14°40′E*
99 K22 **Nassogne** Luxembourg, SE Belgium *50°08′N 05°19′E*
12 J6 **Nastapoka Islands** *island group* Northwest Territories, C Canada
93 M19 **Nastola** Etelä-Suomi, S Finland *60°57′N 25°56′E*
171 O4 **Nasugbu** Luzon, N Philippines *14°03′N 120°39′E*
94 N11 **Näsviken** Gävleborg, C Sweden *61°46′N 16°55′E*
Naszód see Năsăud
83 I17 **Nata** Central, NE Botswana *20°11′S 26°10′E*
54 E11 **Natagaima** Tolima, C Colombia *03°38′N 75°07′W*
59 Q14 **Natal** *state capital* Rio Grande do Norte, E Brazil *05°46′S 35°15′W*
168 I11 **Natal** Sumatera, N Indonesia *0°32′N 99°07′E*
Natal see KwaZulu/Natal
173 L10 **Natal Basin** *var.* Mozambique Basin. *undersea feature* W Indian Ocean *30°00′S 40°00′E*
25 R12 **Natalia** Texas, SW USA *29°11′N 98°51′W*
67 W15 **Natal Valley** *undersea feature* SW Indian Ocean *31°00′S 33°15′E*
Natanya see Netanya
143 O7 **Naţanz** Eşfahān, C Iran *33°31′N 51°55′E*
13 Q11 **Natashquan** Québec, E Canada *50°10′N 61°50′W*
13 Q10 **Natashquan** ⤳ Newfoundland and Labrador/Québec, E Canada
22 J7 **Natchez** Mississippi, S USA *31°34′N 91°24′W*
22 G6 **Natchitoches** Louisiana, S USA *31°45′N 93°05′W*
108 E10 **Naters** Valais, S Switzerland *46°22′N 08°00′E*
Nathanya see Netanya
92 O3 **Nathorst Land** *physical region* W Svalbard
186 E9 **National Capital District** ◆ *province* S Papua New Guinea
35 U17 **National City** California, W USA *32°40′N 117°06′W*
184 M10 **National Park** Manawatu-Wanganui, North Island, New Zealand *39°11′S 175°22′E*
77 R14 **Natitingou** NW Benin *10°21′N 01°26′E*
40 B5 **Natividad, Isla** *island* NW Mexico
165 Q10 **Natori** Miyagi, Honshū, C Japan *38°12′N 140°51′E*
18 C14 **Natrona Heights** Pennsylvania, NE USA *40°37′N 79°42′W*
81 H20 **Natron, Lake** ◎ Kenya/Tanzania
Natsrat see Natzrat
166 L7 **Nattalin** Bago, C Burma (Myanmar) *18°25′N 95°34′E*
92 J12 **Nattavaara** *Lapp.* Nahtavárr. Norrbotten, N Sweden *66°45′N 20°58′E*
109 S3 **Natternbach** Oberösterreich, N Austria *48°26′N 13°44′E*
95 M22 **Nättraby** Blekinge, S Sweden *56°12′N 15°30′E*
169 P10 **Natuna Besar, Pulau** *island* Kepulauan Natuna, W Indonesia
Natuna Islands see Natuna, Kepulauan
169 O9 **Natuna, Kepulauan** *var.* Natuna Islands. *island group* W Indonesia
169 N9 **Natuna, Laut** *Eng.* Natuna Sea. *sea* W Indonesia
Natuna Sea see Natuna, Laut
21 N6 **Natural Bridge** *tourist site* Kentucky, C USA
173 V11 **Naturaliste Fracture Zone** *tectonic feature* E Indian Ocean
174 J10 **Naturaliste Plateau** *undersea feature* E Indian Ocean
138 G9 **Natzrat** *var.* Natsrat, *Ar.* En Nazira, *Eng.* Nazareth; *prev.* Nazerat. Northern, N Israel *32°42′N 35°18′E*
Nau see Nov
103 O14 **Naucelle** Aveyron, S France *44°10′N 02°19′E*
83 D20 **Nauchas** Hardap, C Namibia *23°40′S 16°19′E*
108 K9 **Nauders** Tirol, W Austria *46°52′N 10°31′E*
Naugard see Nowogard
153 N11 **Naugarh** Uttar Pradesh, N India *24°50′N 83°17′E*
118 F12 **Naujamiestis** Panevėžys, C Lithuania *55°42′N 24°10′E*
118 E10 **Naujoji Akmenė** Šiaulai, NW Lithuania *56°20′N 22°57′E*
149 R16 **Naukot** *var.* Naokot. Sind, SE Pakistan *24°52′N 69°27′E*
101 L16 **Naumburg** *var.* Naumburg an der Saale. Sachsen-Anhalt, C Germany *51°09′N 11°48′E*
Naumburg am Queis see Nowogrodziec
Naumburg an der Saale see Naumburg
191 W15 **Naunau** *ancient monument* Easter Island, Chile, E Pacific Ocean
Nauparha see Nūāparha
138 G10 **Nā'ūr** 'Ammān, W Jordan *31°52′N 35°50′E*
189 Q8 **Nauru** *off.* Republic of Nauru; *prev.* Pleasant Island. ◆ *republic* W Pacific Ocean
175 P5 **Nauru** *island* W Pacific Ocean
189 Q9 **Nauru International** ✈ S Nauru
Nauru, Republic of see Nauru
Nausari see Navsāri
19 Q12 **Nauset Beach** *beach* Massachusetts, NE USA
Naushahra see Nowshera
149 P14 **Naushahro Fīroz** Sind, SE Pakistan *26°51′N 68°11′E*
Naushara see Nowshera
187 X14 **Nausori** Viti Levu, W Fiji *18°01′S 178°31′E*
56 F9 **Nauta** Loreto, N Peru *04°31′S 73°36′W*
153 O12 **Nautanwa** Uttar Pradesh, N India *27°26′N 83°25′E*
41 R13 **Nautla** Veracruz-Llave, E Mexico *20°15′N 96°45′W*
Nauzad see Now Zād
41 N6 **Nava** Coahuila, NE Mexico *28°28′N 100°45′W*
Navabad see Navobod
104 L6 **Nava del Rey** Castilla-León, N Spain *41°19′N 05°04′W*
153 S15 **Navadwīp** *prev.* Nabadwip. West Bengal, NE India *23°24′N 88°23′E*
104 M9 **Navahermosa** Castilla-La Mancha, C Spain *39°39′N 04°25′W*
119 I16 **Navahrudak** *Pol.* Nowogródek, *Rus.* Novogrudok. Hrodzyenskaya Voblasts', W Belarus *53°36′N 25°50′E*
119 I16 **Navahrudskaye Wzvyshsha** ▲ W Belarus
36 M8 **Navajo Mount** ▲ Utah, W USA *37°00′N 110°52′W*
37 Q9 **Navajo Reservoir** ⊠ New Mexico, SW USA
104 K9 **Navalmoral de la Mata** Extremadura, W Spain *39°54′N 05°33′W*
104 K10 **Navalvillar de Pelea** Extremadura, W Spain *39°05′N 05°27′W*
97 F17 **Navan** *Ir.* An Uaimh. E Ireland *53°39′N 06°41′W*
Navanagar see Jāmnagar
118 L12 **Navapolatsk** *Rus.* Novopolotsk. Vitsyebskaya Voblasts', N Belarus *55°34′N 28°35′E*
149 P6 **Nāvar, Dasht-e** *Pash.* Dasht-i-Nawar. *desert* C Afghanistan
123 W6 **Navarin, Mys** *headland* NE Russian Federation *62°18′N 179°06′E*
63 I25 **Navarino, Isla** *island* S Chile
105 Q4 **Navarra** *Eng./Fr.* Navarre. ◆ *autonomous community* N Spain
Navarre see Navarra
105 P4 **Navarrete** La Rioja, N Spain *42°26′N 02°34′W*
61 C20 **Navarro** Buenos Aires, E Argentina *35°00′S 59°15′W*
105 O12 **Navas de San Juan** Andalucía, S Spain *38°11′N 03°19′W*
127 N4 **Navashino** Nizhegorodskaya Oblast', W Russian Federation *55°33′N 42°15′E*
25 V10 **Navasota** Texas, SW USA *30°23′N 96°05′W*
25 U9 **Navasota River** ⤳ Texas, SW USA
44 I9 **Navassa Island** ◇ *US unincorporated territory* C West Indies
119 L19 **Navasyolki** *Rus.* Novosëlki. Homyel'skaya Voblasts', SE Belarus *52°24′N 28°33′E*
119 H17 **Navasyel'nya** *Pol.* Nowojelnia, *Rus.* Novoyel'nya. Hrodzyenskaya Voblasts', W Belarus *53°28′N 25°35′E*
171 Y13 **Naver** Papua, E Indonesia *03°27′S 139°45′E*
118 H5 **Navesti** ⤳ C Estonia
104 J1 **Navia** Asturias, N Spain *43°33′N 06°43′W*
104 J2 **Navia** ⤳ NW Spain
59 I21 **Naviraí** Mato Grosso do Sul, SW Brazil *23°01′S 54°09′W*
126 I6 **Navlya** Bryanskaya Oblast', W Russian Federation *52°47′N 34°28′E*
187 X13 **Navoalevu** Vanua Levu, N Fiji *16°22′S 179°28′E*
147 R12 **Navobod** *Rus.* Navabad, Novabad. C Tajikistan *39°00′N 70°06′E*
147 P13 **Navobod** *Rus.* Navabad. W Tajikistan *38°37′N 68°42′E*
Navoi see Navoiy
146 M11 **Navoiy** *Rus.* Navoi. Navoiy Viloyati, C Uzbekistan *40°05′N 65°23′E*
Navoiyskaya Oblast' see Navoiy Viloyati
146 K8 **Navoiy Viloyati** *Rus.* Navoiyskaya Oblast'. ◆ *province* N Uzbekistan
40 G7 **Navojoa** Sonora, NW Mexico *27°04′N 109°28′W*
Navolat see Navolato
40 H9 **Navolato** *var.* Navolat. Sinaloa, C Mexico *24°46′N 107°42′W*
187 Q13 **Navonda** Ambae, C Vanuatu *15°21′S 167°58′E*
Návpaktos see Náfpaktos
Návplion see Náfplio
77 P14 **Navrongo** N Ghana *10°51′N 01°03′W*
154 D12 **Navsāri** *var.* Nausari. Gujarāt, W India *20°55′N 72°55′E*
187 X15 **Navua** Viti Levu, W Fiji *18°15′S 178°10′E*
138 H8 **Nawá** Dar'ā, S Syria *32°53′N 36°03′E*
Nawabashah see Nawābshāh
153 S14 **Nawabganj** Rajshahi, NW Bangladesh *24°35′N 88°21′E*
153 S14 **Nawābganj** Uttar Pradesh, N India *26°52′N 82°09′E*
149 Q15 **Nawābshāh** *var.* Nawabashah. Sind, S Pakistan *26°15′N 68°26′E*
153 P14 **Nawāda** Bihār, N India *24°54′N 85°33′E*
152 H11 **Nawalgarh** Rājasthān, N India *27°48′N 75°21′E*
Nawāl, Sabkhat an see Noual, Sebkhet en
Nawapara see Nūāparha
Nawar, Dasht-i- see Nāvar, Dasht-e
167 N4 **Nawnghkio** *var.* Nawngkio. Shan State, C Burma (Myanmar) *22°17′N 96°50′E*
Nawngkio see Nawnghkio
137 U13 **Naxçıvan** *Rus.* Nakhichevan'. SW Azerbaijan *39°14′N 45°24′E*
160 I10 **Naxi** Sichuan, C China *28°50′N 105°20′E*
115 K21 **Náxos** *var.* Naxos. Náxos, Kykládes, Greece, Aegean Sea *36°07′N 25°24′E*
115 K21 **Náxos** *island* Kykládes, Greece, Aegean Sea
40 J11 **Nayarit** ◆ *state* C Mexico
187 Y14 **Nayau** *island* Lau Group, E Fiji
143 S8 **Nāy Band** Yazd, E Iran *32°26′N 57°30′E*
165 T2 **Nayoro** Hokkaidō, NE Japan *44°22′N 142°27′E*
104 F9 **Nazaré** *var.* Nazare. Leiria, C Portugal *39°36′N 09°04′W*
Nazare see Nazaré
24 M4 **Nazareth** Texas, SW USA *34°32′N 102°06′W*
Nazareth see Natzrat
173 O8 **Nazareth Bank** *undersea feature* W Indian Ocean
40 K9 **Nazas** Durango, C Mexico *25°15′N 104°06′W*
57 F16 **Nazca** Ica, S Peru *14°53′S 74°54′W*
0 L17 **Nazca Plate** *tectonic feature*
193 U9 **Nazca Ridge** *undersea feature* E Pacific Ocean *22°00′S 82°00′W*
165 V15 **Naze** *var.* Nase. Kagoshima, Amami-ōshima, SW Japan *28°21′N 129°30′E*
Nazerat see Natzrat
137 R14 **Nazik Gölü** ◎ E Turkey
136 C15 **Nazilli** Aydın, SW Turkey *37°55′N 28°20′E*
137 P14 **Nazimiye** Tunceli, E Turkey *39°12′N 39°51′E*
Nazinon see Red Volta
10 L15 **Nazko** British Columbia, SW Canada *52°57′N 123°44′W*
127 O16 **Nazran'** Respublika Ingushetiya, SW Russian Federation *43°14′N 44°47′E*
80 J13 **Nazrēt** *var.* Adama, Hadama. Oromīya, C Ethiopia *08°31′N 39°20′E*
Nazwāh see Nizwa
82 J13 **Nchanga** Copperbelt, C Zambia *12°30′S 27°53′E*
82 J11 **Nchelenge** Luapula, N Zambia *09°20′S 28°50′E*
Ncheu see Ntcheu
83 J25 **Nciba** *Eng.* Great Kei; *prev.* Groot-Kei. ⤳ S South Africa
Ndaghamcha, Sebkra de see Te-n-Dghâmcha, Sebkhet
81 G21 **Ndala** Tabora, C Tanzania *04°45′S 33°15′E*
82 B11 **N'Dalatando** *Port.* Salazar, Vila Salazar. Cuanza Norte, NW Angola *09°19′S 14°48′E*
77 S14 **Ndali** C Benin *09°50′N 02°46′E*
81 E18 **Ndeke** SW Uganda *0°11′S 30°04′E*
78 J13 **Ndélé** Bamingui-Bangoran, N Central African Republic *08°24′N 20°41′E*
79 E19 **Ndendé** Ngounié, S Gabon *02°21′S 11°20′E*
79 E20 **Ndindi** Nyanga, S Gabon *03°47′S 11°06′E*
78 G11 **Ndjamena** *var.* N'Djamena; *prev.* Fort-Lamy. ● (Chad) Chari-Baguirmi, W Chad *12°08′N 15°02′E*
78 G11 **Ndjamena** ✈ Chari-Baguirmi, W Chad *12°09′N 15°00′E*
N'Djamena see Ndjamena
79 D18 **Ndjolé** Moyen-Ogooué, W Gabon *0°07′S 10°45′E*
82 J13 **Ndola** Copperbelt, C Zambia *12°59′S 28°35′E*
Ndrhamcha, Sebkha de see Te-n-Dghâmcha, Sebkhet
79 L15 **Ndu** Orientale, N Dem. Rep. Congo *04°36′N 22°49′E*
81 H21 **Nduguti** Singida, C Tanzania *04°19′S 34°40′E*
186 M9 **Nduindui** Guadalcanal, C Solomon Islands *09°46′S 159°54′E*
Nduke see Kolombangara
Ndzouani see Anjouan
115 F16 **Néa Anchiálos** *var.* Nea Anhialos, Néa Ankhíalos. Thessalía, C Greece *39°16′N 22°49′E*
Nea Anhialos/Néa Ankhíalos see Néa Anchiálos
115 H18 **Néa Artáki** Évvoia, C Greece *38°31′N 23°39′E*
97 F15 **Neagh, Lough** ◎ E Northern Ireland, United Kingdom
32 F7 **Neah Bay** Washington, NW USA *48°21′N 124°39′W*
115 J22 **Nea Kaméni** *island* Kykládes, Greece, Aegean Sea
181 O8 **Neale, Lake** ◎ Northern Territory, C Australia
182 G2 **Neales River** *seasonal river* South Australia
115 G14 **Néa Moudanía** *var.* Néa Moudhaniá. Kentrikí Makedonía, N Greece *40°14′N 23°17′E*
Néa Moudhaniá see Néa Moudanía
116 K10 **Neamţ** ◆ *county* NE Romania
Neapel see Napoli
115 D14 **Neápoli** *prev.* Neápolis. Dytikí Makedonía, N Greece *40°19′N 21°23′E*
115 K25 **Neápoli** Kríti, Greece, E Mediterranean Sea *35°15′N 25°37′E*

◆ Country ● Country Capital ◇ Dependent Territory ○ Dependent Territory Capital ◆ Administrative Regions ✈ International Airport ▲ Mountain ▲ Mountain Range ⛰ Volcano ⤳ River ◎ Lake ⊠ Reservoir

115 G22 **Neápoli** Pelopónnisos, S Greece 36°29′N 23°05′E
Neápolis *see* Neápoli, Greece
Neapolis *see* Napoli, Italy
Neapolis *see* Nablus, West Bank
38 D16 **Near Islands** *island group* Aleutian Islands, Alaska, USA
97 J21 **Neath** S Wales, United Kingdom 51°40′N 03°48′W
114 H13 **Néa Zíchni** *var.* Néa Zíkhni; *prev.* Néa Zíkhna. Kentrikí Makedonía, NE Greece 41°02′N 23°50′E
Néa Zíkhna/Néa Zíkhni *see* Néa Zíchni
42 C5 **Nebaj** Quiché, W Guatemala 15°25′N 91°05′W
77 P13 **Nebbou** S Burkina 11°22′N 01°49′W
Nebitdag *see* Balkanabat
54 M13 **Neblina, Pico da** ▲ NW Brazil 0°49′N 66°31′W
124 I13 **Nebolchi** Novgorodskaya Oblast', W Russian Federation 59°08′N 33°19′E
36 L4 **Nebo, Mount** ▲ Utah, W USA 39°47′N 111°46′W
28 L14 **Nebraska** *off.* State of Nebraska, ***also known as*** Blackwater State, Cornhusker State, Tree Planters State. ◈ *state* C USA
29 S16 **Nebraska City** Nebraska, C USA 40°38′N 95°52′W
107 K23 **Nebrodi, Monti** *var.* Monti Caronie. ▲▲ Sicilia, Italy, C Mediterranean Sea
10 L14 **Nechako** British Columbia, SW Canada
29 Q2 **Neche** North Dakota, N USA 48°57′N 97°33′W
25 V8 **Neches** Texas, SW USA 31°51′N 95°28′W
25 W8 **Neches River** Texas, SW USA
101 H20 **Neckar** SW Germany
101 H20 **Neckarsulm** Baden-Württemberg, SW Germany 49°12′N 09°13′E
192 L5 **Necker Island** *island* C British Virgin Islands
175 U3 **Necker Ridge** *undersea feature* N Pacific Ocean
61 D23 **Necochea** Buenos Aires, E Argentina 38°34′S 58°42′W
104 H2 **Neda** Galicia, NW Spain 43°29′N 08°09′W
115 E20 **Néda** *var.* Nédas. S Greece
Nédas *see* Néda
114 J12 **Nedelino** Smolyan, S Bulgaria 41°27′N 25°05′E
25 Y11 **Nederland** Texas, SW USA 29°58′N 93°59′W
Nederland *see* Netherlands
98 K12 **Neder Rijn** *Eng.* Lower Rhine. C Netherlands
99 L16 **Nederweert** Limburg, SE Netherlands 51°17′N 05°45′E
159 N17 **Nêdong** *var.* Zêtang. Xizang Zizhiqu, W China 29°11′N 91°48′E
95 G16 **Nedre Tokke** ◎ S Norway
Nedrigaylov *see* Nedryhayliv
117 S3 **Nedryhayliv** *Rus.* Nedrigaylov. Sums'ka Oblast', NE Ukraine 50°51′N 33°54′E
98 O11 **Neede** Gelderland, E Netherlands 52°08′N 06°36′E
33 T13 **Needle Mountain** ▲ Wyoming, C USA 44°03′N 109°33′W
35 Y14 **Needles** California, W USA 34°50′N 114°37′W
97 M24 **Needles, The** *rocks* S England, United Kingdom
62 O7 **Ñeembucú** *off.* Departamento de Ñeembucú. ◈ *department* SW Paraguay
Ñeembucú, Departamento de *see* Ñeembucú
30 M7 **Neenah** Wisconsin, N USA 44°09′N 88°26′W
11 W16 **Neepawa** Manitoba, S Canada 50°14′N 99°29′W
99 K16 **Neerpelt** Limburg, NE Belgium 51°13′N 05°26′E
74 M6 **Nefta** ✈ W Tunisia 34°03′N 08°05′E
126 L15 **Neftegorsk** Krasnodarskiy Kray, SW Russian Federation 44°21′N 39°40′E
127 S6 **Neftegorsk** Samarskaya Oblast', W Russian Federation 52°48′N 51°04′E
127 U3 **Neftekamsk** Respublika Bashkortostan, W Russian Federation 56°07′N 54°13′E
127 O14 **Neftekumsk** Stavropol'skiy Kray, SW Russian Federation 44°45′N 45°00′E
Neftezavodsk *see* Seýdi
82 C10 **Negage** *var.* N'Gage. Uíge, NW Angola 07°47′S 15°27′E
Negapatam/Negapattinam *see* Nāgappattinam
169 T17 **Negara** Bali, Indonesia 08°21′S 114°35′E
169 T13 **Negara** Borneo, C Indonesia 02°40′S 115°05′E
Negara Brunei Darussalam *see* Brunei
31 N4 **Negaunee** Michigan, N USA 46°30′N 87°36′W
81 J15 **Negēlē** *var.* Negelli, *It.* Neghelli. Oromīya, C Ethiopia 05°13′N 39°43′E
Negelli *see* Negēlē
Negeri Pahang Darul Makmur *see* Pahang
Negeri Selangor Darul Ehsan *see* Selangor
168 K9 **Negeri Sembilan** *var.* Negri Sembilan. ◈ *state* Peninsular Malaysia
92 P3 **Negerpynten** *headland* S Svalbard 77°15′N 22°40′E
Negev *see* HaNegev
Neghelli *see* Negēlē
116 I12 **Negoiu** *var.* Negoiul. ▲ S Romania 45°34′N 24°34′E
Negoiul *see* Negoiu
82 P13 **Negomane** *var.* Negomano. Cabo Delgado, N Mozambique 11°22′S 38°32′E
Negomano *see* Negomane
155 J25 **Negombo** Western Province, SW Sri Lanka 07°13′N 79°51′E
Negoreloye *see* Nyeharelaye
112 P12 **Negotin** Serbia, E Serbia 44°14′N 22°31′E
113 P19 **Negotino** C Macedonia 41°29′N 22°04′E
56 A10 **Negra, Punto** *headland* NW Peru 06°03′S 81°08′W
104 G3 **Negreira** Galicia, NW Spain 42°54′N 08°46′W
116 L10 **Negrești** Vaslui, E Romania 46°50′N 27°28′E
Negrești *see* Negrești-Oaș
116 H8 **Negrești-Oaș** *Hung.* Avasfelsőfalu; *prev.* Negrești. Satu Mare, NE Romania 47°56′N 23°22′E
44 H12 **Negril** W Jamaica 18°16′N 78°21′W
Negri Sembilan *see* Negeri Sembilan
63 K15 **Negro, Río** E Argentina
62 N7 **Negro, Río** NE Argentina
57 N17 **Negro, Río** E Bolivia
48 F6 **Negro, Rio** N South America
61 E18 **Negro, Río** Brazil/Uruguay
62 O5 **Negro, Río** C Paraguay
Negro, Río *see* Chixoy, Río, Guatemala/Mexico
Negro, Río *see* Sico Tinto, Río, Honduras
171 P6 **Negros** *island* C Philippines
116 M15 **Negru Vodă** Constanța, SE Romania 43°49′N 28°12′E
13 P13 **Neguac** New Brunswick, SE Canada 47°16′N 65°04′W
14 B7 **Negwazu, Lake** ◎ Ontario, S Canada
Négyfalu *see* Săcele
32 F10 **Nehalem** Oregon, NW USA 45°42′N 123°55′W
32 F10 **Nehalem River** Oregon, NW USA
Nehavend *see* Nahāvand
143 V9 **Nehbandān** Khorāsān, E Iran 31°00′N 60°00′E
163 V6 **Nehe** Heilongjiang, NE China 48°28′N 124°52′E
193 Y14 **Neiafu** 'Uta Vava'u, N Tonga 18°36′S 173°58′W
45 N9 **Neiba** *var.* Neyba. SW Dominican Republic 18°31′N 71°25′W
Néid, Carn Uí *see* Mizen Head
92 M9 **Neiden** Finnmark, N Norway 69°41′N 29°23′E
Neidín *see* Kenmare
Néifinn *see* Nephin
103 S10 **Neige, Crêt de la** ▲ E France 46°18′N 05°58′E
173 O16 **Neiges, Piton des** ▲ C Réunion 21°05′S 55°28′E
15 R9 **Neiges, Rivière des** Québec, SE Canada
160 I10 **Neijiang** Sichuan, C China 29°32′N 105°03′E
30 K6 **Neillsville** Wisconsin, N USA 44°34′N 90°36′W
Nei Monggol Zizhiqu/Nei Mongol *see* Nei Mongol Zizhiqu
163 Q10 **Nei Mongol Gaoyuan** *plateau* NE China
163 O12 **Nei Mongol Zizhiqu** *var.* Nei Mongol, *Eng.* Inner Mongolia, Inner Mongolian Autonomous Region; *prev.* Nei Monggol Zizhiqu. ◈ *autonomous region* N China
161 O4 **Neiqiu** Hebei, E China 37°22′N 114°34′E
Neiriz *see* Neyrīz
101 Q16 **Neisse** *Cz.* Lužická Nisa *Pol.* Nisa, *Ger.* Lausitzer Neisse, Nysa Łużycka. C Europe
Neisse *see* Nysa
54 E11 **Neiva** Huila, S Colombia 02°58′N 75°15′W
160 M7 **Neixiang** Henan, C China 33°08′N 111°50′E
Nejafabad *see* Najafābād
11 V9 **Nejanilini Lake** ◎ Manitoba, C Canada
Nejd *see* Najd
80 I13 **Nek'emtē** *var.* Lakemti, Nakamti. Oromīya, C Ethiopia 09°06′N 36°31′E
126 M9 **Nekhayevskaya** Volgogradskaya Oblast', SW Russian Federation 50°25′N 41°44′E
30 K7 **Nekoosa** Wisconsin, N USA 44°19′N 89°54′W
Neksø Bornholm *see* Nexø
104 H7 **Nelas** Viseu, N Portugal 40°32′N 07°52′W
124 H16 **Nelidovo** Tverskaya Oblast', W Russian Federation 56°13′N 32°45′E
29 P13 **Neligh** Nebraska, C USA 42°07′N 98°01′W
123 R11 **Nel'kan** Khabarovskiy Kray, E Russian Federation 57°44′N 136°09′E
92 M10 **Nellim** *var.* Nellimö, *Lapp.* Njellim. Lappi, N Finland 68°49′N 28°18′E
Nellimö *see* Nellim
155 J18 **Nellore** Andhra Pradesh, E India 14°29′N 80°E
61 B17 **Nelson** Santa Fe, C Argentina 31°16′S 60°45′W
11 O17 **Nelson** British Columbia, SW Canada 49°29′N 117°17′W
185 I14 **Nelson** Nelson, South Island, New Zealand 41°17′S 173°17′E
97 L17 **Nelson** NW England, United Kingdom 53°51′N 02°13′W
29 P17 **Nelson** Nebraska, C USA 40°12′N 98°04′W
185 J14 **Nelson** ◈ *unitary authority* South Island, New Zealand
11 X12 **Nelson** Manitoba, C Canada
183 U8 **Nelson Bay** New South Wales, SE Australia 32°48′S 152°10′E
182 K13 **Nelson, Cape** *headland* Victoria, SE Australia 38°25′S 141°33′E
63 G23 **Nelson, Estrecho** *strait* SE Pacific Ocean
11 W12 **Nelson House** Manitoba, C Canada 55°49′N 98°51′W
30 J4 **Nelson Lake** ◎ Wisconsin, N USA
31 T14 **Nelsonville** Ohio, N USA 39°27′N 82°13′W
27 S2 **Nelsoon River** Iowa/Missouri, C USA
83 K21 **Nelspruit** Mpumalanga, NE South Africa 25°28′S 30°58′E
76 L10 **Néma** Hodh ech Chargui, SE Mauritania 16°32′N 07°12′W
118 D13 **Neman** *Ger.* Ragnit. Kaliningradskaya Oblast', W Russian Federation 55°01′N 22°00′E
84 I9 **Neman** *Bel.* Nyoman, *Ger.* Memel, *Lith.* Nemunas, *Pol.* Niemen. NE Europe
Nemausus *see* Nîmes
115 F19 **Neméa** Pelopónnisos, S Greece 37°49′N 22°40′E
Německý Brod *see* Havlíčkův Brod
14 D7 **Nemegosenda** Ontario, S Canada
14 D8 **Nemegosenda Lake** ◎ Ontario, S Canada
119 H14 **Nemencinė** Vilnius, SE Lithuania 54°50′N 25°29′E
Nemetocenna *see* Arras
Nemirov *see* Nemyriv
103 O6 **Nemours** Seine-et-Marne, N France 48°16′N 02°41′E
Nemunas *see* Neman
165 W4 **Nemuro** Hokkaidō, NE Japan 43°20′N 145°35′E
165 W4 **Nemuro-hantō** *peninsula* Hokkaidō, NE Japan
165 W3 **Nemuro-kaikyō** *strait* Japan/Russian Federation
165 W4 **Nemuro-wan** *bay* N Japan
116 H5 **Nemyriv** *Rus.* Nemirov. L'vivs'ka Oblast', NW Ukraine 50°08′N 23°28′E
117 N7 **Nemyriv** *Rus.* Nemirov. Vinnyts'ka Oblast', C Ukraine 48°58′N 28°50′E
97 D19 **Nenagh** *Ir.* An tAonach. Tipperary, C Ireland 52°52′N 08°12′W
39 R9 **Nenana** Alaska, USA 64°33′N 149°05′W
39 R9 **Nenana River** Alaska, USA
187 P10 **Nendö** *var.* Swallow Island. *island* Santa Cruz Islands, E Solomon Islands
97 O19 **Nene** E England, United Kingdom
125 R4 **Nenetskiy Avtonomnyy Okrug** ◈ *autonomous district* Arkhangel'skaya Oblast', NW Russian Federation
191 W11 **Nengonengo** *atoll* Îles Tuamotu, C French Polynesia
163 V6 **Nenjiang** Heilongjiang, NE China 49°11′N 125°18′E
163 U6 **Nen Jiang** *var.* Nonni. NE China
189 P16 **Neoch** *atoll* Caroline Islands, C Micronesia
115 D18 **Neochóri** Dytikí Ellás, C Greece 38°23′N 21°14′E
27 Q7 **Neodesha** Kansas, C USA 37°25′N 95°40′W
29 S14 **Neola** Iowa, C USA 41°27′N 95°40′W
115 E16 **Néo Monastíri** *var.* Néon Monastiri. Thessalía, C Greece 39°22′N 21°55′E
Néon Karlovasi/Néon Karlovásion *see* Karlovási
Néon Monastiri *see* Néo Monastíri
27 R8 **Neosho** Missouri, C USA 36°53′N 94°24′W
27 Q7 **Neosho River** Kansas/Oklahoma, C USA
123 N12 **Nepa** C Russian Federation
153 N10 **Nepal** *off.* Nepal. ◆ *monarchy* S Asia
Nepal *see* Nepal
152 M11 **Nepālganj** Mid Western, SW Nepal 28°04′N 81°37′E
14 L13 **Nepean** Ontario, SE Canada 45°19′N 75°54′W
36 L4 **Nephi** Utah, W USA 39°43′N 111°50′W
97 B16 **Nephin** *Ir.* Néifinn. ▲ W Ireland 54°00′N 09°21′W
67 T9 **Nepoko** NE Dem. Rep. Congo
18 K15 **Neptune** New Jersey, NE USA 40°10′N 74°03′W
182 G10 **Neptune Islands** *island group* South Australia
107 I14 **Nera** *anc.* Nar. C Italy
102 L14 **Nérac** Lot-et-Garonne, SW France 44°08′N 00°21′E
111 D16 **Neratovice** *Ger.* Neratowitz. Středocesky Kraj, C Czech Republic 50°16′N 14°31′E
Neratowitz *see* Neratovice
123 O13 **Nercha** S Russian Federation
123 O13 **Nerchinsk** Chitinskaya Oblast', S Russian Federation 52°01′N 116°25′E
123 P14 **Nerchinskiy Zavod** Chitinskaya Oblast', S Russian Federation 51°13′N 119°25′E
124 M15 **Nerekhta** Kostromskaya Oblast', NW Russian Federation 57°27′N 40°33′E
118 H10 **Nereta** Aizkraukle, S Latvia 56°12′N 25°18′E
106 K13 **Nereto** Abruzzo, C Italy 42°49′N 13°50′E
113 H15 **Neretva** Bosnia and Herzegovina/Croatia
115 C17 **Nerikós** *ruins* Lefkáda, Iónia Nísiá, Greece, C Mediterranean Sea
83 F15 **Neriquinha** Cuando Cubango, SE Angola 15°44′S 21°34′E
118 I13 **Neris** *Bel.* Viliya, *Pol.* Wilia; *prev. Pol.* Wilja. Belarus/Lithuania
Neris *see* Viliya
105 N15 **Nerja** Andalucía, S Spain 36°45′N 03°35′W
124 L16 **Nerl'** W Russian Federation
105 P12 **Nerpio** Castilla-La Mancha, C Spain 38°08′N 02°18′W
104 J13 **Nerva** Andalucía, S Spain 37°40′N 06°31′W
98 L4 **Nes** Friesland, N Netherlands 53°28′N 05°46′E
94 G13 **Nesbyen** Buskerud, S Norway 60°36′N 09°35′E
114 M9 **Nesebŭr** Burgas, E Bulgaria 42°40′N 27°43′E
92 L2 **Neskaupstadhur** Austurland, E Iceland 65°08′N 13°45′W
92 F13 **Nesna** Nordland, C Norway 66°11′N 12°54′E
26 K5 **Ness City** Kansas, C USA 38°27′N 99°54′W
Nesselsdorf *see* Kopřivnice
108 H7 **Nesslau** Sankt Gallen, NE Switzerland 47°13′N 09°12′E
96 I9 **Ness, Loch** ◎ N Scotland, United Kingdom
Nesterov *see* Zhovkva
114 I12 **Néstos** *Bul.* Mesta, *Turk.* Kara Su. Bulgaria/Greece *see also* Mesta
Néstos *see* Mesta
95 C14 **Nesttun** Hordaland, S Norway 60°19′N 05°16′E
Nesvizh *see* Nyasvizh
138 F9 **Netanya** *var.* Natanya, Nathanya. Central, C Israel 32°20′N 34°51′E
98 I9 **Netherlands** *off.* Kingdom of the Netherlands, *var.* Holland, *Dut.* Koninkrijk der Nederlanden, Nederland. ◆ *monarchy* NW Europe
45 S9 **Netherlands Antilles** *prev.* Dutch West Indies. ◇ *Dutch autonomous region* S Caribbean Sea
Netherlands East Indies *see* Indonesia
Netherlands Guiana *see* Surinam
Netherlands, Kingdom of the *see* Netherlands
Netherlands New Guinea *see* Papua
116 L4 **Netishyn** Khmel'nyts'ka Oblast', W Ukraine 50°20′N 26°38′E
138 E11 **Netivot** Southern, S Israel 31°26′N 34°36′E
107 O21 **Neto** S Italy
9 Q6 **Nettilling Lake** ◎ Baffin Island, Nunavut, N Canada
29 V3 **Nett Lake** ◎ Minnesota, N USA
107 I16 **Nettuno** Lazio, C Italy 41°27′N 12°40′E
Netum *see* Noto
41 U16 **Netzahualcóyotl, Presa** ⊠ SE Mexico
Netze *see* Noteć
Neu Amerika *see* Puławy
Neubetsche *see* Novi Bečej
Neubidschow *see* Nový Bydžov
Neubistritz *see* Nová Bystřice
100 N9 **Neubrandenburg** Mecklenburg-Vorpommern, NE Germany 53°33′N 13°16′E
101 K22 **Neuburg an der Donau** Bayern, S Germany 48°43′N 11°10′E
108 C8 **Neuchâtel** *Ger.* Neuenburg. Neuchâtel, W Switzerland 46°59′N 06°55′E
108 C8 **Neuchâtel** *Ger.* Neuenburg. ◈ *canton* W Switzerland
108 C8 **Neuchâtel, Lac de** *Ger.* Neuenburger See. ◎ W Switzerland
Neudorf *see* Spišská Nová Ves
100 L10 **Neue Elde** *canal* N Germany
Neuenburg *see* Neuchâtel
Neuenburg an der Elbe *see* Nymburk
Neuenburger See *see* Neuchâtel, Lac de
108 F7 **Neuenhof** Aargau, N Switzerland 47°27′N 08°17′E
100 H11 **Neuenland** ✈ (Bremen) Bremen, NW Germany 53°03′N 08°46′E
Neuenstadt *see* La Neuveville
101 C18 **Neuerburg** Rheinland-Pfalz, W Germany 50°01′N 06°13′E
99 K24 **Neufchâteau** Luxembourg, SE Belgium 49°50′N 05°26′E
103 S6 **Neufchâteau** Vosges, NE France 48°21′N 05°42′E
102 M3 **Neufchâtel-en-Bray** Seine-Maritime, N France 49°44′N 01°26′E
109 S3 **Neufelden** Oberösterreich, N Austria 48°27′N 14°01′E
Neugradisk *see* Nova Gradiška
Neuhaus *see* Jindřichův Hradec
Neuhäusel *see* Nové Zámky
108 G6 **Neuhausen** *var.* Neuhausen am Rheinfall. Schaffhausen, N Switzerland 47°24′N 08°37′E
Neuhausen am Rheinfall *see* Neuhausen
101 I17 **Neuhof** Hessen, C Germany 50°26′N 09°34′E
Neuhof *see* Zgierz
Neukuhren *see* Pionerskiy
Neu-Langenburg *see* Tukuyu
109 W4 **Neulengbach** Niederösterreich, NE Austria 48°10′N 15°53′E
113 G15 **Neum** Federacija Bosna I Hercegovina, S Bosnia and Herzegovina 42°57′N 17°33′E
Neumark *see* Nowy Targ, Małopolskie, Poland
Neumark *see* Nowe Miasto Lubawskie, Warmińsko-Mazurskie, Poland
Neumarkt *see* Neumarkt im Hausruckkreis, Oberösterreich, Austria
Neumarkt *see* Neumarkt am Wallersee, Salzburg, Austria
Neumarkt *see* Sroda Śląska, Dolnośląskie, Poland
Neumarkt *see* Târgu Secuiesc, Covasna, Romania
Neumarkt *see* Târgu Mureș
109 Q5 **Neumarkt am Wallersee** *var.* Neumarkt. Salzburg, NW Austria 47°55′N 13°16′E
109 R4 **Neumarkt im Hausruckkreis** *var.* Neumarkt. Oberösterreich, N Austria 48°16′N 13°40′E
101 L20 **Neumarkt in der Oberpfalz** Bayern, SE Germany 49°16′N 11°28′E
Neumarktl *see* Tržič
Neumoldowa *see* Moldova Nouă
100 J8 **Neumünster** Schleswig-Holstein, N Germany 54°04′N 09°59′E
109 X5 **Neunkirchen** *var.* Neunkirchen am Steinfeld. Niederösterreich, E Austria 47°44′N 16°05′E
101 E20 **Neunkirchen** Saarland, SW Germany 49°21′N 07°11′E
Neunkirchen am Steinfeld *see* Neunkirchen
Neuoderberg *see* Bohumín
63 I15 **Neuquén** Neuquén, SE Argentina 39°03′S 68°36′W
63 H14 **Neuquén** *off.* Provincia de Neuquén. ◈ *province* W Argentina
Neuquén, Provincia de *see* Neuquén
63 H14 **Neuquén, Río** W Argentina
Neurode *see* Nowa Ruda
100 N11 **Neuruppin** Brandenburg, NE Germany 52°56′N 12°49′E
Neusalz an der Oder *see* Nowa Sól
Neu Sandec *see* Nowy Sącz
101 K22 **Neusäss** Bayern, S Germany 48°24′N 10°49′E
Neusatz *see* Novi Sad
Neuschliss *see* Gherla
21 N8 **Neuse River** North Carolina, SE USA
109 Z5 **Neusiedl am See** Burgenland, E Austria 47°58′N 16°51′E
111 G22 **Neusiedler See** *Hung.* Fertő. ◎ Austria/Hungary
Neusohl *see* Banská Bystrica
101 D15 **Neuss** *anc.* Novaesium, Novesium. Nordrhein-Westfalen, W Germany 51°12′N 06°42′E
Neuss *see* Nyon
Neustadt *see* Neustadt bei Coburg, Bayern, Germany
Neustadt *see* Neustadt an der Aisch, Bayern, Germany
Neustadt *see* Prudnik, Opole, Poland
Neustadt *see* Baia Mare, Maramureș, Romania
100 I12 **Neustadt am Rübenberge** Niedersachsen, N Germany 52°30′N 09°28′E
101 J19 **Neustadt an der Aisch** *var.* Neustadt. Bayern, C Germany 49°34′N 10°36′E
Neustadt an der Haardt *see* Neustadt an der Weinstrasse
101 F20 **Neustadt an der Weinstrasse** *prev.* Neustadt an der Haardt, *hist.* Niewenstat; *anc.* Nova Civitas. Rheinland-Pfalz, SW Germany 49°21′N 08°09′E
101 K18 **Neustadt bei Coburg** *var.* Neustadt. Bayern, C Germany 50°19′N 11°06′E
Neustadt bei Pinne *see* Lwówek
Neustadt in Oberschlesien *see* Prudnik
Neustadtl *see* Novo mesto
Neustadtl in Mähren *see* Nové Město na Moravě
Neustettin *see* Szczecinek
108 M8 **Neustift im Stubaital** *var.* Stubaital. Tirol, W Austria 47°07′N 11°26′E
100 N10 **Neustrelitz** Mecklenburg-Vorpommern, NE Germany 53°22′N 13°05′E
Neutitschein *see* Nový Jičín
Neutra *see* Nitra
101 J22 **Neu-Ulm** Bayern, S Germany 48°23′N 10°02′E
Neuveville *see* La Neuveville
103 N12 **Neuvic** Corrèze, C France 45°23′N 02°16′E
Neuwarp *see* Nowe Warpno
100 G9 **Neuwerk** *island* NW Germany
101 E17 **Neuwied** Rheinland-Pfalz, W Germany 50°26′N 07°28′E
Neuzen *see* Terneuzen
124 H12 **Neva** NW Russian Federation
29 V14 **Nevada** Iowa, C USA 42°01′N 93°27′W
27 R6 **Nevada** Missouri, C USA 37°51′N 94°22′W
35 R5 **Nevada** *off.* State of Nevada, ***also known as*** Battle Born State, Sagebrush State, Silver State. ◈ *state* W USA
35 P6 **Nevada City** California, W USA 39°15′N 121°02′W
105 O14 **NevadaSierra** ▲▲ S Spain
35 P6 **Nevada, Sierra** ▲▲ W USA
62 I13 **Nevado, Sierra del** ▲▲ W Argentina
124 G16 **Nevel'** Pskovskaya Oblast', W Russian Federation 56°01′N 29°54′E
123 T14 **Nevel'sk** Ostrov Sakhalin, Sakhalinskaya Oblast', SE Russian Federation 46°41′N 141°54′E
123 Q13 **Never** Amurskaya Oblast', SE Russian Federation 53°58′N 124°04′E
127 Q6 **Neverkino** Penzenskaya Oblast', W Russian Federation 52°53′N 46°46′E
103 P9 **Nevers** *anc.* Noviodunum. Nièvre, C France 47°N 03°09′E
18 J12 **Neversink River** New York, NE USA
183 Q6 **Nevertire** New South Wales, SE Australia 31°52′S 147°42′E
113 H15 **Nevesinje** ◈ Republika Srpska, S Bosnia and Herzegovina
118 G12 **Nevežis** C Lithuania
138 F11 **Neve Zohar** *prev.* Newé Zohar. Southern, E Israel 31°07′N 35°23′E
126 M14 **Nevinnomyssk** Stavropol'skiy Kray, SW Russian Federation 44°39′N 41°57′E
45 W10 **Nevis** *island* Saint Kitts and Nevis
Nevoso, Monte *see* Veliki Snežnik
Nevrokop *see* Gotse Delchev
136 J14 **Nevșehir** *var.* Nevshehr. Nevșehir, C Turkey 38°38′N 34°43′E
136 J14 **Nevșehir** *var.* Nevshehr. ◈ *province* C Turkey
Nevshehr *see* Nevșehir
122 G10 **Nev'yansk** Sverdlovskaya Oblast', C Russian Federation 57°26′N 60°15′E
81 J25 **Newala** Mtwara, SE Tanzania 10°59′S 39°18′E
31 P16 **New Albany** Indiana, N USA 38°17′N 85°50′W
22 M2 **New Albany** Mississippi, S USA 34°29′N 89°00′W
29 Y11 **New Albin** Iowa, C USA 43°30′N 91°17′W
55 U8 **New Amsterdam** E Guyana 06°17′N 57°31′W
183 Q4 **New Angledool** New South Wales, SE Australia 29°06′S 147°54′E
21 Y2 **Newark** Delaware, NE USA 39°42′N 75°45′W
18 K14 **Newark** New Jersey, NE USA 40°42′N 74°12′W
18 G10 **Newark** New York, NE USA 43°01′N 77°04′W
31 T13 **Newark** Ohio, N USA 40°03′N 82°24′W
Newark *see* Newark-on-Trent
35 W5 **Newark Lake** ◎ Nevada, W USA
97 N18 **Newark-on-Trent** *var.* Newark. C England, United Kingdom 53°05′N 00°49′W
22 M7 **New Augusta** Mississippi, S USA 31°12′N 89°03′W
19 P12 **New Bedford** Massachusetts, NE USA 41°38′N 70°55′W
32 G11 **Newberg** Oregon, NW USA 45°18′N 122°58′W
21 X10 **New Bern** North Carolina, SE USA 35°05′N 77°04′W
20 F8 **Newbern** Tennessee, S USA 36°06′N 89°15′W
31 P4 **Newberry** Michigan, N USA 46°21′N 85°30′W
21 Q12 **Newberry** South Carolina, SE USA 34°17′N 81°39′W
18 F15 **New Bloomfield** Pennsylvania, NE USA 40°24′N 77°08′W
25 X5 **New Boston** Texas, SW USA 33°27′N 94°25′W
25 S11 **New Braunfels** Texas, SW USA 29°43′N 98°09′W
31 Q13 **New Bremen** Ohio, N USA 40°26′N 84°22′W
97 F18 **Newbridge** *Ir.* An Droichead Nua. Kildare, C Ireland 53°11′N 06°48′W
18 B14 **New Brighton** Pennsylvania, NE USA 40°44′N 80°18′W
18 M12 **New Britain** Connecticut, NE USA 41°37′N 72°45′W
186 G7 **New Britain** *island* E Papua New Guinea
192 I8 **New Britain Trench** *undersea feature* W Pacific Ocean
18 J15 **New Brunswick** New Jersey, NE USA 40°29′N 74°27′W
15 V8 **New Brunswick** *Fr.* Nouveau-Brunswick. ◈ *province* SE Canada
18 K13 **Newburgh** New York, NE USA 41°30′N 74°00′W
97 M22 **Newbury** S England, United Kingdom 51°25′N 01°20′W
19 P10 **Newburyport** Massachusetts, NE USA 42°49′N 70°53′W
77 T14 **New Bussa** Niger, W Nigeria 09°50′N 04°32′E
187 O17 **New Caledonia** *var.* Kanaky, *Fr.* Nouvelle-Calédonie. ◇ *French overseas territory* SW Pacific Ocean
187 O15 **New Caledonia** *island* SW Pacific Ocean
175 O10 **New Caledonia Basin** *undersea feature* W Pacific Ocean
183 T8 **Newcastle** New South Wales, SE Australia 32°55′S 151°46′E
13 O14 **Newcastle** New Brunswick, SE Canada 47°01′N 65°36′W
14 I15 **Newcastle** Ontario, SE Canada 43°55′N 78°35′W
83 K22 **Newcastle** KwaZulu/Natal, E South Africa 27°45′S 29°55′E
97 G16 **Newcastle** *Ir.* An Caisleán Nua. SE Northern Ireland, United Kingdom 54°12′N 05°54′W
31 P13 **New Castle** Indiana, N USA 39°56′N 85°21′W
20 L5 **New Castle** Kentucky, S USA 38°28′N 85°10′W
27 N11 **Newcastle** Oklahoma, C USA 35°15′N 97°36′W
18 B13 **New Castle** Pennsylvania, NE USA 41°00′N 80°22′W
25 R6 **Newcastle** Texas, SW USA 33°11′N 98°44′W
36 J7 **Newcastle** Utah, W USA 37°40′N 113°31′W
21 S6 **New Castle** Virginia, NE USA 37°31′N 80°09′W
33 Z13 **Newcastle** Wyoming, C USA 43°52′N 104°14′W
45 W10 **Newcastle** ✈ Nevis, Saint Kitts and Nevis 17°08′N 62°36′W
97 L14 **Newcastle** ✈ NE England, United Kingdom 55°03′N 01°42′W
Newcastle *see* Newcastle upon Tyne
97 L18 **Newcastle-under-Lyme** C England, United Kingdom 53°N 02°14′W
97 M14 **Newcastle upon Tyne** *var.* Newcastle, *hist.* Monkchester, *Lat.* Pons Aelii. NE England, United Kingdom 54°59′N 01°35′W
181 Q4 **Newcastle Waters** Northern Territory, N Australia 17°20′S 133°26′E
Newchwang *see* Yingkou
18 K13 **New City** New York, NE USA 41°08′N 73°57′W
31 U13 **Newcomerstown** Ohio, N USA 40°16′N 81°36′W
18 G15 **New Cumberland** Pennsylvania, NE USA 40°13′N 76°52′W
21 R1 **New Cumberland** West Virginia, NE USA 40°30′N 80°35′W
152 I10 **New Delhi** ● (India) Delhi, N India 28°35′N 77°15′E
11 O17 **New Denver** British Columbia, SW Canada 49°58′N 117°21′W
28 J9 **Newell** South Dakota, N USA 44°42′N 103°25′W
21 Q13 **New Ellenton** South Carolina, SE USA 33°25′N 81°41′W
22 J6 **Newellton** Louisiana, S USA 32°04′N 91°14′W
28 K6 **New England** North Dakota, N USA 46°32′N 102°52′W
19 P8 **New England** *cultural region* NE USA
New England of the West *see* Minnesota
183 U5 **New England Range** ▲▲ New South Wales, SE Australia
64 G9 **New England Seamounts** *var.* Bermuda-New England Seamount Arc. *undersea feature* W Atlantic Ocean 38°00′N 61°00′W
38 M14 **Newenham, Cape** *headland* Alaska, USA 58°39′N 162°10′W
Newé Zohar *see* Neve Zohar
18 D9 **Newfane** New York, NE USA 43°16′N 78°40′W
97 M23 **New Forest** *physical region* S England, United Kingdom
13 T12 **Newfoundland** *Fr.* Terre-Neuve. *island* Newfoundland and Labrador, SE Canada
13 R9 **Newfoundland and Labrador** *Fr.* Terre Neuve. ◈ *province* E Canada
65 J8 **Newfoundland Basin** *undersea feature* NW Atlantic Ocean 45°00′N 40°00′W
64 I8 **Newfoundland Ridge** *undersea feature* NW Atlantic Ocean
64 J8 **Newfoundland Seamounts** *undersea feature* N Sargasso Sea
18 G16 **New Freedom** Pennsylvania, NE USA 39°43′N 76°41′W
186 K9 **New Georgia** *island* New Georgia Islands, NW Solomon Islands
186 K8 **New Georgia Islands** *island group* NW Solomon Islands
186 L8 **New Georgia Sound** *var.* The Slot. *sound* E Solomon Sea
30 L9 **New Glarus** Wisconsin, N USA 42°50′N 89°38′W
13 Q15 **New Glasgow** Nova Scotia, SE Canada 45°36′N 62°38′W
New Goa *see* Panaji
186 A6 **New Guinea** *Dut.* Nieuw Guinea, *Ind.* Irian. *island* Indonesia/Papua New Guinea
192 H8 **New Guinea Trench** *undersea feature* SW Pacific Ocean
32 I6 **Newhalem** Washington, NW USA 48°40′N 121°18′W
39 P13 **Newhalen** Alaska, USA 59°43′N 154°54′W
29 X13 **Newhall** Iowa, C USA 42°00′N 91°58′W
14 F16 **New Hamburg** Ontario, S Canada 43°24′N 80°37′W
19 N9 **New Hampshire** *off.* State of New Hampshire, ***also known as*** Granite State. ◈ *state* NE USA
29 W12 **New Hampton** Iowa, C USA 43°03′N 92°19′W
186 G5 **New Hanover** *island* NE Papua New Guinea
97 P23 **Newhaven** SE England, United Kingdom 50°48′N 00°00′E
18 M13 **New Haven** Connecticut, NE USA 41°18′N 72°55′W
31 Q12 **New Haven** Indiana, N USA 41°02′N 84°59′W
27 W5 **New Haven** Missouri, C USA 38°34′N 91°15′W
10 K13 **New Hazelton** British Columbia, SW Canada 55°15′N 127°30′W
New Hebrides *see* Vanuatu
175 P9 **New Hebrides Trench** *undersea feature* N Coral Sea
18 H15 **New Holland** Pennsylvania, NE USA 40°06′N 76°05′W
22 I9 **New Iberia** Louisiana, S USA 30°00′N 91°51′W
186 G5 **New Ireland** ◈ *province* NE Papua New Guinea
186 G5 **New Ireland** *island* NE Papua New Guinea
65 A24 **New Island** *island* W Falkland Islands
18 J15 **New Jersey** *off.* State of New Jersey, ***also known as*** The Garden State. ◈ *state* NE USA
18 C14 **New Kensington** Pennsylvania, NE USA 40°33′N 79°45′W
21 W6 **New Kent** Virginia, NE USA 37°32′N 76°59′W
27 O8 **Newkirk** Oklahoma, C USA 36°54′N 97°03′W
21 Q9 **Newland** North Carolina, SE USA 36°04′N 81°50′W
28 L6 **New Leipzig** North Dakota, N USA 46°21′N 101°54′W
14 H9 **New Liskeard** Ontario, S Canada 47°31′N 79°41′W
22 G7 **Newllano** Louisiana, S USA 31°06′N 93°16′W
19 N13 **New London** Connecticut, NE USA 41°21′N 72°04′W
29 Y15 **New London** Iowa, C USA 40°55′N 91°24′W
29 T8 **New London** Minnesota, N USA 45°18′N 94°56′W
27 V3 **New London** Missouri, C USA 39°34′N 91°24′W
30 M7 **New London** Wisconsin, N USA 44°25′N 88°44′W
27 Y8 **New Madrid** Missouri, C USA 36°34′N 89°32′W
180 J8 **Newman** Western Australia 23°18′S 119°45′E
194 M13 **Newman Island** *island* Antarctica
14 H15 **Newmarket** Ontario, S Canada 44°03′N 79°27′W
97 P20 **Newmarket** E England, United Kingdom 52°18′N 00°28′E
19 P10 **Newmarket** New Hampshire, NE USA 43°04′N 70°53′W
21 U4 **New Market** Virginia, NE USA 38°39′N 78°40′W
21 R2 **New Martinsville** West Virginia, NE USA 39°39′N 80°52′W
31 U14 **New Matamoras** Ohio, N USA 39°32′N 81°04′W
32 M12 **New Meadows** Idaho, NW USA 44°57′N 116°16′W
26 R12 **New Mexico** *off.* State of New Mexico, ***also known as*** Land of Enchantment, Sunshine State. ◈ *state* SW USA
149 V6 **New Mīrpur** *var.* Mīrpur. Sind, SE Pakistan 33°11′N 73°46′E
151 N15 **New Moore Island** *Island* E India
23 S4 **Newnan** Georgia, SE USA 33°22′N 84°48′W
183 P17 **New Norfolk** Tasmania, SE Australia 42°46′S 147°02′E
22 K9 **New Orleans** Louisiana, S USA 30°00′N 90°01′W
22 K9 **New Orleans** ✈ Louisiana, S USA 29°59′N 90°17′W
18 K12 **New Paltz** New York, NE USA 41°44′N 74°04′W
31 U12 **New Philadelphia** Ohio, N USA 40°29′N 81°27′W
184 K10 **New Plymouth** Taranaki, North Island, New Zealand 39°04′S 174°06′E
97 M24 **Newport** S England, United Kingdom 50°42′N 01°18′W
97 K22 **Newport** SE Wales, United Kingdom 51°35′N 03°W
27 W10 **Newport** Arkansas, C USA 35°36′N 91°16′W
31 N13 **Newport** Indiana, N USA 39°52′N 87°24′W
20 M3 **Newport** Kentucky, S USA 39°05′N 84°27′W
29 W9 **Newport** Minnesota, N USA 44°52′N 93°00′W
32 F12 **Newport** Oregon, NW USA 44°39′N 124°04′W
19 O13 **Newport** Rhode Island, NE USA 41°29′N 71°17′W
21 O9 **Newport** Tennessee, S USA 35°58′N 83°13′W
19 N6 **Newport** Vermont, NE USA 44°56′N 72°13′W
32 M7 **Newport** Washington, NW USA 48°08′N 117°05′W
21 X7 **Newport News** Virginia, NE USA 36°59′N 76°26′W
97 N20 **Newport Pagnell** SE England, United Kingdom 52°05′N 00°44′W
23 U12 **New Port Richey** Florida, SE USA 28°14′N 82°42′W

◆ Country
● Country Capital
◇ Dependent Territory
○ Dependent Territory Capital
◈ Administrative Regions
✈ International Airport
▲ Mountain
▲▲ Mountain Range
Volcano
River
◎ Lake
⊠ Reservoir

29 V9 **New Prague** Minnesota, N USA *44°32′N 93°34′W*
44 H3 **New Providence** *island* N Bahamas
97 I20 **New Quay** SW Wales, United Kingdom *52°13′N 04°22′W*
97 H24 **Newquay** SW England, United Kingdom *50°27′N 05°03′W*
29 V10 **New Richland** Minnesota, N USA *43°53′N 93°29′W*
15 X7 **New-Richmond** Québec, SE Canada *48°12′N 65°52′W*
31 R15 **New Richmond** Ohio, N USA *38°57′N 84°16′W*
30 I5 **New Richmond** Wisconsin, N USA *45°09′N 92°31′W*
42 G1 **New River** ≈ N Belize
55 T12 **New River** ≈ SE Guyana
21 R6 **New River** ≈ West Virginia, NE USA
42 G1 **New River Lagoon** ◎ N Belize
22 J8 **New Roads** Louisiana, S USA *30°42′N 91°26′W*
18 L14 **New Rochelle** New York, NE USA *40°55′N 73°44′W*
29 O4 **New Rockford** North Dakota, N USA *47°40′N 99°08′W*
97 P23 **New Romney** SE England, United Kingdom *50°58′N 00°56′E*
97 F20 **New Ross** ***Ir.*** Ros Mhic Thriúin. Wexford, SE Ireland *52°24′N 06°56′W*
97 F16 **Newry** ***Ir.*** An tIúr. SE Northern Ireland, United Kingdom *54°11′N 06°20′W*
28 M5 **New Salem** North Dakota, N USA *46°51′N 101°24′W*
New Sarum ***see*** Salisbury
29 W14 **New Sharon** Iowa, C USA *41°28′N 92°39′W*
New Siberian Islands ***see*** Novosibirskiye Ostrova
23 X11 **New Smyrna Beach** Florida, SE USA *29°01′N 80°55′W*
183 O7 **New South Wales** ◐ *state* SE Australia
39 O13 **New Stuyahok** Alaska, USA *59°27′N 157°18′W*
21 N8 **New Tazewell** Tennessee, S USA *36°26′N 83°36′W*
New Tehri ***see*** Tehri
38 M12 **Newtok** Alaska, USA *60°56′N 164°37′W*
23 S7 **Newton** Georgia, SE USA *31°18′N 84°20′W*
29 W14 **Newton** Iowa, C USA *41°42′N 93°03′W*
27 N6 **Newton** Kansas, C USA *38°02′N 97°22′W*
19 O11 **Newton** Massachusetts, NE USA *42°19′N 71°10′W*
22 M5 **Newton** Mississippi, S USA *32°19′N 89°09′W*
18 J14 **Newton** New Jersey, NE USA *41°03′N 74°45′W*
21 R9 **Newton** North Carolina, SE USA *35°42′N 81°14′W*
25 Y9 **Newton** Texas, SW USA *30°51′N 93°45′W*
97 J24 **Newton Abbot** SW England, United Kingdom *50°33′N 03°34′W*
96 K13 **Newton St Boswells** SE Scotland, United Kingdom *55°34′N 02°40′W*
97 I14 **Newton Stewart** S Scotland, United Kingdom *54°58′N 04°30′W*
92 O2 **Newtontoppen** ▲ C Svalbard *78°57′N 17°34′E*
97 J20 **Newtown** E Wales, United Kingdom *52°32′N 03°19′W*
28 K3 **New Town** North Dakota, N USA *47°58′N 102°30′W*
97 G15 **Newtownabbey** ***Ir.*** Baile na Mainistreach. E Northern Ireland, United Kingdom *54°40′N 05°57′W*
97 G15 **Newtownards** ***Ir.*** Baile Nua na hArda. SE Northern Ireland, United Kingdom *54°36′N 05°41′W*
29 U10 **New Ulm** Minnesota, N USA *44°20′N 94°28′W*
28 K10 **New Underwood** South Dakota, N USA *44°05′N 102°46′W*
25 V10 **New Waverly** Texas, SW USA *30°32′N 95°28′W*
18 K14 **New York** New York, NE USA *40°45′N 73°57′W*
18 G10 **New York** ◐ *state* NE USA
35 X13 **New York Mountains** ▲▲ California, W USA
184 K12 **New Zealand** ◆ *commonwealth republic* SW Pacific Ocean
95 M24 **Nexø** ***var.*** Neksø Bornholm. E Denmark *55°04′N 15°09′E*
125 O15 **Neya** Kostromskaya Oblast′, NW Russian Federation *58°19′N 43°51′E*
Neyba ***see*** Neiba
143 Q12 **Neyrīz** ***var.*** Neiriz, Niriz. Fārs, S Iran *29°14′N 54°18′E*
143 T4 **Neyshābūr** ***var.*** Nishapur. Khorāsān-Razavī, NE Iran *36°15′N 58°47′E*
155 J21 **Neyveli** Tamil Nādu, SE India *11°36′N 79°26′E*
Nezhin ***see*** Nizhyn
33 N10 **Nezperce** Idaho, NW USA *46°14′N 116°15′W*
22 H8 **Nezpique, Bayou** ≈ Louisiana, S USA
77 Y13 **Ngadda** ≈ NE Nigeria
N'Gage ***see*** Negage
185 G16 **Ngahere** West Coast, South Island, New Zealand *42°22′S 171°29′E*
77 Z12 **Ngala** Borno, NE Nigeria *12°19′N 14°11′E*
158 K16 **Ngamring** Xizang Zizhiqu, W China *29°16′N 87°10′E*
81 K19 **Ngangerabeli Plain** *plain* SE Kenya
158 I14 **Ngangla Ringco** ◎ W China
158 H13 **Nganglong Kangri** ▲ W China *32°55′N 81°00′E*
158 K15 **Ngangzê Co** ◎ W China
79 F14 **Ngaoundéré** ***var.*** N'Gaoundéré. Adamaoua, N Cameroon *07°20′N 13°35′E*
N'Gaoundéré ***see*** Ngaoundéré
81 E20 **Ngara** Kagera, NW Tanzania *02°30′S 30°40′E*
188 F8 **Ngardmau Bay** *bay* Babeldaob, N Palau
188 F7 **Ngaregur** *island* Palau Islands, N Palau
Ngarrab ***see*** Gyaca
184 L7 **Ngaruawahia** Waikato, North Island, New Zealand *37°41′S 175°10′E*
184 N11 **Ngaruroro** ≈ North Island, New Zealand
190 I16 **Ngatangiia** Rarotonga, S Cook Islands *21°14′S 159°44′W*
184 M6 **Ngatea** Waikato, North Island, New Zealand *37°16′S 175°29′E*
166 L8 **Ngathainggyaung** Ayeyarwady, SW Burma (Myanmar) *17°22′N 95°04′E*
Ngatik ***see*** Ngetik Atoll
Ngau ***see*** Gau
Ngawa ***see*** Aba
172 G12 **Ngazidja** ***Fr.*** Grande-Comore. *island* NW Comoros
188 C7 **Ngcheangel** ***var.*** Kayangel Islands. *island* Palau Islands, N Palau
188 E10 **Ngchemiangel** Babeldaob, N Palau
188 C8 **Ngeaur** ***var.*** Angaur. *island* Palau Islands, S Palau
188 E10 **Ngerkeai** Babeldaob, N Palau
188 F9 **Ngermechau** Babeldaob, N Palau *07°35′N 134°39′E*
188 C8 **Ngeruktabel** ***prev.*** Urukthapel. *island* Palau Islands, S Palau
188 F8 **Ngetbong** Babeldaob, N Palau *07°37′N 134°35′E*
189 T17 **Ngetik Atoll** ***var.*** Ngatik; ***prev.*** Los Jardines. *atoll* Caroline Islands, E Micronesia
188 E10 **Ngetkip** Babeldaob, N Palau
Nghia Dan ***see*** Thai Hoa
83 C16 **N'Giva** ***var.*** Ondjiva, ***Port.*** Vila Pereira de Eça. Cunene, S Angola *17°02′S 15°42′E*
79 G20 **Ngo** Plateaux, SE Congo *02°28′S 15°43′E*
43 P16 **Ngöbe-Buglé** ◐ *special territory* W Panama
167 S7 **Ngoc Lac** Thanh Hoa, N Vietnam *20°06′N 105°21′E*
79 G17 **Ngoko** ≈ Cameroon/Congo
81 H19 **Ngorengore** Rift Valley, SW Kenya *01°01′S 35°26′E*
159 Q11 **Ngoring Hu** ◎ C China
Ngorolaka ***see*** Banifing
81 H20 **Ngorongoro Crater** *crater* N Tanzania
79 D19 **Ngounié** ***off.*** Province de la Ngounié, ***var.*** La Ngounié. ◐ *province* S Gabon
79 D19 **Ngounié** ≈ Congo/Gabon
Ngounié, Province de la ***see*** Ngounié
78 H10 **Ngoura** ***var.*** NGoura. Chari-Baguirmi, W Chad *12°52′N 16°27′E*
NGoura ***see*** Ngoura
78 G10 **Ngouri** ***var.*** NGouri; ***prev.*** Fort-Millot. Lac, W Chad *13°42′N 15°19′E*
NGouri ***see*** Ngouri
77 Y10 **Ngourti** Diffa, E Niger *15°22′N 13°13′E*
77 Y11 **Nguigmi** ***var.*** N'Guigmi. Diffa, SE Niger *14°17′N 13°07′E*
N'Guigmi ***see*** Nguigmi
Nguimbo ***see*** Lumbala N'Guimbo
188 F15 **Ngulu Atoll** *atoll* Caroline Islands, W Micronesia
187 R14 **Nguna** *island* C Vanuatu
N'Gunza ***see*** Sumbe
169 U17 **Ngurah Rai** ✈ (Bali) Bali, S Indonesia *8°40′S 115°14′E*
77 W12 **Nguru** Yobe, NE Nigeria *12°55′N 10°31′E*
Ngwaketze ***see*** Southern
83 I16 **Ngweze** ≈ S Zambia
83 M17 **Nhamatanda** Sofala, C Mozambique *19°16′S 34°10′E*
58 G12 **Nhamundá, Rio** ***var.*** Jamundá, Yamundá. ≈ N Brazil
60 J7 **Nhandeara** São Paulo, S Brazil *20°40′S 50°03′W*
82 D12 **Nharêa** ***var.*** N'Harea, Nhareia. Bié, W Angola *11°38′S 16°58′E*
N'Harea ***see*** Nharêa
Nhareia ***see*** Nharêa
167 V12 **Nha Trang** Khanh Hoa, S Vietnam *12°15′N 109°10′E*
182 L11 **Nhill** Victoria, SE Australia *36°21′S 141°38′E*
83 L22 **Nhlangano** ***prev.*** Goedgegun. SW Swaziland *27°06′S 31°12′E*
181 S1 **Nhulunbuy** Northern Territory, N Australia *12°16′S 136°46′E*
77 N10 **Niafounké** Tombouctou, W Mali *15°54′N 03°58′W*
31 N5 **Niagara** Wisconsin, N USA *45°45′N 87°57′W*
14 H16 **Niagara** ≈ Ontario, S Canada
14 G15 **Niagara Escarpment** *hill range* Ontario, S Canada
14 H16 **Niagara Falls** Ontario, S Canada *43°05′N 79°06′W*
18 D9 **Niagara Falls** New York, NE USA *43°06′N 79°04′W*
14 H16 **Niagara Falls** *waterfall* Canada/USA
76 K12 **Niagassola** ***var.*** Nyagassola. Haute-Guinée, NE Guinea *12°24′N 09°03′W*
77 R12 **Niamey** ● (Niger) Niamey, SW Niger *13°28′N 02°03′E*
77 R12 **Niamey** ✈ Niamey, SW Niger *13°28′N 02°14′E*
77 R14 **Niamtougou** N Togo *09°50′N 01°08′E*
79 O16 **Niangara** Orientale, NE Dem. Rep. Congo *03°45′N 27°54′E*
77 O10 **Niangay, Lac** ◎ E Mali
77 N14 **Niangoloko** SW Burkina *10°15′N 04°53′W*
27 U6 **Niangua River** ≈ Missouri, C USA
79 O17 **Nia-Nia** Orientale, NE Dem. Rep. Congo *01°26′N 27°38′E*
19 N13 **Niantic** Connecticut, NE USA *41°19′N 72°11′W*
163 U7 **Nianzishan** Heilongjiang, NE China *47°31′N 122°53′E*
79 E20 **Niari** ◐ *province* SW Congo
168 H10 **Nias, Pulau** *island* W Indonesia
82 O13 **Niassa** ***off.*** Província do Niassa. ◐ *province* N Mozambique
Niassa, Província do ***see*** Niassa
191 U10 **Niau** *island* Îles Tuamotu, C French Polynesia
95 G20 **Nibe** Nordjylland, N Denmark *56°59′N 09°39′E*
189 Q8 **Nibok** N Nauru *0°31′S 166°55′E*
118 C10 **Nīca** Liepāja, W Latvia *56°21′N 21°03′E*
Nicaea ***see*** Nice
42 J9 **Nicaragua** ***off.*** Republic of Nicaragua. ◆ *republic* Central America
42 K11 **Nicaragua, Lago de** ***var.*** Cocibolca, Gran Lago, ***Eng.*** Lake Nicaragua. ◎ S Nicaragua
Nicaragua, Lake ***see*** Nicaragua, Lago de
64 D11 **Nicaraguan Rise** *undersea feature* NW Caribbean Sea *16°00′N 80°00′W*
Nicaragua, Republic of ***see*** Nicaragua
Nicaria ***see*** Ikaría
107 N21 **Nicastro** Calabria, SW Italy *38°59′N 16°20′E*
103 V15 **Nice** ***It.*** Nizza; ***anc.*** Nicaea. Alpes-Maritimes, SE France *43°43′N 07°13′E*
Nice ***see*** Côte d'Azur
Nicephorium ***see*** Ar Raqqah
12 M9 **Nichicun, Lac** ◎ Québec, E Canada
164 D16 **Nichinan** ***var.*** Nitinan. Miyazaki, Kyūshū, SW Japan *31°36′N 131°23′E*
44 E4 **Nicholas Channel** *channel* N Cuba
Nicholas II Land ***see*** Severnaya Zemlya
149 U2 **Nicholas Range** ***Pash.*** Selselehye Kuhe Vākhān, ***Taj.*** Qatorkŭhi Vakhon. ▲▲ Afghanistan/Tajikistan
20 M6 **Nicholasville** Kentucky, S USA *37°52′N 84°34′W*
44 G2 **Nicholls Town** Andros Island, NW Bahamas *25°07′N 78°01′W*
21 U12 **Nichols** South Carolina, SE USA *34°13′N 79°09′W*
55 U9 **Nickerie** ◐ *district* NW Surinam
55 V9 **Nickerie Rivier** ≈ NW Surinam
151 P22 **Nicobar Islands** *island group* India, E Indian Ocean
116 L9 **Nicolae Bălcescu** Botoşani, NE Romania *47°33′N 26°52′E*
15 P11 **Nicolet** Québec, SE Canada *46°13′N 72°37′W*
15 Q12 **Nicolet** ≈ Québec, SE Canada
31 Q4 **Nicolet, Lake** ◎ Michigan, N USA
29 U10 **Nicollet** Minnesota, N USA *44°16′N 94°11′W*
61 F19 **Nico Pérez** Florida, S Uruguay *33°30′S 55°10′W*
Nicopolis ***see*** Nikopol, Bulgaria
Nicopolis ***see*** Nikópoli, Greece
121 P2 **Nicosia** ***Gk.*** Lefkosía, ***Turk.*** Lefkoşa. ● (Cyprus) C Cyprus *35°10′N 33°23′E*
107 K24 **Nicosia** Sicilia, Italy, C Mediterranean Sea *37°45′N 14°24′E*
107 N22 **Nicotera** Calabria, SW Italy *38°33′N 15°55′E*
42 K13 **Nicoya** Guanacaste, W Costa Rica *10°09′N 85°26′W*
42 L14 **Nicoya, Golfo de** *gulf* W Costa Rica
42 L14 **Nicoya, Península de** *peninsula* NW Costa Rica
Nictheroy ***see*** Niterói
118 B12 **Nida** ***Ger.*** Nidden. Klaipėda, SW Lithuania *55°20′N 21°00′E*
111 L15 **Nida** ≈ S Poland
Nidaros ***see*** Trondheim
108 D8 **Nidau** Bern, W Switzerland *47°07′N 07°15′E*
101 H17 **Nidda** ≈ W Germany
Nidden ***see*** Nida
95 F17 **Nidelva** ≈ S Norway
110 L9 **Nidzica** ***Ger.*** Niedenburg. Warmińsko-Mazurskie, NE Poland *53°22′N 20°27′E*
100 H6 **Niebüll** Schleswig-Holstein, N Germany *54°47′N 08°51′E*
Niedenburg ***see*** Nidzica
99 N25 **Niederanven** Luxembourg, C Luxembourg *49°39′N 06°15′E*
103 V4 **Niederbronn-les-Bains** Bas-Rhin, NE France *48°57′N 07°37′E*
Niederdonau ***see*** Niederösterreich
109 S7 **Niedere Tauern** ▲▲ C Austria
101 P14 **Niederlausitz** ***Eng.*** Lower Lusatia, ***Lus.*** Donja Łužica. *physical region* E Germany
109 U5 **Niederösterreich** ***off.*** Land Niederösterreich, ***Eng.*** Lower Austria, ***Ger.*** Niederdonau; ***prev.*** Lower Danube. ◐ *state* NE Austria
Niederösterreich, Land ***see*** Niederösterreich
100 G12 **Niedersachsen** ***Eng.*** Lower Saxony, ***Fr.*** Basse-Saxe. ◐ *state* NW Germany
79 D17 **Niefang** ***var.*** Sevilla de Niefang. NW Equatorial Guinea *01°52′N 10°12′E*
83 G23 **Niekerkshoop** Northern Cape, W South Africa *29°21′S 22°49′E*
99 G17 **Niel** Antwerpen, N Belgium *51°07′N 04°20′E*
Niélé ***see*** Niellé
76 M14 **Niellé** ***var.*** Niélé. N Ivory Coast *10°12′N 05°38′W*
79 O22 **Niemba** Katanga, E Dem. Rep. Congo *05°58′S 28°24′E*
111 G15 **Niemcza** ***Ger.*** Nimptsch. Dolnośląskie, SW Poland *50°45′N 16°52′E*
Niemen ***see*** Neman
92 J13 **Niemisel** Norrbotten, N Sweden *66°00′N 22°00′E*
111 H15 **Niemodlin** ***Ger.*** Falkenberg. Opolskie, SW Poland *50°37′N 17°45′E*
76 M13 **Niéna** Sikasso, SW Mali *11°24′N 06°20′W*
100 H12 **Nienburg** Niedersachsen, N Germany *52°37′N 09°12′E*
100 N13 **Nieplitz** ≈ NE Germany
111 L16 **Niepołomice** Malopolskie, S Poland *50°02′N 20°12′E*
101 D14 **Niers** ≈ Germany/Netherlands
101 Q15 **Niesky** ***Lus.*** Niska. Sachsen, E Germany *51°16′N 14°49′E*
Nieśwież ***see*** Nyasvizh
Nieuport ***see*** Nieuwpoort
98 O8 **Nieuw-Amsterdam** Drenthe, NE Netherlands *52°43′N 06°52′E*
55 W9 **Nieuw Amsterdam** Commewijne, NE Surinam *05°53′N 55°05′W*
99 M14 **Nieuw-Bergen** Limburg, SE Netherlands *51°36′N 06°04′E*
98 O7 **Nieuw-Buinen** Drenthe, NE Netherlands *52°57′N 06°55′E*
98 J12 **Nieuwegein** Utrecht, C Netherlands *52°03′N 05°06′E*
98 P6 **Nieuwe Pekela** Groningen, NE Netherlands *53°04′N 06°58′E*
98 P5 **Nieuweschans** Groningen, NE Netherlands *53°10′N 07°10′E*
Nieuw Guinea ***see*** New Guinea
98 I11 **Nieuwkoop** Zuid-Holland, C Netherlands *52°09′N 04°46′E*
98 M9 **Nieuwleusen** Overijssel, S Netherlands *52°34′N 06°16′E*
98 J11 **Nieuw-Loosdrecht** Noord-Holland, C Netherlands *52°12′N 05°08′E*
55 U9 **Nieuw Nickerie** Nickerie, NW Surinam *05°56′N 57°W*
98 P5 **Nieuwolda** Groningen, NE Netherlands *53°15′N 06°58′E*
99 B17 **Nieuwpoort** ***var.*** Nieuport. West-Vlaanderen , W Belgium *51°08′N 02°45′E*
99 G14 **Nieuw-Vossemeer** Noord-Brabant, S Netherlands *51°34′N 04°13′E*
98 P7 **Nieuw-Weerdinge** Drenthe, NE Netherlands *52°51′N 07°00′E*
40 L10 **Nieves** Zacatecas, C Mexico *24°00′N 102°57′W*
64 O11 **Nieves, Pico de las** ▲ Gran Canaria, Islas Canarias, Spain, NE Atlantic Ocean *27°58′N 15°34′W*
103 P8 **Nièvre** ◐ *department* C France
Niewenstat ***see*** Neustadt an der Weinstrasse
136 J15 **Niğde** Niğde, C Turkey *37°58′N 34°42′E*
136 J15 **Niğde** ◐ *province* C Turkey
83 J21 **Nigel** Gauteng, NE South Africa *26°25′S 28°28′E*
77 V10 **Niger** ***off.*** Republic of Niger. ◆ *republic* W Africa
77 T14 **Niger** ◐ *state* C Nigeria
67 P8 **Niger** ≈ W Africa
Niger Cone ***see*** Niger Fan
67 P9 **Niger Delta** *delta* S Nigeria
67 P9 **Niger Fan** ***var.*** Niger Cone. *undersea feature* E Atlantic Ocean *04°15′N 05°00′E*
77 T13 **Nigeria** ***off.*** Federal Republic of Nigeria. ◆ *federal republic* W Africa
Nigeria, Federal Republic of ***see*** Nigeria
77 T17 **Niger, Mouths of the** *delta* S Nigeria
Niger, Republic of ***see*** Niger
185 C24 **Nightcaps** Southland, South Island, New Zealand *45°58′S 168°03′E*
14 F7 **Night Hawk Lake** ◎ Ontario, S Canada
65 M19 **Nightingale Island** *island* S Tristan da Cunha, S Atlantic Ocean
38 M12 **Nightmute** Alaska, USA *60°28′N 164°43′W*
114 G13 **Nigríta** Kentrikí Makedonía, NE Greece *40°54′N 23°29′E*
148 J15 **Nihing** ***Per.*** Rūd-e Nahang. ≈ Iran/Pakistan
191 V10 **Nihiru** *atoll* Îles Tuamotu, C French Polynesia
Nihommatsu ***see*** Nihonmatsu
Nihon ***see*** Japan
165 P11 **Nihonmatsu** ***var.*** Nihommatsu, Nihonmatu. Fukushima, Honshū, C Japan *37°34′N 140°25′E*
Nihonmatu ***see*** Nihonmatsu
62 I12 **Nihuil, Embalse del** ◎ W Argentina
165 O10 **Niigata** Niigata, Honshū, C Japan *37°55′N 139°01′E*
165 O11 **Niigata** ***off.*** Niigata-ken. ◐ *prefecture* Honshū, C Japan
Niigata-ken ***see*** Niigata
165 G14 **Niihama** Ehime, Shikoku, SW Japan *33°57′N 133°15′E*
38 A8 **Ni'ihau** ***var.*** Niihau. *island* Hawai'i, USA, C Pacific Ocean
165 X12 **Nii-jima** *island* E Japan
165 H12 **Niimi** Okayama, Honshū, SW Japan *35°00′N 133°27′E*
165 O10 **Niitsu** ***var.*** Niitu. Niigata, Honshū, C Japan *37°48′N 139°09′E*
Niitu ***see*** Niitsu
105 P15 **Nijar** Andalucía, S Spain *36°57′N 02°13′W*
98 K11 **Nijkerk** Gelderland, C Netherlands *52°13′N 05°30′E*
99 H16 **Nijlen** Antwerpen, N Belgium *51°10′N 04°40′E*
98 L13 **Nijmegen** ***Ger.*** Nimwegen; ***anc.*** Noviomagus. Gelderland, SE Netherlands *51°50′N 05°52′E*
98 N10 **Nijverdal** Overijssel, E Netherlands *52°22′N 06°28′E*
190 G16 **Nikao** Rarotonga, S Cook Islands
Nikaria ***see*** Ikaría
124 I2 **Nikel'** ***Finn.*** Kolosjoki. Murmanskaya Oblast′, NW Russian Federation *69°25′N 30°12′E*
171 Q17 **Nikiniki** Timor, S Indonesia *10°S 124°30′E*
129 Q15 **Nikitin Seamount** *undersea feature* E Indian Ocean *05°48′S 84°48′E*
77 S14 **Nikki** E Benin *09°55′N 03°12′E*
Niklasmarkt ***see*** Gheorgheni
39 P10 **Nikolai** Alaska, USA *63°00′N 154°22′W*
Nikolaiken ***see*** Mikołajki
Nikolainkaupunki ***see*** Vaasa
Nikolayev ***see*** Mykolayiv
145 O6 **Nikolayevka** Severnyy Kazakhstan, N Kazakhstan
Nikolayevka ***see*** Zhetigen
127 P9 **Nikolayevsk** Volgogradskaya Oblast′, SW Russian Federation *50°03′N 45°30′E*
Nikolayevskaya Oblast' ***see*** Mykolayivs'ka Oblast'
123 S12 **Nikolayevsk-na-Amure** Khabarovskiy Kray, SE Russian Federation *53°04′N 140°39′E*
127 P6 **Nikol'sk** Penzenskaya Oblast′, W Russian Federation *53°46′N 46°03′E*
125 O13 **Nikol'sk** Vologodskaya Oblast′, NW Russian Federation *59°35′N 45°31′E*
Nikol'sk ***see*** Ussuriysk
38 K17 **Nikolski** Umnak Island, Alaska, USA *52°56′N 168°52′W*
Nikol'skiy ***see*** Satpayev
127 V7 **Nikol'skoye** Orenburgskaya Oblast′, W Russian Federation *52°01′N 55°48′E*
Nikol'sk-Ussuriyskiy ***see*** Ussuriysk
114 J7 **Nikopol** ***anc.*** Nicopolis. Pleven, N Bulgaria *43°43′N 24°55′E*
117 S9 **Nikopol'** Dnipropetrovs'ka Oblast′, SE Ukraine *47°34′N 34°23′E*
115 C17 **Nikópoli** ***anc.*** Nicopolis. *site of ancient city* Ípeiros, W Greece
136 M12 **Niksar** Tokat, N Turkey *40°35′N 36°59′E*
143 V14 **Nīkshahr** Sīstān va Balūchestān, SE Iran *26°15′N 60°10′E*
113 J16 **Nikšić** C Montenegro *42°47′N 18°56′E*
191 R4 **Nikumaroro** ; ***prev.*** Gardner Island. *atoll* Phoenix Islands, C Kiribati
191 P3 **Nikunau** ***var.*** Nukunau; ***prev.*** Byron Island. *atoll* Tungaru, W Kiribati
155 G21 **Nilambūr** Kerala, SW India *11°17′N 76°15′E*
35 X16 **Niland** California, W USA *33°14′N 115°31′W*
80 G8 **Nile** *former province* NW Uganda
67 T3 **Nile** ***Ar.*** Nahr an Nīl. ≈ N Africa
75 W7 **Nile Delta** *delta* N Egypt
67 T3 **Nile Fan** *undersea feature* E Mediterranean Sea *33°00′N 31°00′E*
31 O11 **Niles** Michigan, N USA *41°49′N 86°15′W*
31 V11 **Niles** Ohio, N USA *41°10′N 80°46′W*
155 F20 **Nīleswaram** Kerala, SW India *12°18′N 75°07′E*
14 K10 **Nilgaut, Lac** ◎ Québec, SE Canada
149 O6 **Nīlī** Dāykondī, C Afghanistan *33°43′N 66°07′E*
158 I5 **Nilka** Xinjiang Uygur Zizhiqu, NW China *43°46′N 82°33′E*
Nīl, Nahr an ***see*** Nile
93 N16 **Nilsiä** Itä-Suomi, C Finland *63°13′N 28°00′E*
154 F9 **Nimach** Madhya Pradesh, C India *24°27′N 74°56′E*
152 G14 **Nimbāhera** Rājasthān, N India *24°38′N 74°45′E*
76 L15 **Nimba, Monts** ***var.*** Nimba Mountains. ▲▲ W Africa
Nimba Mountains ***see*** Nimba, Monts
Nimburg ***see*** Nymburk
103 Q15 **Nîmes** ***anc.*** Nemausus, Nismes. Gard, S France *43°49′N 04°20′E*
152 H11 **Nīm ka Thāna** Rājasthān, N India *27°42′N 75°50′E*
183 R11 **Nimmitabel** New South Wales, SE Australia *36°34′S 149°18′E*
Nimptsch ***see*** Niemcza
195 R11 **Nimrod Glacier** *glacier* Antarctica
Nimroze ***see*** Nīmrūz
148 K8 **Nīmrūz** ***var.*** Nimroze; ***prev.*** Chakhānsūr. ◐ *province* SW Afghanistan
81 F16 **Nimule** Eastern Equatoria, S Sudan *03°35′N 32°03′E*
Nimwegen ***see*** Nijmegen
139 P3 **Nīnawá** ◐ *governorate* NW Iraq
155 C23 **Nine Degree Channel** *channel* India/Maldives
18 G9 **Ninemile Point** *headland* New York, NE USA *43°31′N 76°22′W*
173 S8 **Ninetyeast Ridge** *undersea feature* E Indian Ocean *04°00′S 90°00′E*
183 P13 **Ninety Mile Beach** *beach* Victoria, SE Australia
184 I2 **Ninety Mile Beach** *beach* North Island, New Zealand
21 P12 **Ninety Six** South Carolina, SE USA *34°10′N 82°01′W*
163 Y9 **Ning'an** Heilongjiang, NE China *44°20′N 129°28′E*
161 S9 **Ningbo** ***var.*** Ning-po, Yin-hsien; ***prev.*** Ninghsien. Zhejiang, SE China *29°54′N 121°33′E*
161 U12 **Ningde** Fujian, SE China *26°48′N 119°33′E*
161 P12 **Ningdu** ***var.*** Meijiang. Jiangxi, S China *26°28′N 115°53′E*
Ning'er ***see*** Pu'er
186 A7 **Ningerum** Western, SW Papua New Guinea *05°40′S 141°10′E*
161 R9 **Ningguo** Anhui, E China *30°33′N 118°58′E*
161 S9 **Ninghai** Zhejiang, SE China *29°18′N 121°26′E*
Ning-hsia ***see*** Ningxia
Ninghsien ***see*** Ningbo
159 S15 **Ningjing Shan** ▲▲ W China
160 J15 **Ningming** ***var.*** Chengzhong. Guangxi Zhuangzu Zizhiqu, S China *22°07′N 106°43′E*
160 H11 **Ningnan** ***var.*** Pisha. Sichuan, C China *26°59′N 102°49′E*
Ning-po ***see*** Ningbo
Ningsia/Ningsia Hui/ Ningsia Hui Autonomous Region ***see*** Ningxia
160 J5 **Ningxia** ***off.*** Ningxia Huizu Zizhiqu, ***var.*** Ning-hsia, Ningsia, ***Eng.*** Ningsia Hui, Ningsia Hui Autonomous Region. ◐ *autonomous region* N China
Ningxia Huizu Zizhiqu ***see*** Ningxia
159 X10 **Ningxian** ***var.*** Xinning. Gansu, N China *35°30′N 108°05′E*
167 T7 **Ninh Binh** Ninh Binh, N Vietnam *20°14′N 106°00′E*
167 V12 **Ninh Hoa** Khanh Hoa, S Vietnam *12°28′N 109°07′E*
186 C4 **Ninigo Group** *island group* N Papua New Guinea
39 Q12 **Ninilchik** Alaska, USA *60°03′N 151°40′W*
27 N7 **Ninnescah River** ≈ Kansas, C USA
195 U16 **Ninnis Glacier** *glacier* Antarctica
165 R8 **Ninohe** Iwate, Honshū, C Japan *40°16′N 141°18′E*
99 F18 **Ninove** Oost-Vlaanderen, C Belgium *50°50′N 04°02′E*
171 O4 **Ninoy Aquino** ✈ (Manila) Luzon, N Philippines *14°26′N 121°00′E*
Nio ***see*** Íos
29 P12 **Niobrara** Nebraska, C USA *42°43′N 97°59′W*
28 M12 **Niobrara River** ≈ Nebraska/Wyoming, C USA
79 I20 **Nioki** Bandundu, W Dem. Rep. Congo *02°44′S 17°42′E*
76 M11 **Niono** Ségou, C Mali *14°18′N 05°59′W*
76 K11 **Nioro** ***var.*** Nioro du Sahel. Kayes, W Mali *15°13′N 09°39′W*
76 G11 **Nioro du Rip** SW Senegal *13°44′N 15°48′W*
Nioro du Sahel ***see*** Nioro
102 K10 **Niort** Deux-Sèvres, W France *46°21′N 00°25′W*
172 H14 **Nioumachoua** Mohéli, S Comoros *12°21′S 43°43′E*
186 C7 **Nipa** Southern Highlands, W Papua New Guinea *06°11′S 143°27′E*
11 U14 **Nipawin** Saskatchewan, S Canada *52°23′N 104°01′W*
12 D12 **Nipigon** Ontario, S Canada *49°02′N 88°15′W*
12 D11 **Nipigon, Lake** ◎ Ontario, S Canada
11 S13 **Nipin** ≈ Saskatchewan, C Canada
14 G11 **Nipissing, Lake** ◎ Ontario, S Canada
35 P13 **Nipomo** California, W USA *35°02′N 120°28′W*
Nippon ***see*** Japan
138 K6 **Niqniqīyah, Jabal an** ▲▲ C Syria
62 I9 **Niquivil** San Juan, W Argentina *30°25′S 68°42′W*
171 Y13 **Nirabotong** Papua, E Indonesia *02°35′S 140°08′E*
Niriz ***see*** Neyrīz
163 U7 **Nirji** ***var.*** Morin Dawa Daurzu Zizhiqi. Nei Mongol Zizhiqu, N China *48°21′N 124°32′E*
155 I14 **Nirmal** Andhra Pradesh, C India *19°04′N 78°21′E*
153 Q13 **Nirmāli** Bihār, NE India *26°18′N 86°35′E*
113 O14 **Niš** ***Eng.*** Nish, ***Ger.*** Nisch; ***anc.*** Naissus. Serbia, SE Serbia *43°21′N 21°53′E*
104 H9 **Nisa** Portalegre, C Portugal *39°31′N 07°39′W*
Nisa ***see*** Neisse
141 P4 **Nişab** Al Ḩudūd ash Shamālīyah, N Saudi Arabia *29°11′N 44°43′E*
141 Q15 **Nişāb** ***var.*** Anşāb. SW Yemen *14°24′N 46°47′E*
113 P14 **Nišava** ***Bul.*** Nishava. ≈ Bulgaria/Serbia ***see also*** Nishava
Nišava ***see*** Nishava
107 K25 **Niscemi** Sicilia, Italy, C Mediterranean Sea *37°09′N 14°23′E*
Nisch/Nish ***see*** Niš
165 R4 **Niseko** Hokkaidō, NE Japan *42°50′N 140°43′E*
Nishapur ***see*** Neyshābūr
114 G9 **Nishava** ***var.*** Nišava. ≈ Bulgaria/Serbia ***see also*** Nišava
Nishava ***see*** Nišava
118 L11 **Nishcha** ≈ N Belarus
165 C17 **Nishinoomote** Kagoshima, Tanega-shima, SW Japan *30°42′N 130°59′E*
165 X15 **Nishino-shima** ***Eng.*** Rosario. *island* Ogasawara-shotō, SE Japan
165 I13 **Nishiwaki** ***var.*** Nisiwaki. Hyōgo, Honshū, SW Japan *34°59′N 134°58′E*
141 U14 **Nishtūn** SE Yemen *15°47′N 52°08′E*
Nisibin ***see*** Nusaybin
Nisiros ***see*** Nísyros
Nisiwaki ***see*** Nishiwaki
Niska ***see*** Niesky
113 O14 **Niška Banja** Serbia, SE Serbia *43°18′N 22°01′E*
12 D6 **Niskibi** ≈ Ontario, C Canada
111 O15 **Nisko** Podkrapackie, SE Poland *50°31′N 22°09′E*
10 H7 **Nisling** ≈ Yukon Territory, W Canada
99 H22 **Nismes** Namur, S Belgium *50°04′N 04°31′E*
Nismes ***see*** Nîmes
116 M10 **Nisporeni** ***Rus.*** Nisporeny. W Moldova *47°04′N 28°10′E*
Nisporeny ***see*** Nisporeni
95 K20 **Nissan** ≈ S Sweden
Nissan Islands ***see*** Green Islands
95 F16 **Nisser** ◎ S Norway
95 E21 **Nissum Bredning** *inlet* NW Denmark
29 U6 **Nisswa** Minnesota, N USA *46°31′N 94°17′W*
Nistru ***see*** Dniester
115 M22 **Nísyros** ***var.*** Nisiros. *island* Dodekánisa, Greece, Aegean Sea
118 H8 **Nītaure** Cēsis, C Latvia *57°05′N 25°12′E*
60 P10 **Niterói** ***prev.*** Nictheroy. Rio de Janeiro, SE Brazil *22°54′S 43°06′W*
14 F16 **Nith** ≈ Ontario, S Canada
96 J13 **Nith** ≈ S Scotland, United Kingdom
Nitinan ***see*** Nichinan
111 I21 **Nitra** ***Ger.*** Neutra, ***Hung.*** Nyitra. Nitriansky Kraj, SW Slovakia *48°20′N 18°05′E*
111 I20 **Nitra** ***Ger.*** Neutra, ***Hung.*** Nyitra. ≈ W Slovakia
111 I21 **Nitriansky Kraj** ◐ *region* SW Slovakia
21 Q5 **Nitro** West Virginia, NE USA *38°24′N 81°50′W*
95 H14 **Nittedal** Akershus, S Norway *60°08′N 10°45′E*
Niuatobutabu ***see*** Niuatoputapu
193 X13 **Niuatoputapu** ***var.*** Niuatobutabu; ***prev.*** Keppel Island. *island* N Tonga
193 U15 **Niu'Aunofa** *headland* Tongatapu, S Tonga *21°03′S 175°19′W*
Niuchwang ***see*** Yingkou
190 B16 **Niue** ◇ *self-governing territory in free association with New Zealand* S Pacific Ocean
190 F10 **Niulakita** ***var.*** Nurakita. *atoll* S Tuvalu
190 E6 **Niutao** *atoll* NW Tuvalu
93 L15 **Nivala** Oulu, C Finland *63°56′N 25°00′E*
102 I15 **Nive** ≈ SW France
99 G19 **Nivelles** Walloon Brabant, C Belgium *50°36′N 04°04′E*
103 P8 **Nivernais** *cultural region* C France
15 N8 **Niverville, Lac** ◎ Québec, SE Canada
27 T7 **Nixa** Missouri, C USA *37°02′N 93°17′W*
35 R5 **Nixon** Nevada, W USA *39°48′N 119°24′W*
25 S12 **Nixon** Texas, SW USA *29°16′N 97°45′W*
Niya ***see*** Minfeng
Niyazov ***see*** Nyýazow
155 H14 **Nizāmābād** Andhra Pradesh, C India *18°40′N 78°05′E*
155 H15 **Nizām Sāgar** ◎ C India
125 N16 **Nizhegorodskaya Oblast'** ◐ *province* W Russian Federation
Nizhnegorskiy ***see*** Nyzhn'ohirs'kyy
127 S4 **Nizhnekamsk** Respublika Tatarstan, W Russian Federation *55°36′N 51°45′E*
127 U3 **Nizhnekamskoye Vodokhranilishche** ⊠ W Russian Federation
123 S14 **Nizhneleninskoye** Yevreyskaya Avtonomnaya Oblast′, SE Russian Federation *47°50′N 132°30′E*
122 L13 **Nizhneudinsk** Irkutskaya Oblast′, S Russian Federation *54°48′N 98°51′E*
122 I10 **Nizhnevartovsk** Khanty-Mansiyskiy Avtonomnyy Okrug-Yugra, C Russian Federation *60°57′N 76°40′E*
123 Q7 **Nizhneyansk** Respublika Sakha (Yakutiya), NE Russian Federation *71°25′N 135°59′E*
127 Q11 **Nizhniy Baskunchak** Astrakhanskaya Oblast′, SW Russian Federation *48°15′N 46°49′E*
127 O6 **Nizhniy Lomov** Penzenskaya Oblast′, W Russian Federation *53°32′N 43°39′E*
127 P3 **Nizhniy Novgorod** ***prev.*** Gor'kiy. Nizhegorodskaya Oblast′, W Russian Federation *56°17′N 44°E*
125 T8 **Nizhniy Odes** Respublika Komi, NW Russian Federation *63°42′N 54°59′E*
Nizhniy Pyandzh ***see*** Panji Poyon
122 G10 **Nizhniy Tagil** Sverdlovskaya Oblast′, C Russian Federation *57°57′N 59°51′E*
127 T4 **Nizhnyaya Maktama** Respublika Tatarstan, W Russian Federation *54°51′N 52°22′E*
125 T9 **Nizhnyaya-Omra** Respublika Komi, NW Russian Federation *62°46′N 55°54′E*
125 P5 **Nizhnyaya Pesha** Nenetskiy Avtonomnyy Okrug, NW Russian Federation *66°54′N 47°37′E*
117 Q3 **Nizhyn** ***Rus.*** Nezhin. Chernihivs'ka Oblast′, NE Ukraine *51°03′N 31°54′E*
136 M17 **Nizip** Gaziantep, S Turkey *37°02′N 37°47′E*
141 X8 **Nizwa** ***var.*** Nazwāh. NE Oman *23°00′N 57°50′E*
Nizza ***see*** Nice
106 C9 **Nizza Monferrato** Piemonte, NE Italy *44°47′N 08°22′E*
Njávdám ***see*** Näätämöjoki
Njellim ***see*** Nellim
81 H24 **Njombe** Iringa, S Tanzania *09°20′S 34°47′E*
81 G23 **Njombe** ≈ C Tanzania
Njuk, Ozero ***see*** Nyuk, Ozero
Njuksenica ***see*** Nyuksenitsa
92 I10 **Njunis** ▲ N Norway *68°47′N 19°24′E*
93 H17 **Njurunda** Västernorrland, C Sweden *62°15′N 17°24′E*
94 N11 **Njutånger** Gävleborg, C Sweden *61°37′N 17°04′E*
79 D14 **Nkambe** Nord-Ouest, NW Cameroon *06°35′N 10°44′E*
Nkata Bay ***see*** Nkhata Bay
79 F21 **Nkayi** ***prev.*** Jacob. Bouenza, S Congo *04°11′S 13°17′E*
83 J17 **Nkayi** Matabeleland North, W Zimbabwe *19°00′S 28°54′E*
82 N13 **Nkhata Bay** ***var.*** Nkata Bay. Northern, N Malawi *11°37′S 34°20′E*
81 E22 **Nkonde** Kigoma, N Tanzania *06°16′S 30°17′E*
79 D15 **Nkongsamba** ***var.*** N'Kongsamba. Littoral, W Cameroon *04°59′N 09°53′E*
N'Kongsamba ***see*** Nkongsamba
83 E16 **Nkurenkuru** Okavango, N Namibia *17°38′S 18°39′E*
77 Q15 **Nkwanta** E Ghana *08°18′N 00°27′E*
167 O2 **Nmai Hka** ***var.*** Me Hka. ≈ N Burma (Myanmar)
Noardwâlde ***see*** Noordwolde
39 N7 **Noatak** Alaska, USA *67°34′N 162°58′W*
39 N7 **Noatak River** ≈ Alaska, USA
164 E15 **Nobeoka** Miyazaki, Kyūshū, SW Japan *32°34′N 131°37′E*
27 N11 **Noble** Oklahoma, C USA *35°08′N 97°23′W*
31 P13 **Noblesville** Indiana, N USA *40°03′N 86°00′W*
165 R5 **Noboribetsu** ***var.*** Noboribetu. Hokkaidō, NE Japan *42°27′N 141°08′E*
Noboribetu ***see*** Noboribetsu
59 H18 **Nobres** Mato Grosso, W Brazil *14°44′S 56°15′W*
107 N21 **Nocera Terinese** Calabria, S Italy *39°03′N 16°10′E*
41 Q16 **Nochixtlán** ***var.*** Asunción Nochixtlán. Oaxaca, SE Mexico *17°29′N 97°17′W*
25 S5 **Nocona** Texas, SW USA *33°47′N 97°43′W*
63 K21 **Nodales, Bahía de los** *bay* S Argentina
27 Q2 **Nodaway River** ≈ Iowa/Missouri, C USA
27 R8 **Noel** Missouri, C USA *36°33′N 94°29′W*
40 H3 **Nogales** Chihuahua, NW Mexico *18°50′N 97°12′W*
40 F3 **Nogales** Sonora, NW Mexico *31°17′N 110°53′W*
36 M17 **Nogales** Arizona, SW USA *31°20′N 110°55′W*
Nogal Valley ***see*** Dooxo Nugaaleed
102 K15 **Nogaro** Gers, S France *43°46′N 00°01′W*
110 J7 **Nogat** ≈ N Poland
164 D12 **Nōgata** Fukuoka, Kyūshū, SW Japan *33°46′N 130°42′E*
127 P15 **Nogayskaya Step'** *steppe* SW Russian Federation
102 M6 **Nogent-le-Rotrou** Eure-et-Loir, C France *48°19′N 00°50′E*

◆ Country
● Country Capital
◇ Dependent Territory
○ Dependent Territory Capital
◐ Administrative Regions
✈ International Airport
▲ Mountain
▲▲ Mountain Range
Volcano
≈ River
◎ Lake
⊠ Reservoir

103 O4 Nogent-sur-Oise Oise, N France 49°16′N 02°28′E
103 P6 Nogent-sur-Seine Aube, N France 48°30′N 03°31′E
122 L10 Noginsk Evenkiyskiy Avtonomnyy Okrug, N Russian Federation 64°28′N 91°09′E
126 L3 Noginsk Moskovskaya Oblast', W Russian Federation 55°51′N 38°23′E
123 T12 Nogliki Ostrov Sakhalin, Sakhalinskaya Oblast', SE Russian Federation 51°44′N 143°14′E
164 K12 Nōgōhaku-san ▲ Honshū, SW Japan 35°46′N 136°30′E
162 D5 Nogoonnuur Bayan-Ölgiy, NW Mongolia 49°31′N 89°48′E
61 C18 Nogoyá Entre Ríos, E Argentina 32°25′S 59°50′W
111 K21 Nógrád off. Nógrád Megye. ◆ county N Hungary
Nógrád Megye see Nógrád
105 U5 Noguera Pallaresa ≈ NE Spain
105 U4 Noguera Ribagorçana ≈ NE Spain
101 E19 Nohfelden Saarland, SW Germany 49°35′N 07°08′E
38 A8 Nohili Point headland Kaua'i, Hawai'i, USA 22°03′N 159°48′W
104 G3 Noia Galicia, NW Spain 42°48′N 08°52′W
103 N16 Noire, Montagne ▲▲ S France
14 J10 Noire, Rivière ≈ Québec, SE Canada
15 P12 Noire, Rivière ≈ Québec, SE Canada
Noire, Rivi`ere see Black River
102 G6 Noires, Montagnes ▲▲ NW France
102 H8 Noirmoutier-en-l'Île Vendée, NW France 47°00′N 02°15′W
102 H8 Noirmoutier, Île de island NW France
187 Q10 Noka Nendö, E Solomon Islands 10°42′S 165°57′E
83 G17 Nokaneng North West, NW Botswana 19°40′S 22°12′E
93 L18 Nokia Länsi-Suomi, W Finland 61°29′N 23°30′E
148 K11 Nok Kundi Baluchistän, SW Pakistan 28°49′N 62°39′E
30 L14 Nokomis Illinois, N USA 39°18′N 89°17′W
30 K5 Nokomis, Lake ⊠ Wisconsin, N USA
78 G9 Nokou Kanem, W Chad 14°36′N 14°45′E
187 Q12 Nokuku Espiritu Santo, W Vanuatu 14°56′S 166°34′E
95 J18 Nol Västra Götaland, S Sweden 57°55′N 12°03′E
79 H16 Nola Sangha-Mbaéré, SW Central African Republic 03°29′N 16°05′E
25 P7 Nolan Texas, SW USA 32°15′N 100°15′W
125 R15 Nolinsk Kirovskaya Oblast', NW Russian Federation 57°35′N 49°54′E
Nolsø see Nólsoy
95 B19 Nólsoy Dan. Nolsø. island E Faeroe Islands
186 B7 Nomad Western, SW Papau New Guinea 06°11′S 142°13′E
164 B16 Noma-zaki Kyūshū, SW Japan
40 K10 Nombre de Dios Durango, C Mexico 23°51′N 104°14′W
42 I5 Nombre de Dios, Cordillera ▲▲ N Honduras
38 M9 Nome Alaska, USA 64°30′N 165°24′W
29 Q6 Nome North Dakota, N USA 46°39′N 97°49′W
38 M9 Nome, Cape headland Alaska, USA 64°25′N 165°00′W
162 K11 Nomgon var. Sangiyn Dalay. Ömnögovĭ, S Mongolia 42°50′N 105°04′E
14 M11 Nominingue, Lac ◎ Québec, SE Canada
Nomoi Islands see Mortlock Islands
164 B16 Nomo-zaki headland Kyūshū, SW Japan 32°34′N 129°45′E
162 G6 Nömrög var. Hödrögö. Dzavhan, N Mongolia 48°51′N 96°48′E
193 X15 Nomuka island Nomuka Group, C Tonga
193 X15 Nomuka Group island group W Tonga
189 Q15 Nomwin Atoll atoll Hall Islands, C Micronesia
8 L10 Nonacho Lake ◎ Northwest Territories, NW Canada
Nondaburi see Nonthaburi
39 P12 Nondalton Alaska, USA 59°58′N 154°51′W
163 V10 Nong'an Jilin, NE China 44°25′N 125°10′E
169 P10 Nong Bua Khok Nakhon Ratchasima, C Thailand 15°23′N 101°51′E
167 Q9 Nong Bua Lamphu Udon Thani, E Thailand 17°11′N 102°27′E
167 R7 Nông Hèt Xiangkhoang, N Laos 19°27′N 104°02′E
Nongkaya see Nong Khai
167 Q8 Nong Khai var. Mi Chai, Nongkaya. Nong Khai, E Thailand 17°52′N 102°44′E
167 N15 Nong Met Surat Thani, SW Thailand 09°27′N 99°09′E
83 L22 Nongoma KwaZulu/Natal, E South Africa 27°54′S 31°40′E
167 P9 Nong Phai Phetchabun, C Thailand 15°58′N 101°02′E
153 U13 Nongstoin Meghālaya, NE India 25°24′N 91°19′E
83 C19 Nonidas Erongo, N Namibia 22°36′S 14°40′E
Nonni see Nen Jiang
40 I7 Nonoava Chihuahua, N Mexico 27°24′N 106°18′W
191 O3 Nonouti prev. Sydenham Island. atoll Tungaru, W Kiribati
167 O11 Nonthaburi var. Nondaburi, Nontha Buri. Nonthaburi, C Thailand 13°48′N 100°11′E
Nontha Buri see Nonthaburi
102 L11 Nontron Dordogne, SW France 45°34′N 00°41′E
181 P1 Noonamah Northern Territory, N Australia 12°46′S 131°08′E
28 K2 Noonan North Dakota, N USA 48°51′N 102°57′W
Noonu see South Miladhunmadulu Atoll
99 E14 Noord-Beveland var. North Beveland. island SW Netherlands
99 J14 Noord-Brabant Eng. North Brabant. ◈ province S Netherlands
98 H7 Noorder Haaks spit NW Netherlands
98 H9 Noord-Holland Eng. North Holland. ◈ province NW Netherlands
Noordhollandsch Kanaal see Noordhollands Kanaal
98 H8 Noordhollands Kanaal var. Noordhollandsch Kanaal. canal NW Netherlands
Noord-Kaap see Northern Cape
98 L8 Noordoostpolder island N Netherlands
45 P16 Noordpunt headland Curaçao, C Netherlands Antilles 12°21′N 69°08′W
98 I8 Noord-Scharwoude Noord-Holland, NW Netherlands 52°42′N 04°48′E
Noordwes see North-West
98 G11 Noordwijk aan Zee Zuid-Holland, W Netherlands 52°15′N 04°25′E
98 H11 Noordwijkerhout Zuid-Holland, W Netherlands 52°16′N 04°30′E
98 M7 Noordwolde Fris. Noardwâlde. Friesland, N Netherlands 52°54′N 06°10′E
Noordzee see North Sea
98 H10 Noordzee-Kanaal canal NW Netherlands
93 K18 Noormarkku Swe. Norrmark. Länsi-Suomi, SW Finland 61°35′N 21°54′E
39 N8 Noorvik Alaska, USA 66°50′N 161°01′W
10 J17 Nootka Sound inlet British Columbia, W Canada
82 A9 Nóqui Dem. Rep. Congo, NW Angola 05°54′S 13°30′E
95 L15 Nora Örebro, C Sweden 59°31′N 15°02′E
147 Q13 Norak Rus. Nurek. W Tajikistan 38°23′N 69°14′E
13 I13 Noranda Québec, SE Canada 48°16′N 79°03′W
29 W12 Nora Springs Iowa, C USA 43°08′N 93°00′W
95 M14 Norberg Västmanland, C Sweden 60°04′N 15°56′E
14 K13 Norcan Lake ◎ Ontario, SE Canada
197 R12 Nord Avannaarsua, N Greenland 81°38′N 12°51′W
78 F13 Nord Eng. North. ◈ province N Cameroon
103 P2 Nord ◈ department N France
92 P1 Nordaustlandet island NE Svalbard
95 G24 Nordborg Ger. Nordburg. Sønderjylland, SW Denmark 55°04′N 09°41′E
Nordburg see Nordborg
95 F23 Nordby Ribe, W Denmark 55°27′N 08°25′E
11 P15 Nordegg Alberta, SW Canada 52°27′N 116°06′W
100 E9 Norden Niedersachsen, NW Germany 53°36′N 07°12′E
100 G10 Nordenham Niedersachsen, NW Germany 53°30′N 08°29′E
122 M6 Nordenshel'da, Arkhipelag island group N Russian Federation
92 O3 Nordenskiold Land physical region W Svalbard
100 E9 Norderney island NW Germany
100 J9 Norderstedt Schleswig-Holstein, N Germany 53°42′N 09°59′E
94 D11 Nordfjord fjord S Norway
94 C11 Nordfjord physical region S Norway
94 D11 Nordfjordeid Sogn og Fjordane, S Norway 61°54′N 06°E
92 G11 Nordfold Nordland, C Norway 67°48′N 15°16′E
Nordfriesische Inseln see North Frisian Islands
100 H7 Nordfriesland cultural region N Germany
101 K15 Nordhausen Thüringen, C Germany 51°31′N 10°48′E
25 T13 Nordheim Texas, SW USA 28°55′N 97°36′W
94 C13 Nordhordland physical region S Norway
100 E12 Nordhorn Niedersachsen, NW Germany 52°26′N 07°04′E
92 I1 Nordhurfjördhur Vestfirdhir, NW Iceland 66°01′N 21°33′W
92 J1 Nordhurland Eystra ◈ region N Iceland
92 I2 Nordhurland Vestra ◈ region N Iceland
172 H16 Nord, Île du island Inner Islands, NE Seychelles
95 F20 Nordjylland var. Nordjyllands Amt. ◈ county N Denmark
Nordjyllands Amt see Nordjylland
92 K7 Nordkapp Eng. North Cape. headland N Norway 25°47′E 71°10′N
92 O1 Nordkapp headland N Svalbard 80°31′N 19°58′E
92 L7 Nordkinn headland N Norway 71°07′N 27°40′E
79 N19 Nord-Kivu off. Région du Nord Kivu. ◈ region E Dem. Rep. Congo
Nord Kivu, Région du see Nord-Kivu
92 G12 Nordland ◈ county C Norway
101 J21 Nördlingen Bayern, S Germany 48°49′N 10°28′E
93 I16 Nordmaling Västerbotten, N Sweden 63°35′N 19°30′E
95 K15 Nordmark Värmland, C Sweden 59°52′N 14°04′E
Nord, Mer du see North Sea
94 F8 Nordmøre physical region S Norway
100 I8 Nord-Ostee-Kanal canal N Germany
0 J3 Nordøstrundingen cape NE Greenland
79 D14 Nord-Ouest Eng. North-West. ◈ province NW Cameroon
Nord-Ouest, Territoires du see Northwest Territories
103 N2 Nord-Pas-de-Calais ◈ region N France
101 F19 Nordpfälzer Bergland ▲▲ W Germany
Nord, Pointe see Fatua, Pointe
187 P16 Nord, Province ◈ province C New Caledonia
101 D14 Nordrhein-Westfalen Eng. North Rhine-Westphalia, Fr. Rhénanie du Nord-Westphalie. ◈ state W Germany
Nordsee/Nordsjøen/Nordsøen see North Sea
100 H7 Nordstrand island N Germany
93 E15 Nord-Trøndelag ◈ county C Norway
97 E19 Nore Ir. An Fheoir. ≈ S Ireland
29 Q14 Norfolk Nebraska, C USA 42°01′N 97°25′W
21 X7 Norfolk Virginia, NE USA 36°51′N 76°17′W
97 P19 Norfolk cultural region E England, United Kingdom
192 K10 Norfolk Island ◇ Australian external territory SW Pacific Ocean
175 P9 Norfolk Ridge undersea feature W Pacific Ocean
27 U8 Norfork Lake ⊠ Arkansas/Missouri, C USA
98 N6 Norg Drenthe, NE Netherlands 53°04′N 06°28′E
Norge see Norway
95 D14 Norheimsund Hordaland, S Norway 60°22′N 06°09′E
25 S16 Norias Texas, SW USA 26°47′N 97°45′W
164 L12 Norikura-dake ▲ Honshū, S Japan 36°06′N 137°33′E
122 K8 Noril'sk Taymyrskiy (Dolgano-Nenetskiy) Avtonomnyy Okrug, N Russian Federation 69°21′N 88°02′E
14 I13 Norland Ontario, SE Canada 44°46′N 78°48′W
21 V8 Norlina North Carolina, SE USA 36°26′N 78°11′W
30 L13 Normal Illinois, N USA 40°30′N 88°59′W
27 N11 Norman Oklahoma, C USA 35°13′N 97°27′W
Norman see Tulita
186 G9 Normanby Island island SE Papua New Guinea
Normandes, Îles see Channel Islands
58 G9 Normandia Roraima, N Brazil 03°57′N 59°39′W
102 L5 Normandie Eng. Normandy. cultural region N France
102 J5 Normandie, Collines de hill range NW France
Normandy see Normandie
25 V9 Normangee Texas, SW USA 31°01′N 96°06′W
21 Q10 Norman, Lake ⊠ North Carolina, SE USA
44 K13 Norman Manley ✈ (Kingston) E Jamaica 17°55′N 76°46′W
181 U5 Norman River ≈ Queensland, NE Australia
181 U4 Normanton Queensland, NE Australia 17°49′S 141°08′E
8 I8 Norman Wells Northwest Territories, NW Canada 65°18′N 126°42′W
12 H12 Normétal Québec, S Canada 48°59′N 79°23′W
163 O7 Norovlin var. Uldz. Hentiy, NE Mongolia 48°47′N 112°01′E
11 V15 Norquay Saskatchewan, S Canada 51°51′N 102°04′W
94 N11 Norra Dellen ◎ C Sweden
93 G15 Norråker Jämtland, C Sweden 64°25′N 15°40′E
94 N12 Norrala Gävleborg, C Sweden 61°22′N 17°04′E
Norra Ny see Stöllet
92 G13 Norra Storfjället ▲ N Sweden 65°57′N 15°15′E
92 I13 Norrbotten ◈ county N Sweden
95 G23 Nørre Aaby var. Nørre Åby. Fyn, C Denmark 55°28′N 09°53′E
Nørre Åby see Nørre Aaby
95 I24 Nørre Alslev Storstrøm, SE Denmark 54°54′N 11°53′E
95 E23 Nørre Nebel Ribe, W Denmark 55°45′N 08°16′E
95 G20 Nørresundby Nordjylland, N Denmark 57°05′N 09°55′E
21 N8 Norris Lake ⊠ Tennessee, S USA
18 I15 Norristown Pennsylvania, NE USA 40°07′N 75°20′W
95 N17 Norrköping Östergötland, S Sweden 58°35′N 16°10′E
Norrmark see Noormarkku
94 N13 Norrsundet Gävleborg, C Sweden 60°55′N 17°09′E
95 P15 Norrtälje Stockholm, C Sweden 59°46′N 18°42′E
180 L12 Norseman Western Australia 32°16′S 121°46′E
93 I14 Norsjö Västerbotten, N Sweden 64°55′N 19°30′E
95 G16 Norsjø ◎ S Norway
123 R13 Norsk Amurskaya Oblast', SE Russian Federation 52°20′N 129°57′E
Norske Havet see Norwegian Sea
187 Q13 Norsup Malekula, C Vanuatu 16°05′S 167°24′E
191 V15 Norte, Cabo headland Easter Island, Chile, E Pacific Ocean 27°03′S 109°24′W
54 F7 Norte de Santander off. Departamento de Norte de Santander. ◈ province N Colombia
Norte de Santander, Departamento de see Norte de Santander
61 E21 Norte, Punta headland E Argentina 36°17′S 56°46′W
21 R13 North South Carolina, SE USA 33°37′N 81°06′W
North see Nord
18 L10 North Adams Massachusetts, NE USA 42°40′N 73°06′W
113 L17 North Albanian Alps Alb. Bjeshkët e Namuna, SCr. Prokletije. ▲▲ SE Europe
97 M15 Northallerton N England, United Kingdom 54°20′N 01°26′W
180 J12 Northam Western Australia 31°40′S 116°40′E
83 J20 Northam Northern, N South Africa 24°56′S 27°18′E
1 North America continent
1 N12 North American Basin undersea feature W Sargasso Sea 30°00′N 60°00′W
0 C5 North American Plate tectonic feature
18 M11 North Amherst Massachusetts, NE USA 42°24′N 72°31′W
97 N20 Northampton C England, United Kingdom 52°14′N 00°54′W
97 M20 Northamptonshire cultural region C England, United Kingdom
151 P18 North Andaman island Andaman Islands, India, NE Indian Ocean
65 D25 North Arm East Falkland, Falkland Islands 52°06′S 59°21′W
21 Q13 North Augusta South Carolina, SE USA 33°30′N 81°58′W
173 W8 North Australian Basin Fr. Bassin Nord de l' Australie. undersea feature E Indian Ocean
31 R11 North Baltimore Ohio, N USA 41°10′N 83°40′W
11 T15 North Battleford Saskatchewan, S Canada 52°47′N 108°19′W
14 H11 North Bay Ontario, S Canada 46°20′N 79°28′W
12 H6 North Belcher Islands island group Belcher Islands, Nunavut, C Canada
29 R15 North Bend Nebraska, C USA 41°27′N 96°46′W
32 E14 North Bend Oregon, NW USA 43°24′N 124°13′W
96 K12 North Berwick SE Scotland, United Kingdom 56°04′N 02°44′W
North Beveland see Noord-Beveland
North Borneo see Sabah
183 P5 North Bourke New South Wales, SE Australia 30°03′S 145°56′E
North Brabant see Noord-Brabant
182 F2 North Branch Neales seasonal river South Australia
44 M6 North Caicos island NW Turks and Caicos Islands
26 L10 North Canadian River ≈ Oklahoma, C USA
31 U12 North Canton Ohio, N USA 40°52′N 81°24′W
13 R13 North, Cape headland Cape Breton Island, Nova Scotia, SE Canada 47°06′N 60°24′W
184 I1 North Cape headland North Island, New Zealand 34°23′S 173°02′E
186 G5 North Cape headland New Ireland, NE Papua New Guinea 02°33′S 150°48′E
North Cape see Nordkapp
18 J17 North Cape May New Jersey, NE USA 38°59′N 74°55′W
12 C9 North Caribou Lake ◎ Ontario, C Canada
21 U10 North Carolina off. State of North Carolina, also known as Old North State, Tar Heel State, Turpentine State. ◈ state SE USA
North Celebes see Sulawesi Utara
155 J24 North Central ◈ province N Sri Lanka
31 S4 North Channel lake channel Canada/USA
97 G14 North Channel strait Northern Ireland/Scotland, United Kingdom
21 S14 North Charleston South Carolina, SE USA 32°53′N 79°59′W
31 N10 North Chicago Illinois, N USA 42°19′N 87°50′W
195 Y10 Northcliffe Glacier glacier Antarctica
31 Q14 North College Hill Ohio, N USA 39°13′N 84°33′W
25 O8 North Concho River ≈ Texas, SW USA
19 O8 North Conway New Hampshire, NE USA 44°03′N 71°06′W
27 V14 North Crossett Arkansas, C USA 33°10′N 91°56′W
28 L4 North Dakota off. State of North Dakota, also known as Flickertail State, Peace Garden State, Sioux State. ◈ state N USA
North Devon Island see Devon Island
97 O22 North Downs hill range SE England, United Kingdom
18 C11 North East Pennsylvania, NE USA 42°13′N 79°49′W
83 I18 North East ◈ district NE Botswana
65 G15 North East Bay bay Ascension Island, C Atlantic Ocean
38 L10 Northeast Cape headland Saint Lawrence Island, Alaska, USA 63°16′N 168°50′W
81 J17 North Eastern ◈ province Kenya
North East Frontier Agency/North East Frontier Agency of Assam see Arunāchal Pradesh
189 V11 Northeast Island island Chuuk, C Micronesia
44 L6 Northeast Point headland Great Inagua, S Bahamas 21°18′N 73°01′W
44 K5 Northeast Point headland Acklins Island, SE Bahamas 22°43′N 73°50′W
44 L12 North East Point headland E Jamaica 18°09′N 76°19′W
191 Z2 Northeast Point headland Kiritimati, E Kiribati 10°23′S 105°45′E
44 H2 Northeast Providence Channel channel N Bahamas
101 J14 Northeim Niedersachsen, C Germany 51°42′N 10°E
29 X14 North English Iowa, C USA 41°30′N 92°04′W
138 G8 Northern ◈ district N Israel
82 M12 Northern ◈ region N Malawi
186 F8 Northern ◈ province S Papua New Guinea
155 J23 Northern ◈ province N Sri Lanka
80 D7 Northern ◈ state N Sudan
82 K12 Northern ◈ province NE Zambia
Northern see Limpopo
80 B13 Northern Bahr el Ghazal ◈ state SW Sudan
Northern Border Region see Al Ḥudūd ash Shamālīyah
83 F24 Northern Cape off. Northern Cape Province, Afr. Noord-Kaap. ◈ province W South Africa
Northern Cape Province see Northern Cape
190 K14 Northern Cook Islands island group N Cook Islands
80 B8 Northern Darfur ◈ state NW Sudan
Northern Dvina see Severnaya Dvina
97 F14 Northern Ireland var. The Six Counties. cultural region Northern Ireland, United Kingdom
97 F14 Northern Ireland var. The Six Counties. ◈ political division Northern Ireland, United Kingdom
80 D9 Northern Kordofan ◈ state C Sudan
187 Z14 Northern Lau Group island group Lau Group, NE Fiji
188 K3 Northern Mariana Islands ◇ US commonwealth territory W Pacific Ocean
Northern Rhodesia see Zambia
Northern Sporades see Vóreies Sporádes
182 D1 Northern Territory ◈ territory N Australia
Northern Transvaal see Limpopo
Northern Ural Hills see Severnyye Uvaly
84 I9 North European Plain plain N Europe
27 V2 North Fabius River ≈ Missouri, C USA
65 D24 North Falkland Sound sound N Falkland Islands
29 V9 Northfield Minnesota, N USA 44°27′N 93°10′W
19 O9 Northfield New Hampshire, NE USA 43°26′N 71°34′W
175 Q8 North Fiji Basin undersea feature N Coral Sea
97 Q22 North Foreland headland SE England, United Kingdom 51°22′N 01°26′E
35 P6 North Fork American River ≈ California, W USA
39 R7 North Fork Chandalar River ≈ Alaska, USA
28 K7 North Fork Grand River ≈ North Dakota/South Dakota, N USA
21 O6 North Fork Kentucky River ≈ Kentucky, S USA
39 Q7 North Fork Koyukuk River ≈ Alaska, USA
39 Q10 North Fork Kuskokwim River ≈ Alaska, USA
26 K11 North Fork Red River ≈ Oklahoma/Texas, SW USA
26 K3 North Fork Solomon River ≈ Kansas, C USA
23 W14 North Fort Myers Florida, SE USA 26°40′N 81°52′W
31 P5 North Fox Island island Michigan, N USA
100 G6 North Frisian Islands var. Nordfriesische Inseln. island group N Germany
197 N9 North Geomagnetic Pole pole Arctic Ocean
18 M13 North Haven Connecticut, NE USA 41°25′N 72°51′W
184 J5 North Head headland North Island, New Zealand 36°23′S 174°01′E
18 L6 North Hero Vermont, NE USA 44°49′N 73°14′W
35 O7 North Highlands California, W USA 38°40′N 121°25′W
North Holland see Noord-Holland
81 I16 North Horr Eastern, N Kenya 03°17′N 37°08′E
151 K21 North Huvadhu Atoll var. Gaafu Alifu Atoll. atoll S Maldives
184 N9 North Island island N New Zealand
21 U14 North Island island South Carolina, SE USA
31 O11 North Judson Indiana, N USA 41°12′N 86°44′W
North Kazakhstan see Severnyy Kazakhstan
31 V10 North Kingsville Ohio, N USA 41°54′N 80°41′W
163 Y13 North Korea off. Democratic People's Republic of Korea, Kor. Chosŏn-minjujuŭi-inmin-kanghwaguk. ◆ republic E Asia
153 X11 North Lakhimpur Assam, NE India 27°10′N 94°00′E
184 J3 Northland off. Northland Region. ◈ region North Island, New Zealand
192 K11 Northland Plateau undersea feature S Pacific Ocean
Northland Region see Northland
35 X11 North Las Vegas Nevada, W USA 36°12′N 115°07′W
31 O11 North Liberty Indiana, N USA 41°36′N 86°22′W
29 X14 North Liberty Iowa, C USA 41°45′N 91°36′W
27 V12 North Little Rock Arkansas, C USA 34°46′N 92°15′W
28 M13 North Loup River ≈ Nebraska, C USA
151 K18 North Maalhosmadulu Atoll var. North Malosmadulu Atoll, Raa Atoll. atoll N Maldives
31 U10 North Madison Ohio, N USA 41°48′N 81°03′W
North Malosmadulu Atoll see North Maalhosmadulu Atoll
31 P12 North Manchester Indiana, N USA 41°00′N 85°45′W
31 P6 North Manitou Island island Michigan, N USA
29 U10 North Mankato Minnesota, N USA 44°11′N 94°03′W
23 Z15 North Miami Florida, SE USA 25°54′N 80°11′W
151 K18 North Miladhunmadulu Atoll var. Shaviyani Atoll. atoll N Maldives
North Minch see Minch, The
23 W15 North Naples Florida, SE USA 26°13′N 81°47′W
175 P8 North New Hebrides Trench undersea feature N Coral Sea
23 Y15 North New River Canal ≈ Florida, SE USA
151 K20 North Nilandhe Atoll atoll C Maldives
36 L2 North Ogden Utah, W USA 41°18′N 111°57′W
North Ossetia see Severnaya Osetiya-Alaniya, Respublika
35 S10 North Palisade ▲ California, W USA 37°06′N 118°31′W
189 U11 North Pass passage Chuuk Islands, C Micronesia
28 M15 North Platte Nebraska, C USA 41°07′N 100°46′W
33 X17 North Platte River ≈ C USA
65 G14 North Point headland Ascension Island, C Atlantic Ocean
172 I16 North Point headland Mahé, NE Seychelles 04°23′S 55°28′E
31 R5 North Point headland Michigan, N USA 45°21′N 83°30′W
31 S6 North Point headland Michigan, N USA 45°01′N 83°16′W
39 S9 North Pole Alaska, USA 64°42′N 147°09′W
197 R9 North Pole pole Arctic Ocean
23 O4 Northport Alabama, S USA 33°13′N 87°34′W
23 W14 North Port Florida, SE USA 27°03′N 82°15′W
32 L6 Northport Washington, NW USA 48°54′N 117°48′W
32 L12 North Powder Oregon, NW USA 45°00′N 117°56′W
29 U13 North Raccoon River ≈ Iowa, C USA
North Rhine-Westphalia see Nordrhein-Westfalen
97 M16 North Riding cultural region N England, United Kingdom
96 G5 North Rona island NW Scotland, United Kingdom
96 K4 North Ronaldsay island NE Scotland, United Kingdom
36 L2 North Salt Lake Utah, W USA 40°51′N 111°54′W
11 P15 North Saskatchewan ≈ Alberta/Saskatchewan, S Canada
35 X5 North Schell Peak ▲ Nevada, W USA 39°25′N 114°34′W
North Scotia Ridge see South Georgia Ridge
86 D10 North Sea Dan. Nordsøen, Dut. Noordzee, Fr. Mer du Nord, Ger. Nordsee, Nor. Nordsjøen; prev. German Ocean, Lat. Mare Germanicum. sea NW Europe
35 T6 North Shoshone Peak ▲ Nevada, W USA 39°08′N 117°28′W
North Siberian Lowland/North Siberian Plain see Severo-Sibirskaya Nizmennost'
29 R13 North Sioux City South Dakota, N USA 42°31′N 96°28′W
96 K4 North Sound, The sound N Scotland, United Kingdom
183 T4 North Star New South Wales, SE Australia 28°55′S 150°25′E
North Star State see Minnesota
183 V3 North Stradbroke Island island Queensland, E Australia
North Sulawesi see Sulawesi Utara
North Sumatra see Sumatera Utara
14 D17 North Sydenham ≈ Ontario, S Canada
18 H9 North Syracuse New York, NE USA 43°07′N 76°07′W
184 K9 North Taranaki Bight gulf North Island, New Zealand
12 H9 North Twin Island island Nunavut, C Canada
96 E8 North Uist island NW Scotland, United Kingdom
97 L14 Northumberland cultural region N England, United Kingdom
181 Y7 Northumberland Isles island group Queensland, NE Australia
13 Q14 Northumberland Strait strait SE Canada
32 G14 North Umpqua River ≈ Oregon, NW USA
45 Q13 North Union Saint Vincent, Saint Vincent and the Grenadines 13°15′N 61°07′W
10 L17 North Vancouver British Columbia, SW Canada 49°21′N 123°05′W
18 K9 Northville New York, NE USA 43°13′N 74°08′W
97 Q19 North Walsham E England, United Kingdom 52°49′N 01°22′E
39 T10 Northway Alaska, USA 62°57′N 141°56′W
149 R7 North Wazīristān ◈ federally administered tribal area NW Pakistan
83 G17 North-West ◈ district NW Botswana
83 G21 North-West off. North-West Province, Afr. Noordwes. ◈ province N South Africa
North-West see Nord-Ouest
64 I6 Northwest Atlantic Mid-Ocean Canyon undersea feature N Atlantic Ocean
180 G8 North West Cape cape Western Australia
38 J9 Northwest Cape headland Saint Lawrence Island, Alaska, USA 63°46′N 171°45′W
155 J24 North Western ◈ province W Sri Lanka
82 H13 North Western ◈ province W Zambia
149 U4 North-West Frontier Province ◈ province NW Pakistan
96 H8 North West Highlands ▲▲ N Scotland, United Kingdom
192 J4 Northwest Pacific Basin undersea feature NW Pacific Ocean 40°00′N 150°00′E
191 Y2 Northwest Point headland Kiritimati, E Kiribati 10°25′S 105°35′E
44 G1 Northwest Providence Channel channel N Bahamas
North-West Province see North-West
13 Q8 North West River Newfoundland and Labrador, E Canada 53°30′N 60°10′W
8 J9 Northwest Territories Fr. Territoires du Nord-Ouest. ◈ territory NW Canada
97 K18 Northwich C England, United Kingdom 53°16′N 02°32′W
25 Q5 North Wichita River ≈ Texas, SW USA
18 J17 North Wildwood New Jersey, NE USA 39°00′N 74°45′W
21 R9 North Wilkesboro North Carolina, SE USA 36°09′N 81°09′W
19 P8 North Windham Maine, NE USA 43°51′N 70°25′W
197 Q6 Northwind Plain undersea feature Arctic Ocean
29 V11 Northwood Iowa, C USA 43°26′N 93°13′W
29 Q4 Northwood North Dakota, N USA 47°43′N 97°34′W
97 M15 North York Moors moorland N England, United Kingdom
25 V9 North Zulch Texas, SW USA 30°54′N 96°06′W
26 K2 Norton Kansas, C USA 39°51′N 99°53′W
31 S13 Norton Ohio, N USA 40°25′N 83°04′W
21 P7 Norton Virginia, NE USA 36°56′N 82°37′W
39 N9 Norton Bay bay Alaska, USA
Norton de Matos see Balombo
31 O9 Norton Shores Michigan, N USA 43°10′N 86°15′W
38 M10 Norton Sound inlet Alaska, USA
27 Q3 Nortonville Kansas, C USA 39°25′N 95°19′W
102 I8 Nort-sur-Erdre Loire-Atlantique, NW France 47°27′N 01°30′W
195 N2 Norvegia, Cape headland Antarctica 71°16′S 12°25′W
18 L13 Norwalk Connecticut, NE USA 41°08′N 73°28′W
29 V14 Norwalk Iowa, C USA 41°28′N 93°40′W
31 S11 Norwalk Ohio, N USA 41°14′N 82°37′W
19 P7 Norway Maine, NE USA 44°13′N 70°30′W
31 N5 Norway Michigan, N USA 45°47′N 87°54′W
93 E17 Norway off. Kingdom of Norway, Nor. Norge. ◆ monarchy N Europe
11 X13 Norway House Manitoba, C Canada 53°59′N 97°50′W
Norway, Kingdom of see Norway
197 R16 Norwegian Basin undersea feature NW Norwegian Sea 68°00′N 02°00′W
84 D6 Norwegian Sea var. Norske Havet. sea NE Atlantic Ocean
197 S17 Norwegian Trench undersea feature NE North Sea 59°00′N 04°30′E
14 F16 Norwich Ontario, S Canada 42°57′N 80°37′W
97 Q19 Norwich E England, United Kingdom 52°38′N 01°18′E
19 N13 Norwich Connecticut, NE USA 41°30′N 72°02′W
18 I11 Norwich New York, NE USA 42°31′N 75°31′W
29 U9 Norwood Minnesota, N USA 44°46′N 93°55′W
31 Q15 Norwood Ohio, N USA 39°07′N 84°27′W
14 H11 Nosbonsing, Lake ◎ Ontario, S Canada
Nösen see Bistriţa
165 T1 Noshappu-misaki headland Hokkaidō, NE Japan 45°26′N 141°38′E
165 P7 Noshiro var. Nosiro; prev. Noshirominato. Akita, Honshū, C Japan 40°11′N 140°02′E
Noshirominato/Nosiro see Noshiro
117 Q3 Nosivka Rus. Nosovka. Chernihivs'ka Oblast', NE Ukraine 50°55′N 31°37′E
67 T14 Nosop var. Nossob, Nossop. ≈ Botswana/Namibia
83 E20 Nossop ≈ E Namibia
125 S4 Nosovaya Nenetskiy Avtonomnyy Okrug, NW Russian Federation 68°12′N 54°33′E
Nosovka see Nosivka
143 V11 Nosratābād Sīstān va Balūchestān, E Iran 29°53′N 59°57′E
95 J18 Nossebro Västra Götaland, S Sweden 58°12′N 12°42′E
96 K6 Noss Head headland N Scotland, United Kingdom 58°29′N 03°03′W
Nossi-Bé see Be, Nosy
81 E20 Nossob ≈ Namibia
Nossob/Nossop see Nosop
172 J2 Nosy Be ✈ Antsirānana, N Madagascar 23°36′S 47°36′E
172 J6 Nosy Varika Fianarantsoa, SE Madagascar 20°36′S 48°31′E
14 L10 Notawassi ≈ Québec, SE Canada
14 M9 Notawassi, Lac ◎ Québec, SE Canada
36 J5 Notch Peak ▲ Utah, W USA 39°08′N 113°24′W
110 G10 Noteć Ger. Netze. ≈ NW Poland
Nóties Sporádes see Dodekánisa
115 J22 Nótion Aigaíon Eng. Aegean South. ◈ region E Greece
115 H18 Nótios Evvoïkós Kólpos gulf E Greece
115 B16 Nótio Stenó Kérkyras strait W Greece
107 L25 Noto anc. Netum. Sicilia, Italy, C Mediterranean Sea 36°53′N 15°05′E
164 M10 Noto Ishikawa, Honshū, SW Japan 37°18′N 137°11′E
95 G15 Notodden Telemark, S Norway 59°35′N 09°18′E
107 L25 Noto, Golfo di gulf Sicilia, Italy, C Mediterranean Sea
164 L10 Noto-hantō peninsula Honshū, SW Japan
164 L11 Noto-jima island SW Japan
13 T11 Notre Dame Bay bay Newfoundland, Newfoundland and Labrador, E Canada
15 P6 Notre-Dame-de-Lorette Québec, SE Canada 49°05′N 72°24′W
14 L11 Notre-Dame-de-Pontmain Québec, SE Canada 46°18′N 75°37′W
15 T8 Notre-Dame-du-Lac Québec, SE Canada 47°36′N 68°48′W

◆ Country ● Country Capital ◇ Dependent Territory ○ Dependent Territory Capital ◈ Administrative Regions ✈ International Airport ▲ Mountain ▲▲ Mountain Range ☌ Volcano ≈ River ◎ Lake ⊠ Reservoir

15 Q6 **Notre-Dame-du-Rosaire** Québec, SE Canada *48°48′N 71°27′W*
15 U8 **Notre-Dame, Monts** ▲▲ Québec, S Canada
77 R16 **Notsé** S Togo *06°59′N 01°12′E*
14 G14 **Nottawasaga** ≈ Ontario, S Canada
14 G14 **Nottawasaga Bay** *lake bay* Ontario, S Canada
12 I11 **Nottaway** ≈ Québec, SE Canada
23 S1 **Nottely Lake** ▣ Georgia, SE USA
95 H16 **Nøtterøy** *island* S Norway
97 M19 **Nottingham** C England, United Kingdom *52°58′N 01°10′W*
9 E14 **Nottingham Island** *island* Nunavut, NE Canada
97 N18 **Nottinghamshire** *cultural region* C England, United Kingdom
21 V7 **Nottoway** Virginia, NE USA *37°07′N 78°03′W*
21 V7 **Nottoway River** ≈ Virginia, NE USA
76 G7 **Nouâdhibou** *prev.* Port-Étienne. Dakhlet Nouâdhibou, W Mauritania *20°54′N 17°01′W*
76 G7 **Nouâdhibou** ✈ Dakhlet Nouâdhibou, W Mauritania *20°59′N 17°02′W*
76 F7 **Nouâdhibou, Dakhlet** *prev.* Baie du Lévrier. *bay* W Mauritania
76 F7 **Nouâdhibou, Râs** *prev.* Cap Blanc. *headland* NW Mauritania *20°48′N 17°03′W*
76 G9 **Nouakchott** ● (Mauritania) Nouakchott District, SW Mauritania *18°09′N 15°58′W*
76 G9 **Nouakchott** ✈ Trarza, SW Mauritania *18°18′N 15°54′W*
120 J11 **Noual, Sebkhet en** *var.* Sabkhat an Nawāl. *salt flat* C Tunisia
76 G8 **Nouâmghâr** *var.* Nouamrhar. Dakhlet Nouâdhibou, W Mauritania *19°22′N 16°31′W*
Nouamrhar *see* Nouâmghâr
Nouă Sulița *see* Novoselytsya
187 Q17 **Nouméa** ○ (New Caledonia) Province Sud, S New Caledonia *22°13′S 166°29′E*
79 E15 **Noun** ≈ C Cameroon
77 N12 **Nouna** W Burkina *12°44′N 03°54′W*
83 H24 **Noupoort** Northern Cape, C South Africa *31°11′S 24°57′E*
Nouveau-Brunswick *see* New Brunswick
Nouveau-Comptoir *see* Wemindji
15 T4 **Nouvel, Lacs** ◎ Québec, SE Canada
15 W7 **Nouvelle** Québec, SE Canada *48°07′N 66°16′W*
15 W7 **Nouvelle** ≈ Québec, SE Canada
Nouvelle-Calédonie *see* New Caledonia
Nouvelle Écosse *see* Nova Scotia
103 R3 **Nouzonville** Ardennes, N France *49°49′N 04°45′E*
147 Q11 **Nov** *Rus.* Nau. NW Tajikistan *40°10′N 69°16′E*
59 I21 **Nova Alvorada** Mato Grosso do Sul, SW Brazil *21°25′S 54°19′W*
Novabad *see* Navobod
111 D19 **Nová Bystřice** *Ger.* Neubistritz. Jihočeský Kraj, S Czech Republic *49°N 15°05′E*
116 H13 **Novaci** Gorj, SW Romania *45°07′N 23°37′E*
Nova Civitas *see* Neustadt an der Weinstrasse
Novaesium *see* Neuss
60 H10 **Nova Esperança** Paraná, S Brazil *23°09′S 52°13′W*
106 H11 **Novafeltria** Marche, C Italy *43°54′N 12°18′E*
60 Q9 **Nova Friburgo** Rio de Janeiro, SE Brazil *22°16′S 42°34′W*
82 D12 **Nova Gaia** *var.* Cambundi-Catembo. Malanje, NE Angola *10°09′S 17°31′E*
109 S12 **Nova Gorica** W Slovenia *45°57′N 13°40′E*
112 G10 **Nova Gradiška** *Ger.* Neugradisk, *Hung.* Újgradiska. Brod-Posavina, NE Croatia *45°15′N 17°23′E*
60 K7 **Nova Granada** São Paulo, S Brazil *20°33′S 49°19′W*
60 O10 **Nova Iguaçu** Rio de Janeiro, SE Brazil *22°31′S 44°05′W*
117 S10 **Nova Kakhovka** *Rus.* Novaya Kakhovka. Khersons'ka Oblast', SE Ukraine *46°45′N 33°20′E*
Nová Karvinná *see* Karviná
Nova Lamego *see* Gabú
Nova Lisboa *see* Huambo
112 C11 **Novalja** Lika-Senj, W Croatia *44°33′N 14°53′E*
119 M14 **Novalukoml'** *Rus.* Novolukoml'. Vitsyebskaya Voblasts', N Belarus *54°40′N 29°09′E*
Nova Mambone *see* Mambone
83 P16 **Nova Nabúri** Zambézia, NE Mozambique *16°47′S 38°55′E*
117 Q9 **Nova Odesa** *var.* Novaya Odessa. Mykolayivs'ka Oblast', S Ukraine *47°19′N 31°45′E*
60 H10 **Nova Olímpia** Paraná, S Brazil *23°28′S 53°12′W*
61 I15 **Nova Prata** Rio Grande do Sul, S Brazil *28°45′S 51°37′W*
14 H12 **Novar** Ontario, S Canada *45°26′N 79°14′W*
106 C7 **Novara** *anc.* Novaria. Piemonte, NW Italy *45°27′N 08°36′E*
Novaria *see* Novara
117 P7 **Novarkanels'k** Kirovohrads'ka Oblast', C Ukraine *48°39′N 30°48′E*
13 P15 **Nova Scotia** *Fr.* Nouvelle Écosse. ◈ *province* SE Canada
0 M9 **Nova Scotia** *physical region* SE Canada
34 M8 **Novato** California, W USA *38°06′N 122°35′W*
192 M7 **Nova Trough** *undersea feature* W Pacific Ocean
116 L7 **Nova Ushtsya** Khmel'nyts'ka Oblast', W Ukraine *48°50′N 27°16′E*
83 M17 **Nova Vanduzi** Manica, C Mozambique *18°54′S 33°18′E*
117 U5 **Nova Vodolaha** *Rus.* Novaya Vodolaga. Kharkivs'ka Oblast', E Ukraine *49°43′N 35°49′E*
123 O12 **Novaya Chara** Chitinskaya Oblast', S Russian Federation *56°45′N 117°58′E*
122 M12 **Novaya Igirma** Irkutskaya Oblast', C Russian Federation *57°08′N 103°52′E*
Novaya Kakhovka *see* Nova Kakhovka
144 E10 **Novaya Kazanka** Zapadnyy Kazakhstan, W Kazakhstan *48°57′N 49°34′E*
124 I12 **Novaya Ladoga** Leningradskaya Oblast', NW Russian Federation *60°03′N 32°15′E*
127 R5 **Novaya Malykla** Ul'yanovskaya Oblast', W Russian Federation *54°13′N 49°55′E*
Novaya Odessa *see* Nova Odesa
123 Q5 **Novaya Sibir', Ostrov** *island* Novosibirskiye Ostrova, NE Russian Federation
Novaya Vodolaga *see* Nova Vodolaha
119 P17 **Novaya Yel'nya** Mahilyowskaya Voblasts', E Belarus *53°16′N 31°14′E*
122 I6 **Novaya Zemlya** *island group* N Russian Federation
Novaya Zemlya Trough *see* East Novaya Zemlya Trough
114 K10 **Nova Zagora** Sliven, C Bulgaria *42°29′N 26°00′E*
105 S12 **Novelda** País Valenciano, E Spain *38°24′N 00°45′W*
111 H19 **Nové Mesto nad Váhom** *Ger.* Waagneustadtl, *Hung.* Vágújhely. Trenčiansky Kraj, W Slovakia *48°46′N 17°50′E*
111 F17 **Nové Město na Moravě** *Ger.* Neustadtl in Mähren. Vysočina, C Czech Republic *49°34′N 16°05′E*
Novesium *see* Neuss
111 I21 **Nové Zámky** *Ger.* Neuhäusel, *Hung.* Érsekújvár. Nitriansky Kraj, SW Slovakia *49°00′N 18°10′E*
Novgorod *see* Velikiy Novgorod
Novgorod-Severskiy *see* Novhorod-Sivers'kyy
122 C7 **Novgorodskaya Oblast'** ◈ *province* W Russian Federation
117 R8 **Novhorodka** Kirovohrads'ka Oblast', C Ukraine *48°21′N 32°38′E*
117 R2 **Novhorod-Sivers'kyy** *Rus.* Novgorod-Severskiy. Chernihivs'ka Oblast', NE Ukraine *52°00′N 33°15′E*
31 R10 **Novi** Michigan, N USA *42°28′N 83°28′W*
Novi *see* Novi Vinodolski
112 L9 **Novi Bečej** *prev.* Új-Becse, Vološinovo, *Ger.* Neubetsche, *Hung.* Törökbecse. Vojvodina, N Serbia *45°36′N 20°09′E*
116 M3 **Novi Bilokorovychi** *Rus.* Belokorovichi. Zhytomyrs'ka Oblast', N Ukraine *51°07′N 28°02′E*
25 Q8 **Novice** Texas, SW USA *32°00′N 99°38′W*
112 A9 **Novigrad** Istra, NW Croatia *45°19′N 13°33′E*
Novi Grad *see* Bosanski Novi
114 G9 **Novi Iskŭr** Sofiya-Grad, W Bulgaria *42°46′N 23°19′E*
106 C9 **Novi Ligure** Piemonte, NW Italy *44°46′N 08°47′E*
99 L22 **Noville** Luxembourg, SE Belgium *50°04′N 05°46′E*
194 I10 **Noville Peninsula** *peninsula* Thurston Island, Antarctica
Noviodunum *see* Soissons, Aisne, France
Noviodunum *see* Nevers, Nièvre, France
Noviodunum *see* Nyon, Vaud, Switzerland
Noviomagus *see* Lisieux, Calvados, France
Noviomagus *see* Nijmegen, Netherlands
114 M8 **Novi Pazar** Shumen, NE Bulgaria *43°20′N 27°12′E*
113 M15 **Novi Pazar** *Turk.* Yenipazar. Serbia, S Serbia *43°09′N 20°31′E*
112 K10 **Novi Sad** *Ger.* Neusatz, *Hung.* Újvidék. Vojvodina, N Serbia *45°16′N 19°49′E*
117 T6 **Novi Sanzhary** Poltavs'ka Oblast', C Ukraine *49°21′N 34°18′E*
112 H12 **Novi Travnik** *prev.* Pučarevo. Federacija Bosna I Hercegovina, C Bosnia and Herzegovina *44°12′N 17°39′E*
112 B10 **Novi Vinodolski** *var.* Novi. Primorje-Gorski Kotar, NW Croatia *45°08′N 14°46′E*
58 F12 **Novo Airão** Amazonas, N Brazil *02°06′S 61°20′W*
Novoalekseyevka *see* Khobda
127 N9 **Novoanninskiy** Volgogradskaya Oblast', SW Russian Federation *50°31′N 42°43′E*
58 F13 **Novo Aripuanã** Amazonas, N Brazil *05°05′S 60°20′W*
117 Y6 **Novoaydar** Luhans'ka Oblast', E Ukraine *49°00′N 39°00′E*
117 X9 **Novoazovs'k** *Rus.* Novoazovsk. Donets'ka Oblast', E Ukraine *47°07′N 38°06′E*
123 R14 **Novobureyskiy** Amurskaya Oblast', SE Russian Federation *49°42′N 129°46′E*
127 Q3 **Novocheboksarsk** Chuvashskaya Respublika, W Russian Federation *56°07′N 47°33′E*
127 R5 **Novocheremshansk** Ul'yanovskaya Oblast', W Russian Federation *54°23′N 50°08′E*
126 L12 **Novocherkassk** Rostovskaya Oblast', SW Russian Federation *47°23′N 40°E*
127 R6 **Novodevich'ye** Samarskaya Oblast', W Russian Federation *53°33′N 48°51′E*
124 M8 **Novodvinsk** Arkhangel'skaya Oblast', NW Russian Federation *64°22′N 40°49′E*
Novograd-Volynskiy *see* Novohrad-Volyns'kyy
Novogrudok *see* Navahrudak
61 I15 **Novo Hamburgo** Rio Grande do Sul, S Brazil *29°42′S 51°07′W*
59 H16 **Novo Horizonte** Mato Grosso, W Brazil *11°19′S 57°11′W*
60 K8 **Novo Horizonte** São Paulo, S Brazil *21°27′S 49°14′W*
116 M4 **Novohrad-Volyns'kyy** *Rus.* Novograd-Volynskiy. Zhytomyrs'ka Oblast', N Ukraine *50°34′N 27°32′E*
145 O7 **Novoishimskiy** *prev.* Kuybyshevskiy. Severnyy Kazakhstan, N Kazakhstan *53°15′N 66°51′E*
Novokazalinsk *see* Ayteke Bi
126 M8 **Novokhopersk** Voronezhskaya Oblast', W Russian Federation *51°09′N 41°34′E*
127 R6 **Novokuybyshevsk** Samarskaya Oblast', W Russian Federation *53°06′N 49°56′E*
122 J13 **Novokuznetsk** *prev.* Stalinsk. Kemerovskaya Oblast', S Russian Federation *53°45′N 87°12′E*
195 R1 **Novolazarevskaya** *Russian research station* Antarctica *70°42′S 11°31′E*
Novolukoml' *see* Novalukoml'
109 V12 **Novo mesto** *Ger.* Rudolfswert; *prev. Ger.* Neustadtl. SE Slovenia *45°49′N 15°09′E*
126 K15 **Novomikhaylovskiy** Krasnodarskiy Kray, SW Russian Federation *44°18′N 38°49′E*
112 L8 **Novo Miloševo** Vojvodina, N Serbia *45°43′N 20°20′E*
Novomirgorod *see* Novomyrhorod
126 L5 **Novomoskovsk** Tul'skaya Oblast', W Russian Federation *54°05′N 38°23′E*
117 U7 **Novomoskovs'k** *Rus.* Novomoskovsk. Dnipropetrovs'ka Oblast', E Ukraine *48°38′N 35°15′E*
117 V8 **Novomykolayivka** Zaporiz'ka Oblast', SE Ukraine *47°58′N 35°54′E*
117 Q7 **Novomyrhorod** *Rus.* Novomirgorod. Kirovohrads'ka Oblast', S Ukraine *48°46′N 31°39′E*
127 N8 **Novonikolayevskiy** Volgogradskaya Oblast', SW Russian Federation *50°55′N 42°24′E*
127 P10 **Novonikol'skoye** Volgogradskaya Oblast', SW Russian Federation *49°23′N 45°06′E*
127 X7 **Novoorsk** Orenburgskaya Oblast', W Russian Federation *51°21′N 59°03′E*
126 M13 **Novopokrovskaya** Krasnodarskiy Kray, SW Russian Federation *45°58′N 40°43′E*
Novopolotsk *see* Navapolatsk
117 Y5 **Novopskov** Luhans'ka Oblast', E Ukraine *49°33′N 39°07′E*
Novoradomsk *see* Radomsko
Novo Redondo *see* Sumbe
127 R8 **Novorepnoye** Saratovskaya Oblast', W Russian Federation *51°04′N 48°34′E*
126 K14 **Novorossiysk** Krasnodarskiy Kray, SW Russian Federation *44°50′N 37°38′E*
Novorossiyskiy/ Novorossiyskoye *see* Akzhar
124 F15 **Novorzhev** Pskovskaya Oblast', W Russian Federation *57°01′N 29°19′E*
Novoselitsa *see* Novoselytsya
117 S12 **Novoselivs'ke** Respublika Krym, S Ukraine *45°26′N 33°37′E*
Novosëlki *see* Navasyolki
114 G6 **Novo Selo** Vidin, NW Bulgaria *44°08′N 22°48′E*
113 M14 **Novo Selo** Serbia, C Serbia *43°39′N 20°54′E*
116 K8 **Novoselytsya** *Rom.* Nouă Sulița, *Rus.* Novoselitsa. Chernivets'ka Oblast', W Ukraine *48°14′N 26°18′E*
127 U7 **Novosergiyevka** Orenburgskaya Oblast', W Russian Federation *52°04′N 53°40′E*
126 L11 **Novoshakhtinsk** Rostovskaya Oblast', SW Russian Federation *47°48′N 39°51′E*
122 J12 **Novosibirsk** Novosibirskaya Oblast', C Russian Federation *55°04′N 83°05′E*
122 J12 **Novosibirskaya Oblast'** ◈ *province* C Russian Federation
122 M4 **Novosibirskiye Ostrova** *Eng.* New Siberian Islands. *island group* N Russian Federation
126 K6 **Novosil'** Orlovskaya Oblast', W Russian Federation *53°00′N 37°59′E*
124 G16 **Novosokol'niki** Pskovskaya Oblast', W Russian Federation *56°21′N 30°07′E*
127 Q6 **Novospasskoye** Ul'yanovskaya Oblast', W Russian Federation *53°08′N 47°48′E*
Novotroickoje *see* Brlik
127 X8 **Novotroitsk** Orenburgskaya Oblast', W Russian Federation *51°10′N 58°18′E*
Novotroitskoye *see* Brlik, Kazakhstan
Novotroitskoye *see* Novotroyits'ke, Ukraine
117 T11 **Novotroyits'ke** *Rus.* Novotroitskoye. Khersons'ka Oblast', S Ukraine *46°21′N 34°21′E*
Novoukrainka *see* Novoukrayinka
117 Q8 **Novoukrayinka** *Rus.* Novoukrainka. Kirovohrads'ka Oblast', C Ukraine *48°19′N 31°33′E*
127 Q5 **Novoul'yanovsk** Ul'yanovskaya Oblast', W Russian Federation *54°10′N 48°19′E*
127 W8 **Novoural'sk** Orenburgskaya Oblast', W Russian Federation *51°19′N 56°57′E*
Novo-Urgench *see* Urganch
127 Q9 **Novouzensk** Saratovskaya Oblast', W Russian Federation *50°28′N 48°07′E*
116 I4 **Novovolyns'k** *Rus.* Novovolynsk. Volyns'ka Oblast', NW Ukraine *50°46′N 24°09′E*
117 S9 **Novovorontsovka** Khersons'ka Oblast', S Ukraine *47°28′N 33°55′E*
147 Y7 **Novovoznesenovka** Issyk-Kul'skaya Oblast', E Kyrgyzstan *42°36′N 78°44′E*
125 R14 **Novovyatsk** Kirovskaya Oblast', NW Russian Federation *58°30′N 49°42′E*
Novoyel'nya *see* Navayel'nya
117 O6 **Novozhyvotiv** Vinnyts'ka Oblast', C Ukraine *49°16′N 29°31′E*
126 H6 **Novozybkov** Bryanskaya Oblast', W Russian Federation *52°36′N 31°58′E*
112 F9 **Novska** Sisak-Moslavina, NE Croatia *45°20′N 16°58′E*
Nový Bohumín *see* Bohumín
111 D15 **Nový Bor** *Ger.* Haida; *prev.* Bor u České Lípy, Hajda. Liberecký Kraj, N Czech Republic *50°46′N 14°32′E*
111 E16 **Nový Bydžov** *Ger.* Neubidschow. Královéhradecký Kraj, N Czech Republic *50°15′N 15°27′E*
119 G18 **Novy Dvor** *Rus.* Novyy Dvor. Hrodzyenskaya Voblasts', W Belarus *53°48′N 24°34′E*
111 I17 **Nový Jičín** *Ger.* Neutitschein. Moravskoslezský Kraj, E Czech Republic *49°36′N 18°00′E*
118 K12 **Novy Pahost** *Rus.* Novyy Pogost. Vitsyebskaya Voblasts', NW Belarus *55°30′N 27°29′E*
Novyy Bug *see* Novyy Buh
117 R9 **Novyy Buh** *Rus.* Novyy Bug. Mykolayivs'ka Oblast', S Ukraine *47°40′N 32°30′E*
117 Q4 **Novyy Bykiv** Chernihivs'ka Oblast', N Ukraine *50°36′N 31°39′E*
Novyy Dvor *see* Novy Dvor
Novyye Aneny *see* Anenii Noi
127 P7 **Novyye Burasy** Saratovskaya Oblast', W Russian Federation *52°10′N 46°00′E*
Novyy Margilan *see* Farg'ona
126 K8 **Novyy Oskol** Belgorodskaya Oblast', W Russian Federation *50°43′N 37°55′E*
Novyy Pogost *see* Novy Pahost
127 R2 **Novyy Tor"yal** Respublika Mariy El, W Russian Federation *56°59′N 48°53′E*
123 N12 **Novyy Uoyan** Respublika Buryatiya, S Russian Federation *56°06′N 111°27′E*
122 J9 **Novyy Urengoy** Yamalo-Nenetskiy Avtonomnyy Okrug, N Russian Federation *66°06′N 76°25′E*
Novyy Uzen' *see* Zhanaozen
111 N16 **Nowa Dęba** Podkarpackie, SE Poland *50°31′N 21°53′E*
111 G15 **Nowa Ruda** *Ger.* Neurode. Dolnośląskie, SW Poland *50°34′N 16°30′E*
110 F12 **Nowa Sól** *var.* Nowasól, *Ger.* Neusalz an der Oder. Lubuskie, W Poland *51°47′N 15°43′E*
Nowasól *see* Nowa Sól
27 Q8 **Nowata** Oklahoma, C USA *36°42′N 95°36′W*
142 M6 **Nowbarān** Markazī, W Iran *35°07′N 49°51′E*
110 J8 **Nowe** Kujawski-pomorskie, N Poland *53°40′N 18°44′E*
110 K9 **Nowe Miasto Lubawskie** *Ger.* Neumark. Warmińsko-Mazurskie, NE Poland *53°24′N 19°36′E*
110 L13 **Nowe Miasto nad Pilicą** Mazowieckie, C Poland *51°37′N 20°34′E*
110 D8 **Nowe Warpno** *Ger.* Neuwarp. Zachodnio-pomorskie, NW Poland *53°52′N 14°12′E*
Nowgong *see* Nagaon
110 E8 **Nowogard** *var.* Nowógard, *Ger.* Naugard. Zachodnio-pomorskie, NW Poland *53°41′N 15°09′E*
110 N9 **Nowogród** Podlaskie, NE Poland *53°14′N 21°52′E*
Nowogródek *see* Navahrudak
111 E14 **Nowogrodziec** *Ger.* Naumburg am Queis. Dolnośląskie, SW Poland *51°12′N 15°24′E*
Nowojelnia *see* Navayel'nya
Nowo-Minsk *see* Mińsk Mazowiecki
33 V13 **Nowood River** ≈ Wyoming, C USA
Nowo-Święciany *see* Švenčionėliai
183 S10 **Nowra-Bomaderry** New South Wales, SE Australia *34°51′S 150°41′E*
Nowrangapur *see* Nabarangapur
149 T5 **Nowshera** *var.* Naushahra, Naushara. North-West Frontier Province, NE Pakistan *34°00′N 72°00′E*
110 J7 **Nowy Dwór Gdański** *Ger.* Tiegenhof. Pomorskie, N Poland *54°12′N 19°03′E*
110 L11 **Nowy Dwór Mazowiecki** Mazowieckie, C Poland *52°26′N 20°43′E*
111 M17 **Nowy Sącz** *Ger.* Neu Sandec. Małopolskie, S Poland *49°36′N 20°42′E*
111 L18 **Nowy Targ** *Ger.* Neumark. Małopolskie, S Poland *49°28′N 20°00′E*
110 F11 **Nowy Tomyśl** *var.* Nowy Tomysl. Wielkopolskie, C Poland *52°18′N 16°07′E*
Nowy Tomysl *see* Nowy Tomyśl
148 M7 **Now Zād** *var.* Nauzad. Helmand, S Afghanistan *32°22′N 64°32′E*
23 N4 **Noxubee River** ≈ Alabama/Mississippi, S USA
122 I10 **Noyabr'sk** Yamalo-Nenetskiy Avtonomnyy Okrug, N Russian Federation *63°08′N 75°19′E*
102 L8 **Noyant** Maine-et-Loire, NW France *47°28′N 00°08′W*
39 X14 **Noyes Island** *island* Alexander Archipelago, Alaska, USA
103 O3 **Noyon** Oise, N France *49°35′N 03°E*
102 I7 **Nozay** Loire-Atlantique, NW France *47°34′N 01°36′W*
82 L12 **Nsando** Northern, NE Zambia *10°22′S 31°14′E*
83 N16 **Nsanje** Southern, S Malawi *16°57′S 35°10′E*
77 Q17 **Nsawam** SE Ghana *05°47′N 00°19′W*
79 E16 **Nsimalen** ✈ Centre, C Cameroon *19°15′N 81°22′E*
82 K12 **Nsombo** Northern, NE Zambia *10°35′S 29°58′E*
82 H13 **Ntambu** North Western, NW Zambia *12°21′S 25°03′E*
83 N14 **Ntcheu** *var.* Ncheu. Central, S Malawi *14°49′S 34°37′E*
79 D17 **Ntem** *prev.* Campo, Kampo. ≈ Cameroon/Equatorial Guinea
83 I14 **Ntemwa** North Western, NW Zambia *14°03′S 26°13′E*
Ntlenyana, Mount *see* Thabana Ntlenyana
79 I19 **Ntomba, Lac** *var.* Lac Tumba. ◎ NW Dem. Rep. Congo
115 I19 **Ntóro, Kávo** *prev.* Akrotírio Kafiréas. *cape* Évvoia, C Greece
81 E19 **Ntungamo** SW Uganda *0°54′S 30°16′E*
81 E18 **Ntusi** SW Uganda *0°05′N 31°13′E*
83 H18 **Ntwetwe Pan** *salt lake* NE Botswana
154 L13 **Nūāparha** *var.* Nauparha, Nawapara. Orissa, SW India *20°43′N 82°42′E*
93 M15 **Nuasjärvi** ◎ C Finland
80 F11 **Nuba Mountains** ▲▲ C Sudan
68 J9 **Nubian Desert** *desert* NE Sudan
116 G10 **Nucet** *Hung.* Diófás. Bihor, W Romania *46°28′N 22°35′E*
Nu Chiang *see* Salween
145 U9 **Nuclear Testing Ground** *nuclear site* Pavlodar, E Kazakhstan
56 E9 **Nucuray, Río** ≈ N Peru
25 R14 **Nueces River** ≈ Texas, SW USA
9 V9 **Nueltin Lake** ◎ Manitoba/Northwest Territories, C Canada
99 K15 **Nuenen** Noord-Brabant, S Netherlands *51°29′N 05°36′E*
62 G6 **Nuestra Señora, Bahía** *bay* N Chile
61 D14 **Nuestra Señora Rosario de Caa Catí** Corrientes, NE Argentina *27°48′S 57°42′W*
54 J9 **Nueva Antioquia** Vichada, E Colombia *06°04′N 69°30′W*
Nueva Caceres *see* Naga
41 O7 **Nueva Ciudad Guerrera** Tamaulipas, C Mexico *26°32′N 99°13′W*
55 N4 **Nueva Esparta** *off.* Estado Nueva Esparta. ◈ *state* NE Venezuela
Nueva Esparta, Estado *see* Nueva Esparta
44 C5 **Nueva Gerona** Isla de la Juventud, S Cuba *21°49′N 82°49′W*
42 H8 **Nueva Guadalupe** San Miguel, E El Salvador *13°30′N 88°21′W*
42 M11 **Nueva Guinea** Región Autónoma Atlántico Sur, SE Nicaragua *11°40′N 84°22′W*
61 D19 **Nueva Helvecia** Colonia, SW Uruguay *34°16′S 57°53′W*
63 J25 **Nueva, Isla** *island* S Chile
40 M14 **Nueva Italia** Michoacán, SW Mexico *19°01′N 102°06′W*
56 D6 **Nueva Loja** *var.* Lago Agrio. Sucumbíos, NE Ecuador
42 F6 **Nueva Ocotepeque** *prev.* Ocotepeque. Ocotepeque, W Honduras *14°25′N 89°10′W*
61 D19 **Nueva Palmira** Colonia, SW Uruguay *33°53′S 58°25′W*
41 N6 **Nueva Rosita** Coahuila, NE Mexico *27°58′N 101°11′W*
42 E7 **Nueva San Salvador** *prev.* Santa Tecla. La Libertad, SW El Salvador *13°40′N 89°18′W*
42 J8 **Nueva Segovia** ◈ *department* NW Nicaragua
Nueva Tabarca *see* Plana, Isla
Nueva Villa de Padilla *see* Nuevo Padilla
61 B21 **Nueve de Julio** Buenos Aires, E Argentina *35°29′S 60°52′W*
44 H6 **Nuevitas** Camagüey, E Cuba *21°34′N 77°18′W*
61 D18 **Nuevo Berlín** Río Negro, W Uruguay *32°59′S 58°03′W*
40 I4 **Nuevo Casas Grandes** Chihuahua, N Mexico *30°23′N 107°54′W*
43 T14 **Nuevo Chagres** Colón, C Panama *09°14′N 80°05′W*
41 W15 **Nuevo Coahuila** Campeche, E Mexico *17°53′N 90°46′W*
63 K17 **Nuevo, Golfo** *gulf* S Argentina
41 O7 **Nuevo Laredo** Tamaulipas, NE Mexico *27°28′N 99°32′W*
41 N8 **Nuevo León** ◈ *state* NE Mexico
41 P10 **Nuevo Padilla** *var.* Nueva Villa de Padilla. Tamaulipas, C Mexico *24°01′N 98°48′W*
56 E6 **Nuevo Rocafuerte** Orellana, E Ecuador *0°59′S 75°27′W*
Nuga *see* Dzavhanmandal
80 O13 **Nugaal** *off.* Gobolka Nugaal. ◈ *region* N Somalia
Nugaal, Gobolka *see* Nugaal
185 E24 **Nugget Point** *headland* South Island, New Zealand *46°26′S 169°49′E*
186 J5 **Nuguria Islands** *island group* E Papua New Guinea
184 P10 **Nuhaka** Hawke's Bay, North Island, New Zealand *39°03′S 177°43′E*
138 M10 **Nuhaydayn, Wādī an** *dry watercourse* W Iraq
190 E7 **Nui Atoll** *atoll* W Tuvalu
Nu Jiang *see* Salween
Nûk *see* Nuuk
182 G7 **Nukey Bluff** *hill* South Australia
Nukha *see* Şäki
123 T9 **Nukh Yablonevyy, Gora** ▲ E Russian Federation *60°26′N 151°45′E*
186 K7 **Nukiki** Choiseul Island, NW Solomon Islands *06°45′S 156°30′E*
186 B6 **Nuku** Sandaun, NW Papua New Guinea *03°48′S 142°23′E*
193 W15 **Nuku** *island* Tongatapu Group, NE Tonga
193 Y16 **Nuku'alofa** ● (Tonga) Tongatapu, S Tonga *21°08′S 175°13′W*
193 U15 **Nuku'alofa** Tongatapu, S Tonga *21°09′S 175°14′W*
190 G12 **Nukuatea** *island* N Wallis and Futuna
190 F7 **Nukufetau Atoll** *atoll* C Tuvalu
190 G12 **Nukuhifala** *island* E Wallis and Futuna
191 W7 **Nuku Hiva** *island* Îles Marquises, NE French Polynesia
191 W7 **Nuku Hiva Island** *island* Îles Marquises, N French Polynesia
190 F9 **Nukulaelae Atoll** *var.* Nukulailai. *atoll* E Tuvalu
Nukulailai *see* Nukulaelae Atoll
190 G11 **Nukuloa** *island* N Wallis and Futuna
186 L6 **Nukumanu Islands** *prev.* Tasman Group. *island group* NE Papua New Guinea
Nukunau *see* Nikunau
190 J9 **Nukunonu Atoll** *island* C Tokelau
190 J9 **Nukunonu Village** Nukunonu Atoll, C Tokelau
189 S18 **Nukuoro Atoll** *atoll* Caroline Islands, S Micronesia
146 H8 **Nukus** Qoraqalpog'iston Respublikasi, W Uzbekistan *42°29′N 59°32′E*
190 G11 **Nukutapu** *island* N Wallis and Futuna
39 O9 **Nulato** Alaska, USA *64°43′N 158°06′W*
39 O10 **Nulato Hills** ▲▲ Alaska, USA
105 T9 **Nules** País Valenciano, E Spain *39°52′N 00°10′W*
Nuling *see* Sultan Kudarat
182 C6 **Nullarbor** South Australia *31°28′S 130°57′E*
180 M11 **Nullarbor Plain** *plateau* South Australia/Western Australia
163 S12 **Nulu'erhu Shan** ▲▲ N China
77 X14 **Numan** Adamawa, E Nigeria *09°26′N 11°58′E*
165 S3 **Numata** Hokkaidō, NE Japan *43°48′N 141°55′E*
81 C15 **Numatinna** ≈ W Sudan
95 F14 **Numedalen** *valley* S Norway
95 G14 **Numedalslågen** *var.* Laagen. ≈ S Norway
93 L19 **Nummela** Etelä-Suomi, S Finland *60°21′N 24°20′E*
183 O11 **Numurkah** Victoria, SE Australia *36°04′S 145°28′E*
196 L16 **Nunap Isua** *var.* Uummannarsuaq, *Dan.* Kap Farvel, *Eng.* Cape Farewell. *cape* S Greenland
9 N8 **Nunavut** ◈ *territory* N Canada
54 H9 **Nunchia** Casanare, C Colombia *05°37′N 72°13′W*
97 M20 **Nuneaton** C England, United Kingdom *52°32′N 01°28′W*
153 W14 **Nungba** Manipur, NE India *24°46′N 93°25′E*
38 L12 **Nunivak Island** *island* Alaska, USA
152 I5 **Nun Kun** ▲ NW India *34°01′N 76°04′E*
98 L10 **Nunspeet** Gelderland, E Netherlands *52°21′N 05°45′E*
107 C18 **Nuoro** Sardegna, Italy, C Mediterranean Sea *40°20′N 09°20′E*
75 R12 **Nuqayy, Jabal** *hill range* S Libya
54 C9 **Nuquí** Chocó, W Colombia *05°44′N 77°16′W*
143 O4 **Nūr** Māzandarān, N Iran *36°32′N 52°00′E*
145 Q9 **Nura** ≈ N Kazakhstan
143 N11 **Nūrābād** Fārs, C Iran *30°08′N 51°30′E*
Nurakita *see* Niulakita
Nurata *see* Nurota
Nuratau, Khrebet *see* Nurota Tizmasi
136 L17 **Nur Dağları** ▲▲ S Turkey
Nurek *see* Norak
Nuremberg *see* Nürnberg
149 S4 **Nūrestān** ◈ *province* C Afghanistan
136 M15 **Nurhak** Kahramanmaraş, S Turkey *37°57′N 37°21′E*
182 J9 **Nuriootpa** South Australia *34°28′S 139°00′E*
127 S5 **Nurlat** Respublika Tatarstan, W Russian Federation *54°26′N 50°48′E*
93 N15 **Nurmes** Itä-Suomi, E Finland *63°31′N 29°10′E*
101 K20 **Nürnberg** *Eng.* Nuremberg. Bayern, S Germany *49°27′N 11°05′E*
101 K20 **Nürnberg** ✈ Bayern, SE Germany *49°29′N 11°04′E*
146 M10 **Nurota** *Rus.* Nurata. Navoiy Viloyati, C Uzbekistan *40°41′N 65°43′E*
147 N10 **Nurota Tizmasi** *Rus.* Khrebet Nuratau. ▲▲ C Uzbekistan
149 T8 **Nūrpur** Punjab, E Pakistan *31°54′N 71°55′E*
183 P6 **Nurri, Mount** *hill* New South Wales, SE Australia
25 T13 **Nursery** Texas, SW USA *28°55′N 97°05′W*
169 V17 **Nusa Tenggara Barat** *off.* Propinsi Nusa Tenggara Barat, *Eng.* West Nusa Tenggara. ◈ *province* S Indonesia
Nusa Tenggara Barat, Propinsi *see* Nusa Tenggara Barat
171 O16 **Nusa Tenggara Timur** *off.* Propinsi Nusa Tenggara Timur, *Eng.* East Nusa Tenggara. ◈ *province* S Indonesia
Nusa Tenggara Timur, Propinsi *see* Nusa Tenggara Timur
171 U14 **Nusawulan** Papua, E Indonesia *04°03′S 132°56′E*
137 Q16 **Nusaybin** *var.* Nisibin. Manisa, SE Turkey *37°08′N 41°11′E*
39 O14 **Nushagak Bay** *bay* Alaska, USA
39 O13 **Nushagak Peninsula** *headland* Alaska, USA *58°39′N 159°03′W*
39 O13 **Nushagak River** ≈ Alaska, USA
160 E11 **Nu Shan** ▲▲ SW China
149 N11 **Nushki** Baluchistān, SW Pakistan *29°33′N 66°01′E*
Nussdorf *see* Năsăud
112 J9 **Nuštar** Vukovar-Srijem, E Croatia *45°20′N 18°48′E*
99 L18 **Nuth** Limburg, SE Netherlands *50°55′N 05°52′E*
100 N13 **Nuthe** ≈ NE Germany
Nutmeg State *see* Connecticut
39 T10 **Nutzotin Mountains** ▲▲ Alaska, USA
64 I5 **Nuuk** *var.* Nûk, *Dan.* Godthaab, Godthåb. ○ (Greenland) Kitaa, SW Greenland *64°15′N 51°35′W*
92 L13 **Nuupas** Lappi, NW Finland *66°01′N 26°19′E*
191 O7 **Nuupere, Pointe** *headland* Moorea, W French Polynesia *17°35′S 149°47′W*
191 O7 **Nuuroa, Pointe** *headland* Tahiti, W French Polynesia
Nüürst *see* Baganuur
Nuwara *see* Nuwara Eliya
155 K25 **Nuwara Eliya** *var.* Nuwara. Central Province, S Sri Lanka *06°58′N 80°46′E*
182 E7 **Nuyts Archipelago** *island group* South Australia
83 F17 **Nxaunxau** North West, NW Botswana *18°57′S 21°18′E*
39 N12 **Nyac** Alaska, USA *61°00′N 159°56′W*
122 H9 **Nyagan'** Khanty-Mansiyskiy Avtonomnyy Okrug-Yugra, N Russian Federation *62°10′N 65°32′E*
Nyagassola *see* Niagassola
Nyagquka *see* Yajiang
81 I18 **Nyahururu** Central, W Kenya *0°04′N 36°22′E*
182 M10 **Nyah West** Victoria, SE Australia *35°14′S 143°18′E*
158 M15 **Nyainqêntanglha Feng** ▲ W China *30°20′N 90°28′E*
159 N15 **Nyainqêntanglha Shan** ▲▲ W China
159 O13 **Nyainrong** Xizang Zizhiqu, W China *32°02′N 92°20′E*
80 B11 **Nyala** Southern Darfur, W Sudan *12°01′N 24°50′E*
158 J17 **Nyalam** Xizang Zizhiqu, SW China *28°10′N 85°57′E*
83 M16 **Nyamapanda** Mashonaland East, NE Zimbabwe *16°59′S 32°52′E*
81 H25 **Nyamtumbo** Ruvuma, S Tanzania *10°33′S 36°08′E*
Nyanda *see* Masvingo
124 M11 **Nyandoma** Arkhangel'skaya Oblast', NW Russian Federation *61°39′N 40°10′E*
83 M16 **Nyanga** *prev.* Inyanga. Manicaland, E Zimbabwe *18°13′S 32°46′E*
79 D20 **Nyanga** *off.* Province de la Nyanga, *var.* La Nyanga. ◈ *province* SW Gabon
79 E20 **Nyanga** ≈ Congo/Gabon
Nyanga, Province de la *see* Nyanga
81 F20 **Nyantakara** Kagera, NW Tanzania *03°05′S 31°23′E*
81 G19 **Nyanza** ◈ *province* W Kenya
81 E21 **Nyanza-Lac** S Burundi *04°16′S 29°38′E*
68 J14 **Nyasa, Lake** *var.* Lake Malawi; *prev.* Lago Nyassa. ◎ E Africa
Nyasaland/Nyasaland Protectorate *see* Malawi
Nyassa, Lago *see* Nyasa, Lake
119 J17 **Nyasvizh** *Pol.* Nieśwież, *Rus.* Nesvizh. Minskaya Voblasts', C Belarus *53°13′N 26°40′E*
166 M8 **Nyaunglebin** Bago, SW Burma (Myanmar) *17°59′N 94°44′E*
166 M5 **Nyaung-u** Magway, C Burma (Myanmar) *21°03′N 95°44′E*
95 H24 **Nyborg** Fyn, C Denmark *55°19′N 10°48′E*
95 N21 **Nybro** Kalmar, S Sweden *56°45′N 15°54′E*
119 J16 **Nyeharelaye** *Rus.* Negoreloye. Minskaya Voblasts', C Belarus *53°36′N 27°04′E*
158 M16 **Nyêmo** *var.* Tarrong. Xizang Zizhiqu, W China *29°25′N 90°10′E*
195 W3 **Nye Mountains** ▲▲ Antarctica
81 I19 **Nyeri** Central, C Kenya *0°25′S 36°56′E*
118 M11 **Nyeshcharda, Vozyera** ◎ N Belarus
92 O2 **Ny-Friesland** *physical region* N Svalbard
95 L14 **Nyhammar** Dalarna, C Sweden *60°19′N 14°55′E*
160 F7 **Nyikog Qu** ≈ C China
158 K14 **Nyima** Xizang Zizhiqu, W China *31°56′N 87°16′E*
83 L14 **Nyimba** Eastern, E Zambia *14°33′S 30°49′E*
159 P15 **Nyingchi** *var.* Pula. Xizang Zizhiqu, W China *29°34′N 94°33′E*
159 P15 **Nyingchi** Xizang Zizhiqu, W China *29°27′N 94°43′E*
Nyinma *see* Maqu
111 O21 **Nyírbátor** Szabolcs-Szatmár-Bereg, E Hungary *47°50′N 22°09′E*
111 N21 **Nyíregyháza** Szabolcs-Szatmár-Bereg, NE Hungary *47°57′N 21°43′E*
Nyiro *see* Ewaso Ng'iro
Nyitra *see* Nitra
Nyitrabánya *see* Handlová
93 K16 **Nykarleby** *Fin.* Uusikaarlepyy. Länsi-Suomi, W Finland *63°22′N 22°30′E*
95 I25 **Nykøbing** Storstrøm, SE Denmark *54°47′N 11°53′E*
95 I22 **Nykøbing** Vestsjælland, C Denmark *55°56′N 11°41′E*
95 F21 **Nykøbing** Viborg, NW Denmark *56°48′N 08°52′E*
95 N17 **Nyköping** Södermanland, S Sweden *58°45′N 17°03′E*
95 L15 **Nykroppa** Värmland, C Sweden *59°37′N 14°18′E*
Nylstroom *see* Modimolle
183 P7 **Nymagee** New South Wales, SE Australia *32°06′S 146°19′E*
183 V5 **Nymboida** New South Wales, SE Australia *29°57′S 152°45′E*
183 U5 **Nymboida River** ≈ New South Wales, SE Australia

◆ Country
● Country Capital
◇ Dependent Territory
○ Dependent Territory Capital
◈ Administrative Regions
✈ International Airport
▲ Mountain
▲▲ Mountain Range
Volcano
≈ River
◎ Lake
▣ Reservoir

111 D16 **Nymburk** var. Neuenburg an der Elbe, Ger. Nimburg. Středočesky Kraj, C Czech Republic 50°12′N 15°00′E
95 O16 **Nynäshamn** Stockholm, C Sweden 58°54′N 17°55′E
183 Q6 **Nyngan** New South Wales, SE Australia 31°36′S 147°07′E
Nyoman see Neman
108 A10 **Nyon** Ger. Neuss; anc. Noviodunum. Vaud, SW Switzerland 46°23′N 06°15′E
79 D16 **Nyong** ≈ SW Cameroon
103 S14 **Nyons** Drôme, E France 44°22′N 05°06′E
79 D14 **Nyos, Lac** Eng. Lake Nyos. ◎ NW Cameroon
Nyos, Lake see Nyos, Lac
125 U11 **Nyrob** var. Nyrov. Permskaya Oblast', NW Russian Federation 60°41′N 56°42′E
Nyrov see Nyrob
111 H15 **Nysa** Ger. Neisse. Opolskie, S Poland 50°28′N 17°20′E
32 M13 **Nyssa** Oregon, NW USA 43°52′N 116°59′W
Nysa Łużycka see Neisse
Nyslott see Savonlinna
Nystad see Uusikaupunki
95 I25 **Nysted** Storstrøm, SE Denmark 54°40′N 11°41′E
125 U14 **Nytva** Permskaya Oblast', NW Russian Federation 57°56′N 55°22′E
165 P8 **Nyūdō-zaki** headland Honshū, C Japan 39°59′N 139°40′E
125 P9 **Nyukhcha** Arkhangel'skaya Oblast', NW Russian Federation 63°24′N 46°34′E
124 H8 **Nyuk, Ozero** var. Ozero Njuk. ◎ NW Russian Federation
125 O12 **Nyuksenitsa** var. Njuksenica. Vologodskaya Oblast', NW Russian Federation 60°25′N 44°12′E
79 O22 **Nyunzu** Katanga, SE Dem. Rep. Congo 05°55′S 28°00′E
123 O10 **Nyurba** Respublika Sakha (Yakutiya), NE Russian Federation 63°17′N 118°15′E
123 O11 **Nyuya** Respublika Sakha (Yakutiya), NE Russian Federation 60°33′N 116°10′E
146 K12 **Nyýazow** Rus. Niyazov. Lebap Welaýaty, NE Turkmenistan 39°13′N 63°16′E
117 T10 **Nyzhni Sirohozy** Khersons'ka Oblast', S Ukraine 46°49′N 34°21′E
117 U12 **Nyzhn'ohirs'kyy** Rus. Nizhnegorskiy. Respublika Krym, S Ukraine 45°26′N 34°42′E
NZ see New Zealand
81 G21 **Nzega** Tabora, C Tanzania 04°13′S 33°11′E
76 K15 **Nzérékoré** SE Guinea 07°45′N 08°49′W
82 A10 **N'Zeto** prev. Ambrizete. Zaire, NW Angola 07°14′S 12°52′E
79 M24 **Nzilo, Lac** prev. Lac Delcommune. ◎ SE Dem. Rep. Congo
Nzwani see Anjouan

O

29 O11 **Oacoma** South Dakota, N USA 43°49′N 99°25′W
29 N9 **Oahe Dam** dam South Dakota, N USA
28 M9 **Oahe, Lake** ⊠ North Dakota/South Dakota, N USA
38 C9 **Oʻahu** var. Oahu. island Hawaiʻian Islands, Hawaiʻi, USA
165 V4 **O-Akan-dake** ▲ Hokkaidō, NE Japan 43°26′N 144°09′E
182 K8 **Oakbank** South Australia 33°07′S 140°36′E
19 P13 **Oak Bluffs** Martha's Vineyard, New York, NE USA 41°25′N 70°32′W
36 K4 **Oak City** Utah, W USA 39°22′N 112°19′W
37 R3 **Oak Creek** Colorado, C USA 40°16′N 106°57′W
35 P8 **Oakdale** California, W USA 37°46′N 120°51′W
22 H8 **Oakdale** Louisiana, S USA 30°49′N 92°39′W
29 P7 **Oakes** North Dakota, N USA 46°08′N 98°05′W
22 J4 **Oak Grove** Louisiana, S USA 32°51′N 91°25′W
97 N19 **Oakham** C England, United Kingdom 52°41′N 00°45′W
32 H7 **Oak Harbor** Washington, NW USA 48°17′N 122°38′W
21 R5 **Oak Hill** West Virginia, NE USA 37°59′N 81°09′W
35 N8 **Oakland** California, W USA 37°48′N 122°16′W
29 T15 **Oakland** Iowa, C USA 41°18′N 95°22′W
19 Q7 **Oakland** Maine, NE USA 44°32′N 69°43′W
21 T3 **Oakland** Maryland, NE USA 39°24′N 79°25′W
29 R14 **Oakland** Nebraska, C USA 41°50′N 96°28′W
31 N11 **Oak Lawn** Illinois, N USA 41°43′N 87°45′W
33 P16 **Oakley** Idaho, NW USA 42°13′N 113°54′W
26 I4 **Oakley** Kansas, C USA 39°08′N 100°53′W
31 N10 **Oak Park** Illinois, N USA 41°53′N 87°46′W
11 X16 **Oak Point** Manitoba, S Canada 50°23′N 97°00′W
32 G13 **Oakridge** Oregon, NW USA 43°45′N 122°27′W
20 M9 **Oak Ridge** Tennessee, S USA 36°02′N 84°12′W
184 K10 **Oakura** Taranaki, North Island, New Zealand 39°07′S 173°58′E
22 L7 **Oak Vale** Mississippi, S USA 31°26′N 89°57′W
14 G16 **Oakville** Ontario, S Canada 43°27′N 79°41′W
25 V8 **Oakwood** Texas, SW USA 31°34′N 95°51′W
185 F22 **Oamaru** Otago, South Island, New Zealand 45°10′S 170°51′E
96 F13 **Oa, Mull of** headland W Scotland, United Kingdom 55°35′N 06°20′W
171 O11 **Oan** Sulawesi, N Indonesia 01°16′N 121°25′E
185 J17 **Oaro** Canterbury, South Island, New Zealand 42°29′S 173°30′E
35 X2 **Oasis** Nevada, W USA 41°01′N 114°29′W
195 S15 **Oates Land** physical region Antarctica
183 P17 **Oatlands** Tasmania, SE Australia 42°21′S 147°23′E
36 I11 **Oatman** Arizona, SW USA 35°03′N 114°19′W
41 R16 **Oaxaca** var. Oaxaca de Juárez; prev. Antequera. Oaxaca, SE Mexico 17°04′N 96°41′W
41 Q16 **Oaxaca** ◐ state SE Mexico
Oaxaca de Juárez see Oaxaca
122 I19 **Ob'** ≈ C Russian Federation
14 G9 **Obabika Lake** ◎ Ontario, S Canada
Obagan see Ubagan
118 M12 **Obal'** Rus. Obol'. Vitsyebskaya Voblasts', N Belarus 55°22′N 29°17′E
79 E16 **Obala** Centre, SW Cameroon 04°09′N 11°32′E
14 C6 **Oba Lake** ◎ Ontario, S Canada
164 J12 **Obama** Fukui, Honshū, SW Japan 35°32′N 135°45′E
96 H11 **Oban** W Scotland, United Kingdom 56°25′N 05°29′W
Oban see Halfmoon Bay
Obando see Puerto Inírida
104 I4 **O Barco** var. El Barco, El Barco de Valdeorras, O Barco de Valdeorras. Galicia, NW Spain 42°24′N 07°00′W
O Barco de Valdeorras see O Barco
Obbia see Hobyo
93 J16 **Obbola** Västerbotten, N Sweden 63°41′N 20°16′E
Obbrovazzo see Obrovac
Obchuga see Abchuha
Obdorsk see Salekhard
Óbecse see Bečej
118 I11 **Obeliai** Panevėžys, NE Lithuania 55°57′N 25°47′E
60 F13 **Oberá** Misiones, NE Argentina 27°29′S 55°08′W
108 E8 **Oberburg** Bern, W Switzerland 47°00′N 07°37′E
109 Q9 **Oberdrauburg** Salzburg, S Austria 46°45′N 12°59′E
Oberglogau see Głogówek
109 W4 **Ober Grafendorf** Niederösterreich, NE Austria 48°09′N 15°33′E
101 E15 **Oberhausen** Nordrhein-Westfalen, W Germany 51°27′N 06°50′E
Oberhollabrunn see Tulln
Oberlaibach see Vrhnika
101 Q15 **Oberlausitz** var. Hornja Łužica. physical region E Germany
26 J2 **Oberlin** Kansas, C USA 39°49′N 100°33′W
22 H8 **Oberlin** Louisiana, S USA 30°37′N 92°45′W
31 T11 **Oberlin** Ohio, N USA 41°17′N 82°13′W
103 U5 **Obernai** Bas-Rhin, NE France 48°28′N 07°30′E
109 R4 **Obernberg am Inn** Oberösterreich, N Austria 48°19′N 13°20′E
Oberndorf see Oberndorf am Neckar
101 G23 **Oberndorf am Neckar** var. Oberndorf. Baden-Württemberg, SW Germany 48°18′N 08°32′E
109 Q5 **Oberndorf bei Salzburg** Salzburg, W Austria 47°57′N 12°57′E
Obernestadtl see Kysucké Nové Mesto
183 S8 **Oberon** New South Wales, SE Australia 33°42′S 149°50′E
109 Q4 **Oberösterreich** off. Land Oberösterreich, Eng. Upper Austria. ◐ state NW Austria
Oberösterreich, Land see Oberösterreich
Oberpahlen see Põltsamaa
101 M19 **Oberpfälzer Wald** ▲▲ SE Germany
109 Y6 **Oberpullendorf** Burgenland, E Austria 47°32′N 16°30′E
Oberradkersburg see Gornja Radgona
101 G18 **Oberursel** Hessen, W Germany 50°12′N 08°34′E
109 Q8 **Obervellach** Salzburg, S Austria 46°56′N 13°10′E
109 X7 **Oberwart** Burgenland, SE Austria 47°18′N 16°12′E
Oberwischau see Vişeu de Sus
109 T7 **Oberwölz** var. Oberwölz-Stadt. Steiermark, SE Austria 47°12′N 14°20′E
Oberwölz-Stadt see Oberwölz
31 S13 **Obetz** Ohio, N USA 39°52′N 82°57′W
Ob', Gulf of see Obskaya Guba
54 G8 **Obia** Santander, C Colombia 06°16′N 73°18′W
58 H12 **Óbidos** Pará, NE Brazil 01°52′S 55°30′W
104 F10 **Óbidos** Leiria, C Portugal 39°21′N 09°09′W
Obidovichi see Abidavichy
147 Q13 **Obigarm** W Tajikistan 38°42′N 69°34′E
165 T2 **Obihiro** Hokkaidō, NE Japan 42°56′N 143°10′E
Obi-Khingou see Khingov
147 P13 **Obikiik** SW Tajikistan 38°07′N 68°36′E
Obilić see Obiliq
113 N16 **Obiliq** Serb. Obilić. N Kosovo 42°50′N 20°57′E
127 O12 **Obil'noye** Respublika Kalmykiya, SW Russian Federation 47°31′N 44°24′E
20 F8 **Obion** Tennessee, S USA 36°15′N 89°11′W
20 F8 **Obion River** ≈ Tennessee, S USA
171 S12 **Obi, Pulau** island Maluku, E Indonesia
165 S2 **Obira** Hokkaidō, NE Japan 44°01′N 141°39′E
127 N11 **Oblivskaya** Rostovskaya Oblast', SW Russian Federation 48°34′N 42°31′E
123 R14 **Obluch'ye** Yevreyskaya Avtonomnaya Oblast', SE Russian Federation 48°59′N 131°18′E
126 K4 **Obninsk** Kaluzhskaya Oblast', W Russian Federation 55°06′N 36°40′E
114 J8 **Obnova** Pleven, N Bulgaria 43°26′N 25°04′E
79 N15 **Obo** Haut-Mbomou, E Central African Republic 05°20′N 26°29′E
159 T9 **Obo** Qinghai, C China 37°57′N 101°03′E
80 M11 **Obock** E Djibouti 11°57′N 43°09′E
Obol' see Obal'
Obolyanka see Abalyanka
171 V13 **Obome** Papua, E Indonesia 03°42′S 133°21′E
110 G11 **Oborniki** Wielkolpolskie, W Poland 52°38′N 16°48′E
79 G19 **Obouya** Cuvette, C Congo 0°56′S 15°41′E
126 J8 **Oboyan'** Kurskaya Oblast', W Russian Federation 51°12′N 36°15′E
124 M9 **Obozerskiy** Arkhangel'skaya Oblast', NW Russian Federation 63°26′N 40°20′E
112 L11 **Obrenovac** Serbia, N Serbia 44°39′N 20°12′E
112 D12 **Obrovac** It. Obbrovazzo. Zadar, SW Croatia 44°12′N 15°40′E
Obrovo see Abrova
35 Q3 **Observation Peak** ▲ California, W USA 40°48′N 120°07′W
122 J8 **Obskaya Guba** Eng. Gulf of Ob. gulf N Russian Federation
173 N13 **Ob' Tablemount** undersea feature S Indian Ocean 50°16′S 51°59′E
173 T10 **Ob' Trench** undersea feature E Indian Ocean
77 P16 **Obuasi** S Ghana 06°15′N 01°36′W
117 P5 **Obukhiv** Rus. Obukhov. Kyyivs'ka Oblast', N Ukraine 50°05′N 30°37′E
Obukhov see Obukhiv
125 U14 **Obva** ≈ NW Russian Federation
Obdur see Xuddur
117 V10 **Obytichna Kosa** spit SE Ukraine
117 V10 **Obytichna Zatoka** gulf SE Ukraine
114 N9 **Obzor** Burgas, E Bulgaria 42°52′N 27°53′E
105 O3 **Oca** ≈ N Spain
23 W10 **Ocala** Florida, SE USA 29°11′N 82°08′W
40 M7 **Ocampo** Coahuila, NE Mexico 27°18′N 102°24′W
54 G7 **Ocaña** Norte de Santander, N Colombia 08°16′N 73°21′W
105 N9 **Ocaña** Castilla-La Mancha, C Spain 39°57′N 03°30′W
104 H4 **O Carballiño** Cast. Carballiño. Galicia, NW Spain 42°26′N 08°05′W
37 T9 **Ocate** New Mexico, SW USA 36°09′N 105°03′W
Ocavango see Okavango
57 D14 **Occidental, Cordillera** ▲▲ W South America
21 Q6 **Oceana** West Virginia, NE USA 37°41′N 81°37′W
21 Z4 **Ocean City** Maryland, NE USA 38°20′N 75°05′W
18 J17 **Ocean City** New Jersey, NE USA 39°15′N 74°33′W
10 K15 **Ocean Falls** British Columbia, SW Canada 52°24′N 127°42′W
Ocean Island see Banaba
Ocean Island see Kure Atoll
64 J9 **Oceanographer Fracture Zone** tectonic feature NW Atlantic Ocean
35 U17 **Oceanside** California, W USA 33°12′N 117°23′W
22 M9 **Ocean Springs** Mississippi, S USA 30°24′N 88°49′W
Ocean State see Rhode Island
25 O9 **O C Fisher Lake** ⊠ Texas, SW USA
117 Q10 **Ochakiv** Rus. Ochakov. Mykolayivs'ka Oblast', S Ukraine 46°36′N 31°33′E
Ochakov see Ochakiv
Ochamchira see Och'amch'ire
137 Q9 **Och'amch'ire** Rus. Ochamchira. W Georgia 42°45′N 41°30′E
Ochansk see Okhansk
125 T15 **Ochër** Permskaya Oblast', NW Russian Federation 57°54′N 54°40′E
115 I19 **Óchi** ▲ Évvoia, C Greece 38°03′N 24°27′E
165 W4 **Ochiishi-misaki** headland Hokkaidō, NE Japan 43°10′N 145°29′E
23 S9 **Ochlockonee River** ≈ Florida/Georgia, SE USA
44 K12 **Ocho Rios** C Jamaica 18°24′N 77°06′W
Ochrida see Ohrid
Ochrida, Lake see Ohrid, Lake
101 J19 **Ochsenfurt** Bayern, C Germany 49°39′N 10°03′E
23 U7 **Ocilla** Georgia, SE USA 31°35′N 83°15′W
94 N13 **Ockelbo** Gävleborg, C Sweden 60°51′N 16°46′E
Ocker see Oker
95 I19 **Öckerö** Västra Götaland, S Sweden 57°43′N 11°39′E
23 U6 **Ocmulgee River** ≈ Georgia, SE USA
116 H11 **Ocna Mureş** Hung. Marosújvár; prev. Ocna Mureşului, prev. Hung. Marosújvárakna. Alba, C Romania 46°25′N 23°53′E
Ocna Mureşului see Ocna Mureş
116 H11 **Ocna Sibiului** Ger. Salzburg, Hung. Vizakna. Sibiu, C Romania 45°52′N 23°59′E
116 H13 **Ocnele Mari** prev. Vioara. Vâlcea, S Romania 45°03′N 24°18′E
116 L7 **Ocniţa** Rus. Oknitsa. N Moldova 48°25′N 27°30′E
23 U4 **Oconee, Lake** ⊠ Georgia, SE USA
23 U5 **Oconee River** ≈ Georgia, SE USA
30 M9 **Oconomowoc** Wisconsin, N USA 43°06′N 88°29′W
30 M6 **Oconto** Wisconsin, N USA 44°55′N 87°52′W
30 M6 **Oconto Falls** Wisconsin, N USA 44°52′N 88°06′W
30 M6 **Oconto River** ≈ Wisconsin, N USA
104 I3 **O Corgo** Galicia, NW Spain 42°56′N 07°25′W
41 V16 **Ocosingo** Chiapas, SE Mexico 17°04′N 92°15′W
42 J8 **Ocotal** Nueva Segovia, NW Nicaragua 13°38′N 86°28′W
42 F6 **Ocotepeque** ◐ department W Honduras
Ocotepeque see Nueva Ocotepeque
40 L13 **Ocotlán** Jalisco, SW Mexico 20°21′N 102°42′W
41 R16 **Ocotlán** var. Ocotlán de Morelos. Oaxaca, SE Mexico 16°49′N 96°49′W
Ocotlán de Morelos see Ocotlán
41 U16 **Ocozocuautla** Chiapas, SE Mexico 16°46′N 93°22′W
21 Y10 **Ocracoke Island** island North Carolina, SE USA
102 I3 **Octeville** Manche, N France 49°37′N 01°39′W
October Revolution Island see Oktyabr'skoy Revolyutsii, Ostrov
43 R17 **Ocú** Herrera, S Panama 07°55′N 80°43′W
83 Q14 **Ocua** Cabo Delgado, NE Mozambique 13°37′S 39°44′E
Ocumare see Ocumare del Tuy
54 M5 **Ocumare del Tuy** var. Ocumare. Miranda, N Venezuela 10°07′N 66°47′W
77 P17 **Oda** SE Ghana 05°55′N 00°56′W
165 G12 **Ōda** var. Oda. Shimane, Honshū, SW Japan 35°10′N 132°29′E
92 K3 **Ódadhahraun** lava flow C Iceland
165 Q7 **Ōdate** Akita, Honshū, C Japan 40°18′N 140°34′E
165 N14 **Odawara** Kanagawa, Honshū, S Japan 35°15′N 139°08′E
95 D14 **Odda** Hordaland, S Norway 60°03′N 06°34′E
95 G22 **Odder** Århus, C Denmark 55°59′N 10°10′E
Oddur see Xuddur
29 T13 **Odebolt** Iowa, C USA 42°18′N 95°15′W
104 H14 **Odeleite** Faro, S Portugal 37°02′N 07°29′W
25 Q4 **Odell** Texas, SW USA 34°19′N 99°24′W
25 T14 **Odem** Texas, SW USA 27°57′N 97°34′W
104 F13 **Odemira** Beja, S Portugal 37°35′N 08°38′W
136 C14 **Ödemiş** İzmir, SW Turkey 38°11′N 27°58′E
Ödenburg see Sopron
83 I22 **Odendaalsrus** Free State, C South Africa 27°52′S 26°42′E
Odenpäh see Otepää
95 H23 **Odense** Fyn, C Denmark 55°24′N 10°23′E
101 H19 **Odenwald** ▲▲ W Germany
84 H10 **Oder** Cz./Pol. Odra. ≈ C Europe
Oderberg see Bohumín
100 P11 **Oderbruch** wetland Germany/Poland
Oderhaff see Szczeciński, Zalew
100 O11 **Oder-Havel-Kanal** canal NE Germany
Oderhellen see Odorheiu Secuiesc
100 P13 **Oder-Spree-Kanal** canal NE Germany
Odertal see Zdzieszowice
106 I7 **Oderzo** Veneto, NE Italy 45°48′N 12°33′E
177 P10 **Odesa** Rus. Odessa. Odes'ka Oblast', SW Ukraine 46°29′N 30°44′E
24 M8 **Odessa** Texas, SW USA 31°51′N 102°22′W
32 K8 **Odessa** Washington, NW USA 47°19′N 118°41′W
Odessa see Odes'ka Oblast'
95 K18 **Ödeshög** Östergötland, S Sweden 58°13′N 14°40′E
117 O9 **Odes'ka Oblast'** var. Odesa, Rus. Odesskaya Oblast'. ◐ province SW Ukraine
Odessa see Odesa
Odesskaya Oblast' see Odes'ka Oblast'
122 H12 **Odesskoye** Omskaya Oblast', C Russian Federation 54°15′N 72°45′E
Odessus see Varna
102 F6 **Odet** ≈ NW France
104 I14 **Odiel** ≈ SW Spain
76 L14 **Odienné** NW Ivory Coast 09°32′N 07°35′W
171 O4 **Odiongan** Tablas Island, C Philippines 12°23′N 122°01′E
116 L12 **Odobeşti** Vrancea, E Romania 45°46′N 27°06′E
110 H13 **Odolanów** Ger. Adelnau. Wielkopolskie, C Poland 51°35′N 17°42′E
167 R13 **Ŏdôngk** Kâmpóng Spoe, S Cambodia 11°48′N 104°45′E
25 N6 **O'donnell** Texas, SW USA 32°57′N 101°49′W
98 O7 **Odoorn** Drenthe, NE Netherlands 52°52′N 06°49′E
Odorhei see Odorheiu Secuiesc
116 J11 **Odorheiu Secuiesc** Ger. Oderhellen, Hung. Vámosudvarhely; prev. Odorhei, Ger. Hofmarkt. Harghita, C Romania 46°18′N 25°19′E
Odra see Oder
112 J9 **Odžaci** Ger. Hodschag, Hung. Hodság. Vojvodina, NW Serbia 45°31′N 19°15′E
59 N14 **Oeiras** Piauí, E Brazil 07°00′S 42°07′W
104 F11 **Oeiras** Lisboa, C Portugal 38°41′N 09°18′W
101 G14 **Oelde** Nordrhein-Westfalen, W Germany 51°49′N 08°09′E
28 J11 **Oelrichs** South Dakota, N USA 43°08′N 103°13′W
101 M17 **Oelsnitz** Sachsen, E Germany 50°22′N 12°12′E
Oels/Oels in Schlesien see Oleśnica
29 X12 **Oelwein** Iowa, C USA 42°40′N 91°54′W
Oeniadae see Oiniádes
191 N17 **Oeno Island** atoll Pitcairn Islands, C Pacific Ocean
Oesel see Saaremaa
108 L7 **Oetz** var. Ötz. Tirol, W Austria 47°15′N 10°56′E
137 P11 **Of** Trabzon, NE Turkey 40°57′N 40°17′E
30 K15 **O'Fallon** Illinois, N USA 38°35′N 89°54′W
27 W4 **O'Fallon** Missouri, C USA 38°54′N 90°31′W
107 N16 **Ofanto** ≈ S Italy
97 D18 **Offaly** Ir. Ua Uíbh Fhailí; prev. King's County. cultural region C Ireland
101 H18 **Offenbach** var. Offenbach am Main. Hessen, W Germany 50°06′N 08°46′E
Offenbach am Main see Offenbach
101 F22 **Offenburg** Baden-Württemberg, SW Germany 48°28′N 07°57′E
182 C2 **Officer Creek** seasonal river South Australia
Oficina María Elena see María Elena
Oficina Pedro de Valdivia see Pedro de Valdivia
115 K22 **Ofidoússa** island Kykládes, Greece, Aegean Sea
Ofiral see Sharm ash Shaykh
92 H10 **Ofotfjorden** fjord N Norway
192 L16 **Ofu** island Manua Islands, E American Samoa
165 R9 **Ōfunato** Iwate, Honshū, C Japan 39°04′N 141°43′E
165 P8 **Oga** Akita, Honshū, C Japan 39°56′N 139°47′E
Ogaadeen see Ogaden
165 Q9 **Ogachi** Akita, Honshū, C Japan 39°03′N 140°26′E
165 P9 **Ogachi-tōge** pass Honshū, C Japan
81 N14 **Ogaden** Som. Ogaadeen. plateau Ethiopia/Somalia
165 P8 **Oga-hantō** peninsula Honshū, C Japan
165 K13 **Ōgaki** Gifu, Honshū, SW Japan 35°22′N 136°35′E
28 L15 **Ogallala** Nebraska, C USA 41°09′N 101°44′W
168 M14 **Ogan, Air** ≈ Sumatera, W Indonesia
165 Y15 **Ogasawara-shotō** Eng. Bonin Islands. island group SE Japan
14 J9 **Ogascanane, Lac** ◎ Québec, SE Canada
165 R7 **Ogawara-ko** ◎ Honshū, C Japan
77 T15 **Ogbomosho** var. Ogmoboso. Oyo, W Nigeria 08°10′N 04°16′E
29 U13 **Ogden** Iowa, C USA 42°03′N 94°01′W
36 L2 **Ogden** Utah, W USA 41°09′N 111°58′W
18 I6 **Ogdensburg** New York, NE USA 44°42′N 75°25′W
23 W5 **Ogeechee River** ≈ Georgia, SE USA
Oger see Ogre
165 N10 **Ogi** Niigata, Sado, C Japan 37°49′N 138°16′E
10 H5 **Ogilvie** Yukon Territory, NW Canada 63°34′N 139°44′W
10 H4 **Ogilvie** ≈ Yukon Territory, NW Canada
10 H5 **Ogilvie Mountains** ▲▲ Yukon Territory, NW Canada
Oginskiy Kanal see Ahinski Kanal
162 J7 **Ögiynuur** var. Dzegstey. Arhangay, C Mongolia 47°38′N 102°31′E
146 F6 **Og'iyon Sho'rxogi** wetland NW Uzbekistan
146 B10 **Oglanly** Balkan Welaýaty, W Turkmenistan 39°56′N 54°25′E
23 T5 **Oglethorpe** Georgia, SE USA 32°17′N 84°03′W
23 T2 **Oglethorpe, Mount** ▲ Georgia, SE USA 34°29′N 84°19′W
106 F7 **Oglio** anc. Ollius. ≈ N Italy
Ogmoboso see Ogbomosho
103 T8 **Ognon** ≈ E France
123 R13 **Ogodzha** Amurskaya Oblast', S Russian Federation 52°51′N 132°49′E
77 W16 **Ogoja** Cross River, S Nigeria 06°37′N 08°48′E
12 C10 **Ogoki** ≈ Ontario, S Canada
12 D11 **Ogoki Lake** ◎ Ontario, C Canada
Ögöömör see Hanhongor
79 F19 **Ogooué** ≈ Congo/Gabon
79 E18 **Ogooué-Ivindo** off. Province de l'Ogooué-Ivindo, var. L'Ogooué-Ivindo. ◐ province N Gabon
Ogooué-Ivindo, Province de l' see Ogooué-Ivindo
79 E19 **Ogooué-Lolo** off. Province de l'Ogooué-Lolo, var. L'Ogooué-Lolo. ◐ province C Gabon
Ogooué-Lolo, Province de l' see Ogooué-Lolo
79 C19 **Ogooué-Maritime** off. Province de l'Ogooué-Maritime, var. L'Ogooué-Maritime. ◐ province W Gabon
Ogooué-Maritime, Province de l' see Ogooué-Maritime
165 D14 **Ogōri** Fukuoka, Kyūshū, SW Japan 33°24′N 130°34′E
114 H7 **Ogosta** ≈ NW Bulgaria
113 Q19 **Ogražden** Bul. Ograzhden. ▲ Bulgaria/FYR Macedonia see also Ograzhden
114 G12 **Ograzhden** Mac. Ogražden. ▲ Bulgaria/FYR Macedonia see also Ogražden
Ograzhden see Ogražden
118 G9 **Ogre** Ger. Oger. Ogre, C Latvia 56°49′N 24°36′E
118 H9 **Ogre** ≈ C Latvia
112 C10 **Ogulin** Karlovac, NW Croatia 45°15′N 15°13′E
77 S16 **Ogun** ◐ state SW Nigeria
Ogurdzhaly, Ostrov see Ogurjaly Adasy
146 A12 **Ogurjaly Adasy** Rus. Ogurdzhaly, Ostrov. island W Turkmenistan
77 U16 **Ogwashi-Uku** Delta, S Nigeria 06°08′N 06°38′E
185 B23 **Ohai** Southland, South Island, New Zealand 45°56′S 167°59′E
147 Q10 **Ohangaron** Rus. Akhangaran. Toshkent Viloyati, E Uzbekistan 40°56′N 69°37′E
147 Q10 **Ohangaron** Rus. Akhangaran. ≈ E Uzbekistan
83 C16 **Ohangwena** ◐ district N Namibia
30 M10 **O'Hare** ✈ (Chicago) Illinois, N USA 41°59′N 87°56′W
165 R6 **Ōhata** Aomori, Honshū, C Japan 41°23′N 141°09′E
184 L13 **Ohau** Manawatu-Wanganui, North Island, New Zealand 40°40′S 175°15′E
185 E20 **Ohau, Lake** ◎ South Island, New Zealand
Ohcejohka see Utsjoki
99 J20 **Ohey** Namur, SE Belgium 50°26′N 05°07′E
191 X15 **O'Higgins, Cabo** headland Easter Island, Chile, E Pacific Ocean 27°05′S 109°15′W
O'Higgins, Lago see San Martín, Lago
31 S12 **Ohio** off. State of Ohio, also known as Buckeye State. ◐ state N USA
0 L10 **Ohio River** ≈ N USA
Ohlau see Oława
101 H16 **Ohm** ≈ C Germany
193 W16 **Ohonua** 'Eua, E Tonga 21°20′S 174°57′W
23 V5 **Ohoopee River** ≈ Georgia, SE USA
100 L12 **Ohre** Ger. Eger. ≈ Czech Republic/Germany
Ohri see Ohrid
113 M20 **Ohrid** Turk. Ochrida, Ohri. SW FYR Macedonia 41°07′N 20°48′E
113 M20 **Ohrid, Lake** var. Lake Ochrida, Alb. Liqeni i Ohrit, Mac. Ohridsko Ezero. ◎ Albania/FYR Macedonia
Ohridsko Ezero/Ohrit, Liqeni i see Ohrid, Lake
184 L9 **Ohura** Manawatu-Wanganui, North Island, New Zealand 38°51′S 174°58′E
58 J9 **Oiapoque** Amapá, E Brazil 03°54′N 51°46′W
58 J10 **Oiapoque, Rio** var. Fleuve l'Oyapok, Oyapock. ≈ Brazil/French Guiana see also Oyapok, Fleuve l'
Oiapoque, Rio see Oyapok, Fleuve l'
15 O9 **Oies, Île aux** island Québec, SE Canada
92 L13 **Oijärvi** Oulu, C Finland 65°38′N 26°05′E
92 L12 **Oikarainen** Lappi, N Finland 66°30′N 25°46′E
188 F10 **Oikuul** Babeldaob, N Palau
18 C13 **Oil City** Pennsylvania, NE USA 41°25′N 79°42′W
18 C12 **Oil Creek** ≈ Pennsylvania, NE USA
35 R13 **Oildale** California, W USA 35°25′N 119°01′W
Oileán Ciarral see Castleisland
Oil Islands see Chagos Archipelago
115 D18 **Oiniádes** anc. Oeniadae. site of ancient city Dytikí Ellás, W Greece
115 L18 **Oinoússes** island E Greece
Oírr, Inis see Inisheer
99 J15 **Oirschot** Noord-Brabant, S Netherlands 51°30′N 05°18′E
103 N4 **Oise** ◐ department N France
103 P3 **Oise** ≈ N France
99 J14 **Oisterwijk** Noord-Brabant, S Netherlands 51°35′N 05°12′E
45 O14 **Oistins** S Barbados 13°04′N 59°33′W
165 E4 **Ōita** Ōita, Kyūshū, SW Japan 33°15′N 131°35′E
165 D14 **Ōita** off. Ōita-ken. ◐ prefecture Kyūshū, SW Japan
Ōita-ken see Ōita
115 E17 **Oíti** ▲ C Greece 38°48′N 22°12′E
165 S4 **Oiwake** Hokkaidō, NE Japan 42°54′N 141°49′E
35 R14 **Ojai** California, W USA 34°25′N 119°15′W
94 K13 **Öje** Dalarna, C Sweden 60°49′N 13°54′E
93 J14 **Öjebyn** Norrbotten, N Sweden 65°20′N 21°26′E
165 B13 **Ojika-jima** island SW Japan
40 K5 **Ojinaga** Chihuahua, N Mexico 29°31′N 104°26′W
40 M11 **Ojo Caliente** var. Ojocaliente. Zacatecas, C Mexico 22°35′N 102°18′W
Ojocaliente see Ojo Caliente
40 D6 **Ojo de Liebre, Laguna** var. Laguna Scammon, Scammon Lagoon. lagoon NW Mexico
62 I7 **Ojos del Salado, Cerro** ▲ W Argentina 27°04′S 68°34′W
105 R7 **Ojos Negros** Aragón, NE Spain 40°43′N 01°30′W
40 M12 **Ojuelos de Jalisco** Aguascalientes, C Mexico 21°52′N 101°40′W
127 N4 **Oka** ≈ W Russian Federation
83 D19 **Okahandja** Otjozondjupa, C Namibia 21°58′S 16°55′E
184 L9 **Okahukura** Manawatu-Wanganui, North Island, New Zealand 38°48′S 175°13′E
184 J3 **Okaihau** Northland, North Island, New Zealand 35°19′S 173°45′E
83 D18 **Okakarara** Otjozondjupa, N Namibia 20°33′S 17°20′E
13 P5 **Okak Islands** island group Newfoundland and Labrador, E Canada
10 M17 **Okanagan** ≈ British Columbia, SW Canada
11 N17 **Okanagan Lake** ◎ British Columbia, SW Canada
Ókanizsa see Kanjiža
83 C16 **Okankolo** Otjikoto, N Namibia 17°57′S 16°28′E
32 K6 **Okanogan River** ≈ Washington, NW USA
83 D18 **Okaputa** Otjozondjupa, N Namibia 20°09′S 16°56′E
149 V9 **Okāra** Punjab, E Pakistan 30°49′N 73°31′E
26 M10 **Okarche** Oklahoma, C USA 35°43′N 97°58′W
Okarem see Ekerem
189 X14 **Okat Harbor** harbor Kosrae, E Micronesia
22 M5 **Okatibbee Creek** ≈ Mississippi, S USA
83 C17 **Okaukuejo** Kunene, N Namibia 19°10′S 15°23′E
Okavanggo see Cubango/Okavango
83 E17 **Okavango** ◐ district NW Namibia
83 G17 **Okavango** var. Cubango, Kavango, Kavengo, Kubango, Okavanggo, Port. Ocavango. ≈ S Africa see also Cubango
Okavango see Cubango
83 G17 **Okavango Delta** wetland N Botswana
164 M12 **Okaya** Nagano, Honshū, S Japan 36°03′N 138°00′E
164 H13 **Okayama** Okayama, Honshū, SW Japan 34°40′N 133°54′E
164 H13 **Okayama** off. Okayama-ken. ◐ prefecture Honshū, SW Japan
Okayama-ken see Okayama
164 L14 **Okazaki** Aichi, Honshū, C Japan 34°58′N 137°10′E
110 M12 **Okęcie** ✈ (Warszawa) Mazowieckie, C Poland 52°08′N 20°57′E
23 Y13 **Okeechobee** Florida, SE USA 27°14′N 80°49′W
23 Y14 **Okeechobee, Lake** ◎ Florida, SE USA
26 M9 **Okeene** Oklahoma, C USA 36°07′N 98°19′W
23 V8 **Okefenokee Swamp** wetland Georgia, SE USA
97 J24 **Okehampton** SW England, United Kingdom 50°44′N 04°W
27 P10 **Okemah** Oklahoma, C USA 35°25′N 96°20′W
77 U16 **Okene** Kogi, S Nigeria 07°31′N 06°15′E
100 K13 **Oker** var. Ocker. ≈ NW Germany
101 J14 **Oker-Stausee** ◎ C Germany
123 T12 **Okha** Ostrov Sakhalin, Sakhalinskaya Oblast', SE Russian Federation 53°33′N 142°55′E
125 U15 **Okhansk** var. Ochansk. Permskaya Oblast', NW Russian Federation 57°44′N 55°20′E
123 S10 **Okhotsk** Khabarovskiy Kray, E Russian Federation 59°21′N 143°15′E
192 J2 **Okhotsk, Sea of** sea NW Pacific Ocean
117 T4 **Okhtyrka** Rus. Akhtyrka. Sums'ka Oblast', NE Ukraine 50°19′N 34°54′E
83 E23 **Okiep** Northern Cape, W South Africa 29°39′S 17°53′E
Oki-guntō see Oki-shotō
164 H11 **Oki-kaikyō** strait SW Japan
165 P16 **Okinawa** Okinawa, SW Japan 26°20′N 127°47′E
165 S16 **Okinawa** off. Okinawa-ken. ◐ prefecture Okinawa, SW Japan
165 S16 **Okinawa** island SW Japan
Okinawa-ken see Okinawa
165 U16 **Okinoerabu-jima** island Nansei-shotō, SW Japan
164 F15 **Okino-shima** island SW Japan
164 H11 **Oki-shotō** var. Oki-guntō. island group SW Japan
77 T16 **Okitipupa** Ondo, SW Nigeria 06°33′N 04°43′E
166 L8 **Okkan** Bago, SW Burma (Myanmar) 17°30′N 95°52′E
27 N10 **Oklahoma** off. State of Oklahoma, also known as The Sooner State. ◐ state C USA
27 N11 **Oklahoma City** state capital Oklahoma, C USA 35°28′N 97°31′W
25 Q4 **Oklaunion** Texas, SW USA 34°07′N 99°07′W
23 W10 **Oklawaha River** ≈ Florida, SE USA
27 P10 **Okmulgee** Oklahoma, C USA 35°38′N 95°59′W
Oknitsa see Ocniţa
22 M3 **Okolona** Mississippi, S USA 34°00′N 88°45′W
165 U2 **Okoppe** Hokkaidō, NE Japan 44°27′N 143°06′E
11 Q16 **Okotoks** Alberta, SW Canada 50°46′N 113°57′W
80 H6 **Oko, Wadi** ≈ NE Sudan
79 G19 **Okoyo** Cuvette, W Congo 01°28′S 15°04′E
77 S15 **Okpara** ≈ Benin/Nigeria
92 J8 **Øksfjord** Finnmark, N Norway 70°13′N 22°22′E
125 R4 **Oksino** Nenetskiy Avtonomnyy Okrug, NW Russian Federation 67°33′N 52°15′E
92 G13 **Oksskolten** ▲ C Norway 66°00′N 14°18′E
Oksu see Ogsu
144 M8 **Oktaybr'skiy** Kostanay, N Kazakhstan
186 B7 **Ok Tedi** Western, W Papua New Guinea
Oktemberyan see Armavir
166 M7 **Oktwin** Bago, C Burma (Myanmar) 18°47′N 96°21′E
127 R6 **Oktyabr'sk** Samarskaya Oblast', W Russian Federation 53°13′N 48°36′E
Oktyabr'sk see Kandyagash
125 N12 **Oktyabr'skiy** Arkhangel'skaya Oblast', NW Russian Federation 61°03′N 43°16′E
122 E10 **Oktyabr'skiy** Kamchatskaya Oblast', E Russian Federation 52°35′N 156°18′E
127 T5 **Oktyabr'skiy** Respublika Bashkortostan, W Russian Federation 54°28′N 53°29′E
127 O11 **Oktyabr'skiy** Volgogradskaya Oblast', SW Russian Federation 48°00′N 43°35′E
Oktyabr'skiy see Aktsyabrski
127 V7 **Oktyabr'skoye** Orenburgskaya Oblast', W Russian Federation 52°22′N 55°39′E
122 M5 **Oktyabr'skoy Revolyutsii, Ostrov** Eng. October Revolution Island. island Severnaya Zemlya, N Russian Federation
164 C15 **Ōkuchi** var. Ōkuti. Kagoshima, Kyūshū, SW Japan 32°04′N 130°36′E
124 I14 **Okulovka** var. Okulovka. Novgorodskaya Oblast', W Russian Federation 58°24′N 33°16′E
Okulovka see Okulovka
165 Q4 **Okushiri-tō** var. Okusiri Tô. island NE Japan
Okusiri Tô see Okushiri-tō
77 S15 **Okuta** Kwara, W Nigeria 09°18′N 03°09′E
Ōkuti see Ōkuchi
83 F19 **Okwa** var. Chapman's. ≈ Botswana/Namibia
123 T10 **Ola** Magadanskaya Oblast', E Russian Federation 59°36′N 151°18′E
27 T11 **Ola** Arkansas, C USA 35°01′N 93°13′W
Ola see Ala
35 T11 **Olacha Peak** ▲ California, W USA 36°15′N 118°07′W
92 J1 **Ólafsfjördhur** Nordhurland Eystra, N Iceland 66°04′N 18°36′W
92 H3 **Ólafsvík** Vesturland, W Iceland 64°52′N 23°45′W
Oláhbrettye see Bretea-Română
Oláhszentgyörgy see Sângeorz-Băi

◆ Country ● Country Capital ◇ Dependent Territory ○ Dependent Territory Capital ◐ Administrative Regions ✈ International Airport ▲ Mountain ▲▲ Mountain Range Volcano ≈ River ◎ Lake ⊠ Reservoir

Oláh-Toplicza *see* Toplița
35 T11 **Olancha** California, W USA 36°16′N 118°00′W
42 J5 **Olanchito** Yoro, C Honduras 15°30′N 86°34′W
42 J6 **Olancho** ⬖ *department* E Honduras
95 O20 **Öland** *island* S Sweden
95 O19 **Ölands norra udde** *headland* S Sweden 57°21′N 17°06′E
95 N22 **Ölands södra udde** *headland* S Sweden 56°12′N 16°26′E
182 K7 **Olary** South Australia 32°18′S 140°16′E
27 R4 **Olathe** Kansas, C USA 38°52′N 94°50′W
61 C22 **Olavarría** Buenos Aires, E Argentina 36°57′S 60°20′W
92 O2 **Olav V Land** *physical region* C Svalbard
111 H14 **Oława** *Ger.* Ohlau. Dolnośląskie, SW Poland 50°57′N 17°18′E
107 D17 **Olbia** *prev.* Terranova Pausania. Sardegna, Italy, C Mediterranean Sea 40°55′N 09°30′E
44 G5 **Old Bahama Channel** *channel* Bahamas/Cuba
Old Bay State/Old Colony State *see* Massachusetts
10 H2 **Old Crow** Yukon Territory, NW Canada 67°34′N 139°55′W
Old Dominion *see* Virginia
Oldeberkeap *see* Oldeberkoop
98 M7 **Oldeberkoop** *Fris.* Oldeberkeap. Friesland, N Netherlands 52°55′N 06°07′E
98 L10 **Oldebroek** Gelderland, E Netherlands 52°27′N 05°54′E
98 L8 **Oldemarkt** Overijssel, N Netherlands 52°49′N 05°58′E
94 E11 **Olden** Sogn Og Fjordane, C Norway 61°52′N 06°44′E
100 G10 **Oldenburg** Niedersachsen, NW Germany 53°09′N 08°13′E
100 K8 **Oldenburg** *var.* Oldenburg in Holstein. Schleswig-Holstein, N Germany 54°17′N 10°55′E
Oldenburg in Holstein *see* Oldenburg
98 P10 **Oldenzaal** Overijssel, E Netherlands 52°19′N 06°53′E
Olderfjord *see* Leaibevuotna
18 J8 **Old Forge** New York, NE USA 43°42′N 74°59′W
Old Goa *see* Goa
97 L17 **Oldham** NW England, United Kingdom 53°36′N 02°W
39 Q14 **Old Harbor** Kodiak Island, Alaska, USA 57°12′N 153°18′W
44 J13 **Old Harbour** C Jamaica 17°56′N 77°06′W
97 C22 **Old Head of Kinsale** *Ir.* An Seancheann. *headland* SW Ireland 51°37′N 08°33′W
20 J8 **Old Hickory Lake** ⊠ Tennessee, S USA
Old Line State *see* Maryland
Old North State *see* North Carolina
81 I17 **Ol Doinyo Lengeyo** ▲▲ C Kenya
11 Q16 **Olds** Alberta, SW Canada 51°50′N 114°06′W
19 O7 **Old Speck Mountain** ▲ Maine, NE USA 44°34′N 70°55′W
19 S6 **Old Town** Maine, NE USA 44°55′N 68°39′W
11 T17 **Old Wives Lake** ◎ Saskatchewan, S Canada
162 J7 **Öldziyt** *var.* Höshööt. Arhangay, C Mongolia 48°06′N 102°34′E
162 I8 **Öldziyt** *var.* Ulaan-Uul. Bayanhongor, C Mongolia 46°03′N 100°52′E
162 L10 **Öldziyt** *var.* Rashaant. Dundgovĭ, C Mongolia 44°54′N 106°32′E
162 K8 **Öldziyt** *var.* Sangiyn Dalay. Övörhangay, C Mongolia 46°35′N 103°18′E
Öldziyt *see* Erdenemandal, Arhangay, Mongolia
Öldziyt *see* Sayhandulaan, Dornogovĭ, Mongolia
188 H6 **Oleai** *var.* San Jose. Saipan, S Northern Mariana Islands
18 E11 **Olean** New York, NE USA 42°04′N 78°24′W
110 O7 **Olecko** *Ger.* Treuburg. Warmińsko-Mazurskie, NE Poland 54°02′N 22°29′E
106 C7 **Oleggio** Piemonte, NE Italy 45°36′N 08°37′E
123 P11 **Olëkma** Amurskaya Oblast′, SE Russian Federation 57°00′N 120°27′E
123 P12 **Olëkma** ≈ C Russian Federation
123 P11 **Olëkminsk** Respublika Sakha (Yakutiya), NE Russian Federation 60°25′N 120°25′E
117 W7 **Oleksandrivka** Donets′ka Oblast′, E Ukraine 48°42′N 36°56′E
117 R7 **Oleksandrivka** *Rus.* Aleksandrovka. Kirovohrads′ka Oblast′, C Ukraine 48°59′N 32°14′E
117 Q9 **Oleksandrivka** Mykolayivs′ka Oblast′, S Ukraine 47°42′N 31°17′E
117 S7 **Oleksandriya** *Rus.* Aleksandriya. Kirovohrads′ka Oblast′, C Ukraine 48°42′N 33°07′E
93 B20 **Ølen** Hordaland, S Norway 59°36′N 05°48′E
124 J4 **Olenegorsk** Murmanskaya Oblast′, NW Russian Federation 68°06′N 33°15′E
123 N9 **Olenëk** Respublika Sakha (Yakutiya), NE Russian Federation 68°28′N 112°18′E
123 N9 **Olenëk** ≈ NE Russian Federation
123 O7 **Olenëkskiy Zaliv** *bay* N Russian Federation
124 K6 **Olenitsa** Murmanskaya Oblast′, NW Russian Federation 66°27′N 35°21′E
102 I11 **Oléron, Île d′** *island* W France
111 H14 **Oleśnica** *Ger.* Oels, Oels in Schlesien. Dolnośląskie, SW Poland 51°13′N 17°20′E
111 I15 **Olesno** *Ger.* Rosenberg. Opolskie, S Poland 50°53′N 18°23′E
116 M3 **Olevs′k** *Rus.* Olevsk. Zhytomyrs′ka Oblast′, N Ukraine 51°12′N 27°38′E
Olevsk *see* Olevs′k
123 S15 **Ol′ga** Primorskiy Kray, SE Russian Federation 43°41′N 135°06′E
Olga, Mount *see* Kata Tjuta
92 P2 **Olgastretet** *strait* E Svalbard
162 D5 **Ölgiy** Bayan-Ölgiy, W Mongolia 48°57′N 89°59′E
95 F23 **Ølgod** Ribe, W Denmark 55°44′N 08°37′E
104 H14 **Olhão** Faro, S Portugal 37°01′N 07°50′W
93 L14 **Olhava** Oulu, C Finland 65°28′N 25°25′E
112 B12 **Olib** *It.* Ulbo. *island* W Croatia
83 B16 **Olifa** Kunene, NW Namibia 17°25′S 14°27′E
83 E20 **Olifants** *var.* Elephant River. ≈ E Namibia
83 E25 **Olifants** *var.* Elefantes. ≈ SW South Africa
83 I20 **Olifants Drift** *var.* Oliphants Drift. Kgatleng, SE Botswana 24°13′S 26°52′E
83 G22 **Olifantshoek** Northern Cape, N South Africa 27°56′S 22°45′E
188 L15 **Olimarao Atoll** *atoll* Caroline Islands, C Micronesia
Ólimbos *see* Ólympos
Olimpo *see* Fuerte Olimpo
59 Q15 **Olinda** Pernambuco, E Brazil 08°S 34°51′W
Olinthos *see* Ólynthos
Oliphants Drift *see* Olifants Drift
Olisipo *see* Lisboa
Olita *see* Alytus
105 Q4 **Olite** Navarra, N Spain 42°29′N 01°40′W
62 K10 **Oliva** Córdoba, C Argentina 32°03′S 63°34′W
105 T11 **Oliva** País Valenciano, E Spain 38°55′N 00°09′W
Oliva *see* La Oliva
104 I12 **Oliva de la Frontera** Extremadura, W Spain 38°17′N 06°54′W
Olivares *see* Olivares de Júcar
62 H9 **Olivares, Cerro de** ▲ N Chile 30°25′S 69°52′W
105 P9 **Olivares de Júcar** *var.* Olivares. Castilla-La Mancha, C Spain 39°45′N 02°21′W
22 L1 **Olive Branch** Mississippi, S USA 34°58′N 89°49′W
21 O5 **Olive Hill** Kentucky, S USA 38°18′N 83°10′W
35 O6 **Olivehurst** California, W USA 39°05′N 121°33′W
104 G7 **Oliveira de Azeméis** Aveiro, N Portugal 40°49′N 08°29′W
104 I11 **Olivenza** Extremadura, W Spain 38°41′N 07°06′W
11 N17 **Oliver** British Columbia, SW Canada 49°10′N 119°37′W
103 N7 **Olivet** Loiret, C France 47°53′N 01°53′E
29 Q12 **Olivet** South Dakota, N USA 43°14′N 97°40′W
29 T9 **Olivia** Minnesota, N USA 44°46′N 94°59′W
185 C20 **Olivine Range** ▲▲ South Island, New Zealand
108 H10 **Olivone** Ticino, S Switzerland 46°32′N 08°55′E
Ölkeyek *see* Ul′kayak
127 O9 **Ol′khovka** Volgogradskaya Oblast′, SW Russian Federation 49°54′N 44°36′E
111 K16 **Olkusz** Małopolskie, S Poland 50°18′N 19°33′E
22 I6 **Olla** Louisiana, S USA 31°54′N 92°14′W
62 I4 **Ollagüe, Volcán** *var.* Oyahue, Volcán Oyahue. ⟁ N Chile 21°25′S 68°10′W
189 U13 **Ollan** *island* Chuuk, C Micronesia
188 F7 **Ollei** Babeldaob, N Palau 07°43′N 134°37′E
Ollius *see* Oglio
108 C10 **Ollon** Vaud, W Switzerland 46°19′N 07°00′E
147 Q10 **Olmaliq** *Rus.* Almalyk. Toshkent Viloyati, E Uzbekistan 40°51′N 69°39′E
104 M6 **Olmedo** Castilla-León, N Spain 41°17′N 04°41′W
56 B10 **Olmos** Lambayeque, W Peru 06°00′S 79°43′W
Olmütz *see* Olomouc
30 M15 **Olney** Illinois, N USA 38°43′N 88°05′W
25 R5 **Olney** Texas, SW USA 33°22′N 98°45′W
95 L22 **Olofström** Blekinge, S Sweden 56°16′N 14°33′E
187 N9 **Olomburi** Malaita, N Solomon Islands 09°00′S 161°09′E
111 H17 **Olomouc** *Ger.* Olmütz, *Pol.* Ołomuniec. Olomoucký Kraj, E Czech Republic 49°36′N 17°13′E
111 H18 **Olomoucký Kraj** ⬖ *region* E Czech Republic
Ołomuniec *see* Olomouc
122 D7 **Olonets** Respublika Kareliya, NW Russian Federation 60°58′N 33°01′E
171 N3 **Olongapo** *off.* Olongapo City. Luzon, N Philippines 14°52′N 120°16′E
Olongapo City *see* Olongapo
102 J16 **Oloron-Ste-Marie** Pyrénées-Atlantiques, SW France 43°12′N 00°35′W
192 L16 **Olosega** *island* Manua Islands, E American Samoa
105 W4 **Olot** Cataluña, NE Spain 42°11′N 02°30′E
146 K12 **Olot** *Rus.* Alat. Buxoro Viloyati, C Uzbekistan 39°22′N 63°42′E
112 I12 **Olovo** Federacija Bosna I Hercegovina, E Bosnia and Herzegovina 44°08′N 18°35′E
123 O14 **Olovyannaya** Chitinskaya Oblast′, S Russian Federation 50°59′N 115°24′E
123 T7 **Oloy** ≈ NE Russian Federation
101 F16 **Olpe** Nordrhein-Westfalen, W Germany 51°02′N 07°51′E
109 N8 **Olperer** ▲ SW Austria 47°03′N 11°36′E
Olshanka *see* Vil′shanka
Ol′shany *see* Al′shany
Olsnitz *see* Murska Sobota
98 M10 **Olst** Overijssel, E Netherlands 52°19′N 06°06′E
110 L8 **Olsztyn** *Ger.* Allenstein. Warmińsko-Mazurskie, N Poland 53°46′N 20°28′E
110 L8 **Olsztynek** *Ger.* Hohenstein in Ostpreussen. Warmińsko-Mazurskie, N Poland 53°35′N 20°17′E
116 I14 **Olt** ⬖ *county* SW Romania
116 I14 **Olt** *var.* Oltul, *Ger.* Alt. ≈ S Romania
108 E7 **Olten** Solothurn, NW Switzerland 47°22′N 07°55′E
116 K14 **Oltenița** *prev. Eng.* Oltenitsa; *anc.* Constantiola. Călărași, SE Romania 44°05′N 26°40′E
Oltenitsa *see* Oltenița
116 H14 **Olteț** ≈ S Romania
24 M4 **Olton** Texas, SW USA 34°10′N 102°07′W
137 R12 **Oltu** Erzurum, NE Turkey 40°34′N 41°59′E
Oltul *see* Olt
146 G7 **Oltynko‘l** Qoraqalpog‘iston Respublikasi, NW Uzbekistan 43°04′N 58°51′E
161 S15 **Oluan Pi** *Eng.* Cape Olwanpi. *headland* S Taiwan 21°57′N 120°48′E
Ólubló *see* Stará L′ubovňa
137 R11 **Olur** Erzurum, NE Turkey 40°49′N 42°08′E
104 L15 **Olvera** Andalucía, S Spain 36°56′N 05°15′W
Ol′viopol′ *see* Pervomays′k
Olwanpi, Cape *see* Oluan Pi
115 D20 **Olympía** Dytikí Ellás, S Greece 37°39′N 21°36′E
32 G9 **Olympia** *state capital* Washington, NW USA 47°02′N 122°54′W
182 H5 **Olympic Dam** South Australia 30°25′S 136°56′E
32 F7 **Olympic Mountains** ▲▲ Washington, NW USA
121 O3 **Ólympos** *var.* Troodos, *Eng.* Mount Olympus. ▲ C Cyprus 34°55′N 32°49′E
115 F15 **Ólympos** *var.* Ólimbos, *Eng.* Mount Olympus. ▲ N Greece 40°04′N 22°24′E
115 L17 **Ólympos** ▲ Lésvos, E Greece 39°03′N 26°20′E
16 C5 **Olympus, Mount** ▲ Washington, NW USA 47°48′N 123°42′W
Olympus, Mount *see* Ólympos
115 G14 **Ólynthos** *var.* Olinthos; *anc.* Olynthus. *site of ancient city* Kentrikí Makedonía, N Greece
Olynthus *see* Ólynthos
117 Q3 **Olyshivka** Chernihivs′ka Oblast′, N Ukraine 51°13′N 31°19′E
123 W8 **Olyutorskiy, Mys** *headland* E Russian Federation 59°56′N 170°22′E
123 V8 **Olyutorskiy Zaliv** *bay* E Russian Federation
186 M10 **Om** ≈ W Papua New Guinea
129 S6 **Om′** ≈ N Russian Federation
158 I13 **Oma** Xizang Zizhiqu, W China 32°30′N 83°14′E
165 R6 **Ōma** Aomori, Honshū, C Japan 41°31′N 140°54′E
125 P6 **Oma** ≈ NW Russian Federation
164 M12 **Ōmachi** *var.* Ômati. Nagano, Honshū, S Japan 36°30′N 137°51′E
165 Q8 **Ōmagari** Akita, Honshū, C Japan 39°29′N 140°29′E
97 E15 **Omagh** *Ir.* An Ómaigh. W Northern Ireland, United Kingdom 54°36′N 07°18′W
29 S15 **Omaha** Nebraska, C USA 41°14′N 95°57′W
83 E19 **Omaheke** ⬖ *district* W Namibia
141 W10 **Oman** *off.* Sultanate of Oman, *Ar.* Salṭanat ‘Umān; *prev.* Muscat and Oman. ◆ *monarchy* SW Asia
129 O10 **Oman Basin** *var.* Bassin d′Oman. *undersea feature* N Indian Ocean 23°20′N 63°00′E
Oman, Bassin d′ *see* Oman Basin
129 N10 **Oman, Gulf of** *Ar.* Khalīj ‘Umān. *gulf* N Arabian Sea
Oman, Sultanate of *see* Oman
184 J3 **Omapere** Northland, North Island, New Zealand 35°32′S 173°24′E
185 E20 **Omarama** Canterbury, South Island, New Zealand 44°29′S 169°57′E
112 F11 **Omarska** ⬖ Republika Srpska, NW Bosnia and Herzegovina
83 C18 **Omaruru** Erongo, NW Namibia 21°28′S 15°56′E
83 C19 **Omaruru** ≈ W Namibia
83 E17 **Omatako** ≈ NE Namibia
Ômati *see* Ōmachi
83 E18 **Omawewozonyanda** Omaheke, E Namibia 21°30′S 19°34′E
165 R6 **Ōma-zaki** *headland* Honshū, C Japan 41°32′N 140°53′E
Omba *see* Ambae
Ombai *see* Alor, Pulau
83 C16 **Ombalantu** Omusati, N Namibia 17°33′S 14°58′E
79 H15 **Ombella-Mpoko** ⬖ *prefecture* S Central African Republic
Ombetsu *see* Onbetsu
83 B17 **Ombombo** Kunene, NW Namibia 18°43′S 13°53′E
79 D19 **Omboué** Ogooué-Maritime, W Gabon 01°38′S 09°20′E
106 G13 **Ombrone** ≈ C Italy
80 F9 **Omdurman** *var.* Umm Durmān. Khartoum, C Sudan 15°37′N 32°29′E
165 N13 **Ōme** Tōkyō, Honshū, S Japan 35°48′N 139°17′E
106 C6 **Omegna** Piemonte, NE Italy 45°54′N 08°25′E
183 P12 **Omeo** Victoria, SE Australia 37°09′S 147°36′E
138 F11 **Omer** Southern, C Israel 31°16′N 34°51′E
41 P16 **Ometepec** Guerrero, S Mexico 16°39′N 98°23′W
42 K11 **Ometepe, Isla de** *island* S Nicaragua
Om Hager *see* Om Ḥajer
80 I10 **Om Ḥajer** *var.* Om Hager. SW Eritrea 14°19′N 36°46′E
142 L10 **Omīdīyeh** Khūzestān, SW Iran 30°45′N 49°42′E
165 J13 **Ōmi-Hachiman** *var.* Ômihachiman. Shiga, Honshū, SW Japan 35°08′N 136°04′E
Ômihachiman *see* Ōmi-Hachiman
10 L12 **Omineca Mountains** ▲▲ British Columbia, W Canada
113 F14 **Omiš** *It.* Almissa. Split-Dalmacija, S Croatia 43°27′N 16°41′E
112 B10 **Omišalj** Primorje-Gorski Kotar, NW Croatia 45°10′N 14°33′E
83 D19 **Omitara** Khomas, C Namibia 22°18′S 18°01′E
41 O16 **Omitlán, Río** ≈ S Mexico
39 X14 **Ommaney, Cape** *headland* Baranof Island, Alaska, USA 56°10′N 134°40′W
98 N9 **Ommen** Overijssel, E Netherlands 52°31′N 06°25′E
163 N7 **Ömnödelger** *var.* Bayanbulag. Hentiy, C Mongolia 47°54′N 109°51′E
162 K11 **Ömnögovĭ** ⬖ *province* S Mongolia
191 X7 **Omoa** Fatu Hira, NE French Polynesia 10°30′S 138°41′E
Omo Botego *see* Omo Wenz
Ómoldova *see* Moldova Veche
123 T7 **Omolon** Chukotskiy Avtonomnyy Okrug, NE Russian Federation 65°11′N 160°33′E
123 T7 **Omolon** ≈ NE Russian Federation
123 Q8 **Omoloy** ≈ NE Russian Federation
165 P8 **Omono-gawa** ≈ Honshū, C Japan
81 I14 **Omo Wenz** *var.* Omo Botego. ≈ Ethiopia/Kenya
122 H12 **Omsk** Omskaya Oblast′, C Russian Federation 55°N 73°22′E
122 H11 **Omskaya Oblast′** ⬖ *province* C Russian Federation
165 U2 **Ōmu** Hokkaidō, NE Japan 44°36′N 142°55′E
110 M9 **Omulew** ≈ NE Poland
116 J12 **Omul, Vârful** *prev.* Vîrful Omu. ▲ C Romania 45°24′N 25°26′E
83 D16 **Omundaungilo** Ohangwena, N Namibia 17°28′S 16°39′E
164 C14 **Ōmura** Nagasaki, Kyūshū, SW Japan 32°56′N 129°58′E
83 B17 **Omusati** ⬖ *district* N Namibia
164 C14 **Ōmuta** Fukuoka, Kyūshū, SW Japan 33°01′N 130°27′E
125 S14 **Omutninsk** Kirovskaya Oblast′, NW Russian Federation 58°37′N 52°08′E
Omu, Vîrful *see* Omul, Vârful
29 V7 **Onamia** Minnesota, N USA 46°04′N 93°40′W
21 Y5 **Onancock** Virginia, NE USA 37°42′N 75°45′W
14 E10 **Onaping Lake** ◎ Ontario, S Canada
30 M12 **Onarga** Illinois, N USA 40°39′N 88°00′W
15 R6 **Onatchiway, Lac** ◎ Québec, SE Canada
29 S14 **Onawa** Iowa, C USA 42°01′N 96°06′W
165 U5 **Onbetsu** *var.* Ombetsu. Hokkaidō, NE Japan 42°52′N 143°54′E
83 B16 **Oncócua** Cunene, SW Angola 16°37′S 13°23′E
105 S9 **Onda** País Valenciano, E Spain 39°58′N 00°17′W
111 N18 **Ondava** ≈ NE Slovakia
Ondjiva *see* N′Giva
77 T16 **Ondo** Ondo, SW Nigeria 07°07′N 04°50′E
77 T16 **Ondo** ⬖ *state* SW Nigeria
163 N8 **Öndörhaan** *var.* Undur Khan; *prev.* Tsetsen Khan. Hentiy, E Mongolia 47°21′N 110°42′E
162 M9 **Öndörshil** *var.* Böhöt. Dundgovĭ, C Mongolia 45°13′N 108°12′E
162 L8 **Öndörshireet** *var.* Bayshint. Töv, C Mongolia 47°22′N 105°04′E
162 I7 **Öndör-Ulaan** *var.* Teel. Arhangay, C Mongolia 48°01′N 100°30′E
83 D18 **Ondundazongonda** Otjozondjupa, N Namibia 20°28′S 18°00′E
151 K21 **One and Half Degree Channel** *channel* S Maldives
187 Z15 **Oneata** *island* Lau Group, E Fiji
124 L9 **Onega** Arkhangel′skaya Oblast′, NW Russian Federation 63°54′N 37°59′E
124 L9 **Onega** ≈ NW Russian Federation
Onega Bay *see* Onezhskaya Guba
Onega, Lake *see* Onezhskoye Ozero
18 I10 **Oneida** New York, NE USA 43°05′N 75°39′W
20 M8 **Oneida** Tennessee, S USA 36°30′N 84°30′W
18 H9 **Oneida Lake** ◎ New York, NE USA
29 P13 **O′Neill** Nebraska, C USA 42°28′N 98°38′W
123 V12 **Onekotan, Ostrov** *island* Kuril′skiye Ostrova, SE Russian Federation
23 P3 **Oneonta** Alabama, S USA 33°57′N 86°28′W
18 J11 **Oneonta** New York, NE USA 42°27′N 75°03′W
190 I16 **Oneroa** *island* S Cook Islands
116 K11 **Onești** *Hung.* Onyest; *prev.* Gheorghe Gheorghiu-Dej. Bacău, E Romania 46°14′N 26°46′E
193 V15 **Onevai** *island* Tongatapu Group, S Tonga
108 A11 **Onex** Genève, SW Switzerland 46°12′N 06°04′E
124 K8 **Onezhskaya Guba** *Eng.* Onega Bay. *bay* NW Russian Federation
122 D7 **Onezhskoye Ozero** *Eng.* Lake Onega. ◎ NW Russian Federation
83 C16 **Ongandjera** Omusati, N Namibia 17°49′S 15°06′E
184 N12 **Ongaonga** Hawke′s Bay, North Island, New Zealand 39°57′S 176°21′E
Ongi *see* Sayhan-Ovoo, Dundgovĭ, Mongolia
Ongi *see* Uyanga
163 W14 **Ongjin** SW North Korea 37°56′N 125°22′E
155 J17 **Ongole** Andhra Pradesh, E India 15°33′N 80°03′E
Ongon *see* Bürd
Ongtüstik Qazaqstan Oblysy *see* Yuzhnyy Kazakhstan
99 I21 **Onhaye** Namur, S Belgium 50°15′N 04°51′E
166 M8 **Onhne** Bago, SW Burma (Myanmar) 17°02′N 96°28′E
137 S9 **Oni** N Georgia 42°36′N 43°13′E
29 N9 **Onida** South Dakota, N USA 44°42′N 100°03′W
164 F15 **Onigajō-yama** ▲ Shikoku, SW Japan 33°10′N 132°37′E
172 H7 **Onilahy** ≈ S Madagascar
77 U16 **Onitsha** Anambra, S Nigeria 06°09′N 06°48′E
164 K12 **Ōno** Fukui, Honshū, SW Japan 35°59′N 136°30′E
164 I13 **Ono** Hyōgo, Honshū, SW Japan 34°52′N 134°55′E
187 K15 **Ono** *island* SW Fiji
164 E13 **Onoda** Yamaguchi, Honshū, SW Japan 34°00′N 131°11′E
187 Z16 **Ono-i-lau** *island* SE Fiji
164 D13 **Ōnojō** *var.* Ônozyô. Fukuoka, Kyūshū, SW Japan 33°34′N 130°29′E
163 O7 **Onon Gol** ≈ N Mongolia
Ononte *see* Orontes
55 N6 **Onoto** Anzoátegui, NE Venezuela 09°36′N 65°12′W
191 O3 **Onotoa** *prev.* Clerk Island. *atoll* Tungaru, W Kiribati
Ônozyô *see* Ōnojō
95 I19 **Onsala** Halland, S Sweden 57°25′N 12°00′E
83 E23 **Onseepkans** Northern Cape, W South Africa 28°44′S 19°18′E
104 F4 **Ons, Illa de** *island* NW Spain
180 H7 **Onslow** Western Australia 21°42′S 115°08′E
21 W11 **Onslow Bay** *bay* North Carolina, E USA
98 P6 **Onstwedde** Groningen, NE Netherlands 53°01′N 07°04′E
164 C16 **On-take** ▲ Kyūshū, SW Japan 31°35′N 130°39′E
35 T15 **Ontario** California, W USA 34°03′N 117°39′W
32 M13 **Ontario** Oregon, NW USA 44°01′N 116°57′W
12 D10 **Ontario** ⬖ *province* S Canada
11 P14 **Ontario, Lake** ◎ Canada/USA
0 L9 **Ontario Peninsula** *peninsula* Canada/USA
Onteniente *see* Ontinyent
105 S11 **Ontinyent** *var.* Onteniente. País Valenciano, E Spain 38°49′N 00°37′W
93 N15 **Ontojärvi** ◎ E Finland
30 L3 **Ontonagon** Michigan, N USA 46°52′N 89°18′W
30 L3 **Ontonagon River** ≈ Michigan, N USA
186 M7 **Ontong Java Atoll** *prev.* Lord Howe Island. *atoll* N Solomon Islands
175 N5 **Ontong Java Rise** *undersea feature* W Pacific Ocean 01°00′N 157°00′E
Onuba *see* Huelva
55 W9 **Onverwacht** Para, N Surinam 05°36′N 55°12′W
Onyest *see* Onești
Oodeypore *see* Udaipur
182 J7 **Oodla Wirra** South Australia 32°52′S 139°05′E
182 F2 **Oodnadatta** South Australia 27°34′S 135°27′E
182 C5 **Ooldea** South Australia 30°29′S 131°50′E
27 Q8 **Oologah Lake** ⊠ Oklahoma, C USA
Oos-Kaap *see* Eastern Cape
Oos-Londen *see* East London
99 E17 **Oostakker** Oost-Vlaanderen, NW Belgium 51°06′N 03°46′E
99 D15 **Oostburg** Zeeland, SW Netherlands 51°20′N 03°30′E
98 K9 **Oostelijk-Flevoland** *polder* C Netherlands
99 B16 **Oostende** *Eng.* Ostend, *Fr.* Ostende. West-Vlaanderen, NW Belgium 51°13′N 02°55′E
99 B16 **Oostende** ✈ West-Vlaanderen, NW Belgium 51°12′N 02°55′E
98 L12 **Oosterbeek** Gelderland, SE Netherlands 51°59′N 05°51′E
99 I14 **Oosterhout** Noord-Brabant, S Netherlands 51°38′N 04°51′E
98 O6 **Oostermoers Vaart** *var.* Hunze. ≈ NE Netherlands
99 F14 **Oosterschelde** *Eng.* Eastern Scheldt. *inlet* SW Netherlands
99 E14 **Oosterscheldedam** *dam* SW Netherlands
98 M7 **Oosterwolde** *Fris.* Easterwâlde. Friesland, N Netherlands 53°01′N 06°15′E
98 I9 **Oosthuizen** Noord-Holland, NW Netherlands 52°34′N 05°00′E
99 H16 **Oostmalle** Antwerpen, N Belgium 51°18′N 04°44′E
Oos-Transvaal *see* Mpumalanga
99 E15 **Oost-Souburg** Zeeland, SW Netherlands 51°28′N 03°36′E
99 E17 **Oost-Vlaanderen** *Eng.* East Flanders. ⬖ *province* NW Belgium
98 J5 **Oost-Vlieland** Friesland, N Netherlands 53°19′N 05°02′E
98 F12 **Oostvoorne** Zuid-Holland, SW Netherlands 51°55′N 04°06′E
Ootacamund *see* Udagamandalam
98 O10 **Ootmarsum** Overijssel, E Netherlands 52°25′N 06°55′E
10 K14 **Ootsa Lake** ⊠ British Columbia, SW Canada
Ooty *see* Udagamandalam
114 L8 **Opaka** Tŭrgovishte, N Bulgaria 43°26′N 26°12′E
79 M18 **Opala** Orientale, C Dem. Rep. Congo 0°40′S 24°20′E
125 Q13 **Oparino** Kirovskaya Oblast′, NW Russian Federation 59°52′N 48°14′E
14 H8 **Opasatica, Lac** ◎ Québec, SE Canada
112 B9 **Opatija** *It.* Abbazia. Primorje-Gorski Kotar, NW Croatia 45°18′N 14°15′E
111 N15 **Opatów** Świętokrzyskie, C Poland 50°45′N 21°27′E
111 I17 **Opava** *Ger.* Troppau. Moravskoslezský Kraj, E Czech Republic 49°56′N 17°53′E
111 H16 **Opava** *Ger.* Oppa. ≈ NE Czech Republic
Ópazova *see* Stara Pazova
Ópécska *see* Pecica
14 E8 **Opeepeesway Lake** ◎ Ontario, S Canada
23 R5 **Opelika** Alabama, S USA 32°39′N 85°22′W
22 I8 **Opelousas** Louisiana, S USA 30°31′N 92°04′W
186 G6 **Open Bay** *bay* New Britain, E Papua New Guinea
14 I12 **Opeongo Lake** ◎ Ontario, SE Canada
99 K17 **Opglabbeek** Limburg, NE Belgium 51°04′N 05°39′E
33 W6 **Opheim** Montana, NW USA 48°50′N 106°24′W
39 P10 **Ophir** Alaska, USA 63°08′N 156°31′W
Ophiusa *see* Formentera
79 N18 **Opienge** Orientale, E Dem. Rep. Congo 0°15′N 27°25′E
185 G20 **Opihi** ≈ South Island, New Zealand
12 J9 **Opinaca** ≈ Québec, C Canada
12 J10 **Opinaca, Réservoir** ⊠ Québec, E Canada
117 T5 **Opishnya** *Rus.* Oposhnya. Poltavs′ka Oblast′, NE Ukraine 49°58′N 34°37′E
98 I8 **Opmeer** Noord-Holland, NW Netherlands 52°43′N 04°56′E
77 V17 **Opobo** Akwa Ibom, S Nigeria 04°36′N 07°37′E
124 F16 **Opochka** Pskovskaya Oblast′, W Russian Federation 56°42′N 28°40′E
110 L13 **Opoczno** Łodzkie, C Poland 51°24′N 20°18′E
111 I15 **Opole** *Ger.* Oppeln. Opolskie, S Poland 50°40′N 17°56′E
111 H15 **Opolskie** ⬖ *province* S Poland
Opornyy *see* Borankul
104 G4 **O Porriño** *var.* Porriño. Galicia, NW Spain 42°10′N 08°38′W
Oporto *see* Porto
Oposhnya *see* Opishnya
184 P8 **Opotiki** Bay of Plenty, North Island, New Zealand 38°02′S 177°18′E
23 Q7 **Opp** Alabama, S USA 31°16′N 86°14′W
Oppa *see* Opava
94 G9 **Oppdal** Sør-Trøndelag, S Norway 62°36′N 09°41′E
Oppeln *see* Opole
107 N23 **Oppido Mamertina** Calabria, SW Italy 38°17′N 15°58′E
Oppidum Ubiorum *see* Köln
94 F12 **Oppland** ⬖ *county* S Norway
118 J12 **Opsa** Vitsyebskaya Voblasts′, NW Belarus 55°32′N 26°50′E
26 I8 **Optima Lake** ⊠ Oklahoma, C USA
184 J11 **Opunake** Taranaki, North Island, New Zealand 39°27′S 173°52′E
191 N6 **Opunohu, Baie d′** *bay* Moorea, W French Polynesia
83 B17 **Opuwo** Kunene, NW Namibia 18°03′S 13°54′E
146 H6 **Oqqal′a** *var.* Akkala, *Rus.* Karakala. Qoraqalpog‘iston Respublikasi, NW Uzbekistan 43°43′N 59°25′E
147 V13 **Oqsu** *Rus.* Oksu. ≈ SE Tajikistan
147 P14 **Oqtogh, Qatorkŭhi** *Rus.* Khrebet Aktau. ▲▲ SW Tajikistan
146 M11 **Oqtosh** *Rus.* Aktash. Samarqand Viloyati, C Uzbekistan 39°23′N 65°46′E
147 N11 **Oqtov Tizmasi** *var.* Khrebet Aktau. ▲▲ C Uzbekistan
30 J12 **Oquawka** Illinois, N USA 40°56′N 90°56′W
144 J10 **Or′** *Kaz.* Or. ≈ Kazakhstan/Russian Federation
36 M15 **Oracle** Arizona, SW USA 32°36′N 110°46′W
147 N13 **O‘radaryo** *Rus.* Uradar′ya. ≈ S Uzbekistan
116 F9 **Oradea** *prev.* Oradea Mare, *Ger.* Grosswardein, *Hung.* Nagyvárad. Bihor, NW Romania 47°03′N 21°56′E
Oradea Mare *see* Oradea
Orahovac *see* Rahovec
112 H9 **Orahovica** Virovitica-Podravina, NE Croatia 45°33′N 17°54′E
152 K13 **Orai** Uttar Pradesh, N India 26°00′N 79°26′E
92 K12 **Orajärvi** Lappi, NW Finland 66°54′N 24°04′E
138 F9 **Or′Akiva** *prev.* Or ‘Aqiva. Haifa, W Israel 32°40′N 34°58′E
Oral *see* Ural′sk
74 I5 **Oran** *var.* Ouahran, Wahran. NW Algeria 35°42′N 00°37′W
183 R8 **Orange** New South Wales, SE Australia 33°16′S 149°06′E
103 R14 **Orange** *anc.* Arausio. Vaucluse, SE France 44°06′N 04°52′E
25 Y10 **Orange** Texas, SW USA 30°05′N 93°43′W
21 V5 **Orange** Virginia, NE USA 38°14′N 78°07′W
21 R13 **Orangeburg** South Carolina, SE USA 33°28′N 80°53′W
58 J9 **Orange, Cabo** *headland* NE Brazil 04°24′N 51°33′W
29 S12 **Orange City** Iowa, C USA 43°00′N 96°03′W
Orange Cone *see* Orange Fan
172 J10 **Orange Fan** *var.* Orange Cone. *undersea feature* SW Indian Ocean 32°00′S 12°00′E
Orange Free State *see* Free State
25 S14 **Orange Grove** Texas, SW USA 27°57′N 97°56′W
18 K13 **Orange Lake** New York, NE USA 41°32′N 74°06′W
23 V10 **Orange Lake** ◎ Florida, SE USA
Orange Mouth/Orangemund *see* Oranjemund
23 W9 **Orange Park** Florida, SE USA 30°10′N 81°42′W
83 E23 **Orange River** *Afr.* Oranjerivier. ≈ S Africa
14 G15 **Orangeville** Ontario, S Canada 43°55′N 80°06′W
36 M5 **Orangeville** Utah, W USA 39°14′N 111°03′W
42 G1 **Orange Walk** Orange Walk, N Belize 18°06′N 88°30′W
42 F1 **Orange Walk** ⬖ *district* NW Belize
100 N11 **Oranienburg** Brandenburg, NE Germany 52°46′N 13°15′E
98 O7 **Oranjekanaal** *canal* NE Netherlands
83 D23 **Oranjemund** *var.* Orangemund; *prev.* Orange Mouth. Karas, SW Namibia 28°33′S 16°28′E
Oranjerivier *see* Orange River
45 N16 **Oranjestad** ○ (Aruba) W Aruba 12°31′N 70°W
Oranje Vrystaat *see* Free State
Orany *see* Varėna
83 H18 **Orapa** Central, C Botswana 21°16′S 25°22′E
Or ‘Aqiva *see* Or′Akiva
112 I10 **Orašje** ⬖ Federacija Bosna I Herecegovina, N Bosnia and Herzegovina
116 G11 **Orăștie** *Ger.* Broos, *Hung.* Szászváros. Hunedoara, W Romania 45°50′N 23°11′E
Orașul Stalin *see* Brașov
111 K18 **Orava** *Hung.* Árva, *Pol.* Orawa. ≈ N Slovakia
Oravainen *see* Oravais
93 K16 **Oravais** *Fin.* Oravainen. Länsi-Suomi, W Finland 63°18′N 22°25′E
Oravicabánya *see* Oravița
116 F13 **Oravița** *Ger.* Orawitza, *Hung.* Oravicabánya. Caraș-Severin, SW Romania 45°02′N 21°43′E
Orawa *see* Orava
185 B24 **Orawia** Southland, South Island, New Zealand 46°03′S 167°49′E
Orawitza *see* Oravița
103 P16 **Orb** ≈ S France
106 C9 **Orba** ≈ NW Italy
158 H12 **Orba Co** ◎ W China
108 B9 **Orbe** Vaud, W Switzerland 46°42′N 06°28′E
107 G14 **Orbetello** Toscana, C Italy 42°28′N 11°15′E
104 K3 **Orbigo** ≈ NW Spain
183 Q12 **Orbost** Victoria, SE Australia 37°44′S 148°28′E
95 O14 **Örbyhus** Uppsala, C Sweden 60°15′N 17°43′E
194 I1 **Orcadas** *Argentinian research station* South Orkney Islands, Antarctica 60°37′S 44°48′W
105 P12 **Orcera** Andalucía, S Spain 38°20′N 02°36′W
33 P9 **Orchard Homes** Montana, NW USA 46°52′N 114°01′W
37 P5 **Orchard Mesa** Colorado, C USA 39°02′N 108°33′W
18 D10 **Orchard Park** New York, NE USA 42°46′N 78°44′W
Orchid Island *see* Lan Yü
115 G18 **Orchómenos** *var.* Orhomenos, Orkhómenos, *prev.* Skripón; *anc.* Orchomenus. Stereá Ellás, C Greece 38°29′N 22°58′E
Orchomenus *see* Orchómenos
106 B7 **Orco** ≈ NW Italy
103 R8 **Or, Côte d′** *physical region* C France
29 O14 **Ord** Nebraska, C USA 41°36′N 98°55′W
119 O15 **Ordats′** *Rus.* Ordat′. Mahilyowskaya Voblasts′, E Belarus 54°10′N 30°42′E
36 K8 **Orderville** Utah, W USA 37°16′N 112°38′W
104 H2 **Ordes** Galicia, NW Spain 43°04′N 08°25′W
35 V14 **Ord Mountain** ▲ California, W USA 34°41′N 116°46′W
163 N14 **Ordos** *prev.* Dongsheng. Nei Mongol Zizhiqu, N China 39°51′N 110°00′E
Ordos Desert *see* Mu Us Shadi
188 B16 **Ordot** C Guam
137 N11 **Ordu** *anc.* Cotyora. Ordu, N Turkey 41°N 37°52′E
136 M11 **Ordu** ⬖ *province* N Turkey
137 V14 **Ordubad** SW Azerbaijan 38°55′N 46°00′E
Orduña *see* Urduña
37 U6 **Ordway** Colorado, C USA 38°13′N 103°45′W
117 T9 **Ordzhonikidze** Dnipropetrovs′ka Oblast′, E Ukraine 47°39′N 34°08′E
Ordzhonikidze *see* Denisovka, Kazakhstan
Ordzhonikidze *see* Vladikavkaz, Russian Federation
Ordzhonikidze *see* Yenakiyeve, Ukraine
Ordzhonikidzeabad *see* Kofarnihon
55 U9 **Orealla** E Guyana 05°13′N 57°17′W
113 G15 **Orebić** *It.* Sabbioncello. Dubrovnik-Neretva, S Croatia 42°58′N 17°12′E
95 M16 **Örebro** Örebro, C Sweden 59°18′N 15°12′E
95 L16 **Örebro** ⬖ *county* C Sweden
25 W6 **Ore City** Texas, SW USA 32°48′N 94°43′W
30 L10 **Oregon** Illinois, N USA 42°00′N 89°19′W
27 Q2 **Oregon** Missouri, C USA 39°59′N 95°08′W
31 R11 **Oregon** Ohio, N USA 41°38′N 83°29′W
32 H13 **Oregon** *off.* State of Oregon, *also known as* Beaver State, Sunset State, Valentine State, Webfoot State. ⬖ *state* NW USA
32 G11 **Oregon City** Oregon, NW USA 45°21′N 122°36′W
Oregon, State of *see* Oregon
95 P14 **Öregrund** Uppsala, C Sweden 60°19′N 18°30′E
Orekhov *see* Orikhiv
126 L3 **Orekhovo-Zuyevo** Moskovskaya Oblast′, W Russian Federation 55°46′N 39°01′E
Orekhovsk *see* Arekhawsk
126 J6 **Orël** Orlovskaya Oblast′, W Russian Federation 52°57′N 36°06′E
Orel *see* Oril′
56 E11 **Orellana** Loreto, N Peru 06°53′S 75°10′W
56 E6 **Orellana** ⬖ *province* NE Ecuador
104 L11 **Orellana, Embalse de** ⊠ W Spain
36 L3 **Orem** Utah, W USA 40°18′N 111°42′W
Ore Mountains *see* Erzgebirge/Krušné Hory
127 V7 **Orenburg** *prev.* Chkalov. Orenburgskaya Oblast′, W Russian Federation 51°46′N 55°12′E

◆ Country
● Country Capital
◇ Dependent Territory
○ Dependent Territory Capital
⬖ Administrative Regions
✈ International Airport
▲ Mountain
▲▲ Mountain Range
⟁ Volcano
≈ River
◎ Lake
⊠ Reservoir

127 V7 **Orenburg** ✈ Orenburgskaya Oblast', W Russian Federation 51°54′N 55°15′E
127 T7 **Orenburgskaya Oblast'** ◈ *province* W Russian Federation
Orense *see* Ourense
188 C8 **Oreor** *var.* Koror. *island* N Palau
185 B24 **Orepuki** Southland, South Island, New Zealand 46°17′S 167°45′E
114 L12 **Orestiáda** *prev.* Orestiás. Anatolikí Makedonía kai Thráki, NE Greece 41°30′N 26°31′E
Orestiás *see* Orestiáda
Öresund/Øresund *see* Sound, The
185 C23 **Oreti** ≈ South Island, New Zealand
184 L5 **Orewa** Auckland, North Island, New Zealand 36°34′S 174°43′E
65 A25 **Orford, Cape** *headland* West Falkland, Falkland Islands 52°00′S 61°04′W
44 B5 **Órganos, Sierra de los** ▲▲ W Cuba
37 R15 **Organ Peak** ▲ New Mexico, SW USA 32°17′N 106°35′W
105 N9 **Orgaz** Castilla-La Mancha, C Spain 39°39′N 03°52′W
Orgeyev *see* Orhei
Orgil *see* Jargalant
105 O15 **Orgiva** *var.* Orjiva. Andalucía, S Spain 36°54′N 03°25′W
163 O10 **Örgön** *var.* Senj. Dornogovĭ, SE Mongolia 44°34′N 110°58′E
Örgön *see* Bayangovĭ
Orgraždеn *see* Ograzhden
117 N9 **Orhei** *var.* Orheiu, *Rus.* Orgeyev. N Moldova 47°25′N 28°48′E
Orheiu *see* Orhei
105 R3 **Orhi** *var.* Orhy, Pico de Orhy, Pic d'Orhy. ▲ France/Spain 42°55′N 01°01′W *see also* Orhy
Orhi *see* Orhy
Orhomenos *see* Orchómenos
162 K6 **Orhon** ◈ *province* N Mongolia
162 L6 **Orhon Gol** ≈ N Mongolia
102 J16 **Orhy** *var.* Orhi, Pico de Orhy, Pic d'Orhy. ▲ France/Spain 43°00′N 01°00′W *see also* Orhi
Orhy *see* Orhi
Orhy, Pic d'/Orhy, Pico de *see* Orhi/Orhy
34 L2 **Orick** California, W USA 41°16′N 124°03′W
32 L6 **Orient** Washington, NW USA 48°51′N 118°14′W
48 D6 **Oriental, Cordillera** ▲▲ Bolivia/Peru
48 D6 **Oriental, Cordillera** ▲▲ C Colombia
57 H16 **Oriental, Cordillera** ▲▲ C Peru
63 M15 **Oriente** Buenos Aires, E Argentina 38°45′S 60°37′W
105 R12 **Orihuela** País Valenciano, E Spain 38°05′N 00°56′W
117 V9 **Orikhiv** *Rus.* Orekhov. Zaporiz'ka Oblast', SE Ukraine 47°32′N 35°48′E
113 K22 **Orikum** *var.* Orikumi. Vlorë, SW Albania 40°20′N 19°28′E
Orikumi *see* Orikum
117 V6 **Oril'** *Rus.* Orel. ≈ E Ukraine
14 H14 **Orillia** Ontario, S Canada 44°36′N 79°26′W
93 M19 **Orimattila** Etelä-Suomi, S Finland 60°48′N 25°40′E
33 Y15 **Orin** Wyoming, C USA 42°39′N 105°10′W
47 R4 **Orinoco, Río** ≈ Colombia/Venezuela
186 C9 **Oriomo** Western, SW Papua New Guinea 08°53′S 143°13′E
30 K11 **Orion** Illinois, N USA 41°21′N 90°22′W
29 Q5 **Oriska** North Dakota, N USA 46°54′N 97°46′W
153 P17 **Orissa** ◈ *state* NE India
Orissaar *see* Orissaare
118 E5 **Orissaare** *Ger.* Orissaar. Saaremaa, W Estonia 58°34′N 23°05′E
107 B19 **Oristano** Sardegna, Italy, C Mediterranean Sea 39°54′N 08°35′E
107 A19 **Oristano, Golfo di** *gulf* Sardegna, Italy, C Mediterranean Sea
54 D13 **Orito** Putumayo, SW Colombia 0°49′N 76°57′W
93 L18 **Orivesi** Häme, W Finland 61°39′N 24°21′E
93 N17 **Orivesi** ◎ Länsi-Suomi, SE Finland
58 H12 **Oriximiná** Pará, NE Brazil 01°45′S 55°50′W
41 Q14 **Orizaba** Veracruz-Llave, E Mexico 18°51′N 97°08′W
41 Q14 **Orizaba, Volcán Pico de** *var.* Citlaltépetl. ▲ S Mexico 19°00′N 97°15′W
95 I16 **Ørje** Østfold, S Norway 59°28′N 11°40′E
113 I16 **Orjen** ▲▲ Bosnia and Herzegovina/Montenegro
Orjiva *see* Orgiva
Orjonikidzeobod *see* Kofarnihon
94 G8 **Orkanger** Sør-Trøndelag, S Norway 63°17′N 09°52′E
94 G8 **Orkdalen** *valley* S Norway
95 K22 **Örkelljunga** Skåne, S Sweden 56°17′N 13°20′E
Orkhaniye *see* Botevgrad
Orkhómenos *see* Orchómenos
94 H9 **Orkla** ≈ S Norway
Orkney *see* Orkney Islands
65 J22 **Orkney Deep** *undersea feature* Scotia Sea/Weddell Sea
96 J4 **Orkney Islands** *var.* Orkney, Orkneys. *island group* N Scotland, United Kingdom
Orkneys *see* Orkney Islands
24 K8 **Orla** Texas, SW USA 31°48′N 103°55′W
35 N5 **Orland** California, W USA 39°43′N 122°12′W
23 X11 **Orlando** Florida, SE USA 28°32′N 81°23′W
23 X12 **Orlando** ✈ Florida, SE USA 28°24′N 81°16′W
107 K23 **Orlando, Capo d'** *headland* Sicilia, Italy, C Mediterranean Sea 38°10′N 14°44′E
Orlau *see* Orlová
103 N6 **Orléanais** *cultural region* C France
103 N7 **Orléans** *anc.* Aurelianum. Loiret, C France 47°54′N 01°53′E
34 L2 **Orleans** California, W USA 41°16′N 123°36′W
19 Q12 **Orleans** Massachusetts, NE USA 41°48′N 69°57′W
15 R10 **Orléans, Île d'** *island* Québec, SE Canada
Orléansville *see* Chlef
111 F16 **Orlice** *Ger.* Adler. ≈ NE Czech Republic
122 L13 **Orlik** Respublika Buryatiya, S Russian Federation 52°32′N 99°36′E
125 Q14 **Orlov** *prev.* Khalturin. Kirovskaya Oblast', NW Russian Federation 58°34′N 48°57′E
111 I17 **Orlová** *Ger.* Orlau, *Pol.* Orłowa. Moravskoslezský Kraj, E Czech Republic 49°50′N 18°21′E
Orlov, Mys *see* Orlovskiy, Mys
126 I6 **Orlovskaya Oblast'** ◈ *province* W Russian Federation
124 M5 **Orlovskiy, Mys** *var.* Mys Orlov. *headland* NW Russian Federation 67°14′N 41°17′E
Orłowa *see* Orlová
103 O5 **Orly** ✈ (Paris) Essonne, N France 48°43′N 02°24′E
119 G16 **Orlya** Hrodzyenskaya Voblasts', W Belarus 53°30′N 24°59′E
114 M7 **Orlyak** *prev.* Makenzen, Trubchular, *Rom.* Trupcilar. Dobrich, NE Bulgaria 43°39′N 27°21′E
148 L16 **Ormāra** Baluchistān, SW Pakistan 25°14′N 64°36′E
171 P5 **Ormoc** *off.* Ormoc City, *var.* MacArthur. Leyte, C Philippines 11°02′N 124°35′E
Ormoc City *see* Ormoc
23 X10 **Ormond Beach** Florida, SE USA 29°16′N 81°04′W
109 X10 **Ormož** *Ger.* Friedau. NE Slovenia 46°24′N 16°09′E
14 J13 **Ormsby** Ontario, SE Canada 44°52′N 77°45′W
97 K17 **Ormskirk** NW England, United Kingdom 53°35′N 02°54′W
Ormsö *see* Vormsi
15 N13 **Ormstown** Québec, SE Canada 45°08′N 73°57′W
Ormuz, Strait of *see* Hormuz, Strait of
103 T8 **Ornans** Doubs, E France 47°06′N 06°06′E
102 K5 **Orne** ◈ *department* N France
102 K5 **Orne** ≈ N France
92 G12 **Ørnes** Nordland, C Norway 66°51′N 13°43′E
110 L7 **Orneta** Warmińsko-Mazurskie, NE Poland 54°07′N 20°10′E
95 P16 **Ornö** Stockholm, C Sweden 59°03′N 18°28′E
37 Q3 **Orno Peak** ▲ Colorado, C USA 40°06′N 107°06′W
93 I16 **Örnsköldsvik** Västernorrland, C Sweden 63°16′N 18°45′E
163 X13 **Oro** E North Korea 39°59′N 127°27′E
45 T6 **Orocovis** C Puerto Rico 18°13′N 66°22′W
54 H10 **Orocué** Casanare, E Colombia 04°51′N 71°21′W
77 N13 **Orodara** SW Burkina 11°00′N 04°54′W
105 S4 **Oroel, Peña de** ▲ N Spain 42°30′N 00°31′W
33 N10 **Orofino** Idaho, NW USA 46°28′N 116°15′W
162 I9 **Orog Nuur** ◎ S Mongolia
35 U14 **Oro Grande** California, W USA 34°36′N 117°19′W
37 S15 **Orogrande** New Mexico, SW USA 32°24′N 106°04′W
191 Q7 **Orohena, Mont** ⛰ Tahiti, W French Polynesia 17°37′S 149°27′W
Orolaunum *see* Arlon
Orol Dengizi *see* Aral Sea
189 S15 **Oroluk Atoll** *atoll* Caroline Islands, C Micronesia
80 J13 **Oromīya** ◈ *federal region* C Ethiopia
Oromo *see* Goba
13 O15 **Oromocto** New Brunswick, SE Canada 45°50′N 66°28′W
191 S4 **Orona** *prev.* Hull Island. *atoll* Phoenix Islands, C Kiribati
191 V17 **Orongo** *ancient monument* Easter Island, Chile, E Pacific Ocean
138 I3 **Orontes** *var.* Ononte, Nahr el Aassi, *Ar.* Nahr al 'Aṣī. ≈ SW Asia
104 L9 **Oropesa** Castilla-La Mancha, C Spain 39°55′N 05°10′W
Oropesa *see* Oropesa del Mar
105 T8 **Oropesa del Mar** *var.* Oropesa, *Cat.* Orpes. País Valenciano, E Spain 40°06′N 00°07′E
Oropeza *see* Cochabamba
Oroqen Zizhiqi *see* Alihe
171 P7 **Oroquieta** *var.* Oroquieta City. Mindanao, S Philippines 08°27′N 123°46′E
Oroquieta City *see* Oroquieta
40 J8 **Oro, Río del** ≈ C Mexico
59 O14 **Orós, Açude** ▣ E Brazil
107 D18 **Orosei, Golfo di** *gulf* Tyrrhenian Sea, C Mediterranean Sea
111 M24 **Orosháza** Békés, SE Hungary 46°33′N 20°40′E
Orosirá Rodhópis *see* Rhodope Mountains
111 I22 **Oroszlány** Komárom-Esztergom, W Hungary 47°28′N 18°16′E
188 B16 **Orote Peninsula** *peninsula* W Guam
123 T9 **Orotukan** Magadanskaya Oblast', E Russian Federation 62°18′N 150°46′E
35 O5 **Oroville** California, W USA 39°29′N 121°35′W
32 K6 **Oroville** Washington, NW USA 48°56′N 119°25′W
35 O5 **Oroville, Lake** ▣ California, W USA
0 G15 **Orozco Fracture Zone** *tectonic feature* E Pacific Ocean
Orpes *see* Oropesa del Mar
64 I7 **Orphan Knoll** *undersea feature* NW Atlantic Ocean 51°00′N 47°00′W
29 V3 **Orr** Minnesota, N USA 48°03′N 92°48′W
95 M21 **Orrefors** Kalmar, S Sweden 56°48′N 15°45′E
182 I7 **Orroroo** South Australia 32°46′S 138°38′E
31 T12 **Orrville** Ohio, N USA 40°50′N 81°45′W
94 L12 **Orsa** Dalarna, C Sweden 61°07′N 14°40′E
Orschowa *see* Orşova
Orschütz *see* Orzyc
119 O14 **Orsha** Vitsyebskaya Voblasts', NE Belarus 54°30′N 30°26′E
127 Q2 **Orshanka** Respublika Mariy El, W Russian Federation 56°54′N 47°54′E
108 C11 **Orsières** Valais, SW Switzerland 46°00′N 07°09′E
127 X8 **Orsk** Orenburgskaya Oblast', W Russian Federation 51°13′N 58°35′E
116 F13 **Orşova** *Ger.* Orschowa, *Hung.* Orsova. Mehedinţi, SW Romania 44°42′N 22°22′E
94 D10 **Ørsta** Møre og Romsdal, S Norway 62°12′N 06°09′E
95 O15 **Örsundsbro** Uppsala, C Sweden 59°45′N 17°19′E
136 D16 **Ortaca** Muğla, SW Turkey 36°49′N 28°43′E
83 I21 **O.R. Tambo** ✈ (Johannesburg) Gauteng, NE South Africa 26°08′S 28°01′E
107 M16 **Orta Nova** Puglia, SE Italy 41°20′N 15°43′E
136 I17 **Orta Toroslar** ▲▲ S Turkey
54 E11 **Ortega** Tolima, W Colombia 03°57′N 75°11′W
104 H1 **Ortegal, Cabo** *headland* NW Spain 43°46′N 07°54′W
Ortelsburg *see* Szczytno
102 J15 **Orthez** Pyrénées-Atlantiques, SW France 43°29′N 00°46′W
57 K14 **Orthon, Río** ≈ N Bolivia
60 J10 **Ortigueira** Paraná, S Brazil 24°10′S 50°55′W
104 H1 **Ortigueira** Galicia, NW Spain 43°40′N 07°50′W
106 H5 **Ortisei** *Ger.* Sankt-Ulrich. Trentino-Alto Adige, N Italy 46°35′N 11°42′E
40 F6 **Ortiz** Sonora, NW Mexico 28°18′N 110°40′W
54 L5 **Ortiz** Guárico, N Venezuela 09°37′N 67°20′W
Ortler *see* Ortles
106 F5 **Ortles** *Ger.* Ortler. ▲ N Italy 46°29′N 10°33′E
107 K14 **Ortona** Abruzzo, C Italy 42°21′N 14°24′E
29 R8 **Ortonville** Minnesota, N USA 45°18′N 96°26′W
147 W8 **Orto-Tokoy** Issyk-Kul'skaya Oblast', NE Kyrgyzstan 42°20′N 76°03′E
93 I15 **Örträsk** Västerbotten, N Sweden 64°10′N 19°00′E
100 J12 **Örtze** ≈ NW Germany
Oruba *see* Aruba
142 I3 **Orūmīyeh** *var.* Rizaiyeh, Urmia, Urmiyeh; *prev.* Reẕā'īyeh. Āẕarbāyjān-e Gharbī, NW Iran 37°33′N 45°06′E
142 J3 **Orūmīyeh, Daryācheh-ye** *var.* Matianus, Sha Hi, Urumi Yeh, *Eng.* Lake Urmia; *prev.* Daryācheh-ye Reẕā'īyeh. ◎ NW Iran
57 K19 **Oruro** Oruro, W Bolivia 17°58′S 67°06′W
57 J19 **Oruro** ◈ *department* W Bolivia
95 I18 **Orust** *island* S Sweden
149 O7 **Orūzgān** *var.* Oruzgān, *Pash.* Ūrūzgān. Orūzgān, C Afghanistan 32°58′N 66°39′E
149 N6 **Orūzgān** *Pash.* Urūzgān. ◈ *province* C Afghanistan
106 H13 **Orvieto** *anc.* Velsuna. Umbria, C Italy 42°43′N 12°06′E
194 K7 **Orville Coast** *physical region* Antarctica
114 H7 **Oryakhovo** Vratsa, NW Bulgaria 43°44′N 23°58′E
Oryokko *see* Yalu
117 R5 **Orzhytsya** Poltavs'ka Oblast', C Ukraine 49°48′N 32°40′E
110 M9 **Orzyc** *Ger.* Orschütz. ≈ NE Poland
110 N8 **Orzysz** *Ger.* Arys. Warmińsko-Mazurskie, NE Poland 53°49′N 21°54′E
98 K13 **Oss** Noord-Brabant, S Netherlands 51°46′N 05°32′E
94 I10 **Os** Hedmark, S Norway 62°29′N 11°14′E
125 U15 **Osa** Permskaya Oblast', NW Russian Federation 57°16′N 55°22′E
115 F15 **Óssa** ▲▲ C Greece
104 H11 **Ossa** ▲ S Portugal 38°43′N 07°33′W
29 W11 **Osage** Iowa, C USA 43°16′N 92°48′W
27 U5 **Osage Beach** Missouri, C USA 38°09′N 92°37′W
27 P5 **Osage City** Kansas, C USA 38°37′N 95°49′W
27 U7 **Osage Fork River** ≈ Missouri, C USA
27 U5 **Osage River** ≈ Missouri, C USA
164 J13 **Ōsaka** *hist.* Naniwa. Ōsaka, Honshū, SW Japan 34°38′N 135°28′E
164 I13 **Ōsaka** *off.* Ōsaka-fu, *var.* Ōsaka Hu. ◈ *urban prefecture* Honshū, SW Japan
Ōsaka-fu/Ōsaka Hu *see* Ōsaka
145 R10 **Osakarovka** Karaganda, C Kazakhstan 50°32′N 72°39′E
Ōsaki *see* Furukawa
29 T7 **Osakis** Minnesota, N USA 45°51′N 95°08′W
43 N16 **Osa, Península de** *peninsula* S Costa Rica
60 M10 **Osasco** São Paulo, S Brazil 23°32′S 46°46′W
27 R5 **Osawatomie** Kansas, C USA 38°30′N 94°57′W
26 L3 **Osborne** Kansas, C USA 39°26′N 98°42′W
173 S8 **Osborn Plateau** *undersea feature* E Indian Ocean
95 L21 **Osby** Skåne, S Sweden 56°24′N 14°00′E
Osca *see* Huesca
92 N2 **Oscar II Land** *physical region* W Svalbard
27 Y10 **Osceola** Arkansas, C USA 35°43′N 89°58′W
29 V15 **Osceola** Iowa, C USA 41°01′N 93°45′W
27 S6 **Osceola** Missouri, C USA 38°01′N 93°41′W
29 Q15 **Osceola** Nebraska, C USA 41°09′N 97°28′W
101 N15 **Oschatz** Sachsen, E Germany 51°17′N 13°10′E
100 K13 **Oschersleben** Sachsen-Anhalt, C Germany 52°02′N 11°14′E
31 R7 **Oscoda** Michigan, N USA 44°25′N 83°19′W
Ösel *see* Saaremaa
94 H6 **Osen** Sør-Trøndelag, S Norway 64°17′N 10°29′E
94 I12 **Osensjøen** ◎ S Norway
164 A14 **Ōse-zaki** Fukue-jima, SW Japan
147 T10 **Osh** Oshskaya Oblast', SW Kyrgyzstan 40°34′N 72°46′E
83 C16 **Oshakati** Oshana, N Namibia 17°46′S 15°43′E
83 C16 **Oshana** ◈ *district* N Namibia
14 H15 **Oshawa** Ontario, SE Canada 43°54′N 78°50′W
165 R10 **Oshika-hantō** *peninsula* Honshū, C Japan
83 C16 **Oshikango** Ohangwena, N Namibia 17°29′S 15°54′E
Oshikoto *see* Otjikoto
165 P5 **Ō-shima** *island* NE Japan
165 N14 **Ō-shima** *island* S Japan
165 Q5 **Oshima-hantō** ▲▲ Hokkaidō, NE Japan
83 D17 **Oshivelo** Otjikoto, N Namibia 18°37′S 17°10′E
28 K14 **Oshkosh** Nebraska, C USA 41°25′N 102°21′W
30 M7 **Oshkosh** Wisconsin, N USA 44°01′N 88°32′W
Oshmyany *see* Ashmyany
Osh Oblasty *see* Oshskaya Oblast'
77 T16 **Oshogbo** *var.* Osogbo. Osun, W Nigeria 07°42′N 04°31′E
147 S11 **Oshskaya Oblast'** *Kir.* Osh Oblasty. ◈ *province* SW Kyrgyzstan
Ōshū *see* Mizusawa
Oshun *see* Osun
79 J20 **Oshwe** Bandundu, C Dem. Rep. Congo 03°24′S 19°32′E
Osiek *see* Osijek
112 I9 **Osijek** *prev.* Osiek, Osjek, *Ger.* Esseg, *Hung.* Eszék. Osijek-Baranja, E Croatia 45°33′N 18°41′E
112 I9 **Osijek-Baranja** *off.* Osječko-Baranjska Županija. ◈ *province* E Croatia
106 J12 **Osimo** Marche, C Italy 43°28′N 13°29′E
122 M12 **Osinovka** Irkutskaya Oblast', C Russian Federation 56°19′N 101°55′E
Osintorf *see* Asintorf
112 N11 **Osipaonica** Serbia, NE Serbia 44°34′N 21°00′E
Osipenko *see* Berdyans'k
Osipovichi *see* Asipovichy
Osječko-Baranjska Županija *see* Osijek-Baranja
Osjek *see* Osijek
29 W15 **Oskaloosa** Iowa, C USA 41°17′N 92°38′W
27 Q4 **Oskaloosa** Kansas, C USA 39°14′N 95°21′W
95 N20 **Oskarshamn** Kalmar, S Sweden 57°16′N 16°25′E
95 J21 **Oskarström** Halland, S Sweden 56°48′N 13°00′E
14 M8 **Oskélanéo** Québec, SE Canada 48°06′N 75°12′W
Öskemen *see* Ust'-Kamenogorsk
117 W5 **Oskil** *Rus.* Oskil. ≈ Russian Federation/Ukraine
Oskil *see* Oskil
93 D20 **Oslo** *prev.* Christiania, Kristiania. ● (Norway) Oslo, S Norway 59°54′N 10°44′E
93 D20 **Oslo** ◈ *county* S Norway
93 D21 **Oslofjorden** *fjord* S Norway
155 G15 **Osmānābād** Mahārāshtra, C India 18°09′N 76°06′E
136 J11 **Osmancık** Çorum, N Turkey 40°58′N 34°50′E
136 L16 **Osmaniye** Osmaniye, S Turkey 37°04′N 36°15′E
136 L16 **Osmaniye** ◈ *province* S Turkey
95 O16 **Ösmo** Stockholm, C Sweden 58°58′N 17°55′E
118 E3 **Osmussaar** *island* W Estonia
100 G13 **Osnabrück** Niedersachsen, NW Germany 52°09′N 07°42′E
110 D11 **Ośno Lubuskie** *Ger.* Drossen. Lubuskie, W Poland 52°28′N 14°51′E
Osogbo *see* Oshogbo
113 P19 **Osogov Mountains** *var.* Osogovske Planine, Osogovski Planina, *Mac.* Osogovski Planini. ▲▲ Bulgaria/FYR Macedonia
Osogovske Planine/Osogovski Planina/Osogovski Planini *see* Osogov Mountains
165 R6 **Osore-zan** ▲ Honshū, C Japan 41°18′N 141°06′E
Oşorhei *see* Târgu Mureş
61 J16 **Osório** Rio Grande do Sul, S Brazil 29°53′S 50°17′W
63 G16 **Osorno** Los Lagos, C Chile 40°39′S 73°05′W
104 M4 **Osorno** Castilla-León, N Spain 42°24′N 04°22′W
11 N17 **Osoyoos** British Columbia, SW Canada 49°02′N 119°31′W
95 C14 **Osøyro** Hordaland, S Norway 60°11′N 05°30′E
54 J6 **Ospino** Portuguesa, N Venezuela 09°17′N 69°26′W
23 X6 **Ossabaw Island** *island* Georgia, SE USA
23 X6 **Ossabaw Sound** *sound* Georgia, SE USA
183 O16 **Ossa, Mount** ▲ Tasmania, SE Australia 41°55′S 146°03′E
104 H11 **Ossa, Serra d'** ▲▲ SE Portugal
77 U16 **Osse** ≈ S Nigeria
30 J6 **Osseo** Wisconsin, N USA 44°33′N 91°13′W
109 S9 **Ossiacher See** ◎ S Austria
18 K13 **Ossining** New York, NE USA 41°10′N 73°50′W
123 V9 **Ossora** Koryakskiy Avtonomnyy Okrug, E Russian Federation 59°16′N 163°02′E
124 I15 **Ostashkov** Tverskaya Oblast', W Russian Federation 57°08′N 33°10′E
100 H9 **Oste** ≈ NW Germany
Ostee *see* Baltic Sea
Ostend/Ostende *see* Oostende
117 P3 **Oster** Chernihivs'ka Oblast', N Ukraine 50°57′N 30°55′E
95 O14 **Österbybruk** Uppsala, C Sweden 60°13′N 17°55′E
95 M19 **Österbymo** Östergotland, S Sweden 57°49′N 15°15′E
94 K12 **Österdalälven** ≈ C Sweden
94 I12 **Østerdalen** *valley* S Norway
95 L18 **Östergötland** ◈ *county* S Sweden
100 H10 **Osterholz-Scharmbeck** Niedersachsen, NW Germany 53°13′N 08°46′E
Östermark *see* Teuva
Östermyra *see* Seinäjoki
Østerø *see* Eysturoy
101 J14 **Osterode am Harz** Niedersachsen, C Germany 51°43′N 10°15′E
Osterode/Osterode in Ostpreussen *see* Ostróda
94 C13 **Osterøy** *island* S Norway
Österreich *see* Austria
93 G16 **Östersund** Jämtland, C Sweden 63°10′N 14°44′E
95 N14 **Östervåla** Västmanland, C Sweden 60°10′N 17°13′E
101 H22 **Ostfildern** Baden-Württemberg, SW Germany 48°43′N 09°16′E
95 H16 **Østfold** ◈ *county* S Norway
100 E9 **Ostfriesische Inseln** *Eng.* East Frisian Islands. *island group* NW Germany
100 F10 **Ostfriesland** *historical region* NW Germany
95 P14 **Östhammar** Uppsala, C Sweden 60°15′N 18°25′E
Ostia Aterni *see* Pescara
106 G8 **Ostiglia** Lombardia, N Italy 45°04′N 11°09′E
95 J14 **Östmark** Värmland, C Sweden 60°15′N 12°45′E
95 K22 **Östra Ringsjön** ◎ S Sweden
111 I17 **Ostrava** Moravskoslezský Kraj, E Czech Republic 49°50′N 18°15′E
Ostravský Kraj *see* Moravskoslezský Kraj
94 J11 **Østrehogna** *Swe.* Härjahågnen, Härjehågna. ▲ Norway/Sweden 61°43′N 12°07′E
110 K8 **Ostróda** *Ger.* Osterode, Osterode in Ostpreussen. Warmińsko-Mazurskie, NE Poland 53°42′N 19°59′E
Ostrog/Ostróg *see* Ostroh
126 L8 **Ostrogozhsk** Voronezhskaya Oblast', W Russian Federation 50°52′N 39°00′E
116 L4 **Ostroh** *Pol.* Ostróg, *Rus.* Ostrog. Rivnens'ka Oblast', NW Ukraine 50°20′N 26°29′E
110 N9 **Ostrołęka** *Ger.* Wiesenhof, *Rus.* Ostrolenka. Mazowieckie, C Poland 53°06′N 21°34′E
Ostrolenka *see* Ostrołęka
111 A16 **Ostrov** *Ger.* Schlackenwerth. Karlovarský Kraj, W Czech Republic 50°18′N 12°56′E
124 F15 **Ostrov** *Latv.* Austrava. Pskovskaya Oblast', W Russian Federation 57°21′N 28°18′E
Ostrovets *see* Ostrowiec Świętokrzyski
113 M21 **Ostrovicës, Mali i** ▲ SE Albania 40°36′N 20°25′E
165 Z2 **Ostrov Iturup** *island* NE Russian Federation
124 M4 **Ostrovnoy** Murmanskaya Oblast', NW Russian Federation 68°00′N 39°40′E
114 L7 **Ostrovo** *prev.* Golema Ada. Razgrad, N Bulgaria 43°40′N 26°37′E
125 N15 **Ostrovskoye** Kostromskaya Oblast', NW Russian Federation 57°46′N 42°18′E
Ostrów *see* Ostrów Wielkopolski
Ostrowiec *see* Ostrowiec Świętokrzyski
111 M14 **Ostrowiec Świętokrzyski** *var.* Ostrowiec, *Rus.* Ostrovets. Świętokrzyskie, C Poland 50°55′N 21°23′E
110 P13 **Ostrów Lubelski** Lubelskie, E Poland 51°29′N 22°57′E
110 N10 **Ostrów Mazowiecka** *var.* Ostrów Mazowiecki. Mazowieckie, NE Poland 52°49′N 21°53′E
Ostrów Mazowiecki *see* Ostrów Mazowiecka
Ostrowo *see* Ostrów Wielkopolski
110 H13 **Ostrów Wielkopolski** *var.* Ostrów, *Ger.* Ostrowo. Wielkopolskie, C Poland 51°40′N 17°47′E
Ostryna *see* Astryna
110 I13 **Ostrzeszów** Wielkopolskie, C Poland 51°25′N 17°55′E
107 P18 **Ostuni** Puglia, SE Italy 40°44′N 17°35′E
Ostyako-Voguls'k *see* Khanty-Mansiysk
114 I9 **Osŭm** ≈ N Bulgaria
Osum *see* Osumit, Lumi i
164 C17 **Ōsumi-hantō** ▲▲ Kyūshū, SW Japan
164 C17 **Ōsumi-kaikyō** *strait* SW Japan
113 L22 **Osumit, Lumi i** *var.* Osum. ≈ SE Albania
77 T16 **Osun** *var.* Oshun. ◈ *state* SW Nigeria
104 L14 **Osuna** Andalucía, S Spain 37°14′N 05°06′W
60 J8 **Osvaldo Cruz** São Paulo, S Brazil 21°49′S 50°52′W
Osveya *see* Asvyeya
18 J7 **Oswegatchie River** ≈ New York, NE USA
27 Q7 **Oswego** Kansas, C USA 37°11′N 95°10′W
18 H9 **Oswego** New York, NE USA 43°27′N 76°13′W
97 K19 **Oswestry** W England, United Kingdom 52°51′N 03°06′W
111 J16 **Oświęcim** *Ger.* Auschwitz. Małopolskie, S Poland 50°02′N 19°11′E
185 E22 **Otago** *off.* Otago Region. ◈ *region* South Island, New Zealand
185 F23 **Otago Peninsula** *peninsula* South Island, New Zealand
Otago Region *see* Otago
165 F13 **Ōtake** Hiroshima, Honshū, SW Japan 34°13′N 132°12′E
184 L13 **Otaki** Wellington, North Island, New Zealand 40°46′S 175°08′E
93 M15 **Otanmäki** Oulu, C Finland 64°07′N 27°04′E
145 T15 **Otar** Zhambyl, SE Kazakhstan 43°30′N 75°13′E
165 R4 **Otaru** Hokkaidō, NE Japan 43°14′N 140°59′E
185 C24 **Otatara** Southland, South Island, New Zealand 46°26′S 168°18′E
185 C24 **Otautau** Southland, South Island, New Zealand 46°10′S 168°01′E
93 M18 **Otava** Itä-Suomi, E Finland 61°37′N 27°07′E
111 B18 **Otava** *Ger.* Wottawa. ≈ SW Czech Republic
56 C6 **Otavalo** Imbabura, N Ecuador 0°13′N 78°15′W
83 D17 **Otavi** Otjozondjupa, N Namibia 19°35′S 17°25′E
165 P12 **Ōtawara** Tochigi, Honshū, S Japan 36°52′N 140°01′E
83 B16 **Otchinjau** Cunene, SW Angola 16°31′S 13°54′E
116 F12 **Oţelu Roşu** *Ger.* Ferdinandsberg, *Hung.* Nándorhgy. Caras-Severin, SW Romania 45°30′N 22°22′E
185 E21 **Otematata** Canterbury, South Island, New Zealand 44°37′S 170°12′E
118 I6 **Otepää** *Ger.* Odenpäh. Valgamaa, SE Estonia 58°01′N 26°30′E
162 H7 **Otgon** *var.* Buyant. Dzavhan, C Mongolia 47°14′N 97°14′E
32 K9 **Othello** Washington, NW USA 46°49′N 119°10′W
115 A15 **Othonoí** *island* Iónia Nisiá, Greece, C Mediterranean Sea
Othris *see* Óthrys
115 F17 **Óthrys** *var.* Othris. ▲▲ C Greece
77 Q14 **Oti** ≈ N Togo
40 K10 **Otinapa** Durango, C Mexico 24°01′N 104°58′W
185 G17 **Otira** West Coast, South Island, New Zealand 42°52′S 171°33′E
37 V3 **Otis** Colorado, C USA 40°09′N 102°57′W
12 L10 **Otish, Monts** ▲▲ Québec, E Canada
83 C17 **Otjikondo** Kunene, N Namibia 19°50′S 15°23′E
83 C17 **Otjikoto** *var.* Oshikoto. ◈ *district* N Namibia
83 E18 **Otjinene** Omaheke, NE Namibia 21°10′S 18°43′E
83 D18 **Otjiwarongo** Otjozondjupa, N Namibia 20°29′S 16°36′E
83 D18 **Otjosondu** *var.* Otjosundu. Otjozondjupa, C Namibia 21°19′S 17°51′E
Otjosundu *see* Otjosondu
83 D18 **Otjozondjupa** ◈ *district* C Namibia
112 C11 **Otočac** Lika-Senj, W Croatia 44°52′N 15°13′E
Otog Qi *see* Ulan
112 J10 **Otok** Vukovar-Srijem, E Croatia 45°10′N 18°52′E
116 K14 **Otopeni** ✈ (Bucureşti) Ilfov, S Romania 44°34′N 26°09′E
184 L8 **Otorohanga** Waikato, North Island, New Zealand 38°10′S 175°14′E
12 D9 **Otoskwin** ≈ Ontario, C Canada
165 G14 **Ōtoyo** Kōchi, Shikoku, SW Japan 33°45′N 133°42′E
95 E16 **Otra** ≈ S Norway
107 R19 **Otranto** Puglia, SE Italy 40°08′N 18°28′E
Otranto, Canale d' *see* Otranto, Strait of
107 Q18 **Otranto, Strait of** *It.* Canale d'Otranto. *strait* Albania/Italy
111 H18 **Otrokovice** *Ger.* Otrokowitz. Zlínský Kraj, E Czech Republic 49°13′N 17°33′E
Otrokowitz *see* Otrokovice
31 P10 **Otsego** Michigan, N USA 42°27′N 85°42′W
31 Q6 **Otsego Lake** ◎ Michigan, N USA
18 I11 **Otselic River** ≈ New York, NE USA
164 J14 **Ōtsu** *var.* Ôtu. Shiga, Honshū, SW Japan 35°03′N 135°49′E
94 G11 **Otta** Oppland, S Norway 61°46′N 09°33′E
189 U13 **Otta** *island* Chuuk, C Micronesia
94 F11 **Otta** ≈ S Norway
189 U13 **Otta Pass** *passage* Chuuk Islands, C Micronesia
95 J22 **Ottarp** Skåne, S Sweden 55°55′N 12°55′E
14 L12 **Ottawa** ● (Canada) Ontario, SE Canada 45°24′N 75°41′W
30 L11 **Ottawa** Illinois, N USA 41°21′N 88°50′W
27 Q5 **Ottawa** Kansas, C USA 38°35′N 95°16′W
31 R12 **Ottawa** Ohio, N USA 41°01′N 84°03′W
14 L12 **Ottawa** *var.* Uplands. ✈ Ontario, SE Canada 45°19′N 75°39′W
14 M12 **Ottawa** *Fr.* Outaouais. ≈ Ontario/Québec, SE Canada
9 R10 **Ottawa Islands** *island group* Nunavut, C Canada
18 L8 **Otter Creek** ≈ Vermont, NE USA
36 L6 **Otter Creek Reservoir** ▣ Utah, W USA
98 L11 **Otterlo** Gelderland, E Netherlands 52°06′N 05°46′E
94 D9 **Otterøya** *island* S Norway
29 S6 **Otter Tail Lake** ◎ Minnesota, N USA
29 R7 **Otter Tail River** ≈ Minnesota, C USA
95 H23 **Otterup** Fyn, C Denmark 55°31′N 10°25′E
99 H19 **Ottignies** Wallon Brabant, C Belgium 50°40′N 04°34′E
101 L23 **Ottobrunn** Bayern, SE Germany 48°02′N 11°40′E
29 X15 **Ottumwa** Iowa, C USA 41°00′N 92°24′W
Ôtu *see* Ōtsu
83 B16 **Otuazuma** Kunene, NW Namibia 17°52′S 13°16′E
77 V16 **Oturkpo** Benue, S Nigeria 07°12′N 08°06′E
193 Y15 **Otu Tolu Group** *island group* SE Tonga
182 M13 **Otway, Cape** *headland* Victoria, SE Australia 38°52′S 143°31′E
63 H24 **Otway, Seno** *inlet* S Chile
Ötz *see* Oetz
108 L8 **Ötztaler Ache** ≈ W Austria
108 L9 **Ötztaler Alpen** *It.* Alpi Venoste. ▲▲ SW Austria
27 T12 **Ouachita, Lake** ▣ Arkansas, C USA
27 R11 **Ouachita Mountains** ▲▲ Arkansas/Oklahoma, C USA
27 U13 **Ouachita River** ≈ Arkansas/Louisiana, C USA
Ouadaï *see* Ouaddaï
76 J7 **Ouadâne** *var.* Ouadane. Adrar, C Mauritania 20°57′N 11°35′W
78 K13 **Ouadda** Haute-Kotto, N Central African Republic 08°02′N 22°22′E
78 J10 **Ouaddaï** *off.* Préfecture du Ouaddaï, *var.* Ouadaï, Wadai. ◈ *prefecture* SE Chad
Ouaddaï, Préfecture du *see* Ouaddaï
77 P13 **Ouagadougou** *var.* Wagadugu. ● (Burkina) C Burkina 12°20′N 01°32′W
77 P13 **Ouagadougou** ✈ C Burkina 12°21′N 01°27′W
77 O12 **Ouahigouya** NW Burkina 13°31′N 02°20′W
Ouahran *see* Oran
79 J14 **Ouaka** ◈ *prefecture* C Central African Republic
79 J15 **Ouaka** ≈ S Central African Republic
Oualam *see* Ouallam
76 M9 **Oualâta** *var.* Oualata. Hodh ech Chargui, SE Mauritania 17°18′N 07°00′W
77 R11 **Ouallam** *var.* Oualam. Tillabéri, W Niger 14°23′N 02°09′E
172 H14 **Ouanani** Mohéli, S Comoros 12°19′S 93°98′E
55 Z10 **Ouanary** E French Guiana 04°11′N 51°40′W
78 L13 **Ouanda Djallé** Vakaga, NE Central African Republic 08°53′N 22°47′E
79 N14 **Ouando** Haut-Mbomou, SE Central African Republic 05°57′N 25°57′E
79 L15 **Ouango** Mbomou, S Central African Republic 04°19′N 22°30′E
77 N14 **Ouangolodougou** *var.* Wangolodougou. N Ivory Coast 09°58′N 05°09′W
172 I13 **Ouani** Anjouan, SE Comoros
79 M15 **Ouara** ≈ E Central African Republic
76 K7 **Ouarâne** *desert* C Mauritania
15 O11 **Ouareau** ≈ Québec, SE Canada
74 K7 **Ouargla** *var.* Wargla. NE Algeria 32°N 05°16′E
74 F8 **Ouarzazate** S Morocco 30°54′N 06°55′W
77 Q11 **Ouatagouna** Gao, E Mali 15°06′N 00°41′E
74 G6 **Ouazzane** *var.* Ouezzane, *Ar.* Wazan, Wazzan. N Morocco 34°52′N 05°35′W
Oubangui *see* Ubangi
Oubangui-Chari *see* Central African Republic
Oubangui-Chari, Territoire de l' *see* Central African Republic
Oubari, Edeyen d' *see* Awbāri, Idhān
98 G13 **Oud-Beijerland** Zuid-Holland, SW Netherlands 51°50′N 04°25′E
98 F13 **Ouddorp** Zuid-Holland, SW Netherlands 51°49′N 03°55′E
77 P9 **Oudeïka** *oasis* C Mali
98 G13 **Oude Maas** ≈ SW Netherlands
99 E18 **Oudenaarde** *Fr.* Audenarde. Oost-Vlaanderen, SW Belgium 50°50′N 03°37′E
99 H14 **Oudenbosch** Noord-Brabant, S Netherlands 51°35′N 04°32′E
98 P6 **Oude Pekela** Groningen, NE Netherlands 53°06′N 07°00′E
Ouderkerk *see* Ouderkerk aan den Amstel
98 I10 **Ouderkerk aan den Amstel** *var.* Ouderkerk. Noord-Holland, C Netherlands 52°18′N 04°54′E
98 I6 **Oudeschild** Noord-Holland, NW Netherlands 53°01′N 04°51′E
99 G14 **Oude-Tonge** Zuid-Holland, SW Netherlands 51°40′N 04°13′E
98 I12 **Oudewater** Utrecht, C Netherlands 52°02′N 04°54′E
Oudjda *see* Oujda
98 L5 **Oudkerk** Friesland, N Netherlands 53°16′N 05°52′E
102 J7 **Oudon** ≈ NW France
98 I9 **Oudorp** Noord-Holland, NW Netherlands 52°39′N 04°47′E
83 G25 **Oudtshoorn** Western Cape, SW South Africa 33°35′S 22°14′E
99 I16 **Oud-Turnhout** Antwerpen, N Belgium 51°19′N 05°01′E
74 F7 **Oued-Zem** C Morocco 32°53′N 06°30′W
187 P16 **Ouégoa** Province Nord, C New Caledonia 20°22′S 164°25′E
76 L13 **Ouéléssébougou** *var.* Ouolossébougou. Koulikoro, SW Mali 11°58′N 07°51′W
77 N16 **Ouéllé** E Ivory Coast 07°18′N 04°01′W
77 R16 **Ouémé** ≈ C Benin
77 O13 **Ouessa** S Burkina 11°02′N 02°44′W
102 D5 **Ouessant, Île d'** *Eng.* Ushant. *island* NW France
79 H17 **Ouésso** Sangha, NW Congo 01°38′N 16°03′E
79 D15 **Ouest** *Eng.* West. ◈ *province* W Cameroon
190 G11 **Ouest, Baie del'** *bay* Îles Wallis, E Wallis and Futuna
15 Y7 **Ouest, Pointe de l'** *headland* Québec, SE Canada 48°08′N 64°57′W
Ouezzane *see* Ouazzane
99 K20 **Ouffet** Liège, E Belgium 50°30′N 05°31′E
79 H14 **Ouham** ◈ *prefecture* NW Central African Republic
78 I13 **Ouham** ≈ Central African Republic/Chad
79 G14 **Ouham-Pendé** ◈ *prefecture* W Central African Republic
77 R16 **Ouidah** *Eng.* Whydah, Wida. S Benin 06°23′N 02°08′E

◆ Country
● Country Capital
◇ Dependent Territory
○ Dependent Territory Capital
◈ Administrative Regions
✈ International Airport
▲ Mountain
▲▲ Mountain Range
⛰ Volcano
≈ River
◎ Lake
▣ Reservoir

74 H6 **Oujda** *Ar.* Oudjda, Ujda. NE Morocco 34°45′N 01°53′W
76 I7 **Oujeft** Adrar, C Mauritania 20°05′N 13°00′W
93 L15 **Oulainen** Oulu, C Finland 64°14′N 24°50′E
Ould Yanja *see* Ould Yenjé
76 J10 **Ould Yenjé** *var.* Ould Yanja. Guidimaka, S Mauritania 15°33′N 11°43′W
93 L14 **Oulu** *Swe.* Uleåborg. Oulu, C Finland 65°01′N 25°28′E
93 M14 **Oulu** *Swe.* Uleåborg. ◈ *province* N Finland
93 L15 **Oulujärvi** *Swe.* Uleträsk. ◎ C Finland
93 M14 **Oulujoki** *Swe.* Uleälv. ↝ C Finland
93 L14 **Oulunsalo** Oulu, C Finland 64°55′N 25°19′E
106 A8 **Oulx** Piemonte, NE Italy 45°05′N 06°41′E
78 J9 **Oum-Chalouba** Borkou-Ennedi-Tibesti, NE Chad 15°48′N 20°46′E
76 M16 **Oumé** C Ivory Coast 06°25′N 05°23′W
74 F7 **Oum er Rbia** ↝ C Morocco
78 J10 **Oum-Hadjer** Batha, E Chad 13°18′N 19°41′E
92 K10 **Ounasjoki** ↝ N Finland
78 J7 **Ounianga Kébir** Borkou-Ennedi-Tibesti, N Chad 19°06′N 20°29′E
Ouolossébougou *see* Ouéléssébougou
Oup *see* Auob
99 K19 **Oupeye** Liège, E Belgium 50°42′N 05°38′E
99 N21 **Our** ↝ NW Europe
37 Q7 **Ouray** Colorado, C USA 38°01′N 107°40′W
103 R7 **Ource** ↝ C France
104 G9 **Ourém** Santarém, C Portugal 39°40′N 08°32′W
104 H4 **Ourense** *Cast.* Orense, *Lat.* Aurium. Galicia, NW Spain 42°20′N 07°52′W
104 I4 **Ourense** *Cast.* Orense. ◈ *province* Galicia, NW Spain
59 O15 **Ouricuri** Pernambuco, E Brazil 07°51′S 40°05′W
60 J9 **Ourinhos** São Paulo, S Brazil 22°59′S 49°52′W
104 G13 **Ourique** Beja, S Portugal 37°38′N 08°13′W
59 M20 **Ouro Preto** Minas Gerais, NE Brazil 20°25′S 43°30′W
Ours, Grand Lac de l' *see* Great Bear Lake
99 K20 **Ourthe** ↝ E Belgium
165 Q9 **Ōu-sanmyaku** ▲▲ Honshū, C Japan
97 M17 **Ouse** ↝ N England, United Kingdom
Ouse *see* Great Ouse
102 H7 **Oust** ↝ NW France
Outaouais *see* Ottawa
15 T4 **Outardes Quatre, Réservoir** ⊠ Québec, SE Canada
15 T5 **Outardes, Rivière aux** ↝ Québec, SE Canada
96 E8 **Outer Hebrides** *var.* Western Isles. *island group* NW Scotland, United Kingdom
30 K3 **Outer Island** *island* Apostle Islands, Wisconsin, N USA
35 S16 **Outer Santa Barbara Passage** *passage* California, SW USA
104 G3 **Outes** Galicia, NW Spain 42°50′N 08°54′W
83 C18 **Outjo** Kunene, N Namibia 20°08′S 16°08′E
11 T16 **Outlook** Saskatchewan, S Canada 51°30′N 107°03′W
93 N16 **Outokumpu** Itä-Suomi, E Finland 62°43′N 29°05′E
96 M2 **Out Skerries** *island group* NE Scotland, United Kingdom
187 Q16 **Ouvéa** *island* Îles Loyauté, NE New Caledonia
103 S14 **Ouvèze** ↝ SE France
182 L9 **Ouyen** Victoria, SE Australia 35°07′S 142°19′E
39 Q14 **Ouzinkie** Kodiak Island, Alaska, USA 57°54′N 152°27′W
137 O13 **Ovacık** Tunceli, E Turkey 39°23′N 39°13′E
106 C9 **Ovada** Piemonte, NE Italy 44°41′N 08°39′E
187 X14 **Ovalau** *island* C Fiji
62 G9 **Ovalle** Coquimbo, N Chile 30°33′S 71°16′W
83 C17 **Ovamboland** *physical region* N Namibia
54 L10 **Ovana, Cerro** ▲ S Venezuela 04°41′N 66°54′W
104 G7 **Ovar** Aveiro, N Portugal 40°52′N 08°38′W
114 L10 **Ovcharitsa, Yazovir** ⊠ SE Bulgaria
54 E6 **Ovejas** Sucre, NW Colombia 09°32′N 75°14′W
101 E16 **Overath** Nordrhein-Westfalen, W Germany 50°55′N 07°16′E
98 F13 **Overflakkee** *island* SW Netherlands
99 H19 **Overijse** Vlaams Brabant, C Belgium 50°46′N 04°32′E
98 N10 **Overijssel** ◈ *province* E Netherlands
98 M9 **Overijssels Kanaal** *canal* E Netherlands
92 K13 **Överkalix** Norrbotten, N Sweden 66°19′N 22°49′E
27 R4 **Overland Park** Kansas, C USA 38°57′N 94°41′W
99 L14 **Overloon** Noord-Brabant, SE Netherlands 51°35′N 05°54′E
99 K16 **Overpelt** Limburg, NE Belgium 51°13′N 05°24′E
35 Y10 **Overton** Nevada, W USA 36°32′N 114°25′W
25 W7 **Overton** Texas, SW USA 32°16′N 94°58′W
92 K13 **Övertorneå** Norrbotten, N Sweden 66°22′N 23°40′E
95 N18 **Överum** Kalmar, S Sweden 57°58′N 16°20′E
92 G13 **Överuman** ◎ N Sweden
117 P11 **Ovidiopol'** Odes'ka Oblast', SW Ukraine 46°15′N 30°27′E
116 M14 **Ovidiu** Constanța, SE Romania 44°16′N 28°34′E
45 N10 **Oviedo** SW Dominican Republic 17°47′N 71°22′W
104 K2 **Oviedo** *anc.* Asturias. Asturias, NW Spain 43°21′N 05°50′W
104 K2 **Oviedo** ✕ Asturias, N Spain 43°21′N 05°50′W
Ovilava *see* Wels
118 D7 **Ovišī** Ventspils, W Latvia 57°34′N 21°43′E
146 K10 **Ovminzatovo Tog'lari** *Rus.* Gory Auminzatau. ▲▲ N Uzbekistan
Övögdiy *see* Telmen
Ovoot *see* Dariganga
157 O4 **Övörhangay** ◈ *province* C Mongolia
94 E12 **Øvre Årdal** Sogn Og Fjordane, S Norway 61°18′N 07°48′E
95 J14 **Övre Fryken** ◎ C Sweden
92 J11 **Övre Soppero** *Lapp.* Badje-Sohppar. Norrbotten, N Sweden 68°07′N 21°40′E
117 N3 **Ovruch** Zhytomyrs'ka Oblast', N Ukraine 51°20′N 28°50′E
Övt *see* Bat-Öldziy
185 E24 **Owaka** Otago, South Island, New Zealand 46°27′S 169°42′E
79 H18 **Owando** *prev.* Fort Rousset. Cuvette, C Congo 0°29′S 15°55′E
164 J14 **Owase** Mie, Honshū, SW Japan 34°04′N 136°11′E
27 P9 **Owasso** Oklahoma, C USA 36°16′N 95°51′W
29 V10 **Owatonna** Minnesota, N USA 44°04′N 93°13′W
173 O4 **Owen Fracture Zone** *tectonic feature* W Arabian Sea
185 H15 **Owen, Mount** ▲ South Island, New Zealand 41°32′S 172°33′E
185 H15 **Owen River** Tasman, South Island, New Zealand 41°40′S 172°28′E
44 D8 **Owen Roberts** ✕ Grand Cayman, Cayman Islands 19°15′N 81°22′W
20 I6 **Owensboro** Kentucky, S USA 37°46′N 87°07′W
35 T11 **Owens Lake** *salt flat* California, W USA
14 F14 **Owen Sound** Ontario, S Canada 44°34′N 80°56′W
14 F13 **Owen Sound** ◎ Ontario, S Canada
35 T10 **Owens River** ↝ California, W USA
186 F9 **Owen Stanley Range** ▲▲ S Papua New Guinea
27 V5 **Owensville** Missouri, C USA 38°21′N 91°30′W
20 M4 **Owenton** Kentucky, S USA 38°33′N 84°50′W
77 U17 **Owerri** Imo, S Nigeria 05°19′N 07°07′E
184 M10 **Owhango** Manawatu-Wanganui, North Island, New Zealand 39°01′S 175°22′E
21 N5 **Owingsville** Kentucky, S USA 38°09′N 83°46′W
77 T16 **Owo** Ondo, SW Nigeria 07°10′N 05°31′E
31 R9 **Owosso** Michigan, N USA 43°00′N 84°10′W
35 V1 **Owyhee** Nevada, W USA 41°57′N 116°07′W
32 L14 **Owyhee, Lake** ◎ Oregon, NW USA
32 L15 **Owyhee River** ↝ Idaho/Oregon, NW USA
92 K1 **Öxarfjörður** *var.* Axarfjördhur. *fjord* N Iceland
94 K12 **Oxberg** Dalarna, C Sweden 61°07′N 14°10′E
11 V17 **Oxbow** Saskatchewan, S Canada 49°16′N 102°12′W
95 O17 **Oxelösund** Södermanland, S Sweden 58°40′N 17°10′E
185 H18 **Oxford** Canterbury, South Island, New Zealand 43°18′S 172°10′E
97 M21 **Oxford** *Lat.* Oxonia. S England, United Kingdom 51°46′N 01°15′W
23 Q3 **Oxford** Alabama, S USA 33°36′N 85°50′W
22 L2 **Oxford** Mississippi, S USA 34°23′N 89°30′W
29 N16 **Oxford** Nebraska, C USA 40°15′N 99°37′W
18 I11 **Oxford** New York, NE USA 42°21′N 75°39′W
21 U8 **Oxford** North Carolina, SE USA 36°22′N 78°37′W
31 Q14 **Oxford** Ohio, N USA 39°30′N 84°45′W
18 H16 **Oxford** Pennsylvania, NE USA 39°46′N 75°57′W
11 X12 **Oxford House** Manitoba, C Canada 54°55′N 95°13′W
29 Y13 **Oxford Junction** Iowa, C USA 41°58′N 90°57′W
11 X12 **Oxford Lake** ◎ Manitoba, C Canada
97 M21 **Oxfordshire** *cultural region* S England, United Kingdom
Oxia *see* Oxyá
41 X12 **Oxkutzcab** Yucatán, SE Mexico 20°18′N 89°26′W
35 R15 **Oxnard** California, W USA 34°12′N 119°10′W
Oxonia *see* Oxford
14 I12 **Oxtongue** ↝ Ontario, SE Canada
Oxus *see* Amu Darya
115 E15 **Oxyá** *var.* Oxia. ▲ C Greece 39°46′N 21°56′E
164 L11 **Oyabe** Toyama, Honshū, SW Japan 36°42′N 136°52′E
Oyahue/Oyahue, Volcán *see* Ollagüe, Volcán
165 O12 **Oyama** Tochigi, Honshū, S Japan 36°19′N 139°46′E
47 U5 **Oyapock** ↝ E French Guiana
Oyapock *see* Oiapoque, Rio/Oyapok, Fleuve l'
55 Z10 **Oyapok, Baie de L'** *bay* Brazil/French Guiana South America W Atlantic Ocean
55 Z11 **Oyapok, Fleuve l'** *var.* Rio Oiapoque, Oyapock. ↝ Brazil/French Guiana *see also* Oiapoque, Rio
Oyapok, Fleuve l' *see* Oiapoque, Rio
79 E17 **Oyem** Woleu-Ntem, N Gabon 01°34′N 11°31′E
11 R16 **Oyen** Alberta, SW Canada 51°20′N 110°28′W
95 I15 **Øyeren** ◎ S Norway
Oygon *see* Tüdevtey
96 I7 **Oykel** ↝ N Scotland, United Kingdom
123 R9 **Oymyakon** Respublika Sakha (Yakutiya), NE Russian Federation 63°28′N 142°22′E
79 H19 **Oyo** Cuvette, C Congo 01°17′S 16°00′E
77 S15 **Oyo** Oyo, W Nigeria 07°51′N 03°57′E
77 S15 **Oyo** ◈ *state* SW Nigeria
56 D13 **Oyón** Lima, C Peru 10°39′S 76°44′W
103 S10 **Oyonnax** Ain, E France 46°16′N 05°39′E
146 L10 **Oyoqog'itma** *Rus.* Ayakagytma. Buxoro Viloyati, C Uzbekistan 40°37′N 64°26′E
146 M9 **Oyoqquduq** *Rus.* Ayakkuduk. Navoiy Viloyati, N Uzbekistan 41°16′N 65°12′E
32 F9 **Oysterville** Washington, NW USA 46°33′N 124°03′W
95 D14 **Øystese** Hordaland, S Norway 60°23′N 06°13′E
145 S16 **Oytal** Zhambyl, S Kazakhstan 42°54′N 73°21′E
147 U10 **Oy-Tal** Oshskaya Oblast', SW Kyrgyzstan 40°23′N 74°04′E
147 T10 **Oy-Tal** ↝ SW Kyrgyzstan
Oyyl *see* Uil
Ozarichi *see* Azarychy
23 R7 **Ozark** Alabama, S USA 31°27′N 85°38′W
27 S10 **Ozark** Arkansas, C USA 35°30′N 93°50′W
27 T8 **Ozark** Missouri, C USA 37°01′N 93°12′W
27 T8 **Ozark Plateau** *plain* Arkansas/Missouri, C USA
27 T6 **Ozarks, Lake of the** ⊠ Missouri, C USA
192 L10 **Ozbourn Seamount** *undersea feature* W Pacific Ocean 26°00′S 174°49′W
111 L20 **Ózd** Borsod-Abaúj-Zemplén, NE Hungary 48°15′N 20°18′E
112 D11 **Ozeblin** ▲ C Croatia 44°37′N 15°52′E
123 V11 **Ozernovskiy** Kamchatskaya Oblast', E Russian Federation 51°28′N 156°32′E
144 M7 **Ozërnoye** *var.* Ozërnyy. Kostanay, N Kazakhstan 53°29′N 63°14′E
124 J15 **Ozërnyy** Tverskaya Oblast', W Russian Federation 57°55′N 33°45′E
Ozërnyy *see* Ozërnoye
115 D18 **Ozerós, Límni** ◎ W Greece
122 G11 **Ozërsk** Chelyabinskaya Oblast', C Russian Federation 55°44′N 60°59′E
119 D14 **Ozersk** *prev.* Darkehnen, *Ger.* Angerapp. Kaliningradskaya Oblast', W Russian Federation 54°23′N 21°59′E
126 L4 **Ozery** Moskovskaya Oblast', W Russian Federation 54°51′N 38°37′E
Özgön *see* Uzgen
107 C17 **Ozieri** Sardegna, Italy, C Mediterranean Sea 40°35′N 09°01′E
111 I15 **Ozimek** *Ger.* Malapane. Opolskie, SW Poland 50°41′N 18°16′E
127 R8 **Ozinki** Saratovskaya Oblast', W Russian Federation 51°16′N 49°45′E
25 O10 **Ozona** Texas, SW USA 30°43′N 101°13′W
Ozorkov *see* Ozorków
110 J12 **Ozorków** *Rus.* Ozorkov. Łódź, C Poland 52°00′N 19°17′E
164 F14 **Ōzu** Ehime, Shikoku, SW Japan 33°30′N 132°33′E
137 R10 **Ozurget'i** *prev.* Makharadze. W Georgia 41°57′N 42°01′E

P

99 J17 **Paal** Limburg, NE Belgium 51°03′N 05°08′E
196 M14 **Paamiut** *var.* Pâmiut, *Dan.* Frederikshåb. S Greenland 62°22′N 49°52′W
Pa-an *see* Hpa-an
101 L22 **Paar** ↝ SE Germany
83 E26 **Paarl** Western Cape, SW South Africa 33°45′S 18°58′E
93 L15 **Paavola** Oulu, C Finland 64°34′N 25°15′E
96 E8 **Pabbay** *island* NW Scotland, United Kingdom
153 T15 **Pabna** Rajshahi, W Bangladesh 24°02′N 89°15′E
109 U4 **Pabneukirchen** Oberösterreich, N Austria 48°19′N 14°49′E
118 H13 **Pabradė** *Pol.* Podbrodzie. Vilnius, SE Lithuania 54°58′N 25°43′E
56 L13 **Pacahuaras, Río** ↝ N Bolivia
Pacaraima, Sierra/Pacaraím, Serra *see* Pakaraima Mountains
56 B11 **Pacasmayo** La Libertad, W Peru 07°27′S 79°33′W
42 D6 **Pacaya, Volcán de** ▲ S Guatemala 14°19′N 90°36′W
115 K23 **Pacheía** *var.* Pachía. *island* Kykládes, Greece, Aegean Sea
Pachía *see* Pacheía
107 L26 **Pachino** Sicilia, Italy, C Mediterranean Sea 36°43′N 15°06′E
56 F12 **Pachitea, Río** ↝ C Peru
154 I11 **Pachmarhi** Madhya Pradesh, C India 22°36′N 78°18′E
121 P3 **Páchna** *var.* Pakhna. SW Cyprus 34°47′N 32°48′E
115 H25 **Páchnes** ▲ Kríti, Greece, E Mediterranean Sea 35°19′N 24°00′E
54 F9 **Pacho** Cundinamarca, C Colombia 05°09′N 74°08′W
154 F12 **Pāchora** Mahārāshtra, C India 20°52′N 75°28′E
41 P13 **Pachuca** *var.* Pachuca de Soto. Hidalgo, C Mexico 20°05′N 98°46′W
Pachuca de Soto *see* Pachuca
27 W5 **Pacific** Missouri, C USA 38°28′N 90°44′W
192 L14 **Pacific-Antarctic Ridge** *undersea feature* S Pacific Ocean 62°00′S 157°00′W
32 F8 **Pacific Beach** Washington, NW USA 47°09′N 124°12′W
35 N10 **Pacific Grove** California, W USA 36°35′N 121°54′W
29 S15 **Pacific Junction** Iowa, C USA 41°01′N 95°48′W
192-193 **Pacific Ocean** *ocean*
129 Z10 **Pacific Plate** *tectonic feature*
113 J15 **Pačir** ▲ N Montenegro 43°19′N 19°07′E
182 L5 **Packsaddle** New South Wales, SE Australia 30°42′S 141°55′E
32 H9 **Packwood** Washington, NW USA 46°37′N 121°38′W
Padalung *see* Phatthalung
168 J12 **Padang** Sumatera, W Indonesia 01°S 100°21′E
168 L9 **Padang Endau** Pahang, Peninsular Malaysia 02°38′N 103°37′E
Padangpandjang *see* Padangpanjang
168 I11 **Padangpanjang** *prev.* Padangpandjang. Sumatera, W Indonesia 0°30′S 100°26′E
168 I10 **Padangsidempuan** *prev.* Padangsidimpoean. Sumatera, W Indonesia 01°23′N 99°15′E
Padangsidimpoean *see* Padangsidempuan
124 I9 **Padany** Respublika Kareliya, NW Russian Federation 63°18′N 33°20′E
93 M18 **Padasjoki** Etelä-Suomi, S Finland 61°20′N 25°21′E
57 M22 **Padcaya** Tarija, S Bolivia 21°52′S 64°46′W
101 H14 **Paderborn** Nordrhein-Westfalen, NW Germany 51°43′N 08°45′E
Padeșul/Padeş, Vîrful *see* Padeș, Vârful
116 F12 **Padeș, Vârful** *var.* Padeşul; *prev.* Virful Padeş. ▲ W Romania 45°39′N 22°19′E
112 L10 **Padinska Skela** Serbia, N Serbia 44°58′N 20°25′E
153 S14 **Padma** *var.* Ganges. ↝ Bangladesh/India *see also* Ganges
Padma *see* Brahmaputra
Padma *see* Ganges
106 H8 **Padova** *Eng.* Padua; *anc.* Patavium. Veneto, NE Italy 45°24′N 11°52′E
82 A10 **Padrão, Ponta do** *headland* NW Angola 06°06′S 12°18′E
25 T16 **Padre Island** *island* Texas, SW USA
104 G3 **Padrón** Galicia, NW Spain 42°44′N 08°40′W
118 K13 **Padsvillye** *Rus.* Podsvil'ye. Vitsyebskaya Voblasts', N Belarus 55°09′N 27°58′E
182 K11 **Padthaway** South Australia 36°39′S 140°30′E
Padua *see* Padova
20 G7 **Paducah** Kentucky, S USA 37°03′N 88°36′W
25 P4 **Paducah** Texas, SW USA 34°01′N 100°18′W
105 N15 **Padul** Andalucía, S Spain 37°02′N 03°37′W
191 P8 **Paea** Tahiti, W French Polynesia 17°41′S 149°35′W
185 L14 **Paekakariki** Wellington, North Island, New Zealand 41°00′S 174°58′E
163 X11 **Paektu-san** *var.* Baitou Shan. ▲ China/North Korea 42°00′N 128°03′E
163 V15 **Paengnyŏng-do** *island* NW South Korea
184 M7 **Paeroa** Waikato, North Island, New Zealand 37°23′S 175°39′E
54 D12 **Páez** Cauca, SW Colombia 02°37′N 76°00′W
121 O3 **Páfos** *var.* Paphos. W Cyprus 34°46′N 32°26′E
121 O3 **Páfos** ✕ SW Cyprus 34°46′N 32°25′E
83 L19 **Pafúri** Gaza, SW Mozambique 22°27′S 31°21′E
112 C12 **Pag** *It.* Pago. Lika-Senj, SW Croatia 44°26′N 15°01′E
112 B11 **Pag** *It.* Pago. *island* Zadar, C Croatia
171 P7 **Pagadian** Mindanao, S Philippines 07°47′N 123°22′E
168 I13 **Pagai Selatan, Pulau** *island* Kepulauan Mentawai, W Indonesia
168 J13 **Pagai Utara, Pulau** *island* Kepulauan Mentawai, W Indonesia
188 K4 **Pagan** *island* C Northern Mariana Islands
115 G16 **Pagasitikós Kólpos** *gulf* E Greece
36 L8 **Page** Arizona, SW USA 36°54′N 111°28′W
29 Q5 **Page** North Dakota, N USA 47°09′N 97°33′W
118 D13 **Pagėgiai** *Ger.* Pogegen. Tauragė, SW Lithuania 55°08′N 21°54′E
21 S11 **Pageland** South Carolina, SE USA 34°46′N 80°23′W
81 G16 **Pager** ↝ NE Uganda
149 Q5 **Paghmān** Kābol, E Afghanistan 34°33′N 68°55′E
Pago *see* Pag
188 C16 **Pago Bay** *bay* E Guam, W Pacific Ocean
115 M20 **Pagóndas** *var.* Pagóndhas. Sámos, Dodekánisa, Greece, Aegean Sea 37°41′N 26°50′E
Pagóndhas *see* Pagóndas
192 J16 **Pago Pago** ○ (American Samoa) Tutuila, W American Samoa 14°16′S 170°43′W
37 R8 **Pagosa Springs** Colorado, C USA 37°13′N 107°01′W
Pagqên *see* Gadê
38 H12 **Pāhala** *var.* Pahala. Hawaii, USA, C Pacific Ocean 19°12′N 155°28′W
168 K8 **Pahang** *var.* Negeri Pahang Darul Makmur. ◈ *state* Peninsular Malaysia
Pahang *see* Pahang, Sungai
168 L8 **Pahang, Sungai** *var.* Pahang, Sungei Pahang. ↝ Peninsular Malaysia
149 S8 **Pahārpur** North-West Frontier Province, NW Pakistan 32°06′N 71°00′E
185 B24 **Pahia Point** *headland* South Island, New Zealand 46°19′S 167°42′E
184 M13 **Pahiatua** Manawatu-Wanganui, North Island, New Zealand 40°30′S 175°49′E
38 H12 **Pāhoa** *var.* Pahoa. Hawaii, USA, C Pacific Ocean 19°29′N 154°56′W
23 Y14 **Pahokee** Florida, SE USA 26°49′N 80°40′W
35 X9 **Pahranagat Range** ▲▲ Nevada, W USA
35 W11 **Pahrump** Nevada, W USA 36°11′N 115°58′W
Pahsien *see* Chongqing
35 V9 **Pahute Mesa** ▲ Nevada, W USA
167 N7 **Pai** Mae Hong Son, NW Thailand 19°24′N 98°26′E
38 F10 **Pa'ia** *var.* Paia. Maui, Hawaii, USA, C Pacific Ocean 20°54′N 156°22′W
Paia *see* Pa'ia
Pai-ch'eng *see* Baicheng
118 H4 **Paide** *Ger.* Weissenstein. Järvamaa, N Estonia 58°55′N 25°36′E
97 J24 **Paignton** SW England, United Kingdom 50°26′N 03°34′W
184 K3 **Paihia** Northland, North Island, New Zealand 35°18′S 174°06′E
93 M18 **Päijänne** ◎ S Finland
114 F13 **Páïko** ▲ N Greece
57 M17 **Paila, Río** ↝ C Bolivia
167 Q12 **Pailin** Bătdâmbâng, W Cambodia 12°51′N 102°34′E
Pailing *see* Chun'an
54 F6 **Pailitas** Cesar, N Colombia 08°58′N 73°38′W
38 F9 **Pailolo Channel** *channel* Hawai'i, USA, C Pacific Ocean
93 K19 **Paimio** *Swe.* Pemar. Länsi-Suomi, SW Finland 60°27′N 22°42′E
165 O16 **Paimi-saki** *var.* Yaeme-saki. *headland* Iriomote-jima, SW Japan 24°18′N 123°40′E
102 G5 **Paimpol** Côtes d'Armor, NW France 48°47′N 03°03′W
168 J12 **Painan** Sumatera, W Indonesia 01°22′S 100°33′E
155 G23 **Paināvu** Kerala, SW India 09°50′N 76°56′E
63 G23 **Paine, Cerro** ▲ S Chile 51°01′S 72°57′W
31 U11 **Painesville** Ohio, N USA 41°43′N 81°15′W
31 S14 **Paint Creek** ↝ Ohio, N USA
36 L10 **Painted Desert** *desert* Arizona, SW USA
Paint Hills *see* Wemindji
30 M4 **Paint River** ↝ Michigan, N USA
25 P8 **Paint Rock** Texas, SW USA 31°32′N 99°56′W
21 O6 **Paintsville** Kentucky, S USA 37°48′N 82°48′W
Paisance *see* Piacenza
96 I12 **Paisley** W Scotland, United Kingdom 55°50′N 04°26′W
32 I15 **Paisley** Oregon, NW USA 42°40′N 120°31′W
105 R10 **País Valenciano** *var.* Valencia, *Cat.* València; *anc.* Valentia. ◈ *autonomous community* NE Spain
105 O3 **País Vasco** *Basq.* Euskadi, *Eng.* The Basque Country, *Sp.* Provincias Vascongadas. ◈ *autonomous community* N Spain
56 A9 **Paita** Piura, NW Peru 05°11′S 81°09′W
169 V6 **Paitan, Teluk** *bay* Sabah, East Malaysia
104 H7 **Paiva, Rio** ↝ N Portugal
92 K12 **Pajala** Norrbotten, N Sweden 67°12′N 23°19′E
104 K3 **Pajares, Puerto de** *pass* NW Spain
54 G9 **Pajarito** Boyacá, C Colombia 05°18′N 72°43′W
54 G4 **Pajaro** La Guajira, S Colombia 11°41′N 72°37′W
Pakanbaru *see* Pekanbaru
55 Q10 **Pakaraima Mountains** *var.* Serra Pacaraim, Sierra Pacaraima. ▲▲ N South America
153 S14 **Pakaur** *var.* Pakur. Jharkhand, N India 24°48′N 87°14′E
167 P10 **Pak Chong** Nakhon Ratchasima, C Thailand 14°38′N 101°22′E
123 V8 **Pakhachi** Koryakskiy Avtonomnyy Okrug, E Russian Federation 60°36′N 168°59′E
Pakhna *see* Páchna
189 U16 **Pakin Atoll** *atoll* Caroline Islands, E Micronesia
149 Q12 **Pakistan** *off.* Islamic Republic of Pakistan, *var.* Islami Jamhuriya e Pakistan. ◆ *republic* S Asia
Pakistan, Islamic Republic of *see* Pakistan
Pakistan, Islami Jamhuriya e *see* Pakistan
167 P8 **Pak Lay** *var.* Muang Pak Lay. Xaignabouli, C Laos 18°06′N 101°21′E
Paknam *see* Samut Prakan
166 L5 **Pakokku** Magway, C Burma (Myanmar) 21°20′N 95°05′E
110 I10 **Pakość** *Ger.* Pakosch. Kujawski-pomorskie, C Poland 52°47′N 18°03′E
Pakosch *see* Pakość
149 V10 **Pākpattan** Punjab, E Pakistan 30°20′N 73°27′E
167 O15 **Pak Phanang** *var.* Ban Pak Phanang. Nakhon Si Thammarat, SW Thailand 08°20′N 100°10′E
112 G9 **Pakrac** *Hung.* Pakrácz. Požega-Slavonija, NE Croatia 45°26′N 17°09′E
Pakrácz *see* Pakrac
118 F11 **Pakruojis** Šiaulai, N Lithuania 56°N 23°51′E
111 J24 **Paks** Tolna, S Hungary 46°38′N 18°51′E
Pak Sane *see* Pakxan
Paksé *see* Pakxé
167 Q10 **Pak Thong Chai** Nakhon Ratchasima, C Thailand 14°43′N 102°01′E
149 R6 **Paktīā** ◈ *province* SE Afghanistan
149 Q7 **Paktīkā** ◈ *province* SE Afghanistan
171 N12 **Pakuli** Sulawesi, C Indonesia 01°14′S 119°55′E
Pakur *see* Pakaur
81 F17 **Pakwach** NW Uganda 02°28′N 31°28′E
167 R8 **Pakxan** *var.* Muang Pakxan, Pak Sane. Bolikhamxai, C Laos 18°27′N 103°38′E
167 S10 **Pakxé** *var.* Paksé. Champasak, S Laos 15°09′N 105°49′E
78 G12 **Pala** Mayo-Kébbi, SW Chad 09°22′N 14°54′E
61 A17 **Palacios** Santa Fe, C Argentina 30°43′S 61°37′W
25 V13 **Palacios** Texas, SW USA 28°42′N 96°13′W
105 X5 **Palafrugell** Cataluña, NE Spain 41°55′N 03°10′E
107 L24 **Palagonia** Sicilia, Italy, C Mediterranean Sea 37°20′N 14°45′E
113 E17 **Palagruža** *It.* Pelagosa. *island* SW Croatia
115 G20 **Palaiá Epídavros** Pelopónnisos, S Greece 37°38′N 23°09′E
121 P3 **Palaichóri** *var.* Palekhori. C Cyprus 34°55′N 33°06′E
115 H25 **Palaiochóra** Kríti, Greece, E Mediterranean Sea 35°14′N 23°37′E
115 A15 **Palaiolastritsa** *religious building* Kérkyra, Iónia Nisiá, Greece, C Mediterranean Sea
115 J19 **Palaiópoli** Ándros, Kykládes, Greece, Aegean Sea 37°49′N 24°49′E
103 N5 **Palaiseau** Essonne, N France 48°41′N 02°14′E
155 G21 **Palakkad** *var.* Pālghāt. Kerala, SW India 10°46′N 76°42′E *see also* Pālghāt
154 N11 **Pāla Laharha** Orissa, E India 21°25′N 85°18′E
83 G19 **Palamakoloi** Ghanzi, C Botswana 23°10′S 22°22′E
115 E16 **Palamás** Thessalía, C Greece 39°28′N 22°05′E
105 X5 **Palamós** Cataluña, NE Spain 41°51′N 03°06′E
118 J5 **Palamuse** *Ger.* Sankt-Bartholomäi. Jõgevamaa, E Estonia 58°41′N 26°35′E
183 Q14 **Palana** Tasmania, SE Australia 39°48′S 147°54′E
123 U9 **Palana** Koryakskiy Avtonomnyy Okrug, E Russian Federation 59°05′N 159°59′E
118 C11 **Palanga** *Ger.* Polangen. Klaipėda, NW Lithuania 05°54′N 21°05′E
143 V10 **Palangān, Kūh-e** ▲▲ E Iran
Palangkaraja *see* Palangkaraya
169 T12 **Palangkaraya** *prev.* Palangkaraja. Borneo, C Indonesia 02°16′S 113°55′E
155 H22 **Palani** Tamil Nādu, SE India 10°30′N 77°24′E
Palanka *see* Bačka Palanka
154 D9 **Pālanpur** Gujarāt, W India 24°12′N 72°29′E
Palantia *see* Palencia
83 I19 **Palapye** Central, SE Botswana 22°37′S 27°06′E
155 J19 **Pālār** ↝ SE India
104 H3 **Palas de Rei** Galicia, NW Spain 42°52′N 07°51′W
123 T9 **Palatka** Magadanskaya Oblast', E Russian Federation 60°09′N 150°33′E
23 W10 **Palatka** Florida, SE USA 29°39′N 81°38′W
188 B9 **Palau** *var.* Belau. ◆ *republic* W Pacific Ocean
Palau *see* Palau Islands
129 Y14 **Palau Islands** *var.* Palau. *island group* N Palau
192 G16 **Palauli Bay** *bay* Savai'i, C Samoa, C Pacific Ocean
167 N11 **Palaw** Tanintharyi, S Burma (Myanmar) 12°57′N 98°39′E
170 M6 **Palawan** *island* W Philippines
171 N6 **Palawan Passage** *passage* W Philippines
192 E7 **Palawan Trough** *undersea feature* S South China Sea 07°00′N 115°00′E
155 H23 **Pālayankottai** Tamil Nādu, SE India 08°42′N 77°46′E
107 L25 **Palazzola Acreide** *anc.* Acrae. Sicilia, Italy, C Mediterranean Sea 37°04′N 14°54′E
118 G3 **Paldiski** *prev.* Baltiski, *Eng.* Baltic Port, *Ger.* Baltischport. Harjumaa, NW Estonia 59°22′N 24°08′E
112 I13 **Pale** Republika Srpska, SE Bosnia and Herzegovina 43°49′N 18°35′E
Palekhori *see* Palaichóri
168 L13 **Palembang** Sumatera, W Indonesia 02°59′S 104°45′E
63 G18 **Palena** Los Lagos, S Chile 43°40′S 71°50′W
63 G18 **Palena, Río** ↝ S Chile
104 M5 **Palencia** *anc.* Palantia, Pallantia. Castilla-León, NW Spain 42°23′N 04°32′W
104 M3 **Palencia** ◈ *province* Castilla-León, N Spain
35 X15 **Palen Dry Lake** ◎ California, W USA
41 V15 **Palenque** Chiapas, SE Mexico 17°32′N 91°59′W
41 V15 **Palenque** *var.* Ruinas de Palenque. *ruins* Chiapas, SE Mexico
45 O9 **Palenque, Punta** *headland* S Dominican Republic 18°13′N 70°08′W
Palenque, Ruinas de *see* Palenque
Palerme *see* Palermo
107 I23 **Palermo** *Fr.* Palerme; *anc.* Panhormus, Panormus. Sicilia, Italy, C Mediterranean Sea 38°08′N 13°23′E
25 V8 **Palestine** Texas, SW USA 31°45′N 95°39′W
25 V7 **Palestine, Lake** ⊠ Texas, SW USA
107 I15 **Palestrina** Lazio, C Italy 41°49′N 12°53′E
166 K5 **Paletwa** Chin State, W Burma (Myanmar) 21°25′N 92°49′E
155 G21 **Pālghāt** *var.* Palakkad. Kerala, SW India 10°46′N 76°42′E *see also* Palakkad
152 F13 **Pāli** Rājasthān, N India 25°48′N 73°21′E
167 N16 **Palian** Trang, SW Thailand 07°10′N 99°40′E
189 O12 **Palikir** ● (Micronesia) Pohnpei, E Micronesia 06°58′N 158°13′E
Palimé *see* Kpalimé
107 L19 **Palinuro, Capo** *headland* S Italy 40°02′N 15°16′E
115 H15 **Paliouri, Akrotírio** *var.* Akrotírio Kanestron. *headland* N Greece 39°55′N 23°45′E
33 R14 **Palisades Reservoir** ⊠ Idaho, NW USA
99 J23 **Paliseul** Luxembourg, SE Belgium 49°55′N 05°09′E
154 C11 **Pālitāna** Gujarāt, W India 21°30′N 71°50′E
118 F4 **Palivere** Läänemaa, W Estonia 58°59′N 23°58′E
41 V14 **Palizada** Campeche, SE Mexico 18°15′N 92°03′W
93 L18 **Pälkäne** Länsi-Suomi, W Finland 61°22′N 24°16′E
155 J22 **Palk Strait** *strait* India/Sri Lanka
155 J23 **Pallai** Northern Province, NW Sri Lanka 09°35′N 80°20′E
Pallantia *see* Palencia
106 C6 **Pallanza** Piemonte, NE Italy 45°57′N 08°32′E
127 Q9 **Pallasovka** Volgogradskaya Oblast', SW Russian Federation 50°06′N 46°52′E
Pallene/Pallíni *see* Kassándra
185 L15 **Palliser Bay** *bay* North Island, New Zealand
185 L15 **Palliser, Cape** *headland* North Island, New Zealand 41°37′S 175°16′E
191 U9 **Palliser, Îles** *island group* Îles Tuamotu, C French Polynesia
82 Q12 **Palma** Cabo Delgado, N Mozambique 10°46′S 40°30′E
105 X9 **Palma** *var.* Palma de Mallorca. Mallorca, Spain, W Mediterranean Sea 39°35′N 02°39′E
105 X9 **Palma** ✕ Mallorca, Spain, W Mediterranean Sea
105 X10 **Palma, Badia de** *bay* Mallorca, Spain, W Mediterranean Sea
104 L13 **Palma del Río** Andalucía, S Spain 37°42′N 05°16′W
Palma de Mallorca *see* Palma
107 J25 **Palma di Montechiaro** Sicilia, Italy, C Mediterranean Sea 37°12′N 13°46′E
106 J7 **Palmanova** Friuli-Venezia Giulia, NE Italy 45°54′N 13°20′E
54 J7 **Palmarito** Apure, C Venezuela 07°36′N 70°08′W
43 N15 **Palmar Sur** Puntarenas, SE Costa Rica 08°54′N 83°27′W
60 I12 **Palmas** Paraná, S Brazil 26°29′S 52°00′W
59 K16 **Palmas** *var.* Palmas do Tocantins. Tocantins, C Brazil 10°24′S 48°19′W
76 L18 **Palmas, Cape** *Fr.* Cap des Palmès. *headland* SW Ivory Coast 04°18′N 07°31′W
Palmas do Tocantins *see* Palmas
54 D11 **Palmaseca** ✕ (Cali) Valle del Cauca, SW Colombia 03°31′N 76°27′W
107 B21 **Palmas, Golfo di** *gulf* Sardegna, Italy, C Mediterranean Sea
44 I7 **Palma Soriano** Santiago de Cuba, E Cuba 20°10′N 76°00′W
23 Y12 **Palm Bay** Florida, SE USA 28°01′N 80°35′W
35 T14 **Palmdale** California, W USA 34°34′N 118°07′W
61 H14 **Palmeira das Missões** Rio Grande do Sul, S Brazil 27°54′S 53°20′W
82 A11 **Palmeirinhas, Ponta das** *headland* NW Angola 09°04′S 13°02′E
39 R11 **Palmer** Alaska, USA 61°36′N 149°06′W
19 N11 **Palmer** Massachusetts, NE USA 42°09′N 72°19′W
25 U7 **Palmer** Texas, SW USA 32°25′N 96°40′W
194 H4 **Palmer** *US research station* Antarctica 64°37′S 64°01′W
15 R11 **Palmer** ↝ Québec, SE Canada
37 T5 **Palmer Lake** Colorado, C USA 39°07′N 104°55′W
194 J6 **Palmer Land** *physical region* Antarctica
14 F15 **Palmerston** Ontario, SE Canada 43°51′N 80°49′W
185 F22 **Palmerston** Otago, South Island, New Zealand 45°27′S 170°42′E
190 K15 **Palmerston** *island* S Cook Islands
Palmerston *see* Darwin
184 M12 **Palmerston North** Manawatu-Wanganui, North Island, New Zealand 40°20′S 175°52′E
23 V13 **Palmetto** Florida, SE USA 27°31′N 82°34′W
The Palmetto State *see* South Carolina
107 M22 **Palmi** Calabria, SW Italy 38°21′N 15°51′E
54 D11 **Palmira** Valle del Cauca, W Colombia 03°33′N 76°17′W
56 F8 **Palmira, Río** ↝ N Peru
61 D19 **Palmitas** Soriano, SW Uruguay 33°27′S 57°48′W
Palmnicken *see* Yantarnyy
35 V15 **Palm Springs** California, W USA 33°48′N 116°33′W
27 V2 **Palmyra** Missouri, C USA 39°48′N 91°31′W
18 G10 **Palmyra** New York, NE USA 43°02′N 77°13′W
18 G15 **Palmyra** Pennsylvania, NE USA 40°18′N 76°35′W
21 V5 **Palmyra** Virginia, NE USA 37°53′N 78°17′W
Palmyra *see* Tudmur
192 L7 **Palmyra Atoll** ◇ *US privately owned unincorporated territory* C Pacific Ocean
154 P12 **Palmyras Point** *headland* E India 20°46′N 87°00′E
35 N9 **Palo Alto** California, W USA 37°26′N 122°08′W
25 O1 **Palo Duro Creek** ↝ Texas, SW USA
Paloe *see* Denpasar, Bali, C Indonesia
Paloe *see* Palu
168 L9 **Paloh** Johor, Peninsular Malaysia 02°10′N 103°11′E
80 F12 **Paloich** Upper Nile, SE Sudan 10°29′N 32°31′E
40 I3 **Palomas** Chihuahua, N Mexico 31°45′N 107°38′W
107 I15 **Palombara Sabina** Lazio, C Italy 42°04′N 12°45′E
105 S13 **Palos, Cabo de** *headland* SE Spain 37°38′N 00°42′W
104 I14 **Palos de la Frontera** Andalucía, S Spain 37°14′N 06°53′W
60 G11 **Palotina** Paraná, S Brazil 24°16′S 53°49′W
32 M9 **Palouse** Washington, NW USA 46°54′N 117°04′W
32 L9 **Palouse River** ↝ Washington, NW USA
35 Y16 **Palo Verde** California, W USA 33°25′N 114°43′W
57 E16 **Palpa** Ica, W Peru 14°35′S 75°09′W
95 M16 **Pålsboda** Örebro, C Sweden 59°04′N 15°21′E
93 M15 **Paltamo** Oulu, C Finland 64°25′N 27°50′E
171 N12 **Palu** *prev.* Paloe. Sulawesi, C Indonesia 0°54′S 119°52′E
137 P14 **Palu** Elazığ, E Turkey 38°43′N 39°56′E
152 I11 **Palwal** Haryāna, N India 28°15′N 77°18′E
123 U6 **Palyavaam** ↝ NE Russian Federation
77 Q13 **Pama** SE Burkina 11°13′N 00°46′E

◆ Country ● Country Capital ◇ Dependent Territory ○ Dependent Territory Capital ◈ Administrative Regions ✕ International Airport ▲ Mountain ▲▲ Mountain Range Volcano ↝ River ◎ Lake ⊠ Reservoir

172 J14 **Pamandzi** ✈ (Mamoudzou) Petite-Terre, E Mayotte
Pamangkat see Pemangkat
143 R11 **Pā Mazār** Kermān, C Iran
83 N19 **Pambarra** Inhambane, SE Mozambique 21°57′S 35°06′E
171 X12 **Pamdai** Papua, E Indonesia 01°58′S 137°19′E
103 N16 **Pamiers** Ariège, S France 43°07′N 01°37′E
147 T14 **Pamir** var. Daryā-ye Pāmīr, Taj. Dar"yoi Pomir. ≈ Afghanistan/Tajikistan see also Pāmīr, Daryā-ye
Pamir see Pāmīr, Daryā-ye
149 U1 **Pāmīr, Daryā-ye** var. Pamir, Taj. Dar"yoi Pomir. ≈ Afghanistan/Tajikistan see also Pamir
Pāmīr, Daryā-ye see Pamir
Pāmīr-e Khord see Little Pamir
Pamir/Pāmīr, Daryā-ye see Pamirs
129 Q8 **Pamirs** Pash. Daryā-ye Pāmīr, Rus. Pamir. ▲▲ C Asia
Pāmiut see Paamiut
21 X10 **Pamlico River** ≈ North Carolina, SE USA
21 Y10 **Pamlico Sound** sound North Carolina, SE USA
25 O2 **Pampa** Texas, SW USA 35°32′N 100°58′W
Pampa Aullagas, Lago see Poopó, Lago
61 B21 **Pampa Húmeda** grassland E Argentina
56 A10 **Pampa las Salinas** salt lake NW Peru
57 F15 **Pampas** Huancavelica, C Peru 12°22′S 74°53′W
63 K13 **Pampas** plain C Argentina
55 O4 **Pampatar** Nueva Esparta, NE Venezuela 11°03′N 63°51′W
Pampeluna see Pamplona
104 H8 **Pampilhosa da Serra** var. Pampilhosa de Serra. Coimbra, N Portugal 40°03′N 07°58′W
173 Y15 **Pamplemousses** N Mauritius 20°06′S 57°34′E
54 G7 **Pamplona** Norte de Santander, N Colombia 07°24′N 72°38′W
105 Q3 **Pamplona** Basq. Iruña, prev. Pampeluna; anc. Pompaelo. Navarra, N Spain 42°49′N 01°39′W
114 I11 **Pamporovo** prev. Vasil Kolarov. Smolyan, S Bulgaria 41°39′N 24°45′E
136 D15 **Pamukkale** Denizli, W Turkey 37°51′N 29°13′E
21 W5 **Pamunkey River** ≈ Virginia, NE USA
152 K5 **Pamzal** Jammu and Kashmir, NW India 34°17′N 78°50′E
30 L14 **Pana** Illinois, N USA 39°23′N 89°04′W
41 Y11 **Panabá** Yucatán, SE Mexico 21°20′N 88°16′W
35 Y8 **Panaca** Nevada, W USA 37°47′N 114°24′W
115 E19 **Panachaikó** ▲▲ S Greece
14 F11 **Panache Lake** ◎ Ontario, S Canada
114 I10 **Panagyurishte** Pazardzhik, C Bulgaria 42°30′N 24°11′E
168 M16 **Panaitan, Pulau** island S Indonesia
115 D18 **Panaitolikó** ▲▲ C Greece
155 E17 **Panaji** var. Pangim, Panjim, New Goa. state capital Goa, W India 15°31′N 73°52′E
43 T15 **Panamá** var. Ciudad de Panamá, Eng. Panama City. ● (Panama) Panamá, C Panama 08°57′N 79°33′W
43 T14 **Panama** off. Republic of Panama. ◆ republic Central America
43 U14 **Panamá** off. Provincia de Panamá. ◐ province E Panama
43 U15 **Panamá, Bahía de** bay N Gulf of Panama
193 T7 **Panama Basin** undersea feature E Pacific Ocean 05°00′N 83°30′W
43 T15 **Panama Canal** canal E Panama
23 R9 **Panama City** Florida, SE USA 30°09′N 85°39′W
43 T14 **Panama City** ✈ Panamá, C Panama 09°02′N 79°24′W
Panama City see Panamá
23 Q9 **Panama City Beach** Florida, SE USA 30°10′N 85°48′W
43 T17 **Panamá, Golfo de** var. Gulf of Panama. gulf S Panama
Panama, Gulf of see Panamá, Golfo de
Panama, Isthmus of see Panamá, Istmo de
43 T15 **Panamá, Istmo de** Eng. Isthmus of Panama; prev. Isthmus of Darien. isthmus E Panama
Panamá, Provincia de see Panamá
Panama, Republic of see Panama
35 U11 **Panamint Range** ▲▲ California, W USA
107 L22 **Panarea, Isola** island Isole Eolie, S Italy
106 G9 **Panaro** ≈ N Italy
171 P5 **Panay Island** island C Philippines
35 W7 **Pancake Range** ▲▲ Nevada, W USA
112 M11 **Pančevo** Ger. Pantschowa, Hung. Pancsova. Vojvodina, N Serbia 44°53′N 20°40′E
113 M15 **Pančićev Vrh** ▲ SW Serbia 43°16′N 20°49′E
116 L12 **Panciu** Vrancea, E Romania 45°54′N 27°08′E
116 F10 **Pâncota** Hung. Pankota; prev. Pîncota. Arad, W Romania 46°20′N 21°45′E
Pancsova see Pančevo
83 N20 **Panda** Inhambane, SE Mozambique 24°02′S 34°45′E
171 X12 **Pandaidori, Kepulauan** island group E Indonesia
25 N11 **Pandale** Texas, SW USA 30°09′N 101°34′W
169 P12 **Pandang Tikar, Pulau** island N Indonesia
61 F20 **Pan de Azúcar** Maldonado, S Uruguay 34°45′S 55°14′W
118 H11 **Pandėlys** Panevėžys, NE Lithuania 56°04′N 25°18′E
155 F15 **Pandharpur** Mahārāshtra, W India 17°42′N 75°24′E
182 J1 **Pandie Pandie** South Australia 26°06′S 139°26′E
171 O12 **Pandiri** Sulawesi, C Indonesia 01°32′S 120°47′E
61 F20 **Pando** Canelones, S Uruguay 34°44′S 55°58′W
57 J14 **Pando** ◐ department N Bolivia
192 K9 **Pandora Bank** undersea feature W Pacific Ocean
95 G20 **Pandrup** Nordjylland, N Denmark 57°14′N 09°42′E
79 J15 **Pandu** Equateur, NW Dem. Rep. Congo 05°03′N 19°14′E
153 V12 **Pandu** Assam, NE India 26°08′N 91°37′E
Paneas see Bāniyās
59 F15 **Panelas** Mato Grosso, W Brazil 09°06′S 60°41′W
118 G12 **Panevėžys** Panevėžys, C Lithuania 55°44′N 24°21′E
118 G11 **Panevėžys** ◐ province NW Lithuania
Panfilov see Zharkent
127 N9 **Panfilovo** Volgogradskaya Oblast', SW Russian Federation 50°25′N 42°55′E
79 N17 **Panga** Orientale, N Dem. Rep. Congo 01°52′N 26°18′E
193 Y15 **Pangai** Lifuka, C Tonga 19°50′S 174°23′W
114 H13 **Pangaío** ▲▲ N Greece
79 G20 **Pangala** Pool, S Congo 03°26′S 14°38′E
81 J22 **Pangani** Tanga, E Tanzania 05°27′S 39°00′E
81 I21 **Pangani** ≈ NE Tanzania
186 K8 **Panggoe** Choiseul Island, NW Solomon Islands 07°00′S 157°05′E
79 N20 **Pangi** Maniema, E Dem. Rep. Congo 03°12′S 26°39′E
Pangim see Panaji
168 H8 **Pangkalanbrandan** Sumatera, W Indonesia 04°00′N 98°15′E
Pangkalanbun see Pangkalanbuun
169 R13 **Pangkalanbuun** var. Pangkalanbun. Borneo, C Indonesia 02°43′S 111°38′E
169 N12 **Pangkalpinang** Pulau Bangka, W Indonesia 02°05′S 106°09′E
11 U17 **Pangman** Saskatchewan, S Canada 49°37′N 104°33′W
Pang-Nga see Phang-Nga
9 S6 **Pangnirtung** Baffin Island, Nunavut, NE Canada 66°05′N 65°45′W
152 K6 **Pangong Tso** var. Bangong Co. ◎ China/India see also Bangong Co
Pangong Tso see Banggong Co
36 K7 **Panguitch** Utah, W USA 37°49′N 112°26′W
186 J7 **Panguna** Bougainville Island, NE Papua New Guinea 06°22′S 155°20′E
171 N8 **Pangutaran Group** island group Sulu Archipelago, SW Philippines
25 N2 **Panhandle** Texas, SW USA 35°21′N 101°24′W
Panhormus see Palermo
171 W14 **Paniai, Danau** ◎ Papua, E Indonesia
79 L21 **Pania-Mutombo** Kasai-Oriental, C Dem. Rep. Congo 05°09′S 23°49′E
187 P16 **Panié, Mont** ▲ C New Caledonia 20°33′S 164°41′E
Panikoilli see Jājapur
152 I10 **Pānīpat** Haryāna, N India 29°18′N 77°00′E
147 Q14 **Panj** Rus. Pyandzh; prev. Kirovabad. SW Tajikistan 37°39′N 69°55′E
147 P15 **Panj** Rus. Pyandzh. ≈ Afghanistan/Tajikistan
149 O5 **Panjāb** Bāmīān, C Afghanistan 34°21′N 67°00′E
147 O12 **Panjakent** Rus. Pendzhikent. W Tajikistan 39°28′N 67°33′E
148 L14 **Panjgūr** Baluchistān, SW Pakistan 26°58′N 64°05′E
Panjim see Panaji
163 U12 **Panjin** Liaoning, NE China 41°11′N 122°05′E
147 P14 **Panji Poyon** Rus. Nizhniy Pyandzh. SW Tajikistan 37°14′N 68°32′E
149 S4 **Panjshīr** ◐ province NE Afghanistan
149 Q4 **Panjshīr** ≈ E Afghanistan
Pankota see Pâncota
77 W14 **Pankshin** Plateau, C Nigeria 09°21′N 09°27′E
163 Y10 **Pan Ling** ▲▲ N China
Panlong Jiang see Lô, Sông
154 J9 **Panna** Madhya Pradesh, C India 24°43′N 80°11′E
99 M16 **Panningen** Limburg, SE Netherlands 51°20′N 05°59′E
149 R13 **Pāno Āqil** Sind, SE Pakistan 27°55′N 69°18′E
121 P3 **Páno Léfkara** S Cyprus 34°52′N 33°18′E
121 O3 **Páno Panagiá** var. Pano Panayia. W Cyprus 34°55′N 32°38′E
Pano Panayia see Páno Panagiá
Panopolis see Akhmīm
29 U14 **Panora** Iowa, C USA 41°41′N 94°21′W
60 I8 **Panorama** São Paulo, S Brazil 21°22′S 51°51′W
115 I24 **Pánormos** Kríti, Greece, E Mediterranean Sea 35°24′N 24°42′E
Panormus see Palermo
163 W11 **Panshi** Jilin, NE China 42°56′N 126°02′E
59 H19 **Pantanal** var. Pantanalmato-Grossense. swamp SW Brazil
Pantanalmato-Grossense see Pantanal
61 H16 **Pântano Grande** Rio Grande do Sul, S Brazil 30°12′S 52°24′W
171 Q16 **Pantar, Pulau** island Kepulauan Alor, S Indonesia
21 X9 **Pantego** North Carolina, SE USA 35°34′N 76°39′E
107 G25 **Pantelleria** anc. Cossyra, Cosyra. Sicilia, Italy, C Mediterranean Sea 36°47′N 12°00′E
107 G25 **Pantelleria, Isola di** island SW Italy
Pante Makasar/Pante Macassar/Pante Makassar see Ponte Macassar
152 K10 **Pantnagar** Uttarakhand, N India 29°00′N 79°28′E
115 A15 **Pantokrátoras** ▲ Kérkyra, Iónia Nisiá, Greece, C Mediterranean Sea 39°45′N 19°51′E
Pantschowa see Pančevo
41 P11 **Pánuco** Veracruz-Llave, E Mexico 22°01′N 98°13′W
41 P11 **Pánuco, Río** ≈ C Mexico
160 I12 **Panxian** Guizhou, S China 25°45′N 104°39′E
168 I10 **Panyabungan** Sumatera, N Indonesia 0°55′N 99°30′E
77 W14 **Panyam** Plateau, C Nigeria 09°28′N 09°13′E
157 N13 **Panzhihua** prev. Dukou, Tu-k'ou. Sichuan, C China 26°35′N 101°41′E
79 I22 **Panzi** Bandundu, SW Dem. Rep. Congo 07°10′S 17°55′E
42 E5 **Panzós** Alta Verapaz, E Guatemala 15°21′N 89°40′W
Pao-chi/Paoki see Baoji
Pao-king see Shaoyang
107 N20 **Paola** Calabria, SW Italy 39°21′N 16°03′E
121 P16 **Paola** E Malta 35°52′N 14°30′E
27 R5 **Paola** Kansas, C USA 38°34′N 94°54′W
31 O15 **Paoli** Indiana, N USA 38°35′N 86°25′W
187 R14 **Paonangisu** Éfaté, C Vanuatu 17°33′S 168°23′E
171 S13 **Paoni** var. Pauni. Pulau Seram, E Indonesia 02°48′S 129°03′E
37 Q5 **Paonia** Colorado, C USA 38°52′N 107°35′W
191 O7 **Paopao** Moorea, W French Polynesia 17°28′S 149°48′W
Pao-shan see Baoshan
Pao-ting see Baoding
Pao-t'ou/Paotow see Baotou
79 H14 **Paoua** Ouham-Pendé, W Central African Republic 07°22′N 16°25′E
Pap see Pop
111 H23 **Pápa** Veszprém, W Hungary 47°20′N 17°29′E
42 J12 **Papagayo, Golfo de** gulf NW Costa Rica
38 H11 **Pāpa'ikou** var. Papaikou. Hawaii, USA, C Pacific Ocean 19°45′N 155°06′W
41 R15 **Papaloapan, Río** ≈ S Mexico
184 L6 **Papakura** Auckland, North Island, New Zealand 37°03′S 174°57′E
41 Q13 **Papantla** var. Papantla de Olarte. Veracruz-Llave, E Mexico 20°30′N 97°21′W
Papantla de Olarte see Papantla
191 P8 **Papara** Tahiti, W French Polynesia 17°45′S 149°33′W
184 K4 **Paparoa** Northland, North Island, New Zealand 36°06′S 174°12′E
185 G16 **Paparoa Range** ▲▲ South Island, New Zealand
115 K20 **Pápas, Akrotírio** headland Ikaría, Dodekánisa, Greece, Aegean Sea 37°31′N 25°58′E
96 L2 **Papa Stour** island NE Scotland, United Kingdom
184 L6 **Papatoetoe** Auckland, North Island, New Zealand 36°58′S 174°52′E
185 E25 **Papatowai** Otago, South Island, New Zealand 46°33′S 169°33′E
96 K4 **Papa Westray** island NE Scotland, United Kingdom
191 T10 **Papeete** ○ (French Polynesia) Tahiti, W French Polynesia 17°32′S 149°34′W
100 F11 **Papenburg** Niedersachsen, NW Germany 53°04′N 07°24′E
98 H13 **Papendrecht** Zuid-Holland, SW Netherlands 51°50′N 04°42′E
191 Q7 **Papenoo** Tahiti, W French Polynesia 17°29′S 149°25′W
191 Q7 **Papenoo Rivière** ≈ Tahiti, W French Polynesia
191 N7 **Papetoai** Moorea, W French Polynesia 17°29′S 149°52′W
92 L3 **Papey** island E Iceland
Paphos see Páfos
40 H5 **Papigochic, Río** ≈ NW Mexico
118 E10 **Papilė** Šiauliai, NW Lithuania 56°08′N 22°51′E
29 S15 **Papillion** Nebraska, C USA 41°09′N 96°02′W
15 T5 **Papinachois** ≈ Québec, SE Canada
171 X13 **Papua** var. Irian Barat, West Irian, West New Guinea, West Papua; prev. Dutch New Guinea, Irian Jaya, Netherlands New Guinea. ◐ province E Indonesia
Papua and New Guinea, Territory of see Papua New Guinea
186 C9 **Papua, Gulf of** gulf S Papua New Guinea
186 C8 **Papua New Guinea** off. Independent State of Papua New Guinea; prev. Territory of Papua and New Guinea. ◆ commonwealth republic NW Melanesia
Papua New Guinea, Independent State of see Papua New Guinea
192 H8 **Papua Plateau** undersea feature N Coral Sea
112 G9 **Papuk** ▲▲ NE Croatia
167 N8 **Papun** Kayin State, S Burma (Myanmar) 18°05′N 97°26′E
42 L14 **Paquera** Puntarenas, W Costa Rica 09°52′N 84°56′W
58 I13 **Pará** off. Estado do Pará. ◐ state NE Brazil
55 V9 **Para** ◐ district N Surinam
Pará see Belém
180 I8 **Paraburdoo** Western Australia 23°07′S 117°40′E
57 E16 **Paracas, Península de** peninsula W Peru
59 L19 **Paracatu** Minas Gerais, NE Brazil 17°14′S 46°52′W
192 E6 **Paracel Islands** ◇ disputed territory SE Asia
182 I6 **Parachilna** South Australia 31°09′S 138°23′E
149 R6 **Pārachinār** North-West Frontier Province, NW Pakistan 33°56′N 70°04′E
112 N13 **Paraćin** Serbia, C Serbia 43°51′N 21°25′E
14 K8 **Paradis** Québec, SE Canada 48°13′N 76°36′W
39 N11 **Paradise** var. Paradise Hill. Alaska, USA 62°28′N 160°09′W
35 O5 **Paradise** California, W USA 39°42′N 121°39′W
35 X11 **Paradise** Nevada, W USA 36°05′N 115°10′W
Paradise Hill see Paradise
37 R11 **Paradise Hills** New Mexico, SW USA 35°12′N 106°42′W
Paradise of the Pacific see Hawai'i
36 L13 **Paradise Valley** Arizona, SW USA 33°31′N 111°56′W
35 T2 **Paradise Valley** Nevada, W USA 41°30′N 117°30′W
115 O22 **Paradisi** ✈ (Ródos) Ródos, Dodekánisa, Greece, Aegean Sea 36°24′N 28°08′E
154 P12 **Pārādwīp** Orissa, E India 20°17′N 86°42′E
Pará, Estado do see Pará
Paraetonium see Mersā Matrūh
117 R4 **Parafiyivka** Chernihivs'ka Oblast', N Ukraine 50°53′N 32°40′E
36 K7 **Paragonah** Utah, W USA 37°53′N 112°46′W
27 X9 **Paragould** Arkansas, C USA 36°02′N 90°30′W
47 X8 **Paraguaçu** var. Paraguassú. ≈ E Brazil
60 J9 **Paraguaçu Paulista** São Paulo, S Brazil 22°22′S 50°35′W
54 H4 **Paraguaipoa** Zulia, NW Venezuela 11°21′N 71°58′W
62 O6 **Paraguarí** Paraguarí, S Paraguay 25°36′S 57°06′W
62 O7 **Paraguarí** off. Departamento de Paraguarí. ◐ department S Paraguay
Paraguarí, Departamento de see Paraguarí
57 O16 **Paraguá, Río** ≈ NE Bolivia
55 O8 **Paragua, Río** ≈ SE Venezuela
Paraguassú see Paraguaçu
62 N5 **Paraguay** ◆ republic C South America
47 U10 **Paraguay** var. Río Paraguay. ≈ C South America
Paraguay, Río see Paraguay
Parahiba/Parahyba see Paraíba
59 P15 **Paraíba** off. Estado da Paraíba; prev. Parahiba, Parahyba. ◐ state E Brazil
Paraíba see João Pessoa
60 P9 **Paraíba do Sul, Rio** ≈ SE Brazil
Paraíba, Estado da see Paraíba
Parainen see Pargas
43 N14 **Paraíso** Cartago, C Costa Rica 09°51′N 83°50′W
41 U14 **Paraíso** Tabasco, SE Mexico 18°26′N 93°10′W
57 O17 **Paraíso, Río** ≈ E Bolivia
Parajd see Praid
77 S14 **Parakou** C Benin 09°23′N 02°40′E
115 F20 **Paralía Tyrou** Pelopónnisos, S Greece 37°17′N 22°50′E
121 Q2 **Paralímni** E Cyprus 35°02′N 34°00′E
115 G18 **Paralímni, Límni** ◎ C Greece
55 W8 **Paramaribo** ● (Surinam) Paramaribo, N Surinam 05°52′N 55°14′W
55 W9 **Paramaribo** ◐ district N Surinam
55 W9 **Paramaribo** ✈ Paramaribo, N Surinam 05°52′N 55°14′W
Paramithiá see Paramythiá
56 C13 **Paramonga** Lima, W Peru 10°42′S 77°50′W
123 V12 **Paramushir, Ostrov** island SE Russian Federation
115 C16 **Paramythiá** var. Paramithiá. Ípeiros, W Greece 39°28′N 20°31′E
62 M10 **Paraná** Entre Ríos, E Argentina 31°48′S 60°29′W
60 H11 **Paraná** off. Estado do Paraná. ◐ state S Brazil
47 U11 **Paraná** var. Alto Paraná. ≈ C South America
Paraná, Estado do see Paraná
60 K12 **Paranaguá** Paraná, S Brazil 25°32′S 48°36′W
59 J20 **Paranaíba, Rio** ≈ E Brazil
61 C19 **Paraná Ibicuy, Río** ≈ E Argentina
59 H15 **Paranaíta** Mato Grosso, W Brazil 09°35′S 57°01′W
60 H9 **Paranapanema, Rio** ≈ S Brazil
60 K11 **Paranapiacaba, Serra do** ▲▲ S Brazil
60 H9 **Paranavaí** Paraná, S Brazil 23°02′S 52°36′W
143 N5 **Parandak** Markazī, W Iran 35°19′N 50°40′E
114 I12 **Paranésti** var. Paranestio. Anatolikí Makedonía kai Thráki, NE Greece 41°16′N 24°31′E
Paranestio see Paranésti
191 W11 **Paraoa** atoll Îles Tuamotu, C French Polynesia
184 L13 **Paraparaumu** Wellington, North Island, New Zealand 40°55′S 175°01′E
57 N20 **Parapetí, Río** ≈ SE Bolivia
54 L10 **Paraque, Cerro** ▲ W Venezuela 06°00′S 67°00′W
154 I11 **Parāsiya** Madhya Pradesh, C India 22°11′N 78°50′E
115 M23 **Paraspóri, Akrotírio** headland Kárpathos, SE Greece 35°54′N 27°15′E
60 O10 **Parati** Rio de Janeiro, SE Brazil 23°15′S 44°42′W
59 K14 **Parauapebas** Pará, N Brazil 06°03′S 49°48′W
103 Q10 **Paray-le-Monial** Saône-et-Loire, C France 46°27′N 04°07′E
Parbatsar see Parvatsar
154 G13 **Parbhani** Mahārāshtra, C India 19°16′N 76°51′E
100 L10 **Parchim** Mecklenburg-Vorpommern, N Germany 53°26′N 11°51′E
Parchwitz see Prochowice
110 P13 **Parczew** Lubelskie, E Poland 51°40′N 23°E
60 L8 **Pardo, Rio** ≈ S Brazil
111 E16 **Pardubice** Ger. Pardubitz. Pardubický Kraj, C Czech Republic 50°01′N 15°47′E
111 E17 **Pardubický Kraj** ◐ region N Czech Republic
Pardubitz see Pardubice
119 F16 **Parechcha** Pol. Porzecze, Rus. Porech'ye. Hrodzyenskaya Voblasts', W Belarus 53°53′N 24°08′E
59 F17 **Parecis, Chapada dos** var. Serra dos Parecis. ▲▲ W Brazil
Parecis, Serra dos see Parecis, Chapada dos
104 M4 **Paredes de Nava** Castilla-León, N Spain 42°09′N 04°42′W
189 U12 **Parem** island Chuuk, C Micronesia
189 O12 **Parem Island** island E Micronesia
184 I1 **Parengarenga Harbour** inlet North Island, New Zealand
15 N8 **Parent** Québec, SE Canada 47°55′N 74°36′W
102 J14 **Parentis-en-Born** Landes, SW France 44°22′N 01°04′W
Parenzo see Poreč
185 G20 **Pareora** Canterbury, South Island, New Zealand 44°28′S 171°12′E
171 N14 **Parepare** Sulawesi, C Indonesia 04°S 119°40′E
115 B16 **Párga** Ípeiros, W Greece 39°18′N 20°19′E
93 K20 **Pargas** Swe. Parainen. Länsi-Suomi, SW Finland 60°18′N 22°20′E
64 O5 **Pargo, Ponta do** headland Madeira, Portugal, NE Atlantic Ocean 32°48′N 17°17′W
Paria, Golfo de see Paria, Gulf of
55 N6 **Pariaguán** Anzoátegui, NE Venezuela 08°51′N 64°43′W
45 X17 **Paria, Gulf of** var. Golfo de Paria. gulf Trinidad and Tobago/Venezuela
57 I15 **Pariamanu, Río** ≈ E Peru
36 L8 **Paria River** ≈ Utah, W USA
Parichi see Parychy
40 M14 **Paricutín, Volcán** Ѫ C Mexico 19°25′N 102°20′W
43 P16 **Parida, Isla** island SW Panama
55 T8 **Parika** NE Guyana 06°51′N 58°25′W
93 O18 **Parikkala** Etelä-Suomi, SE Finland 61°33′N 29°34′E
58 E10 **Parima, Serra** var. Sierra Parima. ▲▲ Brazil/Venezuela see also Parima, Sierra
55 N11 **Parima, Sierra** var. Serra Parima. ▲▲ Brazil/Venezuela see also Parima, Serra
57 F17 **Parinacochas, Laguna** ◎ SW Peru
56 A9 **Pariñas, Punta** headland NW Peru 04°45′S 81°22′W
58 H12 **Parintins** Amazonas, N Brazil 02°38′S 56°45′W
103 O5 **Paris** anc. Lutetia, Lutetia Parisiorum, Parisii. ● (France) Paris, N France 48°52′N 02°19′E
191 Y2 **Paris** Kiritimati, E Kiribati 01°55′N 157°30′W
27 S11 **Paris** Arkansas, C USA 35°17′N 93°46′W
33 S16 **Paris** Idaho, NW USA 42°14′N 111°24′W
31 N14 **Paris** Illinois, N USA 39°36′N 87°42′W
20 M5 **Paris** Kentucky, S USA 38°13′N 84°15′W
27 V3 **Paris** Missouri, C USA 39°28′N 92°00′W
20 H8 **Paris** Tennessee, S USA 36°19′N 88°20′W
25 V5 **Paris** Texas, SW USA 33°41′N 95°33′W
Parisii see Paris
43 S16 **Parita** Herrera, S Panama 08°01′N 80°30′W
43 S16 **Parita, Bahía de** bay S Panama
93 K18 **Parkano** Länsi-Suomi, W Finland 62°03′N 23°E
Parkan/Párkány see Štúrovo
27 N6 **Park City** Kansas, C USA 37°48′N 97°19′W
36 L3 **Park City** Utah, W USA 40°39′N 111°30′W
36 I12 **Parker** Arizona, SW USA 34°07′N 114°16′W
23 R9 **Parker** Florida, SE USA 30°07′N 85°36′W
29 R11 **Parker** South Dakota, N USA 43°24′N 97°08′W
35 Z14 **Parker Dam** California, W USA 34°17′N 114°08′W
29 W13 **Parkersburg** Iowa, C USA 42°34′N 92°47′W
21 Q3 **Parkersburg** West Virginia, NE USA 39°17′N 81°33′W
29 T7 **Parkers Prairie** Minnesota, N USA 46°09′N 95°19′W
171 P8 **Parker Volcano** Ѫ Mindanao, S Philippines 06°09′N 124°52′E
181 W13 **Parkes** New South Wales, SE Australia 33°10′S 148°10′E
30 K4 **Park Falls** Wisconsin, N USA 45°57′N 90°25′W
Parkhar see Farkhor
14 E16 **Parkhill** Ontario, S Canada 43°11′N 81°39′W
29 T5 **Park Rapids** Minnesota, N USA 46°55′N 95°03′W
29 Q3 **Park River** North Dakota, N USA 48°24′N 97°44′W
29 Q11 **Parkston** South Dakota, N USA 43°24′N 97°58′W
10 L17 **Parksville** Vancouver Island, British Columbia, SW Canada 49°13′N 124°13′W
37 S3 **Parkview Mountain** ▲ Colorado, C USA 40°19′N 106°08′W
105 N8 **Parla** Madrid, C Spain 40°13′N 03°48′W
155 N14 **Parlākimidi** Andhra Pradesh, E India 18°46′N 84°05′E
29 S8 **Parle, Lac qui** ◎ Minnesota, N USA
155 G14 **Parli Vaijnāth** Mahārāshtra, C India 18°53′N 76°36′E
106 F9 **Parma** Emilia-Romagna, N Italy 44°50′N 10°20′E
31 T11 **Parma** Ohio, N USA 41°24′N 81°43′W
Parnahyba see Parnaíba
58 N13 **Parnaíba** var. Parnahyba. Piauí, E Brazil 02°58′S 41°46′W
65 J14 **Parnaíba Ridge** undersea feature C Atlantic Ocean
58 N13 **Parnaíba, Rio** ≈ NE Brazil
115 F18 **Parnassós** ▲▲ C Greece
185 J17 **Parnassus** Canterbury, South Island, New Zealand 42°41′S 173°18′E
182 H10 **Parndana** South Australia 35°48′S 137°13′E
115 H19 **Párnitha** ▲▲ C Greece
Parnon see Párnonas
115 F21 **Párnonas** var. Parnon. ▲▲ S Greece
118 G5 **Pärnu** Ger. Pernau, Latv. Pērnava; prev. Rus. Pernov. Pärnumaa, SW Estonia 58°24′N 24°32′E
118 G6 **Pärnu** var. Parnu Jõgi, Ger. Pernau. ≈ SW Estonia
118 G5 **Pärnu-Jaagupi** Ger. Sankt-Jakobi. Pärnumaa, SW Estonia 58°36′N 24°30′E
Parnu Jõgi see Pärnu
118 G5 **Pärnu Laht** Ger. Pernauer Bucht. bay SW Estonia
118 F5 **Pärnumaa** var. Pärnu Maakond. ◐ province SW Estonia
Pärnu Maakond see Pärnumaa
153 T11 **Paro** W Bhutan 27°23′N 89°31′E
153 T11 **Paro** ✈ (Thimphu) W Bhutan 27°23′N 89°31′E
185 G17 **Paroa** West Coast, South Island, New Zealand 42°31′S 171°10′E
163 X14 **P'aro-ho** var. Hwach'ŏn-chŏsuji. ⊠ N South Korea
115 J21 **Pároikiá** prev. Páros. Páros, Kykládes, Greece, Aegean Sea 37°04′N 25°06′E
183 N6 **Paroo River** seasonal river New South Wales/Queensland, SE Australia
Paropamisus Range see Sefīd Kūh, Selseleh-ye
Paropamisus Range see Sefīd Kūh, Selseleh-ye
115 J21 **Páros** island Kykládes, Greece, Aegean Sea
Páros see Pároikiá
36 K7 **Parowan** Utah, W USA 37°50′N 112°49′W
103 U13 **Parpaillon** ▲▲ SE France
108 I9 **Parpan** Graubünden, S Switzerland 46°46′N 09°32′E
62 G13 **Parral** Maule, C Chile 36°08′S 71°52′W
Parral see Hidalgo del Parral
183 T9 **Parramatta** New South Wales, SE Australia 33°49′S 150°59′E
21 Y6 **Parramore Island** island Virginia, NE USA
40 M8 **Parras** var. Parras de la Fuente. Coahuila, NE Mexico 25°26′N 102°07′W
Parras de la Fuente see Parras
42 M14 **Parrita** Puntarenas, S Costa Rica 09°30′N 84°20′W
Parry group see Mukojima-rettō
14 G13 **Parry Island** island Ontario, S Canada
197 O9 **Parry Islands** island group Nunavut, NW Canada
14 G12 **Parry Sound** Ontario, S Canada 45°21′N 80°03′W
110 F7 **Parsęta** Ger. Persante. ≈ NW Poland
28 L3 **Parshall** North Dakota, N USA 47°57′N 102°07′W
27 Q7 **Parsons** Kansas, C USA 37°20′N 95°15′W
20 H9 **Parsons** Tennessee, S USA 35°39′N 88°07′W
21 T3 **Parsons** West Virginia, NE USA 39°06′N 79°43′W
Parsonstown see Birr
100 P11 **Parsteiner See** ◎ NE Germany
107 I24 **Partanna** Sicilia, Italy, C Mediterranean Sea 37°43′N 12°54′E
108 J8 **Partenen** Graubünden, E Switzerland 46°58′N 10°01′E
102 K9 **Parthenay** Deux-Sèvres, W France 46°39′N 00°13′W
95 J19 **Partille** Västra Götaland, S Sweden 57°43′N 12°12′E
107 I23 **Partinico** Sicilia, Italy, C Mediterranean Sea 38°03′N 13°07′E
111 I20 **Partizánske** prev. Simonovany, Hung. Simony. Trenčiansky Kraj, W Slovakia 48°35′N 18°23′E
58 H11 **Paru de Oeste, Rio** ≈ N Brazil
182 K9 **Paruna** South Australia 34°45′S 140°43′E
58 I11 **Paru, Rio** ≈ N Brazil
149 Q5 **Parvān** Pash. Parwān. ◐ province E Afghanistan
155 M14 **Pārvatipuram** Andhra Pradesh, E India 17°01′N 81°47′E
152 G12 **Parvatsar** prev. Parbatsar. Rājasthān, N India 26°52′N 74°49′E
Parwān see Parvān
158 I15 **Paryang** Xizang Zizhiqu, W China 30°04′N 83°28′E
119 M18 **Parychy** Rus. Parichi. Homyel'skaya Voblasts', SE Belarus 52°48′N 29°25′E
83 J21 **Parys** Free State, C South Africa 26°55′S 27°28′E
35 T15 **Pasadena** California, W USA 34°09′N 118°09′W
25 W11 **Pasadena** Texas, SW USA 29°41′N 95°13′W
56 B8 **Pasaje** El Oro, SW Ecuador 03°23′S 79°50′W
137 T9 **P'asanauri** N Georgia 42°21′N 44°40′E
168 I13 **Pasapuat** Pulau Pagai Utara, W Indonesia 02°36′S 99°58′E
167 N7 **Pasawng** Kayah State, C Burma (Myanmar) 18°50′N 97°16′E
114 L13 **Paşayiğit** Edirne, NW Turkey 40°58′N 26°38′E
23 N9 **Pascagoula** Mississippi, S USA 30°21′N 88°32′W
22 M8 **Pascagoula River** ≈ Mississippi, S USA
116 F12 **Paşcani** Hung. Páskán. Iaşi, NE Romania 47°14′N 26°46′E
109 T4 **Pasching** Oberösterreich, N Austria 48°16′N 14°10′E
32 K10 **Pasco** Washington, NW USA 46°13′N 119°06′W
56 E13 **Pasco** off. Departamento de Pasco. ◐ department C Peru
Pasco, Departamento de see Pasco
191 N11 **Pascua, Isla de** var. Rapa Nui, Easter Island. island E Pacific Ocean
63 G21 **Pascua, Río** ≈ S Chile
103 N1 **Pas-de-Calais** ◐ department N France
100 P10 **Pasewalk** Mecklenburg-Vorpommern, NE Germany 53°31′N 13°59′E
11 T10 **Pasfield Lake** ◎ Saskatchewan, C Canada
Pa-shih Hai-hsia see Bashi Channel
Pashkeni see Bolyarovo
Pashmakli see Smolyan
153 X10 **Pāsighāt** Arunāchal Pradesh, NE India 28°08′N 95°13′E
137 Q12 **Pasinler** Erzurum, NE Turkey 39°59′N 41°41′E
Pasi Oloy, Qatorkŭhi see Zaalayskiy Khrebet
42 E3 **Pasión, Río de la** ≈ N Guatemala
168 J12 **Pasirganting** Sumatera, W Indonesia 02°04′S 100°51′E
Pasirpangarayan see Bagansiapiapi
168 K6 **Pasir Puteh** var. Pasir Putih. Kelantan, Peninsular Malaysia 05°50′N 102°24′E
Pasir Putih see Pasir Puteh
169 R9 **Pasir, Tanjung** headland East Malaysia 02°24′N 111°12′E
95 N20 **Påskallavik** Kalmar, S Sweden 57°10′N 16°25′E
Páskán see Paşcani
Paskevicha, Zaliv see Tushchybas, Zaliv
110 K7 **Pasłęk** Ger. Preußisch Holland. Warmińsko-Mazurskie, NE Poland 54°03′N 19°40′E
110 K7 **Pasłęka** Ger. Passarge. ≈ N Poland
148 K16 **Pasni** Baluchistān, SW Pakistan 25°13′N 63°30′E
63 I18 **Paso de Indios** Chubut, S Argentina 43°52′S 69°06′W
54 L7 **Paso del Caballo** Guárico, N Venezuela 08°19′N 67°08′W
61 E15 **Paso de los Libres** Corrientes, NE Argentina 29°43′S 57°09′W
61 E18 **Paso de los Toros** Tacuarembó, C Uruguay 32°45′S 56°30′W
Pasoeroean see Pasuruan
35 P12 **Paso Robles** California, W USA 35°37′N 120°42′W
15 Y7 **Paspébiac** Québec, SE Canada 48°03′N 65°10′W
11 U14 **Pasquia Hills** ▲▲ Saskatchewan, S Canada
149 W7 **Pasrūr** Punjab, E Pakistan 32°12′N 74°42′E
30 M1 **Passage Island** island Michigan, N USA
65 B24 **Passage Islands** island group W Falkland Islands
8 K5 **Passage Point** headland Banks Island, Northwest Territories, NW Canada 73°31′N 115°12′W
Passarge see Pasłęka
115 C15 **Passarón** ancient monument Ípeiros, W Greece
Passarowitz see Požarevac
101 O22 **Passau** Bayern, SE Germany 48°34′N 13°28′E
22 M9 **Pass Christian** Mississippi, S USA 30°19′N 89°15′W
107 L26 **Passero, Capo** headland Sicilia, Italy, C Mediterranean Sea 36°40′N 15°09′E
171 P5 **Passi** Panay Island, C Philippines 11°05′N 122°37′E
61 H14 **Passo Fundo** Rio Grande do Sul, S Brazil 28°16′S 52°20′W
60 H13 **Passo Fundo, Barragem de** ⊠ S Brazil
61 H15 **Passo Real, Barragem de** ⊠ S Brazil
59 L20 **Passos** Minas Gerais, NE Brazil 20°45′S 46°38′W
167 X10 **Passu Keah** island S Paracel Islands
118 J13 **Pastavy** Pol. Postawy, Rus. Postavy. Vitsyebskaya Voblasts', NW Belarus 55°07′N 26°50′E
56 D7 **Pastaza** ◐ province E Ecuador
56 D9 **Pastaza, Río** ≈ Ecuador/Peru
61 A21 **Pasteur** Buenos Aires, E Argentina 35°10′S 62°14′W
15 V3 **Pasteur** ≈ Québec, SE Canada
147 Q12 **Pastigav** Rus. Pastigov. W Tajikistan 39°27′N 69°16′E
Pastigov see Pastigav
54 C13 **Pasto** Nariño, SW Colombia 01°12′N 77°17′W
38 M10 **Pastol Bay** bay Alaska, USA
37 O8 **Pastora Peak** ▲ Arizona, SW USA 36°48′N 109°10′W
105 O8 **Pastrana** Castilla-La Mancha, C Spain 40°24′N 02°55′W
169 S16 **Pasuruan** prev. Pasoeroean. Jawa, C Indonesia 07°38′S 112°44′E
118 F11 **Pasvalys** Panevėžys, N Lithuania 56°03′N 24°24′E
111 K21 **Pásztó** Nógrád, N Hungary 47°57′N 19°41′E
189 U12 **Pata** var. Patta. atoll Chuuk Islands, C Micronesia
36 M16 **Patagonia** Arizona, SW USA 31°32′N 110°45′W
63 H20 **Patagonia** physical region Argentina/Chile
Patalung see Phatthalung
154 D9 **Pātan** Gujarāt, W India 23°51′N 72°11′E
154 J10 **Pātan** Madhya Pradesh, C India 23°19′N 79°41′E
171 S11 **Patani** Pulau Halmahera, E Indonesia 0°19′N 128°46′E
Patani see Pattani
15 V7 **Patapédia Est** ≈ Québec, SE Canada
116 K13 **Pătâriagele** prev. Pătîriagele. Buzău, SE Romania 45°19′N 26°21′E
Patavium see Padova
182 I5 **Patawarta Hill** ▲ South Australia 30°57′S 138°42′E
182 L10 **Patchewollock** Victoria, SE Australia 35°24′S 142°11′E
184 K11 **Patea** Taranaki, North Island, New Zealand 39°48′S 174°35′E
184 K11 **Patea** ≈ North Island, New Zealand
77 U15 **Pategi** Kwara, C Nigeria 08°39′N 05°46′E
81 K20 **Pate Island** var. Patta Island. island SE Kenya
105 S10 **Paterna** País Valenciano, E Spain 39°30′N 00°24′W
109 R9 **Paternion** Slvn. Špatrjan. Kärnten, S Austria 46°40′N 13°43′E
107 L24 **Paternò** anc. Hybla, Hybla Major. Sicilia, Italy, C Mediterranean Sea 37°34′N 14°55′E
32 J7 **Pateros** Washington, NW USA 48°01′N 119°55′W
18 J14 **Paterson** New Jersey, NE USA 40°55′N 74°12′W
32 J10 **Paterson** Washington, NW USA 45°56′N 119°37′W
185 C25 **Paterson Inlet** inlet Stewart Island, New Zealand
98 N6 **Paterswolde** Drenthe, NE Netherlands 53°07′N 06°32′E
155 G24 **Pathanāmthitta** Kerala, SW India 9°05′N 76°38′E
152 H7 **Pathānkot** Himāchal Pradesh, N India 32°16′N 75°43′E

◆ Country ● Country Capital ◇ Dependent Territory ○ Dependent Territory Capital ◐ Administrative Regions ✈ International Airport ▲ Mountain ▲▲ Mountain Range Ѫ Volcano ≈ River ◎ Lake ⊠ Reservoir

166 K8 **Pathein** *var.* Bassein. Ayeyarwady, SW Burma (Myanmar) *16°46′N 94°45′E*
33 W15 **Pathfinder Reservoir** ▣ Wyoming, C USA
167 O11 **Pathum Thani** *var.* Patumdhani, Prathum Thani. Pathum Thani, C Thailand *14°03′N 100°29′E*
54 C12 **Patía** *var.* El Bordo. Cauca, SW Colombia *02°07′N 76°57′W*
152 I9 **Patiāla** *var.* Puttiala. Punjab, NW India *30°21′N 76°27′E*
54 B12 **Patía, Río** ≈ SW Colombia
188 D15 **Pati Point** *headland* NE Guam *13°36′N 144°39′E*
Pâtiriagele *see* Pătîriagele
56 C13 **Pativilca** Lima, W Peru *10°44′S 77°45′W*
166 M1 **Pātkai Bum** *var.* Patkai Range. ▲▲ Burma (Myanmar)/India
Patkai Range *see* Pātkai Bum
115 L20 **Pátmos** Pátmos, Dodekánisa, Greece, Aegean Sea *37°18′N 26°32′E*
115 L20 **Pátmos** *island* Dodekánisa, Greece, Aegean Sea
153 P13 **Patna** *var.* Azimabad. *state capital* Bihār, N India *25°36′N 85°11′E*
154 M12 **Patnāgarh** Orissa, E India *20°42′N 83°12′E*
171 O5 **Patnongon** Panay Island, C Philippines *10°56′N 122°03′E*
137 S13 **Patnos** Ağrı, E Turkey *39°14′N 42°52′E*
60 H12 **Pato Branco** Paraná, S Brazil *26°20′S 52°40′W*
31 O16 **Patoka Lake** ◎ Indiana, N USA
92 L9 **Patoniva** *Lapp.* Buoddobohki. Lappi, N Finland *69°44′N 27°01′E*
113 K21 **Patos** *var.* Patosi. Fier, SW Albania *40°40′N 19°37′E*
Patos *see* Patos de Minas
59 K19 **Patos de Minas** *var.* Patos. Minas Gerais, NE Brazil *18°35′S 46°32′W*
Patosi *see* Patos
61 I17 **Patos, Lagoa dos** *lagoon* S Brazil
62 J9 **Patquía** La Rioja, C Argentina *30°02′S 66°54′W*
115 E19 **Pátra** *Eng.* Patras; *prev.* Pátrai. Dytikí Ellás, S Greece *38°14′N 21°45′E*
115 D18 **Patraïkós Kólpos** *gulf* S Greece
Pátrai/Patras *see* Pátra
92 G2 **Patreksfjördhur** Vestfirdhir, W Iceland *65°33′N 23°54′W*
24 M7 **Patricia** Texas, SW USA *32°34′N 102°00′W*
63 F21 **Patricio Lynch, Isla** *island* S Chile
Patta *see* Pata
Patta Island *see* Pate Island
167 O16 **Pattani** *var.* Patani. Pattani, SW Thailand *06°50′N 101°20′E*
167 P12 **Pattaya** Chon Buri, S Thailand *12°57′N 100°53′E*
19 S4 **Patten** Maine, NE USA *45°58′N 68°27′W*
35 O9 **Patterson** California, W USA *37°27′N 121°07′W*
22 J10 **Patterson** Louisiana, S USA *29°41′N 91°18′W*
35 R7 **Patterson, Mount** ▲ California, W USA *38°27′N 119°16′W*
31 P4 **Patterson, Point** *headland* Michigan, N USA *45°58′N 85°39′W*
107 L23 **Patti** Sicilia, Italy, C Mediterranean Sea *38°08′N 14°58′E*
107 L23 **Patti, Golfo di** *gulf* Sicilia, Italy
93 L14 **Pattijoki** Oulu, W Finland *64°41′N 24°40′E*
193 Q4 **Patton Escarpment** *undersea feature* E Pacific Ocean
27 S2 **Pattonsburg** Missouri, C USA *40°03′N 94°08′W*
0 D6 **Patton Seamount** *undersea feature* NE Pacific Ocean *54°40′N 150°30′W*
10 J12 **Pattullo, Mount** ▲ British Columbia, W Canada *56°18′N 129°43′W*
153 U16 **Patuakhali** *var.* Patukhali. Barisal, S Bangladesh *22°20′N 90°20′E*
42 M5 **Patuca, Río** ≈ E Honduras
Patukhali *see* Patuakhali
Patumdhani *see* Pathum Thani
40 M14 **Pátzcuaro** Michoacán, SW Mexico *19°30′N 101°38′W*
42 C6 **Patzicía** Chimaltenango, S Guatemala *14°38′N 90°52′W*
102 K16 **Pau** Pyrénées-Atlantiques, SW France *43°18′N 00°22′W*
102 J12 **Pauillac** Gironde, SW France *45°12′N 00°44′W*
166 L5 **Pauk** Magway, W Burma (Myanmar) *21°25′N 94°30′E*
8 I6 **Paulatuk** Northwest Territories, NW Canada *69°23′N 124°W*
42 K5 **Paulayá, Río** ≈ NE Honduras
22 M6 **Paulding** Mississippi, S USA *32°01′N 89°01′W*
31 Q12 **Paulding** Ohio, N USA *41°08′N 84°34′W*
29 S12 **Paullina** Iowa, C USA *42°58′N 95°41′W*
59 P15 **Paulo Afonso** Bahia, E Brazil *09°21′S 38°14′W*
38 M16 **Pauloff Harbor** *var.* Pavlor Harbour. Sanak Island, Alaska, USA *54°26′N 162°43′W*
27 N12 **Pauls Valley** Oklahoma, C USA *34°46′N 97°14′W*
166 L7 **Paungde** Bago, C Burma (Myanmar) *18°30′N 95°30′E*
Pauni *see* Paoni
152 K9 **Pauri** Uttaranchal, N India *30°08′N 78°48′E*
Pautalia *see* Kyustendil
142 J5 **Pāveh** Kermānshāhān, NW Iran *35°02′N 46°15′E*
114 I9 **Pavel Banya** Stara Zagora, C Bulgaria *42°35′N 25°19′E*
126 L5 **Pavelets** Ryazanskaya Oblast', W Russian Federation *53°47′N 39°22′E*
106 D8 **Pavia** *anc.* Ticinum. Lombardia, N Italy *45°10′N 09°10′E*
118 C9 **Pāvilosta** Liepāja, W Latvia *56°52′N 21°12′E*
125 P14 **Pavino** Kostromskaya Oblast', NW Russian Federation *59°10′N 46°09′E*
114 J8 **Pavlikeni** Veliko Tŭrnovo, N Bulgaria *43°14′N 25°20′E*
145 T8 **Pavlodar** Pavlodar, NE Kazakhstan *52°21′N 76°59′E*
145 S9 **Pavlodar** *off.* Pavlodarskaya Oblast', *Kaz.* Pavlodar Oblysy. ◈ *province* NE Kazakhstan
Pavlodar Oblysy/Pavlodarskaya Oblast' *see* Pavlodar
Pavlograd *see* Pavlohrad
117 U7 **Pavlohrad** *Rus.* Pavlograd. Dnipropetrovs'ka Oblast', E Ukraine *48°32′N 35°50′E*
Pavlor Harbour *see* Pauloff Harbor
145 R9 **Pavlovka** Akmola, C Kazakhstan *51°22′N 72°35′E*
127 V4 **Pavlovka** Respublika Bashkortostan, W Russian Federation *55°28′N 56°36′E*
127 Q7 **Pavlovka** Ul'yanovskaya Oblast', W Russian Federation *52°40′N 47°08′E*
127 N3 **Pavlovo** Nizhegorodskaya Oblast', W Russian Federation *55°59′N 43°03′E*
126 L9 **Pavlovsk** Voronezhskaya Oblast', W Russian Federation *50°26′N 40°08′E*
126 L13 **Pavlovskaya** Krasnodarskiy Kray, SW Russian Federation *46°06′N 39°52′E*
117 S7 **Pavlysh** Kirovohrads'ka Oblast', C Ukraine *48°54′N 33°20′E*
106 F10 **Pavullo nel Frignano** Emilia-Romagna, C Italy *44°19′N 10°52′E*
27 P8 **Pawhuska** Oklahoma, C USA *36°42′N 96°21′W*
21 U13 **Pawleys Island** South Carolina, SE USA *33°27′N 79°07′W*
167 N6 **Pawn** ≈ C Burma (Myanmar)
30 K14 **Pawnee** Illinois, N USA *39°35′N 89°34′W*
27 O9 **Pawnee** Oklahoma, C USA *36°21′N 96°50′W*
37 U2 **Pawnee Buttes** ▲ Colorado, C USA *40°49′N 103°58′W*
29 S17 **Pawnee City** Nebraska, C USA *40°06′N 96°09′W*
26 K5 **Pawnee River** ≈ Kansas, C USA
31 O10 **Paw Paw** Michigan, N USA *42°12′N 86°09′W*
31 O10 **Paw Paw Lake** Michigan, N USA *42°12′N 86°16′W*
19 O12 **Pawtucket** Rhode Island, NE USA *41°52′N 71°22′W*
Pax Augusta *see* Badajoz
115 I25 **Paximádia** *island* SE Greece
Pax Julia *see* Beja
115 B16 **Paxoí** *island* Iónia Nisiá, Greece, C Mediterranean Sea
39 S10 **Paxson** Alaska, USA *62°58′N 145°27′W*
147 O11 **Paxtakor** Jizzax Viloyati, C Uzbekistan *40°21′N 67°54′E*
30 M13 **Paxton** Illinois, N USA *40°27′N 88°06′W*
124 J11 **Pay** Respublika Kareliya, NW Russian Federation *61°10′N 34°24′E*
166 M8 **Payagyi** Bago, SW Burma (Myanmar) *17°28′N 96°32′E*
108 C9 **Payerne** *Ger.* Peterlingen. Vaud, W Switzerland *46°49′N 06°57′E*
32 M13 **Payette** Idaho, NW USA *44°04′N 116°55′W*
32 M13 **Payette River** ≈ Idaho, NW USA
125 V2 **Pay-Khoy, Khrebet** ▲▲ NW Russian Federation
Payne *see* Kangirsuk
12 K4 **Payne, Lac** ◎ Québec, NE Canada
29 T8 **Paynesville** Minnesota, N USA *45°22′N 94°42′W*
169 S8 **Payong, Tanjung** *cape* East Malaysia
Payo Obispo *see* Chetumal
61 D18 **Paysandú** Paysandú, W Uruguay *32°21′S 58°05′W*
61 D17 **Paysandú** ◈ *department* W Uruguay
102 I7 **Pays de la Loire** ◈ *region* NW France
36 L12 **Payson** Arizona, SW USA *34°13′N 111°19′W*
36 L4 **Payson** Utah, W USA *40°02′N 111°43′W*
125 W4 **Payyer, Gora** ▲ NW Russian Federation *66°49′N 64°33′E*
Payzawat *see* Jiashi
137 Q11 **Pazar** Rize, NE Turkey *41°10′N 40°53′E*
136 F10 **Pazarbaşı Burnu** *headland* NW Turkey *41°12′N 30°18′E*
136 M16 **Pazarcık** Kahramanmaraş, S Turkey *37°31′N 37°19′E*
114 I10 **Pazardzhik** *prev.* Tatar Pazardzhik. Pazardzhik, SW Bulgaria *42°11′N 24°21′E*
64 H11 **Pazardzhik** ◈ *province* C Bulgaria
54 H9 **Paz de Ariporo** Casanare, E Colombia *05°54′N 71°52′W*
112 A10 **Pazin** *Ger.* Mitterburg, *It.* Pisino. Istra, NW Croatia *45°14′N 13°56′E*
42 D7 **Paz, Río** ≈ El Salvador/Guatemala
113 O18 **Pčinja** ≈ N Macedonia
193 V15 **Pea** Tongatapu, S Tonga *21°10′S 175°14′W*
27 O6 **Peabody** Kansas, C USA *38°10′N 97°06′W*
11 O12 **Peace** ≈ Alberta/British Columbia, W Canada
Peace Garden State *see* North Dakota
11 Q10 **Peace Point** Alberta, C Canada *59°11′N 112°12′W*
11 O12 **Peace River** Alberta, W Canada *56°15′N 117°18′W*
23 W13 **Peace River** ≈ Florida, SE USA
11 N17 **Peachland** British Columbia, SW Canada *49°49′N 119°48′W*
36 J10 **Peach Springs** Arizona, SW USA *35°33′N 113°27′W*
Peach State *see* Georgia
23 S4 **Peachtree City** Georgia, SE USA *33°24′N 84°36′W*
189 Y13 **Peacock Point** *point* SE Wake Island
97 M18 **Peak District** *physical region* C England, United Kingdom
183 Q7 **Peak Hill** New South Wales, SE Australia *32°39′S 148°12′E*
65 G15 **Peak, The** ▲ C Ascension Island
105 O13 **Peal de Becerro** Andalucía, S Spain *37°55′N 03°08′W*
189 X11 **Peale Island** *island* N Wake Island
37 O6 **Peale, Mount** ▲ Utah, W USA *38°26′N 109°13′W*
39 O4 **Peard Bay** *bay* Alaska, USA
23 Q7 **Pea River** ≈ Alabama/Florida, S USA
25 W11 **Pearland** Texas, SW USA *29°33′N 95°17′W*
38 D9 **Pearl City** O'ahu, Hawaii, USA, C Pacific Ocean *21°24′N 157°58′W*
38 D9 **Pearl Harbor** *inlet* O'ahu, Hawai'i, USA, C Pacific Ocean
Pearl Islands *see* Perlas, Archipiélago de las
Pearl Lagoon *see* Perlas, Laguna de
22 M5 **Pearl River** ≈ Louisiana/Mississippi, S USA
25 Q13 **Pearsall** Texas, SW USA *28°54′N 99°07′W*
23 U7 **Pearson** Georgia, SE USA *31°18′N 82°51′W*
25 P4 **Pease River** ≈ Texas, SW USA
12 F7 **Peawanuk** Ontario, C Canada *54°55′N 85°31′W*
12 E8 **Peawanuk** ≈ Ontario, S Canada
83 P16 **Pebane** Zambézia, NE Mozambique *17°14′S 38°10′E*
65 C23 **Pebble Island** *island* N Falkland Islands
Peć *see* Pejë
25 R8 **Pecan Bayou** ≈ Texas, SW USA
22 H10 **Pecan Island** Louisiana, S USA *29°39′N 92°26′W*
60 L12 **Peças, Ilha das** *island* S Brazil
30 L10 **Pecatonica River** ≈ Illinois/Wisconsin, N USA
108 G10 **Peccia** Ticino, S Switzerland *46°24′N 08°39′E*
Pechenegi *see* Pechenihy
Pechenezhskoye Vodokhranilishche *see* Pechenizhs'ke Vodoskhovyshche
124 I2 **Pechenga** *Fin.* Petsamo. Murmanskaya Oblast', NW Russian Federation *69°34′N 31°14′E*
117 V5 **Pechenihy** *Rus.* Pechenegi. Kharkivs'ka Oblast', E Ukraine *49°49′N 36°57′E*
117 V5 **Pechenizhs'ke Vodoskhovyshche** *Rus.* Pechenezhskoye Vodokhranilishche. ▣ E Ukraine
125 U7 **Pechora** Respublika Komi, NW Russian Federation *65°09′N 57°09′E*
125 R6 **Pechora** ≈ NW Russian Federation
Pechora Bay *see* Pechorskaya Guba
Pechora Sea *see* Pechorskoye More
125 S3 **Pechorskaya Guba** *Eng.* Pechora Bay. *bay* NW Russian Federation
122 H7 **Pechorskoye More** *Eng.* Pechora Sea. *sea* NW Russian Federation
124 F14 **Pechory** *Est.* Petseri. Pskovskaya Oblast', W Russian Federation *57°49′N 27°37′E*
116 E11 **Pecica** *Ger.* Petschka, *Hung.* Ópécska. Arad, W Romania *46°09′N 21°06′E*
24 K8 **Pecos** Texas, SW USA *31°25′N 103°30′W*
25 N11 **Pecos River** ≈ New Mexico/Texas, SW USA
111 I25 **Pécs** *Ger.* Fünfkirchen, *Lat.* Sopianae. Baranya, SW Hungary *46°05′N 18°11′E*
43 T17 **Pedasí** Los Santos, S Panama *07°36′N 80°04′W*
Pedde *see* Pedja
183 O17 **Pedder, Lake** ◎ Tasmania, SE Australia
44 M10 **Pedernales** SW Dominican Republic *18°02′N 71°41′W*
55 Q5 **Pedernales** Delta Amacuro, NE Venezuela *09°58′N 62°15′W*
25 R10 **Pedernales River** ≈ Texas, SW USA
62 H6 **Pedernales, Salar de** *salt lake* N Chile
Pedhoulas *see* Pedoulás
55 X11 **Pédima** *var.* Malavate. SW French Guiana *03°15′N 54°08′W*
182 F1 **Pedirka** South Australia *26°41′S 135°11′E*
171 S11 **Pediwang** Pulau Halmahera, E Indonesia *01°29′N 127°57′E*
118 I5 **Pedja** *var.* Pedja Jõgi, *Ger.* Pedde. ≈ E Estonia
Pedja Jõgi *see* Pedja
121 O3 **Pedoulás** *var.* Pedhoulas. W Cyprus *34°58′N 32°51′E*
59 N18 **Pedra Azul** Minas Gerais, NE Brazil *16°02′S 41°17′W*
104 I3 **Pedrafita, Porto de** *var.* Puerto de Piedrafita. *pass* NW Spain
76 E9 **Pedra Lume** Sal, NE Cape Verde *16°47′N 22°54′W*
43 P16 **Pedregal** Chiriquí, W Panama *09°04′N 79°25′W*
54 J4 **Pedregal** Falcón, N Venezuela *11°04′N 70°08′W*
40 L9 **Pedriceña** Durango, C Mexico *25°08′N 103°46′W*
60 L11 **Pedro Barros** São Paulo, S Brazil *24°12′S 47°22′W*
39 Q13 **Pedro Bay** Alaska, USA *59°47′N 154°06′W*
62 H4 **Pedro de Valdivia** *var.* Oficina Pedro de Valdivia. Antofagasta, N Chile *22°33′S 69°38′W*
62 P4 **Pedro Juan Caballero** Amambay, E Paraguay *22°34′S 55°41′W*
63 L15 **Pedro Luro** Buenos Aires, E Argentina *39°30′S 62°38′W*
105 O10 **Pedro Muñoz** Castilla-La Mancha, C Spain *39°25′N 02°56′W*
155 J22 **Pedro, Point** *headland* NW Sri Lanka *09°54′N 80°08′E*
182 K9 **Peebinga** South Australia *34°56′S 140°56′E*
96 J13 **Peebles** SE Scotland, United Kingdom *55°40′N 03°15′W*
31 S15 **Peebles** Ohio, N USA *38°57′N 83°23′W*
96 J12 **Peebles** *cultural region* SE Scotland, United Kingdom
18 K13 **Peekskill** New York, NE USA *41°17′N 73°54′W*
97 I16 **Peel** W Isle of Man *54°13′N 04°04′W*
8 G7 **Peel** ≈ Northwest Territories/Yukon Territory, NW Canada
8 K5 **Peel Point** *headland* Victoria Island, Northwest Territories, NW Canada *73°22′N 114°33′W*
8 M5 **Peel Sound** *passage* Nunavut, N Canada
100 N9 **Peene** ≈ NE Germany
99 K17 **Peer** Limburg, NE Belgium *51°08′N 05°29′E*
14 H14 **Pefferlaw** Ontario, S Canada *44°18′N 79°11′W*
185 I18 **Pegasus Bay** *bay* South Island, New Zealand
121 O3 **Pégeia** *var.* Peyia. SW Cyprus *34°52′N 32°24′E*
109 V7 **Peggau** Steiermark, SE Austria *47°10′N 15°20′E*
101 L19 **Pegnitz** Bayern, SE Germany *49°45′N 11°33′E*
101 L19 **Pegnitz** ≈ SE Germany
105 T11 **Pego** País Valenciano, E Spain *38°51′N 00°08′W*
Pegu *see* Bago
Pegu *see* Bago
189 N13 **Pehleng** Pohnpei, E Micronesia
114 M12 **Pehlivanköy** Kırklareli, NW Turkey *41°21′N 26°55′E*
77 R14 **Péhonko** C Benin *10°14′N 01°57′E*
61 B21 **Pehuajó** Buenos Aires, E Argentina *35°48′S 61°53′W*
Pei-ching *see* Beijing/Beijing Shi
100 J13 **Peine** Niedersachsen, C Germany *52°19′N 10°14′E*
Pei-p'ing *see* Beijing/Beijing Shi
Peipsi Järv/Peipus-See *see* Peipus, Lake
118 J5 **Peipus, Lake** *Est.* Peipsi Järv, *Ger.* Peipus-See, *Rus.* Chudskoye Ozero. ◎ Estonia/Russian Federation
115 H19 **Peiraías** *prev.* Piraiévs, *Eng.* Piraeus. Attikí, C Greece *37°57′N 23°42′E*
Peisern *see* Pyzdry
60 I8 **Peixe, Rio do** ≈ S Brazil
59 I16 **Peixoto de Azevedo** Mato Grosso, W Brazil *10°18′S 55°03′W*
168 O11 **Pejantan, Pulau** *island* W Indonesia
113 L16 **Pejë** *Serb.* Peć. W Kosovo *42°40′N 20°19′E*
167 R7 **Pèk** *var.* Xieng Khouang; *prev.* Xiangkhoang. Xiangkhoang, N Laos *19°19′N 103°23′E*
112 N11 **Pek** ≈ E Serbia
169 Q16 **Pekalongan** Jawa, C Indonesia *06°54′S 109°37′E*
168 K11 **Pekanbaru** *var.* Pakanbaru. Sumatera, W Indonesia *0°31′N 101°27′E*
30 L12 **Pekin** Illinois, N USA *40°34′N 89°38′W*
Peking *see* Beijing/Beijing Shi
Pelabohan Kelang/Pelabuhan Kelang *see* Pelabuhan Klang
168 J9 **Pelabuhan Klang** *var.* Kuala Pelabohan Kelang, Pelabohan Kelang, Pelabuhan Kelang, Port Klang, Port Swettenham. Selangor, Peninsular Malaysia *02°57′N 101°24′E*
120 L11 **Pelagie, Isole** *island group* SW Italy
Pelagosa *see* Palagruža
22 L5 **Pelahatchie** Mississippi, S USA *32°19′N 89°48′W*
169 T14 **Pelaihari** *var.* Pleihari. Borneo, C Indonesia *03°48′S 114°45′E*
103 U14 **Pelat, Mont** ▲ SE France *44°16′N 06°46′E*
116 F12 **Peleaga, Vârful** *prev.* Vîrful Peleaga. ▲ W Romania *45°23′N 22°52′E*
Peleaga, Vîrful *see* Peleaga, Vârful
123 O11 **Peleduy** Respublika Sakha (Yakutiya), NE Russian Federation *59°39′N 112°36′E*
14 C18 **Pelee Island** *island* Ontario, S Canada
45 Q11 **Pelée, Montagne** ▲ N Martinique *14°47′N 61°10′W*
14 D18 **Pelee, Point** *headland* Ontario, S Canada *41°56′N 82°30′W*
171 P12 **Pelei** Pulau Peleng, N Indonesia *01°26′S 123°27′E*
Peleliu *see* Beliliou
171 P12 **Peleng, Pulau** *island* Kepulauan Banggai, N Indonesia
23 T7 **Pelham** Georgia, SE USA *31°07′N 84°09′W*
111 E18 **Pelhřimov** *Ger.* Pilgram. Vysočina, C Czech Republic *49°26′N 15°14′E*
39 W13 **Pelican** Chichagof Island, Alaska, USA *57°52′N 136°05′W*
191 Z3 **Pelican Lagoon** ◎ Kiritimati, E Kiribati
29 U6 **Pelican Lake** ◎ Minnesota, N USA
29 V3 **Pelican Lake** ◎ Minnesota, N USA
30 L5 **Pelican Lake** ◎ Wisconsin, N USA
44 G1 **Pelican Point** Grand Bahama Island, N Bahamas *26°39′N 78°09′W*
83 B19 **Pelican Point** *headland* W Namibia *22°55′S 14°25′E*
29 S6 **Pelican Rapids** Minnesota, N USA *46°34′N 96°04′W*
Pelican State *see* Louisiana
11 U13 **Pelikan Narrows** Saskatchewan, C Canada *55°11′N 102°51′W*
115 L18 **Pelinaío** ▲ Chíos, E Greece *38°31′N 26°01′E*
Pelinnaeum *see* Pelinnaío
115 E16 **Pelinnaío** *anc.* Pelinnaeum. *ruins* Thessalía, C Greece
113 N20 **Pelister** ▲ SW FYR Macedonia *41°00′N 21°12′E*
113 G15 **Pelješac** *peninsula* S Croatia
92 M12 **Pelkosenniemi** Lappi, NE Finland *67°06′N 27°30′E*
29 W15 **Pella** Iowa, C USA *41°24′N 92°55′W*
114 F13 **Pélla** *site of ancient city* Kentrikí Makedonía, N Greece
23 Q3 **Pell City** Alabama, S USA *33°35′N 86°17′W*
61 A22 **Pellegrini** Buenos Aires, E Argentina *36°16′S 63°07′W*
92 K12 **Pello** Lappi, NW Finland *66°47′N 24°E*
100 G7 **Pellworm** *island* N Germany
10 H6 **Pelly** ≈ Yukon Territory, NW Canada
Pelly Bay *see* Kugaaruk
10 I8 **Pelly Mountains** ▲▲ Yukon Territory, W Canada
Pélmonostor *see* Beli Manastir
37 P13 **Pelona Mountain** ▲ New Mexico, SW USA *33°40′N 108°06′W*
Peloponnese/Peloponnesus *see* Pelopónnisos
115 E20 **Pelopónnisos** *Eng.* Peloponnese. ◈ *region* S Greece
115 E20 **Pelopónnisos** *var.* Morea, *Eng.* Peloponnese; *anc.* Peloponnesus. *peninsula* S Greece
107 L23 **Peloritani, Monti** *anc.* Pelorus and Neptunius. ▲▲ Sicilia, Italy, C Mediterranean Sea
107 M22 **Peloro, Capo** *var.* Punta del Faro. *headland* S Italy *38°15′N 15°39′E*
Pelorus and Neptunius *see* Peloritani, Monti
61 H17 **Pelotas** Rio Grande do Sul, S Brazil *31°45′S 52°20′W*
61 I14 **Pelotas, Rio** ≈ S Brazil
92 K10 **Peltovuoma** *Lapp.* Bealdovuopmi. Lappi, N Finland *68°23′N 24°12′E*
19 R4 **Pemadumcook Lake** ◎ Maine, NE USA
169 Q16 **Pemalang** Jawa, C Indonesia *06°53′S 109°07′E*
169 P10 **Pemangkat** *var.* Pamangkat. Borneo, C Indonesia *01°11′N 109°00′E*
Pemar *see* Paimio
168 I9 **Pematangsiantar** Sumatera, W Indonesia *02°59′N 99°01′E*
83 Q14 **Pemba** *prev.* Port Amelia, Porto Amélia. Cabo Delgado, NE Mozambique *13°S 40°35′E*
81 J22 **Pemba** ◈ *region* E Tanzania
81 K21 **Pemba** *island* E Tanzania
83 Q14 **Pemba, Baia de** *inlet* NE Mozambique
81 J21 **Pemba Channel** *channel* E Tanzania
81 J22 **Pemba North** ◈ *region* E Tanzania
81 J22 **Pemba South** ◈ *region* E Tanzania
180 J14 **Pemberton** Western Australia *34°27′S 116°09′E*
10 M16 **Pemberton** British Columbia, SW Canada *50°19′N 122°49′W*
29 Q2 **Pembina** North Dakota, N USA *48°58′N 97°14′W*
11 P15 **Pembina** ≈ Alberta, SW Canada
29 Q2 **Pembina** ≈ Canada/USA
171 X16 **Pembre** Papua, E Indonesia *07°49′S 138°01′E*
14 K12 **Pembroke** Ontario, SE Canada *45°49′N 77°08′W*
97 H21 **Pembroke** SW Wales, United Kingdom *51°41′N 04°55′W*
23 W6 **Pembroke** Georgia, SE USA *32°09′N 81°35′W*
21 U11 **Pembroke** North Carolina, SE USA *34°40′N 79°12′W*
21 R7 **Pembroke** Virginia, NE USA *37°19′N 80°38′W*
97 H21 **Pembroke** *cultural region* SW Wales, United Kingdom
Pembuang, Sungai *see* Seruyan, Sungai
43 S15 **Peña Blanca, Cerro** ▲ C Panama *08°39′N 80°39′W*
104 K8 **Peña de Francia, Sierra de la** ▲▲ W Spain
104 G6 **Penafiel** *var.* Peñafiel. Porto, N Portugal *41°12′N 08°17′W*
105 N6 **Peñafiel** Castilla-León, N Spain *41°36′N 04°07′W*
Peñafiel *see* Penafiel
105 S8 **Peñagolosa** ▲ E Spain *40°10′N 00°15′W*
105 N7 **Peñalara, Pico de** ▲ C Spain *40°52′N 03°55′W*
171 X16 **Penambo, Banjaran** *var.* Banjaran Tama Abu, Penambo Range. ▲▲ Indonesia/Malaysia
Penambo Range *see* Penambo, Banjaran
41 O10 **Peña Nevada, Cerro** ▲ C Mexico *23°46′N 99°52′W*
Penang *see* Pinang
Penang *see* George Town
Penang *see* Pinang, Pulau, Peninsular Malaysia
60 J8 **Penápolis** São Paulo, S Brazil *21°23′S 50°02′W*
104 L7 **Peñaranda de Bracamonte** Castilla-León, N Spain *40°54′N 05°13′W*
105 S8 **Peñarroya** ▲ E Spain *40°24′N 00°42′W*
104 L12 **Peñarroya-Pueblonuevo** Andalucía, S Spain *38°21′N 05°18′W*
97 K22 **Penarth** S Wales, United Kingdom *51°27′N 03°11′W*
104 K1 **Peñas, Cabo de** *headland* N Spain *43°39′N 05°52′W*
63 F20 **Penas, Golfo de** *gulf* S Chile
Pen-ch'i *see* Benxi
79 H14 **Pendé** *var.* Logone Oriental. ≈ Central African Republic/Chad
76 I14 **Pendembu** E Sierra Leone *09°06′N 12°12′W*
29 R13 **Pender** Nebraska, C USA *42°06′N 96°42′W*
Penderma *see* Bandırma
32 K11 **Pendleton** Oregon, NW USA *45°40′N 118°47′W*
32 M7 **Pend Oreille, Lake** ◎ Idaho, NW USA
32 M7 **Pend Oreille River** ≈ Idaho/Washington, NW USA
Pendzhikent *see* Panjakent
Peneius *see* Pineiós
104 G8 **Penela** Coimbra, N Portugal *40°02′N 08°23′W*
14 G13 **Penetanguishene** Ontario, S Canada *44°45′N 79°55′W*
151 H15 **Penganga** ≈ C India
161 T12 **P'engchia Yu** *island* N Taiwan
79 M21 **Penge** Kasai-Oriental, C Dem. Rep. Congo *05°29′S 24°38′E*
Penghu Archipelago/P'enghu Ch'üntao/Penghu Islands *see* P'enghu Liehtao
161 R14 **P'enghu Liehtao** *var.* P'enghu Ch'üntao, Penghu Islands, *Eng.* Penghu Archipelago, Pescadores, *Jap.* Hoko-guntō, Hoko-shotō. *island group* W Taiwan
Penghu Shuidao/P'enghu Shuitao *see* Pescadores Channel
161 R4 **Penglai** *var.* Dengzhou. Shandong, E China *37°50′N 120°45′E*
Peng-pu *see* Bengbu
Penhsihu *see* Benxi
Penibético, Sistema *see* Béticos, Sistemas
104 F10 **Peniche** Leiria, W Portugal *39°21′N 09°23′W*
169 U17 **Penida, Nusa** *island* S Indonesia
Peninsular State *see* Florida
105 T8 **Peñíscola** País Valenciano, E Spain *40°22′N 00°24′E*
40 M13 **Pénjamo** Guanajuato, C Mexico *20°26′N 101°44′W*
Penki *see* Benxi
102 F7 **Penmarch, Pointe de** *headland* NW France *47°46′N 04°34′W*
107 L15 **Penna, Punta della** *headland* C Italy *42°10′N 14°43′E*
107 K14 **Penne** Abruzzo, C Italy *42°28′N 13°57′E*
Penner *see* Penneru
155 J18 **Penneru** *var.* Penner. ≈ C India
182 I10 **Penneshaw** South Australia *35°45′S 137°57′E*
18 C14 **Penn Hills** Pennsylvania, NE USA *40°28′N 79°53′W*
Penninae, Alpes/Pennine, Alpi *see* Pennine Alps
108 D11 **Pennine Alps** *Fr.* Alpes Pennines, *It.* Alpi Pennine, *Lat.* Alpes Penninae. ▲▲ Italy/Switzerland
Pennine Chain *see* Pennines
97 L15 **Pennines** *var.* Pennine Chain. ▲▲ N England, United Kingdom
Pennines, Alpes *see* Pennine Alps
21 O8 **Pennington Gap** Virginia, NE USA *36°45′N 83°01′W*
18 I16 **Penns Grove** New Jersey, NE USA *39°42′N 75°27′W*
18 I16 **Pennsville** New Jersey, NE USA *39°37′N 75°29′W*
18 E14 **Pennsylvania** *off.* Commonwealth of Pennsylvania, *also known as* Keystone State. ◈ *state* NE USA
18 G10 **Penn Yan** New York, NE USA *42°39′N 77°02′W*
124 H16 **Peno** Tverskaya Oblast', W Russian Federation *56°55′N 32°44′E*
19 R7 **Penobscot Bay** *bay* Maine, NE USA
19 S5 **Penobscot River** ≈ Maine, NE USA
182 K12 **Penola** South Australia *37°24′S 140°50′E*
40 K9 **Peñón Blanco** Durango, C Mexico *25°12′N 100°50′W*
182 E7 **Penong** South Australia *31°57′S 133°01′E*
43 S16 **Penonomé** Coclé, C Panama *08°29′N 80°22′W*
190 L13 **Penrhyn** *atoll* N Cook Islands
192 M9 **Penrhyn Basin** *undersea feature* C Pacific Ocean
183 S9 **Penrith** New South Wales, SE Australia *33°45′S 150°48′E*
97 K15 **Penrith** NW England, United Kingdom *54°40′N 02°44′W*
23 O9 **Pensacola** Florida, SE USA *30°25′N 87°13′W*
23 O9 **Pensacola Bay** *bay* Florida, SE USA
195 N7 **Pensacola Mountains** ▲▲ Antarctica
182 L12 **Penshurst** Victoria, SE Australia *37°54′S 142°19′E*
187 R13 **Pentecost** *Fr.* Pentecôte. *island* C Vanuatu
15 V4 **Pentecôte** ≈ Québec, SE Canada
Pentecôte *see* Pentecost
15 V4 **Pentecôte, Lac** ◎ Québec, SE Canada
8 H15 **Penticton** British Columbia, SW Canada *49°29′N 119°38′W*
96 J6 **Pentland Firth** *strait* N Scotland, United Kingdom
96 J12 **Pentland Hills** *hill range* S Scotland, United Kingdom
171 Q12 **Penu** Pulau Taliabu, E Indonesia *01°43′S 125°09′E*
155 H18 **Penukonda** Andhra Pradesh, E India *14°04′N 77°38′E*
166 L7 **Penwegon** Bago, C Burma (Myanmar) *18°14′N 96°34′E*
24 M8 **Penwell** Texas, SW USA *31°45′N 102°32′W*
97 J21 **Pen y Fan** ▲ SE Wales, United Kingdom *51°52′N 03°25′W*
97 L16 **Pen-y-ghent** ▲ N England, United Kingdom *54°11′N 02°15′W*
127 O6 **Penza** Penzenskaya Oblast', W Russian Federation *53°11′N 45°E*
97 G25 **Penzance** SW England, United Kingdom *50°08′N 05°33′W*
127 N6 **Penzenskaya Oblast'** ◈ *province* W Russian Federation
123 U7 **Penzhina** ≈ E Russian Federation
123 U9 **Penzhinskaya Guba** *bay* E Russian Federation
Penzig *see* Pieńsk
36 K13 **Peoria** Arizona, SW USA *33°34′N 112°14′W*
30 L12 **Peoria** Illinois, N USA *40°42′N 89°35′W*
30 L12 **Peoria Heights** Illinois, N USA *40°45′N 89°34′W*
31 N11 **Peotone** Illinois, N USA *41°19′N 87°47′W*
18 J11 **Pepacton Reservoir** ▣ New York, NE USA
76 I15 **Pepel** W Sierra Leone *08°39′N 13°04′W*
30 I6 **Pepin, Lake** ▣ Minnesota/Wisconsin, N USA
99 L20 **Pepinster** Liège, E Belgium *50°34′N 05°49′E*
113 L20 **Peqin** *var.* Peqini. Elbasan, C Albania *41°03′N 19°46′E*
Peqini *see* Peqin
40 D7 **Pequeña, Punta** *headland* NW Mexico *26°13′N 112°34′W*
168 J8 **Perak** ◈ *state* Peninsular Malaysia
105 R7 **Perales del Alfambra** Aragón, NE Spain *40°38′N 01°00′W*
115 C15 **Pérama** *var.* Perama. Ípeiros, W Greece *39°42′N 20°51′E*
Perama *see* Pérama
155 I22 **Perambalūr** Tamil Nādu, SE India *11°14′N 78°51′E*
92 M13 **Perä-Posio** Lappi, NE Finland *66°10′N 27°56′E*
15 Z6 **Percé** Québec, SE Canada *48°32′N 64°14′W*
15 Z6 **Percé, Rocher** *island* Québec, S Canada
102 L5 **Perche, Collines de** ▲ N France
109 X4 **Perchtoldsdorf** Niederösterreich, NE Austria *48°06′N 16°16′E*
180 L6 **Percival Lakes** *lakes* Western Australia
105 T3 **Perdido, Monte** ▲ NE Spain *42°41′N 00°01′E*
23 O8 **Perdido River** ≈ Alabama/Florida, S USA
Perece Vela Basin *see* West Mariana Basin
116 G7 **Perechyn** Zakarpats'ka Oblast', W Ukraine *48°45′N 22°28′E*
54 E10 **Pereira** Risaralda, W Colombia *04°47′N 75°46′W*
60 I7 **Pereira Barreto** São Paulo, S Brazil *20°37′S 51°07′W*
59 G15 **Pereirinha** Pará, N Brazil *08°18′S 57°30′W*
127 N10 **Perelazovskiy** Volgogradskaya Oblast', SW Russian Federation *49°10′N 42°30′E*
127 S7 **Perelyub** Saratovskaya Oblast', W Russian Federation *51°52′N 50°19′E*
31 P7 **Pere Marquette River** ≈ Michigan, N USA
Peremyshl *see* Przemyśl
116 I5 **Peremyshlyany** L'vivs'ka Oblast', W Ukraine *49°42′N 24°33′E*
Pereshchepino *see* Pereshchepyne
116 L9 **Pereshchepyne** *Rus.* Pereshchepino. Dnipropetrovs'ka Oblast', E Ukraine *48°59′N 35°22′E*
124 L16 **Pereslavl'-Zalesskiy** Yaroslavskaya Oblast', W Russian Federation *56°42′N 38°45′E*
117 Y7 **Pereval's'k** Luhans'ka Oblast', E Ukraine *48°28′N 38°54′E*
127 U7 **Perevolotskiy** Orenburgskaya Oblast', W Russian Federation *51°54′N 54°05′E*
Pereyaslav-Khmel'nitskiy *see* Pereyaslav-Khmel'nyts'kyy
117 Q5 **Pereyaslav-Khmel'nyts'kyy** *Rus.* Pereyaslav-Khmel'nitskiy. Kyyivs'ka Oblast', N Ukraine *50°05′N 31°28′E*
109 U4 **Perg** Oberösterreich, N Austria *48°15′N 14°38′E*
61 B19 **Pergamino** Buenos Aires, E Argentina *33°56′S 60°38′W*
106 G6 **Pergine Valsugana** *Ger.* Persen. Trentino-Alto Adige, N Italy *46°04′N 11°13′E*
29 S6 **Perham** Minnesota, N USA *46°35′N 95°34′W*
93 L16 **Perho** Länsi-Suomi, W Finland *63°15′N 24°25′E*
116 E11 **Periam** *Ger.* Perjamosch, *Hung.* Perjámos. Timiş, W Romania *46°02′N 20°54′E*
15 Q6 **Péribonca** ≈ Québec, SE Canada
12 L11 **Péribonca, Lac** ◎ Québec, SE Canada
15 Q6 **Péribonca, Petite Rivière** ≈ Québec, SE Canada
15 Q7 **Péribonka** Québec, SE Canada *48°45′N 72°01′W*
40 I9 **Pericos** Sinaloa, C Mexico *25°03′N 107°42′W*
169 Q10 **Perigi** Borneo, C Indonesia
102 L12 **Périgueux** *anc.* Vesuna. Dordogne, SW France *45°12′N 00°41′E*
54 G5 **Perijá, Serranía de** ▲▲ Columbia/Venezuela
115 H17 **Peristéra** *island* Vóreies Sporádes, Greece, Aegean Sea
63 H20 **Perito Moreno** Santa Cruz, S Argentina *46°35′S 71°W*
155 G22 **Periyal** *var.* Periyār. ≈ SW India
Periyār *see* Periyal
155 G23 **Periyār Lake** ◎ S India
Perjámos/Perjamosch *see* Periam
27 O9 **Perkins** Oklahoma, C USA *35°58′N 97°01′W*
116 L7 **Perkivtsi** Chernivets'ka Oblast', W Ukraine *48°28′N 26°48′E*
43 U15 **Perlas, Archipiélago de las** *Eng.* Pearl Islands. *island group* SE Panama
43 O10 **Perlas, Cayos de** *reef* SE Nicaragua
43 N9 **Perlas, Laguna de** *Eng.* Pearl Lagoon. *lagoon* E Nicaragua
43 N10 **Perlas, Punta de** *headland* E Nicaragua *12°22′N 83°30′W*
100 L11 **Perleberg** Brandenburg, N Germany *53°04′N 11°52′E*
Perlepe *see* Prilep
168 I6 **Perlis** ◈ *state* Peninsular Malaysia
125 U14 **Perm'** *prev.* Molotov. Permskaya Oblast', NW Russian Federation *58°01′N 56°10′E*
113 M22 **Përmet** *var.* Përmeti, Prëmet. Gjirokastër, S Albania *40°12′N 20°24′E*
Përmeti *see* Përmet
125 U15 **Permskaya Oblast'** ◈ *province* NW Russian Federation
59 P15 **Pernambuco** *off.* Estado de Pernambuco. ◈ *state* E Brazil
Pernambuco *see* Recife
Pernambuco Abyssal Plain *see* Pernambuco Plain
Pernambuco, Estado de *see* Pernambuco
47 Y6 **Pernambuco Plain** *var.* Pernambuco Abyssal Plain. *undersea feature* E Atlantic Ocean *07°30′S 27°00′W*
65 K15 **Pernambuco Seamounts** *undersea feature* C Atlantic Ocean
182 H6 **Pernatty Lagoon** *salt lake* South Australia
Pernau *see* Pärnu
Pernauer Bucht *see* Pärnu Laht
Pērnava *see* Pärnu
114 G9 **Pernik** *prev.* Dimitrovo. Pernik, W Bulgaria *42°36′N 23°02′E*
114 G10 **Pernik** ◈ *province* W Bulgaria
93 K20 **Perniö** *Swe.* Bjärnå. Länsi-Suomi, SW Finland *60°13′N 23°10′E*

◆ Country
● Country Capital
◇ Dependent Territory
○ Dependent Territory Capital
◈ Administrative Regions
✈ International Airport
▲ Mountain
▲▲ Mountain Range
Volcano
≈ River
◎ Lake
▣ Reservoir

109 *X5* **Pernitz** Niederösterreich, E Austria *47°54′N 15°58′E*
Pernov *see* Pärnu
103 *O3* **Péronne** Somme, N France *49°56′N 02°57′E*
14 *L8* **Péronne, Lac** ◎ Québec, SE Canada
106 *A8* **Perosa Argentina** Piemonte, NE Italy *45°02′N 07°10′E*
41 *Q14* **Perote** Veracruz-Llave, E Mexico *19°32′N 97°16′W*
Pérouse *see* Perugia
191 *W15* **Pérouse, Bahía de la** *bay* Easter Island, Chile, E Pacific Ocean
Perovsk *see* Kzylorda
103 *O17* **Perpignan** Pyrénées-Orientales, S France *42°41′N 02°53′E*
113 *M20* **Përrenjas** *var.* Përrenjasi, Prenjas, Prenjasi. Elbasan, E Albania *41°04′N 20°34′E*
Përrenjasi *see* Përrenjas
92 *O2* **Perriertoppen** ▲ C Svalbard *79°10′N 17°01′E*
25 *S6* **Perrin** Texas, SW USA *32°59′N 98°03′W*
23 *Y16* **Perrine** Florida, SE USA *25°36′N 80°21′W*
37 *S12* **Perro, Laguna del** ◎ New Mexico, SW USA
102 *G5* **Perros-Guirec** Côtes d'Armor, NW France *48°49′N 03°28′W*
23 *T9* **Perry** Florida, SE USA *30°07′N 83°34′W*
23 *T5* **Perry** Georgia, SE USA *32°27′N 83°43′W*
29 *U14* **Perry** Iowa, C USA *41°50′N 94°06′W*
18 *E10* **Perry** New York, NE USA *42°43′N 78°00′W*
27 *N9* **Perry** Oklahoma, C USA *36°17′N 97°18′W*
27 *Q3* **Perry Lake** ▣ Kansas, C USA
31 *R11* **Perrysburg** Ohio, N USA *41°33′N 83°37′W*
25 *O1* **Perryton** Texas, SW USA *36°23′N 100°48′W*
39 *O15* **Perryville** Alaska, USA *55°55′N 159°08′W*
27 *U11* **Perryville** Arkansas, C USA *35°00′N 92°48′W*
27 *Y6* **Perryville** Missouri, C USA *37°43′N 89°51′W*
Persante *see* Parsęta
Persen *see* Pergine Valsugana
Pershay *see* Pyarshai
117 *V7* **Pershotravens'k** Dnipropetrovs'ka Oblast', E Ukraine *48°19′N 36°22′E*
Pershotravneve *see* Manhush
Persia *see* Iran
141 *T5* **Persian Gulf** *var.* The Gulf, *Ar.* Khalīj al 'Arabī, *Per.* Khalīj-e Fars. *Gulf* SW Asia *see also* Gulf, The
Persis *see* Fārs
95 *K22* **Perstorp** Skåne, S Sweden *56°08′N 13°23′E*
137 *O14* **Pertek** Tunceli, C Turkey *38°53′N 39°19′E*
183 *P16* **Perth** Tasmania, SE Australia *41°39′S 147°11′E*
180 *I13* **Perth** *state capital* Western Australia *31°58′S 115°49′E*
14 *L13* **Perth** Ontario, SE Canada *44°54′N 76°15′W*
96 *J11* **Perth** C Scotland, United Kingdom *56°24′N 03°28′W*
96 *J10* **Perth** *cultural region* C Scotland, United Kingdom
180 *I12* **Perth** ✈ Western Australia *31°51′S 116°06′E*
173 *V10* **Perth Basin** *undersea feature* SE Indian Ocean *28°30′S 110°00′E*
103 *S15* **Pertuis** Vaucluse, SE France *43°42′N 05°30′E*
103 *Y16* **Pertusato, Capo** *headland* Corse, France, C Mediterranean Sea *41°22′N 09°10′E*
30 *L11* **Peru** Illinois, N USA *41°18′N 89°09′W*
31 *P12* **Peru** Indiana, N USA *40°45′N 86°04′W*
57 *E13* **Peru** *off.* Republic of Peru. ◆ *republic* W South America
Peru *see* Beru
193 *T9* **Peru Basin** *undersea feature* E Pacific Ocean *15°00′S 85°00′W*
193 *U8* **Peru-Chile Trench** *undersea feature* E Pacific Ocean *20°00′S 73°00′W*
112 *F13* **Perućko Jezero** ◎ S Croatia
106 *H13* **Perugia** *Fr.* Pérouse; *anc.* Perusia. Umbria, C Italy *43°06′N 12°24′E*
Perugia, Lake of *see* Trasimeno, Lago
61 *D15* **Perugorría** Corrientes, NE Argentina *29°21′S 58°35′W*
60 *M11* **Peruíbe** São Paulo, S Brazil *24°18′S 47°01′W*
155 *B21* **Perumalpār** *reef* India, N Indian Ocean
Peru, Republic of *see* Peru
Perusia *see* Perugia
99 *D20* **Péruwelz** Hainaut, SW Belgium *50°30′N 03°35′E*
137 *R15* **Pervari** Siirt, SE Turkey *37°55′N 42°32′E*
127 *O4* **Pervomaysk** Nizhegorodskaya Oblast', W Russian Federation *54°52′N 43°49′E*
117 *X7* **Pervomays'k** Luhans'ka Oblast', E Ukraine *48°38′N 38°36′E*
117 *P8* **Pervomays'k** *prev.* Ol'viopol'. Mykolayivs'ka Oblast', S Ukraine *48°02′N 30°51′E*
117 *S12* **Pervomays'ke** Respublika Krym, S Ukraine *45°43′N 33°49′E*
127 *V7* **Pervomayskiy** Orenburgskaya Oblast', W Russian Federation *51°32′N 54°58′E*
126 *M6* **Pervomayskiy** Tambovskaya Oblast', W Russian Federation *53°15′N 40°20′E*
117 *V6* **Pervomays'kyy** Kharkivs'ka Oblast', E Ukraine *49°24′N 36°12′E*
122 *F10* **Pervoural'sk** Sverdlovskaya Oblast', C Russian Federation *56°58′N 59°50′E*
123 *V11* **Pervyy Kuril'skiy Proliv** *strait* E Russian Federation
99 *I19* **Perwez** Walloon Brabant, C Belgium *50°39′N 04°49′E*
106 *I11* **Pesaro** *anc.* Pisaurum. Marche, C Italy *43°55′N 12°53′E*
35 *N9* **Pescadero** California, W USA *37°15′N 122°23′W*
Pescadores *see* P'enghu Liehtao
161 *S14* **Pescadores Channel** *var.* Penghu Shuidao, P'enghu Shuitao. *channel* W Taiwan
107 *K14* **Pescara** *anc.* Aternum, Ostia Aterni. Abruzzo, C Italy *42°28′N 14°13′E*
107 *K15* **Pescara** ≈ C Italy
106 *F11* **Pescia** Toscana, C Italy *43°54′N 10°41′E*
108 *C8* **Peseux** Neuchâtel, W Switzerland *46°59′N 06°53′E*
125 *P6* **Pësha** ≈ NW Russian Federation
149 *T5* **Peshāwar** North-West Frontier Province, N Pakistan *34°01′N 71°33′E*
149 *T6* **Peshāwar** ✈ North-West Frontier Province, N Pakistan *34°01′N 71°40′E*
113 *M19* **Peshkopi** *var.* Peshkopia, Peshkopija. Dibër, NE Albania *41°40′N 20°25′E*
Peshkopia/Peshkopija *see* Peshkopi
114 *I11* **Peshtera** Pazardzhik, C Bulgaria *42°02′N 24°18′E*
31 *N6* **Peshtigo** Wisconsin, N USA *45°04′N 87°43′W*
31 *N6* **Peshtigo River** ≈ Wisconsin, N USA
Peski *see* Pyeski
125 *S13* **Peskovka** Kirovskaya Oblast', NW Russian Federation *59°04′N 52°17′E*
103 *S8* **Pesmes** Haute-Saône, E France *47°17′N 05°33′E*
104 *H6* **Peso da Régua** *var.* Pêso da Regua. Vila Real, N Portugal *41°10′N 07°47′W*
40 *F5* **Pesqueira** Sonora, NW Mexico *29°22′N 110°58′W*
102 *J13* **Pessac** Gironde, SW France *44°46′N 00°42′W*
111 *J23* **Pest** *off.* Pest Megye. ◐ *county* C Hungary
Pest Megye *see* Pest
124 *J14* **Pestovo** Novgorodskaya Oblast', W Russian Federation *58°37′N 35°48′E*
40 *M15* **Petacalco, Bahía** *bay* W Mexico
Petach-Tikva *see* Petah Tikva
138 *F10* **Petah Tikva** *var.* Petach-Tikva, Petah Tiqva, Petakh Tikva; *prev.* Petah Tiqwa. Tel Aviv, C Israel *32°05′N 34°53′E*
Petah Tiqwa *see* Petah Tikva
93 *L17* **Petäjävesi** Länsi-Suomi, C Finland *62°17′N 25°10′E*
Petakh Tikva/Petah Tiqva *see* Petah Tikva
22 *M7* **Petal** Mississippi, S USA *31°21′N 89°15′W*
115 *I19* **Petalioí** *island* C Greece
115 *H19* **Petalión, Kólpos** *gulf* E Greece
115 *J19* **Pétalo** ▲ Ándros, Kykládes, Greece, Aegean Sea *37°51′N 24°50′E*
34 *M8* **Petaluma** California, W USA *38°15′N 122°37′W*
99 *L25* **Pétange** Luxembourg, SW Luxembourg *49°33′N 05°53′E*
54 *M5* **Petare** Miranda, N Venezuela *10°31′N 66°50′W*
41 *N16* **Petatlán** Guerrero, S Mexico *17°31′N 101°16′W*
83 *L14* **Petauke** Eastern, E Zambia *14°12′S 31°16′E*
14 *J12* **Petawawa** Ontario, SE Canada *45°54′N 77°18′W*
14 *J11* **Petawawa** ≈ Ontario, SE Canada
Petchaburi *see* Phetchaburi
42 *D2* **Petén** *off.* Departamento del Petén. ◐ *department* N Guatemala
Petén, Departamento del *see* Petén
42 *D2* **Petén Itzá, Lago** *var.* Lago de Flores. ◎ N Guatemala
30 *K7* **Petenwell Lake** ▣ Wisconsin, N USA
14 *D6* **Peterbell** Ontario, S Canada *48°34′N 83°19′W*
182 *I7* **Peterborough** South Australia *32°59′S 138°51′E*
14 *I14* **Peterborough** Ontario, SE Canada *44°19′N 78°20′W*
97 *N20* **Peterborough** *prev.* Medeshamstede. E England, United Kingdom *52°35′N 00°15′W*
19 *N10* **Peterborough** New Hampshire, NE USA *42°51′N 71°54′W*
96 *L8* **Peterhead** NE Scotland, United Kingdom *57°30′N 01°46′W*
Peterhof *see* Luboń
Peter I øy *see* Peter I Øy
193 *Q14* **Peter I Øy** ◇ *Norwegian dependency* Antarctica
194 *H9* **Peter I Øy** *var.* Peter I øy. *island* Antarctica
97 *M14* **Peterlee** N England, United Kingdom *54°45′N 01°18′W*
Peterlingen *see* Payerne
197 *P14* **Petermann Bjerg** ▲ C Greenland *73°16′N 27°59′W*
11 *S12* **Peter Pond Lake** ◎ Saskatchewan, C Canada
39 *X13* **Petersburg** Mytkof Island, Alaska, USA *56°43′N 132°51′W*
30 *K13* **Petersburg** Illinois, N USA *40°01′N 89°52′W*
31 *N16* **Petersburg** Indiana, N USA *38°30′N 87°16′W*
29 *Q3* **Petersburg** North Dakota, N USA *47°59′N 97°59′W*
25 *N5* **Petersburg** Texas, SW USA *33°52′N 101°36′W*
21 *V7* **Petersburg** Virginia, NE USA *37°14′N 77°24′W*
21 *T4* **Petersburg** West Virginia, NE USA *39°01′N 79°09′W*
100 *H12* **Petershagen** Nordrhein-Westfalen, NW Germany *52°22′N 08°58′E*
55 *S9* **Peters Mine** *var.* Peter's Mine. N Guyana *06°13′N 59°18′W*
107 *O21* **Petilia Policastro** Calabria, SW Italy *39°07′N 16°48′E*
44 *M9* **Pétionville** S Haiti *18°29′N 72°16′W*
45 *X6* **Petit-Bourg** Basse Terre, C Guadeloupe *16°12′N 61°36′W*
15 *Y5* **Petit-Cap** Québec, SE Canada *49°00′N 64°26′W*
45 *Y6* **Petit Cul-de-Sac Marin** *bay* C Guadeloupe
44 *M9* **Petite-Rivière-de-l'Artibonite** C Haiti *19°10′N 72°30′W*
173 *X16* **Petite Rivière Noire, Piton de la** ▲ C Mauritius
15 *R9* **Petite-Rivière-St-François** Québec, SE Canada *47°18′N 70°34′W*
44 *L9* **Petit-Goâve** S Haiti *18°27′N 72°51′W*
Petitjean *see* Sidi-Kacem
13 *N10* **Petit Lac Manicouagan** ◎ Québec, E Canada
19 *T7* **Petit Manan Point** *headland* Maine, NE USA *44°23′N 67°54′W*
Petit Mécatina, Rivière du *see* Little Mecatina
11 *N10* **Petitot** ≈ Alberta/British Columbia, W Canada
45 *S12* **Petit Piton** ▲ SW Saint Lucia *13°49′N 61°03′W*
Petit-Popo *see* Aného
Petit St-Bernard, Col du *see* Little Saint Bernard Pass
13 *O8* **Petitsikapau Lake** ◎ Newfoundland and Labrador, E Canada
92 *L11* **Petkula** Lappi, N Finland *67°41′N 26°44′E*
41 *X12* **Peto** Yucatán, SE Mexico *20°09′N 88°55′W*
62 *G10* **Petorca** Valparaíso, C Chile *32°18′S 70°49′W*
31 *Q5* **Petoskey** Michigan, N USA *45°51′N 88°03′W*
138 *G14* **Petra** *archaeological site* Ma'ān, W Jordan
Petra *see* Wādī Mūsā
115 *F14* **Pétras, Sténa** *pass* N Greece
123 *S16* **Petra Velikogo, Zaliv** *bay* SE Russian Federation
Petrel *see* Petrer
14 *K15* **Petre, Point** *headland* Ontario, SE Canada *43°49′N 77°07′W*
105 *S12* **Petrer** *var.* Petrel. País Valenciano, E Spain *38°28′N 00°46′W*
125 *U11* **Petretsovo** Permskaya Oblast', NW Russian Federation *61°22′N 57°21′E*
114 *G12* **Petrich** Blagoevgrad, SW Bulgaria *41°25′N 23°12′E*
187 *P15* **Petrie, Récif** *reef* N New Caledonia
37 *N11* **Petrified Forest** *prehistoric site* Arizona, SW USA
Petrikau *see* Piotrków Trybunalski
Petrikov *see* Pyetrykaw
116 *H12* **Petrila** *Hung.* Petrilla. Hunedoara, W Romania *45°27′N 23°25′E*
Petrilla *see* Petrila
112 *E9* **Petrinja** Sisak-Moslavina, C Croatia *45°27′N 16°14′E*
Petroaleksandrovsk *see* To'rtkok'l
Petrőcz *see* Bački Petrovac
124 *G12* **Petrodvorets** *Fin.* Pietarhovi. Leningradskaya Oblast', NW Russian Federation *59°53′N 29°52′E*
Petrograd *see* Sankt-Peterburg
Petrokov *see* Piotrków Trybunalski
54 *G6* **Petrólea** Norte de Santander, NE Colombia *08°30′N 72°35′W*
14 *D16* **Petrolia** Ontario, S Canada *42°54′N 82°07′W*
25 *S4* **Petrolia** Texas, SW USA *34°00′N 98°13′W*
59 *O15* **Petrolina** Pernambuco, E Brazil *09°22′S 40°30′W*
45 *T6* **Petrona, Punta** *headland* C Puerto Rico *17°57′N 66°23′W*
Petropavl *see* Petropavlovsk
117 *V7* **Petropavlivka** Dnipropetrovs'ka Oblast', E Ukraine *48°28′N 36°28′E*
145 *P6* **Petropavlovsk** *Kaz.* Petropavl. Severnyy Kazakhstan, N Kazakhstan *54°47′N 69°06′E*
123 *V11* **Petropavlovsk-Kamchatskiy** Kamchatskaya Oblast', E Russian Federation *53°03′N 158°43′E*
60 *P9* **Petrópolis** Rio de Janeiro, SE Brazil *22°30′S 43°28′W*
116 *H12* **Petroşani** *var.* Petroşeni, *Ger.* Petroschen, *Hung.* Petrozsény. Hunedoara, W Romania *45°25′N 23°22′E*
Petroschen/Petroşeni *see* Petroşani
Petroskoi *see* Petrozavodsk
112 *N12* **Petrovac** Serbia, E Serbia *42°22′N 21°25′E*
Petrovac *see* Bosanski Petrovac
113 *J17* **Petrovac na Moru** S Montenegro *42°11′N 19°00′E*
Petrovac/Petrovácz *see* Bački Petrovac
117 *S8* **Petrove** Kirovohrads'ka Oblast', C Ukraine *48°22′N 33°12′E*
113 *O18* **Petrovec** C FYR Macedonia *41°57′N 21°37′E*
Petrovgrad *see* Zrenjanin
127 *P7* **Petrovsk** Saratovskaya Oblast', W Russian Federation *52°20′N 45°23′E*
Petrovsk-Port *see* Makhachkala
127 *P9* **Petrov Val** Volgogradskaya Oblast', SW Russian Federation *50°10′N 45°16′E*
124 *J11* **Petrozavodsk** *Fin.* Petroskoi. Respublika Kareliya, NW Russian Federation *61°46′N 34°19′E*
Petrozsény *see* Petroşani
83 *D20* **Petrusdal** Hardap, C Namibia *23°42′S 17°23′E*
117 *T7* **Petrykivka** Dnipropetrovs'ka Oblast', E Ukraine *48°44′N 34°42′E*
Petsamo *see* Pechenga
Petschka *see* Pecica
Petseri *see* Pechory
Pettau *see* Ptuj
109 *S5* **Pettenbach** Oberösterreich, C Austria *47°58′N 14°03′E*
25 *S13* **Pettus** Texas, SW USA *28°34′N 97°49′W*
122 *G12* **Petukhovo** Kurganskaya Oblast', C Russian Federation *55°04′N 67°49′E*
Petuna *see* Songyuan
109 *R4* **Peuerbach** Oberösterreich, N Austria *48°19′N 13°45′E*
62 *G12* **Peumo** Libertador, C Chile *34°20′S 71°12′W*
123 *T6* **Pevek** Chukotskiy Avtonomnyy Okrug, NE Russian Federation *69°41′N 170°19′E*
27 *X5* **Pevely** Missouri, C USA *38°16′N 90°24′W*
Peyia *see* Pégeia
102 *J15* **Peyrehorade** Landes, SW France *43°33′N 01°05′W*
124 *J14* **Peza** ≈ NW Russian Federation
103 *P16* **Pézenas** Hérault, S France *43°28′N 03°25′E*
111 *H20* **Pezinok** *Ger.* Bösing, *Hung.* Bazin. Bratislavský Kraj, W Slovakia *48°17′N 17°15′E*
101 *L22* **Pfaffenhofen an der Ilm** Bayern, SE Germany *48°31′N 11°30′E*
108 *G7* **Pfäffikon** Schwyz, C Switzerland *47°11′N 08°46′E*
101 *F20* **Pfälzer Wald** *hill range* W Germany
101 *N22* **Pfarrkirchen** Bayern, SE Germany *48°25′N 12°56′E*
101 *G21* **Pforzheim** Baden-Württemberg, SW Germany *48°53′N 08°42′E*
101 *H24* **Pfullendorf** Baden-Württemberg, S Germany *47°55′N 09°16′E*
108 *K8* **Pfunds** Tirol, W Austria *46°56′N 10°30′E*
101 *G19* **Pfungstadt** Hessen, W Germany *49°48′N 08°36′E*
83 *L20* **Phalaborwa** Limpopo, NE South Africa *23°59′S 31°04′E*
152 *E11* **Phalodi** Rājasthān, NW India *27°06′N 72°22′E*
152 *E12* **Phalsund** Rājasthān, NW India *26°22′N 71°56′E*
155 *E15* **Phaltan** Mahārāshtra, W India *18°01′N 74°31′E*
167 *O7* **Phan** *var.* Muang Phan. Chiang Rai, NW Thailand *19°34′N 99°44′E*
167 *O14* **Phangan, Ko** *island* SW Thailand
166 *M15* **Phang-Nga** *var.* Pang-Nga, Phangnga. Phangnga, SW Thailand *08°29′N 98°31′E*
Phangnga *see* Phang-Nga
Phan Rang/Phanrang *see* Phan Rang-Thap Cham
167 *V13* **Phan Rang-Thap Cham** *var.* Phanrang, Phan Rang, Phan Rang Thap Cham. Ninh Thuân, S Vietnam *11°34′N 109°00′E*
167 *U13* **Phan Ri** Binh Thuân, S Vietnam *11°11′N 108°31′E*
167 *U13* **Phan Thiêt** Binh Thuân, S Vietnam *10°56′N 108°06′E*
Pharnacia *see* Giresun
25 *S17* **Pharr** Texas, SW USA *26°11′N 98°10′W*
Pharus *see* Hvar
167 *N16* **Phatthalung** *var.* Padalung, Patalung. Phatthalung, SW Thailand *07°38′N 100°04′E*
167 *O7* **Phayao** *var.* Muang Phayao. Phayao, NW Thailand *19°10′N 99°55′E*
11 *U10* **Phelps Lake** ◎ Saskatchewan, C Canada
21 *X9* **Phelps Lake** ◎ North Carolina, SE USA
23 *R5* **Phenix City** Alabama, S USA *32°28′N 85°00′W*
167 *T8* **Pheo** Quang Binh, C Vietnam *17°42′N 105°58′E*
Phet Buri *see* Phetchaburi
167 *O11* **Phetchaburi** *var.* Bejraburi, Petchaburi, Phet Buri. Phetchaburi, SW Thailand *13°05′N 99°58′E*
167 *O9* **Phichit** *var.* Bichitra, Muang Phichit, Pichit. Phichit, C Thailand *16°29′N 100°21′E*
22 *M5* **Philadelphia** Mississippi, S USA *32°45′N 89°06′W*
18 *I7* **Philadelphia** New York, NE USA *44°10′N 75°40′W*
18 *I16* **Philadelphia** Pennsylvania, NE USA *40°N 75°10′W*
18 *I16* **Philadelphia** ✈ Pennsylvania, NE USA *39°51′N 75°13′W*
Philadelphia *see* 'Ammān
28 *L10* **Philip** South Dakota, N USA *44°02′N 101°39′W*
99 *H22* **Philippeville** Namur, S Belgium *50°12′N 04°33′E*
Philippeville *see* Skikda
21 *S3* **Philippi** West Virginia, NE USA *39°08′N 80°03′W*
Philippi *see* Fílippoi
195 *Y9* **Philippi Glacier** *glacier* Antarctica
192 *G6* **Philippine Basin** *undersea feature* W Pacific Ocean *17°00′N 132°00′E*
129 *X12* **Philippine Plate** *tectonic feature*
171 *O5* **Philippines** *off.* Republic of the Philippines. ◆ *republic* SE Asia
129 *X13* **Philippines** *island group* W Pacific Ocean
171 *P3* **Philippine Sea** *sea* W Pacific Ocean
Philippines, Republic of the *see* Philippines
192 *F6* **Philippine Trench** *undersea feature* W Philippine Sea
83 *H23* **Philippolis** Free State, C South Africa *30°16′S 25°16′E*
Philippopolis *see* Plovdiv
Philippopolis *see* Shahbā', Syria
45 *V9* **Philipsburg** Sint Maarten, N Netherlands Antilles *17°58′N 63°02′W*
33 *P10* **Philipsburg** Montana, NW USA *46°19′N 113°17′W*
39 *R6* **Philip Smith Mountains** ▲▲ Alaska, USA
152 *H8* **Phillaur** Punjab, N India *31°02′N 75°50′E*
183 *N13* **Phillip Island** *island* Victoria, SE Australia
25 *N2* **Phillips** Texas, SW USA *35°39′N 101°21′W*
30 *K5* **Phillips** Wisconsin, N USA *45°42′N 90°23′W*
26 *K3* **Phillipsburg** Kansas, C USA *39°45′N 99°19′W*
18 *I14* **Phillipsburg** New Jersey, NE USA *40°39′N 75°09′W*
21 *S7* **Philpott Lake** ▣ Virginia, NE USA
Phintias *see* Licata
167 *P9* **Phitsanulok** *var.* Bisnulok, Muang Phitsanulok, Pitsanulok. Phitsanulok, C Thailand *16°49′N 100°15′E*
Phlórina *see* Flórina
Phnom Penh *see* Phnum Penh
167 *S13* **Phnum Penh** *var.* Phnom Penh. ● (Cambodia) Phnum Penh, S Cambodia *11°35′N 104°55′E*
167 *S11* **Phnum Tbêng Meanchey** Preăh Vihéar, N Cambodia *13°45′N 104°58′E*
36 *K13* **Phoenix** *state capital* Arizona, SW USA *33°27′N 112°04′W*
Phoenix Island *see* Rawaki
191 *R3* **Phoenix Islands** *island group* C Kiribati
18 *I15* **Phoenixville** Pennsylvania, NE USA *40°07′N 75°31′W*
83 *K22* **Phofung** *var.* Mont-aux-Sources. ▲ N Lesotho *28°47′S 28°52′E*
167 *Q10* **Phon** Khon Kaen, E Thailand *15°47′N 102°35′E*
167 *Q5* **Phôngsali** *var.* Phong Saly. Phôngsali, N Laos *21°40′N 102°04′E*
Phong Saly *see* Phôngsali
167 *Q8* **Phônhông** C Laos *18°29′N 102°26′E*
167 *R5* **Phô Rang** *var.* Bao Yèn. Lao Cai, N Vietnam *22°12′N 104°27′E*
Phort Láirge, Cuan *see* Waterford Harbour
167 *N10* **Phra Chedi Sam Ong** Kanchanaburi, W Thailand *15°18′N 98°26′E*
167 *O8* **Phrae** *var.* Muang Phrae, Prae. Phrae, NW Thailand *18°07′N 100°09′E*
Phra Nakhon Si Ayutthaya *see* Ayutthaya
167 *M14* **Phra Thong, Ko** *island* SW Thailand
Phu Cŭơng *see* Thu Dâu Môt
166 *M15* **Phuket** *var.* Bhuket, Puket, *Mal.* Ujung Salang; *prev.* Junkseylon, Salang. Phuket, SW Thailand *07°52′N 98°22′E*
166 *M15* **Phuket** ✈ Phuket, SW Thailand *08°03′N 98°16′E*
166 *M15* **Phuket, Ko** *island* SW Thailand
154 *N12* **Phulabāni** *prev.* Phulbani. Orissa, E India *20°30′N 84°18′E*
Phulbani *see* Phulabāni
167 *U9* **Phu Lôc** Th,a Thiên-Huê, C Vietnam *16°13′N 107°53′E*
167 *S13* **Phumĭ Banam** Prey Vêng, S Cambodia *11°14′N 105°18′E*
167 *R13* **Phumĭ Chŏâm** Kâmpóng Spœ, SW Cambodia *11°42′N 103°58′E*
167 *T11* **Phumĭ Kalêng** Stœ̆ng Trêng, NE Cambodia *13°57′N 106°17′E*
167 *S12* **Phumĭ Kâmpóng Trâbêk** *prev.* Phum Kompong Trabek. Kâmpóng Thum, C Cambodia *13°06′N 105°16′E*
167 *Q11* **Phumĭ Koŭk Kduŏch** Bătdâmbâng, NW Cambodia *13°16′N 103°08′E*
167 *T11* **Phumĭ Labăng** Rôtânôkiri, NE Cambodia *13°51′N 107°01′E*
167 *S11* **Phumĭ Mlu Prey** Preăh Vihéar, N Cambodia *13°48′N 105°16′E*
167 *R11* **Phumĭ Moŭng** Siĕmréab, NW Cambodia *13°45′N 103°35′E*
167 *Q12* **Phumĭ Prâmaôy** Poŭthĭsăt, W Cambodia *12°13′N 103°05′E*
167 *Q13* **Phumĭ Samĭt** Kaôh Kông, SW Cambodia *10°54′N 103°09′E*
167 *R11* **Phumĭ Sâmraông** *prev.* Phum Samrong. Siĕmréab, NW Cambodia *14°11′N 103°31′E*
167 *S12* **Phumĭ Siĕmbok** Stœ̆ng Trêng, N Cambodia *13°28′N 105°59′E*
167 *S11* **Phumĭ Thalabârĭvăt** Stœ̆ng Trêng, N Cambodia *13°34′N 105°57′E*
167 *R13* **Phumĭ Veal Renh** Kâmpôt, SW Cambodia *10°43′N 103°49′E*
167 *P13* **Phumĭ Yeay Sên** Kaôh Kông, SW Cambodia *11°09′N 103°09′E*
Phum Kompong Trabek *see* Phumĭ Kâmpóng Trâbêk
Phum Samrong *see* Phumĭ Sâmraông
167 *V11* **Phu My** Binh Đinh, C Vietnam *14°07′N 109°05′E*
167 *S14* **Phung Hiêp** Cân Thơ, S Vietnam *09°50′N 105°48′E*
153 *T12* **Phuntsholing** SW Bhutan *26°52′N 89°26′E*
167 *R15* **Phươc Long** Minh Hai, S Vietnam *09°27′N 105°25′E*
Phươc Sơn *see* Khâm Đưc
167 *R14* **Phu Quôc, Đao** *var.* Phu Quoc Island. *island* S Vietnam
Phu Quoc Island *see* Phu Quôc, Đao
167 *S6* **Phu Tho** Vinh Phu, N Vietnam *21°23′N 105°13′E*
Phu Vinh *see* Tra Vinh
166 *M7* **Phyu** *var.* Hpyu, Pyu. Bago, C Burma (Myanmar) *18°29′N 96°28′E*
189 *T13* **Piaanu Pass** *passage* Chuuk Islands, C Micronesia
106 *E8* **Piacenza** *Fr.* Paisance; *anc.* Placentia. Emilia-Romagna, N Italy *45°02′N 09°42′E*
107 *K14* **Pianella** Abruzzo, C Italy *42°23′N 14°04′E*
107 *M15* **Pianosa, Isola** *island* Archipelago Toscano, C Italy
171 *U13* **Piar** Papua, E Indonesia *02°49′S 132°46′E*
45 *U14* **Piarco** *var.* Port of Spain. ✈ (Port-of-Spain) Trinidad, Trinidad and Tobago *10°36′N 61°21′W*
110 *M12* **Piaseczno** Mazowieckie, C Poland *52°03′N 21°00′E*
116 *I15* **Piatra** Teleorman, S Romania *43°49′N 25°10′E*
116 *L10* **Piatra-Neamţ** *Hung.* Karácsonkő. Neamţ, NE Romania *46°54′N 26°23′E*
Piauhy *see* Piauí
59 *N15* **Piauí** *off.* Estado do Piauí; *prev.* Piauhy. ◐ *state* E Brazil
Piauí, Estado do *see* Piauí
106 *I7* **Piave** ≈ NE Italy
107 *K24* **Piazza Armerina** *var.* Chiazza. Sicilia, Italy, C Mediterranean Sea *37°23′N 14°22′E*
81 *G14* **Pibor** *Amh.* Pībor Wenz. ≈ Ethiopia/Sudan
81 *G14* **Pibor Post** Jonglei, SE Sudan *06°50′N 33°06′E*
Pībor Wenz *see* Pibor
Pibrans *see* Příbram
36 *K11* **Picacho Butte** ▲ Arizona, SW USA *35°12′N 112°44′W*
40 *D4* **Picachos, Cerro** ▲ NW Mexico *29°15′N 114°04′W*
103 *O4* **Picardie** *Eng.* Picardy. ◐ *region* N France
Picardy *see* Picardie
22 *L8* **Picayune** Mississippi, S USA *30°31′N 89°40′W*
Piccolo San Bernardo, Colle di *see* Little Saint Bernard Pass
PicdeBälaitous *see* Balaïtous
62 *K5* **Pichanal** Salta, N Argentina *23°18′S 64°10′W*
147 *P12* **Pichandar** W Tajikistan *38°44′N 68°51′E*
27 *R8* **Picher** Oklahoma, C USA *36°59′N 94°49′W*
62 *G12* **Pichilemu** Libertador, C Chile *34°25′S 72°00′W*
40 *F9* **Pichilingue** Baja California Sur, NW Mexico *24°20′N 110°17′W*
56 *B6* **Pichincha** ◐ *province* N Ecuador
56 *C6* **Pichincha** ▲ N Ecuador *0°12′S 78°39′W*
Pichit *see* Phichit
41 *U15* **Pichucalco** Chiapas, SE Mexico *17°32′N 93°07′W*
22 *L5* **Pickens** Mississippi, S USA *32°52′N 89°58′W*
21 *O11* **Pickens** South Carolina, SE USA *34°53′N 82°42′W*
14 *G11* **Pickerel** ≈ Ontario, S Canada
14 *H15* **Pickering** Ontario, S Canada *43°50′N 79°03′W*
97 *N16* **Pickering** N England, United Kingdom *54°14′N 00°47′W*
31 *S13* **Pickerington** Ohio, N USA *39°52′N 82°45′W*
12 *C10* **Pickle Lake** Ontario, C Canada *51°30′N 90°10′W*
29 *P12* **Pickstown** South Dakota, N USA *43°02′N 98°31′W*
25 *V6* **Pickton** Texas, SW USA *33°01′N 95°19′W*
23 *N1* **Pickwick Lake** ▣ S USA
64 *N2* **Pico** *var.* Ilha do Pico. *island* Azores, Portugal, NE Atlantic Ocean
63 *J19* **Pico de Salamanca** Chubut, SE Argentina *45°26′S 67°26′W*
1 *P9* **Pico Fracture Zone** *tectonic feature* NW Atlantic Ocean
Pico, Ilha do *see* Pico
59 *O14* **Picos** Piauí, E Brazil *07°05′S 41°24′W*
63 *I20* **Pico Truncado** Santa Cruz, SE Argentina *46°45′S 68°00′W*
183 *S9* **Picton** New South Wales, SE Australia *34°12′S 150°36′E*
14 *K15* **Picton** Ontario, SE Canada *43°59′N 77°09′W*
185 *K14* **Picton** Marlborough, South Island, New Zealand *41°18′S 174°00′E*
63 *H15* **Picún Leufú, Arroyo** ≈ SW Argentina
Pidálion *see* Gkréko, Akrotíri
155 *K25* **Pidurutalagala** ▲ S Sri Lanka *07°03′N 80°47′E*
116 *K6* **Pidvolochys'k** Ternopil's'ka Oblast', W Ukraine *49°31′N 26°09′E*
107 *K16* **Piedimonte Matese** Campania, S Italy *41°20′N 14°30′E*
27 *X7* **Piedmont** Missouri, C USA *37°09′N 90°42′W*
21 *P11* **Piedmont** South Carolina, SE USA *34°42′N 82°27′W*
17 *S12* **Piedmont** *escarpment* E USA
Piedmont *see* Piemonte
31 *U13* **Piedmont Lake** ▣ Ohio, N USA
104 *M11* **Piedrabuena** Castilla-La Mancha, C Spain *39°02′N 04°10′W*
Piedrafita, Puerto de *see* Pedrafita, Porto de
104 *L8* **Piedrahita** Castilla-León, N Spain *40°27′N 05°20′W*
41 *N6* **Piedras Negras** *var.* Ciudad Porfirio Díaz. Coahuila, NE Mexico *28°40′N 100°32′W*
61 *E21* **Piedras, Punta** *headland* E Argentina *35°27′S 57°04′W*
57 *I14* **Piedras, Río de las** ≈ E Peru
111 *J16* **Piekary Śląskie** Śląskie, S Poland *50°24′N 18°58′E*
93 *M17* **Pieksämäki** Itä-Suomi, E Finland *62°18′N 27°10′E*
109 *V5* **Pielach** ≈ NE Austria
93 *M16* **Pielavesi** Itä-Suomi, C Finland *63°14′N 26°45′E*
93 *M16* **Pielavesi** ◎ C Finland
93 *N16* **Pielinen** *var.* Pielisjärvi. ◎ E Finland
Pielisjärvi *see* Pielinen
106 *A8* **Piemonte** *Eng.* Piedmont. ◐ *region* NW Italy
111 *L18* **Pieniny** ▲▲ S Poland
111 *E14* **Pieńsk** *Ger.* Penzig. Dolnośląskie, SW Poland *51°14′N 15°03′E*
29 *Q13* **Pierce** Nebraska, C USA *42°12′N 97°31′W*
11 *R14* **Pierceland** Saskatchewan, C Canada
115 *E14* **Piéria** ▲▲ N Greece
29 *N10* **Pierre** *state capital* South Dakota, N USA *44°22′N 100°21′W*
102 *K16* **Pierrefitte-Nestalas** Hautes-Pyrénées, S France *42°57′N 00°04′W*
103 *R14* **Pierrelatte** Drôme, E France *44°22′N 04°40′E*
15 *P11* **Pierreville** Québec, SE Canada *46°05′N 72°48′W*
15 *O7* **Pierriche** ≈ Québec, SE Canada
111 *H20* **Piešt'any** *Ger.* Pistyan, *Hung.* Pöstyén. Tranavský Kraj, W Slovakia *48°37′N 17°48′E*
109 *X5* **Piesting** ≈ E Austria
Pietarhovi *see* Petrodvorets
Pietari *see* Sankt-Peterburg
Pietarsaari *see* Jakobstad
83 *K23* **Pietermaritzburg** *var.* Maritzburg. KwaZulu/Natal, E South Africa *29°35′S 30°23′E*
Pietersburg *see* Polokwane
107 *K24* **Pietraperzia** Sicilia, Italy, C Mediterranean Sea *37°25′N 14°08′E*
107 *N22* **Pietra Spada, Passo della** *pass* SW Italy
83 *K22* **Piet Retief** Mpumalanga, E South Africa *27°00′S 30°49′E*
116 *J10* **Pietrosul, Vârful** *prev.* Vîrful Pietrosu. ▲ N Romania *47°06′N 25°09′E*
106 *I6* **Pieve di Cadore** Veneto, NE Italy *46°27′N 12°22′E*
14 *C18* **Pigeon Bay** *lake bay* Ontario, S Canada
27 *X8* **Piggott** Arkansas, C USA *36°22′N 90°11′W*
83 *L21* **Piggs Peak** NW Swaziland *25°58′S 31°17′E*
Pigs, Bay of *see* Cochinos, Bahía de
61 *A23* **Pigüé** Buenos Aires, E Argentina *37°38′S 62°27′W*
41 *O12* **Piguícas** ▲ C Mexico *21°08′N 99°37′W*
193 *W15* **Piha Passage** *passage* S Tonga
Pihkva Järv *see* Pskov, Lake
93 *N18* **Pihlajavesi** ◎ SE Finland
93 *J18* **Pihlava** Länsi-Suomi, SW Finland *61°33′N 21°36′E*
93 *L16* **Pihtipudas** Länsi-Suomi, C Finland *63°20′N 25°37′E*
40 *L14* **Pihuamo** Jalisco, SW Mexico *19°20′N 103°21′W*
189 *U11* **Piis Moen** *var.* Pis. *atoll* Chuuk Islands, C Micronesia
41 *U17* **Pijijiapán** Chiapas, SE Mexico *15°42′N 93°12′W*
98 *G12* **Pijnacker** Zuid-Holland, W Netherlands *52°01′N 04°26′E*
42 *H5* **Pijol, Pico** ▲ NW Honduras *15°07′N 87°39′W*
Pikaar *see* Bikar Atoll
124 *I13* **Pikalevo** Leningradskaya Oblast', NW Russian Federation *59°33′N 34°04′E*
188 *M15* **Pikelot** *island* Caroline Islands, C Micronesia
30 *M5* **Pike River** ≈ Wisconsin, N USA
37 *T5* **Pikes Peak** ▲ Colorado, C USA *38°51′N 105°06′W*
21 *P6* **Pikeville** Kentucky, S USA *37°29′N 82°33′W*
20 *L9* **Pikeville** Tennessee, S USA *35°35′N 85°11′W*
Pikinni *see* Bikini Atoll
79 *H18* **Pikounda** Sangha, C Congo *0°30′N 16°44′E*
110 *G9* **Piła** *Ger.* Schneidemühl. Wielkopolskie, C Poland *53°09′N 16°44′E*
62 *N6* **Pilagá, Riacho** ≈ NE Argentina
61 *D20* **Pilar** Buenos Aires, E Argentina *34°28′S 58°55′W*
62 *N7* **Pilar** *var.* Villa del Pilar. Ñeembucú, S Paraguay *26°55′S 58°20′W*
62 *N6* **Pilcomayo, Rio** ≈ C South America
147 *R12* **Pildon** *Rus.* Pil'don. C Tajikistan *39°10′N 71°00′E*
Piles *see* Pylés
Pilgram *see* Pelhřimov
152 *L10* **Pīlībhīt** Uttar Pradesh, N India *28°37′N 79°48′E*
110 *M13* **Pilica** ≈ C Poland
115 *G16* **Pílio** ▲▲ C Greece
111 *J22* **Pilisvörösvár** Pest, N Hungary *47°38′N 18°55′E*
65 *G15* **Pillar Bay** *bay* Ascension Island, C Atlantic Ocean
183 *P17* **Pillar, Cape** *headland* Tasmania, SE Australia *43°13′S 147°58′E*
Pillau *see* Baltiysk
183 *R5* **Pilliga** New South Wales, SE Australia *30°22′S 148°53′E*
44 *H8* **Pilón** Granma, E Cuba *19°54′N 77°20′W*
Pilos *see* Pýlos
11 *W17* **Pilot Mound** Manitoba, S Canada *49°12′N 98°49′W*
21 *S8* **Pilot Mountain** North Carolina, SE USA *36°23′N 80°28′W*
39 *O14* **Pilot Point** Alaska, USA *57°33′N 157°34′W*
25 *T5* **Pilot Point** Texas, SW USA *33°24′N 96°57′W*
32 *K11* **Pilot Rock** Oregon, NW USA *45°28′N 118°49′W*
38 *M11* **Pilot Station** Alaska, USA *61°56′N 162°52′W*
Pilsen *see* Plzeň
111 *K18* **Pilsko** ▲ N Slovakia *49°31′N 19°21′E*
Pilten *see* Piltene
118 *D8* **Piltene** *Ger.* Pilten. Ventspils, W Latvia *57°14′N 21°41′E*
111 *M16* **Pilzno** Podkarpackie, SE Poland *49°58′N 21°18′E*
Pilzno *see* Plzeň
37 *N14* **Pima** Arizona, SW USA *32°49′N 109°50′W*
58 *H13* **Pimenta** Pará, N Brazil *04°32′S 56°17′W*
59 *F16* **Pimenta Bueno** Rondônia, W Brazil *11°40′S 61°14′W*
56 *B11* **Pimentel** Lambayeque, W Peru *06°51′S 79°53′W*
105 *S6* **Pina** Aragón, NE Spain *41°28′N 00°31′W*
119 *I20* **Pina** ≈ SW Belarus
40 *E2* **Pinacate, Sierra del** ▲ NW Mexico *31°49′N 113°30′W*
63 *H22* **Pináculo, Cerro** ▲ S Argentina *50°46′S 72°07′W*
191 *X11* **Pinaki** *atoll* Îles Tuamotu, E French Polynesia
37 *N15* **Pinaleno Mountains** ▲▲ Arizona, SW USA
171 *P4* **Pinamalayan** Mindoro, N Philippines *13°00′N 121°30′E*
169 *Q10* **Pinang** Borneo, C Indonesia *0°36′N 109°11′W*
168 *J7* **Pinang** *var.* Penang. ◐ *state* Peninsular Malaysia
Pinang *see* Pinang, Pulau, Peninsular Malaysia
Pinang *see* George Town
168 *J7* **Pinang, Pulau** *var.* Penang, Pinang; *prev.* Prince of Wales Island. *island* Peninsular Malaysia
44 *B5* **Pinar del Río** Pinar del Río, W Cuba *22°24′N 83°42′W*
114 *N11* **Pınarhisar** Kırklareli, NW Turkey *41°37′N 27°32′E*
171 *O3* **Pinatubo, Mount** 🌋 Luzon, N Philippines *15°08′N 120°21′E*
11 *Y16* **Pinawa** Manitoba, S Canada *50°09′N 95°52′W*
11 *Q17* **Pincher Creek** Alberta, SW Canada *49°31′N 113°53′W*
30 *L16* **Pinckneyville** Illinois, N USA *38°04′N 89°22′W*
Pîncota *see* Pâncota
111 *L15* **Pińczów** Świętokrzyskie, C Poland *50°30′N 20°30′E*
149 *U7* **Pind Dādan Khān** Punjab, E Pakistan *32°36′N 73°07′E*
Píndhos/Píndhos Óros *see* Píndos
149 *V8* **Pindi Bhattiān** Punjab, E Pakistan *31°54′N 73°20′E*
149 *U6* **Pindi Gheb** Punjab, E Pakistan *33°16′N 72°21′E*
115 *D15* **Píndos** *var.* Píndhos Óros, *Eng.* Pindus Mountains; *prev.* Píndhos. ▲▲ C Greece
Pindus Mountains *see* Píndos

◆ Country
● Country Capital
◇ Dependent Territory
○ Dependent Territory Capital
◐ Administrative Regions
✈ International Airport
▲ Mountain
▲▲ Mountain Range
🌋 Volcano
≈ River
◎ Lake
▣ Reservoir

18 J16 **Pine Barrens** physical region New Jersey, NE USA
27 V12 **Pine Bluff** Arkansas, C USA 34°15′N 92°00′W
23 X11 **Pine Castle** Florida, SE USA 28°28′N 81°22′W
29 V7 **Pine City** Minnesota, N USA 45°49′N 92°55′W
181 P2 **Pine Creek** Northern Territory, N Australia 13°51′S 131°51′E
35 V4 **Pine Creek** Nevada, W USA
18 F13 **Pine Creek** Pennsylvania, NE USA
27 Q13 **Pine Creek Lake** Oklahoma, C USA
33 T15 **Pinedale** Wyoming, C USA 42°52′N 109°51′W
11 X15 **Pine Dock** Manitoba, S Canada 51°34′N 96°47′W
11 Y16 **Pine Falls** Manitoba, S Canada 50°29′N 96°12′W
35 R10 **Pine Flat Lake** California, W USA
125 N8 **Pinega** Arkhangel'skaya Oblast', NW Russian Federation 64°40′N 43°24′E
125 N8 **Pinega** NW Russian Federation
15 N12 **Pine Hill** Québec, SE Canada 45°44′N 74°30′W
11 T12 **Pinehouse Lake** Saskatchewan, C Canada
21 T10 **Pinehurst** North Carolina, SE USA 35°12′N 79°28′W
115 D19 **Pineiós** S Greece
115 E16 **Pineiós** var. Piniós; anc. Peneius. C Greece
29 W10 **Pine Island** Minnesota, N USA 44°12′N 92°39′W
23 V15 **Pine Island** island Florida, SE USA
194 K10 **Pine Island Glacier** glacier Antarctica
25 X9 **Pineland** Texas, SW USA 31°15′N 93°58′W
23 V13 **Pinellas Park** Florida, SE USA 27°50′N 82°42′W
10 M13 **Pine Pass** pass British Columbia, W Canada
8 J10 **Pine Point** Northwest Territories, W Canada 60°52′N 114°30′W
28 K12 **Pine Ridge** South Dakota, N USA 43°01′N 102°33′W
29 U6 **Pine River** Minnesota, N USA 46°43′N 94°24′W
31 Q8 **Pine River** Michigan, N USA
30 M4 **Pine River** Wisconsin, N USA
106 A8 **Pinerolo** Piemonte, NE Italy 44°56′N 07°21′E
115 I15 **Pínes, Akrotírio** var. Akrotírio Pínnes. headland N Greece 40°06′N 24°19′E
25 W6 **Pines, Lake O' the** Texas, SW USA
Pines, The Isle of the see Juventud, Isla de la
Pine Tree State see Maine
21 N7 **Pineville** Kentucky, S USA 36°47′N 83°43′W
22 H7 **Pineville** Louisiana, S USA 31°19′N 92°25′W
27 R8 **Pineville** Missouri, C USA 36°36′N 94°23′W
21 R10 **Pineville** North Carolina, SE USA 35°04′N 80°53′W
21 Q6 **Pineville** West Virginia, NE USA 37°35′N 81°34′W
33 V8 **Piney Buttes** physical region Montana, NW USA
163 W9 **Ping'an** Jilin, NE China 44°36′N 127°13′E
160 H14 **Pingbian** var. Pingbian Miaozu Zizhixian, Yuping. Yunnan, SW China 22°51′N 103°28′E
Pingbian Miaozu Zizhixian see Pingbian
157 S9 **Pingdingshan** Henan, C China 33°52′N 113°20′E
161 R4 **Pingdu** Shandong, E China 36°50′N 119°55′E
189 W16 **Pingelap Atoll** atoll Caroline Islands, E Micronesia
160 K14 **Pingguo** var. Matou. Guangxi Zhuangzu Zizhiqu, S China 23°24′N 107°30′E
161 Q13 **Pinghe** var. Xiaoxi. Fujian, SE China 24°30′N 117°19′E
P'ing-hsiang see Pingxiang
161 N10 **Pingjiang** Hunan, S China 28°44′N 113°33′E
Pingkiang see Harbin
160 L8 **Pingli** Shaanxi, C China 32°27′N 109°21′E
159 W10 **Pingliang** var. Kongtong, P'ing-liang. Gansu, C China 35°27′N 106°38′E
P'ing-liang see Pingliang
159 W8 **Pingluo** Ningxia, N China 38°55′N 106°31′E
Pingma see Tiandong
167 O7 **Ping, Mae Nam** W Thailand
161 Q1 **Pingquan** Hebei, E China 41°02′N 118°35′E
29 P5 **Pingree** North Dakota, N USA 47°07′N 98°54′W
Pingsiang see Pingxiang
161 S14 **P'ingtung** Jap. Heitō. S Taiwan 22°40′N 120°30′E
160 I8 **Pingwu** var. Long'an. Sichuan, C China 32°33′N 104°32′E
160 J15 **Pingxiang** Guangxi Zhuangzu Zizhiqu, S China 22°03′N 106°44′E
161 O11 **Pingxiang** var. P'ing-hsiang; prev. Pingsiang. Jiangxi, S China 27°42′N 113°50′E
Pingxiang see Tongwei
161 S11 **Pingyang** var. Kunyang. Zhejiang, SE China 27°46′N 120°37′E
161 P5 **Pingyi** Shandong, E China 35°30′N 117°38′E
161 P5 **Pingyin** Shandong, E China 36°18′N 116°24′E
60 H13 **Pinhalzinho** Santa Catarina, S Brazil 26°53′S 52°57′W
60 I12 **Pinhão** Paraná, S Brazil 25°46′S 51°32′W
61 H17 **Pinheiro Machado** Rio Grande do Sul, S Brazil 31°34′S 53°22′W
104 I7 **Pinhel** Guarda, N Portugal 40°47′N 07°03′W
Piniós see Pineiós
168 I11 **Pini, Pulau** island Kepulauan Batu, W Indonesia
109 Y7 **Pinka** SE Austria
109 X7 **Pinkafeld** Burgenland, SE Austria 47°23′N 16°08′E
Pinkiang see Harbin
10 M12 **Pink Mountain** British Columbia, W Canada 57°10′N 122°36′W
166 M3 **Pinlebu** Sagaing, N Burma (Myanmar) 24°02′N 95°21′E
38 J12 **Pinnacle Island** island Alaska, USA
180 I12 **Pinnacles, The** tourist site Western Australia
182 K10 **Pinnaroo** South Australia 35°17′S 140°54′E
Pinne see Pniewy
100 I9 **Pinneberg** Schleswig-Holstein, N Germany 53°40′N 09°49′E
Pínnes, Akrotírio see Píńes, Akrotírio
Pinos, Isla de see Juventud, Isla de la
35 R14 **Pinos, Mount** ▲ California, W USA 34°48′N 119°09′W
105 R12 **Pinoso** País Valenciano, E Spain 38°25′N 01°02′W
105 N14 **Pinos-Puente** Andalucía, S Spain 37°16′N 03°46′W
41 Q17 **Pinotepa Nacional** var. Santiago Pinotepa Nacional. Oaxaca, SE Mexico 16°20′N 98°02′W
114 F13 **Pínovo** ▲ N Greece 41°06′N 22°19′E
187 R17 **Pins, Île des** var. Kunyé. island E New Caledonia
119 I20 **Pinsk** Pol. Pińsk. Brestskaya Voblasts', SW Belarus 52°07′N 26°07′E
14 D18 **Pins, Pointe aux** headland Ontario, S Canada 42°14′N 81°53′W
57 B16 **Pinta, Isla** var. Abingdon. island Galapagos Islands, Ecuador, E Pacific Ocean
125 Q12 **Pinyug** Kirovskaya Oblast', NW Russian Federation 60°12′N 47°45′E
57 B17 **Pinzón, Isla** var. Duncan Island. island Galapagos Islands, Ecuador, E Pacific Ocean
35 Y8 **Pioche** Nevada, W USA 37°57′N 114°30′W
106 F13 **Piombino** Toscana, C Italy 42°54′N 10°30′E
0 C9 **Pioneer Fracture Zone** tectonic feature NE Pacific Ocean
122 L5 **Pioner, Ostrov** island Severnaya Zemlya, N Russian Federation
118 A13 **Pionerskiy** Ger. Neukuhren. Kaliningradskaya Oblast', W Russian Federation 54°57′N 20°16′E
110 N13 **Pionki** Mazowieckie, C Poland 51°30′N 21°27′E
184 L9 **Piopio** Waikato, North Island, New Zealand 38°27′S 175°00′E
110 K13 **Piotrków Trybunalski** Ger. Petrikau, Rus. Petrokov. Łodzkie, C Poland 51°25′N 19°42′E
152 F12 **Pīpār Road** Rājasthān, N India 26°25′N 73°29′E
115 I16 **Pipéri** island Vóreies Sporádes, Greece, Aegean Sea
29 S10 **Pipestone** Minnesota, N USA 44°00′N 96°19′W
12 C9 **Pipestone** Ontario, C Canada
61 E21 **Pipinas** Buenos Aires, E Argentina 35°32′S 57°20′W
149 T7 **Piplān** prev. Liaqatabad. Punjab, E Pakistan 32°17′N 71°24′E
15 R5 **Pipmuacan, Réservoir** Québec, SE Canada
Piqan see Shanshan
31 R13 **Piqua** Ohio, N USA 40°08′N 84°14′W
105 P5 **Piqueras, Puerto de** pass N Spain
60 H11 **Piquiri, Rio** S Brazil
60 L9 **Piracicaba** São Paulo, S Brazil 22°45′S 47°40′W
Piraeus/Piraiévs see Peiraías
60 K10 **Piraju** São Paulo, S Brazil 23°12′S 49°24′W
60 K9 **Pirajuí** São Paulo, S Brazil 21°58′S 49°27′W
63 G21 **Pirámide, Cerro** ▲ S Chile 49°06′S 73°32′W
Piramiva see Pyramíva
109 R13 **Piran** It. Pirano. SW Slovenia 45°35′N 13°35′E
62 N6 **Pirané** Formosa, N Argentina 25°42′S 59°06′W
59 J18 **Piranhas** Goiás, S Brazil 16°24′S 51°51′W
Pirano see Piran
142 I4 **Pīrānshahr** Āžarbāyjān-e Gharbī, NW Iran 36°41′N 45°08′E
59 M19 **Pirapora** Minas Gerais, NE Brazil 17°20′S 44°54′W
60 I9 **Pirapòzinho** São Paulo, S Brazil 22°17′S 51°31′W
61 G19 **Piraraja** Lavalleja, S Uruguay 33°44′S 54°45′W
60 L9 **Pirassununga** São Paulo, S Brazil 21°58′S 47°23′W
45 V6 **Pirata, Monte** ▲ E Puerto Rico 18°06′N 65°33′W
60 I13 **Piratuba** Santa Catarina, S Brazil 27°26′S 51°47′W
114 I9 **Pirdop** prev. Strednogorie. Sofiya, W Bulgaria 42°44′N 24°09′E
191 P7 **Pirea** Tahiti, W French Polynesia
59 K18 **Pirenópolis** Goiás, S Brazil 15°48′S 49°00′W
153 S13 **Pirganj** Rajshahi, NW Bangladesh 25°51′N 88°25′E
Pirgi see Pyrgí
Pírgos see Pýrgos
61 F20 **Piriápolis** Maldonado, S Uruguay 34°51′S 55°15′W
114 G11 **Pirin** ▲▲ SW Bulgaria
Pirineos see Pyrenees
58 N13 **Piripiri** Piauí, E Brazil 04°15′S 41°46′W
118 H4 **Pirita** var. Pirita Jõgi. NW Estonia
Pirita Jõgi see Pirita
54 J6 **Píritu** Portuguesa, N Venezuela 09°21′N 69°16′W
93 L18 **Pirkkala** Länsi-Suomi, W Finland 61°27′N 23°47′E
101 F20 **Pirmasens** Rheinland-Pfalz, SW Germany 49°12′N 07°37′E
101 P16 **Pirna** Sachsen, E Germany 50°57′N 13°56′E
Piroe see Piru
113 Q15 **Pirot** Serbia, SE Serbia 43°12′N 22°34′E
152 H6 **Pīr Panjāl Range** ▲▲ NE India
43 W16 **Pirre, Cerro** ▲ SE Panama 07°54′N 77°42′W
137 Y11 **Pirsaat** Rus. Pirsagat. E Azerbaijan
Pirsagat see Pirsaat
143 V11 **Pīr Shūrān, Selseleh-ye** ▲▲ SE Iran
92 M12 **Pirttikoski** Lappi, N Finland 66°20′N 27°08′E
Pirttikylä see Pörtom
171 R13 **Piru** prev. Piroe. Pulau Seram, E Indonesia 03°01′S 128°10′E
Piryatin see Pyryatyn
Pis see Piis Moen
106 F11 **Pisa** var. Pisae. Toscana, C Italy 43°43′N 10°23′E
Pisae see Pisa
189 V12 **Pisar** atoll Chuuk Islands, C Micronesia
Pisaurum see Pesaro
14 M10 **Piscatosine, Lac** Québec, SE Canada
109 W7 **Pischeldorf** Steiermark, SE Austria 47°11′N 15°48′E
Pischk see Simeria
107 L19 **Pisciotta** Campania, S Italy 40°07′N 15°13′E
57 E16 **Pisco** Ica, SW Peru 13°46′S 76°12′W
116 G9 **Pişcolt** Hung. Piskolt. Satu Mare, NW Romania 47°35′N 22°18′E
57 E16 **Pisco, Río** E Peru
111 C18 **Písek** Budějovický Kraj, S Czech Republic 49°19′N 14°07′E
31 R14 **Pisgah** Ohio, N USA 39°19′N 84°22′W
Pisha see Ningnan
158 F9 **Pishan** var. Guma. Xinjiang Uygur Zizhiqu, NW China 37°36′N 78°45′E
117 N8 **Pishchanka** Vinnyts'ka Oblast', C Ukraine 48°12′N 28°52′E
113 K21 **Pishë** Fier, SW Albania 40°40′N 19°22′E
143 X14 **Pīshīn** Sīstān va Balūchestān, SE Iran 26°05′N 61°46′E
149 O9 **Pishīn** North-West Frontier Province, NW Pakistan 30°33′N 67°01′E
149 N11 **Pishin Lora** var. Psein Lora, Pash. Pseyn Bowr. SW Pakistan
Pishma see Pizhma
Pishpek see Bishkek
171 O14 **Pising** Pulau Kabaena, C Indonesia 05°07′S 121°50′E
Pisino see Pazin
Piski see Simeria
Piskolt see Pişcolt
147 Q9 **Piskom** Rus. Pskem. E Uzbekistan
Piskom Tizmasi see Pskemskiy Khrebet
35 P13 **Pismo Beach** California, W USA 35°08′N 120°38′W
77 P12 **Pissila** C Burkina 13°07′N 00°51′W
62 H8 **Pissis, Monte** ▲ N Argentina 27°45′S 68°43′W
41 X12 **Piste** Yucatán, E Mexico 20°40′N 88°34′W
107 O18 **Pisticci** Basilicata, S Italy 40°23′N 16°33′E
106 F11 **Pistoia** anc. Pistoria, Pistoriæ. Toscana, C Italy 43°57′N 10°53′E
32 E15 **Pistol River** Oregon, NW USA 42°13′N 124°23′W
Pistoria/Pistoriæ see Pistoia
15 U5 **Pistuacanis** Québec, SE Canada
Pistyan see Piešt'any
104 M5 **Pisuerga** N Spain
110 N8 **Pisz** Ger. Johannisburg. Warmińsko-Mazurskie, NE Poland 53°37′N 21°49′E
76 I13 **Pita** NW Guinea 11°05′N 12°15′W
54 D12 **Pitalito** Huila, S Colombia 01°51′N 76°01′W
60 I11 **Pitanga** Paraná, S Brazil 24°45′S 51°43′W
182 M9 **Pitarpunga Lake** salt lake New South Wales, SE Australia
193 P10 **Pitcairn Island** island S Pitcairn Islands
193 P10 **Pitcairn Islands** ◇ UK dependent territory C Pacific Ocean
93 J14 **Piteå** Norrbotten, N Sweden 65°19′N 21°30′E
92 I13 **Piteälven** N Sweden
116 I13 **Piteşti** Argeş, S Romania 44°53′N 24°49′E
Pithagorio see Pythagóreio
180 I12 **Pithara** Western Australia 30°31′S 116°38′E
103 N6 **Pithiviers** Loiret, C France 48°10′N 02°15′E
152 L9 **Pithorāgarh** Uttarakhand, N India 29°35′N 80°12′E
188 B16 **Piti** W Guam 13°28′N 144°42′E
106 G13 **Pitigliano** Toscana, C Italy 42°38′N 11°40′E
40 F3 **Pitiquito** Sonora, NW Mexico 30°39′N 112°00′W
Pitkäranta see Pitkyaranta
38 M11 **Pitkas Point** Alaska, USA 62°01′N 163°17′W
124 H11 **Pitkyaranta** Fin. Pitkäranta. Respublika Kareliya, NW Russian Federation 61°34′N 31°27′E
96 J10 **Pitlochry** C Scotland, United Kingdom 56°47′N 03°48′W
18 I16 **Pitman** New Jersey, NE USA 39°43′N 75°06′W
146 I9 **Pitnak** var. Drujba, Rus. Druzhba. Xorazm Viloyati, W Uzbekistan 41°14′N 61°13′E
112 G8 **Pitomača** Virovitica-Podravina, NE Croatia 45°57′N 17°14′E
35 O2 **Pit River** California, W USA
63 G15 **Pitrufquén** Araucanía, S Chile 38°59′S 72°40′W
Pitsanulok see Phitsanulok
Pitschen see Byczyna
Pitsunda see Bichvint'a
109 X6 **Pitten** E Austria
10 J14 **Pitt Island** island British Columbia, W Canada
Pitt Island see Makin
22 M3 **Pittsboro** Mississippi, S USA 33°55′N 89°20′W
21 T9 **Pittsboro** North Carolina, SE USA 35°46′N 79°12′W
27 R7 **Pittsburg** Kansas, C USA 37°24′N 94°42′W
25 W6 **Pittsburg** Texas, SW USA 33°00′N 94°58′W
18 B14 **Pittsburgh** Pennsylvania, NE USA 40°26′N 80°W
30 J14 **Pittsfield** Illinois, N USA 39°36′N 90°48′W
19 R6 **Pittsfield** Maine, NE USA 44°46′N 69°22′W
18 L11 **Pittsfield** Massachusetts, NE USA 42°27′N 73°15′W
183 U3 **Pittsworth** Queensland, E Australia 27°43′S 151°36′E
62 I8 **Pituil** La Rioja, NW Argentina 28°33′S 67°24′W
56 A10 **Piura** Piura, NW Peru 05°11′S 80°41′W
56 A9 **Piura** off. Departamento de Piura. department NW Peru
Piura, Departamento de see Piura
35 S13 **Piute Peak** ▲ California, W USA 35°27′N 118°24′W
113 J15 **Piva** NW Montenegro
117 V5 **Pivdenne** Kharkivs'ka Oblast', E Ukraine 49°52′N 36°04′E
117 P8 **Pivdennyy Buh** Rus. Yuzhnyy Bug. S Ukraine
54 F5 **Pivijay** Magdalena, N Colombia 10°31′N 74°36′W
109 T13 **Pivka** prev. Šent Peter, Ger. Sankt Peter, It. San Pietro del Carso. SW Slovenia 45°41′N 14°12′E
117 U13 **Pivnichno-Kryms'kyy Kanal** canal S Ukraine
113 J15 **Pivsko Jezero** NW Montenegro
111 M18 **Piwniczna** Małopolskie, S Poland 49°26′N 20°43′E
35 R12 **Pixley** California, W USA 35°58′N 119°18′W
125 Q15 **Pizhma** var. Pishma. NW Russian Federation
13 U13 **Placentia** Newfoundland, Newfoundland and Labrador, SE Canada 47°12′N 53°58′W
Placentia see Piacenza
13 U13 **Placentia Bay** inlet Newfoundland, Newfoundland and Labrador, SE Canada
171 P5 **Placer** Masbate, N Philippines 11°54′N 123°54′E
35 P7 **Placerville** California, W USA 38°42′N 120°48′W
44 F5 **Placetas** Villa Clara, C Cuba 22°18′N 79°40′W
113 Q18 **Plačkovica** ▲▲ E Macedonia
36 L2 **Plain City** Utah, W USA 41°18′N 112°05′W
22 G4 **Plain Dealing** Louisiana, S USA 32°54′N 93°42′W
31 O14 **Plainfield** Indiana, N USA 39°42′N 86°18′W
18 K14 **Plainfield** New Jersey, NE USA 40°37′N 74°25′W
33 O8 **Plains** Montana, NW USA 47°27′N 114°52′W
24 L6 **Plains** Texas, SW USA 33°12′N 102°50′W
29 X10 **Plainview** Minnesota, N USA 44°10′N 92°10′W
29 Q13 **Plainview** Nebraska, C USA 42°21′N 97°47′W
25 N4 **Plainview** Texas, SW USA 34°12′N 101°43′W
26 K4 **Plainville** Kansas, C USA 39°13′N 99°18′W
115 I22 **Pláka** var. Mílos. Mílos, Kykládes, Greece, Aegean Sea 36°44′N 24°25′E
115 J15 **Pláka, Akrotírio** headland Límnos, E Greece 40°02′N 25°25′E
113 N19 **Plakenska Planina** ▲▲ SW Macedonia
44 K5 **Plana Cays** islets SE Bahamas
105 S12 **Plana, Isla** var. Nueva Tabarca. island E Spain
59 L18 **Planaltina** Goiás, S Brazil 15°35′S 47°28′W
83 O14 **Planalto Moçambicano** plateau N Mozambique
112 N10 **Plandište** Vojvodina, NE Serbia 45°13′N 21°07′E
100 N13 **Plane** NE Germany
54 E6 **Planeta Rica** Córdoba, NW Colombia 08°24′N 75°39′W
29 P11 **Plankinton** South Dakota, N USA 43°43′N 98°28′W
30 M11 **Plano** Illinois, N USA 41°39′N 88°32′W
25 U6 **Plano** Texas, SW USA 33°01′N 96°42′W
23 W12 **Plant City** Florida, SE USA 28°01′N 82°06′W
22 J9 **Plaquemine** Louisiana, S USA 30°17′N 91°13′W
104 K9 **Plasencia** Extremadura, W Spain 40°02′N 06°05′W
110 P7 **Płaska** Podlaskie, NE Poland 53°55′N 23°18′E
112 C10 **Plaški** Karlovac, C Croatia 45°04′N 15°21′E
113 N19 **Plasnica** SW FYR Macedonia 41°28′N 21°07′E
13 N14 **Plaster Rock** New Brunswick, SE Canada 46°55′N 67°24′W
107 J24 **Platani** anc. Halycus. Sicilia, Italy, C Mediterranean Sea
115 G17 **Plataniá** Thessalía, C Greece 39°09′N 23°15′E
115 G24 **Plátanos** Kríti, Greece, E Mediterranean Sea 35°27′N 23°34′E
65 H18 **Plata, Río de la** var. River Plate. estuary Argentina/Uruguay
77 V15 **Plateau** state C Nigeria
79 G19 **Plateaux** var. Région des Plateaux. province C Congo
Plateaux, Région des see Plateaux
Plate, Île see Flat Island
92 P1 **Platen, Kapp** headland NE Svalbard 80°30′N 22°46′E
Plate, River see Plata, Río de la
99 G22 **Plate Taille, Lac de la** var. L'Eau d'Heure. SE Belgium
Plathe see Płoty
39 N13 **Platinum** Alaska, USA 59°01′N 161°49′W
54 F5 **Plato** Magdalena, N Colombia 09°47′N 74°47′W
29 O11 **Platte** South Dakota, N USA 43°20′N 98°51′W
27 R3 **Platte City** Missouri, C USA 39°22′N 94°47′W
Plattensee see Balaton
27 R3 **Platte River** Iowa/Missouri, USA
29 Q15 **Platte River** Nebraska, C USA
37 T3 **Platteville** Colorado, C USA 40°13′N 104°49′W
30 K9 **Platteville** Wisconsin, N USA 42°44′N 90°27′W
101 N21 **Plattling** Bayern, SE Germany 48°45′N 12°52′E
27 R3 **Plattsburg** Missouri, C USA 39°33′N 94°27′W
18 L6 **Plattsburgh** New York, NE USA 44°42′N 73°29′W
29 S15 **Plattsmouth** Nebraska, C USA 41°00′N 95°52′W
101 M17 **Plauen** var. Plauen im Vogtland. Sachsen, E Germany 50°31′N 12°08′E
Plauen im Vogtland see Plauen
100 M10 **Plauer See** NE Germany
113 L16 **Plav** E Montenegro 42°36′N 19°57′E
118 I10 **Pļaviņas** Ger. Stockmannshof. Aizkraukle, S Latvia 56°37′N 25°40′E
126 K5 **Plavsk** Tul'skaya Oblast', W Russian Federation 53°42′N 37°21′E
41 Z12 **Playa del Carmen** Quintana Roo, E Mexico 20°37′N 87°04′W
40 J12 **Playa Los Corchos** Nayarit, SW Mexico 21°91′N 105°28′W
37 P16 **Playas Lake** New Mexico, SW USA
41 S15 **Playa Vicenté** Veracruz-Llave, SE Mexico 17°42′N 95°01′W
167 U11 **Plây Cu** var. Pleiku. Gia Lai, C Vietnam 13°57′N 108°01′E
28 L3 **Plaza** North Dakota, N USA 48°00′N 102°00′W
63 I15 **Plaza Huincul** Neuquén, C Argentina 38°55′S 69°14′W
36 L3 **Pleasant Grove** Utah, W USA 40°21′N 111°44′W
29 V14 **Pleasant Hill** Iowa, C USA 41°34′N 93°31′W
27 R4 **Pleasant Hill** Missouri, C USA 38°47′N 94°16′W
Pleasant Island see Nauru
36 K13 **Pleasant, Lake** Arizona, SW USA
19 P8 **Pleasant Mountain** ▲ Maine, NE USA 44°01′N 70°47′W
27 R5 **Pleasanton** Kansas, C USA 38°09′N 94°43′W
25 R12 **Pleasanton** Texas, SW USA 28°58′N 98°28′W
185 G20 **Pleasant Point** Canterbury, South Island, New Zealand 44°16′S 171°09′E
19 R5 **Pleasant River** Maine, NE USA
18 J17 **Pleasantville** New Jersey, NE USA 39°22′N 74°31′W
103 N12 **Pléaux** Cantal, C France 45°08′N 02°10′E
111 B19 **Plechý** var. Plöckenstein. ▲ Austria/Czech Republic 48°45′N 13°50′E
Pleebo see Plibo
Pleihari see Pelaihari
Pleiku see Plây Cu
101 M16 **Pleisse** E Germany
Plencia see Plentzia
184 O7 **Plenty, Bay of** bay North Island, New Zealand
33 Y6 **Plentywood** Montana, NW USA 48°46′N 104°33′W
105 O2 **Plentzia** var. Plencia. País Vasco, N Spain 43°25′N 02°56′W
102 H5 **Plérin** Côtes d'Armor, NW France 48°33′N 02°46′W
124 M10 **Plesetsk** Arkhangel'skaya Oblast', NW Russian Federation 62°41′N 40°14′E
Pleshchenitsy see Plyeshchanitsy
Pleskau see Pskov
Pleskauer See see Pskov, Lake
Pleskava see Pskov
112 E8 **Pleso International** (Zagreb) Zagreb, NW Croatia 45°45′N 16°00′E
Pless see Pszczyna
15 Q11 **Plessisville** Québec, SE Canada 46°14′N 71°46′W
110 H12 **Pleszew** Wielkopolskie, C Poland 51°54′N 17°47′E
12 L10 **Plétipi, Lac** Québec, SE Canada
101 F15 **Plettenberg** Nordrhein-Westfalen, W Germany 51°13′N 07°52′E
114 I8 **Pleven** prev. Plevna. Pleven, N Bulgaria 43°25′N 24°36′E
114 I8 **Pleven** province N Bulgaria
Plevlja/Plevlje see Pljevlja
Plevna see Pleven
Plezzo see Bovec
Pliberk see Bleiburg
76 L17 **Plibo** var. Pleebo. SE Liberia 04°38′N 07°41′W
121 R11 **Pliny Trench** undersea feature C Mediterranean Sea
118 K13 **Plisa** Rus. Plissa. Vitsyebskaya Voblasts', N Belarus 55°13′N 27°57′E
Plissa see Plisa
112 D11 **Plitvica Selo** Lika-Senj, W Croatia 44°53′N 15°36′E
112 D11 **Plješevica** ▲▲ C Croatia
113 K14 **Pljevlja** prev. Plevlja, Plevlje. N Montenegro 43°21′N 19°21′E
Ploça see Plocë
Plocce see Ploče
113 K22 **Plocë** var. Ploça. Vlorë, SW Albania 40°24′N 19°41′E
113 G15 **Ploče** It. Plocce; prev. Kardeljevo. Dubrovnik-Neretva, SE Croatia 43°02′N 17°25′E
110 K11 **Płock** Ger. Plozk. Mazowieckie, C Poland 52°32′N 19°40′E
109 Q10 **Plöcken Pass** Ger. Plöckenpass, It. Passo di Monte Croce Carnico. pass SW Austria
Plöckenpass see Plöcken Pass
Plöckenstein see Plechý
99 B19 **Ploegsteert** Hainaut, W Belgium 50°45′N 02°52′E
102 H6 **Ploërmel** Morbihan, NW France 47°57′N 02°24′W
Ploeşti see Ploieşti
116 K13 **Ploieşti** prev. Ploeşti. Prahova, SE Romania 44°56′N 26°03′E
115 L17 **Plomári** prev. Plomárion. Lésvos, E Greece 38°58′N 26°24′E
Plomárion see Plomári
103 O12 **Plomb du Cantal** ▲ C France 45°03′N 02°48′E
183 V6 **Plomer, Point** headland New South Wales, SE Australia 31°19′S 153°00′E
100 J8 **Plön** Schleswig-Holstein, N Germany 54°10′N 10°25′E
110 L11 **Płońsk** Mazowieckie, C Poland 52°38′N 20°23′E
119 J20 **Plotnitsa** Brestskaya Voblasts', SW Belarus 52°03′N 26°39′E
110 E8 **Płoty** Ger. Plathe. Zachodnio-pomorskie, NW Poland 53°48′N 15°16′E
102 G7 **Plouay** Morbihan, NW France 47°54′N 03°14′W
111 D15 **Ploučnice** Ger. Polzen. NE Czech Republic
114 I10 **Plovdiv** prev. Eumolpias; anc. Evmolpia, Philippopolis, Lat. Trimontium. Plovdiv, C Bulgaria 42°09′N 24°47′E
114 I11 **Plovdiv** province C Bulgaria
30 L6 **Plover** Wisconsin, N USA 44°30′N 89°33′W
Plozk see Płock
27 U11 **Plumerville** Arkansas, C USA 35°09′N 92°38′W
19 P10 **Plum Island** island Massachusetts, NE USA
32 M9 **Plummer** Idaho, NW USA 47°19′N 116°54′W
83 J18 **Plumtree** Matabeleland South, SW Zimbabwe 20°30′S 27°50′E
118 D11 **Plungė** Telšiai, W Lithuania 55°55′N 21°53′E
113 J15 **Plužine** NW Montenegro 43°08′N 18°49′E
119 K14 **Plyeshchanitsy** Rus. Pleshchenitsy. Minskaya Voblasts', N Belarus 54°25′N 27°50′E
45 V10 **Plymouth** ○ (Montserrat) SW Montserrat 16°44′N 62°14′W
97 I24 **Plymouth** SW England, United Kingdom 50°23′N 04°10′W
31 O11 **Plymouth** Indiana, N USA 41°20′N 86°19′W
19 P12 **Plymouth** Massachusetts, NE USA 41°57′N 70°40′W
19 N8 **Plymouth** New Hampshire, NE USA 43°43′N 71°39′W
21 X9 **Plymouth** North Carolina, SE USA 35°53′N 76°46′W
30 M8 **Plymouth** Wisconsin, N USA 43°48′N 87°58′W
97 J20 **Plynlimon** ▲ C Wales, United Kingdom 52°27′N 03°48′W
124 G14 **Plyussa** Pskovskaya Oblast', W Russian Federation 58°27′N 29°21′E
111 B17 **Plzeň** Ger. Pilsen, Pol. Pilzno. Plzeňský Kraj, W Czech Republic 49°45′N 13°23′E
111 B17 **Plzeňský Kraj** region W Czech Republic
110 F11 **Pniewy** Ger. Pinne. Wielkolpolskie, W Poland 52°31′N 16°14′E
77 P13 **Pô** S Burkina 11°11′N 01°10′W
106 D8 **Po** N Italy
42 M13 **Poás, Volcán** NW Costa Rica 10°12′N 84°12′W
77 S16 **Pobè** S Benin 07°00′N 02°41′E
123 S8 **Pobeda, Gora** ▲ NE Russian Federation 65°28′N 145°44′E
Pobeda Peak see Pobedy, Pik/Tomur Feng
147 Z7 **Pobedy, Pik** Chin. Tomür Feng. ▲ China/Kyrgyzstan 42°02′N 80°02′E see also Tomür Feng
Pobedy, Pik see Tomür Feng
110 H11 **Pobiedziska** Ger. Pudewitz. Wielkolpolskie, C Poland 52°30′N 17°19′E
Po, Bocche del see Po, Foci del
27 W9 **Pocahontas** Arkansas, C USA 36°15′N 91°00′W
29 U12 **Pocahontas** Iowa, C USA 42°44′N 94°40′W
33 Q15 **Pocatello** Idaho, NW USA 42°52′N 112°27′W
167 S13 **Pochentong** (Phnum Penh) Phnum Penh, S Cambodia 11°24′N 104°52′E
126 I6 **Pochep** Bryanskaya Oblast', W Russian Federation 52°56′N 33°20′E
126 H4 **Pochinok** Smolenskaya Oblast', W Russian Federation 54°21′N 32°29′E
41 R17 **Pochutla** var. San Pedro Pochutla. Oaxaca, SE Mexico 15°45′N 96°30′W
62 I6 **Pocitos, Salar** var. Salar Quiróm. salt lake NW Argentina
101 O22 **Pocking** Bayern, SE Germany 48°22′N 13°17′E
186 I10 **Pocklington Reef** reef SE Papua New Guinea
59 P15 **Poço da Cruz, Açude** E Brazil
27 R11 **Pocola** Oklahoma, C USA 35°13′N 94°28′W
21 Y5 **Pocomoke City** Maryland, NE USA 38°04′N 75°34′W
59 L21 **Poços de Caldas** Minas Gerais, NE Brazil 21°48′S 46°33′W
124 H14 **Podberez'ye** Novgorodskaya Oblast', NW Russian Federation 58°42′N 31°22′E
Podbrodzie see Pabradė
125 U8 **Podcher'ye** Respublika Komi, NW Russian Federation 63°55′N 57°34′E
111 E16 **Poděbrady** Ger. Podiebrad. Středočeský Kraj, C Czech Republic 50°10′N 15°06′E
126 L9 **Podgorenskiy** Voronezhskaya Oblast', W Russian Federation 50°22′N 39°43′E
113 J17 **Podgorica** prev. Titograd. ● S Montenegro 42°25′N 19°16′E
113 K17 **Podgorica** S Montenegro 42°22′N 19°16′E
109 T13 **Podgrad** SW Slovenia 45°31′N 14°09′E
Podiebrad see Poděbrady
116 M5 **Podil's'ka Vysochina** plateau W Ukraine
Podium Anicensis see le Puy
122 L11 **Podkamennaya Tunguska** Eng. Stony Tunguska. C Russian Federation
111 N17 **Podkarpackie** province SW Poland
Pod Klošter see Arnoldstein
110 P9 **Podlaskie** province Mazowieckie, C Poland
127 Q8 **Podlesnoye** Saratovskaya Oblast', W Russian Federation 51°51′N 47°03′E
126 K4 **Podol'sk** Moskovskaya Oblast', W Russian Federation 55°24′N 37°30′E
76 H10 **Podor** N Senegal 16°40′N 14°57′W
125 P12 **Podosinovets** Kirovskaya Oblast', NW Russian Federation 60°15′N 47°06′E
124 I12 **Podporozh'ye** Leningradskaya Oblast', NW Russian Federation 60°52′N 34°00′E
Podravska Slatina see Slatina
112 J13 **Podromanlja** Republika Srpska, SE Bosnia and Herzegovina 43°55′N 18°46′E
Podsvil'ye see Padsvillye
116 L9 **Podu Iloaiei** prev. Podul Iloaiei. Iaşi, NE Romania 47°13′N 27°16′E
113 N15 **Podujevë** Serb. Podujevo. N Kosovo 42°56′N 21°13′E
Podujevo see Podujevë
Podul Iloaiei see Podu Iloaiei
Podunajská Rovina see Little Alföld
124 M12 **Podyuga** Arkhangel'skaya Oblast', NW Russian Federation 61°04′N 40°46′E
56 A9 **Poechos, Embalse** NW Peru
55 W10 **Poeketi** Sipaliwini, E Surinam
100 L8 **Poel** island N Germany
83 M20 **Poelela, Lagoa** S Mozambique
Poerwodadi see Purwodadi
Poerwokerto see Purwokerto
Poerworedjo see Purworejo
Poetovio see Ptuj
83 E23 **Pofadder** Northern Cape, W South Africa 29°09′S 19°25′E
106 I9 **Po, Foci del** var. Bocche del Po. NE Italy
116 E12 **Pogăniş** W Romania
Pogegen see Pagėgiai
106 G12 **Poggibonsi** Toscana, C Italy 43°28′N 11°09′E
107 I14 **Poggio Mirteto** Lazio, C Italy 42°17′N 12°42′E
109 V4 **Pöggstall** Niederösterreich, N Austria 48°19′N 15°10′E
116 L13 **Pogoanele** Buzău, SE Romania 44°55′N 27°00′E
Pogónion see Delvináki
113 M21 **Pogradec** var. Pogradeci. Korçë, SE Albania 40°54′N 20°40′E
Pogradeci see Pogradec
123 S15 **Pogranichnyy** Primorskiy Kray, SE Russian Federation 44°18′N 131°33′E
38 M16 **Pogromni Volcano** ▲ Unimak Island, Alaska, USA 54°34′N 164°41′W
163 Z15 **P'ohang** Jap. Hokō. E South Korea 36°02′N 129°20′E
15 T9 **Pohénégamook, Lac** Québec, SE Canada
93 L20 **Pohja** Swe. Pojo. Etelä-Suomi, SW Finland 60°07′N 23°30′E
Pohjanlahti see Bothnia, Gulf of
189 U16 **Pohnpei** state E Micronesia
189 O12 **Pohnpei** Pohnpei, E Micronesia
189 O12 **Pohnpei** prev. Ponape Ascension Island. island E Micronesia
111 F19 **Pohořelice** Ger. Pohrlitz. Jihomoravský Kraj, SE Czech Republic 48°58′N 16°30′E
109 V10 **Pohorje** Ger. Bacher. ▲▲ N Slovenia
117 N6 **Pohrebyshche** Vinnyts'ka Oblast', C Ukraine 49°31′N 29°16′E
Pohrlitz see Pohořelice
161 P9 **Po Hu** E China
116 G15 **Poiana Mare** Dolj, S Romania 43°55′N 23°02′E
Poictiers see Poitiers
127 N6 **Poim** Penzenskaya Oblast', W Russian Federation 53°03′N 43°11′E
159 N15 **Poindo** Xigzang Zizhiqu, W China 29°58′N 91°20′E
195 Y13 **Poinsett, Cape** headland Antarctica 65°35′S 113°00′E
29 R9 **Poinsett, Lake** South Dakota, N USA
22 I10 **Point Au Fer Island** island Louisiana, S USA
39 X14 **Point Baker** Prince of Wales Island, Alaska, USA 56°19′N 133°31′W
25 U13 **Point Comfort** Texas, SW USA 28°40′N 96°33′W
Point de Galle see Galle
44 K10 **Pointe à Gravois** headland SW Haiti 18°00′N 73°53′W
22 L10 **Pointe a la Hache** Louisiana, S USA 29°34′N 89°48′W
45 Y6 **Pointe-à-Pitre** Grande Terre, C Guadeloupe 16°14′N 61°32′W
15 U7 **Pointe-au-Père** Québec, SE Canada 48°31′N 68°27′W
15 V5 **Pointe-aux-Anglais** Québec, SE Canada 49°40′N 67°09′W
45 T10 **Pointe Du Cap** headland N Saint Lucia 14°06′N 60°56′W
79 E21 **Pointe-Noire** Kouilou, S Congo 04°46′S 11°53′E
45 X6 **Pointe Noire** Basse Terre, W Guadeloupe 16°14′N 61°47′W
79 E21 **Pointe-Noire** Kouilou, S Congo 04°45′S 11°55′E
45 U15 **Point Fortin** Trinidad, Trinidad and Tobago 10°12′N 61°41′W
38 M6 **Point Hope** Alaska, USA 68°21′N 166°48′W
39 N5 **Point Lay** Alaska, USA 69°42′N 162°57′W
18 B16 **Point Marion** Pennsylvania, NE USA 39°44′N 79°53′W
18 K16 **Point Pleasant** New Jersey, NE USA 40°04′N 74°00′W
21 P4 **Point Pleasant** West Virginia, NE USA 38°53′N 82°07′W
45 R14 **Point Salines** (St. George's) SW Grenada 12°00′N 61°47′W
102 L9 **Poitiers** prev. Poictiers; anc. Limonum. Vienne, W France 46°35′N 00°19′E
102 K9 **Poitou** cultural region W France
102 K10 **Poitou-Charentes** region W France
103 N3 **Poix-de-Picardie** Somme, N France 49°47′N 01°58′E
Pojo see Pohja
37 S10 **Pojoaque** New Mexico, SW USA 35°52′N 106°01′W
152 E11 **Pokaran** Rājasthān, NW India 26°55′N 71°55′E
183 R4 **Pokataroo** New South Wales, SE Australia 29°37′S 148°43′E
119 P18 **Pokats'** Rus. Pokot'. SE Belarus
29 V5 **Pokegama Lake** Minnesota, N USA
184 L6 **Pokeno** Waikato, North Island, New Zealand 37°15′S 175°01′E
153 O11 **Pokharā** Western, C Nepal 28°14′N 84°E

◆ Country
● Country Capital
◇ Dependent Territory
○ Dependent Territory Capital
Administrative Regions
International Airport
▲ Mountain
▲▲ Mountain Range
Volcano
River
Lake
Reservoir

127 T6 Pokhvistnevo Samarskaya Oblast', W Russian Federation 53°38′N 52°07′E
55 W10 Pokigron Sipaliwini, C Surinam 04°31′N 55°23′W
92 L10 Pokka Lapp. Pohkkä. Lappi, N Finland 68°11′N 25°45′E
79 N16 Poko Orientale, NE Dem. Rep. Congo 03°08′N 26°52′E
Pokot' see Pokats'
Po-ko-to Shan see Bogda Shan
147 S7 Pokrovka Talasskaya Oblast', NW Kyrgyzstan 42°45′N 71°33′E
Pokrovka see Kyzyl-Suu
117 V8 Pokrovs'ke Rus. Pokrovskoye. Dnipropetrovs'ka Oblast', E Ukraine 47°58′N 36°15′E
Pokrovskoye see Pokrovs'ke
Pola see Pula
37 N10 Polacca Arizona, SW USA 35°49′N 110°21′W
104 L2 Pola de Laviana Asturias, N Spain 43°15′N 05°33′W
104 K2 Pola de Lena Asturias, N Spain 43°10′N 05°49′W
104 L2 Pola de Siero Asturias, N Spain 43°24′N 05°39′W
191 Y3 Poland Kiritimati, E Kiribati 01°52′N 157°33′W
110 H12 Poland off. Republic of Poland, var. Polish Republic, Pol. Polska, Rzeczpospolita Polska; prev. Pol. Polska Rzeczpospolita Ludowa, The Polish People's Republic. ◆ republic C Europe
Poland, Republic of see Poland
Polangen see Palanga
110 G7 Polanów Ger. Pollnow. Zachodnio-pomorskie, NW Poland 54°07′N 16°38′E
136 H13 Polatlı Ankara, C Turkey 39°34′N 32°08′E
118 L12 Polatsk Rus. Polotsk. Vitsyebskaya Voblasts', N Belarus 55°29′N 28°47′E
125 U14 Polazna Permskaya Oblast', NW Russian Federation 58°18′N 56°22′E
110 F8 Połczyn-Zdrój Ger. Bad Polzin. Zachodnio-pomorskie, NW Poland 53°44′N 16°02′E
149 R5 Pol-e-'Alam Logar, E Afghanistan 33°59′N 69°02′E
Polekhatum see Pulhatyn
149 Q3 Pol-e Khomrī var. Pul-i-Khumri. Baghlān, NE Afghanistan 35°55′N 68°45′E
197 S10 Pole Plain undersea feature Arctic Ocean
Pol-e-Safid see Pol-e Sefid
143 P5 Pol-e Sefid var. Pol-e-Safid, Pul-i-Sefid. Māzandarān, N Iran 36°05′N 53°01′E
118 B13 Polessk Ger. Labiau. Kaliningradskaya Oblast', W Russian Federation 54°52′N 21°06′E
Polesskoye see Polis'ke
171 N13 Polewali Sulawesi, C Indonesia 03°26′S 119°23′E
114 G11 Polezhan ▲ SW Bulgaria 41°42′N 23°28′E
78 F13 Poli Nord, N Cameroon 09°31′N 13°10′E
Poli see Pólis
107 M19 Policastro, Golfo di gulf S Italy
110 D8 Police Ger. Politz. Zachodnio-pomorskie, NW Poland 53°34′N 14°34′E
172 I17 Police, Pointe headland Mahé, NE Seychelles 04°48′S 55°31′E
115 L17 Polichnitos var. Polihnitos, Polikhnitos. Lésvos, E Greece 39°04′N 26°10′E
Poligiros see Polýgyros
107 P17 Polignano a Mare Puglia, SE Italy 40°59′N 17°13′E
103 S9 Poligny Jura, E France 46°51′N 05°42′E
Polihnitos see Polichnitos
Polikastro/Políkastron see Polýkastro
Políkhnitos see Polichnitos
171 O3 Polillo Islands island group N Philippines
109 Q9 Polinik ▲ SW Austria 46°54′N 13°10′E
115 J15 Políochni var. Polýochni. site of ancient city Límnos, E Greece
121 O2 Pólis var. Poli. W Cyprus 35°02′N 32°27′E
Polish People's Republic, The see Poland
Polish Republic see Poland
117 O3 Polis'ke Rus. Polesskoye. Kyyivs'ka Oblast', N Ukraine 51°16′N 29°27′E
107 N22 Polistena Calabria, SW Italy 38°25′N 16°05′E
Politz see Police
Políyiros see Polýgyros
29 V14 Polk City Iowa, C USA 41°46′N 93°42′W
110 F13 Polkowice Ger. Heerwegen. Dolnośląskie, W Poland 51°32′N 16°06′E
155 G22 Pollāchi Tamil Nādu, SE India 10°38′N 77°00′E
109 W7 Pöllau Steiermark, SE Austria 47°18′N 15°46′E
189 T13 Polle atoll Chuuk Islands, C Micronesia
105 X9 Pollença Mallorca, Spain, W Mediterranean Sea 39°52′N 03°01′E
Pollnow see Polanów
29 N7 Pollock South Dakota, N USA 45°53′N 100°15′W
92 L8 Polmak Finnmark, N Norway 70°01′N 28°04′E
30 L10 Polo Illinois, N USA 41°59′N 89°34′W
193 Y15 Poloa island Tongatapu Group, N Tonga
42 E5 Polochic, Río ≈ C Guatemala
Pologi see Polohy
117 V9 Polohy Rus. Pologi. Zaporiz'ka Oblast', SE Ukraine 47°30′N 36°18′E
83 K20 Polokwane prev. Pietersburg. Limpopo, NE South Africa 23°54′S 29°23′E
14 M10 Polonais, Lac des ◎ Québec, SE Canada
61 G20 Polonio, Cabo headland E Uruguay 34°22′S 53°46′W
155 K24 Polonnaruwa North Central Province, C Sri Lanka 07°56′N 81°02′E
116 L5 Polonne Rus. Polonnoye. Khmel'nyts'ka Oblast', NW Ukraine 50°10′N 27°30′E
Polonnoye see Polonne
Polotsk see Polatsk
Polovinka see Ugleural'skiy
109 T7 Pöls var. Pölsbach. ≈ E Austria
Pölsbach see Pöls
Polska/Polska, Rzeczpospolita/Polska Rzeczpospolita Ludowa see Poland
114 L10 Polski Gradets Stara Zagora, C Bulgaria 42°12′N 26°06′E
114 K8 Polski Trŭmbesh Ruse, N Bulgaria 43°22′N 25°38′E
33 P8 Polson Montana, NW USA 47°41′N 114°09′W
117 T6 Poltava Poltavs'ka Oblast', NE Ukraine 49°33′N 34°32′E
Poltava see Poltavs'ka Oblast'
117 R5 Poltavs'ka Oblast' var. Poltava, Rus. Poltavskaya Oblast'. ◐ province NE Ukraine
Poltavskaya Oblast' see Poltavs'ka Oblast'
Poltoratsk see Aşgabat
118 I5 Põltsamaa Ger. Oberpahlen. Jõgevamaa, E Estonia 58°40′N 26°00′E
118 I4 Põltsamaa var. Põltsamaa Jõgi. ≈ C Estonia
Põltsamaa Jõgi see Põltsamaa
122 I8 Poluy ≈ N Russian Federation
118 J6 Põlva Ger. Põlwe. Põlvamaa, SE Estonia 58°04′N 27°06′E
93 N16 Polvijärvi Itä-Suomi, SE Finland 62°53′N 29°20′E
Põlwe see Põlva
115 I22 Polýaigos island Kykládes, Greece, Aegean Sea
115 I22 Polyaigou Folégandrou, Stenó strait Kykládes, Greece, Aegean Sea
124 J3 Polyarnyy Murmanskaya Oblast', NW Russian Federation 69°10′N 33°21′E
124 I5 Polyarnyye Zori Murmanskaya Oblast', NW Russian Federation 67°22′N 32°31′E
125 W5 Polyarnyy Ural ▲▲ NW Russian Federation
115 G14 Polýgyros var. Poligiros, Políyiros. Kentrikí Makedonía, N Greece 40°21′N 23°27′E
114 F13 Polýkastro var. Polikastro; prev. Políkastron. Kentrikí Makedonía, N Greece 41°01′N 22°33′E
193 O9 Polynesia island group C Pacific Ocean
Polýochni see Políochni
41 Y13 Polyuc Quintana Roo, E Mexico
109 V10 Polzela C Slovenia 46°18′N 15°04′E
Polzen see Ploučnice
56 D12 Pomabamba Ancash, C Peru 08°48′S 77°30′W
185 D23 Pomahaka ≈ South Island, New Zealand
106 F12 Pomarance Toscana, C Italy 43°19′N 10°53′E
104 G9 Pombal Leiria, C Portugal 39°55′N 08°38′W
76 D9 Pombas Santo Antão, NW Cape Verde 17°09′N 25°02′W
83 N19 Pomene Inhambane, SE Mozambique 22°57′S 35°34′E
110 G8 Pomerania cultural region Germany/Poland
110 D7 Pomeranian Bay Ger. Pommersche Bucht, Pol. Zatoka Pomorska. bay Germany/Poland
31 T15 Pomeroy Ohio, N USA 39°01′N 82°01′W
32 L10 Pomeroy Washington, NW USA 46°28′N 117°36′W
117 Q8 Pomichna Kirovohrads'ka Oblast', C Ukraine 48°07′N 31°25′E
186 H7 Pomio New Britain, E Papua New Guinea 05°31′S 151°30′E
Pomir, Dar"yoi see Pamir/Pāmīr, Daryā-ye
27 T6 Pomme de Terre Lake ⊠ Missouri, C USA
29 S8 Pomme de Terre River ≈ Minnesota, N USA
Pommersche Bucht see Pomeranian Bay
35 T15 Pomona California, W USA 34°03′N 117°45′W
114 N9 Pomorie Burgas, E Bulgaria 42°32′N 27°39′E
Pomorska, Zatoka see Pomeranian Bay
110 H8 Pomorskie ◐ province N Poland
125 Q4 Pomorskiy Proliv strait NW Russian Federation
125 T10 Pomozdino Respublika Komi, NW Russian Federation 62°11′N 54°13′E
Pompaelo see Pamplona
23 Z15 Pompano Beach Florida, SE USA 26°14′N 80°06′W
107 K18 Pompei Campania, S Italy 40°45′N 14°27′E
33 V10 Pompeys Pillar Montana, NW USA 45°58′N 107°55′W
Ponape Ascension Island see Pohnpei
29 R13 Ponca Nebraska, C USA 42°35′N 96°42′W
27 O8 Ponca City Oklahoma, C USA 36°41′N 97°04′W
45 T6 Ponce C Puerto Rico 18°01′N 66°36′W
23 X10 Ponce de Leon Inlet inlet Florida, SE USA
22 K8 Ponchatoula Louisiana, S USA 30°26′N 90°26′W
26 M8 Pond Creek Oklahoma, C USA 36°40′N 97°48′W
155 J20 Pondicherry var. Puduchcheri, Fr. Pondichéry. Pondicherry, SE India 11°59′N 79°50′E
151 I20 Pondicherry var. Puduchcheri, Fr. Pondichéry. ◐ union territory India
Pondichéry see Pondicherry
197 N11 Pond Inlet Baffin Island, Nunavut, NE Canada 72°37′N 77°56′W
187 P16 Ponérihouen Province Nord, C New Caledonia 21°04′S 165°24′E
104 J4 Ponferrada Castilla-León, NW Spain 42°33′N 06°35′W
184 N13 Pongaroa Manawatu-Wanganui, North Island, New Zealand 40°36′S 176°08′E
167 Q12 Pong Nam Ron Chanthaburi, S Thailand 12°55′N 102°15′E
81 C14 Pongo ≈ S Sudan
152 I7 Pong Reservoir ⊠ N India
111 N14 Poniatowa Lubelskie, E Poland 51°11′N 22°05′E
167 R12 Pônley Kâmpóng Chhnăng, C Cambodia 12°26′N 104°25′E
155 J20 Ponnaiyār ≈ SE India
11 Q15 Ponoka Alberta, SW Canada 52°42′N 113°33′W
127 U6 Ponomarevka Orenburgskaya Oblast', W Russian Federation 53°16′N 54°10′E
169 Q17 Ponorogo Jawa, C Indonesia 07°51′S 111°30′E
124 M5 Ponoy Murmanskaya Oblast', NW Russian Federation 67°00′N 41°06′E
122 F6 Ponoy ≈ NW Russian Federation
102 K11 Pons Charente-Maritime, W France 45°31′N 00°31′W
Pons see Ponts
Pons Aelii see Newcastle upon Tyne
Pons Vetus see Pontevedra
99 G20 Pont-à-Celles Hainaut, S Belgium 50°31′N 04°21′E
102 K16 Pontacq Pyrénées-Atlantiques, SW France 43°11′N 00°06′W
64 P3 Ponta Delgada São Miguel, Azores, Portugal, NE Atlantic Ocean 37°29′N 25°40′W
64 P3 Ponta Delgado ✈ São Miguel, Azores, Portugal, NE Atlantic Ocean 37°28′N 25°40′W
64 N2 Ponta do Pico ▲ Pico, Azores, Portugal, NE Atlantic Ocean 38°28′N 28°25′W
60 J11 Ponta Grossa Paraná, S Brazil 25°07′S 50°09′W
103 S5 Pont-à-Mousson Meurthe-et-Moselle, NE France 48°55′N 06°03′E
103 T9 Pontarlier Doubs, E France 46°54′N 06°20′E
106 G11 Pontassieve Toscana, C Italy 43°46′N 11°28′E
102 L4 Pont-Audemer Eure, N France 49°22′N 00°31′E
22 K9 Pontchartrain, Lake ◎ Louisiana, S USA
102 I8 Pontchâteau Loire-Atlantique, NW France 47°26′N 02°04′W
103 R10 Pont-de-Vaux Ain, E France 46°25′N 04°57′E
104 G4 Ponteareas Galicia, NW Spain 42°11′N 08°29′W
106 J6 Pontebba Friuli-Venezia Giulia, NE Italy 46°32′N 13°18′E
104 G4 Ponte Caldelas Galicia, NW Spain 42°23′N 08°30′W
107 J16 Pontecorvo Lazio, C Italy 41°27′N 13°40′E
104 G5 Ponte da Barca Viana do Castelo, N Portugal 41°48′N 08°25′W
104 G5 Ponte de Lima Viana do Castelo, N Portugal 41°46′N 08°35′W
106 F11 Pontedera Toscana, C Italy 43°40′N 10°38′E
104 H10 Ponte de Sor Portalegre, C Portugal 39°15′N 08°01′W
104 H2 Pontedeume Galicia, NW Spain 43°22′N 08°09′W
106 F6 Ponte di Legno Lombardia, N Italy 46°16′N 10°31′E
11 T17 Ponteix Saskatchewan, S Canada 49°43′N 107°22′W
171 Q16 Ponte Macassar var. Pante Macassar, Pante Makasar. W East Timor 09°11′S 124°27′E
59 N20 Ponte Nova Minas Gerais, NE Brazil 20°25′S 42°54′W
59 G18 Pontes e Lacerda Mato Grosso, W Brazil 15°14′S 59°21′W
104 G4 Pontevedra anc. Pons Vetus. Galicia, NW Spain 42°25′N 08°39′W
104 G3 Pontevedra ◐ province Galicia, NW Spain
104 G4 Pontevedra, Ría de estuary NW Spain
30 M12 Pontiac Illinois, N USA 40°54′N 88°36′W
31 R9 Pontiac Michigan, N USA 42°38′N 83°17′W
169 P11 Pontianak Borneo, C Indonesia 0°05′S 109°16′E
107 I16 Pontino, Agro plain C Italy
Pontisarae see Pontoise
102 H6 Pontivy Morbihan, NW France 48°04′N 02°58′W
102 F6 Pont-l'Abbé Finistère, NW France 47°52′N 04°14′W
103 N4 Pontoise anc. Briva Isarae, Cergy-Pontoise, Pontisarae. Val-d'Oise, N France 49°03′N 02°05′E
11 W13 Ponton Manitoba, C Canada 54°36′N 99°02′W
102 J5 Pontorson Manche, N France 48°33′N 01°31′W
22 M2 Pontotoc Mississippi, S USA 34°15′N 89°00′W
25 R9 Pontotoc Texas, SW USA 30°52′N 98°57′W
106 E10 Pontremoli Toscana, C Italy 44°24′N 09°55′E
108 J10 Pontresina Graubünden, S Switzerland 46°29′N 09°52′E
105 U5 Ponts var. Pons. Cataluña, NE Spain 41°55′N 01°12′E
103 R14 Pont-St-Esprit Gard, S France 44°15′N 04°37′E
97 K21 Pontypool Wel. Pontypŵl. SE Wales, United Kingdom 51°43′N 03°02′W
97 J22 Pontypridd S Wales, United Kingdom 51°37′N 03°22′W
Pontypŵl see Pontypool
43 R17 Ponuga Veraguas, SE Panama 07°50′N 80°58′W
184 L6 Ponui Island island N New Zealand
119 K14 Ponya ≈ N Belarus
107 I17 Ponza, Isola di Island Isole Ponziane, S Italy
107 I17 Ponziane, Isole island C Italy
182 F7 Poochera South Australia 32°45′S 134°51′E
97 L24 Poole S England, United Kingdom 50°43′N 01°59′W
25 S6 Poolville Texas, SW USA 33°00′N 97°55′W
Poona see Pune
182 M8 Pooncarie New South Wales, SE Australia 33°26′S 142°37′E
183 N6 Poopelloe Lake seasonal lake New South Wales, SE Australia
57 K19 Poopó Oruro, C Bolivia 18°23′S 66°58′W
57 K19 Poopó, Lago var. Lago Pampa Aullagas. ◎ W Bolivia
184 L3 Poor Knights Islands island N New Zealand
39 P10 Poorman Alaska, USA 64°05′N 155°34′W
182 E3 Pootnoura South Australia 28°31′S 134°09′E
147 R10 Pop Rus. Pap. Namangan Viloyati, E Uzbekistan 40°49′N 71°06′E
117 X7 Popasna Rus. Popasnaya. Luhans'ka Oblast', E Ukraine 48°38′N 38°24′E
Popasnaya see Popasna
54 D12 Popayán Cauca, SW Colombia 02°27′N 76°32′W
99 B18 Poperinge West-Vlaanderen, W Belgium 50°52′N 02°44′E
123 N7 Popigay Taymyrskiy (Dolgano-Nenetskiy) Avtonomnyy Okrug, N Russian Federation 71°54′N 110°45′E
123 N7 Popigay ≈ N Russian Federation
117 O5 Popil'nya Zhytomyrs'ka Oblast', N Ukraine 49°57′N 29°24′E
182 K8 Popiltah Lake seasonal lake New South Wales, SE Australia
33 X7 Poplar Montana, NW USA 48°06′N 105°12′W
11 Y14 Poplar ≈ Manitoba, C Canada
27 X8 Poplar Bluff Missouri, C USA 36°45′N 90°23′W
33 X6 Poplar River ≈ Montana, NW USA
41 P14 Popocatépetl ⛰ S Mexico 18°59′N 98°37′W
79 H21 Popokabaka Bandundu, SW Dem. Rep. Congo 05°42′S 16°35′E
107 J15 Popoli Abruzzo, C Italy 42°09′N 13°51′E
186 F9 Popondetta Northern, S Papua New Guinea 08°45′S 148°15′E
112 F9 Popovača Sisak-Moslavina, NE Croatia 45°35′N 16°37′E
114 L8 Popovo Tŭrgovishte, N Bulgaria 43°20′N 26°14′E
Popovo see Iskra
Popper see Poprad
30 M5 Popple River ≈ Wisconsin, N USA
111 L19 Poprad Ger. Deutschendorf, Hung. Poprád. Prešovský Kraj, E Slovakia 49°04′N 20°16′E
111 L18 Poprad Ger. Popper, Hung. Poprád. ≈ Poland/Slovakia
111 L19 Poprad-Tatry ✈ (Poprad) Prešovský Kraj, E Slovakia 49°04′N 20°21′E
21 X7 Poquoson Virginia, NE USA 37°08′N 76°21′W
149 O15 Porāli ≈ SW Pakistan
184 N12 Porangahau Hawke's Bay, North Island, New Zealand 40°19′S 176°36′E
59 K17 Porangatu Goiás, C Brazil 13°28′S 49°14′W
119 G18 Porazava Pol. Porozow, Rus. Porozovo. Hrodzyenskaya Voblasts', W Belarus 52°56′N 24°22′E
154 A11 Porbandar Gujarāt, W India 21°40′N 69°40′E
10 I13 Porcher Island island British Columbia, SW Canada
104 M13 Porcuna Andalucía, S Spain 37°52′N 04°12′W
14 F7 Porcupine Ontario, S Canada 48°31′N 81°07′W
64 M6 Porcupine Bank undersea feature N Atlantic Ocean
11 V15 Porcupine Hills ▲▲ Manitoba/Saskatchewan, S Canada
30 L3 Porcupine Mountains hill range Michigan, N USA
64 M7 Porcupine Plain undersea feature E Atlantic Ocean 16°00′W 49°00′N
8 G7 Porcupine River ≈ Canada/USA
106 I7 Pordenone anc. Portenau. Friuli-Venezia Giulia, NE Italy 45°58′N 12°39′E
54 H9 Pore Casanare, E Colombia 05°42′N 71°59′W
112 A9 Poreč It. Parenzo. Istra, NW Croatia 45°16′N 13°36′E
60 I9 Porecatu Paraná, S Brazil 22°46′S 51°22′W
Porech'ye see Parechcha
127 P4 Poretskoye Chuvashskaya Respublika, W Russian Federation 55°12′N 46°20′E
77 Q13 Porga N Benin 11°04′N 00°58′E
186 B7 Porgera Enga, W Papua New Guinea 05°32′S 143°08′E
93 K18 Pori Swe. Björneborg. Länsi-Suomi, SW Finland 61°28′N 21°50′E
185 L14 Porirua Wellington, North Island, New Zealand 41°08′S 174°51′E
92 I12 Porjus Lapp. Bårjås. Norrbotten, N Sweden 66°55′N 19°55′E
124 G14 Porkhov Pskovskaya Oblast', W Russian Federation 57°46′N 29°27′E
55 O4 Porlamar Nueva Esparta, NE Venezuela 10°57′N 63°51′W
102 I8 Pornic Loire-Atlantique, NW France 47°07′N 02°07′W
186 B7 Poroma Southern Highlands, W Papua New Guinea 06°15′S 143°34′E
123 T13 Poronaysk Ostrov Sakhalin, Sakhalinskaya Oblast', SE Russian Federation 49°15′N 143°00′E
115 G20 Póros Póros, S Greece 37°30′N 23°27′E
115 C19 Póros Kefallinía, Iónia Nisiá, Greece, C Mediterranean Sea 38°09′N 20°46′E
115 G20 Póros island S Greece
81 G24 Poroto Mountains ▲▲ SW Tanzania
112 B10 Porozina Primorje-Gorski Kotar, NW Croatia 45°07′N 14°17′E
Porozovo/Porozow see Porazava
195 X15 Porpoise Bay bay Antarctica
65 G15 Porpoise Point headland NE Ascension Island 07°54′S 14°22′W
108 C6 Porrentruy Jura, NW Switzerland 47°25′N 07°06′E
106 F10 Porretta Terme Emilia-Romagna, C Italy 44°10′N 11°01′E
Porriño see O Porriño
Pors see Porsangenfijorden
92 L7 Porsangenfijorden Lapp. Pors. fjord N Norway
92 K8 Porsangerhalvøya peninsula N Norway
95 G16 Porsgrunn Telemark, S Norway 59°08′N 09°38′E
136 E13 Porsuk Çayı ≈ C Turkey
Porsy see Boldumsaz
57 N18 Portachuelo Santa Cruz, C Bolivia 17°21′S 63°24′W
182 I9 Port Adelaide South Australia 34°49′S 138°31′E
97 F15 Portadown Ir. Port An Dúnáin. S Northern Ireland, United Kingdom 54°26′N 06°27′W
31 P10 Portage Michigan, N USA 42°12′N 85°34′W
18 D15 Portage Pennsylvania, NE USA 40°23′N 78°40′W
30 K8 Portage Wisconsin, N USA 43°33′N 89°29′W
30 M3 Portage Lake ◎ Michigan, N USA
11 X16 Portage la Prairie Manitoba, S Canada 49°58′N 98°20′W
31 R11 Portage River ≈ Ohio, N USA
27 Y8 Portageville Missouri, C USA 36°25′N 89°42′W
28 L2 Portal North Dakota, N USA 48°57′N 102°33′W
10 L17 Port Alberni Vancouver Island, British Columbia, SW Canada 49°11′N 124°49′W
14 E15 Port Albert Ontario, S Canada 43°51′N 81°42′W
104 I10 Portalegre anc. Ammaia, Amoea. Portalegre, E Portugal 39°17′N 07°25′W
104 H10 Portalegre ◐ district C Portugal
37 V12 Portales New Mexico, SW USA 34°11′N 103°19′W
39 X14 Port Alexander Baranof Island, Alaska, USA 56°15′N 134°39′W
83 I25 Port Alfred Eastern Cape, S South Africa 33°31′S 26°55′E
10 J16 Port Alice Vancouver Island, British Columbia, SW Canada 50°23′N 127°24′W
22 J8 Port Allen Louisiana, S USA 30°27′N 91°12′W
Port Amelia see Pemba
Port An Dúnáin see Portadown
32 G7 Port Angeles Washington, NW USA 48°06′N 123°26′W
44 L12 Port Antonio NE Jamaica 18°10′N 76°27′W
115 D16 Pórta Panagiá religious building Thessalía, C Greece
25 T14 Port Aransas Texas, SW USA 27°49′N 97°03′W
97 E18 Portarlington Ir. Cúil an tSúdaire. Laois/Offaly, C Ireland 53°10′N 07°11′W
183 P17 Port Arthur Tasmania, SE Australia 43°09′S 147°51′E
25 Y11 Port Arthur Texas, SW USA 29°55′N 93°56′W
96 G12 Port Askaig W Scotland, United Kingdom 55°51′N 06°06′W
182 I7 Port Augusta South Australia 32°29′S 137°44′E
44 M9 Port-au-Prince ● (Haiti) C Haiti 18°33′N 72°20′W
44 M9 Port-au-Prince ✈ E Haiti 18°38′N 72°13′W
22 I8 Port Barre Louisiana, S USA 30°33′N 91°57′W
Port-Bergé see Boriziny
151 Q19 Port Blair Andaman and Nicobar Islands, SE India 11°40′N 92°44′E
25 X12 Port Bolivar Texas, SW USA 29°21′N 94°45′W
105 X4 Portbou Cataluña, NE Spain 42°26′N 03°10′E
77 N17 Port Bouet ✈ (Abidjan) SE Ivory Coast 05°17′N 03°55′W
182 I8 Port Broughton South Australia 33°39′S 137°55′E
14 F17 Port Burwell Ontario, S Canada 42°39′N 80°47′W
12 G17 Port Burwell Québec, NE Canada 60°25′N 64°49′W
182 M13 Port Campbell Victoria, SE Australia 38°37′S 143°00′E
15 V4 Port-Cartier Québec, SE Canada 50°00′N 66°55′W
185 F23 Port Chalmers Otago, South Island, New Zealand 45°46′S 170°37′E
23 W14 Port Charlotte Florida, SE USA 27°00′N 82°07′W
38 L9 Port Clarence Alaska, USA 65°15′N 166°51′W
10 I13 Port Clements Graham Island, British Columbia, SW Canada 53°37′N 132°12′W
31 S11 Port Clinton Ohio, N USA 41°30′N 82°56′W
14 H17 Port Colborne Ontario, S Canada 42°51′N 79°16′W
15 Y7 Port-Daniel Québec, SE Canada 48°10′N 64°58′W
Port Darwin see Darwin
183 O17 Port Davey headland Tasmania, SE Australia 43°19′S 145°54′E
44 K8 Port-de-Paix NW Haiti 19°56′N 72°52′W
181 W4 Port Douglas Queensland, NE Australia 16°33′S 145°27′E
10 J13 Port Edward British Columbia, SW Canada 54°11′N 130°16′W
83 K24 Port Edward KwaZulu/Natal, SE South Africa 31°03′S 30°14′E
58 J12 Portel Pará, NE Brazil 01°58′S 50°45′W
104 H12 Portel Évora, S Portugal 38°18′N 07°42′W
14 E14 Port Elgin Ontario, S Canada 44°26′N 81°22′W
45 Y14 Port Elizabeth Bequia, Saint Vincent and the Grenadines 13°01′N 61°15′W
83 I26 Port Elizabeth Eastern Cape, S South Africa 33°58′S 25°36′E
96 G13 Port Ellen W Scotland, United Kingdom 55°37′N 06°12′W
Portenau see Pordenone
97 H16 Port Erin SW Isle of Man 54°05′N 04°47′W
45 Q13 Porter Point headland Saint Vincent, Saint Vincent and the Grenadines 13°22′N 61°10′W
185 G18 Porters Pass pass South Island, New Zealand
83 E25 Porterville Western Cape, SW South Africa 33°03′S 19°00′E
35 R12 Porterville California, W USA 36°03′N 119°03′W
Port-Étienne see Nouâdhibou
182 L13 Port Fairy Victoria, SE Australia 38°24′S 142°13′E
184 M4 Port Fitzroy Great Barrier Island, Auckland, NE New Zealand 36°10′S 175°21′E
Port Florence see Kisumu
Port-Francqui see Ilebo
79 C18 Port-Gentil Ogooué-Maritime, W Gabon 0°40′S 08°50′E
182 I7 Port Germein South Australia 33°02′S 138°01′E
22 J6 Port Gibson Mississippi, S USA 31°57′N 90°58′W
39 Q13 Port Graham Alaska, USA 59°21′N 151°49′W
77 U17 Port Harcourt Rivers, S Nigeria 04°43′N 07°02′E
10 J16 Port Hardy Vancouver Island, British Columbia, SW Canada 50°41′N 127°30′W
Port Harrison see Inukjuak
13 R14 Port Hawkesbury Cape Breton Island, Nova Scotia, SE Canada 45°36′N 61°22′W
180 I6 Port Hedland Western Australia 20°23′S 118°40′E
39 O15 Port Heiden Alaska, USA 56°54′N 158°40′W
97 I19 Porthmadog var. Portmadoc. NW Wales, United Kingdom 52°55′N 04°08′W
14 I15 Port Hope Ontario, SE Canada 43°58′N 78°18′W
13 S9 Port Hope Simpson Newfoundland and Labrador, E Canada 52°30′N 56°18′W
65 C24 Port Howard Settlement West Falkland, Falkland Islands
31 T9 Port Huron Michigan, N USA 42°58′N 82°25′W
107 K17 Portici Campania, S Italy 40°48′N 14°20′E
137 Y13 Port-Iliç Rus. Port Il'ich. SE Azerbaijan 38°54′N 48°49′E
Port Il'ich see Port-Iliç
104 G14 Portimão var. Vila Nova de Portimão. Faro, S Portugal 37°08′N 08°32′W
25 T17 Port Isabel Texas, SW USA 26°04′N 97°13′W
18 J13 Port Jervis New York, NE USA 41°22′N 74°39′W
55 S7 Port Kaituma NW Guyana 07°42′N 59°52′W
126 K12 Port Katon Rostovskaya Oblast', SW Russian Federation 46°52′N 38°46′E
183 S9 Port Kembla New South Wales, SE Australia 34°30′S 150°54′E
182 F8 Port Kenny South Australia 33°09′S 134°38′E
Port Klang see Pelabuhan Klang
Port Láirge see Waterford
183 S8 Portland New South Wales, SE Australia 33°24′S 150°00′E
182 L13 Portland Victoria, SE Australia 38°21′S 141°38′E
184 K4 Portland Northland, North Island, New Zealand 35°48′S 174°19′E
31 Q13 Portland Indiana, N USA 40°25′N 84°58′W
19 P8 Portland Maine, NE USA 43°41′N 70°16′W
31 Q9 Portland Michigan, N USA 42°51′N 84°52′W
29 Q4 Portland North Dakota, N USA 47°28′N 97°22′W
32 G11 Portland Oregon, NW USA 45°31′N 122°41′W
20 J8 Portland Tennessee, S USA 36°34′N 86°31′W
25 T14 Portland Texas, SW USA 27°52′N 97°19′W
32 G11 Portland ✈ Oregon, NW USA 45°36′N 122°34′W
182 L13 Portland Bay bay Victoria, SE Australia
44 K13 Portland Bight bay S Jamaica
97 L24 Portland Bill var. Bill of Portland. headland S England, United Kingdom 50°31′N 02°28′W
Portland, Bill of see Portland Bill
183 P15 Portland, Cape headland Tasmania, SE Australia 40°46′S 147°58′E
10 J12 Portland Inlet inlet British Columbia, W Canada
184 P11 Portland Island island E New Zealand
65 F15 Portland Point headland SW Ascension Island
44 J13 Portland Point headland C Jamaica 17°42′N 77°10′W
103 P16 Port-la-Nouvelle Aude, S France 43°01′N 03°04′E
Portlaoighise see Port Laoise
97 E18 Port Laoise var. Portlaoise, Ir. Portlaoighise; prev. Maryborough. C Ireland 53°02′N 07°17′W
Portlaoise see Port Laoise
25 U13 Port Lavaca Texas, SW USA 28°36′N 96°39′W
182 G9 Port Lincoln South Australia 34°43′S 135°49′E
39 Q14 Port Lions Kodiak Island, Alaska, USA 57°55′N 152°48′W
76 I15 Port Loko W Sierra Leone 08°50′N 12°50′W
65 E24 Port Louis East Falkland, Falkland Islands 51°31′S 58°07′W
45 Y5 Port-Louis Grande Terre, N Guadeloupe 16°25′N 61°32′W
173 X16 Port Louis ● (Mauritius) NW Mauritius 20°10′S 57°30′E
Port Louis see Scarborough
Port-Lyautey see Kénitra
182 K12 Port MacDonnell South Australia 38°04′S 140°40′E
183 U7 Port Macquarie New South Wales, SE Australia 31°26′S 152°55′E
Portmadoc see Porthmadog
Port Mahon see Mahón
44 K12 Port Maria C Jamaica 18°22′N 76°54′W
10 K16 Port McNeill Vancouver Island, British Columbia, SW Canada 50°34′N 127°06′W
13 P11 Port-Menier Île d'Anticosti, Québec, E Canada 49°49′N 64°19′W
39 N15 Port Moller Alaska, USA 56°00′N 160°31′W
44 L13 Port Morant E Jamaica 17°53′N 76°20′W
44 K13 Portmore C Jamaica 17°58′N 76°52′W
186 D9 Port Moresby ● (Papua New Guinea) Central/National Capital District, SW Papua New Guinea 09°28′S 147°12′E
Port Natal see Durban
25 Y11 Port Neches Texas, SW USA 29°59′N 93°57′W
182 G9 Port Neill South Australia 34°06′S 136°19′E
15 S6 Portneuf ≈ Québec, SE Canada
15 R6 Portneuf, Lac ◎ Québec, SE Canada
83 D23 Port Nolloth Northern Cape, W South Africa 29°17′S 16°51′E
18 J17 Port Norris New Jersey, NE USA 39°13′N 75°00′W
Port-Nouveau-Québec see Kangiqsualujjuaq
104 G6 Porto Eng. Oporto; anc. Portus Cale. Porto, NW Portugal 41°09′N 08°37′W
104 G6 Porto var. Pôrto. ◐ district N Portugal
104 G6 Porto ✈ Porto, W Portugal 41°09′N 08°37′W
Pôrto see Porto
61 I16 Porto Alegre var. Pôrto Alegre. state capital Rio Grande do Sul, S Brazil 30°03′S 51°10′W
Porto Alexandre see Tombua
82 B12 Porto Amboim Cuanza Sul, NW Angola 10°47′S 13°43′E
Porto Amélia see Pemba
Porto Bello see Portobelo
43 T14 Portobelo var. Porto Bello, Puerto Bello. Colón, N Panama 09°33′N 79°37′W
60 G10 Pôrto Camargo Paraná, S Brazil 23°23′S 53°47′W
25 U13 Port O'Connor Texas, SW USA 28°26′N 96°26′W
Pôrto de Mós see Porto de Moz
58 J12 Porto de Moz var. Pôrto de Mós. Pará, NE Brazil 01°45′S 52°15′W
64 O5 Porto do Moniz Madeira, Portugal, NE Atlantic Ocean
59 H16 Porto dos Gaúchos Mato Grosso, W Brazil 11°32′S 57°16′W
Porto Edda see Sarandë
107 J24 Porto Empedocle Sicilia, Italy, C Mediterranean Sea 37°18′N 13°32′E
59 H20 Porto Esperança Mato Grosso do Sul, SW Brazil 19°36′S 57°24′W
106 E13 Portoferraio Toscana, C Italy 42°49′N 10°18′E
96 G6 Port of Ness NW Scotland, United Kingdom 58°29′N 06°15′W
45 U14 Port-of-Spain ● (Trinidad and Tobago) Trinidad, Trinidad and Tobago 10°39′N 61°30′W
Port of Spain see Piarco
103 X15 Porto, Golfe de gulf Corse, France, C Mediterranean Sea
Porto Grande see Mindelo
106 I7 Portogruaro Veneto, NE Italy 45°46′N 12°50′E
35 P5 Portola California, W USA 39°48′N 120°28′W
187 Q13 Port-Olry Espiritu Santo, C Vanuatu 15°03′S 167°04′E
93 J17 Pörtom Fin. Pirttikylä. Länsi-Suomi, W Finland 62°42′N 21°40′E
Port Omna see Portumna
59 G21 Porto Murtinho Mato Grosso do Sul, SW Brazil 21°42′S 57°52′W
59 K16 Porto Nacional Tocantins, C Brazil 10°41′S 48°19′W
77 S16 Porto-Novo ● (Benin) S Benin 06°29′N 02°37′E
23 X10 Port Orange Florida, SE USA 29°06′N 80°59′W
32 G8 Port Orchard Washington, NW USA 47°32′N 122°38′W
Porto Re see Kraljevica
32 E15 Port Orford Oregon, NW USA 42°45′N 124°30′W
Porto Rico see Puerto Rico
106 J13 Porto San Giorgio Marche, C Italy 43°10′N 13°47′E
107 F14 Porto San Stefano Toscana, C Italy 42°26′N 11°09′E
64 P5 Porto Santo var. Vila Baleira. Porto Santo, Madeira, Portugal, NE Atlantic Ocean 33°04′N 16°20′W
64 Q5 Porto Santo ✈ Porto Santo, Madeira, Portugal, NE Atlantic Ocean 33°04′N 16°20′W
64 P5 Porto Santo var. Ilha do Porto Santo. island Madeira, Portugal, NE Atlantic Ocean
Porto Santo, Ilha do see Porto Santo
60 H9 Porto São José Paraná, S Brazil 22°43′S 53°10′W
59 O19 Porto Seguro Bahia, E Brazil 16°25′S 39°07′W
107 B17 Porto Torres Sardegna, Italy, C Mediterranean Sea 40°50′N 08°23′E
59 J23 Porto União Santa Catarina, S Brazil 26°15′S 51°04′W
103 Y16 Porto-Vecchio Corse, France, C Mediterranean Sea 41°35′N 09°17′E
59 E15 Porto Velho var. Velho. state capital Rondônia, W Brazil 08°45′S 63°54′W
56 A6 Portoviejo var. Puertoviejo. Manabí, W Ecuador 01°03′S 80°31′W
185 B26 Port Pegasus bay Stewart Island, New Zealand
14 H15 Port Perry Ontario, SE Canada 44°08′N 78°57′W
183 N12 Port Phillip Bay harbour Victoria, SE Australia
182 I8 Port Pirie South Australia 33°11′S 138°01′E
96 G9 Portree N Scotland, United Kingdom 57°26′N 06°12′W
Port Rex see East London
Port Rois see Portrush

◆ Country
● Country Capital
◇ Dependent Territory
○ Dependent Territory Capital
◐ Administrative Regions
✈ International Airport
▲ Mountain
▲▲ Mountain Range
⛰ Volcano
≈ River
◎ Lake
⊠ Reservoir

44 K13 **Port Royal** E Jamaica *17°55′N 76°52′W*
21 R15 **Port Royal** South Carolina, SE USA *32°22′N 80°41′W*
21 R15 **Port Royal Sound** *inlet* South Carolina, SE USA
97 F14 **Portrush** *Ir.* Port Rois. N Northern Ireland, United Kingdom *55°12′N 06°40′W*
Port Said *see* Būr Sa'īd
23 R9 **Port Saint Joe** Florida, SE USA *29°49′N 85°18′W*
23 Y11 **Port Saint John** Florida, SE USA *28°28′N 80°46′W*
103 R16 **Port-St-Louis-du-Rhône** Bouches-du-Rhône, SE France *43°22′N 04°48′E*
44 K10 **Port Salut** SW Haiti *18°04′N 73°55′W*
65 E24 **Port Salvador** *inlet* East Falkland, Falkland Islands
65 D24 **Port San Carlos** East Falkland, Falkland Islands *51°30′S 58°59′W*
13 S10 **Port Saunders** Newfoundland, Newfoundland and Labrador, SE Canada *50°40′N 57°17′W*
83 K24 **Port Shepstone** KwaZulu/Natal, E South Africa *30°44′S 30°28′E*
45 O11 **Portsmouth** *var.* Grand-Anse. NW Dominica *15°34′N 61°27′W*
97 N24 **Portsmouth** S England, United Kingdom *50°48′N 01°05′W*
19 P10 **Portsmouth** New Hampshire, NE USA *43°04′N 70°47′W*
31 S15 **Portsmouth** Ohio, N USA *38°43′N 83°00′W*
21 X7 **Portsmouth** Virginia, NE USA *36°50′N 76°18′W*
14 E17 **Port Stanley** Ontario, S Canada *42°39′N 81°12′W*
Port Stanley *see* Stanley
65 B25 **Port Stephens** *inlet* West Falkland, Falkland Islands
65 B25 **Port Stephens Settlement** West Falkland, Falkland Islands
97 F14 **Portstewart** *Ir.* Port Stíobhaird. N Northern Ireland, United Kingdom *55°11′N 06°43′W*
Port Stíobhaird *see* Portstewart
83 K24 **Port St. Johns** Eastern Cape, SE South Africa *31°37′S 29°32′E*
80 I7 **Port Sudan** Red Sea, NE Sudan *19°37′N 37°14′E*
22 L10 **Port Sulphur** Louisiana, S USA *29°28′N 89°41′W*
Port Swettenham *see* Klang/Pelabuhan Klang
97 J22 **Port Talbot** S Wales, United Kingdom *51°36′N 03°47′W*
92 L11 **Porttipahdan Tekojärvi** ◎ N Finland
32 G7 **Port Townsend** Washington, NW USA *48°07′N 122°45′W*
104 H9 **Portugal** *off.* Portuguese Republic. ◆ *republic* SW Europe
105 O2 **Portugalete** País Vasco, N Spain *43°19′N 03°01′W*
54 J6 **Portuguesa** *off.* Estado Portuguesa. ◐ *state* N Venezuela
Portuguesa, Estado *see* Portuguesa
Portuguese East Africa *see* Mozambique
Portuguese Guinea *see* Guinea-Bissau
Portuguese Republic *see* Portugal
Portuguese Timor *see* East Timor
Portuguese West Africa *see* Angola
97 D18 **Portumna** *Ir.* Port Omna. Galway, W Ireland *53°06′N 08°13′W*
Portus Cale *see* Porto
Portus Magnus *see* Almería
Portus Magonis *see* Mahón
103 P17 **Port-Vendres** *var.* Port Vendres. Pyrénées-Orientales, S France *42°31′N 03°06′E*
182 H9 **Port Victoria** South Australia *34°34′S 137°31′E*
187 Q14 **Port-Vila** *var.* Vila. ● (Vanuatu) Éfaté, C Vanuatu *17°45′S 168°21′E*
Port Vila *see* Bauer Field
182 I9 **Port Wakefield** South Australia *34°13′S 138°10′E*
31 N8 **Port Washington** Wisconsin, N USA *43°23′N 87°54′W*
57 J14 **Porvenir** Pando, NW Bolivia *11°15′S 68°43′W*
63 I24 **Porvenir** Magallanes, S Chile *53°18′S 70°22′W*
61 D18 **Porvenir** Paysandú, W Uruguay *32°23′S 57°59′W*
93 M19 **Porvoo** *Swe.* Borgå. Etelä-Suomi, S Finland *60°25′N 25°40′E*
Porzecze *see* Parechcha
104 M10 **Porzuna** Castilla-La Mancha, C Spain *39°10′N 04°10′W*
61 E14 **Posadas** Misiones, NE Argentina *27°27′S 55°52′W*
104 L13 **Posadas** Andalucía, S Spain *37°48′N 05°06′W*
Poschega *see* Požega
108 J11 **Poschiavino** ≈ Italy/Switzerland
108 J10 **Poschiavo** *Ger.* Puschlav. Graubünden, S Switzerland *46°19′N 10°02′E*
112 D12 **Posedarje** Zadar, SW Croatia *44°12′N 15°27′E*
Posen *see* Poznań
124 L14 **Poshekhon'ye** Yaroslavskaya Oblast', W Russian Federation *58°31′N 39°07′E*
92 M13 **Posio** Lappi, NE Finland *66°06′N 28°16′E*
Poskam *see* Zepu
Posnania *see* Poznań
1713 O12 **Poso** Sulawesi, C Indonesia *01°23′S 120°45′E*
171 O12 **Poso, Danau** ◎ Sulawesi, C Indonesia
137 R10 **Posof** Ardahan, NE Turkey *41°30′N 42°33′E*
25 R6 **Possum Kingdom Lake** ⊠ Texas, SW USA
25 N6 **Post** Texas, SW USA *33°14′N 101°24′W*
Postavy/Postawy *see* Pastavy
12 I7 **Poste-de-la-Baleine** Québec, NE Canada *55°13′N 77°54′W*
99 M17 **Posterholt** Limburg, SE Netherlands *51°07′N 06°02′E*
83 G22 **Postmasburg** Northern Cape, N South Africa *28°20′S 23°05′E*
Pôsto Diuarum *see* Campo de Diauarum
59 I16 **Pôsto Jacaré** Mato Grosso, W Brazil *12°S 53°27′W*
109 T12 **Postojna** *Ger.* Adelsberg, *It.* Postumia. SW Slovenia *45°48′N 14°12′E*
Postumia *see* Postojna
29 X12 **Postville** Iowa, C USA *43°04′N 91°34′W*
Pöstyén *see* Piešťany
113 G14 **Posušje** Federacija Bosna I Hercegovina, SW Bosnia and Herzegovina *43°28′N 17°20′E*
171 O16 **Pota** Flores, C Indonesia *08°21′S 120°50′E*
115 G23 **Potamós** Antikýthira, S Greece *35°53′N 23°17′E*
55 S9 **Potaru River** ≈ C Guyana
83 I21 **Potchefstroom** North-West, N South Africa *26°42′S 27°06′E*
27 R11 **Poteau** Oklahoma, C USA *35°03′N 94°36′W*
25 R12 **Poteet** Texas, SW USA *29°02′N 98°34′W*
115 G14 **Poteídaia** *site of ancient city* Kentrikí Makedonía, N Greece
Potentia *see* Potenza
107 M18 **Potenza** *anc.* Potentia. Basilicata, S Italy *40°40′N 15°50′E*
185 A24 **Poteriteri, Lake** ◎ South Island, New Zealand
104 M2 **Potes** Cantabria, N Spain *43°10′N 04°41′W*
Potgietersrus *see* Mokopane
25 S12 **Poth** Texas, SW USA *29°04′N 98°04′W*
32 J9 **Potholes Reservoir** ⊠ Washington, NW USA
137 Q9 **P'ot'i** W Georgia *42°10′N 41°42′E*
77 X13 **Potiskum** Yobe, NE Nigeria *11°38′N 11°07′E*
Potkozarje *see* Ivanjska
32 M9 **Potlatch** Idaho, NW USA *46°55′N 116°51′W*
33 N9 **Pot Mountain** ▲ Idaho, NW USA *46°44′N 115°24′W*
113 H14 **Potoci** Federacija Bosna I Hercegovina, S Bosnia and Herzegovina *43°24′N 17°52′E*
21 V3 **Potomac River** ≈ NE USA
57 L20 **Potosí** Potosí, S Bolivia *19°35′S 65°51′W*
42 H9 **Potosí** Chinandega, NW Nicaragua *12°58′N 87°30′W*
27 W6 **Potosi** Missouri, C USA *37°57′N 90°49′W*
57 K21 **Potosí** ◐ *department* SW Bolivia
62 H7 **Potrerillos** Atacama, N Chile *26°30′S 69°25′W*
42 H5 **Potrerillos** Cortés, NW Honduras *15°10′N 87°58′W*
62 H8 **Potro, Cerro del** ▲ N Chile *28°22′S 69°34′W*
100 N12 **Potsdam** Brandenburg, NE Germany *52°24′N 13°04′E*
18 J7 **Potsdam** New York, NE USA *44°40′N 74°58′W*
109 X5 **Pottendorf** Niederösterreich, E Austria *47°55′N 16°23′E*
109 X5 **Pottenstein** Niederösterreich, E Austria *47°58′N 16°07′E*
18 I15 **Pottstown** Pennsylvania, NE USA *40°15′N 75°39′W*
18 H14 **Pottsville** Pennsylvania, NE USA *40°40′N 76°10′W*
155 L25 **Pottuvil** Eastern Province, SE Sri Lanka *06°53′N 81°49′E*
149 U6 **Potwar Plateau** *plateau* NE Pakistan
102 J7 **Pouancé** Maine-et-Loire, W France *47°46′N 01°11′W*
15 R6 **Poulin de Courval, Lac** ◎ Québec, SE Canada
18 L9 **Poultney** Vermont, NE USA *43°31′N 73°12′W*
187 O16 **Poum** Province Nord, W New Caledonia *20°15′S 164°03′E*
59 L21 **Pouso Alegre** Minas Gerais, NE Brazil *22°13′S 45°56′W*
192 I16 **Poutasi** Upolu, SE Samoa *14°00′S 171°43′W*
167 R12 **Poŭthĭsăt** *prev.* Pursat. Poŭthĭsăt, W Cambodia *12°32′N 103°55′E*
167 R12 **Poŭthĭsăt, Stœng** *prev.* Pursat. ≈ W Cambodia
102 J9 **Pouzauges** Vendée, NW France *46°47′N 00°54′W*
Po, Valle del *see* Po Valley
106 F8 **Po Valley** *It.* Valle del Po. *valley* N Italy
111 I19 **Považská Bystrica** *Ger.* Waagbistritz, *Hung.* Vágbeszterce. Trenčiansky Kraj, W Slovakia *49°07′N 18°26′E*
124 J10 **Povenets** Respublika Kareliya, NW Russian Federation *62°50′N 34°47′E*
184 Q9 **Poverty Bay** *inlet* North Island, New Zealand
112 K12 **Povlen** ▲ W Serbia
104 G6 **Póvoa de Varzim** Porto, NW Portugal *41°22′N 08°46′W*
127 N8 **Povorino** Voronezhskaya Oblast', W Russian Federation *51°10′N 42°16′E*
Povungnituk *see* Puvirnituq
12 J3 **Povungnituk, Rivière de** ≈ Québec, NE Canada
14 H11 **Powassan** Ontario, S Canada *46°05′N 79°21′W*
35 U17 **Poway** California, W USA *32°57′N 117°02′W*
33 W14 **Powder River** Wyoming, C USA *43°01′N 106°57′W*
33 Y10 **Powder River** ≈ Montana/Wyoming, NW USA
32 L12 **Powder River** ≈ Oregon, NW USA
33 W13 **Powder River Pass** *pass* Wyoming, C USA
33 U12 **Powell** Wyoming, C USA *44°45′N 108°45′W*
65 I22 **Powell Basin** *undersea feature* NW Weddell Sea
36 M8 **Powell, Lake** ◎ Utah, W USA
37 R4 **Powell, Mount** ▲ Colorado, C USA *39°25′N 106°20′W*
10 L17 **Powell River** British Columbia, SW Canada *49°54′N 124°34′W*
31 N5 **Powers** Michigan, N USA *45°40′N 87°29′W*
28 K2 **Powers Lake** North Dakota, N USA *48°33′N 102°37′W*
21 V6 **Powhatan** Virginia, NE USA *37°33′N 77°56′W*
31 V13 **Powhatan Point** Ohio, N USA *39°49′N 80°49′W*
97 J20 **Powys** *cultural region* E Wales, United Kingdom
187 P17 **Poya** Province Nord, C New Caledonia *21°19′S 165°07′E*
161 P10 **Poyang Hu** ◎ S China
30 L7 **Poygan, Lake** ◎ Wisconsin, N USA
109 Y2 **Poysdorf** Niederösterreich, NE Austria *48°40′N 16°38′E*
112 N11 **Požarevac** *Ger.* Passarowitz. Serbia, NE Serbia *44°37′N 21°11′E*
41 Q13 **Poza Rica** *var.* Poza Rica de Hidalgo. Veracruz-Llave, E Mexico *20°34′N 97°26′W*
Poza Rica de Hidalgo *see* Poza Rica
112 L13 **Požega** *prev.* Slavonska Požega, *Ger.* Poschega, *Hung.* Pozsega. Požega-Slavonija, NE Croatia *45°19′N 17°42′E*
112 H9 **Požega-Slavonija** *off.* Požeško-Slavonska Županija. ◐ *province* NE Croatia
Požeško-Slavonska Županija *see* Požega-Slavonija
125 U13 **Pozhva** Komi-Permyatskiy Avtonomnyy Okrug, NW Russian Federation *59°07′N 56°04′E*
110 G11 **Poznań** *Ger.* Posen, Posnania. Wielkolpolskie, C Poland *52°24′N 16°56′E*
105 O13 **Pozo Alcón** Andalucía, S Spain *37°43′N 02°55′W*
62 H3 **Pozo Almonte** Tarapacá, N Chile *20°16′S 69°50′W*
104 L12 **Pozoblanco** Andalucía, S Spain *38°23′N 04°48′W*
105 Q11 **Pozo Cañada** Castilla-La Mancha, C Spain *38°49′N 01°45′W*
62 N5 **Pozo Colorado** Presidente Hayes, C Paraguay *23°26′S 58°51′W*
63 J20 **Pozos, Punta** *headland* S Argentina *47°55′S 65°46′W*
Pozsega *see* Požega
Pozsony *see* Bratislava
55 N5 **Pozuelos** Anzoátegui, NE Venezuela *10°11′N 64°39′W*
107 L26 **Pozzallo** Sicilia, Italy, C Mediterranean Sea *36°44′N 14°51′E*
107 K17 **Pozzuoli** *anc.* Puteoli. Campania, S Italy *40°49′N 14°07′E*
77 P17 **Pra** ≈ S Ghana
111 C19 **Prachatice** *Ger.* Prachatitz. Jihočeský Kraj, S Czech Republic *49°01′N 14°02′E*
Prachatitz *see* Prachatice
167 P11 **Prachin Buri** *var.* Prachinburi. Prachin Buri, C Thailand *14°05′N 101°23′E*
Prachinburi *see* Prachin Buri
Prachuab Girikhand *see* Prachuap Khiri Khan
167 O12 **Prachuap Khiri Khan** *var.* Prachuab Girikhand. Prachuap Khiri Khan, SW Thailand *11°50′N 99°49′E*
111 H16 **Praděd** *Ger.* Altvater. ▲ NE Czech Republic *50°06′N 17°14′E*
54 D11 **Pradera** Valle del Cauca, SW Colombia *03°23′N 76°11′W*
103 O17 **Prades** Pyrénées-Orientales, S France *42°36′N 02°22′E*
59 O19 **Prado** Bahia, SE Brazil *17°13′S 39°15′W*
54 E11 **Prado** Tolima, C Colombia *03°45′N 74°55′W*
Prado del Ganso *see* Goose Green
Prae *see* Phrae
95 J24 **Præstø** Storstrøm, SE Denmark *55°08′N 12°03′E*
Prag/Praga/Prague *see* Praha
27 O10 **Prague** Oklahoma, C USA *35°29′N 96°40′W*
111 D16 **Praha** *Eng.* Prague, *Ger.* Prag, *Pol.* Praga. ● (Czech Republic) Středočeský Kraj, NW Czech Republic *50°06′N 14°26′E*
116 J13 **Prahova** ◐ *county* SE Romania
116 J13 **Prahova** ≈ S Romania
76 E10 **Praia** ● (Cape Verde) Santiago, S Cape Verde *14°55′N 23°31′W*
83 M21 **Praia do Bilene** Gaza, S Mozambique *25°18′S 33°10′E*
83 M20 **Praia do Xai-Xai** Gaza, S Mozambique *25°04′S 33°43′E*
116 J10 **Praid** *Hung.* Parajd. Harghita, C Romania *46°33′N 25°06′E*
26 J3 **Prairie Dog Creek** ≈ Kansas/Nebraska, C USA
30 J9 **Prairie du Chien** Wisconsin, N USA *43°02′N 91°08′W*
27 S9 **Prairie Grove** Arkansas, C USA *35°58′N 94°19′W*
31 P10 **Prairie River** ≈ Michigan, N USA
Prairie State *see* Illinois
25 V11 **Prairie View** Texas, SW USA *30°05′N 95°59′W*
167 Q10 **Prakhon Chai** Buri Ram, E Thailand *14°36′N 103°04′E*
109 R4 **Pram** ≈ N Austria
109 S4 **Prambachkirchen** Oberösterreich, N Austria *48°18′N 13°50′E*
118 H2 **Prangli** *island* N Estonia
154 J13 **Prānhita** ≈ C India
127 O14 **Praskoveya** Stavropol'skiy Kray, SW Russian Federation *44°45′N 44°11′E*
172 I15 **Praslin** *island* Inner Islands, NE Seychelles
115 O23 **Prasonísi, Akrotírio** *cape* Ródos, Dodekánisa, Greece, Aegean Sea
111 I14 **Praszka** Opolskie, S Poland *51°05′N 18°29′E*
152 M13 **Pratāpgarh** Uttar Pradesh, N India *25°53′N 81°56′E*
Pratas Island *see* Tungsha Tao
119 M18 **Pratasy** *Rus.* Protasy. Homyel'skaya Voblasts', SE Belarus *52°47′N 29°05′E*
167 Q10 **Prathai** Nakhon Ratchasima, E Thailand *15°31′N 102°42′E*
Prathet Thai *see* Thailand
Prathum Thani *see* Pathum Thani
63 F21 **Prat, Isla** *island* S Chile
106 G11 **Prato** Toscana, C Italy *43°53′N 11°05′E*
103 O17 **Prats-de-Mollo-la-Preste** Pyrénées-Orientales, S France *42°25′N 02°28′E*
26 L6 **Pratt** Kansas, C USA *37°40′N 98°45′W*
108 E6 **Pratteln** Basel-Land, NW Switzerland *47°32′N 07°42′E*
193 O2 **Pratt Seamount** *undersea feature* N Pacific Ocean *56°09′N 142°30′W*
23 P5 **Prattville** Alabama, S USA *32°27′N 86°27′W*
Praust *see* Pruszcz Gdański
119 B14 **Pravdinsk** *Ger.* Friedland. Kaliningradskaya Oblast', W Russian Federation *54°26′N 21°01′E*
104 K2 **Pravia** Asturias, N Spain *43°30′N 06°06′W*
118 L12 **Prazaroki** *Rus.* Prozoroki. Vitsyebskaya Voblasts', N Belarus *55°18′N 28°13′E*
Prázsmár *see* Prejmer
167 S11 **Preăh Vihéar** Preăh Vihéar, N Cambodia *13°57′N 104°48′E*
116 J12 **Predeal** *Hung.* Predeál. Brașov, C Romania *45°30′N 25°31′E*
109 S8 **Predlitz** Steiermark, SE Austria *47°04′N 13°54′E*
11 V15 **Preeceville** Saskatchewan, S Canada *51°58′N 102°40′W*
Preenkuln *see* Priekule
102 K6 **Pré-en-Pail** Mayenne, NW France *48°27′N 00°15′W*
109 T4 **Pregarten** Oberösterreich, N Austria *48°21′N 14°31′E*
54 H7 **Pregonero** Táchira, NW Venezuela *08°02′N 71°35′W*
118 J10 **Preiļi** *Ger.* Preli. Preiļi, SE Latvia *56°17′N 26°52′E*
116 J12 **Prejmer** *Ger.* Tartlau, *Hung.* Prázsmár. Brașov, S Romania *45°42′N 25°49′E*
113 J16 **Prekornica** ▲▲ C Montenegro
Preli *see* Preiļi
Prëmet *see* Përmet
100 M12 **Premnitz** Brandenburg, NE Germany *52°33′N 12°22′E*
25 S15 **Premont** Texas, SW USA *27°21′N 98°07′W*
113 H14 **Prenj** ▲▲ S Bosnia and Herzegovina
Prenjas/Prenjasi *see* Përrenjas
22 L7 **Prentiss** Mississippi, S USA *31°36′N 89°52′W*
Preny *see* Prienai
100 O10 **Prenzlau** Brandenburg, NE Germany *53°19′N 13°52′E*
123 N11 **Preobrazhenka** Irkutskaya Oblast', C Russian Federation *60°01′N 108°00′E*
166 J9 **Preparis Island** *island* SW Burma (Myanmar)
Prerau *see* Přerov
111 H18 **Přerov** *Ger.* Prerau. Olomoucký Kraj, E Czech Republic *49°27′N 17°27′E*
Preschau *see* Prešov
14 M14 **Prescott** Ontario, SE Canada *44°43′N 75°33′W*
36 K12 **Prescott** Arizona, SW USA *34°33′N 112°26′W*
27 T13 **Prescott** Arkansas, C USA *33°49′N 93°25′W*
32 L10 **Prescott** Washington, NW USA *46°17′N 118°21′W*
30 H6 **Prescott** Wisconsin, N USA *44°46′N 92°45′W*
185 A24 **Preservation Inlet** *inlet* South Island, New Zealand
112 O7 **Preševo** Serbia, SE Serbia *42°20′N 21°38′E*
29 N10 **Presho** South Dakota, N USA *43°54′N 100°03′W*
58 M13 **Presidente Dutra** Maranhão, E Brazil *05°17′S 44°30′W*
60 I8 **Presidente Epitácio** São Paulo, S Brazil *21°45′S 52°07′W*
62 N5 **Presidente Hayes** *off.* Departamento de Presidente Hayes. ◐ *department* C Paraguay
Presidente Hayes, Departamento de *see* Presidente Hayes
60 I9 **Presidente Prudente** São Paulo, S Brazil *22°09′S 51°24′W*
Presidente Stroessner *see* Ciudad del Este
Presidente Vargas *see* Itabira
60 I8 **Presidente Venceslau** São Paulo, S Brazil *21°52′S 51°51′W*
193 O10 **President Thiers Seamount** *undersea feature* C Pacific Ocean *24°39′S 145°50′W*
24 J11 **Presidio** Texas, SW USA *29°33′N 104°22′W*
Preslav *see* Veliki Preslav
111 M19 **Prešov** *var.* Preschau, *Ger.* Eperies, *Hung.* Eperjes. Prešovský Kraj, E Slovakia *49°N 21°14′E*
111 M19 **Prešovský Kraj** ◐ *region* E Slovakia
113 N20 **Prespa, Lake** *Alb.* Liqen i Prespës, *Gk.* Límni Megáli Préspa, Limni Prespa, *Mac.* Prespansko Ezero, *Serb.* Prespansko Jezero. ◎ SE Europe
Prespa, Limni/Prespansko Ezero/Prespansko Jezero/Prespës, Liqen i *see* Prespa, Lake
19 S2 **Presque Isle** Maine, NE USA *46°40′N 68°01′W*
18 B11 **Presque Isle** *headland* Pennsylvania, NE USA *42°09′N 80°06′W*
Pressburg *see* Bratislava
77 P17 **Prestea** SW Ghana *05°22′N 02°07′W*
111 B17 **Přeštice** *Ger.* Pschestitz. Plzeňský Kraj, W Czech Republic *49°36′N 13°19′E*
97 K17 **Preston** NW England, United Kingdom *53°46′N 02°42′W*
23 S6 **Preston** Georgia, SE USA *32°03′N 84°32′W*
33 R16 **Preston** Idaho, NW USA *42°06′N 111°52′W*
29 Z13 **Preston** Iowa, C USA *42°03′N 90°24′W*
29 X11 **Preston** Minnesota, N USA *43°41′N 92°06′W*
21 O6 **Prestonsburg** Kentucky, S USA *37°40′N 82°46′W*
96 I13 **Prestwick** W Scotland, United Kingdom *55°31′N 04°39′W*
83 145 **Pretoria** *var.* Epitoli, Tshwane. ● Gauteng, NE South Africa *25°41′S 28°12′E* ***see also*** Tshwane
Pretoria-Witwatersrand-Vereeniging *see* Gauteng
Pretusha *see* Pretushë
113 M21 **Pretushë** *var.* Pretusha. Korçë, SE Albania *40°50′N 20°45′E*
Preussisch Eylau *see* Bagrationovsk
Preußisch Holland *see* Pasłęk
Preussisch-Stargard *see* Starogard Gdański
115 C17 **Préveza** Ípeiros, W Greece *38°59′N 20°44′E*
37 V3 **Prewitt Reservoir** ⊠ Colorado, C USA
167 S13 **Prey Vêng** Prey Vêng, S Cambodia *11°30′N 105°20′E*
144 M12 **Priaral'skiye Karakumy, Peski** *desert* SW Kazakhstan
123 P14 **Priargunsk** Chitinskaya Oblast', S Russian Federation *50°25′N 119°12′E*
38 K14 **Pribilof Islands** *island group* Alaska, USA
113 K14 **Priboj** Serbia, W Serbia *43°34′N 19°33′E*
111 C17 **Příbram** *Ger.* Pibrans. Středočeský Kraj, W Czech Republic *49°41′N 14°02′E*
36 M4 **Price** Utah, W USA *39°35′N 110°49′W*
37 N5 **Price River** ≈ Utah, W USA
23 N8 **Prichard** Alabama, S USA *30°44′N 88°04′W*
25 R8 **Priddy** Texas, SW USA *31°39′N 98°30′W*
105 P8 **Priego** Castilla-La Mancha, C Spain *40°26′N 02°19′W*
104 M14 **Priego de Córdoba** Andalucía, S Spain *37°27′N 04°12′W*
118 C10 **Priekule** *Ger.* Preenkuln. Liepāja, SW Latvia *56°26′N 21°36′E*
118 C12 **Priekulė** *Ger.* Prökuls. Klaipėda, W Lithuania *55°36′N 21°16′E*
119 F14 **Prienai** *Pol.* Preny. Kaunas, S Lithuania *54°37′N 23°56′E*
83 G23 **Prieska** Northern Cape, C South Africa *29°40′S 22°45′E*
32 M7 **Priest Lake** ◎ Idaho, NW USA
32 M7 **Priest River** Idaho, NW USA *48°10′N 117°02′W*
104 M3 **Prieta, Peña** ▲ N Spain *43°01′N 04°42′W*
40 J10 **Prieto, Cerro** ▲ C Mexico *24°10′N 105°21′W*
111 J19 **Prievidza** *var.* Priewitz, *Ger.* Priwitz, *Hung.* Privigye. Trenčiansky Kraj, W Slovakia *48°47′N 18°35′E*
Priewitz *see* Prievidza
112 F10 **Prijedor** ◐ Republika Srpska, NW Bosnia and Herzegovina
113 K14 **Prijepolje** Serbia, W Serbia *43°24′N 19°39′E*
Prikaspiyskaya Nizmennost' *see* Caspian Depression
113 O19 **Prilep** *Turk.* Perlepe. S FYR Macedonia *41°21′N 21°34′E*
108 B9 **Prilly** Vaud, SW Switzerland *46°32′N 06°38′E*
Priluki *see* Pryluky
62 L10 **Primero, Río** ≈ C Argentina
29 S12 **Primghar** Iowa, C USA *43°05′N 95°37′W*
112 B9 **Primorje-Gorski Kotar** *off.* Primorsko-Goranska Županija. ◐ *province* NW Croatia
118 A13 **Primorsk** *Ger.* Fischhausen. Kaliningradskaya Oblast', W Russian Federation *54°45′N 20°00′E*
124 G12 **Primorsk** *Fin.* Koivisto. Leningradskaya Oblast', NW Russian Federation *60°20′N 28°39′E*
123 S14 **Primorskiy Kray** *prev. Eng.* Maritime Territory. ◐ *territory* SE Russian Federation
114 N10 **Primorsko** *prev.* Keupriya. Burgas, E Bulgaria *42°15′N 27°45′E*
126 K13 **Primorsko-Akhtarsk** Krasnodarskiy Kray, SW Russian Federation *46°03′N 38°44′E*
Primorsko-Goranska Županija *see* Primorje-Gorski Kotar
Primorsk/Primorskoye *see* Prymors'k
117 U13 **Primors'kyy** Respublika Krym, S Ukraine *45°09′N 35°33′E*
113 D14 **Primošten** Šibenik-Knin, S Croatia *43°34′N 15°57′E*
11 R13 **Primrose Lake** ◎ Saskatchewan, C Canada
11 T14 **Prince Albert** Saskatchewan, S Canada *53°09′N 105°43′W*
83 G25 **Prince Albert** Western Cape, SW South Africa *33°13′S 22°03′E*
8 J5 **Prince Albert Peninsula** *peninsula* Victoria Island, Northwest Territories, NW Canada
8 J6 **Prince Albert Sound** *inlet* Northwest Territories, N Canada
J5 8 **Prince Alfred, Cape** *headland* Northwest Territories, NW Canada
9 P6 **Prince Charles Island** *island* Nunavut, NE Canada
195 W6 **Prince Charles Mountains** ▲▲ Antarctica
Prince-Édouard, Île-du *see* Prince Edward Island
172 M13 **Prince Edward Fracture Zone** *tectonic feature* SW Indian Ocean
13 P14 **Prince Edward Island** *Fr.* Île-du Prince-Édouard. ◐ *province* SE Canada
13 Q14 **Prince Edward Island** *Fr.* Île-du Prince-Édouard. *island* SE Canada
173 M12 **Prince Edward Islands** *island group* S South Africa
21 X4 **Prince Frederick** Maryland, NE USA *38°32′N 76°35′W*
10 M14 **Prince George** British Columbia, SW Canada *53°55′N 122°49′W*
21 W6 **Prince George** Virginia, NE USA *37°13′N 77°13′W*
197 O8 **Prince Gustaf Adolf Sea** *sea* Nunavut, N Canada
197 Q3 **Prince of Wales, Cape** *headland* Alaska, USA *65°39′N 168°12′W*
181 V1 **Prince of Wales Island** *island* Queensland, E Australia
8 L5 **Prince of Wales Island** *island* Queen Elizabeth Islands, Nunavut, NW Canada
39 Y14 **Prince of Wales Island** *island* Alexander Archipelago, Alaska, USA
Prince of Wales Island *see* Pinang, Pulau
8 J5 **Prince of Wales Strait** *strait* Northwest Territories, N Canada
197 O8 **Prince Patrick Island** *island* Parry Islands, Northwest Territories, NW Canada
9 N5 **Prince Regent Inlet** *channel* Nunavut, N Canada
10 J13 **Prince Rupert** British Columbia, SW Canada *54°18′N 130°17′W*
Prince's Island *see* Príncipe
21 Y5 **Princess Anne** Maryland, NE USA *38°12′N 75°42′W*
181 W2 **Princess Charlotte Bay** *bay* Queensland, NE Australia
195 W7 **Princess Elizabeth Land** *physical region* Antarctica
10 J14 **Princess Royal Island** *island* British Columbia, SW Canada
45 U15 **Princes Town** Trinidad, Trinidad and Tobago *10°16′N 61°23′W*
11 N17 **Princeton** British Columbia, SW Canada *49°25′N 120°35′W*
30 L11 **Princeton** Illinois, N USA *41°22′N 89°27′W*
31 N16 **Princeton** Indiana, N USA *38°21′N 87°33′W*
29 Z14 **Princeton** Iowa, C USA *41°40′N 90°21′W*
20 H7 **Princeton** Kentucky, S USA *37°06′N 87°52′W*
29 V8 **Princeton** Minnesota, N USA *45°34′N 93°34′W*
27 S1 **Princeton** Missouri, C USA *40°22′N 93°37′W*
18 J15 **Princeton** New Jersey, NE USA *40°21′N 74°39′W*
21 R6 **Princeton** West Virginia, NE USA *37°23′N 81°06′W*
39 S12 **Prince William Sound** *inlet* Alaska, USA
67 P9 **Príncipe** *var.* Príncipe Island, *Eng.* Prince's Island. *island* N Sao Tome and Principe
Príncipe Island *see* Príncipe
32 I13 **Prineville** Oregon, NW USA *44°19′N 120°50′W*
28 J11 **Pringle** South Dakota, N USA *43°34′N 103°34′W*
25 N1 **Pringle** Texas, SW USA *35°55′N 101°28′W*
99 H14 **Prinsenbeek** Noord-Brabant, S Netherlands *51°36′N 04°42′E*
98 L6 **Prinses Margriet Kanaal** *canal* N Netherlands
195 R1 **Prinsesse Astrid Kyst** *physical region* Antarctica
195 T2 **Prinsesse Ragnhild Kyst** *physical region* Antarctica
195 U2 **Prins Harald Kyst** *physical region* Antarctica
92 N2 **Prins Karls Forland** *island* W Svalbard
43 N8 **Prinzapolka** Región Autónoma Atlántico Norte, NE Nicaragua *13°19′N 83°35′W*
42 L8 **Prinzapolka, Río** ≈ NE Nicaragua
122 H9 **Priob'ye** Khanty-Mansiyskiy Avtonomnyy Okrug-Yugra, N Russian Federation *62°25′N 65°36′E*
104 H1 **Prior, Cabo** *headland* NW Spain *43°33′N 08°21′W*
29 V9 **Prior Lake** Minnesota, N USA *44°42′N 93°25′W*
124 H11 **Priozersk** *Fin.* Käkisalmi. Leningradskaya Oblast', NW Russian Federation *61°02′N 30°07′E*
119 J20 **Pripet** *Bel.* Prypyats', *Ukr.* Pryp"yat'. ≈ Belarus/Ukraine
119 J20 **Pripet Marshes** *wetland* Belarus/Ukraine
113 N16 **Prishtinë** *Eng.* Pristina, *Serb.* Priština. C Kosovo *42°40′N 21°10′E*
126 J8 **Pristen'** Kurskaya Oblast', W Russian Federation *51°15′N 36°47′E*
Priština *see* Prishtinë
Pristina *see* Prishtinë
100 M10 **Pritzwalk** Brandenburg, NE Germany *53°10′N 12°11′E*
103 R13 **Privas** Ardèche, E France *44°45′N 04°35′E*
107 I16 **Priverno** Lazio, C Italy *41°28′N 13°11′E*
Privigye *see* Prievidza
112 C12 **Privlaka** Zadar, SW Croatia *44°15′N 15°07′E*
124 M15 **Privolzhsk** Ivanovskaya Oblast', NW Russian Federation *57°24′N 41°16′E*
127 P7 **Privolzhskaya Vozvyshennost'** *var.* Volga Uplands. ▲▲ W Russian Federation
127 P8 **Privolzhskiy** Saratovskaya Oblast', W Russian Federation *51°24′N 46°02′E*
127 P8 **Privolzhskoye** Saratovskaya Oblast', W Russian Federation *51°08′N 45°57′E*
Priwitz *see* Prievidza
127 N13 **Priyutnoye** Respublika Kalmykiya, SW Russian Federation *46°08′N 43°33′E*
127 U5 **Priyutovo** Respublika Bashkortostan, W Russian Federation *53°54′N 53°56′E*
113 M17 **Prizren** S Kosovo *42°14′N 20°46′E*
107 I24 **Prizzi** Sicilia, Italy, C Mediterranean Sea *37°44′N 13°26′E*
113 P18 **Probištip** NE FYR Macedonia *42°00′N 22°06′E*
169 S16 **Probolinggo** Jawa, C Indonesia *07°45′S 113°12′E*
Probstberg *see* Wyszków
111 F14 **Prochowice** *Ger.* Parchwitz. Dolnośląskie, SW Poland *51°15′N 16°22′E*
29 W5 **Proctor** Minnesota, N USA *46°46′N 92°13′W*
25 R8 **Proctor** Texas, SW USA *31°57′N 98°25′W*
25 R8 **Proctor Lake** ⊠ Texas, SW USA
155 I18 **Proddatūr** Andhra Pradesh, E India *14°45′N 78°34′E*
104 H9 **Proença-a-Nova** *var.* Proença a Nova. Castelo Branco, C Portugal *39°45′N 07°56′W*
Proença a Nova *see* Proença-a-Nova
99 I21 **Profondeville** Namur, SE Belgium *50°22′N 04°52′E*
41 W11 **Progreso** Yucatán, SE Mexico *21°14′N 89°41′W*
123 R14 **Progress** Amurskaya Oblast', SE Russian Federation *49°40′N 129°30′E*
127 O15 **Prokhladnyy** Kabardino-Balkarskaya Respublika, SW Russian Federation *43°48′N 44°02′E*
Prokletije *see* North Albanian Alps
Prōkuls *see* Priekulė
113 O15 **Prokuplje** Serbia, SE Serbia *43°15′N 21°35′E*
124 H14 **Proletariy** Novgorodskaya Oblast', W Russian Federation *58°24′N 31°40′E*
126 M12 **Proletarsk** Rostovskaya Oblast', SW Russian Federation *46°42′N 41°48′E*
127 N13 **Proletarskoye Vodokhranilishche** *salt lake* SW Russian Federation
Prome *see* Pyay
60 J8 **Promissão** São Paulo, S Brazil *21°33′S 49°51′W*
60 J8 **Promissão, Represa de** ⊠ S Brazil
125 V4 **Promyshlennyy** Respublika Komi, NW Russian Federation *67°36′N 64°E*
119 O16 **Pronya** ≈ E Belarus
10 M11 **Prophet River** British Columbia, W Canada *58°07′N 122°39′W*
30 K11 **Prophetstown** Illinois, N USA *41°40′N 89°56′W*
Propinsi Kepulauan Riau *see* Kepulauan Riau
59 P16 **Propriá** Sergipe, E Brazil *10°15′S 36°51′W*
103 X16 **Propriano** Corse, France, C Mediterranean Sea *41°41′N 08°54′E*
Prościejów *see* Prostějov
Proskurov *see* Khmel'nyts'kyy
114 H12 **Prosotsáni** Anatolikí Makedonía kai Thráki, NE Greece *41°11′N 23°59′E*
171 Q7 **Prosperidad** Mindanao, S Philippines *08°36′N 125°54′E*
32 J10 **Prosser** Washington, NW USA *46°12′N 119°46′W*
Prossnitz *see* Prostějov
111 G18 **Prostějov** *Ger.* Prossnitz, *Pol.* Prościejów. Olomoucký Kraj, E Czech Republic *49°29′N 17°08′E*
117 V8 **Prosyana** Dnipropetrovs'ka Oblast', E Ukraine *48°07′N 36°22′E*
111 L16 **Proszowice** Małopolskie, S Poland *50°12′N 20°15′E*
Protasy *see* Pratasy
172 J11 **Protea Seamount** *undersea feature* SW Indian Ocean *36°50′S 18°05′E*
115 D21 **Próti** *island* S Greece
114 N8 **Provadiya** Varna, E Bulgaria *43°10′N 27°29′E*
103 T14 **Provence** *cultural region* SE France
103 S15 **Provence** *prev.* Marseille-Marigrane. ✈ (Marseille) Bouches-du-Rhône, SE France *43°25′N 05°15′E*
103 T14 **Provence-Alpes-Côte d'Azur** ◐ *region* SE France
20 H6 **Providence** Kentucky, S USA *37°23′N 87°47′W*
19 N12 **Providence** *state capital* Rhode Island, NE USA *41°50′N 71°26′W*
36 L1 **Providence** Utah, W USA *41°42′N 111°49′W*
Providence *see* Fort Providence
Providence *see* Providence Atoll
67 X10 **Providence Atoll** *var.* Providence. *atoll* S Seychelles
14 D12 **Providence Bay** Manitoulin Island, Ontario, S Canada *45°39′N 82°16′W*
23 R6 **Providence Canyon** *valley* Alabama/Georgia, S USA
22 I5 **Providence, Lake** ◎ Louisiana, S USA
35 X13 **Providence Mountains** ▲▲ California, W USA
43 Q7 **Providencia, Isla de** *island* NW Colombia, Caribbean Sea
44 L6 **Providenciales** *island* W Turks and Caicos Islands
19 Q12 **Provincetown** Massachusetts, NE USA *42°01′N 70°10′W*
103 P5 **Provins** Seine-et-Marne, N France *48°34′N 03°18′E*
36 L3 **Provo** Utah, W USA *40°14′N 111°39′W*
11 R15 **Provost** Alberta, SW Canada *52°24′N 110°16′W*
112 G13 **Prozor** Federacija Bosna I Hercegovina, SW Bosnia and Herzegovina *43°46′N 17°38′E*
Prozoroki *see* Prazaroki
60 I11 **Prudentópolis** Paraná, S Brazil *25°12′S 50°58′W*
39 R5 **Prudhoe Bay** Alaska, USA *70°16′N 148°18′W*
39 R4 **Prudhoe Bay** *bay* Alaska, USA
111 H16 **Prudnik** *Ger.* Neustadt, Neustadt in Oberschlesien. Opole, SW Poland *50°20′N 17°34′E*
119 J16 **Prudy** Minskaya Voblasts', C Belarus *53°47′N 26°32′E*
101 D18 **Prüm** Rheinland-Pfalz, W Germany *50°15′N 06°27′E*
101 D18 **Prüm** ≈ W Germany
Prusa *see* Bursa
110 J7 **Pruszcz Gdański** *Ger.* Praust. Pomorskie, N Poland *54°16′N 18°36′E*
110 M12 **Pruszków** *Ger.* Kaltdorf. Mazowieckie, C Poland *52°09′N 20°49′E*
116 K8 **Prut** *Ger.* Pruth. ≈ E Europe
Pruth *see* Prut
108 L8 **Prutz** Tirol, W Austria *47°07′N 10°42′E*
Pružana *see* Pruzhany
119 G19 **Pruzhany** *Pol.* Prużana. Brestskaya Voblasts', SW Belarus *52°33′N 24°28′E*
124 I11 **Pryazha** Respublika Kareliya, NW Russian Federation *61°42′N 33°39′E*
117 U10 **Pryazovs'ke** Zaporiz'ka Oblast', SE Ukraine *46°43′N 35°39′E*
Prychornomor'ska Nyzovyna *see* Black Sea Lowland
Prydniprovs'ka Nyzovyna/Prydnyaprowskaya Nizina *see* Dnieper Lowland
195 Y7 **Prydz Bay** *bay* Antarctica

◆ Country ● Country Capital ◇ Dependent Territory ○ Dependent Territory Capital ◐ Administrative Regions ✈ International Airport ▲ Mountain ▲▲ Mountain Range ♨ Volcano ≈ River ◎ Lake ⊠ Reservoir

117 R4 **Pryluky** *Rus.* Priluki. Chernihivs'ka Oblast', NE Ukraine 50°35′N 32°23′E
117 V10 **Prymors'k** *Rus.* Primorsk; *prev.* Primorskoye. Zaporiz'ka Oblast', SE Ukraine 46°44′N 36°19′E
27 Q9 **Pryor** Oklahoma, C USA 36°19′N 95°19′W
33 U11 **Pryor Creek** ≈ Montana, NW USA
Pryp"yat'/Prypyats' *see* Pripet
110 M10 **Przasnysz** Mazowieckie, C Poland 53°01′N 20°51′E
111 K14 **Przedbórz** Łodzkie, S Poland 51°04′N 19°51′E
111 P17 **Przemyśl** *Rus.* Peremyshl. Podkarpackie, C Poland 49°47′N 22°47′E
111 O16 **Przeworsk** Podkarpackie, SE Poland 50°04′N 22°30′E
Przheval'sk *see* Karakol
110 L13 **Przysucha** Mazowieckie, SE Poland 51°22′N 20°36′E
115 H18 **Psachná** *var.* Psahna, Psakhná. Évvoia, C Greece 38°35′N 23°39′E
Psahna/Psakhná *see* Psachná
115 K18 **Psará** *island* E Greece
115 I16 **Psathoúra** *island* Vóreies Sporádes, Greece, Aegean Sea
Pschestitz *see* Přeštice
Psein Lora *see* Pishin Lora
117 S5 **Psel** *Rus.* Psël. ≈ Russian Federation/Ukraine
Psël *see* Psel
115 M21 **Psérimos** *island* Dodekánisa, Greece, Aegean Sea
Pseyn Bowr *see* Pishin Lora
Pskem *see* Piskom
147 R8 **Pskemskiy Khrebet** *Uzb.* Piskom Tizmasi. ▲▲ Kyrgyzstan/Uzbekistan
124 F14 **Pskov** *Ger.* Pleskau, *Latv.* Pleskava. Pskovskaya Oblast', W Russian Federation 58°32′N 31°15′E
118 K6 **Pskov, Lake** *Est.* Pihkva Järv, *Ger.* Pleskauer See, *Rus.* Pskovskoye Ozero. ◎ Estonia/Russian Federation
124 F15 **Pskovskaya Oblast'** ◈ *province* W Russian Federation
Pskovskoye Ozero *see* Pskov, Lake
112 G9 **Psunj** ▲▲ NE Croatia
111 J17 **Pszczyna** *Ger.* Pless. Śląskie, S Poland 49°59′N 18°54′E
Ptačnik/Ptacsnik *see* Vtáčnik
115 D17 **Ptéri** ▲ C Greece 39°08′N 21°32′E
Ptich' *see* Ptsich
115 E14 **Ptolemaïda** *prev.* Ptolemaïs. Dytikí Makedonía, N Greece 40°34′N 21°42′E
Ptolemaïs *see* Ptolemaïda, Greece
Ptolemaïs *see* 'Akko, Israel
119 M19 **Ptsich** *Rus.* Ptich'. Homyel'skaya Voblasts', SE Belarus 52°11′N 28°49′E
119 M18 **Ptsich** *Rus.* Ptich'. ≈ SE Belarus
109 X10 **Ptuj** *Ger.* Pettau; *anc.* Poetovio. NE Slovenia 46°26′N 15°54′E
61 A23 **Puán** Buenos Aires, E Argentina 37°35′S 62°45′W
192 H15 **Pu'apu'a** Savai'i, C Samoa 13°32′S 172°09′W
192 G15 **Puava, Cape** *headland* Savai'i, NW Samoa
Pubao *see* Baingoin
56 F12 **Pucallpa** Ucayali, C Peru 08°21′S 74°33′W
57 J17 **Pucarani** La Paz, NW Bolivia 16°25′S 68°29′W
Pučarevo *see* Novi Travnik
157 U12 **Pucheng** Shaanxi, SE China 35°00′N 109°34′E
160 L6 **Pucheng** *var.* Nanpu. Fujian, C China 27°59′N 118°31′E
125 N16 **Puchezh** Ivanovskaya Oblast', W Russian Federation 56°58′N 41°08′E
111 I19 **Púchov** *Hung.* Puhó. Trenčiansky Kraj, W Slovakia 49°08′N 18°15′E
116 J13 **Pucioasa** Dâmbovița, S Romania 45°04′N 25°23′E
110 I6 **Puck** Pomorskie, N Poland 54°43′N 18°24′E
30 L8 **Puckaway Lake** ◎ Wisconsin, N USA
63 G15 **Pucón** Araucanía, S Chile 39°18′S 71°52′W
93 M14 **Pudasjärvi** Oulu, C Finland 65°20′N 27°02′E
148 L8 **Pūdeh Tal, Shelleh-ye** ≈ SW Afghanistan
127 S1 **Pudem** Udmurtskaya Respublika, NW Russian Federation 58°18′N 52°08′E
Pudewitz *see* Pobiedziska
124 K11 **Pudozh** Respublika Kareliya, NW Russian Federation 61°48′N 36°30′E
97 M17 **Pudsey** N England, United Kingdom 53°48′N 01°40′W
Puduchcheri *see* Pondicherry
151 H21 **Pudukkottai** Tamil Nādu, SE India 10°23′N 78°47′E
171 Z13 **Pue** Papua, E Indonesia 02°42′S 140°36′E
41 P14 **Puebla** *var.* Puebla de Zaragoza. Puebla, S Mexico 19°02′N 98°13′W
41 P15 **Puebla** ◈ *state* S Mexico
104 L11 **Puebla de Alcocer** Extremadura, W Spain 38°59′N 05°14′W
Puebla de Don Fabrique *see* Puebla de Don Fadrique
105 P13 **Puebla de Don Fadrique** *var.* Puebla de Don Fabrique. Andalucía, S Spain 37°58′N 02°25′W
104 J11 **Puebla de la Calzada** Extremadura, W Spain 38°54′N 06°38′W
104 J5 **Puebla de Sanabria** Castilla-León, N Spain 42°04′N 06°38′W
Puebla de Trives *see* A Pobla de Trives
Puebla de Zaragoza *see* Puebla
37 T6 **Pueblo** Colorado, C USA 38°15′N 104°37′W
37 N10 **Pueblo Colorado Wash** *valley* Arizona, SW USA
61 C16 **Pueblo Libertador** Corrientes, NE Argentina 30°13′S 59°23′W
40 J10 **Pueblo Nuevo** Durango, C Mexico 23°24′N 105°21′W
42 J8 **Pueblo Nuevo** Estelí, NW Nicaragua 13°21′N 86°30′W
54 J3 **Pueblo Nuevo** Falcón, N Venezuela 11°59′N 69°57′W
42 B6 **Pueblo Nuevo Tiquisate** *var.* Tiquisate. Escuintla, SW Guatemala 14°16′N 91°21′W
41 Q11 **Pueblo Viejo, Laguna de** *lagoon* E Mexico
63 J14 **Puelches** La Pampa, C Argentina 38°08′S 65°56′W
104 L14 **Puente-Genil** Andalucía, S Spain 37°23′N 04°45′W
105 Q3 **Puente la Reina** *Bas.* Gares. Navarra, N Spain 42°40′N 01°49′W
104 L12 **Puente Nuevo, Embalse de** ⊠ S Spain
57 D14 **Puente Piedra** Lima, W Peru 11°49′S 77°01′W
160 F14 **Pu'er** *var.* Ning'er. Yunnan, SW China 23°09′N 100°58′E
45 V6 **Puerca, Punta** *headland* E Puerto Rico 18°13′N 65°36′W
37 R12 **Puerco, Rio** ≈ New Mexico, SW USA
57 J17 **Puerto Acosta** La Paz, W Bolivia 15°33′S 69°15′W
63 G19 **Puerto Aisén** Aisén, S Chile 45°24′S 72°42′W
41 R17 **Puerto Ángel** Oaxaca, SE Mexico 15°39′N 96°29′W
Puerto Argentino *see* Stanley
41 T17 **Puerto Arista** Chiapas, SE Mexico 15°55′N 93°47′W
43 O16 **Puerto Armuelles** Chiriquí, SW Panama 08°19′N 82°51′W
Puerto Arrecife *see* Arrecife
54 D14 **Puerto Asís** Putumayo, SW Colombia 0°31′N 76°31′W
54 L9 **Puerto Ayacucho** Amazonas, SW Venezuela 05°45′N 67°37′W
57 C18 **Puerto Ayora** Galapagos Islands, Ecuador, E Pacific Ocean 0°45′S 90°19′W
57 C18 **Puerto Baquerizo Moreno** *var.* Baquerizo Moreno. Galapagos Islands, Ecuador, E Pacific Ocean 0°54′S 89°37′W
42 G4 **Puerto Barrios** Izabal, E Guatemala 15°42′N 88°34′W
Puerto Bello *see* Portobelo
54 F8 **Puerto Berrío** Antioquia, C Colombia 06°28′N 74°28′W
54 F9 **Puerto Boyaca** Boyacá, C Colombia 05°58′N 74°36′W
54 K4 **Puerto Cabello** Carabobo, N Venezuela 10°29′N 68°02′W
43 N7 **Puerto Cabezas** *var.* Bilwi. Región Autónoma Atlántico Norte, NE Nicaragua 14°05′N 83°22′W
54 L9 **Puerto Carreño** Vichada, E Colombia 06°08′N 67°30′W
54 E4 **Puerto Colombia** Atlántico, N Colombia 10°59′N 74°57′W
42 H4 **Puerto Cortés** Cortés, NW Honduras 15°50′N 87°55′W
54 J4 **Puerto Cumarebo** Falcón, N Venezuela 11°29′N 69°21′W
Puerto de Cabras *see* Puerto del Rosario
55 Q5 **Puerto de Hierro** Sucre, NE Venezuela 10°40′N 62°03′W
64 O11 **Puerto de la Cruz** Tenerife, Islas Canarias, Spain, NE Atlantic Ocean 28°24′N 16°33′W
64 Q11 **Puerto del Rosario** *var.* Puerto de Cabras. Fuerteventura, Islas Canarias, Spain, NE Atlantic Ocean 28°29′N 13°52′W
63 J20 **Puerto Deseado** Santa Cruz, SE Argentina 47°46′S 65°53′W
40 F8 **Puerto Escondido** Baja California Sur, NW Mexico 25°48′N 111°20′W
41 R17 **Puerto Escondido** Oaxaca, SE Mexico 15°48′N 96°57′W
60 G12 **Puerto Esperanza** Misiones, NE Argentina 26°01′S 54°39′W
54 H10 **Puerto Gaitán** Meta, C Colombia 04°20′N 72°10′W
Puerto Gallegos *see* Río Gallegos
60 G12 **Puerto Iguazú** Misiones, NE Argentina 25°39′S 54°35′W
56 F12 **Puerto Inca** Huánuco, N Peru 09°22′S 74°54′W
54 L11 **Puerto Inírida** *var.* Obando. Guainía, E Colombia 03°48′N 67°54′W
42 K13 **Puerto Jesús** Guanacaste, NW Costa Rica 10°08′N 85°26′W
41 Z11 **Puerto Juárez** Quintana Roo, SE Mexico 21°06′N 86°46′W
55 N5 **Puerto La Cruz** Anzoátegui, NE Venezuela 10°14′N 64°40′W
54 E14 **Puerto Leguízamo** Putumayo, S Colombia 0°14′N 74°45′W
43 N5 **Puerto Lempira** Gracias a Dios, E Honduras 15°14′N 83°48′W
Puerto Libertad *see* La Libertad
54 I11 **Puerto Limón** Meta, E Colombia 04°00′N 71°09′W
54 D13 **Puerto Limón** Putumayo, SW Colombia 01°02′N 76°30′W
Puerto Limón *see* Limón
105 N11 **Puertollano** Castilla-La Mancha, C Spain 38°41′N 04°07′W
63 K17 **Puerto Lobos** Chubut, SE Argentina 42°00′S 64°58′W
54 I3 **Puerto López** La Guajira, N Colombia 11°54′N 71°21′W
105 Q14 **Puerto Lumbreras** Murcia, SE Spain 37°35′N 01°49′W
41 V17 **Puerto Madero** Chiapas, SE Mexico 14°44′N 92°25′W
63 K17 **Puerto Madryn** Chubut, S Argentina 42°45′S 65°02′W
Puerto Magdalena *see* Bahía Magdalena
57 J15 **Puerto Maldonado** Madre de Dios, E Peru 12°37′S 69°11′W
Puerto Masachapa *see* Masachapa
Puerto México *see* Coatzacoalcos
63 G17 **Puerto Montt** Los Lagos, C Chile 41°28′S 72°57′W
41 Z12 **Puerto Morelos** Quintana Roo, SE Mexico 20°47′N 86°54′W
54 L10 **Puerto Nariño** Vichada, E Colombia 04°57′N 67°51′W
63 H23 **Puerto Natales** Magallanes, S Chile 51°42′S 72°28′W
43 X15 **Puerto Obaldía** Kuna Yala, NE Panama 08°38′N 77°26′W
44 H6 **Puerto Padre** Las Tunas, E Cuba 21°13′N 76°35′W
54 L9 **Puerto Páez** Apure, C Venezuela 06°10′N 67°30′W
40 E3 **Puerto Peñasco** Sonora, NW Mexico 31°20′N 113°35′W
55 N5 **Puerto Píritu** Anzoátegui, NE Venezuela 10°04′N 65°00′W
45 N8 **Puerto Plata** *var.* San Felipe de Puerto Plata. N Dominican Republic 19°46′N 70°42′W
45 N8 **Puerto Plata** ✈ N Dominican Republic 19°43′N 70°43′W
Puerto Presidente Stroessner *see* Ciudad del Este
171 N6 **Puerto Princesa** *off.* Puerto Princesa City. Palawan, W Philippines 09°48′N 118°43′E
Puerto Princesa City *see* Puerto Princesa
Puerto Príncipe *see* Camagüey
Puerto Quellón *see* Quellón
60 F13 **Puerto Rico** Misiones, NE Argentina 26°48′S 54°59′W
57 K14 **Puerto Rico** Pando, N Bolivia 11°07′S 67°32′W
54 E12 **Puerto Rico** Caquetá, S Colombia 01°54′N 75°13′W
45 U5 **Puerto Rico** *off.* Commonwealth of Puerto Rico; *prev.* Porto Rico. ◇ US *commonwealth territory* C West Indies
64 F11 **Puerto Rico** *island* C West Indies
Puerto Rico, Commonwealth of *see* Puerto Rico
64 G11 **Puerto Rico Trench** *undersea feature* NE Caribbean Sea
54 I8 **Puerto Rondón** Arauca, E Colombia 06°16′N 71°05′W
Puerto San José *see* San José
63 J21 **Puerto San Julián** *var.* San Julián. Santa Cruz, SE Argentina 49°14′S 67°41′W
63 I22 **Puerto Santa Cruz** *var.* Santa Cruz. Santa Cruz, SE Argentina 50°05′S 68°31′W
Puerto Sauce *see* Juan L. Lacaze
57 Q20 **Puerto Suárez** Santa Cruz, E Bolivia 18°59′S 57°47′W
54 D13 **Puerto Umbría** Putumayo, SW Colombia 0°52′N 76°36′W
40 J13 **Puerto Vallarta** Jalisco, SW Mexico 20°36′N 105°15′W
63 G16 **Puerto Varas** Los Lagos, C Chile 41°20′S 73°00′W
42 M13 **Puerto Viejo** Heredia, NE Costa Rica 10°27′N 84°00′W
Puertoviejo *see* Portoviejo
57 B18 **Puerto Villamil** *var.* Villamil. Galapagos Islands, Ecuador, E Pacific Ocean 0°57′S 91°00′W
54 F8 **Puerto Wilches** Santander, N Colombia 07°22′N 73°53′W
63 H20 **Pueyrredón, Lago** *var.* Lago Cochrane. ◎ S Argentina
127 R7 **Pugachëv** Saratovskaya Oblast', W Russian Federation 52°06′N 48°50′E
127 T3 **Pugachëvo** Udmurtskaya Respublika, NW Russian Federation 56°38′N 53°03′E
32 H8 **Puget Sound** *sound* Washington, NW USA
107 O17 **Puglia** *var.* Le Puglie, *Eng.* Apulia. ◈ *region* SE Italy
107 N17 **Puglia, Canosa di** *anc.* Canusium. Puglia, SE Italy 41°13′N 16°04′E
118 I6 **Puhja** *Ger.* Kawelecht. Tartumaa, SE Estonia 58°20′N 26°19′E
Puhó *see* Púchov
105 V4 **Puigcerdà** Cataluña, NE Spain 42°25′N 01°53′E
Puigmal *see* Puigmal d'Err
103 N17 **Puigmal d'Err** *var.* Puigmal. ▲ S France 42°24′N 02°07′E
76 I16 **Pujehun** S Sierra Leone 07°23′N 11°44′W
Puka *see* Pukë
185 E20 **Pukaki, Lake** ◎ South Island, New Zealand
38 F10 **Pukalani** Maui, Hawaii, USA, C Pacific Ocean 20°50′N 156°20′W
190 J13 **Pukapuka** *atoll* N Cook Islands
191 X9 **Pukapuka** *atoll* Îles Tuamotu, E French Polynesia
Pukari Neem *see* Purekkari Neem
191 X11 **Pukarua** *var.* Pukaruha. *atoll* Îles Tuamotu, E French Polynesia
Pukaruha *see* Pukarua
14 A7 **Pukaskwa** ≈ Ontario, S Canada
11 V12 **Pukatawagan** Manitoba, C Canada 55°46′N 101°14′W
191 X16 **Pukatikei, Maunga** ⛰ Easter Island, Chile, E Pacific Ocean
182 C1 **Pukatja** *var.* Ernabella. South Australia 26°18′S 132°13′E
163 Y12 **Pukch'ŏng** E North Korea 40°13′N 128°20′E
113 L18 **Pukë** *var.* Puka. Shkodër, N Albania 42°03′N 19°53′E
184 L6 **Pukekohe** Auckland, North Island, New Zealand 37°12′S 174°54′E
184 L7 **Pukemiro** Waikato, North Island, New Zealand 37°37′S 175°02′E
190 D12 **Puke, Mont** ▲ Île Futuna, W Wallis and Futuna
Puket *see* Phuket
185 C20 **Puketeraki Range** ▲▲ South Island, New Zealand
184 N13 **Puketoi Range** ▲▲ North Island, New Zealand
185 F21 **Pukeuri Junction** Otago, South Island, New Zealand 45°01′S 171°01′E
119 L16 **Pukhavichy** *Rus.* Pukhovichi. Minskaya Voblasts', C Belarus 53°32′N 28°15′E
Pukhovichi *see* Pukhavichy
124 M10 **Puksoozero** Arkhangel'skaya Oblast', NW Russian Federation 62°37′N 40°29′E
112 A10 **Pula** *It.* Pola; *prev.* Pulj. Istra, NW Croatia 44°53′N 13°51′E
Pula *see* Nyingchi
163 U14 **Pulandian** *var.* Xinjin. Liaoning, NE China 39°25′N 121°58′E
163 T14 **Pulandian Wan** *bay* NE China
189 O15 **Pulap Atoll** *atoll* Caroline Islands, C Micronesia
18 H9 **Pulaski** New York, NE USA 43°34′N 76°06′W
20 I10 **Pulaski** Tennessee, S USA 35°11′N 87°00′W
21 R7 **Pulaski** Virginia, NE USA 37°03′N 80°47′W
171 Y14 **Pulau, Sungai** ≈ Papua, E Indonesia
110 N13 **Puławy** *Ger.* Neu Amerika. Lubelskie, E Poland 51°25′N 21°57′E
146 I16 **Pulhatyn** *Rus.* Polekhatum; *prev.* Pul'-I-Khatum. Ahal Welaýaty, S Turkmenistan 36°01′N 61°08′E
101 E16 **Pulheim** Nordrhein-Westfalen, W Germany 51°00′N 06°48′E
155 J19 **Pulicat Lake** *lagoon* SE India
Pul'-I-Khatum *see* Pulhatyn
Pul-i-Khumri *see* Pol-e Khomrī
Pul-i-Sefid *see* Pol-e Sefid
Pulj *see* Pula
109 W2 **Pulkau** ≈ NE Austria
93 L15 **Pulkkila** Oulu, C Finland 64°15′N 25°53′E
122 C7 **Pulkovo** ✈ (Sankt-Peterburg) Leningradskaya Oblast', NW Russian Federation 60°06′N 30°23′E
32 M9 **Pullman** Washington, NW USA 46°43′N 117°10′W
108 B10 **Pully** Vaud, SW Switzerland 46°31′N 06°40′E
40 F7 **Púlpita, Punta** *headland* NW Mexico 26°30′N 111°28′W
110 M10 **Pułtusk** Mazowieckie, C Poland 52°41′N 21°04′E
158 H10 **Pulu** Xinjiang Uygur Zizhiqu, W China 36°10′N 81°29′E
137 P13 **Pülümür** Tunceli, E Turkey 39°30′N 39°54′E
189 N16 **Pulusuk** *island* Caroline Islands, C Micronesia
189 N16 **Puluwat Atoll** *atoll* Caroline Islands, C Micronesia
25 N11 **Pumpville** Texas, SW USA 39°55′N 101°43′W
191 P7 **Punaauia** *var.* Hakapehi. Tahiti, W French Polynesia 17°38′S 149°37′W
56 B8 **Puná, Isla** *island* SW Ecuador
185 G16 **Punakaiki** West Coast, South Island, New Zealand 42°07′S 171°21′E
153 T11 **Punakha** C Bhutan 27°38′N 89°50′E
57 L18 **Punata** Cochabamba, C Bolivia 17°32′S 65°50′W
155 E14 **Pune** *prev.* Poona. Mahārāshtra, W India 18°32′N 73°52′E
83 M17 **Pungoè, Rio** *var.* Púnguè, Pungwe. ≈ C Mozambique
21 X10 **Pungo River** ≈ North Carolina, SE USA
Púnguè/Pungwe *see* Pungoè, Rio
79 N19 **Punia** Maniema, E Dem. Rep. Congo 01°28′S 26°25′E
62 H8 **Punilla, Sierra de la** ▲▲ W Argentina
161 P14 **Puning** Guangdong, S China 23°24′N 116°14′E
62 G10 **Punitaqui** Coquimbo, C Chile 30°50′S 71°29′W
149 T9 **Punjab** *prev.* West Punjab, Western Punjab. ◈ *province* E Pakistan
152 H8 **Punjab** *state* NW India
129 Q9 **Punjab Plains** *plain* N India
93 O17 **Punkaharju** *var.* Punkasalmi. Itä-Suomi, E Finland 61°45′N 29°21′E
Punkasalmi *see* Punkaharju
57 I17 **Puno** Puno, SE Peru 15°53′S 70°03′W
57 H17 **Puno** *off.* Departamento de Puno. ◈ *department* S Peru
Puno, Departamento de *see* Puno
61 B24 **Punta Alta** Buenos Aires, E Argentina 38°54′S 62°01′W
63 H24 **Punta Arenas** *prev.* Magallanes. Magallanes, S Chile 53°10′S 70°56′W
45 T6 **Punta, Cerro de** ▲ C Puerto Rico 18°10′N 66°36′W
43 T15 **Punta Chame** Panamá, C Panama 08°39′N 79°42′W
57 G17 **Punta Colorada** Arequipa, SW Peru 16°17′S 72°31′W
40 F9 **Punta Coyote** Baja California Sur, NW Mexico
62 G8 **Punta de Díaz** Atacama, N Chile 28°03′S 70°36′W
61 G20 **Punta del Este** Maldonado, S Uruguay 34°59′S 54°58′W
63 K17 **Punta Delgada** Chubut, SE Argentina 42°46′S 63°40′W
55 O5 **Punta de Mata** Monagas, NE Venezuela 09°48′N 63°38′W
55 O4 **Punta de Piedras** Nueva Esparta, NE Venezuela 10°57′N 64°06′W
42 F4 **Punta Gorda** Toledo, SE Belize 16°07′N 88°47′W
43 N11 **Punta Gorda** Región Autónoma Atlántico Sur, SE Nicaragua 11°31′N 83°46′W
23 W14 **Punta Gorda** Florida, SE USA 26°55′N 82°03′W
42 M11 **Punta Gorda, Río** ≈ SE Nicaragua
62 H6 **Punta Negra, Salar de** *salt lake* N Chile
40 D5 **Punta Prieta** Baja California Norte, NW Mexico 28°56′N 114°11′W
42 L13 **Puntarenas** Puntarenas, W Costa Rica 09°58′N 84°50′W
42 L13 **Puntarenas** *off.* Provincia de Puntarenas. ◈ *province* W Costa Rica
Puntarenas, Provincia de *see* Puntarenas
80 P13 **Puntland** *cultural region* NE Somalia
54 J4 **Punto Fijo** Falcón, N Venezuela 11°42′N 70°13′W
105 S4 **Puntón de Guara** ▲ N Spain 42°18′N 00°13′W
18 D14 **Punxsutawney** Pennsylvania, NE USA 40°55′N 78°57′W
93 M14 **Puolanka** Oulu, C Finland 64°51′N 27°42′E
57 J17 **Pupuya, Nevado** ▲ W Bolivia 15°04′S 69°01′W
Puqi *see* Chibi
57 F16 **Puquio** Ayacucho, S Peru 14°44′S 74°07′W
122 J9 **Pur** ≈ N Russian Federation
186 D7 **Purari** ≈ S Papua New Guinea
27 N11 **Purcell** Oklahoma, C USA 35°00′N 97°21′W
11 O16 **Purcell Mountains** ▲▲ British Columbia, SW Canada
105 P14 **Purchena** Andalucía, S Spain 37°21′N 02°21′W
27 S8 **Purdy** Missouri, C USA 36°49′N 93°55′W
118 I2 **Purekkari Neem** *prev.* Pukari Neem. *headland* N Estonia 59°33′N 24°49′E
37 U7 **Purgatoire River** ≈ Colorado, C USA
Purgstall *see* Purgstall an der Erlauf
109 V5 **Purgstall an der Erlauf** *var.* Purgstall. Niederösterreich, NE Austria 48°01′N 15°08′E
154 O13 **Puri** *var.* Jagannath. Orissa, E India 19°52′N 85°49′E
Puriramya *see* Buriram
109 X4 **Purkersdorf** Niederösterreich, NE Austria 48°13′N 16°12′E
98 I9 **Purmerend** Noord-Holland, C Netherlands 52°30′N 04°56′E
151 G16 **Pūrna** ≈ C India
Purnea *see* Pūrnia
153 R13 **Pūrnia** *prev.* Purnea. Bihār, NE India 25°47′N 87°28′E
Pursat *see* Poŭthĭsăt, Stœ̆ng, W, Cambodia
Pursat *see* Poŭthĭsăt, Poŭthĭsăt, W Cambodia
Purulia *see* Puruliya
150 L13 **Puruliya** *prev.* Purulia. West Bengal, NE India 23°20′N 86°24′E
47 G7 **Purus, Rio** *var.* Río Purús. ≈ Brazil/Peru
186 C9 **Purutu Island** *island* SW Papua New Guinea
93 N17 **Puruvesi** ◎ SE Finland
22 L7 **Purvis** Mississippi, S USA 31°08′N 89°24′W
114 J11 **Pŭrvomay** *prev.* Borisovgrad. Plovdiv, C Bulgaria 42°06′N 25°13′E
169 R16 **Purwodadi** *prev.* Poerwodadi. Jawa, C Indonesia 07°05′S 110°53′E
169 P16 **Purwokerto** *prev.* Poerwokerto. Jawa, C Indonesia 07°25′S 109°14′E
169 P16 **Purworejo** *prev.* Poerworedjo. Jawa, C Indonesia 07°45′S 110°04′E
20 H8 **Puryear** Tennessee, S USA 36°25′N 88°21′W
154 H13 **Pusad** Mahārāshtra, C India 19°56′N 77°40′E
163 Z16 **Pusan** *off.* Pusan-gwangyŏksi, *var.* Busan, *Jap.* Fusan. SE South Korea 35°11′N 129°04′E
Pusan *see* Kim Hae
Pusan-gwangyŏksi *see* Pusan
168 H7 **Pusatgajo, Pegunungan** ▲▲ Sumatera, NW Indonesia
Puschlav *see* Poschiavo
124 G13 **Pushkin** *prev.* Tsarskoye Selo. Leningradskaya Oblast', NW Russian Federation 59°42′N 30°24′E
126 L3 **Pushkino** Moskovskaya Oblast', W Russian Federation 55°57′N 37°45′E
127 Q8 **Pushkino** Saratovskaya Oblast', W Russian Federation 51°09′N 47°00′E
Pushkino *see* Biläsuvar
111 M22 **Püspökladány** Hajdú-Bihar, E Hungary 47°20′N 21°05′E
118 J3 **Püssi** *Ger.* Isenhof. Ida-Virumaa, NE Estonia 59°22′N 27°04′E
116 I5 **Pustomyty** L'vivs'ka Oblast', W Ukraine 49°43′N 23°55′E
124 F16 **Pustoshka** Pskovskaya Oblast', W Russian Federation 56°21′N 29°16′E
Pusztakalán *see* Călan
167 N1 **Putao** *prev.* Fort Hertz. Kachin State, N Burma (Myanmar) 27°22′N 97°24′E
184 M8 **Putaruru** Waikato, North Island, New Zealand 38°03′S 175°48′E
Puteoli *see* Pozzuoli
161 R12 **Putian** Fujian, SE China 25°32′N 119°02′E
107 O17 **Putignano** Puglia, SE Italy 40°51′N 17°08′E
Puting *see* De'an
Putivl' *see* Putyvl'
41 Q16 **Putla** *var.* Putla de Guerrero. Oaxaca, SE Mexico 17°01′N 97°56′W
Putla de Guerrero *see* Putla
19 N12 **Putnam** Connecticut, NE USA 41°56′N 71°52′W
25 Q7 **Putnam** Texas, SW USA 32°22′N 99°11′W
18 M10 **Putney** Vermont, NE USA 42°59′N 72°30′W
111 L20 **Putnok** Borsod-Abaúj-Zemplén, NE Hungary 48°18′N 20°25′E
Putorana, Gory/Putorana Mountains *see* Putorana, Plato
122 L8 **Putorana, Plato** *var.* Gory Putorana, *Eng.* Putorana Mountains. ▲▲ N Russian Federation
168 K9 **Putrajaya** ● (Malaysia) Kuala Lumpur, Peninsular Malaysia 02°57′N 101°42′E
62 H2 **Putre** Tarapacá, N Chile 18°11′S 69°30′W
155 J24 **Puttalam** North Western Province, W Sri Lanka 08°02′N 79°55′E
155 J24 **Puttalam Lagoon** *lagoon* W Sri Lanka
99 H17 **Putte** Antwerpen, C Belgium 51°04′N 04°39′E
94 E10 **Puttegga** ▲ S Norway 62°13′N 07°40′E
98 K11 **Putten** Gelderland, C Netherlands 52°15′N 05°36′E
100 K7 **Puttgarden** Schleswig-Holstein, N Germany 54°30′N 11°13′E
Puttiala *see* Patiāla
101 D20 **Püttlingen** Saarland, SW Germany 49°16′N 06°52′E
54 D14 **Putumayo** *off.* Intendencia del Putumayo. ◈ *province* S Colombia
Putumayo, Intendencia del *see* Putumayo
48 E7 **Putumayo, Río** *var.* Içá, Rio. ≈ NW South America *see also* Içá, Rio
Putumayo, Río *see* Içá, Rio
169 P11 **Putus, Tanjung** *headland* Borneo, N Indonesia 0°27′S 109°04′E
116 J8 **Putyla** Chernivets'ka Oblast', W Ukraine 47°59′N 25°04′E
117 S3 **Putyvl'** *Rus.* Putivl'. Sums'ka Oblast', NE Ukraine 51°21′N 33°53′E
93 M18 **Puula** ◎ SE Finland
93 N18 **Puumala** Itä-Suomi, E Finland 61°31′N 28°12′E
118 I5 **Puurmani** *Ger.* Talkhof. Jõgevamaa, E Estonia 58°36′N 26°17′E
99 G17 **Puurs** Antwerpen, N Belgium 51°05′N 04°17′E
38 F10 **Pu'u 'Ula'ula** *var.* Red Hill. ▲ Maui, Hawai'i, USA 20°42′N 156°16′W
38 A8 **Pu'uwai** *var.* Puuwai. Ni'ihau, Hawaii, USA, C Pacific Ocean 21°54′N 160°11′W
12 J4 **Puvirnituq** *prev.* Povungnituk. Québec, NE Canada 60°10′N 77°20′W
32 H8 **Puyallup** Washington, NW USA 47°11′N 122°17′W
161 O5 **Puyang** Henan, C China 35°40′N 115°00′E
161 R9 **Puyang Jiang** *var.* Tsien Tang. ≈ SE China
103 O11 **Puy-de-Dôme** ◈ *department* C France
103 N15 **Puylaurens** Tarn, S France 43°33′N 02°01′E
102 M13 **Puy-l'Evêque** Lot, S France 44°31′N 01°10′E
103 N17 **Puymorens, Col de** *pass* S France
56 C7 **Puyo** Pastaza, C Ecuador 01°30′S 77°58′W
185 A24 **Puysegur Point** *headland* South Island, New Zealand 46°09′S 166°38′E
148 J8 **Pūzak, Hāmūn-e** *Pash.* Hāmūn-i-Puzak. ◎ SW Afghanistan
Puzak, Hāmūn-i- *see* Pūzak, Hāmūn-e
81 J23 **Pwani** *Eng.* Coast. ◈ *region* E Tanzania
79 O23 **Pweto** Katanga, SE Dem. Rep. Congo 08°28′S 28°52′E
97 I19 **Pwllheli** NW Wales, United Kingdom 52°54′N 04°23′W
189 O14 **Pwok** Pohnpei, E Micronesia
122 I9 **Pyakupur** ≈ N Russian Federation
124 M6 **Pyalitsa** Murmanskaya Oblast', NW Russian Federation 66°17′N 39°56′E
124 K10 **Pyal'ma** Respublika Kareliya, NW Russian Federation 62°24′N 35°56′E
Pyandzh *see* Panj
124 I6 **Pyaozero, Ozero** ◎ NW Russian Federation
166 L9 **Pyapon** Ayeyarwady, SW Burma (Myanmar) 16°15′N 95°40′E
119 J15 **Pyarshai** *Rus.* Pershay. Minskaya Voblasts', C Belarus 54°02′N 26°41′E
122 K8 **Pyasina** ≈ N Russian Federation
114 I10 **Pyasŭchnik, Yazovir** ⊠ C Bulgaria
Pyatikhatki *see* P"yatykhatky
117 S7 **P"yatykhatky** *Rus.* Pyatikhatki. Dnipropetrovs'ka Oblast', E Ukraine 48°23′N 33°43′E
166 M6 **Pyawbwe** Mandalay, C Burma (Myanmar) 20°39′N 96°04′E
166 L7 **Pyay** *var.* Prome, Pye. Bago, C Burma (Myanmar) 18°50′N 95°14′E
127 T3 **Pychas** Udmurtskaya Respublika, NW Russian Federation 56°30′N 52°33′E
Pye *see* Pyay
166 K6 **Pyechin** Chin State, W Burma (Myanmar) 20°01′N 93°36′E
119 G17 **Pyeski** *Rus.* Peski. Hrodzyenskaya Voblasts', W Belarus 53°21′N 24°38′E
119 L19 **Pyetrykaw** *Rus.* Petrikov. Homyel'skaya Voblasts', SE Belarus 52°08′N 28°30′E
93 O17 **Pyhäjärvi** ◎ SE Finland
93 M16 **Pyhajärvi** ◎ C Finland
93 L15 **Pyhäjoki** Oulu, W Finland 64°28′N 24°15′E
93 L15 **Pyhäjoki** ≈ W Finland
93 M15 **Pyhäntä** Oulu, C Finland 64°07′N 26°19′E
93 M16 **Pyhäsalmi** Oulu, C Finland 63°38′N 26°E
93 O17 **Pyhäselkä** ◎ SE Finland
93 M19 **Pyhtää** *Swe.* Pyttis. Etelä-Suomi, S Finland 60°29′N 26°40′E
166 M5 **Pyin-Oo-Lwin** *var.* Maymyo. Mandalay, C Burma (Myanmar) 22°03′N 96°30′E
115 N24 **Pylés** *var.* Piles. Kárpathos, SE Greece 35°31′N 27°08′E
115 D21 **Pýlos** *var.* Pilos. Pelopónnisos, S Greece 36°55′N 21°42′E
18 B12 **Pymatuning Reservoir** ⊠ Ohio/Pennsylvania, NE USA
163 X15 **P'yŏngt'aek** NW South Korea 37°00′N 127°04′E
163 V14 **P'yŏngyang** *var.* P'yŏngyang-si, *Eng.* Pyongyang. ● (North Korea) SW North Korea 39°04′N 125°46′E
P'yŏngyang-si *see* P'yŏngyang
35 Q4 **Pyramid Lake** ◎ Nevada, W USA
37 P15 **Pyramid Mountains** ▲▲ New Mexico, SW USA
37 R5 **Pyramid Peak** ▲ Colorado, C USA 39°04′N 106°57′W
115 D17 **Pyramíva** *var.* Piramiva. ▲ C Greece 39°08′N 21°18′E
Pyrenaei Montes *see* Pyrenees
86 B12 **Pyrenees** *Fr.* Pyrénées, *Sp.* Pirineos; *anc.* Pyrenaei Montes. ▲▲ SW Europe
102 J16 **Pyrénées-Atlantiques** ◈ *department* SW France
103 N17 **Pyrénées-Orientales** ◈ *department* S France
115 L19 **Pyrgí** *var.* Pirgi. Chíos, E Greece 38°13′N 26°01′E
115 D20 **Pýrgos** *var.* Pírgos. Dytikí Ellás, S Greece 37°40′N 21°27′E
Pyritz *see* Pyrzyce
115 E19 **Pýrros** ≈ S Greece
117 R4 **Pyryatyn** *Rus.* Piryatin. Poltavs'ka Oblast', NE Ukraine 50°14′N 32°31′E
110 D9 **Pyrzyce** *Ger.* Pyritz. Zachodnio-pomorskie, NW Poland 53°09′N 14°53′E
124 F15 **Pytalovo** *Latv.* Abrene; *prev.* Jaunlatgale. Pskovskaya Oblast', W Russian Federation 57°06′N 27°55′E
115 M20 **Pythagóreio** *var.* Pithagorio. Sámos, Dodekánisa, Greece, Aegean Sea 37°42′N 26°57′E
14 L11 **Pythonga, Lac** ◎ Québec, SE Canada
Pyttis *see* Pyhtää
Pyu *see* Phyu
166 M8 **Pyuntaza** Bago, SW Burma (Myanmar) 17°51′N 96°44′E
153 N11 **Pyuthān** Mid Western, W Nepal 28°09′N 82°50′E
110 H12 **Pyzdry** *Ger.* Peisern. Wielkopolskie, C Poland 52°10′N 17°42′E

Q

138 H13 **Qā' al Jafr** ◎ S Jordan
197 O11 **Qaanaaq** *var.* Qânâq, *Dan.* Thule. ◈ Avannaarsua, N Greenland
Qabanbay *see* Kabanbay
138 G7 **Qabb Eliâs** E Lebanon 33°46′N 35°49′E
Qabil *see* Al Qābil
Qabırrı *see* Iori
Qābis *see* Gabès
Qābis, Khalīj *see* Gabès, Golfe de
Qabqa *see* Gonghe
141 S14 **Qabr Hūd** C Yemen 16°02′N 49°36′E
Qacentina *see* Constantine
148 L4 **Qādes** Bādghīs, NW Afghanistan 34°48′N 63°26′E
139 T11 **Qādisīyah** Al Qādisīyah, S Iraq 31°43′N 44°28′E
139 Q6 **Qādisīyah, Buḥayrat al** ⊠ NW Iraq
143 O4 **Qā'emshahr** *prev.* 'Alīābad, Shāhī. Māzandarān, N Iran 36°31′N 52°49′E
143 U7 **Qā'en** *var.* Qain, Qāyen. Khorāsān-Razavī, E Iran 33°43′N 59°07′E
141 U13 **Qafa** *spring/well* SW Oman 17°46′N 52°55′E
Qafṣah *see* Gafsa
163 Q12 **Qagan Nur** *var.* Xulun Hobot Qagan, Zhengxiangbai Qi. Nei Mongol Zizhiqu, N China 42°10′N 114°57′E
163 V9 **Qagan Nur** ◎ NE China
163 Q11 **Qagan Nur** ◎ N China
Qagan Us *see* Dulan
158 H13 **Qagcaka** Xizang Zizhiqu, W China 32°32′N 81°52′E
Qagchêng *see* Xiangcheng
Qahremānshahr *see* Kermānshāh
159 Q10 **Qaidam He** ≈ C China
156 L8 **Qaidam Pendi** *basin* C China
Qain *see* Qā'en
Qala Āhangarān *see* Chaghcharān
139 U3 **Qalạ Diza** *var.* Qal 'at Dīzah. As Sulaymānīyah, NE Iraq 36°11′N 45°07′E
Qal'ah Sālih *see* Qal'at Ṣāliḥ
147 R13 **Qal'aikhum** *Rus.* Kalaikhum. S Tajikistan 38°28′N 70°49′E
Qala Nau *see* Qal'eh-ye Now
141 V17 **Qalansīyah** Suquṭrā, W Yemen 12°40′N 53°30′E
Qala Panja *see* Qal'eh-ye Panjeh
Qala Shāhar *see* Qal'eh Shahr
149 O8 **Qalāt** *Per.* Kalāt. Zābol, S Afghanistan 32°10′N 66°54′E
139 W9 **Qal'at Aḥmad** Maysān, E Iraq 32°24′N 46°46′E
141 N11 **Qal'at Bīshah** 'Asīr, SW Saudi Arabia 19°59′N 42°38′E
138 H4 **Qal'at Burzay** Ḥamāh, W Syria 35°37′N 36°16′E
Qal 'at Dīzah *see* Qalạ Diza
139 W9 **Qal'at Huṣayn** Maysān, E Iraq 32°19′N 46°46′E
139 V10 **Qal'at Majnūnah** Al Qādisīyah, S Iraq 31°39′N 45°44′E
139 X11 **Qal'at Ṣāliḥ** *var.* Qal'ah Sālih. Maysān, E Iraq 31°30′N 47°24′E
139 V10 **Qal'at Sukkar** Dhī Qār, SE Iraq 31°52′N 46°05′E
Qalba Zhotasy *see* Kalbinskiy Khrebet
143 Q12 **Qal'eh Bīābān** Fārs, S Iran
149 N4 **Qal'eh Shahr** *Pash.* Qala Shāhar. Sar-e Pol, N Afghanistan 35°34′N 65°38′E
148 L4 **Qal'eh-ye Now** *var.* Qala Nau. Bādghīs, NW Afghanistan 35°N 63°08′E
149 T2 **Qal'eh-ye Panjeh** *var.* Qala Panja. Badakhshān, NE Afghanistan 36°56′N 72°15′E
Qalqaman *see* Kalkaman
Qalzhat *see* Kol'zhat
Qamar Bay *see* Qamar, Ghubbat al
141 U14 **Qamar, Ghubbat al** *Eng.* Qamar Bay. *bay* Oman/Yemen
141 V13 **Qamar, Jabal al** ▲▲ SW Oman
147 N12 **Qamashi** Qashqadaryo Viloyati, S Uzbekistan 38°52′N 66°30′E
Qambar *see* Kambar
159 R14 **Qamdo** Xizang Zizhiqu, W China 31°09′N 97°09′E
75 R7 **Qamīnis** NE Libya 31°48′N 20°04′E
Qamishly *see* Al Qāmishlī
Qânâq *see* Qaanaaq
Qandahār *see* Kandahār
80 Q11 **Qandala** Bari, NE Somalia 11°30′N 50°00′E
Qandyaghash *see* Kandyagash
138 L2 **Qanṭārī** Ar Raqqah, N Syria 36°24′N 39°16′E
Qapiciğ Dağı *see* Qazangödağ
158 H5 **Qapqal** *var.* Qapqal Xibe Zizhixian. Xinjiang Uygur Zizhiqu, NW China 43°46′N 81°09′E
Qapqal Xibe Zizhixian *see* Qapqal

◆ Country
● Country Capital
◇ Dependent Territory
○ Dependent Territory Capital
◈ Administrative Regions
✈ International Airport
▲ Mountain
▲▲ Mountain Range
⛰ Volcano
≈ River
◎ Lake
⊠ Reservoir

Qapshagay Böyeni *see* Kapchagayskoye Vodokhranilishche
Qapshaghay *see* Kapchagay
Qapugtang *see* Zadoi
196 M15 **Qaqortoq** *Dan.* Julianehåb. ⬖ Kitaa, S Greenland
139 T4 **Qara Anjīr** At Ta’mīn, N Iraq 35°30′N 44°37′E
Qarabāgh *see* Qarah Bāgh
Qarabaū *see* Karabau
Qaraböget *see* Karaboget
Qarabulaq *see* Karabulak
Qarabutaq *see* Karabutak
Qaraghandy/Qaraghandy Oblysy *see* Karaganda
Qaraghayly *see* Karagayly
139 U4 **Qara Gol** As Sulaymānīyah, NE Iraq 35°21′N 45°38′E
75 U8 **Qārah** *var.* Qâra. NW Egypt 29°34′N 26°28′E
Qārah *see* Qārah
148 J4 **Qarah Bāgh** *var.* Qarabāgh. Herāt, NW Afghanistan 35°06′N 61°33′E
138 G7 **Qaraoun, Lac de** *var.* Buḩayrat al Qir‘awn. ◎ S Lebanon
Qaraoy *see* Karaoy
Qaraqoyyn *see* Karakoyyn, Ozero
Qara Qum *see* Garagum
Qarasū *see* Karasu
Qaratal *see* Karatal
Qarataū *see* Karatau, Khrebet, Kazakhstan
Qarataū *see* Karatau, Zhambyl, Kazakhstan
Qaraton *see* Karaton
Qarazhal *see* Karazhal
80 P13 **Qardho** *var.* Kardh, *It.* Gardo. Bari, N Somalia 09°34′N 49°30′E
142 M6 **Qareh Chāy** ≈ N Iran
142 K2 **Qareh Sū** ≈ NW Iran
Qariateïne *see* Al Qaryatayn
Qarkilik *see* Ruoqiang
147 O13 **Qarluq** *Rus.* Karluk. Surkhondaryo Viloyati, S Uzbekistan 38°17′N 67°39′E
147 U12 **Qarokŭl** *Rus.* Karakul’. E Tajikistan 39°07′N 73°33′E
147 T12 **Qarokŭl** *Rus.* Ozero Karakul’. ◎ E Tajikistan
Qarqan *see* Qiemo
158 K9 **Qarqan He** ≈ NW China
Qarqannah, Juzur *see* Kerkenah, Îles de
Qarqaraly *see* Karkaralinsk
149 O1 **Qarqīn** Jowzjān, N Afghanistan 37°25′N 66°03′E
Qars *see* Kars
Qarsaqbay *see* Karsakpay
146 M12 **Qarshi** *Rus.* Karshi; *prev.* Bek-Budi. Qashqadaryo Viloyati, S Uzbekistan 38°54′N 65°48′E
146 L12 **Qarshi Cho‘li** *Rus.* Karshinskaya Step. *grassland* S Uzbekistan
146 M13 **Qarshi Kanali** *Rus.* Karshinskiy Kanal. *canal* Turkmenistan/Uzbekistan
Qaryatayn *see* Al Qaryatayn
Qāsh, Nahr al *see* Gash
146 M12 **Qashqadaryo Viloyati** *Rus.* Kashkadar’inskaya Oblast’. ⬖ *province* S Uzbekistan
Qasigianguit *see* Qasigiannguit
197 N13 **Qasigiannguit** *var.* Qasigianguit, *Dan.* Christianshåb. ⬖ Kitaa, C Greenland
Qaşīm, Minţaqat *see* Al Qaşīm
75 V10 **Qaşr al Farāfirah** *var.* Qasr Farâfra. W Egypt 27°00′N 27°59′E
139 P8 **Qaşr ‘Amīj** Al Anbār, C Iraq 33°30′N 41°52′E
139 R9 **Qaşr Darwīshāh** Karbalā’, C Iraq 32°36′N 43°27′E
142 J6 **Qaşr-e Shīrīn** Kermānshāhān, W Iran 34°32′N 45°36′E
Qasr Farâfra *see* Qaşr al Farāfirah
Qassim *see* Al Qaşīm
141 O16 **Qa‘ţabah** SW Yemen 13°51′N 44°42′E
138 H7 **Qaţanā** *var.* Katana. Dimashq, S Syria 33°27′N 36°04′E
143 N15 **Qatar** *off.* State of Qatar, *Ar.* Dawlat Qaţar. ◆ *monarchy* SW Asia
Qatar, State of *see* Qatar
Qatrana *see* Al Qaţrānah
143 Q12 **Qaţrūyeh** Fārs, S Iran 29°08′N 54°42′E
Qattara Depression/Qaţţārah, Munkhafaḑ al *see* Qaţţārah, Munkhafaḑ al
75 U8 **Qaţţārah, Munkhafaḑ al** *var.* Munkhafaḑ al Qaţţārah *var.* Monkhafad el Qaţţâra, *Eng.* Qattara Depression. *desert* NW Egypt
Qaţţâra, Monkhafad el *see* Qaţţārah, Munkhafaḑ al
Qattinah, Buhayrat *see* Ḩimş, Buḩayrat
Qausuittuq *see* Resolute
Qaydār *see* Qeydār
Qāyen *see* Qā’en
Qaynar *see* Kaynar
147 Q11 **Qayroqqum** *Rus.* Kayrakkum. NW Tajikistan 40°16′N 69°46′E
147 Q10 **Qayroqqum, Obanbori** *Rus.* Kayrakkumskoye Vodokhranilishche. ⊠ NW Tajikistan
159 O17 **Qayü** Xizang Zizhiqu, W China 28°17′N 92°46′E
137 V13 **Qazangödağ** *Rus.* Gora Kapydzhik, *Turk.* Qapiciğ Dağı. ▲ SW Azerbaijan 39°18′N 46°00′E
139 U7 **Qazānīyah** *var.* Dhū Shaykh. Diyālá, E Iraq 33°39′N 45°33′E
Qazaqstan/Qazaqstan Respublikasy *see* Kazakhstan
137 T9 **Qazbegi** *Rus.* Kazbegi. NE Georgia 42°39′N 44°36′E
149 P15 **Qāzi Ahmad** *var.* Kazi Ahmad. Sind, SE Pakistan 26°19′N 68°08′E
137 Y12 **Qazimämmäd** *Rus.* Kazi Magomed. SE Azerbaijan 40°03′N 48°56′E
Qazris *see* Cáceres
142 M4 **Qazvīn** *var.* Kazvin. Qazvīn, N Iran 36°16′N 50°E
142 M5 **Qazvīn** ⬖ *province* N Iran
187 Z13 **Qelelevu Lagoon** *lagoon* NE Fiji
Qena *see* Qinā
113 L23 **Qeparo** Vlorë, S Albania 40°04′N 19°49′E
Qeqertarssuaq *see* Qeqertarsuaq
197 N13 **Qeqertarsuaq** *var.* Qeqertarssuaq, *Dan.* Godhavn. ⬖ Kitaa, S Greenland
196 M13 **Qeqertarsuaq** *island* W Greenland
197 N13 **Qeqertarsuup Tunua** *Dan.* Disko Bugt. *inlet* W Greenland
Qerveh *see* Qorveh
143 S14 **Qeshm** Hormozgān, S Iran 26°58′N 56°17′E
143 R14 **Qeshm** *var.* Jazīreh-ye Qeshm, Qeshm Island. *island* S Iran
Qeshm Island/Qeshm, Jazīreh-ye *see* Qeshm
Qey *see* Kīsh, Jazīreh-ye
142 L4 **Qeydār** *var.* Qaydār. Zanjān, NW Iran 36°50′N 47°40′E
142 K5 **Qezel Owzan, Rūd-e** *var.* Ki Zil Uzen, Qi Zil Uzun. ≈ NW Iran
Qian *see* Guizhou
161 Q2 **Qian’an** Hebei, E China 40°01′N 118°43′E
Qiandao Hu *see* Xin’anjiang Shuiku
Qiandaohu *see* Chun’an
Qian Gorlo/Qian Gorlos/Qian Gorlos Mongolzu Zizhixian/Quianguozhen *see* Qianguo
163 V9 **Qianguo** *var.* Qian Gorlo, Qian Gorlos, Qian Gorlos Mongolzu Zizhixian, Quianguozhen. Jilin, NE China 45°05′N 124°52′E
161 N9 **Qianjiang** Hubei, C China 30°23′N 112°58′E
160 K10 **Qianjiang** Sichuan, C China 29°30′N 108°45′E
160 L14 **Qian Jiang** ≈ S China
160 G9 **Qianning** *var.* Gartar. Sichuan, C China 30°27′N 101°24′E
163 U13 **Qian Shan** ▲▲ NE China
160 H10 **Qianwei** *var.* Yujin. Sichuan, C China 29°15′N 103°52′E
160 J11 **Qianxi** Guizhou, S China 27°00′N 106°01′E
Qiaotou *see* Datong
Qiaowa *see* Muli
159 Q7 **Qiaowan** Gansu, N China 40°37′N 96°40′E
Qibilī *see* Kebili
158 K9 **Qiemo** *var.* Qarqan. Xinjiang Uygur Zizhiqu, NW China 38°09′N 85°30′E
160 J10 **Qijiang** *var.* Gunan. Chongqing Shi, C China 29°01′N 106°40′E
159 N5 **Qijiaojing** Xinjiang Uygur Zizhiqu, NW China 43°29′N 91°35′E
Qike *see* Xunke
9 R5 **Qikiqtarjuaq** *prev.* Broughton Island. Nunavut, NE Canada 67°35′N 63°55′W
149 P9 **Qila Saifullāh** Baluchistān, SW Pakistan 30°45′N 68°08′E
159 S9 **Qilian** *var.* Babao. Qinghai, C China 38°09′N 100°08′E
159 N8 **Qilian Shan** *var.* Kilien Mountains. ▲▲ N China
197 O11 **Qimusseriarsuaq** *Dan.* Melville Bugt, *Eng.* Melville Bay. *bay* NW Greenland
75 X10 **Qinā** *var.* Qena; *anc.* Caene, Caenepolis. E Egypt 26°12′N 32°49′E
159 W11 **Qin’an** Gansu, C China 34°49′N 105°50′E
159 X10 **Qingcheng** Gansu, N China 36°01′N 107°53′E
Qincheng *see* Nanfeng
Qing *see* Qinghai
163 W7 **Qing’an** Heilongjiang, NE China 46°53′N 127°29′E
161 R5 **Qingdao** *var.* Ching-Tao, Ch’ing-tao, Tsingtao, Tsintao, *Ger.* Tsingtau. Shandong, E China 36°31′N 120°55′E
163 V8 **Qinggang** Heilongjiang, NE China 46°41′N 126°05′E
Qinggil *see* Qinghe
159 P11 **Qinghai** *var.* Chinghai, Koko Nor, Qing, Qinghai Sheng, Tsinghai. ⬖ *province* C China
159 S10 **Qinghai Hu** *var.* Ch’ing Hai, Tsing Hai, *Mong.* Koko Nor. ◎ C China
Qinghai Sheng *see* Qinghai
158 M3 **Qinghe** *var.* Qinggil. Xinjiang Uygur Zizhiqu, NW China 46°42′N 90°19′E
160 L4 **Qingjian** *var.* Kuanzhou; *prev.* Xiuyan. Shaanxi, C China 37°10′N 110°09′E
160 L9 **Qing Jiang** ≈ C China
Qingjiang *see* Huai’an
Qingkou *see* Ganyu
160 I12 **Qinglong** *var.* Liancheng. Guizhou, S China 25°49′N 105°10′E
161 Q2 **Qinglong** Hebei, E China 40°24′N 118°57′E
Qingshan *see* Wudalianchi
159 R12 **Qingshuihe** Qinghai, C China 33°47′N 97°10′E
159 X10 **Qingyang** *var.* Xifeng. Gansu, C China 35°46′N 107°35′E
Qingyang *see* Jinjiang
161 N14 **Qingyuan** Guangdong, S China 23°42′N 113°02′E
163 V11 **Qingyuan** *var.* Qingyuan Manzu Zizhixian. Liaoning, NE China 42°08′N 124°55′E
Qingyuan *see* Shandan
Qingyuan *see* Weiyuan
Qingyuan Manzu Zizhixian *see* Qingyuan
158 L13 **Qingzang Gaoyuan** *var.* Xizang Gaoyuan, *Eng.* Plateau of Tibet. *plateau* W China
161 Q4 **Qingzhou** *prev.* Yidu. Shandong, E China 36°41′N 118°29′E
157 R9 **Qin He** ≈ C China
161 Q2 **Qinhuangdao** Hebei, E China 39°57′N 119°31′E
160 K7 **Qin Ling** ▲▲ C China
161 N5 **Qinxian** *var.* Dingchang, Qin Xian. Shanxi, C China 36°46′N 112°42′E
Qin Xian *see* Qinxian
161 N6 **Qinyang** Henan, C China 35°05′N 112°56′E
160 K15 **Qinzhou** Guangxi Zhuangzu Zizhiqu, S China 22°09′N 108°36′E
Qiong *see* Hainan
160 L17 **Qionghai** *prev.* Jiaji. Hainan, S China 19°12′N 110°26′E
160 H9 **Qionglai** Sichuan, C China 30°24′N 103°28′E
160 H8 **Qionglai Shan** ▲▲ C China
Qiongxi *see* Hongyuan
160 L17 **Qiongzhou Haixia** *var.* Hainan Strait. *strait* S China
163 U7 **Qiqihar** *var.* Ch’i-ch’i-ha-erh, Tsitsihar; *prev.* Lungkiang. Heilongjiang, NE China 47°23′N 124°E
Qir *see* Qīr-va-Kārzīn
158 H10 **Qira** Xinjiang Uygur Zizhiqu, NW China 37°05′N 80°45′E
Qir‘awn, Buḩayrat al *see* Qaraoun, Lac de
143 P12 **Qīr-va-Kārzīn** *var.* Qir. Fārs, S Iran 28°27′N 53°04′E
Qiryat Gat *see* Kyriat Gat
Qiryat Shemona *see* Kiryat Shmona
Qishlaq *see* Garmsār
141 U14 **Qishn** SE Yemen 15°29′N 51°44′E
Qishon, Naḩal *see* Kishon, Nahal
Qita Ghazzah *see* Gaza Strip
156 K5 **Qitai** Xinjiang Uygur Zizhiqu, NW China 44°N 89°34′E
163 Y8 **Qitaihe** Heilongjiang, NE China 45°45′N 130°53′E
141 W12 **Qitbīt, Wādī** *dry watercourse* S Oman
161 O5 **Qixian** *var.* Qi Xian, Zhaoge. Henan, C China 35°35′N 114°10′E
Qi Xian *see* Qixian
Qīzān *see* Jīzān
Qizil Orda *see* Kzylorda
Qizil Qum/Qizilqum *see* Kyzyl Kum
147 V14 **Qizilrabot** *Rus.* Kyzylrabot. SE Tajikistan 37°29′N 74°44′E
146 J10 **Qizilravote** *Rus.* Kyzylrabat. Buxoro Viloyati, C Uzbekistan 40°35′N 62°09′E
Qi Zil Uzun *see* Qezel Owzan, Rūd-e
139 S4 **Qizil Yār** At Ta’mīn, N Iraq 35°26′N 44°12′E
Qoghaly *see* Kugaly
Qogir Feng *see* K2
143 N6 **Qom** *var.* Kum, Qum. Qom, N Iran 34°43′N 50°54′E
143 N6 **Qom** ⬖ *province* N Iran
Qomisheh *see* Shahreẕā
Qomolangma Feng *see* Everest, Mount
142 M7 **Qom, Rūd-e** ≈ C Iran
Qomsheh *see* Shahreẕā
Qomul *see* Hami
Qondūz *see* Kondoz
159 N16 **Qonggyai** Xizang Zizhiqu, W China 29°01′N 91°39′E
146 G7 **Qo‘ng‘irot** *Rus.* Kungrad. Qoraqalpog‘iston Respublikasi, NW Uzbekistan 43°01′N 58°49′E
Qongyrat *see* Konyrat
Qoqek *see* Tacheng
147 R10 **Qo‘qon** *var.* Khokand, *Rus.* Kokand. Farg’ona Viloyati, E Uzbekistan 40°34′N 70°55′E
Qorabowur Kirlari *see* Karabaur’, Uval
Qoradaryo *see* Karadar’ya
146 G6 **Qorajar** *Rus.* Karadzhar. Qoraqalpog‘iston Respublikasi, NW Uzbekistan 43°34′N 58°35′E
146 K12 **Qorako‘l** *Rus.* Karakul’. Buxoro Viloyati, C Uzbekistan 39°27′N 63°45′E
146 H7 **Qorao‘zak** *Rus.* Karauzyak. Qoraqalpog‘iston Respublikasi, NW Uzbekistan 43°07′N 60°03′E
146 E5 **Qoraqalpog‘iston** *Rus.* Karakalpakya. Qoraqalpog‘iston Respublikasi, NW Uzbekistan 44°45′N 56°06′E
146 G7 **Qoraqalpog‘iston Respublikasi** *Rus.* Respublika Karakalpakstan. ⬖ *autonomous republic* NW Uzbekistan
Qorghalzhyn *see* Korgalzhyn
138 H6 **Qornet es Saouda** ▲ NE Lebanon 36°06′N 34°06′E
146 L12 **Qorowulbozor** *Rus.* Karaulbazar. Buxoro Viloyati, C Uzbekistan 39°28′N 64°49′E
142 K5 **Qorveh** *var.* Qerveh, Qurveh. Kordestān, W Iran 35°09′N 47°48′E
147 N11 **Qo‘shrabot** *Rus.* Kushrabat. Samarqand Viloyati, C Uzbekistan 40°15′N 66°40′E
Qosköl *see* Koskol’
Qosshaghyl *see* Koschagyl
Qostanay/Qostanay Oblysy *see* Kostanay
143 P12 **Qoţbābād** Fārs, S Iran 28°52′N 53°40′E
143 R13 **Qoţbābād** Hormozgān, S Iran 27°49′N 56°00′E
138 H6 **Qoubaïyât** *var.* Al Qubayyāt. N Lebanon 37°00′N 34°30′E
Qoussantîna *see* Constantine
Qowowuyag *see* Cho Oyu
147 O11 **Qo‘ytosh** *Rus.* Koytash. Jizzax Viloyati, C Uzbekistan 40°13′N 67°19′E
146 G7 **Qozonketkan** *Rus.* Kazanketken. Qoraqalpog‘iston Respublikasi, W Uzbekistan 42°59′N 59°21′E
146 H6 **Qozoqdaryo** *Rus.* Kazakdar’ya. Qoraqalpog‘iston Respublikasi, NW Uzbekistan 43°26′N 59°47′E
19 N11 **Quabbin Reservoir** ⊠ Massachusetts, NE USA
100 F12 **Quakenbrück** Niedersachsen, NW Germany 52°41′N 07°57′E
18 I15 **Quakertown** Pennsylvania, NE USA 40°26′N 75°17′W
182 M10 **Quambatook** Victoria, SE Australia 35°52′S 143°28′E
25 Q4 **Quanah** Texas, SW USA 34°17′N 99°46′W
167 V10 **Quang Ngai** *var.* Quangngai, Quang Nghia. Quang Ngai, C Vietnam 15°09′N 108°50′E
Quangngai *see* Quang Ngai
Quang Nghia *see* Quang Ngai
167 T9 **Quang Tri** *var.* Trièu Hai. Quang Tri, C Vietnam 16°46′N 107°11′E
Quanjiang *see* Suichuan
Quan Long *see* Ca Mau
152 L4 **Quanshuigou** China/India 35°40′N 79°28′E
161 R13 **Quanzhou** *var.* Ch’uan-chou, Tsinkiang; *prev.* Chin-chiang. Fujian, SE China 24°56′N 118°31′E
160 M12 **Quanzhou** Guangxi Zhuangzu Zizhiqu, S China 25°59′N 111°02′E
11 V16 **Qu’Appelle** ≈ Saskatchewan, S Canada
12 M3 **Quaqtaq** *prev.* Koartac. Québec, NE Canada 60°50′N 69°30′W
61 E16 **Quaraí** Rio Grande do Sul, S Brazil 30°38′S 56°25′W
59 H24 **Quaraí, Rio** *Sp.* Río Cuareim. ≈ Brazil/Uruguay *see also* Cuareim, Río
Quaraí, Rio *see* Cuareim, Río
171 N13 **Quarles, Pegunungan** ▲▲ Sulawesi, C Indonesia
Quarnero *see* Kvarner
107 C20 **Quartu Sant’ Elena** Sardegna, Italy, C Mediterranean Sea 39°15′N 09°12′E
29 X13 **Quasqueton** Iowa, C USA 42°23′N 91°45′W
173 X16 **Quatre Bornes** W Mauritius 20°15′S 57°28′E
172 I17 **Quatre Bornes** Mahé, NE Seychelles
137 X10 **Quba** *Rus.* Kuba. N Azerbaijan 41°22′N 48°30′E
Qubba *see* Ba‘qūbah
143 T3 **Qūchān** *var.* Kuchan. Khorāsān-Razavī, NE Iran 37°12′N 58°28′E
183 R10 **Queanbeyan** New South Wales, SE Australia 35°24′S 149°17′E
15 Q10 **Québec** *var.* Quebec. *province capital* Québec, SE Canada 46°50′N 71°15′W
14 K10 **Québec** *var.* Quebec. ⬖ *province* SE Canada
61 D17 **Quebracho** Paysandú, W Uruguay 31°58′S 57°53′W
43 P16 **Quebrada Guabo** Ngöbe-Buglé, W Panama 08°19′N 81°50′W
101 K14 **Quedlinburg** Sachsen-Anhalt, C Germany 51°48′N 11°09′E
138 H10 **Queen Alia** ✕ (‘Ammān) ‘Ammān, C Jordan
10 L16 **Queen Bess, Mount** ▲ British Columbia, SW Canada 51°15′N 124°29′W
10 I14 **Queen Charlotte** British Columbia, SW Canada 53°18′N 132°04′W
65 B24 **Queen Charlotte Bay** *bay* West Falkland, W Falkland Islands
10 H14 **Queen Charlotte Islands** *Fr.* Îles de la Reine-Charlotte. *island group* British Columbia, SW Canada
10 I15 **Queen Charlotte Sound** *sea area* British Columbia, W Canada
10 J16 **Queen Charlotte Strait** *strait* British Columbia, W Canada
27 U1 **Queen City** Missouri, C USA 40°24′N 92°34′W
25 X5 **Queen City** Texas, SW USA 33°09′N 94°09′W
197 O9 **Queen Elizabeth Islands** *Fr.* Îles de la Reine-Élisabeth. *island group* Nunavut, N Canada
195 Y10 **Queen Mary Coast** *physical region* Antarctica
65 N24 **Queen Mary’s Peak** ▲ C Tristan da Cunha
196 M8 **Queen Maud Gulf** *gulf* Arctic Ocean
195 P11 **Queen Maud Mountains** ▲▲ Antarctica
Queen’s County *see* Laois
181 U7 **Queensland** ⬖ *state* N Australia
192 I9 **Queensland Plateau** *undersea feature* N Coral Sea
183 O16 **Queenstown** Tasmania, SE Australia 42°06′S 145°33′E
185 C22 **Queenstown** Otago, South Island, New Zealand 45°01′S 168°44′E
83 I24 **Queenstown** Eastern Cape, S South Africa 31°52′S 26°50′E
Queenstown *see* Cobh
32 F8 **Queets** Washington, NW USA 47°31′N 124°19′W
61 D18 **Queguay Grande, Río** ≈ W Uruguay
59 O16 **Queimadas** Bahia, E Brazil 10°59′S 39°38′W
82 D11 **Quela** Malanje, NW Angola 09°18′S 17°07′E
83 O16 **Quelimane** *var.* Kilimane, Kilmain, Quilimane. Zambézia, NE Mozambique 17°53′S 36°51′E
63 G18 **Quellón** *var.* Puerto Quellón. Los Lagos, S Chile 43°05′S 73°38′W
Quelpart *see* Cheju-do
37 P12 **Quemado** New Mexico, SW USA 34°18′N 108°29′W
25 O12 **Quemado** Texas, SW USA 28°58′N 100°36′W
44 K7 **Quemado, Punta de** *headland* E Cuba 20°13′N 74°07′W
Quemoy *see* Chinmen Tao
62 K13 **Quemú Quemú** La Pampa, E Argentina 36°03′S 63°36′W
155 E17 **Quepem** Goa, W India 15°13′N 74°03′E
42 M14 **Quepos** Puntarenas, S Costa Rica 09°28′N 84°10′W
Que Que *see* Kwekwe
61 D23 **Quequén** Buenos Aires, E Argentina 38°30′S 58°44′W
61 D23 **Quequén Grande, Río** ≈ E Argentina
61 C23 **Quequén Salado, Río** ≈ E Argentina
Quera *see* Chur
41 N13 **Querétaro** Querétaro de Arteaga, C Mexico 20°36′N 100°24′W
40 F4 **Querobabi** Sonora, NW Mexico 30°02′N 111°02′W
42 M13 **Quesada** *var.* Ciudad Quesada, San Carlos. Alajuela, N Costa Rica 10°19′N 84°26′W
105 O13 **Quesada** Andalucía, S Spain 37°52′N 03°05′W
161 O7 **Queshan** Henan, C China 32°48′N 114°03′E
10 M15 **Quesnel** British Columbia, SW Canada 52°59′N 122°30′W
37 S9 **Questa** New Mexico, SW USA 36°41′N 105°37′W
102 H7 **Questembert** Morbihan, NW France 47°39′N 02°24′W
57 K22 **Quetena, Río** ≈ SW Bolivia
149 O10 **Quetta** Baluchistān, SW Pakistan 30°15′N 67°E
Quetzalcoalco *see* Coatzacoalcos
Quetzaltenango *see* Quezaltenango
56 B6 **Quevedo** Los Ríos, C Ecuador 01°02′S 79°27′W
42 B6 **Quezaltenango** *var.* Quetzaltenango. Quezaltenango, W Guatemala 14°50′N 91°30′W
42 A2 **Quezaltenango** *off.* Departamento de Quezaltenango, *var.* Quetzaltenango. ⬖ *department* SW Guatemala
Quezaltenango, Departamento de *see* Quezaltenango
42 E6 **Quezaltepeque** Chiquimula, SE Guatemala 14°38′N 89°25′W
170 M6 **Quezon** Palawan, W Philippines 09°13′N 118°01′E
161 P5 **Qufu** Shandong, E China 35°37′N 117°05′E
82 B12 **Quibala** Cuanza Sul, NW Angola 10°44′S 14°58′E
82 B11 **Quibaxe** *var.* Quibaxi. Cuanza Norte, NW Angola 08°30′S 14°36′E
Quibaxi *see* Quibaxe
54 D9 **Quibdó** Chocó, W Colombia 05°40′N 76°38′W
102 G7 **Quiberon** Morbihan, NW France 47°30′N 03°07′W
102 G7 **Quiberon, Baie de** *bay* NW France
54 J5 **Quíbor** Lara, N Venezuela 09°55′N 69°35′W
42 C4 **Quiché** *off.* Departamento del Quiché. ⬖ *department* W Guatemala
Quiché, Departamento del *see* Quiché
99 E21 **Quiévrain** Hainaut, S Belgium 50°25′N 03°41′E
40 I9 **Quila** Sinaloa, C Mexico 24°24′N 107°11′W
83 B14 **Quilengues** Huíla, SW Angola 14°09′S 14°04′E
Quilimane *see* Quelimane
57 G15 **Quillabamba** Cusco, C Peru 12°49′S 72°41′W
57 L18 **Quillacollo** Cochabamba, C Bolivia 17°26′S 66°16′W
62 H4 **Quillagua** Antofagasta, N Chile 21°33′S 69°32′W
103 N17 **Quillan** Aude, S France 42°52′N 02°11′E
11 U15 **Quill Lakes** ◎ Saskatchewan, S Canada
62 G11 **Quillota** Valparaíso, C Chile 32°54′S 71°16′W
155 G23 **Quilon** *var.* Kollam. Kerala, SW India 08°57′N 76°37′E *see also* Kollam
181 V9 **Quilpie** Queensland, C Australia 26°39′S 144°15′E
149 O4 **Quil-Qala** Bāmīān, N Afghanistan 35°13′N 67°02′E
62 L7 **Quimilí** Santiago del Estero, C Argentina 27°35′S 62°25′W
57 O19 **Quimome** Santa Cruz, E Bolivia 17°45′S 61°15′W
102 F6 **Quimper** *anc.* Quimper Corentin. Finistère, NW France 48°00′N 04°05′W
Quimper Corentin *see* Quimper
102 G7 **Quimperlé** Finistère, NW France 47°52′N 03°33′W
32 F8 **Quinault** Washington, NW USA 47°27′N 123°53′W
32 F8 **Quinault River** ≈ Washington, NW USA
35 P5 **Quincy** California, W USA 39°56′N 120°56′W
23 S8 **Quincy** Florida, SE USA 30°35′N 84°34′W
30 I13 **Quincy** Illinois, N USA 39°56′N 91°24′W
19 O11 **Quincy** Massachusetts, NE USA 42°15′N 71°00′W
32 J9 **Quincy** Washington, NW USA 47°13′N 119°51′W
54 E10 **Quindío** *off.* Departamento del Quindío. ⬖ *province* C Colombia
54 E10 **Quindío, Nevado del** ▲ C Colombia 04°42′N 75°25′W
62 J10 **Quines** San Luis, C Argentina 32°15′S 65°46′W
39 N13 **Quinhagak** Alaska, USA 59°45′N 161°55′W
76 G13 **Quinhámel** W Guinea-Bissau 11°52′N 15°52′W
Qui Nhon/Quinhon *see* Quy Nhơn
Quinindé *see* Rosa Zárate
25 U6 **Quinlan** Texas, SW USA 32°54′N 96°08′W
61 H17 **Quinta** Rio Grande do Sul, S Brazil 32°05′S 52°18′W
105 O10 **Quintanar de la Orden** Castilla-La Mancha, C Spain 39°36′N 03°03′W
41 X13 **Quintana Roo** ⬖ *state* SE Mexico
105 S6 **Quinto** Aragón, NE Spain 41°25′N 00°31′W
108 G10 **Quinto** Ticino, S Switzerland 46°32′N 08°44′E
27 Q11 **Quinton** Oklahoma, C USA 35°07′N 95°22′W
62 K12 **Quinto, Río** ≈ C Argentina
82 A10 **Quinzau** Dem. Rep. Congo, NW Angola 06°50′S 12°48′E
14 H8 **Quinze, Lac des** ◎ Québec, SE Canada
83 B15 **Quipungo** Huíla, C Angola 14°49′S 14°29′E
62 G13 **Quirihue** Bío Bío, C Chile 36°15′S 72°35′W
82 D12 **Quirima** Malanje, NW Angola 10°51′S 18°06′E
183 T6 **Quirindi** New South Wales, SE Australia 31°29′S 150°40′E
55 P5 **Quiriquire** Monagas, NE Venezuela 09°59′N 63°14′W
14 D10 **Quirke Lake** ◎ Ontario, S Canada
61 B21 **Quiroga** Buenos Aires, E Argentina 35°18′S 61°22′W
104 I4 **Quiroga** Galicia, NW Spain 42°28′N 07°15′W
Quiróm, Salar *see* Pocitos, Salar
56 B9 **Quiroz, Río** ≈ NW Peru
82 Q13 **Quissanga** Cabo Delgado, NE Mozambique 12°24′S 40°33′E
83 M20 **Quissico** Inhambane, S Mozambique 24°42′S 34°44′E
25 O4 **Quitaque** Texas, SW USA 34°22′N 101°03′W
82 Q13 **Quiterajo** Cabo Delgado, NE Mozambique 11°37′S 40°22′E
23 T6 **Quitman** Georgia, SE USA 30°46′N 83°33′W
22 M6 **Quitman** Mississippi, S USA 32°02′N 88°43′W
25 V6 **Quitman** Texas, SW USA 32°37′N 95°26′W
56 C6 **Quito** ● (Ecuador) Pichincha, N Ecuador 0°14′S 78°30′W
Quito *see* Mariscal Sucre
58 P13 **Quixadá** Ceará, E Brazil 04°57′S 39°04′W
83 Q15 **Quixaxe** Nampula, NE Mozambique 15°15′S 40°07′E
161 N13 **Qujiang** *var.* Maba. Guangdong, S China 24°47′N 113°34′E
160 J9 **Qu Jiang** ≈ C China
161 R10 **Qu Jiang** ≈ SE China
160 H12 **Qujing** Yunnan, SW China 25°39′N 103°52′E
Qulan *see* Kulan
163 T8 **Qulin Gol** *prev.* Chaor He. ≈ NE China
146 L10 **QuljuqtovTog‘lari** *Rus.* Gory Kul’dzhuktau. ▲▲ C Uzbekistan
Qulsary *see* Kul’sary
Qulyndy Zhazyghy *see* Kulunda Steppe
Qum *see* Qom
Qumälisch *see* Lubartów
159 P11 **Qumar He** ≈ C China
159 Q12 **Qumarlêb** *var.* Yuegai; *prev.* Yuegaitan. Qinghai, C China 34°06′N 95°54′E
159 Q15 **Qumdo** Xizang Zizhiqu, W China 30°03′N 95°33′E
Qumisheh *see* Shahreẕā
147 O14 **Qumqo‘rg‘on** *Rus.* Kumkurgan. Surkhondaryo Viloyati, S Uzbekistan 37°54′N 67°31′E
Qunaytirah/Qunayţirah, Muḩāfaẓat al *see* Al Qunayţirah
189 V12 **Quoi** *island* Chuuk, C Micronesia
9 N8 **Quoich** ≈ Nunavut, NE Canada
83 E26 **Quoin Point** *headland* SW South Africa 34°48′S 19°39′E
182 I7 **Quorn** South Australia 32°22′S 138°03′E
Qurein *see* Al Kuwayt
147 P14 **Qŭrghonteppa** *Rus.* Kurgan-Tyube. SW Tajikistan 37°51′N 68°42′E
Qurlurtuuq *see* Kugluktuk
Qurveh *see* Qorveh
Quryq *see* Kuryk
Qusair *see* Al Quşayr
137 X10 **Qusar** *Rus.* Kusary. NE Azerbaijan 41°26′N 48°27′E
Quşayr *see* Al Quşayr
Quseir *see* Al Quşayr
142 I2 **Qūshchī** Āžarbāyjān-e Gharbi, N Iran 37°59′N 45°05′E
Qusmuryn *see* Kushmurun, Kostanay, Kazakhstan
Qusmuryn *see* Kushmurun, Ozero
159 O16 **Qusum** Xizang Zizhiqu, W China 29°02′N 92°09′E
Quţayfah/Qutayfe/Quteife *see* Al Quţayfah
Quthing *see* Moyeni
147 S10 **Quvasoy** *Rus.* Kuvasay. Farg’ona Viloyati, E Uzbekistan 40°17′N 71°53′E
Quwair *see* Guwêr
Quxar *see* Lhazê
Qu Xian *see* Quzhou
159 N16 **Qüxü** *var.* Xoi. Xizang Zizhiqu, W China 29°25′N 90°48′E
Quyang *see* Jingzhou
167 V13 **Quy Chanh** Ninh Thuân, S Vietnam 11°28′N 108°53′E
167 V11 **Quy Nhơn** *var.* Quinhon, Qui Nhon. Binh Đinh, C Vietnam 13°47′N 109°11′E
161 R10 **Quzhou** *var.* Qu Xian. Zhejiang, SE China 28°55′N 118°54′E
Qyteti Stalin *see* Kuçovë
Qyzylaghash *see* Kyzylagash
Qyzylorda *see* Kzylorda
Qyzyltū *see* Kishkenekol’
Qyzylzhar *see* Kyzylzhar

R

Raa Atoll *see* North Maalhosmadulu Atoll
109 R4 **Raab** Oberösterreich, N Austria 48°19′N 13°40′E
109 X8 **Raab** *Hung.* Rába. ≈ Austria/Hungary *see also* Rába
Raab *see* Rába
Raab *see* Győr
109 V2 **Raabs an der Thaya** Niederösterreich, E Austria 48°51′N 15°28′E
93 L14 **Raahe** *Swe.* Brahestad. Oulu, W Finland 64°42′N 24°31′E
98 M10 **Raalte** Overijssel, E Netherlands 52°23′N 06°16′E
99 I14 **Raamsdonksveer** Noord-Brabant, S Netherlands 51°42′N 04°54′E
92 L12 **Raanujärvi** Lappi, NW Finland 66°39′N 24°40′E
96 G9 **Raasay** *island* NW Scotland, United Kingdom
118 H3 **Raasiku** *Ger.* Rasik. Harjumaa, NW Estonia 59°22′N 25°11′E
112 B11 **Rab** *It.* Arbe. Primorje-Gorski Kotar, NW Croatia 44°46′N 14°46′E
112 B11 **Rab** *It.* Arbe. *island* NW Croatia
171 N16 **Raba** Sumbawa, S Indonesia 08°27′S 118°45′E
111 G22 **Rába** *Ger.* Raab. ≈ Austria/Hungary *see also* Raab
Rába *see* Raab
112 A10 **Rabac** Istra, NW Croatia 45°03′N 14°09′E
104 I2 **Rábade** Galicia, NW Spain 43°07′N 07°37′W
80 F10 **Rabak** White Nile, C Sudan 13°12′N 32°44′E
186 G9 **Rabaraba** Milne Bay, SE Papua New Guinea 10°00′S 149°50′E
102 K16 **Rabastens-de-Bigorre** Hautes-Pyrénées, S France 43°23′N 00°10′E
121 O16 **Rabat** W Malta 35°51′N 14°25′E
74 F6 **Rabat** *var.* al Dar al Baida. ● (Morocco) NW Morocco 34°02′N 06°51′W
Rabat *see* Victoria
186 H6 **Rabaul** New Britain, E Papua New Guinea 04°13′S 152°11′E
Rabbah Ammon/Rabbath Ammon *see* ‘Ammān
28 K8 **Rabbit Creek** ≈ South Dakota, N USA
14 H10 **Rabbit Lake** ◎ Ontario, S Canada
187 Y14 **Rabi** *prev.* Rambi. *island* N Fiji
140 K9 **Rābigh** Makkah, W Saudi Arabia 22°51′N 39°E
42 D5 **Rabinal** Baja Verapaz, C Guatemala 15°05′N 90°26′W
168 G9 **Rabi, Pulau** *island* NW Indonesia, East Indies
111 L17 **Rabka** Małopolskie, S Poland 49°38′N 20°E
155 F16 **Rabkavi** Karnātaka, W India 16°40′N 75°03′E
Râbniţa *see* Rîbniţa
109 Y6 **Rabnitz** ≈ E Austria
124 J7 **Rabocheostrovsk** Respublika Kareliya, NW Russian Federation 64°58′N 34°46′E
23 U1 **Rabun Bald** ▲ Georgia, SE USA 34°58′N 83°18′W
75 S11 **Rabyānah** SE Libya 24°07′N 21°58′E
75 S11 **Rabyānah, Ramlat** *var.* Rebiana Sand Sea, Şaḩrā’ Rabyānah. *desert* SE Libya
Rabyānah, Şaḩrā’ *see* Rabyānah, Ramlat
116 L11 **Răcăciuni** Bacău, E Romania 46°20′N 27°00′E
Racaka *see* Riwoqê
107 J24 **Racalmuto** Sicilia, Italy, C Mediterranean Sea 37°25′N 13°44′E
116 J14 **Răcari** Dâmboviţa, SE Romania 44°37′N 25°43′E
Răcari *see* Durankulak
116 F13 **Răcăşdia** *Hung.* Rakasd. Caraş-Severin, SW Romania 44°58′N 21°36′E
106 B9 **Racconigi** Piemonte, NE Italy 44°45′N 07°41′E
31 T15 **Raccoon Creek** ≈ Ohio, N USA
13 V13 **Race, Cape** *headland* Newfoundland, Newfoundland and Labrador, E Canada 46°40′N 53°05′W
22 K10 **Raceland** Louisiana, S USA 29°43′N 90°36′W
19 Q12 **Race Point** *headland* Massachusetts, NE USA 42°03′N 70°14′W
167 S14 **Rach Gia** Kiên Giang, S Vietnam 10°01′N 105°05′E
167 S14 **Rach Gia, Vinh** *bay* S Vietnam
76 J8 **Rachid** Tagant, C Mauritania 18°48′N 11°41′W
110 L10 **Raciąż** Mazowieckie, C Poland 52°46′N 20°04′E
111 I16 **Racibórz** *Ger.* Ratibor. Śląskie, S Poland 50°05′N 18°10′E
31 N9 **Racine** Wisconsin, N USA 42°42′N 87°50′W
14 D7 **Racine Lake** ◎ Ontario, S Canada
111 J23 **Ráckeve** Pest, C Hungary 47°10′N 18°58′E
Rácz-Becse *see* Bečej
141 O15 **Radā’** *var.* Ridā’. W Yemen 14°24′N 44°49′E
113 O15 **Radan** ▲ SE Serbia 42°59′N 21°31′E
63 J19 **Rada Tilly** Chubut, SE Argentina 45°54′S 67°33′W
116 K8 **Rădăuţi** *Ger.* Radautz, *Hung.* Rádóc. Suceava, N Romania 47°49′N 25°58′E
116 L8 **Rădăuţi-Prut** Botoşani, NE Romania 48°14′N 26°47′E
Radautz *see* Rădăuţi
Radbusa *see* Radbuza
111 A17 **Radbuza** *Ger.* Radbusa. ≈ SE Czech Republic
20 K6 **Radcliff** Kentucky, S USA 37°50′N 85°57′W
139 O2 **Radd, Wādī ar** *dry watercourse* N Syria
95 H16 **Råde** Østfold, S Norway 59°21′N 10°53′E
101 N17 **Radebeul** Sachsen, E Germany 51°06′N 13°41′E
109 V11 **Radeče** *Ger.* Ratschach. C Slovenia 46°01′N 15°10′E
Radein *see* Radenci
116 J4 **Radekhiv** *Pol.* Radziechów, *Rus.* Radekhov. L’vivs’ka Oblast’, W Ukraine 50°17′N 24°39′E
Radekhov *see* Radekhiv
109 X9 **Radenci** *Ger.* Radein; *prev.* Radinci. NE Slovenia 46°36′N 16°02′E
109 S9 **Radenthein** Kärnten, S Austria 46°48′N 13°42′E
Rádeyilikóé *see* Fort Good Hope
21 R7 **Radford** Virginia, NE USA 37°07′N 80°34′W
154 C9 **Rādhanpur** Gujarāt, W India 23°52′N 71°49′E
Radinci *see* Radenci
127 Q6 **Radishchevo** Ul’yanovskaya Oblast’, W Russian Federation 52°49′N 47°54′E
12 I9 **Radisson** Québec, E Canada 53°47′N 77°35′W
11 P16 **Radium Hot Springs** British Columbia, SW Canada 50°39′N 116°09′W
116 F11 **Radna** *Hung.* Máriaradna. Arad, W Romania 46°05′N 21°41′E
114 K10 **Radnevo** Stara Zagora, C Bulgaria 42°17′N 25°58′E
97 J20 **Radnor** *cultural region* E Wales, United Kingdom
Radnót *see* Iernut
Rádóc *see* Rădăuţi
101 H24 **Radolfzell am Bodensee** Baden-Württemberg, S Germany 47°43′N 08°58′E
110 M13 **Radom** Mazowieckie, C Poland 51°23′N 21°08′E
116 I14 **Radomireşti** Olt, S Romania 44°06′N 25°00′E
111 K14 **Radomsko** *Rus.* Novoradomsk. Łódzkie, C Poland 51°04′N 19°25′E
117 N4 **Radomyshl’** Zhytomyrs’ka Oblast’, N Ukraine 50°30′N 29°16′E
113 P19 **Radoviš** *prev.* Radovište. E Macedonia 41°39′N 22°26′E
Radovište *see* Radoviš
94 B13 **Radøy** *island* S Norway
109 R7 **Radstadt** Salzburg, NW Austria 47°24′N 13°31′E
182 E8 **Radstock, Cape** *headland* South Australia 33°11′S 134°18′E
109 U10 **Raduha** ▲ N Slovenia 46°24′N 14°46′E
119 G15 **Radun’** Hrodzyenskaya Voblasts’, W Belarus 54°03′N 25°00′E

◆ Country
● Country Capital
◇ Dependent Territory
○ Dependent Territory Capital
⬖ Administrative Regions
✕ International Airport
▲ Mountain
▲▲ Mountain Range
Volcano
≈ River
◎ Lake
⊠ Reservoir

126 M3 **Raduzhnyy** Vladimirskaya Oblast', W Russian Federation 55°59′N 40°15′E
118 F11 **Radviliškis** Šiaulai, N Lithuania 55°48′N 23°32′E
11 U17 **Radville** Saskatchewan, S Canada 49°28′N 104°19′W
140 K7 **Raḍwá, Jabal** ▲ W Saudi Arabia 24°31′N 38°21′E
111 P16 **Radymno** Podkarpackie, SE Poland 49°57′N 22°49′E
116 J5 **Radyvyliv** Rivnens'ka Oblast', NW Ukraine 50°07′N 25°12′E
Radziechów *see* Radekhiv
110 I11 **Radziejów** Kujawskio-pomorskie, C Poland 52°36′N 18°33′E
110 O12 **Radzyń Podlaski** Lubelskie, E Poland 51°48′N 22°37′E
8 J7 **Rae** ≈ Nunavut, NW Canada
152 M13 **Rāe Bareli** Uttar Pradesh, N India 26°14′N 81°14′E
Rae-Edzo *see* Edzo
21 T11 **Raeford** North Carolina, SE USA 34°59′N 79°15′W
99 M19 **Raeren** Liège, E Belgium 50°42′N 06°06′E
9 N7 **Rae Strait** *strait* Nunavut, N Canada
184 L11 **Raetihi** Manawatu-Wanganui, North Island, New Zealand 39°29′S 175°16′E
Raevavae *see* Raivavae
Rafa *see* Rafah
62 M10 **Rafaela** Santa Fe, E Argentina 31°16′S 61°25′W
138 E11 **Rafah** *var.* Rafa, Rafaḥ, ***Heb.*** Rafiaḥ, Raphiah. SW Gaza Strip 31°18′N 34°15′E
79 L15 **Rafaï** Mbomou, SE Central African Republic 05°01′N 23°51′E
141 O4 **Rafḥah** Al Ḥudūd ash Shamālīyah, N Saudi Arabia 29°41′N 43°29′E
Rafiaḥ *see* Rafah
143 R10 **Rafsanjān** Kermān, C Iran 30°25′N 56°E
80 B13 **Raga** Western Bahr el Ghazal, SW Sudan 08°28′N 25°41′E
19 S8 **Ragged Island** *island* Maine, NE USA
44 I5 **Ragged Island Range** *island group* S Bahamas
184 L7 **Raglan** Waikato, North Island, New Zealand 37°48′S 174°54′E
22 G8 **Ragley** Louisiana, S USA 30°31′N 93°13′W
Ragnit *see* Neman
107 K25 **Ragusa** Sicilia, Italy, C Mediterranean Sea 36°56′N 14°42′E
Ragusa *see* Dubrovnik
Ragusavecchia *see* Cavtat
171 P14 **Raha** Pulau Muna, C Indonesia 04°50′S 122°43′E
119 N17 **Rahachow** *Rus.* Rogachëv. Homyel'skaya Voblasts', SE Belarus 53°03′N 30°03′E
67 U6 **Rahad** *var.* Nahr ar Rahad. ≈ W Sudan
Rahad, Nahr ar *see* Rahad
Rahaeng *see* Tak
138 F11 **Rahat** Southern, C Israel 31°20′N 34°43′E
140 L8 **Rahaṭ, Ḥarrat** *lava flow* W Saudi Arabia
149 S12 **Rahīmyār Khān** Punjab, SE Pakistan 28°27′N 70°21′E
95 I14 **Råholt** Akershus, S Norway 60°16′N 11°10′E
113 M17 **Rahovec** *Serb.* Orahovac. W Kosovo 42°24′N 20°40′E
191 S10 **Raiatea** *island* Îles Sous le Vent, W French Polynesia
155 H16 **Rāichūr** Karnātaka, C India 16°15′N 77°20′E
Raidestos *see* Tekirdağ
153 S13 **Rāiganj** West Bengal, NE India 25°38′N 88°11′E
154 M11 **Raigarh** Chhattīsgarh, C India 21°53′N 83°28′E
183 O16 **Railton** Tasmania, SE Australia 41°24′S 146°28′E
36 L8 **Rainbow Bridge** *natural arch* Utah, W USA
23 Q3 **Rainbow City** Alabama, S USA 33°57′N 86°02′W
11 N11 **Rainbow Lake** Alberta, W Canada 58°30′N 119°24′W
21 R5 **Rainelle** West Virginia, NE USA 37°57′N 80°46′W
32 G10 **Rainier** Oregon, NW USA 46°05′N 122°55′W
32 H9 **Rainier, Mount** ⛰ Washington, NW USA 46°51′N 121°45′W
23 Q2 **Rainsville** Alabama, S USA 34°29′N 85°51′W
12 B11 **Rainy Lake** ◎ Canada/USA
12 A11 **Rainy River** Ontario, C Canada 48°44′N 94°33′W
Raippaluoto *see* Replot
154 K12 **Raipur** Chhattīsgarh, C India 21°16′N 81°42′E
154 H10 **Raisen** Madhya Pradesh, C India 23°21′N 77°49′E
15 N13 **Raisin** ≈ Ontario, SE Canada
31 R11 **Raisin, River** ≈ Michigan, N USA
191 U13 **Raivavae** *var.* Raevavae. Îles Australes, SW French Polynesia
149 W9 **Rāiwind** Punjab, E Pakistan 31°14′N 74°10′E
171 T12 **Raja Ampat, Kepulauan** *island group* E Indonesia
155 L16 **Rājahmundry** Andhra Pradesh, E India 17°05′N 81°42′E
155 I18 **Rājampet** Andhra Pradesh, E India 14°09′N 79°10′E
Rajang *see* Rajang, Batang
169 S9 **Rajang, Batang** *var.* Rajang. ≈ East Malaysia
149 S11 **Rājanpur** Punjab, E Pakistan 29°05′N 70°25′E
155 H23 **Rājapālaiyam** Tamil Nādu, SE India 09°26′N 77°36′E
152 E12 **Rājasthān** ◐ *state* NW India
153 T15 **Rajbari** Dhaka, C Bangladesh 23°47′N 89°39′E
153 R12 **Rajbiraj** Eastern, E Nepal 26°34′N 86°52′E
154 G9 **Rājgarh** Madhya Pradesh, C India 24°01′N 76°42′E
152 H10 **Rājgarh** Rājasthān, NW India 28°38′N 75°21′E
153 P14 **Rājgīr** Bihār, N India 25°01′N 85°26′E
110 O8 **Rajgród** Podlaskie, NE Poland 53°43′N 22°40′E
154 L12 **Rājim** Chhattīsgarh, C India 20°57′N 81°58′E
112 C11 **Rajinac, Mali** ▲ W Croatia 44°47′N 15°04′E
154 B10 **Rājkot** Gujarāt, W India 22°18′N 70°47′E
153 R14 **Rājmahal** Jhārkhand, NE India 25°03′N 87°49′E
153 Q14 **Rājmahāl Hills** *hill range* N India
154 K12 **Rāj Nāndgaon** Chhattīsgarh, C India 21°06′N 81°02′E
154 E12 **Rājpīpla** Gujarāt, W India 21°49′N 73°36′E
152 I8 **Rājpura** Punjab, NW India 30°29′N 76°40′E
152 E14 **Rājsamand** Rājasthān, N India 23°04′N 73.53°00′E
153 S14 **Rajshahi** *prev.* Rampur Boalia. Rajshahi, W Bangladesh 24°24′N 88°40′E
153 S13 **Rajshahi** ◐ *division* NW Bangladesh
158 J16 **Raka** Xizang Zizhiqu, W China 29°27′N 85°48′E
190 K13 **Rakahanga** *atoll* N Cook Islands
185 H19 **Rakaia** Canterbury, South Island, New Zealand 43°45′S 172°02′E
185 G19 **Rakaia** ≈ South Island, New Zealand
152 H3 **Rakaposhi** ▲ N India 36°06′N 74°31′E
Rakasd *see* Răcăşdia
169 N15 **Rakata, Pulau** *var.* Pulau Krakatau. *island* S Indonesia
141 U10 **Rakbah, Qalamat ar** *well* SE Saudi Arabia
Rakhine State *see* Arakan State
116 I8 **Rakhiv** Zakarpats'ka Oblast', W Ukraine 48°05′N 24°15′E
141 V13 **Rakhyūt** SW Oman 16°41′N 53°09′E
192 K9 **Rakiraki** Viti Levu, W Fiji 17°22′S 178°10′E
126 J8 **Rakitnoye** Belgorodskaya Oblast', W Russian Federation 50°50′N 35°51′E
Rakka *see* Ar Raqqah
118 I4 **Rakke** Lääne-Virumaa, NE Estonia 58°58′N 26°14′E
95 I16 **Rakkestad** Østfold, S Norway 59°25′N 11°17′E
110 F12 **Rakoniewice** *Ger.* Rakwitz. Wielkopolskie, C Poland 52°09′N 16°10′E
Rakonitz *see* Rakovník
83 H18 **Rakops** Central, C Botswana 21°01′S 24°20′E
111 C16 **Rakovník** *Ger.* Rakonitz. Středočeský Kraj, W Czech Republic 50°07′N 13°44′E
114 J10 **Rakovski** Plovdiv, C Bulgaria 42°16′N 24°58′E
Rakutō-kō *see* Naktong-gang
118 I3 **Rakvere** *Ger.* Wesenberg. Lääne-Virumaa, N Estonia 59°21′N 26°20′E
Rakwitz *see* Rakoniewice
22 L6 **Raleigh** Mississippi, S USA 32°01′N 89°30′W
21 U9 **Raleigh** *state capital* North Carolina, SE USA 35°46′N 78°38′W
21 Y11 **Raleigh Bay** *bay* North Carolina, SE USA
21 U9 **Raleigh-Durham** ✕ North Carolina, SE USA 35°54′N 78°45′W
189 S6 **Ralik Chain** *island group* Ralik Chain, W Marshall Islands
25 N5 **Ralls** Texas, SW USA 33°40′N 101°23′W
18 G13 **Ralston** Pennsylvania, NE USA 41°29′N 76°57′W
141 O16 **Ramādah** W Yemen 13°35′N 43°50′E
Ramadi *see* Ar Ramādī
105 N2 **Ramales de la Victoria** Cantabria, N Spain 43°15′N 03°28′W
138 F10 **Ramallah** C West Bank 31°55′N 35°12′E
61 C19 **Ramallo** Buenos Aires, E Argentina 33°30′S 60°01′W
155 H20 **Rāmanagaram** Karnātaka, E India 12°45′N 77°16′E
155 I23 **Rāmanāthapuram** Tamil Nādu, SE India 09°23′N 78°53′E
154 N12 **Rāmapur** Orissa, E India 21°48′N 84°00′E
155 I14 **Rāmāreddi** *var.* Kāmāreddi, Kamareddy. Andhra Pradesh, C India 18°19′N 78°23′E
138 F10 **Ramat Gan** Tel Aviv, W Israel 32°04′N 34°48′E
103 T6 **Rambervillers** Vosges, NE France 48°15′N 06°50′E
Rambi *see* Rabi
103 N5 **Rambouillet** Yvelines, N France 48°39′N 01°50′E
186 E5 **Rambutyo Island** *island* N Papua New Guinea
153 Q12 **Ramechhāp** Central, C Nepal 27°20′N 86°05′E
183 R12 **Rame Head** *headland* Victoria, SE Australia 37°48′S 149°30′E
126 L4 **Ramenskoye** Moskovskaya Oblast', W Russian Federation 55°31′N 38°24′E
124 J15 **Rameshki** Tverskaya Oblast', W Russian Federation 57°21′N 36°05′E
153 P14 **Rāmgarh** Jhārkhand, N India 23°37′N 85°32′E
152 D11 **Rāmgarh** Rājasthān, NW India 27°29′N 70°38′E
142 M9 **Rāmhormoz** *var.* Ram Hormuz, Ramuz. Khūzestān, SW Iran 31°15′N 49°38′E
Ram Hormuz *see* Rāmhormoz
Ram, Jebel *see* Ramm, Jabal
138 F10 **Ramla** *var.* Ramle, Ramleh, *Ar.* Er Ramle. Central, C Israel 31°56′N 34°52′E
Ramle/Ramleh *see* Ramla
138 F14 **Ramm, Jabal** *var.* Jebel Ram. ▲ SW Jordan 29°34′N 35°24′E
152 K10 **Rāmnagar** Uttarakhand, N India 29°23′N 79°07′E
95 N15 **Ramnäs** Västmanland, C Sweden 59°46′N 16°16′E
Râmnicul-Sărat *see* Râmnicu Sărat
116 L12 **Râmnicu Sărat** *prev.* Râmnicul-Sărat, Rîmnicu-Sărat. Buzău, E Romania 45°24′N 27°06′E
116 I13 **Râmnicu Vâlcea** *prev.* Rîmnicu Vîlcea. Vâlcea, C Romania 45°04′N 24°32′E
Ramokgwebana *see* Ramokgwebane
83 J18 **Ramokgwebane** *var.* Ramokgwebana. Central, NE Botswana 20°38′S 27°40′E
126 L7 **Ramon'** Voronezhskaya Oblast', W Russian Federation 51°51′N 39°18′E
35 V17 **Ramona** California, W USA 33°02′N 116°52′W
56 A10 **Ramón, Laguna** ◎ NW Peru
14 G7 **Ramore** Ontario, S Canada 48°26′N 80°19′W
40 M11 **Ramos** San Luis Potosí, C Mexico 22°48′N 101°55′W
41 N8 **Ramos Arizpe** Coahuila, NE Mexico 25°35′N 100°59′W
40 J9 **Ramos, Río de** ≈ C Mexico
83 J21 **Ramotswa** South East, S Botswana 24°56′S 25°50′E
39 R8 **Rampart** Alaska, USA 65°30′N 150°10′W
8 H8 **Ramparts** ≈ Northwest Territories, NW Canada
152 K10 **Rāmpur** Uttar Pradesh, N India 28°48′N 79°03′E
154 F9 **Rāmpura** Madhya Pradesh, C India 24°30′N 75°32′E
Rampura *see* Rudrapur
Rampur Boalia *see* Rajshahi
166 K6 **Ramree Island** *island* W Burma (Myanmar)
141 W6 **Rams** *var.* Ar Rams. Ra's al Khaymah, NE United Arab Emirates 25°52′N 56°01′E
143 N4 **Rāmsar** *prev.* Sakhtsar. Māzandarān, N Iran 36°55′N 50°39′E
93 H16 **Ramsele** Västernorrland, N Sweden 63°33′N 16°35′E
21 T9 **Ramseur** North Carolina, SE USA 35°43′N 79°39′W
97 I16 **Ramsey** NE Isle of Man 54°19′N 04°24′W
97 I16 **Ramsey Bay** *bay* NE Isle of Man
14 E9 **Ramsey Lake** ◎ Ontario, S Canada
97 Q22 **Ramsgate** SE England, United Kingdom 51°20′N 01°25′E
94 M10 **Ramsjö** Gävleborg, C Sweden 62°10′N 15°40′E
154 I12 **Rāmtek** Mahārāshtra, C India 21°28′N 79°28′E
Ramtha *see* Ar Ramthā
Ramuz *see* Rāmhormoz
118 G12 **Ramygala** Panevėžys, C Lithuania 55°30′N 24°18′E
152 H14 **Rāna Pratāp Sāgar** ◎ N India
169 V7 **Ranau** Sabah, East Malaysia 05°56′N 116°43′E
168 L14 **Ranau, Danau** ◎ Sumatera, W Indonesia
62 H12 **Rancagua** Libertador, C Chile 34°10′S 70°45′W
99 G22 **Rance** Hainaut, S Belgium 50°09′N 04°16′E
102 H6 **Rance** ≈ NW France
60 J9 **Rancharia** São Paulo, S Brazil 22°13′S 50°53′W
153 P15 **Rānchi** Jhārkhand, N India 23°22′N 85°20′E
61 D21 **Ranchos** Buenos Aires, E Argentina 35°32′S 58°22′W
37 S9 **Ranchos De Taos** New Mexico, SW USA 36°21′N 105°36′W
63 G16 **Ranco, Lago** ◎ C Chile
95 C16 **Randaberg** Rogaland, S Norway 59°00′N 05°38′E
29 U7 **Randall** Minnesota, N USA 46°05′N 94°30′W
107 L23 **Randazzo** Sicilia, Italy, C Mediterranean Sea 37°52′N 14°57′E
95 G21 **Randers** Århus, C Denmark 56°28′N 10°03′E
92 I12 **Randijaure** ◎ N Sweden
21 T9 **Randleman** North Carolina, SE USA 35°49′N 79°48′W
19 O11 **Randolph** Massachusetts, NE USA 42°09′N 71°02′W
29 Q13 **Randolph** Nebraska, C USA 42°25′N 97°05′W
36 M1 **Randolph** Utah, W USA 41°40′N 111°10′W
100 P9 **Randow** ≈ NE Germany
95 H14 **Randsfjorden** ◎ S Norway
92 K13 **Råneå** Norrbotten, N Sweden 65°52′N 22°17′E
92 G12 **Ranelva** ≈ C Norway
93 F15 **Ranemsletta** Nord-Trøndelag, C Norway 64°36′N 11°55′E
76 H10 **Ranérou** C Senegal 15°17′N 14°00′W
Ráneš *see* Ringvassøya
185 E22 **Ranfurly** Otago, South Island, New Zealand 45°07′S 170°06′E
167 P17 **Rangae** Narathiwat, SW Thailand 06°15′N 101°45′E
153 V16 **Rangamati** Chittagong, SE Bangladesh 22°40′N 92°10′E
184 I2 **Rangaunu Bay** *bay* North Island, New Zealand
19 P6 **Rangeley** Maine, NE USA 44°58′N 70°37′W
37 O4 **Rangely** Colorado, C USA 40°05′N 108°48′W
25 R7 **Ranger** Texas, SW USA 32°28′N 98°40′W
14 C9 **Ranger Lake** Ontario, S Canada 46°51′N 83°34′W
14 C9 **Ranger Lake** ◎ Ontario, S Canada
153 V12 **Rangia** Assam, NE India 26°26′N 91°38′E
185 I18 **Rangiora** Canterbury, South Island, New Zealand 43°19′S 172°34′E
191 T9 **Rangiroa** *atoll* Îles Tuamotu, W French Polynesia
184 N9 **Rangitaiki** ≈ North Island, New Zealand
185 F19 **Rangitata** ≈ South Island, New Zealand
184 M12 **Rangitikei** ≈ North Island, New Zealand
184 L6 **Rangitoto Island** *island* N New Zealand
Rangkasbitoeng *see* Rangkasbitung
169 N16 **Rangkasbitung** *prev.* Rangkasbitoeng. Jawa, SW Indonesia 06°21′S 106°12′E
167 P9 **Rang, Khao** ▲ C Thailand 16°13′N 99°03′E
147 V13 **Rangkŭl** *Rus.* Rangkul'. SE Tajikistan 38°30′N 74°24′E
Rangkul' *see* Rangkŭl
Rangoon *see* Yangon
153 T13 **Rangpur** Rajshahi, N Bangladesh 25°46′N 89°20′E
155 F18 **Rānibennur** Karnātaka, W India 14°36′N 75°39′E
153 R15 **Rāniganj** West Bengal, NE India 23°34′N 87°13′E
149 Q13 **Rānīpur** Sind, SE Pakistan 27°17′N 68°34′E
Rāniyah *see* Ṛānya
25 N9 **Rankin** Texas, SW USA 31°14′N 101°56′W
9 O9 **Rankin Inlet** Nunavut, C Canada 62°52′N 92°14′W
183 P8 **Rankins Springs** New South Wales, SE Australia 33°51′S 146°16′E
Rankovićevo *see* Kraljevo
108 I7 **Rankweil** Vorarlberg, W Austria 47°17′N 09°40′E
Rann *see* Brežice
127 T8 **Ranneye** Orenburgskaya Oblast', W Russian Federation 51°28′N 52°29′E
96 I10 **Rannoch, Loch** ◎ C Scotland, United Kingdom
191 U17 **Rano Kau** *var.* Rano Kao. *crater* Easter Island, Chile, E Pacific Ocean
167 N14 **Ranong** Ranong, SW Thailand 09°59′N 98°40′E
186 J8 **Ranongga** *var.* Ghanongga. *island* NW Solomon Islands
191 W16 **Rano Raraku** *ancient monument* Easter Island, Chile, E Pacific Ocean
171 V12 **Ransiki** Papua, E Indonesia 01°27′S 134°12′E
92 K12 **Rantajärvi** Norrbotten, N Sweden 66°45′N 23°39′E
93 N17 **Rantasalmi** Itä-Suomi, SE Finland 62°02′N 28°22′E
169 U13 **Rantau** Borneo, C Indonesia 02°56′S 115°09′E
168 L10 **Rantau, Pulau** *var.* Pulau Tebingtinggi. *island* W Indonesia
171 N13 **Rantepao** Sulawesi, C Indonesia 02°58′S 119°58′E
30 M13 **Rantoul** Illinois, N USA 40°19′N 88°08′W
93 L15 **Rantsila** Oulu, C Finland 64°31′N 25°40′E
92 L13 **Ranua** Lappi, NW Finland 65°55′N 26°34′E
139 T3 **Ṛānya** *var.* Rāniyah. As Sulaymānīyah, NE Iraq 36°15′N 44°53′E
157 X3 **Raohe** Heilongjiang, NE China 46°49′N 134°00′E
74 H9 **Raoui, Erg er** *desert* W Algeria
193 O10 **Rapa** *island* Îles Australes, S French Polynesia
191 V14 **Rapa Iti** *island* Îles Australes, SW French Polynesia
106 D10 **Rapallo** Liguria, NW Italy 44°21′N 09°13′E
Rapa Nui *see* Pascua, Isla de
Raphiah *see* Rafah
21 V5 **Rapidan River** ≈ Virginia, NE USA
28 J10 **Rapid City** South Dakota, N USA 44°05′N 103°14′W
15 P8 **Rapide-Blanc** Québec, SE Canada 47°48′N 72°57′W
14 I8 **Rapide-Deux** Québec, SE Canada 47°56′N 78°33′W
118 K6 **Räpina** *Ger.* Rappin. Põlvamaa, SE Estonia 58°06′N 27°27′E
118 G4 **Rapla** *Ger.* Rappel. Raplamaa, NW Estonia 59°00′N 24°46′E
118 G4 **Raplamaa** *var.* Rapla Maakond. ◐ *province* NW Estonia
Rapla Maakond *see* Raplamaa
21 X6 **Rappahonnock River** ≈ Virginia, NE USA
Rappel *see* Rapla
108 G7 **Rapperswil** Sankt Gallen, NE Switzerland 47°14′N 08°50′E
Rappin *see* Räpina
153 N12 **Rāpti** ≈ N India
57 K16 **Rapulo, Río** ≈ E Bolivia
Raqqah/Raqqah, Muḥāfaẓat al *see* Ar Raqqah
18 J8 **Raquette Lake** ◎ New York, NE USA
18 J6 **Raquette River** ≈ New York, NE USA
191 V10 **Raraka** *atoll* Îles Tuamotu, C French Polynesia
191 V10 **Raroia** *atoll* Îles Tuamotu, C French Polynesia
190 H15 **Rarotonga** ✕ Rarotonga, S Cook Islands, C Pacific Ocean 21°15′S 159°45′W
190 H16 **Rarotonga** *island* S Cook Islands, C Pacific Ocean
147 P12 **Rarz** W Tajikistan 39°23′N 68°43′E
Ras al'Ain *see* Ra's al 'Ayn
139 N2 **Ra's al 'Ayn** *var.* Ras al'Ain. Al Ḥasakah, N Syria 36°52′N 40°05′E
138 H3 **Ra's al Basīṭ** Al Lādhiqīyah, W Syria 35°57′N 35°55′E
Ra's al-Hafǧī *see* Ra's al Khafjī
141 R5 **Ra's al Khafjī** *var.* Ra's al-Hafǧī. Ash Sharqīyah, NE Saudi Arabia 28°22′N 48°30′E
Ras al-Khaimah/Ras al Khaimah *see* Ra's al Khaymah
143 R15 **Ra's al Khaymah** *var.* Ras al Khaimah. Ra's al Khaymah, NE United Arab Emirates 25°44′N 55°55′E
143 R15 **Ra's al Khaymah** *var.* Ras al-Khaimah. ✕ Ra's al Khaymah, NE United Arab Emirates 25°37′N 55°51′E
138 G13 **Ra's an Naqb** Ma'ān, S Jordan 30°00′N 35°29′E
61 B26 **Rasa, Punta** *headland* E Argentina 40°50′S 62°15′W
171 V12 **Rasawi** Papua, E Indonesia 02°04′S 134°02′E
Râşcani *see* Rîşcani
80 J10 **Ras Dashen Terara** ▲ N Ethiopia 13°12′N 38°09′E
Rasdhoo Atoll *see* Rasdu Atoll
151 K19 **Rasdu Atoll** *var.* Rasdhoo Atoll. *atoll* C Maldives
118 E12 **Raseiniai** Kaunas, C Lithuania 55°23′N 23°06′E
75 X8 **Ra's Ghārib** *var.* Râs Ghârib. E Egypt 28°16′N 33°01′E
Râs Ghârib *see* Ra's Ghārib
162 J6 **Rashaant** Hövsgöl, N Mongolia 49°08′N 101°27′E
Rashaant *see* Delüün, Bayan-Ölgiy, Mongolia
Rashaant *see* Öldziyt, Dundgovĭ, Mongolia
80 F12 **Rashad** Southern Kordofan, C Sudan 11°55′N 31°05′E
75 V7 **Rashīd** *Eng.* Rosetta. N Egypt 31°25′N 30°25′E
139 Y11 **Rashīd** Al Başrah, E Iraq 31°15′N 47°31′E
142 M3 **Rasht** *var.* Resht. Gīlān, NW Iran 37°18′N 49°38′E
139 S2 **Ṛashwan** Arbīl, N Iraq 36°28′N 43°54′E
Rasik *see* Raasiku
143 W14 **Rāsk** Sīstān va Balūchestān, SE Iran 26°13′N 61°25′E
113 M15 **Raška** Serbia, C Serbia 43°18′N 20°37′E
119 P15 **Rasna** *Rus.* Ryasna. Mahilyowskaya Voblasts', E Belarus 54°01′N 31°12′E
116 J12 **Râşnov** *prev.* Rîşno, Rozsnyó, ***Hung.*** Barcarozsnyó. Braşov, C Romania 45°35′N 25°27′E
118 L11 **Rasony** *Rus.* Rossony. Vitsyebskaya Voblasts', N Belarus 55°53′N 28°50′E
Ra's Shamrah *see* Ugarit
127 N7 **Rasskazovo** Tambovskaya Oblast', W Russian Federation 52°42′N 41°45′E
119 O16 **Rasta** ≈ E Belarus
Rastadt *see* Rastatt
Rastâne *see* Ar Rastān
141 S6 **Ra's Tannūrah** *Eng.* Ras Tanura. Ash Sharqīyah, NE Saudi Arabia 26°44′N 50°04′E
Ras Tanura *see* Ra's Tannūrah
101 G21 **Rastatt** *var.* Rastadt. Baden-Württemberg, SW Germany 48°51′N 08°13′E
Rastenburg *see* Kętrzyn
149 V7 **Rasūlnagar** Punjab, E Pakistan 32°20′N 73°51′E
189 U6 **Ratak Chain** *island group* Ratak Chain, E Marshall Islands
119 K15 **Ratamka** *Rus.* Ratomka. Minskaya Voblasts', C Belarus 53°56′N 27°21′E
93 G17 **Ratän** Jämtland, C Sweden 62°28′N 14°35′E
152 G11 **Ratangarh** Rājasthān, NW India 28°02′N 74°39′E
Rat Buri *see* Ratchaburi
167 O11 **Ratchaburi** *var.* Rat Buri. Ratchaburi, W Thailand 13°30′N 99°50′E
29 W15 **Rathbun Lake** ⊠ Iowa, C USA
Ráth Caola *see* Rathkeale
166 K5 **Rathedaung** Rakhine State, W Burma (Myanmar) 20°30′N 92°48′E
100 M12 **Rathenow** Brandenburg, NE Germany 52°37′N 12°21′E
97 C19 **Rathkeale** *Ir.* Ráth Caola. Limerick, SW Ireland 52°32′N 08°56′W
96 F13 **Rathlin Island** *Ir.* Reachlainn. *island* N Northern Ireland, United Kingdom
97 C20 **Ráth Luirc** *Ir.* An Ráth. Cork, SW Ireland 52°22′N 08°44′W
Ratibor *see* Racibórz
Ratisbon/Ratisbona/Ratisbonne *see* Regensburg
Rätische Alpen *see* Rhaetian Alps
38 E17 **Rat Island** *island* Aleutian Islands, Alaska, USA
38 E17 **Rat Islands** *island group* Aleutian Islands, Alaska, USA
154 F10 **Ratlām** *prev.* Rutlam. Madhya Pradesh, C India 23°23′N 75°04′E
155 D15 **Ratnāgiri** Mahārāshtra, W India 17°00′N 73°20′E
155 K26 **Ratnapura** Sabaragamuwa Province, S Sri Lanka 06°41′N 80°25′E
Ratne *see* Ratno
116 J2 **Ratno** *var.* Ratne. Volyns'ka Oblast', NW Ukraine 51°40′N 24°33′E
Ratomka *see* Ratamka
37 U8 **Raton** New Mexico, SW USA 36°54′N 104°27′W
139 O7 **Ratqah, Wādī ar** *dry watercourse* W Iraq
Ratschach *see* Radeče
167 O16 **Rattaphum** Songkhla, SW Thailand 07°07′N 100°16′E
26 L6 **Rattlesnake Creek** ≈ Kansas, C USA
94 L13 **Rättvik** Dalarna, C Sweden 60°53′N 15°12′E
100 K9 **Ratzeburg** Mecklenburg-Vorpommern, N Germany 53°41′N 10°48′E
100 K9 **Ratzeburger See** ◎ N Germany
10 J10 **Ratz, Mount** ▲ British Columbia, SW Canada 57°22′N 132°17′W
61 D22 **Rauch** Buenos Aires, E Argentina 36°45′S 59°05′W
41 U16 **Raudales** Chiapas, SE Mexico
Raudhatain *see* Ar Rawḍatayn
Raudnitz an der Elbe *see* Roudnice nad Labem
92 K1 **Raufarhöfn** Nordhurland Eystra, NE Iceland 66°27′N 15°58′W
94 H13 **Raufoss** Oppland, S Norway 60°44′N 10°39′E
Raukawa *see* Cook Strait
184 Q8 **Raukumara** ▲ North Island, New Zealand 37°46′S 178°07′E
192 K11 **Raukumara Plain** *undersea feature* N Coral Sea
184 P8 **Raukumara Range** ▲▲ North Island, New Zealand
154 N11 **Rāulakela** *var.* Raurkela; *prev.* Rourkela. Orissa, E India 22°13′N 84°53′E
95 F15 **Rauland** Telemark, S Norway 59°41′N 07°57′E
93 J19 **Rauma** *Swe.* Raumo. Länsi-Suomi, SW Finland 61°09′N 21°30′E
94 F10 **Rauma** ≈ S Norway
Raumo *see* Rauma
118 H8 **Rauna** Cēsis, C Latvia 57°19′N 25°34′E
169 T17 **Raung, Gunung** ▲ Jawa, S Indonesia 08°00′S 114°07′E
Raurkela *see* Rāulakela
95 J22 **Raus** Skåne, S Sweden 56°01′N 12°48′E
165 W3 **Rausu** Hokkaidō, NE Japan 44°00′N 145°06′E
165 W3 **Rausu-dake** ▲ Hokkaidō, NE Japan 44°06′N 145°04′E
116 M9 **Răut** *var.* Răuţel. ≈ C Moldova
93 M17 **Rautalampi** Itä-Suomi, C Finland 62°37′N 26°48′E
93 N16 **Rautavaara** Itä-Suomi, C Finland 63°30′N 28°19′E
Răuţel *see* Răut
93 O18 **Rautjärvi** Etelä-Suomi, SE Finland 61°21′N 29°20′E
Rautu *see* Sosnovo
191 V11 **Ravahere** *atoll* Îles Tuamotu, C French Polynesia
107 J25 **Ravanusa** Sicilia, Italy, C Mediterranean Sea 37°16′N 13°59′E
143 S9 **Rāvar** Kermān, C Iran 31°15′N 56°51′E
147 Q11 **Ravat** Batkenskaya Oblast', SW Kyrgyzstan 39°54′N 70°06′E
18 K11 **Ravena** New York, NE USA 42°28′N 73°49′W
106 H10 **Ravenna** Emilia-Romagna, N Italy 44°28′N 12°15′E
29 O15 **Ravenna** Nebraska, C USA 41°01′N 98°54′W
31 U11 **Ravenna** Ohio, N USA 41°09′N 81°14′W
101 I24 **Ravensburg** Baden-Württemberg, S Germany 47°47′N 09°37′E
181 W4 **Ravenshoe** Queensland, NE Australia 17°29′S 145°28′E
180 K13 **Ravensthorpe** Western Australia 33°37′S 120°03′E
21 Q4 **Ravenswood** West Virginia, NE USA 38°57′N 81°45′W
149 U9 **Rāvi** ≈ India/Pakistan
112 C9 **Ravna Gora** Primorje-Gorski Kotar, NW Croatia 45°20′N 14°54′E
109 U10 **Ravne na Koroškem** *Ger.* Gutenstein. N Slovenia 46°33′N 14°57′E
139 P6 **Rāwah** Al Anbār, W Iraq 34°32′N 41°54′E
191 T4 **Rawaki** *prev.* Phoenix Island. *atoll* Phoenix Islands, C Kiribati
149 U6 **Rāwalpindi** Punjab, NE Pakistan 33°38′N 73°06′E
110 L13 **Rawa Mazowiecka** Łódzkie, C Poland 51°47′N 20°16′E
139 T2 **Ṛawāndiz** *var.* Rawandoz, Rawāndūz. Arbīl, N Iraq 36°38′N 44°32′E
Rawandoz/Rawāndūz *see* Ṛawāndiz
171 U12 **Rawas** Papua, E Indonesia 01°07′S 132°12′E
139 O4 **Rawḍah** ◎ E Syria
110 G13 **Rawicz** *Ger.* Rawitsch. Wielkopolskie, C Poland 51°37′N 16°51′E
Rawitsch *see* Rawicz
180 M11 **Rawlinna** Western Australia 31°01′S 125°36′E
33 W16 **Rawlins** Wyoming, C USA 41°47′N 107°14′W
63 K17 **Rawson** Chubut, SE Argentina 43°22′S 65°01′W
159 R16 **Rawu** Xizang Zizhiqu, W China 29°30′N 96°42′E
153 P12 **Raxaul** Bihār, N India 26°58′N 84°51′E
28 K3 **Ray** North Dakota, N USA 48°19′N 103°11′W
169 S11 **Raya, Bukit** ▲ Borneo, C Indonesia 0°40′S 112°40′E
155 I18 **Rāyachoti** Andhra Pradesh, E India 14°03′N 78°43′E
Rāyadrug *see* Rāyagada
155 M14 **Rāyagada** *prev.* Rāyadrug. Orissa, E India 19°10′N 83°28′E
138 H7 **Rayak** *var.* Rayaq, Riyāq. E Lebanon 33°51′N 36°03′E
Rayaq *see* Rayak
139 T2 **Ṛāyat** Arbīl, E Iraq 36°39′N 44°56′E
169 N12 **Raya, Tanjung** *cape* Pulau Bangka, W Indonesia
13 R13 **Ray, Cape** *headland* Newfoundland, Newfoundland and Labrador, E Canada 47°38′N 59°15′W
123 Q13 **Raychikhinsk** Amurskaya Oblast', SE Russian Federation 49°47′N 129°19′E
127 U5 **Rayevskiy** Respublika Bashkortostan, W Russian Federation 54°04′N 54°58′E
11 Q17 **Raymond** Alberta, SW Canada 49°30′N 112°41′W
22 K6 **Raymond** Mississippi, S USA 32°15′N 90°25′W
32 F9 **Raymond** Washington, NW USA 46°41′N 123°43′W
183 T8 **Raymond Terrace** New South Wales, SE Australia 32°47′S 151°45′E
25 T17 **Raymondville** Texas, SW USA 26°30′N 97°48′W
11 U16 **Raymore** Saskatchewan, S Canada 51°24′N 104°34′W
39 Q8 **Ray Mountains** ▲▲ Alaska, USA
22 H9 **Rayne** Louisiana, S USA 30°13′N 92°15′W
41 O12 **Rayón** San Luis Potosí, C Mexico 21°54′N 99°33′W
40 G4 **Rayón** Sonora, NW Mexico 29°45′N 110°33′W
167 P12 **Rayong** Rayong, S Thailand 12°42′N 101°17′E
25 T5 **Ray Roberts, Lake** ◎ Texas, SW USA
18 E15 **Raystown Lake** ⊠ Pennsylvania, NE USA
141 V13 **Raysūt** SW Oman 16°58′N 54°02′E
27 R4 **Raytown** Missouri, C USA 39°00′N 94°27′W
22 I5 **Rayville** Louisiana, S USA 32°29′N 91°45′W
142 L5 **Razan** Hamadān, W Iran 35°22′N 48°58′E
139 S9 **Razāzah, Buḥayrat ar** *var.* Baḥr al Milḥ. ◎ C Iraq
114 L9 **Razboyna** ▲ E Bulgaria 42°54′N 26°31′E
Razdan *see* Hrazdan
Razdolnoye *see* Rozdol'ne
Razelm, Lacul *see* Razim, Lacul
139 U2 **Ṛazga** As Sulaymānīyah, E Iraq 36°25′N 45°06′E
114 L8 **Razgrad** Razgrad, N Bulgaria 43°33′N 26°31′E
114 L8 **Razgrad** ◐ *province* NE Bulgaria
117 N13 **Razim, Lacul** *prev.* Lacul Razelm. *lagoon* NW Black Sea
114 G11 **Razlog** Blagoevgrad, SW Bulgaria 41°53′N 23°28′E
118 K10 **Rāznas Ezers** ◎ SE Latvia
102 E6 **Raz, Pointe du** *headland* NW France 48°06′N 04°52′W
Reachlainn *see* Rathlin Island
Reachrainn *see* Lambay Island
97 N22 **Reading** S England, United Kingdom 51°28′N 00°59′W
18 H15 **Reading** Pennsylvania, NE USA 40°20′N 75°55′W
48 C7 **Real, Cordillera** ▲▲ C Ecuador
62 K12 **Realicó** La Pampa, C Argentina 35°02′S 64°14′W
25 R15 **Realitos** Texas, SW USA 27°26′N 98°31′W
108 G9 **Realp** Uri, C Switzerland 46°36′N 08°32′E
167 Q12 **Reăng Kesei** Bătdâmbâng, W Cambodia 12°57′N 103°15′E
191 Y11 **Reao** *atoll* Îles Tuamotu, E French Polynesia
Reate *see* Rieti
Greater Antarctica *see* East Antarctica
180 L11 **Rebecca, Lake** ◎ Western Australia
Rebiana Sand Sea *see* Rabyānah, Ramlat
124 H8 **Reboly** *Finn.* Repola. Respublika Kareliya, NW Russian Federation 63°51′N 30°49′E
165 S1 **Rebun** Rebun-tō, NE Japan 45°19′N 141°02′E
165 S1 **Rebun-tō** *island* NE Japan
106 J12 **Recanati** Marche, C Italy 43°23′N 13°34′E
Rechitsa *see* Rechytsa
109 Y7 **Rechnitz** Burgenland, SE Austria 47°19′N 16°26′E
119 J20 **Rechytsa** *Rus.* Rechitsa. Brestskaya Voblasts', SW Belarus 51°51′N 26°48′E
119 O19 **Rechytsa** *Rus.* Rechitsa. Homyel'skaya Voblasts', SE Belarus 52°22′N 30°23′E
59 Q15 **Recife** *prev.* Pernambuco. *state capital* Pernambuco, E Brazil 08°06′S 34°53′W
83 I26 **Recife, Cape** *Afr.* Kaap Recife. *headland* S South Africa 34°03′S 25°37′E
Recife, Kaap *see* Recife, Cape
172 I16 **Récifs, Îles aux** *island* Inner Islands, NE Seychelles
101 E14 **Recklinghausen** Nordrhein-Westfalen, W Germany 51°37′N 07°12′E
100 M8 **Recknitz** ≈ NE Germany
99 K23 **Recogne** Luxembourg, SE Belgium 49°56′N 05°20′E
61 C15 **Reconquista** Santa Fe, C Argentina 29°08′S 59°38′W
195 O6 **Recovery Glacier** *glacier* Antarctica
59 G15 **Recreio** Mato Grosso, W Brazil 08°13′S 58°15′W
27 X9 **Rector** Arkansas, C USA 36°15′N 90°17′W
110 E9 **Recz** *Ger.* Reetz Neumark. Zachodnio-pomorskie, NW Poland 53°16′N 15°32′E
99 L24 **Redange** *var.* Redange-sur-Attert. Diekirch, W Luxembourg 49°46′N 05°53′E
Redange-sur-Attert *see* Redange
18 C13 **Redbank Creek** ≈ Pennsylvania, NE USA
13 S9 **Red Bay** Québec, E Canada 51°40′N 56°37′W
23 N2 **Red Bay** Alabama, S USA 34°26′N 88°08′W
35 N4 **Red Bluff** California, W USA 40°09′N 122°14′W
24 J8 **Red Bluff Reservoir** ◎ New Mexico/Texas, SW USA
30 K16 **Red Bud** Illinois, N USA 38°12′N 89°59′W
30 J5 **Red Cedar River** ≈ Wisconsin, N USA
11 R17 **Redcliff** Alberta, SW Canada 50°06′N 110°48′W
83 K17 **Redcliff** Midlands, C Zimbabwe 19°00′S 29°49′E
182 L9 **Red Cliffs** Victoria, SE Australia 34°21′S 142°12′E
29 P17 **Red Cloud** Nebraska, C USA 40°05′N 98°31′W
22 L8 **Red Creek** ≈ Mississippi, S USA
11 P15 **Red Deer** Alberta, SW Canada 52°15′N 113°48′W
11 Q16 **Red Deer** ≈ Alberta, SW Canada
39 O11 **Red Devil** Alaska, USA 61°45′N 157°18′W
35 N3 **Redding** California, W USA 40°33′N 122°26′W
97 L20 **Redditch** W England, United Kingdom 52°19′N 01°56′W
29 P9 **Redfield** South Dakota, N USA 44°51′N 98°31′W
24 J12 **Redford** Texas, SW USA 29°31′N 104°19′W
45 V13 **Redhead** Trinidad, Trinidad and Tobago 10°44′N 60°58′W
182 I8 **Red Hill** South Australia 33°34′S 138°13′E
Red Hill *see* Pu'u 'Ula'ula
26 K7 **Red Hills** *hill range* Kansas, C USA
13 T12 **Red Indian Lake** ◎ Newfoundland, Newfoundland and Labrador, E Canada
124 J16 **Redkino** Tverskaya Oblast', W Russian Federation 56°41′N 36°07′E
12 A10 **Red Lake** Ontario, C Canada 51°00′N 93°55′W
36 I10 **Red Lake** *salt flat* Arizona, SW USA
29 S4 **Red Lake Falls** Minnesota, N USA 47°52′N 96°16′W
29 R4 **Red Lake River** ≈ Minnesota, N USA
35 U15 **Redlands** California, W USA 34°03′N 117°10′W
18 G16 **Red Lion** Pennsylvania, NE USA 39°53′N 76°36′W
33 U11 **Red Lodge** Montana, NW USA 45°11′N 109°15′W
32 H13 **Redmond** Oregon, NW USA 44°16′N 121°10′W
36 L5 **Redmond** Utah, W USA 39°00′N 111°51′W
32 H8 **Redmond** Washington, NW USA 47°40′N 122°07′W
Rednitz *see* Regnitz
29 T15 **Red Oak** Iowa, C USA 41°00′N 95°10′W
18 K12 **Red Oaks Mill** New York, NE USA 41°39′N 73°52′W
102 I7 **Redon** Ille-et-Vilaine, NW France 47°39′N 02°05′W
45 W10 **Redonda** *island* SW Antigua and Barbuda
104 G4 **Redondela** Galicia, NW Spain 42°17′N 08°36′W
104 H11 **Redondo** Évora, S Portugal 38°38′N 07°32′W
39 Q12 **Redoubt Volcano** ▲ Alaska, USA 60°29′N 152°44′W
11 Y16 **Red River** ≈ Canada/USA
129 U12 **Red River** *var.* Yuan, *Chin.* Yuan Jiang, *Vtn.* Sông Hông Hà. ≈ China/Vietnam
25 W4 **Red River** ≈ S USA
22 H7 **Red River** ≈ Louisiana, S USA
30 M6 **Red River** ≈ Wisconsin, N USA

◆ Country
● Country Capital
◇ Dependent Territory
○ Dependent Territory Capital
◐ Administrative Regions
✕ International Airport
▲ Mountain
▲▲ Mountain Range
⛰ Volcano
≈ River
◎ Lake
⊠ Reservoir

Red Rock, Lake *see* Red Rock Reservoir
29 *W14* **Red Rock Reservoir** *var.* Lake Red Rock. ⊠ Iowa, C USA
80 *H7* **Red Sea** ◐ *state* NE Sudan
75 *Y9* **Red Sea** *var.* Sinus Arabicus. *sea* Africa/Asia
21 *T11* **Red Springs** North Carolina, SE USA *34°49′N 79°10′W*
8 *I9* **Redstone** ≈ Northwest Territories, NW Canada
11 *V17* **Redvers** Saskatchewan, S Canada *49°31′N 101°33′W*
77 *P13* **Red Volta** *var.* Nazinon, *Fr.* Volta Rouge. ≈ Burkina/Ghana
11 *Q14* **Redwater** Alberta, SW Canada *53°57′N 113°06′W*
28 *M16* **Red Willow Creek** ≈ Nebraska, C USA
29 *W9* **Red Wing** Minnesota, N USA *44°33′N 92°31′W*
35 *N9* **Redwood City** California, W USA *37°29′N 122°13′W*
29 *T9* **Redwood Falls** Minnesota, N USA *44°33′N 95°07′W*
31 *P7* **Reed City** Michigan, N USA *43°52′N 85°30′W*
28 *K6* **Reeder** North Dakota, N USA *46°03′N 102°55′W*
35 *R11* **Reedley** California, W USA *36°35′N 119°27′W*
33 *T11* **Reedpoint** Montana, NW USA *45°41′N 109°33′W*
30 *K8* **Reedsburg** Wisconsin, N USA *43°33′N 90°03′W*
32 *E13* **Reedsport** Oregon, NW USA *43°42′N 124°06′W*
187 *Q9* **Reef Islands** *island group* Santa Cruz Islands, E Solomon Islands
185 *H16* **Reefton** West Coast, South Island, New Zealand *42°07′S 171°53′E*
20 *F8* **Reelfoot Lake** ◎ Tennessee, S USA
97 *D17* **Ree, Lough** *Ir.* Loch Rí. ◎ C Ireland
Reengus *see* Rīngas
35 *U4* **Reese River** ≈ Nevada, W USA
98 *M8* **Reest** ≈ E Netherlands
Reetz Neumark *see* Recz
Reevhtse *see* Røsvatnet
137 *N13* **Refahiye** Erzincan, C Turkey *39°54′N 38°45′E*
23 *N4* **Reform** Alabama, S USA *33°22′N 88°01′W*
95 *K20* **Reftele** Jönköping, S Sweden *57°10′N 13°34′E*
25 *T14* **Refugio** Texas, SW USA *28°19′N 97°18′W*
110 *E8* **Rega** ≈ NW Poland
Regar *see* Tursunzoda
101 *O21* **Regen** Bayern, SE Germany *48°57′N 13°10′E*
101 *M20* **Regen** ≈ SE Germany
101 *M21* **Regensburg** *Eng.* Ratisbon, *Fr.* Ratisbonne, *hist.* Ratisbona; *anc.* Castra Regina, Reginum. Bayern, SE Germany *49°01′N 12°06′E*
101 *M21* **Regenstauf** Bayern, SE Germany *49°06′N 12°07′E*
74 *I10* **Reggane** C Algeria *26°46′N 00°09′E*
98 *N9* **Regge** ≈ E Netherlands
Reggio *see* Reggio nell'Emilia
Reggio Calabria *see* Reggio di Calabria
107 *M23* **Reggio di Calabria** *var.* Reggio Calabria, *Gk.* Rhegion; *anc.* Regium, Rhegium. Calabria, SW Italy *38°06′N 15°39′E*
Reggio Emilia *see* Reggio nell'Emilia
106 *F9* **Reggio nell'Emilia** *var.* Reggio Emilia, *abbrev.* Reggio; *anc.* Regium Lepidum. Emilia-Romagna, N Italy *44°42′N 10°37′E*
116 *I10* **Reghin** *Ger.* Sächsisch-Reen, *Hung.* Szászrégen; *prev.* Reghinul Săsesc, *Ger.* Sächsisch-Regen. Mureş, C Romania *46°46′N 24°41′E*
Reghinul Săsesc *see* Reghin
11 *U16* **Regina** *province capital* Saskatchewan, S Canada *50°25′N 104°39′W*
55 *Z10* **Régina** E French Guiana *04°20′N 52°07′W*
11 *U16* **Regina** ✕ Saskatchewan, S Canada *50°21′N 104°43′W*
11 *U16* **Regina Beach** Saskatchewan, S Canada *50°44′N 105°03′W*
Reginum *see* Regensburg
Région du Haut-Congo *see* Haut-Congo
Registan *see* Rīgestān
60 *L11* **Registro** São Paulo, S Brazil *24°30′S 47°50′W*
Regium *see* Reggio di Calabria
Regium Lepidum *see* Reggio nell'Emilia
101 *K19* **Regnitz** *var.* Rednitz. ≈ SE Germany
40 *K10* **Regocijo** Durango, W Mexico *23°35′N 105°11′W*
104 *H12* **Reguengos de Monsaraz** Évora, S Portugal *38°25′N 07°32′W*
101 *M18* **Rehau** Bayern, E Germany *50°15′N 12°03′E*
83 *D19* **Rehoboth** Hardap, C Namibia *23°18′S 17°03′E*
21 *Z4* **Rehoboth Beach** Delaware, NE USA *38°42′N 75°03′W*
138 *F10* **Rehovot** ; *prev.* Reḥovot. Central, C Israel *31°54′N 34°49′E*
Reḥovot *see* Rehovot
81 *J20* **Rei** *spring/well* S Kenya *03°24′S 39°18′E*
Reichenau *see* Rychnov nad Kněžnou
Reichenau *see* Bogatynia, Poland
101 *M17* **Reichenbach** *var.* Reichenbach im Vogtland. Sachsen, E Germany *50°36′N 12°18′E*
Reichenbach *see* Dzierżoniów
Reichenbach im Vogtland *see* Reichenbach
Reichenberg *see* Liberec
181 *O11* **Reid** Western Australia *30°49′S 128°24′E*
23 *V6* **Reidsville** Georgia, SE USA *32°05′N 82°07′W*
21 *T8* **Reidsville** North Carolina, SE USA *36°21′N 79°39′W*
Reifnitz *see* Ribnica
97 *O22* **Reigate** SE England, United Kingdom *51°14′N 00°13′W*
Reikjavik *see* Reykjavík
102 *I10* **Ré, Île de** *island* W France
37 *N15* **Reiley Peak** ▲ Arizona, SW USA *32°24′N 110°09′W*
103 *Q4* **Reims** *Eng.* Rheims; *anc.* Durocortorum, Remi. Marne, N France *49°16′N 04°01′E*
63 *G23* **Reina Adelaida, Archipiélago** *island group* S Chile
45 *O16* **Reina Beatrix** ✕ (Oranjestad) C Aruba *12°30′N 69°57′W*
108 *F7* **Reinach** Aargau, W Switzerland *47°16′N 08°12′E*
108 *E6* **Reinach** Basel-Land, NW Switzerland *47°30′N 07°36′E*
64 *O11* **Reina Sofía** ✕ (Tenerife) Tenerife, Islas Canarias, Spain, NE Atlantic Ocean
29 *W13* **Reinbeck** Iowa, C USA *42°19′N 92°36′W*
100 *J10* **Reinbek** Schleswig-Holstein, N Germany *53°31′N 10°15′E*
11 *U12* **Reindeer** ≈ Saskatchewan, C Canada
11 *U11* **Reindeer Lake** ◎ Manitoba/Saskatchewan, C Canada
Reine-Charlotte, Îles de la *see* Queen Charlotte Islands
Reine-Élisabeth, Îles de la *see* Queen Elizabeth Islands
94 *F13* **Reineskarvet** ▲ S Norway *60°38′N 07°48′E*
184 *H1* **Reinga, Cape** *headland* North Island, New Zealand *34°24′S 172°40′E*
105 *N3* **Reinosa** Cantabria, N Spain *43°01′N 04°09′W*
109 *R8* **Reisseck** ▲ S Austria *46°57′N 13°21′E*
21 *W3* **Reisterstown** Maryland, NE USA *39°27′N 76°46′W*
Reisui *see* Yŏsu
98 *N5* **Reitdiep** ≈ NE Netherlands
191 *V10* **Reitoru** *atoll* Îles Tuamotu, C French Polynesia
95 *M17* **Rejmyre** Östergötland, S Sweden *58°49′N 15°55′E*
Reka *see* Rijeka
Reka Ili *see* Ile/Ili He
95 *N16* **Rekarne** Västmanland, C Sweden *59°25′N 16°04′E*
Rekhovot *see* Rehovot
8 *K9* **Reliance** Northwest Territories, C Canada *62°45′N 109°08′W*
33 *U16* **Reliance** Wyoming, C USA *41°42′N 109°13′W*
74 *I5* **Relizane** *var.* Ghelîzâne, Ghilizane. NW Algeria *35°45′N 00°33′E*
182 *I7* **Remarkable, Mount** ▲ South Australia *32°46′S 138°08′E*
54 *E8* **Remedios** Antioquia, N Colombia *07°02′N 74°42′W*
43 *Q16* **Remedios** Veraguas, W Panama *08°13′N 81°48′W*
42 *D8* **Remedios, Punta** *headland* SW El Salvador *13°31′N 89°48′W*
Remi *see* Reims
99 *N25* **Remich** Grevenmacher, SE Luxembourg *49°33′N 06°23′E*
99 *J19* **Remicourt** Liège, E Belgium *50°40′N 05°19′E*
14 *H8* **Rémigny, Lac** ◎ Québec, SE Canada
55 *Z10* **Rémire** NE French Guiana *04°52′N 52°16′W*
127 *N13* **Remontnoye** Rostovskaya Oblast', SW Russian Federation *46°35′N 43°38′E*
171 *U14* **Remoon** Pulau Kur, E Indonesia *05°18′S 131°59′E*
99 *L20* **Remouchamps** Liège, E Belgium *50°29′N 05°43′E*
103 *R15* **Remoulins** Gard, S France *43°56′N 04°34′E*
173 *X16* **Rempart, Mont du** *hill* W Mauritius
101 *E15* **Remscheid** Nordrhein-Westfalen, W Germany *51°10′N 07°11′E*
29 *S12* **Remsen** Iowa, C USA *42°48′N 95°58′W*
94 *I12* **Rena** Hedmark, S Norway *61°08′N 11°21′E*
94 *I11* **Renåa** ≈ S Norway
Renaix *see* Ronse
118 *H7* **Rencēni** Valmiera, N Latvia *57°43′N 25°25′E*
118 *D9* **Renda** Kuldīga, W Latvia *57°04′N 22°18′E*
107 *N20* **Rende** Calabria, SW Italy *39°19′N 16°10′E*
99 *K21* **Rendeux** Luxembourg, SE Belgium *50°15′N 05°28′E*
Rendina *see* Rentína
30 *L16* **Rend Lake** ⊠ Illinois, N USA
186 *K9* **Rendova** *island* New Georgia Islands, NW Solomon Islands
100 *I8* **Rendsburg** Schleswig-Holstein, N Germany *54°18′N 09°40′E*
108 *B9* **Renens** Vaud, SW Switzerland *46°32′N 06°36′E*
14 *K12* **Renfrew** Ontario, SE Canada *45°28′N 76°44′W*
96 *I12* **Renfrew** *cultural region* SW Scotland, United Kingdom
168 *L11* **Rengat** Sumatera, W Indonesia *0°26′S 102°38′E*
153 *W12* **Rengma Hills** ▲▲ NE India
62 *H12* **Rengo** Libertador, C Chile *34°24′S 70°50′W*
116 *M12* **Reni** Odes'ka Oblast', SW Ukraine *45°30′N 28°18′E*
80 *F11* **Renk** Upper Nile, E Sudan *11°48′N 32°49′E*
93 *L19* **Renko** Etelä-Suomi, S Finland *60°52′N 24°16′E*
98 *L12* **Renkum** Gelderland, SE Netherlands *51°58′N 05°43′E*
182 *K9* **Renmark** South Australia *34°12′S 140°43′E*
186 *L10* **Rennell** *var.* Mu Nggava. *island* S Solomon Islands
181 *Q4* **Renner Springs Roadhouse** Northern Territory, N Australia *18°12′S 133°48′E*
102 *I6* **Rennes** *Bret.* Roazon; *anc.* Condate. Ille-et-Vilaine, NW France *48°08′N 01°40′W*
195 *S16* **Rennick Glacier** *glacier* Antarctica
11 *Y16* **Rennie** Manitoba, S Canada *49°51′N 95°28′W*
35 *Q5* **Reno** Nevada, W USA *39°32′N 119°49′W*
106 *H10* **Reno** ≈ N Italy
35 *Q5* **Reno-Cannon** ✕ Nevada, W USA *39°26′N 119°42′W*
83 *F24* **Renoster** ≈ SW South Africa
15 *T5* **Renouard, Lac** ◎ Québec, SE Canada
18 *F13* **Renovo** Pennsylvania, NE USA *41°19′N 77°42′W*
161 *O3* **Renqiu** Hebei, E China *38°49′N 116°02′E*
160 *I9* **Renshou** Sichuan, C China *30°02′N 104°09′E*
31 *N12* **Rensselaer** Indiana, N USA *40°57′N 87°09′W*
18 *L11* **Rensselaer** New York, NE USA *42°38′N 73°44′W*
Rentería *see* Errenteria
115 *E17* **Rentína** *var.* Rendina. Thessalía, C Greece *39°04′N 21°58′E*
29 *T9* **Renville** Minnesota, N USA *44°48′N 95°13′W*
77 *O13* **Réo** W Burkina *12°20′N 02°28′W*
15 *O12* **Repentigny** Québec, SE Canada *45°42′N 73°28′W*
146 *K13* **Repetek** Lebap Welaýaty, E Turkmenistan *38°40′N 63°12′E*
93 *J16* **Replot** *Fin.* Raippaluoto. *island* W Finland
Repola *see* Reboly
Reppen *see* Rzepin
Reps *see* Rupea
27 *T7* **Republic** Missouri, C USA *37°07′N 93°28′W*
32 *K7* **Republic** Washington, NW USA *48°39′N 118°44′W*
27 *N3* **Republican River** ≈ Kansas/Nebraska, C USA
9 *O7* **Repulse Bay** Northwest Terretories, N Canada *66°35′N 86°20′W*
56 *F9* **Requena** Loreto, NE Peru *05°05′S 73°52′W*
105 *R10* **Requena** País Valenciano, E Spain *39°29′N 01°08′W*
103 *O14* **Réquista** Aveyron, S France *44°00′N 02°31′E*
136 *M12* **Reşadiye** Tokat, N Turkey *40°24′N 37°19′E*
Reschenpass *see* Resia, Passo di
Reschitza *see* Reşiţa
113 *N20* **Resen** *Turk.* Resne. SW FYR Macedonia *41°07′N 21°00′E*
60 *J11* **Reserva** Paraná, S Brazil *24°40′S 50°52′W*
11 *V15* **Reserve** Saskatchewan, S Canada *52°24′N 102°37′W*
37 *P13* **Reserve** New Mexico, SW USA *33°42′N 108°45′W*
Reshetilovka *see* Reshetylivka
117 *S6* **Reshetylivka** *Rus.* Reshetilovka. Poltavs'ka Oblast', NE Ukraine *49°34′N 34°05′E*
Resht *see* Rasht
106 *F5* **Resia, Passo di** *Ger.* Reschenpass. *pass* Austria/Italy
Resicabánya *see* Reşiţa
62 *N7* **Resistencia** Chaco, NE Argentina *27°27′S 58°56′W*
116 *F12* **Reşiţa** *Ger.* Reschitza, *Hung.* Resicabánya. Caraş-Severin, W Romania *45°14′N 21°58′E*
Resne *see* Resen
197 *N9* **Resolute** *Inuit* Qausuittuq. Cornwallis Island, Nunavut, N Canada *74°41′N 94°54′W*
Resolution *see* Fort Resolution
9 *T7* **Resolution Island** *island* Nunavut, NE Canada
185 *A23* **Resolution Island** *island* SW New Zealand
15 *W7* **Restigouche** Québec, SE Canada *48°02′N 66°42′W*
11 *W17* **Reston** Manitoba, S Canada *49°33′N 101°03′W*
14 *H11* **Restoule Lake** ◎ Ontario, S Canada
54 *F10* **Restrepo** Meta, C Colombia *04°20′N 73°29′W*
42 *B6* **Retalhuleu** Retalhuleu, SW Guatemala *14°31′N 91°40′W*
42 *A1* **Retalhuleu** *off.* Departamento de Retalhuleu. ◐ *department* SW Guatemala
Retalhuleu, Departamento de *see* Retalhuleu
97 *N18* **Retford** C England, United Kingdom *53°18′N 00°52′W*
103 *Q3* **Rethel** Ardennes, N France *49°31′N 04°22′E*
Rethimno/Réthimnon *see* Réthymno
115 *I25* **Réthymno** *prev.* Rethimno, Réthimnon. Kríti, Greece, E Mediterranean Sea *35°21′N 24°29′E*
Retiche, Alpi *see* Rhaetian Alps
99 *J16* **Retie** Antwerpen, N Belgium *51°18′N 05°05′E*
111 *J21* **Rétság** Nógrád, N Hungary *47°57′N 19°08′E*
109 *W2* **Retz** Niederösterreich, NE Austria *48°46′N 15°58′E*
173 *N15* **Réunion** *off.* La Réunion. ◇ *French overseas department* W Indian Ocean
128 *L17* **Réunion** *island* W Indian Ocean
105 *U6* **Reus** Cataluña, E Spain *41°10′N 01°06′E*
108 *F7* **Reuss** ≈ NW Switzerland
99 *J15* **Reusel** Noord-Brabant, S Netherlands *51°21′N 05°10′E*
Reuţel *see* Ciuhuru
101 *H22* **Reutlingen** Baden-Württemberg, S Germany *48°30′N 09°13′E*
108 *L7* **Reutte** Tirol, W Austria *47°30′N 10°44′E*
99 *M16* **Reuver** Limburg, SE Netherlands *51°17′N 06°05′E*
28 *K7* **Reva** South Dakota, N USA *45°30′N 103°03′W*
Reval/Revel *see* Tallinn
124 *J4* **Revda** Murmanskaya Oblast', NW Russian Federation *67°57′N 34°29′E*
122 *F6* **Revda** Sverdlovskaya Oblast', C Russian Federation *56°48′N 59°42′E*
103 *N16* **Revel** Haute-Garonne, S France *43°27′N 01°59′E*
11 *O16* **Revelstoke** British Columbia, SW Canada *51°02′N 118°12′W*
43 *N13* **Reventazón, Río** ≈ E Costa Rica
106 *G9* **Revere** Lombardia, N Italy *45°03′N 11°07′E*
39 *Y14* **Revillagigedo Island** *island* Alexander Archipelago, Alaska, USA
193 *R7* **Revillagigedo Islands** Mexico
103 *R3* **Revin** Ardennes, N France *49°57′N 04°39′E*
92 *O3* **Revnosa** *headland* C Svalbard *78°03′N 18°52′E*
Revolyutsii, Pik *see* Revolyutsiya, Qullai
147 *T13* **Revolyutsiya, Qullai** *Rus.* Pik Revolyutsii. ▲ SE Tajikistan *38°40′N 72°26′E*
111 *L19* **Revúca** *Ger.* Grossrauschenbach, *Hung.* Nagyrőce. Banskobystrický Kraj, C Slovakia *48°40′N 20°10′E*
154 *K9* **Rewa** Madhya Pradesh, C India *24°32′N 81°18′E*
152 *I11* **Rewāri** Haryāna, N India *28°14′N 76°38′E*
33 *R14* **Rexburg** Idaho, NW USA *43°49′N 111°47′W*
78 *G13* **Rey Bouba** Nord, NE Cameroon *08°40′N 14°11′E*
92 *L3* **Reydharfjördhur** Austurland, E Iceland *65°02′N 14°12′W*
57 *K16* **Reyes** Beni, NW Bolivia *14°17′S 67°18′W*
34 *L8* **Reyes, Point** *headland* California, W USA *37°59′N 123°01′W*
54 *B12* **Reyes, Punta** *headland* SW Colombia *02°44′N 78°08′W*
136 *L17* **Reyhanlı** Hatay, S Turkey *36°16′N 36°35′E*
43 *U16* **Rey, Isla del** *island* Archipiélago de las Perlas, SE Panama
92 *H2* **Reykhólar** Vestfirdhir, W Iceland *65°28′N 22°12′W*
92 *K2* **Reykjahlídh** Nordhurland Eystra, NE Iceland *65°37′N 16°54′W*
92 *I4* **Reykjanes** ◐ *region* SW Iceland
197 *O16* **Reykjanes Basin** *var.* Irminger Basin. *undersea feature* N Atlantic Ocean *62°30′N 33°30′W*
197 *N17* **Reykjanes Ridge** *undersea feature* N Atlantic Ocean *62°00′N 27°00′W*
92 *H4* **Reykjavík** *var.* Reikjavik. ● (Iceland) Höfudhborgarsvaedhi, W Iceland *64°08′N 21°54′W*
18 *D13* **Reynoldsville** Pennsylvania, NE USA *41°04′N 78°51′W*
41 *P8* **Reynosa** Tamaulipas, C Mexico *26°03′N 98°19′W*
Reẕa'īyeh *see* Orūmīyeh
Reẕā'īyeh, Daryācheh-ye *see* Orūmīyeh, Daryācheh-ye
102 *I8* **Rezé** Loire-Atlantique, NW France *47°10′N 01°36′W*
118 *K10* **Rēzekne** *Ger.* Rositten; *prev. Rus.* Rezhitsa. Rēzekne, SE Latvia *56°31′N 27°22′E*
Rezhitsa *see* Rēzekne
117 *N9* **Rezina** NE Moldova *47°44′N 28°58′E*
114 *N11* **Rezovo** *Turk.* Rezve. Burgas, E Bulgaria *42°00′N 28°00′E*
114 *N11* **Rezovska Reka** *Turk.* Rezve Deresi. ≈ Bulgaria/Turkey *see also* Rezve Deresi
Rezovska Reka *see* Rezve Deresi
Rezve *see* Rezovo
114 *N11* **Rezve Deresi** *Bul.* Rezovska Reka. ≈ Bulgaria/Turkey *see also* Rezovska Reka
Rezve Deresi *see* Rezovska Reka
Rhadames *see* Ghadāmis
Rhaedestus *see* Tekirdağ
108 *J10* **Rhaetian Alps** *Fr.* Alpes Rhétiques, *Ger.* Rätische Alpen, *It.* Alpi Retiche. ▲▲ C Europe
108 *I8* **Rhätikon** ▲▲ C Europe
101 *G14* **Rheda-Wiedenbrück** Nordrhein-Westfalen, W Germany *51°51′N 08°17′E*
98 *M12* **Rheden** Gelderland, E Netherlands *52°01′N 06°03′E*
Rhegion/Rhegium *see* Reggio di Calabria
Rheims *see* Reims
Rhein *see* Rhine
101 *E17* **Rheinbach** Nordrhein-Westfalen, W Germany *50°37′N 06°57′E*
100 *F13* **Rheine** *var.* Rheine in Westfalen. Nordrhein-Westfalen, NW Germany *52°17′N 07°27′E*
Rheine in Westfalen *see* Rheine
Rheinfeld *see* Rheinfelden
101 *F24* **Rheinfelden** Baden-Württemberg, S Germany *47°34′N 07°46′E*
108 *E6* **Rheinfelden** *var.* Rheinfeld. Aargau, N Switzerland *47°33′N 07°47′E*
101 *E17* **Rheinisches Schiefergebirge** *var.* Rhine State Uplands, *Eng.* Rhenish Slate Mountains. ▲▲ W Germany
101 *D18* **Rheinland-Pfalz** *Eng.* Rhineland-Palatinate, *Fr.* Rhénanie-Palatinat. ◐ *state* W Germany
101 *G18* **Rhein Main** ✕ (Frankfurt am Main) Hessen, W Germany *50°03′N 08°33′E*
Rhénanie du Nord-Westphalie *see* Nordrhein-Westfalen
Rhénanie-Palatinat *see* Rheinland-Pfalz
98 *K12* **Rhenen** Utrecht, C Netherlands *52°01′N 06°02′E*
Rhenish Slate Mountains *see* Rheinisches Schiefergebirge
Rhétiques, Alpes *see* Rhaetian Alps
100 *N10* **Rhin** ≈ NE Germany
Rhin *see* Rhine
84 *F10* **Rhine** *Dut.* Rijn, *Fr.* Rhin, *Ger.* Rhein. ≈ W Europe
30 *L5* **Rhinelander** Wisconsin, N USA *45°39′N 89°23′W*
Rhineland-Palatinate *see* Rheinland-Pfalz
Rhine State Uplands *see* Rheinisches Schiefergebirge
100 *N11* **Rhinkanal** *canal* NE Germany
81 *F17* **Rhino Camp** NW Uganda *02°58′N 31°24′E*
74 *D7* **Rhir, Cap** *headland* W Morocco *30°40′N 09°54′W*
106 *D7* **Rho** Lombardia, N Italy *45°32′N 09°02′E*
19 *N12* **Rhode Island** *off.* State of Rhode Island and Providence Plantations, *also known as* Little Rhody, Ocean State. ◐ *state* NE USA
19 *O13* **Rhode Island** *island* Rhode Island, NE USA
19 *O13* **Rhode Island Sound** *sound* Maine/Rhode Island, NE USA
Rhodes *see* Ródos
Rhode-Saint-Genèse *see* Sint-Genesius-Rode
84 *L14* **Rhodes Basin** *undersea feature* E Mediterranean Sea *35°55′N 28°30′E*
Rhodesia *see* Zimbabwe
114 *I12* **Rhodope Mountains** *var.* Rodhópi Óri, *Bul.* Rhodope Planina, Rodopi, *Gk.* Orosirá Rodhópis, *Turk.* Dospad Dagh. ▲▲ Bulgaria/Greece
Rhodope Planina *see* Rhodope Mountains
101 *I18* **Rhön** ▲▲ C Germany
103 *Q10* **Rhône** ◐ *department* E France
86 *C12* **Rhône** ≈ France/Switzerland
103 *R12* **Rhône-Alpes** ◐ *region* E France
98 *G13* **Rhoon** Zuid-Holland, SW Netherlands *51°52′N 04°25′E*
96 *G9* **Rhum** *var.* Rum. *island* W Scotland, United Kingdom
Rhuthun *see* Ruthin
97 *J18* **Rhyl** NE Wales, United Kingdom *53°19′N 03°28′W*
59 *K18* **Rialma** Goiás, S Brazil *15°22′S 49°35′W*
104 *L3* **Riaño** Castilla-León, N Spain *42°59′N 05°00′W*
105 *O9* **Riansáres** ≈ C Spain
152 *H6* **Riāsi** Jammu and Kashmir, NW India *33°03′N 74°51′E*
168 *K10* **Riau** *off.* Propinsi Riau. ◐ *province* W Indonesia
Riau Archipelago *see* Riau, Kepulauan
168 *M11* **Riau, Kepulauan** *var.* Riau Archipelago, *Dut.* Riouw-Archipel. *island group* W Indonesia
Riau, Propinsi *see* Riau
105 *O6* **Riaza** Castilla-León, N Spain *41°17′N 03°29′W*
105 *N6* **Riaza** ≈ N Spain
81 *K17* **Riba** *spring/well* NE Kenya *01°56′N 40°38′E*
104 *H4* **Ribadavia** Galicia, NW Spain *42°17′N 08°08′W*
104 *J2* **Ribadeo** Galicia, NW Spain *43°32′N 07°04′W*
104 *L2* **Ribadesella** Asturias, N Spain *43°27′N 05°04′W*
104 *G10* **Ribatejo** *former province* C Portugal
83 *P15* **Ribáuè** Nampula, N Mozambique *14°56′S 38°19′E*
97 *K17* **Ribble** ≈ NW England, United Kingdom
95 *F23* **Ribe** Ribe, W Denmark *55°20′N 08°47′E*
95 *F23* **Ribe** *off.* Ribe Amt, *var.* Ripen. ◐ *county* W Denmark
Ribe Amt *see* Ribe
104 *G3* **Ribeira** Galicia, NW Spain *42°33′N 09°01′W*
64 *O5* **Ribeira Brava** Madeira, Portugal, NE Atlantic Ocean *32°39′N 17°04′W*
64 *P3* **Ribeira Grande** São Miguel, Azores, Portugal, NE Atlantic Ocean *37°34′N 25°32′W*
60 *L8* **Ribeirão Preto** São Paulo, S Brazil *21°09′S 47°48′W*
60 *L11* **Ribeira, Rio** ≈ S Brazil
107 *I24* **Ribera** Sicilia, Italy, C Mediterranean Sea *37°31′N 13°16′E*
57 *L14* **Riberalta** Beni, N Bolivia *11°01′S 66°04′W*
105 *W4* **Ribes de Freser** Cataluña, NE Spain *42°18′N 02°11′E*
30 *L6* **Rib Mountain** ▲ Wisconsin, N USA *44°55′N 89°41′W*
109 *U12* **Ribnica** *Ger.* Reifnitz. S Slovenia *45°46′N 14°40′E*
117 *N9* **Rîbniţa** *var.* Râbniţa, *Rus.* Rybnitsa. NE Moldova *47°46′N 29°01′E*
100 *M8* **Ribnitz-Damgarten** Mecklenburg-Vorpommern, NE Germany *54°14′N 12°25′E*
111 *D16* **Říčany** *Ger.* Ritschan. Středočesky Kraj, W Czech Republic *49°59′N 14°40′E*
29 *U7* **Rice** Minnesota, N USA *45°42′N 94°10′W*
30 *J5* **Rice Lake** Wisconsin, N USA *45°33′N 91°43′W*
14 *I15* **Rice Lake** ◎ Ontario, SE Canada
14 *E8* **Rice Lake** ◎ Ontario, S Canada
23 *V3* **Richard B. Russell Lake** ⊠ Georgia, SE USA
25 *U6* **Richardson** Texas, SW USA *32°55′N 96°44′W*
11 *R11* **Richardson** ≈ Alberta, C Canada
10 *I3* **Richardson Mountains** ▲▲ Yukon Territory, NW Canada
185 *C21* **Richardson Mountains** ▲▲ South Island, New Zealand
42 *F3* **Richardson Peak** ▲ SE Belize *16°34′N 88°46′W*
76 *G10* **Richard Toll** N Senegal *16°28′N 15°44′W*
28 *L5* **Richardton** North Dakota, N USA *46°52′N 102°19′W*
14 *F13* **Rich, Cape** *headland* Ontario, S Canada *44°42′N 80°37′W*
102 *L8* **Richelieu** Indre-et-Loire, C France *47°01′N 00°18′E*
33 *P15* **Richfield** Idaho, NW USA *43°03′N 114°11′W*
36 *K5* **Richfield** Utah, W USA *38°45′N 112°05′W*
18 *J10* **Richfield Springs** New York, NE USA *42°52′N 74°57′W*
18 *M6* **Richford** Vermont, NE USA *44°59′N 72°37′W*
27 *R6* **Rich Hill** Missouri, C USA *38°06′N 94°22′W*
13 *P14* **Richibucto** New Brunswick, SE Canada *46°42′N 64°54′W*
108 *G8* **Richisau** Glarus, NE Switzerland *47°00′N 08°54′E*
23 *S6* **Richland** Georgia, SE USA *32°05′N 84°40′W*
27 *U6* **Richland** Missouri, C USA *37°51′N 92°24′W*
25 *U8* **Richland** Texas, SW USA *31°55′N 96°25′W*
32 *K10* **Richland** Washington, NW USA *46°17′N 119°16′W*
30 *K8* **Richland Center** Wisconsin, N USA *43°22′N 90°24′W*
21 *W11* **Richlands** North Carolina, SE USA *34°52′N 77°33′W*
21 *Q7* **Richlands** Virginia, NE USA *37°05′N 81°47′W*
25 *R9* **Richland Springs** Texas, SW USA *31°16′N 98°56′W*
183 *S8* **Richmond** New South Wales, SE Australia *33°36′S 150°44′E*
10 *L17* **Richmond** British Columbia, SW Canada *49°07′N 123°09′W*
14 *L13* **Richmond** Ontario, SE Canada *45°12′N 75°49′W*
15 *Q12* **Richmond** Québec, SE Canada *45°39′N 72°07′W*
185 *I14* **Richmond** Tasman, South Island, New Zealand *41°25′S 173°04′E*
35 *N8* **Richmond** California, W USA *37°57′N 122°22′W*
31 *Q14* **Richmond** Indiana, N USA *39°50′N 84°51′W*
20 *M6* **Richmond** Kentucky, S USA *37°45′N 84°19′W*
27 *S4* **Richmond** Missouri, C USA *39°15′N 93°59′W*
25 *V11* **Richmond** Texas, SW USA *29°36′N 95°48′W*
36 *L1* **Richmond** Utah, W USA *41°55′N 111°51′W*
21 *W6* **Richmond** *state capital* Virginia, NE USA *37°33′N 77°28′W*
14 *H15* **Richmond Hill** Ontario, S Canada *43°51′N 79°24′W*
185 *J15* **Richmond Range** ▲▲ South Island, New Zealand
27 *S12* **Rich Mountain** ▲ Arkansas, C USA *34°37′N 94°17′W*
31 *S13* **Richwood** Ohio, N USA *40°25′N 83°18′W*
21 *R5* **Richwood** West Virginia, NE USA *38°13′N 80°31′W*
104 *K5* **Ricobayo, Embalse de** ⊠ NW Spain
Ricomagus *see* Riom
Ridā' *see* Radā'
145 *X9* **Ridder** *Kaz.* Leningor. Vostochnyy Kazakhstan, E Kazakhstan *50°20′N 83°34′E*
98 *H13* **Ridderkerk** Zuid-Holland, SW Netherlands *51°52′N 04°35′E*
33 *N16* **Riddle** Idaho, NW USA *42°07′N 116°09′W*
32 *F14* **Riddle** Oregon, NW USA *42°57′N 123°21′W*
14 *L13* **Rideau** ≈ Ontario, SE Canada
35 *T12* **Ridgecrest** California, W USA *35°37′N 117°40′W*
18 *L13* **Ridgefield** Connecticut, NE USA *41°16′N 73°30′W*
22 *K5* **Ridgeland** Mississippi, S USA *32°25′N 90°07′W*
21 *R15* **Ridgeland** South Carolina, SE USA *32°30′N 80°59′W*
20 *F8* **Ridgely** Tennessee, S USA *36°15′N 89°29′W*
14 *D17* **Ridgetown** Ontario, S Canada *42°27′N 81°52′W*
21 *R12* **Ridgeway** South Carolina, SE USA *34°17′N 80°56′W*
Ridgeway *see* Ridgway
18 *D13* **Ridgway** *var.* Ridgeway. Pennsylvania, NE USA *41°24′N 78°40′W*
11 *W16* **Riding Mountain** ▲▲ Manitoba, S Canada
Ried *see* Ried im Innkreis
109 *R4* **Ried im Innkreis** *var.* Ried. Oberösterreich, NW Austria *48°13′N 13°29′E*
109 *X8* **Riegersburg** Steiermark, SE Austria *47°03′N 15°52′E*
108 *E6* **Riehen** Basel-Stadt, NW Switzerland *47°35′N 07°39′E*
92 *J9* **Riehppegáisá** *var.* Rieppe. ▲ N Norway *69°38′N 21°31′E*
99 *K18* **Riemst** Limburg, NE Belgium *50°49′N 05°36′E*
Rieppe *see* Riehppegáisá
101 *O15* **Riesa** Sachsen, E Germany *51°18′N 13°18′E*
63 *H24* **Riesco, Isla** *island* S Chile
107 *K25* **Riesi** Sicilia, Italy, C Mediterranean Sea *37°17′N 14°05′E*
83 *F25* **Riet** ≈ SW South Africa
83 *I23* **Riet** ≈ SW South Africa
118 *D11* **Rietavas** Telšiai, W Lithuania *55°43′N 21°56′E*
83 *F19* **Rietfontein** Omaheke, E Namibia *21°58′S 20°58′E*
107 *I14* **Rieti** *anc.* Reate. Lazio, C Italy *42°24′N 12°51′E*
84 *D14* **Rif** *var.* Riff, Er Rif, Er Riff. ▲▲ N Morocco
Riff *see* Rif
37 *Q4* **Rifle** Colorado, C USA *39°30′N 107°46′W*
31 *R7* **Rifle River** ≈ Michigan, N USA
81 *H18* **Rift Valley** ◐ *province* Kenya
Rift Valley *see* Great Rift Valley
118 *F9* **Rīga** *Eng.* Riga. ● (Latvia) Rīga, C Latvia *56°57′N 24°08′E*
Rigaer Bucht *see* Riga, Gulf of
118 *F6* **Riga, Gulf of** *Est.* Liivi Laht, *Ger.* Rigaer Bucht, *Latv.* Rīgas Jūras Līcis, *Rus.* Rizhskiy Zaliv; *prev. Est.* Riia Laht. *gulf* Estonia/Latvia
Rīgas Jūras Līcis *see* Riga, Gulf of
15 *N12* **Rigaud** ≈ Ontario/Québec, SE Canada
33 *R14* **Rigby** Idaho, NW USA *43°40′N 111°54′W*
148 *M10* **Rīgestān** *var.* Registan. *desert region* S Afghanistan
32 *M11* **Riggins** Idaho, NW USA *45°24′N 116°18′W*
13 *R8* **Rigolet** Newfoundland and Labrador, NE Canada *51°10′N 58°25′W*
78 *G9* **Rig-Rig** Kanem, W Chad *14°16′N 14°21′E*
118 *F4* **Riguldi** Läänemaa, W Estonia *59°07′N 23°34′E*
Riia Laht *see* Riga, Gulf of
93 *L19* **Riihimäki** Etelä-Suomi, S Finland *60°45′N 24°45′E*
195 *O2* **Riiser-Larsenisen** *ice shelf* Antarctica
195 *U2* **Riiser-Larsen Peninsula** *peninsula* Antarctica
65 *P22* **Riiser-Larsen Sea** *sea* Antarctica
40 *D2* **Riíto** Sonora, NW Mexico *32°06′N 114°57′W*
112 *B9* **Rijeka** *Ger.* Sankt Veit am Flaum, *It.* Fiume, *Slvn.* Reka; *anc.* Tarsatica. Primorje-Gorski Kotar, NW Croatia *45°20′N 14°26′E*
99 *I14* **Rijen** Noord-Brabant, S Netherlands *51°35′N 04°55′E*
99 *H15* **Rijkevorsel** Antwerpen, N Belgium *51°23′N 04°43′E*
Rijn *see* Rhine
98 *G11* **Rijnsburg** Zuid-Holland, W Netherlands *52°12′N 04°27′E*
Rijssel *see* Lille
98 *N10* **Rijssen** Overijssel, E Netherlands *52°19′N 06°30′E*
98 *G12* **Rijswijk** *Eng.* Ryswick. Zuid-Holland, W Netherlands *52°03′N 04°20′E*
92 *I10* **Riksgränsen** Norrbotten, N Sweden *68°24′N 18°15′E*
165 *U4* **Rikubetsu** Hokkaidō, NE Japan *43°30′N 143°43′E*
165 *R9* **Rikuzen-Takata** Iwate, Honshū, C Japan *39°03′N 141°38′E*
27 *O4* **Riley** Kansas, C USA *39°18′N 96°49′W*
99 *I17* **Rillaar** Vlaams Brabant, C Belgium *50°58′N 04°58′E*
Rí, Loch *see* Ree, Lough
114 *G11* **Rilska Reka** ≈ W Bulgaria
77 *T12* **Rima** ≈ N Nigeria
141 *N7* **Rimah, Wādī ar** *var.* Wādī ar Rummah. *dry watercourse* C Saudi Arabia
Rimaszombat *see* Rimavská Sobota
191 *R12* **Rimatara** *island* Îles Australes, SW French Polynesia
111 *L20* **Rimavská Sobota** *Ger.* Gross-Steffelsdorf, *Hung.* Rimaszombat. Bankobystrický Kraj, C Slovakia *48°24′N 20°01′E*
11 *Q15* **Rimbey** Alberta, SW Canada *52°39′N 114°10′W*
95 *P15* **Rimbo** Stockholm, C Sweden *59°44′N 18°21′E*
95 *M18* **Rimforsa** Östergötland, S Sweden *58°06′N 15°40′E*
106 *I11* **Rimini** *anc.* Ariminum. Emilia-Romagna, N Italy *44°03′N 12°33′E*
Rîmnicu-Sărat *see* Râmnicu Sărat
Rîmnicu Vîlcea *see* Râmnicu Vâlcea
149 *Y3* **Rimo Muztāgh** ▲▲ India/Pakistan
15 *U7* **Rimouski** Québec, SE Canada *48°26′N 68°32′W*
158 *M16* **Rinbung** Xizang Zizhiqu, W China *29°15′N 89°40′E*
Rinchinlhumbe *see* Dzöölön
62 *I5* **Rincón, Cerro** ▲ N Chile *24°01′S 67°19′W*
104 *M15* **Rincón de la Victoria** Andalucía, S Spain *36°43′N 04°18′W*
Rincón del Bonete, Lago Artificial de *see* Río Negro, Embalse del
105 *Q4* **Rincón de Soto** La Rioja, N Spain *42°15′N 01°50′W*
94 *G8* **Rindal** Møre og Romsdal, S Norway *63°02′N 09°09′E*
115 *J20* **Ríneia** *island* Kykládes, Greece, Aegean Sea
152 *H11* **Rīngas** *prev.* Reengus, Rīngus. Rājasthān, N India *27°18′N 75°27′E*
95 *H24* **Ringe** Fyn, C Denmark *55°14′N 10°30′E*
94 *H11* **Ringebu** Oppland, S Norway *61°31′N 10°09′E*
Ringen *see* Rõngu
186 *K8* **Ringgi** Kolombangara, NW Solomon Islands *08°03′S 157°08′E*
23 *R1* **Ringgold** Georgia, SE USA *34°55′N 85°06′W*
22 *G5* **Ringgold** Louisiana, S USA *32°19′N 93°16′W*
25 *S5* **Ringgold** Texas, SW USA *33°47′N 97°56′W*
95 *E22* **Ringkøbing** Ringkøbing, W Denmark *56°04′N 08°22′E*
95 *E21* **Ringkøbing** *var.* Ringkøbing Amt. ◐ *county* W Denmark
Ringkøbing Amt *see* Ringkøbing
95 *E22* **Ringkøbing Fjord** *fjord* W Denmark
33 *S10* **Ringling** Montana, NW USA *46°15′N 110°48′W*
27 *N13* **Ringling** Oklahoma, C USA *34°12′N 97°35′W*
94 *H13* **Ringsaker** Hedmark, S Norway *60°54′N 10°45′E*
95 *I23* **Ringsted** Vestsjælland, E Denmark *55°28′N 11°48′E*
Rīngus *see* Rīngas
92 *I9* **Ringvassøya** *Lapp.* Ráneš. *island* N Norway
18 *K13* **Ringwood** New Jersey, NE USA *41°06′N 74°15′W*
Rinn Duáin *see* Hook Head
100 *H13* **Rinteln** Niedersachsen, NW Germany *52°10′N 09°04′E*
115 *E18* **Río** Dytikí Ellás, S Greece *38°18′N 21°48′E*
Rio *see* Rio de Janeiro
56 *C7* **Riobamba** Chimborazo, C Ecuador *01°44′S 78°40′W*
60 *P9* **Rio Bonito** Rio de Janeiro, SE Brazil *22°42′S 42°38′W*
59 *C16* **Rio Branco** *state capital* Acre, W Brazil *09°59′S 67°49′W*
61 *H18* **Río Branco** Cerro Largo, NE Uruguay *32°32′S 53°28′W*
Rio Branco, Território de *see* Roraima
41 *P8* **Río Bravo** Tamaulipas, C Mexico *25°57′N 98°03′W*
63 *G16* **Río Bueno** Los Lagos, C Chile *40°20′S 72°55′W*
55 *P5* **Río Caribe** Sucre, NE Venezuela *10°43′N 63°06′W*
54 *M5* **Río Chico** Miranda, N Venezuela *10°18′N 66°00′W*
63 *H18* **Río Cisnes** Aisén, S Chile *44°29′S 71°15′W*
60 *L9* **Rio Claro** São Paulo, S Brazil *22°19′S 47°35′W*
45 *V14* **Rio Claro** Trinidad, Trinidad and Tobago *10°18′N 61°11′W*
54 *J5* **Río Claro** Lara, N Venezuela *09°54′N 69°23′W*
63 *K15* **Rio Colorado** Río Negro, E Argentina *39°01′S 64°05′W*
62 *K11* **Río Cuarto** Córdoba, C Argentina *33°06′S 64°20′W*
60 *P10* **Rio de Janeiro** *var.* Rio. *state capital* Rio de Janeiro, SE Brazil *22°53′S 43°17′W*
60 *P9* **Rio de Janeiro** *off.* Estado do Rio de Janeiro. ◐ *state* SE Brazil
Rio de Janeiro, Estado do *see* Rio de Janeiro
43 *R17* **Río de Jesús** Veraguas, S Panama *07°58′N 81°01′W*
34 *K3* **Rio Dell** California, W USA *40°30′N 124°07′W*

◆ Country ● Country Capital ◇ Dependent Territory ○ Dependent Territory Capital ◐ Administrative Regions ✕ International Airport ▲ Mountain ▲▲ Mountain Range Volcano ≈ River ◎ Lake ⊠ Reservoir

60 K13 **Rio do Sul** Santa Catarina, S Brazil *27°15′S 49°37′W*
63 I23 **Río Gallegos** *var.* Gallegos, Puerto Gallegos. Santa Cruz, S Argentina *51°40′S 69°21′W*
63 J24 **Río Grande** Tierra del Fuego, S Argentina *53°45′S 67°46′W*
61 I18 **Rio Grande** *var.* São Pedro do Rio Grande do Sul. Rio Grande do Sul, S Brazil *32°03′S 52°08′W*
40 L10 **Río Grande** Zacatecas, C Mexico *23°50′N 103°20′W*
42 J9 **Río Grande** León, NW Nicaragua *12°59′N 86°34′W*
45 V5 **Río Grande** E Puerto Rico *18°23′N 65°51′W*
24 I9 **Rio Grande** ≈ Texas, SW USA
25 R17 **Rio Grande City** Texas, SW USA *26°24′N 98°50′W*
59 P14 **Rio Grande do Norte** *off.* Estado do Rio Grande do Norte. ⬖ *state* E Brazil
Rio Grande do Norte, Estado do *see* Rio Grande do Norte
61 G15 **Rio Grande do Sul** *off.* Estado do Rio Grande do Sul. ⬖ *state* S Brazil
Rio Grande do Sul, Estado do *see* Rio Grande do Sul
65 M17 **Rio Grande Fracture Zone** *tectonic feature* C Atlantic Ocean
65 J18 **Rio Grande Gap** *undersea feature* S Atlantic Ocean
Rio Grande Plateau *see* Rio Grande Rise
65 J18 **Rio Grande Rise** *var.* Rio Grande Plateau. *undersea feature* SW Atlantic Ocean *31°00′S 35°00′W*
54 G4 **Riohacha** La Guajira, N Colombia *11°23′N 72°47′W*
43 S16 **Río Hato** Coclé, C Panama *08°21′N 80°10′W*
25 T17 **Rio Hondo** Texas, SW USA *26°14′N 97°34′W*
56 D10 **Rioja** San Martín, N Peru *06°02′S 77°10′W*
41 Y11 **Río Lagartos** Yucatán, SE Mexico *21°35′N 88°08′W*
103 P11 **Riom** *anc.* Ricomagus. Puy-de-Dôme, C France *45°54′N 03°06′E*
104 F10 **Rio Maior** Santarém, C Portugal *39°20′N 08°55′W*
103 O12 **Riom-ès-Montagnes** Cantal, C France *45°15′N 02°39′E*
60 J12 **Rio Negro** Paraná, S Brazil *26°06′S 49°46′W*
63 I15 **Río Negro** *off.* Provincia de Río Negro. ⬖ *province* C Argentina
61 D18 **Río Negro** ⬖ *department* W Uruguay
47 V12 **Río Negro, Embalse del** *var.* Lago Artificial de Rincón del Bonete. ⊡ C Uruguay
Río Negro, Provincia de *see* Río Negro
107 M17 **Rionero in Vulture** Basilicata, S Italy *40°55′N 15°40′E*
137 S9 **Rioni** ≈ W Georgia
105 P12 **Riópar** Castilla-La Mancha, C Spain *38°31′N 02°27′W*
61 H16 **Rio Pardo** Rio Grande do Sul, S Brazil *29°41′S 52°25′W*
37 R11 **Rio Rancho Estates** New Mexico, SW USA *35°14′N 106°40′W*
42 L11 **Río San Juan** ⬖ *department* S Nicaragua
54 E9 **Ríosucio** Caldas, W Colombia *05°26′N 75°44′W*
54 C7 **Ríosucio** Chocó, NW Colombia *07°25′N 77°05′W*
62 K10 **Río Tercero** Córdoba, C Argentina *32°15′S 64°08′W*
42 K5 **Río Tinto, Sierra** ⛰ NE Honduras
54 J5 **Río Tocuyo** Lara, N Venezuela *10°18′N 70°00′W*
Riouw-Archipel *see* Riau, Kepulauan
59 J19 **Rio Verde** Goiás, C Brazil *17°50′S 50°55′W*
41 O12 **Río Verde** *var.* Rioverde. San Luis Potosí, C Mexico *21°58′N 100°W*
Rioverde *see* Río Verde
35 O8 **Rio Vista** California, W USA *38°09′N 121°42′W*
112 M11 **Ripanj** Serbia, N Serbia *44°37′N 20°30′E*
106 J13 **Ripatransone** Marche, C Italy *43°00′N 13°45′E*
Ripen *see* Ribe
22 M2 **Ripley** Mississippi, S USA *34°43′N 88°57′W*
31 R15 **Ripley** Ohio, N USA *38°45′N 83°51′W*
20 F9 **Ripley** Tennessee, S USA *35°43′N 89°30′W*
21 Q4 **Ripley** West Virginia, NE USA *38°49′N 81°44′W*
105 W4 **Ripoll** Cataluña, NE Spain *42°12′N 02°12′E*
97 M16 **Ripon** N England, United Kingdom *54°07′N 01°31′W*
30 M7 **Ripon** Wisconsin, N USA *43°52′N 88°48′W*
107 L24 **Riposto** Sicilia, Italy, C Mediterranean Sea *37°44′N 15°13′E*
99 L14 **Rips** Noord-Brabant, SE Netherlands *51°31′N 05°49′E*
54 D9 **Risaralda** *off.* Departamento de Risaralda. ⬖ *province* C Colombia
Risaralda, Departamento de *see* Risaralda
116 L8 **Rîşcani** *var.* Râşcani, *Rus.* Ryshkany. NW Moldova *47°55′N 27°31′E*
152 J9 **Rishikesh** Uttarakhand, N India *30°06′N 78°16′E*
165 S1 **Rishiri-tō** *var.* Risiri Tô. *island* NE Japan
165 S1 **Rishiri-yama** ⩕ Rishiri-tō, NE Japan *45°11′N 141°11′E*
25 R7 **Rising Star** Texas, SW USA *32°06′N 98°57′W*
31 Q15 **Rising Sun** Indiana, N USA *38°58′N 84°53′W*
Risiri Tô *see* Rishiri-tō
102 L4 **Risle** ≈ N France
Rišno *see* Râşnov
27 V13 **Rison** Arkansas, C USA *33°58′N 92°11′W*
95 G17 **Risør** Aust-Agder, S Norway *58°44′N 09°15′E*
92 H10 **Risøyhamn** Nordland, C Norway *69°00′N 15°37′E*
101 I23 **Riss** ≈ S Germany
118 G4 **Risti** *Ger.* Kreuz. Läänemaa, W Estonia *59°01′N 24°01′E*
15 V8 **Ristigouche** ≈ Québec, SE Canada
93 N18 **Ristiina** Itä-Suomi, E Finland *61°32′N 27°15′E*
93 N14 **Ristijärvi** Oulu, C Finland *64°30′N 28°15′E*
188 C14 **Ritidian Point** *headland* N Guam *13°39′N 144°51′E*
Ritschan *see* Říčany
35 R9 **Ritter, Mount** ▲ California, W USA *37°40′N 119°10′W*
31 T12 **Rittman** Ohio, N USA *40°58′N 81°46′W*
32 L9 **Ritzville** Washington, NW USA *47°07′N 118°22′W*
Riva *see* Riva del Garda
61 A21 **Rivadavia** Buenos Aires, E Argentina *35°29′S 62°59′W*
106 F7 **Riva del Garda** *var.* Riva. Trentino-Alto Adige, N Italy *45°54′N 10°50′E*
106 B8 **Rivarolo Canavese** Piemonte, W Italy *45°21′N 07°42′E*
42 K11 **Rivas** Rivas, SW Nicaragua *11°26′N 85°50′W*
42 J11 **Rivas** ⬖ *department* SW Nicaragua
103 R11 **Rive-de-Gier** Loire, E France *45°31′N 04°36′E*
61 A22 **Rivera** Buenos Aires, E Argentina *37°13′S 63°14′W*
61 F16 **Rivera** Rivera, NE Uruguay *30°54′S 55°31′W*
61 F17 **Rivera** ⬖ *department* NE Uruguay
35 P9 **Riverbank** California, W USA *37°43′N 120°59′W*
76 K17 **River Cess** SW Liberia *05°28′N 09°32′W*
28 M4 **Riverdale** North Dakota, N USA *47°29′N 101°22′W*
30 I6 **River Falls** Wisconsin, N USA *44°52′N 92°38′W*
11 T16 **Riverhurst** Saskatchewan, S Canada *50°52′N 106°49′W*
183 O10 **Riverina** *physical region* New South Wales, SE Australia
80 G8 **River Nile** ⬖ *state* NE Sudan
63 F19 **Rivero, Isla** *island* Archipiélago de los Chonos, S Chile
11 W16 **Rivers** Manitoba, S Canada *50°02′N 100°14′W*
77 U17 **Rivers** ⬖ *state* S Nigeria
185 D23 **Riversdale** Southland, South Island, New Zealand *45°54′S 168°44′E*
83 F26 **Riversdale** Western Cape, SW South Africa *34°05′S 21°15′E*
35 U15 **Riverside** California, W USA *33°58′N 117°25′W*
25 W9 **Riverside** Texas, SW USA *30°51′N 95°24′W*
37 U3 **Riverside Reservoir** ⊡ Colorado, C USA
10 K15 **Rivers Inlet** British Columbia, SW Canada *51°43′N 127°19′W*
10 K15 **Rivers Inlet** *inlet* British Columbia, SW Canada
11 X15 **Riverton** Manitoba, S Canada *51°00′N 97°00′W*
185 C24 **Riverton** Southland, South Island, New Zealand *46°20′S 168°02′E*
30 L13 **Riverton** Illinois, N USA *39°50′N 89°31′W*
36 L3 **Riverton** Utah, W USA *40°32′N 111°57′W*
33 V15 **Riverton** Wyoming, C USA *43°01′N 108°22′W*
14 G10 **River Valley** Ontario, S Canada *46°36′N 80°09′W*
13 P14 **Riverview** New Brunswick, SE Canada *46°03′N 64°47′W*
103 O17 **Rivesaltes** Pyrénées-Orientales, S France *42°46′N 02°48′E*
36 H11 **Riviera** Arizona, SW USA *35°06′N 114°36′W*
25 S15 **Riviera** Texas, SW USA *27°15′N 97°48′W*
23 Z14 **Riviera Beach** Florida, SE USA *26°46′N 80°03′W*
15 Q10 **Rivière-à-Pierre** Québec, SE Canada *46°59′N 72°12′W*
15 T9 **Rivière-Bleue** Québec, SE Canada *47°26′N 69°02′W*
15 T8 **Rivière-du-Loup** Québec, SE Canada *47°49′N 69°32′W*
173 Y15 **Rivière du Rempart** NE Mauritius *20°06′S 57°41′E*
45 R12 **Rivière-Pilote** S Martinique *14°29′N 60°54′W*
173 O17 **Rivière St-Etienne, Point de la** *headland* SW Réunion
13 S10 **Rivière-St-Paul** Québec, E Canada *51°26′N 57°52′W*
Rivière Sèche *see* Bel Air
116 K4 **Rivne** *Pol.* Równe, *Rus.* Rovno. Rivnens'ka Oblast', NW Ukraine *50°37′N 26°16′E*
Rivne *see* Rivnens'ka Oblast'
116 K3 **Rivnens'ka Oblast'** *var.* Rivne, *Rus.* Rovenskaya Oblast'. ⬖ *province* NW Ukraine
106 B8 **Rivoli** Piemonte, NW Italy *45°04′N 07°31′E*
159 Q14 **Riwoqê** *var.* Racaka. Xizang Zizhiqu, W China *31°10′N 96°25′E*
99 H19 **Rixensart** Walloon Brabant, C Belgium *50°43′N 04°32′E*
Riyadh/Riyāḍ, Minṭaqat ar *see* Ar Riyāḍ
Riyāq *see* Rayak
Rizaiyeh *see* Orūmīyeh
137 P11 **Rize** Rize, NE Turkey *41°03′N 40°33′E*
137 P11 **Rize** *prev.* Çoruh. ⬖ *province* NE Turkey
161 R5 **Rizhao** Shandong, E China *35°23′N 119°31′E*
Rizhskiy Zaliv *see* Riga, Gulf of
Rizokarpaso/Rizokárpason *see* Dipkarpaz
107 O21 **Rizzuto, Capo** *headland* S Italy *38°54′N 17°05′E*
95 F15 **Rjukan** Telemark, S Norway *59°54′N 08°33′E*
95 D16 **Rjuven** ⛰ S Norway
76 H9 **Rkîz** Trarza, W Mauritania *16°50′N 15°20′W*
115 Q23 **Ro** *prev.* Ágios Geórgios. *island* SE Greece
95 H14 **Roa** Oppland, S Norway *60°16′N 10°38′E*
105 N5 **Roa** Castilla-León, N Spain *41°42′N 03°55′W*
45 T9 **Road Town** ○ (British Virgin Islands) Tortola, C British Virgin Islands *18°28′N 64°39′W*
96 F6 **Roag, Loch** *inlet* NW Scotland, United Kingdom
37 O5 **Roan Cliffs** *cliff* Colorado/Utah, W USA
21 P9 **Roan High Knob** *var.* Roan Mountain. ▲ North Carolina/Tennessee, SE USA *36°09′N 82°07′W*
Roan Mountain *see* Roan High Knob
103 Q10 **Roanne** *anc.* Rodunma. Loire, E France *46°03′N 04°04′E*
23 R4 **Roanoke** Alabama, S USA *33°09′N 85°22′W*
21 S7 **Roanoke** Virginia, NE USA *37°16′N 79°57′W*
21 Z9 **Roanoke Island** *island* North Carolina, SE USA
21 W8 **Roanoke Rapids** North Carolina, SE USA *36°27′N 77°39′W*
21 X9 **Roanoke River** ≈ North Carolina/Virginia, SE USA
37 O4 **Roan Plateau** *plain* Utah, W USA
37 R5 **Roaring Fork River** ≈ Colorado, C USA
25 O5 **Roaring Springs** Texas, SW USA *33°54′N 100°51′W*
42 J4 **Roatán** *var.* Coxen Hole, Coxin Hole. Islas de la Bahía, N Honduras *16°19′N 86°33′W*
42 I4 **Roatán, Isla de** *island* Islas de la Bahía, N Honduras
Roat Kampuchea *see* Cambodia
Roazon *see* Rennes
143 T7 **Robāţ-e Chāh Gonbad** Yazd, E Iran *33°24′N 57°43′E*
143 R7 **Robāţ-e Khān** Yazd, C Iran *33°24′N 56°04′E*
143 T7 **Robāţ-e Khvosh Āb** Yazd, E Iran
143 R8 **Robāţ-e Posht-e Bādām** Yazd, NE Iran *33°01′N 55°34′E*
143 Q8 **Robāţ-e Rīzāb** Yazd, C Iran
175 S8 **Robbie Ridge** *undersea feature* W Pacific Ocean
21 T10 **Robbins** North Carolina, SE USA *35°25′N 79°35′W*
183 N15 **Robbins Island** *island* Tasmania, SE Australia
21 N10 **Robbinsville** North Carolina, SE USA *35°18′N 83°49′W*
182 J12 **Robe** South Australia *37°11′S 139°48′E*
21 W9 **Robersonville** North Carolina, SE USA *35°49′N 77°15′W*
25 P8 **Robert Lee** Texas, SW USA *31°50′N 100°30′W*
35 V5 **Roberts Creek Mountain** ▲ Nevada, W USA *39°52′N 116°16′W*
93 J15 **Robertsfors** Västerbotten, N Sweden *64°12′N 20°50′E*
153 N14 **Robertsganj** Uttar Pradesh, N India *24°41′N 83°04′E*
27 R11 **Robert S. Kerr Reservoir** ⊡ Oklahoma, C USA
38 L12 **Roberts Mountain** ▲ Nunivak Island, Alaska, USA *60°01′N 166°15′W*
83 F26 **Robertson** Western Cape, SW South Africa *33°48′S 19°53′E*
194 H4 **Robertson Island** *island* Antarctica
76 J16 **Robertsport** W Liberia *06°45′N 11°15′W*
182 J8 **Robertstown** South Australia *34°00′S 139°04′E*
Robert Williams *see* Caála
15 P7 **Roberval** Québec, SE Canada *48°31′N 72°16′W*
31 N15 **Robinson** Illinois, N USA *39°00′N 87°44′W*
193 U11 **Róbinson Crusoe, Isla** *island* Islas Juan Fernández, Chile, E Pacific Ocean
180 J9 **Robinson Range** ⛰ Western Australia
182 M9 **Robinvale** Victoria, SE Australia *34°37′S 142°45′E*
105 P11 **Robledo** Castilla-La Mancha, C Spain *38°45′N 02°27′W*
54 G5 **Robles** *var.* La Paz, Robles La Paz. Cesar, N Colombia *10°24′N 73°11′W*
Robles La Paz *see* Robles
11 V15 **Roblin** Manitoba, S Canada *51°15′N 101°20′W*
11 S17 **Robsart** Saskatchewan, S Canada *49°22′N 109°15′W*
11 N15 **Robson, Mount** ▲ British Columbia, SW Canada *53°09′N 119°16′W*
25 T14 **Robstown** Texas, SW USA *27°47′N 97°40′W*
25 P6 **Roby** Texas, SW USA *32°42′N 100°23′W*
104 E11 **Roca, Cabo da** *cape* C Portugal
Rocadas *see* Xangongo
41 S14 **Roca Partida, Punta** *headland* C Mexico *18°43′N 95°11′W*
47 X6 **Rocas, Atol das** *island* E Brazil
107 L18 **Roccadaspide** *var.* Rocca d'Aspide. Campania, S Italy *40°25′N 15°12′E*
Rocca d'Aspide *see* Roccadaspide
107 K15 **Roccaraso** Abruzzo, C Italy *41°49′N 14°01′E*
106 H10 **Rocca San Casciano** Emilia-Romagna, C Italy *44°06′N 11°51′E*
106 G13 **Roccastrada** Toscana, C Italy *43°00′N 11°09′E*
61 G20 **Rocha** Rocha, E Uruguay *34°30′S 54°22′W*
61 G19 **Rocha** ⬖ *department* E Uruguay
97 L17 **Rochdale** NW England, United Kingdom *53°38′N 02°09′W*
102 L11 **Rochechouart** Haute-Vienne, C France *45°49′N 00°49′E*
99 J22 **Rochefort** Namur, SE Belgium *50°10′N 05°13′E*
102 J11 **Rochefort** *var.* Rochefort sur Mer. Charente-Maritime, W France *45°57′N 00°58′W*
Rochefort sur Mer *see* Rochefort
125 N10 **Rochegda** Arkhangel'skaya Oblast', NW Russian Federation *62°37′N 43°21′E*
30 L10 **Rochelle** Illinois, N USA *41°54′N 89°03′W*
25 Q9 **Rochelle** Texas, SW USA *31°13′N 99°10′W*
15 V3 **Rochers Ouest, Rivière aux** ≈ Québec, SE Canada
97 O22 **Rochester** *anc.* Durobrivae. SE England, United Kingdom *51°24′N 00°30′E*
31 O12 **Rochester** Indiana, N USA *41°03′N 86°13′W*
29 W10 **Rochester** Minnesota, N USA *44°01′N 92°28′W*
19 O9 **Rochester** New Hampshire, NE USA *43°18′N 70°58′W*
18 F9 **Rochester** New York, NE USA *43°09′N 77°37′W*
25 P5 **Rochester** Texas, SW USA *33°19′N 99°51′W*
31 S9 **Rochester Hills** Michigan, N USA *42°39′N 83°04′W*
Rocheuses, Montagnes/Rockies *see* Rocky Mountains
64 M6 **Rockall** *island* N Atlantic Ocean, United Kingdom
64 L6 **Rockall Bank** *undersea feature* N Atlantic Ocean
84 B8 **Rockall Rise** *undersea feature* N Atlantic Ocean *59°00′N 14°00′W*
84 C9 **Rockall Trough** *undersea feature* N Atlantic Ocean *57°00′N 12°00′W*
35 U2 **Rock Creek** ≈ Nevada, W USA
25 T10 **Rockdale** Texas, SW USA *30°39′N 96°58′W*
195 N12 **Rockefeller Plateau** *plateau* Antarctica
30 K11 **Rock Falls** Illinois, N USA *41°46′N 89°41′W*
23 Q5 **Rockford** Alabama, S USA *32°53′N 86°11′W*
30 L10 **Rockford** Illinois, N USA *42°16′N 89°06′W*
15 Q12 **Rock Forest** Québec, SE Canada *45°21′N 71°58′W*
11 T17 **Rockglen** Saskatchewan, S Canada *49°11′N 105°57′W*
181 Y8 **Rockhampton** Queensland, E Australia *23°31′S 150°31′E*
21 R11 **Rock Hill** South Carolina, SE USA *34°55′N 81°01′W*
180 I13 **Rockingham** Western Australia *32°16′S 115°21′E*
21 T11 **Rockingham** North Carolina, SE USA *34°56′N 79°47′W*
30 J11 **Rock Island** Illinois, N USA *41°30′N 90°34′W*
25 U12 **Rock Island** Texas, SW USA *29°31′N 96°33′W*
14 C10 **Rock Lake** Ontario, S Canada *46°25′N 83°49′W*
29 O2 **Rock Lake** North Dakota, N USA *48°45′N 99°12′W*
14 I12 **Rock Lake** ◎ Ontario, SE Canada
14 M12 **Rockland** Ontario, SE Canada *45°33′N 75°16′W*
19 R7 **Rockland** Maine, NE USA *44°08′N 69°06′W*
182 L11 **Rocklands Reservoir** ⊡ Victoria, SE Australia
35 O7 **Rocklin** California, W USA *38°48′N 121°13′W*
23 R3 **Rockmart** Georgia, SE USA *34°00′N 85°02′W*
31 N16 **Rockport** Indiana, N USA *37°53′N 87°04′W*
27 Q1 **Rock Port** Missouri, C USA *40°26′N 95°30′W*
25 T14 **Rockport** Texas, SW USA *28°02′N 99°04′W*
32 I7 **Rockport** Washington, NW USA *48°28′N 121°36′W*
29 S11 **Rock Rapids** Iowa, C USA *43°25′N 96°10′W*
30 K11 **Rock River** ≈ Illinois/Wisconsin, N USA
44 I3 **Rock Sound** Eleuthera Island, C Bahamas *24°52′N 76°10′W*
25 P11 **Rocksprings** Texas, SW USA *30°02′N 100°14′W*
33 U17 **Rock Springs** Wyoming, C USA *41°35′N 109°12′W*
55 T9 **Rockstone** C Guyana *05°58′N 58°33′W*
29 S12 **Rock Valley** Iowa, C USA *43°12′N 96°17′W*
31 N14 **Rockville** Indiana, N USA *39°45′N 87°15′W*
21 W3 **Rockville** Maryland, NE USA *39°05′N 77°10′W*
25 U6 **Rockwall** Texas, SW USA *32°56′N 96°27′W*
29 U13 **Rockwell City** Iowa, C USA *42°24′N 94°37′W*
31 S10 **Rockwood** Michigan, N USA *42°04′N 83°15′W*
20 M9 **Rockwood** Tennessee, S USA *35°52′N 84°41′W*
25 Q8 **Rockwood** Texas, SW USA *31°29′N 99°23′W*
37 U6 **Rocky Ford** Colorado, C USA *38°03′N 103°45′W*
14 D9 **Rocky Island Lake** ◎ Ontario, S Canada
21 V9 **Rocky Mount** North Carolina, SE USA *35°56′N 77°48′W*
21 S7 **Rocky Mount** Virginia, NE USA *37°00′N 79°53′W*
33 Q8 **Rocky Mountain** ▲ Montana, NW USA *47°45′N 112°46′W*
11 P15 **Rocky Mountain House** Alberta, SW Canada *52°24′N 114°52′W*
37 T3 **Rocky Mountain National Park** *national park* Colorado, C USA
2 E12 **Rocky Mountains** *var.* Rockies, *Fr.* Montagnes Rocheuses. ⛰ Canada/USA
42 H1 **Rocky Point** *headland* NE Belize *18°21′N 88°04′W*
83 A17 **Rocky Point** *headland* NW Namibia *19°01′S 12°27′E*
95 F14 **Rødberg** Buskerud, S Norway *60°16′N 09°00′E*
95 I25 **Rødby** Storstrøm, SE Denmark *54°42′N 11°24′E*
95 I25 **Rødbyhavn** Storstrøm, SE Denmark *54°39′N 11°24′E*
13 T10 **Roddickton** Newfoundland, Newfoundland and Labrador, SE Canada *50°51′N 56°03′W*
95 F23 **Rødding** Sønderjylland, SW Denmark *55°22′N 09°04′E*
95 M22 **Rödeby** Blekinge, S Sweden *56°16′N 15°35′E*
98 N6 **Roden** Drenthe, NE Netherlands *53°08′N 06°26′E*
62 H9 **Rodeo** San Juan, W Argentina *30°12′S 69°06′W*
103 O14 **Rodez** *anc.* Segodunum. Aveyron, S France *44°21′N 02°34′E*
Rodholívos *see* Rodolívos
Rodhópi Óri *see* Rhodope Mountains
Ródhos/Rodi *see* Ródos
107 N15 **Rodi Gargancio** Puglia, SE Italy *41°54′N 15°51′E*
101 N20 **Roding** Bayern, SE Germany *49°12′N 12°30′E*
113 J19 **Rodinit, Kepi i** *headland* W Albania *41°35′N 19°27′E*
116 I9 **Rodnei, Munţii** ⛰ N Romania
184 L4 **Rodney, Cape** *headland* North Island, New Zealand *36°16′S 174°48′E*
38 L9 **Rodney, Cape** *headland* Alaska, USA *64°39′N 166°24′W*
124 M16 **Rodniki** Ivanovskaya Oblast', W Russian Federation *57°04′N 41°45′E*
119 Q16 **Rodnya** Mahilyowskaya Voblasts', E Belarus *53°31′N 32°07′E*
Rodó *see* José Enrique Rodó
114 H13 **Rodolívos** *var.* Rodholívos. Kentrikí Makedonía, NE Greece *40°55′N 24°00′E*
Rodopi *see* Rhodope Mountains
115 O22 **Ródos** *var.* Ródhos, *Eng.* Rhodes, *It.* Rodi. Ródos, Dodekánisa, Greece, Aegean Sea *36°26′N 28°14′E*
115 O22 **Ródos** *var.* Ródhos, *Eng.* Rhodes, *It.* Rodi; *anc.* Rhodos. *island* Dodekánisa, Greece, Aegean Sea
Rodosto *see* Tekirdağ
59 A14 **Rodrigues** Amazonas, W Brazil *06°50′S 73°45′W*
173 P8 **Rodrigues** *var.* Rodriquez. *island* E Mauritius
Rodriquez *see* Rodrigues
Rodunma *see* Roanne
180 I7 **Roebourne** Western Australia *20°49′S 117°04′E*
83 J20 **Roedtan** Limpopo, NE South Africa *24°37′S 29°05′E*
98 H11 **Roelofarendsveen** Zuid-Holland, W Netherlands *52°12′N 04°37′E*
Roepat *see* Rupat, Pulau
Roer *see* Rur
99 M16 **Roermond** Limburg, SE Netherlands *51°12′N 06°E*
99 C18 **Roeselare** *Fr.* Roulers; *prev.* Rousselaere. West-Vlaanderen, W Belgium *50°57′N 03°08′E*
9 P8 **Roes Welcome Sound** *strait* Nunavut, N Canada
Roeteng *see* Ruteng
Rofreit *see* Rovereto
Rogachëv *see* Rahachow
57 L15 **Rogagua, Laguna** ◎ NW Bolivia
95 C16 **Rogaland** ⬖ *county* S Norway
25 Y9 **Roganville** Texas, SW USA *30°49′N 93°54′W*
109 W11 **Rogaška Slatina** *Ger.* Rohitsch-Sauerbrunn; *prev.* Rogatec-Slatina. E Slovenia *46°13′N 15°38′E*
Rogatec-Slatina *see* Rogaška Slatina
112 J13 **Rogatica** Republika Srpska, SE Bosnia and Herzegovina *43°50′N 18°55′E*
Rogatin *see* Rohatyn
93 F17 **Rogen** ◎ C Sweden
27 S9 **Rogers** Arkansas, C USA *36°19′N 94°07′W*
29 P5 **Rogers** North Dakota, N USA *47°03′N 98°12′W*
25 T9 **Rogers** Texas, SW USA *30°53′N 97°10′W*
31 R5 **Rogers City** Michigan, N USA *45°25′N 83°49′W*
Roger Simpson Island *see* Abemama
35 T14 **Rogers Lake** *salt flat* California, W USA
21 Q8 **Rogers, Mount** ▲ Virginia, NE USA *36°39′N 81°32′W*
33 O16 **Rogerson** Idaho, NW USA *42°11′N 114°36′W*
11 O16 **Rogers Pass** *pass* British Columbia, SW Canada
21 O8 **Rogersville** Tennessee, S USA *36°26′N 83°01′W*
99 L16 **Roggel** Limburg, SE Netherlands *51°16′N 05°55′E*
Roggeveen *see* Roggewein, Cabo
193 R10 **Roggeveen Basin** *undersea feature* E Pacific Ocean *31°30′S 95°30′W*
191 X16 **Roggewein, Cabo** *var.* Roggeveen. *headland* Easter Island, Chile, E Pacific Ocean *27°07′S 109°15′W*
103 Y13 **Rogliano** Corse, France, C Mediterranean Sea *42°58′N 09°25′E*
107 N21 **Rogliano** Calabria, SW Italy *39°09′N 16°18′E*
92 G12 **Rognan** Nordland, C Norway *67°04′N 15°21′E*
100 K10 **Rögnitz** ≈ N Germany
Rogozhina/Rogozhinë *see* Rrogozhinë
110 G10 **Rogoźno** Wielkopolskie, C Poland *52°46′N 16°58′E*
32 E15 **Rogue River** ≈ Oregon, NW USA
116 I6 **Rohatyn** *Rus.* Rogatin. Ivano-Frankivs'ka Oblast', W Ukraine *49°25′N 24°35′E*
189 O14 **Rohi** Pohnpei, E Micronesia
Rohitsch-Sauerbrunn *see* Rogaška Slatina
149 Q13 **Rohri** Sind, SE Pakistan *27°39′N 68°57′E*
152 I10 **Rohtak** Haryāna, N India *28°57′N 76°38′E*
Roi Ed *see* Roi Et
167 R9 **Roi Et** *var.* Muang Roi Et, Roi Ed. Roi Et, E Thailand *16°05′N 103°38′E*
191 U9 **Roi Georges, Îles du** *island group* Îles Tuamotu, C French Polynesia
153 Y10 **Roing** Arunāchal Pradesh, NE India *28°06′N 95°46′E*
118 E7 **Roja** Talsi, NW Latvia *57°31′N 22°44′E*
61 B20 **Rojas** Buenos Aires, E Argentina *34°10′S 60°45′W*
149 R12 **Rojhān** Punjab, E Pakistan *28°39′N 70°00′E*
41 Q12 **Rojo, Cabo** *headland* C Mexico *21°33′N 97°19′W*
45 Q10 **Rojo, Cabo** *headland* W Puerto Rico *17°57′N 67°10′W*
168 K10 **Rokan Kiri, Sungai** ≈ Sumatera, W Indonesia
118 I11 **Rokiškis** Panevėžys, NE Lithuania *55°58′N 25°35′E*
165 R7 **Rokkasho** Aomori, Honshū, C Japan *40°59′N 141°22′E*
111 B17 **Rokycany** *Ger.* Rokytzan. Plzeňský Kraj, W Czech Republic *49°45′N 13°36′E*
117 P6 **Rokytne** Kyyivs'ka Oblast', N Ukraine *49°40′N 30°29′E*
116 L3 **Rokytne** Rivnens'ka Oblast', NW Ukraine *51°19′N 27°09′E*
Rokytzan *see* Rokycany
158 L11 **Rola Co** ◎ W China
29 V13 **Roland** Iowa, C USA *42°10′N 93°30′W*
95 D15 **Røldal** Hordaland, S Norway *59°52′N 06°49′E*
98 O7 **Rolde** Drenthe, NE Netherlands *52°58′N 06°39′E*
29 O2 **Rolette** North Dakota, N USA *48°39′N 99°50′W*
27 V6 **Rolla** Missouri, C USA *37°56′N 91°47′W*
29 O2 **Rolla** North Dakota, N USA *48°51′N 99°37′W*
108 A10 **Rolle** Vaud, W Switzerland *46°27′N 06°19′E*
181 X8 **Rolleston** Queensland, E Australia *24°30′S 148°36′E*
185 H19 **Rolleston** Canterbury, South Island, New Zealand *43°34′S 172°24′E*
185 G18 **Rolleston Range** ⛰ South Island, New Zealand
14 H8 **Rollet** Québec, SE Canada *47°56′N 79°14′W*
22 J4 **Rolling Fork** Mississippi, S USA *32°54′N 90°52′W*
20 L6 **Rolling Fork** ≈ Kentucky, S USA
14 J11 **Rolphton** Ontario, SE Canada *46°09′N 77°43′W*
Röm *see* Rømø
181 X10 **Roma** Queensland, E Australia *26°32′S 148°54′E*
107 I15 **Roma** *Eng.* Rome. ● (Italy) Lazio, C Italy *41°53′N 12°30′E*
95 P19 **Roma** Gotland, SE Sweden *57°31′N 18°28′E*
21 T14 **Romain, Cape** *headland* South Carolina, SE USA *33°00′N 79°21′W*
13 P11 **Romaine** ≈ Newfoundland and Labrador/Québec, E Canada
25 R17 **Roma Los Saenz** Texas, SW USA *26°24′N 99°01′W*
114 H8 **Roman** Vratsa, NW Bulgaria *43°09′N 23°56′E*
116 L10 **Roman** *Hung.* Románvásár. Neamţ, NE Romania *46°46′N 26°56′E*
64 M13 **Romanche Fracture Zone** *tectonic feature* E Atlantic Ocean
61 C15 **Romang** Santa Fe, C Argentina *29°30′S 59°46′W*
171 R15 **Romang, Pulau** *var.* Pulau Roma. *island* Kepulauan Damar, E Indonesia
171 R15 **Romang, Selat** *strait* Nusa Tenggara, S Indonesia
116 J11 **Romania** *Bul.* Rumŭniya, *Ger.* Rumänien, *Hung.* Románia, *Rom.* România, *SCr.* Rumunjska, *Ukr.* Rumuniya, *prev.* Republica Socialistă România, Roumania, Rumania, Socialist Republic of Romania, *prev.Rom.* Romînia. ◆ *republic* SE Europe
România, Republica Socialistă *see* Romania
Romania, Socialist Republic of *see* Romania
117 T7 **Romaniv** *Rus.* Dniprodzerzhinsk, *prev.* Dniprodzerzhyns'k, *prev.* Kamenskoye. Dnipropetrovs'ka Oblast', E Ukraine *48°30′N 34°35′E*
23 W16 **Romano, Cape** *headland* Florida, SE USA *25°51′N 81°40′W*
44 G5 **Romano, Cayo** *island* C Cuba
123 O13 **Romanovka** Respublika Buryatiya, S Russian Federation *53°10′N 112°34′E*
127 N8 **Romanovka** Saratovskaya Oblast', W Russian Federation *51°45′N 42°45′E*
108 I6 **Romanshorn** Thurgau, NE Switzerland *47°34′N 09°23′E*
103 R12 **Romans-sur-Isère** Drôme, E France *45°03′N 05°03′E*
189 U12 **Romanum** *island* Chuuk, C Micronesia
Románvásár *see* Roman
39 S5 **Romanzof Mountains** ⛰ Alaska, USA
Roma, Pulau *see* Romang, Pulau
103 S4 **Rombas** Moselle, NE France *49°15′N 06°04′E*
23 R2 **Rome** Georgia, SE USA *34°01′N 85°02′W*
18 I9 **Rome** New York, NE USA *43°13′N 75°28′W*
Rome *see* Roma
31 S9 **Romeo** Michigan, N USA *42°48′N 83°00′W*
Römerstadt *see* Rýmařov
Rometan *see* Romiton
103 P5 **Romilly-sur-Seine** Aube, N France *48°31′N 03°44′E*
Rominia *see* Romania
146 L11 **Romiton** *Rus.* Rometan. Buxoro Viloyati, C Uzbekistan *39°56′N 64°21′E*
21 U3 **Romney** West Virginia, NE USA *39°21′N 78°44′W*
117 S4 **Romny** Sums'ka Oblast', NE Ukraine *50°45′N 33°30′E*
95 E24 **Rømø** *Ger.* Röm. *island* SW Denmark
117 S5 **Romodan** Poltavs'ka Oblast', NE Ukraine *50°00′N 33°20′E*
127 P5 **Romodanovo** Respublika Mordoviya, W Russian Federation *54°25′N 45°24′E*
Romorantin *see* Romorantin-Lanthenay
103 N8 **Romorantin-Lanthenay** *var.* Romorantin. Loir-et-Cher, C France *47°22′N 01°44′E*
94 F9 **Romsdal** *physical region* S Norway
94 F10 **Romsdalen** *valley* S Norway
94 E9 **Romsdalsfjorden** *fjord* S Norway
33 P8 **Ronan** Montana, NW USA *47°31′N 114°06′W*
59 M14 **Roncador** Maranhão, E Brazil *05°48′S 45°08′W*
186 M7 **Roncador Reef** *reef* N Solomon Islands
59 J17 **Roncador, Serra do** ⛰ C Brazil
21 S6 **Ronceverte** West Virginia, NE USA *37°45′N 80°27′W*
107 H14 **Ronciglione** Lazio, C Italy *42°16′N 12°15′E*
104 L15 **Ronda** Andalucía, S Spain *36°45′N 05°10′W*
94 G11 **Rondane** ⛰ S Norway
104 L15 **Ronda, Serranía de** ⛰ S Spain
95 H22 **Rønde** Århus, C Denmark *56°18′N 10°28′E*
Ronde, Île *see* Round Island
Rōndik *see* Rongrik Atoll
59 E16 **Rondônia** *off.* Estado de Rondônia; *prev.* Território de Rondônia. ⬖ *state* W Brazil
Rondônia, Estado de *see* Rondônia
Rondônia, Território de *see* Rondônia
59 I18 **Rondonópolis** Mato Grosso, W Brazil *16°29′S 54°37′W*
94 G11 **Rondslottet** ▲ S Norway *61°54′N 09°48′E*
95 P20 **Ronehamn** Gotland, SE Sweden *57°10′N 18°30′E*
160 L13 **Rong'an** *var.* Chang'an, Rongan. Guangxi Zhuangzu Zizhiqu, S China *25°14′N 109°20′E*
Rongan *see* Rong'an
Rongcheng *see* Rongxian, Guangxi, China
Rongcheng *see* Jianli, Hubei, China
189 R4 **Rongelap Atoll** *var.* Rōnlap. *atoll* Ralik Chain, NW Marshall Islands
Rongerik *see* Rongrik Atoll
160 K12 **Rongjiang** *var.* Guzhou. Guizhou, S China *25°59′N 108°27′E*
160 L13 **Rong Jiang** ≈ S China
Rongjiang *see* Nankang
Rong, Kas *see* Rŭng, Kaôh
167 P8 **Rong Kwang** Phrae, NW Thailand *18°19′N 100°18′E*
189 T4 **Rongrik Atoll** *var.* Rōndik, Rongerik. *atoll* Ralik Chain, N Marshall Islands
189 X2 **Rongrong** *island* SE Marshall Islands
160 L13 **Rongshui** *var.* Rongshui Miaozu Zizhixian. Guangxi Zhuangzu Zizhiqu, S China *25°05′N 109°09′E*
Rongshui Miaozu Zizhixian *see* Rongshui
118 I6 **Rõngu** *Ger.* Ringen. Tartumaa, SE Estonia *58°10′N 26°17′E*
Rongwo *see* Tongren
160 L15 **Rongxian** *var.* Rongzhou; *prev.* Rongcheng. Guangxi Zhuangzu Zizhiqu, S China *22°52′N 110°33′E*
Rongzhag *see* Danba
Rongzhou *see* Rongxian
Roniu *see* Ronui, Mont
189 N13 **Ronkiti** Pohnpei, E Micronesia *06°48′N 158°10′E*
Rōnlap *see* Rongelap Atoll
95 L24 **Rønne** Bornholm, E Denmark *55°07′N 14°43′E*
95 M22 **Ronneby** Blekinge, S Sweden *56°12′N 15°18′E*
194 J7 **Ronne Entrance** *inlet* Antarctica
194 L6 **Ronne Ice Shelf** *ice shelf* Antarctica
99 E19 **Ronse** *Fr.* Renaix. Oost-Vlaanderen, SW Belgium *50°45′N 03°36′E*
191 R8 **Ronui, Mont** *var.* Roniu. ⩕ Tahiti, W French Polynesia *17°49′S 149°12′W*
30 K14 **Roodhouse** Illinois, N USA *39°28′N 90°22′W*
83 C19 **Rooibank** Erongo, W Namibia *23°04′S 14°34′E*
Rooke Island *see* Umboi Island
65 N24 **Rookery Point** *headland* NE Tristan da Cunha *37°03′S 12°15′W*
171 V13 **Roon, Pulau** *island* E Indonesia
173 V7 **Roo Rise** *undersea feature* E Indian Ocean
152 J9 **Roorkee** Uttarakhand, N India *29°51′N 77°54′E*
99 H15 **Roosendaal** Noord-Brabant, S Netherlands *51°32′N 04°29′E*
25 P10 **Roosevelt** Texas, SW USA *30°28′N 100°06′W*
37 N3 **Roosevelt** Utah, W USA *40°18′N 109°59′W*
47 T8 **Roosevelt** ≈ W Brazil
195 O13 **Roosevelt Island** *island* Antarctica
10 L10 **Roosevelt, Mount** ▲ British Columbia, W Canada *58°28′N 125°22′W*
11 P17 **Rooslville** British Columbia, SW Canada *48°59′N 115°03′W*
29 X10 **Root River** ≈ Minnesota, N USA
Ropar *see* Rūpnagar
111 N16 **Ropczyce** Podkarpackie, SE Poland *50°04′N 21°31′E*
181 Q3 **Roper Bar** Northern Territory, N Australia *14°45′S 134°30′E*
24 M5 **Ropesville** Texas, SW USA *33°24′N 102°09′W*
102 K14 **Roquefort** Landes, SW France *44°01′N 00°18′W*
61 C21 **Roque Pérez** Buenos Aires, E Argentina *35°25′S 59°24′W*
58 E10 **Roraima** *off.* Estado de Roraima; *prev.* Território de Rio Branco, Território de Roraima. ⬖ *state* N Brazil
Roraima, Estado de *see* Roraima
58 F9 **Roraima, Mount** ▲ N South America *05°10′N 60°36′W*
Roraima, Território de *see* Roraima
94 I9 **Røros** Sør-Trøndelag, S Norway *62°37′N 11°25′E*
108 I7 **Rorschach** Sankt Gallen, NE Switzerland *47°28′N 09°30′E*
93 E14 **Rørvik** Nord-Trøndelag, C Norway *64°54′N 11°15′E*
119 G17 **Ros'** *Rus.* Ross'. Hrodzyenskaya Voblasts', W Belarus *53°25′N 24°24′E*
185 F17 **Ross** West Coast, South Island, New Zealand *42°54′S 170°52′E*
119 G17 **Ros'** *Rus.* Ross'. ≈ W Belarus
10 J7 **Ross** ≈ Yukon Territory, W Canada
117 O6 **Ros'** ≈ N Ukraine
44 K7 **Rosa, Lake** ◎ Great Inagua, S Bahamas
32 M9 **Rosalia** Washington, NW USA *47°14′N 117°22′W*
191 W15 **Rosalia, Punta** *headland* Easter Island, Chile, E Pacific Ocean *27°04′S 109°19′W*
45 P12 **Rosalie** E Dominica *15°22′N 61°15′W*

◆ Country ● Country Capital ◇ Dependent Territory ○ Dependent Territory Capital ⬖ Administrative Regions ✈ International Airport ▲ Mountain ⛰ Mountain Range ⩕ Volcano ≈ River ◎ Lake ⊡ Reservoir

35 T14 **Rosamond** California, W USA 34°51′N 118°09′W
35 S14 **Rosamond Lake** *salt flat* California, W USA
96 H8 **Ross and Cromarty** *cultural region* N Scotland, United Kingdom
61 B18 **Rosario** Santa Fe, C Argentina 32°56′S 60°39′W
40 J11 **Rosario** Sinaloa, C Mexico 23°00′N 105°51′W
40 G6 **Rosario** Sonora, NW Mexico 27°53′N 109°18′W
62 O6 **Rosario** San Pedro, C Paraguay 24°26′S 57°06′W
61 E20 **Rosario** Colonia, SW Uruguay 34°20′S 57°26′W
54 H5 **Rosario** Zulia, NW Venezuela 10°18′N 72°19′W
Rosario *see* Nishino-shima
Rosario *see* Rosarito
40 B4 **Rosario, Bahía del** *bay* NW Mexico
62 K6 **Rosario de la Frontera** Salta, N Argentina 25°50′S 65°00′W
61 C18 **Rosario del Tala** Entre Ríos, E Argentina 32°20′S 59°10′W
61 F16 **Rosário do Sul** Rio Grande do Sul, S Brazil 30°15′S 54°55′W
59 H18 **Rosário Oeste** Mato Grosso, W Brazil 14°50′S 56°25′W
40 B1 **Rosarito** *var.* Rosario. Baja California Norte, NW Mexico 32°25′N 117°04′W
40 D5 **Rosarito** Baja California Norte, NW Mexico 28°27′N 113°58′W
40 F7 **Rosarito** Baja California Sur, NW Mexico 26°28′N 111°41′W
104 L9 **Rosarito, Embalse del** ⊠ W Spain
107 N22 **Rosarno** Calabria, SW Italy 38°29′N 15°59′E
56 B5 **Rosa Zárate** *var.* Quinindé. Esmeraldas, SW Ecuador 0°14′N 79°28′W
Roscianum *see* Rossano
29 O8 **Roscoe** South Dakota, N USA 45°24′N 99°19′W
25 P7 **Roscoe** Texas, SW USA 32°27′N 100°32′W
102 F5 **Roscoff** Finistère, NW France 48°43′N 04°00′W
Ros Comáin *see* Roscommon
97 C17 **Roscommon** *Ir.* Ros Comáin. C Ireland 53°38′N 08°11′W
31 Q7 **Roscommon** Michigan, N USA 44°30′N 84°35′W
97 C17 **Roscommon** *Ir.* Ros Comáin. *cultural region* C Ireland
Ros. Cré *see* Roscrea
97 D19 **Roscrea** *Ir.* Ros. Cré. C Ireland 52°57′N 07°47′W
14 H13 **Rosseau** Ontario, S Canada 45°15′N 79°38′W
45 X12 **Roseau** *prev.* Charlotte Town. ● (Dominica) SW Dominica 15°17′N 61°23′W
29 S2 **Roseau** Minnesota, N USA 48°51′N 95°45′W
173 Y16 **Rose Belle** SE Mauritius 20°24′S 57°36′E
183 O16 **Rosebery** Tasmania, SE Australia 41°51′S 145°33′E
21 U11 **Roseboro** North Carolina, SE USA 34°58′N 78°31′W
25 T9 **Rosebud** Texas, SW USA 31°04′N 96°58′W
33 W10 **Rosebud Creek** ≈ Montana, NW USA
32 F14 **Roseburg** Oregon, NW USA 43°13′N 123°21′W
22 J3 **Rosedale** Mississippi, S USA 33°51′N 91°01′W
99 H21 **Rosée** Namur, S Belgium 50°15′N 04°43′E
55 U8 **Rose Hall** E Guyana 06°14′N 57°30′W
173 X16 **Rose Hill** W Mauritius 20°14′S 57°29′E
80 H12 **Roseires, Reservoir** *var.* Lake Rusayris. ⊠ E Sudan
Rosenau *see* Rožnov pod Radhoštěm
Rosenau *see* Rožňava
25 V11 **Rosenberg** Texas, SW USA 29°33′N 95°48′W
Rosenberg *see* Olesno, Poland
Rosenberg *see* Ružomberok, Slovakia
100 I10 **Rosengarten** Niedersachsen, N Germany 53°24′N 09°54′E
101 M24 **Rosenheim** Bayern, S Germany 47°51′N 12°08′E
Rosenhof *see* Zilupe
105 X4 **Roses** Cataluña, NE Spain 42°15′N 03°11′E
105 X4 **Roses, Golf de** *gulf* NE Spain
107 K14 **Roseto degli Abruzzi** Abruzzo, C Italy 42°39′N 14°01′E
11 S16 **Rosetown** Saskatchewan, S Canada 51°34′N 107°59′W
Rosetta *see* Rashīd
35 O7 **Roseville** California, W USA 38°44′N 121°16′W
30 J12 **Roseville** Illinois, N USA 40°42′N 90°40′W
29 V8 **Roseville** Minnesota, N USA 45°00′N 93°09′W
29 R7 **Rosholt** South Dakota, N USA 45°51′N 96°42′W
106 F12 **Rosignano Marittimo** Toscana, C Italy 43°24′N 10°28′E
116 I14 **Roşiori de Vede** Teleorman, S Romania 44°06′N 25°00′E
114 K8 **Rositsa** ≈ N Bulgaria
Rositten *see* Rēzekne
95 J23 **Roskilde** Roskilde, E Denmark 55°39′N 12°07′E
95 I23 **Roskilde** *off.* Roskilde Amt. ◐ *county* E Denmark
Roskilde Amt *see* Roskilde
Ros Láir *see* Rosslare
126 H5 **Roslavl'** Smolenskaya Oblast', W Russian Federation 54°N 32°57′E
124 J3 **Roslyakovo** Murmanskaya Oblast', NW Russian Federation 69°03′N 33°12′E
32 I8 **Roslyn** Washington, NW USA 47°13′N 120°52′W
99 K14 **Rosmalen** Noord-Brabant, S Netherlands 51°43′N 05°21′E
Ros Mhic Thriúin *see* New Ross
113 P19 **Rosoman** C FYR Macedonia 41°31′N 21°55′E
102 F6 **Rosporden** Finistère, NW France 47°58′N 03°54′W
Ross' *see* Ros'
107 O20 **Rossano** *anc.* Roscianum. Calabria, SW Italy 39°35′N 16°38′E
22 L5 **Ross Barnett Reservoir** ⊠ Mississippi, S USA
11 W16 **Rossburn** Manitoba, S Canada 50°42′N 100°49′W
14 H13 **Rosseau, Lake** ◎ Ontario, S Canada
186 I10 **Rossel Island** *prev.* Yela Island. *island* SE Papua New Guinea
195 P12 **Ross Ice Shelf** *ice shelf* Antarctica
13 P16 **Rossignol, Lake** ◎ Nova Scotia, SE Canada
83 C19 **Rössing** Erongo, W Namibia 22°31′S 14°52′E
195 Q14 **Ross Island** *island* Antarctica
Rossitten *see* Rybachiy
Rossiyskaya Federatsiya *see* Russian Federation
11 N17 **Rossland** British Columbia, SW Canada 49°03′N 117°49′W
97 F20 **Rosslare** *Ir.* Ros Láir. Wexford, SE Ireland 52°16′N 06°23′W
97 F20 **Rosslare Harbour** Wexford, SE Ireland 52°15′N 06°20′W
101 M14 **Rosslau** Sachsen-Anhalt, E Germany 51°52′N 12°15′E
76 G10 **Rosso** Trarza, SW Mauritania 16°36′N 15°50′W
103 X14 **Rosso, Cap** *headland* Corse, France, C Mediterranean Sea 42°25′N 08°22′E
93 H16 **Rossön** Jämtland, C Sweden 63°54′N 16°21′E
97 K21 **Ross-on-Wye** W England, United Kingdom 51°55′N 02°34′W
Rossony *see* Rasony
126 L9 **Rossosh'** Voronezhskaya Oblast', W Russian Federation 50°10′N 39°34′E
181 Q7 **Ross River** Northern Territory, N Australia 23°36′S 134°30′E
10 J7 **Ross River** Yukon Territory, W Canada 61°57′N 132°26′W
195 O15 **Ross Sea** *sea* Antarctica
92 G13 **Røsvatnet** *Lapp.* Reevhtse. ◎ C Norway
23 R1 **Rossville** Georgia, SE USA 34°59′N 85°22′W
Rostak *see* Ar Rustāq
143 P14 **Rostāq** Hormozgān, S Iran 26°48′N 53°50′E
117 N5 **Rostavytsya** ≈ N Ukraine
11 T15 **Rosthern** Saskatchewan, S Canada 52°40′N 106°20′W
100 M8 **Rostock** Mecklenburg-Vorpommern, NE Germany 54°05′N 12°08′E
124 L16 **Rostov** Yaroslavskaya Oblast', W Russian Federation 57°11′N 39°19′E
Rostov *see* Rostov-na-Donu
126 L12 **Rostov-na-Donu** *var.* Rostov, *Eng.* Rostov-on-Don. Rostovskaya Oblast', SW Russian Federation 47°16′N 39°45′E
Rostov-on-Don *see* Rostov-na-Donu
126 L10 **Rostovskaya Oblast'** ◐ *province* SW Russian Federation
93 J14 **Rosvik** Norrbotten, N Sweden 65°26′N 21°48′E
23 S3 **Roswell** Georgia, SE USA 34°01′N 84°21′W
37 U14 **Roswell** New Mexico, SW USA 33°23′N 104°31′W
94 K12 **Rot** Dalarna, C Sweden 61°16′N 14°04′E
101 I23 **Rot** ≈ S Germany
104 J15 **Rota** Andalucía, S Spain 36°39′N 06°20′W
188 K9 **Rota** *island* S Northern Mariana Islands
25 P6 **Rotan** Texas, SW USA 32°51′N 100°28′W
Rotcher Island *see* Tamana
100 I11 **Rotenburg** Niedersachsen, NW Germany 53°06′N 09°25′E
Rotenburg *see* Rotenburg an der Fulda
101 I16 **Rotenburg an der Fulda** *var.* Rotenburg. Thüringen, C Germany 51°00′N 09°43′E
101 L18 **Roter Main** ≈ E Germany
101 K20 **Roth** Bayern, SE Germany 49°15′N 11°06′E
101 G16 **Rothaargebirge** ▲▲ W Germany
Rothenburg *see* Rothenburg ob der Tauber
101 J20 **Rothenburg ob der Tauber** *var.* Rothenburg. Bayern, S Germany 49°23′N 10°10′E
194 H6 **Rothera** *UK research station* Antarctica 67°28′S 68°31′W
185 I17 **Rotherham** Canterbury, South Island, New Zealand 42°42′S 172°56′E
97 M17 **Rotherham** N England, United Kingdom 53°26′N 01°20′W
96 H12 **Rothesay** W Scotland, United Kingdom 55°49′N 05°03′W
108 E7 **Rothrist** Aargau, N Switzerland 47°18′N 07°54′E
194 H6 **Rothschild Island** *island* Antarctica
171 P17 **Roti, Pulau** *island* S Indonesia
183 O8 **Roto** New South Wales, SE Australia 33°04′S 145°27′E
184 N8 **Rotoiti, Lake** ◎ North Island, New Zealand
Rotomagus *see* Rouen
107 N19 **Rotondella** Basilicata, S Italy 40°12′N 16°30′E
103 X15 **Rotondo, Monte** ▲ Corse, France, C Mediterranean Sea 42°15′N 09°03′E
185 I15 **Rotoroa, Lake** ◎ South Island, New Zealand
184 N8 **Rotorua** Bay of Plenty, North Island, New Zealand 38°10′S 176°14′E
184 N8 **Rotorua, Lake** ◎ North Island, New Zealand
101 N22 **Rott** ≈ SE Germany
108 F10 **Rotten** ≈ S Switzerland
109 T6 **Rottenmann** Steiermark, E Austria 47°31′N 14°18′E
98 H12 **Rotterdam** Zuid-Holland, SW Netherlands 51°55′N 04°30′E
18 K10 **Rotterdam** New York, NE USA 42°46′N 73°57′W
95 M21 **Rottnen** ◎ S Sweden
98 N4 **Rottumeroog** *island* Waddeneilanden, NE Netherlands
98 N4 **Rottumerplaat** *island* Waddeneilanden, NE Netherlands
101 G23 **Rottweil** Baden-Württemberg, S Germany 48°10′N 08°38′E
191 O7 **Rotui, Mont** 🌋 Moorea, W French Polynesia 17°30′S 149°50′W
103 P1 **Roubaix** Nord, N France 50°42′N 03°10′E
111 C15 **Roudnice nad Labem** *Ger.* Raudnitz an der Elbe. Ústecký Kraj, NW Czech Republic 50°25′N 14°14′E
102 M4 **Rouen** *anc.* Rotomagus. Seine-Maritime, N France 49°26′N 01°05′E
171 X13 **Rouffaer Reserves** *reserve* Papua, E Indonesia
15 N10 **Rouge, Rivière** ≈ Québec, SE Canada
20 J6 **Rough River** ≈ Kentucky, S USA
20 J6 **Rough River Lake** ⊠ Kentucky, S USA
Rouhaïbé *see* Ar Ruḩaybah
102 K11 **Rouillac** Charente, W France 45°46′N 00°04′W
Roulers *see* Roeselare
Roumania *see* Romania
173 Y15 **Round Island** *var.* Île Ronde. *island* NE Mauritius
14 J12 **Round Lake** ◎ Ontario, SE Canada
35 U7 **Round Mountain** Nevada, W USA 38°42′N 117°04′W
25 R10 **Round Mountain** Texas, SW USA 30°25′N 98°20′W
183 U5 **Round Mountain** ▲ New South Wales, SE Australia 30°22′S 152°13′E
25 S10 **Round Rock** Texas, SW USA 30°30′N 97°40′W
33 U10 **Roundup** Montana, NW USA 46°27′N 108°32′W
55 Y10 **Roura** NE French Guiana 04°44′N 52°16′W
Rourkela *see* Rāulakela
96 J4 **Rousay** *island* N Scotland, United Kingdom
Rousselaere *see* Roeselare
103 O17 **Roussillon** *cultural region* S France
15 V7 **Routhierville** Québec, SE Canada 48°09′N 67°07′W
99 K25 **Rouvroy** Luxembourg, SE Belgium 49°33′N 05°28′E
14 I7 **Rouyn-Noranda** Québec, SE Canada 48°16′N 79°03′W
Rouyuan *see* Huachi
Rouyuanchengzi *see* Huachi
92 L12 **Rovaniemi** Lappi, N Finland 66°29′N 25°40′E
106 E7 **Rovato** Lombardia, N Italy 45°34′N 10°03′E
125 N11 **Rovdino** Arkhangel'skaya Oblast', NW Russian Federation 61°36′N 42°28′E
Roven'ki *see* Roven'ky
117 Y8 **Roven'ky** *var.* Roven'ki. Luhans'ka Oblast', E Ukraine 48°05′N 39°20′E
Rovenskaya Oblast' *see* Rivnens'ka Oblast'
Rovenskaya Sloboda *see* Rovyenskaya Slabada
106 G7 **Rovereto** *Ger.* Rofreit. Trentino-Alto Adige, N Italy 45°53′N 11°03′E
167 S12 **Rôviĕng Tbong** Preăh Vihéar, N Cambodia 13°18′N 105°06′E
Rovigno *see* Rovinj
106 H8 **Rovigo** Veneto, NE Italy 45°04′N 11°48′E
112 A10 **Rovinj** *It.* Rovigno. Istra, NW Croatia 45°06′N 13°39′E
54 E10 **Rovira** Tolima, C Colombia 04°15′N 75°15′W
Rovno *see* Rivne
127 P9 **Rovnoye** Saratovskaya Oblast', W Russian Federation 50°43′N 46°03′E
82 Q12 **Rovuma, Rio** *var.* Ruvuma. ≈ Mozambique/Tanzania *see also* Ruvuma
Rovuma, Rio *see* Ruvuma
119 O19 **Rovyenskaya Slabada** *Rus.* Rovenskaya Sloboda. Homyel'skaya Voblasts', SE Belarus 52°13′N 30°19′E
183 R5 **Rowena** New South Wales, SE Australia 29°51′S 148°55′E
21 T11 **Rowland** North Carolina, SE USA 34°32′N 79°17′W
9 P5 **Rowley** ≈ Baffin Island, Nunavut, NE Canada
9 P6 **Rowley Island** *island* Nunavut, NE Canada
173 W8 **Rowley Shoals** *reef* NW Australia
Równe *see* Rivne
171 O4 **Roxas** Mindoro, N Philippines 12°36′N 121°29′E
171 P5 **Roxas City** Panay Island, C Philippines 11°33′N 122°43′E
21 U8 **Roxboro** North Carolina, SE USA 36°24′N 79°00′W
185 D23 **Roxburgh** Otago, South Island, New Zealand 45°32′S 169°18′E
96 K13 **Roxburgh** *cultural region* SE Scotland, United Kingdom
182 H5 **Roxby Downs** South Australia 30°29′S 136°56′E
95 M17 **Roxen** ◎ S Sweden
25 V5 **Roxton** Texas, SW USA 33°33′N 95°43′W
15 P12 **Roxton-Sud** Québec, SE Canada 45°30′N 72°35′W
33 U8 **Roy** Montana, NW USA 47°19′N 108°55′W
37 U10 **Roy** New Mexico, SW USA 35°56′N 104°12′W
97 E17 **Royal Canal** *Ir.* An Chanáil Ríoga. *canal* C Ireland
30 L1 **Royale, Isle** *island* Michigan, N USA
37 S6 **Royal Gorge** *valley* Colorado, C USA
97 M20 **Royal Leamington Spa** *var.* Leamington, Leamington Spa. C England, United Kingdom 52°18′N 01°31′W
97 O23 **Royal Tunbridge Wells** *var.* Tunbridge Wells. SE England, United Kingdom 51°08′N 00°16′E
24 L9 **Royalty** Texas, SW USA 31°21′N 102°51′W
102 J11 **Royan** Charente-Maritime, W France 45°37′N 01°01′W
65 B24 **Roy Cove Settlement** West Falkland, Falkland Islands 51°32′S 60°23′W
103 O3 **Roye** Somme, N France 49°42′N 02°46′E
95 H15 **Røyken** Buskerud, S Norway 59°47′N 10°21′E
93 F14 **Røyrvik** Nord-Trøndelag, C Norway 64°53′N 13°30′E
25 U6 **Royse City** Texas, SW USA 32°58′N 96°19′W
97 O21 **Royston** E England, United Kingdom 52°05′N 00°01′W
23 U2 **Royston** Georgia, SE USA 34°17′N 83°06′W
114 L10 **Roza** *prev.* Gyulovo. Yambol, E Bulgaria 42°29′N 26°30′E
113 L16 **Rožaje** E Montenegro 42°51′N 20°11′E
110 M10 **Różan** Mazowieckie, C Poland 52°36′N 21°27′E
117 O10 **Rozdil'na** Odes'ka Oblast', SW Ukraine 46°51′N 30°03′E
117 S12 **Rozdol'ne** *Rus.* Razdolnoye. Respublika Krym, S Ukraine 45°45′N 33°27′E
145 Q9 **Rozhdestvenka** Akmola, C Kazakhstan 50°51′N 71°25′E
116 I6 **Rozhnyativ** Ivano-Frankivs'ka Oblast', W Ukraine 48°58′N 24°07′E
116 J3 **Rozhyshche** Volyns'ka Oblast', NW Ukraine 50°54′N 25°16′E
Roznau am Radhost *see* Rožnov pod Radhoštěm
111 L19 **Rožňava** *Ger.* Rosenau, *Hung.* Rozsnyó. Košický Kraj, E Slovakia 48°41′N 20°32′E
116 K10 **Roznov** Neamţ, NE Romania 46°47′N 26°33′E
111 I18 **Rožnov pod Radhoštěm** *Ger.* Rosenau, Roznau am Radhost. Zlínský Kraj, E Czech Republic 49°28′N 18°09′E
Rózsahegy *see* Ružomberok
Rozsnyó *see* Râşnov, Romania
Rozsnyó *see* Rožňava, Slovakia
113 K18 **Rranxë** Shkodër, NW Albania 41°58′N 19°27′E
113 L18 **Rrëshen** *var.* Rresheni, Rrshen. Lezhë, C Albania 41°46′N 19°54′E
Rresheni *see* Rrëshen
Rrogozhina *see* Rrogozhinë
113 K20 **Rrogozhinë** *var.* Rogozhina, Rogozhinë, Rrogozhina. Tiranë, W Albania 41°04′N 19°40′E
Rrshen *see* Rrëshen
112 O13 **Rtanj** ▲ E Serbia 43°45′N 21°54′E
127 O7 **Rtishchevo** Saratovskaya Oblast', W Russian Federation 52°16′N 43°46′E
184 N12 **Ruahine Range** *var.* Ruarine. ▲▲ North Island, New Zealand
185 L14 **Ruamahanga** ≈ North Island, New Zealand
Ruanda *see* Rwanda
184 M10 **Ruapehu, Mount** 🌋 North Island, New Zealand 39°15′S 175°33′E
185 C25 **Ruapuke Island** *island* SW New Zealand
Ruarine *see* Ruahine Range
184 O9 **Ruatahuna** Bay of Plenty, North Island, New Zealand 38°38′S 176°56′E
184 Q8 **Ruatoria** Gisborne, North Island, New Zealand 37°54′S 178°18′E
184 K4 **Ruawai** Northland, North Island, New Zealand 36°08′S 174°04′E
15 N8 **Ruban** ≈ Québec, SE Canada
81 I22 **Rubeho Mountains** ▲▲ C Tanzania
165 U3 **Rubeshibe** Hokkaidō, NE Japan 43°49′N 143°37′E
Rubezhnoye *see* Rubizhne
113 L18 **Rubik** Lezhë, C Albania 41°46′N 19°48′E
54 H7 **Rubio** Táchira, W Venezuela 07°42′N 72°23′W
117 X6 **Rubizhne** *Rus.* Rubezhnoye. Luhans'ka Oblast', E Ukraine 49°01′N 38°22′E
81 F20 **Rubondo Island** *island* N Tanzania
122 I13 **Rubtsovsk** Altayskiy Kray, S Russian Federation 51°34′N 81°11′E
39 P9 **Ruby** Alaska, USA 64°44′N 155°29′W
35 W3 **Ruby Dome** ▲ Nevada, W USA 40°35′N 115°25′W
35 W4 **Ruby Lake** ◎ Nevada, W USA
35 W4 **Ruby Mountains** ▲▲ Nevada, W USA
33 Q12 **Ruby Range** ▲▲ Montana, NW USA
118 C10 **Rucava** Liepāja, SW Latvia 56°09′N 21°10′E
143 S13 **Rūdān** *var.* Dehbārez. Hormozgān, S Iran 27°30′N 57°10′E
Rudelstadt *see* Ciechanowiec
Rudensk *see* Rudzyensk
119 G14 **Rūdiškės** Vilnius, S Lithuania 54°31′N 24°49′E
95 H24 **Rudkøbing** Fyn, C Denmark 54°57′N 10°43′E
125 S13 **Rudnichnyy** Kirovskaya Oblast', NW Russian Federation 59°37′N 52°28′E
Rūdnīchnyy *see* Koksu
Rudny *see* Rudnyy
126 H4 **Rudnya** Smolenskaya Oblast', W Russian Federation 54°55′N 31°10′E
127 O8 **Rudnya** Volgogradskaya Oblast', SW Russian Federation 50°54′N 44°27′E
144 M7 **Rudnyy** *var.* Rudny. Kostanay, N Kazakhstan 53°N 63°05′E
122 K3 **Rudol'fa, Ostrov** *island* Zemlya Frantsa-Iosifa, NW Russian Federation
Rudolf, Lake *see* Turkana, Lake
Rudolfswert *see* Novo mesto
101 L17 **Rudolstadt** Thüringen, C Germany 50°44′N 11°20′E
152 K9 **Rudraprayāg** Uttarakhand, N India 28°51′N 79°01′E
152 K10 **Rudrapur** *var.* Rampura. Uttarakhand, N India 28°58′N 79°23′E
31 Q4 **Rudyard** Michigan, N USA 46°15′N 84°36′W
33 S7 **Rudyard** Montana, NW USA 48°33′N 110°37′W
119 K16 **Rudzyensk** *Rus.* Rudensk. Minskaya Voblasts', C Belarus 53°36′N 27°52′E
104 L6 **Rueda** Castilla-León, N Spain 41°24′N 04°58′W
114 F10 **Ruen** ▲ Bulgaria/FYR Macedonia 42°10′N 22°31′E
80 G10 **Rufa'a** Gezira, C Sudan 14°49′N 33°21′E
102 L10 **Ruffec** Charente, W France 46°01′N 00°10′E
21 R14 **Ruffin** South Carolina, SE USA 33°00′N 80°48′W
81 J23 **Rufiji** ≈ E Tanzania
61 A20 **Rufino** Santa Fe, C Argentina 34°16′S 62°45′W
76 F11 **Rufisque** W Senegal 14°44′N 17°18′W
83 K14 **Rufunsa** Lusaka, C Zambia 15°02′S 29°35′E
118 J9 **Rugāji** Balvi, E Latvia 57°01′N 27°07′E
161 R7 **Rugao** Jiangsu, E China 32°27′N 120°35′E
97 M20 **Rugby** C England, United Kingdom 52°22′N 01°18′W
29 N3 **Rugby** North Dakota, N USA 48°24′N 100°00′W
100 N7 **Rügen** *headland* NE Germany 54°25′N 13°21′E
Ruhaybeh *see* Ar Ruḩaybah
81 E19 **Ruhengeri** NW Rwanda 01°39′S 29°16′E
Ruhja *see* Rūjiena
100 M10 **Ruhner Berg** *hill* N Germany
118 F7 **Ruhnu** *var.* Ruhnu Saar, *Swe.* Runö. *island* SW Estonia
Ruhnu Saar *see* Ruhnu
101 G15 **Ruhr** ≈ W Germany
91 W6 **Ruhr Valley** *industrial region* W Germany
161 S11 **Rui'an** *var.* Rui an. Zhejiang, SE China 27°51′N 120°39′E
Rui an *see* Rui'an
161 P10 **Ruichang** Jiangxi, S China 29°46′N 115°37′E
24 J11 **Ruidosa** Texas, SW USA 30°00′N 104°40′W
37 S14 **Ruidoso** New Mexico, SW USA 33°19′N 105°40′W
161 P12 **Ruijin** Jiangxi, S China 25°52′N 116°01′E
160 D13 **Ruili** Yunnan, SW China 24°04′N 97°49′E
98 N8 **Ruinen** Drenthe, NE Netherlands 52°46′N 06°19′E
99 D17 **Ruiselede** West-Vlaanderen, W Belgium 51°03′N 03°21′E
64 P5 **Ruivo de Santana, Pico** ▲ Madeira, Portugal, NE Atlantic Ocean 32°46′N 16°57′W
40 J12 **Ruiz** Nayarit, SW Mexico 22°00′N 105°09′W
54 E10 **Ruiz, Nevado del** 🌋 W Colombia 04°53′N 75°22′W
138 J9 **Rujaylah, Ḩarrat ar** *salt lake* N Jordan
Rujen *see* Rūjiena
118 H7 **Rūjiena** *Est.* Ruhja, *Ger.* Rujen. Valmiera, N Latvia 57°54′N 25°22′E
79 I18 **Ruki** ≈ W Dem. Rep. Congo
81 E22 **Rukwa** ◐ *region* SW Tanzania
81 F23 **Rukwa, Lake** ◎ SE Tanzania
25 P6 **Rule** Texas, SW USA 33°10′N 99°53′W
22 K3 **Ruleville** Mississippi, S USA 33°43′N 90°33′W
Rum *see* Rhum
112 K10 **Ruma** Vojvodina, N Serbia 45°02′N 19°51′E
Rumadiya *see* Ar Ramādī
141 Q7 **Rumāḩ** Ar Riyāḑ, C Saudi Arabia 25°35′N 47°09′E
Rumaitha *see* Ar Rumaythah
Rumania/Rumänien *see* Romania
Rumänisch-Sankt-Georgen *see* Sângeorz-Băi
139 Y13 **Rumaylah** Al Başrah, SE Iraq 30°16′N 47°22′E
139 P2 **Rumaylah, Wādī** *dry watercourse* NE Syria
171 U13 **Rumbati** Papua, E Indonesia 02°44′S 132°04′E
81 E14 **Rumbek** El Buhayrat, S Sudan 06°50′N 29°42′E
Rumburg *see* Rumburk
111 D14 **Rumburk** *Ger.* Rumburg. Ústecký Kraj, NW Czech Republic 50°58′N 14°35′E
44 J4 **Rum Cay** *island* C Bahamas
99 M26 **Rumelange** Luxembourg, S Luxembourg 49°28′N 06°02′E
99 D20 **Rumes** Hainaut, SW Belgium 50°33′N 03°19′E
19 P7 **Rumford** Maine, NE USA 44°31′N 70°31′W
110 I6 **Rumia** Pomorskie, N Poland 54°36′N 18°21′E
113 J17 **Rumija** ▲▲ S Montenegro
103 T11 **Rumilly** Haute-Savoie, E France 45°52′N 05°57′E
139 O6 **Rūmiyah** Al Anbār, W Iraq 34°28′N 41°17′E
Rummah, Wādī ar *see* Rimah, Wādī ar
Rummelsburg in Pommern *see* Miastko
165 S3 **Rumoi** Hokkaidō, NE Japan 43°57′N 141°40′E
82 M12 **Rumphi** *var.* Rumpi. Northern, N Malawi 11°00′S 33°51′E
Rumpi *see* Rumphi
29 V7 **Rum River** ≈ Minnesota, N USA
188 F16 **Rumung** *island* Caroline Islands, W Micronesia
Rumuniya/Rumŭniya/Rumunjska *see* Romania
185 G16 **Runanga** West Coast, South Island, New Zealand 42°25′S 171°15′E
184 P7 **Runaway, Cape** *headland* North Island, New Zealand 37°33′S 177°59′E
97 K18 **Runcorn** C England, United Kingdom 53°20′N 02°44′W
118 K10 **Rundāni** *var.* Rundāni. Ludza, E Latvia 56°19′N 27°51′E
Rundāni *see* Rundāni
83 L18 **Runde** *var.* Lundi. ≈ SE Zimbabwe
83 E16 **Rundu** *var.* Runtu. Okavango, NE Namibia 17°55′S 19°45′E
93 I16 **Rundvik** Västerbotten, N Sweden 63°31′N 19°22′E
81 G20 **Runere** Mwanza, N Tanzania 03°06′S 33°18′E
25 S13 **Runge** Texas, SW USA 28°52′N 97°42′W
167 Q13 **Rŭng, Kaôh** *prev.* Kas Rong. *island* SW Cambodia
79 O16 **Rungu** Orientale, NE Dem. Rep. Congo 03°11′N 27°52′E
81 F23 **Rungwa** Rukwa, W Tanzania 07°18′S 31°40′E
81 G22 **Rungwa** Singida, C Tanzania 06°54′S 33°33′E
94 M14 **Runn** ◎ C Sweden
24 M4 **Running Water Draw** *valley* New Mexico/Texas, SW USA
Runö *see* Ruhnu
Runtu *see* Rundu
189 V12 **Ruo** *island* Caroline Islands, C Micronesia
158 L9 **Ruoqiang** *var.* Jo-ch'iang, *Uigh.* Charkhlik, Charkhliq, Qarkilik. Xinjiang Uygur Zizhiqu, NW China 38°59′N 88°08′E
159 S7 **Ruo Shui** ≈ N China
92 L8 **Ruostekfielbmá** *var.* Rustefjelbma Finnmark. Finnmark, N Norway 70°25′N 28°10′E
93 L18 **Ruovesi** Länsi-Suomi, W Finland 61°59′N 24°05′E
112 B9 **Rupa** Primorje-Gorski Kotar, NW Croatia 45°29′N 14°15′E
182 M11 **Rupanyup** Victoria, SE Australia 36°38′S 142°37′E
168 K9 **Rupat, Pulau** *prev.* Roepat. *island* W Indonesia
168 K10 **Rupat, Selat** *strait* Sumatera, W Indonesia
116 J11 **Rupea** *Ger.* Reps, *Hung.* Kőhalom; *prev.* Cohalm. Braşov, C Romania 46°02′N 25°13′E
99 G17 **Rupel** ≈ N Belgium
Rupella *see* la Rochelle
33 P15 **Rupert** Idaho, NW USA 42°37′N 113°40′W
21 R5 **Rupert** West Virginia, NE USA 37°57′N 80°40′W
Rupert House *see* Waskaganish
12 J10 **Rupert, Rivière de** ≈ Québec, C Canada
152 I8 **Rūpnagar** *var.* Ropar. Punjab, India
194 M13 **Ruppert Coast** *physical region* Antarctica
100 N11 **Ruppiner Kanal** *canal* NE Germany
55 S11 **Rupununi River** ≈ S Guyana
101 D16 **Rur** *Dut.* Roer. ≈ Germany/Netherlands
58 H13 **Rurópolis Presidente Medici** Pará, N Brazil 04°05′S 55°26′W
191 S12 **Rurutu** *island* Îles Australes, SW French Polynesia
Rusaddir *see* Melilla
83 L17 **Rusape** Manicaland, E Zimbabwe 18°32′S 32°07′E
Rusayris, Lake *see* Roseires, Reservoir
Ruschuk/Rusçuk *see* Ruse
114 K7 **Ruse** *var.* Ruschuk, Rustchuk, *Turk.* Rusçuk. Ruse, N Bulgaria 43°50′N 25°59′E
109 W10 **Ruše** NE Slovenia 46°31′N 15°30′E
114 L7 **Ruse** ◐ *province* N Bulgaria
114 K7 **Rusenski Lom** ≈ N Bulgaria
97 G17 **Rush** *Ir.* An Ros. Dublin, E Ireland 53°32′N 06°06′W
161 S4 **Rushan** *var.* Xiacun. Shandong, E China 36°55′N 121°26′E
Rushan *see* Rŭshon
Rushanskiy Khrebet *see* Rushon, Qatorkŭhi
29 V7 **Rush City** Minnesota, N USA 45°41′N 92°56′W
37 V5 **Rush Creek** ≈ Colorado, C USA
29 X10 **Rushford** Minnesota, N USA 43°48′N 91°45′W
154 N13 **Rushikulya** ≈ E India
14 D8 **Rush Lake** ◎ Ontario, S Canada
30 M7 **Rush Lake** ◎ Wisconsin, N USA
28 J10 **Rushmore, Mount** ▲ South Dakota, N USA 43°52′N 103°27′W
147 S13 **Rŭshon** *Rus.* Rushan. S Tajikistan 37°58′N 71°31′E
147 S14 **Rushon, Qatorkŭhi** *Rus.* Rushanskiy Khrebet. ▲▲ SE Tajikistan
26 M12 **Rush Springs** Oklahoma, C USA 34°46′N 97°57′W
45 V15 **Rushville** Trinidad, Trinidad and Tobago 10°07′N 61°03′W
30 J13 **Rushville** Illinois, N USA 40°07′N 90°33′W
28 K12 **Rushville** Nebraska, C USA 42°41′N 102°28′W
183 O11 **Rushworth** Victoria, SE Australia 36°36′S 145°03′E
25 W8 **Rusk** Texas, SW USA 31°49′N 95°11′W
93 I14 **Rusksele** Västerbotten, N Sweden 64°49′N 18°55′E
118 C12 **Rusnė** Klaipėda, W Lithuania 55°18′N 21°19′E
114 M10 **Rusokastrenska Reka** ≈ E Bulgaria
Russadir *see* Melilla
109 X3 **Russbach** ≈ NE Austria
11 V16 **Russell** Manitoba, S Canada 50°47′N 101°17′W
184 K2 **Russell** Northland, North Island, New Zealand 35°17′S 174°07′E
26 L4 **Russell** Kansas, C USA 38°54′N 98°51′W
21 O4 **Russell** Kentucky, S USA 38°30′N 82°43′W
20 L7 **Russell Springs** Kentucky, S USA 37°02′N 85°03′W
23 O2 **Russellville** Alabama, S USA 34°30′N 87°43′W
27 T11 **Russellville** Arkansas, C USA 35°17′N 93°06′W
20 J7 **Russellville** Kentucky, S USA 36°50′N 86°54′W
101 G18 **Rüsselsheim** Hessen, W Germany 50°00′N 08°25′E
Russia *see* Russian Federation
Russian America *see* Alaska
122 J11 **Russian Federation** *off.* Russian Federation, *var.* Russia, *Latv.* Krievija, *Rus.* Rossiyskaya Federatsiya. ◆ *republic* Asia/Europe
Russian Federation *see* Russian Federation
39 N11 **Russian Mission** Alaska, USA 61°48′N 161°23′W
34 M7 **Russian River** ≈ California, W USA
122 J5 **Russkaya Gavan'** Novaya Zemlya, Arkhangel'skaya Oblast', N Russian Federation 76°13′N 62°48′E
122 J5 **Russkiy, Ostrov** *island* N Russian Federation
109 Y5 **Rust** Burgenland, E Austria 47°48′N 16°42′E
Rustaq *see* Ar Rustāq
137 U10 **Rust'avi** SE Georgia 41°36′N 45°00′E
21 T7 **Rustburg** Virginia, NE USA 37°17′N 79°07′W
Rustchuk *see* Ruse
Rustefjelbma Finnmark *see* Ruostekfielbmá
83 I21 **Rustenburg** North-West, N South Africa 25°40′S 27°15′E
22 H5 **Ruston** Louisiana, S USA 32°31′N 92°38′W
81 E21 **Rutana** SE Burundi 04°01′S 30°01′E
62 I4 **Rutana, Volcán** 🌋 N Chile 22°43′S 67°52′W
Rutanzige, Lake *see* Edward, Lake
Rutba *see* Ar Ruţbah
104 M14 **Rute** Andalucía, S Spain 37°20′N 04°23′W
171 N16 **Ruteng** *prev.* Roeteng. Flores, C Indonesia 08°35′S 120°28′E
194 L8 **Rutford Ice Stream** *ice feature* Antarctica
35 X6 **Ruth** Nevada, W USA 39°15′N 115°00′W
101 G15 **Rüthen** Nordrhein-Westfalen, W Germany 51°30′N 08°28′E
14 D17 **Rutherford** Ontario, S Canada 42°39′N 82°06′W
21 Q10 **Rutherfordton** North Carolina, SE USA 35°23′N 81°57′W
97 J18 **Ruthin** *Wel.* Rhuthun. NE Wales, United Kingdom 53°05′N 03°18′W
108 G7 **Rüti** Zürich, N Switzerland 47°16′N 08°51′E
Rutlam *see* Ratlām
18 M9 **Rutland** Vermont, NE USA 43°37′N 72°59′W
97 N19 **Rutland** *cultural region* C England, United Kingdom
21 N8 **Rutledge** Tennessee, S USA 36°16′N 83°31′W
158 G12 **Rutog** *var.* Rutög, Rutok. Xizang Zizhiqu, W China 33°27′N 79°43′E
Rutok *see* Rutog
79 P19 **Rutshuru** Nord-Kivu, E Dem. Rep. Congo 01°11′S 29°28′E
98 L8 **Rutten** Flevoland, N Netherlands 52°49′N 05°44′E
127 Q17 **Rutul** Respublika Dagestan, SW Russian Federation 41°35′N 47°30′E
93 L14 **Ruukki** Oulu, C Finland 64°40′N 25°35′E
98 N11 **Ruurlo** Gelderland, E Netherlands 52°04′N 06°27′E
143 S15 **Ru'ūs al Jibāl** *cape* Oman/United Arab Emirates
138 I7 **Ru'ūs aţ Ţiwāl, Jabal** ▲▲ W Syria
81 H23 **Ruvuma** ◐ *region* SE Tanzania
81 I25 **Ruvuma** *var.* Rio Rovuma. ≈ Mozambique/Tanzania *see also* Rovuma, Rio
Ruvuma *see* Rovuma, Rio
Ruwais *see* Ar Ruways
138 L9 **Ruwayshid, Wadi ar** *dry watercourse* NE Jordan
141 Z10 **Ruways, Ra's ar** *headland* E Oman 20°58′N 59°00′E
79 P18 **Ruwenzori** ▲▲ Dem. Rep. Congo/Uganda
141 Y8 **Ruwī** NE Oman 23°33′N 58°31′E
114 F9 **Ruy** ▲ Bulgaria/Serbia 42°52′N 22°35′E
Ruya *see* Luia, Rio
81 E20 **Ruyigi** E Burundi 03°28′S 30°19′E
127 P5 **Ruzayevka** Respublika Mordoviya, W Russian Federation 54°04′N 44°56′E
119 G18 **Ruzhany** Brestskaya Voblasts', SW Belarus 52°52′N 24°53′E
114 I10 **Rŭzhevo Konare** Plovdiv, C Bulgaria 42°16′N 24°58′E
Ruzhin *see* Ruzhyn
114 G7 **Ruzhintsi** Vidin, NW Bulgaria 43°38′N 22°50′E
161 N6 **Ruzhou** Henan, C China 34°10′N 112°51′E
117 N5 **Ruzhyn** *Rus.* Ruzhin. Zhytomyrs'ka Oblast', N Ukraine 49°42′N 29°01′E
111 K19 **Ružomberok** *Ger.* Rosenberg, *Hung.* Rózsahegy. Žilinský Kraj, N Slovakia 49°04′N 19°19′E
111 C16 **Ruzyně** ✕ (Praha) Praha, C Czech Republic
81 D19 **Rwanda** *off.* Rwandese Republic; *prev.* Ruanda. ◆ *republic* C Africa
Rwandese Republic *see* Rwanda
95 G22 **Ry** Århus, C Denmark 56°06′N 09°46′E
Ryasna *see* Rasna
126 L5 **Ryazan'** Ryazanskaya Oblast', W Russian Federation 54°37′N 39°37′E
126 L5 **Ryazanskaya Oblast'** ◐ *province* W Russian Federation
126 M6 **Ryazhsk** Ryazanskaya Oblast', W Russian Federation 53°42′N 40°09′E
118 B13 **Rybachiy** *Ger.* Rossitten. Kaliningradskaya Oblast', W Russian Federation 55°09′N 20°49′E
124 J2 **Rybachiy, Poluostrov** *peninsula* NW Russian Federation
Rybach'ye *see* Balykchy
124 L15 **Rybinsk** *prev.* Andropov. Yaroslavskaya Oblast', W Russian Federation 58°03′N 38°53′E
124 K14 **Rybinskoye Vodokhranilishche** *Eng.* Rybinsk Reservoir, Rybinsk Sea. ⊠ W Russian Federation
Rybinsk Reservoir/Rybinsk Sea *see* Rybinskoye Vodokhranilishche
111 I16 **Rybnik** Śląskie, S Poland 50°05′N 18°31′E
Rybnitsa *see* Rîbniţa

◆ Country ● Country Capital ◇ Dependent Territory ○ Dependent Territory Capital ◐ Administrative Regions ✕ International Airport ▲ Mountain ▲▲ Mountain Range 🌋 Volcano ≈ River ◎ Lake ⊠ Reservoir

111 *F16* **Rychnov nad Kněžnou** *Ger.* Reichenau. Královéhradecký Kraj, N Czech Republic *50°10′N 16°17′E*
110 *I12* **Rychwał** Wielkopolskie, C Poland *52°04′N 18°10′E*
11 *O13* **Rycroft** Alberta, W Canada *55°45′N 118°42′W*
95 *L21* **Ryd** Kronoberg, S Sweden *56°27′N 14°44′E*
95 *L20* **Rydaholm** Jönköping, S Sweden *56°57′N 14°19′E*
194 *I8* **Rydberg Peninsula** *peninsula* Antarctica
97 *P23* **Rye** SE England, United Kingdom *50°57′N 00°42′E*
33 *T10* **Ryegate** Montana, NW USA *46°21′N 109°12′W*
35 *S3* **Rye Patch Reservoir** ⊠ Nevada, W USA
95 *D15* **Ryfylke** *physical region* S Norway
95 *H16* **Rygge** Østfold, S Norway *59°22′N 10°45′E*
110 *N13* **Ryki** Lubelskie, E Poland *51°38′N 21°57′E*
Rykovo *see* Yenakiyeve
126 *I7* **Ryl′sk** Kurskaya Oblast′, W Russian Federation *51°34′N 34°41′E*
183 *S8* **Rylstone** New South Wales, SE Australia *32°48′S 149°58′E*
111 *H17* **Rýmařov** *Ger.* Römerstadt. Moravskoslezský Kraj, E Czech Republic *49°56′N 17°15′E*
144 *E11* **Ryn-Peski** *desert* W Kazakhstan
165 *N10* **Ryōtsu** *var.* Ryôtu. Niigata, Sado, C Japan *38°06′N 138°28′E*
Ryôtu *see* Ryōtsu
110 *K10* **Rypin** Kujawsko-pomorskie, C Poland *53°03′N 19°25′E*
Ryshkany *see* Rîșcani
Ryssel *see* Lille
Ryswick *see* Rijswijk
95 *M24* **Rytterknægten** *hill* E Denmark
Ryukyu Islands *see* Nansei-shotō
192 *G5* **Ryukyu Trench** *var.* Nansei Syotō Trench. *undersea feature* S East China Sea *24°45′N 128°00′E*
110 *D11* **Rzepin** *Ger.* Reppen. Lubuskie, W Poland *52°20′N 14°48′E*
111 *N16* **Rzeszów** Podkarpackie, SE Poland *50°03′N 22°01′E*
124 *I16* **Rzhev** Tverskaya Oblast′, W Russian Federation *56°17′N 34°22′E*
Rzhishchev *see* Rzhyshchiv
117 *P5* **Rzhyshchiv** *Rus.* Rzhishchev. Kyyivs′ka Oblast′, N Ukraine *49°58′N 31°02′E*

S

138 *E11* **Sa′ad** Southern, W Israel *31°27′N 34°31′E*
109 *P7* **Saalach** ⇝ W Austria
101 *L14* **Saale** ⇝ C Germany
101 *L17* **Saalfeld** *var.* Saalfeld an der Saale. Thüringen, C Germany *50°39′N 11°22′E*
Saalfeld *see* Zalewo
Saalfeld an der Saale *see* Saalfeld
108 *C8* **Saane** ⇝ W Switzerland
101 *D19* **Saar** *Fr.* Sarre. ⇝ France/ Germany
101 *E20* **Saarbrücken** *Fr.* Sarrebruck. Saarland, SW Germany *49°13′N 07°01′E*
Saarburg *see* Sarrebourg
118 *D6* **Sääre** *var.* Sjar. Saaremaa, W Estonia *57°57′N 21°53′E*
Saare *see* Saaremaa
118 *D5* **Saaremaa** *off.* Saare Maakond. ◆ *province* W Estonia
118 *E6* **Saaremaa** *Ger.* Oesel, Ösel; *prev.* Saare. *island* W Estonia
Saare Maakond *see* Saaremaa
92 *L12* **Saarenkylä** Lappi, N Finland *66°31′N 25°51′E*
Saargemund *see* Sarreguemines
93 *L17* **Saarijärvi** Länsi-Suomi, C Finland *62°42′N 25°16′E*
Saar in Mähren *see* Žd′ár nad Sázavou
92 *M10* **Saariselkä** *Lapp.* Suoločielgi. Lappi, N Finland *68°27′N 27°29′E*
92 *L10* **Saariselkä** *hill range* NE Finland
101 *D20* **Saarland** *Fr.* Sarre. ◆ *state* SW Germany
Saarlautern *see* Saarlouis
101 *D20* **Saarlouis** *prev.* Saarlautern. Saarland, SW Germany *49°19′N 06°45′E*
108 *E11* **Saaser Vispa** ⇝ S Switzerland
137 *X12* **Saatlı** *Rus.* Saatly. C Azerbaijan *39°57′N 48°24′E*
Saatly *see* Saatlı
Saaz *see* Žatec
45 *V9* **Saba** *island* N Netherlands Antilles
138 *J7* **Sab′ Ābār** *var.* Sab′a Biyar, Sa′b Bi′ār. Ḥimṣ, C Syria *33°46′N 37°41′E*
Sab′a Biyar *see* Sab′ Ābār
112 *K11* **Šabac** Serbia, W Serbia *44°45′N 19°42′E*
105 *W5* **Sabadell** Cataluña, E Spain *41°33′N 02°07′E*
164 *K12* **Sabae** Fukui, Honshū, SW Japan *36°00′N 136°12′E*
169 *V7* **Sabah** *prev.* British North Borneo, North Borneo. ◆ *state* East Malaysia
168 *J8* **Sabak** *var.* Sabak Bernam. Selangor, Peninsular Malaysia *03°45′N 100°59′E*
Sabak Bernam *see* Sabak
38 *D16* **Sabak, Cape** *headland* Agattu Island, Alaska, USA *52°21′N 173°43′E*
81 *J20* **Sabaki** ⇝ S Kenya
142 *L2* **Sabalān, Kuhhā-ye** ▲ NW Iran *38°21′N 47°47′E*
154 *H7* **Sabalgarh** Madhya Pradesh, C India *26°18′N 77°28′E*
44 *E4* **Sabana, Archipiélago de** *island group* C Cuba
42 *H7* **Sabanagrande** *var.* Sabana Grande. Francisco Morazán, S Honduras *13°48′N 87°15′W*
Sabana Grande *see* Sabanagrande
54 *E5* **Sabanalarga** Atlántico, N Colombia *10°38′N 74°55′W*
41 *W14* **Sabancuy** Campeche, SE Mexico *18°58′N 91°11′W*
45 *N8* **Sabaneta** NW Dominican Republic *19°30′N 71°21′W*
54 *J4* **Sabaneta** Falcón, N Venezuela *11°17′N 70°00′W*
188 *H4* **Sabaneta, Puntan** *prev.* Ushi Point. *headland* Saipan, S Northern Mariana Islands *15°17′N 145°49′E*
171 *X14* **Sabang** Papua, E Indonesia *04°33′S 138°42′E*
116 *L10* **Săbăoani** Neamț, NE Romania *47°01′N 26°51′E*
155 *J26* **Sabaragamuwa** ◆ *province* C Sri Lanka
Sabaria *see* Szombathely
154 *D10* **Sābarmati** ⇝ NW India
171 *S10* **Sabatai** Pulau Morotai, E Indonesia *02°04′N 128°23′E*
141 *Q15* **Sab′atayn, Ramlat as** *desert* C Yemen
107 *I16* **Sabaudia** Lazio, C Italy *41°17′N 13°02′E*
57 *J19* **Sabaya** Oruro, S Bolivia *19°09′S 68°21′W*
Sa′b Bi′ār *see* Sab′ Ābār
Sabbioncello *see* Orebić
148 *I8* **Şāberī, Hāmūn-e** *var.* Daryācheh-ye Hāmun, Daryācheh-ye Sīstān. ◎ Afghanistan/Iran *see also* Sīstān, Daryācheh-ye
Şāberī, Hāmūn-e *see* Sīstān, Daryācheh-ye
27 *P2* **Sabetha** Kansas, C USA *39°54′N 95°48′W*
75 *P10* **Sabhā** C Libya *27°02′N 14°26′E*
67 *V13* **Sabi** *var.* Save. ⇝ Mozambique/Zimbabwe *see also* Save
Sabi *see* Save
118 *E8* **Sabile** *Ger.* Zabeln. Talsi, NW Latvia *57°03′N 22°33′E*
31 *R14* **Sabina** Ohio, N USA *39°29′N 83°38′W*
40 *I3* **Sabinal** Chihuahua, N Mexico *30°59′N 107°29′W*
25 *Q12* **Sabinal** Texas, SW USA *29°19′N 99°28′W*
25 *Q11* **Sabinal River** ⇝ Texas, SW USA
105 *S4* **Sabiñánigo** Aragón, NE Spain *42°31′N 00°22′W*
41 *N6* **Sabinas** Coahuila, NE Mexico *27°52′N 101°04′W*
41 *O8* **Sabinas Hidalgo** Nuevo León, NE Mexico *26°29′N 100°09′W*
41 *N6* **Sabinas, Río** ⇝ NE Mexico
22 *F9* **Sabine Lake** ◎ Louisiana/ Texas, S USA
92 *O3* **Sabine Land** *physical region* C Svalbard
25 *W7* **Sabine River** ⇝ Louisiana/ Texas, SW USA
137 *X12* **Sabirabad** C Azerbaijan *40°00′N 48°27′E*
Sabkha *see* As Sabkhah
171 *O4* **Sablayan** Mindoro, N Philippines *12°48′N 120°48′E*
13 *P16* **Sable, Cape** *headland* Newfoundland and Labrador, SE Canada *43°21′N 65°40′W*
23 *X17* **Sable, Cape** *headland* Florida, SE USA *25°12′N 81°06′W*
13 *R16* **Sable Island** *island* Nova Scotia, SE Canada
14 *L11* **Sables, Lac des** ◎ Québec, SE Canada
14 *E10* **Sables, Rivière aux** ⇝ Ontario, S Canada
102 *K7* **Sable-sur-Sarthe** Sarthe, NW France *47°49′N 00°19′W*
125 *U7* **Sablya, Gora** ▲ NW Russian Federation *64°46′N 58°52′E*
77 *U14* **Sabon Birnin Gwari** Kaduna, C Nigeria *10°43′N 06°39′E*
77 *V11* **Sabon Kafi** Zinder, C Niger *14°37′N 08°46′E*
104 *I6* **Sabor, Rio** ⇝ N Portugal
14 *J8* **Sabourin, Lac** ◎ Québec, SE Canada
102 *J14* **Sabres** Landes, SW France *44°07′N 00°46′W*
195 *X13* **Sabrina Coast** *physical region* Antarctica
140 *M11* **Sabt al Ulāyā** ′Asīr, SW Saudi Arabia *19°33′N 41°58′E*
104 *I8* **Sabugal** Guarda, N Portugal *40°20′N 07°05′W*
29 *Z13* **Sabula** Iowa, C USA *42°04′N 90°10′W*
141 *N13* **Şabyā** Jīzān, SW Saudi Arabia *17°50′N 42°50′E*
Sabzawar *see* Sabzevār
Sabzawaran *see* Jiroft
143 *S4* **Sabzevār** *var.* Sabzawar. Khorāsān-Razavī, NE Iran *36°13′N 57°38′E*
Sabzvārān *see* Jiroft
Sacajawea Peak *see* Matterhorn
82 *C9* **Sacandica** Uíge, NW Angola *06°01′S 15°57′E*
42 *A2* **Sacatepéquez** *off.* Departamento de Sacatepéquez. ◆ *department* S Guatemala
Sacatepéquez, Departamento de *see* Sacatepéquez
104 *F11* **Sacavém** Lisboa, W Portugal *38°47′N 09°06′W*
29 *T13* **Sac City** Iowa, C USA *42°25′N 94°59′W*
105 *P8* **Sacedón** Castilla-La Mancha, C Spain *40°29′N 02°44′W*
116 *J12* **Săcele** *Ger.* Vierdörfer, *Hung.* Négyfalu; *prev. Ger.* Sieben Dörfer, *Hung.* Hétfalu. Brașov, C Romania *45°36′N 25°40′E*
12 *C8* **Sachigo** Ontario, C Canada *53°52′N 92°16′W*
12 *C7* **Sachigo** ⇝ Ontario, C Canada
12 *C8* **Sachigo Lake** ◎ Ontario, C Canada
163 *Y16* **Sach′ŏn** *Jap.* Sansenhō; *prev.* Sanch′ŏnpŏ. S South Korea *34°55′N 128°07′E*
101 *O15* **Sachsen** *Eng.* Saxony, *Fr.* Saxe. ◆ *state* E Germany
101 *K14* **Sachsen-Anhalt** *Eng.* Saxony-Anhalt. ◆ *state* C Germany
109 *R9* **Sachsenburg** Salzburg, S Austria *46°49′N 13°23′E*
Sachsenfeld *see* Žalec
8 *I5* **Sachs Harbour** *var.* Ikaahuk. Banks Island, Northwest Territories, N Canada *72°N 125°14′W*
Sächsisch-Reen/Sächsisch-Regen *see* Reghin
18 *H8* **Sackets Harbor** New York, NE USA *43°57′N 76°06′W*
13 *P14* **Sackville** New Brunswick, SE Canada *45°54′N 64°23′W*
19 *P9* **Saco** Maine, NE USA *43°32′N 70°25′W*
19 *P8* **Saco River** ⇝ Maine/New Hampshire, NE USA
35 *O7* **Sacramento** *state capital* California, W USA *38°35′N 121°30′W*
37 *T14* **Sacramento Mountains** ▲ New Mexico, SW USA
35 *N6* **Sacramento River** ⇝ California, W USA
35 *N5* **Sacramento Valley** *valley* California, W USA
36 *I10* **Sacramento Wash** *valley* Arizona, SW USA
105 *N15* **Sacratif, Cabo** *headland* S Spain *36°41′N 03°30′W*
116 *F9* **Săcueni** *prev.* Săcuieni, *Hung.* Székelyhíd. Bihor, W Romania *47°20′N 22°05′E*
Săcuieni *see* Săcueni
105 *R4* **Sádaba** Aragón, NE Spain *42°15′N 01°16′W*
Sá da Bandeira *see* Lubango
138 *I6* **Şadad** Ḥimṣ, W Syria *34°19′N 36°52′E*
141 *O13* **Şa′dah** NW Yemen *16°59′N 43°45′E*
167 *O16* **Sadao** Songkhla, SW Thailand *06°39′N 100°30′E*
142 *L8* **Sadd-e Dez, Daryācheh-ye** ◎ W Iran
19 *S3* **Saddleback Mountain** *hill* Maine, NE USA
19 *P6* **Saddleback Mountain** ▲ Maine, NE USA *44°57′N 70°27′W*
141 *W13* **Sadḥ** S Oman *17°11′N 55°08′E*
76 *J11* **Sadiola** Kayes, W Mali *13°48′N 11°47′W*
149 *R12* **Sādiqābād** Punjab, E Pakistan *28°16′N 70°10′E*
153 *Y10* **Sadiya** Assam, NE India *27°49′N 95°38′E*
139 *W9* **Sa′dīyah, Hawr as** ◎ E Iraq
165 *N9* **Sado** *var.* Sadoga-shima. *island* C Japan
Sadoga-shima *see* Sado
104 *F12* **Sado, Rio** ⇝ S Portugal
114 *I8* **Sadovets** Pleven, N Bulgaria *43°19′N 24°21′E*
114 *J11* **Sadovo** Plovdiv, C Bulgaria *42°07′N 24°56′E*
127 *O11* **Sadovoye** Respublika Kalmykiya, SW Russian Federation *47°51′N 44°34′E*
105 *W9* **Sa Dragonera** *var.* Isla Dragonera. *island* Islas Baleares, Spain, W Mediterranean Sea
105 *P9* **Saelices** Castilla-La Mancha, C Spain *39°55′N 02°49′W*
Saena Julia *see* Siena
Saetabicula *see* Alzira
114 *O12* **Safaalan** Tekirdağ, NW Turkey *41°26′N 28°07′E*
Safad *see* Tsefat
Şafāqis *see* Sfax
143 *P10* **Şafāshahr** *var.* Deh Bīd. Fārs, C Iran *30°50′N 53°50′E*
192 *I16* **Safata Bay** *bay* Upolu, Samoa, C Pacific Ocean
Safed *see* Tsefat
139 *X11* **Şaffāf, Ḩawr aş** *marshy lake* S Iraq
95 *J16* **Säffle** Värmland, C Sweden *59°08′N 12°55′E*
37 *N15* **Safford** Arizona, SW USA *32°46′N 109°41′W*
74 *E7* **Safi** W Morocco *32°19′N 09°14′W*
126 *J4* **Safonovo** Smolenskaya Oblast′, W Russian Federation *55°05′N 33°12′E*
136 *H11* **Safranbolu** Karabük, NW Turkey *41°16′N 32°41′E*
139 *Y13* **Safwān** Al Başrah, SE Iraq *30°06′N 47°44′E*
158 *J16* **Saga** *var.* Gya′gya. Xizang Zizhiqu, W China *29°22′N 85°19′E*
164 *C14* **Saga** Saga, Kyūshū, SW Japan *33°14′N 130°16′E*
164 *C13* **Saga** *off.* Saga-ken. ◆ *prefecture* Kyūshū, SW Japan
165 *P10* **Sagae** Yamagata, Honshū, C Japan *38°22′N 140°12′E*
166 *L3* **Sagaing** Sagaing, C Burma (Myanmar) *21°55′N 95°56′E*
166 *L5* **Sagaing** ◆ *division* N Burma (Myanmar)
Saga-ken *see* Saga
165 *N13* **Sagamihara** Kanagawa, Honshū, S Japan *35°34′N 139°22′E*
165 *N14* **Sagami-nada** *inlet* SW Japan
Sagan *see* Żagań
29 *Y3* **Saganaga Lake** ◎ Minnesota, N USA
155 *F18* **Sāgar** Karnātaka, W India *14°09′N 75°02′E*
154 *I9* **Sāgar** *prev.* Saugor. Madhya Pradesh, C India *23°53′N 78°46′E*
15 *S8* **Sagard** Québec, SE Canada *48°01′N 70°03′W*
Sagarmāthā *see* Everest, Mount
Sagebrush State *see* Nevada
143 *V11* **Sāghand** Yazd, C Iran *32°33′N 55°12′E*
19 *N14* **Sag Harbor** Long Island, New York, NE USA *40°59′N 72°15′W*
Saghez *see* Saqqez
Saghyz *see* Sagiz
31 *R8* **Saginaw** Michigan, N USA *43°25′N 83°57′W*
31 *R8* **Saginaw Bay** *lake bay* Michigan, N USA
144 *H11* **Sagiz** *Kaz.* Saghyz. Atyrau, W Kazakhstan *48°12′N 54°56′E*
64 *H6* **Saglek Bank** *undersea feature* W Labrador Sea
13 *P5* **Saglek Bay** *bay* SW Labrador Sea
Saglouc/Sagluk *see* Salluit
103 *X15* **Sagone, Golfe de** *gulf* Corse, France, C Mediterranean Sea
105 *P13* **Sagra** ▲ S Spain *37°59′N 02°33′W*
104 *F14* **Sagres** Faro, S Portugal *37°01′N 08°56′W*
37 *S7* **Saguache** Colorado, C USA *38°05′N 106°05′W*
44 *J7* **Sagua de Tánamo** Holguín, E Cuba *20°38′N 75°14′W*
44 *E5* **Sagua la Grande** Villa Clara, C Cuba *22°48′N 80°06′W*
15 *R7* **Saguenay** ⇝ Québec, SE Canada
74 *C9* **Saguia al Hamra** *var.* As Saqia al Hamra. ⇝ N Western Sahara
105 *S9* **Sagunto** *Cat.* Sagunt, *Ar.* Murviedro; *anc.* Saguntum. País Valenciano, E Spain *39°40′N 00°17′W*
Sagunt/Saguntum *see* Sagunto
158 *L16* **Sa′gya** Xizang Zizhiqu, W China *28°51′N 88°00′E*
138 *H10* **Saḩāb** ′Ammān, NW Jordan *31°52′N 36°00′E*
54 *E6* **Sahagún** Córdoba, NW Colombia *08°58′N 75°30′W*
104 *L4* **Sahagún** Castilla-León, N Spain *42°23′N 05°02′W*
141 *X8* **Şaḩam** N Oman *24°06′N 56°52′E*
68 *F9* **Sahara** *desert* Libya/Algeria
Sahara el Gharbîya *see* Şaḩrā′ al Gharbīyah
75 *X9* **Sahara el Sharqîya** *var.* Aş Şaḩrā′ ash Sharqīyah, *Eng.* Arabian Desert, Eastern Desert. *desert* E Egypt
Saharan Atlas *see* Atlas Saharien
152 *J9* **Sahāranpur** Uttar Pradesh, N India *29°58′N 77°33′E*
64 *L10* **Saharan Seamounts** *var.* Saharian Seamounts. *undersea feature* E Atlantic Ocean *25°00′N 20°00′W*
Saharian Seamounts *see* Saharan Seamounts
153 *Q13* **Saharsa** Bihār, NE India *25°54′N 86°36′E*
67 *O7* **Sahel** *physical region* C Africa
153 *R14* **Sāhibganj** Jhārkhand, NE India *25°15′N 87°40′E*
80 *N12* **Sahil** *off.* Gobolka Sahil. ◆ *region* N Somalia
139 *Q7* **Şaḩīlīyah** Al Anbār, C Iraq *33°43′N 42°42′E*
138 *H4* **Şaḩīlīyah, Jibāl as** ▲ NW Syria
114 *M13* **Şahin** Tekirdağ, NW Turkey *41°01′N 26°51′E*
149 *U8* **Sāhīwāl** Punjab, E Pakistan *31°57′N 72°22′E*
149 *U9* **Sāhīwāl** *prev.* Montgomery. Punjab, E Pakistan *30°40′N 73°05′E*
141 *W11* **Şaḩmah, Ramlat as** *desert* C Oman
75 *U9* **Şaḩrā′ al Gharbīyah** *var.* Sahara el Gharbîya, *Eng.* Western Desert. *desert* C Egypt
139 *T13* **Şaḩrā′ al Ḩijārah** *desert* S Iraq
40 *H5* **Sahuaripa** Sonora, NW Mexico *29°02′N 109°14′W*
36 *M16* **Sahuarita** Arizona, SW USA *31°24′N 110°55′W*
40 *L13* **Sahuayo** *var.* Sahuayo de José María Morelos; *prev.* Sahuayo de Díaz, Sahuayo de Porfirio Díaz. Michoacán, SW Mexico *20°05′N 102°42′W*
Sahuayo de Díaz/Sahuayo de José Mariá Morelos/ Sahuayo de Porfirio Díaz *see* Sahuayo
173 *W8* **Sahul Shelf** *undersea feature* N Timor Sea
167 *P17* **Sai Buri** Pattani, SW Thailand *06°42′N 101°37′E*
74 *I6* **Saïda** NW Algeria *34°50′N 00°10′E*
138 *G7* **Saïda** *var.* Şaydā, Sayida; *anc.* Sidon. W Lebanon *33°20′N 35°24′E*
Sa′īdābād *see* Sīrjān
80 *B13* **Sa′id Bundas** Western Bahr el Ghazal, SW Sudan *08°24′N 24°53′E*
186 *E7* **Saidor** Madang, N Papua New Guinea *05°38′S 146°28′E*
153 *S13* **Saidpur** *var.* Syedpur. Rajshahi, NW Bangladesh *25°48′N 89°E*
149 *U5* **Saidu Sharif** *var.* Mingora, Mongora. North-West Frontier Province, N Pakistan *34°45′N 72°21′E*
108 *C7* **Saignelégier** Jura, NW Switzerland *47°18′N 07°03′E*
164 *H11* **Saigō** Shimane, Dōgo, SW Japan *36°12′N 133°18′E*
Saigon *see* Hô Chi Minh
163 *P11* **SaihanTal** *var.* Sonid Youqi. Nei Mongol Zizhiqu, N China *42°45′N 112°36′E*
162 *I12* **Saihan Toroi** Nei Mongol Zizhiqu, N China *41°44′N 100°29′E*
Sai Hun *see* Syr Darya
92 *M11* **Saija** Lappi, NE Finland *67°07′N 28°46′E*
164 *G14* **Saijō** Ehime, Shikoku, SW Japan *33°55′N 133°10′E*
164 *E15* **Saiki** Ōita, Kyūshū, SW Japan *32°57′N 131°52′E*
93 *N18* **Saimaa** ◎ SE Finland
93 *N18* **Saimaa Canal** *Fin.* Saimaan Kanava, *Rus.* Saymenskiy Kanal. *canal* Finland/Russian Federation
Saimaan Kanava *see* Saimaa Canal
40 *L10* **San Alto** Zacatecas, C Mexico *23°36′N 103°14′W*
96 *L12* **St Abb′s Head** *headland* SE Scotland, United Kingdom *55°54′N 02°07′W*
11 *Y16* **St. Adolphe** Manitoba, S Canada *49°39′N 96°55′W*
103 *O15* **St-Affrique** Aveyron, S France *43°57′N 02°52′E*
15 *Q10* **St-Agapit** Québec, SE Canada *46°22′N 71°37′W*
97 *O21* **St Albans** *anc.* Verulamium. E England, United Kingdom *51°46′N 00°21′W*
18 *L6* **Saint Albans** Vermont, NE USA *44°49′N 73°07′W*
21 *Q5* **Saint Albans** West Virginia, NE USA *38°21′N 81°47′W*
St. Alban′s Head *see* St Aldhelm′s Head
11 *Q14* **St. Albert** Alberta, SW Canada *53°38′N 113°38′W*
97 *M24* **St Aldhelm′s Head** *var.* St. Alban′s Head. *headland* S England, United Kingdom *50°34′N 02°04′W*
15 *O11* **St-Alexis-des-Monts** Québec, SE Canada *46°30′N 73°08′W*
103 *P2* **St-Amand-les-Eaux** Nord, N France *50°27′N 03°25′E*
103 *O9* **St-Amand-Montrond** *var.* St-Amand-Mont-Rond. Cher, C France *46°43′N 02°29′E*
173 *P16* **St-André** NE Réunion
14 *M12* **St-André-Avellin** Québec, SE Canada *45°45′N 75°04′W*
Saint-André, Cap *see* Vilanandro, Tanjona
102 *K12* **St-André-de-Cubzac** Gironde, SW France *45°01′N 00°26′W*
96 *K11* **St Andrews** E Scotland, United Kingdom *56°20′N 02°49′W*
23 *Q9* **Saint Andrews Bay** *bay* Florida, SE USA
23 *W7* **Saint Andrew Sound** *sound* Georgia, SE USA
Saint Anna Trough *see* Svyataya Anna Trough
44 *J11* **St. Ann′s Bay** C Jamaica *18°26′N 77°12′W*
13 *T10* **St. Anthony** Newfoundland and Labrador, SE Canada *51°22′N 55°34′W*
33 *R13* **Saint Anthony** Idaho, NW USA *43°56′N 111°38′W*
182 *M11* **Saint Arnaud** Victoria, SE Australia *36°39′S 143°15′E*
185 *I15* **St.Arnaud Range** ▲ South Island, New Zealand
13 *R10* **St-Augustin** Québec, E Canada *51°13′N 58°39′W*
23 *X9* **Saint Augustine** Florida, SE USA *29°54′N 81°19′W*
97 *H24* **St Austell** SW England, United Kingdom *50°21′N 04°47′W*
103 *T4* **St-Avold** Moselle, NE France *49°06′N 06°43′E*
103 *N17* **St-Barthélemy** ▲ S France
102 *L17* **St-Béat** Haute-Garonne, S France *42°55′N 00°39′E*
97 *I15* **St Bees Head** *headland* NW England, United Kingdom *54°30′N 03°39′W*
173 *P16* **St-Benoit** E Réunion
103 *T13* **St-Bonnet** Hautes-Alpes, SE France *44°41′N 06°04′E*
St.Botolph′s Town *see* Boston
97 *G21* **St Brides Bay** *inlet* SW Wales, United Kingdom
102 *H5* **St-Brieuc** Côtes d′Armor, NW France *48°31′N 02°45′W*
102 *H5* **St-Brieuc, Baie de** *bay* NW France
102 *L7* **St-Calais** Sarthe, NW France *47°55′N 00°48′E*
15 *Q10* **St-Casimir** Québec, SE Canada *46°40′N 72°05′W*
14 *H16* **St. Catharines** Ontario, S Canada *43°10′N 79°15′W*
45 *R14* **St. Catherine, Mount** ▲ N Grenada *12°10′N 61°41′W*
64 *C11* **St Catherine Point** *headland* E Bermuda
23 *X6* **Saint Catherines Island** *island* Georgia, SE USA
97 *M24* **St Catherine′s Point** *headland* S England, United Kingdom *50°34′N 01°17′W*
103 *N13* **St-Céré** Lot, S France *44°52′N 01°53′E*
108 *A10* **St. Cergue** Vaud, W Switzerland *46°25′N 06°10′E*
103 *R11* **St-Chamond** Loire, E France *45°29′N 04°32′E*
33 *S16* **Saint Charles** Idaho, NW USA *42°05′N 111°23′W*
27 *X4* **Saint Charles** Missouri, C USA *38°48′N 90°29′W*
103 *P13* **St-Chély-d′Apcher** Lozère, S France *44°51′N 03°16′E*
Saint Christopher and Nevis, Federation of *see* Saint Kitts and Nevis
Saint Christopher-Nevis *see* Saint Kitts and Nevis
31 *S9* **Saint Clair** Michigan, N USA *42°49′N 82°29′W*
183 *O17* **St. Clair, Lake** ◎ Tasmania, SE Australia
14 *C17* **St. Clair, Lake** *var.* Lac à L′Eau Claire. ◎ Canada/USA
31 *S10* **Saint Clair Shores** Michigan, N USA *42°30′N 82°53′W*
103 *S10* **St-Claude** *anc.* Condate. Jura, E France *46°23′N 05°52′E*
45 *X6* **St-Claude** Basse Terre, SW Guadeloupe *16°02′N 61°42′W*
23 *X12* **Saint Cloud** Florida, SE USA *28°15′N 81°15′W*
29 *U8* **Saint Cloud** Minnesota, N USA *45°34′N 94°10′W*
45 *T9* **Saint Croix** *island* S Virgin Islands (US)
30 *J4* **Saint Croix Flowage** ⊠ Wisconsin, N USA
19 *T5* **Saint Croix River** ⇝ Canada/USA
29 *W7* **Saint Croix River** ⇝ Minnesota/Wisconsin, N USA
45 *S14* **St.David′s** SE Grenada *12°01′N 61°40′W*
97 *H21* **St David′s** SW Wales, United Kingdom *51°53′N 05°16′W*
97 *G21* **St David′s Head** *headland* SW Wales, United Kingdom *51°54′N 05°19′W*
64 *C12* **St David′s Island** *island* E Bermuda
173 *O16* **St-Denis** ○ (Réunion) NW Réunion *20°55′S 14°34′E*
103 *U6* **St-Dié** Vosges, NE France *48°17′N 06°57′E*
103 *R5* **St-Dizier** *anc.* Desiderii Fanum. Haute-Marne, N France *48°39′N 05°00′E*
15 *N11* **St-Donat** Québec, SE Canada *46°19′N 74°15′W*
15 *N11* **Ste-Adèle** Québec, SE Canada *45°58′N 74°10′W*
15 *N11* **Ste-Agathe-des-Monts** Québec, SE Canada *46°03′N 74°19′W*
11 *Y16* **Ste. Anne** Manitoba, S Canada *49°40′N 96°40′W*
45 *R12* **Ste-Anne** Grande Terre, E Guadeloupe *16°13′N 61°23′W*
45 *Y6* **Ste-Anne** SE Martinique *14°26′N 60°53′W*
15 *Q10* **Ste-Anne** ⇝ Québec, SE Canada
172 *I16* **Sainte Anne** *island* Inner Islands, NE Seychelles
15 *W6* **Ste-Anne-des-Monts** Québec, SE Canada *49°07′N 66°29′W*
14 *M10* **Ste-Anne-du-Lac** Québec, SE Canada *46°51′N 75°20′W*
15 *S10* **Ste-Apolline** Québec, SE Canada *46°47′N 70°15′W*
15 *R10* **Ste-Claire** Québec, SE Canada *46°30′N 70°40′W*
15 *Q10* **Ste-Croix** Québec, SE Canada *46°36′N 71°42′W*
108 *B8* **Ste. Croix** Vaud, SW Switzerland *46°50′N 06°31′E*
103 *P14* **Ste-Énimie** Lozère, S France *44°21′N 03°26′E*
27 *Y6* **Sainte Genevieve** Missouri, C USA *37°57′N 90°01′W*
103 *S12* **St-Egrève** Isère, E France *45°15′N 05°41′E*
39 *T12* **Saint Elias, Cape** *headland* Kayak Island, Alaska, USA *59°48′N 144°36′W*
39 *U11* **St Elias, Mount** ▲ Alaska, USA *60°18′N 140°57′W*
10 *G8* **Saint Elias Mountains** ▲ Canada/USA
55 *Y10* **St-Élie** N French Guiana *04°50′N 53°21′W*
103 *O10* **St-Eloy-les-Mines** Puy-de-Dôme, C France *46°07′N 02°50′E*
15 *R10* **Ste-Marie** Québec, SE Canada *46°28′N 71°00′W*
45 *Q11* **Ste-Marie** NE Martinique *14°47′N 61°00′W*
173 *P16* **Ste-Marie** NE Réunion
103 *U6* **Ste-Marie-aux-Mines** Haut-Rhin, NE France *48°16′N 07°12′E*
Sainte Marie, Cap *see* Vohimena, Tanjona
102 *L8* **Ste-Maure-de-Touraine** Indre-et-Loire, C France *47°06′N 00°38′E*
103 *R4* **Ste-Menehould** Marne, NE France *49°06′N 04°54′E*
Ste-Perpétue *see* Ste-Perpétue-de-l′Islet
15 *S9* **Ste-Perpétue-de-l′Islet** *var.* Ste-Perpétue. Québec, SE Canada *47°02′N 69°58′W*
45 *X11* **Ste-Rose** Basse Terre, N Guadeloupe *16°20′N 61°42′W*
173 *P16* **Ste-Rose** E Réunion
11 *W15* **Ste. Rose du Lac** Manitoba, S Canada *51°04′N 99°31′W*
102 *J11* **Saintes** *anc.* Mediolanum. Charente-Maritime, W France *45°45′N 00°37′W*
45 *X7* **Saintes, Canal des** *channel* SW Guadeloupe
Saintes, Îles des *see* les Saintes
173 *P16* **Ste-Suzanne** N Réunion
15 *P10* **Ste-Thècle** Québec, SE Canada *46°48′N 72°31′W*
103 *Q12* **St-Étienne** Loire, E France *45°26′N 04°23′E*
102 *M4* **St-Étienne-du-Rouvray** Seine-Maritime, N France *49°22′N 01°07′E*
Saint Eustatius *see* Sint Eustatius
15 *R7* **Ste-Marguerite** ⇝ Québec, SE Canada
14 *M11* **Ste-Véronique** Québec, SE Canada *46°30′N 74°58′W*
15 *P7* **St-Félicien** Québec, SE Canada *48°38′N 72°29′W*
15 *O11* **St-Félix-de-Valois** Québec, SE Canada *46°10′N 73°26′W*
103 *Y14* **St-Florent** Corse, France, C Mediterranean Sea *42°41′N 09°19′E*
103 *Y14* **St-Florent, Golfe de** *gulf* Corse, France, C Mediterranean Sea
103 *P6* **St-Florentin** Yonne, C France *48°00′N 03°46′E*
103 *N9* **St-Florent-sur-Cher** Cher, C France *47°00′N 02°13′E*
103 *P12* **St-Flour** Cantal, C France *45°02′N 03°05′E*
26 *H2* **Saint Francis** Kansas, C USA *39°45′N 101°31′W*
83 *H26* **St. Francis, Cape** *headland* S South Africa *34°11′S 24°45′E*
27 *X10* **Saint Francis River** ⇝ Arkansas/Missouri, C USA
22 *J8* **Saint Francisville** Louisiana, S USA *30°46′N 91°22′W*
45 *Y6* **St-François** Grande Terre, E Guadeloupe *16°15′N 61°17′W*
15 *Q12* **St-François** ⇝ Québec, SE Canada
27 *X7* **Saint Francois Mountains** ▲ Missouri, C USA
Saint Gall *see* St-Gall/Saint Gall/ St.Gallen
St-Gall/Saint Gall/St. Gallen *see* Sankt Gallen
102 *L16* **St-Gaudens** Haute-Garonne, S France *43°07′N 00°43′E*
15 *R12* **St-Gédéon** Québec, SE Canada *45°51′N 70°36′W*
181 *X10* **Saint George** Queensland, E Australia *28°05′S 148°40′E*
64 *B12* **St George** N Bermuda *32°24′N 64°42′W*
38 *K15* **Saint George** Saint George Island, Alaska, USA *56°34′N 169°30′W*
21 *S14* **Saint George** South Carolina, SE USA *33°12′N 80°34′W*
36 *J8* **Saint George** Utah, W USA *37°06′N 113°35′W*
13 *R12* **St. George, Cape** *headland* Newfoundland and Labrador, E Canada *48°26′N 59°17′W*
186 *I6* **St. George, Cape** *headland* New Ireland, NE Papua New Guinea *04°49′S 152°52′E*
38 *J15* **Saint George Island** *island* Pribilof Islands, Alaska, USA
23 *S10* **Saint George Island** *island* Florida, SE USA
99 *J19* **Saint-Georges** Liège, E Belgium *50°36′N 05°20′E*
15 *R11* **St-Georges** Québec, SE Canada *46°08′N 70°40′W*
55 *Z11* **St-Georges** E French Guiana *03°55′N 51°49′W*
45 *R14* **St. George′s** ● (Grenada) SW Grenada *12°04′N 61°45′W*
13 *R12* **St. George′s Bay** *inlet* Newfoundland and Labrador, E Canada
97 *G21* **Saint George′s Channel** *channel* Ireland/Wales, United Kingdom
186 *H6* **St. George′s Channel** *channel* NE Papua New Guinea
64 *B11* **St George′s Island** *island* E Bermuda
99 *I21* **Saint-Gérard** Namur, S Belgium *50°20′N 04°47′E*
St-Germain *see* St-Germain-en-Laye
15 *P12* **St-Germain-de-Grantham** Québec, SE Canada *45°49′N 72°32′W*
103 *N5* **St-Germain-en-Laye** *var.* St-Germain. Yvelines, N France *48°53′N 02°04′E*
102 *H8* **St-Gildas, Pointe du** *headland* NW France *47°09′N 02°25′W*
103 *R15* **St-Gilles** Gard, S France *43°41′N 04°24′E*
102 *I9* **St-Gilles-Croix-de-Vie** Vendée, NW France *46°41′N 01°55′W*
173 *O16* **St-Gilles-les-Bains** W Réunion *21°02′S 55°14′E*
102 *M16* **St-Girons** Ariège, S France *42°58′N 01°07′E*
Saint Gotthard *see* Szentgotthárd
108 *G9* **St. Gotthard Tunnel** *tunnel* Ticino, S Switzerland
97 *H22* **St Govan′s Head** *headland* SW Wales, United Kingdom *51°35′N 04°55′W*
34 *M7* **Saint Helena** California, W USA *38°29′N 122°30′W*
65 *F24* **Saint Helena** ◇ UK *dependent territory* C Atlantic Ocean
67 *O12* **Saint Helena** *island* C Atlantic Ocean
65 *M16* **Saint Helena Fracture Zone** *tectonic feature* C Atlantic Ocean
34 *M7* **Saint Helena, Mount** ▲ California, W USA *38°40′N 122°39′W*
21 *S15* **Saint Helena Sound** *inlet* South Carolina, SE USA
31 *Q7* **Saint Helen, Lake** ◎ Michigan, N USA
183 *Q16* **Saint Helens** Tasmania, SE Australia *41°21′S 148°15′E*
97 *K18* **St Helens** NW England, United Kingdom *53°28′N 02°44′W*
32 *G10* **Saint Helens** Oregon, NW USA *45°54′N 122°50′W*
32 *H10* **Saint Helens, Mount** ⌂ Washington, NW USA *46°24′N 121°49′W*
97 *L26* **St Helier** ○ (Jersey) S Jersey, Channel Islands *49°12′N 02°07′W*
15 *S9* **St-Hilarion** Québec, SE Canada *47°34′N 70°24′W*
99 *K22* **Saint-Hubert** Luxembourg, SE Belgium *50°02′N 05°23′E*
15 *P12* **St-Hyacinthe** Québec, SE Canada *45°38′N 72°57′W*
St.Iago de la Vega *see* Spanish Town
31 *Q4* **Saint Ignace** Michigan, N USA *45°53′N 84°44′W*
15 *O10* **St-Ignace-du-Lac** Québec, SE Canada *46°43′N 73°49′W*
12 *D12* **St. Ignace Island** *island* Ontario, S Canada
108 *C7* **St. Imier** Bern, W Switzerland *47°09′N 06°55′E*
97 *G25* **St Ives** SW England, United Kingdom *50°12′N 05°29′W*
29 *U10* **Saint James** Minnesota, N USA *44°00′N 94°36′W*
10 *I15* **St. James, Cape** *headland* Graham Island, British Columbia, SW Canada *51°57′N 131°04′W*
15 *O13* **St-Jean** *var.* St-Jean-sur-Richelieu. Québec, SE Canada *45°15′N 73°16′W*
55 *X9* **St-Jean** NW French Guiana *05°25′N 54°05′W*
Saint-Jean-d′Acre *see* Akko
102 *K11* **St-Jean-d′Angély** Charente-Maritime, W France *45°57′N 00°31′W*
103 *N7* **St-Jean-de-Braye** Loiret, C France *47°54′N 01°58′E*
102 *I16* **St-Jean-de-Luz** Pyrénées-Atlantiques, SW France *43°24′N 01°40′W*
103 *T12* **St-Jean-de-Maurienne** Savoie, E France *45°17′N 06°21′E*
102 *I9* **St-Jean-de-Monts** Vendée, NW France *46°45′N 02°00′W*
103 *Q14* **St-Jean-du-Gard** Gard, S France *44°06′N 03°49′E*
15 *Q7* **St-Jean, Lac** ◎ Québec, SE Canada
102 *I16* **St-Jean-Pied-de-Port** Pyrénées-Atlantiques, SW France *43°10′N 01°14′W*
15 *S9* **St-Jean-Port-Joli** Québec, SE Canada *47°13′N 70°16′W*
St-Jean-sur-Richelieu *see* St-Jean
15 *N12* **St-Jérôme** Québec, SE Canada *45°47′N 74°01′W*
25 *T5* **Saint Jo** Texas, SW USA *33°42′N 97°33′W*
13 *O15* **St. John** New Brunswick, SE Canada *45°16′N 66°03′W*
26 *L6* **Saint John** Kansas, C USA *37°59′N 98°44′W*
19 *Q2* **Saint John** *Fr.* Saint-John. ⇝ Canada/USA
76 *K16* **Saint John** ⇝ C Liberia
45 *T9* **Saint John** *island* C Virgin Islands (US)
Saint-John *see* Saint John
22 *I6* **Saint John, Lake** ◎ Louisiana, S USA
45 *W10* **St John′s** ● (Antigua and Barbuda) Antigua, Antigua and Barbuda *17°06′N 61°50′W*
13 *V12* **St. John′s** *province capital* Newfoundland and Labrador, E Canada *47°34′N 52°41′W*
37 *O12* **Saint Johns** Arizona, SW USA *34°28′N 109°22′W*
31 *Q9* **Saint Johns** Michigan, N USA *43°01′N 84°31′W*
13 *V12* **St. John′s** ✕ Newfoundland and Labrador, E Canada *47°22′N 52°45′W*
23 *X11* **Saint Johns River** ⇝ Florida, SE USA
103 *Q11* **St-Just-St-Rambert** Loire, E France *45°30′N 04°13′E*
45 *N12* **St. Joseph** W Dominica *15°24′N 61°26′W*
173 *P17* **St-Joseph** S Réunion
22 *J6* **Saint Joseph** Louisiana, S USA *31°56′N 91°14′W*
31 *O10* **Saint Joseph** Michigan, N USA *42°05′N 86°30′W*
27 *R3* **Saint Joseph** Missouri, C USA *39°46′N 94°49′W*
20 *I10* **Saint Joseph** Tennessee, S USA *35°02′N 87°29′W*
22 *R9* **Saint Joseph Bay** *bay* Florida, SE USA
15 *R11* **St-Joseph-de-Beauce** Québec, SE Canada *46°20′N 70°52′W*
12 *C10* **St. Joseph, Lake** ◎ Ontario, C Canada

◆ Country ● Country Capital ◇ Dependent Territory ○ Dependent Territory Capital ◆ Administrative Regions ✕ International Airport ▲ Mountain ▲ Mountain Range ⌂ Volcano ⇝ River ◎ Lake ⊠ Reservoir

31 Q11 **Saint Joseph River** N USA
14 C11 **Saint Joseph's Island** *island* Ontario, S Canada
15 N11 **St-Jovite** Québec, SE Canada *46°07′N 74°35′W*
121 P16 **St Julian's** N Malta *35°55′N 14°29′E*
St-Julien *see* St-Julien-en-Genevois
103 T10 **St-Julien-en-Genevois** *var.* St-Julien. Haute-Savoie, E France *46°07′N 06°06′E*
102 M11 **St-Junien** Haute-Vienne, C France *45°52′N 00°54′E*
96 D8 **St Kilda** *island* NW Scotland, United Kingdom
45 V10 **Saint Kitts** *island* Saint Kitts and Nevis
45 U10 **Saint Kitts and Nevis** *off.* Federation of Saint Christopher and Nevis, *var.* Saint Christopher-Nevis. ◆ *commonwealth republic* E West Indies
11 X16 **St. Laurent** Manitoba, S Canada *50°20′N 97°55′W*
St-Laurent *see* St-Laurent-du-Maroni
55 X9 **St-Laurent-du-Maroni** *var.* St-Laurent. NW French Guiana *05°29′N 54°03′W*
St-Laurent, Fleuve *see* St. Lawrence
102 J12 **St-Laurent-Médoc** Gironde, SW France *45°11′N 00°50′W*
13 N12 **St. Lawrence** *Fr.* Fleuve St-Laurent. Canada/USA
13 Q12 **St. Lawrence, Gulf of** *gulf* NW Atlantic Ocean
38 K10 **Saint Lawrence Island** *island* Alaska, USA
14 M14 **Saint Lawrence River** Canada/USA
99 L25 **Saint-Léger** Luxembourg, SE Belgium *49°36′N 05°39′E*
13 N14 **St. Léonard** New Brunswick, SE Canada *47°10′N 67°55′W*
15 P11 **St-Léonard** Québec, SE Canada *46°06′N 72°18′W*
173 O17 **St-Leu** W Réunion *21°09′S 55°17′E*
102 J4 **St-Lô** *anc.* Briovera, Laudus. Manche, N France *49°07′N 01°08′W*
11 T15 **St. Louis** Saskatchewan, S Canada *52°50′N 105°43′W*
103 V7 **St-Louis** Haut-Rhin, NE France *47°35′N 07°34′E*
173 O17 **St-Louis** S Réunion
76 G10 **Saint Louis** NW Senegal *15°59′N 16°30′W*
27 X4 **Saint Louis** Missouri, C USA *38°38′N 90°15′W*
29 W5 **Saint Louis River** Minnesota, N USA
103 T7 **St-Loup-sur-Semouse** Haute-Saône, E France *47°53′N 06°15′E*
15 O12 **St-Luc** Québec, SE Canada *45°19′N 73°18′W*
45 X13 **Saint Lucia** ◆ *commonwealth republic* SE West Indies
47 S3 **Saint Lucia** *island* SE West Indies
83 L22 **St. Lucia, Cape** *headland* E South Africa *28°29′S 32°26′E*
45 Y13 **Saint Lucia Channel** *channel* Martinique/Saint Lucia
23 Y14 **Saint Lucie Canal** *canal* Florida, SE USA
23 Z13 **Saint Lucie Inlet** *inlet* Florida, SE USA
96 L2 **St Magnus Bay** *bay* N Scotland, United Kingdom
102 K10 **St-Maixent-l'École** Deux-Sèvres, W France *46°24′N 00°13′W*
11 Y16 **St. Malo** Manitoba, S Canada *49°16′N 96°58′W*
102 I5 **St-Malo** Ille-et-Vilaine, NW France *48°39′N 02°W*
102 H4 **St-Malo, Golfe de** *gulf* NW France
44 L9 **St-Marc** C Haiti *19°08′N 72°41′W*
44 L9 **St-Marc, Canal de** *channel* W Haiti
103 S12 **St-Marcellin-le-Mollard** Isère, E France *45°12′N 05°18′E*
55 Y12 **Saint-Marcel, Mont** ▲ S French Guiana *2°32′N 53°00′E*
96 K5 **St Margaret's Hope** NE Scotland, United Kingdom *58°50′N 02°57′W*
32 M9 **Saint Maries** Idaho, NW USA *47°19′N 116°37′W*
23 T9 **Saint Marks** Florida, SE USA *30°09′N 84°12′W*
108 D11 **St. Martin** Valais, SW Switzerland *46°09′N 07°27′E*
Saint Martin *see* Sint Maarten
31 O5 **Saint Martin Island** *island* Michigan, N USA
22 I9 **Saint Martinville** Louisiana, S USA *30°09′N 91°51′W*
185 E20 **St. Mary, Mount** ▲ South Island, New Zealand *44°16′S 169°42′E*
186 E8 **St. Mary, Mount** ▲ S Papua New Guinea *08°06′S 147°00′E*
182 I6 **Saint Mary Peak** ▲ South Australia *31°25′S 138°39′E*
183 Q16 **Saint Marys** Tasmania, SE Australia *41°34′S 148°13′E*
14 E16 **St. Marys** Ontario, S Canada *43°15′N 81°08′W*
38 M11 **Saint Marys** Alaska, USA *62°03′N 163°10′W*
23 W8 **Saint Marys** Georgia, SE USA *30°44′N 81°30′W*
27 P4 **Saint Marys** Kansas, C USA *39°09′N 96°00′W*
31 Q4 **Saint Marys** Ohio, N USA *40°31′N 84°22′W*
21 R3 **Saint Marys** West Virginia, NE USA *39°24′N 81°13′W*
23 W8 **Saint Marys River** Florida/Georgia, SE USA
31 Q4 **Saint Marys River** Michigan, N USA
102 D6 **St-Mathieu, Pointe** *headland* NW France *48°17′N 04°56′W*
38 J12 **Saint Matthew Island** *island* Alaska, USA
21 R13 **Saint Matthews** South Carolina, SE USA *33°40′N 80°44′W*
St.Matthew's Island *see* Zadetkyi Kyun
186 G4 **St.Matthias Group** *island group* NE Papua New Guinea
108 C11 **St. Maurice** Valais, SW Switzerland *46°09′N 07°28′E*
15 P9 **St-Maurice** Québec, SE Canada
102 J13 **St-Médard-en-Jalles** Gironde, SW France *44°54′N 00°43′W*
39 N10 **Saint Michael** Alaska, USA *63°28′N 162°02′W*
15 N10 **St-Michel-des-Saints** Québec, SE Canada *46°39′N 73°54′W*
103 S5 **St-Mihiel** Meuse, NE France *48°57′N 05°33′E*
108 J10 **St. Moritz** *Ger.* Sankt Moritz, *Rmsch.* San Murezzan. Graubünden, SE Switzerland *46°30′N 09°51′E*
102 H8 **St-Nazaire** Loire-Atlantique, NW France *47°17′N 02°12′W*
Saint Nicholas *see* São Nicolau
Saint-Nicolas *see* Sint-Niklaas
103 N1 **St-Omer** Pas-de-Calais, N France *50°45′N 02°15′E*
102 J11 **Saintonge** *cultural region* W France
15 S9 **St-Pacôme** Québec, SE Canada *47°22′N 69°56′W*
15 S10 **St-Pamphile** Québec, SE Canada *46°57′N 69°46′W*
15 S9 **St-Pascal** Québec, SE Canada *47°32B 69°48′W*
14 J11 **St-Patrice, Lac** ◎ Québec, SE Canada
11 R14 **St. Paul** Alberta, SW Canada *54°00′N 111°18′W*
173 O16 **St-Paul** NW Réunion
38 K14 **Saint Paul** Saint Paul Island, Alaska, USA *57°08′N 170°13′W*
29 V8 **Saint Paul** *state capital* Minnesota, N USA *45°N 93°10′W*
29 P15 **Saint Paul** Nebraska, C USA *41°13′N 98°26′W*
21 P7 **Saint Paul** Virginia, NE USA *36°53′N 82°18′W*
77 Q17 **Saint Paul, Cape** *headland* S Ghana *05°44′N 00°55′E*
103 O17 **St-Paul-de-Fenouillet** Pyrénées-Orientales, S France *42°49′N 02°29′E*
65 K14 **Saint Paul Fracture Zone** *tectonic feature* E Atlantic Ocean
38 J14 **Saint Paul Island** *island* Pribilof Islands, Alaska, USA
102 J15 **St-Paul-les-Dax** Landes, SW France *43°45′N 01°01′W*
21 U11 **Saint Pauls** North Carolina, SE USA *34°45′N 78°56′W*
Saint Paul's Bay *see* San Pawl il-Baħar
191 R16 **St Paul's Point** *headland* Pitcairn Island, Pitcairn Islands
29 U10 **Saint Peter** Minnesota, N USA *44°21′N 93°58′W*
97 L26 **St Peter Port** ○ (Guernsey) C Guernsey, Channel Islands *49°28′N 02°33′W*
23 V13 **Saint Petersburg** Florida, SE USA *27°47′N 82°37′W*
Saint Petersburg *see* Sankt-Peterburg
23 V13 **Saint Petersburg Beach** Florida, SE USA *27°43′N 82°43′W*
173 P17 **St-Philippe** SE Réunion *21°21′S 55°46′E*
45 Q11 **St-Pierre** NW Martinique *14°44′N 61°11′W*
173 O17 **St-Pierre** SW Réunion
13 S13 **St-Pierre and Miquelon** *Fr.* Îles St-Pierre et Miquelon. ◇ *French territorial collectivity* NE North America
15 P11 **St-Pierre, Lac** ◎ Québec, SE Canada
102 F5 **St-Pol-de-Léon** Finistère, NW France *48°42′N 04°00′W*
103 O2 **St-Pol-sur-Ternoise** Pas-de-Calais, N France *50°22′N 02°21′E*
St. Pons *see* St-Pons-de-Thomières
103 O16 **St-Pons-de-Thomières** *var.* St. Pons. Hérault, S France *43°28′N 02°48′E*
103 P10 **St-Pourçain-sur-Sioule** Allier, C France *46°19′N 03°16′E*
15 S11 **St-Prosper** Québec, SE Canada *46°14′N 70°28′W*
103 P3 **St-Quentin** Aisne, N France *49°51′N 03°17′E*
15 R10 **St-Raphaël** Québec, SE Canada *46°47′N 70°46′W*
103 U15 **St-Raphaël** Var, SE France *43°26′N 06°46′E*
15 Q10 **St-Raymond** Québec, SE Canada *46°53′N 71°49′W*
33 O9 **Saint Regis** Montana, NW USA *47°18′N 115°06′W*
18 J7 **Saint Regis River** New York, NE USA
103 R15 **St-Rémy-de-Provence** Bouches-du-Rhône, SE France *43°48′N 04°49′E*
102 M9 **St-Savin** Vienne, W France *46°34′N 00°53′E*
Saint-Sébastien,Cap *see* Anorontany, Tanjona
23 X7 **Saint Simons Island** *island* Georgia, SE USA
191 Y2 **Saint Stanislas Bay** *bay* Kiritimati, E Kiribati
13 O15 **St. Stephen** New Brunswick, SE Canada *45°12′N 67°18′W*
39 X12 **Saint Terese** Alaska, USA *58°28′N 134°46′W*
14 E17 **St. Thomas** Ontario, S Canada *42°46′N 81°12′W*
29 Q2 **Saint Thomas** North Dakota, N USA *48°37′N 97°28′W*
45 T9 **Saint Thomas** *island* W Virgin Islands (US)
Saint Thomas *see* São Tomé, Sao Tome and Principe
Saint Thomas *see* Charlotte Amalie, Virgin Islands (US)
15 P10 **St-Tite** Québec, SE Canada *46°42′N 72°32′W*
Saint-Trond *see* Sint-Truiden
103 U16 **St-Tropez** Var, SE France *43°16′N 06°39′E*
Saint Ubes *see* Setúbal
102 L3 **St-Valéry-en-Caux** Seine-Maritime, N France *49°53′N 00°42′E*
103 Q9 **St-Vallier** Saône-et-Loire, C France *46°39′N 04°19′E*
106 B7 **St-Vincent** Valle d'Aosta, NW Italy *45°47′N 07°42′E*
45 Q14 **Saint Vincent** *island* N Saint Vincent and the Grenadines
Saint Vincent *see* São Vicente
45 W14 **Saint Vincent and the Grenadines** ◆ *commonwealth republic* SE West Indies
Saint-Vincent, Cap *see* Ankaboa, Tanjona
Saint Vincent, Cape *see* São Vicente, Cabo de
102 I15 **St-Vincent-de-Tyrosse** Landes, SW France *43°39′N 01°16′W*
182 I9 **Saint Vincent, Gulf** *gulf* South Australia
23 R10 **Saint Vincent Island** *island* Florida, SE USA
45 T12 **Saint Vincent Passage** *passage* Saint Lucia/Saint Vincent and the Grenadines
183 N18 **Saint Vincent, Point** *headland* Tasmania, SE Australia *43°19′S 145°50′E*
Saint-Vith *see* Sankt-Vith
11 S14 **St. Walburg** Saskatchewan, S Canada *53°38′N 109°12′W*
St Wolfgangsee *see* Wolfgangsee
102 M11 **St-Yrieix-la-Perche** Haute-Vienne, C France *45°31′N 01°12′E*
Saint Yves *see* Setúbal
188 H5 **Saipan** *island* ● (Northern Mariana Islands) S Northern Mariana Islands
188 H6 **Saipan Channel** *channel* S Northern Mariana Islands
188 H6 **Saipan International** ✕ Saipan, S Northern Mariana Islands
74 G6 **Sais** ✕ (Fès) C Morocco *33°58′N 04°48′W*
Saishū *see* Cheju-do
Saishū *see* Cheju
102 J16 **Saison** SW France
169 R10 **Sai, Sungai** Borneo, N Indonesia
165 N13 **Saitama** *off.* Saitama-ken. ◐ *prefecture* Honshū, S Japan
Saitama *see* Urawa
Saitama-ken *see* Saitama
Saiyid Abid *see* Sayyid 'Abīd
57 J19 **Sajama, Nevado** ▲ W Bolivia *17°57′S 68°51′W*
141 V13 **Sājir, Ras** *headland* S Oman *16°42′N 53°40′E*
111 M20 **Sajószentpéter** Borsod-Abaúj-Zemplén, NE Hungary *48°13′N 20°43′E*
83 F24 **Sak** SW South Africa
81 J18 **Saka** Coast, E Kenya *0°11′S 39°27′E*
167 P11 **Sa Kaeo** Prachin Buri, C Thailand *13°47′N 102°03′E*
164 J14 **Sakai** Ōsaka, Honshū, SW Japan *34°35′N 135°28′E*
164 H14 **Sakaide** Kagawa, Shikoku, SW Japan *34°19′N 133°50′E*
164 H12 **Sakaiminato** Tottori, Honshū, SW Japan *35°34′N 133°12′E*
140 M3 **Sakākah** Al Jawf, NW Saudi Arabia *29°56′N 40°10′E*
28 L4 **Sakakawea, Lake** ⊠ North Dakota, N USA
12 J9 **Sakami, Lac** ◎ Québec, C Canada
79 O26 **Sakania** Katanga, SE Dem. Rep. Congo *12°44′S 28°34′E*
146 K12 **Sakar** Lebap Welaýaty, E Turkmenistan *38°57′N 63°46′E*
172 H7 **Sakaraha** Toliara, SW Madagascar *22°54′S 44°31′E*
146 I14 **Sakarçäge** *var.* Sakarchäge, *Rus.* Sakar-Chaga. Mary Welaýaty, C Turkmenistan *37°40′N 61°33′E*
Sakar-Chaga/Sakarchäge *see* Sakarçäge
Sak'art'velo *see* Georgia
136 F11 **Sakarya** ◐ *province* NW Turkey
136 F12 **Sakarya Nehri** NW Turkey
165 P9 **Sakata** Yamagata, Honshū, C Japan *38°54′N 139°51′E*
145 S11 **Saken Seyfullin** *Kaz.* Säken Seyfüllīn; *prev.* Zharyk. Karaganda, C Kazakhstan *48°52′N 72°51′E*
Säken Seyfüllīn *see* Saken Seyfullin
123 P9 **Sakha (Yakutiya), Respublika** *var.* Respublika Yakutiya, *Eng.* Yakutia. ◐ *autonomous republic* NE Russian Federation
Sakhalin *see* Sakhalin, Ostrov
192 I3 **Sakhalin, Ostrov** *var.* Sakhalin. *island* SE Russian Federation
123 U12 **Sakhalinskaya Oblast'** ◐ *province* SE Russian Federation
123 T12 **Sakhalinskiy Zaliv** *gulf* E Russian Federation
Sakhnovshchina *see* Sakhnovshchyna
117 U6 **Sakhnovshchyna** *Rus.* Sakhnovshchina. Kharkivs'ka Oblast', E Ukraine *49°08′N 35°52′E*
Sakhon Nakhon *see* Sakon Nakhon
Sakhtsar *see* Rāmsar
137 W10 **Şäki** *Rus.* Sheki; *prev.* Nukha. NW Azerbaijan *41°09′N 47°10′E*
Saki *see* Saky
118 E13 **Šakiai** *Ger.* Schaken. Marijampolė, S Lithuania *54°57′N 23°04′E*
165 O16 **Sakishima-shotō** *var.* Sakisima Syotô. *island group* SW Japan
Sakisima Syotô *see* Sakishima-shotō
Sakiz *see* Saqqez
Sakiz-Adasi *see* Chíos
155 F19 **Sakleshpur** Karnātaka, E India *12°58′N 75°45′E*
167 S9 **Sakon Nakhon** *var.* Muang Sakon Nakhon, Sakhon Nakhon. Sakon Nakhon, E Thailand *17°10′N 104°08′E*
149 P15 **Sakrand** Sind, SE Pakistan *26°06′N 68°20′E*
83 F24 **Sak River** *Afr.* Sakrivier. Northern Cape, W South Africa *30°49′S 20°24′E*
Sakrivier *see* Sak River
Saksaul'skiy *see* Saksaul'skoye
144 K13 **Saksaul'skoye** *var.* Saksaul'skiy, *Kaz.* Sekseūil. Kzylorda, S Kazakhstan *47°07′N 61°06′E*
95 I25 **Sakskøbing** Storstrøm, SE Denmark *54°48′N 11°39′E*
165 N12 **Saku** Nagano, Honshū, S Japan *36°17′N 138°29′E*
117 S13 **Saky** *Rus.* Saki. Respublika Krym, S Ukraine *45°09′N 33°36′E*
76 E9 **Sal** *island* Ilhas de Barlavento, NE Cape Verde
127 N12 **Sal** SW Russian Federation
111 I21 **Sal'a** *Hung.* Sellye, Vágsellye. Nitriansky Kraj, SW Slovakia *48°09′N 17°51′E*
95 N15 **Sala** Västmanland, C Sweden *59°55′N 16°38′E*
15 N13 **Salaberry-de-Valleyfield** *var.* Valleyfield. Québec, SE Canada *45°15′N 74°07′W*
118 G7 **Salacgrīva** *Est.* Salatsi. Limbaži, N Latvia *57°45′N 24°21′E*
107 M18 **Sala Consilina** Campania, S Italy *40°23′N 15°35′E*
40 C2 **Salada, Laguna** ◎ NW Mexico
61 D14 **Saladas** Corrientes, NE Argentina *28°15′S 58°40′W*
61 C21 **Saladillo** Buenos Aires, E Argentina *35°40′S 59°50′W*
61 B16 **Saladillo, Río** C Argentina
25 T9 **Salado** Texas, SW USA *30°57′N 97°32′W*
63 J16 **Salado, Arroyo** SE Argentina
61 D21 **Salado, Río** E Argentina
62 J12 **Salado, Río** C Argentina
41 N7 **Salado, Río** NE Mexico
37 Q12 **Salado, Rio** New Mexico, SW USA
143 N6 **Salafchegān** *var.* Sarafjagān. Quom, N Iran *34°28′N 50°28′E*
77 Q15 **Salaga** C Ghana *08°31′N 00°37′W*
139 S6 **Şalāḩ ad Dīn** ◐ *governorate* C Iraq
192 G5 **Sala'ilua** Savai'i, W Samoa *13°39′S 172°33′W*
116 G9 **Sălaj** ◐ *county* NW Romania
83 H20 **Salajwe** Kweneng, SE Botswana *23°40′S 24°46′E*
78 H9 **Salal** Kanem, W Chad *14°48′N 17°12′E*
80 I6 **Salala** Red Sea, NE Sudan *21°17′N 36°16′E*
141 V13 **Şalālah** SW Oman *17°01′N 54°04′E*
42 D5 **Salamá** Baja Verapaz, C Guatemala *15°06′N 90°18′W*
42 J6 **Salamá** Olancho, C Honduras *14°48′N 86°34′W*
62 G10 **Salamanca** Coquimbo, C Chile *31°47′S 70°58′W*
41 N13 **Salamanca** Guanajuato, C Mexico *20°34′N 101°12′W*
104 K7 **Salamanca** *anc.* Helmantica, Salmantica. Castilla-León, NW Spain *40°58′N 05°40′W*
18 D11 **Salamanca** New York, NE USA *42°09′N 78°43′W*
104 J7 **Salamanca** ◐ *province* Castilla-León, W Spain
63 J19 **Salamanca, Pampa de** *plain* S Argentina
78 J12 **Salamat** *off.* Préfecture du Salamat. ◐ *prefecture* SE Chad
78 I12 **Salamat, Bahr** S Chad
Salamat, Préfecture du *see* Salamat
54 F5 **Salamina** Magdalena, N Colombia *10°30′N 74°48′W*
115 G19 **Salamína** *var.* Salamís. Salamína, C Greece *37°58′N 23°29′E*
115 G19 **Salamína** *island* C Greece
Salamís *see* Salamína
138 I5 **Salamīyah** *var.* As Salamīyah. Ḩamāh, W Syria *35°01′N 37°02′E*
31 P12 **Salamonie Lake** ⊠ Indiana, N USA
31 P12 **Salamonie River** Indiana, N USA
Salang *see* Phuket
192 I16 **Salani** Upolu, SE Samoa *14°00′S 171°35′W*
118 C11 **Salantai** Klaipėda, NW Lithuania *56°05′N 21°36′E*
104 K2 **Salas** Asturias, N Spain *43°25′N 06°15′W*
105 O5 **Salas de los Infantes** Castilla-León, N Spain *42°02′N 03°17′W*
102 M16 **Salat** S France
189 V13 **Salat** *island* Chuuk, C Micronesia
169 Q16 **Salatiga** Jawa, C Indonesia *07°15′S 110°34′E*
189 V13 **Salat Pass** *passage* W Pacific Ocean
Salatsi *see* Salacgrīva
167 T10 **Salavan** *var.* Saravan, Saravane. Salavan, S Laos *15°43′N 106°26′E*
127 V6 **Salavat** Respublika Bashkortostan, W Russian Federation *53°20′N 55°54′E*
56 C12 **Salaverry** La Libertad, N Peru *08°14′S 78°55′W*
171 T12 **Salawati, Pulau** *island* E Indonesia
193 R10 **Sala y Gomez** *island* Chile, E Pacific Ocean
Sala y Gomez Fracture Zone *see* Sala y Gomez Ridge
193 S10 **Sala y Gomez Ridge** *var.* Sala y Gomez Fracture Zone. *tectonic feature* SE Pacific Ocean
61 A22 **Salazar** Buenos Aires, E Argentina *36°20′S 62°11′W*
54 G7 **Salazar** Norte de Santander, N Colombia *07°46′N 72°46′W*
Salazar *see* N'Dalatando
173 P16 **Salazie** C Réunion *21°02′S 55°33′E*
103 N8 **Salbris** Loir-et-Cher, C France *47°25′N 02°02′E*
57 G15 **Salcantay, Nevado** ▲ C Peru *13°21′S 72°31′W*
45 O8 **Salcedo** N Dominican Republic *19°26′N 70°25′W*
39 S9 **Salcha River** Alaska, USA
119 H15 **Šalčininkai** Vilnius, SE Lithuania *54°20′N 25°26′E*
Saldae *see* Béjaïa
54 E11 **Saldaña** Tolima, C Colombia *03°57′N 75°01′W*
104 M4 **Saldaña** Castilla-León, N Spain *42°31′N 04°44′W*
83 E25 **Saldanha** Western Cape, SW South Africa *33°00′S 17°56′E*
Salduba *see* Zaragoza
61 B23 **Saldungaray** Buenos Aires, E Argentina *38°15′S 61°45′W*
118 D9 **Saldus** *Ger.* Frauenburg. Saldus, W Latvia *56°40′N 22°29′E*
183 P13 **Sale** Victoria, SE Australia *38°06′S 147°06′E*
74 F6 **Salé** NW Morocco *34°07′N 06°40′W*
74 F6 **Salé** ✕ (Rabat) W Morocco *34°09′N 06°30′W*
Salehābād *see* Andīmeshk
170 M16 **Saleh, Teluk** *bay* Nusa Tenggara, S Indonesia
122 H8 **Salekhard** *prev.* Obdorsk. Yamalo-Nenetskiy Avtonomnyy Okrug, N Russian Federation *66°33′N 66°35′E*
192 H16 **Sālelologa** Savai'i, C Samoa *13°42′S 172°10′W*
155 H21 **Salem** Tamil Nādu, SE India *11°38′N 78°08′E*
27 V9 **Salem** Arkansas, C USA *36°21′N 91°49′W*
30 L15 **Salem** Illinois, N USA *38°37′N 88°57′W*
31 P15 **Salem** Indiana, N USA *38°38′N 86°06′W*
19 P11 **Salem** Massachusetts, NE USA *42°30′N 70°51′W*
27 V6 **Salem** Missouri, C USA *37°39′N 91°32′W*
18 I16 **Salem** New Jersey, NE USA *39°33′N 75°26′W*
31 U12 **Salem** Ohio, N USA *40°52′N 80°51′W*
32 G12 **Salem** *state capital* Oregon, NW USA *44°57′N 123°01′W*
29 Q11 **Salem** South Dakota, N USA *43°43′N 97°23′W*
36 L4 **Salem** Utah, W USA *40°03′N 111°40′W*
21 S7 **Salem** Virginia, NE USA *37°16′N 80°00′W*
21 R3 **Salem** West Virginia, NE USA *39°15′N 80°32′W*
107 H23 **Salemi** Sicilia, Italy, C Mediterranean Sea *37°48′N 12°48′E*
Salemy *see* As Sālimī
94 K12 **Sälen** Dalarna, C Sweden *61°11′N 13°14′E*
107 Q18 **Salentina, Campi** Puglia, SE Italy *40°23′N 18°01′E*
107 Q18 **Salentina, Penisola** *peninsula* SE Italy
107 L18 **Salerno** *anc.* Salernum. Campania, S Italy *40°40′N 14°44′E*
107 L18 **Salerno, Golfo di** *Eng.* Gulf of Salerno. *gulf* S Italy
Salerno, Gulf of *see* Salerno, Golfo di
Salernum *see* Salerno
97 K17 **Salford** NW England, United Kingdom *53°30′N 02°16′W*
Salgir *see* Salhyr
111 K21 **Salgótarján** Nógrád, N Hungary *48°07′N 19°47′E*
59 O15 **Salgueiro** Pernambuco, E Brazil *08°04′S 39°05′W*
94 C13 **Salhus** Hordaland, S Norway *60°30′N 05°15′E*
117 T12 **Salhyr** *Rus.* Salgir. S Ukraine
171 Q9 **Salibabu, Pulau** *island* N Indonesia
37 S6 **Salida** Colorado, C USA *38°29′N 105°57′W*
102 J15 **Salies-de-Béarn** Pyrénées-Atlantiques, SW France *43°28′N 00°55′W*
136 C14 **Salihli** Manisa, W Turkey *38°29′N 28°08′E*
119 K18 **Salihorsk** *Rus.* Soligorsk. Minskaya Voblasts', S Belarus *52°48′N 27°32′E*
119 K18 **Salihorskaye Vodaskhovishcha** ⊠ C Belarus
83 N14 **Salima** Central, C Malawi *13°44′S 34°21′E*
166 L5 **Salin** Magway, W Burma (Myanmar) *20°30′N 94°40′E*
27 N4 **Salina** Kansas, C USA *38°53′N 97°36′W*
36 L5 **Salina** Utah, W USA *38°57′N 111°54′W*
41 S17 **Salina Cruz** Oaxaca, SE Mexico *16°11′N 95°12′W*
107 L22 **Salina, Isola** *island* Isole Eolie, S Italy
44 J5 **Salina Point** *headland* Acklins Island, SE Bahamas *22°10′N 74°16′W*
56 A7 **Salinas** Guayas, W Ecuador *02°15′S 80°58′W*
40 M11 **Salinas** *var.* Salinas de Hidalgo. San Luis Potosí, C Mexico *22°36′N 101°41′W*
45 T6 **Salinas** C Puerto Rico *17°57′N 66°18′W*
35 O10 **Salinas** California, W USA *36°41′N 121°40′W*
Salinas, Cabo de *see* Salines, Cap de ses
Salinas de Hidalgo *see* Salinas
82 A13 **Salinas, Ponta das** *headland* W Angola *12°50′S 12°57′E*
45 O10 **Salinas, Punta** *headland* S Dominican Republic *18°11′N 70°32′W*
Salinas, Río *see* Chixoy, Río
35 O11 **Salinas River** California, W USA
22 H6 **Saline Lake** ◎ Louisiana, S USA
25 R17 **Salineno** Texas, SW USA *26°29′N 99°06′W*
27 V14 **Saline River** Arkansas, C USA
30 M17 **Saline River** Illinois, N USA
105 X10 **Salines, Cap de ses** *var.* Cabo de Salinas. *headland* Mallorca, Spain, W Mediterranean Sea *39°15′N 03°03′E*
Salisburg *see* Mazsalaca
45 O12 **Salisbury** *var.* Baroui. W Dominica *15°26′N 61°27′W*
97 M23 **Salisbury** *var.* New Sarum. S England, United Kingdom *51°05′N 01°48′W*
21 Y4 **Salisbury** Maryland, NE USA *38°22′N 75°37′W*
27 T3 **Salisbury** Missouri, C USA *39°25′N 92°48′W*
21 S9 **Salisbury** North Carolina, SE USA *35°40′N 80°28′W*
Salisbury *see* Harare
9 Q7 **Salisbury Island** *island* Nunavut, NE Canada
Salisbury, Lake *see* Bisina, Lake
97 L23 **Salisbury Plain** *plain* S England, United Kingdom
21 R14 **Salkehatchie River** South Carolina, SE USA
138 I9 **Şalkhad** As Suwaydā', SW Syria *32°29′N 36°42′E*
92 M12 **Salla** Lappi, NE Finland *66°50′N 28°40′E*
Sállan *see* Sørøya
103 U11 **Sallanches** Haute-Savoie, E France *45°55′N 06°37′E*
105 V5 **Sallent** Cataluña, NE Spain *41°48′N 01°52′E*
61 A22 **Salliqueló** Buenos Aires, E Argentina *36°45′S 62°55′W*
27 R10 **Sallisaw** Oklahoma, C USA *35°27′N 94°49′W*
80 I7 **Sallom** Red Sea, NE Sudan *19°17′N 37°02′E*
12 J2 **Salluit** *prev.* Saglouc, Sagluk. Québec, NE Canada *62°10′N 75°40′W*
Sallyana *see* Şalyān
13 S11 **Sally's Cove** Newfoundland and Labrador, E Canada *49°43′N 58°00′W*
139 W9 **Salmān Bin 'Arāzah** Maysān, E Iraq *32°33′N 46°36′E*
Salmantica *see* Salamanca
142 I2 **Salmās** *prev.* Dilman, Shāpūr. Āzarbāyjān-e Gharbī, NW Iran *38°13′N 44°50′E*
124 I11 **Salmi** Respublika Kareliya, NW Russian Federation *61°21′N 31°55′E*
33 P12 **Salmon** Idaho, NW USA *45°10′N 113°54′W*
11 N16 **Salmon Arm** British Columbia, SW Canada *50°41′N 119°18′W*
192 L5 **Salmon Bank** *undersea feature* N Pacific Ocean *26°55′N 176°28′W*
Salmon Leap *see* Leixlip
34 L2 **Salmon Mountains** ▲▲ California, W USA
14 J15 **Salmon Point** *headland* Ontario, SE Canada *43°51′N 77°15′W*
33 N11 **Salmon River** Idaho, NW USA
18 K6 **Salmon River** New York, NE USA
33 N12 **Salmon River Mountains** ▲▲ Idaho, NW USA
18 I9 **Salmon River Reservoir** ⊠ New York, NE USA
93 K19 **Salo** Länsi-Suomi, SW Finland *60°23′N 23°10′E*
106 F7 **Salò** Lombardia, N Italy *45°37′N 10°30′E*
Salona/Salonae *see* Solin
103 S15 **Salon-de-Provence** Bouches-du-Rhône, SE France *43°39′N 05°05′E*
Salonica/Salonika *see* Thessaloníki
115 I14 **Salonikiós, Akrotírio** *var.* Akrotírio Salonikós. *headland* Thásos, E Greece *40°34′N 24°39′E*
Salonikós, Akrotírio *see* Salonikiós, Akrotírio
116 F10 **Salonta** *Hung.* Nagyszalonta. Bihor, W Romania *46°49′N 21°40′E*
104 I9 **Salor** W Spain
105 U6 **Salou** Cataluña, NE Spain *41°05′N 01°08′E*
76 H11 **Saloum** C Senegal
42 H4 **Sal, Punta** *headland* NW Honduras *15°55′N 87°36′W*
92 N3 **Salpynten** *headland* W Svalbard *78°12′N 12°11′E*
138 I3 **Salqīn** Idlib, W Syria *36°09′N 36°27′E*
93 F14 **Salsbruket** Nord-Trøndelag, C Norway *64°49′N 11°48′E*
126 M13 **Sal'sk** Rostovskaya Oblast', SW Russian Federation *46°30′N 41°31′E*
107 K25 **Salso** Sicilia, Italy, C Mediterranean Sea
107 J25 **Salso** Sicilia, Italy, C Mediterranean Sea
106 E9 **Salsomaggiore Terme** Emilia-Romagna, N Italy *44°49′N 09°58′E*
Salt *see* As Salṭ
62 J6 **Salta** Salta, NW Argentina *24°47′S 65°23′W*
62 K6 **Salta** *off.* Provincia de Salta. ◐ *province* N Argentina
Salta, Provincia de *see* Salta
97 I24 **Saltash** SW England, United Kingdom *50°26′N 04°14′W*
24 I8 **Salt Basin** *basin* Texas, SW USA
11 V16 **Saltcoats** Saskatchewan, S Canada *51°06′N 102°12′W*
30 L13 **Salt Creek** Illinois, N USA
24 J9 **Salt Draw** Texas, SW USA
97 F21 **Saltee Islands** *island group* SE Ireland
92 G12 **Saltfjorden** *inlet* C Norway
24 I8 **Salt Flat** Texas, SW USA *31°43′N 105°05′W*
27 N8 **Salt Fork Arkansas River** Oklahoma, C USA
31 T13 **Salt Fork Lake** ⊠ Ohio, N USA
26 J11 **Salt Fork Red River** Oklahoma/Texas, C USA
95 J23 **Saltholm** *island* E Denmark
41 N8 **Saltillo** Coahuila, NE Mexico *25°30′N 101°W*
182 L5 **Salt Lake** *salt lake* New South Wales, SE Australia
37 V15 **Salt Lake** ◎ New Mexico, SW USA
36 K2 **Salt Lake City** *state capital* Utah, W USA *40°45′N 111°54′W*
61 C20 **Salto** Buenos Aires, E Argentina *34°18′S 60°17′W*
61 D17 **Salto** Salto, N Uruguay *31°23′S 57°58′W*
61 E17 **Salto** ◐ *department* N Uruguay
107 I14 **Salto** C Italy
62 Q6 **Salto del Guairá** Canindeyú, E Paraguay *24°06′S 54°22′W*
61 D17 **Salto Grande, Embalse de** *var.* Lago de Salto Grande. ⊠ Argentina/Uruguay
Salto Grande, Lago de *see* Salto Grande, Embalse de
35 W16 **Salton Sea** ◎ California, W USA
60 I12 **Salto Santiago, Represa de** ⊠ S Brazil
149 U7 **Salt Range** ▲▲ E Pakistan
36 M13 **Salt River** Arizona, SW USA
20 L5 **Salt River** Kentucky, S USA
27 V3 **Salt River** Missouri, C USA
95 F17 **Saltrød** Aust-Agder, S Norway *58°28′N 08°49′E*
95 P16 **Saltsjöbaden** Stockholm, C Sweden *59°15′N 18°20′E*
92 G12 **Saltstraumen** Nordland, C Norway *67°16′N 14°42′E*
21 Q7 **Saltville** Virginia, NE USA *36°52′N 81°48′W*
Saluces/Saluciae *see* Saluzzo
21 Q12 **Saluda** South Carolina, SE USA *34°00′N 81°47′W*
21 X6 **Saluda** Virginia, NE USA *37°36′N 76°36′W*
21 Q12 **Saluda River** South Carolina, SE USA
Salûm *see* As Sallūm
152 F14 **Sālūmbar** Rājasthān, N India *24°16′N 74°04′E*
Salûm, Gulf of *see* Khalīj as Sallūm
171 O11 **Salumpaga** Sulawesi, N Indonesia *01°18′N 120°58′E*
155 M14 **Sālūr** Andhra Pradesh, E India *18°31′N 83°16′E*
55 Y9 **Salut, Îles du** *island group* N French Guiana
106 A9 **Saluzzo** *Fr.* Saluces; *anc.* Saluciae. Piemonte, NW Italy *44°39′N 07°29′E*
63 F23 **Salvación, Bahía** *bay* S Chile
59 P17 **Salvador** *prev.* São Salvador. *state capital* Bahia, E Brazil *12°58′S 38°29′W*
65 E24 **Salvador** East Falkland, Falkland Islands *51°28′S 58°22′W*
22 K10 **Salvador, Lake** ◎ Louisiana, S USA
Salvaleón de Higüey *see* Higüey
104 F10 **Salvaterra de Magos** Santarém, C Portugal *39°01′N 08°47′W*
41 N13 **Salvatierra** Guanajuato, C Mexico *20°14′N 100°52′W*
105 P3 **Salvatierra** *Basq.* Agurain. País Vasco, N Spain *42°52′N 02°23′W*
Salwa/Salwah *see* As Salwā
166 M7 **Salween** *Bur.* Thanlwin, *Chin.* Nu Chiang, Nu Jiang. SE Asia
137 Y12 **Salyan** *Rus.* Sal'yany. SE Azerbaijan *39°36′N 48°57′E*
153 N11 **Şalyān** *var.* Sallyana. Mid Western, W Nepal *28°22′N 82°10′E*
Sal'yany *see* Salyan
21 O6 **Salyersville** Kentucky, S USA *37°43′N 83°06′W*
109 V6 **Salza** E Austria
109 Q7 **Salzach** Austria/Germany
109 Q6 **Salzburg** *anc.* Juvavum. Salzburg, N Austria *47°48′N 13°03′E*
109 O8 **Salzburg** *off.* Land Salzburg. ◐ *state* C Austria
Salzburg *see* Ocna Sibiului
Salzburg Alps *see* Salzburger Kalkalpen
109 Q7 **Salzburger Kalkalpen** *Eng.* Salzburg Alps. ▲▲ C Austria
Salzburg, Land *see* Salzburg
100 J13 **Salzgitter** *prev.* Watenstedt-Salzgitter. Niedersachsen, C Germany *52°07′N 10°24′E*
101 G14 **Salzkotten** Nordrhein-Westfalen, W Germany *51°40′N 08°36′E*
100 K11 **Salzwedel** Sachsen-Anhalt, N Germany *52°51′N 11°10′E*
152 D11 **Sām** Rājasthān, NW India *26°50′N 70°30′E*
Šamac *see* Bosanski Šamac
54 G9 **Samacá** Boyacá, C Colombia *05°28′N 73°33′W*
40 I7 **Samachique** Chihuahua, N Mexico *27°17′N 107°28′W*
141 Y8 **Şamad** NE Oman *22°47′N 58°12′E*
Sama de Langreo *see* Sama, Spain
Samaden *see* Samedan
57 M19 **Samaipata** Santa Cruz, C Bolivia *18°08′S 63°53′W*
167 T10 **Samakhixai** *var.* Attapu, Attopeu. Attapu, S Laos *14°48′N 106°51′E*
Samakov *see* Samokov
42 B6 **Samalá, Río** SW Guatemala
40 J3 **Samalayuca** Chihuahua, N Mexico *31°25′N 106°30′W*
155 L16 **Sāmalkot** Andhra Pradesh, E India *17°03′N 82°15′E*
45 P8 **Samaná** *var.* Santa Bárbara de Samaná. E Dominican Republic *19°14′N 69°20′W*
45 P8 **Samaná, Bahía de** *bay* E Dominican Republic
44 K4 **Samana Cay** *island* SE Bahamas
136 K17 **Samandağı** Hatay, S Turkey *36°07′N 35°55′E*
149 P3 **Samangān** ◐ *province* N Afghanistan
Samangān *see* Āybak
165 T5 **Samani** Hokkaidō, NE Japan *42°07′N 142°57′E*
54 C13 **Samaniego** Nariño, SW Colombia *01°22′N 77°35′W*
171 Q5 **Samar** *island* C Philippines
127 S6 **Samara** *prev.* Kuybyshev. Samarskaya Oblast', W Russian Federation *53°15′N 50°15′E*
127 T7 **Samara** W Russian Federation
127 S6 **Samara** ✕ Samarskaya Oblast', W Russian Federation *53°11′N 50°27′E*
117 V7 **Samara** E Ukraine
186 G10 **Samarai** Milne Bay, SE Papua New Guinea *10°36′S 150°39′E*
Samarang *see* Semarang
123 T14 **Samarga** Khabarovskiy Kray, SE Russian Federation *47°43′N 139°08′E*
138 G9 **Samarian Hills** *hill range* N Israel
54 L9 **Samariapo** Amazonas, C Venezuela *05°16′N 67°43′W*
169 V11 **Samarinda** Borneo, C Indonesia *0°30′S 117°09′E*
Samarkand *see* Samarqand
Samarkandskaya Oblast' *see* Samarqand Viloyati
Samarkandski/Samarkandskoye *see* Temirtau

◆ Country
● Country Capital
◇ Dependent Territory
○ Dependent Territory Capital
◐ Administrative Regions
✕ International Airport
▲ Mountain
▲▲ Mountain Range
Volcano
River
◎ Lake
⊠ Reservoir

Samarobriva see Amiens
147 N11 Samarqand Rus. Samarkand. Samarqand Viloyati, C Uzbekistan 39°40′N 66°56′E
146 M11 Samarqand Viloyati Rus. Samarkandskaya Oblast'. ◆ province C Uzbekistan
139 S6 Sāmarrā' Ṣalāḥ ad Dīn, C Iraq 34°13′N 43°52′E
127 R7 Samarskaya Oblast' prev. Kuybyshevskaya Oblast'. ◆ province W Russian Federation
153 Q13 Samastipur Bihār, N India 25°52′N 85°47′E
76 L14 Samatiguila NW Ivory Coast 09°51′N 07°36′W
Samawa see As Samāwah
137 Y11 Şamaxı Rus. Shemakha. E Azerbaijan 40°38′N 48°34′E
79 K18 Samba Equateur, NW Dem. Rep. Congo 0°13′N 21°17′E
79 N21 Samba Maniema, E Dem. Rep. Congo 04°41′S 26°23′E
152 H6 Samba Jammu and Kashmir, NW India 32°32′N 75°08′E
169 W10 Sambaliung, Pegunungan ▲ Borneo, N Indonesia
154 M11 Sambalpur Orissa, E India 21°28′N 84°04′E
67 X12 Sambao ≈ W Madagascar
169 Q10 Sambas, Sungai ≈ Borneo, N Indonesia
172 K2 Sambava Antsiranana, NE Madagascar 14°16′S 50°10′E
152 J10 Sambhal Uttar Pradesh, N India 28°35′N 78°34′E
152 H12 Sāmbhar Salt Lake ◎ N India
107 N21 Sambiase Calabria, SW Italy 38°58′N 16°16′E
116 H5 Sambir Rus. Sambor. L'vivs'ka Oblast', NW Ukraine 49°31′N 23°10′E
82 C13 Sambo Huambo, C Angola 13°07′S 16°06′E
Sambor see Sambir
61 E21 Samborombón, Bahía bay NE Argentina
99 H20 Sambre ≈ Belgium/France
43 V16 Sambú, Río ≈ SE Panama
163 Z14 Samch'ŏk Jap. Sanchoku. NE South Korea 37°21′N 129°12′E
Samch'ŏnpŏ see Sach'ŏn
81 I21 Same Kilimanjaro, NE Tanzania 04°04′S 37°41′E
108 J10 Samedan Ger. Samaden. Graubünden, S Switzerland 46°31′N 09°51′E
82 K12 Samfya Luapula, N Zambia 11°22′S 29°34′E
141 W13 Samḥān, Jabal ▲ SW Oman
115 C18 Sámi Kefallonía, Iónia Nisiá, Greece, C Mediterranean Sea 38°15′N 20°39′E
56 F10 Samiria, Río ≈ N Peru
Samirum see Semīrom
137 V11 Şämkir Rus. Shamkhor. NW Azerbaijan 40°51′N 46°03′E
167 S7 Sam, Nam Vtn. Sông Chu. ≈ Laos/Vietnam
Samnān see Semnān
Sam Neua see Xam Nua
75 P10 Samnū C Libya 27°19′N 15°01′E
192 H15 Samoa off. Independent State of Western Samoa, var. Sāmoa; prev. Western Samoa. ◆ monarchy W Polynesia
192 L9 Sāmoa island group American Samoa
Sāmoa see Samoa
175 T9 Samoa Basin undersea feature W Pacific Ocean
112 D8 Samobor Zagreb, N Croatia 45°48′N 15°38′E
114 H10 Samokov var. Samakov. Sofiya, W Bulgaria 42°19′N 23°34′E
111 H21 Šamorín Ger. Sommerein, Hung. Somorja. Trnavský Kraj, W Slovakia 48°01′N 17°18′E
115 M19 Sámos prev. Limín Vathéos. Sámos, Dodekánisa, Greece, Aegean Sea 37°45′N 26°58′E
115 M20 Sámos island Dodekánisa, Greece, Aegean Sea
Samosch see Szamos
168 I9 Samosir, Pulau island W Indonesia
Samothrace see Samothráki
115 K14 Samothráki Samothráki, NE Greece 40°28′N 25°31′E
115 J14 Samothráki anc. Samothrace. island NE Greece
115 A15 Samothráki island Iónia Nisiá, Greece, C Mediterranean Sea
Samotschin see Szamocin
Sampê see Xiangcheng
169 S13 Sampit Borneo, C Indonesia 02°30′S 112°30′E
169 S12 Sampit, Sungai ≈ Borneo, N Indonesia
Sampoku see Sanpoku
186 H7 Sampun New Britain, E Papua New Guinea 05°19′S 152°06′E
79 N24 Sampwe Katanga, SE Dem. Rep. Congo 09°17′S 27°22′E
25 X8 Sam Rayburn Reservoir ⊠ Texas, SW USA
158 H15 Samsang Xizang Zizhiqu, W China 30°23′N 82°49′E
167 Q6 Sam Sao, Phou ▲ Laos/Thailand
95 H22 Samsø island E Denmark
95 H23 Samsø Bælt channel E Denmark
167 T7 Sâm Sơn Thanh Hoa, N Vietnam 19°44′N 105°53′E
136 L11 Samsun anc. Amisus. Samsun, N Turkey 41°17′N 36°22′E
136 K11 Samsun ◆ province N Turkey
137 R9 Samtredia W Georgia 42°09′N 42°20′E
59 E15 Samuel, Represa de ⊠ W Brazil
167 O14 Samui, Ko island SW Thailand
Samundari see Samundri
149 U9 Samundri var. Samundari. Punjab, E Pakistan 31°04′N 72°58′E
137 X10 Samur ≈ Azerbaijan/Russian Federation
137 Y11 Samur-Abşeron Kanalı Rus. Sam ur-Apsheronskiy Kanal. canal E Azerbaijan
Sam ur-Apsheronskiy Kanal see Samur-Abşeron Kanalı
167 O11 Samut Prakan var. Muang Samut Prakan, Paknam. Samut Prakan, C Thailand 13°36′N 100°36′E
167 O11 Samut Sakhon var. Maha Chai, Samut Sakorn, Tha Chin. Samut Sakhon, C Thailand 13°31′N 100°15′E
Samut Sakorn see Samut Sakhon
167 O11 Samut Songhram prev. Meklong. Samut Songkhram, SW Thailand 13°25′N 100°01′E
77 N12 San Ségou, C Mali 13°21′N 04°57′W
111 O15 San ≈ SE Poland
141 O15 Ṣan'ā' Eng. Sana. ● (Yemen) W Yemen 15°24′N 44°14′E
112 F11 Sana ≈ NW Bosnia and Herzegovina
80 O12 Sanaag off. Gobolka Sanaag. ◆ region N Somalia
Sanaag, Gobolka see Sanaag
114 J8 Sanadinovo Pleven, N Bulgaria 43°33′N 25°00′E
195 P1 Sanae South African research station Antarctica 70°19′S 01°31′W
139 Y10 Sanāf, Hawr as ◎ S Iraq
79 E15 Sanaga ≈ C Cameroon
54 D12 San Agustín Huila, SW Colombia 01°53′N 76°14′W
171 R8 San Agustin, Cape headland Mindanao, S Philippines 06°17′N 126°12′E
37 Q13 San Agustin, Plains of plain New Mexico, SW USA
38 M16 Sanak Islands island Aleutian Islands, Alaska, USA
San Alessandro see Kita-Iō-jima
193 U10 San Ambrosio, Isla Eng. San Ambrosio Island. island W Chile
San Ambrosio Island see San Ambrosio, Isla
171 Q12 Sanana Pulau Sanana, E Indonesia 02°04′S 125°58′E
171 Q12 Sanana, Pulau island Maluku, E Indonesia
142 K5 Sanandaj prev. Sinneh. Kordestān, W Iran 35°18′N 47°01′E
35 P8 San Andreas California, W USA 38°10′N 120°40′W
2 C13 San Andreas Fault fault W USA
54 G8 San Andrés Santander, C Colombia 06°52′N 72°53′W
61 C20 San Andrés de Giles Buenos Aires, E Argentina 34°27′S 59°27′W
43 Q7 San Andrés, Isla de island NW Colombia, Caribbean Sea
43 Q7 San Andrés y Providencia ◆ province Colombia, Caribbean Sea
37 R14 San Andres Mountains ▲ New Mexico, SW USA
41 S15 San Andrés Tuxtla var. Tuxtla. Veracruz-Llave, E Mexico 18°28′N 95°15′W
25 P8 San Angelo Texas, SW USA 31°28′N 100°26′W
107 A20 San Antioco, Isola di island W Italy
42 F4 San Antonio Toledo, S Belize 16°13′N 89°02′W
62 G11 San Antonio Valparaíso, C Chile 33°35′S 71°38′W
188 H6 San Antonio Saipan, S Northern Mariana Islands
37 R13 San Antonio New Mexico, SW USA 33°53′N 106°52′W
25 R12 San Antonio Texas, SW USA 29°25′N 98°30′W
54 M11 San Antonio Amazonas, S Venezuela 03°31′N 66°47′W
54 I7 San Antonio Barinas, C Venezuela 07°24′N 71°28′W
55 O5 San Antonio Monagas, NE Venezuela 10°03′N 63°45′W
25 S12 San Antonio ✕ Texas, SW USA 29°31′N 98°11′W
San Antonio see San Antonio del Táchira
San Antonio Abad see Sant Antoni de Portmany
25 U13 San Antonio Bay inlet Texas, SW USA
61 E22 San Antonio, Cabo headland E Argentina 36°45′S 56°40′W
44 A5 San Antonio, Cabo de headland W Cuba 21°51′N 84°58′W
105 T11 San Antonio, Cabo de headland E Spain 38°50′N 00°09′E
54 H7 San Antonio de Caparo Táchira, W Venezuela 07°34′N 71°28′W
62 J5 San Antonio de los Cobres Salta, NE Argentina 24°10′S 66°17′W
54 H7 San Antonio del Táchira var. San Antonio. Táchira, W Venezuela 07°48′N 72°28′W
35 T15 San Antonio, Mount ▲ California, W USA 34°18′N 117°37′W
63 K16 San Antonio Oeste Río Negro, E Argentina 40°45′S 64°58′W
25 T13 San Antonio River ≈ Texas, SW USA
55 J5 Sanare Lara, N Venezuela 09°45′N 69°39′W
103 T16 Sanary-sur-Mer Var, SE France 43°07′N 05°48′E
25 X8 San Augustine Texas, SW USA 31°32′N 94°09′W
San Augustine see Minami-Iō-jima
141 T13 Sanāw var. Sanaw. NE Yemen 18°N 51°E
41 O11 San Bartolo San Luis Potosí, C Mexico 22°20′N 100°05′W
107 L16 San Bartolomeo in Galdo Campania, S Italy 41°24′N 15°01′E
106 K13 San Benedetto del Tronto Marche, C Italy 42°57′N 13°53′E
42 E3 San Benito Petén, N Guatemala 16°56′N 89°53′W
25 T17 San Benito Texas, SW USA 26°07′N 97°37′W
54 E6 San Benito Abad Sucre, N Colombia 08°56′N 75°02′W
35 P11 San Benito Mountain ▲ California, W USA 36°21′N 120°37′W
35 O10 San Benito River ≈ California, W USA
108 H10 San Bernardino Graubünden, S Switzerland 46°21′N 09°13′E
35 U15 San Bernardino California, W USA 34°06′N 117°15′W
35 U15 San Bernardino Mountains ▲ California, W USA
62 H11 San Bernardo Santiago, C Chile 33°37′S 70°45′W
40 J8 San Bernardo Durango, C Mexico 25°58′N 105°27′W
164 G12 Sanbe-san ▲ Kyūshū, SW Japan 35°09′N 132°36′E
San Bizenti-Barakaldo see San Vicente de Barakaldo
40 J12 San Blas Nayarit, C Mexico 21°35′N 105°20′W
40 H8 San Blas Sinaloa, C Mexico 26°05′N 108°44′W
San Blas see Kuna Yala
43 U14 San Blas, Archipiélago de island group NE Panama
23 Q10 San Blas, Cape headland Florida, SE USA 29°39′N 85°21′W
43 V14 San Blas, Cordillera de ▲ NE Panama
62 J8 San Blas de los Sauces Catamarca, NW Argentina 28°18′S 67°12′W
106 G8 San Bonifacio Veneto, NE Italy 45°22′N 11°14′E
29 S12 Sanborn Iowa, C USA 43°10′N 95°39′W
40 M7 San Buenaventura Coahuila, NE Mexico 27°04′N 101°32′W
105 S5 San Caprasio ▲ N Spain 41°45′N 00°26′W
62 G13 San Carlos Bío Bío, C Chile 36°25′S 71°58′W
40 E9 San Carlos Baja California Sur, NW Mexico 24°52′N 112°15′W
41 N5 San Carlos Coahuila, NE Mexico 29°00′N 100°51′W
41 P9 San Carlos Tamaulipas, C Mexico 24°36′N 98°42′W
42 L12 San Carlos Río San Juan, S Nicaragua 11°06′N 84°46′W
43 T16 San Carlos Panamá, C Panama 08°29′N 79°58′W
171 N3 San Carlos off. San Carlos City. Luzon, N Philippines 15°57′N 120°18′E
61 G20 San Carlos Maldonado, S Uruguay 34°46′S 54°58′W
36 M14 San Carlos Arizona, SW USA 33°21′N 110°27′W
54 K5 San Carlos Cojedes, N Venezuela 09°39′N 68°35′W
San Carlos see Quesada, Costa Rica
San Carlos see Luba, Equatorial Guinea
61 B17 San Carlos Centro Santa Fe, C Argentina 31°45′S 61°05′W
171 P6 San Carlos City Negros, C Philippines 10°34′N 123°24′E
San Carlos City see San Carlos
San Carlos de Ancud see Ancud
63 H16 San Carlos de Bariloche Río Negro, SW Argentina 41°08′S 71°15′W
61 B21 San Carlos de Bolívar Buenos Aires, E Argentina 36°15′S 61°06′W
54 H6 San Carlos del Zulia Zulia, W Venezuela 09°01′N 71°58′W
54 L12 San Carlos de Río Negro Amazonas, S Venezuela 01°54′N 67°54′W
San Carlos, Estrecho de see Falkland Sound
36 M14 San Carlos Reservoir ⊠ Arizona, SW USA
42 M12 San Carlos, Río ≈ N Costa Rica
65 D24 San Carlos Settlement East Falkland, Falkland Islands
61 C23 San Cayetano Buenos Aires, E Argentina 38°20′S 59°37′W
103 O8 Sancerre Cher, C France 47°19′N 02°53′E
158 G7 Sanchakou Xinjiang Uygur Zizhiqu, NW China 39°56′N 78°28′E
Sanchoku see Samch'ŏk
41 O12 San Ciro San Luis Potosí, C Mexico 21°40′N 99°50′W
105 P10 San Clemente Castilla-La Mancha, C Spain 39°24′N 02°25′W
35 T16 San Clemente California, W USA 33°25′N 117°36′W
61 E21 San Clemente del Tuyú Buenos Aires, E Argentina 36°22′S 56°43′W
35 S17 San Clemente Island island Channel Islands, California, W USA
103 O9 Sancoins Cher, C France 46°49′N 03°00′E
61 B16 San Cristóbal Santa Fe, C Argentina 30°20′S 61°14′W
44 B4 San Cristóbal Pinar del Río, W Cuba 22°43′N 83°03′W
45 O9 San Cristóbal var. Benemérita de San Cristóbal. S Dominican Republic 18°27′N 70°07′W
54 H7 San Cristóbal Táchira, W Venezuela 07°46′N 72°15′W
187 N10 San Cristobal var. Makira. island SE Solomon Islands
San Cristóbal see San Cristóbal de Las Casas
41 U16 San Cristóbal de Las Casas var. San Cristóbal. Chiapas, SE Mexico 16°44′N 92°40′W
187 N10 San Cristóbal, Isla var. Chatham Island. island Galapagos Islands, Ecuador, E Pacific Ocean
42 D5 San Cristóbal Verapaz Alta Verapaz, C Guatemala 15°21′N 90°22′W
44 F6 Sancti Spíritus Sancti Spíritus, C Cuba 21°54′N 79°27′W
103 O11 Sancy, Puy de ▲ C France 45°33′N 02°48′E
95 D15 Sand Rogaland, S Norway 59°28′N 06°16′E
169 W7 Sandakan Sabah, East Malaysia 05°52′N 118°04′E
182 K9 Sandalwood South Australia 34°51′S 140°13′E
Sandalwood Island see Sumba, Pulau
94 D11 Sandane Sogn Og Fjordane, S Norway 61°47′N 06°14′E
114 G12 Sandanski prev. Sveti Vrach. Blagoevgrad, SW Bulgaria 41°36′N 23°19′E
Sandaohezi see Shawan
76 J11 Sandaré Kayes, W Mali 14°36′N 10°22′W
95 J19 Sandared Västra Götaland, S Sweden 57°43′N 12°47′E
94 N12 Sandarne Gävleborg, C Sweden 61°15′N 17°10′E
186 B5 Sandaun prev. West Sepik. ◆ province NW Papua New Guinea
96 K4 Sanday island NE Scotland, United Kingdom
31 P15 Sand Creek ≈ Indiana, N USA
95 H15 Sande Vestfold, S Norway 59°34′N 10°13′E
95 H16 Sandefjord Vestfold, S Norway 59°10′N 10°15′E
77 O15 Sandégué E Ivory Coast 07°59′N 03°33′W
77 P14 Sandema N Ghana 10°42′N 01°17′W
37 O11 Sanders Arizona, SW USA 35°13′N 109°21′W
24 M11 Sanderson Texas, SW USA 30°08′N 102°25′W
23 U4 Sandersville Georgia, SE USA 32°58′N 82°48′W
92 H4 Sandgerdhi Sudhurland, SW Iceland 64°01′N 22°42′W
28 K14 Sand Hills ▲ Nebraska, C USA
25 S14 Sandia Texas, SW USA 27°59′N 97°52′W
35 T17 San Diego California, W USA 32°43′N 117°09′W
25 S14 San Diego Texas, SW USA 27°47′N 98°15′W
136 F14 Sandıklı Afyon, W Turkey 38°28′N 30°17′E
152 L12 Sandila Uttar Pradesh, N India 27°05′N 80°37′E
San Dimitri Point see San Dimitri, Ras
121 N15 San Dimitri, Ras var. San Dimitri Point. headland Gozo, NW Malta 36°04′N 14°12′E
168 J13 Sanding, Selat strait W Indonesia
30 J3 Sand Island island Apostle Islands, Wisconsin, N USA
95 C16 Sandnes Rogaland, S Norway 58°51′N 05°45′E
92 F13 Sandnessjøen Nordland, C Norway 66°00′N 12°37′E
Sando see Sandoy
79 L24 Sandoa Katanga, S Dem. Rep. Congo 09°41′S 22°56′E
111 N15 Sandomierz Rus. Sandomir. Świętokrzyskie, C Poland 50°42′N 21°45′E
Sandomir see Sandomierz
54 C13 Sandoná Nariño, SW Colombia 01°18′N 77°28′W
106 I7 San Donà di Piave Veneto, NE Italy 45°38′N 12°34′E
124 K14 Sandovo Tverskaya Oblast', W Russian Federation 58°26′N 36°30′E
Sandoway see Thandwe
97 M24 Sandown S England, United Kingdom 50°40′N 01°11′W
95 B19 Sandoy Dan. Sandø. island C Faeroe Islands
39 N16 Sand Point Popof Island, Alaska, USA 55°20′N 160°30′W
32 M7 Sandpoint Idaho, NW USA 48°16′N 116°33′W
65 N24 Sand Point headland E Tristan da Cunha
31 R7 Sand Point headland Michigan, N USA 43°54′N 83°24′W
93 H14 Sandsele Västerbotten, N Sweden 65°16′N 17°40′E
10 I14 Sandspit Moresby Island, British Columbia, SW Canada 53°14′N 131°50′W
27 P9 Sand Springs Oklahoma, C USA 36°08′N 96°06′W
29 W7 Sandstone Minnesota, N USA 46°07′N 92°51′W
36 K15 Sand Tank Mountains ▲ Arizona, SW USA
31 S8 Sandusky Michigan, N USA 43°26′N 82°50′W
31 S11 Sandusky Ohio, N USA 41°27′N 82°42′W
31 S12 Sandusky River ≈ Ohio, N USA
83 D22 Sandverhaar Karas, S Namibia 26°50′S 17°25′E
95 L24 Sandvig Bornholm, E Denmark 55°15′N 14°45′E
95 H15 Sandvika Akershus, S Norway 59°54′N 10°29′E
94 N13 Sandviken Gävleborg, C Sweden 60°38′N 16°50′E
30 M11 Sandwich Illinois, N USA 41°39′N 88°37′W
Sandwich Island see Efate
Sandwich Islands see Hawaiian Islands
153 V16 Sandwip island SE Bangladesh
11 U12 Sandy Bay Saskatchewan, C Canada 55°31′N 102°14′W
183 N16 Sandy Cape headland Tasmania, SE Australia 41°27′S 144°43′E
36 L3 Sandy City Utah, W USA 40°36′N 111°53′W
31 U12 Sandy Creek ≈ Ohio, N USA
21 O5 Sandy Hook Kentucky, S USA 38°05′N 83°09′W
18 K15 Sandy Hook headland New Jersey, NE USA 40°27′N 73°59′W
Sandykachi/Sandykgachy see Sandykgaçy
146 J15 Sandykgaçy var. Sandykgachy. Maryyskiy Velayat, S Turkmenistan 36°34′N 62°28′E
Sandykgachy see Sandykgaçy
146 J15 Sandykgaçy var. Sandykgachy, Rus. Sandykachi. Mary Welaýaty, S Turkmenistan 36°34′N 62°28′E
146 L13 Sandykly Gumy Rus. Peski Sandykly. desert E Turkmenistan
Sandykly, Peski see Sandykly Gumy
11 Q13 Sandy Lake Alberta, W Canada 55°50′N 113°30′W
12 B8 Sandy Lake Ontario, C Canada 53°00′N 93°25′W
12 B8 Sandy Lake ◎ Ontario, C Canada
65 N25 Sandy Point headland E Tristan da Cunha
23 S3 Sandy Springs Georgia, SE USA 33°57′N 84°23′W
24 H8 San Elizario Texas, SW USA 31°35′N 106°16′W
99 L25 Sanem Luxembourg, SW Luxembourg 49°33′N 05°56′E
42 K5 San Esteban Olancho, C Honduras 15°19′N 85°52′W
105 O6 San Esteban de Gormaz Castilla-León, N Spain 41°34′N 03°13′W
40 E5 San Esteban, Isla island NW Mexico
San Eugenio/San Eugenio del Cuareim see Artigas
62 H11 San Felipe var. San Felipe de Aconcagua. Valparaíso, C Chile 32°45′S 70°42′W
40 D3 San Felipe Baja California Norte, NW Mexico 31°03′N 114°52′W
40 N12 San Felipe Guanajuato, C Mexico 21°30′N 101°15′W
54 K5 San Felipe Yaracuy, NW Venezuela 10°25′N 68°40′W
44 B5 San Felipe, Cayos de island group W Cuba
San Felipe de Aconcagua see San Felipe
San Felipe de Puerto Plata see Puerto Plata
37 R11 San Felipe Pueblo New Mexico, SW USA 35°25′N 106°27′W
San Feliú de Guixols see Sant Feliu de Guixols
193 T10 San Félix, Isla Eng. San Felix Island. island W Chile
San Felix Island see San Félix, Isla
54 L11 San Fernanado de Atabapo Amazonas, S Venezuela 04°00′N 67°42′W
40 C4 San Fernando var. Misión San Fernando. Baja California Norte, NW Mexico 29°58′N 115°14′W
41 P9 San Fernando Tamaulipas, C Mexico 24°50′N 98°10′W
171 N2 San Fernando Luzon, N Philippines 16°45′N 120°21′E
171 O3 San Fernando Luzon, N Philippines 15°01′N 120°41′E
104 J16 San Fernando prev. Isla de León. Andalucía, S Spain 36°28′N 06°12′W
45 U14 San Fernando Trinidad, Trinidad and Tobago 10°17′N 61°27′W
35 S15 San Fernando California, W USA 34°16′N 118°26′W
54 L7 San Fernando var. San Fernando de Apure. Apure, C Venezuela 07°54′N 67°28′W
San Fernando de Apure see San Fernando
62 L8 San Fernando del Valle de Catamarca var. Catamarca. Catamarca, NW Argentina 28°28′S 65°46′W
San Fernando de Monte Cristi see Monte Cristi
41 P9 San Fernando, Río ≈ C Mexico
23 X11 Sanford Florida, SE USA 28°48′N 81°16′W
19 P9 Sanford Maine, NE USA 43°26′N 70°46′W
21 T10 Sanford North Carolina, SE USA 35°29′N 79°10′W
25 N2 Sanford Texas, SW USA 35°42′N 101°31′W
39 T10 Sanford, Mount ▲ Alaska, USA 62°21′N 144°12′W
42 G8 San Francisco var. Gotera, San Francisco Gotera. Morazán, E El Salvador 13°41′N 88°06′W
43 R16 San Francisco Veraguas, C Panama 08°19′N 80°59′W
171 N2 San Francisco var. Aurora. Luzon, N Philippines 13°22′N 122°31′E
35 L8 San Francisco California, W USA 37°47′N 122°25′W
54 H5 San Francisco Zulia, NW Venezuela 10°36′N 71°39′W
34 M8 San Francisco ✕ California, W USA 37°37′N 122°23′W
35 N9 San Francisco Bay bay California, W USA
61 C24 San Francisco de Bellocq Buenos Aires, E Argentina 38°42′S 60°01′W
40 I6 San Francisco de Borja Chihuahua, N Mexico 27°57′N 106°42′W
42 J6 San Francisco de la Paz Olancho, C Honduras 14°55′N 86°14′W
40 J7 San Francisco del Oro Chihuahua, N Mexico 26°52′N 105°50′W
40 M12 San Francisco del Rincón Jalisco, SW Mexico 21°00′N 101°51′W
45 O8 San Francisco de Macorís C Dominican Republic 19°19′N 70°15′W
San Francisco de Satipo see Satipo
San Francisco Gotera see San Francisco
San Francisco Telixtlahuaca see Telixtlahuaca
107 K23 San Fratello Sicilia, Italy, C Mediterranean Sea 38°00′N 14°35′E
San Fructuoso see Tacuarembó
82 C12 Sanga Cuanza Sul, NW Angola 11°10′S 15°27′E
56 C5 San Gabriel Carchi, N Ecuador 0°35′N 77°48′W
159 S15 Sa'ngain Xizang Zizhiqu, W China 30°47′N 98°45′E
154 E13 Sangamner Mahārāshtra, W India 19°37′N 74°18′E
152 H12 Sāngāner Rājasthān, N India 26°48′N 75°48′E
Sangan, Koh-i- see Sangān, Kūh-e
149 N6 Sangān, Kūh-e Pash. Koh-i-Sangan. ▲ C Afghanistan
123 P10 Sangar Respublika Sakha (Yakutiya), NE Russian Federation 63°48′N 127°37′E
155 H18 Sangāreddi Andhra Pradesh, India 17°37′N 78°04′E
169 V11 Sangasanga Borneo, C Indonesia 0°36′S 117°12′E
103 N1 Sangatte Pas-de-Calais, N France 50°56′N 01°41′E
107 B19 San Gavino Monreale Sardegna, Italy, C Mediterranean Sea 39°33′N 08°47′E
57 D16 Sangayan, Isla island W Peru
30 L14 Sangchris Lake ⊠ Illinois, N USA
171 N16 Sangeang, Pulau island S Indonesia
116 I10 Sângeorgiu de Pădure prev. Erdăt-Sângeorz, Sîngeorgiu de Pădure, Hung. Erdőszentgyörgy. Mureș, C Romania 46°27′N 24°50′E
116 I9 Sângeorz-Băi var. Singeroz Băi, Ger. Rumänisch-Sankt-Georgen, Hung. Oláhszentgyörgy; prev. Sîngeorz-Băi. Bistrița-Năsăud, N Romania 47°24′N 24°40′E
35 R10 Sanger California, W USA 36°42′N 119°33′W
25 T5 Sanger Texas, SW USA 33°21′N 97°10′W
Sângerei see Sîngerei
101 L15 Sangerhausen Sachsen-Anhalt, C Germany 51°29′N 11°18′E
45 S6 San Germán W Puerto Rico 18°05′N 67°02′W
San Germano see Cassino
161 N2 Sanggan He ≈ E China
169 Q11 Sanggau Borneo, C Indonesia 0°08′N 110°35′E
79 G17 Sangha ◆ province N Congo
79 H16 Sangha ≈ Central African Republic/Congo
79 G16 Sangha-Mbaéré ◆ prefecture SW Central African Republic
149 Q15 Sānghar Sind, SE Pakistan 26°10′N 68°59′E
115 F22 Sangiás ▲ S Greece 36°39′N 22°24′E
Sangihe, Kepulauan see Sangir, Kepulauan
171 Q9 Sangihe, Pulau var. Sangir. island N Indonesia
54 G8 San Gil Santander, C Colombia 06°35′N 73°08′W
106 F12 San Gimignano Toscana, C Italy 43°30′N 11°00′E
148 M8 Sangin var. Sangin. Helmand, S Afghanistan 32°03′N 64°50′E
Sangin see Sangin
107 O21 San Giovanni in Fiore Calabria, SW Italy 39°15′N 16°42′E
107 M16 San Giovanni Rotondo Puglia, SE Italy 41°43′N 15°44′E
106 G12 San Giovanni Valdarno Toscana, C Italy 43°34′N 11°31′E
Sangir see Sangihe, Pulau
171 Q10 Sangir, Kepulauan var. Kepulauan Sangihe. island group N Indonesia
Sangiyn Dalay see Erdenedalay, Dundgovĭ, Mongolia
Sangiyn Dalay see Erdene, Govĭ-Altay, Mongolia
Sangiyn Dalay see Nomgon, Ömnögovĭ, Mongolia
Sangiyn Dalay see Öldziyt, Övörhangay, Mongolia
163 Y15 Sangju Jap. Shōshū. C South Korea 36°26′N 128°09′E
167 R11 Sângkha Surin, E Thailand 14°36′N 103°43′E
169 W10 Sangkulirang Borneo, N Indonesia 01°00′N 117°56′E
169 W10 Sangkulirang, Teluk bay Borneo, N Indonesia
155 E16 Sāngli Mahārāshtra, W India 16°55′N 74°37′E
79 E16 Sangmélima Sud, S Cameroon 02°57′N 11°56′E
35 V15 San Gorgonio Mountain ▲ California, W USA 34°06′N 116°50′W
37 T8 Sangre de Cristo Mountains ▲ Colorado/New Mexico, C USA
61 A20 San Gregorio Santa Fe, C Argentina 34°18′S 62°02′W
61 F18 San Gregorio de Polanco Tacuarembó, C Uruguay 32°37′S 55°50′W
45 V14 Sangre Grande Trinidad, Trinidad and Tobago 10°35′N 61°08′W
159 N16 Sangri Xizang Zizhiqu, W China 29°17′N 92°01′E
152 H9 Sangrūr Punjab, NW India 30°16′N 75°52′E
158 K16 Sangsang Xizang Zizhiqu, W China 29°45′N 86°42′E
44 I11 Sangster off. Sir Donald Sangster International Airport, var. Montego Bay. ✕ (Montego Bay) W Jamaica 18°30′N 77°54′W
59 G17 Sangue, Rio do ≈ W Brazil
105 R4 Sangüesa Navarra, N Spain 42°34′N 01°17′W
61 C16 San Gustavo Entre Ríos, E Argentina 30°41′S 59°23′W
Sangyuan see Wuqiao
40 C6 San Hipólito, Punta headland W Mexico 26°57′N 114°00′W
23 W15 Sanibel Sanibel Island, Florida, SE USA 26°27′N 82°01′W
23 V15 Sanibel Island island Florida, SE USA
60 F13 San Ignacio Misiones, NE Argentina 27°15′S 55°32′W
42 F2 San Ignacio prev. Cayo, El Cayo. Cayo, W Belize 17°09′N 89°02′W
57 L16 San Ignacio Beni, N Bolivia 14°54′S 65°35′W
57 O18 San Ignacio Santa Cruz, E Bolivia 16°23′S 60°59′W
42 M14 San Ignacio var. San Ignacio de Acosta. San José, W Costa Rica 09°46′N 84°10′W
40 E6 San Ignacio Baja California Sur, NW Mexico 27°18′N 112°51′W
40 J10 San Ignacio Sinaloa, W Mexico 23°55′N 106°25′W
56 B9 San Ignacio Cajamarca, N Peru 05°09′S 79°00′W
San Ignacio de Acosta see San Ignacio
40 D7 San Ignacio, Laguna lagoon W Mexico
12 I6 Sanikiluaq Belcher Islands, Nunavut, C Canada 55°20′N 77°50′W
171 O3 San Ildefonso Peninsula peninsula Luzon, N Philippines
Saniquillie see Sanniquellie
61 D20 San Isidro Buenos Aires, E Argentina 34°28′S 58°31′W
43 N14 San Isidro var. San Isidro de El General. San José, SE Costa Rica 09°28′N 83°42′W
San Isidro de El General see San Isidro
54 E5 San Jacinto Bolívar, N Colombia 09°53′N 75°06′W
35 U16 San Jacinto California, W USA 33°47′N 116°58′W
35 V15 San Jacinto Peak ▲ California, W USA 33°48′N 116°40′W
61 F14 San Javier Misiones, NE Argentina 27°50′S 55°06′W
61 C16 San Javier Santa Fe, C Argentina 30°35′S 59°59′W
105 S13 San Javier Murcia, SE Spain 37°49′N 00°50′W
61 D18 San Javier Río Negro, W Uruguay 32°41′S 58°08′W
61 C16 San Javier, Río ≈ C Argentina
160 L12 Sanjiang var. Guyi, Sanjiang Dongzu Zizhixian. Guangxi Zhuangzu Zizhiqu, S China 25°46′N 109°26′E
Sanjiang see Jinping, Guizhou
Sanjiang Dongzu Zizhixian see Sanjiang
Sanjiaocheng see Haiyan
165 N11 Sanjō var. Sanzyô. Niigata, Honshū, C Japan 37°39′N 139°00′E
57 M15 San Joaquín Beni, N Bolivia 13°06′S 64°46′W
55 O6 San Joaquín Anzoátegui, NE Venezuela 09°21′N 64°30′W
35 O9 San Joaquin River ≈ California, W USA
35 P10 San Joaquin Valley valley California, W USA
61 A18 San Jorge Santa Fe, C Argentina 31°50′S 61°50′W
40 D3 San Jorge, Bahía de bay NW Mexico
63 J19 San Jorge, Golfo var. Gulf of San Jorge. gulf S Argentina
San Jorge, Gulf of see San Jorge, Golfo
San Jorge, Isla de see Weddell Island
61 F14 San José Misiones, NE Argentina 27°46′S 55°47′W
57 P19 San José var. San José de Chiquitos. Santa Cruz, E Bolivia 14°13′S 68°05′W
42 M14 San José ● (Costa Rica) San José, C Costa Rica 09°55′N 84°05′W
42 C7 San José var. Puerto San José. Escuintla, S Guatemala 14°00′N 90°50′W
40 G6 San José Sonora, NW Mexico 27°32′N 110°09′W
188 K8 San Jose Tinian, S Northern Mariana Islands 15°00′S 145°38′E
105 U11 San José Eivissa, Spain, W Mediterranean Sea 38°55′N 01°18′E
35 N9 San Jose California, W USA 37°18′N 121°53′W
54 H5 San José Zulia, NW Venezuela 10°02′N 72°24′W
42 M14 San José off. Provincia de San José. ◆ province W Costa Rica
61 E19 San José ◆ department S Uruguay
42 M13 San José ✕ Alajuela, C Costa Rica 10°03′N 84°12′W
San José see San José del Guaviare, Colombia
San Jose see Oleai
San Jose see Sant Josep de sa Talaia, Ibiza, Spain
San José see San José de Mayo, Uruguay
171 O3 San Jose City Luzon, N Philippines 15°49′N 120°57′E
San José de Chiquitos see San José
San José de Cúcuta see Cúcuta
61 D16 San José de Feliciano Entre Ríos, E Argentina 30°26′S 58°46′W
55 O6 San José de Guanipa var. El Tigrito. Anzoátegui, NE Venezuela 08°54′N 64°10′W
62 I9 San José de Jáchal San Juan, W Argentina 30°15′S 68°46′W
40 G10 San José del Cabo Baja California Sur, NW Mexico 23°01′N 109°40′W
54 G12 San José del Guaviare var. San José. Guaviare, S Colombia 02°34′N 72°38′W
61 E20 San José de Mayo var. San José. San José, S Uruguay 34°20′S 56°42′W
54 I10 San José de Ocuné Vichada, E Colombia 04°10′N 70°21′W
41 O9 San José de Raíces Nuevo León, NE Mexico 24°32′N 100°15′W
63 K17 San José, Golfo gulf E Argentina
40 F9 San José, Isla island NW Mexico
43 U16 San José, Isla island SE Panama
25 U14 San Jose Island island Texas, SW USA
San José, Provincia de see San José
62 I10 San Juan San Juan, W Argentina 31°37′S 68°27′W
45 N9 San Juan var. San Juan de la Maguana. C Dominican Republic 18°49′N 71°12′W
57 E17 San Juan Ica, S Peru 15°22′S 75°07′W
45 U5 San Juan ○ (Puerto Rico) NE Puerto Rico 18°28′N 66°06′W
62 H10 San Juan off. Provincia de San Juan. ◆ province W Argentina
45 U5 San Juan var. Luis Muñoz Marín. ✕ NE Puerto Rico 18°27′N 66°05′W
San Juan see San Juan de los Morros
62 O7 San Juan Bautista Misiones, S Paraguay 26°40′S 57°08′W
35 O10 San Juan Bautista California, W USA 36°50′N 121°34′W
San Juan Bautista see Villahermosa
San Juan Bautista Cuicatlán see Cuicatlán
San Juan Bautista Tuxtepec see Tuxtepec

◆ Country
● Country Capital
◇ Dependent Territory
○ Dependent Territory Capital
◆ Administrative Regions
✕ International Airport
▲ Mountain
▲ Mountain Range
Volcano
≈ River
◎ Lake
⊠ Reservoir

79 C17 **San Juan, Cabo** *headland* S Equatorial Guinea *01°09′N 09°25′E*
105 S12 **San Juan de Alicante** País Valenciano, E Spain *38°26′N 00°27′W*
54 H7 **San Juan de Colón** Táchira, NW Venezuela *08°02′N 72°17′W*
40 L9 **San Juan de Guadalupe** Durango, C Mexico *25°12′N 100°50′W*
San Juan de la Maguana *see* San Juan
54 G4 **San Juan del Cesar** La Guajira, N Colombia *10°45′N 73°00′W*
40 L15 **San Juan de Lima, Punta** *headland* SW Mexico *18°34′N 103°40′W*
42 I8 **San Juan de Limay** Estelí, NW Nicaragua *13°10′N 86°36′W*
43 N12 **San Juan del Norte** *var.* Greytown. Río San Juan, SE Nicaragua *10°58′N 83°40′W*
54 K4 **San Juan de los Cayos** Falcón, N Venezuela *11°11′N 68°27′W*
40 M12 **San Juan de los Lagos** Jalisco, C Mexico *21°15′N 102°15′W*
54 L5 **San Juan de los Morros** *var.* San Juan. Guárico, N Venezuela *09°53′N 67°23′W*
40 K9 **San Juan del Río** Durango, C Mexico *25°12′N 100°50′W*
41 O13 **San Juan del Río** Querétaro de Arteaga, C Mexico *20°24′N 100°00′W*
42 J11 **San Juan del Sur** Rivas, SW Nicaragua *11°16′N 85°51′W*
54 M9 **San Juan de Manapiare** Amazonas, S Venezuela *05°15′N 66°05′W*
40 E7 **San Juanico** Baja California Sur, NW Mexico
40 D7 **San Juanico, Punta** *headland* NW Mexico *26°01′N 112°17′W*
32 G6 **San Juan Islands** *island group* Washington, NW USA
40 I6 **San Juanito** Chihuahua, N Mexico
40 I12 **San Juanito, Isla** *island* C Mexico
37 R8 **San Juan Mountains** ▲▲ Colorado, C USA
54 E5 **San Juan Nepomuceno** Bolívar, NW Colombia *09°57′N 75°06′W*
44 E5 **San Juan, Pico** ▲ C Cuba *21°58′N 80°10′W*
San Juan, Provincia de *see* San Juan
191 W15 **San Juan, Punta** *headland* Easter Island, Chile, E Pacific Ocean *27°03′S 109°22′W*
42 M12 **San Juan, Río** ≈ Costa Rica/Nicaragua
41 S15 **San Juan, Río** ≈ SE Mexico
37 O8 **San Juan River** ≈ Colorado/Utah, W USA
San Julián *see* Puerto San Julián
61 B17 **San Justo** Santa Fe, C Argentina *30°47′S 60°32′W*
109 W5 **Sankt Aegyd am Neuwalde** Niederösterreich, E Austria *47°51′N 15°34′E*
109 U9 **Sankt Andrä** *Slvn.* Šent Andraž. Kärnten, S Austria *46°46′N 14°49′E*
Sankt Andrä *see* Szentendre
Sankt Anna *see* Sântana
108 K8 **Sankt Anton-am-Arlberg** Vorarlberg, W Austria *47°08′N 10°11′E*
101 E16 **Sankt Augustin** Nordrhein-Westfalen, W Germany *50°46′N 07°10′E*
Sankt-Bartholomäi *see* Palamuse
101 F24 **Sankt Blasien** Baden-Württemberg, SW Germany *47°43′N 08°09′E*
109 R3 **Sankt Florian am Inn** Oberösterreich, N Austria *48°24′N 13°27′E*
108 I7 **Sankt Gallen** *var.* St. Gallen, *Eng.* Saint Gall, *Fr.* St-Gall. Sankt Gallen, NE Switzerland *47°25′N 09°23′E*
108 H8 **Sankt Gallen** *var.* St.Gallen, *Eng.* Saint Gall, *Fr.* St-Gall. ◆ *canton* NE Switzerland
108 J8 **Sankt Gallenkirch** Vorarlberg, W Austria *47°00′N 10°59′E*
109 Q5 **Sankt Georgen** Salzburg, N Austria *47°59′N 12°57′E*
Sankt Georgen *see* Đurđevac
Sankt-Georgen *see* Sfântu Gheorghe
109 R6 **Sankt Gilgen** Salzburg, NW Austria *47°46′N 13°21′E*
Sankt Gotthard *see* Szentgotthárd
101 E20 **Sankt Ingbert** Saarland, SW Germany *49°17′N 07°07′E*
Sankt-Jakobi *see* Viru-Jaagupi, Lääne-Virumaa, Estonia
Sankt-Jakobi *see* Pärnu-Jaagupi, Pärnumaa, Estonia
Sankt Johann *see* Sankt Johann in Tirol
109 T7 **Sankt Johann am Tauern** Steiermark, E Austria *47°20′N 14°27′E*
109 Q7 **Sankt Johann im Pongau** Salzburg, NW Austria *47°22′N 13°13′E*
109 P6 **Sankt Johann in Tirol** *var.* Sankt Johann. Tirol, W Austria *47°32′N 12°26′E*
Sankt-Johannis *see* Järva-Jaani
108 L8 **Sankt Leonhard** Tirol, W Austria *47°05′N 10°53′E*
Sankt Margarethen *see* Sankt Margarethen im Burgenland
109 Y5 **Sankt Margarethen im Burgenland** *var.* Sankt Margarethen. Burgenland, E Austria *47°49′N 16°38′E*
Sankt Martin *see* Martin
109 X8 **Sankt Martin an der Raab** Burgenland, SE Austria *46°59′N 16°12′E*
109 U7 **Sankt Michael in Obersteiermark** Steiermark, SE Austria *47°21′N 14°59′E*
Sankt Michel *see* Mikkeli
Sankt Moritz *see* St. Moritz
108 E11 **Sankt Niklaus** Valais, S Switzerland *46°09′N 07°48′E*
109 S7 **Sankt Nikolai** *var.* Sankt Nikolai im Sölktal. Steiermark, SE Austria *47°18′N 14°04′E*
Sankt Nikolai im Sölktal *see* Sankt Nikolai
109 U9 **Sankt Paul** *var.* Sankt Paul im Lavanttal. Kärnten, S Austria *46°42′N 14°53′E*
Sankt Paul im Lavanttal *see* Sankt Paul
Sankt Peter *see* Pivka
109 W9 **Sankt Peter am Ottersbach** Steiermark, SE Austria *46°49′N 15°48′E*
124 J13 **Sankt-Peterburg** *prev.* Leningrad, Petrograd, *Eng.* Saint Petersburg, *Fin.* Pietari. Leningradskaya Oblast', NW Russian Federation *59°55′N 30°25′E*
100 H8 **Sankt Peter-Ording** Schleswig-Holstein, N Germany *54°18′N 08°37′E*
109 V4 **Sankt Pölten** Niederösterreich, N Austria *48°14′N 15°38′E*
109 W7 **Sankt Ruprecht** *var.* Sankt Ruprecht an der Raab. Steiermark, SE Austria *47°10′N 15°41′E*
Sankt Ruprecht an der Raab *see* Sankt Ruprecht
Sankt-Ulrich *see* Ortisei
109 T4 **Sankt Valentin** Niederösterreich, C Austria *48°11′N 14°33′E*
Sankt Veit am Flaum *see* Rijeka
109 T9 **Sankt Veit an der Glan** *Slvn.* St. Vid. Kärnten, S Austria *46°47′N 14°22′E*
99 M21 **Sankt-Vith** *var.* Saint-Vith. Liège, E Belgium *50°17′N 06°07′E*
101 E20 **Sankt Wendel** Saarland, SW Germany *49°28′N 07°10′E*
109 R6 **Sankt Wolfgang** Salzburg, NW Austria *47°43′N 13°30′E*
79 K21 **Sankuru** ≈ C Dem. Rep. Congo
40 D8 **San Lázaro, Cabo** *headland* NW Mexico *24°46′N 112°15′W*
137 O16 **Şanlıurfa** *prev.* Sanli Urfa, Urfa; *anc.* Edessa. şanlıurfa, S Turkey *37°08′N 38°45′E*
137 O16 **Şanlıurfa** *prev.* Urfa. ◐ *province* SE Turkey
Sanli Urfa *see* Şanlıurfa
137 O16 **Şanlıurfa Yaylası** *plateau* SE Turkey
61 B18 **San Lorenzo** Santa Fe, C Argentina *32°45′S 60°45′W*
57 M21 **San Lorenzo** Tarija, S Bolivia *21°25′S 64°45′W*
56 C5 **San Lorenzo** Esmeraldas, N Ecuador *01°15′N 78°51′W*
42 H8 **San Lorenzo** Valle, S Honduras *13°24′N 87°27′W*
56 A6 **San Lorenzo, Cabo** *headland* W Ecuador *0°57′S 80°49′W*
105 N8 **San Lorenzo de El Escorial** *var.* El Escorial. Madrid, C Spain *40°36′N 04°07′W*
40 E5 **San Lorenzo, Isla** *island* NW Mexico
57 C14 **San Lorenzo, Isla** *island* W Peru
63 G20 **San Lorenzo, Monte** ▲ S Argentina *47°40′S 72°12′W*
40 I9 **San Lorenzo, Río** ≈ C Mexico
104 J15 **Sanlúcar de Barrameda** Andalucía, S Spain *36°46′N 06°21′W*
104 J14 **Sanlúcar la Mayor** Andalucía, S Spain *37°24′N 06°13′W*
40 F11 **San Lucas** Baja California Sur, NW Mexico *22°50′N 109°52′W*
40 E6 **San Lucas** *var.* Cabo San Lucas. Baja California Sur, NW Mexico *27°14′N 112°15′W*
40 G11 **San Lucas, Cabo** *var.* San Lucas Cape. *headland* NW Mexico *22°52′N 109°53′W*
San Lucas Cape *see* San Lucas, Cabo
62 J11 **San Luis** San Luis, C Argentina *33°18′S 66°18′W*
42 E4 **San Luis** Petén, NE Guatemala *16°16′N 89°27′W*
40 D2 **San Luis** *var.* San Luis Río Colorado. Sonora, NW Mexico *32°26′N 114°48′W*
42 M7 **San Luis** Región Autónoma Atlántico Norte, NE Nicaragua *13°59′N 84°10′W*
36 H15 **San Luis** Arizona, SW USA *32°27′N 114°45′W*
37 T8 **San Luis** Colorado, C USA *37°09′N 105°24′W*
54 J4 **San Luis** Falcón, N Venezuela *11°09′N 69°39′W*
62 J11 **San Luis** *off.* Provincia de San Luis. ◐ *province* C Argentina
41 N12 **San Luis de la Paz** Guanajuato, C Mexico *21°15′N 100°33′W*
40 K8 **San Luis del Cordero** Durango, C Mexico *25°25′N 104°09′W*
40 D4 **San Luis, Isla** *island* NW Mexico
42 E6 **San Luis Jilotepeque** Jalapa, SE Guatemala *14°40′N 89°42′W*
57 M16 **San Luis, Laguna de** ◎ NW Bolivia
35 P13 **San Luis Obispo** California, W USA *35°17′N 120°40′W*
37 R7 **San Luis Peak** ▲ Colorado, C USA *37°59′N 106°55′W*
41 N11 **San Luis Potosí** San Luis Potosí, C Mexico *22°10′N 100°57′W*
41 N11 **San Luis Potosí** ◐ *state* C Mexico
San Luis, Provincia de *see* San Luis
35 O10 **San Luis Reservoir** ⊠ California, W USA
San Luis Río Colorado *see* San Luis
37 S8 **San Luis Valley** *basin* Colorado, C USA
107 C19 **Sanluri** Sardegna, Italy, C Mediterranean Sea *39°34′N 08°54′E*
61 D23 **San Manuel** Buenos Aires, E Argentina *37°47′S 58°50′W*
36 M15 **San Manuel** Arizona, SW USA *32°36′N 110°37′W*
106 F11 **San Marcello Pistoiese** Toscana, C Italy *44°03′N 10°46′E*
107 N20 **San Marco Argentano** Calabria, SW Italy *39°31′N 16°07′E*
54 E6 **San Marcos** Sucre, N Colombia *08°38′N 75°10′W*
42 M14 **San Marcos** San José, C Costa Rica *09°39′N 84°00′W*
42 B5 **San Marcos** San Marcos, W Guatemala *14°58′N 91°48′W*
42 F6 **San Marcos** Ocotepeque, SW Honduras *14°23′N 88°57′W*
41 O16 **San Marcos** Guerrero, S Mexico *16°45′N 99°22′W*
25 S11 **San Marcos** Texas, SW USA *29°54′N 97°57′W*
42 A5 **San Marcos** *off.* Departamento de San Marcos. ◐ *department* W Guatemala
San Marcos de Arica *see* Arica
San Marcos, Departamento de *see* San Marcos
40 E6 **San Marcos, Isla** *island* NW Mexico
106 H11 **San Marino** ● (San Marino) C San Marino *43°54′N 12°27′E*
106 I11 **San Marino** *off.* Republic of San Marino. ◆ *republic* S Europe
San Marino, Republic of *see* San Marino
62 I11 **San Martín** Mendoza, C Argentina *33°05′S 68°28′W*
54 F11 **San Martín** Meta, C Colombia *03°43′N 73°42′W*
56 D11 **San Martín** *off.* Departamento de San Martín. ◐ *department* C Peru
194 I5 **San Martín** *Argentinian research station* Antarctica *68°18′S 67°03′W*
63 H16 **San Martín de los Andes** Neuquén, W Argentina *40°11′S 71°22′W*
San Martín, Departamento de *see* San Martín
104 M8 **San Martín de Valdeiglesias** Madrid, C Spain *40°21′N 04°24′W*
63 G21 **San Martín, Lago** *var.* Lago O'Higgins. ◎ S Argentina
106 H6 **San Martino di Castrozza** Trentino-Alto Adige, N Italy *46°16′N 11°50′E*
57 N16 **San Martín, Río** ≈ N Bolivia
San Martin Texmelucan *see* Texmelucan
35 N9 **San Mateo** California, W USA *37°33′N 122°19′W*
55 O6 **San Mateo** Anzoátegui, NE Venezuela *09°48′N 64°36′W*
42 B4 **San Mateo Ixtatán** Huehuetenango, W Guatemala *15°50′N 91°30′W*
57 Q18 **San Matías** Santa Cruz, E Bolivia *16°20′S 58°24′W*
63 K16 **San Matías, Golfo** *var.* Gulf of San Matías. *gulf* E Argentina
San Matías, Gulf of *see* San Matías, Golfo
15 O8 **Sanmaur** Québec, SE Canada *47°52′N 73°47′W*
161 T10 **Sanmen Wan** *bay* E China
160 M6 **Sanmenxia** *var.* Shan Xian. Henan, C China *34°46′N 111°17′E*
Sânmiclăuş Mare *see* Sânnicolau Mare
61 D14 **San Miguel** Corrientes, NE Argentina *28°02′S 57°41′W*
57 L16 **San Miguel** Beni, N Bolivia *16°43′S 61°06′W*
42 G8 **San Miguel** San Miguel, SE El Salvador *13°27′N 88°11′W*
40 L6 **San Miguel** Coahuila, N Mexico *29°10′N 101°28′W*
40 J9 **San Miguel** *var.* San Miguel de Cruces. Durango, C Mexico *24°25′N 105°55′W*
43 U16 **San Miguel** Panamá, SE Panama *08°27′N 78°51′W*
35 P12 **San Miguel** California, W USA *35°45′N 120°42′W*
42 B9 **San Miguel** ◐ *department* E El Salvador
41 N13 **San Miguel de Allende** Guanajuato, C Mexico *20°56′N 100°48′W*
San Miguel de Cruces *see* San Miguel
San Miguel de Ibarra *see* Ibarra
61 D21 **San Miguel del Monte** Buenos Aires, E Argentina *35°26′S 58°50′W*
62 J7 **San Miguel de Tucumán** *var.* Tucumán. Tucumán, N Argentina *26°47′S 65°15′W*
43 V16 **San Miguel, Golfo de** *gulf* S Panama
35 P15 **San Miguel Island** *island* California, W USA
42 L11 **San Miguelito** Río San Juan, S Nicaragua *11°22′N 84°54′W*
43 T15 **San Miguelito** Panamá, C Panama *08°58′N 79°31′W*
57 N18 **San Miguel, Río** ≈ E Bolivia
56 D6 **San Miguel, Río** ≈ Colombia/Ecuador
40 I7 **San Miguel, Río** ≈ N Mexico
42 G8 **San Miguel, Volcán de** Ѫ SE El Salvador *13°27′N 88°18′W*
161 Q12 **Sanming** Fujian, SE China *26°11′N 117°37′E*
106 F11 **San Miniato** Toscana, C Italy *43°40′N 10°53′E*
San Murezzan *see* St. Moritz
Sannār *see* Sennar
107 M15 **Sannicandro Garganico** Puglia, SE Italy *41°50′N 15°32′E*
40 H6 **San Nicolás** Sonora, NW Mexico *28°31′N 109°24′W*
61 C19 **San Nicolás de los Arroyos** Buenos Aires, E Argentina *33°20′S 60°13′W*
35 R16 **San Nicolas Island** *island* Channel Islands, California, W USA
Sânnicolaul-Mare *see* Sânnicolau Mare
116 E11 **Sânnicolau Mare** *var.* Sânnicolaul-Mare, *Hung.* Nagyszentmiklós; *prev.* Sânmiclăuş Mare, Sînnicolau Mare. Timiş, W Romania *46°05′N 20°38′E*
123 Q6 **Sannikova, Proliv** *strait* NE Russian Federation
76 K16 **Sanniquellie** *var.* Saniquillie. NE Liberia *07°24′N 08°45′W*
165 R7 **Sannohe** Aomori, Honshū, C Japan *40°23′N 141°16′E*
Sanntaler Alpen *see* Kamniško-Savinjske Alpe
111 O17 **Sanok** Podkarpackie, SE Poland *49°31′N 22°14′E*
54 E5 **San Onofre** Sucre, NW Colombia *09°45′N 75°33′W*
57 K21 **San Pablo** Potosí, S Bolivia *21°43′S 66°38′W*
171 O4 **San Pablo** *off.* San Pablo City. Luzon, N Philippines *14°04′N 121°16′E*
San Pablo Balleza *see* Balleza
35 N8 **San Pablo Bay** *bay* California, W USA
San Pablo City *see* San Pablo
40 C6 **San Pablo, Punta** *headland* NW Mexico *27°12′N 114°30′W*
43 R16 **San Pablo, Río** ≈ C Panama
171 P4 **San Pascual** Burias Island, C Philippines *13°06′N 122°59′E*
121 Q16 **San Pawl il-Bahar** *Eng.* Saint Paul's Bay. E Malta *35°57′N 14°24′E*
61 C19 **San Pedro** Buenos Aires, E Argentina *33°43′S 59°45′W*
62 K5 **San Pedro** Jujuy, N Argentina *24°12′S 64°55′W*
60 G13 **San Pedro** Misiones, NE Argentina *26°38′S 54°12′W*
42 H1 **San Pedro** Corozal, NE Belize *17°58′N 87°55′W*
76 M17 **San-Pédro** S Ivory Coast *04°45′N 06°37′W*
40 L8 **San Pedro** *var.* San Pedro de las Colonias. Coahuila, NE Mexico *25°47′N 102°57′W*
62 O5 **San Pedro** San Pedro, SE Paraguay *24°08′S 57°08′W*
62 O6 **San Pedro** *off.* Departamento de San Pedro. ◐ *department* C Paraguay
44 G6 **San Pedro** ≈ C Cuba
77 N16 **San Pedro** ✈ (Yamoussoukro) C Ivory Coast *06°49′N 05°14′W*
San Pedro *see* San Pedro del Pinatar
42 D5 **San Pedro Carchá** Alta Verapaz, C Guatemala *15°30′N 90°12′W*
35 S16 **San Pedro Channel** *channel* California, W USA
62 I5 **San Pedro de Atacama** Antofagasta, N Chile *22°52′S 68°10′W*
San Pedro de Durazno *see* Durazno
40 G5 **San Pedro de la Cueva** Sonora, NW Mexico *29°17′N 109°47′W*
San Pedro de las Colonias *see* San Pedro
56 B11 **San Pedro de Lloc** La Libertad, NW Peru *07°26′S 79°31′W*
105 S13 **San Pedro del Pinatar** *var.* San Pedro. Murcia, SE Spain *37°50′N 00°47′W*
45 P9 **San Pedro de Macorís** SE Dominican Republic *18°30′N 69°18′W*
San Pedro, Departamento de *see* San Pedro
40 C3 **San Pedro Mártir, Sierra** ▲▲ NW Mexico
San Pedro Pochutla *see* Pochutla
42 D2 **San Pedro, Río** ≈ Guatemala/Mexico
40 K10 **San Pedro, Río** ≈ C Mexico
104 J10 **San Pedro, Sierra de** ▲▲ W Spain
42 G5 **San Pedro Sula** Cortés, NW Honduras *15°26′N 88°01′W*
San Pedro Tapanatepec *see* Tapanatepec
62 I4 **San Pedro, Volcán** Ѫ N Chile *21°46′S 68°13′W*
106 E7 **San Pellegrino Terme** Lombardia, N Italy *45°53′N 09°42′E*
25 T16 **San Perlita** Texas, SW USA *26°30′N 97°38′W*
San Pietro *see* Supetar
San Pietro del Carso *see* Pivka
107 A20 **San Pietro, Isola di** *island* W Italy
32 K7 **Sanpoil River** ≈ Washington, NW USA
165 O9 **Sanpoku** *var.* Sampoku. Niigata, Honshū, C Japan *38°32′N 139°33′E*
40 C3 **San Quintín** Baja California Norte, NW Mexico *30°28′N 115°58′W*
40 B3 **San Quintín, Bahía de** *bay* NW Mexico
40 B3 **San Quintín, Cabo** *headland* NW Mexico *30°22′N 116°01′W*
62 I12 **San Rafael** Mendoza, W Argentina *34°44′S 68°15′W*
41 N9 **San Rafael** Nuevo León, NE Mexico *25°01′N 100°33′W*
34 M8 **San Rafael** California, W USA *37°58′N 122°31′W*
37 Q11 **San Rafael** New Mexico, SW USA *35°03′N 107°52′W*
54 H4 **San Rafael** *var.* El Moján. Zulia, NW Venezuela *10°58′N 71°45′W*
42 J8 **San Rafael del Norte** Jinotega, NW Nicaragua *13°12′N 86°06′W*
42 J10 **San Rafael del Sur** Managua, SW Nicaragua *11°51′N 86°24′W*
36 M5 **San Rafael Knob** ▲ Utah, W USA *38°46′N 110°45′W*
35 Q14 **San Rafael Mountains** ▲▲ California, W USA
43 M13 **San Ramón** Alajuela, C Costa Rica *10°04′N 84°31′W*
57 E14 **San Ramón** Junín, C Peru *11°08′S 75°18′W*
61 F19 **San Ramón** Canelones, S Uruguay *34°18′S 55°55′W*
62 K5 **San Ramón de la Nueva Orán** Salta, N Argentina *23°08′S 64°20′W*
57 O16 **San Ramón, Río** ≈ E Bolivia
106 B11 **San Remo** Liguria, NW Italy *43°48′N 07°47′E*
54 J3 **San Román, Cabo** *headland* NW Venezuela *12°10′N 70°01′W*
61 C15 **San Roque** Corrientes, NE Argentina *28°35′S 58°45′W*
188 I4 **San Roque** Saipan, S Northern Mariana Islands *15°15′S 145°47′E*
104 K16 **San Roque** Andalucía, S Spain *36°13′N 05°23′W*
25 R9 **San Saba** Texas, SW USA *31°13′N 98°44′W*
25 Q9 **San Saba River** ≈ Texas, SW USA
61 D17 **San Salvador** Entre Ríos, E Argentina *31°38′S 58°30′W*
42 F7 **San Salvador** ● (El Salvador) San Salvador, SW El Salvador *13°42′N 89°12′W*
42 A10 **San Salvador** ◐ *department* C El Salvador
44 K4 **San Salvador** *prev.* Watlings Island. *island* E Bahamas
42 F8 **San Salvador** ✈ La Paz, S El Salvador *13°27′N 89°04′W*
62 J5 **San Salvador de Jujuy** *var.* Jujuy. Jujuy, N Argentina *24°10′S 65°20′W*
57 B18 **San Salvador, Isla** *island* Ecuador
42 F7 **San Salvador, Volcán de** Ѫ C El Salvador *13°58′N 89°14′W*
77 Q14 **Sansanné-Mango** *var.* Mango. N Togo *10°21′N 00°28′E*
45 S5 **San Sebastián** W Puerto Rico *18°21′N 67°00′W*
63 J24 **San Sebastián, Bahía** *bay* S Argentina
Sansenhō *see* Sach'ŏn
106 H12 **Sansepolcro** Toscana, C Italy *43°35′N 12°12′E*
107 M16 **San Severo** Puglia, SE Italy *41°41′N 15°23′E*
112 F11 **Sanski Most** ◐ Federacija Bosna I Hercegovina, NW Bosnia and Herzegovina
171 W12 **Sansundi** Papua, E Indonesia *0°42′S 135°48′E*
162 K9 **Sant** *var.* Mayhan. Övörhangay, C Mongolia *46°02′N 104°00′E*
104 K11 **Santa Amalia** Extremadura, W Spain *39°00′N 06°01′W*
60 F13 **Santa Ana** Misiones, NE Argentina *27°22′S 55°34′W*
57 L16 **Santa Ana** Beni, N Bolivia *13°43′S 65°37′W*
42 E7 **Santa Ana** Santa Ana, NW El Salvador *13°59′N 89°34′W*
40 F4 **Santa Ana** Sonora, NW Mexico *30°31′N 111°08′W*
35 T16 **Santa Ana** California, W USA *33°45′N 117°52′W*
55 N6 **Santa Ana** Nueva Esparta, NE Venezuela *09°15′N 64°39′W*
42 A9 **Santa Ana** ◐ *department* NW El Salvador
Santa Ana de Coro *see* Coro
35 U16 **Santa Ana Mountains** ▲▲ California, W USA
42 E7 **Santa Ana, Volcán de** *var.* La Matepec. Ѫ W El Salvador *13°49′N 89°36′W*
42 G6 **Santa Bárbara** Santa Bárbara, W Honduras *14°56′N 88°11′W*
40 J7 **Santa Barbara** Chihuahua, N Mexico *26°46′N 105°46′W*
35 Q14 **Santa Barbara** California, W USA *34°24′N 119°40′W*
54 L11 **Santa Bárbara** Amazonas, S Venezuela *03°55′N 67°06′W*
54 I7 **Santa Bárbara** Barinas, W Venezuela *07°48′N 71°10′W*
42 F5 **Santa Bárbara** ◐ *department* NW Honduras
Santa Bárbara *see* Iscuandé
35 Q15 **Santa Barbara Channel** *channel* California, W USA
Santa Bárbara de Samaná *see* Samaná
35 R16 **Santa Barbara Island** *island* Channel Islands, California, W USA
54 E5 **Santa Catalina** Bolívar, N Colombia *10°36′N 75°17′W*
43 R15 **Santa Catalina** Ngöbe Bugle, W Panama *08°46′N 81°18′W*
35 T17 **Santa Catalina, Gulf of** *gulf* California, W USA
43 Q7 **Santa Catalina, Isla** *island* NW Colombia, Caribbean Sea
40 F8 **Santa Catalina, Isla** *island* NW Mexico
35 S16 **Santa Catalina Island** *island* Channel Islands, California, W USA
41 N8 **Santa Catarina** Nuevo León, NE Mexico *25°39′N 100°30′W*
60 H13 **Santa Catarina** *off.* Estado de Santa Catarina. ◐ *state* S Brazil
Santa Catarina de Tepehuanes *see* Tepehuanes
Santa Catarina, Estado de *see* Santa Catarina
60 L13 **Santa Catarina, Ilha de** *island* S Brazil
45 Q16 **Santa Catherina** Curaçao, C Netherlands Antilles *12°07′N 68°46′W*
44 E5 **Santa Clara** Villa Clara, C Cuba *22°25′N 78°01′W*
35 N9 **Santa Clara** California, W USA *37°20′N 121°57′W*
36 J8 **Santa Clara** Utah, W USA *37°07′N 113°39′W*
Santa Clara *see* Santa Clara de Olimar
61 F18 **Santa Clara de Olimar** *var.* Santa Clara. Cerro Largo, NE Uruguay *32°50′S 54°54′W*
61 A17 **Santa Clara de Saguier** Santa Fe, C Argentina *31°21′S 61°50′W*
Santa Coloma *see* Santa Coloma de Gramanet
105 X5 **Santa Coloma de Farners** *var.* Santa Coloma de Farnés. Cataluña, NE Spain *41°52′N 02°39′E*
Santa Coloma de Farnés *see* Santa Coloma de Farners
105 W6 **Santa Coloma de Gramanet** *var.* Santa Coloma. Cataluña, NE Spain *41°28′N 02°14′E*
104 G2 **Santa Comba** Galicia, NW Spain *43°02′N 08°49′W*
Santa Comba *see* Uaco Cungo
104 H8 **Santa Comba Dão** Viseu, N Portugal *40°23′N 08°07′W*
82 C10 **Santa Cruz** Uíge, NW Angola *06°56′S 16°25′E*
57 N19 **Santa Cruz** *var.* Santa Cruz de la Sierra. Santa Cruz, C Bolivia *17°49′S 63°11′W*
62 G12 **Santa Cruz** Libertador, C Chile *34°38′S 71°27′W*
42 K13 **Santa Cruz** Guanacaste, W Costa Rica *10°15′N 85°35′W*
44 I12 **Santa Cruz** W Jamaica *18°03′N 77°43′W*
64 P6 **Santa Cruz** Madeira, Portugal, NE Atlantic Ocean *32°43′N 16°47′W*
35 N10 **Santa Cruz** California, W USA *36°58′N 122°01′W*
63 H20 **Santa Cruz** *off.* Provincia de Santa Cruz. ◐ *province* S Argentina
57 O18 **Santa Cruz** ◐ *department* E Bolivia
Santa Cruz *see* Puerto Santa Cruz
Santa Cruz *see* Viru-Viru
Santa Cruz Barillas *see* Barillas
59 O18 **Santa Cruz Cabrália** Bahia, E Brazil *16°17′S 39°03′W*
Santa Cruz de El Seibo *see* El Seibo
64 N11 **Santa Cruz de la Palma** La Palma, Islas Canarias, Spain, NE Atlantic Ocean *28°41′N 17°46′W*
Santa Cruz de la Sierra *see* Santa Cruz
105 O9 **Santa Cruz de la Zarza** Castilla-La Mancha, C Spain *39°59′N 03°10′W*
42 C5 **Santa Cruz del Quiché** Quiché, W Guatemala *15°02′N 91°06′W*
105 N8 **Santa Cruz del Retamar** Castilla-La Mancha, C Spain *40°08′N 04°14′W*
Santa Cruz del Seibo *see* El Seibo
44 G7 **Santa Cruz del Sur** Camagüey, C Cuba *20°44′N 78°00′W*
105 O11 **Santa Cruz de Mudela** Castilla-La Mancha, C Spain *38°37′N 03°27′W*
64 Q11 **Santa Cruz de Tenerife** Tenerife, Islas Canarias, Spain, NE Atlantic Ocean *28°28′N 16°15′W*
64 P11 **Santa Cruz de Tenerife** ◐ *province* Islas Canarias, Spain, NE Atlantic Ocean
60 K9 **Santa Cruz do Rio Pardo** São Paulo, S Brazil *22°52′S 49°37′W*
61 H15 **Santa Cruz do Sul** Rio Grande do Sul, S Brazil *29°42′S 52°25′W*
57 C17 **Santa Cruz, Isla** *var.* Indefatigable Island, Isla Chávez. *island* Galapagos Islands, Ecuador, E Pacific Ocean
40 F8 **Santa Cruz, Isla** *island* NW Mexico
35 Q15 **Santa Cruz Island** *island* California, W USA
187 Q10 **Santa Cruz Islands** *island group* E Solomon Islands
Santa Cruz, Provincia de *see* Santa Cruz
63 I22 **Santa Cruz, Río** ≈ S Argentina
36 L15 **Santa Cruz River** ≈ Arizona, SW USA
61 C17 **Santa Elena** Entre Ríos, E Argentina *30°58′S 59°47′W*
42 F2 **Santa Elena** Cayo, W Belize *17°08′N 89°04′W*
25 R16 **Santa Elena** Texas, SW USA *26°43′N 98°30′W*
56 A7 **Santa Elena, Bahía de** *bay* W Ecuador
55 R10 **Santa Elena de Uairén** Bolívar, E Venezuela *04°40′N 61°03′W*
42 K12 **Santa Elena, Península** *peninsula* NW Costa Rica
56 A7 **Santa Elena, Punta** *headland* W Ecuador *02°11′S 81°00′W*
104 L11 **Santa Eufemia** Andalucía, S Spain *38°36′N 04°54′W*
107 N21 **Santa Eufemia, Golfo di** *gulf* S Italy
105 S4 **Santa Eulalia de Gállego** Aragón, NE Spain *42°16′N 00°46′W*
105 V11 **Santa Eulària del Riu** Ibiza, Spain, W Mediterranean Sea *39°00′N 01°33′E*
61 B17 **Santa Fe** Santa Fe, C Argentina *31°36′S 60°47′W*
44 C6 **Santa Fé** *var.* La Fe. Isla de la Juventud, W Cuba *21°45′N 82°45′W*
43 R16 **Santa Fé** Veraguas, C Panama *08°29′N 80°50′W*
105 N14 **Santa Fe** Andalucía, S Spain *37°11′N 03°43′W*
37 S10 **Santa Fe** *state capital* New Mexico, SW USA *35°41′N 105°56′W*
61 B15 **Santa Fe** *off.* Provincia de Santa Fe. ◐ *province* C Argentina
Santa Fe *see* Bogotá
Santa Fe de Bogotá *see* Bogotá
60 J7 **Santa Fé do Sul** São Paulo, S Brazil *20°13′S 50°56′W*
57 B18 **Santa Fe, Isla** *var.* Barrington Island. *island* Galapagos Islands, Ecuador, E Pacific Ocean
Santa Fe, Provincia de *see* Santa Fe
23 V9 **Santa Fe River** ≈ Florida, SE USA
59 M15 **Santa Filomena** Piauí, E Brazil *09°06′S 45°52′W*
40 G10 **Santa Genoveva** ▲ NW Mexico *23°07′N 109°56′W*
153 S14 **Santahar** Rajshahi, NW Bangladesh *24°45′N 89°03′E*
60 G11 **Santa Helena** Paraná, S Brazil *24°53′S 54°19′W*
54 J5 **Santa Inés** Lara, N Venezuela *10°37′N 69°18′W*
63 G24 **Santa Inés, Isla** *island* S Chile
62 J13 **Santa Isabel** La Pampa, C Argentina *36°11′S 66°59′W*
43 U14 **Santa Isabel** Colón, N Panama *09°31′N 79°12′W*
186 L8 **Santa Isabel** *var.* Bughotu. *island* N Solomon Islands
Santa Isabel *see* Malabo
58 D11 **Santa Isabel do Rio Negro** Amazonas, NW Brazil *0°40′S 64°56′W*
61 C15 **Santa Lucia** Corrientes, NE Argentina *28°58′S 59°05′W*
57 I17 **Santa Lucía** Puno, S Peru *15°45′S 70°34′W*
61 F20 **Santa Lucía** *var.* Santa Lucia. Canelones, S Uruguay *34°26′S 56°25′W*
42 B6 **Santa Lucía Cotzumalguapa** Escuintla, SW Guatemala *14°20′N 91°00′W*
107 L23 **Santa Lucia del Mela** Sicilia, Italy, C Mediterranean Sea *38°08′N 15°17′E*
35 O11 **Santa Lucia Range** ▲▲ California, W USA
40 D9 **Santa Margarita, Isla** *island* NW Mexico
62 J7 **Santa María** Catamarca, N Argentina *26°51′S 66°02′W*
61 G15 **Santa Maria** Rio Grande do Sul, S Brazil *29°41′S 53°48′W*
35 P13 **Santa Maria** California, W USA *34°56′N 120°25′W*
64 Q4 **Santa Maria** ✈ Santa Maria, Azores, Portugal, NE Atlantic Ocean
64 P3 **Santa Maria** *island* Azores, Portugal, NE Atlantic Ocean
Santa Maria *see* Gaua
Santa María Asunción Tlaxiaco *see* Tlaxiaco
40 G9 **Santa María, Bahía** *bay* W Mexico
83 L21 **Santa Maria, Cabo de** *headland* S Mozambique *26°05′S 32°58′E*
104 G15 **Santa Maria, Cabo de** *headland* S Portugal *36°57′N 07°55′W*
44 J4 **Santa Maria, Cape** *headland* Long Island, C Bahamas *23°40′N 75°20′W*
107 J17 **Santa Maria Capua Vetere** Campania, S Italy *41°05′N 14°15′E*
104 G7 **Santa Maria da Feira** Aveiro, N Portugal *40°55′N 08°32′W*
59 M17 **Santa Maria da Vitória** Bahia, E Brazil *13°26′S 44°09′W*
55 N9 **Santa Maria de Erebato** Bolívar, SE Venezuela *05°09′N 64°50′W*
55 N6 **Santa María de Ipire** Guárico, C Venezuela *08°51′N 65°21′W*
Santa María del Buen Aire *see* Buenos Aires
40 J8 **Santa María del Oro** Durango, C Mexico *25°57′N 105°22′W*
41 N12 **Santa María del Río** San Luis Potosí, C Mexico *21°48′N 100°42′W*
Santa Maria di Castellabate *see* Castellabate
107 Q20 **Santa Maria di Leuca, Capo** *headland* SE Italy *39°48′N 18°21′E*
108 K10 **Santa Maria-im-Munstertal** Graubünden, SE Switzerland *46°36′N 10°25′E*
57 B18 **Santa María, Isla** *var.* Isla Floreana, Charles Island. *island* Galapagos Islands, Ecuador, E Pacific Ocean
40 J3 **Santa María, Laguna de** ◎ N Mexico
61 G16 **Santa Maria, Rio** ≈ S Brazil
43 R16 **Santa María, Río** ≈ C Panama
36 J12 **Santa Maria River** ≈ Arizona, SW USA
107 G15 **Santa Marinella** Lazio, C Italy *42°01′N 11°51′E*
54 F4 **Santa Marta** Magdalena, N Colombia *11°14′N 74°13′W*
104 J11 **Santa Marta** Extremadura, W Spain *38°37′N 06°39′W*
54 F4 **Santa Marta, Sierra Nevada de** ▲▲ NE Colombia
Santa Maura *see* Lefkáda
35 S15 **Santa Monica** California, W USA *34°01′N 118°29′W*
116 F10 **Sântana** *Ger.* Sankt Anna, *Hung.* Újszentanna; *prev.* Sintana. Arad, W Romania *46°20′N 21°30′E*
61 F16 **Santana, Coxilha de** *hill range* S Brazil
61 H16 **Santana da Boa Vista** Rio Grande do Sul, S Brazil *30°52′S 53°03′W*
61 F16 **Santana do Livramento** *prev.* Livramento. Rio Grande do Sul, S Brazil *30°52′S 55°30′W*
105 N2 **Santander** Cantabria, N Spain *43°28′N 03°48′W*
54 F8 **Santander** *off.* Departamento de Santander. ◐ *province* C Colombia
Santander, Departamento de *see* Santander
Santander Jiménez *see* Jiménez
Sant'Andrea *see* Svetac
107 B20 **Sant'Antioco** Sardegna, Italy, C Mediterranean Sea *39°03′N 08°28′E*
105 V11 **Sant Antoni de Portmany** *Cas.* San Antonio Abad. Ibiza, Spain, W Mediterranean Sea *38°58′N 01°18′E*
105 Y10 **Santanyí** Mallorca, Spain, W Mediterranean Sea *39°22′N 03°07′E*
104 J13 **Santa Olalla del Cala** Andalucía, S Spain *37°54′N 06°13′W*
35 R15 **Santa Paula** California, W USA *34°21′N 119°03′W*
36 L4 **Santaquin** Utah, W USA *39°58′N 111°46′W*
58 I12 **Santarém** Pará, N Brazil *02°26′S 54°41′W*
104 G10 **Santarém** *anc.* Scalabis. Santarém, W Portugal *39°14′N 08°40′W*
104 G10 **Santarém** ◐ *district* C Portugal
44 F4 **Santaren Channel** *channel* W Bahamas
54 K10 **Santa Rita** Vichada, E Colombia *04°51′N 68°27′W*
188 B16 **Santa Rita** SW Guam
42 H5 **Santa Rita** Cortés, NW Honduras *15°10′N 87°54′W*
40 E9 **Santa Rita** Baja California Sur, NW Mexico *27°29′N 100°33′W*
54 H5 **Santa Rita** Zulia, NW Venezuela *10°35′N 71°30′W*
59 I19 **Santa Rita de Araguaia** Goiás, S Brazil *17°17′S 53°13′W*
Santa Rita de Cassia *see* Cássia
61 D14 **Santa Rosa** Corrientes, NE Argentina *28°18′S 58°04′W*

◆ Country
● Country Capital
◇ Dependent Territory
○ Dependent Territory Capital
◐ Administrative Regions
✈ International Airport
▲ Mountain
▲▲ Mountain Range
Ѫ Volcano
≈ River
◎ Lake
⊠ Reservoir

62 K13 **Santa Rosa** La Pampa, C Argentina 36°38′S 64°15′W
61 G14 **Santa Rosa** Rio Grande do Sul, S Brazil 27°50′S 54°29′W
58 E10 **Santa Rosa** Roraima, N Brazil 03°41′N 62°29′W
56 B8 **Santa Rosa** El Oro, SW Ecuador 03°29′S 79°57′W
57 I16 **Santa Rosa** Puno, S Peru 14°38′S 70°45′W
34 M7 **Santa Rosa** California, W USA 38°27′N 122°42′W
37 U11 **Santa Rosa** New Mexico, SW USA 34°54′N 104°43′W
55 O6 **Santa Rosa** Anzoátegui, NE Venezuela 09°37′N 64°20′W
42 A3 **Santa Rosa** ***off.*** Departamento de Santa Rosa. ◐ *department* SE Guatemala
Santa Rosa *see* Santa Rosa de Copán
63 J15 **Santa Rosa, Bajo de** *basin* E Argentina
42 F6 **Santa Rosa de Copán** ***var.*** Santa Rosa. Copán, W Honduras 14°48′N 88°43′W
54 E8 **Santa Rosa de Osos** Antioquia, C Colombia 06°40′N 75°27′W
Santa Rosa, Departamento de *see* Santa Rosa
35 Q15 **Santa Rosa Island** *island* California, W USA
23 O9 **Santa Rosa Island** *island* Florida, SE USA
40 E6 **Santa Rosalía** Baja California Sur, NW Mexico 27°20′N 112°20′W
54 K6 **Santa Rosalía** Portuguesa, NW Venezuela 09°02′N 69°01′W
188 C15 **Santa Rosa, Mount** ▲ NE Guam
35 V16 **Santa Rosa Mountains** ▲▲ California, W USA
35 T2 **Santa Rosa Range** ▲▲ Nevada, W USA
62 M8 **Santa Sylvina** Chaco, N Argentina 27°49′S 61°09′W
Santa Tecla *see* Nueva San Salvador
61 B19 **Santa Teresa** Santa Fe, C Argentina 33°30′S 60°45′W
59 O20 **Santa Teresa** Espírito Santo, SE Brazil 19°51′S 40°49′W
61 E21 **Santa Teresita** Buenos Aires, E Argentina 36°32′S 56°41′W
61 H19 **Santa Vitória do Palmar** Rio Grande do Sul, S Brazil 33°32′S 53°25′W
35 Q14 **Santa Ynez River** 〰 California, W USA
Sant Carles de la Rápida *see* Sant Carles de la Ràpita
105 U7 **Sant Carles de la Ràpita** ***var.*** Sant Carles de la Rápida. Cataluña, NE Spain 40°37′N 00°36′E
105 W5 **Sant Celoni** Cataluña, NE Spain 41°39′N 02°25′E
35 U17 **Santee** California, W USA 32°50′N 116°58′W
21 T13 **Santee River** 〰 South Carolina, SE USA
40 K15 **San Telmo, Punta** *headland* SW Mexico 18°19′N 103°30′W
107 O17 **Santeramo in Colle** Puglia, SE Italy 40°47′N 16°45′E
107 M23 **San Teresa di Riva** Sicilia, Italy, C Mediterranean Sea 38°00′N 15°25′E
105 X5 **Sant Feliu de Guíxols** ***var.*** San Feliú de Guixols. Cataluña, NE Spain 41°47′N 03°02′E
105 W6 **Sant Feliu de Llobregat** Cataluña, NE Spain 41°22′N 02°00′E
106 C7 **Santhià** Piemonte, NE Italy 45°21′N 08°11′E
61 F15 **Santiago** Rio Grande do Sul, S Brazil 29°11′S 54°52′W
62 H11 **Santiago** ***var.*** Gran Santiago. ● (Chile) Santiago, C Chile 33°30′S 70°40′W
45 N8 **Santiago** ***var.*** Santiago de los Caballeros. N Dominican Republic 19°27′N 70°42′W
40 G10 **Santiago** Baja California Sur, NW Mexico 23°32′N 109°47′W
41 O8 **Santiago** Nuevo León, NE Mexico 25°22′N 100°09′W
43 R16 **Santiago** Veraguas, S Panama 08°06′N 80°59′W
57 E16 **Santiago** Ica, SW Peru 14°14′S 75°44′W
104 G3 **Santiago** ***var.*** Santiago de Compostela, ***Eng.*** Compostella; ***anc.*** Campus Stellae. Galicia, NW Spain 42°52′N 08°33′W
62 H11 **Santiago** ***off.*** Región Metropolitana de Santiago, ***var.*** Metropolitan. ◐ *region* C Chile
76 D10 **Santiago** ***var.*** São Tiago. *island* Ilhas de Sotavento, S Cape Verde
62 H11 **Santiago** ✈ Santiago, C Chile 33°27′S 70°40′W
104 G3 **Santiago** ✈ Galicia, NW Spain
Santiago *see* Santiago de Cuba, Cuba
Santiago *see* Grande de Santiago, Río, Mexico
42 B6 **Santiago Atitlán** Sololá, SW Guatemala 14°39′N 91°12′W
43 Q16 **Santiago, Cerro** ▲ W Panama 08°27′N 81°42′W
Santiago de Compostela *see* Santiago
44 I8 **Santiago de Cuba** ***var.*** Santiago. Santiago de Cuba, E Cuba 20°01′N 75°51′W
Santiago de Guayaquil *see* Guayaquil
62 K8 **Santiago del Estero** Santiago del Estero, C Argentina 27°51′S 64°16′W
61 A15 **Santiago del Estero** ***off.*** Provincia de Santiago del Estero. ◐ *province* N Argentina
Santiago del Estero, Provincia de *see* Santiago del Estero
40 I8 **Santiago de los Caballeros** Sinaloa, W Mexico 25°33′N 107°22′W
Santiago de los Caballeros *see* Santiago, Dominican Republic
Santiago de los Caballeros *see* Ciudad de Guatemala, Guatemala
42 F8 **Santiago de María** Usulután, SE El Salvador 13°28′N 88°28′W
104 F12 **Santiago do Cacém** Setúbal, S Portugal 38°01′N 08°42′W
40 J12 **Santiago Ixcuintla** Nayarit, C Mexico 21°50′N 105°11′W
Santiago Jamiltepec *see* Jamiltepec
24 L11 **Santiago Mountains** ▲▲ Texas, SW USA
40 J9 **Santiago Papasquiaro** Durango, C Mexico 25°00′N 105°27′W
Santiago Pinotepa Nacional *see* Pinotepa Nacional
Santiago, Región Metropolitana de *see* Santiago
56 C8 **Santiago, Río** 〰 N Peru
40 M10 **San Tiburcio** Zacatecas, C Mexico 24°08′N 101°29′W
105 N2 **Santillana** Cantabria, N Spain 43°24′N 04°06′W
54 I5 **San Timoteo** Zulia, NW Venezuela 09°50′N 71°05′W
Santi Quaranta *see* Sarandë
Santissima Trinidad *see* Chilung
105 O12 **Santisteban del Puerto** Andalucía, S Spain 38°15′N 03°11′W
105 U7 **Sant Jordi, Golf de** *gulf* NE Spain
105 U11 **Sant Josep de sa Talaia** ***var.*** San Jose. Ibiza, Spain, W Mediterranean Sea 38°55′N 1°18′E
162 G6 **Santmargats** ***var.*** Holboo. Dzavhan, W Mongolia 48°35′N 95°25′E
105 T8 **Sant Mateu** País Valenciano, E Spain 40°28′N 00°10′E
25 S7 **Santo** Texas, SW USA 32°35′N 98°06′W
Santo *see* Espiritu Santo
60 M10 **Santo Amaro, Ilha de** *island* SE Brazil
61 G14 **Santo Ângelo** Rio Grande do Sul, S Brazil 28°17′S 54°15′W
76 C9 **Santo Antão** *island* Ilhas de Barlavento, N Cape Verde
60 J10 **Santo Antônio da Platina** Paraná, S Brazil 23°20′S 50°05′W
58 C13 **Santo Antônio do Içá** Amazonas, N Brazil 03°05′S 67°56′W
57 Q18 **Santo Corazón, Río** 〰 E Bolivia
44 E5 **Santo Domingo** Villa Clara, C Cuba 22°35′N 80°15′W
45 O9 **Santo Domingo** ***prev.*** Ciudad Trujillo. ● (Dominican Republic) SE Dominican Republic 18°30′N 69°57′W
40 E8 **Santo Domingo** Baja California Sur, NW Mexico 25°34′N 112°00′W
40 M10 **Santo Domingo** San Luis Potosí, C Mexico 23°18′N 101°42′W
42 L10 **Santo Domingo** Chontales, S Nicaragua 12°15′N 84°59′W
105 P4 **Santo Domingo de la Calzada** La Rioja, N Spain 42°26′N 02°57′W
56 B6 **Santo Domingo de los Colorados** Pichincha, NW Ecuador 0°13′S 79°09′W
Santo Domingo Tehuantepec *see* Tehuantepec
55 O6 **San Tomé** Anzoátegui, NE Venezuela 08°58′N 64°08′W
San Tomé de Guayana *see* Ciudad Guayana
105 R13 **Santomera** Murcia, SE Spain 38°03′N 01°05′W
105 O2 **Santoña** Cantabria, N Spain 43°27′N 03°28′W
Santorin *see* Santoríni
115 K22 **Santoríni** ***var.*** Santorin, ***prev.*** Thíra; ***anc.*** Thera. *island* Kykládes, Greece, Aegean Sea
60 M10 **Santos** São Paulo, S Brazil 23°56′S 46°22′W
65 J17 **Santos Plateau** *undersea feature* SW Atlantic Ocean 25°00′S 43°00′W
104 G6 **Santo Tirso** Porto, N Portugal 41°20′N 08°25′W
40 B2 **Santo Tomás** Baja California Norte, NW Mexico 31°32′N 116°26′W
42 L10 **Santo Tomás** Chontales, S Nicaragua 12°04′N 85°02′W
42 G5 **Santo Tomás de Castilla** Izabal, E Guatemala 15°40′N 88°36′W
40 B2 **Santo Tomás, Punta** *headland* NW Mexico 31°30′N 116°40′W
57 H16 **Santo Tomás, Río** 〰 C Peru
57 B18 **Santo Tomás, Volcán** ⛰ Galapagos Islands, Ecuador, E Pacific Ocean 0°46′S 91°01′W
61 F14 **Santo Tomé** Corrientes, NE Argentina 28°31′S 56°03′W
Santo Tomé de Guayana *see* Ciudad Guayana
98 H10 **Santpoort** Noord-Holland, W Netherlands 52°26′N 04°38′E
Santurce *see* Santurtzi
105 O2 **Santurtzi** ***var.*** Santurce, Santurzi. País Vasco, N Spain 43°20′N 03°03′W
Santurzi *see* Santurtzi
63 G20 **San Valentín, Cerro** ▲ S Chile 46°36′S 73°17′W
42 F8 **San Vicente** San Vicente, C El Salvador 13°38′N 88°42′W*
40 C2 **San Vicente** Baja California Norte, NW Mexico 31°20′N 116°15′W
188 H6 **San Vicente** Saipan, S Northern Mariana Islands
42 B9 **San Vicente** ◐ *department* E El Salvador
104 I10 **San Vicente de Alcántara** Extremadura, W Spain 39°21′N 07°07′W
105 N2 **San Vicente de Barakaldo** ***var.*** Baracaldo, ***Basq.*** San Bizenti-Barakaldo. País Vasco, N Spain 43°17′N 02°59′W
57 E15 **San Vicente de Cañete** ***var.*** Cañete. Lima, W Peru 13°06′S 76°23′W
104 M2 **San Vicente de la Barquera** Cantabria, N Spain 43°23′N 04°24′W
54 E12 **San Vicente del Caguán** Caquetá, S Colombia 02°07′N 74°47′W
42 F8 **San Vincente, Volcán de** ⛰ C El Salvador 13°34′N 88°50′W
43 O15 **San Vito** Puntarenas, SE Costa Rica 08°49′N 82°58′W
106 I7 **San Vito al Tagliamento** Friuli-Venezia Giulia, NE Italy 45°54′N 12°55′E
107 H23 **San Vito, Capo** *headland* Sicilia, Italy, C Mediterranean Sea 38°11′N 12°41′E
107 P18 **San Vito dei Normanni** Puglia, SE Italy 40°40′N 17°42′E
160 L17 **Sanya** ***var.*** Ya Xian. Hainan, S China 18°25′N 109°27′E
83 J16 **Sanyati** 〰 N Zimbabwe
25 Q16 **San Ygnacio** Texas, SW USA 27°04′N 99°26′W
160 L6 **Sanyuan** Shaanxi, C China 34°40′N 108°56′E
123 P11 **Sanyyakhtakh** Respublika Sakha (Yakutiya), NE Russian Federation 60°34′N 124°09′E
146 J15 **S. A.Nyýazow Adyndaky** ***Rus.*** Imeni S. A. Niyazova. Maryyskiy Velayat, S Turkmenistan 36°44′N 62°23′E
82 C10 **Sanza Pombo** Uíge, NW Angola 07°20′S 16°00′E
Sanzyô *see* Sanjō
104 G14 **São Bartolomeu de Messines** Faro, S Portugal 37°12′N 08°16′W
60 M10 **São Bernardo do Campo** São Paulo, S Brazil 23°45′S 46°34′W
61 F15 **São Borja** Rio Grande do Sul, S Brazil 28°35′S 56°01′W
104 H14 **São Brás de Alportel** Faro, S Portugal 37°09′N 07°55′W
60 M10 **São Caetano do Sul** São Paulo, S Brazil 23°37′S 46°34′W
60 L9 **São Carlos** São Paulo, S Brazil 22°02′S 47°53′W
59 P16 **São Cristóvão** Sergipe, E Brazil 10°59′S 37°10′W
61 F15 **São Fancisco de Assis** Rio Grande do Sul, S Brazil 29°32′S 55°07′W
58 K13 **São Félix** Pará, NE Brazil 06°43′S 51°56′W
São Félix *see* São Félix do Araguaia
59 J16 **São Félix do Araguaia** ***var.*** São Félix. Mato Grosso, W Brazil 11°36′S 50°40′W
59 J14 **São Félix do Xingu** Pará, NE Brazil 06°38′S 51°59′W
60 Q9 **São Fidélis** Rio de Janeiro, SE Brazil 21°37′S 41°40′W
76 D10 **São Filipe** Fogo, S Cape Verde 14°52′N 24°29′W
60 K12 **São Francisco do Sul** Santa Catarina, S Brazil 26°17′S 48°39′W
60 K12 **São Francisco, Ilha de** *island* S Brazil
59 P16 **São Francisco, Rio** 〰 E Brazil
61 G16 **São Gabriel** Rio Grande do Sul, S Brazil 30°17′S 54°17′W
60 P10 **São Gonçalo** Rio de Janeiro, SE Brazil 22°48′S 43°03′W
81 H23 **Sao Hill** Iringa, S Tanzania 08°19′S 35°11′E
60 R9 **São João da Barra** Rio de Janeiro, SE Brazil 21°39′S 41°04′W
104 G7 **São João da Madeira** Aveiro, N Portugal 40°52′N 08°28′W
58 M12 **São João de Cortes** Maranhão, E Brazil 02°30′S 44°27′W
59 M21 **São João del Rei** Minas Gerais, NE Brazil 21°08′S 44°15′W
59 N15 **São João do Piauí** Piauí, E Brazil 08°21′S 42°14′W
59 N14 **São João dos Patos** Maranhão, E Brazil 06°29′S 43°44′W
58 C11 **São Joaquim** Amazonas, NW Brazil 0°08′S 67°10′W
61 J14 **São Joaquim** Santa Catarina, S Brazil 28°20′S 49°55′W
60 L7 **São Joaquim da Barra** São Paulo, S Brazil 20°36′S 47°50′W
64 N2 **São Jorge** *island* Azores, Portugal, NE Atlantic Ocean
61 K14 **São José** Santa Catarina, S Brazil 27°34′S 48°39′W
60 M8 **São José do Rio Pardo** São Paulo, S Brazil 21°37′S 46°52′W
60 K8 **São José do Rio Preto** São Paulo, S Brazil 20°50′S 49°20′W
60 N10 **São Jose dos Campos** São Paulo, S Brazil 23°07′S 45°52′W
61 I17 **São Lourenço do Sul** Rio Grande do Sul, S Brazil 31°25′S 52°00′W
58 M12 **São Luís** *state capital* Maranhão, NE Brazil 02°34′S 44°16′W
58 F11 **São Luís** Roraima, N Brazil 01°11′N 60°15′W
58 M12 **São Luís, Ilha de** *island* NE Brazil
61 F14 **São Luiz Gonzaga** Rio Grande do Sul, S Brazil 28°24′S 54°58′W
São Mandol *see* São Manuel, Rio
47 U8 **Sao Manuel** 〰 C Brazil
59 H15 **São Manuel, Rio** ***var.*** São Mandol, Teles Pirés. 〰 C Brazil
58 C11 **São Marcelino** Amazonas, NW Brazil 0°53′N 67°16′W
58 N12 **São Marcos, Baía de** *bay* N Brazil
59 O20 **São Mateus** Espírito Santo, SE Brazil 18°44′S 39°53′W
60 J12 **São Mateus do Sul** Paraná, S Brazil 25°58′S 50°29′W
64 P3 **São Miguel** *island* Azores, Portugal, NE Atlantic Ocean
60 G13 **São Miguel d'Oeste** Santa Catarina, S Brazil 26°45′S 53°34′W
45 P9 **Saona, Isla** *island* SE Dominican Republic
172 H12 **Saondzou** ▲ Grande Comore, NW Comoros
103 R10 **Saône** 〰 E France
103 Q9 **Saône-et-Loire** ◐ *department* C France
76 D9 **São Nicolau** ***Eng.*** Saint Nicholas. *island* Ilhas de Barlavento, N Cape Verde
60 M10 **São Paulo** *state capital* São Paulo, S Brazil 23°33′S 46°39′W
60 K9 **São Paulo** ***off.*** Estado de São Paulo. ◐ *state* S Brazil
São Paulo de Loanda *see* Luanda
São Paulo, Estado de *see* São Paulo
São Pedro do Rio Grande do Sul *see* Rio Grande
104 H7 **São Pedro do Sul** Viseu, N Portugal 40°46′N 07°58′W
64 K13 **São Pedro e São Paulo** *undersea feature* C Atlantic Ocean 01°25′N 28°54′W
59 M14 **São Raimundo das Mangabeiras** Maranhão, E Brazil 07°00′S 45°30′W
59 Q14 **São Roque, Cabo de** *headland* E Brazil 05°29′S 35°16′W
São Salvador *see* Salvador, Brazil
São Salvador/São Salvador do Congo *see* M'Banza Congo, Angola
60 N10 **São Sebastião, Ilha de** *island* S Brazil
83 N19 **São Sebastião, Ponta** *headland* C Mozambique 22°09′S 35°33′E
104 F13 **São Teotónio** Beja, S Portugal 37°30′N 08°41′W
São Tiago *see* Santiago
79 B18 **São Tomé** ● (Sao Tome and Principe) São Tomé, S Sao Tome and Principe 0°22′N 06°41′E
79 B18 **São Tomé** ✈ São Tomé, S Sao Tome and Principe 0°24′N 06°39′E
79 B18 **São Tomé** ***Eng.*** Saint Thomas. *island* S Sao Tome and Principe
79 B17 **Sao Tome and Principe** ***off.*** Democratic Republic of Sao Tome and Principe. ◆ *republic* E Atlantic Ocean
Sao Tome and Principe, Democratic Republic of *see* Sao Tome and Principe
74 H9 **Saoura, Oued** 〰 NW Algeria
60 M10 **São Vicente** ***Eng.*** Saint Vincent. São Paulo, S Brazil 23°55′S 46°25′W
64 O5 **São Vicente** Madeira, Portugal, NE Atlantic Ocean 32°48′N 17°03′W
76 C9 **São Vicente** ***Eng.*** Saint Vincent. *island* Ilhas de Barlavento, N Cape Verde
104 F14 **São Vicente, Cabo de** ***Eng.*** Cape Saint Vincent, ***Port.*** Cabode São Vicente. *cape* S Portugal
São Vicente, Cabo de *see* São Vicente, Cabo de
Sápai *see* Sápes
Sapaleri, Cerro *see* Zapaleri, Cerro
Saparoea *see* Saparua
171 S13 **Saparua** ***prev.*** Saparoea. Pulau Saparau, C Indonesia 03°35′S 128°37′E
168 L11 **Sapat** Sumatera, W Indonesia 0°18′S 103°18′E
77 U17 **Sapele** Delta, S Nigeria 05°54′N 05°43′E
23 X7 **Sapelo Island** *island* Georgia, SE USA
23 X7 **Sapelo Sound** *sound* Georgia, SE USA
114 K13 **Sápes** ***var.*** Sápai. Anatolikí Makedonía kai Thráki, NE Greece 41°02′N 25°44′E
Sapiéntza *see* Sapiénza
115 D22 **Sapiénza** ***var.*** Sapiéntza. *island* S Greece
138 F12 **Sapir** ***prev.*** Sappir. Southern, S Israel 30°43′N 35°11′E
61 I15 **Sapiranga** Rio Grande do Sul, S Brazil 29°39′S 50°58′W
114 K13 **Sápka** ▲▲ NE Greece
105 X9 **Sa Pobla** Mallorca, Spain, W Mediterranean Sea 39°46′N 03°03′E
56 D11 **Saposoa** San Martín, N Peru 06°53′S 76°45′W
119 F16 **Sapotskin** ***Pol.*** Sopockinie, ***Rus.*** Sapotskino, Sopotskin. Hrodzyenskaya Voblasts', W Belarus 53°50′N 23°39′E
77 P13 **Sapoui** ***var.*** Sapouy. S Burkina 11°34′N 01°44′W
Sapouy *see* Sapoui
Sappir *see* Sapir
165 S4 **Sapporo** Hokkaidō, NE Japan 43°05′N 141°21′E
107 M19 **Sapri** Campania, S Italy 40°05′N 15°36′E
169 T16 **Sapudi, Pulau** *island* S Indonesia
27 P9 **Sapulpa** Oklahoma, C USA 36°00′N 96°06′W
142 J4 **Saqqez** ***var.*** Saghez, Sakiz, Saqqiz. Kordestān, NW Iran 36°31′N 46°16′E
Saqqiz *see* Saqqez
139 U8 **Sarābādī** Wāsiţ, E Iraq 33°00′N 44°52′E
167 P10 **Sara Buri** ***var.*** Saraburi. Saraburi, C Thailand 14°32′N 100°53′E
Saraburi *see* Sara Buri
Sarafjagān *see* Salafchegān
24 K9 **Saragosa** Texas, SW USA 31°03′N 103°39′W
Saragossa *see* Zaragoza
Saragt *see* Sarahs
56 B8 **Saraguro** Loja, S Ecuador 03°42′S 79°18′W
146 I15 **Sarahs** ***var.*** Saragt, ***Rus.*** Serakhs. Ahal Welaýaty, S Turkmenistan 36°33′N 61°10′E
126 M6 **Sarai** Ryazanskaya Oblast', W Russian Federation 53°43′N 39°59′E
Sarāi *see* Sarāy
154 M12 **Saraipāli** Chhattīsgarh, C India 21°21′N 83°01′E
149 T9 **Sarāi Sidhu** Punjab, E Pakistan 30°35′N 72°02′E
93 M15 **Säräisniemi** Oulu, C Finland 64°25′N 26°50′E
113 I14 **Sarajevo** ● (Bosnia and Herzegovina) Federacija Bosna I Hercegovina, SE Bosnia and Herzegovina 43°53′N 18°24′E
112 I13 **Sarajevo** ✈ Federacija Bosna I Hercegovina, C Bosnia and Herzegovina 43°49′N 18°21′E
143 V4 **Sarakhs** Khorāsān-Razavī, NE Iran 36°50′N 61°00′E
115 H17 **Sarakíniko, Akrotírio** *headland* Évvoia, C Greece 38°46′N 23°43′E
115 I18 **Sarakinó** *island* Vóreies Sporádes, Greece, Aegean Sea
127 V7 **Saraktash** Orenburgskaya Oblast', W Russian Federation 51°46′N 56°23′E
30 L15 **Sara, Lake** ⊠ Illinois, N USA
23 N8 **Saraland** Alabama, S USA 30°49′N 88°04′W
55 V9 **Saramacca** ◐ *district* N Surinam
55 V10 **Saramacca Rivier** 〰 C Surinam
166 M2 **Saramati** ▲ N Burma (Myanmar) 25°46′N 95°01′E
145 R10 **Saran'** ***Kaz.*** Saran. Karaganda, C Kazakhstan 49°47′N 73°02′E
18 K7 **Saranac Lake** New York, NE USA 44°18′N 74°06′W
18 K7 **Saranac River** 〰 New York, NE USA
Saranda *see* Sarandë
113 L23 **Sarandë** ***var.*** Saranda, ***It.*** Porto Edda; ***prev.*** Santi Quaranta. Vlorë, S Albania 39°53′N 20°E
61 H14 **Sarandi** Rio Grande do Sul, S Brazil 27°57′S 52°58′W
61 F19 **Sarandí del Yí** Durazno, C Uruguay 33°18′S 55°38′W
61 F19 **Sarandí Grande** Florida, S Uruguay 33°43′S 56°19′W
171 Q8 **Sarangani Islands** *island group* S Philippines
127 P5 **Saransk** Respublika Mordoviya, W Russian Federation 54°11′N 45°10′E
115 C14 **Sarantáporos** 〰 N Greece
114 H9 **Sarantsi** Sofiya, W Bulgaria 42°43′N 23°46′E
127 T3 **Sarapul** Udmurtskaya Respublika, NW Russian Federation 56°26′N 53°52′E
Sarâqeb *see* Sarāqib
138 I3 **Sarāqib** ***Fr.*** Sarâqeb. Idlib, N Syria 35°52′N 36°48′E
54 J5 **Sarare** Lara, N Venezuela 09°47′N 69°10′W
55 O10 **Sarariña** Amazonas, S Venezuela 04°10′N 64°31′W
143 S10 **Sar Ashk** Kermān, C Iran
23 V13 **Sarasota** Florida, SE USA 27°20′N 82°31′W
117 O11 **Sarata** Odes'ka Oblast', SW Ukraine 46°01′N 29°40′E
116 I10 **Sărăţel** ***Hung.*** Szeretfalva. Bistriţa-Năsăud, N Romania 47°02′N 24°24′E
25 X10 **Saratoga** Texas, SW USA 30°15′N 94°31′W
18 K10 **Saratoga Springs** New York, NE USA 43°04′N 73°47′W
127 P8 **Saratov** Saratovskaya Oblast', W Russian Federation 51°33′N 45°58′E
127 P8 **Saratovskaya Oblast'** ◐ *province* W Russian Federation
127 Q7 **Saratovskoye Vodokhranilishche** ⊠ W Russian Federation
143 X13 **Sarāvān** Sīstān va Balūchestān, SE Iran 27°11′N 62°35′E
Saravan/Saravane *see* Salavan
169 S9 **Sarawak** ◐ *state* East Malaysia
Sarawak *see* Kuching
139 U6 **Sarāy** ***var.*** Sarāi. Diyālá, E Iraq 34°06′N 45°06′E
136 D10 **Saray** Tekirdağ, NW Turkey 41°27′N 27°56′E
76 J12 **Saraya** SE Senegal 12°50′N 11°45′W
143 W14 **Sarbāz** Sīstān va Balūchestān, SE Iran 26°38′N 61°13′E
143 U8 **Sarbīsheh** Khorāsān-e Janūbī, E Iran 32°35′N 59°50′E
111 J24 **Sárbogárd** Fejér, C Hungary 46°54′N 18°36′E
Şărcad *see* Sarkad
27 S7 **Sarcoxie** Missouri, C USA 37°04′N 94°07′W
152 L11 **Sārda** ***Nep.*** Kali. 〰 India/Nepal
152 G10 **Sardārshahr** Rājasthān, NW India 28°30′N 74°30′E
107 C18 **Sardegna** ***Eng.*** Sardinia. ◐ *region* Italy, C Mediterranean Sea
107 A18 **Sardegna** ***Eng.*** Sardinia. *island* Italy, C Mediterranean Sea
42 K13 **Sardinal** Guanacaste, NW Costa Rica 10°30′N 85°38′W
54 G7 **Sardinata** Norte de Santander, N Colombia 08°07′N 72°47′W
Sardinia *see* Sardegna
120 K8 **Sardinia-Corsica Trough** *undersea feature* Tyrrhenian Sea, C Mediterranean Sea
22 L2 **Sardis** Mississippi, S USA 34°25′N 89°55′W
22 L2 **Sardis Lake** ⊠ Mississippi, S USA
27 P12 **Sardis Lake** ⊠ Oklahoma, C USA
92 H12 **Sarek** ▲▲ N Sweden
92 H11 **Sarektjåhkkå** ▲ N Sweden 67°28′N 17°56′E
149 N3 **Sar-e Pol** ***var.*** Sar-i-Pul. Sar-e Pol, N Afghanistan 36°16′N 65°55′E
149 O3 **Sar-e Pol** ◐ *province* N Afghanistan
Sar-e Pol *see* Sar-e Pol-e Žahāb
142 J6 **Sar-e Pol-e Žahāb** ***var.*** Sar-e Pol, Sar-i Pul. Kermānshāhān, W Iran 34°28′N 45°52′E
Sarera, Teluk *see* Cenderawasih, Teluk
147 T13 **Sarez, Kŭli** ***Rus.*** Sarezskoye Ozero. ◎ SE Tajikistan
Sarezskoye Ozero *see* Sarez, Kŭli
64 G10 **Sargasso Sea** *sea* W Atlantic Ocean
149 U8 **Sargodha** Punjab, NE Pakistan 32°06′N 72°48′E
78 I13 **Sarh** ***prev.*** Fort-Archambault. Moyen-Chari, S Chad 09°08′N 18°22′E
143 P4 **Sārī** ***var.*** Sari, Sāri. Māzandarān, N Iran 36°37′N 53°05′E
115 N23 **Saría** *island* SE Greece
Sariasiya *see* Sariosiyo
40 F3 **Saric** Sonora, NW Mexico 31°08′N 111°22′W
188 K6 **Sarigan** *island* C Northern Mariana Islands
136 D14 **Sarıgöl** Manisa, SW Turkey 38°16′N 28°41′E
139 T6 **Sārihah** At Ta'mīn, E Iraq 34°34′N 44°38′E
137 R12 **Sarıkamış** Kars, NE Turkey 40°18′N 42°36′E
169 R9 **Sarikei** Sarawak, East Malaysia 02°07′N 111°30′E
147 U12 **Sarikol Range** ***Rus.*** Sarykol'skiy Khrebet. ▲▲ China/Tajikistan
181 Y7 **Sarina** Queensland, NE Australia 21°34′S 149°12′E
Sarine *see* La Sarine
105 S5 **Sariñena** Aragón, NE Spain 41°47′N 00°10′W
147 O13 **Sariosiyo** ***Rus.*** Sariasiya. Surkhondaryo Viloyati, S Uzbekistan 38°25′N 67°51′E
Sar-i-Pul *see* Sar-e Pol, Afghanistan
Sar-i Pul *see* Sar-e Pol-e Žahāb, Iran
Sariqamish Kŭli *see* Sarygamyş Köli
149 V1 **Sarī Qūl** ***Rus.*** Ozero Zurkul', ***Taj.*** Zŭrkŭl. ◎ Afghanistan/Tajikistan ***see also*** Zŭrkŭl
Sarī Qūl *see* Zŭrkŭl
75 Q12 **Sarīr Tībistī** ***var.*** Serir Tibesti. *desert* S Libya
25 S15 **Sarita** Texas, SW USA 27°14′N 97°48′W
163 W14 **Sariwŏn** SW North Korea 38°30′N 125°52′E
114 P12 **Sarıyer** İstanbul, NW Turkey 41°11′N 29°03′E
97 L26 **Sark** ***Fr.*** Sercq. *island* Channel Islands
111 N24 **Sarkad** ***Rom.*** Şărcad. Békés, SE Hungary 46°44′N 21°25′E
145 W14 **Sarkand** ***Kaz.*** Sarqan. Almaty, SW Kazakhstan 45°24′N 79°55′E
Sarkaņi *see* Krasnogorskoye
152 D11 **Sarkāri Tala** Rājasthān, NW India 27°39′N 70°52′E
136 G15 **Şarkîkaraağaç** ***var.*** Şarki Karaağaç. Isparta, SW Turkey 38°04′N 31°22′E
Şarki Karaağaç *see* Şarkîkaraağaç
136 L13 **Şarkışla** Sivas, C Turkey 39°21′N 36°27′E
136 C11 **Şarköy** Tekirdağ, NW Turkey 40°37′N 27°07′E
Sárköz *see* Livada
Sarlat *see* Sarlat-la-Canéda
102 M13 **Sarlat-la-Canéda** ***var.*** Sarlat. Dordogne, SW France 44°54′N 01°12′E
109 S3 **Sarleinsbach** Oberösterreich, N Austria 48°33′N 13°55′E
Šarma *see* Ash Sharmah
171 Y12 **Sarmi** Papua, E Indonesia 01°51′S 138°45′E
63 I19 **Sarmiento** Chubut, S Argentina 45°38′S 69°07′W
63 H25 **Sarmiento, Monte** ▲ S Chile 54°28′S 70°49′W
94 J11 **Särna** Dalarna, C Sweden 61°40′N 13°10′E
108 F8 **Sarnen** Obwalden, C Switzerland 46°54′N 08°15′E
108 F9 **Sarner See** ◎ C Switzerland
14 D16 **Sarnia** Ontario, S Canada 42°58′N 82°23′W
116 L3 **Sarny** Rivnens'ka Oblast', NW Ukraine 51°20′N 26°35′E
171 O13 **Saroako** Sulawesi, C Indonesia 02°31′S 121°18′E
118 L13 **Sarochyna** ***Rus.*** Sorochino. Vitsyebskaya Voblasts', N Belarus 55°12′N 28°45′E
168 L12 **Sarolangun** Sumatera, W Indonesia 02°17′S 102°39′E
165 U3 **Saroma** Hokkaidō, NE Japan 44°01′N 143°43′E
165 V3 **Saroma-ko** ◎ Hokkaidō, NE Japan
Saronic Gulf *see* Saronikós Kólpos
115 H20 **Saronikós Kólpos** ***Eng.*** Saronic Gulf. *gulf* S Greece
106 D7 **Saronno** Lombardia, N Italy 45°38′N 09°02′E
136 B11 **Saros Körfezi** *gulf* NW Turkey
111 N20 **Sárospatak** Borsod-Abaúj-Zemplén, NE Hungary 48°18′N 21°30′E
127 O4 **Sarov** ***prev.*** Sarova. Respublika Mordoviya, SW Russian Federation 54°39′N 43°09′E
Sarova *see* Sarov
127 P12 **Sarpa** Respublika Kalmykiya, SW Russian Federation 47°00′N 45°42′E
127 P12 **Sarpa, Ozero** ◎ SW Russian Federation
113 M18 **Šar Planina** ▲▲ FYR Macedonia/Serbia
95 I16 **Sarpsborg** Østfold, S Norway 59°16′N 11°07′E
139 U5 **Sarqaļā** At Ta'mīn, N Iraq
Sarqan *see* Sarkand
103 U4 **Sarralbe** Moselle, NE France 49°02′N 07°01′E
Sarre *see* Saar, France/Germany
Sarre *see* Saarland, Germany
103 U5 **Sarrebourg** ***Ger.*** Saarburg. Moselle, NE France 48°43′N 07°03′E
Sarrebruck *see* Saarbrücken
103 U4 **Sarreguemines** ***prev.*** Saargemund. Moselle, NE France 49°06′N 07°04′E
104 I3 **Sarria** Galicia, NW Spain 42°47′N 07°25′W
105 S8 **Sarrión** Aragón, NE Spain 40°09′N 00°49′W
42 F4 **Sarstoon** ***Sp.*** Río Sarstún. 〰 Belize/Guatemala
Sarstún, Río *see* Sarstoon
123 Q9 **Sartang** 〰 NE Russian Federation
103 X16 **Sartène** Corse, France, C Mediterranean Sea 41°38′N 08°58′E
102 K7 **Sarthe** ◐ *department* NW France
102 K7 **Sarthe** 〰 N France
115 H15 **Sárti** Kentrikí Makedonía, N Greece 40°05′N 24°E
Sartu *see* Daqing
165 T1 **Sarufutsu** Hokkaidō, NE Japan 45°20′N 142°03′E
Saruhan *see* Manisa
152 G9 **Sarūpsar** Rājasthān, NW India 29°25′N 73°50′E
137 U13 **Şärur** ***prev.*** Il'ichevsk. SW Azerbaijan 39°30′N 44°59′E
Sarvani *see* Marneuli
111 G23 **Sárvár** Vas, W Hungary 47°15′N 16°59′E
143 P11 **Sarvestān** Fārs, S Iran 29°16′N 53°13′E
171 W12 **Sarwon** Papua, E Indonesia 0°58′S 136°08′E
145 P17 **Saryagash** ***Kaz.*** Saryaghash. Yuzhnyy Kazakhstan, S Kazakhstan 41°29′N 69°10′E
Saryaghash *see* Saryagash
Saryarqa *see* Kazakhskiy Melkosopochnik
147 W8 **Sary-Bulak** Narynskaya Oblast', C Kyrgyzstan 41°56′N 75°44′E
147 U10 **Sary-Bulak** Oshskaya Oblast', SW Kyrgyzstan 40°49′N 73°44′E
117 S14 **Sarych, Mys** *headland* S Ukraine 44°23′N 33°44′E
147 Z7 **Sary-Dzhaz** ***var.*** Aksu He. 〰 China/Kyrgyzstan ***see also*** Aksu He
Sary-Dzhaz *see* Aksu He
146 F8 **Sarygamyş Köli** ***Rus.*** Sarykamyshkoye Ozero, ***Uzb.*** Sariqamish Kŭli. *salt lake* Kazakhstan/Uzbekistan
144 G13 **Sarykamys** ***Kaz.*** Saryqamys. Mangistau, SW Kazakhstan 45°58′N 53°30′E
Sarykamyshkoye Ozero *see* Sarygamyş Köli
145 N7 **Sarykol'** ***prev.*** Uritskiy. Kustanay, N Kazakhstan 53°19′N 65°34′E
Sarykol'skiy Khrebet *see* Sarikol Range
144 M10 **Sarykopa, Ozero** ◎ C Kazakhstan
145 V15 **Saryozek** ***Kaz.*** Saryözek. Almaty, SE Kazakhstan 44°22′N 77°57′E
Saryqamys *see* Sarykamys
145 S13 **Saryshagan** ***Kaz.*** Saryshaghan. Karaganda, SE Kazakhstan 46°05′N 73°38′E
Saryshaghan *see* Saryshagan
145 O13 **Sarysu** 〰 S Kazakhstan
147 T11 **Sary-Tash** Oshskaya Oblast', SW Kyrgyzstan 39°44′N 73°14′E
145 T12 **Saryterek** Karaganda, C Kazakhstan 47°46′N 74°06′E
Saryyazynskoye Vodokhranilishche *see* Saryýazy Suw Howdany
146 J15 **Saryýazy Suw Howdany** ***Rus.*** Saryyazynskoye Vodokhranilishche. ⊠ S Turkmenistan
145 T14 **Saryyesik-Atyrau, Peski** *desert* E Kazakhstan
106 E10 **Sarzana** Liguria, NW Italy 44°07′N 09°59′E
188 B17 **Sasalaguan, Mount** ▲ S Guam
153 O14 **Sasarām** Bihār, N India 24°58′N 84°01′E
186 M8 **Sasari, Mount** ▲ Santa Isabel, N Solomon Islands 08°09′S 159°32′E
164 C13 **Sasebo** Nagasaki, Kyūshū, SW Japan 33°10′N 129°42′E
14 I9 **Saseginaga, Lac** ◎ Québec, SE Canada
Saseno *see* Sazan
11 R13 **Saskatchewan** ◐ *province* SW Canada
11 U14 **Saskatchewan** 〰 Manitoba/Saskatchewan, C Canada
11 T15 **Saskatoon** Saskatchewan, S Canada 52°10′N 106°40′W
11 T15 **Saskatoon** ✈ Saskatchewan, S Canada 52°15′N 107°05′W
123 N7 **Saskylakh** Respublika Sakha (Yakutiya), NE Russian Federation 71°56′N 114°07′E
42 L7 **Saslaya, Cerro** ▲ N Nicaragua 13°52′N 85°06′W
38 G17 **Sasmik, Cape** *headland* Tanaga Island, Alaska, USA 51°36′N 177°55′W
119 N19 **Sasnovy Bor** ***Rus.*** Sosnovyy Bor. Homyel'skaya Voblasts', SE Belarus 52°32′N 29°35′E
127 N5 **Sasovo** Ryazanskaya Oblast', W Russian Federation 54°19′N 41°54′E
25 S12 **Saspamco** Texas, SW USA 29°13′N 98°18′W
109 W9 **Sass** ***var.*** Sassbach. 〰 SE Austria
76 M17 **Sassandra** S Ivory Coast 04°58′N 06°08′W
76 M17 **Sassandra** ***var.*** Ibo, Sassandra Fleuve. 〰 S Ivory Coast
Sassandra Fleuve *see* Sassandra
107 B17 **Sassari** Sardegna, Italy, C Mediterranean Sea 40°44′N 08°33′E
Sassbach *see* Sass
98 H11 **Sassenheim** Zuid-Holland, W Netherlands 52°14′N 04°31′E
Sassmacken *see* Valdemārpils
100 O7 **Sassnitz** Mecklenburg-Vorpommern, NE Germany 54°32′N 13°39′E
99 E16 **Sas van Gent** Zeeland, SW Netherlands 51°13′N 03°48′E
145 W12 **Sasykkol', Ozero** ◎ E Kazakhstan
117 O12 **Sasyk, Ozero** ***Rus.*** Ozero Kunduk. ◎ SW Ukraine
76 J12 **Satadougou** Kayes, SW Mali 12°40′N 11°25′W
164 C17 **Sata-misaki** Kyūshū, SW Japan
26 I7 **Satanta** Kansas, C USA 37°23′N 102°00′W
155 E15 **Sātāra** Mahārāshtra, W India 17°41′N 73°59′E
192 G15 **Sātaua** Savai'i, NW Samoa 13°26′S 172°40′W
188 M16 **Satawal** *island* Caroline Islands, C Micronesia
189 R17 **Satawan Atoll** *atoll* Mortlock Islands, C Micronesia
Sätbaev *see* Satpayev
23 Y12 **Satellite Beach** Florida, SE USA 28°10′N 80°35′W
95 M14 **Säter** Dalarna, C Sweden 60°21′N 15°45′E
Sathmar *see* Satu Mare
23 V7 **Satilla River** 〰 Georgia, SE USA
57 F14 **Satipo** ***var.*** San Francisco de Satipo. Junín, C Peru 11°19′S 74°37′W
122 F11 **Satka** Chelyabinskaya Oblast', C Russian Federation 55°08′N 58°54′E
153 T16 **Satkhira** Khulna, SW Bangladesh 22°43′N 89°06′E

146 J13 **Şatlyk** Rus. Shatlyk. Mary Welaýaty, C Turkmenistan 37°55′N 61°00′E
154 K9 **Satna** prev. Sutna. Madhya Pradesh, C India 24°33′N 80°50′E
103 R11 **Satolas** ✕ (Lyon) Rhône, E France 45°44′N 05°01′E
111 N20 **Sátoraljaújhely** Borsod-Abaúj-Zemplén, NE Hungary 48°24′N 21°39′E
145 O12 **Satpayev** Kaz. Sätbaev; prev. Nikol'skiy. Karaganda, C Kazakhstan 47°59′N 67°27′E
154 G11 **Sātpura Range** ▲ C India
Satsuma-Sendai see Sendai
167 P12 **Sattahip** var. Ban Sattahip, Ban Sattahipp. Chon Buri, S Thailand 12°36′N 100°56′E
92 L11 **Sattanen** Lappi, NE Finland 67°31′N 26°35′E
Satul see Satun
116 H9 **Satulung** Hung. Kővárhosszúfalu. Maramureş, N Romania 47°34′N 23°26′E
Satul-Vechi see Staro Selo
116 G8 **Satu Mare** Ger. Sathmar, Hung. Szatmárrnémeti. Satu Mare, NW Romania 47°46′N 22°55′E
116 G8 **Satu Mare** ◆ county NW Romania
167 N16 **Satun** var. Satul, Setul. Satun, SW Thailand 06°40′N 100°01′E
192 G16 **Satupa'iteau** Savai'i, W Samoa 13°46′S 172°26′W
Sau see Sava
14 F14 **Sauble** ~ Ontario, S Canada
14 F13 **Sauble Beach** Ontario, S Canada 44°36′N 81°15′W
61 C16 **Sauce** Corrientes, NE Argentina 30°05′S 58°46′W
Sauce see Juan L. Lacaze
36 K15 **Sauceda Mountains** ▲ Arizona, SW USA
61 C17 **Sauce de Luna** Entre Ríos, E Argentina 31°15′S 59°09′W
63 L15 **Sauce Grande, Río** ~ E Argentina
40 K6 **Saucillo** Chihuahua, N Mexico 28°01′N 105°17′W
95 D15 **Sauda** Rogaland, S Norway 59°38′N 06°23′E
145 Q16 **Saudakent** Kaz. Saūdakent; prev. Baykadam, Kaz. Bayqadam. Zhambyl, S Kazakhstan 43°49′N 69°56′E
92 J2 **Saudhárkrókur** Nordhurland Vestra, N Iceland 65°45′N 19°39′W
141 P9 **Saudi Arabia** off. Kingdom of Saudi Arabia, Al 'Arabīyah as Su'ūdīyah, Ar. Al Mamlakah al 'Arabīyah as Su'ūdīyah. ◆ monarchy SW Asia
Saudi Arabia, Kingdom of see Saudi Arabia
101 D19 **Sauer** var. Sûre. ~ NW Europe see also Sûre
Sauer see Sûre
101 F15 **Sauerland** forest W Germany
14 F14 **Saugeen** ~ Ontario, S Canada
18 K12 **Saugerties** New York, NE USA 42°04′N 73°55′W
Saugor see Sāgar
10 K15 **Saugstad, Mount** ▲ British Columbia, SW Canada 52°12′N 126°35′W
Sāūjbulāgh see Mahābād
102 J11 **Saujon** Charente-Maritime, W France 45°40′N 00°54′W
29 T7 **Sauk Centre** Minnesota, N USA 45°44′N 94°57′W
30 L8 **Sauk City** Wisconsin, N USA 43°16′N 89°43′W
29 U7 **Sauk Rapids** Minnesota, N USA 45°35′N 94°09′W
55 Y11 **Saül** C French Guiana 03°37′N 53°12′W
103 O7 **Sauldre** ~ C France
101 I23 **Saulgau** Baden-Württemberg, SW Germany 48°03′N 09°28′E
103 Q8 **Saulieu** Côte d'Or, C France 47°15′N 04°15′E
118 G8 **Saulkrasti** Rīga, C Latvia 57°14′N 24°25′E
15 S6 **Sault-aux-Cochons, Rivière du** ~ Québec, SE Canada
31 Q4 **Sault Sainte Marie** Michigan, N USA 46°29′N 84°22′W
12 F14 **Sault Ste. Marie** Ontario, S Canada 46°30′N 84°17′W
145 P7 **Saumalkol'** prev. Volodarskoye. Severnyy Kazakhstan, N Kazakhstan 53°19′N 68°05′E
190 E13 **Sauma, Pointe** headland Île Alofi, W Wallis and Futuna 14°21′S 177°58′W
171 T16 **Saumlaki** var. Saumlakki. Pulau Yamdena, E Indonesia 07°53′S 131°18′E
Saumlakki see Saumlaki
15 R12 **Saumon, Rivière au** ~ Québec, SE Canada
102 K8 **Saumur** Maine-et-Loire, NW France 47°16′N 00°04′W
185 F23 **Saunders, Cape** headland South Island, New Zealand 45°53′S 170°40′E
195 N13 **Saunders Coast** physical region Antarctica
65 C24 **Saunders Island Settlement** Saunders Island, NW Falkland Islands 51°22′S 60°05′W
82 F11 **Saurimo** Port. Henrique de Carvalho, Vila Henrique de Carvalho. Lunda Sul, NE Angola 09°39′S 20°24′E
55 S11 **Sauriwaunawa** S Guyana 03°10′N 59°51′W
82 D12 **Sautar** Malanje, NW Angola 11°10′S 18°26′E
45 S13 **Sauteurs** N Grenada 12°14′N 61°38′W
102 K13 **Sauveterre-de-Guyenne** Gironde, SW France 44°43′N 00°02′W
119 O14 **Sava** Mahilyowskaya Voblasts', E Belarus 54°22′N 30°49′E
42 J5 **Savá** Colón, N Honduras 15°30′N 86°16′W
84 H11 **Sava** Eng. Save, Ger. Sau, Hung. Száva. ~ SE Europe
33 Y8 **Savage** Montana, NW USA 47°28′N 104°17′W
183 N16 **Savage River** Tasmania, SE Australia 41°34′S 145°15′E
77 R15 **Savalou** S Benin 07°59′N 01°58′E
30 K10 **Savanna** Illinois, N USA 42°05′N 90°09′W
23 X6 **Savannah** Georgia, SE USA 32°02′N 81°01′W
27 R2 **Savannah** Missouri, C USA 39°57′N 94°49′W
20 H10 **Savannah** Tennessee, S USA 35°12′N 88°15′W
21 O12 **Savannah River** ~ Georgia/South Carolina, SE USA
Savannakhét see Khanthabouli
44 H12 **Savanna-La-Mar** W Jamaica 18°13′N 78°08′W
12 B10 **Savant Lake** ◎ Ontario, S Canada
155 F17 **Savanūr** Karnātaka, W India 14°58′N 75°19′E
93 J16 **Sävar** Västerbotten, N Sweden 63°52′N 20°33′E
Savaria see Szombathely
154 C11 **Sāvarkundla** var. Kundla. Gujarāt, W India 21°21′N 71°20′E
116 F11 **Săvârşin** Hung. Soborsin; prev. Săvirşin. Arad, W Romania 46°00′N 22°15′E
136 C13 **Savaştepe** Balıkesir, W Turkey 39°20′N 27°38′E
147 P11 **Savat** Rus. Savat. Sirdaryo Viloyati, E Uzbekistan 40°03′N 68°35′E
Savat see Savat
Sāvdijāri see Skaulo
77 R15 **Savè** SE Benin 08°04′N 02°29′E
83 N18 **Save** Inhambane, E Mozambique 21°07′S 34°35′E
102 L16 **Save** ~ S France
83 L17 **Save** var. Sabi. ~ Mozambique/Zimbabwe see also Sabi
Save see Sava
Save see Sabi
142 M6 **Sāveh** Markazī, W Iran 35°00′N 50°22′E
116 L8 **Săveni** Botoşani, NE Romania 47°57′N 26°52′E
103 N16 **Saverdun** Ariège, S France 43°15′N 01°34′E
103 U5 **Saverne** var. Zabern; anc. Tres Tabernae. Bas-Rhin, NE France 48°45′N 07°22′E
106 B9 **Savigliano** Piemonte, NW Italy 44°39′N 07°39′E
Savigsivik see Savissivik
Savinichi see Savinichy
119 Q16 **Savinichy** Rus. Savinichi. Mahilyowskaya Voblasts', E Belarus 53°28′N 31°46′E
109 U10 **Savinja** ~ N Slovenia
106 H11 **Savio** ~ C Italy
Săvirşin see Săvârşin
197 O11 **Savissivik** var. Savigsivik. ◆ Avannaarsua, N Greenland
93 N18 **Savitaipale** Etelä-Suomi, SE Finland 61°12′N 27°43′E
113 J15 **Šavnik** C Montenegro 42°57′N 19°04′E
108 I9 **Savognin** Graubünden, S Switzerland 46°34′N 09°35′E
103 T12 **Savoie** ◆ department E France
106 C10 **Savona** Liguria, NW Italy 44°18′N 08°29′E
93 N17 **Savonlinna** Swe. Nyslott. Itä-Suomi, E Finland 61°51′N 28°56′E
93 N17 **Savonranta** Itä-Suomi, E Finland 62°10′N 29°10′E
38 K10 **Savoonga** Saint Lawrence Island, Alaska, USA 63°40′N 170°29′W
30 M13 **Savoy** Illinois, N USA 40°03′N 88°15′W
117 O8 **Savran'** Odes'ka Oblast', SW Ukraine 48°07′N 30°00′E
137 R11 **Şavşat** Artvin, NE Turkey 41°15′N 42°30′E
95 L19 **Sävsjö** Jönköping, S Sweden 57°25′N 14°40′E
Savu, Kepulauan see Sawu, Kepulauan
92 M11 **Savukoski** Lappi, NE Finland 67°17′N 28°14′E
Savu, Pulau see Sawu, Pulau
187 Y14 **Savusavu** Vanua Levu, N Fiji 16°48′S 179°20′E
171 O17 **Savu Sea** Ind. Laut Sawu. sea S Indonesia
83 H17 **Savute** North-West, N Botswana 18°33′S 24°06′E
139 N7 **Şawāb Uqlat'** well W Iraq
138 M7 **Şawāb, Wādī aş** dry watercourse W Iraq
152 H13 **Sawāi Mādhopur** Rājasthān, N India 26°00′N 76°22′E
Sawakin see Suakin
167 R8 **Sawang Daen Din** Sakon Nakhon, E Thailand 17°28′N 103°27′E
167 O8 **Sawankhalok** var. Swankalok. Sukhothai, NW Thailand 17°19′N 99°50′E
165 P13 **Sawara** Chiba, Honshū, S Japan 35°52′N 140°31′E
37 R5 **Sawatch Range** ▲ Colorado, C USA
141 N12 **Sawdā', Jabal** ▲ SW Saudi Arabia 18°15′N 42°26′E
75 P9 **Sawdā', Jabal as** ▲ C Libya
Sawdirī see Sodiri
97 F14 **Sawel Mountain** ▲ C Northern Ireland, United Kingdom 54°49′N 07°04′W
75 X10 **Sawhāj** var. Sawhāj var. Sohâg, Suliag. C Egypt 26°28′N 31°44′E
Sawhāj see Sawhāj
77 O15 **Sawla** N Ghana 09°14′N 02°26′W
141 X12 **Şawqirah** var. Suqrah. S Oman 18°16′N 56°34′E
141 X12 **Şawqirah, Dawḥat** var. Ghubbat Sawqirah, Sukra Bay, Suqrah Bay. bay S Oman
Sawqirah, Ghubbat see Şawqirah, Dawḥat
183 V5 **Sawtell** New South Wales, SE Australia 30°22′S 153°04′E
138 K7 **Şawt, Wādī aş** dry watercourse S Syria
171 O17 **Sawu, Kepulauan** var. Kepulauan Savu. island group S Indonesia
Sawu, Laut see Savu Sea
171 O17 **Sawu, Pulau** var. Pulau Sawu. island Kepulauan Sawu, S Indonesia
105 S12 **Sax** País Valenciano, E Spain 38°33′N 00°49′W
Saxe see Sachsen
108 C11 **Saxon** Valais, SW Switzerland 46°07′N 07°09′E
Saxony see Sachsen
Saxony-Anhalt see Sachsen-Anhalt
77 R12 **Say** Niamey, SW Niger 13°08′N 02°20′E
15 V7 **Sayabec** Québec, SE Canada 48°33′N 67°42′W
Sayaboury see Xaignabouli
145 U12 **Sayak** Kaz. Sayaq. Karaganda, E Kazakhstan 46°54′N 77°17′E
57 D14 **Sayán** Lima, W Peru 11°10′S 77°08′W
129 T6 **Sayanskiy Khrebet** ▲ S Russian Federation
Sayaq see Sayak
146 K13 **Saýat** Rus. Sayat. Lebap Welaýaty, E Turkmenistan 38°44′N 63°51′E
42 D3 **Sayaxché** Petén, N Guatemala 16°34′N 90°14′W
Şaydā/Sayida see Saïda
162 J7 **Sayhan** var. Hüremt. Bulgan, C Mongolia 48°40′N 102°33′E
163 N10 **Sayhandulaan** var. Öldziyt. Dornogovĭ, SE Mongolia 44°42′N 109°10′E
162 K9 **Sayhan-Ovoo** var. Ongi. Dundgovĭ, C Mongolia 45°27′N 103°58′E
141 T15 **Sayhūt** E Yemen 15°18′N 51°16′E
29 U14 **Saylorville Lake** ⊠ Iowa, C USA
Saymenskiy Kanal see Saimaa Canal
163 N10 **Saynshand** Dornogovĭ, SE Mongolia 44°51′N 110°07′E
Saynshand see Sevrey
Sayn-Ust see Hohmorit
Say-Ötesh see Say-Utës
138 J7 **Şayqal, Baḩr** ◎ S Syria
Sayrab see Sayrob
158 H4 **Sayram Hu** ◎ NW China
26 K11 **Sayre** Oklahoma, C USA 35°18′N 99°38′W
18 H12 **Sayre** Pennsylvania, NE USA 41°57′N 76°30′W
18 K15 **Sayreville** New Jersey, NE USA 40°27′N 74°19′W
147 N13 **Sayrob** Rus. Sayrab. Surkhondaryo Viloyati, S Uzbekistan 38°03′N 66°54′E
40 L13 **Sayula** Jalisco, SW Mexico 19°52′N 103°36′W
141 R14 **Say'ūn** var. Saywūn. C Yemen 15°53′N 48°32′E
144 G14 **Say-Utës** Kaz. Say-Ötesh. Mangistau, SW Kazakhstan 44°20′N 53°32′E
10 K16 **Sayward** Vancouver Island, British Columbia, SW Canada 50°20′N 126°01′W
Saywūn see Say'ūn
Sayyāl see As Sayyāl
139 U8 **Sayyid 'Abīd** var. Saiyid Abid. Wāsiţ, E Iraq 32°51′N 45°07′E
113 J22 **Sazan** var. Ishulli i Sazanit, It. Saseno. island SW Albania
Sazanit, Ishulli i see Sazan
Sazau/Sazawa see Sázava
111 E17 **Sázava** var. Sazau, Ger. Sazawa. ~ C Czech Republic
124 J14 **Sazonovo** Vologodskaya Oblast', NW Russian Federation 59°04′N 35°10′E
102 G6 **Scaër** Finistère, NW France 48°00′N 03°40′W
97 J15 **Scafell Pike** ▲ NW England, United Kingdom 54°26′N 03°10′W
Scalabis see Santarém
96 M2 **Scalloway** N Scotland, United Kingdom 60°10′N 01°17′W
38 M11 **Scammon Bay** Alaska, USA 61°50′N 165°34′W
Scammon Lagoon/ Scammon, Laguna see Ojo de Liebre, Laguna
84 F7 **Scandinavia** geophysical region NW Europe
Scania see Skåne
96 K5 **Scapa Flow** sea basin N Scotland, United Kingdom
107 K26 **Scaramia, Capo** headland Sicilia, Italy, C Mediterranean Sea 36°46′N 14°29′E
14 H15 **Scarborough** Ontario, SE Canada 43°46′N 79°14′W
45 Z16 **Scarborough** prev. Port Louis. Tobago, Trinidad and Tobago 11°11′N 60°45′W
97 N16 **Scarborough** N England, United Kingdom 54°17′N 00°24′W
185 I17 **Scargill** Canterbury, South Island, New Zealand 42°57′S 172°57′E
96 E7 **Scarp** island NW Scotland, United Kingdom
Scarpanto see Kárpathos
Scarpanto Strait see Karpathou, Stenó
107 G25 **Scauri** Sicilia, Italy, C Mediterranean Sea 36°45′N 12°06′E
Scealg, Bá na see Ballinskelligs Bay
Scebeli see Shebeli
100 K10 **Schaale** ~ N Germany
100 K9 **Schaalsee** ◎ N Germany
99 G18 **Schaerbeek** Brussels, C Belgium 50°52′N 04°21′E
108 G6 **Schaffhausen** Fr. Schaffhouse. Schaffhausen, N Switzerland 47°42′N 08°38′E
108 G6 **Schaffhausen** Fr. Schaffhouse. ◆ canton N Switzerland
Schaffhouse see Schaffhausen
98 I8 **Schagen** Noord-Holland, NW Netherlands 52°47′N 04°47′E
Schaken see Šakiai
98 M10 **Schalkhaar** Overijssel, E Netherlands 52°16′N 06°10′E
109 R3 **Schärding** Oberösterreich, N Austria 48°27′N 13°26′E
100 G9 **Scharhörn** island NW Germany
Schässburg see Sighişoara
Schaulen see Šiauliai
30 M10 **Schaumburg** Illinois, N USA 42°01′N 88°04′W
Schebschi Mountains see Shebshi Mountains
98 P6 **Scheemda** Groningen, NE Netherlands 53°10′N 06°58′E
100 I10 **Scheessel** Niedersachsen, NW Germany 53°11′N 09°33′E
13 N8 **Schefferville** Québec, E Canada 54°50′N 67°W
Schelde see Scheldt
99 D18 **Scheldt** Dut. Schelde, Fr. Escaut. ~ W Europe
35 X5 **Schell Creek Range** ▲ Nevada, W USA
18 K10 **Schenectady** New York, NE USA 42°48′N 73°57′W
99 I17 **Scherpenheuvel** Fr. Montaigu. Vlaams Brabant, C Belgium 51°00′N 04°57′E
98 K11 **Scherpenzeel** Gelderland, C Netherlands 52°07′N 05°30′E
25 S12 **Schertz** Texas, SW USA 29°33′N 98°16′W
98 G11 **Scheveningen** Zuid-Holland, W Netherlands 52°07′N 04°18′E
98 G12 **Schiedam** Zuid-Holland, SW Netherlands 51°55′N 04°25′E
99 M24 **Schieren** Diekirch, NE Luxembourg 49°50′N 06°06′E
98 M4 **Schiermonnikoog** Fris. Skiermûntseach. Friesland, N Netherlands 53°28′N 06°09′E
98 M4 **Schiermonnikoog** Fris. Skiermûntseach. island Waddeneilanden, N Netherlands
99 K14 **Schijndel** Noord-Brabant, S Netherlands 51°37′N 05°27′E
Schil see Jiu
99 H16 **Schilde** Antwerpen, N Belgium 51°14′N 04°35′E
Schillen see Zhilino
103 V5 **Schiltigheim** Bas-Rhin, NE France 48°38′N 07°47′E
106 G7 **Schio** Veneto, NE Italy 45°42′N 11°21′E
98 H10 **Schiphol** ✕ (Amsterdam) Noord-Holland, C Netherlands 52°18′N 04°48′E
Schippenbeil see Sępopol
Schiria see Şiria
Schivelbein see Świdwin
115 D22 **Schíza** island S Greece
175 U3 **Schjetman Reef** reef Antarctica
Schlackenwerth see Ostrov
109 R7 **Schladming** Steiermark, SE Austria 47°24′N 13°42′E
Schlan see Slaný
Schlanders see Silandro
100 I7 **Schlei** inlet N Germany
101 D17 **Schleiden** Nordrhein-Westfalen, W Germany 50°31′N 06°30′E
Schlelau see Szydłowiec
100 I7 **Schleswig** Schleswig-Holstein, N Germany 54°31′N 09°34′E
29 T13 **Schleswig** Iowa, C USA 42°10′N 95°27′W
100 H8 **Schleswig-Holstein** ◆ state N Germany
Schlettstadt see Sélestat
108 F7 **Schlieren** Zürich, N Switzerland 47°23′N 08°27′E
Schlochau see Człuchów
Schloppe see Człopa
101 I18 **Schlüchtern** Hessen, C Germany 50°19′N 09°27′E
101 J17 **Schmalkalden** Thüringen, C Germany 50°42′N 10°26′E
109 W2 **Schmida** ~ NE Austria
65 P19 **Schmidt-Ott Seamount** var. Schmitt-Ott Seamount, Schmitt-Ott Tablemount. undersea feature SW Indian Ocean 39°37′S 13°00′E
Schmiegel see Śmigiel
Schmitt-Ott Seamount/ Schmitt-Ott Tablemount see Schmidt-Ott Seamount
15 V3 **Schmon** ~ Québec, SE Canada
101 M18 **Schneeberg** ▲ W Germany 50°03′N 11°51′E
Schneeberg see Veliki Snežnik
Schnee-Eifel see Schneifel
Schneekoppe see Sněžka
Schneidemühl see Piła
101 D18 **Schneifel** var. Schnee-Eifel. plateau W Germany
Schnelle Körös/Schnelle Kreisch see Crişul Repede
100 I11 **Schneverdingen** var. Schneverdingen (Wümme). Niedersachsen, NW Germany 53°07′N 09°48′E
Schneverdingen (Wümme) see Schneverdingen
Schoden see Skuodas
45 Q12 **Schœlcher** W Martinique 14°37′N 61°08′W
18 K10 **Schoharie** New York, NE USA 42°40′N 74°20′W
18 K11 **Schoharie Creek** ~ New York, NE USA
115 J21 **Schoinoússa** island Kykládes, Greece, Aegean Sea
100 L13 **Schönebeck** Sachsen-Anhalt, C Germany 52°01′N 11°45′E
Schöneck see Skarszewy
100 O12 **Schönefeld** ✕ (Berlin) Berlin, NE Germany 52°23′N 13°29′E
101 K24 **Schongau** Bayern, S Germany 47°49′N 10°54′E
100 K13 **Schöningen** Niedersachsen, C Germany 52°07′N 10°58′E
Schönlanke see Trzcianka
Schönsee see Kowalewo Pomorskie
31 P10 **Schoolcraft** Michigan, N USA 42°05′N 85°39′W
98 O8 **Schoonebeek** Drenthe, NE Netherlands 52°39′N 06°57′E
98 I12 **Schoonhoven** Zuid-Holland, C Netherlands 51°57′N 04°51′E
98 H8 **Schoorl** Noord-Holland, NW Netherlands 52°42′N 04°40′E
Schooten see Schoten
101 F24 **Schopfheim** Baden-Württemberg, SW Germany 47°39′N 07°49′E
101 I21 **Schorndorf** Baden-Württemberg, S Germany 48°48′N 09°31′E
100 F10 **Schortens** Niedersachsen, NW Germany 53°31′N 07°57′E
99 H16 **Schoten** var. Schooten. Antwerpen, N Belgium 51°15′N 04°30′E
183 Q17 **Schouten Island** island Tasmania, SE Australia
186 C5 **Schouten Islands** island group NW Papua New Guinea
98 E13 **Schouwen** island SW Netherlands
Schreiberhau see Szklarska Poręba
109 U2 **Schrems** Niederösterreich, E Austria 48°48′N 15°05′E
101 L22 **Schrobenhausen** Bayern, SE Germany 48°33′N 11°14′E
18 L8 **Schroon Lake** ◎ New York, NE USA
108 J8 **Schruns** Vorarlberg, W Austria 47°04′N 09°54′E
Schubin see Szubin
25 U11 **Schulenburg** Texas, SW USA 29°40′N 96°54′W
Schuls see Scuol
108 E8 **Schüpfheim** Luzern, C Switzerland 47°02′N 07°23′E
35 S6 **Schurz** Nevada, W USA 38°55′N 118°48′W
101 I24 **Schussen** ~ S Germany
Schüttenhofen see Sušice
29 R15 **Schuyler** Nebraska, C USA 41°25′N 97°04′W
18 L10 **Schuylerville** New York, NE USA 43°05′N 73°34′W
101 K20 **Schwabach** Bayern, SE Germany 49°20′N 11°02′E
Schwabenalb see Schwäbische Alb
101 I23 **Schwäbische Alb** var. Schwabenalb, Eng. Swabian Jura. ▲ S Germany
101 I22 **Schwäbisch Gmünd** var. Gmünd. Baden-Württemberg, SW Germany 48°49′N 09°48′E
101 I21 **Schwäbisch Hall** var. Hall. Baden-Württemberg, SW Germany 49°07′N 09°45′E
101 H16 **Schwalm** ~ C Germany
109 V9 **Schwanberg** Steiermark, SE Austria 46°46′N 15°12′E
108 H8 **Schwanden** Glarus, E Switzerland 47°02′N 09°04′E
101 M20 **Schwandorf** Bayern, SE Germany 49°20′N 12°07′E
109 S5 **Schwanenstadt** Oberösterreich, NW Austria 48°03′N 13°47′E
169 S11 **Schwaner, Pegunungan** ▲ Borneo, N Indonesia
109 W5 **Schwarza** ~ E Austria
109 P9 **Schwarzach** ~ S Austria
101 M20 **Schwarzach** Cz. Černice. ~ Czech Republic/Germany
Schwarzach see Schwarzach im Pongau
109 Q7 **Schwarzach im Pongau** var. Schwarzach. Salzburg, NW Austria 47°19′N 13°09′E
Schwarzawa see Svratka
101 N14 **Schwarze Elster** ~ E Germany
Schwarze Körös see Crişul Negru
108 D9 **Schwarzenburg** Bern, W Switzerland 46°51′N 07°28′E
83 D21 **Schwarzrand** ▲ S Namibia
101 G23 **Schwarzwald** Eng. Black Forest. ▲ SW Germany
Schwarzwasser see Wda
39 P7 **Schwatka Mountains** ▲ Alaska, USA
109 N7 **Schwaz** Tirol, W Austria 47°21′N 11°44′E
109 Y4 **Schwechat** Niederösterreich, NE Austria 48°09′N 16°29′E
109 Y4 **Schwechat** ✕ (Wien) Wien, E Austria 48°04′N 16°31′E
100 P11 **Schwedt** Brandenburg, NE Germany 53°04′N 14°16′E
101 D19 **Schweich** Rheinland-Pfalz, SW Germany 49°49′N 06°44′E
Schweidnitz see Świdnica
101 J18 **Schweinfurt** Bayern, SE Germany 50°03′N 10°13′E
Schweiz see Switzerland
100 L9 **Schwerin** Mecklenburg-Vorpommern, N Germany 53°38′N 11°25′E
Schwerin see Skwierzyna
100 L9 **Schweriner See** ◎ N Germany
Schwertberg see Świecie
101 F15 **Schwerte** Nordrhein-Westfalen, W Germany 51°27′N 07°34′E
Schwiebus see Świebodzin
100 P13 **Schwielochsee** ◎ NE Germany
Schwihau see Švihov
Schwiz see Schwyz
108 G8 **Schwyz** var. Schwiz. Schwyz, C Switzerland 47°02′N 08°39′E
108 G8 **Schwyz** var. Schwiz. ◆ canton C Switzerland
14 J11 **Schyan** ~ Québec, SE Canada
Schyl see Jiu
107 I24 **Sciacca** Sicilia, Italy, C Mediterranean Sea 37°31′N 13°05′E
Sciasciamana see Shashemenē
107 L26 **Scicli** Sicilia, Italy, C Mediterranean Sea 36°48′N 14°43′E
97 F25 **Scilly, Isles of** island group SW England, United Kingdom
111 H17 **Ščinawa** Ger. Steinau an der Elbe. Dolnośląskie, SW Poland 51°22′N 16°27′E
Scio see Chíos
31 S14 **Scioto River** ~ Ohio, N USA
36 L5 **Scipio** Utah, W USA 39°15′N 112°06′W
33 X6 **Scobey** Montana, NW USA 48°47′N 105°25′W
183 T7 **Scone** New South Wales, SE Australia 32°02′S 150°51′E
Scoresby Sound/ Scoresbysund see Ittoqqortoormiit
Scoresby Sund see Kangertittivaq
Scorno, Punta dello see Caprara, Punta
34 K3 **Scotia** California, W USA 40°34′N 124°07′W
47 Y14 **Scotia Plate** tectonic feature
47 V15 **Scotia Ridge** undersea feature S Atlantic Ocean
194 H2 **Scotia Sea** sea SW Atlantic Ocean
29 Q12 **Scotland** South Dakota, N USA 43°09′N 97°43′W
25 R5 **Scotland** Texas, SW USA 33°37′N 98°27′W
96 H11 **Scotland** ◆ national region Scotland, U K
21 W8 **Scotland Neck** North Carolina, SE USA 36°07′N 77°25′W
195 R13 **Scott Base** NZ research station Antarctica 77°52′S 167°18′E
10 J16 **Scott, Cape** headland Vancouver Island, British Columbia, SW Canada 50°43′N 128°24′W
26 I5 **Scott City** Kansas, C USA 38°28′N 100°55′W
27 Y7 **Scott City** Missouri, C USA 37°13′N 89°31′W
195 R14 **Scott Coast** physical region Antarctica
18 C15 **Scottdale** Pennsylvania, NE USA 40°05′N 79°35′W
195 Y11 **Scott Glacier** glacier Antarctica
195 Q17 **Scott Island** island Antarctica
26 L11 **Scott, Mount** ▲ Oklahoma, USA 34°52′N 98°34′W
32 G15 **Scott, Mount** ▲ Oregon, NW USA 42°53′N 122°06′W
34 M1 **Scott River** ~ California, W USA
28 I13 **Scottsbluff** Nebraska, C USA 41°52′N 103°40′W
23 Q2 **Scottsboro** Alabama, S USA 34°40′N 86°01′W
31 P15 **Scottsburg** Indiana, N USA 38°42′N 85°47′W
183 P16 **Scottsdale** Tasmania, SE Australia 41°13′S 147°30′E
36 L13 **Scottsdale** Arizona, SW USA 33°31′N 111°54′W
45 O12 **Scotts Head Village** var. Cachacrou. S Dominica 15°12′N 61°22′W
192 L14 **Scott Shoal** undersea feature S Pacific Ocean
20 K7 **Scottsville** Kentucky, S USA 36°45′N 86°11′W
29 U14 **Scranton** Iowa, C USA 42°01′N 94°33′W
18 I13 **Scranton** Pennsylvania, NE USA 41°25′N 75°40′W
186 B6 **Screw** ~ NW Papua New Guinea
29 R14 **Scribner** Nebraska, C USA 41°40′N 96°40′W
Scrobesbyrig' see Shrewsbury
14 I14 **Scugog** ~ Ontario, SE Canada
14 I14 **Scugog, Lake** ◎ Ontario, SE Canada
97 N17 **Scunthorpe** E England, United Kingdom 53°35′N 00°39′W
108 K9 **Scuol** Ger. Schuls. Graubünden, E Switzerland 46°51′N 10°21′E
Scupi see Skopje
Scutari see Shkodër
113 K17 **Scutari, Lake** Alb. Liqeni i Shkodrës, SCr. Skadarsko Jezero. ◎ Albania/ Montenegro
Scyros see Skýros
Scythopolis see Bet She'an
138 E11 **Sderot** prev. Sederot. Southern, S Israel 31°31′N 34°35′E
25 U13 **Seadrift** Texas, SW USA 28°25′N 96°42′W
21 Y4 **Seaford** var. Seaford City. Delaware, NE USA 38°39′N 75°35′W
Seaford City see Seaford
14 E15 **Seaforth** Ontario, S Canada 43°33′N 81°25′W
24 M6 **Seagraves** Texas, SW USA 32°56′N 102°33′W
11 X9 **Seal** ~ Manitoba, C Canada
182 M10 **Sea Lake** Victoria, SE Australia 35°34′S 142°51′E
83 G26 **Seal, Cape** headland S South Africa 34°06′S 23°18′E
65 D26 **Sea Lion Islands** island group SE Falkland Islands
19 S8 **Seal Island** island Maine, NE USA
25 V11 **Sealy** Texas, SW USA 29°46′N 96°09′W
35 X12 **Searchlight** Nevada, W USA 35°27′N 114°54′W
27 V11 **Searcy** Arkansas, C USA 35°14′N 91°43′W
19 R7 **Searsport** Maine, NE USA 44°28′N 68°54′W
35 N10 **Seaside** California, W USA 36°36′N 121°51′W
32 F10 **Seaside** Oregon, NW USA 45°57′N 123°55′W
18 K16 **Seaside Heights** New Jersey, NE USA 39°56′N 74°03′W
32 H8 **Seattle** Washington, NW USA 47°35′N 122°20′W
32 H9 **Seattle-Tacoma** ✕ Washington, NW USA 47°04′N 122°27′W
185 J16 **Seaward Kaikoura Range** ▲ South Island, New Zealand
42 J9 **Sébaco** Matagalpa, W Nicaragua 12°51′N 86°08′W
19 P8 **Sebago Lake** ◎ Maine, NE USA
169 S13 **Sebangan, Teluk** bay Borneo, C Indonesia
169 S13 **Sebanganu, Teluk** bay Borneo, C Indonesia
Sebaste/Sebastia see Sivas
23 Y12 **Sebastian** Florida, SE USA 27°55′N 80°31′W
40 C5 **Sebastían Vizcaíno, Bahía** bay NW Mexico
19 R6 **Sebasticook Lake** ◎ Maine, NE USA
34 M7 **Sebastopol** California, W USA 38°22′N 122°50′W
Sebastopol' see Sevastopol'
169 W8 **Sebatik, Pulau** island N Indonesia
19 R5 **Sebec Lake** ◎ Maine, NE USA
76 K12 **Sébékoro** Kayes, W Mali 13°00′N 09°03′W
Sebenico see Šibenik
40 G6 **Seberi, Cerro** ▲ NW Mexico 27°49′N 110°18′W
116 H11 **Sebeş** Ger. Mühlbach, Hung. Szászsebes; prev. Sebeşu Săsesc. Alba, W Romania 45°58′N 23°34′E
Sebes-Körös see Crişul Repede
Sebeşu Săsesc see Sebeş
31 R8 **Sebewaing** Michigan, N USA 43°43′N 83°27′W
124 F16 **Sebezh** Pskovskaya Oblast', W Russian Federation 56°19′N 28°31′E
137 N12 **Şebinkarahisar** Giresun, N Turkey 40°19′N 38°25′E
116 F11 **Sebiş** Hung. Borossebes. Arad, W Romania 46°21′N 22°09′E
Sebkra Azz el Matti see Azzel Matti, Sebkha
19 Q4 **Seboomook Lake** ◎ Maine, NE USA
74 G6 **Sebou** var. Sebu. ~ N Morocco
20 I6 **Sebree** Kentucky, S USA 37°34′N 87°30′W
23 X13 **Sebring** Florida, SE USA 27°30′N 81°26′W
Sebta see Ceuta
Sebu see Sebou
169 U13 **Sebuku, Pulau** island N Indonesia
169 W8 **Sebuku, Teluk** bay Borneo, N Indonesia
106 F10 **Secchia** ~ N Italy
10 L17 **Sechelt** British Columbia, SW Canada 49°25′N 123°37′W
56 C12 **Sechín, Río** ~ W Peru
56 A10 **Sechura, Bahía de** bay NW Peru
185 A22 **Secretary Island** island SW New Zealand
155 I15 **Secunderābād** var. Sikandarabad. Andhra Pradesh, C India 17°30′N 78°33′E
57 L17 **Sécure, Río** ~ C Bolivia
118 D10 **Seda** Telšiai, NW Lithuania 56°10′N 22°04′E
27 T5 **Sedalia** Missouri, C USA 38°42′N 93°15′W
103 R3 **Sedan** Ardennes, N France 49°42′N 04°56′E
27 P7 **Sedan** Kansas, C USA 37°07′N 96°11′W
105 N3 **Sedano** Castilla-León, N Spain 42°43′N 03°43′W
104 H10 **Seda, Ribeira de** stream C Portugal
185 K15 **Seddon** Marlborough, South Island, New Zealand 41°42′S 174°05′E
185 H15 **Seddonville** West Coast, South Island, New Zealand 41°35′S 171°59′E
143 U7 **Sedeh** Khorāsān-e Janūbī, E Iran 33°18′N 59°12′E
Sederot see Sderot
65 B23 **Sedge Island** island NW Falkland Islands
76 G12 **Sédhiou** SW Senegal 12°39′N 15°33′W
11 U16 **Sedley** Saskatchewan, S Canada 50°06′N 103°51′W
Sedlez see Siedlce
117 Q2 **Sedniv** Chernihivs'ka Oblast', N Ukraine 51°39′N 31°34′E
36 L11 **Sedona** Arizona, SW USA 34°52′N 111°45′W
Sedunum see Sion
118 F12 **Šeduva** Šiauliai, N Lithuania 55°45′N 23°46′E
141 Y8 **Seeb** var. Muscat Sīb Airport. ✕ (Masqaţ) NE Oman 23°36′N 58°27′E
Seeb see As Sīb
108 M7 **Seefeld-in-Tirol** Tirol, W Austria 47°19′N 11°16′E
83 E22 **Seeheim Noord** Karas, S Namibia 26°50′S 17°45′E
Seeland see Sjælland
195 N9 **Seelig, Mount** ▲ Antarctica 81°45′S 102°15′W
Seenu Atoll see Addu Atoll
Seeonee see Seoni
Seer see Dörgön
102 L5 **Sées** Orne, N France 48°36′N 00°11′E
101 J14 **Seesen** Niedersachsen, C Germany 51°54′N 10°11′E
Seesker Höhe see Szeska Góra
100 J10 **Seevetal** Niedersachsen, N Germany 53°24′N 10°01′E
109 V6 **Seewiesen** Steiermark, E Austria 47°37′N 15°16′E
136 J13 **Şefaatli** var. Kızılkoca. Yozgat, C Turkey 39°32′N 34°45′E
143 V9 **Sefīdābeh** Khorāsān-e Janūbī, E Iran 31°05′N 60°30′E
149 N3 **Sefid, Darya-ye** Pash. Āb-i-safed. ~ N Afghanistan
148 K5 **Sefīd Kūh, Selseleh-ye** Eng. Paropamisus Range. ▲ W Afghanistan 34°00′N 61°40′E
148 K5 **Sefīd Kūh, Selseleh-ye** Eng. Paropamisus Range. ▲ W Afghanistan
142 M4 **Sefīd, Rūd-e** ~ NW Iran
74 G6 **Sefrou** N Morocco 33°51′N 04°49′W
185 E19 **Sefton, Mount** ▲ South Island, New Zealand 43°43′S 169°58′E
171 S13 **Segaf, Kepulauan** island group E Indonesia
169 W7 **Segama, Sungai** ~ East Malaysia
168 L9 **Segamat** Johor, Peninsular Malaysia 02°30′N 102°48′E
77 S13 **Ségbana** NE Benin 10°56′N 03°42′E
Segestica see Sisak
Segesvár see Sighişoara
171 T12 **Seget** Papua, E Indonesia 01°21′S 131°04′E
Segewold see Sigulda
124 J9 **Segezha** Respublika Kareliya, NW Russian Federation 63°39′N 34°24′E
Seghedin see Szeged
Segna see Senj
107 I16 **Segni** Lazio, C Italy 41°41′N 13°02′E
Segodunum see Rodez
105 S9 **Segorbe** País Valenciano, E Spain 39°51′N 00°30′W
76 M12 **Ségou** var. Segu. Ségou, C Mali 13°26′N 06°12′W
76 M12 **Ségou** ◆ region SW Mali
54 E8 **Segovia** Antioquia, N Colombia 07°08′N 74°39′W
105 N7 **Segovia** Castilla-León, C Spain 40°57′N 04°07′W
104 M6 **Segovia** ◆ province Castilla-León, N Spain
Segoviao Wangkí see Coco, Río
124 J9 **Segozerskoye Vodokhranilishche** ◎ NW Russian Federation
102 J7 **Segré** Maine-et-Loire, NW France 47°41′N 00°51′W
105 U5 **Segre** ~ NE Spain
Segu see Ségou
38 I17 **Seguam Island** island Aleutian Islands, Alaska, USA
38 I17 **Seguam Pass** strait Aleutian Islands, Alaska, USA
77 Y7 **Séguédine** Agadez, NE Niger 20°12′N 13°03′E
76 M15 **Séguéla** W Ivory Coast 07°58′N 06°44′W
25 S11 **Seguin** Texas, SW USA 29°34′N 97°58′W
38 E17 **Segula Island** island Aleutian Islands, Alaska, USA
62 K10 **Segundo, Río** ~ C Argentina
105 Q12 **Segura** ~ S Spain
105 P13 **Segura, Sierra de** ▲ S Spain
83 G18 **Sehithwa** North-West, N Botswana 20°28′S 22°43′E
154 H10 **Sehore** Madhya Pradesh, C India 23°12′N 77°08′E
186 G9 **Sehulea** Normanby Island, S Papua New Guinea 09°55′S 151°10′E
149 P15 **Sehwān** Sind, SE Pakistan 26°26′N 67°52′N

◆ Country ● Country Capital ◇ Dependent Territory ○ Dependent Territory Capital ◆ Administrative Regions ✕ International Airport ▲ Mountain ▲ Mountain Range ⛰ Volcano ~ River ◎ Lake ⊠ Reservoir

109 V8 **Seiersberg** Steiermark, SE Austria 47°01´N 15°22´E
26 L9 **Seiling** Oklahoma, C USA 36°09´N 98°55´W
103 S9 **Seille** ≈ E France
99 J20 **Seilles** Namur, SE Belgium 50°31´N 05°12´E
93 K17 **Seinäjoki** *Swe.* Östermyra. Länsi-Suomi, W Finland 62°45´N 22°55´E
12 B12 **Seine** ≈ Ontario, S Canada
102 M4 **Seine** ≈ N France
102 K4 **Seine, Baie de la** *bay* N France
Seine, Banc de la *see* Seine Seamount
103 O5 **Seine-et-Marne** ◐ *department* N France
102 L3 **Seine-Maritime** ◐ *department* N France
84 B14 **Seine Plain** *undersea feature* E Atlantic Ocean 34°00´N 12°15´W
84 B15 **Seine Seamount** *var.* Banc de la Seine. *undersea feature* E Atlantic Ocean 33°45´N 14°25´W
102 E6 **Sein, Île de** *island* NW France
171 Y14 **Seinma** Papua, E Indonesia 04°10´S 138°54´E
Seisbierrum *see* Sexbierum
109 U5 **Seitenstetten Markt** Niederösterreich, C Austria 48°03´N 14°41´E
Seiyo *see* Uwa
Seiyu *see* Chŏnju
95 H22 **Sejerø** *island* E Denmark
110 P7 **Sejny** Podlaskie, NE Poland 54°09´N 23°21´E
81 G20 **Seke** Shinyanga, N Tanzania 03°16´S 33°31´E
164 L13 **Seki** Gifu, Honshū, SW Japan 35°30´N 136°54´E
161 U12 **Sekibi-sho** *island* China/ Japan/Taiwan
165 U3 **Sekihoku-tōge** *pass* Hokkaidō, NE Japan
Sekondi *see* Sekondi-Takoradi
77 P17 **Sekondi-Takoradi** *var.* Sekondi. S Ghana 04°55´N 01°45´W
80 J11 **Sek'ot'a** Āmara, N Ethiopia 12°41´N 39°05´E
Sekseüil *see* Saksaul'skoye
32 I9 **Selah** Washington, NW USA 46°39´N 120°31´W
168 J8 **Selangor** *var.* Negeri Selangor Darul Ehsan. ◐ *state* Peninsular Malaysia
Selânik *see* Thessaloníki
168 K10 **Selapanjang** Pulau Rantau, W Indonesia 01°00´N 102°44´E
167 R10 **Selaphum** Roi Et, E Thailand 16°00´N 103°54´E
171 T16 **Selaru, Pulau** *island* Kepulauan Tanimbar, E Indonesia
171 U13 **Selassi** Papua, E Indonesia 03°16´S 132°50´E
168 J7 **Selatan, Selat** *strait* Peninsular Malaysia
39 N8 **Selawik** Alaska, USA 66°36´N 160°00´W
39 N8 **Selawik Lake** ◎ Alaska, USA
171 N14 **Selayar, Selat** *strait* Sulawesi, C Indonesia
95 C14 **Selbjørnsfjorden** *fjord* S Norway
94 H8 **Selbusjøen** ◎ S Norway
97 M17 **Selby** N England, United Kingdom 53°49´N 01°06´W
29 N8 **Selby** South Dakota, N USA 45°30´N 100°01´W
21 Z4 **Selbyville** Delaware, NE USA 38°28´N 75°12´W
136 B15 **Selçuk** *var.* Akıncılar. İzmir, SW Turkey 37°56´N 27°25´E
39 Q13 **Seldovia** Alaska, USA 59°26´N 151°42´W
107 M18 **Sele** *anc.* Silarius. ≈ S Italy
83 J19 **Selebi-Phikwe** Central, E Botswana 21°58´S 27°48´E
42 B5 **Selegua, Río** ≈ W Guatemala
129 X7 **Selemdzha** ≈ SE Russian Federation
129 U7 **Selenga** *Mong.* Selenge Mörön. ≈ Mongolia/ Russian Federation
79 I19 **Selenge** Bandundu, W Dem. Rep. Congo 01°58´S 18°11´E
162 K6 **Selenge** *var.* Ingettolgoy. Bulgan, N Mongolia 49°27´N 103°59´E
162 L6 **Selenge** ◐ *province* N Mongolia
Selenge *see* Hyalganat, Bulgan, Mongolia
Selenge *see* Ih-Uul, Hövsgöl, Mongolia
Selenge Mörön *see* Selenga
123 N14 **Selenginsk** Respublika Buryatiya, S Russian Federation 52°00´N 106°40´E
Selenica *see* Selenicë
113 K22 **Selenicë** *var.* Selenica. Vlorë, SW Albania 40°32´N 19°38´E
123 Q8 **Selennyakh** ≈ NE Russian Federation
100 J8 **Selenter See** ◎ N Germany
Sele Sound *see* Soela Väin
103 U6 **Sélestat** *Ger.* Schlettstadt. Bas-Rhin, NE France 48°16´N 07°28´E
Selety *see* Sileti
Seleucia *see* Silifke
92 I4 **Selfoss** Sudhurland, SW Iceland 63°56´N 20°59´W
28 M7 **Selfridge** North Dakota, N USA 46°01´N 100°52´W
76 I15 **Seli** ≈ N Sierra Leone
76 I11 **Sélibabi** *var.* Sélibaby. Guidimaka, S Mauritania 15°14´N 12°11´W
Sélibaby *see* Sélibabi
Selidovka/Selidovo *see* Selydove
124 I15 **Seliger, Ozero** ◎ W Russian Federation
36 J11 **Seligman** Arizona, SW USA 35°20´N 112°56´W
27 S8 **Seligman** Missouri, C USA 36°31´N 93°56´W
80 E6 **Selima Oasis** *oasis* N Sudan
76 L13 **Sélingué, Lac de** ▣ S Mali
Selinoús *see* Kréstena
18 G14 **Selinsgrove** Pennsylvania, NE USA 40°47´N 76°51´W
Selishche *see* Syelishcha
124 I16 **Selizharovo** Tverskaya Oblast', W Russian Federation 56°50´N 33°24´E
94 C10 **Selje** Sogn Og Fjordane, S Norway 62°02´N 05°22´E
11 X16 **Selkirk** Manitoba, S Canada 50°10´N 96°52´W
96 K13 **Selkirk** SE Scotland, United Kingdom 55°36´N 02°48´W
96 K13 **Selkirk** *cultural region* SE Scotland, United Kingdom
11 O16 **Selkirk Mountains** ▲▲ British Columbia, SW Canada
193 T11 **Selkirk Rise** *undersea feature* SE Pacific Ocean
115 F21 **Sellasía** Pelopónnisos, S Greece 37°14´N 22°24´E
44 M9 **Selle, Pic de la** *var.* La Selle. ▲ SE Haiti 18°18´N 71°55´W
102 M8 **Selles-sur-Cher** Loir-et-Cher, C France 47°16´N 01°31´E
36 K16 **Sells** Arizona, SW USA 31°54´N 111°52´W
Sellye *see* Sal'a
23 P5 **Selma** Alabama, S USA 32°24´N 87°01´W
35 Q11 **Selma** California, W USA 36°33´N 119°37´W
20 G10 **Selmer** Tennessee, S USA 35°10´N 88°34´W
173 N17 **Sel, Pointe au** *headland* W Réunion
Selselehye Kuhe Vākhān *see* Nicholas Range
127 S2 **Selty** Udmurtskaya Respublika, NW Russian Federation 57°19´N 52°09´E
Selukwe *see* Shurugwi
62 L9 **Selva** Santiago del Estero, N Argentina 29°46´S 62°02´W
11 T9 **Selwyn Lake** ◎ Northwest Territories/Saskatchewan, C Canada
10 K6 **Selwyn Mountains** ▲▲ Yukon Territory, NW Canada
181 T6 **Selwyn Range** ▲▲ Queensland, C Australia
117 W8 **Selydove** *var.* Selidovka, *Rus.* Selidovo. Donets'ka Oblast', SE Ukraine 48°06´N 37°16´E
Selzaete *see* Zelzate
Seman *see* Semanit, Lumi i
168 M15 **Semangka, Teluk** *bay* Sumatera, SW Indonesia
113 D22 **Semanit, Lumi i** *var.* Seman. ≈ W Albania
169 Q16 **Semarang** *var.* Samarang. Jawa, C Indonesia 06°58´S 110°29´E
169 Q10 **Sematan** Sarawak, East Malaysia 01°50´N 109°44´E
171 P17 **Semau, Pulau** *island* S Indonesia
169 V8 **Sembakung, Sungai** ≈ Borneo, N Indonesia
79 G17 **Sembé** Sangha, NW Congo 01°38´N 14°35´E
169 S13 **Sembulu, Danau** ◎ Borneo, N Indonesia
Semendria *see* Smederevo
117 R1 **Semenivka** Chernihivs'ka Oblast', N Ukraine 52°10´N 32°37´E
117 S6 **Semenivka** *Rus.* Semenovka. Poltavs'ka Oblast', NE Ukraine 49°36´N 33°10´E
127 O3 **Semenov** Nizhegorodskaya Oblast', W Russian Federation 56°47´N 44°27´E
Semenovka *see* Semenivka
169 S17 **Semeru, Gunung** *var.* Mahameru. ▲ Jawa, S Indonesia 08°01´S 112°53´E
Semey *see* Semipalatinsk
Semezhevo *see* Syemyezhava
126 L7 **Semiluki** Voronezhskaya Oblast', W Russian Federation 51°46´N 39°00´E
33 W16 **Seminoe Reservoir** ▣ Wyoming, C USA
27 O11 **Seminole** Oklahoma, C USA 35°13´N 96°40´W
24 M6 **Seminole** Texas, SW USA 32°43´N 102°39´W
23 S8 **Seminole, Lake** ▣ Florida/ Georgia, SE USA
Semiozernoye *see* Auliyekol'
145 V9 **Semipalatinsk** *Kaz.* Semey. Vostochnyy Kazakhstan, E Kazakhstan 50°26´N 80°16´E
143 O9 **Semīrom** *var.* Samirum. Eşfahān, C Iran 31°20´N 51°50´E
38 F17 **Semisopochnoi Island** *island* Aleutian Islands, Alaska, USA
169 R11 **Semitau** Borneo, C Indonesia 0°30´N 111°59´E
81 E18 **Semliki** ≈ Uganda/Dem. Rep. Congo
143 P5 **Semnān** *var.* Samnān. Semnān, N Iran 35°37´N 53°21´E
143 Q5 **Semnān** *off.* Ostān-e Semnān. ◐ *province* N Iran
Semnān, Ostān-e *see* Semnān
99 K24 **Semois** ≈ SE Belgium
108 E8 **Sempacher See** ◎ C Switzerland
Sena *see* Vila de Sena
30 L12 **Senachwine Lake** ◎ Illinois, N USA
59 O14 **Senador Pompeu** Ceará, E Brazil 05°30´S 39°25´W
Sena Gallica *see* Senigallia
59 C15 **Sena Madureira** Acre, W Brazil 09°05´S 68°41´W
155 L25 **Senanayake Samudra** ◎ E Sri Lanka
83 G15 **Senanga** Western, SW Zambia 16°09´S 23°16´E
27 Y9 **Senath** Missouri, C USA 36°07´N 90°09´W
22 L2 **Senatobia** Mississippi, S USA 34°37´N 89°58´W
164 C16 **Sendai** *var.* Satsuma-Sendai. Kagoshima, Kyūshū, SW Japan 31°49´N 130°17´E
165 Q10 **Sendai** Miyagi, Honshū, C Japan 38°16´N 140°52´E
165 Q11 **Sendai-wan** *bay* E Japan
101 J23 **Senden** Bayern, S Germany 48°18´N 10°04´E
154 F11 **Sendhwa** Madhya Pradesh, C India 21°38´N 75°04´E
111 H21 **Senec** *Ger.* Wartberg, *Hung.* Szenc; *prev.* Szempcz. Bratislavský Kraj, W Slovakia 48°14´N 17°24´E
27 P3 **Seneca** Kansas, C USA 39°50´N 96°04´W
27 R8 **Seneca** Missouri, C USA 36°50´N 94°36´W
32 K13 **Seneca** Oregon, NW USA 44°06´N 118°57´W
21 O11 **Seneca** South Carolina, SE USA 34°41´N 82°57´W
18 G11 **Seneca Lake** ◎ New York, NE USA
31 U13 **Senecaville Lake** ▣ Ohio, N USA
76 G11 **Senegal** *off.* Republic of Senegal, *Fr.* Sénégal. ◆ *republic* W Africa
76 H9 **Senegal** *Fr.* Sénégal. ≈ W Africa
Senegal, Republic of *see* Senegal
31 O4 **Seney Marsh** *wetland* Michigan, N USA
101 P14 **Senftenberg** Brandenburg, E Germany 51°31´N 14°01´E
82 L11 **Senga Hill** Northern, NE Zambia 09°26´S 31°12´E
158 G13 **Sênggê Zangbo** ≈ W China
171 Z13 **Senggi** Papua, E Indonesia 03°26´S 140°46´E
127 R5 **Sengiley** Ul'yanovskaya Oblast', W Russian Federation 53°54´N 48°51´E
63 I19 **Senguerr, Río** ≈ S Argentina
83 J16 **Sengwa** ≈ C Zimbabwe
Senia *see* Senj
111 H19 **Senica** *Ger.* Senitz, *Hung.* Szenice. Trnavský Kraj, W Slovakia 48°40´N 17°22´E
Seniça *see* Sjenica
106 J11 **Senigallia** *anc.* Sena Gallica. Marche, C Italy 43°43´N 13°13´E
136 F15 **Senirkent** Isparta, SW Turkey 38°07´N 30°34´E
Senitz *see* Senica
112 C10 **Senj** *Ger.* Zengg, *It.* Segna; *anc.* Senia. Lika-Senj, NW Croatia 44°58´N 14°55´E
Senj *see* Örgön
92 H9 **Senja** *prev.* Senjen. *island* N Norway
Senjen *see* Senja
161 U12 **Senkaku-shotō** *island group* SW Japan
137 R12 **Şenkaya** Erzurum, NE Turkey 40°33´N 42°17´E
83 I16 **Senkobo** Southern, S Zambia 17°38´S 25°58´E
103 O4 **Senlis** Oise, N France 49°13´N 02°33´E
167 T12 **Senmonorom** Môndól Kiri, E Cambodia 12°27´N 107°12´E
80 G10 **Sennar** *var.* Sannār. Sinnar, C Sudan 13°31´N 33°38´E
Senno *see* Syanno
Senones *see* Sens
109 W11 **Senovo** E Slovenia 46°01´N 15°24´E
103 P6 **Sens** *anc.* Agendicum, Senones. Yonne, C France 48°12´N 03°17´E
Sensburg *see* Mrągowo
167 S11 **Sên, Stœng** ≈ C Cambodia
42 F7 **Sensuntepeque** Cabañas, NE El Salvador 13°52´N 88°38´W
112 L8 **Senta** *Hung.* Zenta. Vojvodina, N Serbia 45°57´N 20°04´E
Šent Andraž *see* Sankt Andrä
171 Y13 **Sentani, Danau** ◎ Papua, E Indonesia
28 J5 **Sentinel Butte** ▲ North Dakota, N USA 46°52´N 103°50´W
10 M13 **Sentinel Peak** ▲ British Columbia, W Canada 54°51´N 122°02´W
59 N16 **Sento Sé** Bahia, E Brazil 09°51´S 41°56´W
Šent Peter *see* Pivka
Št. Vid *see* Sankt Veit an der Glan
Seo de Urgel *see* La See d'Urgel
154 I7 **Seondha** Madhya Pradesh, C India 26°09´N 78°47´E
154 J11 **Seoni** *prev.* Seeonee. Madhya Pradesh, C India 22°06´N 79°36´E
Seoul *see* Sŏul
83 I17 **Sepako** Central, NE Botswana 19°50´S 26°29´E
184 I13 **Separation Point** *headland* South Island, New Zealand 40°46´S 172°58´E
169 V10 **Sepasu** Borneo, N Indonesia 0°44´N 117°38´E
186 B6 **Sepik** ≈ Indonesia/Papua New Guinea
Sepone *see* Muang Xépôn
110 M7 **Sępopol** *Ger.* Schippenbeil. Warmińsko-Mazurskie, N Poland 54°16´N 21°09´E
116 F10 **Şepreuş** *Hung.* Seprős. Arad, W Romania 46°34´N 21°44´E
Seprős *see* Şepreuş
Şepşi-Sângeorz/ Sepsiszentgyőrgy *see* Sfântu Gheorghe
15 W4 **Sept-Îles** Québec, SE Canada 50°11´N 66°19´W
105 N6 **Sepúlveda** Castilla-León, N Spain 41°18´N 03°45´W
104 K8 **Sequeros** Castilla-León, N Spain 40°31´N 06°04´W
104 L5 **Sequillo** ≈ NW Spain
32 G7 **Sequim** Washington, NW USA 48°04´N 123°06´W
35 S11 **Sequoia National Park** *national park* California, W USA
137 Q14 **Şerafettin Dağları** ▲▲ E Turkey
127 N10 **Serafimovich** Volgogradskaya Oblast', SW Russian Federation 49°34´N 42°43´E
127 U5 **Serafimovskiy** Respublika Bashkortostan, W Russian Federation 54°26´N 53°49´E
171 Q10 **Serai** Sulawesi, N Indonesia 01°45´N 124°58´E
99 K19 **Seraing** Liège, E Belgium 50°37´N 05°31´E
Sêraitang *see* Baima
Serakhs *see* Sarahs
171 W13 **Serami** Papua, E Indonesia 02°11´S 136°46´E
Seram, Laut *see* Ceram Sea
Serampore/Serampur *see* Shrīrāmpur
171 S13 **Seram, Pulau** *var.* Serang, *Eng.* Ceram. *island* Maluku, E Indonesia
169 N15 **Serang** Jawa, C Indonesia 06°07´S 106°09´E
Serang *see* Seram, Pulau
169 P9 **Serasan, Pulau** *island* Kepulauan Natuna, W Indonesia
169 P9 **Serasan, Selat** *strait* Indonesia/Malaysia
112 M13 **Serbia** *off.* Federal Republic of Serbia; *prev.* Yugoslavia, *SCr.* Jugoslavija. ◆ *federal republic* SE Europe
112 M12 **Serbia** *Ger.* Serbien, *Serb.* Srbija. ◐ *republic* Serbia
Serbia, Federal Republic of *see* Serbia
Serbien *see* Serbia
Sercq *see* Sark
146 D12 **Serdar** *prev. Rus.* Gyzyrlabat, Kizyl-Arvat. Balkan Welaýaty, W Turkmenistan 39°02´N 56°15´E
Serdica *see* Sofiya
Serdobol' *see* Sortavala
127 O7 **Serdobsk** Penzenskaya Oblast', W Russian Federation 52°30´N 44°16´E
145 X9 **Serebryansk** Vostochnyy Kazakhstan, E Kazakhstan 49°44´N 83°16´E
123 Q12 **Serebryanyy Bor** Respublika Sakha (Yakutiya), NE Russian Federation 56°40´N 124°46´E
111 H20 **Sered'** *Hung.* Szered. Trnavský Kraj, W Slovakia 48°19´N 17°45´E
117 S1 **Seredyna-Buda** Sums'ka Oblast', NE Ukraine 52°09´N 34°00´E
118 E13 **Seredžius** Tauragė, C Lithuania 55°04´N 23°24´E
136 I14 **Şereflikoçhisar** Ankara, C Turkey 38°56´N 33°31´E
106 D7 **Seregno** Lombardia, N Italy 45°39´N 09°12´E
103 P7 **Serein** ≈ C France
168 K9 **Seremban** Negeri Sembilan, Peninsular Malaysia 02°42´N 101°54´E
81 H20 **Serengeti Plain** *plain* N Tanzania
82 K13 **Serenje** Central, E Zambia 13°12´S 30°15´E
Seres *see* Sérres
116 J5 **Seret** ≈ W Ukraine
Seret/Sereth *see* Siret
115 I21 **Serfopoúla** *island* Kykládes, Greece, Aegean Sea
127 P4 **Sergach** Nizhegorodskaya Oblast', W Russian Federation 55°31´N 45°29´E
29 S13 **Sergeant Bluff** Iowa, C USA 42°24´N 96°19´W
163 P7 **Sergelen** Dornod, NE Mongolia 48°31´N 114°01´E
Sergelen *see* Tuvshinshiree
168 H8 **Sergeulangit, Pegunungan** ▲▲ Sumatera, NW Indonesia
122 L5 **Sergeya Kirova, Ostrova** *island* N Russian Federation
Sergeyevichi *see* Syarhyeyevichy
145 O7 **Sergeyevka** Severnyy Kazakhstan, N Kazakhstan 53°53´N 67°25´E
Sergiopol *see* Ayagoz
59 P16 **Sergipe** *off.* Estado de Sergipe. ◐ *state* E Brazil
Sergipe, Estado de *see* Sergipe
126 L3 **Sergiyev Posad** Moskovskaya Oblast', W Russian Federation 56°21´N 38°10´E
124 K5 **Sergozero, Ozero** ◎ NW Russian Federation
146 J17 **Serhetabat** *prev. Rus.* Gushgy, Kushka. Mary Welaýaty, S Turkmenistan 35°19´N 62°17´E
169 Q10 **Serian** Sarawak, East Malaysia 01°10´N 110°35´E
115 I21 **Sérifos** *anc.* Seriphos. *island* Kykládes, Greece, Aegean Sea
115 I21 **Sérifou, Stenó** *strait* SE Greece
136 F16 **Serik** Antalya, SW Turkey 36°55´N 31°06´E
106 E7 **Serio** ≈ N Italy
Seriphos *see* Sérifos
Serir Tibesti *see* Sarīr Tībistī
Sêrkog *see* Sêrtar
127 S5 **Sernovodsk** Samarskaya Oblast', W Russian Federation 53°56´N 51°16´E
127 R2 **Sernur** Respublika Mariy El, W Russian Federation 56°55´N 49°09´E
110 M11 **Serock** Mazowieckie, C Poland 52°30´N 21°03´E
61 B18 **Serodino** Santa Fe, C Argentina 32°33´S 60°52´W
Seroei *see* Serui
105 P14 **Serón** Andalucía, S Spain 37°20´N 02°28´W
99 E14 **Serooskerke** Zeeland, SW Netherlands 51°42´N 03°52´E
105 T6 **Seròs** Cataluña, NE Spain 41°27´N 00°24´E
122 G10 **Serov** Sverdlovskaya Oblast', C Russian Federation 59°42´N 60°32´E
83 I19 **Serowe** Central, SE Botswana 22°26´S 26°44´E
104 H13 **Serpa** Beja, S Portugal 37°56´N 07°36´W
Serpa Pinto *see* Menongue
182 A4 **Serpentine Lakes** *salt lake* South Australia
45 T15 **Serpent's Mouth, The** *Sp.* Boca de la Serpiente. *strait* Trinidad and Tobago/ Venezuela
Serpiente, Boca de la *see* Serpent's Mouth, The
126 K4 **Serpukhov** Moskovskaya Oblast', W Russian Federation 54°54´N 37°26´E
104 I10 **Serra de São Mamede** ▲ C Portugal 39°18´N 07°19´W
60 K13 **Serra do Mar** ▲▲
Sérrai *see* Sérres
107 N22 **Serra San Bruno** Calabria, SW Italy 38°32´N 16°18´E
103 S14 **Serres** Hautes-Alpes, SE France 44°26´N 05°42´E
114 H13 **Sérres** *var.* Seres; *prev.* Sérrai. Kentrikí Makedonía, NE Greece 41°03´N 23°33´E
62 J9 **Serrezuela** Córdoba, C Argentina 30°38´S 65°26´W
59 O16 **Serrinha** Bahia, E Brazil 11°38´S 38°56´W
59 M19 **Serro** *var.* Sêrro. Minas Gerais, NE Brazil 18°38´S 43°22´W
Sêrro *see* Serro
Sert *see* Siirt
104 H9 **Sertã** *var.* Sertá. Castelo Branco, C Portugal 39°48´N 08°05´W
Sertá *see* Sertã
60 L8 **Sertãozinho** São Paulo, S Brazil 21°04´S 47°55´W
160 F7 **Sêrtar** *var.* Sêrkog. Sichuan, C China 32°18´N 100°18´E
124 G12 **Sertolovo** Leningradskaya Oblast', NW Russian Federation 60°08´N 30°06´E
171 W13 **Serui** *prev.* Seroei. Papua, E Indonesia 01°53´S 136°15´E
83 J19 **Serule** Central, E Botswana 21°58´S 27°20´E
169 S12 **Seruyan, Sungai** *var.* Sungai Pembuang. ≈ Borneo, N Indonesia
115 E14 **Sérvia** Dytikí Makedonía, N Greece 40°12´N 22°01´E
160 E7 **Sêrxü** *var.* Jugar. Sichuan, C China 32°54´N 98°06´E
123 R13 **Seryshevo** Amurskaya Oblast', SE Russian Federation 51°03´N 128°16´E
Sesana *see* Sežana
169 V8 **Sesayap, Sungai** ≈ Borneo, N Indonesia
Sesdlets *see* Siedlce
79 N17 **Sese** Orientale, N Dem. Rep. Congo 02°13´N 25°52´E
81 F18 **Sese Islands** *island group* S Uganda
83 H16 **Sesheke** *var.* Sesheko. Western, SE Zambia 17°28´S 24°20´E
Sesheko *see* Sesheke
106 C8 **Sesia** *anc.* Sessites. ≈ NW Italy
104 F11 **Sesimbra** Setúbal, S Portugal 38°26´N 09°06´W
115 N22 **Seskliό** *island* Dodekánisa, Greece, Aegean Sea
30 L16 **Sesser** Illinois, N USA 38°05´N 89°03´W
Sessites *see* Sesia
106 G11 **Sesto Fiorentino** Toscana, C Italy 43°50´N 11°12´E
106 E7 **Sesto San Giovanni** Lombardia, N Italy 45°32´N 09°14´E
106 A8 **Sestriere** Piemonte, NE Italy 45°00´N 06°54´E
106 D10 **Sestri Levante** Liguria, NW Italy 44°16´N 09°22´E
124 G12 **Sestroretsk** Leningradskaya Oblast', NW Russian Federation 60°05´N 29°57´E
107 C20 **Sestu** Sardegna, Italy, C Mediterranean Sea 39°15´N 09°06´E
112 E8 **Sesvete** Zagreb, N Croatia 45°50´N 16°03´E
118 G12 **Šeta** Kaunas, C Lithuania 55°17´N 24°16´E
Setabis *see* Xàtiva
165 Q4 **Setana** Hokkaidō, NE Japan 42°27´N 139°52´E
103 Q16 **Sète** *prev.* Cette. Hérault, S France 43°24´N 03°42´E
58 J11 **Sete Ilhas** Amapá, NE Brazil 01°06´N 52°06´W
59 L20 **Sete Lagoas** Minas Gerais, NE Brazil 19°29´S 44°15´W
60 G10 **Sete Quedas, Ilha das** *island* S Brazil
92 I10 **Setermoen** Troms, N Norway 68°51´N 18°20´E
95 E17 **Setesdal** *valley* S Norway
43 W16 **Setetule, Cerro** ▲ SE Panama 07°51´N 77°37´W
21 Q5 **Seth** West Virginia, NE USA 38°06´N 81°40´W
Setia *see* Sezze
74 K5 **Sétif** *var.* Stif. N Algeria 36°11´N 05°24´E
164 L5 **Seto** Aichi, Honshū, SW Japan 35°14´N 137°06´E
164 G13 **Seto-naikai** *Eng.* Inland Sea. *sea* S Japan
165 V16 **Setouchi** *var.* Setoushi. Kagoshima, Amami-Ō-shima, SW Japan 44°19´N 142°58´E
Setoushi *see* Setouchi
74 F6 **Settat** W Morocco 33°03´N 07°37´W
79 D20 **Setté Cama** Ogooué-Maritime, SW Gabon 02°32´S 09°46´E
11 W13 **Setting Lake** ◎ Manitoba, C Canada
97 L16 **Settle** N England, United Kingdom 54°04´N 02°17´W
189 Y12 **Settlement** E Wake Island 19°17´N 166°38´E
104 F11 **Setúbal** *Eng.* Saint Ubes, Saint Yves. Setúbal, W Portugal 38°31´N 08°54´W
104 F11 **Setúbal** ◐ *district* S Portugal
104 F12 **Setúbal, Baía de** *bay* W Portugal
Setul *see* Satun
12 B10 **Seul, Lac** ◎ Ontario, S Canada
103 R8 **Seurre** Côte d'Or, C France 47°00´N 05°09´E
137 U11 **Sevan** C Armenia 40°32´N 44°56´E
137 V12 **Sevana Lich** *Eng.* Lake Sevan, *Rus.* Ozero Sevan. ◎ E Armenia
Sevan, Lake/Sevan, Ozero *see* Sevana Lich
77 N11 **Sévaré** Mopti, C Mali 14°32´N 04°06´W
117 S14 **Sevastopol'** *Eng.* Sebastopol. Respublika Krym, S Ukraine 44°36´N 33°33´E
25 R14 **Seven Sisters** Texas, SW USA 27°57´N 98°34´W
10 K13 **Seven Sisters Peaks** ▲ British Columbia, SW Canada 54°57´N 128°10´W
99 M15 **Sevenum** Limburg, SE Netherlands 51°25´N 06°01´E
103 P14 **Séverac-le-Château** Aveyron, S France 44°18´N 03°03´E
14 H13 **Severn** ≈ Ontario, S Canada
97 L21 **Severn** *Wel.* Hafren. ≈ England/Wales, United Kingdom
125 O11 **Severnaya Dvina** *var.* Northern Dvina. ≈ NW Russian Federation
127 N16 **Severnaya Osetiya-Alaniya, Respublika** *Eng.* North Ossetia; *prev.* Respublika Severnaya Osetiya, Severo-Osetinskaya SSR. ◐ *autonomous republic* SW Russian Federation
Severnaya Osetiya, Respublika *see* Severnaya Osetiya-Alaniya, Respublika
122 M5 **Severnaya Zemlya** *var.* Nicholas II Land. *island group* N Russian Federation
127 T5 **Severnoye** Orenburgskaya Oblast', W Russian Federation 54°03´N 52°31´E
35 S3 **Severn Troughs Range** ▲▲ Nevada, W USA
125 W3 **Severnyy** Respublika Komi, NW Russian Federation 67°38´N 64°13´E
144 I13 **Severnyy Chink Ustyurta** ▲▲ W Kazakhstan
125 Q13 **Severnyye Uvaly** *var.* Northern Ural Hills. *hill range* NW Russian Federation
145 O6 **Severnyy Kazakhstan** *off.* Severo-Kazakhstanskaya Oblast', *var.* North Kazakhstan, *Kaz.* Soltüstik Qazaqstan Oblysy. ◐ *province* N Kazakhstan
125 V9 **Severnyy Ural** ▲▲ NW Russian Federation
Severo-Alichurskiy Khrebet *see* Alichuri Shimolí, Qatorkŭhi
123 N12 **Severobaykal'sk** Respublika Buryatiya, S Russian Federation 55°39´N 109°17´E
Severodonetsk *see* Syeverodonets'k
124 M8 **Severodvinsk** *prev.* Molotov, Sudostroy. Arkhangel'skaya Oblast', NW Russian Federation 64°32´N 39°50´E
Severo-Kazakhstanskaya Oblast' *see* Severnyy Kazakhstan
123 U11 **Severo-Kuril'sk** Sakhalinskaya Oblast', SE Russian Federation 50°38´N 155°57´E
124 J3 **Severomorsk** Murmanskaya Oblast', NW Russian Federation 69°00´N 33°16´E
Severo-Osetinskaya SSR *see* Severnaya Osetiya-Alaniya, Respublika
122 M7 **Severo-Sibirskaya Nizmennost'** *var.* North Siberian Plain, *Eng.* North Siberian Lowland. *lowlands* N Russian Federation
122 G10 **Severoural'sk** Sverdlovskaya Oblast', C Russian Federation 60°09´N 59°58´E
122 L11 **Severo-Yeniseyskiy** Krasnoyarskiy Kray, C Russian Federation 60°29´N 93°13´E
122 J12 **Seversk** Tomskaya Oblast', C Russian Federation 53°37´N 84°47´E
126 M11 **Severskiy Donets** *Ukr.* Sivers'kyy Donets'. ≈ Russian Federation/ Ukraine *see also* Sivers'kyy Donets'
Severskiy Donets *see* Sivers'kyy Donets'
92 M9 **Sevettijärvi** Lappi, N Finland 69°31´N 28°40´E
36 M5 **Sevier Bridge Reservoir** ▣ Utah, W USA
36 J4 **Sevier Desert** *plain* Utah, W USA
36 J5 **Sevier Lake** ◎ Utah, W USA
21 N9 **Sevierville** Tennessee, S USA 35°53´N 83°34´W
104 J14 **Sevilla** *Eng.* Seville; *anc.* Hispalis. Andalucía, SW Spain 37°24´N 05°59´W
104 J13 **Sevilla** ◐ *province* Andalucía, SW Spain
Sevilla de Niefang *see* Niefang
43 O16 **Sevilla, Isla** *island* SW Panama
Seville *see* Sevilla
114 J9 **Sevlievo** Gabrovo, N Bulgaria 43°01´N 25°06´E
Sevluš/Sevlyush *see* Vynohradiv
109 V11 **Sevnica** *Ger.* Lichtenwald. E Slovenia 46°00´N 15°20´E
162 J11 **Sevrey** *var.* Saynshand. Ömnögovĭ, S Mongolia 43°30´N 102°08´E
126 I7 **Sevsk** Bryanskaya Oblast', W Russian Federation 52°03´N 34°31´E
76 J15 **Sewa** ≈ E Sierra Leone
39 R12 **Seward** Alaska, USA 60°06´N 149°26´W
29 R15 **Seward** Nebraska, C USA 40°52´N 97°06´W
10 G8 **Seward Glacier** *glacier* Yukon Territory, W Canada
197 Q3 **Seward Peninsula** *peninsula* Alaska, USA
Seward's Folly *see* Alaska
62 H12 **Sewell** Libertador, C Chile 34°05´S 70°25´W
98 K5 **Sexbierum** *Fris.* Seisbierrum. Friesland, N Netherlands 53°13´N 05°28´E
11 O13 **Sexsmith** Alberta, W Canada 55°18´N 118°45´W
41 W13 **Seybaplaya** Campeche, SE Mexico 19°39´N 90°36´W
173 N6 **Seychelles** *off.* Republic of Seychelles. ◆ *republic* W Indian Ocean
67 Z9 **Seychelles** *island group* NE Seychelles
173 N6 **Seychelles Bank** *var.* Le Banc des Seychelles. *undersea feature* W Indian Ocean 04°45´S 55°30´E
Seychelles, Le Banc des *see* Seychelles Bank
Seychelles, Republic of *see* Seychelles
172 H17 **Seychellois, Morne** ▲ Mahé, NE Seychelles
92 L2 **Seydhisfjördhur** Austurland, E Iceland 65°15´N 14°00´W
146 J12 **Seýdi** *Rus.* Seydi; *prev.* Neftezavodsk. Lebap Welaýaty, E Turkmenistan 39°31´N 62°53´E
136 G16 **Seydişehir** Konya, SW Turkey 37°25´N 31°51´E
136 J13 **Seyfe Gölü** ◎ C Turkey
Seyhan *see* Adana
136 K16 **Seyhan Barajı** ▣ S Turkey
136 K17 **Seyhan Nehri** ≈ S Turkey
136 F13 **Seyitgazi** Eskişehir, W Turkey 39°27´N 30°42´E
126 J7 **Seym** ≈ W Russian Federation
117 S3 **Seym** ≈ N Ukraine
123 T9 **Seymchan** Magadanskaya Oblast', E Russian Federation 62°54´N 152°27´E
114 N12 **Seymen** Tekirdağ, NW Turkey 41°06´N 27°56´E
183 O11 **Seymour** Victoria, SE Australia 37°01´S 145°10´E
83 I25 **Seymour** Eastern Cape, S South Africa 32°33´S 26°46´E
29 W16 **Seymour** Iowa, C USA 40°40´N 93°07´W
27 U7 **Seymour** Missouri, C USA 37°09´N 92°46´W
25 Q5 **Seymour** Texas, SW USA 33°36´N 99°16´W
114 M12 **Şeytan Deresi** ≈ NW Turkey
109 S12 **Sežana** *It.* Sesana. SW Slovenia 45°42´N 13°52´E
103 P5 **Sézanne** Marne, N France 48°43´N 03°41´E
107 I16 **Sezze** *anc.* Setia. Lazio, C Italy 41°29´N 13°04´E
Sfákia *see* Chóra Sfakíon
115 D21 **Sfaktiría** *island* S Greece
116 J11 **Sfântu Gheorghe** *Ger.* Sankt-Georgen, *Hung.* Sepsiszentgyőrgy; *prev.* Şepşi-Sângeorz, Sfîntu Gheorghe. Covasna, C Romania 45°52´N 25°49´E
117 N13 **Sfântu Gheorghe, Braţul** *var.* Gheorghe Braţul. ≈ E Romania
75 N6 **Sfax** *Ar.* Şafāqis. E Tunisia 34°45´N 10°45´E
75 N6 **Sfax** ✈ E Tunisia 34°43´N 10°37´E
Sfîntu Gheorghe *see* Sfântu Gheorghe
98 H13 **'s-Gravendeel** Zuid-Holland, SW Netherlands 51°48´N 04°36´E
98 F11 **'s-Gravenhage** *var.* Den Haag, *Eng.* The Hague, *Fr.* La Haye. ● (Netherlands-seat of government) Zuid-Holland, W Netherlands 52°07´N 04°17´E
98 G12 **'s-Gravenzande** Zuid-Holland, W Netherlands 52°00´N 04°10´E
Shaan/Shaanxi Sheng *see* Shaanxi
159 X11 **Shaanxi** *var.* Shaan, Shaanxi Sheng, Shan-hsi, Shenshi, Shensi. ◐ *province* C China
Shaartuz *see* Shahrtuz
Shaba *see* Katanga
Shabani *see* Zvishavane
81 N17 **Shabeellaha Dhexe** *off.* Gobolka Shabeellaha Dhexe. ◐ *region* E Somalia
Shabeellaha Dhexe, Gobolka *see* Shabeellaha Dhexe
81 L17 **Shabeellaha Hoose** *off.* Gobolka Shabeellaha Hoose. ◐ *region* S Somalia
Shabeellaha Hoose, Gobolka *see* Shabeellaha Hoose
Shabeelle, Webi *see* Shebeli
114 O7 **Shabla** Dobrich, NE Bulgaria 43°33´N 28°31´E
114 O7 **Shabla, Nos** *headland* NE Bulgaria 43°30´N 28°36´E
13 N9 **Shabogama Lake** ◎ Newfoundland and Labrador, E Canada
79 N20 **Shabunda** Sud-Kivu, E Dem. Rep. Congo 02°42´S 27°20´E
141 Q15 **Shabwah** C Yemen 15°09´N 46°46´E
158 F8 **Shache** *var.* Yarkant. Xinjiang Uygur Zizhiqu, NW China 38°27´N 77°16´E
Shacheng *see* Huailai
195 R12 **Shackleton Coast** *physical region* Antarctica
195 Z10 **Shackleton Ice Shelf** *ice shelf* Antarctica
Shaddādī *see* Ash Shadādah
28 K7 **Shadehill Reservoir** ▣ South Dakota, N USA
122 G11 **Shadrinsk** Kurganskaya Oblast', C Russian Federation 56°08´N 63°18´E
31 O12 **Shafer, Lake** ▣ Indiana, N USA
35 R13 **Shafter** California, W USA 35°27´N 119°15´W
24 J11 **Shafter** Texas, SW USA 29°49´N 104°18´W
97 L23 **Shaftesbury** S England, United Kingdom 51°01´N 02°12´W
185 F22 **Shag** ≈ South Island, New Zealand
145 V9 **Shagan** ≈ E Kazakhstan
39 O11 **Shageluk** Alaska, USA 62°40´N 159°33´W
122 K14 **Shagonar** Respublika Tyva, S Russian Federation 51°31´N 93°06´E
185 F22 **Shag Point** *headland* South Island, New Zealand 45°28´S 170°50´E
144 J12 **Shagyray, Plato** *plain* SW Kazakhstan
Shāhābād *see* Eslāmābād
168 K9 **Shah Alam** Selangor, Peninsular Malaysia 03°02´N 101°31´E
117 O12 **Shahany, Ozero** ◎ SW Ukraine
138 H9 **Shahbā'** *anc.* Philippopolis. As Suwaydā', S Syria 32°50´N 36°38´E
Shahbān *see* Ad Dayr
149 P17 **Shāh Bandar** Sind, SE Pakistan 23°59´N 67°54´E
149 P13 **Shahdād Kot** Sind, SW Pakistan 27°49´N 67°49´E
143 T10 **Shahdād, Namakzār-e** *salt pan* E Iran
149 Q15 **Shāhdādpur** Sind, SE Pakistan 25°56´N 68°40´E
154 K10 **Shahdol** Madhya Pradesh, C India 23°19´N 81°26´E
161 N7 **Sha He** ≈ C China
Shahe *see* Linze
Shahepu *see* Linze
153 N13 **Shāhganj** Uttar Pradesh, N India 26°03´N 82°41´E
152 C11 **Shāhgarh** Rājasthān, NW India 27°08´N 69°56´E
Sha Hi *see* Orūmīyeh, Daryācheh-ye
Shāhī *see* Qā'emshahr
Shahjahanabad *see* Delhi
152 L11 **Shāhjahānpur** Uttar Pradesh, N India 27°53´N 79°55´E
149 U7 **Shāhpur** Punjab, E Pakistan 32°15´N 72°32´E
Shāhpur *see* Shāhpur Chākar
152 G13 **Shāhpura** Rājasthān, N India 25°38´N 75°01´E
149 Q15 **Shāhpur Chākar** *var.* Shāhpur. Sind, SE Pakistan 26°11´N 68°44´E
148 M5 **Shahrak** Ghowr, C Afghanistan 34°09´N 64°16´E
143 Q11 **Shahr-e Bābak** Kermān, C Iran 30°08´N 55°04´E
143 N8 **Shahr-e Kord** *var.* Shahr Kord. Chahār MaḨall va Bakhtīārī, C Iran 32°20´N 50°52´E
143 O9 **Shahreẕā** *var.* Qomisheh, Qumisheh, Shahriza; *prev.* Qomsheh. Eşfahān, C Iran 32°01´N 51°51´E

◆ Country
● Country Capital
◇ Dependent Territory
○ Dependent Territory Capital
◐ Administrative Regions
✈ International Airport
▲ Mountain
▲▲ Mountain Range
⛰ Volcano
≈ River
◎ Lake
▣ Reservoir

147 S10 **Shahrikhon** *Rus.* Shakhrikhan. Andijon Viloyati, E Uzbekistan 40°42′N 72°03′E
147 P11 **Shahriston** *Rus.* Shakhristan. NW Tajikistan 39°45′N 68°47′E
Shahriza *see* Shahreẓā
Shahr-i-Zabul *see* Zābol
Shahr Kord *see* Shahr-e Kord
147 P14 **Shahrtuz** *Rus.* Shaartuz. SW Tajikistan 37°13′N 68°05′E
143 Q4 **Shāhrūd** *prev.* Emāmrūd, Emāmshahr. Semnān, N Iran 36°30′N 55°E
Shahsavār/Shahsawar *see* Tonekābon
Shaidara *see* Step' Nardara
Shaikh Ābid *see* Shaykh 'Ābid
Shaikh Fāris *see* Shaykh Fāris
Shaikh Najm *see* Shaykh Najm
138 K5 **Shā'īr, Jabal** ▲ C Syria 34°51′N 37°49′E
154 G10 **Shājāpur** Madhya Pradesh, C India 23°27′N 76°21′E
80 J8 **Shakal, Ras** *headland* NE Sudan 18°04′N 38°34′E
83 G17 **Shakawe** North West, NW Botswana 18°25′S 21°53′E
Shakhdarinskiy Khrebet *see* Shokhdara, Qatorkŭhi
Shakhrikhan *see* Shahrikhon
Shakhrisabz *see* Sharixon
Shakhristan *see* Shahriston
Shakhtërsk *see* Shakhtars'k
145 R10 **Shakhtinsk** Karaganda, C Kazakhstan 49°40′N 72°37′E
126 L11 **Shakhty** Rostovskaya Oblast', SW Russian Federation 47°45′N 40°14′E
127 P2 **Shakhun'ya** Nizhegorodskaya Oblast', W Russian Federation 57°42′N 46°36′E
77 S15 **Shaki** Oyo, W Nigeria 08°37′N 03°25′E
81 J15 **Shakīso** Oromīya, C Ethiopia 05°33′N 38°48′E
117 X8 **Shakhtars'k** *Rus.* Shakhtërsk. Donets'ka Oblast', SE Ukraine 48°02′N 38°18′E
29 V9 **Shakopee** Minnesota, N USA 44°48′N 93°31′W
165 R3 **Shakotan-misaki** *headland* Hokkaidō, NE Japan 43°22′N 140°28′E
39 N9 **Shaktoolik** Alaska, USA 64°19′N 161°05′W
81 J14 **Shala Hāyk'** ◎ C Ethiopia
124 M10 **Shalakusha** Arkhangel'skaya Oblast', NW Russian Federation 62°16′N 40°16′E
145 U8 **Shalday** Pavlodar, NE Kazakhstan 51°57′N 78°51′E
127 P16 **Shali** Chechenskaya Respublika, SW Russian Federation 43°03′N 45°55′E
141 W12 **Shalim** *var.* Shelim. S Oman 18°07′N 55°39′E
Shaliuhe *see* Gangca
144 K12 **Shalkar** *var.* Chelkar. Aktyubinsk, W Kazakhstan 47°50′N 59°29′E
144 F9 **Shalkar, Ozero** *prev.* Chelkar Ozero. ◎ W Kazakhstan
21 V12 **Shallotte** North Carolina, SE USA 33°58′N 78°21′W
25 N5 **Shallowater** Texas, SW USA 33°41′N 102°00′W
124 K11 **Shal'skiy** Respublika Kareliya, NW Russian Federation 61°45′N 36°02′E
160 F9 **Shaluli Shan** ▲▲ C China
81 F22 **Shama** ≈ C Tanzania
11 Z11 **Shamattawa** Manitoba, C Canada 55°52′N 92°05′W
12 F8 **Shamattawa** ≈ Ontario, C Canada
Shām, Bādiyat ash *see* Syrian Desert
Shamiya *see* Ash Shāmīyah
141 X8 **Shām, Jabal ash** *var.* Jebel Sham. ▲ NW Oman 23°21′N 57°08′E
Sham, Jebel *see* Shām, Jabal ash
Shamkhor *see* Şämkir
18 G14 **Shamokin** Pennsylvania, NE USA 40°47′N 76°33′W
25 P2 **Shamrock** Texas, SW USA 35°12′N 100°15′W
Shana *see* Kuril'sk
Sha'nabī, Jabal ash *see* Chambi, Jebel
139 Y12 **Shanāwah** Al Başrah, E Iraq 30°57′N 47°25′E
Shancheng *see* Taining
159 T8 **Shandan** *var.* Qingyuan. Gansu, N China 38°50′N 101°08′E
Shandī *see* Shendi
161 Q5 **Shandong** *var.* Lu, Shandong Sheng, Shantung. ◈ *province* E China
161 R4 **Shandong Bandao** *var.* Shantung Peninsula. *peninsula* E China
Shandong Sheng *see* Shandong
139 U8 **Shandrūkh** Diyālá, E Iraq 33°20′N 45°19′E
83 J17 **Shangani** ≈ W Zimbabwe
161 O15 **Shangchuan Dao** *island* S China
Shangchuankou *see* Minhe
163 P12 **Shangdu** Nei Mongol Zizhiqu, N China 41°32′N 113°33′E
161 O11 **Shanggao** *var.* Aoyang. Jiangxi, S China 28°16′N 114°55′E
Shangguan *see* Daixian
161 S8 **Shanghai** *var.* Shang-hai. Shanghai Shi, E China 31°14′N 121°28′E
161 S8 **Shanghai Shi** *var.* Hu, Shanghai. ◈ *municipality* E China
161 P13 **Shanghang** *var.* Linjiang. Fujian, SE China 25°03′N 116°25′E
160 K14 **Shanglin** *var.* Dafeng. Guangxi Zhuangzu Zizhiqu, S China 23°26′N 108°32′E
160 L7 **Shangluo** *prev.* Shangxian, Shangzhou. Shaanxi, C China 33°51′N 109°55′E
83 G15 **Shangombo** Western, W Zambia 16°28′S 22°10′E
Shangpai/Shangpaihe *see* Feixi
161 O6 **Shangqiu** *var.* Zhuji. Henan, C China 34°24′N 115°37′E
161 Q10 **Shangrao** Jiangxi, S China 28°27′N 117°57′E
Shangxian *see* Shangluo
161 S9 **Shangyu** *var.* Baiguan. Zhejiang, SE China 30°03′N 120°52′E
163 X9 **Shangzhi** Heilongjiang, NE China 45°13′N 127°59′E
Shangzhou *see* Shangluo
Shanhe *see* Zhengning
163 W9 **Shanhetun** Heilongjiang, NE China 44°42′N 127°12′E
Shan-hsi *see* Shaanxi, China
Shan-hsi *see* Shanxi, China
159 O6 **Shankou** Xinjiang Uygur Zizhiqu, W China 42°02′N 94°08′E
184 M13 **Shannon** Manawatu-Wanganui, North Island, New Zealand 40°32′S 175°24′E
97 C17 **Shannon** *Ir.* An tSionainn. ≈ W Ireland
97 B19 **Shannon** ✈ W Ireland 52°42′N 08°57′W
167 N6 **Shan Plateau** *plateau* E Burma (Myanmar)
158 M6 **Shanshan** *var.* Piqan. Xinjiang Uygur Zizhiqu, NW China 42°53′N 90°18′E
Shansi *see* Shanxi
167 N5 **Shan State** ◈ *state* E Burma (Myanmar)
Shantar Islands *see* Shantarskiye Ostrova
123 S12 **Shantarskiye Ostrova** *Eng.* Shantar Islands. *island group* E Russian Federation
161 Q14 **Shantou** *var.* Shan-t'ou, Swatow. Guangdong, S China 23°23′N 116°39′E
Shan-t'ou *see* Shantou
Shantung *see* Shandong
Shantung Peninsula *see* Shandong Bandao
161 O15 **Shanwei** Guangdong, China 22°48′N 115°13′E
163 O14 **Shanxi** *var.* Jin, Shan-hsi, Shansi, Shanxi Sheng. ◈ *province* C China
161 P6 **Shanxian** *var.* Shan Xian. Shandong, E China 34°51′N 116°09′E
Shan Xian *see* Sanmenxia
Shan Xian *see* Shanxian
Shanxi Sheng *see* Shanxi
160 L7 **Shanyang** Shaanxi, C China 33°35′N 109°48′E
161 N13 **Shanyin** *var.* Daiyue. Shanxi, C China E Asia 39°30′N 112°56′E
161 O13 **Shaoguan** *var.* Shao-kuan, *Cant.* Kukong; *prev.* Ch'u-chiang. Guangdong, S China 24°57′N 113°38′E
Shao-kuan *see* Shaoguan
161 Q11 **Shaowu** Fujian, SE China 27°24′N 117°26′E
161 S9 **Shaoxing** Zhejiang, SE China 30°02′N 120°35′E
160 M11 **Shaoyang** *var.* Baoqing, Shao-yang; *prev.* Pao-king. Hunan, S China 27°13′N 111°31′E
160 M12 **Shaoyang** *var.* Tangdukou. Hunan, S China 26°54′N 111°14′E
Shao-yang *see* Shaoyang
96 K5 **Shapinsay** *island* NE Scotland, United Kingdom
125 S4 **Shapkina** ≈ NW Russian Federation
Shāpūr *see* Salmās
158 M4 **Shaqiuhe** Xinjiang Uygur Zizhiqu, W China 45°00′N 88°52′E
139 T2 **Shaqlāwa** *var.* Shaqlāwah. Arbīl, E Iraq 36°24′N 44°21′E
Shaqlāwah *see* Shaqlāwa
138 I8 **Shaqqā** As Suwaydā', S Syria 32°53′N 36°42′E
141 P7 **Shaqrā'** Ar Riyāḍ, C Saudi Arabia 25°11′N 45°08′E
Shaqrā *see* Shuqrah
145 W10 **Shar** *var.* Charsk. Vostochnyy Kazakhstan, E Kazakhstan 49°33′N 81°03′E
149 O6 **Sharan** Dāykondī, SE Afghanistan 33°28′N 66°19′E
149 Q7 **Sharan** *var.* Zareh Sharan. Paktīkā, E Afghanistan 33°08′N 68°47′E
Sharaqpur *see* Sharqpur
Sharbaqty *see* Shcherbakty
141 X12 **Sharbatāt** S Oman 17°57′N 56°14′E
Sharbatāt, Ra's *see* Sharbithāt, Ras
141 X12 **Sharbithāt, Ras** *var.* Ra's Sharbatāt. *headland* S Oman 17°55′N 56°30′E
14 K14 **Sharbot Lake** Ontario, SE Canada 44°45′N 76°46′W
145 P17 **Shardara** *var.* Chardara. Yuzhnyy Kazakhstan, S Kazakhstan 41°15′N 68°01′E
Shardara Dalasy *see* Step' Nardara
162 F8 **Sharga** Govĭ-Altay, W Mongolia 46°16′N 95°32′E
Sharga *see* Tsagaan-Uul
116 M7 **Sharhorod** Vinnyts'ka Oblast', C Ukraine 48°46′N 28°05′E
Sharhulsan *see* Mandal-Ovoo
165 V3 **Shari** Hokkaidō, NE Japan 43°54′N 144°42′E
Shari *see* Chari
139 T6 **Shārī, Buḥayrat** ◎ C Iraq
147 N12 **Sharixon** *Rus.* Shakhrisabz. Qashqadaryo Viloyati, S Uzbekistan 39°01′N 66°45′E
Sharjah *see* Ash Shāriqah
118 K12 **Sharkawshchyna** *var.* Sharkowshchyna, *Pol.* Szarkowszczyzna, *Rus.* Sharkovshchina. Vitsyebskaya Voblasts', NW Belarus 55°27′N 27°28′E
180 G9 **Shark Bay** *bay* Western Australia
141 Y9 **Sharkh** E Oman 21°20′N 59°04′E
Sharkovshchina/Sharkowshchyna *see* Sharkawshchyna
127 U6 **Sharlyk** Orenburgskaya Oblast', W Russian Federation 52°52′N 54°45′E
75 Y9 **Sharm ash Shaykh** *var.* Ofiral, Sharm el Sheikh. E Egypt 27°51′N 34°16′E
Sharm el Sheikh *see* Sharm ash Shaykh
18 B13 **Sharon** Pennsylvania, NE USA 41°12′N 80°28′W
26 H4 **Sharon Springs** Kansas, C USA 38°54′N 101°46′W
31 Q14 **Sharonville** Ohio, N USA 39°16′N 84°24′W
Sharourah *see* Sharūrah
29 O10 **Sharpe, Lake** ⊠ South Dakota, N USA
Sharqī, Al Jabal ash/Sharqi, Jebel esh *see* Anti-Lebanon
Sharqīyah, Al Minṭaqah ash *see* Ash Sharqīyah
138 I6 **Sharqīyat an Nabk, Jabal** ▲▲ W Syria
149 W8 **Sharqpur** *var.* Sharaqpur. Punjab, E Pakistan 31°29′N 74°08′E
141 Q13 **Sharūrah** *var.* Sharourah. Najrān, S Saudi Arabia 17°29′N 47°05′E
125 O14 **Shar'ya** Kostromskaya Oblast', NW Russian Federation 58°22′N 45°30′E
145 V15 **Sharyn** *var.* Charyn. ≈ SE Kazakhstan
Sharyn *see* Charyn
122 K13 **Sharypovo** Krasnoyarskiy Kray, C Russian Federation 55°33′N 89°12′E
83 J18 **Shashe** Central, NE Botswana 21°25′S 27°28′E
83 J18 **Shashe** *var.* Shashi. ≈ Botswana/Zimbabwe
81 J14 **Shashemenē** *var.* Shashemene, Shashhamana, *It.* Sciasciamana. Oromīya, C Ethiopia 07°16′N 38°38′E
Shashemenne/Shashhamana *see* Shashemenē
Shashi *see* Shashe
Shashi/Sha-shih/Shasi *see* Jingzhou, Hubei
35 N3 **Shasta Lake** ⊠ California, W USA
35 N2 **Shasta, Mount** ▲ California, W USA 41°24′N 122°11′W
127 O4 **Shatki** Nizhegorodskaya Oblast', W Russian Federation 55°09′N 44°04′E
Shatlyk *see* Şatlyk
Shatra *see* Ash Shaṭrah
119 K17 **Shatsk** Minskaya Voblasts', C Belarus 53°25′N 27°41′E
127 N5 **Shatsk** Ryazanskaya Oblast', W Russian Federation 54°02′N 41°38′E
26 J9 **Shattuck** Oklahoma, C USA 36°16′N 99°52′W
145 P16 **Shaul'der** Yuzhnyy Kazakhstan, S Kazakhstan 42°45′N 68°21′E
11 S17 **Shaunavon** Saskatchewan, S Canada 49°49′N 108°25′W
Shavat *see* Shovot
Shaviyani Atoll *see* North Miladhunmadulu Atoll
158 K4 **Shawan** *var.* Sandaohezi. Xinjiang Uygur Zizhiqu, NW China 44°21′N 85°37′E
14 G12 **Shawanaga** Ontario, S Canada 45°29′N 80°16′W
30 M6 **Shawano** Wisconsin, N USA 44°46′N 88°38′W
30 M6 **Shawano Lake** ◎ Wisconsin, N USA
15 P10 **Shawinigan** *prev.* Shawinigan Falls. Québec, SE Canada 46°33′N 72°45′W
Shawinigan Falls *see* Shawinigan
15 P10 **Shawinigan-Sud** Québec, SE Canada 46°30′N 72°43′W
138 J5 **Shawmarīyah, Jabal ash** ▲ C Syria
27 O11 **Shawnee** Oklahoma, C USA 35°20′N 96°55′W
14 K12 **Shawville** Québec, SE Canada 45°37′N 76°31′W
145 Q16 **Shayan** *var.* Chayan. Yuzhnyy Kazakhstan, S Kazakhstan 42°59′N 69°22′E
Shaykh *see* Ash Shakk
139 W9 **Shaykh 'Ābid** *var.* Shaikh Ābid. Wāsiţ, E Iraq 32°40′N 46°09′E
139 Y10 **Shaykh Fāris** *var.* Shaikh Fāris. Maysān, E Iraq 32°06′N 47°39′E
139 T7 **Shaykh Ḥātim** Baghdād, E Iraq 33°29′N 44°15′E
Shaykh, Jabal ash *see* Hermon, Mount
139 X10 **Shaykh Najm** *var.* Shaikh Najm. Maysān, E Iraq 32°04′N 46°54′E
139 W9 **Shaykh Sa'd** Maysān, E Iraq 32°35′N 46°16′E
147 T14 **Shazud** SE Tajikistan 37°45′N 72°22′E
119 N18 **Shchadryn** *Rus.* Shchedrin. Homyel'skaya Voblasts', SE Belarus 52°53′N 29°33′E
119 H18 **Shchara** ≈ SW Belarus
Shchedrin *see* Shchadryn
Shcheglovsk *see* Kemerovo
126 K5 **Shchëkino** Tul'skaya Oblast', W Russian Federation 53°57′N 37°33′E
125 S7 **Shchel'yayur** Respublika Komi, NW Russian Federation 65°19′N 53°27′E
145 U8 **Shcherbakty** *Kaz.* Sharbaqty. Pavlodar, E Kazakhstan 52°28′N 78°00′E
126 K7 **Shchigry** Kurskaya Oblast', W Russian Federation 51°53′N 36°49′E
Shchitkovichi *see* Shchytkavichy
117 Q2 **Shchors** Chernihivs'ka Oblast', N Ukraine 51°49′N 31°58′E
117 T8 **Shchors'k** Dnipropetrovs'ka Oblast', E Ukraine 48°20′N 34°07′E
Shchuchin *see* Shchuchyn
145 Q7 **Shchuchinsk** *prev.* Shchuchye. Akmola, N Kazakhstan 52°57′N 70°10′E
Shchuchye *see* Shchuchinsk
119 G16 **Shchuchyn** *Pol.* Szczuczyn Nowogródzki, *Rus.* Shchuchin. Hrodzyenskaya Voblasts', W Belarus 53°36′N 24°45′E
119 K17 **Shchytkavichy** *Rus.* Shchitkovichi. Minskaya Voblasts', C Belarus 53°13′N 27°59′E
122 J13 **Shebalino** Respublika Altay, S Russian Federation 51°16′N 85°41′E
126 J9 **Shebekino** Belgorodskaya Oblast', W Russian Federation 50°25′N 36°55′E
Shebelē Wenz, Wabē *see* Shebeli
81 L14 **Shebeli** *Amh.* Wabē Shebelē Wenz, *It.* Scebeli, *Som.* Webi Shabeelle. ≈ Ethiopia/Somalia
113 M20 **Shebenikut, Maja e** ▲ E Albania 41°13′N 20°27′E
149 N2 **Sheberghān** *var.* Shibarghān, Shiberghan, Shiberghān. Jowzjān, N Afghanistan 36°41′N 65°45′E
144 F14 **Shebir** Mangistau, SW Kazakhstan 44°52′N 52°01′E
31 N8 **Sheboygan** Wisconsin, N USA 43°46′N 87°44′W
77 X15 **Shebshi Mountains** *var.* Schebschi Mountains. ▲▲ E Nigeria
Shechem *see* Nablus
Shedadi *see* Ash Shadādah
13 P14 **Shediac** New Brunswick, SE Canada 46°13′N 64°35′W
126 L15 **Shedok** Krasnodarskiy Kray, SW Russian Federation 44°12′N 40°49′E
80 N12 **Sheekh** Togdheer, N Somalia 10°01′N 45°21′E
38 M11 **Sheenjek River** ≈ Alaska, USA
96 D13 **Sheep Haven** *Ir.* Cuan na gCaorach. *inlet* N Ireland
35 X10 **Sheep Range** ▲▲ Nevada, W USA
98 M13 **'s-Heerenberg** Gelderland, E Netherlands 51°52′N 06°15′E
97 P22 **Sheerness** SE England, United Kingdom 51°27′N 00°45′E
13 Q15 **Sheet Harbour** Nova Scotia, SE Canada 44°56′N 62°31′W
185 H18 **Sheffield** Canterbury, South Island, New Zealand 43°22′S 172°01′E
97 M18 **Sheffield** N England, United Kingdom 53°23′N 01°30′W
23 O2 **Sheffield** Alabama, S USA 34°46′N 87°42′W
29 V12 **Sheffield** Iowa, C USA 42°53′N 93°13′W
25 N10 **Sheffield** Texas, SW USA 30°42′N 101°49′W
63 H22 **Shehuen, Río** ≈ S Argentina
Shekhem *see* Nablus
149 V8 **Shekhūpura** Punjab, NE Pakistan 31°42′N 74°08′E
Sheki *see* Şäki
124 L14 **Sheksna** Vologodskaya Oblast', NW Russian Federation 59°11′N 38°32′E
123 T5 **Shelagskiy, Mys** *headland* NE Russian Federation 70°04′N 170°39′E
27 V3 **Shelbina** Missouri, C USA 39°41′N 92°02′W
13 P16 **Shelburne** Nova Scotia, SE Canada 43°47′N 65°20′W
14 G14 **Shelburne** Ontario, S Canada 44°04′N 80°12′W
33 R7 **Shelby** Montana, NW USA 48°30′N 111°52′W
21 Q10 **Shelby** North Carolina, SE USA 35°15′N 81°34′W
31 S12 **Shelby** Ohio, N USA 40°52′N 82°39′W
30 L14 **Shelbyville** Illinois, N USA 39°24′N 88°47′W
31 P14 **Shelbyville** Indiana, N USA 39°31′N 85°46′W
20 L5 **Shelbyville** Kentucky, S USA 38°13′N 85°12′W
27 V2 **Shelbyville** Missouri, C USA 39°48′N 92°01′W
20 J10 **Shelbyville** Tennessee, S USA 35°29′N 86°30′W
25 X8 **Shelbyville** Texas, SW USA 31°42′N 94°03′W
30 L14 **Shelbyville, Lake** ⊠ Illinois, N USA
29 S12 **Sheldon** Iowa, C USA 43°10′N 95°51′W
38 M11 **Sheldons Point** Alaska, USA 62°31′N 165°03′W
Shelek *see* Chilik
Shelekhov Gulf *see* Shelikhova, Zaliv
123 U9 **Shelikhova, Zaliv** *Eng.* Shelekhov Gulf. *gulf* E Russian Federation
39 P14 **Shelikof Strait** *strait* Alaska, USA
Shelim *see* Shalim
11 T14 **Shellbrook** Saskatchewan, S Canada 53°14′N 106°24′W
28 L3 **Shell Creek** ≈ North Dakota, N USA
Shellif *see* Chelif, Oued
22 I10 **Shell Keys** *island group* Louisiana, S USA
30 I4 **Shell Lake** Wisconsin, N USA 45°44′N 91°56′W
29 W12 **Shell Rock** Iowa, C USA 42°42′N 92°34′W
185 C26 **Shelter Point** *headland* Stewart Island, New Zealand 47°04′S 168°13′E
18 L13 **Shelton** Connecticut, NE USA 41°19′N 73°06′W
32 G8 **Shelton** Washington, NW USA 47°13′N 123°06′W
Shemakha *see* Şamaxı
145 W9 **Shemonaikha** Vostochnyy Kazakhstan, E Kazakhstan 50°38′N 81°55′E
127 Q4 **Shemursha** Chuvashskaya Respublika, W Russian Federation 54°57′N 47°27′E
38 D16 **Shemya Island** *island* Aleutian Islands, Alaska, USA
29 T16 **Shenandoah** Iowa, C USA 40°46′N 95°23′W
21 U4 **Shenandoah** Virginia, NE USA 38°26′N 78°34′W
21 U4 **Shenandoah Mountains** *ridge* West Virginia, NE USA
21 V3 **Shenandoah River** ≈ West Virginia, NE USA
77 W15 **Shendam** Plateau, C Nigeria 08°52′N 09°30′E
80 G8 **Shendi** *var.* Shandī. River Nile, NE Sudan 16°41′N 33°22′E
76 I15 **Shenge** SW Sierra Leone 07°54′N 12°54′W
146 L10 **Shengeldi** *Rus.* Chingildi. Navoiy Viloyati, N Uzbekistan 40°59′N 64°13′E
145 U15 **Shengel'dy** Almaty, SE Kazakhstan 44°04′N 77°31′E
113 K18 **Shëngjin** *var.* Shëngjini. Lezhë, NW Albania 41°49′N 19°34′E
Shëngjini *see* Shëngjin
Shengking *see* Liaoning
Sheng Xian/Shengxian *see* Shengzhou
161 S9 **Shengzhou** *var.* Shengxian, Sheng Xian. Zhejiang, SE China 29°36′N 120°42′E
Shenking *see* Liaoning
125 N11 **Shenkursk** Arkhangel'skaya Oblast', NW Russian Federation 62°10′N 42°58′E
160 L3 **Shenmu** Shaanxi, C China 38°49′N 110°27′E
113 L19 **Shën Noj i Madh** ▲ C Albania 41°23′N 20°07′E
160 L8 **Shennong Ding** ▲ C China 31°24′N 110°16′E
Shenshi/Shensi *see* Shaanxi
163 V12 **Shenyang** *Chin.* Shen-yang, *Eng.* Moukden, Mukden; *prev.* Fengtien. *province capital* Liaoning, NE China 41°50′N 123°26′E
Shen-yang *see* Shenyang
161 O15 **Shenzhen** Guangdong, S China 22°39′N 114°02′E
154 G8 **Sheopur** Madhya Pradesh, C India 25°41′N 76°42′E
116 L5 **Shepetivka** *Rus.* Shepetovka. Khmel'nyts'ka Oblast', NW Ukraine 50°12′N 27°01′E
Shepetovka *see* Shepetivka
25 W10 **Shepherd** Texas, SW USA 30°30′N 95°00′W
187 R14 **Shepherd Islands** *island group* C Vanuatu
20 K5 **Shepherdsville** Kentucky, S USA 38°00′N 85°42′W
183 O11 **Shepparton** Victoria, SE Australia 36°25′S 145°26′E
97 P22 **Sheppey, Isle of** *island* SE England, United Kingdom
Sherabad *see* Sherobod
9 O4 **Sherard, Cape** *headland* Nunavut, N Canada 74°36′N 80°10′W
97 L23 **Sherborne** S England, United Kingdom 50°58′N 02°30′W
76 H16 **Sherbro Island** *island* SW Sierra Leone
15 Q12 **Sherbrooke** Québec, SE Canada 45°23′N 71°55′W
29 T11 **Sherburn** Minnesota, N USA 43°39′N 94°43′W
78 H6 **Sherda** Borkou-Ennedi-Tibesti, N Chad 20°04′N 16°48′E
80 G7 **Shereik** River Nile, N Sudan 18°44′N 33°37′E
126 K3 **Sheremet'yevo** ✈ (Moskva) Moskovskaya Oblast', W Russian Federation 56°05′N 37°10′E
153 P14 **Sherghāti** Bihār, N India 24°35′N 84°51′E
27 U12 **Sheridan** Arkansas, C USA 34°18′N 92°22′W
33 W12 **Sheridan** Wyoming, C USA 44°47′N 106°59′W
182 G8 **Sheringa** South Australia 33°51′S 135°13′E
25 U5 **Sherman** Texas, SW USA 33°39′N 96°35′W
194 J10 **Sherman Island** *island* Antarctica
19 S4 **Sherman Mills** Maine, NE USA 45°51′N 68°23′W
29 O15 **Sherman Reservoir** ⊠ Nebraska, C USA
147 N14 **Sherobod** *Rus.* Sherabad. Surkhondaryo Viloyati, S Uzbekistan 37°43′N 66°59′E
147 O13 **Sherobod** *Rus.* Sherabad. ≈ S Uzbekistan
153 T14 **Sherpur** Dhaka, N Bangladesh 25°00′N 90°01′E
37 T4 **Sherrelwood** Colorado, C USA 39°49′N 105°00′W
99 J14 **'s-Hertogenbosch** *Fr.* Bois-le-Duc, *Ger.* Herzogenbusch. Noord-Brabant, S Netherlands 51°41′N 05°19′E
28 M2 **Sherwood** North Dakota, N USA 48°55′N 101°36′W
11 Q14 **Sherwood Park** Alberta, SW Canada 53°34′N 113°04′W
56 F13 **Sheshea, Río** ≈ E Peru
143 T5 **Sheshtamad** Khorāsān-Razavī, NE Iran 36°03′N 57°45′E
29 S10 **Shetek, Lake** ◎ Minnesota, N USA
96 M2 **Shetland Islands** *island group* NE Scotland, United Kingdom
144 F14 **Shetpe** Mangistau, SW Kazakhstan 44°06′N 52°03′E
154 C11 **Shetrunji** ≈ W India
Shevchenko *see* Aktau
117 W5 **Shevchenkove** Kharkivs'ka Oblast', E Ukraine 49°40′N 37°13′E
81 H14 **Shewa Gīmīra** Southern Nationalities, S Ethiopia 07°12′N 35°49′E
161 Q9 **Shexian** *var.* Huicheng, She Xian. Anhui, E China 29°53′N 118°27′E
She Xian *see* Shexian
161 R6 **Sheyang** *prev.* Hede. Jiangsu, E China 33°49′N 120°13′E
29 O4 **Sheyenne** North Dakota, N USA 47°49′N 99°08′W
29 P4 **Sheyenne River** ≈ North Dakota, N USA
96 G7 **Shiant Islands** *island group* NW Scotland, United Kingdom
123 U12 **Shiashkotan, Ostrov** *island* Kuril'skiye Ostrova, SE Russian Federation
31 R9 **Shiawassee River** ≈ Michigan, N USA
141 R14 **Shibām** C Yemen 15°49′N 48°24′E
Shibarghān *see* Sheberghān
165 O10 **Shibata** *var.* Sibata. Niigata, Honshū, C Japan 37°57′N 139°20′E
Shiberghan/Shiberghān *see* Sheberghān
Shibh Jazīrat Sīnā' *see* Sinai
75 W8 **Shibīn al Kawm** *var.* Shibīn el Kôm. N Egypt 30°33′N 31°00′E
Shibīn el Kôm *see* Shibīn al Kawm
143 O13 **Shīb, Kūh-e** ▲ S Iran
12 D8 **Shibogama Lake** ◎ Ontario, C Canada
Shibotsu-jima *see* Zelënyy, Ostrov
164 B16 **Shibushi** Kagoshima, Kyūshū, SW Japan 31°27′N 131°05′E
189 U13 **Shichiyo Islands** *island group* Chuuk, C Micronesia
Shickshock Mountains *see* Chic-Chocs, Monts
145 S8 **Shiderti** *var.* Shiderty. Pavlodar, NE Kazakhstan 51°40′N 74°50′E
145 S9 **Shiderti** ≈ N Kazakhstan
Shiderty *see* Shiderti
96 G10 **Shiel, Loch** ◎ N Scotland, United Kingdom
164 J13 **Shiga** *off.* Shiga-ken, *var.* Siga. ◈ *prefecture* Honshū, SW Japan
Shiga-ken *see* Shiga
Shigatse *see* Xigazê
141 U13 **Shiḥan** *oasis* NE Yemen
Shih-chia-chuang/Shihmen *see* Shijiazhuang
158 K4 **Shihezi** Xinjiang Uygur Zizhiqu, NW China 44°21′N 85°59′E
Shiichi *see* Shyichy
113 K19 **Shijak** *var.* Shijaku. Durrës, W Albania 41°21′N 19°34′E
Shijaku *see* Shijak
161 O4 **Shijiazhuang** *var.* Shih-chia-chuang; *prev.* Shihmen. *province capital* Hebei, E China 38°04′N 114°28′E
165 R5 **Shikabe** Hokkaidō, NE Japan 42°03′N 140°45′E
149 Q13 **Shikārpur** Sind, S Pakistan 27°59′N 68°39′E
127 Q7 **Shikhany** Saratovskaya Oblast', W Russian Federation 52°07′N 47°13′E
189 V12 **Shiki Islands** *island group* Chuuk, C Micronesia
164 G14 **Shikoku** *var.* Sikoku. *island* SW Japan
192 H5 **Shikoku Basin** *var.* Sikoku Basin. *undersea feature* N Philippine Sea 28°00′N 137°00′E
164 G14 **Shikoku-sanchi** ▲▲ Shikoku, SW Japan
165 X4 **Shikotan, Ostrov** *Jap.* Shikotan-tō. *island* NE Russian Federation
Shikotan-tō *see* Shikotan, Ostrov
165 R4 **Shikotsu-ko** *var.* Sikotu Ko. ◎ Hokkaidō, NE Japan
81 N15 **Shilabo** Sumalē, E Ethiopia 06°05′N 44°48′E
127 X7 **Shil'da** Orenburgskaya Oblast', W Russian Federation 51°46′N 59°48′E
139 V3 **Shilēr, Āw-e** ≈ E Iraq
153 S12 **Shiliguri** *prev.* Siliguri. West Bengal, NE India 26°46′N 88°24′E
Shiliu *see* Changjiang
129 V7 **Shilka** ≈ S Russian Federation
18 H15 **Shillington** Pennsylvania, NE USA 40°18′N 75°57′W
153 V13 **Shillong** *state capital* Meghālaya, NE India 25°37′N 91°54′E
126 M5 **Shilovo** Ryazanskaya Oblast', W Russian Federation 54°18′N 40°53′E
164 C14 **Shimabara** *var.* Simabara. Nagasaki, Kyūshū, SW Japan 32°48′N 130°20′E
164 C14 **Shimabara-wan** *bay* SW Japan
164 F12 **Shimane** *off.* Shimane-ken, *var.* Simane. ◈ *prefecture* Honshū, SW Japan
164 G11 **Shimane-hantō** *peninsula* Honshū, SW Japan
Shimane-ken *see* Shimane
123 Q13 **Shimanovsk** Amurskaya Oblast', SE Russian Federation 52°00′N 127°36′E
Shimanto *see* Nakamura
Shimbir Berris *see* Shimbiris
80 O12 **Shimbiris** *var.* Shimbir Berris. ▲ N Somalia 10°43′N 47°10′E
165 T4 **Shimizu** Hokkaidō, NE Japan 42°58′N 142°54′E
164 M14 **Shimizu** *var.* Simizu. Shizuoka, Honshū, S Japan 35°01′N 138°29′E
152 I8 **Shimla** *prev.* Simla. *state capital* Himāchal Pradesh, N India 31°07′N 77°09′E
165 N14 **Shimoda** *var.* Simoda. Shizuoka, Honshū, S Japan 34°40′N 138°55′E
165 O13 **Shimodate** *var.* Simodate. Ibaraki, Honshū, S Japan 36°20′N 140°00′E
155 F18 **Shimoga** Karnātaka, W India 13°56′N 75°31′E
164 C15 **Shimo-jima** *island* SW Japan
164 B15 **Shimo-Koshiki-jima** *island* SW Japan
81 J21 **Shimoni** Coast, S Kenya 04°40′S 39°22′E
164 D13 **Shimonoseki** *var.* Simonoseki, *hist.* Akamagaseki, Bakan. Yamaguchi, Honshū, SW Japan 33°57′N 130°54′E
124 G14 **Shimsk** Novgorodskaya Oblast', NW Russian Federation 58°12′N 30°43′E
141 W7 **Shināş** N Oman 24°45′N 56°24′E
148 J6 **Shīndand** Herāt, W Afghanistan 33°19′N 62°09′E
Shinei *see* Hsinying
162 H10 **Shinejinst** *var.* Dzalaa. Bayanhongor, C Mongolia 44°29′N 99°19′E
25 T12 **Shiner** Texas, SW USA 29°25′N 97°10′W
167 N1 **Shingbwiyang** Kachin State, N Burma (Myanmar) 26°40′N 96°14′E
145 W11 **Shingozha** Vostochnyy Kazakhstan, E Kazakhstan 47°46′N 80°38′E
164 J15 **Shingū** *var.* Singû. Wakayama, Honshū, SW Japan 33°41′N 135°57′E
14 F8 **Shining Tree** Ontario, S Canada 47°36′N 81°12′W
165 P9 **Shinjō** *var.* Sinzyô. Yamagata, Honshū, C Japan 38°47′N 140°17′E
96 I7 **Shin, Loch** ◎ N Scotland, United Kingdom
21 S3 **Shinnston** West Virginia, NE USA 39°22′N 80°19′W
138 I6 **Shinshār** *Fr.* Chinnchâr. Ḥimş, W Syria 34°36′N 36°45′E
Shinshū *see* Chinju
165 T4 **Shintoku** Hokkaidō, NE Japan 43°03′N 142°50′E
81 G20 **Shinyanga** Shinyanga, NW Tanzania 03°40′S 33°25′E
81 G20 **Shinyanga** ◈ *region* N Tanzania
165 Q10 **Shiogama** *var.* Siogama. Miyagi, Honshū, C Japan 38°19′N 141°00′E
164 M12 **Shiojiri** *var.* Sioziri. Nagano, Honshū, S Japan 36°08′N 137°58′E
164 I15 **Shiono-misaki** *headland* Honshū, SW Japan 33°25′N 135°45′E
165 Q12 **Shioya-zaki** *headland* Honshū, C Japan 37°00′N 140°57′E
114 J9 **Shipchenski Prokhod** *pass* C Bulgaria
160 G14 **Shiping** Yunnan, SW China 23°45′N 102°23′E
13 P13 **Shippagan** *var.* Shippegan. New Brunswick, SE Canada 47°45′N 64°44′W
Shippegan *see* Shippagan
18 F15 **Shippensburg** Pennsylvania, NE USA 40°03′N 77°31′W
37 P9 **Shiprock** New Mexico, SW USA 36°47′N 108°41′W
37 O9 **Ship Rock** ▲ New Mexico, SW USA 36°41′N 108°50′W
15 R6 **Shipshaw** ≈ Québec, SE Canada
123 V10 **Shipunskiy, Mys** *headland* E Russian Federation 53°04′N 159°57′E
160 K7 **Shiquan** Shaanxi, C China 33°05′N 108°15′E
122 K13 **Shira** Respublika Khakasiya, S Russian Federation 54°35′N 89°58′E
Shirajganj Ghat *see* Sirajganj
165 P12 **Shirakawa** *var.* Sirakawa. Fukushima, Honshū, C Japan 37°07′N 140°11′E
164 M13 **Shirane-san** ▲ Honshū, S Japan 35°39′N 138°13′E
165 U14 **Shiranuka** Hokkaidō, NE Japan 42°57′N 144°01′E
195 N12 **Shirase Coast** *physical region* Antarctica
165 U3 **Shirataki** Hokkaidō, NE Japan 43°55′N 143°14′E
143 O11 **Shīrāz** *var.* Shīrāz. Fārs, S Iran 29°38′N 52°34′E
83 N15 **Shire** *var.* Chire. ≈ Malawi/Mozambique
Shiree *see* Tsagaanhayrhan
Shireet *see* Bayandelger
165 W3 **Shiretoko-hantō** *headland* Hokkaidō, NE Japan 44°06′N 145°07′E
165 W3 **Shiretoko-misaki** *headland* Hokkaidō, NE Japan 44°20′N 145°19′E
127 N5 **Shiringushi** Respublika Mordoviya, W Russian Federation 53°50′N 42°49′E
148 M3 **Shīrīn Tagāb** Fāryāb, N Afghanistan 36°49′N 65°01′E
149 N2 **Shīrīn Tagāb** ≈ N Afghanistan
165 R6 **Shiriya-zaki** *headland* Honshū, C Japan 41°24′N 141°27′E
144 I12 **Shirkala, Gryada** *plain* W Kazakhstan
165 P10 **Shiroishi** *var.* Siroisi. Miyagi, Honshū, C Japan 38°00′N 140°38′E
Shirokoye *see* Shyroke
165 O10 **Shirone** *var.* Sirone. Niigata, Honshū, C Japan 37°46′N 139°00′E
164 L12 **Shirotori** Gifu, Honshū, SW Japan 35°53′N 136°52′E
197 T1 **Shirshov Ridge** *undersea feature* W Bering Sea
Shirshütür/Shirshyutyur, Peski *see* Şirşütür Gumy
143 T3 **Shīrvān** *var.* Shirwān. Khorāsān, NE Iran 37°25′N 57°55′E
Shirwa, Lake *see* Chilwa, Lake
Shirwān *see* Shīrvān
159 N5 **Shisanjianfang** Xinjiang Uygur Zizhiqu, W China 43°10′N 91°15′E
38 M16 **Shishaldin Volcano** ▲ Unimak Island, Alaska, USA 54°45′N 163°58′W
Shishchitsy *see* Shyshchytsy
83 G16 **Shishikola** North West, N Botswana 18°09′S 23°08′E
38 M8 **Shishmaref** Alaska, USA 66°15′N 166°04′W
Shisur *see* Ash Shişar
164 L13 **Shitara** Aichi, Honshū, SW Japan 35°06′N 137°33′E
152 D12 **Shiv** Rājasthān, NW India 26°11′N 71°14′E
Shivāji Sāgar *see* Konya Reservoir
154 H8 **Shivpuri** Madhya Pradesh, C India 25°28′N 77°41′E
36 J9 **Shivwits Plateau** *plain* Arizona, SW USA
Shiwalik Range *see* Siwalik Range
160 M8 **Shiyan** Hubei, C China 32°31′N 110°45′E
Shizilu *see* Junan
160 H13 **Shizong** *var.* Danfeng. Yunnan, SW China 24°53′N 104°E
165 R10 **Shizugawa** Miyagi, Honshū, NE Japan 38°40′N 141°26′E
159 W8 **Shizuishan** *var.* Dawukou. Ningxia, N China 39°04′N 106°22′E
165 T5 **Shizunai** Hokkaidō, NE Japan 42°20′N 142°24′E
165 M14 **Shizuoka** *var.* Sizuoka. Shizuoka, Honshū, S Japan 34°59′N 138°20′E
164 M13 **Shizuoka** *off.* Shizuoka-ken, *var.* Sizuoka. ◈ *prefecture* Honshū, S Japan
Shizuoka-ken *see* Shizuoka
Shklov *see* Shklow
119 N15 **Shklow** *Rus.* Shklov. Mahilyowskaya Voblasts', E Belarus 54°13′N 30°18′E
113 K18 **Shkodër** *var.* Shkodra, *It.* Scutari, *SCr.* Skadar. Shkodër, NW Albania 42°03′N 19°31′E
113 K17 **Shkodër** ◈ *district* NW Albania
Shkodra *see* Shkodër
Shkodrës, Liqeni i *see* Scutari, Lake
113 L20 **Shkumbinit, Lumi i** *var.* Shkumbi, Shkumbin. ≈ C Albania
Shkumbî/Shkumbin *see* Shkumbinit, Lumi i
Shligigh, Cuan *see* Sligo Bay
122 L4 **Shmidta, Ostrov** *island* Severnaya Zemlya, N Russian Federation
183 S10 **Shoalhaven River** ≈ New South Wales, SE Australia
11 W16 **Shoal Lake** Manitoba, S Canada 50°28′N 100°36′W
31 O15 **Shoals** Indiana, N USA 38°40′N 86°47′W
164 I13 **Shōdo-shima** *island* SW Japan

◆ Country
● Country Capital
◇ Dependent Territory
○ Dependent Territory Capital
◈ Administrative Regions
✈ International Airport
▲ Mountain
▲▲ Mountain Range
Volcano
≈ River
◎ Lake
⊠ Reservoir

Shōka *see* Changhua
122 M5 **Shokal'skogo, Proliv** *strait* N Russian Federation
147 T14 **Shokhdara, Qatorkŭhi** *Rus.* Shakhdarinskiy Khrebet. ▲▲ SE Tajikistan
145 P15 **Sholakkorgan** *var.* Chulakkurgan. Yuzhnyy Kazakhstan, S Kazakhstan 43°45′N 69°10′E
145 N9 **Sholaksay** Kostanay, N Kazakhstan 51°45′N 64°45′E
Sholāpur *see* Solāpur
Sholdaneshty *see* Şoldăneşti
Shonzhy *see* Chundzha
Shoqpar *see* Chokpar
155 G21 **Shoranūr** Kerala, SW India 10°53′N 76°06′E
155 G16 **Shorāpur** Karnātaka, C India 16°34′N 76°48′E
147 O14 **Sho'rchi** *Rus.* Shurchi. Surkhondaryo Viloyati, S Uzbekistan 37°58′N 67°40′E
30 M11 **Shorewood** Illinois, N USA 41°31′N 88°12′W
Shorkazakhly, Solonchak *see* Kazakhlyshor, Solonchak
145 Q9 **Shortandy** Akmola, C Kazakhstan 51°45′N 71°01′E
Shortepa/Shor Tepe *see* Shūr Tappeh
186 J7 **Shortland Island** *var.* Alu. *island* Shortland Islands, NW Solomon Islands
Shosambetsu *see* Shosanbetsu
165 S2 **Shosanbetsu** *var.* Shosambetsu. Hokkaidō, NE Japan 44°31′N 141°47′E
33 O15 **Shoshone** Idaho, NW USA 42°56′N 114°24′W
35 T6 **Shoshone Mountains** ▲▲ Nevada, W USA
33 U12 **Shoshone River** ≋ Wyoming, C USA
83 I19 **Shoshong** Central, SE Botswana 23°02′S 26°31′E
33 V14 **Shoshoni** Wyoming, C USA 43°13′N 108°06′W
Shōshū *see* Sangju
117 S2 **Shostka** Sums'ka Oblast', NE Ukraine 51°52′N 33°30′E
185 C21 **Shotover** ≋ South Island, New Zealand
146 H9 **Shovot** *Rus.* Shavat. Xorazm Viloyati, W Uzbekistan 41°41′N 60°13′E
37 N12 **Show Low** Arizona, SW USA 34°15′N 110°01′W
Show Me State *see* Missouri
125 O4 **Shoyna** Nenetskiy Avtonomnyy Okrug, NW Russian Federation 67°50′N 44°09′E
124 M11 **Shozhma** Arkhangel'skaya Oblast', NW Russian Federation 61°57′N 40°10′E
117 Q7 **Shpola** Cherkas'ka Oblast', N Ukraine 49°00′N 31°27′E
Shqipëria/Shqipërisë, Republika e *see* Albania
22 G5 **Shreveport** Louisiana, S USA 32°32′N 93°45′W
97 K19 **Shrewsbury** *hist.* Scrobesbyrig'. W England, United Kingdom 52°43′N 02°45′W
152 D11 **Shri Mohangarh** *prev.* Sri Mohangorh. Rājasthān, NW India 27°17′N 71°18′E
153 S16 **Shrīrāmpur** *prev.* Serampore, Serampur. West Bengal, NE India 22°44′N 88°20′E
97 K19 **Shropshire** *cultural region* W England, United Kingdom
113 N17 **Shtime** *Serb.* Štimlje. C Kosovo 42°27′N 21°03′E
145 S16 **Shu** *Kaz.* Shū. Zhambyl, SE Kazakhstan 43°34′N 73°41′E
160 G13 **Shuangbai** *var.* Tuodian. Yunnan, SW China 24°45′N 101°38′E
163 W9 **Shuangcheng** Heilongjiang, NE China 45°20′N 126°21′E
Shuangcheng *see* Zherong
160 E14 **Shuangjiang** *var.* Weiyuan. Yunnan, SW China 23°28′N 99°43′E
Shuangjiang *see* Jiangkou
Shuangjiang *see* Tongdao
163 U10 **Shuangliao** *var.* Zhengjiatun. Jilin, NE China 43°31′N 123°32′E
Shuang-liao *see* Liaoyuan
Shuangshipu *see* Fengxian
163 Y7 **Shuangyashan** *var.* Shuang-ya-shan. Heilongjiang, NE China 46°37′N 131°10′E
Shuang-ya-shan *see* Shuangyashan
Shu'aymiah *see* Shu'aymīyah
141 W12 **Shu'aymīyah** *var.* Shu'aymiah. S Oman 17°55′N 55°39′E
144 I10 **Shubarkuduk** *Kaz.* Shubarqudyq. Aktyubinsk, W Kazakhstan 49°09′N 56°31′E
Shubarqudyq *see* Shubarkuduk
145 N12 **Shubar-Tengiz, Ozero** ⊚ C Kazakhstan
39 S5 **Shublik Mountains** ▲▲ Alaska, USA
Shubrā al Khaymah *see* Shubrâ el Kheima
121 U13 **Shubrâ el Kheima** *var.* Shubrā al Khaymah. N Egypt 30°06′N 31°15′E
158 E8 **Shufu** *var.* Tuokezhake. Xinjiang Uygur Zizhiqu, NW China 39°18′N 75°43′E
147 S14 **Shughnon, Qatorkŭhi** *Rus.* Shugnanskiy Khrebet. ▲▲ SE Tajikistan
Shugnanskiy Khrebet *see* Shughnon, Qatorkŭhi
161 Q6 **Shu He** ≋ E China
Shuicheng *see* Lupanshui
Shuiding *see* Huocheng
Shuidong *see* Dianbai
Shuiji *see* Laixi
Shū-Ile Taūlary *see* Chu-Iliyskiye Gory
Shuilocheng *see* Zhuanglang
Shuiluo *see* Zhuanglang
149 T10 **Shujāābād** Punjab, E Pakistan 29°53′N 71°23′E
Shū, Kazakhstan *see* Shu
Shū, Kazakhstan/Kyrgyzstan *see* Chu
163 W9 **Shulan** Jilin, NE China 44°28′N 126°57′E
158 E8 **Shule** Xinjiang Uygur Zizhiqu, NW China 39°19′N 76°06′E
Shuleh *see* Shule He
159 Q8 **Shule He** *var.* Shuleh, Sulo. ≋ C China
30 K9 **Shullsburg** Wisconsin, N USA 42°37′N 90°12′W
Shulu *see* Xinji
39 N16 **Shumagin Islands** *island group* Alaska, USA
146 G7 **Shumanay** Qoraqalpog'iston Respublikasi, W Uzbekistan 42°42′N 58°56′E
114 M8 **Shumen** Shumen, NE Bulgaria 43°17′N 26°57′E
114 M8 **Shumen** ◈ *province* NE Bulgaria
127 P4 **Shumerlya** Chuvashskaya Respublika, W Russian Federation 55°31′N 46°24′E
122 G11 **Shumikha** Kurganskaya Oblast', C Russian Federation 55°12′N 63°09′E
118 M12 **Shumilina** *Rus.* Shumilino. Vitsyebskaya Voblasts', NE Belarus 55°18′N 29°37′E
Shumilino *see* Shumilina
123 V11 **Shumshu, Ostrov** *island* SE Russian Federation
116 K5 **Shums'k** Ternopil's'ka Oblast', W Ukraine 50°06′N 26°04′E
Shūnan *see* Tokuyama
39 O7 **Shungnak** Alaska, USA 66°53′N 157°08′W
Shunsen *see* Ch'unch'ŏn
Shuoxian *see* Shuozhou
161 N3 **Shuozhou** *var.* Shuoxian. Shanxi, C China 39°20′N 112°25′E
141 P16 **Shuqrah** *var.* Shaqrā. SW Yemen 13°26′N 45°44′E
Shurab *see* Shŭrob
Shurchi *see* Sho'rchi
147 R11 **Shŭrob** *Rus.* Shurab. NW Tajikistan 40°02′N 70°31′E
143 T10 **Shūr, Rūd-e** ≋ E Iran
149 O2 **Shūr Tappeh** *var.* Shortepa, Shor Tepe. Balkh, N Afghanistan 37°22′N 66°49′E
83 K17 **Shurugwi** *prev.* Selukwe. Midlands, C Zimbabwe 19°40′S 30°00′E
142 L8 **Shūsh** *anc.* Susa, *Bibl.* Shushan. Khūzestān, SW Iran 32°12′N 48°20′E
Shushan *see* Shūsh
142 L9 **Shūshtar** *var.* Shustar, Shushter. Khūzestān, SW Iran 32°03′N 48°51′E
Shushter/Shustar *see* Shūshtar
141 T9 **Shuṭfah, Qalamat** *well* E Saudi Arabia
139 V9 **Shuwayjah, Hawr ash** *var.* Hawr as Suwayqiyah. ⊚ E Iraq
124 M16 **Shuya** Ivanovskaya Oblast', W Russian Federation 56°51′N 41°24′E
39 Q14 **Shuyak Island** *island* Alaska, USA
166 M4 **Shwebo** Sagaing, C Burma (Myanmar) 22°35′N 95°42′E
166 L7 **Shwedaung** Bago, W Burma (Myanmar) 18°44′N 95°12′E
166 M7 **Shwegyin** Bago, SW Burma (Myanmar) 17°56′N 96°59′E
167 N4 **Shweli** *Chin.* Longchuan Jiang. ≋ Burma (Myanmar)/China
166 M6 **Shwemyo** Mandalay, C Burma (Myanmar) 20°04′N 96°13′E
Shyghanaq *see* Chiganak
Shyghys Qazagastan Oblysy *see* Vostochnyy Kazakhstan
Shyghys Qongyrat *see* Vostochno-Kounradskiy
Shyghys Qongyrat *see* Shygys Konyrat
145 T12 **Shygys Konyrat** , *Kaz.* Shyghys Qongyrat. Karaganda, C Kazakhstan 47°01′N 75°05′E
119 M19 **Shyichy** *Rus.* Shiichi. Homyel'skaya Voblasts', SE Belarus 52°15′N 29°14′E
145 Q17 **Shymkent** *prev.* Chimkent. Yuzhnyy Kazakhstan, S Kazakhstan 42°19′N 69°36′E
Shyngghyrlaū *see* Chingirlau
152 J5 **Shyok** Jammu and Kashmir, NW India 34°13′N 78°12′E
117 S9 **Shyroke** *Rus.* Shirokoye. Dnipropetrovs'ka Oblast', E Ukraine 47°41′N 33°16′E
117 O9 **Shyryayeve** Odes'ka Oblast', SW Ukraine 47°21′N 30°11′E
117 S5 **Shyshaky** Poltavs'ka Oblast', C Ukraine 49°54′N 34°00′E
119 K17 **Shyshchytsy** *Rus.* Shishchitsy. Minskaya Voblasts', C Belarus 53°13′N 27°33′E
149 Y3 **Siachen Muztāgh** ▲▲ NE Pakistan
Siadehan *see* Tākestān
148 M13 **Siāhān Range** ▲▲ W Pakistan
142 I1 **Sīāh Chashmeh** *var.* Chālderān. Āžarbāyjān-e Gharbī, N Iran 39°02′N 44°22′E
149 W7 **Siālkot** Punjab, NE Pakistan 32°29′N 74°35′E
186 E7 **Sialum** Morobe, C Papua New Guinea 06°02′S 147°37′E
Siam *see* Thailand
Siam, Gulf of *see* Thailand, Gulf of
Sian *see* Xi'an
Siang *see* Brahmaputra
Siangtan *see* Xiangtan
169 N8 **Siantan, Pulau** *island* Kepulauan Anambas, W Indonesia
54 H11 **Siare, Río** ≋ C Colombia
171 R6 **Siargao Island** *island* S Philippines
186 F72 **Siassi** Umboi Island, C Papua New Guinea 05°34′S 147°50′E
115 D14 **Siátista** Dytikí Makedonía, N Greece 40°16′N 21°34′E
166 K4 **Siatlai** Chin State, W Burma (Myanmar) 22°05′N 93°36′E
171 P6 **Siaton** Negros, C Philippines 09°03′N 123°03′E
171 P6 **Siaton Point** *headland* Negros, C Philippines 09°03′N 123°00′E
118 F11 **Šiauliai** *Ger.* Schaulen. Šiauliai, N Lithuania 55°55′N 23°21′E
118 E11 **Šiauliai** ◈ *province* N Lithuania
171 Q10 **Siau, Pulau** *island* N Indonesia
83 J15 **Siavonga** Southern, SE Zambia 16°33′S 28°42′E
Siazan' *see* Siyäzän
Sibah *see* As Sībah
107 N20 **Sibari** Calabria, S Italy 39°45′N 16°26′E
Sibata *see* Shibata
127 X6 **Sibay** Respublika Bashkortostan, W Russian Federation 52°40′N 58°39′E
93 M19 **Sibbo** *Fin.* Sipoo. Etelä-Suomi, S Finland 60°22′N 25°20′E
112 D13 **Šibenik** *It.* Sebenico. Šibenik-Knin, S Croatia 43°43′N 15°54′E
Sibenik *see* Šibenik-Knin
112 E13 **Šibenik-Knin** *off.* Šibenska Županija, *var.* Sibenik. ◈ *province* S Croatia
Šibenik-Knin *see* Drniš
Šibenska Županija *see* Šibenik-Knin
Siberia *see* Sibir'
Siberoet *see* Siberut, Pulau
168 H12 **Siberut, Pulau** *prev.* Siberoet. *island* Kepulauan Mentawai, W Indonesia
168 I12 **Siberut, Selat** *strait* W Indonesia
149 P11 **Sibi** Baluchistān, SW Pakistan 29°31′N 67°54′E
186 B9 **Sibidiri** Western, SW Papua New Guinea 08°58′S 142°14′E
123 N10 **Sibir'** *var.* Siberia. *physical region* NE Russian Federation
79 F20 **Sibiti** Lékoumou, S Congo 03°41′S 13°20′E
81 G21 **Sibiti** ≋ C Tanzania
116 I12 **Sibiu** *Ger.* Hermannstadt, *Hung.* Nagyszeben. Sibiu, C Romania 45°48′N 24°09′E
116 I11 **Sibiu** ◈ *county* C Romania
29 S11 **Sibley** Iowa, C USA 43°24′N 95°45′W
153 X11 **Sibsāgar** Assam, NE India 26°59′N 94°38′E
169 R9 **Sibu** Sarawak, East Malaysia 02°18′N 111°49′E
42 G2 **Sibun** ≋ E Belize
79 I15 **Sibut** *prev.* Fort-Sibut. Kémo, S Central African Republic 05°44′N 19°07′E
171 P4 **Sibuyan Island** *island* C Philippines
189 U1 **Sibylla Island** *island* N Marshall Islands
11 N16 **Sicamous** British Columbia, SW Canada 50°49′N 118°52′W
Sichelburger Gerbirge *see* Gorjanci
167 N14 **Sichon** *var.* Ban Sichon, Si Chon. Nakhon Si Thammarat, SW Thailand 09°03′N 99°51′E
Si Chon *see* Sichon
160 H9 **Sichuan** *var.* Chuan, Sichuan Sheng, Ssu-ch'uan, Szechuan, Szechwan. ◈ *province* C China
160 I9 **Sichuan Pendi** *basin* C China
Sichuan Sheng *see* Sichuan
103 S16 **Sicie, Cap** *headland* SE France 43°03′N 05°50′E
107 J24 **Sicilia** *Eng.* Sicily; *anc.* Trinacria. ◈ *region* Italy, C Mediterranean Sea
107 M24 **Sicilia** *Eng.* Sicily; *anc.* Trinacria. *island* Italy, C Mediterranean Sea
Sicilian Channel *see* Sicily, Strait of
107 H24 **Sicily, Strait of** *var.* Sicilian Channel. *strait* C Mediterranean Sea
42 K5 **Sico Tinto, Río** *var.* Río Negro. ≋ NE Honduras
57 H16 **Sicuani** Cusco, S Peru 14°21′S 71°13′W
112 J10 **Šid** Vojvodina, NW Serbia 45°07′N 19°13′E
115 A15 **Sidári** Kérkyra, Iónia Nisiá, Greece, C Mediterranean Sea 39°47′N 19°43′E
169 Q11 **Sidas** Borneo, C Indonesia 0°24′N 109°46′E
98 O5 **Siddeburen** Groningen, NE Netherlands 53°15′N 06°52′E
154 D9 **Siddhapur** *prev.* Siddhpur, Sidhpur. Gujarāt, W India 23°57′N 72°28′E
Siddhpur *see* Siddhapur
155 I15 **Siddipet** Andhra Pradesh, C India 18°10′N 78°54′E
77 N14 **Sidéradougou** SW Burkina 10°39′N 04°16′W
107 N23 **Siderno** Calabria, SW Italy 38°18′N 16°19′E
Siders *see* Sierre
154 L9 **Sidhi** Madhya Pradesh, C India 24°24′N 81°54′E
Sidhirókastron *see* Sidirókastro
Sidhpur *see* Siddhapur
75 U7 **Sīdī Barrānī** NW Egypt 31°38′N 25°58′E
74 I6 **Sidi Bel Abbès** *var.* Sidi bel Abbès, Sidi-Bel-Abbès. NW Algeria 35°12′N 00°43′W
74 E7 **Sidi-Bennour** W Morocco 32°39′N 08°28′W
74 M6 **Sidi Bouzid** *var.* Gammouda, Sīdī Bu Zayd. C Tunisia 35°05′N 09°20′E
Sīdī Bu Zayd *see* Sidi Bouzid
74 D8 **Sidi-Ifni** SW Morocco 29°33′N 10°04′W
74 G6 **Sidi-Kacem** *prev.* Petitjean. N Morocco 34°21′N 05°46′W
114 G12 **Sidirókastro** *prev.* Sidhirókastron. Kentrikí Makedonía, NE Greece 41°14′N 23°23′E
194 L12 **Sidley, Mount** ▲ Antarctica 76°39′S 124°48′W
29 S16 **Sidney** Iowa, C USA 40°45′N 95°39′W
33 Y7 **Sidney** Montana, NW USA 47°42′N 104°10′W
28 J15 **Sidney** Nebraska, C USA 41°09′N 102°57′W
18 I11 **Sidney** New York, NE USA 42°18′N 75°21′W
31 R13 **Sidney** Ohio, N USA 40°16′N 84°09′W
23 T2 **Sidney Lanier, Lake** ⊠ Georgia, SE USA
Sidon *see* Saïda
122 J9 **Sidorovsk** Yamalo-Nenetskiy Avtonomnyy Okrug, N Russian Federation 66°34′N 82°12′E
Sidra *see* Surt
Sidra/Sidra, Gulf of *see* Surt, Khalīj, N Libya
Siebenbürgen *see* Transylvania
Sieben Dörfer *see* Săcele
110 O12 **Siedlce** *Ger.* Sedlez, *Rus.* Sesdlets. Mazowieckie, C Poland 52°10′N 22°18′E
101 E16 **Sieg** ≋ W Germany
101 F16 **Siegen** Nordrhein-Westfalen, W Germany 50°53′N 08°02′E
109 X4 **Sieghartskirchen** Niederösterreich, E Austria 48°13′N 16°01′E
110 O11 **Siemiatycze** Podlaskie, NE Poland 52°27′N 22°52′E
167 T11 **Siĕmpang** Stœ̆ng Trêng, NE Cambodia 14°07′N 106°24′E
167 R11 **Siĕmréab** *prev.* Siemreap. Siĕmréab, NW Cambodia 13°21′N 103°50′E
Siemreap *see* Siĕmréab
106 G12 **Siena** *Fr.* Sienne; *anc.* Saena Julia. Toscana, C Italy 43°20′N 11°20′E
Sienne *see* Siena
92 K12 **Sieppijärvi** Lappi, NW Finland 67°09′N 23°58′E
110 J13 **Sieradz** Sieradz, C Poland 51°36′N 18°42′E
110 K10 **Sierpc** Mazowieckie, C Poland 52°51′N 19°44′E
24 I9 **Sierra Blanca** Texas, SW USA 31°10′N 105°22′W
37 S14 **Sierra Blanca Peak** ▲ New Mexico, SW USA 33°22′N 105°48′W
35 P5 **Sierra City** California, W USA 39°34′N 120°35′W
63 I16 **Sierra Colorada** Río Negro, S Argentina 40°37′S 67°48′W
63 J16 **Sierra Grande** Río Negro, E Argentina 41°34′S 65°21′W
76 G15 **Sierra Leone** *off.* Republic of Sierra Leone. ◆ *republic* W Africa
64 M13 **Sierra Leone Basin** *undersea feature* E Atlantic Ocean 05°00′N 17°00′W
66 K8 **Sierra Leone Fracture Zone** *tectonic feature* E Atlantic Ocean
Sierra Leone, Republic of *see* Sierra Leone
Sierra Leone Ridge *see* Sierra Leone Rise
64 L13 **Sierra Leone Rise** *var.* Sierra Leone Ridge, Sierra Leone Schwelle. *undersea feature* E Atlantic Ocean 05°30′N 21°00′W
Sierra Leone Schwelle *see* Sierra Leone Rise
40 L7 **Sierra Mojada** Coahuila, NE Mexico 27°13′N 103°42′W
37 N16 **Sierra Vista** Arizona, SW USA 31°33′N 110°18′W
108 D10 **Sierre** *Ger.* Siders. Valais, SW Switzerland 46°18′N 07°33′E
36 L16 **Sierrita Mountains** ▲▲ Arizona, SW USA
Siete Moai *see* Ahu Akivi
76 M15 **Sifié** W Ivory Coast 07°59′N 06°55′W
115 I21 **Sífnos** *anc.* Siphnos. *island* Kykládes, Greece, Aegean Sea
115 I21 **Sífnou, Stenó** *strait* SE Greece
Siga *see* Shiga
103 P16 **Sigean** Aude, S France 43°02′N 02°58′E
Sighet *see* Sighetu Marmației
Sighetul Marmației *see* Sighetu Marmației
116 I8 **Sighetu Marmației** *var.* Sighet, Sighetul Marmației, *Hung.* Máramarossziget. Maramureș, N Romania 47°56′N 23°53′E
116 I11 **Sighișoara** *Ger.* Schässburg, *Hung.* Segesvár. Mureș, C Romania 46°12′N 24°48′E
168 G7 **Sigli** Sumatera, W Indonesia 05°21′N 95°56′E
92 J1 **Siglufjördhur** Nordhurland Vestra, N Iceland 66°09′N 18°56′W
101 H23 **Sigmaringen** Baden-Württemberg, S Germany 48°04′N 09°12′E
101 N20 **Signalberg** ▲ SE Germany 49°30′N 12°34′E
36 I13 **Signal Peak** ▲ Arizona, SW USA 33°20′N 114°03′W
Signan *see* Xi'an
194 H1 **Signy** *UK research station* South Orkney Islands, Antarctica 60°27′S 45°35′W
29 X15 **Sigourney** Iowa, C USA 41°19′N 92°12′W
115 K17 **Sígri, Akrotírio** *headland* Lésvos, E Greece 39°12′N 25°49′E
Sigsbee Deep *see* Mexico Basin
47 N2 **Sigsbee Escarpment** *undersea feature* N Gulf of Mexico 26°00′N 92°30′W
56 C8 **Sigsig** Azuay, S Ecuador 03°04′S 78°50′W
95 O15 **Sigtuna** Stockholm, C Sweden 59°36′N 17°44′E
42 H6 **Siguatepeque** Comayagua, W Honduras 14°39′N 87°48′W
105 P7 **Sigüenza** Castilla-La Mancha, C Spain 41°04′N 02°38′W
105 R4 **Sigües** Aragón, NE Spain 42°39′N 01°00′W
76 K13 **Siguiri** NE Guinea 11°26′N 09°08′W
118 G8 **Sigulda** *Ger.* Segewold. Rīga, C Latvia 57°08′N 24°51′E
Sihanoukville *see* Kâmpóng Saôm
108 G8 **Sihlsee** ⊚ NW Switzerland
93 K18 **Siikainen** Länsi-Suomi, SW Finland 61°52′N 21°49′E
93 M16 **Siilinjärvi** Itä-Suomi, C Finland 63°05′N 27°40′E
137 R15 **Siirt** *var.* Sert; *anc.* Tigranocerta. Siirt, SE Turkey 37°56′N 41°56′E
137 R15 **Siirt** *var.* Sert. ◈ *province* SE Turkey
187 N8 **Sikaiana** *var.* Stewart Islands. *island group* W Solomon Islands
Sikandarabad *see* Secunderābād
152 J11 **Sikandra Rao** Uttar Pradesh, N India 27°42′N 78°21′E
10 M11 **Sikanni Chief** British Columbia, W Canada 57°16′N 122°44′W
10 M11 **Sikanni Chief** ≋ British Columbia, W Canada
152 H11 **Sīkar** Rājasthān, N India 27°33′N 75°12′E
76 M13 **Sikasso** Sikasso, S Mali 11°21′N 05°43′W
76 L13 **Sikasso** ◈ *region* SW Mali
167 N3 **Sikaw** Kachin State, C Burma (Myanmar) 23°50′N 97°04′E
83 H14 **Sikelenge** Western, W Zambia 14°51′S 24°13′E
27 Y7 **Sikeston** Missouri, C USA 36°52′N 89°35′W
93 J14 **Sikfors** Norrbotten, N Sweden 65°29′N 21°17′E
123 T14 **Sikhote-Alin', Khrebet** ▲▲ SE Russian Federation
Siking *see* Xi'an
115 J22 **Síkinos** *island* Kykládes, Greece, Aegean Sea
153 S11 **Sikkim** *Tib.* Denjong. ◈ *state* N India
111 I26 **Siklós** Baranya, SW Hungary 45°51′N 18°18′E
Sikoku *see* Shikoku
Sikoku Basin *see* Shikoku Basin
83 G14 **Sikongo** Western, W Zambia 15°03′S 22°07′E
Sikotu Ko *see* Shikotsu-ko
Sikouri/Sikoúrion *see* Sykoúrio
123 P8 **Siktyakh** Respublika Sakha (Yakutiya), NE Russian Federation 69°45′N 124°42′E
118 D12 **Šilalė** Tauragė, W Lithuania 55°29′N 22°10′E
106 G5 **Silandro** *Ger.* Schlanders. Trentino-Alto Adige, N Italy 46°39′N 10°55′E
41 N12 **Silao** Guanajuato, C Mexico 20°56′N 101°28′W
Silarius *see* Sele
153 W14 **Silchar** Assam, NE India 24°49′N 92°48′E
108 G9 **Silenen** Uri, C Switzerland 46°49′N 08°39′E
21 T9 **Siler City** North Carolina, SE USA 35°43′N 79°27′W
33 U11 **Silesia** Montana, NW USA 45°32′N 108°52′W
110 F13 **Silesia** *physical region* SW Poland
74 K12 **Silet** S Algeria 22°45′N 04°51′E
145 R8 **Sileti** *var.* Selety. ≋ N Kazakhstan
Siletitengiz *see* Siletiteniz, Ozero
145 R7 **Siletiteniz, Ozero** *Kaz.* Siletitengiz. ⊚ N Kazakhstan
172 H16 **Silhouette** *island* Inner Islands, SE Seychelles
136 I17 **Silifke** *anc.* Seleucia. İçel, S Turkey 36°22′N 33°57′E
Siliguri *see* Shiliguri
156 J10 **Siling Co** ⊚ W China
Silinhot *see* Xilinhot
192 G14 **Silisili, Mauga** ▲ Savai'i, C Samoa 13°37′S 172°26′W
114 M6 **Silistra** *var.* Silistria; *anc.* Durostorum. Silistra, NE Bulgaria 44°06′N 27°17′E
114 M7 **Silistra** ◈ *province* NE Bulgaria
Silistria *see* Silistra
136 D10 **Silivri** İstanbul, NW Turkey 41°05′N 28°15′E
94 L13 **Siljan** ⊚ C Sweden
95 G22 **Silkeborg** Århus, C Denmark 56°10′N 09°34′E
108 M8 **Sill** ≋ W Austria
105 S10 **Silla** País Valenciano, E Spain 39°22′N 00°25′W
62 H3 **Sillajguay, Cordillera** ▲ N Chile 19°45′S 68°39′W
118 K3 **Sillamäe** *Ger.* Sillamäggi. Ida-Virumaa, NE Estonia 59°23′N 27°45′E
Sillamäggi *see* Sillamäe
Sillein *see* Žilina
109 P9 **Sillian** Tirol, W Austria 46°45′N 12°25′E
112 B10 **Šilo** Primorje-Gorski Kotar, NW Croatia 45°09′N 14°39′E
27 R9 **Siloam Springs** Arkansas, C USA 36°11′N 94°32′W
25 X10 **Silsbee** Texas, SW USA 30°21′N 94°10′W
143 W15 **Sīlūp, Rūd-e** ≋ SE Iran
118 C12 **Šilutė** *Ger.* Heydekrug. Klaipėda, W Lithuania 55°20′N 21°30′E
137 Q15 **Silvan** Diyarbakır, SE Turkey 38°08′N 41°E
108 J10 **Silvaplana** Graubünden, S Switzerland 46°27′N 09°45′E
Silva Porto *see* Kuito
58 M12 **Silva, Recife do** *reef* E Brazil
154 D12 **Silvassa** Dādra and Nagar Haveli, W India 20°13′N 73°03′E
29 X4 **Silver Bay** Minnesota, N USA 47°17′N 91°15′W
37 P15 **Silver City** New Mexico, SW USA 32°47′N 108°16′W
18 D10 **Silver Creek** New York, NE USA 42°32′N 79°10′W
37 N12 **Silver Creek** ≋ Arizona, SW USA
27 P4 **Silver Lake** Kansas, C USA 39°06′N 95°51′W
32 I14 **Silver Lake** Oregon, NW USA 43°07′N 121°04′W
35 T9 **Silver Peak Range** ▲▲ Nevada, W USA
21 W3 **Silver Spring** Maryland, NE USA 39°00′N 77°01′W
Silver State *see* Colorado
Silver State *see* Nevada
37 Q7 **Silverton** Colorado, C USA 37°48′N 107°39′W
18 K16 **Silverton** New Jersey, NE USA 40°00′N 74°09′W
32 G11 **Silverton** Oregon, NW USA 45°00′N 122°46′W
25 N4 **Silverton** Texas, SW USA 34°28′N 101°18′W
104 G14 **Silves** Faro, S Portugal 37°11′N 08°26′W
54 D12 **Silvia** Cauca, SW Colombia 02°37′N 76°24′W
108 J9 **Silvrettagruppe** ▲▲ Austria/Switzerland
Sily-Vajdej *see* Vulcan
108 L7 **Silz** Tirol, W Austria 47°17′N 11°00′E
172 I13 **Sima** Anjouan, SE Comoros 12°11′S 44°18′E
Simabara *see* Shimabara
83 H15 **Simakando** Western, W Zambia 16°43′S 24°46′E
Simane *see* Shimane
119 L20 **Simanichy** *Rus.* Simonichi. Homyel'skaya Voblasts', SE Belarus 51°53′N 28°05′E
160 F14 **Simao** Yunnan, SW China 22°30′N 101°06′E
153 P12 **Simarā** Central, C Nepal 27°14′N 85°00′E
14 I8 **Simard, Lac** ⊚ Québec, SE Canada
136 D13 **Simav** Kütahya, W Turkey 39°05′N 28°59′E
136 D13 **Simav Çayı** ≋ NW Turkey
79 L18 **Simba** Orientale, N Dem. Rep. Congo 0°46′N 22°54′E
186 C7 **Simbai** Madang, N Papua New Guinea 05°12′S 144°33′E
Simbirsk *see* Ul'yanovsk
14 F17 **Simcoe** Ontario, S Canada 42°50′N 80°19′W
14 H14 **Simcoe, Lake** ⊚ Ontario, S Canada
80 J11 **Sīmēn** ▲▲ N Ethiopia
114 K11 **Simeonovgrad** *prev.* Maritsa. Khaskovo, S Bulgaria 42°03′N 25°36′E
116 G11 **Simeria** *Ger.* Pischk, *Hung.* Piski. Hunedoara, W Romania 45°51′N 23°00′E
107 L24 **Simeto** ≋ Sicilia, Italy, C Mediterranean Sea
168 G9 **Simeulue, Pulau** *island* NW Indonesia
117 T13 **Simferopol'** Respublika Krym, S Ukraine 44°55′N 33°06′E
117 T13 **Simferopol'** ✈ Respublika Krym, S Ukraine 44°55′N 34°04′E
Simi *see* Sými
152 M9 **Simikot** Far Western, NW Nepal 30°02′N 81°49′E
54 F7 **Simití** Bolívar, N Colombia 07°57′N 73°57′W
114 G11 **Simitla** Blagoevgrad, SW Bulgaria 41°57′N 23°06′E
35 S15 **Simi Valley** California, W USA 34°16′N 118°47′W
Simizu *see* Shimizu
Simla *see* Shimla
Şimlăul Silvaniei/Şimleul Silvaniei *see* Şimleu Silvaniei
116 G9 **Şimleu Silvaniei** *Hung.* Szilágysomlyó; *prev.* Şimlăul Silvaniei, Şimleul Silvaniei. Sălaj, NW Romania 47°12′N 22°49′E
Simmer *see* Simmerbach
101 E19 **Simmerbach** *var.* Simmer. ≋ W Germany
101 F18 **Simmern** Rheinland-Pfalz, W Germany 50°00′N 07°30′E
22 I7 **Simmesport** Louisiana, S USA 30°58′N 91°48′W
119 F14 **Simnas** Alytus, S Lithuania 54°23′N 23°40′E
92 L13 **Simo** Lappi, NW Finland 65°40′N 25°04′E
Simoda *see* Shimoda
Simodate *see* Shimodate
92 M13 **Simojärvi** ⊚ N Finland
92 L13 **Simojoki** ≋ NW Finland
41 U15 **Simojovel** *var.* Simojovel de Allende. Chiapas, SE Mexico 17°14′N 92°40′W
Simojovel de Allende *see* Simojovel
56 B7 **Simon Bolivar** *var.* Guayaquil. ✈ (Quayaquil) Guayas, W Ecuador 02°16′S 79°54′W
54 L5 **Simon Bolívar** ✈ (Caracas) Vargas, N Venezuela 10°33′N 66°54′W
Simonichi *see* Simanichy
14 M12 **Simon, Lac** ⊚ Québec, SE Canada
Simonoseki *see* Shimonoseki
Šimonovany *see* Partizánske
Simonstad *see* Simon's Town
83 E26 **Simon's Town** *var.* Simonstad. Western Cape, SW South Africa 34°12′S 18°26′E
Simony *see* Partizánske
Simpeln *see* Simplon
99 M18 **Simpelveld** Limburg, SE Netherlands 50°50′N 05°59′E
108 E11 **Simplon** *var.* Simpeln. Valais, SW Switzerland 46°13′N 08°01′E
108 E11 **Simplon Pass** *pass* S Switzerland
106 C6 **Simplon Tunnel** *tunnel* Italy/Switzerland
Simpson *see* Fort Simpson
182 G1 **Simpson Desert** *desert* Northern Territory/South Australia
10 J9 **Simpson Peak** ▲ British Columbia, W Canada 59°43′N 131°29′W
9 N7 **Simpson Peninsula** *peninsula* Nunavut, NE Canada
21 P11 **Simpsonville** South Carolina, SE USA 34°44′N 82°15′W
95 L23 **Simrishamn** Skåne, S Sweden 55°34′N 14°20′E
123 U13 **Simushir, Ostrov** *island* Kuril'skiye Ostrova, SE Russian Federation
168 G9 **Sinabang** Sumatera, W Indonesia 02°27′N 96°24′E
81 N15 **Sina Dhaqa** Galguduud, C Somalia 05°21′N 46°21′E
75 X8 **Sinai** *var.* Sinai Peninsula, *Ar.* Shibh Jazirat Sīnā', Sīnā. *physical region* NE Egypt
116 J12 **Sinaia** Prahova, SE Romania 45°20′N 25°33′E
188 B16 **Sinajana** C Guam 13°28′N 144°45′E
40 H8 **Sinaloa** ◈ *state* C Mexico
54 H4 **Sinamaica** Zulia, NW Venezuela 11°06′N 71°52′W
163 X14 **Sinan-ni** SE North Korea 38°37′N 127°43′E
Sīnā/Sinai Peninsula *see* Sinai
Sīnāwan *see* Sīnāwin
75 N8 **Sīnāwin** *var.* Sīnāwan. NW Libya 31°00′N 10°37′E
83 J16 **Sinazongwe** Southern, S Zambia 17°14′S 27°27′E
166 L6 **Sinbaungwe** Magway, W Burma (Myanmar) 19°44′N 95°10′E
166 L5 **Sinbyugyun** Magway, W Burma (Myanmar) 20°38′N 94°40′E
54 E6 **Since** Sucre, NW Colombia 09°14′N 75°08′W
54 E6 **Sincelejo** Sucre, NW Colombia 09°17′N 75°23′W
166 J5 **Sinchaingbyin** *var.* Zullapara. Rakhine State, W Burma (Myanmar) 20°51′N 92°23′E
23 U4 **Sinclair, Lake** ⊠ Georgia, SE USA
10 M14 **Sinclair Mills** British Columbia, SW Canada 54°03′N 121°37′W
149 Q14 **Sind** *var.* Sindh. ◈ *province* SE Pakistan
154 I8 **Sind** ≋ N India
95 H19 **Sindal** Nordjylland, N Denmark 57°29′N 10°13′E
171 P7 **Sindañgan** Mindanao, S Philippines 08°09′N 122°59′E
79 D19 **Sindara** Ngounié, W Gabon 01°07′S 10°41′E
152 E13 **Sindari** *prev.* Sindri. Rājasthān, N India 25°32′N 71°58′E
114 N8 **Sindel** Varna, E Bulgaria 43°07′N 27°35′E
101 H22 **Sindelfingen** Baden-Württemberg, SW Germany 48°43′N 09°E
155 G16 **Sindgi** Karnātaka, C India 17°01′N 76°22′E
Sindh *see* Sind
118 G5 **Sindi** *Ger.* Zintenhof. Pärnumaa, SW Estonia 58°28′N 24°41′E
136 C13 **Sındırgı** Balıkesir, W Turkey 39°13′N 28°10′E
77 N14 **Sindou** SW Burkina 10°35′N 05°04′W
Sindri *see* Sindari
149 T9 **Sind Sāgar Doāb** *desert* E Pakistan
126 M11 **Sinegorskiy** Rostovskaya Oblast', SW Russian Federation 48°01′N 40°52′E
123 S9 **Sinegor'ye** Magadanskaya Oblast', E Russian Federation 62°04′N 150°33′E
114 O12 **Sinekli** İstanbul, NW Turkey 41°13′N 28°13′E
104 F12 **Sines** Setúbal, S Portugal 37°58′N 08°52′W
104 F12 **Sines, Cabo de** *headland* S Portugal 37°57′N 08°55′W
92 L12 **Sinettä** Lappi, NW Finland 66°39′N 25°25′E
186 H6 **Sinewit, Mount** ▲ New Britain, C Papua New Guinea 04°42′S 151°58′E
80 G11 **Singa** *var.* Sinja, Sinjah. Sinnar, E Sudan 13°11′N 33°55′E
78 J12 **Singako** Moyen-Chari, S Chad 09°52′N 19°31′E
Singan *see* Xi'an
168 K10 **Singapore** ● (Singapore) S Singapore 01°17′N 103°48′E
168 L10 **Singapore** *off.* Republic of Singapore. ◆ *republic* SE Asia
Singapore, Republic of *see* Singapore
169 U17 **Singaraja** Bali, C Indonesia 08°06′S 115°04′E
167 O10 **Sing Buri** *var.* Singhaburi. Sing Buri, C Thailand 14°56′N 100°21′E
101 H24 **Singen** Baden-Württemberg, S Germany 47°46′N 08°50′E
Sîngeorgiu de Pădure *see* Sângeorgiu de Pădure
Sîngeorz-Băi/Singeroz Băi *see* Sângeorz-Băi
116 M9 **Sîngerei** *var.* Sângerei; *prev.* Lazovsk. N Moldova 47°38′N 28°08′E
Singhaburi *see* Sing Buri
81 H21 **Singida** Singida, C Tanzania 04°45′S 34°48′E
81 G22 **Singida** ◈ *region* C Tanzania
Singidunum *see* Beograd
166 M2 **Singkaling Hkamti** Sagaing, N Burma (Myanmar) 26°00′N 95°43′E
171 N14 **Singkang** Sulawesi, C Indonesia 04°09′S 119°58′E
168 J11 **Singkarak, Danau** ⊚ Sumatera, W Indonesia
169 N10 **Singkawang** Borneo, C Indonesia 0°57′N 108°57′E
168 M11 **Singkep, Pulau** *island* Kepulauan Lingga, W Indonesia
168 H9 **Singkilbaru** Sumatera, W Indonesia 02°18′N 97°47′E
183 T7 **Singleton** New South Wales, SE Australia 32°38′S 151°00′E
Singora *see* Songkhla
Singû *see* Shingū
Sining *see* Xining
107 D17 **Siniscola** Sardegna, Italy, C Mediterranean Sea 40°34′N 09°42′E
113 F14 **Sinj** Split-Dalmacija, SE Croatia 43°41′N 16°37′E
Sinjajevina *see* Sinjavina
139 P3 **Sinjār** Nīnawýa, NW Iraq 36°20′N 41°51′E
139 P2 **Sinjār, Jabal** ▲▲ N Iraq
Sinja/Sinjah *see* Singa
113 K15 **Sinjavina** *var.* Sinjajevina. ▲▲ C Montenegro
80 I7 **Sinkat** Red Sea, NE Sudan 18°52′N 36°51′E
Sinkiang/Sinkiang Uighur Autonomous Region *see* Xinjiang Uygur Zizhiqu
Sînmartin *see* Târnăveni
163 V13 **Sinmi-do** *island* NW North Korea
101 I18 **Sinn** ≋ C Germany
Sinnamarie *see* Sinnamary
55 Y9 **Sinnamary** *var.* Sinnamarie. N French Guiana 05°23′N 53°00′W
80 G11 **Sinnar** ◈ *state* E Sudan
Sinneh *see* Sanandaj
18 E13 **Sinnemahoning Creek** ≋ Pennsylvania, NE USA
Sînnicolau Mare *see* Sânnicolau Mare
Sinoe, Lacul *see* Sinoie, Lacul
Sinoia *see* Chinhoyi
117 N14 **Sinoie, Lacul** *prev.* Lacul Sinoe. *lagoon* SE Romania
59 H16 **Sinop** Mato Grosso, W Brazil 11°38′S 55°27′W
136 K10 **Sinop** *anc.* Sinope. Sinop, N Turkey 42°02′N 35°09′E
136 J10 **Sinop** ◈ *province* N Turkey
136 K10 **Sinop Burnu** *headland* N Turkey 42°02′N 35°12′E
Sinope *see* Sinop
Sino/Sinoe *see* Greenville
163 Y12 **Sinp'o** E North Korea 40°01′N 128°10′E
101 H20 **Sinsheim** Baden-Württemberg, SW Germany 49°15′N 08°53′E
Sîntana *see* Sântana
169 R11 **Sintang** Borneo, C Indonesia 0°03′N 111°31′E
99 F14 **Sint Annaland** Zeeland, SW Netherlands 51°36′N 04°07′E
98 L5 **Sint Annaparochie** Friesland, N Netherlands 53°20′N 05°46′E
45 V9 **Sint Eustatius** *Eng.* Saint Eustatius. *island* N Netherlands Antilles

◆ Country
● Country Capital
◇ Dependent Territory
○ Dependent Territory Capital
◈ Administrative Regions
✈ International Airport
▲ Mountain
▲▲ Mountain Range
Ѫ Volcano
≋ River
⊚ Lake
⊠ Reservoir

99 G19 **Sint-Genesius-Rode** Fr. Rhode-Saint-Genèse. Vlaams Brabant, C Belgium 50°45′N 04°21′E
99 F16 **Sint-Gillis-Waas** Oost-Vlaanderen, N Belgium 51°14′N 04°08′E
99 H17 **Sint-Katelijne-Waver** Antwerpen, C Belgium 51°05′N 04°31′E
99 E18 **Sint-Lievens-Houtem** Oost-Vlaanderen, NW Belgium 50°55′N 03°52′E
45 V9 **Sint Maarten** Eng. Saint Martin. island N Netherlands Antilles
99 F14 **Sint Maartensdijk** Zeeland, SW Netherlands 51°33′N 04°05′E
99 L19 **Sint-Martens-Voeren** Fr. Fouron-Saint-Martin. Limburg, NE Belgium 50°46′N 05°49′E
99 J14 **Sint-Michielsgestel** Noord-Brabant, S Netherlands 51°38′N 05°21′E
Sîn-Miclăuș see Gheorgheni
45 O16 **Sint Nicholaas** S Aruba 12°25′N 69°52′W
99 F16 **Sint-Niklaas** Fr. Saint-Nicolas. Oost-Vlaanderen, N Belgium 51°10′N 04°09′E
99 K14 **Sint-Oedenrode** Noord-Brabant, S Netherlands 51°34′N 05°28′E
25 T14 **Sinton** Texas, SW USA 28°02′N 97°33′W
99 G14 **Sint Philipsland** Zeeland, SW Netherlands 51°37′N 04°11′E
99 G19 **Sint-Pieters-Leeuw** Vlaams Brabant, C Belgium 50°47′N 04°16′E
104 E11 **Sintra** prev. Cintra. Lisboa, W Portugal 38°48′N 09°22′W
99 J18 **Sint-Truiden** Fr. Saint-Trond. Limburg, NE Belgium 50°48′N 05°13′E
99 H14 **Sint Willebrord** Noord-Brabant, S Netherlands 51°33′N 04°35′E
163 V13 **Sinŭiju** W North Korea 40°08′N 124°33′E
80 P13 **Sinujiif** Nugaal, NE Somalia 08°33′N 49°05′E
Sinus Aelaniticus see Aqaba, Gulf of
Sinus Gallicus see Lion, Golfe du
Sinyang see Xinyang
Sinyavka see Sinyawka
119 I18 **Sinyawka** Rus. Sinyavka. Minskaya Voblasts', SW Belarus 52°57′N 26°29′E
Sinying see Hsinying
Sinyukha see Synyukha
Sinzyô see Shinjō
111 I24 **Sió** ≈ W Hungary
171 O7 **Siocon** Mindanao, S Philippines 07°37′N 122°09′E
111 I24 **Siófok** Somogy, Hungary 46°54′N 18°03′E
Siogama see Shiogama
83 G15 **Sioma** Western, SW Zambia 16°39′S 23°36′E
108 D11 **Sion** Ger. Sitten; anc. Sedunum. Valais, SW Switzerland 46°15′N 07°23′E
103 O11 **Sioule** ≈ C France
29 S12 **Sioux Center** Iowa, C USA 43°04′N 96°10′W
29 R13 **Sioux City** Iowa, C USA 42°30′N 96°24′W
29 R11 **Sioux Falls** South Dakota, N USA 43°33′N 96°45′W
12 B11 **Sioux Lookout** Ontario, S Canada 49°27′N 94°06′W
29 T12 **Sioux Rapids** Iowa, C USA 42°53′N 95°09′W
Sioux State see North Dakota
Sioziri see Shiojiri
171 P6 **Sipalay** Negros, C Philippines 09°46′N 122°25′E
55 V11 **Sipaliwini** ◐ district S Surinam
45 U15 **Siparia** Trinidad, Trinidad and Tobago 10°08′N 61°31′W
Siphnos see Sífnos
163 V11 **Siping** var. Ssu-p'ing, Szeping; prev. Ssu-p'ing-chieh. Jilin, NE China 43°09′N 124°22′E
11 X12 **Sipiwesk** Manitoba, C Canada 55°28′N 97°16′W
11 W13 **Sipiwesk Lake** ◎ Manitoba, C Canada
195 O11 **Siple Coast** physical region Antarctica
194 K12 **Siple Island** island Antarctica
194 K13 **Siple, Mount** ▲ Siple Island, Antarctica 73°25′S 126°24′W
Sipoo see Sibbo
112 G12 **Šipovo** Republika Srpska, W Bosnia and Herzegovina 44°16′N 17°05′E
23 O4 **Sipsey River** ≈ Alabama, S USA
168 I13 **Sipura, Pulau** island W Indonesia
0 G16 **Siqueiros Fracture Zone** tectonic feature E Pacific Ocean
42 L10 **Siquia, Río** ≈ SE Nicaragua
43 N13 **Siquirres** Limón, E Costa Rica 10°05′N 83°30′W
54 J5 **Siquisique** Lara, N Venezuela 10°36′N 69°45′W
155 G19 **Sīra** Karnātaka, W India 13°46′N 76°54′E
95 D16 **Sira** ≈ S Norway
167 P12 **Siracha** var. Ban Si Racha, Si Racha. Chon Buri, S Thailand 13°10′N 100°57′E
Si Racha see Siracha
107 L25 **Siracusa** Eng. Syracuse. Sicilia, Italy, C Mediterranean Sea 37°04′N 15°17′E
153 T14 **Sirajganj** var. Shirajganj Ghat. Rajshahi, C Bangladesh 24°27′N 89°42′E
Sirakawa see Shirakawa
11 N14 **Sir Alexander, Mount** ▲ British Columbia, W Canada 54°00′N 120°33′W
137 O12 **Şiran** Gümüşhane, NE Turkey 40°12′N 39°07′E
77 Q12 **Sirba** ≈ E Burkina
143 O17 **Şīr Banī Yās** island W United Arab Emirates
95 D17 **Sirdalsvatnet** ◎ S Norway
Sir Darya/Sirdaryo see Syr Darya
147 P10 **Sirdaryo** Sirdaryo Viloyati, E Uzbekistan 40°46′N 68°34′E
147 O11 **Sirdaryo Viloyati** Rus. Syrdar'inskaya Oblast'. ◐ province E Uzbekistan
Sir Donald Sangster International Airport see Sangster
181 S3 **Sir Edward Pellew Group** island group Northern Territory, NE Australia
116 K8 **Siret** Ger. Sereth, Hung. Szeret. Suceava, N Romania 47°55′N 26°05′E
116 K8 **Siret** var. Siretul, Ger. Sereth, Rus. Seret. ≈ Romania/Ukraine
Siretul see Siret
140 K3 **Sirḥān, Wādī as** dry watercourse Jordan/Saudi Arabia
152 I8 **Sirhind** Punjab, N India 30°39′N 76°28′E
116 F11 **Şiria** Ger. Schiria. Arad, W Romania 46°16′N 21°38′E
Siria see Syria
143 S14 **Sīrīk** Hormozgān, SE Iran 26°32′N 57°07′E
167 P8 **Sirikit Reservoir** ◎ N Thailand
58 K12 **Sirituba, Ilha** island NE Brazil
143 R11 **Sīrjān** prev. Sa'īdābād. Kermān, S Iran 29°29′N 55°39′E
182 H9 **Sir Joseph Banks Group** island group South Australia
92 K11 **Sirkka** Lappi, N Finland 67°49′N 24°48′E
Sirna see Sýrna
137 R16 **Şırnak** Şırnak, SE Turkey 37°33′N 42°27′E
137 S16 **Şırnak** ◐ province SE Turkey
152 E14 **Sirohi** Rājasthān, N India 25°53′N 72°58′E
Siroisi see Shiroishi
155 J14 **Sironcha** Mahārāshtra, C India 18°51′N 80°03′E
Sirone see Shirone
Síros see Sýros
Sirotino see Sirotsina
118 M12 **Sirotsina** Rus. Sirotino. Vitsyebskaya Voblasts', N Belarus 55°23′N 29°37′E
152 H9 **Sirsa** Haryāna, NW India 29°32′N 75°04′E
173 Y17 **Sir Seewoosagur Ramgoolam** ✈ (port Louis) SE Mauritius
155 E18 **Sirsi** Karnātaka, W India 14°46′N 74°49′E
146 K12 **Şirşütür Gumy** var. Shirshütür, Rus. Peski Shirshyutyur. desert E Turkmenistan
Sirte see Surt
182 A2 **Sir Thomas, Mount** ▲ South Australia 27°09′S 129°49′E
Sirti, Gulf of see Surt, Khalīj
142 J5 **Sīrvān, Rūdkhāneh-ye** var. Nahr Diyālá, Sirwan. ≈ Iran/Iraq see also Diyālá, Nahr
Sīrvān, Rudkhaneh-ye see Diyālá, Sirwan Nahr
118 H13 **Širvintos** Vilnius, SE Lithuania 55°01′N 24°58′E
Sīrwān see Diyālá, Nahr/Sīrvān, Rudkhaneh-ye
11 N15 **Sir Wilfrid Laurier, Mount** ▲ British Columbia, SW Canada 52°45′N 119°51′W
14 M10 **Sir-Wilfrid, Mont** ▲ Québec, SE Canada 46°57′N 75°33′W
Sisačko-Moslavačka Županija see Sisak-Moslavina
112 E9 **Sisak** var. Siscia, Ger. Sissek, Hung. Sziszek; anc. Segestica. Sisak-Moslavina, C Croatia 45°28′N 16°21′E
167 R10 **Si Sa Ket** var. Sisaket, Sri Saket. Si Sa Ket, E Thailand 15°08′N 104°18′E
Sisaket see Si Sa Ket
112 E9 **Sisak-Moslavina** off. Sisačko-Moslavačka Županija. ◐ province C Croatia
167 O8 **Si Satchanala** Sukhothai, NW Thailand
Siscia see Sisak
83 G22 **Sishen** Northern Cape, NW South Africa 27°47′S 22°59′E
137 V13 **Sisian** SE Armenia 39°31′N 46°03′E
197 N13 **Sisimiut** var. Holsteinborg, Holsteinsborg, Holstenborg, Holstensborg. Kitaa, S Greenland 67°07′N 53°42′W
30 M1 **Siskiwit Bay** lake bay Michigan, N USA
34 L1 **Siskiyou Mountains** ▲▲ California/Oregon, W USA
167 Q11 **Sisŏphŏn** Bătdâmbâng, NW Cambodia 13°37′N 102°58′E
108 E7 **Sissach** Basel-Land, NW Switzerland 47°28′N 07°48′E
186 B5 **Sissano** Sandaun, NW Papua New Guinea 03°02′S 142°01′E
Sissek see Sisak
29 R7 **Sisseton** South Dakota, N USA 45°39′N 97°03′W
143 W9 **Sīstān, Daryācheh-ye** var. Daryācheh-ye Hāmūn, Hāmūn-e Şāberī. ◎ Afghanistan/Iran see also Şāberī, Hāmūn-e
Sīstān, Daryācheh-ye see Şāberī, Hāmūn-e
143 V12 **Sīstān va Balūchestān** off. Ostān-e Sīstān va Balūchestān, var. Balūchestān va Sīstān. ◐ province SE Iran
Sīstān va Balūchestān, Ostān-e see Sīstān va Balūchestān
103 T14 **Sisteron** Alpes-de-Haute-Provence, SE France 44°12′N 05°55′E
32 H13 **Sisters** Oregon, NW USA 44°17′N 121°33′W
65 G15 **Sisters Peak** ▲ N Ascension Island 07°56′S 14°23′W
21 R3 **Sistersville** West Virginia, NE USA 39°33′N 81°00′W
Sistova see Svishtov
Sitakund see Sitakunda
153 V16 **Sitakunda** var. Sitakund. Chittagong, SE Bangladesh 22°35′N 91°40′E
153 P12 **Sītāmarhi** Bihār, N India 26°36′N 85°30′E
152 L11 **Sītāpur** Uttar Pradesh, N India 27°33′N 80°40′E
Sitaș Cristuru see Cristuru Secuiesc
115 L25 **Siteía** var. Sitía. Kríti, Greece, E Mediterranean Sea 35°13′N 26°06′E
105 V6 **Sitges** Cataluña, NE Spain 41°14′N 01°49′E
115 H15 **Sithoniá** peninsula NE Greece
Sitía see Siteía
54 F4 **Sitionuevo** Magdalena, N Colombia 10°46′N 74°43′W
39 X13 **Sitka** Baranof Island, Alaska, USA 57°03′N 135°19′W
39 Q15 **Sitkinak Island** island Trinity Islands, Alaska, USA
Sittang see Sittoung
99 L17 **Sittard** Limburg, SE Netherlands 51°N 05°52′E
Sitten see Sion
108 H7 **Sitter** ≈ NW Switzerland
109 U10 **Sittersdorf** Kärnten, S Austria 46°31′N 14°34′E
166 M7 **Sittoung** var. Sittang. ≈ S Burma (Myanmar)
166 K6 **Sittwe** var. Akyab. Rakhine State, W Burma (Myanmar) 22°09′N 92°51′E
42 L8 **Siuna** Región Autónoma Atlántico Norte, NE Nicaragua 13°44′N 84°46′W
153 R15 **Siuri** West Bengal, NE India 23°54′N 87°32′E
Siut see Asyūţ
155 I23 **Sivaganga** Tamil Nādu, SE India 09°59′N 78°30′E
123 Q13 **Sivaki** Amurskaya Oblast', SE Russian Federation 52°39′N 126°43′E
136 M13 **Sivas** anc. Sebastia, Sebaste. Sivas, C Turkey 39°44′N 37°01′E
136 M13 **Sivas** ◐ province C Turkey
137 O15 **Siverek** Şanlıurfa, S Turkey 37°46′N 39°19′E
117 X6 **Sivers'k** Donets'ka Oblast', E Ukraine 48°52′N 38°07′E
124 G13 **Siverskiy** Leningradskaya Oblast', NW Russian Federation 59°21′N 30°01′E
117 X6 **Sivers'kyy Donets'** Rus. Severskiy Donets. ≈ Russian Federation/Ukraine see also Severskiy Donets
Sivers'kyy Donets' see Severskiy Donets
125 W5 **Sivomaskinskiy** Respublika Komi, NW Russian Federation 66°42′N 62°33′E
136 G13 **Sivrihisar** Eskişehir, W Turkey 39°29′N 31°32′E
99 F22 **Sivry** Hainaut, S Belgium 50°10′N 04°11′E
123 V9 **Sivuchiy, Mys** headland E Russian Federation 56°45′N 163°13′E
Siwa see Sīwah
75 U9 **Sīwah** var. Siwa. NW Egypt 29°11′N 25°32′E
152 J9 **Siwalik Range** var. Shiwalik Range. ▲▲ India/Nepal
153 O13 **Siwān** Bihār, N India 26°14′N 84°21′E
43 O14 **Sixaola, Río** ≈ Costa Rica/Panama
Six Counties, The see Northern Ireland
103 T16 **Six-Fours-les-Plages** Var, SE France 43°05′N 05°50′E
161 Q7 **Sixian** var. Si Xian. Anhui, E China 33°29′N 117°53′E
Si Xian see Sixian
22 J9 **Six Mile Lake** ◎ Louisiana, S USA
139 V3 **Siyāh Gūz** As Sulaymānīyah, E Iraq 35°49′N 45°45′E
155 L25 **Siyambalanduwa** Uva Province, SE Sri Lanka 06°54′N 81°32′E
137 Y10 **Siyäzän** Rus. Siazan'. NE Azerbaijan 41°05′N 49°05′E
Sizebolu see Sozopol
Sizuoka see Shizuoka
95 I24 **Sjælland** Eng. Zealand, Ger. Seeland. island E Denmark
Sjar see Sääre
113 L15 **Sjenica** Turk. Seniça. Serbia, SW Serbia 43°16′N 20°01′E
94 G11 **Sjoa** ≈ S Norway
95 K23 **Sjöbo** Skåne, S Sweden 55°37′N 13°45′E
94 E9 **Sjøholt** Møre og Romsdal, S Norway 62°29′N 06°50′E
92 O1 **Sjuøyane** island group N Svalbard
Skadar see Shkodër
Skadarsko Jezero see Scutari, Lake
117 R11 **Skadovs'k** Khersons'ka Oblast', S Ukraine 46°07′N 32°53′E
95 I24 **Skælskør** Vestsjælland, E Denmark 55°16′N 11°18′E
92 I2 **Skagaströnd** prev. Höfdhakaupstadhur. Nordhurland Vestra, N Iceland 65°49′N 20°18′W
95 H19 **Skagen** Nordjylland, N Denmark 57°44′N 10°37′E
Skagerak see Skagerrak
95 L16 **Skagern** ◎ C Sweden
197 T17 **Skagerrak** var. Skagerak. channel N Europe
94 G12 **Skaget** ▲ S Norway 61°19′N 09°07′E
32 H7 **Skagit River** ≈ Washington, NW USA
39 W12 **Skagway** Alaska, USA 59°27′N 135°18′W
92 K8 **Skaidi** Finnmark, N Norway 70°26′N 24°31′E
115 F21 **Skála** Pelopónnisos, S Greece 36°51′N 22°39′E
116 K6 **Skalat** Pol. Skałat. Ternopil's'ka Oblast', W Ukraine 49°27′N 25°59′E
95 J22 **Skälderviken** inlet Denmark/Sweden
92 I12 **Skalka** ◎ N Sweden
114 I12 **Skalotí** Anatolikí Makedonía kai Thráki, NE Greece 41°24′N 24°16′E
95 G22 **Skanderborg** Århus, C Denmark 56°02′N 09°57′E
95 K22 **Skåne** prev. Eng. Scania. ◐ county S Sweden
75 N6 **Skanès** ✈ (Sousse) E Tunisia 35°36′N 10°56′E
95 C15 **Skånevik** Hordaland, S Norway 59°43′N 06°35′E
95 M18 **Skänninge** Östergötland, S Sweden 58°24′N 15°05′E
95 J23 **Skanör med Falsterbo** Skåne, S Sweden 55°24′N 12°48′E
115 H17 **Skantzoúra** island Vóreies Sporádes, Greece, Aegean Sea
95 K18 **Skara** Västra Götaland, S Sweden 58°23′N 13°25′E
95 M17 **Skärblacka** Östergötland, S Sweden 58°34′N 15°54′E
152 I5 **Skārdu** Jammu and Kashmīr, India 35°18′N 75°44′E
95 I18 **Skärhamn** Västra Götaland, S Sweden 57°59′N 11°33′E
95 I14 **Skarnes** Hedmark, S Norway 60°14′N 11°41′E
119 M21 **Skarodnaye** Rus. Skorodnoye. Homyel'skaya Voblasts', SE Belarus 51°38′N 28°50′E
110 I8 **Skarszewy** Ger. Schöneck. Pomorskie, NW Poland 54°04′N 18°25′E
111 M14 **Skarżysko-Kamienna** Świętokrzyskie, C Poland 51°07′N 20°52′E
95 K16 **Skattkärr** Värmland, C Sweden 59°25′N 13°42′E
118 D12 **Skaudvilė** Tauragė, SW Lithuania 55°25′N 22°33′E
92 J12 **Skaulo** Lapp. Sávdijári. Norrbotten, N Sweden 67°21′N 21°03′E
111 K17 **Skawina** Małopolskie, S Poland 49°59′N 19°49′E
10 K12 **Skeena** ≈ British Columbia, SW Canada
10 J11 **Skeena Mountains** ▲▲ British Columbia, W Canada
97 O18 **Skegness** E England, United Kingdom 53°10′N 00°21′E
92 J4 **Skeidharársandur** coast S Iceland
93 J15 **Skellefteå** Västerbotten, N Sweden 64°45′N 20°58′E
93 I14 **Skellefteälven** ≈ N Sweden
93 J15 **Skelleftehamn** Västerbotten, N Sweden 64°41′N 21°13′E
25 O2 **Skellytown** Texas, SW USA 35°34′N 101°10′W
95 J19 **Skene** Västra Götaland, S Sweden 57°30′N 12°34′E
97 G17 **Skerries** Ir. Na Sceirí. Dublin, E Ireland 53°35′N 06°07′W
95 H15 **Ski** Akershus, S Norway 59°43′N 10°50′E
115 G17 **Skíathos** Skíathos, Vóreies Sporádes, Greece, Aegean Sea 39°10′N 23°30′E
115 G17 **Skíathos** island Vóreies Sporádes, Greece, Aegean Sea
27 P9 **Skiatook** Oklahoma, C USA 36°22′N 96°00′W
27 P9 **Skiatook Lake** ▣ Oklahoma, C USA
97 B22 **Skibbereen** Ir. An Sciobairín. Cork, SW Ireland 51°33′N 09°15′W
92 I9 **Skibotn** Troms, N Norway 69°22′N 20°18′E
119 F16 **Skidal'** Rus. Skidel'. Hrodzyenskaya Voblasts', W Belarus 53°35′N 24°15′E
97 K15 **Skiddaw** ▲ NW England, United Kingdom 54°37′N 03°07′W
Skidel' see Skidal'
25 T14 **Skidmore** Texas, SW USA 28°13′N 97°40′W
95 G16 **Skien** Telemark, S Norway 59°14′N 09°37′E
Skiermûntseach see Schiermonnikoog
110 L12 **Skierniewice** Łódzkie, C Poland 51°58′N 20°10′E
74 L5 **Skikda** prev. Philippeville. NE Algeria 36°51′N 07°E
30 M16 **Skillet Fork** ≈ Illinois, N USA
95 L19 **Skillingaryd** Jönköping, S Sweden 57°27′N 14°05′E
115 B19 **Skinári, Akrotírio** headland Iónia Nisiá, Greece 37°55′N 20°57′E
95 M15 **Skinnskatteberg** Västmanland, C Sweden 59°50′N 15°41′E
182 M12 **Skipton** Victoria, SE Australia 37°44′S 143°21′E
97 L16 **Skipton** N England, United Kingdom 53°57′N 02°W
Skiropoula see Skyropoúla
Skíros see Skýros
95 F21 **Skive** Viborg, NW Denmark 56°34′N 09°02′E
94 F11 **Skjåk** Oppland, S Norway 61°52′N 08°21′E
92 K2 **Skjálfandafljót** ≈ C Iceland
95 F22 **Skjern** Ringkøbing, W Denmark 55°57′N 08°30′E
95 F22 **Skjern Å** var. Skjern Aa. ≈ W Denmark
Skjern Aa see Skjern Å
92 G12 **Skjerstad** Nordland, C Norway 67°14′N 15°00′E
92 J8 **Skjervøy** Troms, N Norway 70°03′N 20°56′E
92 I10 **Skjold** Troms, N Norway 69°03′N 19°18′E
111 I17 **Skoczów** Śląskie, S Poland 49°49′N 18°45′E
109 T11 **Škofja Loka** Ger. Bischoflack. NW Slovenia 46°12′N 14°16′E
94 N12 **Skog** Gävleborg, C Sweden 61°10′N 16°49′E
95 K16 **Skoghall** Värmland, C Sweden 59°20′N 13°30′E
31 N10 **Skokie** Illinois, N USA 42°01′N 87°43′W
116 H6 **Skole** L'vivs'ka Oblast', W Ukraine 49°04′N 23°29′E
115 D19 **Skóllis** ▲ S Greece 37°58′N 21°33′E
167 S13 **Skon** Kâmpóng Cham, C Cambodia 12°56′N 104°36′E
115 H17 **Skópelos** Skópelos, Vóreies Sporádes, Greece, Aegean Sea 39°07′N 23°43′E
115 H17 **Skópelos** island Vóreies Sporádes, Greece, Aegean Sea
126 L5 **Skopin** Ryazanskaya Oblast', W Russian Federation 53°46′N 39°37′E
113 N18 **Skopje** var. Üsküb, Turk. Üsküp, prev. Skoplje; anc. Scupi. ● (FYR Macedonia) N FYR Macedonia 42°N 21°28′E
113 O18 **Skopje** ✈ N FYR Macedonia 41°58′N 21°35′E
Skoplje see Skopje
110 I8 **Skórcz** Ger. Skurz. Pomorskie, N Poland 53°46′N 18°43′E
Skorodnoye see Skarodnaye
93 H16 **Skorped** Västernorrland, C Sweden 63°23′N 17°55′E
95 G21 **Skørping** Nordjylland, N Denmark 56°50′N 09°55′E
95 K18 **Skövde** Västra Götaland, S Sweden 58°24′N 13°52′E
123 Q13 **Skovorodino** Amurskaya Oblast', SE Russian Federation 54°03′N 123°47′E
19 Q6 **Skowhegan** Maine, NE USA 44°46′N 69°41′W
11 W15 **Skownan** Manitoba, S Canada 51°55′N 99°34′W
94 H13 **Skreia** Oppland, S Norway 60°37′N 11°00′E
Skripón see Orchómenos
118 H9 **Skrīveri** Aizkraukle, S Latvia 56°39′N 25°08′E
118 J11 **Skrudaliena** Daugvapils, SE Latvia 55°50′N 26°42′E
118 D9 **Skrunda** Kuldīga, W Latvia 56°39′N 22°01′E
95 C16 **Skudeneshavn** Rogaland, S Norway 59°10′N 05°16′E
83 L20 **Skukuza** Mpumalanga, NE South Africa 25°01′S 31°35′E
97 B22 **Skull** Ir. An Scoil. SW Ireland 51°32′N 09°34′W
22 L3 **Skuna River** ≈ Mississippi, S USA
29 X15 **Skunk River** ≈ Iowa, C USA
Skuø see Skúvoy
118 C10 **Skuodas** Ger. Schoden, Pol. Szkudy. Klaipėda, NW Lithuania 56°16′N 21°30′E
95 K23 **Skurup** Skåne, S Sweden 55°28′N 13°30′E
Skurz see Skórcz
114 H8 **Skŭt** ≈ NW Bulgaria
94 O13 **Skutskär** Uppsala, C Sweden 60°39′N 17°25′E
95 B19 **Skúvoy** Dan. Skuø. island C Faeroe Islands
Skvira see Skvyra
117 O5 **Skvyra** Rus. Skvira. Kyyivs'ka Oblast', N Ukraine 49°44′N 29°42′E
39 Q11 **Skwentna** Alaska, USA 61°56′N 151°03′W
110 E11 **Skwierzyna** Ger. Schwerin. Lubuskie, W Poland 52°37′N 15°27′E
194 J7 **SkyBlu** UK research station Antarctica74°51′N 71°77′W
96 G9 **Skye, Isle of** island NW Scotland, United Kingdom
36 K13 **Sky Harbor** ✈ (Phoenix) Arizona, SW USA 32°26′N 112°00′W
32 I8 **Skykomish** Washington, NW USA 47°40′N 121°20′W
Skylge see Terschelling
63 F19 **Skyring, Peninsula** peninsula S Chile
63 H24 **Skyring, Seno** inlet S Chile
115 H17 **Skyropoúla** var. Skiropoula. island Vóreies Sporádes, Greece, Aegean Sea
115 I17 **Skýros** var. Skíros. Skńyros, Vóreies Sporádes, Greece, Aegean Sea 38°55′N 24°34′E
115 I17 **Skýros** var. Skíros; anc. Scyros. island Vóreies Sporádes, Greece, Aegean Sea
118 J12 **Slabodka** Rus. Slobodka. Vitsyebskaya Voblasts', NW Belarus 55°41′N 27°11′E
95 I23 **Slagelse** Vestsjælland, E Denmark 55°25′N 11°22′E
93 I14 **Slagnäs** Norrbotten, N Sweden 65°36′N 18°10′E
39 T10 **Slana** Alaska, USA 62°46′N 144°00′W
97 F20 **Slaney** Ir. An tSláine. ≈ SE Ireland
116 J13 **Slănic** Prahova, SE Romania 45°14′N 25°58′E
116 K11 **Slănic Moldova** Bacău, E Romania 46°12′N 26°23′E
113 H16 **Slano** Dubrovnik-Neretva, SE Croatia 42°47′N 17°54′E
124 F13 **Slantsy** Leningradskaya Oblast', NW Russian Federation 59°06′N 28°00′E
111 C16 **Slaný** Ger. Schlan. Střední Čechy, NW Czech Republic 50°14′N 14°05′E
111 K16 **Śląskie** ◐ province S Poland
12 C10 **Slate Falls** Ontario, S Canada 51°11′N 91°32′W
27 T4 **Slater** Missouri, C USA 39°13′N 93°04′W
112 H9 **Slatina** Hung. Szlatina; prev. Podravska Slatina. Virovitica-Podravina, NE Croatia 45°40′N 17°46′E
116 I14 **Slatina** Olt, S Romania 45°27′N 24°21′E
25 N5 **Slaton** Texas, SW USA 33°26′N 101°38′W
95 H14 **Slattum** Akershus, S Norway 60°00′N 10°55′E
11 R10 **Slave** ≈ Alberta/Northwest Territories, C Canada
68 E12 **Slave Coast** coastal region W Africa
11 P13 **Slave Lake** Alberta, SW Canada 55°17′N 114°46′W
122 I13 **Slavgorod** Altayskiy Kray, S Russian Federation 52°55′N 78°46′E
Slavgorod see Slawharad
Slavonia see Slavonija
112 G9 **Slavonija** Eng. Slavonia, Ger. Slawonien, Hung. Szlavonia, Szlavonország. cultural region NE Croatia
112 H10 **Slavonski Brod** Ger. Brod, Hung. Bród; prev. Brod, Brod na Savi. Brod-Posavina, NE Croatia 45°09′N 18°00′E
Slavonski Brod-Posavina see Brod-Posavina
116 L4 **Slavuta** Khmel'nyts'ka Oblast', NW Ukraine 50°18′N 26°52′E
117 P2 **Slavutych** Chernihivs'ka Oblast', N Ukraine 51°31′N 30°47′E
123 R15 **Slavyanka** Primorskiy Kray, SE Russian Federation 42°46′N 131°19′E
114 J8 **Slavyanovo** Pleven, N Bulgaria 43°28′N 24°52′E
Slavyansk see Slov"yans'k
126 K14 **Slavyansk-na-Kubani** Krasnodarskiy Kray, SW Russian Federation 45°16′N 38°09′E
119 N20 **Slavyechna** Rus. Slovechna. ≈ Belarus/Ukraine
119 O16 **Slawharad** Rus. Slavgorod. Mahilyowskaya Voblasts', E Belarus 53°27′N 31°00′E
110 G7 **Sławno** Zachodnio-pomorskie, NW Poland 54°23′N 16°43′E
Slawonien see Slavonija
29 S10 **Slayton** Minnesota, N USA 43°59′N 95°45′W
97 N18 **Sleaford** E England, United Kingdom 52°59′N 00°28′W
97 A20 **Slea Head** Ir. Ceann Sléibhe. headland SW Ireland 52°05′N 10°25′W
96 G9 **Sleat, Sound of** strait NW Scotland, United Kingdom
Sledyuki see Slyedzyuki
12 I5 **Sleeper Islands** island group Nunavut, C Canada
31 O6 **Sleeping Bear Point** headland Michigan, N USA 44°54′N 86°02′W
29 T10 **Sleepy Eye** Minnesota, N USA 44°18′N 94°43′W
39 O11 **Sleetmute** Alaska, USA 61°42′N 157°10′W
Sléibhe, Ceann see Slea Head
Slēmānī see As Sulaymānīyah
195 O5 **Slessor Glacier** glacier Antarctica
22 L9 **Slidell** Louisiana, S USA 30°16′N 89°46′W
18 K12 **Slide Mountain** ▲ New York, NE USA 42°00′N 74°23′W
98 I13 **Sliedrecht** Zuid-Holland, C Netherlands 51°50′N 04°46′E
121 P16 **Sliema** N Malta 35°54′N 14°31′E
97 G16 **Slieve Donard** ▲ SE Northern Ireland, United Kingdom 54°10′N 05°57′W
Sligeach see Sligo
97 D16 **Sligo** Ir. Sligeach. Sligo, NW Ireland 54°17′N 08°28′W
97 C16 **Sligo** Ir. Sligeach. cultural region NW Ireland
97 C15 **Sligo Bay** Ir. Cuan Shligigh. inlet NW Ireland
18 B13 **Slippery Rock** Pennsylvania, NE USA 41°02′N 80°02′W
95 P19 **Slite** Gotland, SE Sweden 57°37′N 18°46′E
114 L9 **Sliven** var. Slivno. Sliven, C Bulgaria 42°42′N 26°21′E
114 L10 **Sliven** ◐ province C Bulgaria
114 G9 **Slivnitsa** Sofiya, W Bulgaria 42°51′N 23°01′E
Slivno see Sliven
114 L7 **Slivo Pole** Ruse, N Bulgaria 43°57′N 26°15′E
29 S13 **Sloan** Iowa, C USA 42°13′N 96°13′W
35 X12 **Sloan** Nevada, W USA 35°56′N 115°13′W
Slobodka see Slabodka
125 R14 **Slobodskoy** Kirovskaya Oblast', NW Russian Federation 58°43′N 50°12′E
Slobodzeya see Slobozia
117 O10 **Slobozia** Rus. Slobodzeya. E Moldova 46°45′N 29°42′E
116 L14 **Slobozia** Ialomiţa, SE Romania 44°34′N 27°23′E
98 O5 **Slochteren** Groningen, NE Netherlands 53°13′N 06°48′E
119 H17 **Slonim** Pol. Słonim. Hrodzyenskaya Voblasts', W Belarus 53°06′N 25°19′E
Słonim see Slonim
98 K7 **Sloter Meer** ◎ N Netherlands
Slot, The see New Georgia Sound
97 N22 **Slough** S England, United Kingdom 51°31′N 00°36′W
111 J20 **Slovakia** off. Slovenská Republika, Ger. Slowakei, Hung. Szlovákia, Slvk. Slovensko. ◆ republic C Europe
Slovak Ore Mountains see Slovenské rudohorie
Slovechna see Slavyechna
109 S12 **Slovenia** off. Republic of Slovenia, Ger. Slowenien, Slvn. Slovenija. ◆ republic SE Europe
Slovenia, Republic of see Slovenia
Slovenija see Slovenia
109 V10 **Slovenj Gradec** Ger. Windischgraz. N Slovenia 46°29′N 15°05′E
109 W10 **Slovenska Bistrica** Ger. Windischfeistritz. NE Slovenia 46°21′N 15°27′E
Slovenská Republika see Slovakia
109 W10 **Slovenske Konjice** E Slovenia 46°21′N 15°28′E
111 K20 **Slovenské rudohorie** Eng. Slovak Ore Mountains, Ger. Slowakisches Erzgebirge, Ungarisches Erzgebirge. ▲▲ C Slovakia
Slovensko see Slovakia
117 Y7 **Slov"yanoserbs'k** Luhans'ka Oblast', E Ukraine 48°41′N 39°00′E
117 W6 **Slov"yans'k** Rus. Slavyansk. Donets'ka Oblast', E Ukraine 48°51′N 37°38′E
Slowakei see Slovakia
Slowakisches Erzgebirge see Slovenské rudohorie
Slowenien see Slovenia
110 D11 **Słubice** Ger. Frankfurt. Lubuskie, W Poland 52°20′N 14°35′E
119 K19 **Sluch** Rus. Sluch'. ≈ C Belarus
116 L4 **Sluch** ≈ NW Ukraine
99 D16 **Sluis** Zeeland, SW Netherlands 51°18′N 03°22′E
112 D10 **Slunj** Hung. Szluin. Karlovac, C Croatia 45°06′N 15°35′E
110 I11 **Słupca** Wielkopolskie, C Poland 52°17′N 17°52′E
110 G6 **Słupia** Ger. Stolpe. ≈ NW Poland
110 G6 **Słupsk** Ger. Stolp. Pomorskie, N Poland 54°28′N 17°01′E
119 K18 **Slutsk** Minskaya Voblasts', S Belarus 53°02′N 27°32′E
119 O16 **Slyedzyuki** Rus. Sledyuki. Mahilyowskaya Voblasts', E Belarus 53°35′N 30°22′E
97 A17 **Slyne Head** Ir. Ceann Léime. headland W Ireland 53°25′N 10°11′W
27 U14 **Smackover** Arkansas, C USA 33°21′N 92°43′W
95 L20 **Småland** cultural region S Sweden
95 K20 **Smålandsstenar** Jönköping, S Sweden 57°10′N 13°24′E
Small Malaita see Maramasike
13 O8 **Smallwood Reservoir** ◎ Newfoundland and Labrador, S Canada
119 N14 **Smalyany** Rus. Smolyany. Vitsyebskaya Voblasts', NE Belarus 54°36′N 30°04′E
119 L15 **Smalyavichy** Rus. Smolevichi. Minskaya Voblasts', C Belarus 54°02′N 28°05′E
74 C9 **Smara** var. Es Semara. N Western Sahara 26°45′N 11°44′W
119 I14 **Smarhon'** Pol. Smorgonie, Rus. Smorgon'. Hrodzyenskaya Voblasts', W Belarus 54°29′N 26°24′E
112 M11 **Smederevo** Ger. Semendria. Serbia, N Serbia 44°41′N 20°56′E
112 M12 **Smederevska Palanka** Serbia, C Serbia 44°24′N 20°56′E
95 M14 **Smedjebacken** Dalarna, C Sweden 60°08′N 15°25′E
116 L13 **Smeeni** Buzău, SE Romania 45°00′N 26°52′E
Smela see Smila
107 D16 **Smeralda, Costa** cultural region Sardegna, Italy, C Mediterranean Sea
111 J22 **Śmigiel** Ger. Schmiegel. Wielkopolskie, C Poland 52°02′N 16°33′E
117 Q6 **Smila** Rus. Smela. Cherkas'ka Oblast', C Ukraine 49°15′N 31°54′E
98 N7 **Smilde** Drenthe, NE Netherlands 52°57′N 06°28′E
11 S16 **Smiley** Saskatchewan, S Canada 51°40′N 109°24′W
25 T12 **Smiley** Texas, SW USA 29°16′N 97°38′W
Smilten see Smiltene
118 I8 **Smiltene** Ger. Smilten. Valka, N Latvia 57°25′N 25°53′E
123 T13 **Smirnykh** Ostrov Sakhalin, Sakhalinskaya Oblast', SE Russian Federation 49°43′N 142°48′E
11 Q13 **Smith** Alberta, W Canada 55°06′N 113°57′W
39 P4 **Smith Bay** bay Alaska, NW USA
12 I3 **Smith, Cape** headland Québec, NE Canada 60°50′N 78°06′W
26 L3 **Smith Center** Kansas, C USA 39°46′N 98°46′W
10 K13 **Smithers** British Columbia, SW Canada 54°45′N 127°10′W
21 V10 **Smithfield** North Carolina, SE USA 35°30′N 78°21′W
36 L1 **Smithfield** Utah, W USA 41°50′N 111°49′W
21 X7 **Smithfield** Virginia, NE USA 36°41′N 76°38′W
12 I3 **Smith Island** island Nunavut, C Canada
Smith Island see Sumisu-jima
20 H7 **Smithland** Kentucky, S USA 37°06′N 88°24′W
21 T7 **Smith Mountain Lake** var. Leesville Lake. ▣ Virginia, NE USA
34 L1 **Smith River** California, W USA 41°54′N 124°09′W
33 R9 **Smith River** ≈ Montana, NW USA
14 L13 **Smiths Falls** Ontario, SE Canada 44°54′N 76°01′W
33 N13 **Smiths Ferry** Idaho, NW USA 44°19′N 116°04′W
20 K7 **Smiths Grove** Kentucky, S USA 37°01′N 86°14′W
183 N15 **Smithton** Tasmania, SE Australia 40°54′S 145°06′E
18 L14 **Smithtown** Long Island, New York, NE USA 40°52′N 73°13′W
20 K9 **Smithville** Tennessee, S USA 35°59′N 85°49′W
25 T11 **Smithville** Texas, SW USA 30°04′N 97°32′W
Šmohor see Hermagor
35 Q4 **Smoke Creek Desert** desert Nevada, W USA
11 O14 **Smoky** ≈ Alberta, W Canada
182 E7 **Smoky Bay** South Australia 32°22′S 133°57′E
183 V6 **Smoky Cape** headland New South Wales, SE Australia 30°54′S 153°06′E
26 L4 **Smoky Hill River** ≈ Kansas, C USA
26 L4 **Smoky Hills** hill range Kansas, C USA
11 Q14 **Smoky Lake** Alberta, SW Canada 54°08′N 112°26′W
94 E8 **Smøla** island W Norway
126 H4 **Smolensk** Smolenskaya Oblast', W Russian Federation 54°48′N 32°08′E
126 H4 **Smolenskaya Oblast'** ◐ province W Russian Federation
Smolensk-Moscow Upland see Smolensko-Moskovskaya Vozvyshennost'
126 J3 **Smolensko-Moskovskaya Vozvyshennost'** var. Smolensk-Moscow Upland. ▲▲ W Russian Federation
Smolevichi see Smalyavichy
115 C15 **Smólikas** var. Smolikás. ▲ W Greece 40°06′N 20°54′E
114 I12 **Smolyan** prev. Pashmakli. Smolyan, S Bulgaria 41°34′N 24°42′E
114 I12 **Smolyan** ◐ province S Bulgaria
Smolyany see Smalyany
33 S15 **Smoot** Wyoming, C USA 42°37′N 110°55′W
12 G12 **Smooth Rock Falls** Ontario, S Canada 49°17′N 81°37′W
Smorgon'/Smorgonie see Smarhon'
114 M9 **Smyadovo** Shumen, NE Bulgaria 43°04′N 27°01′E
95 K23 **Smygehamn** Skåne, S Sweden 55°19′N 13°25′E
194 I7 **Smyley Island** island Antarctica
21 Y3 **Smyrna** Delaware, NE USA 39°18′N 75°36′W
23 S3 **Smyrna** Georgia, SE USA 33°52′N 84°30′W
20 J9 **Smyrna** Tennessee, S USA 36°00′N 86°30′W
Smyrna see İzmir
97 I16 **Snaefell** ▲ C Isle of Man 54°15′N 04°29′W
92 H3 **Snaefellsjökull** ▲ W Iceland 64°51′N 23°51′W
92 J3 **Snækollur** ▲ C Iceland 64°38′N 19°18′W

◆ Country
● Country Capital
◇ Dependent Territory
○ Dependent Territory Capital
◐ Administrative Regions
✈ International Airport
▲ Mountain
▲▲ Mountain Range
Volcano
≈ River
◎ Lake
▣ Reservoir

10 J4 **Snake** ≈ Yukon Territory, NW Canada
29 O8 **Snake Creek** ≈ South Dakota, N USA
183 P13 **Snake Island** *island* Victoria, SE Australia
35 Y6 **Snake Range** ▲▲ Nevada, W USA
32 K10 **Snake River** ≈ NW USA
29 V6 **Snake River** ≈ Minnesota, N USA
28 L12 **Snake River** ≈ Nebraska, C USA
33 Q14 **Snake River Plain** *plain* Idaho, NW USA
93 F15 **Snåsa** Nord-Trøndelag, C Norway 64°16´N 12°25´E
21 O8 **Sneedville** Tennessee, S USA 36°31´N 83°13´W
98 K6 **Sneek** Friesland, N Netherlands 53°02´N 05°40´E
Sneeuw-gebergte *see* Maoke, Pegunungan
95 F22 **Snejbjerg** Ringkøbing, C Denmark 56°08´N 08°55´E
124 J3 **Snezhnogorsk** Murmanskaya Oblast', NW Russian Federation 69°12´N 33°20´E
122 K9 **Snezhnogorsk** Taymyrskiy (Dolgano-Nenetskiy) Avtonomnyy Okrug, N Russian Federation 68°06´N 87°37´E
Snezhnoye *see* Snizhne
111 G15 **Sněžka** *Ger.* Schneekoppe, *Pol.* Śnieżka. ▲ N Czech Republic/Poland 50°42´N 15°55´E
110 N8 **Śniardwy, Jezioro** *Ger.* Spirdingsee. ◎ NE Poland
Sniečkus *see* Visaginas
Śnieżka *see* Sněžka
117 R10 **Snihurivka** Mykolayivs'ka Oblast', S Ukraine 47°05´N 32°48´E
116 I5 **Snilov** ✈ (L'viv) L'vivs'ka Oblast', W Ukraine 49°45´N 23°59´E
111 O19 **Snina** *Hung.* Szinna. Prešovský Kraj, E Slovakia 49°N 22°10´E
117 Y8 **Snizhne** *Rus.* Snezhnoye. Donets'ka Oblast', SE Ukraine 48°01´N 38°46´E
94 G10 **Snøhetta** *var.* Snohetta. ▲ S Norway 62°22´N 09°08´E
92 G12 **Snøtinden** ▲ C Norway 66°39´N 13°50´E
97 I18 **Snowdon** ▲ NW Wales, United Kingdom 53°04´N 04°04´W
97 I18 **Snowdonia** ▲▲ NW Wales, United Kingdom
8 K10 **Snowdrift** ≈ Northwest Territories, NW Canada
Snowdrift *see* Łutselk'e
37 N12 **Snowflake** Arizona, SW USA 34°30´N 110°04´W
21 Y5 **Snow Hill** Maryland, NE USA 38°11´N 75°23´W
21 W10 **Snow Hill** North Carolina, SE USA 35°26´N 77°39´W
194 H3 **Snowhill Island** *island* Antarctica
11 V13 **Snow Lake** Manitoba, C Canada 54°56´N 100°02´W
37 R5 **Snowmass Mountain** ▲ Colorado, C USA 39°07´N 107°04´W
18 M10 **Snow, Mount** ▲ Vermont, NE USA 42°56´N 72°52´W
34 M5 **Snow Mountain** ▲ California, W USA 39°44´N 123°01´W
Snow Mountains *see* Maoke, Pegunungan
33 N7 **Snowshoe Peak** ▲ Montana, NW USA 48°15´N 115°44´W
182 I8 **Snowtown** South Australia 33°49´S 138°13´E
36 K1 **Snowville** Utah, W USA 41°59´N 112°42´W
35 X3 **Snow Water Lake** ◎ Nevada, W USA
183 Q11 **Snowy Mountains** ▲▲ New South Wales/Victoria, SE Australia
183 Q12 **Snowy River** ≈ New South Wales/Victoria, SE Australia
44 K5 **Snug Corner** Acklins Island, SE Bahamas 22°31´N 73°51´W
167 T13 **Snuŏl** Krâchéh, E Cambodia 12°04´N 106°26´E
116 J7 **Snyatyn** Ivano-Frankivs'ka Oblast', W Ukraine 48°30´N 25°50´E
26 L12 **Snyder** Oklahoma, C USA 34°37´N 98°56´W
25 O6 **Snyder** Texas, SW USA 32°43´N 100°54´W
172 H3 **Soalala** Mahajanga, W Madagascar 16°05´S 45°21´E
172 J4 **Soanierana-Ivongo** Toamasina, E Madagascar 16°53´S 49°35´E
171 R11 **Soasiu** *var.* Tidore. Pulau Tidore, E Indonesia 0°40´N 127°25´E
54 G8 **Soatá** Boyacá, C Colombia 06°23´N 72°40´W
172 I5 **Soavinandriana** Antananarivo, C Madagascar 19°09´S 46°43´E
77 V13 **Soba** Kaduna, C Nigeria 10°58´N 08°06´E
163 Y16 **Sobaek-sanmaek** ▲▲ S South Korea
80 F13 **Sobat** ≈ E Sudan
171 Z14 **Sobger, Sungai** ≈ Papua, E Indonesia
171 V13 **Sobiei** Papua, E Indonesia 02°31´S 134°30´E
126 M3 **Sobinka** Vladimirskaya Oblast', W Russian Federation 56°00´N 39°55´E
127 S7 **Sobolevo** Orenburgskaya Oblast', W Russian Federation 51°57´N 51°42´E
Soborsin *see* Săvârşin
164 D15 **Sobo-san** ▲ Kyūshū, SW Japan 32°50´N 131°16´E
111 G14 **Sobótka** Dolnośląskie, SW Poland 50°53´N 16°48´E
59 O15 **Sobradinho** Bahia, E Brazil 09°33´S 40°56´W
Sobradinho, Barragem de *see* Sobradinho, Represa de
59 O16 **Sobradinho, Represa de** *var.* Barragem de Sobradinho. ⊠ E Brazil
58 O13 **Sobral** Ceará, E Brazil 03°45´S 40°20´W
105 T4 **Sobrarbe** *physical region* NE Spain
109 R10 **Soča** *It.* Isonzo. ≈ Italy/Slovenia
110 L11 **Sochaczew** Mazowieckie, C Poland 52°15´N 20°15´E
126 L15 **Sochi** Krasnodarskiy Kray, SW Russian Federation 43°35´N 39°46´E
114 G13 **Sochós** *var.* Sohos, Sokhós. Kentrikí Makedonía, N Greece 40°49´N 23°23´E
191 R11 **Société, Archipel de la** *var.* Archipel de Tahiti, Îles de la Société, *Eng.* Society Islands. *island group* W French Polynesia
Société, Îles de la/Society Islands *see* Société, Archipel de la
21 T11 **Society Hill** South Carolina, SE USA 34°28´N 79°54´W
175 W9 **Society Ridge** *undersea feature* C Pacific Ocean
62 I5 **Socompa, Volcán** ⛰ N Chile 24°18´S 68°03´W
Soconusco, Sierra de *see* Madre, Sierra
54 G8 **Socorro** Santander, C Colombia 06°30´N 73°16´W
37 R13 **Socorro** New Mexico, SW USA 33°58´N 106°55´W
Socotra *see* Suquṭrā
167 S14 **Soc Trăng** *var.* Khanh Hung. Soc Trăng, S Vietnam 09°36´N 105°58´E
105 P10 **Socuéllamos** Castilla-La Mancha, C Spain 39°18´N 02°48´W
35 W13 **Soda Lake** *salt flat* California, W USA
92 L11 **Sodankylä** Lappi, N Finland 67°26´N 26°35´E
Sodari *see* Sodiri
33 R15 **Soda Springs** Idaho, NW USA 42°39´N 111°36´W
Soddo/Soddu *see* Sodo
20 L10 **Soddy Daisy** Tennessee, S USA 35°14´N 85°11´W
95 N14 **Söderfors** Uppsala, C Sweden 60°23´N 17°14´E
94 N12 **Söderhamn** Gävleborg, C Sweden 61°19´N 17°10´E
95 N17 **Söderköping** Östergötland, S Sweden 58°28´N 16°20´E
95 N17 **Södermanland** ⬖ *county* C Sweden
95 O16 **Södertälje** Stockholm, C Sweden 59°11´N 17°39´E
80 D10 **Sodiri** *var.* Sawdirī, Sodari. Northern Kordofan, C Sudan 14°23´N 29°06´E
81 I14 **Sodo** *var.* Soddo, Soddu. Southern Nationalities, S Ethiopia 06°49´N 37°43´E
94 N11 **Södra Dellen** ◎ C Sweden
95 M19 **Södra Vi** Kalmar, S Sweden 57°45´N 15°45´E
18 G9 **Sodus Point** *headland* New York, NE USA 43°16´N 76°59´W
171 Q17 **Soe** *prev.* Soë. Timor, C Indonesia 09°51´S 124°29´E
Soebang *see* Subang
Soekaboemi *see* Sukabumi
169 N15 **Soekarno-Hatta** ✈ (Jakarta) Jawa, S Indonesia
Soëla-Sund *see* Soela Väin
118 E5 **Soela Väin** *prev. Eng.* Sele Sound, *Ger.* Dagden-Sund, Soëla-Sund. *strait* W Estonia
Soemba *see* Sumba, Pulau
Soembawa *see* Sumbawa
Soemenep *see* Sumenep
Soengaipenoeh *see* Sungaipenuh
Soerabaja *see* Surabaya
Soerakarta *see* Surakarta
101 G14 **Soest** Nordrhein-Westfalen, W Germany 51°34´N 08°06´E
98 J11 **Soest** Utrecht, C Netherlands 52°10´N 05°20´E
100 F11 **Soeste** ≈ NW Germany
98 J11 **Soesterberg** Utrecht, C Netherlands 52°07´N 05°17´E
115 E16 **Sofádes** *var.* Sofádhes. Thessalía, C Greece 39°20´N 22°06´E
Sofádhes *see* Sofádes
83 N18 **Sofala** Sofala, C Mozambique 20°04´S 34°43´E
83 N17 **Sofala** ⬖ *province* C Mozambique
83 N18 **Sofala, Baia de** *bay* C Mozambique
172 J3 **Sofia** *seasonal river* NW Madagascar
Sofia *see* Sofiya
115 G19 **Sofikó** Pelopónnisos, S Greece 37°46´N 23°04´E
Sofi-Kurgan *see* Sopu-Korgon
114 G10 **Sofiya** *var.* Sophia, *Eng.* Sofia, *Lat.* Serdica. ● (Bulgaria) Sofiya-Grad, W Bulgaria 42°42´N 23°20´E
114 H9 **Sofiya** ⬖ *province* W Bulgaria
114 G9 **Sofiya** ✈ Sofiya-Grad, W Bulgaria 42°42´N 23°26´E
114 G9 **Sofiya, Grad** ⬖ *municipality* W Bulgaria
Sofiyevka *see* Sofiyivka
117 S8 **Sofiyivka** *Rus.* Sofiyevka. Dnipropetrovs'ka Oblast', E Ukraine 48°04´N 33°55´E
123 R12 **Sofiysk** Khabarovskiy Kray, SE Russian Federation 51°32´N 139°46´E
123 R13 **Sofiysk** Khabarovskiy Kray, SE Russian Federation 52°20´N 133°37´E
124 I6 **Sofporog** Respublika Kareliya, NW Russian Federation 65°48´N 31°30´E
115 L23 **Sofraná** *prev.* Záfora. *island* Kykládes, Greece, Aegean Sea
165 Y14 **Sōfu-gan** *island* Izu-shotō, SE Japan
156 K10 **Sog** Xizang Zizhiqu, W China 31°52´N 93°40´E
54 G9 **Sogamoso** Boyacá, C Colombia 05°43´N 72°56´W
136 I11 **Soğanlı Çayı** ≈ N Turkey
94 E12 **Sogn** *physical region* S Norway
Sogndal *see* Sogndalsfjøra
94 E12 **Sogndalsfjøra** *var.* Sogndal. Sogn Og Fjordane, S Norway 61°13´N 07°05´E
95 E18 **Søgne** Vest-Agder, S Norway 58°05´N 07°49´E
94 D12 **Sognefjorden** *fjord* NE North Sea
94 C12 **Sogn Og Fjordane** ⬖ *county* S Norway
162 I11 **Sogo Nur** ◎ N China
159 T12 **Sogruma** Qinghai, W China 32°32´N 100°52´E
163 X17 **Sŏgwip'o** S South Korea 33°14´N 126°33´E
Sohâg *see* Sawhāj
Sohar *see* Şuḩār
64 H9 **Sohm Plain** *undersea feature* NW Atlantic Ocean
100 H7 **Soholmer Au** ≈ N Germany
Sohos *see* Sochós
Sohrau *see* Żory
99 F20 **Soignies** Hainaut, SW Belgium 50°35´N 04°04´E
159 R15 **Soila** Xizang Zizhiqu, W China 30°40´N 97°07´E
103 P4 **Soissons** *anc.* Augusta Suessionum, Noviodunum. Aisne, N France 49°23´N 03°20´E
164 H13 **Sōja** Okayama, Honshū, SW Japan 34°40´N 133°42´E
152 F13 **Sojat** Rājasthān, N India 25°53´N 73°45´E
163 W13 **Sŏjosŏn-man** *inlet* W North Korea
116 I4 **Sokal'** *Rus.* Sokal. L'vivs'ka Oblast', NW Ukraine 50°29´N 24°17´E
163 Y14 **Sokch'o** N South Korea 38°07´N 128°34´E
136 B15 **Söke** Aydın, SW Turkey 37°46´N 27°24´E
189 N12 **Sokehs Island** *island* E Micronesia
79 M24 **Sokele** Katanga, SE Dem. Rep. Congo 09°54´S 24°38´E
147 R11 **Sokh** *Uzb.* Sŭkh. ≈ Kyrgyzstan/Uzbekistan
Sokh *see* So'x
Sokhós *see* Sochós
137 Q8 **Sokhumi** *Rus.* Sukhumi. NW Georgia 43°02´N 41°01´E
113 O14 **Sokobanja** Serbia, E Serbia 43°39´N 21°51´E
77 R15 **Sokodé** C Togo 08°58´N 01°10´E
123 T10 **Sokol** Magadanskaya Oblast', E Russian Federation 59°51´N 150°56´E
124 M13 **Sokol** Vologodskaya Oblast', NW Russian Federation 59°26´N 40°09´E
110 P9 **Sokółka** Podlaskie, NE Poland 53°24´N 23°31´E
76 M11 **Sokolo** Ségou, W Mali 14°43´N 06°02´W
111 A16 **Sokolov** *Ger.* Falkenau an der Eger; *prev.* Falknov nad Ohří. Karlovarský Kraj, W Czech Republic 50°10´N 12°38´E
111 O16 **Sokołów Małopolski** Podkarpackie, SE Poland 50°12´N 22°07´E
110 O11 **Sokołów Podlaski** Mazowieckie, C Poland 52°26´N 22°14´E
76 G11 **Sokone** W Senegal 13°53´N 16°22´W
77 T12 **Sokoto** Sokoto, NW Nigeria 13°05´N 05°16´E
77 T12 **Sokoto** ⬖ *state* NW Nigeria
77 S12 **Sokoto** ≈ NW Nigeria
Sokotra *see* Suquṭrā
147 U7 **Sokuluk** Chuyskaya Oblast', N Kyrgyzstan 42°53´N 74°19´E
116 L7 **Sokyryany** Chernivets'ka Oblast', W Ukraine 48°28´N 27°25´E
95 C16 **Sola** Rogaland, S Norway 58°53´N 05°36´E
187 R12 **Sola** Vanua Lava, N Vanuatu 13°51´S 167°34´E
95 C17 **Sola** ✈ (Stavanger) Rogaland, S Norway 58°54´N 05°36´E
81 H18 **Solai** Rift Valley, W Kenya 0°02´N 36°03´E
152 I8 **Solan** Himāchal Pradesh, N India 30°54´N 77°06´E
185 A25 **Solander Island** *island* SW New Zealand
Solano *see* Bahía Solano
155 F15 **Solāpur** *var.* Sholāpur. Mahārāshtra, W India 17°43´N 75°54´E
93 H16 **Solberg** Västernorrland, C Sweden 63°48´N 17°40´E
116 K9 **Solca** *Ger.* Solka. Suceava, N Romania 47°40´N 25°50´E
105 O16 **Sol, Costa del** *coastal region* S Spain
106 F5 **Solda** *Ger.* Sulden. Trentino-Alto Adige, N Italy 46°33´N 10°35´E
117 N9 **Şoldăneşti** *Rus.* Sholdaneshty. N Moldova 47°49´N 28°45´E
Soldau *see* Wkra
108 L8 **Sölden** Tirol, W Austria 46°58´N 11°01´E
27 P3 **Soldier Creek** ≈ Kansas, C USA
39 R12 **Soldotna** Alaska, USA 60°29´N 151°03´W
110 I10 **Solec Kujawski** Kujawsko-pomorskie, C Poland 53°04´N 18°09´E
61 B16 **Soledad** Santa Fe, C Argentina 30°38´S 60°52´W
55 E4 **Soledad** Atlántico, N Colombia 10°54´N 74°48´W
35 O11 **Soledad** California, W USA 36°25´N 121°19´W
55 O7 **Soledad** Anzoátegui, NE Venezuela 08°10´N 63°36´W
61 H15 **Soledade** Rio Grande do Sul, S Brazil 28°50´S 52°30´W
Isla Soledad *see* East Falkland
103 Y15 **Solenzara** Corse, France, C Mediterranean Sea 41°55´N 09°24´E
Soleure *see* Solothurn
94 C12 **Solheim** Hordaland, S Norway 60°54´N 05°30´E
125 N14 **Soligalich** Kostromskaya Oblast', NW Russian Federation 59°05´N 42°15´E
Soligorsk *see* Salihorsk
97 L20 **Solihull** C England, United Kingdom 52°25´N 01°45´W
125 U13 **Solikamsk** Permskaya Oblast', NW Russian Federation 59°37´N 56°46´E
127 V8 **Sol'-Iletsk** Orenburgskaya Oblast', W Russian Federation 51°09´N 55°05´E
57 G17 **Solimana, Nevado** ▲ S Peru 15°24´S 72°49´W
58 E13 **Solimões, Rio** ≈ C Brazil
113 E14 **Solin** *It.* Salona; *anc.* Salonae. Split-Dalmacija, S Croatia 43°33´N 16°29´E
101 E15 **Solingen** Nordrhein-Westfalen, W Germany 51°10´N 07°05´E
Solka *see* Solca
93 H16 **Sollefteå** Västernorrland, C Sweden 63°09´N 17°15´E
95 O15 **Sollentuna** Stockholm, C Sweden 59°26´N 17°56´E
105 X9 **Sóller** Mallorca, Spain, W Mediterranean Sea 39°46´N 02°42´E
94 L13 **Sollerön** Dalarna, C Sweden 60°55´N 14°34´E
101 I14 **Solling** *hill range* C Germany
95 O16 **Solna** Stockholm, C Sweden 59°22´N 17°58´E
126 K3 **Solnechnogorsk** Moskovskaya Oblast', W Russian Federation 56°07´N 37°04´E
123 R10 **Solnechnyy** Khabarovskiy Kray, SE Russian Federation 50°41´N 136°42´E
123 S13 **Solnechnyy** Respublika Sakha (Yakutiya), NE Russian Federation 60°13´N 137°42´E
Solo *see* Surakarta
107 L17 **Solofra** Campania, S Italy 40°49´N 14°48´E
168 J11 **Solok** Sumatera, W Indonesia 0°45´S 100°42´E
42 C6 **Sololá** Sololá, W Guatemala 14°46´N 91°09´W
42 A2 **Sololá** *off.* Departamento de Sololá. ⬖ *department* SW Guatemala
Sololá, Departamento de *see* Sololá
81 J16 **Sololo** Eastern, N Kenya 03°31´N 38°39´E
42 C4 **Soloma** Huehuetenango, W Guatemala 15°38´N 91°25´W
38 M9 **Solomon** Alaska, USA 64°33´N 164°26´W
27 N4 **Solomon** Kansas, C USA 38°55´N 97°22´W
187 N9 **Solomon Islands** *prev.* British Solomon Islands Protectorate. ◆ *commonwealth republic* W Solomon Islands N Melanesia W Pacific Ocean
186 L7 **Solomon Islands** *island group* Papua New Guinea/Solomon Islands
26 M3 **Solomon River** ≈ Kansas, C USA
186 H8 **Solomon Sea** *sea* W Pacific Ocean
31 U11 **Solon** Ohio, N USA 41°23´N 81°26´W
117 T8 **Solone** Dnipropetrovs'ka Oblast', E Ukraine 48°12´N 34°49´E
171 P16 **Solor, Kepulauan** *island group* S Indonesia
126 M4 **Solotcha** Ryazanskaya Oblast', W Russian Federation 54°43´N 39°50´E
108 D7 **Solothurn** *Fr.* Soleure. Solothurn, NW Switzerland 47°13´N 07°32´E
108 D7 **Solothurn** *Fr.* Soleure. ⬖ *canton* NW Switzerland
124 J7 **Solovetskiye Ostrova** *island group* NW Russian Federation
105 V5 **Solsona** Cataluña, NE Spain 42°00´N 01°31´E
113 E14 **Šolta** *It.* Solta. *island* S Croatia
Solṭānābād *see* Kāshmar
142 L4 **Solṭānīyeh** Zanjān, NW Iran 36°24´N 48°50´E
100 I11 **Soltau** Niedersachsen, NW Germany 52°59´N 09°50´E
124 G14 **Sol'tsy** Novgorodskaya Oblast', W Russian Federation 58°09´N 30°23´E
Soltūstik Qazaqstan Oblysy *see* Severnyy Kazakhstan
Solun *see* Thessaloníki
113 O19 **Solunska Glava** ▲ C FYR Macedonia 41°43´N 21°24´E
95 L22 **Sölvesborg** Blekinge, S Sweden 56°04´N 14°35´E
97 J15 **Solway Firth** *inlet* England/Scotland, United Kingdom
82 I13 **Solwezi** North Western, NW Zambia 12°11´S 26°23´E
165 Q11 **Sōma** Fukushima, Honshū, C Japan 37°49´N 140°52´E
136 C13 **Soma** Manisa, W Turkey 39°10´N 27°36´E
81 O15 **Somalia** *off.* Somali Democratic Republic, *Som.* Jamuuriyada Demuqraadiga Soomaaliyeed, Soomaaliya; *prev.* Italian Somaliland, Somaliland Protectorate. ◆ *republic* E Africa
173 N6 **Somali Basin** *undersea feature* W Indian Ocean 0°00´N 52°00´E
Somali Democratic Republic *see* Somalia
80 N12 **Somaliland** ⬖ *disputed territory* N Somalia
Somaliland Protectorate *see* Somalia
67 Y8 **Somali Plain** *undersea feature* W Indian Ocean 01°00´N 51°30´E
112 J8 **Sombor** *Hung.* Zombor. Vojvodina, NW Serbia 45°46´N 19°07´E
99 H20 **Sombreffe** Namur, S Belgium 50°32´N 04°39´E
40 L10 **Sombrerete** Zacatecas, C Mexico 23°38´N 103°40´W
45 V8 **Sombrero** *island* N Anguilla
151 Q21 **Sombrero Channel** *channel* Nicobar Islands, India
116 H9 **Şomcuta Mare** *Hung.* Nagysomkút; *prev.* Somcuţa Mare. Maramureş, N Romania 47°29´N 23°30´E
Somcuţa Mare *see* Şomcuta Mare
167 R9 **Somdet** Kalasin, E Thailand 16°41´N 103°44´E
99 L15 **Someren** Noord-Brabant, SE Netherlands 51°23´N 05°42´E
93 L19 **Somero** Länsi-Suomi, SW Finland 60°37´N 23°30´E
33 P7 **Somers** Montana, NW USA 48°04´N 114°16´W
64 A12 **Somerset** *var.* Somerset Village. W Bermuda 32°18´N 64°53´W
37 Q5 **Somerset** Colorado, C USA 38°55´N 107°27´W
20 M7 **Somerset** Kentucky, S USA 37°05´N 84°36´W
19 O12 **Somerset** Massachusetts, NE USA 41°46´N 71°07´W
97 K23 **Somerset** *cultural region* SW England, United Kingdom
Somerset East *see* Somerset-Oos
64 A12 **Somerset Island** *island* W Bermuda
197 N9 **Somerset Island** *island* Queen Elizabeth Islands, Nunavut, NW Canada
Somerset Nile *see* Victoria Nile
83 I25 **Somerset-Oos** *var.* Somerset East. Eastern Cape, S South Africa 32°44´S 25°35´E
Somerset Village *see* Somerset
83 E26 **Somerset-Wes** *var.* Somerset West. Western Cape, SW South Africa 34°05´S 18°51´E
Somerset West *see* Somerset-Wes
Somers Islands *see* Bermuda
18 J17 **Somers Point** New Jersey, NE USA 39°18´N 74°34´W
19 P9 **Somersworth** New Hampshire, NE USA 43°15´N 70°52´W
36 H15 **Somerton** Arizona, SW USA 32°36´N 114°42´W
18 J14 **Somerville** New Jersey, NE USA 40°34´N 74°36´W
20 F10 **Somerville** Tennessee, S USA 35°14´N 89°24´W
25 U10 **Somerville** Texas, SW USA 30°21´N 96°31´W
25 T10 **Somerville Lake** ⊠ Texas, SW USA
Someş/Somesch/Someşul *see* Szamos
103 N2 **Somme** ⬖ *department* N France
103 N2 **Somme** ≈ N France
95 L18 **Sommen** Jönköping, S Sweden 58°07´N 14°58´E
95 M18 **Sommen** ◎ S Sweden
101 K16 **Sömmerda** Thüringen, C Germany 51°10´N 11°07´E
Sommerein *see* Šamorín
Sommerfeld *see* Lubsko
55 Y11 **Sommet Tabulaire** *var.* Mont Itoupé. ▲▲ S French Guiana
111 H25 **Somogy** *off.* Somogy Megye. ⬖ *county* SW Hungary
Somogy Megye *see* Somogy
Somorja *see* Šamorín
105 N7 **Somosierra, Puerto de** *pass* N Spain
187 Y14 **Somosomo** Taveuni, N Fiji 16°46´S 179°57´W
42 I9 **Somotillo** Chinandega, NW Nicaragua 13°01´N 86°53´W
42 I8 **Somoto** Madriz, NW Nicaragua 13°29´N 86°36´W
110 I11 **Sompolno** Wielkopolskie, C Poland 52°24´N 18°30´E
102 J17 **Somport, Col du** *var.* Puerto de Somport, *Sp.* Somport; *anc.* Summus Portus. *pass* France/Spain *see also* Somport
99 K15 **Son** Noord-Brabant, S Netherlands 51°32´N 05°34´E
95 H15 **Son** Akershus, S Norway 59°32´N 10°42´E
154 L9 **Son** *var.* Sone. ≈ C India
43 R16 **Soná** Veraguas, W Panama 08°00´N 81°20´W
Sonag *see* Zêkog
154 M12 **Sonapur** *prev.* Sonepur. Orissa, E India 20°50´N 83°58´E
95 G24 **Sønderborg** *Ger.* Sonderburg. Sønderjylland, SW Denmark 54°55´N 09°48´E
Sonderburg *see* Sønderborg
95 F24 **Sønderjylland** *var.* Sønderjyllands Amt. ⬖ *county* SW Denmark
Sønderjyllands Amt *see* Sønderjylland
101 K15 **Sondershausen** Thüringen, C Germany 51°22´N 10°52´E
Sondre Strømfjord *see* Kangerlussuaq
106 E6 **Sondrio** Lombardia, N Italy 46°11´N 09°52´E
Sone *see* Son
Sonepur *see* Sonapur
57 K22 **Sonequera** ▲ S Bolivia 22°06´S 67°10´W
167 V12 **Sông Câu** Phu Yên, C Vietnam 13°26´N 109°12´E
167 R15 **Sông Đốc** Minh Hai, S Vietnam 09°03´N 104°51´E
81 H25 **Songea** Ruvuma, S Tanzania 10°42´S 35°39´E
163 X10 **Songhua Hu** ◎ NE China
163 Y7 **Songhua Jiang** *var.* Sungari. ≈ NE China
161 S8 **Songjiang** Shanghai Shi, E China 31°01´N 121°14´E
Sŏngjin *see* Kimch'aek
167 O16 **Songkhla** *var.* Songkla, *Mal.* Singora. Songkhla, SW Thailand 07°12´N 100°35´E
Songkla *see* Songkhla
163 T13 **Song Ling** ▲▲ NE China
129 U12 **Sŏng Ma** *Laos* Ma, Nam. ≈ Laos/Vietnam
163 W14 **Songnim** SW North Korea 38°43´N 125°40´E
82 B10 **Songo** Uíge, NW Angola 07°30´S 14°56´E
83 M15 **Songo** Tete, NW Mozambique 15°36´S 32°45´E
79 F21 **Songololo** Bas-Congo, SW Dem. Rep. Congo 05°40´S 14°05´E
160 H7 **Songpan** *var.* Jin'an, *Tib.* Sungpu. Sichuan, C China 32°49´N 103°39´E
163 Y17 **Sŏngsan** S South Korea
161 R11 **Songxi** Fujian, SE China 27°33´N 118°46´E
160 M6 **Songxian** *var.* Song Xian. Henan, C China 34°11´N 112°04´E
Song Xian *see* Songxian
161 R10 **Songyang** *var.* Xiping; *prev.* Songyin. Zhejiang, SE China 28°29´N 119°27´E
Songyin *see* Songyang
163 V9 **Songyuan** *var.* Fu-yü, Petuna; *prev.* Fuyu. Jilin, NE China 45°10´N 124°52´E
Sonid Youqi *see* SaihanTal
Sonid Zuoqi *see* Mandalt
152 I10 **Sonīpat** Haryāna, N India 29°00´N 77°01´E
93 M15 **Sonkajärvi** Itä-Suomi, C Finland 63°40´N 27°30´E
167 R6 **Sơn La** Sơn La, N Vietnam 21°20´N 103°55´E
149 O16 **Sonmiāni** Baluchistān, S Pakistan 25°24´N 66°37´E
149 O16 **Sonmiāni Bay** *bay* S Pakistan
101 K18 **Sonneberg** Thüringen, C Germany 50°22´N 11°10´E
101 N24 **Sonntagshorn** ▲ Austria/Germany 47°40´N 12°42´E
Sonoita *see* Sonoyta
40 E3 **Sonoita, Rio** *var.* Río Sonoyta. ≈ Mexico/USA
35 N7 **Sonoma** California, W USA 38°16´N 122°28´W
35 T3 **Sonoma Peak** ▲ Nevada, W USA 40°50´N 117°34´W
35 P8 **Sonora** California, W USA 37°58´N 120°22´W
25 O10 **Sonora** Texas, SW USA 30°34´N 100°39´W
40 F5 **Sonora** ⬖ *state* NW Mexico
35 X17 **Sonoran Desert** *var.* Desierto de Altar. *desert* Mexico/USA *see also* Altar, Desierto de
40 G5 **Sonora, Río** ≈ NW Mexico
40 E2 **Sonoyta** *var.* Sonoita. Sonora, NW Mexico 31°49´N 112°50´W
Sonoyta, Río *see* Sonoita, Rio
142 K6 **Sonqor** *var.* Sunqur. Kermānshāhān, W Iran 34°45´N 47°39´E
105 N9 **Sonseca** *var.* Sonseca con Casalgordo. Castilla-La Mancha, C Spain 39°40´N 03°59´W
Sonseca con Casalgordo *see* Sonseca
54 E9 **Sonsón** Antioquia, W Colombia 05°45´N 75°18´W
42 E7 **Sonsonate** Sonsonate, W El Salvador 13°44´N 89°43´W
42 A9 **Sonsonate** ⬖ *department* SW El Salvador
188 A10 **Sonsorol Islands** *island group* S Palau
112 J9 **Sonta** *Hung.* Szond; *prev.* Szonta. Vojvodina, NW Serbia 45°34´N 19°06´E
167 S6 **Sơn Tây** *var.* Sontay. Ha Tây, N Vietnam 21°06´N 105°32´E
Sontay *see* Sơn Tây
101 J25 **Sonthofen** Bayern, S Germany 47°31´N 10°16´E
Soochow *see* Suzhou
80 O13 **Sool** *off.* Gobolka Sool. ⬖ *region* N Somalia
Soomaaliya/Soomaaliyeed, Jamuuriyada Demuqraadiga *see* Somalia
Soome Laht *see* Finland, Gulf of
23 V5 **Soperton** Georgia, SE USA 32°22´N 82°35´W
167 S6 **Sop Hao** Houaphan, N Laos 20°33´N 104°25´E
Sophia *see* Sofiya
171 S10 **Sopi** Pulau Morotai, E Indonesia 02°36´N 128°32´E
Sopianae *see* Pécs
171 U13 **Sopinusa** Papua, E Indonesia 03°31´S 132°55´E
81 B14 **Sopo** ≈ W Sudan
Sopockinie/Sopotskin/Sopotskino *see* Sapotskin
114 I9 **Sopot** Plovdiv, C Bulgaria 42°39´N 24°43´E
110 I7 **Sopot** *Ger.* Zoppot. Pomorskie, N Poland 54°26´N 18°33´E
167 O8 **Sop Prap** *var.* Ban Sop Prap. Lampang, NW Thailand 17°55´N 99°20´E
111 G22 **Sopron** *Ger.* Ödenburg. Győr-Moson-Sopron, NW Hungary 47°40´N 16°35´E
147 U11 **Sopu-Korgon** *var.* Sofi-Kurgan. Oshskaya Oblast', SW Kyrgyzstan 40°03´N 73°30´E
152 H5 **Sopur** Jammu and Kashmir, NW India 34°19´N 74°30´E
107 J15 **Sora** Lazio, C Italy 41°43´N 13°37´E
154 N13 **Sorada** Orissa, E India 19°46´N 84°29´E
93 H17 **Söråker** Västernorrland, C Sweden 62°32´N 17°32´E
57 J17 **Sorata** La Paz, W Bolivia 15°47´S 68°38´W
Sorau/Sorau in der Niederlausitz *see* Żary
105 Q14 **Sorbas** Andalucía, S Spain 37°06´N 02°06´W
Sord/Sórd Choluim Chille *see* Swords
15 O11 **Sorel** Québec, SE Canada 46°03´N 73°06´W
183 P17 **Sorell** Tasmania, SE Australia 42°49´S 147°34´E
183 O17 **Sorell, Lake** ◎ Tasmania, SE Australia
106 E8 **Soresina** Lombardia, N Italy 45°17´N 09°51´E
95 D14 **Sørfjorden** *fjord* S Norway
94 N11 **Sörforsa** Gävleborg, C Sweden 61°45´N 17°00´E
103 R14 **Sorgues** Vaucluse, SE France 44°N 04°52´E
136 K13 **Sorgun** Yozgat, C Turkey 39°49´N 35°10´E
105 P5 **Soria** Castilla-León, N Spain 41°47´N 02°26´W
105 P6 **Soria** ⬖ *province* Castilla-León, N Spain
61 D19 **Soriano** Soriano, SW Uruguay 33°25´S 58°21´W
61 D19 **Soriano** ⬖ *department* SW Uruguay
92 O4 **Sørkapp** *headland* SW Svalbard 76°34´N 16°33´E
143 T5 **Sorkh, Kūh-e** ▲▲ NE Iran
95 I23 **Sorø** Vestsjælland, E Denmark 55°26´N 11°34´E
Soro *see* Ghazal, Bahr el
116 M8 **Soroca** *Rus.* Soroki. N Moldova 48°10´N 28°18´E
60 L10 **Sorocaba** São Paulo, S Brazil 23°29´S 47°27´W
Sorochino *see* Sarochyna
127 T7 **Sorochinsk** Orenburgskaya Oblast', W Russian Federation 52°26´N 53°10´E
Soroki *see* Soroca
188 H15 **Sorol** *atoll* Caroline Islands, W Micronesia
171 T12 **Sorong** Papua, E Indonesia 0°49´S 131°16´E
81 G17 **Soroti** C Uganda 01°42´N 33°37´E
Sørøy *see* Sørøya
92 J8 **Sørøya** *var.* Sørøy, *Lapp.* Sállan. *island* N Norway
104 G11 **Sorraia, Rio** ≈ C Portugal
92 I10 **Sørreisa** Troms, N Norway 69°08´N 18°09´E
107 K18 **Sorrento** *anc.* Surrentum. Campania, S Italy 40°37´N 14°23´E
104 H10 **Sor, Ribeira de** *stream* C Portugal
195 T3 **Sør Rondane** ▲▲ Antarctica
93 H14 **Sorsele** Västerbotten, N Sweden 65°31´N 17°34´E
107 B17 **Sorso** Sardegna, Italy, C Mediterranean Sea 40°46´N 08°33´E
171 P4 **Sorsogon** Luzon, N Philippines 12°57´N 124°04´E
105 U4 **Sort** Cataluña, NE Spain 42°25´N 01°07´E
124 H11 **Sortavala** *prev.* Serdobol'. Respublika Kareliya, NW Russian Federation 61°45´N 30°37´E
107 L25 **Sortino** Sicilia, Italy, C Mediterranean Sea 37°10´N 15°02´E
92 G10 **Sortland** Nordland, C Norway 68°44´N 15°25´E
94 G9 **Sør-Trøndelag** ⬖ *county* S Norway
95 I15 **Sørumsand** Akershus, S Norway 59°58´N 11°13´E
118 D6 **Sõrve Säär** *headland* SW Estonia 57°54´N 22°02´E
95 K22 **Sösdala** Skåne, S Sweden 56°00´N 13°36´E
105 R4 **Sos del Rey Católico** Aragón, NE Spain 42°30´N 01°13´W
93 F15 **Sösjöfjällen** ▲ C Sweden 63°51´N 13°15´E
126 K7 **Sosna** ≈ W Russian Federation
62 H12 **Sosneado, Cerro** ▲ W Argentina 34°44´S 69°52´W
125 S9 **Sosnogorsk** Respublika Komi, NW Russian Federation 63°33´N 53°55´E
124 J8 **Sosnovets** Respublika Kareliya, NW Russian Federation 64°25´N 34°23´E
Sosnovets *see* Sosnowiec
127 Q3 **Sosnovka** Chuvashskaya Respublika, W Russian Federation 56°18´N 47°14´E
125 S16 **Sosnovka** Kirovskaya Oblast', NW Russian Federation 56°15´N 51°20´E
124 M6 **Sosnovka** Murmanskaya Oblast', NW Russian Federation 66°28´N 40°31´E
126 M6 **Sosnovka** Tambovskaya Oblast', W Russian Federation 53°14´N 41°19´E
124 H12 **Sosnovo** *Fin.* Rautu. Leningradskaya Oblast', NW Russian Federation 60°30´N 30°13´E
124 G13 **Sosnovyy Bor** Leningradskaya Oblast', NW Russian Federation 59°53´N 29°07´E
127 V3 **Sosnovyy Bor** Respublika Bashkortostan, W Russian Federation 55°51´N 57°09´E
Sosnovyy Bor *see* Sasnovy Bor
111 J16 **Sosnowiec** *Ger.* Sosnowitz, *Rus.* Sosnovets. Śląskie, S Poland 50°16´N 19°07´E
Sosnowitz *see* Sosnowiec
117 R2 **Sosnytsya** Chernihivs'ka Oblast', N Ukraine 51°31´N 32°30´E
109 V10 **Šoštanj** N Slovenia 46°23´N 15°03´E
122 G10 **Sos'va** Sverdlovskaya Oblast', C Russian Federation 59°13´N 61°58´E
54 D12 **Sotará, Volcán** ⛰ S Colombia 02°04´N 76°40´W
76 D10 **Sotavento, Ilhas de** *var.* Leeward Islands. *island group* S Cape Verde
93 N15 **Sotkamo** Oulu, C Finland 64°06´N 28°30´E
109 W11 **Sotla** ≈ E Slovenia
41 P10 **Soto la Marina** Tamaulipas, C Mexico 23°44´N 98°10´W
41 P10 **Soto la Marina, Río** ≈ C Mexico
95 B14 **Sotra** *island* S Norway
41 X12 **Sotuta** Yucatán, SE Mexico 20°34´N 89°00´W
79 F17 **Souanké** Sangha, NW Congo 02°03´N 14°02´E
76 M17 **Soubré** S Ivory Coast 05°50´N 06°35´W
115 H24 **Soúda** *var.* Soúdha, *Eng.* Suda. Kríti, Greece, E Mediterranean Sea 35°29´N 24°04´E
Soúdha *see* Soúda
Soueida *see* As Suwaydā'
114 L12 **Souflí** *prev.* Souflíon. Anatolikí Makedonía kai Thráki, NE Greece 41°12´N 26°18´E
Souflíon *see* Souflí
45 S11 **Soufrière** W Saint Lucia 13°51´N 61°03´W
45 X6 **Soufrière** ⛰ Basse Terre, S Guadeloupe 16°03´N 61°39´W
102 M13 **Souillac** Lot, S France 44°53´N 01°29´E
173 Y17 **Souillac** S Mauritius 20°31´S 57°31´E
74 M5 **Souk Ahras** NE Algeria 36°14´N 08°00´E
Souk el Arba du Rharb/Souk-el-Arba-du-Rharb/Souk-el-Arba-el-Rhab *see* Souk-el-Arba-Rharb
74 E6 **Souk-el-Arba-Rharb** *var.* Souk el Arba du Rharb, Souk-el-Arba-du-Rharb, Souk-el-Arba-el-Rhab. NW Morocco 34°38´N 06°00´W
Soukhné *see* As Sukhnah
163 X14 **Sŏul** *off.* Sŏul-t'ŭkpyŏlsi, *Eng.* Seoul, *Jap.* Keijō; *prev.* Kyŏngsŏng. ● (South Korea) NW South Korea 37°30´N 126°58´E
102 J11 **Soulac-sur-Mer** Gironde, SW France 45°31´N 01°06´W
Sŏul-t'ŭkpyŏlsi *see* Sŏul
99 L19 **Soumagne** Liège, E Belgium 50°36´N 05°48´E
18 M14 **Sound Beach** Long Island, New York, NE USA 40°56´N 72°58´W
95 J22 **Sound, The** *Dan.* Øresund, *Swe.* Öresund. *strait* Denmark/Sweden
115 H20 **Soúnio, Akrotírio** *headland* C Greece 37°39´N 24°01´E
138 F8 **Soûr** *var.* Şūr; *anc.* Tyre. SW Lebanon 33°18´N 35°30´E
Sources, Mont-aux- *see* Phofung
104 G8 **Soure** Coimbra, N Portugal 40°04´N 08°38´W
11 W17 **Souris** Manitoba, S Canada 49°38´N 100°17´W
13 Q14 **Souris** Prince Edward Island, SE Canada 46°22´N 62°16´W

◆ Country
● Country Capital
◇ Dependent Territory
○ Dependent Territory Capital
⬖ Administrative Regions
✈ International Airport
▲ Mountain
▲▲ Mountain Range
⛰ Volcano
≈ River
◎ Lake
⊠ Reservoir

28 L2 **Souris River** var. Mouse River. Canada/USA
25 X10 **Sour Lake** Texas, SW USA 30°08′N 94°24′W
115 F17 **Soúrpi** Thessalía, C Greece 39°07′N 22°55′E
104 H11 **Sousel** Portalegre, C Portugal 38°57′N 07°40′W
75 N6 **Sousse** var. Súsah. NE Tunisia 35°46′N 10°38′E
14 H11 **South** Ontario, S Canada
South see Sud
83 G23 **South Africa** off. Republic of South Africa, Afr. Suid-Afrika. ◆ republic S Africa
South Africa, Republic of see South Africa
46-47 **South America** continent
2 J17 **South American Plate** tectonic feature
97 M23 **Southampton** hist. Hamwih, Lat. Clausentum. S England, United Kingdom 50°54′N 01°23′W
19 N14 **Southampton** Long Island, New York, NE USA 40°52′N 72°22′W
9 P8 **Southampton Island** island Nunavut, NE Canada
151 P20 **South Andaman** island Andaman Islands, India, NE Indian Ocean
13 Q6 **South Aulatsivik Island** island Newfoundland and Labrador, E Canada
182 E4 **South Australia** state S Australia
South Australian Abyssal Plain see South Australian Plain
192 G11 **South Australian Basin** undersea feature SW Indian Ocean 38°00′S 126°00′E
173 X12 **South Australian Plain** var. South Australian Abyssal Plain. undersea feature SE Indian Ocean
37 R13 **South Baldy** ▲ New Mexico, SW USA 33°59′N 107°11′W
23 Y14 **South Bay** Florida, SE USA 26°39′N 80°43′W
14 E12 **South Baymouth** Manitoulin Island, Ontario, S Canada 45°33′N 82°01′W
30 L10 **South Beloit** Illinois, N USA 42°29′N 89°02′W
31 O11 **South Bend** Indiana, N USA 41°40′N 86°15′W
25 R6 **South Bend** Texas, SW USA 32°58′N 98°39′W
32 F9 **South Bend** Washington, NW USA 46°38′N 123°48′W
South Beveland see Zuid-Beveland
South Borneo see Kalimantan Selatan
21 U7 **South Boston** Virginia, NE USA 36°42′N 78°58′W
182 F2 **South Branch Neales** seasonal river South Australia
21 U3 **South Branch Potomac River** West Virginia, NE USA
185 H19 **Southbridge** Canterbury, South Island, New Zealand 43°49′S 172°17′E
19 N12 **Southbridge** Massachusetts, NE USA 42°03′N 72°00′W
183 P17 **South Bruny Island** island Tasmania, SE Australia
18 L7 **South Burlington** Vermont, NE USA 44°27′N 73°08′W
44 M6 **South Caicos** island S Turks and Caicos Islands
South Cape see Ka Lae
23 V3 **South Carolina** off. State of South Carolina, also known as The Palmetto State. state SE USA
South Carpathians see Carpații Meridionalii
South Celebes see Sulawesi Selatan
21 Q5 **South Charleston** West Virginia, NE USA 38°22′N 81°42′W
192 D7 **South China Basin** undersea feature SE South China Sea 15°00′N 115°00′E
169 R8 **South China Sea** Chin. Nan Hai, Ind. Laut Cina Selatan, Vtn. Biên Đông. sea SE Asia
33 Z10 **South Dakota** off. State of South Dakota, also known as The Coyote State, Sunshine State. state N USA
23 X10 **South Daytona** Florida, SE USA 29°09′N 81°01′W
37 R10 **South Domingo Pueblo** New Mexico, SW USA 35°28′N 106°24′W
97 N23 **South Downs** hill range SE England, United Kingdom
83 I21 **South East** district SE Botswana
65 H15 **South East Bay** bay Ascension Island, C Atlantic Ocean
183 O17 **South East Cape** headland Tasmania, SE Australia 43°36′S 146°52′E
38 K10 **Southeast Cape** headland Saint Lawrence Island, Alaska, USA 62°56′N 169°39′W
South-East Celebes see Sulawesi Tenggara
192 G12 **Southeast Indian Ridge** undersea feature Indian Ocean/Pacific Ocean 50°00′S 110°00′E
Southeast Island see Tagula Island
193 P13 **Southeast Pacific Basin** var. Belling Hausen Mulde. undersea feature SE Pacific Ocean 60°00′S 115°00′W
65 H15 **South East Point** headland SE Ascension Island
183 O14 **South East Point** headland Victoria, S Australia 39°10′S 146°21′E
44 L5 **Southeast Point** headland Mayaguana, SE Bahamas 22°15′N 72°44′W
191 Z3 **Southeast Point** headland Kiritimati, NE Kiribati 01°42′N 157°10′W
South-East Sulawesi see Sulawesi Tenggara
11 U12 **Southend** Saskatchewan, C Canada 56°20′N 103°14′W
97 P22 **Southend-on-Sea** E England, United Kingdom 51°33′N 00°43′E
83 H20 **Southern** var. Bangwaketse, Ngwaketze. district SE Botswana
138 E13 **Southern** district S Israel
83 N15 **Southern** region S Malawi
155 J26 **Southern** province S Sri Lanka
83 I15 **Southern** province S Zambia
185 E19 **Southern Alps** ▲ South Island, New Zealand
190 K15 **Southern Cook Islands** island group S Cook Islands
180 K12 **Southern Cross** Western Australia 31°17′S 119°15′E
80 A12 **Southern Darfur** state W Sudan
186 B7 **Southern Highlands** province W Papua New Guinea
11 V11 **Southern Indian Lake** Manitoba, C Canada
80 E11 **Southern Kordofan** state C Sudan
187 Z15 **Southern Lau Group** island group Lau Group, SE Fiji
81 I15 **Southern Nationalities** region S Ethiopia
173 S13 **Southern Ocean** ocean
21 T10 **Southern Pines** North Carolina, SE USA 35°10′N 79°23′W
96 I13 **Southern Uplands** S Scotland, United Kingdom
Southern Urals see Yuzhnyy Ural
183 P16 **South Esk River** Tasmania, SE Australia
11 U16 **Southey** Saskatchewan, S Canada 50°53′N 104°27′W
27 V2 **South Fabius River** Missouri, C USA
31 S10 **Southfield** Michigan, N USA 42°28′N 83°12′W
192 K10 **South Fiji Basin** undersea feature S Pacific Ocean 26°00′S 175°00′E
97 Q22 **South Foreland** headland SE England, United Kingdom 51°08′N 01°22′E
35 P7 **South Fork American River** California, W USA
28 K7 **South Fork Grand River** South Dakota, N USA
35 T12 **South Fork Kern River** California, W USA
39 Q7 **South Fork Koyukuk River** Alaska, USA
39 Q11 **South Fork Kuskokwim River** Alaska, USA
26 H2 **South Fork Republican River** C USA
26 L3 **South Fork Solomon River** Kansas, C USA
31 P5 **South Fox Island** island Michigan, N USA
20 G8 **South Fulton** Tennessee, S USA 36°28′N 88°53′W
195 U10 **South Geomagnetic Pole** pole Antarctica
65 J20 **South Georgia** island South Georgia and the South Sandwich Islands, SW Atlantic Ocean
65 K21 **South Georgia and the South Sandwich Islands** UK Dependent Territory SW Atlantic Ocean
47 Y14 **South Georgia Ridge** var. North Scotia Ridge. undersea feature SW Atlantic Ocean 54°00′S 40°00′W
181 Q1 **South Goulburn Island** island Northern Territory, N Australia
153 U16 **South Hatia Island** island SE Bangladesh
31 O10 **South Haven** Michigan, N USA 42°24′N 86°16′W
21 V7 **South Hill** Virginia, NE USA 36°43′N 78°07′W
South Holland see Zuid-Holland
21 P8 **South Holston Lake** Tennessee/Virginia, S USA
175 N1 **South Honshu Ridge** undersea feature W Pacific Ocean
26 M6 **South Hutchinson** Kansas, C USA 38°01′N 97°56′W
151 K21 **South Huvadhu Atoll** atoll S Maldives
173 U14 **South Indian Basin** undersea feature Indian Ocean/Pacific Ocean 60°00′S 120°00′E
11 W11 **South Indian Lake** Manitoba, C Canada 56°48′N 98°56′W
81 I17 **South Island** island NW Kenya
185 C20 **South Island** island S New Zealand
South Kalimantan see Kalimantan Selatan
South Kazakhstan see Yuzhnyy Kazakhstan
163 X15 **South Korea** off. Republic of Korea, Kor. Taehan Min'guk. ◆ republic E Asia
35 Q6 **South Lake Tahoe** California, W USA 38°56′N 119°57′W
25 N6 **Southland** Texas, SW USA 33°16′N 101°31′W
185 B23 **Southland** off. Southland Region. region South Island, New Zealand
Southland Region see Southland
29 N15 **South Loup River** Nebraska, C USA
151 K19 **South Maalhosmadulu Atoll** atoll N Maldives
14 E15 **South Maitland** Ontario, S Canada
192 E8 **South Makassar Basin** undersea feature E Java Sea
31 O6 **South Manitou Island** island Michigan, N USA
151 K18 **South Miladhunmadulu Atoll** var. Noonu. atoll N Maldives
21 X8 **South Mills** North Carolina, SE USA 36°28′N 76°18′W
8 H9 **South Nahanni** Northwest Territories, NW Canada
39 P13 **South Naknek** Alaska, USA 58°39′N 157°01′W
14 M13 **South Nation** Ontario, SE Canada
44 F9 **South Negril Point** headland W Jamaica 18°14′N 78°21′W
151 K20 **South Nilandhe Atoll** var. Dhaalu Atoll. atoll C Maldives
36 L2 **South Ogden** Utah, W USA 41°09′N 111°58′W
18 M14 **Southold** Long Island, New York, NE USA 41°03′N 72°24′W
194 H1 **South Orkney Islands** island group Antarctica
137 S9 **South Ossetia** former autonomous region SW Georgia
South Pacific Basin see Southwest Pacific Basin
19 P7 **South Paris** Maine, NE USA 44°14′N 70°33′W
189 U13 **South Pass** passage Chuuk Islands, C Micronesia
33 U15 **South Pass** pass Wyoming, C USA
20 K10 **South Pittsburg** Tennessee, S USA 35°00′N 85°42′W
28 K15 **South Platte River** Colorado/Nebraska, C USA
31 T16 **South Point** Ohio, N USA 38°25′N 82°35′W
65 G15 **South Point** headland S Ascension Island
31 R6 **South Point** headland Michigan, N USA 44°51′N 83°17′W
South Point see Ka Lae
195 Q9 **South Pole** pole Antarctica
183 P17 **Southport** Tasmania, SE Australia 43°26′S 146°57′E
97 K17 **Southport** NW England, United Kingdom 53°39′N 03°01′W
21 V12 **Southport** North Carolina, SE USA 33°55′N 78°00′W
19 P8 **South Portland** Maine, NE USA 43°38′N 70°14′W
14 H12 **South River** Ontario, S Canada 45°50′N 79°23′W
21 U11 **South River** North Carolina, SE USA
96 K5 **South Ronaldsay** island NE Scotland, United Kingdom
36 L2 **South Salt Lake** Utah, W USA 40°42′N 111°52′W
65 L21 **South Sandwich Islands** island group SW Atlantic Ocean
65 K21 **South Sandwich Trench** undersea feature SW Atlantic Ocean 56°30′S 25°00′W
11 S16 **South Saskatchewan** Alberta/Saskatchewan, S Canada
65 I21 **South Scotia Ridge** undersea feature S Scotia Sea
11 V10 **South Seal** Manitoba, C Canada
194 G4 **South Shetland Islands** island group Antarctica
65 H22 **South Shetland Trough** undersea feature Atlantic Ocean/Pacific Ocean 61°00′S 59°30′W
97 M14 **South Shields** NE England, United Kingdom 55°N 01°25′W
29 R13 **South Sioux City** Nebraska, C USA 42°28′N 96°24′W
192 J9 **South Solomon Trench** undersea feature W Pacific Ocean
183 V3 **South Stradbroke Island** island Queensland, E Australia
South Sulawesi see Sulawesi Selatan
South Sumatra see Sumatera Selatan
184 K11 **South Taranaki Bight** bight SE Tasman Sea
South Tasmania Plateau see Tasman Plateau
36 M15 **South Tucson** Arizona, SW USA 32°11′N 110°56′W
12 H9 **South Twin Island** island Nunavut, C Canada
96 E9 **South Uist** island NW Scotland, United Kingdom
149 R8 **South Waziristān** federally administered tribal area NW Pakistan
South-West see Sud-Ouest
South-West Africa/South West Africa see Namibia
65 F15 **South West Bay** bay Ascension Island, C Atlantic Ocean
183 N18 **South West Cape** headland Tasmania, SE Australia 43°34′S 146°01′E
185 B26 **South West Cape** headland Stewart Island, New Zealand 47°15′S 167°28′E
38 J10 **Southwest Cape** headland Saint Lawrence Island, Alaska, USA 63°19′N 171°27′W
Southwest Indian Ocean Ridge see Southwest Indian Ridge
173 N11 **Southwest Indian Ridge** var. Southwest Indian Ocean Ridge. undersea feature SW Indian Ocean 43°00′S 40°00′E
192 L10 **Southwest Pacific Basin** var. South Pacific Basin. undersea feature SE Pacific Ocean 40°00′S 150°00′W
44 H2 **Southwest Point** headland Great Abaco, N Bahamas 25°50′N 77°12′W
191 X3 **South West Point** headland Kiritimati, NE Kiribati 01°53′N 157°34′E
65 G25 **South West Point** headland SW Saint Helena 16°00′S 05°48′W
25 P5 **South Wichita River** Texas, SW USA
97 Q20 **Southwold** E England, United Kingdom 52°15′N 01°36′E
19 Q12 **South Yarmouth** Massachusetts, NE USA 41°38′N 70°09′W
116 J10 **Sovata** Hung. Szováta. Mureș, C Romania 46°36′N 25°04′E
107 N22 **Soverato** Calabria, SW Italy 38°40′N 16°31′E
121 O4 **Sovereign Base Area** uk military installation S Cyprus
Sovetabad see Ghafurov
126 C2 **Sovetsk** Ger. Tilsit. Kaliningradskaya Oblast', W Russian Federation 55°04′N 21°52′E
125 Q15 **Sovetsk** Kirovskaya Oblast', NW Russian Federation 57°37′N 49°02′E
127 N10 **Sovetskaya** Rostovskaya Oblast', SW Russian Federation 49°00′N 42°09′E
127 P3 **Sovetskiy** Respublika Mariy El, W Russian Federation 56°45′N 48°30′E
Sovetskoye see Ketchenery
146 I15 **Sovet"yab** prev. Sovet"yap. Ahal Welaýaty, S Turkmenistan 36°29′N 61°13′E
Sovet"yap see Sovet"yab
117 U12 **Sovyets'kyy** Respublika Krym, S Ukraine 45°20′N 34°54′E
83 I18 **Sowa** var. Sua. Central, NE Botswana 20°33′S 26°18′E
83 I18 **Sowa Pan** var. Sua Pan. salt lake NE Botswana
83 J21 **Soweto** Gauteng, NE South Africa 26°08′S 27°54′E
147 R11 **So'x** Rus. Sokh. Farg'ona Viloyati, E Uzbekistan 39°56′N 71°10′E
Sōya-kaikyō see La Perouse Strait
165 T1 **Sōya-misaki** headland Hokkaidō, NE Japan 45°31′N 141°55′E
125 N7 **Soyana** NW Russian Federation
146 A8 **Soye, Mys** var. Mys Suz. headland NW Turkmenistan 41°47′N 52°27′E
82 A10 **Soyo** Dem. Rep. Congo, NW Angola 06°07′S 12°18′E
80 J10 **Soyra** ▲ C Eritrea 14°46′N 39°29′E
Sozaq see Suzak
119 P16 **Sozh** NE Europe
114 N10 **Sozopol** prev. Sizebolu; anc. Apollonia. Burgas, E Bulgaria 42°25′N 27°42′E
99 L20 **Spa** Liège, E Belgium 50°29′N 05°52′E
194 I7 **Spaatz Island** island Antarctica
144 M14 **Space Launching Centre** space station Kzylorda, S Kazakhstan
105 O7 **Spain** off. Kingdom of Spain, Sp. España; anc. Hispania, Iberia, Lat. Hispana. ◆ monarchy SW Europe
Spain, Kingdom of see Spain
Spalato see Split
97 O19 **Spalding** E England, United Kingdom 52°49′N 00°06′W
14 D11 **Spanish** Ontario, S Canada 46°12′N 82°21′W
36 L3 **Spanish Fork** Utah, W USA 40°09′N 111°40′W
64 B12 **Spanish Point** headland C Bermuda 32°18′N 64°49′W
14 E9 **Spanish River** Ontario, S Canada
44 K13 **Spanish Town** hist. St.Iago de la Vega. C Jamaica 18°N 76°57′W
Spánta, Akrotírio see Spátha, Akrotírio
35 Q5 **Sparks** Nevada, W USA 39°32′N 119°45′W
Sparnacum see Épernay
95 N16 **Sparreholm** Södermanland, C Sweden 59°04′N 16°51′E
23 U4 **Sparta** Georgia, SE USA 33°16′N 82°58′W
30 K16 **Sparta** Illinois, N USA 38°07′N 89°42′W
31 P9 **Sparta** Michigan, N USA 43°09′N 85°42′W
21 R8 **Sparta** North Carolina, SE USA 36°30′N 81°07′W
20 L9 **Sparta** Tennessee, S USA 35°55′N 85°30′W
30 I7 **Sparta** Wisconsin, N USA 43°57′N 90°50′W
Sparta see Spárti
21 Q11 **Spartanburg** South Carolina, SE USA 34°56′N 81°57′W
115 F21 **Spárti** Eng. Sparta. Pelopónnisos, S Greece 37°05′N 22°25′E
107 B21 **Spartivento, Capo** headland Sardegna, Italy, C Mediterranean Sea 38°52′N 08°50′E
11 P17 **Sparwood** British Columbia, SW Canada 49°45′N 114°45′W
126 J4 **Spas-Demensk** Kaluzhskaya Oblast', W Russian Federation 54°22′N 34°16′E
126 M4 **Spas-Klepiki** Ryazanskaya Oblast', W Russian Federation 55°08′N 40°15′E
Spasovo see Kulen Vakuf
123 R15 **Spassk-Dal'niy** Primorskiy Kray, SE Russian Federation 44°34′N 132°52′E
126 M5 **Spassk-Ryazanskiy** Ryazanskaya Oblast', W Russian Federation 54°25′N 40°21′E
115 H19 **Spáta** Attikí, C Greece 37°58′N 23°55′E
121 Q11 **Spátha, Akrotírio** var. Akrotírio Spánta. headland Kríti, Greece, E Mediterranean Sea 35°42′N 23°44′E
Špatrjan see Paternion
28 I9 **Spearfish** South Dakota, N USA 44°29′N 103°51′W
25 O1 **Spearman** Texas, SW USA 36°12′N 101°13′W
65 C25 **Speedwell Island** island S Falkland Islands
65 G25 **Speery Island** island S Saint Helena
45 N14 **Speightstown** NW Barbados 13°15′N 59°39′W
106 I13 **Spello** Umbria, C Italy 43°00′N 12°41′E
39 R12 **Spenard** Alaska, USA 61°09′N 150°03′W
Spence Bay see Taloyoak
31 O14 **Spencer** Indiana, N USA 39°18′N 86°46′W
29 T12 **Spencer** Iowa, C USA 43°09′N 95°07′W
29 P12 **Spencer** Nebraska, C USA 42°52′N 98°42′W
21 S9 **Spencer** North Carolina, SE USA 35°41′N 80°26′W
20 L9 **Spencer** Tennessee, S USA 35°46′N 85°27′W
21 Q4 **Spencer** West Virginia, NE USA 38°48′N 81°22′W
30 K6 **Spencer** Wisconsin, N USA 44°46′N 90°17′W
182 G10 **Spencer, Cape** headland South Australia 35°17′S 136°52′E
39 V13 **Spencer, Cape** headland Alaska, USA 58°12′N 136°39′W
182 H9 **Spencer Gulf** gulf South Australia
18 F9 **Spencerport** New York, NE USA 43°11′N 77°48′W
31 Q12 **Spencerville** Ohio, N USA 40°42′N 84°21′W
115 E17 **Spercheiáda** var. Sperhiada, Sperkhiás. Stereá Ellás, C Greece 38°54′N 22°07′E
115 E17 **Spercheiós** C Greece
Sperhiada see Spercheiáda
95 G14 **Sperillen** S Norway
Sperkhiás see Spercheiáda
101 I18 **Spessart** hill range C Germany
Spétsai see Spétses
115 G21 **Spétses** prev. Spétsai. Spétses, S Greece 37°16′N 23°09′E
115 G21 **Spétses** island S Greece
96 J8 **Spey** NE Scotland, United Kingdom
101 G20 **Speyer** Eng. Spires; anc. Civitas Nemetum, Spira. Rheinland-Pfalz, SW Germany 49°18′N 08°26′E
101 G20 **Speyerbach** W Germany
107 N20 **Spezzano Albanese** Calabria, SW Italy 39°40′N 16°17′E
Spice Islands see Maluku
100 F9 **Spiekeroog** island NW Germany
109 W9 **Spielfeld** Steiermark, SE Austria 46°43′N 15°36′E
65 N21 **Spiess Seamount** undersea feature S Atlantic Ocean 53°00′S 02°00′W
108 E9 **Spiez** Bern, W Switzerland 46°42′N 07°41′E
98 G13 **Spijkenisse** Zuid-Holland, SW Netherlands 51°52′N 04°19′E
39 T6 **Spike Mountain** ▲ Alaska, USA 67°42′N 141°39′W
115 I25 **Spíli** Kríti, Greece, E Mediterranean Sea 35°12′N 24°33′E
108 D10 **Spillgerten** ▲ W Switzerland 46°34′N 07°25′E
118 F9 **Spilva** ✕ (Riga) Rīga, C Latvia 56°55′N 24°03′E
107 N17 **Spinazzola** Puglia, SE Italy 40°58′N 16°06′E
149 O9 **Spīn Būldak** Kandahār, S Afghanistan 31°01′N 66°23′E
Spira see Speyer
Spirdingsee see Śniardwy, Jezioro
Spires see Speyer
29 T11 **Spirit Lake** Iowa, C USA 43°25′N 95°06′W
29 T11 **Spirit Lake** Iowa, C USA
11 N13 **Spirit River** Alberta, W Canada 55°46′N 118°51′W
11 S14 **Spiritwood** Saskatchewan, S Canada 53°18′N 107°33′W
27 R11 **Spiro** Oklahoma, C USA 35°14′N 94°37′W
111 L19 **Spišská Nová Ves** Ger. Neudorf, Zipser Neudorf, Hung. Igló. Košický Kraj, E Slovakia 48°58′N 20°35′E
137 T11 **Spitak** NW Armenia 40°51′N 44°17′E
92 O2 **Spitsbergen** island NW Svalbard
Spittal see Spittal an der Drau
109 R9 **Spittal an der Drau** var. Spittal. Kärnten, S Austria 46°48′N 13°30′E
109 V3 **Spitz** Niederösterreich, NE Austria 48°24′N 15°22′E
94 D9 **Spjelkavik** Møre og Romsdal, S Norway 62°28′N 06°22′E
25 W10 **Splendora** Texas, SW USA 30°13′N 95°09′W
113 E14 **Split** It. Spalato. Split-Dalmacija, S Croatia 43°31′N 16°27′E
113 E14 **Split** ✕ Split-Dalmacija, S Croatia 43°33′N 16°19′E
113 E14 **Split-Dalmacija** off. Splitsko-Dalmatinska Županija. province S Croatia
11 X12 **Split Lake** Manitoba, C Canada
Splitsko-Dalmatinska Županija see Split-Dalmacija
108 H10 **Splügen** Graubünden, S Switzerland 46°33′N 09°18′E
Spodnji Dravograd see Dravograd
25 P12 **Spofford** Texas, SW USA 29°10′N 100°24′W
118 J11 **Špoģi** Daugvapils, SE Latvia 56°03′N 26°47′E
32 L8 **Spokane** Washington, NW USA 47°40′N 117°26′W
32 L8 **Spokane River** Washington, NW USA
106 I13 **Spoleto** Umbria, C Italy 42°44′N 12°44′E
30 I4 **Spooner** Wisconsin, N USA 45°51′N 91°49′W
30 K12 **Spoon River** Illinois, N USA
21 W5 **Spotsylvania** Virginia, NE USA 38°12′N 77°35′W
32 L8 **Sprague** Washington, NW USA 47°19′N 117°55′W
170 J5 **Spratly Island** island SW Spratly Islands
192 E6 **Spratly Islands** Chin. Nansha Qundao. ◇ disputed territory SE Asia
32 J12 **Spray** Oregon, NW USA 44°30′N 119°38′W
112 I11 **Spreča** N Bosnia and Herzegovina
100 P13 **Spree** E Germany
100 P13 **Spreewald** wetland NE Germany
101 P14 **Spremberg** Brandenburg, E Germany 51°34′N 14°22′E
25 W11 **Spring** Texas, SW USA 30°03′N 95°24′W
31 Q10 **Spring Arbor** Michigan, N USA 42°12′N 84°33′W
83 E23 **Springbok** Northern Cape, W South Africa 29°44′S 17°56′E
18 I15 **Spring City** Pennsylvania, NE USA 40°10′N 75°33′W
20 L9 **Spring City** Tennessee, S USA 35°41′N 84°51′W
36 L4 **Spring City** Utah, W USA 39°28′N 111°30′W
35 W3 **Spring Creek** Nevada, W USA 40°45′N 115°40′W
27 S9 **Springdale** Arkansas, C USA 36°11′N 94°07′W
31 Q14 **Springdale** Ohio, N USA 39°17′N 84°29′W
100 I13 **Springe** Niedersachsen, N Germany 52°13′N 09°33′E
37 U9 **Springer** New Mexico, SW USA 36°21′N 104°35′W
37 W7 **Springfield** Colorado, C USA 37°24′N 102°36′W
23 W5 **Springfield** Georgia, SE USA 32°21′N 81°20′W
30 K14 **Springfield** state capital Illinois, N USA 39°48′N 89°39′W
20 L6 **Springfield** Kentucky, S USA 37°42′N 85°18′W
18 M12 **Springfield** Massachusetts, NE USA 42°06′N 72°32′W
29 T10 **Springfield** Minnesota, N USA 44°15′N 94°58′W
27 T7 **Springfield** Missouri, C USA 37°13′N 93°18′W
31 R13 **Springfield** Ohio, N USA 39°55′N 83°49′W
32 G13 **Springfield** Oregon, NW USA 44°03′N 123°01′W
29 Q12 **Springfield** South Dakota, N USA 42°51′N 97°54′W
20 J8 **Springfield** Tennessee, S USA 36°30′N 86°54′W
18 M9 **Springfield** Vermont, NE USA 43°18′N 72°27′W
30 K14 **Springfield, Lake** Illinois, N USA
55 T8 **Spring Garden** NE Guyana 06°58′N 58°34′W
30 K8 **Spring Green** Wisconsin, N USA 43°10′N 90°02′W
29 X11 **Spring Grove** Minnesota, N USA 43°33′N 91°38′W
13 P15 **Springhill** Nova Scotia, SE Canada 45°40′N 64°04′W
23 V12 **Spring Hill** Florida, SE USA 28°28′N 82°36′W
27 R4 **Spring Hill** Kansas, C USA 38°44′N 94°49′W
22 G4 **Springhill** Louisiana, S USA 33°01′N 93°27′W
20 I9 **Spring Hill** Tennessee, S USA 35°46′N 86°55′W
21 U10 **Spring Lake** North Carolina, SE USA 35°10′N 78°58′W
24 M4 **Springlake** Texas, SW USA 34°13′N 102°18′W
35 W11 **Spring Mountains** Nevada, W USA
27 W9 **Spring River** Arkansas/Missouri, C USA
27 S7 **Spring River** Missouri/Oklahoma, C USA
83 J21 **Springs** Gauteng, NE South Africa 26°16′S 28°26′E
185 H16 **Springs Junction** West Coast, South Island, New Zealand 42°21′S 172°11′E
181 X8 **Springsure** Queensland, E Australia 24°09′S 148°06′E
29 W11 **Spring Valley** Minnesota, N USA 43°41′N 92°23′W
18 K13 **Spring Valley** New York, NE USA 41°10′N 73°58′W
29 N12 **Springview** Nebraska, C USA 42°49′N 99°45′W
18 D11 **Springville** New York, NE USA 42°27′N 78°52′W
36 L3 **Springville** Utah, W USA 40°10′N 111°36′W
Sprottau see Szprotawa
15 V4 **Sproule, Pointe** headland Québec, SE Canada 49°47′N 67°02′W
11 Q14 **Spruce Grove** Alberta, SW Canada 53°36′N 113°55′W
21 T4 **Spruce Knob** ▲ West Virginia, NE USA 38°40′N 79°37′W
35 X3 **Spruce Mountain** ▲ Nevada, W USA 40°33′N 114°46′W
21 P9 **Spruce Pine** North Carolina, SE USA 35°55′N 82°03′W
98 G13 **Spui** SW Netherlands
107 O19 **Spulico, Capo** headland S Italy 39°57′N 16°38′E
25 O5 **Spur** Texas, SW USA 33°28′N 100°51′W
97 O17 **Spurn Head** headland E England, United Kingdom 53°34′N 00°06′E
99 H20 **Spy** Namur, S Belgium 50°29′N 04°43′E
95 I15 **Spydeberg** Østfold, S Norway 59°36′N 11°04′E
185 J17 **Spy Glass Point** headland South Island, New Zealand 42°33′S 173°31′E
10 L17 **Squamish** British Columbia, SW Canada 49°41′N 123°11′W
19 O8 **Squam Lake** New Hampshire, NE USA
19 S2 **Squa Pan Mountain** ▲ Maine, NE USA 46°36′N 68°09′W
39 N16 **Squaw Harbor** Unga Island, Alaska, USA 55°12′N 160°41′W
14 E11 **Squaw Island** island Ontario, S Canada
107 O22 **Squillace, Golfo di** gulf S Italy
107 Q18 **Squinzano** Puglia, SE Italy 40°26′N 18°03′E
Sráid na Cathrach see Milltown Malbay
167 S11 **Srâlau** Stœng Trêng, N Cambodia 14°03′N 105°46′E
Srath an Urláir see Stranorlar
112 G10 **Srbac** Republika Srpska, N Bosnia and Herzegovina
Srbija see Serbia
Srbinje see Foča
112 K9 **Srbobran** var. Bácsszenttamás, Hung. Szenttamás. Vojvodina, N Serbia 45°33′N 19°46′E
Srbobran see Donji Vakuf
167 R13 **Srê Âmběl** Kaôh Kông, SW Cambodia 11°07′N 103°46′E
112 K13 **Srebrenica** Republika Srpska, E Bosnia and Herzegovina 44°04′N 19°18′E
112 I11 **Srebrenik** Federacija Bosna I Hercegovina, NE Bosnia and Herzegovina 44°42′N 18°30′E
114 K10 **Sredets** prev. Syulemeshlii. Stara Zagora, C Bulgaria 42°16′N 25°40′E
114 M10 **Sredets** prev. Grudovo. Burgas, E Bulgaria
114 M10 **Sredetska Reka** SE Bulgaria
123 U9 **Sredinnyy Khrebet** E Russian Federation
114 N7 **Sredishte** Rom. Beibunar; prev. Knyazhevo. Dobrich, NE Bulgaria 43°51′N 27°30′E
114 I10 **Sredna Gora** C Bulgaria
123 R7 **Srednekolymsk** Respublika Sakha (Yakutiya), NE Russian Federation 67°28′N 153°52′E
126 K7 **Sredne-Russkaya Vozvyshennost'** Eng. Central Russian Upland. W Russian Federation
122 L9 **Srednesibirskoye Ploskogor'ye** var. Central Siberian Uplands, Eng. Central Siberian Plateau. N Russian Federation
125 V13 **Sredniy Ural** NW Russian Federation
167 T12 **Srê Khtŭm** Môndól Kiri, E Cambodia 12°10′N 106°52′E
110 G12 **Śrem** Wielkopolskie, C Poland 52°07′N 17°00′E
112 K10 **Sremska Mitrovica** prev. Mitrovica, Ger. Mitrowitz. Vojvodina, NW Serbia 44°58′N 19°37′E
167 R11 **Srêng, Stœng** NW Cambodia
167 R11 **Srê Noy** Siĕmréab, NW Cambodia 13°47′N 104°03′E
Srepok, Sông see Srêpôk, Tônle
167 T12 **Srêpôk, Tônle** var. Sông Srepok. Cambodia/Vietnam
123 P13 **Sretensk** Chitinskaya Oblast', S Russian Federation 52°14′N 117°33′E
169 R10 **Sri Aman** Sarawak, East Malaysia 01°13′N 111°25′E
117 R4 **Sribne** Chernihivs'ka Oblast', N Ukraine 50°40′N 32°55′E
Sri Jayawardanapura see Sri Jayewardanapura Kotte
155 I25 **Sri Jayewardanapura Kotte** var. Sri Jayawardanapura. Western Province, W Sri Lanka 06°54′N 79°58′E
155 M14 **Srīkākulam** Andhra Pradesh, E India 18°18′N 83°54′E
155 J25 **Sri Lanka** off. Democratic Socialist Republic of Sri Lanka; prev. Ceylon. ◆ republic S Asia
130 F14 **Sri Lanka** island S Asia
Sri Lanka, Democratic Socialist Republic of see Sri Lanka
153 V14 **Srimangal** Sylhet, E Bangladesh 24°19′N 91°40′E
Sri Mohangorh see Shri Mohangarh
152 H5 **Srīnagar** state capital Jammu and Kashmir, N India 34°07′N 74°50′E
167 N10 **Srinagarind Reservoir** W Thailand
155 F19 **Sringeri** Karnātaka, W India 13°26′N 75°13′E
155 K25 **Sri Pada** Eng. Adam's Peak. ▲ S Sri Lanka 06°49′N 80°25′E
Sri Saket see Si Sa Ket
111 G14 **Środa Śląska** Ger. Neumarkt. Dolnośląskie, SW Poland 51°10′N 16°30′E
110 H12 **Środa Wielkopolska** Wielkopolskie, C Poland 52°13′N 17°17′E
Srpska Kostajnica see Bosanska Kostajnica
113 G14 **Srpska, Republika** republic Bosnia and Herzegovina
Srpski Brod see Bosanski Brod
Ssu-ch'uan see Sichuan
Ssu-p'ing/Ssu-p'ing-chieh see Siping
Stablo see Stavelot
99 G15 **Stabroek** Antwerpen, N Belgium 51°21′N 04°22′E
Stackeln see Strenči
96 I5 **Stack Skerry** island N Scotland, United Kingdom
100 I9 **Stade** Niedersachsen, NW Germany 53°36′N 09°29′E
94 C10 **Stadlandet** peninsula S Norway
109 R5 **Stadl-Paura** Oberösterreich, NW Austria 48°05′N 13°52′E
119 L20 **Stadolichy** Rus. Stodolichi. Homyel'skaya Voblasts', SE Belarus 51°44′N 28°30′E
98 P7 **Stadskanaal** Groningen, NE Netherlands 53°N 06°55′E
101 H16 **Stadtallendorf** Hessen, C Germany 50°49′N 09°01′E
101 K23 **Stadtbergen** Bayern, S Germany 48°21′N 10°50′E
108 G7 **Stäfa** Zürich, NE Switzerland 47°14′N 08°45′E
95 K23 **Staffanstorp** Skåne, S Sweden 55°38′N 13°13′E
101 K18 **Staffelstein** Bayern, C Germany 50°05′N 11°00′E
97 L19 **Stafford** C England, United Kingdom 52°48′N 02°07′W
26 L6 **Stafford** Kansas, C USA 37°57′N 98°36′W
21 W4 **Stafford** Virginia, NE USA 38°26′N 77°27′W
97 L19 **Staffordshire** cultural region C England, United Kingdom
19 N12 **Stafford Springs** Connecticut, NE USA 41°57′N 72°18′W
115 H14 **Stágira** Kentrikí Makedonía, N Greece 40°31′N 23°46′E
118 G7 **Staicele** Limbaži, N Latvia 57°52′N 24°48′E
Ştaierdorf-Anina see Anina
109 V8 **Stainz** Steiermark, SE Austria 46°55′N 15°18′E
Stájerlakanina see Anina
117 Y7 **Stakhanov** Luhans'ka Oblast', E Ukraine 48°30′N 38°42′E
108 E11 **Stalden** Valais, SW Switzerland 46°12′N 07°55′E
15 S8 **St-Alexandre** Québec, SE Canada 47°39′N 69°36′W
Stalin see Varna
Stalinabad see Dushanbe
Stalingrad see Volgograd
Staliniri see Ts'khinvali
Stalino see Donets'k
Stalinobod see Dushanbe
Stalinov Štít see Gerlachovský štít
Stalinsk see Novokuznetsk
Stalins'kaya Oblast' see Donets'ka Oblast'
Stalinski Zaliv see Varnenski Zaliv
Stalin, Yazovir see Iskŭr, Yazovir
111 N15 **Stalowa Wola** Podkarpackie, SE Poland 50°35′N 22°02′E
114 I11 **Stamboliyski** Plovdiv, C Bulgaria 42°09′N 24°32′E
114 J8 **Stamboliyski, Yazovir** N Bulgaria
15 Q7 **St-Ambroise** Québec, SE Canada 48°35′N 71°19′W
97 N19 **Stamford** E England, United Kingdom 52°39′N 00°32′W

18 L14 **Stamford** Connecticut, NE USA 41°03′N 73°32′W
25 P6 **Stamford** Texas, SW USA 32°55′N 99°49′W
25 Q6 **Stamford, Lake** ⊡ Texas, SW USA
108 I10 **Stampa** Graubünden, SE Switzerland 46°21′N 09°35′E
Stampalia *see* Astypálaia
27 T14 **Stamps** Arkansas, C USA 33°22′N 93°30′W
92 G11 **Stamsund** Nordland, C Norway 68°07′N 13°50′E
27 R2 **Stanberry** Missouri, C USA 40°12′N 94°33′W
195 O3 **Stancomb-Wills Glacier** *glacier* Antarctica
83 K21 **Standerton** Mpumalanga, E South Africa 26°57′S 29°14′E
31 R7 **Standish** Michigan, N USA 43°59′N 83°58′W
20 M6 **Stanford** Kentucky, S USA 37°30′N 84°40′W
33 S9 **Stanford** Montana, NW USA 47°08′N 110°15′W
95 P19 **Stånga** Gotland, SE Sweden 57°16′N 18°30′E
94 I13 **Stange** Hedmark, S Norway 60°40′N 11°05′E
83 L23 **Stanger** KwaZulu/Natal, E South Africa 29°20′S 31°18′E
Stanimaka *see* Asenovgrad
Stanislau *see* Ivano-Frankivs'k
35 P8 **Stanislaus River** ≈ California, W USA
Stanislav *see* Ivano-Frankivs'k
Stanislavskaya Oblast' *see* Ivano-Frankivs'ka Oblast'
Stanisławów *see* Ivano-Frankivs'k
Stanke Dimitrov *see* Dupnitsa
183 O15 **Stanley** Tasmania, SE Australia 40°48′S 145°18′E
65 E24 **Stanley** *var.* Port Stanley, Puerto Argentino. ○ (Falkland Islands) East Falkland, Falkland Islands 51°45′S 57°56′W
33 O13 **Stanley** Idaho, NW USA 44°12′N 114°58′W
28 L3 **Stanley** North Dakota, N USA 48°19′N 102°23′W
21 U4 **Stanley** Virginia, NE USA 38°34′N 78°30′W
30 J6 **Stanley** Wisconsin, N USA 44°58′N 90°54′W
79 G21 **Stanley Pool** *var.* Pool Malebo. ◎ Congo/Dem. Rep. Congo
155 H20 **Stanley Reservoir** ⊡ S India
Stanleyville *see* Kisangani
42 G3 **Stann Creek** ◐ *district* SE Belize
Stann Creek *see* Dangriga
123 Q12 **Stanovoy Khrebet** ▲▲ SE Russian Federation
108 F8 **Stans** Unterwalden, C Switzerland 46°57′N 08°23′E
97 O21 **Stansted** ✈ (London) Essex, E England, United Kingdom 51°53′N 00°16′E
183 U4 **Stanthorpe** Queensland, E Australia 28°35′S 151°52′E
21 N6 **Stanton** Kentucky, S USA 37°51′N 83°51′W
31 Q8 **Stanton** Michigan, N USA 43°19′N 85°04′W
29 Q14 **Stanton** Nebraska, C USA 41°57′N 97°13′W
28 L5 **Stanton** North Dakota, N USA 47°19′N 101°22′W
25 N7 **Stanton** Texas, SW USA 32°07′N 101°47′W
32 H7 **Stanwood** Washington, NW USA 48°14′N 122°22′W
117 Y7 **Stanychno-Luhans'ke** Luhans'ka Oblast', E Ukraine 48°39′N 39°30′E
108 K7 **Stanzach** Tirol, W Austria 47°24′N 10°36′E
98 M9 **Staphorst** Overijssel, E Netherlands 52°38′N 06°12′E
14 D18 **Staples** Ontario, S Canada 42°09′N 82°34′W
29 T6 **Staples** Minnesota, N USA 46°21′N 94°47′W
28 M14 **Stapleton** Nebraska, C USA 41°29′N 100°40′W
25 S8 **Star** Texas, SW USA 31°27′N 98°16′W
111 M14 **Starachowice** Świętokrzyskie, C Poland 51°04′N 21°02′E
Stara Kanjiža *see* Kanjiža
111 M18 **Stará Ľubovňa** *Ger.* Altlublau, *Hung.* Ólubló. Prešovský Kraj, E Slovakia 49°19′N 20°40′E
112 L10 **Stara Pazova** *Ger.* Altpasua, *Hung.* Ópazova. Vojvodina, N Serbia 44°59′N 20°10′E
Stara Planina *see* Balkan Mountains
114 L9 **Stara Reka** ≈ C Bulgaria
116 M5 **Stara Synyava** Khmel'nyts'ka Oblast', W Ukraine 49°39′N 27°39′E
116 I2 **Stara Vyzhivka** Volyns'ka Oblast', NW Ukraine 51°27′N 24°25′E
Staraya Belitsa *see* Staraya Byelitsa
119 M14 **Staraya Byelitsa** *Rus.* Staraya Belitsa. Vitsyebskaya Voblasts', NE Belarus 54°42′N 29°38′E
127 R5 **Staraya Mayna** Ul'yanovskaya Oblast', W Russian Federation 54°36′N 48°57′E
119 O18 **Staraya Rudnya** Homyel'skaya Voblasts', SE Belarus 52°50′N 30°17′E
124 H14 **Staraya Russa** Novgorodskaya Oblast', W Russian Federation 57°59′N 31°18′E
114 K10 **Stara Zagora** *Lat.* Augusta Trajana. Stara Zagora, C Bulgaria 42°26′N 25°39′E
114 K10 **Stara Zagora** ◐ *province* C Bulgaria
29 S8 **Starbuck** Minnesota, N USA 45°36′N 95°31′W
191 W4 **Starbuck Island** *prev.* Volunteer Island. *island* E Kiribati
27 V13 **Star City** Arkansas, C USA 33°56′N 91°52′W
112 F13 **Staretina** ▲▲ W Bosnia and Herzegovina
Stargard in Pommern *see* Stargard Szczeciński
110 E9 **Stargard Szczeciński** *Ger.* Stargard in Pommern. Zachodnio-pomorskie, NW Poland 53°20′N 15°02′E
187 N10 **Star Harbour** *harbour* San Cristobal, SE Solomon Islands
Stari Bečej *see* Bečej
113 F15 **Stari Grad** *It.* Cittavecchia. Split-Dalmacija, S Croatia 43°11′N 16°36′E
124 J16 **Staritsa** Tverskaya Oblast', W Russian Federation 56°28′N 34°51′E
23 V9 **Starke** Florida, SE USA 29°56′N 82°07′W
22 M4 **Starkville** Mississippi, S USA 33°27′N 88°49′W
186 B7 **Star Mountains** *Ind.* Pegunungan Sterren. ▲▲ Indonesia/Papua New Guinea
101 L23 **Starnberg** Bayern, SE Germany 48°00′N 11°19′E
101 L24 **Starnberger See** ◎ SE Germany
Starobel'sk *see* Starobil's'k
117 X8 **Starobesheve** Donets'ka Oblast', E Ukraine 47°45′N 38°01′E
117 Y6 **Starobil's'k** *Rus.* Starobel'sk. Luhans'ka Oblast', E Ukraine 49°16′N 38°56′E
119 K18 **Starobin** *var.* Starobyn. Minskaya Voblasts', S Belarus 52°44′N 27°28′E
Starobyn *see* Starobin
126 H6 **Starodub** Bryanskaya Oblast', W Russian Federation 52°30′N 32°56′E
110 I8 **Starogard Gdański** *Ger.* Preussisch-Stargard. Pomorskie, N Poland 53°57′N 18°29′E
145 P16 **Staroikan** Yuzhnyy Kazakhstan, S Kazakhstan 43°09′N 68°34′E
Starokonstantinov *see* Starokostyantyniv
116 L5 **Starokostyantyniv** *Rus.* Starokonstantinov. Khmel'nyts'ka Oblast', NW Ukraine 49°43′N 27°13′E
126 K12 **Starominskaya** Krasnodarskiy Kray, SW Russian Federation 46°31′N 39°03′E
114 L7 **Staro Selo** *Rom.* Satul-Vechi; *prev.* Star-Smil. Silistra, NE Bulgaria 43°58′N 26°32′E
126 K12 **Staroshcherbinovskaya** Krasnodarskiy Kray, SW Russian Federation 46°36′N 38°42′E
127 V6 **Starosubkhangulovo** Respublika Bashkortostan, W Russian Federation 53°05′N 57°22′E
35 S4 **Star Peak** ▲ Nevada, W USA 40°31′N 118°09′W
15 T8 **St-Arsène** Québec, SE Canada 47°55′N 69°21′W
Star-Smil *see* Staro Selo
97 J25 **Start Point** *headland* SW England, United Kingdom 50°13′N 03°38′W
Startsy *see* Kirawsk
Starum *see* Stavoren
119 L18 **Staryya Darohi** *Rus.* Staryye Dorogi. Minskaya Voblasts', S Belarus 53°02′N 28°16′E
Staryye Dorogi *see* Staryya Darohi
127 T2 **Staryye Zyattsy** Udmurtskaya Respublika, NW Russian Federation 57°22′N 52°42′E
117 U13 **Staryy Krym** Respublika Krym, S Ukraine 45°03′N 35°06′E
126 K8 **Staryy Oskol** Belgorodskaya Oblast', W Russian Federation 51°21′N 37°52′E
116 H6 **Staryy Sambir** L'vivs'ka Oblast', W Ukraine 49°27′N 23°00′E
101 L14 **Stassfurt** *var.* Staßfurt. Sachsen-Anhalt, C Germany 51°51′N 11°35′E
Staßfurt *see* Stassfurt
111 M15 **Staszów** Świętokrzyskie, C Poland 50°33′N 21°07′E
29 W13 **State Center** Iowa, C USA 42°01′N 93°09′W
18 E14 **State College** Pennsylvania, NE USA 40°48′N 77°52′W
18 K15 **Staten Island** *island* New York, NE USA
Staten Island *see* Estados, Isla de los
23 U8 **Statenville** Georgia, SE USA 30°42′N 83°00′W
23 W5 **Statesboro** Georgia, SE USA 32°28′N 81°47′W
States, The *see* United States of America
21 R9 **Statesville** North Carolina, SE USA 35°46′N 80°54′W
95 G16 **Stathelle** Telemark, S Norway 59°01′N 09°40′E
30 K15 **Staunton** Illinois, N USA 39°00′N 89°47′W
21 T5 **Staunton** Virginia, NE USA 38°10′N 79°05′W
95 C16 **Stavanger** Rogaland, S Norway 58°58′N 05°43′E
99 L21 **Stavelot** *Dut.* Stablo. Liège, E Belgium 50°24′N 05°56′E
95 G16 **Stavern** Vestfold, S Norway 58°58′N 10°01′E
Stavers Island *see* Vostok Island
98 J7 **Stavoren** *Fris.* Starum. Friesland, N Netherlands 52°52′N 05°22′E
115 K21 **Stavrí, Akrotírio** *var.* Akrotírio Stavrós. *headland* Naxos, Kykládes, Greece, Aegean Sea 37°12′N 25°32′E
126 M14 **Stavropol'** *prev.* Voroshilovsk. Stavropol'skiy Kray, SW Russian Federation 45°02′N 41°58′E
Stavropol' *see* Tol'yatti
126 M14 **Stavropol'skaya Vozvyshennost'** ▲▲ SW Russian Federation
126 M14 **Stavropol'skiy Kray** ◐ *territory* SW Russian Federation
115 H14 **Stavrós** Kentrikí Makedonía, N Greece 40°39′N 23°43′E
115 J24 **Stavrós, Akrotírio** *headland* Kríti, Greece, E Mediterranean Sea 35°25′N 24°57′E
Stavrós, Akrotírio *see* Stavrí, Akrotírio
114 I12 **Stavroúpoli** *prev.* Stavroúpolis. Anatolikí Makedonía kai Thráki, NE Greece 41°12′N 24°45′E
Stavroúpolis *see* Stavroúpoli
117 O6 **Stavyshche** Kyyivs'ka Oblast', N Ukraine 49°23′N 30°10′E
182 M11 **Stawell** Victoria, SE Australia 37°06′S 142°52′E
110 N9 **Stawiski** Podlaskie, NE Poland 53°22′N 22°08′E
14 G14 **Stayner** Ontario, S Canada 44°25′N 80°05′W
14 D17 **St. Clair** ≈ Canada/USA
37 R3 **Steamboat Springs** Colorado, C USA 40°28′N 106°51′W
15 U4 **Ste-Anne, Lac** ◎ Québec, SE Canada
20 M8 **Stearns** Kentucky, S USA 36°39′N 84°27′W
39 N10 **Stebbins** Alaska, USA 63°30′N 162°15′W
15 U7 **Ste-Blandine** Québec, SE Canada 48°22′N 68°27′W
108 K7 **Steeg** Tirol, W Austria 47°15′N 10°18′E
27 Y9 **Steele** Missouri, C USA 36°04′N 89°49′W
29 N5 **Steele** North Dakota, N USA 46°51′N 99°55′W
194 J5 **Steele Island** *island* Antarctica
30 K16 **Steeleville** Illinois, N USA 38°00′N 89°39′W
27 W6 **Steelville** Missouri, C USA 37°57′N 91°21′W
99 G14 **Steenbergen** Noord-Brabant, S Netherlands 51°35′N 04°19′E
Steenkool *see* Bintuni
11 O10 **Steen River** Alberta, W Canada 59°37′N 117°17′W
98 M8 **Steenwijk** Overijssel, N Netherlands 52°47′N 06°07′E
174 J8 **Steep Point** *headland* Western Australia 26°09′S 113°11′E
116 L9 **Ştefăneşti** Botoşani, NE Romania 47°44′N 27°15′E
Stefanie, Lake *see* Ch'ew Bahir
8 L5 **Stefansson Island** *island* Nunavut, N Canada
117 O10 **Ştefan Vodă** *Rus.* Suvorovo. SE Moldova 46°33′N 29°39′E
63 H18 **Steffen, Cerro** ▲ S Chile 44°27′S 71°42′W
108 D9 **Steffisburg** Bern, C Switzerland 46°47′N 07°38′E
95 J24 **Stege** Storstrøm, SE Denmark 54°59′N 12°18′E
116 G10 **Ştei** *Hung.* Vaskohsziklás. Bihor, W Romania 46°34′N 22°28′E
Steier *see* Steyr
Steierdorf/Steierdorf-Anina *see* Anina
109 T7 **Steiermark** *off.* Land Steiermark, *Eng.* Styria. ◐ *state* C Austria
Steiermark, Land *see* Steiermark
101 J19 **Steigerwald** *hill range* C Germany
99 L17 **Stein** Limburg, SE Netherlands 50°58′N 05°45′E
Stein *see* Stein an der Donau
Stein *see* Kamnik, Slovenia
108 M8 **Steinach** Tirol, W Austria 47°07′N 11°30′E
Steinamanger *see* Szombathely
109 W3 **Stein an der Donau** *var.* Stein. Niederösterreich, NE Austria 48°25′N 15°35′E
Steinau an der Elbe *see* Ścinawa
11 Y16 **Steinbach** Manitoba, S Canada 49°32′N 96°40′W
Steiner Alpen *see* Kamniško-Savinjske Alpe
99 L24 **Steinfort** Luxembourg, W Luxembourg 49°39′N 05°55′E
100 H12 **Steinhuder Meer** ◎ NW Germany
93 E15 **Steinkjer** Nord-Trøndelag, C Norway 64°01′N 11°29′E
Stejarul *see* Karapelit
99 F16 **Stekene** Oost-Vlaanderen, NW Belgium 51°13′N 04°04′E
83 E26 **Stellenbosch** Western Cape, SW South Africa 33°56′S 18°51′E
98 F13 **Stellendam** Zuid-Holland, SW Netherlands 51°48′N 04°01′E
39 T12 **Steller, Mount** ▲ Alaska, USA 60°36′N 142°49′W
103 Y14 **Stello, Monte** ▲ Corse, France, C Mediterranean Sea 42°49′N 09°24′E
106 F5 **Stelvio, Passo dello** *pass* Italy/Switzerland
15 S7 **Ste-Marguerite Nord-Est** ≈ Québec, SE Canada
15 V4 **Ste-Marguerite, Pointe** *headland* Québec, SE Canada 50°01′N 66°43′W
12 J14 **Ste-Marie, Lac** ⊡ Québec, S Canada
103 R3 **Stenay** Meuse, NE France 49°29′N 05°12′E
100 L12 **Stendal** Sachsen-Anhalt, C Germany 52°36′N 11°52′E
118 E8 **Stende** Talsi, NW Latvia 57°09′N 22°33′E
182 H10 **Stenhouse Bay** South Australia 35°15′S 136°58′E
95 J23 **Stenløse** Frederiksborg, E Denmark 55°47′N 12°13′E
95 L19 **Stensjön** Jönköping, S Sweden 57°36′N 14°42′E
95 K18 **Stenstorp** Västra Götaland, S Sweden 58°15′N 13°45′E
95 I18 **Stenungsund** Västra Götaland, S Sweden 58°05′N 11°49′E
Stepanakert *see* Xankändi
137 T11 **Step'anavan** N Armenia 41°00′N 44°27′E
100 K9 **Stepenitz** ≈ N Germany
29 O10 **Stephan** South Dakota, N USA 44°12′N 99°25′W
29 R3 **Stephen** Minnesota, N USA 48°27′N 96°54′W
27 T14 **Stephens** Arkansas, C USA 33°25′N 93°04′W
184 J13 **Stephens, Cape** *headland* D'Urville Island, Marlborough, SW New Zealand 40°42′S 173°56′E
21 V3 **Stephens City** Virginia, NE USA 39°03′N 78°10′W
182 L6 **Stephens Creek** New South Wales, SE Australia 31°51′S 141°30′E
184 K13 **Stephens Island** *island* C New Zealand
31 N5 **Stephenson** Michigan, N USA 45°27′N 87°36′W
13 S12 **Stephenville** Newfoundland, Newfoundland and Labrador, SE Canada 48°33′N 58°34′W
25 S7 **Stephenville** Texas, SW USA 32°12′N 98°13′W
145 P17 **Step' Nardara** *Kaz.* Shardara Dalasy; *prev.* Shaidara. *grassland* S Kazakhstan
145 R8 **Stepnogorsk** Akmola, C Kazakhstan 52°04′N 72°18′E
127 O15 **Stepnoye** Stavropol'skiy Kray, SW Russian Federation 44°18′N 44°34′E
145 Q8 **Stepnyak** Akmola, N Kazakhstan 52°52′N 70°49′E
192 J17 **Steps Point** *headland* Tutuila, W American Samoa 14°23′S 170°46′W
115 F17 **Stereá Ellás** *Eng.* Greece Central. ◐ *region* C Greece
83 J24 **Sterkspruit** Eastern Cape, SE South Africa 30°31′S 27°22′E
127 U6 **Sterlibashevo** Respublika Bashkortostan, W Russian Federation 53°19′N 55°12′E
39 R12 **Sterling** Alaska, USA 60°32′N 150°51′W
37 V3 **Sterling** Colorado, C USA 40°37′N 103°12′W
30 K11 **Sterling** Illinois, N USA 41°47′N 89°42′W
26 M5 **Sterling** Kansas, C USA 38°12′N 98°12′W
25 O8 **Sterling City** Texas, SW USA 31°50′N 101°00′W
31 S9 **Sterling Heights** Michigan, N USA 42°34′N 83°01′W
21 W3 **Sterling Park** Virginia, NE USA 39°00′N 77°24′W
37 V2 **Sterling Reservoir** ⊡ Colorado, C USA
22 I5 **Sterlington** Louisiana, S USA 32°42′N 92°05′W
127 U6 **Sterlitamak** Respublika Bashkortostan, W Russian Federation 53°39′N 56°00′E
Sternberg *see* Šternberk
111 H17 **Šternberk** *Ger.* Sternberg. Olomoucký Kraj, E Czech Republic 49°45′N 17°20′E
141 V17 **Stēroh** Suquṭrā, S Yemen 12°21′N 53°50′E
Sterren, Pegunungan *see* Star Mountains
110 G11 **Stęszew** Wielkopolskie, C Poland 52°16′N 16°41′E
Stettin *see* Szczecin
Stettiner Haff *see* Szczeciński, Zalew
11 Q15 **Stettler** Alberta, SW Canada 52°21′N 112°40′W
31 V13 **Steubenville** Ohio, N USA 40°21′N 80°37′W
97 O21 **Stevenage** E England, United Kingdom 51°55′N 00°14′W
23 Q1 **Stevenson** Alabama, S USA 34°52′N 85°50′W
32 H11 **Stevenson** Washington, NW USA 45°43′N 121°54′W
182 E1 **Stevenson Creek** *seasonal river* South Australia
39 Q13 **Stevenson Entrance** *strait* Alaska, USA
30 L6 **Stevens Point** Wisconsin, N USA 44°32′N 89°33′W
39 R8 **Stevens Village** Alaska, USA 66°01′N 149°02′W
33 P10 **Stevensville** Montana, NW USA 46°30′N 114°05′W
93 E25 **Stevns Klint** *headland* E Denmark 55°15′N 12°25′E
10 J12 **Stewart** British Columbia, W Canada 55°58′N 129°52′W
10 I6 **Stewart** ≈ Yukon Territory, NW Canada
10 I6 **Stewart Crossing** Yukon Territory, NW Canada 63°22′N 136°37′W
63 H25 **Stewart, Isla** *island* S Chile
185 B25 **Stewart Island** *island* S New Zealand
Stewart Islands *see* Sikaiana
181 W6 **Stewart, Mount** ▲ Queensland, E Australia 20°11′S 145°29′E
10 H6 **Stewart River** Yukon Territory, NW Canada 63°17′N 139°24′W
27 R3 **Stewartsville** Missouri, C USA 39°45′N 94°30′W
11 S16 **Stewart Valley** Saskatchewan, S Canada 50°34′N 107°47′W
29 W10 **Stewartville** Minnesota, N USA 43°51′N 92°29′W
Steyerlak-Anina *see* Anina
109 T5 **Steyr** *var.* Steier. Oberösterreich, N Austria 48°02′N 14°26′E
109 T5 **Steyr** ≈ NW Austria
15 T7 **St-Fabien** Québec, SE Canada 48°19′N 68°51′W
15 R11 **St-François, Lac** ◎ Québec, SE Canada
83 E25 **St. Helena Bay** *bay* SW South Africa
15 T8 **St-Hubert** Québec, SE Canada 47°46′N 69°15′W
29 P11 **Stickney** South Dakota, N USA 43°24′N 98°23′W
98 L5 **Stiens** Friesland, N Netherlands 53°15′N 05°45′E
Stif *see* Sétif
27 Q11 **Stigler** Oklahoma, C USA 35°16′N 95°08′W
107 N18 **Stigliano** Basilicata, S Italy 40°24′N 16°13′E
95 N17 **Stigtomta** Södermanland, C Sweden 58°48′N 16°47′E
10 I11 **Stikine** ≈ British Columbia, W Canada
Stilida/Stilís *see* Stylída
95 G22 **Stilling** Århus, C Denmark 56°04′N 10°00′E
29 W8 **Stillwater** Minnesota, N USA 45°03′N 92°48′W
27 O9 **Stillwater** Oklahoma, C USA 36°07′N 97°03′W
35 S5 **Stillwater Range** ▲▲ Nevada, W USA
18 I8 **Stillwater Reservoir** ⊡ New York, NE USA
107 O22 **Stilo, Punta** *headland* S Italy 38°27′N 16°36′E
27 R10 **Stilwell** Oklahoma, C USA 35°48′N 94°37′W
Štimlje *see* Shtime
25 N1 **Stinnett** Texas, SW USA 35°49′N 101°27′W
113 P18 **Štip** E FYR Macedonia 41°45′N 22°10′E
Stira *see* Stýra
96 J12 **Stirling** C Scotland, United Kingdom 56°07′N 03°57′W
96 I12 **Stirling** *cultural region* C Scotland, United Kingdom
180 J14 **Stirling Range** ▲▲ Western Australia
15 R8 **St-Jean** ≈ Québec, SE Canada
93 E16 **Stjørdalshalsen** Nord-Trøndelag, C Norway 63°27′N 10°57′E
83 L22 **St. Lucia** KwaZulu/Natal, E South Africa 28°22′S 32°25′E
Stochód *see* Stokhid
101 H24 **Stockach** Baden-Württemberg, S Germany 47°51′N 09°01′E
25 S12 **Stockdale** Texas, SW USA 29°14′N 97°57′W
109 X3 **Stockerau** Niederösterreich, NE Austria 48°24′N 16°13′E
93 H20 **Stockholm** ● (Sweden) Stockholm, C Sweden 59°17′N 18°03′E
95 O15 **Stockholm** ◐ *county* C Sweden
Stockmannshof *see* Pļaviņas
97 L18 **Stockport** NW England, United Kingdom 53°25′N 02°10′W
65 K15 **Stocks Seamount** *undersea feature* C Atlantic Ocean 11°42′S 33°48′W
35 O8 **Stockton** California, W USA 37°56′N 121°19′W
26 L3 **Stockton** Kansas, C USA 39°27′N 99°17′W
27 S6 **Stockton** Missouri, C USA 37°43′N 93°49′W
30 K3 **Stockton Island** *island* Apostle Islands, Wisconsin, N USA
27 S7 **Stockton Lake** ⊡ Missouri, C USA
97 M15 **Stockton-on-Tees** *var.* Stockton on Tees. N England, United Kingdom 54°34′N 01°19′W
Stockton on Tees *see* Stockton-on-Tees
24 M10 **Stockton Plateau** *plain* Texas, SW USA
28 M16 **Stockville** Nebraska, C USA 40°33′N 100°20′W
93 H17 **Stöde** Västernorrland, C Sweden 62°27′N 16°34′E
Stodolichi *see* Stadolichy
113 M19 **Stogovo Karaorman** ▲▲ W FYR Macedonia
Stoke *see* Stoke-on-Trent
97 L19 **Stoke-on-Trent** *var.* Stoke. C England, United Kingdom 53°N 02°10′W
182 M15 **Stokes Point** *headland* Tasmania, SE Australia 40°09′S 143°55′E
116 J2 **Stokhid** *Pol.* Stochód, *Rus.* Stokhod. ≈ NW Ukraine
Stokhod *see* Stokhid
92 I4 **Stokkseyri** Sudhurland, SW Iceland 63°49′N 21°00′W
92 G10 **Stokmarknes** Nordland, C Norway 68°34′N 14°55′E
Stol *see* Veliki Krš
113 H15 **Stolac** Federacija Bosna I Hercegovina, S Bosnia and Herzegovina 43°04′N 17°58′E
Stolbce *see* Stowbtsy
101 D16 **Stolberg** *var.* Stolberg im Rheinland. Nordrhein-Westfalen, W Germany 50°45′N 06°15′E
Stolberg im Rheinland *see* Stolberg
123 P6 **Stolbovoy, Ostrov** *island* NE Russian Federation
Stolbtsy *see* Stowbtsy
119 J20 **Stolin** Brestskaya Voblasts', SW Belarus 51°53′N 26°51′E
95 K14 **Stöllet** *var.* Norra Ny. Värmland, C Sweden 60°24′N 13°15′E
Stolp *see* Słupsk
Stolpe *see* Słupia
Stolpmünde *see* Ustka
115 F15 **Stómio** Thessalía, C Greece 39°51′N 22°45′E
14 J11 **Stonecliffe** Ontario, SE Canada 46°12′N 77°58′W
96 L10 **Stonehaven** NE Scotland, United Kingdom 56°59′N 02°14′W
97 M23 **Stonehenge** *ancient monument* Wiltshire, S England, United Kingdom
23 T3 **Stone Mountain** ▲ Georgia, SE USA 33°48′N 84°10′W
11 X16 **Stonewall** Manitoba, S Canada 50°08′N 97°20′W
21 S3 **Stonewood** West Virginia, NE USA 39°15′N 80°18′W
14 D17 **Stoney Point** Ontario, S Canada 42°18′N 82°32′W
92 H10 **Stonglandseidet** Troms, N Norway 69°03′N 17°06′E
65 N25 **Stonybeach Bay** *bay* Tristan da Cunha, SE Atlantic Ocean
35 N5 **Stony Creek** ≈ California, W USA
65 N25 **Stonyhill Point** *headland* S Tristan da Cunha
14 I14 **Stony Lake** ◎ Ontario, SE Canada
11 Q14 **Stony Plain** Alberta, SW Canada 53°31′N 114°04′W
21 R9 **Stony Point** North Carolina, SE USA 35°51′N 81°04′W
18 G8 **Stony Point** *headland* New York, NE USA 43°50′N 76°18′W
11 T10 **Stony Rapids** Saskatchewan, C Canada 59°14′N 105°48′W
39 P11 **Stony River** Alaska, USA 61°48′N 156°37′W
Stony Tunguska *see* Podkamennaya Tunguska
12 G10 **Stooping** ≈ Ontario, C Canada
100 I9 **Stör** ≈ N Germany
95 M15 **Storå** Örebro, S Sweden 59°44′N 15°10′E
95 J16 **Stora Gla** ◎ C Sweden
95 J16 **Stora Le** *Nor.* Store Le. ◎ Norway/Sweden
92 I12 **Stora Lulevatten** ◎ N Sweden
92 H13 **Storavan** ◎ N Sweden
93 I20 **Storby** Åland, SW Finland 60°12′N 19°33′E
94 E10 **Stordalen** Møre og Romsdal, S Norway 62°22′N 07°00′E
95 H23 **Storebælt** *var.* Store Bælt, *Eng.* Great Belt, Storebelt. *channel* Baltic Sea/Kattegat
Store Bælt *see* Storebælt
Storebelt *see* Storebælt
95 M19 **Storebro** Kalmar, S Sweden 57°36′N 15°30′E
95 J24 **Store Heddinge** Storstrøm, SE Denmark 55°19′N 12°24′E
Store Le *see* Stora Le
93 E16 **Støren** Sør-Trøndelag, S Norway 63°02′N 10°16′E
92 O4 **Storfjorden** *fjord* S Norway
95 L15 **Storfors** Värmland, C Sweden 59°33′N 14°16′E
92 G13 **Storforshei** Nordland, C Norway 66°25′N 14°25′E
Storhammer *see* Hamar
100 L10 **Störkanal** *canal* N Germany
93 F16 **Storlien** Jämtland, C Sweden 63°18′N 12°10′E
183 P17 **Storm Bay** *inlet* Tasmania, SE Australia
29 T12 **Storm Lake** Iowa, C USA 42°38′N 95°12′W
29 S13 **Storm Lake** ◎ Iowa, C USA
96 G7 **Stornoway** NW Scotland, United Kingdom 58°13′N 06°23′W
Storojineț *see* Storozhynets'
92 P1 **Storøya** *island* NE Svalbard
125 S10 **Storozhevsk** Respublika Komi, NW Russian Federation 61°56′N 52°18′E
Storozhinets *see* Storozhynets'
116 K8 **Storozhynets'** *Ger.* Storozynetz, *Rom.* Storojineţ, *Rus.* Storozhinets. Chernivets'ka Oblast', W Ukraine 48°11′N 25°42′E
Storozynetz *see* Storozhynets'
92 H11 **Storriten** ▲ C Norway 68°09′N 17°12′E
19 N12 **Storrs** Connecticut, NE USA 41°48′N 72°15′W
94 I11 **Storsjøen** ◎ S Norway
94 N13 **Storsjön** ◎ C Sweden
93 F16 **Storsjön** ◎ C Sweden
92 J9 **Storslett** Troms, N Norway 69°45′N 21°03′E
94 H11 **Storsølnkletten** ▲ S Norway 61°52′N 11°32′E
92 I9 **Storsteinnes** Troms, N Norway 69°13′N 19°14′E
95 I24 **Storstrøm** *var.* Storstrøms Amt. ◐ *county* SE Denmark
Storstrøms Amt *see* Storstrøm
93 J14 **Storsund** Norrbotten, N Sweden 65°36′N 20°40′E
94 I9 **Storsylen** *Swe.* Sylarna. ▲ Norway/Sweden 63°00′N 12°14′E
92 H11 **Stortoppen** ▲ N Sweden 67°33′N 17°27′E
93 H14 **Storuman** Västerbotten, N Sweden 65°05′N 17°10′E
93 H14 **Storuman** ◎ N Sweden
94 N13 **Storvik** Gävleborg, C Sweden 60°37′N 16°30′E
95 O14 **Storvreta** Uppsala, C Sweden 59°58′N 17°42′E
29 V13 **Story City** Iowa, C USA 42°10′N 93°36′W
11 V17 **Stoughton** Saskatchewan, S Canada 49°40′N 103°01′W
19 O11 **Stoughton** Massachusetts, NE USA 42°07′N 71°06′W
30 L9 **Stoughton** Wisconsin, N USA 42°56′N 89°12′W
97 L23 **Stour** ≈ E England, United Kingdom
97 P21 **Stour** ≈ S England, United Kingdom
27 T5 **Stover** Missouri, C USA 38°26′N 92°59′W
95 G21 **Støvring** Nordjylland, N Denmark 56°53′N 09°52′E
119 J17 **Stowbtsy** *Pol.* Stolbce, *Rus.* Stolbtsy. Minskaya Voblasts', C Belarus 53°29′N 26°44′E
25 X11 **Stowell** Texas, SW USA 29°47′N 94°22′W
97 P20 **Stowmarket** E England, United Kingdom 52°05′N 00°54′E
114 N8 **Stozher** Dobrich, NE Bulgaria 43°27′N 27°49′E
97 E14 **Strabane** *Ir.* An Srath Bán. W Northern Ireland, United Kingdom 54°49′N 07°27′W
121 S11 **Strabo Trench** *undersea feature* C Mediterranean Sea
27 T7 **Strafford** Missouri, C USA 37°16′N 93°07′W
183 N17 **Strahan** Tasmania, SE Australia 42°10′S 145°18′E
111 C18 **Strakonice** *Ger.* Strakonitz. Jihočeský Kraj, S Czech Republic 49°14′N 13°55′E
Strakonitz *see* Strakonice
100 N8 **Stralsund** Mecklenburg-Vorpommern, NE Germany 54°18′N 13°06′E
99 L16 **Stramproy** Limburg, SE Netherlands 51°12′N 05°43′E
83 K22 **Strand** Western Cape, SW South Africa 34°06′S 18°50′E
94 E10 **Stranda** Møre og Romsdal, S Norway 62°18′N 06°56′E
97 G15 **Strangford Lough** *Ir.* Loch Cuan. *inlet* E Northern Ireland, United Kingdom
95 N16 **Strängnäs** Södermanland, C Sweden 59°22′N 17°02′E
97 E14 **Stranorlar** *Ir.* Srath an Urláir. NW Ireland 54°48′N 07°46′W
97 H14 **Stranraer** S Scotland, United Kingdom 54°54′N 05°02′W
11 U16 **Strasbourg** Saskatchewan, S Canada 51°05′N 104°58′W
103 V5 **Strasbourg** *Ger.* Strassburg; *anc.* Argentoratum. Bas-Rhin, NE France 48°35′N 07°45′E
109 T8 **Strassburg** Kärnten, S Austria 46°54′N 14°21′E
37 U4 **Strasburg** Colorado, C USA 39°42′N 104°13′W
29 N7 **Strasburg** North Dakota, N USA 46°07′N 100°10′W
31 U12 **Strasburg** Ohio, N USA 40°35′N 81°31′W
21 U3 **Strasburg** Virginia, NE USA 38°59′N 78°21′W
117 N10 **Strășeni** *var.* Strasheny. C Moldova 47°07′N 28°37′E
Strasheny *see* Strășeni
Strassburg *see* Strasbourg, France
Strassburg *see* Aiud, Romania
99 M25 **Strassen** Luxembourg, S Luxembourg 49°37′N 06°05′E
109 R5 **Strasswalchen** Salzburg, C Austria 47°59′N 13°19′E
14 F16 **Stratford** Ontario, S Canada 43°22′N 81°00′W
184 K10 **Stratford** Taranaki, North Island, New Zealand 39°20′S 174°16′E
35 Q11 **Stratford** California, W USA 36°10′N 119°47′W
29 V13 **Stratford** Iowa, C USA 42°16′N 93°55′W
27 O12 **Stratford** Oklahoma, C USA 34°48′N 96°57′W
25 N1 **Stratford** Texas, SW USA 36°21′N 102°05′W
30 K6 **Stratford** Wisconsin, N USA 44°53′N 90°13′W
Stratford *see* Stratford-upon-Avon
97 M20 **Stratford-upon-Avon** *var.* Stratford. C England, United Kingdom 52°12′N 01°41′W
183 O17 **Strathgordon** Tasmania, SE Australia 42°49′S 146°04′E
11 Q16 **Strathmore** Alberta, SW Canada 51°05′N 113°18′W
35 R11 **Strathmore** California, W USA 36°07′N 119°04′W
14 E16 **Strathroy** Ontario, S Canada 42°57′N 81°40′W
96 I6 **Strathy Point** *headland* N Scotland, United Kingdom 58°36′N 04°04′W
37 W4 **Stratton** Colorado, C USA 39°16′N 102°34′W
19 P6 **Stratton** Maine, NE USA 45°08′N 70°25′W
18 M10 **Stratton Mountain** ▲ Vermont, NE USA 43°05′N 72°55′W
101 N21 **Straubing** Bayern, SE Germany 48°53′N 12°35′E
100 O12 **Strausberg** Brandenburg, E Germany 52°34′N 13°52′E
32 K13 **Strawberry Mountain** ▲ Oregon, NW USA 44°18′N 118°43′W
29 X12 **Strawberry Point** Iowa, C USA 42°40′N 91°31′W
36 M3 **Strawberry Reservoir** ⊡ Utah, W USA
36 M4 **Strawberry River** ≈ Utah, W USA
25 R7 **Strawn** Texas, SW USA 32°33′N 98°30′W
113 P17 **Straža** ▲ Bulgaria/FYR Macedonia 42°16′N 22°13′E
111 I19 **Strážov** *Hung.* Sztrazsó. ▲ NW Slovakia 48°59′N 18°29′E
182 F7 **Streaky Bay** South Australia 32°49′S 134°13′E
182 E7 **Streaky Bay** *bay* South Australia
30 L12 **Streator** Illinois, N USA 41°07′N 88°50′W
Streckenbach *see* Świdnik
Strednogorie *see* Pirdop
111 C17 **Středočeský Kraj** ◐ *region* C Czech Republic
29 O6 **Streeter** North Dakota, N USA 46°37′N 99°23′W
25 U8 **Streetman** Texas, SW USA 31°52′N 96°19′W
116 G13 **Strehaia** Mehedinți, SW Romania 44°37′N 23°10′E
Strehlen *see* Strzelin
114 I10 **Strelcha** Pazardzhik, C Bulgaria 42°28′N 24°21′E
122 L12 **Strelka** Krasnoyarskiy Kray, C Russian Federation 58°05′N 92°54′E
124 L6 **Strel'na** ≈ NW Russian Federation
118 H7 **Strenči** *Ger.* Stackeln. Valka, N Latvia 57°38′N 25°42′E
15 V6 **St-René-de-Matane** Québec, SE Canada 48°42′N 67°22′W
108 K8 **Strengen** Tirol, W Austria 47°07′N 10°25′E
106 C6 **Stresa** Piemonte, NE Italy 45°52′N 08°32′E
Streshin *see* Streshyn
119 N18 **Streshyn** *Rus.* Streshin. Homyel'skaya Voblasts', SE Belarus 52°43′N 30°07′E
95 B18 **Streymoy** *Dan.* Strømø. *island* N Faeroe Islands
95 G23 **Strib** Fyn, C Denmark 55°33′N 09°47′E
111 A17 **Stříbro** *Ger.* Mies. Plzeňský Kraj, W Czech Republic 49°44′N 12°55′E
186 B7 **Strickland** ≈ SW Papua New Guinea
Striegau *see* Strzegom
Strigonium *see* Esztergom
98 H13 **Strijen** Zuid-Holland, SW Netherlands 51°45′N 04°34′E
63 H21 **Strobel, Lago** ◎ S Argentina
61 B25 **Stroeder** Buenos Aires, E Argentina 40°11′S 62°35′W
115 C20 **Strofádes** *island* Iónia Nisiá, Greece, C Mediterranean Sea
Strofilia *see* Strofyliá
115 G17 **Strofyliá** *var.* Strofilia. Évvoia, C Greece 38°49′N 23°25′E
100 O10 **Strom** ≈ NE Germany
107 L22 **Stromboli** ⛰ Isola Stromboli, SW Italy 38°48′N 15°13′E
107 L22 **Stromboli, Isola** *island* Isole Eolie, S Italy
96 H9 **Stromeferry** N Scotland, United Kingdom 57°20′N 05°35′W
96 J5 **Stromness** N Scotland, United Kingdom 58°57′N 03°18′W
Strømø *see* Streymoy
94 N11 **Strömsbruk** Gävleborg, C Sweden 61°52′N 17°19′E
29 Q15 **Stromsburg** Nebraska, C USA 41°06′N 97°36′W
95 K21 **Strömsnäsbruk** Kronoberg, S Sweden 56°35′N 13°45′E
95 I17 **Strömstad** Västra Götaland, S Sweden 58°56′N 11°11′E
93 G16 **Strömsund** Jämtland, C Sweden 63°51′N 15°35′E
93 G15 **Ströms Vattudal** *valley* N Sweden
27 V14 **Strong** Arkansas, C USA 33°06′N 92°19′W
Strongilí *see* Strongylí
107 O21 **Strongoli** Calabria, SW Italy 39°17′N 17°03′E
31 T11 **Strongsville** Ohio, N USA 41°18′N 81°50′W
115 Q23 **Strongylí** *var.* Strongilí. *island* SE Greece
96 K5 **Stronsay** *island* NE Scotland, United Kingdom
97 L21 **Stroud** C England, United Kingdom 51°46′N 02°15′W
27 O10 **Stroud** Oklahoma, C USA 35°45′N 96°39′W
18 I14 **Stroudsburg** Pennsylvania, NE USA 40°59′N 75°12′W

95 F21 **Struer** Ringkøbing, W Denmark 56°29′N 08°37′E
113 M20 **Struga** SW FYR Macedonia 41°11′N 20°40′E
Strugi-Kranyse *see* Strugi-Krasnyye
124 G14 **Strugi-Krasnyye** *var.* Strugi-Kranyse. Pskovskaya Oblast', W Russian Federation 58°19′N 29°09′E
114 G11 **Struma** *Gk.* Strymónas. ~ Bulgaria/Greece *see also* Strymónas
Struma *see* Strymónas
97 G21 **Strumble Head** *headland* SW Wales, United Kingdom 52°01′N 05°05′W
Strumeshnitsa *see* Strumica
113 Q19 **Strumica** E FYR Macedonia 41°27′N 22°39′E
113 Q19 **Strumica** *Bulg.* Strumeshnitsa. ~ Bulgaria/FYR Macedonia
114 G11 **Strumyani** Blagoevgrad, SW Bulgaria 41°41′N 23°13′E
31 V12 **Struthers** Ohio, N USA 41°03′N 80°36′W
114 I10 **Stryama** ~ C Bulgaria
114 G13 **Strymónas** *Bul.* Struma. ~ Bulgaria/Greece *see also* Struma
Strymónas *see* Struma
115 H14 **Strymonikós Kólpos** *gulf* N Greece
116 I6 **Stryy** L'vivs'ka Oblast', NW Ukraine 49°16′N 23°51′E
116 H6 **Stryy** ~ W Ukraine
111 F14 **Strzegom** *Ger.* Striegau. Wałbrzych, SW Poland 50°59′N 16°20′E
110 E10 **Strzelce Krajeńskie** *Ger.* Friedeberg Neumark. Lubuskie, W Poland 52°52′N 15°30′E
111 I15 **Strzelce Opolskie** *Ger.* Gross Strehlitz. Opolskie, SW Poland 50°31′N 18°19′E
182 K3 **Strzelecki Creek** *seasonal river* South Australia
182 J3 **Strzelecki Desert** *desert* South Australia
111 G15 **Strzelin** *Ger.* Strehlen. Dolnośląskie, SW Poland 50°48′N 17°03′E
110 I11 **Strzelno** Kujawsko-pomorski, C Poland 52°38′N 18°11′E
111 N17 **Strzyżów** Podkarpackie, SE Poland 49°52′N 21°46′E
15 S8 **St-Siméon** Québec, SE Canada 47°50′N 69°55′W
Stua Laighean *see* Leinster, Mount
23 Y13 **Stuart** Florida, SE USA 27°12′N 80°15′W
29 U14 **Stuart** Iowa, C USA 41°30′N 94°19′W
29 O13 **Stuart** Nebraska, C USA 42°36′N 99°08′W
21 S8 **Stuart** Virginia, NE USA 36°38′N 80°19′W
10 L13 **Stuart** ~ British Columbia, SW Canada
39 N10 **Stuart Island** *island* Alaska, USA
10 L13 **Stuart Lake** ◎ British Columbia, SW Canada
185 B22 **Stuart Mountains** ▲▲ South Island, New Zealand
182 F3 **Stuart Range** *hill range* South Australia
Stubaital *see* Neustift im Stubaital
95 I24 **Stubbekøbing** Storstrøm, SE Denmark 54°53′N 12°04′E
45 P14 **Stubbs** Saint Vincent, Saint Vincent and the Grenadines 13°08′N 61°09′W
109 V6 **Stübming** ~ E Austria
114 J11 **Studen Kladenets, Yazovir** ⊠ S Bulgaria
185 G21 **Studholme** Canterbury, South Island, New Zealand 44°44′S 171°08′E
Stuhlweissenberg *see* Székesfehérvár
Stuhm *see* Sztum
12 C7 **Stull Lake** ◎ Ontario, C Canada
126 L4 **Stupino** Moskovskaya Oblast', W Russian Federation 54°53′N 38°06′E
27 U4 **Sturgeon** Missouri, C USA 39°13′N 92°16′W
14 G10 **Sturgeon** ~ Ontario, S Canada
31 N6 **Sturgeon Bay** Wisconsin, N USA 44°51′N 87°21′W
14 G11 **Sturgeon Falls** Ontario, S Canada 46°22′N 79°57′W
12 C11 **Sturgeon Lake** ◎ Ontario, S Canada
30 M3 **Sturgeon River** ~ Michigan, N USA
20 H6 **Sturgis** Kentucky, S USA 37°33′N 87°58′W
31 P11 **Sturgis** Michigan, N USA 41°48′N 85°25′W
28 J9 **Sturgis** South Dakota, N USA 44°24′N 103°30′W
112 D10 **Šturlić** ◐ Federacija Bosna I Hercegovina, NW Bosnia and Herzegovina
111 J22 **Štúrovo** *Hung.* Párkány; *prev.* Parkan. Nitriansky Kraj, SW Slovakia 47°49′N 18°40′E
182 L4 **Sturt, Mount** *hill* New South Wales, SE Australia
181 P4 **Sturt Plain** *plain* Northern Territory, N Australia
181 T9 **Sturt Stony Desert** *desert* South Australia
83 J25 **Stutterheim** Eastern Cape, S South Africa 32°35′S 27°26′E
101 H21 **Stuttgart** Baden-Württemberg, SW Germany 48°47′N 09°12′E
27 W12 **Stuttgart** Arkansas, C USA 34°30′N 91°32′W
92 H2 **Stykkishólmur** Vesturland, W Iceland 65°04′N 22°43′W
115 F17 **Stylída** *var.* Stilida, Stilís. Stereá Ellás, C Greece 38°55′N 22°37′E
116 K2 **Styr** *Rus.* Styr'. ~ Belarus/Ukraine
115 I19 **Stýra** *var.* Stira. Évvoia, C Greece 38°10′N 24°13′E
Styria *see* Steiermark
15 Y5 **St-Yvon** Québec, SE Canada 49°09′N 64°51′W
Su *see* Jiangsu
Sua *see* Sowa
171 Q17 **Suai** W East Timor 09°19′S 125°16′E
54 G9 **Suaita** Santander, C Colombia 06°07′N 73°30′W
80 I7 **Suakin** *var.* Sawakin. Red Sea, NE Sudan 19°06′N 37°17′E
161 T13 **Suao** *Jap.* Suō. N Taiwan 24°33′N 121°48′E
Suao *see* Suau
Sua Pan *see* Sowa Pan
40 G6 **Suaqui Grande** Sonora, NW Mexico 28°22′N 109°52′W
61 A16 **Suardi** Santa Fe, C Argentina 30°32′S 61°58′W
54 D11 **Suárez** Cauca, SW Colombia 02°55′N 76°41′W
186 G10 **Suau** *var.* Suao. Suaul Island, SE Papua New Guinea 10°39′S 150°03′E
118 G12 **Subačius** Panevėžys, NE Lithuania 55°46′N 24°45′E
168 K9 **Subang** *prev.* Soebang. Jawa, C Indonesia 06°32′S 107°45′E
169 O16 **Subang** ✈ (Kuala Lumpur) Pahang, Peninsular Malaysia
129 S10 **Subansiri** ~ NE India
118 I11 **Subate** Daugvapils, SE Latvia 56°00′N 25°54′E
139 N5 **Subaykhān** Dayr az Zawr, E Syria 34°52′N 40°35′E
Subei/Subei Mongolzu Zizhixian *see* Dangchengwan
169 P9 **Subi Besar, Pulau** *island* Kepulauan Natuna, W Indonesia
Subiyah *see* Aş Şubayḩīyah
26 I7 **Sublette** Kansas, C USA 37°28′N 100°52′W
112 K8 **Subotica** *Ger.* Maria-Theresiopel, *Hung.* Szabadka. Vojvodina, N Serbia 46°06′N 19°41′E
116 K9 **Suceava** *Ger.* Suczawa, *Hung.* Szucsava. Suceava, NE Romania 47°41′N 26°16′E
116 J9 **Suceava** ◐ *county* NE Romania
116 K9 **Suceava** *Ger.* Suczawa. ~ N Romania
112 E12 **Sučevići** Zadar, SW Croatia 44°13′N 16°04′E
111 K17 **Sucha Beskidzka** Małopolskie, S Poland 49°44′N 19°36′E
111 M14 **Suchedniów** Świętokrzyskie, C Poland 51°01′N 20°49′E
42 A2 **Suchitepéquez** *off.* Departamento de Suchitepéquez. ◐ *department* SW Guatemala
Suchitepéquez, Departamento de *see* Suchitepéquez
Su-chou *see* Suzhou
Suchow *see* Xuzhou, Jiangsu, China
Suchow *see* Suzhou, Jiangsu, China
97 D17 **Suck** ~ C Ireland
Sucker State *see* Illinois
186 F9 **Suckling, Mount** ▲ S Papua New Guinea 09°36′S 149°00′E
57 L19 **Sucre** *hist.* Chuquisaca, La Plata. ● (Bolivia-legal capital) Chuquisaca, S Bolivia 18°53′S 65°25′W
54 E6 **Sucre** Santander, N Colombia 08°50′N 74°22′W
56 A7 **Sucre** Manabí, W Ecuador 01°21′S 80°27′W
54 E6 **Sucre** *off.* Departamento de Sucre. ◐ *province* N Colombia
55 O5 **Sucre** *off.* Estado Sucre. ◐ *state* NE Venezuela
Sucre, Departamento de *see* Sucre
Sucre, Estado *see* Sucre
56 D6 **Sucumbíos** ◐ *province* NE Ecuador
113 G15 **Sućuraj** Split-Dalmacija, S Croatia 43°07′N 17°10′E
58 K10 **Sucuriju** Amapá, NE Brazil 01°31′N 50°W
Suczawa *see* Suceava
79 E16 **Sud** *Eng.* South. ◐ *province* S Cameroon
124 K13 **Suda** ~ NW Russian Federation
Suda *see* Soúda
117 U13 **Sudak** Respublika Krym, S Ukraine 44°52′N 34°57′E
24 M4 **Sudan** Texas, SW USA 34°04′N 102°32′W
80 C10 **Sudan** *off.* Republic of Sudan, *Ar.* Jumhuriyat as-Sudan; *prev.* Anglo-Egyptian Sudan. ◆ *republic* N Africa
Sudanese Republic *see* Mali
Sudan, Jumhuriyat as- *see* Sudan
Sudan, Republic of *see* Sudan
14 F10 **Sudbury** Ontario, S Canada 46°29′N 81°W
97 P20 **Sudbury** E England, United Kingdom 52°04′N 00°43′E
Sud, Canal de *see* Gonâve, Canal de la
80 E13 **Sudd** *swamp region* S Sudan
100 K10 **Sude** ~ N Germany
Suderø *see* Suðuroy
Sudest Island *see* Tagula Island
111 E15 **Sudeten** *var.* Sudetes, Sudetic Mountains, *Cz./Pol.* Sudety. ▲▲ Czech Republic/Poland
Sudetes/Sudetic Mountains/Sudety *see* Sudeten
92 G1 **Suðhreyri** Vestfirdhir, NW Iceland 66°08′N 23°31′W
92 J4 **Suðhurland** ◐ *region* S Iceland
95 B19 **Suðuroy** *Dan.* Suderø. *island* S Faeroe Islands
124 M15 **Sudislavl'** Kostromskaya Oblast', NW Russian Federation 57°55′N 41°45′E
Südkarpaten *see* Carpaţii Meridionalii
79 N20 **Sud-Kivu** *off.* Région Sud Kivu. ◐ *region* E Dem. Rep. Congo
Sud Kivu, Région *see* Sud-Kivu
Südliche Morava *see* Južna Morava
100 E12 **Süd-Nord-Kanal** *canal* NW Germany
126 M3 **Sudogda** Vladimirskaya Oblast', W Russian Federation 55°58′N 40°57′E
Sudostroy *see* Severodvinsk
79 C15 **Sud-Ouest** *Eng.* South-West. ◐ *province* W Cameroon
173 X17 **Sud Ouest, Pointe** *headland* SW Mauritius 20°27′S 57°18′E
187 P17 **Sud, Province** ◐ *province* S New Caledonia
126 J8 **Sudzha** Kurskaya Oblast', W Russian Federation 51°12′N 35°19′E
81 D15 **Sue** ~ S Sudan
105 S10 **Sueca** País Valenciano, E Spain 39°13′N 00°19′W
114 I10 **Sŭedinenie** Plovdiv, C Bulgaria 42°14′N 24°36′E
Suero *see* Alzira
75 X8 **Suez** *Ar.* As Suways, El Suweis. NE Egypt 29°59′N 32°33′E
75 W7 **Suez Canal** *Ar.* Qanāt as Suways. *canal* NE Egypt
Suez, Gulf of *see* Khalīj as Suways
11 R17 **Suffield** Alberta, SW Canada 50°15′N 111°05′W
21 X7 **Suffolk** Virginia, NE USA 36°44′N 76°37′W
97 P20 **Suffolk** *cultural region* E England, United Kingdom
142 J2 **Şūfīān** Āzarbāyjān-e Sharqī, N Iran 38°15′N 45°59′E
31 N12 **Sugar Creek** ~ Illinois, N USA
30 L13 **Sugar Creek** ~ Illinois, N USA
31 R3 **Sugar Island** *island* Michigan, N USA
25 V11 **Sugar Land** Texas, SW USA 29°37′N 95°37′W
19 P6 **Sugarloaf Mountain** ▲ Maine, NE USA 45°01′N 70°18′W
65 G24 **Sugar Loaf Point** *headland* N Saint Helena 15°54′S 05°43′W
136 G16 **Suğla Gölü** ◎ SW Turkey
123 T8 **Sugoy** ~ E Russian Federation
158 F7 **Sugun** Xinjiang Uygur Zizhiqu, W China 39°46′N 76°45′E
147 U11 **Sugut, Gora** ▲ SW Kyrgyzstan 39°52′N 73°36′E
169 V6 **Sugut, Sungai** ~ East Malaysia
159 O9 **Suhai Hu** ◎ C China
162 K14 **Suhait** Nei Mongol Zizhiqu, N China 39°29′N 105°11′E
141 X7 **Şuḩār** *var.* Sohar. N Oman 24°20′N 56°43′E
113 M17 **Suharekë** *Serb.* Suva Reka. S Kosovo 42°23′N 20°50′E
162 L6 **Sühbaatar** Selenge, N Mongolia 50°12′N 106°14′E
163 P8 **Sühbaatar** *var.* Haylaastay. Sühbaatar, E Mongolia 46°44′N 113°51′E
163 P9 **Sühbaatar** ◐ *province* E Mongolia
101 K17 **Suhl** Thüringen, C Germany 50°37′N 10°43′E
108 F7 **Suhr** Aargau, N Switzerland 47°23′N 08°05′E
Sui'an *see* Zhangpu
Suicheng *see* Suixi
161 O12 **Suichuan** *var.* Quanjiang. Jiangxi, S China 26°26′N 114°34′E
Suid-Afrika *see* South Africa
160 L4 **Suide** *var.* Mingzhou. Shaanxi, C China 37°30′N 110°10′E
Suidwes-Afrika *see* Namibia
163 Y9 **Suifenhe** Heilongjiang, NE China 44°22′N 131°12′E
Suigen *see* Suwŏn
163 W8 **Suihua** Heilongjiang, NE China 46°40′N 127°00′E
Súilí, Loch *see* Swilly, Lough
161 Q6 **Suining** Jiangsu, E China 33°54′N 117°58′E
160 I9 **Suining** Sichuan, C China 30°31′N 105°33′E
103 Q4 **Suippes** Marne, N France 49°08′N 04°31′E
97 E20 **Suir** *Ir.* An tSiúir. ~ S Ireland
165 J13 **Suita** Ōsaka, Honshū, SW Japan 34°39′N 135°27′E
160 L16 **Suixi** *var.* Suicheng. Guangdong, S China 21°23′N 110°14′E
Sui Xian *see* Suizhou
163 T13 **Suizhong** Liaoning, NE China 40°19′N 120°22′E
161 N8 **Suizhou** *prev.* Sui Xian. Hubei, C China 31°46′N 113°20′E
149 P17 **Sujāwal** Sind, SE Pakistan 24°36′N 68°06′E
169 O16 **Sukabumi** *prev.* Soekaboemi. Jawa, C Indonesia 06°55′S 106°56′E
169 Q12 **Sukadana, Teluk** *bay* Borneo, W Indonesia
165 P11 **Sukagawa** Fukushima, Honshū, C Japan 37°16′N 140°20′E
Sukarnapura *see* Jayapura
Sukarno, Puntjak *see* Jaya, Puncak
Sükh *see* Sokh
114 N8 **Sukha Reka** ~ NE Bulgaria
114 J8 **Sukhindol** Veliko Turnovo, N Bulgaria 43°11′N 24°10′E
126 J5 **Sukhinichi** Kaluzhskaya Oblast', W Russian Federation 54°06′N 35°22′E
Sukhne *see* As Sukhnah
127 S5 **Sukhodol** Samarskaya Oblast', W Russian Federation 53°53′N 51°13′E
129 Q4 **Sukhona** *var.* Tot'ma. ~ NW Russian Federation
167 O8 **Sukhothai** *var.* Sukotai. Sukhothai, W Thailand 17°00′N 99°51′E
Sukhumi *see* Sokhumi
Sukkertoppen *see* Maniitsoq
149 Q13 **Sukkur** Sind, SE Pakistan 27°45′N 68°46′E
Sukotai *see* Sukhothai
Sukra Bay *see* Şawqirah, Dawḩat
125 V15 **Suksun** Permskaya Oblast', NW Russian Federation 57°10′N 57°27′E
165 F15 **Sukumo** Kōchi, Shikoku, SW Japan 32°55′N 132°42′E
94 B12 **Sula** *island* S Norway
125 Q5 **Sula** ~ NW Russian Federation
117 R5 **Sula** ~ N Ukraine
42 H6 **Sulaco, Río** ~ NW Honduras
Sulaimaniya *see* As Sulaymānīyah
149 S10 **Sulaimān Range** ▲▲ C Pakistan
127 Q16 **Sulak** Respublika Dagestan, SW Russian Federation 43°19′N 47°28′E
127 Q16 **Sulak** ~ SW Russian Federation
171 Q13 **Sula, Kepulauan** *island group* C Indonesia
136 I12 **Sulakyurt** *var.* Konur. Kırıkkale, N Turkey 40°10′N 33°42′E
171 P17 **Sulamu** Timor, S Indonesia 09°57′S 123°33′E
96 F5 **Sula Sgeir** *island* NW Scotland, United Kingdom
171 N13 **Sulawesi** *Eng.* Celebes. *island* C Indonesia
Sulawesi, Laut *see* Celebes Sea
171 N14 **Sulawesi Selatan** *off.* Propinsi Sulawesi Selatan, *Eng.* South Celebes, South Sulawesi. ◐ *province* C Indonesia
Sulawesi Selatan, Propinsi *see* Sulawesi Selatan
171 P12 **Sulawesi Tengah** *off.* Propinsi Sulawesi Tengah, *Eng.* Central Celebes, Central Sulawesi. ◐ *province* N Indonesia
Sulawesi Tengah, Propinsi *see* Sulawesi Tengah
171 O14 **Sulawesi Tenggara** *off.* Propinsi Sulawesi Tenggara, *Eng.* South-East Celebes, South-East Sulawesi. ◐ *province* C Indonesia
Sulawesi Tenggara, Propinsi *see* Sulawesi Tenggara
171 P11 **Sulawesi Utara** *off.* Propinsi Sulawesi Utara, *Eng.* North Celebes, North Sulawesi. ◐ *province* N Indonesia
Sulawesi Utara, Propinsi *see* Sulawesi Utara
139 T5 **Sulaymān Beg** At Ta'mīn, N Iraq
Sulaymānīyah, Muḩāfaẓat as *see* As Sulaymānīyah
95 D15 **Suldalsvatnet** ◎ S Norway
Sulden *see* Solda
110 E12 **Sulechów** *Ger.* Züllichau. Lubuskie, W Poland 52°05′N 15°37′E
110 E11 **Sulęcin** Lubuskie, W Poland 52°29′N 15°06′E
77 U14 **Suleja** Niger, C Nigeria 09°15′N 07°10′E
111 K14 **Sulejów** Łodzkie, S Poland 51°21′N 19°57′E
96 I5 **Sule Skerry** *island* N Scotland, United Kingdom
Suliag *see* Sawhāj
76 J16 **Sulima** S Sierra Leone 06°59′N 11°34′W
117 O13 **Sulina** Tulcea, SE Romania 45°07′N 29°40′E
117 N13 **Sulina, Braţul** ~ SE Romania
100 H12 **Sulingen** Niedersachsen, NW Germany 52°40′N 08°48′E
Sulisjielmmá *see* Sulitjelma
92 H12 **Sulisskongen** ▲ C Norway 67°10′N 16°16′E
92 H12 **Sulitjelma** *Lapp.* Sulisjielmmá. Nordland, C Norway 67°10′N 16°05′E
56 A9 **Sullana** Piura, NW Peru 04°54′S 80°42′W
23 N3 **Sulligent** Alabama, S USA 33°54′N 88°07′W
30 M14 **Sullivan** Illinois, N USA 39°36′N 88°36′W
31 N15 **Sullivan** Indiana, N USA 39°05′N 87°24′W
27 W5 **Sullivan** Missouri, C USA 38°12′N 91°09′W
Sullivan Island *see* Lanbi Kyun
96 M1 **Sullom Voe** NE Scotland, United Kingdom 60°24′N 01°09′W
103 O7 **Sully-sur-Loire** Loiret, C France 47°46′N 02°21′E
Sulmo *see* Sulmona
107 K15 **Sulmona** *anc.* Sulmo. Abruzzo, C Italy 42°03′N 13°56′E
Sulo *see* Shule He
114 M11 **Süloğlu** Edirne, NW Turkey 41°46′N 26°55′E
22 G9 **Sulphur** Louisiana, S USA 30°14′N 93°22′W
27 O12 **Sulphur** Oklahoma, C USA 34°31′N 96°58′W
28 K9 **Sulphur Creek** ~ South Dakota, N USA
24 M5 **Sulphur Draw** ~ Texas, SW USA
25 W5 **Sulphur River** ~ Arkansas/Texas, SW USA
25 V6 **Sulphur Springs** Texas, SW USA 33°09′N 95°36′W
24 M6 **Sulphur Springs Draw** ~ Texas, SW USA
14 D8 **Sultan** Ontario, S Canada 47°34′N 82°45′W
Sultānābād *see* Arāk
Sultan Alonto, Lake *see* Lanao, Lake
136 G15 **Sultan Dağları** ▲▲ C Turkey
114 N13 **Sultanköy** Tekirdağ, NW Turkey 41°01′N 27°58′E
171 Q7 **Sultan Kudarat** *var.* Nuling. Mindanao, S Philippines 07°20′N 124°16′E
152 M13 **Sultānpur** Uttar Pradesh, N India 26°15′N 82°04′E
171 O9 **Sulu Archipelago** *island group* SW Philippines
192 F7 **Sulu Basin** *undersea feature* SE South China Sea 08°00′N 121°30′E
Sülüktü *see* Sulyukta
Sulu, Laut *see* Sulu Sea
169 X6 **Sulu Sea** *var.* Laut Sulu. *sea* SW Philippines
145 O15 **Sulutobe** *Kaz.* Sulütöbe. Kzylorda, S Kazakhstan 44°31′N 66°17′E
Sulütöbe *see* Sulutobe
147 Q11 **Sulyukta** *Kir.* Sülüktü. Batkenskaya Oblast', SW Kyrgyzstan 39°57′N 69°31′E
Sulz *see* Sulz am Neckar
101 G22 **Sulz am Neckar** *var.* Sulz. Baden-Württemberg, SW Germany 48°22′N 08°37′E
101 L20 **Sulzbach-Rosenberg** Bayern, SE Germany 49°30′N 11°43′E
195 N13 **Sulzberger Bay** *bay* Antarctica
Sumail *see* Summēl
81 M14 **Sumalē** ◐ *federal region* E Ethiopia
113 F15 **Sumartin** Split-Dalmacija, S Croatia 43°17′N 16°52′E
32 H6 **Sumas** Washington, NW USA 49°00′N 122°15′W
168 J10 **Sumatera** *Eng.* Sumatra. *island* W Indonesia
168 J12 **Sumatera Barat** *off.* Propinsi Sumatera Barat, *Eng.* West Sumatra. ◐ *province* W Indonesia
Sumatera Barat, Propinsi *see* Sumatera Barat
168 L13 **Sumatera Selatan** *off.* Propinsi Sumatera Selatan, *Eng.* South Sumatra. ◐ *province* W Indonesia
Sumatera Selatan, Propinsi *see* Sumatera Selatan
168 H10 **Sumatera Utara** *off.* Propinsi Sumatera Utara, *Eng.* North Sumatra. ◐ *province* W Indonesia
Sumatera Utara, Propinsi *see* Sumatera Utara
Sumatra *see* Sumatera
Šumava *see* Bohemian Forest
Sumayl *see* Summēl
139 U7 **Sumayr al Muḩammad** Diyālá, E Iraq 33°34′N 45°06′E
171 N17 **Sumba, Pulau** *Eng.* Sandalwood Island; *prev.* Soemba. *island* Nusa Tenggara, C Indonesia
146 D12 **Sumbar** ~ W Turkmenistan
192 E9 **Sumbawa** *prev.* Soembawa. *island* Nusa Tenggara, C Indonesia
170 L16 **Sumbawabesar** Sumbawa, S Indonesia 08°30′S 117°25′E
81 F23 **Sumbawanga** Rukwa, W Tanzania 07°57′S 31°37′E
82 B12 **Sumbe** *var.* N'Gunza, *Port.* Novo Redondo. Cuanza Sul, W Angola 11°13′S 13°53′E
96 M3 **Sumburgh Head** *headland* NE Scotland, United Kingdom 59°51′N 01°16′W
111 H23 **Sümeg** Veszprém, W Hungary 47°01′N 17°13′E
80 C12 **Sumeih** Southern Darfur, S Sudan 09°50′N 27°39′E
169 T16 **Sumenep** *prev.* Soemenep. Pulau Madura, C Indonesia 07°01′S 113°51′E
Sumgait *see* Sumqayıtçay, Azerbaijan
Sumgait *see* Sumqayıt, Azerbaijan
165 Y14 **Sumisu-jima** *Eng.* Smith Island. *island* SE Japan
139 Q2 **Summēl** *var.* Sumail, Sumayl. Dahūk, N Iraq 36°52′N 42°51′E
31 O5 **Summer Island** *island* Michigan, N USA
32 H15 **Summer Lake** ◎ Oregon, NW USA
11 N17 **Summerland** British Columbia, SW Canada 49°35′N 119°45′W
13 P14 **Summerside** Prince Edward Island, SE Canada 46°24′N 63°46′W
21 R5 **Summersville** West Virginia, NE USA 38°17′N 80°52′W
21 R5 **Summersville Lake** ⊠ West Virginia, NE USA
21 S13 **Summerton** South Carolina, SE USA 33°36′N 80°21′W
23 R2 **Summerville** Georgia, SE USA 34°28′N 85°21′W
21 S14 **Summerville** South Carolina, SE USA 33°01′N 80°10′W
39 R10 **Summit** Alaska, USA 63°21′N 148°50′W
35 V6 **Summit Mountain** ▲ Nevada, W USA 39°23′N 116°25′W
37 R8 **Summit Peak** ▲ Colorado, C USA 37°21′N 106°42′W
Summus Portus *see* Somport, Col du
29 X12 **Sumner** Iowa, C USA 42°51′N 92°05′W
22 K3 **Sumner** Mississippi, S USA 33°58′N 90°22′W
185 H17 **Sumner, Lake** ◎ South Island, New Zealand
37 U12 **Sumner, Lake** ⊠ New Mexico, SW USA
111 G17 **Šumperk** *Ger.* Mährisch-Schönberg. Olomoucký Kraj, E Czech Republic 49°58′N 17°00′E
42 F7 **Sumpul, Río** ~ El Salvador/Honduras
137 Z11 **Sumqayıt** *Rus.* Sumgait. E Azerbaijan 40°33′N 49°41′E
137 Y11 **Sumqayıtçay** *Rus.* Sumgait. ~ E Azerbaijan
147 R9 **Sumsar** Dzhalal-Abadskaya Oblast', W Kyrgyzstan 41°12′N 71°16′E
117 S3 **Sums'ka Oblast'** *var.* Sumy, *Rus.* Sumskaya Oblast'. ◐ *province* NE Ukraine
Sumskaya Oblast' *see* Sums'ka Oblast'
124 J8 **Sumskiy Posad** Respublika Kareliya, NW Russian Federation 64°12′N 35°22′E
21 S12 **Sumter** South Carolina, SE USA 33°54′N 80°22′W
117 T3 **Sumy** Sums'ka Oblast', NE Ukraine 50°54′N 34°49′E
Sumy *see* Sums'ka Oblast'
159 Q15 **Sumzom** Xizang Zizhiqu, W China 29°45′N 96°14′E
125 R15 **Suna** Kirovskaya Oblast', NW Russian Federation 57°53′N 50°04′E
124 I10 **Suna** ~ NW Russian Federation
165 S3 **Sunagawa** Hokkaidō, NE Japan 43°30′N 141°55′E
153 V13 **Sunamganj** Sylhet, NE Bangladesh 25°04′N 91°24′E
163 W14 **Sunan** ✈ (P'yŏngyang) SW North Korea 39°12′N 125°40′E
Sunan/Sunan Yugurzu Zizhixian *see* Hongwansi
19 N9 **Sunapee Lake** ◎ New Hampshire, NE USA
139 P4 **Sunaysilah** *salt marsh* N Iraq
20 M8 **Sunbright** Tennessee, S USA 36°12′N 84°39′W
33 R6 **Sunburst** Montana, NW USA 48°51′N 111°54′W
183 N12 **Sunbury** Victoria, SE Australia 37°36′S 114°45′E
21 X8 **Sunbury** North Carolina, SE USA 36°27′N 76°34′W
18 G14 **Sunbury** Pennsylvania, NE USA 40°51′N 76°47′W
61 A17 **Sunchales** Santa Fe, C Argentina 30°58′S 61°35′W
163 W13 **Sunch'ŏn** SW North Korea 39°28′N 125°58′E
163 Y16 **Sunch'ŏn** *Jap.* Junten. S South Korea 34°56′N 127°29′E
36 K13 **Sun City** Arizona, SW USA 33°36′N 112°16′W
19 O9 **Suncook** New Hampshire, NE USA 43°07′N 71°25′W
161 P5 **Suncun** *prev.* Xinwen. Shandong, E China 35°49′N 117°36′E
Sunda Islands *see* Greater Sunda Islands
33 Z12 **Sundance** Wyoming, C USA 44°24′N 104°22′W
153 T17 **Sundarbans** *wetland* Bangladesh/India
154 M11 **Sundargarh** Orissa, E India 22°07′N 84°02′E
129 U15 **Sunda Shelf** *undersea feature* S South China Sea 05°00′N 107°00′E
Sunda Trench *see* Java Trench
129 U17 **Sunda Trough** *undersea feature* E Indian Ocean 08°50′S 109°30′E
95 O16 **Sundbyberg** Stockholm, C Sweden 59°22′N 17°58′E
97 M14 **Sunderland** *var.* Wearmouth. NE England, United Kingdom 54°55′N 01°23′W
101 F15 **Sundern** Nordrhein-Westfalen, W Germany 51°19′N 08°00′E
136 F12 **Sündiken Dağları** ▲▲ C Turkey
24 M5 **Sundown** Texas, SW USA 33°27′N 102°29′W
11 P16 **Sundre** Alberta, SW Canada 51°49′N 114°46′W
14 H12 **Sundridge** Ontario, S Canada 45°45′N 79°25′W
93 H17 **Sundsvall** Västernorrland, C Sweden 62°22′N 17°20′E
26 H4 **Sunflower, Mount** ▲ Kansas, C USA 39°01′N 102°02′W
Sunflower State *see* Kansas
169 N14 **Sungaibuntu** Sumatera, SW Indonesia 04°04′S 105°37′E
168 K12 **Sungaidareh** Sumatera, W Indonesia 0°58′S 101°30′E
167 P17 **Sungai Kolok** *var.* Sungai Ko-Lok. Narathiwat, SW Thailand 06°02′N 101°58′E
Sungai Ko-Lok *see* Sungai Kolok
168 K12 **Sungaipenuh** *prev.* Soengaipenoeh. Sumatera, W Indonesia 02°S 101°28′E
169 P11 **Sungaipinyuh** Borneo, C Indonesia 0°16′N 109°06′E
Sungari *see* Songhua Jiang
Sungaria *see* Dzungaria
Sungei Pahang *see* Pahang, Sungai
167 O8 **Sung Men** Phrae, NW Thailand 17°59′N 100°07′E
83 M15 **Sungo** Tete, NW Mozambique 16°31′S 33°58′E
Sungpu *see* Songpan
168 M13 **Sungsang** Sumatera, W Indonesia 02°22′S 104°50′E
114 M9 **Sungurlare** Burgas, E Bulgaria 42°47′N 26°46′E
136 J12 **Sungurlu** Çorum, N Turkey 40°10′N 34°23′E
112 F9 **Sunja** Sisak-Moslavina, C Croatia 45°21′N 16°33′E
153 Q12 **Sun Koshī** ~ E Nepal
94 F9 **Sunndalen** *valley* S Norway
94 F9 **Sunndalsøra** Møre og Romsdal, S Norway 62°39′N 08°37′E
95 K15 **Sunne** Värmland, C Sweden 59°52′N 13°05′E
95 O15 **Sunnersta** Uppsala, C Sweden 59°46′N 17°40′E
94 C11 **Sunnfjord** *physical region* S Norway
95 C15 **Sunnhordland** *physical region* S Norway
94 D10 **Sunnmøre** *physical region* S Norway
37 N4 **Sunnyside** Utah, W USA 39°33′N 110°23′W
32 J10 **Sunnyside** Washington, NW USA 46°01′N 119°58′W
35 N9 **Sunnyvale** California, W USA 37°22′N 122°02′W
30 L8 **Sun Prairie** Wisconsin, N USA 43°12′N 89°12′W
Sunqur *see* Sonqor
25 N1 **Sunray** Texas, SW USA 36°01′N 101°49′W
22 I8 **Sunset** Louisiana, S USA 30°24′N 92°04′W
25 S5 **Sunset** Texas, SW USA 33°24′N 97°45′W
Sunset State *see* Oregon
181 Z10 **Sunshine Coast** *cultural region* Queensland, E Australia
Sunshine State *see* Florida
Sunshine State *see* New Mexico
Sunshine State *see* South Dakota
123 O10 **Suntar** Respublika Sakha (Yakutiya), NE Russian Federation 62°10′N 117°34′E
39 R10 **Suntrana** Alaska, USA 63°51′N 148°51′W
148 J15 **Suntsar** Baluchistān, SW Pakistan 25°30′N 62°03′E
163 W15 **Sunwi-do** *island* SW North Korea
163 W6 **Sunwu** Heilongjiang, NE China 49°29′N 127°15′E
77 O16 **Sunyani** W Ghana 07°22′N 02°18′W
Suō *see* Suao
93 M17 **Suolahti** Länsi-Suomi, C Finland 62°32′N 25°51′E
Suoločielgi *see* Saariselkä
Suomenlahti *see* Finland, Gulf of
Suomen Tasavalta/Suomi *see* Finland
93 N14 **Suomussalmi** Oulu, E Finland 64°54′N 29°05′E
165 E13 **Suō-nada** *sea* SW Japan
93 M17 **Suonenjoki** Itä-Suomi, C Finland 62°36′N 27°07′E
167 S13 **Suŏng** Kâmpóng Cham, C Cambodia 11°53′N 105°41′E
124 I10 **Suoyarvi** Respublika Kareliya, NW Russian Federation 62°02′N 32°24′E
Supanburi *see* Suphan Buri
57 D14 **Supe** Lima, W Peru 10°49′S 77°40′W
15 V7 **Supérieur, Lac** ◎ Québec, SE Canada
Supérieur, Lac *see* Superior, Lake
36 M14 **Superior** Arizona, SW USA 33°17′N 111°06′W
33 O9 **Superior** Montana, NW USA 47°11′N 114°53′W
29 P17 **Superior** Nebraska, C USA 40°01′N 98°04′W
30 I3 **Superior** Wisconsin, N USA 46°42′N 92°04′W
41 S17 **Superior, Laguna** *lagoon* S Mexico
31 N2 **Superior, Lake** *Fr.* Lac Supérieur. ◎ Canada/USA
36 L13 **Superstition Mountains** ▲▲ Arizona, SW USA
113 F14 **Supetar** *It.* San Pietro. Split-Dalmacija, S Croatia 43°22′N 16°34′E
167 O10 **Suphan Buri** *var.* Supanburi. Suphan Buri, W Thailand 14°29′N 100°10′E
171 V12 **Supiori, Pulau** *island* E Indonesia
188 K2 **Supply Reef** *reef* N Northern Mariana Islands
195 O7 **Support Force Glacier** *glacier* Antarctica
137 R10 **Sup'sa** *var.* Supsa. ~ W Georgia
Supsa *see* Sup'sa
Sūq 'Abs *see* 'Abs
139 W12 **Sūq ash Shuyūkh** Dhī Qār, SE Iraq 30°53′N 46°28′E
138 H4 **Şuqaylibīyah** Ḩamāh, W Syria 35°21′N 36°24′E
161 Q6 **Suqian** Jiangsu, E China 33°57′N 118°18′E
Suqrah *see* Şawqirah
Suqrah Bay *see* Şawqirah, Dawḩat
141 V16 **Suquţrā** *var.* Sokotra, *Eng.* Socotra. *island* SE Yemen
141 Z8 **Şūr** NE Oman 22°32′N 59°33′E
Şūr *see* Soûr
127 P5 **Sura** Penzenskaya Oblast', W Russian Federation 53°23′N 45°03′E
127 P4 **Sura** ~ W Russian Federation
149 N12 **Surāb** Baluchistān, SW Pakistan 28°28′N 66°15′E
Surabaja *see* Surabaya
192 E8 **Surabaya** *prev.* Surabaja, Soerabaja. Jawa, C Indonesia 07°14′S 112°45′E
95 N15 **Surahammar** Västmanland, C Sweden 59°43′N 16°13′E
169 Q16 **Surakarta** *Eng.* Solo; *prev.* Soerakarta. Jawa, S Indonesia 07°32′S 110°50′E
Surakhany *see* Suraxanı
137 S10 **Surami** C Georgia 41°59′N 43°36′E
143 X13 **Sūrān** Sīstān va Balūchestān, SE Iran 27°18′N 61°58′E
111 I21 **Šurany** *Hung.* Nagysurány. Nitriansky Kraj, SW Slovakia 48°05′N 18°10′E
154 D12 **Sūrat** Gujarāt, W India 21°10′N 72°54′E
Suratdhani *see* Surat Thani
152 G9 **Sūratgarh** Rājasthān, NW India 29°20′N 73°59′E
167 N14 **Surat Thani** *var.* Suratdhani. Surat Thani, SW Thailand 09°09′N 99°20′E
119 Q16 **Suraw** *Rus.* Surov. ~ E Belarus
137 Z11 **Suraxanı** *Rus.* Surakhany. E Azerbaijan 40°25′N 49°59′E
141 Y11 **Surayr** E Oman 19°56′N 57°47′E
138 K2 **Suraysāt** Ḩalab, N Syria 36°42′N 38°01′E
118 O12 **Surazh** Vitsyebskaya Voblasts', NE Belarus 55°25′N 30°44′E
126 H6 **Surazh** Bryanskaya Oblast', W Russian Federation 53°04′N 32°29′E
191 V17 **Sur, Cabo** *headland* Easter Island, Chile, E Pacific Ocean 27°11′S 109°26′W
112 L11 **Surčin** Serbia, N Serbia 44°48′N 20°19′E
116 H9 **Surduc** *Hung.* Szurduk. Sălaj, NW Romania 47°13′N 23°20′E
113 P16 **Surdulica** Serbia, SE Serbia 42°43′N 22°10′E
99 L24 **Sûre** *var.* Sauer. ~ W Europe *see also* Sauer
Sûre *see* Sauer
154 C10 **Surendranagar** Gujarāt, W India 22°44′N 71°43′E
18 K16 **Surf City** New Jersey, NE USA 39°21′N 74°24′W
183 V3 **Surfers Paradise** Queensland, E Australia 27°54′S 153°18′E
21 U13 **Surfside Beach** South Carolina, SE USA 33°36′N 78°58′W
102 J10 **Surgères** Charente-Maritime, W France 46°07′N 00°44′W
122 H10 **Surgut** Khanty-Mansiyskiy Avtonomnyy Okrug-Yugra, C Russian Federation 61°13′N 73°28′E
122 K10 **Surgutikha** Krasnoyarskiy Kray, N Russian Federation 64°44′N 87°13′E
98 M6 **Surhuisterveen** Friesland, N Netherlands 53°11′N 06°10′E
105 V5 **Súria** Cataluña, NE Spain 41°50′N 01°45′E
143 P10 **Sūrīān** Fārs, S Iran
155 J15 **Suriāpet** Andhra Pradesh, C India 17°10′N 79°42′E
171 Q6 **Surigao** Mindanao, S Philippines 09°43′N 125°31′E
167 R10 **Surin** Surin, E Thailand 14°53′N 103°29′E
55 U11 **Surinam** *off.* Republic of Suriname, *var.* Suriname; *prev.* Dutch Guiana, Netherlands Guiana. ◆ *republic* N South America
Suriname *see* Surinam
Suriname, Republic of *see* Surinam
Sūrīya/Sūrīyah, Al-Jumhūrīyah al-'Arabīyah as- *see* Syria
Surkhab, Darya-i- *see* Kahmard, Daryā-ye
Surkhandar'inskaya Oblast' *see* Surxondaryo Viloyati
Surkhandar'ya *see* Surxondaryo
Surkhet *see* Birendranagar
147 R12 **Surkhob** ~ C Tajikistan
137 P11 **Sürmene** Trabzon, NE Turkey 40°56′N 40°03′E
Surov *see* Suraw
127 N11 **Surovikino** Volgogradskaya Oblast', SW Russian Federation 48°39′N 42°46′E

◆ Country
● Country Capital
◇ Dependent Territory
○ Dependent Territory Capital
◐ Administrative Regions
✈ International Airport
▲ Mountain
▲▲ Mountain Range
Volcano
~ River
◎ Lake
⊠ Reservoir

35 N11 Sur, Point headland California, W USA 36°18′N 121°54′W
187 N15 Surprise, Île island N New Caledonia
61 E22 Sur, Punta headland E Argentina 50°59′S 69°10′W
Surrentum see Sorrento
28 M3 Surrey North Dakota, N USA 48°13′N 101°05′W
97 O22 Surrey cultural region SE England, United Kingdom
21 X7 Surry Virginia, NE USA 37°08′N 81°34′W
108 F8 Sursee Luzern, W Switzerland 47°11′N 08°07′E
127 P6 Sursk Penzenskaya Oblast', W Russian Federation 53°06′N 45°46′E
127 P5 Surskoye Ul'yanovskaya Oblast', W Russian Federation 54°28′N 46°47′E
75 P8 Surt var. Sidra, Sirte. N Libya 31°13′N 16°35′E
95 I19 Surte Västra Götaland, S Sweden 57°49′N 12°01′E
75 Q8 Surt, Khalīj Eng. Gulf of Sidra, Gulf of Sirti, Sidra. gulf N Libya
92 I5 Surtsey island S Iceland
137 N17 Suruç Şanlıurfa, S Turkey 36°58′N 38°24′E
168 L13 Surulangun Sumatera, W Indonesia 02°35′S 102°47′E
147 P13 Surxondaryo Rus. Surkhandar'ya. ≈ Tajikistan/Uzbekistan
147 N13 Surxondaryo Viloyati Rus. Surkhandar'inskaya Oblast'. ◈ province S Uzbekistan
Süs see Susch
106 A8 Susa Piemonte, NE Italy 45°10′N 07°01′E
165 E12 Susa Yamaguchi, Honshū, SW Japan 34°35′N 131°34′E
Susa see Shūsh
113 E16 Sušac It. Cazza. island SW Croatia
Sūsah see Sousse
164 G14 Susaki Kōchi, Shikoku, SW Japan 33°22′N 133°13′E
165 I15 Susami Wakayama, Honshū, SW Japan 33°32′N 135°32′E
142 K9 Sūsangerd var. Susangird. Khūzestān, SW Iran 31°40′N 48°06′E
Susangird see Sūsangerd
35 P4 Susanville California, W USA 40°25′N 120°39′W
108 J9 Susch var. Süs. Graubünden, SE Switzerland 46°45′N 10°04′E
137 N12 Suşehri Sivas, N Turkey 40°11′N 38°06′E
Susiana see Khūzestān
111 B18 Sušice Ger. Schüttenhofen. Plzeňský Kraj, W Czech Republic 49°14′N 13°32′E
39 R11 Susitna Alaska, USA 61°32′N 150°30′W
39 R11 Susitna River ≈ Alaska, USA
127 Q3 Suslonger Respublika Mariy El, W Russian Federation 56°18′N 48°16′E
105 N14 Suspiro del Moro, Puerto del pass S Spain
18 H16 Susquehanna River ≈ New York/Pennsylvania, NE USA
13 O15 Sussex New Brunswick, SE Canada 45°43′N 65°32′W
18 J13 Sussex New Jersey, NE USA 41°12′N 74°34′W
21 W7 Sussex Virginia, NE USA 36°54′N 77°16′W
97 O23 Sussex cultural region S England, United Kingdom
183 S10 Sussex Inlet New South Wales, SE Australia 35°10′S 150°35′E
99 L17 Susteren Limburg, SE Netherlands 51°04′N 05°50′E
10 K12 Sustut Peak ▲ British Columbia, W Canada 56°25′N 126°34′W
123 S9 Susuman Magadanskaya Oblast', E Russian Federation 62°46′N 148°08′E
188 H6 Susupe ● (Northern Mariana Islands-judicial capital) Saipan, S Northern Mariana Islands
136 D12 Susurluk Balıkesir, NW Turkey 39°55′N 28°10′E
114 M13 Susuzmüsellim Tekirdağ, NW Turkey 41°04′N 27°03′E
136 F15 Sütçüler Isparta, SW Turkey 37°31′N 31°00′E
116 L13 Şuţeşti Brăila, SE Romania 45°13′N 27°27′E
83 F25 Sutherland Western Cape, SW South Africa 32°24′S 20°40′E
28 L15 Sutherland Nebraska, C USA 41°09′N 101°07′W
96 I7 Sutherland cultural region N Scotland, United Kingdom
185 B21 Sutherland Falls waterfall South Island, New Zealand
32 F14 Sutherlin Oregon, NW USA 43°23′N 123°18′W
149 V10 Sutlej ≈ India/Pakistan
Sutna see Satna
35 P7 Sutter Creek California, W USA 38°22′N 120°49′W
39 R11 Sutton Alaska, USA 61°42′N 148°53′W
29 Q16 Sutton Nebraska, C USA 40°36′N 97°52′W
21 R4 Sutton West Virginia, NE USA 38°41′N 80°43′W
12 F8 Sutton ≈ Ontario, C Canada
97 M19 Sutton Coldfield C England, United Kingdom 52°34′N 01°48′W
21 R4 Sutton Lake ⊠ West Virginia, NE USA
15 P13 Sutton, Monts hill range Québec, SE Canada
12 F8 Sutton Ridges ▲▲ Ontario, C Canada
165 Q4 Suttsu Hokkaidō, NE Japan 42°46′N 140°12′E
39 P15 Sutwik Island island Alaska, USA
Süüj see Dashinchilen
118 H5 Suure-Jaani Ger. Gross-Sankt-Johannis. Viljandimaa, S Estonia 58°34′N 25°28′E
118 J7 Suur Munamägi var. Munamägi, Ger. Eier-Berg. ▲ SE Estonia 57°42′N 27°03′E
118 F5 Suur Väin Ger. Grosser Sund. strait W Estonia
147 U8 Suusamyr Chuyskaya Oblast', C Kyrgyzstan 42°07′N 73°55′E
187 X14 Suva ● (Fiji) Viti Levu, W Fiji 18°08′S 178°27′E
187 X15 Suva ✈ Viti Levu, C Fiji 18°01′S 178°30′E
113 N18 Suva Gora ▲ W FYR Macedonia
118 H11 Suvainiškis Panevežys, NE Lithuania 56°09′N 25°15′E
Suvalkai/Suvalki see Suwałki
113 P15 Suva Planina ▲▲ SE Serbia
Suva Reka see Suharekë
126 K5 Suvorov Tul'skaya Oblast', W Russian Federation 54°08′N 36°33′E
117 N12 Suvorove Odes'ka Oblast', SW Ukraine 45°35′N 28°58′E
114 M8 Suvorovo Varna, E Bulgaria 43°19′N 27°26′E
Suvorovo see Ştefan Vodă
Suwaik see As Suwayq
Suwaira see Aş Şuwayrah
110 O7 Suwałki Lith. Suvalkai, Rus. Suvalki. Podlaskie, NE Poland 54°06′N 22°56′E
167 R10 Suwannaphum Roi Et, E Thailand 15°36′N 103°46′E
23 V8 Suwannee River ≈ Florida/Georgia, SE USA
Şuwār see Aş Şuwār
190 K14 Suwarrow atoll N Cook Islands
143 R16 Suwaydān var. Sweiham. Abū Ẓaby, E United Arab Emirates 24°30′N 55°19′E
Suwaydá/Suwaydā', Muḥāfaẓat as see As Suwaydā'
Suwayqiyah, Hawr as see Shuwayjah, Hawr ash
Suways, Qanāt as see Suez Canal
Suweida see As Suwaydā'
Suweon see Suwŏn
163 X15 Suwŏn var. Suweon, Jap. Suigen. NW South Korea 37°17′N 127°03′E
Su Xian see Suzhou
143 R14 Sūzā Hormozgān, S Iran 26°50′N 56°05′E
145 P15 Suzak Kaz. Sozaq. Yuzhnyy Kazakhstan, S Kazakhstan 44°09′N 68°28′E
165 N12 Suzaka var. Suzaka. Nagano, Honshū, S Japan 36°38′N 138°20′E
Suzaka see Suzaka
126 M3 Suzdal' Vladimirskaya Oblast', W Russian Federation 56°27′N 40°29′E
161 P7 Suzhou var. Su Xian. Anhui, E China 33°38′N 117°02′E
161 R8 Suzhou var. Soochow, Su-chou, Suchow; prev. Wuhsien. Jiangsu, E China 31°23′N 120°34′E
Suzhou see Jiuquan
163 V12 Suzi He ≈ NE China
Suz, Mys see Soye, Mys
165 M10 Suzu Ishikawa, Honshū, SW Japan 37°24′N 137°12′E
165 K14 Suzuka Mie, Honshū, SW Japan 34°52′N 136°37′E
165 M10 Suzu-misaki headland Honshū, SW Japan 37°31′N 137°19′E
Svågälv see Svågan
94 M10 Svågan var. Svågälv. ≈ C Sweden
Svalava/Svaljava see Svalyava
92 O2 Svalbard ◇ Norwegian dependency Arctic Ocean
92 J2 Svalbardhseyri Nordhurland Eystra, N Iceland 65°43′N 18°03′W
95 K22 Svalöv Skåne, S Sweden 55°55′N 13°06′E
116 H7 Svalyava Cz. Svalava, Svaljava, Hung. Szolyva. Zakarpats'ka Oblast', W Ukraine 48°33′N 23°00′E
92 O2 Svanbergfjellet ▲ C Svalbard 78°40′N 18°10′E
95 M24 Svaneke Bornholm, E Denmark 55°07′N 15°08′E
95 L22 Svängsta Blekinge, S Sweden 56°16′N 14°46′E
95 J16 Svanskog Värmland, C Sweden 59°10′N 12°34′E
95 L16 Svartå Örebro, C Sweden 59°13′N 14°07′E
95 L15 Svartälven ≈ C Sweden
92 G12 Svartisen glacier C Norway
117 X6 Svatove Rus. Svatovo. Luhans'ka Oblast', E Ukraine 49°24′N 38°11′E
Svatovo see Svatove
Sväty Kríž nad Hronom see Žiar nad Hronom
167 Q11 Svay Chék, Stœng ≈ Cambodia/Thailand
167 S13 Svay Riĕng Svay Riĕng, S Cambodia 11°05′N 105°48′E
92 O3 Sveagruva Spitsbergen, W Svalbard 77°53′N 16°42′E
95 K23 Svedala Skåne, S Sweden 55°30′N 13°15′E
118 H12 Svėdesai Utena, NE Lithuania 55°42′N 25°22′E
93 G18 Sveg Jämtland, C Sweden 62°02′N 14°20′E
118 C12 Švėkšna Klaipėda, W Lithuania 55°31′N 21°37′E
94 C11 Svelgen Sogn Og Fjordane, S Norway 61°47′N 05°18′E
95 H15 Svelvik Vestfold, S Norway 59°37′N 10°24′E
118 I13 Švenčionėliai Pol. Nowo-Święciany. Vilnius, SE Lithuania 55°10′N 26°00′E
118 I13 Švenčionys Pol. Swięciany. Vilnius, SE Lithuania 55°08′N 26°08′E
95 H24 Svendborg Fyn, C Denmark 55°04′N 10°38′E
95 K19 Svenljunga Västra Götaland, S Sweden 57°30′N 13°05′E
92 P2 Svenskøya island E Svalbard
93 G17 Svenstavik Jämtland, C Sweden 62°40′N 14°24′E
95 G20 Svenstrup Nordjylland, N Denmark 56°58′N 09°52′E
118 H12 Šventoji ≈ C Lithuania
117 Z8 Sverdlovs'k Rus. Sverdlovsk; prev. Imeni Sverdlova Rudnik. Luhans'ka Oblast', E Ukraine 48°05′N 39°37′E
Sverdlovsk see Yekaterinburg
127 W2 Sverdlovskaya Oblast' ◈ province C Russian Federation
122 K6 Sverdrupa, Ostrov island N Russian Federation
Sverige see Sweden
113 D15 Svetac prev. Sveti Andrea, It. Sant'Andrea. island SW Croatia
Sveti Andrea see Svetac
Sveti Nikola see Svetac
113 O18 Sveti Nikole prev. Sveti Nikola. C FYR Macedonia 41°54′N 21°55′E
Sveti Vrach see Sandanski
123 T14 Svetlaya Primorskiy Kray, SE Russian Federation 46°33′N 138°20′E
126 B2 Svetlogorsk Kaliningradskaya Oblast', W Russian Federation 54°56′N 20°09′E
122 K9 Svetlogorsk Krasnoyarskiy Kray, N Russian Federation 66°51′N 88°29′E
Svetlogorsk see Svyetlahorsk
127 N14 Svetlograd Stavropol'skiy Kray, SW Russian Federation 45°20′N 42°53′E
Svetlovodsk see Svitlovods'k
119 A14 Svetlyy Ger. Zimmerbude. Kaliningradskaya Oblast', W Russian Federation 54°42′N 20°07′E
127 Y8 Svetlyy Orenburgskaya Oblast', W Russian Federation 50°34′N 60°42′E
127 P7 Svetlyy Saratovskaya Oblast', W Russian Federation 51°42′N 45°40′E
124 G11 Svetogorsk Fin. Enso. Leningradskaya Oblast', NW Russian Federation 61°06′N 28°52′E
Svetozarevo see Jagodina
111 B18 Švihov Ger. Schwihau. Plzeňský Kraj, W Czech Republic 49°31′N 13°18′E
112 E13 Svilaja ▲▲ SE Croatia
112 N12 Svilajnac Serbia, C Serbia 44°15′N 21°12′E
114 L11 Svilengrad prev. Mustafa-Pasha. Khaskovo, S Bulgaria 41°45′N 26°14′E
Svinecea Mare, Munte see Svinecea Mare, Vârful
116 F13 Svinecea Mare, Vârful var. Munte Svinecea Mare. ▲ SW Romania 44°47′N 22°10′E
Svinø see Svínoy
95 B18 Svínoy Dan. Svinø. island NE Faeroe Islands
147 N14 Svintsovyy Rudnik Turkm. Swintsowyy Rudnik. Lebap Welaýaty, E Turkmenistan 37°54′N 66°25′E
118 I13 Svir Rus. Svir'. Minskaya Voblasts', NW Belarus 54°51′N 26°24′E
124 I12 Svir' canal NW Russian Federation
Svir', Ozero see Svir, Vozyera
119 I14 Svir, Vozyera Rus. Ozero Svir'. ◎ C Belarus
114 J7 Svishtov prev. Sistova. Veliko Tŭrnovo, N Bulgaria 43°37′N 25°20′E
119 F18 Svislach Pol. Świsłocz, Rus. Svisloch'. Hrodzyenskaya Voblasts', W Belarus 53°02′N 24°06′E
119 M17 Svislach Rus. Svisloch'. Mahilyowskaya Voblasts', E Belarus 53°26′N 28°59′E
119 L17 Svislach Rus. Svisloch'. ≈ E Belarus
Svisloch' see Svislach
111 F17 Svitavy Ger. Zwittau. Pardubický Kraj, C Czech Republic 49°45′N 16°27′E
117 S6 Svitlovods'k Rus. Svetlovodsk. Kirovohrads'ka Oblast', C Ukraine 49°05′N 33°15′E
Svizzera see Switzerland
123 Q13 Svobodnyy Amurskaya Oblast', SE Russian Federation 51°24′N 128°05′E
114 G9 Svoge Sofiya, W Bulgaria 42°58′N 23°20′E
92 G11 Svolvær Nordland, C Norway 68°15′N 14°40′E
111 F18 Svratka Ger. Schwarzawa. ≈ SE Czech Republic
113 P14 Svrljig Serbia, E Serbia 43°26′N 22°07′E
197 U10 Svyataya Anna Trough var. Saint Anna Trough. undersea feature N Kara Sea
124 M4 Svyatoy Nos, Mys headland NW Russian Federation 68°07′N 39°49′E
119 N18 Svyetlahorsk Rus. Svetlogorsk. Homyel'skaya Voblasts', SE Belarus 52°38′N 29°46′E
149 U5 Swābi North-West Frontier Province, N Pakistan 34°07′N 72°28′E
Swabian Jura see Schwäbische Alb
97 P19 Swaffham E England, United Kingdom 52°39′N 00°40′E
23 V5 Swainsboro Georgia, SE USA 32°36′N 82°19′W
83 C19 Swakop ≈ W Namibia
83 C19 Swakopmund Erongo, W Namibia 22°40′S 14°34′E
97 M15 Swale ≈ N England, United Kingdom
Swallow Island see Nendö
99 M16 Swalmen Limburg, SE Netherlands 51°13′N 06°02′E
12 G8 Swan ≈ Ontario, C Canada
97 L24 Swanage S England, United Kingdom 50°37′N 01°59′W
182 M10 Swan Hill Victoria, SE Australia 35°23′S 143°37′E
11 P13 Swan Hills Alberta, W Canada 54°41′N 116°20′W
65 D24 Swan Island island C Falkland Islands
Swankalok see Sawankhalok
29 U10 Swan Lake ◎ Minnesota, N USA
21 Y10 Swanquarter North Carolina, SE USA 35°24′N 76°20′W
182 J9 Swan Reach South Australia 34°39′S 139°35′E
11 V15 Swan River Manitoba, S Canada 52°06′N 101°17′W
183 P17 Swansea Tasmania, SE Australia 42°09′S 148°03′E
97 J22 Swansea Wel. Abertawe. S Wales, United Kingdom 51°38′N 03°57′W
21 R13 Swansea South Carolina, SE USA 33°47′N 81°06′W
19 S7 Swans Island island Maine, NE USA
28 L17 Swanson Lake ⊠ Nebraska, C USA
31 R11 Swanton Ohio, N USA 41°35′N 83°53′W
110 G11 Swarzędz Poznań, W Poland 52°24′N 17°05′E
Swatow see Shantou
83 L22 Swaziland off. Kingdom of Swaziland. ◆ monarchy S Africa
Swaziland, Kingdom of see Swaziland
93 G18 Sweden off. Kingdom of Sweden, Swe. Sverige. ◆ monarchy N Europe
Sweden, Kingdom of see Sweden
Swedru see Agona Swedru
25 V12 Sweeny Texas, SW USA 29°02′N 95°42′W
33 R6 Sweetgrass Montana, NW USA 48°58′N 111°58′W
32 G12 Sweet Home Oregon, NW USA 44°24′N 122°44′W
25 T12 Sweet Home Texas, SW USA 29°21′N 97°04′W
27 T4 Sweet Springs Missouri, C USA 38°57′N 93°24′W
20 M10 Sweetwater Tennessee, S USA 35°36′N 84°27′W
25 P7 Sweetwater Texas, SW USA 32°27′N 100°25′W
33 V15 Sweetwater River ≈ Wyoming, C USA
Sweiham see Suwaydān
83 F26 Swellendam Western Cape, SW South Africa 34°01′S 20°26′E
111 G15 Świdnica Ger. Schweidnitz. Wałbrzych, SW Poland 50°51′N 16°29′E
111 O14 Świdnik Ger. Streckenbach. Lubelskie, E Poland 51°14′N 22°41′E
110 F8 Świdwin Ger. Schivelbein. Zachodnio-pomorskie, NW Poland 53°47′N 15°44′E
111 F15 Świebodzice Ger. Freiburg in Schlesien, Swiebodzice. Wałbrzych, SW Poland 50°54′N 16°23′E
110 E11 Świebodzin Ger. Schwiebus. Lubuskie, W Poland 52°15′N 15°31′E
Święciany see Švenčionys
110 I9 Świecie Ger. Schwertberg. Kujawsko-pomorskie, C Poland 53°24′N 18°24′E
111 L15 Świętokrzyskie ◈ province S Poland
11 T16 Swift Current Saskatchewan, S Canada 50°17′N 107°49′W
98 K9 Swifterbant Flevoland, C Netherlands 52°36′N 05°33′E
183 Q12 Swifts Creek Victoria, SE Australia 37°17′S 147°41′E
96 E13 Swilly, Lough Ir. Loch Súilí. inlet N Ireland
97 M22 Swindon S England, United Kingdom 51°34′N 01°47′W
Swinemünde see Świnoujście
110 D8 Świnoujście Ger. Swinemünde. Zachodnio-pomorskie, NW Poland 53°54′N 14°13′E
Swintsowyy Rudnik see Svintsovyy Rudnik
Świsłocz see Svislach
Swiss Confederation see Switzerland
108 E9 Switzerland off. Swiss Confederation, Fr. La Suisse, Ger. Schweiz, It. Svizzera; anc. Helvetia. ◆ federal republic C Europe
97 F17 Swords Ir. Sord, Sórd Choluim Chille. Dublin, E Ireland 53°28′N 06°13′W
18 H13 Swoyersville Pennsylvania, NE USA 41°18′N 75°48′W
124 I10 Syamozera, Ozero ◎ NW Russian Federation
124 M13 Syamzha Vologodskaya Oblast', NW Russian Federation 60°02′N 41°09′E
118 N13 Syanno Rus. Senno. Vitsyebskaya Voblasts', NE Belarus 54°49′N 29°43′E
119 K16 Syarhyeyevichy Rus. Sergeyevichi. Minskaya Voblasts', C Belarus 53°30′N 27°45′E
124 I12 Syas'stroy Leningradskaya Oblast', NW Russian Federation 60°05′N 32°37′E
Sycaminum see Hefa
30 M10 Sycamore Illinois, N USA 41°59′N 88°41′W
126 J3 Sychëvka Smolenskaya Oblast', W Russian Federation 55°52′N 34°19′E
111 H14 Syców Ger. Gross Wartenberg. Dolnośląskie, SW Poland 51°18′N 17°42′E
14 E17 Sydenham ≈ Ontario, S Canada
Sydenham Island see Nonouti
183 T9 Sydney state capital New South Wales, SE Australia 33°55′S 151°10′E
13 R14 Sydney Cape Breton Island, Nova Scotia, SE Canada 46°10′N 60°10′W
Sydney Island see Manra
13 R14 Sydney Mines Cape Breton Island, Nova Scotia, SE Canada 46°14′N 60°19′W
Sydpur see Saidpur
119 K18 Syelishcha Rus. Selishche. Minskaya Voblasts', C Belarus 53°01′N 27°25′E
119 J18 Syemyezhava Rus. Semezhevo. Minskaya Voblasts', C Belarus 52°58′N 27°00′E
Syene see Aswân
117 X6 Syeverodonets'k Rus. Severodonetsk. Luhans'ka Oblast', E Ukraine 48°59′N 38°28′E
161 T6 Sÿiao Shan island SE China
100 H11 Syke Niedersachsen, NW Germany 52°55′N 08°49′E
94 D10 Sykkylven Møre og Romsdal, S Norway 62°23′N 06°35′E
Sykoúri see Sykoúrio
115 F15 Sykoúrio var. Sikouri, Sykoúri; prev. Sikoúrion. Thessalía, C Greece 39°46′N 22°35′E
125 R11 Syktyvkar prev. Ust'-Sysol'sk. Respublika Komi, NW Russian Federation 61°42′N 50°45′E
23 Q4 Sylacauga Alabama, S USA 33°10′N 86°15′W
Sylarna see Storsylen
153 V14 Sylhet Sylhet, NE Bangladesh 24°53′N 91°51′E
153 V13 Sylhet ◈ division NE Bangladesh
100 G6 Sylt island NW Germany
21 O10 Sylva North Carolina, SE USA 35°23′N 83°13′W
125 V15 Sylva ≈ NW Russian Federation
23 W5 Sylvania Georgia, SE USA 32°45′N 81°38′W
31 R11 Sylvania Ohio, N USA 41°43′N 83°42′W
11 Q15 Sylvan Lake Alberta, SW Canada 52°18′N 114°02′W
33 T13 Sylvan Pass pass Wyoming, C USA
23 T7 Sylvester Georgia, SE USA 31°31′N 83°50′W
25 P6 Sylvester Texas, SW USA 32°42′N 100°15′W
10 L11 Sylvia, Mount ▲ British Columbia, W Canada 58°03′N 124°26′W
122 K11 Sym ≈ C Russian Federation
115 N22 Sými var. Simi. island Dodekánisa, Greece, Aegean Sea
117 U8 Synel'nykove Dnipropetrovs'ka Oblast', E Ukraine 48°19′N 35°32′E
125 U6 Synya Respublika Komi, NW Russian Federation 65°21′N 58°01′E
117 P7 Synyukha Rus. Sinyukha. ≈ S Ukraine
195 V2 Syowa Japanese research station Antarctica 68°58′S 40°07′E
26 H6 Syracuse Kansas, C USA 38°00′N 101°43′W
29 S16 Syracuse Nebraska, C USA 40°39′N 96°11′W
18 H10 Syracuse New York, NE USA 43°03′N 76°09′W
Syracuse see Siracusa
Syrdar'inskaya Oblast' see Sirdaryo Viloyati
Syrdariya see Syr Darya
144 L14 Syr Darya var. Sai Hun, Sir Darya, Syrdarya, Kaz. Syrdariya, Rus. Syrdar'ya, Uzb. Sirdaryo; anc. Jaxartes. ≈ C Asia
Syrdarya see Syr Darya
138 J6 Syria off. Syrian Arab Republic, var. Siria, Syrie, Ar. Al-Jumhūrīyah al-'Arabīyah as-Sūrīyah, Sūrīya. ◆ republic SW Asia
Syrian Arab Republic see Syria
138 L9 Syrian Desert Ar. Al Hamad, Bādiyat ash Shām. desert SW Asia
Syrie see Syria
115 L22 Sýrna var. Sirna. island Kykládes, Greece, Aegean Sea
115 I20 Sýros var. Síros. island Kykládes, Greece, Aegean Sea
93 M18 Sysmä Etelä-Suomi, S Finland 61°28′N 25°37′E
125 R12 Sysola ≈ NW Russian Federation
Syulemeshlii see Sredets
127 S2 Syumsi Udmurtskaya Respublika, NW Russian Federation 57°07′N 51°35′E
114 K10 Syuyutliyka ≈ C Bulgaria
Syvash, Zaliv see Syvash, Zatoka
117 U12 Syvash, Zatoka Rus. Zaliv Syvash. inlet S Ukraine
127 Q6 Syzran' Samarskaya Oblast', W Russian Federation 53°10′N 48°23′E
Szabadka see Subotica
111 N21 Szabolcs-Szatmár-Bereg off. Szabolcs-Szatmár-Bereg Megye. ◈ county E Hungary
Szabolcs-Szatmár-Bereg Megye see Szabolcs-Szatmár-Bereg
110 G10 Szamocin Ger. Samotschin. Wielkopolskie, C Poland 53°02′N 17°04′E
116 H8 Szamos var. Someş, Someşul, Ger. Samosch, Somesch. ≈ Hungary/Romania
Szamosújvár see Gherla
110 G11 Szamotuły Poznań, W Poland 52°35′N 16°36′E
Szarkowszczyzna see Sharkawshchyna
111 M24 Szarvas Békés, SE Hungary 46°51′N 20°35′E
Szászmagyarós see Măieruş
Szászrégen see Reghin
Szászsebes see Sebeş
Szászváros see Orăştie
Szatmárrnémeti see Satu Mare
Száva see Sava
111 P15 Szczebrzeszyn Lubelskie, E Poland 50°43′N 23°00′E
110 D9 Szczecin Eng./Ger. Stettin. Zachodnio-pomorskie, NW Poland 53°25′N 14°32′E
110 G8 Szczecinek Ger. Neustettin. Zachodnio-pomorskie, NW Poland 53°43′N 16°40′E
110 D8 Szczeciński, Zalew var. Stettiner Haff, Ger. Oderhaff. bay Germany/Poland
111 K15 Szczekociny Śląskie, S Poland 50°38′N 19°46′E
110 N8 Szczuczyn Podlaskie, NE Poland 53°34′N 22°17′E
Szczuczyn Nowogródzki see Shchuchyn
110 M8 Szczytno Ger. Ortelsburg. Warmińsko-Mazurskie, NE Poland 53°34′N 21°E
Szechuan/Szechwan see Sichuan
111 K21 Szécsény Nógrád, N Hungary 48°07′N 19°30′E
111 L25 Szeged Ger. Szegedin, Rom. Seghedin. Csongrád, SE Hungary 46°17′N 20°06′E
Szegedin see Szeged
111 N23 Szeghalom Békés, SE Hungary 47°01′N 21°09′E
Székelyhid see Săcueni
Székelykeresztúr see Cristuru Secuiesc
111 I23 Székesfehérvár Ger. Stuhlweissenberg; anc. Alba Regia. Fejér, W Hungary 47°13′N 18°24′E
Szeklerburg see Miercurea-Ciuc
Szekler Neumarkt see Târgu Secuiesc
111 J25 Szekszárd Tolna, S Hungary 46°21′N 18°41′E
Szempcz/Szenc see Senec
Szenice see Senica
Szentágota see Agnita
111 J22 Szentendre Ger. Sankt Andrä. Pest, N Hungary 47°40′N 19°02′E
111 L24 Szentes Csongrád, SE Hungary 46°40′N 20°17′E
111 F23 Szentgotthárd Eng. Saint Gotthard, Ger. Sankt Gotthard. Vas, W Hungary 46°57′N 16°18′E
Szentgyörgy see Đurđevac
Szenttamás see Srbobran
Széphely see Jebel
Szeping see Siping
Szered see Sereď
111 N21 Szerencs Borsod-Abaúj-Zemplén, NE Hungary 48°10′N 21°11′E
Szeret see Siret
Szeretfalva see Sărăţel
110 N7 Szeska Góra var. Szeskie Wygórza, Ger. Seesker Höhe. hill NE Poland
Szeskie Wygórza see Szeska Góra
111 H25 Szigetvár Baranya, SW Hungary 46°01′N 17°50′E
Szilágysomlyó see Şimleu Silvaniei
Szinna see Snina
Sziszek see Sisak
Szitás-Keresztúr see Cristuru Secuiesc
111 E15 Szklarska Poręba Ger. Schreiberhau. Dolnośląskie, SW Poland 50°50′N 15°30′E
Szkudy see Skuodas
Szlatina see Slatina
Szlavonia/Szlavonország see Slavonija
Szlovákia see Slovakia
Szluin see Slunj
111 L23 Szolnok Jász-Nagykun-Szolnok, C Hungary 47°11′N 20°12′E
Szolyva see Svalyava
111 G23 Szombathely Ger. Steinamanger; anc. Sabaria, Savaria. Vas, W Hungary 47°14′N 16°38′E
Szond/Szonta see Sonta
Szováta see Sovata
110 F13 Szprotawa Ger. Sprottau. Lubuskie, W Poland 51°33′N 15°32′E
Sztálinváros see Dunaújváros
Sztrazsó see Strážov
110 J8 Sztum Ger. Stuhm. Pomorskie, N Poland 53°54′N 19°01′E
110 H10 Szubin Ger. Schubin. Kujawsko-pomorskie, C Poland 53°04′N 17°49′E
Szucsava see Suceava
Szurduk see Surduc
111 M14 Szydłowiec Ger. Schlelau. Mazowieckie, C Poland 51°14′N 20°50′E

T

190 I17 Taakoka island S Cook Islands
Taalintehdas see Dalsbruk
171 O4 Taal, Lake ◎ Luzon, NW Philippines
95 J23 Taastrup var. Tåstrup. København, E Denmark 55°39′N 12°19′E
111 I24 Tab Somogy, W Hungary 46°45′N 18°01′E
171 P4 Tabaco Luzon, N Philippines 13°22′N 123°42′E
186 G4 Tabalo Mussau Island, NE Papua New Guinea 01°22′S 149°37′E
104 K5 Tábara Castilla-León, N Spain 41°49′N 05°57′W
186 H5 Tabar Islands island group NE Papua New Guinea
Tabariya, Bahrat see Tiberias, Lake
143 S7 Ṭabas var. Golshan. Yazd, C Iran 33°37′N 56°54′E
43 P15 Tabasará, Serranía de ▲▲ W Panama
41 U15 Tabasco ◈ state SE Mexico
Tabasco see Grijalva, Río
127 Q2 Tabashino Respublika Mariy El, W Russian Federation 57°00′N 47°47′E
58 B13 Tabatinga Amazonas, N Brazil 04°14′S 69°44′W
74 G9 Tabelbala W Algeria 29°22′N 03°01′W
11 Q17 Taber Alberta, SW Canada 49°48′N 112°09′W
171 V15 Taberfane Pulau Trangan, E Indonesia 06°14′S 134°08′E
95 L19 Taberg Jönköping, S Sweden 57°42′N 14°05′E
191 O3 Tabiteuea prev. Drummond Island. atoll Tungaru, W Kiribati
171 O5 Tablas Island island C Philippines
184 Q10 Table Cape headland North Island, New Zealand 39°07′S 178°00′E
13 S13 Table Mountain ▲ Newfoundland, Newfoundland and Labrador, E Canada 47°39′N 59°15′W
173 P17 Table, Pointe de la headland SE Réunion 21°19′S 55°49′E
27 S8 Table Rock Lake ⊠ Arkansas/Missouri, C USA
36 K14 Table Top ▲ Arizona, SW USA 32°45′N 112°07′W
186 D8 Tabletop, Mount ▲ C Papua New Guinea 06°51′S 146°00′E
111 D18 Tábor Jihočeský Kraj, S Czech Republic 49°25′N 14°41′E
123 R7 Tabor Respublika Sakha (Yakutiya), NE Russian Federation 71°14′N 150°23′E
29 S15 Tabor Iowa, C USA 40°54′N 95°40′W
81 F21 Tabora Tabora, W Tanzania 05°04′S 32°49′E
81 F21 Tabora ◈ region C Tanzania
21 U12 Tabor City North Carolina, SE USA 34°09′N 78°52′W
147 Q10 Taboshar NW Tajikistan 40°37′N 69°33′E
76 L18 Tabou var. Tabu. S Ivory Coast 04°28′N 07°20′W
142 J2 Tabrīz var. Tebriz; anc. Tauris. Āzarbāyjān-e Sharqī, NW Iran 38°05′N 46°18′E
Tabu see Tabou
191 W1 Tabuaeran prev. Fanning Island. atoll Line Islands, E Kiribati
171 O2 Tabuk Luzon, N Philippines 17°26′N 121°25′E
140 J4 Tabūk Tabūk, NW Saudi Arabia 28°25′N 36°34′E
140 J5 Tabūk off. Minṭaqat Tabūk. ◈ province NW Saudi Arabia
Tabūk, Minṭaqat see Tabūk
187 Q13 Tabwemasana, Mount ▲ Espiritu Santo, W Vanuatu 15°22′S 166°44′E
95 O15 Täby Stockholm, C Sweden 59°29′N 18°04′E
41 N14 Tacámbaro Michoacán, SW Mexico 19°12′N 101°27′W
42 A5 Tacaná, Volcán ⛰ Guatemala/Mexico 15°07′N 92°06′W
43 X16 Tacarcuna, Cerro ▲ SE Panama 08°08′N 77°15′W
Tachau see Tachov
158 J3 Tacheng var. Qoqek. Xinjiang Uygur Zizhiqu, NW China 46°45′N 82°55′E
54 H7 Táchira off. Estado Táchira. ◈ state W Venezuela
Táchira, Estado see Táchira
161 T13 Tachoshui N Taiwan 24°26′N 121°43′E
111 A17 Tachov Ger. Tachau. Plzeňský Kraj, W Czech Republic 49°48′N 12°38′E
171 Q5 Tacloban off. Tacloban City. Leyte, C Philippines 11°15′N 125°E
Tacloban City see Tacloban
57 I19 Tacna Tacna, SE Peru 18°S 70°15′W
57 H18 Tacna off. Departamento de Tacna. ◈ department S Peru
Tacna, Departamento de see Tacna
32 H8 Tacoma Washington, NW USA 47°15′N 122°27′W
18 L11 Taconic Range ▲▲ NE USA
62 L6 Taco Pozo Formosa, N Argentina 25°35′S 63°15′W
57 M20 Tacsara, Cordillera de ▲▲ S Bolivia
61 F17 Tacuarembó prev. San Fructuoso. Tacuarembó, C Uruguay 31°42′S 56°W
61 E18 Tacuarembó ◈ department C Uruguay
61 F17 Tacuarembó, Río ≈ C Uruguay
83 I14 Taculi North Western, NW Zambia 14°17′S 26°51′E
171 Q8 Tacurong Mindanao, S Philippines 06°42′N 124°40′E
77 V8 Tadek ≈ NW Niger
74 J9 Tademaït, Plateau du plateau C Algeria
187 R17 Tadine Province des Îles Loyauté, E New Caledonia 21°33′S 167°54′E
80 M11 Tadjoura, Golfe de Eng. Gulf of Tajura. inlet E Djibouti
80 L11 Tadjourah E Djibouti 11°47′N 42°51′E
Tadmor/Tadmur see Tudmur
11 W10 Tadoule Lake ◎ Manitoba, C Canada
15 S8 Tadoussac Québec, SE Canada 48°09′N 69°43′W
155 H18 Tādpatri Andhra Pradesh, E India 14°55′N 77°59′E
Tadzhikabad see Tojikobod
Tadzhikistan see Tajikistan
163 Y14 T'aebaek-sanmaek ▲▲ E South Korea
163 V15 Taechŏng-do island NW South Korea
163 X13 Taedong-gang ≈ C North Korea
163 Y16 Taegu off. Taegu-gwangyŏksi, var. Daegu, Jap. Taikyū. SE South Korea 35°55′N 128°33′E
Taegu-gwangyŏksi see Taegu
Taehan-haehyŏp see Korea Strait
Taehan Min'guk see South Korea
163 Y15 Taejŏn off. Taejŏn-gwangyŏksi, Jap. Taiden. C South Korea 36°20′N 127°28′E
Taejŏn-gwangyŏksi see Taejŏn
193 Z13 Tafahi island N Tonga
105 Q4 Tafalla Navarra, N Spain 42°32′N 01°41′W
77 W7 Tafassâsset, Ténéré du desert N Niger
75 M12 Tafassâsset, Oued ≈ SE Algeria
55 U11 Tafelberg ▲ S Surinam 03°55′N 56°09′W
97 J21 Taff ≈ SE Wales, United Kingdom
Tafila/Ṭafīlah, Muḥāfaẓat aṭ see Aṭ Ṭafīlah
77 N15 Tafiré N Ivory Coast 09°04′N 05°10′W
142 M6 Tafresh Markazi, W Iran 34°40′N 50°00′E
143 Q9 Taft Yazd, C Iran 31°45′N 54°14′E
35 R13 Taft California, W USA 35°08′N 119°27′W
25 T14 Taft Texas, SW USA 27°58′N 97°24′W
143 W12 Taftān, Kūh-e ▲ SE Iran 28°38′N 61°06′E
35 R13 Taft Heights California, W USA 35°06′N 119°29′W
189 Y14 Tafunsak Kosrae, E Micronesia 05°21′N 162°58′E
192 G16 Tāga Savai'i, SW Samoa 13°46′S 172°31′W
149 O6 Tagāb Dāikondī, E Afghanistan 33°53′N 66°23′E
39 O8 Tagagawik River ≈ Alaska, USA
165 Q10 Tagajō var. Tagayô. Miyagi, Honshū, C Japan 38°18′N 140°58′E
126 K12 Taganrog Rostovskaya Oblast', SW Russian Federation 47°10′N 38°55′E
126 K12 Taganrog, Gulf of Rus. Taganrogskiy Zaliv, Ukr. Tahanroz'ka Zatoka. gulf Russian Federation/Ukraine
Taganrogskiy Zaliv see Taganrog, Gulf of
76 J8 Tagant ◈ region C Mauritania

◆ Country
● Country Capital
◇ Dependent Territory
○ Dependent Territory Capital
◈ Administrative Regions
✈ International Airport
▲ Mountain
▲▲ Mountain Range
⛰ Volcano
≈ River
◎ Lake
⊠ Reservoir

148 M14 **Tagas** Baluchistān, SW Pakistan 27°09′N 64°36′E
171 O4 **Tagaytay** Luzon, N Philippines 14°04′N 120°55′E
Tagazyô see Tagajô
171 P6 **Tagbilaran** var. Tagbilaran City. Bohol, C Philippines 09°41′N 123°54′E
Tagbilaran City see Tagbilaran
106 B10 **Taggia** Liguria, NW Italy 43°51′N 07°48′E
77 V9 **Taghouaji, Massif de** ▲ C Niger 17°13′N 08°37′E
107 J15 **Tagliacozzo** Lazio, C Italy 42°03′N 13°15′E
106 J7 **Tagliamento** ≈ NE Italy
149 N3 **Tagow Bāy** var. Bai. Sar-e Pol, N Afghanistan 35°41′N 66°01′E
146 H9 **Tagta** var. Tahta, Rus. Takhta. Daşoguz Welaýaty, N Turkmenistan 41°40′N 59°51′E
146 J16 **Tagtabazar** var. Takhtabazar. Mary Welaýaty, S Turkmenistan 35°57′N 62°49′E
59 L17 **Taguatinga** Tocantins, C Brazil 12°16′S 46°25′W
186 I10 **Tagula** Tagula Island, SE Papua New Guinea 11°21′S 153°11′E
186 I11 **Tagula Island** prev. Southeast Island, Sudest Island. island SE Papua New Guinea
171 Q7 **Tagum** Mindanao, S Philippines 07°22′N 125°51′E
54 C7 **Tagún, Cerro** elevation Colombia/Panama
105 P7 **Tagus** Port. Rio Tejo, Sp. Río Tajo. ≈ Portugal/Spain
64 M9 **Tagus Plain** undersea feature E Atlantic Ocean 37°30′N 12°00′W
191 S10 **Tahaa** island Îles Sous le Vent, W French Polynesia
191 U10 **Tahanea** atoll Îles Tuamotu, C French Polynesia
Tahanroz'ka Zatoka see Taganrog, Gulf of
74 K12 **Tahat** ▲ SE Algeria 23°15′N 05°34′E
163 U4 **Tahe** Heilongjiang, NE China 52°21′N 124°42′E
Tahilt see Tsogt
191 T10 **Tahiti** island Îles du Vent, W French Polynesia
Tahiti, Archipel de see Société, Archipel de la
118 E4 **Tahkuna Nina** headland W Estonia 59°06′N 22°35′E
148 K12 **Tāhlāb** ≈ W Pakistan
148 K12 **Tāhlāb, Dasht-i** desert SW Pakistan
27 R10 **Tahlequah** Oklahoma, C USA 35°57′N 94°58′W
35 Q6 **Tahoe City** California, W USA 39°09′N 120°09′W
35 P6 **Tahoe, Lake** ◎ California/Nevada, W USA
25 N6 **Tahoka** Texas, SW USA 33°10′N 101°47′W
32 F8 **Taholah** Washington, NW USA 47°19′N 124°17′W
77 T11 **Tahoua** Tahoua, W Niger 14°53′N 05°18′E
77 T11 **Tahoua** ◐ department W Niger
31 P3 **Tahquamenon Falls** waterfall Michigan, N USA
31 P4 **Tahquamenon River** ≈ Michigan, N USA
139 V10 **Taḥrīr** Al Qādisīyah, S Iraq 31°58′N 45°34′E
10 K17 **Tahsis** Vancouver Island, British Columbia, SW Canada 49°42′N 126°31′W
75 W9 **Ṭahta** var. Tahta. C Egypt 26°47′N 31°31′E
Tahta see Tagta
136 L15 **Tahtalı Dağları** ▲▲ C Turkey
57 I14 **Tahuamanu, Río** ≈ Bolivia/Peru
56 F13 **Tahuanía, Río** ≈ E Peru
191 X7 **Tahuata** island Îles Marquises, NE French Polynesia
76 L17 **Tai** SW Ivory Coast 05°52′N 07°28′W
161 P5 **Tai'an** Shandong, E China 36°13′N 117°12′E
191 R8 **Taiarapu, Presqu'île de** peninsula Tahiti, W French Polynesia
Taibad see Tāybād
160 K7 **Taibai Shan** ▲ C China 33°57′N 107°31′E
105 Q12 **Taibilla, Sierra de** ▲▲ S Spain
Taibus Qi see Baochang
Taichū see T'aichung
161 S13 **T'aichung** Jap. Taichū; prev. Taiwan. C Taiwan 24°09′N 120°40′E
Taiden see Taejŏn
185 E23 **Taieri** ≈ South Island, New Zealand
115 F21 **Taïgetos** ▲▲ S Greece
161 N4 **Taihang Shan** ▲▲ C China
184 M11 **Taihape** Manawatu-Wanganui, North Island, New Zealand 39°41′S 175°47′E
161 O7 **Taihe** Anhui, E China 33°14′N 115°35′E
161 O12 **Taihe** var. Chengjiang. Jiangxi, S China 26°47′N 114°52′E
Taihoku see T'aipei
161 P9 **Taihu** Anhui, E China 30°22′N 116°20′E
161 R8 **Tai Hu** ◎ E China
159 O9 **Taikang** var. Dorbod, Dorbod Mongolzu Zizhixian. Heilongjiang, NE China 46°50′N 124°25′E
161 O6 **Taikang** Henan, C China 34°01′N 114°59′E
165 T5 **Taiki** Hokkaidō, NE Japan 42°29′N 143°15′E
166 L8 **Taikkyi** Yangon, SW Burma (Myanmar) 17°16′N 95°55′E
Taikyū see Taegu
163 U8 **Tailai** Heilongjiang, NE China 46°25′N 123°25′E
168 I12 **Taileleo** Pulau Siberut, W Indonesia 01°45′S 99°06′E
182 J10 **Tailem Bend** South Australia 35°20′S 139°34′E
96 I8 **Tain** N Scotland, United Kingdom 57°49′N 04°04′W
161 S14 **T'ainan** Jap. Tainan; prev. Dainan. S Taiwan 23°01′N 120°05′E
115 E22 **Taínaro, Akrotírio** cape S Greece
161 Q11 **Taining** var. Shancheng. Fujian, SE China 26°55′N 117°13′E
191 W7 **Taiohae** prev. Madisonville. Nuku Hiva, NE French Polynesia 08°55′S 140°04′W
161 T13 **T'aipei** Jap. Taihoku; prev. Daihoku. ● (Taiwan) N Taiwan 25°02′N 121°28′E
168 J7 **Taiping** Perak, Peninsular Malaysia 04°54′N 100°42′E
Taiping see Chongzuo
163 S8 **Taiping Ling** ▲ NE China 47°27′N 120°27′E
165 Q4 **Taisei** Hokkaidō, NE Japan 42°13′N 139°52′E
165 G12 **Taisha** Shimane, Honshū, SW Japan 35°23′N 132°40′E
109 R4 **Taiskirchen** Oberösterreich, NW Austria 48°15′N 13°33′E
63 F20 **Taitao, Peninsula de** peninsula S Chile
Taitō see T'aitung
161 T14 **T'aitung** Jap. Taitō. S Taiwan 22°43′N 121°10′E
92 M13 **Taivalkoski** Oulu, E Finland 65°35′N 28°20′E
93 K19 **Taivassalo** Länsi-Suomi, SW Finland 60°35′N 21°36′E
161 T14 **Taiwan** off. Republic of China, var. Formosa, Formo'sa. ◆ republic E Asia
192 F5 **Taiwan** var. Formosa. island E Asia
Taiwan see T'aichung
T'aiwan Haihsia/Taiwan Haixia see Taiwan Strait
Taiwan Shan see Chungyang Shanmo
161 R13 **Taiwan Strait** var. Formosa Strait, Chin. T'aiwan Haihsia, Taiwan Haixia. strait China/Taiwan
161 N4 **Taiyuan** var. T'ai-yuan, T'ai-yüan; prev. Yangku. province capital Shanxi, C China 37°48′N 112°33′E
T'ai-yuan/T'ai-yüan see Taiyuan
161 R7 **Taizhou** Jiangsu, E China 32°36′N 119°52′E
161 S10 **Taizhou** var. Jiaojiang; prev. Haimen. Zhejiang, SE China 28°36′N 121°19′E
Taizhou see Linhai
141 O16 **Ta'izz** SW Yemen 13°36′N 44°04′E
141 O16 **Ta'izz** ✕ SW Yemen 13°40′N 44°10′E
75 P12 **Tajarhī** SW Libya 24°21′N 14°28′E
147 P13 **Tajikistan** off. Republic of Tajikistan, Rus. Tadzhikistan, Taj. Jumhurii Tojikiston; prev. Tajik S.S.R. ◆ republic C Asia
Tajikistan, Republic of see Tajikistan
Tajik S.S.R see Tajikistan
165 O11 **Tajima** Fukushima, Honshū, C Japan 37°10′N 139°46′E
Tajoe see Tayu
Tajo, Río see Tagus
42 B5 **Tajumulco, Volcán** Ж W Guatemala 15°04′N 91°50′W
105 P7 **Tajuña** ≈ C Spain
Tajura, Gulf of see Tadjoura, Golfe de
167 O9 **Tak** var. Rahaeng. Tak, W Thailand 16°51′N 99°08′E
189 U4 **Taka Atoll** var. Tōke. atoll Ratak Chain, N Marshall Islands
165 P12 **Takahagi** Ibaraki, Honshū, S Japan 36°42′N 140°42′E
165 H13 **Takahashi** var. Takahasi. Okayama, Honshū, SW Japan 34°48′N 133°38′E
Takahasi see Takahashi
189 P12 **Takaieu Island** island E Micronesia
184 I13 **Takaka** Tasman, South Island, New Zealand 40°52′S 172°49′E
170 M14 **Takalar** Sulawesi, C Indonesia 05°28′S 119°24′E
165 H13 **Takamatsu** var. Takamatu. Kagawa, Shikoku, SW Japan 34°19′N 133°59′E
Takamatu see Takamatsu
165 D14 **Takamori** Kumamoto, Kyūshū, SW Japan 32°50′N 131°08′E
165 D16 **Takanabe** Miyazaki, Kyūshū, SW Japan 32°13′N 131°31′E
170 M16 **Takan, Gunung** ▲ Pulau Sumba, S Indonesia 08°52′S 117°32′E
165 Q7 **Takanosu** var. Kita-Akita. Akita, Honshū, C Japan 40°13′N 140°23′E
Takao see Kaohsiung
165 L11 **Takaoka** Toyama, Honshū, SW Japan 36°44′N 137°02′E
184 N12 **Takapau** Hawke's Bay, North Island, New Zealand 40°01′S 176°21′E
191 U9 **Takapoto** atoll Îles Tuamotu, C French Polynesia
184 L5 **Takapuna** Auckland, North Island, New Zealand 36°48′S 174°46′E
165 J13 **Takarazuka** Hyōgo, Honshū, SW Japan 34°49′N 135°21′E
191 U9 **Takaroa** atoll Îles Tuamotu, C French Polynesia
165 N12 **Takasaki** Gunma, Honshū, S Japan 36°20′N 139°00′E
164 L12 **Takayama** Gifu, Honshū, SW Japan 36°09′N 137°16′E
164 K12 **Takefu** var. Echizen, Takehu. Fukui, Honshū, SW Japan 35°55′N 136°11′E
Takehu see Takefu
164 C14 **Takeo** Saga, Kyūshū, SW Japan 33°13′N 130°00′E
Takeo see Takêv
164 C17 **Take-shima** island Nansei-shotō, SW Japan
142 M5 **Tākestān** var. Takistan; prev. Siadehan. Qazvīn, N Iran 36°02′N 49°40′E
164 D14 **Taketa** Ōita, Kyūshū, SW Japan 33°00′N 131°23′E
167 R13 **Takêv** prev. Takeo. Takêv, S Cambodia 10°59′N 104°47′E
167 O10 **Tak Fah** Nakhon Sawan, C Thailand
139 T13 **Takhādīd** well S Iraq
149 R3 **Takhār** ◐ province NE Afghanistan
Takhiatash see Taxiatosh
167 S13 **Ta Khmau** Kândal, S Cambodia 11°30′N 104°59′E
Takhta see Tagta
Takhtabazar see Tagtabazar
145 O8 **Takhtabrod** Severnyy Kazakhstan, N Kazakhstan 52°35′N 67°37′E
Takhtakupyr see Taxtako'pir
142 M8 **Takht-e Shāh, Kūh-e** ▲ C Iran
77 V12 **Takiéta** Zinder, S Niger 13°43′N 08°33′E
8 J8 **Takijuq Lake** ◎ Nunavut, NW Canada
165 S3 **Takikawa** Hokkaidō, NE Japan 43°35′N 141°54′E
165 U3 **Takinoue** Hokkaidō, NE Japan 44°10′N 143°09′E
Takistan see Tākestān
185 B23 **Takitimu Mountains** ▲▲ South Island, New Zealand
Takkaze see Tekezē
165 R7 **Takko** Aomori, Honshū, C Japan 40°19′N 141°11′E
10 L13 **Takla Lake** ◎ British Columbia, SW Canada
Takla Makan Desert see Taklimakan Shamo
158 H9 **Taklimakan Shamo** Eng. Takla Makan Desert. desert NW China
167 T12 **Takôk** Môndól Kiri, E Cambodia 12°37′N 106°30′E
39 P10 **Takotna** Alaska, USA 62°59′N 156°03′W
Takow see Kaohsiung
123 O12 **Taksimo** Respublika Buryatiya, S Russian Federation 56°18′N 114°53′E
164 C13 **Taku** Saga, Kyūshū, SW Japan 33°19′N 130°06′E
10 I10 **Taku** ≈ British Columbia, W Canada
166 M15 **Takua Pa** var. Ban Takua Pa. Phangnga, SW Thailand 08°55′N 98°20′E
77 W16 **Takum** Taraba, E Nigeria 07°16′N 10°00′E
191 V10 **Takume** atoll Îles Tuamotu, C French Polynesia
190 L16 **Takutea** island S Cook Islands
186 K6 **Takuu Islands** prev. Mortlock Group. island group NE Papua New Guinea
119 L18 **Tal'** Minskaya Voblasts', S Belarus 52°52′N 27°58′E
40 L13 **Tala** Jalisco, C Mexico 20°39′N 103°45′W
61 F19 **Tala** Canelones, S Uruguay 34°24′S 55°45′W
Talabriga see Aveiro, Portugal
Talabriga see Talavera de la Reina, Spain
119 N14 **Talachyn** Rus. Tolochin. Vitsyebskaya Voblasts', NE Belarus 54°25′N 29°42′E
149 U7 **Talagang** Punjab, E Pakistan 32°55′N 72°29′E
105 V11 **Talaiassa** ▲ Ibiza, Spain, W Mediterranean Sea 38°55′N 01°17′E
155 J23 **Talaimannar** Northern Province, NW Sri Lanka 09°05′N 79°43′E
117 R3 **Talalayivka** Chernihivs'ka Oblast', N Ukraine 50°51′N 33°09′E
43 O15 **Talamanca, Cordillera de** ▲▲ S Costa Rica
56 A9 **Talara** Piura, NW Peru 04°31′S 81°17′W
104 L11 **Talarrubias** Extremadura, W Spain 39°03′N 05°14′W
147 S8 **Talas** Talasskaya Oblast', NW Kyrgyzstan 42°29′N 72°21′E
147 S8 **Talas** ≈ NW Kyrgyzstan
186 G7 **Talasea** New Britain, E Papua New Guinea 05°20′S 150°01′E
Talas Oblasty see Talasskaya Oblast'
147 S8 **Talasskaya Oblast'** Kir. Talas Oblasty. ◐ province NW Kyrgyzstan
147 S8 **Talasskiy Alatau, Khrebet** ▲▲ Kazakhstan/Kyrgyzstan
77 U12 **Talata Mafara** Zamfara, NW Nigeria 12°33′N 06°01′E
171 R9 **Talaud, Kepulauan** island group E Indonesia
104 M9 **Talavera de la Reina** anc. Caesarobriga, Talabriga. Castilla-La Mancha, C Spain 39°58′N 04°50′W
104 J11 **Talavera la Real** Extremadura, W Spain 38°53′N 06°46′W
186 F7 **Talawe, Mount** ▲ New Britain, C Papua New Guinea 05°30′S 148°24′E
23 S5 **Talbotton** Georgia, SE USA 32°40′N 84°32′W
183 R7 **Talbragar River** ≈ New South Wales, SE Australia
62 G13 **Talca** Maule, C Chile 35°28′S 71°42′W
62 F13 **Talcahuano** Bío Bío, C Chile 36°43′S 73°07′W
154 N12 **Tālcher** Orissa, E India 20°57′N 85°13′E
25 W5 **Talco** Texas, SW USA 33°21′N 95°06′W
145 V14 **Taldykorgan** Kaz. Taldyqorghan; prev. Taldy-Kurgan. Taldykorgan, SE Kazakhstan 45°N 78°23′E
Taldy-Kurgan/Taldyqorghan see Taldykorgan
147 Y7 **Taldy-Suu** Issyk-Kul'skaya Oblast', E Kyrgyzstan 42°49′N 78°33′E
147 U10 **Taldy-Suu** Oshskaya Oblast', SW Kyrgyzstan 40°33′N 73°52′E
Tal-e Khosravī see Yāsūj
193 Y15 **Taleki Tonga** island Otu Tolu Group, C Tonga
193 Y15 **Taleki Vavu'u** island Otu Tolu Group, C Tonga
102 J13 **Talence** Gironde, SW France 44°49′N 00°35′W
145 U16 **Talgar** Kaz. Talghar. Almaty, SE Kazakhstan 43°17′N 77°15′E
Talghar see Talgar
171 Q12 **Taliabu, Pulau** island Kepulauan Sula, C Indonesia
115 L22 **Taliarós, Akrotírio** headland Astypálaia, Kykládes, Greece, Aegean Sea 36°31′N 26°18′E
Ta-lien see Dalian
27 Q12 **Talihina** Oklahoma, C USA 34°45′N 95°03′W
Talimardzhan see Tollimarjon
137 T12 **Tal'in** Rus. Talin; prev. Verin T'alin. W Armenia 40°23′N 43°51′E
Talin see T'alin
81 E15 **Tali Post** Bahr el Gabel, S Sudan 05°55′N 30°44′E
Taliq-an see Tāloqān
Talış Dağları see Talish Mountains
142 L2 **Talish Mountains** Az. Talış Dağları, Per. Kūhhā-ye Ţavālesh, Rus. Talyshskiye Gory. ▲▲ Azerbaijan/Iran
170 M16 **Taliwang** Sumbawa, C Indonesia 08°45′S 116°55′E
119 L17 **Tal'ka** Minskaya Voblasts', C Belarus 53°22′N 28°21′E
39 R11 **Talkeetna** Alaska, USA 62°19′N 150°06′W
39 R11 **Talkeetna Mountains** ▲▲ Alaska, USA
Talkhof see Puurmani
92 H2 **Tálknafjördhur** Vestfirdhir, W Iceland 65°38′N 23°51′W
139 Q3 **Tall 'Abṭah** Nīnawá, N Iraq 35°52′N 42°40′E
138 M2 **Tall Abyaḍ** var. Tell Abiad. Ar Raqqah, N Syria 36°42′N 38°56′E
23 Q4 **Talladega** Alabama, S USA 33°26′N 86°06′W
139 Q2 **Tall 'Afar** Nīnawýa, N Iraq 36°22′N 42°27′E
23 S8 **Tallahassee** prev. Muskogean. state capital Florida, SE USA 30°26′N 84°17′W
22 L2 **Tallahatchie River** ≈ Mississippi, S USA
Tall al Abyaḍ see At Tall al Abyaḍ
139 W12 **Tall al Laḥm** Dhī Qār, S Iraq 30°46′N 46°22′E
183 P11 **Tallangatta** Victoria, SE Australia 36°15′S 147°13′E
23 R4 **Tallapoosa River** ≈ Alabama/Georgia, S USA
103 T13 **Tallard** Hautes-Alpes, SE France 44°30′N 06°04′E
139 Q3 **Tall ash Sha'īr** Nīnawá, N Iraq 36°11′N 42°26′E
23 Q5 **Tallassee** Alabama, S USA 32°32′N 85°53′W
139 R4 **Tall 'Azbah** Nīnawýa, NW Iraq 35°47′N 43°13′E
138 I5 **Tall Bīsah** Ḥimṣ, W Syria 34°50′N 36°44′E
139 R3 **Tall Ḥassūnah** Al Anbār, N Iraq 36°05′N 43°10′E
139 Q2 **Tall Ḥuqnah** var. Tell Huqnah. Nīnawá, N Iraq 36°33′N 42°34′E
Tallin see Tallinn
118 G3 **Tallinn** Ger. Reval, Rus. Tallin; prev. Revel. ● (Estonia) Harjumaa, NW Estonia 59°26′N 24°42′E
118 H3 **Tallinn** ✕ Harjumaa, NW Estonia 59°23′N 24°52′E
138 H5 **Tall Kalakh** var. Tell Kalakh. Ḥimṣ, C Syria 34°40′N 36°18′E
139 R2 **Tall Kayf** Nīnawýa, NW Iraq 36°30′N 43°08′E
Tall Kūchak see Tall Kūshik
139 P2 **Tall Kūshik** var. Tall Kūchak. Al Ḥasakah, E Syria 36°48′N 42°01′E
31 U12 **Tallmadge** Ohio, N USA 41°06′N 81°26′W
22 J5 **Tallulah** Louisiana, S USA 32°22′N 91°12′W
139 Q2 **Tall 'Uwaynāt** Nīnawýa, NW Iraq 36°43′N 42°18′E
139 Q2 **Tall Ẓāhir** Nīnawá, N Iraq 36°51′N 42°29′E
122 J13 **Tal'menka** Altayskiy Kray, S Russian Federation 53°55′N 83°26′E
122 K8 **Talnakh** Taymyrskiy (Dolgano-Nenetskiy) Avtonomnyy Okrug, N Russian Federation 69°26′N 88°27′E
117 P7 **Tal'ne** Rus. Tal'noye. Cherkas'ka Oblast', C Ukraine 48°55′N 30°40′E
Tal'noye see Tal'ne
80 E12 **Talodi** Southern Kordofan, C Sudan 10°40′N 30°25′E
188 B16 **Talofofo** SE Guam 13°21′N 144°45′E
188 B16 **Talofofo Bay** bay SE Guam
26 L9 **Taloga** Oklahoma, C USA 36°02′N 98°58′W
123 T10 **Talon** Magadanskaya Oblast', E Russian Federation 59°47′N 148°46′E
14 H11 **Talon, Lake** ◎ Ontario, S Canada
149 R2 **Tāloqān** var. Taliq-an. Takhār, NE Afghanistan 36°44′N 69°33′E
126 M8 **Talovaya** Voronezhskaya Oblast', W Russian Federation 51°07′N 40°46′E
9 N6 **Taloyoak** prev. Spence Bay. Nunavut, N Canada 69°30′N 93°25′W
25 Q8 **Talpa** Texas, SW USA 31°46′N 99°42′W
40 K13 **Talpa de Allende** Jalisco, C Mexico 20°22′N 104°51′W
23 S9 **Talquin, Lake** ⊠ Florida, SE USA
Talsen see Talsi
Talshand see Chandmanī
118 E8 **Talsi** Ger. Talsen. Talsi, NW Latvia 57°14′N 22°35′E
143 V11 **Tal Sīāh** Sīstān va Balūchestān, SE Iran 28°19′N 57°43′E
62 G6 **Taltal** Antofagasta, N Chile 25°22′S 70°27′W
8 K10 **Taltson** ≈ Northwest Territories, NW Canada
168 K11 **Taluk** Sumatera, W Indonesia 0°32′S 101°35′E
92 J8 **Talvik** Finnmark, N Norway 70°02′N 22°59′E
182 M7 **Talyawalka Creek** ≈ New South Wales, SE Australia
Talyshskiye Gory see Talish Mountains
29 W14 **Tama** Iowa, C USA 41°58′N 92°34′W
Tama Abu, Banjaran see Penambo, Banjaran
169 U9 **Tamabo, Banjaran** ▲▲ East Malaysia
190 B16 **Tamakautoga** SW Niue 19°05′S 169°55′W
127 N7 **Tamala** Penzenskaya Oblast', W Russian Federation 52°32′N 43°18′E
77 P15 **Tamale** C Ghana 09°21′N 00°54′W
191 P3 **Tamana** prev. Rotcher Island. atoll Tungaru, W Kiribati
74 K12 **Tamanrasset** var. Tamenghest. S Algeria 22°49′N 05°32′E
74 J13 **Tamanrasset** wadi Algeria/Mali
166 M2 **Tamanthi** Sagaing, N Burma (Myanmar) 25°17′N 95°18′E
97 I24 **Tamar** ≈ SW England, United Kingdom
Tamar see Tudmur
54 H9 **Támara** Casanare, C Colombia 05°51′N 72°09′W
54 F7 **Tamar, Alto de** ▲ C Colombia 07°25′N 74°28′W
173 X16 **Tamarin** E Mauritius 20°20′S 57°22′E
105 T5 **Tamarite de Litera** var. Tararite de Llitera. Aragón, NE Spain 41°52′N 00°25′E
111 I24 **Tamási** Tolna, S Hungary 46°39′N 18°17′E
Tamatave see Toamasina
41 O9 **Tamaulipas** ◐ state C Mexico
41 P10 **Tamaulipas, Sierra de** ▲▲ C Mexico
56 F12 **Tamaya, Río** ≈ E Peru
40 I9 **Tamazula** Durango, C Mexico 24°43′N 106°33′W
40 L14 **Tamazula** Jalisco, C Mexico 19°41′N 103°18′W
Tamazulápam see Tamazulapán
41 Q15 **Tamazulapán** var. Tamazulápam. Oaxaca, SE Mexico 17°41′N 97°33′W
41 P12 **Tamazunchale** San Luis Potosí, C Mexico 21°17′N 98°46′W
76 H11 **Tambacounda** SE Senegal 13°44′N 13°43′W
83 M16 **Tambara** Manica, C Mozambique 16°42′S 34°14′E
77 T13 **Tambawel** Sokoto, NW Nigeria 12°24′N 04°42′E
186 M9 **Tambea** Guadalcanal, C Solomon Islands 09°19′S 159°42′E
169 N10 **Tambelan, Kepulauan** island group W Indonesia
57 E15 **Tambo de Mora** Ica, W Peru 13°30′S 76°08′W
170 L16 **Tambora, Gunung** Ж Sumbawa, S Indonesia 08°16′S 117°59′E
61 E17 **Tamborés** Paysandú, W Uruguay 31°50′S 56°17′W
57 F14 **Tambo, Río** ≈ C Peru
56 F7 **Tamboryacu, Río** ≈ N Peru
126 M7 **Tambov** Tambovskaya Oblast', W Russian Federation 52°43′N 41°28′E
126 L6 **Tambovskaya Oblast'** ◐ province W Russian Federation
104 H3 **Tambre** ≈ NW Spain
169 V7 **Tambunan** Sabah, East Malaysia 05°40′N 116°22′E
81 C15 **Tambura** Western Equatoria, SW Sudan 05°38′N 27°30′E
Tamchaket see Tâmchekket
76 J9 **Tâmchekket** var. Tamchaket. Hodh el Gharbi, S Mauritania 17°23′N 10°37′W
167 T7 **Tam Điệp** Ninh Bình, N Vietnam 20°09′N 105°54′E
Tamdybulak see Tomdibuloq
54 H8 **Tame** Arauca, C Colombia 06°27′N 71°42′W
104 H6 **Tâmega, Rio** Sp. Río Támega. ≈ Portugal/Spain
Támega, Río see Tâmega, Rio
115 H20 **Tamélos, Akrotírio** headland Tziá, Kykládes, Greece, Aegean Sea 37°31′N 24°16′E
Tamenghest see Tamanrasset
77 V8 **Tamgak, Adrar** ▲ C Niger 19°10′N 08°39′E
76 I13 **Tamgue** ▲ NW Guinea 12°14′N 12°18′W
41 Q12 **Tamiahua** Veracruz-Llave, E Mexico 21°15′N 97°27′W
41 Q12 **Tamiahua, Laguna de** lagoon E Mexico
23 Y16 **Tamiami Canal** canal Florida, SE USA
188 F17 **Tamil Harbor** harbour Yap, W Micronesia
155 H21 **Tamil Nādu** prev. Madras. ◐ state SE India
Ta'mīm, Muḥāfaẓat at see At Ta'mīm
99 H20 **Tamines** Namur, S Belgium 50°27′N 04°37′E
116 E12 **Tamiš** Ger. Temesch, Hung. Temes. ≈ Romania/Serbia
167 U10 **Tam Ky** Quang Nam-Đa Nẵng, C Vietnam 15°32′N 108°30′E
Tammerfors see Tampere
Tammisaari see Ekenäs
95 N14 **Tämnaren** ◎ C Sweden
191 Q7 **Tamotoe, Passe** passage Tahiti, W French Polynesia
23 V12 **Tampa** Florida, SE USA 27°57′N 82°27′W
23 V12 **Tampa** ✕ Florida, SE USA 27°57′N 82°29′W
23 V13 **Tampa Bay** bay Florida, SE USA
93 L18 **Tampere** Swe. Tammerfors. Länsi-Suomi, W Finland 61°30′N 23°45′E
41 Q11 **Tampico** Tamaulipas, C Mexico 22°18′N 97°52′W
171 P14 **Tampo** Pulau Muna, C Indonesia 04°38′S 122°40′E
167 V11 **Tam Quan** Bình Định, C Vietnam 14°34′N 109°00′E
162 J13 **Tamsag Muchang** Nei Mongol Zizhiqu, N China 40°28′N 102°34′E
Tamsal see Tamsalu
118 I4 **Tamsalu** Ger. Tamsal. Lääne-Virumaa, NE Estonia 59°10′N 26°07′E
109 S8 **Tamsweg** Salzburg, SW Austria 47°08′N 13°49′E
41 P12 **Tamuín** San Luis Potosí, C Mexico 22°00′N 98°44′W
188 C15 **Tamuning** NW Guam 13°29′N 144°47′E
183 T6 **Tamworth** New South Wales, SE Australia 31°07′S 150°54′E
97 M19 **Tamworth** C England, United Kingdom 52°39′N 01°40′W
81 K19 **Tana** ≈ SE Kenya
Tana see Deatnu/Tana
164 I15 **Tanabe** Wakayama, Honshū, SW Japan 33°43′N 135°22′E
92 L8 **Tana Bru** Finnmark, N Norway 70°11′N 28°06′E
39 T10 **Tanacross** Alaska, USA 63°30′N 143°21′W
92 L7 **Tanafjorden** Lapp. Deanuvuotna. fjord N Norway
38 G17 **Tanaga Island** island Aleutian Islands, Alaska, USA
38 G17 **Tanaga Volcano** ▲ Tanaga Island, Alaska, USA 51°53′N 178°08′W
107 M18 **Tanagro** ≈ S Italy
80 H11 **T'ana Hāyk'** var. Lake Tana. ◎ NW Ethiopia
168 H11 **Tanahbela, Pulau** island Kepulauan Batu, W Indonesia
171 H15 **Tanahjampea, Pulau** island W Indonesia
168 H11 **Tanahmasa, Pulau** island Kepulauan Batu, W Indonesia
Tanais see Don
152 L10 **Tanakpur** Uttarakhand, N India 29°04′N 80°06′E
Tana, Lake see T'ana Hāyk'
181 P5 **Tanami Desert** desert Northern Territory, N Australia
167 T14 **Tân An** Long An, S Vietnam 10°32′N 106°24′E
39 Q9 **Tanana** Alaska, USA 65°12′N 152°00′W
Tananarive see Antananarivo
39 Q9 **Tanana River** ≈ Alaska, USA
95 C16 **Tananger** Rogaland, S Norway 58°55′N 05°34′E
188 H5 **Tanapag** Saipan, S Northern Mariana Islands 15°14′S 145°45′E
188 H5 **Tanapag, Puetton** bay Saipan, S Northern Mariana Islands
106 C9 **Tanaro** ≈ N Italy
163 Y12 **Tanch'ŏn** E North Korea 40°22′N 128°49′E
40 M14 **Tancítaro, Cerro** Ж C Mexico 19°16′N 102°25′W
153 N12 **Tānda** Uttar Pradesh, N India 26°33′N 82°39′E
77 O15 **Tanda** E Ivory Coast 07°48′N 03°10′W
116 L14 **Ţăndărei** Ialomiţa, SE Romania 44°39′N 27°40′E
63 N14 **Tandil** Buenos Aires, E Argentina 37°18′S 59°10′W
78 H12 **Tandjilé** off. Préfecture du Tandjilé. ◐ prefecture SW Chad
Tandjilé, Préfecture du see Tandjilé
Tandjoeng see Tanjung
Tandjoengkarang see Bandar Lampung
Tandjoengpandan see Tanjungpandan
Tandjoengpinang see Tanjungpinang
Tandjoengredeb see Tanjungredeb
149 Q16 **Tando Allāhyār** Sind, SE Pakistan 25°28′N 68°44′E
149 Q17 **Tando Bāgo** Sind, SE Pakistan 24°48′N 68°59′E
149 Q16 **Tando Muhammad Khān** Sind, SE Pakistan 25°07′N 68°35′E
182 L7 **Tandou Lake** seasonal lake New South Wales, SE Australia
94 L11 **Tandsjöborg** Gävleborg, C Sweden 61°40′N 14°40′E
155 H15 **Tāndūr** Andhra Pradesh, C India 17°16′N 77°37′E
164 C17 **Tanega-shima** island Nansei-shotō, SW Japan
165 R7 **Taneichi** Iwate, Honshū, C Japan 40°23′N 141°42′E
Tanen Taunggyi see Tane Range
167 N8 **Tane Range** Bur. Tanen Taunggyi. ▲▲ W Thailand
111 P15 **Tanew** ≈ SE Poland
21 W2 **Taneytown** Maryland, NE USA 39°39′N 77°10′W
74 H12 **Tanezrouft** desert Algeria/Mali
138 L7 **Ţanf, Jabal at** ▲ SE Syria 33°32′N 38°43′E
81 J21 **Tanga** Tanga, E Tanzania 05°07′S 39°05′E
81 I22 **Tanga** ◐ region E Tanzania
153 T14 **Tangail** Dhaka, C Bangladesh 24°15′N 89°55′E
186 I5 **Tanga Islands** island group NE Papua New Guinea
155 K26 **Tangalla** Southern Province, S Sri Lanka 06°02′N 80°47′E
Tanganyika and Zanzibar see Tanzania
68 J13 **Tanganyika, Lake** ◎ E Africa
56 E7 **Tangarana, Río** ≈ N Peru
191 V16 **Tangaroa, Maunga** Ж Easter Island, Chile, E Pacific Ocean
Tangdukou see Shaoyang
74 G5 **Tanger** var. Tangiers, Tangier, Fr./Ger. Tangerk, Sp. Tánger; anc. Tingis. NW Morocco 35°49′N 05°49′W
169 N15 **Tangerang** Jawa, C Indonesia 06°14′S 106°36′E
Tangerk see Tanger
100 M12 **Tangermünde** Sachsen-Anhalt, C Germany 52°35′N 11°57′E
159 O12 **Tanggulashan** var. Togton Heyan, Tuotuoheyan. Qinghai, C China 34°13′N 92°25′E
156 K10 **Tanggula Shan** var. Dangla, Tangla Range. ▲▲ W China
159 N13 **Tanggula Shan** ▲ W China 33°18′N 91°10′E
156 K10 **Tanggula Shankou** Tib. Dang La. pass W China
161 N7 **Tanghe** Henan, C China 32°40′N 112°53′E
149 T5 **Tāngi** North-West Frontier Province, NW Pakistan 34°18′N 71°42′E
Tangier see Tanger
21 Y5 **Tangier Island** island Virginia, NE USA
Tangiers see Tanger
22 K8 **Tangipahoa River** ≈ Louisiana, S USA
Tangla Range see Tanggula Shan
164 J12 **Tango-hantō** peninsula Honshū, SW Japan
156 I10 **Tangra Yumco** var. Tangro Tso. ◎ W China
Tangro Tso see Tangra Yumco
157 T7 **Tangshan** var. T'ang-shan. Hebei, E China 39°39′N 118°15′E
T'ang-shan see Tangshan
77 R14 **Tanguiéta** NW Benin 10°35′N 01°19′E
163 X7 **Tangwang He** ≈ NE China
163 X7 **Tangyuan** Heilongjiang, NE China 46°45′N 129°52′E
92 M11 **Tanhua** Lappi, N Finland 67°31′N 27°30′E
159 R15 **Taniantaweng Shan** ▲▲ W China
171 U16 **Tanimbar, Kepulauan** island group Maluku, E Indonesia
Tanintharyi see Tenasserim
139 U4 **Tānjarō** ≈ E Iraq
129 T15 **Tanjong Piai** headland Peninsular Malaysia
Tanjore see Thanjāvūr
169 U12 **Tanjung** prev. Tandjoeng. Borneo, C Indonesia 02°08′S 115°23′E
169 W9 **Tanjungbatu** Borneo, N Indonesia 02°19′N 118°03′E
Tanjungkarang/Tanjungkarang-Telukbetung see Bandar Lampung
169 N13 **Tanjungpandan** prev. Tandjoengpandan. Pulau Belitung, W Indonesia 02°44′S 107°36′E
168 M10 **Tanjungpinang** prev. Tandjoengpinang. Pulau Bintan, W Indonesia 0°55′N 104°28′E
169 V9 **Tanjungredeb** var. Tanjungredep; prev. Tandjoengredeb. Borneo, C Indonesia 02°09′N 117°29′E
Tanjungredep see Tanjungredeb
149 S8 **Tānk** North-West Frontier Province, NW Pakistan 32°14′N 70°29′E
187 S15 **Tanna** island S Vanuatu
93 F17 **Tännäs** Jämtland, C Sweden 62°27′N 12°40′E
Tannenhof see Krynica
108 K7 **Tannheim** Tirol, W Austria 47°30′N 10°32′E
Tannu-Tuva see Tyva, Respublika
171 Q12 **Tano** Pulau Taliabu, E Indonesia 01°51′S 124°55′E
77 O17 **Tano** ≈ S Ghana
152 D10 **Tanot** Rājasthān, NW India 27°44′N 70°17′E
77 V11 **Tanout** Zinder, C Niger 14°58′N 08°54′E
Tan Phu see Định Quan
41 P12 **Tanquián** San Luis Potosí, C Mexico 21°38′N 98°39′W
77 R13 **Tansarga** E Burkina 11°51′N 01°51′E
167 T13 **Tan Son Nhat** ✕ (Hô Chi Minh) Tây Ninh, S Vietnam 10°52′N 106°38′E
75 V8 **Ţanţā** var. Tanta, Tantâ. N Egypt 30°42′N 31°00′E
74 D9 **Tan-Tan** SW Morocco 28°30′N 11°11′W
41 P12 **Tantoyuca** Veracruz-Llave, E Mexico 21°21′N 98°12′W
152 J12 **Tāntpur** Uttar Pradesh, N India 26°51′N 77°29′E
Tan-tung see Dandong
38 M12 **Tanunak** Alaska, USA 60°35′N 165°15′W
166 L5 **Ta-nyaung** Magway, W Burma (Myanmar) 20°49′N 94°40′E
167 S5 **Tân Yên** Tuyên Quang, N Vietnam 22°08′N 104°58′E
81 F22 **Tanzania** off. United Republic of Tanzania, Swa. Jamhuri ya Muungano wa Tanzania; prev. German East Africa, Tanganyika and Zanzibar. ◆ republic E Africa
Tanzania, Jamhuri ya Muungano wa see Tanzania
Tanzania, United Republic of see Tanzania
Tao'an see Taonan
163 T8 **Tao'er He** ≈ NE China
159 U11 **Tao He** ≈ C China
163 U9 **Taonan** var. Tao'an. Jilin, NE China 45°20′N 122°46′E
T'aon-an see Baicheng
Taongi see Bokaak Atoll
107 M23 **Taormina** anc. Tauromenium. Sicilia, Italy, C Mediterranean Sea 37°54′N 15°18′E
37 S9 **Taos** New Mexico, SW USA 36°24′N 105°35′W
Taoudenit see Taoudenni
77 O6 **Taoudenni** var. Taoudenit. Tombouctou, N Mali 22°46′N 03°54′W
74 G6 **Taounate** N Morocco 34°33′N 04°39′N
Taoyang see Lintao
161 S13 **T'aoyüan** Jap. Tōen. N Taiwan 25°00′N 121°15′E
118 I3 **Tapa** Ger. Taps. Lääne-Virumaa, NE Estonia 59°15′N 26°E
41 V17 **Tapachula** Chiapas, SE Mexico 14°53′N 92°18′W
Tapaiu see Gvardeysk
59 H14 **Tapajós, Rio** var. Tapajóz. ≈ NW Brazil
Tapajóz see Tapajós, Rio
61 C21 **Tapalqué** var. Tapalquén. Buenos Aires, E Argentina 36°21′S 60°01′W
Tapalquén see Tapalqué
Tapanahoni see Tapanahony Rivier
55 W11 **Tapanahony Rivier** var. Tapanahoni. ≈ E Surinam
41 T16 **Tapanatepec** var. San Pedro Tapanatepec. Oaxaca, SE Mexico 16°23′N 94°09′W
185 D23 **Tapanui** Otago, South Island, New Zealand 45°55′S 169°16′E
59 E14 **Tapauá** Amazonas, N Brazil 05°42′S 64°15′W
47 R7 **Tapauá, Rio** ≈ W Brazil
185 I14 **Tapawera** Tasman, South Island, New Zealand 41°24′S 172°50′E
61 I16 **Tapes** Rio Grande do Sul, S Brazil 30°40′S 51°25′W
76 K16 **Tapeta** C Liberia 06°36′N 08°52′W
154 H11 **Tāpi** prev. Tāpti. ≈ W India
104 J2 **Tapia de Casariego** Asturias, N Spain 43°34′N 06°56′W
56 F10 **Tapiche, Río** ≈ N Peru
167 N15 **Tapi, Mae Nam** var. Luang. ≈ SW Thailand
186 E8 **Tapini** Central, S Papua New Guinea 08°16′S 146°09′E
Tapirapecó, Serra see Tapirapecó, Sierra

◆ Country ● Country Capital ◇ Dependent Territory ○ Dependent Territory Capital ◐ Administrative Regions ✕ International Airport ▲ Mountain ▲▲ Mountain Range Ж Volcano ≈ River ◎ Lake ⊠ Reservoir

55 N13 **Tapirapecó, Sierra** *Port.* Serra Tapirapecó. ▲▲ Brazil/Venezuela
77 R13 **Tapoa** ≈ Benin/Niger
188 H5 **Tapochau, Mount** ▲ Saipan, S Northern Mariana Islands
111 H24 **Tapolca** Veszprém, W Hungary *46°54′N 17°29′E*
21 X5 **Tappahannock** Virginia, NE USA *37°55′N 76°54′W*
31 U13 **Tappan Lake** ⊠ Ohio, N USA
165 Q6 **Tappi-zaki** *headland* Honshū, C Japan *41°15′N 140°19′E*
Taps *see* Tapa
Tāpti *see* Tāpi
Tapuaemanu *see* Maiao
185 J16 **Tapuaenuku** ▲ South Island, New Zealand *42°00′S 173°39′E*
171 N8 **Tapul Group** *island group* Sulu Archipelago, SW Philippines
58 E11 **Tapurmcuará** *var.* Tapuruquara. Amazonas, NW Brazil *0°17′S 65°00′W*
Tapuruquara *see* Tapurmcuará
192 J17 **Taputapu, Cape** *headland* Tutuila, W American Samoa *14°20′S 170°51′W*
141 W13 **Ţāqah** S Oman *17°02′N 54°23′E*
139 T3 **Taqtaq** Arbīl, N Iraq *35°54′N 44°36′E*
61 J15 **Taquara** Rio Grande do Sul, S Brazil *29°36′S 50°46′W*
59 H19 **Taquari, Rio** ≈ C Brazil
60 L8 **Taquaritinga** São Paulo, S Brazil *21°22′S 48°29′W*
122 I11 **Tara** Omskaya Oblast', C Russian Federation *56°54′N 74°17′E*
83 I16 **Tara** Southern, S Zambia *16°56′S 26°50′E*
113 J15 **Tara** ≈ Montenegro
112 K13 **Tara** ▲▲ W Serbia
77 W15 **Taraba** ◐ *state* E Nigeria
77 X15 **Taraba** ≈ E Nigeria
75 O7 **Ţarābulus** *var.* Ţarābulus al Gharb, *Eng.* Tripoli. ● (Libya) NW Libya *32°54′N 13°11′E*
75 O7 **Tarābulus** ✈ NW Libya *32°37′N 13°07′E*
Ţarābulus al Gharb *see* Ţarābulus
Tarābulus/Ţarābulus ash Shām *see* Tripoli
105 O7 **Taracena** Castilla-La Mancha, C Spain *40°39′N 03°08′W*
117 N12 **Taraclia** *Rus.* Tarakilya. S Moldova *45°55′N 28°40′E*
139 V10 **Tarād al Kahf** Dhī Qār, SE Iraq *31°58′N 45°58′E*
183 R10 **Tarago** New South Wales, SE Australia *35°04′S 149°40′E*
162 J8 **Taragt** *var.* Hüremt. Övörhangay, C Mongolia *46°18′N 102°27′E*
169 V8 **Tarakan** Borneo, C Indonesia *03°20′N 117°38′E*
169 V9 **Tarakan, Pulau** *island* N Indonesia
Tarakilya *see* Taraclia
165 P16 **Tarama-jima** *island* Sakishima-shotō, SW Japan
184 K10 **Taranaki** *off.* Taranaki Region. ◐ *region* North Island, New Zealand
184 K10 **Taranaki, Mount** *var.* Egmont. ⋀ North Island, New Zealand *39°16′S 174°04′E*
Taranaki Region *see* Taranaki
105 O9 **Tarancón** Castilla-La Mancha, C Spain *40°01′N 03°01′W*
188 M15 **Tarang Reef** *reef* C Micronesia
96 E7 **Taransay** *island* NW Scotland, United Kingdom
107 P18 **Taranto** *var.* Tarentum. Puglia, SE Italy *40°30′N 17°11′E*
107 O19 **Taranto, Golfo di** *Eng.* Gulf of Taranto. *gulf* S Italy
Taranto, Gulf of *see* Taranto, Golfo di
62 G3 **Tarapacá** *off.* Región de Tarapacá. ◐ *region* N Chile
Tarapacá, Región de *see* Tarapacá
187 N9 **Tarapaina** Maramasike Island, N Solomon Islands *09°28′S 161°24′E*
56 D10 **Tarapoto** San Martín, N Peru *06°31′S 76°23′W*
138 M6 **Ţaraq an Na'jah** *hill range* E Syria
138 M6 **Ţaraq Sidāwī** *hill range* E Syria
103 Q11 **Tarare** Rhône, E France *45°54′N 04°26′E*
Tararite de Llitera *see* Tamarite de Litera
184 M13 **Tararua Range** ▲▲ North Island, New Zealand
151 Q22 **Tarāsa Dwīp** *island* Nicobar Islands, India, NE Indian Ocean
103 Q15 **Tarascon** Bouches-du-Rhône, SE France *43°48′N 04°39′E*
102 M17 **Tarascon-sur-Ariège** Ariège, S France *42°51′N 01°35′E*
117 P6 **Tarashcha** Kyyivs'ka Oblast', N Ukraine *49°34′N 30°31′E*
57 L18 **Tarata** Cochabamba, C Bolivia *17°35′S 66°04′W*
57 I18 **Tarata** Tacna, SW Peru *17°30′S 70°00′W*
190 H2 **Taratai** *atoll* Tungaru, W Kiribati
59 B15 **Tarauacá** Acre, W Brazil *08°06′S 70°45′W*
59 B15 **Tarauacá, Rio** ≈ NW Brazil
191 Q8 **Taravao** Tahiti, W French Polynesia *17°44′S 149°19′W*
191 R8 **Taravao, Baie de** *bay* Tahiti, W French Polynesia
191 Q8 **Taravao, Isthme de** *isthmus* Tahiti, W French Polynesia
103 X16 **Taravo** ≈ Corse, France, C Mediterranean Sea
190 J3 **Tarawa** ✈ Tarawa, W Kiribati *0°53′S 169°32′E*
190 H2 **Tarawa** *atoll* Tungaru, W Kiribati
184 N10 **Tarawera** Hawke's Bay, North Island, New Zealand *39°03′S 176°34′E*
184 N8 **Tarawera, Lake** ◎ North Island, New Zealand
184 N8 **Tarawera, Mount** ▲ North Island, New Zealand *38°13′S 176°29′E*
105 S8 **Tarayuela** ▲ N Spain *40°28′N 00°22′W*
145 R16 **Taraz** *prev.* Aulie Ata, Auliye-Ata, Dzhambul, Zhambyl. Zhambyl, S Kazakhstan *42°55′N 71°27′E*
105 Q5 **Tarazona** Aragón, NE Spain *41°54′N 01°44′W*
105 Q10 **Tarazona de la Mancha** Castilla-La Mancha, C Spain *39°16′N 01°55′W*
145 X12 **Tarbagatay, Khrebet** ▲▲ China/Kazakhstan
96 J8 **Tarbat Ness** *headland* N Scotland, United Kingdom *57°51′N 03°48′W*
149 U5 **Tarbela Reservoir** ⊠ N Pakistan
96 H12 **Tarbert** W Scotland, United Kingdom *55°52′N 05°26′W*
96 F7 **Tarbert** NW Scotland, United Kingdom *57°54′N 06°48′W*
102 K16 **Tarbes** *anc.* Bigorra. Hautes-Pyrénées, S France *43°14′N 00°04′E*
21 W9 **Tarboro** North Carolina, SE USA *35°54′N 77°34′W*
Tarca *see* Torysa
106 J6 **Tarcento** Friuli-Venezia Giulia, NE Italy *46°13′N 13°13′E*
182 F5 **Tarcoola** South Australia *30°44′S 134°34′E*
105 S5 **Tardienta** Aragón, NE Spain *41°58′N 00°31′W*
102 L11 **Tardoire** ≈ W France
183 U7 **Taree** New South Wales, SE Australia *31°56′S 152°29′E*
92 K12 **Tärendö** *Lapp.* Deargget. Norrbotten, N Sweden *67°10′N 22°40′E*
Tarentum *see* Taranto
74 C9 **Tarfaya** SW Morocco *27°56′N 12°55′W*
116 J13 **Târgovişte** *prev.* Tîrgovişte. Dâmboviţa, S Romania *44°54′N 25°29′E*
Tărgovište *see* Tŭrgovishte
116 M12 **Târgu Bujor** *prev.* Tîrgu Bujor. Galaţi, E Romania *45°52′N 27°55′E*
116 H13 **Târgu Cărbuneşti** *prev.* Tîrgu. Gorj, SW Romania *44°57′N 23°32′E*
116 L9 **Târgu Frumos** *prev.* Tîrgu Frumos. Iaşi, NE Romania *47°12′N 27°00′E*
116 H13 **Targu Jiu** *prev.* Tîrgu Jiu. Gorj, W Romania *45°03′N 23°20′E*
116 H9 **Târgu Lăpuş** *prev.* Tîrgu Lăpuş. Maramureş, N Romania *47°28′N 23°54′E*
Târgul-Neamţ *see* Târgu-Neamţ
Târgul-Săcuiesc *see* Târgu Secuiesc
116 I10 **Târgu Mureş** *prev.* Oşorhei, Tîrgu Mures, *Ger.* Neumarkt, *Hung.* Marosvásárhely. Mureş, C Romania *46°33′N 24°36′E*
116 K9 **Târgu-Neamţ** *var.* Târgul-Neamţ; *prev.* Tîrgu-Neamţ. Neamţ, NE Romania *47°12′N 26°25′E*
116 K11 **Târgu Ocna** *Hung.* Aknavásár; *prev.* Tîrgu Ocna. Bacău, E Romania *46°17′N 26°37′E*
116 K11 **Târgu Secuiesc** *Ger.* Neumarkt, Szekler Neumarkt, *Hung.* Kezdivásárhely; *prev.* Chezdi-Oşorheiu, Târgul-Săcuiesc, Tîrgu Secuiesc. Covasna, E Romania *46°00′N 26°08′E*
145 X10 **Targyn** Vostochnyy Kazakhstan, E Kazakhstan *49°32′N 82°47′E*
Tar Heel State *see* North Carolina
186 C7 **Tari** Southern Highlands, W Papua New Guinea *05°52′S 142°58′E*
162 J6 **Tarialan** *var.* Badrah. Hövsgöl, N Mongolia *49°33′N 101°58′E*
162 I7 **Tariat** *var.* Horgo. Arhangay, C Mongolia *48°06′N 99°52′E*
143 P17 **Ţarīf** Abū Z̧aby, C United Arab Emirates *24°02′N 53°47′E*
104 K16 **Tarifa** Andalucía, S Spain *36°01′N 05°36′W*
84 C14 **Tarifa, Punta de** *headland* SW Spain *36°01′N 05°39′W*
57 M21 **Tarija** Tarija, S Bolivia *21°33′S 64°42′W*
57 M21 **Tarija** ◐ *department* S Bolivia
141 R14 **Tarīm** C Yemen *16°N 48°50′E*
Tarim Basin *see* Tarim Pendi
81 G19 **Tarime** Mara, N Tanzania *01°20′S 34°24′E*
129 S8 **Tarim He** ≈ NW China
159 H8 **Tarim Pendi** *Eng.* Tarim Basin. *basin* NW China
149 N7 **Tarīn Kowt** *var.* Terinkot. Orūzgān, C Afghanistan *32°38′N 65°52′E*
171 O12 **Taripa** Sulawesi, C Indonesia *01°51′S 120°46′E*
117 Q12 **Tarkhankut, Mys** *headland* S Ukraine *45°20′N 32°32′E*
27 Q1 **Tarkio** Missouri, C USA *40°25′N 95°24′W*
122 J9 **Tarko-Sale** Yamalo-Nenetskiy Avtonomnyy Okrug, N Russian Federation *64°55′N 77°34′E*
77 P17 **Tarkwa** S Ghana *05°16′N 01°59′W*
171 O3 **Tarlac** Luzon, N Philippines *15°29′N 120°34′E*
95 F22 **Tarm** Ringkøbing, W Denmark *55°55′N 08°32′E*
57 E14 **Tarma** Junín, C Peru *11°28′S 75°41′W*
103 N15 **Tarn** ◐ *department* S France
102 M15 **Tarn** ≈ S France
111 L22 **Tarna** ≈ C Hungary
92 G13 **Tärnaby** Västerbotten, N Sweden *65°44′N 15°20′E*
149 P8 **Tarnak Rūd** ≈ SE Afghanistan
116 J11 **Târnava Mare** *Ger.* Grosse Kokel, *Hung.* Nagy-Küküllő; *prev.* Tîrnava Mare. ≈ S Romania
116 I11 **Târnava Mică** *Ger.* Kleine Kokel, *Hung.* Kis-Küküllo; *prev.* Tîrnava Mică. ≈ C Romania
116 I11 **Târnăveni** *Ger.* Marteskirch, Martinskirch, *Hung.* Dicsőszentmárton; *prev.* Sînmartin, Tîrnăveni. Mureş, C Romania *46°20′N 24°17′E*
102 L14 **Tarn-et-Garonne** ◐ *department* S France
111 P18 **Tarnica** ▲ SE Poland *49°05′N 22°43′E*
111 N15 **Tarnobrzeg** Podkarpackie, SE Poland *50°35′N 21°40′E*
125 N12 **Tarnogskiy Gorodok** Vologodskaya Oblast', NW Russian Federation *60°28′N 43°45′E*
Tarnopol *see* Ternopil'
111 M16 **Tarnów** Małopolskie, S Poland *50°01′N 20°59′E*
Tarnowice/Tarnowitz *see* Tarnowskie Góry
111 J16 **Tarnowskie Góry** *var.* Tarnowice, Tarnowskie Gory, *Ger.* Tarnowitz. Śląskie, S Poland *50°27′N 18°52′E*
95 N14 **Tärnsjö** Västmanland, C Sweden *60°10′N 16°57′E*
106 E9 **Taro** ≈ NW Italy
186 I6 **Taron** New Ireland, NE Papua New Guinea *04°22′S 153°04′E*
74 E8 **Taroudannt** *var.* Taroudant. SW Morocco *30°31′N 08°50′W*
Taroudant *see* Taroudannt
23 V12 **Tarpon, Lake** ◎ Florida, SE USA
23 V12 **Tarpon Springs** Florida, SE USA *28°09′N 82°45′W*
107 G14 **Tarquinia** *anc.* Tarquinii, *hist.* Corneto. Lazio, C Italy *42°23′N 11°45′E*
Tarquinii *see* Tarquinia
Tarraco *see* Tarragona
76 D10 **Tarrafal** Santiago, S Cape Verde *15°16′N 23°45′W*
105 V6 **Tarragona** *anc.* Tarraco. Cataluña, E Spain *41°07′N 01°15′E*
105 T7 **Tarragona** ◐ *province* Cataluña, NE Spain
183 O17 **Tarraleah** Tasmania, SE Australia *42°11′S 146°29′E*
23 P3 **Tarrant City** Alabama, S USA *33°34′N 86°45′W*
185 D21 **Tarras** Otago, South Island, New Zealand *44°48′S 169°25′E*
Tarrasa *see* Terrassa
105 U5 **Tàrrega** *var.* Tarrega. Cataluña, NE Spain *41°39′N 01°09′E*
21 W9 **Tar River** ≈ North Carolina, SE USA
Tarrong *see* Nyêmo
Tarsatica *see* Rijeka
136 J17 **Tarsus** İçel, S Turkey *36°52′N 34°52′E*
62 K4 **Tartagal** Salta, N Argentina *22°32′S 63°50′W*
137 V12 **Tärtär** *Rus.* Terter. ≈ SW Azerbaijan
102 J15 **Tartas** Landes, SW France *43°52′N 00°45′W*
Tartlau *see* Prejmer
Tartous/Tartouss *see* Ţarţūs
118 J5 **Tartu** *Ger.* Dorpat; *prev. Rus.* Yurev, Yury'ev. Tartumaa, SE Estonia *58°20′N 26°44′E*
118 I5 **Tartumaa** *off.* Tartu Maakond. ◐ *province* E Estonia
Tartu Maakond *see* Tartumaa
138 H5 **Ţarţūs** *Fr.* Tartouss; *anc.* Tortosa. Tarţūs, W Syria *34°55′N 35°52′E*
138 H5 **Ţarţūs** *off.* Muḩāfaz̧at Ţarţūs, *var.* Tartous, Tartus. ◐ *governorate* W Syria
Ţarţūs, Muḩāfaz̧at *see* Ţarţūs
164 C16 **Tarumizu** Kagoshima, Kyūshū, SW Japan *31°30′N 130°40′E*
126 K4 **Tarusa** Kaluzhskaya Oblast', W Russian Federation *54°45′N 37°10′E*
117 N11 **Tarutyne** Odes'ka Oblast', SW Ukraine *46°11′N 29°09′E*
162 I7 **Tarvagatyn Nuruu** ▲▲ N Mongolia
106 J6 **Tarvisio** Friuli-Venezia Giulia, NE Italy *46°31′N 13°33′E*
Tarvisium *see* Treviso
57 O16 **Tarvo, Río** ≈ E Bolivia
14 G8 **Tarzwell** Ontario, S Canada *48°00′N 79°58′W*
40 K5 **Tasajera, Sierra de la** ▲▲ N Mexico
145 S13 **Tasaral** Karaganda, C Kazakhstan *46°17′N 73°54′E*
Tasböget *see* Tasbuget
145 N15 **Tasbuget** *Kaz.* Tasböget. Kzylorda, S Kazakhstan *44°46′N 65°38′E*
108 E11 **Tasch** Valais, SW Switzerland *46°04′N 07°43′E*
Tasek Kenyir *see* Kenyir, Tasik
122 J14 **Tashanta** Respublika Altay, S Russian Federation *49°42′N 89°15′E*
Tashauz *see* Daşoguz
Tashi Chho Dzong *see* Thimphu
153 U11 **Tashigang** E Bhutan *27°19′N 91°33′E*
137 T11 **Tashir** *prev.* Kalinino. N Armenia *41°07′N 44°16′E*
143 Q11 **Ţashk, Daryācheh-ye** ◎ C Iran
Tashkent *see* Toshkent
Tashkentskaya Oblast' *see* Toshkent Viloyati
Tashkepri *see* Daşköpri
Tash-Kömür *see* Tash-Kumyr
147 S9 **Tash-Kumyr** *Kir.* Tash-Kömür. Dzhalal-Abadskaya Oblast', W Kyrgyzstan *41°22′N 72°09′E*
127 T7 **Tashla** Orenburgskaya Oblast', W Russian Federation *51°42′N 52°33′E*
Tashqurghan *see* Kholm
122 J13 **Tashtagol** Kemerovskaya Oblast', S Russian Federation *52°49′N 88°00′E*
95 H24 **Tåsinge** *island* C Denmark
12 M5 **Tasiujaq** Québec, E Canada *58°43′N 69°58′W*
77 W11 **Tasker** Zinder, C Niger *15°06′N 10°42′E*
145 W12 **Taskesken** Vostochnyy Kazakhstan, E Kazakhstan *47°15′N 80°45′E*
136 J10 **Taşköprü** Kastamonu, N Turkey *41°30′N 34°12′E*
Taskuduk, Peski *see* Tosquduq Qumlari
186 G5 **Taskul** New Ireland, NE Papua New Guinea *02°34′S 150°25′E*
137 S13 **Taşlıçay** Ağrı, E Turkey *39°37′N 43°23′E*
185 H14 **Tasman** *off.* Tasman District. ◐ *unitary authority* South Island, New Zealand
192 J12 **Tasman Basin** *var.* East Australian Basin. *undersea feature* S Tasman Sea
185 I14 **Tasman Bay** *inlet* South Island, New Zealand
Tasman District *see* Tasman
192 I13 **Tasman Fracture Zone** *tectonic feature* S Indian Ocean
185 E19 **Tasman Glacier** *glacier* South Island, New Zealand
Tasman Group *see* Nukumanu Islands
183 N15 **Tasmania** *prev.* Van Diemen's Land. ◐ *state* SE Australia
183 Q16 **Tasmania** *island* SE Australia
185 H14 **Tasman Mountains** ▲▲ South Island, New Zealand
183 P17 **Tasman Peninsula** *peninsula* Tasmania, SE Australia
192 I11 **Tasman Plain** *undersea feature* W Tasman Sea
192 I12 **Tasman Plateau** *var.* South Tasmania Plateau. *undersea feature* SW Tasman Sea
192 I11 **Tasman Sea** *sea* SW Pacific Ocean
116 G9 **Tăşnad** *Ger.* Trestenberg, Trestendorf, *Hung.* Tasnád. Satu Mare, NW Romania *47°30′N 22°33′E*
136 L11 **Taşova** Amasya, N Turkey *40°45′N 36°20′E*
77 T10 **Tassara** Tahoua, W Niger *16°40′N 05°34′E*
12 K4 **Tassialouc, Lac** ◎ Québec, C Canada
Tassili du Hoggar *see* Tassili ta-n-Ahaggar
74 L11 **Tassili-n-Ajjer** *plateau* E Algeria
74 K14 **Tassili ta-n-Ahaggar** *var.* Tassili du Hoggar. *plateau* S Algeria
59 M15 **Tasso Fragoso** Maranhão, E Brazil *08°22′S 45°53′W*
Tåstrup *see* Taastrup
145 O9 **Tasty-Taldy** Akmola, C Kazakhstan *50°47′N 66°31′E*
143 W10 **Tāsūkī** Sīstān va Balūchestān, SE Iran
111 I22 **Tata** *Ger.* Totis. Komárom-Esztergom, NW Hungary *47°39′N 18°19′E*
74 E8 **Tata** SW Morocco *29°38′N 08°04′W*
Tataaihoa, Pointe *see* Vénus, Pointe
111 I22 **Tatabánya** Komárom-Esztergom, NW Hungary *47°33′N 18°23′E*
191 X10 **Tatakoto** *atoll* Îles Tuamotu, E French Polynesia
75 N7 **Tataouine** *var.* Taţāwīn. SE Tunisia *32°48′N 10°27′E*
55 O5 **Tataracual, Cerro** ▲ NE Venezuela *10°13′N 64°20′W*
117 O12 **Tatarbunary** Odes'ka Oblast', SW Ukraine *45°50′N 29°37′E*
119 M17 **Tatarka** Mahilyowskaya Voblasts', E Belarus *53°15′N 28°50′E*
Tatar Pazardzhik *see* Pazardzhik
122 I12 **Tatarsk** Novosibirskaya Oblast', C Russian Federation *55°08′N 75°58′E*
Tatarskaya ASSR *see* Tatarstan, Respublika
123 T13 **Tatarskiy Proliv** *Eng.* Tatar Strait. *strait* SE Russian Federation
127 R4 **Tatarstan, Respublika** *prev.* Tatarskaya ASSR. ◐ *autonomous republic* W Russian Federation
Tatar Strait *see* Tatarskiy Proliv
Taţāwīn *see* Tataouine
171 N12 **Tate** Sulawesi, N Indonesia *0°12′S 119°44′E*
141 N11 **Tathlīth** 'Asīr, S Saudi Arabia *19°38′N 43°32′E*
141 O11 **Tathlīth, Wādī** *dry watercourse* S Saudi Arabia
183 R11 **Tathra** New South Wales, SE Australia *36°46′S 149°58′E*
127 P8 **Tatishchevo** Saratovskaya Oblast', W Russian Federation *51°43′N 45°35′E*
39 S12 **Tatitlek** Alaska, USA *60°49′N 146°29′W*
10 L15 **Tatla Lake** British Columbia, SW Canada *51°54′N 124°39′W*
121 Q2 **Tatlısu** *Gk.* Akanthoú. N Cyprus *35°21′N 33°45′E*
11 Z10 **Tatnam, Cape** *headland* Manitoba, C Canada *57°16′N 91°03′W*
111 K18 **Tatra Mountains** *Ger.* Tatra, *Hung.* Tátra, *Pol./Slvk.* Tatry. ▲▲ Poland/Slovakia
Tatra/Tátra *see* Tatra Mountains
Tatry *see* Tatra Mountains
164 I13 **Tatsuno** *var.* Tatuno. Hyōgo, Honshū, SW Japan *34°54′N 134°30′E*
145 S16 **Tatti** *var.* Tatty. Zhambyl, S Kazakhstan *43°11′N 73°22′E*
Tatty *see* Tatti
60 L10 **Tatuí** São Paulo, S Brazil *23°21′S 47°49′W*
37 V14 **Tatum** New Mexico, SW USA *33°15′N 103°19′W*
25 X7 **Tatum** Texas, SW USA *32°19′N 94°31′W*
Ta-t'ung/Tatung *see* Datong
Tatuno *see* Tatsuno
137 R14 **Tatvan** Bitlis, SE Turkey *38°31′N 42°15′E*
95 C16 **Tau** Rogaland, S Norway *59°04′N 05°55′E*
192 L17 **Ta'ū** *var.* Tau. *island* Manua Islands, E American Samoa
193 W15 **Tau** *island* Tongatapu Group, N Tonga
59 O14 **Tauá** Ceará, E Brazil *06°04′S 40°26′W*
60 N10 **Taubaté** São Paulo, S Brazil *23°S 45°36′W*
101 I19 **Tauber** ≈ SW Germany
101 I19 **Tauberbiscofsheim** Baden-Württemberg, C Germany *49°37′N 09°39′E*
144 E14 **Tauchik** *Kaz.* Taūshyq. Mangistau, SW Kazakhstan *44°17′N 51°22′E*
191 W10 **Tauere** *atoll* Îles Tuamotu, C French Polynesia
101 H17 **Taufstein** ▲ C Germany *50°31′N 09°18′E*
190 I17 **Taukoka** *island* SE Cook Islands
145 T15 **Taukum, Peski** *desert* SE Kazakhstan
184 L10 **Taumarunui** Manawatu-Wanganui, North Island, New Zealand *38°52′S 175°14′E*
59 A15 **Taumaturgo** Acre, W Brazil *08°54′S 72°48′W*
27 X6 **Taum Sauk Mountain** ▲ Missouri, C USA *37°34′N 90°43′W*
83 H22 **Taung** North-West, N South Africa *27°32′S 24°48′E*
166 L6 **Taungdwingyi** Magway, C Burma (Myanmar) *20°01′N 95°20′E*
166 M6 **Taunggyi** Shan State, C Burma (Myanmar) *20°47′N 97°00′E*
166 M7 **Taungoo** Bago, C Burma (Myanmar) *18°57′N 96°26′E*
166 L5 **Taungtha** Mandalay, C Burma (Myanmar) *21°16′N 95°25′E*
166 K7 **Taungup** Rakhine State, W Burma (Myanmar) *18°50′N 94°14′E*
149 S9 **Taunsa** Punjab, E Pakistan *30°43′N 70°41′E*
97 K23 **Taunton** SW England, United Kingdom *51°01′N 03°06′W*
19 O12 **Taunton** Massachusetts, NE USA *41°54′N 71°03′W*
101 F18 **Taunus** ▲▲ W Germany
101 G18 **Taunusstein** Hessen, W Germany *50°09′N 08°09′E*
184 N9 **Taupo** Waikato, North Island, New Zealand *38°42′S 176°05′E*
184 M9 **Taupo, Lake** ◎ North Island, New Zealand
109 R8 **Taurach** *var.* Taurachbach. ≈ E Austria
Taurachbach *see* Taurach
118 D12 **Tauragė** *Ger.* Tauroggen. Tauragė, SW Lithuania *55°16′N 22°17′E*
118 D13 **Tauragė** ◐ *province* Lithuania
54 G10 **Tauramena** Casanare, C Colombia *05°02′N 72°43′W*
184 N7 **Tauranga** Bay of Plenty, North Island, New Zealand *37°42′S 176°09′E*
15 O10 **Taureau, Réservoir** ⊠ Québec, SE Canada
107 N22 **Taurianova** Calabria, SW Italy *38°22′N 16°01′E*
Tauris *see* Tabrīz
184 I2 **Tauroa Point** *headland* North Island, New Zealand *35°09′S 173°02′E*
Tauroggen *see* Tauragė
Tauromenium *see* Taormina
Taurus Mountains *see* Toros Dağları
Taus *see* Domažlice
Taūshyq *see* Tauchik
105 R5 **Tauste** Aragón, NE Spain *41°55′N 01°15′W*
191 V16 **Tautara, Motu** *island* Easter Island, Chile, E Pacific Ocean
191 R8 **Tautira** Tahiti, W French Polynesia *17°45′S 149°10′W*
Tauz *see* Tovuz
Ţavālesh, Kūhhā-ye *see* Talish Mountains
136 D15 **Tavas** Denizli, SW Turkey *37°33′N 29°04′E*
Tavastehus *see* Hämeenlinna
Tavau *see* Davos
122 G10 **Tavda** Sverdlovskaya Oblast', C Russian Federation *58°01′N 65°07′E*
122 G10 **Tavda** ≈ C Russian Federation
105 T11 **Tavernes de la Valldigna** País Valenciano, E Spain *39°03′N 00°13′W*
81 I20 **Taveta** Coast, S Kenya *03°23′S 37°40′E*
187 Y14 **Taveuni** *island* N Fiji
147 R13 **Tavildara** *Rus.* Tavil'dara, Tovil'-Dora. C Tajikistan *38°42′N 70°27′E*
Tavin *see* Adaatsag
104 H14 **Tavira** Faro, S Portugal *37°07′N 07°39′W*
97 I24 **Tavistock** SW England, United Kingdom *50°33′N 04°08′W*
Tavoy *see* Dawei
Tavoy Island *see* Mali Kyun
115 E16 **Tavropoú, Techníti Límni** ⊠ C Greece
136 E13 **Tavşanlı** Kütahya, NW Turkey *39°34′N 29°28′E*
187 X14 **Tavua** Viti Levu, W Fiji *17°27′S 177°51′E*
97 J23 **Taw** ≈ SW England, United Kingdom
185 L14 **Tawa** Wellington, North Island, New Zealand *41°10′S 174°50′E*
25 V6 **Tawakoni, Lake** ⊠ Texas, SW USA
153 V11 **Tawang** Arunāchal Pradesh, NE India *27°34′N 91°54′E*
169 R17 **Tawang, Teluk** *bay* Jawa, S Indonesia
31 R7 **Tawas Bay** ◎ Michigan, N USA
31 R7 **Tawas City** Michigan, N USA *44°16′N 83°33′W*
169 V8 **Tawau** Sabah, East Malaysia *04°16′N 117°54′E*
141 U10 **Ţawīl, Qalamat aţ** *well* SE Saudi Arabia
171 N9 **Tawitawi** *island* Tawitawi Group, SW Philippines
Ţawkar *see* Tokar
Tāwūq *see* Dāqūq
Tawzar *see* Tozeur
41 O15 **Taxco** *var.* Taxco de Alarcón. Guerrero, S Mexico *18°32′N 99°37′W*
Taxco de Alarcón *see* Taxco
146 H8 **Taxiatosh** *Rus.* Takhiatash. Qoraqalpog'iston Respublikasi, W Uzbekistan *42°27′N 59°27′E*
158 D9 **Taxkorgan** *var.* Taxkorgan Tajik Zizhixian. Xinjiang Uygur Zizhiqu, NW China *37°43′N 75°13′E*
Taxkorgan Tajik Zizhixian *see* Taxkorgan
146 H7 **Taxtako'pir** *Rus.* Takhtakupyr. Qoraqalpog'iston Respublikasi, NW Uzbekistan *43°04′N 60°23′E*
96 J10 **Tay** ≈ C Scotland, United Kingdom
143 V6 **Tāybād** *var.* Taibad, Tāyybād, Tayyebāt. Khorāsān-Razavī, NE Iran *34°48′N 60°46′E*
Taybert at Turkz *see* Ţayyibat at Turkī
124 J3 **Taybola** Murmanskaya Oblast', NW Russian Federation *68°30′N 33°18′E*
81 M16 **Tayeeglow** Bakool, C Somalia *04°01′N 44°25′E*
96 K11 **Tay, Firth of** *inlet* E Scotland, United Kingdom
122 J12 **Tayga** Kemerovskaya Oblast', S Russian Federation *56°02′N 85°26′E*
Taygan *see* Delger
123 T9 **Taygonos, Mys** *headland* E Russian Federation *60°36′N 160°09′E*
96 I11 **Tay, Loch** ◎ C Scotland, United Kingdom
11 N12 **Taylor** British Columbia, W Canada *56°09′N 120°43′W*
29 O14 **Taylor** Nebraska, C USA *41°47′N 99°23′W*
18 I13 **Taylor** Pennsylvania, NE USA *41°22′N 75°41′W*
25 T10 **Taylor** Texas, SW USA *30°34′N 97°24′W*
37 Q11 **Taylor, Mount** ▲ New Mexico, SW USA *35°14′N 107°36′W*
37 R5 **Taylor Park Reservoir** ⊠ Colorado, C USA
37 R6 **Taylor River** ≈ Colorado, C USA
21 P11 **Taylors** South Carolina, SE USA *34°55′N 82°18′W*
20 L5 **Taylorsville** Kentucky, S USA *38°01′N 85°21′W*
21 R6 **Taylorsville** North Carolina, SE USA *35°56′N 81°10′W*
30 L14 **Taylorville** Illinois, N USA *39°33′N 89°17′W*
140 K5 **Taymā'** Tabūk, NW Saudi Arabia *27°39′N 38°32′E*
122 M10 **Taymura** ≈ C Russian Federation
123 O7 **Taymylyr** Respublika Sakha (Yakutiya), NE Russian Federation *72°32′N 121°54′E*
122 L7 **Taymyr, Ozero** ◎ N Russian Federation
122 M6 **Taymyr, Poluostrov** *peninsula* N Russian Federation
122 L8 **Taymyrskiy (Dolgano-Nenetskiy) Avtonomnyy Okrug** ◐ *autonomous district* Krasnoyarskiy Kray, N Russian Federation
167 S13 **Tây Ninh** Tây Ninh, S Vietnam *11°21′N 106°07′E*
122 L12 **Tayshet** Irkutskaya Oblast', S Russian Federation *55°51′N 98°04′E*
162 G8 **Tayshir** *var.* Tsagaan-Olom. Govĭ-Altay, C Mongolia *46°42′N 96°30′E*
171 N5 **Taytay** Palawan, W Philippines *10°49′N 119°30′E*
169 Q16 **Tayu** *prev.* Tajoe. Jawa, C Indonesia *06°32′S 111°02′E*
Tāyybād/Tayyebāt *see* Tāybād
138 L5 **Ţayyibah** *var.* At Taybé. Ḩimş, C Syria *35°13′N 38°51′E*
138 I4 **Ţayyibat at Turkī** *var.* Taybert at Turkz. Ḩamāh, W Syria *35°16′N 36°55′E*
145 P7 **Tayynsha** *prev.* Krasnoarmeysk. Severnyy Kazakhstan, N Kazakhstan *53°52′N 69°51′E*
122 J10 **Taz** ≈ N Russian Federation
74 G6 **Taza** NE Morocco *34°13′N 04°06′W*
139 T4 **Tāza Khurmātū** At Ta'mīn, E Iraq *35°18′N 44°22′E*
165 Q8 **Tazawa-ko** ◎ Honshū, C Japan
21 N8 **Tazewell** Tennessee, S USA *36°27′N 83°34′W*
21 Q7 **Tazewell** Virginia, NE USA *37°08′N 81°34′W*
75 S11 **Tāzirbū** SE Libya *25°43′N 21°16′E*
39 S11 **Tazlina Lake** ◎ Alaska, USA
122 J8 **Tazovskiy** Yamalo-Nenetskiy Avtonomnyy Okrug, N Russian Federation *67°33′N 78°21′E*
137 U10 **T'bilisi** *Eng.* Tiflis. ● (Georgia) SE Georgia *41°41′N 44°55′E*
137 T10 **T'bilisi** ✈ S Georgia *41°43′N 44°49′E*
79 E14 **Tchabal Mbabo** ▲ NW Cameroon *07°12′N 12°16′E*
Tchad *see* Chad
Tchad, Lac *see* Chad, Lake
77 S15 **Tchaourou** E Benin *08°58′N 02°40′E*
79 E20 **Tchibanga** Nyanga, S Gabon *02°49′S 11°00′E*
Tchien *see* Zwedru
77 Z6 **Tchigaï, Plateau du** ▲▲ NE Niger
77 V9 **Tchighozérine** Agadez, C Niger *17°15′N 07°48′E*
77 T10 **Tchin-Tabaradene** Tahoua, W Niger *15°57′N 05°49′E*
78 G13 **Tcholliré** Nord, NE Cameroon *08°48′N 14°00′E*
Tchongking *see* Chongqing
22 K4 **Tchula** Mississippi, S USA *33°10′N 90°13′W*
110 I7 **Tczew** *Ger.* Dirschau. Pomorskie, N Poland *54°05′N 18°46′E*
116 I10 **Teaca** *Ger.* Tekendorf, *Hung.* Teke; *prev. Ger.* Teckendorf. Bistriţa-Năsăud, N Romania *46°55′N 24°30′E*
40 J11 **Teacapán** Sinaloa, C Mexico *22°33′N 105°44′W*
190 A10 **Teafuafou** *island* Funafuti Atoll, C Tuvalu
25 U8 **Teague** Texas, SW USA *31°37′N 96°16′W*
191 R9 **Teahupoo** Tahiti, W French Polynesia *17°51′S 149°15′W*
190 H15 **Te Aiti Point** *headland* Rarotonga, S Cook Islands *21°11′S 59°47′W*
185 B22 **Te Anau** Southland, South Island, New Zealand *45°25′S 167°45′E*
185 B22 **Te Anau, Lake** ◎ South Island, New Zealand
41 U15 **Teapa** Tabasco, SE Mexico *17°36′N 92°57′W*
184 Q7 **Te Araroa** Gisborne, North Island, New Zealand *37°37′S 178°21′E*
184 M7 **Te Aroha** Waikato, North Island, New Zealand *37°32′S 175°58′E*
Teate *see* Chieti
190 A9 **Te Ava Fuagea** *channel* Funafuti Atoll, SE Tuvalu
190 B8 **Te Ava I Te Lape** *channel* Funafuti Atoll, SE Tuvalu
190 B9 **Te Ava Pua Pua** *channel* Funafuti Atoll, SE Tuvalu
184 M8 **Te Awamutu** Waikato, North Island, New Zealand *38°00′S 177°18′E*
171 X12 **Teba** Papua, E Indonesia *01°27′S 137°54′E*
104 L15 **Teba** Andalucía, S Spain *36°59′N 04°54′W*
126 M15 **Teberda** Karachayevo-Cherkesskaya Respublika, SW Russian Federation *43°28′N 41°45′E*
74 M6 **Tébessa** NE Algeria *35°21′N 08°06′E*
62 O7 **Tebicuary, Río** ≈ S Paraguay
168 I8 **Tebingtinggi** Sumatera, N Indonesia *03°20′N 99°08′E*
168 L13 **Tebingtinggi** Sumatera, W Indonesia *03°33′S 103°00′E*
Tebingtinggi, Pulau *see* Rantau, Pulau
Tebriz *see* Tabrīz
137 U9 **Tebulosmta** *Rus.* Gora Tebulosmta. ▲ Georgia/Russian Federation *42°33′N 45°21′E*
Tebulosmta, Gora *see* Tebulosmta
41 Q14 **Tecamachalco** Puebla, S Mexico *18°52′N 97°44′W*
40 B1 **Tecate** Baja California Norte, NW Mexico *32°33′N 116°38′W*
136 M13 **Tecer Dağları** ▲▲ C Turkey
103 O17 **Tech** ≈ S France
77 P16 **Techiman** W Ghana *07°35′N 01°56′W*
117 N15 **Techirghiol** Constanţa, SE Romania *44°03′N 28°37′E*
74 A12 **Techla** *var.* Techlé. SW Western Sahara *21°39′N 14°57′W*
Techlé *see* Techla
63 H18 **Tecka, Sierra de** ▲▲ SW Argentina
Teckendorf *see* Teaca
40 K13 **Tecolotlán** Jalisco, SW Mexico *20°10′N 104°07′W*
40 K14 **Tecomán** Colima, SW Mexico *18°53′N 103°54′W*
35 V12 **Tecopa** California, W USA *35°51′N 116°14′W*
40 G5 **Tecoripa** Sonora, NW Mexico *28°38′N 109°58′W*
41 N16 **Tecpan** *var.* Tecpan de Galeana. Guerrero, S Mexico *17°12′N 100°39′W*
Tecpan de Galeana *see* Tecpan
40 J11 **Tecuala** Nayarit, C Mexico *22°24′N 105°30′W*
116 L12 **Tecuci** Galaţi, E Romania *45°50′N 27°27′E*
31 R10 **Tecumseh** Michigan, N USA *42°00′N 83°57′W*
29 S16 **Tecumseh** Nebraska, C USA *40°22′N 96°12′W*
27 O11 **Tecumseh** Oklahoma, C USA *35°15′N 96°56′W*
Tedzhen *see* Harīrūd/Tejen
Tedzhen *see* Tejen
146 H15 **Tedzhenstroy** *Turkm.* Tejenstroy. Ahal Welaýaty, S Turkmenistan *36°57′N 60°49′E*
Teel *see* Öndör-Ulaan
97 L15 **Tees** ≈ N England, United Kingdom
14 E15 **Teeswater** Ontario, S Canada *44°00′N 81°17′W*
190 A10 **Tefala** *island* Funafuti Atoll, C Tuvalu
58 D13 **Tefé** Amazonas, N Brazil *03°24′S 64°45′W*
74 K11 **Tefedest** ▲▲ S Algeria
136 E16 **Tefenni** Burdur, SW Turkey *37°19′N 29°45′E*
58 D13 **Tefé, Rio** ≈ NW Brazil
169 P16 **Tegal** Jawa, C Indonesia *06°52′S 109°07′E*
100 O12 **Tegel** ✈ (Berlin) Berlin, NE Germany *52°33′N 13°16′E*
99 M15 **Tegelen** Limburg, SE Netherlands *51°20′N 06°09′E*
101 L24 **Tegernsee** ◎ SE Germany
107 M18 **Teggiano** Campania, S Italy *40°25′N 15°28′E*
77 U14 **Tegina** Niger, C Nigeria *10°06′N 06°10′E*
42 I7 **Tegucigalpa** ● (Honduras) Francisco Morazán, SW Honduras *14°04′N 87°11′W*
42 H7 **Tegucigalpa** ✈ Central District, C Honduras *14°03′N 87°20′W*
Tegucigalpa *see* Central District
Tegucigalpa *see* Francisco Morazán
77 U9 **Teguidda-n-Tessoumt** Agadez, C Niger *17°27′N 06°40′E*
64 Q11 **Teguise** Lanzarote, Islas Canarias, Spain, NE Atlantic Ocean *29°04′N 13°38′W*
122 K12 **Tegul'det** Tomskaya Oblast', C Russian Federation *57°16′N 87°58′E*
35 S13 **Tehachapi** California, W USA *35°07′N 118°27′W*
35 S13 **Tehachapi Mountains** ▲▲ California, W USA
Tehama *see* Tihāmah
Teheran *see* Tehrān
77 O14 **Téhini** NE Ivory Coast *09°36′N 03°40′W*
143 N5 **Tehrān** *var.* Teheran. ● (Iran) Tehrān, N Iran *35°44′N 51°27′E*
143 N6 **Tehrān** *off.* Ostān-e Tehrān, *var.* Tehran. ◐ *province* N Iran
Tehrān, Ostān-e *see* Tehrān
152 K9 **Tehri** *var.* New Tehri. Uttarakhand, N India *30°12′N 78°29′E*

◆ Country
● Country Capital
◇ Dependent Territory
○ Dependent Territory Capital
◐ Administrative Regions
✈ International Airport
▲ Mountain
▲▲ Mountain Range
⋀ Volcano
≈ River
◎ Lake
⊠ Reservoir

Tehri see Tīkamgarh
41 Q15 **Tehuacán** Puebla, S Mexico 18°29′N 97°24′W
41 S17 **Tehuantepec** var. Santo Domingo Tehuantepec. Oaxaca, SE Mexico 16°18′N 95°14′W
41 S17 **Tehuantepec, Golfo de** var. Gulf of Tehuantepec. gulf S Mexico
Tehuantepec, Gulf of see Tehuantepec, Golfo de
Tehuantepec, Isthmus of see Tehuantepec, Istmo de
41 T16 **Tehuantepec, Istmo de** var. Isthmus of Tehuantepec. isthmus SE Mexico
0 I16 **Tehuantepec Ridge** undersea feature E Pacific Ocean 13°30′N 98°00′W
41 S16 **Tehuantepec, Río** SE Mexico
191 W10 **Tehuata** atoll Îles Tuamotu, C French Polynesia
64 O11 **Teide, Pico del** ▲ Gran Canaria, Islas Canarias, Spain, NE Atlantic Ocean 28°16′N 16°39′W
97 I21 **Teifi** SW Wales, United Kingdom
80 B9 **Teiga Plateau** plateau W Sudan
97 J24 **Teignmouth** SW England, United Kingdom 50°34′N 03°29′W
Teisen see Chech'ŏn
116 H1 **Teiuş** Ger. Dreikirchen, Hung. Tövis. Alba, C Romania 46°12′N 23°40′E
169 U17 **Tejakula** Bali, C Indonesia 08°09′S 115°19′E
146 H14 **Tejen** Rus. Tedzhen. Ahal Welaýaty, S Turkmenistan 37°24′N 60°29′E
146 I15 **Tejen** Per. Harīrūd, Rus. Tedzhen. Afghanistan/Iran see also Harīrūd
Tejen see Harīrūd
Tejenstroy see Tedzhenstroy
35 S14 **Tejon Pass** pass California, W USA
Tejo, Rio see Tagus
41 O14 **Tejupilco** var. Tejupilco de Hidalgo. México, S Mexico 18°55′N 100°10′W
Tejupilco de Hidalgo see Tejupilco
184 P7 **Te Kaha** Bay of Plenty, North Island, New Zealand 37°45′S 177°42′E
29 S14 **Tekamah** Nebraska, C USA 41°46′N 96°13′W
184 I1 **Te Kao** Northland, North Island, New Zealand 34°40′S 172°57′E
185 F20 **Tekapo** South Island, New Zealand
185 F19 **Tekapo, Lake** ◎ South Island, New Zealand
184 P9 **Te Karaka** Gisborne, North Island, New Zealand 38°30′S 177°52′E
184 L7 **Te Kauwhata** Waikato, North Island, New Zealand 37°22′S 175°07′E
41 X12 **Tekax** var. Tekax de Álvaro Obregón. Yucatán, SE Mexico 20°07′N 89°10′W
Tekax de Álvaro Obregón see Tekax
136 A14 **Teke Burnu** headland W Turkey 38°06′N 26°35′E
114 M12 **Teke Deresi** NW Turkey
146 D10 **Tekedzhik, Gory** hill range NW Turkmenistan
145 V14 **Tekeli** Almaty, SE Kazakhstan 44°50′N 78°47′E
145 R7 **Teke, Ozero** ◎ N Kazakhstan
158 I5 **Tekes** Xinjiang Uygur Zizhiqu, NW China 43°15′N 81°43′E
145 W16 **Tekes** Almaty, SE Kazakhstan 42°40′N 80°01′E
Tekes see Tekes He
158 H5 **Tekes He** Rus. Tekes. China/Kazakhstan
Teke/Tekendorf see Teaca
80 I10 **Tekezē** var. Takkaze. Eritrea/Ethiopia
Tekhtin see Tsyakhtsin
136 C10 **Tekirdağ** It. Rodosto; anc. Bisanthe, Raidestos, Rhaedestus. Tekirdağ, NW Turkey 40°59′N 27°31′E
136 C10 **Tekirdağ** ⬖ province NW Turkey
155 N14 **Tekkali** Andhra Pradesh, E India 18°37′N 84°15′E
115 K15 **Tekke Burnu** Turk. İlyasbaba Burnu. headland NW Turkey 40°03′N 26°12′E
137 Q13 **Tekman** Erzurum, NE Turkey 39°39′N 41°31′E
32 M9 **Tekoa** Washington, NW USA 47°13′N 117°05′W
190 H16 **Te Kou** ▲ Rarotonga, S Cook Islands 21°14′S 159°46′W
Tekrit see Tikrīt
171 P12 **Teku** Sulawesi, N Indonesia 0°46′S 123°25′E
184 L9 **Te Kuiti** Waikato, North Island, New Zealand 38°21′S 175°10′E
42 H4 **Tela** Atlántida, NW Honduras 15°46′N 87°25′W
138 F12 **Telalim** Southern, S Israel 30°58′N 34°47′E
Telanaipura see Jambi
137 U10 **T'elavi** E Georgia 41°55′N 45°29′E
138 F10 **Tel Aviv** ⬖ district W Israel
Tel Aviv-Jaffa see Tel Aviv-Yafo
138 F10 **Tel Aviv-Yafo** var. Tel Aviv-Jaffa. Tel Aviv, C Israel 32°05′N 34°46′E
111 E18 **Telč** Ger. Teltsch. Vysočina, C Czech Republic 49°10′N 15°28′E
186 B6 **Telefomin** Sandaun, NW Papua New Guinea 05°08′S 141°31′E
10 J10 **Telegraph Creek** British Columbia, W Canada 57°56′N 131°10′W
190 B10 **Telele** island Funafuti Atoll, C Tuvalu
60 J11 **Telêmaco Borba** Paraná, S Brazil 24°20′S 50°44′W
95 E15 **Telemark** ⬖ county S Norway
62 J13 **Telén** La Pampa, C Argentina 36°20′S 65°31′W
Teleneshty see Teleneşti
116 M9 **Teleneşti** Rus. Teleneshty. C Moldova 47°35′N 28°20′E
104 J4 **Teleno, El** ▲ NW Spain 42°19′N 06°21′W
116 I15 **Teleorman** ⬖ county S Romania
116 I14 **Teleorman** S Romania
25 V5 **Telephone** Texas, SW USA 33°48′N 96°00′W
35 U11 **Telescope Peak** ▲ California, W USA 36°09′N 117°03′W
Teles Pirés see São Manuel, Rio
97 L19 **Telford** W England, United Kingdom 52°42′N 02°28′W
108 L7 **Telfs** Tirol, W Austria 47°19′N 11°05′E
42 I9 **Telica** León, NW Nicaragua 12°30′N 86°52′W
42 J6 **Telica, Río** C Honduras
76 I13 **Télimélé** W Guinea 10°45′N 13°02′W
43 O14 **Telire, Río** Costa Rica/Panama
114 I8 **Telish** prev. Azizie. Pleven, N Bulgaria 43°20′N 24°15′E
41 R16 **Telixtlahuaca** var. San Francisco Telixtlahuaca. Oaxaca, SE Mexico 17°18′N 96°54′W
10 K13 **Telkwa** British Columbia, SW Canada 54°39′N 126°51′W
25 P4 **Tell** Texas, SW USA 34°18′N 100°20′W
Tell Abiad see Tall Abyaḍ
Tell Abiad/Tell Abyad see At Tall al Abyaḍ
31 O16 **Tell City** Indiana, N USA 37°56′N 86°47′W
38 M9 **Teller** Alaska, USA 65°15′N 166°21′W
Tell Huqnah see Tall Ḥuqnah
155 F20 **Tellicherry** var. Thalashsheri, Thalassery. Kerala, SW India 11°44′N 75°29′E see also Thalassery
20 M10 **Tellico Plains** Tennessee, S USA 35°19′N 84°18′W
Tell Kalakh see Tall Kalakh
Tell Mardīkh see Ebla
54 E11 **Tello** Huila, C Colombia 03°06′N 75°08′W
Tell Shedadi see Ash Shadādah
37 Q7 **Telluride** Colorado, C USA 37°56′N 107°48′W
117 X9 **Tel'manove** Donets'ka Oblast', E Ukraine 47°24′N 38°03′E
Tel'man/Tel'mansk see Gubadag
162 H6 **Telmen** var. Övögdiy. Dzavhan, C Mongolia 48°38′N 97°39′E
162 H6 **Telmen Nuur** ◎ NW Mongolia
Teloekbetoeng see Bandar Lampung
41 O15 **Teloloapán** Guerrero, S Mexico 18°21′N 99°52′W
Telo Martius see Toulon
125 V8 **Telposiz, Gora** ▲ NW Russian Federation 63°52′N 59°15′E
Telschen see Telšiai
63 J17 **Telsen** Chubut, S Argentina 42°27′S 66°59′W
118 D11 **Telšiai** Ger. Telschen. Telšiai, NW Lithuania 55°59′N 22°21′E
118 D11 **Telšiai** ⬖ province NW Lithuania
Teltsch see Telč
Telukbetung see Bandar Lampung
168 H10 **Telukdalam** Pulau Nias, W Indonesia 0°34′N 97°47′E
14 H9 **Temagami** Ontario, S Canada 47°03′N 79°47′W
14 G9 **Temagami, Lake** ◎ Ontario, S Canada
190 H16 **Te Manga** ▲ Rarotonga, S Cook Islands 21°13′S 159°45′W
191 W12 **Tematangi** atoll Îles Tuamotu, S French Polynesia
41 X11 **Temax** Yucatán, SE Mexico 21°10′N 88°53′W
171 E14 **Tembagapura** Papua, E Indonesia 04°10′S 137°19′E
129 U5 **Tembenchi** N Russian Federation
55 P6 **Temblador** Monagas, NE Venezuela 08°59′N 62°44′W
105 N9 **Tembleque** Castilla-La Mancha, C Spain 39°41′N 03°30′W
Temboni see Mitemele, Río
35 U16 **Temecula** California, W USA 33°29′N 117°09′W
168 K7 **Temengor, Tasik** ◎ Peninsular Malaysia
112 L9 **Temerin** Vojvodina, N Serbia 45°25′N 19°54′E
Temeschburg/Temeschwar see Timişoara
Temes-Kubin see Kovin
Temes/Temesch see Tamiš
Temesvár/Temeswar see Timişoara
Teminaboean see Teminabuan
171 U12 **Teminabuan** prev. Teminaboean. Papua, E Indonesia 01°30′S 131°59′E
145 P17 **Temirlanovka** Yuzhnyy Kazakhstan, S Kazakhstan 42°36′N 69°17′E
145 R10 **Temirtau** prev. Samarkandski, Samarkandskoye. Karaganda, C Kazakhstan 50°05′N 72°55′E
14 H10 **Témiscaming** Québec, SE Canada 46°40′N 79°04′W
Témiscamingue, Lac see Timiskaming, Lake
15 T8 **Témiscouata, Lac** ◎ Québec, SE Canada
127 N5 **Temnikov** Respublika Mordoviya, W Russian Federation 54°39′N 43°09′E
191 Y13 **Temoe** island Îles Gambier, E French Polynesia
183 Q9 **Temora** New South Wales, SE Australia 34°28′S 147°33′E
40 H7 **Témoris** Chihuahua, W Mexico 27°16′N 108°15′W
40 I5 **Temósachic** Chihuahua, N Mexico 28°55′N 107°42′W
187 Q10 **Temotu** var. Temotu Province. ⬖ province E Solomon Islands
Temotu Province see Temotu
36 L14 **Tempe** Arizona, SW USA 33°24′N 111°54′W
Tempelburg see Czaplinek
107 C17 **Tempio Pausania** Sardegna, Italy, C Mediterranean Sea 40°55′N 09°07′E
42 K12 **Tempisque, Río** NW Costa Rica
25 T9 **Temple** Texas, SW USA 31°06′N 97°22′W
100 O12 **Templehof** ✈ (Berlin) Berlin, NE Germany 52°28′N 13°24′E
97 D19 **Templemore** Ir. An Teampall Mór. Tipperary, C Ireland 52°48′N 07°50′W
100 O11 **Templin** Brandenburg, NE Germany 53°07′N 13°31′E
41 P12 **Tempoal** var. Tempoal de Sánchez. Veracruz-Llave, E Mexico 21°32′N 98°23′W
Tempoal de Sánchez see Tempoal
41 P13 **Tempoal, Río** C Mexico
83 E14 **Tempué** Moxico, C Angola 13°36′S 18°56′E
126 J14 **Temryuk** Krasnodarskiy Kray, SW Russian Federation 45°15′N 37°26′E
99 G17 **Temse** Oost-Vlaanderen, N Belgium 51°08′N 04°13′E
63 F15 **Temuco** Araucanía, C Chile 38°45′S 72°37′W
185 G20 **Temuka** Canterbury, South Island, New Zealand 44°14′S 171°17′E
189 P13 **Temwen Island** island E Micronesia
56 C6 **Tena** Napo, C Ecuador 01°00′S 77°48′W
41 W13 **Tenabo** Campeche, E Mexico 20°02′N 90°12′W
Tenaghau see Aola
25 X7 **Tenaha** Texas, SW USA 31°56′N 94°14′W
39 X13 **Tenake** Chichagof Island, Alaska, USA 57°46′N 135°13′W
155 K16 **Tenāli** Andhra Pradesh, E India 16°13′N 80°36′E
Tenan see Ch'ŏnan
41 O14 **Tenancingo** var. Tenencingo de Degollado. México, S Mexico 18°57′N 99°39′W
191 X12 **Tenararo** island Groupe Actéon, SE French Polynesia
167 N12 **Tenasserim** Tanintharyi, S Burma (Myanmar) 12°05′N 99°00′E
167 N11 **Tenasserim** var. Tanintharyi. ⬖ division S Burma (Myanmar)
98 O5 **Ten Boer** Groningen, NE Netherlands 53°16′N 06°42′E
97 I21 **Tenby** SW Wales, United Kingdom 51°41′N 04°43′W
80 K11 **Tendaho** Āfar, NE Ethiopia 11°39′N 40°59′E
103 V14 **Tende** Alpes Maritimes, SE France 44°04′N 07°34′E
151 Q20 **Ten Degree Channel** strait Andaman and Nicobar Islands, India, E Indian Ocean
80 F11 **Tendelti** White Nile, E Sudan 13°01′N 31°55′E
76 G8 **Te-n-Dghâmcha, Sebkhet** var. Sebkha de Ndrhamcha, Sebkra de Ndaghamcha. salt lake W Mauritania
165 P10 **Tendō** Yamagata, Honshū, C Japan 38°22′N 140°22′E
74 H7 **Tendrara** NE Morocco 33°06′N 01°58′W
117 Q11 **Tendrivs'ka Kosa** spit S Ukraine
117 Q11 **Tendrivs'ka Zatoka** gulf S Ukraine
Tenencingo de Degollado see Tenancingo
77 N11 **Ténenkou** Mopti, C Mali 14°28′N 04°55′W
77 W9 **Ténéré** physical region C Niger
77 W9 **Ténére, Erg du** desert C Niger
64 O11 **Tenerife** island Islas Canarias, Spain, NE Atlantic Ocean
74 J5 **Ténès** NW Algeria 36°35′N 01°18′E
170 M15 **Tengah, Kepulauan** island group C Indonesia
Tengcheng see Tengxian
169 V11 **Tenggarong** Borneo, C Indonesia 0°23′S 117°00′E
162 J15 **Tengger Shamo** desert N China
168 L8 **Tenggul, Pulau** island Peninsular Malaysia
Tengiz Köl see Tengiz, Ozero
145 P9 **Tengiz, Ozero** Kaz. Tengiz Köl. salt lake C Kazakhstan
76 M14 **Tengréla** var. Tingréla. N Ivory Coast 10°26′N 06°20′W
160 M14 **Tengxian** var. Tengcheng, Tengxian, Teng Xian. Guangxi Zhuangzu Zizhiqu, S China 23°24′N 110°49′E
Teng Xian see Tengxian
Tengxian see Tengxian
155 H23 **Teni** var. Theni. Tamil Nādu, SE India 10°00′N 77°29′E
194 H2 **Teniente Rodolfo Marsh** Chilean research station South Shetland Islands, Antarctica 61°57′S 58°23′W
32 G9 **Tenino** Washington, NW USA 46°51′N 122°51′W
112 I9 **Tenja** Osijek-Baranja, E Croatia 45°30′N 18°45′E
188 B16 **Tenjo, Mount** ▲ W Guam
155 H23 **Tenkāsi** Tamil Nādu, SE India 08°58′N 77°22′E
79 N24 **Tenke** Katanga, SE Dem. Rep. Congo 10°34′S 26°12′E
Tenke see Tinca
123 Q7 **Tenkeli** Respublika Sakha (Yakutiya), NE Russian Federation 70°09′N 140°39′E
27 R10 **Tenkiller Ferry Lake** ⊡ Oklahoma, C USA
77 Q13 **Tenkodogo** S Burkina 11°54′N 00°19′W
181 Q5 **Tennant Creek** Northern Territory, C Australia 19°40′S 134°16′E
20 G9 **Tennessee** off. State of Tennessee, also known as The Volunteer State. ⬖ state SE USA
37 R5 **Tennessee Pass** pass Colorado, C USA
20 H10 **Tennessee River** S USA
23 N2 **Tennessee Tombigbee Waterway** canal Alabama/Mississippi, S USA
99 K22 **Tenneville** Luxembourg, SE Belgium 50°05′N 05°31′E
92 M11 **Tenniöjoki** NE Finland
92 L9 **Tenojoki** Lapp. Deatnu, Nor. Tana. Finland/Norway see also Deatnu
169 U7 **Tenom** Sabah, East Malaysia 05°07′N 115°57′E
Tenos see Tínos
41 V15 **Tenosique** var. Tenosique de Pino Suárez. Tabasco, SE Mexico 17°30′N 91°24′W
Tenosique de Pino Suárez see Tenosique
22 I6 **Tensas River** Louisiana, S USA
23 O8 **Tensaw River** Alabama, S USA
74 E7 **Tensift** seasonal river W Morocco
171 O12 **Tentena** var. Tenteno. Sulawesi, C Indonesia 01°46′S 120°40′E
Tenteno see Tentena
183 U4 **Tenterfield** New South Wales, SE Australia 29°04′S 152°02′E
23 X16 **Ten Thousand Islands** island group Florida, SE USA
60 H9 **Teodoro Sampaio** São Paulo, S Brazil 22°30′S 52°13′W
59 N19 **Teófilo Otoni** var. Theophilo Ottoni. Minas Gerais, NE Brazil 17°52′S 41°31′W
116 K5 **Teofipol'** Khmel'nyts'ka Oblast', W Ukraine 50°00′N 26°22′E
191 Q8 **Teohatu** Tahiti, W French Polynesia
41 P14 **Teotihuacán** ruins México, S Mexico
Teotilán see Teotitlán del Camino
41 Q15 **Teotitlán del Camino** var. Teotilán. Oaxaca, S Mexico 18°10′N 97°08′W
190 G12 **Tepa** Île Uvea, E Wallis and Futuna 13°19′S 176°09′W
191 P8 **Tepaee, Récif** reef Tahiti, W French Polynesia
40 L14 **Tepalcatepec** Michoacán, SW Mexico 19°11′N 102°50′W
190 A16 **Tepa Point** headland SW Niue 19°07′S 169°56′E
40 L13 **Tepatitlán** var. Tepatitlán de Morelos. Jalisco, SW Mexico 20°50′N 102°46′W
Tepatitlán de Morelos see Tepatitlán
40 J9 **Tepehuanes** var. Santa Catarina de Tepehuanes. Durango, C Mexico 25°22′N 105°42′W
Tepelena see Tepelenë
113 L22 **Tepelenë** var. Tepelena, It. Tepeleni. Gjirokastër, S Albania 40°18′N 20°00′E
Tepeleni see Tepelenë
40 K12 **Tepic** Nayarit, C Mexico 21°30′N 104°55′W
111 C15 **Teplice** Ger. Teplitz; prev. Teplice-Šanov, Teplitz-Schönau. Ústecký Kraj, NW Czech Republic 50°38′N 13°49′E
Teplice-Šanov/Teplitz/Teplitz-Schönau see Teplice
117 O7 **Teplyk** Vinnyts'ka Oblast', C Ukraine 48°40′N 29°46′E
123 R10 **Teplyy Klyuch** Respublika Sakha (Yakutiya), NE Russian Federation 62°46′N 137°01′E
40 E5 **Tepoca, Cabo** headland NW Mexico 29°19′N 112°24′W
191 W9 **Tepoto** island Îles du Désappointement, C French Polynesia
92 L11 **Tepsa** Lappi, N Finland 67°34′N 25°36′E
190 B8 **Tepuka** atoll Funafuti Atoll, C Tuvalu
184 N7 **Te Puke** Bay of Plenty, North Island, New Zealand 37°48′S 176°19′E
40 L13 **Tequila** Jalisco, SW Mexico 20°52′N 103°48′W
41 O13 **Tequisquiapan** Querétaro de Arteaga, C Mexico 20°34′N 99°52′W
77 Q12 **Téra** Tillabéri, W Niger 14°01′N 00°45′E
104 J5 **Tera** NW Spain
191 V1 **Teraina** prev. Washington Island. atoll Line Islands, E Kiribati
81 F15 **Terakeka** Bahr el Gabel, S Sudan 05°26′N 31°45′E
107 J14 **Teramo** anc. Interamna. Abruzzi, C Italy 42°40′N 13°43′E
98 P7 **Ter Apel** Groningen, NE Netherlands 52°52′N 07°05′E
104 H11 **Tera, Ribeira de** S Portugal
185 K14 **Terawhiti, Cape** headland North Island, New Zealand 41°17′S 174°36′E
98 N12 **Terborg** Gelderland, E Netherlands 51°55′N 06°22′E
137 P13 **Tercan** Erzincan, NE Turkey 39°47′N 40°23′E
64 O2 **Terceira** ✈ Terceira, Azores, Portugal, NE Atlantic Ocean 38°43′N 27°13′W
64 O2 **Terceira** var. Ilha Terceira. island Azores, Portugal, NE Atlantic Ocean
Terceira, Ilha see Terceira
116 K6 **Terebovlya** Ternopil's'ka Oblast', W Ukraine 49°18′N 25°44′E
127 O15 **Terek** SW Russian Federation
Terekhovka see Tsyerakhowka
147 R9 **Terek-Say** Dzhalal-Abadskaya Oblast', W Kyrgyzstan 41°28′N 71°06′E
145 Z10 **Terekty** prev. Alekseevka, Alekseyevka. Vostochnyy Kazakhstan, E Kazakhstan 48°25′N 85°38′E
168 L7 **Terengganu** var. Trengganu. ⬖ state Peninsular Malaysia
127 X7 **Terensay** Orenburgskaya Oblast', W Russian Federation 51°35′N 59°28′E
58 N13 **Teresina** var. Therezina. state capital Piauí, NE Brazil 05°09′S 42°46′W
60 P9 **Teresópolis** Rio de Janeiro, SE Brazil 22°25′S 42°59′W
110 P12 **Terespol** Lubelskie, E Poland 52°05′N 23°37′E
191 V16 **Terevaka, Maunga** Easter Island, Chile, E Pacific Ocean 27°05′S 109°23′W
103 P3 **Tergnier** Aisne, N France 49°39′N 03°18′E
43 O14 **Teribe, Río** NW Panama
124 K3 **Teriberka** Murmanskaya Oblast', NW Russian Federation 69°10′N 35°18′E
Terinkot see Tarīn Kowt
Terisaqqan see Tersakkan
24 K12 **Terlingua** Texas, SW USA 29°18′N 103°36′W
24 K11 **Terlingua Creek** Texas, SW USA
62 K7 **Termas de Río Hondo** Santiago del Estero, N Argentina 27°29′S 64°52′W
136 M11 **Terme** Samsun, N Turkey 41°12′N 37°00′E
Termez see Termiz
Termia see Kýthnos
107 J23 **Termini Imerese** anc. Thermae Himerenses. Sicilia, Italy, C Mediterranean Sea 37°59′N 13°42′E
41 V14 **Términos, Laguna de** lagoon SE Mexico
77 X10 **Termit-Kaoboul** Zinder, C Niger 15°34′N 11°31′E
147 O14 **Termiz** Rus. Termez. Surkhondaryo Viloyati, S Uzbekistan 37°17′N 67°12′E
107 L15 **Termoli** Molise, C Italy 42°00′N 14°58′E
Termonde see Dendermonde
98 P5 **Termunten** Groningen, NE Netherlands 53°18′N 07°02′E
171 R11 **Ternate** Pulau Ternate, E Indonesia 0°48′N 127°23′E
109 T5 **Ternberg** Oberösterreich, N Austria 47°57′N 14°22′E
99 E15 **Terneuzen** var. Neuzen. Zeeland, SW Netherlands 51°20′N 03°50′E
123 T14 **Terney** Primorskiy Kray, SE Russian Federation 45°03′N 136°43′E
107 I14 **Terni** anc. Interamna Nahars. Umbria, C Italy 42°34′N 12°38′E
109 X6 **Ternitz** Niederösterreich, E Austria 47°43′N 16°02′E
117 V7 **Ternivka** Dnipropetrovs'ka Oblast', E Ukraine 48°30′N 36°05′E
116 K6 **Ternopil'** Pol. Tarnopol, Rus. Ternopol'. Ternopil's'ka Oblast', W Ukraine 49°32′N 25°38′E
Ternopil' see Ternopil's'ka Oblast'
116 I6 **Ternopil's'ka Oblast'** var. Ternopil', Rus. Ternopol'skaya Oblast'. ⬖ province NW Ukraine
Ternopol' see Ternopil'
Ternopol'skaya Oblast' see Ternopil's'ka Oblast'
123 U13 **Terpeniya, Mys** headland Ostrov Sakhalin, SE Russian Federation 48°37′N 144°40′E
Térraba, Río see Grande de Térraba, Río
10 J13 **Terrace** British Columbia, W Canada 54°31′N 128°32′W
12 D12 **Terrace Bay** Ontario, S Canada 48°47′N 87°06′W
107 I16 **Terracina** Lazio, C Italy 41°18′N 13°13′E
93 F14 **Terråk** Troms, N Norway 65°03′N 12°22′E
26 M13 **Terral** Oklahoma, C USA 33°55′N 97°54′W
107 B19 **Terralba** Sardegna, Italy, C Mediterranean Sea 39°47′N 08°35′E
Terranova di Sicilia see Gela
Terranova Pausania see Olbia
105 W5 **Terrassa** Cast. Tarrasa. Cataluña, E Spain 41°34′N 02°01′E
15 O12 **Terrebonne** Québec, SE Canada 45°42′N 73°37′W
22 J11 **Terrebonne Bay** bay Louisiana, SE USA
31 N14 **Terre Haute** Indiana, N USA 39°27′N 87°24′W
25 U6 **Terrell** Texas, SW USA 32°44′N 96°16′W
Terre Neuve see Newfoundland and Labrador
33 Q14 **Terreton** Idaho, NW USA 43°49′N 112°25′W
103 T7 **Territoire-de-Belfort** ⬖ department E France
33 X9 **Terry** Montana, NW USA 46°46′N 105°16′W
28 I9 **Terry Peak** ▲ South Dakota, N USA 44°19′N 103°49′W
136 H14 **Tersakan Gölü** ◎ C Turkey
145 O10 **Tersakkan** Kaz. Terisaqqan. C Kazakhstan
98 J4 **Terschelling** Fris. Skylge. island Waddeneilanden, N Netherlands
78 H10 **Tersef** Chari-Baguirmi, C Chad 12°55′N 16°49′E
147 X8 **Terskey Ala-Too, Khrebet** ▲▲ Kazakhstan/Kyrgyzstan
Terter see Tärtär
105 R8 **Teruel** anc. Turba. Aragón, E Spain 40°21′N 01°06′W
105 R7 **Teruel** ⬖ province Aragón, E Spain
114 M7 **Tervel** prev. Kurtbunar, Rom. Curtbunar. Dobrich, NE Bulgaria 43°45′N 27°25′E
93 M16 **Tervo** Itä-Suomi, C Finland 62°57′N 26°48′E
92 L13 **Tervola** Lappi, NW Finland 66°04′N 24°49′E
Tervueren see Tervuren
99 H18 **Tervuren** var. Tervueren. Vlaams Brabant, C Belgium 50°48′N 04°28′E
162 G5 **Tes** var. Dzür. Dzavhan, W Mongolia 49°37′N 95°46′E
112 H11 **Tešanj** Federacija Bosna I Hercegovina, N Bosnia and Herzegovina 44°37′N 18°00′E
Teschen see Cieszyn
83 M19 **Tesenane** Inhambane, S Mozambique 22°48′S 34°02′E
80 I9 **Teseney** var. Tessenei. W Eritrea 15°05′N 36°42′E
39 P5 **Teshekpuk Lake** ◎ Alaska, USA
162 K6 **Teshig** Bulgan, N Mongolia 49°51′N 102°45′E
165 T2 **Teshio** Hokkaidō, NE Japan 44°49′N 141°46′E
165 T2 **Teshio-sanchi** ▲▲ Hokkaidō, NE Japan
14 L7 **Tessier, Lac** ◎ Québec, SE Canada
Těšín see Cieszyn
Tesiyn Gol see Tes-Khem
129 T7 **Tes-Khem** var. Tesiyn Gol. Mongolia/Russian Federation
112 H11 **Teslić** Republika Srpska, N Bosnia and Herzegovina 44°35′N 17°50′E
10 I9 **Teslin** Yukon Territory, W Canada 60°12′N 132°44′W
10 I8 **Teslin** British Columbia/Yukon Territory, W Canada
77 Q8 **Tessalit** Kidal, NE Mali 20°12′N 00°58′E
77 V12 **Tessaoua** Maradi, S Niger 13°46′N 07°55′E
99 J17 **Tessenderlo** Limburg, NE Belgium 51°05′N 05°04′E
Tessenei see Teseney
Tessin see Ticino
97 M23 **Test** S England, United Kingdom
Testama see Tõstamaa
55 P4 **Testigos, Islas los** island group N Venezuela
37 S10 **Tesuque** New Mexico, SW USA 35°45′N 105°55′W
103 O17 **Têt** var. Tet. S France
Tet see Têt
54 G5 **Tetas, Cerro de las** ▲ NW Venezuela 09°58′N 73°00′W
83 M15 **Tete** Tete, NW Mozambique 16°14′S 33°34′E
83 M15 **Tete** off. Província de Tete. ⬖ province NW Mozambique
11 N15 **Tête Jaune Cache** British Columbia, SW Canada 52°52′N 119°22′W
184 O8 **Te Teko** Bay of Plenty, North Island, New Zealand 38°03′S 176°48′E
186 K9 **Tetepare** island New Georgia Islands, NW Solomon Islands
Tete, Província de see Tete
Teterev see Teteriv
116 M5 **Teteriv** Rus. Teterev. N Ukraine
100 M9 **Teterow** Mecklenburg-Vorpommern, NE Germany 53°47′N 12°34′E
114 I9 **Teteven** Lovech, N Bulgaria 42°54′N 24°18′E
191 T10 **Tetiaroa** atoll Îles du Vent, W French Polynesia
105 P14 **Tetica de Bacares** ▲ S Spain 37°15′N 02°24′W
Tetiyev see Tetiyiv
117 O6 **Tetiyiv** Rus. Tetiyev. Kyyivs'ka Oblast', N Ukraine 49°21′N 29°40′E
39 T10 **Tetlin** Alaska, USA 63°08′N 142°31′W
33 R8 **Teton River** Montana, NW USA
74 G5 **Tétouan** var. Tetouan, Tetuán. N Morocco 35°33′N 05°22′W
Tetova/Tetovë see Tetovo
114 L7 **Tetovo** Razgrad, N Bulgaria 43°49′N 26°21′E
113 N18 **Tetovo** Alb. Tetova, Tetovë, Turk. Kalkandelen. NW FYR Macedonia 42°01′N 20°58′E
115 E20 **Tetrázio** ▲▲ S Greece
Tetschen see Děčín
Tetuán see Tétouan
191 Q8 **Tetufera, Mont** ▲ Tahiti, W French Polynesia 17°40′S 149°26′W
127 R4 **Tetyushi** Respublika Tatarstan, W Russian Federation 54°55′N 48°46′E
108 I7 **Teufen** Sankt Gallen, NE Switzerland 47°24′N 09°24′E
40 L12 **Teul** var. Teul de Gonzáles Ortega. Zacatecas, C Mexico 21°30′N 103°28′W
107 B21 **Teulada** Sardegna, Italy, C Mediterranean Sea 38°58′N 08°46′E
Teul de Gonzáles Ortega see Teul
11 X16 **Teulon** Manitoba, S Canada 50°20′N 97°14′W
42 I7 **Teupasenti** El Paraíso, S Honduras 14°13′N 86°42′W
165 S2 **Teuri-tō** island NE Japan
100 G13 **Teutoburger Wald** Eng. Teutoburg Forest. hill range NW Germany
Teutoburg Forest see Teutoburger Wald
93 K17 **Teuva** Swe. Östermark. Länsi-Suomi, W Finland 62°29′N 21°45′E
107 H15 **Tevere** Eng. Tiber. C Italy
Teverya see Tverya
96 K13 **Teviot** SE Scotland, United Kingdom
Tevli see Tewli
122 H11 **Tevriz** Omskaya Oblast', C Russian Federation 57°30′N 72°13′E
185 B24 **Te Waewae Bay** bay South Island, New Zealand
97 L21 **Tewkesbury** C England, United Kingdom 51°59′N 02°09′W
119 F19 **Tewli** Rus. Tevli. Brestskaya Voblasts', SW Belarus 52°20′N 24°15′E
159 U12 **Têwo** var. Dêngka; prev. Dêngkagoin. Gansu, C China 34°05′N 103°15′E
Tewulike see Hoxud
25 U12 **Texana, Lake** ◎ Texas, SW USA
27 S14 **Texarkana** Arkansas, C USA 33°26′N 94°02′W
25 X5 **Texarkana** Texas, SW USA 33°26′N 94°03′W
25 N9 **Texas** off. State of Texas, also known as Lone Star State. ⬖ state S USA
25 W12 **Texas City** Texas, SW USA 29°23′N 94°55′W
41 P14 **Texcoco** México, C Mexico 19°32′N 98°52′W
98 I6 **Texel** island Waddeneilanden, NW Netherlands
26 H8 **Texhoma** Oklahoma, C USA 36°30′N 101°46′W
25 N1 **Texhoma** Texas, SW USA 36°30′N 101°46′W
37 W12 **Texico** New Mexico, SW USA 34°23′N 103°03′W
24 L1 **Texline** Texas, SW USA 36°22′N 103°01′W
41 P14 **Texmelucan** var. San Martín Texmelucan. Puebla, S Mexico 19°46′N 98°53′W
27 O13 **Texoma, Lake** ⊡ Oklahoma/Texas, C USA
25 N9 **Texon** Texas, SW USA 31°13′N 101°42′W
83 J23 **Teyateyaneng** NW Lesotho 29°04′S 27°51′E
124 M16 **Teykovo** Ivanovskaya Oblast', W Russian Federation 56°49′N 40°31′E
124 M16 **Teza** W Russian Federation
41 Q13 **Teziutlán** Puebla, S Mexico 19°49′N 97°22′W
153 W12 **Tezpur** Assam, NE India 26°39′N 92°47′E
153 Y11 **Tezu** Arunāchal Pradesh, NE India 27°55′N 96°09′E
Thaa Atoll see Kolhumadulu
9 N10 **Tha-Anne** Nunavut, NE Canada
83 K23 **Thabana Ntlenyana** var. Thabantshonyana, Mount Ntlenyana. ▲ E Lesotho 29°26′S 29°16′E
Thabantshonyana see Thabana Ntlenyana
83 J23 **Thaba Putsoa** ▲ C Lesotho 29°48′S 27°46′E
167 Q8 **Tha Bo** Nong Khai, E Thailand 17°52′N 102°34′E
103 T12 **Thabor, Pic du** ▲ E France 45°07′N 06°34′E
Tha Chin see Samut Sakhon
166 M7 **Thagaya** Bago, C Burma (Myanmar) 19°19′N 96°16′E
Thai, Ao see Thailand, Gulf of
167 T6 **Thai Binh** Thai Binh, N Vietnam 20°27′N 106°20′E
167 S7 **Thai Hoa** var. Nghia Dan. Nghê An, N Vietnam 19°21′N 105°26′E
167 P9 **Thailand** off. Kingdom of Thailand, Th. Prathet Thai; prev. Siam. ◆ monarchy SE Asia
167 P13 **Thailand, Gulf of** var. Gulf of Siam, Th. Ao Thai, Vtn. Vinh Thai Lan. gulf SE Asia
Thailand, Kingdom of see Thailand
Thai Lan, Vinh see Thailand, Gulf of
167 T6 **Thai Nguyên** Băc Thai, N Vietnam 21°36′N 105°50′E
167 S8 **Thakhèk** var. Muang Khammouan. Khammouan, C Laos 17°25′N 104°51′E
153 S13 **Thakurgaon** Rajshahi, NW Bangladesh 26°05′N 88°34′E
149 S6 **Thal** North-West Frontier Province, NW Pakistan 33°24′N 70°32′E
166 M15 **Thalang** Phuket, SW Thailand 08°00′N 98°21′E
Thalashsheri see Tellicherry/Thalassery
155 F20 **Thalassery** var. Tellicherry, Thalashsheri. Kerala, SW India 11°44′N 75°29′E see also Tellicherry
167 Q10 **Thalat Khae** Nakhon Ratchasima, C Thailand 15°15′N 102°24′E
109 Q5 **Thalgau** Salzburg, NW Austria 47°49′N 13°19′E
108 G7 **Thalwil** Zürich, NW Switzerland 47°17′N 08°35′E
83 I20 **Thamaga** Kweneng, SE Botswana 24°41′S 25°31′E
Thamarīd see Thamarīt
141 V13 **Thamarīt** var. Thamarīd, Thumrayt. SW Oman 17°39′N 54°02′E
141 P16 **Thamar, Jabal** ▲ SW Yemen 13°46′N 45°32′E
184 M6 **Thames** Waikato, North Island, New Zealand 37°10′S 175°33′E
14 D17 **Thames** Ontario, S Canada
97 O22 **Thames** S England, United Kingdom
184 M6 **Thames, Firth of** gulf North Island, New Zealand
14 D17 **Thamesville** Ontario, S Canada 42°33′N 81°58′W
141 S13 **Thamūd** N Yemen 17°18′N 49°57′E
167 N9 **Thanbyuzayat** Mon State, S Burma (Myanmar) 15°58′N 97°44′E
166 K7 **Thandwe** var. Sandoway. Rakhine State, W Burma (Myanmar) 18°28′N 94°20′E
152 I9 **Thānesar** Haryāna, NW India 29°58′N 76°48′E
167 T7 **Thanh Hoa** Thanh Hoa, N Vietnam 19°49′N 105°48′E
Thanintari Taungdan see Bilauktaung Range
155 I21 **Thanjāvūr** prev. Tanjore. Tamil Nādu, SE India 10°46′N 79°09′E
Thanlwin see Salween
103 U7 **Thann** Haut-Rhin, NE France 47°51′N 07°04′E
167 O16 **Tha Nong Phrom** Phatthalung, SW Thailand 07°24′N 100°04′E
167 N13 **Thap Sakae** var. Thap Sakau. Prachuap Khiri Khan, SW Thailand 11°30′N 99°35′E
Thap Sakau see Thap Sakae
98 L10 **'t Harde** Gelderland, E Netherlands 52°25′N 05°53′E
152 D11 **Thar Desert** var. Great Indian Desert, Indian Desert. desert India/Pakistan
181 V10 **Thargomindah** Queensland, C Australia 28°00′S 143°47′E
150 D11 **Thar Pārkar** desert SE Pakistan
139 S7 **Tharthār al Furāt, Qanāt ath** canal C Iraq
139 R7 **Tharthār, Buḥayrat ath** ◎ C Iraq
139 R5 **Tharthār, Wādī ath** dry watercourse N Iraq
167 N13 **Tha Sae** Chumphon, SW Thailand
167 N15 **Tha Sala** Nakhon Si Thammarat, SW Thailand 08°43′N 99°54′E
114 I13 **Thásos** Thásos, E Greece 40°47′N 24°43′E
115 I14 **Thásos** island E Greece
37 N14 **Thatcher** Arizona, SW USA 32°47′N 109°46′W
167 T5 **Thât Khê** var. Trâng Dinh. Lang Sơn, N Vietnam 22°15′N 106°26′E
166 M8 **Thaton** Mon State, S Burma (Myanmar) 16°56′N 97°20′E
167 S9 **That Phanom** Nakhon Phanom, E Thailand 16°52′N 104°41′E
167 R10 **Tha Tum** Surin, E Thailand 15°18′N 103°39′E
103 P16 **Thau, Bassin de** var. Étang de Thau. ◎ S France

◆ Country
● Country Capital
◇ Dependent Territory
○ Dependent Territory Capital
⬖ Administrative Regions
✈ International Airport
▲ Mountain
▲▲ Mountain Range
Volcano
River
◎ Lake
⊡ Reservoir

Thau, Étang de *see* Thau, Bassin de
166 *L3* **Thaungdut** Sagaing, N Burma (Myanmar) *24°26′N 94°45′E*
167 *O8* **Thaungyin** *Th.* Mae Nam Moei. Burma (Myanmar)/Thailand
167 *R8* **Tha Uthen** Nakhon Phanom, E Thailand *17°32′N 104°34′E*
109 *W2* **Thaya** *var.* Dyje. Austria/Czech Republic *see also* Dyje
Thaya *see* Dyje
27 *V8* **Thayer** Missouri, C USA *36°31′N 91°34′W*
166 *L6* **Thayetmyo** Magway, C Burma (Myanmar) *19°20′N 95°10′E*
33 *S15* **Thayne** Wyoming, C USA *42°54′N 111°01′W*
166 *M5* **Thazi** Mandalay, C Burma (Myanmar) *20°50′N 96°04′E*
Thebes *see* Thíva
44 *L5* **The Carlton** *var.* Abraham Bay. Mayaguana, SE Bahamas *22°21′N 72°56′W*
45 *O14* **The Crane** *var.* Crane. S Barbados *13°06′N 59°27′W*
32 *I11* **The Dalles** Oregon, NW USA *45°36′N 121°10′W*
28 *M14* **Thedford** Nebraska, C USA *41°59′N 100°32′W*
The Flatts Village *see* Flatts Village
The Hague *see* 's-Gravenhage
Theiss *see* Tisa/Tisza
8 *M9* **Thelon** Northwest Territories, N Canada
Theni *see* Teni
11 *V15* **Theodore** Saskatchewan, S Canada *51°25′N 103°01′W*
23 *N8* **Theodore** Alabama, S USA *30°33′N 88°10′W*
36 *L13* **Theodore Roosevelt Lake** Arizona, SW USA
Theodosia *see* Feodosiya
Theophilo Ottoni *see* Teófilo Otoni
11 *V13* **The Pas** Manitoba, C Canada *53°49′N 101°09′W*
31 *T14* **The Plains** Ohio, N USA *39°22′N 82°07′W*
Thera *see* Santoríni
172 *H17* **Thérèse, Île** *island* Inner Islands, NE Seychelles
Therezina *see* Teresina
115 *L20* **Thérma** Ikaría, Dodekánisa, Greece, Aegean Sea *37°37′N 26°18′E*
Thermae Himerenses *see* Termini Imerese
Thermae Pannonicae *see* Baden
Thermaic Gulf/Thermaicus Sinus *see* Thermaïkós Kólpos
121 *Q8* **Thermaïkós Kólpos** *Eng.* Thermaic Gulf; *anc.* Thermaicus Sinus. *gulf* N Greece
Thermiá *see* Kýthnos
115 *L17* **Thermís** Lésvos, E Greece *39°08′N 26°32′E*
115 *E18* **Thérmo** Dytikí Elláda, C Greece *38°32′N 21°42′E*
33 *V14* **Thermopolis** Wyoming, C USA *43°39′N 108°12′W*
183 *P10* **The Rock** New South Wales, SE Australia *35°18′S 147°07′E*
195 *O5* **Theron Mountains** Antarctica
The Sooner State *see* Oklahoma
115 *G18* **Thespiés** Stereá Ellás, C Greece *38°18′N 23°08′E*
115 *E16* **Thessalía** *Eng.* Thessaly. *region* C Greece
14 *C10* **Thessalon** Ontario, S Canada *46°15′N 83°34′W*
115 *G14* **Thessaloníki** *Eng.* Salonica, Salonika, *SCr.* Solun, *Turk.* Selânik. Kentrikí Makedonía, N Greece *40°38′N 22°58′E*
115 *G14* **Thessaloníki** ✕ Kentrikí Makedonía, N Greece *40°30′N 22°58′E*
Thessaly *see* Thessalía
84 *B12* **Theta Gap** *undersea feature* E Atlantic Ocean *12°40′W 43°30′N*
97 *P20* **Thetford** E England, United Kingdom *52°25′N 00°45′E*
15 *R11* **Thetford-Mines** Québec, SE Canada *46°07′N 71°16′W*
113 *K17* **Theth** *var.* Thethi. Shkodër, N Albania *42°25′N 19°45′E*
Thethi *see* Theth
99 *L20* **Theux** Liège, E Belgium *50°33′N 05°48′E*
45 *V9* **The Valley** (Anguilla) E Anguilla *18°13′N 63°00′W*
27 *N10* **The Village** Oklahoma, C USA *35°33′N 97°33′W*
The Volunteer State *see* Tennessee
25 *W10* **The Woodlands** Texas, SW USA *30°09′N 95°27′E*
Thiamis *see* Kalamás
Thian Shan *see* Tien Shan
Thibet *see* Xizang Zizhiqu
22 *J9* **Thibodaux** Louisiana, S USA *29°48′N 90°49′W*
29 *S3* **Thief Lake** Minnesota, N USA
29 *S3* **Thief River** Minnesota, N USA
29 *S3* **Thief River Falls** Minnesota, N USA *48°07′N 96°10′W*
Thièle *see* La Thielle
32 *G14* **Thielsen, Mount** Oregon, NW USA *43°09′N 122°04′W*
Thielt *see* Tielt
106 *G7* **Thiene** Veneto, NE Italy *45°43′N 11°29′E*
Thienen *see* Tienen
103 *P11* **Thiers** Puy-de-Dôme, C France *45°51′N 03°33′E*
76 *F11* **Thiès** W Senegal *14°49′N 16°52′W*
81 *I19* **Thika** Central, S Kenya *01°03′S 37°05′E*
Thikombia *see* Cikobia
151 *K18* **Thiladhunmathi Atoll** *var.* Tiladummati Atoll. *atoll* N Maldives
Thimbu *see* Thimphu
153 *T11* **Thimphu** *var.* Thimbu; *prev.* Tashi Chho Dzong. ● (Bhutan) W Bhutan *27°28′N 89°37′E*
92 *H2* **Thingeyri** Vestfirdhir, NW Iceland *65°52′N 23°28′W*
92 *I3* **Thingvellir** Sudhurland, SW Iceland *64°15′N 21°06′W*
187 *Q17* **Thio** Province Sud, C New Caledonia *21°37′S 166°13′E*
103 *T4* **Thionville** *Ger.* Diedenhofen. Moselle, NE France *49°22′N 06°11′E*
77 *O12* **Thiou** NW Burkina *13°42′N 02°34′W*
115 *K22* **Thíra** Santoríni, Kykládes, Greece, Aegean Sea *36°25′N 25°26′E*
Thíra *see* Santoríni
115 *J22* **Thirasía** *island* Kykládes, Greece, Aegean Sea
97 *M16* **Thirsk** N England, United Kingdom *54°07′N 01°17′W*
14 *F12* **Thirty Thousand Islands** *island group* Ontario, S Canada
155 *G24* **Thiruvanathapuram** *var.* Tiruvantapuram, Trivandrum. *state capital* Kerala, SW India *08°30′N 76°57′E*
155 *H22* **Thiruvārūr** *var.* Tiruvarur. Tamil Nādu, SE India *10°46′N 79°39′E*
95 *F20* **Thisted** Viborg, NW Denmark *56°58′N 08°42′E*
Thistil Fjord *see* Thistilfjördhur
92 *L1* **Thistilfjördhur** *var.* Thistil Fjord. *fjord* NE Iceland
182 *G9* **Thistle Island** *island* South Australia
Thithia *see* Cicia
Thiukhaoluang Phrahang *see* Luang Prabang Range
115 *G18* **Thíva** *Eng.* Thebes; *prev.* Thívai. Stereá Ellás, C Greece *38°19′N 23°19′E*
Thívai *see* Thíva
102 *M12* **Thiviers** Dordogne, SW France *45°24′N 00°54′E*
92 *J4* **Thjórsá** C Iceland
9 *N10* **Thlewiaza** Nunavut, NE Canada
8 *L10* **Thoa** Northwest Territories, NW Canada
99 *G14* **Tholen** Zeeland, SW Netherlands *51°31′N 04°13′E*
99 *F14* **Tholen** *island* SW Netherlands
26 *L10* **Thomas** Oklahoma, C USA *35°44′N 98°45′W*
21 *T3* **Thomas** West Virginia, NE USA *39°09′N 79°28′W*
27 *U3* **Thomas Hill Reservoir** Missouri, C USA
23 *S5* **Thomaston** Georgia, SE USA *32°53′N 84°19′W*
19 *R7* **Thomaston** Maine, NE USA *44°06′N 69°10′W*
25 *T12* **Thomaston** Texas, SW USA *28°56′N 97°07′W*
23 *O6* **Thomasville** Alabama, S USA *31°54′N 87°42′W*
23 *T8* **Thomasville** Georgia, SE USA *30°49′N 83°57′W*
21 *S9* **Thomasville** North Carolina, SE USA *35°52′N 80°04′W*
35 *N5* **Thomes Creek** California, W USA
11 *W12* **Thompson** Manitoba, C Canada *55°45′N 97°54′W*
29 *R4* **Thompson** North Dakota, N USA *47°45′N 97°07′W*
0 *F8* **Thompson** Alberta/British Columbia, SW Canada
33 *O8* **Thompson Falls** Montana, NW USA *47°36′N 115°20′W*
29 *Q10* **Thompson, Lake** South Dakota, N USA
34 *M3* **Thompson Peak** California, W USA *41°00′N 123°01′W*
27 *S2* **Thompson River** Missouri, C USA
185 *A22* **Thompson Sound** *sound* South Island, New Zealand
8 *J5* **Thomsen** Banks Island, Northwest Territories, NW Canada
23 *V4* **Thomson** Georgia, SE USA *33°28′N 82°30′W*
103 *T10* **Thonon-les-Bains** Haute-Savoie, E France *46°22′N 06°30′E*
103 *O15* **Thoré** *var.* Thore. S France
Thore *see* Thoré
37 *P11* **Thoreau** New Mexico, SW USA *35°24′N 108°13′W*
Thorenburg *see* Turda
92 *J3* **Thórisvatn** C Iceland
92 *P4* **Thor, Kapp** *headland* S Svalbard *76°25′N 25°01′E*
92 *I4* **Thorlákshöfn** Sudhurland, SW Iceland *63°52′N 21°24′W*
Thorn *see* Toruń
25 *T10* **Thorndale** Texas, SW USA *30°36′N 97°12′W*
14 *H10* **Thorne** Ontario, S Canada *46°38′N 79°04′W*
97 *J14* **Thornhill** S Scotland, United Kingdom *55°13′N 03°46′W*
25 *U8* **Thornton** Texas, SW USA *31°24′N 96°34′W*
Thornton Island *see* Millennium Island
14 *H16* **Thorold** Ontario, S Canada *43°07′N 79°15′W*
32 *I9* **Thorp** Washington, NW USA *47°03′N 120°40′W*
Thorshavn *see* Tórshavn
195 *S3* **Thorshavnheiane** *physical region* Antarctica
92 *L1* **Thórshöfn** Nordhurland Eystra, NE Iceland *66°09′N 15°18′W*
Thospitis *see* Van Gölü
167 *S14* **Thôt Nôt** Cân Thơ, S Vietnam *10°17′N 105°31′E*
102 *K8* **Thouars** Deux-Sèvres, W France *46°59′N 00°13′W*
153 *X14* **Thoubal** Manipur, NE India *24°40′N 94°00′E*
102 *K9* **Thouet** W France
Thoune *see* Thun
18 *H7* **Thousand Islands** *island* Canada/USA
35 *S15* **Thousand Oaks** California, W USA *34°10′N 118°50′W*
114 *L12* **Thrace** *cultural region* SE Europe
114 *J13* **Thracian Sea** *Gk.* Thrakikó Pélagos; *anc.* Thracium Mare. *sea* Greece/Turkey
Thracium Mare/Thrakikó Pélagos *see* Thracian Sea
Thrá Lí, Bá *see* Tralee Bay
33 *R11* **Three Forks** Montana, NW USA *45°53′N 111°34′W*
162 *M8* **Three Gorges Dam** *dam* Hubei, C China
160 *L9* **Three Gorges Reservoir** C China
11 *Q16* **Three Hills** Alberta, SW Canada *51°43′N 113°15′W*
183 *N15* **Three Hummock Island** *island* Tasmania, SE Australia
184 *H1* **Three Kings Islands** *island group* N New Zealand
175 *P10* **Three Kings Rise** *undersea feature* W Pacific Ocean
77 *O18* **Three Points, Cape** *headland* S Ghana *04°43′N 02°03′W*
31 *P10* **Three Rivers** Michigan, N USA *41°56′N 85°37′W*
25 *S13* **Three Rivers** Texas, SW USA *28°27′N 98°10′W*
83 *G24* **Three Sisters** Northern Cape, SW South Africa *31°51′S 23°04′E*
32 *H13* **Three Sisters** Oregon, NW USA *44°08′N 121°46′W*
187 *N10* **Three Sisters Islands** *island group* SE Solomon Islands
155 *G22* **Thrissur** *var.* Trichūr. Kerala, SW India *10°32′N 76°14′E* *see also* Trichūr
25 *Q6* **Throckmorton** Texas, SW USA *33°11′N 99°12′W*
180 *M10* **Throssell, Lake** *salt lake* Western Australia
115 *K25* **Thryptis** *var.* Thrýptis. Kríti, Greece, E Mediterranean Sea *35°06′N 25°51′E*
167 *T13* **Thu Dâu Môt** *var.* Phu Cu'ong. Sông Be, S Vietnam *10°58′N 106°40′E*
167 *S6* **Thu Do** ✕ (Ha Nôi) Ha Nôi, N Vietnam *21°13′N 105°46′E*
99 *G21* **Thuin** Hainaut, S Belgium *50°21′N 04°18′E*
149 *Q12* **Thul** Sind, SE Pakistan *28°14′N 68°50′E*
Thule *see* Qaanaaq
83 *J18* **Thuli** *var.* Tuli. S Zimbabwe
Thumrayt *see* Thamarīt
108 *D9* **Thun** *Fr.* Thoune. Bern, W Switzerland *46°46′N 07°38′E*
14 *C17* **Thunder Bay** Ontario, S Canada *48°27′N 89°12′W*
30 *M1* **Thunder Bay** *lake bay* S Canada
31 *R6* **Thunder Bay** *lake bay* Michigan, N USA
31 *R6* **Thunder Bay River** Michigan, N USA
27 *N11* **Thunderbird, Lake** Oklahoma, C USA
28 *L8* **Thunder Butte Creek** South Dakota, N USA
108 *E9* **Thuner See** C Switzerland
167 *N15* **Thung Song** *var.* Cha Mai. Nakhon Si Thammarat, SW Thailand *08°10′N 99°41′E*
108 *H7* **Thur** N Switzerland
108 *G6* **Thurgau** *Fr.* Thurgovie. *canton* NE Switzerland
Thurgovie *see* Thurgau
Thuringe *see* Thüringen
108 *J7* **Thüringen** Vorarlberg, W Austria *47°12′N 09°48′E*
101 *J17* **Thüringen** *Eng.* Thuringia, *Fr.* Thuringe. *state* C Germany
101 *J17* **Thüringer Wald** *Eng.* Thuringian Forest. C Germany
Thuringia *see* Thüringen
Thuringian Forest *see* Thüringer Wald
97 *D19* **Thurles** *Ir.* Durlas. S Ireland *52°41′N 07°49′W*
21 *W2* **Thurmont** Maryland, NE USA *39°36′N 77°22′W*
Thurø *see* Thurø By
95 *H24* **Thurø By** *var.* Thurø. Fyn, C Denmark *55°03′N 10°43′E*
14 *M12* **Thurso** Québec, SE Canada *45°36′N 75°13′W*
96 *J6* **Thurso** N Scotland, United Kingdom *58°35′N 03°32′W*
194 *I10* **Thurston Island** *island* Antarctica
108 *I9* **Thusis** Graubünden, S Switzerland *46°40′N 09°27′E*
Thýamis *see* Kalamás
95 *E21* **Thyborøn** *var.* Tyborøn. Ringkøbing, W Denmark *56°40′N 08°12′E*
195 *U3* **Thyer Glacier** *glacier* Antarctica
115 *L20* **Thýmaina** *island* Dodekánisa, Greece, Aegean Sea
83 *N15* **Thyolo** *var.* Cholo. Southern, S Malawi *16°03′S 35°11′E*
183 *U6* **Tia** New South Wales, SE Australia *31°14′S 151°51′E*
54 *H5* **Tía Juana** Zulia, NW Venezuela *10°18′N 71°24′W*
Tiancheng *see* Chongyang
160 *J14* **Tiandong** *var.* Pingma. Guangxi Zhuangzu Zizhiqu, S China *23°37′N 107°06′E*
161 *O3* **Tianjin** *var.* Tientsin. Tianjin Shi, E China *39°13′N 117°06′E*
Tianjin *see* Tianjin Shi
161 *P3* **Tianjin Shi** *var.* Jin, Tianjin, T'ien-ching, Tientsin. *municipality* E China
159 *S10* **Tianjun** *var.* Xinyuan. Qinghai, C China *37°16′N 99°03′E*
160 *J13* **Tianlin** *var.* Leli. Guangxi Zhuangzu Zizhiqu, S China *24°27′N 106°03′E*
Tian Shan *see* Tien Shan
159 *W11* **Tianshui** Gansu, C China *34°33′N 105°51′E*
150 *I7* **Tianshuihai** Xinjiang Uygur Zizhiqu, W China *35°17′N 79°30′E*
161 *S10* **Tiantai** Zhejiang, SE China *29°11′N 121°01′E*
160 *J14* **Tianyang** *var.* Tianzhou. Guangxi Zhuangzu Zizhiqu, S China *23°50′N 106°52′E*
Tianzhou *see* Tianyang
159 *U9* **Tianzhu** *var.* Huazangsi, Tianzhu Zangzu Zizhixian. Gansu, C China *37°01′N 103°04′E*
Tianzhu Zangzu Zizhixian *see* Tianzhu
191 *Q7* **Tiarei** Tahiti, W French Polynesia *17°32′S 149°20′W*
74 *J6* **Tiaret** *var.* Tihert. NW Algeria *35°20′N 01°20′E*
77 *N17* **Tiassalé** S Ivory Coast *05°54′N 04°50′W*
192 *I16* **Ti'avea** Upolu, SE Samoa *13°58′S 171°30′W*
Tiba *see* Chiba
60 *J11* **Tibagi** *var.* Tibagy. Paraná, S Brazil *24°29′S 50°29′W*
60 *J10* **Tibagi, Rio** *var.* Rio Tibají. S Brazil
Tibají *see* Tibagi
Tibají, Rio *see* Tibagi, Rio
139 *Q9* **Tibal, Wādī** *dry watercourse* S Iraq
54 *G9* **Tibaná** Boyacá, C Colombia *05°19′N 73°25′W*
79 *F14* **Tibati** Adamaoua, N Cameroon *06°25′N 12°33′E*
76 *K15* **Tibé, Pic de** SE Guinea *08°39′N 08°58′W*
Tiber *see* Tevere, Italy
Tiber *see* Tivoli, Italy
Tiberias *see* Tverya
138 *G8* **Tiberias, Lake** *var.* Chinnereth, Sea of Bahr Tabariya, Sea of Galilee, *Ar.* Bahrat Tabariya, *Heb.* Yam Kinneret. N Israel
67 *Q5* **Tibesti** *var.* Tibesti Massif, *Ar.* Tibistī. N Africa
Tibesti Massif *see* Tibesti
Tibet *see* Xizang Zizhiqu
Tibetan Autonomous Region *see* Xizang Zizhiqu
Tibet, Plateau of *see* Qingzang Gaoyuan
Tibistī *see* Tibesti
14 *K7* **Tiblemont, Lac** Québec, SE Canada
139 *X9* **Tīb, Nahr aṭ** S Iraq
Tībnī *see* At Tibnī
182 *L4* **Tibooburra** New South Wales, SE Australia *29°24′S 142°01′E*
95 *L18* **Tibro** Västra Götaland, S Sweden *58°25′N 14°11′E*
40 *E5* **Tiburón, Isla** *var.* Isla del Tiburón. *island* NW Mexico
Tiburón, Isla del *see* Tiburón, Isla
23 *W14* **Tice** Florida, SE USA *26°40′N 81°49′W*
Tichau *see* Tychy
114 *L8* **Ticha, Yazovir** NE Bulgaria
76 *K9* **Tichît** *var.* Tichitt. Tagant, C Mauritania *18°26′N 09°31′W*
Tichitt *see* Tichît
108 *G11* **Ticino** *Fr./Ger.* Tessin. *canton* S Switzerland
106 *D8* **Ticino** Italy/Switzerland
108 *H11* **Ticino** *Ger.* Tessin. SW Switzerland
Ticinum *see* Pavia
41 *X12* **Ticul** Yucatán, SE Mexico *20°22′N 89°30′W*
95 *K18* **Tidaholm** Västra Götaland, S Sweden *58°12′N 13°55′E*
Tidjikdja *see* Tidjikja
76 *J8* **Tidjikja** *var.* Tidjikdja; *prev.* Fort-Cappolani. Tagant, C Mauritania *18°31′N 11°24′W*
Tidore *see* Soasiu
171 *R11* **Tidore, Pulau** *island* E Indonesia
Tîdra, Île *see* Et Tîdra
77 *N16* **Tiébissou** *var.* Tiebissou. C Ivory Coast *07°10′N 05°10′W*
Tiebissou *see* Tiébissou
Tiefa *see* Diaobingshan
108 *I9* **Tiefencastel** Graubünden, S Switzerland *46°40′N 09°33′E*
Tiegenhof *see* Nowy Dwór Gdański
T'ieh-ling *see* Tieling
98 *K13* **Tiel** Gelderland, C Netherlands *51°53′N 05°26′E*
163 *W7* **Tieli** Heilongjiang, NE China *46°57′N 128°01′E*
163 *V11* **Tieling** *var.* T'ieh-ling. Liaoning, NE China *42°19′N 123°52′E*
152 *L4* **Tielongtan** China/India *35°10′N 79°32′E*
99 *D17* **Tielt** *var.* Thielt. West-Vlaanderen, W Belgium *51°00′N 03°20′E*
T'ien-ching *see* Tianjin Shi
99 *I18* **Tienen** *var.* Thienen, *Fr.* Tirlemont. Vlaams Brabant, C Belgium *50°48′N 04°56′E*
Tiên Giang, Sông *see* Mekong
147 *X9* **Tien Shan** *Chin.* Thian Shan, Tian Shan, T'ien Shan, *Rus.* Tyan'-Shan'. C Asia
Tientsin *see* Tianjin
167 *U6* **Tiên Yên** Quang Ninh, N Vietnam *21°19′N 107°24′E*
95 *O14* **Tierp** Uppsala, C Sweden *60°20′N 17°30′E*
62 *H7* **Tierra Amarilla** Atacama, N Chile *27°28′S 70°17′W*
37 *R9* **Tierra Amarilla** New Mexico, SW USA *36°42′N 106°31′W*
41 *R15* **Tierra Blanca** Veracruz-Llave, E Mexico *18°28′N 96°21′W*
41 *O16* **Tierra Colorada** Guerrero, S Mexico *17°10′N 99°30′W*
63 *J17* **Tierra Colorada, Bajo de la** *basin* SE Argentina
63 *I25* **Tierra del Fuego** *off.* Provincia de la Tierra del Fuego. *province* S Argentina
63 *J24* **Tierra del Fuego** *island* Argentina/Chile
Tierra del Fuego, Provincia de la *see* Tierra del Fuego
54 *D7* **Tierralta** Córdoba, NW Colombia *08°10′N 76°04′W*
104 *K9* **Tiétar** W Spain
60 *L10* **Tietê** São Paulo, S Brazil *23°04′S 47°41′W*
60 *J8* **Tietê, Rio** S Brazil
32 *I9* **Tieton** Washington, NW USA *46°41′N 120°43′W*
32 *J6* **Tiffany Mountain** Washington, NW USA *48°40′N 119°55′W*
31 *S12* **Tiffin** Ohio, N USA *41°06′N 83°10′W*
31 *Q11* **Tiffin River** Ohio, N USA
Tiflis *see* T'bilisi
23 *U7* **Tifton** Georgia, SE USA *31°27′N 83°31′W*
171 *R13* **Tifu** Pulau Buru, E Indonesia *03°46′S 126°36′E*
38 *L17* **Tigalda Island** *island* Aleutian Islands, Alaska, USA
115 *I15* **Tigáni, Akrotírio** *headland* Límnos, E Greece *39°50′N 25°03′E*
169 *V6* **Tiga Tarok** Sabah, East Malaysia *06°57′N 117°07′E*
117 *O10* **Tighina** *Rus.* Bendery; *prev.* Bender. E Moldova *46°51′N 29°28′E*
145 *X9* **Tigiretskiy Khrebet** E Kazakhstan
79 *F14* **Tignère** Adamaoua, N Cameroon *07°24′N 12°35′E*
13 *P14* **Tignish** Prince Edward Island, SE Canada *46°58′N 64°03′W*
Tigranocerta *see* Siirt
80 *I11* **Tigray** *federal region* N Ethiopia
41 *O11* **Tigre, Cerro del** C Mexico *23°06′N 99°13′W*
56 *F8* **Tigre, Río** N Peru
139 *X10* **Tigris** *Ar.* Dijlah, *Turk.* Dicle. Iraq/Turkey
76 *G9* **Tiguent** Trarza, SW Mauritania *17°15′N 16°00′W*
74 *M10* **Tiguentourine** E Algeria *27°59′N 09°16′E*
77 *V10* **Tiguidit, Falaise de** *ridge* C Niger
141 *N13* **Tihāmah** *var.* Tehama. *plain* Saudi Arabia/Yemen
Tihert *see* Tiaret
Ti-hua/Tihwa *see* Ürümqi
41 *Q13* **Tihuatlán** Veracruz-Llave, E Mexico *20°44′N 97°30′W*
40 *B1* **Tijuana** Baja California Norte, NW Mexico *32°32′N 117°01′W*
42 *E2* **Tikal** Petén, N Guatemala *17°11′N 89°36′W*
154 *I9* **Tīkamgarh** *prev.* Tehri. Madhya Pradesh, C India *24°44′N 78°50′E*
158 *L7* **Tikanlik** Xinjiang Uygur Zizhiqu, NW China *40°34′N 87°37′E*
77 *P12* **Tikaré** N Burkina *13°16′N 01°39′W*
39 *O12* **Tikchik Lakes** *lakes* Alaska, USA
191 *T9* **Tikehau** *atoll* Îles Tuamotu, C French Polynesia
191 *V9* **Tikei** *island* Îles Tuamotu, C French Polynesia
126 *L13* **Tikhoretsk** Krasnodarskiy Kray, SW Russian Federation *45°51′N 40°07′E*
124 *I13* **Tikhvin** Leningradskaya Oblast', NW Russian Federation *59°37′N 33°30′E*
193 *P9* **Tiki Basin** *undersea feature* S Pacific Ocean
76 *K13* **Tikinsso** NE Guinea
184 *Q8* **Tikitiki** Gisborne, North Island, New Zealand *37°49′S 178°23′E*
79 *D16* **Tiko** Sud-Ouest, SW Cameroon *04°02′N 09°19′E*
139 *S6* **Tikrīt** *var.* Tekrit. Ṣalāḥ ad Dīn, N Iraq *34°36′N 43°42′E*
124 *I8* **Tiksha** Respublika Kareliya, NW Russian Federation *64°07′N 32°31′E*
124 *I6* **Tikshozero, Ozero** NW Russian Federation
123 *P7* **Tiksi** Respublika Sakha (Yakutiya), NE Russian Federation *71°40′N 128°47′E*
Tiladummati Atoll *see* Thiladhunmathi Atoll
42 *A6* **Tilapa** San Marcos, SW Guatemala *14°31′N 92°11′W*
42 *L13* **Tilarán** Guanacaste, NW Costa Rica *10°28′N 84°57′W*
99 *J14* **Tilburg** Noord-Brabant, S Netherlands *51°34′N 05°05′E*
14 *D17* **Tilbury** Ontario, S Canada *42°15′N 82°26′W*
182 *K4* **Tilcha** South Australia *29°37′S 140°52′E*
Tilcha Creek *see* Callabonna Creek
29 *Q14* **Tilden** Nebraska, C USA *42°03′N 97°49′W*
25 *R13* **Tilden** Texas, SW USA *28°27′N 98°43′W*
14 *H10* **Tilden Lake** Ontario, S Canada *46°35′N 79°36′W*
116 *G9* **Tileagd** *Hung.* Mezőtelegd. Bihor, W Romania *47°03′N 22°11′E*
77 *Q8* **Tîlemsi, Vallée de** C Mali
123 *V8* **Tilichiki** Koryakskiy Avtonomnyy Okrug, E Russian Federation *60°25′N 165°55′E*
Tiligul *see* Tilihul
Tiligul'skiy Liman *see* Tilihul's'kyy Lyman
117 *P9* **Tilihul** *Rus.* Tiligul. SW Ukraine
117 *P10* **Tilihul's'kyy Lyman** *Rus.* Tiligul'skiy Liman. S Ukraine
Tilimsen *see* Tlemcen
Tilio Martius *see* Toulon
77 *R11* **Tillabéri** *var.* Tillabéry. Tillabéri, W Niger *14°13′N 01°27′E*
77 *R11* **Tillabéri** *department* SW Niger
Tillabéry *see* Tillabéri
32 *F11* **Tillamook** Oregon, NW USA *45°28′N 123°50′W*
32 *E11* **Tillamook Bay** *inlet* Oregon, NW USA
151 *Q22* **Tillanchāng Dwīp** *island* Nicobar Islands, India, NE Indian Ocean
95 *N15* **Tillberga** Västmanland, C Sweden *59°41′N 16°37′E*
Tillenberg *see* Dyleň
21 *S10* **Tillery, Lake** North Carolina, SE USA
77 *T10* **Tillia** Tahoua, W Niger *16°13′N 04°51′E*
23 *N8* **Tillmans Corner** Alabama, S USA *30°35′N 88°10′W*
14 *F17* **Tillsonburg** Ontario, S Canada *42°53′N 80°44′W*
115 *N22* **Tílos** *island* Dodekánisa, Greece, Aegean Sea
183 *N5* **Tilpa** New South Wales, SE Australia *30°56′S 144°24′E*
Tilsit *see* Sovetsk
31 *N13* **Tilton** Illinois, N USA *40°06′N 87°39′W*
126 *K7* **Tim** Kurskaya Oblast', W Russian Federation *51°39′N 37°11′E*
54 *D12* **Timaná** Huila, S Colombia *01°58′N 75°55′W*
Timan Ridge *see* Timanskiy Kryazh
125 *Q6* **Timanskiy Kryazh** *Eng.* Timan Ridge. *ridge* NW Russian Federation
185 *G20* **Timaru** Canterbury, South Island, New Zealand *44°23′S 171°15′E*
127 *S6* **Timashevo** Samarskaya Oblast', W Russian Federation *53°22′N 51°13′E*
126 *K13* **Timashevsk** Krasnodarskiy Kray, SW Russian Federation *45°37′N 38°57′E*
Timbaki/Timbákion *see* Tympáki
22 *K10* **Timbalier Bay** *bay* Louisiana, S USA
22 *K11* **Timbalier Island** *island* Louisiana, S USA
76 *L10* **Timbedgha** *var.* Timbédra. Hodh ech Chargui, SE Mauritania *16°17′N 08°14′W*
Timbédra *see* Timbedgha
32 *G10* **Timber** Oregon, NW USA *45°42′N 123°19′W*
181 *O3* **Timber Creek** Northern Territory, N Australia *15°35′S 130°21′E*
28 *M8* **Timber Lake** South Dakota, N USA *45°25′N 101°01′W*
54 *D12* **Timbío** Cauca, SW Colombia *02°20′N 76°40′W*
54 *C12* **Timbiquí** Cauca, SW Colombia *02°43′N 77°45′W*
83 *O17* **Timbue, Ponta** *headland* C Mozambique *18°49′S 36°22′E*
Timbuktu *see* Tombouctou
169 *W8* **Timbun Mata, Pulau** *island* E Malaysia
77 *P8* **Timétrine** *var.* Ti-n-Kâr. *oasis* C Mali
Timfi *see* Týmfi
Timfristos *see* Tymfristós
77 *V9* **Timia** Agadez, C Niger *18°07′N 08°49′E*
171 *X14* **Timika** Papua, E Indonesia *04°39′S 137°15′E*
74 *I9* **Timimoun** C Algeria *29°18′N 00°21′E*
Timiris, Cap *see* Timirist, Râs
76 *F8* **Timirist, Râs** *var.* Cap Timiris. *headland* NW Mauritania *19°18′N 16°28′W*
145 *O7* **Timiryazevo** Severnyy Kazakhstan, N Kazakhstan *53°45′N 66°33′E*
116 *E11* **Timiș** *county* SW Romania
14 *H9* **Timiskaming, Lake** *Fr.* Lac Témiscamingue. Ontario/Québec, SE Canada
116 *E11* **Timișoara** *Ger.* Temeschwar, Temeswar, *Hung.* Temesvár; *prev.* Temeschburg. Timiș, W Romania *45°46′N 21°17′E*
116 *E11* **Timișoara** ✕ Timiș, SW Romania *45°50′N 21°21′E*
Timkovichi *see* Tsimkavichy
77 *U8* **Ti-m-Meghsoï** NW Niger
100 *K8* **Timmerdorfer Strand** Schleswig-Holstein, N Germany *53°59′N 10°50′E*
14 *F7* **Timmins** Ontario, S Canada *48°09′N 80°01′W*
21 *S12* **Timmonsville** South Carolina, SE USA *34°07′N 79°56′W*
30 *K5* **Timms Hill** Wisconsin, N USA *45°27′N 90°12′W*
112 *P12* **Timok** E Serbia
58 *N13* **Timon** Maranhão, E Brazil *05°08′S 42°52′W*
171 *Q17* **Timor Sea** *sea* E Indian Ocean
Timor Timur *see* East Timor
Timor Trench *see* Timor Trough
192 *G8* **Timor Trough** *var.* Timor Trench. *undersea feature* NE Timor Sea
61 *A21* **Timote** Buenos Aires, E Argentina *35°22′S 62°13′W*
54 *I6* **Timotes** Mérida, NW Venezuela *08°57′N 70°46′W*
25 *X8* **Timpson** Texas, SW USA *31°54′N 94°24′W*
123 *Q11* **Timpton** NE Russian Federation
93 *H17* **Timrå** Västernorrland, C Sweden *62°29′N 17°20′E*
20 *J10* **Tims Ford Lake** Tennessee, S USA
168 *L7* **Timur, Banjaran** Peninsular Malaysia
149 *T4* **Timurgara** North-West Frontier Province, N Pakistan *34°50′N 71°55′E*
171 *Q8* **Tinaca Point** *headland* Mindanao, S Philippines *05°35′N 125°18′E*
54 *K5* **Tinaco** Cojedes, N Venezuela *09°44′N 68°28′W*
64 *Q11* **Tinajo** Lanzarote, Islas Canarias, Spain, NE Atlantic Ocean *29°03′N 13°41′W*
187 *P10* **Tinakula** *island* Santa Cruz Islands, E Solomon Islands
54 *K5* **Tinaquillo** Cojedes, N Venezuela *09°57′N 68°20′W*
116 *F10* **Tinca** *Hung.* Tenke. Bihor, W Romania *46°46′N 21°58′E*
155 *J20* **Tindivanam** Tamil Nādu, SE India *12°15′N 79°41′E*
74 *E9* **Tindouf** W Algeria *27°43′N 08°09′W*
74 *E9* **Tindouf, Sebkha de** *salt lake* W Algeria
104 *J2* **Tineo** Asturias, N Spain *43°20′N 06°25′W*
77 *R9* **Ti-n-Essako** Kidal, E Mali *18°30′N 02°27′E*
183 *T5* **Tingha** New South Wales, SE Australia *29°56′S 151°13′E*
Tingis *see* Tanger
Tinglett *see* Tinglev
95 *F24* **Tinglev** *Ger.* Tinglett. Sønderjylland, SW Denmark *54°57′N 09°15′E*
56 *E12* **Tingo María** Huánuco, C Peru *09°10′S 76°00′W*
Tingréla *see* Tengréla
158 *K16* **Tingri** *var.* Xêgar. Xizang Zizhiqu, W China *28°40′N 87°04′E*
95 *M21* **Tingsryd** Kronoberg, S Sweden *56°30′N 15°E*
95 *P19* **Tingstäde** Gotland, SE Sweden *57°45′N 18°36′E*
62 *H12* **Tinguiririca, Volcán** C Chile *34°52′S 70°24′W*
94 *F9* **Tingvoll** Møre og Romsdal, S Norway *62°55′N 08°13′E*
188 *K8* **Tinian** *island* S Northern Mariana Islands
Ti-n-Kâr *see* Timétrine
Tinnevelly *see* Tirunelveli
95 *G15* **Tinnoset** Telemark, S Norway *59°43′N 09°03′E*
95 *F15* **Tinnsjø** S Norway
Tino *see* Chino
115 *J20* **Tínos** Tínos, Kykládes, Greece, Aegean Sea *37°33′N 25°08′E*
115 *J20* **Tínos** *anc.* Tenos. *island* Kykládes, Greece, Aegean Sea
153 *R14* **Tinpahar** Jhārkhand, NE India *25°00′N 87°43′E*
153 *X11* **Tinsukia** Assam, NE India *27°28′N 95°20′E*
76 *K10* **Tintâne** Hodh el Gharbi, S Mauritania *16°25′N 10°08′W*
62 *L7* **Tintina** Santiago del Estero, N Argentina *27°00′S 62°45′W*
182 *K10* **Tintinara** South Australia *35°54′S 140°04′E*
104 *I14* **Tinto** SW Spain
77 *S8* **Ti-n-Zaouâtene** Kidal, NE Mali *19°56′N 02°45′E*
Tiobraid Árann *see* Tipperary
28 *K3* **Tioga** North Dakota, N USA *48°24′N 102°56′W*
18 *G12* **Tioga** Pennsylvania, NE USA *41°54′N 77°07′W*
25 *T5* **Tioga** Texas, SW USA *33°28′N 96°55′W*
35 *Q8* **Tioga Pass** *pass* California, W USA
18 *G12* **Tioga River** New York/Pennsylvania, NE USA
Tioman Island *see* Tioman, Pulau
168 *M9* **Tioman, Pulau** *var.* Tioman Island. *island* Peninsular Malaysia
18 *C12* **Tionesta** Pennsylvania, NE USA *41°31′N 79°30′W*
18 *D12* **Tionesta Creek** Pennsylvania, NE USA
168 *J13* **Tiop** Pulau Pagai Selatan, W Indonesia *03°12′S 100°21′E*
18 *H11* **Tioughnioga River** New York, NE USA
74 *J5* **Tipasa** *var.* Tipaza. N Algeria *36°35′N 02°27′E*
Tipaza *see* Tipasa
42 *J10* **Tipitapa** Managua, W Nicaragua *12°08′N 86°04′W*
31 *R13* **Tipp City** Ohio, N USA *39°57′N 84°10′W*
31 *O12* **Tippecanoe River** Indiana, N USA
97 *D20* **Tipperary** *Ir.* Tiobraid Árann. S Ireland *52°29′N 08°10′W*
97 *D19* **Tipperary** *Ir.* Tiobraid Árann. *cultural region* S Ireland
35 *R12* **Tipton** California, W USA *36°02′N 119°19′W*
31 *P13* **Tipton** Indiana, N USA *40°19′N 86°00′W*
29 *Y14* **Tipton** Iowa, C USA *41°46′N 91°07′W*
27 *U5* **Tipton** Missouri, C USA *38°39′N 92°46′W*
36 *I10* **Tipton, Mount** Arizona, SW USA *35°32′N 114°11′W*
20 *F8* **Tiptonville** Tennessee, S USA *36°21′N 89°30′W*
12 *E12* **Tip Top Mountain** Ontario, S Canada *48°18′N 86°06′W*
155 *G19* **Tiptūr** Karnātaka, W India *13°17′N 76°31′E*
Tiquisate *see* Pueblo Nuevo Tiquisate
58 *L13* **Tiracambu, Serra do** E Brazil
Tirana *see* Tiranë
113 *K19* **Tirana Rinas** ✕ Durrës, W Albania *41°25′N 19°41′E*
113 *L20* **Tiranë** *var.* Tirana. ● (Albania) Tiranë, C Albania *41°20′N 19°50′E*
113 *K20* **Tiranë** *district* W Albania
140 *I5* **Tīrān, Jazīrat** *island* Egypt/Saudi Arabia
106 *F6* **Tirano** Lombardia, N Italy *46°13′N 10°10′E*
182 *I2* **Tirari Desert** *desert* South Australia
117 *O10* **Tiraspol** *Rus.* Tiraspol'. E Moldova *46°50′N 29°35′E*
Tiraspol' *see* Tiraspol
184 *M8* **Tirau** Waikato, North Island, New Zealand *37°59′S 175°44′E*
136 *C14* **Tire** İzmir, SW Turkey *38°04′N 27°45′E*
137 *O11* **Tirebolu** Giresun, N Turkey *41°01′N 38°49′E*
96 *F11* **Tiree** *island* W Scotland, United Kingdom
Tîrgoviște *see* Târgoviște
Tîrgu *see* Târgu Cărbunești
Tîrgu Bujor *see* Târgu Bujor
Tîrgu Frumos *see* Târgu Frumos
Tîrgu Jiu *see* Targu Jiu
Tîrgu Lăpuș *see* Târgu Lăpuș
Tîrgu Mures *see* Târgu Mureș
Tîrgu-Neamț *see* Târgu-Neamț
Tîrgu Ocna *see* Târgu Ocna
Tîrgu Secuiesc *see* Târgu Secuiesc
149 *T3* **Tirich Mīr** NW Pakistan *36°12′N 71°51′E*
76 *J5* **Tiris Zemmour** *region* N Mauritania
Tirlemont *see* Tienen
127 *W5* **Tirlyanskiy** Respublika Bashkortostan, W Russian Federation *54°09′N 58°32′E*
Tîrnava Mare *see* Târnava Mare
Tîrnava Mică *see* Târnava Mică
Tîrnăveni *see* Târnăveni
Tírnavos *see* Týrnavos
Tîrnovo *see* Veliko Tŭrnovo
154 *J11* **Tirodi** Madhya Pradesh, C India *21°40′N 79°44′E*
108 *K8* **Tirol** *off.* Land Tirol, *var.* Tyrol, *It.* Tirolo. *state* W Austria
Tirol, Land *see* Tirol
Tirolo *see* Tirol
Tirreno, Mare *see* Tyrrhenian Sea
107 *B19* **Tirso** Sardegna, Italy, C Mediterranean Sea
95 *H22* **Tirstrup** ✕ (Århus) Århus, C Denmark *56°17′N 10°36′E*
155 *I21* **Tiruchchirāppalli** *prev.* Trichinopoly. Tamil Nādu, SE India *10°50′N 78°43′E*
155 *H23* **Tirunelveli** *var.* Tinnevelly. Tamil Nādu, SE India *08°45′N 77°43′E*
155 *J19* **Tirupati** Andhra Pradesh, E India *13°39′N 79°25′E*
155 *I20* **Tiruppattūr** Tamil Nādu, SE India *12°28′N 78°31′E*
155 *H21* **Tiruppur** Tamil Nādu, SW India *11°05′N 77°20′E*
155 *J20* **Tiruvallūr** *var.* Tirvellore. Tamil Nādu, SE India *13°08′N 79°54′E*
Tiruvantapuram *see* Thiruvanathapuram/Trivandrum
Tiruvarur *see* Thiruvārūr
155 *I20* **Tiruvannāmalai** Tamil Nādu, SE India *12°13′N 79°07′E*
Tirvellore *see* Tiruvallūr
112 *L10* **Tisa** *Ger.* Theiss, *Hung.* Tisza, *Rus.* Tissa, *Ukr.* Tysa. SE Europe *see also* Tisza

◆ Country
● Country Capital
◇ Dependent Territory
○ Dependent Territory Capital
◆ Administrative Regions
✕ International Airport
▲ Mountain
▲ Mountain Range
Volcano
River
Lake
Reservoir

Tisa *see* Tisza
Tischnowitz *see* Tišnov
11 U14 **Tisdale** Saskatchewan, S Canada *52°51′N 104°01′W*
27 O13 **Tishomingo** Oklahoma, C USA *34°15′N 96°41′W*
95 M17 **Tisnaren** ◎ S Sweden
111 F18 **Tišnov** *Ger.* Tischnowitz. Jihomoravský Kraj, SE Czech Republic *49°22′N 16°24′E*
Tissa *see* Tisa/Tisza
74 J6 **Tissemsilt** N Algeria *35°37′N 01°48′E*
153 S12 **Tista** ≈ NE India
112 L8 **Tisza** *Ger.* Theiss, *Rom./Slvn./SCr.* Tisa, *Rus.* Tissa, *Ukr.* Tysa. ≈ SE Europe *see also* Tisa
Tisza *see* Tisa
111 L23 **Tiszaföldvár** Jász-Nagykun-Szolnok, E Hungary *47°00′N 20°16′E*
111 M22 **Tiszafüred** Jász-Nagykun-Szolnok, E Hungary *47°38′N 20°45′E*
111 L23 **Tiszakécske** Bács-Kiskun, C Hungary *46°56′N 20°04′E*
111 M21 **Tiszaújváros** *prev.* Leninváros. Borsod-Abaúj-Zemplén, NE Hungary *47°56′N 21°03′E*
111 N21 **Tiszavasvári** Szabolcs-Szatmár-Bereg, NE Hungary *47°56′N 21°21′E*
57 I17 **Titicaca, Lake** ◎ Bolivia/Peru
190 H17 **Titikaveka** Rarotonga, S Cook Islands *21°16′S 159°45′W*
154 M13 **Titilāgarh** *var.* Titlagarh. Orissa, E India *20°18′N 83°09′E*
168 K8 **Titiwangsa, Banjaran** ▲▲ Peninsular Malaysia
Titlagarh *see* Titilāgarh
Titograd *see* Podgorica
Titose *see* Chitose
Titova Mitrovica *see* Mitrovicë
Titovo Užice *see* Užice
113 M18 **Titov Vrv** ▲ NW FYR Macedonia *41°58′N 20°49′E*
94 F7 **Titran** Sør-Trøndelag, S Norway *63°40′N 08°20′E*
31 Q8 **Tittabawassee River** ≈ Michigan, N USA
116 J13 **Titu** Dâmbovița, S Romania *44°40′N 25°32′E*
79 M16 **Titule** Orientale, N Dem. Rep. Congo *03°20′N 25°23′E*
23 X11 **Titusville** Florida, SE USA *28°37′N 80°50′W*
18 C12 **Titusville** Pennsylvania, NE USA *41°36′N 79°39′W*
76 G11 **Tivaouane** W Senegal *14°59′N 16°50′W*
113 I17 **Tivat** SW Montenegro *42°25′N 18°43′E*
14 E14 **Tiverton** Ontario, S Canada *44°15′N 81°31′W*
97 J23 **Tiverton** SW England, United Kingdom *50°54′N 03°30′W*
19 O12 **Tiverton** Rhode Island, NE USA *41°38′N 71°10′W*
107 I15 **Tivoli** *anc.* Tiber. Lazio, C Italy *41°58′N 12°45′E*
25 U13 **Tivoli** Texas, SW USA *28°26′N 96°54′W*
141 Z8 **Ţīwī** NE Oman *22°43′N 59°20′E*
41 Y11 **Tizimín** Yucatán, SE Mexico *21°10′N 88°09′W*
74 K5 **Tizi Ouzou** *var.* Tizi-Ouzou. N Algeria *36°44′N 04°06′E*
Tizi-Ouzou *see* Tizi Ouzou
74 D8 **Tiznit** SW Morocco *29°43′N 09°39′W*
95 F23 **Tjæreborg** Ribe, W Denmark *55°28′N 08°35′E*
113 I14 **Tjentište** Republika Srpska, SE Bosnia and Herzegovina *43°23′N 18°42′E*
98 L7 **Tjeukemeer** ◎ N Netherlands
Tjiamis *see* Ciamis
Tjiandjoer *see* Cianjur
Tjilatjap *see* Cilacap
Tjirebon *see* Cirebon
95 I18 **Tjörn** *island* S Sweden
92 O3 **Tjuvfjorden** *fjord* S Svalbard
Tkvarcheli *see* Tqvarch'eli
40 L8 **Tlahualillo** Durango, N Mexico *26°06′N 103°25′W*
41 P14 **Tlalnepantla** México, C Mexico *19°34′N 99°12′W*
41 Q13 **Tlapacoyán** Veracruz-Llave, E Mexico *19°58′N 97°13′W*
41 P16 **Tlapa de Comonfort** Guerrero, S Mexico *17°33′N 98°33′W*
40 L13 **Tlaquepaque** Jalisco, C Mexico *20°36′N 103°19′W*
Tlascala *see* Tlaxcala
41 P14 **Tlaxcala** *var.* Tlascala, Tlaxcala de Xicohténcatl. Tlaxcala, C Mexico *19°17′N 98°16′W*
41 P14 **Tlaxcala** ◐ *state* S Mexico
Tlaxcala de Xicohténcatl *see* Tlaxcala
41 P14 **Tlaxco** *var.* Tlaxco de Morelos. Tlaxcala, S Mexico *19°38′N 98°06′W*
Tlaxco de Morelos *see* Tlaxco
41 Q16 **Tlaxiaco** *var.* Santa María Asunción Tlaxiaco. Oaxaca, S Mexico *17°18′N 97°42′W*
74 I6 **Tlemcen** *var.* Tilimsen, Tlemsen. NW Algeria *34°53′N 01°21′W*
Tlemsen *see* Tlemcen
138 L4 **Tlété Ouâte Rharbi, Jebel** ▲ N Syria
116 J7 **Tlumach** Ivano-Frankivs'ka Oblast', W Ukraine *48°53′N 25°00′E*
127 P17 **Tlyarata** Respublika Dagestan, SW Russian Federation *42°10′N 46°30′E*
116 K10 **Toaca, Vârful** *prev.* Vîrful Toaca. ▲ NE Romania *46°58′N 25°55′E*
Toaca, Vîrful *see* Toaca, Vârful
187 R13 **Toak** Ambrym, C Vanuatu *16°21′S 168°16′E*
172 J4 **Toamasina** *var.* Tamatave. Toamasina, E Madagascar *18°10′S 49°23′E*
172 J4 **Toamasina** ◐ *province* E Madagascar
172 J4 **Toamasina** ✕ Toamasina, E Madagascar *18°10′S 49°23′E*
21 X6 **Toano** Virginia, NE USA *37°22′N 76°46′W*
191 U10 **Toau** *atoll* Îles Tuamotu, C French Polynesia
45 T6 **Toa Vaca, Embalse** ▣ C Puerto Rico
62 K13 **Toay** La Pampa, C Argentina *36°43′S 64°22′W*
159 R14 **Toba** Xizang Zizhiqu, W China *31°17′N 97°37′E*
164 K14 **Toba** Mie, Honshū, SW Japan *34°29′N 136°51′E*
168 I9 **Toba, Danau** ◎ Sumatera, W Indonesia
45 Y16 **Tobago** *island* NE Trinidad and Tobago
149 Q9 **Toba Kākar Range** ▲▲ NW Pakistan
105 Q12 **Tobarra** Castilla-La Mancha, C Spain *38°36′N 01°41′W*
149 U9 **Toba Tek Singh** Punjab, E Pakistan *30°54′N 72°30′E*
171 R11 **Tobelo** Pulau Halmahera, E Indonesia *01°45′N 127°59′E*
14 E12 **Tobermory** Ontario, S Canada *45°15′N 81°39′W*
96 G10 **Tobermory** W Scotland, United Kingdom *56°37′N 06°12′W*
165 S4 **Tōbetsu** Hokkaidō, NE Japan *43°12′N 141°28′E*
180 M6 **Tobin Lake** ◎ Western Australia
11 U14 **Tobin Lake** ◎ Saskatchewan, C Canada
35 T4 **Tobin, Mount** ▲ Nevada, W USA *40°25′N 117°28′W*
165 O9 **Tobi-shima** *island* C Japan
169 N13 **Toboali** Pulau Bangka, W Indonesia *03°00′S 106°30′E*
144 M8 **Tobol** *Kaz.* Tobyl. Kustanay, N Kazakhstan *52°42′N 62°36′E*
144 L8 **Tobol** *Kaz.* Tobyl. ≈ Kazakhstan/Russian Federation
122 H11 **Tobol'sk** Tyumenskaya Oblast', C Russian Federation *58°15′N 68°12′E*
Tobruch/Tobruk *see* Ţubruq
125 R3 **Tobseda** Nenetskiy Avtonomnyy Okrug, NW Russian Federation *68°37′N 52°24′E*
Tobyl *see* Tobol
125 Q6 **Tobysh** ≈ NW Russian Federation
54 F10 **Tocaima** Cundinamarca, C Colombia *04°30′N 74°38′W*
59 K16 **Tocantins** *off.* Estado do Tocantins. ◐ *state* C Brazil
Tocantins, Estado do *see* Tocantins
59 K15 **Tocantins, Rio** ≈ N Brazil
23 T2 **Toccoa** Georgia, SE USA *34°34′N 83°19′W*
165 O12 **Tochigi** *off.* Tochigi-ken, *var.* Totigi. ◐ *prefecture* Honshū, S Japan
Tochigi-ken *see* Tochigi
165 O11 **Tochio** *var.* Totio. Niigata, Honshū, C Japan *37°27′N 139°00′E*
95 I15 **Töcksfors** Värmland, C Sweden *59°30′N 11°49′E*
42 J5 **Tocoa** Colón, N Honduras *15°40′N 86°01′W*
62 H4 **Tocopilla** Antofagasta, N Chile *22°06′S 70°08′W*
62 I4 **Tocorpuri, Cerro de** ▲ Bolivia/Chile *22°26′S 67°53′W*
183 O10 **Tocumwal** New South Wales, SE Australia *35°53′S 145°35′E*
54 K4 **Tocuyo de La Costa** Falcón, NW Venezuela *11°04′N 68°23′W*
152 H13 **Toda Rāisingh** Rājasthān, N India *26°02′N 75°35′E*
106 H13 **Todi** Umbria, C Italy *42°47′N 12°25′E*
108 G9 **Tödi** ▲ NE Switzerland *46°52′N 08°53′E*
171 T12 **Todlo** Papua, E Indonesia *0°46′S 130°50′E*
165 S9 **Todoga-saki** *headland* Honshū, C Japan *39°33′N 142°02′E*
59 P17 **Todos os Santos, Baía de** *bay* E Brazil
40 F10 **Todos Santos** Baja California Sur, NW Mexico *23°28′N 110°14′W*
40 B2 **Todos Santos, Bahía de** *bay* NW Mexico
Toeban *see* Tuban
Toekang Besi Eilanden *see* Tukangbesi, Kepulauan
Toeloengagoeng *see* Tulungagung
Tōen *see* T'aoyüan
185 D25 **Toetoes Bay** *bay* South Island, New Zealand
11 Q14 **Tofield** Alberta, SW Canada *53°22′N 112°39′W*
10 K17 **Tofino** Vancouver Island, British Columbia, SW Canada *49°05′N 125°51′W*
189 X17 **Tofol** Kosrae, E Micronesia
95 J20 **Tofta** Halland, S Sweden *57°10′N 12°19′E*
95 H15 **Tofte** Buskerud, S Norway *59°31′N 10°33′E*
95 F24 **Toftlund** Sønderjylland, SW Denmark *55°12′N 09°04′E*
193 X15 **Tofua** *island* Ha'apai Group, C Tonga
187 Q12 **Toga** *island* Torres Islands, N Vanuatu
80 N13 **Togdheer** *off.* Gobolka Togdheer. ◐ *region* NW Somalia
Togdheer, Gobolka *see* Togdheer
Toghyzaq *see* Toguzak
164 L11 **Togi** Ishikawa, Honshū, SW Japan *37°06′N 136°44′E*
39 N13 **Togiak** Alaska, USA *59°03′N 160°31′W*
171 O11 **Togian, Kepulauan** *island group* C Indonesia
77 Q15 **Togo** *off.* Togolese Republic; *prev.* French Togoland. ◆ *republic* W Africa
Togolese Republic *see* Togo
162 F8 **Tögrög** Govĭ-Altay, SW Mongolia *45°51′N 95°04′E*
162 F8 **Tögrög** *var.* Hoolt. Övörhangay, C Mongolia *45°31′N 103°06′E*
Tögrög *see* Manhan
159 N12 **Togton He** *var.* Tuotuo He. ≈ C China
Togton Heyan *see* Tanggulashan
144 L7 **Toguzak** *Kaz.* Toghyzaq. ≈ Kazakhstan/Russian Federation
37 P10 **Tohatchi** New Mexico, SW USA *35°51′N 108°45′W*
191 O7 **Tohiea, Mont** Ѫ Moorea, W French Polynesia *17°33′S 149°48′W*
137 N14 **Tohma Çayı** ≈ C Turkey
93 O17 **Tohmajärvi** Itä-Suomi, SE Finland *62°12′N 30°19′E*
93 L16 **Toholampi** Länsi-Suomi, W Finland *63°46′N 24°15′E*
Töhöm *see* Mandah
23 X12 **Tohopekaliga, Lake** ◎ Florida, SE USA
164 M14 **Toi** Shizuoka, Honshū, S Japan *34°55′N 138°45′E*
190 B15 **Toi** N Niue *18°57′S 169°51′W*
93 L19 **Toijala** Länsi-Suomi, SW Finland *61°09′N 23°51′E*
171 P12 **Toima** Sulawesi, N Indonesia *0°48′S 122°21′E*
164 D17 **Toi-misaki** Kyūshū, SW Japan
171 Q17 **Toineke** Timor, S Indonesia *10°06′S 124°22′E*
Toirc, Inis *see* Inishturk
35 U6 **Toiyabe Range** ▲▲ Nevada, W USA
Tojikiston, Jumhurii *see* Tajikistan
147 R12 **Tojikobod** *Rus.* Tadzhikabad. C Tajikistan *39°08′N 70°54′E*
164 G12 **Tōjō** Hiroshima, Honshū, SW Japan *34°54′N 133°15′E*
39 T10 **Tok** Alaska, USA *63°20′N 142°59′W*
164 K13 **Tōkai** Aichi, Honshū, SW Japan *35°01′N 136°51′E*
111 N21 **Tokaj** Borsod-Abaúj-Zemplén, NE Hungary *48°08′N 21°25′E*
165 N11 **Tōkamachi** Niigata, Honshū, C Japan *37°08′N 138°44′E*
185 D25 **Tokanui** Southland, South Island, New Zealand *46°33′S 169°02′E*
80 I7 **Tokar** *var.* Ţawkar. Red Sea, NE Sudan *18°27′N 37°41′E*
136 L12 **Tokat** Tokat, N Turkey *40°20′N 36°35′E*
136 L12 **Tokat** ◐ *province* N Turkey
163 X15 **Tŏkchŏk-kundo** *island group* NW South Korea
Tōke *see* Taka Atoll
190 J9 **Tokelau** ◇ *NZ overseas territory* W Polynesia
Tőketerebes *see* Trebišov
Tokhtamyshbek *see* Tŭkhtamish
24 M6 **Tokio** Texas, SW USA *33°09′N 102°31′W*
Tokio *see* Tōkyō
189 W11 **Toki Point** *point* NW Wake Island
Tokkuztara *see* Gongliu
147 V7 **Tokmak** *Kir.* Tokmok. Chuyskaya Oblast', N Kyrgyzstan *42°50′N 75°18′E*
117 V9 **Tokmak** *var.* Velykyy Tokmak. Zaporiz'ka Oblast', SE Ukraine *47°13′N 35°43′E*
Tokmok *see* Tokmak
184 Q8 **Tokomaru Bay** Gisborne, North Island, New Zealand *38°10′S 178°18′E*
184 M8 **Tokoroa** Waikato, North Island, New Zealand *38°14′S 175°52′E*
76 K14 **Tokounou** C Guinea *09°43′N 09°46′W*
38 M12 **Toksook Bay** Alaska, USA *60°33′N 165°01′W*
Toksu *see* Xinhe
Toksum *see* Toksun
158 L6 **Toksun** *var.* Toksum. Xinjiang Uygur Zizhiqu, NW China *42°47′N 88°38′E*
147 T8 **Toktogul** Talasskaya Oblast', NW Kyrgyzstan *41°51′N 72°56′E*
147 T9 **Toktogul'skoye Vodokhranilishche** ▣ W Kyrgyzstan
Toktomush *see* Tŭkhtamish
193 Y14 **Toku** *island* Vava'u Group, N Tonga
165 U16 **Tokunoshima** Kagoshima, Tokuno-shima, SW Japan
165 U16 **Tokuno-shima** *island* Nansei-shotō, SW Japan
164 I14 **Tokushima** *var.* Tokusima. Tokushima, Shikoku, SW Japan *34°04′N 134°28′E*
164 H14 **Tokushima** *off.* Tokushima-ken, *var.* Tokusima. ◐ *prefecture* Shikoku, SW Japan
Tokushima-ken *see* Tokushima
Tokusima *see* Tokushima
164 E13 **Tokuyama** *var.* Shūnan. Yamaguchi, Honshū, SW Japan *34°04′N 131°48′E*
165 N13 **Tōkyō** *var.* Tokio. ● (Japan) Tōkyō, Honshū, S Japan *35°40′N 139°45′E*
165 O13 **Tōkyō** *off.* Tōkyō-to. ◐ *capital district* Honshū, S Japan
Tōkyō-to *see* Tōkyō
145 T12 **Tokyrau** ≈ C Kazakhstan
149 O3 **Tokzār** *Pash.* Tukzār. Sar-e Pol, N Afghanistan *35°47′N 66°28′E*
145 W13 **Tokzhaylau** *prev.* Dzerzhinskoye. Almaty, SE Kazakhstan *45°49′N 81°04′E*
145 W13 **Tokzhaylau** *var.* Dzerzhinskoye. Taldykorgan, SE Kazakhstan *45°49′N 81°04′E*
189 U12 **Tol** *atoll* Chuuk Islands, C Micronesia
184 Q9 **Tolaga Bay** Gisborne, North Island, New Zealand *38°22′S 178°17′E*
172 I7 **Tôlañaro** *prev.* Faradofay, Fort-Dauphin. Toliara, SE Madagascar
162 D6 **Tolbo** Bayan-Ölgiy, W Mongolia *48°22′N 90°22′E*
Tolbukhin *see* Dobrich
60 G11 **Toledo** Paraná, S Brazil *24°45′S 53°41′W*
54 G8 **Toledo** Norte de Santander, N Colombia *07°16′N 72°28′W*
105 N9 **Toledo** *anc.* Toletum. Castilla-La Mancha, C Spain *39°52′N 04°02′W*
30 M14 **Toledo** Illinois, N USA *39°16′N 88°15′W*
29 W13 **Toledo** Iowa, C USA *42°00′N 92°34′W*
31 R11 **Toledo** Ohio, N USA *41°40′N 83°33′W*
32 F12 **Toledo** Oregon, NW USA *44°37′N 123°56′W*
32 G9 **Toledo** Washington, NW USA *46°27′N 122°49′W*
42 F3 **Toledo** ◐ *district* S Belize
104 M9 **Toledo** ◐ *province* Castilla-La Mancha, C Spain
25 Y7 **Toledo Bend Reservoir** ▣ Louisiana/Texas, SW USA
104 M10 **Toledo, Montes de** ▲▲ C Spain
106 J12 **Tolentino** Marche, C Italy *43°08′N 13°17′E*
Toletum *see* Toledo
94 H10 **Tolga** Hedmark, S Norway *62°25′N 11°00′E*
158 J3 **Toli** Xinjiang Uygur Zizhiqu, NW China *45°55′N 83°33′E*
172 H7 **Toliara** *var.* Toliary; *prev.* Tuléar. Toliara, SW Madagascar *23°20′S 43°41′E*
172 H7 **Toliara** ◐ *province* SW Madagascar
Toliary *see* Toliara
54 D11 **Tolima** *off.* Departamento del Tolima. ◐ *province* C Colombia
Tolima, Departamento del *see* Tolima
171 N11 **Tolitoli** Sulawesi, C Indonesia *01°05′N 120°50′E*
95 K22 **Tollarp** Skåne, S Sweden *55°55′N 14°00′E*
100 N9 **Tollense** ≈ NE Germany
100 N10 **Tollensesee** ◎ NE Germany
36 K13 **Tolleson** Arizona, SW USA *33°25′N 112°15′W*
146 M13 **Tollimarjon** *Rus.* Talimardzhan. Qashqadaryo Viloyati, S Uzbekistan *38°22′N 65°31′E*
Tolmein *see* Tolmin
106 J6 **Tolmezzo** Friuli-Venezia Giulia, NE Italy *46°27′N 13°01′E*
109 S11 **Tolmin** *Ger.* Tolmein, *It.* Tolmino. W Slovenia *46°12′N 13°39′E*
Tolmino *see* Tolmin
111 J25 **Tolna** *Ger.* Tolnau. Tolna, S Hungary *46°26′N 18°47′E*
111 I24 **Tolna** *off.* Tolna Megye. ◐ *county* SW Hungary
Tolna Megye *see* Tolna
Tolnau *see* Tolna
79 I20 **Tolo** Bandundu, W Dem. Rep. Congo *02°57′S 18°35′E*
Tolochin *see* Talachyn
190 D12 **Toloke** Île Futuna, W Wallis and Futuna
30 M13 **Tolono** Illinois, N USA *39°59′N 88°16′W*
105 Q3 **Tolosa** País Vasco, N Spain *43°09′N 02°04′W*
Tolosa *see* Toulouse
171 O13 **Tolo, Teluk** *bay* Sulawesi, C Indonesia
39 R9 **Tolovana River** ≈ Alaska, USA
123 U10 **Tolstoy, Mys** *headland* E Russian Federation *59°12′N 155°04′E*
63 G15 **Toltén** Araucanía, C Chile *39°13′S 73°15′W*
63 G15 **Toltén, Río** ≈ S Chile
54 E6 **Tolú** Sucre, NW Colombia *09°32′N 75°34′W*
41 O14 **Toluca** *var.* Toluca de Lerdo. México, S Mexico *19°20′N 99°40′W*
Toluca de Lerdo *see* Toluca
41 O14 **Toluca, Nevado de** Ѫ C Mexico *19°05′N 99°45′W*
127 R6 **Tol'yatti** *prev.* Stavropol'. Samarskaya Oblast', W Russian Federation *53°32′N 49°27′E*
77 O12 **Toma** NW Burkina *12°46′N 02°51′W*
30 K7 **Tomah** Wisconsin, N USA *43°59′N 90°31′W*
30 L5 **Tomahawk** Wisconsin, N USA *45°27′N 89°40′W*
117 T8 **Tomakivka** Dnipropetrovs'ka Oblast', E Ukraine *47°47′N 34°45′E*
165 S4 **Tomakomai** Hokkaidō, NE Japan *42°38′N 141°32′E*
165 S2 **Tomamae** Hokkaidō, NE Japan *44°18′N 141°38′E*
104 G9 **Tomar** Santarém, W Portugal *39°36′N 08°25′W*
123 T13 **Tomari** Ostrov Sakhalin, Sakhalinskaya Oblast', SE Russian Federation *47°47′N 142°09′E*
115 C16 **Tómaros** ▲ W Greece *39°31′N 20°45′E*
Tomaschow *see* Tomaszów Mazowiecki
Tomaschow *see* Tomaszów Lubelski
61 E16 **Tomás Gomensoro** Artigas, N Uruguay *30°28′S 57°28′W*
117 N7 **Tomashpil'** Vinnyts'ka Oblast', C Ukraine *48°32′N 28°31′E*
Tomaszów *see* Tomaszów Mazowiecki
111 P15 **Tomaszów Lubelski** *Ger.* Tomaschow. Lubelskie, E Poland *50°29′N 23°23′E*
Tomaszów Mazowiecka *see* Tomaszów Mazowiecki
110 L13 **Tomaszów Mazowiecki** *var.* Tomaszów Mazowiecka; *prev.* Tomaszów, *Ger.* Tomaschow. Łódzkie, C Poland *51°33′N 20°E*
40 J13 **Tomatlán** Jalisco, C Mexico *19°53′N 105°18′W*
81 F15 **Tombe** Jonglei, S Sudan *05°52′N 31°40′E*
23 N4 **Tombigbee River** ≈ Alabama/Mississippi, S USA
82 A10 **Tomboco** Dem. Rep. Congo, NW Angola *06°50′S 13°20′E*
77 O10 **Tombouctou** *Eng.* Timbuktu. Tombouctou, N Mali *16°47′N 03°03′W*
77 N9 **Tombouctou** ◐ *region* W Mali
37 N16 **Tombstone** Arizona, SW USA *31°42′N 110°04′W*
83 A15 **Tombua** *Port.* Porto Alexandre. Namibe, SW Angola *15°49′S 11°53′E*
83 J19 **Tom Burke** Limpopo, NE South Africa *23°07′S 28°01′E*
146 L9 **Tomdibuloq** *Rus.* Tamdybulak. Navoiy Viloyati, N Uzbekistan *41°48′N 64°33′E*
146 L9 **Tomditov-Tog'lari** ▲▲ N Uzbekistan
62 G13 **Tomé** Bío Bío, C Chile *36°38′S 72°57′W*
58 L12 **Tomé-Açu** Pará, NE Brazil *02°25′S 48°09′W*
95 L23 **Tomelilla** Skåne, S Sweden *55°33′N 14°00′E*
105 O10 **Tomelloso** Castilla-La Mancha, C Spain *39°09′N 03°01′W*
14 H10 **Tomiko Lake** ◎ Ontario, S Canada
77 N12 **Tominian** Ségou, C Mali *13°18′N 04°39′W*
171 N12 **Tomini, Gulf of** *var.* Teluk Tomini; *prev.* Teluk Gorontalo. *bay* Sulawesi, C Indonesia
Tomini, Teluk *see* Tomini, Gulf of
165 Q11 **Tomioka** Fukushima, Honshū, C Japan *37°19′N 140°57′E*
113 G14 **Tomislavgrad** Federacija Bosna I Hercegovina, SW Bosnia and Herzegovina *43°43′N 17°15′E*
181 O9 **Tomkinson Ranges** ▲▲ South Australia/Western Australia
123 Q11 **Tommot** Respublika Sakha (Yakutiya), NE Russian Federation *58°57′N 126°24′E*
171 Q11 **Tomohon** Sulawesi, N Indonesia *01°19′N 124°49′E*
54 K9 **Tomo, Río** ≈ E Colombia
113 L21 **Tomorrit, Mali i** ▲ S Albania *40°43′N 20°12′E*
11 S17 **Tompkins** Saskatchewan, S Canada *50°03′N 108°49′W*
20 K8 **Tompkinsville** Kentucky, S USA *36°43′N 85°41′W*
171 N11 **Tompo** Sulawesi, N Indonesia *0°56′N 120°16′E*
180 I8 **Tom Price** Western Australia *22°48′S 117°49′E*
122 J12 **Tomsk** Tomskaya Oblast', C Russian Federation *56°30′N 85°05′E*
122 I11 **Tomskaya Oblast'** ◐ *province* C Russian Federation
18 K16 **Toms River** New Jersey, NE USA *39°56′N 74°09′W*
Tom Steed Lake *see* Tom Steed Reservoir
26 L12 **Tom Steed Reservoir** *var.* Tom Steed Lake. ▣ Oklahoma, C USA
171 U13 **Tomu** Papua, E Indonesia *02°07′S 133°01′E*
158 H6 **Tomür Feng** *var.* Pobeda Peak, *Rus.* Pik Pobedy. ▲ China/Kyrgyzstan *42°02′N 80°07′E* *see also* Pobedy, Pik
Tomür Feng *see* Pobedy, Pik
189 N13 **Tomworoahlang** Pohnpei, E Micronesia
41 U17 **Tonalá** Chiapas, SE Mexico *16°08′N 93°41′W*
106 F6 **Tonale, Passo del** *pass* N Italy
164 I11 **Tonami** Toyama, Honshū, SW Japan *36°40′N 136°55′E*
58 C12 **Tonantins** Amazonas, W Brazil *02°58′S 67°30′W*
32 K6 **Tonasket** Washington, NW USA *48°41′N 119°27′W*
55 Y9 **Tonate** *var.* Macouria. N French Guiana *05°00′N 52°28′W*
18 D10 **Tonawanda** New York, NE USA *43°00′N 78°51′W*
171 Q11 **Tondano** Sulawesi, C Indonesia *01°19′N 124°56′E*
104 H7 **Tondela** Viseu, N Portugal *40°31′N 08°05′W*
95 F24 **Tønder** *Ger.* Tondern. Sønderjylland, SW Denmark *54°57′N 08°53′E*
Tondern *see* Tønder
143 N4 **Tonekābon** *var.* Shahsawar, Tonkābon; *prev.* Shahsavār. Māzandarān, N Iran *36°40′N 51°25′E*
Tonezh *see* Tonyezh
193 Y14 **Tonga** *off.* Kingdom of Tonga, *var.* Friendly Islands. ◆ *monarchy* SW Pacific Ocean
175 R9 **Tonga** *island group* SW Pacific Ocean
83 K23 **Tongaat** KwaZulu/Natal, E South Africa *29°35′S 31°07′E*
Tonga, Kingdom of *see* Tonga
161 Q13 **Tong'an** *var.* Datong, Tong an. Fujian, SE China *24°43′N 118°07′E*
Tong an *see* Tong'an
27 Q4 **Tonganoxie** Kansas, C USA *39°06′N 95°05′W*
39 Y13 **Tongass National Forest** *reserve* Alaska, USA
193 Y16 **Tongatapu** ✕ Tongatapu, S Tonga *21°10′S 175°10′W*
193 Y16 **Tongatapu** *island* Tongatapu Group, S Tonga
193 Y16 **Tongatapu Group** *island group* S Tonga
175 S9 **Tonga Trench** *undersea feature* S Pacific Ocean
161 N8 **Tongbai Shan** ▲▲ C China
161 P8 **Tongcheng** Anhui, E China *31°16′N 117°00′E*
160 L6 **Tongchuan** Shaanxi, C China *35°10′N 109°03′E*
160 L12 **Tongdao** *var.* Tongdao Dongzu Zizhixian; *prev.* Shuangjiang. Hunan, S China *26°06′N 109°46′E*
Tongdao Dongzu Zizhixian *see* Tongdao
159 T11 **Tongde** *var.* Gabasumdo. Qinghai, C China *35°13′N 100°39′E*
99 K19 **Tongeren** *Fr.* Tongres. Limburg, NE Belgium *50°47′N 05°28′E*
163 Y14 **Tonghae** NE South Korea *37°26′N 129°09′E*
160 G13 **Tonghai** *var.* Xiushan. Yunnan, SW China *24°06′N 102°45′E*
163 X8 **Tonghe** Heilongjiang, NE China *46°00′N 128°45′E*
163 W11 **Tonghua** Jilin, NE China *41°45′N 125°50′E*
163 Z6 **Tongjiang** Heilongjiang, NE China *47°39′N 132°29′E*
163 Y13 **Tongjosŏn-man** *prev.* Broughton Bay. *bay* E North Korea
163 V7 **Tongken He** ≈ NE China
167 T7 **Tongking, Gulf of** *Chin.* Beibu Wan, *Vtn.* Vinh Băc Bô. *gulf* China/Vietnam
163 U10 **Tongliao** Nei Mongol Zizhiqu, N China *43°37′N 122°15′E*
161 Q9 **Tongling** Anhui, E China *30°55′N 117°50′E*
161 R9 **Tonglu** Zhejiang, SE China *29°50′N 119°38′E*
187 R14 **Tongoa** *island* Shepherd Islands, S Vanuatu
62 G9 **Tongoy** Coquimbo, C Chile *30°16′S 71°31′W*
160 L11 **Tongren** *var.* Rongwo. Guizhou, S China *27°44′N 109°10′E*
159 T11 **Tongren** *var.* Rongwo. Qinghai, C China *35°31′N 101°58′E*
Tongres *see* Tongeren
153 U11 **Tongsa** *var.* Tongsa Dzong. C Bhutan *27°33′N 90°30′E*
Tongsa Dzong *see* Tongsa
Tongshan *see* Fuding, Fujian, China
Tongshan *see* Xuzhou, Jiangsu, China
Tongshi *see* Wuzhishan
159 P12 **Tongtian He** ≈ C China
96 I6 **Tongue** N Scotland, United Kingdom *58°30′N 04°25′W*
44 H3 **Tongue of the Ocean** *strait* C Bahamas
33 X10 **Tongue River** ≈ Montana, NW USA
33 W11 **Tongue River Resevoir** ▣ Montana, NW USA
159 V11 **Tongwei** *var.* Pingxiang. Gansu, C China *35°09′N 105°15′E*
159 W9 **Tongxin** Ningxia, N China *37°00′N 105°41′E*
163 U9 **Tongyu** *var.* Kaitong. Jilin, NE China *44°49′N 123°08′E*
160 J11 **Tongzi** *var.* Loushanguan. Guizhou, S China *28°08′N 106°49′E*
162 F8 **Tonhil** *var.* Dzüyl. Govĭ-Altay, SW Mongolia *46°09′N 93°55′E*
40 G5 **Tónichi** Sonora, NW Mexico *28°37′N 109°34′W*
81 D14 **Tonj** Warab, SW Sudan *07°18′N 28°41′E*
152 H13 **Tonk** Rājasthān, N India *26°10′N 75°50′E*
Tonkābon *see* Tonekābon
27 N8 **Tonkawa** Oklahoma, C USA *36°40′N 97°18′W*
167 Q12 **Tônlé Sap** *Eng.* Great Lake. ◎ W Cambodia
102 L14 **Tonneins** Lot-et-Garonne, SW France *44°21′N 00°21′E*
103 Q7 **Tonnerre** Yonne, C France *47°50′N 04°00′E*
Tonoas *see* Dublon
35 U8 **Tonopah** Nevada, W USA *38°04′N 117°13′W*
164 H13 **Tonoshō** Okayama, Shōdo-shima, SW Japan *34°29′N 134°10′E*
43 S17 **Tonosí** Los Santos, S Panama *07°23′N 80°26′W*
95 H16 **Tønsberg** Vestfold, S Norway *59°16′N 10°25′E*
39 T11 **Tonsina** Alaska, USA *61°39′N 145°10′W*
95 D17 **Tonstad** Vest-Agder, S Norway *58°40′N 06°42′E*
193 X15 **Tonumea** *island* Nomuka Group, W Tonga
137 O11 **Tonya** Trabzon, NE Turkey *40°52′N 39°17′E*
119 K20 **Tonyezh** *Rus.* Tonezh. Homyel'skaya Voblasts', SE Belarus *51°50′N 27°48′E*
36 L3 **Tooele** Utah, W USA *40°32′N 112°18′W*
122 L13 **Toora-Khem** Respublika Tyva, S Russian Federation *52°25′N 96°01′E*
183 O5 **Toorale East** New South Wales, SE Australia *30°29′S 145°25′E*
83 H25 **Toorberg** ▲ S South Africa *32°02′S 24°02′E*
118 G5 **Tootsi** Pärnumaa, SW Estonia *58°34′N 24°43′E*
183 U3 **Toowoomba** Queensland, E Australia *27°35′S 151°54′E*
27 Q4 **Topeka** *state capital* Kansas, C USA *39°03′N 95°41′W*
122 J12 **Topki** Kemerovskaya Oblast', S Russian Federation *55°12′N 85°40′E*
111 M18 **Topl'a** *Hung.* Toplya. ≈ NE Slovakia
Toplicza *see* Toplița
116 J10 **Toplița** *Ger.* Töplitz, *Hung.* Marosheviz; *prev.* Toplița Română, *Hung.* Oláh-Toplicza, Toplicza. Harghita, C Romania *45°56′N 25°20′E*
Toplița Română/Töplitz *see* Toplița
Toplya *see* Topl'a
111 I20 **Topoľčany** *Hung.* Nagytapolcsány. Nitriansky Kraj, W Slovakia *48°33′N 18°10′E*
40 G8 **Topolobampo** Sinaloa, C Mexico *25°36′N 109°04′W*
116 I13 **Topoloveni** Argeș, S Romania *44°49′N 25°02′E*
114 L11 **Topolovgrad** *prev.* Kavakli. Khaskovo, S Bulgaria *42°06′N 26°20′E*
Topolya *see* Bačka Topola
124 I6 **Topozero, Ozero** ◎ NW Russian Federation
32 J10 **Toppenish** Washington, NW USA *46°22′N 120°18′W*
181 P4 **Top Springs Roadhouse** Northern Territory, N Australia *16°37′S 131°49′E*
189 U11 **Tora** *island* Chuuk, C Micronesia
Toraigh *see* Tory Island
189 U11 **Tora Island Pass** *passage* Chuuk Islands, C Micronesia
143 U5 **Torbat-e Ḩeydarīyeh** *var.* Turbat-i-Haidari. Khorāsān-Razavī, NE Iran *35°18′N 59°12′E*
143 V5 **Torbat-e Jām** *var.* Turbat-i-Jam. Khorāsān-Razavī, NE Iran *35°16′N 60°36′E*
39 Q11 **Torbert, Mount** ▲ Alaska, USA *61°30′N 152°15′W*
31 P6 **Torch Lake** ◎ Michigan, N USA
Törcsvár *see* Bran
Torda *see* Turda
104 L6 **Tordesillas** Castilla-León, N Spain *41°30′N 05°00′W*
92 K13 **Töre** Norrbotten, N Sweden *65°55′N 22°40′E*
95 L17 **Töreboda** Västra Götaland, S Sweden *58°41′N 14°07′E*
95 J21 **Torekov** Skåne, S Sweden *56°25′N 12°39′E*
92 O3 **Torell Land** *physical region* SW Svalbard
117 Y8 **Torez** Donets'ka Oblast', SE Ukraine *48°00′N 38°38′E*
101 N14 **Torgau** Sachsen, E Germany *51°34′N 13°01′E*
Torgay *see* Turgay
Torgay Üstirti *see* Turgayskaya Stolovaya Strana
Torghay *see* Turgay
95 N22 **Torhamn** Blekinge, S Sweden *56°04′N 15°49′E*
99 C17 **Torhout** West-Vlaanderen, W Belgium *51°04′N 03°06′E*
106 B8 **Torino** *Eng.* Turin. Piemonte, NW Italy *45°03′N 07°39′E*
165 U15 **Tori-shima** *island* Izu-shotō, SE Japan
81 F16 **Torit** Eastern Equatoria, S Sudan *04°27′N 32°31′E*
186 H6 **Toriu** New Britain, E Papua New Guinea *04°39′S 151°42′E*
148 M4 **Torkestān, Selseleh-ye Band-e** *var.* Bandi-i Turkistan. ▲▲ NW Afghanistan
104 L7 **Tormes** ≈ W Spain
Tornacum *see* Tournai
Torneå *see* Tornio
92 K12 **Torneälven** *var.* Torniojoki, *Fin.* Tornionjoki. ≈ Finland/Sweden
92 I11 **Torneträsk** ◎ N Sweden
13 O4 **Torngat Mountains** ▲▲ Newfoundland and Labrador, NE Canada
24 H8 **Tornillo** Texas, SW USA *31°26′N 106°06′W*
92 K13 **Tornio** *Swe.* Torneå. Lappi, NW Finland *65°50′N 24°18′E*
Torniojoki/Tornionjoki *see* Torneälven
61 B23 **Tornquist** Buenos Aires, E Argentina *38°08′S 62°15′W*
104 L6 **Toro** Castilla-León, N Spain *41°31′N 05°24′W*
62 H9 **Toro, Cerro del** ▲ N Chile *29°10′S 69°43′W*
77 R12 **Torodi** Tillabéri, SW Niger *13°05′N 01°46′E*
Törökbecse *see* Novi Bečej
186 J7 **Torokina** Bougainville Island, NE Papua New Guinea *06°12′S 155°04′E*
111 L23 **Törökszentmiklós** Jász-Nagykun-Szolnok, E Hungary *47°11′N 20°26′E*
42 G7 **Torola, Río** ≈ El Salvador/Honduras
Toronaíos, Kólpos *see* Kassándras, Kólpos
14 H15 **Toronto** *province capital* Ontario, S Canada *43°42′N 79°25′W*
31 V12 **Toronto** Ohio, N USA *40°27′N 80°36′W*
Toronto *see* Lester B. Pearson
27 P6 **Toronto Lake** ▣ Kansas, C USA
35 V16 **Toro Peak** ▲ California, W USA *33°31′N 116°25′W*
124 H16 **Toropets** Tverskaya Oblast', W Russian Federation *56°29′N 31°37′E*
81 G18 **Tororo** E Uganda *0°42′N 34°12′E*
136 H16 **Toros Dağları** *Eng.* Taurus Mountains. ▲▲ S Turkey
183 N13 **Torquay** Victoria, SE Australia *38°21′S 144°18′E*
97 J24 **Torquay** SW England, United Kingdom *50°28′N 03°30′W*
104 M5 **Torquemada** Castilla-León, N Spain *42°02′N 04°17′W*
35 S16 **Torrance** California, W USA *33°50′N 118°20′W*
104 G12 **Torrão** Setúbal, S Portugal *38°18′N 08°13′W*
104 H8 **Torre, Alto da** ▲ C Portugal *40°21′N 07°31′W*
107 K18 **Torre Annunziata** Campania, S Italy *40°45′N 14°27′E*
105 T8 **Torreblanca** País Valenciano, E Spain *40°14′N 00°12′E*
104 L15 **Torrecilla** ▲ S Spain *36°38′N 04°54′W*
105 P4 **Torrecilla en Cameros** La Rioja, N Spain *42°18′N 02°33′W*
105 N13 **Torredelcampo** Andalucía, S Spain *37°45′N 03°52′W*
107 K17 **Torre del Greco** Campania, S Italy *40°46′N 14°22′E*
104 I6 **Torre de Moncorvo** *var.* Moncorvo, Tôrre de Moncorvo. Bragança, N Portugal *41°10′N 07°03′W*
104 J9 **Torrejoncillo** Extremadura, W Spain *39°54′N 06°28′W*
105 O8 **Torrejón de Ardoz** Madrid, C Spain *40°27′N 03°29′W*
105 N7 **Torrelaguna** Madrid, C Spain *40°50′N 03°33′W*
105 N2 **Torrelavega** Cantabria, N Spain *43°21′N 04°03′W*
107 M16 **Torremaggiore** Puglia, SE Italy *41°42′N 15°17′E*
104 M15 **Torremolinos** Andalucía, S Spain *36°38′N 04°30′W*
182 I6 **Torrens, Lake** *salt lake* South Australia
105 S10 **Torrent** *Cas.* Torrente, *var.* Torrent de l'Horta. País Valenciano, E Spain *39°27′N 00°28′W*
Torrent de l'Horta/Torrente *see* Torrent
40 L8 **Torreón** Coahuila, NE Mexico *25°47′N 103°21′W*
105 R13 **Torre Pacheco** Murcia, SE Spain *37°43′N 00°57′W*
106 A8 **Torre Pellice** Piemonte, NE Italy *44°49′N 07°12′E*
105 O13 **Torreperogil** Andalucía, S Spain *38°02′N 03°17′W*
61 J15 **Torres** Rio Grande do Sul, S Brazil *29°20′S 49°43′W*
Torrès, Îles *see* Torres Islands
187 Q11 **Torres Islands** *Fr.* Îles Torrès. *island group* N Vanuatu
104 G9 **Torres Novas** Santarém, C Portugal *39°28′N 08°32′W*
181 V1 **Torres Strait** *strait* Australia/Papua New Guinea
104 F10 **Torres Vedras** Lisboa, C Portugal *39°05′N 09°15′W*
105 S13 **Torrevieja** País Valenciano, E Spain *37°59′N 00°40′W*
186 B6 **Torricelli Mountains** ▲▲ NW Papua New Guinea
96 G8 **Torridon, Loch** *inlet* NW Scotland, United Kingdom
106 D9 **Torriglia** Liguria, NW Italy *44°31′N 09°08′E*
104 M9 **Torrijos** Castilla-La Mancha, C Spain *39°59′N 04°18′W*
18 L12 **Torrington** Connecticut, NE USA *41°48′N 73°07′W*

◆ Country
● Country Capital
◇ Dependent Territory
○ Dependent Territory Capital
◐ Administrative Regions
✕ International Airport
▲ Mountain
▲▲ Mountain Range
Ѫ Volcano
≈ River
◎ Lake
▣ Reservoir

33 Z15 **Torrington** Wyoming, C USA *42°04′N 104°10′W*
Torröjen *see* Torrön
94 F16 **Torrön** *prev.* Torröjen. ◎ C Sweden
105 N15 **Torrox** Andalucía, S Spain *36°45′N 03°58′W*
94 N13 **Torsåker** Gävleborg, C Sweden *60°31′N 16°30′E*
95 N21 **Torsås** Kalmar, S Sweden *56°24′N 16°00′E*
95 J14 **Torsby** Värmland, C Sweden *60°07′N 13°E*
95 N16 **Torshälla** Södermanland, C Sweden *59°25′N 16°28′E*
95 B19 **Tórshavn** *Dan.* Thorshavn. ○ Faeroe Islands *62°02′N 06°47′W*
Torshiz *see* Kāshmar
146 I9 **To'rtkok'l** *var.* Türtkül, *Rus.* Turtkul'; *prev.* Petroaleksandrovsk. Qoraqalpog'iston Respublikasi, W Uzbekistan *41°35′N 61°E*
Tortoise Islands *see* Colón, Archipiélago de
45 T9 **Tortola** *island* C British Virgin Islands
106 D9 **Tortona** *anc.* Dertona. Piemonte, NW Italy *44°54′N 08°52′E*
107 L23 **Tortorici** Sicilia, Italy, C Mediterranean Sea *38°02′N 14°49′E*
105 U7 **Tortosa** *anc.* Dertosa. Cataluña, E Spain *40°49′N 00°31′E*
Tortosa *see* Ṭarṭūs
105 U7 **Tortosa, Cap** *cape* E Spain
44 L8 **Tortue, Île de la** *var.* Tortuga Island. *island* N Haiti
55 Y10 **Tortue, Montagne** ▲▲ C French Guiana
Tortuga, Isla *see* La Tortuga, Isla
Tortuga Island *see* Tortue, Île de la
54 C11 **Tortugas, Golfo** *gulf* W Colombia
45 T5 **Tortuguero, Laguna** *lagoon* N Puerto Rico
137 Q12 **Tortum** Erzurum, NE Turkey *40°20′N 41°36′E*
Torugart, Pereval *see* Turugart Shankou
137 O12 **Torul** Gümüşhane, NE Turkey *40°35′N 39°18′E*
110 J10 **Toruń** *Ger.* Thorn. Toruń, Kujawsko-pomorskie, C Poland *53°02′N 18°36′E*
95 K20 **Torup** Halland, S Sweden *56°57′N 13°04′E*
118 I6 **Tõrva** *Ger.* Törwa. Valgamaa, S Estonia *58°00′N 25°54′E*
Törwa *see* Tõrva
96 D13 **Tory Island** *Ir.* Toraigh. *island* NW Ireland
111 N19 **Torysa** *Hung.* Tarca. ≈ NE Slovakia
Torzburg *see* Bran
124 J16 **Torzhok** Tverskaya Oblast', W Russian Federation *57°04′N 34°55′E*
164 F15 **Tosa-Shimizu** *var.* Tosasimizu. Kōchi, Shikoku, SW Japan *32°47′N 132°58′E*
Tosasimizu *see* Tosa-Shimizu
164 G15 **Tosa-wan** *bay* SW Japan
83 H21 **Tosca** North-West, N South Africa *25°51′S 23°56′E*
106 F12 **Toscana** *Eng.* Tuscany. ◈ *region* C Italy
107 E14 **Toscano, Archipelago** *Eng.* Tuscan Archipelago. *island group* C Italy
106 G10 **Tosco-Emiliano, Appennino** *Eng.* Tuscan-Emilian Mountains. ▲▲ C Italy
Tösei *see* Tungshih
165 N15 **To-shima** *island* Izu-shotō, SE Japan
147 Q9 **Toshkent** *Eng./Rus.* Tashkent. ● Toshkent Viloyati, E Uzbekistan *41°19′N 69°17′E*
147 Q9 **Toshkent** ✕ Toshkent Viloyati, E Uzbekistan *41°13′N 69°15′E*
147 P9 **Toshkent Viloyati** *Rus.* Tashkentskaya Oblast'. ◈ *province* E Uzbekistan
124 H13 **Tosno** Leningradskaya Oblast', NW Russian Federation *59°34′N 30°48′E*
159 Q10 **Toson Hu** ◎ C China
162 H6 **Tosontsengel** Dzavhan, NW Mongolia *48°42′N 98°14′E*
162 J6 **Tosontsengel** *var.* Tsengel. Hövsgöl, N Mongolia *49°29′N 101°09′E*
146 I8 **Tosquduq Qumlari** *var.* Goshquduq Qum, Taskuduk, Peski. *desert* W Uzbekistan
105 U4 **Tossal de l'Orri** *var.* Llorri. ▲ NE Spain *42°24′N 01°15′E*
61 A15 **Tostado** Santa Fe, C Argentina *29°15′S 61°45′W*
118 F6 **Tõstamaa** *Ger.* Testama. Pärnumaa, SW Estonia *58°20′N 23°59′E*
100 I10 **Tostedt** Niedersachsen, NW Germany *53°16′N 09°42′E*
136 J11 **Tosya** Kastamonu, N Turkey *41°02′N 34°02′E*
95 F15 **Totak** ◎ S Norway
105 R13 **Totana** Murcia, SE Spain *37°45′N 01°30′W*
94 H13 **Toten** *physical region* S Norway
83 G18 **Toteng** North-West, C Botswana *20°25′S 23°00′E*
102 M3 **Tôtes** Seine-Maritime, N France *49°40′N 01°02′E*
Totigi *see* Tochigi
Totio *see* Tochio
Totis *see* Tata
189 U13 **Totiw** *island* Chuuk, C Micronesia
125 N13 **Tot'ma** *var.* Totma. Vologodskaya Oblast', NW Russian Federation *59°58′N 42°42′E*
Tot'ma *see* Sukhona
55 V9 **Totness** Coronie, N Surinam *05°53′N 56°19′W*
42 C5 **Totonicapán** Totonicapán, W Guatemala *14°58′N 91°12′W*
42 A2 **Totonicapán** *off.* Departamento de Totonicapán. ◈ *department* W Guatemala
Totonicapán, Departamento de *see* Totonicapán
61 B18 **Totoras** Santa Fe, C Argentina *32°35′S 61°11′W*
187 Y15 **Totoya** *island* S Fiji
183 Q7 **Tottenham** New South Wales, SE Australia *32°16′S 147°23′E*
164 I12 **Tottori** Tottori, Honshū, SW Japan *35°29′N 134°14′E*
164 H12 **Tottori** *off.* Tottori-ken. ◈ *prefecture* Honshū, SW Japan
Tottori-ken *see* Tottori
76 I6 **Touâjîl** Tiris Zemmour, N Mauritania *22°03′N 12°40′W*
76 L15 **Touba** W Ivory Coast *08°17′N 07°41′W*
76 G11 **Touba** W Senegal *14°55′N 15°53′W*
74 E7 **Toubkal, Jbel** ▲ W Morocco *31°00′N 07°50′W*
32 K10 **Touchet** Washington, NW USA *46°03′N 118°40′W*
103 P7 **Toucy** Yonne, C France *47°45′N 03°18′E*
77 O12 **Tougan** W Burkina *13°06′N 03°03′W*
74 L7 **Touggourt** NE Algeria *33°08′N 06°04′E*
77 Q12 **Tougouri** N Burkina *13°22′N 00°25′W*
76 J13 **Tougué** NW Guinea *11°29′N 11°48′W*
76 K12 **Toukoto** Kayes, W Mali *13°27′N 09°52′W*
103 S5 **Toul** Meurthe-et-Moselle, NE France *48°41′N 05°54′E*
76 L16 **Toulépleu** *var.* Toulobli. W Ivory Coast *06°37′N 08°27′W*
161 S14 **Touliu** C Taiwan *23°44′N 120°27′E*
15 U3 **Toulnustouc** ≈ Québec, SE Canada
Toulobli *see* Toulépleu
103 T16 **Toulon** *anc.* Telo Martius, Tilio Martius. Var, SE France *43°07′N 05°56′E*
30 K12 **Toulon** Illinois, N USA *41°05′N 89°54′W*
102 M15 **Toulouse** *anc.* Tolosa. Haute-Garonne, S France *43°37′N 01°25′E*
102 M15 **Toulouse** ✕ Haute-Garonne, S France *43°38′N 01°19′E*
77 N16 **Toumodi** C Ivory Coast *06°34′N 05°01′W*
74 G9 **Tounassine, Hamada** *hill range* W Algeria
Toungoo *see* Taungoo
102 L8 **Touraine** *cultural region* C France
Tourane *see* Đà Nẵng
103 P1 **Tourcoing** Nord, N France *50°44′N 03°10′E*
104 F2 **Touriñán, Cabo** *headland* NW Spain *43°02′N 09°20′W*
76 J6 **Tourine** Tiris Zemmour, N Mauritania *22°23′N 11°50′W*
102 J3 **Tourlaville** Manche, N France *49°38′N 01°34′W*
99 D19 **Tournai** *var.* Tournay, *Dut.* Doornik; *anc.* Tornacum. Hainaut, SW Belgium *50°36′N 03°24′E*
102 L16 **Tournay** Hautes-Pyrénées, S France *43°10′N 00°16′E*
Tournay *see* Tournai
103 R12 **Tournon** Ardèche, E France *45°05′N 04°49′E*
103 R9 **Tournus** Saône-et-Loire, C France *46°33′N 04°53′E*
59 Q14 **Touros** Rio Grande do Norte, E Brazil *05°10′S 35°29′W*
102 L8 **Tours** *anc.* Caesarodunum, Turoni. Indre-et-Loire, C France *47°22′N 00°40′E*
183 Q17 **Tourville, Cape** *headland* Tasmania, SE Australia *42°09′S 148°20′E*
162 L8 **Töv** ◈ *province* C Mongolia
54 H7 **Tovar** Mérida, NW Venezuela *08°22′N 71°50′W*
126 L5 **Tovarkovskiy** Tul'skaya Oblast', W Russian Federation *53°41′N 38°18′E*
Tovil'-Dora *see* Tavildara
Tövis *see* Teiuş
137 V11 **Tovuz** *Rus.* Tauz. W Azerbaijan *40°58′N 45°41′E*
165 R7 **Towada** Aomori, Honshū, C Japan *40°35′N 141°13′E*
184 K3 **Towai** Northland, North Island, New Zealand *35°29′S 174°06′E*
18 H12 **Towanda** Pennsylvania, NE USA *41°45′N 76°25′W*
29 W4 **Tower** Minnesota, N USA *47°48′N 92°16′W*
171 N12 **Towera** Sulawesi, N Indonesia *0°29′S 120°01′E*
Tower Island *see* Genovesa, Isla
180 M13 **Tower Peak** ▲ Western Australia *33°23′S 123°27′E*
35 U11 **Towne Pass** *pass* California, W USA
29 N3 **Towner** North Dakota, N USA *48°20′N 100°27′W*
33 R10 **Townsend** Montana, NW USA *46°19′N 111°31′W*
181 X6 **Townsville** Queensland, NE Australia *19°24′S 146°53′E*
Towoeti Meer *see* Towuti, Danau
148 K4 **Towraghoudī** Herāt, NW Afghanistan *35°13′N 62°19′E*
21 X3 **Towson** Maryland, NE USA *39°25′N 76°36′W*
171 O13 **Towuti, Danau** *Dut.* Towoeti Meer. ◎ Sulawesi, C Indonesia
Toxkan He *see* Ak-say
24 K9 **Toyah** Texas, SW USA *31°18′N 103°47′W*
165 R4 **Tōya-ko** ◎ Hokkaidō, NE Japan
164 L11 **Toyama** Toyama, Honshū, SW Japan *36°41′N 137°13′E*
164 L11 **Toyama** *off.* Toyama-ken. ◈ *prefecture* Honshū, SW Japan
Toyama-ken *see* Toyama
164 L11 **Toyama-wan** *bay* W Japan
164 H15 **Tōyo** Kōchi, Shikoku, SW Japan *33°22′N 134°18′E*
Toyohara *see* Yuzhno-Sakhalinsk
164 L14 **Toyohashi** *var.* Toyohasi. Aichi, Honshū, SW Japan *34°46′N 137°22′E*
Toyohasi *see* Toyohashi
164 L14 **Toyokawa** Aichi, Honshū, SW Japan *34°47′N 137°24′E*
164 I14 **Toyooka** Hyōgo, Honshū, SW Japan *35°35′N 134°48′E*
164 L13 **Toyota** Aichi, Honshū, SW Japan *35°04′N 137°09′E*
165 T1 **Toyotomi** Hokkaidō, NE Japan *45°07′N 141°45′E*
147 Q10 **To'ytepa** *Rus.* Toytepa. Toshkent Viloyati, E Uzbekistan *41°04′N 69°22′E*
Toytepa *see* To'ytepa
74 M6 **Tozeur** *var.* Tawzar. W Tunisia *34°00′N 08°09′E*
39 Q8 **Tozi, Mount** ▲ Alaska, USA *65°45′N 151°01′W*
137 Q9 **Tqvarch'eli** *Rus.* Tkvarcheli. NW Georgia *42°51′N 41°42′E*
Trâblous *see* Tripoli
137 O11 **Trabzon** *Eng.* Trebizond; *anc.* Trapezus. Trabzon, NE Turkey *41°N 39°43′E*
137 O11 **Trabzon** *Eng.* Trebizond. ◈ *province* NE Turkey
13 P13 **Tracadie** New Brunswick, SE Canada *47°32′N 64°57′W*
Trachenberg *see* Żmigród
15 O11 **Tracy** Québec, SE Canada *45°59′N 73°07′W*
35 O8 **Tracy** California, W USA *37°43′N 121°27′W*
29 S10 **Tracy** Minnesota, N USA *44°14′N 95°37′W*
20 K10 **Tracy City** Tennessee, S USA *35°15′N 85°44′W*
106 D7 **Tradate** Lombardia, N Italy *45°43′N 08°57′E*
84 F6 **Traena Bank** *undersea feature* E Norwegian Sea *66°15′N 09°45′E*
29 W13 **Traer** Iowa, C USA *42°11′N 92°28′W*
104 J16 **Trafalgar, Cabo de** *headland* SW Spain *36°10′N 06°03′W*
Traiectum ad Mosam/ Traiectum Tungorum *see* Maastricht
Tráigh Mhór *see* Tramore
11 O17 **Trail** British Columbia, SW Canada *49°94′N 117°39′W*
58 B11 **Traíra, Serra do** ▲▲ NW Brazil
109 V5 **Traisen** Niederösterreich, NE Austria *48°03′N 15°37′E*
109 W4 **Traisen** ≈ NE Austria
109 X4 **Traiskirchen** Niederösterreich, NE Austria *48°01′N 16°18′E*
Trajani Portus *see* Civitavecchia
Trajectum ad Rhenum *see* Utrecht
119 H14 **Trakai** *Ger.* Traken, *Pol.* Troki. Vilnius, SE Lithuania *54°39′N 24°58′E*
Traken *see* Trakai
97 B20 **Tralee** *Ir.* Trá Lí. SW Ireland *52°16′N 09°42′W*
97 A20 **Tralee Bay** *Ir.* Bá Thrá Lí. *bay* SW Ireland
Trá Lí *see* Tralee
Trälleborg *see* Trelleborg
Tralles Aydin *see* Aydın
61 J16 **Tramandaí** Rio Grande do Sul, S Brazil *30°01′S 50°11′W*
108 C7 **Tramelan** Bern, W Switzerland *47°13′N 07°07′E*
Trá Mhór *see* Tramore
97 E20 **Tramore** *Ir.* Tráigh Mhór, Trá Mhór. Waterford, S Ireland *52°10′N 07°10′W*
95 L18 **Tranås** Jönköping, S Sweden *58°03′N 15°00′E*
62 J7 **Trancas** Tucumán, N Argentina *26°11′S 65°20′W*
104 I7 **Trancoso** Guarda, N Portugal *40°46′N 07°21′W*
95 H22 **Tranebjerg** Århus, C Denmark *55°51′N 10°36′E*
95 K19 **Tranemo** Västra Götaland, S Sweden *57°30′N 13°20′E*
167 N16 **Trang** Trang, S Thailand *07°33′N 99°36′E*
171 V15 **Trangan, Pulau** *island* Kepulauan Aru, E Indonesia
Trâng Dinh *see* Thât Khê
183 Q7 **Trangie** New South Wales, SE Australia *32°01′S 147°58′E*
94 K12 **Trängslet** Dalarna, C Sweden *61°22′N 13°43′E*
107 N16 **Trani** Puglia, SE Italy *41°17′N 16°25′E*
61 F17 **Tranqueras** Rivera, NE Uruguay *31°13′S 55°45′W*
63 G17 **Tranqui, Isla** *island* S Chile
39 V6 **Trans-Alaska pipeline** *oil pipeline* Alaska, USA
195 Q10 **Transantarctic Mountains** ▲▲ Antarctica
Transcarpathian Oblast *see* Zakarpats'ka Oblast'
122 E9 **Trans-Siberian Railway** *railway* Russian Federation
Transilvania *see* Transylvania
Transilvaniei, Alpi *see* Carpaţii Meridionalii
Transjordan *see* Jordan
172 L11 **Transkei Basin** *undersea feature* SW Indian Ocean *35°30′S 29°00′E*
117 O10 **Transnistria** *cultural region* E Moldavia
Transsylvanische Alpen/ Transylvanian Alps *see* Carpaţii Meridionalii
94 K12 **Transtrand** Dalarna, C Sweden *61°06′N 13°19′E*
116 G10 **Transylvania** *Eng.* Ardeal, Transilvania, *Ger.* Siebenbürgen, *Hung.* Erdély. *cultural region* NW Romania
167 S14 **Tra Ôn** Vinh Long, S Vietnam *09°58′N 105°58′E*
107 H23 **Trapani** *anc.* Drepanum. Sicilia, Italy, C Mediterranean Sea *38°02′N 12°32′E*
167 S12 **Trâpeăng Vêng** Kâmpóng Thum, C Cambodia *12°37′N 104°58′E*
Trapezus *see* Trabzon
114 L9 **Trapoklovo** Sliven, C Bulgaria *42°40′N 26°36′E*
183 P13 **Traralgon** Victoria, SE Australia *38°15′S 146°36′E*
76 H9 **Trarza** ◈ *region* SW Mauritania
Trasimenischersee *see* Trasimeno, Lago
106 H12 **Trasimeno, Lago** *Eng.* Lake of Perugia, *Ger.* Trasimenischersee. ◎ C Italy
95 J20 **Träslövsläge** Halland, S Sweden *57°02′N 12°18′E*
Trás-os-Montes *see* Cucumbi
104 I6 **Trás-os-Montes e Alto Douro** *former province* N Portugal
167 Q12 **Trat** *var.* Bang Phra. Trat, S Thailand *12°16′N 102°30′E*
Trá Tholl, Inis *see* Inishtrahull
Traù *see* Trogir
109 T4 **Traun** Oberösterreich, N Austria *48°14′N 14°15′E*
109 S5 **Traun** ≈ N Austria
Traun, Lake *see* Traunsee
101 N23 **Traunreut** Bayern, SE Germany *47°58′N 12°36′E*
109 S5 **Traunsee** *var.* Gmundner See, *Eng.* Lake Traun. ◎ N Austria
Trautenau *see* Trutnov
21 P11 **Travelers Rest** South Carolina, SE USA *34°58′N 82°26′W*
182 L8 **Travellers Lake** *seasonal lake* New South Wales, SE Australia
31 P6 **Traverse City** Michigan, N USA *44°45′N 85°37′W*
29 R7 **Traverse, Lake** ◎ Minnesota/South Dakota, N USA
185 I16 **Travers, Mount** ▲ South Island, New Zealand *42°01′S 172°46′E*
11 P17 **Travers Reservoir** ⊠ Alberta, SW Canada
167 T14 **Tra Vinh** *var.* Phu Vinh. Tra Vinh, S Vietnam *09°57′N 106°20′E*
25 S10 **Travis, Lake** ⊠ Texas, SW USA
112 H12 **Travnik** Federacija Bosna I Hercegovina, C Bosnia and Herzegovina *44°14′N 17°40′E*
109 V11 **Trbovlje** *Ger.* Trifail. C Slovenia *46°10′N 15°03′E*
23 V13 **Treasure Island** Florida, SE USA *27°46′N 82°46′W*
Treasure State *see* Montana
186 I8 **Treasury Islands** *island group* NW Solomon Islands
106 D9 **Trebbia** *anc.* Trebia. ≈ NW Italy
100 N8 **Trebel** ≈ NE Germany
103 O16 **Trèbes** Aude, S France *43°12′N 02°26′E*
Trebia *see* Trebbia
111 F18 **Třebíč** *Ger.* Trebitsch. Vysočina, C Czech Republic *49°13′N 15°52′E*
113 I16 **Trebinje** Republika Srpska, S Bosnia and Herzegovina *42°42′N 18°19′E*
Trebišnica *see* Trebišnjica
113 H16 **Trebišnjica** *var.* Trebišnica. ≈ S Bosnia and Herzegovina
111 N20 **Trebišov** *Hung.* Tőketerebes. Košický Kraj, E Slovakia *48°37′N 21°44′E*
Trebitsch *see* Třebíč
Trebizond *see* Trabzon
Trebnitz *see* Trzebnica
109 V12 **Trebnje** SE Slovenia *45°54′N 15°01′E*
111 D19 **Třeboň** *Ger.* Wittingau. Jihočeský Kraj, S Czech Republic *49°00′N 14°46′E*
104 J15 **Trebujena** Andalucía, S Spain *36°52′N 06°11′W*
100 I7 **Treene** ≈ N Germany
Tree Planters State *see* Nebraska
109 S9 **Treffen** Kärnten, S Austria *46°40′N 13°51′E*
Trefynwy *see* Monmouth
102 G5 **Tréguier** Côtes d'Armor, NW France *48°50′N 03°12′W*
61 G18 **Treinta y Tres** Treinta y Tres, E Uruguay *33°16′S 54°17′W*
61 F18 **Treinta y Tres** ◈ *department* E Uruguay
122 F11 **Trëkhgornyy** Chelyabinskaya Oblast', C Russian Federation *54°42′N 58°25′E*
114 F9 **Treklyanska Reka** ≈ W Bulgaria
102 K8 **Trélazé** Maine-et-Loire, NW France *47°27′N 00°28′W*
63 K17 **Trelew** Chubut, SE Argentina *43°13′S 65°15′W*
95 K23 **Trelleborg** *var.* Trälleborg. Skåne, S Sweden *55°22′N 13°10′E*
113 P15 **Trem** ▲ SE Serbia *43°10′N 22°12′E*
15 N11 **Tremblant, Mont** ▲ Québec, SE Canada *46°13′N 74°34′W*
99 H17 **Tremelo** Vlaams Brabant, C Belgium *51°N 04°34′E*
107 M15 **Tremiti, Isole** *island group* SE Italy
30 K12 **Tremont** Illinois, N USA *40°30′N 89°31′W*
36 L1 **Tremonton** Utah, W USA *41°42′N 112°09′W*
105 U4 **Tremp** Cataluña, NE Spain *42°09′N 00°53′E*
30 J7 **Trempealeau** Wisconsin, N USA *44°00′N 91°25′W*
15 P8 **Trenche** ≈ Québec, SE Canada
15 O7 **Trenche, Lac** ◎ Québec, SE Canada
111 I20 **Trenčiansky Kraj** ◈ *region* W Slovakia
111 I19 **Trenčín** *Ger.* Trentschin, *Hung.* Trencsén. Trenčiansky Kraj, W Slovakia *48°54′N 18°03′E*
Trencsén *see* Trenčín
Trengganu *see* Terengganu
Trengganu, Kuala *see* Kuala Terengganu
61 A21 **Trenque Lauquen** Buenos Aires, E Argentina *36°01′S 62°47′W*
14 J14 **Trent** ≈ Ontario, SE Canada
97 N18 **Trent** ≈ C England, United Kingdom
Trent *see* Trento
106 F5 **Trentino-Alto Adige** *prev.* Venezia Tridentina. ◈ *region* N Italy
106 G6 **Trento** *Eng.* Trent, *Ger.* Trient; *anc.* Tridentum. Trentino-Alto Adige, N Italy *46°05′N 11°08′E*
14 J15 **Trenton** Ontario, SE Canada *44°07′N 77°34′W*
23 V10 **Trenton** Florida, SE USA *29°36′N 82°49′W*
23 R1 **Trenton** Georgia, SE USA *34°52′N 85°27′W*
31 S10 **Trenton** Michigan, N USA *42°08′N 83°10′W*
27 S2 **Trenton** Missouri, C USA *40°04′N 93°37′W*
28 M17 **Trenton** Nebraska, C USA *40°10′N 101°00′W*
18 J15 **Trenton** *state capital* New Jersey, NE USA *40°13′N 74°45′W*
21 W10 **Trenton** North Carolina, SE USA *35°03′N 77°20′W*
20 G9 **Trenton** Tennessee, S USA *35°59′N 88°59′W*
36 L1 **Trenton** Utah, W USA *41°53′N 111°57′W*
Trentschin *see* Trenčín
Treptow an der Rega *see* Trzebiatów
61 C23 **Tres Arroyos** Buenos Aires, E Argentina *38°22′S 60°17′W*
61 J15 **Três Cachoeiras** Rio Grande do Sul, S Brazil *29°21′S 49°48′W*
106 E7 **Trescore Balneario** Lombardia, N Italy *45°43′N 09°52′E*
41 V17 **Tres Cruces, Cerro** ▲ SE Mexico *15°28′N 92°27′W*
57 K18 **Tres Cruces, Cordillera** ▲▲ W Bolivia
113 N18 **Treska** ≈ NW FYR Macedonia
113 I14 **Treskavica** ▲▲ SE Bosnia and Herzegovina
59 J20 **Três Lagoas** Mato Grosso do Sul, SW Brazil *20°46′S 51°43′W*
40 H12 **Tres Marías, Islas** *island group* C Mexico
59 M19 **Três Marias, Represa** ⊠ SE Brazil
63 F20 **Tres Montes, Península** *headland* S Chile *46°49′S 75°29′W*
105 O3 **Trespaderne** Castilla-León, N Spain *42°47′N 03°24′W*
60 G13 **Três Passos** Rio Grande do Sul, S Brazil *27°33′S 53°55′W*
61 A23 **Tres Picos, Cerro** ▲ E Argentina *38°10′S 61°54′W*
63 G17 **Tres Picos, Cerro** ▲ SW Argentina *42°22′S 71°51′W*
60 I12 **Três Pinheiros** Paraná, S Brazil *25°25′S 51°57′W*
59 M21 **Três Pontas** Minas Gerais, SE Brazil *21°33′S 45°18′W*
Tres Puntas, Cabo *see* Manabique, Punta
60 P9 **Três Rios** Rio de Janeiro, SE Brazil *22°06′S 43°15′W*
Tres Tabernae *see* Saverne
Trestenberg/Trestendorf *see* Tăşnad
41 R15 **Tres Valles** Veracruz-Llave, SE Mexico *18°14′N 96°03′W*
94 H12 **Tretten** Oppland, S Norway *61°19′N 10°19′E*
Treuburg *see* Olecko
101 K21 **Treuchtlingen** Bayern, S Germany *48°57′N 10°55′E*
100 N13 **Treuenbrietzen** Brandenburg, E Germany *52°06′N 12°52′E*
95 F16 **Treungen** Telemark, S Norway *59°00′N 08°34′E*
63 H17 **Trevelín** Chubut, SW Argentina *43°02′S 71°27′W*
Treves/Trèves *see* Trier
106 I13 **Trevi** Umbria, C Italy *42°52′N 12°46′E*
106 E7 **Treviglio** Lombardia, N Italy *45°32′N 09°35′E*
104 J4 **Trevinca, Peña** ▲ NW Spain *42°10′N 06°49′W*
105 P3 **Treviño** Castilla-León, N Spain *42°45′N 02°41′W*
106 I7 **Treviso** *anc.* Tarvisium. Veneto, NE Italy *45°40′N 12°15′E*
97 G24 **Trevose Head** *headland* SW England, United Kingdom *50°33′N 05°03′W*
Trg *see* Feldkirchen in Kärnten
183 P17 **Triabunna** Tasmania, SE Australia *42°33′S 147°55′E*
21 W4 **Triangle** Virginia, NE USA *38°30′N 77°17′W*
83 L18 **Triangle** Masvingo, SE Zimbabwe *20°58′S 31°28′E*
115 L23 **Tría Nisía** *island* Kykládes, Greece, Aegean Sea
Triberg *see* Triberg im Schwarzwald
101 G23 **Triberg im Schwarzwald** *var.* Triberg. Baden-Württemberg, SW Germany *48°07′N 08°13′E*
153 P11 **Tribhuvan** ✕ (Kathmandu) Central, C Nepal
54 C9 **Tribugá, Golfo de** *gulf* W Colombia
181 W4 **Tribulation, Cape** *headland* Queensland, NE Australia *16°14′S 145°48′E*
108 M8 **Tribulaun** ▲ SW Austria *46°59′N 11°18′E*
11 U17 **Tribune** Saskatchewan, S Canada *49°16′N 103°50′W*
26 H5 **Tribune** Kansas, C USA *38°27′N 101°46′W*
107 N18 **Tricarico** Basilicata, S Italy *40°37′N 16°09′E*
107 Q19 **Tricase** Puglia, SE Italy *39°56′N 18°21′E*
Trichinopoly *see* Tiruchchirāppalli
115 D18 **Trichonída, Límni** ◎ C Greece
155 G22 **Trichūr** *var.* Thrissur. Kerala, SW India *10°32′N 76°14′E* *see also* Thrissur
Tricorno *see* Triglav
183 O8 **Trida** New South Wales, SE Australia *33°02′S 145°03′E*
35 S1 **Trident Peak** ▲ Nevada, W USA *41°52′N 118°22′W*
Tridentum/Trient *see* Trento
109 T6 **Trieben** Steiermark, SE Austria *47°29′N 14°30′E*
101 D19 **Trier** *Eng.* Treves, *Fr.* Trèves; *anc.* Augusta Treverorum. Rheinland-Pfalz, SW Germany *49°45′N 06°39′E*
106 K7 **Trieste** *Slvn.* Trst. Friuli-Venezia Giulia, NE Italy *45°39′N 13°45′E*
Trieste, Golfo di/Triest, Golf von *see* Trieste, Gulf of
106 J8 **Trieste, Gulf of** *Cro.* Tršćanski Zaljev, *Ger.* Golf von Triest, *It.* Golfo di Trieste, *Slvn.* Tržaški Zaliv. *gulf* S Europe
109 W4 **Triesting** ≈ W Austria
Triêu Hai *see* Quang Tri
Trifail *see* Trbovlje
116 L9 **Trifeşti** Iaşi, NE Romania *47°30′N 27°31′E*
109 S10 **Triglav** *It.* Tricorno. ▲ NW Slovenia *46°22′N 13°40′E*
104 I14 **Trigueros** Andalucía, S Spain *37°24′N 06°50′W*
115 E16 **Tríkala** *prev.* Trikkala. Thessalía, C Greece *39°33′N 21°46′E*
115 E17 **Trikeriótis** ≈ C Greece
Trikkala *see* Tríkala
Trikomo/Tríkomon *see* Iskele
97 F17 **Trim** *Ir.* Baile Átha Troim. Meath, E Ireland *53°34′N 06°47′W*
108 E7 **Trimbach** Solothurn, NW Switzerland *47°22′N 07°53′E*
109 Q5 **Trimmelkam** Oberösterreich, N Austria *48°02′N 12°55′E*
29 U11 **Trimont** Minnesota, N USA *43°45′N 94°42′W*
Trimontium *see* Plovdiv
Trinacria *see* Sicilia
155 K24 **Trincomalee** *var.* Trinkomali. Eastern Province, NE Sri Lanka *08°34′N 81°13′E*
65 K16 **Trindade, Ilha da** *island* Brazil, W Atlantic Ocean
47 Y9 **Trindade Spur** *undersea feature* SW Atlantic Ocean *21°00′S 35°00′W*
111 J17 **Třinec** *Ger.* Trzynietz. Moravskoslezský Kraj, E Czech Republic *49°41′N 18°39′E*
57 M16 **Trinidad** Beni, N Bolivia *14°52′S 64°54′W*
54 H9 **Trinidad** Casanare, E Colombia *05°25′N 71°39′W*
44 E6 **Trinidad** Sancti Spíritus, C Cuba *21°48′N 80°00′W*
61 E19 **Trinidad** Flores, S Uruguay *33°35′S 56°54′W*
37 U8 **Trinidad** Colorado, C USA *37°11′N 104°31′W*
45 Y17 **Trinidad** *island* C Trinidad and Tobago
Trinidad *see* Jose Abad Santos
45 Y16 **Trinidad and Tobago** *off.* Republic of Trinidad and Tobago. ◆ *republic* SE West Indies
Trinidad and Tobago, Republic of *see* Trinidad and Tobago
63 F22 **Trinidad, Golfo** *gulf* S Chile
61 B24 **Trinidad, Isla** *island* E Argentina
107 N16 **Trinitapoli** Puglia, SE Italy *41°22′N 16°06′E*
55 X10 **Trinité, Montagnes de la** ▲▲ C French Guiana
25 W9 **Trinity** Texas, SW USA *30°57′N 95°22′W*
13 U12 **Trinity Bay** *inlet* Newfoundland, Newfoundland and Labrador, E Canada
39 P15 **Trinity Islands** *island group* Alaska, USA
35 N2 **Trinity Mountains** ▲▲ California, W USA
35 S4 **Trinity Peak** ▲ Nevada, W USA *40°13′N 118°43′W*
35 S5 **Trinity Range** ▲▲ Nevada, W USA
35 N2 **Trinity River** ≈ California, W USA
25 V8 **Trinity River** ≈ Texas, SW USA
Trinkomali *see* Trincomalee
173 Y15 **Triolet** NW Mauritius *20°05′S 57°32′E*
107 O20 **Trionto, Capo** *headland* S Italy *39°37′N 16°46′E*
Tripiti, Ákra *see* Trypití, Akrotírio
115 F20 **Trípoli** *prev.* Trípolis. Pelopónnisos, S Greece *37°31′N 22°22′E*
138 G6 **Tripoli** *var.* Tarābulus, Ṭarābulus ash Shām, Trâblous; *anc.* Tripolis. N Lebanon *34°30′N 35°42′E*
29 X12 **Tripoli** Iowa, C USA *42°48′N 92°15′W*
Tripoli *see* Ṭarābulus
Trípolis *see* Trípoli, Greece
Tripolis *see* Tripoli, Lebanon
75 O8 **Tripolitania** ◈ *cultural region* NW Libya
29 Q12 **Tripp** South Dakota, N USA *43°12′N 97°57′W*
153 V15 **Tripura** *var.* Hill Tippera. ◈ *state* NE India
108 K8 **Trisanna** ≈ W Austria
100 H8 **Trischen** *island* NW Germany
65 M24 **Tristan da Cunha** ◇ *dependency of Saint Helena* SE Atlantic Ocean
67 P15 **Tristan da Cunha** *island* SE Atlantic Ocean
65 L18 **Tristan da Cunha Fracture Zone** *tectonic feature* S Atlantic Ocean
167 S14 **Tri Tôn** An Giang, S Vietnam *10°26′N 105°01′E*
167 W10 **Triton Island** *island* S Paracel Islands
155 G24 **Trivandrum** *var.* Thiruvanathapuram, Tiruvantapuram. *state capital* Kerala, SW India *08°30′N 76°57′E*
111 H20 **Trnava** *Ger.* Tyrnau, *Hung.* Nagyszombat. Trnavský Kraj, W Slovakia *48°22′N 17°36′E*
111 H20 **Trnavský Kraj** ◈ *region* W Slovakia
Trnovo *see* Veliko Tŭrnovo
Trobriand Island *see* Kiriwina Island
Trobriand Islands *see* Kiriwina Islands
11 Q16 **Trochu** Alberta, SW Canada *51°48′N 113°12′W*
109 U7 **Trofaiach** Steiermark, SE Austria *47°25′N 15°01′E*
93 F14 **Trofors** Troms, N Norway *65°31′N 13°19′E*
113 E14 **Trogir** *It.* Traù. Split-Dalmacija, S Croatia *43°32′N 16°13′E*
112 F13 **Troglav** ▲ Bosnia and Herzegovina/Croatia *44°00′N 16°36′E*
107 M16 **Troia** Puglia, SE Italy *41°21′N 15°19′E*
107 K24 **Troina** Sicilia, Italy, C Mediterranean Sea *37°47′N 14°37′E*
173 O16 **Trois-Bassins** W Réunion *21°05′S 55°18′E*
101 E17 **Troisdorf** Nordrhein-Westfalen, W Germany *50°49′N 07°09′E*
74 H5 **Trois Fourches, Cap des** *headland* NE Morocco *35°27′N 02°58′W*
15 T8 **Trois-Pistoles** Québec, SE Canada *48°08′N 69°10′W*
99 L21 **Trois-Ponts** Liège, E Belgium *50°22′N 05°52′E*
15 P11 **Trois-Rivières** Québec, SE Canada *46°21′N 72°34′W*
55 Y12 **Trois Sauts** S French Guiana *02°15′N 52°52′W*
99 M22 **Troisvierges** Diekirch, N Luxembourg *50°07′N 06°00′E*
122 F11 **Troitsk** Chelyabinskaya Oblast', S Russian Federation *54°04′N 61°31′E*
125 T9 **Troitsko-Pechorsk** Respublika Komi, NW Russian Federation *62°39′N 56°06′E*
127 V7 **Troitskoye** Orenburgskaya Oblast', W Russian Federation *52°23′N 56°24′E*
Troki *see* Trakai
94 F9 **Trolla** ▲ S Norway *62°41′N 09°47′E*
95 J18 **Trollhättan** Västra Götaland, S Sweden *58°17′N 12°20′E*
94 G9 **Trollheimen** ▲▲ S Norway
94 E9 **Trolltindane** ▲ S Norway *62°30′N 07°43′E*
58 H11 **Trombetas, Rio** ≈ NE Brazil
128 L16 **Tromelin, Île** *island* N Réunion
92 I9 **Troms** ◈ *county* N Norway
92 I9 **Tromsø** *Fin.* Tromssa. Troms, N Norway *69°39′N 19°01′E*
84 F5 **Tromsøflaket** *undersea feature* W Barents Sea *18°30′E 71°30′N*
Tromssa *see* Tromsø
94 H10 **Tron** ▲ S Norway *62°12′N 10°46′E*
35 U12 **Trona** California, W USA *35°46′N 117°21′W*
63 G16 **Tronador, Cerro** ▲ S Chile *41°12′S 71°51′W*
94 H8 **Trondheim** *Ger.* Drontheim; *prev.* Nidaros, Trondhjem. Sør-Trøndelag, S Norway *63°25′N 10°24′E*
94 H7 **Trondheimsfjorden** *fjord* S Norway
Trondhjem *see* Trondheim
107 J14 **Tronto** ≈ C Italy
121 P3 **Troódos** *var.* Troodos Mountains. ▲▲ C Cyprus
Troodos *see* Ólympos
Troodos Mountains *see* Troódos
96 I13 **Troon** W Scotland, United Kingdom *55°32′N 04°41′W*
107 M22 **Tropea** Calabria, SW Italy *38°40′N 15°52′E*
36 L7 **Tropic** Utah, W USA *37°37′N 112°04′W*
64 L10 **Tropic Seamount** *var.* Banc du Tropique. *undersea feature* E Atlantic Ocean *23°50′N 20°40′W*
Tropique, Banc du *see* Tropic Seamount
Tropoja *see* Tropojë
113 L17 **Tropojë** *var.* Tropoja. Kukës, N Albania *42°25′N 20°09′E*
Troppau *see* Opava
95 O16 **Trosa** Södermanland, C Sweden *58°54′N 17°35′E*
118 H12 **Troškūnai** Utena, E Lithuania *55°36′N 24°55′E*
101 G23 **Trossingen** Baden-Württemberg, SW Germany *48°04′N 08°37′E*
117 T4 **Trostyanets'** *Rus.* Trostyanets. Sums'ka Oblast', NE Ukraine *50°30′N 34°59′E*
117 N7 **Trostyanets'** *Rus.* Trostyanets. Vinnyts'ka Oblast', C Ukraine *48°35′N 29°10′E*
Trostyanets *see* Trostyanets'
116 L11 **Trotuş** ≈ E Romania
44 M8 **Trou-du-Nord** N Haiti *19°34′N 71°57′W*
25 W7 **Troup** Texas, SW USA *32°08′N 95°07′W*
8 I10 **Trout** ≈ Northwest Territories, NW Canada
33 N8 **Trout Creek** Montana, NW USA *47°51′N 115°40′W*
32 H10 **Trout Lake** Washington, NW USA *45°59′N 121°33′W*
12 B9 **Trout Lake** ◎ Ontario, S Canada
33 T12 **Trout Peak** ▲ Wyoming, C USA *44°36′N 109°33′W*
102 L4 **Trouville** Calvados, N France *49°21′N 00°07′E*
97 L22 **Trowbridge** S England, United Kingdom *51°20′N 02°13′W*
23 Q6 **Troy** Alabama, S USA *31°48′N 85°58′W*
27 Q3 **Troy** Kansas, C USA *39°45′N 95°06′W*
27 W4 **Troy** Missouri, C USA *38°59′N 90°59′W*
18 L10 **Troy** New York, NE USA *42°43′N 73°37′W*
21 S10 **Troy** North Carolina, SE USA *35°23′N 79°54′W*
31 R13 **Troy** Ohio, N USA *40°02′N 84°12′W*
25 T9 **Troy** Texas, SW USA *31°12′N 97°18′W*
114 I9 **Troyan** Lovech, N Bulgaria *42°52′N 24°42′E*
114 I9 **Troyanski Prokhod** *pass* N Bulgaria
145 N6 **Troyebratskiy** Severnyy Kazakhstan, N Kazakhstan *54°25′N 66°03′E*
103 Q6 **Troyes** *anc.* Augustobona Tricassium. Aube, N France *48°18′N 04°04′E*
117 X5 **Troyits'ke** Luhans'ka Oblast', E Ukraine *49°55′N 38°18′E*
35 W7 **Troy Peak** ▲ Nevada, W USA *38°18′N 115°27′W*
113 G15 **Trpanj** Dubrovnik-Neretva, S Croatia *43°00′N 17°18′E*
Tršćanski Zaljev *see* Trieste, Gulf of
Trst *see* Trieste
113 N14 **Trstenik** Serbia, C Serbia *43°38′N 21°01′E*
126 I6 **Trubchevsk** Bryanskaya Oblast', W Russian Federation *52°33′N 33°45′E*
Trubchular *see* Orlyak
37 S10 **Truchas Peak** ▲ New Mexico, SW USA *35°57′N 105°38′W*

143 P16 Trucial Coast physical region C United Arab Emirates
Trucial States see United Arab Emirates
35 Q6 Truckee California, W USA 39°18′N 120°10′W
35 R5 Truckee River Nevada, W USA
127 Q13 Trudfront Astrakhanskaya Oblast', SW Russian Federation 45°56′N 47°42′E
14 I9 Truite, Lac à la ◎ Québec, SE Canada
42 K4 Trujillo Colón, NE Honduras 15°59′N 85°54′W
56 C12 Trujillo La Libertad, NW Peru 08°04′S 79°02′W
104 K10 Trujillo Extremadura, W Spain 39°28′N 05°53′W
54 I6 Trujillo Trujillo, NW Venezuela 09°20′N 70°38′W
54 I6 Trujillo off. Estado Trujillo. ◐ state W Venezuela
Trujillo, Estado see Trujillo
Truk see Chuuk
Truk Islands see Chuuk Islands
29 U10 Truman Minnesota, N USA 43°49′N 94°26′W
27 X10 Trumann Arkansas, C USA 35°40′N 90°30′W
36 J9 Trumbull, Mount ▲ Arizona, SW USA 36°22′N 113°09′W
114 F9 Trŭn Pernik, W Bulgaria 42°51′N 22°37′E
183 Q8 Trundle New South Wales, SE Australia 32°55′S 147°43′E
129 U13 Trung Phân physical region S Vietnam
Trupcilar see Orlyak
13 Q15 Truro Nova Scotia, SE Canada 45°24′N 63°18′W
97 H25 Truro SW England, United Kingdom 50°16′N 05°03′W
25 P5 Truscott Texas, SW USA 33°43′N 99°48′W
116 K9 Truşeşti Botoşani, NE Romania 47°45′N 27°01′E
116 H6 Truskavets' L'vivs'ka Oblast', W Ukraine 49°15′N 23°30′E
95 H22 Trustrup Århus, C Denmark 56°20′N 10°46′E
10 M11 Trutch British Columbia, W Canada 57°42′N 123°00′W
37 Q14 Truth Or Consequences New Mexico, SW USA 33°07′N 107°15′W
111 F15 Trutnov Ger. Trautenau. Královéhradecký Kraj, N Czech Republic 50°34′N 15°55′E
103 P13 Truyère C France
114 K9 Tryavna Lovech, N Bulgaria 42°52′N 25°30′E
28 M14 Tryon Nebraska, C USA 41°33′N 100°57′W
115 J16 Trypití, Akrotírio var. Ákra Tripití. headland Ágios Efstrátios, E Greece 39°28′N 24°58′E
94 J12 Trysil Hedmark, S Norway 61°18′N 12°16′E
94 I11 Trysilelva S Norway
112 D10 Tržac Federacija Bosna I Hercegovina, NW Bosnia and Herzegovina 44°58′N 15°48′E
Tržaški Zaliv see Trieste, Gulf of
110 G10 Trzcianka Ger. Schönlanke. Pila, Wielkopolskie, C Poland 53°02′N 16°24′E
110 E7 Trzebiatów Ger. Treptow an der Rega. Zachodnio-pomorskie, NW Poland 54°04′N 15°14′E
111 G14 Trzebnica Ger. Trebnitz. Dolnośląskie, SW Poland 51°19′N 17°03′E
109 T10 Tržič Ger. Neumarktl. NW Slovenia 46°22′N 14°17′E
Trzynietz see Třinec
83 G21 Tsabong var. Tshabong. Kgalagadi, SW Botswana 26°03′S 22°27′E
162 G7 Tsagaanchuluut Dzavhan, C Mongolia 47°06′N 96°40′E
162 M8 Tsagaandelger var. Haraat. Dundgovĭ, C Mongolia 46°30′N 107°39′E
Tsagaanders see Bayantümen
162 G7 Tsagaanhayrhan var. Shiree. Dzavhan, W Mongolia 47°30′N 96°48′E
Tsagaannuur see Halhgol
Tsagaan-Olom see Tayshir
Tsagaan-Ovoo see Nariynteel
Tsagaantüngi see Altantsögts
162 H6 Tsagaan-Uul var. Sharga. Hövsgöl, N Mongolia 49°33′N 98°36′E
162 J5 Tsagaan-Üür var. Bulgan. Hövsgöl, N Mongolia 50°30′N 101°28′E
127 P12 Tsagan Aman Respublika Kalmykiya, SW Russian Federation 47°37′N 46°43′E
23 V11 Tsala Apopka Lake ◎ Florida, SE USA
Tsamkong see Zhanjiang
Tsangpo see Brahmaputra
Tsant see Deren
Tsao see Tsau
172 I4 Tsaratanana Mahajanga, C Madagascar 16°46′S 47°40′E
114 N10 Tsarevo prev. Michurin. Burgas, E Bulgaria 42°10′N 27°51′E
Tsarigrad see Istanbul
Tsaritsyn see Volgograd
114 K7 Tsar Kaloyan Ruse, N Bulgaria 43°36′N 26°14′E
Tsarskoye Selo see Pushkin
117 T7 Tsarychanka Dnipropetrovs'ka Oblast', E Ukraine 48°56′N 34°29′E
83 H21 Tsatsu Southern, S Botswana 25°21′S 24°45′E
83 G17 Tsau var. Tsao. North-West, NW Botswana 20°08′S 22°29′E
81 J20 Tsavo Coast, S Kenya 02°59′S 38°28′E
83 E21 Tsawisis Karas, S Namibia 26°18′S 18°09′E
Tschakathurn see Čakovec
Tschaslau see Čáslav
Tschenstochau see Częstochowa
Tschernembl see Črnomelj
28 K6 Tschida, Lake ⊠ North Dakota, N USA
Tschorna see Mustvee
162 G8 Tseel Govĭ-Altay, SW Mongolia 45°45′N 95°54′E
138 G8 Tsefat var. Safed, Ar. Safad; prev. Zefat. Northern, N Israel 32°57′N 35°27′E
126 M13 Tselina Rostovskaya Oblast', SW Russian Federation 46°31′N 41°01′E
Tselinograd see Astana
Tselinogradskaya Oblast see Akmola
Tsengel see Tosontsengel
162 J8 Tsenher var. Altan-Ovoo. Arhangay, C Mongolia 47°24′N 101°51′E
Tsenher see Mönhhayrhan
163 N8 Tsenhermandal var. Modot. Hentiy, C Mongolia 47°45′N 109°03′E
Tsentral'nyye Nizmennyye Garagumy see Merkezi Garagumy
83 E21 Tses Karas, S Namibia 25°58′S 18°08′E
Tseshevlya see Tsyeshawlya
162 E7 Tsetseg var. Tsetsegnuur. Hovd, W Mongolia 46°30′N 93°16′E
Tsetsegnuur see Tsetseg
Tsetsen Khan see Öndörhaan
162 J8 Tsetserleg Arhangay, C Mongolia 47°29′N 101°19′E
162 H6 Tsetserleg var. Halban. Hövsgöl, N Mongolia 49°30′N 97°33′E
162 J8 Tsetserleg var. Hujirt. Övörhangay, C Mongolia 46°50′N 102°38′E
77 R16 Tsévié S Togo 06°25′N 01°13′E
Tshabong see Tsabong
83 G20 Tshane Kgalagadi, SW Botswana 24°05′S 21°54′E
Tshangalele, Lac see Lufira, Lac de Retenue de la
83 H17 Tshauxaba Central, C Botswana 19°56′S 25°09′E
79 F21 Tshela Bas-Congo, W Dem. Rep. Congo 04°56′S 13°02′E
79 K22 Tshibala Kasai-Occidental, S Dem. Rep. Congo 06°53′S 22°01′E
79 J22 Tshikapa Kasai-Occidental, SW Dem. Rep. Congo 06°23′S 20°47′E
79 L22 Tshilenge Kasai Oriental , S Dem. Rep. Congo 06°17′S 23°48′E
79 L24 Tshimbalanga Katanga, S Dem. Rep. Congo 09°42′S 23°04′E
79 L22 Tshimbulu Kasai-Occidental, S Dem. Rep. Congo 06°27′S 22°54′E
Tshiumbe see Chiumbe
79 M21 Tshofa Kasai-Oriental, C Dem. Rep. Congo 05°13′S 25°13′E
79 K18 Tshuapa C Dem. Rep. Congo
83 J21 Tshwane var. Epitoli; prev. Pretoria. ● Gauteng, NE South Africa 25°41′S 28°12′E see also Pretoria
114 G7 Tsibritsa NW Bulgaria
Tsien Tang see Puyang Jiang
114 I12 Tsiganska Gradishte ▲ Bulgaria/Greece 41°24′N 24°41′E
Tsihombe see Tsiombe
8 H7 Tsiigehtchic prev. Arctic Red River. Northwest Territories, NW Canada 67°24′N 133°40′W
125 Q7 Tsil'ma NW Russian Federation
119 J17 Tsimkavichy Rus. Timkovichi. Minskaya Voblasts', C Belarus 53°04′N 26°59′E
126 M11 Tsimlyansk Rostovskaya Oblast', SW Russian Federation 47°39′N 42°05′E
127 N11 Tsimlyanskoye Vodokhranilishche var. Tsimlyansk Vodoskhovshche, Eng. Tsimlyansk Reservoir. ⊠ SW Russian Federation
Tsimlyansk Reservoir see Tsimlyanskoye Vodokhranilishche
Tsimlyansk Vodoskhovshche see Tsimlyanskoye Vodokhranilishche
Tsinan see Jinan
Tsing Hai see Qinghai Hu, China
Tsinghai see Qinghai, China
Tsingtao/Tsingtau see Qingdao
Tsingyuan see Baoding
Tsinkiang see Quanzhou
Tsintao see Qingdao
83 D17 Tsintsabis Otjikoto, N Namibia 18°45′S 17°51′E
172 H8 Tsiombe var. Tsihombe. Toliara, S Madagascar 25°16′S 45°29′E
123 O13 Tsipa S Russian Federation
172 H5 Tsiribihina W Madagascar
172 I5 Tsiroanomandidy Antananarivo, C Madagascar 18°44′S 46°02′E
189 U13 Tsis island Chuuk, C Micronesia
Tsitsihar see Qiqihar
127 Q3 Tsivil'sk Chuvashskaya Respublika, W Russian Federation 55°51′N 47°30′E
137 T9 Ts'khinvali prev. Staliniri. C Georgia 42°12′N 43°58′E
119 J19 Tsna SW Belarus
124 I15 Tsna var. Zna. W Russian Federation
162 G9 Tsogt var. Tahilt. Govĭ-Altay, W Mongolia 45°20′N 96°42′E
162 K10 Tsogt-Ovoo var. Doloon. Ömnögovĭ, S Mongolia 44°28′N 105°22′E
162 L10 Tsogttsetsiy var. Baruunsuu. Ömnögovĭ, S Mongolia 43°46′N 105°28′E
Tsoohor see Hürmen
164 K14 Tsu var. Tu. Mie, Honshū, SW Japan 34°41′N 136°30′E
165 O10 Tsubame var. Tubame. Niigata, Honshū, C Japan 37°40′N 138°56′E
165 V3 Tsubetsu Hokkaidō, NE Japan 43°43′N 144°01′E
165 O13 Tsuchiura var. Tutiura. Ibaraki, Honshū, S Japan 36°05′N 140°11′E
165 Q6 Tsugaru-kaikyō strait N Japan
164 E14 Tsukumi var. Tukumi. Ōita, Kyūshū, SW Japan 33°00′N 131°51′E
Tsul-Ulaan see Bayannuur
Tsul-Ulaan see Bayannuur
83 D17 Tsumeb Otjikoto, N Namibia 19°13′S 17°42′E
83 F17 Tsumkwe Otjozondjupa, NE Namibia 19°37′S 20°30′E
164 D15 Tsuno Miyazaki, Kyūshū, SW Japan 32°43′N 131°32′E
164 D12 Tsuno-shima island SW Japan
164 K12 Tsuruga var. Turuga. Fukui, Honshū, SW Japan 35°38′N 136°01′E
164 H12 Tsurugi-san ▲ Shikoku, SW Japan 33°50′N 134°04′E
165 P9 Tsuruoka var. Turuoka. Yamagata, Honshū, C Japan 38°44′N 139°48′E
164 C12 Tsushima var. Tsushima-tô. island group SW Japan
Tsushima-tô see Tsushima
164 H12 Tsuyama var. Tuyama. Okayama, Honshū, SW Japan 35°04′N 134°01′E
83 G19 Tswaane Ghanzi, W Botswana 22°21′S 21°52′E
119 N16 Tsyakhtsin Rus. Tekhtin. Mahilyowskaya Voblasts', E Belarus 53°51′N 29°44′E
119 P19 Tsyerakhowka Rus. Terekhovka. Homyel'skaya Voblasts', SE Belarus 52°13′N 31°24′E
119 I17 Tsyeshawlya Rus. Cheshevlya, Tseshevlya. Brestskaya Voblasts', SW Belarus 53°14′N 25°49′E
Tsyurupinsk see Tsyurupyns'k
117 R10 Tsyurupyns'k Rus. Tsyurupinsk. Khersons'ka Oblast', S Ukraine 46°35′N 32°43′E
Tu see Tsu
186 C7 Tua C Papua New Guinea
Tuaim see Tuam
184 L6 Tuakau Waikato, North Island, New Zealand 37°16′S 174°56′E
97 C17 Tuam Ir. Tuaim. Galway, W Ireland 53°31′N 08°50′W
185 K14 Tuamarina Marlborough, South Island, New Zealand 41°27′S 174°00′E
Tuamotu, Archipel des see Tuamotu, Îles
193 Q9 Tuamotu Fracture Zone tectonic feature E Pacific Ocean
191 W9 Tuamotu, Îles var. Archipel des Tuamotu, Dangerous Archipelago, Tuamotu Islands. island group N French Polynesia
Tuamotu Islands see Tuamotu, Îles
175 X10 Tuamotu Ridge undersea feature C Pacific Ocean
167 R5 Tuân Giao Lai Châu, N Vietnam 21°34′N 103°24′E
171 O2 Tuao Luzon, N Philippines 17°42′N 121°25′E
190 B15 Tuapa NW Niue 18°57′S 169°59′W
43 N7 Tuapí Región Autónoma Atlántico Norte, NE Nicaragua 14°10′N 83°20′W
126 K15 Tuapse Krasnodarskiy Kray, SW Russian Federation 44°08′N 39°07′E
169 U6 Tuaran Sabah, East Malaysia 06°12′N 116°12′E
104 I6 Tua, Rio N Portugal
192 H15 Tuasivi Savai'i, C Samoa 13°38′S 172°08′W
185 B24 Tuatapere Southland, South Island, New Zealand 46°09′S 167°43′E
36 M9 Tuba City Arizona, SW USA 36°08′N 111°14′W
138 H11 Ţūbah, Qaşr aţ castle 'Ammān, C Jordan
Tubame see Tsubame
169 R16 Tuban prev. Toeban. Jawa, C Indonesia 06°55′S 112°01′E
141 O16 Tuban, Wādī dry watercourse SW Yemen
61 K14 Tubarão Santa Catarina, S Brazil 28°29′S 49°00′W
98 O10 Tubbergen Overijssel, E Netherlands 52°25′N 06°46′E
Tubeke see Tubize
101 H22 Tübingen var. Tuebingen. Baden-Württemberg, SW Germany 48°32′N 09°04′E
127 W6 Tubinskiy Respublika Bashkortostan, W Russian Federation 52°48′N 58°18′E
99 G19 Tubize Dut. Tubeke. Walloon Brabant, C Belgium 50°43′N 04°14′E
76 J16 Tubmanburg NW Liberia 06°50′N 10°53′W
75 T7 Tubruq Eng. Tobruk, It. Tobruch. NE Libya 32°05′N 23°59′E
191 T13 Tubuai island Îles Australes, SW French Polynesia
Tubuai, Îles/Tubuai Islands see Australes, Îles
Tubuai-Manu see Maiao
40 F3 Tubutama Sonora, NW Mexico 30°51′N 111°31′W
54 K4 Tucacas Falcón, N Venezuela 10°50′N 68°22′W
59 P16 Tucano Bahia, E Brazil 10°52′S 38°48′W
57 P19 Tucavaca, Río E Bolivia
110 H8 Tuchola Kujawsko-pomorskie, C Poland 53°36′N 17°50′E
111 M17 Tuchów Małopolskie, S Poland 49°53′N 21°04′E
23 S3 Tucker Georgia, SE USA 33°53′N 84°10′W
27 W10 Tuckerman Arkansas, C USA 35°43′N 91°12′W
64 B12 Tucker's Town E Bermuda 32°20′N 64°42′W
Tuckum see Tukums
36 M15 Tucson Arizona, SW USA 32°14′N 111°01′W
62 J7 Tucumán off. Provincia de Tucumán. ◐ province N Argentina
Tucumán see San Miguel de Tucumán
Tucumán, Provincia de see Tucumán
37 V11 Tucumcari New Mexico, SW USA 35°10′N 103°43′W
58 H13 Tucunaré Pará, N Brazil 05°15′S 55°49′W
55 Q6 Tucupita Delta Amacuro, NE Venezuela 09°02′N 62°04′W
58 K13 Tucuruí, Represa de ⊠ NE Brazil
110 F9 Tuczno Zachodnio-pomorskie, NW Poland 53°12′N 16°08′E
Tuddo see Tudu
105 Q5 Tudela Basq. Tutera; anc. Tutela. Navarra, N Spain 42°04′N 01°37′W
104 M6 Tudela de Duero Castilla-León, N Spain 41°35′N 04°34′W
162 G6 Tüdevtey var. Oygon. Dzavhan, N Mongolia 48°57′N 96°33′E
138 K6 Tudmur var. Tadmur, Tamar, Gk. Palmyra, Bibl. Tadmor. Ḩimş, C Syria 34°36′N 38°15′E
118 J4 Tudu Ger. Tuddo. Lääne-Virumaa, NE Estonia 59°12′N 26°52′E
Tuebingen see Tübingen
122 J14 Tuekta Respublika Altay, S Russian Federation 50°51′N 85°52′E
104 I5 Tuela, Rio N Portugal
153 X12 Tuensang Nāgāland, NE India 26°16′N 94°45′E
136 L15 Tufanbeyli Adana, C Turkey 38°15′N 36°13′E
Tüffer see Laško
186 F9 Tufi Northern, S Papua New Guinea 09°08′S 149°20′E
193 O3 Tufts Plain undersea feature N Pacific Ocean
Tugalan see Kolkhozobod
67 V14 Tugela SE South Africa
21 P6 Tug Fork S USA
39 P15 Tugidak Island island Trinity Islands, Alaska, USA
171 O2 Tuguegarao Luzon, N Philippines 17°37′N 121°48′E
123 S12 Tugur Khabarovskiy Kray, SE Russian Federation 53°43′N 137°00′E
161 P4 Tuhai He E China
104 G4 Tui Galicia, NW Spain 42°02′N 08°37′W
77 O13 Tui var. Grand Balé. W Burkina
57 J16 Tuichi, Río W Bolivia
64 Q11 Tuineje Fuerteventura, Islas Canarias, Spain, NE Atlantic Ocean 28°18′N 14°03′W
43 X16 Tuira, Río SE Panama
Tuisarkan see Tūysarkān
Tujiabu see Yongxiu
127 W5 Tukan Respublika Bashkortostan, W Russian Federation 53°58′N 57°29′E
171 P14 Tukangbesi, Kepulauan Dut. Toekang Besi Eilanden. island group C Indonesia
147 V13 Tükhtamish Rus. Toktomush; prev. Tokhtamyshbek. SE Tajikistan 37°51′N 74°41′E
184 O12 Tukituki North Island, New Zealand
Tu-k'ou see Panzhihua
121 P12 Tūkrah NE Libya 32°32′N 20°35′E
8 H6 Tuktoyaktuk Northwest Territories, NW Canada 69°27′N 133°W
168 I9 Tuktuk Pulau Samosir, W Indonesia 02°32′N 98°43′E
Tukumi see Tsukumi
118 E9 Tukums Ger. Tuckum. W Latvia 56°58′N 23°12′E
81 G24 Tukuyu prev. Neu-Langenburg. Mbeya, S Tanzania 09°14′S 33°39′E
Tukzār see Tokzār
41 O13 Tula var. Tula de Allende. Hidalgo, C Mexico 20°01′N 99°21′W
41 O11 Tula Tamaulipas, C Mexico 22°59′N 99°43′W
126 K5 Tula Tul'skaya Oblast', W Russian Federation 54°11′N 37°39′E
Tulach Mhór see Tullamore
Tula de Allende see Tula
186 M9 Tulaghi var. Tulagi. Florida Islands, C Solomon Islands 09°04′S 160°09′E
Tulagi see Tulaghi
159 N10 Tulagt Ar Gol W China
41 P13 Tulancingo Hidalgo, C Mexico 20°34′N 98°25′W
35 R11 Tulare California, W USA 36°12′N 119°21′W
29 P9 Tulare South Dakota, N USA 44°43′N 98°29′W
35 Q12 Tulare Lake Bed salt flat California, W USA
37 S14 Tularosa New Mexico, SW USA 33°04′N 106°01′W
37 P13 Tularosa Mountains ▲▲ New Mexico, SW USA
37 S15 Tularosa Valley basin New Mexico, SW USA
83 E25 Tulbagh Western Cape, SW South Africa 33°17′S 19°09′E
56 C5 Tulcán Carchi, N Ecuador 0°44′N 77°43′W
117 N13 Tulcea Tulcea, E Romania 45°11′N 28°49′E
117 N13 Tulcea ◐ county SE Romania
Tul'chin see Tul'chyn
117 N7 Tul'chyn Rus. Tul'chin. Vinnyts'ka Oblast', C Ukraine 48°40′N 28°49′E
Tuléar see Toliara
35 O1 Tulelake California, W USA 41°57′N 121°30′W
116 J10 Tulgheş Hung. Gyergyótölgyes. Harghita, C Romania 46°57′N 25°46′E
Tuli see Thuli
25 N4 Tulia Texas, SW USA 34°32′N 101°46′W
8 I9 Tulita prev. Fort Norman, Norman. Northwest Territories, NW Canada 64°55′N 125°29′W
20 J10 Tullahoma Tennessee, S USA 35°21′N 86°12′W
183 N12 Tullamarine ✕ (Melbourne) Victoria, SE Australia 37°40′S 144°46′E
183 Q7 Tullamore New South Wales, SE Australia 32°39′S 147°35′E
97 E18 Tullamore Ir. Tulach Mhór. Offaly, C Ireland 53°16′N 07°30′W
103 N12 Tulle anc. Tutela. Corrèze, C France 45°16′N 01°46′E
109 X3 Tulln var. Oberhollabrunn. Niederösterreich, NE Austria 48°20′N 16°02′E
109 W4 Tulln NE Austria
22 H6 Tullos Louisiana, S USA 31°48′N 92°19′W
97 F19 Tullow Ir. An Tullach. Carlow, SE Ireland 52°48′N 06°44′W
181 W5 Tully Queensland, NE Australia 18°03′S 145°56′E
124 J3 Tuloma NW Russian Federation
27 P9 Tulsa Oklahoma, C USA 36°09′N 96°W
153 N11 Tulsipur Mid Western, W Nepal 28°01′N 82°22′E
126 K6 Tul'skaya Oblast' ◐ province W Russian Federation
126 L14 Tul'skiy Respublika Adygeya, SW Russian Federation 44°26′N 40°12′E
186 E5 Tulu Manus Island, N Papua New Guinea 01°58′S 146°50′E
54 D10 Tuluá Valle del Cauca, W Colombia 04°01′N 76°16′W
116 M12 Tulucești Galați, E Romania 45°35′N 28°01′E
39 N12 Tuluksak Alaska, USA 61°06′N 160°57′W
41 Z12 Tulum, Ruinas de ruins Quintana Roo, SE Mexico
169 R17 Tulungagung prev. Toeloengagoeng. Jawa, C Indonesia 08°03′S 111°54′E
186 J6 Tulun Islands var. Kilinailau Islands; prev. Carteret Islands. island group NE Papua New Guinea
126 M4 Tuma Ryazanskaya Oblast', W Russian Federation 55°09′N 40°27′E
54 B12 Tumaco Nariño, SW Colombia 01°51′N 78°46′W
54 B12 Tumaco, Bahía de bay SW Colombia
Tuman-gang see Tumen
42 L8 Tuma, Río N Nicaragua
95 O16 Tumba Stockholm, C Sweden 59°12′N 17°49′E
Tumba, Lac see Ntomba, Lac
169 S12 Tumbangsenamang Borneo, C Indonesia 01°17′S 112°21′E
183 Q10 Tumbarumba New South Wales, SE Australia 35°47′S 148°03′E
56 A8 Tumbes Tumbes, NW Peru 03°33′S 80°27′W
56 A9 Tumbes off. Departamento de Tumbes. ◐ department NW Peru
Tumbes, Departamento de see Tumbes
19 P5 Tumbledown Mountain ▲ Maine, NE USA 45°27′N 70°28′W
11 N13 Tumbler Ridge British Columbia, W Canada 55°06′N 120°51′W
167 Q12 Tumbŏt, Phnum ▲ W Cambodia 12°23′N 102°57′E
182 G9 Tumby Bay South Australia 34°22′S 136°05′E
163 Y10 Tumen Jilin, NE China 42°56′N 129°47′E
163 Y11 Tumen Chin. Tumen Jiang, Kor. Tuman-gang, Rus. Tumyn'tszyan. E Asia
Tumen Jiang see Tumen
55 Q8 Tumeremo Bolívar, E Venezuela 07°17′N 61°30′W
155 G19 Tumkūr Karnātaka, W India 13°20′N 77°06′E
96 I10 Tummel C Scotland, United Kingdom
188 B15 Tumon Bay bay W Guam
77 P14 Tumu NW Ghana 10°55′N 01°59′W
58 I10 Tumuc-Humac Mountains var. Serra Tumucumaque. ▲▲ South America
Tumucumaque, Serra see Tumuc-Humac Mountains
183 Q10 Tumut New South Wales, SE Australia 35°20′S 148°14′E
158 F7 Tumxuk var. Urad Qianqi. Xinjiang Uygur Zizhiqu, NW China 78°40′N 39°54′E
Tumyn'tszyan see Tumen
Tün see Ferdows
45 U14 Tunapuna Trinidad, Trinidad and Tobago 10°38′N 61°23′W
60 K11 Tunas Paraná, S Brazil 24°57′S 49°05′W
Tunbridge Wells see Royal Tunbridge Wells
114 L11 Tunca Nehri Bul. Tundzha. Bulgaria/Turkey see also Tundzha
Tunca Nehri see Tundzha
137 O14 Tunceli var. Kalan. Tunceli, E Turkey 39°07′N 39°34′E
137 O14 Tunceli ◐ province C Turkey
152 J12 Tūndla Uttar Pradesh, N India 27°13′N 78°14′E
81 I25 Tunduru Ruvuma, S Tanzania 11°08′S 37°21′E
114 L10 Tundzha Turk. Tunca Nehri. Bulgaria/Turkey see also Tunca Nehri
Tundzha see Tunca Nehri
162 I6 Tünel var. Bulag. Hövsgöl, N Mongolia 49°51′N 100°41′E
155 H17 Tungabhadra S India
155 F17 Tungabhadra Reservoir ⊠ S India
191 P2 Tungaru prev. Gilbert Islands. island group W Kiribati
171 P7 Tungawan Mindanao, S Philippines 07°33′N 122°22′E
Tungdor see Mainling
T'ung-shan see Xuzhou
161 Q16 Tungsha Tao Chin. Dongsha Qundao, Eng. Pratas Island. island S Taiwan
161 S13 Tungshih Jap. Tōsei. N Taiwan 24°13′N 120°54′E
8 H9 Tungsten Northwest Territories, W Canada 62°N 128°09′W
Tung-t'ing Hu see Dongting Hu
56 A13 Tungurahua ◐ province C Ecuador
95 F14 Tunhovdfjorden ◎ S Norway
22 K2 Tunica Mississippi, S USA 34°40′N 90°22′W
75 N5 Tunis var. Tûnis. ● (Tunisia) NE Tunisia 36°53′N 10°10′E
75 N5 Tunis, Golfe de Ar. Khalīj Tūnis. gulf NE Tunisia
75 N6 Tunisia off. Tunisian Republic, Ar. Al Jumhūrīyah at Tūnisīyah, Fr. République Tunisienne. ◆ republic N Africa
Tunisian Republic see Tunisia
Tunisienne, République see Tunisia
Tūnisīyah, Al Jumhūrīyah at see Tunisia
Tūnis, Khalīj see Tunis, Golfe de
54 G9 Tunja Boyacá, C Colombia 05°33′N 73°23′W
93 F14 Tunnsjøen Lapp. Dåtnejaevrie. ◎ C Norway
39 N12 Tuntutuliak Alaska, USA 60°21′N 162°40′W
197 P14 Tunu ◐ province E Greenland
147 U8 Tunuk Chuyskaya Oblast', C Kyrgyzstan 42°11′N 73°55′E
13 Q6 Tunungayualok Island island Newfoundland and Labrador, E Canada
62 H11 Tunuyán Mendoza, W Argentina 33°35′S 69°00′W
62 I11 Tunuyán, Río W Argentina
Tunxi see Huangshan
Tuodian see Shuangbai
Tuoji see Zhongba
Tuokezhake see Shufu
35 P9 Tuolumne River California, W USA
Tuong Buong see Tương Đương
167 R7 Tương Đương var. Tuong Buong. Nghê An, N Vietnam 19°15′N 104°30′E
160 I13 Tuoniang Jiang S China
Tuotiereke see Jeminay
Tuotuo He see Togton He
Tuotuoheyan see Tanggulashan
Tüp see Tyup
60 J9 Tupã São Paulo, S Brazil 21°57′S 50°28′W
191 S10 Tupai var. Motu Iti. atoll Îles Sous le Vent, W French Polynesia
61 G15 Tupanciretã Rio Grande do Sul, S Brazil 29°06′S 53°48′W
22 M2 Tupelo Mississippi, S USA 34°15′N 88°42′W
59 K18 Tupiraçaba Goiás, S Brazil 14°33′S 48°40′W
57 L21 Tupiza Potosí, S Bolivia 21°27′S 65°45′W
11 N13 Tupper British Columbia, W Canada 55°30′N 119°59′W
18 J8 Tupper Lake ◎ New York, NE USA
146 J10 Tuproqqal'a Khorazm Viloyati, W Uzbekistan 40°52′N 62°00′E
146 J10 Tuproqqal'a Rus. Turpakkla. Xorazm Viloyati, W Uzbekistan 40°52′N 62°00′E
62 H11 Tupungato, Volcán ▲ W Argentina 33°27′S 69°42′W
163 T9 Tuquan Nei Mongol Zizhiqu, N China 45°21′N 121°36′E
54 C13 Túquerres Nariño, SW Colombia 01°06′N 77°37′W
153 U13 Tura Meghālaya, NE India 25°33′N 90°14′E
122 M10 Tura Evenkiyskiy Avtonomnyy Okrug, N Russian Federation 64°20′N 100°17′E
122 G10 Tura C Russian Federation
140 M10 Turabah Makkah, W Saudi Arabia 22°00′N 42°00′E
55 O8 Turagua, Cerro ▲ C Venezuela 06°59′N 64°34′W
184 L12 Turakina Manawatu-Wanganui, North Island, New Zealand 40°03′S 175°13′E
185 K15 Turakirae Head headland North Island, New Zealand 41°26′S 174°54′E
186 B8 Turama S Papua New Guinea
122 K13 Turan Respublika Tyva, S Russian Federation 52°11′N 93°40′E
184 M10 Turangi Waikato, North Island, New Zealand 39°01′S 175°47′E
146 F11 Turan Lowland var. Turan Plain, Kaz. Turan Oypaty, Rus. Turanskaya Nizmennost', Turk. Turan Pesligi, Uzb. Turan Pasttekisligi. plain C Asia
Turan Oypaty/Turan Pesligi/Turan Plain/Turanskaya Nizmennost' see Turan Lowland
Turan Pasttekisligi see Turan Lowland
138 K7 Ţuraq al 'Ilab hill range S Syria
119 K20 Turaw Rus. Turov. Homyel'skaya Voblasts', SE Belarus 52°04′N 27°44′E
140 L2 Turayf Al Ḩudūd ash Shamālīyah, NW Saudi Arabia 31°43′N 38°40′E
Turba see Teruel
54 E5 Turbaco Bolívar, N Colombia 10°20′N 75°25′W
148 K15 Turbat Baluchistān, SW Pakistan 26°02′N 62°56′E
Turbat-i-Haidari see Torbat-e Ḩeydarīyeh
Turbat-i-Jam see Torbat-e Jām
54 D7 Turbo Antioquia, NW Colombia 08°06′N 76°44′W
Turčianský Svätý Martin see Martin
116 H10 Turda Ger. Thorenburg, Hung. Torda. Cluj, NW Romania 46°35′N 23°50′E
142 M7 Ţureh Markazī, W Iran
191 X12 Tureia atoll Îles Tuamotu, SE French Polynesia
110 I12 Turek Wielkopolskie, C Poland 52°01′N 18°30′E
93 L19 Turenki Etelä-Suomi, SW Finland 60°55′N 24°38′E
Turfan see Turpan
145 R8 Turgay Kaz. Torghay. Akmola, W Kazakhstan 51°46′N 72°45′E
145 N10 Turgay Kaz. Torgay. C Kazakhstan
144 M8 Turgayskaya Stolovaya Strana Kaz. Torgay Üstirti. plateau Kazakhstan/Russian Federation
Turgel see Türi
114 L8 Tŭrgovishte prev. Eski Dzhumaya, Tărgovište. Tŭrgovishte, N Bulgaria 43°15′N 26°34′E
114 L8 Tŭrgovishte ◐ province N Bulgaria
136 C14 Turgutlu Manisa, W Turkey 38°30′N 27°43′E
136 L12 Turhal Tokat, N Turkey 40°23′N 36°05′E
118 H4 Türi Ger. Turgel. Järvamaa, N Estonia 58°48′N 25°28′E
105 S9 Turia E Spain
58 M12 Turiaçu Maranhão, E Brazil 01°40′S 45°22′W
Turin see Torino
116 I3 Turiys'k Volyns'ka Oblast', NW Ukraine 51°05′N 24°31′E
Turja see Tur"ya
116 H6 Turka L'vivs'ka Oblast', W Ukraine 49°07′N 23°01′E
81 H16 Turkana, Lake var. Lake Rudolf. ◎ N Kenya
145 P16 Turkestan Kaz. Türkistan. Yuzhnyy Kazakhstan, S Kazakhstan 43°18′N 68°18′E
147 Q12 Turkestan Range Rus. Turkestanskiy Khrebet. ▲▲ C Asia
Turkestanskiy Khrebet see Turkestan Range
111 M23 Túrkeve Jász-Nagykun-Szolnok, E Hungary 47°06′N 20°42′E
25 O4 Turkey Texas, SW USA 34°23′N 100°54′W
136 H14 Turkey off. Republic of Turkey, Turk. Türkiye Cumhuriyeti. ◆ republic SW Asia
181 N4 Turkey Creek Western Australia 16°54′S 128°12′E
26 M9 Turkey Creek Oklahoma, C USA
37 T9 Turkey Mountains ▲▲ New Mexico, SW USA
Turkey, Republic of see Turkey
29 X11 Turkey River Iowa, C USA
127 N7 Turki Saratovskaya Oblast', W Russian Federation 52°00′N 43°16′E
121 O1 Turkish Republic of Northern Cyprus ◇ disputed territory Cyprus
Türkistan see Turkestan
Turkistan, Bandi-i see Torkestān, Selseleh-ye Band-e
Türkiye Cumhuriyeti see Turkey
146 K12 Türkmenabat prev. Rus. Chardzhev, Chardzhou, Chardzhui, Lenin-Turkmenski, Turkm. Chärjew. Lebap Welaýaty, E Turkmenistan 39°07′N 63°30′E
146 A11 Türkmen Aylagy Rus. Turkmenskiy Zaliv. lake gulf W Turkmenistan
Turkmenbashi see Türkmenbaşy
146 A10 Türkmenbaşy Rus. Turkmenbashi; prev. Krasnovodsk. Balkan Welaýaty, W Turkmenistan 40°N 53°04′E
146 A10 Türkmenbaşy Aylagy prev. Rus. Krasnovodskiy Zaliv, Turkm. Krasnowodsk Aylagy. lake Gulf W Turkmenistan
146 J14 Türkmengala Rus. Turkmen-kala; prev. Turkmen-Kala. Mary Welaýaty, S Turkmenistan 37°25′N 62°19′E
146 G13 Turkmenistan ; prev. Turkmenskaya Soviet Socialist Republic. ◆ republic C Asia
Turkmen-kala/Turkmen-Kala see Türkmengala
Turkmenskaya Soviet Socialist Republic see Turkmenistan
Turkmenskiy Zaliv see Türkmen Aylagy
136 L16 Türkoğlu Kahramanmaraş, S Turkey 37°24′N 36°49′E
44 L6 Turks and Caicos Islands ◇ UK dependent territory N West Indies
64 G10 Turks and Caicos Islands UK dependant territory N West Indies
45 N6 Turks Islands island group SE Turks and Caicos Islands
93 K19 Turku Swe. Åbo. Länsi-Suomi, SW Finland 60°27′N 22°17′E
81 H17 Turkwel seasonal river NW Kenya
27 P9 Turley Oklahoma, C USA 36°14′N 95°58′W
35 P9 Turlock California, W USA 37°29′N 120°52′W
118 I12 Turmantas Utena, NE Lithuania 55°41′N 26°27′E
Turmberg see Wieżyca
54 L5 Turmero Aragua, N Venezuela South America 10°14′N 66°40′W
184 N13 Turnagain, Cape headland North Island, New Zealand 40°30′S 176°36′E
Turnau see Turnov
42 H2 Turneffe Islands island group E Belize
18 M11 Turners Falls Massachusetts, NE USA 42°36′N 72°31′W
11 P16 Turner Valley Alberta, SW Canada 50°43′N 114°19′W
99 I16 Turnhout Antwerpen, N Belgium 51°19′N 04°57′E
109 V5 Türnitz Niederösterreich, E Austria 47°56′N 15°26′E
11 S12 Turnor Lake ◎ Saskatchewan, C Canada
111 E15 Turnov Ger. Turnau. Liberecký Kraj, N Czech Republic 50°36′N 15°10′E
Tŭrnovo see Veliko Tŭrnovo
116 I15 Turnu Măgurele var. Turnu-Măgurele. Teleorman, S Romania 43°44′N 24°53′E
Turnu Severin see Drobeta-Turnu Severin
Turócszentmárton see Martin
Turoni see Tours
Turov see Turaw
Turpakkla see Tuproqqal'a
158 M6 Turpan var. Turfan. Xinjiang Uygur Zizhiqu, NW China 42°55′N 89°06′E
Turpan Depression see Turpan Pendi

◆ Country
● Country Capital
◇ Dependent Territory
○ Dependent Territory Capital
◐ Administrative Regions
✕ International Airport
▲ Mountain
▲▲ Mountain Range
Volcano
River
◎ Lake
⊠ Reservoir

158 M6 **Turpan Pendi** *Eng.* Turpan Depression. *depression* NW China
158 M5 **Turpan Zhan** Xinjiang Uygur Zizhiqu, W China 43°10′N 89°06′E
Turpentine State *see* North Carolina
44 H8 **Turquino, Pico** ▲ E Cuba 19°54′N 76°55′W
27 Y10 **Turrell** Arkansas, C USA 35°22′N 90°13′W
43 N14 **Turrialba** Cartago, E Costa Rica 09°56′N 83°40′W
96 K8 **Turriff** NE Scotland, United Kingdom 57°32′N 02°28′W
139 V7 **Tursāq** Diyālá, E Iraq 33°27′N 45°47′E
Turshiz *see* Kāshmar
Tursunzade *see* Tursunzoda
147 P13 **Tursunzoda** *Rus.* Tursunzade; *prev.* Regar. W Tajikistan 38°30′N 68°10′E
Turt *see* Hanh
Türtkŭl/Turtkul' *see* To'rtkok'l
29 O9 **Turtle Creek** ≈ South Dakota, N USA
30 K4 **Turtle Flambeau Flowage** ⊠ Wisconsin, N USA
11 S14 **Turtleford** Saskatchewan, S Canada 53°21′N 108°48′W
28 M4 **Turtle Lake** North Dakota, N USA 47°31′N 100°53′W
92 K12 **Turtola** Lappi, NW Finland 66°39′N 23°55′E
122 M10 **Turu** ≈ N Russian Federation
Turuga *see* Tsuruga
147 V10 **Turugart Pass** *pass* China/Kyrgyzstan
158 E7 **Turugart Shankou** *var.* Pereval Torugart. *pass* China/Kyrgyzstan
122 K9 **Turukhan** ≈ N Russian Federation
122 K9 **Turukhansk** Krasnoyarskiy Kray, N Russian Federation 65°50′N 87°48′E
139 N3 **Ţurumbah** *well* NE Syria
Turuoka *see* Tsuruoka
144 H14 **Turush** Mangistau, SW Kazakhstan 45°24′N 56°02′E
60 K7 **Turvo, Rio** ≈ S Brazil
116 J2 **Tur"ya** *Pol.* Turja, *Rus.* Tur'ya. ≈ NW Ukraine
23 O4 **Tuscaloosa** Alabama, S USA 33°13′N 87°34′W
23 O4 **Tuscaloosa, Lake** ⊚ Alabama, S USA
Tuscan Archipelago *see* Toscano, Archipelago
Tuscan-Emilian Mountains *see* Tosco-Emiliano, Appennino
Tuscany *see* Toscana
35 V2 **Tuscarora** Nevada, W USA 41°16′N 116°13′W
18 F15 **Tuscarora Mountain** *ridge* Pennsylvania, NE USA
30 M14 **Tuscola** Illinois, N USA 39°46′N 88°19′W
25 P7 **Tuscola** Texas, SW USA 32°12′N 99°48′W
23 O2 **Tuscumbia** Alabama, S USA 34°43′N 87°42′W
92 O4 **Tusenøyane** *island group* S Svalbard
144 K13 **Tushchybas, Zaliv** *prev.* Zaliv Paskevicha. *lake gulf* SW Kazakhstan
Tusima *see* Tsushima
171 Y15 **Tusirah** Papua, E Indonesia 06°46′S 140°19′E
23 Q5 **Tuskegee** Alabama, S USA 32°25′N 85°41′W
94 E8 **Tustna** *island* S Norway
39 R12 **Tustumena Lake** ⊚ Alaska, USA
110 K13 **Tuszyn** Łódzkie, C Poland 51°36′N 19°31′E
137 S13 **Tutak** Ağrı, E Turkey 39°34′N 42°48′E
185 C20 **Tutamoe Range** ▲▲ North Island, New Zealand
Tutasev *see* Tutayev
124 L15 **Tutayev** *var.* Tutasev. Yaroslavskaya Oblast', W Russian Federation 57°51′N 39°29′E
Tutela *see* Tulle, France
Tutela *see* Tudela, Spain
Tutera *see* Tudela
155 H23 **Tuticorin** Tamil Nādu, SE India 08°48′N 78°10′E
113 L15 **Tutin** Serbia, S Serbia 43°00′N 20°20′E
184 O10 **Tutira** Hawke's Bay, North Island, New Zealand 39°14′S 176°53′E
Tutiura *see* Tsuchiura
122 K10 **Tutonchny** Evenkiyskiy Avtonomnyy Okrug, N Russian Federation 64°12′N 93°52′E
114 L6 **Tutrakan** Silistra, NE Bulgaria 44°03′N 26°38′E
29 N5 **Tuttle** North Dakota, N USA 47°07′N 99°58′W
26 M11 **Tuttle** Oklahoma, C USA 35°17′N 97°48′W
27 O3 **Tuttle Creek Lake** ⊠ Kansas, C USA
101 H23 **Tuttlingen** Baden-Württemberg, S Germany 47°59′N 08°49′E
171 R16 **Tutuala** East Timor 08°23′S 127°12′E
192 K17 **Tutuila** *island* W American Samoa
83 I18 **Tutume** Central, E Botswana 20°26′S 27°02′E
39 N7 **Tututalak Mountain** ▲ Alaska, USA 67°51′N 161°27′W
22 K3 **Tutwiler** Mississippi, S USA 34°00′N 90°25′W
162 L8 **Tuul Gol** ≈ N Mongolia
93 O16 **Tuupovaara** Itä-Suomi, E Finland 62°30′N 30°40′E
Tuva *see* Tyva, Respublika
190 E7 **Tuvalu** *prev.* Ellice Islands. ◆ *commonwealth republic* SW Pacific Ocean
Tuvinskaya ASSR *see* Tyva, Respublika
163 O9 **Tuvshinshiree** *var.* Sergelen. Sühbaatar, E Mongolia 46°12′N 111°48′E
141 P9 **Ţuwayq, Jabal** ▲▲ C Saudi Arabia
138 H13 **Ţuwayyil ash Shihāq** *desert* S Jordan
11 U16 **Tuxford** Saskatchewan, S Canada 50°33′N 105°32′W
167 U12 **Tu Xoay** Đăc Lăc, S Vietnam 12°18′N 107°33′E
40 L14 **Tuxpan** Jalisco, C Mexico 19°33′N 103°21′W
40 J12 **Tuxpan** Nayarit, C Mexico 21°57′N 105°12′W
41 Q12 **Tuxpán** *var.* Tuxpán de Rodríguez Cano. Veracruz-Llave, E Mexico 20°58′N 97°23′W
Tuxpán de Rodríguez Cano *see* Tuxpán
41 R15 **Tuxtepec** *var.* San Juan Bautista Tuxtepec. Oaxaca, S Mexico 18°02′N 96°05′W
41 U16 **Tuxtla** *var.* Tuxtla Gutiérrez. Chiapas, SE Mexico 16°44′N 93°03′W
Tuxtla *see* San Andrés Tuxtla
Tuxtla Gutiérrez *see* Tuxtla
Tuyama *see* Toyama
167 T5 **Tuyên Quang** Tuyên Quang, N Vietnam 21°48′N 105°18′E
167 U13 **Tuy Hoa** Binh Thuân, S Vietnam 11°03′N 108°12′E
167 V12 **Tuy Hoa** Phu Yên, S Vietnam 13°02′N 109°15′E
127 U5 **Tuymazy** Respublika Bashkortostan, W Russian Federation 54°36′N 53°40′E
Tuy Phong *see* Liên Hương
142 L6 **Tūysarkān** *var.* Tuisarkan, Tuyserkān. Hamadān, W Iran 34°31′N 48°30′E
Tūyserkān *see* Tūysarkān
145 W16 **Tuyuk** *Kaz.* Tuyyq. Taldykorgan, SE Kazakhstan 43°07′N 79°24′E
Tuyyq *see* Tuyuk
136 I14 **Tuz Gölü** ⊚ C Turkey
125 Q15 **Tuzha** Kirovskaya Oblast', NW Russian Federation 57°37′N 48°02′E
113 K17 **Tuzi** S Montenegro 42°22′N 19°21′E
139 T5 **Tūz Khurmātū** At Ta'mīn, N Iraq 34°56′N 44°38′E
112 I11 **Tuzla** Federacija Bosna I Hercegovina, NE Bosnia and Herzegovina 44°33′N 18°40′E
117 N15 **Tuzla** Constanţa, SE Romania 43°58′N 28°38′E
137 T12 **Tuzluca** Iğdır, E Turkey 40°02′N 43°39′E
95 J20 **Tvååker** Halland, S Sweden 57°04′N 12°25′E
95 F17 **Tvedestrand** Aust-Agder, S Norway 58°36′N 08°55′E
124 J16 **Tver'** *prev.* Kalinin. Tverskaya Oblast', W Russian Federation 56°53′N 35°52′E
126 I15 **Tverskaya Oblast'** ◆ *province* W Russian Federation
124 I15 **Tvertsa** ≈ W Russian Federation
138 G9 **Tverya** *var.* Tiberias; *prev.* Teverya. Northern, N Israel 32°48′N 35°32′E
110 H13 **Twardogóra** *Ger.* Festenberg. Dolnośląskie, SW Poland 51°21′N 17°27′E
14 J14 **Tweed** Ontario, SE Canada 44°29′N 77°19′W
96 K13 **Tweed** ≈ England/Scotland, United Kingdom
98 O7 **Tweede-Exloërmond** Drenthe, NE Netherlands 52°55′N 06°55′E
183 V3 **Tweed Heads** New South Wales, SE Australia 28°10′S 153°32′E
98 M11 **Twello** Gelderland, E Netherlands 52°14′N 06°07′E
35 W15 **Twentynine Palms** California, W USA 34°08′N 116°03′W
25 P9 **Twin Buttes Reservoir** ⊠ Texas, SW USA
33 O15 **Twin Falls** Idaho, NW USA 42°34′N 114°28′W
39 N13 **Twin Hills** Alaska, USA 59°06′N 160°21′W
11 O11 **Twin Lakes** Alberta, W Canada 57°47′N 117°30′W
33 O12 **Twin Peaks** ▲ Idaho, NW USA 44°37′N 114°24′W
185 I14 **Twins, The** ▲ South Island, New Zealand 41°14′S 172°38′E
29 S5 **Twin Valley** Minnesota, N USA 47°15′N 96°15′W
100 G11 **Twistringen** Niedersachsen, NW Germany 52°48′N 08°39′E
185 E20 **Twizel** Canterbury, South Island, New Zealand 44°04′S 171°12′E
29 X5 **Two Harbors** Minnesota, N USA 47°01′N 91°40′W
11 R14 **Two Hills** Alberta, SW Canada 53°40′N 111°43′W
31 N7 **Two Rivers** Wisconsin, N USA 44°10′N 87°33′W
116 H8 **Tyachiv** Zakarpats'ka Oblast', W Ukraine 48°02′N 23°35′E
Tyan'-Shan' *see* Tien Shan
166 L3 **Tyao** ≈ Burma (Myanmar)/India
117 R6 **Tyasmyn** ≈ N Ukraine
23 X6 **Tybee Island** Georgia, SE USA 32°00′N 80°51′W
Tyborøn *see* Thyborøn
111 J16 **Tychy** *Ger.* Tichau. Śląskie, S Poland 50°12′N 19°01′E
111 O16 **Tyczyn** Podkarpackie, SE Poland 49°58′N 22°03′E
94 I8 **Tydal** Sør-Trøndelag, S Norway 63°01′N 11°36′E
115 H24 **Tyflós** ≈ Kríti, Greece, E Mediterranean Sea
21 S3 **Tygart Lake** ⊠ West Virginia, NE USA
123 Q13 **Tygda** Amurskaya Oblast', SE Russian Federation 53°07′N 126°12′E
21 Q11 **Tyger River** ≈ South Carolina, SE USA
32 I11 **Tygh Valley** Oregon, NW USA 45°15′N 121°12′W
94 F12 **Tyin** ⊚ S Norway
29 S10 **Tyler** Minnesota, N USA 44°18′N 96°07′W
25 W7 **Tyler** Texas, SW USA 32°21′N 95°18′W
25 W7 **Tyler, Lake** ⊠ Texas, SW USA
22 K7 **Tylertown** Mississippi, S USA 31°07′N 90°08′W
117 P10 **Tylihuls'kyy Lyman** ⊚ SW Ukraine
Tylos *see* Bahrain
115 C15 **Tymfi** *var.* Timfi. ▲ W Greece 39°58′N 20°51′E
115 E17 **Tymfristós** *var.* Timfristos. ▲ C Greece 38°57′N 21°49′E
115 J25 **Tympáki** *var.* Timbaki; *prev.* Timbákion. Kríti, Greece, E Mediterranean Sea 35°04′N 24°47′E
123 Q12 **Tynda** Amurskaya Oblast', SE Russian Federation 55°09′N 124°44′E
29 Q12 **Tyndall** South Dakota, N USA 42°57′N 97°52′W
97 L14 **Tyne** ≈ N England, United Kingdom
97 M14 **Tynemouth** NE England, United Kingdom 55°01′N 01°24′W
97 L14 **Tyneside** *cultural region* NE England, United Kingdom
94 H10 **Tynset** Hedmark, S Norway 61°45′N 10°49′E
39 Q12 **Tyonek** Alaska, USA 61°04′N 151°08′W
Työsi *see* Chōshi
Tyras *see* Dniester
Tyras *see* Bilhorod-Dnistrovs'kyy
Tyre *see* Soûr
95 G14 **Tyrifjorden** ⊚ S Norway
95 K22 **Tyringe** Skåne, S Sweden 56°09′N 13°35′E
123 R13 **Tyrma** Khabarovskiy Kray, SE Russian Federation 50°00′N 132°04′E
Tyrnau *see* Trnava
115 F15 **Týrnavos** *var.* Tirnavos. Thessalía, C Greece 39°45′N 22°18′E
127 N16 **Tyrnyauz** Kabardino-Balkarskaya Respublika, SW Russian Federation 43°19′N 42°55′E
Tyrol *see* Tirol
18 E14 **Tyrone** Pennsylvania, NE USA 40°41′N 78°12′W
97 E15 **Tyrone** *cultural region* W Northern Ireland, United Kingdom
Tyros *see* Bahrain
182 M10 **Tyrrell, Lake** *salt lake* Victoria, SE Australia
84 H14 **Tyrrhenian Basin** *undersea feature* Tyrrhenian Sea, C Mediterranean Sea 39°30′N 13°00′E
120 L8 **Tyrrhenian Sea** *It.* Mare Tirreno. *sea* N Mediterranean Sea
94 J12 **Tyrsil** ≈ Hedmark, S Norway
Tysa *see* Tisa/Tisza
116 J7 **Tysmenytsya** Ivano-Frankivs'ka Oblast', W Ukraine 48°54′N 24°50′E
95 C14 **Tysnesøya** *island* S Norway
95 C14 **Tysse** Hordaland, S Norway 60°23′N 05°46′E
95 D14 **Tyssedal** Hordaland, S Norway 60°07′N 06°36′E
95 O17 **Tystberga** Södermanland, C Sweden 58°51′N 17°15′E
118 E12 **Tytuvėnai** Šiaulai, C Lithuania 55°36′N 23°14′E
144 D14 **Tyub-Karagan, Mys** *headland* SW Kazakhstan 44°40′N 50°19′E
147 W8 **Tyugel'-Say** Narynskaya Oblast', C Kyrgyzstan 41°57′N 74°40′E
122 H11 **Tyukalinsk** Omskaya Oblast', C Russian Federation 55°56′N 72°02′E
127 V7 **Tyul'gan** Orenburgskaya Oblast', W Russian Federation 52°27′N 56°08′E
122 G11 **Tyumen'** Tyumenskaya Oblast', C Russian Federation 57°11′N 65°29′E
122 H11 **Tyumenskaya Oblast'** ◆ *province* C Russian Federation
147 Y7 **Tyup** *Kir.* Tüp. Issyk-Kul'skaya Oblast', NE Kyrgyzstan 42°44′N 78°18′E
122 L14 **Tyva, Respublika** *prev.* Tannu-Tuva, Tuva, Tuvinskaya ASSR. ◆ *autonomous republic* C Russian Federation
117 N7 **Tyvriv** Vinnyts'ka Oblast', C Ukraine 49°01′N 28°28′E
97 J21 **Tywi** ≈ S Wales, United Kingdom
97 I19 **Tywyn** W Wales, United Kingdom 52°35′N 04°06′W
83 K20 **Tzaneen** Limpopo, NE South Africa 23°50′S 30°09′E
Tzekung *see* Zigong
115 I20 **Tziá** *prev.* Kéa, Kéos; *anc.* Ceos. *island* Kykládes, Greece, Aegean Sea
41 X12 **Tzucacab** Yucatán, SE Mexico 20°04′N 89°03′W

U

82 B12 **Uaco Cungo** *var.* Waku Kungo, *Port.* Santa Comba. Cuanza Sul, C Angola 11°21′S 15°04′E
UAE *see* United Arab Emirates
191 X7 **Ua Huka** *island* Îles Marquises, NE French Polynesia
58 E10 **Uaiacás** Roraima, N Brazil 03°28′N 63°13′W
Uamba *see* Wamba
Uanle Uen *see* Wanlaweyn
191 W7 **Ua Pu** *island* Îles Marquises, NE French Polynesia
81 L17 **Uar Garas** *spring/well* SW Somalia 01°19′N 41°22′E
58 G12 **Uatumã, Rio** ≈ C Brazil
Ua Uíbh Fhailí *see* Offaly
58 C11 **Uaupés, Rio** *var.* Río Vaupés. ≈ Brazil/Colombia *see also* Vaupés, Río
Uaupés, Rio *see* Vaupés, Río
145 X9 **Uba** ≈ E Kazakhstan
145 N6 **Ubagan** *Kaz.* Obagan. ≈ Kazakhstan/Russian Federation
186 G7 **Ubai** New Britain, E Papua New Guinea 05°38′S 150°45′E
79 J15 **Ubangi** *Fr.* Oubangui. ≈ C Africa
Ubangi-Shari *see* Central African Republic
116 M3 **Ubarts'** *Ukr.* Ubort'. ≈ Belarus/Ukraine *see also* Ubort'
Ubarts' *see* Ubort'
54 F9 **Ubaté** Cundinamarca, C Colombia 05°20′N 73°50′W
60 N10 **Ubatuba** São Paulo, S Brazil 23°26′S 45°04′W
149 R12 **Ubauro** Sind, SE Pakistan 28°08′N 69°43′E
171 Q6 **Ubay** Bohol, C Philippines 10°02′N 124°29′E
103 U14 **Ubaye** ≈ SE France
Ubayid, Wadi al *see* Ubayyiḍ, Wādī al
139 N8 **Ubaylah** Al Anbār, W Iraq 33°06′N 40°13′E
139 O10 **Ubayyiḍ, Wādī al** *var.* Wadi al Ubayid. *dry watercourse* SW Iraq
98 L13 **Ubbergen** Gelderland, E Netherlands 51°49′N 05°54′E
164 E13 **Ube** Yamaguchi, Honshū, SW Japan 33°57′N 131°15′E
105 O13 **Ubeda** Andalucía, S Spain 38°01′N 03°22′W
109 V7 **Übelbach** *var.* Markt-Übelbach. Steiermark, SE Austria 47°13′N 15°15′E
59 L20 **Uberaba** Minas Gerais, SE Brazil 19°47′S 47°57′W
57 Q19 **Uberaba, Laguna** ⊚ E Bolivia
59 K19 **Uberlândia** Minas Gerais, SE Brazil 18°17′S 48°17′W
101 H24 **Überlingen** Baden-Württemberg, S Germany 47°46′N 09°10′E
77 U16 **Ubiaja** Edo, S Nigeria 06°39′N 06°23′E
104 K3 **Ubiña, Peña** ▲ NW Spain 43°01′N 05°58′W
57 H17 **Ubinas, Volcán** ⩚ S Peru 16°16′S 70°49′W
Ubol Rajadhani/Ubol Ratchathani *see* Ubon Ratchathani
167 P9 **Ubolratna Reservoir** ⊠ C Thailand
167 S10 **Ubon Ratchathani** *var.* Muang Ubon, Ubol Rajadhani, Ubol Ratchathani, Udon Ratchathani. Ubon Ratchathani, E Thailand 15°15′N 104°50′E
119 L20 **Ubort'** *Bel.* Ubarts'. ≈ Belarus/Ukraine *see also* Ubarts'
Ubort' *see* Ubarts'
104 K15 **Ubrique** Andalucía, S Spain 36°42′N 05°27′W
Ubsu-Nur, Ozero *see* Uvs Nuur
79 M18 **Ubundu** Orientale, C Dem. Rep. Congo 0°24′S 25°30′E
146 J13 **Üçajy** *var.* Uchajy, *Rus.* Uch-Adzhi. Mary Welaýaty, C Turkmenistan 38°06′N 62°44′E
137 X11 **Ucar** *Rus.* Udzhary. C Azerbaijan 40°31′N 47°40′E
56 G13 **Ucayali** *off.* Departamento de Ucayali. ◆ *department* E Peru
Ucayali, Departamento de *see* Ucayali
56 F10 **Ucayali, Río** ≈ C Peru
Uccle *see* Ukkel
Uch-Adzhi/Üchajy *see* Üçajy
127 X4 **Uchaly** Respublika Bashkortostan, W Russian Federation 54°19′N 59°33′E
145 W13 **Ucharal** *Kaz.* Üsharal. Almaty, E Kazakhstan 46°08′N 80°55′E
164 C17 **Uchinoura** Kagoshima, Kyūshū, SW Japan 31°16′N 131°04′E
165 R5 **Uchiura-wan** *bay* NW Pacific Ocean
Uchkuduk *see* Uchquduq
147 S9 **Uchqo'rg'on** *Rus.* Uchkurghan. Namangan Viloyati, E Uzbekistan 41°06′N 72°04′E
146 K8 **Uchquduq** *Rus.* Uchkuduk. Navoiy Viloyati, N Uzbekistan 42°12′N 63°27′E
Uchsay *see* Uchsoy
146 G6 **Uchsoy** *Rus.* Uchsay. Qoraqalpog'iston Respublikasi, NW Uzbekistan 43°51′N 58°51′E
Uchtagan Gumy/Uchtagan, Peski *see* Uçtagan Gumy
123 R11 **Uchur** ≈ E Russian Federation
100 O10 **Uckermark** *cultural region* E Germany
10 K17 **Ucluelet** Vancouver Island, British Columbia, SW Canada 48°55′N 123°34′W
146 D10 **Uçtagan Gumy** *var.* Uchtagan Gumy, *Rus.* Peski Uchtagan. *desert* NW Turkmenistan
122 M13 **Uda** ≈ S Russian Federation
123 R12 **Uda** ≈ E Russian Federation
123 N6 **Udachnyy** Respublika Sakha (Yakutiya), NE Russian Federation 66°27′N 112°18′E
155 G21 **Udagamandalam** *var.* Ooty, Udhagamandalam; *prev.* Ootacamund. Tamil Nādu, SW India 11°28′N 76°42′E
152 F14 **Udaipur** *prev.* Oodeypore. Rājasthān, N India 24°35′N 73°41′E
Udayadhani *see* Uthai Thani
143 N16 **'Udayd, Khawr al** *var.* Khor al Udeid. *inlet* Qatar/Saudi Arabia
112 D11 **Udbina** Lika-Senj, W Croatia 44°33′N 15°46′E
95 I18 **Uddevalla** Västra Götaland, S Sweden 58°20′N 11°56′E
Uddjaur *see* Uddjaure
92 H13 **Uddjaure** *var.* Uddjaur. ⊚ N Sweden
Udeid, Khor al *see* 'Udayd, Khawr al
99 K14 **Uden** Noord-Brabant, SE Netherlands 51°40′N 05°37′E
Uden *see* Udenhout
99 J14 **Udenhout** *var.* Uden. Noord-Brabant, S Netherlands 51°37′N 05°09′E
155 H14 **Udgīr** Mahārāshtra, C India 18°23′N 77°06′E
Udhagamandalam *see* Udagamandalam
152 H6 **Udhampur** Jammu and Kashmir, NW India 32°55′N 75°07′E
139 X14 **'Udhaybah, 'Uqlat al** *well* S Iraq
106 J7 **Udine** *anc.* Utina. Friuli-Venezia Giulia, NE Italy 46°05′N 13°10′E
175 T14 **Udintsev Fracture Zone** *tectonic feature* S Pacific Ocean
Udipi *see* Udupi
Udmurtia *see* Udmurtskaya Respublika
127 S2 **Udmurtskaya Respublika** *Eng.* Udmurtia. ◆ *autonomous republic* NW Russian Federation
124 J15 **Udomlya** Tverskaya Oblast', W Russian Federation 57°53′N 34°59′E
Udon Ratchathani *see* Ubon Ratchathani
167 Q8 **Udon Thani** *var.* Ban Mak Khaeng, Udorndhani. Udon Thani, N Thailand 17°25′N 102°45′E
Udorndhani *see* Udon Thani
189 U12 **Udot** *atoll* Chuuk Islands, C Micronesia
123 S12 **Udskaya Guba** *bay* E Russian Federation
123 R12 **Udskoye** Khabarovskiy Kray, SE Russian Federation 54°32′N 134°26′E
155 E19 **Udupi** *var.* Udipi. Karnātaka, SW India 13°18′N 74°46′E
Udzhary *see* Ucar
100 O9 **Uecker** ≈ NE Germany
100 P9 **Ueckermünde** Mecklenburg-Vorpommern, NE Germany 53°43′N 14°03′E
164 M12 **Ueda** *var.* Uyeda. Nagano, Honshū, S Japan 36°27′N 138°13′E
79 L16 **Uele** *var.* Welle. ≈ NE Dem. Rep. Congo
123 W5 **Uelen** Chukotskiy Avtonomnyy Okrug, NE Russian Federation 66°01′N 169°52′W
Uele (upper course) *see* Kibali, Dem. Rep. Congo
Uele (upper course) *see* Uolo, Río, Equatorial Guinea/Gabon
100 J11 **Uelzen** Niedersachsen, N Germany 52°58′N 10°34′E
164 J14 **Ueno** Mie, Honshū, SW Japan 34°45′N 136°08′E
127 V4 **Ufa** Respublika Bashkortostan, W Russian Federation 54°46′N 56°02′E
127 V4 **Ufa** ≈ W Russian Federation
Ufra *see* Kenar
83 C18 **Ugab** ≈ C Namibia
118 D8 **Ugāle** Ventspils, NW Latvia 57°16′N 21°58′E
81 F17 **Uganda** *off.* Republic of Uganda. ◆ *republic* E Africa
Uganda, Republic of *see* Uganda
138 G4 **Ugarit** *Ar.* Ra's Shamrah. *site of ancient city* Al Lādhiqīyah, NW Syria
39 O14 **Ugashik** Alaska, USA 57°30′N 157°24′W
107 Q19 **Ugento** Puglia, SE Italy 39°53′N 18°09′E
105 O15 **Ugíjar** Andalucía, S Spain 36°58′N 03°03′W
103 T11 **Ugine** Savoie, E France 45°45′N 06°25′E
123 R13 **Uglegorsk** Amurskaya Oblast', S Russian Federation 51°40′N 128°05′E
Ugleural'sk *see* Ugleural'skiy
125 V13 **Ugleural'skiy** *var.* Ugleural'sk, *earlier* Polovinka. Permskaya Oblast', NW Russian Federation 58°57′N 57°37′E
124 L15 **Uglich** Yaroslavskaya Oblast', W Russian Federation 57°33′N 38°23′E
126 I4 **Ugra** ≈ W Russian Federation
147 V9 **Ugyut** Narynskaya Oblast', C Kyrgyzstan 41°22′N 74°49′E
111 H19 **Uherské Hradiště** *Ger.* Ungarisch-Hradisch. Zlínský Kraj, E Czech Republic 49°05′N 17°26′E
111 H19 **Uherský Brod** *Ger.* Ungarisch-Brod. Zlínský Kraj, E Czech Republic 49°01′N 17°40′E
111 B17 **Úhlava** *Ger.* Angel. ≈ W Czech Republic
Uhorshchyna *see* Hungary
31 T13 **Uhrichsville** Ohio, N USA 40°23′N 81°21′W
Uhuru Peak *see* Kilimanjaro
96 G8 **Uig** N Scotland, United Kingdom 57°35′N 06°22′W
82 B10 **Uíge** *Port.* Carmona, Vila Marechal Carmona. Uíge, NW Angola 07°37′S 15°02′E
82 B10 **Uíge** ◆ *province* N Angola
193 Y15 **Uiha** *island* Ha'apai Group, C Tonga
189 U13 **Uijec** *island* Chuuk, C Micronesia
163 X14 **Uijŏngbu** *Jap.* Giseifu. NW South Korea 37°42′N 127°02′E
144 H10 **Uil** *Kaz.* Oyyl. Aktyubinsk, W Kazakhstan 49°06′N 54°41′E
144 H10 **Uil** *Kaz.* Oyyl. ≈ W Kazakhstan
36 M3 **Uinta Mountains** ▲▲ Utah, W USA
83 C18 **Uis** Erongo, NW Namibia 21°08′S 14°49′E
83 I25 **Uitenhage** Eastern Cape, S South Africa 33°44′S 25°27′E
98 H9 **Uitgeest** Noord-Holland, W Netherlands 52°32′N 04°43′E
98 I11 **Uithoorn** Noord-Holland, C Netherlands 52°14′N 04°50′E
98 O4 **Uithuizen** Groningen, NE Netherlands 53°24′N 06°40′E
98 O4 **Uithuizermeeden** Groningen, NE Netherlands 53°25′N 06°43′E
189 R6 **Ujae Atoll** *var.* Wūjae. *atoll* Ralik Chain, W Marshall Islands
Ujain *see* Ujjain
111 I16 **Ujazd** Opolskie, S Poland 50°22′N 18°20′E
Új-Becse *see* Novi Bečej
Ujda *see* Oujda
189 N5 **Ujelang Atoll** *var.* Wujlān. *atoll* Ralik Chain, W Marshall Islands
111 N21 **Újfehértó** Szabolcs-Szatmár-Bereg, E Hungary 47°48′N 21°40′E
Ujgradiska *see* Nova Gradiška
164 J13 **Uji** *var.* Uzi. Kyōto, Honshū, SW Japan 34°54′N 135°48′E
81 E21 **Ujiji** Kigoma, W Tanzania 04°55′S 29°39′E
154 G10 **Ujjain** *prev.* Ujain. Madhya Pradesh, C India 23°11′N 75°50′E
'Ujmān *see* 'Ajmān
Újmoldova *see* Moldova Nouă
Újszentanna *see* Sântana
Ujungpandang *see* Makassar
Ujung Salang *see* Phuket
Újvidék *see* Novi Sad
UK *see* United Kingdom
154 E11 **Ukāi Reservoir** ⊠ W India
81 G19 **Ukara Island** *island* N Tanzania
'Ukash, Wādī *see* 'Akāsh, Wādī
81 F19 **Ukerewe Island** *island* N Tanzania
139 S9 **Ukhaydir** Al Anbār, C Iraq 32°28′N 43°36′E
153 X13 **Ukhrul** Manipur, NE India 25°08′N 94°24′E
125 S9 **Ukhta** Respublika Komi, NW Russian Federation 63°31′N 53°48′E
34 L6 **Ukiah** California, W USA 39°07′N 123°14′W
32 K12 **Ukiah** Oregon, NW USA 45°06′N 118°57′W
99 G18 **Ukkel** *Fr.* Uccle. Brussels, C Belgium 50°47′N 04°19′E
118 G13 **Ukmergė** *Pol.* Wiłkomierz. Vilnius, C Lithuania 55°16′N 24°46′E
Ukraina *see* Ukraine
116 L6 **Ukraine** *off.* Ukraine, *Rus.* Ukraina, *Ukr.* Ukrayina; *prev.* Ukrainian Soviet Socialist Republic, Ukrainskay S.S.R. ◆ *republic* SE Europe
Ukraine *see* Ukraine
Ukrainian Soviet Socialist Republic *see* Ukraine
Ukrainskay S.S.R/Ukrayina *see* Ukraine
82 B13 **Uku** Cuanza Sul, NW Angola 11°25′S 14°18′E
164 B13 **Uku-jima** *island* Gotō-rettō, SW Japan
83 F20 **Ukwi** Kgalagadi, SW Botswana 23°41′S 20°26′E
118 M13 **Ula** *Rus.* Ulla. Vitsyebskaya Voblasts', N Belarus 55°14′N 29°15′E
136 C16 **Ula** Muğla, SW Turkey 37°08′N 28°25′E
118 M13 **Ula** *Rus.* Ulla. ≈ N Belarus
162 L7 **Ulaanbaatar** *Eng.* Ulan Bator; *prev.* Urga. ● (Mongolia) Töv, C Mongolia 47°55′N 106°57′E
Ulaan-Ereg *see* Bayanmönh
162 E5 **Ulaangom** Uvs, NW Mongolia 49°56′N 92°06′E
162 D5 **Ulaanhus** *var.* Bilüü. Bayan-Ölgiy, W Mongolia 48°54′N 89°40′E
Ulaantolgoy *see* Möst
Ulaan-Uul *see* Öldziyt, Bayanhongor, Mongolia
Ulaan-Uul *see* Erdene, Dornogovĭ, Mongolia
162 M14 **Ulan** *var.* Otog Qi. Nei Mongol Zizhiqu, N China 39°05′N 107°58′E
159 R10 **Ulan** *var.* Xireg; *prev.* Xiligou. Qinghai, C China 36°59′N 98°21′E
Ulan Bator *see* Ulaanbaatar
162 L13 **Ulan Buh Shamo** *desert* N China
Ulanhad *see* Chifeng
163 T8 **Ulanhot** Nei Mongol Zizhiqu, N China 46°02′N 122°E
127 Q14 **Ulan Khol** Respublika Kalmykiya, SW Russian Federation 45°27′N 46°48′E
163 P13 **Ulan Qab** *var.* Jining. Nei Mongol Zizhiqu, N China 40°59′N 113°08′E
162 M13 **Ulansuhai Nur** ⊚ N China
123 N14 **Ulan-Ude** *prev.* Verkhneudinsk. Respublika Buryatiya, S Russian Federation 51°55′N 107°40′E
159 N12 **Ulan Ul Hu** ⊚ C China
187 N9 **Ulawa Island** *island* SE Solomon Islands
138 J7 **'Ulayyānīyah, Bi'r al** *var.* Al Hilbeh. *well* S Syria
123 S12 **Ul'banskiy Zaliv** *strait* E Russian Federation
Ulbo *see* Olib
113 J18 **Ulcinj** S Montenegro 41°56′N 19°14′E
Uldz *see* Norovlin
Uleåborg *see* Oulu
Uleälv *see* Oulujoki
95 G16 **Ulefoss** Telemark, S Norway 59°17′N 09°15′E
Uleträsk *see* Oulujärvi
113 L19 **Ulëz** *var.* Ulëza. Dibër, C Albania 41°42′N 19°52′E
Ulëza *see* Ulëz
95 F22 **Ulfborg** Ringkøbing, W Denmark 56°16′N 08°21′E
98 N13 **Ulft** Gelderland, E Netherlands 51°53′N 06°23′E
162 G7 **Uliastay** *prev.* Jibhalanta. Dzavhan, W Mongolia 47°47′N 96°53′E
188 F8 **Ulimang** Babeldaob, N Palau
67 T10 **Ulindi** ≈ W Dem. Rep. Congo
188 H14 **Ulithi Atoll** *atoll* Caroline Islands, W Micronesia
112 N10 **Uljma** Vojvodina, NE Serbia 45°04′N 21°08′E
144 L11 **Ul'kayak** *Kaz.* Ölkeyek. ≈ C Kazakhstan
145 Q7 **Ul'ken-Karoy, Ozero** ⊚ N Kazakhstan
Ülkenözen *see* Bol'shoy Uzen'
Ülkenqobda *see* Bol'shaya Khobda
104 G3 **Ulla** ≈ NW Spain
Ulla *see* Ula
183 S10 **Ulladulla** New South Wales, SE Australia 35°21′S 150°25′E
153 T14 **Ullapara** Rajshahi, W Bangladesh 24°20′N 89°34′E
96 H7 **Ullapool** N Scotland, United Kingdom 57°54′N 05°10′W
95 J20 **Ullared** Halland, S Sweden 57°07′N 12°45′E
105 T7 **Ulldecona** Cataluña, NE Spain 40°36′N 00°27′E
92 I9 **Ullsfjorden** *fjord* N Norway
97 K15 **Ullswater** ⊚ NW England, United Kingdom
101 I22 **Ulm** Baden-Württemberg, S Germany 48°24′N 09°59′E
33 R8 **Ulm** Montana, NW USA 47°27′N 111°32′W
183 V5 **Ulmarra** New South Wales, SE Australia 29°37′S 153°06′E
116 K13 **Ulmeni** Buzău, C Romania 45°08′N 26°43′E
116 K14 **Ulmeni** Călărași, S Romania 44°08′N 26°43′E
42 L7 **Ulmukhuás** Región Autónoma Atlántico Norte, NE Nicaragua 14°20′N 84°30′W
188 C8 **Ulong** *var.* Aulong. *island* Palau Islands, N Palau
83 N14 **Ulonguè** *var.* Ulongwé. Tete, NW Mozambique 14°34′S 34°21′E
Ulongwé *see* Ulonguè
95 K19 **Ulricehamn** Västra Götaland, S Sweden 57°47′N 13°25′E
98 N5 **Ulrum** Groningen, NE Netherlands 53°24′N 06°20′E
163 Z16 **Ulsan** *Jap.* Urusan. SE South Korea 35°33′N 129°19′E
94 D10 **Ulsteinvik** Møre og Romsdal, S Norway 62°21′N 05°53′E
97 D15 **Ulster** ◆ *province* Northern Ireland, United Kingdom/Ireland
171 Q10 **Ulu** Pulau Siau, N Indonesia 02°46′N 125°22′E
123 Q11 **Ulu** Respublika Sakha (Yakutiya), NE Russian Federation 60°18′N 127°27′E
42 H5 **Ulúa, Río** ≈ NW Honduras
136 D12 **Ulubat Gölü** ⊚ NW Turkey
136 E12 **Uludağ** ▲ NW Turkey 40°08′N 29°13′E
158 D7 **Ulugqat** Xinjiang Uygur Zizhiqu, W China 39°45′N 74°10′E
136 J16 **Ulukışla** Niğde, S Turkey 37°33′N 34°29′E
189 O15 **Ulul** *island* Caroline Islands, C Micronesia
83 L22 **Ulundi** KwaZulu/Natal, E South Africa 28°18′S 31°26′E
158 M3 **Ulungur He** ≈ NW China
158 K2 **Ulungur Hu** ⊚ NW China
181 P8 **Uluru** *var.* Ayers Rock. *monolith* Northern Territory, C Australia
97 K16 **Ulverston** NW England, United Kingdom 54°13′N 03°08′W
183 O16 **Ulverstone** Tasmania, SE Australia 41°09′S 146°10′E
94 D13 **Ulvik** Hordaland, S Norway 60°34′N 06°53′E
93 J18 **Ulvila** Länsi-Suomi, W Finland 61°26′N 21°55′E
117 O8 **Ul'yanivka** *Rus.* Ul'yanovka. Kirovohrads'ka Oblast', C Ukraine 48°18′N 30°15′E
Ul'yanovka *see* Ul'yanivka
127 Q5 **Ul'yanovsk** *prev.* Simbirsk. Ul'yanovskaya Oblast', W Russian Federation 54°17′N 48°21′E
127 Q5 **Ul'yanovskaya Oblast'** ◆ *province* W Russian Federation
145 S10 **Ul'yanovskiy** Karaganda, C Kazakhstan 50°05′N 73°45′E
Ul'yanovskiy Kanal *see* Ul'yanow Kanali
146 M13 **Ul'yanow Kanali** *Rus.* Ul'yanovskiy Kanal. *canal* Turkmenistan/Uzbekistan
Ulyshylanshyq *see* Uly-Zhylanshyk
26 H6 **Ulysses** Kansas, C USA 37°36′N 101°23′W
145 O12 **Ulytau, Gory** ▲ C Kazakhstan
145 N11 **Uly-Zhylanshyk** *Kaz.* Ulyshylanshyq. ≈ C Kazakhstan
112 A9 **Umag** *It.* Umago. Istra, NW Croatia 45°25′N 13°32′E
Umago *see* Umag
41 W12 **Umán** Yucatán, SE Mexico 20°51′N 89°43′W
117 O7 **Uman'** *Rus.* Uman. Cherkas'ka Oblast', C Ukraine 48°45′N 30°10′E
189 V13 **Uman** *atoll* Chuuk Islands, C Micronesia
Uman *see* Uman'
Umanak/Umanaq *see* Uummannaq
'Umān, Khalīj *see* Oman, Gulf of
'Umān, Salṭanat *see* Oman
154 K10 **Umaria** Madhya Pradesh, C India 23°34′N 80°49′E
149 R16 **Umarkot** Sind, SE Pakistan 25°22′N 69°48′E
188 B17 **Umatac** SW Guam 13°17′N 144°40′E
188 A17 **Umatac Bay** *bay* SW Guam
139 S6 **Umayqah** Şalāḥ ad Dīn, C Iraq 34°32′N 43°45′E
124 J5 **Umba** Murmanskaya Oblast', NW Russian Federation 66°39′N 34°24′E
138 I8 **Umbāshī, Khirbat al** *ruins* As Suwaydā', S Syria
80 A12 **Umbelasha** ≈ W Sudan
106 H12 **Umbertide** Umbria, C Italy 43°16′N 12°21′E
61 B17 **Umberto** *var.* Humberto. Santa Fe, C Argentina 30°52′S 61°19′W
186 E7 **Umboi Island** *var.* Rooke Island. *island* C Papua New Guinea
124 J4 **Umbozero, Ozero** ⊚ NW Russian Federation
106 H13 **Umbria** ◆ *region* C Italy
Umbrian-Machigian Mountains *see* Umbro-Marchigiano, Appennino
106 I12 **Umbro-Marchigiano, Appennino** *Eng.* Umbrian-Machigian Mountains. ▲▲ C Italy
93 J16 **Umeå** Västerbotten, N Sweden 63°50′N 20°15′E
93 H14 **Umeälven** ≈ N Sweden
39 Q5 **Umiat** Alaska, USA 69°22′N 152°09′W
83 K23 **Umlazi** KwaZulu/Natal, E South Africa 29°58′S 30°50′E
139 X10 **Umm al Baqar, Hawr** *var.* Birkat ad Dawaymah. *spring* S Iraq
139 Q5 **Umm al Faṭūr** *var.* Umm al Tūz. Şalāḥ ad Dīn, C Iraq 34°53′N 42°42′E
141 U12 **Umm al Ḥayt, Wādī** *var.* Wādī Amilḥayt. *seasonal river* SW Oman
Umm al Qaiwain *see* Umm al Qaywayn
143 R15 **Umm al Qaywayn** *var.* Umm al Qaiwain. Umm al Qaywayn, NE United Arab Emirates 25°43′N 55°55′E
Umm al Tūz *see* Umm al Faṭūr
138 J3 **Umm 'Āmūd** Ḥalab, N Syria 35°57′N 37°39′E
141 Y10 **Umm ar Ruşāş** *var.* Umm Ruşayş. W Oman 20°26′N 58°48′E
141 X9 **Ummas Samīn** *salt flat* C Oman

◆ Country
● Country Capital
◇ Dependent Territory
○ Dependent Territory Capital
◆ Administrative Regions
✈ International Airport
▲ Mountain
▲▲ Mountain Range
⩚ Volcano
≈ River
⊚ Lake
⊠ Reservoir

141 V9 **Umm az Zumūl** *oasis* E Saudi Arabia
80 A9 **Umm Buru** Western Darfur, W Sudan 15°01′N 23°36′E
80 A12 **Umm Dafag** Southern Darfur, W Sudan 10°28′N 23°20′E
Umm Durmān *see* Omdurman
138 F9 **Umm el Fahm** Haifa, N Israel 32°30′N 35°06′E
80 F9 **Umm Inderab** Northern Kordofan, C Sudan 15°12′N 31°54′E
80 C10 **Umm Keddada** Northern Darfur, W Sudan 13°36′N 26°42′E
140 J7 **Umm Lajj** Tabūk, W Saudi Arabia 25°02′N 37°19′E
138 L10 **Umm Maḥfur** ≈ N Jordan
139 Y13 **Umm Qaṣr** Al Baṣrah, SE Iraq 30°02′N 47°55′E
Umm Ruṣayṣ *see* Umm ar Ruṣāṣ
80 F11 **Umm Ruwaba** *var.* Umm Ruwābah, Um Ruwāba. Northern Kordofan, C Sudan 12°54′N 31°13′E
Umm Ruwābah *see* Umm Ruwaba
143 N16 **Umm Saʿīd** *var.* Musayʿīd. S Qatar 24°57′N 51°32′E
139 Y10 **Umm Sawān, Hawr** ◎ S Iraq
138 K10 **Umm Ṭuways, Wādī** *dry watercourse* N Jordan
38 J17 **Umnak Island** *island* Aleutian Islands, Alaska, USA
32 F13 **Umpqua River** ≈ Oregon, NW USA
82 D13 **Umpulo** Bié, C Angola 12°43′S 17°42′E
154 I12 **Umred** Mahārāshtra, C India 20°54′N 79°19′E
Um Ruwāba *see* Umm Ruwaba
Umtali *see* Mutare
83 J24 **Umtata** Eastern Cape, SE South Africa 31°33′S 28°47′E
77 V17 **Umuahia** Abia, SW Nigeria 05°30′N 07°33′E
60 H10 **Umuarama** Paraná, S Brazil 23°45′S 53°20′W
Umvuma *see* Mvuma
83 K18 **Umzingwani** ≈ S Zimbabwe
112 D11 **Una** ≈ Bosnia and Herzegovina/Croatia
Una *see* Unna
112 E12 **Unac** ≈ W Bosnia and Herzegovina
23 T6 **Unadilla** Georgia, SE USA 32°15′N 83°44′W
18 I10 **Unadilla River** ≈ New York, NE USA
59 L18 **Unaí** Minas Gerais, SE Brazil 16°24′S 46°49′W
39 N10 **Unalakleet** Alaska, USA 63°52′N 160°47′W
38 K17 **Unalaska Island** *island* Aleutian Islands, Alaska, USA
185 I16 **Una, Mount** ▲ South Island, New Zealand 42°12′S 172°34′E
82 N13 **Unango** Niassa, N Mozambique 12°45′S 35°28′E
Unao *see* Unnāo
92 L12 **Unari** Lappi, N Finland 67°07′N 25°37′E
141 O6 **ʿUnayzah** *var.* Anaiza. Al Qaṣīm, C Saudi Arabia 26°03′N 44°00′E
138 L10 **ʿUnayzah, Jabal** ▲ Jordan/Saudi Arabia 32°09′N 39°11′E
Unci *see* Almería
57 K19 **Uncía** Potosí, C Bolivia 18°30′S 66°29′W
37 Q7 **Uncompahgre Peak** ▲ Colorado, C USA 38°04′N 107°27′W
37 P6 **Uncompahgre Plateau** *plain* Colorado, C USA
95 L17 **Unden** ◎ S Sweden
28 M4 **Underwood** North Dakota, N USA 47°25′N 101°09′W
171 T13 **Undur** Pulau Seram, E Indonesia 03°41′S 130°38′E
Undur Khan *see* Öndörhaan
126 H6 **Unecha** Bryanskaya Oblast', W Russian Federation 52°51′N 32°38′E
39 N16 **Unga** Unga Island, Alaska, USA 55°14′N 160°34′W
Ungaria *see* Hungary
183 P8 **Ungarie** New South Wales, SE Australia 33°39′S 146°54′E
Ungarisch-Brod *see* Uherský Brod
Ungarisches Erzgebirge *see* Slovenské rudohorie
Ungarisch-Hradisch *see* Uherské Hradiště
Ungarn *see* Hungary
12 M4 **Ungava Bay** *bay* Québec, E Canada
12 J2 **Ungava, Péninsule d'** *peninsula* Québec, SE Canada
Ungeny *see* Ungheni
116 M9 **Ungheni** *Rus.* Ungeny. W Moldova 47°13′N 27°48′E
Unguja *see* Zanzibar
146 G10 **Üngüz Angyrsyndaky Garagum** *Rus.* Zaunguzskiye Garagumy. *desert* N Turkmenistan
146 H11 **Unguz, Solonchakovyye Vpadiny** *salt marsh* C Turkmenistan
Ungvár *see* Uzhhorod
60 I12 **União da Vitória** Paraná, S Brazil 26°13′S 51°05′W
111 G17 **Uničov** *Ger.* Mährisch-Neustadt. Olomoucký Kraj, E Czech Republic 49°48′N 17°05′E
110 J12 **Uniejów** Łódzkie, C Poland 51°58′N 18°46′E
112 A11 **Unije** *island* W Croatia
38 L16 **Unimak Island** *island* Aleutian Islands, Alaska, USA
38 L16 **Unimak Pass** *strait* Aleutian Islands, Alaska, USA
62 J12 **Unión** San Luis, C Argentina 35°09′S 65°55′W
27 W5 **Union** Missouri, C USA 38°27′N 91°01′W
32 L12 **Union** Oregon, NW USA 45°12′N 117°51′W
21 Q11 **Union** South Carolina, SE USA 34°42′N 81°37′W
21 R6 **Union** West Virginia, NE USA 37°36′N 80°34′W
61 B25 **Unión, Bahía** *bay* E Argentina
31 Q13 **Union City** Indiana, N USA 40°12′N 84°50′W
31 Q10 **Union City** Michigan, N USA 42°03′N 85°06′W
18 C12 **Union City** Pennsylvania, NE USA 41°54′N 79°51′W
20 G8 **Union City** Tennessee, S USA 36°26′N 89°03′W
32 G14 **Union Creek** Oregon, NW USA 42°54′N 122°26′W
83 G25 **Uniondale** Western Cape, SW South Africa 33°40′S 23°07′E
40 K13 **Unión de Tula** Jalisco, SW Mexico 19°58′N 104°16′W
30 M9 **Union Grove** Wisconsin, N USA 42°39′N 88°03′W
45 Y15 **Union Island** *island* S Saint Vincent and the Grenadines
Union of Myanmar *see* Burma
46 K5 **Union Reefs** *reef* SW Mexico
0 D7 **Union Seamount** *undersea feature* NE Pacific Ocean 49°35′N 132°45′W
23 Q6 **Union Springs** Alabama, S USA 32°08′N 85°43′W
20 H6 **Uniontown** Kentucky, S USA 37°46′N 87°55′W
18 C16 **Uniontown** Pennsylvania, NE USA 39°54′N 79°44′W
27 T1 **Unionville** Missouri, C USA 40°28′N 93°00′W
141 V8 **United Arab Emirates** *Ar.* Al Imārāt al ʿArabīyah al Muttaḥidah, *abbrev.* UAE; *prev.* Trucial States. ◆ *federation* SW Asia
United Arab Republic *see* Egypt
97 H14 **United Kingdom** *off.* United Kingdom of Great Britain and Northern Ireland, *abbrev.* UK. ◆ *monarchy* NW Europe
United Kingdom of Great Britain and Northern Ireland *see* United Kingdom
United Mexican States *see* Mexico
United Provinces *see* Uttar Pradesh
16 L10 **United States of America** *off.* United States of America, *var.* America, The States, *abbrev.* U.S., USA. ◆ *federal republic* North America
United States of America *see* United States of America
124 J10 **Unitsa** Respublika Kareliya, NW Russian Federation 62°31′N 34°31′E
11 S15 **Unity** Saskatchewan, S Canada 52°27′N 109°10′W
Unity State *see* Wahda
105 Q8 **Universales, Montes** ▲▲ C Spain
27 X4 **University City** Missouri, C USA 38°40′N 90°19′W
187 Q13 **Unmet** Malekula, C Vanuatu 16°09′S 167°16′E
101 F15 **Unna** Nordrhein-Westfalen, W Germany 51°32′N 07°41′E
152 H8 **Unna** *var.* Una. Uttarakhand, N India 31°27′N 76°16′E
Unnan *see* Kisuki
152 L12 **Unnão** *prev.* Unao. Uttar Pradesh, N India 26°32′N 80°30′E
187 R15 **Unpongkor** Erromango, S Vanuatu 18°48′S 169°01′E
Unruhstadt *see* Kargowa
96 M1 **Unst** *island* NE Scotland, United Kingdom
101 K16 **Unstrut** ≈ C Germany
Unterdrauburg *see* Dravograd
Unterlimbach *see* Lendava
101 L23 **Unterschleissheim** Bayern, SE Germany 48°16′N 11°34′E
101 H24 **Untersee** ◎ Germany/Switzerland
100 O10 **Unterueckersee** ◎ NE Germany
108 F9 **Unterwalden** ◐ *canton* C Switzerland
55 N12 **Unturán, Sierra de** ▲▲ Brazil/Venezuela
159 N11 **Unuli Horog** Qinghai, W China 35°10′N 91°50′E
136 M11 **Ünye** Ordu, W Turkey 41°08′N 37°14′E
Unza *see* Unzha
125 O14 **Unzha** *var.* Unza. ≈ NW Russian Federation
79 E17 **Uolo, Río** *var.* Eyo (lower course), Mbini, Uele (upper course), Woleu; *prev.* Benito. ≈ Equatorial Guinea/Gabon
55 Q10 **Uonán** Bolívar, SE Venezuela 04°33′N 62°10′W
161 T12 **Uotsuri-shima** *island* China/Japan/Taiwan
165 M11 **Uozu** Toyama, Honshū, SW Japan 36°50′N 137°25′E
42 L12 **Upala** Alajuela, NW Costa Rica 10°52′N 85°W
55 P7 **Upata** Bolívar, E Venezuela 08°02′N 62°25′W
79 M23 **Upemba, Lac** ◎ SE Dem. Rep. Congo
197 O12 **Upernavik** *var.* Upernivik. Kitaa, C Greenland 73°06′N 55°42′W
Upernivik *see* Upernavik
83 F22 **Upington** Northern Cape, W South Africa 28°28′S 21°14′E
Uplands *see* Ottawa
192 I16 **ʿUpolu** *island* SE Samoa
38 G11 **ʿUpolu Point** *var.* Upolu Point. *headland* Hawaiʿi, USA, C Pacific Ocean 20°15′N 155°51′W
Upper Austria *see* Oberösterreich
Upper Bann *see* Bann
14 M13 **Upper Canada Village** *tourist site* Ontario, SE Canada
18 I16 **Upper Darby** Pennsylvania, NE USA 39°57′N 75°15′W
28 L2 **Upper Des Lacs Lake** ⊠ North Dakota, N USA
185 L14 **Upper Hutt** Wellington, North Island, New Zealand 41°06′S 175°06′E
29 X11 **Upper Iowa River** ≈ Iowa, C USA
32 H15 **Upper Klamath Lake** ◎ Oregon, NW USA
34 M6 **Upper Lake** California, W USA 39°07′N 122°53′W
35 Q1 **Upper Lake** ◎ California, W USA
10 K9 **Upper Liard** Yukon Territory, W Canada 60°01′N 128°59′W
97 E16 **Upper Lough Erne** ◎ SW Northern Ireland, United Kingdom
80 F12 **Upper Nile** ◐ *state* E Sudan
29 T3 **Upper Red Lake** ◎ Minnesota, N USA
31 S12 **Upper Sandusky** Ohio, N USA 40°49′N 83°16′W
Upper Volta *see* Burkina
95 O15 **Upplandsväsby** *var.* Upplands Väsby. Stockholm, C Sweden 59°29′N 18°04′E
Upplands Väsby *see* Upplandsväsby
95 O15 **Uppsala** Uppsala, C Sweden 59°52′N 17°38′E
95 O14 **Uppsala** ◐ *county* C Sweden
38 J12 **Upright Cape** *headland* Saint Matthew Island, Alaska, USA 60°19′N 172°15′W
20 K6 **Upton** Kentucky, S USA 37°25′N 85°53′W
33 Y13 **Upton** Wyoming, C USA 44°06′N 104°37′W
141 N7 **ʿUqlat aṣ Ṣuqūr** Al Qaṣīm, W Saudi Arabia 25°51′N 42°13′E
Uqsuqtuuq *see* Gjoa Haven
Uqturpan *see* Wushi
54 C7 **Urabá, Golfo de** *gulf* NW Colombia
Uracas *see* Farallon de Pajaros
uradqianqi *see* Wulashan, N China
Uradar'ya *see* Oʻradaryo
Urad Qianqi *see* Xishanzui, N China
165 U5 **Urahoro** Hokkaidō, NE Japan 42°47′N 143°41′E
165 T5 **Urakawa** Hokkaidō, NE Japan 42°11′N 142°42′E
127 X6 **Ural** *Kaz.* Zayyq. ≈ Kazakhstan/Russian Federation
183 T6 **Uralla** New South Wales, SE Australia 30°39′S 151°30′E
Ural Mountains *see* Ural'skiye Gory
144 F8 **Ural'sk** *Kaz.* Oral. Zapadnyy Kazakhstan, NW Kazakhstan 51°12′N 51°17′E
Ural'skaya Oblast' *see* Zapadnyy Kazakhstan
127 W5 **Ural'skiye Gory** *var.* Ural'skiy Khrebet, *Eng.* Ural Mountains. ▲▲ Kazakhstan/Russian Federation
Ural'skiy Khrebet *see* Ural'skiye Gory
138 I3 **Urām aṣ Ṣughrá** Ḥalab, N Syria 36°10′N 36°55′E
183 P10 **Urana** New South Wales, SE Australia 35°22′S 146°16′E
11 S10 **Uranium City** Saskatchewan, C Canada 59°30′N 108°46′W
58 F10 **Uraricoera** Roraima, N Brazil 03°26′N 60°54′W
47 S5 **Uraricoera, Rio** ≈ N Brazil
Ura-Tyube *see* Ŭroteppa
165 O13 **Urawa** *var.* Saitama. Saitama, Honshū, S Japan 35°52′N 139°40′E
122 H10 **Uray** Khanty-Mansiyskiy Avtonomnyy Okrug-Yugra, C Russian Federation 60°07′N 64°38′E
141 R7 **ʿUrayʿirah** Ash Sharqīyah, E Saudi Arabia 25°59′N 48°52′E
30 M13 **Urbana** Illinois, N USA 40°06′N 88°12′W
31 R13 **Urbana** Ohio, N USA 40°04′N 83°46′W
29 V14 **Urbandale** Iowa, C USA 41°37′N 93°42′W
106 I11 **Urbania** Marche, C Italy 43°40′N 12°33′E
106 I11 **Urbino** Marche, C Italy 43°45′N 12°38′E
57 H16 **Urcos** Cusco, S Peru 13°40′S 71°38′W
144 D10 **Urda** Zapadnyy Kazakhstan, W Kazakhstan 48°52′N 47°31′E
105 N10 **Urda** Castilla-La Mancha, C Spain 39°25′N 03°43′W
Urdgol *see* Chandmanī
105 O3 **Urduña** *var.* Orduña. País Vasco, N Spain 43°00′N 03°00′W
Urdunn *see* Jordan
145 X12 **Urdzhar** *Kaz.* Ürzhar. Vostochnyy Kazakhstan, E Kazakhstan 47°06′N 81°33′E
97 L16 **Ure** ≈ N England, United Kingdom
119 K18 **Urechcha** *Rus.* Urech'ye. Minskaya Voblasts', S Belarus 52°57′N 27°54′E
Urech'ye *see* Urechcha
127 P2 **Uren'** Nizhegorodskaya Oblast', W Russian Federation 57°30′N 45°48′E
122 J9 **Urengoy** Yamalo-Nenetskiy Avtonomnyy Okrug, N Russian Federation 65°52′N 78°42′E
184 K10 **Urenui** Taranaki, North Island, New Zealand 38°59′S 174°25′E
187 Q12 **Ureparapara** *island* Banks Islands, N Vanuatu
40 G5 **Ures** Sonora, NW Mexico 29°26′N 110°24′W
Urfa *see* Şanlıurfa
Urga *see* Ulaanbaatar
162 F6 **Urgamal** *var.* Hungiy. Dzavhan, W Mongolia 48°31′N 94°15′E
146 H9 **Urganch** *Rus.* Urgench; *prev.* Novo-Urgench. Xorazm Viloyati, W Uzbekistan 41°40′N 60°32′E
Urgench *see* Urganch
136 J14 **Ürgüp** Nevşehir, C Turkey 38°39′N 34°55′E
147 O12 **Urgut** Samarqand Viloyati, C Uzbekistan 39°26′N 67°15′E
158 K3 **Urho** Xinjiang Uygur Zizhiqu, W China 46°05′N 84°51′E
152 G5 **Uri** Jammu and Kashmir, NW India 34°05′N 74°03′E
108 G9 **Uri** ◐ *canton* C Switzerland
54 F11 **Uribe** Meta, C Colombia 03°01′N 74°33′W
54 H4 **Uribia** La Guajira, N Colombia 11°45′N 72°19′W
116 G12 **Uricani** *Hung.* Hobicaurikány. Hunedoara, SW Romania 45°18′N 23°03′E
57 M21 **Uriondo** Tarija, S Bolivia 21°43′S 64°40′W
40 I7 **Urique** Chihuahua, N Mexico 27°16′N 107°51′W
40 I7 **Urique, Río** ≈ N Mexico
56 E9 **Urityacu, Río** ≈ N Peru
Uritskiy *see* Sarykol'
98 K8 **Urk** Flevoland, N Netherlands 52°40′N 05°35′E
136 B14 **Urla** İzmir, W Turkey 38°19′N 26°47′E
116 K13 **Urlaţi** Prahova, SE Romania 44°59′N 26°15′E
127 V4 **Urman** Respublika Bashkortostan, W Russian Federation 54°53′N 56°52′E
147 P12 **Urmetan** W Tajikistan 39°27′N 68°13′E
Urmia *see* Orūmīyeh
Urmia, Lake *see* Orūmīyeh, Daryācheh-ye
Urmiyeh *see* Orūmīyeh
Uroševac *see* Ferizaj
147 P11 **Ŭroteppa** *Rus.* Ura-Tyube. NW Tajikistan 39°55′N 68°57′E
54 D8 **Urrao** Antioquia, W Colombia 06°16′N 76°10′W
Ursat'yevskaya *see* Xovos
Urt *see* Gurvantes
127 X7 **Urtazym** Orenburgskaya Oblast', W Russian Federation 52°12′N 58°48′E
59 K18 **Uruaçu** Goiás, C Brazil 14°38′S 49°06′W
40 M14 **Uruapan** *var.* Uruapan del Progreso. Michoacán, SW Mexico 19°26′N 102°04′W
Uruapan del Progreso *see* Uruapan
57 G15 **Urubamba, Cordillera** ▲▲ C Peru
57 G14 **Urubamba, Río** ≈ C Peru
58 G12 **Urucará** Amazonas, N Brazil 02°30′S 57°45′W
61 E16 **Uruguaiana** Rio Grande do Sul, S Brazil 29°45′S 57°05′W
Uruguai, Rio *see* Uruguay
61 E18 **Uruguay** *off.* Oriental Republic of Uruguay; *prev.* La Banda Oriental. ◆ *republic* E South America
61 E15 **Uruguay** *var.* Rio Uruguai, Río Uruguay. ≈ E South America
Uruguay, Oriental Republic of *see* Uruguay
Uruguay, Río *see* Uruguay
Urukthapel *see* Ngeruktabel
Urumchi *see* Ürümqi
Urumi Yeh *see* Orūmīyeh, Daryācheh-ye
158 L5 **Ürümqi** *var.* Tihwa, Urumchi, Urumqi, Urumtsi, Wu-lu-k'o-mu-shi, Wu-lu-mu-ch'i; *prev.* Ti-hua. Xinjiang Uygur Zizhiqu, NW China 43°52′N 87°31′E
Urumtsi *see* Ürümqi
Urundi *see* Burundi
183 V6 **Urunga** New South Wales, SE Australia 30°33′S 152°58′E
188 C15 **Uruno Point** *headland* NW Guam 13°37′N 144°50′E
123 U13 **Urup, Ostrov** *island* Kuril'skiye Ostrova, SE Russian Federation
141 P11 **ʿUruq al Mawārid** *desert* S Saudi Arabia
Urusan *see* Ulsan
127 O16 **Urus-Martan** Chechenskaya Respublika, SW Russian Federation 43°08′N 45°33′E
127 T5 **Urussu** Respublika Tatarstan, W Russian Federation 54°34′N 53°23′E
184 K10 **Uruti** Taranaki, North Island, New Zealand 38°57′S 174°32′E
57 K19 **Uru Uru, Lago** ◎ W Bolivia
55 P9 **Uruyén** Bolívar, SE Venezuela 05°40′N 62°26′W
Ürūzgān *see* Orūzgān
165 T3 **Uryū-gawa** ≈ Hokkaidō, NE Japan
165 T2 **Uryū-ko** ◎ Hokkaidō, NE Japan
127 N8 **Uryupinsk** Volgogradskaya Oblast', SW Russian Federation 50°51′N 41°59′E
Ürzhar *see* Urdzhar
125 R16 **Urzhum** Kirovskaya Oblast', NW Russian Federation 57°09′N 49°56′E
116 K13 **Urziceni** Ialomiţa, SE Romania 44°43′N 26°39′E
164 E14 **Usa** Ōita, Kyūshū, SW Japan 33°31′N 131°22′E
119 L16 **Usa** ≈ C Belarus
125 T6 **Usa** ≈ NW Russian Federation
136 E14 **Uşak** *prev.* Ushak. Uşak, W Turkey 38°42′N 29°25′E
136 D14 **Uşak** *var.* Ushak. ◐ *province* W Turkey
83 C19 **Usakos** Erongo, W Namibia 22°01′S 15°32′E
81 J21 **Usambara Mountains** ▲▲ NE Tanzania
81 G23 **Usangu Flats** *wetland* SW Tanzania
65 D24 **Usborne, Mount** ▲ East Falkland, Falkland Islands 51°35′S 58°57′W
100 O8 **Usedom** *island* NE Germany
99 M24 **Useldange** Diekirch, C Luxembourg 49°47′N 05°59′E
Ushachi *see* Ushachy
118 L13 **Ushachy** *Rus.* Ushachi. Vitsyebskaya Voblasts', N Belarus 55°11′N 28°37′E
Ushak *see* Uşak
122 L4 **Ushakova, Ostrov** *island* Severnaya Zemlya, N Russian Federation
Ushant *see* Ouessant, Île d'
Üsharal *see* Ucharal
164 B15 **Ushibuka** *var.* Usibuka. Kumamoto, Shimo-jima, SW Japan 32°12′N 130°00′E
Ushi Point *see* Sabaneta, Puntan
145 V14 **Ushtobe** *Kaz.* Üshtöbe. Almaty, SE Kazakhstan 45°15′N 77°59′E
Üshtöbe *see* Ushtobe
63 I25 **Ushuaia** Tierra del Fuego, S Argentina 54°48′S 68°19′W
39 R10 **Usibelli** Alaska, USA 63°54′N 148°41′W
Usibuka *see* Ushibuka
186 D7 **Usino** Madang, N Papua New Guinea 05°40′S 145°31′E
125 U6 **Usinsk** Respublika Komi, NW Russian Federation 66°01′N 57°37′E
97 K22 **Usk** *Wel.* Wysg. ≈ SE Wales, United Kingdom
Uskočke Planine/Uskokengebirge *see* Gorjanci
Uskoplje *see* Gornji Vakuf
Üsküb/Üsküp *see* Skopje
114 M11 **Üsküpdere** Kırklareli, NW Turkey 41°41′N 27°21′E
126 L7 **Usman'** Lipetskaya Oblast', W Russian Federation 52°04′N 39°41′E
118 D8 **Usmas Ezers** ◎ NW Latvia
125 U13 **Usol'ye** Permskaya Oblast', NW Russian Federation 59°27′N 56°33′E
41 T16 **Uspanapa, Río** ≈ SE Mexico
145 R11 **Uspenskiy** Karaganda, C Kazakhstan 48°45′N 72°46′E
103 O11 **Ussel** Corrèze, C France 45°33′N 02°18′E
163 Z6 **Ussuri** *var.* Usuri, Wusuri, *Chin.* Wusuli Jiang. ≈ China/Russian Federation
123 S15 **Ussuriysk** *prev.* Nikol'sk, Nikol'sk-Ussuriyskiy, Voroshilov. Primorskiy Kray, SE Russian Federation 43°48′N 131°59′E
136 J10 **Usta Burnu** *headland* N Turkey 41°58′N 34°30′E
149 P13 **Usta Muhammad** Baluchistān, SW Pakistan 28°07′N 68°00′E
123 V11 **Ust'-Bol'sheretsk** Kamchatskaya Oblast', E Russian Federation 52°48′N 156°12′E
127 N9 **Ust'-Buzulukskaya** Volgogradskaya Oblast', SW Russian Federation 50°12′N 42°06′E
111 C16 **Ustecký Kraj** ◐ *region* NW Czech Republic
108 G7 **Uster** Zürich, NE Switzerland 47°21′N 08°49′E
107 I22 **Ustica, Isola d'** *island* S Italy
122 M11 **Ust'-Ilimsk** Irkutskaya Oblast', C Russian Federation 57°57′N 102°30′E
111 C15 **Ústí nad Labem** *Ger.* Aussig. Ústecký Kraj, NW Czech Republic 50°41′N 14°04′E
111 F17 **Ústí nad Orlicí** *Ger.* Wildenschwert. Pardubický Kraj, C Czech Republic 49°58′N 16°24′E
Ustinov *see* Izhevsk
113 J14 **Ustiprača** ◐ Republika Srpska, SE Bosnia and Herzegovina
122 H11 **Ust'-Ishim** Omskaya Oblast', C Russian Federation 57°42′N 70°58′E
110 G6 **Ustka** *Ger.* Stolpmünde. Pomorskie, N Poland 54°35′N 16°50′E
123 V9 **Ust'-Kamchatsk** Kamchatskaya Oblast', E Russian Federation 56°14′N 162°28′E
145 X9 **Ust'-Kamenogorsk** *Kaz.* Öskemen. Vostochnyy Kazakhstan, E Kazakhstan 49°58′N 82°36′E
123 T10 **Ust'-Khayryuzovo** Koryakskiy Avtonomnyy Okrug, E Russian Federation 57°07′N 156°37′E
122 I14 **Ust'-Koksa** Respublika Altay, S Russian Federation 50°15′N 85°45′E
125 S11 **Ust'-Kulom** Respublika Komi, NW Russian Federation 61°42′N 53°42′E
123 Q8 **Ust'-Kuyga** Respublika Sakha (Yakutiya), NE Russian Federation 69°59′N 135°27′E
126 L14 **Ust'-Labinsk** Krasnodarskiy Kray, SW Russian Federation 44°40′N 40°46′E
123 R10 **Ust'-Maya** Respublika Sakha (Yakutiya), NE Russian Federation 60°27′N 134°28′E
123 R9 **Ust'-Nera** Respublika Sakha (Yakutiya), NE Russian Federation 64°28′N 143°01′E
123 P12 **Ust'-Nyukzha** Amurskaya Oblast', S Russian Federation 56°30′N 121°32′E
123 O7 **Ust'-Olenëk** Respublika Sakha (Yakutiya), NE Russian Federation 73°03′N 119°34′E
123 T9 **Ust'-Omchug** Magadanskaya Oblast', E Russian Federation 61°07′N 149°17′E
122 M13 **Ust'-Ordynskiy** Ust'-Ordynskiy Buryatskiy Avtonomnyy Okrug, S Russian Federation 52°50′N 104°42′E
122 M13 **Ust'-Ordynskiy Buryatskiy Avtonomnyy Okrug** ◐ *autonomous district* S Russian Federation
125 N8 **Ust'-Pinega** Arkhangel'skaya Oblast', NW Russian Federation 64°09′N 41°55′E
122 K8 **Ust'-Port** Taymyrskiy (Dolgano-Nenetskiy) Avtonomnyy Okrug, N Russian Federation 69°42′N 84°25′E
114 L11 **Ustrem** *prev.* Vakav. Yambol, E Bulgaria 42°01′N 26°28′E
111 O18 **Ustrzyki Dolne** Podkarpackie, SE Poland 49°26′N 22°36′E
Ust'-Sysol'sk *see* Syktyvkar
125 R7 **Ust'-Tsil'ma** Respublika Komi, NW Russian Federation 65°25′N 52°09′E
Ust Urt *see* Ustyurt Plateau
125 O11 **Ust'ya** ≈ NW Russian Federation
124 K6 **Ust'ye Varzugi** Murmanskaya Oblast', NW Russian Federation 66°16′N 36°47′E
123 V10 **Ust'yevoye** *prev.* Kirovskiy. Kamchatskaya Oblast', E Russian Federation 54°06′N 155°48′E
117 R8 **Ustynivka** Kirovohrads'ka Oblast', C Ukraine 47°58′N 32°32′E
144 H15 **Ustyurt Plateau** *var.* Ust Urt, *Uzb.* Ustyurt Platosi. *plateau* Kazakhstan/Uzbekistan
Ustyurt Platosi *see* Ustyurt Plateau
124 K14 **Ustyuzhna** Vologodskaya Oblast', NW Russian Federation 58°50′N 36°25′E
158 J4 **Usu** Xinjiang Uygur Zizhiqu, NW China 44°27′N 84°37′E
171 O13 **Usu** Sulawesi, C Indonesia 02°34′S 120°58′E
164 E14 **Usuki** Ōita, Kyūshū, SW Japan 33°07′N 131°48′E
42 G8 **Usulután** Usulután, SE El Salvador 13°20′N 88°26′W
42 B9 **Usulután** ◐ *department* SE El Salvador
41 W16 **Usumacinta, Río** ≈ Guatemala/Mexico
Usumbura *see* Bujumbura
Usuri *see* Ussuri
U.S./USA *see* United States of America
171 W14 **Uta** Papua, E Indonesia 04°28′S 136°03′E
36 K5 **Utah** *off.* State of Utah, *also known as* Beehive State, Mormon State. ◐ *state* W USA
36 L3 **Utah Lake** ◎ Utah, W USA
Utaidhani *see* Uthai Thani
93 M14 **Utajärvi** Oulu, C Finland 64°45′N 26°25′E
Utamboni *see* Mitemele, Río
Utaradit *see* Uttaradit
165 T3 **Utashinai** *var.* Utasinai. Hokkaidō, NE Japan 43°32′N 142°03′E
Utasinai *see* Utashinai
193 Y14 **ʿUta Vavaʿu** *island* Vavaʿu Group, N Tonga
37 V9 **Ute Creek** ≈ New Mexico, SW USA
118 H12 **Utena** Utena, E Lithuania 55°30′N 25°34′E
118 H12 **Utena** ◐ *province* Lithuania
37 V10 **Ute Reservoir** ⊠ New Mexico, SW USA
167 O10 **Uthai Thani** *var.* Muang Uthai Thani, Udayadhani, Utaidhani. Uthai Thani, W Thailand 15°22′N 100°03′E
149 O15 **Uthal** Baluchistān, SW Pakistan 25°53′N 66°37′E
18 I10 **Utica** New York, NE USA 43°06′N 75°15′W
105 R10 **Utiel** País Valenciano, E Spain 39°33′N 01°13′W
11 O13 **Utikuma Lake** ◎ Alberta, W Canada
42 I4 **Utila, Isla de** *island* Islas de la Bahía, N Honduras
Utina *see* Udine
59 O17 **Utinga** Bahia, E Brazil 12°05′S 41°07′W
Utirik *see* Utrik Atoll
95 M22 **Utlängan** *island* S Sweden
117 U11 **Utlyuts'kyy Lyman** *bay* S Ukraine
95 P16 **Utö** Stockholm, C Sweden 58°55′N 18°19′E
25 Q12 **Utopia** Texas, SW USA 29°30′N 99°31′W
98 J11 **Utrecht** *Lat.* Trajectum ad Rhenum. Utrecht, C Netherlands 52°06′N 05°07′E
83 K22 **Utrecht** KwaZulu/Natal, E South Africa 27°40′S 30°20′E
98 I11 **Utrecht** ◐ *province* C Netherlands
104 K14 **Utrera** Andalucía, S Spain 37°10′N 05°47′W
189 V4 **Utrik Atoll** *var.* Utirik, Utrōk, Utrōnk. *atoll* Ratak Chain, N Marshall Islands
Utrōk/Utrōnk *see* Utrik Atoll
95 B16 **Utsira** *island* SW Norway
92 L8 **Utsjoki** *var.* Ohcejohka. Lappi, N Finland 69°54′N 27°01′E
165 O12 **Utsunomiya** *var.* Utunomiya. Tochigi, Honshū, S Japan 36°36′N 139°53′E
127 P13 **Utta** Respublika Kalmykiya, SW Russian Federation 46°22′N 46°03′E
167 O8 **Uttaradit** *var.* Utaradit. Uttaradit, N Thailand 17°38′N 100°05′E
152 J9 **Uttarakhand** ◐ *state* N India
152 J8 **Uttarkāshi** Uttarakhand, N India 30°45′N 78°19′E
152 K11 **Uttar Pradesh** *prev.* United Provinces, United Provinces of Agra and Oudh. ◐ *state* N India
45 T5 **Utuado** C Puerto Rico 18°17′N 66°41′W
158 K3 **Utubulak** Xinjiang Uygur Zizhiqu, W China 46°50′N 86°15′E
39 N5 **Utukok River** ≈ Alaska, USA
Utunomiya *see* Utsunomiya
187 P10 **Utupua** *island* Santa Cruz Islands, E Solomon Islands
144 G9 **Utva** ≈ NW Kazakhstan
189 Y15 **Utwe** Kosrae, E Micronesia
189 X15 **Utwe Harbor** *harbour* Kosrae, E Micronesia
Uubulan *see* Hayrhan
163 O8 **Uulbayan** *var.* Dzüünbulag. Sühbaatar, E Mongolia 46°30′N 112°22′E
118 G6 **Uulu** Pärnumaa, SW Estonia 58°15′N 24°32′E
197 N13 **Uummannaq** *var.* Umanak, Umanaq. ◐ Kitaa, C Greenland
Uummannarsuaq *see* Nunap Isua
162 E4 **Üüreg Nuur** ◎ NW Mongolia
Uusikaarlepyy *see* Nykarleby
93 J19 **Uusikaupunki** *Swe.* Nystad. Länsi-Suomi, SW Finland 60°48′N 21°25′E
127 S2 **Uva** Udmurtskaya Respublika, NW Russian Federation 56°41′N 52°15′E
155 K25 **Uva** ◐ *province* SE Sri Lanka
113 L14 **Uvac** ≈ W Serbia
25 Q12 **Uvalde** Texas, SW USA 29°14′N 99°49′W
119 O18 **Uvaravichy** *Rus.* Uvarovichi. Homyel'skaya Voblasts', SE Belarus 52°36′N 30°44′E
54 J11 **Uvá, Río** ≈ E Colombia
Uvarovichi *see* Uvaravichy
127 N7 **Uvarovo** Tambovskaya Oblast', W Russian Federation 51°58′N 42°13′E
122 H10 **Uvat** Tyumenskaya Oblast', C Russian Federation 59°11′N 68°37′E
190 G12 **Uvea, Île** *island* N Wallis and Futuna
81 E21 **Uvinza** Kigoma, W Tanzania 05°08′S 30°23′E
79 O20 **Uvira** Sud-Kivu, E Dem. Rep. Congo 03°24′S 29°05′E
162 E5 **Uvs** ◐ *province* NW Mongolia
162 F5 **Uvs Nuur** *var.* Ozero Ubsu-Nur. ◎ Mongolia/Russian Federation
Uxin Qi *see* Galutu, N China
164 F14 **Uwa** *var.* Seiyo. Ehime, Shikoku, SW Japan 33°22′N 132°29′E
164 F14 **Uwajima** *var.* Uwazima. Ehime, Shikoku, SW Japan 33°13′N 132°32′E
80 B5 **ʿUwaynāt, Jabal al** *var.* Jebel Uweinat. ▲ Libya/Sudan 21°51′N 25°01′E
Uwazima *see* Uwajima
Uweinat, Jebel *see* ʿUwaynāt, Jabal al
14 H14 **Uxbridge** Ontario, S Canada 44°07′N 79°07′W
Uxellodunum *see* Issoudun
Uxin Qi *see* Dabqig, N China
41 X12 **Uxmal, Ruinas** *ruins* Yucatán, SE Mexico
129 Q5 **Uy** ≈ Kazakhstan/Russian Federation
144 K15 **Uyaly** Kzylorda, S Kazakhstan 44°22′N 61°16′E
123 R8 **Uyandina** ≈ NE Russian Federation
162 J8 **Uyanga** *var.* Ongi. Övörhangay, C Mongolia 46°30′N 102°18′E
Üydzen *see* Manlay
Uyeda *see* Ueda
122 K5 **Uyedineniya, Ostrov** *island* N Russian Federation
77 V17 **Uyo** Akwa Ibom, S Nigeria 05°00′N 07°57′E
162 D8 **Üyönch** Hovd, W Mongolia 46°04′N 92°05′E
145 Q15 **Uyuk** Zhambyl, S Kazakhstan 43°46′N 70°55′E
141 V13 **ʿUyūn** SW Oman 17°19′N 53°50′E
57 K20 **Uyuni** Potosí, W Bolivia 20°27′S 66°48′W
57 J20 **Uyuni, Salar de** *wetland* SW Bolivia
146 I9 **Uzbekistan** *off.* Republic of Uzbekistan. ◆ *republic* C Asia
Uzbekistan, Republic of *see* Uzbekistan
158 D8 **Uzbel Shankou** *Rus.* Pereval Kyzyl-Dzhiik. *pass* China/Tajikistan
146 B11 **Uzboý** *prev. Rus.* Imeni 26 Bakinskikh Komissarov, *Turkm.* 26 Baku Komissarlary Adyndaky. Balkan Welaýaty, W Turkmenistan 39°24′N 54°04′E
119 J17 **Uzda** Minskaya Voblasts', C Belarus 53°29′N 27°10′E
103 N12 **Uzerche** Corrèze, C France 45°24′N 01°35′E
103 R14 **Uzès** Gard, S France 44°00′N 04°25′E
147 T10 **Uzgen** *Kir.* Özgön. Oshskaya Oblast', SW Kyrgyzstan 40°42′N 73°17′E
117 O3 **Uzh** ≈ N Ukraine
Uzhgorod *see* Uzhhorod
116 G7 **Uzhhorod** *Rus.* Uzhgorod; *prev.* Ungvár. Zakarpats'ka Oblast', W Ukraine 48°36′N 22°19′E
Uzi *see* Uji
112 K13 **Užice** *prev.* Titovo Užice. Serbia, W Serbia 43°52′N 19°51′E
Uzin *see* Uzyn
126 L5 **Uzlovaya** Tul'skaya Oblast', W Russian Federation 54°01′N 38°15′E
108 H7 **Uznach** Sankt Gallen, NE Switzerland 47°12′N 09°00′E
145 U16 **Uzunagach** Almaty, SE Kazakhstan 43°08′N 76°20′E
136 B10 **Uzunköprü** Edirne, NW Turkey 41°18′N 26°40′E
118 D11 **Užventis** Šiaulai, C Lithuania 55°49′N 22°38′E
117 P5 **Uzyn** *Rus.* Uzin. Kyyivs'ka Oblast', N Ukraine 49°52′N 30°27′E
145 N7 **Uzynkol'** Kostanay, N Kazakhstan
145 N7 **Uzynkol'** *prev.* Lenīn, Leninskoye. Kustanay, N Kazakhstan 54°05′N 65°23′E

V

Vääksy *see* Asikkala
83 H23 **Vaal** ≈ C South Africa
93 M14 **Vaala** Oulu, C Finland 64°34′N 26°49′E
93 N19 **Vaalimaa** Etelä-Suomi, SE Finland 60°34′N 27°49′E
99 M19 **Vaals** Limburg, SE Netherlands 50°46′N 06°01′E
93 J16 **Vaasa** *Swe.* Vasa; *prev.* Nikolainkaupunki. Länsi-Suomi, W Finland 63°07′N 21°39′E
98 L10 **Vaassen** Gelderland, E Netherlands 52°18′N 05°59′E
118 G11 **Vabalninkas** Panevėžys, NE Lithuania 55°59′N 24°45′E
Vabkent *see* Vobkent
111 J22 **Vác** *Ger.* Waitzen. Pest, N Hungary 47°46′N 19°08′E
61 I14 **Vacaria** Rio Grande do Sul, S Brazil 28°31′S 50°52′W
35 N7 **Vacaville** California, W USA 38°21′N 121°59′W
103 R15 **Vaccarès, Étang de** ◎ SE France
44 L10 **Vache, Île à** *island* SW Haiti
173 Y16 **Vacoas** W Mauritius 20°18′S 57°29′E
155 F21 **Vadakara** *var.* Badagara. Kerala, SW India 11°36′N 75°34′E **see also** Badagara
32 G10 **Vader** Washington, NW USA 46°23′N 122°58′W
94 D12 **Vadheim** Sogn Og Fjordane, S Norway 61°12′N 05°48′E
154 D11 **Vadodara** *prev.* Baroda. Gujarāt, W India 22°19′N 73°14′E
92 M8 **Vadsø** *Fin.* Vesisaari. Finnmark, N Norway 70°07′N 29°47′E
95 L17 **Vadstena** Östergötland, S Sweden 58°26′N 14°55′E
108 I8 **Vaduz** ● (Liechtenstein) W Liechtenstein 47°08′N 09°32′E
Vág *see* Váh
125 N12 **Vaga** ≈ NW Russian Federation
94 G11 **Vågåmo** Oppland, S Norway 61°52′N 09°06′E
112 D12 **Vaganski Vrh** ▲ W Croatia 44°24′N 15°32′E
95 A19 **Vágar** *Dan.* Vågø. *island* W Faeroe Islands
Vágbeszterce *see* Považská Bystrica
95 L19 **Vaggeryd** Jönköping, S Sweden 57°30′N 14°10′E
137 T12 **Vagharshapat** *var.* Ejmiadzin, Ejmiatsin, Etchmiadzin, *Rus.* Echmiadzin. W Armenia 40°10′N 44°17′E
95 O16 **Vagnhärad** Södermanland, C Sweden 58°57′N 17°32′E
Vågø *see* Vágar

◆ Country ● Country Capital ◇ Dependent Territory ○ Dependent Territory Capital ◐ Administrative Regions ✈ International Airport ▲ Mountain ▲▲ Mountain Range Volcano ≈ River ◎ Lake ⊠ Reservoir

104 G7 **Vagos** Aveiro, N Portugal 40°33′N 08°42′W
Vágsellye see Sal'a
92 H10 **Vågsfjorden** fjord N Norway
94 C10 **Vågsøy** island S Norway
Vágújhely see Nové Mesto nad Váhom
111 I21 **Váh** Ger. Waag, Hung. Vág. ≈ W Slovakia
93 K16 **Vähäkyrö** Länsi-Suomi, W Finland 63°04′N 22°05′E
191 X11 **Vahitahi** atoll Îles Tuamotu, E French Polynesia
Váhtjer see Gällivare
Vaidei see Vulcan
22 L4 **Vaiden** Mississippi, S USA 33°19′N 89°42′W
155 I23 **Vaigai** ≈ SE India
191 V16 **Vaihu** Easter Island, Chile, E Pacific Ocean 27°10′S 109°22′W
118 I6 **Väike Emajõgi** ≈ S Estonia
118 I4 **Väike-Maarja** Ger. Klein-Marien. Lääne-Virumaa, NE Estonia 59°07′N 26°16′E
Väike-Salatsi see Mazsalaca
37 R4 **Vail** Colorado, C USA 39°36′N 106°20′W
193 V15 **Vaina** Tongatapu, S Tonga 21°12′S 175°10′W
118 E5 **Väinameri** prev. Muhu Väin, Ger. Moon-Sund. sea E Baltic Sea
93 N18 **Vainikkala** Etelä-Suomi, SE Finland 60°54′N 28°18′E
118 D10 **Vaiņode** Liepāja, SW Latvia 56°25′N 21°52′E
155 H23 **Vaippār** ≈ SE India
191 W11 **Vairaatea** atoll Îles Tuamotu, C French Polynesia
191 R8 **Vairao** Tahiti, W French Polynesia 17°48′S 149°17′W
103 R14 **Vaison-la-Romaine** Vaucluse, SE France 44°15′N 05°04′E
190 G11 **Vaitupu** Île Uvea, E Wallis and Futuna 13°14′S 176°09′W
190 F7 **Vaitupu** atoll C Tuvalu
Vajdahunyad see Hunedoara
Vajdej see Vulcan
78 K12 **Vakaga** ◆ prefecture NE Central African Republic
114 H10 **Vakarel** Sofiya, W Bulgaria 42°35′N 23°40′E
Vakav see Ustrem
137 O11 **Vakfıkebir** Trabzon, NE Turkey 41°03′N 39°19′E
122 J10 **Vakh** ≈ C Russian Federation
Vakhon, Qatorkŭhi see Nicholas Range
147 P14 **Vakhsh** SW Tajikistan 37°46′N 68°48′E
147 Q12 **Vakhsh** ≈ SW Tajikistan
127 P1 **Vakhtan** Nizhegorodskaya Oblast', W Russian Federation 58°00′N 46°43′E
94 C13 **Vaksdal** Hordaland, S Norway 60°29′N 05°45′E
125 O8 **Vaksha** ≈ NW Russian Federation
Valachia see Wallachia
108 D11 **Valais** Ger. Wallis. ◆ canton SW Switzerland
113 M21 **Valamarës, Mali i** ▲ SE Albania 40°48′N 20°31′E
127 S2 **Valamaz** Udmurtskaya Respublika, NW Russian Federation 57°36′N 52°07′E
113 Q19 **Valandovo** SE FYR Macedonia 41°20′N 22°33′E
111 I18 **Valašské Meziříčí** Ger. Wallachisch-Meseritsch, Pol. Wałeckie Międzyrzecze. Zlínský Kraj, E Czech Republic 49°29′N 17°57′E
115 I17 **Valáxa** island Vóreies Sporádes, Greece, Aegean Sea
95 K16 **Vålberg** Värmland, C Sweden 59°24′N 13°12′E
116 H12 **Vâlcea** prev. Vîlcea. ◆ county SW Romania
63 J16 **Valcheta** Río Negro, E Argentina 40°42′S 66°08′W
15 P12 **Valcourt** Québec, SE Canada 45°28′N 72°18′W
Valdai Hills see Valdayskaya Vozvyshennost'
104 M3 **Valdavia** ≈ N Spain
124 I15 **Valday** Novgorodskaya Oblast', W Russian Federation 57°57′N 33°20′E
124 I15 **Valdayskaya Vozvyshennost'** var. Valdai Hills. hill range W Russian Federation
104 L9 **Valdecañas, Embalse de** ⊠ W Spain
118 E8 **Valdemārpils** Ger. Sassmacken. Talsi, NW Latvia 57°23′N 22°36′E
95 N18 **Valdemarsvik** Östergötland, S Sweden 58°13′N 16°35′E
105 N8 **Valdemoro** Madrid, C Spain 40°12′N 03°40′W
105 O11 **Valdepeñas** Castilla-La Mancha, C Spain 38°46′N 03°24′W
104 L5 **Valderaduey** ≈ NE Spain
104 L5 **Valderas** Castilla-León, N Spain 42°05′N 05°27′W
105 T7 **Valderrobres** var. Vall-de-roures. Aragón, NE Spain 40°53′N 00°08′E
63 K17 **Valdés, Península** peninsula SE Argentina
56 C5 **Valdéz** var. Limones. Esmeraldas, NW Ecuador 01°13′N 79°00′W
39 S11 **Valdez** Alaska, USA 61°08′N 146°21′W
Valdia see Weldiya
103 U11 **Val d'Isère** Savoie, E France 45°27′N 07°03′E
63 G15 **Valdivia** Los Lagos, C Chile 39°50′S 73°13′W
Valdivia Bank see Valdivia Seamount
65 P17 **Valdivia Seamount** var. Valdivia Bank. undersea feature E Atlantic Ocean 26°15′S 06°25′E
103 N4 **Val-d'Oise** ◆ department N France
14 J8 **Val-d'Or** Québec, SE Canada 48°06′N 77°42′W
23 U8 **Valdosta** Georgia, SE USA 30°49′N 83°16′W
95 G13 **Valdres** physical region S Norway
32 L13 **Vale** Oregon, NW USA 43°59′N 117°15′W
116 F9 **Valea lui Mihai** Hung. Érmihályfalva. Bihor, NW Romania 47°31′N 22°08′E
11 N15 **Valemount** British Columbia, SW Canada 52°46′N 119°17′W
59 O17 **Valença** Bahia, E Brazil 13°22′S 39°06′W
104 F4 **Valença do Minho** Viana do Castelo, N Portugal 42°02′N 08°38′W
59 N14 **Valença do Piauí** Piauí, E Brazil 06°26′S 41°46′W
103 N8 **Valençay** Indre, C France 47°10′N 01°31′E
103 R13 **Valence** anc. Valentia, Valentia Julia, Ventia. Drôme, E France 44°56′N 04°54′E
105 S10 **Valencia** País Valenciano, E Spain 39°29′N 00°24′W
54 K5 **Valencia** Carabobo, N Venezuela 10°12′N 68°02′W
105 R10 **Valencia** Cat. València. ◆ province País Valenciano, E Spain
105 S10 **Valencia** ✈ Valencia, E Spain
104 I10 **Valencia de Alcántara** Extremadura, W Spain 39°25′N 07°14′W
104 L4 **Valencia de Don Juan** Castilla-León, N Spain 42°17′N 05°31′W
105 U9 **Valencia, Golfo de** var. Gulf of Valencia. gulf E Spain
Valencia, Gulf of see Valencia, Golfo de
97 A21 **Valencia Island** Ir. Dairbhre. island SW Ireland
Valencia/València see País Valenciano
103 P2 **Valenciennes** Nord, N France 50°21′N 03°32′E
116 K13 **Vălenii de Munte** Prahova, SE Romania 45°11′N 26°02′E
Valentia see Valence, France
Valentia see País Valenciano
Valentia Julia see Valence
103 T8 **Valentigney** Doubs, E France 47°27′N 06°49′E
28 M12 **Valentine** Nebraska, C USA 42°53′N 100°31′W
24 J10 **Valentine** Texas, SW USA 30°35′N 104°30′W
Valentine State see Oregon
106 C8 **Valenza** Piemonte, NW Italy 45°01′N 08°37′E
94 I13 **Våler** Hedmark, S Norway 60°39′N 11°52′E
54 I6 **Valera** Trujillo, NW Venezuela 09°21′N 70°38′W
192 M11 **Valerie Guyot Seamount** undersea feature S Pacific Ocean 33°00′S 164°00′W
Valetta see Valletta
118 I7 **Valga** Ger. Walk, Latv. Valka. Valgamaa, S Estonia 57°48′N 26°04′E
118 I7 **Valgamaa** var. Valga Maakond. ◆ province S Estonia
Valga Maakond see Valgamaa
43 Q15 **Valiente, Península** peninsula NW Panama
103 X16 **Valinco, Golfe de** gulf Corse, France, C Mediterranean Sea
112 L12 **Valjevo** Serbia, W Serbia 44°17′N 19°54′E
Valjok see Válljohka
118 I7 **Valka** Ger. Walk. Valka, N Latvia 57°48′N 26°01′E
Valka see Valga
93 L18 **Valkeakoski** Länsi-Suomi, W Finland 61°17′N 24°05′E
93 M19 **Valkeala** Etelä-Suomi, S Finland 60°55′N 26°49′E
99 L18 **Valkenburg** Limburg, SE Netherlands 50°52′N 05°50′E
99 K15 **Valkenswaard** Noord-Brabant, S Netherlands 51°21′N 05°29′E
119 G15 **Valkininkai** Alytus, S Lithuania 54°22′N 24°51′E
117 U5 **Valky** Kharkivs'ka Oblast', E Ukraine 49°51′N 35°40′E
41 Y12 **Valladolid** Yucatán, SE Mexico 20°39′N 88°13′W
104 M5 **Valladolid** Castilla-León, NW Spain 41°39′N 04°45′W
104 L5 **Valladolid** ◆ province Castilla-León, N Spain
103 U15 **Vallauris** Alpes-Maritimes, SE France 43°34′N 07°03′E
Vall-de-roures see Valderrobres
Vall D'Uxó see La Vall d'Uixó
95 E16 **Valle** Aust-Agder, S Norway 59°13′N 07°33′E
105 N2 **Valle** Cantabria, N Spain 43°14′N 04°16′W
42 H8 **Valle** ◆ department S Honduras
105 N8 **Vallecas** Madrid, C Spain 40°23′N 03°37′W
37 Q8 **Vallecito Reservoir** ⊠ Colorado, C USA
106 A7 **Valle d'Aosta** ◆ region NW Italy
41 O14 **Valle de Bravo** México, S Mexico 19°19′N 100°08′W
55 N5 **Valle de Guanape** Anzoátegui, N Venezuela 09°54′N 65°41′W
54 M6 **Valle de La Pascua** Guárico, N Venezuela 09°15′N 66°00′W
54 B11 **Valle del Cauca** off. Departamento del Valle del Cauca. ◆ province W Colombia
Valle del Cauca, Departamento del see Valle del Cauca
41 N13 **Valle de Santiago** Guanajuato, C Mexico 20°25′N 101°15′W
40 J7 **Valle de Zaragoza** Chihuahua, N Mexico 27°25′N 105°50′W
54 G5 **Valledupar** Cesar, N Colombia 10°31′N 73°16′W
76 G10 **Vallée de Ferlo** ≈ NW Senegal
57 M19 **Vallegrande** Santa Cruz, C Bolivia 18°30′S 64°06′W
41 P8 **Valle Hermoso** Tamaulipas, C Mexico 25°39′N 97°49′W
35 N8 **Vallejo** California, W USA 38°08′N 122°16′W
62 G8 **Vallenar** Atacama, N Chile 28°35′S 70°44′W
95 O15 **Vallentuna** Stockholm, C Sweden 59°32′N 18°05′E
121 P16 **Valletta** prev. Valetta. ● (Malta) E Malta 35°54′N 14°31′E
27 N6 **Valley Center** Kansas, C USA 37°49′N 97°22′W
29 Q5 **Valley City** North Dakota, N USA 46°57′N 97°58′W
32 I15 **Valley Falls** Oregon, NW USA 42°28′N 120°16′W
Valleyfield see Salaberry-de-Valleyfield
21 S4 **Valley Head** West Virginia, NE USA 38°33′N 80°01′W
25 T8 **Valley Mills** Texas, SW USA 31°36′N 97°27′W
75 W10 **Valley of the Kings** ancient monument E Egypt
29 R11 **Valley Springs** South Dakota, N USA 43°34′N 96°28′W
20 K5 **Valley Station** Kentucky, S USA 38°06′N 85°52′W
11 O13 **Valleyview** Alberta, W Canada 55°02′N 117°17′W
25 T5 **Valley View** Texas, SW USA 33°27′N 97°08′W
61 C21 **Vallimanca, Arroyo** ≈ E Argentina
92 L9 **Válljohka** var. Valjok. Finnmark, N Norway 69°40′N 25°52′E
107 M19 **Vallo della Lucania** Campania, S Italy 40°13′N 15°15′E
108 B9 **Vallorbe** Vaud, W Switzerland 46°43′N 06°21′E
105 V6 **Valls** Cataluña, NE Spain 41°18′N 01°15′E
94 N11 **Vallsta** Gävleborg, C Sweden 61°30′N 16°25′E
94 N12 **Vallvik** Gävleborg, C Sweden 61°10′N 17°15′E
11 T17 **Val Marie** Saskatchewan, S Canada 49°15′N 107°44′W
118 H7 **Valmiera** Est. Volmari, Ger. Wolmar. Valmiera, N Latvia 57°34′N 25°26′E
105 N3 **Valnera** ▲ N Spain 43°08′N 03°39′W
102 J3 **Valognes** Manche, N France 49°31′N 01°28′W
Valona see Vlorë
Valona Bay see Vlorës, Gjiri i
104 G6 **Valongo** var. Valongo de Gaia. Porto, N Portugal 41°11′N 08°30′W
Valongo de Gaia see Valongo
104 M5 **Valoria la Buena** Castilla-León, N Spain 41°48′N 04°33′W
119 J15 **Valozhyn** Pol. Wołożyn, Rus. Volozhin. Minskaya Voblasts', C Belarus 54°05′N 26°32′E
104 I5 **Valpaços** Vila Real, N Portugal 41°36′N 07°17′W
62 G11 **Valparaíso** Valparaíso, C Chile 33°05′S 71°18′W
40 L11 **Valparaíso** Zacatecas, C Mexico 22°49′N 103°28′W
23 P8 **Valparaiso** Florida, SE USA 30°30′N 86°28′W
31 N11 **Valparaiso** Indiana, N USA 41°28′N 87°04′W
62 G11 **Valparaíso** off. Región de Valparaíso. ◆ region C Chile
Valparaíso, Región de see Valparaíso
Valpo see Valpovo
112 I9 **Valpovo** Hung. Valpó. Osijek-Baranja, E Croatia 45°40′N 18°25′E
103 R14 **Valréas** Vaucluse, SE France 44°22′N 05°00′E
Vals see Vals-Platz
154 D12 **Valsād** prev. Bulsar. Gujarāt, W India 20°40′N 72°55′E
Valsbaai see False Bay
171 T12 **Valse Pisang, Kepulauan** island group E Indonesia
108 H9 **Vals-Platz** var. Vals. Graubünden, S Switzerland 46°39′N 09°09′E
171 X16 **Vals, Tanjung** headland Papua, SE Indonesia 08°26′S 137°35′E
93 N15 **Valtimo** Itä-Suomi, E Finland 63°39′N 28°49′E
115 D17 **Váltou** ▲ C Greece
127 O12 **Valuyevka** Rostovskaya Oblast', SW Russian Federation 46°48′N 43°49′E
126 K9 **Valuyki** Belgorodskaya Oblast', W Russian Federation 50°11′N 38°07′E
36 L2 **Val Verda** Utah, W USA 40°51′N 111°53′W
64 N12 **Valverde** Hierro, Islas Canarias, Spain, NE Atlantic Ocean 27°48′N 17°55′W
104 I13 **Valverde del Camino** Andalucía, S Spain 37°35′N 06°45′W
95 G23 **Vamdrup** Vejle, C Denmark 55°26′N 09°18′E
94 L12 **Våmhus** Dalarna, C Sweden 61°07′N 14°30′E
93 K18 **Vammala** Länsi-Suomi, SW Finland 61°20′N 22°55′E
Vámosudvarhely see Odorheiu Secuiesc
137 S14 **Van** Van, E Turkey 38°30′N 43°23′E
25 V7 **Van** Texas, SW USA 32°31′N 95°38′W
137 T14 **Van** ◆ province E Turkey
137 T11 **Vanadzor** prev. Kirovakan. N Armenia 40°49′N 44°29′E
25 U5 **Van Alstyne** Texas, SW USA 33°25′N 96°34′W
33 W10 **Vananda** Montana, NW USA 46°22′N 106°58′W
116 I11 **Vânători** Hung. Héjjasfalva; prev. Vînători. Mureș, C Romania 46°14′N 24°56′E
191 W12 **Vanavana** atoll Îles Tuamotu, SE French Polynesia
Vana-Vändra see Vändra
122 M11 **Vanavara** Evenkiyskiy Avtonomnyy Okrug, C Russian Federation 60°19′N 102°19′E
15 Q8 **Van Bruyssel** Québec, SE Canada 47°56′N 72°08′W
27 R10 **Van Buren** Arkansas, C USA 35°28′N 94°25′W
19 S1 **Van Buren** Maine, NE USA 47°07′N 67°57′W
27 W7 **Van Buren** Missouri, C USA 37°00′N 91°00′W
19 T5 **Vanceboro** Maine, NE USA 45°31′N 67°25′W
21 W10 **Vanceboro** North Carolina, SE USA 35°16′N 77°06′W
21 O4 **Vanceburg** Kentucky, S USA 38°36′N 84°40′W
Vanch see Vanj
10 L17 **Vancouver** British Columbia, SW Canada 49°13′N 123°06′W
32 G11 **Vancouver** Washington, NW USA 45°38′N 122°39′W
10 L17 **Vancouver** ✈ British Columbia, SW Canada 49°03′N 123°00′W
10 K16 **Vancouver Island** island British Columbia, SW Canada
Vanda see Vantaa
171 X13 **Van Daalen** ≈ Papua, E Indonesia
30 L15 **Vandalia** Illinois, N USA 38°57′N 89°05′W
27 V3 **Vandalia** Missouri, C USA 39°18′N 91°29′W
31 R13 **Vandalia** Ohio, N USA 39°53′N 84°12′W
25 U13 **Vanderbilt** Texas, SW USA 28°45′N 96°37′W
31 Q10 **Vandercook Lake** Michigan, N USA 42°11′N 84°23′W
10 L14 **Vanderhoof** British Columbia, SW Canada 53°54′N 124°00′W
18 K8 **Vanderwhacker Mountain** ▲ New York, NE USA 43°54′N 74°06′W
181 P1 **Van Diemen Gulf** gulf Northern Territory, N Australia
Van Diemen's Land see Tasmania
118 H5 **Vändra** Ger. Fennern; prev. Vana-Vändra. Pärnumaa, SW Estonia 58°39′N 25°00′E
Vandsburg see Więcbork
34 L4 **Van Duzen River** ≈ California, W USA
119 G15 **Vandžiogala** Kaunas, C Lithuania 55°07′N 23°55′E
41 N10 **Vanegas** San Luis Potosí, C Mexico 23°53′N 100°55′W
Vaner, Lake see Vänern
95 K17 **Vänern** Eng. Lake Vaner; prev. Lake Vener. ◎ S Sweden
95 J18 **Vänersborg** Västra Götaland, S Sweden 58°16′N 12°22′E
94 F12 **Vang** Oppland, S Norway 61°07′N 08°34′E
172 I7 **Vangaindrano** Fianarantsoa, SE Madagascar 23°21′S 47°35′E
137 S14 **Van Gölü** Eng. Lake Van; anc. Thospitis. salt lake E Turkey
186 L9 **Vangunu** island New Georgia Islands, NW Solomon Islands
24 J9 **Van Horn** Texas, SW USA 31°03′N 104°51′W
187 Q11 **Vanikolo** var. Vanikoro. island Santa Cruz Islands, E Solomon Islands
Vanikoro see Vanikolo
186 A5 **Vanimo** Sandaun, NW Papua New Guinea 02°40′S 141°17′E
123 T13 **Vanino** Khabarovskiy Kray, SE Russian Federation 49°10′N 140°18′E
155 G19 **Vānīvilāsa Sāgara** ◎ SW India
147 S13 **Vanj** Rus. Vanch. S Tajikistan 38°22′N 71°27′E
116 G14 **Vânju Mare** prev. Vînju Mare. Mehedinți, SW Romania 44°25′N 22°52′E
15 N12 **Vankleek Hill** Ontario, SE Canada 45°32′N 74°39′W
Van, Lake see Van Gölü
93 I16 **Vännäs** Västerbotten, N Sweden 63°54′N 19°43′E
93 I15 **Vännäsby** Västerbotten, N Sweden 63°55′N 19°53′E
102 H7 **Vannes** anc. Dariorigum. Morbihan, NW France 47°40′N 02°45′W
92 I8 **Vannøya** island N Norway
103 T12 **Vanoise, Massif de la** ▲ E France
83 E24 **Vanrhynsdorp** Western Cape, SW South Africa 31°36′S 18°45′E
21 P7 **Vansant** Virginia, NE USA 37°13′N 82°03′W
94 L13 **Vansbro** Dalarna, C Sweden 60°32′N 14°15′E
95 D18 **Vanse** Vest-Agder, S Norway 58°04′N 06°40′E
9 P7 **Vansittart Island** island Nunavut, NE Canada
93 M20 **Vantaa** Swe. Vanda. Etelä-Suomi, S Finland 60°18′N 25°01′E
93 L19 **Vantaa** ✈ (Helsinki) Etelä-Suomi, S Finland 60°18′N 25°01′E
32 J9 **Vantage** Washington, NW USA 46°55′N 119°55′W
187 Z14 **Vanua Balavu** prev. Vanua Mbalavu. island Lau Group, E Fiji
187 R12 **Vanua Lava** island Banks Islands, N Vanuatu
187 Y13 **Vanua Levu** island N Fiji
Vanua Mbalavu see Vanua Balavu
187 R12 **Vanuatu** off. Republic of Vanuatu; prev. New Hebrides. ◆ republic SW Pacific Ocean
175 P8 **Vanuatu** island group SW Pacific Ocean
Vanuatu, Republic of see Vanuatu
31 Q12 **Van Wert** Ohio, N USA 40°52′N 84°34′W
187 Q17 **Vao** Province Sud, S New Caledonia 22°40′S 167°29′E
Vapincum see Gap
117 N7 **Vapnyarka** Vinnyts'ka Oblast', C Ukraine 48°31′S 28°44′E
103 T15 **Var** ◆ department SE France
103 U14 **Var** ≈ SE France
95 J18 **Vara** Västra Götaland, S Sweden 58°16′N 12°57′E
Varadinska Županija see Varaždin
118 J10 **Varakļāni** Madona, C Latvia 56°36′N 26°40′E
106 C7 **Varallo** Piemonte, NE Italy 45°51′N 08°16′E
143 O5 **Varāmīn** var. Veramin. Tehrān, N Iran 35°19′N 51°40′E
153 N14 **Vārānasi** prev. Banaras, Benares, hist. Kasi. Uttar Pradesh, N India 25°20′N 83°E
125 T3 **Varandey** Nenetskiy Avtonomnyy Okrug, NW Russian Federation 68°48′N 57°54′E
92 M8 **Varangerbotn** Finnmark, N Norway 70°09′N 28°28′E
92 M8 **Varangerfjorden** Lapp. Várjjatvuotna. fjord N Norway
92 M8 **Varangerhalvøya** Lapp. Várnjárga. peninsula N Norway
Varannó see Vranov nad Topľou
107 M15 **Varano, Lago di** ◎ SE Italy
118 J13 **Varapayeva** Rus. Voropayevo. Vitsyebskaya Voblasts', NW Belarus 55°09′N 27°13′E
Varasd see Varaždin
112 E7 **Varaždin** Ger. Warasdin, Hung. Varasd. Varaždin, N Croatia 46°18′N 16°21′E
112 E7 **Varaždin** off. Varadinska Županija. ◆ province N Croatia
106 C10 **Varazze** Liguria, NW Italy 44°21′N 08°35′E
95 J20 **Varberg** Halland, S Sweden 57°06′N 12°15′E
149 P5 **Vardak** var. Wardak, Pash. Wardag. ◆ province E Afghanistan
113 Q19 **Vardar** Gk. Axiós. ≈ FYR Macedonia/Greece see also Axiós
Vardar see Axiós
95 F23 **Varde** Ribe, W Denmark 55°38′N 08°31′E
137 V12 **Vardenis** E Armenia 40°11′N 45°43′E
92 N8 **Vardø** Fin. Vuoreija. Finnmark, N Norway 70°22′N 31°06′E
115 E18 **Vardoúsia** ▲ C Greece
Vareia see Logroño
100 G10 **Varel** Niedersachsen, NW Germany 53°24′N 08°07′E
119 G15 **Varėna** Pol. Orany. Alytus, S Lithuania 54°13′N 24°35′E
15 O12 **Varennes** Québec, SE Canada 45°42′N 73°25′W
103 P10 **Varennes-sur-Allier** Allier, C France 46°17′N 03°24′E
112 I12 **Vareš** Federacija Bosna I Hercegovina, E Bosnia and Herzegovina 44°12′N 18°19′E
106 D7 **Varese** Lombardia, N Italy 45°49′N 08°50′E
116 J12 **Vârful Moldoveanu** var. Moldoveanul; prev. Vîrful Moldoveanu. ▲ C Romania 45°35′N 24°48′E
Varganzi see Warganza
95 J18 **Vårgårda** Västra Götaland, S Sweden 58°00′N 12°49′E
54 L4 **Vargas** off. Estado Vargas. ◆ state N Venezuela
95 J18 **Vargön** Västra Götaland, S Sweden 58°21′N 12°22′E
95 C17 **Varhaug** Rogaland, S Norway 58°37′N 05°39′E
Várjjatvuotna see Varangerfjorden
93 N17 **Varkaus** Itä-Suomi, C Finland 62°20′N 27°50′E
92 J2 **Varmahlídh** Nordhurland Vestra, N Iceland 65°32′N 19°33′W
95 J15 **Värmland** ◆ county C Sweden
95 K16 **Värmlandsnäs** peninsula S Sweden
114 N8 **Varna** prev. Stalin; anc. Odessus. Varna, E Bulgaria 43°14′N 27°56′E
114 N8 **Varna** ◆ province E Bulgaria
114 N8 **Varna** ✈ Varna, E Bulgaria 43°16′N 27°52′E
95 L20 **Värnamo** Jönköping, S Sweden 57°11′N 14°03′E
114 N8 **Varnenski Zaliv** prev. Stalinski Zaliv. bay E Bulgaria
114 N8 **Varnensko Ezero** estuary E Bulgaria
118 D11 **Varniai** Telšiai, W Lithuania 55°45′N 22°22′E
Várnjárga see Varangerhalvøya
Varnoúntas see Baba
111 D14 **Varnsdorf** Ger. Warnsdorf. Ústecký Kraj, NW Czech Republic 50°57′N 14°35′E
111 I23 **Várpalota** Veszprém, W Hungary 47°12′N 18°08′E
Varshava see Warszawa
118 K6 **Värska** Põlvamaa, SE Estonia 57°58′N 27°37′E
98 N12 **Varsseveld** Gelderland, E Netherlands 51°55′N 06°28′E
115 D19 **Vartholomió** prev. Vartholomión. Dytikí Ellás, S Greece 37°52′N 21°12′E
Vartholomión see Vartholomió
137 Q14 **Varto** Muş, E Turkey 39°10′N 41°28′E
95 K18 **Vartofta** Västra Götaland, S Sweden 58°06′N 13°40′E
93 O17 **Värtsilä** Itä-Suomi, E Finland 62°10′N 30°35′E
Värtsilä see Vyartsilya
117 R4 **Varva** Chernihivs'ka Oblast', NE Ukraine 50°31′N 32°43′E
59 H18 **Várzea Grande** Mato Grosso, SW Brazil 15°39′S 56°08′W
106 D9 **Varzi** Lombardia, N Italy 44°51′N 09°13′E
Varzimanor Ayni see Ayní
124 K5 **Varzuga** ≈ NW Russian Federation
103 P8 **Varzy** Nièvre, C France 47°22′N 03°22′E
111 G23 **Vas** off. Vas Megye. ◆ county W Hungary
190 A9 **Vasafua** island Funafuti Atoll, C Tuvalu
111 O21 **Vásárosnamény** Szabolcs-Szatmár-Bereg, E Hungary 48°10′N 22°18′E
104 H13 **Vascão, Ribeira de** ≈ S Portugal
116 G10 **Vașcău** Hung. Vaskoh. Bihor, NE Romania 46°28′N 22°30′E
Vascongadas, Provincias see País Vasco
Vashess Bay see Vaskess Bay
Vāsht see Khāsh
Vasilevichi see Vasilyevichy
115 G14 **Vasilikí** Kentrikí Makedonía, NE Greece 40°28′N 23°08′E
115 C18 **Vasilikí** Lefkáda, Iónia Nisiá, Greece, C Mediterranean Sea 38°36′N 20°37′E
115 K25 **Vasilikí** Kríti, Greece, E Mediterranean Sea 35°04′N 25°49′E
119 G16 **Vasilishki** Pol. Wasiliszki. Hrodzyenskaya Voblasts', W Belarus 53°47′N 24°51′E
Vasil Kolarov see Pamporovo
Vasil'kov see Vasyl'kiv
119 N19 **Vasilyevichy** Rus. Vasilevichi. Homyel'skaya Voblasts', SE Belarus 52°15′N 29°50′E
191 Y3 **Vaskess Bay** var. Vashess Bay. bay Kiritimati, E Kiribati
Vaskoh see Vașcău
Vaskohsziklás see Ștei
116 M10 **Vaslui** Vaslui, C Romania 46°38′N 27°44′E
116 L11 **Vaslui** ◆ county NE Romania
Vas Megye see Vas
31 R8 **Vassar** Michigan, N USA 43°22′N 83°34′W
95 E15 **Vassdalsegga** ▲ S Norway 59°47′N 07°07′E
60 P9 **Vassouras** Rio de Janeiro, SE Brazil 22°24′S 43°38′W
95 N15 **Västerås** Västmanland, C Sweden 59°37′N 16°33′E
93 G15 **Västerbotten** ◆ county N Sweden
94 K12 **Västerdalälven** ≈ C Sweden
95 O16 **Västerhaninge** Stockholm, C Sweden 59°07′N 18°06′E
94 M10 **Västernorrland** ◆ county C Sweden
95 N19 **Västervik** Kalmar, S Sweden 57°44′N 16°40′E
95 M15 **Västmanland** ◆ county C Sweden
107 L15 **Vasto** anc. Histonium. Abruzzo, C Italy 42°07′N 14°43′E
95 J19 **Västra Götaland** ◆ county S Sweden
95 J16 **Västra Silen** ◎ S Sweden
111 G23 **Vasvár** Ger. Eisenburg. Vas, W Hungary 47°03′N 16°48′E
117 U9 **Vasylivka** Zaporiz'ka Oblast', SE Ukraine 47°26′N 35°18′E
117 O5 **Vasyl'kiv** var. Vasil'kov. Kyyivs'ka Oblast', N Ukraine 50°12′N 30°18′E
122 I11 **Vasyugan** ≈ C Russian Federation
103 N8 **Vatan** Indre, C France 47°06′N 01°49′E
Vaté see Efate
115 C18 **Vathy** prev. Itháki. Itháki, Iónia Nisiá, Greece, C Mediterranean Sea 38°22′N 20°43′E
107 G15 **Vatican City** off. Vatican City. ◆ papal state S Europe
Vatican City see Vatican City
107 M22 **Vaticano, Capo** headland S Italy 38°37′N 15°49′E
92 K3 **Vatnajökull** glacier SE Iceland
95 P15 **Vätö** Stockholm, C Sweden 59°48′N 18°55′E
187 Z16 **Vatoa** island Lau Group, SE Fiji
172 J5 **Vatomandry** Toamasina, E Madagascar 19°20′S 48°58′E
116 J9 **Vatra Dornei** Ger. Dorna Watra. Suceava, NE Romania 47°20′N 25°21′E
116 J9 **Vatra Moldoviței** Suceava, NE Romania 47°37′N 25°36′E
Vatter, Lake see Vättern
95 L18 **Vättern** Eng. Lake Vatter; prev. Lake Vetter. ◎ S Sweden
187 X5 **Vatulele** island SW Fiji
117 P7 **Vatutine** Cherkas'ka Oblast', C Ukraine 49°01′N 31°04′E
187 W15 **Vatu Vara** island Lau Group, E Fiji
103 R14 **Vaucluse** ◆ department SE France
103 S5 **Vaucouleurs** Meuse, NE France 48°37′N 05°38′E
108 B9 **Vaud** Ger. Waadt. ◆ canton SW Switzerland
15 N12 **Vaudreuil** Québec, SE Canada 45°24′N 74°01′W
37 T12 **Vaughn** New Mexico, SW USA 34°36′N 105°12′W
54 I14 **Vaupés** off. Comisaría del Vaupés. ◆ province SE Colombia
Vaupés, Comisaría del see Vaupés
54 J13 **Vaupés, Río** var. Rio Uaupés. ≈ Brazil/Colombia see also Uaupés, Rio
Vaupés, Río see Uaupés, Rio
103 Q15 **Vauvert** Gard, S France 43°42′N 04°16′E
11 R17 **Vauxhall** Alberta, SW Canada 50°05′N 112°09′W
99 K23 **Vaux-sur-Sûre** Luxembourg, SE Belgium 49°55′N 05°34′E
172 J4 **Vavatenina** Toamasina, E Madagascar 17°25′S 49°11′E
193 Y14 **Vava'u Group** island group N Tonga
76 M16 **Vavoua** W Ivory Coast 07°23′N 06°29′W
127 S2 **Vavozh** Udmurtskaya Respublika, NW Russian Federation 56°48′N 51°53′E
155 K23 **Vavuniya** Northern Province, N Sri Lanka 08°45′N 80°30′E
119 G17 **Vawkavysk** Pol. Wołkowysk, Rus. Volkovysk. Hrodzyenskaya Voblasts', W Belarus 53°10′N 24°28′E
119 F17 **Vawkavyskaye Wzvyshsha** Rus. Volkovyskiye Vysoty. hill range W Belarus
95 P15 **Vaxholm** Stockholm, C Sweden 59°25′N 18°21′E
95 L21 **Växjö** var. Vexiö. Kronoberg, S Sweden 56°52′N 14°50′E
125 T1 **Vaygach, Ostrov** island NW Russian Federation
137 V13 **Vayk'** prev. Azizbekov. SE Armenia 39°41′N 45°28′E
Vazáš see Vittangi
125 P8 **Vazhgort** prev. Chasovo. Respublika Komi, NW Russian Federation 64°06′N 46°44′E
45 V10 **V. C. Bird** ✈ (St. John's) Antigua, Antigua and Barbuda 17°07′N 61°49′W
95 C16 **Veavågen** Rogaland, S Norway 59°18′N 5°13′E
29 Q7 **Veblen** South Dakota, N USA 45°50′N 97°17′W
98 N9 **Vecht** Ger. Vechte. ≈ Germany/Netherlands see also Vechte
Vecht see Vechte
100 G12 **Vechta** Niedersachsen, NW Germany 52°44′N 08°16′E
100 E12 **Vechte** Dut. Vecht. ≈ Germany/Netherlands see also Vecht
Vechte see Vecht
118 I8 **Vecpiebalga** Cēsis, C Latvia 57°03′N 25°47′E
118 G9 **Vecumnieki** Bauska, C Latvia 56°36′N 24°30′E
Vedāvati see Hagari
95 J20 **Veddige** Halland, S Sweden 57°16′N 12°19′E
116 J15 **Vedea** ≈ S Romania
127 P16 **Vedeno** Chechenskaya Respublika, SW Russian Federation 42°57′N 46°02′E
95 C16 **Vedvågen** Rogaland, S Norway 59°18′N 05°13′E
98 O6 **Veendam** Groningen, NE Netherlands 53°05′N 06°53′E
98 K12 **Veenendaal** Utrecht, C Netherlands 52°03′N 05°33′E
99 E14 **Veere** Zeeland, SW Netherlands 51°33′N 03°40′E
24 M2 **Vega** Texas, SW USA 35°14′N 102°26′W
92 E13 **Vega** island C Norway
45 T5 **Vega Baja** C Puerto Rico 18°27′N 66°23′W
38 D17 **Vega Point** headland Kiska Island, Alaska, USA 51°49′N 177°19′E
95 F17 **Vegår** ◎ S Norway
99 K14 **Veghel** Noord-Brabant, S Netherlands 51°37′N 05°33′E
Veglia see Krk
114 E13 **Vegorítida, Límni** var. Límni Vegorítis. ◎ N Greece
Vegorítis, Límni see Vegorítida, Límni
11 Q14 **Vegreville** Alberta, SW Canada 53°30′N 112°02′W
95 K21 **Veinge** Halland, S Sweden 56°33′N 13°04′E
61 B21 **Veinticinco de Mayo** var. 25 de Mayo. Buenos Aires, E Argentina 35°27′S 60°11′W
63 I14 **Veinticinco de Mayo** La Pampa, C Argentina 37°45′S 67°40′W
119 F15 **Veisiejai** Alytus, S Lithuania 54°06′N 23°42′E
95 F23 **Vejen** Ribe, W Denmark 55°29′N 09°13′E
104 K16 **Vejer de la Frontera** Andalucía, S Spain 36°15′N 05°58′W
95 G23 **Vejle** Vejle, C Denmark 55°43′N 09°33′E
95 F23 **Vejle** off. Vejle Amt. ◆ county C Denmark
Vejle Amt see Vejle
114 M7 **Vekilski** Shumen, NE Bulgaria 43°33′N 27°19′E
54 G3 **Vela, Cabo de la** headland NE Colombia 12°14′N 72°13′W
Vela Goa see Goa
113 F15 **Vela Luka** Dubrovnik-Neretva, S Croatia 42°57′N 16°43′E
61 G19 **Velázquez** Rocha, E Uruguay 34°05′S 54°16′W
101 E15 **Velbert** Nordrhein-Westfalen, W Germany 51°22′N 07°03′E
109 S9 **Velden** Kärnten, S Austria 46°37′N 13°59′E
Veldes see Bled
99 K15 **Veldhoven** Noord-Brabant, S Netherlands 51°24′N 05°24′E
112 C11 **Velebit** ▲ C Croatia
114 N11 **Veleka** ≈ SE Bulgaria
109 V10 **Velenje** Ger. Wöllan. N Slovenia 46°22′N 15°07′E
190 E12 **Vele, Pointe** headland Île Futuna, S Wallis and Futuna
113 O18 **Veles** Turk. Köprülü. C FYR Macedonia 41°43′N 21°49′E
113 M20 **Velešta** SW FYR Macedonia 41°16′N 20°37′E
115 F16 **Velestíno** prev. Velestínon. Thessalía, C Greece 39°23′N 22°45′E
Velestínon see Velestíno
Velevshchina see Vyelyewshchyna
54 F9 **Vélez** Santander, C Colombia 06°02′N 73°43′W
105 Q13 **Vélez Blanco** Andalucía, S Spain 37°43′N 02°07′W
104 M17 **Vélez de la Gomera, Peñon de** island group S Spain
105 N15 **Vélez-Málaga** Andalucía, S Spain 36°47′N 04°06′W
105 Q13 **Vélez Rubio** Andalucía, S Spain 37°39′N 02°04′W
Velha Goa see Goa
Velho see Porto Velho
112 E8 **Velika Gorica** Zagreb, N Croatia 45°43′N 16°03′E
112 C9 **Velika Kapela** ▲ NW Croatia
Velika Kikinda see Kikinda
112 D10 **Velika Kladuša** Federacija Bosna I Hercegovina, NW Bosnia and Herzegovina 45°10′N 15°48′E
112 N11 **Velika Morava** var. Glavn'a Morava, Morava, Ger. Grosse Morava. ≈ C Serbia
112 N12 **Velika Plana** Serbia, C Serbia 44°20′N 21°01′E
109 U10 **Velika Raduha** ▲ N Slovenia 46°24′N 14°46′E
123 V7 **Velikaya** ≈ NE Russian Federation
124 F15 **Velikaya** ≈ W Russian Federation
Velikaya Berestovitsa see Vyalikaya Byerastavitsa
Velikaya Lepetikha see Velyka Lepetykha
Veliki Bečkerek see Zrenjanin
112 P12 **Veliki Krš** var. Stol. ▲ E Serbia 44°10′N 22°09′E
114 L8 **Veliki Preslav** prev. Preslav. Shumen, NE Bulgaria 43°09′N 26°50′E
112 B9 **Veliki Risnjak** ▲ NW Croatia 45°30′N 14°31′E
109 T13 **Veliki Snežnik** Ger. Schneeberg, It. Monte Nevoso. ▲ SW Slovenia 45°36′N 14°25′E
112 J13 **Veliki Stolac** ▲ E Bosnia and Herzegovina 43°55′N 19°15′E
Velikiy Bor see Vyaliki Bor
124 G16 **Velikiye Luki** Pskovskaya Oblast', W Russian Federation 56°20′N 30°27′E
124 H14 **Velikiy Novgorod** prev. Novgorod. Novgorodskaya Oblast', W Russian Federation 58°32′N 31°15′E
125 P12 **Velikiy Ustyug** Vologodskaya Oblast', NW Russian Federation 60°46′N 46°18′E
112 N11 **Veliko Gradište** Serbia, NE Serbia 44°46′N 21°28′E
155 I18 **Velikonda Range** ▲ SE India

◆ Country
● Country Capital
◇ Dependent Territory
○ Dependent Territory Capital
◆ Administrative Regions
✈ International Airport
▲ Mountain
▲ Mountain Range
Volcano
≈ River
◎ Lake
⊠ Reservoir

114 *K9* **Veliko Tŭrnovo** *prev.* Tirnovo, Trnovo, Tŭrnovo. Veliko Tŭrnovo, N Bulgaria *43°05′N 25°40′E*
114 *K8* **Veliko Tŭrnovo** ⬖ *province* N Bulgaria
Velikovec *see* Völkermarkt
125 *R5* **Velikovisochnoye** Nenetskiy Avtonomnyy Okrug, NW Russian Federation *67°13′N 52°00′E*
76 *H12* **Vélingara** C Senegal *15°00′N 14°39′W*
76 *H11* **Vélingara** S Senegal *13°12′N 14°05′W*
114 *H11* **Velingrad** Pazardzhik, C Bulgaria *42°01′N 24°00′E*
126 *H3* **Velizh** Smolenskaya Oblast', W Russian Federation *55°30′N 31°06′E*
111 *F16* **Velká Deštná** *var.* Deštná, Grosskoppe, ***Ger.*** Deschnaer Koppe. ▲ NE Czech Republic *50°18′N 16°25′E*
111 *F18* **Velké Meziříčí** ***Ger.*** Grossmeseritsch. Vysočina, C Czech Republic *49°22′N 16°02′E*
92 *N1* **Velkomstpynten** *headland* NW Svalbard *79°51′N 11°37′E*
111 *K21* **Veľký Krtíš** Banskobystrický Kraj, C Slovakia *48°13′N 19°21′E*
186 *J8* **Vella Lavella** *var.* Mbilua. *island* New Georgia Islands, NW Solomon Islands
107 *I15* **Velletri** Lazio, C Italy *41°41′N 12°47′E*
95 *K23* **Vellinge** Skåne, S Sweden *55°29′N 13°00′E*
155 *I19* **Vellore** Tamil Nādu, SE India *12°56′N 79°09′E*
Velobriga *see* Viana do Castelo
115 *G21* **Velopoúla** *island* S Greece
98 *M12* **Velp** Gelderland, SE Netherlands *52°00′N 05°59′E*
Velsen *see* Velsen-Noord
98 *H9* **Velsen-Noord** *var.* Velsen. Noord-Holland, W Netherlands *52°27′N 04°40′E*
125 *N12* **Vel'sk** *var.* Velsk. Arkhangel'skaya Oblast', NW Russian Federation *61°03′N 42°01′E*
Velsuna *see* Orvieto
98 *K10* **Veluwemeer** *lake channel* C Netherlands
28 *M3* **Velva** North Dakota, N USA *48°03′N 100°55′W*
Velvendos/Velvendós *see* Velventós
115 *E14* **Velventós** *var.* Velvendos, Velvendós. Dytikí Makedonía, N Greece *40°15′N 22°04′E*
117 *S5* **Velyka Bahachka** Poltavs'ka Oblast', C Ukraine *49°46′N 33°44′E*
117 *S9* **Velyka Lepetykha** ***Rus.*** Velikaya Lepetikha. Khersons'ka Oblast', S Ukraine *47°09′N 33°59′E*
117 *O10* **Velyka Mykhaylivka** Odes'ka Oblast', SW Ukraine *47°07′N 29°49′E*
117 *W8* **Velyka Novosilka** Donets'ka Oblast', E Ukraine *47°49′N 36°49′E*
117 *S9* **Velyka Oleksandrivka** Khersons'ka Oblast', S Ukraine *47°17′N 33°16′E*
117 *T4* **Velyka Pysarivka** Sums'ka Oblast', NE Ukraine *50°25′N 35°28′E*
116 *G6* **Velykyy Bereznyy** Zakarpats'ka Oblast', W Ukraine *48°54′N 22°27′E*
117 *W4* **Velykyy Burluk** Kharkivs'ka Oblast', E Ukraine *50°04′N 37°25′E*
Velykyy Tokmak *see* Tokmak
173 *P7* **Vema Fracture Zone** *tectonic feature* W Indian Ocean
65 *P18* **Vema Seamount** *undersea feature* SW Indian Ocean *31°38′S 08°19′E*
93 *F17* **Vemdalen** Jämtland, C Sweden *62°26′N 13°50′E*
95 *N19* **Vena** Kalmar, S Sweden *57°31′N 16°00′E*
41 *N11* **Venado** San Luis Potosí, C Mexico *22°56′N 101°05′W*
62 *L11* **Venado Tuerto** Entre Ríos, E Argentina *33°45′S 61°56′W*
61 *A19* **Venado Tuerto** Santa Fe, C Argentina *33°46′S 61°57′W*
107 *K16* **Venafro** Molise, C Italy *41°28′N 14°03′E*
55 *Q9* **Venamo, Cerro** ▲ E Venezuela *05°56′N 61°25′W*
106 *B8* **Venaria** Piemonte, NW Italy *45°09′N 07°40′E*
103 *U15* **Vence** Alpes-Maritimes, SE France *43°45′N 07°07′E*
104 *H5* **Venda Nova** Vila Real, N Portugal *41°40′N 07°58′W*
104 *G11* **Vendas Novas** Évora, S Portugal *38°41′N 08°27′W*
102 *J9* **Vendée** ⬖ *department* NW France
103 *Q6* **Vendeuvre-sur-Barse** Aube, NE France *48°08′N 04°17′E*
102 *M7* **Vendôme** Loir-et-Cher, C France *47°48′N 01°04′E*
Venedig *see* Venezia
Vener, Lake *see* Vänern
106 *I8* **Veneta, Laguna** *lagoon* NE Italy
Venetia *see* Venezia
39 *S7* **Venetie** Alaska, USA *67°00′N 146°25′W*
106 *H8* **Veneto** *var.* Venezia Euganea. ⬖ *region* NE Italy
114 *M7* **Venets** Shumen, NE Bulgaria *43°33′N 26°56′E*
126 *L5* **Venev** Tul'skaya Oblast', W Russian Federation *54°18′N 38°16′E*
106 *I8* **Venezia** ***Eng.*** Venice, ***Fr.*** Venise, ***Ger.*** Venedig; ***anc.*** Venetia. Veneto, NE Italy *45°26′N 12°20′E*
Venezia Euganea *see* Veneto
Venezia, Golfo di *see* Venice, Gulf of
Venezia Tridentina *see* Trentino-Alto Adige
54 *K8* **Venezuela** ***off.*** Republic of Venezuela; ***prev.*** Estados Unidos de Venezuela, United States of Venezuela. ◆ *republic* N South America
Venezuela, Cordillera de *see* Costa, Cordillera de la
Venezuela, Estados Unidos de *see* Venezuela
54 *I4* **Venezuela, Golfo de** ***Eng.*** Gulf of Maracaibo, Gulf of Venezuela. *gulf* NW Venezuela
Venezuela, Gulf of *see* Venezuela, Golfo de
64 *F11* **Venezuelan Basin** *undersea feature* E Caribbean Sea
Venezuela, Republic of *see* Venezuela
Venezuela, United States of *see* Venezuela
155 *D16* **Vengurla** Mahārāshtra, W India *15°55′N 73°39′E*
39 *O15* **Veniaminof, Mount** ▲ Alaska, USA *56°12′N 159°24′W*
23 *V14* **Venice** Florida, SE USA *27°06′N 82°27′W*
22 *L10* **Venice** Louisiana, S USA *29°15′N 89°20′W*
Venice *see* Venezia
106 *J8* **Venice, Gulf of** ***It.*** Golfo di Venezia, ***Slvn.*** Beneški Zaliv. *gulf* N Adriatic Sea
Venise *see* Venezia
94 *K13* **Venjan** Dalarna, C Sweden *60°58′N 13°55′E*
94 *K13* **Venjansjön** ◎ C Sweden
155 *J18* **Venkatagiri** Andhra Pradesh, E India *14°00′N 79°39′E*
99 *M15* **Venlo** ***prev.*** Venloo. Limburg, SE Netherlands *51°22′N 06°11′E*
Venloo *see* Venlo
95 *E18* **Vennesla** Vest-Agder, S Norway *58°15′N 08°00′E*
107 *M17* **Venosa** ***anc.*** Venusia. Basilicata, S Italy *40°57′N 15°49′E*
Venoste, Alpi *see* Ötztaler Alpen
Venraij *see* Venray
99 *M14* **Venray** *var.* Venraij. Limburg, SE Netherlands *51°32′N 05°59′E*
118 *C8* **Venta** ***Ger.*** Windau. ≈ Latvia/Lithuania
Venta Belgarum *see* Winchester
40 *G9* **Ventana, Punta Arena de la** *var.* Punta de la Ventana. *headland* NW Mexico *24°03′N 109°49′W*
Ventana, Punta de la *see* Ventana, Punta Arena de la
61 *B23* **Ventana, Sierra de la** *hill range* E Argentina
Ventia *see* Valence
191 *S11* **Vent, Îles du** *var.* Windward Islands. *island group* Archipel de la Société, W French Polynesia
191 *R10* **Vent, Îles Sous le** *var.* Leeward Islands. *island group* Archipel de la Société, W French Polynesia
106 *B11* **Ventimiglia** Liguria, NW Italy *43°47′N 07°37′E*
97 *M24* **Ventnor** S England, United Kingdom *50°36′N 01°11′W*
18 *J17* **Ventnor City** New Jersey, NE USA *39°19′N 74°27′W*
103 *S14* **Ventoux, Mont** ▲ SE France *44°12′N 05°21′E*
118 *C8* **Ventspils** ***Ger.*** Windau. Ventspils, NW Latvia *57°22′N 21°34′E*
54 *M10* **Ventuari, Río** ≈ S Venezuela
35 *R15* **Ventura** California, W USA *34°15′N 119°18′W*
182 *F8* **Venus Bay** South Australia *33°15′S 134°42′E*
Venusia *see* Venosa
191 *P7* **Vénus, Pointe** *var.* Pointe Tataaihoa. *headland* Tahiti, W French Polynesia *17°28′S 149°29′W*
41 *V16* **Venustiano Carranza** Chiapas, SE Mexico *16°21′N 92°33′W*
41 *N7* **Venustiano Carranza, Presa** ⊠ NE Mexico
61 *B15* **Vera** Santa Fe, C Argentina *29°28′S 60°10′W*
105 *Q14* **Vera** Andalucía, S Spain *37°15′N 01°51′W*
63 *K18* **Vera, Bahía** *bay* E Argentina
41 *R14* **Veracruz** *var.* Veracruz Llave. Veracruz-Llave, E Mexico *19°10′N 96°09′W*
Veracruz *see* Veracruz-Llave
41 *Q13* **Veracruz-Llave** *var.* Veracruz. ⬖ *state* E Mexico
Veracruz Llave *see* Veracruz
43 *Q16* **Veraguas** ***off.*** Provincia de Veraguas. ⬖ *province* W Panama
Veraguas, Provincia de *see* Veraguas
Veramin *see* Varāmīn
154 *B12* **Verāval** Gujarāt, W India *20°54′N 70°22′E*
106 *C6* **Verbania** Piemonte, NW Italy *45°56′N 08°34′E*
107 *N20* **Verbicaro** Calabria, SW Italy *39°44′N 15°51′E*
108 *D11* **Verbier** Valais, SW Switzerland *46°06′N 07°14′E*
Vercellae *see* Vercelli
106 *C8* **Vercelli** ***anc.*** Vercellae. Piemonte, NW Italy *45°19′N 08°25′E*
103 *S13* **Vercors** *physical region* E France
Verdal *see* Verdalsøra
93 *E16* **Verdalsøra** *var.* Verdal. Nord-Trøndelag, C Norway *63°47′N 11°27′E*
Verde, Cabo *see* Cape Verde
44 *J5* **Verde, Cape** *headland* Long Island, C Bahamas *22°51′N 75°50′W*
104 *M2* **Verde, Costa** *coastal region* N Spain
Verde Grande, Río/Verde Grande y de Belem, Río *see* Verde, Río
100 *H11* **Verden** Niedersachsen, NW Germany *52°55′N 09°14′E*
57 *P16* **Verde, Río** ≈ Bolivia/Brazil
59 *J19* **Verde, Rio** ≈ SE Brazil
40 *M12* **Verde, Río** *var.* Río Verde Grande, Río Verde Grande y de Belem. ≈ C Mexico
41 *Q16* **Verde, Río** ≈ SE Mexico
36 *L13* **Verde River** ≈ Arizona, SW USA
Verdhikoúsa/Verdhikoússa *see* Verdikoússa
27 *Q8* **Verdigris River** ≈ Kansas/Oklahoma, C USA
115 *E15* **Verdikoússa** *var.* Verdhikoúsa, Verdhikoússa. Thessalía, C Greece *39°47′N 21°59′E*
103 *S15* **Verdon** ≈ SE France
15 *O12* **Verdun** Québec, SE Canada *45°27′N 73°36′W*
103 *S4* **Verdun** *var.* Verdun-sur-Meuse; ***anc.*** Verodunum. Meuse, NE France *49°09′N 05°25′E*
Verdun-sur-Meuse *see* Verdun
83 *J21* **Vereeniging** Gauteng, NE South Africa *26°41′S 27°56′E*
Veremeyki *see* Vyeramyeyki
125 *T14* **Vereshchagino** Permskaya Oblast', NW Russian Federation *58°06′N 54°38′E*
76 *G14* **Verga, Cap** *headland* W Guinea *10°12′N 14°27′W*
61 *G18* **Vergara** Treinta y Tres, E Uruguay *32°58′S 53°54′W*
108 *G11* **Vergeletto** Ticino, S Switzerland *46°13′N 08°34′E*
18 *L8* **Vergennes** Vermont, NE USA *44°09′N 73°13′W*
Veria *see* Véroia
104 *I5* **Verín** Galicia, NW Spain *41°55′N 07°26′W*
Verin T'alin *see* T'alin
118 *K6* **Veriora** Põlvamaa, SE Estonia *57°57′N 27°23′E*
117 *T7* **Verkhivtseve** Dnipropetrovs'ka Oblast', E Ukraine *48°27′N 34°15′E*
Verkhnedvinsk *see* Vyerkhnyadzvinsk
122 *K10* **Verkhneimbatsk** Krasnoyarskiy Kray, N Russian Federation *63°06′N 88°03′E*
124 *I3* **Verkhnetulomskiy** Murmanskaya Oblast', NW Russian Federation *68°37′N 31°46′E*
124 *I3* **Verkhnetulomskoye Vodokhranilishche** ⊠ NW Russian Federation
Verkhneudinsk *see* Ulan-Ude
123 *P10* **Verkhnevilyuysk** Respublika Sakha (Yakutiya), NE Russian Federation *63°44′N 119°59′E*
127 *W5* **Verkhniy Avzyan** Respublika Bashkortostan, W Russian Federation *53°31′N 57°26′E*
127 *Q11* **Verkhniy Baskunchak** Astrakhanskaya Oblast', SW Russian Federation *48°14′N 46°43′E*
127 *W3* **Verkhniye Kigi** Respublika Bashkortostan, W Russian Federation *55°25′N 58°40′E*
117 *T9* **Verkhniy Rohachyk** Khersons'ka Oblast', S Ukraine *47°16′N 34°16′E*
123 *Q11* **Verkhnyaya Amga** Respublika Sakha (Yakutiya), NE Russian Federation *59°34′N 127°07′E*
125 *V6* **Verkhnyaya Inta** Respublika Komi, NW Russian Federation *65°55′N 60°07′E*
125 *O10* **Verkhnyaya Toyma** Arkhangel'skaya Oblast', NW Russian Federation *62°12′N 44°57′E*
126 *K6* **Verkhov'ye** Orlovskaya Oblast', W Russian Federation *52°49′N 37°20′E*
116 *I8* **Verkhovyna** Ivano-Frankivs'ka Oblast', W Ukraine *48°09′N 24°48′E*
123 *P8* **Verkhoyanskiy Khrebet** ▲▲ NE Russian Federation
117 *T7* **Verkn'odniprovs'k** Dnipropetrovs'ka Oblast', E Ukraine *48°40′N 34°17′E*
101 *G14* **Verl** Nordrhein-Westfalen, NW Germany *51°52′N 08°30′E*
92 *N1* **Verlegenhuken** *headland* N Svalbard *80°03′N 16°15′E*
82 *A9* **Vermelha, Ponta** *headland* NW Angola *05°40′S 12°09′E*
103 *P7* **Vermenton** Yonne, C France *47°40′N 03°43′E*
11 *R14* **Vermilion** Alberta, SW Canada *53°21′N 110°52′W*
31 *T11* **Vermilion** Ohio, N USA *41°25′N 82°21′W*
22 *I10* **Vermilion Bay** *bay* Louisiana, S USA
29 *V4* **Vermilion Lake** ◎ Minnesota, N USA
14 *F9* **Vermilion River** ≈ Ontario, S Canada
30 *L12* **Vermilion River** ≈ Illinois, N USA
29 *R12* **Vermillion** South Dakota, N USA *42°46′N 96°55′W*
29 *R12* **Vermillion River** ≈ South Dakota, N USA
15 *O9* **Vermillon, Rivière** ≈ Québec, SE Canada
115 *E14* **Vérmio** ▲▲ N Greece
18 *L8* **Vermont** ***off.*** State of Vermont, ***also known as*** Green Mountain State. ⬖ *state* NE USA
113 *K16* **Vermosh** *var.* Vermoshi. Shkodër, N Albania *42°37′N 19°42′E*
Vermoshi *see* Vermosh
37 *O3* **Vernal** Utah, W USA *40°27′N 109°31′W*
14 *G11* **Verner** Ontario, S Canada *46°24′N 80°04′W*
102 *M5* **Verneuil-sur-Avre** Eure, N France *48°44′N 00°55′E*
114 *D13* **Vérno** ▲▲ N Greece
11 *N17* **Vernon** British Columbia, SW Canada *50°17′N 119°19′W*
102 *M4* **Vernon** Eure, N France *49°04′N 01°28′E*
23 *N3* **Vernon** Alabama, S USA *33°45′N 88°06′W*
31 *P15* **Vernon** Indiana, N USA *38°59′N 85°39′W*
25 *Q4* **Vernon** Texas, SW USA *34°11′N 99°17′W*
32 *G10* **Vernonia** Oregon, NW USA *45°51′N 123°11′W*
14 *G12* **Vernon, Lake** ◎ Ontario, S Canada
22 *G7* **Vernon Lake** ⊠ Louisiana, S USA
23 *Y13* **Vero Beach** Florida, SE USA *27°38′N 80°24′W*
Verőcze *see* Virovitica
Verodunum *see* Verdun
115 *E14* **Véroia** *var.* Veria, Vérroia, ***Turk.*** Karaferiye. Kentrikí Makedonía, N Greece *40°32′N 22°11′E*
106 *E8* **Verolanuova** Lombardia, N Italy *45°20′N 10°06′E*
14 *K14* **Verona** Ontario, SE Canada *44°30′N 76°42′W*
106 *G8* **Verona** Veneto, NE Italy *45°27′N 11°E*
29 *P6* **Verona** North Dakota, N USA *46°19′N 98°03′W*
30 *L9* **Verona** Wisconsin, N USA *42°59′N 89°33′W*
61 *E20* **Verónica** Buenos Aires, E Argentina *35°25′S 57°16′W*
22 *J9* **Verret, Lake** ◎ Louisiana, S USA
Vérroia *see* Véroia
103 *N5* **Versailles** Yvelines, N France *48°48′N 02°08′E*
31 *P15* **Versailles** Indiana, N USA *39°04′N 85°16′W*
20 *M5* **Versailles** Kentucky, S USA *38°02′N 84°45′W*
27 *U5* **Versailles** Missouri, C USA *38°25′N 92°51′W*
31 *Q13* **Versailles** Ohio, N USA *40°13′N 84°28′W*
Versecz *see* Vršac
108 *A10* **Versoix** Genève, SW Switzerland *46°17′N 06°10′E*
15 *Z6* **Verte, Pointe** *headland* Québec, SE Canada *48°36′N 64°10′W*
111 *I22* **Vértes** ▲▲ NW Hungary
44 *G6* **Vertientes** Camagüey, C Cuba *21°18′N 78°11′W*
114 *G13* **Vertískos** ▲▲ N Greece
102 *I8* **Vertou** Loire-Atlantique, NW France *47°10′N 01°28′W*
Verulamium *see* St Albans
99 *L19* **Verviers** Liège, E Belgium *50°36′N 05°52′E*
103 *Y14* **Vescovato** Corse, France, C Mediterranean Sea *42°30′N 09°27′E*
99 *L20* **Vesdre** ≈ E Belgium
117 *U10* **Vesele** ***Rus.*** Veseloye. Zaporiz'ka Oblast', S Ukraine *47°00′N 34°52′E*
111 *D18* **Veselí nad Lužnicí** *var.* Weseli an der Lainsitz, ***Ger.*** Frohenbruck. Jihočeský Kraj, S Czech Republic *49°11′N 14°40′E*
114 *M9* **Veselinovo** Shumen, NE Bulgaria *43°01′N 27°02′E*
126 *L12* **Veselovskoye Vodokhranilishche** ⊠ SW Russian Federation
Veseloye *see* Vesele
117 *Q9* **Veselynove** Mykolayivs'ka Oblast', S Ukraine *47°21′N 31°15′E*
Veseya *see* Vyasyeya
126 *M10* **Veshenskaya** Rostovskaya Oblast', SW Russian Federation *49°37′N 41°43′E*
127 *Q5* **Veshkayma** Ul'yanovskaya Oblast', W Russian Federation *54°04′N 47°06′E*
Vesisaari *see* Vadsø
Vesontio *see* Besançon
103 *T7* **Vesoul** ***anc.*** Vesulium, Vesulum. Haute-Saône, E France *47°37′N 06°09′E*
95 *J20* **Vessigebro** Halland, S Sweden *56°58′N 12°40′E*
95 *D17* **Vest-Agder** ⬖ *county* S Norway
23 *P4* **Vestavia Hills** Alabama, S USA *33°27′N 86°47′W*
84 *F6* **Vesterålen** *island* NW Norway
92 *G10* **Vesterålen** *island group* N Norway
87 *V3* **Vestervig** Viborg, NW Denmark *56°46′N 08°20′E*
92 *H2* **Vestfirdhir** ⬖ *region* NW Iceland
92 *G11* **Vestfjorden** *fjord* C Norway
95 *G16* **Vestfold** ⬖ *county* S Norway
Vestmanhavn *see* Vestmanna
95 *B18* **Vestmanna** ***Dan.*** Vestmanhavn. Streymoy, N Faeroe Islands *62°09′N 07°11′W*
92 *I4* **Vestmannaeyjar** Sudhurland, S Iceland *63°26′N 20°14′W*
94 *E9* **Vestnes** Møre og Romsdal, S Norway *62°39′N 07°00′E*
95 *I23* **Vestsjælland** ***off.*** Vestsjællands Amt. ⬖ *county* E Denmark
Vestsjællands Amt *see* Vestsjælland
92 *H3* **Vesturland** ⬖ *region* W Iceland
92 *G11* **Vestvågøya** *island* C Norway
Vesulium/Vesulum *see* Vesoul
Vesuna *see* Périgueux
107 *K17* **Vesuvio** ***Eng.*** Vesuvius. ✲ S Italy *40°48′N 14°29′E*
Vesuvius *see* Vesuvio
124 *K14* **Ves'yegonsk** Tverskaya Oblast', W Russian Federation *58°40′N 37°13′E*
111 *I23* **Veszprém** ***Ger.*** Veszprim. Veszprém, W Hungary *47°06′N 17°54′E*
111 *H23* **Veszprém** ***off.*** Veszprém Megye. ⬖ *county* W Hungary
Veszprém Megye *see* Veszprém
Veszprim *see* Veszprém
Vetka *see* Vyetka
95 *M19* **Vetlanda** Jönköping, S Sweden *57°26′N 15°05′E*
127 *P1* **Vetluga** Nizhegorodskaya Oblast', W Russian Federation *57°51′N 45°45′E*
125 *P14* **Vetluga** ≈ NW Russian Federation
125 *O14* **Vetluzhskiy** Kostromskaya Oblast', NW Russian Federation *58°21′N 45°25′E*
127 *P2* **Vetluzhskiy** Nizhegorodskaya Oblast', W Russian Federation *57°10′N 45°07′E*
114 *K7* **Vetovo** Ruse, N Bulgaria *43°42′N 26°16′E*
107 *H14* **Vetralla** Lazio, C Italy *42°18′N 12°03′E*
Vetrino *see* Vyetryna
122 *L7* **Vetrovaya, Gora** ▲ N Russian Federation *73°54′N 95°00′E*
Vetter, Lake *see* Vättern
106 *J13* **Vettore, Monte** ▲ C Italy *42°49′N 13°15′E*
99 *A17* **Veurne** *var.* Furnes. West-Vlaanderen, W Belgium *51°04′N 02°40′E*
31 *Q15* **Vevay** Indiana, N USA *38°45′N 85°08′W*
108 *C10* **Vevey** ***Ger.*** Vivis; ***anc.*** Vibiscum. Vaud, SW Switzerland *46°28′N 06°51′E*
Vexiö *see* Växjö
103 *S13* **Veynes** Hautes-Alpes, SE France *44°33′N 05°51′E*
103 *N11* **Vézère** ≈ W France
114 *I9* **Vezhen** ▲ C Bulgaria *42°45′N 24°22′E*
136 *K11* **Vezirköprü** Samsun, N Turkey *41°09′N 35°27′E*
57 *J18* **Viacha** La Paz, W Bolivia *16°40′S 68°17′W*
27 *R10* **Vian** Oklahoma, C USA *35°30′N 94°56′W*
Viana de Castelo *see* Viana do Castelo
104 *H12* **Viana do Alentejo** Évora, S Portugal *38°20′N 08°00′W*
104 *I4* **Viana do Bolo** Galicia, NW Spain *42°10′N 07°06′W*
104 *G5* **Viana do Castelo** *var.* Viana de Castelo; ***anc.*** Velobriga. Viana do Castelo, NW Portugal *41°41′N 08°50′W*
104 *G5* **Viana do Castelo** *var.* Viana de Castelo. ⬖ *district* N Portugal
98 *J12* **Vianen** Utrecht, C Netherlands *52°N 05°06′E*
167 *Q8* **Viangchan** ***Eng./Fr.*** Vientiane. ● (Laos) C Laos *17°58′N 102°38′E*
167 *P6* **Viangphoukha** *var.* Vieng Pou Kha. Louang Namtha, N Laos *20°41′N 101°03′E*
104 *K13* **Viar** ≈ SW Spain
106 *E11* **Viareggio** Toscana, C Italy *43°52′N 10°15′E*
103 *O14* **Viaur** ≈ S France
Vibiscum *see* Vevey
95 *G21* **Viborg** Viborg, NW Denmark *56°28′N 09°25′E*
29 *R12* **Viborg** South Dakota, N USA *43°10′N 97°04′W*
95 *F21* **Viborg** ***off.*** Viborg Amt. ⬖ *county* NW Denmark
Viborg Amt *see* Viborg
107 *N22* **Vibo Valentia** ***prev.*** Monteleone di Calabria; ***anc.*** Hipponium. Calabria, SW Italy *38°40′N 16°06′E*
105 *W5* **Vic** *var.* Vich; ***anc.*** Ausa, Vicus Ausonensis. Cataluña, NE Spain *41°56′N 02°16′E*
102 *K16* **Vic-en-Bigorre** Hautes-Pyrénées, S France *43°23′N 00°04′E*
40 *K10* **Vicente Guerrero** Durango, C Mexico *23°30′N 104°24′W*
41 *P10* **Vicente Guerrero, Presa** *var.* Presa de las Adjuntas. ⊠ NE Mexico
Vicentia *see* Vicenza
106 *G8* **Vicenza** ***anc.*** Vicentia. Veneto, NE Italy *45°32′N 11°31′E*
Vich *see* Vic
54 *J10* **Vichada** ***off.*** Comisaría del Vichada. ⬖ *province* E Colombia
Vichada, Comisaría del *see* Vichada
54 *K10* **Vichada, Río** ≈ E Colombia
61 *G17* **Vichadero** Rivera, NE Uruguay *31°45′S 54°41′W*
Vichegda *see* Vychegda
124 *M16* **Vichuga** Ivanovskaya Oblast', W Russian Federation *57°13′N 41°51′E*
103 *P10* **Vichy** Allier, C France *46°08′N 03°26′E*
26 *K9* **Vici** Oklahoma, C USA *36°09′N 99°18′W*
31 *P10* **Vicksburg** Michigan, N USA *42°07′N 85°31′W*
22 *J5* **Vicksburg** Mississippi, S USA *32°21′N 90°52′W*
103 *O12* **Vic-sur-Cère** Cantal, C France *45°00′N 02°36′E*
59 *I21* **Víctor** Mato Grosso do Sul, SW Brazil *21°39′S 53°21′W*
29 *X14* **Victor** Iowa, C USA *41°45′N 92°18′W*
182 *I10* **Victor Harbor** South Australia *35°33′S 138°37′E*
61 *C18* **Victoria** Entre Ríos, E Argentina *32°40′S 60°10′W*
10 *L17* **Victoria** *province capital* Vancouver Island, British Columbia, SW Canada *48°25′N 123°22′W*
45 *R14* **Victoria** NW Grenada *12°12′N 61°42′W*
42 *H6* **Victoria** Yoro, NW Honduras *15°01′N 87°28′W*
121 *O15* **Victoria** *var.* Rabat. Gozo, NW Malta *36°02′N 14°14′E*
116 *I12* **Victoria** ***Ger.*** Viktoriastadt. Brașov, C Romania *45°44′N 24°41′E*
172 *H17* **Victoria** ● (Seychelles) Mahé, SW Seychelles *04°38′S 28°28′E*
25 *U13* **Victoria** Texas, SW USA *28°47′N 96°59′W*
183 *N12* **Victoria** ⬖ *state* SE Australia
174 *K7* **Victoria** ≈ Western Australia
Victoria *see* Labuan, East Malaysia
Victoria *see* Masvingo, Zimbabwe
Victoria Bank *see* Vitória Seamount
11 *Y15* **Victoria Beach** Manitoba, S Canada *50°40′N 96°30′W*
Victoria de Durango *see* Durango
Victoria de las Tunas *see* Las Tunas
83 *I16* **Victoria Falls** Matabeleland North, W Zimbabwe *17°55′S 25°51′E*
83 *I16* **Victoria Falls** *waterfall* Zambia/Zimbabwe
83 *I16* **Victoria Falls** ✈ Matabeleland North, W Zimbabwe *18°03′S 25°48′E*
Victoria Falls *see* Iguaçu, Salto do
63 *F19* **Victoria, Isla** *island* Archipiélago de los Chonos, S Chile
8 *K6* **Victoria Island** *island* Northwest Territories/Nunavut, NW Canada
182 *L8* **Victoria, Lake** ◎ New South Wales, SE Australia
68 *I12* **Victoria, Lake** *var.* Victoria Nyanza. ◎ E Africa
195 *S13* **Victoria Land** *physical region* Antarctica
187 *X14* **Victoria, Mount** ▲ Viti Levu, W Fiji *17°37′S 178°00′E*
166 *L5* **Victoria, Mount** ▲ W Burma (Myanmar) *21°13′N 93°53′E*
186 *E9* **Victoria, Mount** ▲ S Papua New Guinea *08°51′S 147°36′E*
81 *F17* **Victoria Nile** *var.* Somerset Nile. ≈ C Uganda
Victoria Nyanza *see* Victoria, Lake
42 *G3* **Victoria Peak** ▲ SE Belize *16°50′N 88°38′W*
185 *H16* **Victoria Range** ▲▲ South Island, New Zealand
181 *O3* **Victoria River** ≈ Northern Territory, N Australia
181 *P3* **Victoria River Roadhouse** Northern Territory, N Australia *15°37′S 131°07′E*
15 *Q11* **Victoriaville** Québec, SE Canada *46°04′N 71°57′W*
Victoria-Wes *see* Victoria West
83 *G24* **Victoria West** ***Afr.*** Victoria-Wes. Northern Cape, W South Africa *31°25′S 23°08′E*
62 *J13* **Victorica** La Pampa, C Argentina *36°15′S 65°25′W*
Victor, Mount *see* Belgicafjella
35 *U14* **Victorville** California, W USA *34°32′N 117°17′W*
62 *G9* **Vicuña** Coquimbo, N Chile *30°00′S 70°44′W*
62 *K11* **Vicuña Mackenna** Córdoba, C Argentina *33°53′S 64°25′W*
Vicus Ausonensis *see* Vic
Vicus Elbii *see* Viterbo
33 *X7* **Vida** Montana, NW USA *47°52′N 105°30′W*
23 *V6* **Vidalia** Georgia, SE USA *32°13′N 82°24′W*
22 *J7* **Vidalia** Louisiana, S USA *31°34′N 91°25′W*
95 *F22* **Videbæk** Ringkøbing, C Denmark *56°08′N 08°38′E*
60 *I13* **Videira** Santa Catarina, S Brazil *27°00′S 51°08′W*
116 *J14* **Videle** Teleorman, S Romania *44°15′N 25°27′E*
Videm-Krško *see* Krško
Vídeň *see* Wien
104 *H12* **Vidigueira** Beja, S Portugal *38°12′N 07°48′W*
114 *J9* **Vidima** ≈ N Bulgaria
114 *G7* **Vidin** ***anc.*** Bononia. Vidin, NW Bulgaria *44°00′N 22°52′E*
114 *F8* **Vidin** ⬖ *province* NW Bulgaria
154 *H10* **Vidisha** Madhya Pradesh, C India *23°30′N 77°50′E*
25 *Y10* **Vidor** Texas, SW USA *30°07′N 94°01′W*
95 *L20* **Vidöstern** ◎ S Sweden
92 *J13* **Vidsel** Norrbotten, N Sweden *65°49′N 20°31′E*
118 *H9* **Vidzemes Augstiene** ▲▲ C Latvia
118 *J12* **Vidzy** Vitsyebskaya Voblasts', NW Belarus *55°24′N 26°38′E*
63 *L16* **Viedma** Río Negro, E Argentina *40°50′S 62°58′W*
63 *H22* **Viedma, Lago** ◎ S Argentina
45 *O11* **Vieille Case** *var.* Itassi. N Dominica *15°36′N 61°24′W*
104 *M2* **Vieja, Peña** ▲ N Spain *43°09′N 04°47′W*
24 *J10* **Vieja, Sierra** ▲▲ Texas, SW USA
40 *E4* **Viejo, Cerro** ▲ NW Mexico *30°16′N 112°18′W*
56 *B9* **Viejo, Cerro** ▲ N Peru *04°54′S 79°24′W*
118 *E10* **Viekšniai** Telšiai, NW Lithuania *56°14′N 22°33′E*
105 *U3* **Vielha** *var.* Viella. Cataluña, NE Spain *42°41′N 00°47′E*
Viella *see* Vielha
99 *L21* **Vielsalm** Luxembourg, E Belgium *50°17′N 05°55′E*
Vieng Pou Kha *see* Viangphoukha
23 *T6* **Vienna** Georgia, SE USA *32°05′N 83°48′W*
30 *L17* **Vienna** Illinois, N USA *37°24′N 88°55′W*
27 *V5* **Vienna** Missouri, C USA *38°12′N 91°59′W*
21 *Q3* **Vienna** West Virginia, NE USA *39°19′N 81°33′W*
Vienna *see* Wien, Austria
Vienna *see* Vienne, France
103 *R11* **Vienne** ***anc.*** Vienna. Isère, E France *45°32′N 04°53′E*
102 *L10* **Vienne** ⬖ *department* W France
102 *L9* **Vienne** ≈ W France
Vientiane *see* Viangchan
Vientos, Paso de los *see* Windward Passage
45 *V6* **Vieques** *var.* Isabel Segunda. E Puerto Rico *18°08′N 65°25′W*
45 *V6* **Vieques, Isla de** *island* E Puerto Rico
45 *V6* **Vieques, Pasaje de** *passage* E Puerto Rico
45 *V5* **Vieques, Sonda de** *sound* E Puerto Rico
Vierdörfer *see* Săcele
93 *M15* **Vieremä** Itä-Suomi, C Finland *63°42′N 27°02′E*
99 *M14* **Vierlingsbeek** Noord-Brabant, SE Netherlands *51°36′N 06°01′E*
101 *G20* **Viernheim** Hessen, W Germany *49°32′N 08°35′E*
101 *D15* **Viersen** Nordrhein-Westfalen, W Germany *51°16′N 06°24′E*
108 *G8* **Vierwaldstätter See** ***Eng.*** Lake of Lucerne. ◎ C Switzerland
103 *N8* **Vierzon** Cher, C France *47°13′N 02°04′E*
40 *L8* **Viesca** Coahuila, NE Mexico *25°25′N 102°45′W*
118 *H10* **Viesīte** ***Ger.*** Eckengraf. Jēkabpils, S Latvia *56°21′N 25°30′E*
107 *N15* **Vieste** Puglia, SE Italy *41°52′N 16°11′E*
167 *T8* **Vietnam** ***off.*** Socialist Republic of Vietnam, ***Vtn.*** Công Hoa Xa Hôi Chu Nghia Viêt Nam. ◆ *republic* SE Asia
Vietnam, Socialist Republic of *see* Vietnam
167 *S5* **Viêt Quang** Ha Giang, N Vietnam *22°24′N 104°48′E*
Vietri *see* Viêt Tri
167 *S6* **Viêt Tri** *var.* Vietri. Vinh Phu, N Vietnam *21°20′N 105°26′E*
30 *L4* **Vieux Desert, Lac** ◎ Michigan/Wisconsin, N USA
45 *Y13* **Vieux Fort** S Saint Lucia *13°43′N 60°57′W*
45 *X6* **Vieux-Habitants** Basse Terre, SW Guadeloupe *16°04′N 61°45′W*
119 *G14* **Vievis** Vilnius, S Lithuania *54°46′N 24°51′E*
171 *N2* **Vigan** Luzon, N Philippines *17°34′N 102°21′E*
106 *D8* **Vigevano** Lombardia, N Italy *45°19′N 08°51′E*
107 *N18* **Viggiano** Basilicata, S Italy *40°21′N 15°54′E*
58 *L12* **Vigia** Pará, NE Brazil *0°50′S 48°07′W*
41 *Y12* **Vigía Chico** Quintana Roo, SE Mexico *19°49′N 87°31′W*
45 *T11* **Vigie** ***prev.*** George F L Charles. ✈ (Castries) NE Saint Lucia *14°01′N 60°59′W*
102 *K17* **Vignemale** *var.* Pic de Vignemale. ▲ France/Spain *42°48′N 00°06′W*
Vignemale, Pic de *see* Vignemale
106 *G10* **Vignola** Emilia-Romagna, C Italy *44°28′N 11°00′E*
104 *G4* **Vigo** Galicia, NW Spain *42°15′N 08°44′W*
104 *G4* **Vigo, Ría de** *estuary* NW Spain
94 *D9* **Vigra** *island* S Norway
95 *C17* **Vigrestad** Rogaland, S Norway *58°34′N 05°42′E*
93 *L15* **Vihanti** Oulu, C Finland *64°29′N 25°E*
149 *U10* **Vihāri** Punjab, E Pakistan *30°03′N 72°32′E*
102 *K8* **Vihiers** Maine-et-Loire, NW France *47°09′N 00°37′W*
111 *O19* **Vihorlat** ▲ E Slovakia *48°54′N 22°09′E*
93 *L19* **Vihti** Etelä-Suomi, S Finland *60°25′N 24°16′E*
Viipuri *see* Vyborg
93 *M16* **Viitasaari** Länsi-Suomi, C Finland *63°05′N 25°52′E*
118 *K3* **Viivikonna** Ida-Virumaa, NE Estonia *59°19′N 27°41′E*
155 *K16* **Vijayawāda** ***prev.*** Bezwada. Andhra Pradesh, SE India *16°34′N 80°40′E*
Vijosa/Vijosë *see* Aóos, Albania/Greece
Vijosa/Vijosë *see* Vjosës, Lumi i, Albania/Greece
92 *J4* **Vík** Sudhurland, S Iceland *63°25′N 18°58′W*
Vik *see* Vikøyri
94 *L13* **Vika** Dalarna, C Sweden *60°55′N 14°30′E*
92 *L12* **Vikajärvi** Lappi, N Finland *66°37′N 26°10′E*
94 *L13* **Vikarbyn** Dalarna, C Sweden *60°57′N 15°00′E*
95 *J22* **Viken** Skåne, S Sweden *56°09′N 12°36′E*
95 *L17* **Viken** ◎ C Sweden
95 *G15* **Vikersund** Buskerud, S Norway *59°58′N 09°59′E*
114 *G11* **Vikhren** ▲ SW Bulgaria *41°45′N 23°24′E*
11 *R15* **Viking** Alberta, SW Canada *53°07′N 111°50′W*
84 *E7* **Viking Bank** *undersea feature* N North Sea *60°35′N 02°35′E*
95 *M14* **Vikmanshyttan** Dalarna, C Sweden *60°19′N 15°55′E*
94 *D12* **Vikøyri** *var.* Vik. Sogn Og Fjordane, S Norway *61°04′N 06°34′E*
93 *H17* **Viksjö** Västernorrland, C Sweden *62°45′N 17°30′E*
Viktoriastadt *see* Victoria
Vila *see* Port-Vila
Vila Arriaga *see* Bibala
Vila Artur de Paiva *see* Cubango
Vila Baleira *see* Porto Santo
Vila Bela da Santissima Trindade *see* Mato Grosso
58 *B12* **Vila Bittencourt** Amazonas, NW Brazil *01°25′S 69°24′W*
Vila da Ponte *see* Cubango
64 *O2* **Vila da Praia da Vitória** Terceira, Azores, Portugal, NE Atlantic Ocean *38°44′N 27°04′W*
Vila de Aljustrel *see* Cangamba
Vila de Almoster *see* Chiange
Vila de João Belo *see* Xai-Xai
Vila de Macia *see* Macia
Vila de Manhiça *see* Manhiça
Vila de Manica *see* Manica
Vila de Mocímboa da Praia *see* Mocímboa da Praia
83 *N16* **Vila de Sena** *var.* Sena. Sofala, C Mozambique *17°25′S 34°59′E*
104 *F14* **Vila do Bispo** Faro, S Portugal *37°05′N 08°53′W*
104 *G6* **Vila do Conde** Porto, NW Portugal *41°21′N 08°45′W*
Vila do Maio *see* Maio
64 *P3* **Vila do Porto** Santa Maria, Azores, Portugal, NE Atlantic Ocean *36°57′N 25°10′W*
83 *K15* **Vila do Zumbo** ***prev.*** Vila do Zumbu, Zumbo. Tete, NW Mozambique *15°36′S 30°30′E*
Vila do Zumbu *see* Vila do Zumbo
104 *I6* **Vila Flor** *var.* Vila Flôr. Bragança, N Portugal *41°18′N 07°09′W*
105 *V6* **Vilafranca del Penedès** *var.* Villafranca del Panadés. Cataluña, NE Spain *41°21′N 01°42′E*
104 *F10* **Vila Franca de Xira** *var.* Vilafranca de Xira. Lisboa, C Portugal *38°57′N 08°59′W*
Vila Gago Coutinho *see* Lumbala N'Guimbo
104 *G3* **Vilagarcía de Arousa** *var.* Villagarcía de Arosa. Galicia, NW Spain *42°35′N 08°45′W*
Vila General Machado *see* Camacupa
Vila Henrique de Carvalho *see* Saurimo
102 *I7* **Vilaine** ≈ NW France
Vila João de Almeida *see* Chibia
118 *K8* **Viļaka** ***Ger.*** Marienhausen. Balvi, NE Latvia *57°12′N 27°43′E*
104 *I2* **Vilalba** Galicia, NW Spain *43°17′N 07°41′W*
Vila Marechal Carmona *see* Uíge

◆ Country
● Country Capital
◇ Dependent Territory
○ Dependent Territory Capital
⬖ Administrative Regions
✈ International Airport
▲ Mountain
▲▲ Mountain Range
✲ Volcano
≈ River
◎ Lake
⊠ Reservoir

Vila Mariano Machado *see* Ganda
172 *G3* **Vilanandro, Tanjona** *Fr.* Cap Saint-André. *headland* W Madagascar *16°10′S 44°27′E*
Vilanculos *see* Vilankulo
118 *J10* **Viļāni** Rēzekne, E Latvia *56°33′N 26°55′E*
83 *N19* **Vilankulo** *var.* Vilanculos. Inhambane, E Mozambique *22°01′S 35°19′E*
Vila Norton de Matos *see* Balombo
104 *G6* **Vila Nova de Famalicão** *var.* Vila Nova de Famalicao. Braga, N Portugal *41°24′N 08°31′W*
104 *I6* **Vila Nova de Foz Côa** *var.* Vila Nova de Fozcôa. Guarda, N Portugal *41°05′N 07°09′W*
Vila Nova de Fozcôa *see* Vila Nova de Foz Côa
104 *F6* **Vila Nova de Gaia** Porto, NW Portugal *41°08′N 08°37′W*
Vila Nova de Portimão *see* Portimão
105 *V6* **Vilanova i La Geltrú** Cataluña, NE Spain *41°15′N 01°42′E*
Vila Pereira de Eça *see* N'Giva
104 *H6* **Vila Pouca de Aguiar** Vila Real, N Portugal *41°30′N 07°38′W*
104 *H6* **Vila Real** *var.* Vila Rial. Vila Real, N Portugal *41°17′N 07°45′W*
104 *H6* **Vila Real** ◐ *district* N Portugal
Vila-real de los Infantes *see* Villarreal
104 *H14* **Vila Real de Santo António** Faro, S Portugal *37°12′N 07°25′W*
104 *J7* **Vilar Formoso** Guarda, N Portugal *40°37′N 06°50′W*
Vila Rial *see* Vila Real
59 *J15* **Vila Rica** Mato Grosso, W Brazil *09°52′S 50°44′W*
Vila Robert Williams *see* Caála
Vila Salazar *see* N'Dalatando
Vila Serpa Pinto *see* Menongue
Vila Teixeira da Silva *see* Bailundo
Vila Teixeira de Sousa *see* Luau
104 *H9* **Vila Velha de Ródão** Castelo Branco, C Portugal *39°39′N 07°40′W*
104 *G5* **Vila Verde** Braga, N Portugal *41°39′N 08°27′W*
104 *H11* **Vila Viçosa** Évora, S Portugal *38°46′N 07°25′W*
57 *G15* **Vilcabamba, Cordillera de** ⛰ C Peru
Vîlcea *see* Vâlcea
122 *J4* **Vil'cheka, Zemlya** *Eng.* Wilczek Land. *island* Zemlya Frantsa-Iosifa, NW Russian Federation
95 *F22* **Vildbjerg** Ringkøbing, C Denmark *56°12′N 08°47′E*
Vileyka *see* Vilyeyka
93 *H15* **Vilhelmina** Västerbotten, N Sweden *64°38′N 16°40′E*
59 *F17* **Vilhena** Rondônia, W Brazil *12°40′S 60°08′W*
115 *G19* **Vília** Attikí, C Greece *38°09′N 23°21′E*
119 *I14* **Viliya** *Lith.* Neris. ≈ W Belarus
Viliya *see* Neris
118 *H5* **Viljandi** *Ger.* Fellin. Viljandimaa, S Estonia *58°22′N 25°30′E*
118 *H5* **Viljandimaa** *var.* Viljandi Maakond. ◐ *province* SW Estonia
Viljandi Maakond *see* Viljandimaa
119 *E14* **Vilkaviškis** *Pol.* Wyłkowyszki. Marijampolė, SW Lithuania *54°39′N 23°03′E*
118 *F13* **Vilkija** Kaunas, C Lithuania *55°02′N 23°36′E*
197 *V9* **Vil'kitskogo, Proliv** *strait* N Russian Federation
Vilkovo *see* Vylkove
57 *L21* **Villa Abecia** Chuquisaca, S Bolivia *21°00′S 65°18′W*
41 *N5* **Villa Acuña** *var.* Ciudad Acuña. Coahuila, NE Mexico *29°18′N 100°58′W*
40 *J4* **Villa Ahumada** Chihuahua, N Mexico *30°38′N 106°30′W*
45 *O9* **Villa Altagracia** C Dominican Republic *18°43′N 70°13′W*
56 *L13* **Villa Bella** Beni, N Bolivia *10°21′S 65°25′W*
104 *J3* **Villablino** Castilla-León, N Spain *42°55′N 06°21′W*
54 *K6* **Villa Bruzual** Portuguesa, N Venezuela *09°20′N 69°06′W*
105 *O9* **Villacañas** Castilla-La Mancha, C Spain *39°38′N 03°20′W*
105 *O12* **Villacarrillo** Andalucía, S Spain *38°07′N 03°05′W*
104 *M7* **Villacastín** Castilla-León, N Spain *40°46′N 04°25′W*
Villa Cecilia *see* Ciudad Madero
109 *S9* **Villach** *Slvn.* Beljak. Kärnten, S Austria *46°36′N 13°49′E*
107 *B20* **Villacidro** Sardegna, Italy, C Mediterranean Sea *39°28′N 08°43′E*
Villa Concepción *see* Concepción
104 *L4* **Villada** Castilla-León, N Spain *42°15′N 04°59′W*
40 *M10* **Villa de Cos** Zacatecas, C Mexico *23°20′N 102°20′W*
54 *L5* **Villa de Cura** *var.* Cura. Aragua, N Venezuela *10°00′N 67°30′W*
Villa del Nevoso *see* Ilirska Bistrica
Villa del Pilar *see* Pilar
104 *M13* **Villa del Río** Andalucía, S Spain *37°59′N 04°17′W*
Villa de Méndez *see* Méndez
42 *H6* **Villa de San Antonio** Comayagua, W Honduras *14°24′N 87°37′W*
105 *N4* **Villadiego** Castilla-León, N Spain *42°31′N 04°01′W*
105 *T8* **Villafames** País Valenciano, E Spain *40°07′N 00°03′W*
41 *U16* **Villa Flores** Chiapas, SE Mexico *16°12′N 93°16′W*
104 *J3* **Villafranca del Bierzo** Castilla-León, N Spain *42°36′N 06°49′W*
105 *S8* **Villafranca del Cid** País Valenciano, E Spain *40°25′N 00°15′W*
104 *J11* **Villafranca de los Barros** Extremadura, W Spain *38°34′N 06°20′W*
105 *N10* **Villafranca de los Caballeros** Castilla-La Mancha, C Spain *39°26′N 03°21′W*
Villafranca del Panadés *see* Vilafranca del Penedès
106 *F8* **Villafranca di Verona** Veneto, NE Italy *45°22′N 10°51′E*
107 *J23* **Villafrati** Sicilia, Italy, C Mediterranean Sea *37°53′N 13°30′E*
Villagarcía de Arosa *see* Vilagarcía de Arousa
41 *O9* **Villagrán** Tamaulipas, C Mexico *24°29′N 99°30′W*
61 *C17* **Villaguay** Entre Ríos, E Argentina *31°55′S 59°01′W*
62 *O6* **Villa Hayes** Presidente Hayes, S Paraguay *25°05′S 57°25′W*
41 *U15* **Villahermosa** *prev.* San Juan Bautista. Tabasco, SE Mexico *17°56′N 92°50′W*
105 *O11* **Villahermosa** Castilla-La Mancha, C Spain *38°46′N 02°52′W*
64 *O11* **Villahermoso** Gomera, Islas Canarias, Spain, NE Atlantic Ocean *38°46′N 02°52′W*
Villa Hidalgo *see* Hidalgo
105 *T12* **Villajoyosa** *Cat.* La Vila Joíosa. País Valenciano, E Spain *38°31′N 00°14′W*
Villa Juárez *see* Juárez
Villalba *see* Collado Villalba
41 *N8* **Villaldama** Nuevo León, NE Mexico *26°29′N 100°27′W*
104 *L5* **Villalón de Campos** Castilla-León, N Spain *42°05′N 05°03′W*
61 *A25* **Villalonga** Buenos Aires, E Argentina *39°55′S 62°35′W*
104 *L5* **Villalpando** Castilla-León, N Spain *41°51′N 05°25′W*
40 *K9* **Villa Madero** *var.* Francisco I. Madero. Durango, C Mexico *24°28′N 104°20′W*
41 *O9* **Villa Mainero** Tamaulipas, C Mexico *24°32′N 99°39′W*
Villamaña *see* Villamañán
104 *L4* **Villamañán** *var.* Villamaña. Castilla-León, N Spain *42°19′N 05°35′W*
62 *L10* **Villa María** Córdoba, C Argentina *32°23′S 63°15′W*
61 *C17* **Villa María Grande** Entre Ríos, E Argentina *31°39′S 59°54′W*
57 *K21* **Villa Martín** Potosí, SW Bolivia *20°46′S 67°45′W*
104 *K15* **Villamartín** Andalucía, S Spain *36°52′N 05°38′W*
62 *J8* **Villa Mazán** La Rioja, NW Argentina *28°43′S 66°25′W*
62 *J11* **Villa Mercedes** *var.* Mercedes. San Luis, C Argentina *33°40′S 65°25′W*
Villamil *see* Puerto Villamil
Villa Nador *see* Nador
54 *G5* **Villanueva** La Guajira, N Colombia *10°37′N 72°58′W*
42 *H5* **Villanueva** Cortés, NW Honduras *15°14′N 88°00′W*
40 *L11* **Villanueva** Zacatecas, C Mexico *22°24′N 102°53′W*
42 *I9* **Villa Nueva** Chinandega, NW Nicaragua *12°58′N 86°46′W*
37 *T11* **Villanueva** New Mexico, SW USA *35°18′N 105°20′W*
104 *M12* **Villanueva de Córdoba** Andalucía, S Spain *38°20′N 04°38′W*
105 *O12* **Villanueva del Arzobispo** Andalucía, S Spain *38°10′N 03°00′W*
104 *K11* **Villanueva de la Serena** Extremadura, W Spain *38°58′N 05°48′W*
104 *L5* **Villanueva del Campo** Castilla-León, N Spain *41°59′N 05°25′W*
105 *O11* **Villanueva de los Infantes** Castilla-La Mancha, C Spain *38°45′N 03°01′W*
61 *C14* **Villa Ocampo** Santa Fe, C Argentina *28°28′S 59°22′W*
40 *J8* **Villa Ocampo** Durango, C Mexico *26°29′N 105°30′W*
40 *J7* **Villa Orestes Pereyra** Durango, C Mexico *26°30′N 105°38′W*
105 *N3* **Villarcayo** Castilla-León, N Spain *42°56′N 03°34′W*
104 *L5* **Villardefrades** Castilla-León, N Spain *41°43′N 05°15′W*
105 *S9* **Villar del Arzobispo** País Valenciano, E Spain *39°44′N 00°50′W*
105 *Q6* **Villaroya de la Sierra** Aragón, NE Spain *41°28′N 01°46′W*
105 *T9* **Villarreal** *var.* Vila-real de los Infantes. País Valenciano, E Spain *39°56′N 00°08′W*
62 *P6* **Villarrica** Guairá, SE Paraguay *25°45′S 56°28′W*
63 *G15* **Villarrica, Volcán** 🌋 S Chile *39°28′S 71°57′W*
105 *P10* **Villarrobledo** Castilla-La Mancha, C Spain *39°16′N 02°36′W*
105 *N10* **Villarrubia de los Ojos** Castilla-La Mancha, C Spain *39°14′N 03°36′W*
18 *J17* **Villas** New Jersey, NE USA *39°01′N 74°54′W*
105 *O3* **Villasana de Mena** Castilla-León, N Spain *43°05′N 03°16′W*
107 *M23* **Villa San Giovanni** Calabria, S Italy *38°12′N 15°39′E*
61 *D18* **Villa San José** Entre Ríos, E Argentina *32°01′S 58°20′W*
Villa Sanjurjo *see* Al-Hoceïma
105 *P6* **Villasayas** Castilla-León, N Spain *41°19′N 02°36′W*
107 *C20* **Villasimius** Sardegna, Italy, C Mediterranean Sea *39°10′N 09°30′E*
41 *N6* **Villa Unión** Coahuila, NE Mexico *28°18′N 100°43′W*
40 *K10* **Villa Unión** Durango, C Mexico *23°59′N 104°01′W*
40 *J10* **Villa Unión** Sinaloa, C Mexico *23°10′N 106°12′W*
62 *K12* **Villa Valeria** Córdoba, C Argentina *34°21′S 64°56′W*
105 *N8* **Villaverde** Madrid, C Spain *40°21′N 03°43′W*
54 *F10* **Villavicencio** Meta, C Colombia *04°09′N 73°38′W*
104 *L2* **Villaviciosa** Asturias, N Spain *43°29′N 05°26′W*
104 *L12* **Villaviciosa de Córdoba** Andalucía, S Spain *38°04′N 05°00′W*
57 *L22* **Villazón** Potosí, S Bolivia *22°05′S 65°35′W*
14 *J8* **Villebon, Lac** ◎ Québec, SE Canada
Ville de Kinshasa *see* Kinshasa
102 *J5* **Villedieu-les-Poêles** Manche, N France *48°51′N 01°12′W*
Villefranche *see* Villefranche-sur-Saône
103 *N16* **Villefranche-de-Lauragais** Haute-Garonne, S France *43°24′N 01°42′E*
103 *N14* **Villefranche-de-Rouergue** Aveyron, S France *44°21′N 02°02′E*
103 *R10* **Villefranche-sur-Saône** *var.* Villefranche. Rhône, E France *46°00′N 04°40′E*
14 *H9* **Ville-Marie** Québec, SE Canada *47°21′N 79°26′W*
102 *M15* **Villemur-sur-Tarn** Haute-Garonne, S France *43°50′N 01°32′E*
105 *S11* **Villena** País Valenciano, E Spain *38°39′N 00°52′W*
Villeneuve-d'Agen *see* Villeneuve-sur-Lot
102 *L13* **Villeneuve-sur-Lot** *var.* Villeneuve-d'Agen, *hist.* Gajac. Lot-et-Garonne, SW France *44°24′N 00°43′E*
103 *P6* **Villeneuve-sur-Yonne** Yonne, C France *48°04′N 03°21′E*
22 *H8* **Ville Platte** Louisiana, S USA *30°41′N 92°16′W*
103 *R11* **Villeurbanne** Rhône, E France *45°46′N 04°54′E*
101 *G23* **Villingen-Schwenningen** Baden-Württemberg, S Germany *48°04′N 08°27′E*
29 *T15* **Villisca** Iowa, C USA *40°55′N 94°58′W*
Villmanstrand *see* Lappeenranta
Vilna *see* Vilnius
119 *H15* **Vilnius** ◐ *province* Lithuania
119 *H14* **Vilnius** *Pol.* Wilno, *Ger.* Wilna; *prev. Rus.* Vilna. ● (Lithuania) Vilnius, SE Lithuania *54°41′N 25°20′E*
119 *H14* **Vilnius** ✈ Vilnius, SE Lithuania *54°33′N 25°17′E*
117 *S7* **Vil'nohirs'k** Dnipropetrovs'ka Oblast', E Ukraine *48°31′N 34°01′E*
117 *U8* **Vil'nyans'k** Zaporiz'ka Oblast', SE Ukraine *47°56′N 35°22′E*
93 *L17* **Vilppula** Länsi-Suomi, W Finland *62°02′N 24°30′E*
101 *M20* **Vils** ≈ SE Germany
118 *C5* **Vilsandi** *island* W Estonia
117 *P8* **Vil'shanka** *Rus.* Olshanka. Kirovohrads'ka Oblast', C Ukraine *48°12′N 30°54′E*
101 *O22* **Vilshofen** Bayern, SE Germany *48°36′N 13°10′E*
155 *J20* **Viluppuram** Tamil Nādu, SE India *12°54′N 79°40′E*
113 *I16* **Vilusi** W Montenegro *42°44′N 18°34′E*
99 *G18* **Vilvoorde** *Fr.* Vilvorde. Vlaams Brabant, C Belgium *50°56′N 04°25′E*
Vilvorde *see* Vilvoorde
119 *J14* **Vilyeyka** *Pol.* Wilejka, *Rus.* Vileyka. Minskaya Voblasts', NW Belarus *54°30′N 26°55′E*
122 *V11* **Vilyuchinsk** Kamchatskaya Oblast', E Russian Federation *52°55′N 158°28′E*
123 *P10* **Vilyuy** ≈ NE Russian Federation
123 *P10* **Vilyuysk** Respublika Sakha (Yakutiya), NE Russian Federation *63°42′N 121°20′E*
123 *N10* **Vilyuyskoye Vodokhranilishche** ⊠ NE Russian Federation
104 *G2* **Vimianzo** Galicia, NW Spain *43°06′N 09°03′W*
95 *M19* **Vimmerby** Kalmar, S Sweden *57°40′N 15°50′E*
102 *L5* **Vimoutiers** Orne, N France *48°56′N 00°10′E*
93 *L16* **Vimpeli** Länsi-Suomi, W Finland *63°10′N 23°50′E*
79 *G14* **Vina** ≈ Cameroon/Chad
62 *G11* **Viña del Mar** Valparaíso, C Chile *33°02′S 71°35′W*
19 *R8* **Vinalhaven Island** *island* Maine, NE USA
105 *T8* **Vinaròs** País Valenciano, E Spain *40°29′N 00°28′E*
Vînători *see* Vânători
31 *N15* **Vincennes** Indiana, N USA *38°42′N 87°30′W*
195 *Y12* **Vincennes Bay** *bay* Antarctica
25 *O7* **Vincent** Texas, SW USA *32°30′N 101°10′W*
95 *H24* **Vindeby** Fyn, C Denmark *54°55′N 11°09′E*
93 *I15* **Vindeln** Västerbotten, N Sweden *64°11′N 19°45′E*
95 *F21* **Vinderup** Ringkøbing, C Denmark *56°29′N 08°48′E*
Vindhya Mountains *see* Vindhya Range
153 *N14* **Vindhya Range** *var.* Vindhya Mountains. ⛰ N India
Vindobona *see* Wien
20 *K6* **Vine Grove** Kentucky, S USA *37°48′N 85°58′W*
18 *J17* **Vineland** New Jersey, NE USA *39°29′N 75°02′W*
116 *E11* **Vinga** Arad, W Romania *46°00′N 21°14′E*
95 *M16* **Vingåker** Södermanland, C Sweden *59°02′N 15°52′E*
167 *S8* **Vinh** Nghê An, N Vietnam *18°42′N 105°41′E*
104 *I5* **Vinhais** Bragança, N Portugal *41°50′N 07°00′W*
167 *T9* **Vinh Linh** Quang Tri, C Vietnam *17°02′N 107°03′E*
Vinh Loi *see* Bac Liêu
167 *S14* **Vinh Long** *var.* Vinhlong. Vinh Long, S Vietnam *10°15′N 105°59′E*
Vinhlong *see* Vinh Long
113 *Q18* **Vinica** NE FYR Macedonia *41°53′N 22°30′E*
109 *V13* **Vinica** SE Slovenia *45°28′N 15°12′E*
114 *G8* **Vinishte** Montana, NW Bulgaria *43°30′N 23°04′E*
27 *Q8* **Vinita** Oklahoma, C USA *36°38′N 95°09′W*
Vinju Mare *see* Vânju Mare
98 *I11* **Vinkeveen** Utrecht, C Netherlands *52°13′N 04°55′E*
116 *L6* **Vin'kivtsi** Khmel'nyts'ka Oblast', W Ukraine *49°02′N 27°13′E*
112 *I10* **Vinkovci** *Ger.* Winkowitz, *Hung.* Vinkovcze. Vukovar-Srijem, E Croatia *45°18′N 18°45′E*
Vinkovcze *see* Vinkovci
Vinnitsa *see* Vinnytsya
Vinnitskaya Oblast'/Vinnytsya *see* Vinnyts'ka Oblast'
116 *M7* **Vinnyts'ka Oblast'** *var.* Vinnytsya, *Rus.* Vinnitskaya Oblast'. ◐ *province* C Ukraine
117 *N6* **Vinnytsya** *Rus.* Vinnitsa. Vinnyts'ka Oblast', C Ukraine *49°14′N 28°30′E*
117 *N6* **Vinnytsya** ✈ Vinnyts'ka Oblast', N Ukraine *49°13′N 28°40′E*
Vinogradov *see* Vynohradiv
194 *L8* **Vinson Massif** ▲ Antarctica *78°45′S 85°19′W*
94 *G11* **Vinstra** Oppland, S Norway *61°36′N 09°45′E*
116 *K12* **Vintilă Vodă** Buzău, SE Romania *45°28′N 26°43′E*
29 *X13* **Vinton** Iowa, C USA *42°10′N 92°01′W*
22 *F9* **Vinton** Louisiana, S USA *30°10′N 93°37′W*
155 *J17* **Vinukonda** Andhra Pradesh, E India *16°03′N 79°41′E*
Vioara *see* Ocnele Mari
83 *E23* **Vioolsdrif** Northern Cape, SW South Africa *28°50′S 17°38′E*
109 *S12* **Vipava** ≈ Italy/Slovenia
82 *M13* **Viphya Mountains** ⛰ C Malawi
171 *Q4* **Virac** Catanduanes Island, N Philippines *13°39′N 124°17′E*
124 *K8* **Virandozero** Respublika Kareliya, NW Russian Federation *63°59′N 36°00′E*
137 *P16* **Viranşehir** Şanlıurfa, SE Turkey *37°13′N 39°32′E*
154 *D13* **Virār** Mahārāshtra, W India *19°30′N 72°48′E*
11 *W16* **Virden** Manitoba, S Canada *49°50′N 100°57′W*
30 *K14* **Virden** Illinois, N USA *39°30′N 89°46′W*
Virdois *see* Virrat
102 *J5* **Vire** Calvados, N France *48°50′N 00°53′W*
102 *J4* **Vire** ≈ N France
83 *A15* **Virei** Namibe, SW Angola *15°43′S 12°54′E*
Vîrful Moldoveanu *see* Vârful Moldoveanu
35 *R5* **Virgina Peak** ▲ Nevada, W USA *39°46′N 119°26′W*
45 *U9* **Virgin Gorda** *island* C British Virgin Islands
83 *I22* **Virginia** Free State, C South Africa *28°06′S 26°53′E*
30 *K13* **Virginia** Illinois, N USA *39°57′N 90°12′W*
29 *W4* **Virginia** Minnesota, N USA *47°31′N 92°32′W*
21 *T6* **Virginia** *off.* Commonwealth of Virginia, *also known as* Mother of Presidents, Mother of States, Old Dominion. ◐ *state* NE USA
21 *Y7* **Virginia Beach** Virginia, NE USA *36°51′N 75°59′W*
33 *R11* **Virginia City** Montana, NW USA *45°17′N 111°54′W*
35 *Q6* **Virginia City** Nevada, W USA *39°19′N 119°39′W*
14 *H8* **Virginiatown** Ontario, S Canada *48°09′N 79°35′W*
Virgin Islands *see* British Virgin Islands
45 *T9* **Virgin Islands (US)** *var.* Virgin Islands of the United States; *prev.* Danish West Indies. ◇ *US unincorporated territory* E West Indies
Virgin Islands of the United States *see* Virgin Islands (US)
45 *T9* **Virgin Passage** *passage* Puerto Rico/Virgin Islands (US)
35 *Y10* **Virgin River** ≈ Nevada/Utah, W USA
Virihaur *see* Virihaure
92 *H12* **Virihaure** *var.* Virihaur. ◎ N Sweden
167 *T11* **Virôchey** Rôtânôkiri, NE Cambodia *13°59′N 106°49′E*
93 *N19* **Virolahti** Etelä-Suomi, S Finland *60°33′N 27°37′E*
30 *J8* **Viroqua** Wisconsin, N USA *43°33′N 90°54′W*
112 *G8* **Virovitica** *Ger.* Virovititz, *Hung.* Verőcze; *prev. Ger.* Werowitz. Virovitica-Podravina, NE Croatia *45°49′N 17°25′E*
112 *G8* **Virovitica-Podravina** *off.* Virovitičko-Podravska Županija. ◐ *province* NE Croatia
Virovitičko-Podravska Županija *see* Virovitica-Podravina
Virovititz *see* Virovitica
113 *J17* **Virpazar** S Montenegro *42°15′N 19°06′E*
93 *L17* **Virrat** *Swe.* Virdois. Länsi-Suomi, W Finland *62°14′N 23°50′E*
95 *M20* **Virserum** Kalmar, S Sweden *57°17′N 15°18′E*
99 *K25* **Virton** Luxembourg, SE Belgium *49°34′N 05°32′E*
118 *F5* **Virtsu** *Ger.* Werder. Läänemaa, W Estonia *58°35′N 23°33′E*
56 *C12* **Virú** La Libertad, C Peru *08°24′S 78°40′W*
Virudhunagar *see* Virudunagar
155 *H23* **Virudunagar** *var.* Virudhunagar; *prev.* Virudupatti. Tamil Nādu, SE India *09°35′N 77°57′E*
Virudupatti *see* Virudunagar
118 *I3* **Viru-Jaagupi** *Ger.* Sankt-Jakobi. Lääne-Virumaa, NE Estonia *59°14′N 26°29′E*
57 *N19* **Viru-Viru** *var.* Santa Cruz. ✈ (Santa Cruz) Santa Cruz, C Bolivia *17°49′S 63°12′W*
113 *E15* **Vis** *It.* Lissa; *anc.* Issa. *island* S Croatia
Vis *see* Fish
118 *I12* **Visaginas** *prev.* Sniečkus. Utena, E Lithuania *55°36′N 26°22′E*
155 *M15* **Visākhapatnam** *var.* Vishakhapatnam. Andhra Pradesh, SE India *17°45′N 83°19′E*
35 *R11* **Visalia** California, W USA *36°19′N 119°19′W*
Vişău *see* Vişeu
95 *P19* **Visby** *Ger.* Wisby. Gotland, SE Sweden *57°37′N 18°20′E*
197 *N9* **Viscount Melville Sound** *prev.* Melville Sound. *sound* Northwest Territories, N Canada
99 *L19* **Visé** Liège, E Belgium *50°44′N 05°42′E*
112 *K13* **Višegrad** Republika Srpska, SE Bosnia and Herzegovina *43°46′N 19°18′E*
58 *L12* **Viseu** Pará, NE Brazil *01°10′S 46°09′W*
104 *H7* **Viseu** *prev.* Vizeu. Viseu, N Portugal *40°40′N 07°55′W*
104 *H7* **Viseu** *var.* Vizeu. ◐ *district* N Portugal
116 *I8* **Vişeu** *Hung.* Visó; *prev.* Vişău. ≈ NW Romania
116 *I8* **Vişeu de Sus** *var.* Vişeul de Sus, *Ger.* Oberwischau, *Hung.* Felsővisó. Maramureş, N Romania *47°43′N 23°24′E*
Vişeul de Sus *see* Vişeu de Sus
Vishakhapatnam *see* Visākhapatnam
125 *R10* **Vishera** ≈ NW Russian Federation
95 *J19* **Viskafors** Västra Götaland, S Sweden *57°37′N 12°50′E*
95 *J20* **Viskan** ≈ S Sweden
95 *L21* **Vislanda** Kronoberg, S Sweden *56°46′N 14°30′E*
Vislinskiy Zaliv *see* Vistula Lagoon
Visó *see* Vişeu
112 *H13* **Visoko** ◐ Federacija Bosna I Hercegovina, C Bosnia and Herzegovina
106 *A9* **Viso, Monte** ▲ NW Italy *44°42′N 07°04′E*
108 *E10* **Visp** Valais, SW Switzerland *46°18′N 07°53′E*
108 *E10* **Vispa** ≈ S Switzerland
95 *M21* **Vissefjärda** Kalmar, S Sweden *56°31′N 15°34′E*
100 *I11* **Visselhövede** Niedersachsen, NW Germany *52°58′N 09°36′E*
95 *G23* **Vissenbjerg** Fyn, C Denmark *55°23′N 10°08′E*
35 *U17* **Vista** California, W USA *33°12′N 117°14′W*
58 *C11* **Vista Alegre** Amazonas, NW Brazil *01°23′N 68°13′W*
114 *J13* **Vistonída, Límni** ◎ NE Greece
92 *K12* **Visttasjohka** ≈ N Sweden
Vistula *see* Wisła
119 *A14* **Vistula Lagoon** *Ger.* Frisches Haff, *Pol.* Zalew Wiślany, *Rus.* Vislinskiy Zaliv. *lagoon* Poland/Russian Federation
114 *I8* **Vit** ≈ NW Bulgaria
Vitebsk *see* Vitsyebsk
Vitebskaya Oblast' *see* Vitsyebskaya Voblasts'
107 *H14* **Viterbo** *anc.* Vicus Elbii. Lazio, C Italy *42°25′N 12°08′E*
112 *H12* **Vitez** Federacija Bosna I Hercegovina, C Bosnia and Herzegovina *44°08′N 17°47′E*
167 *S14* **Vi Thanh** Cân Thơ, S Vietnam *09°45′N 105°28′E*
Viti *see* Fiji
186 *E7* **Vitiaz Strait** *strait* NE Papua New Guinea
104 *J7* **Vitigudino** Castilla-León, N Spain *41°00′N 06°26′W*
187 *W15* **Viti Levu** *island* W Fiji
123 *O11* **Vitim** ≈ C Russian Federation
123 *O12* **Vitimskiy** Irkutskaya Oblast', C Russian Federation *58°12′N 113°10′E*
109 *V2* **Vitis** Niederösterreich, N Austria *48°45′N 15°09′E*
59 *O20* **Vitória** *state capital* Espírito Santo, SE Brazil *20°19′S 40°21′W*
Vitoria *see* Vitoria-Gasteiz
Vitoria Bank *see* Vitória Seamount
59 *N18* **Vitória da Conquista** Bahia, E Brazil *14°53′S 40°52′W*
105 *P3* **Vitoria-Gasteiz** *var.* Vitoria, *Eng.* Vittoria. País Vasco, N Spain *42°51′N 02°40′W*
65 *J16* **Vitória Seamount** *var.* Victoria Bank, Vitoria Bank. *undersea feature* C Atlantic Ocean *18°48′S 37°24′W*
112 *F13* **Vitorog** ▲ SW Bosnia and Herzegovina *44°06′N 17°03′E*
102 *J6* **Vitré** Ille-et-Vilaine, NW France *48°07′N 01°12′W*
103 *R5* **Vitry-le-François** Marne, N France *48°43′N 04°36′E*
114 *D13* **Vítsi** *var.* Vítsoi. ▲ N Greece *40°39′N 21°23′E*
Vítsoi *see* Vítsi
118 *N13* **Vitsyebsk** *Rus.* Vitebsk. Vitsyebskaya Voblasts', NE Belarus *55°11′N 30°10′E*
118 *K13* **Vitsyebskaya Voblasts'** *prev. Rus.* Vitebskaya Oblast'. ◐ *province* N Belarus
92 *J11* **Vittangi** *Lapp.* Vazáš. Norrbotten, N Sweden *67°40′N 21°39′E*
103 *R8* **Vitteaux** Côte d'Or, C France *47°24′N 04°31′E*
103 *S6* **Vittel** Vosges, NE France *48°13′N 05°57′E*
95 *N15* **Vittinge** Västmanland, C Sweden *59°52′N 17°04′E*
107 *K25* **Vittoria** Sicilia, Italy, C Mediterranean Sea *36°56′N 14°30′E*
Vittoria *see* Vitoria-Gasteiz
106 *I7* **Vittorio Veneto** Veneto, NE Italy *45°59′N 12°18′E*
175 *Q9* **Vitu Levu** *island* W Fiji
175 *Q7* **Vityaz Trench** *undersea feature* W Pacific Ocean
108 *G8* **Vitznau** Luzern, W Switzerland *47°01′N 08°28′E*
104 *I1* **Viveiro** Galicia, NW Spain *43°39′N 07°35′W*
105 *S9* **Viver** País Valenciano, E Spain *39°55′N 00°36′W*
103 *Q13* **Viverais, Monts du** ⛰ C France
122 *L9* **Vivi** ≈ N Russian Federation
22 *F4* **Vivian** Louisiana, S USA *32°52′N 93°59′W*
29 *N10* **Vivian** South Dakota, N USA *43°53′N 100°16′W*
103 *R13* **Viviers** Ardèche, E France *44°31′N 04°40′E*
Vivis *see* Vevey
83 *K19* **Vivo** Limpopo, NE South Africa *22°58′S 29°13′E*
102 *L10* **Vivonne** Vienne, W France *46°25′N 00°15′E*
Vizakna *see* Ocna Sibiului
105 *O2* **Vizcaya** *Basq.* Bizkaia. ◐ *province* País Vasco, N Spain
Vizcaya, Golfo de *see* Biscay, Bay of
136 *C10* **Vize** Kırklareli, NW Turkey *41°34′N 27°45′E*
122 *K4* **Vize, Ostrov** *island* Severnaya Zemlya, N Russian Federation
Vizeu *see* Viseu
155 *M15* **Vizianagaram** *var.* Vizianagram. Andhra Pradesh, E India *18°07′N 83°25′E*
Vizianagram *see* Vizianagaram
103 *S12* **Vizille** Isère, E France *45°05′N 05°46′E*
125 *R11* **Vizinga** Respublika Komi, NW Russian Federation *61°06′N 50°09′E*
116 *M13* **Viziru** Brăila, SE Romania *45°00′N 27°43′E*
113 *K21* **Vjosës, Lumi i** *var.* Vijosa, Vijosë, *Gk.* Aóos. ≈ Albania/Greece *see also* Aóos
Vjosës, Lumi i *see* Aóos
99 *H18* **Vlaams Brabant** ◐ *province* C Belgium
Vlaanderen *see* Flanders
98 *G12* **Vlaardingen** Zuid-Holland, SW Netherlands *51°55′N 04°21′E*
116 *F10* **Vlădeasa, Vârful** *prev.* Vîrful Vlădeasa. ▲ NW Romania *46°45′N 22°46′E*
Vlădeasa, Vîrful *see* Vlădeasa, Vârful
113 *P16* **Vladičin Han** Serbia, SE Serbia *42°44′N 22°04′E*
127 *O16* **Vladikavkaz** *prev.* Dzaudzhikau, Ordzhonikidze. Respublika Severnaya Osetiya, SW Russian Federation *42°58′N 44°41′E*
126 *M3* **Vladimir** Vladimirskaya Oblast', W Russian Federation *56°09′N 40°21′E*
144 *M7* **Vladimirovka** Kostanay, N Kazakhstan *53°30′N 64°02′E*
Vladimirovka *see* Yuzhno-Sakhalinsk
126 *L3* **Vladimirskaya Oblast'** ◐ *province* W Russian Federation
126 *I3* **Vladimirskiy Tupik** Smolenskaya Oblast', W Russian Federation *55°45′N 33°25′E*
Vladimir-Volynskiy *see* Volodymyr-Volyns'kyy
123 *Q7* **Vladivostok** Primorskiy Kray, SE Russian Federation *43°09′N 131°53′E*
117 *U13* **Vladyslavivka** Respublika Krym, S Ukraine *45°09′N 35°25′E*
98 *P6* **Vlagtwedde** Groningen, NE Netherlands *53°02′N 07°07′E*
Vlajna *see* Kukavica
112 *J12* **Vlasenica** ◐ Republika Srpska, E Bosnia and Herzegovina
112 *G12* **Vlašić** ▲ C Bosnia and Herzegovina *44°18′N 17°40′E*
111 *D17* **Vlašim** *Ger.* Wlaschim. Středočeský Kraj, C Czech Republic *49°42′N 14°54′E*
113 *P15* **Vlasotince** Serbia, SE Serbia *42°58′N 22°07′E*
123 *Q7* **Vlasovo** Respublika Sakha (Yakutiya), NE Russian Federation *70°41′N 134°49′E*
98 *I11* **Vleuten** Utrecht, C Netherlands *52°07′N 05°01′E*
98 *I5* **Vlieland** *Fris.* Flylân. *island* Waddeneilanden, N Netherlands
98 *I5* **Vliestroom** *strait* NW Netherlands
99 *J14* **Vlijmen** Noord-Brabant, S Netherlands *51°42′N 05°14′E*
99 *E15* **Vlissingen** *Eng.* Flushing, *Fr.* Flessingue. Zeeland, SW Netherlands *51°26′N 03°34′E*
Vlodava *see* Włodawa
Vlonë/Vlora *see* Vlorë
113 *K22* **Vlorë** *prev.* Vlonë, *It.* Valona, Vlora. Vlorë, SW Albania *40°28′N 19°31′E*
113 *K22* **Vlorë** ◐ *district* SW Albania
113 *K22* **Vlorës, Gjiri i** *var.* Valona Bay. *bay* SW Albania
Vlotslavsk *see* Włocławek
111 *C16* **Vltava** *Ger.* Moldau. ≈ W Czech Republic
126 *K3* **Vnukovo** ✈ (Moskva) Gorod Moskva, W Russian Federation *55°30′N 36°52′E*
146 *L11* **Vobkent** *Rus.* Vabkent. Buxoro Viloyati, C Uzbekistan *40°01′N 64°25′E*
25 *Q9* **Voca** Texas, SW USA *30°58′N 99°09′W*
109 *R5* **Vöcklabruck** Oberösterreich, NW Austria *48°01′N 13°38′E*
112 *D13* **Vodice** Šibenik-Knin, S Croatia *43°46′N 15°46′E*
124 *K10* **Vodlozero, Ozero** ◎ NW Russian Federation
112 *A10* **Vodnjan** *It.* Dignano d'Istria. Istra, NW Croatia *44°57′N 13°51′E*
125 *S9* **Vodnyy** Respublika Komi, NW Russian Federation *63°31′N 53°21′E*
95 *G20* **Vodskov** Nordjylland, N Denmark *57°07′N 10°02′E*
92 *H4* **Vogar** Sudhurland, SW Iceland *63°58′N 22°20′W*
Vogelkop *see* Doberai, Jazirah
77 *X15* **Vogel Peak** *prev.* Dimlang. ▲ E Nigeria *08°16′N 11°44′E*
101 *H17* **Vogelsberg** ⛰ C Germany
106 *D8* **Voghera** Lombardia, N Italy *44°59′N 09°01′E*
112 *I13* **Vogošća** Federacija Bosna I Hercegovina, SE Bosnia and Herzegovina *43°55′N 18°20′E*
101 *M17* **Vogtland** *historical region* E Germany
125 *V12* **Vogul'skiy Kamen', Gora** ▲ NW Russian Federation *60°10′N 58°41′E*
187 *P16* **Voh** Province Nord, C New Caledonia *20°57′S 164°41′E*
Vohémar *see* Iharaña
172 *H8* **Vohimena, Tanjona** *Fr.* Cap Sainte Marie. *headland* S Madagascar *25°20′S 45°06′E*
172 *J6* **Vohipeno** Fianarantsoa, SE Madagascar *22°21′S 47°51′E*
118 *H5* **Võhma** *Ger.* Wöchma. Viljandimaa, S Estonia *58°37′N 25°34′E*
81 *J20* **Voi** Coast, S Kenya *03°23′S 38°35′E*
76 *K15* **Voinjama** N Liberia *08°25′N 09°42′W*
103 *S12* **Voiron** Isère, E France *45°22′N 05°35′E*
109 *V8* **Voitsberg** Steiermark, SE Austria *47°04′N 15°09′E*
95 *F24* **Vojens** *Ger.* Woyens. Sønderjylland, SW Denmark *55°15′N 09°19′E*
112 *K9* **Vojvodina** *Ger.* Wojwodina. Vojvodina, N Serbia
15 *S6* **Volant** ≈ Québec, SE Canada
Volaterrae *see* Volterra
43 *P15* **Volcán** *var.* Hato del Volcán. Chiriquí, W Panama *08°45′N 82°38′W*
Volcano Islands *see* Kazan-rettō
Volchansk *see* Vovchans'k
Volchya *see* Vovcha
94 *D10* **Volda** Møre og Romsdal, S Norway *62°07′N 06°04′E*
98 *J9* **Volendam** Noord-Holland, C Netherlands *52°30′N 05°04′E*
124 *L15* **Volga** Yaroslavskaya Oblast', W Russian Federation *57°56′N 38°23′E*
29 *R10* **Volga** South Dakota, N USA *44°19′N 96°55′W*
122 *C11* **Volga** ≈ NW Russian Federation
Volga-Baltic Waterway *see* Volgo-Baltiyskiy Kanal
Volga Uplands *see* Privolzhskaya Vozvyshennost'
124 *L13* **Volgo-Baltiyskiy Kanal** *var.* Volga-Baltic Waterway. *canal* NW Russian Federation
126 *M12* **Volgodonsk** Rostovskaya Oblast', SW Russian Federation *47°35′N 42°03′E*
127 *O10* **Volgograd** *prev.* Stalingrad, Tsaritsyn. Volgogradskaya Oblast', SW Russian Federation *48°42′N 44°29′E*
127 *N9* **Volgogradskaya Oblast'** ◐ *province* SW Russian Federation
127 *P10* **Volgogradskoye Vodokhranilishche** ⊠ SW Russian Federation
101 *J19* **Volkach** Bayern, C Germany *49°51′N 10°15′E*
109 *U9* **Völkermarkt** *Slvn.* Velikovec. Kärnten, S Austria *46°40′N 14°38′E*
124 *I12* **Volkhov** Leningradskaya Oblast', NW Russian Federation *59°56′N 32°19′E*
101 *D20* **Völklingen** Saarland, SW Germany *49°15′N 06°51′E*
Volkovysk *see* Vawkavysk
Volkovyskiye Vysoty *see* Vawkavyskaye Wzvyshsha
83 *K22* **Volksrust** Mpumalanga, E South Africa *27°22′S 29°54′E*
98 *L8* **Vollenhove** Overijssel, N Netherlands *52°40′N 05°58′E*
119 *L16* **Volma** ≈ C Belarus
Volmari *see* Valmiera
117 *W9* **Volnovakha** Donets'ka Oblast', SE Ukraine *47°36′N 37°32′E*
116 *K6* **Volochys'k** Khmel'nyts'ka Oblast', W Ukraine *49°32′N 26°14′E*
117 *O6* **Volodarka** Kyyivs'ka Oblast', N Ukraine *49°31′N 29°55′E*
117 *W9* **Volodars'ke** Donets'ka Oblast', E Ukraine *47°11′N 37°19′E*
127 *R13* **Volodarskiy** Astrakhanskaya Oblast', SW Russian Federation *46°23′N 48°39′E*
Volodarskoye *see* Saumalkol'
117 *N8* **Volodars'k-Volyns'kyy** Zhytomyrs'ka Oblast', N Ukraine *50°37′N 28°28′E*
116 *K3* **Volodymerets'** Rivnens'ka Oblast', NW Ukraine *51°24′N 25°52′E*
116 *I3* **Volodymyr-Volyns'kyy** *Pol.* Włodzimierz, *Rus.* Vladimir-Volynskiy. Volyns'ka Oblast', NW Ukraine *50°51′N 24°19′E*
124 *L14* **Vologda** Vologodskaya Oblast', W Russian Federation *59°10′N 39°55′E*
124 *L12* **Vologodskaya Oblast'** ◐ *province* NW Russian Federation
126 *K3* **Volokolamsk** Moskovskaya Oblast', W Russian Federation *56°03′N 35°57′E*
126 *K9* **Volokonovka** Belgorodskaya Oblast', W Russian Federation *50°30′N 37°54′E*
115 *G16* **Vólos** Thessalía, C Greece *39°21′N 22°58′E*
124 *M11* **Voloshka** Arkhangel'skaya Oblast', NW Russian Federation *61°19′N 40°06′E*
Vološinovo *see* Novi Bečej
116 *H7* **Volovets'** Zakarpats'ka Oblast', W Ukraine *48°42′N 23°12′E*
Volozhin *see* Valozhyn
127 *Q7* **Vol'sk** Saratovskaya Oblast', W Russian Federation *52°04′N 47°20′E*
77 *Q17* **Volta** ≈ SE Ghana
Volta Blanche *see* White Volta
77 *P16* **Volta, Lake** ⊠ SE Ghana
Volta Noire *see* Black Volta
60 *O9* **Volta Redonda** Rio de Janeiro, SE Brazil *22°31′S 44°05′W*
Volta Rouge *see* Red Volta

◆ Country
● Country Capital
◇ Dependent Territory
○ Dependent Territory Capital
◐ Administrative Regions
✈ International Airport
▲ Mountain
⛰ Mountain Range
🌋 Volcano
≈ River
◎ Lake
⊠ Reservoir

106 *F12* **Volterra** *anc.* Volaterrae. Toscana, C Italy *43°23´N 10°52´E*
107 *K17* **Volturno** ≈ S Italy
113 *I15* **Volujak** ▲▲ NW Montenegro
Volunteer Island *see* Starbuck Island
114 *H13* **Vólvi, Límni** ◎ N Greece
Volyn *see* Volyns'ka Oblast'
116 *I3* **Volyns'ka Oblast'** *var.* Volyn, ***Rus.*** Volynskaya Oblast'. ◈ *province* NW Ukraine
Volynskaya Oblast' *see* Volyns'ka Oblast'
127 *Q3* **Volzhsk** Respublika Mariy El, W Russian Federation *55°53´N 48°21´E*
127 *O10* **Volzhskiy** Volgogradskaya Oblast', SW Russian Federation *48°49´N 44°40´E*
172 *I7* **Vondrozo** Fianarantsoa, SE Madagascar *22°50´S 47°20´E*
39 *P10* **Von Frank Mountain** ▲ Alaska, USA *63°36´N 154°29´W*
115 *C17* **Vónitsa** Dytikí Ellás, W Greece *38°55´N 20°53´E*
118 *J6* **Võnnu** ***Ger.*** Wendau. Tartumaa, SE Estonia *58°17´N 27°06´E*
98 *G12* **Voorburg** Zuid-Holland, W Netherlands *52°04´N 04°22´E*
98 *H11* **Voorschoten** Zuid-Holland, W Netherlands *52°08´N 04°26´E*
98 *M11* **Voorst** Gelderland, E Netherlands *52°10´N 06°10´E*
98 *K11* **Voorthuizen** Gelderland, C Netherlands *52°12´N 05°36´E*
92 *L2* **Vopnafjördhur** Austurland, E Iceland *65°45´N 14°51´W*
92 *L2* **Vopnafjördhur** *bay* E Iceland
Vora *see* Vorë
119 *H15* **Voranava** ***Pol.*** Werenów, ***Rus.*** Voronovo. Hrodzyenskaya Voblasts', W Belarus *54°09´N 25°19´E*
108 *I8* **Vorarlberg** ***off.*** Land Vorarlberg. ◈ *state* W Austria
Vorarlberg, Land *see* Vorarlberg
109 *X7* **Vorau** Steiermark, E Austria *47°22´N 15°55´E*
98 *N11* **Vorden** Gelderland, E Netherlands *52°07´N 06°18´E*
108 *H9* **Vorderrhein** ≈ SE Switzerland
92 *J2* **Vordhufell** ▲ N Iceland *65°42´N 18°45´W*
95 *I24* **Vordingborg** Storstrøm, SE Denmark *55°01´N 11°55´E*
113 *K19* **Vorë** *var.* Vora. Tiranë, W Albania *41°23´N 19°37´E*
115 *H17* **Vóreies Sporádes** *var.* Vóreioi Sporádes, Vórioi Sporádhes, ***Eng.*** Northern Sporades. *island group* E Greece
Vóreioi Sporádes *see* Vóreies Sporádes
115 *J17* **Vóreion Aigaíon** ***Eng.*** Aegean North. ◈ *region* SE Greece
115 *G18* **Vóreios Evvoïkós Kólpos** *var.* Voreiós Evvoïkós Kólpos. *gulf* E Greece
197 *S16* **Voring Plateau** *undersea feature* N Norwegian Sea *67°00´N 04°00´E*
Vórioi Sporádhes *see* Vóreies Sporádes
125 *W4* **Vorkuta** Respublika Komi, NW Russian Federation *67°27´N 64°E*
95 *I14* **Vorma** ≈ S Norway
118 *E4* **Vormsi** *var.* Vormsi Saar, ***Ger.*** Worms, ***Swed.*** Ormsö. *island* W Estonia
Vormsi Saar *see* Vormsi
127 *N7* **Vorona** ≈ W Russian Federation
126 *L7* **Voronezh** Voronezhskaya Oblast', W Russian Federation *51°40´N 39°13´E*
126 *L7* **Voronezh** ≈ W Russian Federation
126 *K8* **Voronezhskaya Oblast'** ◈ *province* W Russian Federation
Voronovitsya *see* Voronovytsya
Voronovo *see* Voranava
117 *N6* **Voronovytsya** ***Rus.*** Voronovitsya. Vinnyts'ka Oblast', C Ukraine *49°06´N 28°49´E*
122 *K7* **Vorontsovo** Taymyrskiy (Dolgano-Nenetskiy) Avtonomnyy Okrug, N Russian Federation *71°45´N 83°31´E*
124 *K3* **Voron'ya** ≈ NW Russian Federation
Voropayevo *see* Varapayeva
Voroshilov *see* Ussuriysk
Voroshilovgrad *see* Luhans'ka Oblast', Ukraine
Voroshilovgrad *see* Luhans'k, Ukraine
Voroshilovgradskaya Oblast' *see* Luhans'ka Oblast'
Voroshilovsk *see* Stavropol', Russian Federation
Voroshilovsk *see* Alchevs'k
137 *V13* **Vorotan** ***Az.*** Bärguşad. ≈ Armenia/Azerbaijan
127 *P3* **Vorotynets** Nizhegorodskaya Oblast', W Russian Federation *56°06´N 46°06´E*
117 *S3* **Vorozhba** Sums'ka Oblast', NE Ukraine *51°10´N 34°15´E*
117 *T5* **Vorskla** ≈ Russian Federation/Ukraine
99 *I17* **Vorst** Antwerpen, N Belgium *51°06´N 05°01´E*
83 *G21* **Vorstershoop** North-West, N South Africa *25°46´S 22°57´E*
118 *H6* **Võrtsjärv** ***Ger.*** Wirz-See. ◎ SE Estonia
118 *J7* **Võru** ***Ger.*** Werro. Võrumaa, SE Estonia *57°51´N 27°01´E*
147 *R11* **Vorukh** N Tajikistan *39°51´N 70°34´E*
118 *I7* **Võrumaa** ***off.*** Võru Maakond. ◈ *province* SE Estonia
Võru Maakond *see* Võrumaa
83 *G24* **Vosburg** Northern Cape, W South Africa *30°35´S 22°52´E*
147 *Q14* **Vose'** ***Rus.*** Vose; ***prev.*** Aral. SW Tajikistan *37°51´N 69°31´E*
103 *S6* **Vosges** ◈ *department* NE France
103 *U6* **Vosges** ▲▲ NE France
124 *K13* **Voskresenkoye** Vologodskaya Oblast', NW Russian Federation *59°25´N 37°56´E*
126 *L4* **Voskresensk** Moskovskaya Oblast', W Russian Federation *55°19´N 38°42´E*
127 *P2* **Voskresenskoye** Nizhegorodskaya Oblast', W Russian Federation *57°00´N 45°33´E*
127 *V6* **Voskresenskoye** Respublika Bashkortostan, W Russian Federation *53°07´N 56°07´E*
94 *D13* **Voss** Hordaland, S Norway *60°38´N 06°25´E*
94 *D13* **Voss** *physical region* S Norway
99 *I16* **Vosselaar** Antwerpen, N Belgium *51°19´N 04°55´E*
94 *D13* **Vosso** ≈ S Norway
Vostochno-Kazakhstanskaya Oblast' *see* Vostochnyy Kazakhstan
145 *T12* **Vostochno-Kounradskiy** ***Kaz.*** Shyghys Qongyrat. Zhezkazgan, C Kazakhstan
123 *S5* **Vostochno-Sibirskoye More** ***Eng.*** East Siberian Sea. *sea* Arctic Ocean
145 *X10* **Vostochnyy Kazakhstan** ***off.*** Vostochno-Kazakhstanskaya Oblast', ***var.*** East Kazakhstan, ***Kaz.*** Shyghys Qazagastan Oblysy. ◈ *province* E Kazakhstan
Vostochnyy Sayan *see* Eastern Sayans
Vostock Island *see* Vostok Island
195 *U10* **Vostok** *Russian research station* Antarctica *77°18´S 105°32´E*
191 *X5* **Vostok Island** *var.* Vostock Island; ***prev.*** Stavers Island. *island* Line Islands, SE Kiribati
127 *T2* **Votkinsk** Udmurtskaya Respublika, NW Russian Federation *57°04´N 54°00´E*
125 *U15* **Votkinskoye Vodokhranilishche** *var.* Votkinsk Reservoir. ▨ NW Russian Federation
Votkinsk Reservoir *see* Votkinskoye Vodokhranilishche
60 *J7* **Votuporanga** São Paulo, S Brazil *20°26´S 49°53´W*
104 *H7* **Vouga, Rio** ≈ N Portugal
115 *E14* **Voúrinos** ▲▲ N Greece
115 *G24* **Voúxa, Akrotírio** *headland* Kríti, Greece, E Mediterranean Sea *35°37´N 23°34´E*
103 *R4* **Vouziers** Ardennes, N France *49°24´N 04°42´E*
117 *V7* **Vovcha** ***Rus.*** Volchya. ≈ E Ukraine
117 *V4* **Vovchans'k** ***Rus.*** Volchansk. Kharkivs'ka Oblast', E Ukraine *50°19´N 36°55´E*
103 *N6* **Voves** Eure-et-Loir, C France *48°18´N 01°39´E*
79 *M14* **Vovodo** ≈ S Central African Republic
94 *M12* **Voxna** Gävleborg, C Sweden *61°21´N 15°35´E*
94 *L11* **Voxnan** ≈ C Sweden
114 *F7* **Voynishka Reka** ≈ NW Bulgaria
125 *T9* **Voyvozh** Respublika Komi, NW Russian Federation *62°54´N 54°52´E*
124 *M12* **Vozhega** Vologodskaya Oblast', NW Russian Federation *60°27´N 40°11´E*
124 *L12* **Vozhe, Ozero** ◎ NW Russian Federation
117 *Q9* **Voznesens'k** ***Rus.*** Voznesensk. Mykolayivs'ka Oblast', S Ukraine *47°34´N 31°21´E*
124 *J12* **Voznesen'ye** Leningradskaya Oblast', NW Russian Federation *61°00´N 35°24´E*
144 *J14* **Vozrozhdeniya, Ostrov** ***Uzb.*** Wozrojdeniye Oroli. *island* Kazakhstan/Uzbekistan
95 *G20* **Vrå** *var.* Vraa. Nordjylland, N Denmark *57°21´N 09°57´E*
Vraa *see* Vrå
114 *H9* **Vrachesh** Sofiya, W Bulgaria *42°52´N 23°45´E*
115 *C19* **Vrachíonas** ▲ Zákynthos, Iónia Nisiá, Greece, C Mediterranean Sea *37°49´N 20°43´E*
117 *P8* **Vradiyivka** Mykolayivs'ka Oblast', S Ukraine *47°51´N 30°37´E*
113 *G14* **Vran** ▲ SW Bosnia and Herzegovina *43°35´N 17°30´E*
116 *K12* **Vrancea** ◈ *county* E Romania
147 *T14* **Vrang** SE Tajikistan *37°03´N 72°26´E*
123 *T4* **Vrangelya, Ostrov** ***Eng.*** Wrangel Island. *island* NE Russian Federation
112 *H13* **Vranica** ▲ C Bosnia and Herzegovina *43°57´N 17°43´E*
113 *O16* **Vranje** Serbia, SE Serbia *42°33´N 21°55´E*
Vranov *see* Vranov nad Topl'ou
111 *N19* **Vranov nad Topl'ou** *var.* Vranov, ***Hung.*** Varannó. Prešovský Kraj, E Slovakia *48°54´N 21°41´E*
114 *H8* **Vratsa** Vratsa, NW Bulgaria *43°13´N 23°34´E*
114 *H8* **Vratsa** ◈ *province* NW Bulgaria
114 *F10* **Vrattsa** ***prev.*** Mirovo. Kyustendil, W Bulgaria *42°15´N 22°33´E*
112 *G11* **Vrbanja** ≈ NW Bosnia and Herzegovina
112 *K9* **Vrbas** Vojvodina, NW Serbia *45°34´N 19°39´E*
112 *G13* **Vrbas** ≈ N Bosnia and Herzegovina
112 *E8* **Vrbovec** Zagreb, N Croatia *45°53´N 16°24´E*
112 *C9* **Vrbovsko** Primorje-Gorski Kotar, NW Croatia *45°22´N 15°06´E*
111 *E15* **Vrchlabí** ***Ger.*** Hohenelbe. Královéhradecký Kraj, N Czech Republic *50°38´N 15°35´E*
83 *J22* **Vrede** Free State, E South Africa *27°25´S 29°10´E*
100 *E13* **Vreden** Nordrhein-Westfalen, NW Germany *52°01´N 06°50´E*
83 *E25* **Vredenburg** Western Cape, SW South Africa *32°55´S 18°00´E*
99 *I23* **Vresse-sur-Semois** Namur, SE Belgium *49°52´N 04°56´E*
95 *L16* **Vretstorp** Örebro, C Sweden *59°03´N 14°51´E*
113 *G15* **Vrgorac** ***prev.*** Vrhgorac. Split-Dalmacija, SE Croatia *43°10´N 17°24´E*
Vrhgorac *see* Vrgorac
109 *T12* **Vrhnika** ***Ger.*** Oberlaibach. W Slovenia *45°57´N 14°18´E*
155 *I21* **Vriddhāchalam** Tamil Nādu, SE India *11°33´N 79°18´E*
98 *N6* **Vries** Drenthe, NE Netherlands *53°04´N 06°34´E*
98 *O10* **Vriezenveen** Overijssel, E Netherlands *52°25´N 06°37´E*
95 *L20* **Vrigstad** Jönköping, S Sweden *57°19´N 14°30´E*
108 *H9* **Vrin** Graubünden, S Switzerland *46°40´N 09°06´E*
112 *E13* **Vrlika** Split-Dalmacija, S Croatia *43°54´N 16°24´E*
113 *M14* **Vrnjačka Banja** Serbia, C Serbia *43°36´N 20°55´E*
Vrondádhes/Vrondados *see* Vrontádos
115 *L18* **Vrontádos** *var.* Vrondados; ***prev.*** Vrondádhes. Chíos, E Greece *38°25´N 26°08´E*
98 *N9* **Vroomshoop** Overijssel, E Netherlands *52°28´N 06°35´E*
112 *N10* **Vršac** ***Ger.*** Werschetz, ***Hung.*** Versecz. Vojvodina, NE Serbia *45°08´N 21°18´E*
112 *M10* **Vršački Kanal** *canal* N Serbia
83 *H21* **Vryburg** North-West, N South Africa *26°57´S 24°44´E*
83 *K22* **Vryheid** KwaZulu/Natal, E South Africa *27°45´S 30°48´E*
111 *I18* **Vsetín** ***Ger.*** Wsetin. Zlínský Kraj, E Czech Republic *49°21´N 17°57´E*
111 *J20* **Vtáčnik** ***Hung.*** Madaras, Ptacsnik; ***prev.*** Ptačnik. ▲ W Slovakia *48°38´N 18°38´E*
Vuadil' *see* Wodil
114 *I11* **Vŭcha** ≈ SW Bulgaria
Vučitrn *see* Vushtrri
99 *J14* **Vught** Noord-Brabant, S Netherlands *51°37´N 05°19´E*
117 *W8* **Vuhledar** Donets'ka Oblast', E Ukraine *47°48´N 37°11´E*
112 *I9* **Vuka** ≈ E Croatia
113 *K17* **Vukël** *var.* Vukli. Shkodër, N Albania *42°29´N 19°39´E*
Vukli *see* Vukël
112 *J9* **Vukovar** ***Hung.*** Vukovár. Vukovar-Srijem, E Croatia *45°18´N 18°45´E*
Vukovarsko-Srijemska Županija *see* Vukovar-Srijem
112 *I10* **Vukovar-Srijem** ***off.*** Vukovarsko-Srijemska Županija. ◈ *province* E Croatia
125 *U8* **Vuktyl** Respublika Komi, NW Russian Federation *63°49´N 57°07´E*
11 *Q17* **Vulcan** Alberta, SW Canada *50°27´N 113°12´W*
116 *G12* **Vulcan** ***Ger.*** Wulkan, ***Hung.*** Zsilyvajdevulkán; ***prev.*** Crivadia Vulcanului, Vaidei, ***Hung.*** Sily-Vajdej, Vajdej. Hunedoara, W Romania *45°22´N 23°16´E*
116 *M12* **Vulcănești** ***Rus.*** Vulkaneshty. S Moldova *45°41´N 28°25´E*
107 *L22* **Vulcano, Isola** *island* Isole Eolie, S Italy
114 *G7* **Vŭlchedrŭm** Montana, NW Bulgaria *43°42´N 23°25´E*
114 *N8* **Vŭlchidol** ***prev.*** Kurt-Dere. Varna, E Bulgaria *43°25´N 27°33´E*
Vulkaneshty *see* Vulcănești
123 *V11* **Vulkannyy** Kamchatskaya Oblast', R Russian Federation *53°01´N 158°26´E*
36 *J13* **Vulture Mountains** ▲▲ Arizona, SW USA
167 *T14* **Vung Tau** ***prev. Fr.*** Cape Saint Jacques, Cap Saint-Jacques. Ba Ria-Vung Tau, S Vietnam *10°21´N 107°04´E*
187 *X15* **Vunisea** Kadavu, SE Fiji *19°04´S 178°10´E*
Vuohčču *see* Vuotso
93 *N15* **Vuokatti** Oulu, C Finland *64°08´N 28°16´E*
93 *M15* **Vuolijoki** Oulu, C Finland *64°09´N 27°00´E*
Vuolleriebme *see* Vuollerim
92 *J13* **Vuollerim** ***Lapp.*** Vuolleriebme. Norrbotten, N Sweden *66°24´N 20°36´E*
Vuoreija *see* Vardø
92 *L10* **Vuotso** ***Lapp.*** Vuohčču. Lappi, N Finland *68°04´N 27°05´E*
114 *J11* **Vŭrbitsa** ***prev.*** Filevo. Khaskovo, S Bulgaria *42°02´N 25°25´E*
114 *J12* **Vŭrbitsa** ≈ S Bulgaria
127 *Q4* **Vurnary** Chuvashskaya Respublika, W Russian Federation *55°30´N 46°59´E*
114 *G8* **Vŭrshets** Montana, NW Bulgaria *43°14´N 23°20´E*
113 *N16* **Vushtrri** ***Serb.*** Vučitrn. N Kosovo *42°49´N 21°00´E*
119 *F17* **Vyalikaya Byerastavitsa** ***Pol.*** Brzostowica Wielka, ***Rus.*** Bol'shaya Berëstovitsa; ***prev.*** Velikaya Berestovitsa. Hrodzyenskaya Voblasts', SW Belarus *53°12´N 24°03´E*
119 *N20* **Vyaliki Bor** ***Rus.*** Velikiy Bor. Homyel'skaya Voblasts', SE Belarus *52°02´N 29°56´E*
119 *J18* **Vyaliki Rozhan** ***Rus.*** Bol'shoy Rozhan. Minskaya Voblasts', S Belarus *52°46´N 27°07´E*
124 *H10* **Vyartsilya** ***Fin.*** Värtsilä. Respublika Kareliya, NW Russian Federation *62°07´N 30°43´E*
119 *K17* **Vyasyeya** ***Rus.*** Veseya. Minskaya Voblasts', C Belarus *53°04´N 27°41´E*
125 *R15* **Vyatka** ≈ NW Russian Federation
Vyatka *see* Kirov
125 *S16* **Vyatskiye Polyany** Kirovskaya Oblast', NW Russian Federation *56°15´N 51°06´E*
123 *S14* **Vyazemskiy** Khabarovskiy Kray, SE Russian Federation *47°28´N 134°39´E*
126 *I4* **Vyaz'ma** Smolenskaya Oblast', W Russian Federation *55°09´N 34°20´E*
127 *N3* **Vyazniki** Vladimirskaya Oblast', W Russian Federation *56°15´N 42°06´E*
127 *O8* **Vyazovka** Volgogradskaya Oblast', SW Russian Federation *50°57´N 43°57´E*
119 *J14* **Vyazyn'** Minskaya Voblasts', NW Belarus *54°25´N 27°10´E*
124 *G11* **Vyborg** ***Fin.*** Viipuri. Leningradskaya Oblast', NW Russian Federation *60°44´N 28°47´E*
125 *P11* **Vychegda** *var.* Vichegda. ≈ NW Russian Federation
125 *P11* **Vychegodskiy** Arkhangel'skaya Oblast', NW Russian Federation *61°14´N 46°53´E*
119 *L14* **Vyelyewshchyna** ***Rus.*** Velevshchina. Vitsyebskaya Voblasts', N Belarus *54°44´N 28°35´E*
119 *P16* **Vyeramyeyki** ***Rus.*** Veremeyki. Mahilyowskaya Voblasts', E Belarus *53°46´N 31°17´E*
118 *K11* **Vyerkhnyadzvinsk** ***Rus.*** Verkhnedvinsk. Vitsyebskaya Voblasts', N Belarus *55°47´N 27°56´E*
119 *P18* **Vyetka** ***Rus.*** Vetka. Homyel'skaya Voblasts', SE Belarus *52°33´N 31°10´E*
118 *L12* **Vyetryna** ***Rus.*** Vetrino. Vitsyebskaya Voblasts', N Belarus *55°25´N 28°28´E*
Vygonovskoye, Ozero *see* Vyhanawskaye, Vozyera
124 *J9* **Vygozero, Ozero** ◎ NW Russian Federation
Vyhanashchanskaye Vozyera *see* Vyhanawskaye, Vozyera
119 *I18* **Vyhanawskaye, Vozyera** *var.* Vyhanashchanskaye Vozyera, ***Rus.*** Ozero Vygonovskoye. ◎ SW Belarus
127 *N4* **Vyksa** Nizhegorodskaya Oblast', W Russian Federation *55°21´N 42°10´E*
117 *O12* **Vylkove** ***Rus.*** Vilkovo. Odes'ka Oblast', SW Ukraine *45°24´N 29°37´E*
125 *R9* **Vym'** ≈ NW Russian Federation
116 *H8* **Vynohradiv** ***Cz.*** Sevluš, ***Hung.*** Nagyszöllös, ***Rus.*** Vinogradov; ***prev.*** Sevlyush. Zakarpats'ka Oblast', W Ukraine *48°09´N 23°01´E*
124 *G13* **Vyritsa** Leningradskaya Oblast', NW Russian Federation *59°25´N 30°20´E*
97 *J19* **Vyrnwy** ***Wel.*** Afon Efyrnwy. ≈ E Wales, United Kingdom
145 *X9* **Vyshe Ivanovskiy Belak, Gora** ▲ E Kazakhstan *50°16´N 83°46´E*
117 *P4* **Vyshhorod** Kyyivs'ka Oblast', N Ukraine *50°36´N 30°28´E*
124 *I15* **Vyshniy Volochek** Tverskaya Oblast', W Russian Federation *57°37´N 34°33´E*
111 *G18* **Vyškov** ***Ger.*** Wischau. Jihomoravský Kraj, SE Czech Republic *49°17´N 17°01´E*
111 *E18* **Vysočina** ***prev.*** Jihlavský Kraj. ◈ *region* N Czech Republic
119 *E19* **Vysokaye** ***Rus.*** Vysokoye. Brestskaya Voblasts', SW Belarus *52°20´N 23°18´E*
111 *F17* **Vysoké Mýto** ***Ger.*** Hohenmauth. Pardubický Kraj, C Czech Republic *49°57´N 16°10´E*
117 *S9* **Vysokopillya** Khersons'ka Oblast', S Ukraine *47°28´N 33°30´E*
126 *K3* **Vysokovsk** Moskovskaya Oblast', W Russian Federation *56°12´N 36°42´E*
Vysokoye *see* Vysokaye
124 *K12* **Vytegra** Vologodskaya Oblast', NW Russian Federation *60°59´N 36°27´E*
116 *J8* **Vyzhnytsya** Chernivets'ka Oblast', W Ukraine *48°14´N 25°10´E*

W

77 *O14* **Wa** NW Ghana *10°07´N 02°28´W*
Waadt *see* Vaud
Waag *see* Váh
Waagbistritz *see* Považská Bystrica
Waagneustadtl *see* Nové Mesto nad Váhom
81 *M16* **Waajid** Gedo, SW Somalia *03°37´N 43°19´E*
98 *L13* **Waal** ≈ S Netherlands
187 *O16* **Waala** Province Nord, W New Caledonia *19°46´S 163°41´E*
99 *I14* **Waalwijk** Noord-Brabant, S Netherlands *51°42´N 05°04´E*
99 *E16* **Waarschoot** Oost-Vlaanderen, NW Belgium *51°09´N 03°35´E*
186 *C7* **Wabag** Enga, W Papua New Guinea *05°28´S 143°40´E*
15 *N7* **Wabano** ≈ Québec, SE Canada
11 *P11* **Wabasca** ≈ Alberta, SW Canada
31 *P12* **Wabash** Indiana, N USA *40°47´N 85°48´W*
29 *X9* **Wabasha** Minnesota, N USA *44°22´N 92°01´W*
31 *N13* **Wabash River** ≈ N USA
14 *C7* **Wabatongushi Lake** ◎ Ontario, S Canada
81 *L15* **Wabē Gestro Wenz** ≈ SE Ethiopia
14 *B9* **Wabos** Ontario, S Canada *46°48´N 84°06´W*
11 *W13* **Wabowden** Manitoba, C Canada *54°57´N 98°38´W*
110 *J9* **Wąbrzeźno** Kujawsko-pomorskie, C Poland *53°18´N 18°55´E*
21 *U12* **Waccamaw River** ≈ South Carolina, SE USA
23 *U11* **Waccasassa Bay** *bay* Florida, SE USA
99 *F16* **Wachtebeke** Oost-Vlaanderen, NW Belgium *51°10´N 03°52´E*
25 *T8* **Waco** Texas, SW USA *31°33´N 97°10´W*
26 *M3* **Waconda Lake** *var.* Great Elder Reservoir. ▨ Kansas, C USA
Wadai *see* Ouaddaï
Wad Al-Hajarah *see* Guadalajara
164 *I12* **Wadayama** Hyōgo, Honshū, SW Japan *35°19´N 134°51´E*
80 *D10* **Wad Banda** Western Kordofan, C Sudan *13°08´N 27°56´E*
75 *P9* **Waddān** NW Libya *29°10´N 16°08´E*
98 *J4* **Waddeneilanden** ***Eng.*** West Frisian Islands. *island group* N Netherlands
98 *J6* **Waddenzee** *var.* Wadden Zee. *sea* SE North Sea
Wadden Zee *see* Waddenzee
10 *L16* **Waddington, Mount** ▲ British Columbia, SW Canada *51°17´N 125°16´W*
98 *H12* **Waddinxveen** Zuid-Holland, C Netherlands *52°03´N 04°38´E*
11 *U15* **Wadena** Saskatchewan, S Canada *51°57´N 103°48´W*
29 *T6* **Wadena** Minnesota, N USA *46°27´N 95°07´W*
108 *G7* **Wädenswil** Zürich, N Switzerland *47°14´N 08°41´E*
21 *S11* **Wadesboro** North Carolina, SE USA *34°59´N 80°03´W*
155 *G16* **Wādi** Karnātaka, C India *17°00´N 76°58´E*
138 *G10* **Wādī as Sīr** *var.* Wadi es Sir. 'Ammān, NW Jordan *31°57´N 35°49´E*
Wadi es Sir *see* Wādī as Sīr
80 *F5* **Wadi Halfa** *var.* Wādī Ḥalfā'. Northern, N Sudan *21°46´N 31°17´E*
138 *G13* **Wādī Mūsā** *var.* Petra. Ma'ān, S Jordan *30°19´N 35°29´E*
23 *V4* **Wadley** Georgia, SE USA *32°52´N 82°24´W*
Wad Madanī *see* Wad Medani
80 *G10* **Wad Medani** *var.* Wad Madanī. Gezira, C Sudan *14°24´N 33°30´E*
80 *F10* **Wad Nimr** White Nile, C Sudan *14°32´N 32°10´E*
165 *U16* **Wadomari** Kagoshima, Okinoerabu-jima, SW Japan *27°25´N 128°40´E*
111 *K17* **Wadowice** Małopolskie, S Poland *49°54´N 19°29´E*
35 *R5* **Wadsworth** Nevada, W USA *39°39´N 119°16´W*
31 *T12* **Wadsworth** Ohio, N USA *41°01´N 81°43´W*
25 *T11* **Waelder** Texas, SW USA *29°42´N 97°16´W*
Waereghem *see* Waregem
163 *U13* **Wafangdian** *var.* Fuxian, Fu Xian. Liaoning, NE China *39°36´N 122°00´E*
171 *R13* **Waflia** Pulau Buru, E Indonesia *03°10´S 126°05´E*
Wagadugu *see* Ouagadougou
98 *K12* **Wageningen** Gelderland, SE Netherlands *51°58´N 05°40´E*
55 *V9* **Wageningen** Nickerie, NW Surinam *05°44´N 56°45´W*
9 *O8* **Wager Bay** *inlet* Nunavut, N Canada
183 *P10* **Wagga Wagga** New South Wales, SE Australia *35°11´S 147°22´E*
180 *J13* **Wagin** Western Australia *33°16´S 117°26´E*
108 *H8* **Wägitaler See** ◎ SW Switzerland
29 *P12* **Wagner** South Dakota, N USA *43°04´N 98°17´W*
27 *Q9* **Wagoner** Oklahoma, C USA *35°58´N 92°23´W*
37 *U10* **Wagon Mound** New Mexico, SW USA *36°00´N 104°42´W*
32 *J14* **Wagontire** Oregon, NW USA *43°15´N 119°51´W*
110 *H10* **Wągrowiec** Wielkopolskie, C Poland *52°49´N 17°11´E*
149 *U6* **Wāh** Punjab, NE Pakistan *33°50´N 72°44´E*
171 *S13* **Wahai** Pulau Seram, E Indonesia *02°48´S 129°29´E*
169 *V10* **Wahau, Sungai** ≈ Borneo, C Indonesia
Wahaybah, Ramlat Al *see* Wahībah, Ramlat Āl
80 *D13* **Wahda** *var.* Unity State. ◈ *state* S Sudan
38 *D9* **Wahiawā** *var.* Wahiawa. O'ahu, Hawaii, USA, C Pacific Ocean *21°30´N 158°01´W*
Wahībah, Ramlat Ahl *see* Wahībah, Ramlat Āl
141 *Y9* **Wahībah, Ramlat Āl** *var.* Ramlat Ahl Wahībah, Ramlat Al Wahaybah, ***Eng.*** Wahībah Sands. *desert* N Oman
Wahībah Sands *see* Wahībah, Ramlat Āl
101 *E16* **Wahn** ✕ (Köln) Nordrhein-Westfalen, W Germany *50°51´N 07°09´E*
29 *R15* **Wahoo** Nebraska, C USA *41°12´N 96°37´W*
29 *R6* **Wahpeton** North Dakota, N USA *46°16´N 96°36´W*
Wahran *see* Oran
36 *J6* **Wah Wah Mountains** ▲▲ Utah, W USA
38 *D9* **Waialua** O'ahu, Hawaii, USA, C Pacific Ocean *21°34´N 158°07´W*
38 *D9* **Wai'anae** *var.* Waianae. O'ahu, Hawaii, USA, C Pacific Ocean *21°26´N 158°11´W*
184 *Q8* **Waiapu** ≈ North Island, New Zealand
185 *I17* **Waiau** Canterbury, South Island, New Zealand *42°39´S 173°03´E*
185 *I17* **Waiau** ≈ South Island, New Zealand
185 *B23* **Waiau** ≈ South Island, New Zealand
101 *H21* **Waiblingen** Baden-Württemberg, S Germany *48°49´N 09°19´E*
Waidhofen *see* Waidhofen an der Thaya, Niederösterreich, Austria
Waidhofen *see* Waidhofen an der Ybbs, Niederösterreich, Austria
109 *V2* **Waidhofen an der Thaya** *var.* Waidhofen. Niederösterreich, NE Austria *48°49´N 15°17´E*
109 *U5* **Waidhofen an der Ybbs** *var.* Waidhofen. Niederösterreich, E Austria *47°58´N 14°47´E*
171 *T11* **Waigeo, Pulau** *island* Maluku, E Indonesia
184 *L5* **Waiheke Island** *island* N New Zealand
184 *M7* **Waihi** Waikato, North Island, New Zealand *37°22´S 175°51´E*
185 *C20* **Waihou** ≈ North Island, New Zealand
Waikaboebak *see* Waikabubak
171 *N17* **Waikabubak** ***prev.*** Waikaboebak. Pulau Sumba, C Indonesia *09°40´S 119°25´E*
185 *D23* **Waikaia** ≈ South Island, New Zealand
185 *D23* **Waikaka** Southland, South Island, New Zealand *45°55´S 168°59´E*
184 *L13* **Waikanae** Wellington, North Island, New Zealand *40°52´S 175°03´E*
184 *M7* **Waikare, Lake** ◎ North Island, New Zealand
184 *O9* **Waikaremoana, Lake** ◎ North Island, New Zealand
185 *I17* **Waikari** Canterbury, South Island, New Zealand *42°50´S 172°41´E*
184 *L8* **Waikato** ***off.*** Waikato Region. ◈ *region* North Island, New Zealand
184 *M8* **Waikato** ≈ North Island, New Zealand
Waikato Region *see* Waikato
182 *J9* **Waikerie** South Australia *34°12´S 139°57´E*
185 *F23* **Waikouaiti** Otago, South Island, New Zealand *45°36´S 170°39´E*
38 *H11* **Wailea** Hawaii, USA, C Pacific Ocean *19°53´N 155°07´W*
38 *F10* **Wailuku** Maui, Hawaii, USA, C Pacific Ocean *20°53´N 156°30´W*
185 *H18* **Waimakariri** ≈ South Island, New Zealand
38 *D9* **Waimānalo Beach** *var.* Waimanalo Beach. O'ahu, Hawaii, USA, C Pacific Ocean *21°20´N 157°42´W*
185 *G15* **Waimangaroa** West Coast, South Island, New Zealand *41°41´S 171°49´E*
185 *G21* **Waimate** Canterbury, South Island, New Zealand *44°44´S 171°03´E*
38 *G11* **Waimea** *var.* Kamuela. Hawaii, USA, C Pacific Ocean *20°02´N 155°20´W*
38 *D9* **Waimea** *var.* Maunawai. O'ahu, Hawaii, USA, C Pacific Ocean *21°39´N 158°04´W*
38 *B8* **Waimea** Kaua'i, Hawaii, USA, C Pacific Ocean *21°57´N 159°40´W*
99 *M20* **Waimes** Liège, E Belgium *50°25´N 06°10´E*
154 *J11* **Wainganga** *var.* Wain River. ≈ C India
Waingapoe *see* Waingapu
171 *N17* **Waingapu** ***prev.*** Waingapoe. Pulau Sumba, C Indonesia *09°40´S 120°16´E*
55 *S7* **Waini** ≈ N Guyana
55 *S7* **Waini Point** *headland* NW Guyana *08°24´N 59°48´W*
Wain River *see* Wainganga
11 *R15* **Wainwright** Alberta, SW Canada *52°50´N 110°51´W*
39 *O5* **Wainwright** Alaska, USA *70°38´N 160°02´W*
184 *K4* **Waiotira** Northland, North Island, New Zealand *35°56´S 174°11´E*
184 *M11* **Waiouru** Manawatu-Wanganui, North Island, New Zealand *39°28´S 175°41´E*
171 *W14* **Waipa** Papua, E Indonesia *03°47´S 136°16´E*
184 *L8* **Waipa** ≈ North Island, New Zealand
184 *P9* **Waipaoa** ≈ North Island, New Zealand
185 *D25* **Waipapa Point** *headland* South Island, New Zealand *46°39´S 168°51´E*
185 *I18* **Waipara** Canterbury, South Island, New Zealand *43°04´S 172°45´E*
184 *N12* **Waipawa** Hawke's Bay, North Island, New Zealand *39°57´S 176°36´E*
184 *K4* **Waipu** Northland, North Island, New Zealand *35°58´S 174°25´E*
184 *N12* **Waipukurau** Hawke's Bay, North Island, New Zealand *40°01´S 176°34´E*
171 *U14* **Wair** Pulau Kai Besar, E Indonesia *05°16´S 133°09´E*
Wairakai *see* Wairakei
184 *N9* **Wairakei** *var.* Wairakai. Waikato, North Island, New Zealand *38°37´S 176°05´E*
185 *M14* **Wairarapa, Lake** ◎ North Island, New Zealand
185 *J15* **Wairau** ≈ South Island, New Zealand
184 *P10* **Wairoa** Hawke's Bay, North Island, New Zealand *39°03´S 177°26´E*
184 *P10* **Wairoa** ≈ North Island, New Zealand
184 *J4* **Wairoa** ≈ North Island, New Zealand
184 *N9* **Waitahanui** Waikato, North Island, New Zealand *38°48´S 176°04´E*
184 *M6* **Waitakaruru** Waikato, North Island, New Zealand *37°14´S 175°22´E*
185 *F21* **Waitaki** ≈ South Island, New Zealand
184 *K10* **Waitara** Taranaki, North Island, New Zealand *39°01´S 174°14´E*
184 *M7* **Waitoa** Waikato, North Island, New Zealand *37°36´S 175°37´E*
184 *L8* **Waitomo Caves** Waikato, North Island, New Zealand *38°17´S 175°06´E*
184 *L11* **Waitotara** Taranaki, North Island, New Zealand *39°49´S 174°43´E*
184 *L11* **Waitotara** ≈ North Island, New Zealand
32 *L10* **Waitsburg** Washington, NW USA *46°16´N 118°09´W*
Waitzen *see* Vác
184 *L6* **Waiuku** Auckland, North Island, New Zealand *37°15´S 174°45´E*
164 *L10* **Wajima** *var.* Wazima. Ishikawa, Honshū, SW Japan *37°23´N 136°53´E*
81 *K17* **Wajir** North Eastern, NE Kenya *01°46´N 40°05´E*
79 *J17* **Waka** Equateur, NW Dem. Rep. Congo *01°04´N 20°11´E*
81 *I14* **Waka** Southern Nationalities, S Ethiopia *07°12´N 37°19´E*
14 *D9* **Wakami Lake** ◎ Ontario, S Canada
164 *I12* **Wakasa** Tottori, Honshū, SW Japan *35°18´N 134°25´E*
164 *J12* **Wakasa-wan** *bay* C Japan
185 *C22* **Wakatipu, Lake** ◎ South Island, New Zealand
11 *T15* **Wakaw** Saskatchewan, S Canada *52°40´N 105°45´W*
164 *I14* **Wakayama** Wakayama, Honshū, SW Japan *34°12´N 135°09´E*
164 *I15* **Wakayama** ***off.*** Wakayama-ken. ◈ *prefecture* Honshū, SW Japan
Wakayama-ken *see* Wakayama
26 *K4* **Wa Keeney** Kansas, C USA *39°02´N 99°53´W*
185 *I14* **Wakefield** Tasman, South Island, New Zealand *41°24´S 173°03´E*
97 *M17* **Wakefield** N England, United Kingdom *53°42´N 01°29´W*
27 *O4* **Wakefield** Kansas, C USA *39°12´N 97°00´W*
30 *L4* **Wakefield** Michigan, N USA *46°27´N 89°55´W*
21 *U9* **Wake Forest** North Carolina, SE USA *35°58´N 78°30´W*
Wakeham Bay *see* Kangiqsujuaq
189 *Y11* **Wake Island** ◇ *US unincorporated territory* NW Pacific Ocean
189 *Y12* **Wake Island** ✕ NW Pacific Ocean
189 *Y12* **Wake Island** *atoll* NW Pacific Ocean
189 *X12* **Wake Lagoon** *lagoon* Wake Island, NW Pacific Ocean
166 *L8* **Wakema** Ayeyarwady, SW Burma (Myanmar) *16°36´N 95°11´E*
Wakhan *see* Khandūd
164 *H14* **Waki** Tokushima, Shikoku, SW Japan *34°04´N 134°10´E*
165 *T1* **Wakkanai** Hokkaidō, NE Japan *45°25´N 141°39´E*
83 *K22* **Wakkerstroom** Mpumalanga, E South Africa *27°21´S 30°10´E*
14 *C10* **Wakomata Lake** ◎ Ontario, S Canada
183 *N10* **Wakool** New South Wales, SE Australia *35°30´S 144°22´E*
Wakra *see* Al Wakrah
Waku Kungo *see* Uaco Cungo
186 *J7* **Wakunai** Bougainville Island, NE Papua New Guinea *05°52´S 155°10´E*
Walachei/Walachia *see* Wallachia
155 *K26* **Walawe Ganga** ≈ S Sri Lanka
111 *F15* **Wałbrzych** ***Ger.*** Waldenburg, Waldenburg in Schlesien. Dolnośląskie, SW Poland *50°45´N 16°20´E*
183 *T6* **Walcha** New South Wales, SE Australia *31°01´S 151°38´E*
101 *K24* **Walchensee** ◎ SE Germany
99 *D14* **Walcheren** *island* SW Netherlands
29 *Z14* **Walcott** Iowa, C USA *41°34´N 90°46´W*
33 *W16* **Walcott** Wyoming, C USA *41°46´N 106°46´W*
99 *G21* **Walcourt** Namur, S Belgium *50°16´N 04°26´E*
110 *G9* **Wałcz** ***Ger.*** Deutsch Krone. Zachodnio-pomorskie, NW Poland *53°17´N 16°29´E*
108 *H7* **Wald** Zürich, N Switzerland *47°17´N 08°56´E*
109 *U3* **Waldaist** ≈ N Austria
180 *I9* **Waldburg Range** ▲▲ Western Australia
37 *R3* **Walden** Colorado, C USA *40°43´N 106°16´W*
18 *K13* **Walden** New York, NE USA *41°35´N 74°09´W*
Waldenburg/Waldenburg in Schlesien *see* Wałbrzych
11 *T15* **Waldheim** Saskatchewan, S Canada *52°38´N 106°35´W*
Waldia *see* Weldiya
101 *M23* **Waldkraiburg** Bayern, SE Germany *48°10´N 12°23´E*
27 *T14* **Waldo** Arkansas, C USA *33°21´N 93°18´W*
23 *V9* **Waldo** Florida, SE USA *29°47´N 82°07´W*
19 *R7* **Waldoboro** Maine, NE USA *44°06´N 69°22´W*
21 *W4* **Waldorf** Maryland, NE USA *38°36´N 76°54´W*
32 *F12* **Waldport** Oregon, NW USA *44°25´N 124°04´W*
27 *S11* **Waldron** Arkansas, C USA *34°54´N 94°09´W*
195 *Y13* **Waldron, Cape** *headland* Antarctica *66°08´S 116°00´E*
101 *F24* **Waldshut-Tiengen** Baden-Württemberg, S Germany *47°37´N 08°13´E*
171 *P12* **Walea, Selat** *strait* Sulawesi, C Indonesia
Wałeckie Międzyrzecze *see* Valašské Meziříčí
108 *H8* **Walensee** ◎ NW Switzerland
38 *L8* **Wales** Alaska, USA *65°36´N 168°03´W*
97 *J20* **Wales** ***Wel.*** Cymru. ◈ *national region* Wales, United Kingdom
9 *O7* **Wales Island** *island* Nunavut, NE Canada
77 *P14* **Walewale** N Ghana *10°21´N 00°48´W*
99 *M24* **Walferdange** Luxembourg, C Luxembourg *49°39´N 06°08´E*
183 *Q5* **Walgett** New South Wales, SE Australia *30°02´S 148°14´E*
194 *K10* **Walgreen Coast** *physical region* Antarctica
29 *Q2* **Walhalla** North Dakota, N USA *48°55´N 97°55´W*
21 *O11* **Walhalla** South Carolina, SE USA *34°46´N 83°05´W*
79 *O19* **Walikale** Nord-Kivu, E Dem. Rep. Congo *01°29´S 28°05´E*
Walk *see* Valga, Estonia

◆ Country
● Country Capital
◇ Dependent Territory
○ Dependent Territory Capital
◈ Administrative Regions
✕ International Airport
▲ Mountain
▲▲ Mountain Range
Volcano
≈ River
◎ Lake
▨ Reservoir

Walk *see* Valka, Latvia
29 U5 **Walker** Minnesota, N USA 47°06′N 94°35′W
15 V4 **Walker, Lac** ◎ Québec, SE Canada
35 S7 **Walker Lake** ◎ Nevada, W USA
35 R6 **Walker River** ≈ Nevada, W USA
28 K10 **Wall** South Dakota, N USA 43°58′N 102°12′W
173 U9 **Wallaby Plateau** *undersea feature* E Indian Ocean
33 N8 **Wallace** Idaho, NW USA 47°28′N 115°55′W
21 V11 **Wallace** North Carolina, SE USA 34°42′N 77°59′W
14 D17 **Wallaceburg** Ontario, S Canada 42°34′N 82°22′W
22 F5 **Wallace Lake** ⊠ Louisiana, S USA
11 P13 **Wallace Mountain** ▲ Alberta, W Canada 54°50′N 115°57′W
116 J14 **Wallachia** *var.* Walachia, *Ger.* Walachei, *Rom.* Valachia. *cultural region* S Romania
Wallachisch-Meseritsch *see* Valašské Meziříčí
183 U4 **Wallangarra** New South Wales, SE Australia 28°56′S 151°57′E
182 I8 **Wallaroo** South Australia 33°56′S 137°38′E
32 L10 **Walla Walla** Washington, NW USA 46°03′N 118°20′W
45 V9 **Wall Blake** ✕ (The Valley) C Anguilla 18°12′N 63°02′W
101 H19 **Walldürn** Baden-Württemberg, SW Germany 49°34′N 09°22′E
100 F12 **Wallenhorst** Niedersachsen, NW Germany 52°21′N 08°01′E
Wallenthal *see* Haţeg
109 S4 **Wallern** Oberösterreich, N Austria 48°13′N 13°58′E
Wallern *see* Wallern im Burgenland
109 Z5 **Wallern im Burgenland** *var.* Wallern. Burgenland, E Austria 47°44′N 16°57′E
18 M9 **Wallingford** Vermont, NE USA 43°27′N 72°56′W
25 V11 **Wallis** Texas, SW USA 29°38′N 96°05′W
Wallis *see* Valais
192 K9 **Wallis and Futuna** *Fr.* Territoire de Wallis et Futuna. ◇ *French overseas territory* C Pacific Ocean
108 G7 **Wallisellen** Zürich, N Switzerland 47°25′N 08°36′E
Wallis et Futuna, Territoire de *see* Wallis and Futuna
190 H11 **Wallis, Îles** *island group* N Wallis and Futuna
31 Q5 **Walloon Lake** ◎ Michigan, N USA
32 K10 **Wallula** Washington, NW USA 46°03′N 118°54′W
32 K10 **Wallula, Lake** ◎ Washington, NW USA
21 S8 **Walnut Cove** North Carolina, SE USA 36°18′N 80°08′W
35 N8 **Walnut Creek** California, W USA 37°52′N 122°04′W
26 K5 **Walnut Creek** ≈ Kansas, C USA
27 W9 **Walnut Ridge** Arkansas, C USA 36°06′N 90°56′W
25 S7 **Walnut Springs** Texas, SW USA 32°05′N 97°42′W
182 L10 **Walpeup** Victoria, SE Australia 35°09′S 142°01′E
187 R17 **Walpole, Île** *island* SE New Caledonia
39 N13 **Walrus Islands** *island group* Alaska, USA
97 L19 **Walsall** C England, United Kingdom 52°35′N 01°58′W
37 T7 **Walsenburg** Colorado, C USA 37°37′N 104°46′W
11 S17 **Walsh** Alberta, SW Canada 49°58′N 110°03′W
37 W7 **Walsh** Colorado, C USA 37°20′N 102°17′W
100 I11 **Walsrode** Niedersachsen, NW Germany 52°52′N 09°36′E
Waltenberg *see* Zalău
21 R14 **Walterboro** South Carolina, SE USA 32°54′N 80°21′W
Walter F.George Lake *see* Walter F. George Reservoir
23 R6 **Walter F. George Reservoir** *var.* Walter F.George Lake. ⊠ Alabama/Georgia, SE USA
26 M12 **Walters** Oklahoma, C USA 34°22′N 98°18′W
101 J16 **Waltershausen** Thüringen, C Germany 50°53′N 10°33′E
173 N10 **Walters Shoal** *var.* Walters Shoals. *reef* S Madagascar
Walters Shoals *see* Walters Shoal
22 M3 **Walthall** Mississippi, S USA 33°36′N 89°16′W
20 M4 **Walton** Kentucky, S USA 38°52′N 84°36′W
18 J11 **Walton** New York, NE USA 42°10′N 75°07′W
159 R16 **Walung** Xizang Zizhiqu, W China 28°07′N 97°00′E
79 O20 **Walungu** Sud-Kivu, E Dem. Rep. Congo 02°40′S 28°37′E
Walvisbaai *see* Walvis Bay
83 C19 **Walvis Bay** *Afr.* Walvisbaai. Erongo, NW Namibia 22°59′S 14°34′E
83 B19 **Walvis Bay** *bay* NW Namibia
Walvish Ridge *see* Walvis Ridge
65 O17 **Walvis Ridge** *var.* Walvish Ridge. *undersea feature* E Atlantic Ocean 28°00′S 03°00′E
171 X16 **Wamal** Papua, E Indonesia 08°00′S 139°06′E
171 U15 **Wamar, Pulau** *island* Kepulauan Aru, E Indonesia
79 O17 **Wamba** Orientale, NE Dem. Rep. Congo 02°10′N 27°59′E
77 V15 **Wamba** Nassarawa, C Nigeria 08°57′N 08°35′E
79 H22 **Wamba** *var.* Uamba. ≈ Angola/Dem. Rep. Congo
27 P4 **Wamego** Kansas, C USA 39°12′N 96°18′W
18 I10 **Wampsville** New York, NE USA 43°03′N 75°40′W
42 K6 **Wampú, Río** ≈ E Honduras
171 X16 **Wan** Papua, E Indonesia 08°15′S 138°00′E
Wan *see* Anhui
183 N4 **Wanaaring** New South Wales, SE Australia 29°42′S 144°07′E
185 D21 **Wanaka** Otago, South Island, New Zealand 44°42′S 169°09′E
185 D20 **Wanaka, Lake** ◎ South Island, New Zealand
171 W14 **Wanapiri** Papua, E Indonesia 04°21′S 135°52′E
14 F9 **Wanapitei** ≈ Ontario, S Canada
14 F10 **Wanapitei Lake** ◎ Ontario, S Canada
18 K14 **Wanaque** New Jersey, NE USA 41°02′N 74°17′W
171 U12 **Wanau** Papua, E Indonesia 01°20′S 132°40′E
185 F22 **Wanbrow, Cape** *headland* South Island, New Zealand 45°07′S 170°59′E
Wancheng *see* Wanning
Wanchuan *see* Zhangjiakou
171 W13 **Wandai** *var.* Komeyo. Papua, E Indonesia 03°35′S 136°15′E
163 Z8 **Wanda Shan** ▲▲ NE China
197 R11 **Wandel Sea** *sea* Arctic Ocean
160 D13 **Wanding** *var.* Wandingzhen. Yunnan, SW China 24°01′N 98°00′E
Wandingzhen *see* Wanding
99 H20 **Wanfercée-Baulet** Hainaut, S Belgium 50°27′N 04°37′E
184 L12 **Wanganui** Manawatu-Wanganui, North Island, New Zealand 39°56′S 175°02′E
184 L11 **Wanganui** ≈ North Island, New Zealand
183 P11 **Wangaratta** Victoria, SE Australia 36°22′S 146°17′E
160 J8 **Wangcang** *var.* Donghe; *prev.* Fengjiaba, Hongjiang. Sichuan, C China 32°15′N 106°16′E
Wangda *see* Zogang
101 I24 **Wangen im Allgäu** Baden-Württemberg, S Germany 47°40′N 09°49′E
Wangerin *see* Węgorzyno
100 F9 **Wangerooge** *island* NW Germany
171 W13 **Wanggar** Papua, E Indonesia 03°22′S 135°15′E
160 J13 **Wangmo** *var.* Fuxing. Guizhou, S China 25°08′N 106°08′E
Wangolodougou *see* Ouangolodougou
161 S9 **Wangpan Yang** *sea* E China
163 Y10 **Wangqing** Jilin, NE China 43°19′N 129°42′E
167 P8 **Wang Saphung** Loei, C Thailand 17°18′N 101°45′E
167 O6 **Wan Hsa-la** Shan State, E Burma (Myanmar) 20°27′N 98°39′E
55 W9 **Wanica** ◐ *district* N Surinam
79 M18 **Wanie-Rukula** Orientale, C Dem. Rep. Congo 0°13′N 25°34′E
Wankie *see* Hwange
Wanki, Río *see* Coco, Río
81 N17 **Wanlaweyn** *var.* Wanle Weyn, *It.* Uanle Uen. Shabeellaha Hoose, SW Somalia 02°36′N 44°47′E
Wanle Weyn *see* Wanlaweyn
180 I12 **Wanneroo** Western Australia 31°40′S 115°35′E
160 L17 **Wanning** *var.* Wancheng. Hainan, S China 18°55′N 110°27′E
167 Q8 **Wanon Niwat** Sakon Nakhon, E Thailand 17°39′N 103°45′E
155 H16 **Wanparti** Andhra Pradesh, C India 16°19′N 78°06′E
Wansen *see* Wiązów
160 L11 **Wanshan** Guizhou, S China 27°45′N 109°12′E
99 M14 **Wanssum** Limburg, SE Netherlands 51°31′N 06°04′E
184 N12 **Wanstead** Hawke's Bay, North Island, New Zealand 40°09′S 176°31′E
Wanxian *see* Wanzhou
188 F16 **Wanyaan** Yap, Micronesia
160 K8 **Wanyuan** Sichuan, C China 32°05′N 108°08′E
161 O11 **Wanzai** *var.* Kangle. Jiangxi, S China 28°06′N 114°27′E
99 J20 **Wanze** Liège, E Belgium 50°32′N 05°16′E
160 K9 **Wanzhou** *var.* Wanxian. Chongqing Shi, C China 30°48′N 108°21′E
31 R12 **Wapakoneta** Ohio, N USA 40°34′N 84°11′W
12 D7 **Wapaseese** ≈ Ontario, C Canada
32 I10 **Wapato** Washington, NW USA 46°27′N 120°25′W
29 Y15 **Wapello** Iowa, C USA 41°10′N 91°13′W
11 N13 **Wapiti** ≈ Alberta/British Columbia, SW Canada
27 X7 **Wappapello Lake** ⊠ Missouri, C USA
18 K13 **Wappingers Falls** New York, NE USA 41°36′N 73°54′W
29 X13 **Wapsipinicon River** ≈ Iowa, C USA
14 L9 **Wapus** ≈ Québec, SE Canada
160 H7 **Waqên** Sichuan, C China 33°05′N 102°34′E
21 Q7 **War** West Virginia, NE USA 37°18′N 81°39′W
80 D13 **Warab** Warab, SW Sudan 08°08′N 28°37′E
81 D14 **Warab** ◐ *state* SW Sudan
155 J15 **Warangal** Andhra Pradesh, C India 18°N 79°35′E
Warasdin *see* Varaždin
183 O16 **Waratah** Tasmania, SE Australia 41°28′S 145°34′E
183 O14 **Waratah Bay** *bay* Victoria, SE Australia
101 H15 **Warburg** Nordrhein-Westfalen, W Germany 51°30′N 09°11′E
182 I1 **Warburton Creek** *seasonal river* South Australia
180 M9 **Warbuton** Western Australia 26°17′S 126°18′E
99 M20 **Warche** ≈ E Belgium
Wardag/Wardak *see* Vardak
32 K9 **Warden** Washington, NW USA 46°58′N 119°02′W
154 I12 **Wardha** Mahārāshtra, W India 20°41′N 78°40′E
Wardija Point *see* Wardija, Ras il-
121 N15 **Wardija, Ras il-** *var.* Wardija Point. *headland* Gozo, NW Malta 36°03′N 14°11′E
139 P3 **Wardīyah** Nīnawá, N Iraq 36°18′N 41°45′E
185 E19 **Ward, Mount** ▲ South Island, New Zealand 43°49′S 169°54′E
10 L11 **Ware** British Columbia, W Canada 57°26′N 125°41′W
99 D18 **Waregem** *var.* Waereghem. West-Vlaanderen, W Belgium 50°53′N 03°26′E
99 J19 **Waremme** Liège, E Belgium 50°41′N 05°15′E
100 N10 **Waren** Mecklenburg-Vorpommern, NE Germany 53°32′N 12°42′E
171 W13 **Waren** Papua, E Indonesia 02°13′S 136°21′E
101 F14 **Warendorf** Nordrhein-Westfalen, W Germany 51°57′N 08°00′E
21 P12 **Ware Shoals** South Carolina, SE USA 34°24′N 82°15′W
98 N4 **Warffum** Groningen, NE Netherlands 53°22′N 06°34′E
81 O15 **Wargalo** Mudug, E Somalia 06°06′N 47°40′E
146 M12 **Warganza** *Rus.* Varganzi. Qashqadaryo Viloyati, S Uzbekistan 39°18′N 66°00′E
Wargla *see* Ouargla
183 T4 **Warialda** New South Wales, SE Australia 29°34′S 150°35′E
154 F13 **Wāri Godri** Mahārāshtra, C India 19°28′N 75°43′E
167 R10 **Warin Chamrap** Ubon Ratchathani, E Thailand 15°11′N 104°51′E
25 R11 **Waring** Texas, SW USA 29°56′N 98°48′W
39 O8 **Waring Mountains** ▲▲ Alaska, USA
110 M12 **Warka** Mazowieckie, E Poland 51°45′N 21°12′E
184 L5 **Warkworth** Auckland, North Island, New Zealand 36°23′S 174°42′E
171 U12 **Warmandi** Papua, E Indonesia 0°21′S 132°38′E
83 E22 **Warmbad** Karas, S Namibia 28°29′S 18°41′E
98 H8 **Warmenhuizen** Noord-Holland, NW Netherlands 52°43′N 04°45′E
110 M8 **Warmińsko-Mazurskie** ◐ *province* C Poland
97 L22 **Warminster** S England, United Kingdom 51°13′N 02°12′W
18 I15 **Warminster** Pennsylvania, NE USA 40°11′N 75°04′W
35 V8 **Warm Springs** Nevada, W USA 38°10′N 116°21′W
32 H12 **Warm Springs** Oregon, NW USA 44°51′N 121°24′W
21 S5 **Warm Springs** Virginia, NE USA 38°03′N 79°48′W
100 M8 **Warnemünde** Mecklenburg-Vorpommern, NE Germany 54°10′N 12°03′E
27 Q10 **Warner** Oklahoma, C USA 35°29′N 95°18′W
35 Q2 **Warner Mountains** ▲▲ California, W USA
23 T5 **Warner Robins** Georgia, SE USA 32°38′N 83°38′W
57 N18 **Warnes** Santa Cruz, C Bolivia 17°30′S 63°11′W
100 M9 **Warnow** ≈ NE Germany
Warnsdorf *see* Varnsdorf
98 M11 **Warnsveld** Gelderland, E Netherlands 52°08′N 06°14′E
154 I13 **Warora** Mahārāshtra, C India 20°12′N 79°01′E
182 L11 **Warracknabeal** Victoria, SE Australia 36°17′S 142°26′E
183 O13 **Warragul** Victoria, SE Australia 38°11′S 145°55′E
183 O4 **Warrego River** *seasonal river* New South Wales/Queensland, E Australia
183 Q6 **Warren** New South Wales, SE Australia 31°41′S 147°51′E
11 X16 **Warren** Manitoba, S Canada 50°05′N 97°33′W
27 V14 **Warren** Arkansas, C USA 33°38′N 92°05′W
31 S10 **Warren** Michigan, N USA 42°29′N 83°02′W
29 R3 **Warren** Minnesota, N USA 48°12′N 96°46′W
31 U11 **Warren** Ohio, N USA 41°14′N 80°49′W
18 D12 **Warren** Pennsylvania, NE USA 41°52′N 79°09′W
25 X10 **Warren** Texas, SW USA 30°33′N 94°24′W
97 G16 **Warrenpoint** *Ir.* An Pointe. SE Northern Ireland, United Kingdom 54°07′N 06°16′W
27 S4 **Warrensburg** Missouri, C USA 38°46′N 93°44′W
83 H22 **Warrenton** Northern Cape, N South Africa 28°07′S 24°51′E
23 U4 **Warrenton** Georgia, SE USA 33°24′N 82°39′W
27 W4 **Warrenton** Missouri, C USA 38°48′N 91°08′W
21 V8 **Warrenton** North Carolina, SE USA 36°24′N 78°11′W
21 V4 **Warrenton** Virginia, NE USA 38°43′N 77°48′W
77 U17 **Warri** Delta, S Nigeria 05°26′N 05°34′E
97 L18 **Warrington** C England, United Kingdom 53°24′N 02°37′W
23 O9 **Warrington** Florida, SE USA 30°22′N 87°16′W
23 P3 **Warrior** Alabama, S USA 33°49′N 86°49′W
182 L13 **Warrnambool** Victoria, SE Australia 38°23′S 142°30′E
29 T2 **Warroad** Minnesota, N USA 48°55′N 95°18′W
183 S6 **Warrumbungle Range** ▲▲ New South Wales, SE Australia
154 J12 **Wārsa** Mahārāshtra, C India 20°42′N 79°58′E
31 P11 **Warsaw** Indiana, N USA 41°13′N 85°52′W
20 L4 **Warsaw** Kentucky, S USA 38°47′N 84°55′W
27 T5 **Warsaw** Missouri, C USA 38°14′N 93°23′W
18 E10 **Warsaw** New York, NE USA 42°44′N 78°06′W
21 V10 **Warsaw** North Carolina, SE USA 35°00′N 78°05′W
21 X5 **Warsaw** Virginia, NE USA 37°57′N 76°46′W
Warsaw/Warschau *see* Warszawa
81 N17 **Warshiikh** Shabeellaha Dhexe, C Somalia 02°22′N 45°52′E
101 G15 **Warstein** Nordrhein-Westfalen, W Germany 51°27′N 08°21′E
110 M11 **Warszawa** *Eng.* Warsaw, *Ger.* Warschau, *Rus.* Varshava. ● (Poland) Mazowieckie, C Poland 52°15′N 21°E
110 J13 **Warta** Sieradz, C Poland 51°43′N 18°37′E
110 D11 **Warta** *Ger.* Warthe. ≈ W Poland
Wartberg *see* Senec
20 M9 **Wartburg** Tennessee, S USA 36°08′N 84°37′W
108 J7 **Warth** Vorarlberg, NW Austria 47°16′N 10°11′E
Warthe *see* Warta
169 U12 **Waru** Borneo, C Indonesia 01°24′S 116°37′E
171 T13 **Waru** Pulau Seram, E Indonesia 03°24′S 130°38′E
139 N6 **Wa'r, Wādī al** *dry watercourse* E Syria
183 U3 **Warwick** Queensland, E Australia 28°12′S 152°E
15 Q11 **Warwick** Québec, SE Canada 45°55′N 72°00′W
97 M20 **Warwick** C England, United Kingdom 52°17′N 01°34′W
18 K13 **Warwick** New York, NE USA 41°15′N 74°21′W
29 P4 **Warwick** North Dakota, N USA 47°49′N 98°42′W
19 O12 **Warwick** Rhode Island, NE USA 41°40′N 71°21′W
97 L20 **Warwickshire** *cultural region* C England, United Kingdom
14 G14 **Wasaga Beach** Ontario, S Canada 44°30′N 80°00′W
77 U13 **Wasagu** Kebbi, NW Nigeria 11°25′N 05°48′E
36 M2 **Wasatch Range** ▲▲ W USA
35 R12 **Wasco** California, W USA 35°34′N 119°20′W
29 V10 **Waseca** Minnesota, N USA 44°04′N 93°30′W
14 H13 **Washago** Ontario, S Canada 44°46′N 78°48′W
19 S2 **Washburn** Maine, NE USA 46°46′N 68°08′W
28 M5 **Washburn** North Dakota, N USA 47°15′N 101°02′W
30 K3 **Washburn** Wisconsin, N USA 46°41′N 90°53′W
31 S14 **Washburn Hill** *hill* Ohio, N USA
154 H13 **Wāshīm** Mahārāshtra, C India 20°06′N 77°08′E
97 M14 **Washington** NE England, United Kingdom 54°54′N 01°31′W
23 U3 **Washington** Georgia, SE USA 33°44′N 82°44′W
30 L12 **Washington** Illinois, N USA 40°42′N 89°24′W
31 N15 **Washington** Indiana, N USA 38°40′N 87°10′W
29 X15 **Washington** Iowa, C USA 41°18′N 91°41′W
27 O3 **Washington** Kansas, C USA 39°49′N 97°03′W
27 W5 **Washington** Missouri, C USA 38°31′N 91°01′W
21 X9 **Washington** North Carolina, SE USA 35°33′N 77°04′W
18 B15 **Washington** Pennsylvania, NE USA 40°11′N 80°16′W
25 V10 **Washington** Texas, SW USA 30°18′N 96°08′W
36 J8 **Washington** Utah, W USA 37°07′N 113°30′W
21 V4 **Washington** Virginia, NE USA 38°43′N 78°11′W
32 I9 **Washington** *off.* State of Washington, *also known as* Chinook State, Evergreen State. ◐ *state* NW USA
Washington *see* Washington Court House
31 S14 **Washington Court House** *var.* Washington. Ohio, NE USA 39°32′N 83°29′W
21 W4 **Washington DC** ● (USA) District of Columbia, NE USA 38°54′N 77°02′W
31 O5 **Washington Island** *island* Wisconsin, N USA
Washington Island *see* Teraina
19 O7 **Washington, Mount** ▲ New Hampshire, NE USA 44°16′N 71°18′W
26 M11 **Washita River** ≈ Oklahoma/Texas, C USA
97 O18 **Wash, The** *inlet* E England, United Kingdom
32 L9 **Washtucna** Washington, NW USA 46°44′N 118°19′W
Wasiliszki *see* Vasilishki
110 P9 **Wasilków** Podlaskie, NE Poland 53°12′N 23°15′E
39 R11 **Wasilla** Alaska, USA 61°34′N 149°26′W
139 V9 **Wāsiţ** ◐ *governorate* E Iraq
55 U9 **Wasjabo** Sipaliwini, NW Surinam 05°09′N 57°09′W
12 I10 **Waskaganish** *prev.* Fort Rupert, Rupert House. Québec, SE Canada 51°30′N 79°45′W
11 X11 **Waskaiowaka Lake** ◎ Manitoba, C Canada
11 T14 **Waskesiu Lake** Saskatchewan, C Canada 53°56′N 106°05′W
25 X7 **Waskom** Texas, SW USA 32°28′N 94°03′W
110 G13 **Wąsosz** Dolnośląskie, SW Poland 51°36′N 16°30′E
42 M6 **Waspam** *var.* Waspán. Región Autónoma Atlántico Norte, NE Nicaragua 14°41′N 84°04′W
Waspán *see* Waspam
165 T3 **Wassamu** Hokkaidō, NE Japan 44°01′N 142°25′E
108 G9 **Wassen** Uri, C Switzerland 46°42′N 08°34′E
98 G11 **Wassenaar** Zuid-Holland, W Netherlands 52°09′N 04°23′E
99 N24 **Wasserbillig** Grevenmacher, E Luxembourg 49°43′N 06°30′E
Wasserburg *see* Wasserburg am Inn
101 M23 **Wasserburg am Inn** *var.* Wasserburg. Bayern, SE Germany 48°02′N 12°12′E
101 I17 **Wasserkuppe** ▲ C Germany 50°30′N 09°55′E
103 R5 **Wassy** Haute-Marne, N France 48°32′N 04°54′E
171 N14 **Watampone** *var.* Bone. Sulawesi, C Indonesia 04°33′S 120°20′E
171 R13 **Watawa** Pulau Buru, E Indonesia 03°36′S 127°13′E
Watenstedt-Salzgitter *see* Salzgitter
18 M13 **Waterbury** Connecticut, NE USA 41°33′N 73°01′W
21 R11 **Wateree Lake** ⊠ South Carolina, SE USA
21 R12 **Wateree River** ≈ South Carolina, SE USA
97 E20 **Waterford** *Ir.* Port Láirge. Waterford, S Ireland 52°15′N 07°08′W
31 S9 **Waterford** Michigan, N USA 42°42′N 83°24′W
97 E20 **Waterford** *Ir.* Port Láirge. *cultural region* S Ireland
97 E21 **Waterford Harbour** *Ir.* Cuan Phort Láirge. *inlet* S Ireland
98 G12 **Wateringen** Zuid-Holland, W Netherlands 52°02′N 04°16′E
99 G19 **Waterloo** Walloon Brabant, C Belgium 50°43′N 04°24′E
14 F16 **Waterloo** Ontario, S Canada 43°28′N 80°32′W
15 P12 **Waterloo** Québec, SE Canada 45°20′N 72°28′W
30 K16 **Waterloo** Illinois, N USA 38°20′N 90°09′W
29 X13 **Waterloo** Iowa, C USA 42°31′N 92°16′W
18 G10 **Waterloo** New York, NE USA 42°54′N 76°51′W
30 L4 **Watersmeet** Michigan, N USA 46°16′N 89°10′W
23 V9 **Watertown** Florida, SE USA 30°11′N 82°36′W
18 I8 **Watertown** New York, NE USA 43°37′N 75°56′W
29 R9 **Watertown** South Dakota, N USA 44°54′N 97°07′W
30 M8 **Watertown** Wisconsin, N USA 43°12′N 88°44′W
22 L3 **Water Valley** Mississippi, S USA 34°09′N 89°37′W
27 O3 **Waterville** Kansas, C USA 39°41′N 96°45′W
17 V6 **Waterville** Maine, NE USA 44°34′N 69°41′W
29 V10 **Waterville** Minnesota, N USA 44°13′N 93°34′W
18 I10 **Waterville** New York, NE USA 42°55′N 75°18′W
14 E16 **Watford** Ontario, S Canada 42°57′N 81°51′W
97 N21 **Watford** E England, United Kingdom 51°39′N 00°24′W
28 K4 **Watford City** North Dakota, N USA 47°48′N 103°16′W
141 X12 **Wāţif** S Oman 18°34′N 56°31′E
18 G11 **Watkins Glen** New York, NE USA 42°23′N 76°53′W
Watlings Island *see* San Salvador
171 U15 **Watnil** Pulau Kai Kecil, E Indonesia 05°45′S 132°39′E
26 M10 **Watonga** Oklahoma, C USA 35°52′N 98°26′W
11 T16 **Watrous** Saskatchewan, S Canada 51°40′N 105°29′W
37 T10 **Watrous** New Mexico, SW USA 35°48′N 104°58′W
79 P16 **Watsa** Orientale, NE Dem. Rep. Congo 03°00′N 29°31′E
31 N12 **Watseka** Illinois, N USA 40°46′N 87°44′W
79 J19 **Watsikengo** Equateur, C Dem. Rep. Congo 0°49′S 20°34′E
182 C5 **Watson** South Australia 30°32′S 131°29′E
11 U15 **Watson** Saskatchewan, S Canada 52°13′N 104°30′W
195 O10 **Watson Escarpment** ▲▲ Antarctica
10 K9 **Watson Lake** Yukon Territory, W Canada 60°05′N 128°47′W
35 N10 **Watsonville** California, W USA 36°53′N 121°43′W
167 Q8 **Wattay** ✕ (Viangchan) Viangchan, C Laos 18°03′N 102°36′E
109 N7 **Wattens** Tirol, W Austria 47°18′N 11°37′E
20 M9 **Watts Bar Lake** ⊠ Tennessee, S USA
108 H7 **Wattwil** Sankt Gallen, NE Switzerland 47°18′N 09°06′E
171 T14 **Watubela, Kepulauan** *island group* E Indonesia
101 N24 **Watzmann** ▲ SE Germany 47°32′N 12°56′E
186 E8 **Wau** Morobe, C Papua New Guinea 07°22′S 146°40′E
81 D14 **Wau** *var.* Wāw. Western Bahr el Ghazal, S Sudan 07°43′N 28°01′E
29 Q8 **Waubay** South Dakota, N USA 45°19′N 97°18′W
29 Q8 **Waubay Lake** ◎ South Dakota, N USA
183 U7 **Wauchope** New South Wales, SE Australia 31°30′S 152°46′E
23 W13 **Wauchula** Florida, SE USA 27°33′N 81°48′W
30 M10 **Wauconda** Illinois, N USA 42°15′N 88°08′W
182 J7 **Waukaringa** South Australia 32°19′S 139°27′E
31 N10 **Waukegan** Illinois, N USA 42°21′N 87°50′W
30 M9 **Waukesha** Wisconsin, N USA 43°01′N 88°14′W
29 X11 **Waukon** Iowa, C USA 43°16′N 91°28′W
30 L8 **Waunakee** Wisconsin, N USA 43°13′N 89°28′W
30 L7 **Waupaca** Wisconsin, N USA 44°23′N 89°04′W
30 M8 **Waupun** Wisconsin, N USA 43°40′N 88°43′W
26 M13 **Waurika** Oklahoma, C USA 34°10′N 98°00′W
26 M12 **Waurika Lake** ⊠ Oklahoma, C USA
30 L6 **Wausau** Wisconsin, N USA 44°58′N 89°40′W
31 R11 **Wauseon** Ohio, N USA 41°33′N 84°08′W
30 L7 **Wautoma** Wisconsin, N USA 44°05′N 89°17′W
30 M9 **Wauwatosa** Wisconsin, N USA 43°03′N 88°03′W
22 L9 **Waveland** Mississippi, S USA 30°17′N 89°22′W
97 Q20 **Waveney** ≈ E England, United Kingdom
184 L11 **Waverley** Taranaki, North Island, New Zealand 39°45′S 174°35′E
29 W12 **Waverly** Iowa, C USA 42°43′N 92°28′W
27 T4 **Waverly** Missouri, C USA 39°12′N 93°31′W
29 R15 **Waverly** Nebraska, C USA 40°56′N 96°27′W
18 G12 **Waverly** New York, NE USA 42°00′N 76°33′W
20 H8 **Waverly** Tennessee, S USA 36°04′N 87°49′W
21 W7 **Waverly** Virginia, NE USA 37°02′N 77°06′W
99 H19 **Wavre** Walloon Brabant, C Belgium 50°43′N 04°37′E
166 M8 **Waw** Bago, SW Burma (Myanmar) 17°26′N 96°40′E
Wāw *see* Wau
14 B7 **Wawa** Ontario, S Canada 47°59′N 84°43′W
77 T14 **Wawa** Niger, W Nigeria 09°52′N 04°33′E
75 Q11 **Wāw al Kabīr** S Libya 25°21′N 16°41′E
43 N7 **Wawa, Río** *var.* Rio Huahua. ≈ NE Nicaragua
186 B8 **Wawoi** ≈ SW Papua New Guinea
25 T7 **Waxahachie** Texas, SW USA 32°23′N 96°52′W
158 L9 **Waxxari** Xinjiang Uygur Zizhiqu, NW China 38°43′N 87°11′E
Wayaobu *see* Zichang
23 V7 **Waycross** Georgia, SE USA 31°13′N 82°21′W
180 K10 **Way, Lake** ◎ Western Australia
31 P9 **Wayland** Michigan, N USA 42°40′N 85°38′W
29 R13 **Wayne** Nebraska, C USA 42°13′N 97°01′W
18 K14 **Wayne** New Jersey, NE USA 40°57′N 74°16′W
21 P5 **Wayne** West Virginia, NE USA 38°14′N 82°27′W
23 V4 **Waynesboro** Georgia, SE USA 33°04′N 82°01′W
22 M7 **Waynesboro** Mississippi, S USA 31°40′N 88°39′W
20 H10 **Waynesboro** Tennessee, S USA 35°20′N 87°49′W
21 U5 **Waynesboro** Virginia, NE USA 38°04′N 78°54′W
18 B16 **Waynesburg** Pennsylvania, NE USA 39°51′N 80°10′W
27 U6 **Waynesville** Missouri, C USA 37°48′N 92°11′W
21 O10 **Waynesville** North Carolina, SE USA 35°29′N 82°59′W
26 L8 **Waynoka** Oklahoma, C USA 36°36′N 98°53′W
Wazan *see* Ouazzane
Wazima *see* Wajima
149 V7 **Wazīrābād** Punjab, NE Pakistan 32°28′N 74°04′E
Wazzan *see* Ouazzane
110 I8 **Wda** *var.* Czarna Woda, *Ger.* Schwarzwasser. ≈ N Poland
187 Q16 **Wé** Province des Îles Loyauté, E New Caledonia 20°55′S 167°15′E
97 O23 **Weald, The** *lowlands* SE England, United Kingdom
186 A9 **Weam** Western, SW Papua New Guinea 08°33′S 141°10′E
97 L15 **Wear** ≈ N England, United Kingdom
Wearmouth *see* Sunderland
26 L10 **Weatherford** Oklahoma, C USA 35°31′N 98°42′W
25 S6 **Weatherford** Texas, SW USA 32°47′N 97°48′W
34 M3 **Weaverville** California, W USA 40°42′N 122°57′W
27 R7 **Webb City** Missouri, C USA 37°07′N 94°28′W
192 G8 **Weber Basin** *undersea feature* S Ceram Sea
Webfoot State *see* Oregon
18 F9 **Webster** New York, NE USA 43°12′N 77°25′W
29 Q8 **Webster** South Dakota, N USA 45°19′N 97°31′W
29 V13 **Webster City** Iowa, C USA 42°28′N 93°49′W
27 X5 **Webster Groves** Missouri, C USA 38°32′N 90°20′W
21 S4 **Webster Springs** *var.* Addison. West Virginia, NE USA 38°29′N 80°52′W
171 S11 **Weda, Teluk** *bay* Pulau Halmahera, E Indonesia
65 B25 **Weddell Island** *var.* Isla de San Jorge. *island* W Falkland Islands
65 K22 **Weddell Plain** *undersea feature* SW Atlantic Ocean 65°00′S 40°00′W
65 K23 **Weddell Sea** *sea* SW Atlantic Ocean
182 M11 **Wedderburn** Victoria, SE Australia 36°26′S 143°37′E
100 I9 **Wedel** Schleswig-Holstein, N Germany 53°35′N 09°42′E
92 N3 **Wedel Jarlsberg Land** *physical region* SW Svalbard
100 I12 **Wedemark** Niedersachsen, NW Germany 52°33′N 09°43′E
10 M17 **Wedge Mountain** ▲ British Columbia, SW Canada 50°10′N 122°43′W
23 R4 **Wedowee** Alabama, S USA 33°16′N 85°28′W
171 U15 **Weduar** Pulau Kai Besar, E Indonesia 05°55′S 132°51′E
35 N2 **Weed** California, W USA 41°26′N 122°24′W
15 Q12 **Weedon Centre** Québec, SE Canada 45°40′N 71°28′W
18 E13 **Weedville** Pennsylvania, NE USA 41°15′N 78°28′W
100 F10 **Weener** Niedersachsen, NW Germany 53°09′N 07°19′E
29 S16 **Weeping Water** Nebraska, C USA 40°52′N 96°08′W
99 L16 **Weert** Limburg, SE Netherlands 51°15′N 05°43′E
98 I10 **Weesp** Noord-Holland, C Netherlands 52°18′N 05°03′E
183 S5 **Wee Waa** New South Wales, SE Australia 30°16′S 149°27′E
110 N7 **Węgorzewo** *Ger.* Angerburg. Warmińsko-Mazurskie, NE Poland 54°12′N 21°49′E
110 E9 **Węgorzyno** *Ger.* Wangerin. Zachodnio-pomorskie, NW Poland 53°34′N 15°35′E
110 N11 **Węgrów** *Ger.* Bingerau. Mazowieckie, C Poland 52°22′N 22°00′E
98 N5 **Wehe-Den Hoorn** Groningen, NE Netherlands 53°20′N 06°29′E
98 M12 **Wehl** Gelderland, E Netherlands 51°58′N 06°13′E
Wehlau *see* Znamensk
168 F7 **Weh, Pulau** *island* NW Indonesia
Wei *see* Weifang
161 P1 **Weichang** *prev.* Zhuizishan. Hebei, E China 41°55′N 117°45′E
Weichang *see* Weishan
Weichsel *see* Wisła
101 M16 **Weida** Thüringen, C Germany 50°46′N 12°05′E
Weiden *see* Weiden in der Oberpfalz
101 M19 **Weiden in der Oberpfalz** *var.* Weiden. Bayern, SE Germany 49°40′N 12°10′E
161 Q4 **Weifang** *var.* Wei, Wei-fang; *prev.* Weihsien. Shandong, E China 36°44′N 119°10′E
161 S4 **Weihai** Shandong, E China 37°30′N 122°04′E
160 K6 **Wei He** ≈ C China
Weihsien *see* Weifang
101 G17 **Weilburg** Hessen, W Germany 50°31′N 08°18′E
101 K24 **Weilheim in Oberbayern** Bayern, SE Germany 47°50′N 11°09′E
183 P4 **Weilmoringle** New South Wales, SE Australia 29°13′S 146°51′E
101 L16 **Weimar** Thüringen, C Germany 50°59′N 11°20′E
25 U11 **Weimar** Texas, SW USA 29°42′N 96°46′W
160 L6 **Weinan** Shaanxi, C China 34°30′N 109°30′E
108 H6 **Weinfelden** Thurgau, NE Switzerland 47°33′N 09°09′E
101 I24 **Weingarten** Baden-Württemberg, S Germany 47°49′N 09°37′E
101 G20 **Weinheim** Baden-Württemberg, SW Germany 49°33′N 08°40′E
160 H11 **Weining** *var.* Caohai, Weining Yizu Huizu Miaozu Zizhixian. Guizhou, S China 26°51′N 104°16′E
Weining Yizu Huizu Miaozu Zizhixian *see* Weining
181 V2 **Weipa** Queensland, NE Australia 12°43′S 142°01′E
11 Y11 **Weir River** Manitoba, C Canada 56°44′N 94°06′W
21 R1 **Weirton** West Virginia, NE USA 40°24′N 80°37′W
32 M13 **Weiser** Idaho, NW USA 44°15′N 116°58′W
160 F12 **Weishan** *var.* Weichang. Yunnan, SW China 25°22′N 100°19′E
161 P6 **Weishan Hu** ◎ E China
101 M15 **Weisse Elster** *Eng.* White Elster. ≈ Czech Republic/Germany
Weisse Körös/Weisse Kreisch *see* Crişul Alb
108 L7 **Weissenbach am Lech** Tirol, W Austria 47°27′N 10°39′E
Weissenburg *see* Wissembourg, France
Weissenburg *see* Alba Iulia, Romania
101 K21 **Weissenburg in Bayern** Bayern, SE Germany 49°02′N 10°59′E
101 M15 **Weissenfels** *var.* Weißenfels. Sachsen-Anhalt, C Germany 51°12′N 11°58′E
109 R9 **Weissensee** ◎ S Austria
Weissenstein *see* Paide
108 E11 **Weisshorn** *var.* Flüela Wisshorn. ▲ SW Switzerland 46°06′N 07°43′E
Weisskirchen *see* Bela Crkva
23 R3 **Weiss Lake** ⊠ Alabama, S USA
101 Q14 **Weisswasser** *Lus.* Běla Woda. Sachsen, E Germany 51°30′N 14°37′E
99 M22 **Weiswampach** Diekirch, N Luxembourg 50°08′N 06°05′E
109 U2 **Weitra** Niederösterreich, N Austria 48°41′N 14°54′E
161 O4 **Weixian** *var.* Wei Xian. Hebei, E China 36°59′N 115°15′E
Wei Xian *see* Weixian
159 V11 **Weiyuan** *var.* Qingyuan. Gansu, C China 35°07′N 104°12′E
Weiyuan *see* Shuangjiang
160 F14 **Weiyuan Jiang** ≈ SW China
109 W7 **Weiz** Steiermark, SE Austria 47°13′N 15°38′E
Weizhou *see* Wenchuan
160 K16 **Weizhou Dao** *island* S China
110 I6 **Wejherowo** Pomorskie, NW Poland 54°36′N 18°12′E
27 Q8 **Welch** Oklahoma, C USA 36°52′N 95°06′W
24 M6 **Welch** Texas, SW USA 32°52′N 102°06′W
21 Q6 **Welch** West Virginia, NE USA 37°26′N 81°36′W
45 O14 **Welchman Hall** C Barbados 13°10′N 59°34′W
80 J11 **Weldiya** *var.* Waldia, *It.* Valdia. Āmara, N Ethiopia 11°45′N 39°39′E
21 W8 **Weldon** North Carolina, SE USA 36°25′N 77°36′W
25 V9 **Weldon** Texas, SW USA 31°00′N 95°33′W
99 M19 **Welkenraedt** Liège, E Belgium 50°40′N 05°58′E
193 O2 **Welker Seamount** *undersea feature* N Pacific Ocean 55°07′N 140°18′W
83 I22 **Welkom** Free State, C South Africa 27°59′S 26°44′E
14 H16 **Welland** Ontario, S Canada 45°59′N 79°14′W
14 G16 **Welland** ≈ Ontario, S Canada
97 O19 **Welland** ≈ C England, United Kingdom
14 H17 **Welland Canal** *canal* Ontario, S Canada
155 K25 **Wellawaya** Uva Province, SE Sri Lanka 06°44′N 81°07′E
Welle *see* Uele
181 T4 **Wellesley Islands** *island group* Queensland, N Australia
99 J22 **Wellin** Luxembourg, SE Belgium 50°06′N 05°05′E
97 N20 **Wellingborough** C England, United Kingdom 52°19′N 00°42′W

◆ Country
● Country Capital
◇ Dependent Territory
○ Dependent Territory Capital
◐ Administrative Regions
✕ International Airport
▲ Mountain
▲▲ Mountain Range
Volcano
≈ River
◎ Lake
⊠ Reservoir

183 R7 **Wellington** New South Wales, SE Australia 32°33´S 148°59´E
14 J15 **Wellington** Ontario, SE Canada 43°59´N 77°21´W
185 L14 **Wellington** ● Wellington, North Island, New Zealand 41°17´S 174°47´E
83 E26 **Wellington** Western Cape, SW South Africa 33°39´S 19°00´E
37 T2 **Wellington** Colorado, C USA 40°42´N 105°00´W
27 N7 **Wellington** Kansas, C USA 37°17´N 97°25´W
35 R7 **Wellington** Nevada, W USA 38°45´N 119°22´W
31 T11 **Wellington** Ohio, N USA 41°10´N 82°13´W
25 P3 **Wellington** Texas, SW USA 34°52´N 100°13´W
36 M4 **Wellington** Utah, W USA 39°31´N 110°45´W
185 M14 **Wellington** *off.* Wellington Region. ◈ *region* (New Zealand) North Island, New Zealand
185 L14 **Wellington** ✈ Wellington, North Island, New Zealand 41°19´S 174°48´E
Wellington *see* Wellington, Isla
63 F22 **Wellington, Isla** *var.* Wellington. *island* S Chile
183 P12 **Wellington, Lake** ◎ Victoria, SE Australia
Wellington Region *see* Wellington
29 X14 **Wellman** Iowa, C USA 41°27´N 91°50´W
24 M6 **Wellman** Texas, SW USA 33°03´N 102°25´W
97 K22 **Wells** SW England, United Kingdom 51°13´N 02°39´W
29 V11 **Wells** Minnesota, N USA 43°45´N 93°43´W
35 X2 **Wells** Nevada, W USA 41°07´N 114°58´W
25 W8 **Wells** Texas, SW USA 31°28´N 94°54´W
18 F12 **Wellsboro** Pennsylvania, NE USA 41°43´N 77°39´W
21 R1 **Wellsburg** West Virginia, NE USA 40°15´N 80°37´W
184 K4 **Wellsford** Auckland, North Island, New Zealand 36°17´S 174°30´E
180 L9 **Wells, Lake** ◎ Western Australia
181 N4 **Wells, Mount** ▲ Western Australia 17°39´S 127°08´E
97 P18 **Wells-next-the-Sea** E England, United Kingdom 52°58´N 00°48´E
31 T15 **Wellston** Ohio, N USA 39°07´N 82°31´W
27 O10 **Wellston** Oklahoma, C USA 35°41´N 97°03´W
18 E11 **Wellsville** New York, NE USA 42°06´N 77°55´W
31 V12 **Wellsville** Ohio, N USA 40°36´N 80°39´W
36 L1 **Wellsville** Utah, W USA 41°38´N 111°55´W
36 I14 **Wellton** Arizona, SW USA 32°40´N 114°09´W
109 S4 **Wels** *anc.* Ovilava. Oberösterreich, N Austria 48°10´N 14°02´E
99 K15 **Welschap** ✈ (Eindhoven) Noord-Brabant, S Netherlands 51°27´N 05°22´E
100 P10 **Welse** ~ NE Germany
22 H9 **Welsh** Louisiana, S USA 30°12´N 92°49´W
97 K19 **Welshpool** *Wel.* Y Trallwng. E Wales, United Kingdom 52°38´N 03°06´W
97 O21 **Welwyn Garden City** E England, United Kingdom 51°48´N 00°13´W
79 K18 **Wema** Equateur, NW Dem. Rep. Congo 0°25´S 21°33´E
81 G21 **Wembere** ~ C Tanzania
11 N13 **Wembley** Alberta, W Canada 55°07´N 119°12´W
12 I9 **Wemindji** *prev.* Nouveau-Comptoir , Paint Hills. Québec, C Canada 53°00´N 78°42´W
99 G18 **Wemmel** Vlaams Brabant, C Belgium 50°54´N 04°18´E
32 J8 **Wenatchee** Washington, NW USA 47°50´N 120°48´W
160 M17 **Wenchang** Hainan, S China 19°34´N 110°46´E
161 R11 **Wencheng** *var.* Daxue. Zhejiang, SE China 27°48´N 120°01´E
77 P16 **Wenchi** W Ghana 07°45´N 02°02´W
Wen-chou/Wenchow *see* Wenzhou
160 H8 **Wenchuan** *var.* Weizhou. Sichuan, C China 31°29´N 103°39´E
Wendau *see* Võnnu
Wenden *see* Cēsis
161 S4 **Wendeng** Shandong, E China 37°10´N 122°00´E
81 J14 **Wendo** Southern Nationalities, S Ethiopia 06°34´N 38°28´E
36 J2 **Wendover** Utah, W USA 40°41´N 114°00´W
14 D9 **Wenebegon** ~ Ontario, S Canada
14 D8 **Wenebegon Lake** ◎ Ontario, S Canada
108 E9 **Wengen** Bern, W Switzerland 46°38´N 07°57´E
161 O13 **Wengyuan** *var.* Longxian. Guangdong, S China 24°22´N 114°06´E
189 P15 **Weno** *prev.* Moen. Chuuk, C Micronesia
189 V12 **Weno** *prev.* Moen. *atoll* Chuuk Islands, C Micronesia
158 N13 **Wenquan** Qinghai, C China 33°16´N 91°44´E
159 H4 **Wenquan** *var.* Arixang, Bogeda'er. Xinjiang Uygur Zizhiqu, NW China 45°00´N 81°02´E
Wenquan *see* Yingshan
160 H14 **Wenshan** *var.* Kaihua. Yunnan, SW China 23°22´N 104°21´E
158 H6 **Wensu** Xinjiang Uygur Zizhiqu, W China 41°15´N 80°11´E
182 L8 **Wentworth** New South Wales, SE Australia 34°04´S 141°53´E
27 W4 **Wentzville** Missouri, C USA 38°48´N 90°51´W
159 V12 **Wenxian** *var.* Wen Xian. Gansu, C China 32°57´N 104°42´E
Wen Xian *see* Wenxian
161 S10 **Wenzhou** *var.* Wen-chou, Wenchow. Zhejiang, SE China 28°02´N 120°36´E
34 L4 **Weott** California, W USA 40°19´N 123°57´W
99 I20 **Wépion** Namur, SE Belgium 50°24´N 04°53´E
100 O11 **Werbellinsee** ◎ NE Germany
99 L21 **Werbomont** Liège, E Belgium 50°22´N 05°43´E
83 G20 **Werda** Kgalagadi, S Botswana 25°13´S 23°16´E
81 N14 **Werdër** Sumalē, E Ethiopia 06°59´N 45°20´E
Werder *see* Virtsu
Werenów *see* Voranava
171 U13 **Weri** Papua, E Indonesia 03°10´S 132°39´E
98 I13 **Werkendam** Noord-Brabant, S Netherlands 51°48´N 04°54´E
101 M20 **Wernberg-Köblitz** Bayern, SE Germany 49°31´N 12°10´E
101 J18 **Werneck** Bayern, C Germany 50°00´N 10°06´E
101 K14 **Wernigerode** Sachsen-Anhalt, C Germany 51°51´N 10°48´E
Werowitz *see* Virovitica
101 J16 **Werra** ~ C Germany
183 N12 **Werribee** Victoria, SE Australia 37°55´S 144°39´E
183 T6 **Werris Creek** New South Wales, SE Australia 31°22´S 150°40´E
Werro *see* Võru
Werschetz *see* Vršac
101 K23 **Wertach** ~ S Germany
101 I19 **Wertheim** Baden-Württemberg, SW Germany 49°45´N 09°31´E
98 J8 **Wervershoof** Noord-Holland, NW Netherlands 52°43´N 05°09´E
Wervicq *see* Wervik
99 C18 **Wervik** *var.* Wervicq, Werwick. West-Vlaanderen, W Belgium 50°47´N 03°03´E
Werwick *see* Wervik
101 D14 **Wesel** Nordrhein-Westfalen, W Germany 51°39´N 06°37´E
Weseli an der Lainsitz *see* Veselí nad Lužnicí
Wesenberg *see* Rakvere
100 H12 **Weser** ~ NW Germany
Wes-Kaap *see* Western Cape
25 S17 **Weslaco** Texas, SW USA 26°09´N 97°59´W
14 J13 **Weslemkoon Lake** ◎ Ontario, SE Canada
181 R1 **Wessel Islands** *island group* Northern Territory, N Australia
29 P9 **Wessington** South Dakota, N USA 44°27´N 98°40´W
29 P10 **Wessington Springs** South Dakota, N USA 44°02´N 98°33´W
25 T8 **West** Texas, SW USA 31°48´N 97°05´W
West *see* Ouest
30 M9 **West Allis** Wisconsin, N USA 43°01´N 88°00´W
182 E8 **Westall, Point** *headland* South Australia 32°54´S 134°04´E
194 M10 **West Antarctica** *var.* Lesser Antarctica. *physical region* Antarctica
14 G11 **West Arm** Ontario, S Canada 46°16´N 80°25´W
West Australian Basin *see* Wharton Basin
West Azerbaijan *see* Āžarbāyjān-e Gharbī
11 N17 **Westbank** British Columbia, SW Canada 49°50´N 119°37´W
138 F10 **West Bank** *disputed region* SW Asia
14 E11 **West Bay** Manitoulin Island, Ontario, S Canada 45°48´N 82°09´W
22 L11 **West Bay** *bay* Louisiana, S USA
30 M8 **West Bend** Wisconsin, N USA 43°26´N 88°13´W
153 R16 **West Bengal** ◈ *state* NE India
West Borneo *see* Kalimantan Barat
29 Y14 **West Branch** Iowa, C USA 41°40´N 91°21´W
31 R7 **West Branch** Michigan, N USA 44°16´N 84°14´W
18 F13 **West Branch Susquehanna River** ~ Pennsylvania, NE USA
97 L20 **West Bromwich** C England, United Kingdom 52°29´N 01°59´W
19 P8 **Westbrook** Maine, NE USA 43°42´N 70°21´W
29 T10 **Westbrook** Minnesota, N USA 44°02´N 95°26´W
29 Y15 **West Burlington** Iowa, C USA 40°49´N 91°09´W
96 L2 **West Burra** *island* NE Scotland, United Kingdom
30 J8 **Westby** Wisconsin, N USA 43°39´N 90°52´W
44 L6 **West Caicos** *island* W Turks and Caicos Islands
185 A24 **West Cape** *headland* South Island, New Zealand 45°51´S 166°26´E
174 L4 **West Caroline Basin** *undersea feature* SW Pacific Ocean 04°00´N 138°00´E
18 I16 **West Chester** Pennsylvania, NE USA 39°56´N 75°35´W
185 E18 **West Coast** *off.* West Coast Region. ◈ *region* South Island, New Zealand
West Coast Region *see* West Coast
25 V12 **West Columbia** Texas, SW USA 29°08´N 95°39´W
29 W10 **West Concord** Minnesota, N USA 44°09´N 92°54´W
29 V14 **West Des Moines** Iowa, C USA 41°33´N 93°42´W
37 Q6 **West Elk Peak** ▲ Colorado, C USA 38°43´N 107°12´W
44 F1 **West End** Grand Bahama Island, N Bahamas 26°36´N 78°55´W
44 F1 **West End Point** *headland* Grand Bahama Island, N Bahamas 26°40´N 78°58´W
98 O7 **Westerbork** Drenthe, NE Netherlands 52°49´N 06°36´E
98 N3 **Westereems** *strait* Germany/Netherlands
98 O9 **Westerhaar-Vriezenveensewijk** Overijssel, E Netherlands 52°28´N 06°38´E
100 G6 **Westerland** Schleswig-Holstein, N Germany 54°54´N 08°19´E
99 I17 **Westerlo** Antwerpen, N Belgium 51°05´N 04°55´E
19 N13 **Westerly** Rhode Island, NE USA 41°22´N 71°45´W
81 G18 **Western** ◈ *province* W Kenya
153 N11 **Western** ◈ *zone* C Nepal
186 A8 **Western** ◈ *province* SW Papua New Guinea
186 J8 **Western** *off.* Western Province. ◈ *province* NW Solomon Islands
155 J26 **Western** ◈ *province* SW Sri Lanka
83 G15 **Western** ◈ *province* SW Zambia
180 K8 **Western Australia** ◈ *state* W Australia
80 A13 **Western Bahr el Ghazal** ◈ *state* SW Sudan
Western Bug *see* Bug
83 F25 **Western Cape** *off.* Western Cape Province, *Afr.* Wes-Kaap. ◈ *province* SW South Africa
Western Cape Province *see* Western Cape
80 A11 **Western Darfur** ◈ *state* W Sudan
Western Desert *see* Şaḩrā' al Gharbīyah
118 G9 **Western Dvina** *Bel.* Dzvina, *Ger.* Düna, *Latv.* Daugava, *Rus.* Zapadnaya Dvina. ~ W Europe
81 D15 **Western Equatoria** ◈ *state* SW Sudan
155 E16 **Western Ghats** ▲▲ SW India
186 C7 **Western Highlands** ◈ *province* C Papua New Guinea
Western Isles *see* Outer Hebrides
80 C12 **Western Kordofan** ◈ *state* C Sudan
21 T3 **Westernport** Maryland, NE USA 39°29´N 79°03´W
Western Province *see* Western
Western Punjab *see* Punjab
74 B10 **Western Sahara** ◇ *disputed territory* N Africa
Western Samoa *see* Samoa
Western Samoa, Independent State of *see* Samoa
Western Sayans *see* Zapadnyy Sayan
Western Scheldt *see* Westerschelde
Western Sierra Madre *see* Madre Occidental, Sierra
99 E15 **Westerschelde** *Eng.* Western Scheldt; *prev.* Honte. *inlet* S North Sea
31 S13 **Westerville** Ohio, N USA 40°07´N 82°55´W
101 F17 **Westerwald** ▲▲ W Germany
65 C25 **West Falkland** *var.* Gran Malvina, Isla Gran Malvina. *island* W Falkland Islands
29 R5 **West Fargo** North Dakota, N USA 46°49´N 96°51´W
188 M15 **West Fayu Atoll** *atoll* Caroline Islands, C Micronesia
18 C11 **Westfield** New York, NE USA 42°18´N 79°34´W
30 L7 **Westfield** Wisconsin, N USA 43°56´N 89°31´W
West Flanders *see* West-Vlaanderen
27 S10 **West Fork** Arkansas, C USA 35°55´N 94°11´W
29 P16 **West Fork Big Blue River** ~ Nebraska, C USA
29 U12 **West Fork Des Moines River** ~ Iowa/Minnesota, C USA
25 S5 **West Fork Trinity River** ~ Texas, SW USA
30 L16 **West Frankfort** Illinois, N USA 37°54´N 88°55´W
98 I8 **West-Friesland** *physical region* NW Netherlands
West Frisian Islands *see* Waddeneilanden
19 T5 **West Grand Lake** ◎ Maine, NE USA
18 M12 **West Hartford** Connecticut, NE USA 41°44´N 72°45´W
18 M13 **West Haven** Connecticut, NE USA 41°16´N 72°57´W
27 X12 **West Helena** Arkansas, C USA 34°33´N 90°38´W
28 M2 **Westhope** North Dakota, N USA 48°54´N 101°01´W
195 Y8 **West Ice Shelf** *ice shelf* Antarctica
47 R2 **West Indies** *island group* SE North America
West Irian *see* Papua
West Java *see* Jawa Barat
36 L3 **West Jordan** Utah, W USA 40°37´N 111°55´W
West Kalimantan *see* Kalimantan Barat
99 D14 **Westkapelle** Zeeland, SW Netherlands 51°32´N 03°26´E
West Kazakhstan *see* Zapadnyy Kazakhstan
31 O13 **West Lafayette** Indiana, N USA 40°24´N 86°54´W
31 T13 **West Lafayette** Ohio, N USA 40°16´N 81°45´W
West Lake *see* Kagera
29 Y14 **West Liberty** Iowa, C USA 41°34´N 91°15´W
21 O5 **West Liberty** Kentucky, S USA 37°56´N 83°16´W
Westliche Morava *see* Zapadna Morava
10 J13 **Westlock** Alberta, SW Canada 54°12´N 113°50´W
14 E17 **West Lorne** Ontario, S Canada 42°36´N 81°35´W
96 J12 **West Lothian** *cultural region* S Scotland, United Kingdom
99 H16 **Westmalle** Antwerpen, N Belgium 51°18´N 04°40´E
192 G6 **West Mariana Basin** *var.* Perece Vela Basin. *undersea feature* W Pacific Ocean 15°00´N 137°00´E
97 E17 **Westmeath** *Ir.* An Iarmhí, Na H-Iarmhidhe. *cultural region* C Ireland
27 Y11 **West Memphis** Arkansas, C USA 35°09´N 90°11´W
21 W2 **Westminster** Maryland, NE USA 39°34´N 77°00´W
21 O11 **Westminster** South Carolina, SE USA 34°39´N 83°06´W
22 I5 **West Monroe** Louisiana, S USA 32°31´N 92°09´W
18 D15 **Westmont** Pennsylvania, NE USA 40°16´N 78°55´W
27 O3 **Westmoreland** Kansas, C USA 39°23´N 96°30´W
35 W17 **Westmorland** California, W USA 33°02´N 115°37´W
186 E6 **West New Britain** ◈ *province* E Papua New Guinea
West New Guinea *see* Papua
83 K18 **West Nicholson** Matabeleland South, S Zimbabwe 21°06´S 29°25´E
29 T14 **West Nishnabotna River** ~ Iowa, C USA
175 P11 **West Norfolk Ridge** *undersea feature* W Pacific Ocean
25 P12 **West Nueces River** ~ Texas, SW USA
West Nusa Tenggara *see* Nusa Tenggara Barat
29 T11 **West Okoboji Lake** ◎ Iowa, C USA
33 R16 **Weston** Idaho, NW USA 42°01´N 119°29´W
21 R4 **Weston** West Virginia, NE USA 39°03´N 80°28´W
97 J22 **Weston-super-Mare** SW England, United Kingdom 51°21´N 02°59´W
23 Z14 **West Palm Beach** Florida, SE USA 26°43´N 80°03´W
West Papua *see* Papua
188 E9 **West Passage** *passage* Babeldaob, N Palau
23 O9 **West Pensacola** Florida, SE USA 30°25´N 87°16´W
27 V8 **West Plains** Missouri, C USA 36°44´N 91°51´W
35 P7 **West Point** California, W USA 38°21´N 120°33´W
23 R5 **West Point** Georgia, SE USA 32°52´N 85°10´W
22 M3 **West Point** Mississippi, S USA 33°36´N 88°39´W
29 R14 **West Point** Nebraska, C USA 41°50´N 96°42´W
21 X6 **West Point** Virginia, NE USA 37°31´N 76°48´W
182 G10 **West Point** *headland* South Australia 35°01´S 135°58´E
23 R4 **West Point Lake** ⊡ Alabama/Georgia, SE USA
97 B16 **Westport** *Ir.* Cathair na Mart. Mayo, W Ireland 53°48´N 09°32´W
185 G15 **Westport** West Coast, South Island, New Zealand 41°46´S 171°37´E
32 F10 **Westport** Oregon, NW USA 46°07´N 123°22´W
32 F9 **Westport** Washington, NW USA 46°53´N 124°06´W
31 S15 **West Portsmouth** Ohio, N USA 38°45´N 83°01´W
West Punjab *see* Punjab
11 V14 **Westray** Manitoba, C Canada 53°30´N 101°19´W
96 J4 **Westray** *island* NE Scotland, United Kingdom
14 F9 **Westree** Ontario, S Canada 47°25´N 81°32´W
97 L16 **West Riding** *cultural region* N England, United Kingdom
West River *see* Xi Jiang
30 J7 **West Salem** Wisconsin, N USA 43°54´N 91°04´W
65 H21 **West Scotia Ridge** *undersea feature* W Scotia Sea
West Sepik *see* Sandaun
173 N4 **West Sheba Ridge** *undersea feature* W Indian Ocean 12°45´N 48°15´E
West Siberian Plain *see* Zapadno-Sibirskaya Ravnina
31 S11 **West Sister Island** *island* Ohio, N USA
West-Skylge *see* West-Terschelling
West Sumatra *see* Sumatera Barat
98 J5 **West-Terschelling** *Fris.* West-Skylge. Friesland, N Netherlands 53°23´N 05°15´E
64 J7 **West Thulean Rise** *undersea feature* N Atlantic Ocean
29 X12 **West Union** Iowa, C USA 42°57´N 91°48´W
31 R15 **West Union** Ohio, N USA 38°47´N 83°33´W
21 R3 **West Union** West Virginia, NE USA 39°18´N 80°47´W
31 N13 **Westville** Illinois, N USA 40°02´N 87°38´W
21 R3 **West Virginia** *off.* State of West Virginia, *also known as* Mountain State. ◈ *state* NE USA
99 A17 **West-Vlaanderen** *Eng.* West Flanders. ◈ *province* W Belgium
35 R7 **West Walker River** ~ California/Nevada, W USA
35 P4 **Westwood** California, W USA 40°18´N 121°02´W
183 P9 **West Wyalong** New South Wales, SE Australia 33°56´S 147°10´E
171 Q16 **Wetar, Pulau** *island* Kepulauan Damar, E Indonesia
Wetar, Selat *see* Wetar Strait
171 R16 **Wetar Strait** *var.* SelatWetar. *strait* Nusa Tenggara, S Indonesia
11 Q15 **Wetaskiwin** Alberta, SW Canada 52°57´N 113°20´W
81 K21 **Wete** Pemba, E Tanzania 05°03´S 39°41´E
166 M4 **Wetlet** Sagaing, C Burma (Myanmar) 22°43´N 95°22´E
37 T6 **Wet Mountains** ▲▲ Colorado, C USA
101 E15 **Wetter** Nordrhein-Westfalen, W Germany 51°22´N 07°24´E
101 H17 **Wetter** ~ W Germany
99 F17 **Wetteren** Oost-Vlaanderen, NW Belgium 51°06´N 03°59´E
108 F7 **Wettingen** Aargau, N Switzerland 47°28´N 08°20´E
27 P11 **Wetumka** Oklahoma, C USA 35°14´N 96°14´W
23 Q5 **Wetumpka** Alabama, S USA 32°32´N 86°12´W
108 G7 **Wetzikon** Zürich, N Switzerland 47°19´N 08°48´E
101 G17 **Wetzlar** Hessen, W Germany 50°33´N 08°30´E
99 C18 **Wevelgem** West-Vlaanderen, W Belgium 50°48´N 03°12´E
38 M6 **Wevok** *var.* Wewuk. Alaska, USA 68°52´N 166°05´W
23 R9 **Wewahitchka** Florida, SE USA 30°06´N 85°12´W
186 C6 **Wewak** East Sepik, NW Papua New Guinea 03°35´S 143°35´E
27 O11 **Wewoka** Oklahoma, C USA 35°09´N 96°30´W
Wewuk *see* Wevok
97 F20 **Wexford** *Ir.* Loch Garman. SE Ireland 52°21´N 06°31´W
97 F20 **Wexford** *Ir.* Loch Garman. *cultural region* SE Ireland
30 L7 **Weyauwega** Wisconsin, N USA 44°16´N 88°54´W
11 U17 **Weyburn** Saskatchewan, S Canada 49°39´N 103°51´W
Weyer *see* Weyer Markt
109 U5 **Weyer Markt** *var.* Weyer. Oberösterreich, N Austria 47°52´N 14°39´E
100 H11 **Weyhe** Niedersachsen, NW Germany 53°00´N 08°52´E
97 L24 **Weymouth** S England, United Kingdom 50°36´N 02°28´W
19 P11 **Weymouth** Massachusetts, NE USA 42°13´N 70°56´W
99 H18 **Wezembeek-Oppem** Vlaams Brabant, C Belgium 50°51´N 04°28´E
98 M9 **Wezep** Gelderland, E Netherlands 52°28´N 06°E
184 M9 **Whakamaru** Waikato, North Island, New Zealand 38°27´S 175°48´E
184 O8 **Whakatane** Bay of Plenty, North Island, New Zealand 37°58´S 177°E
184 O8 **Whakatane** ~ North Island, New Zealand
9 O9 **Whale Cove** Nunavut, C Canada 62°14´N 92°10´W
96 M2 **Whalsay** *island* NE Scotland, United Kingdom
184 L11 **Whangaehu** ~ North Island, New Zealand
184 M6 **Whangamata** Waikato, North Island, New Zealand 37°13´S 175°54´E
184 Q9 **Whangara** Gisborne, North Island, New Zealand 38°34´S 178°12´E
184 K3 **Whangarei** Northland, North Island, New Zealand 35°44´S 174°18´E
184 K3 **Whangaruru Harbour** *inlet* North Island, New Zealand
25 V12 **Wharton** Texas, SW USA 29°19´N 96°08´W
173 U8 **Wharton Basin** *var.* West Australian Basin. *undersea feature* E Indian Ocean
185 E18 **Whataroa** West Coast, South Island, New Zealand 43°17´S 170°20´E
8 J9 **Wha Ti** Northwest Territories, W Canada 63°10´N 117°12´W
8 K10 **Wha Ti** *prev.* Lac la Martre. Northwest Territories, W Canada 63°10´N 117°12´W
184 K6 **Whatipu** Auckland, North Island, New Zealand 37°17´S 174°44´E
33 Y16 **Wheatland** Wyoming, C USA 42°03´N 104°57´W
14 D18 **Wheatley** Ontario, S Canada 42°06´N 82°27´W
30 M10 **Wheaton** Illinois, N USA 41°52´N 88°06´W
29 R7 **Wheaton** Minnesota, N USA 45°48´N 96°30´W
37 T4 **Wheat Ridge** Colorado, C USA 39°44´N 105°06´W
25 P2 **Wheeler** Texas, SW USA 35°26´N 100°17´W
23 O2 **Wheeler Lake** ⊡ Alabama, S USA
35 Y6 **Wheeler Peak** ▲ Nevada, W USA 39°00´N 114°17´W
37 T9 **Wheeler Peak** ▲ New Mexico, SW USA 36°34´N 105°25´W
31 S15 **Wheelersburg** Ohio, N USA 38°43´N 82°51´W
21 R2 **Wheeling** West Virginia, NE USA 40°05´N 80°43´W
97 L16 **Whernside** ▲ N England, United Kingdom 54°13´N 02°27´W
182 F9 **Whidbey, Point** *headland* South Australia 34°36´S 135°08´E
180 I7 **Whim Creek** Western Australia 20°51´S 117°54´E
10 L17 **Whistler** British Columbia, SW Canada 50°07´N 122°57´W
21 W8 **Whitakers** North Carolina, SE USA 36°06´N 77°43´W
14 H15 **Whitby** Ontario, S Canada 43°52´N 78°56´W
97 N15 **Whitby** N England, United Kingdom 54°29´N 00°37´W
10 G6 **White** ~ Yukon Territory, W Canada
13 T11 **White Bay** *bay* Newfoundland, Newfoundland and Labrador, E Canada
20 I8 **White Bluff** Tennessee, S USA 36°06´N 87°13´W
28 J6 **White Butte** ▲ North Dakota, N USA 46°23´N 103°18´W
19 R5 **White Cap Mountain** ▲ Maine, NE USA 45°33´N 69°15´W
22 J9 **White Castle** Louisiana, S USA 30°10´N 91°09´W
182 M5 **White Cliffs** New South Wales, SE Australia 30°52´S 143°04´E
31 P8 **White Cloud** Michigan, N USA 43°34´N 85°47´W
11 P14 **Whitecourt** Alberta, SW Canada 54°10´N 115°38´W
25 O2 **White Deer** Texas, SW USA 35°26´N 101°10´W
White Elster *see* Weisse Elster
24 M5 **Whiteface** Texas, SW USA 33°36´N 102°36´W
18 K7 **Whiteface Mountain** ▲ New York, NE USA 44°22´N 73°54´W
29 W5 **Whiteface Reservoir** ⊡ Minnesota, N USA
33 O7 **Whitefish** Montana, NW USA 48°24´N 114°20´W
31 N9 **Whitefish Bay** Wisconsin, N USA 43°09´N 87°54´W
31 Q3 **Whitefish Bay** *lake bay* Canada/USA
14 E11 **Whitefish Falls** Ontario, S Canada 46°06´N 81°42´W
14 B7 **Whitefish Lake** ◎ Ontario, S Canada
29 U6 **Whitefish Lake** ◎ Minnesota, C USA
31 Q3 **Whitefish Point** *headland* Michigan, N USA 46°46´N 84°57´W
31 O4 **Whitefish River** ~ Michigan, N USA
25 O4 **Whiteflat** Texas, SW USA 34°06´N 100°55´W
27 V12 **White Hall** Arkansas, C USA 34°18´N 92°05´W
30 K14 **White Hall** Illinois, N USA 39°26´N 90°24´W
31 O8 **Whitehall** Michigan, N USA 43°24´N 86°21´W
18 L9 **Whitehall** New York, NE USA 43°33´N 73°24´W
31 S13 **Whitehall** Ohio, N USA 39°58´N 82°53´W
30 J7 **Whitehall** Wisconsin, N USA 44°22´N 91°20´W
97 J15 **Whitehaven** NW England, United Kingdom 54°33´N 03°35´W
10 I8 **Whitehorse** *territory capital* Yukon Territory, W Canada 60°41´N 135°08´W
184 O7 **White Island** *island* NE New Zealand
14 K13 **White Lake** ◎ Ontario, SE Canada
22 H10 **White Lake** ◎ Louisiana, S USA
186 G7 **Whiteman Range** ▲▲ New Britain, E Papua New Guinea
183 Q15 **Whitemark** Tasmania, SE Australia 40°10´S 148°01´E
35 S9 **White Mountains** ▲▲ California/Nevada, W USA
19 N7 **White Mountains** ▲▲ Maine/New Hampshire, NE USA
80 F11 **White Nile** ◈ *state* C Sudan
67 U7 **White Nile** *var.* Bahr el Jebel. ~ S Sudan
81 E14 **White Nile** *Ar.* Al Baḩr al Abyaḑ, An Nīl al Abyaḑ, Bahr el Jebel. ~ SE Sudan
25 W5 **White Oak Creek** ~ Texas, SW USA
10 H9 **White Pass** *pass* Canada/USA
32 I9 **White Pass** *pass* Washington, NW USA
21 O9 **White Pine** Tennessee, S USA 36°06´N 83°17´W
18 K14 **White Plains** New York, NE USA 41°01´N 73°45´W
37 N13 **Whiteriver** Arizona, SW USA 33°50´N 109°57´W
28 M11 **White River** South Dakota, N USA 43°34´N 100°45´W
27 W12 **White River** ~ Arkansas, SE USA
37 P3 **White River** ~ Colorado/Utah, C USA
31 N15 **White River** ~ Indiana, N USA
31 O8 **White River** ~ Michigan, N USA
28 K11 **White River** ~ South Dakota, N USA
25 O5 **White River** ~ Texas, SW USA
18 M8 **White River** ~ Vermont, NE USA
25 O5 **White River Lake** ⊡ Texas, SW USA
32 H11 **White Salmon** Washington, NW USA 45°43´N 121°29´W
18 I10 **Whitesboro** New York, NE USA 43°07´N 75°17´W
25 T5 **Whitesboro** Texas, SW USA 33°39´N 96°54´W
21 O7 **Whitesburg** Kentucky, S USA 37°07´N 82°52´W
White Sea *see* Beloye More
White Sea-Baltic Canal/White Sea Canal *see* Belomorsko-Baltiyskiy Kanal
63 I25 **Whiteside, Canal** *channel* S Chile
33 S10 **White Sulphur Springs** Montana, NW USA 46°33´N 110°54´W
21 R6 **White Sulphur Springs** West Virginia, NE USA 37°48´N 80°18´W
20 J6 **Whitesville** Kentucky, S USA 37°40´N 86°48´W
32 I10 **White Swan** Washington, NW USA 46°22´N 120°46´W
21 U12 **Whiteville** North Carolina, SE USA 34°20´N 78°42´W
20 F10 **Whiteville** Tennessee, S USA 35°19´N 89°09´W
77 Q13 **White Volta** *var.* Nakambé, *Fr.* Volta Blanche. ~ Burkina/Ghana
30 M9 **Whitewater** Wisconsin, N USA 42°51´N 88°43´W
37 P14 **Whitewater Baldy** ▲ New Mexico, SW USA 33°19´N 108°38´W
23 X17 **Whitewater Bay** *bay* Florida, SE USA
31 Q14 **Whitewater River** ~ Indiana/Ohio, N USA
11 V16 **Whitewood** Saskatchewan, S Canada 50°19´N 102°16´W
28 J9 **Whitewood** South Dakota, N USA 44°27´N 103°38´W
25 U5 **Whitewright** Texas, SW USA 33°30´N 96°23´W
97 I15 **Whithorn** S Scotland, United Kingdom 54°44´N 04°26´W
184 M6 **Whitianga** Waikato, North Island, New Zealand 36°50´S 175°42´E
19 N11 **Whitinsville** Massachusetts, NE USA 42°06´N 71°40´W
20 M8 **Whitley City** Kentucky, S USA 36°45´N 84°29´W
21 Q11 **Whitmire** South Carolina, SE USA 34°30´N 81°36´W
31 R10 **Whitmore Lake** Michigan, N USA 42°26´N 83°44´W
195 N9 **Whitmore Mountains** ▲▲ Antarctica
14 I12 **Whitney** Ontario, SE Canada 45°29´N 78°11´W
25 T8 **Whitney** Texas, SW USA 31°56´N 97°20´W
25 S8 **Whitney, Lake** ⊡ Texas, SW USA
35 S11 **Whitney, Mount** ▲ California, W USA 37°45´N 119°55´W
181 Y6 **Whitsunday Group** *island group* Queensland, E Australia
25 S6 **Whitt** Texas, SW USA 32°55´N 98°01´W
29 U12 **Whittemore** Iowa, C USA 43°03´N 94°25´W
39 R12 **Whittier** Alaska, USA 60°46´N 148°40´W
35 T15 **Whittier** California, W USA 33°58´N 118°01´W
83 I25 **Whittlesea** Eastern Cape, S South Africa 32°08´S 26°51´E
20 K10 **Whitwell** Tennessee, S USA 35°12´N 85°31´W
8 L10 **Wholdaia Lake** ◎ Northwest Territories, NW Canada
182 H7 **Whyalla** South Australia 33°04´S 137°34´E
Whydah *see* Ouidah
14 F13 **Wiarton** Ontario, S Canada 44°44´N 81°10´W
171 O13 **Wiau** Sulawesi, C Indonesia 03°08´S 121°22´E
111 H15 **Wiązów** *Ger.* Wansen. Dolnośląskie, SW Poland 50°49´N 17°13´E
33 Y8 **Wibaux** Montana, NW USA 46°57´N 104°11´W
27 N6 **Wichita** Kansas, C USA 37°42´N 97°20´W
25 R5 **Wichita Falls** Texas, SW USA 33°55´N 98°30´W
26 L11 **Wichita Mountains** ▲▲ Oklahoma, C USA
25 R5 **Wichita River** ~ Texas, SW USA
96 K6 **Wick** N Scotland, United Kingdom 58°26´N 03°06´W
36 K13 **Wickenburg** Arizona, SW USA 33°57´N 112°41´W
24 L8 **Wickett** Texas, SW USA 31°34´N 103°00´W
180 I7 **Wickham** Western Australia 20°40´S 117°11´E
182 M14 **Wickham, Cape** *headland* Tasmania, SE Australia 39°36´S 143°55´E
20 G7 **Wickliffe** Kentucky, S USA 36°58´N 89°04´W
97 G19 **Wicklow** *Ir.* Cill Mhantáin. E Ireland 52°59´N 06°03´W
97 F19 **Wicklow** *Ir.* Cill Mhantáin. *cultural region* E Ireland
97 G19 **Wicklow Head** *Ir.* Ceann Chill Mhantáin. *headland* E Ireland 52°57´N 06°00´W
97 F18 **Wicklow Mountains** *Ir.* Sléibhte Chill Mhantáin. ▲▲ E Ireland
14 H10 **Wicksteed Lake** ◎ Ontario, S Canada
Wida *see* Ouidah
65 G15 **Wideawake Airfield** ✈ (Georgetown) SW Ascension Island
97 K18 **Widnes** NW England, United Kingdom 53°22´N 02°44´W
110 H9 **Więcbork** *Ger.* Vandsburg. Kujawsko-pomorskie, C Poland 53°21´N 17°31´E
101 E17 **Wied** ~ W Germany
101 F16 **Wiehl** Nordrhein-Westfalen, W Germany 50°57´N 07°33´E
111 L17 **Wieliczka** Małopolskie, S Poland 50°N 20°02´E
110 H12 **Wielkopolskie** ◈ *province* SW Poland
111 J14 **Wieluń** Sieradz, C Poland 51°14´N 18°33´E
109 X4 **Wien** *Eng.* Vienna, *Hung.* Bécs, *Slvk.* Vídeň, *Slvn.* Dunaj; *anc.* Vindobona. ● (Austria) Wien, NE Austria 48°13´N 16°22´E
109 X4 **Wien** *off.* Land Wien, *Eng.* Vienna. ◈ *state* NE Austria
109 X5 **Wiener Neustadt** Niederösterreich, E Austria 47°49´N 16°08´E
Wien, Land *see* Wien
110 G7 **Wieprza** *Ger.* Wipper. ~ NW Poland
98 O10 **Wierden** Overijssel, E Netherlands 52°22´N 06°35´E
98 I7 **Wieringerwerf** Noord-Holland, NW Netherlands 52°51´N 05°01´E
Wieruschow *see* Wieruszów
111 I14 **Wieruszów** *Ger.* Wieruschow. Łódzkie, C Poland 51°18´N 18°09´E
109 V9 **Wies** Steiermark, SE Austria 46°40´N 15°16´E
Wiesbachhorn *see* Grosses Weiesbachhorn
101 G18 **Wiesbaden** Hessen, W Germany 50°06´N 08°14´E
Wieselburg and Ungarisch-Altenburg/Wieselburg-Ungarisch-Altenburg *see* Mosonmagyaróvár
Wiesenhof *see* Ostrołęka
101 G20 **Wiesloch** Baden-Württemberg, SW Germany 49°18´N 08°42´E
100 F10 **Wiesmoor** Niedersachsen, NW Germany 53°22´N 07°46´E
110 I7 **Wieżyca** *Ger.* Turmberg. *hill* Pomorskie, N Poland
97 L17 **Wigan** NW England, United Kingdom 53°33´N 02°38´W
37 U3 **Wiggins** Colorado, C USA 40°11´N 104°03´W
22 M8 **Wiggins** Mississippi, S USA 30°50´N 89°09´W
Wigorna Ceaster *see* Worcester
97 I14 **Wigtown** S Scotland, United Kingdom 54°53´N 04°27´W
97 H14 **Wigtown** *cultural region* SW Scotland, United Kingdom
97 I15 **Wigtown Bay** *bay* SW Scotland, United Kingdom
98 L13 **Wijchen** Gelderland, SE Netherlands 51°48´N 05°44´E
92 N1 **Wijdefjorden** *fjord* NW Svalbard
98 M10 **Wijhe** Overijssel, E Netherlands 52°22´N 06°07´E
98 J12 **Wijk bij Duurstede** Utrecht, C Netherlands 51°58´N 05°21´E
98 J13 **Wijk en Aalburg** Noord-Brabant, S Netherlands 51°46´N 05°06´E
99 H16 **Wijnegem** Antwerpen, N Belgium 51°13´N 04°32´E
14 E11 **Wikwemikong** Manitoulin Island, Ontario, S Canada 45°46´N 81°43´W
108 H7 **Wil** Sankt Gallen, NE Switzerland 47°28´N 09°03´E
29 R16 **Wilber** Nebraska, C USA 40°28´N 96°57´W
32 K8 **Wilbur** Washington, NW USA 47°45´N 118°42´W
27 Q11 **Wilburton** Oklahoma, C USA 34°57´N 95°20´W
182 M6 **Wilcannia** New South Wales, SE Australia 31°34´S 143°23´E
18 D12 **Wilcox** Pennsylvania, NE USA 41°34´N 78°40´W
Wilczek Land *see* Vil'cheka, Zemlya

◆ Country
● Country Capital
◇ Dependent Territory
○ Dependent Territory Capital
◈ Administrative Regions
✈ International Airport
▲ Mountain
▲▲ Mountain Range
△ Volcano
~ River
◎ Lake
⊡ Reservoir

109 U6 **Wildalpen** Steiermark, E Austria *47°40′N 14°54′E*

31 O13 **Wildcat Creek** ⇝ Indiana, N USA

108 L9 **Wilde Kreuzspitze** *It.* Picco di Croce. ▲ Austria/Italy *46°53′N 10°51′E*

Wildenschwert *see* Ústí nad Orlicí

98 O6 **Wildervank** Groningen, NE Netherlands *53°04′N 06°52′E*

100 G11 **Wildeshausen** Niedersachsen, NW Germany *52°54′N 08°26′E*

108 D10 **Wildhorn** ▲ SW Switzerland *46°21′N 07°22′E*

11 R17 **Wild Horse** Alberta, SW Canada *49°00′N 110°19′W*

27 N12 **Wildhorse Creek** ⇝ Oklahoma, C USA

28 L14 **Wild Horse Hill** ▲ Nebraska, C USA *41°52′N 101°56′W*

109 W8 **Wildon** Steiermark, SE Austria *46°53′N 15°29′E*

24 M2 **Wildorado** Texas, SW USA *35°12′N 102°10′W*

29 R6 **Wild Rice River** ⇝ Minnesota/North Dakota, N USA

Wilejka *see* Vilyeyka

195 Y9 **Wilhelm II Coast** *physical region* Antarctica

195 X9 **Wilhelm II Land** *physical region* Antarctica

55 U11 **Wilhelmina Gebergte** ▲▲ C Surinam

18 B13 **Wilhelm, Lake** ⊠ Pennsylvania, NE USA

92 O2 **Wilhelmøya** *island* C Svalbard

Wilhelm-Pieck-Stadt *see* Guben

109 W4 **Wilhelmsburg** Niederösterreich, E Austria *48°07′N 15°37′E*

100 G10 **Wilhelmshaven** Niedersachsen, NW Germany *53°31′N 08°07′E*

Wilia/Wilja *see* Neris

18 H13 **Wilkes Barre** Pennsylvania, NE USA *41°15′N 75°50′W*

21 R9 **Wilkesboro** North Carolina, SE USA *36°08′N 81°09′W*

195 W15 **Wilkes Coast** *physical region* Antarctica

189 W12 **Wilkes Island** *island* N Wake Island

195 X12 **Wilkes Land** *physical region* Antarctica

11 S15 **Wilkie** Saskatchewan, S Canada *52°27′N 108°42′W*

194 I6 **Wilkins Ice Shelf** *ice shelf* Antarctica

182 D4 **Wilkinsons Lakes** *salt lake* South Australia

Wiłkomierz *see* Ukmergė

182 K11 **Willalooka** South Australia *36°24′S 140°20′E*

32 G11 **Willamette River** ⇝ Oregon, NW USA

183 O8 **Willandra Billabong Creek** *seasonal river* New South Wales, SE Australia

32 F9 **Willapa Bay** *inlet* Washington, NW USA

27 T7 **Willard** Missouri, C USA *37°18′N 93°25′W*

37 S12 **Willard** New Mexico, SW USA *34°36′N 106°01′W*

31 S12 **Willard** Ohio, N USA *41°03′N 82°43′W*

36 L1 **Willard** Utah, W USA *41°23′N 112°01′W*

186 G6 **Willaumez Peninsula** *headland* New Britain, E Papua New Guinea *05°03′S 150°04′E*

37 N15 **Willcox** Arizona, SW USA *32°13′N 109°49′W*

37 N16 **Willcox Playa** *salt flat* Arizona, SW USA

99 G17 **Willebroek** Antwerpen, C Belgium *51°04′N 04°22′E*

99 G14 **Willemstad** Noord-Brabant, S Netherlands *51°40′N 04°27′E*

45 P16 **Willemstad** ○ (Netherlands Antilles) Curaçao, Netherlands Antilles *12°07′N 68°54′W*

11 S11 **William** ⇝ Saskatchewan, C Canada

23 O6 **William "Bill" Dannelly Reservoir** ⊠ Alabama, S USA

182 G3 **William Creek** South Australia *28°55′S 136°23′E*

181 T15 **William, Mount** ▲ South Australia

36 K11 **Williams** Arizona, SW USA *35°15′N 112°11′W*

29 X14 **Williamsburg** Iowa, C USA *41°39′N 92°00′W*

20 M8 **Williamsburg** Kentucky, S USA *36°44′N 84°10′W*

31 R15 **Williamsburg** Ohio, N USA *39°00′N 84°02′W*

21 X6 **Williamsburg** Virginia, NE USA *37°17′N 76°43′W*

10 M15 **Williams Lake** British Columbia, SW Canada *52°08′N 122°09′W*

21 P6 **Williamson** West Virginia, NE USA *37°42′N 82°16′W*

31 N13 **Williamsport** Indiana, N USA *40°18′N 87°18′W*

18 G13 **Williamsport** Pennsylvania, NE USA *41°16′N 77°03′W*

21 W9 **Williamston** North Carolina, SE USA *35°53′N 77°05′W*

21 P11 **Williamston** South Carolina, SE USA *34°37′N 82°28′W*

20 M4 **Williamstown** Kentucky, S USA *38°39′N 84°32′W*

18 L10 **Williamstown** Massachusetts, NE USA *42°41′N 73°11′W*

18 J16 **Willingboro** New Jersey, NE USA *40°01′N 74°52′W*

11 Q14 **Willingdon** Alberta, SW Canada *53°49′N 112°08′W*

25 W10 **Willis** Texas, SW USA *30°25′N 95°28′W*

108 F8 **Willisau** Luzern, W Switzerland *47°07′N 08°00′E*

83 F24 **Williston** Northern Cape, W South Africa *31°20′S 20°52′E*

23 V10 **Williston** Florida, SE USA *29°23′N 82°27′W*

28 J3 **Williston** North Dakota, N USA *48°07′N 103°37′W*

21 Q13 **Williston** South Carolina, SE USA *33°24′N 81°25′W*

10 L12 **Williston Lake** ⊠ British Columbia, W Canada

34 L5 **Willits** California, W USA *39°24′N 123°22′W*

29 T8 **Willmar** Minnesota, N USA *45°07′N 95°02′W*

10 K11 **Will, Mount** ▲ British Columbia, W Canada *57°31′N 128°48′W*

31 T11 **Willoughby** Ohio, N USA *41°38′N 81°24′W*

11 U17 **Willow Bunch** Saskatchewan, S Canada *49°30′N 105°41′W*

32 J11 **Willow Creek** ⇝ Oregon, NW USA

39 R11 **Willow Lake** Alaska, USA *61°44′N 150°02′W*

8 I9 **Willowlake** ⇝ Northwest Territories, NW Canada

83 H25 **Willowmore** Eastern Cape, S South Africa *33°18′S 23°30′E*

30 L5 **Willow Reservoir** ⊠ Wisconsin, N USA

35 N5 **Willows** California, W USA *39°28′N 122°12′W*

27 V7 **Willow Springs** Missouri, C USA *36°59′N 91°58′W*

182 I7 **Wilmington** South Australia *32°42′S 138°08′E*

21 Y2 **Wilmington** Delaware, NE USA *39°45′N 75°33′W*

21 V12 **Wilmington** North Carolina, SE USA *34°14′N 77°55′W*

31 R14 **Wilmington** Ohio, N USA *39°27′N 83°49′W*

20 M6 **Wilmore** Kentucky, S USA *37°51′N 84°39′W*

29 R8 **Wilmot** South Dakota, N USA *45°24′N 96°51′W*

Wilna/Wilno *see* Vilnius

101 G16 **Wilnsdorf** Nordrhein-Westfalen, W Germany *50°49′N 08°06′E*

99 G16 **Wilrijk** Antwerpen, N Belgium *51°11′N 04°25′E*

100 I10 **Wilseder Berg** *hill* NW Germany

67 Z12 **Wilshaw Ridge** *undersea feature* W Indian Ocean *17°30′S 56°30′E*

21 V9 **Wilson** North Carolina, SE USA *35°43′N 77°56′W*

25 N5 **Wilson** Texas, SW USA *33°21′N 101°44′W*

182 A7 **Wilson Bluff** *headland* South Australia/Western Australia *31°41′S 129°01′E*

35 Y7 **Wilson Creek Range** ▲▲ Nevada, W USA

23 O1 **Wilson Lake** ⊠ Alabama, S USA

26 M4 **Wilson Lake** ⊠ Kansas, SE USA

37 P7 **Wilson, Mount** ▲ Colorado, C USA *37°50′N 107°59′W*

183 P13 **Wilsons Promontory** *peninsula* Victoria, SE Australia

29 Y14 **Wilton** Iowa, C USA *41°35′N 91°01′W*

19 P7 **Wilton** Maine, NE USA *44°35′N 70°15′W*

28 M5 **Wilton** North Dakota, N USA *47°09′N 100°46′W*

97 L22 **Wiltshire** *cultural region* S England, United Kingdom

99 M23 **Wiltz** Diekirch, NW Luxembourg *49°58′N 05°56′E*

180 K9 **Wiluna** Western Australia *26°34′S 120°14′E*

99 M23 **Wilwerwiltz** Diekirch, NE Luxembourg *49°59′N 06°00′E*

29 P5 **Wimbledon** North Dakota, N USA *47°08′N 98°25′W*

42 K7 **Wina** *var.* Güina. Jinotega, N Nicaragua *14°00′N 85°14′W*

31 O12 **Winamac** Indiana, N USA *41°03′N 86°37′W*

81 G19 **Winam Gulf** *var.* Kavirondo Gulf. *gulf* SW Kenya

83 I22 **Winburg** Free State, C South Africa *28°31′S 27°01′E*

19 N10 **Winchendon** Massachusetts, NE USA *42°41′N 72°01′W*

14 M13 **Winchester** Ontario, SE Canada *45°07′N 75°19′W*

97 M23 **Winchester** *hist.* Wintanceaster, *Lat.* Venta Belgarum. S England, United Kingdom *51°04′N 01°19′W*

32 M10 **Winchester** Idaho, NW USA *46°13′N 116°35′W*

30 J14 **Winchester** Illinois, N USA *39°38′N 90°28′W*

31 Q13 **Winchester** Indiana, N USA *40°11′N 84°57′W*

20 M5 **Winchester** Kentucky, S USA *38°00′N 84°10′W*

18 M10 **Winchester** New Hampshire, NE USA *42°46′N 72°21′W*

20 K10 **Winchester** Tennessee, S USA *35°11′N 86°06′W*

21 V3 **Winchester** Virginia, NE USA *39°11′N 78°12′W*

99 L22 **Wincrange** Diekirch, NW Luxembourg *50°03′N 05°55′E*

10 I5 **Wind** ⇝ Yukon Territory, NW Canada

183 S8 **Windamere, Lake** ◎ New South Wales, SE Australia

Windau *see* Ventspils, Latvia

Windau *see* Venta, Latvia/Lithuania

18 D15 **Windber** Pennsylvania, NE USA *40°12′N 78°47′W*

23 T3 **Winder** Georgia, SE USA *33°59′N 83°43′W*

97 K15 **Windermere** NW England, United Kingdom *54°24′N 02°54′W*

14 C7 **Windermere Lake** ◎ Ontario, S Canada

31 U11 **Windham** Ohio, N USA *41°14′N 81°03′W*

83 D19 **Windhoek** *Ger.* Windhuk. ● (Namibia) Khomas, C Namibia *22°34′S 17°06′E*

83 D20 **Windhoek** ✕ Khomas, C Namibia *22°31′S 17°04′E*

Windhuk *see* Windhoek

15 O8 **Windigo** Québec, SE Canada *47°45′N 73°19′W*

15 O8 **Windigo** ⇝ Québec, SE Canada

Windischfeistritz *see* Slovenska Bistrica

109 T6 **Windischgarsten** Oberösterreich, W Austria *47°42′N 14°21′E*

Windischgraz *see* Slovenj Gradec

37 T16 **Wind Mountain** ▲ New Mexico, SW USA *32°01′N 105°35′W*

29 T10 **Windom** Minnesota, N USA *43°52′N 95°07′W*

37 Q7 **Windom Peak** ▲ Colorado, C USA *37°37′N 107°35′W*

181 U9 **Windorah** Queensland, C Australia *25°25′S 142°41′E*

37 O10 **Window Rock** Arizona, SW USA *35°40′N 109°03′W*

31 N9 **Wind Point** *headland* Wisconsin, N USA *42°46′N 87°46′W*

33 U14 **Wind River** ⇝ Wyoming, C USA

13 P15 **Windsor** Nova Scotia, SE Canada *45°00′N 64°09′W*

14 C17 **Windsor** Ontario, S Canada *42°18′N 83°W*

15 Q12 **Windsor** Québec, SE Canada *45°34′N 72°00′W*

97 N22 **Windsor** S England, United Kingdom *51°29′N 00°39′W*

37 T3 **Windsor** Colorado, C USA *40°28′N 104°54′W*

18 M12 **Windsor** Connecticut, NE USA *41°51′N 72°38′W*

27 T5 **Windsor** Missouri, C USA *38°31′N 93°31′W*

21 X9 **Windsor** North Carolina, SE USA *36°00′N 76°57′W*

18 M12 **Windsor Locks** Connecticut, NE USA *41°55′N 72°37′W*

25 R5 **Windthorst** Texas, SW USA *33°34′N 98°26′W*

45 Z14 **Windward Islands** *island group* E West Indies

Windward Islands *see* Barlavento, Ilhas de, Cape Verde

Windward Islands *see* Vent, Îles du, Archipel de la Société, French Polynesia

44 K8 **Windward Passage** *Sp.* Paso de los Vientos. *channel* Cuba/Haiti

55 T9 **Wineperu** C Guyana *06°10′N 58°34′W*

23 O3 **Winfield** Alabama, S USA *33°55′N 87°49′W*

29 Y15 **Winfield** Iowa, C USA *41°07′N 91°26′W*

27 O7 **Winfield** Kansas, C USA *37°14′N 97°00′W*

25 W6 **Winfield** Texas, SW USA *33°10′N 95°06′W*

21 Q4 **Winfield** West Virginia, NE USA *38°30′N 81°54′W*

29 N5 **Wing** North Dakota, N USA *47°06′N 100°16′W*

183 U7 **Wingham** New South Wales, SE Australia *31°52′S 152°24′E*

12 G16 **Wingham** Ontario, S Canada *43°54′N 81°19′W*

33 T8 **Winifred** Montana, NW USA *47°33′N 109°26′W*

12 E9 **Winisk Lake** ◎ Ontario, C Canada

24 L8 **Wink** Texas, SW USA *31°45′N 103°09′W*

36 M14 **Winkelman** Arizona, SW USA *32°59′N 110°46′W*

11 X17 **Winkler** Manitoba, S Canada *49°12′N 97°55′W*

109 Q9 **Winklern** Tirol, W Austria *46°54′N 12°54′E*

Winkowitz *see* Vinkovci

32 G9 **Winlock** Washington, NW USA *46°29′N 122°56′W*

77 P17 **Winneba** SE Ghana *05°22′N 00°38′W*

29 U11 **Winnebago** Minnesota, N USA *43°46′N 94°10′W*

29 R13 **Winnebago** Nebraska, C USA *42°14′N 96°28′W*

30 M7 **Winnebago, Lake** ◎ Wisconsin, N USA

30 M7 **Winneconne** Wisconsin, N USA *44°07′N 88°44′W*

35 T3 **Winnemucca** Nevada, W USA *40°59′N 117°44′W*

35 R4 **Winnemucca Lake** ◎ Nevada, W USA

101 H21 **Winnenden** Baden-Württemberg, SW Germany *48°52′N 09°22′E*

29 N11 **Winner** South Dakota, N USA *43°22′N 99°51′W*

33 U9 **Winnett** Montana, NW USA *47°00′N 108°18′W*

14 I9 **Winneway** Québec, SE Canada *47°35′N 78°33′W*

22 H6 **Winnfield** Louisiana, S USA *31°55′N 92°38′W*

29 U4 **Winnibigoshish, Lake** ◎ Minnesota, N USA

25 X11 **Winnie** Texas, SW USA *29°49′N 94°22′W*

11 Y16 **Winnipeg** *province capital* Manitoba, S Canada *49°53′N 97°10′W*

11 X16 **Winnipeg** ✕ Manitoba, S Canada *49°56′N 97°16′W*

0 J8 **Winnipeg** ⇝ Manitoba, S Canada

11 X16 **Winnipeg Beach** Manitoba, S Canada *50°25′N 96°59′W*

11 W14 **Winnipeg, Lake** ◎ Manitoba, C Canada

11 W15 **Winnipegosis** Manitoba, S Canada *51°36′N 99°59′W*

11 W15 **Winnipegosis, Lake** ◎ Manitoba, C Canada

19 O8 **Winnipesaukee, Lake** ◎ New Hampshire, NE USA

22 I6 **Winnsboro** Louisiana, S USA *32°09′N 91°43′W*

21 R12 **Winnsboro** South Carolina, SE USA *34°22′N 81°05′W*

25 W6 **Winnsboro** Texas, SW USA *33°01′N 95°16′W*

29 X10 **Winona** Minnesota, N USA *44°03′N 91°37′W*

22 L4 **Winona** Mississippi, S USA *33°30′N 89°42′W*

27 W7 **Winona** Missouri, C USA *37°00′N 91°19′W*

25 W7 **Winona** Texas, SW USA *32°29′N 95°10′W*

18 M7 **Winooski River** ⇝ Vermont, NE USA

98 P6 **Winschoten** Groningen, NE Netherlands *53°09′N 07°03′E*

100 J10 **Winsen** Niedersachsen, N Germany *53°22′N 10°13′E*

36 M11 **Winslow** Arizona, SW USA *35°01′N 110°42′W*

19 Q7 **Winslow** Maine, NE USA *44°33′N 69°35′W*

18 M12 **Winsted** Connecticut, NE USA *41°55′N 73°03′W*

32 F14 **Winston** Oregon, NW USA *43°07′N 123°24′W*

21 S9 **Winston Salem** North Carolina, SE USA *36°06′N 80°15′W*

98 N5 **Winsum** Groningen, NE Netherlands *53°20′N 06°31′E*

Wintanceaster *see* Winchester

23 W11 **Winter Garden** Florida, SE USA *28°34′N 81°35′W*

10 J16 **Winter Harbour** Vancouver Island, British Columbia, SW Canada *50°28′N 128°03′W*

23 W12 **Winter Haven** Florida, SE USA *28°01′N 81°43′W*

23 X11 **Winter Park** Florida, SE USA *28°36′N 81°20′W*

25 P8 **Winters** Texas, SW USA *31°57′N 99°57′W*

29 U15 **Winterset** Iowa, C USA *41°19′N 94°00′W*

98 O12 **Winterswijk** Gelderland, E Netherlands *51°58′N 06°44′E*

108 G6 **Winterthur** Zürich, NE Switzerland *47°30′N 08°43′E*

29 U9 **Winthrop** Minnesota, N USA *44°32′N 94°22′W*

32 J7 **Winthrop** Washington, NW USA *48°28′N 120°13′W*

181 V7 **Winton** Queensland, E Australia *22°22′S 143°04′E*

185 C24 **Winton** Southland, South Island, New Zealand *46°08′S 168°20′E*

21 X8 **Winton** North Carolina, SE USA *36°24′N 76°57′W*

101 K15 **Wipper** ⇝ C Germany

101 K14 **Wipper** ⇝ C Germany

Wipper *see* Wieprza

182 G6 **Wirraminna** South Australia *31°10′S 136°13′E*

182 F4 **Wirrida** South Australia *29°34′S 134°33′E*

182 F7 **Wirrulla** South Australia *32°27′S 134°33′E*

Wirsitz *see* Wyrzysk

Wirz-See *see* Võrtsjärv

97 O19 **Wisbech** E England, United Kingdom *52°39′N 00°08′E*

Wisby *see* Visby

19 Q8 **Wiscasset** Maine, NE USA *44°01′N 69°41′W*

Wischau *see* Vyškov

30 J5 **Wisconsin** *off.* State of Wisconsin, ***also known as*** Badger State. ◐ *state* N USA

30 L8 **Wisconsin Dells** Wisconsin, N USA *43°37′N 89°43′W*

30 L8 **Wisconsin, Lake** ⊠ Wisconsin, N USA

30 L7 **Wisconsin Rapids** Wisconsin, N USA *44°24′N 89°50′W*

30 L7 **Wisconsin River** ⇝ Wisconsin, N USA

33 P11 **Wisdom** Montana, NW USA *45°36′N 113°27′W*

21 P7 **Wise** Virginia, NE USA *37°00′N 82°36′W*

39 Q7 **Wiseman** Alaska, USA *67°24′N 150°06′W*

96 J12 **Wishaw** W Scotland, United Kingdom *55°47′N 03°56′W*

29 O6 **Wishek** North Dakota, N USA *46°12′N 99°33′W*

32 I11 **Wishram** Washington, NW USA *45°40′N 120°53′W*

111 J17 **Wisła** Śląskie, S Poland *49°39′N 18°50′E*

110 K11 **Wisła** *Eng.* Vistula, *Ger.* Weichsel. ⇝ C Poland

Wiślany, Zalew *see* Vistula Lagoon

111 M16 **Wisłoka** ⇝ SE Poland

100 L9 **Wismar** Mecklenburg-Vorpommern, N Germany *53°54′N 11°28′E*

29 R14 **Wisner** Nebraska, C USA *41°59′N 96°54′W*

103 V4 **Wissembourg** *var.* Weissenburg. Bas-Rhin, NE France *49°03′N 07°57′E*

30 J6 **Wissota, Lake** ⊠ Wisconsin, N USA

97 O18 **Witham** ⇝ E England, United Kingdom

97 O17 **Withernsea** E England, United Kingdom *53°46′N 00°01′W*

37 Q13 **Withington, Mount** ▲ New Mexico, SW USA *33°52′N 107°29′W*

23 U8 **Withlacoochee River** ⇝ Florida/Georgia, SE USA

110 H11 **Witkowo** Wielkopolskie, C Poland *52°27′N 17°49′E*

97 M21 **Witney** S England, United Kingdom *51°47′N 01°30′W*

101 E15 **Witten** Nordrhein-Westfalen, W Germany *51°25′N 07°19′E*

101 N14 **Wittenberg** Sachsen-Anhalt, E Germany *51°53′N 12°39′E*

30 L6 **Wittenberg** Wisconsin, N USA *44°53′N 89°20′W*

100 L11 **Wittenberge** Brandenburg, N Germany *52°59′N 11°45′E*

103 U7 **Wittenheim** Haut-Rhin, NE France *47°49′N 07°19′E*

180 I7 **Wittenoom** Western Australia *22°17′S 118°22′E*

Wittingau *see* Třeboň

100 K12 **Wittingen** Niedersachsen, C Germany *52°42′N 10°43′E*

101 E18 **Wittlich** Rheinland-Pfalz, SW Germany *49°59′N 06°54′E*

100 F9 **Wittmund** Niedersachsen, NW Germany *53°34′N 07°46′E*

100 M10 **Wittstock** Brandenburg, NE Germany *53°10′N 12°29′E*

186 F6 **Witu Islands** *island group* E Papua New Guinea

110 O7 **Wiżajny** Podlaskie, NE Poland *54°22′N 22°51′E*

55 W10 **W. J. van Blommesteinmeer** ⊠ E Surinam

110 L11 **Wkra** *Ger.* Soldau. ⇝ C Poland

110 I6 **Władysławowo** Pomorskie, N Poland *54°48′N 18°25′E*

Wlaschim *see* Vlašim

111 E14 **Wleń** *Ger.* Lähn. Dolnośląskie, SW Poland *51°00′N 15°39′E*

110 J11 **Włocławek** *Ger./Rus.* Vlotslavsk. Kujawsko-pomorskie, C Poland *52°39′N 19°03′E*

110 P13 **Włodawa** *Rus.* Vlodava. Lubelskie, SE Poland *51°33′N 23°31′E*

Włodzimierz *see* Volodymyr-Volyns'kyy

111 K15 **Włoszczowa** Świętokrzyskie, C Poland *50°51′N 19°58′E*

83 C19 **Wlotzkasbaken** Erongo, W Namibia *22°26′S 14°30′E*

15 R12 **Woburn** Québec, SE Canada *45°22′N 70°52′W*

19 O11 **Woburn** Massachusetts, NE USA *42°28′N 71°09′W*

Wocheiner Feistritz *see* Bohinjska Bistrica

Wöchma *see* Võhma

147 S11 **Wodil** *var.* Vuadil'. Farg'ona Viloyati, E Uzbekistan *40°10′N 71°43′E*

181 V14 **Wodonga** Victoria, SE Australia *36°11′S 146°55′E*

111 I17 **Wodzisław Śląski** *Ger.* Loslau. Śląskie, S Poland *49°59′N 18°27′E*

98 I11 **Woerden** Zuid-Holland, C Netherlands *52°06′N 04°54′E*

98 I8 **Wognum** Noord-Holland, NW Netherlands *52°40′N 05°01′E*

Wohlau *see* Wołów

108 F7 **Wohlen** Aargau, NW Switzerland *47°21′N 08°17′E*

195 R2 **Wohlthat Massivet** ▲▲ Antarctica

Wojerecy *see* Hoyerswerda

Wōjjā *see* Wotje Atoll

Wojwodina *see* Vojvodina

171 V15 **Wokam, Pulau** *island* Kepulauan Aru, E Indonesia

97 N22 **Woking** SE England, United Kingdom *51°20′N 00°34′W*

Woldenberg Neumark *see* Dobiegniew

188 K15 **Woleai Atoll** *atoll* Caroline Islands, W Micronesia

Woleu *see* Uolo, Río

79 E17 **Woleu-Ntem** *off.* Province du Woleu-Ntem, *var.* Le Woleu-Ntem. ◐ *province* W Gabon

Woleu-Ntem, Province du *see* Woleu-Ntem

32 F15 **Wolf Creek** Oregon, NW USA *42°40′N 123°22′W*

26 K9 **Wolf Creek** ⇝ Oklahoma/Texas, SW USA

37 R7 **Wolf Creek Pass** *pass* Colorado, C USA

19 O9 **Wolfeboro** New Hampshire, NE USA *43°34′N 71°10′W*

25 U5 **Wolfe City** Texas, SW USA *33°22′N 96°04′W*

14 L15 **Wolfe Island** *island* Ontario, SE Canada

101 M14 **Wolfen** Sachsen-Anhalt, E Germany *51°40′N 12°16′E*

100 J13 **Wolfenbüttel** Niedersachsen, C Germany *52°10′N 10°33′E*

109 T4 **Wolfern** Oberösterreich, N Austria *48°06′N 14°16′E*

109 Q6 **Wolfgangsee** *var.* Abersee, St Wolfgangsee. ◎ N Austria

39 P9 **Wolf Mountain** ▲ Alaska, USA *65°20′N 154°08′W*

33 X7 **Wolf Point** Montana, NW USA *48°05′N 105°40′W*

22 L8 **Wolf River** ⇝ Mississippi, S USA

30 M7 **Wolf River** ⇝ Wisconsin, N USA

109 U9 **Wolfsberg** Kärnten, SE Austria *46°50′N 14°50′E*

100 K12 **Wolfsburg** Niedersachsen, N Germany *52°25′N 10°47′E*

57 B17 **Wolf, Volcán** ⛰ Galapagos Islands, Ecuador, E Pacific Ocean *0°01′N 91°22′W*

100 O8 **Wolgast** Mecklenburg-Vorpommern, NE Germany *54°04′N 13°47′E*

108 F8 **Wolhusen** Luzern, W Switzerland *47°04′N 08°06′E*

110 D8 **Wolin** *Ger.* Wollin. Zachodnio-pomorskie, NW Poland *53°52′N 14°35′E*

109 Y3 **Wolkersdorf** Niederösterreich, NE Austria *48°24′N 16°31′E*

Wołkowysk *see* Vawkavysk

Wöllan *see* Velenje

8 J6 **Wollaston, Cape** *headland* Victoria Island, Northwest Territories, NW Canada *71°00′N 118°21′W*

63 J25 **Wollaston, Isla** *island* S Chile

11 U11 **Wollaston Lake** Saskatchewan, C Canada *58°05′N 103°38′W*

11 T10 **Wollaston Lake** ◎ Saskatchewan, C Canada

8 J6 **Wollaston Peninsula** *peninsula* Victoria Island, Northwest Territories/Nunavut NW Canada

Wollin *see* Wolin

183 S9 **Wollongong** New South Wales, SE Australia *34°25′S 150°52′E*

Wolmar *see* Valmiera

100 L13 **Wolmirstedt** Sachsen-Anhalt, C Germany *52°15′N 11°37′E*

110 M11 **Wołomin** Mazowieckie, C Poland *52°20′N 21°11′E*

110 G!3 **Wołów** *Ger.* Wohlau. Dolnośląskie, SW Poland *51°21′N 16°40′E*

Wołożyn *see* Valozhyn

14 G11 **Wolseley Bay** Ontario, S Canada *46°05′N 80°16′W*

29 P10 **Wolsey** South Dakota, N USA *44°22′N 98°28′W*

110 F12 **Wolsztyn** Wielkopolskie, C Poland *52°07′N 16°07′E*

98 M7 **Wolvega** *Fris.* Wolvegea. Friesland, N Netherlands *52°53′N 06°E*

Wolvegea *see* Wolvega

97 K19 **Wolverhampton** C England, United Kingdom *52°36′N 02°08′W*

Wolverine State *see* Michigan

99 G18 **Wolvertem** Vlaams Brabant, C Belgium *50°55′N 04°19′E*

99 H16 **Wommelgem** Antwerpen, N Belgium *51°12′N 04°32′E*

186 D7 **Wonenara** *var.* Wonerara. Eastern Highlands, C Papua New Guinea *06°46′S 145°54′E*

Wonerara *see* Wonenara

Wongalara Lake *see* Wongalarroo Lake

183 N6 **Wongalarroo Lake** *var.* Wongalara Lake. *seasonal lake* New South Wales, SE Australia

163 Y15 **Wŏnju** *Jap.* Genshū. N South Korea *37°21′N 127°57′E*

10 M12 **Wonowon** British Columbia, W Canada *56°46′N 121°54′W*

163 X13 **Wŏnsan** SE North Korea *39°11′N 127°21′E*

183 O13 **Wonthaggi** Victoria, SE Australia *38°38′S 145°37′E*

23 N2 **Woodall Mountain** ▲ Mississippi, S USA *34°47′N 88°14′W*

23 W7 **Woodbine** Georgia, SE USA *30°58′N 81°43′W*

29 S14 **Woodbine** Iowa, C USA *41°44′N 95°42′W*

18 J17 **Woodbine** New Jersey, NE USA *39°12′N 74°47′W*

21 W4 **Woodbridge** Virginia, NE USA *38°40′N 77°17′W*

183 V4 **Woodburn** New South Wales, SE Australia *29°07′S 153°23′E*

32 G11 **Woodburn** Oregon, NW USA *45°08′N 122°51′W*

20 K9 **Woodbury** Tennessee, S USA *35°49′N 86°06′W*

183 V5 **Wooded Bluff** *headland* New South Wales, SE Australia *29°24′S 153°22′E*

183 V3 **Woodenbong** New South Wales, SE Australia *28°24′S 152°39′E*

35 R11 **Woodlake** California, W USA *36°24′N 119°06′W*

35 N7 **Woodland** California, W USA *38°41′N 121°46′W*

19 T5 **Woodland** Maine, NE USA *45°10′N 67°25′W*

32 G10 **Woodland** Washington, NW USA *45°54′N 122°44′W*

37 T5 **Woodland Park** Colorado, C USA *38°59′N 105°03′W*

186 I9 **Woodlark Island** *var.* Murua Island. *island* SE Papua New Guinea

Woodle Island *see* Kuria

11 T17 **Wood Mountain** ▲▲ Saskatchewan, S Canada

30 K15 **Wood River** Illinois, N USA *38°51′N 90°06′W*

29 P16 **Wood River** Nebraska, C USA *40°48′N 98°33′W*

39 R9 **Wood River** ⇝ Alaska, USA

39 O13 **Wood River Lakes** *lakes* Alaska, USA

182 C1 **Woodroffe, Mount** ▲ South Australia *26°19′S 131°42′E*

21 P11 **Woodruff** South Carolina, SE USA *34°44′N 82°02′W*

30 K4 **Woodruff** Wisconsin, N USA *45°55′N 89°41′W*

25 T14 **Woodsboro** Texas, SW USA *28°14′N 97°19′W*

31 U13 **Woodsfield** Ohio, N USA *39°45′N 81°07′W*

181 P4 **Woods, Lake** ◎ Northern Territory, N Australia

11 Z16 **Woods, Lake of the** *Fr.* Lac des Bois. ◎ Canada/USA

25 Q6 **Woodson** Texas, SW USA *33°00′N 99°01′W*

13 N14 **Woodstock** New Brunswick, SE Canada *46°10′N 67°38′W*

14 F16 **Woodstock** Ontario, S Canada *43°07′N 80°46′W*

30 M10 **Woodstock** Illinois, N USA *42°18′N 88°27′W*

18 M9 **Woodstock** Vermont, NE USA *43°37′N 72°33′W*

21 U4 **Woodstock** Virginia, NE USA *38°55′N 78°31′W*

19 N8 **Woodsville** New Hampshire, NE USA *44°08′N 72°02′W*

184 M12 **Woodville** Manawatu-Wanganui, North Island, New Zealand *40°22′S 175°59′E*

22 J7 **Woodville** Mississippi, S USA *31°06′N 91°18′W*

25 X9 **Woodville** Texas, SW USA *30°47′N 94°26′W*

26 K9 **Woodward** Oklahoma, C USA *36°26′N 99°25′W*

29 O5 **Woodworth** North Dakota, N USA *47°06′N 99°19′W*

171 W12 **Wool** Papua, E Indonesia *01°38′S 135°34′E*

183 V5 **Woolgoolga** New South Wales, E Australia *30°04′S 153°09′E*

182 H6 **Woomera** South Australia *31°12′S 136°52′E*

19 O12 **Woonsocket** Rhode Island, NE USA *41°58′N 71°27′W*

29 P10 **Woonsocket** South Dakota, N USA *44°03′N 98°16′W*

31 T12 **Wooster** Ohio, N USA *40°48′N 81°56′W*

80 L12 **Woqooyi Galbeed** *off.* Gobolka Woqooyi Galbeed. ◐ *region* NW Somalia

Woqooyi Galbeed, Gobolka *see* Woqooyi Galbeed

108 E8 **Worb** Bern, C Switzerland *46°54′N 07°36′E*

83 F26 **Worcester** Western Cape, SW South Africa *33°41′S 19°22′E*

97 L20 **Worcester** *hist.* Wigorna Ceaster. W England, United Kingdom *52°11′N 02°13′W*

19 N11 **Worcester** Massachusetts, NE USA *42°17′N 71°48′W*

97 L20 **Worcestershire** *cultural region* C England, United Kingdom

32 H16 **Worden** Oregon, NW USA *42°04′N 121°50′W*

109 O6 **Wörgl** Tirol, W Austria *47°29′N 12°04′E*

171 V15 **Workai, Pulau** *island* Kepulauan Aru, E Indonesia

97 J15 **Workington** NW England, United Kingdom *54°39′N 03°33′W*

98 K7 **Workum** Friesland, N Netherlands *52°58′N 05°25′E*

33 V13 **Worland** Wyoming, C USA *44°01′N 107°57′W*

see São João de Cortes

Wormatia *see* Worms

99 N25 **Wormeldange** Grevenmacher, E Luxembourg *49°37′N 06°25′E*

98 I9 **Wormer** Noord-Holland, C Netherlands *52°30′N 04°50′E*

101 G19 **Worms** *anc.* Augusta Vangionum, Borbetomagus, Wormatia. Rheinland-Pfalz, SW Germany *49°38′N 08°22′E*

Worms *see* Vormsi

101 K21 **Wörnitz** ⇝ S Germany

25 U8 **Wortham** Texas, SW USA *31°47′N 96°27′W*

101 G21 **Wörth am Rhein** Rheinland-Pfalz, SW Germany *49°04′N 08°16′E*

109 S9 **Wörther See** ◎ S Austria

97 O23 **Worthing** SE England, United Kingdom *50°48′N 00°23′W*

29 S11 **Worthington** Minnesota, N USA *43°37′N 95°37′W*

31 S13 **Worthington** Ohio, N USA *40°05′N 83°01′W*

35 W8 **Worthington Peak** ▲ Nevada, W USA *37°57′N 115°32′W*

171 Y13 **Wosi** Papua, E Indonesia *03°55′S 138°54′E*

171 V13 **Wosimi** Papua, E Indonesia *02°44′S 134°34′E*

189 R5 **Wotho Atoll** *var.* Wōtto. *atoll* Ralik Chain, W Marshall Islands

189 V5 **Wotje Atoll** *var.* Wōjjā. *atoll* Ratak Chain, E Marshall Islands

Wotoe *see* Wotu

Wottawa *see* Otava

Wōtto *see* Wotho Atoll

171 O13 **Wotu** *prev.* Wotoe. Sulawesi, C Indonesia *02°34′S 120°46′E*

98 K11 **Woudenberg** Utrecht, C Netherlands *52°05′N 05°25′E*

98 I13 **Woudrichem** Noord-Brabant, S Netherlands *51°49′N 05°E*

43 N8 **Wounta** *var.* Huaunta. Región Autónoma Atlántico Norte, NE Nicaragua *13°30′N 83°32′W*

171 P14 **Wowoni, Pulau** *island* C Indonesia

81 J17 **Woyamdero Plain** *plain* E Kenya

Woyens *see* Vojens

Wozrojdeniye Oroli *see* Vozrozhdeniya, Ostrov

Wrangel Island *see* Vrangelya, Ostrov

39 Y13 **Wrangell** Wrangell Island, Alaska, USA *56°28′N 132°22′W*

38 C15 **Wrangell, Cape** *headland* Attu Island, Alaska, USA *52°55′N 172°28′E*

39 S11 **Wrangell, Mount** ▲ Alaska, USA *62°00′N 144°01′W*

39 T11 **Wrangell Mountains** ▲▲ Alaska, USA

197 S7 **Wrangel Plain** *undersea feature* Arctic Ocean

96 H6 **Wrath, Cape** *headland* N Scotland, United Kingdom *58°37′N 05°01′W*

37 W3 **Wray** Colorado, C USA *40°01′N 102°12′W*

44 K13 **Wreck Point** *headland* C Jamaica *17°50′N 76°55′W*

83 C23 **Wreck Point** *headland* W South Africa *28°52′S 16°17′E*

23 V4 **Wrens** Georgia, SE USA *33°12′N 82°23′W*

97 K18 **Wrexham** NE Wales, United Kingdom *53°03′N 03°W*

27 R13 **Wright City** Oklahoma, C USA *34°03′N 95°00′W*

194 J12 **Wright Island** *island* Antarctica

13 N9 **Wright, Mont** ▲ Québec, E Canada *52°36′N 67°40′W*

25 X5 **Wright Patman Lake** ⊠ Texas, SW USA

36 M16 **Wrightson, Mount** ▲ Arizona, SW USA *31°42′N 110°51′W*

23 U5 **Wrightsville** Georgia, SE USA *32°43′N 82°43′W*

21 W12 **Wrightsville Beach** North Carolina, SE USA *34°12′N 77°48′W*

35 T15 **Wrightwood** California, W USA *34°21′N 117°37′W*

8 H9 **Wrigley** Northwest Territories, W Canada *63°16′N 123°39′W*

111 G14 **Wrocław** *Eng./Ger.* Breslau. Dolnośląskie, SW Poland *51°07′N 17°01′E*

110 F10 **Wronki** *Ger.* Fronicken. Wielkopolskie, C Poland *52°42′N 16°22′E*

110 H11 **Września** Wielkopolskie, C Poland *52°19′N 17°34′E*

110 F12 **Wschowa** Lubuskie, W Poland *51°49′N 16°15′E*

Wsetin *see* Vsetín

161 O5 **Wu'an** Hebei, E China *36°45′N 114°12′E*

180 I12 **Wubin** Western Australia *30°05′S 116°43′E*

163 W9 **Wuchang** Heilongjiang, NE China *44°55′N 127°13′E*

Wuchang *see* Wuhan

Wu-chou/Wuchow *see* Wuzhou

160 M16 **Wuchuan** *var.* Meilu. Guangdong, S China *21°28′N 110°49′E*

160 K10 **Wuchuan** *var.* Duru, Gelaozu Miaozu Zhizhixian. Guizhou, S China *28°40′N 108°04′E*

163 O13 **Wuchuan** Nei Mongol Zizhiqu, N China *41°04′N 111°28′E*

163 V6 **Wudalianchi** *var.* Qingshan; *prev.* Dedu. Heilongjiang, NE China *48°40′N 126°06′E*

159 O11 **Wudaoliang** Qinghai, C China *35°16′N 93°03′E*

141 Q13 **Wuday'ah** *spring/well* S Saudi Arabia *17°03′N 47°06′E*

77 V13 **Wudil** Kano, N Nigeria *11°46′N 08°49′E*

160 G12 **Wuding** *var.* Jincheng. Yunnan, SW China *25°30′N 102°21′E*

182 G8 **Wudinna** South Australia *33°06′S 135°30′E*

Wudu *see* Longnan

160 L9 **Wufeng** Hubei, C China *30°09′N 110°31′E*

161 O11 **Wugong Shan** ▲▲ S China

157 P7 **Wuhai** *var.* Haibowan. Nei Mongol Zizhiqu, N China *39°40′N 106°48′E*

161 O9 **Wuhan** *var.* Han-kou, Han-k'ou, Hanyang, Wuchang, Wu-han; *prev.* Hankow. *province capital* Hubei, C China *30°35′N 114°19′E*

Wu-han *see* Wuhan

161 Q7 **Wuhe** Anhui, E China *33°05′N 117°55′E*

Wuhsien *see* Suzhou

Wuhsi/Wu-his *see* Wuxi

161 Q8 **Wuhu** *var.* Wu-na-mu. Anhui, E China *31°23′N 118°25′E*

Wūjae *see* Ujae Atoll

160 K11 **Wu Jiang** ⇝ C China

158 L5 **Wujiaqu** Xinjiang Uygur Zizhiqu, NW China *44°11′N 87°30′E*

Wujlān *see* Ujelang Atoll

77 W15 **Wukari** Taraba, E Nigeria *07°51′N 09°49′E*

Wulan *see* Jingyuan

152 H4 **Wular Lake** ◎ NE India

162 M13 **Wulashan** Nei Mongol Zizhiqu, N China *40°43′N 108°45′E*

160 H11 **Wulian Feng** ▲▲ SW China

160 F13 **Wuliang Shan** ▲▲ SW China

160 K11 **Wuling Shan** ▲▲ S China

109 Y5 **Wulka** ⇝ E Austria

◆ Country ● Country Capital ◇ Dependent Territory ○ Dependent Territory Capital ◐ Administrative Regions ✕ International Airport ▲ Mountain ▲▲ Mountain Range ⛰ Volcano ⇝ River ◎ Lake ⊠ Reservoir

Wulkan *see* Vulcan
109 T3 **Wullowitz** Oberösterreich, N Austria 48°37'N 14°27'E
Wu-lu-k'o-mu-shi/Wu-lu-mu-ch'i *see* Ürümqi
79 D14 **Wum** Nord-Ouest, NE Cameroon 06°24'N 10°04'E
160 H12 **Wumeng Shan** ▲▲ SW China
160 K14 **Wuming** Guangxi Zhuangzu Zizhiqu, S China 23°12'N 108°11'E
100 I10 **Wümme** ~ NW Germany
Wu-na-mu *see* Wuhu
171 X13 **Wunen** Papua, E Indonesia 03°40'S 138°31'E
12 D9 **Wunnummin Lake** ◎ Ontario, C Canada
80 D13 **Wun Rog** Warab, S Sudan 09°00'N 28°20'E
101 M18 **Wunsiedel** Bayern, E Germany 50°02'N 12°00'E
100 I12 **Wunstorf** Niedersachsen, NW Germany 52°25'N 09°25'E
166 M3 **Wuntho** Sagaing, N Burma (Myanmar) 23°52'N 95°43'E
101 F15 **Wupper** ~ W Germany
101 E15 **Wuppertal** *prev.* Barmen-Elberfeld. Nordrhein-Westfalen, W Germany 51°16'N 07°12'E
160 K5 **Wuqi** Shaanxi, C China 36°57'N 108°15'E
158 E7 **Wuqia** Xinjiang Uygur Zizhiqu, NW China 39°50'N 75°19'E
161 P4 **Wuqiao** *var.* Sangyuan. Hebei, E China 37°40'N 116°21'E
101 L23 **Würm** ~ SE Germany
77 T12 **Wurno** Sokoto, NW Nigeria 13°15'N 05°24'E
101 I19 **Würzburg** Bayern, SW Germany 49°48'N 09°56'E
101 N15 **Wurzen** Sachsen, E Germany 51°21'N 12°48'E
159 V11 **Wushan** Gansu, C China 34°42'N 104°53'E
160 L9 **Wu Shan** ▲▲ C China
158 G7 **Wushi** *var.* Uqturpan. Xinjiang Uygur Zizhiqu, NW China 41°07'N 79°09'E
Wusih *see* Wuxi
65 N18 **Wüst Seamount** *undersea feature* S Atlantic Ocean 32°00'S 00°06'E
Wusuli Jiang/Wusuri *see* Ussuri
161 N3 **Wutai Shan** *var.* Beitai Ding. ▲ C China 39°00'N 114°00'E
160 H10 **Wutongqiao** Sichuan, C China 29°21'N 103°48'E
159 P6 **Wutongwozi Quan** *spring* NW China
99 H15 **Wuustwezel** Antwerpen, N Belgium 51°24'N 04°34'E
186 B4 **Wuvulu Island** *island* NW Papua New Guinea
159 U9 **Wuwei** *var.* Liangzhou. Gansu, C China 37°58'N 102°40'E
161 R8 **Wuxi** *var.* Wuhsi, Wu-hsi, Wusih. Jiangsu, E China 31°35'N 120°19'E
Wuxing *see* Huzhou
160 L14 **Wuxuan** Guangxi Zhuangzu Zizhiqu, S China 23°40'N 109°41'E
Wuyang *see* Zhenyuan
160 K11 **Wuyang He** ~ S China
163 X6 **Wuyiling** Heilongjiang, NE China 48°36'N 129°24'E
161 Q11 **Wuyishan** *prev.* Chong'an. Fujian, SE China 27°48'N 118°03'E
157 T12 **Wuyi Shan** ▲▲ SE China
162 M13 **Wuyuan** Nei Mongol Zizhiqu, N China 41°05'N 108°15'E
160 L17 **Wuzhishan** *prev.* Tongshi. Hainan, S China 18°37'N 109°34'E
160 L17 **Wuzhi Shan** ▲ S China 18°52'N 109°36'E
159 W8 **Wuzhong** Ningxia, N China 37°58'N 106°09'E
160 M14 **Wuzhou** *var.* Wu-chou, Wuchow. Guangxi Zhuangzu Zizhiqu, S China 23°30'N 111°21'E
18 H12 **Wyalusing** Pennsylvania, NE USA 41°40'N 76°13'W
182 M10 **Wycheproof** Victoria, SE Australia 36°06'S 143°13'E
97 K21 **Wye** *Wel.* Gwy. ~ England/Wales, United Kingdom
Wyłkowyszki *see* Vilkaviškis
97 P19 **Wymondham** E England, United Kingdom 52°29'N 01°10'E
29 R17 **Wymore** Nebraska, C USA 40°07'N 96°39'W
182 E5 **Wynbring** South Australia 30°34'S 133°27'E
181 N3 **Wyndham** Western Australia 15°28'S 128°08'E
29 R6 **Wyndmere** North Dakota, N USA 46°16'N 97°07'W
27 X11 **Wynne** Arkansas, C USA 35°14'N 90°48'W
27 N12 **Wynnewood** Oklahoma, C USA 34°39'N 97°09'W
183 O15 **Wynyard** Tasmania, SE Australia 40°57'S 145°33'E
11 U15 **Wynyard** Saskatchewan, S Canada 51°46'N 104°10'W
33 V11 **Wyola** Montana, NW USA 45°07'N 107°23'W
182 A4 **Wyola Lake** *salt lake* South Australia
31 P9 **Wyoming** Michigan, N USA 42°54'N 85°42'W
33 V14 **Wyoming** *off.* State of Wyoming, *also known as* Equality State. ◐ *state* C USA
33 S15 **Wyoming Range** ▲▲ Wyoming, C USA
183 T8 **Wyong** New South Wales, SE Australia 33°18'S 151°27'E
110 G9 **Wyrzysk** *Ger.* Wirsitz. Wielkopolskie, C Poland 53°09'N 17°15'E
Wysg *see* Usk
110 O10 **Wysokie Mazowieckie** Łomża, E Poland 52°54'N 22°34'E
110 M11 **Wyszków** *Ger.* Probstberg. Mazowieckie, NE Poland 52°36'N 21°28'E
110 L11 **Wyszogród** Mazowieckie, C Poland 52°24'N 20°14'E
21 R7 **Wytheville** Virginia, NE USA 36°57'N 81°07'W
111 L15 **Wyżyna Małopolska** *plateau*

X

80 Q12 **Xaafuun** *It.* Hafun. Bari, NE Somalia 10°25'N 51°17'E
80 Q12 **Xaafuun, Raas** *var.* Ras Hafun. *cape* NE Somalia
Xàbia *see* Jávea
42 C4 **Xaclbal, Río** *var.* Xalbal. ~ Guatemala/Mexico
137 Y10 **Xaçmaz** *Rus.* Khachmas. N Azerbaijan 41°26'N 48°47'E
80 O12 **Xadeed** *var.* Haded. *physical region* N Somalia
159 O14 **Xagquka** Xizang Zizhiqu, W China 31°47'N 92°46'E
167 Q6 **Xai** *var.* Muang Xay, Muong Sai. Oudômxai, N Laos 20°41'N 102°00'E
158 F10 **Xaidulla** Xinjiang Uygur Zizhiqu, W China 36°27'N 77°46'E
167 Q7 **Xaignabouli** *prev.* Muang Xaignabouri, *Fr.* Sayaboury. Xaignabouli, N Laos 19°16'N 101°43'E
167 R7 **Xai Lai Leng, Phou** ▲ Laos/Vietnam 19°13'N 104°09'E
158 L15 **Xainza** Xizang Zizhiqu, W China 30°54'N 88°36'E
158 L16 **Xaitongmoin** Xizang Zizhiqu, W China 29°27'N 88°13'E
83 F17 **Xaixai** *var.* Caecae. North-West, NW Botswana 19°52'S 21°04'E
83 M20 **Xai-Xai** *prev.* João Belo, Vila de João Belo. Gaza, S Mozambique 25°01'S 33°37'E
Xalbal *see* Xaclbal, Río
80 P13 **Xalin** Sool, N Somalia 09°16'N 49°00'E
146 H7 **Xalqobod** *Rus.* Khalkabad. Qoraqalpog'iston Respublikasi, W Uzbekistan 42°42'N 59°46'E
167 R6 **Xam Nua** *var.* Sam Neua. Houaphan, N Laos 20°24'N 104°03'E
82 D11 **Xá-Muteba** *Port.* Cinco de Outubro. Lunda Norte, NE Angola 09°34'S 17°50'E
Xangda *see* Nangqên
83 C16 **Xangongo** *Port.* Rocadas. Cunene, SW Angola 16°43'S 15°01'E
137 W12 **Xankändi** *Rus.* Khankendi; *prev.* Stepanakert. SW Azerbaijan 39°50'N 46°44'E
137 V11 **Xanlar** *Rus.* Khanlar. NW Azerbaijan 40°37'N 46°18'E
114 J13 **Xánthi** Anatolikí Makedonía kai Thráki, NE Greece 41°09'N 24°54'E
60 H13 **Xanxerê** Santa Catarina, S Brazil 26°52'S 52°25'W
81 O15 **Xarardheere** Mudug, E Somalia 04°45'N 47°54'E
137 Z11 **Xärä Zirä Adası** *Rus.* Ostrov Bulla. *Island* E Azerbaijan
162 K13 **Xar Burd** *prev.* Bayan Nuru. Nei Mongol Zizhiqu, N China 40°09'N 104°48'E
163 T11 **Xar Moron** ~ NE China
163 T11 **Xar Moron** ~ N China
Xarsingma *see* Chomo/Yadong
Xarra *see* Xarrë
113 L23 **Xarrë** *var.* Xarra. Vlorë, S Albania 39°45'N 20°01'E
82 D12 **Xassengue** Lunda Sul, NW Angola 10°28'S 18°32'E
105 S11 **Xàtiva** *Cas.* Xátiva; *anc.* Setabis, *var.* Jativa. País Valenciano, E Spain 39°N 00°32'W
Xauen *see* Chefchaouen
60 K10 **Xavantes, Represa de** *var.* Represa de Chavantes. ⊠ S Brazil
158 I7 **Xayar** Xinjiang Uygur Zizhiqu, W China 41°16'N 82°52'E
Xäzär Dänizi *see* Caspian Sea
167 S8 **Xé Bangfai** ~ C Laos
167 T9 **Xé Banghiang** *var.* Bang Hieng. ~ S Laos
Xêgar *see* Tingri
31 R14 **Xenia** Ohio, N USA 39°40'N 83°55'W
Xeres *see* Jeréz de la Frontera
115 E15 **Xeriás** ~ C Greece
115 G17 **Xeró** ▲ Évvoia, C Greece 38°52'N 23°18'E
Xhumo *see* Cum
161 N15 **Xiachuan Dao** *island* S China
Xiacun *see* Rushan
Xiaguan *see* Dali
159 U11 **Xiahe** *var.* Labrang. Gansu, C China 35°12'N 102°28'E
161 Q13 **Xiamen** *var.* Hsia-men; *prev.* Amoy. Fujian, SE China 24°28'N 118°05'E
160 L6 **Xi'an** *var.* Changan, Sian, Signan, Siking, Singan, Xian. *province capital* Shaanxi, C China 34°16'N 108°54'E
160 L10 **Xianfeng** *var.* Gaoleshan. Hubei, C China 29°45'N 109°10'E
Xiang *see* Hunan
161 N7 **Xiangcheng** Henan, C China 33°51'N'N 113°27'E
160 F10 **Xiangcheng** *var.* Sampê, *Tib.* Qagchêng. Sichuan, C China 28°52'N 99°45'E
160 M8 **Xiangfan** *var.* Xiangyang. Hubei, C China 32°07'N 112°00'E
Xianggang *see* Hong Kong
161 N10 **Xiang Jiang** ~ S China
Xiangkhoang *see* Pèk
167 Q7 **Xiangkhoang, Plateau de** *var.* Plain of Jars. *plateau* N Laos
161 N11 **Xiangtan** *var.* Hsiang-t'an, Siangtan. Hunan, S China 27°53'N 112°55'E
161 N11 **Xiangxiang** Hunan, S China 27°50'N 112°31'E
Xiangyang *see* Xiangfan
161 S10 **Xianju** Zhejiang, SE China 28°53'N 120°41'E
161 O9 **Xianning** Hubei, C China 29°32'N 114°10'E
Xianshui *see* Dawu
160 F8 **Xianshui He** ~ C China
161 N9 **Xiantao** *var.* Mianyang. Hubei, C China 30°20'N 113°31'E
161 R10 **Xianxia Ling** ▲▲ SE China
160 K6 **Xianyang** Shaanxi, C China 34°26'N 118°40'E
158 L5 **Xiaocaohu** Xinjiang Uygur Zizhiqu, W China 45°44'N 90°07'E
161 O9 **Xiaogan** Hubei, C China 30°55'N 113°54'E
Xiaogang *see* Dongxiang
163 W6 **Xiao Hinggan Ling** *Eng.* Lesser Khingan Range. ▲▲ NE China
160 M6 **Xiao Shan** ▲▲ C China
160 M12 **Xiao Shui** ~ S China
Xiaoxi *see* Pinghe
161 P6 **Xiaoxian** *var.* Longcheng, Xiao Xian. Anhui, E China 34°11'N 116°56'E
Xiao Xian *see* Xiaoxian
160 G11 **Xichang** Sichuan, C China 27°52'N 102°16'E
41 P11 **Xicoténcatl** Tamaulipas, C Mexico 22°59'N 98°54'W
Xieng Khouang *see* Pèk
Xieng Ngeun *see* Muong Xiang Ngeun
160 J11 **Xifeng** *var.* Yongjing. Guizhou, S China 27°15'N 106°44'E
Xifeng *see* Qingyang
Xigang *see* Helan
158 L16 **Xigazê** *var.* Jih-k'a-tse, Shigatse, Xigaze. Xizang Zizhiqu, W China 29°18'N 88°50'E
159 W11 **Xihe** *var.* Hanyuan. Gansu, C China 34°00'N 105°24'E
160 I8 **Xi He** ~ C China
Xihuachi *see* Heshui
159 W10 **Xiji** Ningxia, N China 36°02'N 105°33'E
160 M14 **Xi Jiang** *var.* Hsi Chiang, *Eng.* West River. ~ S China
159 Q7 **Xijian Quan** *spring* NW China
160 K15 **Xijin Shuiku** ⊠ S China
Xilaganí *see* Xylaganí
Xiligou *see* Ulan
160 I13 **Xilin** *var.* Bada. Guangxi Zhuangzu Zizhiqu, S China 24°30'N 105°00'E
163 Q10 **Xilinhot** *var.* Silinhot. Nei Mongol Zizhiqu, N China 43°58'N 116°07'E
Xilinji *see* Mohe
Xilokastro *see* Xylókastro
Xin *see* Xinjiang Uygur Zizhiqu
Xin'an *see* Anlong
161 R10 **Xin'anjiang Shuiku** *var.* Qiandao Hu. ⊠ SE China
Xin'anzhen *see* Xinyi
Xin Barag Youqi *see* Altan Emel
Xin Barag Zuoqi *see* Amgalang
163 W12 **Xinbin** *var.* Xinbin Manzu Zizhixian. Liaoning, NE China 41°44'N 125°02'E
Xinbin Manzu Zizhixian *see* Xinbin
161 O7 **Xincai** Henan, C China 32°47'N 114°58'E
Xincheng *see* Zhaojue
Xindu *see* Luhuo
161 O13 **Xinfeng** *var.* Jiading. Jiangxi, S China 25°23'N 114°48'E
161 O14 **Xinfengjiang Shuiku** ⊠ S China
Xing'an *see* Ankang
Xingba *see* Lhünzê
163 T13 **Xingcheng** Liaoning, NE China 40°38'N 120°47'E
Xingcheng *see* Xingning
82 E11 **Xinge** Lunda Norte, NE Angola 09°44'S 19°10'E
161 P12 **Xingguo** *var.* Lianjiang. Jiangxi, S China 26°25'N 115°22'E
159 S11 **Xinghai** *var.* Ziketan. Qinghai, C China 35°12'N 102°28'E
161 R7 **Xinghua** Jiangsu, E China 32°54'N 119°48'E
Xingkai Hu *see* Khanka, Lake
161 P13 **Xingning** *var.* Xingcheng. Guangdong, S China 24°05'N 115°47'E
160 I13 **Xingren** Guizhou, S China 25°26'N 105°08'E
161 O4 **Xingtai** Hebei, E China 37°08'N 114°29'E
59 J14 **Xingu, Rio** ~ C Brazil
159 P6 **Xingxingxia** Xinjiang Uygur Zizhiqu, NW China 41°48'N 95°01'E
160 I13 **Xingyi** Guizhou, S China 25°04'N 104°51'E
158 I6 **Xinhe** *var.* Toksu. Xinjiang Uygur Zizhiqu, NW China 41°32'N 82°39'E
163 Q10 **Xin Hot** Nei Mongol Zizhiqu, N China 43°58'N 114°59'E
Xinhua *see* Funing
163 T12 **Xinhui** *var.* Aohan Qi. Nei Mongol Zizhiqu, N China 42°12'N 119°57'E
159 T10 **Xining** *var.* Hsining, Hsi-ning, Sining. *province capital* Qinghai, C China 36°37'N 101°46'E
161 O4 **Xinji** *prev.* Shulu. Hebei, E China 37°55'N 115°14'E
161 P10 **Xinjian** Jiangxi, S China 28°37'N 115°46'E
Xinjiang *see* Xinjiang Uygur Zizhiqu
162 D8 **Xinjiang Uygur Zizhiqu** *var.* Sinkiang, Sinkiang Uighur Autonomous Region, Xin, Xinjiang. ◐ *autonomous region* NW China
160 H9 **Xinjin** *var.* Meixing, *Tib.* Zainlha. Sichuan, C China 30°27'N 103°46'E
Xinjin *see* Pulandian
Xinjing *see* Jingxi
163 U12 **Xinmin** Liaoning, NE China 41°58'N 122°51'E
160 M12 **Xinning** *var.* Jinshi. Hunan, S China 26°34'N 110°57'E
Xinning *see* Ningxian
Xinning *see* Fusui
Xinpu *see* Lianyungang
Xinshan *see* Anyuan
161 P5 **Xintai** Shandong, E China 35°54'N 117°44'E
Xinwen *see* Suncun
Xin Xian *see* Xinzhou
161 N6 **Xinxiang** Henan, C China 35°13'N 113°48'E
161 O8 **Xinyang** *var.* Hsin-yang, Sinyang. Henan, C China 32°09'N 114°04'E
161 Q6 **Xinyi** *var.* Xin'anzhen. Jiangsu, E China 34°17'N 118°14'E
161 Q6 **Xinyi He** ~ E China
161 O11 **Xinyu** Jiangxi, S China 27°51'N 115°00'E
158 I5 **Xinyuan** *var.* Künes. Xinjiang Uygur Zizhiqu, NW China 43°25'N 83°12'E
Xinyuan *see* Tianjun
162 M13 **Xinzhao Shan** ▲ N China 39°37'N 107°51'E
161 N3 **Xinzhou** *var.* Xin Xian. Shanxi, C China 38°24'N 112°43'E
Xinzhou *see* Longlin
104 H4 **Xinzo de Limia** Galicia, NW Spain 42°05'N 07°45'W
Xions *see* Książ Wielkopolski
161 O7 **Xiping** Henan, C China 33°22'N 114°00'E
Xiping *see* Songyang
159 T11 **Xiqing Shan** ▲▲ C China
59 N16 **Xique-Xique** Bahia, E Brazil 10°47'S 42°44'W
Xireg *see* Ulan
115 E14 **Xirovoúni** ▲ N Greece 40°31'N 21°58'E
162 M13 **Xishanzui** *prev.* Urad Qianqi. Nei Mongol Zizhiqu, N China 40°43'N 108°41'E
160 J11 **Xishui** *var.* Donghuang. Guizhou, S China 28°24'N 106°09'E
Xi Ujimqin Qi *see* Bayan Ul
160 K11 **Xiushan** *var.* Zhonghe. Chongqing Shi, C China 28°23'N 108°52'E
Xiushan *see* Tonghai
161 O10 **Xiu Shui** ~ S China
Xiuyan *see* Qingjian
146 H9 **Xiva** *Rus.* Khiva, Khiwa. Xorazm Viloyati, W Uzbekistan 41°22'N 60°22'E
158 J16 **Xixabangma Feng** ▲ W China 28°25'N 85°47'E
160 M7 **Xixia** Henan, C China 33°30'N 111°25'E
Xixón *see* Gijón
Xixona *see* Jijona
Xizang *see* Xizang Zizhiqu
Xizang Gaoyuan *see* Qingzang Gaoyuan
160 E9 **Xizang Zizhiqu** *var.* Thibet, Tibetan Autonomous Region, Xizang, *Eng.* Tibet. ◐ *autonomous region* W China
163 U14 **Xizhong Dao** *island* N China
Xoi *see* Qüxü
146 H8 **Xo'jayli** *Rus.* Khodzheyli. Qoraqalpog'iston Respublikasi, W Uzbekistan 42°23'N 59°27'E
Xolotlán *see* Managua, Lago de
147 I9 **Xonqa** *var.* Khonqa, *Rus.* Khanka. Xorazm Viloyati, W Uzbekistan 41°31'N 60°39'E
146 H9 **Xorazm Viloyati** *Rus.* Khorezmskaya Oblast'. ◐ *province* W Uzbekistan
159 N9 **Xorkol** Xinjiang Uygur Zizhiqu, NW China 38°45'N 91°07'E
147 P11 **Xovos** *var.* Ursat'yevskaya, *Rus.* Khavast. Sirdaryo Viloyati, E Uzbekistan 40°14'N 68°46'E
41 X14 **Xpujil** Quintana Roo, E Mexico 18°30'N 89°24'W
161 Q8 **Xuancheng** *var.* Xuanzhou. Anhui, E China 30°57'N 118°53'E
167 T9 **Xuân Đuc** Quang Binh, C Vietnam 17°19'N 106°38'E
160 L9 **Xuan'en** *var.* Zhushan. Hubei, C China 30°03'N 109°26'E
160 K8 **Xuanhan** Sichuan, C China 31°25'N 107°41'E
161 O2 **Xuanhua** Hebei, E China 40°36'N 115°01'E
161 P4 **Xuanhui He** ~ E China
H12 **Xuanwei** Yunnan, China 26°08'N 104°04'E
Xuanzhou *see* Xuancheng
161 N7 **Xuchang** Henan, C China 34°03'N 113°48'E
Xucheng *see* Xuwen
137 X10 **Xudat** *Rus.* Khudat. NE Azerbaijan 41°37'N 48°39'E
81 M16 **Xuddur** *var.* Hudur, *It.* Oddur. Bakool, SW Somalia 04°07'N 43°47'E
80 O13 **Xudun** Sool, N Somalia 09°12'N 47°34'E
160 L11 **Xuefeng Shan** ▲▲ S China
147 O13 **Xufar** Surkhondaryo Viloyati, S Uzbekistan 38°31'N 67°45'E
Xulun Hobot Qagan *see* Qagan Nur
42 F2 **Xunantunich** *ruins* Cayo, W Belize
163 W6 **Xun He** ~ NE China
160 L7 **Xun He** ~ C China
160 L14 **Xun Jiang** ~ S China
163 W5 **Xunke** *var.* Bianjing; *prev.* Qike. Heilongjiang, NE China 49°36'N 128°25'E
161 P13 **Xunwu** *var.* Changning. Jiangxi, S China 24°59'N 115°33'E
161 O3 **Xushui** Hebei, E China 39°01'N 115°38'E
160 L16 **Xuwen** *var.* Xucheng. Guangdong, S China 20°21'N 110°09'E
160 I11 **Xuyong** *var.* Yongning. Sichuan, C China 28°17'N 105°21'E
161 P6 **Xuzhou** *var.* Hsu-chou, Suchow, Tongshan; *prev.* T'ung-shan. Jiangsu, E China 34°17'N 117°09'E
114 K13 **Xylaganí** *var.* Xilaganí. Anatolikí Makedonía kai Thráki, NE Greece 40°58'N 25°27'E
115 F19 **Xylókastro** *var.* Xilokastro. Pelopónnisos, S Greece 38°04'N 22°36'E

Y

160 H9 **Ya'an** *var.* Yaan. Sichuan, C China 30°N 102°57'E
182 L10 **Yaapeet** Victoria, SE Australia 35°48'S 142°03'E
79 D15 **Yabassi** Littoral, W Cameroon 04°30'N 09°59'E
81 J15 **Yabēlo** Oromīya, C Ethiopia 04°53'N 38°01'E
114 H9 **Yablanitsa** Lovech, N Bulgaria 43°01'N 24°06'E
43 N7 **Yablis** Región Autónoma Atlántico Norte, NE Nicaragua 14°08'N 83°44'W
123 O14 **Yablonovyy Khrebet** ▲▲ S Russian Federation
162 J14 **Yabrai Shan** ▲▲ NE China
45 U6 **Yabucoa** E Puerto Rico 18°02'N 65°53'W
160 J11 **Yachi He** ~ S China
32 H10 **Yacolt** Washington, NW USA 45°49'N 122°22'W
54 M10 **Yacuaray** Amazonas, S Venezuela 04°12'N 66°30'W
57 M22 **Yacuiba** Tarija, S Bolivia 22°00'S 63°43'W
57 K16 **Yacuma, Río** ~ C Bolivia
155 H16 **Yādgīr** Karnātaka, C India 16°46'N 77°09'E
21 R8 **Yadkin River** ~ North Carolina, SE USA
21 R9 **Yadkinville** North Carolina, SE USA 36°07'N 80°40'W
158 L17 **Yadong** *var.* Xarsingma. Xizang Zizhiqu, W China 27°31'N 88°58'E *see also* Chomo
127 P3 **Yadrin** Chuvashskaya Respublika, W Russian Federation 55°55'N 46°10'E
Yaegama-shotō *see* Yaeyama-shotō
Yaeme-saki *see* Paimi-saki
165 O16 **Yaeyama-shotō** *var.* Yaegama-shotō. *island group* SW Japan
75 O8 **Yafran** NW Libya 32°04'N 12°31'E
165 S2 **Yagashiri-tō** *island* NE Japan
65 H21 **Yaghan Basin** *undersea feature* SE Pacific Ocean
123 S9 **Yagodnoye** Magadanskaya Oblast', E Russian Federation 62°37'N 149°18'E
Yagotin *see* Yahotyn
78 G12 **Yagoua** Extrême-Nord, NE Cameroon 10°23'N 15°13'E
159 Q11 **Yagradagzê Shan** ▲ C China 35°06'N 95°41'E
Yaguachi *see* Yaguachi Nuevo
56 B7 **Yaguachi Nuevo** *var.* Yaguachi. Guayas, W Ecuador 02°06'S 79°43'W
Yaguarón, Río *see* Jaguarão, Rio
117 Q11 **Yahorlyts'kyy Lyman** *bay* S Ukraine
117 Q5 **Yahotyn** *Rus.* Yagotin. Kyyivs'ka Oblast', N Ukraine 50°15'N 31°48'E
40 L12 **Yahualica** Jalisco, SW Mexico 21°11'N 102°29'W
79 L17 **Yahuma** Orientale, N Dem. Rep. Congo 01°12'N 23°00'E
136 K15 **Yahyalı** Kayseri, C Turkey 38°08'N 35°23'E
167 N15 **Yai, Khao** ▲ SW Thailand 08°45'N 99°32'E
164 M14 **Yaizu** Shizuoka, Honshū, S Japan 34°52'N 138°20'E
160 G9 **Yajiang** *var.* Hekou, *Tib.* Nyagquka. Sichuan, C China 30°05'N 100°57'E
119 O14 **Yakawlyevichi** *Rus.* Yakovlevichi. Vitsyebskaya Voblasts', NE Belarus 54°20'N 30°31'E
163 S6 **Yakeshi** Nei Mongol Zizhiqu, N China 49°16'N 120°42'E
32 I9 **Yakima** Washington, NW USA 46°36'N 120°30'W
32 J10 **Yakima River** ~ Washington, NW USA
Yakkabag *see* Yakkabog'
147 N12 **Yakkabog'** *Rus.* Yakkabag. Qashqadaryo Viloyati, S Uzbekistan 38°57'N 66°35'E
148 L12 **Yakmach** Baluchistān, SW Pakistan 28°48'N 63°48'E
77 O12 **Yako** W Burkina 12°59'N 02°15'W
39 W13 **Yakobi Island** *island* Alexander Archipelago, Alaska, USA
79 K16 **Yakoma** Equateur, N Dem. Rep. Congo 04°04'N 22°23'E
114 H11 **Yakoruda** Blagoevgrad, SW Bulgaria 42°01'N 23°40'E
Yakovlevichi *see* Yakawlyevichi
127 T2 **Yakshur-Bod'ya** Udmurtskaya Respublika, NW Russian Federation 57°10'N 53°10'E
165 Q5 **Yakumo** Hokkaidō, NE Japan 42°18'N 140°15'E
164 B17 **Yaku-shima** *island* Nansei-shotō, SW Japan
39 V12 **Yakutat** Alaska, USA 59°33'N 139°44'W
39 U12 **Yakutat Bay** *inlet* Alaska, USA
Yakutia/Yakutiya/Yakutiya, Respublika *see* Sakha (Yakutiya), Respublika
123 Q10 **Yakutsk** Respublika Sakha (Yakutiya), NE Russian Federation 62°10'N 129°50'E
167 O17 **Yala** Yala, SW Thailand 06°32'N 101°19'E
182 D6 **Yalata** South Australia 31°30'S 131°53'E
31 S9 **Yale** Michigan, N USA 43°07'N 82°45'W
180 I11 **Yalgoo** Western Australia 28°23'S 116°43'E
114 O12 **Yalıköy** İstanbul, NW Turkey 41°29'N 28°19'E
79 L14 **Yalinga** Haute-Kotto, C Central African Republic 06°47'N 23°09'E
119 M17 **Yalizava** *Rus.* Yelizovo. Mahilyowskaya Voblasts', E Belarus 53°24'N 29°01'E
44 L13 **Yallahs Hill** ▲ E Jamaica 17°53'N 76°31'W
22 L3 **Yalobusha River** ~ Mississippi, S USA
79 H15 **Yaloké** Ombella-Mpoko, W Central African Republic 05°15'N 17°12'E
160 E7 **Yalong Jiang** ~ C China
136 E11 **Yalova** Yalova, NW Turkey 40°40'N 29°17'E
136 E11 **Yalova** ◐ *province* NW Turkey
Yaloveny *see* Ialoveni
Yalpug *see* Ialpug
Yalpug, Ozero *see* Yalpuh, Ozero
117 N12 **Yalpuh, Ozero** *Rus.* Ozero Yalpug. ◎ SW Ukraine
117 T14 **Yalta** Respublika Krym, S Ukraine 44°30'N 34°09'E
163 W12 **Yalu** *Chin.* Yalu Jiang, *Jap.* Oryokko, *Kor.* Amnok-kang. ~ China/North Korea
Yalu Jiang *see* Yalu
136 F14 **Yalvaç** Isparta, SW Turkey 38°16'N 31°09'E
165 R9 **Yamada** Iwate, Honshū, C Japan 39°27'N 141°56'E
165 D14 **Yamaga** Kumamoto, Kyūshū, SW Japan 33°02'N 130°41'E
165 P10 **Yamagata** Yamagata, Honshū, C Japan 38°15'N 140°19'E
165 P9 **Yamagata** *off.* Yamagata-ken. ◐ *prefecture* Honshū, C Japan
Yamagata-ken *see* Yamagata
164 C16 **Yamagawa** Kagoshima, Kyūshū, SW Japan 31°12'N 130°37'E
164 E13 **Yamaguchi** *var.* Yamaguti. Yamaguchi, Honshū, SW Japan 34°11'N 131°26'E
164 E13 **Yamaguchi** *off.* Yamaguchi-ken, *var.* Yamaguti. ◐ *prefecture* Honshū, SW Japan
Yamaguchi-ken *see* Yamaguchi
Yamaguti *see* Yamaguchi
125 X5 **Yamalo-Nenetskiy Avtonomnyy Okrug** ◐ *autonomous district* N Russian Federation
122 J7 **Yamal, Poluostrov** *peninsula* N Russian Federation
165 N13 **Yamanashi** *off.* Yamanashi-ken, *var.* Yamanasi. ◐ *prefecture* Honshū, S Japan
Yamanashi-ken *see* Yamanashi
Yamanasi *see* Yamanashi
Yamanīyah, Al Jumhūrīyah al *see* Yemen
127 W5 **Yamantau** ▲ W Russian Federation 53°11'N 57°30'E
Yamasaki *see* Yamazaki
15 P12 **Yamaska** ~ Québec, SE Canada
192 G4 **Yamato Ridge** *undersea feature* S Sea of Japan 39°20'N 135°00'E
164 I13 **Yamazaki** *var.* Yamasaki. Hyōgo, Honshū, SW Japan 35°00'N 134°31'E
183 V5 **Yamba** New South Wales, SE Australia 29°28'S 153°22'E
81 D16 **Yambio** *var.* Yambiyo. Western Equatoria, S Sudan 04°34'N 28°21'E
Yambiyo *see* Yambio
114 L10 **Yambol** *Turk.* Yanboli. Yambol, E Bulgaria 42°29'N 26°30'E
114 M11 **Yambol** ◐ *province* E Bulgaria
79 M17 **Yambuya** Orientale, N Dem. Rep. Congo 01°22'N 24°21'E
171 T15 **Yamdena, Pulau** *prev.* Jamdena. *island* Kepulauan Tanimbar, E Indonesia
165 O14 **Yame** Fukuoka, Kyūshū, SW Japan 33°14'N 130°32'E
166 M6 **Yamethin** Mandalay, C Burma (Myanmar) 20°24'N 96°08'E
186 C6 **Yaminbot** East Sepik, NW Papua New Guinea 04°34'S 143°56'E
181 U9 **Yamma Yamma, Lake** ◎ Queensland, C Australia
76 M16 **Yamoussoukro** ● (Ivory Coast) C Ivory Coast 06°51'N 05°21'W
37 P3 **Yampa River** ~ Colorado, C USA
117 S2 **Yampil'** Sums'ka Oblast', NE Ukraine 51°57'N 33°49'E
116 M8 **Yampil'** Vinnyts'ka Oblast', C Ukraine 48°15'N 28°18'E
123 T9 **Yamsk** Magadanskaya Oblast', E Russian Federation 59°33'N 154°04'E
152 J8 **Yamuna** *prev.* Jumna. ~ N India
152 I9 **Yamunānagar** Haryāna, N India 30°07'N 77°17'E
Yamundá *see* Nhamundá, Rio
145 U8 **Yamyshevo** Pavlodar, NE Kazakhstan 51°49'N 77°28'E
159 N16 **Yamzho Yumco** ◎ W China
123 Q8 **Yana** ~ NE Russian Federation
186 H9 **Yanaba Island** *island* SE Papua New Guinea
155 L16 **Yanam** *var.* Yanaon. Pondicherry, E India 16°45'N 82°16'E
160 L5 **Yan'an** *var.* Yanan. Shaanxi, C China 36°35'N 109°27'E
Yanaon *see* Yanam
127 U3 **Yanaul** ▲ Respublika Bashkortostan, W Russian Federation 56°15'N 54°57'E
118 O12 **Yanavichy** *Rus.* Yanovichi. Vitsyebskaya Voblasts', NE Belarus 55°17'N 30°42'E
Yanboli *see* Yambol
140 K8 **Yanbu 'al Baḩr** Al Madīnah, W Saudi Arabia 24°07'N 38°03'E
21 T8 **Yanceyville** North Carolina, SE USA 36°25'N 79°22'W
161 R7 **Yancheng** Jiangsu, E China 33°28'N 120°10'E
159 W8 **Yanchi** Ningxia, N China 37°49'N 107°24'E
160 L5 **Yanchuan** Shaanxi, C China 36°54'N 110°04'E
183 O10 **Yanco Creek** *seasonal river* New South Wales, SE Australia
183 O6 **Yanda Creek** *seasonal river* New South Wales, SE Australia
182 K4 **Yandama Creek** *seasonal river* New South Wales/South Australia
161 S11 **Yandang Shan** ▲▲ SE China
159 O6 **Yandun** Xinjiang Uygur Zizhiqu, W China 42°24'N 94°08'E
76 L13 **Yanfolila** Sikasso, SW Mali 11°08'N 08°12'W
79 M18 **Yangambi** Orientale, N Dem. Rep. Congo 0°46'N 24°24'E
158 M15 **Yangbajain** Xizang Zizhiqu, W China 30°05'N 90°35'E
Yangcheng *see* Yangshan, Guangdong, S China
Yangchow *see* Yangzhou
160 M15 **Yangchun** *var.* Chuncheng. Guangdong, S China 22°16'N 111°49'E
161 N2 **Yanggao** *var.* Longquàn. Shanxi, C China 40°24'N 113°51'E
Yanggeta *see* Yaqeta
Yangiabad *see* Yangiobod
Yangibazar *see* Dzhany-Bazar, Kyrgyzstan
Yangi-Bazar *see* Kofarnihon, Tajikistan
Yangiklshak *see* Yangiqishloq
146 M13 **Yangi-Nishon** *Rus.* Yang-Nishan. Qashqadaryo Viloyati, S Uzbekistan 38°37'N 65°39'E
147 Q9 **Yangiobod** *Rus.* Yangiabad. Toshkent Viloyati, E Uzbekistan 41°10'N 70°10'E
147 O10 **Yangiqishloq** *Rus.* Yangiklshak. Jizzax Viloyati, C Uzbekistan 40°27'N 67°06'E
147 P11 **Yangiyer** Sirdaryo Viloyati, E Uzbekistan 40°19'N 68°48'E
147 P9 **Yangiyo'l** *Rus.* Yangiyul'. Toshkent Viloyati, E Uzbekistan 41°12'N 69°05'E
Yangiyul' *see* Yangiyo'l
160 M15 **Yangjiang** Guangdong, S China 21°50'N 112°02'E
Yangku *see* Taiyuan
Yang-Nishan *see* Yangi-Nishon
166 L8 **Yangon** *Eng.* Rangoon. Yangon, S Burma (Myanmar) 16°50'N 96°11'E
166 M8 **Yangon** *Eng.* Rangoon. ◐ *division* SW Burma (Myanmar)
161 N4 **Yangquan** Shanxi, C China 37°52'N 113°29'E
161 N13 **Yangshan** *var.* Yangcheng. Guangdong, S China 24°32'N 112°36'E
167 U12 **Yang Sin, Chu** ▲ S Vietnam 12°23'N 108°25'E
Yangtze *see* Chang Jiang/Jinsha Jiang
Yangtze *see* Jinsha Jiang
Yangtze Kiang *see* Chang Jiang
161 R7 **Yangzhou** *var.* Yangchow. Jiangsu, E China 32°22'N 119°22'E
160 L5 **Yan He** ~ C China
163 Y10 **Yanji** Jilin, NE China 42°54'N 129°31'E
Yanji *see* Longjing
Yanjing *see* Yanyuan
29 Q12 **Yankton** South Dakota, N USA 42°52'N 97°24'W
161 O12 **Yanling** *prev.* Lingxian, Ling Xian. Hunan, S China 26°32'N 113°48'E
Yannina *see* Ioánnina
123 Q7 **Yano-Indigirskaya Nizmennost'** *plain* NE Russian Federation
Yanovichi *see* Yanavichy
155 K24 **Yan Oya** ~ N Sri Lanka
158 K6 **Yanqi** *var.* Yanqi Huizu Zizhixian. Xinjiang Uygur Zizhiqu, NW China 42°04'N 86°32'E
Yanqi Huizu Zizhixian *see* Yanqi
161 Q10 **Yanshan** *var.* Hekou. Jiangxi, S China 28°18'N 117°43'E
160 H14 **Yanshan** *var.* Jiangna. Yunnan, SW China 23°36'N 104°20'E
161 P2 **Yan Shan** ▲▲ E China
163 X8 **Yanshou** Heilongjiang, NE China 45°27'N 128°19'E
123 Q7 **Yanskiy Zaliv** *bay* N Russian Federation
183 O4 **Yantabulla** New South Wales, SE Australia 29°22'S 145°00'E
161 R4 **Yantai** *var.* Yan-t'ai; *prev.* Chefoo, Chih-fu. Shandong, E China 37°30'N 121°22'E
118 A13 **Yantarnyy** *Ger.* Palmnicken. Kaliningradskaya Oblast', W Russian Federation 54°53'N 19°59'E
114 J9 **Yantra** Gabrovo, N Bulgaria 42°58'N 25°19'E
114 K9 **Yantra** ~ N Bulgaria
160 G11 **Yanyuan** *var.* Yanjing. Sichuan, C China 27°30'N 101°22'E
161 P5 **Yanzhou** Shandong, E China 35°35'N 116°53'E
79 E16 **Yaoundé** *var.* Yaunde. ● (Cameroon) Centre, S Cameroon 03°51'N 11°31'E
188 I14 **Yap** ◐ *state* W Micronesia
188 F16 **Yap** *island* Caroline Islands, W Micronesia
57 M18 **Yapacani, Rio** ~ C Bolivia
171 W14 **Yapa Kopra** Papua, E Indonesia 04°18'S 135°05'E
Yapan *see* Yapen, Selat
Yapanskoye More *see* East Sea/Japan, Sea of
77 P15 **Yapei** N Ghana 09°10'N 01°08'W
12 M10 **Yapeitso, Mont** ▲ Québec, E Canada 52°18'N 70°24'W
171 W12 **Yapen, Pulau** *prev.* Japen. *island* E Indonesia
171 W12 **Yapen, Selat** *var.* Yapan. *strait* Papua, E Indonesia
61 E15 **Yapeyú** Corrientes, NE Argentina 29°28'S 56°50'W
136 I11 **Yapraklı** Çankın, N Turkey 40°45'N 33°46'E
174 M3 **Yap Trench** *var.* Yap Trough. *undersea feature* SE Philippine Sea 08°30'N 138°00'E
Yap Trough *see* Yap Trench
Yapurá *see* Caquetá, Río, Brazil/Colombia
Yapurá *see* Japurá, Rio, Brazil/Colombia
197 I12 **Yaqaga** *island* N Fiji
197 H12 **Yaqeta** *prev.* Yanggeta. *island* Yasawa Group, NW Fiji
40 G6 **Yaqui** Sonora, NW Mexico 27°21'N 109°59'W
32 E12 **Yaquina Bay** *bay* Oregon, NW USA
40 G6 **Yaqui, Río** ~ NW Mexico
54 K5 **Yaracuy** *off.* Estado Yaracuy. ◐ *state* NW Venezuela
Yaracuy, Estado *see* Yaracuy
146 E13 **Yarajy** *Rus.* Yaradzhi. Ahal Welaýaty, C Turkmenistan 38°12'N 57°40'E
Yaradzhi *see* Yarajy
125 Q15 **Yaransk** Kirovskaya Oblast', NW Russian Federation 57°18'N 47°52'E
136 F17 **Yardımcı Burnu** *headland* SW Turkey 36°10'N 30°25'E
97 Q19 **Yare** ~ E England, United Kingdom
125 S9 **Yarega** Respublika Komi, NW Russian Federation 63°27'N 53°28'E
116 I7 **Yaremcha** Ivano-Frankivs'ka Oblast', W Ukraine 48°27'N 24°34'E
189 Q9 **Yaren** SW Nauru 0°33'S 166°54'E
125 Q10 **Yarensk** Arkhangel'skaya Oblast', NW Russian Federation 62°09'N 49°03'E

◆ Country
● Country Capital
◇ Dependent Territory
○ Dependent Territory Capital
◐ Administrative Regions
✈ International Airport
▲ Mountain
▲▲ Mountain Range
Volcano
~ River
◎ Lake
⊠ Reservoir

155 F16 **Yargatti** Karnātaka, W India 16°07′N 75°11′E
164 M12 **Yariga-take** ▲ Honshū, S Japan 36°20′N 137°38′E
141 O15 **Yarim** W Yemen 14°15′N 44°23′E
54 F14 **Yarí, Río** ≈ SW Colombia
54 K5 **Yaritagua** Yaracuy, N Venezuela 10°05′N 69°07′W
Yarkand see Yarkant He
Yarkant see Shache
158 E9 **Yarkant He** var. Yarkand. ≈ NW China
149 U3 **Yarkhūn** ≈ NW Pakistan
Yarlung Zangbo Jiang see Brahmaputra
116 L6 **Yarmolyntsi** Khmel'nyts'ka Oblast', W Ukraine 49°13′N 26°53′E
13 O16 **Yarmouth** Nova Scotia, SE Canada 43°53′N 66°09′W
Yarmouth see Great Yarmouth
Yaroslav see Jarosław
124 L15 **Yaroslavl'** Yaroslavskaya Oblast', W Russian Federation 57°38′N 39°53′E
124 K14 **Yaroslavskaya Oblast'** ◐ province W Russian Federation
123 N11 **Yaroslavskiy** Respublika Sakha (Yakutiya), NE Russian Federation 60°10′N 114°12′E
183 P13 **Yarram** Victoria, SE Australia 38°36′S 146°40′E
183 O11 **Yarrawonga** Victoria, SE Australia 36°04′S 145°58′E
182 L4 **Yarriarraburra Swamp** wetland New South Wales, SE Australia
122 I8 **Yar-Sale** Yamalo-Nenetskiy Avtonomnyy Okrug, N Russian Federation 66°52′N 70°42′E
122 K11 **Yartsevo** Krasnoyarskiy Kray, C Russian Federation 60°15′N 90°09′E
126 I4 **Yartsevo** Smolenskaya Oblast', W Russian Federation 55°03′N 32°46′E
54 E8 **Yarumal** Antioquia, NW Colombia 06°59′N 75°25′W
187 W14 **Yasawa Group** island group NW Fiji
77 V12 **Yashi** Katsina, N Nigeria 12°21′N 07°56′E
77 S14 **Yashikera** Kwara, W Nigeria 09°46′N 03°19′E
147 T14 **Yashilkŭl** Rus. Ozero Yashil'kul'. ◎ SE Tajikistan
Yashil'kul', Ozero see Yashilkŭl
165 P9 **Yashima** Akita, Honshū, C Japan 39°10′N 140°10′E
127 P13 **Yashkul'** Respublika Kalmykiya, SW Russian Federation 46°09′N 45°22′E
146 F13 **Yashlyk** Ahal Welaýaty, C Turkmenistan 37°46′N 58°51′E
Yasinovataya see Yasynuvata
114 N10 **Yasna Polyana** Burgas, E Bulgaria 42°18′N 27°35′E
167 R10 **Yasothon** Yasothon, E Thailand 15°46′N 104°12′E
183 R10 **Yass** New South Wales, SE Australia 34°52′S 148°55′E
Yassy see Iaşi
164 H12 **Yasugi** Shimane, Honshū, SW Japan 35°25′N 133°12′E
143 N10 **Yāsūj** var. Yesuj; prev. Tal-e Khosravī. Kohkīlūyeh va Būyer AHmad, C Iran 30°40′N 51°34′E
136 M11 **Yasun Burnu** headland N Turkey 41°07′N 37°40′E
117 X8 **Yasynuvata** Rus. Yasinovataya. Donets'ka Oblast', SE Ukraine 48°05′N 37°57′E
136 C15 **Yatağan** Muğla, SW Turkey 37°22′N 28°08′E
165 Q7 **Yatate-tōge** pass Honshū, C Japan
187 Q17 **Yaté** Province Sud, S New Caledonia 22°10′S 166°56′E
27 P6 **Yates Center** Kansas, C USA 37°54′N 95°44′W
185 B21 **Yates Point** headland South Island, New Zealand 44°30′S 167°49′E
9 N9 **Yathkyed Lake** ◎ Nunavut, NE Canada
171 T16 **Yatoke** Pulau Babar, E Indonesia 07°51′S 129°49′E
79 M18 **Yatolema** Orientale, N Dem. Rep. Congo 0°25′N 24°35′E
164 C15 **Yatsushiro** var. Yatusiro. Kumamoto, Kyūshū, SW Japan 32°30′N 130°34′E
164 C15 **Yatsushiro-kai** bay SW Japan
138 F11 **Yatta** var. Yuta. S West Bank 31°29′N 35°10′E
81 J20 **Yatta Plateau** plateau SE Kenya
Yatusiro see Yatsushiro
57 F17 **Yauca, Río** ≈ SW Peru
45 S6 **Yauco** W Puerto Rico 18°02′N 66°51′W
Yaunde see Yaoundé
Yavan see Yovon
Yavarí see Javari, Rio
56 G9 **Yavari Mirim, Río** ≈ NE Peru
40 G7 **Yavaros** Sonora, NW Mexico 26°40′N 109°32′W
154 I13 **Yavatmāl** Mahārāshtra, C India 20°22′N 78°11′E
54 M9 **Yaví, Cerro** ▲ C Venezuela 05°43′N 65°51′W
43 W16 **Yaviza** Darién, SE Panama 08°09′N 77°41′W
138 F10 **Yavne** Central, W Israel 31°52′N 34°45′E
116 H5 **Yavoriv** Pol. Jaworów, Rus. Yavorov. L'vivs'ka Oblast', NW Ukraine 49°57′N 23°22′E
Yavorov see Yavoriv
164 F14 **Yawatahama** Ehime, Shikoku, SW Japan 33°27′N 132°24′E
Ya Xian see Sanya
136 L17 **Yayladaği** Hatay, S Turkey 35°55′N 36°00′E
125 V13 **Yayva** Permskaya Oblast', NW Russian Federation 59°19′N 57°15′E
125 V12 **Yayva** ≈ NW Russian Federation
143 Q9 **Yazd** var. Yezd. Yazd, C Iran 31°55′N 54°22′E
143 Q8 **Yazd** off. Ostān-e Yazd, var. Yezd. ◐ province C Iran
Yazd, Ostān-e see Yazd
Yazgulemskiy Khrebet see Yazgulom, Qatorkŭhi
147 S13 **Yazgulom, Qatorkŭhi** Rus. Yazgulemskiy Khrebet. ▲▲ S Tajikistan
22 K5 **Yazoo City** Mississippi, S USA 32°51′N 90°24′W
22 K5 **Yazoo River** ≈ Mississippi, S USA
127 Q5 **Yazykovka** Ul'yanovskaya Oblast', W Russian Federation 54°19′N 47°22′E
109 U4 **Ybbs** Niederösterreich, NE Austria 48°10′N 15°03′E
109 U4 **Ybbs** ≈ C Austria
95 G22 **Yding Skovhøj** hill C Denmark
115 G20 **Ýdra** var. Ídhra, Idra. Ýdra, S Greece 37°20′N 23°28′E
115 G21 **Ýdra** var. Ídhra. island Ýdra, S Greece
115 G20 **Ýdras, Kólpos** strait S Greece
167 N10 **Ye** Mon State, S Burma (Myanmar) 15°15′N 97°50′E
183 O12 **Yea** Victoria, SE Australia 37°15′S 145°27′E
Yebaishou see Jianping
78 I5 **Yebbi-Bou** Borkou-Ennedi-Tibesti, N Chad 21°12′N 17°55′E
158 F9 **Yecheng** var. Kargilik. Xinjiang Uygur Zizhiqu, NW China 37°54′N 77°26′E
105 R11 **Yecla** Murcia, SE Spain 38°36′N 01°07′W
40 H6 **Yécora** Sonora, NW Mexico 28°23′N 108°56′W
Yedintsy see Edineţ
124 J13 **Yefimovskiy** Leningradskaya Oblast', NW Russian Federation 59°32′N 34°34′E
126 K6 **Yefremov** Tul'skaya Oblast', W Russian Federation 53°10′N 38°02′E
159 T11 **Yêgainnyin** var. Henan Mongolzu Zizhixian. Qinghai, C China 34°42′N 101°36′E
137 U12 **Yegbhegis** Rus. Yekhegis. ≈ C Armenia
137 U12 **Yeghegnadzor** C Armenia 39°45′N 45°20′E
145 T10 **Yegindybulak** Kaz. Egindibulaq. Karaganda, C Kazakhstan 49°45′N 75°45′E
126 L4 **Yegor'yevsk** Moskovskaya Oblast', W Russian Federation 55°29′N 39°03′E
Yehuda, Haré see Judaean Hills
81 E15 **Yei** ≈ S Sudan
161 P8 **Yeji** var. Yejiaji. Anhui, E China 31°52′N 115°58′E
Yejiaji see Yeji
122 G10 **Yekaterinburg** prev. Sverdlovsk. Sverdlovskaya Oblast', C Russian Federation 56°52′N 60°35′E
Yekaterinodar see Krasnodar
Yekaterinoslav see Dnipropetrovs'k
123 R13 **Yekaterinoslavka** Amurskaya Oblast', SE Russian Federation 50°23′N 129°03′E
127 O7 **Yekaterinovka** Saratovskaya Oblast', W Russian Federation 52°01′N 44°11′E
76 K16 **Yekepa** NE Liberia 07°35′N 08°32′W
Yekhegis see Yegbhegis
127 T3 **Yelabuga** Respublika Tatarstan, W Russian Federation 55°46′N 52°07′E
Yela Island see Rossel Island
127 O8 **Yelan'** Volgogradskaya Oblast', SW Russian Federation 51°00′N 43°40′E
117 Q9 **Yelanets'** Rus. Yelanets. Mykolayivs'ka Oblast', S Ukraine 47°40′N 31°51′E
126 L7 **Yelets** Lipetskaya Oblast', W Russian Federation 52°37′N 38°29′E
125 W4 **Yeletskiy** Respublika Komi, NW Russian Federation 67°03′N 64°05′E
76 J11 **Yélimané** Kayes, W Mali 15°06′N 10°43′W
Yelisavetpol see Gäncä
Yelizavetgrad see Kirovohrad
123 T12 **Yelizavety, Mys** headland SE Russian Federation 54°20′N 142°39′E
Yelizovo see Yalizava
127 S5 **Yelkhovka** Samarskaya Oblast', W Russian Federation 53°51′N 50°16′E
96 M1 **Yell** island NE Scotland, United Kingdom
155 E17 **Yellāpur** Karnātaka, W India 15°06′N 74°50′E
11 U17 **Yellow Grass** Saskatchewan, S Canada 49°51′N 104°09′W
Yellowhammer State see Alabama
11 O15 **Yellowhead Pass** pass Alberta/British Columbia, SW Canada
8 K10 **Yellowknife** territory capital Northwest Territories, W Canada 62°30′N 114°29′W
8 K9 **Yellowknife** ≈ Northwest Territories, NW Canada
23 P8 **Yellow River** ≈ Alabama/Florida, S USA
30 J6 **Yellow River** ≈ Wisconsin, N USA
30 K7 **Yellow River** ≈ Wisconsin, N USA
30 I4 **Yellow River** ≈ Wisconsin, N USA
Yellow River see Huang He
157 V8 **Yellow Sea** Chin. Huang Hai, Kor. Hwang-Hae. sea E Asia
33 S13 **Yellowstone Lake** ◎ Wyoming, C USA
33 T13 **Yellowstone National Park** national park Wyoming, NW USA
33 Y8 **Yellowstone River** ≈ Montana/Wyoming, NW USA
96 L1 **Yell Sound** strait N Scotland, United Kingdom
27 U9 **Yellville** Arkansas, C USA 36°12′N 92°41′W
126 I4 **Yel'nya** Smolenskaya Oblast', W Russian Federation 54°34′N 33°11′E
122 K10 **Yeloguy** ≈ C Russian Federation
Yëloten see Yolöten
119 M20 **Yel'sk** Homyel'skaya Voblasts', SE Belarus 51°48′N 29°09′E
77 T13 **Yelwa** Kebbi, W Nigeria 10°52′N 04°46′E
21 R15 **Yemassee** South Carolina, SE USA 32°41′N 80°51′W
141 O15 **Yemen** off. Republic of Yemen, Ar. Al Jumhuriyah al Yamaniyah, Al Yaman. ◆ republic SW Asia
Yemen, Republic of see Yemen
116 M4 **Yemil'chyne** Zhytomyrs'ka Oblast', N Ukraine 50°51′N 27°49′E
124 M10 **Yemtsa** Arkhangel'skaya Oblast', NW Russian Federation 63°04′N 40°18′E
124 M10 **Yemtsa** ≈ NW Russian Federation
125 R10 **Yemva** prev. Zheleznodorozhnyy. Respublika Komi, NW Russian Federation 62°38′N 50°59′E
77 U17 **Yenagoa** Bayelsa, S Nigeria 4°58′N 6°16′E
117 X7 **Yenakiyeve** Rus. Yenakiyevo; prev. Ordzhonikidze, Rykovo. Donets'ka Oblast', E Ukraine 48°13′N 38°13′E
Yenakiyevo see Yenakiyeve
166 L6 **Yenangyaung** Magway, W Burma (Myanmar) 20°28′N 94°54′E
167 S5 **Yên Bai** Yên Bai, N Vietnam 21°43′N 104°54′E
183 P9 **Yenda** New South Wales, SE Australia 34°16′S 146°15′E
77 Q14 **Yendi** NE Ghana 09°30′N 00°01′W
Yêndum see Zhag'yab
158 E8 **Yengisar** Xinjiang Uygur Zizhiqu, NW China 38°50′N 76°11′E
136 H11 **Yenice Çayı** var. Filyos Çayı. ≈ N Turkey
121 R1 **Yenierenköy** var. Yialousa, Gk. Agialoúsa. NE Cyprus 35°33′N 34°13′E
Yenipazar see Novi Pazar
136 E12 **Yenişehir** Bursa, NW Turkey 40°17′N 29°38′E
Yenisei Bay see Yeniseyskiy Zaliv
122 K12 **Yeniseysk** Krasnoyarskiy Kray, C Russian Federation 58°23′N 92°06′E
197 W10 **Yeniseyskiy Zaliv** var. Yenisei Bay. bay N Russian Federation
127 Q12 **Yenotayevka** Astrakhanskaya Oblast', SW Russian Federation 47°16′N 47°01′E
124 I4 **Yenozero, Ozero** ◎ NW Russian Federation
Yenping see Nanping
39 Q11 **Yentna River** ≈ Alaska, USA
180 M10 **Yeo, Lake** salt lake Western Australia
183 R7 **Yeoval** New South Wales, SE Australia 32°45′S 148°39′E
97 K23 **Yeovil** SW England, United Kingdom 50°57′N 02°39′W
40 H6 **Yepachic** Chihuahua, N Mexico 28°27′N 108°25′W
181 Y8 **Yeppoon** Queensland, E Australia 23°05′S 150°42′E
126 M5 **Yeraktur** Ryazanskaya Oblast', W Russian Federation 54°45′N 41°09′E
Yeraliyev see Kuryk
146 F12 **Yerbent** Ahal Welaýaty, C Turkmenistan 39°19′N 58°34′E
123 N11 **Yerbogachën** Irkutskaya Oblast', C Russian Federation 61°07′N 108°03′E
137 T12 **Yerevan** Eng. Erivan. ● (Armenia) C Armenia 40°12′N 44°31′E
137 U12 **Yerevan** ✈ C Armenia 40°07′N 44°34′E
145 R9 **Yereymentau** var. Jermentau, Kaz. Ereymentaŭ. Akmola, C Kazakhstan 51°38′N 73°10′E
127 O12 **Yergeni** hill range SW Russian Federation
Yeriho see Jericho
35 R6 **Yerington** Nevada, W USA 38°58′N 119°10′W
136 J13 **Yerköy** Yozgat, C Turkey 39°39′N 34°28′E
114 L13 **Yerlisu** Edirne, NW Turkey 40°45′N 26°38′E
Yermak see Aksu
145 R9 **Yermentau, Gory** ▲▲ C Kazakhstan
125 R5 **Yërmitsa** Respublika Komi, NW Russian Federation 66°57′N 52°15′E
35 V14 **Yermo** California, W USA 34°54′N 116°49′W
123 P13 **Yerofey Pavlovich** Amurskaya Oblast', SE Russian Federation 53°58′N 121°49′E
99 F15 **Yerseke** Zeeland, SW Netherlands 51°30′N 04°03′E
127 Q8 **Yershov** Saratovskaya Oblast', W Russian Federation 51°18′N 48°16′E
125 P9 **Yërtom** Respublika Komi, NW Russian Federation 63°27′N 47°52′E
56 D13 **Yerupaja, Nevado** ▲ C Peru 10°23′S 76°58′W
Yerushalayim see Jerusalem
105 R4 **Yesa, Embalse de** ⊠ NE Spain
144 F9 **Yesensay** Zapadnyy Kazakhstan, NW Kazakhstan 49°59′N 51°19′E
144 F9 **Yesensay** Zapadnyy Kazakhstan, NW Kazakhstan 49°58′N 51°19′E
145 V15 **Yesik** Kaz. Esik; prev. Issyk. Almaty, SE Kazakhstan 42°23′N 77°25′E
145 O8 **Yesil'** Kaz. Esil. Akmola, C Kazakhstan 51°58′N 66°24′E
136 K15 **Yeşilhisar** Kayseri, C Turkey 38°22′N 35°08′E
136 L11 **Yeşilırmak** var. Iris. ≈ N Turkey
37 U12 **Yeso** New Mexico, SW USA 34°25′N 104°36′W
Yeso see Hokkaidō
127 N15 **Yessentuki** Stavropol'skiy Kray, SW Russian Federation 44°06′N 42°51′E
122 M9 **Yessey** Evenkiyskiy Avtonomnyy Okrug, N Russian Federation 68°18′N 101°49′E
105 P12 **Yeste** Castilla-La Mancha, C Spain 38°21′N 02°18′W
Yesuj see Yāsūj
183 T4 **Yetman** New South Wales, SE Australia 28°56′S 150°47′E
76 L4 **Yeti** physical region N Mauritania
166 M4 **Ye-u** Sagaing, C Burma (Myanmar) 22°49′N 95°26′E
102 H9 **Yeu, Île d'** island NW France
Yevlakh see Yevlax
137 W11 **Yevlax** Rus. Yevlakh. C Azerbaijan 40°36′N 47°10′E
117 S13 **Yevpatoriya** Respublika Krym, S Ukraine 45°12′N 33°23′E
Ye Xian see Laizhou
126 K12 **Yeya** ≈ SW Russian Federation
158 I10 **Yeyik** Xinjiang Uygur Zizhiqu, W China 36°44′N 83°14′E
126 K12 **Yeysk** Krasnodarskiy Kray, SW Russian Federation 46°41′N 38°15′E
Yezd see Yazd
Yezerishche see Yezyaryshcha
Yezhou see Jianshi
Yezo see Hokkaidō
118 N11 **Yezyaryshcha** Rus. Yezerishche. Vitsyebskaya Voblasts', NE Belarus 55°50′N 29°59′E
Yialí see Gyali
Yialousa see Yenierenköy
163 V7 **Yi'an** Heilongjiang, NE China 47°52′N 125°13′E
Yiannitsá see Giannitsá
160 I10 **Yibin** Sichuan, C China 28°50′N 104°35′E
158 K13 **Yibug Caka** ◎ W China
160 M9 **Yichang** Hubei, C China 30°37′N 111°02′E
160 L5 **Yichuan** var. Danzhou. Shaanxi, C China 36°05′N 110°02′E
157 W3 **Yichun** Heilongjiang, NE China 47°41′N 129°10′E
161 O11 **Yichun** Jiangxi, S China 27°45′N 114°22′E
160 M9 **Yidu** prev. Zhicheng. Hubei, C China 30°21′N 111°27′E
Yidu see Qingzhou
188 C15 **Yigo** NE Guam 13°33′N 144°53′E
161 Q5 **Yi He** ≈ E China
163 X8 **Yilan** Heilongjiang, NE China 46°18′N 129°36′E
136 C9 **Yıldız Dağları** ▲▲ NW Turkey
136 L13 **Yıldızeli** Sivas, N Turkey 39°52′N 36°37′E
163 U4 **Yilehuli Shan** ▲▲ NE China
163 Z7 **Yimin He** ≈ NE China
159 W8 **Yinchuan** var. Yinch'uan, Yin-ch'uan, Yinchwan. province capital Ningxia, N China 38°30′N 106°19′E
Yinchwan see Yinchuan
Yindu He see Indus
Yingcheng see Yingde
161 N14 **Yingde** var. Yingcheng. Guangdong, S China 24°08′N 113°21′E
161 O7 **Ying He** ≈ E China
163 U13 **Yingkou** var. Ying-k'ou, Yingkow; prev. Newchwang, Niuchwang. Liaoning, NE China 40°40′N 122°17′E
Yingkow see Yingkou
161 P9 **Yingshan** var. Wenquan. Hubei, C China 30°45′N 115°41′E
Yingshan see Guangshui
161 Q10 **Yingtan** Jiangxi, S China 28°17′N 117°03′E
Yin-hsien see Ningbo
158 H5 **Yining** var. I-ning, Uigh. Gulja, Kuldja. Xinjiang Uygur Zizhiqu, NW China 43°53′N 81°18′E
160 K11 **Yinjiang** var. Yinjiang Tujiazu Miaozu Zizhixian. Guizhou, S China 28°22′N 108°07′E
Yinjiang Tujiazu Miaozu Zizhixian see Yinjiang
166 L4 **Yinmabin** Sagaing, C Burma (Myanmar) 22°05′N 94°57′E
163 N13 **Yin Shan** ▲▲ N China
Yin-tu Ho see Indus
159 P15 **Yi'ong Zangbo** ≈ W China
Yioúra see Gyáros
81 J14 **Yirga 'Alem** It. Irgalem. Southern Nationalities, S Ethiopia 06°43′N 38°24′E
61 E19 **Yí, Río** ≈ C Uruguay
81 E14 **Yirol** El Buhayrat, S Sudan 06°34′N 30°33′E
163 S8 **Yirshi** var. Yirxie. Nei Mongol Zizhiqu, N China 47°16′N 119°51′E
Yirxie see Yirshi
Yishan see Guanyun
Yishi see Linyi
161 Q5 **Yishui** Shandong, E China 35°50′N 118°39′E
Yisrael/Yisra'el see Israel
Yíthion see Gýtheio
Yitiaoshan see Jingtai
163 W10 **Yitong** var. Yitong Manzu Zizhixian. Jilin, NE China 43°23′N 125°19′E
Yitong Manzu Zizhixian see Yitong
159 P5 **Yiwu** var. Aratürük. Xinjiang Uygur Zizhiqu, NW China 43°16′N 94°38′E
163 U12 **Yiwulü Shan** ▲ N China
163 T12 **Yixian** var. Yizhou. Liaoning, NE China 41°29′N 121°21′E
161 N10 **Yiyang** Hunan, S China 28°39′N 112°10′E
161 Q10 **Yiyang** Jiangxi, S China 28°21′N 117°23′E
161 N13 **Yizhang** Hunan, S China 25°24′N 112°51′E
Yizhou see Yixian
93 K19 **Yläne** Länsi-Suomi, SW Finland 60°51′N 22°26′E
93 L14 **Yli-Ii** Oulu, C Finland 65°21′N 25°55′E
93 L14 **Ylikiiminki** Oulu, C Finland 65°00′N 26°10′E
92 N13 **Yli-Kitka** ◎ NE Finland
93 K17 **Ylistaro** Länsi-Suomi, W Finland 62°58′N 22°30′E
92 K13 **Ylitornio** Lappi, NW Finland 66°19′N 23°40′E
93 L15 **Ylivieska** Oulu, W Finland 64°05′N 24°30′E
93 L18 **Ylöjärvi** Länsi-Suomi, W Finland 61°31′N 23°37′E
95 N17 **Yngaren** ◎ C Sweden
25 T12 **Yoakum** Texas, SW USA 29°17′N 97°09′W
77 X13 **Yobe** ◐ state NE Nigeria
165 R3 **Yobetsu-dake** ※ Hokkaidō, NE Japan 43°15′N 140°27′E
80 L11 **Yoboki** C Djibouti 11°30′N 42°04′E
22 M4 **Yockanookany River** ≈ Mississippi, S USA
22 L2 **Yocona River** ≈ Mississippi, S USA
171 Y15 **Yodom** Papua, E Indonesia 07°12′S 139°24′E
169 Q16 **Yogyakarta** prev. Djokjakarta, Jogjakarta, Jokyakarta. Jawa, C Indonesia 07°48′S 110°24′E
169 P17 **Yogyakarta** off. Daerah Istimewa Yogyakarta, var. Djokjakarta, Jogjakarta, Jokyakarta. ◐ autonomous district S Indonesia
Yogyakarta, Daerah Istimewa see Yogyakarta
165 Q3 **Yoichi** Hokkaidō, NE Japan 43°11′N 140°45′E
42 G6 **Yojoa, Lago de** ◎ NW Honduras
79 G16 **Yokadouma** Est, SE Cameroon 03°26′N 15°06′E
164 K13 **Yokkaichi** var. Yokkaiti. Mie, Honshū, SW Japan 34°58′N 136°38′E
Yokkaiti see Yokkaichi
79 E15 **Yoko** Centre, C Cameroon 05°29′N 12°19′E
165 V15 **Yokoate-jima** island Nansei-shotō, SW Japan
165 R6 **Yokohama** Aomori, Honshū, C Japan 41°04′N 141°14′E
165 O14 **Yokosuka** Kanagawa, Honshū, S Japan 35°18′N 139°39′E
164 G12 **Yokota** Shimane, Honshū, SW Japan 35°10′N 133°03′E
165 Q9 **Yokote** Akita, Honshū, C Japan 39°20′N 140°33′E
77 Y14 **Yola** Adamawa, E Nigeria 09°08′N 12°24′E
79 L19 **Yolombo** Equateur, C Dem. Rep. Congo 01°36′S 23°13′E
146 J14 **Yolöten** Rus. Yëloten; prev. Iolotan'. Mary Welaýaty, S Turkmenistan 37°15′N 62°18′E
165 Y15 **Yome-jima** island Ogasawara-shotō, SE Japan
76 K16 **Yomou** SE Guinea 07°30′N 09°13′W
171 Y15 **Yomuka** Papua, E Indonesia 07°25′S 138°36′E
188 C16 **Yona** E Guam 13°24′N 144°46′E
164 H12 **Yonago** Tottori, Honshū, SW Japan 35°30′N 134°15′E
165 N16 **Yonaguni** Okinawa, SW Japan 24°29′N 123°00′E
165 N16 **Yonaguni-jima** island Nansei-shotō, SW Japan
165 T16 **Yonaha-dake** ▲ Okinawa, SW Japan 26°43′N 128°13′E
163 X14 **Yŏnan** SW North Korea 37°50′N 126°15′E
165 P10 **Yonezawa** Yamagata, Honshū, C Japan 37°56′N 140°06′E
161 Q12 **Yong'an** var. Yongan. Fujian, SE China 25°58′N 117°26′E
Yongan see Fengjie
159 T9 **Yongchang** Gansu, N China 38°15′N 101°56′E
161 P7 **Yongcheng** Henan, C China 33°56′N 116°21′E
163 Z15 **Yŏngch'ŏn** Jap. Eisen. SE South Korea 35°56′N 128°55′E
160 J10 **Yongchuan** Chongqing Shi, C China 29°27′N 105°56′E
159 U10 **Yongdeng** Gansu, C China 35°58′N 103°27′E
Yongding see Yongren
129 W9 **Yongding He** ≈ E China
161 P11 **Yongfeng** var. Enjiang. Jiangxi, S China 27°19′N 115°23′E
158 L5 **Yongfengqu** Xinjiang Uygur Zizhiqu, W China 43°28′N 87°09′E
160 L13 **Yongfu** Guangxi Zhuangzu Zizhiqu, S China 24°57′N 109°59′E
163 X13 **Yŏnghŭng** E North Korea 39°31′N 127°14′E
159 U10 **Yongjing** var. Liujiaxia. Gansu, C China 36°00′N 103°30′E
Yongjing see Xifeng
163 Y15 **Yŏngju** Jap. Eishū. C South Korea 36°48′N 128°37′E
Yongning see Xuyong
160 E12 **Yongping** Yunnan, SW China 25°30′N 99°28′E
160 G12 **Yongren** var. Yongding. Yunnan, SW China 26°09′N 101°40′E
160 L10 **Yongshun** var. Lingxi. Hunan, S China 29°02′N 109°46′E
161 P10 **Yongxiu** var. Tujiabu. Jiangxi, S China 29°09′N 115°47′E
160 M12 **Yongzhou** var. Lengshuitan. Hunan, S China 26°13′N 111°36′E
Yongzhou see Zhishan
18 K14 **Yonkers** New York, NE USA 40°56′N 73°51′W
103 Q7 **Yonne** ◐ department C France
103 P6 **Yonne** ≈ C France
54 H9 **Yopal** var. El Yopal. Casanare, C Colombia 05°20′N 72°19′W
158 E8 **Yopurga** var. Yukuriawat. Xinjiang Uygur Zizhiqu, NW China 39°13′N 76°44′E
147 S11 **Yordon** var. Iordan, Rus. Jardan. Farg'ona Viloyati, E Uzbekistan 39°59′N 71°44′E
180 J12 **York** Western Australia 31°55′S 116°52′E
97 M16 **York** anc. Eboracum, Eburacum. N England, United Kingdom 53°58′N 01°05′W
23 N5 **York** Alabama, S USA 32°29′N 88°18′W
29 Q15 **York** Nebraska, C USA 40°52′N 97°35′W
18 G16 **York** Pennsylvania, NE USA 39°57′N 76°44′W
21 R11 **York** South Carolina, SE USA 34°59′N 81°14′W
14 J13 **York** ≈ Ontario, SE Canada
15 X6 **York** ≈ Québec, SE Canada
181 V1 **York, Cape** headland Queensland, NE Australia 10°40′S 142°36′E
182 I9 **Yorke Peninsula** peninsula South Australia
182 I9 **Yorketown** South Australia 35°01′S 137°38′E
19 P9 **York Harbor** Maine, NE USA 43°10′N 70°37′W
York, Kap see Innaanganeq
21 X6 **York River** ≈ Virginia, NE USA
97 M16 **Yorkshire** cultural region N England, United Kingdom
97 L16 **Yorkshire Dales** physical region N England, United Kingdom
11 V16 **Yorkton** Saskatchewan, S Canada 51°12′N 102°29′W
25 T12 **Yorktown** Texas, SW USA 28°58′N 97°30′W
21 X6 **Yorktown** Virginia, NE USA 37°14′N 76°32′W
30 M11 **Yorkville** Illinois, N USA 41°38′N 88°27′W
42 I5 **Yoro** Yoro, C Honduras 15°08′N 87°10′W
42 H5 **Yoro** ◐ department N Honduras
165 T16 **Yoron-jima** island Nansei-shotō, SW Japan
77 N13 **Yorosso** Sikasso, S Mali 12°21′N 04°47′W
35 R8 **Yosemite National Park** national park California, W USA
127 Q3 **Yoshkar-Ola** Respublika Mariy El, W Russian Federation 56°38′N 47°54′E
Yösönbulag see Altay
162 K8 **Yösöndzüyl** var. Mönhbulag. Övörhangay, C Mongolia 46°48′N 103°25′E
171 Y16 **Yos Sudarso, Pulau** var. Pulau Dolak, Pulau Kolepom; prev. Jos Sudarso. island E Indonesia
163 Y17 **Yŏsu** Jap. Reisui. S South Korea 34°45′N 127°41′E
165 R4 **Yotei-zan** ▲ Hokkaidō, NE Japan 42°50′N 140°46′E
97 D21 **Youghal** Ir. Eochaill. Cork, S Ireland 51°57′N 07°50′W
97 D21 **Youghal Bay** Ir. Cuan Eochaille. inlet S Ireland
18 C15 **Youghiogheny River** ≈ Pennsylvania, NE USA
160 K14 **You Jiang** ≈ S China
183 Q9 **Young** New South Wales, SE Australia 34°19′S 148°20′E
11 T15 **Young** Saskatchewan, S Canada 51°44′N 105°44′W
61 E18 **Young** Río Negro, W Uruguay 32°44′S 57°36′W
182 G5 **Younghusband, Lake** salt lake South Australia
182 J10 **Younghusband Peninsula** peninsula South Australia
184 Q10 **Young Nicks Head** headland North Island, New Zealand 39°38′S 177°03′E
185 D20 **Young Range** ▲▲ South Island, New Zealand
191 Q15 **Young's Rock** island Pitcairn Island, Pitcairn Islands
11 R16 **Youngstown** Alberta, SW Canada 51°32′N 111°12′W
31 V12 **Youngstown** Ohio, N USA 41°06′N 80°39′W
159 N9 **Youshashan** Qinghai, C China 38°12′N 90°58′E
Youth, Isle of see Juventud, Isla de la
77 N11 **Youvarou** Mopti, C Mali 15°19′N 04°15′W
160 K10 **Youyang** var. Zhongduo. Chongqing Shi, C China 28°48′N 108°48′E
163 Y7 **Youyi** Heilongjiang, NE China 46°51′N 131°54′E
147 P13 **Yovon** Rus. Yavan. SW Tajikistan 38°19′N 69°02′E
136 J13 **Yozgat** Yozgat, C Turkey 39°49′N 34°48′E
136 K13 **Yozgat** ◐ province C Turkey
62 O6 **Ypacaraí** var. Ypacaray. Central, S Paraguay 25°23′S 57°16′W
Ypacaray see Ypacaraí
62 P5 **Ypané, Río** ≈ C Paraguay
Ypres see Ieper
114 I13 **Ypsário** var. Ipsario. ▲ Thásos, E Greece 40°43′N 24°39′E
31 R10 **Ypsilanti** Michigan, N USA 42°12′N 83°36′W
34 M1 **Yreka** California, W USA 41°43′N 122°39′W
Yrendagüé see General Eugenio A. Garay
Yrghyz see Irgiz
186 G5 **Ysabel Channel** channel N Papua New Guinea
14 K8 **Yser, Lac** ◎ Québec, SE Canada
147 Y8 **Yshtyk** Issyk-Kul'skaya Oblast', E Kyrgyzstan 41°34′N 78°21′E
109 U4 **Ysper** ≈ N Austria
Yssel see IJssel
103 Q12 **Yssingeaux** Haute-Loire, C France 45°09′N 04°07′E
95 K23 **Ystad** Skåne, S Sweden 55°25′N 13°51′E
Ysyk-Köl see Issyk-Kul', Ozero
Ysyk-Köl see Balykchy
Ysyk-Köl Oblasty see Issyk-Kul'skaya Oblast'
96 L8 **Ythan** ≈ NE Scotland, United Kingdom
Y Trallwng see Welshpool
94 C13 **Ytre Arna** Hordaland, S Norway 60°28′N 05°25′E
94 B12 **Ytre Sula** island S Norway
93 G17 **Ytterhogdal** Jämtland, C Sweden 62°10′N 14°55′E
Yu see Henan
Yuan see Red River
Yuancheng see Heyuan, Guangdong, S China
Yuan Jiang see Red River
161 S13 **Yüanlin** Jap. Inrin. C Taiwan 23°57′N 120°33′E
161 N3 **Yuanping** Shanxi, C China 38°26′N 112°42′E
Yuanquan see Anxi
Yuanshan see Lianping
161 O11 **Yuan Shui** ≈ S China
35 O6 **Yuba City** California, W USA 39°07′N 121°40′W
35 O6 **Yuba River** ≈ California, W USA
80 H13 **Yubdo** Oromiya, C Ethiopia 09°05′N 35°28′E
41 X12 **Yucatán** ◐ state SE Mexico
47 O3 **Yucatan Basin** var. Yucatan Deep. undersea feature N Caribbean Sea 20°00′N 84°00′W
Yucatán, Canal de see Yucatan Channel
41 Y10 **Yucatan Channel** Sp. Canal de Yucatán. channel Cuba/Mexico
Yucatan Deep see Yucatan Basin
Yucatan Peninsula see Yucatán, Península de
41 X13 **Yucatán, Península de** Eng. Yucatan Peninsula. peninsula Guatemala/Mexico
36 I11 **Yucca** Arizona, SW USA 34°49′N 114°06′W
35 V15 **Yucca Valley** California, W USA 34°06′N 116°30′W
161 P4 **Yucheng** Shandong, E China 37°01′N 116°37′E
Yuci see Jinzhong
129 X5 **Yudoma** ≈ E Russian Federation
161 P12 **Yudu** var. Gongjiang. Jiangxi, C China 26°02′N 115°24′E
Yue see Guangdong
Yuecheng see Yuexi
160 M12 **Yuecheng Ling** ▲▲ S China
Yuegai see Qumarlêb
Yuegaitan see Qumarlêb
181 P7 **Yuendumu** Northern Territory, N Australia 22°19′S 131°51′E
Yue Shan, Tai see Lantau Island
160 H10 **Yuexi** var. Yuecheng. Sichuan, C China 28°50′N 102°36′E
161 N10 **Yueyang** Hunan, S China 29°24′N 113°08′E
125 U14 **Yug** Permskaya Oblast', NW Russian Federation 57°49′N 56°08′E
125 P13 **Yug** ≈ NW Russian Federation
123 R10 **Yugorënok** Respublika Sakha (Yakutiya), NE Russian Federation 59°46′N 137°36′E
122 H9 **Yugorsk** Khanty-Mansiyskiy Avtonomnyy Okrug-Yugra, C Russian Federation 61°17′N 63°25′E
122 H7 **Yugorskiy Poluostrov** peninsula NW Russian Federation
Yugoslavia see Serbia
146 K14 **Yugo-Vostochnyye Garagumy** prev. Yugo-Vostochnyye Karakumy. desert E Turkmenistan
Yugo-Vostochnyye Karakumy see Yugo-Vostochnyye Garagumy
Yuhu see Eryuan
161 S10 **Yuhuan Dao** island SE China
160 L14 **Yu Jiang** ≈ S China
Yujin see Qianwei
123 S7 **Yukagirskoye Ploskogor'ye** plateau NE Russian Federation
118 L11 **Yukhavichy** Rus. Yukhovichi. Vitsyebskaya Voblasts', N Belarus 56°02′N 28°39′E
126 J4 **Yukhnov** Kaluzhskaya Oblast', W Russian Federation 54°43′N 35°15′E
Yukhovichi see Yukhavichy
79 J20 **Yuki** var. Yuki Kengunda. Bandundu, W Dem. Rep. Congo 03°57′S 19°30′E
Yuki Kengunda see Yuki
26 M10 **Yukon** Oklahoma, C USA 35°30′N 97°45′W
0 F4 **Yukon** ≈ Canada/USA
Yukon see Yukon Territory
39 S7 **Yukon Flats** salt flat Alaska, USA
Yukon, Territoire du see Yukon Territory
10 I5 **Yukon Territory** var. Yukon, Fr. Territoire du Yukon. ◐ territory NW Canada
137 T16 **Yüksekova** Hakkâri, SE Turkey 37°35′N 44°17′E
123 N10 **Yukta** Evenkiyskiy Avtonomnyy Okrug, C Russian Federation 63°16′N 106°04′E
165 O13 **Yukuhashi** var. Yukuhasi. Fukuoka, Kyūshū, SW Japan 33°41′N 131°00′E
Yukuhasi see Yukuhashi
Yukuriawat see Yopurga
125 O9 **Yula** ≈ NW Russian Federation
181 P8 **Yulara** Northern Territory, N Australia 25°15′S 130°57′E
127 W6 **Yuldybayevo** Respublika Bashkortostan, W Russian Federation 52°22′N 57°55′E
23 W8 **Yulee** Florida, SE USA 30°37′N 81°36′W
158 K7 **Yuli** var. Lopnur. Xinjiang Uygur Zizhiqu, NW China 41°24′N 86°12′E
161 T14 **Yüli** C Taiwan 23°23′N 121°18′E
160 L15 **Yulin** Guangxi Zhuangzu Zizhiqu, S China 22°37′N 110°08′E
160 L4 **Yulin** Shaanxi, C China 38°14′N 109°48′E
161 T14 **Yüli Shan** ▲ E Taiwan 23°23′N 121°14′E
160 F11 **Yulong Xueshan** ▲ SW China 27°09′N 100°10′E
36 H14 **Yuma** Arizona, SW USA 32°40′N 114°38′W
37 W3 **Yuma** Colorado, C USA 40°07′N 102°43′W
54 K5 **Yumare** Yaracuy, N Venezuela 10°37′N 68°41′W
63 G14 **Yumbel** Bío Bío, C Chile 37°05′S 72°40′W
79 N19 **Yumbi** Maniema, E Dem. Rep. Congo 01°14′S 26°14′E
159 Q7 **Yumen** prev. Yumenzhen. Gansu, N China 40°19′N 97°12′E
Yumenzhen see Yumen
158 J3 **Yumin** var. Karabura. Xinjiang Uygur Zizhiqu, NW China 46°14′N 82°52′E
Yun see Yunnan
136 G14 **Yunak** Konya, W Turkey 38°50′N 31°42′E
45 O8 **Yuna, Río** ≈ E Dominican Republic
38 I17 **Yunaska Island** island Aleutian Islands, Alaska, USA
160 M6 **Yuncheng** Shanxi, C China 35°07′N 110°45′E
Yuncheng see Yunfu
161 N14 **Yunfu** var. Yuncheng. Guangdong, S China 22°56′N 112°02′E

◆ Country ● Country Capital ◇ Dependent Territory ○ Dependent Territory Capital ◐ Administrative Regions ✈ International Airport ▲ Mountain ▲▲ Mountain Range ※ Volcano ≈ River ◎ Lake ⊠ Reservoir

57 L18 Yungas physical region E Bolivia
Yungki see Jilin
Yung-ning see Nanning
160 I12 Yungui Gaoyuan plateau SW China
Yunjinghong see Jinghong
160 M15 Yunkai Dashan ▲▲ S China
Yunki see Jilin
160 E11 Yun Ling ▲▲ SW China
Yunling see Yunxiao
161 N9 Yunmeng Hubei, C China 31°04′N 113°45′E
157 N14 Yunnan var. Yun, Yunnan Sheng, Yünnan, Yun-nan. ◐ province SW China
Yunnan see Kunming
Yunnan Sheng see Yunnan
Yünnan/Yun-nan see Yunnan
165 P15 Yunomae Kumamoto, Kyūshū, SW Japan 32°16′N 131°00′E
161 N8 Yun Shui ≈ C China
182 J7 Yunta South Australia 32°37′S 139°33′E
161 Q14 Yunxiao var. Yunling. Fujian, SE China 23°56′N 117°16′E
160 K9 Yunyang Sichuan, C China 31°03′N 109°43′E
Yunzhong see Huairen
193 S9 Yupanqui Basin undersea feature E Pacific Ocean
Yuping see Libo, Guizhou, China
Yuping see Pingbian, Yunnan, China
Yuratishki see Yuratsishki
119 I15 Yuratsishki Pol. Juraciszki, Rus. Yuratishki. Hrodzyenskaya Voblasts', W Belarus 54°02′N 25°56′E
Yurev see Tartu
122 J12 Yurga Kemerovskaya Oblast', S Russian Federation 55°42′N 84°59′E
Yurihonjō see Honjō
56 E10 Yurimaguas Loreto, N Peru 05°54′S 76°07′W
127 P3 Yurino Respublika Mariy El, W Russian Federation 56°19′N 46°15′E
41 N13 Yuriria Guanajuato, C Mexico 20°12′N 101°09′W
125 T13 Yurla Komi-Permyatskiy Avtonomnyy Okrug, NW Russian Federation 59°18′N 54°19′E
Yuruá, Río see Juruá, Rio
114 M13 Yürük Tekirdağ, NW Turkey 40°58′N 27°09′E
158 G10 Yurungkax He ≈ W China
125 Q14 Yur'ya var. Jarja. Kirovskaya Oblast', NW Russian Federation 59°01′N 49°22′E
Yury'ev see Tartu
125 N16 Yur'yevets Ivanovskaya Oblast', W Russian Federation 57°19′N 43°01′E
126 M3 Yur'yev-Pol'skiy Vladimirskaya Oblast', W Russian Federation 56°28′N 39°39′E
117 V7 Yur"yivka Dnipropetrovs'ka Oblast', E Ukraine 48°45′N 36°01′E
42 I7 Yuscarán El Paraíso, S Honduras 13°55′N 86°51′W
161 P12 Yu Shan ▲ S China
124 I7 Yushkozero Respublika Kareliya, NW Russian Federation 64°46′N 32°13′E
124 I7 Yushkozerskoye Vodokhranilishche var. Ozero Kujto. ◎ NW Russian Federation
169 W9 Yushu Jilin, China E Asia 44°48′N 126°31′E
159 R13 Yushu var. Gyêgu. Qinghai, C China 33°04′N 97°E
127 P12 Yusta Respublika Kalmykiya, SW Russian Federation 47°06′N 46°16′E
124 I10 Yustozero Respublika Kareliya, NW Russian Federation 62°44′N 33°31′E
137 Q11 Yusufeli Artvin, NE Turkey 40°50′N 41°31′E
164 F14 Yusuhara Kōchi, Shikoku, SW Japan 33°22′N 132°52′E
125 T14 Yus'va Permskaya Oblast', NW Russian Federation 58°48′N 54°59′E
Yuta see Yatta
161 P2 Yutian Hebei, E China 39°52′N 117°44′E
158 H10 Yutian var. Keriya, Mugalla. Xinjiang Uygur Zizhiqu, NW China 36°49′N 81°31′E
62 K5 Yuto Jujuy, NW Argentina 23°35′S 64°28′W
62 P7 Yuty Caazapá, S Paraguay 26°31′S 56°20′W
160 G13 Yuxi Yunnan, SW China 24°22′N 102°28′E
161 O2 Yuxian prev. Yu Xian. Hebei, E China 39°50′N 114°33′E
Yu Xian see Yuxian
165 Q9 Yuzawa Akita, Honshū, C Japan 39°11′N 140°29′E
125 N16 Yuzha Ivanovskaya Oblast', W Russian Federation 56°34′N 42°00′E
Yuzhno-Alichurskiy Khrebet see Alichuri Janubí, Qatorkŭhi
Yuzhno-Kazakhstanskaya Oblast' see Yuzhnyy Kazakhstan
123 T13 Yuzhno-Sakhalinsk Jap. Toyohara; prev. Vladimirovka. Ostrov Sakhalin, Sakhalinskaya Oblast', SE Russian Federation 46°58′N 142°45′E
127 P14 Yuzhno-Sukhokumsk Respublika Dagestan, SW Russian Federation 44°43′N 45°32′E
145 Z10 Yuzhnyy Altay, Khrebet ▲▲ E Kazakhstan
Yuzhnyy Bug see Pivdennyy Buh
145 O15 Yuzhnyy Kazakhstan off. Yuzhno-Kazakhstanskaya Oblast', Eng. South Kazakhstan, Kaz. Ongtüstik Qazaqstan Oblysy; prev. Chimkentskaya Oblast'. ◐ province S Kazakhstan
123 U10 Yuzhnyy, Mys headland E Russian Federation 57°44′N 156°49′E
127 W6 Yuzhnyy Ural var. Southern Urals. ▲▲ W Russian Federation
159 V10 Yuzhong Gansu, C China 35°52′N 104°09′E
Yuzhou see Chongqing
103 N5 Yvelines ◐ department N France
108 B9 Yverdon var. Yverdon-les-Bains, Ger. Iferten; anc. Eborodunum. Vaud, W Switzerland 46°47′N 06°38′E
Yverdon-les-Bains see Yverdon
102 M3 Yvetot Seine-Maritime, N France 49°37′N 00°48′E
Ÿylanly see Gurbansoltan Eje

Z

147 T12 Zaalayskiy Khrebet Taj. Qatorkŭhi Pasi Oloy. ▲▲ Kyrgyzstan/Tajikistan
Zaamin see Zomin
Zaandam see Zaanstad
98 I10 Zaanstad prev. Zaandam. Noord-Holland, C Netherlands 52°27′N 04°49′E
Zabadani see Az Zabdānī
119 L18 Zabalatstsye Rus. Zabolot'ye. Homyel'skaya Voblasts', SE Belarus 52°40′N 28°34′E
112 L9 Žabalj Ger. Josefsdorf, Hung. Zsablya; prev. Józseffalva. Vojvodina, N Serbia 45°22′N 20°01′E
Zāb aş Şaghīr, Nahraz see Little Zab
123 P14 Zabaykal'sk Chitinskaya Oblast', S Russian Federation 49°37′N 117°20′E
Zāb-e Kūchek, Rūdkhāneh-ye see Little Zab
Zabeln see Sabile
Zabéré see Zabré
Zabern see Saverne
141 N16 Zabīd W Yemen 14°N 43°E
141 O16 Zabīd, Wādī dry watercourse SW Yemen
Żabinka see Zhabinka
Ząbkowice see Ząbkowice Śląskie
111 G15 Ząbkowice Śląskie var. Ząbkowice, Ger. Frankenstein, Frankenstein in Schlesien. Dolnośląskie, SW Poland 50°35′N 16°48′E
110 P10 Zabłudów Podlaskie, NE Poland 53°00′N 23°21′E
112 D8 Zabok Krapina-Zagorje, N Croatia 46°00′N 15°48′E
143 W9 Zābol var. Shahr-i-Zabul, Zabul; prev. Nasratabad. Sīstān va Balūchestān, E Iran 31°N 61°32′E
149 O7 Zābol Pash. Zābul. ◐ province SE Afghanistan
143 W13 Zābolī Sīstān va Balūchestān, SE Iran 27°09′N 61°32′E
Zabolot'ye see Zabalatstsye
77 Q13 Zabré var. Zabéré. S Burkina 11°13′N 00°34′W
111 G17 Zábřeh Ger. Hohenstadt. Olomoucký Kraj, E Czech Republic 49°52′N 16°53′E
111 J16 Zabrze Ger. Hindenburg, Hindenburg in Oberschlesien. Śląskie, S Poland 50°18′N 18°47′E
Zabul/Zābul see Zābol
42 E6 Zacapa Zacapa, E Guatemala 14°59′N 89°33′W
42 A3 Zacapa off. Departamento de Zacapa. ◐ department E Guatemala
Zacapa, Departamento de see Zacapa
40 M14 Zacapú Michoacán, SW Mexico 19°49′N 101°48′W
41 V14 Zacatal Campeche, SE Mexico 18°40′N 91°52′W
40 M11 Zacatecas Zacatecas, C Mexico 22°46′N 102°33′W
40 L10 Zacatecas ◐ state C Mexico
42 F8 Zacatecoluca La Paz, S El Salvador 13°29′N 88°51′W
41 P15 Zacatepec Morelos, S Mexico 18°40′N 99°11′W
41 Q13 Zacatlán Puebla, S Mexico 19°56′N 97°58′W
144 F8 Zachagansk Kaz. Zashaghan. Zapadnyy Kazakhstan, NW Kazakhstan 51°04′N 51°13′E
115 D20 Zacháro var. Zaharo, Zakháro. Dytikí Elláda, S Greece 37°29′N 21°40′E
22 I8 Zachary Louisiana, S USA 30°39′N 91°09′W
117 U6 Zachepylivka Kharkivs'ka Oblast', E Ukraine 49°13′N 35°15′E
Zachist'ye see Zachystsye
110 E9 Zachodnio-pomorskie ◐ province NW Poland
119 L14 Zachystsye Rus. Zachist'ye. Minskaya Voblasts', NW Belarus 54°24′N 28°45′E
40 L13 Zacoalco var. Zacoalco de Torres. Jalisco, SW Mexico 20°14′N 103°33′W
Zacoalco de Torres see Zacoalco
41 P13 Zacualtipán Hidalgo, C Mexico 20°39′N 98°42′W
112 C12 Zadar It. Zara; anc. Iader. Zadar, SW Croatia 44°07′N 15°15′E
112 C12 Zadar off. Zadarsko-Kninska Županija, Zadar-Knin. ◐ province SW Croatia
Zadar-Knin see Zadar
Zadarsko-Kninska Županija see Zadar
166 M14 Zadetkyi Kyun var. St.Matthew's Island. island Mergui Archipelago, S Burma (Myanmar)
67 Q9 Zadié var. Djadié. ≈ NE Gabon
159 Q13 Zadoi var. Qapugtang. Qinghai, C China 32°56′N 95°21′E
126 L7 Zadonsk Lipetskaya Oblast', W Russian Federation 52°25′N 38°55′E
Za'farāna see Za'farānah
75 X8 Za'farānah var. Za'farāna. E Egypt 29°06′N 32°34′E
149 W7 Zafarwāl Punjab, E Pakistan 32°20′N 74°53′E
121 Q1 Zafer Burnu var. Cape Andreas, Cape Apostolas Andreas, Gk. Akrotíri Apostólou Andréa. cape NE Cyprus
107 J23 Zafferano, Capo headland Sicilia, Italy, C Mediterranean Sea 38°06′N 13°31′E
114 M7 Zafirovo Silistra, NE Bulgaria 44°00′N 26°51′E
Záfora see Sofraná
104 J12 Zafra Extremadura, W Spain 38°25′N 06°27′W
110 E13 Żagań var. Żagań, Żegań, Ger. Sagan. Lubuskie, W Poland 51°37′N 15°20′E
118 F10 Žagarė Pol. Żagory. Šiaulai, N Lithuania 56°22′N 23°16′E
Zagazig see Az Zaqāzīq
74 M5 Zaghouan var. Zaghwān. NE Tunisia 36°26′N 10°05′E
Zaghwān see Zaghouan
115 G16 Zagorá Thessalía, C Greece 39°27′N 23°06′E
Zagorod'ye see Zaharoddzye
Żagory see Žagarė
Zágráb see Zagreb
112 E8 Zagreb Ger. Agram, Hung. Zágráb. ● (Croatia) Zagreb, N Croatia 45°48′N 15°58′E
112 E8 Zagreb prev. Grad Zagreb. ◐ province N Croatia
142 L7 Zāgros, Kūhhā-ye Eng. Zagros Mountains. ▲▲ W Iran
Zagros Mountains see Zāgros, Kūhhā-ye
112 O12 Žagubica Serbia, E Serbia 44°13′N 21°47′E
Zagunao see Lixian
111 L22 Zagyva ≈ N Hungary
Zaharo see Zacháro
119 G19 Zaharoddzye Rus. Zagorod'ye. physical region SW Belarus
143 W11 Zāhedān var. Zahidan; prev. Duzdab. Sīstān va Balūchestān, SE Iran 29°31′N 60°51′E
Zahidan see Zāhedān
Zahlah see Zahlé
138 H7 Zahlé var. Zahlah. C Lebanon 33°51′N 35°54′E
146 J14 Zähmet Rus. Zakhmet. Mary Welaýaty, C Turkmenistan 37°48′N 62°33′E
111 O20 Záhony Szabolcs-Szatmár-Bereg, NE Hungary 48°26′N 22°11′E
141 N13 Zahrān 'Asīr, S Saudi Arabia 17°48′N 43°28′E
139 R12 Zahrat al Baṭn hill range S Iraq
120 H11 Zahrez Chergui var. Zahrez Chergúi. marsh N Algeria
Zainlha see Xinjin
127 S4 Zainsk Respublika Tatarstan, W Russian Federation 55°12′N 52°01′E
82 A10 Zaire prev. Congo. ◐ province NW Angola
Zaire see Congo (river)
Zaire see Congo (Democratic Republic of)
112 P13 Zaječar Serbia, E Serbia 43°54′N 22°16′E
83 L18 Zaka Masvingo, E Zimbabwe 20°20′S 31°29′E
122 M14 Zakamensk Respublika Buryatiya, S Russian Federation 50°18′N 102°57′E
116 G7 Zakarpats'ka Oblast' Eng. Transcarpathian Oblast, Rus. Zakarpatskaya Oblast'. ◐ province W Ukraine
Zakarpatskaya Oblast' see Zakarpats'ka Oblast'
Zakataly see Zaqatala
Zakháro see Zacháro
Zakhidnyy Buh/Zakhodni Buh see Bug
Zakhmet see Zähmet
139 Q1 Zākhō var. Zākhū. Dahūk, N Iraq 37°09′N 42°40′E
Zākhū see Zākhō
Zákinthos see Zákynthos
111 L18 Zakopane Małopolskie, S Poland 49°17′N 19°57′E
78 J12 Zakouma Salamat, S Chad 10°47′N 19°51′E
115 L25 Zákros Kríti, Greece, E Mediterranean Sea 35°06′N 26°12′E
115 C19 Zákynthos var. Zákinthos. Zákynthos, W Greece 37°47′N 20°54′E
115 C20 Zákynthos var. Zákinthos, It. Zante. island Iónia Nísoi, Greece, C Mediterranean Sea
115 C19 Zakýnthou, Porthmós strait SW Greece
111 G24 Zala off. Zala Megye. ◐ county W Hungary
111 G24 Zala ≈ W Hungary
138 M4 Zalābiyah Dayr az Zawr, C Syria 35°39′N 39°51′E
111 G24 Zalaegerszeg Zala, W Hungary 46°51′N 16°49′E
104 K11 Zalamea de la Serena Extremadura, W Spain 38°38′N 05°37′W
104 J13 Zalamea la Real Andalucía, S Spain 37°41′N 06°40′W
Zala Megye see Zala
163 U7 Zalantun var. Butha Qi. Nei Mongol Zizhiqu, N China 47°58′N 122°44′E
111 G23 Zalaszentgrót Zala, SW Hungary 46°57′N 17°05′E
Zalatna see Zlatna
116 G9 Zalău Ger. Waltenberg, Hung. Zilah; prev. Ger. Zillenmarkt. Sălaj, NW Romania 47°11′N 23°03′E
109 V10 Žalec Ger. Sachsenfeld. C Slovenia 46°15′N 15°08′E
110 K8 Zalewo Ger. Saalfeld. Warmińsko-Mazurskie, NE Poland 53°54′N 19°39′E
141 N9 Zalim Makkah, W Saudi Arabia 22°46′N 42°12′E
80 A11 Zalingei var. Zalinje. Western Darfur, W Sudan 12°51′N 23°29′E
Zalinje see Zalingei
116 K7 Zalishchyky Ternopil's'ka Oblast', W Ukraine 48°40′N 25°43′E
Zallah see Zillah
98 J13 Zaltbommel Gelderland, C Netherlands 51°49′N 05°15′E
124 H15 Zaluch'ye Novgorodskaya Oblast', NW Russian Federation 57°40′N 31°45′E
Zamak see Zamakh
141 Q14 Zamakh var. Zamak. N Yemen 16°26′N 47°35′E
136 K15 Zamantı Irmağı ≈ C Turkey
Zambesi/Zambeze see Zambezi
83 G14 Zambezi North Western, W Zambia 13°34′S 23°08′E
83 K15 Zambezi var. Zambesi, Port. Zambeze. ≈ S Africa
83 O15 Zambézia off. Província da Zambézia. ◐ province C Mozambique
Zambézia, Província da see Zambézia
83 I14 Zambia off. Republic of Zambia; prev. Northern Rhodesia. ◆ republic S Africa
Zambia, Republic of see Zambia
171 O8 Zamboanga off. Zamboanga City. Mindanao, S Philippines 06°56′N 122°03′E
Zamboanga City see Zamboanga
54 E5 Zambrano Bolívar, N Colombia 09°45′N 74°50′W
110 N10 Zambrów Łomża, E Poland 52°59′N 22°14′E
83 L14 Zambué Tete, NW Mozambique 15°03′S 30°49′E
77 T13 Zamfara ≈ NW Nigeria
Zamkog see Zamtang
56 C9 Zamora Zamora Chinchipe, S Ecuador 04°04′S 78°52′W
104 K6 Zamora Castilla-León, NW Spain 41°30′N 05°45′W
104 K5 Zamora ◐ province Castilla-León, NW Spain
Zamora see Barinas
56 A13 Zamora Chinchipe ◐ province S Ecuador
40 M13 Zamora de Hidalgo Michoacán, SW Mexico 20°N 102°18′W
111 P15 Zamość Rus. Zamoste. Lubelskie, E Poland 50°44′N 23°16′E
Zamoste see Zamość
160 G7 Zamtang var. Zamkog; prev. Gamba. Sichuan, C China 32°19′N 100°55′E
75 O8 Zamzam, Wādī dry watercourse NW Libya
79 F20 Zanaga Lékoumou, S Congo 02°50′S 13°53′E
41 T16 Zanatepec Oaxaca, SE Mexico 16°28′N 94°24′W
105 P9 Záncara ≈ C Spain
Zancle see Messina
158 G14 Zanda Xizang Zizhiqu, W China 31°29′N 79°50′E
98 H10 Zandvoort Noord-Holland, W Netherlands 52°22′N 04°31′E
39 P8 Zane Hills hill range Alaska, USA
31 T13 Zanesville Ohio, N USA 39°55′N 82°02′W
Zanga see Hrazdan
Zangkaxa see Domar
142 L4 Zanjān var. Zenjan, Zinjan. Zanjān, NW Iran 36°40′N 48°30′E
142 L4 Zanjān off. Ostān-e Zanjān, var. Zenjan, Zinjan. ◐ province NW Iran
Zanjān, Ostān-e see Zanjān
Zante see Zákynthos
81 J22 Zanzibar Zanzibar, E Tanzania 06°10′S 39°12′E
81 J22 Zanzibar ◐ region E Tanzania
81 J22 Zanzibar Swa. Unguja. island E Tanzania
81 J22 Zanzibar Channel channel E Tanzania
81 J23 Zanzibar North ◐ region E Tanzania
81 J23 Zanzibar South ◐ region E Tanzania
81 J23 Zanzibar West ◐ region E Tanzania
161 N8 Zaoyang Hubei, C China 32°10′N 112°45′E
165 P10 Zaō-zan ▲ Honshū, C Japan 38°06′N 140°27′E
124 J2 Zaozërsk Murmanskaya Oblast', NW Russian Federation 69°25′N 32°25′E
161 Q6 Zaozhuang Shandong, E China 34°53′N 117°38′E
28 L4 Zap North Dakota, N USA 47°18′N 101°55′W
112 L13 Zapadna Morava Ger. Westliche Morava. ≈ C Serbia
124 H16 Zapadnaya Dvina Tverskaya Oblast', W Russian Federation 56°17′N 32°03′E
Zapadnaya Dvina see Western Dvina
Zapadno-Kazakhstanskaya Oblast' see Zapadnyy Kazakhstan
122 I9 Zapadno-Sibirskaya Ravnina Eng. West Siberian Plain. plain C Russian Federation
Zapadnyy Bug see Bug
144 E9 Zapadnyy Kazakhstan off. Zapadno-Kazakhstanskaya Oblast', Eng. West Kazakhstan, Kaz. Batys Qazaqstan Oblysy; prev. Ural'skaya Oblast'. ◐ province NW Kazakhstan
122 K13 Zapadnyy Sayan Eng. Western Sayans. ▲▲ S Russian Federation
63 H15 Zapala Neuquén, W Argentina 38°54′S 70°06′W
62 I4 Zapaleri, Cerro var. Cerro Sapaleri. ▲ N Chile 22°51′S 67°10′W
25 Q16 Zapata Texas, SW USA 26°57′N 99°17′W
44 D5 Zapata, Península de peninsula W Cuba
61 G19 Zapicán Lavalleja, S Uruguay 33°31′S 54°55′W
65 J19 Zapiola Ridge undersea feature SW Atlantic Ocean
65 L19 Zapiola Seamount undersea feature S Atlantic Ocean 38°15′S 26°15′W
124 I2 Zapolyarnyy Murmanskaya Oblast', NW Russian Federation 69°24′N 30°53′E
117 U8 Zaporizhzhya Rus. Zaporozh'ye; prev. Aleksandrovsk. Zaporiz'ka Oblast', SE Ukraine 47°47′N 35°12′E
Zaporizhzhya see Zaporiz'ka Oblast'
117 U9 Zaporiz'ka Oblast' var. Zaporizhzhya, Rus. Zaporozhskaya Oblast'. ◐ province SE Ukraine
Zaporozhskaya Oblast' see Zaporiz'ka Oblast'
Zaporozh'ye see Zaporizhzhya
40 L14 Zapotiltic Jalisco, SW Mexico 19°40′N 103°29′W
158 G13 Zapug Xizang Zizhiqu, W China
137 V10 Zaqatala Rus. Zakataly. NW Azerbaijan 41°38′N 46°38′E
159 P13 Zaqên Qinghai, W China 33°23′N 94°31′E
159 Q13 Za Qu ≈ C China
136 M13 Zara Sivas, C Turkey 39°55′N 37°44′E
Zara see Zadar
Zarafshan see Zarafshon
147 P12 Zarafshon Rus. Zeravshan. W Tajikistan 39°12′N 68°36′E
146 L9 Zarafshon Rus. Zarafshan. Navoiy Viloyati, N Uzbekistan 41°33′N 64°09′E
Zarafshon see Zeravshan
147 O12 Zarafshon, Qatorkŭhi Rus. Zeravshanskiy Khrebet, Uzb. Zarafshon Tizmasi. ▲▲ Tajikistan/Uzbekistan
Zarafshon Tizmasi see Zarafshon, Qatorkŭhi
54 E7 Zaragoza Antioquia, N Colombia 07°30′N 74°52′W
40 I5 Zaragoza Chihuahua, N Mexico 29°36′N 107°41′W
41 N6 Zaragoza Coahuila, NE Mexico 28°31′N 100°54′W
41 O10 Zaragoza Nuevo León, NE Mexico 23°59′N 99°49′W
105 R5 Zaragoza Eng. Saragossa; anc. Caesaraugusta, Salduba. Aragón, NE Spain 41°39′N 00°54′W
105 R6 Zaragoza ◐ province Aragón, NE Spain
105 R5 Zaragoza ✈ Aragón, NE Spain 41°38′N 00°53′W
143 S10 Zarand Kermān, C Iran 30°50′N 56°35′E
148 J9 Zaranj Nīmrūz, SW Afghanistan 30°59′N 61°54′E
118 I11 Zarasai Utena, E Lithuania 55°44′N 26°17′E
62 N12 Zárate prev. General José F.Uriburu. Buenos Aires, E Argentina 34°06′S 59°03′W
105 Q2 Zarautz var. Zarauz. País Vasco, N Spain 43°17′N 02°10′W
Zarauz see Zarautz
Zaravecchia see Biograd na Moru
Zarāyīn see Zarēn
126 L4 Zaraysk Moskovskaya Oblast', W Russian Federation 54°48′N 38°54′E
55 N6 Zaraza Guárico, N Venezuela 09°23′N 65°20′W
Zarbdar see Zarbdor
147 P11 Zarbdor Rus. Zarbdar. Jizzax Viloyati, C Uzbekistan 40°04′N 68°10′E
142 M8 Zard Kūh ▲ SW Iran 32°19′N 50°03′E
124 I5 Zarechensk Murmanskaya Oblast', NW Russian Federation 66°39′N 31°27′E
127 P6 Zarechnyy Penzenskaya Oblast', W Russian Federation 53°12′N 45°12′E
Zareh Sharan see Sharan
39 Y14 Zarembo Island island Alexander Archipelago, Alaska, USA
139 V4 Zarēn var. Zarāyīn. As Sulaymānīyah, E Iraq 35°16′N 45°43′E
149 Q7 Zarghūn Shahr var. Katawaz. Paktīkā, SE Afghanistan 32°40′N 68°20′E
77 V13 Zaria Kaduna, C Nigeria 11°06′N 07°42′E
116 K2 Zarichne Rivnens'ka Oblast', NW Ukraine 51°49′N 26°09′E
122 J13 Zarinsk Altayskiy Kray, S Russian Federation 53°34′N 85°22′E
116 J12 Zărneşti Hung. Zernest. Braşov, C Romania 45°34′N 25°18′E
115 J25 Zarós Kríti, Greece, E Mediterranean Sea 35°08′N 24°54′E
100 O9 Zarow ≈ NE Germany
Zarqa see Az Zarqā'
Zarqa/Muḥāfaẓat az Zarqā' see Az Zarqā'
111 G20 Záruby ▲ W Slovakia 48°30′N 17°24′E
56 B8 Zaruma El Oro, SW Ecuador 03°46′S 79°38′W
110 E13 Żary Ger. Sorau, Sorau in der Niederlausitz. Lubuskie, W Poland 51°44′N 15°09′E
54 D10 Zarzal Valle del Cauca, W Colombia 04°24′N 76°01′W
42 I7 Zarzalar, Cerro ▲ S Honduras 14°15′N 86°49′W
Zashaghan see Zachagansk
152 I5 Zāskār ≈ NE India
152 I5 Zāskār Range ▲▲ NE India
119 K15 Zaslawye Minskaya Voblasts', C Belarus 54°01′N 27°16′E
116 K7 Zastavna Chernivets'ka Oblast', W Ukraine 48°30′N 25°51′E
111 B16 Žatec Ger. Saaz. Ústecký Kraj, NW Czech Republic 50°20′N 13°35′E
Zaumgarten see Chrzanów
Zaunguzskiye Garagumy see Üngüz Angyrsyndaky Garagum
25 X9 Zavalla Texas, SW USA 31°09′N 94°25′W
99 H18 Zaventem Vlaams Brabant, C Belgium 50°53′N 04°28′E
99 H18 Zaventem ✈ (Brussel/Bruxelles) Vlaams Brabant, C Belgium 50°55′N 04°28′E
Zavertse see Zawiercie
114 L7 Zavet Razgrad, NE Bulgaria 43°46′N 26°40′E
127 O12 Zavetnoye Rostovskaya Oblast', SW Russian Federation 47°10′N 43°54′E
156 M3 Zavhan Gol ≈ W Mongolia
112 H12 Zavidovići Federacija Bosna I Hercegovina, N Bosnia and Herzegovina 44°26′N 18°07′E
123 R13 Zavitinsk Amurskaya Oblast', SE Russian Federation 50°23′N 128°57′E
Zawia see Az Zāwiyah
111 K15 Zawiercie Rus. Zavertse. Śląskie, S Poland 50°29′N 19°24′E
75 P11 Zawīlah var. Zuwaylah, It. Zueila. C Libya 26°10′N 15°07′E
138 I4 Zāwiyah, Jabal az ▲▲ NW Syria
109 Y3 Zaya ≈ NE Austria
166 M8 Zayatkyi Bago, C Burma (Myanmar) 17°48′N 96°27′E
145 Y11 Zaysan Vostochnyy Kazakhstan, E Kazakhstan 47°30′N 84°55′E
Zaysan Köl see Zaysan, Ozero
145 Y11 Zaysan, Ozero Kaz. Zaysan Köl. ◎ E Kazakhstan
159 R16 Zayü var. Gyigang. Xizang Zizhiqu, W China 28°36′N 97°25′E
Zayyq see Ural
44 F6 Zaza ≈ C Cuba
116 K5 Zbarazh Ternopil's'ka Oblast', W Ukraine 49°40′N 25°47′E
116 J5 Zboriv Ternopil's'ka Oblast', W Ukraine 49°40′N 25°07′E
111 F18 Zbraslav Jihomoravský Kraj, SE Czech Republic 49°13′N 16°19′E
116 K6 Zbruch ≈ W Ukraine
Žďár see Žďár nad Sázavou
111 F17 Žďár nad Sázavou Ger. Saar in Mähren; prev. Žďár. Vysočina, C Czech Republic 49°34′N 16°00′E
116 K4 Zdolbuniv Pol. Zdolbunów, Rus. Zdolbunov. Rivnens'ka Oblast', NW Ukraine 50°33′N 26°15′E
Zdolbunov/Zdolbunów see Zdolbuniv
110 J13 Zduńska Wola Sieradz, C Poland 51°37′N 18°57′E
117 O4 Zdvizh ≈ N Ukraine
Zdzięciół see Dzyatlava
111 I16 Zdzieszowice Ger. Odertal. Opolskie, SW Poland 50°24′N 18°06′E
Zealand see Sjælland
188 K6 Zealandia Bank undersea feature C Pacific Ocean
63 H20 Zeballos, Monte ▲ S Argentina 47°04′S 71°32′W
83 K20 Zebediela Limpopo, NE South Africa 24°16′S 29°21′E
113 L18 Zebë, Mal var. Mali i Zebës. ▲ NE Albania 41°57′N 20°16′E
Zebës, Mali i see Zebë, Mal
21 V9 Zebulon North Carolina, SE USA 35°49′N 78°19′W
112 K8 Žednik Hung. Bácsjózseffalva. Vojvodina, N Serbia 45°58′N 19°40′E
99 C15 Zeebrugge West-Vlaanderen, NW Belgium 51°20′N 03°13′E
183 N16 Zeehan Tasmania, SE Australia 41°54′S 145°19′E
99 L14 Zeeland Noord-Brabant, SE Netherlands 51°42′N 05°40′E
29 N7 Zeeland North Dakota, N USA 45°57′N 99°49′W
99 E14 Zeeland ◐ province SW Netherlands
83 I21 Zeerust North-West, N South Africa 25°33′S 26°06′E
98 K10 Zeewolde Flevoland, C Netherlands 52°20′N 05°32′E
Zefat see Tsefat
Zegań see Żagań
Zehden see Cedynia
100 O11 Zehdenick Brandenburg, NE Germany 52°58′N 13°19′E
Zē-i Bādīnān see Great Zab
Zeiden see Codlea
146 M14 Zeidskoye Vodokhranilishche ▣ E Turkmenistan
Zē-i Kōya see Little Zab
181 P7 Zeil, Mount ▲ Northern Territory, C Australia 23°31′S 132°41′E
98 J12 Zeist Utrecht, C Netherlands 52°05′N 05°15′E
101 M16 Zeitz Sachsen-Anhalt, E Germany 51°03′N 12°08′E
159 T11 Zêkog var. Zequ; prev. Sonag. Qinghai, C China 35°03′N 101°30′E
Zelaya Norte see Atlántico Norte, Región Autónoma
Zelaya Sur see Atlántico Sur, Región Autónoma
99 F17 Zele Oost-Vlaanderen, NW Belgium 51°04′N 04°02′E
110 N12 Żelechów Lubelskie, E Poland 51°49′N 21°57′E
113 H14 Zelena Glava ▲ SE Bosnia and Herzegovina 43°32′N 17°55′E
113 P20 Zelen Breg ▲ S Macedonia 41°10′N 22°14′E
113 I14 Zelengora ▲▲ S Bosnia and Herzegovina
124 I5 Zelenoborskiy Murmanskaya Oblast', NW Russian Federation 66°52′N 32°25′E
127 R3 Zelenodol'sk Respublika Tatarstan, W Russian Federation 55°52′N 48°49′E
117 S9 Zelenodol's'k Dnipropetrovs'ka Oblast', E Ukraine 47°38′N 33°41′E
122 J12 Zelenogorsk Krasnoyarskiy Kray, C Russian Federation 56°08′N 94°29′E
126 K3 Zelenograd Moskovskaya Oblast', W Russian Federation 56°02′N 37°08′E
118 B13 Zelenogradsk Ger. Cranz, Kranz. Kaliningradskaya Oblast', W Russian Federation 54°58′N 20°30′E
127 O15 Zelenokumsk Stavropol'skiy Kray, SW Russian Federation 44°22′N 43°48′E
165 X4 Zelënyy, Ostrov var. Shibotsu-jima. island NE Russian Federation
Železna Kapela see Eisenkappel
Železna Vrata see Demir Kapija
112 L11 Železniki Serbia, N Serbia 44°45′N 20°23′E
98 N12 Zelhem Gelderland, E Netherlands 52°00′N 06°21′E
113 N18 Želino NW FYR Macedonia 42°00′N 21°06′E
113 M14 Željin ▲ C Serbia
101 K17 Zella-Mehlis Thüringen, C Germany 50°40′N 10°40′E
109 P7 Zell am See var. Zell-am-See. Salzburg, S Austria 47°19′N 12°47′E
Zell-am-See see Zell am See
109 N7 Zell am Ziller Tirol, W Austria 47°13′N 11°52′E
Zelle see Celle
109 W2 Zellerndorf Niederösterreich, NE Austria 48°40′N 15°57′E
109 U7 Zeltweg Steiermark, S Austria 47°12′N 14°46′E
119 G17 Zel'va Pol. Zelwa. Hrodzyenskaya Voblasts', W Belarus 53°09′N 24°49′E
118 H13 Želva Vilnius, C Lithuania 55°13′N 25°07′E
Zelwa see Zel'va
99 E16 Zelzate var. Selzaete. Oost-Vlaanderen, NW Belgium 51°12′N 03°49′E
118 E11 Žemaičių Aukštumas physical region W Lithuania
118 C12 Žemaičių Naumiestis Klaipėda, SW Lithuania 55°22′N 21°39′E
119 L14 Zembin var. Zyembin. Minskaya Voblasts', C Belarus 54°22′N 28°13′E
127 N6 Zemetchino Penzenskaya Oblast', W Russian Federation 53°31′N 42°35′E
79 M15 Zémio Haut-Mbomou, E Central African Republic 05°04′N 25°07′E
41 R16 Zempoaltepec, Cerro ▲ SE Mexico 17°04′N 95°54′W
99 G17 Zemst Vlaams Brabant, C Belgium 50°59′N 04°28′E
112 L11 Zemun Serbia, N Serbia 44°52′N 20°25′E
Zendajan see Zendeh Jan
148 J5 Zendeh Jan var. Zendajan, Zindajān. Herāt, NW Afghanistan 34°55′N 61°53′E
Zengg see Senj
112 H12 Zenica Federacija Bosna I Hercegovina, C Bosnia and Herzegovina 44°12′N 17°53′E
Zenjan see Zanjān
Zen'kov see Zin'kiv
Zenshū see Chŏnju
Zenta see Senta
82 B11 Zenza do Itombe Cuanza Norte, NW Angola 09°22′S 14°10′E
112 H12 Žepče Federacija Bosna I Hercegovina, N Bosnia and Herzegovina 44°26′N 18°00′E
23 W12 Zephyrhills Florida, SE USA 28°13′N 82°10′W
158 F9 Zepu var. Poskam. Xinjiang Uygur Zizhiqu, NW China 38°10′N 77°18′E
Zequ see Zêkog
147 Q12 Zeravshan Taj./Uzb. Zarafshon. ≈ Tajikistan/Uzbekistan
Zeravshan see Zarafshon
Zeravshanskiy Khrebet see Zarafshon, Qatorkŭhi
101 M14 Zerbst Sachsen-Anhalt, E Germany 51°57′N 12°05′E
145 P8 Zerenda Akmola, N Kazakhstan 52°56′N 69°09′E
110 H12 Żerków Wielkopolskie, C Poland 52°03′N 17°33′E
108 E11 Zermatt Valais, SW Switzerland 46°00′N 07°45′E
Zernest see Zărneşti
108 J9 Zernez Graubünden, SE Switzerland 46°42′N 10°06′E
126 L12 Zernograd Rostovskaya Oblast', SW Russian Federation 46°52′N 40°13′E
Zestafoni see Zestap'oni
137 S9 Zestap'oni Rus. Zestafoni. C Georgia 42°09′N 43°00′E
98 H12 Zestienhoven ✈ (Rotterdam) Zuid-Holland, SW Netherlands 51°57′N 04°30′E
113 J16 Zeta ≈ C Montenegro
8 L6 Zeta Lake ◎ Victoria Island, Northwest Territories, N Canada
Zētang see Nêdong
98 L12 Zetten Gelderland, SE Netherlands 51°55′N 05°43′E
101 M17 Zeulenroda Thüringen, C Germany 50°40′N 11°58′E
100 H10 Zeven Niedersachsen, NW Germany 53°17′N 09°16′E
98 M12 Zevenaar Gelderland, SE Netherlands 51°55′N 06°05′E
99 H14 Zevenbergen Noord-Brabant, S Netherlands 51°39′N 04°36′E
129 X6 Zeya ≈ SE Russian Federation
Zeya Reservoir see Zeyskoye Vodokhranilishche
143 T11 Zeynalābād Kermān, C Iran 29°56′N 57°29′E
123 R12 Zeyskoye Vodokhranilishche Eng. Zeya Reservoir. ▣ SE Russian Federation
104 H8 Zêzere, Rio ≈ C Portugal
Zgerzh see Zgierz
138 H6 Zgharta N Lebanon 34°24′N 35°54′E
110 K12 Zgierz Ger. Neuhof, Rus. Zgerzh. Łódź, C Poland 51°55′N 19°20′E
111 E14 Zgorzelec Ger. Görlitz. Dolnośląskie, SW Poland 51°10′N 15°E
119 F19 Zhabinka Pol. Żabinka. Brestskaya Voblasts', SW Belarus 52°12′N 24°01′E
Zhaggo see Luhuo
159 R15 Zhag'yab var. Yêndum. Xizang Zizhiqu, W China 30°42′N 97°33′E
144 L9 Zhailma Kaz. Zhayylma. Kostanay, N Kazakhstan 51°34′N 61°39′E
Zhalagash see Dzhalagash
145 V16 Zhalanash Almaty, SE Kazakhstan 43°04′N 78°08′E
145 S7 Zhalauly, Ozero ◎ NE Kazakhstan
144 E9 Zhalpaktal Kaz. Zhalpaqtal; prev. Furmanovo. Zapadnyy Kazakhstan, W Kazakhstan 49°43′N 49°28′E
Zhalpaqtal see Zhalpaktal
119 G16 Zhaludok Rus. Zheludok. Hrodzyenskaya Voblasts', W Belarus 53°36′N 24°59′E
Zhaman-Akkol', Ozero see Akkol', Ozero
145 Q14 Zhambyl off. Zhambylskaya Oblast', Kaz. Zhambyl Oblysy; prev. Dzhambulskaya Oblast'. ◐ province S Kazakhstan
Zhambyl see Taraz
Zhambyl Oblysy/Zhambylskaya Oblast' see Zhambyl
Zhamo see Bomi
145 S12 Zhamshy ≈ C Kazakhstan
144 M15 Zhanadar'ya Kyzylorda, S Kazakhstan 44°41′N 64°39′E

◆ Country
● Country Capital
◇ Dependent Territory
○ Dependent Territory Capital
◐ Administrative Regions
✈ International Airport
▲ Mountain
▲▲ Mountain Range
Volcano
≈ River
◎ Lake
▣ Reservoir